2010 College

HANDBOOK

2010 College HANDBOOK

CollegeBoard

Forty-Seventh Edition

The College Board, New York

The College Board

The College Board is a not-for-profit membership association whose mission is to connect students to college success and opportunity. Founded in 1900, the College Board is composed of more than 5,600 schools, colleges, universities and other educational organizations. Each year, the College Board serves seven million students and their parents, 23,000 high schools, and 3,800 colleges through major programs and services in college readiness, college admissions, guidance, assessment, financial aid, enrollment, and teaching and learning. Among its best-known programs are the SAT®, the PSAT/NMSQT® and the Advanced Placement Program® (AP®). The College Board is committed to the principles of excellence and equity, and that commitment is embodied in all of its programs, services, activities and concerns.

For further information, visit www.collegeboard.com.

Editorial inquiries concerning this book should be directed to College Planning Services, The College Board, 45 Columbus Avenue, New York, NY 10023-6992; or telephone 212-713-8000.

Copies of this book are available from your local bookseller or may be ordered from College Board Publications, P.O. Box 869010, Plano, TX 75074-0998. The book may also be ordered online through the College Board Store at www.collegeboard.com. The price is $29.95.

ISBN: 978-0-87447-846-4

Printed in the United States of America

Contents

Preface ... vii

What's in this book ... 1

About accreditation ... 10

Selecting colleges ... 13

Applying to colleges ... 23

Taking college admissions and placement tests ... 29

Life on campus ... 38

Glossary ... 40

Four-year colleges
- College descriptions by state ... 49

Two-year colleges
- College descriptions by state ... 1365

Early Decision and Early Action table ... 2083

Wait list table ... 2095

Indexes
- College type
  - Liberal arts ... 2103
  - Upper-division ... 2105
  - Agricultural and technical ... 2106
  - Art/music ... 2106
  - Bible ... 2106
  - Business ... 2107
  - Culinary ... 2108
  - Engineering ... 2108
  - Maritime ... 2108
  - Military ... 2108
  - Nursing and health science ... 2108
  - Schools of mortuary science ... 2109
  - Seminary/rabbinical ... 2109
  - Teachers ... 2110
  - Technical and career ... 2110

Special characteristics
- Colleges for men 2113
- Colleges for women 2113
- Affiliated with a religion 2113
- Historically black colleges 2115
- Hispanic-serving colleges 2115
- Tribal colleges 2116

Undergraduate enrollment size
- Very small 2117
- Small 2119
- Medium 2122
- Large 2125
- Very large 2126

Admission selectivity
- Admit under 50% of applicants 2128
- Admit 50 to 75% of applicants 2129
- Admit over 75% of applicants 2131
- Open admission 2133

Admissions/placement policies
- No closing date 2139
- SAT Subject Tests™ required for admission 2146
- SAT Subject Tests recommended for admission 2146
- Colleges that offer ROTC
  - Air Force 2148
  - Army 2150
  - Naval 2154

NCAA sports by division 2155

Alphabetical index of colleges 2196

Preface

When the *College Handbook* first appeared in 1941, students and parents had little access to college information of any kind. Now, in this Internet age, many find the amount of available information to be overwhelming.

What's needed is a single, trusted source where the key facts about colleges can be compared and contrasted on a consistent basis. From its inception, the *Handbook* has met this need by providing college-bound students and their advisers with the authoritative, reliable and up-to-date facts necessary to make informed college decisions.

This edition of the *Handbook* presents facts about 3,845 colleges, universities and technical schools. To be included, an institution must be accredited by a national or regional accrediting association recognized by the U.S. Department of Education and offer some undergraduate degree programs — at least an associate degree.

Throughout the *Handbook*, information is presented in accordance with the Common Data Set initiative, in which the College Board has taken a leading role. The goal of this collaborative effort with other publishers and college administrators is to provide students with the most accurate, consistently comparable data available.

The college descriptions are based primarily on information supplied by the colleges themselves in response to the College Board's Annual Survey of Colleges 2009, with some data supplied by federal and state agencies. The survey was completed by participating colleges in spring 2009. Several thousand college administrators across the country participated in this effort. Without their continued cooperation, publication of the *Handbook* would not be possible.

A staff of data editors verified the facts to be certain that all descriptions are as complete and accurate as possible. Although the College Board makes every effort to ensure that the information about colleges is correct and up to date, we urge students to confirm facts with the colleges themselves.

The enormous task of data collection, management and verification was directed by Connie Betterton and Stan Bernstein, with the assistance of Cathy Serico, Andrew Costello, Renée Gernand, Roger Harris, Doris Chow and Ralph Hockens. Jennifer Donato, Rachael Mason, Aimee McDermott and Andrea Morabito compiled, edited and verified the data.

We thank our readers — you and the many students, parents and counselors whose comments and suggestions over the years have helped to make this the most widely used college directory in the nation. We welcome your suggestions on how the *Handbook* can continue to meet the ever-changing needs of future generations of college-bound students.

Tom Vanderberg
Senior Editor, College Planning Services

What's in this book

If you're beginning your college search feeling a bit overwhelmed and intimidated by the sheer number of choices, you're not alone. Just about everyone starts out feeling that way. But even the most daunting job can be easily handled with the right tools and a plan, and the *College Handbook* gives you both.

Getting Started

The *College Handbook* is the best place to begin your college search, and you will no doubt find yourself returning to this source as your search progresses and evolves. You should not, however, rely on this book exclusively. Take advantage of the other resources available to you — the Internet, campus visits and interviews, college fairs and viewbooks, your school counselor, family and friends — before you make your final decision. Don't be dismayed if you find that you must change directions more than once as you learn about the colleges. This only means that you are learning more about yourself as well.

The *Handbook* is divided into four major sections. The first (where you are now) contains guidance materials to help you plan for college. Four-year college descriptions are in the second section, two-year college descriptions are in the third, and the last section contains tables and indexes. Margin tabs help you to quickly move from section to section.

Although you might be eager to dive right into the college descriptions, it is far better to start your college search with a basic idea of what you want to look for. Take the time to go through the guidance materials in the first section to get on the right track. Read the articles, ranging from college admissions and placement tests to dorm life. The valuable insights you gain will give you confidence as you continue your college search.

Once you can identify your needs and preferences with regard to college size and type and have an idea of what other characteristics are important to you, the indexes at the end of the book will help you locate colleges that fit the bill.

KNOW THE LINGO

You'll find sidebars like this throughout the first part of this book highlighting and defining key terms. There's also a comprehensive glossary beginning on page 40.

For a complete explanation of the various index categories, see "Tables and Indexes" beginning on page 7.

The heart and soul of the *Handbook*, of course, are the descriptions of four-year and two-year colleges. These follow standard formats to make it easy to find a particular item of information in any description and to compare one college with another. Read "The College Descriptions" below to see what the descriptions contain and how the information is presented. If you are not sure of the meaning of a term found in the *Handbook* descriptions or guidance materials, check the glossary beginning on page 40.

GOOD TO KNOW

The chapter "Selecting colleges" has broad advice on using the college profiles and indexes to find colleges you're interested in and assess your chances of being admitted when you apply. The information in this chapter, on the other hand, defines exactly what's covered in every college description.

The College Descriptions

The college. Each description begins with the college's official name — which isn't always the one in popular use. The heading also includes the college's city, state and Web site address. Most colleges now have Web sites that are invaluable resources in your college search. The designation "CB member" after the college's name indicates that the college is a member of the College Board; the four-digit CB code should be used when requesting that SAT® scores or Advanced Placement® (AP®) grades be sent to the college.

Key facts. The bulleted list highlights information that you may want to compare across colleges and that you'll need if you decide to apply. This information includes:

- Type of institution (e.g., liberal arts college, university) and whether it has a religious affiliation.
- Whether the campus is urban, suburban or rural, and whether it is primarily a residential or a commuter campus.
- Total number of undergraduate students; profile of the undergraduate student body (percent part-time, women, minority breakdown, international); total number of graduate students on campus. *Two-year undergraduate data are included under Student Profile.*
- Percentage of applicants admitted to the freshman class, which gives you some idea of how competitive the college is. *Four-year colleges only.*
- Admissions requirements for fall 2010: tests, essay, interview (if required of all applicants).
- Percentage of students who graduate within six years (most students take more than four years to earn a bachelor's degree). Caveat: This figure is based on students who enrolled as freshmen and remained to graduate; it does not include students who transferred into or out of the college during that period.

GOOD TO KNOW

The College Board's **Web-based College Search** (www.collegeboard.com/collegesearch) is a powerful, fast and easy tool for creating your list of colleges to investigate. The intuitive interface helps you find colleges that match your requirements, do side-by-side comparisons and find additional colleges that may also fit the bill. You can also go directly to any college's Web site. With the *College Handbook* as your companion desk reference, you can quickly cut your college search down to size.

General information. The date the college was founded, the type of institutional accreditation it has, the number and type of degrees awarded in 2007-08, and whether the college has an ROTC program will give you a sense of the academic life on campus. Whether the college organizes its calendar on a semester, trimester, quarter or some other schedule indicates the way the college structures its courses.

Pay particular attention to the faculty information. The total number of faculty and its makeup are important to your everyday experience at an institution. Class size information, showing percentages of classes with few or many students, is another indication of a college's learning environment. Colleges were also invited to provide a list of special facilities (from arboretums to zoos) or additional unique information about their institutions in this section.

For two-year colleges only: This is where you will find total enrollment figures for both degree-seeking and non-degree-seeking students, and information about partnerships with other schools or organizations.

KNOW THE LINGO

Campus — The physical location of a college or university. Includes classroom buildings, libraries, research facilities, dormitories, dining halls and administration buildings.

Branch campus — A part of a college, university or community college that is geographically separate from the main campus, has its own faculty and administration, and may have separate admissions requirements and degree programs.

Freshman class profile. (*Four-year colleges*) This provides a snapshot of the college's 2008 freshman class and is presented in tabular format to make it easily accessible. This is the best source of information about whether your own profile fits in with that of students currently attending the college, and whether you'd be comfortable if admitted.

- Number who applied, were admitted and enrolled.
- Mid-50 percent of enrolled freshmen's SAT/ACT test scores. This is the score range for half the freshman class. (Remember that 25 percent of enrolled freshmen scored below and 25 percent above the reported figures.)
- Information about high school GPA and class rank.
- Percentage who completed the year in good standing and returned as sophomores.
- Percentage who come from out of state, live on campus, are international students, and join fraternities or sororities.

Student profile. (*Two-year colleges*) This is similar to the freshman class profile for four-year colleges, but the data presented covers the entire undergraduate student body.

- Percentage enrolled in transfer or vocational programs. Number admitted and enrolled as first-time, first-year students. Percentage who already have a bachelor's degree or higher. Number who transferred from other institutions.
- Percentage of the total undergraduate student body who are part-time students, live on campus, are women, come from out of state, are minorities and are international students.

Transfer out. (*Two-year colleges*)

- Percentage of students in transfer programs who go on to four-year colleges.
- Colleges to which most students transferred in 2008.

Basis for selection. This is where you can find the details of a college's admissions policies, including factors the college considers most important in deciding whether or not to offer you admission. If it says "Open admission," that means the college accepts anyone with a high school or GED diploma, space permitting. Special requirements for homeschooled and learning-disabled students are also reported here.

High school preparation. Almost all colleges listed in the *Handbook* require a high school diploma or its equivalent. Some colleges have very specific requirements in terms of education background and high school courses taken. The required and recommended number of course units that applicants should have taken in high school is listed here. Where a range is given, the lower number represents the required units; the higher number is a recommendation.

2009-10 annual costs. You should estimate and anticipate the total annual costs for each college you are considering. In doing so, the elements listed below need to be considered. Unless otherwise noted, the reported figures reflect the costs for the 2009-10 academic year.

- *Tuition/fees* include the cost of instruction and mandated fees for all students. For public colleges, both in-state and out-of-state costs are listed. If the college combines tuition, fees, and room and board expenses, that single figure is given as a comprehensive fee.
- *Room/board* figures are for a student living on campus in a double room with a full meal plan. Single rooms or rooms for three or more could cost a lot more or less than the figure reported here. Many colleges have a range of meal plans with fewer meals per week, which would lower your board cost.
- *Books/supplies* expenses can vary depending on the program you take. Some fields, such as art or architecture, may require more expensive supplies.
- *Personal expenses* include items such as clothing, laundry, entertainment and furnishings. Personal expenses will vary widely depending on your lifestyle. Transportation costs are not included.
- *Per-credit-hour tuition* (two-year colleges only) is of particular interest to students planning to attend college part time.

Financial aid. This information provides a summary of financial aid awarded for the academic year(s) indicated, and describes financial aid award policies for need-based and non-need-based aid. This information will give you an idea of how first-year and undergraduate student assistance has been awarded and will help you compare financial aid policies among the colleges. You should always contact the admissions or financial aid office for complete information and for answers to any questions you might have regarding eligibility and award policies.

Application procedures. This is where you can find out about the college's application procedures and deadlines for both admissions and financial aid.

- *Admissions.* Most colleges require an application fee, noted here, but will waive it for applicants with need. Take note of any "priority dates" — after which qualified applicants are considered on a first-come, first-served basis, and only for as long as slots are available.

KNOW THE LINGO

College — The generic term for an institution of higher education. Also a term used to designate divisions within a university.

Liberal arts college — A college that emphasizes the liberal arts in its core curriculum and academic offerings and does not offer vocational, professional or preprofessional programs.

University — An institution of higher education that is divided into several colleges, schools or institutes. Generally, university students take classes in the college to which they were accepted, but they may be allowed to take some courses offered by other colleges within the university, and can use shared facilities such as libraries and laboratories.

KEEP IN MIND

The "required" units listed under **"high school preparation"** are just that — the minimum requirement. **For your application to be competitive,** you should strive to complete the recommended units as well.

GOOD TO KNOW

The figures for the **costs of books and supplies and personal expenses** are averages from across the entire student population. **Your own costs may be much higher or lower**, depending on how heavy your course load is, what kind of classes you take, and your lifestyle. For more information on the different components of college costs, read the articles in the "Pay for College" section of www.collegeboard.com, or see the College Board's *Getting Financial Aid*.

- *Financial aid.* Required forms plus priority, closing, notification and reply dates are listed for fall-term financial aid applications. The Free Application for Federal Student Aid (FAFSA) is required by every college offering federal financial aid. If the college requires the CSS/Financial Aid PROFILE® to determine your eligibility for nonfederal funds, it is noted here. "Institutional form" means the college has a form of its own. Pay special attention to priority dates and deadlines; if the college indicates "no deadline" for financial aid, it means it will continue to process requests as long as funds are available. You should always apply as early as possible to obtain the best consideration for financial aid awards.

Academics. Many colleges offer a range of special study options that can enrich or enhance your education experience. Special academic programs are listed in this section. Check the glossary for brief descriptions of each of the programs listed.

College policies on granting credit or advanced placement through the College Board's Advanced Placement Program® and College-Level Examination Program® (CLEP®), and/or other placement programs and institutional tests are listed next. Most colleges have a maximum number of credit hours by examination that may be counted toward a degree, which is also listed.

Academic support services list the programs the college provides to assist students in succeeding academically. Preadmission summer programs, special counselors, tutoring, learning disabled programs and study skills assistance are some of the options offered.

Honors college/program. If a college has a separate undergraduate honors college or a program with different admissions and academic offerings from those available to regular students, this section will tell you what's available and how to apply.

Majors. Only majors leading to a bachelor's degree (for four-year colleges) or an associate degree (for two-year colleges) are included here. They are listed alphabetically by general category. The majors listed here are based on the U.S. Department of Education's Classification of Instructional Programs; colleges were asked to match the majors they offer to this list. Many colleges additionally offer concentrations within a major, which are not reflected here.

Most popular majors. This will give you an idea of whether a substantial number of students are completing a major in an area that is of interest to you. This list is based on the percentage of students who were awarded degrees in each of the general categories listed in the 2007-08 academic year.

Computing on campus. Whether you bring your own computer to campus, or plan on using college-provided workstations, you'll want to know what technological support the college provides for student use, and whether the college requires you to bring your own PC or laptop. This section lists the number of workstations available for student use and where they're located; whether dorms are wired for high-speed Internet access and/or linked to the campus network; if there is a wireless network; if there's online course registration, an online library or student Web hosting; and whether commuter students can link to the campus network.

Student life. If you attend the college, you will need to know if it requires enrollees to attend freshman orientation, and if it has policies and regulations governing student behavior.

If on-campus housing is available — whether it's in the form of dormitories, apartments, fraternity/sorority housing or cooperative housing — it will be indicated here. Most dormitories today are coeducational, but many colleges offer single-sex accommodations either in separate buildings or separate floors. Some colleges are now also offering "substance-free" or "wellness" dormitories, whose residents pledge not to use alcohol, tobacco or any illegal drugs. This section also indicates if on-campus housing is guaranteed for freshmen, or for all four years; and the policies and deadlines for deposits.

Most colleges have provided a selective list of student activities sponsored by the institution. Read the list carefully to see if it reflects the type of student organizations and opportunities of interest to you.

Athletics. Intercollegiate and intramural sports available at the college are listed here, along with the team name. Sports offered for men or women only are indicated by (M) or (W). The athletic association to which the college belongs also is indicated. If you want to know which colleges play in the NCAA and at what division level, see the index at the back of this book titled "NCAA sports by division," where you'll see each college listed by sport.

Student services. This section lists the college's basic range of services for students. Among these are health, personal counseling, services for adult students, student employment services, placement service for graduates, veterans' counseling and on-campus day care. This section also lists special services/facilities for learning disabled students and those with visual, speech or hearing impairments.

Contact. The last item in each description provides the admissions office's e-mail address, telephone and fax numbers, the name and/or title of the admissions director, and the mailing address of the college office to contact for further information and applications.

KNOW THE LINGO

NCAA — The National Collegiate Athletic Association. This is the largest collegiate athletic association, and it oversees the most athletic scholarship money. The NCAA governs league play in 23 championship sports.

NAIA — The National Association of Intercollegiate Athletics. Its members are mostly small colleges, offering 13 sports.

NJCAA — The National Junior College Athletic Association. NJCAA members are all two-year community or junior colleges.

USCAA — United States Collegiate Athletic Association. USCAA's members are primarily very small colleges.

NCCAA — National Christian College Athletic Association. NCCAA sponsors league play among Bible colleges and other Christian-oriented institutions.

Brief Descriptions

The 383 colleges that did not respond to our Annual Survey of Colleges are described in brief with the following information: name, city, state, college type, accreditation, location and calendar. Annual costs and financial aid information are provided, if available. The addresses to contact for further information are also listed.

Tables and Indexes

The tables and indexes in the back of this book are a useful tool to find colleges quickly and zero in on the schools that interest you.

Early Application and Wait-List Outcomes

If you are considering applying to a college early, the Early Decision and Early Action table on page 2083 shows application deadlines and notification dates for early application programs, as well as the number of students who applied and were admitted last year under those policies.

If you find that you have been placed on a college's wait list for acceptance, consult the wait list table on page 2095. It will give you a sense of your chances, by showing how many students were placed on the wait list last year, how many accepted their place on the list, and how many were eventually admitted from the list.

College Indexes

You can use the college indexes to quickly find schools that interest you. In most of the indexes, colleges are listed alphabetically by state because, for many students, geographic location is a primary requirement. Colleges that are part of a system are listed alphabetically under the system name.

The following explanation of index terms may help you decide whether a certain type of college or a special program or policy interests you.

College type

KNOW THE LINGO

There are so many **types of specialized colleges** that we didn't have room to describe them all here. If you'd like to know more about a specific type of college, see the glossary that begins on page 40.

Liberal arts. Sometimes known as arts and sciences. The study of liberal arts is intended to develop general knowledge and reasoning ability as opposed to specific preparation for a career. Most liberal arts colleges are privately controlled. They generally don't offer as many majors in the technical or scientific disciplines as comprehensive colleges or universities.

Upper-division. Offer the last two years of undergraduate study (junior and senior courses only), usually in specialized programs leading to the bachelor's degree. Students generally transfer to upper-division colleges after completing an associate degree or after finishing their second year of study at a four-year college.

Specialized. Concentrate their offerings in one or two specific areas, such as business or engineering. Students who enroll at specialized colleges generally have a precise idea of what they want to study.

Special characteristics

Colleges for men/women. Some of these colleges may enroll a few women or men, but their student bodies are predominantly of one sex.

Colleges with religious affiliations. Lists each college under the official name of the denomination with which it is affiliated. Student life at some colleges is greatly influenced by the religious affiliation. At other colleges, the affiliation may be historic only, having little influence on college life.

Historically black colleges. Identifies historically or predominantly black colleges that are committed to educating African American students. The information was obtained from the National Association for Equal Opportunity in Higher Education and the U.S. government.

Hispanic-serving colleges. Identifies colleges where Hispanic students comprise at least 25 percent of the total full-time undergraduate enrollment. The information was obtained from the Hispanic Association of Colleges and Universities (HACU).

Tribal colleges. Identifies colleges committed to serving geographically isolated populations of Native Americans. The information was obtained from the Carnegie Classification of Institutions of Higher Education.

Undergraduate enrollment size

The number of students at a college helps determine its environment.

Very small. Fewer than 750 undergraduates.

Small. 750 to 1,999 undergraduates.

Medium to large. 2,000 to 7,499 undergraduates.

Large. 7,500 to 14,999 undergraduates.

Very large. 15,000 or more undergraduates.

Admissions selectivity

Admit under 50 percent, 50-75 percent, over 75 percent. Colleges in three categories of selectivity that limit admission to applicants who meet specific requirements.

Open admissions. Colleges that admit virtually all applicants with a high school diploma or its equivalent, as long as space is available.

Many public institutions offer open admissions to state residents but have selective admissions requirements for out-of-state students or to selected programs; check the college descriptions to see what applies.

Admissions/placement policies

No closing date. These colleges will accept applications up to the time of registration.

SAT Subject Test required/recommended. These two indexes list colleges that require or recommend that applicants take one or more

SAT Subject Tests™ for admission. The college descriptions provide more detailed information.

Colleges that offer ROTC

The U.S. armed forces offer Reserve Officers' Training Corps programs that prepare candidates for commissions in the Air Force, Army and Navy (Naval ROTC includes the Marine Corps). These programs are offered either at the colleges listed in the index or at cooperating institutions. ROTC programs may take either two or four years to complete. Use this index, organized by branch of service, to find colleges that offer the ROTC program of interest to you.

KEEP IN MIND

The **NCAA sports indexes** only list colleges that offer sports for which the NCAA holds a championship. There are NCAA sports that don't have a championship, such as men's rowing. And remember that many colleges offer sports through a different association (NAIA or NJCAA), or offer intramural play.

Colleges with NCAA sports

Lists National Collegiate Athletic Association (NCAA) championship sports by division level and the colleges, state by state, that offer them. Also indicates whether each sport is available for men only or for women only. (Crew is an NCAA sport for women only; use the college search on collegeboard.com to find colleges that offer crew for men.) To be an NCAA member, colleges must offer at least four sports and have at least one in each season (fall, winter and spring).

Alphabetical index of colleges

Lists the name and state abbreviation for every institution in the *Handbook*. If a name has changed, the old name is cross-referenced to the new name.

About accreditation

Every college and university in this book is accredited by an agency recognized by the U.S. Department of Education. That means you can trust that any of them will give you an education that meets basic standards for college-level study, that your studies will qualify for federal need-based financial aid and/or federal education tax breaks, and that the degree you will earn at the end of your studies will be recognized by future employers.

What Is Accreditation?

Accreditation is a voluntary process of peer review and self-regulation. The standards for each accrediting agency are slightly different but, generally, each agency ensures that its members meet basic standards in their administrative procedures, physical facilities and the quality of their academic programs.

The agencies listed on page 12 are *regional* and *national* agencies that accredit entire institutions. In majors that lead to a professional certification — such as nursing, engineering or teacher education — there may also be *specialized* agencies that accredit just one program, department or school at the college. For example, the Accreditation Board for Engineering and Technology (ABET) accredits engineering and engineering technology programs. In addition to guaranteeing the academic quality of programs, these specialized agencies often have a guidance component that helps university students make the transition to professional careers. You can find more information about specialized accrediting agencies in the College Board's *Book of Majors*, or at the Council for Higher Education Accreditation's Web site (www.chea.org).

GOOD TO KNOW

Every college contained in the *College Handbook* and collegeboard.com's College Search has been accredited by either a national or regional accrediting agency recognized by the U.S. Department of Education.

What Does Accreditation Mean to Me?

GOOD TO KNOW

Only colleges that are accredited by an agency recognized by the U.S. Department of Education may distribute **federal financial aid** to their students.

If you attend an accredited college, you can be sure that:

- You will be able to use federal student aid (Title IV money) to help pay for your costs if you qualify based on financial need.
- Your tuition will qualify you for federal income tax deductions and/or credits (if you meet other conditions).
- Academic credits you earn there are eligible to transfer to another accredited college.
- Employers and professional licensing boards will recognize the degree you earn as an academic credential, as will graduate schools and other academic institutions to which you may apply.

You should, however, understand what accreditation *doesn't* mean:

- There's no guarantee that you will receive federal need-based financial aid just by attending any college, even if it's accredited.
- Regional and national accreditation ensures that every academic program at the college meets standards, but that doesn't mean that the quality of every program at the college is equal.
- If you're applying for transfer from one undergraduate institution to another, there's no guarantee that all your credits will count toward the graduation requirements of the college where you plan to finish your degree. If you plan to attend a lower-division college for your first two years of study and then go on to earn a bachelor's degree, be sure to talk to the transfer counselor there before enrolling in courses.
- Similarly, there's no guarantee that graduate schools or employers will see your undergraduate course of study as appropriate preparation for the demands of their program or job requirements.

REGIONAL ACCREDITING ASSOCIATIONS

Middle States Commission on Higher Education
3624 Market Street
Philadelphia, PA 19104-2680
www.msche.org

Delaware, District of Columbia, Maryland, New Jersey, New York, Pennsylvania, Puerto Rico, Virgin Islands

New England Association of Schools and Colleges
209 Burlington Road, Suite 201
Bedford, MA 01730-1433
www.neasc.org

Connecticut, Maine, Massachusetts, New Hampshire, Rhode Island, Vermont

North Central Association of Colleges and Schools
30 North LaSalle Street, Suite 2400
Chicago, IL 60602-2504
www.ncahigherlearningcommission.org

Arizona, Arkansas, Colorado, Illinois, Indiana, Iowa, Kansas, Michigan, Minnesota, Missouri, Nebraska, New Mexico, North Dakota, Ohio, Oklahoma, South Dakota, West Virginia, Wisconsin, Wyoming

Northwest Association of Accredited Schools
1510 Robert Street, Suite 103
Boise, ID 83705-5194
www.northwestaccreditation.org

Alaska, Idaho, Montana, Nevada, Oregon, Utah, Washington

Southern Association of Colleges and Schools
1866 Southern Lane
Decatur, GA 30033-4097
www.sacs.org

Alabama, Florida, Georgia, Kentucky, Louisiana, Mississippi, North Carolina, South Carolina, Tennessee, Texas, Virginia

Western Association of Schools and Colleges
Accrediting Commission for Senior Colleges and Universities
985 Atlantic Avenue, Suite 100
Alameda, CA 94501
www.wascsenior.org

Accrediting Commission for Community and Junior Colleges
10 Commercial Boulevard, Suite 204
Novato, CA 94949
www.accjc.org

American Samoa, California, Guam, Hawaii, Trust Territory of the Pacific

New York Board of Regents
Office of College and University Evaluation
New York State Education Department
5 North Mezzanine
Albany, NY 12234
www.regents.nysed.gov

NATIONAL ACCREDITING ASSOCIATIONS

ACICS — **Accrediting Council for Independent Colleges and Schools**
750 First Street NE, Suite 980
Washington, DC 20002-4241
www.acics.org

ACCSCT — **Accrediting Commission of Career Schools/Colleges of Technology**
2101 Wilson Boulevard, Suite 302
Arlington, VA 22201
www.accsct.org

ABHE — **Association for Biblical Higher Education**
5575 S. Semoran Boulevard, Suite 26
Orlando, FL 32822-1781
www.abhe.org

AARTS — **Association of Advanced Rabbinical and Talmudic Schools**
11 Broadway, Suite 405
New York, NY 10004

ATS — **Association of Theological Schools in the United States and Canada**
10 Summit Park Drive
Pittsburgh, PA 15275-1110
www.ats.edu

DETC — **Distance Education and Training Council**
1601 18th Street NW, Suite 2
Washington, DC 20009
www.detc.org

Selecting colleges

There are more than 3,800 accredited colleges in the United States. This book will help you get an idea of the types of colleges you're interested in attending and learn more about colleges that fall into those categories. From there, you can create a list of colleges you would like to learn more about, and start requesting information from them, visiting their Web sites, and (if you can) visiting their campuses. By December of your senior year, you should have your choices narrowed down to a final list of four to eight colleges to which you want to apply.

KNOW THE LINGO

"Target" school — a college you'd like to attend that will be somewhat difficult for you to get in. Usually a college where your GPA and standardized test scores would be about average. Most students apply to between two and four target schools.

"Reach" school — a college you'd like to attend, but will be difficult for you to get in. Your GPA and test scores may be below average for this school, but some other aspect of your application may make up for that. You should apply to one or two reach schools.

"Safety" school — a college you'd like to attend that's also sure to accept you. You should apply to at least one safety school.

Finding Your Fit

Every college is unique in some way. And everybody has different interests, ambitions and needs. When investigating colleges, you will probably look for different things than your friends, parents and siblings did when they applied. But there are some "big picture" elements that everyone, including you, should consider.

Colleges fall into broad categories — small and large, liberal arts and professionally oriented, academically selective and open admissions. There are also personal criteria you need to consider, such as whether a college is in your hometown or a thousand miles away.

Type of Institution

This will give you a sense of how the college organizes its academic departments. Different types of institutions include:

Liberal arts colleges offer a broad base of courses in the humanities, social sciences and natural sciences. Most are private and focus mainly on undergraduate students. Classes tend to be small, and personal attention is available. An education at a liberal arts college will prepare you for a broad range of career and graduate school options.

Community and junior colleges offer a degree after the completion of two years of full-time study. They frequently offer technical programs that prepare you for immediate entry into the job market. To learn more about the benefits of attending a community college, read "About Community Colleges" on page 20.

Agricultural colleges, technical schools and professional institutes emphasize preparation for specific careers. Examples include art institutes and music conservatories, Bible colleges, business colleges, schools of health science, seminaries and rabbinical yeshivas, and teachers colleges.

Universities are generally bigger than colleges and offer more majors and research facilities. Classes in introductory subjects may have hundreds of students, and some classes may be taught by graduate students.

Most universities are subdivided into colleges or schools. For example, a state university might have a large college of liberal arts, a school of engineering and applied sciences, a small school of nursing, a teachers college and several graduate schools all on the same campus.

Different universities have different rules for whether you can, for example, take a computer science course offered by the engineering school while enrolled in the liberal arts college. Generally, the different colleges of a university share campus facilities (such as dorms and dining halls) and some research facilities (such as libraries), and a university-wide administration handles admissions, financial aid and similar services for the various colleges.

GOOD TO KNOW

When **applying to a university**, applicants typically have to **choose a specific college** to which they want to apply. Each college may have its own admissions requirements. Not all colleges within a university will admit applicants coming out of high school — some may be for graduate study only, and some may be upper-division colleges.

Size of the Student Body and Faculty

Size will affect many of your opportunities and experiences, including:

- the range of academic majors offered;
- the possibilities for extracurricular activities and athletics;
- the amount of personal attention you'll receive from faculty, administrators and other students; and
- the availability and size of academic facilities such as laboratories, libraries and art studios.

When considering size, be sure to look beyond the raw number of students attending. For example, perhaps you're considering a large university, but you'll be applying to its much smaller school of health sciences.

Also remember to investigate not just the number of faculty, but also how accessible faculty members are to students. You can get a rough sense of this from the "class size" entry in the *Handbook* descriptions, but if you are already interested in a particular major or department, it really helps to visit the campus and talk to students who are enrolled in that program.

Location

Do you want to go home frequently, or do you see this as a time to experience a new part of the country? Perhaps you like an urban environment with access to museums, ethnic food or major league ball games. Or maybe you hope for easy access to the outdoors or the serenity of a small town.

Academic Quality

The easiest way to measure a school's quality and the satisfaction of its students is to learn the percentage of students who return after the first year and the percentage of entering students who remain to graduate. Comparatively good retention and graduation rates are indicators that responsible academic, social and financial support systems exist for most students. These figures are reported in the *Handbook* descriptions. On average nationwide, 55 percent of four-year college students graduate from the same institution within six years or less.

One of the best ways to research a college's reputation is by talking to people who are familiar with colleges or the fields that interest you. Ask your parents if anyone they know went to one of the colleges on your short list. Talk to your school counselor — he or she probably knows quite a bit about local colleges and nationally known universities. Talk to your teachers — they might know the academic reputations of departments that relate to their teaching field. You can also research the reputations of colleges on the Internet, but beware — not everyone on the Internet is an expert, and sometimes rumors get passed along as fact.

If you already know what subjects you want to study, research the strengths of those schools or departments at the colleges and universities in which you're interested. One way to do this is to look at their departmental Web sites for the following:

- Are there a lot of courses offered, or just a few?
- Do the courses offered concentrate on one subfield within the major? This is not necessarily a bad thing, but it could tell you that the department is strong in some areas and weak in others.
- Do most of the professors have terminal degrees in their field? Usually the Ph.D. is the terminal degree, but in some fields, it's another graduate degree.
- The Web site may also tell you about research and scholarship that professors are doing, work that undergraduate students are doing, or the careers of recent alumni.

These are general questions that would apply to any department. For questions to ask colleges about a specific major, see the College Board's *Book of Majors*. It contains profiles of undergraduate majors, and each profile has a list of things to look for in a department offering that major.

GOOD TO KNOW

If you're still **undecided about your college major**, relax — just pick an academically balanced institution that offers a range of majors and programs, and take courses in subjects you find intriguing. Most colleges offer advising or mentoring to help you find a focus.

Campus Life

Consider what your college life will be like beyond the classroom. Aim for a balance between academics, activities and social life. In your research, try to learn the answers to these questions:

- What extracurricular activities, athletics and special activities are available?
- Does the community around the college offer interesting outlets for students?
- Are students welcomed by the surrounding community?
- Is there a congregation of my faith on campus? Are there student groups based around my ethnic group or national culture?
- Is the college religiously affiliated? If so, how does that affiliation affect student life — for example, is attendance at services required?
- How do fraternities and sororities influence campus life?
- Is housing guaranteed? How are dorms assigned? (For more about housing options, see page 38.)

You can learn the answers to many of these questions by reading the college profiles in this book, but for others, you may have to do more in-depth research, such as visiting the college's Web site or its campus.

Can I Afford this College?

Today's college price tags make cost an important consideration for most students. At the same time, most colleges work to ensure that academically qualified students from every economic circumstance can find financial aid. Be sure to look beyond the price tag in considering cost. The *Handbook* descriptions give you a general idea of the college's cost and its financial aid packages. For more detailed "cost profiles" of the colleges, and for general advice about financial aid, see the College Board's *Getting Financial Aid*, which is a companion volume to this book.

EXPERT ADVICE

"Students should look at a school because it's the right fit for them academically, socially, spiritually and geographically. **Is cost an important part?** Yes. It's a consideration, but only one among many."

— Bonnie Lee Behm, Director of Financial Assistance, Villanova University

Where Can I Get In?

Of course, finding a college that's the right fit for you is only half of the equation. Unless you're applying to a college with an open admissions policy, you also have to convince the admissions reviewers that you really are a good fit.

What Are Colleges Looking For?

When they review your application, college admissions officers want to see, foremost, "students who have challenged themselves academically," says Martha Pitts, the director of admissions at the University of Oregon. But they don't just want to see good grades; they also want to make sure that candidates will add something positive to the campus community. Mike Sexton,

Where to Find More Information

Once you've created a list of colleges you'd like to learn more about, you should try to get information from as many sources as possible. Different people will tell you different things about colleges, so the more the merrier!

✔ **Your school counselor** can tell you about colleges and let you know when college fairs or visits from admissions recruiters are coming to your school. He or she may also have a file of college course catalogs, viewbooks and other literature.

✔ **Visiting admissions staff** who come to your school — either by themselves or as part of a large college fair — can tell you more about the college they represent and its application process.

✔ **College Web sites and guidebooks** offer a wealth of information about majors offered, activities and life on campus.

✔ **Returning graduates** who went to your school and come home for breaks will probably be eager to tell you all about their experiences.

✔ **Campus visits** are a chance to see the campus and its dorms, libraries and other facilities in person; talk to admissions officers (whether informally or in an interview); observe classes and talk to students; and much more. Try to visit the campus while classes are in session. For tips on planning a visit, read the articles in the "Find a College" section of www.collegeboard.com, or get *Campus Visits & College Interviews* by Zola Dincin Schneider (College Board, 2002).

the dean of admissions at Lewis & Clark College, puts it this way: He looks at the applications for "a spark that tells us they'll be good roommates, good lab partners, good to have in class."

One thing you should never do is try to guess what the admissions committee is looking for and try to tailor your application to it. Admissions officers read thousands of applications every year, and they can almost instantly tell feigned interest in a college or a false presentation of oneself from the real thing.

Your transcript is the most important thing

There it is, in large type, but it bears repeating: Your high school transcript is the most important thing for your application success. Colleges want to see that you've challenged yourself academically throughout high school and that you are willing to put academics first for the next two to four years.

Be aware that admissions staff won't just look at the grades on your transcript. They will look at which courses you took, and the grade trend over four years. For example, if you barely passed Intro to Biology as a freshman, but then turned around and got a B in AP Biology as a junior, colleges will consider that a plus. On the other hand, if you've been getting steady C's in English for the last three years, colleges may wonder why you haven't improved.

EXPERT ADVICE

"**If students try to force themselves to look like a fit** to the admissions committee, that's like putting square pegs in round holes — they will be unhappy."

— Deren Finks, former Dean of Admission and Financial Aid, Harvey Mudd College

A related factor that admissions officers look for is an upward trend in the difficulty of your course work. Sexton says he becomes concerned when students "start taking a lighter load senior year. I can see why they would do it sometimes, but for some people, it's going to close doors." Don't feel you need to suffocate yourself with too many courses and extracurriculars, but don't try to cruise through your senior year either.

EXPERT ADVICE

"**The first thing most colleges and universities will consider** will be the high school courses a student chose. Are they challenging? Are they college-prep, honors or AP courses?"

— Mary Ellen Anderson, Director of Admissions, Indiana University-Bloomington

Test scores are just part of the picture

Your scores on the admissions tests can be important, but generally they're not as important as your high school transcript. Most often, admissions officers will use your test scores to supplement your transcript or help them interpret it.

Although grades earned in high school courses are very important, they don't always mean the same thing. An A earned in the same course taught by different teachers in your school may not represent exactly the same amount of work, the same teaching or the same level of learning. Likewise, an A earned in the same course but in different schools and different parts of the country may not really be the same. That's where standardized tests can help.

If you've already taken an admissions test (e.g., the SAT), look at your scores the same way the admissions committee will look at them — objectively. They don't represent all that you've achieved or will achieve. The scores are one indicator of how far along you are right now in developing the skills you need for college and a career. In deciding where to apply to college, it's helpful to compare your scores to those of the mid-50 percent score range of freshmen who enrolled the previous year in the colleges you're considering. You'll find this information in the section titled "freshman class profile" of each four-year college description. If your scores compare favorably, you're on your way to finding the right match. But if your scores are higher or lower, it's not necessarily a mismatch. Only 50 out of every 100 freshmen had scores in that range, which means 25 had higher scores and 25 had lower scores. You may be well suited for this college in other important ways. You'll be better able to decide after reading the entire college description, visiting the college's Web site and (if possible) visiting the campus.

Personality can go a long way

Very few colleges assess applications using just transcripts and test scores. Most will ask for information about your involvement in extracurricular activities, recommendations from your teachers, a recommendation from your counselor, and a brief application essay. Some will ask for an interview as well. A few will ask for recommendations from someone who is not on your school faculty, for example, a minister, employer or friend.

What all of these application components have in common is that they help admissions officers look "beyond the numbers" and see what kind of person you are, and how you might contribute to their campus community. They won't be the first, or most important, thing the college looks at, but they can help round out your application and may help the admissions committee decide between you and several equally qualified candidates.

Here's a closer look at each of the personal factors colleges usually look at:

Recommendations. Recommendations will give the college a sense of your overall attitude toward learning, your character and the context for the grades on your transcript. Do you have a real passion for mathematics? Did you try really hard and improve over the year to get that "B" in U.S. History? Or could you have been an "A" student if you had taken the class more seriously? For tips on choosing which teachers to ask for recommendations, and how to ask them, see pages 27 and 28.

GOOD TO KNOW

You can use the college descriptions in this *Handbook* to learn their course requirements and what they recommend beyond these requirements. **This is your best indication of whether you can get in:** Do you have the lab science courses and foreign language study they require? Have you settled for the required minimum of history and social sciences, or have you taken their full recommendation? You can also learn about the high school GPAs of last year's entering class, and how those students were ranked in their high schools.

Extracurriculars. Your involvement in extracurricular activities — whether they're sports, a part-time job, volunteering in your community, the school play, the yearbook or something entirely different — will tell the college about how active you are in your community. From that, they'll have a good picture of your leadership potential and how likely you are to contribute to their own campus community. They'll also have a sense of how much time you spend on nonschool work, which gives them a context for reading your grades. Generally, it's best to dedicate yourself to a few extracurricular activities in which you're really interested. Making minor contributions to 10 different activities doesn't look as impressive as becoming a leader of one club that you're passionate about. Similarly, changing activities every semester makes you look fickle; it's better to show some consistency.

Essays. Admissions officers use application essays to learn how creative you are, how well you can write and, sometimes, whether you're truly interested in attending their college. They are the most subjective of all the components of an application, but they are also the one component over which you have total control. For more about how applications are used by admissions officials, and tips on writing your essays, read *The College Application Essay* by Sarah Myers McGinty (College Board, 2004).

GOOD TO KNOW

Your school counselor will send the colleges to which you apply a **profile of your high school**, which will list what courses are offered, describe high school diploma requirements and generally give admissions officers an overview of the academic program at your school. From this, **colleges will know whether you haven't taken the most rigorous courses available** — or, for that matter, if you've done extremely well despite a gap in your school's academic program.

Interviews. Interviews are rarely required and usually don't carry a great deal of weight in the overall application. If you are asked to come to an interview, you should look at it as an opportunity to put a personal face on your application, tell the college more about yourself, and learn more about whether the college would be a good fit for you. If you are shy, don't worry — no one ever gets rejected by a college because of a bad interview. For more about interviews, including checklists of questions to expect and questions you should ask, read *Campus Visits & College Interviews* by Zola Dincin Schneider (College Board, 2002).

How "interested" are you?

As college admissions have become more competitive, colleges have begun to weigh an additional factor along with the other parts of the application: "demonstrated interest." What this means is that admissions officials try to determine whether, if they accept you, you will enroll at their college.

Interest in a college is not something you should try to fake — if you have to pretend to want to go to a college, you won't be happy going there, so your application is a waste of time. If you really want to go to a college, your interest will show itself naturally, and colleges will be able to tell. That said, here are some things that colleges usually look for when they try to gauge your level of interest:

- Is your application essay customized to their college, or does it seem like a generic essay that you could have sent to any college?
- Did you write the college asking for information about their programs?
- Have you talked to any admissions officers from the college — at your high school, via e-mail, or when visiting the campus?
- If you interview with the college, do you ask basic questions that you could have answered by reading their Web site, or do you ask in-depth questions that show that you've already researched the college?

Like the personal factors, your level of interest in the college isn't nearly as important as the courses you've taken, your grades or your test scores. But if the admissions committee is trying to decide between you and another equally qualified candidate, it could tip your application one way or the other.

About Community Colleges

Do you want a quick start to a career path? Do you need to cut the cost of a four-year college degree? Do you want to sharpen your study skills before enrolling at a university? Do you need to attend classes at night or on weekends? Do you want to attend a college close to home?

If you said yes to even one question above, check out your options at a community college (CC). You won't be alone — 45 percent of all first-time freshmen go to two-year colleges. One reason: These institutions offer two kinds of learning.

- If your goal is a four-year degree, you can earn a two-year associate degree at a low-cost community college, then transfer to a four-year college as a junior.
- If your goal is career training, you can earn an occupational degree or certificate in two years or less, then start working immediately in many high-demand fields (like health care or computer technology).

A STUDENT'S STORY

"I'm getting the basics out of the way at an inexpensive cost," says Samantha Mattioli, a freshman at Westchester Community College in Valhalla, N.Y. Sam, who is majoring in business management, says, "**I won't have a lot of debt** when I finish my associate degree." That will free up funds for her second degree, in massage therapy — step two toward Sam's goal of running her own massage therapy business.

Fit Your Education to Your Needs

A community college offers many advantages in terms of academic preparation for upper-division university work.

If you need more academic preparation, a community college can offer a leg up to achieving your goals. New students usually take placement tests in reading, writing and math. Those who need to build skills can take catch-up courses, then — over time — move into a regular academic program.

If your high school grades aren't the greatest, but a four-year college is your goal, taking community college courses — and building a record of good grades — can polish your academic record. Then you can transfer. (But don't expect it to be easy — community college courses are no different than four-year college courses.)

If you're achievement oriented, community colleges offer challenging honors courses. Honors programs not only stimulate you but also offer mentoring and networking opportunities. They will also make you a strong candidate for transfer to a four-year college.

If English is your second language, community colleges have special programs that will help you build your English skills.

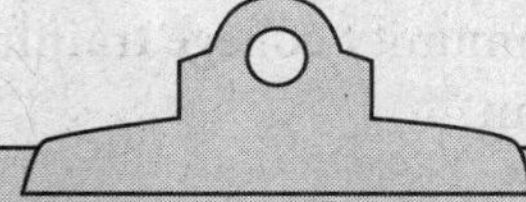

Keep on Track at a Community College

If you go to a community college or junior college, it's important for you to keep your goals in mind as you choose courses.

PLANNING TO TRANSFER TO A FOUR-YEAR COLLEGE?

- ✔ Talk to advisers at the community college. Most public CCs offer two-year course plans that fulfill requirements at nearby colleges. To transfer without losing credits, follow those plans!
- ✔ Talk to advisers at the four-year college you hope to attend, too. They may have inside info.
- ✔ Make sure you've fulfilled requirements to declare a major at the four-year college — not just the general admissions requirements. For example, Biology 101 at your CC may transfer, but might not be enough preparation for you to take the junior-level courses in the chemistry major.
- ✔ Don't self-advise! If you're not sure whether a course will transfer, ask. Wrong courses waste your time and money, and that's discouraging.
- ✔ Keep going. Don't "gap" your education, taking time out between semesters or colleges. Once you begin, keep at it — that's the path to getting your four-year degree.

TRAINING FOR AN OCCUPATION?

Make sure your degree or certificate can lead to employment.

- ✔ Talk to advisers at your community college, but don't just accept claims that when you graduate, you'll get a job.
- ✔ Ask how many students have gone straight from the college to the workforce in recent years, what jobs they got, and with which employers.
- ✔ Before you enroll, talk to potential employers in the outside world, too.

Learn on Your Schedule

Many CC students have jobs and family responsibilities. Scheduling classes may be a big challenge. So community colleges tend to offer day, night and weekend courses. They have pioneered new teaching methods, too. Some offer online courses (distance learning), combine Internet and classroom learning, give interactive TV courses, condense semester courses into a shorter time frame, and more.

Community College Can Be a Ticket to Hot Job Markets

With two years or less of community college training, you can earn an occupational degree or certificate in

- Fast-growing health fields
- The computer world
- New and emerging fields

A community college may be the best route to many high-demand jobs that require two-year degrees not available at four-year colleges. Look for CC courses in construction technology, culinary arts, law enforcement and biotechnology. With homeland security in the news, colleges are training many first responders.

Many community colleges also have certificate options that provide intensive training in a specialized field like computer-assisted drafting, food service technology or paralegal studies. These certificates usually take six months to a year to complete.

CCs often focus on preparing people to work in local industries.

Do you want work in your area? Look for programs like these in local community colleges:

Joliet, Ill. Joliet Junior College is nationally known for its agriculture and horticulture programs. Farming is big business in the Midwest, and Joliet grads have job offers waiting. Students learn at a 100-acre college farm and do paid internships for credit.

Tucson, Az. Home to many air-industry businesses, Pima Community College boasts an FAA-certified aviation tech program that prepares students to repair the structure, "airframe" and power plants of commercial jetliners. Pima's job placement record for successful grads of the program is over 95 percent.

Not bad! But also, not the case at every CC or in every field. So research your CC and your local job markets like crazy — just as you'd research a four-year college.

GOOD TO KNOW

Income and career results: Researchers from the University of Illinois at Chicago and Penn State compared college grads from similar backgrounds who began college in two-year and in four-year institutions. On average, the two groups ended up with similar salaries in careers that offered similar job prestige, stability and satisfaction.

Applying to colleges

After you've gone through some exploration and preliminary research, it's time to sit down and apply! In order to successfully apply, you'll need to budget and manage your time, follow each college's instructions to a T and, most important, take a good hard look at yourself and your interests.

Managing Your Time

Most deadlines for regular admissions applications are due in early January or February, and most early application deadlines are in November. For any application, you'll need to fill out forms and request that your transcript and standardized test scores be sent to the college. For most applications to selective colleges, you'll also need to ask teachers and your counselor for recommendations, write an essay or personal statement, and maybe even schedule an interview with the admissions office. You may also want to take the SAT or SAT Subject Tests in November or December. Meanwhile, you'll be in the middle of your senior year, with academic, extracurricular and social commitments all over your calendar.

The first thing you should do once you decide to which colleges you're applying is to make a checklist of all the deadlines and tasks you'll have to accomplish for the applications. Remember to budget time for other people to do things. Teachers won't write recommendations overnight, and testing organizations will need a few weeks to send official score reports to colleges.

For some sample checklists and a college application calendar, read the articles in the "Apply to College" section of www.collegeboard.com. For more help, use the My Organizer feature of the site, which will help you plan and remind you of upcoming deadlines, or read *Get It Together for College: A Planner to Help You Get Organized and Get In* (College Board, 2008).

JUNIOR YEAR CALENDAR

THE SUMMER BEFORE

- **Read** interesting books — no matter what you select as a major in college, you'll need a good vocabulary and strong reading comprehension skills. Reading is also one of the best ways to get ready.
- **Get a social security number** if you don't already have one — you'll need it for your college applications.
- **Think about yourself.** What are you curious about — nature and animals? People and places? Math and science? What do you like to do — working with your hands or with computers? Helping people? Being outdoors? Knowing the basics about yourself will help you make the right college choices.
- **Talk to your family and friends** about college and your goals. They know you best and will have good insights.

SEPTEMBER

- **Meet with your school counselor** to make sure you are taking the courses that colleges look for.
- **Resolve to get the best grades** you can this year. The payoff will be more colleges to choose from, and a better chance for scholarship money.
- **Pick up the *Official Student Guide to the PSAT/NMSQT®*** from your guidance office and take the practice test (you'll take the real test in October).
- Get involved in an **extracurricular activity**.
- Find out if your school will have a **college night**.

OCTOBER

- Take the **PSAT/NMSQT**.
- Attend a **college fair**.
- Begin looking through the *College Handbook* — **start a preliminary list of colleges** that might interest you.
- Start to **learn about financial aid**. Use the College Board's *Getting Financial Aid* to learn how it works, and the financial aid calculators at **www.collegeboard.com** to estimate how much aid you might receive.

NOVEMBER

- Begin to **research scholarships** — use the College Board's *Scholarship Handbook* to find out about deadlines and eligibility requirements.
- **Learn about the SAT**. Go to collegeboard.com. Also, pick up the SAT Registration Guide at your guidance office.
- If you are planning to major in the arts (drama, music, fine art), ask your teachers about requirements for a **portfolio or audition**.

DECEMBER

- Review your **PSAT/NMSQT Score Report** with your school counselor. Sign up for your free My College QuickStart™ account on collegeboard.com/quickstart.
- Spend time over the holidays to **think about what kind of college** you want. Big or small? Far away or close to home? **Make a list** of the college features that are important to you.
- **Begin preparing for the SAT.** Learn more about **SAT** practice tools on **collegeboard.com**.

JANUARY

- **Meet with your school counselor** to talk about the colleges in which you are interested, what entrance exams you should take, and when you should take them.
- If English is not your primary language, decide when to take the **TOEFL** test.
- Start thinking about **what you want to study in college**. Use resources like the College Board's *Book of Majors* and My College QuickStart™.
- **Register for the SAT** if you want to take it in **March**.

FEBRUARY

- Think about which teachers you will ask to write **letters of recommendation**.
- If you're in Advanced Placement® (AP®) courses, **register for AP Exams** given in May.
- Ask your counselor or teacher about taking the **SAT Subject Tests™** in the spring. You should take them while course material is still fresh in your mind.

MARCH

- **Register for the SAT and/or SAT Subject Tests** if you want to take them in **May**.
- **Narrow your college list** to a reasonable number. Explore the colleges' Web sites, read their brochures and catalogues, and talk to your family and friends.
- **Practice the SAT**. Ask your school counselor for the **SAT Preparation Booklet™** — it's free and offers sample question for the SAT Subject Tests. Download a free official practice test from **collegeboard.com**.

APRIL

- **Register for the SAT and/or SAT Subject Tests** if you want to take them in **June**.
- **Plan courses for your senior year.** Make sure you are going to meet the high school course requirements for your top-choice colleges.
- **Plan campus visits.** It's best to go when classes are in session. Start with colleges that are close by.

MAY

- If you are considering **military academies or ROTC** scholarships, contact your counselor before leaving school for the summer.
- Talk to your counselor about **NCAA requirements** if you want to play Division I or II sports in college.
- Start looking for a **summer job or volunteer work** — the good ones go fast.

SENIOR YEAR CALENDAR

THE SUMMER BEFORE

- **Register for the SAT and/or SAT Subject Tests** if you want to take them in **October or November**.
- If you want to play a NCAA Division I or II sport in college, **register with the NCAA Eligibility Center (www.ncaaclearinghouse.net)**.
- **Visit colleges** on your list. Call ahead for the campus tour schedule.
- Begin working on your **college application essays**.
- Find out about **local scholarships** offered by church groups, civic associations and businesses in your area.
- **Write a résumé** (accomplishments, activities and work experiences) to help you later with your college applications.
- **Request college application forms** if you aren't going to apply online.

SEPTEMBER

- Meet with your school counselor to **finalize your list of colleges**. Be sure your list includes "safety," "reach" and "target" schools.
- **Start a checklist** of all application requirements, deadlines, fees, etc.
- If you can't afford SAT application fees, your counselor can help you request a **fee waiver**.
- Set up **final campus visits and interviews**; attend open houses at colleges that interest you.
- Find out if there will be a **family financial aid night** at your school or elsewhere in your area this fall, and put it on your calendar.

OCTOBER

- **Register for the SAT and/or SAT Subject Tests** if you want to take them in **December or January**.
- If you are going to apply under an **Early Decision or Early Action** plan, get started now.
- **Ask for letters of recommendation** from your counselor, teachers, coaches or employers.
- Write **first drafts of your college essays** and ask your parents and teachers to review them.
- If you need to fill out the **CSS/Financial Aid PROFILE®**, you can do so on collegeboard.com starting Oct. 1.

NOVEMBER

- **Finish your application essays**. Proofread them rigorously for mistakes.
- **Apply to colleges with rolling admission** (first-come, first-served) as early as possible. Keep hard copies.
- Make sure your **admissions test (e.g., SAT) scores** will be sent by the testing agency to each one of your colleges.
- Give your school counselor the proper **forms to send transcripts** to your colleges at least two weeks in advance.
- **Get PINs for the FAFSA** for both yourself and for one of your parents from **www.pin.ed.gov**.

DECEMBER

- Try to **wrap up college applications** before winter break. Make copies for yourself and your school counselor.
- If you applied for **Early Decision**, you should have an answer by Dec. 15. If you are denied or deferred, submit applications now to other colleges.
- **Apply for scholarships** in time to meet application deadlines.
- Start gathering what you need to complete the FAFSA. **Visit FAFSA on the Web** for a list of needed documents.
- **Contact the financial aid office** at the colleges on your list to see if they require any **other financial aid forms**.

JANUARY

- **Submit your FAFSA** as soon as you can. If a college to which you're applying has a financial aid priority date of Feb. 1, use estimates based on your end-of-year pay stubs and last year's tax returns.
- **Submit other financial aid forms** that may be required — such as PROFILE or the college's own forms. Keep copies.
- If a college wants to see your **midyear grades**, give the form to your school counselor.
- If you have any **new honors or accomplishments** that were not in your original application, let your colleges know.

FEBRUARY

- **Contact your colleges** to confirm that all application materials have been received.
- Correct or update your **Student Aid Report (SAR)** that follows the FAFSA.
- If any **special circumstances** affect your family's financial situation, alert each college's financial aid office.
- **File income tax returns early.** Some colleges want copies of your family's returns before finalizing financial aid offers.
- **Register for AP Exams** you want to take. (If you are homeschooled or your school does not offer AP, you must contact AP Services by March 1.)

MARCH

- **Admissions decisions start arriving.** Read everything you receive carefully, as some documents may require prompt action on your part.
- **Revisit colleges** that accepted you if it's hard to make a choice.
- **Don't get senioritis!** Colleges want to see strong grades in the second half of your senior year.

APRIL

- **Carefully compare financial aid award letters** from the colleges that accept you — it might not be clear which is the better offer. If you have questions, contact the college's financial aid office or talk to your school counselor.
- **If you don't get enough aid**, consider your options, which include appealing the award.
- Make a final decision, **accept the aid package, and mail a deposit check** to the college you select before May 1 (the acceptance deadline for most schools).
- **Notify the other colleges** that you won't be attending (so another student can have your spot).

MAY

- AP Exams are given. Make sure your **AP Grade Report** is sent to your college.
- **Study hard for final exams**. Most admissions offers are contingent on your final grades.
- **Thank everyone** who wrote you recommendations or otherwise helped with your college applications.
- If you plan on playing a Division I or II college sport, have your school counselor send your **final transcript to the NCAA Eligibility Center**.
- **If you weren't accepted** anywhere, don't give up — you still have options. Talk to your school counselor about them.

Filling Out the Application

A typical application will ask you to provide some personal information; a list of schools you have attended; brief descriptions of your extracurricular activities, jobs and any academic honors you have earned; and standardized test scores. They will also ask for information about your family and their education background, which colleges may use to determine whether you merit special consideration as a first-generation college student or a "legacy" applicant. Finally, most applications give you the option of affiliating yourself with a race or ethnic group. If you choose to do so, colleges may take that into consideration when reviewing your application; however, your answer won't hurt your chances of admission.

Finally, all applications will ask whether and when you plan to file for financial aid. Checking this box does not mean you have applied for financial aid! It just lets the admissions office know that they should coordinate with the financial aid office later on. For more information on financial aid and how to apply for it, read the articles in the "Pay for College" section of www.collegeboard.com, or get the College Board's book, *Getting Financial Aid*.

PLANNING AHEAD

In addition to the traditional typed or handwritten application, many schools today accept **online applications** (if they do, it will say so in their *Handbook* description). You may also be able to fill out the **Common Application** and send it to several schools — though you should be aware that some Common Application subscribers also require a supplementary form of their own.

What Goes with Your Application

Besides the application form, there are several things that need to be included with your application. You will have to send some of them with the form; others will be sent to the college by other people.

Application fee

The average college application fee is around $25. (Some colleges charge up to $60, while others don't have an application fee at all.) The fee is usually nonrefundable, even if you're not offered admission. Many colleges offer fee waivers for applicants from low-income families. If you need a fee waiver, call the college's admissions office for more information.

High school transcript

This form is filled out by an official of your high school. If it comes with your admissions materials, you should give it to the guidance office to complete as early as possible. Some colleges send this form directly to your school after receiving your application.

Admissions test scores

If you need to submit standardized test scores, you must make sure the testing agency itself sends an official score report. Writing your scores on your application or sending a photocopy of your own personal score report will not suffice. When you take the SAT, you are entitled to four free official score reports, which are sent to the colleges you choose. This service is included in the fee you pay to take the test.

KEEP IN MIND

If you apply online, remember to print your applications and proofread them before you submit them, just as you would with a printed application. Also, be sure to tell your school counselor that you've applied online — your school will still need to send your transcript to the college.

PLANNING AHEAD

In many cases, you'll be able to **reuse the same essay for several college applications** (and maybe even use it for a scholarship application or two as well). If you do this, be sure that the essay you want to use really does answer the question on each application, and that you change any references to the college from application to application.

Letters of recommendation

Some colleges ask you to submit one or more letters of recommendation from a teacher, counselor or other adult who knows you well. Usually the person writing the letter will send it directly to the college, though sometimes your school counselor will assemble the letters and send them with your transcript.

Essays short and long

If you're applying to selective colleges, your essay often plays a very important role. Whether you're writing an autobiographical statement or an essay on a specific theme, take the opportunity to express your individuality in a way that sets you apart from other applicants.

Some applications will ask you to attach a separate essay of one or two pages, others will ask you to fill in some one-paragraph short responses directly on the application form, and others will ask for both. Whichever type of question you're answering, give it some thought. Draft, revise and edit your response before putting it with the application, and be sure to type or (if you must) print legibly. (The "fun" fonts that came with your word processor are usually not legible.)

Your parents, school counselors and teachers may have some helpful insights into things you should talk about in your essays. For tips and strategies on how to approach different types of essay questions, general advice on the writing process, and information about how admissions officers evaluate essays, obtain a copy of Sarah Myers McGinty's *The College Application Essay* (College Board, 2004).

Interview

An interview is required or recommended by some colleges. Even if it's not required, it's a good idea to set up an interview because it gives you a chance to make a personal connection with someone who will have a voice in deciding whether or not you'll be offered admission. If you're too far away for an on-campus interview, try to arrange to meet with an alumnus in your community.

Try to schedule interviews early in your senior year — if you wait until December you may not have time to make the appointment before the application is due. Also, scheduling an interview late in the year may make the college think that your decision to apply was an afterthought. Many students feel most comfortable scheduling their first interviews with colleges they feel confident about getting into. That way, they can experience interview situations and build their confidence before going to "high stakes" interviews with their "reach" schools.

For tips on preparing for interviews and getting the most out of them, obtain a copy of Zola Dincin Schneider's *Campus Visits & College Interviews* (College Board, 2002), or read the articles in the "Apply to College" section of the College Board Web site.

How to ask for recommendations

The key to getting a great recommendation is to be a great student. But showing good manners helps.

- ✔ Be sure to *ask* for a recommendation — don't demand one.
- ✔ Respect the time constraints of those you're asking for this favor. Mary Lee Hoganson, a former counselor at Homewood-Flossmoor High School in Illinois, says that "teachers should always receive a minimum of two weeks' notice."
- ✔ Provide teachers and counselors with a deadline for each recommendation that you are requesting, especially noting the earliest deadline.
- ✔ Offer them a "brag sheet" or résumé reminding them of your accomplishments over the years. They might know your work in their classes very well, but they might not remember that you were also responsible for organizing the school talent show your junior year.
- ✔ Include addressed and stamped envelopes for each school to which you're applying.
- ✔ On the application form, waive your right to view recommendation letters. This makes the recommendation more credible in the eyes of the college.
- ✔ Follow up with your recommendation writers a week or so before your first deadline.
- ✔ Once you have decided which college to attend, write thank-you notes to everyone who provided a recommendation and tell them where you've decided to go to college. Be sure to do this before you leave high school.

EXPERT ADVICE

"Be sure to **ask for recommendations in a way that allows a teacher to decline** comfortably if he or she does not have time to do an adequate job. For example: 'Do you feel you know me well enough, and do you have enough time to write a supportive letter of recommendation?'"

— Mary Lee Hoganson, former counselor, Homewood-Flossmoor High School, Flossmoor, Ill.

Auditions, portfolios and other supplementary materials

If you're applying for a fine or performing arts program in music, studio art or graphic design, you may have to document prior work by auditioning on campus or submitting an audiotape, slides or some other sample of your work to demonstrate your ability. Talk to a teacher or mentor in your subject for advice on both how to assemble a portfolio and which of your pieces to include. Be sure to check the deadlines for auditions — they are often different from the deadlines for applications.

In some cases, a college will ask all students to submit an academic writing sample, either instead of or in addition to a personal statement. You should send a graded essay, presentation or lab report that you did well on, preferably a copy that has your teacher's comments and the grade you received on it.

Taking college admissions and placement tests

In your junior or senior year of high school, you will probably have to take a college admissions test to satisfy the admissions requirements at the colleges you are considering.

You may also want to take college-level exams in specific subjects in order to strengthen your application portfolio, place out of introductory college courses, get college credit for your high school work, or all three. At the end of this chapter, you'll find an introduction to the two most widely recognized college credit-by-exam programs.

College Admissions Tests: Why You Should Take Them

This chapter will give you advice on how to get ready and register for the standardized tests that satisfy the admissions requirements at the colleges you are considering. You may also want to take the college-level exams in specific subjects in order to strengthen your application portfolio, place out of introductory college courses, get college credit for your high school work, or all three.

Some colleges also require one or more SAT Subject Tests in addition to, or instead of, the SAT. These requirements are all spelled out in the *Handbook* descriptions for each college.

The SAT

The College Board's SAT tests your knowledge of subjects that are necessary for college success: reading, writing and mathematics. It tells you how well you use the skills and knowledge you have attained in and outside of the classroom — including how you think, solve problems and communicate. The SAT is an important resource for colleges, and it is the best predictor of how well you'll do in college when used with high school grades. The SAT is a fair and unbiased test that is geared to all students. Each question goes through a rigorous review to ensure that it's fair for students from all backgrounds.

What Are SAT Subject Tests™?

SAT Subject Tests are one-hour exams offered in 20 subjects that measure your achievement in foreign languages, mathematics, sciences, history and literature.

If your grades in college-preparatory courses are good, you may want to take one or several of these tests to demonstrate the content mastery you've achieved. The best time to take a Subject Test is after you have completed, or nearly completed, all the courses in that subject. A number of colleges use SAT Subject Test scores for various purposes:

Admission: Some colleges require Subject Tests for admission for all students. Others require them only for certain applicants, such as students who were homeschooled in high school. If they do, their *Handbook* descriptions will indicate this in the bulleted list of key facts and in the "Basis for selection" section.

Placement in honors programs: A college might require Subject Tests for placement in an honors college or other special program.

Scholarship awards: Merit scholarships may be awarded partly on the basis of Subject Test scores. Information about each college's merit scholarships and their requirements is included in the College Board's *Getting Financial Aid.*

Advanced placement: Some colleges will allow you to skip introductory courses if your Subject Test score is sufficient.

For help practicing for your test(s), visit the SAT Subject Tests Learning Center on www.collegeboard.com, or get *The Official Study Guide for all SAT Subject Tests™*, which is available in bookstores and libraries everywhere.

KNOW THE LINGO

The SAT — A measure of the critical thinking skills you'll need for academic success in college. The SAT assesses how well you analyze and solve problems — skills you learned in high school that you'll need in college. It consists of three sections: mathematics, critical reading and writing. The writing section includes both multiple-choice questions and a short essay.

SAT Subject Tests — Tests designed to measure mastery of specific subjects like English, history, mathematics, science and language. The tests are independent of any particular textbook or method of instruction. Depending on the subject, an SAT Subject Test may include multiple-choice questions, an essay or (for some foreign language tests) a listening section.

2009-2010 SAT® PROGRAM TEST CALENDAR

Test Dates	Oct. 5*	Nov. 7	Dec. 5	Jan. 23*	Mar. 13	May 1*	June 5
Registration Deadlines							
Regular	Sept. 9	Oct. 1	Oct. 30	Dec. 15	Feb. 4	Mar. 25	Apr. 29
Late	Sept. 23	Oct. 15	Nov. 12	Dec. 30	Feb. 18	Apr. 8	May 13
SAT Reasoning Test™	■	■	■	■	■	■	■
SAT Subject Tests™							
Literature	■	■	■	■		■	■
United States (U.S.) History	■	■		■		■	■
World History			■				■
Mathematics Level 1†	■	■	■	■		■	■
Mathematics Level 2†	■	■	■	■		■	■
Biology E/M (Ecological/Molecular)	■	■	■	■		■	■
Chemistry	■	■	■	■		■	■
Physics	■	■	■	■		■	■
Languages: Reading Only							
French	■		■	■		■	■
German							■
Modern Hebrew							■
Italian			■				
Latin			■				■
Spanish	■		■	■		■	■
Languages: Reading and Listening							
Chinese		■					
French		■					
German		■					
Japanese		■					
Korean		■					
Spanish		■					

*Question-and-Answer Service available.
†Calculator required.
NOTE: Sunday test dates follow each Saturday test date for students who cannot test on Saturday because of a religious observance.

Services for Students with Disabilities

Students may receive accommodations (extended time, large print, etc.) on College Board exams if they submit an eligibility form and meet the eligibility requirements. **Students must: 1)** have a disability that requires testing accommodations; **2)** have documentation on file that supports the need for accommodations; **and 3)** receive and use the requested accommodations for school-based tests. (See program material regarding the Guidelines for Documentation, and for exceptions to the above requirements.)

SSD Contacts
(all College Board programs):

Voice 609-771-7137
TTY 609-882-4118
Fax 609-771-7944
E-mail sat.ssd@ets.org
www.collegeboard.com/ssd

Getting Ready for the SAT

The best way to get ready for the SAT is to take challenging courses, study hard and familiarize yourself with the test. College admissions staff are more impressed by an academic record that shows real effort and achievement than they are by test scores alone.

Before taking the SAT, you should:

- Take the PSAT/NMSQT®.
- Become familiar with the test's format, directions, answer sheet and question types.
- Understand the skills tested on the SAT using the Skills Insight™ tool on collegeboard.com.
- Review algebra and geometry.
- Practice reading critically.
- Read and write as much as possible, in and out of school.

PLANNING AHEAD

Most students take the SAT in the spring of their junior year and again in the fall of their senior year. Students who take SAT Subject Tests usually do so either in June of their junior year or in November or December of their senior year.

When you know which test(s) to take, you'll find a schedule of registration and administration dates on page 31. Your school counselor can tell you where the SAT will be administered close to your home and school. You can also find SAT information and preparation tools at **www.collegeboard.com/sat**.

The PSAT/NMSQT®

Taking the PSAT/NMSQT (Preliminary SAT/National Merit Scholarship Qualifying Test) is the best way to practice for the SAT. For many students, the PSAT/NMSQT is also the first official step on the road to college. It assesses skills developed through years of study in a wide range of courses as well as through experiences outside the classroom. Students taking the test in their junior year also may be eligible to enter National Merit Scholarship Corporation competitions and other scholarship programs.

All students who take the test receive free online access to My College QuickStart™ until they graduate from high school. This personalized planning kit, based on your test results, features:

- An online PSAT/NMSQT Score Report, including projected SAT score ranges, state percentiles and the power to sort answer explanations by difficulty and question type.
- Personalized lists of colleges, majors and careers.
- MyRoad™ — the College Board's majors, college and career exploration program.
- A customized SAT study plan, including a guided review of PSAT/NMSQT test results, skill improvement advice, SAT practice questions, a full-length SAT practice test and SAT essay preparation.

For more information about the PSAT/NMSQT, **visit www.collegeboard.com/psat.**

Practice Materials

To help students get ready for the SAT and college success, the College Board offers many free and low-cost online test practice tools. Available at collegeboard.com, the leading Web site for SAT and college planning information, these resources can help you get familiar with and practice for the SAT.

- **The Official SAT Question of the Day™**: Practice a different question each day with the College Board's popular SAT Question of the Day. Visit our Web site or sign up to receive free daily test questions via e-mail.
- **The Official SAT Practice Test:** Print or enter your answers online as you take a free official SAT practice test. See how you score and get detailed answer explanations to help you better understand where you need to improve.
- **SAT Skills Insight™**: A free online tool that shows you the skills you know and highlights those you need to know better, including:
  - Skills tested on the SAT.
  - Skills typical of students who score within a particular score band.
  - Suggestions for how to sharpen those skills.
  - Real SAT questions and answers.
- **The Official SAT Study Guide™**: This best seller helps students practice for the SAT by providing:
  - 10 official practice tests, focused sets of practice questions and practice essay prompts.
  - A review of concepts and test-taking approaches.
  - Chapters on the PSAT/NMSQT and the SAT essay.
  - Exclusive access to free online practice-test score reports and answer explanations.
- **The Official SAT Online Course™**: This service is available anytime from any computer with Internet access. It features:
  - 18 interactive lessons that cover all SAT sections and the PSAT/NMSQT.
  - 6 practice tests and 600+ practice questions.
  - Powerful reporting tools for educators and detailed reports for students.
  - Answer explanations and immediate essay scoring.

Taking the Test

When should I take the test?

Many students decide that the end of their junior year is a logical point at which to take a college admissions test for the first time. By then, you've been studying English, math, science, social studies, and other courses for more than 11 years! You've been reading, studying and taking tests regularly during that time. And if you took the PSAT/NMSQT in October of your junior year, your memory will be fresh from the experience.

How many times should I take the test?

Research shows that many students see modest increases in their score upon taking the test a second time. Most students who repeat the test take it once in the spring of their junior year and once in the fall of their senior year. There is no evidence that taking the test more than twice is beneficial to your score.

Remember: All of the work you've done in school — including your reading, writing and math — is what really helps you do your best on the test and be better prepared for college.

How to register

The best way to register is online. It's fast and easy, and it helps you avoid late fees or missed postmark deadlines. You can even register for next year's tests over the summer. SAT registration may be completed at www.collegeboard.com.

To register for the SAT by mail, complete the paper registration form included with the *SAT Registration Guide* and send it with your test fee payment. You can get a *Registration Guide* in your school's guidance office. Registration deadlines are about four and a half weeks before the test date. There are also late registration deadlines, and it's possible to register on a standby basis. Both of these involve an additional fee.

Score Choice™

The College Board has introduced Score Choice™, a new feature that gives you the option to choose the SAT scores you send to colleges by test date — in accordance with each college's or university's score-use practice. Designed to reduce your stress and improve the test-day experience, Score Choice gives you an opportunity to show colleges the scores you feel best represent your abilities.

Score Choice is optional, so if you don't actively choose to use it, all of your scores will be sent automatically. Since most colleges only consider your best scores, you should still feel comfortable reporting scores from all of your test dates.

Each college, university and scholarship program has different score-use practices. Our new easy-to-use score-reporting process displays score-use practices for each participating institution, but you should also check with colleges to ensure that you are following their score-reporting requirements. E-mail reminders will be sent to you if you have not sent SAT scores to any colleges by the typical deadlines.

Remember:

- Scores from an entire SAT test (critical reading, writing and mathematics sections) will be sent — scores of individual sections from different test dates cannot be selected independently.
- You can send any or all scores to a college on a single report — it will not cost more to send one, multiple or all test scores.
- You receive four free score reports with your registration. We continue to recommend that you take full advantage of these reports.
- Score Choice is available via the Web or by calling Customer Service (toll free within the United States).

Earning College Credit by Examination

Most colleges allow you to place out of introductory courses in subject areas where you have already done college-level work, either in high school or through your own life experiences. For example, you might be able to skip the first year of college Spanish and go straight to intermediate-level courses. In order to demonstrate your knowledge, the college usually requires you to either take a nationally offered standardized test, such as an AP Examination or a CLEP exam, or to take an exam offered by the college on campus. (You often have a choice of doing either — that is, if you haven't taken the AP Spanish Language Exam, you can take the college's Spanish placement test as an alternative.)

If you take an AP or CLEP exam, many colleges also allow you to earn credit based on your exam score. To use the same example as above, you wouldn't just place into second-year Spanish; you would also earn credits toward graduation as if you had taken first-year Spanish there on campus. If you have qualifying scores on enough exams, some colleges will even grant you "sophomore standing," meaning you are treated as a sophomore for academic purposes such as when you get to register for courses. (You still have to obey the college's other rules for freshmen, though, so don't expect to be given a single dorm room and a parking permit just because you have sophomore standing through AP.)

KNOW THE LINGO

Advanced placement — The ability to skip an introductory course in a subject. Many colleges offer advanced placement in appropriate subjects for AP Exams, CLEP or SAT Subject Tests. You may also qualify for advanced placement by taking the college's own placement exam.

Credit by exam — College credit earned for prior knowledge, usually demonstrated on either an AP Exam or a CLEP exam.

Sophomore standing — If a college grants an incoming student the equivalent of 30 semester hours of credit by exam, they may allow the student to be considered a sophomore for academic purposes, such as when the student registers for courses or can declare a major.

AP Course Calendar

Spring before starting an AP course	Well ahead of time, you need to start thinking about what AP courses you might want to take. Discuss your plans with your parents, teachers and school counselor.
Summer	Some AP teachers require you to complete work (like reading) during the summer months to prepare for their courses. For example, for AP English Literature you may be given a reading list. Make sure you complete these assignments so that you're up to speed when the class begins.
January	Talk to your AP teachers and/or AP Coordinator about taking the exams. Contact the disabilities (SSD) coordinator at your school if you will need testing accommodations.
February	Deadlines for students with disabilities whose eligibility forms require Documentation Review.
March	Deadlines for homeschooled students and students whose schools do not offer AP to arrange for testing at a nearby school. Deadlines for students with disabilities whose eligibility forms do not require Documentation Review.
May 3-7 and May 10-14, 2009	Exam dates.
June 15, 2009	Deadline for receipt of requests for grade withholding, grade cancellation or a change in a college grade report recipient.
July	AP Grade Reports released to designated colleges, and to students and their high schools.

GOOD TO KNOW

Many colleges grant credit or advanced placement to incoming freshmen who have qualifying grades on AP Exams. Some even grant sophomore standing if you've earned qualifying grades on a requisite number of exams. You can find out specific AP policies for each exam at more than 1,000 colleges at **www.collegeboard.com/ap/creditpolicy**.

More About Advanced Placement®

The AP Program offers a wide range of college-level courses that are taught in high schools by high school teachers; a national exam is given for each subject every May. AP courses give you a chance to do college-level work while still in high school. Research studies have shown that students with AP experience succeed in college at a rate significantly higher than the average student.

In all, there are more than 30 courses in a wide variety of subject areas. Even if an AP course is not offered at your school, you may still be able to take the exam if you make arrangements with your school's AP Coordinator (usually a school counselor or a teacher). If your school doesn't offer AP at all, or you are homeschooled, you can still make arrangements to take an AP Exam at a nearby school that offers AP.

AP courses are challenging — after all, you're doing college-level work in high school! They can also be very rewarding. If you're not sure whether you should take an AP course, talk to your teachers, your school counselor and your parents. You might also want to look at the College Board publications *Choose AP* or the bilingual *Get with the Program/Avanza con el Programa*. Your school should be able to order copies of these for you and your parents.

More About the College-Level Examination Program® (CLEP®)

CLEP, as the program is familiarly known, is the most widely accepted college credit-by-examination program in the country. Approximately 2,900 accredited colleges and universities award credit for qualifying scores on CLEP exams.

Unlike AP Exams, CLEP exams do not correspond to courses that you take in high school. Rather, CLEP offers 34 exams in the areas of business, English composition and literature, foreign languages, history and social studies, and science and mathematics. You can take a CLEP exam at any time during your college career, and the exams are offered year-round. You can find out if your college grants credit for CLEP exams by using the CLEP college search at www.collegeboard.com/clepcolleges.

CLEP is computer based, allowing for instant score reports, so you know that day if you will be awarded credit for your performance. To find out more about CLEP exams, to see a list of suggested textbooks and online resources for each exam, and to download study guides, visit www.collegeboard.com/clep.

Life on campus

A college isn't just a place where you'll take classes for two or four years. You'll also be spending most of your time there — and, if you're a residential student, you'll even be living there. When you're deciding where to go, academics should come first, but you should also consider how comfortable the campus feels. Some things to take into account are the housing options, local transit, whether the campus feels safe, and the social life of the campus.

Housing Options

At most colleges, you'll have lots of choices about where to live. You may live in an on-campus dorm, an off-campus house or apartment building, or a fraternity/sorority house. At some colleges, you won't have as many choices your freshman year, but even then you may have a choice of several freshman dorms.

Typically, after you accept an offer of admission, the college's housing office will ask you to submit a form stating your housing preferences. You should use this form not only to state your preference of what dorm in which they will place you, but also to help them find you a roommate who will be compatible. Are you a quiet person? What times do you usually wake up and go to bed? Are you messy or neat? Do you smoke? The housing office will try to find someone whose answers to those questions were similar to your own.

Living in Dorms

College dormitories have changed a lot over the years. While they were once bare-bones facilities that offered little more than a place to sleep, today most dorms offer a complete living and learning environment. It's not uncommon to find study areas, TV lounges, computer labs, small kitchens or even fast-food take-out restaurants built into modern dorms. While some dorms are still built on the traditional floor plan of a hallway of double rooms sharing a bathroom, others are based around suites or apartments.

KNOW THE LINGO

Dorm — short for "dormitory." An on-campus building with rooms for students. Sometimes called a "residence hall."

Single — a dorm room for one student. On some campuses, these are not available for freshmen.

Double — a dorm room shared by two students.

Suite — a set of rooms in a dorm or apartment building that adjoin a common living area.

GOOD TO KNOW

Most colleges will require you to live on campus your freshman year, unless you can live with your parents and commute to class. But even if you are required to live on campus, you may still have a wide variety of housing options, ranging from dorms to apartment suites with built-in kitchens.

Some colleges offer theme-related residences for both freshmen and upperclassmen. These programs give you the opportunity to live with other students who share similar interests in a field of study, culture, hobby or personal value. Students in theme residences not only live together, but often they also eat together and participate in social events related around the dorm's theme. Some theme residences will also have a member of the faculty who lives in the dorm and advises its students. Examples of theme residences include:

- *Diversity programs,* where the residents come from a wide variety of cultural backgrounds
- *Honors residences,* where all the students are on merit scholarships
- *Discipline-based residences,* such as a dorm for engineering and science majors
- *Foreign language immersion dorms,* where all the residents study and speak a particular foreign language
- *Substance-free housing* (a.k.a. "wellness" or "positive choice" housing), where all the residents pledge not to drink, smoke or do drugs

EXPERT ADVICE

"**Be honest on your housing preferences form**. If you've been pretty quiet throughout high school and always go to bed at 10 p.m., don't say you party a lot and stay up past midnight. Random roommate placement is tricky enough without stacking the deck against yourself."

— *Caitlin, student, Puget Sound University*

Roommate issues

Most roommate situations work out OK; often, freshman roommates become good friends. But there are cases when roommates just don't get along.

The best way to avoid this is to communicate with your roommates. At the beginning of the semester, tell them what you expect in terms of when you'll go to bed, when you'll get up in the mornings, when it's OK to have friends visit the room, and whether you'll be able to sleep while they work on their computer. Remember that communication is a two-way street: You should also ask your roommates about their own expectations, and listen to what they tell you.

As the semester goes on, be sure to let your roommates know if something is bothering you. Don't ignore problems or obnoxious behavior — they will only get worse if you don't speak up. Similarly, if your roommate complains about your own habits, try to correct them.

If worse comes to worst, it's not unknown for colleges to reassign roommates in midsemester. But because of space issues, this isn't always possible, and when it is possible, it's not always ideal. You'll probably find yourself living in a new dorm, away from all the friends you've already made. You might also find yourself as the new third roommate who is squeezed into a room that had previously slept two.

Glossary

Definitions of commonly used terms vary from college to college. Consult specific college catalogs or their Web sites for more detailed information.

Accelerated study. A college program of study completed in less time than is usually required, most often by attending classes in the summer or by taking extra courses during the regular academic terms. Completion of a bachelor's degree program in three years is an example of acceleration.

Accreditation. Recognition by an accrediting organization or agency that a college meets certain acceptable standards in its education programs, services and facilities. Regional accreditation applies to a college as a whole and not to any particular programs or courses of study. Accreditation of specific types of schools, such as Bible colleges or trade and technical schools, may also be determined by a national organization. Institutional accreditation by regional accrediting associations and by national accrediting organizations is included in the *Handbook*'s descriptions of colleges. See pages 10-12 for more information about accreditation and the names and addresses of the national and regional accrediting associations.

ACT. A college entrance examination given at test centers in the United States and other countries on specified dates. Please visit the organization's Web site for further information.

Advanced placement. Admission or assignment of a freshman to an advanced course in a certain subject on the basis of evidence that the student has already completed the equivalent of the college's freshman course in that subject.

Advanced Placement Program (AP). An academic program of the College Board that provides high school students with the opportunity to study and learn at the college level. The AP Program offers more than 30 courses and exams in a wide variety of subject areas. High schools offer the courses and administer the exams to interested students. Most colleges and universities in the United States accept qualifying AP Exam grades for credit, advanced placement or both.

Agricultural college. A college or university that primarily trains students in the agricultural sciences and agribusiness operations.

Articulation agreement. A formal agreement between two higher education institutions, stating specific policies relating to transfer and recognition of academic achievement in order to facilitate the successful transfer of students without duplication of course work.

Associate degree. A degree granted by a college or university after the satisfactory completion of the equivalent of a two-year, full-time program of study. In general, the associate of arts (A.A.) or associate of science (A.S.) degree is granted after completing a program of study similar to the first two years of a four-year college curriculum. The associate in applied science (A.A.S.) is awarded by many colleges on completion of technological or vocational programs of study.

Bachelor's, or baccalaureate, degree. A degree received after the satisfactory completion of a four- or five-year, full-time program of study (or its part-time equivalent) at a college or university. The bachelor of arts (B.A.), bachelor of science (B.S.) and bachelor of fine arts (B.F.A.) are the most common baccalaureates. Policies concerning their award vary from college to college.

Bible college. An undergraduate institution whose program, in addition to a general education in the liberal arts, includes a significant element of Bible study. Most Bible colleges seek to prepare their students for vocational or lay Christian ministry.

Branch campus. A part of a college, university or community college that is geographically separate from the main campus, has its own faculty and administration, and may have separate admissions requirements and degree programs.

Business college. A college that primarily prepares students to work in an office or entrepreneurial setting. The curriculum may focus on management, clerical positions or both.

Campus. The physical location of a college or university. Includes classroom buildings, libraries, research facilities, dormitories, dining halls and administration buildings.

Calendar. The system by which an institution divides its year into shorter periods for instruction and awarding credit. The most common calendars are those based on the semester, trimester, quarter and 4-1-4.

Candidates Reply Date Agreement (CRDA). A college subscribing to this College Board-sponsored agreement will not require any applicants offered admission as freshmen to notify the college of their decision to attend (or to accept an offer of financial aid) before May 1 of the year the applicants apply. The purpose of the agreement is to give applicants time to hear from all the colleges to which they have applied before having to make a commitment to any of them.

CB code. A four-digit College Board code number that students use to designate colleges or scholarship programs to receive their SAT score reports.

Certificate. An award for completing a particular program or course of study, usually given by two-year colleges or vocational or technical schools for nondegree programs of a year or less.

College. The generic term for an institution of higher education. Also a term used to designate divisions within a university.

College-Level Examination Program (CLEP). Thirty-four examinations in undergraduate college courses that provide students of any age the opportunity to demonstrate college-level achievement, thereby reducing costs and time to degree completion. The examinations, which are sponsored by the College Board, are administered at colleges year-round via computer, providing test-takers with instant score results.

College-preparatory subjects. A term used to describe subjects required for admission to, or recommended as preparation for, college. It is usually understood to mean subjects from the fields of English, history and social studies, foreign languages, mathematics, science and the arts.

College Scholarship Service® (CSS®). A unit of the College Board that assists postsecondary institutions, state scholarship programs and private scholarship organizations in the equitable and efficient distribution of student financial aid funds.

Combined bachelor's/graduate degree. A program in which students complete a bachelor's degree and a master's degree or first-professional degree in less than the usual amount of time. In most programs, students apply to the graduate program during their first three years of undergraduate study, and begin the graduate program in their fourth year of college. Successful completion results in awarding of both a bachelor's degree and a graduate degree. At some colleges, this option is called a joint degree program.

Common Application. The standard application form distributed by the National Association of Secondary School Principals to colleges who are subscribers to the Common Application Group.

Community/junior college. A college that offers only the first two years of undergraduate study. Community colleges are public institutions, whereas junior colleges are privately operated on a not-for-profit basis. Both usually offer terminal (or "vocational") programs and transfer programs.

Consortium. A group of colleges and universities that share a common geographic location. Consortiums of colleges in the same town often allow students at one institution to take classes at other consortium colleges and use facilities (such as libraries) at the member colleges. Larger consortiums, on the state or regional level, may allow for "visiting semesters" or offer in-state tuition to out-of-state students.

Cooperative education (co-op). A program that provides for alternative class attendance and employment in business, industry or government. Students are typically paid for their work. Under a cooperative plan, five years are normally required to complete a bachelor's degree, but graduates have the advantage of about a year's practical work experience in addition to their studies.

Cooperative housing. College-owned, operated or affiliated housing in which students share room and board expenses and participate in household chores to reduce their living expenses.

Credit hour. A unit of measure representing an hour (50 minutes) of instruction over a 15-week period in a semester or trimester system, or over a 10-week period in a quarter system. It is applied toward the total number of hours needed for completing the requirements of a degree, diploma, certificate or other formal award.

Credit/placement by examination. Academic credit or placement out of introductory courses granted by a college to entering students who have demonstrated proficiency in college-level studies through examinations such as those administered by the College Board's AP and CLEP programs.

Cross-registration. The practice, through agreements between colleges, of permitting students enrolled at one college or university to enroll in courses at another institution without formally applying for admission to the second institution.

CSS/Financial Aid PROFILE®. An application and service offered by the College Board, which is used by some colleges, universities and private scholarship programs to award their own private financial aid funds. Students pay a fee to send reports to institutions and programs that use PROFILE. Students register with PROFILE on www.collegeboard.com. PROFILE provides a customized application for each registrant, based on the individual's information and the requirements of the colleges and programs from which she or he is seeking aid. Students complete and submit the customized application to the College Board for processing and reporting to institutions. The PROFILE is not a federal form and may not be used to apply for federal student aid.

Culinary school. A vocational college that primarily prepares students to work as chefs or caterers.

Deferred admission. The practice of permitting students to postpone enrollment, usually for one year, after acceptance to the college.

Degree. An award given by a college or university certifying that a student has completed a course of study. *See* bachelor's degree, associate degree, graduate degree. *See also* Certificate.

Distance learning. An option for earning course credit off campus via cable television, the Internet, satellite classes, videotapes, correspondence courses or other means. *See also* Virtual university.

Doctoral degree (doctorate). *See* Graduate degree.

Dormitory. *See* Residence hall.

Double major. Any program in which a student concurrently completes the requirements of two majors.

Dual enrollment. The practice of students enrolling in college courses while still in high school.

Early Action (EA). Students who apply under a college's Early Action plan receive a decision earlier than the standard response date but are not required to accept the admissions offer or to make a deposit prior to May 1. See the Early Decision/Early Action table for a list of colleges that offer Early Action plans, including application deadlines and notification dates.

Early admission. The policy of some colleges of admitting certain students who have not completed high school — usually students of exceptional ability who have completed their junior year. These students are enrolled full-time in college.

Early Decision (ED). Students who apply under Early Decision make a commitment to enroll at the college if admitted and offered a satisfactory financial aid package. Application deadlines are usually in November or December with a mid-to-late-December notification date. Some colleges have two rounds of Early Decision. See the Early Decision/Early Action table for details.

Engineering college/institute/school. An institution of higher education that primarily prepares students for careers as licensed professional engineers or engineering technologists.

Exchange student program. Any arrangement that permits a student to study for a semester or more at another college in the United States without extending the amount of time required for a degree.

External degree program. A system of study whereby a student earns credit toward a degree through independent study, college courses, proficiency examinations and personal experience. External degree colleges generally have no campus or classroom facilities.

FAFSA. *See* Free Application for Federal Student Aid (FAFSA).

First-professional degree. A degree granted upon completion of academic requirements to become licensed in a recognized profession. The programs of study require at least two years of previous college work for entrance, and at least six years of total college work for completion. The medical doctorate (M.D.) is one kind of first-professional degree.

For-profit college. A private institution operated by its owners as a profit-making enterprise.

4-1-4 calendar. A variation of the semester calendar system, the 4-1-4 calendar consists of two terms of about 16 weeks each, separated by a one-month intersession used for intensive short courses, independent study, off-campus work or other types of instruction.

Free Application for Federal Student Aid (FAFSA). A form completed by all applicants for federal student aid. In many states, completion of the FAFSA is also sufficient to establish eligibility for state-sponsored aid programs. There is no charge to students for completing the FAFSA. The online form may be filed any time after Jan. 1 of the year for which one is seeking aid (e.g., after Jan. 1, 2010, for academic year 2010-11 assistance).

General Educational Development (GED). A series of tests that individuals who did not complete high school may take through their state education system to qualify for a high school equivalency certificate.

Grade point average (GPA) or ratio. A system used by many schools for evaluating the overall scholastic performance of students. Grade points are determined by first multiplying the number of hours given for a course by the numerical value of the grade and then dividing the sum of all grade points by the total number of hours carried. The most common system of numerical values for grades is A = 4, B = 3, C = 2, D = 1, and E or F = 0. Also called quality point average or ratio.

Graduate degree. A degree pursued after a student has earned a bachelor's degree. The master's degree, which requires one to three years of study, is usually the degree earned after the bachelor's. The doctoral degree requires further study. First-professional degrees are also graduate degrees.

Health sciences college. An institution of higher education that primarily prepares students to enter work in a clinic, hospital or private medical practice.

Hispanic-serving college. A college where Hispanic students compose at least 25 percent of the full-time undergraduate enrollment.

Historically black college. An institution founded before 1964 whose mission was historically, and remains, the education of African Americans.

Homeschooled. For purposes of the application requirements described in the "basis for selection" entries of the college descriptions, this refers to homeschooling during the four years of secondary school (grades 9-12).

Honors program. Any special program for very able students that offers the opportunity for education enrichment, independent study, acceleration or some combination of these.

Independent student. For financial aid purposes, a student who is not dependent on financial support from his or her parents. Also called a self-supporting student.

Independent study. Academic work chosen or designed by the student under an instructor's supervision. This work is usually undertaken outside of the regular classroom structure.

International Baccalaureate (IB). A high school curriculum offered by some schools in the United States and other countries. Some colleges award credit for completion of this curriculum. Please visit the organization's Web site for further information.

Internship. A short-term, supervised work experience, usually related to a student's major field, for which the student earns academic credit. The work can be full or part time, on or off campus, paid or unpaid. Student teaching and apprenticeships are examples.

Intersession term. A short term offered between semesters. *See also* 4-1-4 calendar.

Junior college. *See* Community/junior college.

Liberal arts. The study of the humanities (literature, the arts and philosophy), history, foreign languages, social sciences, mathematics and natural sciences. Study of the liberal arts and humanities prepares students to develop general knowledge and reasoning ability rather than specific skills.

Liberal arts/career combination. A program of study in which a student typically completes three years of study in a liberal arts field followed by two years of professional/technical study (for example, engineering) at the end of which the student is awarded bachelor of arts and bachelor of science degrees. The combination is also referred to as a 3+2 program.

Liberal arts college. A college that emphasizes the liberal arts in its core curriculum and academic offerings and does not offer vocational or professional programs.

Lower division. The freshman and sophomore years of college study.

Major. A student's academic field of specialization. In general, most courses in the major are taken during the junior and senior years.

Maritime college/institute/academy. An institution of higher education that prepares students to operate commercial shipping or fishing vessels. Upon graduation, students of most maritime academies are commissioned as officers in the United States Merchant Marine, and simultaneously commissioned as officers in the U.S. Navy Reserve.

Master's degree. *See* Graduate degree.

Military college/institute/academy. An institution of higher education that prepares students (who are called "cadets" while enrolled) to become active-duty officers in the armed services. The curriculum usually combines a study of the liberal arts, military science and engineering. Cadets usually participate in military training assignments during the summer term in addition to attending the college in the fall and spring semesters.

Minor. Course work that is not as extensive as that in a major but gives students some specialized knowledge of a second field.

NAIA. The National Association of Intercollegiate Athletics. NAIA members are mostly small colleges. Championships are offered in 13 sports.

NCAA. The National Collegiate Athletics Association. The largest collegiate athletic association, it oversees the most athletic scholarship money. The NCAA governs league play in 23 championship sports.

NCCAA. National Christian College Athletic Association. NCCAA sponsors league play among Bible colleges and other Christian-oriented institutions.

NJCAA. The National Junior College Athletic Association. NJCAA members are two-year junior or community colleges.

Need-based financial aid. Financial aid given to students who have demonstrated financial need, which is calculated by subtracting the student's expected family contribution from a college's total costs. The expected family contribution is derived from a need analysis of the family's overall financial circumstances, using either a Federal Methodology to determine a student's eligibility for federal student aid, or an Institutional Methodology to determine eligibility for nonfederal financial aid.

Nondegree study. A college-level course of study that does not lead to a degree. Nondegree study may or may not be part of a program leading to a certificate.

Nursing college. An institution of higher education that primarily prepares students to become registered nurses (RNs) or licensed practical nurses (LPNs).

Open admissions. The college admissions policy of admitting high school graduates and other adults generally without regard to conventional academic qualifications, such as high school subjects, high school grades and admissions test scores. Virtually all applicants with high school diplomas or their equivalent are accepted, space permitting.

Placement by examination. *See* Credit/placement by examination.

Private college. Institutions described in this book as "private" are operated on a not-for-profit basis. They may be independent or church affiliated. *See also* Proprietary college.

PROFILE. *See* CSS/Financial Aid PROFILE.

Priority date. The date by which an application, whether for admission, housing or financial aid, must be received to be given the strongest possible consideration. After that date, applicants are considered on a first-come, first-served basis.

Proprietary college. *See* For-profit college.

PSAT/NMSQT® (Preliminary SAT/National Merit Scholarship Qualifying Test). A preparatory tool for the SAT that is administered by high schools to sophomores and juniors each year in October. The PSAT/NMSQT serves as the qualifying test for scholarships awarded by the National Merit Scholarship Corporation.

Public college/university. An institution that is supported by taxes and other public revenue and governed by a county, state or federal government agency.

Quality point average. *See* Grade point average (GPA) or ratio.

Quarter. An academic calendar period of about 12 weeks. Four quarters make up an academic year, but at colleges using the quarter system, students make normal academic progress by attending three quarters each year. In some colleges, students can accelerate their programs by attending all four quarters in one or more years.

Rabbinical college. *See* Seminary/rabbinical college.

Regional accreditation. *See* Accreditation.

Regular admission. Admission during the college's normal calendar for admissions, as opposed to Early Decision or Early Action admissions.

Reserve Officers' Training Corps (ROTC). Programs conducted by certain colleges in cooperation with the United States Air Force, Army and Navy. Navy ROTC includes the Marine Corps (the Coast Guard and Merchant Marine do not sponsor ROTC programs). Local recruiting offices of the services themselves can supply detailed information about these programs, as can participating colleges.

Residence hall. An on-campus living facility. Also known as a dormitory (or "dorm").

Residency requirement. The minimum number of terms that a student must spend taking courses on campus (as opposed to independent study, transfer credits from other colleges, or credit by examination) to be eligible for graduation. Can also refer to the minimum amount of time a student must have lived in-state in order to qualify for the in-state tuition rate at a public college or university.

Rolling admissions. An admissions procedure by which the college considers each student's application as soon as all the required credentials, such as school records and test scores, have been received. The college usually notifies an applicant of its decision without delay. At many colleges, rolling admissions allows for early notification and works much like nonbinding Early Action programs.

Room and board. The cost of housing and meals for students who reside on campus and/or dine in college-operated meal halls.

The SAT. The College Board's test of critical reading, writing and mathematics skills is given on specified dates throughout the year at test centers in the United States and other countries. The SAT is used by most colleges and sponsors of financial aid programs.

SAT Subject Tests. College Board tests in specific subjects are given at test centers in the United States and other countries on specified dates throughout the year. The tests are used by colleges for help in both evaluating applicants for admission and determining course placement, and exemption of enrolled first-year students.

Semester. A period of about 16 weeks. Colleges on a semester system offer two semesters of instruction a year; there may be an additional summer session.

Semester at sea. A program for credit, usually for students with majors in oceanography or marine-related fields, in which students live on a ship, frequently a research vessel, for part of a semester. Academic courses are generally taken in conjunction with the sea experience.

Seminary/rabbinical college. An institution that prepares its student for professional religious ministry. Most seminaries are graduate-only institutions that offer first-professional degrees in divinity or rabbinical studies. The seminaries described in this book also offer undergraduate programs in philosophy, theology, Bible studies or other related liberal arts.

Sophomore standing. Consideration of a student as a sophomore for academic purposes such as registering for classes and declaring a major. A college may grant sophomore standing to incoming freshmen if they have enough credits from AP, CLEP or IB exams.

Student Aid Report (SAR). A report produced by the U.S. Department of Education and sent to students in response to their having filed the Free Application for Federal Student Aid (FAFSA). The SAR contains information the student provided on the FAFSA as well as the federally calculated result, which the financial aid office will use in determining the student's eligibility for a Federal Pell Grant and other federal student aid programs.

Student-designed major. An academic program that allows a student to construct a major field of study not formally offered by the college. Often nontraditional and interdisciplinary in nature, the major is developed by the student with the approval of a designated college officer or committee.

Study abroad. Any arrangement by which a student completes part of the college program — typically the junior year but sometimes only a semester or a summer — by studying in another country. A college may operate a campus abroad, or it may have a cooperative agreement with some other U.S. college or an institution of the other country.

Teacher certification. A college program designed to prepare students to meet the requirements for certification as teachers in elementary and secondary schools.

Teachers college. A college that specializes in preparing students to teach in elementary or secondary schools. Most teachers colleges offer a curriculum that combines a study of the liberal arts with the study of pedagogy.

Technical college/school. A college that offers a wide variety of vocational programs to students.

Term. The shorter period into which colleges divide the school year. *See* Calendar.

Terminal degree. The highest degree level attainable in a particular field. For most teaching faculty this is a doctoral degree. In certain fields, however, a master's degree is the highest level.

Terminal program. An education program designed to prepare students for immediate employment. These programs usually can be completed in less than four years beyond high school and are available in most community colleges and vocational-technical institutes.

Test of English as a Foreign Language (TOEFL). A test generally used by international students to demonstrate their English language proficiency at the advanced level required for study at colleges and universities in the United States. Please visit the organization's Web site for further information.

Transcript. A copy of a student's official academic record listing all courses taken and grades received.

Transfer program. An education program in a two-year college (or a four-year college that offers associate degrees), primarily for students who plan to continue their studies in a four-year college or university.

Transfer student. A student who has attended another college for any period, which may be defined by various colleges as any time from a single term up to three years. A transfer student may receive credit for all or some of the courses successfully completed before the transfer.

Trimester. An academic calendar period of about 15 weeks. Three trimesters make up one year. Students normally progress by attending two of the trimesters each year and in some colleges can accelerate their programs by attending all three trimesters in one or more years.

Tuition. The price of instruction at a college. Tuition may be charged per term or per credit hour.

Two-year college. *See* Community/junior college; Upper-division college.

United Nations semester. A program in which students take courses at a college in New York City while interning at the United Nations.

University. An institution of higher education that is divided into several colleges, schools or institutes. When applying to a university, students typically have to apply for admission to a specific college, which may have its own admissions requirements. Not all colleges within a university will admit applicants who are high school graduates — some may be for graduate study only, and some may be upper-division colleges. Generally, university students take classes in the college to which they were accepted, but they may be allowed to take some courses offered by other colleges within the university and can use shared facilities such as libraries and laboratories.

Upper division. The junior and senior years of study.

Upper-division college. A college offering bachelor's degree programs that begin with the junior year. Entering students must have completed their freshman and sophomore years at other colleges.

Urban semester. A program for credit in which students spend a semester in a major city and experience the complexities of an urban center through course work, seminars and/or internships related to their major.

USCAA. United States Collegiate Athletic Association. USCAA's members are primarily very small colleges.

Virtual university. A degree-granting, accredited institution wherein all courses are delivered by distance learning, with no physical campus.

Vocational program. *See* Terminal program.

Wait list. A list of students who meet the admissions requirements, but will only be offered a place in the class if space becomes available. See the wait-list table in the back of this book for a list of colleges that placed students on a wait list last year, along with the number of students who were eventually accepted from that list.

Washington semester. A program in which students intern with a government agency or department in the Washington, D.C., metropolitan area. Students earn field service credit for their work and frequently take courses at area colleges.

Weekend college. A program that allows students to take a complete course of study and attend classes only on weekends. These programs are generally restricted to a few areas of study at a college and require more than the traditional number of years to complete.

Work-study. An arrangement by which a student combines employment and college study. The employment may be an integral part of the academic program (as in cooperative education and internships) or simply a means of paying for college (as in the Federal Work-Study Program).

Four-year colleges

Alabama

Alabama Agricultural and Mechanical University

Huntsville, Alabama — **CB member**
www.aamu.edu — **CB code: 1003**

- Public 4-year university and agricultural college
- Residential campus in small city
- 4,290 degree-seeking undergraduates: 6% part-time, 54% women, 96% African American, 2% international
- 827 degree-seeking graduate students
- 49% of applicants admitted
- SAT or ACT (ACT writing optional) required
- 33% graduate within 6 years

General. Founded in 1875. Regionally accredited. Campus located near Redstone Arsenal-Defense Research/Space Research Center. **Degrees:** 628 bachelor's awarded; master's, doctoral offered. **ROTC:** Army. **Location:** 2 miles from downtown, 95 miles from Birmingham. **Calendar:** Semester, extensive summer session. **Full-time faculty:** 309 total; 45% have terminal degrees, 53% minority, 39% women. **Part-time faculty:** 76 total; 18% have terminal degrees, 63% minority, 63% women. **Class size:** 48% < 20, 37% 20-39, 9% 40-49, 6% 50-99, less than 1% >100. **Special facilities:** State black archives research center and museum.

Freshman class profile. 3,961 applied, 1,941 admitted, 1,046 enrolled.

Mid 50% test scores		**Out-of-state:**	40%
ACT composite:	14-21	**Live on campus:**	91%

Basis for selection. 2.0 GPA required. Test scores important, but may be waived dependent upon evaluation of GPA and other achievements. Interview, essay recommended. **Homeschooled:** Must meet Alabama State Department of Education requirements.

High school preparation. Required units include English 4, mathematics 4 and science 2.

2008-2009 Annual costs. Tuition/fees: $4,930; $9,220 out-of-state. Part-time student required fees are $440. Room/board: $3,592.

Financial aid. **Non-need-based:** Scholarships awarded for athletics, minority status.

Application procedures. **Admission:** Priority date 5/1; deadline 7/15 (receipt date). $25 fee, may be waived for applicants with need. Admission notification on a rolling basis. **Financial aid:** FAFSA, institutional form required. Applicants notified on a rolling basis; must reply within 2 week(s) of notification.

Academics. Bachelor of Technical Studies available to adult learners in nontraditional fields. **Special study options:** Cooperative education, distance learning, double major, dual enrollment of high school students, exchange student, honors, independent study, internships, study abroad, teacher certification program, Washington semester, weekend college. **Credit/placement by examination:** AP, CLEP, SAT, ACT, institutional tests. 9 credit hours maximum toward bachelor's degree. Scores from DANTES, CLEP, ACE, and similar tests, and work experiences considered for credit toward degree. **Support services:** Learning center, reduced course load, remedial instruction, study skills assistance, tutoring.

Honors college/program. Second semester freshmen with 20-21 ACT (SAT 1030) may be considered with 3.5 college GPA, 12 credit hours completed at the university, and 3.3 high school GPA. The academic program consists of honors core courses.

Majors. **Agriculture:** Economics. **Architecture:** Urban/community planning. **Biology:** General. **Business:** General, accounting, business admin, finance, marketing, office management, public finance. **Communications:** Journalism. **Communications technology:** General, graphic/printing. **Computer sciences:** General. **Education:** General, business, early childhood, elementary, music, physical, school counseling, secondary, special, speech impaired. **Engineering:** Civil, mechanical. **Engineering technology:** Civil. **Family/consumer sciences:** General. **Math:** General. **Physical sciences:** Chemistry, physics. **Psychology:** General. **Public administration:** Social work. **Social sciences:** Political science, sociology. **Visual/performing arts:** Art, conducting, music performance.

Most popular majors. Biology 10%, business/marketing 24%, education 12%, engineering/engineering technologies 13%, psychology 7%, public administration/social services 7%.

Computing on campus. 928 workstations in dormitories, library, computer center, student center. Dormitories linked to campus network. Commuter students can connect to campus network. Helpline available.

Student life. **Freshman orientation:** Mandatory, $100 fee. Preregistration for classes offered. **Housing:** Guaranteed on-campus for all undergraduates. Single-sex dorms available. $100 deposit, deadline 8/1. **Activities:** Bands, choral groups, dance, drama, literary magazine, music ensembles, radio station, student government, student newspaper, TV station, Christian student organization, honor society, service clubs, NAACP, African-American political club, Baptist student union, Islamic association, Caribbean students association, International Association of Nigerian Students.

Athletics. NCAA. **Intercollegiate:** Baseball M, basketball, bowling W, cross-country, football (tackle) M, golf, soccer, softball W, tennis, track and field, volleyball W. **Intramural:** Basketball, football (tackle) M, soccer W, softball, volleyball. **Team name:** Bulldogs.

Student services. Adult student services, career counseling, student employment services, health services, personal counseling, placement for graduates, veterans' counselor. **Physically disabled:** Services for visually, speech, hearing impaired.

Contact. E-mail: juan.alexander@aamu.edu
Phone: (256) 372-5245 Toll-free number: (256) 372-5245
Fax: (256) 372-5249
Juan Alexander, Director of Admissions, Alabama Agricultural and Mechanical University, Box 908, Normal, AL 35762

Alabama State University

Montgomery, Alabama — **CB member**
www.alasu.edu — **CB code: 1006**

- Public 4-year university
- Residential campus in small city
- 4,695 degree-seeking undergraduates: 11% part-time, 58% women, 98% African American
- 949 degree-seeking graduate students
- 46% of applicants admitted
- Interview required

General. Founded in 1867. Regionally accredited. **Degrees:** 457 bachelor's awarded; master's, doctoral, first professional offered. **ROTC:** Army, Air Force. **Location:** 91 miles from Birmingham, 162 miles from Atlanta. **Calendar:** Semester, limited summer session. **Full-time faculty:** 243 total; 65% have terminal degrees, 64% minority, 56% women. **Part-time faculty:** 168 total; 27% have terminal degrees, 81% minority, 60% women. **Class size:** 39% < 20, 52% 20-39, 4% 40-49, 5% 50-99. **Special facilities:** Black history collection, E. D. Nixon papers from civil rights movement of 1960's.

Freshman class profile. 8,510 applied, 3,936 admitted, 1,383 enrolled.

Mid 50% test scores			
SAT critical reading:	360-440	GPA 2.0-2.99:	71%
SAT math:	360-450	Rank in top quarter:	11%
ACT composite:	15-18	Rank in top tenth:	2%
GPA 3.75 or higher:	4%	Return as sophomores:	54%
GPA 3.50-3.74:	6%	Out-of-state:	47%
GPA 3.0-3.49:	19%	Live on campus:	70%

Basis for selection. School record and GPA very important. 2.2 GPA from accredited high school required. Interview and essay recommended. Audition required of music majors. Portfolio recommended for art majors. **Homeschooled:** Transcript of courses and grades required. 20 ACT required. **Learning Disabled:** Must submit appropriate documentation in order to be given special consideration.

High school preparation. College-preparatory program recommended. 15 units required. Required units include English 4, mathematics 3, history 3, science 3, foreign language 1, computer science 1 and visual/performing arts 1.

2008-2009 Annual costs. Tuition/fees: $5,460; $10,068 out-of-state. Room/board: $4,600. Books/supplies: $1,000. Personal expenses: $1,380.

2008-2009 Financial aid. Need-based: Average need met was 66%. Average scholarship/grant was $4,673; average loan $3,508. 40% of total undergraduate aid awarded as scholarships/grants, 60% as loans/jobs. **Non-need-based:** Scholarships awarded for academics, alumni affiliation, art, athletics, job skills, leadership, minority status, music/drama, ROTC, state residency.

Application procedures. Admission: Closing date 7/30 (postmark date). $25 fee, may be waived for applicants with need. Admission notification on a rolling basis beginning on or about 9/1. **Financial aid:** Priority date 4/1; no closing date. FAFSA required. Applicants notified on a rolling basis starting 5/15.

Academics. Special study options: Combined bachelor's/graduate degree, cooperative education, cross-registration, double major, honors, independent study, internships, teacher certification program. **Credit/placement by examination:** AP, CLEP, ACT, institutional tests. 45 credit hours maximum toward bachelor's degree. Students must have approval of the academic advisor, department head, dean and vice president for academic affairs prior to taking CLEP exam. **Support services:** Learning center, remedial instruction, study skills assistance, tutoring, writing center.

Honors college/program. 3.3 GPA and 24 ACT or 1100 SAT required; 34 freshmen admitted.

Majors. Biology: General, marine. **Business:** Accounting, business admin, finance, marketing. **Communications:** General. **Computer sciences:** Computer science, information systems. **Education:** Early childhood, elementary, music, physical, secondary, special. **Health:** Medical records admin. **History:** General. **Math:** General. **Parks/recreation:** Facilities management. **Physical sciences:** Chemistry, physics. **Protective services:** Criminal justice. **Psychology:** General. **Public administration:** Social work. **Social sciences:** Political science, sociology. **Visual/performing arts:** Art, dramatic.

Most popular majors. Biology 6%, business/marketing 14%, communications/journalism 6%, computer/information sciences 12%, education 22%, psychology 7%, public administration/social services 9%, security/protective services 8%, visual/performing arts 6%.

Computing on campus. 405 workstations in library, computer center. Online course registration, online library, helpline, wireless network available.

Student life. Freshman orientation: Mandatory, $55 fee. Preregistration for classes offered. **Housing:** Single-sex dorms, special housing for disabled available. $200 deposit, deadline 5/31. Housing for nontraditional students available. **Activities:** Bands, campus ministries, choral groups, dance, drama, international student organizations, music ensembles, Model UN, musical theater, radio station, student government, student newspaper, Student Christian Association.

Athletics. NCAA. **Intercollegiate:** Baseball M, basketball, bowling W, cross-country, football (tackle) M, golf, soccer W, softball W, tennis, track and field, volleyball W. **Intramural:** Baseball M, basketball, softball, swimming, tennis, track and field, volleyball W. **Team name:** Hornets.

Student services. Adult student services, alcohol/substance abuse counseling, career counseling, services for economically disadvantaged, student employment services, financial aid counseling, health services, minority student services, personal counseling, placement for graduates, veterans' counselor. **Physically disabled:** Services for visually impaired. **Learning disabled:** Comprehensive services available.

Contact. E-mail: mpettway@alasu.edu
Phone: (334) 229-4291 Toll-free number: (800) 253-5037
Fax: (334) 229-4984
Martha Pettway, Director of Admissions and Recruitment, Alabama State University, PO Box 271, Montgomery, AL 36101-0271

Amridge University
Montgomery, Alabama
www.amridgeuniversity.edu **CB code: 7001**

- Private 4-year university and seminary college affiliated with Church of Christ
- Commuter campus in small city
- 356 degree-seeking undergraduates: 35% part-time, 50% women, 35% African American, 1% Asian American, 5% Hispanic American
- 353 degree-seeking graduate students

General. Founded in 1967. Regionally accredited. **Degrees:** 105 bachelor's awarded; master's, doctoral, first professional offered. **Location:** 100 miles from Birmingham, 150 miles from Atlanta. **Calendar:** Semester, extensive summer session. **Full-time faculty:** 58 total. **Part-time faculty:** 37 total.

Basis for selection. Open admission, but selective for some programs. Students admitted under conditional admission must earn a 2.0 during the first 24 semester hours attempted. **Homeschooled:** Transcript of courses and grades, interview required.

High school preparation. 15 units recommended.

2008-2009 Annual costs. Books/supplies: $800. Personal expenses: $1,739.

2007-2008 Financial aid. Non-need-based: Scholarships awarded for academics, leadership.

Application procedures. Admission: No deadline. $75 fee. Admission notification on a rolling basis. **Financial aid:** Priority date 5/1, closing date 6/30. FAFSA, institutional form required. Applicants notified by 6/30; must reply by 8/15 or within 2 week(s) of notification.

Academics. Special study options: Accelerated study, distance learning, double major, independent study, internships. Participant in the U.S. Department of Education's Distance Education Demonstration Program and in eArmyU and GoArmyEd initiatives. **Credit/placement by examination:** CLEP. 36 credit hours maximum toward bachelor's degree. **Support services:** Tutoring.

Majors. Business: Business admin. **Computer sciences:** General. **Liberal arts:** Arts/sciences. **Theology:** Bible.

Most popular majors. Liberal arts 61%, theological studies 38%.

Computing on campus. PC or laptop required. 25 workstations in library, computer center. Online course registration, online library, helpline available.

Student life. Freshman orientation: Available. Online orientation available at any time.

Student services. Financial aid counseling, placement for graduates, veterans' counselor.

Contact. E-mail: admissions@amridgeuniversity.edu
Phone: (334) 387-7425 Toll-free number: (800) 351-4040 ext. 7524
Fax: (334) 387-3878
Ora Davis, Admissions Officer, Amridge University, PO Box 240240, Montgomery, AL 36124-0240

Andrew Jackson University
Birmingham, Alabama
www.aju.edu **CB code: 3877**

- For-profit 4-year virtual liberal arts college
- Very large city
- 532 degree-seeking undergraduates

General. Accredited by DETC. **Degrees:** 26 bachelor's, 8 associate awarded; master's offered. **Calendar:** Continuous, extensive summer session. **Part-time faculty:** 50 total.

Basis for selection. Open admission. **Homeschooled:** State high school equivalency certificate, letter of recommendation (nonparent) required.

2008-2009 Annual costs. Books/supplies: $750.

Application procedures. Admission: No deadline. $75 fee. Admission notification on a rolling basis. Must reply by May 1 or within 12 week(s) if notified thereafter.

Academics. Special study options: Accelerated study, distance learning, independent study. **Credit/placement by examination:** AP, CLEP. 15 credit hours maximum toward associate degree, 30 toward bachelor's. **Support services:** Reduced course load.

Majors. Business: General. **Communications:** General. **Protective services:** Criminal justice.

Most popular majors. Business/marketing 11%, public administration/social services 89%.

Computing on campus. PC or laptop required.

Student life. Freshman orientation: Available.

Athletics. Team name: Generals.

Contact. E-mail: admissions@aju.edu
Phone: (205) 871-9288 Toll-free number: (800) 429-9300
Fax: (205) 871-9294
Tammy Kassner, Director of Student Affairs, Andrew Jackson University, 2919 John Hawkins Parkway, Birmingham, AL 35244

Athens State University
Athens, Alabama
www.athens.edu **CB code: 0706**

- Public two-year upper-division business, liberal arts and teachers college
- Commuter campus in large town
- 88% of applicants admitted

General. Founded in 1822. Regionally accredited. **Degrees:** 805 bachelor's awarded. **Articulation:** Agreements with state schools through the Alabama Articulation and General Studies Committee. **Location:** 14 miles from Decatur, 24 miles from Huntsville. **Calendar:** Semester, extensive summer session. **Full-time faculty:** 70 total. **Part-time faculty:** 90 total. **Class size:** 44% < 20, 44% 20-39, 4% 40-49, 3% 50-99, 5% >100.

Student profile. 3,114 degree-seeking undergraduates. 1,069 applied as first time-transfer students, 943 admitted, 753 enrolled. 81% transferred from two-year, 19% transferred from four-year institutions.

Women:	68%	**Out-of-state:**	4%
Part-time:	53%	**25 or older:**	90%

Basis for selection. College transcript required. Transfer accepted as juniors, seniors.

2009-2010 Annual costs. Tuition/fees: $4,350; $7,950 out-of-state. Books/supplies: $800.

Financial aid. Need-based: 98% of total undergraduate aid awarded as scholarships/grants, 2% as loans/jobs. **Non-need-based:** Scholarships awarded for academics, alumni affiliation, art, athletics, leadership, minority status.

Application procedures. Admission: Rolling admission. $30 fee. **Financial aid:** FAFSA required.

Academics. Special study options: Cooperative education, distance learning, double major, dual enrollment of high school students, honors, independent study, internships, liberal arts/career combination, study abroad, teacher certification program, weekend college. **Credit/placement by examination:** AP, CLEP.

Majors. Biology: General. **Business:** Accounting, business admin, human resources, information resources management. **Computer sciences:** General. **Education:** General, biology, chemistry, early childhood, elementary, English, history, mathematics, middle, physical, physics, science, secondary, social science, social studies, special, trade/industrial. **Engineering technology:** Instrumentation. **History:** General. **Interdisciplinary:** Behavioral sciences. **Liberal arts:** Arts/sciences. **Math:** General. **Philosophy/religion:** Religion. **Physical sciences:** Chemistry, physics. **Protective services:** Criminal justice. **Psychology:** General. **Social sciences:** Political science, sociology. **Visual/performing arts:** Art.

Most popular majors. Business/marketing 31%, computer/information sciences 6%, education 34%, interdisciplinary studies 6%, liberal arts 6%.

Computing on campus. 341 workstations in library, computer center, student center. Commuter students can connect to campus network. Online library available.

Student life. Housing: Coed dorms available. **Activities:** Campus ministries, drama, literary magazine, student government, student newspaper, African-American history association, Centurions, Athenian hosts/hostesses, TKE, Tau Kappa Epsilon, Wesley Fellowship campus ministries, Pi tau Chi, pre-law society, council for exceptional children.

Athletics. Team name: Bears.

Student services. Career counseling, student employment services, financial aid counseling, minority student services, placement for graduates, veterans' counselor. **Physically disabled:** Services for visually, speech, hearing impaired.

Contact. E-mail: admissions@athens.edu
Phone: (256) 233-8220 Toll-free number: (800) 522-0272
Fax: (256) 233-6565
Necedah Henderson, Coordinator of Admissions, Athens State University, 300 North Beaty Street, Athens, AL 35611

Auburn University
Auburn, Alabama **CB member**
www.auburn.edu **CB code: 1005**

- Public 4-year university
- Commuter campus in large town
- 20,031 degree-seeking undergraduates: 8% part-time, 49% women, 8% African American, 2% Asian American, 2% Hispanic American, 1% Native American, 1% international
- 4,455 degree-seeking graduate students
- 71% of applicants admitted
- SAT or ACT (ACT writing optional), application essay required
- 64% graduate within 6 years

General. Founded in 1856. Regionally accredited. **Degrees:** 3,763 bachelor's awarded; master's, doctoral, first professional offered. **ROTC:** Army, Naval, Air Force. **Location:** 55 miles from Montgomery, 110 miles from Atlanta. **Calendar:** Semester, extensive summer session. **Full-time faculty:** 1,176 total; 18% minority, 30% women. **Part-time faculty:** 147 total; 5% minority, 45% women. **Class size:** 27% < 20, 54% 20-39, 5% 40-49, 9% 50-99, 5% >100. **Special facilities:** Space power institute, electron microscopes, rhizotron, nuclear science center, arboretum, torsatron, center for arts and humanities, sports museum.

Freshman class profile. 17,068 applied, 12,085 admitted, 3,984 enrolled.

Mid 50% test scores		**Rank in top quarter:**	60%
SAT critical reading:	520-620	**Rank in top tenth:**	31%
SAT math:	550-650	**Return as sophomores:**	87%
SAT writing:	520-620	**Out-of-state:**	43%
ACT composite:	23-28	**Live on campus:**	41%
GPA 3.75 or higher:	47%	**International:**	1%
GPA 3.50-3.74:	20%	**Fraternities:**	25%
GPA 3.0-3.49:	28%	**Sororities:**	43%
GPA 2.0-2.99:	5%		

Basis for selection. Each student evaluated based on combination of standardized test scores, GPA, and additional information required on application.

High school preparation. College-preparatory program required. 12 units required; 15 recommended. Required and recommended units include English 4, mathematics 3, social studies 3-4, science 2-3 (laboratory 1) and foreign language 1. Math must include algebra I, algebra II, and either geometry, trigonometry, calculus or analysis. Science must include biology and a physical science.

2008-2009 Annual costs. Tuition/fees: $6,500; $18,260 out-of-state. Room/board: $8,260. Books/supplies: $1,100. Personal expenses: $2,398.

2007-2008 Financial aid. Need-based: 2,133 full-time freshmen applied for aid; 1,179 were judged to have need; 1,179 of these received aid.

Average need met was 58%. Average scholarship/grant was $5,555; average loan $3,872. 37% of total undergraduate aid awarded as scholarships/grants, 63% as loans/jobs. **Non-need-based:** Awarded to 2,727 full-time undergraduates, including 985 freshmen. **Additional information:** State of Alabama has pre-paid college tuition plan for residents.

Application procedures. Admission: $40 fee, may be waived for applicants with need. Admission notification on a rolling basis beginning on or about 10/1. **Financial aid:** No deadline. FAFSA, institutional form required. Applicants notified on a rolling basis.

Academics. Special study options: Accelerated study, cooperative education, distance learning, double major, dual enrollment of high school students, ESL, honors, independent study, internships, liberal arts/career combination, study abroad, teacher certification program. DVM/Master's in veterinary specialty, dual option program in education/subject areas. **Credit/placement by examination:** AP, CLEP, SAT, ACT, institutional tests. **Support services:** Learning center, reduced course load, study skills assistance, tutoring, writing center.

Honors college/program. 29 ACT/1280 SAT (exclusive of Writing) and 3.5 GPA required (3.4 GPA may be considered). Approximately 200 freshmen accepted last year.

Majors. Agriculture: Animal sciences, aquaculture, economics, horticultural science, poultry, soil science. **Architecture:** Architecture, environmental design, interior. **Biology:** General, bacteriology, biochemistry, botany, entomology, marine, molecular, zoology. **Business:** Accounting, business admin, communications, finance, human resources, international, logistics, managerial economics, marketing, operations. **Communications:** Journalism, public relations, radio/tv. **Computer sciences:** General. **Conservation:** Environmental science, forest sciences, wildlife. **Education:** Adult/continuing, early childhood, elementary, English, foreign languages, health, mathematics, music, physical, science, social science, special, voc/tech. **Engineering:** Aerospace, agricultural, architectural, chemical, civil, computer, electrical, materials, mechanical, software, textile. **Family/consumer sciences:** Apparel marketing, family studies, food/nutrition, housing. **Foreign languages:** French, German, Spanish. **Health:** Audiology/speech pathology, communication disorders, health care admin, nursing (RN), premedicine. **History:** General. **Math:** General, applied. **Parks/recreation:** Exercise sciences. **Philosophy/religion:** Philosophy, religion. **Physical sciences:** Chemistry, geology, physics. **Psychology:** General. **Public administration:** General, social work. **Science technology:** Biological. **Social sciences:** Anthropology, economics, geography, political science, sociology. **Transportation:** Aviation management. **Visual/performing arts:** Design, dramatic, industrial design, studio arts.

Most popular majors. Biology 6%, business/marketing 25%, education 10%, engineering/engineering technologies 13%, social sciences 7%.

Computing on campus. 600 workstations in dormitories, library, computer center, student center. Dormitories linked to campus network. Commuter students can connect to campus network. Online course registration, online library, helpline, repair service available.

Student life. Freshman orientation: Available, $75 fee. Preregistration for classes offered. **Housing:** Coed dorms, single-sex dorms, special housing for disabled, apartments, fraternity/sorority housing, wellness housing available. Honors housing available. **Activities:** Bands, campus ministries, choral groups, dance, drama, film society, international student organizations, literary magazine, music ensembles, musical theater, opera, radio station, student government, student newspaper, symphony orchestra, TV station, over 300 religious, political, ethnic, and social service organizations.

Athletics. NCAA. **Intercollegiate:** Baseball M, basketball, cross-country, diving, equestrian W, football (tackle) M, golf, gymnastics W, soccer W, softball W, swimming, tennis, track and field, volleyball W. **Intramural:** Badminton, basketball, bowling, cheerleading, football (non-tackle), golf, gymnastics, lacrosse, racquetball, rugby, skiing, soccer, softball, swimming, table tennis, tennis, track and field, volleyball, wrestling M. **Team name:** Tigers.

Student services. Adult student services, alcohol/substance abuse counseling, career counseling, student employment services, financial aid counseling, health services, minority student services, personal counseling, placement for graduates, veterans' counselor, women's services. **Physically disabled:** Services for visually, speech, hearing impaired.

Contact. E-mail: admissions@auburn.edu
Phone: (334) 844-4080 Toll-free number: (800) 282-8769
Fax: (334) 844-6436
Cindy Singley, Director of University Recruitment, Auburn University, Quad Center, Auburn, AL 36849-5111

Auburn University at Montgomery

Montgomery, Alabama — **CB member**
www.aum.edu — **CB code: 1036**

- Public 4-year university
- Commuter campus in small city
- 4,323 degree-seeking undergraduates: 33% part-time, 62% women, 31% African American, 2% Asian American, 1% Hispanic American, 2% international
- 797 degree-seeking graduate students
- 91% of applicants admitted
- SAT or ACT (ACT writing optional) required

General. Founded in 1967. Regionally accredited. **Degrees:** 678 bachelor's awarded; master's, doctoral offered. **ROTC:** Army, Air Force. **Location:** 100 miles from Auburn, 90 miles from Birmingham. **Calendar:** Semester, extensive summer session. **Full-time faculty:** 201 total; 19% minority, 42% women. **Part-time faculty:** 159 total; 18% minority, 56% women. **Class size:** 49% < 20, 47% 20-39, 2% 40-49, 1% 50-99, less than 1% >100.

Freshman class profile. 1,621 applied, 1,470 admitted, 766 enrolled.

Mid 50% test scores		**Live on campus:**	22%
ACT composite:	18-22		

Basis for selection. GPA and ACT/SAT scores considered for admission. Provisional admission may be available for students who do not meet requirements for regular admission. C average after 18 hours of academic courses required for provisional students to become regular students.

High school preparation. College-preparatory program recommended. 4 units recommended. Recommended units include English 3, mathematics 2, social studies 2, history 2, science 2 (laboratory 2), foreign language 2 and academic electives 2.

2008-2009 Annual costs. Tuition/fees: $5,580; $16,200 out-of-state. Room only: $3,420.

2008-2009 Financial aid. Need-based: 23% of total undergraduate aid awarded as scholarships/grants, 77% as loans/jobs. **Non-need-based:** Scholarships awarded for academics, alumni affiliation, art, athletics, job skills, leadership, minority status, music/drama, religious affiliation, ROTC.

Application procedures. Admission: $25 fee. Admission notification on a rolling basis. **Financial aid:** Priority date 3/15; no closing date. FAFSA required. Applicants notified on a rolling basis starting 5/1; must reply within 2 week(s) of notification.

Academics. Interdisciplinary Master of Liberal Arts available. **Special study options:** Accelerated study, cooperative education, cross-registration, distance learning, double major, dual enrollment of high school students, ESL, honors, independent study, internships, liberal arts/career combination, study abroad, teacher certification program, weekend college. Joint Ph.D. in public administration with Auburn University; cooperative doctoral program in educational leadership with Auburn University (Ed.D.). **Credit/placement by examination:** AP, CLEP, IB, SAT, ACT, institutional tests. 64 credit hours maximum toward bachelor's degree. **Support services:** Learning center, reduced course load, remedial instruction, tutoring.

Majors. Biology: General. **Business:** General, accounting, business admin, finance, human resources, management information systems, managerial economics, marketing. **Communications:** General. **Education:** Elementary, secondary. **Foreign languages:** General. **Health:** Nursing (RN). **History:** General. **Liberal arts:** Arts/sciences. **Math:** General. **Physical sciences:** General. **Protective services:** Criminal justice. **Psychology:** General. **Social sciences:** Political science, sociology. **Visual/performing arts:** Art.

Most popular majors. Biology 8%, business/marketing 34%, education 13%, health sciences 14%, psychology 6%, security/protective services 6%.

Computing on campus. 500 workstations in dormitories, library, computer center, student center. Dormitories wired for high-speed internet access and linked to campus network. Commuter students can connect to campus network. Online course registration, online library, helpline, repair service, student web hosting, wireless network available.

Student life. Freshman orientation: Mandatory, $50 fee. Preregistration for classes offered. Two sessions, 1 hour each, morning and evening. Programs held 2 days before start of each semester. **Policies:** Students required to conform to all policies and regulations of the university by October registration. **Housing:** Coed dorms, special housing for disabled, apartments available. $100 nonrefundable deposit. **Activities:** Campus ministries, choral groups, drama, film society, international student organizations, student government, student newspaper, American Humanics, S.A.L.T, Chinese association, Young African American Against Media Stereotypes.

Athletics. NAIA. **Intercollegiate:** Baseball M, basketball, soccer, softball W, tennis. **Intramural:** Baseball, basketball M, bowling, football (non-tackle), softball, tennis, volleyball. **Team name:** Senators.

Student services. Adult student services, career counseling, student employment services, health services, personal counseling, placement for graduates, veterans' counselor, women's services. **Physically disabled:** Services for visually, speech, hearing impaired.

Contact. E-mail: admitme@aum.edu
Phone: (334) 244-3616 Toll-free number: (800) 227-2649
Fax: (334) 244-3795
Valerie Crawford, Director of Admissions, Auburn University at Montgomery, 7400 East Drive, Room 139 Taylor Center, Montgomery, AL 36124-4023

Birmingham-Southern College

Birmingham, Alabama — **CB member**
www.bsc.edu — **CB code: 1064**

- Private 4-year liberal arts college affiliated with United Methodist Church
- Residential campus in very large city
- 1,412 degree-seeking undergraduates: 2% part-time, 51% women, 8% African American, 3% Asian American, 1% Hispanic American
- 46 degree-seeking graduate students
- 69% of applicants admitted
- SAT or ACT (ACT writing recommended), application essay required
- 66% graduate within 6 years; 50% enter graduate study

General. Founded in 1856. Regionally accredited. **Degrees:** 290 bachelor's awarded; master's offered. **ROTC:** Army, Air Force. **Location:** 3 miles from downtown. **Calendar:** 4-1-4, limited summer session. **Full-time faculty:** 104 total; 94% have terminal degrees, 2% minority, 43% women. **Part-time faculty:** 34 total; 24% have terminal degrees, 47% women. **Class size:** 65% < 20, 33% 20-39, 1% 40-49, 1% 50-99. **Special facilities:** Planetarium, southern environmental center and interactive museum, ecoscape garden.

Freshman class profile. 2,101 applied, 1,447 admitted, 451 enrolled.

Mid 50% test scores			
SAT critical reading:	520-640	Rank in top quarter:	53%
SAT math:	510-630	Rank in top tenth:	32%
ACT composite:	23-28	End year in good standing:	95%
GPA 3.75 or higher:	33%	Return as sophomores:	75%
GPA 3.50-3.74:	18%	Out-of-state:	43%
GPA 3.0-3.49:	24%	Live on campus:	97%
GPA 2.0-2.99:	25%	Fraternities:	43%
		Sororities:	46%

Basis for selection. High school record most important, followed by test scores, recommendations, and required essay. Interview required for early admission, recommended for borderline applicants. Auditions required for music, theatre, dance majors. **Homeschooled:** Interviews recommended.

High school preparation. College-preparatory program required. 16 units required. Required and recommended units include English 4, mathematics 4, social studies 2, history 2, science 4 (laboratory 2), foreign language 2 and academic electives 10.

2008-2009 Annual costs. Tuition/fees: $25,586. Room/board: $8,595. Books/supplies: $1,000. Personal expenses: $500.

2008-2009 Financial aid. Need-based: 299 full-time freshmen applied for aid; 236 were judged to have need; 236 of these received aid. Average need met was 99%. Average scholarship/grant was $4,857; average loan $3,395. 86% of total undergraduate aid awarded as scholarships/grants, 14% as loans/jobs. **Non-need-based:** Awarded to 1,315 full-time undergraduates, including 424 freshmen. Scholarships awarded for academics, alumni affiliation, art, job skills, leadership, minority status, music/drama, religious affiliation, state residency. **Additional information:** Auditions required for music, theatre, dance applicants seeking scholarships. Portfolios required for art applicants seeking scholarships, and essays recommended for all applicants seeking scholarships.

Application procedures. Admission: Priority date 1/1; no deadline. $40 fee, may be waived for applicants with need. Admission notification on a rolling basis beginning on or about 7/1. **Financial aid:** Closing date 3/1. FAFSA required. Applicants notified on a rolling basis starting 3/1; must reply by 8/21.

Academics. Special study options: Combined bachelor's/graduate degree, cooperative education, cross-registration, double major, dual enrollment of high school students, exchange student, honors, independent study, internships, semester at sea, student-designed major, study abroad, teacher certification program, Washington semester. 4-1-4 in nursing with Vanderbilt; 3-2 in engineering with Washington University, Columbia University, University of Alabama, and Auburn University; 3-2 in environment studies with Duke University. **Credit/placement by examination:** AP, CLEP, IB, SAT, ACT, institutional tests. 64 credit hours maximum toward bachelor's degree. **Support services:** Learning center, pre-admission summer program, reduced course load, study skills assistance, tutoring, writing center.

Majors. Biology: General. **Business:** General, accounting, business admin, finance, international, marketing. **Computer sciences:** General, computer science. **Conservation:** Environmental studies. **Education:** General, art, early childhood, elementary, music, secondary, special. **Foreign languages:** French, German, Spanish. **History:** General. **Interdisciplinary:** Math/computer science. **Math:** General. **Philosophy/religion:** Philosophy, religion. **Physical sciences:** Chemistry, physics. **Psychology:** General. **Social sciences:** Economics, political science, sociology. **Theology:** Sacred music. **Visual/performing arts:** General, art, art history/conservation, dance, dramatic, drawing, music history, music theory/composition, painting, photography, piano/organ, sculpture, voice/opera.

Most popular majors. Biology 10%, business/marketing 21%, education 6%, English 10%, interdisciplinary studies 9%, psychology 10%, social sciences 8%, visual/performing arts 10%.

Computing on campus. 252 workstations in dormitories, library, computer center, student center. Dormitories wired for high-speed internet access and linked to campus network. Commuter students can connect to campus network. Online course registration, online library, helpline, student web hosting, wireless network available.

Student life. Freshman orientation: Mandatory. Preregistration for classes offered. One-day mini-session in June and 4-day session prior to beginning of fall classes. **Housing:** Guaranteed on-campus for all undergraduates. Single-sex dorms, special housing for disabled, apartments, fraternity/sorority housing, wellness housing available. $200 nonrefundable deposit, deadline 5/1. Handicapped students accommodated on individual basis. **Activities:** Bands, campus ministries, choral groups, dance, drama, international student organizations, literary magazine, music ensembles, musical theater, opera, student government, student newspaper, Fellowship of Christian Athletes, Young Republicans, Young Democrats, black student union, Allies, Students Offering Support, Conservancy, Wesley Fellowship, Intervarsity Christian Fellowship.

Athletics. NCAA. **Intercollegiate:** Baseball M, basketball, cheerleading, cross-country, football (tackle) M, golf, lacrosse, rifle W, soccer, softball W, tennis, track and field, volleyball W. **Intramural:** Basketball, football (non-tackle), racquetball, soccer, softball, table tennis, volleyball, water polo. **Team name:** Panthers.

Student services. Alcohol/substance abuse counseling, chaplain/spiritual director, career counseling, student employment services, financial aid counseling, health services, personal counseling, placement for graduates, veterans' counselor.

Contact. E-mail: admission@bsc.edu
Phone: (205) 226-4696 Toll-free number: (800) 523-5793
Fax: (205) 226-3074
Sheri Salmon, Dean for Enrollment Management, Birmingham-Southern College, 900 Arkadelphia Road, Birmingham, AL 35254

Columbia Southern University

Orange Beach, Alabama
www.columbiasouthern.edu — **CB code: 3878**

- For-profit 4-year virtual business college
- Commuter campus in small town
- 10,850 degree-seeking undergraduates
- 3,207 graduate students

General. Accredited by DETC. **Degrees:** 451 bachelor's, 124 associate awarded; master's, doctoral offered. **Location:** 60 miles from Mobile. **Calendar:** Continuous. **Full-time faculty:** 22 total; 91% have terminal degrees. **Part-time faculty:** 105 total; 41% have terminal degrees.

Freshman class profile. 65 enrolled.

Basis for selection. Open admission.

2009-2010 Annual costs. Tuition/fees (projected): $4,730.

Application procedures. Admission: No deadline. $25 fee. **Financial aid:** FAFSA, institutional form required.

Academics. Special study options: Distance learning. **Credit/placement by examination:** CLEP.

Majors. Business: Business admin, hospitality admin, human resources, marketing, tourism/travel. **Computer sciences:** Information technology. **Health:** Health care admin. **Protective services:** Firefighting, law enforcement admin. **Psychology:** General. **Other:** Occupational Safety and Health.

Most popular majors. Business/marketing 49%, health sciences 6%, natural resources/environmental science 6%, security/protective services 29%.

Computing on campus. PC or laptop required. Commuter students can connect to campus network. Online course registration, online library available.

Student life. Freshman orientation: Mandatory, $195 fee. Online course. **Activities:** Student newspaper.

Student services. Financial aid counseling.

Contact. E-mail: admissions@columbiasouthern.edu
Phone: (251) 981-3771 ext. 521 Toll-free number: (800) 977-8449 ext. 521
Fax: (251) 981-3815
Kathy Cole, Director of Admissions/Enrollments, Columbia Southern University, 25326 Canal Road, Orange Beach, AL 36561

Concordia College

Selma, Alabama
www.concordiaselma.edu **CB code: 1989**

- Private 4-year liberal arts college affiliated with Lutheran Church - Missouri Synod
- Residential campus in large town

General. Founded in 1922. Regionally accredited. **Location:** 50 miles from Montgomery. **Calendar:** Semester.

Annual costs/financial aid. Tuition/fees (2008-2009): $6,300. Room/board: $3,200. Books/supplies: $600. Need-based financial aid available to full-time and part-time students.

Contact. Phone: (334) 874-5700
Director of Admissions, 1804 Green Street, Selma, AL 36701

Faulkner University

Montgomery, Alabama
www.faulkner.edu **CB code: 1034**

- Private 4-year university and liberal arts college affiliated with Church of Christ
- Residential campus in large city
- 2,483 degree-seeking undergraduates: 19% part-time, 62% women
- 441 degree-seeking graduate students
- 59% of applicants admitted
- SAT or ACT (ACT writing optional) required

General. Founded in 1942. Regionally accredited. **Degrees:** 601 bachelor's, 20 associate awarded; master's, doctoral, first professional offered. **ROTC:** Army, Air Force. **Calendar:** Semester, limited summer session. **Full-time faculty:** 105 total; 67% have terminal degrees, 11% minority, 32% women. **Part-time faculty:** 50 total; 44% have terminal degrees, 14% minority, 40% women. **Class size:** 77% < 20, 18% 20-39, 3% 40-49, 2% 50-99, less than 1% >100.

Freshman class profile. 875 applied, 518 admitted, 221 enrolled.

Mid 50% test scores			
SAT critical reading:	400-550	**GPA 3.0-3.49:**	36%
SAT math:	370-530	**GPA 2.0-2.99:**	34%
ACT composite:	18-22	**Rank in top quarter:**	18%
GPA 3.75 or higher:	15%	**Rank in top tenth:**	10%
GPA 3.50-3.74:	14%	**Out-of-state:**	34%
		Live on campus:	62%

Basis for selection. Academic record, test scores, and personal or career goals most important. Interview, essay recommended.

High school preparation. College-preparatory program recommended. 15 units required. 9 units from among social sciences, foreign language, mathematics and science required.

2008-2009 Annual costs. Tuition/fees: $12,770. Room/board: $6,350. Books/supplies: $1,500. Personal expenses: $1,200.

2008-2009 Financial aid. Need-based: Average need met was 60%. Average scholarship/grant was $2,650; average loan $3,500. 31% of total undergraduate aid awarded as scholarships/grants, 69% as loans/jobs. **Non-need-based:** Scholarships awarded for academics, alumni affiliation, art, athletics, leadership, music/drama, religious affiliation, ROTC, state residency.

Application procedures. Admission: Priority date 2/15; no deadline. $10 fee, may be waived for applicants with need. Admission notification on a rolling basis beginning on or about 8/15. **Financial aid:** Priority date 5/1; no closing date. FAFSA, institutional form required. Applicants notified on a rolling basis starting 6/1; must reply within 3 week(s) of notification.

Academics. Full-time students required to take Bible course each semester. **Special study options:** Accelerated study, combined bachelor's/graduate degree, cross-registration, distance learning, double major, dual enrollment of high school students, honors, independent study, internships, liberal arts/career combination, study abroad, teacher certification program, weekend college. **Credit/placement by examination:** AP, CLEP, IB, SAT, ACT, institutional tests. 16 credit hours maximum toward associate degree, 32 toward bachelor's. **Support services:** Learning center, reduced course load, remedial instruction, study skills assistance, tutoring, writing center.

Majors. Biology: General, biomedical sciences. **Business:** General, accounting/finance, business admin, human resources, management information systems, management science, marketing. **Communications:** Journalism. **Computer sciences:** General, computer science, information systems. **Education:** General, biology, drama/dance, elementary, English, history, mathematics, middle, multi-level teacher, physical, science, secondary, social science, social studies. **Family/consumer sciences:** Communication, family/community services. **Health:** Community health services, marriage/family therapy, mental health counseling, predental, premedicine, prenursing, prepharmacy, preveterinary. **History:** General. **Legal studies:** General, paralegal, prelaw. **Liberal arts:** Arts/sciences, humanities. **Math:** General. **Parks/recreation:** Health/fitness, sports admin. **Philosophy/religion:** Christian, religion. **Protective services:** Criminal justice. **Psychology:** General. **Social sciences:** General. **Theology:** Bible, missionary, theology, youth ministry. **Visual/performing arts:** Dramatic, theater arts management, theater design.

Computing on campus. 250 workstations in dormitories, library, computer center, student center. Dormitories wired for high-speed internet access and linked to campus network. Online library, helpline, wireless network available.

Student life. Freshman orientation: Mandatory. Preregistration for classes offered. **Policies:** Religious observance required. **Housing:** Guaranteed on-campus for freshmen. Single-sex dorms, special housing for disabled, apartments available. $50 nonrefundable deposit. **Activities:** Campus ministries, choral groups, drama, literary magazine, music ensembles, musical theater, student government, student newspaper, minister's club, service organizations, religious organizations.

Athletics. NAIA, NCCAA. **Intercollegiate:** Baseball M, basketball M, cheerleading, cross-country, football (tackle) M, golf M, softball W, volleyball W. **Intramural:** Badminton, basketball, bowling, football (non-tackle), racquetball, softball, table tennis, tennis, track and field, volleyball. **Team name:** Eagles.

Student services. Adult student services, chaplain/spiritual director, career counseling, student employment services, financial aid counseling, health services, personal counseling, placement for graduates, veterans' counselor. **Physically disabled:** Services for visually, speech, hearing impaired. **Learning disabled:** Comprehensive services available.

Contact. E-mail: admissions@faulkner.edu
Phone: (334) 386-7200 Toll-free number: (800) 879-9816 ext. 7200
Fax: (334) 386-7137
Keith Mock, Director of Admissions, Faulkner University, 5345 Atlanta Highway, Montgomery, AL 36109-3398

Heritage Christian University

Florence, Alabama
www.hcu.edu **CB code: 0805**

- Private 4-year Bible college affiliated with Church of Christ
- Commuter campus in large town
- 73 degree-seeking undergraduates
- 83% of applicants admitted

General. Founded in 1971. Accredited by ABHE. **Degrees:** 12 bachelor's, 4 associate awarded; master's offered. **Location:** 125 miles from Birmingham, 50 miles from Huntsville. **Calendar:** Semester, limited summer session. **Full-time faculty:** 5 total. **Part-time faculty:** 14 total. **Class size:** 96% < 20, 4% 20-39.

Freshman class profile. 6 applied, 5 admitted, 4 enrolled.

Out-of-state:	40%	**Live on campus:**	10%

Basis for selection. Religious affiliation and recommendations very important, school achievement considered. Interview recommended.

2008-2009 Annual costs. Tuition/fees: $10,140. Room only: $3,000. Books/supplies: $800. Personal expenses: $600.

Application procedures. Admission: No deadline. $25 fee. Admission notification on a rolling basis. **Financial aid:** Priority date 6/1; no closing date. FAFSA required. Applicants notified on a rolling basis starting 6/1; must reply by 7/28 or within 2 week(s) of notification.

Academics. Special study options: Accelerated study, distance learning, dual enrollment of high school students, independent study, internships. **Credit/placement by examination:** AP, CLEP, institutional tests. 24 credit hours maximum toward associate degree, 24 toward bachelor's. **Support services:** Reduced course load, remedial instruction, study skills assistance, tutoring.

Majors. Theology: Bible.

Computing on campus. 12 workstations in library, computer center. Wireless network available.

Student life. Freshman orientation: Mandatory. Preregistration for classes offered. **Housing:** Guaranteed on-campus for freshmen. Single-sex dorms, apartments, wellness housing available. **Activities:** Student government, Christian service program, mission club.

Student services. Career counseling, student employment services, personal counseling, placement for graduates, veterans' counselor.

Contact. E-mail: hcu@hcu.edu
Phone: (256) 766-6610 Toll-free number: (800) 367-3565
Fax: (256) 766-9289
Travis Harmon, Director of Enrollment Services, Heritage Christian University, 3625 Helton Drive, Florence, AL 35630

Herzing College
Birmingham, Alabama
www.herzing.edu — **CB code: 2851**

- For-profit 4-year business and technical college
- Very large city

General. Regionally accredited. **Calendar:** Semester.

Annual costs/financial aid. $350 to $385 per credit hour depending on program. Need-based financial aid available for full-time students.

Contact. Phone: (205) 916-2800
Director of Admissions, 280 West Valley Avenue, Birmingham, AL 35209

Huntingdon College
Montgomery, Alabama — **CB member**
www.huntingdon.edu — **CB code: 1303**

- Private 4-year liberal arts college affiliated with United Methodist Church
- Residential campus in small city
- 1,076 degree-seeking undergraduates: 21% part-time, 51% women, 17% African American, 1% Hispanic American, 1% international
- 65% of applicants admitted
- SAT or ACT (ACT writing optional) required
- 51% graduate within 6 years

General. Founded in 1854. Regionally accredited. Numerous locations throughout central and south Alabama. **Degrees:** 194 bachelor's awarded. **ROTC:** Army, Air Force. **Location:** 90 miles from Birmingham, 180 miles from Atlanta. **Calendar:** Semester, limited summer session. **Full-time faculty:** 44 total; 84% have terminal degrees, 11% minority, 39% women. **Part-time faculty:** 72 total; 40% have terminal degrees, 17% minority, 42% women. **Class size:** 65% < 20, 31% 20-39, 3% 40-49, less than 1% 50-99.

Special facilities: Recital hall with individual practice studios, ecological center, sports medicine and athletic training facilities, United Methodist Church archives.

Freshman class profile. 1,098 applied, 713 admitted, 254 enrolled.

Mid 50% test scores		**Rank in top quarter:**	33%
SAT critical reading:	430-560	**Rank in top tenth:**	9%
SAT math:	450-540	**End year in good standing:**	84%
SAT writing:	440-570	**Return as sophomores:**	67%
ACT composite:	19-24	**Out-of-state:**	5%
GPA 3.75 or higher:	19%	**Live on campus:**	75%
GPA 3.50-3.74:	19%	**Fraternities:**	16%
GPA 3.0-3.49:	36%	**Sororities:**	34%
GPA 2.0-2.99:	25%		

Basis for selection. Applicants must have 2.25 GPA and 20 ACT (930 SAT). Interview, essay recommended. Audition required of music majors; portfolio recommended for art majors. **Learning Disabled:** Students meet with Center for Learning Enrichment to assign appropriate academic assistance and services, which take effect upon matriculation.

High school preparation. College-preparatory program recommended. 14 units recommended. Recommended units include English 4, mathematics 3, social studies 3, science 2 and foreign language 2. 3 credit hours can be taken in history or social studies.

2008-2009 Annual costs. Tuition/fees: $20,020. Room/board: $6,950. Books/supplies: $1,000. Personal expenses: $1,045.

2008-2009 Financial aid. Need-based: 218 full-time freshmen applied for aid; 187 were judged to have need; 187 of these received aid. Average need met was 92%. Average scholarship/grant was $6,264; average loan $3,650. 45% of total undergraduate aid awarded as scholarships/grants, 55% as loans/jobs. **Non-need-based:** Awarded to 792 full-time undergraduates, including 253 freshmen. Scholarships awarded for academics, alumni affiliation, music/drama, religious affiliation, ROTC, state residency.

Application procedures. Admission: Priority date 5/15; deadline 8/21 (receipt date). $20 fee, may be waived for applicants with need. Admission notification on a rolling basis beginning on or about 9/2. **Financial aid:** Priority date 4/14; no closing date. Institutional form required. Applicants notified on a rolling basis starting 3/14; must reply by 5/14 or within 2 week(s) of notification.

Academics. Special study options: Combined bachelor's/graduate degree, cross-registration, double major, honors, independent study, internships, liberal arts/career combination, student-designed major, study abroad, teacher certification program. Adult Degree Completion Program; dual engineering degree with Auburn University and exchange student program with universities in Ireland; travel opportunities to all full-time juniors and seniors within regular educational costs or for nominal additional fees. **Credit/placement by examination:** AP, CLEP, IB, SAT, ACT, institutional tests. 30 credit hours maximum toward bachelor's degree. No credit will be granted on examinations taken after the student has entered college. In any one discipline, maximum of 12 credit hours may be earned. $25 recording fee per awarded credit hour is assessed. **Support services:** Learning center, reduced course load, remedial instruction, study skills assistance, tutoring, writing center.

Majors. Biology: General, cellular/anatomical. **Business:** General, accounting, business admin. **Communications:** General. **Education:** Chemistry, elementary, English, history, music. **Health:** Athletic training. **History:** General. **Math:** General. **Parks/recreation:** Exercise sciences, sports admin. **Philosophy/religion:** Religion. **Physical sciences:** Chemistry. **Psychology:** General. **Social sciences:** Political science. **Theology:** Religious ed. **Visual/performing arts:** Music performance, studio arts.

Most popular majors. Biology 12%, business/marketing 44%, communications/journalism 6%, parks/recreation 6%.

Computing on campus. PC or laptop required. 13 workstations in library. Dormitories wired for high-speed internet access and linked to campus network. Commuter students can connect to campus network. Online library, repair service, student web hosting, wireless network available.

Student life. Freshman orientation: Mandatory. Preregistration for classes offered. Held 3 times during the summer prior to fall semester (June, July, August). **Housing:** Guaranteed on-campus for all undergraduates. Coed dorms, special housing for disabled available. $50 fully refundable deposit, deadline 5/1. **Activities:** Bands, campus ministries, choral groups, drama, international student organizations, literary magazine, music ensembles, Model UN, musical theater, student government, student newspaper, Fellowship of Christian Athletes, Conservative club, Democratic club, Young Republicans, Habitat for Humanity, international students association, student government association, Sigma Nu, Chi Omega, Phi Mu.

Athletics. NCAA. **Intercollegiate:** Baseball M, basketball, cross-country, football (tackle) M, golf, soccer, softball W, tennis, volleyball W. **Intramural:** Basketball, football (non-tackle), soccer, softball, table tennis, tennis, volleyball. **Team name:** Hawks.

Student services. Adult student services, chaplain/spiritual director, career counseling, student employment services, financial aid counseling, health services, placement for graduates. **Physically disabled:** Services for visually, hearing impaired.

Contact. E-mail: admiss@huntingdon.edu
Phone: (334) 833-4497 Toll-free number: (800) 763-0313
Fax: (334) 833-4347
Joseph Miller, Director, Office of Admission, Huntingdon College, 1500 East Fairview Avenue, Montgomery, AL 36106-2148

Huntsville Bible College
Huntsville, Alabama
www.hbc1.edu

- Private 4-year Bible college
- Small city
- 62 degree-seeking undergraduates

General. Accredited by ABHE. **Degrees:** 7 bachelor's, 2 associate awarded. **Location:** 87 miles from Birmingham; 100 miles from Nashville, Tennessee. **Calendar:** Semester. **Part-time faculty:** 13 total.

Freshman class profile. 17 applied, 17 admitted, 15 enrolled.

Basis for selection. Open admission.

2008-2009 Annual costs. Tuition/fees: $3,080.

Application procedures. Admission: Closing date 9/1. $10 fee. **Financial aid:** Priority date 4/1, closing date 6/30.

Academics. Credit/placement by examination: CLEP.

Majors. Theology: Bible, theology.

Student life. Freshman orientation: Mandatory. Preregistration for classes offered.

Contact. E-mail: students@hbc1.edu
Phone: (256) 539-0834 Fax: (256) 539-0854
Willie Brown, Director of Admissions, Huntsville Bible College, 904 Oakwood Avenue, Huntsville, AL 35811

ITT Technical Institute: Birmingham
Bessemer, Alabama
www.itt-tech.edu **CB code: 2696**

- For-profit 4-year technical college
- Commuter campus in very large city

General. Accredited by ACICS. **Calendar:** Quarter.

Contact. Phone: (205) 991-5410
Director of Recruitment, 6270 Park South Drive, Bessemer, AL 35022

Jacksonville State University
Jacksonville, Alabama
www.jsu.edu **CB code: 1736**

- Public 4-year university
- Commuter campus in small town
- 7,522 degree-seeking undergraduates: 21% part-time, 58% women, 28% African American, 1% Asian American, 1% Hispanic American, 1% Native American, 2% international
- 1,563 degree-seeking graduate students
- 86% of applicants admitted
- SAT or ACT (ACT writing optional) required
- 38% graduate within 6 years

General. Founded in 1883. Regionally accredited. **Degrees:** 1,049 bachelor's awarded; master's offered. **ROTC:** Army. **Location:** 75 miles from Birmingham, 100 miles from Atlanta. **Calendar:** Semester, extensive summer session. **Full-time faculty:** 322 total; 65% have terminal degrees, 12% minority, 45% women. **Part-time faculty:** 131 total; 17% have terminal degrees, 12% minority, 64% women. **Class size:** 35% < 20, 51% 20-39, 8% 40-49, 6% 50-99, less than 1% >100. **Special facilities:** Space observatory, Little River Canyon field school.

Freshman class profile. 3,456 applied, 2,971 admitted, 2,013 enrolled.

Mid 50% test scores			
SAT critical reading:	410-500	Rank in top quarter:	13%
SAT math:	410-500	Rank in top tenth:	3%
ACT composite:	17-22	Return as sophomores:	69%
GPA 3.75 or higher:	10%	Out-of-state:	26%
GPA 3.50-3.74:	20%	Live on campus:	60%
GPA 3.0-3.49:	40%	Fraternities:	9%
GPA 2.0-2.99:	26%	Sororities:	9%

Basis for selection. High school record and test scores very important. 16 ACT or 750 SAT (exclusive of Writing) required for conditional admission. 19 ACT or 900 SAT (exclusive of Writing) required for unconditional admission. SAT/ACT scores must be submitted by beginning of term.

High school preparation. 15 units required. Required units include English 3 and academic electives 4. 8 units required in math, science, foreign language, social studies/history.

2008-2009 Annual costs. Tuition/fees: $5,700; $11,400 out-of-state. Room/board: $4,215. Books/supplies: $1,100. Personal expenses: $2,903.

2007-2008 Financial aid. Non-need-based: Scholarships awarded for academics, alumni affiliation, art, athletics, music/drama, ROTC.

Application procedures. Admission: No deadline. $30 fee. Admission notification on a rolling basis. **Financial aid:** Priority date 3/15; no closing date. FAFSA, institutional form required. Applicants notified on a rolling basis starting 5/15; must reply within 2 week(s) of notification.

Academics. Special study options: Accelerated study, combined bachelor's/graduate degree, cooperative education, distance learning, double major, dual enrollment of high school students, ESL, honors, independent study, internships, teacher certification program. **Credit/placement by examination:** AP, CLEP, SAT, ACT, institutional tests. 46 credit hours maximum toward bachelor's degree. Maximum credit hours awarded through CLEP examinations: 31 for general tests, 15 through subject tests. **Support services:** Learning center, pre-admission summer program, remedial instruction, tutoring.

Majors. Biology: General. **Business:** Accounting, business admin, finance, managerial economics, marketing. **Communications:** Radio/tv. **Computer sciences:** General. **Education:** Elementary, health, physical, secondary, special. **Engineering technology:** Electrical, manufacturing, occupational safety. **Family/consumer sciences:** General. **Foreign languages:** General. **Health:** Nursing (RN). **History:** General. **Liberal arts:** Arts/sciences. **Math:** General. **Parks/recreation:** General. **Physical sciences:** Chemistry, physics. **Protective services:** Criminal justice. **Psychology:** General. **Public administration:** Social work. **Social sciences:** Economics, geography, political science, sociology. **Visual/performing arts:** Art, dramatic.

Most popular majors. Business/marketing 14%, education 16%, health sciences 14%, public administration/social services 8%, security/protective services 7%, social sciences 6%.

Computing on campus. 330 workstations in library, computer center, student center. Dormitories linked to campus network. Commuter students can connect to campus network. Online course registration, helpline, wireless network available.

Student life. Freshman orientation: Available, $40 fee. Preregistration for classes offered. **Housing:** Coed dorms, single-sex dorms, apartments, fraternity/sorority housing, wellness housing available. $100 deposit. **Activities:** Bands, choral groups, drama, international student organizations, music ensembles, musical theater, opera, radio station, student government, student newspaper, symphony orchestra, TV station, Panhellenic council, adult learners forum, peer counselors, African American association, book club.

Athletics. NCAA. **Intercollegiate:** Baseball M, basketball, cross-country, football (tackle) M, golf, rifle, soccer W, softball W, tennis, track and field, volleyball W. **Intramural:** Basketball, bowling, football (tackle) M, racquetball, rugby M, softball, tennis, track and field, volleyball. **Team name:** Gamecocks.

Student services. Career counseling, student employment services, financial aid counseling, health services, minority student services, on-campus daycare, personal counseling, placement for graduates, veterans' counselor. **Physically disabled:** Services for visually, speech, hearing impaired.

Contact. E-mail: info@jsucc.jsu.edu
Phone: (256) 782-5268 Toll-free number: (800) 231-5291
Fax: (256) 782-5121
Martha Mitchell, Director of Admissions, Jacksonville State University, 700 Pelham Road North, Jacksonville, AL 36265-1602

Judson College
Marion, Alabama
www.judson.edu **CB code: 1349**

- Private 4-year liberal arts college for women affiliated with Baptist faith
- Residential campus in small town
- 313 degree-seeking undergraduates: 16% part-time, 97% women, 12% African American, 1% Hispanic American, 1% Native American, 1% international
- 84% of applicants admitted
- Interview required
- 49% graduate within 6 years; 21% enter graduate study

General. Founded in 1838. Regionally accredited. Men accepted for distance learning program only. **Degrees:** 50 bachelor's awarded. **ROTC:** Army. **Location:** 75 miles from Birmingham and Montgomery. **Calendar:** Semester, limited summer session. **Full-time faculty:** 18 total; 78% have terminal degrees, 39% women. **Part-time faculty:** 23 total; 35% have terminal degrees, 61% women. **Class size:** 79% < 20, 21% 20-39. **Special facilities:** Alabama Women's Hall of Fame, Baptist missionary memorabilia, equestrian facilities.

Freshman class profile. 306 applied, 256 admitted, 96 enrolled.

Mid 50% test scores		**GPA 3.0-3.49:**	30%
SAT critical reading:	540-590	**GPA 2.0-2.99:**	22%
SAT math:	470-590	**Rank in top quarter:**	22%
SAT writing:	520-630	**End year in good standing:**	81%
ACT composite:	19-26	**Return as sophomores:**	79%
GPA 3.75 or higher:	37%	**Out-of-state:**	24%
GPA 3.50-3.74:	11%	**Live on campus:**	96%

Basis for selection. Academic record, recommendations, test scores considered. Interview required.

High school preparation. College-preparatory program recommended. 16 units required; 20 recommended. Required and recommended units include English 4, mathematics 2-4, social studies 3-4, history 2, science 2-4, foreign language 2 and academic electives 5.

2009-2010 Annual costs. Tuition/fees (projected): $12,547. Room/board: $7,969. Books/supplies: $1,200. Personal expenses: $1,600.

2008-2009 Financial aid. Need-based: 87 full-time freshmen applied for aid; 73 were judged to have need; 73 of these received aid. Average need met was 79%. Average scholarship/grant was $10,923; average loan $3,440. 71% of total undergraduate aid awarded as scholarships/grants, 29% as loans/jobs. **Non-need-based:** Scholarships awarded for academics, alumni affiliation, art, athletics, music/drama, religious affiliation, state residency.

Application procedures. Admission: Priority date 8/1; no deadline. $35 fee, may be waived for applicants with need. Admission notification on a rolling basis beginning on or about 8/1. **Financial aid:** Priority date 3/1; no closing date. FAFSA, institutional form required. Applicants notified on a rolling basis starting 3/1; must reply within 2 week(s) of notification.

Academics. Special study options: Accelerated study, cross-registration, distance learning, double major, dual enrollment of high school students, independent study, internships, student-designed major, study abroad, teacher certification program, Washington semester. **Credit/placement by examination:** AP, CLEP, IB, ACT, institutional tests. 30 credit hours maximum toward bachelor's degree. No student may receive more than 30 semester hours of non-attendance credit from all sources, or more than six semester hours in any one department. Maximum permitted from CLEP General Examinations is 15 of 30 hours. **Support services:** Reduced course load, remedial instruction, study skills assistance, tutoring, writing center.

Majors. Biology: General. **Business:** Business admin. **Education:** Elementary, English, mathematics, music, science, social science. **Foreign languages:** General. **History:** General. **Math:** General. **Philosophy/religion:** Religion. **Physical sciences:** Chemistry. **Protective services:** Law enforcement admin. **Psychology:** General. **Visual/performing arts:** Art.

Most popular majors. Biology 12%, business/marketing 8%, education 10%, English 6%, history 10%, physical sciences 6%, psychology 20%, visual/performing arts 16%.

Computing on campus. 59 workstations in library, computer center. Commuter students can connect to campus network. Online library, helpline, wireless network available.

Student life. Freshman orientation: Mandatory, $105 fee. Preregistration for classes offered. Orientation includes placement tests, academic registration. **Housing:** Guaranteed on-campus for all undergraduates. Wellness housing available. $110 nonrefundable deposit, deadline 8/15. **Activities:** Campus ministries, choral groups, drama, literary magazine, music ensembles, musical theater, student government, student newspaper, Students in Free Enterprise, College Democrats, College Republicans, psych-key club, Cahaba River society, Judson Ambassadors.

Athletics. USCAA. **Intercollegiate:** Basketball W, equestrian W, soccer W, softball W, tennis W, volleyball W. **Intramural:** Basketball W, equestrian W, field hockey W, soccer W, softball W, swimming W, table tennis W, tennis W, volleyball W. **Team name:** Lady Eagles.

Student services. Adult student services, alcohol/substance abuse counseling, chaplain/spiritual director, career counseling, student employment services, financial aid counseling, health services, personal counseling.

Contact. E-mail: admissions@judson.edu
Phone: (334) 683-5110 Toll-free number: (800) 447-9472
Fax: (334) 683-5282
Charlotte Clements, Vice President for Admissions and Financial Aid, Judson College, 302 Bibb Street, Marion, AL 36756

Miles College
Birmingham, Alabama
www.miles.edu **CB code: 1468**

- Private 4-year liberal arts college affiliated with Christian Methodist Episcopal Church
- Commuter campus in very large city
- 1,800 degree-seeking undergraduates

General. Founded in 1905. Regionally accredited. **Degrees:** 185 bachelor's awarded. **ROTC:** Army, Air Force. **Location:** 6 miles from downtown. **Calendar:** Semester, limited summer session. **Full-time faculty:** 92 total. **Part-time faculty:** 40 total. **Special facilities:** African-American materials center, learning research center.

Basis for selection. Open admission, but selective for some programs. Admission to education program based on 2.0 high school GPA, ACT composite score of 16 and recommendations; 3 letters of recommendation required of all.

High school preparation. 20 units recommended. Recommended units include English 4, mathematics 4, social studies 4, history 4 and science 4. 4 units math and science recommended, particularly, for natural science applicants.

2008-2009 Annual costs. Tuition/fees: $7,968. Room/board: $5,516. Books/supplies: $400. Personal expenses: $1,000.

2007-2008 Financial aid. All financial aid based on need.

Application procedures. Admission: Closing date 7/15. No application fee. Admission notification on a rolling basis. **Financial aid:** Priority date 4/15; no closing date. FAFSA required. Applicants notified on a rolling basis starting 7/15; must reply within 2 week(s) of notification.

Academics. Special study options: Cooperative education, cross-registration, double major, dual enrollment of high school students, exchange student, honors, independent study, internships, teacher certification program. **Credit/placement by examination:** CLEP, institutional tests. **Support services:** Reduced course load, remedial instruction, study skills assistance, tutoring, writing center.

Majors. Biology: General. **Business:** Accounting, business admin, purchasing. **Communications:** General. **Computer sciences:** General. **Conservation:** Environmental science. **Education:** Elementary, English, instructional media, mathematics, science, secondary, social science, social studies. **History:** General. **Math:** General. **Physical sciences:** Chemistry. **Public administration:** Social work. **Social sciences:** Political science. **Visual/performing arts:** Music pedagogy, music performance.

Computing on campus. 150 workstations in dormitories, library, computer center. Commuter students can connect to campus network.

Student life. Freshman orientation: Available, $100 fee. Preregistration for classes offered. Week-long program held one week prior to the start of classes. **Policies:** Students must maintain 2.0 GPA to participate in student activities that are not co-curricular on campus. **Housing:** Single-sex dorms, apartments, wellness housing available. $150 nonrefundable deposit. **Activities:** Marching band, choral groups, dance, drama, music ensembles, musical theater, radio station, student government, student newspaper, TV station, interdenominational ministerial association.

Athletics. NCAA. **Intercollegiate:** Baseball M, basketball, cross-country, football (tackle) M, softball W, volleyball. **Intramural:** Badminton, basketball, softball, tennis, volleyball. **Team name:** Golden Bears.

Student services. Adult student services, chaplain/spiritual director, career counseling, services for economically disadvantaged, student employment services, financial aid counseling, health services, personal counseling, placement for graduates.

Contact. E-mail: admissions@miles.edu
Phone: (205) 929-1655 Fax: (205) 923-9292
Christopher Robertson, Director of Admissions and Recruitment, Miles College, 5500 Myron-Massey Boulevard, Fairfield, AL 35064

Oakwood University

Huntsville, Alabama — **CB member**
www.oakwood.edu — **CB code: 1586**

- Private 4-year liberal arts college affiliated with Seventh-day Adventists
- Residential campus in small city
- 1,789 degree-seeking undergraduates: 6% part-time, 59% women, 91% African American, 1% Hispanic American, 6% international
- 49 degree-seeking graduate students
- 56% of applicants admitted
- SAT or ACT (ACT writing optional) required

General. Founded in 1896. Regionally accredited. **Degrees:** 259 bachelor's, 5 associate awarded; master's offered. **Location:** 5 miles from Huntsville. **Calendar:** Semester, limited summer session. **Full-time faculty:** 105 total. **Part-time faculty:** 80 total. **Class size:** 52% < 20, 39% 20-39, 5% 40-49, 4% 50-99, less than 1% >100.

Freshman class profile. 1,775 applied, 996 admitted, 487 enrolled.

Mid 50% test scores		**GPA 2.0-2.99:**	44%
SAT critical reading:	400-530	**Rank in top quarter:**	26%
SAT math:	360-490	**Rank in top tenth:**	8%
ACT composite:	16-21	**Out-of-state:**	89%
GPA 3.75 or higher:	13%	**Live on campus:**	94%
GPA 3.50-3.74:	13%	**International:**	2%
GPA 3.0-3.49:	26%		

Basis for selection. Applicants with 2.0 GPA considered for acceptance. Special consideration for exceptional applicants. **Homeschooled:** Transcript of courses and grades, letter of recommendation (nonparent) required.

High school preparation. 18 units recommended. Recommended units include English 4, mathematics 2, social studies 1, history 1, science 2 (laboratory 1) and foreign language 2.

2008-2009 Annual costs. Tuition/fees: $13,174. Room/board: $7,458.

Financial aid. Non-need-based: Scholarships awarded for academics, leadership, religious affiliation, state residency.

Application procedures. Admission: Priority date 6/30; no deadline. $25 fee, may be waived for applicants with need. Admission notification on a rolling basis beginning on or about 12/1. **Financial aid:** Priority date 3/31; no closing date. FAFSA required. Applicants notified on a rolling basis starting 4/1.

Academics. Special study options: Double major, honors, internships, study abroad, teacher certification program. **Credit/placement by examination:** AP, CLEP, SAT, ACT, institutional tests. **Support services:** Learning center, reduced course load, remedial instruction, study skills assistance, tutoring, writing center.

Majors. Biology: General, biochemistry, biomedical sciences. **Business:** Accounting, business admin, finance, marketing. **Communications:** General. **Computer sciences:** General, computer science, information technology. **Education:** Biology, business, chemistry, elementary, English, family/consumer sciences, history, mathematics, music, physical, science, social science. **Family/consumer sciences:** General, family studies, food/nutrition. **Foreign languages:** French, Spanish. **Health:** Cytotechnology. **History:** General. **Interdisciplinary:** Math/computer science, natural sciences. **Liberal arts:** Arts/sciences. **Math:** General, applied. **Parks/recreation:** Health/fitness. **Philosophy/religion:** Religion. **Physical sciences:** Chemistry. **Psychology:** General. **Public administration:** Social work. **Theology:** Religious ed, theology.

Most popular majors. Biology 20%, business/marketing 22%, health sciences 9%, psychology 9%, theological studies 7%.

Computing on campus. 300 workstations in dormitories, library. Dormitories wired for high-speed internet access and linked to campus network. Commuter students can connect to campus network. Helpline, wireless network available.

Student life. Freshman orientation: Mandatory. **Policies:** Students sit on most faculty and administrative committees. Religious observance required. **Housing:** Single-sex dorms, apartments available. **Activities:** Choral groups, music ensembles, radio station, student government, student newspaper, Outreach, NAACP.

Athletics. Intramural: Baseball M, basketball, golf, gymnastics, soccer, softball, tennis, volleyball. **Team name:** Ambassadors.

Student services. Adult student services, chaplain/spiritual director, career counseling, student employment services, financial aid counseling, health services, on-campus daycare, personal counseling, placement for graduates, veterans' counselor.

Contact. E-mail: admission@oakwood.edu
Phone: (256) 726-7030 Toll-free number: (800) 824-5312
Fax: (256) 726-7154
Jason McCracken, Director of Enrollment Management, Oakwood University, 7000 Adventist Boulevard, NW, Huntsville, AL 35896

Samford University

Birmingham, Alabama — **CB member**
www.samford.edu — **CB code: 1302**

- Private 4-year university affiliated with Southern Baptist Convention
- Residential campus in small city
- 2,824 degree-seeking undergraduates: 7% part-time, 64% women
- 1,587 degree-seeking graduate students
- 89% of applicants admitted
- SAT or ACT (ACT writing recommended), application essay required
- 76% graduate within 6 years

General. Founded in 1841. Regionally accredited. Students taught to integrate Christian faith with learning and living. **Degrees:** 607 bachelor's, 5 associate awarded; master's, doctoral, first professional offered. **ROTC:** Army, Air Force. **Location:** 6 miles from downtown. **Calendar:** 4-1-4, extensive summer session. **Full-time faculty:** 290 total; 83% have terminal degrees, 9% minority, 45% women. **Part-time faculty:** 147 total; 42% have terminal degrees, 5% minority, 53% women. **Class size:** 66% < 20, 30% 20-39, 2% 40-49, 1% 50-99. **Special facilities:** Computer-assisted journalism laboratory, geographic information system, observatory, global center, planetarium, conservatory.

Freshman class profile. 2,153 applied, 1,924 admitted, 708 enrolled.

Mid 50% test scores		**Rank in top tenth:**	36%
SAT critical reading:	510-660	**End year in good standing:**	81%
SAT math:	500-610	**Return as sophomores:**	84%
ACT composite:	22-27	**Out-of-state:**	56%
GPA 3.75 or higher:	45%	**Live on campus:**	96%
GPA 3.50-3.74:	16%	**International:**	1%
GPA 3.0-3.49:	26%	**Fraternities:**	9%
GPA 2.0-2.99:	13%	**Sororities:**	28%
Rank in top quarter:	59%		

Basis for selection. High school GPA, courses selected and rigor, test scores, recommendations, essay, academic content and trend of high school grades important. Interview recommended. Audition required for music majors. Portfolio recommended for art and journalism majors. **Homeschooled:** Statement describing homeschool structure and mission, transcript of courses and grades, letter of recommendation (nonparent) required. Leadership resume required.

High school preparation. College-preparatory program required. 4 units required. Required and recommended units include English 4, mathematics 3, social studies 2, history 2, science 3 (laboratory 2) and foreign language 2.

2008-2009 Annual costs. Tuition/fees: $19,520. Room/board: $6,294. Books/supplies: $1,200. Personal expenses: $3,000.

2007-2008 Financial aid. **Need-based:** 427 full-time freshmen applied for aid; 277 were judged to have need; 277 of these received aid. Average need met was 82%. Average scholarship/grant was $10,669; average loan $4,068. 50% of total undergraduate aid awarded as scholarships/grants, 50% as loans/jobs. **Non-need-based:** Awarded to 1,771 full-time undergraduates, including 476 freshmen. Scholarships awarded for academics, athletics, leadership, music/drama, religious affiliation, ROTC, state residency. **Additional information:** Consideration for merit scholarships automatically given to students with admission files completed by December 15.

Application procedures. **Admission:** Priority date 3/1; no deadline. $35 fee, may be waived for applicants with need. Admission notification on a rolling basis beginning on or about 11/1. Must reply by May 1 or within 2 week(s) if notified thereafter. **Financial aid:** Priority date 3/1; no closing date. FAFSA required. Applicants notified by 4/1; must reply by 5/1.

Academics. **Special study options:** Accelerated study, combined bachelor's/graduate degree, cooperative education, cross-registration, distance learning, double major, dual enrollment of high school students, exchange student, honors, independent study, internships, liberal arts/career combination, student-designed major, study abroad, teacher certification program. Semester offered at Samford London Study Center. **Credit/placement by examination:** AP, CLEP, IB, SAT, ACT, institutional tests. 30 credit hours maximum toward associate degree, 30 toward bachelor's. **Support services:** Learning center, reduced course load, study skills assistance, tutoring, writing center.

Majors. **Area/ethnic studies:** Asian, Latin American. **Biology:** General, biochemistry, marine. **Business:** General, accounting, business admin, entrepreneurial studies, finance, human resources, international, managerial economics, marketing, training/development. **Communications:** General, journalism. **Computer sciences:** Computer science. **Conservation:** Environmental science, environmental studies. **Education:** Biology, English, history, multi-level teacher, music, physical, science, social science, speech. **Engineering:** Physics. **Family/consumer sciences:** Family studies. **Foreign languages:** General, ancient Greek, classics, French, German, Latin, Spanish. **Health:** Athletic training, nursing (RN). **History:** General. **Interdisciplinary:** Classical/archaeology, nutrition sciences, science/society. **Math:** General. **Parks/recreation:** Exercise sciences, health/fitness. **Philosophy/religion:** Philosophy, religion. **Physical sciences:** Chemistry, physics. **Psychology:** General, counseling. **Public administration:** General. **Social sciences:** Cartography, geography, international relations, political science, sociology. **Theology:** Sacred music. **Visual/performing arts:** Art, dramatic, graphic design, interior design, music pedagogy, music performance, music theory/composition, piano/organ, voice/opera.

Most popular majors. Biology 9%, business/marketing 19%, communications/journalism 7%, education 6%, health sciences 14%, social sciences 6%, visual/performing arts 11%.

Computing on campus. 203 workstations in library, computer center, student center. Dormitories wired for high-speed internet access and linked to campus network. Commuter students can connect to campus network. Online library, helpline, repair service, wireless network available.

Student life. **Freshman orientation:** Mandatory, $150 fee. Preregistration for classes offered. Four sessions lasting 1 and a half days in summer; includes parents. **Policies:** Student code of values observed. Religious observance required. **Housing:** Guaranteed on-campus for freshmen. Single-sex dorms, special housing for disabled, fraternity/sorority housing, wellness housing available. $250 nonrefundable deposit, deadline 5/1. **Activities:** Bands, campus ministries, choral groups, dance, drama, international student organizations, literary magazine, music ensembles, Model UN, musical theater, radio station, student government, student newspaper, symphony orchestra, Amnesty International, Circle K, Habitat for Humanity, Gamma Sigma Sigma, Alpha Phi Omega, College Republicans, international club, Samford Ambassadors, Beta Beta Beta, Ville Crew.

Athletics. NCAA. **Intercollegiate:** Baseball M, basketball, cross-country, football (tackle) M, golf, soccer W, softball W, tennis, track and field, volleyball W. **Intramural:** Basketball, bowling, cheerleading, football (non-tackle) M, football (tackle), golf, racquetball, soccer, softball, table tennis, tennis, volleyball, water polo. **Team name:** Bulldogs.

Student services. Adult student services, chaplain/spiritual director, career counseling, student employment services, financial aid counseling, health services, personal counseling, placement for graduates. **Physically disabled:** Services for visually, speech, hearing impaired. **Learning disabled:** Comprehensive services available.

Contact. E-mail: admiss@samford.edu
Phone: (205) 726-3673 Toll-free number: (800) 888-7218
Fax: (205) 726-2171
R. Philip Kimrey, Dean of Admission, Samford University, 800 Lakeshore Drive, Birmingham, AL 35229

Selma University

Selma, Alabama
www.selmauniversity.org **CB code: 1792**

- Private 4-year university affiliated with Baptist faith
- Large town
- 125 degree-seeking undergraduates

General. Founded in 1878. Candidate for regional accreditation; also accredited by ABHE. **Degrees:** 16 bachelor's, 4 associate awarded; master's offered. **Location:** 50 miles from Montgomery. **Calendar:** Semester, limited summer session. **Full-time faculty:** 3 total. **Part-time faculty:** 15 total.

Basis for selection. Open admission. Students with deficient high school record or low test scores must take remedial courses.

2008-2009 Annual costs. Tuition/fees: $4,600. Books/supplies: $600. Personal expenses: $600.

2008-2009 Financial aid. **Need-based:** 50% of total undergraduate aid awarded as scholarships/grants, 50% as loans/jobs.

Application procedures. **Admission:** No deadline. $10 fee, may be waived for applicants with need. Admission notification on a rolling basis beginning on or about 8/1. **Financial aid:** Priority date 9/15; no closing date. FAFSA required. Applicants notified on a rolling basis starting 8/23; must reply within 2 week(s) of notification.

Academics. **Credit/placement by examination:** CLEP, institutional tests. **Support services:** Reduced course load, remedial instruction, tutoring.

Student life. **Housing:** Single-sex dorms available. **Activities:** Choral groups, drama, music ensembles, student government, student newspaper, Baptist student union.

Athletics. NJCAA. **Intercollegiate:** Baseball M, basketball, volleyball M. **Intramural:** Basketball, softball, table tennis, volleyball.

Student services. Career counseling, personal counseling.

Contact. Phone: (334) 872-2533 Fax: (334) 872-7746
Leila Millhouse, Registrar, Selma University, 1501 Lapsley Street, Selma, AL 36701

South University: Montgomery

Montgomery, Alabama
www.southuniversity.edu **CB code: 3947**

- For-profit 4-year business and health science college
- Commuter campus in small city
- 513 degree-seeking undergraduates: 45% part-time, 78% women
- 48 graduate students
- SAT or ACT (ACT writing recommended), interview required

General. Founded in 1887. Regionally accredited. **Degrees:** 30 bachelor's, 55 associate awarded; master's offered. **Location:** 100 miles from Birmingham, 160 miles from Atlanta. **Calendar:** Quarter, extensive summer session. **Full-time faculty:** 16 total. **Part-time faculty:** 36 total. **Class size:** 69% < 20, 31% 20-39.

Basis for selection. High school diploma or GED required. Entrance test most important. CPT (school-administered entrance test) may be provided in place of SAT/ACT.

2008-2009 Annual costs. Tuition/fees: $14,085. Books/supplies: $1,200. Personal expenses: $3,279.

2007-2008 Financial aid. All financial aid based on need.

Application procedures. **Admission:** No deadline. $50 fee. Admission notification on a rolling basis. **Financial aid:** No deadline. FAFSA required. Applicants notified on a rolling basis starting 6/1.

Academics. **Special study options:** Distance learning, double major, internships. **Credit/placement by examination:** CLEP, institutional tests. **Support services:** Remedial instruction, study skills assistance, tutoring.

Majors. **Business:** Business admin. **Computer sciences:** Information technology. **Legal studies:** General.

Computing on campus. 58 workstations in library, computer center. Online library, repair service, wireless network available.

Student life. Freshman orientation: Mandatory. Preregistration for classes offered.

Student services. Career counseling, financial aid counseling, personal counseling, placement for graduates, veterans' counselor.

Contact. E-mail: apearson@southuniversity.edu
Phone: (334) 395-8800 Fax: (334) 395-8859
Anna Pearson, Director of Admissions, South University: Montgomery, 5355 Vaughn Road, Montgomery, AL 36116-1120

Southeastern Bible College

Birmingham, Alabama
www.sebc.edu **CB code: 1723**

- Private 4-year Bible college affiliated with nondenominational tradition
- Commuter campus in very large city
- 197 degree-seeking undergraduates: 18% part-time, 36% women, 28% African American, 1% Asian American, 2% international
- 98% of applicants admitted
- SAT or ACT (ACT writing optional), application essay required

General. Founded in 1935. Accredited by ABHE. **Degrees:** 46 bachelor's, 2 associate awarded. **Location:** 10 miles from downtown. **Calendar:** Semester, limited summer session. **Full-time faculty:** 8 total; 100% have terminal degrees. **Part-time faculty:** 20 total; 30% have terminal degrees, 5% minority, 30% women. **Class size:** 86% < 20, 10% 20-39, 3% 40-49, 1% 50-99.

Freshman class profile. 48 applied, 47 admitted, 19 enrolled.

Mid 50% test scores		**GPA 2.0-2.99:**	39%
ACT composite:	16-22	**Return as sophomores:**	65%
GPA 3.75 or higher:	17%	**Live on campus:**	53%
GPA 3.50-3.74:	17%	**International:**	5%
GPA 3.0-3.49:	11%		

Basis for selection. High school GPA and SAT or ACT test scores important. Christian character evaluated through 2 recommendations, one from church and the other a personal recommendation. Autobiography and statement of agreement with college's principle doctrines required. **Learning Disabled:** Students should meet with equity coordinator if desired.

High school preparation. College-preparatory program recommended. 24 units recommended. Recommended units include English 4, mathematics 4, social studies 4, science 4, computer science .5.

2008-2009 Annual costs. Tuition/fees: $10,610. Room only: $2,450. Books/supplies: $800.

2008-2009 Financial aid. Need-based: 24% of total undergraduate aid awarded as scholarships/grants, 76% as loans/jobs. **Non-need-based:** Scholarships awarded for academics, leadership, music/drama, state residency.

Application procedures. Admission: Closing date 8/1 (postmark date). $30 fee. Admission notification on a rolling basis. **Financial aid:** No deadline. FAFSA, institutional form required.

Academics. Special study options: Double major, internships. Adult degree completion program with classes one night per week. **Credit/placement by examination:** AP, CLEP, IB, institutional tests. **Support services:** Reduced course load, study skills assistance.

Majors. Theology: Bible. **Other:** Leadership ministries.

Computing on campus. 25 workstations in library, computer center. Dormitories wired for high-speed internet access. Wireless network available.

Student life. Freshman orientation: Mandatory. Preregistration for classes offered. One-day session held the day before registration. **Policies:** Religious observance required. **Housing:** Single-sex dorms, wellness housing available. **Activities:** Choral groups, music ensembles, student government, student missions fellowship.

Athletics. NCCAA. **Intercollegiate:** Basketball M. **Team name:** Sabers.

Student services. Adult student services, chaplain/spiritual director, financial aid counseling, personal counseling. **Physically disabled:** Services for speech, hearing impaired.

Contact. E-mail: info@sebc.edu
Phone: (205) 970-9210 Toll-free number: (800) 749-8878
Fax: (205) 970-9207
Lynn Gannett-Malick, Director of Enrollment Management, Southeastern Bible College, 2545 Valleydale Road, Birmingham, AL 35244-2083

Spring Hill College

Mobile, Alabama **CB member**
www.shc.edu **CB code: 1733**

- Private 4-year liberal arts college affiliated with Roman Catholic Church
- Residential campus in large city
- 1,308 degree-seeking undergraduates: 11% part-time, 65% women, 18% African American, 1% Asian American, 7% Hispanic American, 1% Native American
- 192 degree-seeking graduate students
- 58% of applicants admitted
- SAT or ACT (ACT writing recommended), application essay required
- 63% graduate within 6 years; 32% enter graduate study

General. Founded in 1830. Regionally accredited. **Degrees:** 232 bachelor's, 1 associate awarded; master's offered. **ROTC:** Army, Air Force. **Location:** 140 miles from New Orleans. **Calendar:** Semester, limited summer session. **Full-time faculty:** 82 total; 84% have terminal degrees, 7% minority, 44% women. **Part-time faculty:** 74 total; 35% have terminal degrees, 7% minority, 53% women. **Class size:** 56% < 20, 41% 20-39, 3% 40-49. **Special facilities:** National historic buildings, public radio broadcasting station, 450-acre wooded campus, 18-hole golf course.

Freshman class profile. 3,377 applied, 1,942 admitted, 347 enrolled.

Mid 50% test scores		**GPA 2.0-2.99:**	15%
SAT critical reading:	500-600	**Rank in top quarter:**	57%
SAT math:	470-610	**Rank in top tenth:**	24%
SAT writing:	490-590	**End year in good standing:**	79%
ACT composite:	21-26	**Return as sophomores:**	77%
GPA 3.75 or higher:	37%	**Out-of-state:**	54%
GPA 3.50-3.74:	19%	**Live on campus:**	87%
GPA 3.0-3.49:	29%		

Basis for selection. Evaluation based on grades, test scores, and achievements/accomplishments outside the classroom. Interview recommended; portfolio recommended of art majors. **Homeschooled:** Statement describing homeschool structure and mission, transcript of courses and grades, interview required. Portfolio should include thorough explanation of all coursework, how it was graded, comprehensive reading list, documentation of any program affiliation, and personal assessments provided by both the student and the primary teacher. Information on any independent research project, community outreach, or unique experience that enriched the home schooling experience may be included.

High school preparation. College-preparatory program recommended. 16 units recommended. Recommended units include English 4, mathematics 3, social studies 2, history 1, science 3 (laboratory 1), foreign language 2 and academic electives 1.

2008-2009 Annual costs. Tuition/fees: $24,240. Room/board: $9,260.

2008-2009 Financial aid. Need-based: 303 full-time freshmen applied for aid; 265 were judged to have need; 265 of these received aid. Average need met was 85%. Average scholarship/grant was $17,302; average loan $4,325. 71% of total undergraduate aid awarded as scholarships/grants, 29% as loans/jobs. **Non-need-based:** Awarded to 1,006 full-time undergraduates, including 278 freshmen. Scholarships awarded for academics, alumni affiliation, athletics, job skills, leadership, minority status, state residency.

Application procedures. Admission: Priority date 1/15; deadline 7/15 (postmark date). $25 fee, may be waived for applicants with need, free for online applicants. Admission notification on a rolling basis beginning on or about 11/1. Must reply by May 1 or within 2 week(s) if notified thereafter. **Financial aid:** Priority date 3/1; no closing date. FAFSA required. Applicants notified on a rolling basis starting 2/15; must reply by 5/1 or within 2 week(s) of notification.

Academics. Special study options: Accelerated study, combined bachelor's/graduate degree, distance learning, double major, dual enrollment of high school students, honors, independent study, internships, student-designed major, study abroad, teacher certification program, Washington semester. Marine biology majors take credit courses at the Dauphin Island Sea Laboratory of the Marine Environmental Sciences Consortium; 3-2 engineering with Auburn University, University of Alabama at Birmingham, Marquette University, University of Florida, and Texas A&M University. **Credit/**

placement by examination: AP, CLEP, IB, SAT, ACT, institutional tests. 30 credit hours maximum toward bachelor's degree. **Support services:** Remedial instruction, study skills assistance, tutoring.

Majors. **Biology:** General, biochemistry. **Business:** Business admin. **Communications:** General. **Education:** Early childhood, elementary, secondary. **Engineering:** General. **Foreign languages:** Spanish. **Health:** Art therapy, nursing (RN). **History:** General. **Interdisciplinary:** Biopsychology. **Liberal arts:** Humanities. **Math:** General. **Philosophy/religion:** Philosophy. **Physical sciences:** Chemistry. **Psychology:** General. **Social sciences:** General, international relations, political science, sociology. **Theology:** Theology. **Visual/performing arts:** Arts management, dramatic, graphic design, studio arts.

Most popular majors. Biology 10%, business/marketing 19%, communications/journalism 10%, health sciences 10%, liberal arts 6%, psychology 11%, social sciences 7%, visual/performing arts 6%.

Computing on campus. 200 workstations in dormitories, library, computer center, student center. Dormitories wired for high-speed internet access and linked to campus network. Commuter students can connect to campus network. Online course registration, online library, helpline, student web hosting, wireless network available.

Student life. **Freshman orientation:** Mandatory, $200 fee. Preregistration for classes offered. Weekend program held in the summer for students and parents. **Housing:** Guaranteed on-campus for all undergraduates. Coed dorms, single-sex dorms, apartments available. $150 fully refundable deposit, deadline 6/1. **Activities:** Campus ministries, choral groups, dance, drama, literary magazine, student government, student newspaper, Amnesty International, Circle K, College Democrats, College Republicans, multicultural student union, political and international studies club, SHAPe Community, students for justice, students for life, TAG3.

Athletics. NAIA. **Intercollegiate:** Baseball M, basketball, cross-country, golf, soccer, softball W, tennis, volleyball W. **Intramural:** Basketball, football (non-tackle), racquetball, soccer, volleyball. **Team name:** Badgers.

Student services. Adult student services, alcohol/substance abuse counseling, chaplain/spiritual director, career counseling, student employment services, financial aid counseling, health services, personal counseling, placement for graduates.

Contact. E-mail: admit@shc.edu
Phone: (251) 380-3030 Toll-free number: (800) 742-6704
Fax: (251) 460-2186
Steven Pochard, Dean of Admission and Financial Aid, Spring Hill College, 4000 Dauphin Street, Mobile, AL 36608-1791

Stillman College

Tuscaloosa, Alabama — CB member
www.stillman.edu — CB code: 1739

- Private 4-year liberal arts college affiliated with Presbyterian Church (USA)
- Residential campus in small city

General. Founded in 1876. Regionally accredited. **Location:** 60 miles from Birmingham. **Calendar:** Semester.

Annual costs/financial aid. Tuition/fees (2008-2009): $12,712. Room/board: $5,994. Need-based financial aid available to full-time and part-time students.

Contact. Phone: (205) 366-8814
Director of Admissions, 3600 Stillman Boulevard, Tuscaloosa, AL 35403

Talladega College

Talladega, Alabama
www.talladega.edu — CB code: 1800

- Private 4-year liberal arts college affiliated with United Church of Christ
- Residential campus in large town
- 631 degree-seeking undergraduates: 15% part-time, 67% women
- Application essay required

General. Founded in 1867. Regionally accredited. **Degrees:** 43 bachelor's awarded. **ROTC:** Army. **Location:** 55 miles from Birmingham, 120 miles from Atlanta. **Calendar:** Semester, limited summer session. **Full-time faculty:** 29 total. **Part-time faculty:** 9 total. **Class size:** 33% < 20, 47% 20-39, 13% 40-49, 7% 50-99. **Special facilities:** Amistad murals.

Freshman class profile.

End year in good standing:	45%	**Out-of-state:**	20%
Return as sophomores:	54%		

Basis for selection. Open admission, but selective for some programs. SAT or ACT recommended for applicants to bachelor's degree program in education. Test scores considered for scholarships. Audition required of music majors. **Homeschooled:** Transcript of courses and grades, state high school equivalency certificate required.

High school preparation. 22 units required. Required units include English 4, mathematics 2, social studies 3, science 2 and academic electives 2. 2 units required in health/physical education.

2008-2009 Annual costs. Tuition/fees: $7,348. Room/board: $4,420. Books/supplies: $1,178. Personal expenses: $1,100.

2008-2009 Financial aid. All financial aid based on need.

Application procedures. **Admission:** No deadline. $25 fee, may be waived for applicants with need. Admission notification on a rolling basis. **Financial aid:** Priority date 4/15; no closing date. FAFSA, institutional form, CSS PROFILE required. Applicants notified on a rolling basis; must reply within 2 week(s) of notification.

Academics. **Special study options:** Combined bachelor's/graduate degree, cooperative education, double major, dual enrollment of high school students, independent study, internships, teacher certification program. Dual degree linkage programs with other colleges in nursing, engineering, pharmacy, veterinary sciences, geology, and allied health. **Credit/placement by examination:** AP, CLEP, institutional tests. 12 credit hours maximum toward bachelor's degree. **Support services:** Learning center, pre-admission summer program, reduced course load, remedial instruction, study skills assistance, tutoring, writing center.

Majors. **Area/ethnic studies:** African-American. **Biology:** General. **Business:** Accounting, business admin, finance, managerial economics, marketing. **Communications:** Journalism, media studies. **Computer sciences:** General. **Education:** Biology, chemistry, English, French, history, mathematics, music, secondary. **Foreign languages:** French, Spanish. **History:** General. **Legal studies:** Prelaw. **Math:** General. **Physical sciences:** Chemistry, physics. **Psychology:** General. **Public administration:** General, social work. **Social sciences:** Economics, sociology. **Visual/performing arts:** Piano/organ, studio arts, voice/opera.

Most popular majors. Biology 28%, computer/information sciences 8%, psychology 16%, social sciences 19%.

Computing on campus. 200 workstations in dormitories, library, computer center. Dormitories wired for high-speed internet access and linked to campus network. Commuter students can connect to campus network. Online library available.

Student life. **Freshman orientation:** Mandatory. Preregistration for classes offered. Held one week prior to school opening. **Policies:** Religious observance required. **Housing:** Guaranteed on-campus for freshmen. Single-sex dorms, wellness housing available. $200 deposit. Dorms for honors students, seniors, athletes. **Activities:** Concert band, choral groups, dance, drama, student government, Arna Bontempts Historical Society, biology club, business and economics club, chemistry club, debate club, Faith Outreach Campus Ministry, foreign language club, math club, National Association of Negro Musicians, psychology club.

Athletics. USCAA. **Intercollegiate:** Baseball M, basketball, cheerleading W, golf M, volleyball W. **Intramural:** Softball W, table tennis, tennis, volleyball W. **Team name:** Tornadoes.

Student services. Alcohol/substance abuse counseling, chaplain/spiritual director, career counseling, student employment services, financial aid counseling, health services, personal counseling, placement for graduates, veterans' counselor. **Physically disabled:** Services for visually, hearing impaired.

Contact. E-mail: admissions@talladega.edu
Phone: (205) 761-6235 Toll-free number: (800) 633-2440
Fax: (205) 362-0274
Floretta Dortch, Director of Admissions, Talladega College, 627 West Battle Street, Talladega, AL 35160

Troy University

Troy, Alabama — CB member
www.troy.edu — CB code: 1738

- Public 4-year university
- Residential campus in large town

- 20,899 degree-seeking undergraduates: 51% part-time, 59% women, 38% African American, 1% Asian American, 3% Hispanic American, 1% Native American, 2% international
- 7,118 degree-seeking graduate students
- 66% of applicants admitted
- SAT or ACT (ACT writing optional) required

General. Founded in 1887. Regionally accredited. **Degrees:** 2,842 bachelor's, 422 associate awarded; master's offered. **ROTC:** Army, Air Force. **Location:** 50 miles from Montgomery. **Calendar:** Semester, extensive summer session. **Full-time faculty:** 452 total; 15% minority, 40% women. **Part-time faculty:** 1,177 total; 16% minority, 41% women. **Class size:** 50% < 20, 40% 20-39, 6% 40-49, 2% 50-99, less than 1% >100. **Special facilities:** Rosa Parks library and museum, planetarium, performing arts theatre.

Freshman class profile. 5,999 applied, 3,974 admitted, 2,908 enrolled.

GPA 3.75 or higher:	17%	**Return as sophomores:**	67%
GPA 3.50-3.74:	10%	**Out-of-state:**	32%
GPA 3.0-3.49:	27%	**Live on campus:**	26%
GPA 2.0-2.99:	42%	**International:**	4%

Basis for selection. 2.0 GPA and 18 ACT required. Audition required of music education majors.

High school preparation. 15 units required. Required units include English 3.

2008-2009 Annual costs. Tuition/fees: $5,410; $10,900 out-of-state. Room/board: $5,286. Books/supplies: $920. Personal expenses: $2,214.

2008-2009 Financial aid. **Need-based:** Average scholarship/grant was $3,760; average loan $3,459. 15% of total undergraduate aid awarded as scholarships/grants, 85% as loans/jobs. **Non-need-based:** Scholarships awarded for academics, alumni affiliation, art, athletics, leadership, minority status, music/drama, ROTC.

Application procedures. **Admission:** No deadline. $30 fee. Admission notification on a rolling basis. **Financial aid:** Closing date 5/1. FAFSA, institutional form required. Applicants notified on a rolling basis starting 5/1; must reply within 2 week(s) of notification.

Academics. **Special study options:** Distance learning, double major, dual enrollment of high school students, ESL, external degree, honors, independent study, internships, study abroad, teacher certification program, weekend college. **Credit/placement by examination:** AP, CLEP, SAT, ACT, institutional tests. 45 credit hours maximum toward associate degree, 90 toward bachelor's. **Support services:** Learning center, pre-admission summer program, reduced course load, remedial instruction, study skills assistance, tutoring, writing center.

Majors. **Biology:** General, marine. **Business:** General, accounting, business admin, finance, management information systems, marketing. **Communications:** Journalism, radio/tv. **Computer sciences:** General. **Conservation:** Environmental science. **Education:** Early childhood, elementary, multi-level teacher, secondary. **Engineering technology:** Electrical, surveying. **Foreign languages:** General, translation. **Health:** Athletic training, nursing (RN). **History:** General. **Liberal arts:** Arts/sciences. **Math:** General. **Parks/recreation:** Sports admin. **Physical sciences:** General, chemistry. **Protective services:** Criminal justice. **Psychology:** General. **Public administration:** Human services, social work. **Social sciences:** General, political science, sociology. **Visual/performing arts:** Art. **Other:** Rehabilitation, Resources and technology management.

Most popular majors. Business/marketing 43%, education 7%, psychology 11%, security/protective services 13%, social sciences 11%.

Computing on campus. 1,570 workstations in library, computer center, student center. Online course registration, online library, helpline available.

Student life. **Freshman orientation:** Mandatory, $55 fee. Preregistration for classes offered. Two-day sessions held during summer. During spring and summer terms, new students can attend orientation session prior to registration for classes. **Housing:** Coed dorms, single-sex dorms, apartments, fraternity/sorority housing, wellness housing available. $100 partly refundable deposit. Substance-abuse-free housing, honor student housing available. **Activities:** Bands, choral groups, dance, drama, music ensembles, musical theater, student government, student newspaper, TV station, religious, service, and professional organizations; honor societies; Young Democrats; Young Republicans.

Athletics. NCAA. **Intercollegiate:** Baseball M, basketball, cheerleading, cross-country, football (tackle) M, golf, rodeo, soccer W, softball W, tennis, track and field, volleyball W. **Intramural:** Basketball, cross-country, diving, field hockey W, golf, softball, swimming, tennis, track and field, volleyball W. **Team name:** Trojans.

Student services. Chaplain/spiritual director, career counseling, student employment services, financial aid counseling, health services, on-campus daycare, personal counseling, placement for graduates, veterans' counselor, women's services. **Physically disabled:** Services for visually, hearing impaired.

Contact. E-mail: bstar@troy.edu
Phone: (334) 670-3179 Toll-free number: (800) 551-9716
Fax: (334) 670-3733
Buddy Starling, Dean of Enrollment Management, Troy University, University Avenue, Adams Administration 111, Troy, AL 36082

Tuskegee University

Tuskegee, Alabama — **CB member**
www.tuskegee.edu — **CB code: 1813**

- Private 4-year university and liberal arts college
- Residential campus in small town
- 2,541 degree-seeking undergraduates: 3% part-time, 56% women
- 207 degree-seeking graduate students
- 58% of applicants admitted
- SAT or ACT (ACT writing optional) required

General. Founded in 1881. Regionally accredited. **Degrees:** 333 bachelor's awarded; master's, doctoral, first professional offered. **ROTC:** Army, Air Force. **Location:** 30 miles from Montgomery, 162 miles from Atlanta. **Calendar:** Semester, limited summer session. **Full-time faculty:** 269 total; 77% have terminal degrees, 77% minority, 38% women. **Part-time faculty:** 32 total; 50% have terminal degrees, 75% minority, 41% women. **Class size:** 55% < 20, 27% 20-39, 8% 40-49, 10% 50-99, less than 1% >100. **Special facilities:** George Washington Carver museum, aerospace science and health education center.

Freshman class profile. 2,827 applied, 1,635 admitted, 723 enrolled.

Mid 50% test scores		**GPA 3.0-3.49:**	29%
SAT critical reading:	390-500	**GPA 2.0-2.99:**	49%
SAT math:	380-490	**Rank in top quarter:**	59%
ACT composite:	16-21	**Rank in top tenth:**	20%
GPA 3.75 or higher:	12%	**Out-of-state:**	70%
GPA 3.50-3.74:	10%	**Live on campus:**	98%

Basis for selection. School achievement record and test scores important. Minimum SAT combined score of 800 (exclusive of Writing) or equivalent ACT required for engineering and nursing applicants, 700 for other applicants. National League for Nursing Guidance Examination required of nursing applicants. Essay recommended; interview recommended for veterinary medicine majors.

High school preparation. 16 units required. Required units include English 4, mathematics 3, social studies 3, science 2 and academic electives 4.

2009-2010 Annual costs. Tuition/fees (projected): $16,160. Room/board: $7,350. Books/supplies: $949. Personal expenses: $1,596.

2008-2009 Financial aid. **Need-based:** 37% of total undergraduate aid awarded as scholarships/grants, 63% as loans/jobs. **Non-need-based:** Scholarships awarded for academics, athletics, ROTC, state residency.

Application procedures. **Admission:** Priority date 5/15; deadline 7/15. $25 fee. Admission notification on a rolling basis beginning on or about 3/1. Must reply by May 1 or within 2 week(s) if notified thereafter. **Financial aid:** Closing date 3/31. FAFSA, institutional form, CSS PROFILE required. Applicants notified on a rolling basis starting 5/15; must reply within 2 week(s) of notification.

Academics. **Special study options:** Combined bachelor's/graduate degree, cooperative education, double major, honors, independent study, internships, liberal arts/career combination, teacher certification program. Engineering program with 2-year colleges. **Credit/placement by examination:** AP, CLEP, SAT, ACT. Credit-by-examination policies determined individually by dean. **Support services:** Learning center, pre-admission summer program, reduced course load, remedial instruction, study skills assistance, tutoring.

Majors. **Agriculture:** Animal sciences, plant sciences, poultry, soil science. **Architecture:** Architecture. **Biology:** General, ecology. **Business:** Accounting, business admin, finance, hospitality admin, management science. **Computer sciences:** General. **Conservation:** General, forestry. **Education:** General, biology, early childhood, elementary, mathematics, mentally handicapped, physical, science, voc/tech. **Engineering:** Aerospace, chemical, electrical, mechanical. **Engineering technology:** Construction. **Family/consumer sciences:** Food/nutrition. **Health:** Clinical lab science. **History:**

General. **Math:** General. **Physical sciences:** Chemistry, physics. **Psychology:** General. **Public administration:** Social work. **Social sciences:** Economics, political science, sociology.

Most popular majors. Agriculture 10%, biology 10%, business/marketing 26%, engineering/engineering technologies 12%, psychology 9%, social sciences 8%.

Computing on campus. 1,000 workstations in dormitories, library, computer center, student center. Dormitories wired for high-speed internet access and linked to campus network. Commuter students can connect to campus network. Online course registration, online library, helpline, repair service, wireless network available.

Student life. Freshman orientation: Available. **Housing:** Single-sex dorms, apartments available. $300 deposit. Honors dormitories available. Freshmen and sophomores not living with parents or guardians required to reside on campus. **Activities:** Bands, choral groups, dance, drama, film society, student government, student newspaper.

Athletics. NCAA. **Intercollegiate:** Baseball M, basketball, cross-country, football (tackle) M, softball W, tennis, track and field, volleyball W. **Intramural:** Basketball M, rifle. **Team name:** Golden Tigers.

Student services. Chaplain/spiritual director, career counseling, financial aid counseling, health services, on-campus daycare, personal counseling, placement for graduates, veterans' counselor.

Contact. E-mail: adm@tuskegee.edu
Phone: (334) 727-8500 Toll-free number: (800) 622-6531
Fax: (334) 724-4402
Robert Laney, Vice President/Director of Admissions and Enrollment Management, Tuskegee University, 102 Old Administration Building, Tuskegee, AL 36088

United States Sports Academy
Daphne, Alabama
www.ussa.edu

- Private two-year upper-division university
- Large town
- Application essay required

General. Regionally accredited. **Degrees:** 6 bachelor's awarded; master's, doctoral offered. **Articulation:** Agreements with Alabama Southern CC, American River College, Andrew College, Barstow CC, Bishop State CC, Camden County College, City College of San Francisco, Columbus State CC, Consumes River College, Cuyahoga CC, Dakota County Technical College, Dallas County CC, East Mississippi CC, Eastern Iowa CC, Eastern Oklahoma State College, Faulkner State CC, Finger Lakes CC, Gadsden State CC, Hagerstown CC, Herkimer County CC, Hillsborough CC, Hiwassee College, Hudson Valley CC, Jamestown CC, Jones County Junior College, Jefferson Davis CC, Manatee CC, Monroe CC, Northern Virginia CC, Ocean County CC, Pensacola Junior College, Saddleback CC, Sufolk County CC. **Location:** 7 miles from Mobile. **Calendar:** Semester. **Full-time faculty:** 10 total. **Part-time faculty:** 20 total.

Student profile. 110 degree-seeking undergraduates.

Basis for selection. Open admission. College transcript, application essay required. Transfer accepted as juniors, seniors.

2008-2009 Annual costs. Tuition/fees: $8,350. Books/supplies: $1,250.

Application procedures. Admission: Rolling admission. $50 fee. Application must be submitted online.

Academics. Special study options: Distance learning, internships, student-designed major. **Credit/placement by examination:** CLEP.

Majors. Parks/recreation: Sports admin. **Other:** Sports studies.

Computing on campus. PC or laptop required. Commuter students can connect to campus network. Online library, wireless network available.

Student services. Adult student services, financial aid counseling. **Physically disabled:** Services for visually, speech, hearing impaired. **Learning disabled:** Comprehensive services available.

Contact. E-mail: admissions@ussa.edu
Phone: (251) 626-3303 Toll-free number: (800) 223-2668
Queint Higgins, Registrar, United States Sports Academy, One Academy Drive, Daphne, AL 36526

University of Alabama
Tuscaloosa, Alabama **CB member**
www.ua.edu **CB code: 1830**

- Public 4-year university
- Residential campus in small city
- 22,046 degree-seeking undergraduates: 7% part-time, 53% women, 11% African American, 1% Asian American, 2% Hispanic American, 1% Native American, 1% international
- 4,506 degree-seeking graduate students
- 60% of applicants admitted
- SAT or ACT with writing required
- 65% graduate within 6 years

General. Founded in 1831. Regionally accredited. Services available for learning impaired students. **Degrees:** 3,398 bachelor's awarded; master's, doctoral, first professional offered. **ROTC:** Army, Air Force. **Location:** 60 miles from Birmingham. **Calendar:** Semester, extensive summer session. **Full-time faculty:** 1,028 total; 89% have terminal degrees, 15% minority, 41% women. **Part-time faculty:** 339 total; 58% have terminal degrees, 8% minority, 50% women. **Class size:** 43% < 20, 36% 20-39, 6% 40-49, 9% 50-99, 6% >100. **Special facilities:** Museum of natural history, arboretum, marine science laboratory, archeological park, observatory, access to CRAY X-UP/24 supercomputer in Huntsville, simulated coal mine setting, concert hall.

Freshman class profile. 18,500 applied, 11,172 admitted, 5,116 enrolled.

Mid 50% test scores		**Rank in top quarter:**	55%
SAT critical reading:	490-600	**Rank in top tenth:**	42%
SAT math:	500-610	**Return as sophomores:**	84%
ACT composite:	21-27	**Out-of-state:**	37%
GPA 3.75 or higher:	29%	**Live on campus:**	89%
GPA 3.50-3.74:	16%	**International:**	1%
GPA 3.0-3.49:	34%	**Fraternities:**	33%
GPA 2.0-2.99:	21%	**Sororities:**	39%

Basis for selection. Admissions based on ACT/SAT, GPA, and course schedule. Typically, students with 21 ACT or 990 SAT (exclusive of Writing) and 3.0 GPA will be admitted. Interview required by any student who appeals admission type or reject decision. Audition required for some performance programs. **Homeschooled:** Statement describing homeschool structure and mission, state high school equivalency certificate required. Students who do not present certified transcripts must take the GED and meet the UA GED admission policy. **Learning Disabled:** Documentation concerning disability should be submitted to the Office of Disability Services upon admission.

High school preparation. College-preparatory program required. 15 units required. Required units include English 4, mathematics 3, social studies 3, history 1, science 3 (laboratory 2), foreign language 1 and academic electives 5.

2008-2009 Annual costs. Tuition/fees: $6,400; $18,000 out-of-state. Room/board: $6,430. Books/supplies: $1,000. Personal expenses: $2,170.

2007-2008 Financial aid. Need-based: 2,170 full-time freshmen applied for aid; 1,429 were judged to have need; 1,378 of these received aid. Average need met was 73%. Average scholarship/grant was $4,119; average loan $3,596. 33% of total undergraduate aid awarded as scholarships/grants, 67% as loans/jobs. **Non-need-based:** Awarded to 7,843 full-time undergraduates, including 2,392 freshmen. Scholarships awarded for academics, alumni affiliation, art, athletics, leadership, minority status, music/drama, ROTC, state residency.

Application procedures. Admission: $35 fee, may be waived for applicants with need. Admission notification on a rolling basis beginning on or about 8/1. **Financial aid:** Priority date 3/1; no closing date. FAFSA required. Applicants notified on a rolling basis starting 4/1; must reply within 3 week(s) of notification.

Academics. Special study options: Accelerated study, combined bachelor's/graduate degree, cooperative education, cross-registration, distance learning, double major, dual enrollment of high school students, ESL, exchange student, external degree, honors, independent study, internships, liberal arts/career combination, student-designed major, study abroad, teacher certification program, Washington semester, weekend college. **Credit/placement by examination:** AP, CLEP, IB, institutional tests. **Support services:** Learning center, pre-admission summer program, remedial instruction, study skills assistance, tutoring, writing center.

Honors college/program. Students with 28 ACT/1240 SAT (exclusive of Writing) eligible to apply. Approximately 1000 first-time freshman enroll.

Majors. Area/ethnic studies: American, Asian, Latin American. **Biology:** General, marine, microbiology. **Business:** Accounting, business admin, finance, management information systems, management science, managerial economics, marketing, restaurant/food services. **Communications:** General, advertising, journalism, public relations, radio/tv. **Computer sciences:** General. **Conservation:** Environmental science. **Education:** Early childhood, elementary, music, physical, secondary, special. **Engineering:** Aerospace, chemical, civil, construction, electrical, mechanical, metallurgical. **Family/consumer sciences:** General, clothing/textiles, family resources, family studies. **Foreign languages:** General, Spanish. **Health:** Athletic training, audiology/speech pathology, dietetics, facilities admin, health services, nursing (RN). **History:** General. **Interdisciplinary:** Intercultural. **Math:** General. **Philosophy/religion:** Philosophy, religion. **Physical sciences:** Chemistry, geology, physics. **Protective services:** Criminal justice. **Psychology:** General. **Public administration:** Social work. **Social sciences:** Anthropology, geography, international relations, political science, sociology. **Visual/performing arts:** Art history/conservation, dance, dramatic, interior design, studio arts.

Most popular majors. Business/marketing 27%, communications/journalism 12%, education 6%, engineering/engineering technologies 6%, family/consumer sciences 7%, health sciences 10%.

Computing on campus. 2,200 workstations in dormitories, library, computer center, student center. Dormitories wired for high-speed internet access and linked to campus network. Commuter students can connect to campus network. Online course registration, online library, helpline, repair service, student web hosting, wireless network available.

Student life. Freshman orientation: Mandatory, $120 fee. Preregistration for classes offered. Two freshman Honors Express sessions, 15 freshman sessions available. **Policies:** Academic integrity policies guided by our Capstone Creed and administered through student honors council. Living/learning program offered. **Housing:** Guaranteed on-campus for freshmen. Coed dorms, single-sex dorms, special housing for disabled, apartments, fraternity/sorority housing available. $250 partly refundable deposit, deadline 3/1. Apartments for visiting scholars available. **Activities:** Bands, campus ministries, choral groups, dance, drama, film society, international student organizations, literary magazine, music ensembles, Model UN, musical theater, opera, radio station, student government, student newspaper, symphony orchestra, TV station, College Republicans, College Democrats, NAACP, African American association, Golden Key, National Society of Black Engineers.

Athletics. NCAA. **Intercollegiate:** Baseball M, basketball, cheerleading, cross-country, diving, football (tackle) M, golf, gymnastics W, rowing (crew) W, soccer W, softball W, swimming, tennis, track and field, volleyball W. **Intramural:** Badminton, basketball, bowling, football (non-tackle), golf, racquetball, soccer, softball, swimming, table tennis, tennis, volleyball. **Team name:** Crimson Tide.

Student services. Adult student services, alcohol/substance abuse counseling, chaplain/spiritual director, career counseling, services for economically disadvantaged, student employment services, financial aid counseling, health services, legal services, minority student services, on-campus daycare, personal counseling, placement for graduates, veterans' counselor, women's services. **Physically disabled:** Services for visually, speech, hearing impaired.

Contact. E-mail: admissions@ua.edu
Phone: (205) 348-5666 Toll-free number: (800) 933-2262
Fax: (205) 348-9046
Mary Spiegel, Executive Director of Undergraduate Admissions, University of Alabama, Box 870132, Tuscaloosa, AL 35487-0132

University of Alabama at Birmingham

Birmingham, Alabama — **CB member**
www.uab.edu — **CB code: 1856**

- Public 4-year university
- Commuter campus in very large city
- 9,989 degree-seeking undergraduates: 25% part-time, 60% women
- 5,224 degree-seeking graduate students
- 85% of applicants admitted
- SAT or ACT (ACT writing optional) required

General. Founded in 1969. Regionally accredited. **Degrees:** 1,907 bachelor's awarded; master's, doctoral, first professional offered. **ROTC:** Army, Air Force. **Location:** Downtown. **Calendar:** Semester, extensive summer session. **Full-time faculty:** 823 total; 87% have terminal degrees, 18% minority, 41% women. **Part-time faculty:** 72 total; 76% have terminal degrees, 12% minority, 36% women. **Class size:** 37% < 20, 41% 20-39, 9% 40-49, 9% 50-99, 4% >100. **Special facilities:** Alabama Museum of Health Sciences.

Freshman class profile. 3,257 applied, 2,756 admitted, 1,277 enrolled.

Mid 50% test scores		**Rank in top tenth:**	30%
ACT composite:	21-27	**Return as sophomores:**	75%
GPA 3.75 or higher:	39%	**Out-of-state:**	8%
GPA 3.50-3.74:	13%	**Live on campus:**	59%
GPA 3.0-3.49:	21%	**International:**	1%
GPA 2.0-2.99:	27%	**Fraternities:**	17%
Rank in top quarter:	56%	**Sororities:**	12%

Basis for selection. Admission decisions based on ACT/SAT, high school GPA, and college preparatory curriculum. Nontraditional students (typically older students) not required to submit standardized test scores for admission. **Homeschooled:** Statement describing homeschool structure and mission required.

High school preparation. 17 units required. Required units include English 4, mathematics 3, social studies 3, science 3 (laboratory 2), foreign language 1 and academic electives 3.

2008-2009 Annual costs. Tuition/fees: $5,696; $12,806 out-of-state. Room/board: $7,500. Books/supplies: $900. Personal expenses: $1,500.

2007-2008 Financial aid. Need-based: 885 full-time freshmen applied for aid; 632 were judged to have need; 619 of these received aid. Average need met was 43%. Average scholarship/grant was $4,087; average loan $3,776. 38% of total undergraduate aid awarded as scholarships/grants, 62% as loans/jobs. **Non-need-based:** Awarded to 2,456 full-time undergraduates, including 731 freshmen. Scholarships awarded for academics, alumni affiliation, art, athletics, leadership, minority status, music/drama, ROTC.

Application procedures. Admission: Closing date 3/1 (receipt date). $35 fee, may be waived for applicants with need. Admission notification on a rolling basis beginning on or about 9/1. **Financial aid:** Priority date 4/1; no closing date. FAFSA, institutional form required. Applicants notified on a rolling basis starting 4/1; must reply within 4 week(s) of notification.

Academics. Combined bachelors/masters program also available in Biology. **Special study options:** Combined bachelor's/graduate degree, cooperative education, cross-registration, distance learning, double major, dual enrollment of high school students, honors, independent study, internships, student-designed major, study abroad, teacher certification program, weekend college. **Credit/placement by examination:** AP, CLEP, IB, SAT, ACT, institutional tests. 45 credit hours maximum toward bachelor's degree. **Support services:** Learning center, reduced course load, remedial instruction, study skills assistance, tutoring, writing center.

Honors college/program. Additional application required. Honors Academy comprised of a University Honors Program, Science and Technology Honors Program, and Global and Community Leadership Honors Program. Each program enrolls 50 freshmen each year for a total of 150 entering freshmen, and either replaces the standard core curriculum with honors seminars or offers a tailored curriculum based on the program?s theme.

Majors. Area/ethnic studies: African-American. **Biology:** General. **Business:** Accounting, business admin, finance, management information systems, managerial economics, marketing, sales/distribution. **Communications:** General. **Computer sciences:** General. **Education:** Early childhood, elementary, health, physical, secondary, special. **Engineering:** Biomedical, civil, electrical, materials, mechanical. **Foreign languages:** General. **Health:** Clinical lab science, cytotechnology, medical radiologic technology/radiation therapy, medical records admin, nuclear medical technology, nursing (RN), respiratory therapy technology. **History:** General. **Interdisciplinary:** Biological/physical sciences, global studies, natural sciences. **Math:** General. **Philosophy/religion:** Philosophy. **Physical sciences:** Chemistry, physics. **Protective services:** Criminal justice. **Psychology:** General. **Public administration:** Social work. **Social sciences:** Anthropology, political science, sociology. **Visual/performing arts:** Art, dramatic. **Other:** Industrial distribution.

Most popular majors. Biology 8%, business/marketing 17%, communications/journalism 7%, education 7%, engineering/engineering technologies 6%, health sciences 21%, psychology 8%.

Computing on campus. 550 workstations in dormitories, library, computer center, student center. Dormitories wired for high-speed internet access and linked to campus network. Commuter students can connect to campus network. Online course registration, online library, helpline, student web hosting, wireless network available.

Student life. Freshman orientation: Mandatory, $150 fee. Preregistration for classes offered. Two-day program offered various times between

June and August. **Housing:** Coed dorms, single-sex dorms, apartments available. $250 deposit, deadline 5/1. **Activities:** Bands, campus ministries, choral groups, dance, drama, international student organizations, literary magazine, music ensembles, musical theater, opera, radio station, student government, student newspaper, Young Democrats, College Republicans, campus civitan club, veterans student organization, Catholic student association, Muslim student association, Chinese student association, African student association.

Athletics. NCAA. **Intercollegiate:** Baseball M, basketball, cross-country W, football (tackle) M, golf, rifle, soccer, softball W, synchronized swimming W, tennis, track and field W, volleyball W. **Intramural:** Badminton, basketball, bowling, football (non-tackle), racquetball, skiing, soccer, softball, squash, swimming, table tennis, tennis, track and field, volleyball, water polo, wrestling M. **Team name:** Blazers.

Student services. Adult student services, career counseling, student employment services, financial aid counseling, health services, minority student services, on-campus daycare, personal counseling, placement for graduates, veterans' counselor, women's services. **Physically disabled:** Services for visually, speech, hearing impaired.

Contact. E-mail: undergradadmit@uab.edu
Phone: (205) 934-8221 Toll-free number: (800) 421-8743
Fax: (205) 975-7114
Chenise Ryan, Director of Admission, University of Alabama at Birmingham, HUC 260, 1530 Third Avenue South, Birmingham, AL 35294-1150

University of Alabama in Huntsville

Huntsville, Alabama — **CB member**
www.uah.edu — **CB code: 1854**

- Public 4-year university
- Commuter campus in small city
- 5,689 degree-seeking undergraduates: 24% part-time, 47% women, 15% African American, 3% Asian American, 2% Hispanic American, 2% Native American, 3% international
- 1,397 degree-seeking graduate students
- 89% of applicants admitted
- SAT or ACT (ACT writing optional) required
- 48% graduate within 6 years

General. Founded in 1950. Regionally accredited. **Degrees:** 889 bachelor's awarded; master's, doctoral offered. **ROTC:** Army. **Location:** 100 miles from Birmingham; 100 miles from Nashville, Tennessee. **Calendar:** Semester, extensive summer session. **Full-time faculty:** 302 total; 91% have terminal degrees, 20% minority, 38% women. **Part-time faculty:** 154 total; 32% have terminal degrees, 7% minority, 42% women. **Class size:** 34% < 20, 42% 20-39, 11% 40-49, 11% 50-99, 2% >100. **Special facilities:** Centers for applied optics, micro-gravity research, robotics, solar research, space plasma, aeronomic research; observatory with vector magnetograph.

Freshman class profile. 1,875 applied, 1,672 admitted, 797 enrolled.

Mid 50% test scores			
SAT critical reading:	480-620	Rank in top tenth:	23%
SAT math:	500-630	End year in good standing:	90%
ACT composite:	22-27	Return as sophomores:	77%
GPA 3.75 or higher:	30%	Out-of-state:	16%
GPA 3.50-3.74:	19%	Live on campus:	49%
GPA 3.0-3.49:	30%	International:	2%
GPA 2.0-2.99:	21%	Fraternities:	3%
Rank in top quarter:	48%	Sororities:	12%

Basis for selection. School achievement record and test scores are the most important factors for admission. Conditional admission may be available for applicants with evidence of a serious commitment to academic pursuits who do not meet requirements for regular admission. **Homeschooled:** Official high school record of courses completed should contain the titles of courses in each subject area, beginning with grade nine; record should contain annotation of the general content in the academic courses and the textbooks used; teaching credentials of the home school teacher should also be included with the application for admission.

High school preparation. College-preparatory program required. 20 units required. Required and recommended units include English 4, mathematics 3-4, social studies 4, science 3-4 (laboratory 2), foreign language 2 and academic electives 6. 4 credits required in either history or social studies.

2008-2009 Annual costs. Tuition/fees: $5,952; $13,092 out-of-state. Per-credit-hour rate decreases as number of hours registered increases. Room/board: $6,100. Books/supplies: $1,042. Personal expenses: $1,928.

2008-2009 Financial aid. Need-based: 680 full-time freshmen applied for aid; 317 were judged to have need; 316 of these received aid. Average need met was 68%. Average scholarship/grant was $5,054; average loan $4,521. 33% of total undergraduate aid awarded as scholarships/grants, 67% as loans/jobs. **Non-need-based:** Awarded to 1,139 full-time undergraduates, including 340 freshmen. Scholarships awarded for academics, art, athletics, leadership, minority status, music/drama, ROTC.

Application procedures. Admission: Closing date 8/15. $30 fee, may be waived for applicants with need. Admission notification on a rolling basis. **Financial aid:** Priority date 4/1, closing date 7/31. FAFSA required. Applicants notified on a rolling basis starting 4/1; must reply within 2 week(s) of notification.

Academics. Special study options: Combined bachelor's/graduate degree, cooperative education, cross-registration, distance learning, double major, dual enrollment of high school students, ESL, honors, independent study, internships, study abroad, teacher certification program. 3-2 program in engineering. Research centers employ undergraduate students on campus and in the community. Co-op program with U.S. Army Redstone Arsenal, NASA Marshall Space Flight Center, U.S. Army Missile Command, over 50 Fortune 500 companies. Intensive English Program (IEP) for nonnative speakers of English available prior to enrollment in a degree program. **Credit/placement by examination:** AP, CLEP, IB, SAT, ACT, institutional tests. 32 credit hours maximum toward bachelor's degree. **Support services:** Learning center, reduced course load, remedial instruction, study skills assistance, tutoring, writing center.

Majors. Biology: General. **Business:** Accounting, business admin, finance, management information systems, marketing, purchasing. **Computer sciences:** General. **Education:** Elementary. **Engineering:** Chemical, civil, computer, electrical, industrial, mechanical. **Foreign languages:** General. **Health:** Nursing (RN). **History:** General. **Math:** General. **Philosophy/religion:** Philosophy. **Physical sciences:** Chemistry, physics. **Psychology:** General. **Social sciences:** Political science, sociology. **Visual/performing arts:** Art. **Other:** Earth System Science.

Most popular majors. Biology 6%, business/marketing 23%, engineering/engineering technologies 25%, English 6%, health sciences 16%.

Computing on campus. 1,153 workstations in dormitories, library, computer center, student center. Dormitories wired for high-speed internet access and linked to campus network. Commuter students can connect to campus network. Online course registration, online library, helpline, repair service, student web hosting, wireless network available.

Student life. Freshman orientation: Mandatory, $95 fee. Preregistration for classes offered. Five 2-day sessions running from June to August for new students. **Housing:** Guaranteed on-campus for freshmen. Coed dorms, special housing for disabled, apartments, fraternity/sorority housing available. $125 partly refundable deposit, deadline 5/1. Pets allowed in dorm rooms. Athletic team housing. **Activities:** Bands, campus ministries, choral groups, dance, drama, international student organizations, literary magazine, music ensembles, Model UN, musical theater, student government, student newspaper, symphony orchestra, black student association, Campus Crusade for Christ, Chinese student & scholar association, College Democrats, Students for Change, Indian student organization, Invisible Children United, National Society of Black Engineers, Reformed University Fellowship.

Athletics. NCAA. **Intercollegiate:** Baseball M, basketball, cross-country, ice hockey M, soccer, softball W, tennis, track and field, volleyball W. **Intramural:** Badminton, basketball, football (non-tackle), golf, racquetball, soccer, softball, table tennis, volleyball. **Team name:** Chargers.

Student services. Adult student services, alcohol/substance abuse counseling, chaplain/spiritual director, career counseling, student employment services, financial aid counseling, health services, minority student services, personal counseling, veterans' counselor, women's services. **Physically disabled:** Services for visually, speech, hearing impaired.

Contact. E-mail: admitme@uah.edu
Phone: (256) 824-6070 Toll-free number: (800) 824-2255
Fax: (256) 824-6073
Sandra Patterson, Director of Admissions, University of Alabama in Huntsville, UAH Office of Undergraduate Admissions, Huntsville, AL 35899

University of Mobile

Mobile, Alabama
www.umobile.edu — **CB code: 1515**

- Private 4-year university and liberal arts college affiliated with Baptist faith
- Commuter campus in small city

- 1,422 degree-seeking undergraduates: 11% part-time, 66% women, 21% African American, 1% Asian American, 1% Hispanic American, 3% Native American, 2% international
- 175 degree-seeking graduate students
- 56% of applicants admitted
- SAT or ACT (ACT writing optional) required
- 47% graduate within 6 years

General. Founded in 1961. Regionally accredited. **Degrees:** 311 bachelor's, 37 associate awarded; master's offered. **ROTC:** Army, Air Force. **Location:** 12 miles from downtown, 140 miles from New Orleans. **Calendar:** Semester, limited summer session. **Full-time faculty:** 83 total; 65% have terminal degrees, 6% minority, 49% women. **Part-time faculty:** 79 total; 22% have terminal degrees, 13% minority, 53% women. **Class size:** 50% < 20, 48% 20-39, 2% 40-49, less than 1% 50-99. **Special facilities:** Forest resource learning center, nature trails.

Freshman class profile. 1,853 applied, 1,035 admitted, 251 enrolled.

Mid 50% test scores		**Return as sophomores:**	77%
SAT critical reading:	500-700	**Out-of-state:**	25%
SAT math:	450-650	**Live on campus:**	73%
SAT writing:	500-700	**International:**	3%
ACT composite:	20-25		

Basis for selection. Admission decisions based on test scores, high school record. SAT Subject Tests recommended. Interview recommended for nursing majors, audition recommended for music majors, portfolio recommended for art majors. **Homeschooled:** Statement describing homeschool structure and mission required.

High school preparation. College-preparatory program recommended. 22 units recommended. Recommended units include English 4, mathematics 3, social studies 3 and foreign language 2.

2008-2009 Annual costs. Tuition/fees: $13,970. Room/board: $7,170.

2008-2009 Financial aid. **Need-based:** 194 full-time freshmen applied for aid; 194 were judged to have need; 193 of these received aid. Average need met was 70%. Average scholarship/grant was $8,469; average loan $3,302. 70% of total undergraduate aid awarded as scholarships/grants, 30% as loans/jobs. **Non-need-based:** Scholarships awarded for academics, alumni affiliation, athletics, music/drama, religious affiliation, ROTC, state residency.

Application procedures. **Admission:** Closing date 8/1. $50 fee. Admission notification on a rolling basis. **Financial aid:** Priority date 2/28; no closing date. FAFSA, institutional form required. Applicants notified on a rolling basis starting 2/1; must reply within 2 week(s) of notification.

Academics. **Special study options:** Accelerated study, combined bachelor's/graduate degree, double major, honors, independent study, internships, teacher certification program. **Credit/placement by examination:** AP, CLEP, IB, SAT, ACT, institutional tests. 30 credit hours maximum toward associate degree, 30 toward bachelor's. **Support services:** Learning center, pre-admission summer program, reduced course load, remedial instruction, study skills assistance, tutoring, writing center.

Majors. **Biology:** General, marine. **Business:** Accounting, business admin. **Communications:** General. **Computer sciences:** General. **Conservation:** Environmental science. **Education:** Biology, early childhood, elementary, English, history, mathematics, music, physical, social science. **Health:** Athletic training, nursing (RN). **History:** General. **Liberal arts:** Humanities. **Math:** General. **Parks/recreation:** Health/fitness. **Philosophy/religion:** Religion. **Psychology:** General. **Social sciences:** General, political science, sociology. **Theology:** Sacred music. **Visual/performing arts:** Art, dramatic, voice/opera.

Most popular majors. Business/marketing 17%, communications/journalism 8%, education 19%, health sciences 16%, liberal arts 10%, philosophy/religious studies 13%.

Computing on campus. 110 workstations in library, computer center. Dormitories wired for high-speed internet access. Commuter students can connect to campus network. Online course registration, online library, wireless network available.

Student life. **Freshman orientation:** Mandatory, $100 fee. Preregistration for classes offered. **Policies:** Religious observance required. **Housing:** Guaranteed on-campus for freshmen. Single-sex dorms available. $250 nonrefundable deposit, deadline 4/30. **Activities:** Bands, campus ministries, choral groups, drama, music ensembles, musical theater, opera, student government, campus activities board, student government association, Ministerial association, swing club, various honor societies, various academic clubs, Fellowship of Christian Athletes.

Athletics. NAIA. **Intercollegiate:** Baseball M, basketball, cheerleading, cross-country, golf, soccer, softball W, tennis, volleyball W. **Intramural:** Basketball, football (non-tackle), softball, volleyball. **Team name:** Rams.

Student services. Adult student services, chaplain/spiritual director, career counseling, student employment services, financial aid counseling, health services, personal counseling, placement for graduates, veterans' counselor.

Contact. E-mail: admininfo@umobile.edu
Phone: (251) 442-2273 Toll-free number: (800) 946-7267
Fax: (251) 442-2498
Kim Leousis, Vice President for Enrollment Management, University of Mobile, 5735 College Parkway, Mobile, AL 36613-2842

University of Montevallo

Montevallo, Alabama — **CB member**
www.montevallo.edu — **CB code: 1004**

- Public 4-year university and liberal arts college
- Residential campus in small town
- 2,558 degree-seeking undergraduates
- 453 graduate students
- 69% of applicants admitted
- SAT or ACT (ACT writing optional) required
- 51% graduate within 6 years

General. Founded in 1896. Regionally accredited. **Degrees:** 411 bachelor's awarded; master's offered. **ROTC:** Army, Air Force. **Location:** 35 miles from Birmingham. **Calendar:** Semester, extensive summer session. **Full-time faculty:** 140 total. **Part-time faculty:** 80 total. **Special facilities:** Foreign language laboratory, child development center, mass communication production center, traffic safety center, swamp, observatory.

Basis for selection. High school record and test scores essential factors in individual evaluation. Interview recommended. Audition required of music majors; portfolio required of art majors. **Homeschooled:** Transcript of courses and grades required. **Learning Disabled:** Conditional admission may be granted if standard requirements not met. Reasonable accommodations will be provided as necessary. Enrolled students needing disability accommodations and services must provide current documentation and make requests through the Services for Students with Disabiltiies Office.

High school preparation. 16 units required. Required and recommended units include English 4, mathematics 2-3, social studies 2, history 2, science 2-3, foreign language 2 and academic electives 4.

2008-2009 Annual costs. Tuition/fees: $6,620; $12,770 out-of-state. Room/board: $4,356. Books/supplies: $900. Personal expenses: $1,980.

2007-2008 Financial aid. **Need-based:** 269 full-time freshmen applied for aid; 205 were judged to have need; 198 of these received aid. Average need met was 70%. Average scholarship/grant was $3,995; average loan $3,275. 44% of total undergraduate aid awarded as scholarships/grants, 56% as loans/jobs. **Non-need-based:** Awarded to 1,087 full-time undergraduates, including 275 freshmen. Scholarships awarded for academics, art, athletics, job skills, leadership, minority status, music/drama, religious affiliation, ROTC.

Application procedures. **Admission:** Closing date 8/20. $25 fee, may be waived for applicants with need. Admission notification on a rolling basis. **Financial aid:** Priority date 4/1; no closing date. FAFSA required. Applicants notified by 5/10; must reply within 2 week(s) of notification.

Academics. Academic support programs available to all first-generation college students from low-income families and students with disabilities. **Special study options:** Accelerated study, combined bachelor's/graduate degree, cross-registration, double major, dual enrollment of high school students, exchange student, honors, independent study, internships, study abroad, teacher certification program. **Credit/placement by examination:** AP, CLEP, IB, institutional tests. 45 credit hours maximum toward bachelor's degree. **Support services:** Learning center, pre-admission summer program, reduced course load, remedial instruction, study skills assistance, tutoring, writing center.

Majors. **Biology:** General. **Business:** Accounting, business admin, finance, management information systems, marketing. **Communications:** Radio/tv. **Education:** Early childhood, elementary. **Family/consumer sciences:** General. **Foreign languages:** General. **Health:** Audiology/hearing, speech pathology. **History:** General. **Math:** General. **Parks/recreation:** Health/fitness. **Physical sciences:** Chemistry. **Psychology:** General. **Public administration:** Social work. **Social sciences:** General, political science, sociology. **Visual/performing arts:** Art, dramatic, music pedagogy.

Most popular majors. Business/marketing 17%, education 11%, English 8%, family/consumer sciences 10%, history 6%, psychology 6%, visual/performing arts 12%.

Computing on campus. 340 workstations in dormitories, library, computer center. Dormitories wired for high-speed internet access and linked to campus network. Commuter students can connect to campus network. Online course registration, online library, helpline, wireless network available.

Student life. **Freshman orientation:** Mandatory. Preregistration for classes offered. Two preregistration sessions during the summer and orientation immediately prior to beginning of fall semester. **Housing:** Guaranteed on-campus for freshmen. Coed dorms, single-sex dorms, apartments available. $100 fully refundable deposit. Several rooms are handicapped accessible. **Activities:** Bands, campus ministries, choral groups, dance, drama, international student organizations, literary magazine, music ensembles, Model UN, musical theater, student government, student newspaper, TV station, African American Society, Young Republicans, Young Democrats, campus outreach, Episcopal Student Fellowship, Feminine Majority Leadership Alliance.

Athletics. NCAA. **Intercollegiate:** Baseball M, basketball, cross-country W, golf, soccer, tennis W, volleyball W. **Intramural:** Basketball, soccer, softball, volleyball. **Team name:** Falcons.

Student services. Adult student services, alcohol/substance abuse counseling, chaplain/spiritual director, career counseling, student employment services, financial aid counseling, health services, minority student services, personal counseling, placement for graduates, veterans' counselor. **Physically disabled:** Services for visually, speech, hearing impaired.

Contact. E-mail: admissions@montevallo.edu
Phone: (205) 665-6030 Toll-free number: (800) 292-4349
Fax: (205) 665-6032
Ira Gurganus, Director of Admissions, University of Montevallo, Station 6030, Montevallo, AL 35115-6030

University of North Alabama

Florence, Alabama — CB member
www.una.edu — CB code: 1735

- Public 4-year university
- Commuter campus in large town
- 5,486 degree-seeking undergraduates
- 1,287 graduate students
- 82% of applicants admitted
- SAT or ACT required

General. Founded in 1830. Regionally accredited. **Degrees:** 642 bachelor's awarded; master's offered. **ROTC:** Army. **Location:** 116 miles from Birmingham. **Calendar:** Semester, extensive summer session. **Full-time faculty:** 242 total. **Part-time faculty:** 99 total. **Class size:** 45% <20, 38% 20-39, 12% 40-49, 4% 50-99, less than 1% >100. **Special facilities:** Planetarium-observatory, laboratory school.

Freshman class profile. 2,437 applied, 2,005 admitted, 1,020 enrolled.

Mid 50% test scores		Out-of-state:	15%
ACT composite:	18-24		

Basis for selection. 18 ACT or 700 SAT (exclusive of Writing), or rank in upper 50% of class required. If submitting GED, 35 on each section or average of 45 on all GED test sections required. Auditions required of music majors. Interviews recommended for education, nursing, social work, preprofessional programs. Portfolios recommended for art majors.

High school preparation. 13 units required. Required units include English 4, mathematics 2, social studies 3, science 2 and foreign language 2.

2008-2009 Annual costs. Tuition/fees: $5,598; $10,188 out-of-state. Room/board: $4,658. Books/supplies: $1,100.

2007-2008 Financial aid. **Non-need-based:** Scholarships awarded for academics, art, athletics, leadership, minority status, music/drama, ROTC, state residency.

Application procedures. **Admission:** Priority date 8/1; no deadline. $25 fee. Admission notification on a rolling basis beginning on or about 6/15. **Financial aid:** Priority date 4/1; no closing date. FAFSA required. Applicants notified on a rolling basis starting 5/31; must reply within 2 week(s) of notification.

Academics. **Special study options:** Accelerated study, cooperative education, distance learning, double major, dual enrollment of high school students, ESL, honors, independent study, internships, student-designed major, teacher certification program, weekend college. **Credit/placement by examination:** AP, CLEP, institutional tests. 34 credit hours maximum toward bachelor's degree. **Support services:** Learning center, pre-admission summer program, reduced course load, remedial instruction, study skills assistance, tutoring.

Majors. **Biology:** General, marine. **Business:** Accounting, business admin, finance, management information systems, managerial economics, marketing. **Computer sciences:** General. **Education:** Elementary, multi-level teacher, secondary. **Family/consumer sciences:** General. **Foreign languages:** General. **Health:** Nursing (RN). **History:** General. **Math:** General. **Parks/recreation:** General. **Physical sciences:** Chemistry, geology, physics. **Protective services:** Law enforcement admin. **Psychology:** General. **Public administration:** Social work. **Social sciences:** Geography, political science, sociology. **Visual/performing arts:** Studio arts.

Most popular majors. Business/marketing 25%, education 8%, English 9%, health sciences 21%, social sciences 7%.

Computing on campus. 600 workstations in dormitories, library, computer center, student center. Dormitories wired for high-speed internet access and linked to campus network. Commuter students can connect to campus network. Online course registration, online library, helpline available.

Student life. **Freshman orientation:** Mandatory, $25 fee. Preregistration for classes offered. Two-day sessions in June and July include academic advisement. **Housing:** Coed dorms, single-sex dorms, apartments, fraternity/sorority housing available. $100 deposit. **Activities:** Bands, choral groups, drama, literary magazine, music ensembles, musical theater, radio station, student government, student newspaper, Young Democrats, Young Republicans, Circle-K, Gold Triangle, black student alliance, Christian student fellowship.

Athletics. NCAA. **Intercollegiate:** Baseball M, basketball, cross-country, football (tackle) M, golf M, soccer W, softball W, tennis, volleyball W. **Intramural:** Badminton, baseball M, basketball, bowling, cross-country, football (tackle) M, golf M, racquetball, softball W, swimming, table tennis, tennis, volleyball. **Team name:** Lions.

Student services. Adult student services, alcohol/substance abuse counseling, chaplain/spiritual director, career counseling, student employment services, financial aid counseling, health services, minority student services, on-campus daycare, personal counseling, placement for graduates, veterans' counselor, women's services. **Physically disabled:** Services for visually, speech, hearing impaired.

Contact. E-mail: admissions@una.edu
Phone: (256) 765-4608 Toll-free number: (800) 825-5862
Fax: (256) 765-4329
Kim Mauldin, Director of Admissions, University of North Alabama, One Harrison Plaza, UNA Box 5011, Florence, AL 35632-0001

University of South Alabama

Mobile, Alabama
www.southalabama.edu — CB code: 1880

- Public 4-year university
- Commuter campus in small city
- 10,701 degree-seeking undergraduates: 25% part-time, 59% women, 19% African American, 3% Asian American, 2% Hispanic American, 1% Native American, 5% international
- 3,016 degree-seeking graduate students
- 90% of applicants admitted
- SAT or ACT required

General. Founded in 1963. Regionally accredited. **Degrees:** 1,559 bachelor's awarded; master's, doctoral, first professional offered. **ROTC:** Army, Air Force. **Location:** 10 miles from downtown, 150 miles from New Orleans. **Calendar:** Semester, extensive summer session. **Full-time faculty:** 795 total; 75% have terminal degrees, 42% women. **Part-time faculty:** 404 total; 56% women. **Special facilities:** Sea laboratory.

Freshman class profile. 3,473 applied, 3,134 admitted, 1,617 enrolled.

Mid 50% test scores		Return as sophomores:	67%
SAT critical reading:	440-570	International:	2%
SAT math:	460-580	Fraternities:	10%
ACT composite:	19-24	Sororities:	10%

Basis for selection. School achievement record and test scores important. Auditions required of music majors. **Learning Disabled:** Submit required documentation to special student services office if requesting services.

High school preparation. 16 units recommended. Recommended units include English 4, mathematics 3, social studies 2, science 2 and academic electives 2.

2008-2009 Annual costs. Tuition/fees: $5,512; $9,922 out-of-state. Room/board: $5,308. Books/supplies: $1,200.

2007-2008 Financial aid. Non-need-based: Scholarships awarded for academics, alumni affiliation, art, athletics, minority status, music/drama, ROTC, state residency.

Application procedures. Admission: Closing date 8/10. $35 fee. Application must be submitted on paper. Admission notification on a rolling basis. **Financial aid:** Priority date 5/1; no closing date. FAFSA, institutional form required. Applicants notified on a rolling basis starting 5/15.

Academics. Students in entry-level programming courses must own a laptop. **Special study options:** Combined bachelor's/graduate degree, cooperative education, distance learning, double major, ESL, honors, independent study, internships, student-designed major, study abroad, teacher certification program, weekend college. **Credit/placement by examination:** AP, CLEP, institutional tests. Maximum of 32 credit hours can be awarded under any combination of AP and CLEP examination credits. **Support services:** Learning center, remedial instruction, study skills assistance, tutoring, writing center.

Majors. Biology: General, biomedical sciences. **Business:** General, accounting, business admin, e-commerce, finance, marketing. **Communications:** General. **Computer sciences:** General. **Education:** Early childhood, elementary, health, physical, secondary, special. **Engineering:** Chemical, civil, computer, electrical, mechanical. **Foreign languages:** General. **Health:** Audiology/speech pathology, clinical lab science, medical radiologic technology/radiation therapy, nursing (RN), respiratory therapy technology. **History:** General. **Liberal arts:** Arts/sciences. **Math:** Statistics. **Parks/recreation:** General. **Philosophy/religion:** Philosophy. **Physical sciences:** Atmospheric science, chemistry, geology, physics. **Protective services:** Criminal justice. **Psychology:** General. **Social sciences:** Anthropology, geography, political science, sociology. **Visual/performing arts:** Art, dramatic.

Most popular majors. Biology 6%, business/marketing 16%, education 16%, health sciences 22%.

Computing on campus. 500 workstations in library, computer center, student center. Dormitories wired for high-speed internet access and linked to campus network. Commuter students can connect to campus network. Online course registration, online library, helpline available.

Student life. Freshman orientation: Mandatory, $75 fee. **Housing:** Coed dorms, special housing for disabled, apartments, fraternity/sorority housing available. $150 deposit. **Activities:** Bands, choral groups, dance, drama, film society, literary magazine, music ensembles, musical theater, opera, student government, student newspaper, symphony orchestra, TV station.

Athletics. NCAA. **Intercollegiate:** Baseball M, basketball, cross-country, football (tackle) M, golf, soccer W, softball W, tennis, track and field, volleyball W. **Intramural:** Basketball, bowling, football (non-tackle), golf, racquetball, soccer, softball, table tennis, tennis, volleyball, water polo. **Team name:** Jaguars.

Student services. Adult student services, alcohol/substance abuse counseling, chaplain/spiritual director, career counseling, services for economically disadvantaged, student employment services, financial aid counseling, health services, minority student services, personal counseling, placement for graduates, veterans' counselor. **Physically disabled:** Services for visually, speech, hearing impaired.

Contact. E-mail: admiss@usouthal.edu
Phone: (251) 460-6141 Toll-free number: (800) 872-5247
Fax: (251) 460-7876
Norma Tanner, Director of Admissions, University of South Alabama, Meisler Hall, Suite 2500, Mobile, AL 36688-0002

University of West Alabama

Livingston, Alabama
www.uwa.edu **CB code: 1737**

- Public 4-year university
- Residential campus in small town
- 1,867 degree-seeking undergraduates: 10% part-time, 60% women, 52% African American, 1% Hispanic American
- 3,020 degree-seeking graduate students
- 68% of applicants admitted
- ACT (writing recommended) required

General. Founded in 1835. Regionally accredited. **Degrees:** 204 bachelor's, 49 associate awarded; master's offered. **ROTC:** Air Force. **Location:** 60 miles from Tuscaloosa. **Calendar:** Semester, limited summer session. **Full-time faculty:** 102 total; 72% have terminal degrees, 20% minority, 50% women. **Part-time faculty:** 89 total; 81% have terminal degrees, 14% minority, 71% women. **Class size:** 61% < 20, 34% 20-39, 2% 40-49, 3% 50-99. **Special facilities:** Nature trail, herbarium, greenhouses, wildflower gardens, bluebird trail.

Freshman class profile. 885 applied, 604 admitted, 303 enrolled.

Mid 50% test scores		Return as sophomores:	56%
ACT composite:	15-22	Out-of-state:	19%

Basis for selection. School achievement record and test scores most important.

High school preparation. 15 units required. Required units include English 3, mathematics 3, social studies 3, science 3 and academic electives 3.

2008-2009 Annual costs. Tuition/fees: $5,200; $9,800 out-of-state. Room/board: $4,104. Personal expenses: $1,200.

2008-2009 Financial aid. Need-based: Average need met was 68%. Average scholarship/grant was $3,102; average loan $3,116. 1% of total undergraduate aid awarded as scholarships/grants, 99% as loans/jobs. **Non-need-based:** Scholarships awarded for academics, alumni affiliation, athletics, leadership, music/drama, state residency.

Application procedures. Admission: No deadline. $20 fee. Admission notification on a rolling basis. **Financial aid:** Priority date 4/1; no closing date. FAFSA required. Applicants notified on a rolling basis starting 6/1; must reply within 2 week(s) of notification.

Academics. Special study options: Accelerated study, cooperative education, distance learning, double major, dual enrollment of high school students, honors, internships, teacher certification program. **Credit/placement by examination:** AP, CLEP, SAT, ACT, institutional tests. 15 credit hours maximum toward associate degree, 30 toward bachelor's. **Support services:** Learning center, reduced course load, remedial instruction, study skills assistance, tutoring, writing center.

Majors. Biology: General, marine. **Business:** Accounting, business admin, management information systems. **Conservation:** General. **Education:** Early childhood, elementary, physical, secondary, special. **Engineering technology:** Manufacturing. **Health:** Athletic training. **History:** General. **Math:** General. **Physical sciences:** Chemistry. **Psychology:** General. **Social sciences:** Sociology.

Most popular majors. Biology 7%, business/marketing 21%, education 34%, engineering/engineering technologies 8%, history 7%, psychology 10%, social sciences 6%.

Computing on campus. 310 workstations in dormitories, library, computer center, student center. Dormitories wired for high-speed internet access and linked to campus network. Commuter students can connect to campus network. Online library, helpline, wireless network available.

Student life. Freshman orientation: Mandatory, $40 fee. Preregistration for classes offered. **Housing:** Guaranteed on-campus for all undergraduates. Coed dorms, single-sex dorms, apartments, wellness housing available. $100 deposit. **Activities:** Bands, campus ministries, choral groups, drama, student government, student newspaper, Wesley Foundation, campus outreach, Fellowship of Christian Athletes, student support services club, African-American cultural association.

Athletics. NCAA. **Intercollegiate:** Baseball M, basketball, cross-country, football (tackle) M, rodeo, softball W, tennis, volleyball W. **Intramural:** Basketball, softball, table tennis, tennis, volleyball, wrestling M. **Team name:** Tigers.

Student services. Career counseling, student employment services, health services, personal counseling, placement for graduates, veterans' counselor. **Physically disabled:** Services for visually, hearing impaired.

Contact. E-mail: admissions@uwa.edu
Phone: (205) 652-3578 Toll-free number: (888) 636-8800
Fax: (205) 652-3708
Richard Hester, Director of Admissions, University of West Alabama, Station 4, Livingston, AL 35470

Virginia College
Birmingham, Alabama
www.vc.edu **CB code: 2596**

- For-profit 4-year technical college
- Commuter campus in very large city

General. Founded in 1975. Accredited by ACICS. **Calendar:** Quarter.

Annual costs/financial aid. Per-credit-hour charge ranges from $302 to $385 and includes fees and books. Personal expenses: $100.

Contact. Phone: (205) 802-1200
Director of Admissions, Box 19249, Birmingham, AL 35219

Virginia College at Huntsville
Huntsville, Alabama
www.vc.edu **CB code: 3451**

- For-profit 4-year business and technical college
- Small city

General. Accredited by ACICS. **Calendar:** Continuous.

Annual costs/financial aid. Students taking 13-16 hours pay $4,320 per quarter; additional fees vary according to program of study. Personal expenses: $2,978. Need-based financial aid available to full-time and part-time students.

Contact. Phone: (256) 533-7387
Vice President of Enrollment, 2800 Bob Wallace Avenue, Huntsville, AL 35805

Four-Year Colleges

Alaska

Alaska Bible College
Glennallen, Alaska
www.akbible.edu **CB code: 1237**

- Private 4-year Bible college affiliated with nondenominational tradition
- Residential campus in rural community
- 26 degree-seeking undergraduates
- SAT or ACT, application essay, interview required

General. Founded in 1966. Accredited by ABHE. **Degrees:** 5 bachelor's, 1 associate awarded. **Location:** 187 miles from Anchorage, 250 miles from Fairbanks. **Calendar:** Semester. **Full-time faculty:** 3 total. **Part-time faculty:** 4 total. **Class size:** 100% < 20. **Special facilities:** Largest theological library collection in Alaska, Alaskan book collection.

Freshman class profile. 13 applied, 13 admitted, 13 enrolled.

Out-of-state:	50%	**Live on campus:**	83%

Basis for selection. Open admission, but selective for some programs. Applicants considered on a case-by-case basis. References and indications of religious commitment most important, followed by school grade record. Test scores and extracurricular activities also considered. **Homeschooled:** Applicants must have documentation of high school equivalence.

High school preparation. College-preparatory program required. Recommended units include English 4, mathematics 4, social studies 4, history 4, science 4 and foreign language 2.

2009-2010 Annual costs. Tuition/fees (projected): $7,524. Room/board: $5,540. Books/supplies: $425. Personal expenses: $1,000.

2008-2009 Financial aid. All financial aid based on need.

Application procedures. Admission: Closing date 7/1 (postmark date). $35 fee. Application must be submitted on paper. Admission notification on a rolling basis beginning on or about 7/1. Must reply by 7/15. **Financial aid:** Priority date 4/30, closing date 8/1. Institutional form required. Applicants notified on a rolling basis; must reply within 2 week(s) of notification.

Academics. Special study options: Double major, dual enrollment of high school students, independent study, internships. **Credit/placement by examination:** AP, CLEP, institutional tests. **Support services:** Remedial instruction, tutoring.

Majors. Theology: Bible.

Computing on campus. 11 workstations in library, computer center, student center.

Student life. Freshman orientation: Mandatory. Preregistration for classes offered. 4-5 day program held immediately before beginning of school year. **Policies:** Religious observance required. **Housing:** Guaranteed on-campus for freshmen. Single-sex dorms, apartments, wellness housing available. $150 fully refundable deposit, deadline 7/1. **Activities:** Radio station, student government.

Student services. Chaplain/spiritual director, financial aid counseling, health services.

Contact. E-mail: info@akbible.edu
Phone: (907) 822-3201 ext. 224 Toll-free number: (800) 478-7884
Fax: (907) 822-5027
Bill Lambert, Director of Admissions, Alaska Bible College, Box 289, Glennallen, AK 99588-0289

Alaska Pacific University
Anchorage, Alaska
www.alaskapacific.edu **CB code: 4201**

- Private 4-year university and liberal arts college
- Commuter campus in large city
- 493 degree-seeking undergraduates: 34% part-time, 67% women, 4% African American, 3% Asian American, 6% Hispanic American, 18% Native American
- 190 degree-seeking graduate students
- 35% of applicants admitted
- SAT or ACT (ACT writing optional), application essay required
- 40% graduate within 6 years

General. Founded in 1957. Regionally accredited. **Degrees:** 84 bachelor's, 2 associate awarded; master's offered. **ROTC:** Air Force. **Calendar:** Differs by program, limited summer session. **Full-time faculty:** 53 total; 58% have terminal degrees, 4% minority, 57% women. **Part-time faculty:** 44 total; 18% have terminal degrees, 2% minority, 50% women. **Class size:** 94% < 20, 6% 20-39. **Special facilities:** Climbing wall, walking trails, lake for canoeing and kayaking, Alaskana collection.

Freshman class profile. 1,353 applied, 471 admitted, 65 enrolled.

Mid 50% test scores		**GPA 2.0-2.99:**	25%
SAT critical reading:	510-630	**Rank in top quarter:**	50%
SAT math:	490-600	**Rank in top tenth:**	24%
ACT composite:	22-26	**End year in good standing:**	80%
GPA 3.75 or higher:	20%	**Return as sophomores:**	80%
GPA 3.50-3.74:	16%	**Out-of-state:**	85%
GPA 3.0-3.49:	39%	**Live on campus:**	88%

Basis for selection. High school record, level of involvement in school and community activities, test scores, writing samples, recommendations most important. **Learning Disabled:** Documentation verifying the disability condition required.

High school preparation. 14 units recommended. Recommended units include English 4, mathematics 3, social studies 1, history 1, science 2 (laboratory 1) and foreign language 2.

2008-2009 Annual costs. Tuition/fees: $22,610. Room/board: $8,884. Books/supplies: $1,000. Personal expenses: $2,700.

2008-2009 Financial aid. Need-based: Average need met was 89%. Average scholarship/grant was $7,500; average loan $3,375. 40% of total undergraduate aid awarded as scholarships/grants, 60% as loans/jobs. **Non-need-based:** Scholarships awarded for academics, alumni affiliation, leadership, religious affiliation, state residency.

Application procedures. Admission: Priority date 12/1; deadline 8/15. $25 fee, may be waived for applicants with need. Admission notification on a rolling basis beginning on or about 1/15. **Financial aid:** Priority date 4/15; no closing date. FAFSA required. Applicants notified on a rolling basis starting 2/1; must reply within 4 week(s) of notification.

Academics. Special study options: Accelerated study, combined bachelor's/graduate degree, distance learning, double major, independent study, internships, liberal arts/career combination, student-designed major, study abroad, teacher certification program. Eco-League exchange program for Environmental Sciences with Prescott College, Northland College, College of the Atlantic, Antioch College, Green Mountain College. **Credit/placement by examination:** AP, CLEP, IB, SAT, ACT, institutional tests. 22 credit hours maximum toward associate degree, 45 toward bachelor's. Sophomore standing available through AP and IB examinations by earning equivalent of 32 semester hours. **Support services:** Learning center, reduced course load, remedial instruction, study skills assistance, tutoring, writing center.

Majors. Biology: Marine. **Business:** Accounting/business management, business admin. **Conservation:** Environmental science, environmental studies, management/policy. **Education:** Elementary, middle. **Health:** Health care admin. **Liberal arts:** Arts/sciences. **Parks/recreation:** Facilities management. **Physical sciences:** Geology. **Psychology:** General. **Public administration:** Human services.

Most popular majors. Business/marketing 36%, education 8%, natural resources/environmental science 19%, parks/recreation 12%, psychology 11%.

Computing on campus. 85 workstations in dormitories, library, computer center, student center. Dormitories wired for high-speed internet access. Online course registration, online library, helpline, student web hosting, wireless network available.

Student life. Freshman orientation: Mandatory. Usually 10 days long, includes outdoor camping events. **Policies:** Student representation on faculty committees and councils stressed. **Housing:** Guaranteed on-campus for freshmen. Coed dorms, cooperative housing, wellness housing available. $300 deposit, deadline 4/30. **Activities:** Campus ministries, choral groups, drama, international student organizations, literary magazine, music ensembles, student government, student newspaper, art club, business club, environmental club, photography club, psychology club, service club, soccer club, volleyball club.

Athletics. Team name: Moose.

Student services. Chaplain/spiritual director, career counseling, student employment services, financial aid counseling, minority student services, personal counseling.

Contact. E-mail: admissions@alaskapacific.edu
Phone: (907) 564-8248 Toll-free number: (800) 252-7528
Fax: (907) 564-8317
Jennifer Jensen, Director of Admissions, Alaska Pacific University, 4101 University Drive, Anchorage, AK 99508

Charter College

Anchorage, Alaska
www.chartercollege.edu **CB code: 3453**

- Private 4-year junior and technical college
- Commuter campus in large city

General. Accredited by ACICS. **Calendar:** Continuous.

Annual costs/financial aid. Total cost for program resulting in an Associate degree ranges from $21,500 to $30,500; $43,500 to $59,500 for a Bachelor's degree. Costs vary by program and full- or part-time status; includes books and supplies. Books/supplies: $700. Need-based financial aid available to full-time and part-time students.

Contact. Phone: (907) 277-1000
Admissions Director, 2221 East Northern Lights Boulevard, Suite 120, Anchorage, AK 99508

University of Alaska Anchorage

Anchorage, Alaska **CB member**
www.uaa.alaska.edu **CB code: 4896**

- Public 4-year university
- Residential campus in large city
- 10,854 degree-seeking undergraduates: 41% part-time, 60% women, 4% African American, 8% Asian American, 5% Hispanic American, 11% Native American, 1% international
- 907 degree-seeking graduate students

General. Founded in 1954. Regionally accredited. **Degrees:** 871 bachelor's, 680 associate awarded; master's offered. **ROTC:** Air Force. **Location:** 3 miles from downtown. **Calendar:** Semester, extensive summer session. **Full-time faculty:** 593 total; 53% have terminal degrees, 12% minority, 54% women. **Part-time faculty:** 665 total; 2% have terminal degrees, 11% minority, 58% women. **Class size:** 55% < 20, 37% 20-39, 5% 40-49, 3% 50-99, less than 1% >100. **Special facilities:** Centers of justice, rural health, supply chain integration, small business development center, alcohol and addiction studies, community engagement and learning, economic education, economic development, psychological services; institutes of environment and natural resources, circumpolar health studies, social and economic research; North Pacific Fisheries Observer Training Center, American Russian Center.

Freshman class profile. 3,539 applied, 2,534 admitted, 1,594 enrolled.

Mid 50% test scores		**GPA 3.0-3.49:**	29%
SAT critical reading:	420-540	**GPA 2.0-2.99:**	43%
SAT math:	420-570	**Rank in top quarter:**	30%
ACT composite:	17-24	**Rank in top tenth:**	11%
GPA 3.75 or higher:	15%	**Return as sophomores:**	70%
GPA 3.50-3.74:	10%	**Out-of-state:**	3%

Basis for selection. Open admission, but selective for some programs. For acceptance into bachelor's program, applications must have high school GPA of at least 2.5 and either SAT, ACT or UAA-approved test scores; high school graduates with GPAs between 2.0 and 2.49 will be admitted on probation. Alternatively, applicants must have successful completion of the GED and either SAT, ACT or UAA-approved test scores. Interviews and essays vary according to program. **Homeschooled:** Transcript of courses and grades required. **Learning Disabled:** Make an appointment with DSS, provide current diagnostic and evaluative reports, and request reasonable accommodations that are supported by documentation.

High school preparation. Requirements vary by program.

2008-2009 Annual costs. Tuition/fees: $4,580; $14,000 out-of-state. Room/board: $7,982. Books/supplies: $990. Personal expenses: $1,427.

Financial aid. Non-need-based: Scholarships awarded for academics, athletics.

Application procedures. Admission: Closing date 7/1. $50 fee, may be waived for applicants with need. Admission notification on a rolling basis. Freshman early admit plan allows students to apply early but wait as long as 2 years to enroll. **Financial aid:** Priority date 4/1, closing date 8/1. FAFSA, institutional form required. Applicants notified on a rolling basis starting 3/15; must reply within 4 week(s) of notification.

Academics. Many programs to assist nontraditional and/or at-risk students for college success. **Special study options:** Combined bachelor's/graduate degree, cooperative education, cross-registration, distance learning, double major, dual enrollment of high school students, ESL, exchange student, honors, independent study, internships, liberal arts/career combination, semester at sea, student-designed major, study abroad, teacher certification program, Washington semester. **Credit/placement by examination:** AP, CLEP, IB, institutional tests. Credit by examination is considered non-resident credit, and non-resident credit policies apply. **Support services:** Learning center, reduced course load, remedial instruction, study skills assistance, tutoring, writing center.

Majors. Biology: General. **Business:** Accounting, business admin, construction management, entrepreneurial studies, finance, hospitality admin, hospitality/recreation, logistics, management information systems, management science, marketing, restaurant/food services. **Communications:** Journalism. **Computer sciences:** Computer science. **Education:** Early childhood, elementary. **Engineering:** General, civil. **Engineering technology:** Electrical, surveying. **Family/consumer sciences:** General. **Foreign languages:** General, French, German, Japanese, Russian, Spanish. **Health:** Health services. **History:** General. **Interdisciplinary:** Biological/physical sciences, math/computer science, natural sciences. **Liberal arts:** Arts/sciences. **Math:** General. **Mechanic/repair:** Aircraft. **Parks/recreation:** Health/fitness. **Philosophy/religion:** Philosophy. **Physical sciences:** Chemistry. **Psychology:** General. **Public administration:** General. **Social sciences:** Anthropology, economics, political science, sociology. **Transportation:** General, air traffic control, airline/commercial pilot, aviation, aviation management. **Visual/performing arts:** Art, dramatic, studio arts.

Most popular majors. Business/marketing 19%, health sciences 17%, history 6%, psychology 9%.

Computing on campus. Dormitories wired for high-speed internet access and linked to campus network. Commuter students can connect to campus network. Online course registration, online library, helpline, repair service, student web hosting, wireless network available.

Student life. Freshman orientation: Available. Preregistration for classes offered. **Housing:** Coed dorms, special housing for disabled, apartments, wellness housing available. $200 deposit. Separate floors for: Alaska natives studying engineering, nursing students, honor students, language and cultures, first-year students under age 20, healthy lifestyle, quiet lifestyle, WWAMI program, Far East exchange program. **Activities:** Jazz band, campus ministries, choral groups, dance, drama, international student organizations, literary magazine, music ensembles, Model UN, opera, radio station, student government, student newspaper, Alaska Native student organization, African American student associations, Baha'i club, College Republicans, Korean Campus Crusade for Christ, Intervarsity Christian Fellowship, disability awareness club, Student Organization Against Racism.

Athletics. NCAA. **Intercollegiate:** Basketball, cross-country, gymnastics W, ice hockey M, skiing, track and field, volleyball W. **Intramural:** Basketball, ice hockey, soccer, volleyball. **Team name:** Seawolves.

Student services. Adult student services, alcohol/substance abuse counseling, career counseling, services for economically disadvantaged, student employment services, financial aid counseling, health services, legal services, minority student services, on-campus daycare, personal counseling, veterans' counselor. **Physically disabled:** Services for visually, speech, hearing impaired. **Learning disabled:** Comprehensive services available.

Contact. E-mail: enroll@uaa.alaska.edu
Phone: (907) 786-1480 Fax: (907) 786-4888
Cecile Mitchell, Director of Admissions, University of Alaska Anchorage, P0 Box 141629, Anchorage, AK 99514-1629

University of Alaska Fairbanks

Fairbanks, Alaska **CB member**
www.uaf.edu **CB code: 4866**

- Public 4-year university
- Commuter campus in small city
- 4,883 degree-seeking undergraduates: 33% part-time, 57% women, 3% African American, 4% Asian American, 4% Hispanic American, 19% Native American, 2% international
- 1,024 degree-seeking graduate students

- 71% of applicants admitted
- 31% graduate within 6 years

General. Founded in 1917. Regionally accredited. Extensive ski trail system located on campus; University of the Arctic participating institution. **Degrees:** 444 bachelor's, 238 associate awarded; master's, doctoral offered. **ROTC:** Army. **Location:** 4 miles from downtown. **Calendar:** Semester, limited summer session. **Full-time faculty:** 332 total; 51% have terminal degrees, 19% minority, 42% women. **Part-time faculty:** 715 total; 32% have terminal degrees, 15% minority, 44% women. **Class size:** 64% < 20, 28% 20-39, 4% 40-49, 3% 50-99, 1% >100. **Special facilities:** Museum of the north, geophysical institute, bioscience library, institute of arctic biology, arctic region supercomputing center, international arctic research center, boreal forest research range, Alaska Native language center, institute of marine sciences, institute of northern engineering, rocketry research range.

Freshman class profile. 1,934 applied, 1,370 admitted, 1,059 enrolled.

Mid 50% test scores		**GPA 2.0-2.99:**	36%
SAT critical reading:	520-580	**Rank in top quarter:**	35%
SAT math:	500-580	**Rank in top tenth:**	13%
SAT writing:	430-540	**Return as sophomores:**	73%
ACT composite:	17-24	**Out-of-state:**	9%
GPA 3.75 or higher:	18%	**Live on campus:**	44%
GPA 3.50-3.74:	14%	**International:**	1%
GPA 3.0-3.49:	29%		

Basis for selection. GED not accepted. Minimum 2.0 high school GPA; 2.5 GPA in 16 core classes, for bachelor's degree-seeking students. Open admissions for associate degree applicants over age 18. Some students may be required to take ASSET and/or COMPASS tests for additional course placement. **Homeschooled:** Transcript of courses and grades, state high school equivalency certificate required. Students who have gone through a state-recognized program and have a valid high school diploma may be admitted to a baccalaureate program. All others admitted via individual review by the UAF admissions office. **Learning Disabled:** Contact UAF Disability Services for assistance.

High school preparation. College-preparatory program required. 16 units required. Required and recommended units include English 4, mathematics 3, social studies 3, science 3 (laboratory 1), foreign language 2 and academic electives 3. Mathematics should include 3 from algebra, geometry and trigonometry, precalculus or calculus.

2008-2009 Annual costs. Tuition/fees: $4,828; $14,248 out-of-state. UA has a tiered tuition rate. For 2009-10, lower division (100, 200) tuition is $141/credit, and upper division (300, 400) tuition is $159/credit. Course and lab fee estimate is $500 for the 2009-10 academic year. Room/board: $7,190. Books/supplies: $1,300. Personal expenses: $2,070.

2007-2008 Financial aid. Need-based: 617 full-time freshmen applied for aid; 346 were judged to have need; 326 of these received aid. Average need met was 55%. Average scholarship/grant was $4,999; average loan $8,604. **Non-need-based:** Awarded to 1,073 full-time undergraduates, including 253 freshmen. Scholarships awarded for academics, art, athletics, leadership, music/drama, ROTC, state residency.

Application procedures. Admission: Priority date 2/15; deadline 7/1 (postmark date). $50 fee, may be waived for applicants with need. Admission notification 9/1. Admission notification on a rolling basis beginning on or about 1/1. **Financial aid:** Priority date 2/15, closing date 7/1. FAFSA required. Applicants notified on a rolling basis starting 3/1; must reply within 2 week(s) of notification.

Academics. Student support services program (federally funded) for students with qualified at-risk status. **Special study options:** Accelerated study, cooperative education, distance learning, double major, dual enrollment of high school students, exchange student, external degree, honors, independent study, internships, semester at sea, student-designed major, study abroad, teacher certification program. **Credit/placement by examination:** AP, CLEP, IB, institutional tests. 15 credit hours maximum toward associate degree, 30 toward bachelor's. 25% of degree requirements awarded for prior work or life experience. Credit awarded for CEEB Advanced Placement Test scores of 3 or greater CLEP, DANTES-DSST, local credit by exam. **Support services:** Learning center, pre-admission summer program, remedial instruction, study skills assistance, tutoring, writing center.

Honors college/program. High school minimum GPA of 3.6 and minimum composite SAT of 1250 (or 1875 including Writing section) or composite ACT 29 for incoming freshmen. University GPA greater than 3.5 required for first-semester college sophomores.

Majors. Area/ethnic studies: Native American, Russian/Slavic. **Biology:** General. **Business:** Accounting, business admin, managerial economics. **Communications:** General, journalism. **Computer sciences:** Computer science. **Conservation:** General, fisheries, forestry, management/policy, wildlife. **Education:** General, music, physical. **Engineering:** Civil, electrical, geological, geotechnical, industrial, mechanical, mining, petroleum. **Foreign languages:** General, Japanese, linguistics, Native American, Russian. **History:** General. **Interdisciplinary:** Biological/physical sciences. **Liberal arts:** Arts/sciences. **Math:** General, applied, statistics. **Philosophy/religion:** Philosophy. **Physical sciences:** Chemistry, geology, physics. **Protective services:** Criminal justice. **Psychology:** General. **Public administration:** Community org/advocacy, social work. **Social sciences:** Anthropology, economics, geography, political science, sociology. **Visual/performing arts:** Art, dramatic, music performance, theater design.

Most popular majors. Biology 10%, business/marketing 12%, engineering/engineering technologies 10%, psychology 9%, public administration/social services 6%, social sciences 7%, visual/performing arts 6%.

Computing on campus. 100 workstations in dormitories, library, computer center. Dormitories wired for high-speed internet access and linked to campus network. Commuter students can connect to campus network. Online course registration, online library, helpline, repair service, student web hosting, wireless network available.

Student life. Freshman orientation: Mandatory, $75 fee. Preregistration for classes offered. Held over the three days immediately proceeding start of class each fall and spring term. **Policies:** Student organizations must be officially recognized on an annual basis by the UAF Student Activities Office. **Housing:** Coed dorms, special housing for disabled, apartments, wellness housing available. $350 nonrefundable deposit, deadline 8/1. Alaska Native cultural housing. **Activities:** Bands, campus ministries, choral groups, dance, drama, international student organizations, literary magazine, music ensembles, Model UN, radio station, student government, student newspaper, symphony orchestra, TV station, American Indian Science and Engineering Society, Black Awareness Student Union, Club Francais, Japanese club, Latin dance club, Namaste India, Inu-Yupiaq Dance Group, Northern Star Chinese Association, University Women's Association, Caribbean music and culture club.

Athletics. NCAA. **Intercollegiate:** Basketball, cross-country, ice hockey M, rifle, skiing, swimming W, volleyball W. **Intramural:** Badminton, basketball, bowling, football (non-tackle), ice hockey, lacrosse, racquetball, soccer, softball, swimming, table tennis, tennis, volleyball, water polo. **Team name:** Nanooks.

Student services. Alcohol/substance abuse counseling, chaplain/spiritual director, career counseling, services for economically disadvantaged, student employment services, financial aid counseling, health services, legal services, minority student services, on-campus daycare, personal counseling, placement for graduates, women's services. **Physically disabled:** Services for visually, speech, hearing impaired.

Contact. E-mail: admissions@uaf.edu
Phone: (907) 474-7500 Toll-free number: (800) 478-1823
Fax: (907) 474-5379
Lael Oldmixon, Admissions Director, University of Alaska Fairbanks, PO Box 757480, Fairbanks, AK 99775-7480

University of Alaska Southeast

Juneau, Alaska — **CB member**
www.uas.alaska.edu — **CB code: 4897**

- Public 4-year university and liberal arts college
- Commuter campus in large town
- 1,145 degree-seeking undergraduates: 50% part-time, 67% women
- 270 degree-seeking graduate students
- 90% of applicants admitted
- SAT or ACT (ACT writing recommended) required

General. Founded in 1972. Regionally accredited. All campuses accessible only by ferry or air. **Degrees:** 93 bachelor's, 65 associate awarded; master's offered. **Location:** Downtown. **Calendar:** Semester, limited summer session. **Full-time faculty:** 107 total; 44% have terminal degrees, 6% minority, 46% women. **Part-time faculty:** 117 total; 3% have terminal degrees, 14% minority, 62% women. **Class size:** 76% < 20, 23% 20-39, less than 1% 40-49, less than 1% 50-99. **Special facilities:** Juneau ice field, Mendenhall glacier, Tongass national forest.

Freshman class profile. 236 applied, 212 admitted, 212 enrolled.

Mid 50% test scores			
SAT critical reading:	440-580	GPA 3.0-3.49:	28%
SAT math:	430-560	GPA 2.0-2.99:	42%
SAT writing:	400-530	Rank in top quarter:	20%
ACT composite:	17-23	Rank in top tenth:	11%
GPA 3.75 or higher:	14%	Return as sophomores:	44%
GPA 3.50-3.74:	8%	Out-of-state:	9%

Basis for selection. High school record most important. Students not meeting BA requirements counseled to AA or certificate program with possibility of later transfer to BA program. Some BA programs admit students as pre-majors and upon satisfying prerequisites may be admitted to major. Financial statement and immunization records required of international applicants as well as a statement of educational equivalency written in English. **Homeschooled:** Student must graduate from accredited home school program or obtain GED.

High school preparation. College-preparatory program recommended. Recommended units include English 4, mathematics 2, social studies 3, science 1 (laboratory 1).

2008-2009 Annual costs. Tuition/fees: $4,303; $11,839 out-of-state. Tuition reported is for lower division offerings; for upper division, $123 per credit. Room/board: $7,583. Books/supplies: $550. Personal expenses: $1,643.

2008-2009 Financial aid. Need-based: Average need met was 45%. Average scholarship/grant was $3,517; average loan $3,264. 38% of total undergraduate aid awarded as scholarships/grants, 62% as loans/jobs. **Non-need-based:** Scholarships awarded for academics, leadership. **Additional information:** Transfer, continuing, and freshman scholarship deadline March 1.

Application procedures. Admission: Priority date 8/1; no deadline. $40 fee, may be waived for applicants with need. Admission notification on a rolling basis. Housing deposit refundable if written letter of cancellation provided prior to July 1. **Financial aid:** Priority date 6/1; no closing date. FAFSA required. Applicants notified on a rolling basis starting 2/15; must reply within 3 week(s) of notification.

Academics. Special study options: Combined bachelor's/graduate degree, cooperative education, distance learning, dual enrollment of high school students, exchange student, external degree, independent study, internships, study abroad, teacher certification program. **Credit/placement by examination:** AP, CLEP, institutional tests. 15 credit hours maximum toward associate degree, 30 toward bachelor's. **Support services:** Learning center, preadmission summer program, remedial instruction, study skills assistance, tutoring, writing center.

Majors. Biology: General, marine. **Business:** General, accounting, management science, marketing. **Communications:** General. **Computer sciences:** Networking. **Conservation:** Environmental science. **Education:** Elementary. **Liberal arts:** Arts/sciences. **Math:** General. **Social sciences:** General, political science. **Visual/performing arts:** Art.

Most popular majors. Biology 8%, business/marketing 30%, liberal arts 40%, social sciences 8%.

Computing on campus. 225 workstations in dormitories, library, computer center, student center. Dormitories wired for high-speed internet access and linked to campus network. Commuter students can connect to campus network. Online course registration, online library, helpline, repair service, student web hosting, wireless network available.

Student life. Freshman orientation: Mandatory, $75 fee. Preregistration for classes offered. Three-day orientation includes outdoor experiences. **Housing:** Coed dorms, special housing for disabled, apartments, wellness housing available. $200 deposit, deadline 4/1. **Activities:** Dance, student government, student newspaper, global connections club, Amnesty International, backcountry skiing club, gay organization, swing dancing club, rock climbing club, English club, Wooch Een Native student organization.

Athletics. Intramural: Badminton, basketball, football (non-tackle) M, racquetball, skiing, softball, tennis, volleyball, weight lifting.

Student services. Adult student services, alcohol/substance abuse counseling, career counseling, student employment services, financial aid counseling, health services, minority student services, personal counseling, placement for graduates, veterans' counselor. **Physically disabled:** Services for visually, hearing impaired.

Contact. E-mail: admissions@uas.alaska.edu
Phone: (907) 796-6100 Toll-free number: (877) 465-4827
Fax: (907) 796-6365
Shontay King, Admissions Director, University of Alaska Southeast, 11120 Glacier Highway, Juneau, AK 99801-8681

Arizona

American Indian College of the Assemblies of God

Phoenix, Arizona
www.aicag.edu **CB code: 2597**

- Private 4-year Bible and teachers college affiliated with Assemblies of God
- Residential campus in very large city
- 50 degree-seeking undergraduates: 14% part-time, 68% women
- 87% of applicants admitted
- SAT or ACT (ACT writing optional), application essay required

General. Founded in 1957. Regionally accredited. **Degrees:** 21 bachelor's awarded. **Location:** 15 miles from downtown. **Calendar:** Semester. **Full-time faculty:** 8 total; 38% have terminal degrees, 25% women. **Part-time faculty:** 15 total; 13% have terminal degrees, 40% minority, 40% women.

Freshman class profile. 52 applied, 45 admitted, 37 enrolled.

End year in good standing:	68%	**Out-of-state:**	45%
Return as sophomores:	66%	**Live on campus:**	78%

Basis for selection. Applicants must show Christian commitment, willingness to abide by Student Handbook, and favorable reference from home pastor. Must also show ability to complete college-level instruction through SAT/ACT score and transcripts. ACT/SAT requirement may be waived by approval of Academic Dean when other evidence of student ability available. **Homeschooled:** Favorable pastoral reference required.

2008-2009 Annual costs. Tuition/fees: $7,174. Room/board: $5,232. Books/supplies: $500. Personal expenses: $2,570.

Application procedures. Admission: No deadline. No application fee. Admission notification on a rolling basis. Students admitted with proper paperwork through first week of semester. **Financial aid:** Priority date 4/1; no closing date. FAFSA required. Applicants notified on a rolling basis starting 7/15.

Academics. Special study options: Double major, ESL, independent study, internships, liberal arts/career combination, teacher certification program. **Credit/placement by examination:** CLEP, institutional tests. **Support services:** Learning center, pre-admission summer program, reduced course load, remedial instruction, study skills assistance, tutoring.

Majors. Education: Elementary. **Theology:** Theology.

Most popular majors. Education 27%, theological studies 73%.

Computing on campus. 39 workstations in library, computer center, student center.

Student life. Freshman orientation: Mandatory. Preregistration for classes offered. Pre-registration orientation session. **Policies:** Religious observance required. **Housing:** Guaranteed on-campus for freshmen. Single-sex dorms, special housing for disabled available. Pets allowed in dorm rooms. **Activities:** Choral groups, music ensembles, student government, associated student body, campus missions fellowship.

Athletics. Intercollegiate: Basketball. **Intramural:** Basketball. **Team name:** Warriors.

Student services. Adult student services, chaplain/spiritual director, career counseling, student employment services, financial aid counseling, personal counseling, placement for graduates.

Contact. E-mail: aicadm@aicag.edu
Phone: (602) 943-335 ext. 232 Toll-free number: (800) 933-3828 ext. 232
Fax: (602) 943-8299
Sandra Gonzales, Director of Enrollment Management, American Indian College of the Assemblies of God, 10020 North 15th Avenue, Phoenix, AZ 85021-2199

Arizona State University

Tempe, Arizona **CB member**
www.asu.edu **CB code: 4007**

- Public 4-year university
- Commuter campus in very large city
- 52,883 degree-seeking undergraduates: 19% part-time, 52% women, 5% African American, 6% Asian American, 15% Hispanic American, 2% Native American, 2% international
- 12,186 degree-seeking graduate students
- 90% of applicants admitted
- SAT or ACT (ACT writing recommended) required
- 56% graduate within 6 years

General. Founded in 1885. Regionally accredited. ASU is comprised of four campuses located in Phoenix and the vicinity: historic flagship campus in Tempe, Polytechnic (East Valley), West (northwest Phoenix), and Downtown (heart of Phoenix). **Degrees:** 10,706 bachelor's awarded; master's, doctoral, first professional offered. **ROTC:** Army, Air Force. **Calendar:** Semester, extensive summer session. **Class size:** 46% < 20, 34% 20-39, 6% 40-49, 9% 50-99, 4% >100. **Special facilities:** Biodesign institute, global institute of sustainability, skysong.

Freshman class profile. 27,089 applied, 24,473 admitted, 9,707 enrolled.

Mid 50% test scores		**GPA 2.0-2.99:**	20%
SAT critical reading:	470-600	**Rank in top quarter:**	58%
SAT math:	480-610	**Rank in top tenth:**	31%
ACT composite:	20-26	**Return as sophomores:**	80%
GPA 3.75 or higher:	30%	**Out-of-state:**	30%
GPA 3.50-3.74:	19%	**Live on campus:**	57%
GPA 3.0-3.49:	31%	**International:**	2%

Basis for selection. Rank in top 25% of class, 3.0 GPA, 22 ACT/1040 SAT (exclusive of writing) required for in-state applicants. In-state requirements plus 24 ACT/1110 SAT (exclusive of Writing) required for out-of-state applicants. Additional requirements for some programs. Auditions required of music, dance, theater majors. Portfolios required of graphic design, architecture, environmental design majors. **Homeschooled:** Affidavit of Completion of Secondary School Education required.

High school preparation. College-preparatory program required. 16 units required. Required units include English 4, mathematics 4, social studies 1, history 1, science 3 (laboratory 3) and foreign language 2. 1 unit U.S. history recommended, 1 fine arts required. 2 of the same foreign languages recommended for College of Liberal Arts and Sciences. 1 each physics and chemistry required for nursing. 4 math, including calculus, recommended for engineering.

2008-2009 Annual costs. Tuition/fees: $5,661; $17,949 out-of-state. Room/board: $8,790.

2007-2008 Financial aid. Need-based: 5,188 full-time freshmen applied for aid; 3,472 were judged to have need; 3,472 of these received aid. Average need met was 63%. Average scholarship/grant was $7,181; average loan $3,098. 51% of total undergraduate aid awarded as scholarships/grants, 49% as loans/jobs. **Non-need-based:** Awarded to 7,851 full-time undergraduates, including 2,538 freshmen. Scholarships awarded for academics, art, athletics, leadership, music/drama, ROTC.

Application procedures. Admission: $25 fee ($50 out-of-state). Admission notification on a rolling basis. Apply for housing as soon as admitted. **Financial aid:** Priority date 3/1; no closing date. FAFSA required. Applicants notified on a rolling basis.

Academics. Special study options: Accelerated study, cooperative education, cross-registration, distance learning, double major, exchange student, honors, independent study, internships, semester at sea, study abroad, teacher certification program, Washington semester. **Credit/placement by examination:** AP, CLEP, IB, SAT, ACT, institutional tests. 60 credit hours maximum toward bachelor's degree. **Support services:** Learning center, study skills assistance, tutoring, writing center.

Honors college/program. Rank in top 5% of high school class, 1300 SAT (exclusive of writing) or 29 ACT required. Separate application required. Dual enrollment in college of student's disciplinary major.

Majors. Agriculture: Business. **Architecture:** Architecture, interior, landscape, urban/community planning. **Area/ethnic studies:** African-American, American, Hispanic-American/Latino/Chicano, Native American, women's. **Biology:** General, biochemistry, botany, conservation, microbiology, molecular. **Business:** Accounting, business admin, construction management, finance, international, management information systems, marketing, nonprofit/

public, operations, purchasing, real estate, tourism/travel. **Communications:** General, journalism. **Communications technology:** Graphics. **Computer sciences:** Computer science, systems analysis. **Education:** Art, biology, business, chemistry, drama/dance, early childhood, elementary, English, family/consumer sciences, foreign languages, French, geography, German, history, mathematics, music, physical, physics, secondary, social studies, Spanish, special. **Engineering:** General, aerospace, biomedical, chemical, civil, computer, electrical, environmental, industrial, materials, mechanical. **Engineering technology:** Computer, electrical, industrial, manufacturing, mechanical. **Family/consumer sciences:** Aging, family resources, food/nutrition. **Foreign languages:** East Asian, French, German, Italian, Russian, Spanish. **Health:** Clinical lab science, communication disorders, music therapy, nursing (RN). **History:** General. **Interdisciplinary:** Global studies, science/society. **Legal studies:** Prelaw. **Liberal arts:** Arts/sciences, humanities. **Math:** General, applied, computational. **Parks/recreation:** General, exercise sciences. **Philosophy/religion:** Philosophy, religion. **Physical sciences:** Chemistry, geology, physics. **Protective services:** Criminal justice, law enforcement admin. **Psychology:** General. **Public administration:** Social work. **Social sciences:** General, anthropology, economics, geography, political science, sociology, urban studies. **Transportation:** Air traffic control, aviation. **Visual/performing arts:** General, art, dance, dramatic, graphic design, industrial design, music performance, music theory/composition.

Most popular majors. Business/marketing 18%, communications/journalism 7%, education 10%, engineering/engineering technologies 7%, interdisciplinary studies 10%, social sciences 7%.

Computing on campus. Dormitories wired for high-speed internet access and linked to campus network. Commuter students can connect to campus network. Online course registration, online library, helpline, wireless network available.

Student life. Freshman orientation: Available. Preregistration for classes offered. **Housing:** Coed dorms, special housing for disabled, apartments, fraternity/sorority housing available. $125 nonrefundable deposit. **Activities:** Bands, campus ministries, choral groups, dance, drama, film society, international student organizations, literary magazine, music ensembles, Model UN, musical theater, opera, radio station, student government, student newspaper, symphony orchestra, TV station, 654 organizations available.

Athletics. NCAA. **Intercollegiate:** Baseball M, basketball, cross-country, diving W, football (tackle) M, golf, gymnastics W, soccer W, softball W, swimming, tennis W, track and field, volleyball W, water polo W, wrestling M. **Intramural:** Badminton, basketball, football (non-tackle), golf, racquetball, soccer, table tennis, tennis, volleyball. **Team name:** Sun Devils.

Student services. Adult student services, career counseling, student employment services, health services, legal services, minority student services, on-campus daycare, personal counseling, placement for graduates, veterans' counselor. **Physically disabled:** Services for visually, speech, hearing impaired.

Contact. E-mail: ugradinq@asu.edu
Phone: (480) 965-7788 Fax: (480) 965-3610
Martha Byrd, Dean, Undergraduate Admissions, Arizona State University, Box 870112, Tempe, AZ 85287-0112

Art Center Design College

Tucson, Arizona
www.theartcenter.edu **CB code: 3037**

- For-profit 4-year visual arts college
- Commuter campus in very large city
- 346 degree-seeking undergraduates
- 80% of applicants admitted
- SAT or ACT (ACT writing optional), application essay, interview required

General. Degrees: 44 bachelor's, 4 associate awarded. **Calendar:** Semester, extensive summer session. **Full-time faculty:** 18 total. **Part-time faculty:** 30 total. **Class size:** 3% < 20, 97% 20-39.

Freshman class profile. 81 applied, 65 admitted, 40 enrolled.

Mid 50% test scores			
SAT critical reading:	440-550	ACT composite:	16-22
SAT math:	360-540	Out-of-state:	3%

Basis for selection. High school transcripts, ACT/SAT scores, essay, interview, personal statement form required. Admissions based on an evaluation of strengths, academic preparedness and communication skills. Art work required for illustration, fine arts, animation and graphic design programs.

High school preparation. College-preparatory program recommended.

2008-2009 Annual costs. Tuition/fees: $16,320. Books/supplies: $1,250. Personal expenses: $3,204.

Financial aid. All financial aid based on need.

Application procedures. Admission: No deadline. $25 fee. Admission notification on a rolling basis. **Financial aid:** No deadline. FAFSA required.

Academics. Special study options: Double major, independent study, internships, liberal arts/career combination. **Credit/placement by examination:** AP, CLEP, IB, SAT, ACT, institutional tests. **Support services:** Learning center, reduced course load, remedial instruction, study skills assistance, tutoring, writing center.

Majors. Architecture: Landscape. **Business:** Marketing. **Communications:** Advertising. **Communications technology:** Animation/special effects. **Visual/performing arts:** Graphic design, illustration, interior design, photography, studio arts.

Computing on campus. 125 workstations in library, computer center, student center. Online course registration, online library, helpline, student web hosting, wireless network available.

Student life. Freshman orientation: Mandatory. Preregistration for classes offered.

Student services. Adult student services, career counseling, student employment services, financial aid counseling, personal counseling, placement for graduates, veterans' counselor.

Contact. E-mail: inquire@theartcenter.edu
Phone: (520) 325-0123 Toll-free number: (800) 825-8753
Colleen Gimbel-Froebe, Director of Enrollment Management, Art Center Design College, 2525 North Country Club Road, Tucson, AZ 85716

Art Institute of Phoenix

Phoenix, Arizona
www.artinstitutes.edu/phoenix **CB code: 4003**

- For-profit 3-year culinary school and visual arts college
- Commuter campus in very large city
- 1,125 degree-seeking undergraduates
- Application essay, interview required

General. Accredited by ACICS. **Degrees:** 235 bachelor's, 40 associate awarded. **Calendar:** Quarter, extensive summer session. **Full-time faculty:** 46 total. **Part-time faculty:** 48 total. **Special facilities:** Culinary labs, video studio, computer labs, editing suites, sound lab.

Basis for selection. High school diploma or GED required; high school GPA considered.

2008-2009 Annual costs. Tuition/fees: $20,405.

Application procedures. Admission: Closing date 10/13 (receipt date). $50 fee. Admission notification on a rolling basis. **Financial aid:** No deadline. FAFSA required.

Academics. Special study options: Distance learning, independent study, internships, study abroad. **Credit/placement by examination:** AP, CLEP, IB, SAT, ACT, institutional tests. **Support services:** Learning center, reduced course load, remedial instruction, tutoring.

Majors. BACHELOR'S. Communications technology: Animation/special effects. **Computer sciences:** Web page design, webmaster. **Personal/culinary services:** Culinary arts. **Visual/performing arts:** Cinematography, commercial/advertising art, graphic design, interior design. **ASSOCIATE. Personal/culinary services:** Culinary arts. **Visual/performing arts:** Graphic design.

Student life. Freshman orientation: Mandatory. Preregistration for classes offered. **Housing:** Apartments available. $150 fully refundable deposit, deadline 10/13. **Activities:** Film society.

Student services. Adult student services, career counseling, student employment services, financial aid counseling, personal counseling, placement for graduates.

Contact. E-mail: aipxadm@aii.edu
Phone: (602) 331-7500 Toll-free number: (800) 474-2479
Fax: (602) 331-5301
Denise Patterson, Director of Admissions, Art Institute of Phoenix, 2233 West Dunlap Avenue, Phoenix, AZ 85021-2859

Art Institute of Tucson
Tucson, Arizona
www.tucsondesigncollege.edu

- For-profit 4-year liberal arts and technical college
- Residential campus in very large city
- 130 full-time, degree-seeking undergraduates
- Application essay, interview required

General. Accredited by ACICS. Free book loan program. **Degrees:** 1 bachelor's, 67 associate awarded. **Location:** 115 miles from Phoenix. **Calendar:** Quarter, limited summer session. **Full-time faculty:** 7 total. **Part-time faculty:** 9 total. **Special facilities:** Fully equipped fashion design lab with industrial sewing machines, sergers, dress forms, computer pattern making software, fully stocked interior design resource room.

Basis for selection. Open admission, but selective for some programs. Artwork portfolio required. **Homeschooled:** Transcript of courses and grades, interview required.

2008-2009 Annual costs. Tuition per-credit-hour charge, $431; cost of starting kit (containing supplies and books) depends upon program.

Application procedures. Admission: No deadline. $35 fee. Application must be submitted on paper. Admission notification on a rolling basis.

Academics. Special study options: Accelerated study. **Credit/placement by examination:** AP, CLEP. **Support services:** Tutoring.

Majors. Visual/performing arts: Interior design.

Computing on campus. 33 workstations in library, computer center. Online library available.

Student life. Freshman orientation: Mandatory. Held the Saturday morning before classes begin. **Activities:** American Society of Interior Designers student chapter.

Student services. Career counseling, student employment services, financial aid counseling, personal counseling, placement for graduates, veterans' counselor.

Contact. Phone: (520) 881-2900 Fax: (520) 881-4234
Director of Academics, Art Institute of Tucson, 1030 North Alvernon Way, Tucson, AZ 85711

Brown Mackie College: Tucson
Tucson, Arizona
www.chap-col.edu **CB code: 3458**

- For-profit 4-year career college
- Commuter campus in very large city
- 325 degree-seeking undergraduates
- Interview required

General. Accredited by ACICS. **Degrees:** 68 bachelor's, 52 associate awarded. **Calendar:** Continuous. **Full-time faculty:** 20 total. **Part-time faculty:** 5 total; 20% minority, 20% women.

Basis for selection. Open admission. **Homeschooled:** State high school equivalency certificate required.

2008-2009 Annual costs. Undergraduates in general curriculum pay $260 per credit hour; $275 per-credit-hour charge for surgical technology program; $260 per-credit-hour charge for occupational therapy assistant courses; all students pay $15 per-credit-hour fee.

Application procedures. Admission: No deadline. No application fee.

Academics. Special study options: Internships. **Credit/placement by examination:** CLEP. **Support services:** Remedial instruction, tutoring.

Majors. Business: Accounting, business admin. **Computer sciences:** Computer science.

Computing on campus. 200 workstations in library.

Student services. Career counseling, financial aid counseling, personal counseling, placement for graduates, veterans' counselor.

Contact. Phone: (520) 327-6866
Holly Helscher, President, Brown Mackie College: Tucson, 4585 East Speedway Boulevard, Suite 204, Tucson, AZ 85712

College of the Humanities and Sciences
Tempe, Arizona
www.chumsci.edu/

- For-profit 4-year liberal arts college
- Small city
- 25 degree-seeking undergraduates
- 90 graduate students

General. Accredited by DETC. **Degrees:** 10 bachelor's awarded; master's, doctoral, first professional offered. **Location:** 12 miles from Phoenix. **Calendar:** Continuous, extensive summer session.

Basis for selection. Open admission.

2008-2009 Annual costs. Per-credit-hour charge (tuition only) is $225.

Application procedures. Admission: No deadline. $50 fee. Application must be submitted on paper. Admission notification on a rolling basis.

Academics. Special study options: Distance learning, student-designed major. **Credit/placement by examination:** CLEP.

Majors. Liberal arts: Arts/sciences, humanities.

Contact. E-mail: information@chumsci.edu
Phone: (877) 248-6724 Toll-free number: (877) 248-6724
Fax: (800) 762-1622
Susan Chiaramonte, Registrar, College of the Humanities and Sciences, 1105 East Broadway Road, Tempe, AZ 85282

Collins College
Tempe, Arizona
www.collinscollege.edu **CB code: 2174**

- For-profit 4-year visual arts and technical college
- Commuter campus in small city
- 1,500 degree-seeking undergraduates
- Application essay, interview required

General. Founded in 1978. Accredited by ACCSCT. Satellite campus in west Phoenix. **Degrees:** 328 bachelor's, 189 associate awarded. **Location:** 5 miles from Phoenix. **Calendar:** Continuous, extensive summer session. **Full-time faculty:** 60 total. **Part-time faculty:** 20 total. **Special facilities:** Photography and video studio with 2 full edit bays.

Basis for selection. Open admission.

2008-2009 Annual costs. Tuition/fees: $14,925. Required fees vary by program.

Application procedures. Admission: No deadline. $50 fee. Admission notification on a rolling basis.

Academics. Special study options: Liberal arts/career combination. **Credit/placement by examination:** CLEP. **Support services:** Tutoring.

Majors. Communications technology: Animation/special effects. **Computer sciences:** LAN/WAN management, system admin, web page design. **Visual/performing arts:** Commercial/advertising art.

Student life. Freshman orientation: Mandatory. **Activities:** TV station.

Student services. Career counseling, student employment services, placement for graduates.

Contact. Phone: (480) 966-3000 Toll-free number: (800) 876-7070
Fax: (480) 902-0663
Vice President of Admissions and Marketing, Collins College, 1140 South Priest Drive, Tempe, AZ 85281

DeVry University: Phoenix
Phoenix, Arizona
www.devry.edu **CB code: 4277**

- For-profit 4-year university
- Commuter campus in large city
- 1,081 degree-seeking undergraduates: 37% part-time, 25% women, 9% African American, 5% Asian American, 21% Hispanic American, 5% Native American, 1% international

- 193 degree-seeking graduate students
- 91% of applicants admitted
- Interview required

General. Founded in 1967. Regionally accredited. **Degrees:** 194 bachelor's, 35 associate awarded; master's offered. **ROTC:** Air Force. **Calendar:** Semester, extensive summer session. **Full-time faculty:** 34 total; 21% women. **Part-time faculty:** 68 total; 13% minority, 34% women.

Freshman class profile. 520 applied, 471 admitted, 270 enrolled.

Basis for selection. Applicants must have high school diploma or equivalent or a degree from accredited postsecondary institution, demonstrate proficiency in basic college-level skills through SAT or ACT scores or institution-administered placement exams, and be at least 17 years of age on the first day of classes. New students may enter at beginning of any semester. CPT accepted.

High school preparation. Required units include mathematics 1.

2008-2009 Annual costs. Tuition/fees: $14,130. Books/supplies: $1,300. Personal expenses: $5,082.

2007-2008 Financial aid. All financial aid based on need.

Application procedures. Admission: No deadline. $50 fee. Admission notification on a rolling basis. **Financial aid:** No deadline. FAFSA required. Applicants notified on a rolling basis.

Academics. Special study options: Accelerated study, cooperative education, distance learning, weekend college. **Credit/placement by examination:** CLEP, institutional tests. **Support services:** Learning center, remedial instruction, tutoring.

Majors. Biology: Biomedical sciences. **Business:** Business admin, human resources, management information systems, operations. **Computer sciences:** General, information systems, networking, security. **Engineering technology:** General, computer, electrical.

Most popular majors. Business/marketing 44%, computer/information sciences 31%, engineering/engineering technologies 25%.

Computing on campus. 436 workstations in library, computer center. Online course registration, online library, helpline available.

Student life. Freshman orientation: Mandatory. **Housing:** Private apartments, student-plan housing, private rooms. **Activities:** Student government, student newspaper, Institute of Electrical and Electronics Engineers, Campus Crusaders for Christ, travel club, Sigma Beta Delta, computer society, inventors club, sports compact car club, Tau Alpha Pi, hockey league.

Athletics. Intramural: Field hockey M, golf, softball.

Student services. Career counseling, student employment services, financial aid counseling, placement for graduates, veterans' counselor. **Physically disabled:** Services for visually, hearing impaired.

Contact. E-mail: admissions@phx.devry.edu
Phone: (602) 870-9201 Toll-free number: (800) 528-0250
Fax: (602) 331-1494
Jerry Driskill, Director of Admissions, DeVry University: Phoenix, 2149 West Dunlap Avenue, Phoenix, AZ 85021-2995

Embry-Riddle Aeronautical University: Prescott Campus

Prescott, Arizona
www.embryriddle.edu **CB code: 4305**

- Private 4-year university
- Residential campus in large town
- 1,672 degree-seeking undergraduates: 8% part-time, 18% women, 2% African American, 7% Asian American, 8% Hispanic American, 1% Native American, 4% international
- 29 degree-seeking graduate students
- 86% of applicants admitted
- SAT or ACT (ACT writing optional) required
- 56% graduate within 6 years; 2% enter graduate study

General. Founded in 1978. Regionally accredited. Eastern residential campus in Daytona Beach, Florida. More than 130 continuing education centers located throughout the United States and Europe. **Degrees:** 343 bachelor's awarded; master's offered. **ROTC:** Army, Air Force. **Location:** 100 miles from Phoenix. **Calendar:** Semester, extensive summer session. **Full-time faculty:** 98 total; 70% have terminal degrees, 8% minority, 18% women. **Part-time faculty:** 32 total; 22% have terminal degrees, 3% minority, 44% women. **Class size:** 52% < 20, 46% 20-39, 2% 40-49, less than 1% 50-99. **Special facilities:** Supersonic wind tunnel, fleet of 40 aircraft, engineering and technical center, aviation safety center.

Freshman class profile. 1,148 applied, 990 admitted, 418 enrolled.

Mid 50% test scores		**Rank in top quarter:**	52%
SAT critical reading:	470-600	**Rank in top tenth:**	25%
SAT math:	500-640	**Return as sophomores:**	79%
ACT composite:	22-28	**Out-of-state:**	83%
GPA 3.75 or higher:	31%	**Live on campus:**	96%
GPA 3.50-3.74:	21%	**International:**	4%
GPA 3.0-3.49:	30%	**Fraternities:**	9%
GPA 2.0-2.99:	18%	**Sororities:**	12%

Basis for selection. High school GPA, class rank, test scores most important. Specific requirements vary by degree program. Flight program applicants must pass medical examination for Class I or II Federal Aviation Administration Medical Certificate at least 60 calendar days prior to enrollment. Interview and essay recommended.

High school preparation. College-preparatory program recommended. 16 units required; 18 recommended. Required and recommended units include English 4, mathematics 3-4, social studies 2, history 1, science 2-3 (laboratory 2-3), foreign language 2 and academic electives 4.

2009-2010 Annual costs. Tuition/fees (projected): $27,740. Room/board: $8,008. Books/supplies: $1,040. Personal expenses: $1,448.

2008-2009 Financial aid. Need-based: 347 full-time freshmen applied for aid; 295 were judged to have need; 294 of these received aid. Average scholarship/grant was $12,678; average loan $4,294. 54% of total undergraduate aid awarded as scholarships/grants, 46% as loans/jobs. **Non-need-based:** Awarded to 60 full-time undergraduates, including 15 freshmen. Scholarships awarded for academics, alumni affiliation, athletics, leadership, ROTC.

Application procedures. Admission: Priority date 1/15; no deadline. $50 fee, may be waived for applicants with need. Admission notification on a rolling basis beginning on or about 11/1. Must reply by May 1 or within 2 week(s) if notified thereafter. Application closing date 60 days prior to start of term. Early application encouraged; available facilities limit enrollment in some programs. **Financial aid:** No deadline. FAFSA required. Applicants notified on a rolling basis starting 3/1; must reply within 4 week(s) of notification.

Academics. Special study options: Accelerated study, cooperative education, distance learning, double major, dual enrollment of high school students, ESL, exchange student, honors, independent study, internships. Flight training. **Credit/placement by examination:** AP, CLEP, IB, SAT, ACT, institutional tests. 15 credit hours maximum toward associate degree, 30 toward bachelor's. **Support services:** Remedial instruction, study skills assistance, tutoring.

Majors. Engineering: General, aerospace, computer, electrical, software. **Interdisciplinary:** Science/society. **Physical sciences:** Physics. **Social sciences:** International relations. **Transportation:** Airline/commercial pilot, aviation.

Most popular majors. Engineering/engineering technologies 26%, interdisciplinary studies 7%, physical sciences 7%, social sciences 14%, trade and industry 42%.

Computing on campus. 470 workstations in library, computer center, student center. Dormitories linked to campus network. Helpline available.

Student life. Freshman orientation: Available. Preregistration for classes offered. **Housing:** Guaranteed on-campus for freshmen. Coed dorms, apartments available. $250 fully refundable deposit, deadline 7/15. **Activities:** Dance, literary magazine, music ensembles, radio station, student government, student newspaper, Rangers (Army ROTC), student activities association, Angel Flight/Silver Wings, residence halls association, Arnold Air Society, Golden Eagles flight team, Greeks, aerobatic club, Japanese anime/manga.

Athletics. NAIA. **Intercollegiate:** Soccer, volleyball W, wrestling M. **Intramural:** Basketball, bowling, cross-country, football (non-tackle), golf, racquetball, soccer, softball, swimming, table tennis, tennis, track and field, volleyball, weight lifting. **Team name:** Eagles.

Student services. Adult student services, career counseling, student employment services, health services, personal counseling, placement for graduates, veterans' counselor. **Physically disabled:** Services for visually, speech, hearing impaired.

Contact. E-mail: pradmit@erau.edu
Phone: (928) 777-6600 Toll-free number: (800) 888-3728
Fax: (928) 777-6606
Debra Cates, Interim Director of Admissions, Embry-Riddle Aeronautical University: Prescott Campus, 3700 Willow Creek Road, Prescott, AZ 86301-3720

Grand Canyon University
Phoenix, Arizona
www.gcu.edu/clgbrd **CB code: 4331**

- For-profit 4-year university
- Commuter campus in very large city
- 4,800 degree-seeking undergraduates
- 8,600 graduate students
- 100% of applicants admitted

General. Founded in 1949. Regionally accredited. **Degrees:** 595 bachelor's awarded; master's, doctoral offered. **ROTC:** Army. **Calendar:** Semester, limited summer session. **Full-time faculty:** 52 total; 14% minority, 62% women. **Part-time faculty:** 1,509 total; 1% minority, 56% women. **Class size:** 64% < 20, 35% 20-39, less than 1% 40-49, less than 1% 50-99. **Special facilities:** Cadaver laboratory.

Freshman class profile. 2,785 applied, 2,781 admitted, 1,144 enrolled.

Basis for selection. Admissions based on graduation from high school (or GED) and academic potential demonstrated by high school GPA of at least 2.25 or standardized test scores. Any student willing to uphold the University's vision and mission and open to the possibility of spiritual as well as intellectual development is encouraged to apply. **Homeschooled:** Transcript of courses and grades required.

High school preparation. College-preparatory program recommended. Recommended units include English 4, mathematics 4, social studies 2, science 3 (laboratory 1) and foreign language 1.

2008-2009 Annual costs. Tuition/fees: $16,030. Room/board: $8,064. Books/supplies: $1,680.

2008-2009 Financial aid. **Need-based:** 15% of total undergraduate aid awarded as scholarships/grants, 85% as loans/jobs. **Non-need-based:** Scholarships awarded for academics, alumni affiliation, athletics, leadership, religious affiliation, ROTC.

Application procedures. **Admission:** Closing date 8/22 (receipt date). $175 fee, may be waived for applicants with need. Admission notification on a rolling basis. **Financial aid:** No deadline. FAFSA required. Applicants notified on a rolling basis.

Academics. **Special study options:** Accelerated study, combined bachelor's/graduate degree, distance learning, double major, dual enrollment of high school students, exchange student, honors, independent study, internships, liberal arts/career combination, study abroad, teacher certification program. **Credit/placement by examination:** AP, CLEP, IB, institutional tests. 30 credit hours maximum toward bachelor's degree. **Support services:** Learning center, reduced course load, remedial instruction, tutoring, writing center.

Majors. **Biology:** General, biochemistry. **Business:** Accounting, business admin, entrepreneurial studies, marketing. **Communications:** General, public relations. **Education:** General, biology, chemistry, elementary, English, mathematics, physical, secondary, special. **Health:** Athletic training, nursing (RN). **History:** General. **Parks/recreation:** General, sports admin. **Philosophy/religion:** Religion. **Protective services:** Criminal justice, firefighting. **Psychology:** General. **Social sciences:** Sociology. **Theology:** Bible. **Other:** Medical imaging.

Most popular majors. Business/marketing 21%, education 8%, health sciences 53%.

Computing on campus. 65 workstations in library, computer center. Dormitories wired for high-speed internet access and linked to campus network. Commuter students can connect to campus network. Online course registration, online library, helpline, wireless network available.

Student life. **Freshman orientation:** Mandatory. Preregistration for classes offered. Held the week before classes. **Policies:** No alcohol and/or candles are allowed. Smoking allowed outdoors only. **Housing:** Guaranteed on-campus for all undergraduates. Coed dorms, special housing for disabled, apartments available. **Activities:** Concert band, campus ministries, choral groups, international student organizations, literary magazine, music ensembles, student government, student newspaper, international student organizations, honors organizations, professional clubs, Christ-purposed relationships, ethnic diversity in Christ, wildlife society, student health advocates.

Athletics. NCAA. **Intercollegiate:** Baseball M, basketball, bowling W, cheerleading M, cross-country, golf, lacrosse M, soccer, softball W, swimming, tennis, volleyball, water polo W, wrestling M. **Intramural:** Basketball, bowling, football (non-tackle), softball, volleyball. **Team name:** Lopes.

Student services. Alcohol/substance abuse counseling, chaplain/spiritual director, career counseling, student employment services, financial aid counseling, health services, personal counseling, placement for graduates, veterans' counselor, women's services. **Physically disabled:** Services for visually, speech, hearing impaired.

Contact. E-mail: admissionsonline@gcu.edu
Phone: (888) 261-2393 Toll-free number: (888) 261-2393
Fax: (602) 589-2017
Karilyn VanOosten, Director of Admissions, Grand Canyon University, 3300 West Camelback Road, Phoenix, AZ 85017

International Baptist College
Tempe, Arizona
www.ibconline.edu

- Private 4-year Bible and seminary college
- Very large city
- 72 degree-seeking undergraduates: 12% part-time, 57% women
- 30 graduate students

General. Regionally accredited. **Degrees:** 12 bachelor's, 1 associate awarded; master's, doctoral offered. **Calendar:** Semester. **Full-time faculty:** 7 total. **Part-time faculty:** 5 total.

Basis for selection. Open admission, but selective for some programs.

2008-2009 Annual costs. Tuition/fees: $8,220.

Application procedures. **Admission:** No deadline. **Financial aid:** Priority date 8/18; no closing date.

Academics. **Credit/placement by examination:** CLEP.

Majors. **Theology:** Missionary, pastoral counseling, religious ed, sacred music.

Most popular majors. Education 62%, theological studies 48%.

Contact. E-mail: torrey.jaspers@ibconline.edu
Phone: (480) 838-7070 ext. 235 Toll-free number: (800) 422-4858 ext. 235
Torrey Jaspers, Enrollment Director, International Baptist College, 2150 East Southern Avenue, Tempe, AZ 85282

International Import-Export Institute
Phoenix, Arizona
www.iiei.edu

- For-profit 4-year virtual career college
- Commuter campus in very large city
- 50 degree-seeking undergraduates

General. Accredited by DETC. **Degrees:** 6 bachelor's awarded. **Calendar:** Semester, extensive summer session. **Part-time faculty:** 60 total.

Basis for selection. Open admission.

2008-2009 Annual costs. Three-week courses: $470; Six-week courses: $845; Nine-week courses: $1,125.

Application procedures. **Admission:** No deadline. $50 fee. Admission notification on a rolling basis.

Academics. **Special study options:** Accelerated study. **Credit/placement by examination:** CLEP, IB.

Majors. **Business:** International.

Computing on campus. PC or laptop required. Online library, helpline available.

Student life. **Activities:** Student newspaper.

Contact. E-mail: iadmissions@expandglobal.com
Phone: (602) 648-5750 Toll-free number: (800) 474-8013
Fax: (62) 648-5755
International Import-Export Institute, 11225 North 28th Drive Suite B201, Phoenix, AZ 85029

ITT Technical Institute: Tempe
Tempe, Arizona

- For-profit 4-year technical college
- Commuter campus in small city

General. Accredited by ACICS. **Calendar:** Quarter.

Contact. Phone: (602) 437-7500
Director of Recruitment, 5005 South Wendler Drive, Tempe, AZ 85282

ITT Technical Institute: Tucson
Tucson, Arizona
www.itt-tech.edu **CB code: 3598**

- For-profit 4-year technical college
- Commuter campus in large city

General. Founded in 1984. Accredited by ACICS. **Calendar:** Quarter.

Contact. Phone: (520) 408-7488
Director of Recruitment, 1455 West River Road, Tucson, AZ 85704

Northcentral University
Prescott Valley, Arizona
www.ncu.edu **CB code: 3883**

- For-profit 4-year virtual university
- Commuter campus in large town
- 361 degree-seeking undergraduates

General. Regionally accredited. All courses and programs offered via distance education. **Degrees:** 34 bachelor's awarded; master's, doctoral offered. **Location:** 12 miles from Prescott, 92 miles from Phoenix. **Calendar:** Continuous, extensive summer session. **Full-time faculty:** 8 total. **Part-time faculty:** 411 total.

Basis for selection. Open admission.

2008-2009 Annual costs. Students pay $275 per semester credit. Books/supplies: $1,200.

Application procedures. Admission: No deadline. $50 fee. Application must be submitted online. Admission notification on a rolling basis. **Financial aid:** No deadline. Must reply within 4 week(s) of notification.

Academics. Programs are 100% online, with one-on-one faculty mentoring and no residency requirement. **Special study options:** Distance learning. **Credit/placement by examination:** AP, CLEP, IB. **Support services:** Reduced course load, writing center.

Majors. Business: General, accounting, business admin, e-commerce, international, management science, marketing. **Computer sciences:** General. **Health:** Health care admin. **Protective services:** Law enforcement admin. **Psychology:** General. **Public administration:** General.

Most popular majors. Business/marketing 63%, psychology 37%.

Computing on campus. Commuter students can connect to campus network. Online course registration, online library, helpline available.

Student life. Freshman orientation: Available. Preregistration for classes offered.

Student services. Financial aid counseling.

Contact. E-mail: info@ncu.edu
Phone: (928) 776-0331 Toll-free number: (866) 776-0331
Fax: (928) 541-7817
Brent Passey, Executive Director of Enrollment, Northcentral University, 10000 East University, Prescott Valley, AZ 86314

Northern Arizona University
Flagstaff, Arizona **CB member**
www.nau.edu **CB code: 4006**

- Public 4-year university
- Residential campus in small city
- 16,887 degree-seeking undergraduates: 16% part-time, 60% women, 3% African American, 3% Asian American, 13% Hispanic American, 6% Native American, 2% international
- 5,362 degree-seeking graduate students
- 74% of applicants admitted

General. Founded in 1899. Regionally accredited. **Degrees:** 2,918 bachelor's awarded; master's, doctoral offered. **ROTC:** Army, Air Force. **Location:** 140 miles from Phoenix. **Calendar:** Semester, extensive summer session. **Full-time faculty:** 774 total; 76% have terminal degrees, 13% minority, 45% women. **Part-time faculty:** 726 total; 37% have terminal degrees, 13% minority, 61% women. **Class size:** 38% < 20, 44% 20-39, 8% 40-49, 8% 50-99, 2% >100. **Special facilities:** 400-acre forest, observatory, high altitude (7,000 feet) training center for athletes.

Freshman class profile. 20,109 applied, 14,847 admitted, 3,588 enrolled.

Mid 50% test scores		**GPA 3.0-3.49:**	36%
SAT critical reading:	490-590	**GPA 2.0-2.99:**	19%
SAT math:	500-600	**Return as sophomores:**	69%
SAT writing:	480-570	**Out-of-state:**	30%
ACT composite:	20-25	**Live on campus:**	89%
GPA 3.75 or higher:	27%	**International:**	2%
GPA 3.50-3.74:	18%		

Basis for selection. 3.0 GPA, class rank in top quarter, 22 ACT (24 out-of-state) or 1040 SAT (1110 out-of-state) required for unconditional admission. Conditional admission with 2.5-2.99 GPA, class rank in upper half, and test scores below requirements for unconditional admission. Audition required of music, music education majors. **Homeschooled:** Transcript of courses and grades, state high school equivalency certificate required.

High school preparation. Required units include English 4, mathematics 4, social studies 2, history 1, science 3 (laboratory 1) and foreign language 2. Math must include 2 algebra, 1 geometry and 1 year of math after algebra II. One social science must be US history. 1 fine arts required.

2008-2009 Annual costs. Tuition/fees: $5,446; $16,544 out-of-state. Room/board: $7,086. Books/supplies: $830. Personal expenses: $2,148.

2007-2008 Financial aid. Need-based: 2,217 full-time freshmen applied for aid; 1,339 were judged to have need; 1,296 of these received aid. Average need met was 72%. Average scholarship/grant was $5,537; average loan $3,144. 46% of total undergraduate aid awarded as scholarships/grants, 54% as loans/jobs. **Non-need-based:** Awarded to 4,751 full-time undergraduates, including 1,476 freshmen. Scholarships awarded for academics, alumni affiliation, art, athletics, leadership, minority status, music/drama, ROTC, state residency.

Application procedures. Admission: Priority date 3/1; no deadline. $25 fee. Admission notification on a rolling basis. Applicants encouraged to apply early. **Financial aid:** Priority date 2/14; no closing date. FAFSA required. Applicants notified on a rolling basis starting 3/15.

Academics. Special study options: Accelerated study, cooperative education, distance learning, double major, dual enrollment of high school students, ESL, exchange student, honors, independent study, internships, study abroad, teacher certification program. **Credit/placement by examination:** AP, CLEP, IB, SAT, ACT, institutional tests. 30 credit hours maximum toward bachelor's degree. **Support services:** Learning center, pre-admission summer program, reduced course load, remedial instruction, study skills assistance, tutoring, writing center.

Honors college/program. Applicants must complete separate application and have 29 ACT, 1290 SAT (exclusive of Writing), or graduate in top 5% of high school class. Students who do not meet criteria can petition for admission to honors program by submitting completed application and unofficial high school transcript, letter of recommendation, and essay.

Majors. Area/ethnic studies: American, Native American, women's. **Biology:** General, animal behavior, aquatic, bacteriology, botany, cell/histology, cellular/molecular, ecology, microbiology, molecular, physiology, wildlife, zoology. **Business:** Accounting, business admin, construction management, fashion, finance, hospitality admin, hotel/motel admin, management information systems, managerial economics, marketing. **Communications:** General, advertising, broadcast journalism, digital media, journalism, public relations, radio/tv. **Computer sciences:** General, computer science. **Conservation:** Environmental science, environmental studies, forest sciences, forestry, wildlife. **Education:** General, art, biology, chemistry, drama/dance, elementary, English, French, German, health, history, mathematics, music, physical, physics, Spanish, special, speech, technology/industrial arts, trade/industrial, voc/tech. **Engineering:** General, civil, computer, electrical, environmental, mechanical, physics. **Engineering technology:** Computer systems, construction. **Foreign languages:** General, French, German, Spanish. **Health:** Athletic training, dental hygiene, health care admin, nursing

(RN), premedicine, preveterinary. **History:** General. **Interdisciplinary:** Behavioral sciences, biological/physical sciences. **Legal studies:** Prelaw. **Liberal arts:** Arts/sciences, humanities. **Math:** General, probability. **Parks/recreation:** General, exercise sciences, facilities management, health/fitness. **Philosophy/religion:** Philosophy, religion. **Physical sciences:** General, astronomy, astrophysics, chemistry, geochemistry, geology, hydrology, paleontology, physics, planetary, theoretical physics. **Protective services:** Criminal justice, law enforcement admin. **Psychology:** General. **Public administration:** Policy analysis, social work. **Social sciences:** General, anthropology, cartography, economics, geography, international relations, political science, sociology, U.S. government. **Visual/performing arts:** General, art, art history/conservation, arts management, ceramics, design, dramatic, interior design, metal/jewelry, music history, music performance, painting, photography, printmaking, sculpture, studio arts, voice/opera.

Most popular majors. Business/marketing 18%, education 20%, health sciences 7%, liberal arts 9%, social sciences 9%, visual/performing arts 6%.

Computing on campus. Dormitories wired for high-speed internet access and linked to campus network. Commuter students can connect to campus network. Online course registration, online library, helpline, repair service, student web hosting, wireless network available.

Student life. **Freshman orientation:** Available, $150 fee. Preregistration for classes offered. **Policies:** Organizations required to register annually, have 12 or more members with 2.0 GPA to start club, have constitution and bylaws, be approved by ASNAU Senate and Office of Student Life, and officers must have 2.25 GPA. **Housing:** Guaranteed on-campus for all undergraduates. Coed dorms, single-sex dorms, special housing for disabled, apartments, fraternity/sorority housing available. $150 partly refundable deposit, deadline 5/1. Honor halls, floors for students 21 years of age and older available. **Activities:** Bands, campus ministries, choral groups, dance, drama, international student organizations, music ensembles, Model UN, radio station, student government, student newspaper, symphony orchestra, TV station, Campus Crusade for Christ, Baptist Student Ministry, Holy Trinity Catholic Newman Center, Hillel at NAU, Episcopal Canterbury Fellowship, Hispanic honor society, African students organization, Asian Americans United, Japanese association.

Athletics. NCAA. **Intercollegiate:** Basketball, cross-country, diving W, football (tackle) M, golf W, soccer W, swimming W, tennis, track and field, volleyball W. **Intramural:** Archery, badminton, baseball M, basketball, bowling, cross-country, football (non-tackle), ice hockey M, lacrosse, racquetball, rugby, skiing, soccer, softball, swimming, table tennis, tennis, track and field, volleyball, water polo M. **Team name:** Lumberjacks.

Student services. Alcohol/substance abuse counseling, chaplain/spiritual director, career counseling, student employment services, financial aid counseling, health services, minority student services, personal counseling, placement for graduates, veterans' counselor. **Physically disabled:** Services for visually, speech, hearing impaired.

Contact. E-mail: undergraduate.admissions@nau.edu
Phone: (928) 523-5511 Toll-free number: (888) 628-2968
Fax: (928) 523-0226
Paul Orscheln, Director of Admissions, Northern Arizona University, PO Box 4084, Flagstaff, AZ 86011-4084

Prescott College

Prescott, Arizona — **CB member**
www.prescott.edu — **CB code: 0484**

- Private 4-year liberal arts college
- Commuter campus in large town
- 717 degree-seeking undergraduates: 11% part-time, 60% women, 2% African American, 1% Asian American, 7% Hispanic American, 1% Native American, 1% international
- 302 degree-seeking graduate students
- 77% of applicants admitted
- SAT or ACT (ACT writing optional), application essay required
- 40% graduate within 6 years

General. Founded in 1966. Regionally accredited. **Degrees:** 228 bachelor's awarded; master's, doctoral offered. **Location:** 100 miles from Phoenix. **Calendar:** Semester, limited summer session. **Full-time faculty:** 62 total; 50% have terminal degrees, 6% minority, 50% women. **Part-time faculty:** 23 total; 44% have terminal degrees, 9% minority, 56% women. **Class size:** 97% < 20, 3% 20-39. **Special facilities:** Facility for marine studies at Kino Bay, Mexico.

Freshman class profile. 365 applied, 280 admitted, 89 enrolled.

Mid 50% test scores		**GPA 2.0-2.99:**	42%
SAT critical reading:	460-660	**Rank in top quarter:**	32%
SAT math:	430-600	**Rank in top tenth:**	11%
SAT writing:	470-610	**End year in good standing:**	81%
ACT composite:	18-27	**Return as sophomores:**	75%
GPA 3.75 or higher:	15%	**Out-of-state:**	79%
GPA 3.50-3.74:	17%	**Live on campus:**	35%
GPA 3.0-3.49:	20%		

Basis for selection. Essay and GPA most important. Letters of recommendation, any personal additions important. College visit, interview recommended. **Homeschooled:** Documentation consistent with requirements in state of residence.

High school preparation. 16 units recommended. Recommended units include English 4, mathematics 3, social studies 1, history 2, science 2 and foreign language 3. One arts unit recommended.

2008-2009 Annual costs. Tuition/fees: $21,792. Room only: $3,400. Books/supplies: $624. Personal expenses: $1,248.

2008-2009 Financial aid. **Need-based:** Average need met was 53%. Average scholarship/grant was $10,256; average loan $3,422. 35% of total undergraduate aid awarded as scholarships/grants, 65% as loans/jobs. **Non-need-based:** Scholarships awarded for academics, alumni affiliation, minority status, state residency.

Application procedures. **Admission:** Priority date 3/1; deadline 8/15 (postmark date). $25 fee, may be waived for applicants with need. Admission notification on a rolling basis beginning on or about 1/1. Must reply by May 1 or within 4 week(s) if notified thereafter. **Financial aid:** Priority date 4/1; no closing date. FAFSA required. Applicants notified on a rolling basis starting 3/15; must reply within 12 week(s) of notification.

Academics. **Special study options:** Cross-registration, distance learning, double major, exchange student, external degree, independent study, internships, liberal arts/career combination, student-designed major, teacher certification program. Adult degree program designed for working adults to obtain degree on year-round, part-time basis. Master of arts self-study program available. Programs also available at center in Tucson. **Credit/placement by examination:** AP, CLEP, IB, institutional tests. 30 credit hours maximum toward bachelor's degree. **Support services:** Learning center, reduced course load, tutoring.

Majors. **Agriculture:** General, agronomy, food science, plant breeding, soil science. **Architecture:** Environmental design. **Area/ethnic studies:** Latin American, regional, women's. **Biology:** General, botany, conservation, ecology, marine. **Business:** General, accounting, business admin, human resources, nonprofit/public, office management. **Communications:** General, journalism, media studies, photojournalism, radio/tv. **Computer sciences:** General, information systems. **Conservation:** General, environmental science, environmental studies, management/policy, wildlife. **Education:** General, adult/continuing, art, bilingual, biology, curriculum, drama/dance, early childhood, early childhood special, elementary, emotionally handicapped, English, foreign languages, history, learning disabled, mathematics, mentally handicapped, multi-level teacher, music, physical, school counseling, science, secondary, social science, social studies, Spanish, special, technology/industrial arts, voc/tech. **Family/consumer sciences:** Child development. **Foreign languages:** Comparative lit, Spanish. **Health:** Art therapy, communication disorders, community health services, dance therapy, health care admin, health services, public health ed, recreational therapy. **History:** General. **Interdisciplinary:** Behavioral sciences, biological/physical sciences, natural sciences, peace/conflict. **Liberal arts:** Arts/sciences, humanities. **Math:** General. **Parks/recreation:** General, facilities management. **Philosophy/religion:** Religion. **Physical sciences:** Geology, planetary. **Psychology:** General, cognitive, community, counseling, developmental, environmental, geropsychology, industrial, medical, social. **Public administration:** Community org/advocacy, human services, policy analysis, social work. **Social sciences:** General, anthropology, geography, international economic development, international relations, political science, sociology. **Visual/performing arts:** General, ceramics, cinematography, crafts, dance, dramatic, film/cinema, interior design, painting, photography, play/screenwriting, sculpture, studio arts. **Other:** Alpine geomorphology, Cultural studies, Ethnobotany, Food studies, Gender across cultures, Human and organizational development, Human science, Integrated studies of culture, healing, and environment, Management in early childhood education, Natural history, Rehabilitation/therapeutic professions, Somatic psychology, Sound arts.

Most popular majors. Biology 8%, education 34%, natural resources/environmental science 9%, psychology 19%, visual/performing arts 6%.

Computing on campus. 50 workstations in dormitories, library, computer center, student center. Dormitories wired for high-speed internet access and linked to campus network. Online library, helpline, wireless network available.

Student life. **Freshman orientation:** Mandatory, $900 fee. Wilderness backpacking orientation offered. Water-based wilderness orientations and community-based orientations offered to those who cannot participate in backpacking session. **Housing:** Coed dorms available. $150 fully refundable deposit, deadline 4/15. **Activities:** Dance, drama, film society, international student organizations, literary magazine, radio station, student government, student newspaper, student environmental network, student chapter of Amnesty International, gender and sexuality alliance, peace and justice center, Aztlan center, service learning program, Maasai community project, student arts council, African-inspired dance gatherings.

Student services. Adult student services, career counseling, financial aid counseling, personal counseling, placement for graduates. **Physically disabled:** Services for visually, speech, hearing impaired.

Contact. E-mail: admissions@prescott.edu
Phone: (928) 350-2100 Toll-free number: (877) 350-2100
Fax: (928) 776-5242
Tim Robison, Dean of Enrollment Management, Prescott College, 220 Grove Avenue, Prescott, AZ 86301

Southwestern College

Phoenix, Arizona
www.swcaz.edu **CB code: 4736**

- Private 4-year Bible and liberal arts college affiliated with Baptist faith
- Residential campus in very large city
- 365 degree-seeking undergraduates
- SAT or ACT (ACT writing optional), application essay required

General. Founded in 1960. Regionally accredited. **Degrees:** 55 bachelor's awarded. **ROTC:** Naval, Air Force. **Calendar:** Semester, limited summer session. **Full-time faculty:** 10 total. **Part-time faculty:** 37 total.

Basis for selection. School achievement record and recommendations very important. Written testimony of conversion experience required for admission. **Homeschooled:** Transcript of courses and grades required. Must present ACT or SAT scores for admission.

High school preparation. Recommended units include English 4, mathematics 3, social studies 3, science 2 and foreign language 2.

2008-2009 Annual costs. Tuition/fees: $14,364. Room/board: $5,046. Books/supplies: $800. Personal expenses: $1,300.

Financial aid. **Non-need-based:** Scholarships awarded for academics, alumni affiliation, athletics, leadership, minority status, music/drama, religious affiliation.

Application procedures. **Admission:** Priority date 4/30; deadline 8/15. $30 fee, may be waived for applicants with need. Admission notification on a rolling basis. **Financial aid:** Priority date 3/15, closing date 8/31. FAFSA, institutional form required. Applicants notified on a rolling basis.

Academics. Off-campus, noncredit Christian internship work required during each semester. **Special study options:** Internships, teacher certification program. **Credit/placement by examination:** AP, CLEP, SAT, ACT. 30 credit hours maximum toward bachelor's degree. **Support services:** Reduced course load, remedial instruction, tutoring.

Majors. **Education:** Elementary, music, secondary. **Philosophy/religion:** Religion. **Psychology:** Family. **Theology:** Bible, missionary, religious ed, sacred music, theology. **Other:** Behavioral health.

Computing on campus. 60 workstations in dormitories, library, computer center. Dormitories wired for high-speed internet access. Online library available.

Student life. **Freshman orientation:** Mandatory. Preregistration for classes offered. **Policies:** Religious observance required. **Housing:** Guaranteed on-campus for all undergraduates. Single-sex dorms, apartments available. $100 nonrefundable deposit, deadline 4/30. **Activities:** Jazz band, choral groups, drama, music ensembles, musical theater, student government, student newspaper, symphony orchestra.

Athletics. NAIA, NCCAA. **Intercollegiate:** Basketball, cross-country, golf, soccer, volleyball W. **Intramural:** Football (tackle) M, table tennis, tennis, volleyball. **Team name:** Eagles.

Student services. Student employment services, financial aid counseling, health services, personal counseling, veterans' counselor.

Contact. E-mail: admissions@swcaz.edu
Phone: (602) 386-5300 ext. 100 Toll-free number: (800) 247-2697
Fax: (602) 404-2159
Heather Kim, Chief Enrollment Officer, Southwestern College, 2625 East Cactus Road, Phoenix, AZ 85032-7042

University of Advancing Technology

Tempe, Arizona
www.uat.edu **CB code: 3608**

- For-profit 4-year university
- Residential campus in very large city
- 1,152 degree-seeking undergraduates: 9% women, 5% African American, 4% Asian American, 6% Hispanic American, 1% Native American
- 65 degree-seeking graduate students
- 45% graduate within 6 years

General. Founded in 1983. Accredited by ACICS. Bachelor's degree can be earned in 2 2/3 years. **Degrees:** 158 bachelor's, 14 associate awarded; master's offered. **Location:** 7 miles from Phoenix. **Calendar:** Semester, extensive summer session. **Full-time faculty:** 28 total. **Part-time faculty:** 26 total. **Class size:** 68% < 20, 27% 20-39, 2% 40-49, 3% 50-99. **Special facilities:** Technology lab, motion capture studio, robotics lab, digital video studio.

Freshman class profile.

Return as sophomores:	54%	**Out-of-state:**	80%

Basis for selection. Academic achievements, leadership experience, career aspirations, hobbies and community and extra-curricular involvement considered. Acceptance based on previous education, test scores (ACT/SAT), the student's match with university culture and a passion for technology. SAT or ACT recommended. Test scores considered during admissions process, but not required unless GPA is not satisfactory. **Homeschooled:** Transcript of courses and grades, state high school equivalency certificate required.

2009-2010 Annual costs. Tuition/fees (projected): $17,900. Room/board: $10,548. Books/supplies: $1,000. Personal expenses: $2,900.

2007-2008 Financial aid. **Need-based:** 31% of total undergraduate aid awarded as scholarships/grants, 69% as loans/jobs.

Application procedures. **Admission:** No deadline. No application fee. Admission notification on a rolling basis. **Financial aid:** Priority date 4/15; no closing date. FAFSA required. Applicants notified on a rolling basis; must reply within 2 week(s) of notification.

Academics. **Special study options:** Accelerated study, distance learning, double major, independent study, internships, student-designed major. **Credit/placement by examination:** AP, CLEP, IB, institutional tests. **Support services:** Learning center, tutoring.

Majors. **Communications technology:** Animation/special effects. **Computer sciences:** A.i./robotics, computer forensics, LAN/WAN management, networking, security, web page design, webmaster. **Engineering:** Software. **Engineering technology:** Robotics. **Other:** Technology management.

Computing on campus. 400 workstations in dormitories, library, computer center, student center. Dormitories wired for high-speed internet access and linked to campus network. Commuter students can connect to campus network. Online course registration, online library, helpline, student web hosting, wireless network available.

Student life. **Freshman orientation:** Mandatory. Preregistration for classes offered. **Housing:** Guaranteed on-campus for freshmen. Coed dorms, apartments available. $550 partly refundable deposit. **Activities:** Dance, film society, student government, student newspaper, Bible study club.

Athletics. **Intercollegiate:** Fencing.

Student services. Career counseling, student employment services, financial aid counseling, personal counseling, placement for graduates.

Contact. E-mail: admissions@uat.edu
Phone: (602) 383-8228 Toll-free number: (800) 658-5744
Fax: (602) 383-8222
Chrys Pistillo, Dean of Student Affairs and Admissions, University of Advancing Technology, 2625 West Baseline Road, Tempe, AZ 85283-1056

Four-Year Colleges

University of Arizona
Tucson, Arizona — **CB member**
www.arizona.edu — **CB code: 4832**

- Public 4-year university
- Residential campus in very large city
- 29,340 degree-seeking undergraduates: 12% part-time, 52% women, 3% African American, 7% Asian American, 17% Hispanic American, 2% Native American, 3% international
- 7,549 degree-seeking graduate students
- 81% of applicants admitted
- Application essay required
- 57% graduate within 6 years

General. Founded in 1885. Regionally accredited. Sierra Vista campus offers credit-bearing classes in general studies and education. **Degrees:** 5,612 bachelor's awarded; master's, doctoral, first professional offered. **ROTC:** Army, Naval, Air Force. **Location:** 111 miles from Phoenix. **Calendar:** Semester, extensive summer session. **Full-time faculty:** 1,593 total; 92% have terminal degrees, 16% minority, 36% women. **Part-time faculty:** 470 total; 60% have terminal degrees, 11% minority, 46% women. **Class size:** 42% < 20, 43% 20-39, 4% 40-49, 6% 50-99, 5% >100. **Special facilities:** Geological museum, state anthropological museum, planetarium, observatory, center for creative photography.

Freshman class profile. 22,544 applied, 18,158 admitted, 6,709 enrolled.

Mid 50% test scores			
SAT critical reading:	480-600	GPA 2.0-2.99:	29%
SAT math:	500-620	Rank in top quarter:	61%
ACT composite:	21-26	Rank in top tenth:	32%
GPA 3.75 or higher:	19%	Return as sophomores:	79%
GPA 3.50-3.74:	16%	Out-of-state:	38%
GPA 3.0-3.49:	35%	Live on campus:	80%
		International:	2%

Basis for selection. Applicants must be in top 25% of class or have 3.0 GPA, 1110 SAT (1040 in-state) or 24 ACT (22 in-state). Conditional admission may be offered to in-state applicants who meet 1 or more of following: top half of class or 2.5 GPA and no more than 1 deficiency in any 2 required subjects, (deficiency not allowed in both math and science). SAT scores exclusive of Writing. SAT or ACT recommended. Auditions required of applied music and all performance majors. Portfolios required for studio art majors. **Homeschooled:** Course work completion information required. **Learning Disabled:** Separate application for fee-based program (SALT).

High school preparation. 16 units required. Required and recommended units include English 4, mathematics 3, social studies 1-2, history 1, science 3 (laboratory 3), foreign language 2 and academic electives 1. One unit fine arts required.

2008-2009 Annual costs. Tuition/fees: $5,531; $18,665 out-of-state. Room/board: $8,058. Books/supplies: $1,000. Personal expenses: $2,368.

2007-2008 Financial aid. Need-based: 3,798 full-time freshmen applied for aid; 2,374 were judged to have need; 2,255 of these received aid. Average need met was 66%. Average scholarship/grant was $6,706; average loan $3,515. 54% of total undergraduate aid awarded as scholarships/grants, 46% as loans/jobs. **Non-need-based:** Awarded to 6,856 full-time undergraduates, including 2,539 freshmen. Scholarships awarded for academics, art. **Additional information:** Arizona Assurance Program: provides housing, books, and tuition for all new, incoming resident freshmen; must be Pell-eligible with combined family income less than $42,500; funding provided as grants, scholarships, and federal work-study.

Application procedures. Admission: Closing date 5/1 (postmark date). $25 fee ($65 out-of-state), may be waived for applicants with need. Admission notification on a rolling basis beginning on or about 11/1. Must reply by May 1 or within 4 week(s) if notified thereafter. **Financial aid:** Priority date 3/1; no closing date. FAFSA required. Applicants notified on a rolling basis starting 4/1; must reply within 3 week(s) of notification.

Academics. Special study options: Accelerated study, combined bachelor's/graduate degree, cooperative education, cross-registration, distance learning, double major, dual enrollment of high school students, ESL, exchange student, external degree, honors, independent study, internships, liberal arts/career combination, semester at sea, study abroad, teacher certification program, weekend college. **Credit/placement by examination:** AP, CLEP, IB, SAT, ACT, institutional tests. 60 credit hours maximum toward bachelor's degree. **Support services:** Learning center, pre-admission summer program, reduced course load, study skills assistance, tutoring, writing center.

Majors. Agriculture: General, agronomy, animal sciences, economics, plant sciences, soil science. **Architecture:** Architecture, urban/community planning. **Area/ethnic studies:** East Asian, Hispanic-American/Latino/Chicano, Latin American, Near/Middle Eastern, women's. **Biology:** General, animal physiology, bacteriology, biochemistry, cell/histology, ecology. **Business:** General, accounting, entrepreneurial studies, finance, human resources, management information systems, managerial economics, marketing, operations. **Communications:** General, journalism, radio/tv. **Computer sciences:** General. **Conservation:** General, environmental studies. **Education:** Art, biology, chemistry, drama/dance, elementary, English, family/consumer sciences, foreign languages, French, German, history, kindergarten/preschool, mathematics, music, physical, physics, science, secondary, social science, social studies, Spanish, special, speech. **Engineering:** General, aerospace, agricultural, chemical, civil, computer, electrical, geological, industrial, materials science, mechanical, mining, physics, systems, water resource. **Engineering technology:** Industrial management. **Family/consumer sciences:** Consumer economics, family studies. **Foreign languages:** Classics, French, German, Italian, linguistics, Russian, Spanish. **Health:** Clinical lab science, communication disorders, health care admin, nursing (RN), preveterinary, speech pathology. **History:** General. **Interdisciplinary:** Nutrition sciences. **Math:** General. **Philosophy/religion:** Judaic, philosophy, religion. **Physical sciences:** Astronomy, chemistry, geology, hydrology, optics, physics. **Protective services:** Law enforcement admin. **Psychology:** General. **Public administration:** General. **Social sciences:** Anthropology, applied economics, economics, geography, political science, sociology. **Visual/performing arts:** General, art history/conservation, dance, dramatic, music performance, studio arts, theater design. **Other:** Applied science, Engineering mathematics.

Most popular majors. Biology 9%, business/marketing 14%, communications/journalism 8%, education 7%, engineering/engineering technologies 7%, psychology 8%, social sciences 10%.

Computing on campus. 2,000 workstations in dormitories, library, computer center, student center. Dormitories wired for high-speed internet access and linked to campus network. Commuter students can connect to campus network. Online course registration, online library, helpline, repair service, student web hosting, wireless network available.

Student life. Freshman orientation: Mandatory, $100 fee. Preregistration for classes offered. Two-day program. **Housing:** Coed dorms, single-sex dorms, special housing for disabled, apartments, fraternity/sorority housing available. $300 partly refundable deposit, deadline 5/1. Special housing for honors students available. **Activities:** Bands, campus ministries, choral groups, dance, drama, international student organizations, literary magazine, music ensembles, Model UN, musical theater, opera, radio station, student government, student newspaper, symphony orchestra, TV station, over 350 clubs and organizations available.

Athletics. NCAA. **Intercollegiate:** Baseball M, basketball, cross-country, diving, football (tackle) M, golf, gymnastics W, lacrosse M, soccer W, softball W, swimming, tennis, track and field, volleyball W. **Intramural:** Badminton, basketball, bowling, cross-country, diving, football (non-tackle), golf, racquetball, soccer, softball, swimming, table tennis, tennis, track and field, volleyball. **Team name:** Wildcats.

Student services. Adult student services, alcohol/substance abuse counseling, chaplain/spiritual director, career counseling, services for economically disadvantaged, student employment services, financial aid counseling, health services, legal services, minority student services, personal counseling, placement for graduates, veterans' counselor, women's services. **Physically disabled:** Services for visually, speech, hearing impaired. **Learning disabled:** Comprehensive services available.

Contact. E-mail: appinfo@arizona.edu
Phone: (520) 621-3237 Fax: (520) 621-9799
Paul Kohn, Dean of Admissions, University of Arizona, Robert L. Nugent Building, Tucson, AZ 85721-0040

University of Phoenix
Phoenix, Arizona — **CB member**
www.phoenix.edu — **CB code: 1024**

- For-profit 4-year virtual university
- Commuter campus in very large city
- 174,818 degree-seeking undergraduates: 68% women
- 75,811 graduate students

General. Founded in 1976. Regionally accredited. Classes are offered in classroom environment and on-line in 39 states, Puerto Rico, Washington DC, Vancouver, British Columbia, Mexico and Europe. **Degrees:** 28,364 bachelor's, 13,846 associate awarded; master's, doctoral offered. **Calendar:** Continuous, extensive summer session. **Full-time faculty:** 1,410 total; 32%

have terminal degrees, 20% minority, 46% women. **Part-time faculty:** 22,965 total; 20% have terminal degrees, 64% minority, 49% women.

Basis for selection. Open admission, but selective for some programs.

2008-2009 Annual costs. Tuition/fees: $10,849. Books/supplies: $750.

Application procedures. **Admission:** No deadline. No application fee. Admission notification on a rolling basis. **Financial aid:** No deadline. FAFSA, institutional form required. Applicants notified on a rolling basis.

Academics. Online library. **Special study options:** Accelerated study, distance learning, independent study, internships, teacher certification program. **Credit/placement by examination:** AP, CLEP, IB. 30 credit hours maximum toward associate degree, 30 toward bachelor's. **Support services:** Remedial instruction, writing center.

Majors. **Business:** Accounting, business admin, communications, finance, hospitality admin, international, management information systems, management science, marketing, retailing. **Computer sciences:** General, database management, networking, programming, webmaster. **Education:** Elementary. **Health:** Facilities admin, health care admin, health services, medical records technology. **Protective services:** Security management. **Public administration:** General.

Most popular majors. Business/marketing 47%, computer/information sciences 10%, health sciences 11%, interdisciplinary studies 22%.

Computing on campus. Commuter students can connect to campus network. Online library, helpline available.

Student life. **Freshman orientation:** Available. **Activities:** International student organizations.

Student services. Adult student services, financial aid counseling, personal counseling.

Contact. E-mail: Kim.breitbach@phoenix.edu
Phone: (866) 766-0766 Toll-free number: (866) 766-0766
Kim Breitbach, Director of Operations and Evaluation Services, University of Phoenix, 4035 South Riverpoint Parkway, Phoenix, AZ 85040-0723

Western International University
Phoenix, Arizona
www.wintu.edu **CB code: 1316**

- For-profit 4-year university and business college
- Commuter campus in very large city
- 1,980 degree-seeking undergraduates: 65% women, 10% African American, 2% Asian American, 13% Hispanic American, 3% Native American, 1% international
- 638 degree-seeking graduate students

General. Founded in 1978. Regionally accredited. Adult student body. Portfolio evaluation of relevant experience for course credit. **Degrees:** 399 bachelor's, 26 associate awarded; master's offered. **Calendar:** Semester, extensive summer session. **Part-time faculty:** 290 total; 36% women.

Basis for selection. Open admission. Interview and essay recommended.

High school preparation. Recommended units include English 4, mathematics 3, social studies 2 and science 2.

2008-2009 Annual costs. Tuition/fees: $10,950. Books/supplies: $1,000.

2007-2008 Financial aid. All financial aid based on need.

Application procedures. **Admission:** No deadline. $85 fee. Admission notification on a rolling basis. **Financial aid:** No deadline. FAFSA, institutional form required. Applicants notified on a rolling basis.

Academics. **Special study options:** Accelerated study, distance learning, double major, dual enrollment of high school students, honors, independent study, study abroad. **Credit/placement by examination:** AP, CLEP, IB, institutional tests. 24 credit hours maximum toward associate degree, 60 toward bachelor's. Maximum of 60 credits by examination and/or assessment may be counted toward degree; 36 hour residency requirement. **Support services:** Learning center, tutoring, writing center.

Majors. **Business:** General, accounting, business admin, finance, international, management information systems, marketing. **Computer sciences:** General. **Liberal arts:** Arts/sciences.

Most popular majors. Business/marketing 79%, computer/information sciences 9%, liberal arts 13%.

Computing on campus. PC or laptop required. 195 workstations in library, computer center. Commuter students can connect to campus network. Online course registration, online library, helpline, wireless network available.

Student life. **Freshman orientation:** Mandatory. Preregistration for classes offered. **Policies:** Cultural activities and special seminars/workshops available. **Activities:** International student organizations, student government, Delta Mu Delta, Upsilon Pi Epsilon, Golden Key Honor Societies.

Student services. Adult student services, career counseling, financial aid counseling, veterans' counselor.

Contact. Phone: (602) 943-2311 Toll-free number: (866) 948-4636
Fax: (602) 371-8637
Jo Arney, Director of University Student Services, Western International University, 9215 North Black Canyon Highway, Phoenix, AZ 85021

Four-Year Colleges

Arkansas

Arkansas Baptist College

Little Rock, Arkansas
www.arkansasbaptist.edu **CB code: 7301**

- Private 4-year liberal arts college affiliated with American Baptist Churches in the USA
- Residential campus in large city
- 625 degree-seeking undergraduates

General. Founded in 1884. Regionally accredited. **Degrees:** 15 bachelor's, 27 associate awarded. **Calendar:** Semester, limited summer session. **Full-time faculty:** 20 total. **Part-time faculty:** 26 total. **Special facilities:** African American leadership institute, literacy writing center.

Basis for selection. Open admission. Academically borderline applicants may be admitted provisionally but must earn 2.0 GPA by end of first semester to continue in good academic standing. **Homeschooled:** Statement describing homeschool structure and mission, interview required.

High school preparation. 18 units recommended. Recommended units include English 4, mathematics 4, social studies 1 and science 2. Vocational and agriculture courses also recommended.

2008-2009 Annual costs. Tuition/fees: $5,700. Room/board: $6,710. Books/supplies: $700. Personal expenses: $850.

Financial aid. All financial aid based on need.

Application procedures. Admission: No deadline. $25 fee. Admission notification on a rolling basis beginning on or about 6/30. **Financial aid:** Closing date 5/1. FAFSA required. Applicants notified on a rolling basis starting 6/15.

Academics. Special study options: Double major, independent study. **Credit/placement by examination:** CLEP, institutional tests. **Support services:** Remedial instruction, tutoring, writing center.

Majors. Business: Business admin. **Education:** Elementary. **Social sciences:** General.

Student life. Freshman orientation: Mandatory, $10 fee. Preregistration for classes offered. Held in August and in January each year. **Policies:** Religious observance required. **Housing:** Single-sex dorms available. **Activities:** Choral groups, student government, student newspaper, Baptist Student Union, student teacher organization.

Athletics. NJCAA. **Intercollegiate:** Basketball, cheerleading M, football (tackle) M. **Team name:** Buffaloes.

Student services. Career counseling, student employment services, health services, on-campus daycare, personal counseling, placement for graduates, veterans' counselor.

Contact. E-mail: admissions@arkansasbaptist.edu
Phone: (501) 244-5104 Toll-free number: (866) 920-4222
Vivian Doyne, Director of Enrollment Management, Arkansas Baptist College, 1621 Dr. Martin Luther King Drive, Little Rock, AR 72202

Arkansas State University

State University, Arkansas **CB member**
www.astate.edu **CB code: 6011**

- Public 4-year university
- Commuter campus in small city
- 9,200 degree-seeking undergraduates: 18% part-time, 59% women, 18% African American, 1% Asian American, 1% Hispanic American, 2% international
- 1,673 degree-seeking graduate students
- 82% of applicants admitted
- SAT or ACT (ACT writing optional) required
- 39% graduate within 6 years; 14% enter graduate study

General. Founded in 1909. Regionally accredited. **Degrees:** 1,362 bachelor's, 197 associate awarded; master's, doctoral offered. **ROTC:** Army. **Location:** 70 miles from Memphis. **Calendar:** Semester, extensive summer session. **Full-time faculty:** 461 total; 62% have terminal degrees, 16% minority, 51% women. **Part-time faculty:** 169 total; 7% have terminal degrees, 8% minority, 61% women. **Class size:** 42% < 20, 46% 20-39, 6% 40-49, 5% 50-99, less than 1% >100. **Special facilities:** Environmental ecotoxicology research facility, electron microscope facility, geographic information center facility, equine center, plantation.

Freshman class profile. 4,288 applied, 3,511 admitted, 1,902 enrolled.

Mid 50% test scores		**Rank in top quarter:**	39%
SAT critical reading:	460-520	**Rank in top tenth:**	20%
SAT math:	480-580	**End year in good standing:**	75%
SAT writing:	410-490	**Return as sophomores:**	68%
ACT composite:	18-24	**Out-of-state:**	15%
GPA 3.75 or higher:	20%	**Live on campus:**	54%
GPA 3.50-3.74:	14%	**International:**	4%
GPA 3.0-3.49:	27%	**Fraternities:**	16%
GPA 2.0-2.99:	35%	**Sororities:**	10%

Basis for selection. For unconditional admission, must have a minimum of 18 on ACT scores composite, English, math, reading or comparable scores on the SAT, ASSET, or COMPASS or a minimum 2.35 high school GPA. Proof of immunization is required. Proof of registration with selective service is required for all males 18 to 25. Students with no ACT or SAT scores may submit ASSET scores. SAT, SAT Subject Tests, ACT scores must be received by first day of classes for fall term admission. Auditions required of music majors; portfolios required of art majors. **Homeschooled:** Must have overall GPA of 2.35 or ACT score of 18. Minimum GED score for restricted admission is 500.

High school preparation. College-preparatory program recommended. 16 units recommended. Recommended units include English 4, mathematics 4, social studies 1, history 2, science 3 (laboratory 3) and foreign language 2.

2008-2009 Annual costs. Tuition/fees: $6,370; $14,290 out-of-state. Room/board: $5,406. Books/supplies: $1,000. Personal expenses: $3,130.

2008-2009 Financial aid. Need-based: 1,576 full-time freshmen applied for aid; 1,558 were judged to have need; 1,558 of these received aid. Average need met was 63%. Average scholarship/grant was $6,800; average loan $3,400. 54% of total undergraduate aid awarded as scholarships/grants, 46% as loans/jobs. **Non-need-based:** Awarded to 3,140 full-time undergraduates, including 682 freshmen. Scholarships awarded for academics, alumni affiliation, art, athletics, leadership, minority status, music/drama, ROTC, state residency.

Application procedures. Admission: Closing date 8/24 (receipt date). $15 fee. Admission notification on a rolling basis. **Financial aid:** Priority date 2/15, closing date 7/1. FAFSA, institutional form required. Applicants notified on a rolling basis starting 6/1; must reply within 2 week(s) of notification.

Academics. Of the first 59 hours completed in college, students allowed to repeat courses with final grade of less than C. No more than 18 semester hours of course work may be repeated. **Special study options:** Accelerated study, distance learning, double major, dual enrollment of high school students, ESL, exchange student, honors, independent study, internships, study abroad, teacher certification program. **Credit/placement by examination:** AP, CLEP, SAT, ACT, institutional tests. 15 credit hours maximum toward associate degree, 30 toward bachelor's. **Support services:** Reduced course load, remedial instruction, study skills assistance, tutoring.

Honors college/program. Students must have a score of 27 or higher on the ACT or a high school GPA of 3.5 or higher.

Majors. Agriculture: General, agribusiness operations, animal sciences, plant sciences. **Biology:** General. **Business:** Accounting, business admin, finance, international, managerial economics, marketing, transportation. **Communications:** Digital media, journalism, radio/tv. **Communications technology:** Graphic/printing. **Computer sciences:** General, data processing. **Conservation:** Wildlife. **Education:** Agricultural, art, biology, business, chemistry, early childhood, English, French, health, mathematics, middle, music, physical, physics, social science, Spanish, special, speech. **Engineering:** General, civil, electrical, mechanical. **Engineering technology:** General. **Foreign languages:** French, Spanish. **Health:** Athletic training, audiology/speech pathology, clinical lab science, medical radiologic technology/radiation therapy, nursing (RN). **History:** General. **Math:** General. **Parks/recreation:** Exercise sciences, health/fitness, sports admin. **Philosophy/religion:** Philosophy. **Physical sciences:** Chemistry, physics. **Protective services:** Forensics. **Psychology:** General. **Public administration:** Social work. **Social sciences:** Criminology, economics, geography, political science, sociology. **Visual/performing arts:** Art, commercial/advertising art, dramatic, music performance. **Other:** Applied science.

Most popular majors. Business/marketing 18%, education 18%, health sciences 13%, liberal arts 7%.

Computing on campus. 510 workstations in dormitories, library, computer center, student center. Dormitories linked to campus network. Commuter students can connect to campus network. Online course registration, helpline, wireless network available.

Student life. Freshman orientation: Mandatory. Preregistration for classes offered. All day session held on various dates for students to meet academic advisor, register for classes and learn about the university. **Housing:** Coed dorms, single-sex dorms, apartments, fraternity/sorority housing, wellness housing available. $100 fully refundable deposit. Honors quarters available. **Activities:** Bands, choral groups, dance, drama, international student organizations, music ensembles, Model UN, musical theater, opera, radio station, student government, student newspaper, symphony orchestra, TV station, Fellowship of Christian Athletes, Habitat for Humanity, Interfaith Christian Student Union, nontraditional adult student organization, Model UN, student leadership board, Colleges Against Cancer, international student association, Black student association, College Democrats.

Athletics. NCAA. **Intercollegiate:** Baseball M, basketball, bowling W, cross-country, football (tackle) M, golf, soccer W, tennis W, track and field, volleyball W. **Intramural:** Basketball, bowling, football (non-tackle), golf, racquetball, soccer, softball, table tennis, tennis, volleyball. **Team name:** Red Wolves.

Student services. Adult student services, career counseling, student employment services, financial aid counseling, health services, minority student services, personal counseling, placement for graduates, veterans' counselor. **Physically disabled:** Services for visually, speech, hearing impaired.

Contact. E-mail: admissions@astate.edu
Phone: (870) 972-3024 Toll-free number: (800) 382-3030
Fax: (870) 972-3406
Tammy Fowler, Director of Admissions, Arkansas State University, PO Box 1630, State University, AR 72467-1630

Arkansas Tech University

Russellville, Arkansas
www.atu.edu **CB code: 6010**

- Public 4-year university and liberal arts college
- Commuter campus in large town
- 6,581 degree-seeking undergraduates: 13% part-time, 53% women, 5% African American, 2% Asian American, 3% Hispanic American, 2% Native American, 3% international
- 512 degree-seeking graduate students
- 92% of applicants admitted
- SAT or ACT (ACT writing optional) required
- 39% graduate within 6 years

General. Founded in 1909. Regionally accredited. **Degrees:** 834 bachelor's, 100 associate awarded; master's offered. **ROTC:** Army. **Location:** 75 miles from Little Rock, 85 miles from Fort Smith. **Calendar:** Semester, extensive summer session. **Full-time faculty:** 288 total; 62% have terminal degrees, 8% minority, 47% women. **Part-time faculty:** 130 total; 8% have terminal degrees, 3% minority, 60% women. **Class size:** 39% < 20, 48% 20-39, 6% 40-49, 7% 50-99. **Special facilities:** Energy center, observatory, technology center.

Freshman class profile. 2,957 applied, 2,731 admitted, 1,543 enrolled.

Mid 50% test scores		**Rank in top quarter:**	45%
SAT critical reading:	420-480	**Rank in top tenth:**	19%
SAT math:	450-530	**Return as sophomores:**	68%
ACT composite:	19-26	**Out-of-state:**	4%
GPA 3.75 or higher:	23%	**Live on campus:**	55%
GPA 3.50-3.74:	16%	**International:**	1%
GPA 3.0-3.49:	28%	**Fraternities:**	3%
GPA 2.0-2.99:	31%	**Sororities:**	8%

Basis for selection. Secondary school record and standardized test scores are very important; class rank is considered. **Homeschooled:** Documentation of home school completion with a composite ACT of 19 or greater.

High school preparation. College-preparatory program recommended. 22 units recommended. Recommended units include English 4, mathematics 4, social studies 1, history 2, science 3 (laboratory 3), foreign language 2, visual/performing arts .5 and academic electives 4.

2008-2009 Annual costs. Tuition/fees: $5,430; $10,260 out-of-state. Room/board: $4,888. Books/supplies: $1,350. Personal expenses: $2,440.

2007-2008 Financial aid. Need-based: 1,208 full-time freshmen applied for aid; 846 were judged to have need; 814 of these received aid. Average need met was 68%. Average scholarship/grant was $4,000; average loan $2,750. 51% of total undergraduate aid awarded as scholarships/grants, 49% as loans/jobs. **Non-need-based:** Awarded to 2,172 full-time undergraduates, including 888 freshmen. Scholarships awarded for academics, athletics, leadership, music/drama, ROTC, state residency.

Application procedures. Admission: No deadline. No application fee. Admission notification on a rolling basis. **Financial aid:** Priority date 4/15; no closing date. FAFSA required. Applicants notified on a rolling basis starting 5/1; must reply within 2 week(s) of notification.

Academics. Special study options: Distance learning, double major, dual enrollment of high school students, ESL, honors, independent study, internships, study abroad, teacher certification program. **Credit/placement by examination:** AP, CLEP, IB, SAT, ACT, institutional tests. 30 credit hours maximum toward associate degree, 30 toward bachelor's. **Support services:** Learning center, reduced course load, remedial instruction, study skills assistance, tutoring.

Honors college/program. Minimum GPA of 3.5 and ACT score of 23. Target of 23 students per year. Honors students required to take honors classes throughout their stay at ATU.

Majors. Agriculture: Agribusiness operations. **Biology:** General. **Business:** Accounting, business admin, hospitality admin. **Communications:** Journalism. **Computer sciences:** General, information technology, systems analysis. **Conservation:** General. **Education:** Art, biology, business, chemistry, early childhood, elementary, English, foreign languages, mathematics, middle, music, physical, science, social studies, speech. **Engineering:** Electrical, mechanical, physics. **Foreign languages:** General. **Health:** Clinical lab science, medical records admin, nursing (RN). **History:** General. **Interdisciplinary:** Global studies. **Math:** General. **Parks/recreation:** Facilities management. **Physical sciences:** General, chemistry, geology. **Protective services:** Emergency management/homeland security. **Psychology:** General. **Social sciences:** Economics, sociology. **Visual/performing arts:** Art.

Most popular majors. Business/marketing 14%, education 21%, English 6%, health sciences 14%.

Computing on campus. 700 workstations in dormitories, library, computer center, student center. Dormitories wired for high-speed internet access and linked to campus network. Commuter students can connect to campus network. Online course registration, online library, helpline, wireless network available.

Student life. Freshman orientation: Mandatory. Preregistration for classes offered. **Housing:** Guaranteed on-campus for freshmen. Coed dorms, single-sex dorms, apartments, fraternity/sorority housing available. $25 nonrefundable deposit. **Activities:** Bands, campus ministries, choral groups, dance, drama, international student organizations, literary magazine, musical theater, radio station, student government, student newspaper, symphony orchestra, TV station.

Athletics. NCAA. **Intercollegiate:** Baseball M, basketball, cross-country W, football (tackle) M, golf, softball W, tennis W, volleyball W. **Intramural:** Basketball, bowling, cheerleading, cross-country, football (tackle), golf, racquetball, soccer, softball, swimming, table tennis, tennis, volleyball. **Team name:** Wonder Boys, Golden Suns.

Student services. Adult student services, alcohol/substance abuse counseling, career counseling, services for economically disadvantaged, student employment services, financial aid counseling, health services, minority student services, personal counseling, placement for graduates, veterans' counselor. **Physically disabled:** Services for visually, speech, hearing impaired.

Contact. E-mail: tech.enroll@atu.edu
Phone: (479) 968-0343 Toll-free number: (800) 582-6953
Fax: (479) 964-0522
Shauna Donnell, Assistant Vice President for Enrollment Management, Arkansas Tech University, 1605 Coliseum Diver Suite 141, Russellville, AR 72801-2222

Central Baptist College

Conway, Arkansas
www.cbc.edu **CB code: 0788**

- Private 4-year Bible and junior college affiliated with Baptist faith
- Residential campus in large town
- 547 degree-seeking undergraduates: 19% part-time, 47% women, 17% African American, 1% Asian American, 3% Hispanic American, 1% Native American, 2% international
- 83% of applicants admitted

- ACT (writing optional) required
- 37% graduate within 6 years

General. Founded in 1952. Regionally accredited. **Degrees:** 65 bachelor's, 25 associate awarded. **ROTC:** Army. **Location:** 30 miles from Little Rock. **Calendar:** Semester, limited summer session. **Full-time faculty:** 18 total; 44% have terminal degrees, 6% minority, 39% women. **Part-time faculty:** 37 total; 11% have terminal degrees, 14% minority, 43% women.

Freshman class profile. 176 applied, 146 admitted, 108 enrolled.

Mid 50% test scores		International:	3%
ACT composite:	19-23		

Basis for selection. Religious commitment most important, followed by school achievement record. Interview recommended. **Homeschooled:** Statement describing homeschool structure and mission, transcript of courses and grades required.

High school preparation. College-preparatory program recommended. 15 units recommended. Recommended units include English 4, mathematics 2, social studies 2 and science 2.

2008-2009 Annual costs. Tuition/fees: $9,650. Room/board: $5,000. Books/supplies: $600. Personal expenses: $800.

Financial aid. Non-need-based: Scholarships awarded for academics, athletics, music/drama, religious affiliation.

Application procedures. Admission: Closing date 8/15 (postmark date). $25 fee. Admission notification on a rolling basis. **Financial aid:** Priority date 7/1, closing date 8/1. FAFSA required. Applicants notified on a rolling basis starting 4/1.

Academics. Special study options: Internships. **Credit/placement by examination:** AP, CLEP, ACT, institutional tests. 15 credit hours maximum toward associate degree, 27 toward bachelor's. **Support services:** Learning center, reduced course load, remedial instruction, study skills assistance, tutoring.

Majors. Biology: General, biotechnology. **Business:** Business admin, marketing, organizational behavior. **Computer sciences:** Data processing. **Health:** Health services. **Public administration:** Social work. **Theology:** Bible, sacred music.

Most popular majors. Business/marketing 40%, computer/information sciences 7%, social sciences 17%, theological studies 29%.

Computing on campus. 52 workstations in library, computer center. Online library available.

Student life. Freshman orientation: Mandatory. Preregistration for classes offered. **Policies:** Religious observance required. **Housing:** Guaranteed on-campus for freshmen. Single-sex dorms, wellness housing available. $100 partly refundable deposit, deadline 8/15. **Activities:** Concert band, choral groups, music ensembles, student government, student newspaper, Association of Baptist Students, College Republicans.

Athletics. NCCAA. **Intercollegiate:** Baseball M, basketball, golf, softball W, volleyball W. **Intramural:** Basketball, football (non-tackle), softball, table tennis, tennis, volleyball. **Team name:** Mustangs.

Student services. Career counseling, financial aid counseling, health services, personal counseling, veterans' counselor.

Contact. E-mail: jwilson@cbc.edu
Phone: (501) 329-6872 Toll-free number: (501) 208-6872
Fax: (501) 329-2941
Jonathan Wilson, Director of Admissions, Central Baptist College, 1501 College Avenue, Conway, AR 72034

Ecclesia College
Springdale, Arkansas
www.ecollege.edu

- Private 4-year liberal arts college affiliated with interdenominational tradition
- Residential campus in large town
- 126 degree-seeking undergraduates
- ACT (writing optional), application essay required

General. Accredited by ABHE. **Degrees:** 19 bachelor's, 3 associate awarded. **Location:** 10 miles from Fayetteville. **Calendar:** Semester, limited summer session. **Full-time faculty:** 1 total. **Part-time faculty:** 43 total; 37% have terminal degrees, 5% minority, 26% women.

Freshman class profile. 65 applied, 51 admitted, 40 enrolled.

Out-of-state:	25%	Live on campus:	75%

Basis for selection. Open admission, but selective for some programs. Recommendations and personal character very important. **Homeschooled:** Interview required.

High school preparation. College-preparatory program recommended. Recommended units include English 4, mathematics 3, social studies 3, science 3 and foreign language 1.

2008-2009 Annual costs. Tuition/fees: $15,050. Full-time students not living on campus may be subject to additional $750 nonresidents fee/semester. Room/board: $5,010. Books/supplies: $500. Personal expenses: $875.

2007-2008 Financial aid. Non-need-based: Scholarships awarded for academics, athletics, leadership, music/drama.

Application procedures. Admission: Closing date 8/22 (receipt date). $35 fee. Application must be submitted on paper. Admission notification on a rolling basis. **Financial aid:** No deadline. FAFSA required. Applicants notified on a rolling basis starting 7/1.

Academics. Special study options: Double major, dual enrollment of high school students, independent study, internships. **Credit/placement by examination:** CLEP, ACT, institutional tests. **Support services:** Remedial instruction, tutoring.

Majors. Business: Business admin. **Theology:** Bible, missionary, pastoral counseling, preministerial, religious ed, sacred music, theology, youth ministry. **Other:** Communication ministries.

Computing on campus. 15 workstations in library, computer center. Dormitories wired for high-speed internet access. Online library, wireless network available.

Student life. Freshman orientation: Mandatory. Preregistration for classes offered. **Policies:** Religious observance required. **Housing:** Single-sex dorms, apartments, wellness housing available. **Activities:** Campus ministries, choral groups, drama, music ensembles, student government.

Athletics. NCCAA. **Intercollegiate:** Baseball M, basketball, golf, track and field. **Team name:** Royals.

Student services. Alcohol/substance abuse counseling, chaplain/spiritual director, career counseling, financial aid counseling, personal counseling, placement for graduates. **Physically disabled:** Services for visually impaired.

Contact. E-mail: admissions@ecollege.edu
Phone: (479) 248-7236 ext. 223 Toll-free number: (800) 735-9926
Fax: (479) 248-1455
Titus Hofer, Director of Admissions, Ecclesia College, 9653 Nations Drive, Springdale, AR 72762

Harding University
Searcy, Arkansas
www.harding.edu **CB code: 6267**

- Private 4-year university affiliated with Church of Christ
- Residential campus in large town
- 4,132 degree-seeking undergraduates: 6% part-time, 54% women, 4% African American, 1% Asian American, 2% Hispanic American, 1% Native American, 5% international
- 1,113 degree-seeking graduate students
- 74% of applicants admitted
- SAT or ACT (ACT writing optional) required
- 61% graduate within 6 years; 36% enter graduate study

General. Founded in 1924. Regionally accredited. **Degrees:** 787 bachelor's awarded; master's, doctoral, first professional offered. **Location:** 50 miles from Little Rock, 105 miles from Memphis. **Calendar:** Semester, extensive summer session. **Full-time faculty:** 239 total; 66% have terminal degrees, 3% minority, 30% women. **Part-time faculty:** 196 total; 31% have terminal degrees, 3% minority, 36% women. **Class size:** 50% < 20, 32% 20-39, 6% 40-49, 12% 50-99, less than 1% >100.

Freshman class profile. 1,874 applied, 1,382 admitted, 986 enrolled.

Mid 50% test scores		**Rank in top tenth:**	29%
SAT critical reading:	500-640	**End year in good standing:**	89%
SAT math:	500-640	**Return as sophomores:**	82%
ACT composite:	22-28	**Out-of-state:**	74%
GPA 3.75 or higher:	45%	**Live on campus:**	95%
GPA 3.50-3.74:	19%	**International:**	4%
GPA 3.0-3.49:	25%	**Fraternities:**	40%
GPA 2.0-2.99:	10%	**Sororities:**	42%
Rank in top quarter:	54%		

Basis for selection. Test scores, academic record, references, interview important. Selective admission with limited openings, students must apply early. Students are encouraged to take rigorous classes in high school. Audition recommended for music majors, portfolio for art majors.

High school preparation. College-preparatory program recommended. 15 units required; 20 recommended. Required and recommended units include English 4, mathematics 3-4, social studies 3-4, science 2-4, foreign language 2 and academic electives 3.

2008-2009 Annual costs. Tuition/fees: $13,130. Room/board: $5,700. Books/supplies: $900. Personal expenses: $1,400.

2007-2008 Financial aid. **Non-need-based:** Scholarships awarded for academics, art, athletics, music/drama, religious affiliation, ROTC, state residency. **Additional information:** Music scholarships available, audition required.

Application procedures. **Admission:** No deadline. $35 fee. Admission notification on a rolling basis. Early application encouraged. **Financial aid:** Priority date 4/1; no closing date. FAFSA, institutional form required. Applicants notified on a rolling basis starting 2/15; must reply within 2 week(s) of notification.

Academics. **Special study options:** Accelerated study, cooperative education, distance learning, double major, dual enrollment of high school students, ESL, honors, independent study, internships, liberal arts/career combination, study abroad, teacher certification program. **Credit/placement by examination:** AP, CLEP, IB, SAT, ACT, institutional tests. 32 credit hours maximum toward bachelor's degree. **Support services:** Learning center, reduced course load, remedial instruction, study skills assistance, tutoring, writing center.

Honors college/program. Honors students are eligible with an ACT score of 27 or higher, or SAT of 1200 or higher. There are approximately 175 Honors Students who begin as freshmen each fall. Honors scholars (40 freshmen each fall) must be National Merit finalists or Trustee Scholarship recipients. The Trustee scholarship recipients are selected from a pool of students with an ACT score of 31 or higher, or an SAT of 1330 or higher.

Majors. **Area/ethnic studies:** American. **Biology:** General, biochemistry, Biochemistry/biophysics and molecular biology. **Business:** Accounting, business admin, fashion, finance, human resources, international, marketing, sales/distribution. **Communications:** General, advertising, broadcast journalism, digital media, journalism, public relations. **Computer sciences:** Computer science, information technology. **Education:** Art, biology, chemistry, early childhood, early childhood special, elementary, English, family/consumer sciences, foreign languages, French, health, mathematics, middle, multi-level teacher, music, physical, science, social studies, Spanish, special, speech. **Engineering:** Computer, electrical, mechanical. **Family/consumer sciences:** General. **Foreign languages:** French, Spanish. **Health:** Art therapy, athletic training, clinical lab science, communication disorders, dietetics, health care admin, nursing (RN), predental, premedicine, prepharmacy, preveterinary, speech pathology. **History:** General. **Interdisciplinary:** Global studies. **Legal studies:** Prelaw. **Liberal arts:** Humanities. **Math:** General. **Parks/recreation:** Exercise sciences, sports admin. **Physical sciences:** Chemistry, physics. **Protective services:** Criminal justice. **Psychology:** General. **Public administration:** General, social work. **Social sciences:** General, economics, political science. **Theology:** Bible, missionary, religious ed, theology, youth ministry. **Visual/performing arts:** Art, dramatic, graphic design, interior design, painting, studio arts.

Most popular majors. Business/marketing 21%, education 14%, health sciences 12%, liberal arts 8%, theological studies 6%.

Computing on campus. 465 workstations in library, computer center, student center. Dormitories wired for high-speed internet access and linked to campus network. Commuter students can connect to campus network. Online course registration, online library, helpline, repair service, wireless network available.

Student life. **Freshman orientation:** Available, $95 fee. Preregistration for classes offered. Three days of orientation immediately before the start of the fall semester. Includes all activities and meals, plus a t-shirt and academic planner. **Policies:** Religious observance required. **Housing:** Guaranteed on-campus for freshmen. Single-sex dorms, special housing for disabled, apartments, wellness housing available. $125 fully refundable deposit, deadline 5/1. Approved off-campus housing. **Activities:** Bands, campus ministries, choral groups, drama, international student organizations, music ensembles, radio station, student government, student newspaper, symphony orchestra, TV station, College Republicans, College Democrats, Good News Singers, Timothy Club, religious mission campaigns, Multi-cultural Student Action Committee, Harding Athletes as Role Models, Harding in Action.

Athletics. NCAA. **Intercollegiate:** Baseball M, basketball, cheerleading M, cross-country, football (tackle) M, golf, soccer, tennis, track and field, volleyball W. **Intramural:** Archery M, basketball, cross-country M, football (non-tackle), golf M, racquetball, soccer, softball, swimming, table tennis M, tennis, track and field, volleyball, weight lifting M. **Team name:** Bisons.

Student services. Adult student services, chaplain/spiritual director, career counseling, student employment services, financial aid counseling, health services, minority student services, personal counseling, placement for graduates. **Physically disabled:** Services for visually, speech, hearing impaired.

Contact. E-mail: admissions@harding.edu
Phone: (501) 279-4407 Toll-free number: (800) 477-4407
Fax: (501) 279-4129
Glenn Dillard, Assistant Vice President for Enrollment Management,
Harding University, 915 East Market Avenue, Searcy, AR 72149-2255

Henderson State University

Arkadelphia, Arkansas — **CB member**
www.getreddie.com — **CB code: 6272**

- Public 4-year university and liberal arts college
- Commuter campus in large town
- 2,833 degree-seeking undergraduates
- 481 graduate students
- 67% of applicants admitted
- SAT or ACT (ACT writing optional) required

General. Founded in 1890. Regionally accredited. **Degrees:** 447 bachelor's awarded; master's offered. **ROTC:** Army. **Location:** 67 miles from Little Rock. **Calendar:** Semester, limited summer session. **Full-time faculty:** 156 total; 69% have terminal degrees, 12% minority, 37% women. **Part-time faculty:** 74 total; 18% have terminal degrees, 5% minority, 70% women. **Class size:** 55% < 20, 38% 20-39, 5% 40-49, 2% 50-99, less than 1% >100. **Special facilities:** Planetarium.

Freshman class profile. 2,361 applied, 1,577 admitted, 748 enrolled.

Mid 50% test scores		**GPA 3.0-3.49:**	31%
SAT critical reading:	430-580	**GPA 2.0-2.99:**	36%
SAT math:	460-570	**Rank in top quarter:**	39%
ACT composite:	18-25	**Rank in top tenth:**	16%
GPA 3.75 or higher:	17%	**Out-of-state:**	18%
GPA 3.50-3.74:	14%	**Live on campus:**	79%

Basis for selection. Applicants must have ACT composite of 19 and minimum 2.5 GPA for unconditional admission. Those not meeting GPA requirement admitted conditionally. Applicants who do not meet minimum test score standards may be admitted through appeal process. Deadline for applying for appeal is July 15. ACT recommended. Test scores must be on file with Admissions prior to registering for classes. Audition recommended for music and theater arts majors. **Homeschooled:** Minimum ACT composite score of 18, transcript required. Completion of college prep curriculum encouraged. **Learning Disabled:** Student Support Disability Services assesses needs of students with learning disabilities.

High school preparation. 14 units required; 22 recommended. Required and recommended units include English 4, mathematics 4, social studies 2, history 1 and science 3. Required: 1/2 oral comm, 1/2 fine art, 6 career focus.

2008-2009 Annual costs. Tuition/fees: $6,024; $10,944 out-of-state. Room/board: $4,790. Books/supplies: $1,200. Personal expenses: $2,000.

2007-2008 Financial aid. **Non-need-based:** Scholarships awarded for academics, alumni affiliation, art, athletics, leadership, minority status, music/drama, state residency.

Application procedures. **Admission:** No deadline. No application fee. Admission notification on a rolling basis beginning on or about 9/1. Application closing date July 15 for applicants with ACT score under 18. **Financial aid:** Priority date 6/1; no closing date. FAFSA required. Applicants notified on a rolling basis starting 4/1; must reply within 2 week(s) of notification.

Academics. **Special study options:** Cross-registration, distance learning, honors, internships, liberal arts/career combination, teacher certification program. **Credit/placement by examination:** AP, CLEP, SAT, ACT, institutional tests. 30 credit hours maximum toward bachelor's degree. **Support services:** Learning center, remedial instruction, study skills assistance, tutoring.

Honors college/program. Freshmen must have composite ACT of 26 or higher. Approximately 90 admitted. Sophomores must have cumulative GPA of 3.25 or higher to petition committee for admission.

Majors. **Biology:** General. **Business:** General, accounting, management information systems. **Communications:** Journalism. **Computer sciences:** General. **Education:** Art, biology, business, early childhood, elementary, English, middle, social science. **Family/consumer sciences:** General. **Foreign languages:** Spanish. **Health:** Athletic training, clinical lab science, nursing (RN). **History:** General. **Math:** General. **Parks/recreation:** Facilities management. **Physical sciences:** Chemistry, physics. **Psychology:** General. **Public administration:** General, social work. **Social sciences:** Political science, sociology. **Transportation:** Airline/commercial pilot. **Visual/performing arts:** Art, dramatic, music performance.

Most popular majors. Business/marketing 16%, education 20%, English 7%, health sciences 8%, psychology 7%, social sciences 6%.

Computing on campus. 125 workstations in dormitories, library, computer center, student center. Dormitories linked to campus network. Commuter students can connect to campus network. Helpline available.

Student life. **Freshman orientation:** Mandatory. Preregistration for classes offered. Day-long program for students and parents includes preregistration, signing up for ID and e-mail address. Program held for week in June, again in July if necessary. **Housing:** Guaranteed on-campus for freshmen. Coed dorms, single-sex dorms, cooperative housing, wellness housing available. $50 deposit. Special hall for Honors College participants, special floor for freshman interest groups available. On-campus apartments leased by outside firm available. Two residence halls are co-ed. **Activities:** Bands, choral groups, dance, drama, literary magazine, music ensembles, radio station, student government, student newspaper, TV station, College Republicans, Young Democrats, Student Foundation, Heart & Key service organization, several religious organizations.

Athletics. NCAA. **Intercollegiate:** Baseball M, basketball, cross-country W, football (tackle) M, golf, softball W, swimming, tennis W, volleyball W. **Intramural:** Soccer M. **Team name:** Reddies.

Student services. Career counseling, student employment services, health services, personal counseling, placement for graduates, veterans' counselor. **Physically disabled:** Services for visually, speech, hearing impaired.

Contact. E-mail: admissions@hsu.edu
Phone: (870) 230-5028 Toll-free number: (800) 228-7333
Fax: (870) 230-5066
Vikita Hardwrick, Director of Admissions, Henderson State University, 1100 Henderson Street, Arkadelphia, AR 71999-0001

Hendrix College

Conway, Arkansas — **CB member**
www.hendrix.edu — **CB code: 6273**

- Private 4-year liberal arts college affiliated with United Methodist Church
- Residential campus in small city
- 1,341 degree-seeking undergraduates: 1% part-time, 55% women, 4% African American, 3% Asian American, 4% Hispanic American, 1% Native American, 2% international
- 8 degree-seeking graduate students
- 94% of applicants admitted
- SAT or ACT (ACT writing optional), application essay required
- 69% graduate within 6 years; 92% enter graduate study

General. Founded in 1876. Regionally accredited. **Degrees:** 192 bachelor's awarded; master's offered. **ROTC:** Army. **Location:** 30 miles from Little Rock. **Calendar:** Semester. **Full-time faculty:** 103 total; 94% have terminal degrees, 10% minority, 39% women. **Part-time faculty:** 28 total; 39% have terminal degrees, 11% minority, 61% women. **Class size:** 63% < 20, 34% 20-39, 2% 40-49, 1% 50-99. **Special facilities:** Teaching theater, two pipe organs, access to elephant farm for research and volunteer service, arboretum, ring laser, hybrid rocket lab.

Freshman class profile. 1,420 applied, 1,339 admitted, 433 enrolled.

Mid 50% test scores		**Rank in top quarter:**	75%
SAT critical reading:	580-690	**Rank in top tenth:**	41%
SAT math:	550-660	**End year in good standing:**	95%
ACT composite:	25-31	**Return as sophomores:**	85%
GPA 3.75 or higher:	55%	**Out-of-state:**	59%
GPA 3.50-3.74:	17%	**Live on campus:**	98%
GPA 3.0-3.49:	20%	**International:**	3%
GPA 2.0-2.99:	8%		

Basis for selection. Academic competence, scholastic potential, motivation, character, and high school leadership important. Interview may be required. **Homeschooled:** Interview required. Portfolio required.

High school preparation. College-preparatory program required. 14 units recommended. Recommended units include English 4, mathematics 3, social studies 3, science 2 and foreign language 2.

2008-2009 Annual costs. Tuition/fees: $26,080. Room/board: $7,950. Books/supplies: $900. Personal expenses: $1,903.

2008-2009 Financial aid. **Need-based:** 365 full-time freshmen applied for aid; 250 were judged to have need; 250 of these received aid. Average need met was 87%. Average scholarship/grant was $17,774; average loan $4,301. 75% of total undergraduate aid awarded as scholarships/grants, 25% as loans/jobs. **Non-need-based:** Awarded to 749 full-time undergraduates, including 271 freshmen. Scholarships awarded for academics, art, leadership, music/drama, religious affiliation.

Application procedures. **Admission:** Priority date 2/1; deadline 8/1 (postmark date). $40 fee, may be waived for applicants with need, free for online applicants. Admission notification on a rolling basis beginning on or about 11/1. Must reply by May 1 or within 4 week(s) if notified thereafter. **Financial aid:** Priority date 2/15; no closing date. FAFSA required. Applicants notified on a rolling basis starting 2/15; must reply by 5/1 or within 4 week(s) of notification.

Academics. **Special study options:** Combined bachelor's/graduate degree, cooperative education, double major, ESL, exchange student, independent study, internships, student-designed major, study abroad, teacher certification program, Washington semester. Hendrix-in-Brussels (Belgium), Hendrix-in-Costa Rica, Hendrix-in-Heilongjiang (China), Hendrix-in-Graz (Austria), Hendrix-in-London (UK), Hendrix-in-Madrid (Spain), Hendrix-in-Oxford (UK), Academia dell 'Arte, other programs with 140 colleges and universities on 6 continents including countries such as Australia, Finland, France, Ghana, Japan. **Credit/placement by examination:** AP, CLEP, IB, SAT, ACT, institutional tests. 6 credit hours maximum toward bachelor's degree. **Support services:** Pre-admission summer program, study skills assistance, tutoring, writing center.

Majors. **Area/ethnic studies:** American. **Biology:** General, Biochemistry/biophysics and molecular biology. **Business:** Accounting, managerial economics. **Computer sciences:** Computer science. **Conservation:** Environmental studies. **Education:** Elementary. **Foreign languages:** French, German, Spanish. **Health:** Health services. **History:** General. **Liberal arts:** Arts/sciences. **Math:** General. **Parks/recreation:** Exercise sciences. **Philosophy/religion:** Philosophy, religion. **Physical sciences:** Chemical physics, chemistry, physics. **Psychology:** General. **Social sciences:** Anthropology, economics, international relations, political science, sociology. **Visual/performing arts:** Art, dramatic. **Other:** Philosophy/religious studies.

Most popular majors. Biology 9%, English 10%, history 8%, philosophy/religious studies 8%, physical sciences 7%, psychology 9%, social sciences 22%, visual/performing arts 7%.

Computing on campus. 75 workstations in dormitories, library, computer center. Dormitories wired for high-speed internet access and linked to campus network. Commuter students can connect to campus network. Online course registration, helpline, repair service, student web hosting, wireless network available.

Student life. **Freshman orientation:** Mandatory. 7-day program prior to fall term. **Housing:** Guaranteed on-campus for freshmen. Coed dorms, single-sex dorms, special housing for disabled, apartments available. $350 partly refundable deposit, deadline 5/1. Co-educational foreign language house (Spanish, German, French) available; suite-style small houses; ecology house. **Activities:** Bands, campus ministries, choral groups, dance, drama, film society, international student organizations, literary magazine, music ensembles, Model UN, radio station, student government, student newspaper, Students for Black Culture, College Republicans, Young Democrats, environmental group, Amnesty International, BACCHUS, Hendrix Peace Links, religious life council, volunteer action center, Students Promoting the Education of Asian Cultures, Hillel.

Athletics. NCAA. **Intercollegiate:** Baseball M, basketball, cross-country, diving, field hockey W, golf, lacrosse M, soccer, softball W, swimming, tennis, track and field, volleyball W. **Intramural:** Badminton, basketball, cheerleading, football (non-tackle), football (tackle), racquetball, soccer, softball, table tennis, tennis. **Team name:** Warriors.

Student services. Alcohol/substance abuse counseling, chaplain/spiritual director, career counseling, student employment services, financial aid counseling, health services, minority student services, personal counseling, placement for graduates. **Physically disabled:** Services for visually impaired.

Contact. E-mail: adm@hendrix.edu
Phone: (501) 450-1362 Toll-free number: (800) 277-9017
Fax: (501) 450-3843
Laura Martin, Director of Admission, Hendrix College, 1600 Washington Avenue, Conway, AR 72032-3080

ITT Technical Institute: Little Rock

Little Rock, Arkansas
www.itt-tech.edu **CB code: 2721**

- For-profit 4-year technical college
- Commuter campus in small city

General. Accredited by ACICS. **Calendar:** Quarter.

Contact. Phone: (501) 565-5550
Director of Recruitment, 4520 S. University Avenue, Little Rock, AR 72204

John Brown University

Siloam Springs, Arkansas
www.jbu.edu **CB code: 6321**

- Private 4-year liberal arts college affiliated with interdenominational tradition
- Residential campus in large town
- 1,674 degree-seeking undergraduates: 5% part-time, 54% women
- 308 degree-seeking graduate students
- 74% of applicants admitted
- SAT or ACT (ACT writing optional), application essay required

General. Founded in 1919. Regionally accredited. **Degrees:** 487 bachelor's, 4 associate awarded; master's offered. **ROTC:** Army, Air Force. **Location:** 30 miles from Fayetteville, 75 miles from Tulsa, Oklahoma. **Calendar:** Semester, limited summer session. **Full-time faculty:** 81 total; 75% have terminal degrees, 4% minority, 22% women. **Part-time faculty:** 74 total; 27% have terminal degrees, 3% minority, 36% women. **Class size:** 49% < 20, 43% 20-39, 7% 40-49, less than 1% 50-99. **Special facilities:** Cadaver lab, cathedral, historical cabin.

Freshman class profile. 896 applied, 662 admitted, 310 enrolled.

Mid 50% test scores		**GPA 3.0-3.49:**	21%
SAT critical reading:	520-650	**GPA 2.0-2.99:**	9%
SAT math:	530-650	**Rank in top quarter:**	67%
ACT composite:	22-29	**Rank in top tenth:**	38%
GPA 3.75 or higher:	49%	**Out-of-state:**	70%
GPA 3.50-3.74:	20%	**Live on campus:**	95%

Basis for selection. Test scores, secondary school record, recommendations, essay, interview most important. Special talents, class rank considered. Combined SAT score of 950 (exclusive of Writing), ACT score of 20 or above. Interview recommended. Audition required of music majors; portfolio recommended for art majors. **Homeschooled:** Transcript of courses and grades required.

High school preparation. Recommended units include English 4, mathematics 3, social studies 2, history 1, science 2 (laboratory 1) and foreign language 2. 4 units of mathematics, 3 science for science and engineering majors; 2 foreign language recommended for home educated students.

2008-2009 Annual costs. Tuition/fees: $18,066. Room/board: $6,580. Books/supplies: $700. Personal expenses: $1,350.

2008-2009 Financial aid. Need-based: 51% of total undergraduate aid awarded as scholarships/grants, 49% as loans/jobs. **Non-need-based:** Scholarships awarded for academics, alumni affiliation, art, athletics, leadership, music/drama, ROTC.

Application procedures. Admission: Priority date 5/1; no deadline. $25 fee, may be waived for applicants with need. Admission notification on a rolling basis beginning on or about 12/1. Must reply by May 1 or within 2 week(s) if notified thereafter. **Financial aid:** Priority date 3/1; no closing date. FAFSA, institutional form required. Applicants notified on a rolling basis starting 3/1; must reply within 4 week(s) of notification.

Academics. Special study options: Accelerated study, distance learning, double major, dual enrollment of high school students, ESL, exchange student, honors, independent study, internships, study abroad, teacher certification program, Washington semester. **Credit/placement by examination:** AP, CLEP, IB, SAT, ACT. 15 credit hours maximum toward associate degree, 30 toward bachelor's. **Support services:** Learning center, reduced course load, remedial instruction, study skills assistance, tutoring, writing center.

Honors college/program. Selected by admissions office/honors committee, requirements are high school GPA, SAT/ACT score and interview.

Majors. Biology: General, biochemistry. **Business:** Accounting, business admin, construction management, international, marketing. **Communications:** Broadcast journalism, digital media, journalism, public relations. **Computer sciences:** Computer science. **Conservation:** General. **Education:** Biology, chemistry, early childhood, English, mathematics, middle, music, social studies. **Engineering:** General. **Family/consumer sciences:** Family/community services. **Foreign languages:** Spanish. **Health:** Athletic training. **History:** General. **Interdisciplinary:** Global studies. **Math:** General. **Parks/recreation:** Exercise sciences, sports admin. **Physical sciences:** Chemistry. **Psychology:** General. **Social sciences:** Political science. **Theology:** Missionary, sacred music, theology, youth ministry. **Visual/performing arts:** Graphic design, illustration, music performance. **Other:** Leadership and management.

Most popular majors. Business/marketing 59%, education 7%, theological studies 6%, visual/performing arts 6%.

Computing on campus. 200 workstations in dormitories, library, computer center, student center. Dormitories wired for high-speed internet access and linked to campus network. Commuter students can connect to campus network. Online course registration, online library, helpline, wireless network available.

Student life. Freshman orientation: Mandatory, $75 fee. Preregistration for classes offered. **Policies:** No alcohol, drugs, or tobacco allowed on campus; all applicants required to sign community covenant each year. Religious observance required. **Housing:** Guaranteed on-campus for freshmen. Coed dorms, single-sex dorms, special housing for disabled, apartments, wellness housing available. $200 deposit. **Activities:** Pep band, choral groups, drama, music ensembles, musical theater, opera, radio station, student government, student newspaper, council to assist in the unity of student evangelism, Young Republicans, Young Democrats, Young Life, Boys & Girls Club volunteer opportunities.

Athletics. NAIA. **Intercollegiate:** Basketball, soccer, swimming W, tennis, volleyball W. **Intramural:** Baseball M, basketball, football (non-tackle), football (tackle) M, racquetball, soccer, softball, tennis, volleyball. **Team name:** Golden Eagles.

Student services. Chaplain/spiritual director, career counseling, student employment services, financial aid counseling, health services, personal counseling, placement for graduates. **Physically disabled:** Services for visually, hearing impaired.

Contact. E-mail: jbuinfo@jbu.edu
Phone: (479) 524-7286 Toll-free number: (877) 528-4636
Fax: (479) 524-4196
Don Crandall, Vice President for Enrollment Management, John Brown University, 2000 West University Street, Siloam Springs, AR 72761-2121

Lyon College

Batesville, Arkansas **CB member**
www.lyon.edu **CB code: 6009**

- Private 4-year liberal arts college affiliated with Presbyterian Church (USA)
- Residential campus in small town
- 453 degree-seeking undergraduates: 4% part-time, 54% women, 4% African American, 1% Asian American, 2% Hispanic American, 2% Native American, 2% international
- 67% of applicants admitted
- SAT or ACT (ACT writing optional) required
- 64% graduate within 6 years; 33% enter graduate study

General. Founded in 1872. Regionally accredited. **Degrees:** 98 bachelor's awarded. **Location:** 90 miles from Little Rock. **Calendar:** Semester, limited summer session. **Full-time faculty:** 44 total; 93% have terminal degrees, 9% minority, 23% women. **Part-time faculty:** 16 total; 6% have terminal degrees, 12% minority, 81% women. **Class size:** 78% < 20, 21% 20-39, 1% 40-49. **Special facilities:** Ozark Regional Studies Center.

Freshman class profile. 847 applied, 569 admitted, 109 enrolled.

Mid 50% test scores			
SAT critical reading:	550-620	Rank in top quarter:	54%
SAT math:	550-610	Rank in top tenth:	27%
ACT composite:	22-27	End year in good standing:	93%
GPA 3.75 or higher:	39%	Return as sophomores:	70%
GPA 3.50-3.74:	20%	Out-of-state:	32%
GPA 3.0-3.49:	32%	Live on campus:	94%
GPA 2.0-2.99:	9%	International:	1%

Basis for selection. High school academic performance and standardized test scores are the most important. Personal essays and letters of recommendation are considered on a case by case basis. Math proficiency and placement are judged with ACT math subscores. Auditions or portfolios required for fine arts.

High school preparation. College-preparatory program recommended. 16 units required; 18 recommended. Required and recommended units include English 4, mathematics 3-4, social studies 1, history 2, science 3-4 (laboratory 2), foreign language 2 and academic electives 1.

2009-2010 Annual costs. Tuition/fees: $19,968. Room/board: $7,340. Books/supplies: $1,000. Personal expenses: $1,000.

2008-2009 Financial aid. Need-based: 93 full-time freshmen applied for aid; 79 were judged to have need; 79 of these received aid. Average need met was 82%. Average scholarship/grant was $13,609; average loan $3,863. 77% of total undergraduate aid awarded as scholarships/grants, 23% as loans/jobs. **Non-need-based:** Awarded to 532 full-time undergraduates, including 129 freshmen. Scholarships awarded for academics, art, athletics, leadership, minority status, music/drama, religious affiliation, state residency.

Application procedures. Admission: Priority date 1/15; no deadline. $25 fee, may be waived for applicants with need. Admission notification on a rolling basis. Must reply by May 1 or within 2 week(s) if notified thereafter. **Financial aid:** Priority date 3/15; no closing date. FAFSA required. Applicants notified on a rolling basis starting 3/1; must reply by 8/15.

Academics. Academic honor code administered by peer-elected student honor council. **Special study options:** Accelerated study, combined bachelor's/graduate degree, cross-registration, double major, dual enrollment of high school students, independent study, internships, student-designed major, study abroad, teacher certification program, Washington semester. **Credit/placement by examination:** AP, CLEP, IB, SAT, ACT, institutional tests. 33 credit hours maximum toward bachelor's degree. **Support services:** Learning center, study skills assistance, tutoring, writing center.

Majors. Biology: General, biochemistry. **Business:** Accounting, business admin. **Computer sciences:** Computer science. **Education:** Early childhood. **Foreign languages:** Spanish. **History:** General. **Math:** General. **Philosophy/religion:** Philosophy, religion. **Physical sciences:** Chemistry. **Psychology:** General. **Social sciences:** Economics, political science. **Visual/performing arts:** Art, dramatic.

Most popular majors. Biology 11%, business/marketing 26%, education 7%, English 7%, history 9%, psychology 10%, social sciences 15%.

Computing on campus. 100 workstations in dormitories, library, computer center, student center. Dormitories wired for high-speed internet access and linked to campus network. Commuter students can connect to campus network. Online course registration, online library, helpline, repair service, wireless network available.

Student life. Freshman orientation: Mandatory, $135 fee. Preregistration for classes offered. **Policies:** Social code administered by peer-elected student social council. **Housing:** Guaranteed on-campus for all undergraduates. Coed dorms, single-sex dorms, apartments, wellness housing available. $100 fully refundable deposit. Limited college-owned off-campus housing is available. **Activities:** Concert band, campus ministries, choral groups, drama, international student organizations, literary magazine, music ensembles, Model UN, student government, student newspaper, Black students association, Fellowship of Christian Athletes.

Athletics. NAIA. **Intercollegiate:** Baseball M, basketball, cheerleading, cross-country, golf, soccer, softball W, volleyball W. **Intramural:** Badminton, basketball, football (non-tackle), softball, table tennis, tennis, volleyball. **Team name:** Scots (M), Pipers (W).

Student services. Chaplain/spiritual director, career counseling, financial aid counseling, health services, personal counseling, placement for graduates.

Contact. E-mail: admissions@lyon.edu
Phone: (870) 307-7250 Toll-free number: (800) 423-2542
Fax: (870) 307-7542
David Heringer, Vice President for Enrollment Services, Lyon College, PO Box 2317, Batesville, AR 72503-2317

Ouachita Baptist University

Arkadelphia, Arkansas
www.obu.edu **CB code: 6549**

- Private 4-year liberal arts college affiliated with Southern Baptist Convention
- Residential campus in large town
- 1,437 degree-seeking undergraduates: 1% part-time, 54% women, 6% African American, 2% Hispanic American, 1% Native American, 3% international
- 66% of applicants admitted
- SAT or ACT (ACT writing optional) required
- 61% graduate within 6 years; 40% enter graduate study

General. Founded in 1886. Regionally accredited. Strong emphasis on global awareness, international study opportunities, missions, and volunteer service. **Degrees:** 263 bachelor's awarded. **ROTC:** Army. **Location:** 65 miles from Little Rock. **Calendar:** Semester, extensive summer session. **Full-time faculty:** 118 total; 72% have terminal degrees, less than 1% minority, 31% women. **Part-time faculty:** 27 total; 7% have terminal degrees, 78% women. **Class size:** 58% < 20, 41% 20-39, less than 1% 40-49, less than 1% 50-99.

Freshman class profile. 1,569 applied, 1,036 admitted, 404 enrolled.

Mid 50% test scores			
SAT critical reading:	470-600	Rank in top tenth:	39%
SAT math:	490-590	End year in good standing:	90%
ACT composite:	21-27	Return as sophomores:	74%
GPA 3.75 or higher:	41%	Out-of-state:	49%
GPA 3.50-3.74:	17%	Live on campus:	99%
GPA 3.0-3.49:	26%	International:	3%
GPA 2.0-2.99:	16%	Fraternities:	35%
Rank in top quarter:	60%	Sororities:	50%

Basis for selection. Test scores and school achievement record most important. Minimum high school GPA of 2.75 required, ACT score of 20 or higher. Interview recommended. Portfolio recommended for studio art majors.

High school preparation. 15 units required; 19 recommended. Required and recommended units include English 4, mathematics 2-3, social studies 1, history 2, science 2-3, foreign language 2 and academic electives 4.

2009-2010 Annual costs. Tuition/fees (projected): $18,940. Room/board: $5,660. Books/supplies: $1,000. Personal expenses: $1,500.

2008-2009 Financial aid. Non-need-based: Scholarships awarded for academics, alumni affiliation, athletics, job skills, leadership, minority status, music/drama, religious affiliation, ROTC, state residency.

Application procedures. Admission: No deadline. No application fee. Admission notification on a rolling basis. **Financial aid:** Priority date 1/15, closing date 6/1. FAFSA required. Applicants notified on a rolling basis starting 11/1; must reply by 5/1.

Academics. Classes in Arkansas Folkways taught at Old Washington State Park. International exchange programs in Australia, Austria, China, Costa Rica, England, France, Germany, Hong Kong, Indonesia, Japan, Morocco, Russia, Scotland, and South Africa. **Special study options:** Cross-registration, distance learning, double major, ESL, honors, independent study, internships, study abroad, teacher certification program. **Credit/placement by examination:** AP, CLEP, IB, ACT, institutional tests. 24 credit hours maximum toward bachelor's degree. **Support services:** Learning center, reduced course load, remedial instruction, study skills assistance, tutoring, writing center.

Majors. Biology: General. **Business:** Accounting, business admin. **Communications:** Media studies. **Computer sciences:** Computer science. **Education:** General, art, biology, business, chemistry, drama/dance, early childhood, English, foreign languages, French, health, history, mathematics, middle, music, physical, physics, science, secondary, social studies, Spanish, speech. **Foreign languages:** French, Russian, Spanish. **Health:** Athletic training, audiology/speech pathology, dietetics, predental, premedicine, prenursing, prepharmacy, preveterinary. **History:** General. **Math:** General. **Parks/recreation:** Exercise sciences. **Philosophy/religion:** Philosophy. **Physical**

sciences: Chemistry, physics. **Psychology:** General. **Social sciences:** Political science, sociology. **Theology:** Bible, missionary, pastoral counseling, sacred music, theology, youth ministry. **Visual/performing arts:** Dramatic, graphic design, music history, music performance, music theory/composition, piano/organ, studio arts, voice/opera. **Other:** Software engineering.

Most popular majors. Biology 10%, business/marketing 14%, education 11%, health sciences 8%, psychology 8%, theological studies 10%, visual/performing arts 10%.

Computing on campus. 250 workstations in dormitories, library, computer center, student center. Dormitories wired for high-speed internet access and linked to campus network. Commuter students can connect to campus network. Online library, helpline, student web hosting, wireless network available.

Student life. Freshman orientation: Mandatory. Preregistration for classes offered. Three-part program: day-long pre-registration and orientation session for students and parents; 3-day weekend program prior to registration with one session for parents; optional 3-day summer retreat. **Policies:** Students under 22 must live in campus housing unless commuting. Only local fraternities and sororities are permitted. Religious observance required. **Housing:** Guaranteed on-campus for all undergraduates. Single-sex dorms, special housing for disabled, apartments, wellness housing available. $50 fully refundable deposit, deadline 6/1. **Activities:** Bands, campus ministries, choral groups, drama, international student organizations, literary magazine, music ensembles, Model UN, musical theater, opera, student government, student newspaper, Fellowship of Christian Athletes, Ouachita student foundation, Pew College Society, ROMS, Young Democrats, College Republicans.

Athletics. NCAA. **Intercollegiate:** Baseball M, basketball, cheerleading, cross-country W, diving, football (tackle) M, golf M, soccer, softball W, swimming, tennis, volleyball W. **Intramural:** Basketball, football (non-tackle), handball, racquetball, soccer, softball, table tennis, volleyball. **Team name:** Tigers.

Student services. Alcohol/substance abuse counseling, chaplain/spiritual director, career counseling, services for economically disadvantaged, student employment services, financial aid counseling, health services, minority student services, personal counseling, placement for graduates, veterans' counselor. **Physically disabled:** Services for visually, speech, hearing impaired.

Contact. E-mail: pittmank@obu.edu
Phone: (870) 245-5110 Toll-free number: (800) 342-5628
Fax: (870) 245-5500
Judy Jones, Director of Admissions/Registrar, Ouachita Baptist University, OBU Box 3776, Arkadelphia, AR 71998-0001

Philander Smith College

Little Rock, Arkansas — **CB member**
www.philander.edu — **CB code: 6578**

- Private 4-year liberal arts college affiliated with United Methodist Church
- Commuter campus in small city
- 587 degree-seeking undergraduates
- 84% of applicants admitted
- SAT or ACT (ACT writing recommended) required

General. Founded in 1877. Regionally accredited. **Degrees:** 108 bachelor's awarded. **ROTC:** Army. **Calendar:** Semester, limited summer session. **Full-time faculty:** 49 total. **Part-time faculty:** 36 total.

Freshman class profile. 981 applied, 825 admitted, 145 enrolled.

Mid 50% test scores			
SAT critical reading:	320-430	GPA 3.50-3.74:	3%
SAT math:	270-440	GPA 3.0-3.49:	29%
SAT writing:	350-430	GPA 2.0-2.99:	58%
ACT composite:	15-21	Rank in top quarter:	33%
GPA 3.75 or higher:	6%	Rank in top tenth:	14%
		Out-of-state:	27%

Basis for selection. High school GPA of 2.5 and ACT Composite of 17 along with rigor of high school record. Students admitted without ACT scores are administered COMPASS test for placement purposes. Students who score below placement cut-off scores in writing, English, or math also required to take COMPASS test.

High school preparation. Recommended units include English 3, mathematics 3, social studies 2, science 3 (laboratory 1) and foreign language 2.

2008-2009 Annual costs. Tuition/fees: $8,740. Room/board: $6,650. Books/supplies: $900. Personal expenses: $1,540.

2008-2009 Financial aid. All financial aid based on need.

Application procedures. Admission: Priority date 3/1; deadline 6/1. $25 fee, may be waived for applicants with need. Admission notification on a rolling basis. **Financial aid:** Priority date 3/1; no closing date. FAFSA, institutional form required. Applicants notified on a rolling basis starting 5/1; must reply within 2 week(s) of notification.

Academics. Special study options: Cooperative education, independent study, internships, liberal arts/career combination, study abroad, teacher certification program. **Credit/placement by examination:** AP, CLEP, SAT, ACT. 30 credit hours maximum toward bachelor's degree. **Support services:** Learning center, reduced course load, remedial instruction, tutoring.

Majors. Biology: General. **Business:** Administrative services, business admin. **Computer sciences:** Computer science. **Education:** Business. **Interdisciplinary:** Math/computer science. **Math:** General. **Philosophy/religion:** Philosophy, religion. **Physical sciences:** Chemistry. **Psychology:** General. **Public administration:** Social work. **Social sciences:** Political science, sociology.

Computing on campus. 72 workstations in dormitories, library, computer center. Dormitories wired for high-speed internet access and linked to campus network. Commuter students can connect to campus network. Online library, wireless network available.

Student life. Freshman orientation: Mandatory, $150 fee. **Housing:** Single-sex dorms available. $245 nonrefundable deposit, deadline 7/10. **Activities:** Choral groups, drama, student government, student newspaper.

Athletics. Intercollegiate: Baseball M, basketball, volleyball W. **Intramural:** Badminton, basketball, tennis. **Team name:** Panthers.

Student services. Career counseling, student employment services, health services, personal counseling, veterans' counselor. **Physically disabled:** Services for visually, hearing impaired.

Contact. E-mail: admissions@philander.edu
Phone: (501) 370-5221 Toll-free number: (800) 446-6772
Fax: (501) 370-5225
George Gray, Director of Admissions, Philander Smith College, One Trudie Kibbe Reed Drive, Little Rock, AR 72202-3718

Southern Arkansas University

Magnolia, Arkansas
www.saumag.edu — **CB code: 6661**

- Public 4-year university
- Residential campus in large town
- 2,546 degree-seeking undergraduates: 12% part-time, 59% women, 30% African American, 1% Asian American, 2% Hispanic American, 1% Native American, 5% international
- 443 graduate students
- 73% of applicants admitted
- SAT or ACT (ACT writing optional) required
- 32% graduate within 6 years

General. Founded in 1909. Regionally accredited. **Degrees:** 427 bachelor's, 97 associate awarded; master's offered. **Location:** 53 miles from Texarkana, Texas, 70 miles from Shreveport, Louisiana. **Calendar:** Semester, extensive summer session. **Full-time faculty:** 151 total; 13% minority, 40% women. **Part-time faculty:** 62 total; 10% minority, 68% women. **Class size:** 55% < 20, 35% 20-39, 6% 40-49, 4% 50-99. **Special facilities:** University farm.

Freshman class profile. 1,921 applied, 1,397 admitted, 626 enrolled.

Mid 50% test scores		Return as sophomores:	56%
SAT critical reading:	350-540	Out-of-state:	27%
SAT math:	400-630	Live on campus:	80%
ACT composite:	17-24	International:	7%

Basis for selection. For unconditional admission, applicants must have ACT of 19 or higher. ACT of 16 to 18 allows conditional admission. TOEFL required for non-native English speakers. Interview required of nursing majors.

High school preparation. Recommended units include English 4, mathematics 4, social studies 3, science 3 (laboratory 3) and foreign language 2. 0.5 computer science also recommended.

2008-2009 Annual costs. Tuition/fees: $5,760; $8,220 out-of-state. Room/board: $4,200. Books/supplies: $1,000. Personal expenses: $2,200.

2007-2008 Financial aid. **Need-based:** 40% of total undergraduate aid awarded as scholarships/grants, 60% as loans/jobs. **Non-need-based:** Scholarships awarded for academics, alumni affiliation, art, athletics, leadership, minority status, music/drama, state residency.

Application procedures. **Admission:** Closing date 8/30 (receipt date). No application fee. Admission notification on a rolling basis. **Financial aid:** Priority date 7/1; no closing date. FAFSA required. Applicants notified on a rolling basis starting 4/15; must reply within 2 week(s) of notification.

Academics. **Special study options:** Combined bachelor's/graduate degree, cross-registration, distance learning, double major, dual enrollment of high school students, honors, independent study, internships, teacher certification program. **Credit/placement by examination:** AP, CLEP, SAT, ACT. 15 credit hours maximum toward associate degree, 30 toward bachelor's. **Support services:** Learning center, reduced course load, remedial instruction, tutoring, writing center.

Honors college/program. Composite ACT score of 26 or higher.

Majors. **Agriculture:** Business. **Biology:** General. **Business:** General, accounting. **Communications:** Journalism. **Computer sciences:** General. **Education:** Agricultural, art, business, chemistry, early childhood, English, mathematics, middle, music, physical, science, social studies, Spanish. **Engineering technology:** Industrial. **Foreign languages:** Spanish. **Health:** Athletic training, clinical lab science, nursing (RN). **History:** General. **Interdisciplinary:** Biological/physical sciences. **Math:** General. **Parks/recreation:** Exercise sciences. **Physical sciences:** Chemistry, physics. **Protective services:** Criminal justice. **Psychology:** General. **Public administration:** Community org/advocacy, social work. **Social sciences:** General, political science, sociology. **Visual/performing arts:** Art, dramatic, studio arts. **Other:** Interdisciplinary studies.

Most popular majors. Biology 7%, business/marketing 36%, education 27%.

Computing on campus. 202 workstations in dormitories, library, computer center. Dormitories wired for high-speed internet access and linked to campus network. Commuter students can connect to campus network. Online library, helpline, wireless network available.

Student life. **Freshman orientation:** Mandatory, $25 fee. Preregistration for classes offered. **Policies:** Freshmen required to live on campus unless commuting or living with parents. **Housing:** Guaranteed on-campus for all undergraduates. Coed dorms, single-sex dorms, apartments, wellness housing available. $50 fully refundable deposit. **Activities:** Bands, choral groups, drama, music ensembles, musical theater, radio station, student government, student newspaper, More than 80 student organizations.

Athletics. NCAA. **Intercollegiate:** Baseball M, basketball, cross-country, football (tackle) M, golf M, softball W, tennis W, track and field, volleyball W. **Intramural:** Badminton, basketball, football (tackle) M, golf M, softball, table tennis, tennis, volleyball. **Team name:** Muleriders.

Student services. Alcohol/substance abuse counseling, career counseling, services for economically disadvantaged, student employment services, financial aid counseling, health services, minority student services, personal counseling, placement for graduates, veterans' counselor, women's services. **Physically disabled:** Services for visually, hearing impaired.

Contact. E-mail: sejennings@saumag.edu
Phone: (870) 235-4040 Toll-free number: (800) 332-7286
Fax: (870) 235-4931
Sarah Jennings, Dean of Enrollment Services, Southern Arkansas University, Box 9382, Magnolia, AR 71754-9382

University of Arkansas

Fayetteville, Arkansas — **CB member**
www.uark.edu — **CB code: 6866**

- Public 4-year university
- Residential campus in small city
- 14,861 degree-seeking undergraduates: 13% part-time, 49% women
- 3,590 degree-seeking graduate students
- 58% of applicants admitted
- SAT or ACT (ACT writing optional) required
- 57% graduate within 6 years

General. Founded in 1871. Regionally accredited. Arkansas Center for Space and Planetary Sciences, GENESIS Technology Incubator program provides tech-based companies with research and development support. **Degrees:** 2,343 bachelor's awarded; master's, doctoral, first professional offered. **ROTC:** Army, Air Force. **Location:** 192 miles from Little Rock, 120 miles from Tulsa, Oklahoma. **Calendar:** Semester, limited summer session. **Full-time faculty:** 899 total; 89% have terminal degrees, 12% minority, 34% women. **Part-time faculty:** 88 total; 57% have terminal degrees, 4% minority, 43% women. **Class size:** 33% < 20, 45% 20-39, 7% 40-49, 11% 50-99, 5% >100. **Special facilities:** Arts center, poultry science center, equine pavilion, animal science center.

Freshman class profile. 12,045 applied, 6,945 admitted, 3,011 enrolled.

Mid 50% test scores		**Rank in top quarter:**	60%
SAT critical reading:	500-630	**Rank in top tenth:**	30%
SAT math:	520-640	**Return as sophomores:**	81%
ACT composite:	23-28	**Out-of-state:**	36%
GPA 3.75 or higher:	39%	**Live on campus:**	88%
GPA 3.50-3.74:	22%	**Fraternities:**	18%
GPA 3.0-3.49:	31%	**Sororities:**	33%
GPA 2.0-2.99:	8%		

Basis for selection. Secondary school record, class rank, test scores, evidence of commitment to success most important. As mandated by state law, those with ACT subscore of 18 or less in English, Mathematics or Reading are assigned developmental coursework or required to take institutional placement test. University policies are more restrictive than the state of Arkansas' policies.

High school preparation. College-preparatory program required. 16 units required. Required and recommended units include English 4, mathematics 4, social studies 3, science 3 (laboratory 2), foreign language 2 and academic electives 2. Mathematics must include algebra I or 2 units applied math, and 3 units chosen from algebra II, geometry, calculus/trigonometry, and statistics. 2 foreign languages strongly recommended.

2008-2009 Annual costs. Tuition/fees: $6,400; $15,278 out-of-state. Room/board: $7,422. Books/supplies: $966. Personal expenses: $1,954.

2007-2008 Financial aid. **Need-based:** 1,642 full-time freshmen applied for aid; 1,089 were judged to have need; 1,063 of these received aid. Average need met was 78%. Average scholarship/grant was $6,656; average loan $3,590. 43% of total undergraduate aid awarded as scholarships/grants, 57% as loans/jobs. **Non-need-based:** Awarded to 2,979 full-time undergraduates, including 819 freshmen. Scholarships awarded for academics, alumni affiliation, art, athletics, leadership, minority status, music/drama, ROTC, state residency.

Application procedures. **Admission:** Priority date 2/1; deadline 8/15 (receipt date). $40 fee, may be waived for applicants with need. Admission notification on a rolling basis beginning on or about 10/1. **Financial aid:** Priority date 3/15; no closing date. FAFSA required. Applicants notified on a rolling basis starting 4/1; must reply within 4 week(s) of notification.

Academics. **Special study options:** Accelerated study, combined bachelor's/graduate degree, cooperative education, distance learning, double major, dual enrollment of high school students, ESL, honors, independent study, internships, liberal arts/career combination, student-designed major, study abroad, teacher certification program, United Nations semester. **Credit/placement by examination:** AP, CLEP, IB, SAT, ACT, institutional tests. **Support services:** Learning center, reduced course load, remedial instruction, study skills assistance, tutoring, writing center.

Honors college/program. Student must be admitted to an honors program in the college of major. Must have a minimum 28 ACT or SAT equivalent and a minimum high school GPA of 3.5. Walton College of Business requires a 28 ACT or SAT equivalent and a minimum high school GPA of 3.75.

Majors. **Agriculture:** Agribusiness operations, agronomy, animal sciences, food science, ornamental horticulture, poultry. **Architecture:** Architecture, landscape. **Area/ethnic studies:** American. **Biology:** General, bacteriology. **Business:** General, accounting, business admin, finance, international, logistics, managerial economics, marketing. **Communications:** General, journalism. **Computer sciences:** General, data processing. **Conservation:** Environmental science. **Education:** Agricultural, elementary, kindergarten/preschool, middle, trade/industrial. **Engineering:** Agricultural, chemical, civil, computer, electrical, industrial, mechanical. **Family/consumer sciences:** Clothing/textiles, family studies, food/nutrition, housing. **Foreign languages:** Classics, French, German, Spanish. **Health:** Audiology/speech pathology, nursing (RN). **History:** General. **Math:** General. **Parks/recreation:** General, health/fitness. **Philosophy/religion:** Philosophy. **Physical sciences:** Chemistry, geology, physics. **Protective services:** Criminal justice. **Psychology:** General. **Public administration:** General, social work. **Social sciences:** Anthropology, economics, geography, international relations, political science, sociology. **Visual/performing arts:** Art, dramatic, music performance.

Most popular majors. Business/marketing 20%, communications/journalism 8%, education 8%, engineering/engineering technologies 9%, social sciences 8%.

Computing on campus. 2,405 workstations in dormitories, library, computer center, student center. Dormitories wired for high-speed internet access and linked to campus network. Commuter students can connect to campus network. Online course registration, online library, helpline, repair service, student web hosting, wireless network available.

Student life. Freshman orientation: Mandatory, $80 fee. Preregistration for classes offered. 2-day orientation session held in summer for students and parents. **Housing:** Coed dorms, single-sex dorms, apartments, fraternity/sorority housing available. $235 partly refundable deposit. Living/learning communities, suites with private bedrooms, first year experience program area, adaptable housing for disabled students, thematic first-year learning communities. **Activities:** Bands, campus ministries, choral groups, dance, drama, film society, international student organizations, literary magazine, music ensembles, musical theater, opera, radio station, student government, student newspaper, symphony orchestra, TV station, More than 200 organizations available.

Athletics. NCAA. **Intercollegiate:** Baseball M, basketball, cheerleading, cross-country, diving W, football (tackle) M, golf, gymnastics W, soccer W, softball W, swimming W, tennis, track and field, volleyball W. **Intramural:** Badminton, basketball, bowling, racquetball, soccer, softball, tennis, volleyball W. **Team name:** Razorbacks.

Student services. Adult student services, alcohol/substance abuse counseling, chaplain/spiritual director, career counseling, student employment services, financial aid counseling, health services, legal services, minority student services, personal counseling, placement for graduates, veterans' counselor. **Physically disabled:** Services for visually, speech, hearing impaired. **Learning disabled:** Comprehensive services available.

Contact. E-mail: uofa@uark.edu
Phone: (479) 575-5346 Toll-free number: (800) 377-8632
Fax: (479) 575-7515
Karen Hodges, Interim Director of Admissions, University of Arkansas, 232 Silas Hunt Hall, Fayetteville, AR 72701

University of Arkansas at Fort Smith

Fort Smith, Arkansas — **CB member**
www.uafortsmith.edu — **CB code: 6220**

- Public 4-year university
- Commuter campus in small city
- 6,110 degree-seeking undergraduates: 27% part-time, 60% women

General. Founded in 1928. Regionally accredited. **Degrees:** 403 bachelor's, 310 associate awarded. **ROTC:** Army, Air Force. **Location:** 150 miles from Little Rock, 120 miles from Tulsa, Oklahoma. **Calendar:** Semester, limited summer session. **Full-time faculty:** 217 total; 43% have terminal degrees, 11% minority, 48% women. **Part-time faculty:** 172 total; 23% have terminal degrees, 6% minority, 49% women. **Class size:** 40% < 20, 53% 20-39, 4% 40-49, 3% 50-99. **Special facilities:** Art galleries.

Freshman class profile. 3,280 applied, 2,029 admitted, 1,282 enrolled.

Mid 50% test scores		**Rank in top tenth:**	10%
ACT composite:	19-24	**End year in good standing:**	68%
GPA 3.75 or higher:	15%	**Return as sophomores:**	61%
GPA 3.50-3.74:	14%	**Out-of-state:**	9%
GPA 3.0-3.49:	30%	**Live on campus:**	16%
GPA 2.0-2.99:	30%	**Fraternities:**	3%
Rank in top quarter:	33%	**Sororities:**	7%

Basis for selection. Open admission, but selective for some programs. Special criteria for health career and education programs. Pre-admission exams are required for all health science programs. Teacher education applicants must take PRAXIS I exam, have grade of C or B in specific English and Rhetoric courses. COMPASS required for placement if ACT/SAT not submitted, or if scores below acceptable minimum (18 on ACT). Interview required of nursing, radiology, surgical technology, paramedic, and dental hygiene majors, as well as teacher education programs. **Homeschooled:** Any private school, home school, or GED student who graduates after May 1, 2002, must have achieved a composite score of 19 on the ACT or the equivalent score on the SAT or COMPASS for unconditional admission to UA Fort Smith. **Learning Disabled:** In order to be considered for accommodations, a student must first submit verification of his or her condition based on Student ADA Services' guidelines and meet with the Student ADA Services coordinator to discuss an accommodation request.

High school preparation. College-preparatory program recommended. 14 units recommended. Recommended units include English 4, mathematics 4, social studies 3, science 3 (laboratory 3).

2008-2009 Annual costs. Tuition/fees: $4,410; $9,600 out-of-state. Room only: $4,282. Books/supplies: $950. Personal expenses: $1,695.

2007-2008 Financial aid. Need-based: 812 full-time freshmen applied for aid; 460 were judged to have need; 443 of these received aid. Average need met was 60%. Average scholarship/grant was $3,849; average loan $2,732. 56% of total undergraduate aid awarded as scholarships/grants, 44% as loans/jobs. **Non-need-based:** Awarded to 1,095 full-time undergraduates, including 511 freshmen. Scholarships awarded for academics, athletics, job skills, leadership, music/drama.

Application procedures. Admission: No deadline. No application fee. Admission notification on a rolling basis. Early applications advised for financial aid. **Financial aid:** Priority date 6/15; no closing date. FAFSA required. Applicants notified on a rolling basis starting 3/1; must reply within 4 week(s) of notification.

Academics. Special study options: Distance learning, double major, dual enrollment of high school students, external degree, honors, independent study, internships, liberal arts/career combination, student-designed major, study abroad, teacher certification program. Associate of Art through distance learning. **Credit/placement by examination:** AP, CLEP, institutional tests. 30 credit hours maximum toward associate degree, 30 toward bachelor's. Prior work/life experience credits awarded for military transcripts only; maximum 30 hours. **Support services:** Learning center, pre-admission summer program, reduced course load, remedial instruction, study skills assistance, tutoring, writing center.

Majors. Biology: General. **Business:** Accounting, business admin. **Computer sciences:** General. **Education:** Biology, chemistry, early childhood, English, history, mathematics, middle, music, social studies, Spanish. **Foreign languages:** Spanish. **Health:** Nursing (RN), sonography. **History:** General. **Interdisciplinary:** Science/society. **Liberal arts:** Arts/sciences. **Math:** General. **Physical sciences:** Chemistry. **Protective services:** Law enforcement admin. **Psychology:** General. **Visual/performing arts:** Graphic design.

Most popular majors. Business/marketing 31%, education 26%, English 7%, history 6%, psychology 10%.

Computing on campus. 590 workstations in dormitories, library, computer center, student center. Dormitories wired for high-speed internet access and linked to campus network. Commuter students can connect to campus network. Online course registration, online library, helpline, wireless network available.

Student life. Freshman orientation: Available. Preregistration for classes offered. **Housing:** Apartments, wellness housing available. $300 fully refundable deposit. **Activities:** Bands, campus ministries, choral groups, drama, international student organizations, literary magazine, music ensembles, student government, symphony orchestra, Future Educators Organization, Students Together Effectively Progressing, First Generation, international club, drama club, Lions for Christ, math club, Sigma Tau Delta, Ozark Mountain Adventure club, organization for adult and returning students.

Athletics. NJCAA. **Intercollegiate:** Baseball M, basketball, golf, tennis, volleyball W. **Intramural:** Basketball, bowling, football (non-tackle), softball, table tennis, volleyball. **Team name:** Lions.

Student services. Adult student services, career counseling, services for economically disadvantaged, student employment services, financial aid counseling, health services, personal counseling, placement for graduates, veterans' counselor. **Physically disabled:** Services for visually, speech, hearing impaired.

Contact. E-mail: information@uafortsmith.edu
Phone: (479) 788-7120 Toll-free number: (888) 512-5466
Fax: (479) 788-7402
Mark Lloyd, Director of Admissions, University of Arkansas at Fort Smith, PO Box 3649, Fort Smith, AR 72913-3649

University of Arkansas at Little Rock

Little Rock, Arkansas — **CB member**
www.ualr.edu — **CB code: 6368**

- Public 4-year university
- Commuter campus in small city
- 9,195 degree-seeking undergraduates
- 88% of applicants admitted
- ACT (writing optional) required

General. Founded in 1927. Regionally accredited. **Degrees:** 1,038 bachelor's, 179 associate awarded; master's, doctoral, first professional offered. **ROTC:** Army. **Calendar:** Semester, limited summer session. **Full-time faculty:** 526 total. **Part-time faculty:** 318 total. **Special facilities:** Planetarium, observatory, government documents depository.

Freshman class profile. 772 applied, 676 admitted, 676 enrolled.

Mid 50% test scores	ACT composite:	17-24

Basis for selection. Unconditional admission based on minimum ACT score of 21 or above, or combined verbal/mathematics SAT score of 990 or above, high school GPA of 2.5 or above, and completion of college preparatory curriculum. Students must meet 2 of 3 basic criteria. All students born after January 1, 1957 required to show Arkansas Certificate of Immunization for Institutions of Higher Education. Interview recommended for academically weak applicants.

High school preparation. 15 units required. Required units include English 4, mathematics 3, social studies 3, science 2 (laboratory 2) and foreign language 2. Social studies should include 1 unit each of American history, world history, and civics or American government.

2008-2009 Annual costs. Tuition/fees: $6,121; $14,304 out-of-state. Room only: $3,100. Books/supplies: $1,000. Personal expenses: $800.

Application procedures. Admission: No deadline. No application fee. Admission notification on a rolling basis. **Financial aid:** Closing date 8/1. FAFSA required. Applicants notified on a rolling basis starting 5/1.

Academics. Special study options: Accelerated study, cooperative education, distance learning, double major, dual enrollment of high school students, ESL, exchange student, honors, independent study, internships, student-designed major, study abroad, teacher certification program, weekend college. **Credit/placement by examination:** AP, CLEP, ACT, institutional tests. 30 credit hours maximum toward associate degree, 30 toward bachelor's. Credit obtained through examination is recorded as approved hours on the official permanent record without grade or grade points. **Support services:** Learning center, reduced course load, remedial instruction, tutoring, writing center.

Majors. Biology: General. **Business:** Accounting, business admin, finance, international, management information systems, managerial economics, marketing. **Communications:** General, advertising, journalism. **Computer sciences:** General, information systems. **Education:** Early childhood, elementary, middle. **Engineering:** Systems. **Engineering technology:** Construction. **Foreign languages:** French, German, sign language interpretation, Spanish. **Health:** Audiology/speech pathology, environmental health. **History:** General. **Interdisciplinary:** Biological/physical sciences. **Liberal arts:** Arts/sciences. **Math:** General, applied. **Philosophy/religion:** Philosophy. **Physical sciences:** Chemistry, geology, physics. **Protective services:** Criminal justice. **Psychology:** General. **Public administration:** Social work. **Social sciences:** Economics, international relations, political science, sociology. **Visual/performing arts:** Art, art history/conservation, dramatic. **Other:** Applied technology.

Computing on campus. 500 workstations in dormitories, library, computer center. Dormitories wired for high-speed internet access and linked to campus network. Commuter students can connect to campus network. Online course registration, online library, wireless network available.

Student life. Freshman orientation: Available. **Housing:** Coed dorms available. $100 fully refundable deposit. **Activities:** Bands, choral groups, dance, drama, literary magazine, music ensembles, musical theater, opera, radio station, student government, student newspaper, TV station, Baptist Student Union, University Republicans, Methodist student club, Muslim students association, Young Democrats, Association for Minority Students Education Needs and Development (AMEND), Advocates for People with Disabilities.

Athletics. NCAA. **Intercollegiate:** Baseball M, basketball, cross-country, golf, soccer, swimming, tennis, track and field, volleyball W. **Intramural:** Badminton, basketball, bowling, football (tackle) M, golf, softball, swimming, table tennis M, tennis, volleyball. **Team name:** Trojans.

Student services. Adult student services, career counseling, student employment services, health services, personal counseling, placement for graduates, veterans' counselor. **Physically disabled:** Services for visually, speech, hearing impaired.

Contact. Phone: (501) 569-3127 Toll-free number: (800) 482-8892
Fax: (501) 569-8956
Tammy Harrison, Director of Admissions and Financial Aid, University of Arkansas at Little Rock, 2801 South University Avenue, Little Rock, AR 72204

University of Arkansas at Monticello

Monticello, Arkansas
www.uamont.edu **CB code: 6007**

- Public 4-year university and technical college
- Commuter campus in large town
- 2,616 degree-seeking undergraduates: 18% part-time, 60% women, 31% African American, 1% Hispanic American, 1% Native American
- 109 degree-seeking graduate students
- 50% of applicants admitted
- 34% graduate within 6 years

General. Founded in 1909. Regionally accredited. **Degrees:** 293 bachelor's, 259 associate awarded; master's offered. **ROTC:** Army. **Location:** 100 miles from Little Rock, 50 miles from Pine Bluff. **Calendar:** Semester, extensive summer session. **Full-time faculty:** 169 total; 47% have terminal degrees, 13% minority, 47% women. **Part-time faculty:** 59 total; 8% have terminal degrees, 14% minority, 61% women. **Class size:** 64% < 20, 29% 20-39, 4% 40-49, 3% 50-99, less than 1% >100. **Special facilities:** Museum of natural history, extensive research forest, planetarium, farm.

Freshman class profile. 1,783 applied, 897 admitted, 722 enrolled.

Mid 50% test scores		End year in good standing:	58%
ACT composite:	17-22	Return as sophomores:	47%
GPA 3.75 or higher:	12%	Out-of-state:	10%
GPA 3.50-3.74:	11%	Live on campus:	38%
GPA 3.0-3.49:	24%	Fraternities:	10%
GPA 2.0-2.99:	44%	Sororities:	10%

Basis for selection. Admissions based on entrance exam scores (ACT, SAT, ASSET, or COMPASS) and complete high school transcript. **Home-schooled:** Transcript of courses and grades required. ACT or SAT for placement and not for admission.

High school preparation. Recommended units include English 4, mathematics 4, social studies 3, science 3 and foreign language 2.

2008-2009 Annual costs. Tuition/fees: $4,600; $8,770 out-of-state. Room/board: $3,870. Books/supplies: $800. Personal expenses: $1,980.

2007-2008 Financial aid. Need-based: 59% of total undergraduate aid awarded as scholarships/grants, 41% as loans/jobs. **Non-need-based:** Scholarships awarded for academics, athletics, job skills, leadership, music/drama, ROTC, state residency.

Application procedures. Admission: Priority date 8/10; no deadline. No application fee. Admission notification on a rolling basis. **Financial aid:** Priority date 5/1; no closing date. FAFSA, institutional form required. Applicants notified on a rolling basis starting 4/1; must reply within 2 week(s) of notification.

Academics. Special study options: Combined bachelor's/graduate degree, cross-registration, distance learning, double major, dual enrollment of high school students, independent study, internships, liberal arts/career combination, study abroad, teacher certification program. **Credit/placement by examination:** AP, CLEP, IB, institutional tests. 9 credit hours maximum toward bachelor's degree. **Support services:** Learning center, pre-admission summer program, reduced course load, remedial instruction, study skills assistance, tutoring, writing center.

Majors. Agriculture: Agribusiness operations. **Biology:** General. **Business:** General, accounting, business admin, management information systems. **Conservation:** Forestry, wildlife. **Education:** Kindergarten/preschool, middle, music, physical. **Engineering technology:** Surveying. **Health:** Nursing (RN). **History:** General. **Interdisciplinary:** Biological/physical sciences. **Math:** General. **Parks/recreation:** Health/fitness. **Physical sciences:** Chemistry. **Protective services:** Criminal justice. **Psychology:** General. **Public administration:** Social work. **Social sciences:** General, political science. **Visual/performing arts:** Art. **Other:** Applied science.

Most popular majors. Business/marketing 33%, education 12%, health sciences 7%, parks/recreation 6%.

Computing on campus. 400 workstations in dormitories, library, computer center, student center. Dormitories wired for high-speed internet access and linked to campus network. Commuter students can connect to campus network. Online course registration, wireless network available.

Student life. Freshman orientation: Mandatory. Preregistration for classes offered. One day, beginning of semester. **Housing:** Guaranteed on-campus for all undergraduates. Single-sex dorms, special housing for disabled, apartments, wellness housing available. $60 fully refundable deposit, deadline 8/15. **Activities:** Bands, choral groups, drama, literary magazine, music ensembles, musical theater, student government, student newspaper, Baptist

Student Union, Missionary Baptist Student Fellowship, Wesley Foundation, Christians in Action, Catholic Weevils, Chi Alpha.

Athletics. NCAA. **Intercollegiate:** Baseball M, basketball, cross-country, football (tackle) M, golf, rodeo, softball W, tennis W, volleyball W. **Intramural:** Archery, badminton, baseball M, basketball, bowling, boxing M, cross-country, football (tackle) M, golf, handball, racquetball, soccer, softball, swimming, table tennis, tennis, track and field, volleyball. **Team name:** Boll Weevils.

Student services. Alcohol/substance abuse counseling, chaplain/spiritual director, career counseling, student employment services, financial aid counseling, health services, personal counseling, placement for graduates, veterans' counselor. **Physically disabled:** Services for visually, speech, hearing impaired.

Contact. E-mail: whitingm@uamont.edu
Phone: (870) 460-1026 Toll-free number: (800) 844-1826
Fax: (870) 460-1926
Mary Whiting, Director of Admissions, University of Arkansas at Monticello, Box 3600, Monticello, AR 71656

University of Arkansas at Pine Bluff

Pine Bluff, Arkansas — **CB member**
www.uapb.edu — **CB code: 6004**

- Public 4-year university
- Commuter campus in small city
- 3,352 degree-seeking undergraduates: 10% part-time, 58% women, 95% African American, 1% international
- 128 degree-seeking graduate students
- 58% of applicants admitted
- SAT or ACT (ACT writing optional) required
- 33% graduate within 6 years

General. Founded in 1873. Regionally accredited. **Degrees:** 365 bachelor's awarded; master's offered. **ROTC:** Army. **Location:** 42 miles from Little Rock. **Calendar:** Semester, limited summer session. **Full-time faculty:** 167 total; 65% have terminal degrees, 46% women. **Part-time faculty:** 79 total; 24% have terminal degrees, 49% women. **Class size:** 47% < 20, 42% 20-39, 5% 40-49, 6% 50-99. **Special facilities:** 220-acre farm, aquaculture fisheries.

Freshman class profile. 2,616 applied, 1,527 admitted, 980 enrolled.

Mid 50% test scores			
SAT critical reading:	340-440	Return as sophomores:	60%
SAT math:	340-460	Out-of-state:	42%
ACT composite:	14-18	Live on campus:	78%
		International:	2%

Basis for selection. Admission credentials for entering freshmen must include formal application, high school transcript, ACT test information and scores (SAT is accepted) and immunization record.

High school preparation. 21 units required. Required units include English 4, mathematics 3, social studies 1, history 2, science 3 (laboratory 2), foreign language 2 and academic electives 4.

2008-2009 Annual costs. Tuition/fees: $4,676; $9,236 out-of-state. Room/board: $6,100. Books/supplies: $800. Personal expenses: $800.

2007-2008 Financial aid. **Non-need-based:** Scholarships awarded for academics, alumni affiliation, art, athletics, leadership, minority status, music/drama, religious affiliation, ROTC, state residency.

Application procedures. **Admission:** Priority date 8/1; no deadline. No application fee. Admission notification on a rolling basis. **Financial aid:** Priority date 4/15; no closing date. FAFSA required. Applicants notified on a rolling basis starting 3/1.

Academics. **Special study options:** Cooperative education, cross-registration, distance learning, double major, dual enrollment of high school students, honors, internships, study abroad, teacher certification program. **Credit/placement by examination:** AP, CLEP, IB, SAT, ACT. 25 credit hours maximum toward bachelor's degree. **Support services:** Learning center, reduced course load, remedial instruction, study skills assistance, tutoring.

Majors. **Agriculture:** Agribusiness operations. **Biology:** General. **Business:** Accounting, business admin. **Communications:** Journalism. **Computer sciences:** General. **Conservation:** General, fisheries. **Education:** General, agricultural, art, business, early childhood, English, family/consumer sciences, mathematics, middle, physical, science, social science, social studies, special, trade/industrial. **Family/consumer sciences:** General, family studies. **Health:** Nursing (RN). **History:** General. **Interdisciplinary:** Gerontology. **Math:** General, applied. **Parks/recreation:** General. **Physical sciences:** Chemistry, physics. **Protective services:** Criminal justice. **Psychology:** General. **Public administration:** Social work. **Social sciences:** Political science, sociology. **Visual/performing arts:** Art. **Other:** Agricultural regulations.

Most popular majors. Biology 7%, business/marketing 16%, engineering/engineering technologies 6%, family/consumer sciences 12%, liberal arts 7%, psychology 7%, security/protective services 7%.

Computing on campus. 1,000 workstations in dormitories, library, computer center, student center. Dormitories linked to campus network. Commuter students can connect to campus network. Online library, helpline, repair service available.

Student life. **Freshman orientation:** Mandatory. Preregistration for classes offered. **Housing:** Single-sex dorms available. $100 deposit. **Activities:** Bands, choral groups, drama, music ensembles, radio station, student government, student newspaper, TV station, Baptist Student Union, political science/prelaw club, Church of God in Christ, Wesley Foundation, criminal justice club.

Athletics. NCAA. **Intercollegiate:** Baseball M, basketball, bowling W, cross-country, football (tackle) M, golf, soccer W, softball W, tennis, track and field, volleyball W. **Intramural:** Baseball M, basketball, bowling, cross-country M, football (tackle), golf, gymnastics, handball, racquetball, softball, swimming, table tennis, tennis, volleyball, weight lifting. **Team name:** Golden Lions.

Student services. Adult student services, alcohol/substance abuse counseling, chaplain/spiritual director, career counseling, services for economically disadvantaged, student employment services, financial aid counseling, health services, on-campus daycare, personal counseling, placement for graduates, veterans' counselor.

Contact. E-mail: fultone@uapb.edu
Phone: (870) 575-8493 Toll-free number: (800) 264-6585
Fax: (870) 575-4608
Mary Jones, Registrar, University of Arkansas at Pine Bluff, 1200 North University Drive, Mail Slot 4981, Pine Bluff, AR 71601-2799

University of Arkansas for Medical Sciences

Little Rock, Arkansas
www.uams.edu — **CB code: 0424**

- Public 4-year university and health science college
- Commuter campus in large city
- 900 degree-seeking undergraduates
- 1,752 graduate students

General. Founded in 1876. Regionally accredited. University has 5 colleges: medicine, nursing, pharmacy, health-related professions, graduate. **Degrees:** 333 bachelor's, 86 associate awarded; master's, doctoral, first professional offered. **Location:** One mile from downtown. **Calendar:** Semester, limited summer session. **Full-time faculty:** 1,230 total.

Basis for selection. Most incoming students must have prior college credit.

2008-2009 Annual costs. In-state students pay $190 per credit hour for the following programs: dental hygiene, diagnostic medical sonography, nuclear medicine imaging sciences and radiologic technology. In-state students pay $180 per credit hour for the following programs: cytotechnology, health information management, medical dosimetry, medical technology, ophthalmic medical technology, radiation therapy, respiratory care and surgical technology. All out-of-state students pay tuition of $436 per credit hour for programs. Emergency medical sciences/paramedic students pay according to program: 4-semester program, $905 tuition; 5-semester program, $724 tuition. Additional required fees vary by program. Books/supplies: $500. Personal expenses: $1,800.

Application procedures. **Admission:** No application fee. Admission notification on a rolling basis. Must reply by May 1 or within 2 week(s) if notified thereafter. Application closing dates vary by program. **Financial aid:** No deadline. FAFSA required. Applicants notified on a rolling basis starting 5/1; must reply within 2 week(s) of notification.

Academics. **Special study options:** Combined bachelor's/graduate degree, distance learning, double major, dual enrollment of high school students, independent study. **Credit/placement by examination:** CLEP.

Majors. Health: Clinical lab science, cytotechnology, dental hygiene, medical radiologic technology/radiation therapy, nuclear medical technology, nursing (RN).

Student life. Freshman orientation: Mandatory. **Housing:** Coed dorms, special housing for disabled, apartments available. **Activities:** Campus ministries, student government.

Student services. Alcohol/substance abuse counseling, chaplain/spiritual director, career counseling, financial aid counseling, health services, minority student services, personal counseling. **Physically disabled:** Services for visually, hearing impaired.

Contact. Phone: (501) 686-5000 Fax: (501) 686-5905
University of Arkansas for Medical Sciences, 4301 West Markham Street, Little Rock, AR 72205

University of Central Arkansas

Conway, Arkansas — **CB member**
www.uca.edu — **CB code: 6012**

- Public 4-year university
- Residential campus in small city
- 9,669 degree-seeking undergraduates: 9% part-time, 57% women, 16% African American, 2% Asian American, 2% Hispanic American, 1% Native American, 3% international
- 1,926 degree-seeking graduate students
- 58% of applicants admitted
- SAT or ACT (ACT writing optional) required
- 54% graduate within 6 years

General. Founded in 1907. Regionally accredited. **Degrees:** 1,480 bachelor's, 24 associate awarded; master's, doctoral offered. **ROTC:** Army. **Location:** 30 miles from Little Rock. **Calendar:** Semester, extensive summer session. **Full-time faculty:** 510 total. **Part-time faculty:** 186 total. **Class size:** 50% < 20, 40% 20-39, 7% 40-49, 2% 50-99, less than 1% >100. **Special facilities:** Observatory, greenhouse, honors center, visual arts center, nature preserve, 24-hour study center, fitness center, human anatomy lab, herbarium, planetarium.

Freshman class profile. 5,848 applied, 3,393 admitted, 2,111 enrolled.

Mid 50% test scores		**GPA 2.0-2.99:**	30%
ACT composite:	20-28	**Return as sophomores:**	72%
GPA 3.75 or higher:	24%	**Out-of-state:**	6%
GPA 3.50-3.74:	16%	**Live on campus:**	77%
GPA 3.0-3.49:	29%	**International:**	4%

Basis for selection. Test scores and high school GPA, along with class rank are important. **Learning Disabled:** Eligibility for services determined individually based on documentation of need. Prospective students encouraged to meet with DSS staff.

High school preparation. Recommended units include English 4, mathematics 4, social studies 1, history 2, science 3 and academic electives 10.

2008-2009 Annual costs. Tuition/fees: $6,505; $11,605 out-of-state. Room/board: $4,740. Books/supplies: $1,000. Personal expenses: $2,360.

2007-2008 Financial aid. Need-based: 39% of total undergraduate aid awarded as scholarships/grants, 61% as loans/jobs. **Non-need-based:** Scholarships awarded for academics, art, athletics, leadership, minority status, music/drama, ROTC, state residency. **Additional information:** Room and board may be paid monthly.

Application procedures. Admission: Priority date 5/1; no deadline. No application fee. Admission notification on a rolling basis. **Financial aid:** Priority date 4/15, closing date 7/1. FAFSA required. Applicants notified on a rolling basis starting 5/4.

Academics. Special study options: Accelerated study, combined bachelor's/graduate degree, cooperative education, distance learning, double major, dual enrollment of high school students, ESL, honors, independent study, internships, liberal arts/career combination, study abroad, teacher certification program. 5-year professional programs in physical therapy and occupational therapy. **Credit/placement by examination:** AP, CLEP, IB, SAT, institutional tests. 30 credit hours maximum toward associate degree, 30 toward bachelor's. **Support services:** Learning center, pre-admission summer program, remedial instruction, study skills assistance, tutoring, writing center.

Honors college/program. Special honors courses and minor in interdisciplinary studies offered. 27 ACT and 3.6 GPA minimum.

Majors. Area/ethnic studies: African-American. **Biology:** General. **Business:** General, accounting, business admin, finance, insurance, management information systems, marketing. **Communications:** Advertising, journalism, public relations. **Computer sciences:** General. **Conservation:** Environmental studies. **Education:** Business, family/consumer sciences, kindergarten/preschool, mathematics, middle, physical, science, social studies. **Family/consumer sciences:** General, food/nutrition. **Foreign languages:** French, Spanish. **Health:** Athletic training, audiology/speech pathology, clinical lab science, community health services, health services, medical radiologic technology/radiation therapy, nuclear medical technology, nursing (RN), substance abuse counseling. **History:** General. **Interdisciplinary:** Biological/physical sciences, global studies. **Liberal arts:** Arts/sciences. **Math:** General. **Parks/recreation:** Exercise sciences. **Philosophy/religion:** Philosophy, religion. **Physical sciences:** Chemistry, physics. **Psychology:** General. **Public administration:** General. **Social sciences:** Economics, geography, political science, sociology. **Visual/performing arts:** Art, cinematography, dramatic, interior design, music performance. **Other:** Leadership studies.

Most popular majors. Biology 6%, business/marketing 21%, education 12%, family/consumer sciences 6%, health sciences 22%.

Computing on campus. 608 workstations in dormitories, library, computer center, student center. Dormitories wired for high-speed internet access and linked to campus network. Commuter students can connect to campus network. Online course registration, online library, helpline, repair service, wireless network available.

Student life. Freshman orientation: Available. Preregistration for classes offered. **Housing:** Guaranteed on-campus for freshmen. Coed dorms, single-sex dorms, special housing for disabled, apartments, fraternity/sorority housing available. $100 deposit. **Activities:** Bands, campus ministries, choral groups, dance, drama, film society, international student organizations, literary magazine, music ensembles, Model UN, radio station, student government, student newspaper, symphony orchestra, TV station, Baptist student union, Methodist student union, Newman Club, Young Democrats, College Republicans, Students for Propagation of Black Culture, Association of Baptist Students, Catholic Campus Ministries, ORBIS.

Athletics. NCAA. **Intercollegiate:** Baseball M, basketball, cross-country, football (tackle) M, golf, soccer, softball W, tennis W, track and field, volleyball W. **Intramural:** Badminton, basketball, bowling, cross-country, football (non-tackle), golf, racquetball, soccer, softball, table tennis, tennis, volleyball. **Team name:** Bears.

Student services. Alcohol/substance abuse counseling, chaplain/spiritual director, career counseling, student employment services, financial aid counseling, health services, minority student services, on-campus daycare, personal counseling, placement for graduates, veterans' counselor, women's services. **Physically disabled:** Services for visually, speech, hearing impaired.

Contact. E-mail: admissions@uca.edu
Phone: (501) 450-3128 Toll-free number: (800) 243-8245
Fax: (501) 450-5228
Melissa Goff, Director of Institutional Research & Admissions, University of Central Arkansas, 201 Donaghey Avenue, Conway, AR 72035

University of the Ozarks

Clarksville, Arkansas
www.ozarks.edu — **CB code: 6111**

- Private 4-year university and liberal arts college affiliated with Presbyterian Church (USA)
- Residential campus in small town
- 636 degree-seeking undergraduates: 2% part-time, 55% women, 4% African American, 1% Asian American, 4% Hispanic American, 3% Native American, 18% international
- 96% of applicants admitted
- SAT or ACT (ACT writing optional), application essay required
- 42% graduate within 6 years

General. Founded in 1834. Regionally accredited. **Degrees:** 98 bachelor's awarded. **Location:** 100 miles from Little Rock, 65 miles from Fort Smith. **Calendar:** Semester, limited summer session. **Full-time faculty:** 48 total; 79% have terminal degrees, 10% minority, 33% women. **Part-time faculty:** 30 total; 3% have terminal degrees, 3% minority, 73% women. **Class size:** 75% < 20, 24% 20-39, less than 1% 40-49.

Freshman class profile. 569 applied, 546 admitted, 195 enrolled.

Mid 50% test scores		**GPA 2.0-2.99:**	15%
SAT critical reading:	420-530	**Rank in top quarter:**	54%
SAT math:	420-560	**Rank in top tenth:**	28%
ACT composite:	21-25	**Return as sophomores:**	74%
GPA 3.75 or higher:	31%	**Out-of-state:**	34%
GPA 3.50-3.74:	24%	**Live on campus:**	84%
GPA 3.0-3.49:	29%	**International:**	9%

Basis for selection. School achievement record and test scores most important. Interview required of those with marginal grades, recommended for all applicants.

High school preparation. College-preparatory program recommended. 18 units recommended. Recommended units include English 4, mathematics 4, social studies 1, history 2, science 3 (laboratory 2) and foreign language 2.

2008-2009 Annual costs. Tuition/fees: $17,330. Room/board: $5,725. Books/supplies: $800. Personal expenses: $2,795.

2008-2009 Financial aid. Need-based: 155 full-time freshmen applied for aid; 143 were judged to have need; 143 of these received aid. Average need met was 87%. Average scholarship/grant was $15,183; average loan $6,476. 66% of total undergraduate aid awarded as scholarships/grants, 34% as loans/jobs. **Non-need-based:** Awarded to 204 full-time undergraduates, including 44 freshmen. Scholarships awarded for academics, alumni affiliation, art, leadership, minority status, music/drama, religious affiliation, state residency. **Additional information:** Walton International Scholarship Program provides full scholarships to selected Central American and Mexican residents.

Application procedures. Admission: Priority date 4/1; no deadline. $30 fee, may be waived for applicants with need, free for online applicants. Admission notification on a rolling basis. **Financial aid:** Priority date 2/15; no closing date. FAFSA required. Applicants notified on a rolling basis starting 3/1; must reply within 2 week(s) of notification.

Academics. Special study options: Cooperative education, double major, dual enrollment of high school students, independent study, internships, liberal arts/career combination, study abroad, teacher certification program. **Credit/placement by examination:** AP, CLEP, SAT, ACT, institutional tests. 30 credit hours maximum toward bachelor's degree. **Support services:** Learning center, remedial instruction, study skills assistance, tutoring.

Majors. Biology: General. **Business:** Accounting, business admin, marketing. **Communications:** Broadcast journalism, media studies. **Conservation:** Environmental studies. **Education:** Biology, business, early childhood, elementary, middle, physical, science, special. **Health:** Predental, premedicine, prepharmacy, preveterinary. **History:** General. **Legal studies:** Prelaw. **Math:** General. **Parks/recreation:** Health/fitness. **Philosophy/religion:** Philosophy, religion. **Physical sciences:** Chemistry, physics. **Psychology:** General. **Public administration:** General. **Social sciences:** General, political science, sociology. **Visual/performing arts:** General, art, dramatic.

Most popular majors. Biology 8%, business/marketing 37%, education 9%, liberal arts 10%, social sciences 11%, visual/performing arts 8%.

Computing on campus. 150 workstations in dormitories, library, computer center, student center. Dormitories wired for high-speed internet access and linked to campus network. Commuter students can connect to campus network. Online course registration, online library, helpline, wireless network available.

Student life. Freshman orientation: Mandatory. Preregistration for classes offered. **Housing:** Guaranteed on-campus for freshmen. Coed dorms, single-sex dorms, apartments available. $100 partly refundable deposit, deadline 8/15. **Activities:** Campus ministries, choral groups, drama, film society, international student organizations, literary magazine, radio station, student government, TV station, Ozarks Area Mission, Alpha & Omega, other religious, ethnic, and social service organizations.

Athletics. NCAA. **Intercollegiate:** Baseball M, basketball, cheerleading, cross-country, soccer, softball W, tennis. **Intramural:** Badminton, basketball, bowling, football (non-tackle), racquetball, soccer, softball, tennis, volleyball. **Team name:** Eagles.

Student services. Chaplain/spiritual director, career counseling, student employment services, financial aid counseling, health services, personal counseling, placement for graduates, veterans' counselor. **Learning disabled:** Comprehensive services available.

Contact. E-mail: admiss@ozarks.edu
Phone: (479) 979-1227 Toll-free number: (800) 264-8636
Fax: (479) 979-1417
Kim Myrick, Dean of Enrollment, University of the Ozarks, 415 North College Avenue, Clarksville, AR 72830-2880

Williams Baptist College

Walnut Ridge, Arkansas
www.wbcoll.edu **CB code: 6658**

- Private 4-year liberal arts college affiliated with Southern Baptist Convention
- Residential campus in small town
- 486 degree-seeking undergraduates: 3% part-time, 53% women, 2% African American, 2% Hispanic American, 1% international
- 62% of applicants admitted
- SAT or ACT (ACT writing optional) required
- 39% graduate within 6 years

General. Founded in 1941. Regionally accredited. **Degrees:** 115 bachelor's, 4 associate awarded. **ROTC:** Army. **Location:** 30 miles from Jonesboro, 100 miles from Memphis. **Calendar:** Semester, limited summer session. **Full-time faculty:** 28 total; 61% have terminal degrees, 39% women. **Part-time faculty:** 16 total; 6% have terminal degrees, 6% minority, 75% women. **Class size:** 52% < 20, 47% 20-39, less than 1% 40-49.

Freshman class profile. 515 applied, 319 admitted, 149 enrolled.

Out-of-state:	10%	**International:**	2%
Live on campus:	85%		

Basis for selection. Students must have a 19 composite ACT score and a 2.5 cumulative high school GPA in order to be admitted unconditionally.

High school preparation. Recommended units include English 4, mathematics 4, social studies 3, science 3 (laboratory 3) and foreign language 2.

2008-2009 Annual costs. Tuition/fees: $10,950. Room/board: $5,000. Books/supplies: $980. Personal expenses: $1,250.

2007-2008 Financial aid. Need-based: 122 full-time freshmen applied for aid; 94 were judged to have need; 94 of these received aid. Average scholarship/grant was $3,347; average loan $2,494. 75% of total undergraduate aid awarded as scholarships/grants, 25% as loans/jobs. **Non-need-based:** Awarded to 439 full-time undergraduates, including 143 freshmen. Scholarships awarded for academics, art, athletics, leadership, minority status, music/drama, religious affiliation, state residency. **Additional information:** Art scholarship applicants must submit portfolio.

Application procedures. Admission: No deadline. $20 fee. Admission notification on a rolling basis. **Financial aid:** Priority date 5/1; no closing date. FAFSA required. Applicants notified on a rolling basis starting 4/1; must reply within 2 week(s) of notification.

Academics. Special study options: Double major, dual enrollment of high school students, independent study, internships, study abroad. **Credit/placement by examination:** AP, CLEP, IB. 30 credit hours maximum toward bachelor's degree. **Support services:** Learning center, reduced course load, remedial instruction, study skills assistance, tutoring.

Majors. Biology: General. **Business:** Business admin, finance. **Computer sciences:** General. **Education:** General, art, early childhood, elementary, English, music, physical, secondary, social studies. **History:** General. **Psychology:** General. **Theology:** Bible, missionary, religious ed, sacred music, theology, youth ministry. **Visual/performing arts:** Studio arts.

Most popular majors. Biology 7%, business/marketing 8%, education 34%, psychology 23%, theological studies 20%.

Computing on campus. 70 workstations in library, computer center, student center. Dormitories wired for high-speed internet access and linked to campus network. Commuter students can connect to campus network. Online library, wireless network available.

Student life. Freshman orientation: Mandatory, $75 fee. 2-day program held at beginning of fall semester. **Policies:** Please see on-line Student Handbook. Religious observance required. **Housing:** Guaranteed on-campus for all undergraduates. Single-sex dorms, apartments available. $75 fully refundable deposit, deadline 5/1. All full-time students under 21 required to live in college housing, unless commuting. **Activities:** Campus ministries, choral groups, drama, international student organizations, music ensembles, student government, Fellowship of Christian Athletes, College Republicans, student activities board, Student Ambassadors.

Athletics. NAIA. **Intercollegiate:** Baseball M, basketball, cheerleading, soccer M, softball W, volleyball W. **Intramural:** Baseball M, basketball, football (non-tackle), softball, volleyball. **Team name:** Eagles.

Student services. Alcohol/substance abuse counseling, chaplain/spiritual director, career counseling, financial aid counseling, health services, personal counseling, veterans' counselor.

Contact. E-mail: admissions@wbcoll.edu
Phone: (870) 759-4121 Toll-free number: (800) 722-4434
Fax: (870) 886-3924
Angela Flippo, Vice President for Enrollment, Williams Baptist College, PO Box 3665, Walnut Ridge, AR 72476

California

Academy of Art University

San Francisco, California
www.academyart.edu **CB code: 1981**

- For-profit 4-year university and visual arts college
- Commuter campus in very large city
- 9,400 degree-seeking undergraduates: 36% part-time, 54% women, 6% African American, 11% Asian American, 9% Hispanic American, 1% Native American, 14% international
- 3,466 degree-seeking graduate students
- 35% graduate within 6 years; 7% enter graduate study

General. Founded in 1929. Accredited by ACICS. Equal emphasis on both fine and applied arts. **Degrees:** 663 bachelor's, 70 associate awarded; master's offered. **Calendar:** Semester, extensive summer session. **Full-time faculty:** 184 total; 23% have terminal degrees, 17% minority, 44% women. **Part-time faculty:** 758 total. **Class size:** 82% < 20, 18% 20-39, less than 1% 50-99, less than 1% >100. **Special facilities:** 3 nonprofit galleries, photography darkrooms, Bosch Telecen, green screen stage, interior design resource room, foundry, 50,000-square-foot sculpture center, Final Cut Pro, Media and Avid Express editing stations.

Freshman class profile. 2,873 applied, 2,873 admitted, 2,289 enrolled.

End year in good standing:	71%	**Live on campus:**	31%
Return as sophomores:	62%	**International:**	11%
Out-of-state:	53%		

Basis for selection. Open admission. Continuing education program offered. Interview recommended, and can be in person or over the phone. **Learning Disabled:** Reasonable accomodations made for students with disabilities.

High school preparation. Art and design courses recommended.

2009-2010 Annual costs. Tuition/fees: $22,490. Room/board: $13,400. Books/supplies: $1,566. Personal expenses: $2,214.

2007-2008 Financial aid. Need-based: 512 full-time freshmen applied for aid; 446 were judged to have need; 443 of these received aid. Average need met was 25%. Average scholarship/grant was $4,275; average loan $2,839. 26% of total undergraduate aid awarded as scholarships/grants, 74% as loans/jobs. **Non-need-based:** Awarded to 123 full-time undergraduates, including 43 freshmen. Scholarships awarded for academics, art. **Additional information:** Numerous summer grant programs available.

Application procedures. Admission: No deadline. $100 fee. Admission notification on a rolling basis. Accepted applicants may preregister in mid March. **Financial aid:** Priority date 7/10; no closing date. FAFSA, institutional form required. Applicants notified on a rolling basis.

Academics. Special study options: Combined bachelor's/graduate degree, distance learning, ESL, honors, independent study, internships, student-designed major, teacher certification program. **Credit/placement by examination:** AP, CLEP, IB. Interview, essay recommended for placement. Portfolio recommended for bachelor of arts applicants. **Support services:** Learning center, pre-admission summer program, reduced course load, remedial instruction, study skills assistance, tutoring, writing center.

Majors. Communications: Advertising, media studies. **Communications technology:** Animation/special effects, desktop publishing. **Computer sciences:** Web page design. **Visual/performing arts:** Cinematography, commercial photography, commercial/advertising art, design, drawing, fashion design, fiber arts, graphic design, illustration, industrial design, interior design, metal/jewelry, multimedia, painting, photography, printmaking, sculpture, studio arts.

Most popular majors. Communication technologies 23%, computer/information sciences 6%, visual/performing arts 71%.

Computing on campus. 800 workstations in dormitories, library, computer center. Dormitories wired for high-speed internet access. Commuter students can connect to campus network. Online course registration, online library, helpline, student web hosting, wireless network available.

Student life. Freshman orientation: Mandatory. Preregistration for classes offered. 5-day session week before start of classes. **Housing:** Guaranteed on-campus for freshmen. Coed dorms, single-sex dorms, special housing for disabled, wellness housing available. $500 deposit. **Activities:** Dance, drama, film society, international student organizations, student government, student newspaper, Chinese society, Circle of Nations.

Athletics. Intercollegiate: Baseball M, basketball, cross-country, golf M, soccer, softball W, tennis W, track and field, volleyball W. **Intramural:** Basketball, football (non-tackle), soccer, softball, table tennis, tennis, volleyball. **Team name:** Urban Knights.

Student services. Alcohol/substance abuse counseling, career counseling, student employment services, financial aid counseling, personal counseling. **Physically disabled:** Services for visually, hearing impaired.

Contact. E-mail: info@academyart.edu
Phone: (415) 274-2200 Toll-free number: (800) 544-2787
Fax: (415) 618-6287
Admissions, Academy of Art University, 79 New Montgomery Street, San Francisco, CA 94105-3410

Alliant International University

San Diego, California **CB member**
www.alliant.edu **CB code: 4039**

- Private two-year upper-division university
- Commuter campus in very large city
- 93% of applicants admitted

General. Founded in 1952. Regionally accredited. Focuses on preparing students for professional careers in applied social sciences. Students may enter as transfers after 2 years of undergraduate study at San Diego, and as freshmen or transfers at Mexico City. **Degrees:** 68 bachelor's awarded; master's, doctoral offered. **Articulation:** Agreements with Cuyamaca College, Glendale College, Grossmont College, Imperial Valley College, MiraCosta College, Mt. San Antonio College, Mt. San Jacinto College, Palomar College, Pasadena College, Riverside Community College, Saddleback College, San Diego City College, San Diego Mesa College, San Diego Miramar College, Santa Monica College, Southwestern College, Ventura College. **Location:** 16 miles from downtown. **Calendar:** Semester, limited summer session. **Full-time faculty:** 161 total; 100% have terminal degrees, 17% minority, 43% women. **Part-time faculty:** 405 total; 93% have terminal degrees, 12% minority. **Class size:** 99% < 20, less than 1% 20-39.

Student profile. 192 degree-seeking undergraduates, 4,185 graduate students. 130 applied as first time-transfer students, 121 admitted, 62 enrolled. 45% transferred from two-year, 55% transferred from four-year institutions.

Women:	64%	**International:**	19%
African American:	4%	**Part-time:**	36%
Asian American:	6%	**Out-of-state:**	14%
Hispanic American:	21%	**Live on campus:**	35%
Native American:	1%	**25 or older:**	54%

Basis for selection. High school transcript, college transcript required. Transfer accepted as sophomores, juniors, seniors.

2008-2009 Annual costs. Tuition/fees: $15,210. Room/board: $8,540. Books/supplies: $1,566. Personal expenses: $2,214.

Financial aid. Need-based: 29% of total undergraduate aid awarded as scholarships/grants, 71% as loans/jobs. **Non-need-based:** Scholarships awarded for academics, alumni affiliation, athletics, leadership.

Application procedures. Admission: Priority date 3/2. $45 fee, may be waived for applicants with need. **Financial aid:** FAFSA required.

Academics. Special study options: Combined bachelor's/graduate degree, ESL, honors, independent study, internships, liberal arts/career combination, study abroad. **Credit/placement by examination:** AP, CLEP, IB, institutional tests. 27 credit hours maximum toward bachelor's degree.

Majors. Area/ethnic studies: Latin American. **Business:** Business admin, hospitality/recreation, international, management information systems, tourism promotion. **Communications:** Journalism. **Conservation:** Environmental studies. **Education:** ESL. **Protective services:** Law enforcement admin. **Psychology:** General. **Social sciences:** International relations.

Most popular majors. Business/marketing 52%, liberal arts 13%, psychology 17%, social sciences 15%.

Computing on campus. 100 workstations in library, computer center. Dormitories wired for high-speed internet access and linked to campus network. Commuter students can connect to campus network. Online library, student web hosting available.

Student life. Housing: Guaranteed on-campus for all undergraduates. Coed dorms available. $265 deposit. All dormitories made up of 2-bedroom suites with central living room. **Activities:** International student organizations, Model UN, student government, student newspaper, Indian student association, Latino student organization, Alliant Turk Society.

Athletics. Intramural: Basketball, bowling, soccer, softball, tennis, volleyball.

Student services. Adult student services, alcohol/substance abuse counseling, career counseling, student employment services, financial aid counseling, health services, personal counseling, placement for graduates, veterans' counselor, women's services. **Physically disabled:** Services for visually, speech, hearing impaired.

Contact. E-mail: admissions3@alliant.edu
Phone: (866) 825-5426 Toll-free number: (866) 825-5426
Fax: (858) 635-4555
Louis Cruz, Director of Enrollment Management, Alliant International University, 10455 Pomerado Road, San Diego, CA 92131-1799

American Jewish University
Los Angeles, California
www.ajula.edu **CB code: 4876**

- Private 4-year university and liberal arts college affiliated with Jewish faith
- Residential campus in very large city
- 100 degree-seeking undergraduates
- 100 graduate students
- 65% of applicants admitted
- SAT or ACT (ACT writing recommended), application essay required

General. Founded in 1947. Regionally accredited. **Degrees:** 30 bachelor's awarded; master's, first professional offered. **Location:** 5 miles from Los Angeles. **Calendar:** Semester. **Full-time faculty:** 14 total; 100% have terminal degrees, 36% women. **Part-time faculty:** 44 total; 43% women. **Class size:** 93% < 20, 7% 20-39. **Special facilities:** Sigi Ziering institute, center for Israel studies, Platt & Borstein contemporary art galleries, Whizin center for continuing education, Jewish community documentation center, educational resources center.

Freshman class profile. 125 applied, 81 admitted, 29 enrolled.

Mid 50% test scores		SAT math:	480-610
SAT critical reading:	470-580	SAT writing:	460-600

Basis for selection. Essay, volunteerism/engagement in community, leadership roles and letters of recommendation are most important, followed by GPA and then standardized test scores. Interview recommended. **Homeschooled:** Transcript of courses and grades, state high school equivalency certificate, letter of recommendation (nonparent) required.

High school preparation. 18 units recommended. Recommended units include English 4, mathematics 3, social studies 2, history 2, science 3 (laboratory 2) and foreign language 2.

2008-2009 Annual costs. Tuition/fees: $22,352. Room/board: $11,416. Books/supplies: $1,566. Personal expenses: $2,214.

2008-2009 Financial aid. Non-need-based: Scholarships awarded for academics, leadership.

Application procedures. Admission: Priority date 1/31; deadline 7/31 (receipt date). $35 fee, may be waived for applicants with need. Admission notification on a rolling basis beginning on or about 11/1. Must reply by May 1 or within 4 week(s) if notified thereafter. **Financial aid:** Priority date 3/2; no closing date. FAFSA, institutional form required. Applicants notified on a rolling basis starting 3/15; must reply within 3 week(s) of notification.

Academics. In addition to majors and general education requirements, students take core curriculum of Jewish and Western Civilization classes. **Special study options:** Accelerated study, combined bachelor's/graduate degree, cross-registration, double major, honors, independent study, internships, student-designed major, study abroad. **Credit/placement by examination:** AP, CLEP, IB, institutional tests. **Support services:** Reduced course load, study skills assistance, tutoring.

Majors. Area/ethnic studies: Near/Middle Eastern. **Biology:** General, biomedical sciences. **Business:** General. **Communications:** General, broadcast journalism, digital media, journalism, media studies. **Foreign languages:** Comparative lit. **Health:** Ethics. **Interdisciplinary:** Biological/physical sciences, natural sciences, peace/conflict. **Legal studies:** Prelaw. **Liberal arts:** Arts/sciences. **Philosophy/religion:** Judaic. **Social sciences:** Political science. **Visual/performing arts:** Dramatic, film/cinema. **Other:** Jewish studies.

Computing on campus. 32 workstations in dormitories, library, computer center. Dormitories wired for high-speed internet access and linked to campus network. Commuter students can connect to campus network. Wireless network available.

Student life. Freshman orientation: Mandatory. Preregistration for classes offered. Held 1 week prior to start of class; usually lasts 3 days. **Policies:** Kosher meals on campus. Students required to live on campus unless 21 or living with parents. **Housing:** Guaranteed on-campus for all undergraduates. Coed dorms, apartments available. $100 nonrefundable deposit, deadline 8/15. **Activities:** Choral groups, drama, international student organizations, literary magazine, Model UN, musical theater, student government, student newspaper, Hillel: The Foundation for Jewish Life on Campus, Israel Action, political science club, Repair the World service organization.

Athletics. Team name: Lions.

Student services. Chaplain/spiritual director, career counseling, student employment services, financial aid counseling, health services, personal counseling, placement for graduates. **Physically disabled:** Services for hearing impaired.

Contact. E-mail: admissions@ajula.edu
Phone: (310) 476-9777 ext. 247 Toll-free number: (877) 462-2585
Fax: (310) 471-3657
Matt Spooner, Admissions Director, American Jewish University, 15600 Mulholland Drive, Los Angeles, CA 90077

Antioch University Los Angeles
Culver City, California
www.antiochla.edu **CB code: 1862**

- Private two-year upper-division branch campus and liberal arts college
- Commuter campus in very large city
- Application essay, interview required

General. Founded in 1972. Regionally accredited. **Degrees:** 47 bachelor's awarded; master's offered. **Articulation:** Agreements with UCLA Extension, Santa Monica College, West Los Angeles College, Compton City College. **Location:** 15 miles from Los Angeles. **Calendar:** Quarter, extensive summer session. **Full-time faculty:** 20 total. **Part-time faculty:** 5 total.

Student profile. 110 degree-seeking undergraduates.

Basis for selection. High school transcript, college transcript, application essay, interview required. Admission decision of full or provisional acceptance made by program chair. Transfer accepted as sophomores, juniors, seniors.

2008-2009 Annual costs. Tuition/fees: $16,150. Cost varies with program. Books/supplies: $1,500.

Application procedures. Admission: Deadline 8/1. $60 fee, may be waived for applicants with need. Must reply by 8/15. **Financial aid:** FAFSA, institutional form required.

Academics. Prior experiential learning credits. **Special study options:** Accelerated study, combined bachelor's/graduate degree, cooperative education, cross-registration, double major, independent study, internships, liberal arts/career combination, student-designed major, study abroad, teacher certification program, weekend college. **Credit/placement by examination:** AP, CLEP. 40 credit hours maximum toward bachelor's degree. DANTES examination scores accepted.

Majors. Liberal arts: Arts/sciences.

Computing on campus. 12 workstations in computer center. Commuter students can connect to campus network.

Student life. Activities: Student government.

Athletics. Team name: Radicals.

Student services. Adult student services, career counseling, student employment services, financial aid counseling, personal counseling, veterans' counselor. **Physically disabled:** Services for visually, speech, hearing impaired.

Contact. E-mail: admissions@antiochla.edu
Phone: (800) 726-8462 Toll-free number: (800) 726-8462
Fax: (310) 822-4824
Michael Nee, Director of Admissions, Antioch University Los Angeles, 400 Corporate Pointe, Culver City, CA 90230-7615

Antioch University Santa Barbara

Santa Barbara, California
www.antiochsb.edu **CB code: 3071**

- Private two-year upper-division university and liberal arts college
- Commuter campus in small city
- Application essay, interview required

General. Founded in 1852. Regionally accredited. **Degrees:** 29 bachelor's awarded; master's, doctoral offered. **Articulation:** Agreements with Santa Barbara City College, University of California: Santa Barbara, Ventura Community College, Cuesta Community College, Allen Hancock Community College. **Location:** Downtown. **Calendar:** Quarter, extensive summer session. **Full-time faculty:** 17 total; 65% women. **Part-time faculty:** 53 total; 57% women.

Student profile. 105 degree-seeking undergraduates, 261 degree-seeking graduate students.

Women:	75%	**Native American:**	2%
African American:	4%	**International:**	1%
Asian American:	1%	**Part-time:**	65%
Hispanic American:	35%	**25 or older:**	90%

Basis for selection. Open admission. High school transcript, college transcript, application essay, interview required. Transfer accepted as juniors, seniors.

2008-2009 Annual costs. Tuition/fees: $15,401. Books/supplies: $1,600.

Financial aid. Need-based: 22% of total undergraduate aid awarded as scholarships/grants, 78% as loans/jobs.

Application procedures. Admission: Rolling admission. $60 fee. **Financial aid:** Priority date 4/1, no deadline. FAFSA, institutional form required.

Academics. Special study options: Cross-registration, double major, independent study, internships, liberal arts/career combination, student-designed major, study abroad, teacher certification program, weekend college. **Credit/placement by examination:** CLEP, IB. **Support services:** Remedial instruction.

Majors. Liberal arts: Arts/sciences.

Computing on campus. 10 workstations in computer center. Online library, helpline available.

Student services. Adult student services, career counseling, financial aid counseling, personal counseling, veterans' counselor.

Contact. E-mail: admissions@antiochsb.edu
Phone: (805) 962-8179 Toll-free number: (866) 5-A-NTIOCH
Fax: (805) 962-4786
Antioch University Santa Barbara, 801 Garden Street, Suite 101, Santa Barbara, CA 93101-1581

Art Center College of Design

Pasadena, California **CB member**
www.artcenter.edu **CB code: 4009**

- Private 4-year visual arts college
- Commuter campus in small city
- 1,504 degree-seeking undergraduates
- 60% of applicants admitted
- SAT or ACT, application essay required

General. Founded in 1930. Regionally accredited. **Degrees:** 534 bachelor's awarded; master's offered. **Location:** 15 miles from Los Angeles. **Calendar:** Trimester, extensive summer session. **Full-time faculty:** 65 total. **Part-time faculty:** 340 total. **Class size:** 87% < 20, 12% 20-39, less than 1% 40-49, less than 1% 50-99. **Special facilities:** 3 galleries; state of the art 3-D modelling and industrial design facilities.

Freshman class profile. 696 applied, 415 admitted, 278 enrolled.

Basis for selection. Strength of specific portfolio for one major, academic record, standardized test scores. SAT/ACT required only for students applying while still in high school. Interviews recommended for local applicants.

High school preparation. Art classes recommended.

2008-2009 Annual costs. Tuition/fees: $30,284. Books/supplies: $5,350. Personal expenses: $3,556.

2007-2008 Financial aid. All financial aid based on need. **Additional information:** Students may apply for scholarships after they enroll while progressing through the program.

Application procedures. Admission: Priority date 3/1; no deadline. $50 fee, may be waived for applicants with need. Admission notification on a rolling basis beginning on or about 1/1. Application 4 to 6 months before fall term recommended. **Financial aid:** Priority date 3/1; no closing date. FAFSA required. Applicants notified on a rolling basis starting 5/15; must reply within 4 week(s) of notification.

Academics. Special study options: Cross-registration, independent study, internships, study abroad. **Credit/placement by examination:** AP, CLEP, IB, institutional tests. **Support services:** Tutoring, writing center.

Majors. Architecture: Environmental design. **Communications:** Advertising. **Communications technology:** Animation/special effects, graphics. **Visual/performing arts:** Cinematography, commercial photography, commercial/advertising art, graphic design, illustration, industrial design, interior design, painting, photography, sculpture, studio arts.

Computing on campus. 250 workstations in library, computer center. Online library, wireless network available.

Student life. Freshman orientation: Mandatory. 3-day program including introduction to a mentor and testing. **Activities:** International student organizations, literary magazine, student government, Chroma Contraste, Eco Council, Women in Design, Out Network.

Student services. Alcohol/substance abuse counseling, career counseling, student employment services, financial aid counseling, personal counseling, placement for graduates. **Physically disabled:** Services for hearing impaired.

Contact. E-mail: admissions@artcenter.edu
Phone: (626) 396-2373 Fax: (626) 795-0578
Kit Baron, Vice President, Admissions, Art Center College of Design, 1700 Lida Street, Pasadena, CA 91103

Art Institute of California: Hollywood

Los Angeles, California
www.artinstitutes.edu/hollywood **CB code: 3463**

- For-profit 4-year visual arts, technical and career college
- Commuter campus in very large city
- 918 degree-seeking undergraduates: 46% part-time, 72% women
- Application essay, interview required

General. Accredited by ACICS. **Degrees:** 65 bachelor's, 30 associate awarded. **Location:** Downtown. **Calendar:** Quarter, extensive summer session. **Full-time faculty:** 17 total; 24% have terminal degrees, 53% minority, 65% women. **Part-time faculty:** 64 total; 34% have terminal degrees, 6% minority, 58% women. **Special facilities:** Sewing and construction rooms, interior design resource room.

Freshman class profile. 185 enrolled.

Basis for selection. Open admission. SAT or ACT recommended.

2008-2009 Annual costs. Tuition/fees: $21,835. Cost for 7-quarter continuous enrollment associate degree program $52,118; cost for 12-quarter continuous enrollment bachelor's degree program $88,938. Fees vary by program. Room only: $9,285. Books/supplies: $1,692.

2007-2008 Financial aid. Need-based: 119 full-time freshmen applied for aid; 119 were judged to have need; 119 of these received aid. Average scholarship/grant was $2,376; average loan $5,605. 40% of total undergraduate aid awarded as scholarships/grants, 60% as loans/jobs.

Application procedures. Admission: No deadline. $50 fee. Admission notification on a rolling basis.

Academics. Special study options: Distance learning, honors, independent study, internships, study abroad, weekend college. **Credit/placement by examination:** AP, CLEP, SAT, ACT, institutional tests. **Support services:** Reduced course load, study skills assistance, tutoring.

Majors. Business: Fashion. **Communications technology:** Animation/special effects. **Computer sciences:** Web page design. **Visual/performing arts:** Fashion design, graphic design, industrial design, interior design.

Most popular majors. Business/marketing 34%, visual/performing arts 66%.

Computing on campus. 162 workstations in library, computer center. Online library, helpline, wireless network available.

Student life. Freshman orientation: Mandatory. Preregistration for classes offered. **Housing:** $250 fully refundable deposit, deadline 10/2. **Activities:** Literary magazine, student newspaper.

Student services. Career counseling, student employment services, financial aid counseling, health services, personal counseling, placement for graduates. **Physically disabled:** Services for hearing impaired.

Contact. E-mail: mromero@aii.edu
Phone: (213) 251-3636 Toll-free number: (877) 468-6232
Fax: (213) 385-3545
Melissa Huen, Senior Director of Admissions, Art Institute of California: Hollywood, 3440 Wilshire Boulevard, 10th Floor, Los Angeles, CA 90010

Art Institute of California: Inland Empire

San Bernardino, California
www.artinstitutes.edu

- For-profit 4-year culinary school and visual arts college
- Large city
- 674 degree-seeking undergraduates

General. Regionally accredited; also accredited by ACCSCT. **Calendar:** Quarter. **Full-time faculty:** 22 total. **Part-time faculty:** 53 total.

Freshman class profile. 198 enrolled.

Academics. Credit/placement by examination: CLEP.

Majors. Communications technology: Animation/special effects. **Personal/culinary services:** Restaurant/catering. **Visual/performing arts:** Fashion design, graphic design, interior design, multimedia. **Other:** Fashion and retail management.

Contact. Toll-free number: (800) 353-0812
Art Institute of California: Inland Empire, 630 East Brier Drive, San Bernardino, CA 92408-2800

Art Institute of California: Orange County

Santa Ana, California
www.artinstitutes.edu/orangecounty **CB code: 3831**

- For-profit 3-year culinary school and visual arts college
- Commuter campus in very large city
- 1,694 degree-seeking undergraduates: 23% part-time, 42% women
- 1,694 graduate students
- Application essay, interview required
- 56% graduate within 6 years

General. Accredited by ACICS. **Degrees:** 244 bachelor's, 78 associate awarded. **Location:** 40 miles from Los Angeles, 90 miles from San Diego. **Calendar:** Quarter, extensive summer session. **Full-time faculty:** 93 total. **Part-time faculty:** 21 total. **Special facilities:** 4 professional skills kitchens, 11 computer labs, interior design resource library, interior design studio, industrial design workshop, student dining lab, fashion lab.

Freshman class profile. 1,043 applied, 374 admitted, 358 enrolled.

Basis for selection. Open admission, but selective for some programs. High school record and general appropriateness of educational background to specific program applied for most important. Portfolio, interview also important. Standardized test scores considered if submitted.

2008-2009 Annual costs. Tuition/fees: $23,384. Typical full-time load 16 credit hours per quarter. Culinary lab fee $315 per quarter, online fee $100 per class per quarter. Room only: $3,025. Books/supplies: $1,100. Personal expenses: $2,280.

Financial aid. Non-need-based: Scholarships awarded for academics, art, minority status.

Application procedures. Admission: No deadline. $50 fee. Admission notification on a rolling basis. **Financial aid:** No deadline. FAFSA required. Applicants notified on a rolling basis; must reply within 2 week(s) of notification.

Academics. Special study options: Cooperative education, distance learning, internships. Online courses. **Credit/placement by examination:** CLEP, IB, institutional tests. 3 credit hours maximum toward associate degree, 3 toward bachelor's. **Support services:** Learning center, pre-admission summer program, reduced course load, study skills assistance, tutoring.

Majors. BACHELOR'S. Business: Apparel. **Communications:** Digital media. **Communications technology:** Animation/special effects. **Computer sciences:** Computer graphics, web page design, webmaster. **Personal/culinary services:** Culinary arts, restaurant/catering. **Visual/performing arts:** Commercial/advertising art, fashion design, graphic design, industrial design, interior design. **ASSOCIATE. Communications:** Digital media. **Computer sciences:** Computer graphics, web page design, webmaster. **Personal/culinary services:** Chef training, culinary arts, restaurant/catering. **Visual/performing arts:** Commercial/advertising art, graphic design, interior design.

Computing on campus. 312 workstations in library, computer center, student center. Online course registration, online library, helpline, repair service, wireless network available.

Student life. Freshman orientation: Mandatory. **Housing:** Special housing for disabled, apartments available. School-sponsored housing available. **Activities:** Film society, student newspaper.

Student services. Career counseling, student employment services, financial aid counseling, personal counseling, placement for graduates, veterans' counselor. **Physically disabled:** Services for visually, speech, hearing impaired.

Contact. E-mail: aicaocadm@aii.edu
Phone: (888) 549-3055 Toll-free number: (888) 549-3055
Fax: (714) 556-1923
Tim Hansen, Sr. Director of Admissions, Art Institute of California: Orange County, 3601 West Sunflower Avenue, Santa Ana, CA 92704-7931

Art Institute of California: Sacramento

Sacramento, California
www.artinstitutes.edu/sacramento

- For-profit 3-year culinary school and visual arts college
- Large city

General. Regionally accredited; also accredited by ACICS. **Calendar:** Quarter.

Academics. Credit/placement by examination: CLEP.

Majors. BACHELOR'S. Communications technology: Animation/special effects. **Personal/culinary services:** Restaurant/catering. **Visual/performing arts:** Cinematography, graphic design, interior design, multimedia. **ASSOCIATE. Personal/culinary services:** General. **Visual/performing arts:** Graphic design, multimedia.

Contact. Phone: (800) 477-1957
Art Institute of California: Sacramento, 2850 Gateway Oaks Drive, Suite 100, Sacramento, CA 95833

Art Institute of California: San Diego

San Diego, California
www.artinstitutes.edu/sandiego **CB code: 3036**

- For-profit 3-year visual arts college
- Residential campus in very large city
- 1,974 degree-seeking undergraduates
- Application essay, interview required

General. Accredited by ACCSCT. **Degrees:** 302 bachelor's, 102 associate awarded. **Calendar:** Quarter. **Full-time faculty:** 58 total. **Part-time faculty:** 75 total. **Special facilities:** Dining lab run by culinary students.

Basis for selection. High school record and general appropriateness of educational background to specific program applied for most important. Portfolio, interview, standardized test scores also important. **Learning Disabled:** Students requiring assistance should notify Assistant Director of Admissions.

2008-2009 Annual costs. Tuition/fees: $22,272.

Application procedures. Admission: No deadline. $50 fee. Admission notification on a rolling basis. **Financial aid:** No deadline. FAFSA required.

Academics. Special study options: Accelerated study, distance learning, internships. **Credit/placement by examination:** AP, CLEP. **Support services:** Study skills assistance, tutoring.

Majors. BACHELOR'S. Communications: Advertising. **Computer sciences:** Computer graphics, web page design, webmaster. **Personal/culinary services:** Restaurant/catering. **Visual/performing arts:** Commercial/advertising art, fashion design, graphic design, interior design, multimedia. **Other:** Fashion marketing and management. **ASSOCIATE. Personal/culinary services:** Chef training, restaurant/catering. **Visual/performing arts:** Commercial/advertising art, design, graphic design.

Computing on campus. 300 workstations in library, computer center. Online library, wireless network available.

Student life. Freshman orientation: Mandatory. Preregistration for classes offered. **Housing:** Single-sex dorms, apartments available. **Activities:** Student government, student newspaper.

Student services. Alcohol/substance abuse counseling, career counseling, services for economically disadvantaged, student employment services, financial aid counseling, personal counseling. **Physically disabled:** Services for visually, speech, hearing impaired. **Learning disabled:** Comprehensive services available.

Contact. E-mail: aicaadmin@aii.edu
Phone: (866) 275-2422 Toll-free number: (866) 275-2422
Melissa Garcia, Director of Admissions, Art Institute of California: San Diego, 7650 Mission Valley Road, San Diego, CA 92108-4423

Art Institute of California: San Francisco

San Francisco, California
www.artinstitutes.edu/sanfrancisco **CB code: 4421**

- For-profit 4-year visual arts college
- Commuter campus in very large city
- 1,539 degree-seeking undergraduates
- Application essay required

General. Founded in 1939. Accredited by ACICS. **Degrees:** 288 bachelor's, 16 associate awarded; master's offered. **Location:** Downtown. **Calendar:** Quarter, extensive summer session. **Full-time faculty:** 34 total. **Part-time faculty:** 93 total. **Special facilities:** Computer-aided fashion design and illustration systems, 2D and 3D animation labs, fashion labs, design library, ZBrush.

Basis for selection. High school record and general appropriateness of educational background to specific program applied for most important. Portfolio, interview, standardized test scores also important. Interview and portfolio recommended.

High school preparation. Recommended units include English 1, mathematics 1, social studies 1 and history 1. One art class recommended.

2008-2009 Annual costs. Tuition/fees: $21,375. Starter kits additional $750-$1,300 estimate for all programs. Books/supplies: $1,125.

2007-2008 Financial aid. Need-based: 42% of total undergraduate aid awarded as scholarships/grants, 58% as loans/jobs.

Application procedures. Admission: No deadline. $50 fee. Admission notification on a rolling basis. **Financial aid:** No deadline. FAFSA required. Applicants notified on a rolling basis.

Academics. Special study options: Distance learning, honors, internships, study abroad. **Credit/placement by examination:** AP, CLEP, IB. **Support services:** Reduced course load, remedial instruction, study skills assistance, tutoring.

Majors. Business: Fashion. **Communications technology:** Animation/special effects. **Computer sciences:** Computer graphics, web page design. **Personal/culinary services:** Chef training, restaurant/catering. **Visual/performing arts:** Commercial/advertising art, fashion design, film/cinema, graphic design, interior design.

Student life. Freshman orientation: Mandatory. **Housing:** Coed dorms, apartments available. $300 deposit. **Activities:** Student government, student newspaper, animation club, society of web architects and programmers, fashion salon, graphic design club, game art and design club, anime club, photography club, eco club, student SIGGRAPH chapter, interior design club.

Student services. Career counseling, student employment services, financial aid counseling, personal counseling, placement for graduates. **Physically disabled:** Services for hearing impaired.

Contact. E-mail: aisfadm@aii.edu
Phone: (415) 865-0198 Toll-free number: (888) 493-3261
Fax: (415) 863-6344
Daniel Chew, Senior Director of Admissions, Art Institute of California: San Francisco, 1170 Market Street, San Francisco, CA 94102

Azusa Pacific University

Azusa, California **CB member**
www.apu.edu **CB code: 4596**

- Private 4-year university affiliated with interdenominational tradition
- Residential campus in small city
- 4,858 degree-seeking undergraduates: 16% part-time, 64% women
- 3,656 degree-seeking graduate students
- 63% of applicants admitted
- SAT or ACT (ACT writing optional), application essay required
- 65% graduate within 6 years

General. Founded in 1899. Regionally accredited. **Degrees:** 1,276 bachelor's awarded; master's, doctoral, first professional offered. **ROTC:** Army. **Location:** 30 miles from Los Angeles. **Calendar:** Semester, limited summer session. **Full-time faculty:** 315 total; 73% have terminal degrees, 25% minority, 45% women. **Part-time faculty:** 38 total; 47% have terminal degrees, 8% minority, 53% women. **Class size:** 63% < 20, 33% 20-39, 2% 40-49, 2% 50-99, less than 1% >100.

Freshman class profile. 4,441 applied, 2,780 admitted, 1,093 enrolled.

Mid 50% test scores		**GPA 2.0-2.99:**	9%
SAT critical reading:	490-590	**Rank in top quarter:**	62%
SAT math:	490-600	**Rank in top tenth:**	31%
ACT composite:	21-26	**Return as sophomores:**	82%
GPA 3.75 or higher:	44%	**Out-of-state:**	26%
GPA 3.50-3.74:	18%	**Live on campus:**	93%
GPA 3.0-3.49:	29%	**International:**	2%

Basis for selection. GPA, test scores, references, statement of agreement, essay important. Auditions required for music applicants. Interviews recommended for borderline applicants. **Homeschooled:** SAT or ACT and transcript from organization required.

High school preparation. College-preparatory program recommended. Recommended units include English 4, mathematics 3, social studies 1, history 2, science 2 and foreign language 3.

2009-2010 Annual costs. Tuition/fees: $26,640. Room/board: $7,742. Books/supplies: $1,566. Personal expenses: $2,214.

2007-2008 Financial aid. Need-based: 845 full-time freshmen applied for aid; 541 were judged to have need; 539 of these received aid. Average need met was 56%. Average scholarship/grant was $12,004; average loan $8,271. 76% of total undergraduate aid awarded as scholarships/grants, 24% as loans/jobs. **Non-need-based:** Awarded to 1,249 full-time undergraduates, including 299 freshmen. Scholarships awarded for academics, athletics, leadership, minority status, music/drama, religious affiliation, ROTC.

Application procedures. Admission: Priority date 3/1; deadline 6/1 (postmark date). $45 fee, may be waived for applicants with need. Admission notification on a rolling basis. Must reply by 5/1. Students with 3.0 high school GPA or higher and 1000 SAT score or higher can apply at completion of junior year and/or before January 1 for admission consideration. Housing deposit due by move-in date. **Financial aid:** Priority date 3/2, closing date 7/1. FAFSA, institutional form required. Applicants notified on a rolling basis starting 3/1; must reply within 3 week(s) of notification.

Academics. More than 20 online masters and credential programs offered for library media teaching. All other online programs are part of individual face to face programs with exception of one course offered completely online. **Special study options:** Accelerated study, cooperative education, distance learning, double major, ESL, exchange student, honors, independent study, internships, study abroad, teacher certification program, urban semester, Washington semester. **Credit/placement by examination:** AP, CLEP, IB, institutional tests. 15 credit hours maximum toward bachelor's degree. Essays required for Analysis and Interpretation of Literature and Freshman College Composition. **Support services:** Learning center, reduced course load, remedial instruction, study skills assistance, tutoring, writing center.

Majors. **Biology:** General, biochemistry. **Business:** General, accounting, business admin, finance, management information systems, marketing. **Communications:** General, broadcast journalism, journalism. **Computer sciences:** General, information systems, web page design. **Education:** General, art, business, elementary, middle, multi-level teacher, physical, secondary. **Foreign languages:** Spanish. **Health:** Nurse practitioner, nursing (RN), predental, premedicine. **History:** General. **Liberal arts:** Arts/sciences. **Math:** General. **Philosophy/religion:** Philosophy, religion. **Physical sciences:** General, chemistry, physics. **Psychology:** General. **Public administration:** Social work. **Social sciences:** General, international relations, political science, sociology. **Theology:** Bible, religious ed, sacred music, theology. **Visual/performing arts:** Art, dramatic, music performance, music theory/composition, studio arts.

Most popular majors. Business/marketing 22%, communications/journalism 11%, health sciences 9%, liberal arts 19%, psychology 7%, visual/performing arts 7%.

Computing on campus. 268 workstations in library, computer center, student center. Dormitories wired for high-speed internet access and linked to campus network. Commuter students can connect to campus network. Online course registration, helpline, repair service, wireless network available.

Student life. **Freshman orientation:** Mandatory. Preregistration for classes offered. Class taken during first semester. **Policies:** Students will refrain from activities which may be spiritually or morally destructive. Religious observance required. **Housing:** Coed dorms, single-sex dorms, apartments available. $250 deposit. **Activities:** Bands, choral groups, drama, music ensembles, musical theater, opera, radio station, student government, student newspaper, symphony orchestra, TV station, minority student association.

Athletics. NAIA. **Intercollegiate:** Baseball M, basketball, cross-country, football (tackle) M, soccer, softball W, tennis M, track and field, volleyball W. **Intramural:** Basketball, football (tackle) M, skiing, volleyball. **Team name:** Cougars.

Student services. Chaplain/spiritual director, career counseling, student employment services, financial aid counseling, health services, minority student services, personal counseling, placement for graduates, veterans' counselor. **Physically disabled:** Services for visually, speech, hearing impaired.

Contact. E-mail: admissions@apu.edu
Phone: (626) 812-3016 Toll-free number: (800) 825-5278
Fax: (626) 812-3096
Dave Burke, Director of Undergraduate Admissions, Azusa Pacific University, 901 East Alosta Avenue, Azusa, CA 91702-7000

Bethany University
Scotts Valley, California
www.bethany.edu **CB code: 4021**

- Private 4-year Bible and liberal arts college affiliated with Assemblies of God
- Residential campus in small town
- 441 degree-seeking undergraduates: 13% part-time, 63% women
- 73 degree-seeking graduate students
- 70% of applicants admitted
- SAT or ACT (ACT writing optional), application essay required
- 33% graduate within 6 years

General. Founded in 1919. Regionally accredited. Located in the Monterey Bay/Santa Cruz area. **Degrees:** 95 bachelor's awarded; master's offered. **Location:** 5 miles from Santa Cruz. **Calendar:** Semester, limited summer session. **Full-time faculty:** 25 total; 68% have terminal degrees, 40% women. **Part-time faculty:** 39 total; 59% women. **Class size:** 70% < 20, 25% 20-39, 2% 40-49, 3% 50-99. **Special facilities:** Early childhood learning center, wellness center, student individualized learning center.

Freshman class profile. 307 applied, 215 admitted, 110 enrolled.

Mid 50% test scores			
SAT critical reading:	430-510	Return as sophomores:	65%
SAT math:	310-510	Out-of-state:	17%
ACT composite:	17-21	Live on campus:	82%
		International:	2%

Basis for selection. Evaluation of academic records, and religious affiliation/commitment very important. Interviews recommended. Auditions required for music applicants. **Homeschooled:** State high school equivalency certificate required. **Learning Disabled:** Students with learning disabilities are recommended to contact the Educational Support Services Offices during the admission's process.

2009-2010 Annual costs. Tuition/fees: $18,150. Room/board: $7,450. Books/supplies: $1,200. Personal expenses: $1,300.

2008-2009 Financial aid. **Non-need-based:** Scholarships awarded for academics, alumni affiliation, athletics, leadership, minority status, music/drama, religious affiliation.

Application procedures. **Admission:** Closing date 7/31 (postmark date). $35 fee. Admission notification on a rolling basis. **Financial aid:** Priority date 3/2; no closing date. FAFSA, institutional form required. Applicants notified on a rolling basis starting 4/15; must reply within 2 week(s) of notification.

Academics. **Special study options:** Accelerated study, combined bachelor's/graduate degree, distance learning, double major, external degree, independent study, internships, study abroad, teacher certification program. **Credit/placement by examination:** AP, CLEP, IB, SAT, ACT. 18 credit hours maximum toward associate degree, 18 toward bachelor's. **Support services:** Learning center, reduced course load, remedial instruction, study skills assistance, tutoring.

Majors. **Business:** General, business admin. **Communications:** General, organizational, public relations. **Education:** Early childhood. **Health:** Substance abuse counseling. **Liberal arts:** Arts/sciences. **Psychology:** General. **Social sciences:** General. **Theology:** Bible, missionary, pastoral counseling, sacred music, theology, youth ministry. **Visual/performing arts:** Dramatic.

Most popular majors. Business/marketing 16%, communications/journalism 7%, education 15%, interdisciplinary studies 8%, psychology 21%, social sciences 13%, theological studies 14%.

Computing on campus. 20 workstations in library, computer center, student center. Dormitories wired for high-speed internet access and linked to campus network. Commuter students can connect to campus network. Online library, wireless network available.

Student life. **Freshman orientation:** Mandatory, $125 fee. Preregistration for classes offered. 5-day program before beginning of classes. **Policies:** Student ministry opportunities. Religious observance required. **Housing:** Guaranteed on-campus for freshmen. Single-sex dorms, apartments, wellness housing available. $100 nonrefundable deposit. **Activities:** Concert band, campus ministries, choral groups, drama, international student organizations, music ensembles, musical theater, student government, student newspaper, symphony orchestra.

Athletics. NAIA. **Intercollegiate:** Baseball M, basketball M, cheerleading, cross-country, soccer, softball W, volleyball W. **Intramural:** Basketball, football (non-tackle). **Team name:** Bruins.

Student services. Adult student services, alcohol/substance abuse counseling, chaplain/spiritual director, career counseling, student employment services, financial aid counseling, health services, on-campus daycare, personal counseling, placement for graduates, veterans' counselor.

Contact. E-mail: info@fc.bethany.edu
Phone: (831) 438-3800 ext. 3900 Toll-free number: (800) 843-9410
Fax: (831) 461-1621
Gretchen Mineni, Director of Admission, Bethany University, 800 Bethany Drive, Scotts Valley, CA 95066-2898

Bethesda Christian University
Anaheim, California
www.bcu.edu **CB code: 3895**

- Private 4-year university affiliated with Christian Church
- Commuter campus in large city
- 245 degree-seeking undergraduates
- 81 graduate students
- Application essay, interview required

General. Accredited by ABHE. Extension office in South Korea. **Degrees:** 43 bachelor's awarded; master's, first professional offered. **Location:** 30 miles from Los Angeles. **Calendar:** Semester, limited summer session. **Full-time faculty:** 4 total. **Part-time faculty:** 44 total. **Class size:** 33% < 20, 64% 20-39, 3% 40-49.

Basis for selection. Open admission. GED not accepted. Admissions decision based on recommendations, essay and interview. Secondary school record also important. ESL placement test not required for students who have TOEFL score 550 or higher or have graduated from English-speaking high school. Auditions required for music majors. Portfolio required for design majors. Christian experience essay required. **Homeschooled:** Transcript of courses and grades, state high school equivalency certificate, letter of recommendation (nonparent) required.

High school preparation. College-preparatory program required.

2009-2010 Annual costs. Tuition/fees (projected): $6,580. Books/supplies: $1,000. Personal expenses: $500.

2008-2009 Financial aid. All financial aid based on need.

Application procedures. Admission: Priority date 2/1; deadline 3/1 (receipt date). $35 fee ($80 out-of-state). Application must be submitted on paper. Admission notification on a rolling basis. **Financial aid:** Closing date 3/14. FAFSA, institutional form required. Applicants notified on a rolling basis starting 6/30.

Academics. Special study options: Combined bachelor's/graduate degree, distance learning, dual enrollment of high school students, ESL, external degree, independent study, liberal arts/career combination, study abroad, teacher certification program. **Credit/placement by examination:** CLEP, IB, institutional tests. **Support services:** Reduced course load.

Majors. Computer sciences: Information technology. **Education:** Early childhood. **Foreign languages:** Translation. **Philosophy/religion:** Religion. **Theology:** Bible, missionary, religious ed, sacred music, theology. **Visual/performing arts:** Conducting, design, fashion design, metal/jewelry, music management, music performance, music theory/composition, piano/organ, stringed instruments, voice/opera.

Computing on campus. PC or laptop required. 30 workstations in dormitories, library, computer center, student center. Dormitories wired for high-speed internet access. Online course registration, helpline, repair service, wireless network available.

Student life. Freshman orientation: Mandatory. Preregistration for classes offered. **Policies:** Religious observance required. **Activities:** Student government.

Student services. Chaplain/spiritual director, financial aid counseling, personal counseling.

Contact. E-mail: admission@bcu.edu
Phone: (714) 517-1945 Fax: (714) 517-1948
Jacqueline Ha, Director of Admissions, Bethesda Christian University, 730 North Euclid Street, Anaheim, CA 92801

Biola University

La Mirada, California
www.biola.edu **CB code: 4017**

- Private 4-year university and Bible college affiliated with interdenominational tradition
- Residential campus in large town
- 3,610 degree-seeking undergraduates: 2% part-time, 62% women
- 81% of applicants admitted
- SAT or ACT (ACT writing recommended), application essay required

General. Founded in 1908. Regionally accredited. Biblically centered Christian institution. **Degrees:** 886 bachelor's awarded; master's, doctoral, first professional offered. **ROTC:** Army, Air Force. **Location:** 22 miles from downtown Los Angeles. **Calendar:** 4-1-4, extensive summer session. **Full-time faculty:** 220 total; 74% have terminal degrees, 27% women. **Part-time faculty:** 199 total; 42% women. **Class size:** 47% < 20, 44% 20-39, 4% 40-49, 3% 50-99, 2% >100. **Special facilities:** Concert hall with pipe organ, electron microscope, recording studio, film studio, MIDI lab for music composition, electronic piano lab, archaeological dig site.

Freshman class profile. 2,470 applied, 2,005 admitted, 838 enrolled.

Mid 50% test scores		**GPA 3.0-3.49:**	31%
SAT critical reading:	500-620	**GPA 2.0-2.99:**	11%
SAT math:	490-620	**Rank in top quarter:**	75%
SAT writing:	500-610	**Rank in top tenth:**	43%
ACT composite:	21-26	**Out-of-state:**	28%
GPA 3.75 or higher:	36%	**Live on campus:**	90%
GPA 3.50-3.74:	22%		

Basis for selection. Christian commitment most important; academic record, personal references, test scores next in importance. School, community, church activities helpful. Out-of-state and ethnic students encouraged to apply. Official transcripts, SAT/ACT, pastoral reference form required. No exceptions to SAT/ACT requirement. If more than one SAT score, the best combination of scores accepted. Auditions recommended for music applicants. Portfolios recommended for art applicants. Any body of work recommended for CMA applicants. Some students asked for an interview. **Homeschooled:** Transcript of courses and grades, letter of recommendation (nonparent) required. Applicants advised to go through accreditation agency. **Learning Disabled:** Student must request the services of the ODS and provide documentation supporting the nature and limitations of a disability.

High school preparation. 21 units recommended. Recommended units include English 4, mathematics 3, social studies 3, history 4, science 3 and foreign language 4. 1 algebra and 1 chemistry required of nursing applicants. 2 math, 1 physics, 1 chemistry required of biology applicants. Some deficiencies may be satisfied during freshman year.

2008-2009 Annual costs. Tuition/fees: $26,424. Room/board: $7,410. Books/supplies: $1,314. Personal expenses: $2,088.

2007-2008 Financial aid. Need-based: Average need met was 68%. Average scholarship/grant was $11,339; average loan $1,796. 57% of total undergraduate aid awarded as scholarships/grants, 43% as loans/jobs. **Non-need-based:** Scholarships awarded for academics, alumni affiliation, art, athletics, leadership, minority status, music/drama, state residency.

Application procedures. Admission: Closing date 3/1 (receipt date). $45 fee, may be waived for applicants with need. Admission notification on a rolling basis beginning on or about 4/1. Must reply by 5/1. **Financial aid:** Priority date 1/1; no closing date. FAFSA required. Applicants notified on a rolling basis starting 3/1.

Academics. Special study options: Combined bachelor's/graduate degree, double major, dual enrollment of high school students, ESL, exchange student, honors, internships, New York semester, student-designed major, study abroad, teacher certification program, Washington semester. 3-2 program with Los Angeles College of Chiropractic, 3-2 engineering program with University of Southern California. **Credit/placement by examination:** AP, CLEP, IB, SAT, ACT. Maximum of 32 credits from CLEP, AP, and IB can be counted toward degree. **Support services:** Learning center, reduced course load, remedial instruction, study skills assistance, tutoring, writing center.

Honors college/program. Admission to Torrey Honors Institute by invitation, after application to the university. Through the use of a classical learning style students are trained in rigorous discussion group format, learning high-level writing and critical thinking skills.

Majors. Biology: General, biochemistry. **Business:** Accounting, business admin, international, management information systems, marketing. **Communications:** General, broadcast journalism, journalism, public relations, radio/tv. **Computer sciences:** Computer science. **Education:** General, elementary, music, physical, secondary. **Engineering:** General. **Foreign languages:** Spanish. **Health:** Communication disorders, nursing (RN). **History:** General. **Interdisciplinary:** Intercultural. **Legal studies:** Prelaw. **Liberal arts:** Arts/sciences. **Math:** General. **Parks/recreation:** Exercise sciences, health/fitness. **Philosophy/religion:** Philosophy, religion. **Physical sciences:** Chemistry, physics. **Psychology:** General. **Social sciences:** General, anthropology, sociology. **Theology:** Bible, religious ed, theology. **Visual/performing arts:** Cinematography, commercial/advertising art, dramatic, drawing, music performance, music theory/composition, painting, sculpture, studio arts.

Most popular majors. Business/marketing 26%, communications/journalism 11%, education 9%, health sciences 6%, psychology 8%, social sciences 7%, theological studies 14%, visual/performing arts 8%.

Computing on campus. 225 workstations in library, computer center. Dormitories wired for high-speed internet access and linked to campus network. Commuter students can connect to campus network. Online course registration, online library, helpline, repair service, student web hosting, wireless network available.

Student life. Freshman orientation: Available, $75 fee. Week-long, held week before term begins. Students assigned to core group led by Biola student. **Policies:** All students encouraged to have Christian service assignment. Students adhere to code of conduct. Freshmen and sophomores under 21 required to live on campus unless living with relatives. Use and possession of drugs and/or alcohol is not permitted. All students (both on and off campus) sign a contract. Religious observance required. **Housing:** Guaranteed on-campus for freshmen. Coed dorms, single-sex dorms, special housing for disabled, apartments available. $250 partly refundable deposit, deadline 5/1. Flex-style dorms with single sex floors/wings available. **Activities:** Bands, campus ministries, choral groups, dance, drama, film society, international student organizations, music ensembles, musical theater, opera, radio station, student government, student newspaper, symphony orchestra, TV station, Student Missionary Union, Korean student association, evangelism team, International Justice Mission, theology club, Society of Christian Philosophy, Tijuana Ministry, Bas Bleu (women's issues), Naturally Diverse.

Athletics. NAIA. **Intercollegiate:** Baseball M, basketball, cross-country, diving, golf, soccer, softball W, swimming, tennis, track and field, volleyball W. **Intramural:** Basketball, football (non-tackle), soccer, softball, volleyball. **Team name:** Eagles.

Student services. Adult student services, chaplain/spiritual director, career counseling, student employment services, financial aid counseling, health services, minority student services, personal counseling, placement for graduates, veterans' counselor. **Physically disabled:** Services for speech, hearing impaired.

Contact. E-mail: admissions@biola.edu
Phone: (562) 903-4752 Toll-free number: (800) 652-4652
Fax: (562) 903-4709
Greg Vaughan, Director of Enrollment Management, Biola University, 13800 Biola Avenue, La Mirada, CA 90639-0001

Brooks Institute
Santa Barbara, California
www.brooks.edu **CB code: 4228**

- For-profit 3-year visual arts college
- Commuter campus in small city
- 1,185 degree-seeking undergraduates: 46% women, 2% African American, 5% Asian American, 9% Hispanic American
- 37 degree-seeking graduate students
- Application essay, interview required
- 48% graduate within 6 years

General. Founded in 1945. Accredited by ACICS. **Degrees:** 509 bachelor's, 11 associate awarded; master's offered. **Location:** 90 miles from Los Angeles. **Calendar:** Semester, extensive summer session. **Full-time faculty:** 59 total. **Part-time faculty:** 6 total. **Special facilities:** 123,000 square feet of studio space for 40 set-ups, 90 cubicles for black and white enlarging, digital labs, design lab for visual communication program.

Freshman class profile. 135 enrolled.

Return as sophomores:	65%	**Out-of-state:**	32%

Basis for selection. School achievement record most important. Photographic experience not required for entrance. Advanced standing may be offered to those with 4X5 view camera experience. Evaluation consists of written examination portfolio and review. TOEFL required of students whose first language is not English. Different standards exist based on paper vs. computer scores and for undergraduate and graduate applicants. At time of matriculation, institution will assess English and math proficiencies for students who have not demonstrated proficiency in both at the college level or by receiving minimum standard scores in national tests. Interviews can be conducted via telephone. Interview and photography portfolio required for advanced standing in core courses. **Homeschooled:** GED required if home schooling not recognized by state. **Learning Disabled:** Protocol for students seeking accommodation is mailed to accepted applicants with provisional acceptance letter.

High school preparation. Recommended units include English 4, mathematics 2, social studies 1, science 1 and foreign language 2. College preparatory program recommended.

2008-2009 Annual costs. Tuition/fees: $17,840.

2007-2008 Financial aid. **Need-based:** 28% of total undergraduate aid awarded as scholarships/grants, 72% as loans/jobs.

Application procedures. **Admission:** No deadline. $100 fee. Admission notification on a rolling basis. Students encouraged to apply at least 6 months in advance. **Financial aid:** Priority date 3/2; no closing date. FAFSA, institutional form required. Applicants notified on a rolling basis starting 5/1.

Academics. **Special study options:** Accelerated study, combined bachelor's/graduate degree, distance learning, double major, independent study, internships. Upper-division students can apply to participate in documentary courses in foreign countries; upper-division professional photography students can apply for inclusion in annual undersea photography class. **Credit/placement by examination:** CLEP, institutional tests. 54 credit hours maximum toward bachelor's degree. **Support services:** Tutoring.

Majors. **Communications:** Photojournalism. **Visual/performing arts:** Cinematography, graphic design, photography.

Computing on campus. 20 workstations in library, computer center. Online library, helpline, wireless network available.

Student life. **Freshman orientation:** Mandatory. Immediately prior to matriculation; normally 2-3 days of activities. **Policies:** Car necessary for travel between campuses and to assignment locations. **Activities:** Student government.

Student services. Career counseling, student employment services, financial aid counseling, personal counseling, placement for graduates.

Contact. E-mail: admissions@brooks.edu
Phone: (888) 304-3456 Toll-free number: (888) 304-3456
Fax: (805) 565-1386
Michael Jacobsen, Director of Admissions, Brooks Institute, 27 East Cota Street, Santa Barbara, CA 93101

Brooks Institute: Ventura
Santa Barbara, California
www.brooks.edu

- For-profit 3-year visual arts and career college
- Small city
- 754 degree-seeking undergraduates
- Application essay, interview required

General. Accredited by ACICS. BA degree in 3 years with intensive program consisting of six 8-week sessions per year. **Degrees:** 509 bachelor's, 11 associate awarded; master's offered. **Location:** 90 miles from Los Angeles. **Calendar:** Semester, extensive summer session. **Full-time faculty:** 36 total. **Part-time faculty:** 70 total. **Special facilities:** 27,000 sq ft sound stage and back lot for film production, 3 story studio building for photography with 30 separate studios, separate industry current digital labs for film editing, post production, graphic design, photo editing and sound editing.

Basis for selection. Open admission, but selective for some programs. High school diploma, high school GPA 2.0, must submit application through admissions process, be accepted by Director of Admissions. All students will be tested for English and math compentency using the Accuplacer exam. Students who have college credit for English Composition and or college algebra with a grade of 2.0 or higher are exempt if the college has their official transcripts on file at the time of entry. Portfolio and exam required if applicant wishes to challenge required courses in program for Advanced Standing. **Homeschooled:** State high school equivalency certificate required. We do not recognize home schooling from California since it is not regulated by the State. We require home schooling to be State recognized and if not to have GED or California High School Proficiency Exam. **Learning Disabled:** Must have medical/professional documentation of disability that is less than 3 years old. Must apply for accommodation through college's protocol.

2008-2009 Annual costs. Tuition/fees: $17,840.

Application procedures. **Admission:** No deadline. $100 fee.

Academics. Short intense course of study with student - teacher interaction. Industry internships. Majority of faculty in core program have industry experience, many still active in field. **Special study options:** Combined bachelor's/graduate degree, independent study, internships, liberal arts/career combination, semester at sea. Overseas documentary photography/filmmaking course annually, undersea course, large offering of specific industry related course electives. **Credit/placement by examination:** CLEP. **Support services:** Pre-admission summer program, reduced course load, remedial instruction, study skills assistance, tutoring, writing center.

Majors. **BACHELOR'S. Visual/performing arts:** Photography. **ASSOCIATE. Visual/performing arts:** Photography.

Contact. E-mail: admissions@brooks.edu
Phone: (805) 966-3888 Toll-free number: (888) 304-3456
Fax: (805) 275-5619
Jamie James, Vice President of Marketing and Admissions, Brooks Institute: Ventura, 801 Alston Road, Santa Barbara, CA 93108

California Baptist University
Riverside, California **CB member**
www.calbaptist.edu **CB code: 4094**

- Private 4-year university and liberal arts college affiliated with Southern Baptist Convention
- Residential campus in large city
- 3,072 degree-seeking undergraduates: 12% part-time, 64% women, 8% African American, 4% Asian American, 18% Hispanic American, 1% Native American, 3% international
- 917 degree-seeking graduate students
- 74% of applicants admitted
- SAT or ACT (ACT writing optional), application essay required
- 51% graduate within 6 years

General. Founded in 1950. Regionally accredited. **Degrees:** 567 bachelor's awarded; master's offered. **ROTC:** Army, Air Force. **Location:** 60 miles from Los Angeles. **Calendar:** Semester. 4-4-1 semester system. Extensive summer session. **Full-time faculty:** 147 total; 50% have terminal degrees, 22% minority, 42% women. **Part-time faculty:** 145 total; 20% have terminal degrees, 24% minority, 37% women. **Class size:** 50% < 20, 38% 20-39, 7% 40-49, 4% 50-99, 1% >100. **Special facilities:** Hymnology collection, performance and recording studios, Nie Wieder! holocaust collection, aquatic center.

Freshman class profile. 1,474 applied, 1,092 admitted, 603 enrolled.

Mid 50% test scores		**GPA 2.0-2.99:**	26%
SAT critical reading:	470-560	**Rank in top quarter:**	49%
SAT math:	510-560	**Rank in top tenth:**	20%
SAT writing:	510-550	**End year in good standing:**	86%
ACT composite:	20-23	**Return as sophomores:**	78%
GPA 3.75 or higher:	26%	**Out-of-state:**	10%
GPA 3.50-3.74:	17%	**Live on campus:**	92%
GPA 3.0-3.49:	30%	**International:**	5%

Basis for selection. School achievement record, test scores, essays, recommendations very important. Interviews recommended. Auditions required for music, drama applicants. **Homeschooled:** Transcript of courses and grades, letter of recommendation (nonparent) required.

High school preparation. College-preparatory program recommended. 15 units required; 19 recommended. Required and recommended units include English 4, mathematics 3-4, social studies 2, history 2, science 2-3 (laboratory 1-2), foreign language 2-3 and academic electives 3.

2008-2009 Annual costs. Tuition/fees: $22,330. Room/board: $7,910. Books/supplies: $1,566. Personal expenses: $2,970.

2007-2008 Financial aid. **Non-need-based:** Scholarships awarded for academics, art, athletics, leadership, music/drama, religious affiliation, ROTC.

Application procedures. **Admission:** Priority date 2/1; no deadline. $45 fee, may be waived for applicants with need. Admission notification on a rolling basis beginning on or about 11/19. **Financial aid:** Priority date 3/2; no closing date. FAFSA required. Applicants notified on a rolling basis starting 3/2; must reply by 5/1 or within 3 week(s) of notification.

Academics. **Special study options:** Accelerated study, distance learning, double major, dual enrollment of high school students, ESL, exchange student, honors, internships, liberal arts/career combination, study abroad, teacher certification program, Washington semester, weekend college. **Credit/placement by examination:** AP, CLEP, IB, SAT, ACT, institutional tests. 30 credit hours maximum toward bachelor's degree. Portfolio course available to assist students in documenting work that may be counted for credit by prior learning experiences. **Support services:** Learning center, reduced course load, remedial instruction, study skills assistance, tutoring, writing center.

Majors. **Biology:** General. **Business:** Accounting, business admin, marketing. **Communications:** General, digital media, journalism, media studies. **Education:** General, early childhood, physical. **Engineering:** General, civil, electrical, mechanical. **Foreign languages:** Spanish. **Health:** Health services, nursing (RN). **History:** General. **Interdisciplinary:** Behavioral sciences, intercultural. **Liberal arts:** Arts/sciences. **Math:** General. **Parks/recreation:** Exercise sciences. **Philosophy/religion:** Christian, philosophy. **Protective services:** Law enforcement admin, police science. **Psychology:** General. **Social sciences:** Political science, sociology. **Theology:** Bible, missionary. **Visual/performing arts:** Art, graphic design, music performance, music theory/composition, piano/organ, theater arts management, voice/opera. **Other:** Christian behavioral science, Foundational mathematics, Music education, Organizational leadership, Psychological anthropology.

Most popular majors. Business/marketing 17%, liberal arts 25%, parks/recreation 7%, psychology 9%, social sciences 7%.

Computing on campus. 279 workstations in library, computer center. Dormitories wired for high-speed internet access and linked to campus network. Commuter students can connect to campus network. Online course registration, online library, helpline available.

Student life. **Freshman orientation:** Mandatory, $250 fee. Preregistration for classes offered. Held prior to beginning of semester. **Policies:** Students receiving institutional scholarships required to live in student housing. Religious observance required. **Housing:** Guaranteed on-campus for freshmen. Single-sex dorms, apartments, cooperative housing available. $300 fully refundable deposit, deadline 8/1. **Activities:** Bands, campus ministries, choral groups, drama, international student organizations, music ensembles, musical theater, student government, student newspaper, symphony orchestra, Young Republicans, Young Democrats, Fellowship of Christian Athletes, Black Student Union, Big Brother, Big Sister, active compassion, elderly ministry, homeless ministry.

Athletics. NAIA. **Intercollegiate:** Baseball M, basketball, cheerleading, cross-country, diving, golf, soccer, softball W, swimming, tennis, volleyball, water polo, wrestling M. **Intramural:** Basketball, bowling, football (non-tackle), golf, softball, table tennis, tennis, volleyball. **Team name:** Lancers.

Student services. Adult student services, chaplain/spiritual director, career counseling, student employment services, financial aid counseling, personal counseling, placement for graduates, veterans' counselor.

Contact. E-mail: admissions@calbaptist.edu
Phone: (951) 343-4212 Toll-free number: (877) 228-8866
Fax: (951) 343-4525
Allen Johnson, Associate Dean of Enrollment Services, California Baptist University, 8432 Magnolia Avenue, Riverside, CA 92504-3297

California Coast University

Santa Ana, California
www.calcoast.edu

- For-profit 4-year virtual university, business and health science college
- Large city
- 2,580 degree-seeking undergraduates

General. Accredited by DETC. **Degrees:** 148 bachelor's, 9 associate awarded; master's offered. **Calendar:** Continuous, extensive summer session. **Part-time faculty:** 26 total.

Basis for selection. Open admission.

2008-2009 Annual costs. Distance-learning undergraduate program total costs: $6,600 (associate degree) and $13,860 (bachelor's degree); international students pay $7,800 (associate degree) and $16,380 (bachelor's degree) in total costs per program.

Application procedures. **Admission:** No deadline. $75 fee.

Academics. **Special study options:** Accelerated study, cross-registration, distance learning, external degree, honors, independent study. **Credit/placement by examination:** CLEP.

Majors. **Business:** General, business admin. **Health:** Health care admin. **Psychology:** General. **Social sciences:** Criminology.

Student life. **Activities:** Student newspaper.

Contact. E-mail: admissions@calcoast.edu
Phone: (714) 547-9625
Admissions Director, California Coast University, 700 North Main Street, Santa Ana, CA 92701

California College of the Arts

San Francisco, California — **CB member**
www.cca.edu — **CB code: 4031**

- Private 4-year visual arts college
- Residential campus in very large city
- 1,336 degree-seeking undergraduates: 7% part-time, 62% women, 3% African American, 16% Asian American, 10% Hispanic American, 1% Native American, 9% international
- 357 degree-seeking graduate students
- 77% of applicants admitted
- Application essay required
- 60% graduate within 6 years

General. Founded in 1907. Regionally accredited. 2 campuses located in San Francisco and Oakland. **Degrees:** 234 bachelor's awarded; master's offered. **Location:** 3 miles from downtown. **Calendar:** Semester, limited summer session. **Full-time faculty:** 65 total; 80% have terminal degrees, 22% minority, 43% women. **Part-time faculty:** 330 total; 62% have terminal degrees, 17% minority, 45% women. **Class size:** 92% < 20, 8% 20-39, less than 1% 50-99. **Special facilities:** Center for art and public life, contemporary arts institute, materials resource center.

Freshman class profile. 1,182 applied, 908 admitted, 248 enrolled.

Mid 50% test scores			
SAT critical reading:	490-600	GPA 3.0-3.49:	42%
SAT math:	460-590	GPA 2.0-2.99:	37%
SAT writing:	320-580	Return as sophomores:	78%
ACT composite:	20-25	Out-of-state:	37%
GPA 3.75 or higher:	7%	Live on campus:	81%
GPA 3.50-3.74:	14%	International:	10%

Basis for selection. High school achievement including art/design activities and interests, GPA, personal essay/statement of purpose, interview, and portfolio very important. 2 letters of recommendation required. SAT or ACT recommended. Test scores are primarily used for placement, but may be considered for admission. SAT or ACT scores with Writing highly recommended and used in English course placement. Portfolio of creative work and statement of artistic and professional goals required. **Homeschooled:** Transcript of courses and grades required. Detailed syllabus of courses (equivalent to grades 10-12) and details of curriculum, including community college transcripts (if applicable) required.

High school preparation. College-preparatory program recommended.

2008-2009 Annual costs. Tuition/fees: $31,382. Room only: $6,600. Books/supplies: $1,500. Personal expenses: $2,200.

2008-2009 Financial aid. **Need-based:** 141 full-time freshmen applied for aid; 123 were judged to have need; 123 of these received aid. Average need met was 64%. Average scholarship/grant was $16,391; average loan $3,656. 73% of total undergraduate aid awarded as scholarships/grants, 27% as loans/jobs. **Non-need-based:** Awarded to 509 full-time undergraduates, including 116 freshmen. Scholarships awarded for academics, art. **Additional information:** Application deadline for merit scholarships February 1.

Application procedures. **Admission:** Priority date 2/1; no deadline. $50 fee, may be waived for applicants with need. Admission notification on a rolling basis beginning on or about 1/15. Must reply by May 1 or within 2 week(s) if notified thereafter. Maximum period of postponement is one semester. **Financial aid:** Priority date 3/1; no closing date. FAFSA required. Applicants notified by 4/1; Applicants notified on a rolling basis starting 3/15; must reply by 5/1 or within 3 week(s) of notification.

Academics. **Special study options:** Combined bachelor's/graduate degree, cross-registration, ESL, exchange student, independent study, internships, student-designed major, study abroad. Community service fellowships, annual career expo, summer English second language (ESL) for international students, pre-college program, disability services. **Credit/placement by examination:** AP, CLEP, IB, SAT, ACT, institutional tests. **Support services:** Learning center, pre-admission summer program, reduced course load, remedial instruction, study skills assistance, tutoring, writing center.

Majors. **Architecture:** Architecture, interior. **Visual/performing arts:** Art, ceramics, cinematography, commercial/advertising art, crafts, drawing, fashion design, fiber arts, graphic design, illustration, industrial design, interior design, metal/jewelry, painting, photography, printmaking, sculpture, studio arts.

Most popular majors. Visual/performing arts 95%.

Computing on campus. 251 workstations in dormitories, library, computer center, student center. Dormitories wired for high-speed internet access and linked to campus network. Commuter students can connect to campus network. Online library, helpline, student web hosting, wireless network available.

Student life. **Freshman orientation:** Mandatory. Preregistration for classes offered. Educational and social programs are offered one week before classes start. **Housing:** Coed dorms, apartments, wellness housing available. $750 partly refundable deposit, deadline 5/15. First-year community, transfer community, multi-cultural community service theme halls available. **Activities:** Film society, international student organizations, literary magazine, student government, student newspaper, Quack, Students for Sustainability, Asian Student Association, Salon Collective, Chimera Council, Graduate Student Alliance, Alliance for Multiculturalism in Architecture, Glass League, American Institute of Architecture Students, Ceramics Guild.

Student services. Career counseling, student employment services, financial aid counseling, personal counseling, placement for graduates.

Contact. E-mail: enroll@cca.edu
Phone: (415) 703-9523 Toll-free number: (800) 447-1278
Fax: (415) 703-9539
Robynne Royster, Director of Undergraduate Admission, California College of the Arts, 1111 Eighth Street, San Francisco, CA 94107-2247

California College San Diego
San Diego, California
www.cc-sd.edu **CB code: 3354**

- For-profit 4-year business and health science college
- Very large city
- 650 degree-seeking undergraduates

General. Accredited by ACCSCT. **Degrees:** 34 bachelor's, 112 associate awarded. **Calendar:** Continuous. **Full-time faculty:** 12 total. **Part-time faculty:** 22 total.

Basis for selection. Open admission.

2008-2009 Annual costs. 20-month Associate programs: Respiratory Therapy $41,300; Medical Specialty $35,300. Other Associate programs $35,300. 36-month Bachelor program: Health Care Administration $62,300. 32-month Bachelor programs $67,300.

Application procedures. **Admission:** No deadline.

Academics. **Credit/placement by examination:** CLEP.

Majors. **Business:** Accounting, business admin. **Computer sciences:** Computer science. **Health:** Health care admin, nursing admin, respiratory therapy technology.

Contact. Phone: (619) 295-5785 Fax: (619) 295-5762
Randy Wolford, Director of Admissions, California College San Diego, 2820 Camino del Rio South 300, San Diego, CA 92108

California Institute of Integral Studies
San Francisco, California
www.ciis.edu **CB code: 3609**

- Private two-year upper-division liberal arts college
- Commuter campus in very large city
- 94% of applicants admitted
- Application essay required

General. Regionally accredited. Offers interdisciplinary, cross-cultural, and applied studies in psychology, philosophy, religion, cultural anthropology, transformative studies and leadership, integrative health, women's spirituality, counseling, community mental health, and the arts. **Degrees:** 42 bachelor's awarded; master's, doctoral offered. **Location:** Downtown. **Calendar:** Semester, extensive summer session. **Full-time faculty:** 50 total; 100% have terminal degrees, 18% minority, 42% women. **Part-time faculty:** 10 total. **Class size:** 81% < 20, 19% 20-39.

Student profile. 83 degree-seeking undergraduates, 1,082 degree-seeking graduate students. 53 applied as first time-transfer students, 50 admitted, 38 enrolled.

Women:	71%	Native American:	1%
African American:	10%	Part-time:	13%
Asian American:	8%	Out-of-state:	2%
Hispanic American:	17%	25 or older:	82%

Basis for selection. College transcript, application essay required. Transfer accepted as juniors.

2008-2009 Annual costs. Tuition/fees: $13,720. Cost quoted for 2 semesters; 3-semester attendance mandatory.

Financial aid. **Need-based:** 201 applied for aid; 186 were judged to have need; 67 of these received aid. Average need met was 15%. 20% of total undergraduate aid awarded as scholarships/grants, 80% as loans/jobs. **Non-need-based:** Awarded to 16 undergraduates. Scholarships awarded for academics, alumni affiliation, art, job skills, leadership, minority status, ROTC, state residency.

Application procedures. **Admission:** Priority date 5/1. $65 fee, may be waived for applicants with need. Application priority dates differ by program.

Academics. **Special study options:** Distance learning, dual enrollment of high school students, independent study, internships, weekend college. **Credit/placement by examination:** AP, CLEP. 30 credit hours maximum toward bachelor's degree. **Support services:** Tutoring, writing center.

Majors. **Liberal arts:** Arts/sciences, humanities.

Computing on campus. 20 workstations in computer center. Commuter students can connect to campus network. Online library, helpline, wireless network available.

Student life. Activities: International student organizations, student government, student newspaper, People of Color, Queer at CIIS, Student Alliance, Integral Dialog Group, UNITE!, White People Working Against Racism, International Students & Friends.

Student services. Career counseling, financial aid counseling, minority student services, personal counseling, placement for graduates.

Contact. E-mail: admissions@ciis.edu
Phone: (415) 575-6150
Allyson Werner, Associate Director of Admissions, California Institute of Integral Studies, 1453 Mission Street, San Francisco, CA 94103

California Institute of Technology

Pasadena, California — **CB member**
www.caltech.edu — **CB code: 4034**

- Private 4-year university
- Residential campus in small city
- 921 degree-seeking undergraduates: 34% women
- 1,205 degree-seeking graduate students
- 17% of applicants admitted
- SAT or ACT (ACT writing optional), SAT Subject Tests, application essay required

General. Founded in 1891. Regionally accredited. **Degrees:** 208 bachelor's awarded; master's, doctoral offered. **ROTC:** Army, Air Force. **Location:** 10 miles from downtown Los Angeles. **Calendar:** Quarter. **Full-time faculty:** 304 total; 98% have terminal degrees, 15% minority, 16% women. **Part-time faculty:** 23 total; 56% have terminal degrees, 26% minority, 39% women. **Class size:** 47% < 20, 12% 20-39, 3% 40-49, 36% 50-99, 2% >100. **Special facilities:** Jet propulsion laboratories, observatory, wind and water tunnels, radio observatory, seismological laboratory, marine biological laboratory.

Freshman class profile. 3,957 applied, 687 admitted, 236 enrolled.

Mid 50% test scores		**Rank in top quarter:**	100%
SAT critical reading:	700-760	**Rank in top tenth:**	97%
SAT math:	770-800	**Out-of-state:**	67%
SAT writing:	690-770	**Live on campus:**	100%
ACT composite:	33-35		

Basis for selection. High school preparation and record (particularly in mathematics and science), test scores, extracurricular activities (science and nonscience-related), counselors' and teachers' recommendations, and demonstrated interest in mathematics and science are major considerations. SAT Subject Test requirements: Math level IIC and one science, either biology (environmental or molecular), chemistry, or physics.

High school preparation. College-preparatory program required. Required and recommended units include English 3-4, mathematics 4, social studies 1-3, history 1, science 2-4 (laboratory 1).

2008-2009 Annual costs. Tuition/fees: $34,437. Room/board: $10,146. Books/supplies: $1,194. Personal expenses: $1,881.

2008-2009 Financial aid. Need-based: 166 full-time freshmen applied for aid; 116 were judged to have need; 116 of these received aid. Average need met was 100%. Average scholarship/grant was $28,846; average loan $2,261. 90% of total undergraduate aid awarded as scholarships/grants, 10% as loans/jobs. **Non-need-based:** Awarded to 113 full-time undergraduates, including 9 freshmen. Scholarships awarded for academics.

Application procedures. Admission: Closing date 1/2 (postmark date). $60 fee, may be waived for applicants with need. Admission notification 4/1. Must reply by 5/1. **Financial aid:** Closing date 1/15. FAFSA, institutional form, CSS PROFILE required. Applicants notified by 4/1; must reply by 5/1.

Academics. Remedial services not formally offered. Remediation available for students deficient in basic scientific knowledge or technical skills. **Special study options:** Combined bachelor's/graduate degree, cooperative education, cross-registration, double major, ESL, exchange student, independent study, liberal arts/career combination, student-designed major, study abroad. **Credit/placement by examination:** CLEP, institutional tests. **Support services:** Reduced course load, tutoring.

Majors. Biology: General. **Business:** Managerial economics. **Computer sciences:** Computer science. **Engineering:** General, chemical, computer, electrical, environmental, materials science, mechanical, physics. **History:** General, science/technology. **Interdisciplinary:** Science/society. **Math:** General, applied. **Philosophy/religion:** Philosophy. **Physical sciences:** Astronomy, astrophysics, chemistry, geochemistry, geology, geophysics, physics, planetary. **Social sciences:** General, economics, political science. **Other:** Computational neural systems, Geobiology.

Most popular majors. Biology 14%, computer/information sciences 10%, engineering/engineering technologies 30%, mathematics 9%, physical sciences 34%.

Computing on campus. 112 workstations in dormitories, library, computer center. Dormitories wired for high-speed internet access and linked to campus network. Commuter students can connect to campus network. Online course registration, online library, helpline, repair service, student web hosting, wireless network available.

Student life. Freshman orientation: Mandatory, $500 fee. 3 day camp. **Housing:** Guaranteed on-campus for all undergraduates. Coed dorms, special housing for disabled, apartments available. Pets allowed in dorm rooms. Single-unit houses available. **Activities:** Bands, choral groups, dance, drama, film society, literary magazine, music ensembles, musical theater, opera, student government, student newspaper, symphony orchestra, Caltech Y, Christian fellowship, Newman Club, Hillel, Amnesty International.

Athletics. NCAA. **Intercollegiate:** Baseball M, basketball, cross-country, diving, fencing, soccer M, swimming, tennis, track and field, volleyball W, water polo. **Intramural:** Badminton, baseball M, basketball, cheerleading, cricket M, cross-country, football (tackle) M, soccer, softball, squash, swimming, table tennis, tennis, track and field, volleyball, water polo M. **Team name:** Beavers.

Student services. Alcohol/substance abuse counseling, chaplain/spiritual director, career counseling, student employment services, financial aid counseling, health services, minority student services, on-campus daycare, personal counseling, placement for graduates, women's services. **Physically disabled:** Services for visually, speech, hearing impaired.

Contact. E-mail: ugadmissions@caltech.edu
Phone: (626) 395-6341 Fax: (626) 683-3026
Richard Bischoff, Director of Admissions, California Institute of Technology, 1200 East California Boulevard, MC 1-94, Pasadena, CA 91125

California Institute of the Arts

Valencia, California — **CB member**
www.calarts.edu — **CB code: 4049**

- Private 4-year visual arts and performing arts college
- Residential campus in small city
- 863 degree-seeking undergraduates: 1% part-time, 47% women, 9% African American, 10% Asian American, 11% Hispanic American, 1% Native American, 7% international
- 501 graduate students
- 33% of applicants admitted
- Application essay required
- 57% graduate within 6 years

General. Founded in 1961. Regionally accredited. Single complex of 6 professional schools: art, critical studies, dance, film/video, music and theater. **Degrees:** 189 bachelor's awarded; master's offered. **Location:** 30 miles from Los Angeles. **Calendar:** Semester. **Full-time faculty:** 156 total; 44% women. **Part-time faculty:** 144 total; 37% women. **Class size:** 75% < 20, 22% 20-39, less than 1% 40-49, 3% 50-99. **Special facilities:** Art studios, galleries, animation studios, concert halls, 6 theaters.

Freshman class profile. 1,161 applied, 388 admitted, 172 enrolled.

End year in good standing:	91%	**Live on campus:**	79%
Return as sophomores:	75%	**International:**	8%
Out-of-state:	62%		

Basis for selection. Admission is talent based, evaluated by faculty via group review. Portfolio required for art/design, film/video, music composition majors, and theater design and production. Auditions required for acting, dance, music majors. Music applicants may submit audio tape recordings in lieu of live audition for some programs. Interview required for directing/performance/production studies majors. **Homeschooled:** Transcript of courses and grades, state high school equivalency certificate, letter of recommendation (nonparent) required.

High school preparation. College-preparatory program recommended.

2009-2010 Annual costs. Tuition/fees (projected): $35,406. Room/board: $9,070. Books/supplies: $1,500. Personal expenses: $1,700.

2008-2009 Financial aid. Need-based: 133 full-time freshmen applied for aid; 103 were judged to have need; 102 of these received aid. Average need met was 72%. Average scholarship/grant was $13,917; average loan $4,907. 49% of total undergraduate aid awarded as scholarships/grants, 51% as loans/jobs. **Non-need-based:** Awarded to 76 full-time undergraduates, including 19 freshmen. Scholarships awarded for academics, art, minority status, music/drama.

Application procedures. Admission: Priority date 12/1; deadline 1/5 (receipt date). $70 fee, may be waived for applicants with need. Application must be submitted online. Admission notification on a rolling basis beginning on or about 3/1. Must reply by May 1 or within 2 week(s) if notified thereafter. Some programs remain open after January 5. Please contact the Office of Admissions for more information. **Financial aid:** Priority date 3/2; no closing date. FAFSA required. Applicants notified on a rolling basis starting 4/1; must reply by 5/1 or within 3 week(s) of notification.

Academics. Numerous special programs that cross traditional lines. **Special study options:** Independent study, internships, student-designed major, study abroad. **Credit/placement by examination:** AP, CLEP, IB, institutional tests. 6 credit hours maximum toward bachelor's degree. **Support services:** Learning center, tutoring.

Majors. Communications technology: Animation/special effects. **Computer sciences:** Computer graphics. **Visual/performing arts:** General, acting, art, cinematography, commercial/advertising art, dance, dramatic, film/cinema, graphic design, jazz, music performance, music theory/composition, painting, photography, piano/organ, sculpture, stringed instruments, studio arts, theater arts management, theater design, voice/opera.

Computing on campus. 40 workstations in library, computer center. Dormitories wired for high-speed internet access. Helpline, wireless network available.

Student life. Freshman orientation: Mandatory. Held the week before classes begin each semester. **Housing:** Coed dorms, special housing for disabled, apartments available. $250 nonrefundable deposit, deadline 6/1. **Activities:** Jazz band, dance, drama, film society, literary magazine, music ensembles, opera, radio station, student government, student newspaper, TV station, black student union, Latino student union, GLBT student union, Asian club, political issues club.

Student services. Career counseling, student employment services, financial aid counseling, health services, personal counseling, placement for graduates, veterans' counselor. **Physically disabled:** Services for visually, speech, hearing impaired.

Contact. E-mail: admiss@calarts.edu
Phone: (661) 255-1050 ext. 2185 Toll-free number: (800) 545-2787
Fax: (661) 253-7710
Molly Ryan, Director of Admissions, California Institute of the Arts, 24700 McBean Parkway, Valencia, CA 91355

California Lutheran University

Thousand Oaks, California — **CB member**
www.callutheran.edu — **CB code: 4088**

- Private 4-year university and liberal arts college affiliated with Evangelical Lutheran Church in America
- Residential campus in small city
- 2,199 degree-seeking undergraduates: 9% part-time, 57% women, 3% African American, 6% Asian American, 16% Hispanic American, 1% Native American, 4% international
- 1,249 degree-seeking graduate students
- 65% of applicants admitted
- SAT or ACT (ACT writing optional), application essay required
- 70% graduate within 6 years

General. Founded in 1959. Regionally accredited. **Degrees:** 571 bachelor's awarded; master's, doctoral offered. **ROTC:** Army, Air Force. **Location:** 45 miles from Los Angeles. **Calendar:** Semester, limited summer session. **Full-time faculty:** 137 total; 87% have terminal degrees, 18% minority, 45% women. **Part-time faculty:** 149 total; 38% have terminal degrees, 13% minority, 45% women. **Class size:** 68% < 20, 30% 20-39, 2% 40-49, less than 1% 50-99. **Special facilities:** Sports and fitness center with dance studio, Olympic-size pool, television studio with editing room.

Freshman class profile. 2,803 applied, 1,816 admitted, 482 enrolled.

Mid 50% test scores		**GPA 2.0-2.99:**	15%
SAT critical reading:	490-600	**Rank in top quarter:**	70%
SAT math:	500-610	**Rank in top tenth:**	31%
SAT writing:	500-590	**Return as sophomores:**	81%
ACT composite:	22-27	**Out-of-state:**	24%
GPA 3.75 or higher:	36%	**Live on campus:**	88%
GPA 3.50-3.74:	17%	**International:**	4%
GPA 3.0-3.49:	32%		

Basis for selection. High school achievement record, rank in class, test scores, essay, letters of recommendation very important. Interview recommended. **Homeschooled:** Transcript of courses and grades, letter of recommendation (nonparent) required. Encouraged to submit passing score on GED and complete interview with Admission Counselor. Transcript must include: brief description of courses, textbook (title and author) information for each course, how foreign language verbal component and natural science laboratory requirements were met; official transcripts from other school(s) attended. **Learning Disabled:** Meeting with the Accessibility Resource Coordinator is recommended.

High school preparation. College-preparatory program recommended. Required units include English 4, mathematics 3, social studies 2, science 2 (laboratory 2) and foreign language 2. Math must be through algebra II and preferably 4 years; 2 years of foreign language must be same language; highly recommend 3 years of science.

2008-2009 Annual costs. Tuition/fees: $27,850. Room/board: $9,650. Books/supplies: $1,399. Personal expenses: $2,021.

2008-2009 Financial aid. Need-based: 471 full-time freshmen applied for aid; 317 were judged to have need; 317 of these received aid. Average need met was 79%. Average scholarship/grant was $18,030; average loan $3,440. 64% of total undergraduate aid awarded as scholarships/grants, 36% as loans/jobs. **Non-need-based:** Awarded to 939 full-time undergraduates, including 210 freshmen. Scholarships awarded for academics, alumni affiliation, art, leadership, minority status, music/drama, religious affiliation, state residency.

Application procedures. Admission: Priority date 11/15; deadline 3/15 (postmark date). $45 fee, may be waived for applicants with need. Admission notification 4/15. Admission notification on a rolling basis beginning on or about 1/15. Must reply by May 1 or within 2 week(s) if notified thereafter. **Financial aid:** Priority date 3/1; no closing date. FAFSA required. Applicants notified on a rolling basis starting 3/15; must reply within 2 week(s) of notification.

Academics. Special study options: Accelerated study, cooperative education, double major, dual enrollment of high school students, exchange student, honors, independent study, internships, New York semester, semester at sea, student-designed major, study abroad, teacher certification program, Washington semester. **Credit/placement by examination:** AP, CLEP, IB, SAT, ACT, institutional tests. 30 credit hours maximum toward bachelor's degree. **Support services:** Learning center, reduced course load, study skills assistance, tutoring, writing center.

Majors. Biology: General, biochemistry, molecular. **Business:** General, accounting, business admin, finance, managerial economics, marketing. **Communications:** General, advertising, broadcast journalism, journalism, public relations. **Computer sciences:** General, computer graphics, computer science, information systems, programming. **Conservation:** Environmental science. **Education:** General, art, early childhood, elementary, English, foreign languages, mathematics, middle, music, physical, reading, science, secondary, social science, social studies, special. **Engineering:** Biomedical. **Foreign languages:** General, French, German, Spanish. **Health:** Athletic training, predental, premedicine, prepharmacy, preveterinary. **History:** General. **Interdisciplinary:** Biological/physical sciences, math/computer science. **Legal studies:** Prelaw. **Liberal arts:** Arts/sciences. **Math:** General. **Philosophy/religion:** Philosophy, religion. **Physical sciences:** Chemistry, geology, physics. **Protective services:** Police science. **Psychology:** General. **Science technology:** Biological. **Social sciences:** Criminology, economics, international relations, political science, sociology. **Theology:** Religious ed, theology. **Visual/performing arts:** General, art, commercial/advertising art, dramatic.

Most popular majors. Business/marketing 27%, communications/journalism 13%, liberal arts 6%, parks/recreation 6%, psychology 8%, social sciences 9%.

Computing on campus. 172 workstations in library, computer center, student center. Dormitories wired for high-speed internet access and linked to campus network. Commuter students can connect to campus network. Online library, helpline, wireless network available.

Student life. Freshman orientation: Mandatory. Preregistration for classes offered. **Policies:** No alcohol on campus except in the chapel for communion, drug free campus. **Housing:** Coed dorms, special housing for disabled, apartments available. $195 fully refundable deposit, deadline 5/1. On campus houses available. **Activities:** Bands, campus ministries, choral groups, dance, drama, international student organizations, literary magazine, music ensembles, Model UN, musical theater, radio station, student government, student newspaper, symphony orchestra, TV station, Lutheran Church Congregation, multicultural and international clubs and organizations, Hillel, Habitat for Humanitiy.

Athletics. NCAA. **Intercollegiate:** Baseball M, basketball, cross-country, diving, football (tackle) M, golf M, soccer, softball W, swimming, tennis, track and field, volleyball W, water polo. **Intramural:** Basketball, football (non-tackle), soccer, softball, volleyball, water polo. **Team name:** Kingsmen/Regals.

Student services. Adult student services, alcohol/substance abuse counseling, chaplain/spiritual director, career counseling, services for economically disadvantaged, student employment services, financial aid counseling, health services, minority student services, personal counseling, placement for graduates, veterans' counselor, women's services. **Physically disabled:** Services for visually, hearing impaired. **Learning disabled:** Comprehensive services available.

Contact. E-mail: admissions@callutheran.edu
Phone: (805) 493-3135 Toll-free number: (877) 258-3678
Fax: (805) 493-3114
Matthew Ward, Vice President for Enrollment Management, California Lutheran University, 60 West Olsen Road #1350, Thousand Oaks, CA 91360-2787

California Maritime Academy

Vallejo, California — **CB member**
www.csum.edu — **CB code: 4035**

- Public 4-year university and maritime college
- Residential campus in small city
- 810 degree-seeking undergraduates
- 73% of applicants admitted

General. Founded in 1929. Regionally accredited. Highest job placement in the California State University system. Not a military school. All students participate in at least one 2-month training cruise around Pacific Ocean geared toward their major. **Degrees:** 161 bachelor's awarded. **ROTC:** Naval. **Location:** 30 miles from San Francisco. **Calendar:** Semester, limited summer session. **Full-time faculty:** 50 total. **Part-time faculty:** 25 total. **Special facilities:** 500-foot training ship, computer-aided radar simulators, bridge simulator, steam simulator.

Freshman class profile. 894 applied, 649 admitted, 249 enrolled.

Out-of-state:	17%	**Live on campus:**	90%

Basis for selection. Applicants must meet California State University Eligibility Index requirements and have strong grades in mathematics and sciences. All accepted students must pass physical examination. Applicants must meet California State University Eligibility Index requirements and have strong grades in mathematics and sciences. All accepted students must pass physical examination. Interview recommended; supplemental admission form required.

High school preparation. Required and recommended units include English 4, mathematics 3-4, social studies 1, history 1, science 2 (laboratory 2), foreign language 2-3 and academic electives 1. One additional mathematics course recommended for mechanical engineering applicants. Chemistry or physics required. One visual or performing arts elective required.

2008-2009 Annual costs. Tuition/fees: $4,112; $14,282 out-of-state. Each student participates in at least one cruise and one internship prior to graduation. Some majors have additional cruise requirements. The cost for a cruise is $3,800. The cost for an internship/co-op is $225. Additionally, each incoming student must purchase a uniform. Prices range from $1,550-$1,785 depending on the major. Reduced out-of-state tuition for residents of AK, AZ, CO, HI, ID, MT, NV, NM, ND, OR, SD, UT, WA, WY available under the Western Undergraduate Exchange (WUE) program. WUE students pay one-and-a half the State University Fee ($3,048 this year), which is $4,572. Room/board: $8,830. Books/supplies: $1,656. Personal expenses: $2,826.

Financial aid. All financial aid based on need. **Additional information:** US Maritime Administration provides annual incentive payment of $3,000 per student, with certain conditions. Tuition waiver for children of deceased or disabled California veterans.

Application procedures. Admission: Priority date 11/30; no deadline. $55 fee, may be waived for applicants with need. Admission notification on a rolling basis beginning on or about 2/1. Must reply by May 1 or within 2 week(s) if notified thereafter. **Financial aid:** Priority date 4/2; no closing date. FAFSA required. Applicants notified on a rolling basis starting 4/1.

Academics. Center for Excellence and Learning provides free tutoring/workshops hosted by professors. **Special study options:** Cooperative education, distance learning, double major, ESL, internships. International training cruise onboard ship "Golden Bear". **Credit/placement by examination:** AP, CLEP. 24 credit hours maximum toward bachelor's degree. **Support services:** Learning center, remedial instruction, tutoring.

Majors. Business: Business admin, logistics. **Engineering:** Marine, mechanical. **Engineering technology:** General. **Interdisciplinary:** Global studies. **Social sciences:** Political science. **Other:** Marine transportation.

Computing on campus. 85 workstations in dormitories, library, computer center, student center. Dormitories wired for high-speed internet access and linked to campus network. Helpline, repair service available.

Student life. Freshman orientation: Mandatory, $200 fee. Preregistration for classes offered. Held last week of August. **Policies:** Students required to live on campus except those married or with children. **Housing:** Guaranteed on-campus for all undergraduates. Coed dorms available. $500 deposit, deadline 7/1. **Activities:** Student government, student newspaper.

Athletics. NAIA. **Intercollegiate:** Basketball, rowing (crew), rugby M, sailing, soccer, water polo. **Intramural:** Badminton, baseball M, basketball, boxing M, golf, racquetball, rowing (crew), rugby M, sailing, softball, tennis, volleyball, water polo. **Team name:** Keelhaulers.

Student services. Career counseling, student employment services, financial aid counseling, health services, minority student services, personal counseling, placement for graduates, veterans' counselor.

Contact. E-mail: admission@csum.edu
Phone: (707) 654-1330 Toll-free number: (800) 561-1945
Fax: (707) 654-1336
Marc McGee, Director of Admission, California Maritime Academy, 200 Maritime Academy Drive, Vallejo, CA 94590

California National University for Advanced Studies

Northridge, California
www.cnuas.edu — **CB code: 3894**

- For-profit 4-year virtual university
- Small city
- 180 degree-seeking undergraduates

General. Accredited by DETC. 100% distance learning university. **Degrees:** 19 bachelor's awarded; master's offered. **Calendar:** Continuous. **Part-time faculty:** 80 total.

Basis for selection. Application/portfolio important.

2008-2009 Annual costs. Domestic/Canada undergraduate tuition: $270/unit; international undergraduate tuition $300/unit.

Application procedures. Admission: No deadline. $75 fee.

Academics. Special study options: Distance learning. **Credit/placement by examination:** CLEP.

Majors. Business: Business admin. **Computer sciences:** Computer science. **Engineering:** General.

Contact. E-mail: cnuadms@mail.cnuas.edu
Phone: (818) 830-2411 Toll-free number: (800) 782-2422
Fax: (818) 830-2418
California National University for Advanced Studies, 8550 Balboa Boulevard, Suite 210, Northridge, CA 91325

California Polytechnic State University: San Luis Obispo

San Luis Obispo, California — **CB member**
www.calpoly.edu — **CB code: 4038**

- Public 4-year university
- Residential campus in large town
- 18,400 degree-seeking undergraduates: 4% part-time, 44% women, 1% African American, 11% Asian American, 11% Hispanic American, 1% Native American, 1% international

- 788 degree-seeking graduate students
- 34% of applicants admitted
- SAT or ACT (ACT writing optional) required
- 72% graduate within 6 years

General. Founded in 1901. Regionally accredited. **Degrees:** 3,641 bachelor's awarded; master's offered. **ROTC:** Army. **Location:** 200 miles from Los Angeles, 250 miles from San Francisco. **Calendar:** Quarter, extensive summer session. **Full-time faculty:** 824 total; 82% have terminal degrees, 14% minority, 31% women. **Part-time faculty:** 469 total; 32% have terminal degrees, 10% minority, 40% women. **Class size:** 17% < 20, 59% 20-39, 12% 40-49, 9% 50-99, 4% >100. **Special facilities:** Printing press museum, university farm, dairy products technical center, architectural design institute.

Freshman class profile. 33,352 applied, 11,173 admitted, 3,501 enrolled.

Mid 50% test scores		**Rank in top quarter:**	83%
SAT critical reading:	530-630	**Rank in top tenth:**	47%
SAT math:	570-680	**Return as sophomores:**	89%
ACT composite:	24-29	**Out-of-state:**	7%
GPA 3.75 or higher:	57%	**Live on campus:**	95%
GPA 3.50-3.74:	22%	**International:**	1%
GPA 3.0-3.49:	19%	**Fraternities:**	10%
GPA 2.0-2.99:	2%	**Sororities:**	11%

Basis for selection. Course work, high school GPA, test scores most important. Extracurricular activities considered. Portfolio required for art, design majors.

High school preparation. College-preparatory program required. 15 units required; 22 recommended. Required and recommended units include English 4-5, mathematics 3-4, social studies 2, history 1, science 3-4 (laboratory 1-2), foreign language 2-3, visual/performing arts 1 and academic electives 1. History must be U.S. history/government.

2008-2009 Annual costs. Tuition/fees: $5,043; $15,213 out-of-state. Required fees vary by program. Room/board: $9,369.

2007-2008 Financial aid. Need-based: 2,816 full-time freshmen applied for aid; 1,417 were judged to have need; 1,244 of these received aid. Average need met was 65%. Average scholarship/grant was $1,882; average loan $3,024. 53% of total undergraduate aid awarded as scholarships/grants, 47% as loans/jobs. **Non-need-based:** Awarded to 984 full-time undergraduates, including 316 freshmen. Scholarships awarded for academics, alumni affiliation, art, athletics, job skills, leadership, music/drama, ROTC, state residency. **Additional information:** College-administered financial aid is not available for undergraduate international students.

Application procedures. Admission: Closing date 11/30 (postmark date). $55 fee, may be waived for applicants with need. Admission notification 4/1. Must reply by 5/1. Housing deposit due on first-come, first-served basis. **Financial aid:** Priority date 3/2; no closing date. FAFSA required. Applicants notified on a rolling basis starting 4/15; must reply within 8 week(s) of notification.

Academics. Special study options: Combined bachelor's/graduate degree, cooperative education, distance learning, double major, ESL, exchange student, honors, internships, liberal arts/career combination, semester at sea, study abroad, teacher certification program. **Credit/placement by examination:** AP, CLEP, SAT, ACT, institutional tests. 45 credit hours maximum toward bachelor's degree. **Support services:** Learning center, preadmission summer program, reduced course load, remedial instruction, study skills assistance, tutoring, writing center.

Majors. Agriculture: Agribusiness operations, agronomy, animal sciences, business, dairy, food science, horticultural science, plant protection, soil science. **Architecture:** Architecture, landscape, urban/community planning. **Biology:** General, biochemistry, microbiology. **Business:** Accounting, construction management, finance, management information systems, marketing. **Communications:** General, journalism. **Communications technology:** Graphics. **Computer sciences:** Computer science. **Conservation:** Forestry. **Education:** Agricultural. **Engineering:** General, aerospace, agricultural, architectural, biomedical, civil, electrical, environmental, industrial, manufacturing, materials, mechanical, software. **Family/consumer sciences:** Child development, food/nutrition. **Foreign languages:** General. **History:** General. **Liberal arts:** Arts/sciences. **Math:** General, statistics. **Parks/recreation:** Exercise sciences, facilities management. **Philosophy/religion:** Philosophy. **Physical sciences:** General, chemistry, geology, physics. **Psychology:** General. **Social sciences:** General, economics, political science. **Visual/performing arts:** Art, commercial/advertising art, dramatic. **Other:** Agricultural science, Art and design, Comparative ethnic studies, Environmental management & protection, Industrial technology.

Most popular majors. Agriculture 12%, architecture 7%, business/marketing 16%, engineering/engineering technologies 23%.

Computing on campus. Dormitories wired for high-speed internet access and linked to campus network. Commuter students can connect to campus network. Online course registration, online library, helpline, student web hosting, wireless network available.

Student life. Freshman orientation: Available. Held week prior to start of fall term. **Housing:** Coed dorms, special housing for disabled, apartments available. $1,888 fully refundable deposit. **Activities:** Bands, campus ministries, choral groups, dance, drama, international student organizations, literary magazine, music ensembles, Model UN, musical theater, radio station, student government, student newspaper, symphony orchestra, TV station, MECHA, Society of Black Engineers and Scientists, Minority Engineering Program.

Athletics. NCAA. **Intercollegiate:** Baseball M, basketball, cross-country, diving, football (tackle) M, golf, soccer, softball W, swimming, tennis, track and field, volleyball W, wrestling M. **Intramural:** Badminton, bowling, equestrian, fencing, field hockey, lacrosse, rugby M, sailing, soccer, triathlon, volleyball, water polo. **Team name:** Mustangs.

Student services. Adult student services, alcohol/substance abuse counseling, chaplain/spiritual director, career counseling, student employment services, health services, minority student services, on-campus daycare, personal counseling, placement for graduates, veterans' counselor, women's services. **Physically disabled:** Services for visually, speech, hearing impaired.

Contact. E-mail: admissions@calpoly.edu
Phone: (805) 756-2311 Fax: (805) 756-5400
James Maraviglia, Admissions Officer, California Polytechnic State University: San Luis Obispo, Admissions Office, Cal Poly, San Luis Obispo, CA 93407-0031

California State Polytechnic University: Pomona

Pomona, California — **CB member**
www.csupomona.edu — **CB code: 4082**

- Public 4-year university
- Commuter campus in small city
- 19,220 degree-seeking undergraduates: 17% part-time, 43% women, 4% African American, 28% Asian American, 30% Hispanic American, 5% international
- 1,970 degree-seeking graduate students
- 53% of applicants admitted
- SAT or ACT (ACT writing optional) required
- 51% graduate within 6 years

General. Founded in 1938. Regionally accredited. **Degrees:** 3,768 bachelor's awarded; master's offered. **ROTC:** Army. **Location:** 30 miles from downtown Los Angeles. **Calendar:** Quarter, extensive summer session. **Full-time faculty:** 569 total; 77% have terminal degrees, 34% minority, 40% women. **Part-time faculty:** 456 total; 28% have terminal degrees, 26% minority, 38% women. **Class size:** 15% < 20, 55% 20-39, 16% 40-49, 12% 50-99, 1% >100. **Special facilities:** Electron microscope center, international center, small ruminant center, Arabian horse center, equine research center, land laboratory, ecological reserve, center for regenerative studies, center for community affairs.

Freshman class profile. 24,530 applied, 12,952 admitted, 2,640 enrolled.

Mid 50% test scores		**GPA 2.0-2.99:**	23%
SAT critical reading:	440-550	**End year in good standing:**	78%
SAT math:	470-600	**Return as sophomores:**	84%
ACT composite:	18-24	**Out-of-state:**	1%
GPA 3.75 or higher:	14%	**Live on campus:**	32%
GPA 3.50-3.74:	19%	**International:**	3%
GPA 3.0-3.49:	44%		

Basis for selection. High school GPA, courses, and test scores important.

High school preparation. College-preparatory program required. 15 units required. Required and recommended units include English 4, mathematics 3-4, social studies 1, history 1, science 2 (laboratory 2), foreign language 2, visual/performing arts 1 and academic electives 1.

2008-2009 Annual costs. Tuition/fees: $3,564; $13,734 out-of-state. Room/board: $9,120. Books/supplies: $1,500. Personal expenses: $1,575.

2008-2009 Financial aid. Need-based: 1,853 full-time freshmen applied for aid; 1,260 were judged to have need; 1,195 of these received aid.

Average need met was 76%. Average scholarship/grant was $7,622; average loan $2,926. 60% of total undergraduate aid awarded as scholarships/grants, 40% as loans/jobs. **Non-need-based:** Awarded to 642 full-time undergraduates, including 157 freshmen. Scholarships awarded for academics, alumni affiliation, athletics, leadership, state residency.

Application procedures. Admission: Priority date 11/30; deadline 11/30 (postmark date). $55 fee, may be waived for applicants with need. Admission notification on a rolling basis beginning on or about 10/2. Must reply by May 1 or within 3 week(s) if notified thereafter. Applications for first time freshmen accepted October 1 through November 30. **Financial aid:** Priority date 3/3; no closing date. FAFSA required. Applicants notified on a rolling basis starting 4/1; must reply within 2 week(s) of notification.

Academics. Special study options: Cooperative education, cross-registration, distance learning, double major, dual enrollment of high school students, ESL, exchange student, external degree, honors, internships, study abroad, teacher certification program. Ocean studies institute, desert studies consortium. **Credit/placement by examination:** AP, CLEP, SAT, ACT, institutional tests. 36 credit hours maximum toward bachelor's degree. **Support services:** Learning center, pre-admission summer program, remedial instruction, study skills assistance, tutoring, writing center.

Honors college/program. Incoming freshmen invited to apply to Honors College if they have scores of 550 or higher on both math and critical reading SAT tests and GPA of 3.5 or higher. Incoming transfer students must have GPA of at least 3.5 at previous institution.

Majors. Agriculture: Animal sciences, business, food science, plant protection. **Architecture:** Architecture, landscape, urban/community planning. **Area/ethnic studies:** American. **Biology:** General, biotechnology, botany, environmental, microbiology, zoology. **Business:** Business admin, hospitality admin. **Communications:** General. **Computer sciences:** Computer science. **Education:** Agricultural. **Engineering:** General, aerospace, chemical, civil, computer, electrical, industrial, manufacturing, materials, mechanical. **Engineering technology:** General, construction, electrical. **Family/consumer sciences:** Clothing/textiles. **Foreign languages:** Spanish. **Health:** Dietetics. **History:** General. **Interdisciplinary:** Behavioral sciences. **Liberal arts:** Arts/sciences, humanities. **Math:** General. **Parks/recreation:** Health/fitness. **Philosophy/religion:** Philosophy. **Physical sciences:** Chemistry, geology, physics. **Psychology:** General. **Social sciences:** General, anthropology, economics, geography, political science, sociology. **Visual/performing arts:** Art, dramatic, graphic design. **Other:** Gender, ethnic, multicultural studies, Integrated earth studies.

Most popular majors. Business/marketing 35%, engineering/engineering technologies 18%, liberal arts 6%.

Computing on campus. 280 workstations in library, computer center. Dormitories wired for high-speed internet access and linked to campus network. Commuter students can connect to campus network. Online course registration, helpline, student web hosting available.

Student life. Freshman orientation: Mandatory, $40 fee. Preregistration for classes offered. One-day orientation. **Housing:** Coed dorms, apartments available. $50 fully refundable deposit. **Activities:** Bands, choral groups, dance, drama, literary magazine, music ensembles, musical theater, opera, student government, student newspaper, symphony orchestra, Campus Crusade for Christ, black student union, Hawaiian club, MECHA, Studies of the World, Newman Club, Hillel, Bahai club, Coptic-Orthodox Christian club.

Athletics. NCAA. **Intercollegiate:** Baseball M, basketball, cross-country, soccer, tennis, track and field, volleyball W. **Intramural:** Badminton, basketball, football (non-tackle) M, golf, racquetball, softball, swimming, table tennis, tennis, track and field, volleyball. **Team name:** Broncos.

Student services. Adult student services, career counseling, student employment services, health services, on-campus daycare, personal counseling, placement for graduates, veterans' counselor. **Physically disabled:** Services for visually, speech, hearing impaired.

Contact. E-mail: admissions@csupomona.edu
Phone: (909) 869-3210 Fax: (909) 869-4529
Scott Duncan, Director of Admissions, California State Polytechnic University: Pomona, 3801 West Temple Avenue, Pomona, CA 91768-4019

California State University: Bakersfield

Bakersfield, California — **CB member**
www.csub.edu — **CB code: 4110**

- Public 4-year university and liberal arts college
- Commuter campus in small city
- 6,078 degree-seeking undergraduates
- 61% of applicants admitted

General. Founded in 1965. Regionally accredited. **Degrees:** 1,152 bachelor's awarded; master's offered. **Location:** 112 miles from Los Angeles. **Calendar:** Quarter, limited summer session. **Full-time faculty:** 284 total. **Part-time faculty:** 132 total. **Class size:** 47% < 20, 44% 20-39, 6% 40-49, 2% 50-99, less than 1% >100. **Special facilities:** 40-acre facility for wild animal care, archaeological information center, center for business and economic research, center for economic education, well-sample repository, center for physiological research.

Freshman class profile. 5,159 applied, 3,171 admitted, 925 enrolled.

Mid 50% test scores		**GPA 3.50-3.74:**	10%
SAT critical reading:	380-490	**GPA 3.0-3.49:**	43%
SAT math:	380-510	**GPA 2.0-2.99:**	34%
ACT composite:	13-20	**Out-of-state:**	3%
GPA 3.75 or higher:	12%	**Live on campus:**	12%

Basis for selection. GPA, test scores, and certain honors courses must place applicant in upper third of California high school graduates (upper sixth for out-of-state applicants) using eligibility index table. Minimum test scores slightly higher for out-of-state students. GPA, test scores, and certain honors courses must place applicant in upper third of California high school graduates (upper sixth for out-of-state applicants) using eligibility index table. Minimum test scores slightly higher for out-of-state students.

High school preparation. Required units include English 4, mathematics 3, history 2, science 2 (laboratory 1), foreign language 2 and academic electives 1. One visual and performing arts required; foreign language must be in same language; math must include algebra, geometry, and intermediate algebra; science must include biology and a physical science.

2008-2009 Annual costs. Tuition/fees: $4,077; $14,241 out-of-state. Reduced out-of-state tuition for residents of AK, AZ, CO, HI, ID, MT, NV, NM, ND, OR, SD, UT, WA, WY available under the Western Undergraduate Exchange (WUE) program. WUE students pay one-and-a half the State University Fees plus campus-based fees, which is $5,601 for the 2008/2009 academic year. Room/board: $6,852. Books/supplies: $1,425. Personal expenses: $2,520.

2007-2008 Financial aid. All financial aid based on need. 69% of total undergraduate aid awarded as scholarships/grants, 31% as loans/jobs.

Application procedures. Admission: Priority date 3/1; no deadline. $55 fee, may be waived for applicants with need. Admission notification on a rolling basis beginning on or about 7/1. **Financial aid:** Priority date 3/2, closing date 4/1. FAFSA required. Applicants notified on a rolling basis; must reply within 2 week(s) of notification.

Academics. Most courses are 5 quarter units. Students enrolled in 3 courses are carrying full unit load. **Special study options:** Accelerated study, cooperative education, distance learning, double major, ESL, exchange student, external degree, honors, independent study, internships, liberal arts/career combination, student-designed major, study abroad, teacher certification program. 2+2 at specified locations for liberal studies (teaching) majors. **Credit/placement by examination:** CLEP. Unlimited number of hours of credit by examination may be counted toward degree. **Support services:** Learning center, pre-admission summer program, reduced course load, remedial instruction, study skills assistance, tutoring.

Majors. Biology: General. **Business:** Business admin. **Communications:** General. **Computer sciences:** Computer science. **Conservation:** Land use planning. **Education:** Early childhood. **Foreign languages:** Spanish. **Health:** Nursing (RN). **History:** General. **Liberal arts:** Arts/sciences. **Math:** General. **Philosophy/religion:** Philosophy, religion. **Physical sciences:** Chemistry, geology, physics. **Protective services:** Criminal justice. **Psychology:** General. **Public administration:** General. **Social sciences:** Anthropology, criminology, economics, political science, sociology. **Visual/performing arts:** General, art, dramatic.

Most popular majors. Business/marketing 15%, liberal arts 27%, psychology 10%, security/protective services 6%, social sciences 7%.

Computing on campus. 600 workstations in library, computer center, student center. Dormitories linked to campus network. Commuter students can connect to campus network. Online course registration, online library, helpline, student web hosting available.

Student life. Freshman orientation: Available, $35 fee. Preregistration for classes offered. **Housing:** Guaranteed on-campus for all undergraduates. Coed dorms, single-sex dorms available. $50 deposit. **Activities:** Jazz band, choral groups, dance, drama, literary magazine, music ensembles, musical theater, student government, student newspaper, black student union, Movimiento Estudiantil Chicano de Aztlan, Christian union, student nursing association, Circle-K, Latinos United for Education.

Athletics. NCAA. **Intercollegiate:** Basketball, cheerleading, cross-country W, golf M, soccer, softball W, swimming, tennis W, track and field, volleyball W, water polo W, wrestling M. **Intramural:** Badminton, basketball, golf, handball, racquetball, soccer, softball, tennis, volleyball. **Team name:** Roadrunners.

Student services. Adult student services, alcohol/substance abuse counseling, career counseling, services for economically disadvantaged, student employment services, financial aid counseling, health services, minority student services, on-campus daycare, personal counseling, placement for graduates, veterans' counselor. **Physically disabled:** Services for visually, speech, hearing impaired. **Learning disabled:** Comprehensive services available.

Contact. Phone: (661) 654-3036 Toll-free number: (800) 788-2782
Fax: (661) 654-3389
Jacqueline Mimms, Director of Admissions, California State University: Bakersfield, 9001 Stockdale Highway, Bakersfield, CA 93311-1099

California State University: Channel Islands

Camarillo, California — **CB member**
www.csuci.edu — **CB code: 4128**

- Public 4-year university
- Commuter campus in small city
- 3,482 degree-seeking undergraduates: 18% part-time, 62% women
- 162 degree-seeking graduate students

General. Regionally accredited. **Degrees:** 185 bachelor's awarded; master's offered. **Calendar:** Semester. **Full-time faculty:** 87 total; 100% have terminal degrees. **Part-time faculty:** 140 total; 100% have terminal degrees.

Freshman class profile. 535 enrolled.

Mid 50% test scores		**GPA 3.50-3.74:**	14%
SAT critical reading:	440-550	**GPA 3.0-3.49:**	46%
SAT math:	440-550	**GPA 2.0-2.99:**	32%
ACT composite:	18-23	**Out-of-state:**	1%
GPA 3.75 or higher:	8%	**Live on campus:**	68%

Basis for selection. Academic GPA very important. Rigor of secondary school record and state residency important. Test scores required for students with less than 3.0 HS GPA.

High school preparation. College-preparatory program required. 15 units required. Required units include English 4, mathematics 3, social studies 1, history 1, science 2 (laboratory 2), foreign language 2, visual/performing arts 1 and academic electives 1.

2008-2009 Annual costs. Tuition/fees: $3,758; $13,928 out-of-state. Room/board: $10,200. Books/supplies: $1,400. Personal expenses: $2,400.

Application procedures. Admission: Priority date 11/30; deadline 1/15 (receipt date). $55 fee, may be waived for applicants with need. Admission notification on a rolling basis beginning on or about 1/2. Must reply by 5/1. **Financial aid:** Priority date 3/2; no closing date.

Academics. Special study options: Double major, independent study, study abroad, teacher certification program. **Credit/placement by examination:** AP, CLEP, SAT, ACT, institutional tests. **Support services:** Remedial instruction, tutoring, writing center.

Majors. Biology: General, biotechnology. **Business:** General. **Communications:** General. **Computer sciences:** General. **Conservation:** Environmental science, management/policy. **Education:** Early childhood. **Foreign languages:** Spanish. **History:** General. **Liberal arts:** Arts/sciences. **Math:** General. **Physical sciences:** Chemistry. **Psychology:** General. **Social sciences:** Economics, political science, sociology. **Visual/performing arts:** General, art. **Other:** Chicano studies.

Most popular majors. Biology 6%, business/marketing 21%, liberal arts 19%, psychology 17%, social sciences 8%, visual/performing arts 8%.

Computing on campus. Dormitories wired for high-speed internet access. Commuter students can connect to campus network. Online course registration, online library, helpline, wireless network available.

Student life. Freshman orientation: Mandatory, $120 fee. Preregistration for classes offered. Two-day session in July. **Housing:** Coed dorms, wellness housing available. $1,000 fully refundable deposit, deadline 6/1. **Activities:** Choral groups, student government, student newspaper.

Student services. Alcohol/substance abuse counseling, career counseling, services for economically disadvantaged, student employment services, financial aid counseling, health services, personal counseling, women's services. **Physically disabled:** Services for visually, speech, hearing impaired. **Learning disabled:** Comprehensive services available.

Contact. E-mail: admissionsandrecords@csuci.edu
Phone: (805) 437-8400
Jane Sweetland, Dean of Enrollment, California State University: Channel Islands, One University Drive, Camarillo, CA 93012

California State University: Chico

Chico, California — **CB member**
www.csuchico.edu — **CB code: 4048**

- Public 4-year university and liberal arts college
- Residential campus in small city
- 15,804 degree-seeking undergraduates: 9% part-time, 52% women, 2% African American, 6% Asian American, 13% Hispanic American, 1% Native American, 2% international
- 869 degree-seeking graduate students
- 87% of applicants admitted
- SAT or ACT (ACT writing optional) required
- 52% graduate within 6 years

General. Founded in 1887. Regionally accredited. **Degrees:** 3,005 bachelor's awarded; master's offered. **Location:** 90 miles from Sacramento, 175 miles from San Francisco. **Calendar:** Semester, limited summer session. **Full-time faculty:** 562 total; 84% have terminal degrees, 16% minority, 39% women. **Part-time faculty:** 409 total; 28% have terminal degrees, 9% minority, 55% women. **Class size:** 28% < 20, 43% 20-39, 17% 40-49, 8% 50-99, 3% >100. **Special facilities:** 1,000-acre farm, planetarium, instructional media center, biology field station, anthropology museum, intercultural studies center, computer graphics lab, assistive technology center, media prep lab, recording arts studio, hydrotherapy pool, echocardiography system, gas displacement chamber, two ecological preserves with nearly 4,100 acres, forensics lab, archaeology lab and research center.

Freshman class profile. 15,069 applied, 13,166 admitted, 2,765 enrolled.

Mid 50% test scores		**Rank in top quarter:**	76%
SAT critical reading:	440-550	**Rank in top tenth:**	35%
SAT math:	460-570	**End year in good standing:**	71%
ACT composite:	19-24	**Return as sophomores:**	79%
GPA 3.75 or higher:	10%	**Out-of-state:**	3%
GPA 3.50-3.74:	9%	**Live on campus:**	62%
GPA 3.0-3.49:	44%	**International:**	1%
GPA 2.0-2.99:	37%		

Basis for selection. Eligibility index derived from high school GPA and test scores. First-time freshmen applicants rank order based on characteristics of applicant pool. GPA determined from 10th, 11th, and 12th-grade college prep courses only, excluding physical education. Nursing program open only to state residents. Portfolio required of fine arts majors. **Homeschooled:** Transcript of courses and grades required. Must be able to verify completion of required college preparatory subject requirements and meet institutional eligibility index. **Learning Disabled:** Students must meet established admission criteria.

High school preparation. 15 units required. Required units include English 4, mathematics 3, social studies 2, science 2 (laboratory 2), foreign language 2 and visual/performing arts 1.

2008-2009 Annual costs. Tuition/fees: $4,008; $14,178 out-of-state. Reduced out-of-state tuition for residents of AK, AZ, CO. HI, ID, MT, NV, NM, ND, OR, SD, UT, WA, WY may be available under the Western Undergraduate Exchange (WUE) program. Room/board: $9,300. Books/supplies: $1,656. Personal expenses: $1,950.

2008-2009 Financial aid. Need-based: 1,836 full-time freshmen applied for aid; 1,158 were judged to have need; 1,138 of these received aid. Average need met was 88%. Average scholarship/grant was $7,913; average loan $3,538. 52% of total undergraduate aid awarded as scholarships/grants, 48% as loans/jobs. **Non-need-based:** Awarded to 2,193 full-time undergraduates, including 828 freshmen. Scholarships awarded for academics, art, athletics, leadership, minority status, music/drama, religious affiliation.

Application procedures. Admission: Priority date 10/1; deadline 11/30 (postmark date). $55 fee, may be waived for applicants with need. Admission notification 3/1. Admission notification on a rolling basis. Must reply by May 1 or within 2 week(s) if notified thereafter. Applications for the following majors must be made during priority periods of October and August: nursing, media arts, graphic design, recording arts, and interior design. All first time freshmen fall applicants should apply between October 1 and November 30. **Financial aid:** Priority date 3/2; no closing date. FAFSA required. Applicants notified on a rolling basis starting 3/2.

Academics. **Special study options:** Cooperative education, cross-registration, distance learning, double major, dual enrollment of high school students, ESL, exchange student, external degree, honors, independent study, internships, student-designed major, study abroad, teacher certification program. **Credit/placement by examination:** AP, CLEP, IB, SAT, ACT, institutional tests. 30 credit hours maximum toward bachelor's degree. 6 semester hours awarded for each International Baccalaureate higher level exam passed with score of 4 to 7. **Support services:** Learning center, pre-admission summer program, reduced course load, remedial instruction, study skills assistance, tutoring, writing center.

Majors. **Agriculture:** Agronomy, animal sciences, business, range science. **Architecture:** Urban/community planning. **Area/ethnic studies:** American, Asian, Latin American, women's. **Biology:** General, biochemistry, botany, ecology, microbiology. **Business:** Accounting, business admin, finance, human resources, management information systems, marketing. **Communications:** Journalism, organizational, public relations, radio/tv. **Computer sciences:** Computer graphics, computer science, information technology. **Conservation:** Environmental science, management/policy. **Education:** Agricultural, art, biology, chemistry, early childhood, English, ESL, French, German, health, instructional media, mathematics, music, physical, science, social science, Spanish. **Engineering:** Civil, computer, mechanical. **Engineering technology:** Construction. **Foreign languages:** French, German, linguistics, Spanish. **Health:** Clinical lab science, communication disorders, dietetics, health services, nursing (RN), predental, premedicine, prepharmacy, preveterinary, recreational therapy. **History:** General. **Interdisciplinary:** Accounting/computer science, gerontology, math/computer science. **Legal studies:** Paralegal. **Liberal arts:** Arts/sciences, humanities. **Math:** General, applied, statistics. **Parks/recreation:** General, exercise sciences, facilities management, health/fitness. **Philosophy/religion:** Judaic, philosophy, religion. **Physical sciences:** General, atmospheric science, chemistry, geology, hydrology, physics. **Protective services:** Criminal justice. **Psychology:** General. **Public administration:** General, social work. **Social sciences:** General, anthropology, economics, geography, international economics, international relations, political science, sociology. **Visual/performing arts:** Art, art history/conservation, design, dramatic, graphic design, interior design, music theory/composition, piano/organ, studio arts. **Other:** Concrete industry management, Ecological, evolutionary and organismal biology, Environmental economics, Mechatronics, Music industry and technology, Supply chain management systems.

Most popular majors. Business/marketing 16%, engineering/engineering technologies 8%, health sciences 6%, liberal arts 8%, parks/recreation 7%, psychology 6%, social sciences 10%, visual/performing arts 8%.

Computing on campus. 1,167 workstations in dormitories, library, student center. Dormitories wired for high-speed internet access and linked to campus network. Commuter students can connect to campus network. Online course registration, online library, helpline, repair service, student web hosting, wireless network available.

Student life. **Freshman orientation:** Available, $50 fee. Preregistration for classes offered. June and July sessions for students and parents. One-day session $50, two days $90. Free mini-orientation session in August, or online orientation also offered. **Housing:** Coed dorms, special housing for disabled, apartments, fraternity/sorority housing, wellness housing available. $1,000 fully refundable deposit. **Activities:** Bands, choral groups, dance, drama, film society, literary magazine, music ensembles, musical theater, opera, radio station, student government, student newspaper, symphony orchestra, over 200 organizations.

Athletics. NCAA. **Intercollegiate:** Baseball M, basketball, cross-country, golf, soccer, softball W, track and field, volleyball W. **Intramural:** Badminton, basketball, bowling, football (non-tackle), soccer, softball, volleyball. **Team name:** Wildcats.

Student services. Adult student services, alcohol/substance abuse counseling, career counseling, services for economically disadvantaged, student employment services, financial aid counseling, health services, legal services, minority student services, on-campus daycare, personal counseling, placement for graduates, veterans' counselor, women's services. **Physically disabled:** Services for visually, speech, hearing impaired. **Learning disabled:** Comprehensive services available.

Contact. E-mail: info@csuchico.edu
Phone: (530) 898-4428 Toll-free number: (800) 542-4426
Fax: (530) 898-6456
Rocky Raquel, Director of Admissions Office, California State University: Chico, 400 West First Street, Chico, CA 95929-0722

California State University: Dominguez Hills

Carson, California — **CB member**
www.csudh.edu — **CB code: 4098**

- Public 4-year university
- Commuter campus in small city
- 8,639 degree-seeking undergraduates: 37% part-time, 68% women, 29% African American, 9% Asian American, 39% Hispanic American, 2% international
- 2,675 degree-seeking graduate students
- 90% of applicants admitted
- 34% graduate within 6 years

General. Founded in 1960. Regionally accredited. **Degrees:** 1,565 bachelor's awarded; master's offered. **ROTC:** Army, Air Force. **Location:** 13 miles from Los Angeles. **Calendar:** Semester, extensive summer session. **Full-time faculty:** 284 total; 79% have terminal degrees, 24% minority, 49% women. **Part-time faculty:** 489 total; 36% have terminal degrees, 27% minority, 54% women. **Class size:** 28% < 20, 51% 20-39, 10% 40-49, 10% 50-99, less than 1% >100. **Special facilities:** Nature preserve, greenhouse, observatory, urban community research center, Japanese garden and theatre complex.

Freshman class profile. 6,070 applied, 5,449 admitted, 950 enrolled.

GPA 3.75 or higher:	3%	**Out-of-state:**	1%
GPA 3.50-3.74:	6%	**Live on campus:**	21%
GPA 3.0-3.49:	35%	**International:**	2%
GPA 2.0-2.99:	55%	**Fraternities:**	2%
End year in good standing:	65%	**Sororities:**	1%
Return as sophomores:	65%		

Basis for selection. Academic record and test scores are most important. SAT/ACT required of applicants who do not meet minimum requirement based on admissions eligibility index. Interview required of Educational Opportunity Program applicants. **Homeschooled:** Statement describing homeschool structure and mission, transcript of courses and grades, state high school equivalency certificate required. **Learning Disabled:** Student must show proof of learning disability to Office of Disability Services.

High school preparation. 15 units required. Required units include English 4, mathematics 3, social studies 2, history 1, science 2 (laboratory 2), foreign language 2, visual/performing arts 1 and academic electives 1.

2008-2009 Annual costs. Tuition/fees: $3,663; $13,833 out-of-state. Reduced out-of-state tuition for residents of AK, AZ, CO, HI, ID, MT, NV, NM, ND, OR, SD, UT, WA, WY available under the Western Undergraduate Exchange (WUE) program. Room/board: $8,955.

2007-2008 Financial aid. **Need-based:** 659 full-time freshmen applied for aid; 652 were judged to have need; 647 of these received aid. Average need met was 65%. Average scholarship/grant was $5,980; average loan $2,907. 63% of total undergraduate aid awarded as scholarships/grants, 37% as loans/jobs. **Non-need-based:** Awarded to 372 full-time undergraduates, including 82 freshmen. Scholarships awarded for academics, alumni affiliation, art, athletics, leadership, music/drama.

Application procedures. **Admission:** Priority date 11/1; no deadline. $55 fee, may be waived for applicants with need. Admission notification on a rolling basis beginning on or about 1/7. **Financial aid:** Priority date 3/2, closing date 4/15. FAFSA required. Applicants notified on a rolling basis starting 2/28; must reply within 4 week(s) of notification.

Academics. **Special study options:** Accelerated study, cross-registration, distance learning, double major, dual enrollment of high school students, external degree, honors, independent study, internships, student-designed major, study abroad, teacher certification program, weekend college. **Credit/placement by examination:** AP, CLEP, IB, SAT, ACT, institutional tests. **Support services:** Learning center, pre-admission summer program, reduced course load, remedial instruction, tutoring, writing center.

Majors. **Area/ethnic studies:** African-American, Hispanic-American/Latino/Chicano. **Biology:** General, biochemistry. **Business:** Business admin, labor relations, labor studies. **Communications:** General, digital media. **Computer sciences:** Computer science. **Engineering technology:** Quality control. **Foreign languages:** Spanish. **Health:** Clinical lab science, health services, nursing (RN). **History:** General. **Interdisciplinary:** Behavioral sciences, peace/conflict. **Legal studies:** Prelaw. **Liberal arts:** Arts/sciences. **Math:** General. **Parks/recreation:** General, health/fitness. **Philosophy/religion:** Philosophy. **Physical sciences:** Chemistry, geology, physics. **Protective services:** Criminal justice. **Psychology:** General. **Public administration:** General, human services. **Social sciences:** Anthropology, geography, political science, sociology, urban studies. **Visual/performing arts:** Art, dramatic. **Other:** Interdisciplinary studies.

Most popular majors. Business/marketing 21%, health sciences 12%, liberal arts 18%, psychology 7%, public administration/social services 6%, social sciences 9%.

Computing on campus. 256 workstations in library, computer center. Dormitories wired for high-speed internet access and linked to campus network. Commuter students can connect to campus network. Online course registration, online library, helpline, student web hosting, wireless network available.

Student life. **Freshman orientation:** Available, $50 fee. Preregistration for classes offered. Offered eleven times a year to incoming admitted freshmen and transfer students. **Housing:** Special housing for disabled, apartments available. $300 fully refundable deposit. **Activities:** Bands, choral groups, dance, drama, international student organizations, literary magazine, music ensembles, musical theater, radio station, student government, student newspaper, TV station, Accounting Society, African-American Business Student Association, Dance Club, Literary Club, Phi Alpha Delta, Political Science Club, Science Society, Hispanic Association of Natural and Social Science, Campus Crusade for Christ.

Athletics. NCAA. **Intercollegiate:** Baseball M, basketball, cross-country W, golf M, soccer, softball W, track and field W, volleyball W. **Intramural:** Basketball, cross-country, football (non-tackle), golf, soccer, softball, swimming, tennis, track and field, volleyball, water polo, weight lifting. **Team name:** Toros.

Student services. Career counseling, services for economically disadvantaged, student employment services, financial aid counseling, health services, on-campus daycare, personal counseling, placement for graduates, veterans' counselor, women's services. **Physically disabled:** Services for visually, speech, hearing impaired.

Contact. Phone: (310) 243-3645 Fax: (310) 516-3609
Linda Wise, Associate Director of Admissions, California State University: Dominguez Hills, 1000 East Victoria Street, Carson, CA 90747

California State University: East Bay

Hayward, California — **CB member**
www.csueastbay.edu — **CB code: 4011**

- Public 4-year university
- Commuter campus in small city
- 10,336 degree-seeking undergraduates: 18% part-time, 61% women, 14% African American, 27% Asian American, 15% Hispanic American, 1% Native American, 6% international
- 2,465 degree-seeking graduate students
- 72% of applicants admitted
- 44% graduate within 6 years

General. Founded in 1957. Regionally accredited. Branch campus in Concord and extensive online courses offered. **Degrees:** 2,326 bachelor's awarded; master's offered. **Location:** 30 miles from San Francisco, 30 miles from San Jose. **Calendar:** Quarter, extensive summer session. **Full-time faculty:** 365 total; 37% minority, 48% women. **Part-time faculty:** 448 total; 23% minority, 60% women. **Class size:** 27% < 20, 47% 20-39, 11% 40-49, 13% 50-99, 2% >100. **Special facilities:** Ecological field station, museum of anthropology, marine laboratory, geology summer field camp.

Freshman class profile. 8,054 applied, 5,767 admitted, 1,362 enrolled.

Mid 50% test scores		**GPA 3.50-3.74:**	10%
SAT critical reading:	390-500	**GPA 3.0-3.49:**	33%
SAT math:	390-510	**GPA 2.0-2.99:**	49%
ACT composite:	15-21	**Out-of-state:**	2%
GPA 3.75 or higher:	8%	**International:**	5%

Basis for selection. Eligibility index based on GPA, test results, and 15 units of subject requirements to yield students in top third of California high school graduates. Out-of-state applicants should be in top sixth of high school class. Test scores not required for residents with high school GPA above 3.0, nonresidents with high school GPA above 3.61.

High school preparation. College-preparatory program required. 15 units required. Required units include English 4, mathematics 3, history 2, science 2 (laboratory 2), foreign language 2 and academic electives 1. One visual and performing arts. Math must be algebra, geometry, and intermediate algebra. Science must be biology and a physical science. Foreign language units must be in same language.

2008-2009 Annual costs. Tuition/fees: $3,392; $13,562 out-of-state. Quoted freshman room-only charge is for suite shared by 6 to 8 students. Additional $3,200 advance purchase of flexible retail meal credits required. (Standard meal plans not available). Room/board: $9,228. Books/supplies: $1,566. Personal expenses: $3,024.

2007-2008 Financial aid. **Non-need-based:** Scholarships awarded for music/drama.

Application procedures. **Admission:** Closing date 8/31 (postmark date). $55 fee, may be waived for applicants with need. Admission notification on a rolling basis beginning on or about 10/1. **Financial aid:** Priority date 3/2; no closing date. FAFSA required. Applicants notified on a rolling basis; must reply within 3 week(s) of notification.

Academics. **Special study options:** Accelerated study, cooperative education, cross-registration, distance learning, double major, dual enrollment of high school students, ESL, exchange student, honors, independent study, internships, liberal arts/career combination, student-designed major, study abroad, teacher certification program. **Credit/placement by examination:** AP, CLEP, IB, SAT, ACT, institutional tests. 45 credit hours maximum toward bachelor's degree. 45-unit limitation excludes advanced placement. **Support services:** Learning center, pre-admission summer program, reduced course load, remedial instruction, study skills assistance, tutoring.

Majors. **Area/ethnic studies:** African-American, Asian-American, Hispanic-American/Latino/Chicano, Latin American, Native American. **Biology:** General, biochemistry, biomedical sciences. **Business:** General, accounting, business admin, entrepreneurial studies, finance, human resources, management information systems, managerial economics, marketing, purchasing, real estate. **Communications:** General, advertising, broadcast journalism, journalism, public relations. **Computer sciences:** General, computer science, information systems, networking. **Conservation:** General, environmental studies. **Education:** Mathematics, physical, speech. **Engineering:** Software. **Engineering technology:** Industrial management. **Foreign languages:** French, Spanish. **Health:** Athletic training, audiology/speech pathology, clinical lab technology, environmental health, prenursing, recreational therapy. **History:** General. **Liberal arts:** Arts/sciences. **Math:** General, applied, statistics. **Parks/recreation:** General, exercise sciences, facilities management, health/fitness. **Philosophy/religion:** Philosophy, religion. **Physical sciences:** Chemistry, geology, physics. **Protective services:** Corrections, law enforcement admin. **Psychology:** General. **Public administration:** General, policy analysis, social work. **Social sciences:** Anthropology, archaeology, economics, geography, political science, sociology. **Visual/performing arts:** Art, art history/conservation, arts management, ceramics, commercial/advertising art, dance, dramatic, drawing, painting, photography, printmaking, sculpture, studio arts, theater design.

Most popular majors. Business/marketing 32%, health sciences 7%, liberal arts 9%, social sciences 9%, visual/performing arts 6%.

Computing on campus. 1,062 workstations in dormitories, library, computer center. Dormitories wired for high-speed internet access and linked to campus network. Commuter students can connect to campus network. Online course registration, helpline, student web hosting available.

Student life. **Freshman orientation:** Mandatory, $80 fee. Preregistration for classes offered. 2 day program with overnight lodging on campus optional. **Policies:** Community and campus-based volunteer programs available. **Housing:** Apartments available. $900 deposit, deadline 5/1. Private coeducational dormitory adjacent to campus. **Activities:** Bands, choral groups, dance, drama, literary magazine, music ensembles, musical theater, opera, radio station, student government, student newspaper, symphony orchestra, TV station, 90 campus organizations.

Athletics. NAIA, NCAA. **Intercollegiate:** Baseball M, basketball, cross-country, golf, soccer, softball W, swimming W, track and field, volleyball W, water polo W. **Intramural:** Badminton, basketball, golf, gymnastics M, racquetball, soccer, softball, swimming, tennis, volleyball. **Team name:** Pioneers.

Student services. Adult student services, career counseling, services for economically disadvantaged, student employment services, financial aid counseling, health services, legal services, minority student services, on-campus daycare, personal counseling, placement for graduates, veterans' counselor. **Physically disabled:** Services for visually, speech, hearing impaired.

Contact. E-mail: admissions@csueastbay.edu
Phone: (510) 885-2784 Fax: (510) 885-4059
Gregory Smith, Associate Vice President, Planning and Enrollment Management, California State University: East Bay, 25800 Carlos Bee Boulevard, Hayward, CA 94542-3095

California State University: Fresno

Fresno, California — **CB member**
www.csufresno.edu — **CB code: 4312**

- Public 4-year university
- Commuter campus in very large city
- 19,245 degree-seeking undergraduates: 18% part-time, 57% women, 6% African American, 15% Asian American, 34% Hispanic American, 1% Native American, 1% international
- 2,483 degree-seeking graduate students
- 70% of applicants admitted
- SAT or ACT (ACT writing optional) required

General. Founded in 1911. Regionally accredited. Designated as an arboretum in 1978. **Degrees:** 3,565 bachelor's awarded; master's, doctoral offered. **ROTC:** Army, Air Force. **Location:** 217 miles from Los Angeles, 192 miles from San Francisco. **Calendar:** Semester, limited summer session. **Full-time faculty:** 712 total; 75% have terminal degrees, 32% minority, 41% women. **Part-time faculty:** 607 total; 7% have terminal degrees, 26% minority, 52% women. **Class size:** 23% < 20, 52% 20-39, 16% 40-49, 7% 50-99, 2% >100. **Special facilities:** 1,190-acre university farm, strength and conditioning center, planetarium.

Freshman class profile. 14,537 applied, 10,196 admitted, 2,821 enrolled.

Mid 50% test scores		**GPA 3.0-3.49:**	39%
SAT critical reading:	400-510	**GPA 2.0-2.99:**	28%
SAT math:	410-540	**End year in good standing:**	79%
ACT composite:	16-22	**Return as sophomores:**	82%
GPA 3.75 or higher:	18%	**Live on campus:**	25%
GPA 3.50-3.74:	15%	**International:**	1%

Basis for selection. Academic GPA, standardized test scores, and rigor of secondary school record very important. Tests recommended, but not required, if student has a high school GPA of 3.0 or higher. **Homeschooled:** Transcript of courses and grades required. **Learning Disabled:** Students with learning disabilities should contact Services for Students with Disabilities after submitting their application for consideration.

High school preparation. College-preparatory program required. 15 units required. Required units include English 4, mathematics 3, social studies 1, history 1, science 1 (laboratory 1), foreign language 2, visual/performing arts 1 and academic electives 1.

2008-2009 Annual costs. Tuition/fees: $3,687; $13,857 out-of-state. Room/board: $8,590. Books/supplies: $1,228. Personal expenses: $1,980.

2008-2009 Financial aid. Need-based: 2,220 full-time freshmen applied for aid; 1,825 were judged to have need; 1,775 of these received aid. Average need met was 74%. Average scholarship/grant was $8,599; average loan $3,030. 64% of total undergraduate aid awarded as scholarships/grants, 36% as loans/jobs. **Non-need-based:** Awarded to 2,177 full-time undergraduates, including 588 freshmen. Scholarships awarded for academics, art, athletics, leadership, music/drama, ROTC, state residency.

Application procedures. Admission: Priority date 11/30; deadline 2/1 (receipt date). $55 fee, may be waived for applicants with need. Application must be submitted online. Admission notification on a rolling basis. **Financial aid:** Priority date 3/3; no closing date. FAFSA required. Applicants notified on a rolling basis starting 4/1; must reply within 3 week(s) of notification.

Academics. Special study options: Accelerated study, combined bachelor's/graduate degree, cooperative education, cross-registration, distance learning, double major, dual enrollment of high school students, ESL, exchange student, honors, independent study, internships, student-designed major, study abroad, teacher certification program. **Credit/placement by examination:** AP, CLEP, IB, institutional tests. 30 credit hours maximum toward bachelor's degree. **Support services:** Learning center, pre-admission summer program, reduced course load, remedial instruction, study skills assistance, tutoring, writing center.

Honors college/program. Honors college admits 50 students each year. Must demonstrate intellectual and creative potential to benefit from honors program and have SAT of 1800 (Critical Reading/Math/Writing) or above, be within upper 10 percent of graduating class, or have minimum GPA of 3.6 (through the end of junior year). Honors students participate in 2 general education honors courses and honors colloquium each semester during first two years and 3 upper division honors courses during their junior and senior years. 30 hours of community service required freshmen year with varying requirement each year thereafter.

Majors. Agriculture: General, agronomy, animal health, animal sciences, business, dairy, food science, horticultural science, plant protection, plant sciences. **Area/ethnic studies:** African-American, women's. **Biology:** General, anatomy, bacteriology, cell/histology, ecology, molecular. **Business:** General, accounting, business admin, finance, human resources, international, management information systems, marketing, real estate. **Communications:** General, journalism, public relations. **Computer sciences:** General, computer science, information systems. **Construction:** Maintenance. **Education:** General, Deaf/hearing impaired, physical. **Engineering:** Civil, computer, electrical, mechanical. **Engineering technology:** Civil, construction, electrical, surveying. **Family/consumer sciences:** Child development, food/nutrition. **Foreign languages:** French, linguistics, Spanish. **Health:** Clinical/medical social work, communication disorders, environmental health, health care admin, nursing (RN), occupational health, vocational rehab counseling. **History:** General. **Interdisciplinary:** Natural sciences. **Liberal arts:** Arts/sciences. **Math:** General. **Parks/recreation:** Exercise sciences, facilities management. **Philosophy/religion:** Philosophy, religion. **Physical sciences:** Chemistry, geology, physics. **Psychology:** General. **Public administration:** General, social work. **Social sciences:** Anthropology, criminology, economics, geography, political science, sociology. **Visual/performing arts:** Art, commercial/advertising art, dance, dramatic, interior design, music theory/composition, theater design.

Most popular majors. Business/marketing 15%, engineering/engineering technologies 7%, health sciences 11%, liberal arts 11%, psychology 6%, social sciences 11%.

Computing on campus. PC or laptop required. 1,500 workstations in dormitories, library, computer center, student center. Dormitories linked to campus network. Commuter students can connect to campus network. Online course registration, online library, helpline, repair service, student web hosting, wireless network available.

Student life. Freshman orientation: Mandatory, $45 fee. One day program held during June and July for the fall semester and November and December for the spring semester. **Housing:** Coed dorms, single-sex dorms, fraternity/sorority housing available. $150 partly refundable deposit, deadline 4/1. **Activities:** Bands, choral groups, dance, drama, international student organizations, literary magazine, music ensembles, musical theater, radio station, student government, student newspaper, symphony orchestra, TV station, over 250 student organizations including religious and ethnic groups.

Athletics. NCAA. **Intercollegiate:** Baseball M, basketball, cross-country, equestrian W, football (tackle) M, golf, soccer W, softball W, tennis, track and field, volleyball W, wrestling M. **Intramural:** Basketball, football (non-tackle), racquetball, soccer, softball, tennis, volleyball. **Team name:** Bulldogs.

Student services. Adult student services, career counseling, services for economically disadvantaged, student employment services, financial aid counseling, health services, minority student services, on-campus daycare, personal counseling, placement for graduates, veterans' counselor, women's services. **Physically disabled:** Services for visually, speech, hearing impaired.

Contact. E-mail: admissions@csufresno.edu
Phone: (559) 278-2261 Fax: (559) 278-4812
Vivian Franco, Director, California State University: Fresno, 5150 North Maple Avenue, M/S JA 57, Fresno, CA 93740-8026

California State University: Fullerton

Fullerton, California — **CB member**
www.fullerton.edu — **CB code: 4589**

- Public 4-year university
- Commuter campus in small city
- 29,868 degree-seeking undergraduates: 23% part-time, 58% women, 4% African American, 22% Asian American, 30% Hispanic American, 1% Native American, 3% international
- 5,550 degree-seeking graduate students
- 60% of applicants admitted
- SAT or ACT required
- 49% graduate within 6 years

General. Founded in 1957. Regionally accredited. **Degrees:** 6,344 bachelor's awarded; master's, doctoral offered. **ROTC:** Army. **Location:** 30 miles from Los Angeles. **Calendar:** Semester, extensive summer session. **Full-time faculty:** 887 total; 82% have terminal degrees, 24% minority, 47% women. **Part-time faculty:** 965 total. **Class size:** 24% < 20, 55% 20-39, 11% 40-49, 7% 50-99, 2% >100. **Special facilities:** Wildlife sanctuary, arboretum, desert studies center, twin studies center, center for children who stutter, south central coastal information center, demographic research center, institute of gerontology, center for oral and public history, center for study of religion in American life, center for study of economics of aging.

Freshman class profile. 33,430 applied, 19,923 admitted, 4,697 enrolled.

Mid 50% test scores		**GPA 2.0-2.99:**	29%
SAT critical reading:	430-530	**End year in good standing:**	78%
SAT math:	450-560	**Return as sophomores:**	79%
ACT composite:	18-23	**Out-of-state:**	1%
GPA 3.75 or higher:	10%	**Live on campus:**	7%
GPA 3.50-3.74:	12%	**International:**	2%
GPA 3.0-3.49:	49%		

Basis for selection. Eligibility index consisting of combination of high school GPA and SAT or ACT score. Audition required of music majors.

High school preparation. College-preparatory program required. 15 units required; 16 recommended. Required and recommended units include English 4, mathematics 3, social studies 1, history 1, science 2 (laboratory 2), foreign language 2-3, visual/performing arts 1 and academic electives 1. 1 unit U.S. history/government required.

2008-2009 Annual costs. Tuition/fees: $3,658; $13,828 out-of-state. Room only: $5,608. Books/supplies: $1,568. Personal expenses: $2,700.

2007-2008 Financial aid. **Need-based:** 2,907 full-time freshmen applied for aid; 1,953 were judged to have need; 1,535 of these received aid. Average need met was 59%. Average scholarship/grant was $6,644; average loan $3,237. 71% of total undergraduate aid awarded as scholarships/grants, 29% as loans/jobs. **Non-need-based:** Awarded to 1,903 full-time undergraduates, including 407 freshmen. Scholarships awarded for academics. **Additional information:** Fee waiver for children of veterans killed in action or with service-connected disability whose annual income is $5,000 or less.

Application procedures. **Admission:** Priority date 10/1; deadline 11/30 (postmark date). $55 fee, may be waived for applicants with need. Application must be submitted online. Admission notification on a rolling basis beginning on or about 1/1. Must reply by 5/15. Reply date given on notification letter. **Financial aid:** Priority date 3/2; no closing date. FAFSA required. Applicants notified by 3/31; Applicants notified on a rolling basis starting 3/31; must reply within 4 week(s) of notification.

Academics. **Special study options:** Cross-registration, distance learning, double major, dual enrollment of high school students, honors, independent study, internships, study abroad, teacher certification program. Service Learning. **Credit/placement by examination:** AP, CLEP, IB, SAT, ACT, institutional tests. 30 credit hours maximum toward bachelor's degree. **Support services:** Learning center, pre-admission summer program, reduced course load, remedial instruction, study skills assistance, tutoring, writing center.

Majors. **Area/ethnic studies:** African-American, American, Asian-American, European, Hispanic-American/Latino/Chicano, Latin American, women's. **Biology:** General, biochemistry. **Business:** Accounting, business admin, entrepreneurial studies, finance, international, managerial economics, marketing, tourism/travel. **Communications:** General, advertising, journalism, public relations, radio/tv. **Computer sciences:** Computer science, information technology. **Education:** Early childhood, music. **Engineering:** General, civil, computer, electrical, mechanical, operations research, science. **Foreign languages:** Comparative lit, French, German, Japanese, linguistics, Spanish. **Health:** Communication disorders, health services, nursing (RN), prenursing. **History:** General. **Liberal arts:** Arts/sciences. **Math:** General, applied, statistics. **Parks/recreation:** Health/fitness. **Philosophy/religion:** Philosophy, religion. **Physical sciences:** Chemistry, geology, physics. **Protective services:** Criminal justice. **Psychology:** General. **Public administration:** General, human services. **Social sciences:** Anthropology, economics, geography, political science, sociology. **Visual/performing arts:** Art, art history/conservation, dance, dramatic, music performance, studio arts.

Most popular majors. Business/marketing 25%, communications/journalism 14%, education 7%, psychology 6%, social sciences 7%, visual/performing arts 6%.

Computing on campus. 2,000 workstations in dormitories, library, computer center, student center. Dormitories wired for high-speed internet access and linked to campus network. Commuter students can connect to campus network. Online course registration, online library, helpline, repair service, wireless network available.

Student life. **Freshman orientation:** Mandatory. Preregistration for classes offered. **Housing:** Apartments, fraternity/sorority housing available. **Activities:** Bands, choral groups, dance, drama, international student organizations, music ensembles, Model UN, musical theater, radio station, student government, student newspaper, symphony orchestra, Chinese Christian Fellowship, Christian Student Association, Disabled Student Association, Fellowship of Christian Athletes, Human Services Student Association, Movimiento Estudiantil Chicano de Atlan, New Democratic Movement, Poltical Science Student Association, Asian, Hispanic, and African-American Faculty/Staff Associations.

Athletics. NCAA. **Intercollegiate:** Baseball M, basketball, cross-country, fencing, gymnastics W, soccer, softball W, tennis W, track and field, volleyball W, wrestling M. **Intramural:** Badminton, basketball, bowling, football (non-tackle), gymnastics, handball M, racquetball, rugby M, skiing, soccer M, softball, swimming, table tennis, tennis, volleyball, wrestling M. **Team name:** Titans.

Student services. Adult student services, career counseling, student employment services, financial aid counseling, health services, legal services, on-campus daycare, personal counseling, placement for graduates, veterans' counselor, women's services. **Physically disabled:** Services for visually, speech, hearing impaired.

Contact. E-mail: admissions@fullerton.edu
Phone: (657) 278-2370 Fax: (657) 278-2356
Nancy Dority, Assistant Vice-President of Enrollment Services, California State University: Fullerton, 800 North State College Boulevard, Langsdorf Hall-114, Fullerton, CA 92831-6900

California State University: Long Beach

Long Beach, California — **CB member**
www.csulb.edu — **CB code: 4389**

- Public 4-year university
- Commuter campus in large city
- 31,564 degree-seeking undergraduates: 19% part-time, 60% women, 5% African American, 24% Asian American, 28% Hispanic American, 1% Native American, 4% international
- 4,814 degree-seeking graduate students
- 42% of applicants admitted
- SAT or ACT (ACT writing optional) required
- 55% graduate within 6 years

General. Founded in 1949. Regionally accredited. **Degrees:** 6,567 bachelor's awarded; master's offered. **ROTC:** Army. **Location:** 25 miles from Los Angeles. **Calendar:** Semester, extensive summer session. **Full-time faculty:** 936 total; 88% have terminal degrees, 30% minority, 45% women. **Part-time faculty:** 1,353 total; 29% have terminal degrees, 28% minority, 54% women. **Class size:** 23% < 20, 54% 20-39, 12% 40-49, 6% 50-99, 5% >100. **Special facilities:** Japanese garden, performing arts center, media center.

Freshman class profile. 48,542 applied, 20,391 admitted, 4,606 enrolled.

Mid 50% test scores		**GPA 2.0-2.99:**	12%
SAT critical reading:	440-550	**Rank in top quarter:**	82%
SAT math:	460-580	**End year in good standing:**	86%
ACT composite:	18-24	**Return as sophomores:**	86%
GPA 3.75 or higher:	15%	**Out-of-state:**	2%
GPA 3.50-3.74:	23%	**Live on campus:**	22%
GPA 3.0-3.49:	50%	**International:**	2%

Basis for selection. Admission based on secondary school record and standardized test scores. Audition required of dance, music majors. Portfolio required of art, design majors.

High school preparation. College-preparatory program required. 15 units required. Required units include English 4, mathematics 3, social studies 1, history 1, science 2 (laboratory 2), foreign language 2 and academic electives 1. 1 unit fine arts required.

2008-2009 Annual costs. Tuition/fees: $3,392; $13,562 out-of-state. Room/board: $7,940. Books/supplies: $1,564. Personal expenses: $2,010.

2008-2009 Financial aid. **Need-based:** 3,239 full-time freshmen applied for aid; 2,364 were judged to have need; 2,158 of these received aid. Average need met was 80%. Average scholarship/grant was $5,450; average loan $2,952. 63% of total undergraduate aid awarded as scholarships/grants, 37% as loans/jobs. **Non-need-based:** Awarded to 3,738 full-time undergraduates, including 424 freshmen. Scholarships awarded for academics, art, athletics, music/drama.

Application procedures. **Admission:** Closing date 11/30 (postmark date). $55 fee, may be waived for applicants with need. Admission notification on a rolling basis beginning on or about 12/1. **Financial aid:** Priority date 3/2; no closing date. FAFSA required. Applicants notified on a rolling basis starting 3/30; must reply within 3 week(s) of notification.

Academics. **Special study options:** Accelerated study, cross-registration, distance learning, double major, dual enrollment of high school students, ESL, honors, independent study, internships, student-designed major, study abroad, teacher certification program, Washington semester. Concurrent enrollment at other CSU campuses. **Credit/placement by examination:** AP, CLEP, IB, SAT, ACT, institutional tests. **Support services:** Learning center, pre-admission summer program, reduced course load, remedial instruction, study skills assistance, tutoring, writing center.

Majors. **Architecture:** Interior. **Area/ethnic studies:** African-American, Asian, Hispanic-American/Latino/Chicano, women's. **Biology:** General, bacteriology, biochemistry, botany, cell/histology, molecular. **Business:** General, accounting, fashion, finance, human resources, international, management science, managerial economics, operations, real estate. **Communications:** Broadcast journalism, journalism, public relations. **Computer sciences:** General, computer science, information systems. **Education:** Art, bilingual, elementary, English, family/consumer sciences, foreign languages, physical, science, social science. **Engineering:** General, aerospace, biomedical, chemical, civil, computer, electrical, materials, mechanical. **Engineering technology:** Civil, construction, electrical, manufacturing. **Family/consumer sciences:** General, clothing/textiles, food/nutrition. **Foreign languages:** Classics, comparative lit, French, German, Japanese, Spanish. **Health:** Medical illustrating, medical radiologic technology/radiation therapy, nursing (RN), public health ed. **History:** General. **Liberal arts:** Arts/sciences. **Math:** General, applied, statistics. **Parks/recreation:** Facilities management. **Philosophy/religion:** Philosophy, religion. **Physical sciences:** Chemistry, geology, physics. **Protective services:** Criminal justice. **Psychology:** General. **Public administration:** Social work. **Social sciences:** Anthropology, economics, geography, sociology. **Visual/performing arts:** Art, art history/conservation, ceramics, cinematography, commercial/advertising art, conducting, dance, design, dramatic, drawing, fiber arts, industrial design, interior design, jazz, metal/jewelry, music history, music performance, painting, photography, piano/organ, printmaking, sculpture, studio arts, theater design, voice/opera.

Most popular majors. Business/marketing 18%, English 9%, health sciences 7%, liberal arts 7%, social sciences 8%, visual/performing arts 8%.

Computing on campus. 1,200 workstations in dormitories, library, computer center. Dormitories linked to campus network. Commuter students can connect to campus network. Online course registration available.

Student life. Freshman orientation: Available, $45 fee. One-day pre-semester session. **Housing:** Coed dorms available. **Activities:** Bands, choral groups, dance, drama, film society, literary magazine, music ensembles, musical theater, opera, radio station, student government, student newspaper, symphony orchestra, TV station, more than 150 political, ethnic, and social service organizations.

Athletics. NCAA. **Intercollegiate:** Baseball M, basketball, cross-country, golf, soccer W, softball, tennis W, track and field, volleyball, water polo. **Intramural:** Basketball, handball, racquetball, rugby M, soccer, softball, tennis, volleyball. **Team name:** Forty-Niners.

Student services. Adult student services, alcohol/substance abuse counseling, chaplain/spiritual director, career counseling, services for economically disadvantaged, student employment services, financial aid counseling, health services, minority student services, on-campus daycare, personal counseling, placement for graduates, veterans' counselor, women's services. **Physically disabled:** Services for visually, speech, hearing impaired.

Contact. E-mail: eslb@csulb.edu
Phone: (562) 985-5471 Fax: (562) 985-4973
Thomas Enders, Assistant Vice President for Enrollment Services, California State University: Long Beach, 1250 Bellflower Boulevard, Long Beach, CA 90840-0106

California State University: Los Angeles

Los Angeles, California — **CB member**
www.calstatela.edu/index2.htm — **CB code: 4399**

- Public 4-year university
- Commuter campus in very large city
- 15,588 degree-seeking undergraduates: 25% part-time, 61% women
- 5,155 degree-seeking graduate students
- 77% of applicants admitted
- 31% graduate within 6 years

General. Founded in 1947. Regionally accredited. **Degrees:** 2,681 bachelor's awarded; master's, doctoral offered. **ROTC:** Army, Air Force. **Location:** 5 miles from downtown. **Calendar:** Quarter, extensive summer session. **Full-time faculty:** 585 total; 43% minority, 48% women. **Part-time faculty:** 614 total; 41% minority, 48% women. **Class size:** 39% < 20, 46% 20-39, 9% 40-49, 4% 50-99, 1% >100. **Special facilities:** Baroque pipe organ, 4 megavolt Van de Graaff accelerator.

Freshman class profile. 18,785 applied, 14,372 admitted, 1,942 enrolled.

Mid 50% test scores		**GPA 2.0-2.99:**	42%
SAT critical reading:	370-480	**End year in good standing:**	80%
SAT math:	370-490	**Return as sophomores:**	74%
ACT composite:	15-19	**Out-of-state:**	4%
GPA 3.75 or higher:	6%	**Live on campus:**	13%
GPA 3.50-3.74:	11%	**International:**	4%
GPA 3.0-3.49:	39%		

Basis for selection. Secondary school record and standardized test scores important. SAT/ACT not required if GPA is 3.0 or above. EPT/ELM required for placement; may be waived based on SAT score. **Homeschooled:** Syllabi and written evaluation of courses completed may be required.

High school preparation. 15 units required. Required units include English 4, mathematics 3, social studies 1, history 1, science 2 (laboratory 2), foreign language 2 and academic electives 1. 1 visual and performing arts required.

2008-2009 Annual costs. Tuition/fees: $3,661; $13,831 out-of-state. Room only: $4,050. Books/supplies: $1,566. Personal expenses: $2,826.

Application procedures. Admission: Closing date 6/15 (postmark date). $55 fee, may be waived for applicants with need. Admission notification on a rolling basis beginning on or about 11/1. **Financial aid:** Priority date 3/1; no closing date. FAFSA required. Applicants notified on a rolling basis starting 4/1; must reply within 3 week(s) of notification.

Academics. Special study options: Accelerated study, combined bachelor's/graduate degree, cooperative education, cross-registration, distance learning, double major, dual enrollment of high school students, ESL, exchange student, honors, independent study, internships, student-designed major, study abroad, teacher certification program. **Credit/placement by examination:** AP, CLEP, institutional tests. **Support services:** Learning center, pre-admission summer program, reduced course load, remedial instruction, tutoring.

Majors. Area/ethnic studies: African-American, Hispanic-American/Latino/Chicano, Latin American. **Biology:** General, biochemistry, microbiology. **Business:** Business admin. **Communications:** General, radio/tv. **Computer sciences:** General. **Education:** Kindergarten/preschool, physical, technology/industrial arts, trade/industrial. **Engineering:** General, civil, electrical, mechanical. **Engineering technology:** Industrial. **Family/consumer sciences:** Food/nutrition. **Foreign languages:** Chinese, French, Japanese, Spanish. **Health:** Communication disorders, nursing (RN). **History:** General. **Interdisciplinary:** Natural sciences. **Liberal arts:** Arts/sciences. **Math:** General. **Philosophy/religion:** Philosophy. **Physical sciences:** Chemistry, geology, physics. **Protective services:** Fire services admin, law enforcement admin. **Psychology:** General. **Public administration:** Social work. **Social sciences:** Anthropology, economics, geography, political science, sociology. **Visual/performing arts:** Art, commercial/advertising art, dramatic, music performance.

Most popular majors. Business/marketing 25%, family/consumer sciences 7%, health sciences 15%, psychology 6%, security/protective services 7%, social sciences 6%.

Computing on campus. 1,500 workstations in dormitories, library, computer center, student center. Commuter students can connect to campus network. Online library, helpline, repair service, student web hosting, wireless network available.

Student life. Freshman orientation: Available, $35 fee. Preregistration for classes offered. **Housing:** Coed dorms, apartments available. $100 deposit, deadline 7/2. **Activities:** Jazz band, choral groups, dance, drama, literary magazine, music ensembles, musical theater, opera, student government, student newspaper, symphony orchestra, Chicanos for Creative Medicine, Hispanic business society, society of women engineers, Movimiento Estudiantil Chicanos de Aetlar, Asian student union, black student association, Sisters of the African Star, Vietnamese student association, Latin American society, Chinese American service club.

Athletics. NCAA. **Intercollegiate:** Baseball M, basketball, cross-country W, soccer, tennis W, track and field, volleyball W. **Intramural:** Basketball, bowling, gymnastics, handball, judo, racquetball, skiing, soccer, softball, swimming, synchronized swimming, tennis, track and field, volleyball, water polo, wrestling M. **Team name:** Golden Eagles.

Student services. Career counseling, student employment services, health services, on-campus daycare, personal counseling, placement for graduates, veterans' counselor. **Physically disabled:** Services for visually, speech, hearing impaired. **Learning disabled:** Comprehensive services available.

Contact. E-mail: admission@calstatela.edu
Phone: (323) 343-3901 Fax: (323) 343-3888
Joan Woosley, Director of Admissions and University Registrar, California State University: Los Angeles, 5151 State University Drive SA101, Los Angeles, CA 90032

California State University: Monterey Bay

Seaside, California — **CB member**
www.csumb.edu — **CB code: 1945**

- Public 4-year liberal arts and teachers college
- Residential campus in large town
- 3,889 degree-seeking undergraduates: 10% part-time, 59% women, 5% African American, 7% Asian American, 28% Hispanic American, 1% Native American, 1% international

- 237 degree-seeking graduate students
- 71% of applicants admitted
- 39% graduate within 6 years

General. Founded in 1995. Regionally accredited. Dedicated to serving low-income, adult learner, first-generation, and underrepresented populations. **Degrees:** 622 bachelor's awarded; master's offered. **Location:** 108 miles from San Francisco, 68 miles from San Jose. **Calendar:** Semester, limited summer session. **Full-time faculty:** 111 total; 86% have terminal degrees, 46% minority, 48% women. **Part-time faculty:** 183 total; 21% have terminal degrees, 27% minority, 56% women. **Class size:** 26% < 20, 61% 20-39, 7% 40-49, 5% 50-99, less than 1% >100. **Special facilities:** Watershed facilities to complement earth systems science and policy major, seafloor mapping lab.

Freshman class profile. 9,545 applied, 6,743 admitted, 913 enrolled.

Mid 50% test scores		**GPA 2.0-2.99:**	42%
SAT critical reading:	440-550	**Rank in top quarter:**	32%
SAT math:	440-550	**Rank in top tenth:**	8%
SAT writing:	440-540	**End year in good standing:**	77%
ACT composite:	18-23	**Return as sophomores:**	67%
GPA 3.75 or higher:	8%	**Out-of-state:**	4%
GPA 3.50-3.74:	12%	**Live on campus:**	90%
GPA 3.0-3.49:	38%		

Basis for selection. Students must be high school graduates or GED equivalent, complete the 15-unit "a-g" course pattern of college preparatory study with grades of C or better and earn qualifying eligibility index. SAT/ACT test scores are not required for those students who earn a GPA of 3.00 or above in high school; 3.61 or above for non-residents. **Homeschooled:** Applicants may be asked to provide supplemental information to document completion of CSU eligibility requirements. **Learning Disabled:** Reviewed case-by-case by Student Disability Resources Department.

High school preparation. College-preparatory program required. 15 units required. Required units include English 4, mathematics 3, social studies 1, history 1, science 2 (laboratory 2), foreign language 2, visual/performing arts 1 and academic electives 1. Science lab units must include 1 biological, 1 physical. Language must be the same language both years. History must include U.S. History.

2008-2009 Annual costs. Tuition/fees: $3,301; $13,471 out-of-state. Room/board: $9,152. Books/supplies: $1,386. Personal expenses: $2,520.

2008-2009 Financial aid. Need-based: 691 full-time freshmen applied for aid; 463 were judged to have need; 411 of these received aid. Average need met was 73%. Average scholarship/grant was $7,942; average loan $3,347. 54% of total undergraduate aid awarded as scholarships/grants, 46% as loans/jobs. **Non-need-based:** Awarded to 274 full-time undergraduates, including 85 freshmen. Scholarships awarded for academics, alumni affiliation, athletics, leadership, state residency.

Application procedures. Admission: Closing date 3/1 (postmark date). $55 fee, may be waived for applicants with need. Admission notification on a rolling basis. Must reply by 5/1. Deferral of one semester is permitted. **Financial aid:** Priority date 3/2; no closing date. FAFSA, institutional form required. Applicants notified by 3/1; must reply within 2 week(s) of notification.

Academics. Special study options: Cross-registration, distance learning, double major, exchange student, independent study, internships, semester at sea, student-designed major, study abroad, teacher certification program. Service Learning. **Credit/placement by examination:** AP, CLEP, IB, SAT, ACT, institutional tests. 30 credit hours maximum toward bachelor's degree. **Support services:** Learning center, reduced course load, remedial instruction, study skills assistance, tutoring, writing center.

Majors. Biology: General. **Business:** Business admin. **Communications:** General. **Computer sciences:** Computer science, networking. **Conservation:** Management/policy. **Foreign languages:** General. **Health:** Health services. **Interdisciplinary:** Global studies. **Liberal arts:** Arts/sciences. **Math:** General. **Psychology:** General. **Social sciences:** General. **Visual/performing arts:** Dramatic, studio arts. **Other:** Kinesiology.

Most popular majors. Business/marketing 16%, communications/journalism 9%, computer/information sciences 8%, liberal arts 30%, natural resources/environmental science 8%, social sciences 11%.

Computing on campus. 800 workstations in library, computer center. Dormitories wired for high-speed internet access and linked to campus network. Commuter students can connect to campus network. Online course registration, online library, helpline, student web hosting, wireless network available.

Student life. Freshman orientation: Mandatory. Preregistration for classes offered. **Housing:** Guaranteed on-campus for all undergraduates. Coed dorms, special housing for disabled, apartments, wellness housing available. $125 fully refundable deposit, deadline 5/1. Six-person suite-style living available. **Activities:** Bands, campus ministries, choral groups, dance, drama, film society, music ensembles, radio station, student government, student newspaper, Amnesty International, business club, MECHA, Black Students United, baseball club, Raza Unida, art club, photography club, Asian club, sailing club.

Athletics. NAIA, NCAA. **Intercollegiate:** Baseball M, basketball, cross-country, golf, sailing, soccer, softball W, volleyball W, water polo W. **Intramural:** Basketball, cheerleading, rugby W, sailing, soccer, softball, volleyball. **Team name:** Otters.

Student services. Adult student services, alcohol/substance abuse counseling, chaplain/spiritual director, career counseling, services for economically disadvantaged, student employment services, financial aid counseling, health services, minority student services, on-campus daycare, personal counseling, placement for graduates, veterans' counselor, women's services. **Physically disabled:** Services for visually, speech, hearing impaired.

Contact. E-mail: admissions@csumb.edu
Phone: (831) 582-3738 Fax: (831) 582-3783
David Linnevers, Director of Admissions & Recruitment, California State University: Monterey Bay, 100 Campus Center, Building 47, Seaside, CA 93955-8001

California State University: Northridge
Northridge, California
www.csun.edu **CB code: 4707**

- Public 4-year university
- Commuter campus in very large city
- 30,235 degree-seeking undergraduates: 23% part-time, 57% women, 9% African American, 13% Asian American, 30% Hispanic American, 5% international
- 5,973 degree-seeking graduate students
- 75% of applicants admitted
- SAT or ACT required
- 39% graduate within 6 years

General. Founded in 1958. Regionally accredited. University center in Ventura. **Degrees:** 6,619 bachelor's awarded; master's offered. **ROTC:** Army, Air Force. **Location:** 20 miles from Los Angeles. **Calendar:** Semester, limited summer session. **Full-time faculty:** 814 total; 31% minority, 44% women. **Part-time faculty:** 1,088 total; 23% minority, 53% women. **Class size:** 14% < 20, 56% 20-39, 16% 40-49, 10% 50-99, 4% >100. **Special facilities:** Anthropology museum, art botanical gardens, urban archives center, observatory, map library, center for the study of cancer and development biology, National Center on Deafness, planetarium.

Freshman class profile. 23,293 applied, 17,411 admitted, 4,624 enrolled.

Mid 50% test scores		**Return as sophomores:**	73%
SAT critical reading:	400-520	**Out-of-state:**	2%
SAT math:	400-530	**International:**	3%
ACT composite:	16-21		

Basis for selection. Index using high school GPA and test scores, and completion of subject requirements. In-state applicants should rank in top third of class; out-of-state in the top sixth. Business administration, economics, engineering, computer science, and physical therapy open to California residents only. Applicants with 3.0 GPA not required to submit test scores. ELM score required for math and English placement. Audition required of music majors.

High school preparation. College-preparatory program required. 15 units required. Required units include English 4, mathematics 3, social studies 1, history 1, science 2 (laboratory 2), foreign language 2, visual/performing arts 1 and academic electives 1.

2008-2009 Annual costs. Tuition/fees: $3,702; $13,872 out-of-state. Room/board: $10,152. Books/supplies: $1,564. Personal expenses: $2,720.

2007-2008 Financial aid. Need-based: 2,897 full-time freshmen applied for aid; 2,448 were judged to have need; 2,448 of these received aid. Average scholarship/grant was $5,245; average loan $3,504. 63% of total undergraduate aid awarded as scholarships/grants, 37% as loans/jobs. **Non-need-based:** Awarded to 8,047 full-time undergraduates, including 1,831 freshmen. Scholarships awarded for academics, athletics, state residency.

Application procedures. Admission: Closing date 11/30. $55 fee, may be waived for applicants with need. Admission notification on a rolling basis beginning on or about 3/1. Must reply by May 1 or within 2 week(s) if notified thereafter. Applications must be completed by November 30 for business administration, economics and physical therapy programs. **Financial aid:** Priority date 3/1; no closing date. FAFSA required. Applicants notified on a rolling basis starting 4/1.

Academics. Special study options: Cross-registration, distance learning, double major, dual enrollment of high school students, ESL, exchange student, independent study, internships, student-designed major, study abroad, teacher certification program. Evening degree program, Saturday classes, extended studies, open university, Program for Adult College Education (PACE) available. **Credit/placement by examination:** AP, CLEP, institutional tests. **Support services:** Learning center, pre-admission summer program, remedial instruction, tutoring.

Majors. Area/ethnic studies: African-American, Hispanic-American/Latino/Chicano. **Biology:** General, bacteriology, biochemistry, cell/histology, molecular. **Business:** Banking/financial services, business admin, human resources, management information systems, management science, managerial economics, real estate. **Communications:** Broadcast journalism, journalism. **Computer sciences:** General. **Education:** Art, business, English, family/consumer sciences, foreign languages, health, mathematics, music, physical, social science, social studies, speech impaired. **Engineering:** General, chemical, civil, computer, electrical, materials, mechanical, mechanics. **Family/consumer sciences:** General, business, child care, clothing/textiles, family studies, family/community services, food/nutrition, housing. **Foreign languages:** Comparative lit, French, German, linguistics, Spanish. **Health:** Nursing (RN), speech pathology. **History:** General. **Liberal arts:** Arts/sciences. **Math:** General, applied, statistics. **Parks/recreation:** General. **Philosophy/religion:** Philosophy, religion. **Physical sciences:** Chemistry, geology, geophysics, physics, planetary. **Psychology:** General. **Social sciences:** Anthropology, economics, geography, political science, sociology, urban studies. **Visual/performing arts:** Art, art history/conservation, ceramics, commercial/advertising art, crafts, dance, dramatic, drawing, metal/jewelry, music history, music performance, music theory/composition, painting, printmaking, sculpture.

Most popular majors. Business/marketing 21%, communications/journalism 8%, communication technologies 8%, engineering/engineering technologies 6%, English 6%, liberal arts 9%, psychology 9%, social sciences 13%, visual/performing arts 6%.

Computing on campus. 723 workstations in library, computer center. Dormitories wired for high-speed internet access and linked to campus network. Commuter students can connect to campus network. Online course registration, online library, helpline, student web hosting, wireless network available.

Student life. Freshman orientation: Mandatory. **Housing:** Apartments available. Off campus housing choices available. **Activities:** Bands, choral groups, dance, drama, music ensembles, musical theater, radio station, student government, student newspaper, women's center, communities, various clubs and organizations.

Athletics. NCAA. **Intercollegiate:** Baseball M, basketball, cross-country, diving, golf, soccer, softball W, swimming, tennis W, track and field, volleyball, water polo W. **Intramural:** Badminton, baseball M, basketball, bowling, cross-country, diving, handball, ice hockey M, racquetball, rugby, sailing, skiing, soccer, softball, swimming, table tennis, tennis, track and field, volleyball. **Team name:** Matadors.

Student services. Adult student services, alcohol/substance abuse counseling, career counseling, services for economically disadvantaged, student employment services, financial aid counseling, health services, minority student services, on-campus daycare, personal counseling, placement for graduates, veterans' counselor, women's services. **Physically disabled:** Services for visually, speech, hearing impaired.

Contact. E-mail: admissions.records@csun.edu
Phone: (818) 677-3700 Fax: (818) 677-3766
Eric Forbes, Director of Admissions and Records, California State University: Northridge, 18111 Nordhoff Street, Northridge, CA 91328-8207

California State University: Sacramento

Sacramento, California — **CB member**
www.csus.edu — **CB code: 4671**

- Public 4-year university
- Commuter campus in very large city
- 21,505 degree-seeking undergraduates: 19% part-time, 58% women
- 3,566 degree-seeking graduate students
- 67% of applicants admitted
- 41% graduate within 6 years

General. Founded in 1947. Regionally accredited. **Degrees:** 4,593 bachelor's awarded; master's, doctoral offered. **ROTC:** Army, Air Force. **Location:** 100 miles from San Francisco. **Calendar:** Semester, extensive summer session. **Full-time faculty:** 827 total; 77% have terminal degrees, 28% minority, 46% women. **Part-time faculty:** 753 total; 27% have terminal degrees, 18% minority, 51% women. **Class size:** 20% < 20, 51% 20-39, 14% 40-49, 12% 50-99, 2% >100. **Special facilities:** Aquatic center, anthropology museum, Hellenic collection.

Freshman class profile. 15,699 applied, 10,504 admitted, 2,296 enrolled.

Mid 50% test scores		**GPA 2.0-2.99:**	31%
SAT critical reading:	400-520	**Return as sophomores:**	78%
SAT math:	420-540	**Out-of-state:**	1%
ACT composite:	16-22	**Live on campus:**	27%
GPA 3.75 or higher:	13%	**Fraternities:**	8%
GPA 3.50-3.74:	16%	**Sororities:**	9%
GPA 3.0-3.49:	40%		

Basis for selection. Student must meet admissions requirements.

High school preparation. College-preparatory program required. 15 units required. Required units include English 4, mathematics 3, history 2, science 2 (laboratory 2), foreign language 2, visual/performing arts 1 and academic electives 1. History must be U.S. history/government.

2008-2009 Annual costs. Tuition/fees: $3,854; $14,024 out-of-state. Assumes 30 units per year at $339 per unit, plus $3,048 in-state tuition. Meal plan cited includes 10 meals per week. Room/board: $11,210. Books/supplies: $1,656. Personal expenses: $2,332.

2007-2008 Financial aid. Need-based: 2,499 full-time freshmen applied for aid; 2,163 were judged to have need; 1,411 of these received aid. Average need met was 47%. Average scholarship/grant was $3,828; average loan $1,584. 59% of total undergraduate aid awarded as scholarships/grants, 41% as loans/jobs. **Non-need-based:** Awarded to 763 full-time undergraduates, including 163 freshmen.

Application procedures. Admission: Priority date 11/30; deadline 3/1 (receipt date). $55 fee, may be waived for applicants with need. Admission notification on a rolling basis. **Financial aid:** FAFSA required. Applicants notified on a rolling basis starting 4/1; must reply within 4 week(s) of notification.

Academics. Special study options: Cooperative education, cross-registration, distance learning, double major, dual enrollment of high school students, ESL, exchange student, honors, independent study, internships, student-designed major, study abroad, teacher certification program. **Credit/placement by examination:** AP, CLEP, IB, SAT, ACT, institutional tests. SAT/ACT may be used to exempt students from English/math placement tests. **Support services:** Learning center, remedial instruction, study skills assistance, tutoring, writing center.

Majors. Architecture: Interior. **Area/ethnic studies:** Asian. **Biology:** General, bacteriology, molecular. **Business:** Accounting, business admin, finance, human resources, insurance, international, marketing, operations, real estate. **Communications:** General, journalism. **Computer sciences:** General, information systems. **Conservation:** General, environmental studies. **Education:** General, kindergarten/preschool, mathematics. **Engineering:** Civil, computer, electrical, mechanical. **Engineering technology:** Construction, mechanical. **Family/consumer sciences:** General. **Foreign languages:** American Sign Language, French, Spanish. **Health:** Audiology/speech pathology, clinical lab technology, nursing (RN), prenursing. **History:** General. **Interdisciplinary:** Gerontology. **Liberal arts:** Arts/sciences, humanities. **Math:** General. **Parks/recreation:** General, health/fitness. **Philosophy/religion:** Philosophy, religion. **Physical sciences:** General, chemistry, geology, physics. **Protective services:** Corrections, law enforcement admin. **Psychology:** General. **Public administration:** Social work. **Social sciences:** General, anthropology, economics, geography, political science, sociology. **Visual/performing arts:** Art, cinematography, commercial/advertising art, dramatic, music management, music performance, music theory/composition, photography, voice/opera. **Other:** Ethnic, cultural minority, and gender studies, Multi-interdisciplinary studies, Teacher education and professional development, specific levels and methods.

Most popular majors. Business/marketing 23%, communications/journalism 8%, health sciences 6%, liberal arts 6%, psychology 6%, security/protective services 8%, social sciences 9%.

Computing on campus. 700 workstations in dormitories, library, computer center, student center. Dormitories wired for high-speed internet access and linked to campus network. Commuter students can connect to campus network. Online course registration, online library, helpline, repair service, student web hosting, wireless network available.

Student life. **Freshman orientation:** Mandatory, $50 fee. Preregistration for classes offered. **Housing:** Coed dorms, special housing for disabled available. Suite style housing available. **Activities:** Bands, campus ministries, choral groups, dance, drama, international student organizations, literary magazine, music ensembles, Model UN, musical theater, opera, radio station, student government, student newspaper, symphony orchestra, more than 250 clubs, organizations and special interest groups.

Athletics. NCAA. **Intercollegiate:** Baseball M, basketball, cross-country, football (tackle) M, golf, gymnastics W, rowing (crew) W, soccer, softball W, tennis, track and field, volleyball W. **Intramural:** Badminton, basketball, bowling, football (non-tackle), golf, racquetball, skiing, soccer, tennis, volleyball. **Team name:** Hornets.

Student services. Adult student services, alcohol/substance abuse counseling, career counseling, services for economically disadvantaged, student employment services, financial aid counseling, health services, legal services, on-campus daycare, personal counseling, placement for graduates, veterans' counselor, women's services. **Physically disabled:** Services for visually, speech, hearing impaired.

Contact. E-mail: outreach@csus.edu
Phone: (916) 278-7766 Fax: (916) 278-5603
Emiliano Diaz, Director of Outreach, Admissions & Records, California State University: Sacramento, 6000 J Street, Sacramento, CA 95819-6048

California State University: San Bernardino

San Bernardino, California — **CB member**
www.csusb.edu — **CB code: 4099**

- Public 4-year university and liberal arts college
- Commuter campus in small city
- 13,947 degree-seeking undergraduates: 15% part-time, 65% women, 12% African American, 8% Asian American, 39% Hispanic American, 1% Native American, 3% international
- 3,699 degree-seeking graduate students
- SAT or ACT (ACT writing optional) required

General. Founded in 1962. Regionally accredited. Palm Desert satellite campus offers day and evening courses in degree and credential programs. **Degrees:** 2,626 bachelor's awarded; master's, doctoral offered. **ROTC:** Army, Air Force. **Location:** 60 miles from Los Angeles. **Calendar:** Quarter, limited summer session. **Full-time faculty:** 471 total; 29% minority, 46% women. **Part-time faculty:** 424 total; 27% minority, 52% women. **Class size:** 25% < 20, 50% 20-39, 9% 40-49, 11% 50-99, 5% >100. **Special facilities:** Animal house, greenhouse, desert studies center.

Freshman class profile.

Mid 50% test scores		**GPA 2.0-2.99:**	46%
SAT critical reading:	390-500	**Rank in top quarter:**	37%
SAT math:	400-510	**Rank in top tenth:**	21%
SAT writing:	-460	**Out-of-state:**	1%
ACT composite:	16-20	**Live on campus:**	21%
GPA 3.75 or higher:	9%	**International:**	3%
GPA 3.50-3.74:	10%	**Fraternities:**	9%
GPA 3.0-3.49:	33%	**Sororities:**	11%

Basis for selection. High school GPA and test scores most important. SAT/ACT not required if high school GPA is 3.0 or higher. Entering undergraduates, except those who qualify for exemption, must take CSU entry-level mathematics (ELM) examination and CSU English placement test (EPT) after admission and before they enroll in classes.

High school preparation. 15 units required. Required units include English 4, mathematics 3, social studies 1, history 1, science 2 (laboratory 2), foreign language 2 and academic electives 1. One visual and performing arts unit also required. Students with disabilities may substitute alternate courses for specific subject requirements.

2008-2009 Annual costs. Tuition/fees: $3,779; $13,949 out-of-state. Room/board: $9,624. Books/supplies: $1,413. Personal expenses: $2,292.

Application procedures. **Admission:** No deadline. $55 fee, may be waived for applicants with need. Admission notification on a rolling basis. Students may apply as late as 3 weeks into quarter. **Financial aid:** Priority date 3/2; no closing date. FAFSA required. Applicants notified on a rolling basis starting 4/1.

Academics. **Special study options:** Accelerated study, cooperative education, cross-registration, distance learning, double major, dual enrollment of high school students, exchange student, honors, independent study, internships, study abroad, teacher certification program. School of Social and Behavioral Sciences offers master's in National Security Studies. **Credit/placement by examination:** AP, CLEP, IB, SAT, ACT, institutional tests. 40 credit hours maximum toward bachelor's degree. **Support services:** Learning center, pre-admission summer program, remedial instruction, tutoring, writing center.

Majors. **Area/ethnic studies:** African-American, American, Hispanic-American/Latino/Chicano. **Biology:** General, biochemistry. **Business:** Accounting, business admin, finance, human resources, international, management information systems, managerial economics, marketing, operations, organizational behavior, real estate. **Communications:** General, radio/tv. **Computer sciences:** Computer science, systems analysis. **Conservation:** Environmental studies. **Education:** Physical, trade/industrial. **Family/consumer sciences:** Child development, family studies, food/nutrition. **Foreign languages:** French, Spanish. **Health:** Environmental health, health care admin, nursing (RN), premedicine. **History:** General. **Interdisciplinary:** Museum. **Liberal arts:** Arts/sciences, humanities. **Math:** General. **Parks/recreation:** Exercise sciences. **Philosophy/religion:** Philosophy. **Physical sciences:** Chemistry, geology, physics. **Protective services:** Law enforcement admin. **Psychology:** General. **Public administration:** General, social work. **Social sciences:** General, anthropology, economics, geography, political science, sociology. **Visual/performing arts:** Art, art history/conservation, commercial/advertising art, dramatic, music history, music performance, musicology, studio arts, theater design, theater history.

Most popular majors. Business/marketing 26%, health sciences 9%, liberal arts 13%, psychology 8%, security/protective services 7%, social sciences 12%.

Computing on campus. 600 workstations in dormitories, library, computer center, student center. Dormitories wired for high-speed internet access and linked to campus network. Commuter students can connect to campus network. Online course registration, online library, wireless network available.

Student life. **Freshman orientation:** Available. Preregistration for classes offered. **Housing:** Coed dorms, single-sex dorms, apartments, wellness housing available. $50 deposit. **Activities:** Jazz band, choral groups, dance, drama, music ensembles, musical theater, radio station, student government, student newspaper, TV station, more than 80 clubs and organizations.

Athletics. NCAA. **Intercollegiate:** Baseball M, basketball, cross-country W, golf M, soccer, softball W, swimming, tennis W, volleyball W, water polo. **Intramural:** Basketball, field hockey W, soccer, softball M, volleyball. **Team name:** Coyotes.

Student services. Adult student services, career counseling, student employment services, financial aid counseling, health services, legal services, minority student services, on-campus daycare, personal counseling, placement for graduates, veterans' counselor, women's services. **Physically disabled:** Services for visually, speech, hearing impaired.

Contact. E-mail: moreinfo@mail.csusb.edu
Phone: (909) 537-5188 Fax: (909) 537-7034
Olivia Rosas, Director of Admissions and Student Recruitment, California State University: San Bernardino, 5500 University Parkway, San Bernardino, CA 92407-2397

California State University: San Marcos

San Marcos, California — **CB member**
www.csusm.edu — **CB code: 5677**

- Public 4-year university
- Commuter campus in large town
- 8,064 degree-seeking undergraduates: 25% part-time, 61% women
- 564 degree-seeking graduate students
- 73% of applicants admitted
- 40% graduate within 6 years

General. Founded in 1989. Regionally accredited. **Degrees:** 1,468 bachelor's awarded; master's offered. **ROTC:** Army, Naval, Air Force. **Location:** 30 miles from San Diego. **Calendar:** Semester, limited summer session. **Full-time faculty:** 321 total; 29% minority. **Part-time faculty:** 206 total; 11% minority. **Class size:** 20% < 20, 56% 20-39, 15% 40-49, 8% 50-99, 2% >100.

Freshman class profile. 9,736 applied, 7,088 admitted, 1,574 enrolled.

Mid 50% test scores		**GPA 3.0-3.49:**	45%
SAT critical reading:	430-530	**GPA 2.0-2.99:**	38%
SAT math:	440-550	**Return as sophomores:**	70%
GPA 3.75 or higher:	7%	**Out-of-state:**	1%
GPA 3.50-3.74:	10%	**International:**	1%

Basis for selection. Student eligibility index calculated on GPA and test score combination. SAT scores can be used to meet English or math proficiency requirements. **Learning Disabled:** C or better grades in all college preparatory classes -- Minimum GPA-2.0.

High school preparation. 15 units required; 16 recommended. Required and recommended units include English 4, mathematics 3-4, social studies 1, history 1, science 2 (laboratory 2), foreign language 2, visual/performing arts 1 and academic electives 1.

2008-2009 Annual costs. Tuition/fees: $3,650; $13,820 out-of-state. Room/board: $9,486. Books/supplies: $1,565. Personal expenses: $2,720.

2007-2008 Financial aid. Non-need-based: Scholarships awarded for academics, athletics, leadership, state residency.

Application procedures. Admission: Closing date 11/30. $55 fee, may be waived for applicants with need. Admission notification on a rolling basis beginning on or about 11/1. Must reply by May 1 or within 3 week(s) if notified thereafter.

Academics. Special study options: Cross-registration, distance learning, double major, dual enrollment of high school students, ESL, independent study, internships, student-designed major, study abroad, teacher certification program, weekend college. Evening degree program, Program for Adult College Education (PACE), saturday classes, Air Force ROTC, extended studies, open university, special sessions, including winter. **Credit/placement by examination:** AP, CLEP, IB, institutional tests. 30 credit hours maximum toward bachelor's degree. **Support services:** Learning center, pre-admission summer program, study skills assistance, tutoring, writing center.

Majors. Area/ethnic studies: Women's. **Biology:** General, biochemistry, biotechnology. **Business:** Business admin. **Communications:** General. **Computer sciences:** General, computer science. **Family/consumer sciences:** Family studies. **Foreign languages:** Spanish. **History:** General. **Liberal arts:** Arts/sciences. **Math:** General. **Physical sciences:** Applied physics, chemistry, physics. **Psychology:** General. **Social sciences:** General, economics, political science, sociology. **Visual/performing arts:** General.

Most popular majors. Business/marketing 23%, communications/journalism 12%, liberal arts 22%, psychology 6%, social sciences 19%.

Computing on campus. 1,100 workstations in library, computer center. Commuter students can connect to campus network. Online course registration, helpline, wireless network available.

Student life. Freshman orientation: Mandatory, $70 fee. One-day program. **Housing:** Special housing for disabled, apartments available. $50 nonrefundable deposit, deadline 10/1. **Activities:** Choral groups, dance, drama, music ensembles, student newspaper, American Indian Science Engineering Society, Circle K, InterVarsity Christian Fellowship, Latter-day Saints student association, accounting society, Black Men on Campus, College Democrats, pre-health society, student housing asociation.

Athletics. NAIA. **Intercollegiate:** Baseball M, cross-country, golf, soccer, softball W, track and field. **Team name:** Cougars.

Student services. Adult student services, alcohol/substance abuse counseling, career counseling, services for economically disadvantaged, student employment services, financial aid counseling, health services, on-campus daycare, personal counseling, placement for graduates, veterans' counselor. **Physically disabled:** Services for visually, speech, hearing impaired.

Contact. E-mail: apply@csusm.edu
Phone: (760) 750-4848
Nathan Evans, Director of Admissions and Recruitment, California State University: San Marcos, 333 South Twin Oaks Valley Road, San Marcos, CA 92096-0001

California State University: Stanislaus

Turlock, California — **CB member**
www.csustan.edu — **CB code: 4713**

- Public 4-year business and liberal arts college
- Commuter campus in small city
- 6,559 degree-seeking undergraduates
- 1,695 graduate students
- 66% of applicants admitted
- 53% graduate within 6 years; 79% enter graduate study

General. Founded in 1957. Regionally accredited. **Degrees:** 1,524 bachelor's awarded; master's offered. **Location:** 15 miles from Modesto. **Calendar:** 4-1-4, extensive summer session. **Full-time faculty:** 312 total; 23% minority, 46% women. **Part-time faculty:** 188 total; 14% minority, 49% women. **Class size:** 32% < 20, 51% 20-39, 10% 40-49, 6% 50-99, 1% >100. **Special facilities:** Observatory, interactive television classrooms, laser laboratory, marine sciences station, greenhouse, mainstage theater, bio-ag eco building.

Freshman class profile. 4,751 applied, 3,125 admitted, 965 enrolled.

Mid 50% test scores		**GPA 3.0-3.49:**	41%
SAT critical reading:	420-530	**GPA 2.0-2.99:**	29%
SAT math:	420-540	**End year in good standing:**	76%
SAT writing:	-490	**Out-of-state:**	2%
ACT composite:	17-22	**Live on campus:**	31%
GPA 3.75 or higher:	15%	**International:**	2%
GPA 3.50-3.74:	15%		

Basis for selection. High school GPA, courses taken, and test scores. Special consideration for veterans, low-income, and minority applicants. For non-native English speakers, ELPT can be substituted for TOEFL for placement. Exemptions result from scoring well on other specified tests or completion of appropriate courses. Test scores required if high school GPA is less than 3.0. Interview recommended for theatre arts and music majors. Audition recommended for music majors. Portfolio recommended for art majors. **Homeschooled:** Transcript of courses and grades, interview required. Applicant must submit SAT or ACT scores. **Learning Disabled:** Students with diagnosed learning disability or neurological disorder that significantly impairs academic performance in specified area may be eligible for waiver of General Education Breadth (GEB) requirement. Additional coursework required in lieu of GEB. Contact Disabled Student Services or submit documentation of disability.

High school preparation. College-preparatory program required. 15 units required. Required units include English 4, mathematics 3, history 2, science 2 (laboratory 2), foreign language 2, visual/performing arts 1 and academic electives 1. History units include history/social studies.

2008-2009 Annual costs. Tuition/fees: $3,819; $13,989 out-of-state. Room/board: $8,820. Books/supplies: $1,566. Personal expenses: $2,250.

2008-2009 Financial aid. Need-based: 573 full-time freshmen applied for aid; 447 were judged to have need; 429 of these received aid. Average need met was 68%. Average scholarship/grant was $5,190; average loan $4,309. 64% of total undergraduate aid awarded as scholarships/grants, 36% as loans/jobs. **Non-need-based:** Scholarships awarded for academics, alumni affiliation, art, athletics, leadership, minority status, music/drama, state residency.

Application procedures. Admission: Priority date 11/30; deadline 3/1 (receipt date). $55 fee, may be waived for applicants with need. Admission notification on a rolling basis beginning on or about 10/1. Must reply by May 1 or within 4 week(s) if notified thereafter. **Financial aid:** Priority date 3/2; no closing date. FAFSA required. Applicants notified on a rolling basis starting 3/15; must reply within 3 week(s) of notification.

Academics. Special study options: Cooperative education, distance learning, double major, dual enrollment of high school students, ESL, exchange student, honors, independent study, internships, liberal arts/career combination, student-designed major, study abroad, teacher certification program. **Credit/placement by examination:** AP, CLEP, IB, SAT, ACT, institutional tests. 24 credit hours maximum toward bachelor's degree. Credit by examination does not count toward residency requirement. **Support services:** Learning center, pre-admission summer program, reduced course load, remedial instruction, study skills assistance, tutoring, writing center.

Majors. Agriculture: General. **Biology:** General. **Business:** Business admin. **Communications:** General. **Computer sciences:** Computer science, information technology. **Education:** Early childhood. **Foreign languages:** Spanish. **Health:** Nursing (RN). **History:** General. **Liberal arts:** Arts/sciences. **Math:** General. **Parks/recreation:** Health/fitness. **Philosophy/religion:** Philosophy. **Physical sciences:** General, chemistry, geology, physics. **Protective services:** Criminal justice. **Psychology:** General, cognitive. **Social sciences:** General, anthropology, economics, geography, political science, sociology. **Visual/performing arts:** Art, dramatic, music performance, studio arts. **Other:** Gender studies, Multi-/interdisciplinary studies, other.

Most popular majors. Business/marketing 20%, liberal arts 16%, psychology 10%, security/protective services 8%, social sciences 12%.

Computing on campus. 201 workstations in dormitories, library, computer center, student center. Dormitories wired for high-speed internet access and linked to campus network. Commuter students can connect to campus network. Online course registration, online library, helpline, wireless network available.

Student life. Freshman orientation: Available. Preregistration for classes offered. Held year-round. **Housing:** Coed dorms, apartments available. $340 partly refundable deposit, deadline 4/16. Summer housing available and some housing units can accomodate disabled students. **Activities:** Bands, choral groups, dance, drama, music ensembles, musical theater, opera, radio station, student government, student newspaper, symphony orchestra, M.E.Ch.A., Phi Alpha Theta, Fusion, Chi Alpha, Hunger Network, L.U.L.A.C., Hmong Students Association, A Day of Hope, Monument.

Athletics. NCAA. **Intercollegiate:** Baseball M, basketball, cross-country, golf M, soccer, softball W, tennis W, track and field, volleyball W. **Intramural:** Basketball, football (non-tackle) M, soccer M, softball W, volleyball W. **Team name:** Warriors.

Student services. Adult student services, alcohol/substance abuse counseling, career counseling, services for economically disadvantaged, student employment services, financial aid counseling, health services, minority student services, on-campus daycare, personal counseling, placement for graduates, veterans' counselor, women's services. **Physically disabled:** Services for visually, speech, hearing impaired. **Learning disabled:** Comprehensive services available.

Contact. E-mail: outreach_help_desk@csustan.edu
Phone: (209) 667-3070 Toll-free number: (800) 300-7420
Fax: (209) 667-3788
Lisa Bernardo, Dean of Admissions, California State University: Stanislaus, One University Cirlce, Turlock, CA 95382-0256

California University of Management and Sciences

Anaheim, California
www.calums.edu

- Private 4-year university, business and health science college
- Very large city
- 75 degree-seeking undergraduates: 47% women
- 32 degree-seeking graduate students
- Application essay, interview required

General. Regionally accredited; also accredited by ACICS. **Degrees:** 2 bachelor's, 5 associate awarded; master's offered. **Location:** Downtown. **Calendar:** Quarter. **Full-time faculty:** 7 total; 86% have terminal degrees, 14% women. **Part-time faculty:** 18 total; 72% have terminal degrees, 11% women.

Freshman class profile.

End year in good standing:	98%	**Return as sophomores:**	84%

Basis for selection. School record, GPA, interview most important followed by class rank, test scores, essay and recommendations. Completion of high school education is required among applicants for Associate and Bachelor degree programs. TOEFL test scores, EPAT test scores, and Wonderlic Test scores are used for admission. **Homeschooled:** Transcript of courses and grades, interview required.

2008-2009 Annual costs. Tuition/fees: $5,790.

Application procedures. Admission: Closing date 9/9 (receipt date). $100 fee.

Academics. Special study options: Combined bachelor's/graduate degree, ESL, independent study. **Credit/placement by examination:** AP, CLEP, institutional tests. **Support services:** Remedial instruction, tutoring.

Majors. Business: Business admin. **Computer sciences:** General.

Computing on campus. 20 workstations in computer center. Online library, wireless network available.

Student life. Freshman orientation: Mandatory. Preregistration for classes offered.

Contact. E-mail: helenk@calums.edu
Phone: (714) 533-3946 Fax: (714) 533-7778
Helen Kim, Director of Admissions, California University of Management and Sciences, 721 North Euclid Streeet, Anaheim, CA 92801

Chapman University

Orange, California — **CB member**
www.chapman.edu — **CB code: 4047**

- Private 4-year university and liberal arts college affiliated with Christian Church (Disciples of Christ)
- Residential campus in very large city
- 4,264 degree-seeking undergraduates: 5% part-time, 58% women, 3% African American, 9% Asian American, 10% Hispanic American, 1% Native American, 2% international
- 1,827 degree-seeking graduate students
- 50% of applicants admitted
- SAT or ACT with writing, application essay required
- 67% graduate within 6 years

General. Founded in 1861. Regionally accredited. **Degrees:** 923 bachelor's awarded; master's, doctoral, first professional offered. **ROTC:** Army, Air Force. **Location:** 35 miles from Los Angeles, 60 miles from San Diego. **Calendar:** 4-1-4, limited summer session. **Full-time faculty:** 334 total; 90% have terminal degrees, 14% minority, 37% women. **Part-time faculty:** 281 total; 41% women. **Class size:** 36% < 20, 60% 20-39, 2% 40-49, 2% 50-99, less than 1% >100. **Special facilities:** Albert Schweitzer collection of photographs, artifacts, and memorabilia, holocaust memorial library.

Freshman class profile. 5,356 applied, 2,681 admitted, 965 enrolled.

Mid 50% test scores		**Rank in top quarter:**	92%
SAT critical reading:	550-670	**Rank in top tenth:**	51%
SAT math:	560-670	**End year in good standing:**	95%
SAT writing:	560-670	**Return as sophomores:**	86%
ACT composite:	25-29	**Out-of-state:**	34%
GPA 3.75 or higher:	45%	**Live on campus:**	89%
GPA 3.50-3.74:	21%	**International:**	2%
GPA 3.0-3.49:	26%	**Fraternities:**	12%
GPA 2.0-2.99:	8%	**Sororities:**	16%

Basis for selection. Academic course work plus GPA and test scores most important. Recommendations, essay, extracurricular activities also considered. SAT Subject Tests recommended. Audition required for music, dance, theater majors. Portfolio required for art, film majors. Supplemental application required for all talent-based majors. **Homeschooled:** Statement describing homeschool structure and mission, state high school equivalency certificate, letter of recommendation (nonparent) required. Test scores required.

High school preparation. College-preparatory program required. 11 units required; 16 recommended. Required and recommended units include English 2-4, mathematics 2-3, social studies 3-4, science 2-3 (laboratory 1) and foreign language 2-3.

2008-2009 Annual costs. Tuition/fees: $34,700. Room/board: $11,315.

2007-2008 Financial aid. Non-need-based: Scholarships awarded for academics, alumni affiliation, art, music/drama, religious affiliation, ROTC.

Application procedures. Admission: Closing date 1/15 (postmark date). $55 fee, may be waived for applicants with need. Application must be submitted online. Admission notification on a rolling basis beginning on or about 3/15. Must reply by May 1 or within 2 week(s) if notified thereafter. **Financial aid:** Priority date 3/2; no closing date. FAFSA required. Applicants notified on a rolling basis starting 3/15; must reply within 3 week(s) of notification.

Academics. Special study options: Combined bachelor's/graduate degree, distance learning, double major, ESL, exchange student, honors, independent study, internships, liberal arts/career combination, semester at sea, student-designed major, study abroad, teacher certification program, Washington semester. **Credit/placement by examination:** AP, CLEP, IB, SAT, ACT, institutional tests. 32 credit hours maximum toward bachelor's degree. **Support services:** Learning center, reduced course load, remedial instruction, study skills assistance, tutoring, writing center.

Majors. Biology: General, biochemistry. **Business:** Accounting, business admin, managerial economics. **Communications:** General, advertising, broadcast journalism. **Computer sciences:** General, computer science. **Education:** Music. **Foreign languages:** French, Spanish. **Health:** Athletic training, health services admin, predental, premedicine, preveterinary. **History:** General, American, European. **Interdisciplinary:** Peace/conflict. **Liberal arts:** Arts/sciences. **Math:** General. **Philosophy/religion:** Philosophy, religion. **Physical sciences:** Chemistry. **Psychology:** General. **Public administration:** Social work. **Social sciences:** Political science, sociology. **Visual/performing arts:** Acting, art, art history/conservation, cinematography, conducting, dance, dramatic, film/cinema, graphic design, music performance, music theory/composition, piano/organ, play/screenwriting, studio arts, voice/opera.

Most popular majors. Business/marketing 26%, communications/journalism 15%, psychology 6%, social sciences 6%, visual/performing arts 23%.

Computing on campus. 453 workstations in dormitories, library, computer center. Dormitories wired for high-speed internet access and linked to campus network. Commuter students can connect to campus network. Online course registration, online library, helpline, repair service, student web hosting, wireless network available.

Student life. Freshman orientation: Mandatory, $140 fee. Preregistration for classes offered. 5-day summer program immediately preceding start of semester. **Housing:** Guaranteed on-campus for freshmen. Coed dorms, special housing for disabled, apartments, wellness housing available. $600 nonrefundable deposit, deadline 5/1. Housing for students with dependents available. **Activities:** Bands, campus ministries, choral groups, dance, drama, film society, international student organizations, literary magazine, music ensembles, Model UN, musical theater, opera, radio station, student government, student newspaper, symphony orchestra, Hillel, black student union, Model UN, gay/lesbian/bisexual association, Disciples on Campus, MEChA, Students for Peaceful Empowerment Action and Knowledge, Asian Pacific student association, student organization of Latinos.

Athletics. NCAA. **Intercollegiate:** Baseball M, basketball, cross-country, football (tackle) M, golf M, rowing (crew) W, soccer, softball W, swimming W, tennis, track and field W, volleyball W, water polo. **Intramural:** Basketball, soccer, tennis, volleyball. **Team name:** Panthers.

Student services. Adult student services, alcohol/substance abuse counseling, chaplain/spiritual director, career counseling, student employment services, financial aid counseling, health services, on-campus daycare, personal counseling, placement for graduates, veterans' counselor. **Physically disabled:** Services for visually, speech, hearing impaired.

Contact. E-mail: admit@chapman.edu
Phone: (714) 997-6711 Toll-free number: (888) 282-7759
Fax: (714) 997-6713
Michael Drummy, Assistant Vice President and Chief Admission Officer, Chapman University, One University Drive, Orange, CA 92866

Charles R. Drew University of Medicine and Science

Los Angeles, California
www.cdrewu.edu **CB code: 4982**

- Private 4-year university and health science college
- Commuter campus in very large city
- 213 degree-seeking undergraduates: 34% African American, 20% Asian American, 24% Hispanic American, 1% Native American
- 143 graduate students
- 78% of applicants admitted
- Application essay, interview required
- 93% graduate within 6 years

General. Regionally accredited. **Degrees:** 71 bachelor's, 55 associate awarded; master's offered. **Calendar:** Semester, limited summer session. **Full-time faculty:** 23 total; 83% have terminal degrees, 87% minority, 61% women. **Part-time faculty:** 20 total. **Class size:** 77% < 20, 13% 20-39, 6% 40-49, 4% 50-99. **Special facilities:** Health sciences library, clinical and population-based research facilities.

Freshman class profile. 106 applied, 83 admitted, 77 enrolled.

Basis for selection. High school/college transcripts, performance on institutional examination if required by program, essay if required, all considered.

2008-2009 Annual costs. Tuition $250/unit for associate degree programs, $312/unit for bachelor's degree programs. Required fees vary by program and enrollment.

2008-2009 Financial aid. Need-based: 38% of total undergraduate aid awarded as scholarships/grants, 62% as loans/jobs.

Application procedures. Admission: $35 fee. Application deadlines vary by program.

Academics. Special study options: Accelerated study, combined bachelor's/graduate degree, cross-registration, distance learning, double major, dual enrollment of high school students, independent study, internships, liberal arts/career combination. **Credit/placement by examination:** AP, CLEP, IB, institutional tests. **Support services:** Learning center, pre-admission summer program, reduced course load, remedial instruction, study skills assistance, tutoring, writing center.

Majors. Biology: Biomedical sciences. **Health:** Health services, health services admin, nuclear medical technology, physician assistant, premedicine, radiologic technology/medical imaging, sonography.

Computing on campus. 100 workstations in library, computer center, student center. Commuter students can connect to campus network. Online course registration, online library, helpline, wireless network available.

Student life. Freshman orientation: Mandatory. Preregistration for classes offered. **Housing:** Off-campus housing available via California State University Dominguez Hills.

Contact. E-mail: makaylahall@cdrewu.edu
Phone: (323) 563-5886 Fax: (323) 569-0597
Makayla Hall, Director of Admissions, Charles R. Drew University of Medicine and Science, 1731 East 120th Street, Los Angeles, CA 90059

Claremont McKenna College

Claremont, California **CB member**
www.claremontmckenna.edu **CB code: 4054**

- Private 4-year liberal arts college
- Residential campus in large town
- 1,211 degree-seeking undergraduates: 46% women, 5% African American, 12% Asian American, 11% Hispanic American, 8% international
- 22% of applicants admitted
- SAT or ACT with writing, application essay required
- 91% graduate within 6 years

General. Founded in 1946. Regionally accredited. One of a cluster of 5 undergraduate and 2 graduate schools on adjoining campuses. Campuses share some facilities. Cross-enrollment available at any of the 5 colleges, which include Claremont McKenna, Harvey Mudd, Pitzer, Pomona, and Scripps. **Degrees:** 281 bachelor's awarded; master's offered. **ROTC:** Army, Air Force. **Location:** 35 miles from downtown Los Angeles. **Calendar:** Semester. **Full-time faculty:** 122 total; 99% have terminal degrees, 21% minority, 30% women. **Part-time faculty:** 35 total; 89% have terminal degrees, 14% minority, 31% women. **Class size:** 85% < 20, 13% 20-39, less than 1% 40-49, 1% 50-99. **Special facilities:** 10 research institutes, atheneaum (center of intellectual, cultural, and social activities), science center, leadership laboratory.

Freshman class profile. 3,670 applied, 800 admitted, 320 enrolled.

Mid 50% test scores		End year in good standing:	99%
SAT critical reading:	630-740	Return as sophomores:	98%
SAT math:	660-750	Out-of-state:	63%
Rank in top quarter:	98%	Live on campus:	100%
Rank in top tenth:	85%	International:	8%

Basis for selection. School achievement record and test scores most important. Extracurricular activities, curriculum, recommendations, essays, interview, and motivation considered. There is also an emphasis on leadership which is examined in the high school career. SAT Subject Tests only required for home-schooled students. Interviews recommended. Students can interview on campus or with alumni in their area. **Homeschooled:** Interview required. SAT Subject Tests required in 3 subjects (math, English, and one of choice).

High school preparation. Required and recommended units include English 4, mathematics 3-4, social studies 1, history 1, science 2-3 (laboratory 2) and foreign language 3. Management-engineering candidates and science majors should have had both physics and chemistry.

2008-2009 Annual costs. Tuition/fees: $37,060. Room/board: $11,930. Books/supplies: $1,000. Personal expenses: $1,000.

2008-2009 Financial aid. Need-based: 178 full-time freshmen applied for aid; 145 were judged to have need; 145 of these received aid. Average need met was 100%. Average scholarship/grant was $32,151. 99% of total undergraduate aid awarded as scholarships/grants, 1% as loans/jobs. **Non-need-based:** Awarded to 111 full-time undergraduates, including 111 freshmen. Scholarships awarded for academics.

Application procedures. Admission: Closing date 1/2 (postmark date). $60 fee, may be waived for applicants with need. Admission notification 4/1. Must reply by 5/1. **Financial aid:** Closing date 2/1. FAFSA, CSS PROFILE required. Applicants notified by 4/1; must reply by 5/1.

Academics. Philosophy, Politics and economics (PPE) major patterned after program at Oxford University available to 12-15 new students each year. Students accepted spring of sophomore year. Environment, economics, and politics (EEP) major also offered. **Special study options:** Combined bachelor's/graduate degree, cross-registration, double major, exchange student, independent study, internships, student-designed major, study abroad, Washington semester. **Credit/placement by examination:** AP, CLEP,

IB, institutional tests. 16 credit hours maximum toward bachelor's degree. **Support services:** Tutoring, writing center.

Majors. **Area/ethnic studies:** African, African-American, American, Asian, Asian-American, European, gay/lesbian, Hispanic-American/Latino/Chicano, Latin American, Pacific, regional, South Asian, Southeast Asian, Spanish/Iberian, Western European, women's. **Biology:** General, biochemistry, molecular. **Business:** Accounting, accounting/business management, managerial economics. **Communications:** Media studies. **Computer sciences:** Computer science. **Conservation:** Environmental science, environmental studies. **Engineering:** General. **Foreign languages:** Chinese, classics, French, German, Italian, Japanese, Russian, Spanish. **Health:** Premedicine. **History:** General. **Interdisciplinary:** Math/computer science, neuroscience. **Legal studies:** General, prelaw. **Math:** General. **Philosophy/religion:** Philosophy, religion. **Physical sciences:** Chemistry, physics. **Psychology:** General. **Social sciences:** Economics, international relations, political science. **Visual/performing arts:** Art, dance, dramatic.

Most popular majors. Business/marketing 11%, history 6%, interdisciplinary studies 6%, psychology 10%, social sciences 42%.

Computing on campus. 169 workstations in dormitories, library, computer center, student center. Dormitories wired for high-speed internet access and linked to campus network. Commuter students can connect to campus network. Online library, helpline, repair service, student web hosting, wireless network available.

Student life. **Freshman orientation:** Mandatory. 5-day program. Parents invited for first day. **Policies:** Full-time rabbi, priest, and Protestant minister on campus. Also services for Mormon, Islamic, Christian Science, Quaker, and B'hai faiths. **Housing:** Guaranteed on-campus for all undergraduates. Coed dorms, special housing for disabled, apartments, wellness housing available. $190 fully refundable deposit, deadline 7/1. **Activities:** Choral groups, dance, drama, international student organizations, literary magazine, music ensembles, Model UN, musical theater, radio station, student government, student newspaper, symphony orchestra, TV station, Debate/Forensics, Volunteer Service, Young Republicans, Young Democrats, Pan-African Students Association, MECHA, Asian American Student Alliance, Religious Activities Center, Intervarsity Faith Team (Christian nondenominational), Hillel.

Athletics. NCAA. **Intercollegiate:** Baseball M, basketball, cross-country, diving, football (tackle) M, golf, lacrosse W, soccer, softball W, swimming, tennis, track and field, volleyball W, water polo. **Intramural:** Archery, badminton, basketball, bowling, fencing, racquetball, rugby, sailing, skiing, soccer, softball, squash, swimming, tennis, track and field, volleyball, water polo, weight lifting. **Team name:** Stags (M), Athenas (W).

Student services. Alcohol/substance abuse counseling, chaplain/spiritual director, career counseling, student employment services, financial aid counseling, health services, minority student services, personal counseling, placement for graduates, women's services. **Physically disabled:** Services for visually, speech, hearing impaired. **Learning disabled:** Comprehensive services available.

Contact. E-mail: admission@claremontmckenna.edu
Phone: (909) 621-8088 Fax: (909) 621-8516
Richard Vos, Vice President and Dean of Admission & Financial Aid, Claremont McKenna College, 890 Columbia Avenue, Claremont, CA 91711-6425

Cogswell Polytechnical College
Sunnyvale, California
www.cogswell.edu **CB code: 4057**

- Private 4-year visual arts and engineering college
- Commuter campus in small city
- 224 degree-seeking undergraduates: 52% part-time, 13% women, 4% African American, 13% Asian American, 11% Hispanic American
- 52% of applicants admitted
- Application essay required
- 50% graduate within 6 years

General. Founded in 1887. Regionally accredited. Program fusion of art and engineering. **Degrees:** 54 bachelor's awarded. **Location:** 45 miles from San Francisco, 4 miles from San Jose. **Calendar:** Semester, extensive summer session. **Full-time faculty:** 10 total; 60% have terminal degrees, 20% women. **Part-time faculty:** 36 total; 8% have terminal degrees, 14% women. **Class size:** 99% < 20, 1% 20-39. **Special facilities:** Electronic music laboratories, sound/recording studio, video studio, editing studio, computer imaging laboratories, SGI laboratory, MIDI laboratory, sculpture studio, drawing/painting studio, 2D and 3D animation laboratories.

Freshman class profile. 27 applied, 14 admitted, 14 enrolled.

Mid 50% test scores		**GPA 2.0-2.99:**	62%
SAT math:	310-560	**End year in good standing:**	76%
SAT writing:	450-700	**Return as sophomores:**	67%
GPA 3.50-3.74:	15%	**Out-of-state:**	7%
GPA 3.0-3.49:	23%		

Basis for selection. Motivation, 2.7 GPA in academic subjects, test scores most important. Recommendations, art portfolio required for art programs, personal essay. SAT or ACT recommended. Interview recommended. Portfolio required for all digital art programs. **Homeschooled:** Transcript of courses and grades, state high school equivalency certificate, letter of recommendation (nonparent) required. **Learning Disabled:** Must be documented by medical/psychological professional.

High school preparation. College-preparatory program recommended. 7 units required. Required units include English 3, mathematics 3, science 1, computer science 1 and visual/performing arts 1. 1 algebra, 1 geometry, 1 trigonometry required for engineering program; or 1 algebra, 1 geometry required for art programs.

2008-2009 Annual costs. Tuition/fees: $17,172. Books/supplies: $1,392.

2007-2008 Financial aid. **Need-based:** 11 full-time freshmen applied for aid; 11 were judged to have need; 11 of these received aid. Average scholarship/grant was $2,000; average loan $3,500. 41% of total undergraduate aid awarded as scholarships/grants, 59% as loans/jobs. **Non-need-based:** Awarded to 87 full-time undergraduates, including 11 freshmen. Scholarships awarded for academics.

Application procedures. **Admission:** Closing date 3/1 (postmark date). $55 fee, may be waived for applicants with need. Admission notification on a rolling basis. **Financial aid:** Priority date 3/2; no closing date. FAFSA required. Applicants notified on a rolling basis starting 4/30; must reply within 4 week(s) of notification.

Academics. **Special study options:** Distance learning, double major, internships, student-designed major, study abroad. **Credit/placement by examination:** AP, CLEP, IB, institutional tests. 18 credit hours maximum toward bachelor's degree. **Support services:** Remedial instruction, tutoring.

Majors. **Engineering:** Software. **Protective services:** Fire safety technology, fire services admin. **Other:** Digital arts engineering, Digital audio technology.

Most popular majors. Security/protective services 29%, visual/performing arts 67%.

Computing on campus. 164 workstations in library, computer center. Commuter students can connect to campus network. Online course registration, online library, helpline, wireless network available.

Student life. **Freshman orientation:** Mandatory. Preregistration for classes offered. **Housing:** Apartments available. $300 fully refundable deposit, deadline 7/1. **Activities:** Radio station, student government.

Athletics. **Intramural:** Skiing, table tennis.

Student services. Alcohol/substance abuse counseling, career counseling, student employment services, financial aid counseling, personal counseling, placement for graduates.

Contact. E-mail: admissions@cogswell.edu
Phone: (408) 541-0100 Toll-free number: (800) 264-7955
Fax: (408) 747-0764
Barb Bloom, Dean of Student Life, Cogswell Polytechnical College, 1175 Bordeaux Drive, Sunnyvale, CA 94089-1299

Coleman University
San Diego, California
www.coleman.edu **CB code: 0955**

- Private 4-year technical college
- Commuter campus in large city
- 498 degree-seeking undergraduates
- Interview required

General. Founded in 1963. Accredited by ACICS. **Degrees:** 82 bachelor's, 185 associate awarded; master's offered. **Calendar:** Continuous. **Full-time faculty:** 95 total. **Part-time faculty:** 40 total.

Basis for selection. Open admission, but selective for some programs. Institutional entrance exam important: math, spatial reasoning, and aptitude assessment tested. Test scores recommended for placement and credit. Institutionally administered aptitude test required. Skills test given during interview.

2008-2009 Annual costs. Tuition $31,320 for 13-month associate degree program in computer information science effective September 1, 2008. Costs vary depending on program. Books/supplies: $425. Personal expenses: $1,206.

Financial aid. All financial aid based on need.

Application procedures. Admission: No deadline. $100 fee. Admission notification on a rolling basis. **Financial aid:** Priority date 3/2; no closing date. FAFSA, institutional form required. Applicants notified on a rolling basis.

Academics. College uses inverted curriculum with major taken before general curriculum. Vast majority of students are transfers. **Special study options:** Accelerated study, cooperative education, distance learning, double major. **Credit/placement by examination:** AP, CLEP. 26 credit hours maximum toward associate degree, 36 toward bachelor's. **Support services:** Reduced course load, tutoring.

Majors. Business: Business admin. **Computer sciences:** General. **Engineering:** Computer. **Engineering technology:** Computer. **Visual/performing arts:** Graphic design.

Most popular majors. Computer/information sciences 95%.

Computing on campus. 365 workstations in library, computer center.

Student life. Activities: International student organizations, student government, student newspaper, student activities committee.

Student services. Career counseling, personal counseling, placement for graduates, veterans' counselor.

Contact. E-mail: admis@coleman.edu
Phone: (858) 499-0202 Toll-free number: (800) 430-2030
Fax: (858) 499-0233
Sheryl Ridens, Director of Admissions, Coleman University, 8888 Balboa Avenue, San Diego, CA 92123

Concordia University

Irvine, California — **CB member**
www.cui.edu — **CB code: 4069**

- Private 4-year university and liberal arts college affiliated with Lutheran Church - Missouri Synod
- Residential campus in small city
- 1,331 degree-seeking undergraduates
- 63% of applicants admitted
- SAT or ACT (ACT writing optional), application essay required

General. Founded in 1972. Regionally accredited. **Degrees:** 301 bachelor's awarded; master's offered. **Location:** 40 miles from Los Angeles, 80 miles from San Diego. **Calendar:** Semester, limited summer session. **Full-time faculty:** 95 total; 64% have terminal degrees. **Part-time faculty:** 224 total; 20% have terminal degrees. **Class size:** 57% < 20, 41% 20-39, 2% 40-49, less than 1% 50-99, less than 1% >100.

Freshman class profile. 1,819 applied, 1,153 admitted, 326 enrolled.

Mid 50% test scores		**GPA 3.0-3.49:**	38%
SAT critical reading:	470-570	**GPA 2.0-2.99:**	12%
SAT math:	450-570	**Rank in top quarter:**	54%
ACT composite:	20-24	**Rank in top tenth:**	20%
GPA 3.75 or higher:	31%	**Out-of-state:**	26%
GPA 3.50-3.74:	19%	**Live on campus:**	93%

Basis for selection. Secondary school record, class rank, standardized test scores most important. Recommendations and character/personal qualities also important. Audition required for music majors.

High school preparation. 14 units required. Required and recommended units include English 4, mathematics 3, social studies 2, science 3 and foreign language 2. Biology, chemistry, algebra I and II, and geometry specifically recommended.

2008-2009 Annual costs. Tuition/fees: $23,930. Room/board: $7,650. Books/supplies: $1,500. Personal expenses: $2,430.

2008-2009 Financial aid. Need-based: 76% of total undergraduate aid awarded as scholarships/grants, 24% as loans/jobs. **Non-need-based:** Scholarships awarded for academics, alumni affiliation, art, athletics, leadership, music/drama, religious affiliation.

Application procedures. Admission: No deadline. $50 fee, may be waived for applicants with need, free for online applicants. Admission notification on a rolling basis. Must reply by May 1 or within 4 week(s) if notified thereafter. **Financial aid:** Priority date 3/2; no closing date. FAFSA, institutional form required. Applicants notified on a rolling basis starting 2/1; must reply within 4 week(s) of notification.

Academics. Special study options: Accelerated study, combined bachelor's/graduate degree, cross-registration, distance learning, double major, dual enrollment of high school students, ESL, exchange student, honors, independent study, internships, student-designed major, study abroad, teacher certification program. **Credit/placement by examination:** AP, CLEP, IB, SAT, ACT. 32 credit hours maximum toward bachelor's degree. **Support services:** Learning center, tutoring, writing center.

Majors. Biology: General. **Business:** Business admin. **Communications:** Media studies. **Education:** General. **Foreign languages:** Biblical. **History:** General. **Interdisciplinary:** Behavioral sciences. **Liberal arts:** Arts/sciences, humanities. **Math:** General. **Parks/recreation:** Exercise sciences. **Physical sciences:** Chemistry. **Psychology:** General. **Social sciences:** Political science. **Theology:** Theology. **Visual/performing arts:** Art, dramatic, film/cinema.

Most popular majors. Business/marketing 23%, communications/journalism 7%, education 13%, liberal arts 15%, parks/recreation 7%, social sciences 10%, visual/performing arts 6%.

Computing on campus. 48 workstations in dormitories, library, computer center, student center. Dormitories wired for high-speed internet access and linked to campus network. Commuter students can connect to campus network. Online course registration, online library, helpline, wireless network available.

Student life. Freshman orientation: Available, $75 fee. Preregistration for classes offered. **Housing:** Guaranteed on-campus for freshmen. Single-sex dorms, special housing for disabled available. $300 nonrefundable deposit, deadline 6/30. **Activities:** Bands, campus ministries, choral groups, dance, drama, film society, literary magazine, music ensembles, musical theater, radio station, student government, student newspaper, Nuestra Voz, improve club, Republican club, math club, sports medicine club, Fellowship of Christian Athletes, ethics club, Cross Cultural Link.

Athletics. NAIA. **Intercollegiate:** Baseball M, basketball, cross-country, golf, soccer, softball W, tennis, track and field, volleyball W, water polo M. **Intramural:** Basketball, bowling, football (non-tackle), soccer, softball, table tennis, track and field, volleyball. **Team name:** Eagles.

Student services. Adult student services, alcohol/substance abuse counseling, chaplain/spiritual director, financial aid counseling, health services, minority student services, personal counseling.

Contact. E-mail: admission@cui.edu
Phone: (949) 854-8002 ext. 1106 Toll-free number: (800) 229-1200
Fax: (949) 854-6894
Scott Rhodes, Executive Director Admissions, Concordia University, 1530 Concordia West, Irvine, CA 92612-3299

Design Institute of San Diego

San Diego, California
www.disd.edu — **CB code: 3492**

- For-profit 4-year technical college
- Very large city
- 490 degree-seeking undergraduates
- 57% of applicants admitted
- Application essay, interview required

General. Accredited by ACICS. **Degrees:** 87 bachelor's awarded. **Calendar:** Semester. **Full-time faculty:** 6 total. **Part-time faculty:** 59 total.

Freshman class profile. 260 applied, 147 admitted, 128 enrolled.

Basis for selection. High school/college grades, 2 professional references considered.

2008-2009 Annual costs. Tuition/fees: $15,600. Books/supplies: $800. Personal expenses: $4,626.

Four-Year Colleges

Application procedures. Admission: No deadline. $25 fee. Admission notification on a rolling basis. **Financial aid:** No deadline. Applicants notified on a rolling basis.

Academics. Credit/placement by examination: CLEP.

Majors. Visual/performing arts: Interior design.

Contact. Phone: (858) 566-1200 Toll-free number: (800) 619-4337
Fax: (858) 566-2711
Paula Parrish, Director of Admissions, Design Institute of San Diego, 8555 Commerce Avenue, San Diego, CA 92121

DeVry University: Fremont

Fremont, California
www.devry.edu **CB code: 0520**

- For-profit 4-year university
- Commuter campus in small city
- 1,255 degree-seeking undergraduates: 39% part-time, 27% women, 10% African American, 27% Asian American, 20% Hispanic American, 1% Native American, 1% international
- 191 degree-seeking graduate students

General. Regionally accredited. **Degrees:** 271 bachelor's, 25 associate awarded; master's offered. **Location:** 15 miles from San Jose. **Calendar:** Semester, extensive summer session. **Full-time faculty:** 35 total; 49% minority, 17% women. **Part-time faculty:** 219 total; 4% minority, 40% women.

Freshman class profile.

Out-of-state:	2%	**International:**	1%

Basis for selection. Applicant must have high school diploma or equivalent, degree from accredited postsecondary institution, pass institutional placement examination, or submit acceptable test scores and be 17 years of age. New students may enter at beginning of any semester. SAT/ACT considered but not required for admission. If applicant chooses not to submit either, must take institution-administered admissions test.

2008-2009 Annual costs. Tuition/fees: $14,800. Books/supplies: $1,300. Personal expenses: $5,082.

2007-2008 Financial aid. All financial aid based on need.

Application procedures. Admission: No deadline. $50 fee. Admission notification on a rolling basis. **Financial aid:** No deadline. FAFSA required. Applicants notified on a rolling basis.

Academics. Special study options: Accelerated study, distance learning. **Credit/placement by examination:** CLEP, institutional tests. **Support services:** Learning center, remedial instruction, tutoring.

Majors. Biology: Bioinformatics. **Business:** Business admin. **Computer sciences:** Networking, systems analysis. **Engineering technology:** Biomedical, computer, electrical. **Other:** Technical management.

Most popular majors. Business/marketing 59%, computer/information sciences 14%, engineering/engineering technologies 27%.

Computing on campus. 350 workstations in library, computer center. Online course registration, online library, helpline available.

Student life. Freshman orientation: Mandatory. **Housing:** Private apartments, student-plan housing, private rooms available. **Activities:** Institute of Electronic and Electrical Engineers, Hmong Organization on Technology, network communications club, Tau Alpha Pi national honor society for engineering technologies, women's organization, game development, Latino American student organization, Phi Beta Lambda national organization for business majors, chess club, self-defense club.

Athletics. Intramural: Soccer.

Student services. Career counseling, student employment services, financial aid counseling, placement for graduates, veterans' counselor. **Physically disabled:** Services for visually, hearing impaired.

Contact. Phone: (510) 574-1200 Toll-free number: (888) 393-3879
Marc Martin, Director of Admission, DeVry University: Fremont, 6600 Dumbarton Circle, Fremont, CA 94555-3615

DeVry University: Long Beach

Long Beach, California
www.devry.edu **CB code: 2053**

- For-profit 4-year university
- Commuter campus in large town
- 878 degree-seeking undergraduates: 57% part-time, 34% women, 17% African American, 24% Asian American, 39% Hispanic American
- 235 degree-seeking graduate students
- Interview required

General. Regionally accredited. **Degrees:** 159 bachelor's, 32 associate awarded; master's offered. **Location:** 26 miles from Los Angeles. **Calendar:** Semester, extensive summer session. **Full-time faculty:** 20 total; 30% minority, 15% women. **Part-time faculty:** 80 total; 32% minority, 29% women.

Basis for selection. Applicant must have high school diploma or equivalent, degree from an accredited postsecondary institution, or submit acceptable test scores and be at least 17 years of age on the first day of classes. New students may enter at beginning of any semester. SAT/ACT considered but not required for admission. If applicant chooses not to submit either, must take institution-administered admissions test.

2008-2009 Annual costs. Tuition/fees: $14,130. Books/supplies: $1,300. Personal expenses: $5,082.

2007-2008 Financial aid. All financial aid based on need.

Application procedures. Admission: No deadline. $50 fee. Admission notification on a rolling basis. **Financial aid:** No deadline. FAFSA required. Applicants notified on a rolling basis.

Academics. Special study options: Accelerated study, distance learning. **Credit/placement by examination:** CLEP. **Support services:** Learning center, remedial instruction, tutoring.

Majors. Biology: Bioinformatics. **Business:** Business admin, operations. **Computer sciences:** Information technology, networking, systems analysis. **Engineering technology:** Computer, electrical. **Other:** Technical management.

Most popular majors. Business/marketing 59%, computer/information sciences 29%, engineering/engineering technologies 13%.

Computing on campus. 463 workstations in library, computer center. Online course registration, online library, helpline available.

Student life. Freshman orientation: Mandatory. **Housing:** Private apartments, student-plan housing, private rooms available. **Activities:** Associate Student Body Advocates, Society of Hispanic Professional Engineers, Epsilon Delta Pi, United Islands, Tau Alpha Pi, business and accounting association, National Society of Black Engineers (NSBE), Institute of Electronic and Electrical Engineers (IEEE).

Student services. Career counseling, student employment services, financial aid counseling, placement for graduates, veterans' counselor. **Physically disabled:** Services for visually, hearing impaired.

Contact. Phone: (562) 427-4162 Toll-free number: (800) 597-0444
Elaine Francisco, Director of Admissions, DeVry University: Long Beach, 3880 Kilroy Airport Way, Long Beach, CA 90806

DeVry University: Pomona

Pomona, California
www.devry.edu **CB code: 4214**

- For-profit 4-year university
- Commuter campus in small city
- 1,707 degree-seeking undergraduates: 54% part-time, 30% women, 12% African American, 16% Asian American, 40% Hispanic American, 1% Native American
- 223 degree-seeking graduate students
- Interview required

General. Founded in 1983. Regionally accredited. **Degrees:** 303 bachelor's, 38 associate awarded; master's offered. **Location:** 13 miles from Los Angeles. **Calendar:** Semester, extensive summer session. **Full-time faculty:** 25 total; 44% minority, 8% women. **Part-time faculty:** 131 total; 31% minority, 31% women.

Basis for selection. Applicant must have high school diploma or equivalent, degree from an accredited postsecondary institution, or submit acceptable test scores and be at least 17 years of age on the first day of classes. New students may enter at beginning of any semester. SAT/ACT considered but not required for admission. If applicant chooses not to submit either, must take an institution-administered admissions test.

2008-2009 Annual costs. Tuition/fees: $14,130. Books/supplies: $1,300. Personal expenses: $3,152.

2007-2008 Financial aid. All financial aid based on need.

Application procedures. Admission: No deadline. $50 fee. Admission notification on a rolling basis. **Financial aid:** No deadline. FAFSA required. Applicants notified on a rolling basis.

Academics. Special study options: Accelerated study, distance learning. **Credit/placement by examination:** CLEP, institutional tests. **Support services:** Learning center, remedial instruction, tutoring.

Majors. Business: General. **Computer sciences:** General, networking. **Engineering technology:** Biomedical, computer, electrical. **Other:** Technical management.

Most popular majors. Business/marketing 68%, computer/information sciences 25%, engineering/engineering technologies 7%.

Computing on campus. 517 workstations in library, computer center. Online course registration, online library, helpline available.

Student life. Freshman orientation: Mandatory. **Housing:** Private apartments, student-plan housing, private rooms available. **Activities:** Gaming association, Institute for Electrical and Electronic Engineers, Living in Truth, National Society of Black Engineers, Phi Beta Lambda, Society of Hispanic Professional Engineers, networking professional association, Toastmasters.

Student services. Career counseling, student employment services, financial aid counseling, placement for graduates, veterans' counselor. **Physically disabled:** Services for visually, hearing impaired.

Contact. Phone: (909) 622-8866
Jere Thrasher, Director of Admissions, DeVry University: Pomona, 901 Corporate Center Drive, Pomona, CA 91768-2642

DeVry University: Sherman Oaks

Sherman Oaks, California
www.devry.edu **CB code: 2800**

- For-profit 4-year university
- Commuter campus in large city
- 573 degree-seeking undergraduates: 41% part-time, 28% women, 14% African American, 18% Asian American, 34% Hispanic American, 1% Native American
- 141 degree-seeking graduate students
- Interview required

General. Regionally accredited. **Degrees:** 104 bachelor's, 17 associate awarded; master's offered. **Location:** 30 miles from Los Angeles. **Calendar:** Semester, extensive summer session. **Full-time faculty:** 8 total; 25% minority, 12% women. **Part-time faculty:** 49 total; 20% minority, 18% women.

Basis for selection. Applicant must have high school diploma or equivalent, degree from an accredited postsecondary institution, or submit acceptable test scores and be at least 17 years of age on the first day of classes. New students may enter at beginning of any semester. SAT/ACT tests considered but not required for admission. If applicant chooses not to submit either, must take institution-administered admissions test.

2008-2009 Annual costs. Tuition/fees: $14,130. Books/supplies: $1,300. Personal expenses: $5,082.

2007-2008 Financial aid. All financial aid based on need.

Application procedures. Admission: No deadline. $50 fee. Admission notification on a rolling basis. **Financial aid:** No deadline. FAFSA required. Applicants notified on a rolling basis.

Academics. Special study options: Accelerated study, distance learning. **Credit/placement by examination:** CLEP, institutional tests. **Support services:** Learning center, remedial instruction, tutoring.

Majors. Business: Business admin. **Computer sciences:** Networking. **Engineering technology:** Computer, electrical. **Other:** Technical management.

Most popular majors. Business/marketing 56%, computer/information sciences 29%, engineering/engineering technologies 15%.

Computing on campus. 412 workstations in library, computer center. Online course registration, online library, helpline available.

Student life. Freshman orientation: Mandatory. **Housing:** Private apartments, student-plan housing, private rooms available. **Activities:** Student government, student newspaper, Institution of Electrical & Electronic Engineers, Society of Hispanic Professional Engineers, Students Under Mass Organization, Progressive Advancement in Life, Diverse National Alliance, bowling club, Omega Sigma Phi, Phi Theta Kappa, Epsilon Delta Pi, Japanese anime club.

Athletics. Intramural: Softball.

Student services. Career counseling, student employment services, financial aid counseling, placement for graduates, veterans' counselor. **Physically disabled:** Services for visually, hearing impaired.

Contact. Phone: (818) 587-6227 Toll-free number: (888) 610-0800
Dewey McGuirk, Director of Admissions, DeVry University: Sherman Oaks, 15301 Ventura Boulevard, D-100, Sherman Oaks, CA 91403

Dominican University of California

San Rafael, California **CB member**
www.dominican.edu **CB code: 4284**

- Private 4-year university and liberal arts college affiliated with Roman Catholic Church
- Residential campus in small city
- 1,426 degree-seeking undergraduates: 19% part-time, 75% women, 6% African American, 23% Asian American, 16% Hispanic American, 1% Native American, 2% international
- 611 degree-seeking graduate students
- 53% of applicants admitted
- SAT or ACT with writing, application essay required
- 41% graduate within 6 years

General. Founded in 1890. Regionally accredited. **Degrees:** 302 bachelor's awarded; master's offered. **Location:** 11 miles from San Francisco. **Calendar:** Semester, limited summer session. **Full-time faculty:** 76 total; 80% have terminal degrees, 14% minority, 64% women. **Part-time faculty:** 256 total; 42% have terminal degrees, 6% minority, 62% women. **Class size:** 66% < 20, 31% 20-39, 2% 40-49, 1% 50-99.

Freshman class profile. 2,819 applied, 1,487 admitted, 267 enrolled.

Mid 50% test scores		**GPA 2.0-2.99:**	20%
SAT critical reading:	460-560	**Rank in top quarter:**	50%
SAT math:	470-560	**Rank in top tenth:**	19%
SAT writing:	460-560	**Return as sophomores:**	69%
ACT composite:	20-25	**Out-of-state:**	11%
GPA 3.75 or higher:	22%	**Live on campus:**	89%
GPA 3.50-3.74:	22%	**International:**	2%
GPA 3.0-3.49:	36%		

Basis for selection. School achievement record, test scores, rigor of secondary school record, character/qualities most important. Interview recommended for borderline applicants. Audition recommended for music majors. Portfolio recommended for art majors. **Homeschooled:** State high school equivalency certificate required.

High school preparation. College-preparatory program recommended. 11 units required; 15 recommended. Required and recommended units include English 4, mathematics 2-3, history 1-2, science 1-2 (laboratory 1) and foreign language 2.

2008-2009 Annual costs. Tuition/fees: $32,390. Room/board: $12,560.

2007-2008 Financial aid. Need-based: 255 full-time freshmen applied for aid; 225 were judged to have need; 225 of these received aid. Average need met was 63%. Average scholarship/grant was $17,310; average loan $3,593. 61% of total undergraduate aid awarded as scholarships/grants, 39% as loans/jobs. **Non-need-based:** Awarded to 329 full-time undergraduates, including 82 freshmen. Scholarships awarded for academics, alumni affiliation, athletics, leadership, minority status, music/drama. **Additional information:** 4-year guarantee program.

Four-Year Colleges

Application procedures. **Admission:** Priority date 2/1; no deadline. $40 fee, may be waived for applicants with need, free for online applicants. Admission notification on a rolling basis beginning on or about 10/15. Must reply by 5/1. **Financial aid:** Priority date 3/2; no closing date. FAFSA, institutional form required. Applicants notified on a rolling basis starting 3/15; must reply within 2 week(s) of notification.

Academics. **Special study options:** Accelerated study, combined bachelor's/graduate degree, cross-registration, distance learning, double major, dual enrollment of high school students, exchange student, honors, independent study, internships, semester at sea, student-designed major, study abroad, teacher certification program, Washington semester, weekend college. Pathways program (evening/weekend degree program for working adults), semester available at Aquinas College (MI), St. Thomas Aquinas College (NY), Barry University (FL), cross-registration with University of California, Berkeley, (4 + 1 humanities, occupational therapy, BA - MBA), liberal studies + multiple subject credential. **Credit/placement by examination:** AP, CLEP, IB, SAT, ACT, institutional tests. No more than 30 units can come from one of the following sources: CLEP/Regents College Exams, ACE/PONSI review courses, experiential learning portfolios. No more than 12 units from challenging courses. No more than 38 units from NLN exams. **Support services:** Learning center, reduced course load, remedial instruction, study skills assistance, tutoring, writing center.

Majors. **Area/ethnic studies:** Women's. **Biology:** General. **Business:** General, business admin. **Communications:** General. **Computer sciences:** Computer graphics. **Health:** Nursing (RN). **History:** General. **Liberal arts:** Arts/sciences, humanities. **Philosophy/religion:** Religion. **Psychology:** General. **Social sciences:** Political science. **Visual/performing arts:** Art, art history/conservation, ballet, music performance. **Other:** Sustainable community studies.

Most popular majors. Biology 9%, business/marketing 21%, health sciences 28%, liberal arts 12%, psychology 13%.

Computing on campus. 210 workstations in library, computer center, student center. Dormitories wired for high-speed internet access and linked to campus network. Commuter students can connect to campus network. Helpline, repair service, wireless network available.

Student life. **Freshman orientation:** Available. Preregistration for classes offered. Fall program held week prior to start of classes. **Housing:** Coed dorms, wellness housing available. $500 fully refundable deposit, deadline 5/1. **Activities:** Jazz band, campus ministries, choral groups, dance, drama, international student organizations, literary magazine, music ensembles, musical theater, radio station, student government, student newspaper, STAND, Dominican Republican Women, ASDU, Black Student Union, Latinos of the Americas, Men's Bible Study, BASIC, Women's Bible Study.

Athletics. NAIA. **Intercollegiate:** Basketball, cheerleading M, golf, lacrosse M, soccer, softball W, tennis W, volleyball W. **Team name:** Penguins.

Student services. Adult student services, alcohol/substance abuse counseling, chaplain/spiritual director, career counseling, student employment services, financial aid counseling, health services, personal counseling, veterans' counselor, women's services. **Physically disabled:** Services for visually impaired.

Contact. E-mail: enroll@dominican.edu
Phone: (415) 485-3204 Toll-free number: (888) 323-6763
Fax: (415) 485-3214
Rebecca Finn Kenney, Director of Admissions, Dominican University of California, 50 Acacia Avenue, San Rafael, CA 94901-2298

Everest College: Ontario Metro

Rancho Cucamonga, California
www.everest-college.com

- For-profit 4-year business college
- Commuter campus in small city

General. Accredited by ACICS. **Calendar:** Quarter.

Contact. Phone: (909) 484-4311
Director of Admissions, 9616 Archibald Avenue, Suite 100, Rancho Cucamonga, CA 91730-8525

Ex'pression College for Digital Arts

Emeryville, California
www.expression.edu

- For-profit 4-year visual arts and technical college
- Large town
- 1,110 full-time, degree-seeking undergraduates

General. Accredited by ACCSCT. **Degrees:** 251 bachelor's awarded. **Calendar:** Semester. **Full-time faculty:** 50 total. **Part-time faculty:** 100 total.

2009-2010 Annual costs. Tuition/fees: $18,880.

Application procedures. **Admission:** No deadline. $95 fee.

Academics. **Credit/placement by examination:** CLEP.

Majors. **Communications technology:** Animation/special effects, graphics, photo/film/video. **Visual/performing arts:** Graphic design.

Contact. Phone: (510) 654-2934 Toll-free number: (877) 833-8800
Klint Schahrer, Director of Admissions, Ex'pression College for Digital Arts, 6601 Shellmound Street, Emeryville, CA 94608

Fresno Pacific University

Fresno, California — **CB member**
www.fresno.edu — **CB code: 4616**

- Private 4-year university and liberal arts college affiliated with Mennonite Brethren Church
- Residential campus in large city
- 1,583 degree-seeking undergraduates
- 74% of applicants admitted
- SAT and SAT Subject Tests or ACT (ACT writing optional) required

General. Founded in 1944. Regionally accredited. **Degrees:** 478 bachelor's awarded; master's offered. **Location:** 150 miles from San Francisco. **Calendar:** Semester, limited summer session. **Full-time faculty:** 95 total; 61% have terminal degrees, 10% minority. **Part-time faculty:** 250 total; 5% minority. **Class size:** 71% < 20, 23% 20-39, 4% 40-49, 2% 50-99, less than 1% >100. **Special facilities:** Mennonite brethren studies center, conflict studies and peacemaking center.

Freshman class profile. 535 applied, 394 admitted, 158 enrolled.

Mid 50% test scores		**GPA 3.0-3.49:**	34%
SAT critical reading:	420-550	**GPA 2.0-2.99:**	20%
SAT math:	470-560	**Rank in top quarter:**	61%
SAT writing:	420-540	**Rank in top tenth:**	27%
ACT composite:	17-23	**Out-of-state:**	5%
GPA 3.75 or higher:	34%	**Live on campus:**	66%
GPA 3.50-3.74:	12%		

Basis for selection. School achievement record and test scores very important, minimum 3.1 high school GPA. Recommendations, autobiography also considered. Interview recommended for academically weak applicants. Auditions for music, English (with drama emphasis) majors.

High school preparation. 13 units required. Required units include English 4, mathematics 3, social studies 2, science 1 (laboratory 1) and foreign language 2. One year of visual or performing arts.

2008-2009 Annual costs. Tuition/fees: $23,202. Room/board: $6,800. Books/supplies: $1,566. Personal expenses: $2,214.

2008-2009 Financial aid. **Need-based:** 57% of total undergraduate aid awarded as scholarships/grants, 43% as loans/jobs. **Non-need-based:** Scholarships awarded for academics, athletics, music/drama.

Application procedures. **Admission:** Priority date 12/1; deadline 7/31 (postmark date). $40 fee, may be waived for applicants with need. Admission notification on a rolling basis beginning on or about 12/1. **Financial aid:** Priority date 3/2; no closing date. FAFSA, institutional form required. Applicants notified on a rolling basis starting 3/2; must reply by 7/30 or within 3 week(s) of notification.

Academics. **Special study options:** Accelerated study, distance learning, double major, dual enrollment of high school students, ESL, exchange student, independent study, internships, student-designed major, study abroad, teacher certification program, Washington semester. **Credit/placement by examination:** AP, CLEP, IB. 30 credit hours maximum toward associate degree, 30 toward bachelor's. **Support services:** Learning center, reduced course load, remedial instruction, study skills assistance, tutoring, writing center.

Majors. **Biology:** General. **Business:** General, accounting, business admin, human resources, international, management information systems, marketing, nonprofit/public, organizational behavior. **Communications:** General. **Computer sciences:** Computer science. **Conservation:** Environmental science, environmental studies. **Education:** Biology, business, elementary, English, mathematics, music, physical, science, social science. **Foreign languages:** Spanish. **Health:** Athletic training, premedicine. **History:** General.

Liberal arts: Arts/sciences. **Math:** General, applied. **Parks/recreation:** Health/fitness, sports admin. **Philosophy/religion:** Philosophy. **Physical sciences:** Chemistry. **Protective services:** Criminalistics. **Psychology:** General. **Public administration:** Social work. **Social sciences:** General, political science, sociology. **Theology:** Bible. **Visual/performing arts:** Art, dramatic, music performance, music theory/composition.

Most popular majors. Business/marketing 38%, education 36%.

Computing on campus. 90 workstations in dormitories, library, computer center, student center. Dormitories wired for high-speed internet access and linked to campus network. Commuter students can connect to campus network. Online course registration, helpline, student web hosting, wireless network available.

Student life. Freshman orientation: Mandatory. Preregistration for classes offered. 4-day fall orientation, 1-day spring. **Housing:** Single-sex dorms, special housing for disabled, apartments, wellness housing available. $200 nonrefundable deposit, deadline 6/1. Several college-rented apartments available nearby. Resident freshmen under age 23 required to live on campus. **Activities:** Bands, choral groups, dance, drama, international student organizations, music ensembles, student government, student newspaper, Summer Harvest, Shalom Covenant, Kids Klub, Amigos Unidos, Students In Free Enterprise, student chaplains, Daughters of Christ, Faith Project, social work club.

Athletics. NAIA. **Intercollegiate:** Baseball M, basketball, cross-country, soccer, swimming, tennis, track and field, volleyball W, water polo. **Intramural:** Basketball, bowling, football (non-tackle), racquetball, soccer, table tennis, volleyball. **Team name:** Sunbirds.

Student services. Adult student services, alcohol/substance abuse counseling, chaplain/spiritual director, career counseling, student employment services, financial aid counseling, health services, personal counseling. **Physically disabled:** Services for visually, hearing impaired.

Contact. E-mail: ugadmis@fresno.edu
Phone: (559) 453-2039 Toll-free number: (800) 660-6089
Fax: (559) 453-2007
Rina Campbell, Director of Undergraduate Admissions, Fresno Pacific University, 1717 South Chestnut Avenue, Fresno, CA 93702-4709

Golden Gate University

San Francisco, California
www.ggu.edu **CB code: 4329**

- Private 4-year university
- Commuter campus in very large city
- 413 degree-seeking undergraduates: 84% part-time, 58% women
- 3,071 degree-seeking graduate students
- 100% of applicants admitted

General. Founded in 1853. Regionally accredited. Evening and weekend degree programs available in San Francisco, San Jose, Walnut Creek, Roseville, Monterey Bay, Los Angeles, and Seattle (WA). Program length differs by location. **Degrees:** 148 bachelor's awarded; master's, doctoral, first professional offered. **Calendar:** Trimester, extensive summer session. **Full-time faculty:** 70 total; 29% women. **Part-time faculty:** 757 total; 30% women.

Freshman class profile. 14 applied, 14 admitted, 9 enrolled.

Basis for selection. School achievement record most important. Work history or military service factor in determining admission of adult students. SAT recommended. Interviews recommended for undecided major applicants.

High school preparation. 14 units recommended. Recommended units include English 4, mathematics 3, social studies 1, history 1, science 2 (laboratory 1) and foreign language 2.

2008-2009 Annual costs. Tuition/fees: $16,200.

2008-2009 Financial aid. All financial aid based on need.

Application procedures. Admission: Priority date 7/1; no deadline. $55 fee. Admission notification on a rolling basis. Students may be admitted up to 1 year (3 trimesters) before they intend to enroll. **Financial aid:** Priority date 1/2; no closing date. FAFSA, institutional form required. Applicants notified on a rolling basis starting 4/1; must reply within 3 week(s) of notification.

Academics. Professional degree, certification, and lifelong learning programs in business, law, tax, technology and related professions. **Special study options:** Accelerated study, cooperative education, distance learning, ESL, internships. **Credit/placement by examination:** AP, CLEP, IB, institutional tests. **Support services:** Reduced course load, tutoring, writing center.

Majors. Business: Accounting, business admin, finance, human resources, information resources management, international, marketing, operations. **Computer sciences:** Information technology.

Most popular majors. Business/marketing 82%, computer/information sciences 18%.

Computing on campus. 300 workstations in library, computer center. Commuter students can connect to campus network. Online course registration, online library, wireless network available.

Student life. Activities: Student government, student newspaper, Phi Alpha Delta law fraternity, Chi Pi Alpha, Indonesian students organization, Malayan students association, Chinese students club, student government, Indian student association, Korean student association, American Marketing Association, Toastmasters.

Student services. Adult student services, career counseling, student employment services, personal counseling, veterans' counselor. **Physically disabled:** Services for visually, speech, hearing impaired.

Contact. E-mail: info@ggu.edu
Phone: (415) 442-7800 Fax: (415) 442-7807
Louis Riccardi, Director of Enrollment Services, Golden Gate University, 536 Mission Street, San Francisco, CA 94105-2968

Harvey Mudd College

Claremont, California **CB member**
www.hmc.edu **CB code: 4341**

- Private 4-year engineering and liberal arts college
- Residential campus in small city
- 738 degree-seeking undergraduates: 36% women, 2% African American, 21% Asian American, 8% Hispanic American, 1% Native American, 3% international
- 36% of applicants admitted
- SAT or ACT with writing, SAT Subject Tests, application essay required
- 90% graduate within 6 years; 40% enter graduate study

General. Founded in 1955. Regionally accredited. One of a cluster of 5 undergraduate and 2 graduate schools on adjoining campuses. Campuses share facilities and cross-enrollment is available within the 5 undergraduate colleges, which include Claremont-McKenna, Harvey Mudd, Pitzer, Pomona, and Scripps. **Degrees:** 169 bachelor's awarded. **ROTC:** Army, Air Force. **Location:** 35 miles from Los Angeles. **Calendar:** Semester, limited summer session. **Full-time faculty:** 84 total; 100% have terminal degrees, 21% minority, 33% women. **Part-time faculty:** 9 total; 89% have terminal degrees, 22% minority, 33% women. **Class size:** 59% < 20, 33% 20-39, 2% 40-49, 5% 50-99, 2% >100. **Special facilities:** Observatory, biological field station, high performance parallel processor.

Freshman class profile. 2,190 applied, 787 admitted, 202 enrolled.

Mid 50% test scores		**Rank in top tenth:**	95%
SAT critical reading:	670-770	**Return as sophomores:**	95%
SAT math:	750-800	**Out-of-state:**	65%
SAT writing:	680-760	**Live on campus:**	100%
ACT composite:	33-35	**International:**	5%
Rank in top quarter:	99%		

Basis for selection. School achievement record important, especially in mathematics and science. Test scores, recommendations, school and community activities important, interviews highly recommended. Students who take the SAT or ACT with wrtiting must also submit SAT Subject Tests in Math Level 2 and in another subject of their choice. **Homeschooled:** Portfolio suggested describing texts used, curriculum format, how instruction was given. Recommend lab science and foreign language courses be taken at high school or college.

High school preparation. College-preparatory program required. 15 units required. Required and recommended units include English 4, mathematics 3-4, social studies 2, history 1-2, science 3 (laboratory 2) and foreign language 2. Calculus, 1 year chemistry, 1 year physics also required.

2008-2009 Annual costs. Tuition/fees: $36,635. Room and board expense covers 16-meal plan. Room/board: $11,971. Books/supplies: $800. Personal expenses: $900.

2007-2008 Financial aid. **Need-based:** 139 full-time freshmen applied for aid; 115 were judged to have need; 115 of these received aid. Average need met was 100%. Average scholarship/grant was $26,872; average loan $3,436. 87% of total undergraduate aid awarded as scholarships/grants, 13% as loans/jobs. **Non-need-based:** Awarded to 354 full-time undergraduates, including 106 freshmen. Scholarships awarded for academics.

Application procedures. **Admission:** Closing date 1/2 (postmark date). $60 fee, may be waived for applicants with need. Admission notification 4/1. Must reply by May 1 or within 2 week(s) if notified thereafter. **Financial aid:** Closing date 2/1. FAFSA, CSS PROFILE required. Applicants notified by 4/1; must reply by 5/1 or within 2 week(s) of notification.

Academics. Course work divided equally between technical core, major, and humanities and social sciences. **Special study options:** Combined bachelor's/graduate degree, cross-registration, double major, exchange student, independent study, internships, liberal arts/career combination, student-designed major, study abroad. Applied engineering, mathematics and computer science clinics, 4+1 BS/MBA with Claremont Graduate University. **Credit/placement by examination:** AP, CLEP, institutional tests. **Support services:** Learning center, pre-admission summer program, reduced course load, study skills assistance, tutoring, writing center.

Majors. **Biology:** General. **Computer sciences:** General. **Engineering:** General. **Interdisciplinary:** Biological/physical sciences. **Math:** General, applied. **Physical sciences:** Chemistry, physics.

Most popular majors. Computer/information sciences 13%, engineering/engineering technologies 42%, mathematics 14%, physical sciences 19%.

Computing on campus. 360 workstations in dormitories, library, computer center. Dormitories wired for high-speed internet access and linked to campus network. Commuter students can connect to campus network. Online course registration, online library, helpline, student web hosting, wireless network available.

Student life. **Freshman orientation:** Mandatory. 5-day residential introduction. **Policies:** Student-directed honor code governs academic and nonacademic life on campus. **Housing:** Guaranteed on-campus for freshmen. Coed dorms, apartments available. $150 deposit, deadline 7/1. Pets allowed in dorm rooms. **Activities:** Bands, campus ministries, choral groups, dance, drama, film society, international student organizations, literary magazine, music ensembles, musical theater, radio station, student government, student newspaper, symphony orchestra, TV station, InterVarsity Christian Fellowship, Hillel, Society of Women Engineers, AIDS Awareness, Asian American student alliance, Korean student union, Muslim student association, Society of Hispanic Engineers, National Society of Black Engineers.

Athletics. NCAA. **Intercollegiate:** Baseball M, basketball, cross-country, diving, football (tackle) M, golf M, lacrosse W, soccer, softball W, swimming, tennis, track and field, volleyball W, water polo. **Intramural:** Basketball, soccer, softball, table tennis, tennis, volleyball, water polo. **Team name:** Athenas/Stags.

Student services. Alcohol/substance abuse counseling, chaplain/spiritual director, career counseling, student employment services, financial aid counseling, health services, minority student services, personal counseling, placement for graduates, women's services.

Contact. E-mail: admission@hmc.edu
Phone: (909) 621-8011 Fax: (909) 607-7046
Peter Osgood, Director of Admission, Harvey Mudd College, 301 Platt Boulevard, Claremont, CA 91711-5901

Holy Names University

Oakland, California
www.hnu.edu **CB code: 4059**

- Private 4-year university affiliated with Roman Catholic Church
- Commuter campus in large city
- 669 degree-seeking undergraduates: 22% part-time, 74% women
- 308 degree-seeking graduate students
- 74% of applicants admitted
- SAT or ACT (ACT writing optional), application essay required
- 35% graduate within 6 years

General. Founded in 1868. Regionally accredited. **Degrees:** 105 bachelor's awarded; master's offered. **ROTC:** Army, Air Force. **Location:** 14 miles from San Francisco. **Calendar:** Semester, limited summer session. **Full-time faculty:** 36 total; 81% have terminal degrees, 22% minority, 69% women. **Part-time faculty:** 102 total; 38% have terminal degrees, 29% minority, 60% women. **Class size:** 69% < 20, 30% 20-39, 1% 40-49. **Special facilities:** Folk music collection, institute for learning disabled.

Freshman class profile. 347 applied, 256 admitted, 129 enrolled.

Mid 50% test scores		**GPA 2.0-2.99:**	44%
SAT critical reading:	420-530	**End year in good standing:**	89%
SAT math:	410-500	**Return as sophomores:**	62%
ACT composite:	17-24	**Out-of-state:**	11%
GPA 3.75 or higher:	10%	**Live on campus:**	82%
GPA 3.50-3.74:	12%	**International:**	5%
GPA 3.0-3.49:	34%		

Basis for selection. Overall strength of high school preparation, SAT or ACT scores, personal essay, letter of recommendation, extracurricular activities and individual talents and achievements. For non-native English speakers, ESL Center proficiency report certifying completion of Level 107 or higher may be substituted for TOEFL. Proficiency exams in theory, sight-singing, dictation and piano are required of all students entering the music program. Exams offered during week prior to beginning of each semester. Music major applicant must also audition for a faculty jury. **Home-schooled:** Transcript of courses and grades, letter of recommendation (non-parent) required. Transcript demonstrating completion of basic credit hours for high school along with short evaluation from primary instructor. May require additional portfolio or performance-based assessments to document competency.

High school preparation. College-preparatory program recommended. 15 units required. Required and recommended units include English 4, mathematics 3, history 1, science 1 (laboratory 1), foreign language 2-3 and academic electives 3. U.S. history or government required, plus 1 additional year of math, foreign language, or lab science.

2008-2009 Annual costs. Tuition/fees: $26,300. Room/board: $8,540. Books/supplies: $1,566. Personal expenses: $2,754.

2007-2008 Financial aid. **Need-based:** 63 full-time freshmen applied for aid; 63 were judged to have need; 63 of these received aid. Average need met was 37%. Average scholarship/grant was $17,631; average loan $3,357. 62% of total undergraduate aid awarded as scholarships/grants, 38% as loans/jobs. **Non-need-based:** Awarded to 188 full-time undergraduates, including 45 freshmen. Scholarships awarded for academics, athletics, leadership, music/drama, religious affiliation.

Application procedures. **Admission:** Priority date 3/2; deadline 8/15 (postmark date). $20 fee, may be waived for applicants with need. Admission notification on a rolling basis beginning on or about 10/1. Must reply by May 1 or within 2 week(s) if notified thereafter. **Financial aid:** Priority date 3/2, closing date 6/30. FAFSA required. Applicants notified on a rolling basis starting 9/1; must reply by 5/1 or within 2 week(s) of notification.

Academics. All undergraduate students must satisfy general education requirements. First component is Foundation in Critical Thinking and Communication. Remaining components use thematic and disciplinary approaches to learning. **Special study options:** Accelerated study, cross-registration, distance learning, double major, ESL, exchange student, independent study, internships, liberal arts/career combination, student-designed major, study abroad, teacher certification program, weekend college. **Credit/placement by examination:** AP, CLEP, IB, institutional tests. 6 credit hours maximum toward bachelor's degree. Maximum of 6 credit hours per general exam awarded. **Support services:** Learning center, reduced course load, remedial instruction, study skills assistance, tutoring.

Majors. **Biology:** General. **Business:** Business admin, communications, human resources, marketing. **Communications:** Digital media. **Computer sciences:** Networking. **Foreign languages:** Spanish. **Health:** Nursing (RN). **History:** General. **Interdisciplinary:** Biopsychology. **Liberal arts:** Arts/sciences, humanities. **Philosophy/religion:** Philosophy, religion. **Psychology:** General. **Public administration:** Human services. **Social sciences:** Criminology, international relations, sociology. **Visual/performing arts:** Music pedagogy, music performance.

Most popular majors. Business/marketing 24%, English 7%, health sciences 29%, liberal arts 13%, psychology 7%, public administration/social services 10%, social sciences 6%.

Computing on campus. 80 workstations in dormitories, library, computer center. Dormitories wired for high-speed internet access and linked to campus network. Online library, helpline, student web hosting, wireless network available.

Student life. **Freshman orientation:** Mandatory, $50 fee. Preregistration for classes offered. 2-3 day weekend event prior to start of term. **Housing:** Guaranteed on-campus for all undergraduates. Coed dorms, wellness housing available. $100 fully refundable deposit, deadline 8/18. **Activities:** Campus ministries, choral groups, drama, music ensembles, Model UN, student government, symphony orchestra, Asian Pacific International, Black Student Union, drama club, speech and debate team, Holy Names Construction, Global Outlook, International Village, Latinos Unidos, social justice club.

Athletics. NAIA. **Intercollegiate:** Basketball, cross-country, golf M, soccer, softball W, volleyball. **Team name:** Hawks.

Student services. Adult student services, chaplain/spiritual director, career counseling, student employment services, financial aid counseling, personal counseling. **Physically disabled:** Services for visually impaired.

Contact. E-mail: admission@hnu.edu
Phone: (510) 436-1351 Toll-free number: (800) 430-1321
Fax: (510) 436-1325
Murad Dibbini, Dean of Enrollment Services, Holy Names University, 3500 Mountain Boulevard, Oakland, CA 94619-1699

Hope International University

Fullerton, California
www.hiu.edu **CB code: 4614**

- Private 4-year university and liberal arts college affiliated with Independent Christian Churches and Churches of Christ
- Residential campus in small city
- 652 degree-seeking undergraduates: 6% African American, 6% Asian American, 16% Hispanic American, 1% Native American, 3% international
- 265 graduate students
- 80% of applicants admitted
- SAT or ACT (ACT writing optional), application essay required
- 42% graduate within 6 years

General. Founded in 1928. Regionally accredited; also accredited by ABHE. In addition to the campus in Fullerton, CA, there is an extension site in Corona, CA. **Degrees:** 177 bachelor's, 4 associate awarded; master's offered. **Location:** 35 miles from Los Angeles. **Calendar:** 4-1-4, limited summer session. **Full-time faculty:** 39 total; 64% have terminal degrees, 8% minority, 28% women. **Part-time faculty:** 81 total; 21% have terminal degrees, 6% minority, 54% women. **Class size:** 56% < 20, 33% 20-39, 6% 40-49, 4% 50-99.

Freshman class profile. 254 applied, 203 admitted, 94 enrolled.

Mid 50% test scores		**GPA 2.0-2.99:**	35%
SAT critical reading:	450-550	**Rank in top quarter:**	38%
SAT math:	440-560	**Rank in top tenth:**	17%
SAT writing:	430-530	**Return as sophomores:**	70%
ACT composite:	18-23	**Out-of-state:**	20%
GPA 3.75 or higher:	20%	**Live on campus:**	77%
GPA 3.50-3.74:	8%	**International:**	1%
GPA 3.0-3.49:	37%		

Basis for selection. Prior academic achievement, standardized test scores, statement of purpose essays, commitment to the mission of the institution and recommendations are important. Extracurricular activities are also considered along with all other factors bearing on potential success. Interviews recommended for academically borderline applicants. **Homeschooled:** If schooled under the auspices of an organization that can offer transcripts, the university will accept these transcripts and SAT/ACT scores. If not, a GED score and SAT/ACT scores are required in the application process. **Learning Disabled:** All documentation must be recent, within the past three years of enrollment, and must have been completed by an appropriate professional, e.g., State licensed psychologist or school psychologist. Documentation shall include both appropriate tests of learning abilities as well as interview material.

High school preparation. College-preparatory program recommended. 13.5 units recommended. Recommended units include English 4, mathematics 2, history 1, science 1 (laboratory 1), foreign language 1, computer science .5 and academic electives 3. One half-unit speech and one-half unit computer science or literacy is recommended.

2009-2010 Annual costs. Tuition/fees (projected): $21,885. Room/board: $8,800. Books/supplies: $1,566. Personal expenses: $2,970.

2008-2009 Financial aid. Need-based: 81 full-time freshmen applied for aid; 75 were judged to have need; 74 of these received aid. Average need met was 70%. Average scholarship/grant was $13,837; average loan $3,929. 69% of total undergraduate aid awarded as scholarships/grants, 31% as loans/jobs. **Non-need-based:** Awarded to 67 full-time undergraduates, including 22 freshmen. Scholarships awarded for academics, job skills, leadership, music/drama, state residency.

Application procedures. Admission: Priority date 12/1; no deadline. $40 fee, may be waived for applicants with need. Admission notification on a rolling basis. **Financial aid:** Closing date 3/2. FAFSA, institutional form required. Applicants notified on a rolling basis starting 3/15; must reply within 2 week(s) of notification.

Academics. Emphasis on field-based interactive learning combined with direct professional involvement with students. **Special study options:** Combined bachelor's/graduate degree, distance learning, double major, ESL, exchange student, external degree, internships, liberal arts/career combination, study abroad, teacher certification program. **Credit/placement by examination:** AP, CLEP, IB, institutional tests. The amount of credit for examinations depends upon the applicability of the exam(s) to the specific degree program requirements. **Support services:** Reduced course load, remedial instruction, study skills assistance, tutoring.

Majors. Business: Business admin. **Education:** Elementary, music, social science. **Family/consumer sciences:** Family studies. **Health:** Athletic training. **Psychology:** General. **Public administration:** Human services. **Social sciences:** General. **Theology:** Bible, missionary, sacred music, theology, youth ministry.

Most popular majors. Business/marketing 24%, education 7%, family/consumer sciences 33%, psychology 9%, social sciences 6%, theological studies 22%.

Computing on campus. 53 workstations in library, computer center. Dormitories wired for high-speed internet access. Online library, helpline, repair service, wireless network available.

Student life. Freshman orientation: Mandatory, $75 fee. Preregistration for classes offered. Fall and spring new student orientation held 3 days before beginning of term. **Policies:** No alcohol permitted, smoking discouraged. Religious observance required. **Housing:** Guaranteed on-campus for freshmen. Single-sex dorms, wellness housing available. $100 partly refundable deposit, deadline 7/1. Single students required to live on campus until age 21 or reaching junior standing, unless living at home or given special approval. **Activities:** Choral groups, drama, international student organizations, music ensembles, musical theater, student government, student newspaper, school outreach, minority students association, business club, counseling center, fitness center, University Praise.

Athletics. NAIA. **Intercollegiate:** Basketball, cheerleading, soccer, softball W, tennis, volleyball. **Intramural:** Badminton, basketball, football (non-tackle) W, soccer, volleyball. **Team name:** Royals.

Student services. Adult student services, chaplain/spiritual director, career counseling, student employment services, financial aid counseling, health services, personal counseling, veterans' counselor.

Contact. E-mail: PCCAdmissions@hiu.edu
Phone: (714) 879-3901 ext. 2215 Toll-free number: (866) 722-4673
Fax: (714) 681-7423
Butch Ellis, Director of Undergraduate Admissions, Hope International University, 2500 East Nutwood Avenue, Fullerton, CA 92831-3199

Horizon College of San Diego

San Diego, California
www.horizoncollege.edu

- Private 4-year Bible college
- Very large city
- 15 degree-seeking undergraduates

General. Regionally accredited; also accredited by ABHE. **Calendar:** Differs by program. **Full-time faculty:** 2 total. **Part-time faculty:** 13 total.

Freshman class profile. 2 enrolled.

Academics. Credit/placement by examination: CLEP.

Majors. Theology: Bible.

Contact. E-mail: info@horizoncollege.org
Horizon College of San Diego, 10625 Scripps Ranch Boulevard, Suite F, San Diego, CA 92131

Humboldt State University

Arcata, California **CB member**
www.humboldt.edu **CB code: 4345**

- Public 4-year university and liberal arts college
- Residential campus in large town
- 6,685 degree-seeking undergraduates: 9% part-time, 54% women, 4% African American, 5% Asian American, 11% Hispanic American, 2% Native American

- 763 degree-seeking graduate students
- 75% of applicants admitted
- 43% graduate within 6 years

General. Founded in 1913. Regionally accredited. **Degrees:** 1,305 bachelor's awarded; master's offered. **Location:** 275 miles from San Francisco. **Calendar:** Semester, limited summer session. **Full-time faculty:** 269 total; 100% have terminal degrees, 11% minority, 37% women. **Part-time faculty:** 252 total; 17% have terminal degrees, 14% minority, 61% women. **Class size:** 38% < 20, 44% 20-39, 8% 40-49, 8% 50-99, 2% >100. **Special facilities:** Marine lab, observatory, natural history museum, marsh and wildlife sanctuary, small lakes and ponds, 280-acre sand dune preserve, research vessel, freshwater fish hatchery, small-game animal pen, fungal genetic stock center, 360-acre experimental forest, 170,000 specimen herbarium, center for appropriate technology, energy research center.

Freshman class profile. 9,627 applied, 7,264 admitted, 1,191 enrolled.

Mid 50% test scores		**GPA 2.0-2.99:**	37%
SAT critical reading:	470-590	**Rank in top quarter:**	42%
SAT math:	460-580	**Rank in top tenth:**	18%
SAT writing:	460-570	**End year in good standing:**	70%
ACT composite:	19-25	**Return as sophomores:**	73%
GPA 3.75 or higher:	12%	**Out-of-state:**	16%
GPA 3.50-3.74:	14%	**Live on campus:**	87%
GPA 3.0-3.49:	37%		

Basis for selection. High school GPA and test scores most important. In-state residents with high school GPA of 3.0 or higher or out-of-state applicants with high school GPA over 3.6 do not have to submit test scores for admission. Essay recommended for academically weak, special consideration applicants.

High school preparation. College-preparatory program required. 15 units required. Required units include English 4, mathematics 3, social studies 1, history 1, science 2 (laboratory 2), foreign language 2 and academic electives 1.

2008-2009 Annual costs. Tuition/fees: $4,139; $14,309 out-of-state. Room/board: $8,972. Books/supplies: $1,470. Personal expenses: $2,170.

2007-2008 Financial aid. **Need-based:** 808 full-time freshmen applied for aid; 569 were judged to have need; 535 of these received aid. Average need met was 71%. Average scholarship/grant was $4,403; average loan $222. 56% of total undergraduate aid awarded as scholarships/grants, 44% as loans/jobs. **Non-need-based:** Awarded to 116 full-time undergraduates, including 21 freshmen. Scholarships awarded for academics.

Application procedures. **Admission:** Priority date 10/1; deadline 8/1. $55 fee, may be waived for applicants with need. Admission notification on a rolling basis beginning on or about 11/15. **Financial aid:** Priority date 3/2; no closing date. FAFSA required. Applicants notified on a rolling basis starting 4/15; must reply within 6 week(s) of notification.

Academics. Indian Teacher and Educational Personnel Program, Indian Natural Resources, Sciences and Engineering Program available. **Special study options:** Cooperative education, cross-registration, distance learning, double major, dual enrollment of high school students, ESL, exchange student, honors, independent study, internships, student-designed major, study abroad, teacher certification program. **Credit/placement by examination:** AP, CLEP, IB, SAT, ACT, institutional tests. 30 credit hours maximum toward bachelor's degree. Humboldt grants undergraduate degree credit for successful completion of non-collegiate instruction, either military or civilian, appropriate to the baccalaureate degree. Credit must be recommended by the Commission on Educational Credit and Credentials of the American Council on Education. **Support services:** Learning center, pre-admission summer program, reduced course load, remedial instruction, study skills assistance, tutoring, writing center.

Majors. **Agriculture:** Range science. **Area/ethnic studies:** Native American, women's. **Biology:** General, botany, zoology. **Business:** General, business admin. **Communications:** General, journalism. **Computer sciences:** General, information systems. **Conservation:** General, environmental studies, fisheries, forestry, management/policy, wildlife. **Education:** Early childhood, elementary, physical, trade/industrial. **Engineering:** Science. **Foreign languages:** French, Spanish. **Health:** Kinesiotherapy, nursing (RN). **History:** General. **Interdisciplinary:** Global studies, intercultural. **Liberal arts:** Arts/sciences. **Math:** General. **Parks/recreation:** Facilities management, health/fitness. **Philosophy/religion:** Philosophy, religion. **Physical sciences:** General, chemistry, geology, oceanography, physics. **Psychology:** General. **Public administration:** Social work. **Social sciences:** General, anthropology, economics, geography, political science, sociology. **Visual/performing arts:** Art, dance, dramatic.

Most popular majors. Biology 8%, liberal arts 10%, natural resources/environmental science 10%, psychology 6%, social sciences 12%, visual/performing arts 10%.

Computing on campus. 770 workstations in dormitories, library, computer center, student center. Dormitories wired for high-speed internet access and linked to campus network. Commuter students can connect to campus network. Online course registration, online library, helpline, student web hosting, wireless network available.

Student life. **Freshman orientation:** Mandatory, $50 fee. Preregistration for classes offered. Student-directed program held June, July and August. **Housing:** Guaranteed on-campus for freshmen. Coed dorms, apartments, wellness housing available. $500 partly refundable deposit, deadline 5/2. **Activities:** Bands, choral groups, dance, drama, film society, literary magazine, music ensembles, musical theater, radio station, student government, student newspaper, symphony orchestra, Newman Club, Campus Crusade for Christ, Youth Educational Services, Black Students Union, MECHA, Gay, Lesbian and Bisexual Students Association, Native American Club, Jewish Student Union, Multicultural Center, Veterans Organization.

Athletics. NCAA. **Intercollegiate:** Basketball, cross-country, football (tackle) M, rowing (crew) W, soccer, softball W, track and field, volleyball W. **Intramural:** Badminton, basketball, football (tackle) M, soccer, softball, volleyball. **Team name:** Lumberjacks.

Student services. Adult student services, career counseling, student employment services, financial aid counseling, health services, on-campus daycare, personal counseling, placement for graduates, veterans' counselor. **Physically disabled:** Services for visually, speech, hearing impaired.

Contact. E-mail: hsuinfo@humboldt.edu
Phone: (707) 826-4402 Toll-free number: (866) 850-9556
Fax: (707) 826-6190
Scott Hagg, Director of Admissions and Student Recruitment, Humboldt State University, One Harpst Street, Arcata, CA 95521-8299

Humphreys College
Stockton, California
www.humphreys.edu **CB code: 4346**

- Private 4-year business and liberal arts college
- Residential campus in large city
- 649 degree-seeking undergraduates
- Interview required

General. Founded in 1896. Regionally accredited. **Degrees:** 95 bachelor's, 40 associate awarded; master's, first professional offered. **Location:** 35 miles from Sacramento, California. **Calendar:** Quarter, extensive summer session. **Full-time faculty:** 18 total; 17% have terminal degrees, 28% minority, 44% women. **Part-time faculty:** 44 total; 14% have terminal degrees, 46% minority, 41% women. **Class size:** 80% < 20, 20% 20-39.

Freshman class profile.

Out-of-state:	3%	**Live on campus:**	25%

Basis for selection. Open admission. ACT used for placement only. **Homeschooled:** State high school equivalency certificate required.

2008-2009 Annual costs. Tuition/fees: $12,240. School-controlled apartment housing cost quoted, not including utilities. Room only: $3,150. Books/supplies: $522. Personal expenses: $738.

2008-2009 Financial aid. **Non-need-based:** Scholarships awarded for academics, state residency.

Application procedures. **Admission:** No deadline. $35 fee, may be waived for applicants with need. Application must be submitted on paper. Admission notification on a rolling basis. **Financial aid:** Closing date 6/30. FAFSA required. Applicants notified on a rolling basis; must reply within 2 week(s) of notification.

Academics. **Special study options:** Combined bachelor's/graduate degree, cooperative education, cross-registration, double major, honors, independent study, internships. **Credit/placement by examination:** AP, CLEP, IB, institutional tests. 4 credit hours maximum toward associate degree, 45 toward bachelor's. **Support services:** Learning center, pre-admission summer program, remedial instruction, tutoring, writing center.

Majors. **Business:** General, accounting, administrative services, business admin, office technology, office/clerical. **Computer sciences:** General. **Education:** General. **Health:** Medical secretary. **Legal studies:** Court reporting, legal secretary, paralegal. **Liberal arts:** Arts/sciences. **Public administration:** Community org/advocacy. **Social sciences:** General.

Computing on campus. 25 workstations in library, computer center. Online library, helpline, wireless network available.

Student life. **Freshman orientation:** Available. Preregistration for classes offered. Held on campus the first week of each academic term. **Housing:** Apartments available. $200 partly refundable deposit, deadline 8/20. **Activities:** Student government, student newspaper, business club.

Student services. Career counseling, student employment services, financial aid counseling, on-campus daycare, personal counseling, placement for graduates, veterans' counselor.

Contact. E-mail: ugadmission@humphreys.edu
Phone: (209) 478-0800 Fax: (209) 478-8721
Santa Lopez-Minarte, Admissions Director, Humphreys College, 6650 Inglewood Avenue, Stockton, CA 95207-3896

Interior Designers Institute

Newport Beach, California
www.idi.edu **CB code: 2318**

- For-profit 4-year visual arts college
- Large city
- 515 degree-seeking undergraduates

General. Accredited by ACCSCT. **Degrees:** 71 bachelor's, 71 associate awarded. **Calendar:** Continuous. **Part-time faculty:** 30 total.

Basis for selection. Open admission.

2008-2009 Annual costs. 12-week certificate program: $1,995. Full year associate degree program: $15,950; bachelor's degree program: $14,950. Books/supplies: $1,500.

Application procedures. **Admission:** No deadline. $95 fee. Application must be submitted on paper.

Academics. **Credit/placement by examination:** CLEP.

Majors. **Visual/performing arts:** Interior design.

Contact. E-mail: contact@idi.edu
Phone: (949) 675-4451 Fax: (949) 759-0667
Susan Bell, Office Manager, Interior Designers Institute, 1061 Camelback Road, Newport Beach, CA 92660-3228

International Academy of Design and Technology: Sacramento

Sacramento, California
www.iadtsacramento.com

- For-profit 4-year liberal arts and technical college
- Very large city
- 450 degree-seeking undergraduates
- 100% of applicants admitted

General. Regionally accredited; also accredited by ACICS. **Calendar:** Continuous. **Full-time faculty:** 3 total. **Part-time faculty:** 30 total.

Freshman class profile. 99 applied, 99 admitted, 99 enrolled.

Application procedures. **Admission:** No deadline. **Financial aid:** No deadline.

Academics. **Credit/placement by examination:** CLEP.

Majors. **Visual/performing arts:** Fashion design, interior design. **Other:** Visual communications.

Contact. E-mail: aepperson@iadtsacramento.com
Phone: (916) 285-9468
Miguel Sanchez, Director of Admissions, International Academy of Design and Technology: Sacramento, 2450 Del Paso Road, Sacramento, CA 95834

ITT Technical Institute: Anaheim

Anaheim, California
www.itt-tech.edu **CB code: 3570**

- For-profit 4-year technical college
- Commuter campus in small city

General. Founded in 1983. Accredited by ACICS. **Location:** 15 miles from Los Angeles. **Calendar:** Quarter.

Contact. Phone: (714) 535-3700
Director of Recruitment, 525 North Muller, Anaheim, CA 92801

ITT Technical Institute: Lathrop

Lathrop, California
www.itt-tech.edu **CB code: 2720**

- For-profit 4-year technical college
- Commuter campus in small town

General. Accredited by ACICS. **Calendar:** Quarter.

Contact. Phone: (209) 858-0077
Director of Recruitment, 16916 South Harlan Road, Lathrop, CA 95330

ITT Technical Institute: Oxnard

Oxnard, California
www.itt-tech.edu **CB code: 2744**

- For-profit 4-year technical college
- Commuter campus in small city

General. Accredited by ACICS. **Location:** 34 miles from Santa Barbara, 52 miles from Los Angeles. **Calendar:** Quarter.

Contact. Phone: (805) 988-0143
Director of Recruitment, 2051 Solar Drive, Building B, Oxnard, CA 93036

ITT Technical Institute: Rancho Cordova

Rancho Cordova, California
www.itt-tech.edu **CB code: 3597**

- For-profit 4-year technical college
- Commuter campus in large city

General. Founded in 1954. Accredited by ACICS. **Location:** 11 miles from Sacramento, 87 miles from San Francisco. **Calendar:** Quarter.

Contact. Phone: (916) 366-3900
Director of Recruitment, 10863 Gold Center Drive, Rancho Cordova, CA 95670

ITT Technical Institute: San Bernardino

San Bernardino, California
www.itt-tech.edu **CB code: 7103**

- For-profit 4-year technical college
- Commuter campus in very large city

General. Accredited by ACICS. **Location:** 60 miles from Los Angeles. **Calendar:** Quarter.

Contact. Phone: (800) 888-3801
Director of Recruitment, 670 East Carnegie Drive, San Bernardino, CA 92408-2800

ITT Technical Institute: San Diego

San Diego, California
www.itt-tech.edu **CB code: 0206**

- For-profit 4-year technical college
- Commuter campus in very large city

General. Founded in 1981. Accredited by ACICS. **Calendar:** Quarter.

Contact. Phone: (858) 571-8500
Director of Recruitment, 9680 Granite Ridge Drive, San Diego, CA 92123

ITT Technical Institute: Sylmar

Sylmar, California
www.itt-tech.edu **CB code: 3571**

- For-profit 4-year technical college
- Commuter campus in very large city

Four-Year Colleges

General. Founded in 1982. Accredited by ACICS. **Calendar:** Quarter.

Contact. Phone: (818) 364-5151
Director of Recruitment, 12669 Encinitas Avenue, Sylmar, CA 91342-3664

ITT Technical Institute: Torrance
Torrance, California
www.itt-tech.edu **CB code: 7104**

- For-profit 4-year technical college
- Commuter campus in small city

General. Accredited by ACICS. **Calendar:** Quarter.

Contact. Phone: (310) 380-1555
Director of Recruitment, 20050 South Vermont Avenue, Torrance, CA 90502

John F. Kennedy University
Pleasant Hill, California
www.jfku.edu **CB code: 1362**

- Private two-year upper-division university
- Commuter campus in large town
- Interview required

General. Founded in 1964. Regionally accredited. Undergraduate and graduate degree Linking program. **Degrees:** 57 bachelor's awarded; master's, doctoral, first professional offered. **Articulation:** Agreements with all California community colleges. **Location:** 35 miles from San Francisco. **Calendar:** Quarter, limited summer session. **Full-time faculty:** 55 total. **Part-time faculty:** 194 total. **Class size:** 81% < 20, 19% 20-39.

Student profile. 225 degree-seeking undergraduates, 1,263 degree-seeking graduate students.

Women:	75%	**Out-of-state:**	1%
Part-time:	79%	**25 or older:**	90%

Basis for selection. Open admission. College transcript, interview required. Deadlines for response to admissions decisions vary with programs. Interview required. Applicants must have 45 quarter hours. Transfer accepted as sophomores, juniors, seniors.

2008-2009 Annual costs. Tuition/fees: $15,468. Books/supplies: $1,080.

Financial aid. All financial aid based on need.

Application procedures. Admission: Rolling admission. $55 fee. **Financial aid:** Priority date 4/1. FAFSA, institutional form required.

Academics. Special study options: Combined bachelor's/graduate degree, cross-registration, independent study, internships, teacher certification program. **Credit/placement by examination:** AP, CLEP. 105 credit hours maximum toward bachelor's degree. Maximum of 105 units through combination of CLEP, DANTES, 2-year schools, and military training. **Support services:** Study skills assistance, writing center.

Majors. Business: Business admin. **Legal studies:** General, paralegal. **Liberal arts:** Arts/sciences. **Psychology:** General. **Visual/performing arts:** Studio arts. **Other:** Philosophy and religion.

Most popular majors. Business/marketing 26%, liberal arts 63%, psychology 11%.

Computing on campus. 25 workstations in library, computer center. Commuter students can connect to campus network.

Student life. Activities: Student government, student newspaper.

Student services. Career counseling, student employment services, veterans' counselor. **Physically disabled:** Services for visually, speech, hearing impaired.

Contact. E-mail: proginfo@jfku.edu
Phone: (925) 969-3535 Toll-free number: (800) 696-5358
Fax: (925) 969-3331
Jen Miller-Hogg, Director of Admissions, John F. Kennedy University, 100 Ellinwood Way, Pleasant Hill, CA 94523-4817

The King's College and Seminary
Van Nuys, California
www.kingscollege.edu **CB code: 3896**

- Private 4-year Bible and seminary college affiliated with nondenominational tradition
- Commuter campus in very large city
- 525 degree-seeking undergraduates
- Application essay required

General. Accredited by ABHE. Evangelical institution. **Degrees:** 17 bachelor's, 10 associate awarded; master's, doctoral, first professional offered. **ROTC:** Army, Naval, Air Force. **Calendar:** Quarter, limited summer session. **Full-time faculty:** 14 total. **Part-time faculty:** 39 total.

Basis for selection. Demonstration of commitment to Christian faith required, essays, references important. SAT or ACT recommended. **Homeschooled:** Statement describing homeschool structure and mission, transcript of courses and grades required.

2009-2010 Annual costs. Tuition/fees: $8,385. Seminary students pay $195 per credit hour. Books/supplies: $1,200.

Financial aid. Non-need-based: Scholarships awarded for academics, leadership. **Additional information:** Specific scholarships may require specific essays.

Application procedures. Admission: No deadline. $45 fee. Admission notification on a rolling basis. Must reply within 30 days. **Financial aid:** No deadline. FAFSA required. Applicants notified on a rolling basis.

Academics. Special study options: Distance learning, external degree, independent study, internships, study abroad. **Credit/placement by examination:** AP, CLEP, IB, institutional tests. 45 credit hours maximum toward associate degree, 45 toward bachelor's. **Support services:** Reduced course load, remedial instruction, study skills assistance, tutoring.

Majors. Theology: Bible.

Computing on campus. Online course registration, online library available.

Student life. Freshman orientation: Mandatory. Preregistration for classes offered. **Policies:** Drug- and alcohol-free campus. Religious observance required. **Activities:** Campus ministries, choral groups, music ensembles, student government, student newspaper, C.S. Lewis club, women in ministry group, Delta Epsilon, National Association of Evangelicals.

Athletics. Intramural: Basketball M.

Student services. Alcohol/substance abuse counseling, chaplain/spiritual director, career counseling, financial aid counseling, personal counseling, placement for graduates, veterans' counselor, women's services.

Contact. E-mail: admissions@kingscollege.edu
Phone: (818) 779-8040 Toll-free number: (888) 779-8040
Fax: (818) 779-8429
Marilyn Chappell, Director of Admissions, The King's College and Seminary, 14800 Sherman Way, Van Nuys, CA 91405-2233

LA College International
Los Angeles, California
www.lac.edu **CB code: 3046**

- For-profit 4-year business and technical college
- Commuter campus in very large city
- 247 degree-seeking undergraduates

General. Accredited by ACICS. **Degrees:** 2 bachelor's, 34 associate awarded. **Calendar:** Continuous. **Part-time faculty:** 25 total.

Basis for selection. Open admission. ATB required if no high school diploma.

2009-2010 Annual costs. Tuition/fees: $12,512. Online tuition $325 per credit hour for AA and BS programs in business management. Books/supplies: $1,500.

Application procedures. Admission: No deadline. $35 fee. **Financial aid:** FAFSA, institutional form required.

Academics. Credit/placement by examination: CLEP.

Majors. **Business:** Business admin. **Computer sciences:** General.

Student life. **Freshman orientation:** Available. 4 days before start date. **Activities:** Student government.

Contact. Phone: (213) 381-3333 Toll-free number: (800) 574-6428
Fax: (213) 383-9369
Shavonne Turner, Admissions Director, LA College International, 3200 Wilshire Boulevard, Suite 400, Los Angeles, CA 90010-1308

La Sierra University

Riverside, California — **CB member**
www.lasierra.edu — **CB code: 4380**

- Private 4-year university affiliated with Seventh-day Adventists
- Residential campus in large city
- 1,442 degree-seeking undergraduates: 9% part-time, 59% women, 9% African American, 25% Asian American, 25% Hispanic American, 1% Native American, 12% international
- 347 degree-seeking graduate students
- 55% of applicants admitted
- SAT or ACT (ACT writing optional), application essay required

General. Founded in 1922. Regionally accredited. **Degrees:** 205 bachelor's awarded; master's, doctoral offered. **Location:** 55 miles from Los Angeles. **Calendar:** Quarter, limited summer session. **Full-time faculty:** 96 total; 84% have terminal degrees, 38% minority, 43% women. **Part-time faculty:** 91 total; 24% minority, 42% women. **Class size:** 67% < 20, 24% 20-39, 5% 40-49, 3% 50-99, less than 1% >100. **Special facilities:** Museum of natural history with large freeze-dried collection (reptiles, mammals, birds), mineral spheres collection, arboretum, observatory, women's resource center.

Freshman class profile. 1,153 applied, 637 admitted, 310 enrolled.

Mid 50% test scores		**GPA 2.0-2.99:**	25%
SAT critical reading:	430-540	**Rank in top quarter:**	46%
SAT math:	430-570	**Rank in top tenth:**	17%
ACT composite:	18-22	**Return as sophomores:**	71%
GPA 3.75 or higher:	28%	**Out-of-state:**	14%
GPA 3.50-3.74:	18%	**Live on campus:**	65%
GPA 3.0-3.49:	29%	**International:**	10%

Basis for selection. Secondary school record and GPA, test scores, recommendations, and religious affiliation or commitment important.

High school preparation. College-preparatory program required. 15 units required. Required and recommended units include English 4, mathematics 3-4, social studies 2, science 2-3 (laboratory 2-3), foreign language 2-3, visual/performing arts 1 and academic electives 1.

2009-2010 Annual costs. Tuition/fees (projected): $24,917. Room/board: $6,990. Books/supplies: $1,605. Personal expenses: $2,322.

2007-2008 Financial aid. **Need-based:** 252 full-time freshmen applied for aid; 213 were judged to have need; 213 of these received aid. Average need met was 68%. Average scholarship/grant was $14,683; average loan $3,321. 56% of total undergraduate aid awarded as scholarships/grants, 44% as loans/jobs. **Non-need-based:** Awarded to 426 full-time undergraduates, including 111 freshmen. Scholarships awarded for academics, leadership, music/drama, religious affiliation.

Application procedures. **Admission:** Priority date 2/1; no deadline. $30 fee, may be waived for applicants with need. Admission notification on a rolling basis. **Financial aid:** Priority date 3/2; no closing date. FAFSA required. Applicants notified on a rolling basis starting 4/15; must reply by 9/1.

Academics. **Special study options:** Accelerated study, cross-registration, distance learning, double major, dual enrollment of high school students, ESL, honors, independent study, internships, student-designed major, study abroad, teacher certification program. **Credit/placement by examination:** AP, CLEP, IB, institutional tests. 24 credit hours maximum toward bachelor's degree. **Support services:** Learning center, pre-admission summer program, reduced course load, remedial instruction, study skills assistance, tutoring, writing center.

Honors college/program. High school GPA above 3.25 and ACT above 60th percentile. 25 freshmen admitted per year.

Majors. **Biology:** General, biochemistry, biometrics, biophysics. **Business:** Accounting, business admin, finance, human resources, marketing. **Communications:** General. **Computer sciences:** Computer science, information systems. **Foreign languages:** Spanish. **History:** General. **Interdisciplinary:** Global studies. **Liberal arts:** Arts/sciences. **Math:** General. **Parks/recreation:** Exercise sciences, health/fitness. **Philosophy/religion:** Religion. **Physical sciences:** General, chemistry. **Psychology:** General, psychobiology. **Public administration:** Social work. **Social sciences:** Economics, sociology. **Visual/performing arts:** Art, studio arts.

Most popular majors. Biology 15%, business/marketing 23%, liberal arts 9%, parks/recreation 9%, public administration/social services 7%, visual/performing arts 7%.

Computing on campus. 262 workstations in dormitories, library, computer center. Dormitories wired for high-speed internet access and linked to campus network. Commuter students can connect to campus network. Online course registration, helpline, wireless network available.

Student life. **Freshman orientation:** Mandatory, $200 fee. Preregistration for classes offered. **Policies:** Smoke- and alcohol-free campus. Religious observance required. **Housing:** Guaranteed on-campus for all undergraduates. Single-sex dorms, apartments, wellness housing available. $100 fully refundable deposit. Honors residence hall available. **Activities:** Bands, campus ministries, choral groups, drama, international student organizations, literary magazine, music ensembles, student government, student newspaper, symphony orchestra, black student association, Earth Awareness, Amnesty International, Korean club, Ole club, Students in Free Enterprise, South Asia student association.

Athletics. NCAA. **Intercollegiate:** Baseball M, basketball, golf M, soccer, softball W, tennis, volleyball W. **Intramural:** Badminton, basketball, football (tackle), softball. **Team name:** Golden Eagles.

Student services. Adult student services, chaplain/spiritual director, career counseling, student employment services, financial aid counseling, health services, personal counseling, placement for graduates, women's services.

Contact. E-mail: admissions@lasierra.edu
Phone: (951) 785-2176 Toll-free number: (800) 874-5587
Fax: (951) 785-2477
Faye Swayze, Director of Admissions & Registrar, La Sierra University, 4500 Riverwalk Parkway, Riverside, CA 92515-8247

Laguna College of Art and Design

Laguna Beach, California
www.lagunacollege.edu — **CB code: 7248**

- Private 4-year visual arts college
- Commuter campus in large town
- 346 degree-seeking undergraduates
- SAT or ACT (ACT writing optional) required

General. Founded in 1961. Regionally accredited. **Degrees:** 64 bachelor's awarded; master's offered. **Location:** 50 miles from Los Angeles, 75 miles from San Diego. **Calendar:** Semester, limited summer session. **Full-time faculty:** 10 total. **Part-time faculty:** 80 total.

Basis for selection. Selection based on academic record and overall merit of 10-piece portfolio which includes minimum of 4 observational drawings. Application fee waived for online applications. Portfolios required.

High school preparation. 14 units recommended. Recommended units include English 2, mathematics 2, social studies 2, history 2, science 2, foreign language 2 and academic electives 2. 3 units of studio art, drawing and painting recommended.

2008-2009 Annual costs. Tuition/fees: $20,600. Books/supplies: $2,400. Personal expenses: $3,024.

Financial aid. **Additional information:** Need- and merit-based scholarship deadline March 20.

Application procedures. **Admission:** Priority date 2/2; no deadline. $45 fee, may be waived for applicants with need, free for online applicants. Admission notification on a rolling basis. **Financial aid:** No deadline. FAFSA, institutional form required. Applicants notified on a rolling basis; must reply within 2 week(s) of notification.

Academics. **Special study options:** Cooperative education, double major, exchange student, independent study, internships, New York semester, study abroad. **Credit/placement by examination:** CLEP. **Support services:** Pre-admission summer program, reduced course load, remedial instruction, tutoring.

Majors. **Visual/performing arts:** Commercial/advertising art, drawing, painting.

Computing on campus. 26 workstations in library, computer center.

Student life. Policies: Very strong student government promoting activities on and off campus. Many art-related social gatherings. **Activities:** Student government, student newspaper, foreign student organization, cultural diversity organization.

Student services. Career counseling, personal counseling, veterans' counselor.

Contact. E-mail: admissions@lagunacollege.edu
Phone: (949) 376-6000 Toll-free number: (800) 255-0762
Fax: (949) 376-6009
Mike Rivas, Admissions Director, Laguna College of Art and Design, 2222 Laguna Canyon Road, Laguna Beach, CA 92651-1136

Life Pacific College
San Dimas, California
www.lifepacific.edu **CB code: 4264**

- Private 4-year Bible college affiliated with The Foursquare Church
- Residential campus in large town
- 414 degree-seeking undergraduates: 25% part-time, 48% women, 4% African American, 5% Asian American, 14% Hispanic American, 1% Native American, 1% international
- SAT or ACT with writing, application essay required
- 46% graduate within 6 years

General. Founded in 1925. Candidate for regional accreditation; also accredited by ABHE. **Degrees:** 83 bachelor's, 7 associate awarded. **Location:** 30 miles from Los Angeles. **Calendar:** Differs by program, limited summer session. **Full-time faculty:** 17 total; 24% have terminal degrees, 12% minority, 24% women. **Part-time faculty:** 22 total; 27% have terminal degrees, 23% women. **Class size:** 75% < 20, 20% 20-39, less than 1% 40-49, 5% 50-99.

Freshman class profile. 138 applied, 72 admitted, 58 enrolled.

Mid 50% test scores			
SAT critical reading:	430-550	ACT composite:	16-20
SAT math:	410-550	Return as sophomores:	79%
SAT writing:	420-510	Out-of-state:	47%
		Live on campus:	81%

Basis for selection. Open admission, but selective for some programs. Christian character, motivation, and ability to accord with college's program most important. Cumulative GPA in last school attended and SAT or ACT scores also considered. **Homeschooled:** Must present official transcript with graduation date. SAT or ACT required. **Learning Disabled:** LIFE Challenges Program available to students with learning disabilities. Request information.

2009-2010 Annual costs. Tuition/fees: $12,250. Room/board: $6,000.

2008-2009 Financial aid. Non-need-based: Scholarships awarded for academics, alumni affiliation.

Application procedures. Admission: Priority date 4/1; deadline 5/1 (postmark date). $35 fee. Application must be submitted on paper. Admission notification on a rolling basis. **Financial aid:** Closing date 7/1. FAFSA required. Applicants notified on a rolling basis starting 6/1.

Academics. Bible studies taught from Charismatic/Pentecostal perspective training leaders for ministry. **Special study options:** Cooperative education, distance learning, dual enrollment of high school students, external degree, independent study, internships, study abroad. **Credit/placement by examination:** AP, CLEP, SAT, ACT, institutional tests. 16 credit hours maximum toward associate degree, 16 toward bachelor's. Credit limited by the number of subjects accepted, course by course basis. **Support services:** Reduced course load, remedial instruction, study skills assistance, writing center.

Majors. Theology: Bible, pastoral counseling.

Computing on campus. 45 workstations in dormitories, library, computer center, student center. Dormitories wired for high-speed internet access and linked to campus network. Online course registration, online library, helpline, wireless network available.

Student life. Freshman orientation: Mandatory, $100 fee. Preregistration for classes offered. One full day (meal provided), includes testing. **Policies:** Religious observance required. **Housing:** Guaranteed on-campus for freshmen. Single-sex dorms, wellness housing available. $200 nonrefundable deposit, deadline 6/1. **Activities:** Choral groups, dance, drama, film society, music ensembles, student government, learning center (tutoring for junior high and high school).

Athletics. Team name: Warriors.

Student services. Adult student services, chaplain/spiritual director, career counseling, student employment services, financial aid counseling, minority student services, personal counseling, placement for graduates, veterans' counselor. **Physically disabled:** Services for speech, hearing impaired.

Contact. E-mail: admissions@lifepacific.edu
Phone: (909) 599-5433 ext. 314 Toll-free number: (877) 886-5433 ext. 314
Fax: (909) 706-6690
Dorienne Elston, Recruitment/Admissions Director, Life Pacific College, Attn: Admissions, San Dimas, CA 91773-3203

Lincoln University
Oakland, California
www.lincolnuca.edu **CB code: 4386**

- Private 4-year university and business college
- Commuter campus in very large city
- 89 degree-seeking undergraduates: 25% part-time, 51% women
- 115 degree-seeking graduate students
- 91% of applicants admitted

General. Founded in 1919. Accredited by ACICS. Primarily serves international students. **Degrees:** 6 bachelor's, 4 associate awarded; master's offered. **Location:** 12 miles from San Francisco. **Calendar:** Semester, limited summer session. **Full-time faculty:** 9 total; 44% women. **Part-time faculty:** 13 total; 23% minority, 8% women. **Special facilities:** Language laboratory.

Freshman class profile. 636 applied, 579 admitted, 42 enrolled.

Basis for selection. High school achievement record most important. Prior to enrollment, students take Michigan Test of English Placement. Interview recommended and personal statements encouraged. **Homeschooled:** Transcript of courses and grades, state high school equivalency certificate required.

2009-2010 Annual costs. Tuition/fees: $8,920. Tuition for Intensive English program $2,860 per 16 weeks. MBA $365/unit. Books/supplies: $600. Personal expenses: $2,520.

2007-2008 Financial aid. All financial aid based on need. 9 full-time freshmen applied for aid; 9 were judged to have need; 9 of these received aid. Average need met was 100%. Average scholarship/grant was $4,730; average loan $3,720. 11% of total undergraduate aid awarded as scholarships/grants, 89% as loans/jobs.

Application procedures. Admission: No deadline. $75 fee. Admission notification on a rolling basis. **Financial aid:** Priority date 3/22, closing date 8/22. FAFSA required. Applicants notified by 12/1; must reply by 1/2.

Academics. Special study options: Cross-registration, double major, ESL, internships. **Credit/placement by examination:** CLEP. **Support services:** Reduced course load, tutoring.

Majors. Business: Business admin, international, management information systems, managerial economics.

Computing on campus. 34 workstations in library, computer center. Wireless network available.

Student life. Freshman orientation: Mandatory. Preregistration for classes offered. One hour discussion of procedures, event announcements. Student government provides information on banking, transportation and other related materials. **Activities:** Student government.

Student services. Career counseling, financial aid counseling, personal counseling.

Contact. E-mail: admissions@lincolnuca.edu
Phone: (510) 628-8010 Toll-free number: (888) 810-9998
Fax: (510) 628-8012
Peggy Au, Director of Admissions and Records, Lincoln University, 401 15th Street, Oakland, CA 94612

Loma Linda University
Loma Linda, California
www.llu.edu **CB code: 4062**

- Private 3-year university and health science college affiliated with Seventh-day Adventists
- Commuter campus in large town

- 1,092 degree-seeking undergraduates: 20% part-time, 72% women, 5% African American, 25% Asian American, 18% Hispanic American, 1% Native American, 6% international
- 2,875 degree-seeking graduate students
- Application essay, interview required

General. Founded in 1905. Regionally accredited. Two undergraduate schools: School of Allied Health and School of Nursing, offering sophomore, junior, senior year study. All LLU programs require previous college credit, thus no first-time freshman applicants accepted. Specific programs are applied to rather than generally to the university. **Degrees:** 313 bachelor's, 200 associate awarded; master's, doctoral, first professional offered. **Location:** 60 miles from Los Angeles, 50 miles from Palm Springs. **Calendar:** Quarter, limited summer session. **Full-time faculty:** 377 total. **Part-time faculty:** 1,425 total. **Class size:** 63% < 20, 21% 20-39, 12% 40-49, 3% 50-99, less than 1% >100.

Basis for selection. For nursing program, high school algebra I and II or college intermediate algebra and one year of high school physics or college introduction to physics with 2.0 or better required. Minimum GPA of 3.0 on all college course work. Character and personal qualities also important. No first-time freshman applicants accepted.

2009-2010 Annual costs. Tuition/fees: $25,164. Tuition quoted for nursing program. Full-time tuition for dental hygiene program: $23,833 plus $1,590 fees. For allied health program $450/credit hour; for certificate programs, $338/credit. Application fee may vary by program; tuition may vary by grade level in program. Room only: $2,520. Books/supplies: $1,200. Personal expenses: $1,260.

Application procedures. Admission: No deadline. $60 fee. Application must be submitted online. Notificaion varies by program. Each program is applied to separately and has own requirements and dates. Student must give at least a two-week notice prior to housing entry date in order to receive a full refund; otherwise no refund will be given. **Financial aid:** FAFSA required.

Academics. Special study options: Combined bachelor's/graduate degree, cross-registration, distance learning, double major, independent study, internships, study abroad. **Credit/placement by examination:** AP, CLEP. **Support services:** Study skills assistance.

Majors. BACHELOR'S. Conservation: Environmental science. **Health:** Audiology/speech pathology, clinical lab science, cytotechnology, dental hygiene, dietetics, EMT paramedic, health care admin, health services, medical radiologic technology/radiation therapy, medical records admin, nursing (RN). **Physical sciences:** Geology. **Other:** Health geographics. **ASSOCIATE. Health:** Medical radiologic technology/radiation therapy, nursing (RN), occupational therapy assistant, physical therapy assistant.

Computing on campus. 362 workstations in library, computer center, student center. Dormitories wired for high-speed internet access and linked to campus network. Commuter students can connect to campus network. Online library, helpline, repair service, wireless network available.

Student life. Policies: Students are not allowed to smoke, use alcohol or drugs. Religious observance required. **Housing:** Guaranteed on-campus for all undergraduates. Single-sex dorms, apartments, wellness housing available. $145 fully refundable deposit. **Activities:** Campus ministries, choral groups, international student organizations, music ensembles, student government, student newspaper, Black Health Professional Student Association, Association of Latin American Students, Social Action Corps, Students for International Mission Service.

Athletics. Intramural: Basketball, football (non-tackle), soccer M, softball, tennis, volleyball.

Student services. Alcohol/substance abuse counseling, chaplain/spiritual director, financial aid counseling, health services, on-campus daycare, personal counseling. **Physically disabled:** Services for hearing impaired.

Contact. E-mail: admissions.app@llu.edu
Phone: (909) 651-5029 Toll-free number: (800) 422-4558
Fax: (909) 558-4879
Loma Linda University, Admissions Processing, Loma Linda, CA 92350

Loyola Marymount University

Los Angeles, California — **CB member**
www.lmu.edu — **CB code: 4403**

- Private 4-year university affiliated with Roman Catholic Church
- Residential campus in very large city
- 5,509 degree-seeking undergraduates: 2% part-time, 57% women, 8% African American, 12% Asian American, 20% Hispanic American, 1% Native American, 2% international
- 3,180 degree-seeking graduate students
- 50% of applicants admitted
- SAT or ACT (ACT writing recommended), application essay required
- 80% graduate within 6 years

General. Founded in 1911. Regionally accredited. **Degrees:** 1,417 bachelor's awarded; master's, doctoral, first professional offered. **ROTC:** Army, Air Force. **Location:** 15 miles from downtown. **Calendar:** Semester, extensive summer session. **Full-time faculty:** 498 total; 100% have terminal degrees, 25% minority, 41% women. **Part-time faculty:** 444 total; 19% minority, 45% women. **Class size:** 47% < 20, 51% 20-39, less than 1% 40-49, 1% 50-99, less than 1% >100. **Special facilities:** Fine arts complex with recital hall and recording arts facilities; Baja California marine station.

Freshman class profile. 9,086 applied, 4,553 admitted, 1,261 enrolled.

Mid 50% test scores		**Rank in top quarter:**	69%
SAT critical reading:	530-630	**Rank in top tenth:**	33%
SAT math:	540-640	**Return as sophomores:**	88%
ACT composite:	23-28	**Out-of-state:**	31%
GPA 3.75 or higher:	43%	**Live on campus:**	96%
GPA 3.50-3.74:	27%	**International:**	2%
GPA 3.0-3.49:	27%	**Fraternities:**	11%
GPA 2.0-2.99:	3%	**Sororities:**	33%

Basis for selection. High school GPA, curriculum, test scores, recommendations, essays, activities important. Interview recommended for early admission, disabled, academically weak applicants. Portfolio required for animation major applicants.

High school preparation. College-preparatory program recommended. 18 units recommended. Recommended units include English 4, mathematics 3, social studies 3, science 2 (laboratory 2), foreign language 3 and academic electives 1. 4 math required of engineering, math, and science majors; physics and chemistry required of engineering and science majors; biology and chemistry required (physics recommended) of biology majors.

2008-2009 Annual costs. Tuition/fees: $33,902. Room/board: $11,808.

2007-2008 Financial aid. Need-based: 953 full-time freshmen applied for aid; 669 were judged to have need; 659 of these received aid. Average need met was 70%. Average scholarship/grant was $15,704; average loan $4,658. 81% of total undergraduate aid awarded as scholarships/grants, 19% as loans/jobs. **Non-need-based:** Awarded to 532 full-time undergraduates, including 253 freshmen. Scholarships awarded for academics, alumni affiliation, art, athletics, music/drama, religious affiliation, ROTC.

Application procedures. Admission: No deadline. $60 fee, may be waived for applicants with need. Admission notification on a rolling basis beginning on or about 11/1. Must reply by 5/1. Must reply by May 1 or within 2 week(s) if notified thereafter. Applicants who desire housing or financial aid should apply by January 15. **Financial aid:** Priority date 2/1, closing date 5/15. FAFSA, CSS PROFILE required. Applicants notified on a rolling basis starting 3/15; must reply by 5/1 or within 4 week(s) of notification.

Academics. Special study options: Accelerated study, cross-registration, distance learning, double major, dual enrollment of high school students, ESL, exchange student, honors, independent study, internships, liberal arts/career combination, semester at sea, student-designed major, study abroad, teacher certification program, Washington semester, weekend college. Encore program for adult students. **Credit/placement by examination:** AP, CLEP, IB, institutional tests. **Support services:** Learning center, reduced course load, study skills assistance, tutoring.

Majors. Area/ethnic studies: African-American, Asian, European, Hispanic-American/Latino/Chicano, women's. **Biology:** General, biochemistry. **Business:** General, accounting, business admin. **Communications:** General, radio/tv. **Communications technology:** Animation/special effects, recording arts. **Computer sciences:** General. **Engineering:** General, civil, electrical, mechanical, physics. **Foreign languages:** Ancient Greek, classics, French, German, Latin, modern Greek, Spanish. **Health:** Art therapy. **History:** General. **Interdisciplinary:** Ancient studies, natural sciences. **Liberal arts:** Arts/sciences, humanities. **Math:** General, applied. **Philosophy/religion:** Philosophy. **Physical sciences:** Chemistry, physics. **Psychology:** General. **Public administration:** General. **Social sciences:** Economics, political science, sociology, urban studies. **Theology:** Theology. **Visual/performing arts:** Art, art history/conservation, cinematography, dance, design, dramatic, film/cinema, play/screenwriting, studio arts.

Most popular majors. Business/marketing 27%, communications/journalism 10%, English 6%, psychology 6%, social sciences 10%, visual/performing arts 14%.

Computing on campus. 650 workstations in dormitories, library, computer center, student center. Dormitories wired for high-speed internet access and linked to campus network. Commuter students can connect to campus network. Online course registration, online library, helpline, repair service, student web hosting, wireless network available.

Student life. **Freshman orientation:** Available, $210 fee. **Housing:** Guaranteed on-campus for freshmen. Coed dorms, single-sex dorms, special housing for disabled, apartments, wellness housing available. $400 nonrefundable deposit. **Activities:** Pep band, campus ministries, choral groups, dance, drama, international student organizations, literary magazine, music ensembles, radio station, student government, student newspaper, TV station, more than 130 student organizations, clubs, and associations.

Athletics. NCAA. **Intercollegiate:** Baseball M, basketball, cross-country, golf M, rowing (crew), soccer, softball W, swimming W, tennis, track and field, volleyball W, water polo. **Intramural:** Basketball, football (tackle), soccer, softball, table tennis, tennis, volleyball, water polo. **Team name:** Lions.

Student services. Adult student services, alcohol/substance abuse counseling, chaplain/spiritual director, career counseling, services for economically disadvantaged, student employment services, financial aid counseling, health services, minority student services, on-campus daycare, personal counseling, placement for graduates, veterans' counselor, women's services. **Physically disabled:** Services for visually, speech, hearing impaired.

Contact. E-mail: admissions@lmu.edu
Phone: (310) 338-2750 Toll-free number: (800) 568-4636
Fax: (310) 338-2797
Matthew Fissinger, Director of Admissions, Loyola Marymount University, Admissions, 1 LMU Drive, Los Angeles, CA 90045-8350

The Master's College

Santa Clarita, California
www.masters.edu **CB code: 4411**

- Private 4-year liberal arts and seminary college affiliated with Christian Church
- Residential campus in small city
- 1,039 degree-seeking undergraduates: 14% part-time, 51% women
- 400 degree-seeking graduate students
- 51% of applicants admitted
- SAT or ACT with writing, application essay required
- 57% graduate within 6 years

General. Founded in 1927. Regionally accredited. Branch campus in Israel; very strong overseas summer missions program. **Degrees:** 292 bachelor's awarded; master's, doctoral, first professional offered. **Location:** 40 miles from Los Angeles. **Calendar:** Semester, limited summer session. **Full-time faculty:** 70 total; 76% have terminal degrees, 10% minority, 13% women. **Part-time faculty:** 127 total; 14% have terminal degrees, 5% minority, 31% women. **Class size:** 76% < 20, 17% 20-39, 3% 40-49, 3% 50-99, less than 1% >100. **Special facilities:** Home economics - family and consumer sciences center.

Freshman class profile. 387 applied, 197 admitted, 192 enrolled.

Mid 50% test scores		**Rank in top quarter:**	61%
SAT critical reading:	480-630	**Rank in top tenth:**	33%
SAT math:	480-610	**End year in good standing:**	90%
ACT composite:	22-27	**Return as sophomores:**	78%
GPA 3.75 or higher:	51%	**Out-of-state:**	35%
GPA 3.50-3.74:	19%	**Live on campus:**	90%
GPA 3.0-3.49:	22%	**International:**	5%
GPA 2.0-2.99:	8%		

Basis for selection. School achievement record, references, religious commitment most important. Applications from all individuals who have placed their faith in Jesus Christ as Lord and Savior are welcome. Audition required of music majors. **Homeschooled:** Transcript of courses and grades, letter of recommendation (nonparent) required. **Learning Disabled:** Must speak with human resources department before attending.

High school preparation. College-preparatory program recommended. Required and recommended units include English 4, mathematics 3, history 2, science 2 and academic electives 3.

2009-2010 Annual costs. Tuition/fees: $24,280. Room/board: $8,000. Books/supplies: $1,638. Personal expenses: $2,088.

2007-2008 Financial aid. **Need-based:** 158 full-time freshmen applied for aid; 128 were judged to have need; 128 of these received aid. Average need met was 71%. Average scholarship/grant was $13,042; average loan $3,766. 62% of total undergraduate aid awarded as scholarships/grants, 38% as loans/jobs. **Non-need-based:** Awarded to 153 full-time undergraduates, including 38 freshmen. Scholarships awarded for academics, alumni affiliation, art, athletics, leadership, music/drama.

Application procedures. **Admission:** Priority date 3/2; no deadline. $40 fee, may be waived for applicants with need. Admission notification on a rolling basis beginning on or about 3/15. Must reply by May 1 or within 2 week(s) if notified thereafter. **Financial aid:** Priority date 3/2; no closing date. FAFSA, institutional form required. Applicants notified on a rolling basis starting 2/18; must reply by 5/1 or within 2 week(s) of notification.

Academics. Students who attend 4 years earn a minor in Biblical Studies upon graduation. **Special study options:** Accelerated study, cooperative education, distance learning, double major, independent study, internships, liberal arts/career combination, study abroad, teacher certification program, Washington semester. Israel semester. **Credit/placement by examination:** AP, CLEP, IB, SAT, ACT, institutional tests. 32 credit hours maximum toward bachelor's degree. **Support services:** Reduced course load, remedial instruction, study skills assistance, tutoring.

Majors. **Biology:** General, environmental. **Business:** Accounting, actuarial science, business admin, finance, management information systems. **Communications:** Media studies, public relations, radio/tv. **Computer sciences:** General. **Education:** General, elementary, ESL, middle, music, physical, science, secondary. **Family/consumer sciences:** General, food/nutrition. **Foreign languages:** Biblical. **Health:** Premedicine. **History:** General. **Interdisciplinary:** Biological/physical sciences, natural sciences. **Legal studies:** Prelaw. **Liberal arts:** Arts/sciences. **Math:** General, applied. **Parks/recreation:** Health/fitness. **Philosophy/religion:** Religion. **Physical sciences:** General. **Social sciences:** Political science, U.S. government. **Theology:** Bible, pastoral counseling, religious ed, sacred music, theology. **Visual/performing arts:** Music management, piano/organ, voice/opera.

Most popular majors. Biology 6%, business/marketing 17%, communications/journalism 9%, history 7%, liberal arts 10%, philosophy/religious studies 30%, visual/performing arts 7%.

Computing on campus. PC or laptop required. 57 workstations in library, computer center. Dormitories wired for high-speed internet access and linked to campus network. Commuter students can connect to campus network. Online course registration, online library, helpline, repair service, wireless network available.

Student life. **Freshman orientation:** Mandatory. Preregistration for classes offered. 5-day program before start of classes. **Policies:** Emphasis on Godly lifestyle, character and leadership development, service, learning, cross-cultural education. Religious observance required. **Housing:** Single-sex dorms, wellness housing available. $200 fully refundable deposit, deadline 5/2. **Activities:** Bands, campus ministries, choral groups, drama, music ensembles, opera, student government, symphony orchestra, summer missions, outreach team.

Athletics. NAIA, NCCAA. **Intercollegiate:** Baseball M, basketball, cross-country, golf M, soccer, tennis W, track and field, volleyball W. **Intramural:** Basketball, football (non-tackle), soccer, volleyball. **Team name:** Mustangs.

Student services. Adult student services, chaplain/spiritual director, career counseling, student employment services, financial aid counseling, health services, personal counseling, placement for graduates, veterans' counselor. **Physically disabled:** Services for visually, speech impaired.

Contact. E-mail: admissions@masters.edu
Phone: (661) 259-3540 ext. 3362 Toll-free number: (800) 568-6248 ext. 3362 Fax: (661) 288-1037
Hollie Gorsh, Director of Admissions, The Master's College, 21726 Placerita Canyon Road, Santa Clarita, CA 91321-1200

Menlo College

Atherton, California **CB member**
www.menlo.edu **CB code: 4483**

- Private 4-year business and liberal arts college
- Residential campus in small city
- 593 degree-seeking undergraduates: 4% part-time, 37% women, 6% African American, 9% Asian American, 13% Hispanic American, 11% international
- 59% of applicants admitted
- SAT or ACT (ACT writing recommended), application essay required
- 48% graduate within 6 years

General. Founded in 1927. Regionally accredited. **Degrees:** 140 bachelor's awarded. **ROTC:** Army, Air Force. **Location:** 30 miles from San Francisco, 30 miles from San Jose. **Calendar:** Semester, limited summer session. **Full-time faculty:** 26 total; 73% have terminal degrees, 12% minority, 46% women. **Part-time faculty:** 46 total; 33% have terminal degrees, 15% minority, 44% women. **Class size:** 55% < 20, 44% 20-39, 1% 50-99.

Freshman class profile. 1,015 applied, 596 admitted, 159 enrolled.

Mid 50% test scores		**GPA 2.0-2.99:**	59%
SAT critical reading:	420-520	**Rank in top quarter:**	27%
SAT math:	430-550	**Rank in top tenth:**	6%
SAT writing:	400-500	**End year in good standing:**	57%
ACT composite:	17-22	**Return as sophomores:**	62%
GPA 3.75 or higher:	8%	**Out-of-state:**	39%
GPA 3.50-3.74:	7%	**Live on campus:**	90%
GPA 3.0-3.49:	26%	**International:**	17%

Basis for selection. High school record, test scores (minimum 1000 SAT, exclusive of Writing, or 21 ACT), 1 recommendation, essay, depth of achievement in cocurricular activities considered. **Homeschooled:** Statement describing homeschool structure and mission, transcript of courses and grades, state high school equivalency certificate, letter of recommendation (nonparent) required. **Learning Disabled:** Direct queries to Academic Success Center.

High school preparation. 15 units required; 24 recommended. Required and recommended units include English 4, mathematics 3, social studies 3, science 3 and foreign language 2.

2009-2010 Annual costs. Tuition/fees (projected): $32,136. Room/board: $11,440. Books/supplies: $1,566. Personal expenses: $2,214.

2008-2009 Financial aid. **Need-based:** 91 full-time freshmen applied for aid; 79 were judged to have need; 79 of these received aid. Average need met was 69%. Average scholarship/grant was $22,458; average loan $2,785. 70% of total undergraduate aid awarded as scholarships/grants, 30% as loans/jobs. **Non-need-based:** Awarded to 212 full-time undergraduates, including 56 freshmen. Scholarships awarded for academics.

Application procedures. **Admission:** Priority date 2/1; no deadline. $40 fee, may be waived for applicants with need. Admission notification on a rolling basis beginning on or about 12/1. Must reply by May 1 or within 4 week(s) if notified thereafter. **Financial aid:** Priority date 3/2, closing date 8/1. FAFSA required. Applicants notified on a rolling basis starting 12/15; must reply by 5/1 or within 2 week(s) of notification.

Academics. Transition to College Program offered to help students not achieving at true academic potential to transition to rigors of college academics. Ongoing support and counseling throughout freshman year. **Special study options:** Accelerated study, cooperative education, double major, independent study, internships, student-designed major, study abroad. **Credit/placement by examination:** AP, CLEP, IB, institutional tests. 30 credit hours maximum toward bachelor's degree. **Support services:** Learning center, pre-admission summer program, reduced course load, remedial instruction, study skills assistance, tutoring, writing center.

Majors. **Business:** Business admin. **Communications:** General. **Liberal arts:** Arts/sciences.

Most popular majors. Business/marketing 68%, communications/journalism 15%, liberal arts 17%.

Computing on campus. 350 workstations in library, computer center. Dormitories wired for high-speed internet access and linked to campus network. Commuter students can connect to campus network. Online course registration, online library, helpline, repair service, wireless network available.

Student life. **Freshman orientation:** Mandatory. Preregistration for classes offered. Weekend before classes begin. Workshops for both parents and students. **Housing:** Guaranteed on-campus for all undergraduates. Coed dorms, single-sex dorms, special housing for disabled, wellness housing available. $300 fully refundable deposit, deadline 7/1. **Activities:** Film society, international student organizations, radio station, student government, student newspaper, TV station, International Club, African-American student union, Latino student union, Asia club, Rotaract, Chinese culture research club, women's club, Jewish student organization, Alpha Chi Honor Society, French club.

Athletics. NAIA, NCAA. **Intercollegiate:** Baseball M, basketball, boxing M, cross-country, football (tackle) M, golf M, soccer, softball W, volleyball W, wrestling. **Intramural:** Basketball M, boxing M. **Team name:** Oaks.

Student services. Adult student services, career counseling, student employment services, financial aid counseling, health services, personal counseling, placement for graduates, women's services. **Physically disabled:** Services for visually, hearing impaired.

Contact. E-mail: admissions@menlo.edu
Phone: (650) 543-3753 Toll-free number: (800) 556-3656
Fax: (650) 543-4496
David Placey, Dean of Enrollment Management, Menlo College, 1000 El Camino Real, Atherton, CA 94027

Mills College

Oakland, California — **CB member**
www.mills.edu — **CB code: 4485**

- Private 4-year liberal arts college for women
- Residential campus in large city
- 956 degree-seeking undergraduates: 6% part-time, 100% women, 9% African American, 8% Asian American, 14% Hispanic American, 1% Native American, 3% international
- 493 degree-seeking graduate students
- 55% of applicants admitted
- SAT or ACT (ACT writing optional), application essay required
- 61% graduate within 6 years

General. Founded in 1852. Regionally accredited. Men admitted to graduate programs. **Degrees:** 186 bachelor's awarded; master's, doctoral offered. **Location:** 18 miles from San Francisco, 8 miles from Berkeley. **Calendar:** Semester, limited summer session. **Full-time faculty:** 96 total; 88% have terminal degrees, 26% minority, 62% women. **Part-time faculty:** 103 total; 59% have terminal degrees, 23% minority, 71% women. **Class size:** 78% < 20, 20% 20-39, less than 1% 40-49, less than 1% 50-99, less than 1% >100. **Special facilities:** Electronic collaborative learning center, center for contemporary music, laboratory children's school for student teachers, women's leadership institute, institute for civic leadership, center for the book, nature trail.

Freshman class profile. 1,416 applied, 776 admitted, 205 enrolled.

Mid 50% test scores		**GPA 2.0-2.99:**	6%
SAT critical reading:	520-650	**Rank in top quarter:**	78%
SAT math:	490-590	**Rank in top tenth:**	43%
SAT writing:	520-620	**End year in good standing:**	88%
ACT composite:	20-27	**Return as sophomores:**	74%
GPA 3.75 or higher:	42%	**Out-of-state:**	27%
GPA 3.50-3.74:	23%	**Live on campus:**	96%
GPA 3.0-3.49:	29%	**International:**	3%

Basis for selection. Minimum 3.0 GPA required, school achievement record most important. All credentials considered. SAT Subject Tests recommended. Interview recommended. **Homeschooled:** Statement describing homeschool structure and mission, state high school equivalency certificate, letter of recommendation (nonparent) required.

High school preparation. Required and recommended units include English 4, mathematics 3-4, social studies 2-4, history 2-4, science 2-4 (laboratory 2), foreign language 2-4, visual/performing arts 2 and academic electives 2.

2008-2009 Annual costs. Tuition/fees: $35,190. Room/board: $10,550. Books/supplies: $1,300. Personal expenses: $2,000.

2008-2009 Financial aid. **Need-based:** 184 full-time freshmen applied for aid; 171 were judged to have need; 171 of these received aid. Average need met was 87%. Average scholarship/grant was $27,283; average loan $3,450. 73% of total undergraduate aid awarded as scholarships/grants, 27% as loans/jobs. **Non-need-based:** Awarded to 72 full-time undergraduates, including 21 freshmen. Scholarships awarded for academics, leadership, minority status, music/drama.

Application procedures. **Admission:** Priority date 2/1; deadline 8/1 (postmark date). $50 fee, may be waived for applicants with need. Admission notification on a rolling basis beginning on or about 11/1. Must reply by May 1 or within 2 week(s) if notified thereafter. **Financial aid:** Priority date 2/15; no closing date. FAFSA, institutional form required. Applicants notified on a rolling basis starting 3/1; must reply by 5/1 or within 2 week(s) of notification.

Academics. Cooperative bachelor of science in nursing program with Samuel Merritt College; pre-nursing students in this program receive a pre-nursing certificate from Mills upon completion of two years of study. Certificate pre-medicine program available to postbaccalaureate students. BA/MA in Infant Mental Health offered. **Special study options:** Combined bachelor's/graduate degree, cross-registration, double major, exchange student, independent study, internships, student-designed major, study abroad, teacher certification program, Washington semester. **Credit/placement by examination:** AP, CLEP, IB, institutional tests. 8 credit hours maximum toward bachelor's degree. **Support services:** Learning center, pre-admission summer program, reduced course load, remedial instruction, study skills assistance, tutoring, writing center.

Majors. **Area/ethnic studies:** American, French, Hispanic-American/Latino/Chicano, Latin American, women's. **Biology:** General, biochemistry, molecular biochemistry. **Business:** General, managerial economics. **Computer sciences:** General, computer science. **Conservation:** Environmental science, environmental studies. **Engineering:** General. **Family/consumer sciences:** Child development. **Foreign languages:** Comparative lit, French, Spanish. **History:** General, American. **Interdisciplinary:** Biopsychology. **Legal studies:** General. **Liberal arts:** Arts/sciences. **Math:** General. **Philosophy/religion:** Philosophy. **Physical sciences:** Chemistry. **Psychology:** General. **Public administration:** Policy analysis. **Social sciences:** General, anthropology, economics, international relations, political science, sociology, U.S. government. **Visual/performing arts:** Art, art history/conservation, dance, multimedia, studio arts.

Most popular majors. Area/ethnic studies 7%, biology 7%, English 12%, family/consumer sciences 6%, psychology 13%, social sciences 21%, visual/performing arts 14%.

Computing on campus. 329 workstations in dormitories, library, computer center, student center. Dormitories wired for high-speed internet access and linked to campus network. Commuter students can connect to campus network. Online course registration, online library, helpline, student web hosting, wireless network available.

Student life. **Freshman orientation:** Mandatory. Preregistration for classes offered. 5 days prior to the start of classes. **Housing:** Guaranteed on-campus for all undergraduates. Special housing for disabled, apartments, cooperative housing, wellness housing available. $150 fully refundable deposit, deadline 6/1. Resumer student housing available. **Activities:** Campus ministries, choral groups, dance, drama, literary magazine, music ensembles, Model UN, radio station, student government, student newspaper.

Athletics. NAIA, NCAA. **Intercollegiate:** Cross-country W, rowing (crew) W, soccer W, swimming W, tennis W, track and field W, volleyball W. **Intramural:** Badminton W, basketball W. **Team name:** Cyclones.

Student services. Adult student services, alcohol/substance abuse counseling, chaplain/spiritual director, career counseling, student employment services, financial aid counseling, health services, minority student services, personal counseling, placement for graduates, women's services. **Physically disabled:** Services for visually, speech, hearing impaired. **Learning disabled:** Comprehensive services available.

Contact. E-mail: admission@mills.edu
Phone: (510) 430-2135 Toll-free number: (800) 876-4557
Fax: (510) 430-3314
Giulietta Aquino, Dean of Undergraduate Admission, Mills College, 5000 MacArthur Boulevard, Oakland, CA 94613

Monterey Institute of International Studies

Monterey, California
www.miis.edu **CB code: 4507**

- Private two-year upper-division liberal arts college
- Commuter campus in small city

General. Founded in 1955. Regionally accredited. **Location:** 130 miles from San Francisco, 60 miles from San Jose. **Calendar:** Semester.

Annual costs/financial aid. Tuition/fees (2008-2009): $29,356. Books/supplies: $900. Need-based financial aid available to full-time and part-time students.

Contact. Phone: (831) 647-4123
Director of Admissions, 460 Pierce Street, Monterey, CA 93940

Mount St. Mary's College

Los Angeles, California **CB member**
www.msmc.la.edu **CB code: 4493**

- Private 4-year liberal arts college affiliated with Roman Catholic Church
- Residential campus in very large city
- 1,880 degree-seeking undergraduates: 25% part-time, 92% women, 9% African American, 22% Asian American, 46% Hispanic American
- 460 degree-seeking graduate students
- 84% of applicants admitted
- SAT or ACT (ACT writing recommended), application essay required
- 67% graduate within 6 years; 40% enter graduate study

General. Founded in 1925. Regionally accredited. Mount St. Mary's College is primarily a women's college at the undergraduate level, although men are admitted to undergraduate nursing and music programs, graduate division, weekend college and some summer courses. **Degrees:** 373 bachelor's, 147 associate awarded; master's, doctoral offered. **Location:** 2 miles from Los Angeles. **Calendar:** Semester, limited summer session. **Full-time faculty:** 84 total; 62% have terminal degrees, 12% minority. **Part-time faculty:** 267 total; 52% have terminal degrees, 24% minority. **Class size:** 65% < 20, 34% 20-39, 1% 40-49, less than 1% 50-99.

Freshman class profile. 992 applied, 837 admitted, 395 enrolled.

Mid 50% test scores		**GPA 3.0-3.49:**	34%
SAT critical reading:	470-560	**GPA 2.0-2.99:**	28%
SAT math:	450-550	**Rank in top quarter:**	56%
SAT writing:	470-560	**Rank in top tenth:**	12%
ACT composite:	19-23	**Return as sophomores:**	85%
GPA 3.75 or higher:	21%	**Out-of-state:**	5%
GPA 3.50-3.74:	17%	**Live on campus:**	76%

Basis for selection. Primary emphasis on school academic record, then test scores, essay, and letters of recommendation. School and community activities also considered. Interview important. Admission requirements considered very competitive in baccalaureate program. Interviews recommended. Auditions recommended of music majors. Portfolios recommended of art majors. **Homeschooled:** Statement describing homeschool structure and mission, transcript of courses and grades, state high school equivalency certificate, letter of recommendation (nonparent) required. **Learning Disabled:** Documentation of learning disability required.

High school preparation. College-preparatory program recommended. 25 units required; 30 recommended. Required and recommended units include English 4, mathematics 3-4, social studies 2-3, history 2-3, science 2-3 (laboratory 2-3), foreign language 2-3 and academic electives 2-3. For associate degree applicants, required courses include algebra, geometry, American history/government, and 4 units English.

2008-2009 Annual costs. Tuition/fees: $27,100. Room/board: $9,830. Books/supplies: $648. Personal expenses: $1,170.

2008-2009 Financial aid. **Non-need-based:** Scholarships awarded for academics, alumni affiliation, art, leadership, music/drama.

Application procedures. **Admission:** Priority date 12/1; deadline 2/15 (postmark date). $40 fee, may be waived for applicants with need. Admission notification on a rolling basis beginning on or about 12/1. Must reply by May 1 or within 2 week(s) if notified thereafter. **Financial aid:** Priority date 3/1, closing date 4/30. FAFSA, institutional form required. Applicants notified on a rolling basis starting 2/1.

Academics. **Special study options:** Accelerated study, combined bachelor's/graduate degree, cross-registration, double major, exchange student, honors, independent study, internships, liberal arts/career combination, student-designed major, study abroad, teacher certification program, United Nations semester, Washington semester, weekend college. **Credit/placement by examination:** AP, CLEP, IB, institutional tests. 24 credit hours maximum toward associate degree, 30 toward bachelor's. **Support services:** Learning center, pre-admission summer program, reduced course load, remedial instruction, study skills assistance, tutoring, writing center.

Majors. **Area/ethnic studies:** American. **Biology:** General, biochemistry. **Business:** General, accounting, business admin, international. **Education:** Elementary, middle, secondary. **Foreign languages:** French, Spanish. **Health:** Clinical lab technology, health care admin, nursing (RN), predental, premedicine, preveterinary. **History:** General. **Legal studies:** Prelaw. **Math:** General, applied. **Philosophy/religion:** Philosophy, religion. **Physical sciences:** Chemistry. **Psychology:** General. **Social sciences:** General, political science, sociology. **Theology:** Sacred music. **Visual/performing arts:** Music performance, music theory/composition, studio arts. **Other:** Film and social justice.

Most popular majors. Biology 9%, business/marketing 9%, English 6%, health sciences 38%, psychology 10%, social sciences 16%.

Computing on campus. 168 workstations in dormitories, library, computer center, student center. Dormitories wired for high-speed internet access and linked to campus network. Commuter students can connect to campus network. Online course registration, helpline, student web hosting, wireless network available.

Student life. **Freshman orientation:** Available. Occurs during a weekend, typically in late June. **Policies:** Student resident life largely self-regulated under direction of Residence Council. **Housing:** Guaranteed on-campus for freshmen. Single-sex dorms available. $100 nonrefundable deposit, deadline 5/1. **Activities:** Campus ministries, choral groups, dance, literary magazine, student government, student newspaper, symphony orchestra, various academic, service, cultural and greek organizations and student clubs available.

Athletics. **Intramural:** Badminton, basketball, golf, soccer, swimming, tennis, volleyball. **Team name:** Athenians.

Student services. Adult student services, chaplain/spiritual director, career counseling, student employment services, financial aid counseling, health services, personal counseling, placement for graduates.

Contact. E-mail: admissions@msmc.la.edu
Phone: (310) 954-4250 Toll-free number: (800) 999-9893
Fax: (310) 954-4259
Yvonne Berumen, Director of Admissions, Mount St. Mary's College, 12001 Chalon Road, Los Angeles, CA 90049

Mt. Sierra College

Monrovia, California
www.mtsierra.edu **CB code: 3090**

- For-profit 3-year technical college
- Commuter campus in very large city
- 458 degree-seeking undergraduates: 44% part-time, 28% women, 8% African American, 11% Asian American, 35% Hispanic American, 1% international
- 85% of applicants admitted
- Application essay, interview required

General. Accredited by ACCSCT. **Degrees:** 87 bachelor's awarded. **Calendar:** Quarter. **Full-time faculty:** 12 total. **Part-time faculty:** 59 total. **Class size:** 98% < 20, 2% 20-39.

Freshman class profile. 39 applied, 33 admitted, 31 enrolled.

Basis for selection. High school graduates accepted upon the basis of writing, math, online assessments, and high school and/or college GPA. **Homeschooled:** Transcript of courses and grades, state high school equivalency certificate, interview required.

2008-2009 Annual costs. Tuition/fees: $15,064. Additional lab fees may apply; varies by program of study. Books/supplies: $2,000.

2007-2008 Financial aid. **Need-based:** 11 full-time freshmen applied for aid; 11 were judged to have need; 11 of these received aid. Average need met was 80%. Average scholarship/grant was $8,110; average loan $3,500. 25% of total undergraduate aid awarded as scholarships/grants, 75% as loans/jobs. **Non-need-based:** Awarded to 12 full-time undergraduates, including 11 freshmen.

Application procedures. **Admission:** No deadline. $50 fee, may be waived for applicants with need. Admission notification on a rolling basis. **Financial aid:** FAFSA required.

Academics. **Special study options:** Accelerated study, distance learning, weekend college. **Credit/placement by examination:** CLEP, IB, institutional tests. **Support services:** Learning center, tutoring, writing center.

Majors. **Business:** Business admin, entrepreneurial studies. **Computer sciences:** General, information technology, networking, security, web page design. **Visual/performing arts:** Graphic design, multimedia.

Most popular majors. Business/marketing 6%, computer/information sciences 48%, visual/performing arts 46%.

Computing on campus. PC or laptop required.

Student life. **Freshman orientation:** Available. Held during first week of classes.

Contact. E-mail: pazadian@mtsierra.edu
Phone: (626) 873-2100 Toll-free number: (888) 828-8800
Fax: (626) 359-1378
Patrick Azadian, Director of Admissions, Mt. Sierra College, 101 East Huntington Drive, Monrovia, CA 91016

National Hispanic University

San Jose, California
www.nhu.edu **CB code: 4593**

- Private 4-year university
- Commuter campus in very large city
- 367 degree-seeking undergraduates: 38% part-time, 65% women
- 188 graduate students
- 54% of applicants admitted
- Application essay required

General. Regionally accredited. **Degrees:** 19 bachelor's awarded. **ROTC:** Army, Naval. **Calendar:** Semester, limited summer session. **Full-time faculty:** 11 total; 46% have terminal degrees, 27% minority, 18% women. **Part-time faculty:** 65 total; 48% minority, 52% women. **Class size:** 67% < 20, 33% 20-39.

Freshman class profile. 207 applied, 112 admitted, 58 enrolled.

Basis for selection. High school GPA, transcript, two letters of recommendation required. **Homeschooled:** State high school equivalency certificate required.

2008-2009 Annual costs. Tuition/fees: $6,080. Books/supplies: $1,566. Personal expenses: $2,754.

2007-2008 Financial aid. **Need-based:** 63% of total undergraduate aid awarded as scholarships/grants, 37% as loans/jobs. **Non-need-based:** Scholarships awarded for academics.

Application procedures. **Admission:** No deadline. $50 fee. Application must be submitted on paper. Admission notification on a rolling basis. **Financial aid:** No deadline. FAFSA required.

Academics. **Special study options:** Cross-registration, independent study, teacher certification program. **Credit/placement by examination:** CLEP, IB, institutional tests. **Support services:** Learning center, remedial instruction, tutoring, writing center.

Majors. **Business:** Business admin. **Computer sciences:** General. **Liberal arts:** Arts/sciences.

Most popular majors. Liberal arts 74%.

Computing on campus. 223 workstations in library, computer center, student center. Online library, wireless network available.

Student life. **Freshman orientation:** Mandatory. Preregistration for classes offered. **Activities:** Student government.

Student services. Financial aid counseling.

Contact. Phone: (408) 273-2696 Fax: (408) 254-1369
Pamela Bustillo, Director of Admissions/Registrar, National Hispanic University, 14271 Story Road, San Jose, CA 95127-3823

National University

La Jolla, California **CB member**
www.nu.edu **CB code: 0470**

- Private 4-year university
- Commuter campus in very large city
- 6,092 degree-seeking undergraduates: 64% part-time, 59% women
- 17,771 degree-seeking graduate students
- Interview required

General. Founded in 1971. Regionally accredited. Campuses in 11 major cities throughout California; courses offered both on-site and online. **Degrees:** 1,025 bachelor's, 86 associate awarded; master's offered. **ROTC:** Army, Naval, Air Force. **Calendar:** Continuous, limited summer session. **Full-time faculty:** 240 total; 77% have terminal degrees, 8% minority, 47% women. **Part-time faculty:** 2,573 total; 25% have terminal degrees, 14% minority, 51% women. **Class size:** 73% < 20, 26% 20-39, less than 1% 40-49, less than 1% 50-99. **Special facilities:** Nursing labs, forensics labs, e-book collection.

Freshman class profile. 1,381 applied, 1,381 admitted, 489 enrolled.

Basis for selection. Open admission, but selective for some programs. Interview, previous business and work experience, academic record considered.

2008-2009 Annual costs. Tuition/fees: $10,224. Books/supplies: $1,386. Personal expenses: $3,260.

2007-2008 Financial aid. **Need-based:** 4% of total undergraduate aid awarded as scholarships/grants, 96% as loans/jobs.

Application procedures. Admission: No deadline. $60 fee. Admission notification on a rolling basis. **Financial aid:** No deadline. FAFSA, institutional form required. Applicants notified on a rolling basis.

Academics. Agreements with over 950 public and private schools to place students earning teaching credentials in practicums. **Special study options:** Accelerated study, cross-registration, distance learning, double major, ESL, independent study, internships, liberal arts/career combination, teacher certification program. **Credit/placement by examination:** AP, CLEP, institutional tests. 14 credit hours maximum toward associate degree, 23 toward bachelor's. **Support services:** Learning center, remedial instruction, tutoring, writing center.

Majors. Area/ethnic studies: Chinese, Near/Middle Eastern. **Business:** General, accounting, business admin, construction management, finance, hospitality admin, human resources, operations, organizational behavior. **Communications:** Broadcast journalism, digital media, journalism, media studies, radio/tv. **Computer sciences:** General, computer science, information systems, information technology, security, system admin, systems analysis. **Conservation:** Environmental science, management/policy. **Education:** Early childhood, mathematics, multi-level teacher, secondary. **Engineering:** Construction, systems. **Engineering technology:** Civil drafting, industrial management. **Family/consumer sciences:** Child development. **Foreign languages:** American Sign Language, Arabic, Chinese, Persian. **Health:** Health care admin, licensed practical nurse, preop/surgical nursing. **History:** General. **Interdisciplinary:** Biological/physical sciences, global studies, intercultural. **Legal studies:** General. **Liberal arts:** Arts/sciences. **Math:** General. **Physical sciences:** General, geology. **Protective services:** Criminal justice, law enforcement admin, security services. **Psychology:** General. **Public administration:** General. **Social sciences:** Economics, sociology. **Visual/performing arts:** Multimedia.

Most popular majors. Business/marketing 24%, computer/information sciences 9%, education 12%, interdisciplinary studies 8%, legal studies 12%, liberal arts 8%, psychology 10%.

Computing on campus. 3,100 workstations in library, computer center, student center. Commuter students can connect to campus network. Online course registration, online library, helpline, wireless network available.

Student life. Freshman orientation: Available. Preregistration for classes offered.

Student services. Adult student services, career counseling, services for economically disadvantaged, student employment services, financial aid counseling, minority student services, placement for graduates, veterans' counselor. **Physically disabled:** Services for visually, speech, hearing impaired.

Contact. E-mail: advisor@nu.edu
Phone: (800) 628-8648 Toll-free number: (800) 628-8648
Fax: (858) 541-7792
Dominick Giovanniello, Associate Regional Dean - San Diego, National University, 11255 North Torrey Pines Road, La Jolla, CA 92037-1011

NewSchool of Architecture & Design

San Diego, California
www.newschoolarch.edu **CB code: 2419**

- For-profit 5-year visual arts and liberal arts college
- Commuter campus in very large city
- 309 degree-seeking undergraduates
- 100% of applicants admitted
- Interview required

General. Founded in 1980. Accredited by ACICS. **Degrees:** 25 bachelor's awarded; master's offered. **Location:** 90 miles from Los Angeles, 17 miles from Tijuana, Mexico. **Calendar:** Quarter, extensive summer session. **Full-time faculty:** 17 total. **Part-time faculty:** 40 total. **Special facilities:** Design clinic.

Freshman class profile. 17 applied, 17 admitted, 17 enrolled.

Basis for selection. Resume considered if submitted. Portfolio review required.

2008-2009 Annual costs. Tuition/fees: $19,845. Books/supplies: $700.

2008-2009 Financial aid. Need-based: 15% of total undergraduate aid awarded as scholarships/grants, 85% as loans/jobs. **Non-need-based:** Scholarships awarded for academics.

Application procedures. Admission: No deadline. $75 fee, may be waived for applicants with need. Admission notification on a rolling basis. Must reply by May 1 or within 4 week(s) if notified thereafter. **Financial aid:** No deadline. FAFSA required. Applicants notified on a rolling basis.

Academics. Special study options: Accelerated study, cooperative education, double major, internships, liberal arts/career combination. Cooperative program available at nearby U.S. International University, where students can take ESL and general education classes. **Credit/placement by examination:** AP, CLEP. **Support services:** Pre-admission summer program, tutoring.

Majors. Architecture: Architecture.

Computing on campus. 17 workstations in library, computer center.

Student life. Freshman orientation: Available. Preregistration for classes offered. Held 1-2 days before start of classes in fall. **Housing:** Some housing through US International University. **Activities:** Literary magazine, student government, student newspaper, American Institute of Architects student chapter.

Student services. Career counseling, student employment services, health services, personal counseling, placement for graduates, veterans' counselor.

Contact. E-mail: admissions@newschoolarch.edu
Phone: (619) 235-4100 Fax: (619) 235-4651
Seth Saunders, Director of Admissions, NewSchool of Architecture & Design, 1249 F Street, San Diego, CA 92101

Northwestern Polytechnic University

Fremont, California
www.npu.edu **CB code: 4335**

- Private 4-year business and engineering college
- Commuter campus in small city
- 169 degree-seeking undergraduates: 30% part-time, 43% women
- 881 degree-seeking graduate students

General. Accredited by ACICS. **Degrees:** 33 bachelor's awarded; master's, doctoral offered. **Location:** 42 miles from San Francisco, 7 miles from San Jose. **Calendar:** Trimester, extensive summer session. **Full-time faculty:** 19 total. **Part-time faculty:** 58 total. **Class size:** 62% < 20, 38% 20-39.

Basis for selection. High school record, pre-calculus required. Recommendations and test scores as reference. Interview recommended. English placement exams are given to international students who do not provide standardized English test scores. On-campus English placement exam may replace TOEFL; on-campus freshman exam may replace SAT. Standardized test administered by ETS or on-campus equivalent assessment test acceptable. The test score does not affect the student's admission to the program.

High school preparation. College-preparatory program required. Required and recommended units include English 3, mathematics 2, social studies 1 and science 1. 1 math required for business programs.

2009-2010 Annual costs. Tuition/fees (projected): $11,010. Books/supplies: $800.

Financial aid. Additional information: Work-study, co-op program, internships available. Employment opportunities with local engineering firms help defray costs.

Application procedures. Admission: Priority date 8/3; deadline 9/12 (postmark date). $60 fee. Admission notification on a rolling basis. Must reply by 9/14.

Academics. Curricula designed to meet needs of high-tech industries and global businesses. **Special study options:** ESL. **Credit/placement by examination:** AP, CLEP, IB, institutional tests. 15 credit hours maximum toward bachelor's degree. **Support services:** Learning center, tutoring.

Majors. Business: Business admin. **Engineering:** Electrical, software, systems.

Most popular majors. Business/marketing 63%, engineering/engineering technologies 37%.

Computing on campus. 250 workstations in library, computer center, student center. Dormitories wired for high-speed internet access. Commuter students can connect to campus network. Online library, helpline, repair service, student web hosting, wireless network available.

Student life. Freshman orientation: Mandatory. Preregistration for classes offered. One-day program before start of classes. **Policies:** Students are required to join student association, and encouraged to join student clubs.

Housing: Apartments, wellness housing available. $300 fully refundable deposit, deadline 8/1. **Activities:** Dance, international student organizations, literary magazine, music ensembles, Model UN, student government.

Athletics. Intercollegiate: Table tennis. **Intramural:** Table tennis.

Student services. Adult student services, career counseling, services for economically disadvantaged, student employment services, personal counseling, placement for graduates, veterans' counselor.

Contact. E-mail: admission@npu.edu
Phone: (510) 592-9688 ext. 8 Fax: (510) 657-8975
Judy Weng, Director of Admission, Northwestern Polytechnic University, 47671 Westinghouse Drive, Fremont, CA 94539

Notre Dame de Namur University

Belmont, California — **CB member**
www.ndnu.edu — **CB code: 4063**

- Private 4-year university and liberal arts college affiliated with Roman Catholic Church
- Residential campus in large town
- 799 degree-seeking undergraduates: 35% part-time, 65% women, 6% African American, 14% Asian American, 21% Hispanic American, 1% Native American, 3% international
- 470 degree-seeking graduate students
- 97% of applicants admitted
- SAT or ACT with writing, application essay required
- 55% graduate within 6 years

General. Founded in 1851. Regionally accredited. **Degrees:** 213 bachelor's awarded; master's offered. **Location:** 24 miles from San Francisco. **Calendar:** Semester, limited summer session. **Full-time faculty:** 54 total; 30% minority, 48% women. **Part-time faculty:** 119 total. **Class size:** 76% < 20, 23% 20-39, less than 1% 50-99.

Freshman class profile. 657 applied, 638 admitted, 147 enrolled.

Mid 50% test scores		**GPA 3.0-3.49:**	28%
SAT critical reading:	440-540	**GPA 2.0-2.99:**	57%
SAT math:	430-520	**Return as sophomores:**	77%
SAT writing:	420-540	**Out-of-state:**	32%
ACT composite:	17-23	**Live on campus:**	93%
GPA 3.75 or higher:	5%	**International:**	3%
GPA 3.50-3.74:	9%		

Basis for selection. High school record and GPA most important; test scores also important. Essay, recommendation, and school and community activities considered. **Homeschooled:** Statement describing homeschool structure and mission, transcript of courses and grades, state high school equivalency certificate, interview, letter of recommendation (nonparent) required.

High school preparation. 15 units required. Required and recommended units include English 4, mathematics 2-3, social studies 2, history 1, science 1-2, foreign language 2-3 and academic electives 3. 3 additional units from fine arts, advanced laboratory science, advanced mathematics, or advanced foreign language also recommended.

2009-2010 Annual costs. Tuition/fees: $27,110. Room/board: $11,210. Books/supplies: $1,330. Personal expenses: $3,150.

Financial aid. Non-need-based: Scholarships awarded for academics, alumni affiliation, athletics, leadership, music/drama, religious affiliation.

Application procedures. Admission: Priority date 2/1; no deadline. $50 fee, may be waived for applicants with need. Admission notification on a rolling basis. Must reply by May 1 or within 3 week(s) if notified thereafter. **Financial aid:** Priority date 3/2; no closing date. FAFSA required. CSS PROFILE accepted but not required. Applicants notified on a rolling basis starting 1/15.

Academics. Special study options: Accelerated study, double major, ESL, exchange student, independent study, internships, liberal arts/career combination, student-designed major, study abroad, teacher certification program. **Credit/placement by examination:** AP, CLEP, IB, institutional tests. 30 credit hours maximum toward bachelor's degree. **Support services:** Learning center, reduced course load, remedial instruction, study skills assistance, tutoring, writing center.

Majors. Biology: General, biochemistry. **Business:** Business admin. **Communications:** General. **Computer sciences:** General. **Health:** Predental, premedicine, prepharmacy, preveterinary. **History:** General. **Legal studies:** Prelaw. **Liberal arts:** Arts/sciences. **Parks/recreation:** Exercise sciences. **Philosophy/religion:** Philosophy, religion. **Psychology:** General. **Public administration:** Human services. **Social sciences:** General, political science, sociology. **Visual/performing arts:** Art, dramatic, graphic design, music performance, studio arts, voice/opera.

Most popular majors. Biology 8%, business/marketing 28%, communications/journalism 9%, liberal arts 11%, psychology 7%, public administration/social services 11%, social sciences 10%, visual/performing arts 8%.

Computing on campus. 85 workstations in library, computer center. Dormitories wired for high-speed internet access and linked to campus network. Commuter students can connect to campus network. Helpline, student web hosting, wireless network available.

Student life. Freshman orientation: Mandatory, $175 fee. Preregistration for classes offered. 1 week preceding opening of classes. **Housing:** Guaranteed on-campus for freshmen. Coed dorms, apartments available. $200 nonrefundable deposit. **Activities:** Campus ministries, choral groups, dance, drama, international student organizations, literary magazine, music ensembles, musical theater, opera, student government, student newspaper, symphony orchestra, Hawaiian club, business/career club, Filipino club, Alianza Latina, Black Student Union, outdoor activities club, Amnesty International, science and medical careers club.

Athletics. NCAA. **Intercollegiate:** Basketball, cross-country, golf M, lacrosse M, soccer, softball W, tennis W, volleyball W. **Team name:** Argonauts.

Student services. Adult student services, alcohol/substance abuse counseling, chaplain/spiritual director, career counseling, student employment services, financial aid counseling, health services, personal counseling, placement for graduates. **Learning disabled:** Comprehensive services available.

Contact. E-mail: admiss@ndnu.edu
Phone: (650) 508-3600 Toll-free number: (800) 263-0545
Fax: (650) 508-3426
Rejeetha Gort, Director of Undergraduate Admissions, Notre Dame de Namur University, 1500 Ralston Avenue, Belmont, CA 94002-1908

Occidental College

Los Angeles, California — **CB member**
www.oxy.edu — **CB code: 4581**

- Private 4-year liberal arts college affiliated with nondenominational tradition
- Residential campus in very large city
- 1,834 degree-seeking undergraduates: 56% women, 6% African American, 15% Asian American, 14% Hispanic American, 1% Native American, 2% international
- 16 degree-seeking graduate students
- 39% of applicants admitted
- SAT or ACT with writing, application essay required
- 86% graduate within 6 years

General. Founded in 1887. Regionally accredited. **Degrees:** 508 bachelor's awarded; master's offered. **ROTC:** Army, Air Force. **Location:** 5 miles from downtown. **Calendar:** Semester. **Full-time faculty:** 162 total; 94% have terminal degrees, 32% minority, 47% women. **Class size:** 69% < 20, 29% 20-39, 2% 40-49, less than 1% 50-99. **Special facilities:** Film lab, print studio, marine biology with scuba access, plasma physics and fluid dynamics labs, ornithology collection, geological collection, astronomical instruments collection, vivarium, greenhouses.

Freshman class profile. 5,790 applied, 2,280 admitted, 467 enrolled.

Mid 50% test scores		**GPA 2.0-2.99:**	3%
SAT critical reading:	590-690	**Rank in top quarter:**	91%
SAT math:	590-680	**Rank in top tenth:**	65%
SAT writing:	590-690	**End year in good standing:**	94%
ACT composite:	26-30	**Return as sophomores:**	94%
GPA 3.75 or higher:	34%	**Out-of-state:**	55%
GPA 3.50-3.74:	30%	**Live on campus:**	100%
GPA 3.0-3.49:	33%	**International:**	2%

Basis for selection. Primary consideration given to academic credentials and holistic qualities such as intellectual curiosity, out-of-class interests, and personal character. SAT Subject Tests recommended. Interview recommended. **Homeschooled:** Statement describing homeschool structure and mission, transcript of courses and grades, state high school equivalency certificate, letter of recommendation (nonparent) required. At least 2 SAT Subject Tests recommended.

High school preparation. College-preparatory program required. 20 units recommended. Recommended units include English 4, mathematics 4, social studies 2, history 2, science 3 (laboratory 2), foreign language 3 and academic electives 2.

2008-2009 Annual costs. Tuition/fees: $37,071. Room/board: $10,270. Books/supplies: $988. Personal expenses: $1,312.

2007-2008 Financial aid. Need-based: 307 full-time freshmen applied for aid; 239 were judged to have need; 239 of these received aid. Average need met was 92%. Average scholarship/grant was $25,556; average loan $4,565. 78% of total undergraduate aid awarded as scholarships/grants, 22% as loans/jobs. **Non-need-based:** Awarded to 492 full-time undergraduates, including 147 freshmen. Scholarships awarded for academics, leadership, music/drama, state residency.

Application procedures. Admission: Closing date 1/10 (postmark date). $50 fee, may be waived for applicants with need. Admission notification 4/1. Must reply by May 1 or within 2 week(s) if notified thereafter. **Financial aid:** Priority date 2/1, closing date 2/1. FAFSA, CSS PROFILE required. Applicants notified by 4/1; must reply by 5/1.

Academics. Special study options: Combined bachelor's/graduate degree, cross-registration, double major, exchange student, honors, independent study, internships, student-designed major, study abroad, United Nations semester, Washington semester. **Credit/placement by examination:** AP, CLEP, IB, institutional tests. **Support services:** Learning center, preadmission summer program, study skills assistance, tutoring, writing center.

Majors. Area/ethnic studies: American, Asian. **Biology:** General, biochemistry. **Foreign languages:** General, French, Spanish. **History:** General. **Interdisciplinary:** Cognitive science. **Math:** General. **Parks/recreation:** Exercise sciences. **Philosophy/religion:** Philosophy, religion. **Physical sciences:** Chemistry, geology, geophysics, physics. **Psychology:** General. **Social sciences:** Economics, international relations, political science, sociology. **Visual/performing arts:** Art, art history/conservation, dramatic. **Other:** Critical theory and social justice.

Most popular majors. Biology 7%, English 7%, foreign language 6%, history 7%, physical sciences 8%, psychology 8%, social sciences 32%, visual/performing arts 11%.

Computing on campus. 300 workstations in dormitories, library, computer center. Dormitories linked to campus network. Commuter students can connect to campus network. Online course registration, online library, helpline, wireless network available.

Student life. Freshman orientation: Mandatory. Preregistration for classes offered. Held one week in August before the start of classes. Prior to Orientation, students can choose to participate in one of three experiences: a wilderness trip; community service program; or arts and culture in Los Angeles. **Policies:** All residence halls student-run; freshmen and sophomores are required to live on campus. **Housing:** Guaranteed on-campus for freshmen. Coed dorms, single-sex dorms, fraternity/sorority housing, wellness housing available. **Activities:** Bands, choral groups, dance, drama, film society, international student organizations, literary magazine, music ensembles, musical theater, radio station, student government, student newspaper, symphony orchestra, more than 120 clubs and organizations available.

Athletics. NCAA. **Intercollegiate:** Baseball M, basketball, cross-country, diving, football (tackle) M, golf, soccer, softball W, swimming, tennis, track and field, volleyball W, water polo. **Intramural:** Basketball, football (non-tackle), volleyball. **Team name:** Tigers.

Student services. Adult student services, alcohol/substance abuse counseling, chaplain/spiritual director, career counseling, services for economically disadvantaged, student employment services, financial aid counseling, health services, minority student services, on-campus daycare, personal counseling, women's services. **Physically disabled:** Services for hearing impaired.

Contact. E-mail: admission@oxy.edu
Phone: (323) 259-2700 Toll-free number: (800) 825-5262
Fax: (323) 341-4875
Vince Cuseo, Dean of Admission, Occidental College, 1600 Campus Road, Los Angeles, CA 90041

Otis College of Art and Design

Los Angeles, California — **CB member**
www.otis.edu — **CB code: 4394**

- Private 4-year visual arts college
- Commuter campus in very large city
- 1,139 degree-seeking undergraduates: 2% part-time, 69% women, 3% African American, 29% Asian American, 14% Hispanic American, 15% international
- 65 degree-seeking graduate students
- 53% of applicants admitted
- SAT or ACT (ACT writing optional), application essay required
- 52% graduate within 6 years

General. Founded in 1918. Regionally accredited. **Degrees:** 216 bachelor's awarded; master's offered. **Calendar:** Semester, limited summer session. **Full-time faculty:** 60 total; 8% have terminal degrees, 13% minority, 60% women. **Part-time faculty:** 206 total; 3% have terminal degrees, 18% minority, 45% women. **Class size:** 78% < 20, 20% 20-39, less than 1% 40-49, 1% 50-99. **Special facilities:** Rare art books collection, full foundry and casting facilities, photographic darkroom, fully equipped printmaking studio, fine art book press room, wood and metal working shops, toy design department, digital imaging studio.

Freshman class profile. 1,317 applied, 703 admitted, 226 enrolled.

Mid 50% test scores		**GPA 3.0-3.49:**	35%
SAT critical reading:	430-580	**GPA 2.0-2.99:**	33%
SAT math:	460-590	**Return as sophomores:**	76%
SAT writing:	430-560	**Out-of-state:**	32%
ACT composite:	17-23	**Live on campus:**	58%
GPA 3.75 or higher:	14%	**International:**	19%
GPA 3.50-3.74:	18%		

Basis for selection. Portfolio most important, followed by school achievement record, essay and test scores. Activities, leadership, motivation also considered. Portfolio required. Interview recommended. **Homeschooled:** Documentation that student has solid academic foundation, is socially and intellectually mature, and has passion for the arts.

High school preparation. Required and recommended units include English 4, mathematics 3-4, social studies 1-2, history 2-3, science 2-4 (laboratory 1-4) and foreign language 2. Drawing and as much art as possible recommended.

2008-2009 Annual costs. Tuition/fees: $30,464. Books/supplies: $1,400. Personal expenses: $1,300.

2008-2009 Financial aid. Need-based: 182 full-time freshmen applied for aid; 143 were judged to have need; 143 of these received aid. Average need met was 54%. Average scholarship/grant was $9,089; average loan $3,323. 56% of total undergraduate aid awarded as scholarships/grants, 44% as loans/jobs. **Non-need-based:** Awarded to 278 full-time undergraduates, including 99 freshmen. Scholarships awarded for academics, art.

Application procedures. Admission: Priority date 2/15; no deadline. $50 fee, may be waived for applicants with need. Admission notification on a rolling basis beginning on or about 12/15. Must reply by May 1 or within 2 week(s) if notified thereafter. **Financial aid:** Priority date 2/15; no closing date. FAFSA required. Applicants notified by 3/1; Applicants notified on a rolling basis starting 3/1; must reply within 2 week(s) of notification.

Academics. Approximately one-third of curriculum consists of liberal arts classes. **Special study options:** Cooperative education, ESL, exchange student, honors, internships, study abroad, teacher certification program. **Credit/placement by examination:** AP, CLEP, IB, institutional tests. **Support services:** Pre-admission summer program, reduced course load, remedial instruction, study skills assistance, tutoring.

Majors. Architecture: Architecture, environmental design, interior, landscape. **Communications technology:** Animation/special effects. **Visual/performing arts:** Art, design, fashion design, graphic design, illustration, industrial design, interior design, multimedia, painting, photography, sculpture, studio arts.

Most popular majors. Visual/performing arts 96%.

Computing on campus. 350 workstations in library, computer center. Helpline, wireless network available.

Student life. Freshman orientation: Mandatory. Orientation held in January and August. **Housing:** Apartments available. $550 nonrefundable deposit, deadline 6/1. Otis sponsored off-campus apartments available. **Activities:** International student organizations, student government, literary organization, Campus Crusade.

Student services. Adult student services, alcohol/substance abuse counseling, career counseling, student employment services, financial aid counseling, personal counseling, placement for graduates. **Physically disabled:** Services for hearing impaired.

Contact. E-mail: admissions@otis.edu
Phone: (310) 665-6820 Toll-free number: (800) 527-6847
Fax: (310) 665-6821
Marc Meredith, Dean of Admissions, Otis College of Art and Design, 9045 Lincoln Boulevard, Los Angeles, CA 90045-9785

Pacific Oaks College
Pasadena, California
www.pacificoaks.edu **CB code: 0482**

- Private two-year upper-division teachers college
- Commuter campus in small city
- 86% of applicants admitted
- Application essay required

General. Founded in 1951. Regionally accredited. College and children's school founded by Quaker families as community education center. **Degrees:** 92 bachelor's awarded; master's offered. **Articulation:** Agreements with De Anza College, Glendale City College, College of the Canyons, Pasadena City College, Rio Hondo College, Santa Monica College, Santa Barbara College, East Los Angeles College, El Camino College, Mt. San Antonio College, Citrus College. **Location:** 10 miles from downtown Los Angeles. **Calendar:** Semester, limited summer session. **Full-time faculty:** 27 total; 52% have terminal degrees, 33% minority, 59% women. **Part-time faculty:** 101 total. **Class size:** 72% < 20, 28% 20-39.

Student profile. 239 degree-seeking undergraduates, 825 graduate students. 28 applied as first time-transfer students, 24 admitted, 25 enrolled.

Women:	95%	**Native American:**	1%
African American:	12%	**Part-time:**	95%
Asian American:	6%	**Out-of-state:**	19%
Hispanic American:	40%	**25 or older:**	94%

Basis for selection. College transcript, application essay required. Must have completed equivalent of GED. Transfer accepted as juniors, seniors.

2008-2009 Annual costs. Tuition/fees: $25,830. Books/supplies: $924. Personal expenses: $4,000.

Financial aid. All financial aid based on need.

Application procedures. Admission: Priority date 4/15; deadline 6/1. $55 fee, may be waived for applicants with need. Application must be submitted on paper.

Academics. Special study options: Accelerated study, distance learning, independent study, internships, teacher certification program, weekend college. **Credit/placement by examination:** CLEP. 30 credit hours maximum toward bachelor's degree. Students age 30-35 without a bachelor's degree may earn credit based on life experience.

Majors. Family/consumer sciences: Family studies.

Computing on campus. 17 workstations in library, computer center. Online library available.

Student life. Activities: Teacher education student association; marriage, family therapy student association.

Student services. Adult student services, career counseling, financial aid counseling. **Physically disabled:** Services for visually, speech, hearing impaired.

Contact. E-mail: admissions@pacificoaks.edu
Phone: (626) 397-1349 Toll-free number: (800) 684-0900
Fax: (626) 666-1220
Augusta Pickens, Director of Admissions, Pacific Oaks College, 5 Westmoreland Place, Pasadena, CA 91103

Pacific States University
Los Angeles, California
www.psuca.edu **CB code: 3547**

- Private 4-year university
- Commuter campus in very large city
- 55 degree-seeking undergraduates: 36% women
- 248 degree-seeking graduate students

General. Accredited by ACICS. **Degrees:** 14 bachelor's awarded; master's, doctoral offered. **Location:** 5 miles from downtown. **Calendar:** Quarter, limited summer session. **Full-time faculty:** 7 total; 57% have terminal degrees, 100% minority, 14% women. **Part-time faculty:** 23 total; 44% have terminal degrees, 100% minority, 26% women.

Freshman class profile.

Live on campus:	10%	**International:**	79%

Basis for selection. Open admission, but selective for some programs. High school diploma and English proficiency required. TOEFL required of students whose native language is not English. **Homeschooled:** Transcript of courses and grades, state high school equivalency certificate required.

2009-2010 Annual costs. Tuition/fees: $13,400. Books/supplies: $1,200.

Financial aid. Non-need-based: Scholarships awarded for academics.

Application procedures. Admission: No deadline. $100 fee. Application must be submitted on paper. Admission notification on a rolling basis. **Financial aid:** No deadline. FAFSA, institutional form required.

Academics. Special study options: Combined bachelor's/graduate degree, distance learning, double major, ESL, liberal arts/career combination. **Credit/placement by examination:** CLEP, IB. 8 credit hours maximum toward bachelor's degree.

Majors. Business: Accounting, management information systems, marketing. **Computer sciences:** General.

Computing on campus. 60 workstations in dormitories, library, computer center. Dormitories wired for high-speed internet access. Online library, wireless network available.

Student life. Freshman orientation: Available. Preregistration for classes offered. Held 2 weeks after each quarter starts, lasting 2 hours. **Housing:** Guaranteed on-campus for all undergraduates. Coed dorms, wellness housing available. **Activities:** Literary magazine, TV station.

Student services. Student employment services, financial aid counseling, personal counseling.

Contact. E-mail: admissions@psuca.edu
Phone: (323) 731-2383 ext. 11 Toll-free number: (888) 200-0383
Fax: (323) 731-7276
Seohee Yang, Director of Admissions, Pacific States University, 1516 South Western Avenue, Los Angeles, CA 90006

Pacific Union College
Angwin, California
www.puc.edu **CB code: 4600**

- Private 4-year liberal arts college affiliated with Seventh-day Adventists
- Residential campus in small town
- 1,203 degree-seeking undergraduates
- 76% of applicants admitted
- SAT or ACT (ACT writing recommended) required

General. Founded in 1882. Regionally accredited. **Degrees:** 234 bachelor's, 102 associate awarded; master's offered. **Location:** 30 miles from Napa, 75 miles from San Francisco. **Calendar:** Quarter, limited summer session. **Full-time faculty:** 81 total; 53% have terminal degrees, 24% minority, 41% women. **Part-time faculty:** 10 total; 40% have terminal degrees, 30% minority, 70% women. **Class size:** 69% < 20, 24% 20-39, 3% 40-49, 4% 50-99, less than 1% >100. **Special facilities:** Observatory, airport/flight training, biology museum, Pitcairn Island Study Center, 1500-acre nature preserve.

Freshman class profile. 1,566 applied, 1,195 admitted, 250 enrolled.

Mid 50% test scores		**GPA 3.50-3.74:**	14%
SAT critical reading:	460-580	**GPA 3.0-3.49:**	31%
SAT math:	440-570	**GPA 2.0-2.99:**	29%
ACT composite:	17-24	**Out-of-state:**	18%
GPA 3.75 or higher:	25%	**Live on campus:**	89%

Basis for selection. Minimum GPA of 2.3 and acceptable recommendations. **Homeschooled:** Transcript of courses and grades, state high school equivalency certificate, letter of recommendation (nonparent) required. **Learning Disabled:** Documentation if available.

High school preparation. 8 units required. Required and recommended units include English 4, mathematics 2-3, history 1-2, science 1-3 and foreign language 2. Computer literacy strongly recommended.

2008-2009 Annual costs. Tuition/fees: $22,695. Room/board: $6,315. Books/supplies: $1,386. Personal expenses: $2,142.

2007-2008 Financial aid. **Non-need-based:** Scholarships awarded for leadership, religious affiliation.

Application procedures. **Admission:** No deadline. $30 fee, may be waived for applicants with need, free for online applicants. Admission notification on a rolling basis beginning on or about 1/15. **Financial aid:** No deadline. FAFSA, institutional form required. Applicants notified on a rolling basis; must reply within 3 week(s) of notification.

Academics. **Special study options:** Combined bachelor's/graduate degree, double major, external degree, honors, independent study, internships, study abroad, teacher certification program. **Credit/placement by examination:** AP, CLEP, IB, SAT, ACT, institutional tests. 24 credit hours maximum toward associate degree, 45 toward bachelor's. **Support services:** Learning center, remedial instruction, study skills assistance, tutoring, writing center.

Majors. **Biology:** General, biochemistry, biophysics. **Business:** General, accounting, business admin, finance, international, management information systems, marketing. **Communications:** General, digital media, journalism, public relations. **Computer sciences:** Computer science. **Education:** Early childhood, elementary, English, mathematics, music, physical. **Foreign languages:** French, Spanish. **Health:** Nursing (RN). **History:** General. **Interdisciplinary:** Natural sciences. **Math:** General. **Philosophy/religion:** Religion. **Physical sciences:** Chemistry, physics. **Psychology:** General. **Public administration:** Social work. **Social sciences:** General. **Theology:** Bible, theology. **Transportation:** Aviation. **Visual/performing arts:** Cinematography, commercial/advertising art, music performance, photography, studio arts.

Most popular majors. Biology 8%, business/marketing 18%, communications/journalism 6%, education 7%, foreign language 9%, health sciences 12%, physical sciences 10%, psychology 6%, visual/performing arts 7%.

Computing on campus. 178 workstations in dormitories, library. Dormitories wired for high-speed internet access and linked to campus network. Commuter students can connect to campus network. Online course registration, online library, helpline, repair service, wireless network available.

Student life. **Freshman orientation:** Mandatory. Preregistration for classes offered. **Policies:** Religious observance required. **Housing:** Guaranteed on-campus for freshmen. Single-sex dorms, apartments, wellness housing available. $150 deposit. **Activities:** Bands, choral groups, drama, film society, literary magazine, music ensembles, musical theater, radio station, student government, student newspaper, symphony orchestra, 20 clubs.

Athletics. NAIA. **Intercollegiate:** Basketball, cross-country, soccer, volleyball. **Intramural:** Basketball, football (non-tackle) M, softball, volleyball. **Team name:** Pioneers.

Student services. Adult student services, alcohol/substance abuse counseling, chaplain/spiritual director, career counseling, student employment services, financial aid counseling, health services, on-campus daycare, personal counseling, placement for graduates. **Physically disabled:** Services for visually, speech, hearing impaired.

Contact. E-mail: enroll@puc.edu
Phone: (707) 965-6336 Toll-free number: (800) 862-7080
Fax: (707) 965-6432
Darren Hagen, Director of Enrollment Services, Pacific Union College, One Angwin Avenue, Angwin, CA 94508

Patten University

Oakland, California — **CB member**
www.patten.edu — **CB code: 4620**

- Private 4-year university and liberal arts college affiliated with interdenominational tradition
- Residential campus in very large city
- 525 degree-seeking undergraduates
- SAT or ACT (ACT writing optional), application essay, interview required

General. Founded in 1944. Regionally accredited. **Degrees:** 44 bachelor's, 12 associate awarded; master's offered. **Location:** 18 miles from San Francisco, 30 miles from San Jose. **Calendar:** Semester, limited summer session. **Full-time faculty:** 20 total. **Part-time faculty:** 120 total.

Freshman class profile. 29 enrolled.

Mid 50% test scores			
SAT critical reading:	500-610	ACT composite:	18-25
SAT math:	460-590	Out-of-state:	5%

Basis for selection. Christian commitment most important. High school record, interview, essay, test scores, recommendation important.

High school preparation. 22 units required. Required units include English 4, mathematics 2, social studies 4, history 2, science 2 (laboratory 1), foreign language 1 and academic electives 6.

2008-2009 Annual costs. Tuition/fees: $12,480. Room/board: $6,980. Books/supplies: $550. Personal expenses: $1,100.

Financial aid. **Non-need-based:** Scholarships awarded for academics, athletics, state residency.

Application procedures. **Admission:** Priority date 3/31; deadline 7/31. $30 fee, may be waived for applicants with need. Admission notification on a rolling basis. **Financial aid:** Priority date 3/31; no closing date. FAFSA, institutional form required. Applicants notified on a rolling basis starting 5/31.

Academics. **Special study options:** Accelerated study, double major, dual enrollment of high school students, independent study, teacher certification program, weekend college. **Credit/placement by examination:** AP, CLEP, institutional tests. **Support services:** Learning center, remedial instruction, tutoring, writing center.

Majors. **Business:** Business admin. **Education:** Adult/continuing, early childhood. **Liberal arts:** Arts/sciences. **Philosophy/religion:** Religion. **Psychology:** General. **Theology:** Religious ed, sacred music.

Computing on campus. 30 workstations in library, computer center. Dormitories wired for high-speed internet access. Online library, wireless network available.

Student life. **Freshman orientation:** Mandatory. Preregistration for classes offered. 3-day overview held week before start of classes. **Policies:** Christian service program designed to involve students in practical ministry. Religious observance required. **Housing:** Guaranteed on-campus for all undergraduates. Single-sex dorms, apartments available. $150 deposit, deadline 7/31. **Activities:** Concert band, choral groups, drama, music ensembles, student government, student newspaper, symphony orchestra, Community of Faith groups, prison ministry.

Athletics. NAIA. **Intercollegiate:** Baseball M, softball W. **Team name:** Lions.

Student services. Adult student services, career counseling, student employment services, personal counseling, placement for graduates, veterans' counselor.

Contact. E-mail: admissions@patten.edu
Phone: (510) 261-8500 ext. 7764 Toll-free number: (877) 472-8836
Fax: (510) 534-4344
Kim Guerra, Director of Admissions, Patten University, 2433 Coolidge Avenue, Oakland, CA 94601-2699

Pepperdine University

Malibu, California — **CB member**
www.pepperdine.edu — **CB code: 4630**

- Private 4-year university and liberal arts college affiliated with Church of Christ
- Residential campus in small city
- 3,386 degree-seeking undergraduates
- 34% of applicants admitted
- SAT or ACT with writing, application essay required
- 81% graduate within 6 years

General. Founded in 1937. Regionally accredited. Education, psychology, business graduate campuses in Los Angeles. Educational centers in Long Beach, Irvine, Encino, West Los Angeles, Westlake Village. 5 campuses in Europe (Germany, England, Italy, Spain, France), 1 in Costa Rica. Education center in Hong-Kong. Part-time, evening, weekend classes for business undergrad programs. **Degrees:** 810 bachelor's awarded; master's, doctoral, first professional offered. **ROTC:** Army, Air Force. **Location:** 14 miles from Santa Monica, 30 miles from Los Angeles. **Calendar:** Semester, limited summer session. **Full-time faculty:** 367 total; 89% have terminal degrees, 12% minority, 37% women. **Part-time faculty:** 312 total; 52% have terminal degrees, 13% minority, 47% women. **Class size:** 68% < 20, 28% 20-39, 2% 40-49, 1% 50-99, 1% >100.

Freshman class profile. 6,910 applied, 2,378 admitted, 782 enrolled.

Mid 50% test scores		**GPA 3.0-3.49:**	21%
SAT critical reading:	550-670	**GPA 2.0-2.99:**	3%
SAT math:	560-680	**Rank in top quarter:**	75%
SAT writing:	550-660	**Rank in top tenth:**	40%
ACT composite:	25-30	**Live on campus:**	98%
GPA 3.75 or higher:	51%	**Fraternities:**	16%
GPA 3.50-3.74:	25%	**Sororities:**	27%

Basis for selection. School achievement record and test scores most important. Special talents, school and community activities, letters of recommendation, personal qualities also considered. Audition required for music, theater majors. Portfolio recommended for art majors. **Homeschooled:** Transcript of courses and grades, state high school equivalency certificate required. **Learning Disabled:** Proper documentation from doctor diagnosing learning disability required.

High school preparation. College-preparatory program recommended. 28 units recommended. Recommended units include English 4, mathematics 4, social studies 3, history 3, science 4 (laboratory 3), foreign language 3 and academic electives 3. 1 speech recommended.

2008-2009 Annual costs. Tuition/fees: $36,770. Room/board: $10,480. Books/supplies: $1,000. Personal expenses: $900.

2008-2009 Financial aid. Non-need-based: Scholarships awarded for academics, art, athletics, minority status, music/drama, religious affiliation.

Application procedures. Admission: Closing date 1/15 (postmark date). $65 fee, may be waived for applicants with need. Admission notification 4/1. Must reply by 5/1. **Financial aid:** Closing date 2/15. FAFSA, institutional form required. Applicants notified by 4/15; must reply within 2 week(s) of notification.

Academics. Great books colloquium, freshman seminars and first year faculty mentor program for all students. **Special study options:** Double major, honors, independent study, internships, student-designed major, study abroad, teacher certification program, Washington semester. 3-2 programs in engineering with USC, Washington University, Boston University. **Credit/placement by examination:** AP, CLEP, IB, institutional tests. 32 credit hours maximum toward bachelor's degree. IB credit awarded for higher level exams only: 4 credits for each score of 5 and above; maximum 16. **Support services:** Pre-admission summer program, remedial instruction, tutoring, writing center.

Majors. Area/ethnic studies: Asian, European, Latin American. **Biology:** General, biochemistry. **Business:** Accounting, business admin, finance, international, marketing. **Communications:** General, advertising, broadcast journalism, journalism, organizational, public relations, radio/tv. **Computer sciences:** General. **Education:** General, chemistry, English, music, physical, speech. **Engineering:** General. **Family/consumer sciences:** Food/nutrition. **Foreign languages:** French, German, Spanish. **Health:** Athletic training. **History:** General. **Interdisciplinary:** Global studies, math/computer science, natural sciences, nutrition sciences. **Liberal arts:** Arts/sciences, humanities. **Math:** General. **Parks/recreation:** Exercise sciences, sports admin. **Philosophy/religion:** Philosophy, religion. **Physical sciences:** Chemistry, physics. **Psychology:** General. **Social sciences:** Economics, political science, sociology. **Visual/performing arts:** Acting, art, art history/conservation, dramatic, multimedia, music history, music theory/composition, studio arts, theater design.

Computing on campus. 292 workstations in dormitories, library, computer center, student center. Dormitories wired for high-speed internet access and linked to campus network. Commuter students can connect to campus network. Online library, helpline, repair service, wireless network available.

Student life. Freshman orientation: Mandatory. Orientation held a week before the official start of the Fall semester. **Policies:** Students required to attend weekly convocation. Freshmen and sophomores live on campus or at home with parent or guardian if single and under 21. **Housing:** Guaranteed on-campus for freshmen. Single-sex dorms, special housing for disabled, apartments, cooperative housing available. **Activities:** Bands, campus ministries, choral groups, dance, drama, film society, international student organizations, literary magazine, music ensembles, Model UN, musical theater, opera, radio station, student government, student newspaper, symphony orchestra, TV station, Campus Crusade for Christ, College Republicans, Young Democrats, volunteer center, black student union, Latin student association, Hawaiian club, Korean student association, Japan club.

Athletics. NCAA. **Intercollegiate:** Baseball M, basketball, cross-country, golf, soccer W, swimming W, tennis, track and field W, volleyball, water polo M. **Intramural:** Basketball, football (non-tackle), handball, soccer, swimming, tennis, volleyball. **Team name:** Waves.

Student services. Alcohol/substance abuse counseling, chaplain/spiritual director, career counseling, student employment services, financial aid counseling, health services, personal counseling, placement for graduates, veterans' counselor. **Physically disabled:** Services for visually, hearing impaired.

Contact. E-mail: admission-seaver@pepperdine.edu
Phone: (310) 506-4392 Fax: (310) 506-4861
Mike Trushke, Director of Admission, Pepperdine University, 24255 Pacific Coast Highway, Malibu, CA 90263-4392

Pitzer College

Claremont, California — **CB member**
www.pitzer.edu — **CB code: 4619**

- Private 4-year liberal arts college
- Residential campus in large town
- 1,025 degree-seeking undergraduates: 5% part-time, 59% women, 6% African American, 9% Asian American, 15% Hispanic American, 3% international
- 22% of applicants admitted
- Application essay required
- 70% graduate within 6 years

General. Founded in 1963. Regionally accredited. One of a cluster of 5 undergraduate and 2 graduate institutions on adjoining campuses. Campuses share facilities. Cross-enrollment available at any of the 5 colleges, which include Claremont-McKenna, Harvey Mudd, Pitzer, Pomona, and Scripps. Interdisciplinary curriculum with social responsibility requirement, intercultural education objective; no academic departments. **Degrees:** 231 bachelor's awarded. **ROTC:** Army, Air Force. **Location:** 35 miles from Los Angeles. **Calendar:** Semester, limited summer session. **Full-time faculty:** 71 total; 100% have terminal degrees, 37% minority, 48% women. **Part-time faculty:** 36 total; 72% have terminal degrees, 19% minority, 50% women. **Class size:** 67% < 20, 31% 20-39, 2% 40-49. **Special facilities:** Ecology center, nature reserve, arboretum, organic garden, women's studies center, restored arts and crafts home with poetry reading room, 2 art galleries.

Freshman class profile. 4,031 applied, 899 admitted, 264 enrolled.

Mid 50% test scores		**GPA 2.0-2.99:**	4%
SAT critical reading:	580-690	**Rank in top quarter:**	80%
SAT math:	580-680	**Rank in top tenth:**	51%
ACT composite:	25-30	**Return as sophomores:**	92%
GPA 3.75 or higher:	54%	**Out-of-state:**	56%
GPA 3.50-3.74:	20%	**Live on campus:**	100%
GPA 3.0-3.49:	22%	**International:**	3%

Basis for selection. School record, essays, 3 recommendations, test scores, leadership, community service, work experience, talent, involvement in sports considered. SAT/ACT not required of students graduating in top 10% of class, or those with an unweighted cumulative GPA of 3.50 or higher in academic subjects. Otherwise, one of the following required: ACT or SAT scores; 2 SAT Subject Tests (one in math); 2 or more AP test scores of at least 4 (one English or English Language and one math or science); 2 International Baccalaureate exams (one English 1A and one math); or one recent junior or senior year graded analytical writing sample from a humanities or social science course and one recent graded exam from an advanced math course. The samples must include the teacher's comments, grades, and the assignment. Interview recommended.

High school preparation. College-preparatory program recommended. 21 units required. Required units include English 4, mathematics 3, social studies 3, history 1, science 3 (laboratory 3), foreign language 3 and visual/performing arts 1.

2008-2009 Annual costs. Tuition/fees: $37,870. Part-time tuition: $4,313 per course. Room/board: $10,930. Books/supplies: $1,000. Personal expenses: $1,000.

2008-2009 Financial aid. Need-based: 139 full-time freshmen applied for aid; 107 were judged to have need; 107 of these received aid. Average need met was 100%. Average scholarship/grant was $27,064; average loan $2,613. 84% of total undergraduate aid awarded as scholarships/grants, 16% as loans/jobs. **Non-need-based:** Awarded to 67 full-time undergraduates, including 28 freshmen. Scholarships awarded for academics, leadership.

Application procedures. Admission: Closing date 1/1 (postmark date). $50 fee, may be waived for applicants with need. Admission notification 4/1. Must reply by 5/1. **Financial aid:** Closing date 2/1. FAFSA, CSS PROFILE required. Applicants notified by 4/1; must reply by 5/1.

Four-Year Colleges

Academics. Students may take up to one-third of courses at other Claremont campuses and must take 32 courses for graduation. Can create independent study courses and special majors. **Special study options:** Combined bachelor's/graduate degree, cooperative education, cross-registration, double major, ESL, exchange student, honors, independent study, internships, liberal arts/career combination, student-designed major, study abroad, urban semester. New Resources (for students over age 25 and nontraditional students), joint science program, joint BA/DO program. **Credit/placement by examination:** AP, CLEP, IB, institutional tests. **Support services:** Tutoring, writing center.

Majors. Area/ethnic studies: African-American, American, Asian, Asian-American, Caribbean, European, Hispanic-American/Latino/Chicano, Latin American, women's. **Biology:** General, biochemistry, biophysics, microbiology. **Business:** Organizational behavior. **Conservation:** Environmental science, environmental studies. **Foreign languages:** General, Chinese, classics, French, German, Italian, Japanese, linguistics, Russian, Spanish. **History:** General, American, European. **Interdisciplinary:** Biological/physical sciences, global studies, intercultural, natural sciences, neuroscience, science/society. **Math:** General. **Philosophy/religion:** Philosophy, religion. **Physical sciences:** Chemistry, organic chemistry, physics. **Psychology:** General. **Social sciences:** General, anthropology, economics, international relations, political science, sociology. **Visual/performing arts:** Art, art history/conservation, cinematography, dance, dramatic, film/cinema, studio arts.

Most popular majors. Area/ethnic studies 8%, English 8%, interdisciplinary studies 6%, psychology 14%, social sciences 23%, visual/performing arts 11%.

Computing on campus. 100 workstations in dormitories, library, computer center, student center. Dormitories wired for high-speed internet access and linked to campus network. Commuter students can connect to campus network. Online library, helpline, student web hosting, wireless network available.

Student life. Freshman orientation: Mandatory. Held the week prior to start of fall semester. **Policies:** Strong philosophical framework of social responsibility and self-governance. **Housing:** Guaranteed on-campus for freshmen. Coed dorms, special housing for disabled, cooperative housing available. **Activities:** Campus ministries, choral groups, dance, drama, international student organizations, literary magazine, music ensembles, Model UN, radio station, student government, student newspaper, symphony orchestra, over 75 social service, religious, political, and ethnic organizations.

Athletics. NCAA. **Intercollegiate:** Badminton, baseball M, basketball, cross-country, diving, football (tackle) M, golf, lacrosse, soccer, softball W, swimming, tennis, track and field, volleyball W, water polo. **Intramural:** Archery, badminton, basketball, golf, racquetball, sailing, soccer, softball W, squash, tennis. **Team name:** Sagehens.

Student services. Adult student services, alcohol/substance abuse counseling, chaplain/spiritual director, career counseling, student employment services, financial aid counseling, health services, minority student services, personal counseling, women's services. **Physically disabled:** Services for visually, speech, hearing impaired.

Contact. E-mail: admission@pitzer.edu
Phone: (909) 621-8129 Toll-free number: (800) 748-9371
Fax: (909) 621-8770
Arnaldo Rodriguez, Vice President of Admission and Financial Aid, Pitzer College, 1050 North Mills Avenue, Claremont, CA 91711-6101

Platt College: Ontario

Ontario, California
www.plattcollege.edu **CB code: 3015**

- For-profit 4-year branch campus and technical college
- Commuter campus in small city

General. Accredited by ACCSCT. **Location:** 20 miles from Los Angeles. **Calendar:** Continuous.

Annual costs/financial aid. Annual tuition varies by program: $10,300--$14,230. Need-based financial aid available to full-time and part-time students.

Contact. Phone: (909) 941-9410
Admissions Director, 3700 Inland Empire Boulevard, Ontario, CA 91764

Platt College: San Diego

San Diego, California
www.platt.edu **CB code: 3020**

- For-profit 4-year visual arts and technical college
- Commuter campus in very large city
- 286 degree-seeking undergraduates: 25% women, 4% African American, 10% Asian American, 18% Hispanic American, 3% international
- Application essay, interview required
- 67% graduate within 6 years

General. Accredited by ACCSCT. **Degrees:** 78 bachelor's, 108 associate awarded. **Calendar:** Continuous. **Full-time faculty:** 6 total. **Part-time faculty:** 33 total; 9% have terminal degrees, 15% minority, 54% women. **Class size:** 91% < 20, 9% 20-39.

Freshman class profile. 118 applied, 118 admitted, 118 enrolled.

Basis for selection. Open admission, but selective for some programs and for out-of-state students. Aptitude test used to measure academic preparedness to undertake college-level courses; SAT considered in lieu of test.

2008-2009 Annual costs. Tuition/fees: $15,010. Total program costs range from $17,710 to $35,810, depending on the program chosen. Books/supplies: $1,100.

2007-2008 Financial aid. Need-based: 35% of total undergraduate aid awarded as scholarships/grants, 65% as loans/jobs.

Application procedures. Admission: No deadline. No application fee. Application must be submitted on paper. **Financial aid:** Closing date 3/2. FAFSA, institutional form required. Applicants notified on a rolling basis; must reply within 1 week(s) of notification.

Academics. Special study options: Accelerated study, internships, liberal arts/career combination. **Credit/placement by examination:** AP, CLEP, institutional tests. **Support services:** Study skills assistance, tutoring.

Majors. Visual/performing arts: General, commercial/advertising art.

Computing on campus. 200 workstations in library, computer center. Online library available.

Student life. Freshman orientation: Mandatory. Preregistration for classes offered.

Student services. Career counseling, services for economically disadvantaged, student employment services, financial aid counseling, personal counseling, placement for graduates.

Contact. E-mail: info@platt.edu
Phone: (619) 265-0107 Toll-free number: (866) 752-8826
Fax: (619) 308-0570
Al Medro, Vice President, Platt College: San Diego, 6250 El Cajon Boulevard, San Diego, CA 92115

Point Loma Nazarene University

San Diego, California **CB member**
www.pointloma.edu **CB code: 4605**

- Private 4-year university and liberal arts college affiliated with Church of the Nazarene
- Residential campus in very large city
- 2,385 degree-seeking undergraduates: 3% part-time, 61% women, 2% African American, 6% Asian American, 11% Hispanic American, 1% Native American
- 780 degree-seeking graduate students
- 78% of applicants admitted
- SAT or ACT (ACT writing recommended), application essay, interview required
- 70% graduate within 6 years

General. Founded in 1902. Regionally accredited. **Degrees:** 558 bachelor's awarded; master's offered. **ROTC:** Army, Naval, Air Force. **Location:** 5 miles from downtown. **Calendar:** Semester, limited summer session. **Full-time faculty:** 175 total; 75% have terminal degrees, 11% minority, 39% women. **Part-time faculty:** 176 total. **Class size:** 57% < 20, 34% 20-39, 7% 40-49, 2% 50-99. **Special facilities:** Historical Greek ampitheatre.

Freshman class profile. 1,810 applied, 1,414 admitted, 538 enrolled.

Mid 50% test scores			
SAT critical reading:	510-620	GPA 2.0-2.99:	8%
SAT math:	510-600	Rank in top quarter:	68%
ACT composite:	22-27	Rank in top tenth:	38%
GPA 3.75 or higher:	48%	Return as sophomores:	83%
GPA 3.50-3.74:	19%	Out-of-state:	22%
GPA 3.0-3.49:	25%	Live on campus:	94%

Basis for selection. Moral character, maturity, intellectual ability, and academic achievement important. Preference given to self-directed applicants who appear to share ideals and objectives of college. SAT recommended.

High school preparation. College-preparatory program required. 18 units recommended. Recommended units include English 4, mathematics 3, social studies 2, history 2, science 2 (laboratory 2), foreign language 2 and academic electives 1.

2009-2010 Annual costs. Tuition/fees: $25,840. Room/board: $8,100. Books/supplies: $1,638. Personal expenses: $2,250.

Application procedures. Admission: Closing date 3/1 (postmark date). $50 fee, may be waived for applicants with need. Admission notification 4/1. Admission notification on a rolling basis. Must reply by May 1 or within 2 week(s) if notified thereafter. **Financial aid:** Closing date 3/2. FAFSA, institutional form required. Applicants notified on a rolling basis starting 3/1.

Academics. Special study options: Double major, honors, independent study, internships, semester at sea, study abroad, teacher certification program, United Nations semester, Washington semester. **Credit/placement by examination:** AP, CLEP, IB, SAT, institutional tests. 32 credit hours maximum toward bachelor's degree. Some restrictions apply in special majors. **Support services:** Learning center, reduced course load, remedial instruction, study skills assistance, tutoring, writing center.

Majors. Biology: General, biochemistry. **Business:** Accounting, business admin, communications, management information systems. **Communications:** General, broadcast journalism, journalism, media studies. **Computer sciences:** Computer science. **Conservation:** Environmental science. **Education:** Art, music. **Engineering:** Physics. **Family/consumer sciences:** General, child development, food/nutrition. **Foreign languages:** Romance, Spanish. **Health:** Athletic training, dietetics, nursing (RN). **History:** General. **Interdisciplinary:** Global studies. **Liberal arts:** Arts/sciences. **Math:** General. **Parks/recreation:** Exercise sciences, health/fitness. **Philosophy/religion:** Philosophy. **Physical sciences:** Chemistry, physics. **Psychology:** General, industrial. **Public administration:** Social work. **Social sciences:** General, international economic development, political science, sociology. **Theology:** Bible, preministerial, sacred music, youth ministry. **Visual/performing arts:** Dramatic, fashion design, graphic design, interior design, music performance, music theory/composition, piano/organ, studio arts, voice/opera. **Other:** Philosophy and religious studies.

Most popular majors. Biology 6%, business/marketing 22%, communications/journalism 7%, family/consumer sciences 7%, health sciences 12%, psychology 9%, visual/performing arts 7%.

Computing on campus. 270 workstations in dormitories, library, computer center, student center. Dormitories wired for high-speed internet access and linked to campus network. Commuter students can connect to campus network. Online course registration, online library, helpline, repair service, wireless network available.

Student life. Freshman orientation: Mandatory. **Policies:** Students are expected to exercise self-discipline, sound judgment and manage conduct both on and off campus consistent with agreements made upon application and with University catalog and Student Handbook. Religious observance required. **Housing:** Guaranteed on-campus for freshmen. Single-sex dorms, apartments, wellness housing available. $425 nonrefundable deposit, deadline 5/1. **Activities:** Bands, campus ministries, choral groups, drama, international student organizations, literary magazine, music ensembles, musical theater, radio station, student government, student newspaper, symphony orchestra, TV station, Students for Social Justice, Social Work Club, College Democrats, College Republicans, Brothers and Sisters United, Association of Latin American Students.

Athletics. NAIA. **Intercollegiate:** Baseball M, basketball, cross-country, golf M, soccer, softball W, tennis, track and field, volleyball W. **Intramural:** Badminton, basketball, football (non-tackle), golf, soccer, softball, tennis, track and field, volleyball. **Team name:** Sea Lions.

Student services. Chaplain/spiritual director, career counseling, student employment services, financial aid counseling, health services, minority student services, on-campus daycare, personal counseling, veterans' counselor. **Physically disabled:** Services for visually, speech, hearing impaired.

Contact. E-mail: admissions@pointloma.edu
Phone: (619) 849-2273 Toll-free number: (800) 733-7770
Fax: (619) 849-2601
Eric Groves, Director of Undergraduate Admissions, Point Loma Nazarene University, 3900 Lomaland Drive, San Diego, CA 92106-2899

Pomona College

Claremont, California — **CB member**
www.pomona.edu — **CB code: 4607**

- Private 4-year liberal arts college
- Residential campus in large town
- 1,516 degree-seeking undergraduates: 50% women, 8% African American, 14% Asian American, 11% Hispanic American, 4% international
- 16% of applicants admitted
- SAT and SAT Subject Tests or ACT (ACT writing recommended), application essay required
- 95% graduate within 6 years

General. Founded in 1887. Regionally accredited. One of a cluster of 5 undergraduate and 2 graduate schools on adjoining campuses. Campuses share facilities. Cross-enrollment available at any of the 5 colleges, which include Claremont-McKenna, Harvey Mudd, Pitzer, Pomona, and Scripps. Extensive overseas studies. **Degrees:** 385 bachelor's awarded. **ROTC:** Army, Air Force. **Location:** 35 miles from Los Angeles, 20 miles from Pasadena. **Calendar:** Semester. **Full-time faculty:** 178 total; 99% have terminal degrees, 26% minority, 42% women. **Part-time faculty:** 39 total; 51% have terminal degrees, 28% minority, 56% women. **Class size:** 70% < 20, 27% 20-39, 1% 40-49, less than 1% 50-99. **Special facilities:** Science center, center for modern language and international relations, observatory, biological field station, ecological preserve, botanic garden, social sciences center, Greek theater, multimedia labs.

Freshman class profile. 6,293 applied, 981 admitted, 382 enrolled.

Mid 50% test scores			
SAT critical reading:	700-780	Rank in top tenth:	87%
SAT math:	690-780	Return as sophomores:	97%
SAT writing:	680-770	Out-of-state:	70%
ACT composite:	30-34	Live on campus:	100%
Rank in top quarter:	98%	International:	6%

Basis for selection. School achievement record, test scores, essays, 3 recommendations most important. Special skills in music, art, drama, or athletics; leadership, motivation, and diversity of background also important. Some preference to children of alumni; special consideration for underrepresented groups. School and community activities also considered. Students submitting SAT must also submit 2 SAT Subject Tests in different subject areas. Interview required for early admission applicants, strongly recommended for all applicants. Audition recommended for music, dance, theater majors. Portfolio recommended for studio art majors. **Homeschooled:** SAT and at least 3 SAT Subject Tests required, more recommended. Detailed description of curriculum required.

High school preparation. College-preparatory program required. 19 units required. Required and recommended units include English 4, mathematics 3-4, social studies 2, history 3, science 3-4 (laboratory 2-3) and foreign language 2-3. 3-4 laboratory science recommended for science applicants. Mathematics through calculus recommended for all applicants.

2008-2009 Annual costs. Tuition/fees: $35,625. Room/board: $12,220. Books/supplies: $850. Personal expenses: $1,000.

2007-2008 Financial aid. All financial aid based on need. 241 full-time freshmen applied for aid; 195 were judged to have need; 195 of these received aid. Average need met was 100%. Average scholarship/grant was $34,000; average loan $2,000. 89% of total undergraduate aid awarded as scholarships/grants, 11% as loans/jobs.

Application procedures. Admission: Closing date 1/2 (receipt date). $65 fee, may be waived for applicants with need. Admission notification 4/10. Must reply by May 1 or within 1 week(s) if notified thereafter. **Financial aid:** Closing date 2/1. FAFSA, CSS PROFILE required. Applicants notified by 4/10; must reply by 5/1.

Academics. Special study options: Combined bachelor's/graduate degree, cross-registration, double major, exchange student, independent study, internships, student-designed major, study abroad, Washington semester. 3-2 program in engineering with California Institute of Technology and Washington University (MO), 4-1 education certification program with Claremont Graduate University. **Credit/placement by examination:** AP, CLEP,

IB, SAT, ACT, institutional tests. 2 credit hours maximum toward bachelor's degree. **Support services:** Tutoring, writing center.

Majors. **Area/ethnic studies:** African-American, American, Asian, Asian-American, German, Hispanic-American/Latino/Chicano, Latin American, women's. **Biology:** General, molecular. **Communications:** Media studies. **Computer sciences:** Computer science. **Conservation:** Environmental studies. **Foreign languages:** General, Chinese, classics, French, German, Japanese, linguistics, Russian, Spanish. **History:** General. **Interdisciplinary:** Cognitive science, global studies, math/computer science, neuroscience, science/society. **Math:** General. **Philosophy/religion:** Philosophy, religion. **Physical sciences:** Astronomy, chemistry, geology, physics. **Psychology:** General. **Public administration:** Policy analysis. **Social sciences:** General, anthropology, economics, international relations, political science, sociology. **Visual/performing arts:** General, art, art history/conservation, dance, dramatic, studio arts.

Most popular majors. Interdisciplinary studies 11%, psychology 10%, social sciences 25%.

Computing on campus. 180 workstations in dormitories, library, computer center, student center. Dormitories wired for high-speed internet access and linked to campus network. Commuter students can connect to campus network. Online library, helpline, wireless network available.

Student life. **Freshman orientation:** Mandatory. Held immediately prior to fall semester; preorientation adventure available. **Housing:** Guaranteed on-campus for all undergraduates. Coed dorms available. $500 nonrefundable deposit, deadline 5/1. **Activities:** Bands, campus ministries, choral groups, dance, drama, film society, international student organizations, literary magazine, music ensembles, Model UN, musical theater, radio station, student government, student newspaper, symphony orchestra, TV station, center for religious activities, international peace, Asian students association, Mortar Board (service organization), women's coalition, gay and lesbian student union.

Athletics. NCAA. **Intercollegiate:** Baseball M, basketball, cross-country, diving, football (tackle) M, golf, lacrosse W, soccer, softball W, swimming, tennis, track and field, volleyball W, water polo. **Intramural:** Badminton, basketball, equestrian, handball, racquetball, skiing, soccer, softball, squash, table tennis, track and field, volleyball, water polo. **Team name:** Sagehens.

Student services. Chaplain/spiritual director, career counseling, services for economically disadvantaged, student employment services, financial aid counseling, health services, minority student services, personal counseling, placement for graduates. **Physically disabled:** Services for visually, hearing impaired.

Contact. E-mail: admissions@pomona.edu
Phone: (909) 621-8134 Fax: (909) 621-8952
Bruce Poch, Vice President and Dean of Admissions, Pomona College, 333 North College Way, Claremont, CA 91711-6312

Remington College: San Diego

San Diego, California
www.remingtoncollege.edu **CB code: 2574**

- For-profit 4-year university
- Very large city

General. Accredited by ACICS. **Calendar:** Quarter.

Annual costs/financial aid. Massage Therapy program $13,050; includes books and supplies.

Contact. Phone: (619) 686-8600
Director of Recruitment, 123 Camino de la Reina, Suite 100, North Building, San Diego, CA 92108-3002

St. Mary's College of California

Moraga, California **CB member**
www.stmarys-ca.edu **CB code: 4675**

- Private 4-year liberal arts college affiliated with Roman Catholic Church
- Residential campus in large town
- 2,514 degree-seeking undergraduates: 3% part-time, 62% women, 6% African American, 11% Asian American, 22% Hispanic American, 1% Native American, 2% international
- 1,219 degree-seeking graduate students
- 81% of applicants admitted
- SAT or ACT (ACT writing optional), application essay required
- 65% graduate within 6 years; 38% enter graduate study

General. Founded in 1863. Regionally accredited. **Degrees:** 651 bachelor's awarded; master's, doctoral offered. **ROTC:** Army, Air Force. **Location:** 20 miles from San Francisco. **Calendar:** 4-1-4, limited summer session. **Full-time faculty:** 208 total; 92% have terminal degrees, 16% minority, 51% women. **Part-time faculty:** 270 total; 28% have terminal degrees, 16% minority, 65% women. **Class size:** 52% < 20, 47% 20-39, less than 1% 40-49, less than 1% 50-99. **Special facilities:** Observatory.

Freshman class profile. 3,638 applied, 2,961 admitted, 675 enrolled.

Mid 50% test scores		**GPA 2.0-2.99:**	24%
SAT critical reading:	490-590	**End year in good standing:**	88%
SAT math:	480-590	**Return as sophomores:**	81%
GPA 3.75 or higher:	24%	**Out-of-state:**	16%
GPA 3.50-3.74:	13%	**Live on campus:**	90%
GPA 3.0-3.49:	39%	**International:**	3%

Basis for selection. School achievement record most important. Interview recommended. **Homeschooled:** Transcript of courses and grades, letter of recommendation (nonparent) required.

High school preparation. 16 units required; 19 recommended. Required and recommended units include English 4, mathematics 3-4, social studies 1, history 1, science 2-3 (laboratory 1), foreign language 2-3 and academic electives 2. One unit each of chemistry, physics, advanced algebra, and trigonometry required for applicants to school of science.

2008-2009 Annual costs. Tuition/fees: $33,250. Room/board: $11,680. Books/supplies: $1,224. Personal expenses: $2,286.

2008-2009 Financial aid. **Need-based:** 566 full-time freshmen applied for aid; 489 were judged to have need; 489 of these received aid. Average need met was 86%. Average scholarship/grant was $24,277; average loan $3,979. 65% of total undergraduate aid awarded as scholarships/grants, 35% as loans/jobs. **Non-need-based:** Awarded to 834 full-time undergraduates, including 224 freshmen. Scholarships awarded for academics, alumni affiliation, athletics, leadership.

Application procedures. **Admission:** Priority date 11/15; deadline 2/1 (postmark date). $55 fee, may be waived for applicants with need. Admission notification 3/15. Admission notification on a rolling basis. Must reply by May 1 or within 2 week(s) if notified thereafter. **Financial aid:** Priority date 2/15; no closing date. FAFSA required. Applicants notified on a rolling basis starting 3/15; must reply by 5/1 or within 2 week(s) of notification.

Academics. **Special study options:** Cross-registration, double major, exchange student, independent study, internships, liberal arts/career combination, student-designed major, study abroad, teacher certification program. 4-year interdisciplinary program with Great Books orientation. **Credit/placement by examination:** AP, CLEP, IB, SAT, institutional tests. 30 credit hours maximum toward bachelor's degree. **Support services:** Learning center, study skills assistance, tutoring, writing center.

Majors. **Area/ethnic studies:** European, Latin American, women's. **Biology:** General, biochemistry. **Business:** General, accounting, business admin, finance, international. **Communications:** General. **Foreign languages:** General, classics, French, German, Italian, Japanese, Spanish. **Health:** Health care admin. **History:** General. **Interdisciplinary:** Biopsychology, math/computer science. **Liberal arts:** Arts/sciences. **Math:** General. **Parks/recreation:** Exercise sciences, health/fitness, sports admin. **Philosophy/religion:** Philosophy, religion. **Physical sciences:** Chemistry, physics. **Psychology:** General, developmental, experimental, industrial, social. **Social sciences:** Anthropology, archaeology, economics, political science, sociology. **Visual/performing arts:** General, art, dance, dramatic.

Most popular majors. Business/marketing 25%, communications/journalism 11%, liberal arts 8%, psychology 10%, social sciences 14%.

Computing on campus. 244 workstations in dormitories, library, computer center. Dormitories wired for high-speed internet access and linked to campus network. Commuter students can connect to campus network. Online course registration, online library, helpline, student web hosting, wireless network available.

Student life. **Freshman orientation:** Mandatory, $250 fee. 4 day and one-half sessions. Freshmen attend 1 session plus 4-day weekend of welcome. **Housing:** Guaranteed on-campus for freshmen. Coed dorms, special housing for disabled, apartments available. $350 nonrefundable deposit, deadline 5/1. **Activities:** Bands, campus ministries, choral groups, dance, drama, film society, international student organizations, literary magazine, music ensembles, musical theater, radio station, student government, student newspaper, TV station, Catholic Institute for Lasallian Social Action, Habitat for Humanity, Amnesty International, Lasallian Collegians, Intervarsity Christians, LASA, Black student union, APASA, multicultural club.

Athletics. NCAA. **Intercollegiate:** Baseball M, basketball, cross-country, golf M, lacrosse W, rowing (crew) W, soccer, softball W, tennis, volleyball W. **Intramural:** Basketball, bowling, football (non-tackle), golf, lacrosse, rowing (crew), skiing, soccer, softball, table tennis, tennis, volleyball, water polo. **Team name:** Gaels.

Student services. Alcohol/substance abuse counseling, chaplain/spiritual director, career counseling, services for economically disadvantaged, student employment services, financial aid counseling, health services, personal counseling, placement for graduates, veterans' counselor, women's services. **Physically disabled:** Services for visually, speech, hearing impaired.

Contact. E-mail: smcadmit@stmarys_ca.edu
Phone: (925) 631-4224 Toll-free number: (800) 800-4762
Fax: (925) 376-7193
Dorothy Jones, Dean of Admissions, St. Mary's College of California, Box 4800, Moraga, CA 94575-4800

Samuel Merritt University

Oakland, California — **CB member**
www.samuelmerritt.edu — **CB code: 4750**

- Private two-year upper-division health science and nursing college
- Commuter campus in large city
- 51% of applicants admitted
- Application essay required

General. Founded in 1909. Regionally accredited. Part of Alta Bates Summit Medical Center, a nonprofit, community-based health care organization. Nursing degree offered in partnership with St. Mary's College of California, Holy Names University, and Mills College. **Degrees:** 278 bachelor's awarded; master's, doctoral, first professional offered. **Articulation:** Agreements with Holy Names University, Mills College, Saint Mary's College of California. **ROTC:** Army, Naval, Air Force. **Location:** 15 miles from San Francisco. **Calendar:** Differs by program, limited summer session. **Full-time faculty:** 92 total; 54% have terminal degrees, 24% minority, 70% women. **Part-time faculty:** 135 total; 15% have terminal degrees, 43% minority, 72% women. **Class size:** 7% < 20, 59% 20-39, 34% 40-49. **Special facilities:** Nursing resource laboratory, health education center, health science library, anatomy laboratory, therapeutic exercise laboratory, living skills laboratory, human occupations laboratory, health sciences simulation lab.

Student profile. 441 degree-seeking undergraduates, 802 degree-seeking graduate students. 280 applied as first time-transfer students, 144 admitted, 112 enrolled. 3% entered as juniors. 100% transferred from two-year institutions.

Women:	90%	**Part-time:**	1%
African American:	5%	**Out-of-state:**	2%
Asian American:	24%	**Live on campus:**	4%
Hispanic American:	8%	**25 or older:**	59%
Native American:	1%		

Basis for selection. College transcript, application essay required. Must have UC transferable college-level coursework in chemistry, anatomy, physiology, multicultural psychology, English (2) and humanities (2). Applicants with fewer than 30 semester hours transferable credits admitted as freshmen. Letter of recommendation and experience in health care environment required. Transfer accepted as juniors.

2009-2010 Annual costs. Tuition/fees: $35,886. $2,958 per semester health insurance mandatory unless student covered by existing insurance. Books/supplies: $1,370. Personal expenses: $4,114.

Financial aid. Need-based: 461 applied for aid; 451 were judged to have need; 451 of these received aid. Average need met was 65%. 43% of total undergraduate aid awarded as scholarships/grants, 57% as loans/jobs. **Non-need-based:** Awarded to 90 undergraduates. Scholarships awarded for academics, leadership, minority status. **Additional information:** Ongoing private scholarships available. Students eligible to work in Medical Center (associated with college).

Application procedures. Admission: Priority date 3/1. $50 fee, may be waived for applicants with need. Application must be submitted on paper. Admission notification 4/1. Must reply by 5/1. **Financial aid:** Priority date 3/2, no deadline. Applicants notified on a rolling basis; must reply within 3 weeks of notification.

Academics. Special study options: Accelerated study, combined bachelor's/graduate degree, cooperative education, cross-registration, distance learning, ESL, independent study, internships, liberal arts/career combination. **Credit/placement by examination:** CLEP. 80 credit hours maximum toward bachelor's degree.

Majors. Health: Nursing (RN).

Computing on campus. 78 workstations in dormitories, library, computer center. Online course registration, online library, helpline, wireless network available.

Student life. Housing: Coed dorms available. $100 fully refundable deposit. **Activities:** Student government, student newspaper, multicultural committee, American Physical Therapy Association, California Nursing Students Association, Christian Fellowship, American Occupational Therapy Association, Chi Eta Phi, gay, lesbian, bisexual and transgender group.

Student services. Career counseling, financial aid counseling, health services, personal counseling. **Physically disabled:** Services for visually, speech, hearing impaired.

Contact. E-mail: admission@samuelmerritt.edu
Phone: (510) 869-6576 Toll-free number: (800) 607-6377
Fax: (510) 869-6576
Anne Seed, Director of Admissions, Samuel Merritt University, 370 Hawthorne Avenue, Oakland, CA 94609-9954

San Diego Christian College

El Cajon, California
www.sdcc.edu — **CB code: 4150**

- Private 4-year liberal arts college affiliated with nondenominational tradition
- Residential campus in small city
- 384 degree-seeking undergraduates: 10% part-time, 55% women, 6% African American, 5% Asian American, 15% Hispanic American, 2% Native American, 1% international
- 26 degree-seeking graduate students
- 55% of applicants admitted
- SAT or ACT (ACT writing optional), application essay required
- 40% graduate within 6 years; 33% enter graduate study

General. Founded in 1970. Regionally accredited. **Degrees:** 128 bachelor's awarded. **ROTC:** Army, Air Force. **Location:** 15 miles from downtown San Diego. **Calendar:** Semester, limited summer session. **Full-time faculty:** 24 total; 50% have terminal degrees, 8% minority, 42% women. **Part-time faculty:** 33 total; 15% have terminal degrees, 21% minority, 42% women. **Class size:** 80% < 20, 18% 20-39, 2% 40-49. **Special facilities:** Museum supporting creationist view, aviation school.

Freshman class profile. 175 applied, 96 admitted, 60 enrolled.

Mid 50% test scores		**GPA 2.0-2.99:**	19%
SAT critical reading:	440-550	**Rank in top quarter:**	30%
SAT math:	440-570	**Rank in top tenth:**	17%
SAT writing:	450-550	**End year in good standing:**	55%
ACT composite:	19-24	**Return as sophomores:**	55%
GPA 3.75 or higher:	22%	**Out-of-state:**	20%
GPA 3.50-3.74:	23%	**Live on campus:**	59%
GPA 3.0-3.49:	33%		

Basis for selection. Academic abilities as indicated by school achievement record and test scores. Personal and spiritual qualities as indicated by essays, recommendations, and interview.

High school preparation. 15 units recommended. Recommended units include English 4, mathematics 3, social studies 3, science 3 and foreign language 2.

2009-2010 Annual costs. Tuition/fees (projected): $21,600. Room/board: $7,540. Books/supplies: $1,386. Personal expenses: $2,142.

2008-2009 Financial aid. Need-based: 45 full-time freshmen applied for aid; 33 were judged to have need; 33 of these received aid. Average need met was 85%. Average scholarship/grant was $8,405; average loan $3,500. 42% of total undergraduate aid awarded as scholarships/grants, 58% as loans/jobs. **Non-need-based:** Awarded to 446 full-time undergraduates, including 50 freshmen. Scholarships awarded for academics, alumni affiliation, athletics, leadership, music/drama, state residency.

Application procedures. Admission: Priority date 7/1; deadline 8/1. $25 fee. Admission notification on a rolling basis. Must reply by May 1 or within 4 week(s) if notified thereafter. **Financial aid:** Priority date 3/2, closing date 7/15. FAFSA, institutional form required. Applicants notified on a rolling basis starting 4/1; must reply by 5/1 or within 4 week(s) of notification.

Academics. **Special study options:** Accelerated study, double major, ESL, honors, independent study, internships, liberal arts/career combination, student-designed major, study abroad, teacher certification program. **Credit/placement by examination:** AP, CLEP, IB, institutional tests. 9 credit hours maximum toward bachelor's degree. **Support services:** Learning center, reduced course load, remedial instruction, study skills assistance, tutoring, writing center.

Majors. **Biology:** General. **Business:** Business admin. **Communications:** General. **Education:** General, early childhood, elementary, English, history, mathematics, middle, music, physical, secondary, social science. **Family/consumer sciences:** Family studies. **Health:** Athletic training. **History:** General. **Math:** General. **Psychology:** General. **Social sciences:** General. **Theology:** Bible, missionary. **Visual/performing arts:** Dramatic, music performance.

Most popular majors. Business/marketing 11%, family/consumer sciences 13%, interdisciplinary studies 20%, liberal arts 8%, parks/recreation 6%, psychology 11%, theological studies 11%.

Computing on campus. 48 workstations in library, computer center. Dormitories wired for high-speed internet access and linked to campus network. Commuter students can connect to campus network. Online library, helpline, repair service, wireless network available.

Student life. **Freshman orientation:** Mandatory, $70 fee. Preregistration for classes offered. Takes place within 2 weeks of start of classes in fall. **Policies:** Religious observance required. **Housing:** Guaranteed on-campus for all undergraduates. Single-sex dorms available. $250 deposit, deadline 7/1. **Activities:** Concert band, campus ministries, choral groups, drama, music ensembles, musical theater, student government, student newspaper, flight team, missions club, art club.

Athletics. NAIA. **Intercollegiate:** Baseball M, basketball, cross-country, golf M, soccer, track and field, volleyball W. **Intramural:** Basketball, football (non-tackle) M, soccer, softball, tennis, volleyball. **Team name:** Hawks.

Student services. Adult student services, chaplain/spiritual director, career counseling, student employment services, financial aid counseling, health services, personal counseling, placement for graduates.

Contact. E-mail: admissions@sdcc.edu
Phone: (619) 588-7747 Toll-free number: (800) 676-2242
Fax: (619) 590-1739
Mitchell FIsk, Vice President for Enrollment & Marketing, San Diego Christian College, 2100 Greenfield Drive, El Cajon, CA 92019-1157

San Diego State University

San Diego, California — **CB member**
www.sdsu.edu — **CB code: 4682**

- Public 4-year university
- Commuter campus in very large city
- 29,481 degree-seeking undergraduates: 15% part-time, 57% women, 4% African American, 16% Asian American, 24% Hispanic American, 1% Native American, 3% international
- 6,351 degree-seeking graduate students
- 31% of applicants admitted
- SAT or ACT (ACT writing optional) required
- 53% graduate within 6 years

General. Founded in 1897. Regionally accredited. Branch campus at Calexico in Imperial Valley. **Degrees:** 6,679 bachelor's awarded; master's, doctoral offered. **ROTC:** Army, Naval, Air Force. **Location:** 8 miles from downtown. **Calendar:** Semester, extensive summer session. **Full-time faculty:** 806 total. **Part-time faculty:** 986 total. **Class size:** 20% < 20, 49% 20-39, 10% 40-49, 14% 50-99, 6% >100. **Special facilities:** Observatory, electron microscope facility, open-air theater, aquatic center, international student center, American Language Institute, recital hall, field studies stations (off-campus), multimedia interactive fine arts lab.

Freshman class profile. 50,148 applied, 15,658 admitted, 4,386 enrolled.

Mid 50% test scores		**End year in good standing:**	83%
SAT critical reading:	460-570	**Return as sophomores:**	81%
SAT math:	470-600	**Out-of-state:**	8%
ACT composite:	20-25	**Live on campus:**	52%
GPA 3.75 or higher:	25%	**International:**	2%
GPA 3.50-3.74:	28%	**Fraternities:**	13%
GPA 3.0-3.49:	36%	**Sororities:**	14%
GPA 2.0-2.99:	11%		

Basis for selection. High school GPA and test scores most important; 20% of those admitted selected using faculty-defined criteria, such as socio-economic status, special talent, and San Diego and Imperial County residency. **Homeschooled:** Transcript of courses and grades required. In cases where the Lab Science courses are not completed in at a regular high school or community college, we request course descriptions to ensure the lab component meets the CSU requirement for admission.

High school preparation. College-preparatory program recommended. 15 units required. Required and recommended units include English 4, mathematics 3-4, social studies 1, history 1, science 2 (laboratory 2), foreign language 2 and academic electives 1. One visual and performing arts required. History must be U.S. history or U.S. government. Science must be 1 biology, 1 physical science.

2008-2009 Annual costs. Tuition/fees: $3,754; $13,924 out-of-state. Room/board: $11,266. Books/supplies: $1,566. Personal expenses: $2,540.

2008-2009 Financial aid. **Need-based:** 3,600 full-time freshmen applied for aid; 2,400 were judged to have need; 2,300 of these received aid. Average need met was 67%. Average scholarship/grant was $7,100; average loan $3,100. 53% of total undergraduate aid awarded as scholarships/grants, 47% as loans/jobs. **Non-need-based:** Awarded to 3,800 full-time undergraduates, including 1,050 freshmen. Scholarships awarded for academics, alumni affiliation, art, athletics, leadership, music/drama, ROTC, state residency.

Application procedures. **Admission:** Closing date 11/30 (postmark date). $55 fee, may be waived for applicants with need. Application must be submitted online. Admission notification 3/1. Must reply by 5/1. **Financial aid:** Priority date 3/2; no closing date. FAFSA required. Applicants notified on a rolling basis starting 2/14.

Academics. **Special study options:** Cross-registration, distance learning, double major, dual enrollment of high school students, ESL, exchange student, honors, independent study, internships, student-designed major, study abroad, teacher certification program. **Credit/placement by examination:** AP, CLEP, IB, SAT, ACT, institutional tests. 30 credit hours maximum toward bachelor's degree. Must be registered in at least 1 course, matriculated and in good standing. Approval of department chair and dean of college required. Restricted to regular undergraduate courses. Does not count toward 30-unit minimum residency requirement. **Support services:** Pre-admission summer program, reduced course load, remedial instruction, tutoring.

Majors. **Agriculture:** Business. **Area/ethnic studies:** African-American, American, Asian, Central/Eastern European, European, Hispanic-American/Latino/Chicano, Latin American, Native American, Russian/Slavic, women's. **Biology:** Microbiology. **Business:** General, accounting, business admin, finance, financial planning, hospitality admin, international, marketing, real estate. **Communications:** Advertising, journalism, public relations, radio/tv. **Computer sciences:** General, computer science, information systems, information technology. **Conservation:** General, environmental studies. **Education:** Early childhood, music, trade/industrial. **Engineering:** General, aerospace, civil, computer, electrical, environmental, mechanical. **Engineering technology:** Construction. **Family/consumer sciences:** Child development. **Foreign languages:** Classics, comparative lit, French, German, Japanese, linguistics, Russian, Spanish. **Health:** Communication disorders, health services, nursing (RN). **History:** General. **Interdisciplinary:** Gerontology. **Liberal arts:** Arts/sciences, humanities. **Math:** General, applied, statistics. **Parks/recreation:** General, health/fitness. **Philosophy/religion:** Judaic, philosophy, religion. **Physical sciences:** General, astronomy, chemistry, geology, molecular physics, physics, theoretical physics. **Protective services:** Law enforcement admin. **Psychology:** General. **Public administration:** General, social work. **Social sciences:** General, anthropology, economics, geography, international relations, political science, sociology, urban studies. **Visual/performing arts:** Art history/conservation, dance, design, dramatic, graphic design, interior design, music performance, studio arts. **Other:** Dietetics/food admin/nutrition, Evolutionary biology, Modern Jewish studies, Telecommunications and film.

Most popular majors. Business/marketing 21%, English 6%, psychology 9%, social sciences 12%.

Computing on campus. 400 workstations in dormitories, library, computer center, student center. Dormitories wired for high-speed internet access and linked to campus network. Commuter students can connect to campus network. Online course registration, online library, helpline, repair service, wireless network available.

Student life. **Freshman orientation:** Mandatory, $55 fee. Preregistration for classes offered. One-day academic orientation in July and August. Student life orientation held in August. **Housing:** Coed dorms, apartments, fraternity/sorority housing available. $800 partly refundable deposit. The Housing and Residential Life Office has a website to assist students and families to find off-campus housing. **Activities:** Bands, campus ministries, choral groups, dance, drama, film society, international student organizations, literary magazine, music ensembles, musical theater, opera, radio station, student government, student newspaper, symphony orchestra, TV station, more than 300 academic, recreational, sports, ethnic, political, honor, and service clubs on campus.

Athletics. NCAA. **Intercollegiate:** Baseball M, basketball, cross-country W, diving W, football (tackle) M, golf, rowing (crew) W, soccer, softball W, swimming W, tennis, track and field W, volleyball W, water polo W. **Intramural:** Basketball, bowling, football (non-tackle), golf, racquetball, soccer, softball, swimming, tennis, volleyball. **Team name:** Aztecs.

Student services. Alcohol/substance abuse counseling, chaplain/spiritual director, career counseling, services for economically disadvantaged, student employment services, financial aid counseling, health services, on-campus daycare, personal counseling, placement for graduates, veterans' counselor, women's services. **Physically disabled:** Services for visually, speech, hearing impaired. **Learning disabled:** Comprehensive services available.

Contact. E-mail: admissions@sdsu.edu
Phone: (619) 594-6336
Beverly Arata, Director of Admissions, San Diego State University, 5500 Campanile Drive, San Diego, CA 92182-7455

San Francisco Art Institute

San Francisco, California **CB member**
www.sfai.edu **CB code: 4036**

- Private 4-year visual arts college
- Commuter campus in very large city
- 346 degree-seeking undergraduates: 8% part-time, 52% women, 5% African American, 10% Asian American, 10% Hispanic American, 1% Native American, 5% international
- 231 degree-seeking graduate students
- 74% of applicants admitted
- SAT or ACT (ACT writing optional), application essay required
- 36% graduate within 6 years

General. Founded in 1871. Regionally accredited. SFAI-sponsored lectures, film screenings, and symposium events with visiting artists available to students. **Degrees:** 75 bachelor's awarded; master's offered. **Location:** Downtown. **Calendar:** Semester, limited summer session. **Full-time faculty:** 48 total. **Part-time faculty:** 99 total. **Class size:** 81% < 20, 17% 20-39, 1% 40-49, less than 1% 50-99. **Special facilities:** EARS XXI high definition research lab, Diego Rivera gallery, digital media studio, digital imaging studio, studio production facilities in photography, printmaking, design/technology, and filmmaking, open studio spaces, graffiti art studio.

Freshman class profile. 333 applied, 247 admitted, 66 enrolled.

Mid 50% test scores			
SAT critical reading:	480-590	GPA 3.50-3.74:	9%
SAT math:	410-550	GPA 3.0-3.49:	36%
SAT writing:	460-580	GPA 2.0-2.99:	46%
ACT composite:	20-27	Return as sophomores:	56%
GPA 3.75 or higher:	9%	Live on campus:	77%
		International:	5%

Basis for selection. Admission decisions based on evaluation of portfolio, academic credentials including transcripts and standardized test scores, letters of recommendation, and personal statement. Portfolio of artwork required. Interviews recommended, but not required. **Homeschooled:** State high school equivalency certificate, letter of recommendation (nonparent) required.

High school preparation. College-preparatory program recommended. Recommended units include English 4, mathematics 2, social studies 3, history 2, science 2, foreign language 2 and visual/performing arts 4. Strong background in English, humanities, and social sciences as well as extensive high school and extracurricular art education recommended.

2009-2010 Annual costs. Tuition/fees (projected): $31,700. Room/board: $10,800. Books/supplies: $1,566. Personal expenses: $2,214.

2007-2008 Financial aid. Need-based: 43 full-time freshmen applied for aid; 37 were judged to have need; 36 of these received aid. Average need met was 41%. Average scholarship/grant was $12,477; average loan $3,297. 69% of total undergraduate aid awarded as scholarships/grants, 31% as loans/jobs. **Non-need-based:** Awarded to 45 full-time undergraduates, including 21 freshmen. Scholarships awarded for academics, art.

Application procedures. Admission: Priority date 2/15; no deadline. $65 fee, may be waived for applicants with need. Admission notification on a rolling basis. Must reply by May 1 or within 3 week(s) if notified thereafter. **Financial aid:** Priority date 3/1, closing date 5/31. FAFSA required. Applicants notified on a rolling basis starting 4/15; must reply within 3 week(s) of notification.

Academics. Special study options: Cross-registration, double major, ESL, exchange student, independent study, internships, New York semester, study abroad. **Credit/placement by examination:** AP, CLEP, IB, institutional tests. 20 credit hours maximum toward bachelor's degree. **Support services:** Learning center, remedial instruction, study skills assistance, tutoring, writing center.

Majors. Social sciences: Urban studies. **Visual/performing arts:** Art, art history/conservation, ceramics, cinematography, film/cinema, multimedia, painting, photography, printmaking, sculpture, studio arts. **Other:** Urban studies.

Computing on campus. 71 workstations in dormitories, library, computer center, student center. Dormitories wired for high-speed internet access. Wireless network available.

Student life. Freshman orientation: Mandatory. Preregistration for classes offered. **Housing:** Coed dorms, wellness housing available. $450 nonrefundable deposit, deadline 6/1. **Activities:** Film society, international student organizations, radio station, student government.

Student services. Career counseling, student employment services, financial aid counseling, personal counseling, placement for graduates, veterans' counselor. **Physically disabled:** Services for visually, speech, hearing impaired.

Contact. E-mail: admissions@sfai.edu
Phone: (415) 749-4500 Toll-free number: (800) 345-7324
Fax: (415) 749-4517
Director of Admissions, San Francisco Art Institute, 800 Chestnut Street, San Francisco, CA 94133-2299

San Francisco Conservatory of Music

San Francisco, California
www.sfcm.edu **CB code: 4744**

- Private 4-year music college
- Commuter campus in very large city
- 200 degree-seeking undergraduates: 3% part-time, 46% women
- 174 degree-seeking graduate students
- 44% of applicants admitted
- Application essay required
- 68% graduate within 6 years

General. Founded in 1917. Regionally accredited. A small school of 400 musicians, all conservatory students receive extensive performance opportunities, both on campus and in the San Francisco Bay area. **Degrees:** 48 bachelor's awarded; master's offered. **Location:** Downtown. **Calendar:** Semester. **Full-time faculty:** 31 total; 26% have terminal degrees, 13% minority, 29% women. **Part-time faculty:** 80 total; 19% have terminal degrees, 5% minority, 31% women. **Class size:** 67% < 20, 29% 20-39, 2% 40-49, less than 1% 50-99, 2% >100. **Special facilities:** Concert performance halls, recording studios, listening lab, music library.

Freshman class profile. 272 applied, 119 admitted, 37 enrolled.

End year in good standing:	81%	Out-of-state:	43%
Return as sophomores:	76%	Live on campus:	46%

Basis for selection. Most important criterion is music audition, followed by school achievement record, letters of recommendation, and test scores. Musical needs of institution also influence admission decisions. SAT or ACT recommended. Audition required. **Homeschooled:** Transcript of courses and grades, state high school equivalency certificate, letter of recommendation (nonparent) required. SAT or ACT required.

High school preparation. Recommended units include English 3 and foreign language 3.

2008-2009 Annual costs. Tuition/fees: $32,080. Books/supplies: $580. Personal expenses: $2,000.

2008-2009 Financial aid. Need-based: 30 full-time freshmen applied for aid; 28 were judged to have need; 28 of these received aid. Average need met was 89%. Average scholarship/grant was $11,600; average loan $3,500. 72% of total undergraduate aid awarded as scholarships/grants, 28% as loans/jobs. **Non-need-based:** Awarded to 169 full-time undergraduates, including 40 freshmen. Scholarships awarded for music/drama.

Application procedures. **Admission:** Closing date 12/1 (receipt date). $100 fee. Application must be submitted online. Admission notification on a rolling basis beginning on or about 3/15. Must reply by 5/1. Must reply by May 1 or within 2 week(s) if notified thereafter. **Financial aid:** Priority date 3/1; no closing date. FAFSA, institutional form required. Applicants notified by 4/1; must reply by 5/1 or within 2 week(s) of notification.

Academics. **Special study options:** Independent study. **Credit/placement by examination:** AP, CLEP, institutional tests. **Support services:** Remedial instruction, study skills assistance, tutoring.

Majors. **Visual/performing arts:** Music performance, music theory/composition, piano/organ, stringed instruments, voice/opera.

Computing on campus. 25 workstations in library, computer center. Dormitories wired for high-speed internet access. Student web hosting, wireless network available.

Student life. **Freshman orientation:** Mandatory. **Housing:** Coed dorms available. **Activities:** Choral groups, music ensembles, musical theater, opera, student government, symphony orchestra.

Student services. Financial aid counseling, health services, personal counseling.

Contact. E-mail: admit@sfcm.edu
Phone: (415) 864-7326 Toll-free number: (800) 899-7326
Fax: (415) 503-6299
Alexander Brose, Director of Admission, San Francisco Conservatory of Music, 50 Oak Street, San Francisco, CA 94102

San Francisco State University

San Francisco, California — **CB member**
www.sfsu.edu — **CB code: 4684**

- Public 4-year university
- Commuter campus in very large city
- 24,378 degree-seeking undergraduates: 18% part-time, 59% women, 6% African American, 30% Asian American, 16% Hispanic American, 1% Native American, 6% international
- 4,603 degree-seeking graduate students
- 66% of applicants admitted
- 44% graduate within 6 years

General. Founded in 1899. Regionally accredited. **Degrees:** 5,845 bachelor's awarded; master's, doctoral offered. **ROTC:** Army, Naval, Air Force. **Location:** 10 miles from downtown. **Calendar:** Semester, limited summer session. **Full-time faculty:** 928 total; 77% have terminal degrees, 36% minority, 48% women. **Part-time faculty:** 917 total; 27% have terminal degrees, 28% minority, 55% women. **Class size:** 21% < 20, 46% 20-39, 12% 40-49, 13% 50-99, 8% >100. **Special facilities:** Marine laboratories, environmental studies center, Sierra Nevada field campus, anthropology museum, astronomy facility.

Freshman class profile. 30,792 applied, 20,351 admitted, 3,603 enrolled.

Mid 50% test scores		**GPA 3.0-3.49:**	45%
SAT critical reading:	440-570	**GPA 2.0-2.99:**	36%
SAT math:	450-570	**Return as sophomores:**	76%
SAT writing:	450-560	**Out-of-state:**	2%
ACT composite:	18-24	**Live on campus:**	46%
GPA 3.75 or higher:	8%	**International:**	4%
GPA 3.50-3.74:	11%		

Basis for selection. School achievement record and score on SAT or ACT most important. Students with GPA over 2.0 may be exempted from SAT/ACT. SAT or ACT scores required if applicant's secondary school GPA is lower than 3.0 for California residents or 3.61 for non-residents. **Homeschooled:** Local school district verification of completion of secondary schooling; SAT or ACT scores.

High school preparation. College-preparatory program required. 14 units required. Required and recommended units include English 4, mathematics 3, social studies 1, history 1, science 2 (laboratory 2), foreign language 2, visual/performing arts 1 and academic electives 1.

2008-2009 Annual costs. Tuition/fees: $3,762; $13,932 out-of-state. Room/board: $11,500. Books/supplies: $1,656. Personal expenses: $3,024.

2008-2009 Financial aid. All financial aid based on need.

Application procedures. **Admission:** Priority date 11/30; deadline 12/10. $55 fee, may be waived for applicants with need. Admission notification on a rolling basis beginning on or about 10/15. Must reply by May 1 or within 2 week(s) if notified thereafter. **Financial aid:** Priority date 3/2; no closing date. FAFSA required. Applicants notified on a rolling basis starting 2/1; must reply within 2 week(s) of notification.

Academics. **Special study options:** Cooperative education, cross-registration, distance learning, double major, dual enrollment of high school students, ESL, exchange student, honors, independent study, internships, liberal arts/career combination, student-designed major, study abroad, teacher certification program. **Credit/placement by examination:** AP, CLEP, IB, SAT, ACT, institutional tests. 30 credit hours maximum toward bachelor's degree. **Support services:** Learning center, pre-admission summer program, remedial instruction, study skills assistance, tutoring, writing center.

Majors. **Area/ethnic studies:** African-American, American, Asian-American, Hispanic-American/Latino/Chicano, Native American, women's. **Biology:** General, biochemistry, botany, cell/histology, ecology, marine, microbiology, physiology, zoology. **Business:** Accounting, banking/financial services, business admin, e-commerce, finance, hospitality admin, international, labor studies, management science, marketing, small business admin. **Communications:** Journalism, radio/tv. **Computer sciences:** General, computer science. **Conservation:** Environmental studies. **Education:** Early childhood. **Engineering:** Civil, computer, electrical, mechanical. **Engineering technology:** Industrial. **Family/consumer sciences:** General, clothing/textiles. **Foreign languages:** Chinese, classics, comparative lit, French, German, Italian, Japanese, Spanish. **Health:** Clinical lab science, communication disorders, dietetics, nursing (RN), public health ed. **History:** General. **Liberal arts:** Arts/sciences, humanities. **Math:** General, applied, statistics. **Parks/recreation:** Exercise sciences, facilities management. **Philosophy/religion:** Judaic, philosophy. **Physical sciences:** Atmospheric science, chemistry, geology, physics. **Protective services:** Criminal justice. **Psychology:** General. **Public administration:** Social work. **Social sciences:** Anthropology, economics, geography, international relations, political science, sociology, urban studies. **Visual/performing arts:** Art, dance, dramatic, film/cinema, industrial design, interior design, music performance. **Other:** Interdisciplinary studies, Philosophy and religion.

Most popular majors. Business/marketing 21%, communications/journalism 7%, English 7%, psychology 9%, social sciences 10%, visual/performing arts 8%.

Computing on campus. 500 workstations in library, computer center. Dormitories wired for high-speed internet access and linked to campus network. Online course registration, online library, helpline, repair service, student web hosting, wireless network available.

Student life. **Freshman orientation:** Mandatory, $35 fee. Preregistration for classes offered. **Housing:** Coed dorms, special housing for disabled, apartments, wellness housing available. $200 fully refundable deposit. **Activities:** Bands, choral groups, dance, drama, film society, literary magazine, music ensembles, musical theater, opera, radio station, student government, student newspaper, symphony orchestra, TV station.

Athletics. NCAA. **Intercollegiate:** Baseball M, basketball, cross-country, soccer, softball W, track and field W, volleyball W, wrestling M. **Intramural:** Basketball, soccer, tennis, volleyball W. **Team name:** Gators.

Student services. Adult student services, alcohol/substance abuse counseling, career counseling, services for economically disadvantaged, student employment services, financial aid counseling, health services, on-campus daycare, personal counseling, placement for graduates, veterans' counselor. **Physically disabled:** Services for visually, speech, hearing impaired.

Contact. E-mail: ugadmit@sfsu.edu
Phone: (415) 338-1113 Fax: (415) 338-7196
John Pliska, Director, Undergraduate Admissions, San Francisco State University, 1600 Holloway Avenue, San Francisco, CA 94132

San Jose State University

San Jose, California — **CB member**
www.sjsu.edu — **CB code: 4687**

- Public 4-year university and liberal arts college
- Commuter campus in very large city
- 25,187 degree-seeking undergraduates: 21% part-time, 52% women
- 7,559 degree-seeking graduate students
- 66% of applicants admitted
- 41% graduate within 6 years

General. Founded in 1857. Regionally accredited. **Degrees:** 4,662 bachelor's awarded; master's offered. **ROTC:** Army, Air Force. **Location:** 50 miles from San Francisco. **Calendar:** Semester, limited summer session. **Full-time faculty:** 710 total; 30% minority, 44% women. **Part-time faculty:** 1,178 total; 26% minority, 51% women. **Class size:** 24% < 20, 50%

20-39, 13% 40-49, 12% 50-99, 2% >100. **Special facilities:** Marine laboratory, natural history living museum, nuclear science lab, center for Beethoven studies, Chicano resource center, art metal foundry, deep-sea research ship, electro-acoustic and recording studio.

Freshman class profile. 24,079 applied, 15,941 admitted, 3,594 enrolled.

Mid 50% test scores			
SAT critical reading:	430-540	GPA 3.0-3.49:	45%
SAT math:	450-580	GPA 2.0-2.99:	35%
SAT writing:	430-530	End year in good standing:	81%
ACT composite:	18-24	Return as sophomores:	80%
GPA 3.75 or higher:	8%	Out-of-state:	1%
GPA 3.50-3.74:	12%	Live on campus:	49%

Basis for selection. High school record and test scores most important. SAT or ACT required for applicants with less than 3.0 GPA.

High school preparation. 15 units required; 17 recommended. Required and recommended units include English 4, mathematics 3-4, history 2, science 2-3 (laboratory 2), foreign language 2, visual/performing arts 1 and academic electives 1. History is 2 units in history/social science.

2008-2009 Annual costs. Tuition/fees: $3,992; $14,162 out-of-state. Room/board: $10,153. Books/supplies: $1,656. Personal expenses: $2,786.

2007-2008 Financial aid. All financial aid based on need. 2,311 full-time freshmen applied for aid; 2,112 were judged to have need; 2,035 of these received aid. Average need met was 87%. Average scholarship/grant was $5,864; average loan $5,632. 47% of total undergraduate aid awarded as scholarships/grants, 53% as loans/jobs.

Application procedures. Admission: Closing date 11/30. $55 fee, may be waived for applicants with need. Application must be submitted online. Admission notification 10/1. Must reply by May 1 or within 2 week(s) if notified thereafter. **Financial aid:** Priority date 3/2, closing date 6/12. FAFSA required. Applicants notified on a rolling basis starting 4/10; must reply within 2 week(s) of notification.

Academics. Special study options: Distance learning, double major, dual enrollment of high school students, honors, independent study, internships, student-designed major, study abroad, teacher certification program. **Credit/placement by examination:** AP, CLEP. **Support services:** Learning center, pre-admission summer program, remedial instruction, study skills assistance, tutoring, writing center.

Majors. Area/ethnic studies: African-American. **Biology:** General, biochemistry, conservation, marine, microbiology, molecular, physiology. **Business:** Accounting, business admin, finance, hospitality admin, human resources, international, marketing. **Communications:** Advertising, journalism, public relations, radio/tv. **Computer sciences:** Computer science, information systems, information technology, systems analysis. **Conservation:** Environmental studies. **Education:** Early childhood. **Engineering:** General, aerospace, chemical, civil, computer, electrical, industrial, materials, mechanical, software. **Engineering technology:** Quality control. **Foreign languages:** Chinese, French, German, Japanese, linguistics, Spanish. **Health:** Communication disorders, dietetics, health care admin, health services, nursing (RN). **History:** General. **Interdisciplinary:** Accounting/computer science, behavioral sciences, natural sciences. **Liberal arts:** Arts/sciences, humanities. **Math:** General, applied. **Parks/recreation:** General, health/fitness. **Philosophy/religion:** Philosophy, religion. **Physical sciences:** Chemistry, geology, physics. **Protective services:** Criminal justice, forensics. **Psychology:** General. **Public administration:** Social work. **Social sciences:** General, anthropology, economics, geography, international relations, political science, sociology. **Transportation:** Aviation. **Visual/performing arts:** General, art, art history/conservation, dance, dramatic, graphic design, industrial design, interior design, music performance, studio arts.

Most popular majors. Business/marketing 31%, communications/journalism 6%, engineering/engineering technologies 10%, health sciences 7%, psychology 6%, social sciences 6%, visual/performing arts 8%.

Computing on campus. Dormitories wired for high-speed internet access and linked to campus network. Commuter students can connect to campus network. Online course registration, online library, helpline, repair service, wireless network available.

Student life. Freshman orientation: Mandatory, $135 fee. Preregistration for classes offered. Mandatory overnight program for all first-time freshmen. **Housing:** Coed dorms, single-sex dorms, special housing for disabled, apartments, cooperative housing, fraternity/sorority housing available. $600 partly refundable deposit. **Activities:** Marching band, campus ministries, choral groups, dance, drama, film society, international student organizations, literary magazine, music ensembles, musical theater, radio station, student government, student newspaper, symphony orchestra.

Athletics. NCAA. **Intercollegiate:** Baseball M, basketball, cheerleading, cross-country, diving W, football (tackle) M, golf, gymnastics W, soccer, softball W, swimming W, tennis W, volleyball W, water polo W. **Intramural:** Archery, badminton, baseball M, basketball, bowling, field hockey W, football (non-tackle), lacrosse, racquetball, soccer, softball, swimming, table tennis, tennis, volleyball W, water polo. **Team name:** Spartans.

Student services. Adult student services, alcohol/substance abuse counseling, chaplain/spiritual director, career counseling, services for economically disadvantaged, student employment services, financial aid counseling, health services, legal services, minority student services, on-campus daycare, personal counseling, placement for graduates, veterans' counselor, women's services. **Physically disabled:** Services for visually, speech, hearing impaired.

Contact. E-mail: contact@sjsu.edu
Phone: (408) 283-7500
Fernanda Karp, Undergraduate Admissions Manager, San Jose State University, One Washington Square, San Jose, CA 95192-0011

Santa Clara University

Santa Clara, California — **CB member**
www.scu.edu — **CB code: 4851**

- Private 4-year university affiliated with Roman Catholic Church
- Residential campus in small city
- 5,234 degree-seeking undergraduates: 2% part-time, 53% women, 4% African American, 16% Asian American, 13% Hispanic American, 3% international
- 3,292 degree-seeking graduate students
- 58% of applicants admitted
- SAT or ACT (ACT writing optional), application essay required
- 85% graduate within 6 years; 30% enter graduate study

General. Founded in 1851. Regionally accredited. **Degrees:** 1,316 bachelor's awarded; master's, doctoral, first professional offered. **ROTC:** Army, Air Force. **Location:** 45 miles from San Francisco, 1 mile from San Jose. **Calendar:** Quarter, limited summer session. **Full-time faculty:** 515 total; 88% have terminal degrees, 20% minority, 43% women. **Part-time faculty:** 257 total; 56% have terminal degrees, 19% minority, 36% women. **Class size:** 38% < 20, 54% 20-39, 7% 40-49, 2% 50-99. **Special facilities:** Historic mission church with artifacts dating from California mission era, applied ethics center, observatory, tennis complex, de Saisset museum.

Freshman class profile. 10,124 applied, 5,834 admitted, 1,221 enrolled.

Mid 50% test scores			
SAT critical reading:	550-650	Rank in top quarter:	72%
SAT math:	570-680	Rank in top tenth:	40%
ACT composite:	25-30	End year in good standing:	93%
GPA 3.75 or higher:	27%	Return as sophomores:	93%
GPA 3.50-3.74:	30%	Out-of-state:	40%
GPA 3.0-3.49:	38%	Live on campus:	95%
GPA 2.0-2.99:	5%	International:	2%

Basis for selection. GED not accepted. Rigor of high school curriculum and GPA most important, followed by test scores, teacher's recommendation, personal essay, and extracurricular activities. Ethnicity and alumni affiliations given special consideration. Interviews not recommended. Audition recommended for music, theater arts majors.

High school preparation. College-preparatory program required. 15 units required; 19 recommended. Required and recommended units include English 4, mathematics 3-4, social studies 3, science 2-3, foreign language 2-3, visual/performing arts 1 and academic electives 1. Social studies units include history.

2008-2009 Annual costs. Tuition/fees: $34,950. Room/board: $11,070.

2008-2009 Financial aid. Need-based: 767 full-time freshmen applied for aid; 522 were judged to have need; 513 of these received aid. Average need met was 77%. Average scholarship/grant was $20,490; average loan $3,270. 80% of total undergraduate aid awarded as scholarships/grants, 20% as loans/jobs. **Non-need-based:** Awarded to 2,494 full-time undergraduates, including 694 freshmen. Scholarships awarded for academics, alumni affiliation, athletics, music/drama, ROTC.

Application procedures. Admission: Closing date 1/7 (postmark date). $55 fee, may be waived for applicants with need. Application must be submitted online. Admission notification 4/1. Must reply by 5/1. **Financial aid:** Priority date 2/1; no closing date. FAFSA, CSS PROFILE required. Applicants notified by 4/1; must reply by 5/1 or within 2 week(s) of notification.

Academics. **Special study options:** Combined bachelor's/graduate degree, cooperative education, double major, honors, independent study, internships, student-designed major, study abroad, teacher certification program, Washington semester. **Credit/placement by examination:** AP, CLEP, IB, institutional tests. No credit by examination awarded to new students. Number of credit hours awarded for International Baccalaureate determined on case-by-case basis. **Support services:** Learning center, reduced course load, study skills assistance, tutoring.

Majors. **Area/ethnic studies:** Women's. **Biology:** General, biochemistry. **Business:** Accounting, accounting/business management, finance, management information systems, managerial economics, marketing, organizational behavior. **Communications:** General. **Conservation:** Environmental science, environmental studies. **Engineering:** General, civil, computer, electrical, mechanical, physics. **Foreign languages:** Ancient Greek, classics, French, German, Italian, Latin, Spanish. **History:** General. **Interdisciplinary:** Ancient studies, math/computer science. **Liberal arts:** Arts/sciences. **Math:** General. **Philosophy/religion:** Philosophy, religion. **Physical sciences:** Chemistry, physics. **Psychology:** General. **Social sciences:** Anthropology, economics, political science, sociology. **Visual/performing arts:** Art history/conservation, dramatic, studio arts. **Other:** Combined sciences.

Most popular majors. Business/marketing 37%, communications/journalism 6%, engineering/engineering technologies 7%, psychology 7%, social sciences 13%.

Computing on campus. 800 workstations in dormitories, library, computer center, student center. Dormitories wired for high-speed internet access and linked to campus network. Commuter students can connect to campus network. Online course registration, online library, helpline, repair service, student web hosting, wireless network available.

Student life. **Freshman orientation:** Mandatory, $285 fee. Preregistration for classes offered. 2-day session in summer and 2-day session on weekend before school starts. Parents attend separate program. **Housing:** Guaranteed on-campus for freshmen. Coed dorms, apartments available. $250 nonrefundable deposit, deadline 5/1. **Activities:** Bands, campus ministries, choral groups, dance, drama, international student organizations, literary magazine, music ensembles, Model UN, musical theater, opera, radio station, student government, student newspaper, symphony orchestra, Asian Pacific Student Union, Ka Mana'o O Ḫawaii, community action program, Barkada, MECHA, Chinese student association, CORE Christian Fellowship, Engineers Without Borders, political science student association.

Athletics. NCAA. **Intercollegiate:** Baseball M, basketball, cross-country, golf, rowing (crew), soccer, tennis, track and field, volleyball W, water polo. **Intramural:** Badminton, baseball, football (non-tackle), soccer, softball, table tennis, tennis, volleyball. **Team name:** Broncos.

Student services. Alcohol/substance abuse counseling, chaplain/spiritual director, career counseling, student employment services, financial aid counseling, health services, legal services, minority student services, on-campus daycare, personal counseling, placement for graduates, veterans' counselor. **Physically disabled:** Services for visually, speech, hearing impaired.

Contact. Phone: (408) 554-4700 Fax: (408) 554-5255
Sandra Hayes, Dean of Undergraduate Admissions, Santa Clara University, 500 El Camino Real, Santa Clara, CA 95053

School of Urban Missions: Oakland

Oakland, California
www.sum.edu

- Private 4-year Bible college affiliated with Assemblies of God
- Residential campus in very large city
- 71 degree-seeking undergraduates: 3% part-time, 48% women, 27% African American, 30% Asian American, 25% Hispanic American
- 93% of applicants admitted
- Application essay, interview required
- 46% graduate within 6 years; 10% enter graduate study

General. Regionally accredited; also accredited by ABHE. Extensive hands-on ministry training with 8 hours per week of ministry. Additional campus in New Orleans. **Degrees:** 5 bachelor's, 6 associate awarded. **Location:** Downtown. **Calendar:** Trimester, limited summer session. **Full-time faculty:** 3 total; 33% have terminal degrees, 67% minority, 33% women. **Part-time faculty:** 12 total; 17% have terminal degrees, 33% minority, 33% women. **Class size:** 42% < 20, 58% 20-39.

Freshman class profile. 30 applied, 28 admitted, 24 enrolled.

End year in good standing:	70%	**Live on campus:**	90%
Return as sophomores:	65%		

Basis for selection. Recommendations, interview, character/personal qualities are very important. Academic GPA and application essay are considered. Pastor's recommendation and one general recommendation required. **Homeschooled:** Transcript of courses and grades, state high school equivalency certificate, letter of recommendation (nonparent) required.

High school preparation. College-preparatory program recommended. No academic requirement for high school diploma. Minimum 2.0 GPA preferred. If student is below 2.0, the student may be enrolled but with academic probation.

2009-2010 Annual costs. Tuition/fees (projected): $7,155. Room only: $2,400. Books/supplies: $1,500. Personal expenses: $4,675.

2007-2008 Financial aid. **Need-based:** 69% of total undergraduate aid awarded as scholarships/grants, 31% as loans/jobs. **Non-need-based:** Scholarships awarded for academics, leadership, religious affiliation.

Application procedures. **Admission:** Closing date 8/15 (postmark date). $20 fee. Application must be submitted on paper. Admission notification 8/15. Admission notification on a rolling basis beginning on or about 1/1. **Financial aid:** No deadline. FAFSA, institutional form required.

Academics. **Special study options:** Distance learning. **Credit/placement by examination:** AP, CLEP. No credit for life experience in the academic courses. Field ministry credits can be considered life experience. **Support services:** Reduced course load, remedial instruction, tutoring.

Majors. **Theology:** Bible.

Computing on campus. 5 workstations in library. Dormitories wired for high-speed internet access and linked to campus network. Online course registration, online library, wireless network available.

Student life. **Freshman orientation:** Mandatory. Preregistration for classes offered. **Policies:** 2 hours of Christian service required per week. Religious observance required. **Housing:** Guaranteed on-campus for all undergraduates. Single-sex dorms, apartments, wellness housing available. $100 nonrefundable deposit, deadline 8/15. **Activities:** Campus ministries.

Student services. Chaplain/spiritual director, financial aid counseling, health services, personal counseling.

Contact. E-mail: sum@sum.edu
Phone: (510) 567-6174 Toll-free number: (888) 567-6174
Fax: (510) 568-1024
Rev. Kenneth Searle, Academic Dean, School of Urban Missions: Oakland, 735 105th Avenue, Oakland, CA 94603

Scripps College

Claremont, California — **CB member**
www.scrippscollege.edu — **CB code: 4693**

- Private 4-year liberal arts college for women
- Residential campus in large town
- 944 degree-seeking undergraduates: 100% women, 4% African American, 13% Asian American, 8% Hispanic American, 1% Native American, 1% international
- 18 graduate students
- 43% of applicants admitted
- SAT or ACT (ACT writing optional), application essay required
- 83% graduate within 6 years

General. Founded in 1926. Regionally accredited. One of cluster of 5 undergraduate and 2 graduate schools on adjoining campuses. Campuses share facilities. Cross-enrollment available at any of the Claremont colleges: Claremont-McKenna, Harvey Mudd, Pitzer, Pomona, and Scripps. **Degrees:** 185 bachelor's awarded. **ROTC:** Army, Air Force. **Location:** 35 miles from Los Angeles. **Calendar:** Semester, limited summer session. **Full-time faculty:** 81 total; 99% have terminal degrees, 16% minority, 57% women. **Part-time faculty:** 28 total; 79% have terminal degrees, 7% minority, 75% women. **Class size:** 79% < 20, 21% 20-39, less than 1% >100. **Special facilities:** Art slide library, biological field station, humanities museum.

Freshman class profile. 1,931 applied, 837 admitted, 253 enrolled.

Mid 50% test scores		GPA 2.0-2.99:	2%
SAT critical reading:	640-730	Rank in top quarter:	92%
SAT math:	620-710	Rank in top tenth:	70%
SAT writing:	650-730	End year in good standing:	100%
ACT composite:	28-32	Return as sophomores:	95%
GPA 3.75 or higher:	77%	Out-of-state:	60%
GPA 3.50-3.74:	10%	Live on campus:	100%
GPA 3.0-3.49:	11%	International:	3%

Basis for selection. Rigor of high school curriculum, GPA, class rank, aptitude as reflected in standardized testing most important. Essays, recommendations, required graded writing assignment significant. SAT Subject Tests used for placement in language only; institutional language and math exam used for placement. Interviews recommended. Audition recommended for music, dance majors. Portfolio recommended for art majors. **Homeschooled:** Statement describing homeschool structure and mission, transcript of courses and grades, letter of recommendation (nonparent) required. Interview highly recommended. **Learning Disabled:** Documentation of learning disability required.

High school preparation. College-preparatory program recommended. 16 units required. Required units include English 4, mathematics 3, social studies 3, science 3 and foreign language 3.

2008-2009 Annual costs. Tuition/fees: $37,950. Room/board: $11,500. Books/supplies: $800. Personal expenses: $1,000.

2008-2009 Financial aid. Need-based: 157 full-time freshmen applied for aid; 111 were judged to have need; 111 of these received aid. Average need met was 100%. Average scholarship/grant was $31,650; average loan $2,935. 82% of total undergraduate aid awarded as scholarships/grants, 18% as loans/jobs. **Non-need-based:** Awarded to 288 full-time undergraduates, including 68 freshmen. Scholarships awarded for academics, leadership.

Application procedures. Admission: Closing date 1/1 (postmark date). $50 fee, may be waived for applicants with need. Admission notification 4/1. Must reply by 5/1. **Financial aid:** Priority date 1/15, closing date 5/1. FAFSA, CSS PROFILE required. Applicants notified by 4/1; must reply by 5/1.

Academics. Almost half of junior class elects to study abroad for semester or year. **Special study options:** Accelerated study, combined bachelor's/graduate degree, cross-registration, double major, exchange student, independent study, internships, New York semester, student-designed major, study abroad, United Nations semester, Washington semester. Post-baccalaureate pre-medical certificate program, humanities internship program, 3-2 engineering. **Credit/placement by examination:** AP, CLEP, IB, institutional tests. 32 credit hours maximum toward bachelor's degree. SAT Subject Tests recommended for placement. **Support services:** Reduced course load, tutoring, writing center.

Majors. Area/ethnic studies: African-American, American, Asian, Asian-American, European, French, German, Hispanic-American/Latino/Chicano, Italian, Latin American, Spanish/Iberian, women's. **Biology:** General, biochemistry, molecular. **Business:** Accounting, organizational behavior. **Computer sciences:** Computer science. **Conservation:** Environmental science, environmental studies. **Engineering:** General. **Foreign languages:** General, Chinese, classics, French, German, Italian, Japanese, linguistics, Russian, Spanish. **History:** General. **Interdisciplinary:** Biological/physical sciences, neuroscience, science/society. **Legal studies:** General. **Liberal arts:** Humanities. **Math:** General. **Philosophy/religion:** Judaic, philosophy, religion. **Physical sciences:** Chemistry, geology, physics. **Psychology:** General. **Public administration:** Policy analysis. **Social sciences:** Anthropology, econometrics, economics, political science, sociology. **Visual/performing arts:** Art history/conservation, dance, dramatic, film/cinema, studio arts. **Other:** Film/video and photographic arts.

Most popular majors. Area/ethnic studies 14%, biology 7%, interdisciplinary studies 7%, psychology 13%, social sciences 20%, visual/performing arts 16%.

Computing on campus. 72 workstations in dormitories, library, computer center. Dormitories wired for high-speed internet access and linked to campus network. Commuter students can connect to campus network. Online library, helpline, repair service, student web hosting, wireless network available.

Student life. Freshman orientation: Mandatory. 5-day orientation begins last Thursday in August. **Housing:** Guaranteed on-campus for freshmen. Special housing for disabled, apartments, wellness housing available. Most sophomores, most juniors and all seniors have single rooms. Off-campus houses available to single students. **Activities:** Campus ministries, choral groups, dance, drama, international student organizations, literary magazine, music ensembles, Model UN, radio station, student government, student newspaper, symphony orchestra, Asian American Student Union, Cafe Con Leche, Claremont Colleges Ballroom Dance Team, Claremont Colleges Women's Rugby, Criminal Justice Network, Economic Society, International Club, Office of Black Student Affairs, On The Loose, and Scripps Associated Students.

Athletics. NCAA. **Intercollegiate:** Basketball W, cross-country W, diving W, golf W, lacrosse W, soccer W, softball W, swimming W, tennis W, track and field W, volleyball W, water polo W. **Intramural:** Basketball W, soccer W, softball W, volleyball W, water polo W. **Team name:** Athenas.

Student services. Adult student services, chaplain/spiritual director, career counseling, student employment services, financial aid counseling, health services, minority student services, personal counseling, placement for graduates, women's services.

Contact. E-mail: admission@scrippscollege.edu
Phone: (909) 621-8149 Toll-free number: (800) 770-1333
Fax: (909) 607-7508
Laura Stratton, Associate Director, Scripps College, 1030 Columbia Avenue, Claremont, CA 91711-3905

Shasta Bible College and Graduate School
Redding, California
www.shasta.edu

- Private 4-year Bible college
- Small city
- 82 degree-seeking undergraduates

General. Regionally accredited. **Calendar:** Semester. **Full-time faculty:** 7 total. **Part-time faculty:** 31 total.

Freshman class profile. 12 enrolled.

Application procedures. Admission: Closing date 8/29.

Academics. Credit/placement by examination: CLEP.

Majors. Theology: Theology. **Other:** Christian teacher education.

Contact. E-mail: admissions@shasta.edu
Phone: (530) 221-4275
Shasta Bible College and Graduate School, 2951 Goodwater Avenue, Redding, CA 96002

Silicon Valley University
San Jose, California
www.svuca.edu

- Private 4-year business and technical college
- Very large city

General. Accredited by ACICS. **Calendar:** Semester.

Annual costs/financial aid. Tuition/fees (2008-2009): $7,853. Books/supplies: $700.

Contact. Phone: (408) 435-8989 ext. 106
6201 San Ignacio, San Jose, CA 95119

Simpson University
Redding, California
www.simpsonuniversity.edu **CB code: 4698**

- Private 4-year liberal arts college affiliated with Christian and Missionary Alliance
- Residential campus in small city
- 935 degree-seeking undergraduates: 3% part-time, 65% women, 4% African American, 7% Asian American, 6% Hispanic American, 1% Native American
- 209 degree-seeking graduate students
- 58% of applicants admitted
- Application essay required
- 45% graduate within 6 years

General. Founded in 1921. Regionally accredited. Christ-centered educational community. **Degrees:** 227 bachelor's, 2 associate awarded; master's, first professional offered. **ROTC:** Army. **Location:** 170 miles from Sacramento. **Calendar:** Semester, limited summer session. **Full-time faculty:** 44

total; 61% have terminal degrees, 7% minority, 30% women. **Part-time faculty:** 54 total; 39% have terminal degrees, 6% minority, 41% women. **Class size:** 70% < 20, 24% 20-39, 2% 40-49, 3% 50-99.

Freshman class profile. 660 applied, 383 admitted, 154 enrolled.

Mid 50% test scores		**GPA 3.0-3.49:**	36%
SAT critical reading:	460-600	**GPA 2.0-2.99:**	16%
SAT math:	450-580	**Rank in top quarter:**	53%
SAT writing:	450-580	**Rank in top tenth:**	20%
ACT composite:	19-26	**Return as sophomores:**	69%
GPA 3.75 or higher:	32%	**Out-of-state:**	20%
GPA 3.50-3.74:	16%	**Live on campus:**	78%

Basis for selection. Commitment to Jesus Christ as reflected in personal statement and required references, academic achievement, other recommendations, and standardized test scores important. SAT and SAT Subject Tests or ACT recommended. **Homeschooled:** Transcript of courses and grades required.

High school preparation. College-preparatory program recommended. Recommended units include English 4, mathematics 3, social studies 3, science 2 and foreign language 2. College-preparatory program highly recommended.

2008-2009 Annual costs. Tuition/fees: $19,500. Room/board: $6,700. Books/supplies: $1,392. Personal expenses: $1,968.

2007-2008 Financial aid. Non-need-based: Scholarships awarded for academics, alumni affiliation, athletics, leadership, minority status, music/drama, religious affiliation, state residency. **Additional information:** Work-study programs available.

Application procedures. Admission: No deadline. $40 fee, may be waived for applicants with need. Admission notification on a rolling basis. Must reply by May 1 or within 2 week(s) if notified thereafter. **Financial aid:** Priority date 3/2; no closing date. FAFSA, institutional form required. Applicants notified on a rolling basis starting 3/1; must reply within 4 week(s) of notification.

Academics. 34-semester-hour teacher credential program permits students to earn California Clear Credential for grades K-8 (multiple subjects) or for grades 7-12 (single subject). **Special study options:** Accelerated study, combined bachelor's/graduate degree, distance learning, double major, honors, independent study, internships, student-designed major, study abroad, teacher certification program, Washington semester, weekend college. **Credit/placement by examination:** AP, CLEP, SAT, ACT, institutional tests. 30 credit hours maximum toward bachelor's degree. Credit by examination granted only to enrolled students. Students may take challenge exam for particular course only once. **Support services:** Reduced course load, remedial instruction, study skills assistance, tutoring, writing center.

Majors. Biology: General. **Business:** Accounting, business admin, management information systems, organizational behavior. **Communications:** General. **Education:** Elementary, English, mathematics, music, social science. **Health:** Health care admin. **History:** General. **Liberal arts:** Arts/sciences. **Math:** General. **Parks/recreation:** General. **Philosophy/religion:** Christian, religion. **Psychology:** General. **Social sciences:** General. **Theology:** Bible, missionary, pastoral counseling, theology, youth ministry.

Most popular majors. Business/marketing 24%, health sciences 7%, liberal arts 19%, psychology 26%, theological studies 10%.

Computing on campus. 50 workstations in dormitories, library, computer center. Dormitories wired for high-speed internet access and linked to campus network. Commuter students can connect to campus network. Online course registration, online library, helpline, repair service, wireless network available.

Student life. Freshman orientation: Mandatory. Preregistration for classes offered. Sessions include placement tests. **Policies:** All single undergraduates under 22 required to live on campus. Request for off-campus living must be approved by Vice President for Student Development. Religious observance required. **Housing:** Guaranteed on-campus for all undergraduates. Single-sex dorms, special housing for disabled, apartments, wellness housing available. $100 fully refundable deposit, deadline 9/1. **Activities:** Jazz band, choral groups, dance, drama, film society, music ensembles, student government, student newspaper, symphony orchestra, Asian Fellowship, Hispanic Fellowship, summer missions teams, chapel worship team, spiritual action committee, psychology club, Missionary Kids Association, commuter student association.

Athletics. NAIA, NCCAA. **Intercollegiate:** Baseball M, basketball, cross-country, golf, soccer, softball W, volleyball W. **Intramural:** Basketball, football (non-tackle), soccer. **Team name:** Red Hawks.

Student services. Adult student services, chaplain/spiritual director, career counseling, student employment services, financial aid counseling, health services, minority student services, personal counseling, veterans' counselor. **Physically disabled:** Services for visually, speech, hearing impaired.

Contact. E-mail: admissions@simpsonuniversity.edu
Phone: (530) 226-4606 Toll-free number: (800) 598-2493
Fax: (530) 226-4861
James Herberger, Director of Enrollment Management, Simpson University, 2211 College View Drive, Redding, CA 96003-8606

Soka University of America

Aliso Viejo, California — **CB member**
www.soka.edu — **CB code: 4066**

- Private 4-year university and liberal arts college
- Residential campus in large town
- 388 degree-seeking undergraduates: 63% women, 3% African American, 21% Asian American, 5% Hispanic American, 45% international
- 6 degree-seeking graduate students
- 52% of applicants admitted
- SAT or ACT with writing, application essay required

General. Degrees: 88 bachelor's awarded; master's offered. **Location:** 70 miles from Los Angeles, 75 miles from San Diego. **Calendar:** Semester. **Full-time faculty:** 38 total; 95% have terminal degrees, 32% minority, 45% women. **Part-time faculty:** 17 total; 53% have terminal degrees, 53% minority, 65% women. **Class size:** 100% < 20.

Freshman class profile. 355 applied, 184 admitted, 127 enrolled.

Mid 50% test scores		**GPA 2.0-2.99:**	3%
SAT critical reading:	440-660	**Rank in top quarter:**	80%
SAT math:	520-720	**Rank in top tenth:**	43%
SAT writing:	490-630	**End year in good standing:**	97%
ACT composite:	23-24	**Return as sophomores:**	100%
GPA 3.75 or higher:	37%	**Out-of-state:**	60%
GPA 3.50-3.74:	38%	**Live on campus:**	99%
GPA 3.0-3.49:	22%	**International:**	43%

Basis for selection. GPA and courses most important. Test scores, essay, recommendations, extracurricular activities also important. **Homeschooled:** State high school equivalency certificate required. Program must be accredited by regional, state, or national agency. **Learning Disabled:** Admission decisions do not consider learning disabilities. Special needs discussed only after student has been admitted and has identified need.

High school preparation. 17 units recommended. Recommended units include English 4, mathematics 3, social studies 2, history 2, science 2 (laboratory 2) and foreign language 2.

2009-2010 Annual costs. Tuition/fees: $24,606. Room/board: $9,360. Books/supplies: $1,000. Personal expenses: $1,500.

2007-2008 Financial aid. Need-based: 101 full-time freshmen applied for aid; 101 were judged to have need; 91 of these received aid. Average need met was 85%. Average scholarship/grant was $12,000; average loan $3,500. 82% of total undergraduate aid awarded as scholarships/grants, 18% as loans/jobs. **Non-need-based:** Awarded to 175 full-time undergraduates, including 9 freshmen. Scholarships awarded for academics, athletics.

Application procedures. Admission: Closing date 1/15 (postmark date). $45 fee. Admission notification 3/15. Must reply by 5/1. **Financial aid:** Closing date 3/1. FAFSA required. Applicants notified on a rolling basis starting 3/15; must reply within 4 week(s) of notification.

Academics. Study abroad required of all students during one semester of their junior year. **Special study options:** ESL, independent study, internships, study abroad. **Credit/placement by examination:** CLEP, SAT, ACT, institutional tests. **Support services:** Study skills assistance, tutoring, writing center.

Majors. Liberal arts: Arts/sciences.

Computing on campus. PC or laptop required. 100 workstations in dormitories, library, computer center. Dormitories wired for high-speed internet access and linked to campus network. Commuter students can connect to campus network. Online course registration, online library, helpline, repair service, wireless network available.

Student life. Freshman orientation: Mandatory. Preregistration for classes offered. 4-day orientation period before upperclassmen arrive. **Housing:** Guaranteed on-campus for all undergraduates. Coed dorms, wellness housing available. Students required to live on campus. **Activities:** Jazz band, choral groups, dance, film society, literary magazine, music ensembles, Model UN, student government, student newspaper, Amnesty International, Buena Vista social club, Chinese club, Green Planet, Humanism in Action, orchestra club, Activist Collective, French club.

Athletics. NAIA. **Intercollegiate:** Cross-country, soccer, swimming, track and field. **Intramural:** Badminton, basketball, racquetball, soccer, tennis, volleyball, weight lifting. **Team name:** Lions.

Student services. Alcohol/substance abuse counseling, career counseling, student employment services, financial aid counseling, health services, personal counseling, placement for graduates. **Physically disabled:** Services for visually, hearing impaired.

Contact. E-mail: admission@soka.edu
Phone: (949) 480-4150 Toll-free number: (888) 600-7652
Fax: (949) 480-4151
Christopher Brown, Director of Admission and Financial Aid, Soka University of America, One University Drive, Aliso Viejo, CA 92656-8081

Sonoma State University
Rohnert Park, California
www.sonoma.edu **CB code: 4723**

- Public 4-year university and liberal arts college
- Commuter campus in large town
- 7,709 degree-seeking undergraduates: 11% part-time, 61% women, 2% African American, 5% Asian American, 12% Hispanic American, 1% Native American, 1% international
- 702 degree-seeking graduate students
- 76% of applicants admitted
- SAT or ACT (ACT writing optional) required
- 56% graduate within 6 years

General. Founded in 1960. Regionally accredited. **Degrees:** 1,644 bachelor's awarded; master's offered. **ROTC:** Army, Naval, Air Force. **Location:** 50 miles from San Francisco, 10 miles from Santa Rosa. **Calendar:** Semester, extensive summer session. **Full-time faculty:** 274 total; 90% have terminal degrees, 16% minority, 46% women. **Part-time faculty:** 353 total; 26% have terminal degrees, 10% minority, 60% women. **Class size:** 39% < 20, 44% 20-39, 8% 40-49, 8% 50-99, 2% >100. **Special facilities:** Observatory, performing arts center, nature preserves, information technology center.

Freshman class profile. 12,240 applied, 9,280 admitted, 1,655 enrolled.

Mid 50% test scores		**GPA 3.0-3.49:**	46%
SAT critical reading:	450-550	**GPA 2.0-2.99:**	35%
SAT math:	460-570	**Return as sophomores:**	74%
ACT composite:	20-24	**Out-of-state:**	1%
GPA 3.75 or higher:	7%	**Live on campus:**	92%
GPA 3.50-3.74:	12%	**International:**	1%

Basis for selection. School GPA and test scores most important. SAT, ACT, SAT Subject Tests must be received before start of term. Audition required of music majors. Portfolio required of art majors. RN required for graduate nursing. **Learning Disabled:** Applicants with disabilities strongly encouraged to complete college preparatory course requirements if at all possible. If applicant judged unable to fulfill specific course requirement because of disability, alternative college preparatory courses may be substituted for specific subject requirements.

High school preparation. College-preparatory program required. 15 units required. Required units include English 4, mathematics 3, history 2, science 2 (laboratory 1), foreign language 2, visual/performing arts 1 and academic electives 1. One visual and performing arts, US government required.

2008-2009 Annual costs. Tuition/fees: $4,272; $14,442 out-of-state. Room/board: $10,115. Books/supplies: $1,656. Personal expenses: $2,826.

2007-2008 Financial aid. Need-based: 683 full-time freshmen applied for aid; 413 were judged to have need; 336 of these received aid. Average need met was 65%. Average scholarship/grant was $7,117; average loan $3,100. 53% of total undergraduate aid awarded as scholarships/grants, 47% as loans/jobs. **Non-need-based:** Awarded to 501 full-time undergraduates, including 91 freshmen. Scholarships awarded for academics, alumni affiliation, art, athletics, leadership, minority status, music/drama.

Application procedures. Admission: Priority date 11/30; deadline 11/30 (postmark date). $55 fee, may be waived for applicants with need. Admission notification 3/1. Admission notification on a rolling basis beginning on or about 11/1. Must reply by 5/1. **Financial aid:** Priority date 1/31; no closing date. FAFSA required. Applicants notified on a rolling basis starting 3/15; must reply within 2 week(s) of notification.

Academics. Special study options: Accelerated study, combined bachelor's/graduate degree, cross-registration, distance learning, double major, dual enrollment of high school students, ESL, exchange student, external degree, honors, independent study, internships, liberal arts/career combination, New York semester, semester at sea, student-designed major, study abroad, teacher certification program, United Nations semester, urban semester, Washington semester. Combined degree programs: bachelor's/MBA; bachelor's/MPA. **Credit/placement by examination:** AP, CLEP, SAT, ACT, institutional tests. 30 credit hours maximum toward bachelor's degree. **Support services:** Learning center, pre-admission summer program, reduced course load, remedial instruction, study skills assistance, tutoring, writing center.

Majors. Area/ethnic studies: African-American, Hispanic-American/Latino/Chicano, women's. **Biology:** General, biochemistry. **Business:** Business admin. **Communications:** General. **Computer sciences:** Computer science, programming. **Conservation:** General, environmental studies. **Engineering:** Computer. **Family/consumer sciences:** Family studies. **Foreign languages:** French, German, Spanish. **Health:** Nursing (RN). **History:** General. **Interdisciplinary:** Global studies. **Liberal arts:** Arts/sciences. **Math:** General. **Philosophy/religion:** Philosophy. **Physical sciences:** Chemistry, geology, physics. **Protective services:** Law enforcement admin. **Psychology:** General. **Social sciences:** Anthropology, economics, geography, political science, sociology. **Visual/performing arts:** General, art history/conservation, dramatic, studio arts.

Most popular majors. Business/marketing 19%, communications/journalism 6%, liberal arts 8%, psychology 14%, social sciences 14%, visual/performing arts 6%.

Computing on campus. PC or laptop required. 400 workstations in library, computer center. Dormitories wired for high-speed internet access and linked to campus network. Commuter students can connect to campus network. Online course registration, online library, helpline, student web hosting, wireless network available.

Student life. Freshman orientation: Available. Preregistration for classes offered. 2-day residential program in June. Parents invited. **Housing:** Guaranteed on-campus for freshmen. Coed dorms, apartments, wellness housing available. $1,000 partly refundable deposit. Focus learning communities, freshman seminar, healthy living, women in math/science dorms available. **Activities:** Jazz band, choral groups, dance, drama, literary magazine, music ensembles, Model UN, musical theater, opera, radio station, student government, student newspaper, symphony orchestra, Student Advocates for Education, College Republicans, Asian Pacific Islander Organization, Raza Native American Council, El Movimiento Estudiantil Chicano/a de Aztlan, InterVarsity Christian Fellowship, Hillel, Best Buddies, Student Ambassadors.

Athletics. NCAA. **Intercollegiate:** Baseball M, basketball, golf, soccer, softball W, tennis, track and field W, volleyball W, water polo W. **Intramural:** Basketball, football (non-tackle), soccer, softball, volleyball. **Team name:** Sea Wolves.

Student services. Adult student services, alcohol/substance abuse counseling, career counseling, services for economically disadvantaged, student employment services, financial aid counseling, health services, minority student services, on-campus daycare, personal counseling, placement for graduates, veterans' counselor, women's services. **Physically disabled:** Services for visually, speech, hearing impaired.

Contact. Phone: (707) 664-2778 Fax: (707) 664-2060
Gustavo Flores, Director, Admissions, Sonoma State University, 1801 East Cotati Avenue, Rohnert Park, CA 94928-3609

Southern California Institute of Architecture
Los Angeles, California
www.sciarc.edu **CB code: 1575**

- Private 5-year visual arts college
- Commuter campus in very large city
- 278 degree-seeking undergraduates: 31% women
- 230 degree-seeking graduate students
- 80% of applicants admitted
- SAT or ACT (ACT writing optional), application essay required

General. Founded in 1972. Regionally accredited. **Degrees:** 93 bachelor's awarded; master's offered. **Location:** Downtown. **Calendar:** Semester, limited summer session. **Part-time faculty:** 80 total. **Special facilities:** Media center, architecture gallery, woodshop and modelmaking center, metal fabrication shop, graphics center, CNC Milling, 3D printers, laser cutter.

Freshman class profile. 124 applied, 99 admitted, 42 enrolled.

Basis for selection. School achievement record, test scores, portfolio, recommendations, and statement of purpose. Portfolio required.

High school preparation. College-preparatory program recommended. Art design and architecture courses recommended.

2009-2010 Annual costs. Tuition/fees: $24,000. International student fee (one-time only) $500. International student mandatory health insurance premium $822 per year. Books/supplies: $1,400.

2008-2009 Financial aid. Non-need-based: Scholarships awarded for academics, state residency.

Application procedures. Admission: Closing date 2/1 (postmark date). $60 fee, may be waived for applicants with need. Application must be submitted on paper. Admission notification on a rolling basis beginning on or about 4/1. Applicants must reply within 3 weeks of notification. **Financial aid:** No deadline. FAFSA, institutional form required. Must reply within 2 week(s) of notification.

Academics. Intensive summer session on introduction to architecture offered to graduates and high school students. **Special study options:** Exchange student, internships, study abroad. SCI-Arc study abroad programs in Switzerland and Japan; exchange programs in Japan, Australia, England, Israel, Netherlands, France, Mexico. **Credit/placement by examination:** AP, CLEP, institutional tests. **Support services:** Pre-admission summer program.

Majors. Architecture: Architecture.

Computing on campus. PC or laptop required. 60 workstations in library, computer center. Commuter students can connect to campus network. Online course registration, helpline, wireless network available.

Student life. Freshman orientation: Mandatory. Held right before school begins. **Policies:** Informal weekly gathering of entire school sponsored by student government. **Activities:** Student government, Architects, Designers, and Planners for Social Responsibility, American Institute of Architects student affiliation, Women in Architecture.

Student services. Career counseling, financial aid counseling, personal counseling, veterans' counselor. **Physically disabled:** Services for speech, hearing impaired.

Contact. E-mail: admissions@sciarc.edu
Phone: (213) 613-2200 ext. 320 Fax: (213) 613-2260
J.J. Jackman, Director of Admission, Southern California Institute of Architecture, 960 East Third Street, Los Angeles, CA 90013

Southern California Institute of Technology

Anaheim, California
www.scit-scu.edu **CB code: 3034**

- For-profit 4-year business and engineering college
- Residential campus in large city
- 501 degree-seeking undergraduates
- Interview required

General. Accredited by ACCSCT. **Degrees:** 34 bachelor's, 1 associate awarded. **Calendar:** Continuous, extensive summer session. **Full-time faculty:** 16 total.

Freshman class profile. 254 applied, 214 admitted, 214 enrolled.

Basis for selection. Open admission, but selective for some programs. Interview required. High School Diploma, GED, Official transcripts from other schools attended, standardized entrance exam required. Wonderlic required. **Homeschooled:** Transcript of courses and grades, interview required.

2008-2009 Annual costs. Tuition/fees: $14,670. Tuition and fees quoted for electronic engineering program. Costs vary by program. Books/supplies: $2,500.

2007-2008 Financial aid. Need-based: 36% of total undergraduate aid awarded as scholarships/grants, 64% as loans/jobs.

Application procedures. Admission: No deadline. $100 fee. Application must be submitted on paper.

Academics. Special study options: Accelerated study, combined bachelor's/graduate degree, cooperative education, double major, ESL, liberal arts/career combination. **Credit/placement by examination:** CLEP. **Support services:** Tutoring.

Majors. Business: Business admin. **Engineering:** Electrical.

Student life. Freshman orientation: Available. Preregistration for classes offered.

Student services. Career counseling, financial aid counseling, placement for graduates.

Contact. E-mail: admissions@scit-scu.edu
Phone: (714) 300-0300 Fax: (714) 300-0310
Jodell Pinesett, Dean of Admissions, Southern California Institute of Technology, 222 South Harbor Boulevard, Suite 200, Anaheim, CA 92805

Southern California Seminary

El Cajon, California
www.socalsem.edu

- Private 4-year Bible and seminary college
- Small city
- 69 degree-seeking undergraduates

General. Regionally accredited. **Calendar:** Trimester. **Full-time faculty:** 10 total. **Part-time faculty:** 34 total.

Basis for selection. Open admission, but selective for some programs.

Application procedures. Financial aid: Closing date 8/7.

Academics. Credit/placement by examination: CLEP.

Majors. Theology: Bible.

Contact. E-mail: admissions@socalsem.edu
Phone: (619) 590-2129
Southern California Seminary, 2075 East Madison Avenue, El Cajon, CA 92019

Stanford University

Stanford, California **CB member**
www.stanford.edu **CB code: 4704**

- Private 4-year university
- Residential campus in small city
- 6,502 degree-seeking undergraduates: 49% women, 10% African American, 23% Asian American, 12% Hispanic American, 3% Native American, 7% international
- 8,430 degree-seeking graduate students
- 9% of applicants admitted
- SAT or ACT with writing, application essay required
- 94% graduate within 6 years; 34% enter graduate study

General. Founded in 1885. Regionally accredited. Research university with seven schools: Business, Earth Sciences, Education, Engineering, Humanities and Sciences, Law, and Medicine. **Degrees:** 1,646 bachelor's awarded; master's, doctoral, first professional offered. **ROTC:** Army, Naval, Air Force. **Location:** 29 miles from San Francisco. **Calendar:** Quarter, extensive summer session. **Full-time faculty:** 984 total; 98% have terminal degrees, 18% minority, 24% women. **Part-time faculty:** 18 total; 83% have terminal degrees, 6% women. **Class size:** 72% < 20, 12% 20-39, 4% 40-49, 7% 50-99, 5% >100. **Special facilities:** Linear accelerator, 18 libraries, nature preserve, marine research center, Rodin sculpture garden, two art galleries, observatory, 10 overseas campuses, medical center.

Freshman class profile. 25,299 applied, 2,400 admitted, 1,703 enrolled.

Mid 50% test scores		**GPA 3.0-3.49:**	4%
SAT critical reading:	650-760	**Rank in top quarter:**	99%
SAT math:	680-780	**Rank in top tenth:**	92%
SAT writing:	670-760	**Return as sophomores:**	98%
ACT composite:	30-34	**Out-of-state:**	64%
GPA 3.75 or higher:	87%	**Live on campus:**	100%
GPA 3.50-3.74:	9%	**International:**	7%

Basis for selection. School achievement record, test scores, extracurricular activities, teacher and counselor evaluations, and personal qualifications most important. Rigor and variety of academic program very important. Personal qualities also considered. SAT Subject Tests recommended. Arts students may submit supplementary materials for review. Submissions should have previously received significant recognition at regional, state, national or international level. **Homeschooled:** Statement describing homeschool structure and mission required. Standardized test scores important. Subject tests recommended. **Learning Disabled:** Prospective students with disabilities are encouraged to meet with Disability Resource Center staff members.

High school preparation. 20 units recommended. Recommended units include English 4, mathematics 4, social studies 2, history 1, science 3 (laboratory 3) and foreign language 3.

2008-2009 Annual costs. Tuition/fees: $36,030. Room/board: $11,182. Books/supplies: $1,455. Personal expenses: $2,325.

2007-2008 Financial aid. All financial aid based on need. 1,020 full-time freshmen applied for aid; 761 were judged to have need; 756 of these received aid. Average need met was 100%. Average scholarship/grant was $31,794; average loan $2,401. 92% of total undergraduate aid awarded as scholarships/grants, 8% as loans/jobs.

Application procedures. **Admission:** Closing date 1/1 (postmark date). $75 fee, may be waived for applicants with need. Admission notification 4/1. Must reply by 5/1. Early action candidates may not apply to other schools under any type of early action, early decision, or early notification program, but can apply under regular admissions. **Financial aid:** Priority date 2/15; no closing date. FAFSA, CSS PROFILE required. Applicants notified on a rolling basis starting 4/3; must reply by 5/1.

Academics. Undergraduate academic offerings stress access to senior faculty through small-group learning experiences and research opportunities. **Special study options:** Combined bachelor's/graduate degree, distance learning, double major, exchange student, honors, independent study, internships, student-designed major, study abroad, Washington semester. Summer research college. **Credit/placement by examination:** AP, CLEP, IB, institutional tests. 45 Advanced Placement units allowed. **Support services:** Learning center, pre-admission summer program, study skills assistance, tutoring, writing center.

Majors. **Area/ethnic studies:** African, African-American, American, Asian-American, East Asian, German, Hispanic-American/Latino/Chicano, Native American, women's. **Biology:** General. **Communications:** General. **Computer sciences:** General, computer science. **Conservation:** Environmental science. **Engineering:** General, chemical, civil, electrical, environmental, materials, materials science, mechanical, petroleum. **Engineering technology:** Industrial management. **Foreign languages:** Chinese, classics, comparative lit, French, German, Italian, Japanese, linguistics, Slavic, Spanish. **History:** General. **Interdisciplinary:** Global studies, intercultural, math/computer science, science/society, systems science. **Liberal arts:** Humanities. **Math:** General. **Philosophy/religion:** Philosophy, religion. **Physical sciences:** Chemistry, geology, geophysics, physics. **Psychology:** General. **Public administration:** Policy analysis. **Social sciences:** Anthropology, archaeology, economics, international relations, political science, sociology, urban studies. **Visual/performing arts:** Art, dramatic, studio arts.

Most popular majors. Biology 8%, engineering/engineering technologies 16%, interdisciplinary studies 14%, social sciences 26%.

Computing on campus. 1,000 workstations in dormitories, library, computer center, student center. Dormitories wired for high-speed internet access and linked to campus network. Commuter students can connect to campus network. Online course registration, online library, helpline, repair service, student web hosting, wireless network available.

Student life. **Freshman orientation:** Mandatory, $438 fee. 6-day academically oriented program held in late September. **Housing:** Guaranteed on-campus for all undergraduates. Coed dorms, single-sex dorms, special housing for disabled, apartments, cooperative housing, fraternity/sorority housing available. **Activities:** Bands, campus ministries, choral groups, dance, drama, film society, international student organizations, literary magazine, music ensembles, Model UN, musical theater, opera, radio station, student government, student newspaper, symphony orchestra, TV station, approximately 600 student groups.

Athletics. NCAA. **Intercollegiate:** Baseball M, basketball, cross-country, diving, fencing, field hockey W, football (tackle) M, golf, gymnastics, lacrosse W, rowing (crew), sailing, soccer, softball W, squash W, swimming, synchronized swimming W, tennis, track and field, volleyball, water polo, wrestling M. **Intramural:** Archery, badminton, basketball, bowling, football (non-tackle), handball, soccer, softball, table tennis, tennis, triathlon, volleyball. **Team name:** Cardinal.

Student services. Alcohol/substance abuse counseling, chaplain/spiritual director, career counseling, student employment services, financial aid counseling, health services, legal services, minority student services, on-campus daycare, personal counseling, placement for graduates, women's services. **Physically disabled:** Services for visually, speech, hearing impaired. **Learning disabled:** Comprehensive services available.

Contact. E-mail: admission@stanford.edu
Phone: (650) 723-2091 Fax: (650) 723-6050
Richard Shaw, Dean of Undergraduate Admission and Financial Aid, Stanford University, Montag Hall, Stanford, CA 94305-6106

Thomas Aquinas College

Santa Paula, California
www.thomasaquinas.edu
CB member
CB code: 4828

- Private 4-year liberal arts college affiliated with Roman Catholic Church
- Residential campus in rural community
- 340 degree-seeking undergraduates: 52% women, 3% Asian American, 8% Hispanic American, 2% Native American, 7% international
- 64% of applicants admitted
- SAT or ACT (ACT writing optional), application essay required
- 69% graduate within 6 years; 20% enter graduate study

General. Founded in 1971. Regionally accredited. **Degrees:** 80 bachelor's awarded. **Location:** 5 miles from Santa Paula, 20 miles from Ventura. **Calendar:** Semester. **Full-time faculty:** 27 total; 67% have terminal degrees, 7% women. **Part-time faculty:** 8 total; 50% have terminal degrees. **Class size:** 100% < 20. **Special facilities:** Walking trails, hiking trails into the Los Padres National Forest.

Freshman class profile. 232 applied, 149 admitted, 102 enrolled.

Mid 50% test scores		**GPA 2.0-2.99:**	7%
SAT critical reading:	600-720	**Rank in top quarter:**	75%
SAT math:	550-640	**Rank in top tenth:**	75%
SAT writing:	600-680	**End year in good standing:**	87%
ACT composite:	26-28	**Return as sophomores:**	85%
GPA 3.75 or higher:	52%	**Out-of-state:**	64%
GPA 3.50-3.74:	25%	**Live on campus:**	100%
GPA 3.0-3.49:	16%	**International:**	10%

Basis for selection. Faculty Admission Committee reviews each applicant for evidence of likely success in all parts of 4-year program. Required essays and 3 letters of reference supplement academic records and test scores. Test scores are accepted on a rolling basis throughout the year. Interview recommended for early admissions applicants, for those whose academic preparation is non-traditional, and for those who have been out of high school for a significant period of time. **Homeschooled:** Applicants not home schooled through formal programs must provide written records of all studies from grades 9 through 12.

High school preparation. College-preparatory program recommended. 13 units required; 16 recommended. Required and recommended units include English 4, mathematics 3-4, history 2, science 2-3 (laboratory 2), foreign language 2 and academic electives 3.

2009-2010 Annual costs. Tuition/fees: $22,400. Room/board: $7,400. Books/supplies: $450. Personal expenses: $2,250.

2008-2009 Financial aid. All financial aid based on need. 74 full-time freshmen applied for aid; 68 were judged to have need; 68 of these received aid. Average need met was 100%. Average scholarship/grant was $11,916; average loan $3,036. 62% of total undergraduate aid awarded as scholarships/grants, 38% as loans/jobs.

Application procedures. **Admission:** No deadline. No application fee. Application must be submitted on paper. Admission notification on a rolling basis beginning on or about 10/1. Must reply by May 1 or within 1 week(s) if notified thereafter. **Financial aid:** Closing date 3/2. FAFSA, institutional form required. Applicants notified on a rolling basis starting 1/1; must reply by 5/1 or within 2 week(s) of notification.

Academics. Great Books curriculum. **Special study options:** Cross-disciplinary curriculum of liberal education through reading and analyzing the "Great Books," with special emphasis on theology, philosophy, math, laboratory science, and literature. **Credit/placement by examination:** CLEP. **Support services:** Tutoring.

Majors. **Liberal arts:** Arts/sciences.

Computing on campus. 17 workstations in dormitories, library, computer center, student center. Dormitories linked to campus network.

Student life. **Freshman orientation:** Mandatory. Preregistration for classes offered. 2-day program immediately before classes begin. **Housing:** Guaranteed on-campus for all undergraduates. Single-sex dorms available. All housing is alcohol/drug/smoke-free. **Activities:** Campus ministries, choral groups, dance, drama, literary magazine, music ensembles, musical theater,

Pro-life group, Legion of Mary, Third Order Dominican, Habitat for Humanity.

Athletics. Intramural: Basketball, football (non-tackle) M, soccer, softball, table tennis, tennis, volleyball.

Student services. Alcohol/substance abuse counseling, chaplain/spiritual director, career counseling, financial aid counseling, health services, personal counseling, placement for graduates.

Contact. E-mail: admissions@thomasaquinas.edu
Phone: (805) 525-4417 Toll-free number: (800) 634-9797
Fax: (805) 421-5905
Jonathan Daly, Director of Admission, Thomas Aquinas College, 10000 North Ojai Road, Santa Paula, CA 93060-9621

University of California: Berkeley

Berkeley, California **CB member**
www.berkeley.edu **CB code: 4833**

- Public 4-year university
- Residential campus in small city
- 25,151 degree-seeking undergraduates: 3% part-time, 53% women, 4% African American, 42% Asian American, 12% Hispanic American, 4% international
- 10,245 degree-seeking graduate students
- 22% of applicants admitted
- SAT and SAT Subject Tests or ACT with writing, SAT Subject Tests, application essay required
- 90% graduate within 6 years

General. Founded in 1868. Regionally accredited. **Degrees:** 6,960 bachelor's awarded; master's, doctoral, first professional offered. **ROTC:** Army, Naval, Air Force. **Location:** 10 miles from San Francisco. **Calendar:** Semester, extensive summer session. **Full-time faculty:** 1,630 total. **Part-time faculty:** 593 total. **Class size:** 62% < 20, 21% 20-39, 3% 40-49, 7% 50-99, 7% >100. **Special facilities:** Museums of art, anthropology, archaeology, paleontology and vertebrate zoology, film archive, science museum and research center for K-12 education, botanical garden, libraries of rare books, Western and Latin Americana, seismographic station, herbacia, performing arts facilities.

Freshman class profile. 48,263 applied, 10,454 admitted, 4,261 enrolled.

Mid 50% test scores			
SAT critical reading:	580-710	GPA 3.0-3.49:	3%
SAT math:	630-760	GPA 2.0-2.99:	1%
SAT writing:	600-720	Rank in top quarter:	100%
GPA 3.75 or higher:	93%	Rank in top tenth:	98%
GPA 3.50-3.74:	3%	Out-of-state:	9%
		International:	8%

Basis for selection. Thorough review of academic performance; likely contribution to the intellectual and cultural vitality of the campus; diversity in personal background and experience; demonstrated qualities in leadership, motivation, concern for others and community; non-academic achievement in the performing arts, athletics or employment; demonstrated interest in major. All applicants must complete 2 SAT Subject Tests in different subject areas. If Math SAT Subject Test is taken, must be Level 2. Test scores must meet criteria determined by the applicant's residency and high school GPA.

High school preparation. College-preparatory program required. 15 units required; 18 recommended. Required and recommended units include English 4, mathematics 3-4, history 2, (laboratory 2-3), foreign language 2-3, visual/performing arts 1 and academic electives 1. 2 units in history or social sciences are required.

2008-2009 Annual costs. Tuition/fees: $7,656; $28,264 out-of-state. Room/board: $14,494. Books/supplies: $1,268. Personal expenses: $1,296.

2008-2009 Financial aid. Non-need-based: Scholarships awarded for academics.

Application procedures. Admission: Closing date 11/30. $60 fee, may be waived for applicants with need. Freshman letters mailed by 3/31, and on-line decisions posted on 3/31. Must reply by 5/1. **Financial aid:** Closing date 3/2. FAFSA required. Applicants notified by 4/15.

Academics. All students required to pass one American cultures class. **Special study options:** Accelerated study, cross-registration, double major, dual enrollment of high school students, ESL, exchange student, honors, independent study, internships, student-designed major, study abroad, teacher certification program. Freshman seminar, undergraduate research apprenticeship, university research expeditions. **Credit/placement by examination:** AP, CLEP, institutional tests. **Support services:** Learning center, preadmission summer program, reduced course load, study skills assistance, tutoring.

Majors. Architecture: Architecture, landscape. **Area/ethnic studies:** African-American, American, Asian, Asian-American, Hispanic-American/Latino/Chicano, Latin American, Native American, Near/Middle Eastern, Southeast Asian, women's. **Biology:** General, botany, cellular/molecular, microbiology, toxicology. **Business:** Business admin. **Communications:** Media studies. **Computer sciences:** Computer science. **Conservation:** General, environmental science, environmental studies, forest management, forestry, management/policy. **Engineering:** Biomedical, chemical, civil, electrical, environmental, geological, manufacturing, materials science, mechanical, nuclear, operations research, physics, science. **Foreign languages:** Ancient Greek, Celtic, Chinese, classics, comparative lit, Dutch/Flemish, French, German, Italian, Japanese, Latin, linguistics, Scandinavian, Slavic, Spanish. **History:** General. **Interdisciplinary:** Classical/archaeology, cognitive science, nutrition sciences, peace/conflict. **Legal studies:** General. **Math:** General, applied, statistics. **Philosophy/religion:** Philosophy, religion. **Physical sciences:** General, astrophysics, atmospheric science, chemistry, geology, geophysics, oceanography, physics. **Psychology:** General. **Public administration:** Social work. **Social sciences:** Anthropology, economics, geography, political science, sociology, urban studies. **Visual/performing arts:** Art, art history/conservation, dance, dramatic, film/cinema.

Most popular majors. Biology 13%, engineering/engineering technologies 11%, English 6%, social sciences 20%.

Computing on campus. Dormitories wired for high-speed internet access and linked to campus network. Commuter students can connect to campus network. Online course registration, online library, helpline, repair service available.

Student life. Freshman orientation: Available, $50 fee. Preregistration for classes offered. **Housing:** Guaranteed on-campus for freshmen. Coed dorms, single-sex dorms, special housing for disabled, apartments, cooperative housing, fraternity/sorority housing available. $300 partly refundable deposit, deadline 5/25. **Activities:** Bands, choral groups, dance, drama, film society, international student organizations, literary magazine, music ensembles, Model UN, musical theater, radio station, student government, student newspaper, symphony orchestra, TV station, Asian American Christian fellowship, black recruitment and retention center, hiking and outdoor society, Americorps, forensics, Chabad, lesbian and gay alliance, Raza recruitment and retention center, College Democrats, College Republicans.

Athletics. NCAA. **Intercollegiate:** Baseball M, basketball, cross-country, diving, field hockey W, football (tackle) M, golf, gymnastics, lacrosse W, rowing (crew), rugby M, soccer, softball W, swimming, tennis, track and field, volleyball W, water polo. **Intramural:** Basketball, bowling, fencing, field hockey M, football (tackle), handball, ice hockey, lacrosse, racquetball, rowing (crew), sailing, skiing, soccer, softball, squash, tennis, volleyball M. **Team name:** Bears.

Student services. Adult student services, alcohol/substance abuse counseling, chaplain/spiritual director, career counseling, services for economically disadvantaged, student employment services, financial aid counseling, health services, legal services, minority student services, on-campus daycare, personal counseling, placement for graduates, veterans' counselor, women's services. **Physically disabled:** Services for visually, speech, hearing impaired.

Contact. Phone: (510) 642-3175
Walter Robinson, Director Undergraduate Admissions, University of California: Berkeley, 110 Sproul Hall, #5800, Berkeley, CA 94720-5800

University of California: Davis

Davis, California **CB member**
www.ucdavis.edu **CB code: 4834**

- Public 4-year university
- Residential campus in small city
- 24,017 degree-seeking undergraduates: 1% part-time, 56% women, 3% African American, 40% Asian American, 13% Hispanic American, 1% Native American, 2% international
- 6,359 degree-seeking graduate students
- 53% of applicants admitted
- SAT or ACT with writing, SAT Subject Tests, application essay required
- 81% graduate within 6 years

General. Founded in 1905. Regionally accredited. **Degrees:** 5,785 bachelor's awarded; master's, doctoral, first professional offered. **ROTC:** Army, Naval, Air Force. **Location:** 15 miles from Sacramento, 72 miles from San Francisco. **Calendar:** Quarter, extensive summer session. **Full-time faculty:** 1,586 total; 98% have terminal degrees, 19% minority, 33% women. **Part-time faculty:** 317 total; 98% have terminal degrees, 19% minority, 42% women. **Class size:** 35% < 20, 33% 20-39, 5% 40-49, 14% 50-99, 13% >100. **Special facilities:** 150-acre arboretum, equestrian center, craft center, marine laboratory, nuclear laboratory, California Regional Primate Research Center, natural reserves, raptor center.

Freshman class profile. 40,605 applied, 21,357 admitted, 4,972 enrolled.

Mid 50% test scores		**GPA 2.0-2.99:**	1%
SAT critical reading:	500-630	**Rank in top quarter:**	100%
SAT math:	550-670	**Rank in top tenth:**	96%
SAT writing:	510-640	**Return as sophomores:**	90%
ACT composite:	22-28	**Out-of-state:**	3%
GPA 3.75 or higher:	58%	**Live on campus:**	89%
GPA 3.50-3.74:	24%	**International:**	2%
GPA 3.0-3.49:	17%		

Basis for selection. Scholastic achievement most important, followed by school and community activities, academic interests, special circumstances, special achievements and awards. Two SAT Subject Tests in two different subject areas of student's choice required: history/social science, English literature, mathematics (Level 2), laboratory science or language other than English.

High school preparation. 15 units required; 18 recommended. Required and recommended units include English 4, mathematics 3-4, social studies 2, science 2-3 (laboratory 2-3), foreign language 2-3, visual/performing arts 1 and academic electives 1. History/social science (social studies above) requirement is one year of U.S. history, or one-half year of U.S. history and one-half year of civics or U.S. government; and one year of world history, cultures and geography. For academic elective ("g" requirement): two semesters chosen from the following areas: visual and performing arts (non-introductory-level courses), history, social science, English, advanced mathematics, laboratory science and language other than English.

2008-2009 Annual costs. Tuition/fees: $8,635; $29,243 out-of-state. Students must purchase the Student Health Insurance Plan (SHIP) unless they are able to prove comparable coverage. Room/board: $11,978. Books/supplies: $1,544. Personal expenses: $1,308.

2008-2009 Financial aid. All financial aid based on need.

Application procedures. Admission: Closing date 11/30. $60 fee, may be waived for applicants with need. Admission notification 3/15. Must reply by 5/1. **Financial aid:** Priority date 3/2; no closing date. FAFSA required. Applicants notified on a rolling basis starting 3/15.

Academics. Seventy percent of undergraduates participate in full- and part-time internships. **Special study options:** Accelerated study, cross-registration, double major, dual enrollment of high school students, ESL, honors, independent study, internships, student-designed major, study abroad, teacher certification program, Washington semester. **Credit/placement by examination:** AP, CLEP. 10 credit hours maximum toward bachelor's degree. **Support services:** Learning center, pre-admission summer program, reduced course load, remedial instruction, study skills assistance, tutoring, writing center.

Majors. Agriculture: Agronomy, animal sciences, food science, international, range science, soil science. **Architecture:** Landscape, urban/community planning. **Area/ethnic studies:** African, African-American, American, Asian-American, East Asian, Hispanic-American/Latino/Chicano, Native American, women's. **Biology:** General, biotechnology, botany, cell/histology, entomology, environmental toxicology, exercise physiology, genetics, microbiology, molecular biochemistry, neurobiology/physiology, zoology. **Communications:** General. **Computer sciences:** Computer science. **Conservation:** General, environmental studies, urban forestry. **Engineering:** Aerospace, biomedical, chemical, civil, computer, electrical, materials, mechanical. **Engineering technology:** Laser/optical. **Family/consumer sciences:** Clothing/textiles, family studies. **Foreign languages:** Chinese, comparative lit, French, German, Italian, Japanese, linguistics, Russian, Spanish. **History:** General. **Interdisciplinary:** Classical/archaeology, medieval/Renaissance, natural sciences, nutrition sciences, science/society. **Math:** General, applied, computational, statistics. **Philosophy/religion:** Philosophy, religion. **Physical sciences:** Applied physics, atmospheric science, chemistry, geology, hydrology, physics. **Psychology:** General. **Social sciences:** Anthropology, economics, international relations, political science, sociology. **Visual/performing arts:** Art history/conservation, design, dramatic, film/cinema, studio arts. **Other:** Avian sciences, Computational applied science, Evolution, ecology and biodiversity, Technocultural studies, Wildlife, fish and conservation biology.

Most popular majors. Agriculture 8%, biology 20%, engineering/engineering technologies 8%, psychology 10%, social sciences 19%.

Computing on campus. 544 workstations in dormitories, library, computer center. Dormitories wired for high-speed internet access and linked to campus network. Commuter students can connect to campus network. Online course registration, online library, helpline, repair service, wireless network available.

Student life. Freshman orientation: Available, $215 fee. Preregistration for classes offered. Summer advising June-August. **Housing:** Coed dorms, single-sex dorms, special housing for disabled, apartments, cooperative housing, wellness housing available. $450 fully refundable deposit, deadline 6/9. Special interest housing available. **Activities:** Bands, campus ministries, choral groups, dance, drama, film society, international student organizations, literary magazine, music ensembles, musical theater, radio station, student government, student newspaper, symphony orchestra, TV station, 316 student organizations.

Athletics. NCAA. **Intercollegiate:** Baseball M, basketball, cross-country, diving, football (tackle) M, golf, gymnastics W, lacrosse W, rowing (crew) W, soccer, softball W, swimming, tennis, track and field, volleyball W, water polo, wrestling M. **Intramural:** Badminton, basketball, bowling, golf, racquetball, soccer, softball, squash, table tennis, tennis, volleyball, water polo. **Team name:** Aggies.

Student services. Adult student services, alcohol/substance abuse counseling, chaplain/spiritual director, career counseling, services for economically disadvantaged, student employment services, financial aid counseling, health services, legal services, minority student services, on-campus daycare, personal counseling, placement for graduates, veterans' counselor, women's services. **Physically disabled:** Services for visually, speech, hearing impaired. **Learning disabled:** Comprehensive services available.

Contact. E-mail: undergraduateadmissions@ucdavis.edu
Phone: (530) 752-2971 Fax: (530) 752-1280
Pamela Burnett, Director of Undergraduate Admissions, University of California: Davis, One Shields Ave, Davis, CA 95616

University of California: Irvine

Irvine, California **CB member**
www.uci.edu **CB code: 4859**

- Public 4-year university
- Residential campus in small city
- 22,122 degree-seeking undergraduates: 3% part-time, 53% women, 2% African American, 52% Asian American, 13% Hispanic American, 3% international
- 4,746 degree-seeking graduate students
- 49% of applicants admitted
- SAT and SAT Subject Tests or ACT with writing, application essay required
- 81% graduate within 6 years

General. Founded in 1965. Regionally accredited. **Degrees:** 5,505 bachelor's awarded; master's, doctoral, first professional offered. **ROTC:** Army, Air Force. **Location:** 40 miles from Los Angeles. **Calendar:** Quarter, extensive summer session. **Full-time faculty:** 1,520 total; 98% have terminal degrees, 27% minority, 34% women. **Part-time faculty:** 449 total; 98% have terminal degrees, 23% minority, 44% women. **Class size:** 44% < 20, 33% 20-39, 4% 40-49, 8% 50-99, 10% >100. **Special facilities:** Outdoor laboratory, ecological preserve, freshwater marsh reserve, arboretum, center for art and technology, observatory.

Freshman class profile. 42,414 applied, 20,670 admitted, 4,583 enrolled.

Mid 50% test scores		**Rank in top tenth:**	96%
SAT critical reading:	520-630	**End year in good standing:**	98%
SAT math:	570-670	**Return as sophomores:**	94%
SAT writing:	520-630	**Out-of-state:**	3%
GPA 3.75 or higher:	65%	**Live on campus:**	85%
GPA 3.50-3.74:	31%	**International:**	2%
GPA 3.0-3.49:	3%	**Fraternities:**	5%
GPA 2.0-2.99:	1%	**Sororities:**	7%
Rank in top quarter:	100%		

Basis for selection. Demonstrated record of academic preparation, educational engagement, talent and skills important. Two SAT Subject Tests required: math and student's choice.

High school preparation. College-preparatory program required. 15 units required; 18 recommended. Required and recommended units include English 4, mathematics 3-4, history 2, science 2-3 (laboratory 2-3), foreign language 2-3, visual/performing arts 1 and academic electives 1.

2008-2009 Annual costs. Tuition/fees: $8,046; $28,654 out-of-state. Room/board: $10,527. Books/supplies: $1,601. Personal expenses: $1,544.

2007-2008 Financial aid. **Need-based:** 3,726 full-time freshmen applied for aid; 2,546 were judged to have need; 2,456 of these received aid. Average need met was 82%. Average scholarship/grant was $10,685; average loan $5,897. 74% of total undergraduate aid awarded as scholarships/grants, 26% as loans/jobs. **Non-need-based:** Awarded to 1,098 full-time undergraduates, including 248 freshmen. Scholarships awarded for academics, alumni affiliation, art, athletics, job skills, leadership, music/drama, state residency.

Application procedures. **Admission:** Closing date 11/30 (receipt date). $60 fee, may be waived for applicants with need. Application must be submitted online. Admission notification 3/31. Must reply by 5/1. **Financial aid:** Closing date 3/2. FAFSA required. Applicants notified by 4/1; must reply by 5/1.

Academics. **Special study options:** Accelerated study, combined bachelor's/graduate degree, distance learning, double major, dual enrollment of high school students, ESL, honors, independent study, internships, liberal arts/career combination, semester at sea, study abroad, teacher certification program, Washington semester. **Credit/placement by examination:** AP, CLEP, IB, institutional tests. **Support services:** Learning center, pre-admission summer program, reduced course load, remedial instruction, study skills assistance, tutoring, writing center.

Majors. **Architecture:** Environmental design. **Area/ethnic studies:** African-American, Asian-American, East Asian, European, German, Hispanic-American/Latino/Chicano, women's. **Biology:** General, Biochemistry/biophysics and molecular biology, botany, cell/histology, ecology, genetics. **Communications:** Journalism. **Computer sciences:** General, computer science, information systems. **Engineering:** General, aerospace, biomedical, chemical, civil, computer, electrical, environmental, materials, mechanical. **Foreign languages:** Chinese, classics, comparative lit, French, German, Japanese, Korean, linguistics, Russian, Spanish. **Health:** Nursing (RN). **History:** General. **Interdisciplinary:** Classical/archaeology, global studies, neuroscience. **Liberal arts:** Humanities. **Math:** General, statistics. **Philosophy/religion:** Philosophy. **Physical sciences:** Chemistry, geology, physics. **Psychology:** General. **Social sciences:** General, anthropology, criminology, economics, political science, sociology. **Visual/performing arts:** Art, art history/conservation, dance, dramatic, film/cinema, music performance, studio arts. **Other:** Business information management.

Most popular majors. Biology 14%, engineering/engineering technologies 8%, interdisciplinary studies 8%, psychology 14%, social sciences 28%, visual/performing arts 7%.

Computing on campus. 1,500 workstations in dormitories, library, computer center, student center. Dormitories wired for high-speed internet access and linked to campus network. Commuter students can connect to campus network. Online course registration, online library, helpline, repair service, student web hosting, wireless network available.

Student life. **Freshman orientation:** Available. Preregistration for classes offered. One or three-day program held during summer. **Housing:** Guaranteed on-campus for freshmen. Coed dorms, single-sex dorms, special housing for disabled, apartments, cooperative housing, fraternity/sorority housing, wellness housing available. $350 partly refundable deposit. **Activities:** Bands, choral groups, dance, drama, film society, international student organizations, literary magazine, music ensembles, musical theater, opera, radio station, student government, student newspaper, symphony orchestra.

Athletics. NCAA. **Intercollegiate:** Baseball M, basketball, cheerleading, cross-country, diving, golf, rowing (crew), sailing, soccer, swimming, tennis, track and field, volleyball, water polo. **Intramural:** Badminton, basketball, bowling, football (non-tackle), golf, racquetball, soccer, softball, swimming, table tennis, tennis, track and field, volleyball, water polo, wrestling. **Team name:** Anteaters.

Student services. Alcohol/substance abuse counseling, career counseling, services for economically disadvantaged, student employment services, financial aid counseling, health services, minority student services, on-campus daycare, personal counseling, placement for graduates, veterans' counselor, women's services. **Physically disabled:** Services for visually, speech, hearing impaired.

Contact. E-mail: admissions@uci.edu
Phone: (949) 824-6703 Fax: (949) 824-2711
Brent Yunek, Director of Admissions, Acting, University of California: Irvine, 204 Aldrich Hall, Irvine, CA 92697-1075

University of California: Los Angeles

Los Angeles, California **CB member**
www.ucla.edu **CB code: 4837**

- Public 4-year university
- Residential campus in very large city
- 26,536 degree-seeking undergraduates: 3% part-time, 55% women, 4% African American, 38% Asian American, 15% Hispanic American, 4% international
- 11,686 degree-seeking graduate students
- 23% of applicants admitted
- SAT or ACT with writing, SAT Subject Tests, application essay required
- 89% graduate within 6 years

General. Founded in 1919. Regionally accredited. **Degrees:** 7,083 bachelor's awarded; master's, doctoral, first professional offered. **ROTC:** Army, Naval, Air Force. **Location:** Downtown. **Calendar:** Quarter, extensive summer session. **Full-time faculty:** 1,948 total; 98% have terminal degrees, 23% minority, 31% women. **Part-time faculty:** 706 total; 98% have terminal degrees, 24% minority, 43% women. **Class size:** 54% < 20, 22% 20-39, 4% 40-49, 9% 50-99, 10% >100. **Special facilities:** Museums with specialized collections, centers for cancer research, plasma physics research labs, film and television archive, high power auroral simulation observatory, lab for embedded collaborative systems, research centers for molecular and neuroscience, graphic and animation labs, nanoscience research labs and centers, cell mimetic space exploration center, particle beam physics lab, southern California particle center, ranch for ecological studies, ethnomusicology archive.

Freshman class profile. 55,437 applied, 12,660 admitted, 4,735 enrolled.

Mid 50% test scores			
SAT critical reading:	570-680	**Rank in top quarter:**	100%
SAT math:	600-730	**Rank in top tenth:**	97%
SAT writing:	580-700	**Return as sophomores:**	97%
ACT composite:	25-31	**Out-of-state:**	10%
GPA 3.75 or higher:	92%	**Live on campus:**	94%
GPA 3.50-3.74:	4%	**International:**	3%
GPA 3.0-3.49:	3%	**Fraternities:**	11%
GPA 2.0-2.99:	1%	**Sororities:**	11%

Basis for selection. GPA, test scores, course work, number of and performance in honors and AP courses most important. Essay considered. Strong senior program important. Extracurricular activities, honors and awards also reviewed. Audition required of music, dance, theater majors. Portfolio required of art majors.

High school preparation. College-preparatory program required. 15 units required; 18 recommended. Required and recommended units include English 4, mathematics 3-4, history 2, science 2-3 (laboratory 2-3), foreign language 2-3, visual/performing arts 1 and academic electives 1.

2008-2009 Annual costs. Tuition/fees: $7,551; $28,162 out-of-state. Room/board: $12,891. Books/supplies: $1,551. Personal expenses: $1,503.

2007-2008 Financial aid. **Need-based:** 2,579 full-time freshmen applied for aid; 2,085 were judged to have need; 2,085 of these received aid. Average need met was 80%. Average scholarship/grant was $12,017; average loan $5,360. 73% of total undergraduate aid awarded as scholarships/grants, 27% as loans/jobs. **Non-need-based:** Awarded to 1,676 full-time undergraduates, including 403 freshmen. Scholarships awarded for academics, alumni affiliation, athletics, ROTC.

Application procedures. **Admission:** Closing date 11/30 (postmark date). $60 fee, may be waived for applicants with need. Admission notification 3/31. Must reply by 5/1. **Financial aid:** Priority date 3/2; no closing date. FAFSA required. Applicants notified on a rolling basis starting 3/15; must reply within 3 week(s) of notification.

Academics. **Special study options:** Accelerated study, double major, honors, independent study, internships, liberal arts/career combination, student-designed major, study abroad. **Credit/placement by examination:** AP, CLEP. **Support services:** Learning center, study skills assistance, tutoring, writing center.

Majors. **Architecture:** Architecture. **Area/ethnic studies:** African-American, Asian, Asian-American, East Asian, European, Hispanic-American/Latino/Chicano, Latin American, Native American, Russian/Slavic, Southeast Asian, women's. **Biology:** General, bacteriology, biochemistry, biophysics, biotechnology, botany, cellular/molecular, ecology, immunology, marine, molecular genetics, physiology, systematic. **Business:** Managerial economics.

Computer sciences: General. **Conservation:** Environmental science. **Engineering:** Aerospace, agricultural, chemical, civil, computer, electrical, geological, materials, materials science, mechanical. **Foreign languages:** African, ancient Greek, Arabic, Chinese, comparative lit, East Asian, French, German, Hebrew, Italian, Japanese, Korean, Latin, linguistics, Portuguese, Romance, Russian, Scandinavian, Slavic, Spanish. **History:** General. **Interdisciplinary:** Classical/archaeology, cognitive science, global studies, neuroscience. **Liberal arts:** Arts/sciences. **Math:** General, applied, computational, statistics. **Philosophy/religion:** Philosophy, religion. **Physical sciences:** Astrophysics, chemistry, geology, geophysics, physics. **Psychology:** General, psychobiology. **Social sciences:** Anthropology, economics, geography, international economic development, international economics, political science, sociology. **Visual/performing arts:** Art, art history/conservation, design, dramatic, film/cinema, music history, musicology. **Other:** Middle Eastern and North African studies.

Most popular majors. Biology 14%, engineering/engineering technologies 6%, English 6%, history 8%, psychology 11%, social sciences 28%.

Computing on campus. 4,324 workstations in dormitories, library, computer center, student center. Dormitories wired for high-speed internet access and linked to campus network. Commuter students can connect to campus network. Online course registration, online library, helpline, repair service, student web hosting, wireless network available.

Student life. **Freshman orientation:** Available, $340 fee. Preregistration for classes offered. 3-day, 2-night program. **Housing:** Guaranteed on-campus for freshmen. Coed dorms, special housing for disabled, apartments, cooperative housing, fraternity/sorority housing, wellness housing available. **Activities:** Bands, campus ministries, choral groups, dance, drama, film society, international student organizations, literary magazine, music ensembles, Model UN, musical theater, opera, radio station, student government, student newspaper, symphony orchestra, TV station.

Athletics. NCAA. **Intercollegiate:** Baseball M, basketball, cross-country, diving W, football (tackle) M, golf, gymnastics W, rowing (crew) W, soccer, softball W, swimming W, tennis, track and field, volleyball, water polo. **Intramural:** Badminton, basketball, football (non-tackle), golf, racquetball, soccer, squash, swimming, table tennis, tennis, track and field, volleyball. **Team name:** Bruins.

Student services. Alcohol/substance abuse counseling, chaplain/spiritual director, career counseling, services for economically disadvantaged, student employment services, financial aid counseling, health services, legal services, minority student services, on-campus daycare, personal counseling, placement for graduates, veterans' counselor, women's services. **Physically disabled:** Services for visually, speech, hearing impaired.

Contact. E-mail: ugadm@saonet.ucla.edu
Phone: (310) 825-3101 Fax: (310) 206-1206
Vu Tran, Director of Undergraduate Admissions, University of California: Los Angeles, 1147 Murphy Hall, Los Angeles, CA 90095-1436

University of California: Merced

Merced, California — **CB member**
www.ucmerced.edu — **CB code: 4129**

- Public 4-year university
- Residential campus in small city
- 2,533 degree-seeking undergraduates: 47% women, 6% African American, 33% Asian American, 30% Hispanic American, 1% Native American, 1% international
- 184 degree-seeking graduate students
- 91% of applicants admitted
- SAT or ACT with writing, SAT Subject Tests, application essay required

General. Candidate for regional accreditation. **Degrees:** 71 bachelor's awarded; master's, doctoral offered. **Location:** 120 miles from San Francisco, 60 miles from Fresno. **Calendar:** Semester, limited summer session. **Full-time faculty:** 162 total; 80% have terminal degrees, 27% minority, 40% women. **Part-time faculty:** 40 total; 50% have terminal degrees, 20% minority, 48% women. **Class size:** 44% < 20, 35% 20-39, 4% 40-49, 12% 50-99, 5% >100. **Special facilities:** Sierra Nevada research institute, Yosemite National Park research station, computational biology center, energy research center.

Freshman class profile. 19,116 applied, 17,324 admitted, 925 enrolled.

Mid 50% test scores		**GPA 2.0-2.99:**	8%
SAT critical reading:	440-570	**End year in good standing:**	70%
SAT math:	460-600	**Return as sophomores:**	79%
SAT writing:	440-560	**Out-of-state:**	1%
GPA 3.75 or higher:	18%	**Live on campus:**	82%
GPA 3.50-3.74:	22%	**International:**	1%
GPA 3.0-3.49:	52%		

Basis for selection. Academic record and test scores determine eligibility. **Homeschooled:** If school is not accredited by a regional association, student must meet eligibility by examination alone.

High school preparation. 15 units required; 18 recommended. Required and recommended units include English 4, mathematics 3-4, history 2, science 2-3 (laboratory 2-3), foreign language 2-3, visual/performing arts 1 and academic electives 1. History is 2 units in history/social science.

2008-2009 Annual costs. Tuition/fees: $7,749; $28,357 out-of-state. Room/board: $11,692. Books/supplies: $1,508. Personal expenses: $1,308.

2008-2009 Financial aid. **Non-need-based:** Scholarships awarded for academics.

Application procedures. **Admission:** Priority date 11/30; deadline 11/30 (postmark date). $60 fee, may be waived for applicants with need. Admission notification 3/31. Must reply by May 1 or within 3 week(s) if notified thereafter. **Financial aid:** Priority date 3/2; no closing date. FAFSA required. Applicants notified on a rolling basis starting 3/2.

Academics. **Special study options:** Accelerated study, distance learning, double major, independent study, internships, study abroad, teacher certification program, Washington semester. Research opportunities and internships at Lawrence Livermore National Laboratories and Yosemite National Park. **Credit/placement by examination:** AP, CLEP, IB, institutional tests. Credit by examination with the approval of the instructor giving the examination and the dean of the school involved. Some courses may not be deemed appropriate for obtaining credit by examination. **Support services:** Learning center, study skills assistance, tutoring, writing center.

Majors. **Biology:** General. **Business:** Management science. **Engineering:** Biomedical, computer, environmental, materials, mechanical. **Foreign languages:** Comparative lit. **History:** General. **Interdisciplinary:** Cognitive science. **Math:** General. **Physical sciences:** Chemistry, geology, physics. **Psychology:** General. **Social sciences:** General, anthropology, economics, political science. **Other:** World cultures and history.

Most popular majors. Biology 39%, engineering/engineering technologies 8%, history 8%, psychology 29%, social sciences 6%.

Computing on campus. 157 workstations in dormitories, library, computer center. Dormitories wired for high-speed internet access and linked to campus network. Commuter students can connect to campus network. Online course registration, online library, helpline, wireless network available.

Student life. **Freshman orientation:** Available, $49 fee. Preregistration for classes offered. **Housing:** Coed dorms, special housing for disabled, wellness housing available. $300 partly refundable deposit, deadline 5/31. **Activities:** Marching band, choral groups, dance, film society, radio station, student government, student newspaper, African American student union, liberal activism club, student government advisory committee, Latino students alliance, Filipino student alliance, Circle K International, American Red Cross club, Jewish student union.

Athletics. **Intramural:** Basketball, football (non-tackle), racquetball, soccer, softball, tennis, volleyball. **Team name:** Golden Bobcats.

Student services. Alcohol/substance abuse counseling, career counseling, services for economically disadvantaged, student employment services, financial aid counseling, health services, minority student services, personal counseling, veterans' counselor, women's services. **Physically disabled:** Services for visually, hearing impaired. **Learning disabled:** Comprehensive services available.

Contact. E-mail: admissions@ucmerced.edu
Phone: (209) 228-4682 Toll-free number: (866) 270-7301
Fax: (209) 228-4244
Encarnacion Ruiz, Director, Admissions and Relations with Schools & Colleges, University of California: Merced, 5200 North Lake Road, Merced, CA 95343-5603

University of California: Riverside

Riverside, California — **CB member**
www.ucr.edu — **CB code: 4839**

- Public 4-year university
- Residential campus in large city
- 15,708 degree-seeking undergraduates: 2% part-time, 52% women, 8% African American, 40% Asian American, 28% Hispanic American, 2% international
- 2,327 degree-seeking graduate students
- 79% of applicants admitted
- SAT or ACT with writing, SAT Subject Tests, application essay required
- 64% graduate within 6 years

General. Founded in 1954. Regionally accredited. **Degrees:** 3,555 bachelor's awarded; master's, doctoral offered. **ROTC:** Army, Air Force. **Location:** 60 miles from Los Angeles. **Calendar:** Quarter, limited summer session. **Full-time faculty:** 817 total; 98% have terminal degrees, 30% minority, 37% women. **Part-time faculty:** 116 total; 98% have terminal degrees, 15% minority, 29% women. **Class size:** 39% < 20, 38% 20-39, 4% 40-49, 10% 50-99, 10% >100. **Special facilities:** Botanical gardens, air pollution research center, photography museum, 8 nature preserves, citrus research center and agricultural experiment station, institute of geophysics and planetary physics, water resources center, salinity lab.

Freshman class profile. 22,534 applied, 17,848 admitted, 4,423 enrolled.

Mid 50% test scores			
SAT critical reading:	450-560	GPA 2.0-2.99:	4%
SAT math:	470-550	Rank in top quarter:	100%
SAT writing:	420-540	Rank in top tenth:	94%
ACT composite:	19-24	End year in good standing:	85%
GPA 3.75 or higher:	18%	Return as sophomores:	84%
GPA 3.50-3.74:	24%	Live on campus:	70%
GPA 3.0-3.49:	54%	International:	2%

Basis for selection. Secondary school record, standardized test scores, and completed UC application with essay. Freshmen applicants must submit SAT reasoning or ACT plus writing exam. SAT Subject Tests required from 2 different subject areas. Math Subject Test must be Level 2. **Homeschooled:** Transcript of courses and grades required. Portfolio describing subjects studied and methods of study may be required.

High school preparation. College-preparatory program required. 15 units required; 18 recommended. Required and recommended units include English 4, mathematics 3-4, history 2, science 2-3 (laboratory 2-3), foreign language 2-3, visual/performing arts 1 and academic electives 1. One year of elective units from 1 of the following: visual/performing arts (non-introductory), history, English, advanced mathematics, laboratory science, foreign language, social science, arts. 2 social science units must include 1 U.S. history or .5 history and .5 civics, and 1 world history, cultures, or geography.

2008-2009 Annual costs. Tuition/fees: $7,846; $28,453 out-of-state. Room/board: $10,850. Books/supplies: $1,700. Personal expenses: $1,700.

2008-2009 Financial aid. Need-based: 3,729 full-time freshmen applied for aid; 2,948 were judged to have need; 2,867 of these received aid. Average need met was 89%. Average scholarship/grant was $13,463; average loan $4,463. 71% of total undergraduate aid awarded as scholarships/grants, 29% as loans/jobs. **Non-need-based:** Awarded to 409 full-time undergraduates, including 150 freshmen. Scholarships awarded for academics, art, athletics, job skills, leadership, music/drama, state residency.

Application procedures. Admission: Closing date 11/30 (postmark date). $60 fee, may be waived for applicants with need. Admission notification on a rolling basis beginning on or about 2/1. Must reply by May 1 or within 3 week(s) if notified thereafter. **Financial aid:** Closing date 3/2. FAFSA required. Applicants notified on a rolling basis starting 3/1; must reply by 5/1 or within 3 week(s) of notification.

Academics. Special study options: Accelerated study, cooperative education, cross-registration, double major, dual enrollment of high school students, ESL, honors, independent study, internships, liberal arts/career combination, student-designed major, study abroad, teacher certification program, Washington semester. **Credit/placement by examination:** AP, CLEP, IB, SAT, ACT, institutional tests. **Support services:** Learning center, preadmission summer program, reduced course load, study skills assistance, tutoring, writing center.

Majors. Area/ethnic studies: African-American, Asian, Asian-American, German, Hispanic-American/Latino/Chicano, Latin American, Native American, Russian/Slavic, women's. **Biology:** General, biochemistry, botany, entomology. **Business:** Business admin, managerial economics. **Computer sciences:** Computer science, information systems. **Conservation:** Environmental science. **Engineering:** Biomedical, chemical, computer, electrical, environmental, materials science, mechanical. **Foreign languages:** General, classics, comparative lit, French, linguistics, Spanish. **History:** General. **Interdisciplinary:** Global studies, neuroscience. **Legal studies:** General. **Liberal arts:** Arts/sciences, humanities. **Math:** General, applied, statistics. **Philosophy/religion:** Philosophy, religion. **Physical sciences:** General, chemistry, geology, geophysics, physics. **Psychology:** General. **Public administration:** General, policy analysis. **Social sciences:** Anthropology, economics, international relations, political science, sociology. **Visual/performing arts:** Art, art history/conservation, dance, dramatic, film/cinema, studio arts. **Other:** Asian literatures & cultures, History/administrative studies, Music and culture, Philosophy/law and society, Political science/public service.

Most popular majors. Biology 14%, business/marketing 22%, liberal arts 6%, psychology 9%, social sciences 19%.

Computing on campus. 1,001 workstations in dormitories, library, computer center, student center. Dormitories wired for high-speed internet access and linked to campus network. Commuter students can connect to campus network. Online course registration, online library, helpline, repair service, student web hosting, wireless network available.

Student life. Freshman orientation: Available. 2-day or 1-day summer programs. **Housing:** Guaranteed on-campus for freshmen. Coed dorms, special housing for disabled, apartments available. $250 deposit, deadline 6/1. **Activities:** Bands, choral groups, dance, drama, film society, literary magazine, music ensembles, musical theater, radio station, student government, student newspaper, 250 clubs and organizations available.

Athletics. NCAA. **Intercollegiate:** Baseball M, basketball, cross-country, golf, soccer, softball W, tennis, track and field, volleyball W. **Intramural:** Badminton, basketball, bowling, football (non-tackle), golf, racquetball, soccer, softball, squash, table tennis, tennis, volleyball. **Team name:** Highlanders.

Student services. Adult student services, alcohol/substance abuse counseling, career counseling, student employment services, financial aid counseling, health services, minority student services, on-campus daycare, personal counseling, placement for graduates, veterans' counselor, women's services. **Physically disabled:** Services for visually, speech, hearing impaired.

Contact. E-mail: discover@ucr.edu
Phone: (951) 827-3411 Fax: (951) 827-6344
Merlyn Campos, Director of Undergraduate Admissions, University of California: Riverside, Admissions Office, Riverside, CA 92521

University of California: San Diego

La Jolla, California — **CB member**
www.ucsd.edu — **CB code: 4836**

- Public 4-year university
- Residential campus in large town
- 22,518 degree-seeking undergraduates: 1% part-time, 52% women, 2% African American, 45% Asian American, 12% Hispanic American, 4% international
- 5,002 degree-seeking graduate students
- 42% of applicants admitted
- SAT or ACT with writing, SAT Subject Tests, application essay required

General. Founded in 1959. Regionally accredited. Includes 6 small undergraduate cluster colleges, each with different housing and general education requirements. **Degrees:** 5,337 bachelor's awarded; master's, doctoral, first professional offered. **Location:** 12 miles from San Diego. **Calendar:** Quarter, extensive summer session. **Full-time faculty:** 951 total; 97% have terminal degrees, 23% minority, 25% women. **Part-time faculty:** 201 total; 18% minority, 36% women. **Class size:** 44% < 20, 22% 20-39, 4% 40-49, 11% 50-99, 20% >100. **Special facilities:** Performing arts centers, student-run co-ops, supercomputer center, nature preserves, electron beam lithography facility, center for music experiment, structural engineering lab, aquarium, additional specialty research centers.

Freshman class profile. 47,365 applied, 19,717 admitted, 4,292 enrolled.

Mid 50% test scores		GPA 3.0-3.49:	4%
SAT critical reading:	540-660	Rank in top quarter:	100%
SAT math:	600-710	Rank in top tenth:	100%
SAT writing:	560-670	Out-of-state:	4%
ACT composite:	24-30	Live on campus:	92%
GPA 3.75 or higher:	80%	Fraternities:	10%
GPA 3.50-3.74:	16%	Sororities:	10%

Basis for selection. High school course pattern, GPA, essay and test scores most important. Admission for out-of-state applicants more selective than for residents. All applicants must take 2 SAT Subject Tests in different subject areas. If Math SAT Subject Test is taken, must be Level 2.

High school preparation. 17 units required. Required and recommended units include English 4, mathematics 3-4, history 2, science 2-3 (laboratory 2-3), foreign language 2-3, visual/performing arts 1 and academic electives 1. History is 2 units in history/social science.

2008-2009 Annual costs. Tuition/fees: $8,062; $28,670 out-of-state. Room/board: $10,787. Books/supplies: $1,523. Personal expenses: $1,483.

2007-2008 Financial aid. **Need-based:** 3,243 full-time freshmen applied for aid; 2,440 were judged to have need; 2,344 of these received aid. Average need met was 83%. Average scholarship/grant was $11,343; average loan $4,254. 70% of total undergraduate aid awarded as scholarships/grants, 30% as loans/jobs. **Non-need-based:** Awarded to 1,017 full-time undergraduates, including 240 freshmen. Scholarships awarded for academics, art, leadership, minority status, music/drama.

Application procedures. **Admission:** Closing date 11/30 (receipt date). $60 fee, may be waived for applicants with need. Application must be submitted online. Admission notification 3/31. Admission notification on a rolling basis beginning on or about 3/15. Must reply by 5/1. **Financial aid:** Priority date 3/2; no closing date. FAFSA required. Applicants notified on a rolling basis starting 3/15; must reply within 3 week(s) of notification.

Academics. **Special study options:** Combined bachelor's/graduate degree, double major, dual enrollment of high school students, ESL, exchange student, honors, independent study, internships, student-designed major, study abroad, Washington semester. In-depth academic assignments working in small groups or one-to-one with faculty; research programs. **Credit/placement by examination:** AP, CLEP, IB, institutional tests. **Support services:** Learning center, pre-admission summer program, reduced course load, study skills assistance, tutoring, writing center.

Majors. **Architecture:** Urban/community planning. **Area/ethnic studies:** Chinese, German, Italian, Japanese, Latin American, Russian/Slavic, women's. **Biology:** General, animal physiology, bacteriology, biochemistry, bioinformatics, biophysics, biotechnology, cell/histology, ecology, evolutionary, molecular. **Business:** Management science. **Communications:** General, digital media. **Computer sciences:** General, computer science, information systems, systems analysis. **Conservation:** Environmental science, environmental studies. **Engineering:** Aerospace, biomedical, chemical, computer, electrical, mechanical, mechanics, physics, science, structural, systems. **Engineering technology:** Aerospace. **Family/consumer sciences:** Family studies. **Foreign languages:** General, classics, French, German, Italian, Japanese, linguistics, Russian, Spanish. **History:** General. **Interdisciplinary:** Behavioral sciences, cognitive science, math/computer science, neuroscience. **Math:** General, applied. **Philosophy/religion:** Judaic, philosophy, religion. **Physical sciences:** Chemical physics, chemistry, molecular physics, physics, planetary. **Psychology:** General. **Public administration:** Policy analysis. **Social sciences:** Anthropology, archaeology, economics, political science, sociology, U.S. government, urban studies. **Visual/performing arts:** Art history/conservation, dance, dramatic, studio arts.

Most popular majors. Biology 17%, engineering/engineering technologies 14%, psychology 8%, social sciences 32%.

Computing on campus. 1,500 workstations in library, computer center, student center. Dormitories wired for high-speed internet access and linked to campus network. Commuter students can connect to campus network. Online course registration, online library, helpline, repair service, student web hosting, wireless network available.

Student life. **Freshman orientation:** Mandatory, $125 fee. Preregistration for classes offered. One- to two-day program for freshmen and transfers. **Housing:** Guaranteed on-campus for freshmen. Coed dorms, special housing for disabled, apartments available. $500 partly refundable deposit, deadline 5/3. Language, cultural interest and international houses available. **Activities:** Pep band, choral groups, dance, drama, film society, international student organizations, literary magazine, music ensembles, Model UN, musical theater, radio station, student government, student newspaper, TV station, 450 student organizations.

Athletics. NCAA. **Intercollegiate:** Baseball M, basketball, cross-country, diving, fencing, golf M, rowing (crew), soccer, softball W, swimming, tennis, track and field, volleyball, water polo. **Intramural:** Basketball, soccer, softball, tennis. **Team name:** Tritons.

Student services. Alcohol/substance abuse counseling, career counseling, services for economically disadvantaged, student employment services, financial aid counseling, health services, legal services, minority student services, on-campus daycare, personal counseling, placement for graduates, veterans' counselor, women's services. **Physically disabled:** Services for visually, speech, hearing impaired. **Learning disabled:** Comprehensive services available.

Contact. E-mail: admissionsinfo@ucsd.edu
Phone: (858) 534-4831 Fax: (858) 822-0042
Mae Brown, Assistant Vice Chancellor and Director of Admissions, University of California: San Diego, 9500 Gilman Drive, 0021, La Jolla, CA 92093-0021

University of California: Santa Barbara

Santa Barbara, California — **CB member**
www.ucsb.edu — **CB code: 4835**

- Public 4-year university
- Residential campus in small city
- 18,888 degree-seeking undergraduates: 2% part-time, 54% women, 3% African American, 17% Asian American, 21% Hispanic American, 1% Native American, 1% international
- 2,976 degree-seeking graduate students
- 49% of applicants admitted
- SAT or ACT with writing, SAT Subject Tests, application essay required
- 81% graduate within 6 years

General. Founded in 1909. Regionally accredited. **Degrees:** 5,553 bachelor's awarded; master's, doctoral offered. **ROTC:** Army. **Location:** 10 miles from downtown, 100 miles from Los Angeles. **Calendar:** Quarter, extensive summer session. **Full-time faculty:** 917 total. **Part-time faculty:** 150 total. **Class size:** 49% < 20, 30% 20-39, 4% 40-49, 9% 50-99, 8% >100. **Special facilities:** Several nature preserves with research facilities, seawater laboratories, robotics laboratory, free electron laser laboratory; institutes for polymers and organic solids, neuroscience research, quantum, nuclear particle astrophysics and cosmology, marine science, theoretical physics.

Freshman class profile. 47,083 applied, 23,183 admitted, 4,385 enrolled.

Mid 50% test scores		GPA 3.0-3.49:	12%
SAT critical reading:	530-650	GPA 2.0-2.99:	1%
SAT math:	550-670	Return as sophomores:	91%
SAT writing:	530-650	Out-of-state:	4%
ACT composite:	23-29	Live on campus:	94%
GPA 3.75 or higher:	65%	International:	1%
GPA 3.50-3.74:	22%		

Basis for selection. Eligibility established by high school GPA, course requirement, and SAT scores. Special consideration for disadvantaged students. All applicants must take 2 SAT Subject Tests in different subject areas. If Math SAT Subject Test is taken, must be Level 2. Audition required of music, dance, drama majors. Portfolio required of art majors.

High school preparation. College-preparatory program required. Required and recommended units include English 4, mathematics 3-4, history 2, (laboratory 2-3), foreign language 2-3, visual/performing arts 1 and academic electives 1. 2 history/social science units required, including 1 U.S. history or 1/2 of U.S. history and 1/2 civics or American government and 1 world history, cultures, or geography.

2008-2009 Annual costs. Tuition/fees: $8,386; $28,994 out-of-state. Room/board: $12,485. Books/supplies: $1,549. Personal expenses: $1,758.

2007-2008 Financial aid. **Need-based:** 3,122 full-time freshmen applied for aid; 2,130 were judged to have need; 1,899 of these received aid. Average need met was 80%. Average scholarship/grant was $14,034; average loan $5,398. 73% of total undergraduate aid awarded as scholarships/grants, 27% as loans/jobs. **Non-need-based:** Awarded to 631 full-time undergraduates, including 156 freshmen. Scholarships awarded for academics, athletics.

Application procedures. **Admission:** Closing date 11/30 (postmark date). $60 fee, may be waived for applicants with need. Admission notification 3/15. Admission notification on a rolling basis beginning on or about 3/1. Must reply by 5/1. **Financial aid:** Priority date 3/2, closing date 5/31. FAFSA required. Applicants notified on a rolling basis starting 3/15; must reply within 2 week(s) of notification.

Academics. **Special study options:** Accelerated study, cross-registration, distance learning, double major, dual enrollment of high school students, ESL, exchange student, honors, independent study, internships, student-designed major, study abroad, teacher certification program, Washington semester. Graduate-level classes, off-campus study, freshman seminars, pre-professional programs and advising, academic minors, and undergraduate research, professional studies in school of environmental science and management and school of education. **Credit/placement by examination:** AP, CLEP, institutional tests. **Support services:** Learning center, pre-admission summer program, reduced course load, tutoring.

Majors. **Area/ethnic studies:** African-American, Asian, Hispanic-American/Latino/Chicano, Latin American, women's. **Biology:** General, aquatic, bacteriology, biochemistry, cell/histology, ecology, marine, molecular, pharmacology, zoology. **Business:** Managerial economics. **Communications:** General. **Computer sciences:** General. **Conservation:** Environmental studies. **Engineering:** Chemical, computer, electrical, mechanical. **Foreign languages:** Chinese, classics, comparative lit, French, German, Italian, Japanese, linguistics, Portuguese, Russian, Slavic, Spanish. **History:** General. **Interdisciplinary:** Biological/physical sciences, biopsychology, global studies, medieval/Renaissance. **Legal studies:** General. **Math:** General, statistics. **Philosophy/religion:** Philosophy, religion. **Physical sciences:** Chemistry, geology, geophysics, physics. **Psychology:** General. **Social sciences:** Anthropology, economics, geography, political science, sociology. **Visual/performing arts:** General, art, art history/conservation, cinematography, dance, dramatic, film/cinema, studio arts.

Most popular majors. Biology 7%, business/marketing 12%, communications/journalism 6%, interdisciplinary studies 7%, psychology 7%, social sciences 18%, visual/performing arts 7%.

Computing on campus. Dormitories wired for high-speed internet access.

Student life. **Freshman orientation:** Available. Preregistration for classes offered. Two-day program; includes sessions for parents. **Housing:** Guaranteed on-campus for freshmen. Coed dorms, apartments, cooperative housing, fraternity/sorority housing, wellness housing available. $100 nonrefundable deposit, deadline 9/1. **Activities:** Bands, campus ministries, choral groups, dance, drama, film society, international student organizations, literary magazine, music ensembles, Model UN, musical theater, opera, radio station, student government, student newspaper, symphony orchestra, TV station, Hillel, Catholic Student Organization, Democratic and Republican student organizations, El Congreso, Persian Student Association, Habitat for Humanity.

Athletics. NCAA. **Intercollegiate:** Baseball M, basketball, cross-country, golf M, gymnastics, soccer, softball W, swimming, tennis, track and field, volleyball, water polo. **Intramural:** Badminton, basketball, bowling, cross-country, football (non-tackle), golf, gymnastics, racquetball, rowing (crew), soccer, softball, squash, tennis, volleyball, water polo. **Team name:** Gauchos.

Student services. Adult student services, alcohol/substance abuse counseling, chaplain/spiritual director, career counseling, services for economically disadvantaged, student employment services, financial aid counseling, health services, minority student services, on-campus daycare, personal counseling, placement for graduates, veterans' counselor, women's services. **Physically disabled:** Services for visually, speech, hearing impaired. **Learning disabled:** Comprehensive services available.

Contact. E-mail: admissions@sa.ucsb.edu
Phone: (805) 893-2881 Fax: (805) 893-2676
Christine Van Gieson, Director of Admissions, University of California: Santa Barbara, 1210 Cheadle Hall, Santa Barbara, CA 93106-2014

University of California: Santa Cruz

Santa Cruz, California — **CB member**
www.ucsc.edu — **CB code: 4860**

- Public 4-year university
- Residential campus in small city
- 15,125 degree-seeking undergraduates: 3% part-time, 53% women, 3% African American, 22% Asian American, 17% Hispanic American, 1% Native American, 1% international
- 1,490 degree-seeking graduate students
- 73% of applicants admitted
- SAT or ACT with writing, SAT Subject Tests, application essay required

General. Founded in 1965. Regionally accredited. **Degrees:** 3,419 bachelor's awarded; master's, doctoral offered. **ROTC:** Army, Naval, Air Force. **Location:** 75 miles from San Francisco, 30 miles from San Jose. **Calendar:** Quarter, limited summer session. **Full-time faculty:** 554 total; 95% have terminal degrees, 21% minority, 34% women. **Part-time faculty:** 237 total; 95% have terminal degrees, 13% minority, 53% women. **Class size:** 37% < 20, 38% 20-39, 4% 40-49, 9% 50-99, 12% >100. **Special facilities:** Observatories, arboretum, agroecology farm, campus preserve, nonlinear science center, music center, bilingual research center, institutes of marine sciences, tectonics, particle physics, center for adaptive optics.

Freshman class profile. 27,837 applied, 20,369 admitted, 3,959 enrolled.

Mid 50% test scores		**GPA 3.0-3.49:**	48%
SAT critical reading:	500-620	**GPA 2.0-2.99:**	4%
SAT math:	520-630	**Rank in top quarter:**	100%
SAT writing:	500-620	**Rank in top tenth:**	96%
ACT composite:	21-29	**Out-of-state:**	3%
GPA 3.75 or higher:	23%	**Live on campus:**	99%
GPA 3.50-3.74:	25%		

Basis for selection. Test scores, GPA in required subjects most important. Personal statement very important. All applicants must take 2 SAT Subject Tests in different subject areas. If Math SAT Subject Test is taken, must be Level 2. Audition required for music majors. Portfolio recommended for art majors. **Homeschooled:** Eligibility appraised on basis of entrance examination or previous college-level work. **Learning Disabled:** Any extenuating circumstances should be included in the personal statement.

High school preparation. College-preparatory program required. 15 units required; 18 recommended. Required and recommended units include English 4, mathematics 3-4, social studies 1, history 1, science 2-3 (laboratory 2-3), foreign language 2-3, visual/performing arts 1 and academic electives 1. History is 2 units in history/social science. 2 semesters of approved arts courses from single visual and performing arts discipline: dance, drama/theater, music, or visual art. Required elective includes 2 semesters from following areas: visual and performing arts, history, social science, English, advanced mathematics, laboratory science, and language other than English.

2008-2009 Annual costs. Tuition/fees: $8,200; $28,808 out-of-state. Room/board: $13,038. Books/supplies: $1,356. Personal expenses: $1,470.

2007-2008 Financial aid. **Need-based:** 2,593 full-time freshmen applied for aid; 1,828 were judged to have need; 1,718 of these received aid. Average need met was 87%. Average scholarship/grant was $10,836; average loan $5,326. 65% of total undergraduate aid awarded as scholarships/grants, 35% as loans/jobs. **Non-need-based:** Awarded to 363 full-time undergraduates, including 73 freshmen. Scholarships awarded for academics, alumni affiliation, art, leadership, music/drama.

Application procedures. **Admission:** Closing date 11/30 (postmark date). $60 fee, may be waived for applicants with need. Admission notification 4/30. Admission notification on a rolling basis beginning on or about 3/15. Must reply by 5/1. **Financial aid:** Closing date 3/2. FAFSA required. Applicants notified on a rolling basis starting 4/1; must reply within 4 week(s) of notification.

Academics. **Special study options:** Combined bachelor's/graduate degree, cooperative education, double major, dual enrollment of high school students, ESL, exchange student, independent study, internships, student-designed major, study abroad, teacher certification program, Washington semester. **Credit/placement by examination:** AP, CLEP, IB, institutional tests. **Support services:** Learning center, reduced course load, remedial instruction, study skills assistance, tutoring, writing center.

Majors. **Agriculture:** Plant sciences. **Area/ethnic studies:** American, German, Italian, women's. **Biology:** General, bioinformatics, cellular/molecular, ecology, marine, molecular biochemistry. **Business:** Managerial economics. **Computer sciences:** General, web page design. **Conservation:** Environmental studies. **Engineering:** Biomedical, computer, electrical. **Foreign languages:** General, classics, linguistics. **History:** General. **Interdisciplinary:** Neuroscience. **Legal studies:** General. **Math:** General. **Philosophy/religion:** Philosophy. **Physical sciences:** Astrophysics, chemistry, geology, physics. **Psychology:** General. **Public administration:** Community org/advocacy. **Social sciences:** Anthropology, economics, political science, sociology. **Visual/performing arts:** Art, art history/conservation, dramatic. **Other:** Area, ethnic, cultural, and gender studies, Biological and biomedical sciences, Computer and information sciences and support services.

Most popular majors. Area/ethnic studies 6%, biology 12%, business/marketing 9%, English 7%, psychology 11%, social sciences 17%, visual/performing arts 11%.

Computing on campus. 300 workstations in dormitories, library, computer center, student center. Dormitories wired for high-speed internet access and linked to campus network. Commuter students can connect to campus network. Online course registration, online library, helpline, repair service, student web hosting, wireless network available.

Student life. **Freshman orientation:** Available, $105 fee. Preregistration for classes offered. **Policies:** Students may create own organizations. **Housing:** Guaranteed on-campus for freshmen. Coed dorms, single-sex dorms, apartments, cooperative housing, wellness housing available. $150 partly refundable deposit, deadline 5/1. **Activities:** Jazz band, choral groups, dance, drama, film society, international student organizations, literary magazine, music ensembles, Model UN, musical theater, opera, radio station, student government, student newspaper, symphony orchestra, TV station, More than 100 student organizations.

Athletics. NCAA. **Intercollegiate:** Basketball, cross-country W, diving, golf W, soccer, swimming, tennis, volleyball, water polo. **Intramural:** Basketball, football (non-tackle), soccer, volleyball. **Team name:** Banana Slugs.

Student services. Adult student services, alcohol/substance abuse counseling, career counseling, services for economically disadvantaged, student employment services, financial aid counseling, health services, minority student services, on-campus daycare, personal counseling, veterans' counselor, women's services. **Physically disabled:** Services for visually, speech, hearing impaired.

Contact. E-mail: admissions@ucsc.edu
Phone: (831) 459-4008 Fax: (831) 459-4452
Michelle Whittingham, Director of Admissions, University of California: Santa Cruz, Cook House, 1156 High Street, Santa Cruz, CA 95064

University of La Verne

La Verne, California — **CB member**
www.laverne.edu — **CB code: 4381**

- Private 4-year university and liberal arts college
- Commuter campus in large town
- 1,528 degree-seeking undergraduates: 4% part-time, 62% women, 7% African American, 5% Asian American, 39% Hispanic American, 1% Native American, 2% international
- 2,341 degree-seeking graduate students
- 59% of applicants admitted
- SAT or ACT with writing, application essay required
- 60% graduate within 6 years

General. Founded in 1891. Regionally accredited. Satellite campuses throughout California provide graduate and professional programs to adult students. **Degrees:** 398 bachelor's awarded; master's, doctoral, first professional offered. **ROTC:** Army. **Location:** 35 miles from Los Angeles. **Calendar:** 4-1-4, limited summer session. **Full-time faculty:** 187 total; 82% have terminal degrees, 20% minority, 48% women. **Part-time faculty:** 202 total; 16% minority. **Class size:** 78% < 20, 21% 20-39, less than 1% 40-49. **Special facilities:** Natural science field station, multiple art galleries.

Freshman class profile. 1,657 applied, 982 admitted, 300 enrolled.

Mid 50% test scores		**GPA 2.0-2.99:**	26%
SAT critical reading:	440-540	**Rank in top quarter:**	55%
SAT math:	440-560	**Rank in top tenth:**	24%
SAT writing:	440-530	**Return as sophomores:**	79%
ACT composite:	18-24	**Out-of-state:**	6%
GPA 3.75 or higher:	23%	**Live on campus:**	50%
GPA 3.50-3.74:	18%	**International:**	2%
GPA 3.0-3.49:	33%	**Sororities:**	8%

Basis for selection. Secondary school record, recommendations, standardized test scores, and essay very important; extracurricular activities, character or personal qualities also important. Class rank, interview, special talents or abilities, alumni relationships, volunteer work, work experience may be considered as additional factors. Individual departments may require interview, audition, or portfolio.

High school preparation. College-preparatory program required. 14 units required; 19 recommended. Required and recommended units include English 4, mathematics 3-4, social studies 2, history 3, science 2 (laboratory 1-2), foreign language 2 and academic electives 2.

2009-2010 Annual costs. Tuition/fees: $28,250. Room/board: $11,110. Books/supplies: $1,638. Personal expenses: $2,400.

2008-2009 Financial aid. **Need-based:** 258 full-time freshmen applied for aid; 240 were judged to have need; 239 of these received aid. Average need met was 50%. Average scholarship/grant was $12,209; average loan $4,798. 65% of total undergraduate aid awarded as scholarships/grants, 35% as loans/jobs. **Non-need-based:** Awarded to 1,158 full-time undergraduates, including 215 freshmen. Scholarships awarded for academics, alumni affiliation, art, leadership, minority status, music/drama, religious affiliation.

Application procedures. **Admission:** Priority date 2/1; no deadline. $50 fee, may be waived for applicants with need. Admission notification on a rolling basis beginning on or about 12/1. Must reply by May 1 or within 2 week(s) if notified thereafter. **Financial aid:** Priority date 3/2; no closing date. FAFSA required. Applicants notified on a rolling basis starting 3/17; must reply within 2 week(s) of notification.

Academics. Main Campus offers a traditional-age undergraduate program and an accelerated program for adults in school of continuing education. Off-campus centers available for degree-seeking students in selected majors. **Special study options:** Accelerated study, combined bachelor's/graduate degree, distance learning, double major, ESL, exchange student, honors, independent study, internships, liberal arts/career combination, student-designed major, study abroad, teacher certification program, weekend college. **Credit/placement by examination:** AP, CLEP, institutional tests. 21 credit hours maximum toward associate degree, 44 toward bachelor's. **Support services:** Learning center, reduced course load, study skills assistance, tutoring, writing center.

Majors. **Biology:** General, environmental. **Business:** Accounting, business admin, e-commerce, international, managerial economics. **Communications:** General, journalism, radio/tv. **Computer sciences:** General. **Conservation:** Environmental science. **Education:** General, early childhood, elementary, physical, secondary. **Family/consumer sciences:** Child care. **Foreign languages:** Comparative lit, French, German, Spanish. **Health:** Athletic training, health care admin. **History:** General. **Interdisciplinary:** Behavioral sciences, biological/physical sciences, natural sciences. **Legal studies:** General. **Liberal arts:** Arts/sciences. **Math:** General. **Philosophy/religion:** Philosophy, religion. **Physical sciences:** Chemistry, physics. **Psychology:** General. **Public administration:** General. **Social sciences:** General, anthropology, criminology, economics, international relations, political science, sociology. **Visual/performing arts:** Art, art history/conservation, dramatic.

Most popular majors. Business/marketing 25%, communications/journalism 12%, liberal arts 14%, psychology 9%, social sciences 14%.

Computing on campus. 500 workstations in dormitories, library, computer center. Dormitories wired for high-speed internet access and linked to campus network. Commuter students can connect to campus network. Online course registration, online library, helpline, student web hosting, wireless network available.

Student life. **Freshman orientation:** Available, $50 fee. Preregistration for classes offered. All-day events for both students and parents. Held primarily in August. **Policies:** Students must be in good academic standing to participate in clubs or organizations, including fraternities/sororities. Freshmen not permitted to join fraternities during the Fall term. **Housing:** Coed dorms, single-sex dorms, special housing for disabled available. $300 fully refundable deposit, deadline 5/1. **Activities:** Campus ministries, choral groups, dance, drama, international student organizations, literary magazine, music ensembles, Model UN, musical theater, radio station, student government, student newspaper, TV station, African American student alliance, Latino student forum, Brothers Forum, Sisters Circle, Rainbow Alliance.

Athletics. NCAA. **Intercollegiate:** Baseball M, basketball, cross-country, diving, football (tackle) M, golf M, soccer, softball W, swimming, tennis, track and field, volleyball W, water polo. **Intramural:** Basketball, soccer, softball, table tennis, volleyball. **Team name:** Leopards.

Student services. Adult student services, alcohol/substance abuse counseling, chaplain/spiritual director, career counseling, services for economically disadvantaged, student employment services, financial aid counseling, health services, minority student services, personal counseling, placement for graduates, veterans' counselor. **Physically disabled:** Services for visually, speech, hearing impaired.

Contact. E-mail: admissions@ulv.edu
Phone: (909) 392-2800 Toll-free number: (800) 876-4858
Fax: (909) 392-2714
Ana Liza Zell, Associate Dean of Undergraduate Admissions, University of La Verne, 1950 Third Street, La Verne, CA 91750

University of Redlands

Redlands, California — **CB member**
www.redlands.edu — **CB code: 4848**

- Private 4-year university and liberal arts college
- Residential campus in small city

- 2,335 degree-seeking undergraduates: 1% part-time, 57% women, 2% African American, 5% Asian American, 11% Hispanic American, 2% international
- 98 degree-seeking graduate students
- 68% of applicants admitted
- SAT or ACT (ACT writing recommended), application essay required
- 70% graduate within 6 years; 41% enter graduate study

General. Founded in 1907. Regionally accredited. NASM accredited school of music is within the College of Arts & Sciences. **Degrees:** 637 bachelor's awarded; master's, doctoral offered. **ROTC:** Army, Naval, Air Force. **Location:** 65 miles from Los Angeles, 40 miles from Palm Springs. **Calendar:** 4-1-4. **Full-time faculty:** 173 total; 87% have terminal degrees, 16% minority, 51% women. **Part-time faculty:** 162 total; 28% have terminal degrees. **Class size:** 72% < 20, 27% 20-39, less than 1% 40-49, less than 1% 50-99. **Special facilities:** Anthropology laboratory, geographic information systems laboratory, physics/laser/photonics laboratory, map library.

Freshman class profile. 3,443 applied, 2,327 admitted, 579 enrolled.

Mid 50% test scores			
SAT critical reading:	520-620	Rank in top quarter:	70%
SAT math:	540-620	Rank in top tenth:	31%
ACT composite:	21-27	End year in good standing:	85%
GPA 3.75 or higher:	37%	Return as sophomores:	85%
GPA 3.50-3.74:	21%	Out-of-state:	39%
GPA 3.0-3.49:	29%	Live on campus:	94%
GPA 2.0-2.99:	13%	International:	2%

Basis for selection. Course selection and grades important. Recommendations, test scores, essays, extracurricular activities also considered. Interview required of Johnston Center for Integrated Studies applicants, strongly recommended for others. Audition required of music majors. Portfolio recommended of art (slides only), creative writing majors. **Homeschooled:** Statement describing homeschool structure and mission required. Common application home school supplement required.

High school preparation. College-preparatory program recommended. 15 units required; 17 recommended. Required and recommended units include English 4, mathematics 3, social studies 2, history 1, science 2-3 (laboratory 2) and foreign language 2.

2008-2009 Annual costs. Tuition/fees: $32,294. Room/board: $10,122. Books/supplies: $1,566. Personal expenses: $2,200.

2008-2009 Financial aid. Need-based: 467 full-time freshmen applied for aid; 353 were judged to have need; 353 of these received aid. Average need met was 81%. Average scholarship/grant was $21,661; average loan $5,313. 77% of total undergraduate aid awarded as scholarships/grants, 23% as loans/jobs. **Non-need-based:** Awarded to 318 full-time undergraduates, including 108 freshmen. Scholarships awarded for academics, art, music/drama.

Application procedures. Admission: Priority date 12/15; deadline 6/1 (postmark date). $30 fee, may be waived for applicants with need. Admission notification on a rolling basis beginning on or about 12/1. Must reply by 5/1. **Financial aid:** Priority date 2/15; no closing date. FAFSA required. Applicants notified on a rolling basis starting 2/28; must reply by 5/1.

Academics. Special study options: Cross-registration, double major, exchange student, honors, independent study, internships, liberal arts/career combination, New York semester, student-designed major, study abroad, teacher certification program, United Nations semester, Washington semester. Nontraditional study programs available through Johnston Center for Integrated Studies and schools of business and education. **Credit/placement by examination:** AP, CLEP, IB, SAT, ACT, institutional tests. 16 credit hours maximum toward bachelor's degree. **Support services:** Learning center, preadmission summer program, reduced course load, study skills assistance, tutoring, writing center.

Majors. Area/ethnic studies: Asian, Latin American, women's. **Biology:** General, biochemistry. **Business:** General, accounting, business admin, management information systems, managerial economics. **Computer sciences:** General. **Conservation:** Environmental science, environmental studies, management/policy. **Education:** Elementary, middle, music, secondary, speech impaired. **Foreign languages:** French, German, Spanish. **Health:** Audiology/speech pathology. **History:** General. **Liberal arts:** Arts/sciences. **Math:** General. **Philosophy/religion:** Philosophy, religion. **Physical sciences:** Chemistry, physics. **Psychology:** General. **Social sciences:** Anthropology, economics, international relations, political science, sociology. **Visual/performing arts:** Art, art history/conservation, dramatic, music history, music performance, music theory/composition.

Most popular majors. Business/marketing 20%, English 9%, health sciences 6%, liberal arts 12%, psychology 9%, social sciences 13%, visual/performing arts 8%.

Computing on campus. 655 workstations in dormitories, library, computer center, student center. Dormitories wired for high-speed internet access and linked to campus network. Commuter students can connect to campus network. Online library, helpline, repair service, student web hosting, wireless network available.

Student life. Freshman orientation: Mandatory. One full week preceding academic school year. **Housing:** Guaranteed on-campus for freshmen. Coed dorms, single-sex dorms, special housing for disabled, apartments, fraternity/sorority housing, wellness housing available. **Activities:** Bands, choral groups, dance, drama, literary magazine, music ensembles, musical theater, opera, radio station, student government, student newspaper, symphony orchestra, Associated Students, Intervarsity Christian Fellowship, African American association, Gay, Lesbian, Bisexual student union, women's center, College Republicans, College Democrats, Asian Pacific Islander association, theater association.

Athletics. NCAA. **Intercollegiate:** Baseball M, basketball, cross-country, diving, football (tackle) M, golf, lacrosse W, soccer, softball W, swimming, tennis, track and field, volleyball W, water polo. **Intramural:** Basketball, football (non-tackle), racquetball, soccer, softball, table tennis, tennis, volleyball, water polo. **Team name:** Bulldogs.

Student services. Adult student services, alcohol/substance abuse counseling, chaplain/spiritual director, career counseling, student employment services, financial aid counseling, health services, minority student services, personal counseling, placement for graduates, veterans' counselor, women's services. **Physically disabled:** Services for visually, speech, hearing impaired.

Contact. E-mail: admissions@redlands.edu
Phone: (909) 748-8074 Toll-free number: (800) 455-5064
Fax: (909) 335-4089
Paul Driscoll, Dean of Admissions, University of Redlands, 1200 East Colton Avenue, Redlands, CA 92373-0999

University of San Diego

San Diego, California — **CB member**
www.sandiego.edu — **CB code: 4849**

- Private 4-year university affiliated with Roman Catholic Church
- Residential campus in very large city
- 5,097 degree-seeking undergraduates: 4% part-time, 58% women, 2% African American, 10% Asian American, 15% Hispanic American, 1% Native American, 3% international
- 2,686 degree-seeking graduate students
- 52% of applicants admitted
- SAT or ACT with writing, application essay required
- 75% graduate within 6 years

General. Founded in 1949. Regionally accredited. **Degrees:** 1,137 bachelor's awarded; master's, doctoral, first professional offered. **ROTC:** Army, Naval, Air Force. **Location:** 5 miles from downtown. **Calendar:** 4-1-4, extensive summer session. **Full-time faculty:** 369 total; 94% have terminal degrees, 19% minority, 45% women. **Part-time faculty:** 432 total; 52% have terminal degrees, 16% minority, 53% women. **Class size:** 36% < 20, 60% 20-39, 3% 40-49, less than 1% 50-99.

Freshman class profile. 10,584 applied, 5,519 admitted, 1,260 enrolled.

Mid 50% test scores			
SAT critical reading:	540-630	Rank in top quarter:	78%
SAT math:	560-650	Rank in top tenth:	39%
SAT writing:	550-650	End year in good standing:	95%
ACT composite:	24-29	Return as sophomores:	85%
GPA 3.75 or higher:	54%	Out-of-state:	41%
GPA 3.50-3.74:	26%	Live on campus:	96%
GPA 3.0-3.49:	20%	International:	2%

Basis for selection. School achievement record, test scores, recommendations, and extracurricular activities important. Out-of-state and international applicants welcome. Advanced Placement English examinations (language or literature) with grade of 4 or 5 may also be used for placement. Audition required of choral scholarship applicants. **Learning Disabled:** Must contact Director of Disability Services.

High school preparation. College-preparatory program recommended. 17 units required; 22 recommended. Required and recommended units include English 4, mathematics 3-4, social studies 3-4, science 3-4 (laboratory 2-3) and foreign language 2-3.

2008-2009 Annual costs. Tuition/fees: $34,264. Room/board: $11,870.

2007-2008 Financial aid. **Need-based:** 673 full-time freshmen applied for aid; 523 were judged to have need; 520 of these received aid. Average need met was 72%. Average scholarship/grant was $17,887; average loan $5,098. 66% of total undergraduate aid awarded as scholarships/grants, 34% as loans/jobs. **Non-need-based:** Awarded to 1,896 full-time undergraduates, including 542 freshmen. Scholarships awarded for academics, athletics, leadership, music/drama, religious affiliation, ROTC.

Application procedures. **Admission:** Priority date 1/15; deadline 3/1 (postmark date). $55 fee, may be waived for applicants with need. Admission notification 4/15. Must reply by May 1 or within 2 week(s) if notified thereafter. **Financial aid:** Priority date 3/2; no closing date. FAFSA required. Applicants notified on a rolling basis starting 3/1; must reply by 5/1 or within 3 week(s) of notification.

Academics. **Special study options:** Combined bachelor's/graduate degree, double major, ESL, honors, independent study, internships, liberal arts/career combination, study abroad, teacher certification program, Washington semester. **Credit/placement by examination:** AP, CLEP, IB, institutional tests. **Support services:** Pre-admission summer program, reduced course load, study skills assistance, tutoring, writing center.

Majors. **Biology:** General, marine. **Business:** Accounting, business admin, finance, managerial economics, marketing. **Communications:** General. **Computer sciences:** Computer science. **Engineering:** Electrical, industrial, mechanical. **Foreign languages:** French, Spanish. **Health:** Nursing (RN). **History:** General. **Interdisciplinary:** Intercultural. **Liberal arts:** Humanities. **Math:** General. **Philosophy/religion:** Philosophy, religion. **Physical sciences:** Chemistry, physics. **Psychology:** General. **Social sciences:** Anthropology, economics, international relations, political science, sociology. **Visual/performing arts:** Art history/conservation, dramatic, studio arts.

Most popular majors. Biology 6%, business/marketing 38%, communications/journalism 9%, psychology 8%, social sciences 15%.

Computing on campus. 250 workstations in dormitories, library, computer center, student center. Dormitories wired for high-speed internet access and linked to campus network. Commuter students can connect to campus network. Online course registration, helpline, repair service, student web hosting, wireless network available.

Student life. **Freshman orientation:** Mandatory. Preregistration for classes offered. 4-day program that starts at the beginning of the semester. **Policies:** Freshmen required to live on campus unless living with parents. **Housing:** Guaranteed on-campus for freshmen. Coed dorms, single-sex dorms, special housing for disabled, apartments available. $300 partly refundable deposit, deadline 5/1. **Activities:** Bands, campus ministries, choral groups, dance, drama, international student organizations, literary magazine, music ensembles, Model UN, musical theater, student government, student newspaper, symphony orchestra, TV station, Black Student Union, Asian Student Association, Young Democrats, Young Republicans, Hawaiian Club, MEChA, Filipino Student Association, Multicultural Center.

Athletics. NCAA. **Intercollegiate:** Baseball M, basketball, cross-country, diving W, football (tackle) M, golf M, rowing (crew), soccer, softball W, swimming W, tennis, volleyball W. **Intramural:** Basketball, football (non-tackle), soccer, softball, tennis, volleyball. **Team name:** Toreros.

Student services. Alcohol/substance abuse counseling, chaplain/spiritual director, career counseling, services for economically disadvantaged, student employment services, financial aid counseling, health services, legal services, on-campus daycare, personal counseling, placement for graduates, veterans' counselor, women's services. **Physically disabled:** Services for visually impaired.

Contact. E-mail: admissions@sandiego.edu
Phone: (619) 260-4506 Toll-free number: (800) 248-4873
Fax: (619) 260-6836
Stephen Pultz, Director of Admissions, University of San Diego, 5998 Alcala Park, San Diego, CA 92110

University of San Francisco

San Francisco, California — **CB member**
www.usfca.edu — **CB code: 4850**

- Private 4-year university affiliated with Roman Catholic Church
- Residential campus in very large city
- 4,934 degree-seeking undergraduates: 3% part-time, 64% women, 4% African American, 21% Asian American, 14% Hispanic American, 1% Native American, 8% international
- 3,291 graduate students
- 64% of applicants admitted
- SAT or ACT with writing, application essay required

General. Founded in 1855. Regionally accredited. **Degrees:** 1,230 bachelor's awarded; master's, doctoral, first professional offered. **ROTC:** Army, Air Force. **Location:** 3 miles from downtown. **Calendar:** 4-1-4, extensive summer session. **Full-time faculty:** 380 total; 92% have terminal degrees, 21% minority, 46% women. **Part-time faculty:** 511 total; 21% minority, 58% women. **Class size:** 49% < 20, 40% 20-39, 8% 40-49, 2% 50-99, less than 1% >100. **Special facilities:** Rare book room, institute for Chinese western cultural history, electron microscope, separate law library available to all students.

Freshman class profile. 8,485 applied, 5,399 admitted, 1,044 enrolled.

Mid 50% test scores		**GPA 2.0-2.99:**	7%
SAT critical reading:	510-620	**Rank in top quarter:**	61%
SAT math:	520-620	**Rank in top tenth:**	26%
SAT writing:	510-620	**Out-of-state:**	29%
ACT composite:	22-27	**Live on campus:**	90%
GPA 3.75 or higher:	29%	**International:**	7%
GPA 3.50-3.74:	22%	**Fraternities:**	1%
GPA 3.0-3.49:	42%	**Sororities:**	1%

Basis for selection. School achievement record, test scores, class rank, school attended, recommendations, extracurricular activities, alumni relationship, personal essay important. Require TOEFL for non-native speakers of English. Interviews required for nursing students. **Homeschooled:** Statement describing homeschool structure and mission, letter of recommendation (nonparent) required. Statement from parents on curriculum required if student not evaluated through high school homeschooling program or agency that evaluates home school programs. **Learning Disabled:** After acceptance, students with disabilities must contact Office of Disablity Related Services to request accommodations.

High school preparation. 20 units required. Required units include English 4, mathematics 3, social studies 3, science 2 (laboratory 2), foreign language 2 and academic electives 6. One chemistry and 1 biology or physics required of nursing and science applicants.

2009-2010 Annual costs. Tuition/fees: $34,770. Nursing undergraduate clinical lab $100 per lab, clinical lab malpractice insurance $25 per lab. Room/board: $11,540. Books/supplies: $1,000. Personal expenses: $2,500.

2008-2009 Financial aid. **Non-need-based:** Scholarships awarded for academics, athletics, ROTC. **Additional information:** Individualized installment plans available.

Application procedures. **Admission:** Priority date 1/15; no deadline. $55 fee, may be waived for applicants with need. Notification begins approximately 4 weeks after all materials submitted including fall grades. Must reply by May 1 or within 2 week(s) if notified thereafter. **Financial aid:** Priority date 2/1; no closing date. FAFSA required. Applicants notified on a rolling basis starting 4/1; must reply within 4 week(s) of notification.

Academics. **Special study options:** Accelerated study, combined bachelor's/graduate degree, cooperative education, cross-registration, distance learning, double major, ESL, exchange student, external degree, honors, independent study, internships, liberal arts/career combination, student-designed major, study abroad, teacher certification program, Washington semester. College of Professional Studies for adult degree-seeking students coming back to school to earn undergraduate bachelor's degree; cooperative work study in Computer Science courses. **Credit/placement by examination:** AP, CLEP, IB, SAT, ACT, institutional tests. 30 credit hours maximum toward bachelor's degree. Credit for experiential learning limited to maximum of 30 undergraduate semester units in College of Professional Studies. **Support services:** Learning center, pre-admission summer program, reduced course load, study skills assistance, tutoring, writing center.

Majors. **Architecture:** Urban/community planning. **Area/ethnic studies:** American. **Biology:** General. **Business:** General, accounting, business admin, entrepreneurial studies, finance, hotel/motel admin, international, marketing, organizational behavior, restaurant/food services. **Communications:** General, advertising, media studies. **Computer sciences:** General, information systems. **Conservation:** Environmental science, environmental studies. **Foreign languages:** Comparative lit, French, Japanese, Spanish. **Health:** Nursing (RN). **History:** General. **Interdisciplinary:** Global studies. **Liberal arts:** Arts/sciences. **Math:** General. **Parks/recreation:** Health/fitness. **Philosophy/religion:** Philosophy. **Physical sciences:** Chemistry, physics. **Psychology:** General. **Public administration:** General. **Social sciences:** Economics, international economics, political science, sociology. **Theology:** Theology. **Visual/performing arts:** General, art history/conservation, arts management, commercial/advertising art, studio arts.

Most popular majors. Business/marketing 29%, communications/journalism 7%, computer/information sciences 6%, health sciences 8%, psychology 8%, social sciences 14%, visual/performing arts 6%.

Computing on campus. 320 workstations in dormitories, library, computer center, student center. Dormitories wired for high-speed internet access and linked to campus network. Commuter students can connect to campus network. Online course registration, online library, helpline, repair service, student web hosting, wireless network available.

Student life. **Freshman orientation:** Mandatory. Preregistration for classes offered. Two-day session including placement tests. **Housing:** Guaranteed on-campus for freshmen. Coed dorms, single-sex dorms, special housing for disabled, apartments available. $300 nonrefundable deposit. Freshman and sophomores under 21 required to live in residence halls unless they have permanent address within 20-mile radius of campus. **Activities:** Pep band, choral groups, dance, drama, international student organizations, literary magazine, music ensembles, musical theater, radio station, student government, student newspaper, TV station, St. Ignatius Institute, People Advocating Cultural Endeavors, Phelan multicultural community.

Athletics. NCAA. **Intercollegiate:** Baseball M, basketball, cross-country, golf, rifle, soccer, tennis, track and field, volleyball W. **Intramural:** Basketball, football (non-tackle), racquetball, soccer, softball, swimming, table tennis, tennis, volleyball. **Team name:** Dons.

Student services. Adult student services, alcohol/substance abuse counseling, chaplain/spiritual director, career counseling, student employment services, financial aid counseling, health services, minority student services, personal counseling, placement for graduates. **Physically disabled:** Services for visually, speech, hearing impaired. **Learning disabled:** Comprehensive services available.

Contact. E-mail: admissions@usfca.edu
Phone: (415) 422-6563 Toll-free number: (800) 225-5873
Fax: (415) 422-2217
Michael Hughes, Director of Admissions, University of San Francisco, 2130 Fulton Street, San Francisco, CA 94117-1046

University of Southern California

Los Angeles, California — **CB member**
www.usc.edu — **CB code: 4852**

- Private 4-year university
- Residential campus in very large city
- 16,283 degree-seeking undergraduates: 3% part-time, 50% women, 5% African American, 23% Asian American, 12% Hispanic American, 1% Native American, 9% international
- 16,213 degree-seeking graduate students
- 22% of applicants admitted
- SAT or ACT with writing, application essay required
- 88% graduate within 6 years

General. Founded in 1880. Regionally accredited. Permanent facilities for study in Sacramento available. **Degrees:** 4,528 bachelor's awarded; master's, doctoral, first professional offered. **ROTC:** Army, Naval, Air Force. **Location:** 3 miles from downtown. **Calendar:** Semester, limited summer session. **Full-time faculty:** 1,666 total; 90% have terminal degrees, 24% minority, 34% women. **Part-time faculty:** 1,081 total; 60% have terminal degrees, 27% minority, 36% women. **Class size:** 64% < 20, 19% 20-39, 6% 40-49, 7% 50-99, 4% >100. **Special facilities:** 3 art/architecture galleries, 2 museums, 2 sculpture gardens, marine science center, Gamble House designed by Greene and Greene, Freeman House designed by Frank Lloyd Wright, integrated media systems center, center for digital arts, technical theater laboratory, recording studio, cinematic arts complex.

Freshman class profile. 35,900 applied, 7,875 admitted, 2,766 enrolled.

Mid 50% test scores		Rank in top quarter:	97%
SAT critical reading:	620-720	Rank in top tenth:	87%
SAT math:	650-750	End year in good standing:	97%
SAT writing:	640-730	Return as sophomores:	97%
ACT composite:	28-33	Out-of-state:	47%
GPA 3.75 or higher:	53%	Live on campus:	99%
GPA 3.50-3.74:	29%	International:	6%
GPA 3.0-3.49:	17%	Fraternities:	20%
GPA 2.0-2.99:	1%	Sororities:	24%

Basis for selection. GED not accepted. Academic achievement, curriculum and test scores most important. Recommendations, activities, essays/writing samples are also very important. Audition required of music and theater majors. Portfolio required of fine arts and architecture majors. **Homeschooled:** 3 SAT Subject tests (1 must be in math) and detailed syllabi of courses, names of textbooks, names and applicable credentials of instructors, details of assistance received or curriculum followed through any public or private agency, and any additional information that may be helpful.

High school preparation. College-preparatory program required. 16 units required; 20 recommended. Required and recommended units include English 4, mathematics 3-4, social studies 2-3, science 2-3 (laboratory 2-3), foreign language 2-3 and academic electives 3.

2008-2009 Annual costs. Tuition/fees: $37,844. Room/board: $11,298.

2007-2008 Financial aid. **Need-based:** 1,849 full-time freshmen applied for aid; 1,194 were judged to have need; 1,193 of these received aid. Average need met was 100%. Average scholarship/grant was $23,131; average loan $4,046. 77% of total undergraduate aid awarded as scholarships/grants, 23% as loans/jobs. **Non-need-based:** Awarded to 6,415 full-time undergraduates, including 1,591 freshmen. Scholarships awarded for academics, alumni affiliation, art, athletics, leadership, music/drama, ROTC.

Application procedures. **Admission:** Priority date 12/10; deadline 1/10 (postmark date). $65 fee, may be waived for applicants with need. Admission notification 4/1. Must reply by 5/1. **Financial aid:** Priority date 2/9; no closing date. FAFSA, CSS PROFILE required. Applicants notified on a rolling basis starting 3/15; must reply by 5/1.

Academics. **Special study options:** Combined bachelor's/graduate degree, cooperative education, distance learning, double major, ESL, exchange student, honors, independent study, internships, liberal arts/career combination, student-designed major, study abroad, Washington semester. Learning communities, thematic option, undergraduate research, freshman seminars. **Credit/placement by examination:** AP, CLEP, IB, institutional tests. 32 credit hours maximum toward bachelor's degree. **Support services:** Learning center, reduced course load, study skills assistance, tutoring, writing center.

Majors. **Architecture:** Architecture, landscape. **Area/ethnic studies:** African-American, American, Asian-American, East Asian, Hispanic-American/Latino/Chicano, women's. **Biology:** General, biochemistry, biophysics. **Business:** Accounting, business admin, international. **Communications:** General, broadcast journalism, journalism, public relations, radio/tv. **Computer sciences:** Computer science. **Conservation:** Environmental science, environmental studies. **Engineering:** Aerospace, biomedical, chemical, civil, computer, construction, electrical, environmental, industrial, mechanical, petroleum, polymer, structural, systems. **Foreign languages:** Classics, comparative lit, East Asian, French, Italian, linguistics, Russian, Spanish. **Health:** Dental hygiene. **History:** General. **Interdisciplinary:** Classical/archaeology, gerontology, global studies, neuroscience. **Math:** General, applied. **Parks/recreation:** Exercise sciences. **Philosophy/religion:** Ethics, Judaic, philosophy, religion. **Physical sciences:** General, astronomy, chemistry, geology, physics. **Psychology:** General. **Public administration:** General. **Social sciences:** Anthropology, economics, geography, international relations, political science, sociology. **Visual/performing arts:** Acting, art history/conservation, dramatic, film/cinema, jazz, music management, music performance, music theory/composition, piano/organ, play/screenwriting, stringed instruments, studio arts, theater arts management, theater design, voice/opera. **Other:** Literature and language.

Most popular majors. Business/marketing 27%, communications/journalism 8%, engineering/engineering technologies 8%, social sciences 13%, visual/performing arts 12%.

Computing on campus. 2,700 workstations in dormitories, library, computer center, student center. Dormitories wired for high-speed internet access and linked to campus network. Commuter students can connect to campus network. Online course registration, online library, helpline, repair service, student web hosting, wireless network available.

Student life. **Freshman orientation:** Available, $150 fee. Preregistration for classes offered. **Policies:** Every incoming student required to take online alcohol education course and pass final exam. **Housing:** Guaranteed on-campus for freshmen. Coed dorms, special housing for disabled, apartments, fraternity/sorority housing, wellness housing available. $400 fully refundable deposit. African-American, Jewish, Latino, LGBT, and Muslim floors, faculty-in-residence programs and residential colleges available. **Activities:** Bands, campus ministries, choral groups, dance, drama, film society, international student organizations, literary magazine, music ensembles, Model UN, musical theater, opera, radio station, student government, student newspaper, symphony orchestra, TV station, academic honors assembly, emerging leaders program, minority consortium, religious council, residential community council, student program board, student volunteer center.

Athletics. NCAA. **Intercollegiate:** Baseball M, basketball, cross-country, diving, football (tackle) M, golf, rowing (crew) W, soccer W, swimming, tennis, track and field, volleyball, water polo. **Intramural:** Baseball M, basketball, cross-country, football (non-tackle), golf, racquetball, soccer, softball, table tennis, tennis, track and field, volleyball, water polo. **Team name:** Trojans.

Student services. Alcohol/substance abuse counseling, chaplain/spiritual director, career counseling, services for economically disadvantaged, student employment services, financial aid counseling, health services, legal services, minority student services, on-campus daycare, personal counseling, placement for graduates, veterans' counselor, women's services. **Physically disabled:** Services for visually, speech, hearing impaired. **Learning disabled:** Comprehensive services available.

Contact. E-mail: admitusc@usc.edu
Phone: (213) 740-1111 Fax: (213) 821-0200
Timothy Brunold, Associate Dean and Director of Undergraduate Admission, University of Southern California, Office of Admission, Los Angeles, CA 90089-0911

University of the Pacific

Stockton, California **CB member**
www.pacific.edu **CB code: 4065**

- Private 4-year university
- Residential campus in large city
- 3,443 degree-seeking undergraduates: 3% part-time, 56% women, 4% African American, 34% Asian American, 11% Hispanic American, 1% Native American, 3% international
- 2,773 degree-seeking graduate students
- 69% of applicants admitted
- SAT or ACT (ACT writing optional), application essay required
- 68% graduate within 6 years

General. Founded in 1851. Regionally accredited. School of Dentistry in San Francisco. McGeorge School of Law in Sacramento. **Degrees:** 726 bachelor's awarded; master's, doctoral, first professional offered. **ROTC:** Air Force. **Location:** 80 miles from San Francisco, 40 miles from Sacramento. **Calendar:** Semester, limited summer session. **Full-time faculty:** 426 total; 92% have terminal degrees, 18% minority, 36% women. **Part-time faculty:** 298 total; 61% have terminal degrees, 25% minority, 42% women. **Class size:** 60% < 20, 30% 20-39, 4% 40-49, 5% 50-99, less than 1% >100. **Special facilities:** Recital facilities, center for western studies, John Muir papers collection, music conservatory.

Freshman class profile. 5,450 applied, 3,783 admitted, 882 enrolled.

Mid 50% test scores		**GPA 2.0-2.99:**	13%
SAT critical reading:	500-620	**Rank in top quarter:**	75%
SAT math:	530-670	**Rank in top tenth:**	39%
SAT writing:	500-620	**Return as sophomores:**	82%
ACT composite:	22-28	**Out-of-state:**	18%
GPA 3.75 or higher:	27%	**Live on campus:**	90%
GPA 3.50-3.74:	27%	**International:**	4%
GPA 3.0-3.49:	33%		

Basis for selection. Secondary school record, standardized test scores, recommendations, essay, extracurricular activities important. SAT Subject Tests recommended. Audition required of music/conservatory majors. **Homeschooled:** Standardized test scores weighted heavily.

High school preparation. College-preparatory program recommended. 16 units required. Required and recommended units include English 4, mathematics 3, social studies 2, history 1, (laboratory 2), foreign language 2, visual/performing arts 1 and academic electives 1. 1 fine/performing arts required.

2009-2010 Annual costs. Tuition/fees: $30,880. Room/board: $10,118. Books/supplies: $1,566. Personal expenses: $2,214.

2008-2009 Financial aid. Need-based: 716 full-time freshmen applied for aid; 605 were judged to have need; 605 of these received aid. Average scholarship/grant was $20,548; average loan $3,764. 71% of total undergraduate aid awarded as scholarships/grants, 29% as loans/jobs. **Non-need-based:** Awarded to 574 full-time undergraduates, including 176 freshmen. Scholarships awarded for academics, athletics, leadership, music/drama, religious affiliation.

Application procedures. Admission: Priority date 11/15; deadline 1/5. $60 fee, may be waived for applicants with need, free for online applicants. Admission notification on a rolling basis beginning on or about 3/15. Housing deposit refundable if canceled by May 1. **Financial aid:** Priority date 2/15; no closing date. FAFSA required. Applicants notified on a rolling basis starting 3/15.

Academics. Special study options: Accelerated study, combined bachelor's/graduate degree, cooperative education, double major, dual enrollment of high school students, ESL, exchange student, honors, independent study, internships, liberal arts/career combination, student-designed major, study abroad, teacher certification program, United Nations semester, Washington semester. Practicum, minors, undergraduate research, combination, ethnic studies, environmental science, gender studies, service learning, thematic minors. **Credit/placement by examination:** AP, CLEP, IB, SAT, ACT, institutional tests. 20 credit hours maximum toward bachelor's degree. **Support services:** Learning center, pre-admission summer program, reduced course load, remedial instruction, tutoring, writing center.

Majors. Biology: General, biochemistry. **Business:** Business admin. **Communications:** General. **Computer sciences:** General, computer science, information systems. **Conservation:** Environmental science, environmental studies. **Education:** General, elementary, multi-level teacher, music, secondary. **Engineering:** General, civil, computer, electrical, mechanical, physics. **Engineering technology:** Industrial management. **Foreign languages:** French, German, Japanese, Spanish. **Health:** Dental hygiene, music therapy, speech pathology. **History:** General. **Interdisciplinary:** Biological/physical sciences. **Liberal arts:** Arts/sciences. **Math:** General, applied. **Parks/recreation:** Health/fitness, sports admin. **Philosophy/religion:** Philosophy, religion. **Physical sciences:** Chemistry, geology, physics. **Psychology:** General. **Social sciences:** General, economics, international relations, political science, sociology. **Visual/performing arts:** Art, commercial/advertising art, dramatic, music history, music management, music performance, music theory/composition, piano/organ, studio arts, voice/opera. **Other:** Geosciences.

Most popular majors. Biology 18%, business/marketing 18%, education 7%, engineering/engineering technologies 9%, health sciences 7%, parks/recreation 7%, social sciences 7%.

Computing on campus. 325 workstations in dormitories, library, computer center. Dormitories wired for high-speed internet access and linked to campus network. Commuter students can connect to campus network. Online course registration, online library, helpline, wireless network available.

Student life. Freshman orientation: Mandatory, $120 fee. Preregistration for classes offered. Offered in January, June, July & August, 2-4 days each. **Housing:** Guaranteed on-campus for freshmen. Coed dorms, apartments, fraternity/sorority housing available. $250 fully refundable deposit. Freshmen and sophomores required to live on campus unless living with parents. **Activities:** Bands, campus ministries, choral groups, dance, drama, film society, international student organizations, literary magazine, music ensembles, Model UN, musical theater, opera, radio station, student government, student newspaper, symphony orchestra, 100 student organizations and clubs.

Athletics. NCAA. **Intercollegiate:** Baseball M, basketball, cross-country W, field hockey W, golf M, soccer W, softball W, swimming, tennis, volleyball, water polo. **Intramural:** Badminton, basketball, bowling, football (tackle), golf, racquetball, soccer, softball, swimming, tennis, volleyball, water polo. **Team name:** Tigers.

Student services. Adult student services, alcohol/substance abuse counseling, chaplain/spiritual director, career counseling, services for economically disadvantaged, student employment services, financial aid counseling, health services, personal counseling, placement for graduates, veterans' counselor. **Physically disabled:** Services for visually, speech, hearing impaired.

Contact. E-mail: admissions@pacific.edu
Phone: (209) 946-2211 Toll-free number: (800) 959-2867
Fax: (209) 946-2413
Rich Toledo, Director of Admissions, University of the Pacific, 3601 Pacific Avenue, Stockton, CA 95211-0197

University of the West

Rosemead, California
www.uwest.edu

- Private 4-year university and liberal arts college affiliated with Buddhism
- Commuter campus in small city
- 65 degree-seeking undergraduates

General. WASC-accredited, private, non profit campus, Buddhist founded institution. **Degrees:** 3 bachelor's awarded; master's, doctoral offered. **Calendar:** Semester, limited summer session. **Full-time faculty:** 9 total. **Part-time faculty:** 21 total.

Basis for selection. Open admission. SAT scores are not required for admission, however a score does help in consideration for admission and for determination of scholarship awards. **Homeschooled:** Handled on case-by-case basis.

2008-2009 Annual costs. Tuition/fees: $9,750. Tuition is $265 per unit for all non-business courses; $315 per unit for all business courses. Room/board: $5,720. Books/supplies: $1,314. Personal expenses: $2,826.

Application procedures. Admission: Priority date 3/1; deadline 6/1. $50 fee. Admission notification on a rolling basis. **Financial aid:** No deadline.

Academics. Special study options: Combined bachelor's/graduate degree, ESL, exchange student, independent study, internships, study abroad.

Credit/placement by examination: CLEP, institutional tests. **Support services:** Learning center, remedial instruction, tutoring, writing center.

Majors. Business: Accounting, international. **History:** General. **Philosophy/religion:** Religion. **Psychology:** General.

Most popular majors. Business/marketing 40%, philosophy/religious studies 40%, psychology 8%.

Computing on campus. 30 workstations in dormitories, library, computer center. Dormitories wired for high-speed internet access and linked to campus network. Commuter students can connect to campus network. Online course registration, online library, student web hosting, wireless network available.

Student life. Freshman orientation: Mandatory. **Housing:** Coed dorms available. $200 fully refundable deposit.

Contact. E-mail: admission@uwest.edu
Phone: (626) 571-8811 ext. 120
Grace Hsiao, Admissions Officer, University of the West, 1409 North Walnut Grove Avenue, Rosemead, CA 91770

Vanguard University of Southern California

Costa Mesa, California
www.vanguard.edu **CB code: 4701**

- Private 4-year university and liberal arts college affiliated with Assemblies of God
- Residential campus in small city
- 1,796 degree-seeking undergraduates: 19% part-time, 61% women, 4% African American, 4% Asian American, 17% Hispanic American, 2% Native American, 1% international
- 290 degree-seeking graduate students
- 81% of applicants admitted
- SAT or ACT (ACT writing optional), application essay required
- 53% graduate within 6 years

General. Founded in 1920. Regionally accredited. **Degrees:** 473 bachelor's awarded; master's offered. **ROTC:** Army, Air Force. **Location:** 45 miles from Los Angeles, 70 miles from San Diego. **Calendar:** Semester, limited summer session. **Full-time faculty:** 85 total; 80% have terminal degrees, 15% minority, 41% women. **Part-time faculty:** 14 total; 43% have terminal degrees, 21% minority, 50% women. **Class size:** 57% < 20, 32% 20-39, 5% 40-49, 6% 50-99.

Freshman class profile. 897 applied, 729 admitted, 313 enrolled.

Mid 50% test scores			
SAT critical reading:	440-550	Rank in top quarter:	29%
SAT math:	420-530	Rank in top tenth:	22%
ACT composite:	18-23	End year in good standing:	86%
GPA 3.75 or higher:	26%	Return as sophomores:	81%
GPA 3.50-3.74:	18%	Out-of-state:	17%
GPA 3.0-3.49:	34%	Live on campus:	90%
GPA 2.0-2.99:	21%	International:	1%

Basis for selection. Priority given to students with GPA of 2.8 or higher, Christian commitment essay, academic reference, reference from pastor. Applications from Christian students who desire an education that integrates Christian faith with learning and living encouraged. Interview recommended for borderline applicants. Audition recommended for music, theater majors. **Homeschooled:** Should take GED to qualify for federal financial aid.

High school preparation. Recommended units include English 4, mathematics 2, social studies 3 and science 2.

2009-2010 Annual costs. Tuition/fees: $25,452. Room/board: $7,994. Books/supplies: $1,638. Personal expenses: $2,250.

2007-2008 Financial aid. Need-based: 318 full-time freshmen applied for aid; 235 were judged to have need; 234 of these received aid. Average need met was 82%. Average scholarship/grant was $14,614; average loan $3,036. 66% of total undergraduate aid awarded as scholarships/grants, 34% as loans/jobs. **Non-need-based:** Awarded to 538 full-time undergraduates, including 169 freshmen. Scholarships awarded for academics, athletics, music/drama, religious affiliation.

Application procedures. Admission: Priority date 12/1; no deadline. $45 fee, may be waived for applicants with need. Admission notification on a rolling basis beginning on or about 1/15. Must reply by May 1 or within 3 week(s) if notified thereafter. **Financial aid:** Priority date 3/2, closing date 3/2. FAFSA required. Applicants notified on a rolling basis starting 4/1; must reply within 3 week(s) of notification.

Academics. Special study options: Accelerated study, combined bachelor's/graduate degree, double major, liberal arts/career combination, study abroad, teacher certification program, Washington semester. **Credit/placement by examination:** AP, CLEP, IB, SAT, ACT. 24 credit hours maximum toward bachelor's degree. **Support services:** Learning center, reduced course load, study skills assistance, tutoring, writing center.

Majors. Biology: General, biochemistry. **Business:** General, accounting, business admin, finance, international, marketing. **Communications:** General, digital media. **Computer sciences:** Information technology. **Education:** Music, physical. **Family/consumer sciences:** Family studies. **Health:** Athletic training, nursing (RN), premedicine. **History:** General. **Interdisciplinary:** Biological/physical sciences, intercultural. **Legal studies:** Prelaw. **Liberal arts:** Arts/sciences. **Math:** General. **Parks/recreation:** Exercise sciences, health/fitness. **Philosophy/religion:** Christian, religion. **Physical sciences:** Chemistry. **Psychology:** General. **Social sciences:** General, anthropology, political science, sociology. **Theology:** Bible, missionary, pastoral counseling, religious ed, theology, youth ministry. **Visual/performing arts:** Cinematography, dramatic, music history, music performance, theater design. **Other:** Physical therapy/therapist.

Most popular majors. Business/marketing 29%, communications/journalism 7%, education 10%, psychology 16%, social sciences 8%, theological studies 8%.

Computing on campus. 182 workstations in dormitories, library, computer center. Dormitories wired for high-speed internet access and linked to campus network. Commuter students can connect to campus network. Online course registration, online library, helpline, wireless network available.

Student life. Freshman orientation: Mandatory, $80 fee. Preregistration for classes offered. 4-day program prior to first day of fall semester. **Policies:** Students must be in good standing to live on campus. Religious observance required. **Housing:** Guaranteed on-campus for all undergraduates. Coed dorms, single-sex dorms, apartments, wellness housing available. $400 deposit, deadline 8/9. **Activities:** Bands, campus ministries, choral groups, dance, drama, film society, international student organizations, literary magazine, music ensembles, musical theater, student government, student newspaper, Students for Social Action (SSA), Live 2 Free, Club Mosaic, El Puente, Students in Free Enterprise (SIFE), Invisible Children Club, Acting on AIDS, Prayer Movement, Hands Across the Border (HATB).

Athletics. NAIA. **Intercollegiate:** Baseball M, basketball, cross-country, soccer, softball W, swimming, tennis, track and field, volleyball W. **Intramural:** Basketball. **Team name:** Lions.

Student services. Adult student services, alcohol/substance abuse counseling, chaplain/spiritual director, career counseling, student employment services, financial aid counseling, health services, minority student services, personal counseling, placement for graduates, veterans' counselor, women's services.

Contact. E-mail: admissions@vanguard.edu
Phone: (714) 966-5496 ext. 3901 Toll-free number: (800) 722-6279
Fax: (714) 966-5471
Calli Christenson, Director of Undergraduate Admissions, Vanguard University of Southern California, 55 Fair Drive, Costa Mesa, CA 92626-9601

West Coast University

Los Angeles, California
www.westcoastuniversity.com/ **CB code: 4966**

- For-profit 4-year health science college
- Commuter campus in very large city
- 556 degree-seeking undergraduates
- Interview required

General. Accredited by ACICS. **Degrees:** 13 bachelor's, 235 associate awarded. **Location:** Downtown. **Calendar:** Semester. **Full-time faculty:** 10 total. **Part-time faculty:** 20 total.

Basis for selection. Open admission, but selective for some programs. Incoming students must pass entrance exams for any program where it is required for entry. Academic record is important but not definitive. Interview with admissions and program director required. **Learning Disabled:** Students with disabilities should make a request for accomodations through the University Student Services department.

2009-2010 Annual costs. LVN to RN (associate degree in nursing), 4 semesters, $9,500/semester plus clinical course costs of $4,250 per clinical rotation, books and fees; RN to BSN Bridge Program, 4 semesters, $9,500/semester plus clinical course costs of $4,250 per clinical rotation, books and fees; bachelor of science in nursing, 8 semesters, $9,500/semester plus clinical course costs of $4,250 per clinical rotation, books and fees. Subject to change. Books/supplies: $3,865. Personal expenses: $3,024.

Application procedures. Admission: No deadline.

Academics. Special study options: Accelerated study, distance learning, internships. **Credit/placement by examination:** CLEP, institutional tests. May challenge test-out of 12 semester credits, maximum. Must achieve score of 75% or higher, one attempt only. Must be taken before enrolling in the course in which equivalency is sought. **Support services:** Study skills assistance, tutoring.

Majors. Health: Nursing (RN).

Computing on campus. 23 workstations in library. Online library available.

Student life. Freshman orientation: Mandatory. **Activities:** Student government.

Student services. Adult student services, career counseling, services for economically disadvantaged, student employment services, financial aid counseling, personal counseling, placement for graduates.

Contact. Phone: (877) 505-4928
Herman Whitaker, Admissions Director, West Coast University, 4021 Rosewood Avenue, Los Angeles, CA 90004

Western Career College: Emeryville

Emeryville, California
www.westerncollege.edu

- For-profit 4-year technical college
- Commuter campus in small town

General. Regionally accredited. **Calendar:** Continuous.

Annual costs/financial aid. ADD: tuition $16,092, fees $498; ADD-AS: tuition $24,372, fees $1,372; ASHS: tuition $11,385, fees $1,248; CJD: tuition $24,066, fees $2,052; GD: tuition $20,115, fees $382; GDD: tuition $27,360, fees $1,256; HCA: tuition $16,092, fees $704; HCAD: tuition $27,477, fees $1,952; HIT: tuition $16,092, fees $1,131; HITD: tuition $27,477, fees $2,379; MA: tuition $16,092, fees $387; MAD: tuition $27,477, fees $1,635; MT: tuition $14,751, fees $819; MTD: tuition $26,136, fees $2,067; PTD: tuition $24,066, fees $1,779. Registration fee $100. Need-based financial aid available for full-time students.

Contact. Phone: (510) 601-0133
6001 Shellmound, #145, Emeryville, CA 94608

Westmont College

Santa Barbara, California — **CB member**
www.westmont.edu — **CB code: 4950**

- Private 4-year liberal arts college affiliated with nondenominational tradition
- Residential campus in small city
- 1,327 degree-seeking undergraduates: 1% part-time, 62% women, 2% African American, 10% Asian American, 11% Hispanic American, 2% Native American, 1% international
- 8 graduate students
- 66% of applicants admitted
- SAT or ACT with writing, application essay required
- 80% graduate within 6 years

General. Founded in 1937. Regionally accredited. **Degrees:** 296 bachelor's awarded. **ROTC:** Army, Air Force. **Location:** 90 miles from Los Angeles. **Calendar:** Semester, limited summer session. **Full-time faculty:** 90 total; 92% have terminal degrees, 13% minority, 33% women. **Part-time faculty:** 36 total; 11% minority, 53% women. **Class size:** 59% < 20, 28% 20-39, 11% 40-49, 2% 50-99. **Special facilities:** Arts center with theater, observatory, electronic music lab, physiology lab.

Freshman class profile. 2,078 applied, 1,364 admitted, 109 enrolled.

Mid 50% test scores		**GPA 2.0-2.99:**	3%
SAT critical reading:	560-660	**Rank in top quarter:**	73%
SAT math:	550-660	**Rank in top tenth:**	40%
SAT writing:	550-650	**Return as sophomores:**	86%
ACT composite:	24-29	**Out-of-state:**	30%
GPA 3.75 or higher:	58%	**Live on campus:**	100%
GPA 3.50-3.74:	22%	**International:**	1%
GPA 3.0-3.49:	17%		

Basis for selection. Personal Christian statement, college preparatory high school curriculum, high school rank, test scores, 1 academic recommendation, and essays important. Personal interview, teacher, pastor, and other recommendations may enhance chances. Test scores must be received by November 1 for Early Action applicants. International applicants must submit TOEFL scores if native language is other than English. Personal interviews recommended. **Homeschooled:** Applicants encouraged. Evaluation based on individual merit as well as high school achievement. Greater emphasis may be given to SAT or ACT scores.

High school preparation. College-preparatory program required. 16 units required. Required and recommended units include English 4, mathematics 3, social studies 2, science 3 (laboratory 2), foreign language 2-3 and academic electives 4. Of 3 math credits recommended, 2 algebra, 1 geometry preferred. Applicants should take composition courses at least 1 semester per year.

2009-2010 Annual costs. Tuition/fees: $33,190. Room/board: $10,550. Books/supplies: $1,638. Personal expenses: $2,142.

2008-2009 Financial aid. Need-based: 273 full-time freshmen applied for aid; 223 were judged to have need; 223 of these received aid. Average need met was 72%. Average scholarship/grant was $19,597; average loan $4,440. 70% of total undergraduate aid awarded as scholarships/grants, 30% as loans/jobs. **Non-need-based:** Awarded to 523 full-time undergraduates, including 142 freshmen. Scholarships awarded for academics, art, athletics, leadership, minority status, music/drama.

Application procedures. Admission: Priority date 2/20; no deadline. $50 fee, may be waived for applicants with need. Admission notification on a rolling basis beginning on or about 4/1. Must reply by May 1 or within 2 week(s) if notified thereafter. Candidates not accepted for Early Action may be considered for admission under Regular Decision. This allows time for submission of additional materials that may strengthen overall application. **Financial aid:** Priority date 3/1; no closing date. FAFSA required. Applicants notified by 3/15; Applicants notified on a rolling basis starting 3/15; must reply by 5/1 or within 2 week(s) of notification.

Academics. Special study options: Accelerated study, double major, exchange student, honors, independent study, internships, semester at sea, student-designed major, study abroad, teacher certification program, urban semester, Washington semester. Cross-cultural studies in Western and Eastern Europe, England, Africa, East Asia, Egypt; semester study available in San Francisco, Los Angeles, Mexico and at one of 12 other member colleges of the Christian College Consortium. **Credit/placement by examination:** AP, CLEP, IB, SAT, ACT, institutional tests. 32 credit hours maximum toward bachelor's degree. **Support services:** Learning center, study skills assistance, tutoring, writing center.

Majors. Area/ethnic studies: European. **Biology:** General. **Business:** General. **Communications:** General. **Computer sciences:** Computer science. **Education:** General. **Engineering:** Physics. **Foreign languages:** French, Spanish. **Health:** Predental, premedicine, prenursing, prepharmacy, preveterinary. **History:** General. **Legal studies:** Prelaw. **Math:** General. **Parks/recreation:** Exercise sciences. **Philosophy/religion:** Philosophy, religion. **Physical sciences:** Chemistry, physics. **Psychology:** General. **Social sciences:** General, anthropology, economics, political science, sociology. **Visual/performing arts:** Art, dramatic. **Other:** English and modern languages.

Most popular majors. Biology 11%, business/marketing 11%, communications/journalism 8%, English 10%, parks/recreation 7%, social sciences 14%, visual/performing arts 10%.

Computing on campus. 100 workstations in library, computer center. Dormitories wired for high-speed internet access and linked to campus network. Commuter students can connect to campus network. Online library, helpline, student web hosting, wireless network available.

Student life. Freshman orientation: Mandatory. Preregistration for classes offered. Overnight program in summer. **Policies:** Chapel attendance required on Mondays, Wednesdays, Fridays. Dry, tobacco-free campus. Religious observance required. **Housing:** Guaranteed on-campus for all undergraduates. Coed dorms, single-sex dorms, apartments, wellness housing available. $500 nonrefundable deposit, deadline 5/1. Coed dorms segregated by floors and/or suites. Men and women do not share hallways and bathrooms. Selected visiting hours for members of opposite sex. **Activities:** Jazz band, campus ministries, choral groups, dance, drama, film society, international student organizations, literary magazine, music ensembles, Model UN, musical theater, radio station, student government, student newspaper, symphony orchestra, Amnesty International, Habitat for Humanity, Leadership Development Program, political organizations, Fellowship of Christian Athletes, community service organizations.

Athletics. NAIA. **Intercollegiate:** Baseball M, basketball, cross-country, soccer, tennis, track and field, volleyball W. **Intramural:** Badminton, basketball, cross-country, field hockey W, football (non-tackle), golf, lacrosse W, racquetball, soccer, softball, swimming, table tennis, tennis, volleyball, water polo. **Team name:** Warriors.

Student services. Alcohol/substance abuse counseling, chaplain/spiritual director, career counseling, student employment services, financial aid counseling, health services, minority student services, personal counseling, placement for graduates. **Physically disabled:** Services for visually, speech, hearing impaired.

Contact. E-mail: admissions@westmont.edu
Phone: (805) 565-6200 Toll-free number: (800) 777-9011
Fax: (805) 565-6234
Joyce Luy, Dean of Admission, Westmont College, 955 La Paz Road, Santa Barbara, CA 93108-1089

Westwood College: Anaheim

Anaheim, California
www.westwood.edu

- For-profit 4-year technical college
- Very large city
- 980 degree-seeking undergraduates
- Interview required

General. Accredited by ACCSCT. **Degrees:** 174 bachelor's, 19 associate awarded. **Calendar:** Continuous. **Full-time faculty:** 19 total. **Part-time faculty:** 49 total.

Basis for selection. Admissions decisions based on assessment test and interview.

2008-2009 Annual costs. Associate degree program: $14,229. Bachelor's degree program: $15,331. Costs may vary by specific program.

Application procedures. Admission: $25 fee. Admission notification on a rolling basis. **Financial aid:** FAFSA required. Applicants notified on a rolling basis.

Academics. Credit/placement by examination: AP, CLEP.

Majors. Business: Accounting/finance, business admin, marketing. **Computer sciences:** Networking, security, web page design, webmaster. **Visual/performing arts:** Design.

Contact. Phone: (714) 938-6140 ext. 60100 Toll-free number: (877) 650-6050
Wes Camp, Director of Admissions, Westwood College: Anaheim, 1551 South Douglass Road, Anaheim, CA 92806

Westwood College: Inland Empire

Upland, California
www.westwood.edu

- For-profit 3-year business and technical college
- Commuter campus in small city
- 993 degree-seeking undergraduates
- Interview required

General. Accredited by ACCSCT. **Degrees:** 182 bachelor's, 26 associate awarded. **Location:** 45 miles from Los Angeles, 22 miles from Riverside. **Calendar:** Continuous, extensive summer session. **Full-time faculty:** 15 total. **Part-time faculty:** 70 total. **Class size:** 64% < 20, 36% 20-39.

Basis for selection. Interview required, documentation of prior education and proficiency in basic college-level skills required, English language proficiency required for applicants whose native language is not English. SAT or ACT recommended. If SAT or ACT scores are not submitted or do not meet minimum requirements, students must take campus-administered ACCUPLACER placement exam.

2008-2009 Annual costs. Tuition/fees: $14,061. Books/supplies: $2,012. Personal expenses: $1,840.

Financial aid. Non-need-based: Scholarships awarded for academics.

Application procedures. Admission: Priority date 10/15; deadline 10/21 (receipt date). $25 fee. Admission notification on a rolling basis. **Financial aid:** No deadline. FAFSA, institutional form required. Must reply within 1 week(s) of notification.

Academics. Special study options: Cooperative education, distance learning, honors, independent study, liberal arts/career combination. Hybrid schedules: combination of both campus and online courses. **Credit/placement by examination:** AP, CLEP, IB, institutional tests. Students may test out of required courses by passing proficiency exams. **Support services:** Learning center, reduced course load, remedial instruction, study skills assistance, tutoring.

Majors. BACHELOR'S. Business: E-commerce, marketing. **Communications:** Digital media. **Communications technology:** Animation/special effects. **Computer sciences:** LAN/WAN management, web page design. **Protective services:** Police science. **Visual/performing arts:** Design, interior design. **ASSOCIATE. Communications:** Digital media. **Computer sciences:** Applications programming. **Engineering technology:** Architectural drafting, computer systems, drafting. **Visual/performing arts:** Commercial/advertising art, graphic design.

Computing on campus. 50 workstations in library. Online library available.

Student life. Freshman orientation: Mandatory. **Activities:** Student government, student newspaper.

Student services. Career counseling, services for economically disadvantaged, student employment services, financial aid counseling, placement for graduates, veterans' counselor.

Contact. E-mail: laiinternet@westwood.edu
Phone: (909) 931-7550 Toll-free number: (866) 288-9488
Fax: (909) 931-5962
Alma Salazar, Director of Admissions, Westwood College: Inland Empire, 20 West Seventh Street, Upland, CA 91786

Westwood College: South Bay

Torrance, California
www.westwood.edu

- For-profit 4-year technical college
- Large city
- 600 degree-seeking undergraduates

General. Accredited by ACCSCT. **Degrees:** 119 bachelor's, 16 associate awarded. **Calendar:** Continuous. **Full-time faculty:** 5 total; 60% women. **Part-time faculty:** 54 total.

Basis for selection. High school record and institutional assessment exam most important. Institutional assessment exam required if ACT/SAT not submitted.

Application procedures. Admission: No deadline. $100 fee.

Academics. Credit/placement by examination: CLEP.

Majors. Communications technology: Animation/special effects, graphics. **Computer sciences:** LAN/WAN management, security. **Construction:** General. **Protective services:** Criminal justice. **Visual/performing arts:** Interior design.

Contact. Phone: (310) 965-0888 Fax: (310) 516-8232
Fred Polk, Admissions Director, Westwood College: South Bay, 19700 South Vermont Avenue #100, Torrance, CA 90502

Whittier College

Whittier, California — **CB member**
www.whittier.edu — **CB code: 4952**

- Private 4-year liberal arts college
- Residential campus in small city
- 1,291 degree-seeking undergraduates: 3% African American, 8% Asian American, 30% Hispanic American, 1% Native American, 2% international
- 72% of applicants admitted

- SAT or ACT with writing, application essay required
- 57% graduate within 6 years

General. Founded in 1887. Regionally accredited. Historic affiliation with the Quakers. **Degrees:** 307 bachelor's awarded; master's, first professional offered. **ROTC:** Army, Air Force. **Location:** 18 miles from Los Angeles. **Calendar:** 4-1-4, limited summer session. **Full-time faculty:** 87 total; 100% have terminal degrees, 28% minority, 44% women. **Part-time faculty:** 36 total; 42% have terminal degrees, 61% minority, 64% women. **Class size:** 55% < 20, 42% 20-39, 1% 40-49, 1% 50-99. **Special facilities:** Quaker books and materials collection, John Greenleaf Whittier collection including manuscripts, letters and furniture, collection of Richard M. Nixon gifts, keck image processing laboratory.

Freshman class profile. 2,186 applied, 1,581 admitted, 403 enrolled.

Mid 50% test scores		**Rank in top quarter:**	35%
SAT critical reading:	470-580	**Rank in top tenth:**	21%
SAT math:	460-580	**Return as sophomores:**	78%
SAT writing:	460-580	**Out-of-state:**	31%
ACT composite:	21-25	**Live on campus:**	86%
GPA 3.75 or higher:	7%	**International:**	4%
GPA 3.50-3.74:	11%	**Fraternities:**	11%
GPA 3.0-3.49:	36%	**Sororities:**	18%
GPA 2.0-2.99:	46%		

Basis for selection. GPA, course selection, and class rank most important followed by essays, references, interviews, test scores, activities, and geographic considerations. Interview recommended. **Homeschooled:** Statement describing homeschool structure and mission, transcript of courses and grades, letter of recommendation (nonparent) required.

High school preparation. College-preparatory program required. Required and recommended units include English 3-4, mathematics 2-3, social studies 1-2, science 1-2 (laboratory 1) and foreign language 2-3.

2008-2009 Annual costs. Tuition/fees: $32,270. Room/board: $9,050. Books/supplies: $1,566. Personal expenses: $2,214.

2008-2009 Financial aid. Need-based: 341 full-time freshmen applied for aid; 213 were judged to have need; 210 of these received aid. Average need met was 94%. Average scholarship/grant was $15,995; average loan $6,331. 23% of total undergraduate aid awarded as scholarships/grants, 77% as loans/jobs. **Non-need-based:** Awarded to 853 full-time undergraduates, including 209 freshmen. Scholarships awarded for academics, alumni affiliation, art, leadership, minority status. **Additional information:** Auditions required for talent scholarship applicants in art, music, and theater.

Application procedures. Admission: Priority date 2/1; no deadline. $50 fee, may be waived for applicants with need. Admission notification on a rolling basis beginning on or about 12/30. Must reply by May 1 or within 2 week(s) if notified thereafter. **Financial aid:** Priority date 3/1, closing date 6/30. FAFSA, institutional form, CSS PROFILE required. Applicants notified on a rolling basis starting 2/15; must reply within 2 week(s) of notification.

Academics. Special study options: Combined bachelor's/graduate degree, double major, independent study, internships, liberal arts/career combination, semester at sea, student-designed major, study abroad, teacher certification program, Washington semester. **Credit/placement by examination:** AP, CLEP, IB, SAT, ACT, institutional tests. 30 credit hours maximum toward bachelor's degree. **Support services:** Learning center, study skills assistance, tutoring, writing center.

Majors. Area/ethnic studies: Latin American. **Biology:** General. **Business:** General. **Conservation:** General. **Education:** General, early childhood. **Foreign languages:** General, comparative lit, French, Spanish. **Health:** Athletic training, predental, premedicine, prepharmacy, preveterinary, recreational therapy. **History:** General. **Legal studies:** Prelaw. **Liberal arts:** Arts/sciences. **Math:** General. **Philosophy/religion:** Philosophy, religion. **Physical sciences:** Chemistry, physics. **Psychology:** General. **Public administration:** Social work. **Social sciences:** Anthropology, international relations, political science, sociology, urban studies. **Visual/performing arts:** Art, art history/conservation, dramatic, music history, theater history.

Most popular majors. Biology 11%, business/marketing 15%, parks/recreation 7%, psychology 8%, social sciences 26%, visual/performing arts 6%.

Computing on campus. 165 workstations in dormitories, library, computer center. Dormitories wired for high-speed internet access and linked to campus network. Online course registration, helpline, wireless network available.

Student life. Freshman orientation: Mandatory, $200 fee. Orientation begins over Labor Day weekend. **Housing:** Guaranteed on-campus for freshmen. Coed dorms, single-sex dorms, wellness housing available. $200 nonrefundable deposit, deadline 5/1. Multicultural hall, honors floor, living and learning community available. **Activities:** Jazz band, choral groups, dance, drama, international student organizations, literary magazine, music ensembles, Model UN, musical theater, radio station, student government, student newspaper, national honor societies.

Athletics. NCAA. **Intercollegiate:** Baseball M, basketball, cross-country, diving, football (tackle) M, golf, lacrosse, soccer, softball W, swimming, tennis, track and field, volleyball W, water polo. **Intramural:** Basketball, softball, volleyball. **Team name:** Poets.

Student services. Career counseling, student employment services, health services, on-campus daycare, personal counseling, placement for graduates.

Contact. E-mail: admission@whittier.edu
Phone: (562) 907-4238 Fax: (562) 907-4870
Kieron Miller, Director of Admission, Whittier College, 13406 East Philadelphia Street, Whittier, CA 90608-0634

William Jessup University

Rocklin, California
www.jessup.edu **CB code: 4756**

- Private 4-year Bible and liberal arts college affiliated with nondenominational tradition
- Residential campus in small city
- 453 degree-seeking undergraduates: 21% part-time, 56% women, 5% African American, 6% Asian American, 7% Hispanic American, 2% Native American
- 3 degree-seeking graduate students
- 65% of applicants admitted
- SAT or ACT (ACT writing recommended), application essay required
- 35% graduate within 6 years

General. Founded in 1939. Regionally accredited; also accredited by ABHE. **Degrees:** 170 bachelor's, 1 associate awarded. **Location:** 20 miles from Sacramento. **Calendar:** Semester, limited summer session. **Full-time faculty:** 20 total; 50% have terminal degrees, 5% minority, 45% women. **Part-time faculty:** 53 total; 23% have terminal degrees, 9% minority, 30% women. **Class size:** 82% < 20, 17% 20-39, less than 1% 50-99, less than 1% >100.

Freshman class profile. 164 applied, 106 admitted, 57 enrolled.

Mid 50% test scores		**GPA 3.0-3.49:**	27%
SAT critical reading:	460-590	**GPA 2.0-2.99:**	25%
SAT math:	480-590	**Rank in top quarter:**	47%
SAT writing:	460-610	**Rank in top tenth:**	19%
ACT composite:	19-27	**Return as sophomores:**	79%
GPA 3.75 or higher:	33%	**Out-of-state:**	7%
GPA 3.50-3.74:	14%	**Live on campus:**	88%

Basis for selection. Academic records, supporting documents, moral character, willingness to comply with standards and values of university strongly considered. Interview strongly recommended, may be required. Audition required for music scholarship (majors only). **Homeschooled:** Statement describing homeschool structure and mission required. Extra emphasis placed on SAT/ACT; professional/third-party home educators transcript provider preferred over in-home development of transcripts. **Learning Disabled:** Once voluntarily disclosed, student is asked to provide documentation of learning disability and meet with academic support advisor regularly.

High school preparation. College-preparatory program recommended. 17 units required; 24 recommended. Required and recommended units include English 4, mathematics 3-4, social studies 1-2, history 2-3, science 2-3 (laboratory 1-2), foreign language 2-3 and academic electives 2-3. Religion taken for credit at accredited parochial/Christian high school may be given academic consideration.

2008-2009 Annual costs. Tuition/fees: $20,480. Room/board: $7,470. Books/supplies: $1,566. Personal expenses: $2,214.

2008-2009 Financial aid. Need-based: 54 full-time freshmen applied for aid; 41 were judged to have need; 41 of these received aid. Average need met was 74%. Average scholarship/grant was $10,033; average loan $3,257. 69% of total undergraduate aid awarded as scholarships/grants, 31% as loans/jobs. **Non-need-based:** Awarded to 333 full-time undergraduates, including 71 freshmen. Scholarships awarded for academics, athletics, leadership, minority status, music/drama, religious affiliation.

Application procedures. Admission: Priority date 4/1; deadline 8/25 (postmark date). $35 fee, may be waived for applicants with need. Admission notification on a rolling basis beginning on or about 11/15. Must reply by June 1 or within 2 weeks of notification of admission. $250 confirmation deposit is applied to housing and refundable until June 1 or within 2 weeks if notified thereafter. **Financial aid:** Priority date 3/2; no closing date. FAFSA required. Applicants notified on a rolling basis starting 3/2; must reply within 3 week(s) of notification.

Academics. All church vocation/ministry-based degrees offer dual major in Bible and Theology. Emphasis placed on pastoral training, missions, youth ministry, and Christian education. **Special study options:** Double major, independent study, internships, study abroad, teacher certification program, Washington semester. Adult degree completion program. **Credit/placement by examination:** AP, CLEP, IB, SAT, ACT, institutional tests. 16 credit hours maximum toward associate degree, 16 toward bachelor's. A maximum of 30 units will be awarded for AP, IB, or CLEP. **Support services:** Reduced course load, study skills assistance, tutoring, writing center.

Majors. Business: Business admin. **Education:** Elementary, multi-level teacher. **History:** General. **Psychology:** General. **Public administration:** Policy analysis. **Theology:** Missionary, pastoral counseling, religious ed, theology, youth ministry.

Most popular majors. Business/marketing 12%, psychology 18%, theological studies 63%.

Computing on campus. 35 workstations in library, computer center. Dormitories wired for high-speed internet access and linked to campus network. Commuter students can connect to campus network. Online library, helpline, repair service, wireless network available.

Student life. Freshman orientation: Mandatory. Preregistration for classes offered. 2-day sessions in late spring and summer. **Policies:** Dry campus. Quiet hours but no curfew. No formal dress code, but appropriate dress recommended. Chapel attendance required. Religious observance required. **Housing:** Guaranteed on-campus for freshmen. Coed dorms, single-sex dorms available. **Activities:** Jazz band, campus ministries, choral groups, film society, music ensembles, student government, spiritual formation groups, multicultural fellowship.

Athletics. NAIA. **Intercollegiate:** Basketball, cross-country, golf M, soccer, track and field, volleyball W. **Team name:** Warriors.

Student services. Chaplain/spiritual director, career counseling, financial aid counseling, personal counseling. **Physically disabled:** Services for visually, hearing impaired.

Contact. E-mail: admissions@jessup.edu
Phone: (916) 577-2222 Toll-free number: (800) 355-7522
Fax: (916) 577-2220
Vance Pascua, Director of Admission, William Jessup University, 333 Sunset Boulevard, Rocklin, CA 95765

Woodbury University

Burbank, California — **CB member**
www.woodbury.edu — **CB code: 4955**

- Private 4-year university
- Commuter campus in very large city
- 1,254 degree-seeking undergraduates
- 73% of applicants admitted
- SAT or ACT (ACT writing optional), application essay required

General. Founded in 1884. Regionally accredited. **Degrees:** 305 bachelor's awarded; master's offered. **Location:** 15 miles from downtown Los Angeles. **Calendar:** Semester, limited summer session. **Full-time faculty:** 48 total; 77% have terminal degrees. **Part-time faculty:** 215 total. **Class size:** 83% < 20, 16% 20-39, less than 1% 40-49. **Special facilities:** Design galleries.

Freshman class profile. 494 applied, 360 admitted, 157 enrolled.

Mid 50% test scores			
SAT critical reading:	410-530	Out-of-state:	10%
SAT math:	420-550	Live on campus:	7%
SAT writing:	410-530	Fraternities:	1%
		Sororities:	1%

Basis for selection. Primary emphasis placed on applicant's prior academic record and standardized test scores. Interview recommended. **Homeschooled:** State high school equivalency certificate required.

High school preparation. College-preparatory program recommended. 15 units recommended. Recommended units include English 4, mathematics 3, social studies 3, history 2, science 3 (laboratory 2) and foreign language 2.

2008-2009 Annual costs. Tuition/fees: $26,978. Room/board: $9,093. Books/supplies: $1,566. Personal expenses: $2,214.

2008-2009 Financial aid. Need-based: 58% of total undergraduate aid awarded as scholarships/grants, 42% as loans/jobs. **Non-need-based:** Scholarships awarded for academics.

Application procedures. Admission: No deadline. $35 fee, may be waived for applicants with need. Admission notification on a rolling basis beginning on or about 11/1. Must reply by May 1 or within 4 week(s) if notified thereafter. **Financial aid:** Priority date 3/2; no closing date. FAFSA, institutional form required. Applicants notified on a rolling basis starting 3/15; must reply by 5/1 or within 2 week(s) of notification.

Academics. Combines professional programs in design, architecture, and business with liberal arts components. **Special study options:** Accelerated study, double major, independent study, internships, liberal arts/career combination, student-designed major, study abroad, weekend college. **Credit/placement by examination:** AP, CLEP, IB, institutional tests. Institutional/departmental examinations used for placement or counseling. **Support services:** Learning center, reduced course load, remedial instruction, tutoring.

Majors. Architecture: Architecture, interior. **Business:** Accounting, business admin, fashion, marketing, organizational behavior. **Communications:** Media studies. **Computer sciences:** General. **Psychology:** General. **Visual/performing arts:** Commercial/advertising art, fashion design, graphic design. **Other:** Film/video and photographic arts, Politics and history.

Most popular majors. Architecture 37%, business/marketing 29%, visual/performing arts 20%.

Computing on campus. 135 workstations in library, computer center. Commuter students can connect to campus network. Online course registration, online library, helpline, wireless network available.

Student life. Freshman orientation: Mandatory, $75 fee. Preregistration for classes offered. **Housing:** Coed dorms, apartments, wellness housing available. $150 fully refundable deposit, deadline 5/1. **Activities:** International student organizations, student government, Armenian student association, residence life council.

Athletics. Intramural: Basketball, soccer.

Student services. Adult student services, alcohol/substance abuse counseling, career counseling, services for economically disadvantaged, student employment services, financial aid counseling, health services, personal counseling, placement for graduates. **Physically disabled:** Services for visually, speech, hearing impaired.

Contact. E-mail: admissions@woodbury.edu
Phone: (818) 767-0888 ext. 221 Toll-free number: (800) 784-9663
Fax: (818) 767-7520
Ruth Lorenzana, Director of Admissions, Woodbury University, 7500 Glenoaks Boulevard, Burbank, CA 91510-7846

World Mission University

Los Angeles, California
www.wmu.edu

- Private 4-year Bible and seminary college affiliated with nondenominational tradition
- Very large city
- 108 degree-seeking undergraduates

General. Accredited by ABHE. **Degrees:** 26 bachelor's awarded; master's, first professional offered. **Location:** Downtown. **Calendar:** Semester, limited summer session. **Full-time faculty:** 5 total. **Part-time faculty:** 3 total.

Basis for selection. Admissions criteria include sense of calling for Christian ministry, participation in church community, academic performance, test results, recommendations. Audition and additional supplementary application required for music programs. **Homeschooled:** Statement describing homeschool structure and mission, transcript of courses and grades, letter of recommendation (nonparent) required.

2008-2009 Annual costs. Tuition/fees: $4,600.

Application procedures. Admission: No deadline. $50 fee. Application must be submitted on paper. Admission notification on a rolling basis.

Academics. Special study options: Distance learning, dual enrollment of high school students, ESL. **Credit/placement by examination:** CLEP, IB, institutional tests.

Majors. Theology: Bible.

Computing on campus. Online library, wireless network available.

Student life. Freshman orientation: Mandatory.

Contact. E-mail: wmuoffice@gmail.com
Phone: (213) 385-2322 Fax: (213) 385-2332
Edmund Rhee, Admissions Director, World Mission University, 500 Shatto Place, Los Angeles, CA 90020

Yeshiva Ohr Elchonon Chabad/West Coast Talmudical Seminary
Los Angeles, California

CB code: 1331

- Private 4-year rabbinical college for men affiliated with Jewish faith
- Residential campus in very large city
- 118 degree-seeking undergraduates: 3% Asian American, 11% international
- Interview required

General. Founded in 1953. Accredited by AARTS. Ordination available. **Degrees:** 19 bachelor's awarded; first professional offered. **Calendar:** Semester, limited summer session. **Full-time faculty:** 5 total. **Part-time faculty:** 3 total.

Freshman class profile. 39 applied, 29 admitted, 29 enrolled.

Out-of-state:	30%	**International:**	7%
Live on campus:	100%		

Basis for selection. Open admission, but selective for some programs. Interview, recommendations, religious affiliation or commitment, and test scores most important. Priority given to California residents. **Homeschooled:** Statement describing homeschool structure and mission, interview, letter of recommendation (nonparent) required.

High school preparation. Recommended units include English 3, mathematics 3, social studies 3, history 2, science 3 and foreign language 2.

2009-2010 Annual costs. Tuition/fees: $10,500. Room/board: $6,500. Books/supplies: $100. Personal expenses: $100.

Application procedures. Admission: No deadline. No application fee. Admission notification on a rolling basis. **Financial aid:** Priority date 1/15, closing date 3/1. Institutional form required. Applicants notified by 5/1; must reply by 7/1.

Academics. Special study options: Dual enrollment of high school students, independent study, weekend college. **Credit/placement by examination:** CLEP, institutional tests. 90 credit hours maximum toward bachelor's degree. For transfer students. **Support services:** Pre-admission summer program, remedial instruction, tutoring.

Majors. Theology: Religious ed, Talmudic.

Computing on campus. 18 workstations in dormitories, computer center.

Student life. Freshman orientation: Available. **Policies:** Religious observance required. **Housing:** Guaranteed on-campus for all undergraduates. $300 fully refundable deposit. **Activities:** Literary magazine, student government, student newspaper.

Student services. Career counseling, services for economically disadvantaged, financial aid counseling, personal counseling.

Contact. Phone: (323) 937-3763
Rabbi Chaim Citron, Director of Admissions, Yeshiva Ohr Elchonon Chabad/West Coast Talmudical Seminary, 7215 Waring Avenue, Los Angeles, CA 90046

Colorado

Adams State College
Alamosa, Colorado
www.adams.edu **CB code: 4001**

- Public 4-year liberal arts college
- Residential campus in small town
- 2,110 degree-seeking undergraduates: 21% part-time, 58% women, 6% African American, 2% Asian American, 30% Hispanic American, 2% Native American
- 656 degree-seeking graduate students
- 56% of applicants admitted
- SAT or ACT (ACT writing optional) required

General. Founded in 1921. Regionally accredited. Hispanic-serving institution. **Degrees:** 284 bachelor's, 25 associate awarded; master's offered. **Location:** 225 miles from Denver; 200 miles from Albuquerque, New Mexico. **Calendar:** Semester, limited summer session. **Full-time faculty:** 112 total; 68% have terminal degrees, 18% minority, 47% women. **Part-time faculty:** 163 total; 16% have terminal degrees, 14% minority, 58% women. **Class size:** 67% < 20, 25% 20-39, 7% 40-49, 1% 50-99. **Special facilities:** Observatory, planetarium, natural history museum, geology museum, cross-cultural center.

Freshman class profile. 2,037 applied, 1,150 admitted, 504 enrolled.

Mid 50% test scores		**GPA 2.0-2.99:**	41%
SAT critical reading:	440-540	**Rank in top quarter:**	22%
SAT math:	430-560	**Rank in top tenth:**	5%
SAT writing:	400-510	**End year in good standing:**	93%
ACT composite:	17-22	**Return as sophomores:**	53%
GPA 3.75 or higher:	10%	**Out-of-state:**	21%
GPA 3.50-3.74:	14%	**Live on campus:**	71%
GPA 3.0-3.49:	31%		

Basis for selection. Open admissions for associate degree programs only. Bachelor's degree candidates must have either 2.0 GPA, or rank in top two-thirds of class with average or above average score on ACT or SAT. ACCUPLACER tests for math and English required if SAT or ACT not available. Audition required of music majors. Portfolio required of art majors. **Homeschooled:** Transcript of courses and grades required.

High school preparation. College-preparatory program recommended. 15 units required. Required and recommended units include English 4, mathematics 2, social studies 3, history 1, science 2 and foreign language 2. Computer applications: .5 units recommended. Math should include Algebra I and one advanced math course.

2008-2009 Annual costs. Tuition/fees: $3,790; $12,919 out-of-state. Room/board: $6,640. Books/supplies: $1,312. Personal expenses: $1,233.

2007-2008 Financial aid. Non-need-based: Scholarships awarded for academics, alumni affiliation, art, athletics, leadership, minority status, music/drama, state residency.

Application procedures. Admission: Priority date 8/1; no deadline. $30 fee, may be waived for applicants with need. Admission notification on a rolling basis. **Financial aid:** Priority date 3/1, closing date 4/15. FAFSA required. Applicants notified on a rolling basis starting 4/30; must reply within 4 week(s) of notification.

Academics. Special study options: Accelerated study, distance learning, double major, dual enrollment of high school students, exchange student, external degree, independent study, internships, student-designed major, study abroad, teacher certification program, weekend college. **Credit/placement by examination:** AP, CLEP, IB, SAT, ACT, institutional tests. 30 credit hours maximum toward bachelor's degree. **Support services:** Learning center, pre-admission summer program, remedial instruction, study skills assistance, tutoring, writing center.

Majors. Agriculture: Business. **Biology:** General, bacteriology. **Business:** General, accounting, business admin, finance, management information systems, marketing, small business admin. **Communications:** General, advertising. **Computer sciences:** General. **Conservation:** Management/policy. **Education:** General, art, biology, business, chemistry, elementary, English, history, mathematics, middle, multi-level teacher, music, physical, science, secondary, social science, social studies, Spanish, special, speech. **Foreign languages:** Spanish. **Health:** Health care admin, health services, nursing (RN), predental, premedicine, prenursing, prepharmacy, preveterinary. **History:** General. **Legal studies:** Prelaw. **Liberal arts:** Arts/sciences. **Math:** General. **Parks/recreation:** Exercise sciences, health/fitness. **Physical sciences:** Chemical physics, chemistry, geology, physics. **Psychology:** General. **Social sciences:** Criminology, economics, sociology. **Visual/performing arts:** Art, ceramics, dramatic, drawing, metal/jewelry, music performance, music theory/composition, painting, photography, printmaking, sculpture, studio arts, voice/opera.

Most popular majors. Business/marketing 30%, liberal arts 21%, parks/recreation 6%, social sciences 13%, visual/performing arts 9%.

Computing on campus. 329 workstations in library, student center. Dormitories wired for high-speed internet access and linked to campus network. Commuter students can connect to campus network. Online course registration, online library, helpline, student web hosting, wireless network available.

Student life. Freshman orientation: Mandatory, $50 fee. Preregistration for classes offered. Program held weekend before start of semester. **Housing:** Guaranteed on-campus for freshmen. Coed dorms, single-sex dorms, special housing for disabled, apartments, wellness housing available. $150 partly refundable deposit. Learning community house, freshman interest-group housing, drug and alcohol-free learning community, outdoor adventure community, making the grade community (must maintain 3.5 GPA). **Activities:** Bands, campus ministries, choral groups, dance, drama, literary magazine, music ensembles, Model UN, musical theater, radio station, student government, student newspaper, Circle K, College Republicans, Newman club, student ambassadors, teacher education association, associated students and faculty, Phi Beta Lambda, gay straight alliance, Semillas de la Tierra, El Parnaso.

Athletics. NCAA. **Intercollegiate:** Basketball, cross-country, football (tackle) M, golf, soccer W, softball W, track and field, volleyball W, wrestling M. **Intramural:** Basketball, bowling, racquetball, skiing, soccer, softball, swimming, tennis, volleyball, water polo. **Team name:** Grizzlies.

Student services. Adult student services, chaplain/spiritual director, career counseling, student employment services, financial aid counseling, health services, minority student services, on-campus daycare, personal counseling, placement for graduates, veterans' counselor. **Physically disabled:** Services for visually, hearing impaired.

Contact. E-mail: ascadmit@adams.edu
Phone: (719) 587-7712 Toll-free number: (800) 824-6494
Fax: (719) 587-7522
Eric Carpio, Director for Admissions, Adams State College, 208 Edgemont Boulevard, Alamosa, CO 81102

American Sentinel University
Aurora, Colorado
www.americansentinel.edu **CB code: 3806**

- For-profit 4-year virtual university
- Very large city
- 811 degree-seeking undergraduates
- 235 graduate students

General. Accredited by DETC. **Degrees:** 120 bachelor's awarded; master's offered. **Calendar:** Continuous, extensive summer session. **Full-time faculty:** 5 total. **Part-time faculty:** 70 total.

Basis for selection. Open admission.

2008-2009 Annual costs. Cost of bachelor?s program $8,100 to $32,000 depending on credits required to complete; includes application fee, technology and library fees.

Application procedures. Admission: No deadline. No application fee. Admission notification on a rolling basis.

Academics. Special study options: Accelerated study, distance learning, honors, independent study, liberal arts/career combination. **Credit/placement by examination:** AP, CLEP. 45 credit hours maximum toward associate degree, 90 toward bachelor's. **Support services:** Learning center, reduced course load, tutoring.

Majors. Business: Business admin, e-commerce, human resources, management information systems, marketing. **Computer sciences:** General, computer science, information systems, information technology, security, system admin, web page design. **Health:** Medical records technology, nursing (RN). **Protective services:** Law enforcement admin.

Computing on campus. PC or laptop required.

Student life. Freshman orientation: Mandatory. Preregistration for classes offered. **Activities:** Student newspaper.

Contact. E-mail: admissions@americansentinel.edu
Phone: (866) 922-5690 Toll-free number: (866) 922-5690
Fax: (866) 505-2450
Natalie Nixon, Director of Admissions, American Sentinel University, 500 Century Park South, Suite 202, Birmingham, AL 35226

Art Institute of Colorado

Denver, Colorado
www.aic.artinstitutes.edu **CB code: 7150**

- For-profit 4-year culinary school and visual arts college
- Commuter campus in very large city
- 2,404 degree-seeking undergraduates: 41% part-time, 55% women
- Application essay, interview required

General. Founded in 1952. Accredited by ACICS. **Degrees:** 325 bachelor's, 177 associate awarded. **Location:** Downtown. **Calendar:** Quarter, extensive summer session. **Full-time faculty:** 65 total. **Part-time faculty:** 65 total. **Special facilities:** Teaching restaurant open to the public at the International School of Culinary Arts.

Basis for selection. Commitment to career most important; essay, interview important; high school transcript considered with GPA. Portfolio required of advanced standing applicants. **Homeschooled:** Documentation of grades and official graduation date required.

2008-2009 Annual costs. Tuition/fees: $21,992. Supply kit $585-$1,965 depending on program. Books/supplies: $3,487.

2008-2009 Financial aid. Additional information: Tuition at time of first enrollment guaranteed to students for 4 years providing student maintains continuous attendance and completes program within 150% of program length.

Application procedures. Admission: No deadline. $150 fee. Admission notification on a rolling basis. **Financial aid:** No deadline. FAFSA, institutional form required. Applicants notified on a rolling basis.

Academics. Special study options: Distance learning, independent study, internships, study abroad. **Credit/placement by examination:** CLEP, IB, institutional tests. 30 credit hours maximum toward associate degree. **Support services:** Learning center, remedial instruction, study skills assistance, writing center.

Majors. Business: Apparel. **Communications technology:** Animation/special effects. **Computer sciences:** Computer graphics, web page design. **Personal/culinary services:** Restaurant/catering. **Visual/performing arts:** Cinematography, graphic design, industrial design, interior design, multimedia, photography.

Most popular majors. Communication technologies 23%, computer/information sciences 9%, visual/performing arts 62%.

Computing on campus. 500 workstations in dormitories, library, computer center. Dormitories wired for high-speed internet access. Wireless network available.

Student life. Freshman orientation: Mandatory. Preregistration for classes offered. **Housing:** Coed dorms, wellness housing available. $300 deposit. **Activities:** Student newspaper.

Student services. Alcohol/substance abuse counseling, career counseling, student employment services, financial aid counseling, personal counseling, placement for graduates, veterans' counselor. **Physically disabled:** Services for visually, speech, hearing impaired.

Contact. E-mail: aicadm@aii.edu
Phone: (303) 837-0825 Toll-free number: (800) 275-2420
Fax: (303) 860-8520
Brian Parker, Director of Admissions, Art Institute of Colorado, 1200 Lincoln Street, Denver, CO 80203-2983

Aspen University

Denver, Colorado
www.aspen.edu

- For-profit 4-year virtual business college
- Very large city
- 520 degree-seeking undergraduates
- Application essay required

General. Accredited by DETC. **Degrees:** 2 bachelor's awarded; master's, doctoral offered. **Calendar:** Continuous. **Part-time faculty:** 85 total.

Basis for selection. Open admission. Three letters of recommendation required. **Homeschooled:** State high school equivalency certificate required.

2008-2009 Annual costs. Tuition/fees: $7,500.

Application procedures. Admission: No deadline. $100 fee. Admission notification on a rolling basis. **Financial aid:** No deadline.

Academics. Special study options: Distance learning. **Credit/placement by examination:** CLEP. **Support services:** Remedial instruction.

Majors. Business: Business admin. **Protective services:** Law enforcement admin.

Computing on campus. PC or laptop required.

Contact. E-mail: admissions@aspen.edu
Phone: (303) 333-4224
Amanda Hosking, Director of Admissions, Aspen University, 501 South Cherry Street, Suite 350, Denver, CO 80246

CollegeAmerica: Colorado Springs

Colorado Springs, Colorado
www.collegeamerica.edu

- For-profit 4-year career college
- Commuter campus in large city
- 388 degree-seeking undergraduates: 68% women, 21% African American, 3% Asian American, 16% Hispanic American, 1% Native American
- Application essay, interview required
- 46% graduate within 6 years; 5% enter graduate study

General. Accredited by ACCSCT. **Degrees:** 12 bachelor's, 31 associate awarded. **Calendar:** Continuous. **Full-time faculty:** 4 total; 50% minority, 50% women. **Part-time faculty:** 14 total; 14% have terminal degrees, 64% minority, 43% women. **Class size:** 14% < 20, 71% 20-39, 14% 40-49. **Special facilities:** Computer labs.

Freshman class profile.

End year in good standing:	94%	**Return as sophomores:**	41%

Basis for selection. Open admission. **Homeschooled:** Transcript of courses and grades required.

2008-2009 Annual costs. Tuition ranges from $342 to $392 per quarter credit depending on program. First-year tuition for associates degree is $14,505 and $14,215 for bachelor's degree.

Application procedures. Admission: No deadline. No application fee. Admission notification on a rolling basis. **Financial aid:** No deadline. FAFSA, institutional form required.

Academics. Special study options: Combined bachelor's/graduate degree, distance learning. **Credit/placement by examination:** CLEP. **Support services:** Tutoring.

Majors. Business: Accounting, business admin. **Computer sciences:** Computer graphics, computer science. **Health:** Health care admin.

Computing on campus. 25 workstations in library, computer center. Online library, wireless network available.

Student life. Freshman orientation: Mandatory.

Student services. Placement for graduates.

Contact. E-mail: crenya@collegeamerica.edu
Phone: (719) 637-0600 Toll-free number: (800) 622-2894
Kylie Burwell, Director of Admissions, CollegeAmerica: Colorado Springs, 3645 Citadel Drive South, Colorado Springs, CO 80909

CollegeAmerica: Fort Collins
Fort Collins, Colorado
www.collegeamerica.edu

- For-profit 4-year business, health science and technical college
- Commuter campus in small city
- 260 degree-seeking undergraduates: 67% women

General. Accredited by ACCSCT. **Degrees:** 18 bachelor's, 67 associate awarded; master's offered. **Calendar:** Continuous, extensive summer session. **Full-time faculty:** 3 total; 100% women. **Part-time faculty:** 10 total; 40% women.

Basis for selection. Open admission. **Homeschooled:** Transcript of courses and grades required.

2008-2009 Annual costs. Tuition ranges from $342 to $392 per quarter credit depending on program.

Application procedures. Admission: No deadline. No application fee. **Financial aid:** No deadline.

Academics. Special study options: Accelerated study, combined bachelor's/graduate degree, distance learning, independent study. **Credit/placement by examination:** CLEP. **Support services:** Study skills assistance, tutoring.

Majors. Business: General, accounting. **Computer sciences:** General. **Health:** Health services.

Computing on campus. 50 workstations in library, computer center, student center. Online library, helpline, repair service, wireless network available.

Student life. Freshman orientation: Mandatory. Preregistration for classes offered. **Activities:** Student government.

Student services. Adult student services, career counseling, services for economically disadvantaged, student employment services, financial aid counseling, personal counseling, placement for graduates, veterans' counselor. **Learning disabled:** Comprehensive services available.

Contact. Phone: (970) 223-6060 Toll-free number: (800) 622-2894
Kristy McNear, Director of Admissions, CollegeAmerica: Fort Collins, 4601 South Mason Street, Fort Collins, CO 80525

Colorado Christian University
Lakewood, Colorado — **CB member**
www.ccu.edu — **CB code: 4659**

- Private 4-year university and liberal arts college affiliated with nondenominational tradition
- Residential campus in large city
- 2,024 degree-seeking undergraduates: 38% part-time, 61% women, 5% African American, 2% Asian American, 8% Hispanic American, 1% Native American
- 441 degree-seeking graduate students
- 42% of applicants admitted
- Application essay required

General. Founded in 1914. Regionally accredited. Adult and graduate programs available online and at Colorado Springs, Grand Junction, Loveland, Denver (multiple locations), and Lakewood campuses. **Degrees:** 332 bachelor's, 19 associate awarded; master's offered. **ROTC:** Army, Air Force. **Location:** 10 miles from Denver. **Calendar:** Semester, extensive summer session. **Full-time faculty:** 41 total; 66% have terminal degrees, 5% minority, 42% women. **Part-time faculty:** 288 total; 28% have terminal degrees, 4% minority, 37% women. **Class size:** 82% < 20, 17% 20-39, less than 1% 40-49, less than 1% 50-99.

Freshman class profile. 4,091 applied, 1,701 admitted, 834 enrolled.

Mid 50% test scores		**GPA 3.0-3.49:**	29%
SAT critical reading:	480-580	**GPA 2.0-2.99:**	22%
SAT math:	450-570	**Rank in top quarter:**	45%
SAT writing:	460-570	**Rank in top tenth:**	20%
ACT composite:	20-25	**Out-of-state:**	53%
GPA 3.75 or higher:	31%	**Live on campus:**	76%
GPA 3.50-3.74:	18%		

Basis for selection. Applicants should exemplify vital Christian experience. Decisions based on high academic ability, personal integrity, and desire for Christ-centered community. Applicant's course selection, academic performance, test scores, essays, spiritual recommendation, activities, and work experience carefully considered. Interviews encouraged. Audition required of music and theater majors.

High school preparation. College-preparatory program required. 19 units recommended. Recommended units include English 4, mathematics 3, social studies 3, history 2, science 2 (laboratory 2) and foreign language 2. Recommend 1 unit of computer science.

2009-2010 Annual costs. Tuition/fees (projected): $21,130. Room/board: $8,455. Books/supplies: $1,188. Personal expenses: $4,338.

2007-2008 Financial aid. Need-based: 157 full-time freshmen applied for aid; 117 were judged to have need; 117 of these received aid. Average need met was 35%. Average scholarship/grant was $8,678; average loan $3,326. 63% of total undergraduate aid awarded as scholarships/grants, 37% as loans/jobs. **Non-need-based:** Awarded to 358 full-time undergraduates, including 180 freshmen. Scholarships awarded for academics, athletics, leadership, music/drama.

Application procedures. Admission: Priority date 3/1; deadline 9/1 (receipt date). $30 fee, may be waived for applicants with need. Admission notification on a rolling basis beginning on or about 11/1. Must reply by May 1 or within 4 week(s) if notified thereafter. **Financial aid:** Priority date 3/15; no closing date. FAFSA required. Applicants notified on a rolling basis starting 4/1; must reply by 5/1 or within 4 week(s) of notification.

Academics. Special study options: Accelerated study, cooperative education, distance learning, double major, honors, independent study, internships, semester at sea, student-designed major, study abroad, teacher certification program, urban semester, Washington semester, weekend college. American studies program (Washington, D.C.), host university for Institute for Family Studies; China studies program at various sites in China, Latin American program (Costa Rica), Los Angeles film studies center, Middle East studies (Cairo, Egypt), Oxford honors program (University of Oxford, England), Russian studies program at various sites in Russia, Summer Institute of Journalism (Washington DC). **Credit/placement by examination:** AP, CLEP, IB, ACT, institutional tests. 15 credit hours maximum toward associate degree, 45 toward bachelor's. **Support services:** Learning center, reduced course load, remedial instruction, study skills assistance, tutoring, writing center.

Majors. Biology: General. **Business:** Accounting, business admin, human resources, management information systems, management science, organizational behavior. **Communications:** General. **Computer sciences:** General. **Education:** General, adult/continuing, early childhood, elementary, English, history, mathematics, music, science, secondary. **Health:** Nursing (RN). **History:** General. **Interdisciplinary:** Biological/physical sciences, global studies. **Liberal arts:** Arts/sciences. **Math:** General. **Psychology:** General. **Social sciences:** General. **Theology:** Bible, theology, youth ministry. **Visual/performing arts:** Music performance, studio arts. **Other:** Early childhood educational theory, Music ministry.

Most popular majors. Business/marketing 18%, computer/information sciences 8%, education 28%, psychology 6%, theological studies 6%.

Computing on campus. 186 workstations in dormitories, library, computer center, student center. Dormitories wired for high-speed internet access and linked to campus network. Commuter students can connect to campus network. Online course registration, online library, helpline, wireless network available.

Student life. Freshman orientation: Mandatory. Preregistration for classes offered. Seminars for students and parents held 4 days prior to beginning of classes. **Policies:** Use of alcoholic beverages, illegal drugs, and tobacco prohibited on campus and at college-sponsored activities. Premarital sexual relationships prohibited. Religious observance required. **Housing:** Guaranteed on-campus for freshmen. Coed dorms, single-sex dorms, special housing for disabled, apartments, wellness housing available. $200 fully refundable deposit, deadline 5/1. **Activities:** Bands, campus ministries, choral groups, drama, literary magazine, music ensembles, musical theater, student government, student newspaper, symphony orchestra, world missions, discipleship groups, Fat Boys, Footprints, prayer ministry, refugee family ministry, SALT, Snappers, Westside.

Athletics. NCAA, NCCAA. **Intercollegiate:** Baseball M, basketball, cross-country, golf, soccer, tennis, volleyball W. **Intramural:** Basketball, football (non-tackle), soccer, softball, tennis, volleyball. **Team name:** Cougars.

Student services. Adult student services, chaplain/spiritual director, career counseling, student employment services, financial aid counseling, health services, personal counseling, placement for graduates, veterans' counselor, women's services. **Physically disabled:** Services for visually, speech, hearing impaired.

Contact. E-mail: admission@ccu.edu
Phone: (303) 963-3200 Toll-free number: (800) 443-2484
Fax: (303) 963-3201
Jim McCormick, Vice President of Student Development, Colorado Christian University, 8787 West Alameda Avenue, Lakewood, CO 80226

Colorado College

Colorado Springs, Colorado — **CB member**
www.coloradocollege.edu — **CB code: 4072**

- Private 4-year liberal arts college
- Residential campus in large city
- 1,972 degree-seeking undergraduates: 54% women, 2% African American, 6% Asian American, 7% Hispanic American, 1% Native American, 3% international
- 30 degree-seeking graduate students
- 26% of applicants admitted
- SAT or ACT (ACT writing optional), application essay required
- 87% graduate within 6 years

General. Founded in 1874. Regionally accredited. Mountain cabin located about 35 minutes from campus for class and retreat use. Baca campus in Southern Colorado available for intensive study. **Degrees:** 611 bachelor's awarded; master's offered. **ROTC:** Army. **Location:** 70 miles from Denver. **Calendar:** Semester, extensive summer session. **Full-time faculty:** 175 total; 90% have terminal degrees, 19% minority, 41% women. **Part-time faculty:** 30 total. **Class size:** 63% < 20, 37% 20-39, less than 1% 40-49. **Special facilities:** Electronic music studio, telescope dome, multimedia computer lab, press, herbarium, environmental science van equipped for field research, petrographic microscopes, X-ray diffractometer, Fourier transform nuclear magnetic resonance spectrometer, sedimentology lab, metabolic equipment, hydrostatic weighing equipment, cadaver study in sports science, scanning electron microscope, transmission electron microscope.

Freshman class profile. 5,338 applied, 1,389 admitted, 551 enrolled.

Mid 50% test scores			
SAT critical reading:	620-700	**End year in good standing:**	97%
SAT math:	610-700	**Return as sophomores:**	94%
SAT writing:	620-700	**Out-of-state:**	76%
ACT composite:	28-32	**Live on campus:**	98%
Rank in top quarter:	87%	**International:**	5%
Rank in top tenth:	66%	**Fraternities:**	3%
		Sororities:	14%

Basis for selection. Personal essays, school achievement record most important. Counselor and teacher recommendations, extracurricular activities and test scores also important. Special talents; geographic, socioeconomic, ethnic diversity considered. Challenging curriculum, including honors/AP/IB courses if available, recommended. Interview optional. **Homeschooled:** Letter of recommendation (nonparent) required. Three letters of recommendation from people outside of the family who have some knowledge of student's academic capabilities and interests. Reading lists, curriculum information, teacher narratives about courses of study, and copies of papers or projects can be used in place of traditional transcript.

High school preparation. College-preparatory program recommended. 16 units required; 20 recommended. Required and recommended units include English 4.

2008-2009 Annual costs. Tuition/fees: $35,844. Room/board: $9,096. Books/supplies: $988. Personal expenses: $972.

2008-2009 Financial aid. **Need-based:** 286 full-time freshmen applied for aid; 236 were judged to have need; 236 of these received aid. Average need met was 95%. Average scholarship/grant was $29,371; average loan $1,861. 90% of total undergraduate aid awarded as scholarships/grants, 10% as loans/jobs. **Non-need-based:** Awarded to 420 full-time undergraduates, including 143 freshmen. Scholarships awarded for academics, athletics. **Additional information:** Need-based financial aid available only to students enrolled half-time or more.

Application procedures. **Admission:** Closing date 1/15 (postmark date). $50 fee, may be waived for applicants with need. Admission notification 4/1. Must reply by May 1 or within 2 week(s) if notified thereafter. Campus visit recommended. Separate letter requesting early action and explaining reasons for applying early required for early action. **Financial aid:** Closing date 2/15. FAFSA, CSS PROFILE required. Applicants notified by 3/20; must reply by 5/1.

Academics. **Special study options:** Combined bachelor's/graduate degree, double major, ESL, external degree, independent study, internships, liberal arts/career combination, semester at sea, student-designed major, study abroad, teacher certification program, urban semester, Washington semester. Urban studies, urban arts and urban education (Chicago); science semester (Oak Ridge, Tennessee); tropical field research (Costa Rica); wilderness field station (Wisconsin); ACM London-Florence program; study abroad programs in France, Germany, Mexico, Russia, Japan, India, Sweden, the Netherlands, and Wales; ACM program in Tanzania and Zimbabwe. **Credit/placement by examination:** AP, CLEP, IB, institutional tests. 32 credit hours maximum toward bachelor's degree. **Support services:** Learning center, pre-admission summer program, study skills assistance, tutoring, writing center.

Majors. **Area/ethnic studies:** Asian, French, Hispanic-American/Latino/Chicano, regional, Russian/Slavic, women's. **Biology:** General, biochemistry. **Computer sciences:** Computer science. **Conservation:** Environmental science. **Foreign languages:** Classics, comparative lit, French, German, Italian, Romance, Russian, Spanish. **History:** General. **Interdisciplinary:** Math/computer science, neuroscience. **Liberal arts:** Arts/sciences. **Math:** General. **Philosophy/religion:** Philosophy, religion. **Physical sciences:** Chemistry, geology, physics. **Psychology:** General. **Social sciences:** Anthropology, econometrics, economics, international economics, political science, sociology. **Visual/performing arts:** Art history/conservation, dance, dramatic, film/cinema, studio arts. **Other:** Classics/History/Politics, Political Economy: American.

Most popular majors. Biology 12%, English 7%, history 8%, philosophy/religious studies 8%, social sciences 28%, visual/performing arts 8%.

Computing on campus. 200 workstations in dormitories, library, computer center, student center. Dormitories wired for high-speed internet access and linked to campus network. Commuter students can connect to campus network. Online course registration, online library, helpline, student web hosting, wireless network available.

Student life. **Freshman orientation:** Mandatory. Preregistration for classes offered. One-week program prior to beginning of fall classes. Parents welcome for first 3 days. Includes service trip. **Housing:** Guaranteed on-campus for all undergraduates. Coed dorms, single-sex dorms, apartments, fraternity/sorority housing, wellness housing available. $200 nonrefundable deposit, deadline 3/2. Pets allowed in dorm rooms. **Activities:** Bands, campus ministries, choral groups, dance, drama, film society, international student organizations, literary magazine, music ensembles, musical theater, radio station, student government, student newspaper, Asian American students union, black student union, Chaverim/Hillel, gay, lesbian, and bisexual alliance, community kitchen, environmental action, Shove Chapel Council, Chicano/Latino organization, victim's assistance team, BreakOut-community service trips.

Athletics. NCAA. **Intercollegiate:** Basketball, cross-country, football (tackle) M, ice hockey M, lacrosse, soccer, softball W, swimming, tennis, track and field, volleyball W, water polo W. **Intramural:** Basketball, football (non-tackle), ice hockey, racquetball, soccer, softball, tennis, volleyball. **Team name:** Tigers.

Student services. Alcohol/substance abuse counseling, chaplain/spiritual director, career counseling, student employment services, financial aid counseling, health services, minority student services, on-campus daycare, personal counseling, women's services. **Physically disabled:** Services for visually, speech, hearing impaired.

Contact. E-mail: admission@coloradocollege.edu
Phone: (719) 389-6344 Toll-free number: (800) 542-7214
Fax: (719) 389-6816
Roberto Garcia, Director of Admission, Colorado College, 14 East Cache La Poudre Street, Colorado Springs, CO 80903-9854

Colorado School of Mines

Golden, Colorado — **CB member**
www.mines.edu — **CB code: 4073**

- Public 4-year university and engineering college
- Residential campus in large town
- 3,400 degree-seeking undergraduates: 5% part-time, 24% women, 2% African American, 5% Asian American, 7% Hispanic American, 1% Native American, 6% international
- 936 degree-seeking graduate students
- 61% of applicants admitted
- SAT or ACT (ACT writing optional) required
- 68% graduate within 6 years

General. Founded in 1874. Regionally accredited. **Degrees:** 626 bachelor's awarded; master's, doctoral offered. **ROTC:** Army, Air Force. **Location:** 20 miles from Denver. **Calendar:** Semester, limited summer session. **Full-time faculty:** 250 total; 83% have terminal degrees, 15% minority, 22% women. **Part-time faculty:** 95 total; 10% have terminal degrees, 10%

minority, 27% women. **Class size:** 43% < 20, 38% 20-39, 6% 40-49, 7% 50-99, 6% >100. **Special facilities:** Geology museum, geophysical observatory, experimental mine.

Freshman class profile. 6,797 applied, 4,180 admitted, 851 enrolled.

Mid 50% test scores		**Rank in top tenth:**	52%
SAT critical reading:	550-610	**Return as sophomores:**	85%
SAT math:	650-700	**Out-of-state:**	28%
ACT composite:	26-30	**Live on campus:**	89%
GPA 3.75 or higher:	52%	**International:**	3%
GPA 3.50-3.74:	26%	**Fraternities:**	15%
GPA 3.0-3.49:	22%	**Sororities:**	17%
Rank in top quarter:	85%		

Basis for selection. Applicants should rank in top third of class, must complete 16 or more academic units, and submit test scores. Both scores and academic record considered with heavier weight given to academic record. Interview and essay recommended. **Homeschooled:** Transcript of courses and grades required. More weight given to ACT or SAT scores.

High school preparation. College-preparatory program required. 16 units required. Required and recommended units include English 4, mathematics 4, social studies 3, science 3 (laboratory 3) and academic electives 2. Math units should include 2 algebra, 1 geometry, 1 advanced math (including trigonometry). Science units should include 1 chemistry or physics.

2008-2009 Annual costs. Tuition/fees: $11,238; $25,248 out-of-state. Room/board: $7,626. Books/supplies: $1,300. Personal expenses: $1,800.

2008-2009 Financial aid. Need-based: 605 full-time freshmen applied for aid; 550 were judged to have need; 550 of these received aid. Average need met was 93%. Average scholarship/grant was $8,750; average loan $5,450. 57% of total undergraduate aid awarded as scholarships/grants, 43% as loans/jobs. **Non-need-based:** Awarded to 1,565 full-time undergraduates, including 405 freshmen. Scholarships awarded for academics, alumni affiliation, athletics, music/drama, ROTC.

Application procedures. Admission: Priority date 4/1; deadline 5/1 (postmark date). $45 fee, may be waived for applicants with need. Admission notification on a rolling basis beginning on or about 10/1. Must reply by May 1 or within 4 week(s) if notified thereafter. **Financial aid:** Priority date 2/15; no closing date. FAFSA required. Applicants notified on a rolling basis starting 3/15; must reply by 5/1 or within 2 week(s) of notification.

Academics. Special study options: Accelerated study, combined bachelor's/graduate degree, cooperative education, double major, dual enrollment of high school students, ESL, exchange student, honors, independent study, internships, study abroad. **Credit/placement by examination:** AP, CLEP, IB, institutional tests. **Support services:** Pre-admission summer program, reduced course load, remedial instruction, study skills assistance, tutoring, writing center.

Majors. Computer sciences: General, computer science. **Engineering:** General, chemical, geological, metallurgical, mining, petroleum, physics. **Interdisciplinary:** Math/computer science. **Math:** Applied. **Physical sciences:** Chemistry, geology, geophysics, physics. **Social sciences:** Economics.

Most popular majors. Engineering/engineering technologies 84%, mathematics 7%, social sciences 6%.

Computing on campus. 400 workstations in dormitories, library, computer center, student center. Dormitories wired for high-speed internet access and linked to campus network. Commuter students can connect to campus network. Online course registration, helpline, repair service, wireless network available.

Student life. Freshman orientation: Available. Preregistration for classes offered. 2-day sessions held during summer; one-day session held at start of fall semester. **Housing:** Guaranteed on-campus for freshmen. Coed dorms, single-sex dorms, apartments, fraternity/sorority housing available. $150 partly refundable deposit, deadline 5/1. **Activities:** Bands, campus ministries, choral groups, dance, drama, international student organizations, literary magazine, music ensembles, musical theater, radio station, student government, student newspaper, symphony orchestra, American Indian science and engineering society, Asian student association, National Society of Black Engineers, Society of Hispanic Professional Engineers, religious clubs, Blue Key, Society of Women Engineers.

Athletics. NCAA. **Intercollegiate:** Baseball M, basketball, cross-country, football (tackle) M, golf, soccer, softball W, swimming, track and field, volleyball W, wrestling M. **Intramural:** Badminton, basketball, cross-country, football (non-tackle), handball, racquetball, rugby M, skin diving, soccer, softball, swimming, tennis, track and field, volleyball. **Team name:** Orediggers.

Student services. Alcohol/substance abuse counseling, career counseling, student employment services, financial aid counseling, health services, minority student services, personal counseling, placement for graduates, veterans' counselor. **Physically disabled:** Services for visually, hearing impaired.

Contact. E-mail: admit@mines.edu
Phone: (303) 273-3200 Toll-free number: (888) 446-9488
Fax: (303) 273-3509
Bruce Goetz, Director of Admissions, Colorado School of Mines, Undergraduate Admissions, Golden, CO 80401

Colorado State University

Fort Collins, Colorado — **CB member**
www.colostate.edu — **CB code: 4075**

- Public 4-year university
- Residential campus in small city
- 20,829 degree-seeking undergraduates: 7% part-time, 52% women, 2% African American, 3% Asian American, 6% Hispanic American, 2% Native American, 2% international
- 4,182 degree-seeking graduate students
- 86% of applicants admitted
- SAT or ACT (ACT writing optional), application essay required
- 63% graduate within 6 years

General. Founded in 1870. Regionally accredited. Colorado State University is a Land Grant University. **Degrees:** 4,289 bachelor's awarded; master's, doctoral, first professional offered. **ROTC:** Army, Air Force. **Location:** 60 miles from Denver. **Calendar:** Semester, extensive summer session. **Full-time faculty:** 925 total; 100% have terminal degrees, 13% minority, 32% women. **Part-time faculty:** 43 total; 98% have terminal degrees, 9% minority, 19% women. **Class size:** 37% < 20, 38% 20-39, 7% 40-49, 10% 50-99, 7% >100. **Special facilities:** Concert hall, thrust theatre, music hall, art museum, engineering research center, equine center, veterinary teaching hospital, environmental learning center, plant environmental research center.

Freshman class profile. 12,494 applied, 10,688 admitted, 4,404 enrolled.

Mid 50% test scores		**Rank in top quarter:**	49%
SAT critical reading:	500-610	**Rank in top tenth:**	20%
SAT math:	510-620	**Return as sophomores:**	82%
SAT writing:	480-590	**Out-of-state:**	20%
ACT composite:	22-26	**Live on campus:**	96%
GPA 3.75 or higher:	32%	**International:**	1%
GPA 3.50-3.74:	24%	**Fraternities:**	6%
GPA 3.0-3.49:	38%	**Sororities:**	7%
GPA 2.0-2.99:	6%		

Basis for selection. Priority consideration given to those with 3.25 GPA and 18 recommended high school credits. Applicants with GPA below 2.5 and/or without the recommended high school units encouraged to apply. Essay must be at least 250 words; 1 letter of recommendation required.

High school preparation. College-preparatory program required. 15 units required; 18 recommended. Required and recommended units include English 4, mathematics 3-4, social studies 2, history 1, science 3 (laboratory 2), foreign language 2 and academic electives 2. Individual programs may have additional requirements.

2008-2009 Annual costs. Tuition/fees: $5,874; $21,590 out-of-state. Room/board: $8,134. Books/supplies: $1,126. Personal expenses: $1,692.

2007-2008 Financial aid. Need-based: 2,515 full-time freshmen applied for aid; 1,442 were judged to have need; 1,442 of these received aid. Average need met was 66%. Average scholarship/grant was $5,422; average loan $3,999. 43% of total undergraduate aid awarded as scholarships/grants, 57% as loans/jobs. **Non-need-based:** Awarded to 1,720 full-time undergraduates, including 252 freshmen. Scholarships awarded for academics, art, athletics, leadership, music/drama, ROTC, state residency. **Additional information:** High-need CO residents put into Economically Disadvantaged group, providing scholarships, grants and work study for the first year. CSU Land Grant Award guarantees full-time Pell-eligible CO residents are funded at minimum of tuition and fees.

Application procedures. Admission: Priority date 2/1; deadline 7/1 (receipt date). $50 fee, may be waived for applicants with need. Admission notification on a rolling basis beginning on or about 9/15. Must reply by May 1 or within 2 week(s) if notified thereafter. Early application (once 6th semester transcript is available) encouraged. **Financial aid:** Priority date

3/1; no closing date. FAFSA required. Applicants notified on a rolling basis starting 3/1.

Academics. Special study options: Accelerated study, combined bachelor's/graduate degree, cooperative education, cross-registration, distance learning, double major, dual enrollment of high school students, ESL, exchange student, external degree, honors, independent study, internships, liberal arts/career combination, semester at sea, study abroad, teacher certification program. **Credit/placement by examination:** AP, CLEP, IB, SAT, ACT, institutional tests. **Support services:** Learning center, study skills assistance, tutoring, writing center.

Majors. Agriculture: Agribusiness operations, agronomy, animal sciences, economics, education services, equestrian studies, horticultural science, horticulture, landscaping, range science, soil science. **Architecture:** Landscape. **Biology:** General, biochemistry, biomedical sciences, botany, microbiology, wildlife, zoology. **Business:** Business admin, construction management, restaurant/food services. **Communications:** Journalism. **Computer sciences:** General, information systems. **Conservation:** General, forest sciences, management/policy, water/wetlands/marine, wildlife. **Education:** Agricultural. **Engineering:** Chemical, civil, computer, electrical, environmental, mechanical, science. **Engineering technology:** Computer systems. **Family/consumer sciences:** General, apparel marketing, family studies, food/nutrition, human nutrition. **Foreign languages:** General. **Health:** Environmental health. **History:** General. **Interdisciplinary:** Natural sciences. **Liberal arts:** Arts/sciences. **Math:** General. **Parks/recreation:** Exercise sciences, facilities management. **Philosophy/religion:** Philosophy. **Physical sciences:** Chemistry, geology, physics. **Protective services:** Fire services admin. **Psychology:** General. **Public administration:** Social work. **Social sciences:** Anthropology, economics, political science, sociology. **Visual/performing arts:** Art, dramatic, interior design, studio arts. **Other:** Applied computing technology, Fish, wildlife and conservation biology, Landscape horticulture, Natural resources recreation and tourism.

Most popular majors. Agriculture 6%, biology 8%, business/marketing 14%, engineering/engineering technologies 12%, English 7%, family/consumer sciences 9%, parks/recreation 7%, social sciences 8%.

Computing on campus. 2,700 workstations in dormitories, library, computer center, student center. Dormitories wired for high-speed internet access and linked to campus network. Commuter students can connect to campus network. Online course registration, online library, helpline, repair service, student web hosting, wireless network available.

Student life. Freshman orientation: Available, $90 fee. Preregistration for classes offered. 21 sessions offered from mid-June to mid-July for incoming freshmen, family members, and guests. **Housing:** Guaranteed on-campus for freshmen. Coed dorms, special housing for disabled, apartments, wellness housing available. $150 partly refundable deposit. Special interest floors, special floors for transfer students available. **Activities:** Bands, campus ministries, choral groups, dance, drama, literary magazine, music ensembles, musical theater, opera, radio station, student government, student newspaper, symphony orchestra, TV station, Asian/American student services, black student services, El Centro student services, GLBT student services, Native American student services, Campus Crusade for Christ, Chabad Jewish student alliance, Habitat for Humanity, College Republicans, Young Democrats.

Athletics. NCAA. **Intercollegiate:** Basketball, cross-country, diving W, football (tackle) M, golf, softball W, swimming W, tennis W, track and field, volleyball W, water polo W. **Intramural:** Basketball, bowling, football (non-tackle), golf, racquetball, soccer, softball, volleyball. **Team name:** Rams.

Student services. Adult student services, alcohol/substance abuse counseling, chaplain/spiritual director, career counseling, services for economically disadvantaged, student employment services, financial aid counseling, health services, legal services, minority student services, on-campus daycare, personal counseling, placement for graduates, veterans' counselor, women's services. **Physically disabled:** Services for visually, speech, hearing impaired.

Contact. E-mail: admissions@colostate.edu
Phone: (970) 491-6909 Fax: (970) 491-7799
James Rawlins, Executive Director of Admissions, Colorado State University, Office of Admissions/Colorado State University, Fort Collins, CO 80523-1062

Colorado State University: Pueblo

Pueblo, Colorado
www.colostate-pueblo.edu **CB code: 4611**

- Public 4-year university
- Commuter campus in small city
- 4,401 degree-seeking undergraduates: 21% part-time, 54% women, 8% African American, 3% Asian American, 25% Hispanic American, 2% Native American, 2% international
- 240 degree-seeking graduate students
- 97% of applicants admitted
- SAT or ACT (ACT writing optional) required

General. Founded in 1933. Regionally accredited. **Degrees:** 742 bachelor's awarded; master's offered. **ROTC:** Army. **Location:** 42 miles from Colorado Springs, 100 miles from Denver. **Calendar:** Semester, extensive summer session. **Full-time faculty:** 177 total; 19% minority, 50% women. **Part-time faculty:** 149 total. **Class size:** 49% < 20, 38% 20-39, 5% 40-49, 6% 50-99, 2% >100. **Special facilities:** 3 electron microscopes, golf course, river trail system, automotive service, ropes course, music amphitheater, 1+ megawatt solar system, 6 kilowatt solar system.

Freshman class profile. 3,471 applied, 3,364 admitted, 1,385 enrolled.

Mid 50% test scores			
SAT critical reading:	420-530	Rank in top quarter:	8%
SAT math:	420-550	Rank in top tenth:	2%
ACT composite:	18-22	Return as sophomores:	66%
GPA 3.75 or higher:	11%	Out-of-state:	8%
GPA 3.50-3.74:	14%	Live on campus:	60%
GPA 3.0-3.49:	31%	International:	1%
GPA 2.0-2.99:	42%	Fraternities:	1%
		Sororities:	1%

Basis for selection. High school achievement record and test scores most important. Auditions for music, portfolios for art required for scholarships.

High school preparation. College-preparatory program required. 15 units required. Required and recommended units include English 4, mathematics 3, social studies 2, history 1, science 3 (laboratory 2), foreign language 2 and academic electives 2.

2008-2009 Annual costs. Tuition/fees: $4,667; $14,788 out-of-state. WUE tuition is $2,713 less per semester than out-of-state rate. Differential tuition charged for business, nursing, computer information systems, and engineering courses at $18 more per-credit-hour. Room/board: $6,300. Books/supplies: $1,698. Personal expenses: $2,998.

2008-2009 Financial aid. Need-based: Average need met was 63%. Average scholarship/grant was $5,498; average loan $3,249. 41% of total undergraduate aid awarded as scholarships/grants, 59% as loans/jobs. **Non-need-based:** Scholarships awarded for academics, alumni affiliation, art, athletics, job skills, leadership, minority status, music/drama, ROTC, state residency.

Application procedures. Admission: Closing date 8/1 (receipt date). $25 fee, may be waived for applicants with need. Admission notification on a rolling basis beginning on or about 8/1. **Financial aid:** Priority date 3/1; no closing date. FAFSA, institutional form required. Applicants notified on a rolling basis starting 3/13; must reply within 3 week(s) of notification.

Academics. Structured first-year program for first-time students. **Special study options:** Accelerated study, combined bachelor's/graduate degree, cooperative education, cross-registration, distance learning, double major, dual enrollment of high school students, ESL, exchange student, external degree, honors, independent study, internships, study abroad, teacher certification program, weekend college. **Credit/placement by examination:** AP, CLEP, IB, SAT, ACT, institutional tests. 30 credit hours maximum toward bachelor's degree. **Support services:** Learning center, reduced course load, remedial instruction, study skills assistance, tutoring, writing center.

Majors. Biology: General. **Business:** Accounting, managerial economics. **Communications:** Media studies. **Computer sciences:** Information systems. **Engineering:** General, industrial. **Engineering technology:** Automotive, civil. **Foreign languages:** General. **Health:** Nursing (RN). **History:** General. **Liberal arts:** Arts/sciences. **Math:** General. **Parks/recreation:** Exercise sciences. **Physical sciences:** Chemistry, physics. **Psychology:** General. **Public administration:** Social work. **Social sciences:** Political science, sociology. **Visual/performing arts:** Studio arts. **Other:** Mechatronics.

Most popular majors. Business/marketing 16%, communications/journalism 6%, health sciences 12%, liberal arts 9%, social sciences 18%.

Computing on campus. 702 workstations in dormitories, library, computer center, student center. Dormitories wired for high-speed internet access and linked to campus network. Commuter students can connect to campus network. Online library, helpline, student web hosting, wireless network available.

Student life. Freshman orientation: Mandatory, $50 fee. Preregistration for classes offered. Three-hour session held during summer. **Housing:** Guaranteed on-campus for freshmen. Coed dorms, special housing for disabled, apartments available. $125 partly refundable deposit, deadline 7/1. **Activities:** Bands, campus ministries, choral groups, dance, international student organizations, literary magazine, music ensembles, radio station, student government, student newspaper, symphony orchestra, TV station, Campus Crusade for Christ, Catholic student union, College Republicans, Society of Mexican American Engineers and Scientists, Movimiento Estudiantil Chicano de Aztlan, multicultural center, Tackling Life's Choices.

Athletics. NCAA. **Intercollegiate:** Baseball M, basketball, cross-country W, golf, soccer, softball W, tennis, volleyball W. **Intramural:** Basketball, football (non-tackle), golf, handball, racquetball, soccer, softball, table tennis, volleyball. **Team name:** Thunderwolves.

Student services. Alcohol/substance abuse counseling, chaplain/spiritual director, career counseling, student employment services, financial aid counseling, health services, on-campus daycare, personal counseling, placement for graduates, veterans' counselor. **Physically disabled:** Services for visually, speech, hearing impaired.

Contact. E-mail: info@colostate-pueblo.edu
Phone: (719) 549-2461 Fax: (719) 549-2419
Dana Trujillo, Director of Admissions, Colorado State University: Pueblo, 2200 Bonforte Boulevard, Pueblo, CO 81001-4901

Colorado Technical University

Colorado Springs, Colorado
www.coloradotech.edu **CB code: 4133**

- For-profit 4-year university and technical college
- Commuter campus in large city
- 1,200 degree-seeking undergraduates
- Interview required

General. Founded in 1965. Regionally accredited. **Degrees:** 250 bachelor's, 70 associate awarded; master's, doctoral offered. **ROTC:** Army. **Location:** 63 miles from Denver. **Calendar:** Quarter, extensive summer session. **Full-time faculty:** 14 total. **Part-time faculty:** 250 total. **Class size:** 69% < 20, 31% 20-39. **Special facilities:** Extensive laboratories and computer facilities.

Basis for selection. Secondary school record, test scores, interview important. SAT or ACT recommended.

2008-2009 Annual costs. Tuition/fees: $13,025. Lab fees $30 per lab class. Books/supplies: $1,300. Personal expenses: $1,215.

Financial aid. Non-need-based: Scholarships awarded for academics, ROTC.

Application procedures. Admission: No deadline. $50 fee. Admission notification on a rolling basis. **Financial aid:** No deadline. FAFSA required. Applicants notified on a rolling basis starting 6/30.

Academics. Special study options: Accelerated study, cooperative education, distance learning, double major, internships, weekend college. **Credit/placement by examination:** CLEP, institutional tests. 30 credit hours maximum toward associate degree, 60 toward bachelor's. Course challenge test offered. Credit for life experience based on evaluation by faculty. **Support services:** Learning center, reduced course load, remedial instruction, tutoring.

Majors. Business: Business admin, e-commerce, human resources, information resources management, logistics, management information systems. **Computer sciences:** General, computer science, information systems, information technology, system admin, systems analysis. **Engineering:** Computer, electrical, software. **Engineering technology:** Electrical.

Most popular majors. Business/marketing 34%, computer/information sciences 32%, engineering/engineering technologies 34%.

Computing on campus. 154 workstations in library, computer center. Commuter students can connect to campus network. Online library, helpline, wireless network available.

Student life. Freshman orientation: Mandatory. Preregistration for classes offered. **Policies:** Students must comply with university's standards of conduct. **Activities:** Student government.

Student services. Career counseling, student employment services, financial aid counseling, personal counseling, placement for graduates, veterans' counselor.

Contact. E-mail: cosadmissions@coloradotech.edu
Phone: (719) 598-0200 Fax: (719) 598-3740
Beth Braaten, Vice President of Admissions, Colorado Technical University, 4435 North Chestnut Street, Colorado Springs, CO 80907

DeVry University: Westminster

Westminster, Colorado
www.devry.edu **CB code: 1327**

- For-profit 4-year university
- Commuter campus in very large city
- 718 degree-seeking undergraduates: 59% part-time, 36% women, 7% African American, 4% Asian American, 10% Hispanic American, 1% Native American
- 64 degree-seeking graduate students
- Interview required

General. Founded in 1945. Regionally accredited. **Degrees:** 108 bachelor's, 19 associate awarded; master's offered. **Calendar:** Semester, extensive summer session. **Full-time faculty:** 14 total; 14% minority, 21% women. **Part-time faculty:** 14 total; 14% minority, 36% women.

Basis for selection. Applicants must have high school diploma or equivalent or a degree from an accredited postsecondary institution, demonstrate proficiency in basic college-level skills through SAT or ACT scores or institutional-administered placement exams, and be at least 17 years of age.

High school preparation. Math unit must be algebra or higher.

2008-2009 Annual costs. Tuition/fees: $14,130. Books/supplies: $1,300. Personal expenses: $5,082.

2007-2008 Financial aid. All financial aid based on need.

Application procedures. Admission: No deadline. $50 fee. Admission notification on a rolling basis. **Financial aid:** No deadline. FAFSA required. Applicants notified on a rolling basis.

Academics. Special study options: Accelerated study, distance learning. **Credit/placement by examination:** CLEP, institutional tests. **Support services:** Learning center, tutoring.

Majors. Business: Business admin. **Computer sciences:** Networking, systems analysis. **Engineering:** Software. **Engineering technology:** Computer, electrical. **Other:** Technical management.

Most popular majors. Business/marketing 64%, computer/information sciences 16%, engineering/engineering technologies 19%.

Computing on campus. 308 workstations in library, computer center. Online course registration, online library, helpline available.

Student life. Freshman orientation: Mandatory. **Activities:** Student government, student newspaper.

Athletics. Intramural: Basketball, volleyball.

Student services. Career counseling, student employment services, financial aid counseling, placement for graduates, veterans' counselor.

Contact. E-mail: denver-admissions@den.devry.edu
Phone: (303) 280-7600 Toll-free number: (888) 212-1857
Fax: (303) 280-7606
Rick Rodman, Director of Admissions, DeVry University: Westminster, 1870 West 122 Avenue, Westminster, CO 80234-2010

Fort Lewis College

Durango, Colorado **CB member**
www.fortlewis.edu **CB code: 4310**

- Public 4-year liberal arts college
- Residential campus in large town
- 3,611 degree-seeking undergraduates: 8% part-time, 48% women, 1% African American, 1% Asian American, 5% Hispanic American, 21% Native American, 1% international
- 60% of applicants admitted
- SAT or ACT (ACT writing optional) required
- 30% graduate within 6 years; 14% enter graduate study

General. Regionally accredited. **Degrees:** 699 bachelor's awarded. **Location:** 220 miles from Albuquerque, New Mexico; 342 miles from Denver. **Calendar:** Semester, extensive summer session. **Full-time faculty:** 189 total; 80% have terminal degrees, 11% minority, 46% women. **Part-time faculty:** 80 total. **Class size:** 53% < 20, 41% 20-39, 5% 40-49, less than 1%

50-99. **Special facilities:** Southwest studies center, nuclear magnetic resonance spectrometer, archaeological dig site, community concert hall, separations and spectroscopy lab, mass spectrometer facilities, tissue culture facility, atomic force microscope.

Freshman class profile. 3,434 applied, 2,074 admitted, 800 enrolled.

Mid 50% test scores		**GPA 2.0-2.99:**	30%
SAT critical reading:	470-570	**Rank in top quarter:**	23%
SAT math:	470-590	**Rank in top tenth:**	7%
SAT writing:	450-560	**Return as sophomores:**	59%
ACT composite:	19-24	**Out-of-state:**	36%
GPA 3.75 or higher:	10%	**Live on campus:**	91%
GPA 3.50-3.74:	8%	**International:**	1%
GPA 3.0-3.49:	52%		

Basis for selection. Colorado Commission on Higher Education index score comprised of high school GPA and test scores utilized as part of admission criteria. Essay recommended. **Homeschooled:** Official copy of high school completion records; 1010 SAT (exclusive of Writing), 22 ACT.

High school preparation. College-preparatory program recommended. 15 units required. Required and recommended units include English 4, mathematics 3, social studies 2, history 1, science 3 (laboratory 2), foreign language 1 and academic electives 2.

2008-2009 Annual costs. Tuition/fees: $4,196; $16,512 out-of-state. Room/board: $7,170. Books/supplies: $1,698. Personal expenses: $2,508.

2007-2008 Financial aid. **Need-based:** 646 full-time freshmen applied for aid; 440 were judged to have need; 438 of these received aid. Average need met was 66%. Average scholarship/grant was $3,950; average loan $3,333. 45% of total undergraduate aid awarded as scholarships/grants, 55% as loans/jobs. **Non-need-based:** Awarded to 1,354 full-time undergraduates, including 621 freshmen. Scholarships awarded for academics, alumni affiliation, art, athletics, job skills, leadership, minority status, music/drama, state residency. **Additional information:** Tuition waived for Native Americans of federally recognized tribes; census number and Certificate of Indian Blood must accompany application.

Application procedures. **Admission:** Closing date 8/1 (postmark date). $30 fee, may be waived for applicants with need. Admission notification on a rolling basis beginning on or about 10/15. **Financial aid:** Priority date 2/15; no closing date. FAFSA required. Applicants notified on a rolling basis starting 3/15; must reply within 2 week(s) of notification.

Academics. **Special study options:** Accelerated study, cooperative education, distance learning, double major, dual enrollment of high school students, ESL, exchange student, honors, independent study, internships, liberal arts/career combination, student-designed major, study abroad, teacher certification program. **Credit/placement by examination:** AP, CLEP, IB, SAT, ACT, institutional tests. 24 credit hours maximum toward bachelor's degree. Up to 24 credits may be granted based on CLEP general exam scores. IB diploma holders will receive a minimum of 24 semester credits. **Support services:** Learning center, remedial instruction, study skills assistance, tutoring, writing center.

Majors. **Area/ethnic studies:** Hispanic-American/Latino/Chicano, Native American, women's. **Biology:** General, ecology. **Business:** General, accounting, business admin, marketing, operations. **Computer sciences:** General. **Conservation:** Environmental studies. **Education:** Multicultural. **Foreign languages:** Spanish. **Health:** Athletic training. **History:** General. **Liberal arts:** Arts/sciences, humanities. **Math:** General. **Parks/recreation:** General, exercise sciences. **Philosophy/religion:** Philosophy. **Physical sciences:** Chemistry, geology, physics. **Psychology:** General, counseling, industrial. **Social sciences:** Anthropology, economics, political science, sociology. **Visual/performing arts:** Dramatic, studio arts.

Most popular majors. Biology 7%, business/marketing 28%, English 7%, liberal arts 13%, parks/recreation 7%, psychology 8%, social sciences 10%, visual/performing arts 7%.

Computing on campus. 672 workstations in dormitories, library, computer center, student center. Dormitories wired for high-speed internet access and linked to campus network. Commuter students can connect to campus network. Online course registration, online library, helpline, repair service, student web hosting, wireless network available.

Student life. **Freshman orientation:** Mandatory, $50 fee. Preregistration for classes offered. **Housing:** Guaranteed on-campus for all undergraduates. Coed dorms, special housing for disabled, apartments, wellness housing available. $100 partly refundable deposit, deadline 7/15. **Activities:** Bands, campus ministries, choral groups, drama, literary magazine, music ensembles, radio station, student government, student newspaper, Newman Club, Circle-K International, international friendship club, business club, American Indian business leaders, American Indian science and engineering society, sociology club, Native American club, Habitat for Humanity.

Athletics. NCAA. **Intercollegiate:** Basketball, cross-country, football (tackle) M, golf M, soccer, softball W, volleyball W. **Intramural:** Badminton, basketball, football (tackle), racquetball, soccer, softball, volleyball. **Team name:** Skyhawks.

Student services. Adult student services, alcohol/substance abuse counseling, chaplain/spiritual director, career counseling, services for economically disadvantaged, student employment services, financial aid counseling, health services, legal services, minority student services, on-campus daycare, personal counseling, placement for graduates, veterans' counselor, women's services. **Physically disabled:** Services for visually, speech, hearing impaired.

Contact. E-mail: admission@fortlewis.edu
Phone: (970) 247-7184 Fax: (970) 247-7179
Andrew Burns, Director of Admission, Fort Lewis College, 1000 Rim Drive, Durango, CO 81301-3999

ITT Technical Institute: Thornton

Thornton, Colorado
www.itt-tech.edu **CB code: 3605**

- For-profit 4-year technical college
- Commuter campus in large city

General. Founded in 1984. Accredited by ACICS. **Calendar:** Quarter.

Contact. Phone: (303) 288-4488
Director of Recruitment, 500 East 84th Avenue, Thornton, CO 80229

Johnson & Wales University: Denver

Denver, Colorado
www.jwu.edu **CB code: 3567**

- Private 4-year university
- Residential campus in large city
- 1,454 degree-seeking undergraduates: 3% part-time, 53% women, 4% African American, 4% Asian American, 9% Hispanic American, 1% Native American, 1% international
- 71% of applicants admitted
- 49% graduate within 6 years

General. Regionally accredited. **Degrees:** 252 bachelor's, 320 associate awarded. **Calendar:** Quarter, limited summer session. **Full-time faculty:** 46 total; 9% minority, 28% women. **Part-time faculty:** 29 total; 52% women. **Class size:** 41% < 20, 51% 20-39, 8% 40-49. **Special facilities:** Community leadership institute.

Freshman class profile. 2,651 applied, 1,892 admitted, 400 enrolled.

Mid 50% test scores		**GPA 2.0-2.99:**	40%
SAT critical reading:	420-540	**Return as sophomores:**	70%
SAT math:	440-560	**Out-of-state:**	59%
GPA 3.75 or higher:	14%	**Live on campus:**	79%
GPA 3.50-3.74:	11%	**International:**	1%
GPA 3.0-3.49:	34%		

Basis for selection. Academic record important, including secondary school curriculum, GPA, class rank, test scores. Student motivation and interest given strong consideration. SAT or ACT recommended. SAT or ACT required for students entering honors program only.

High school preparation. College-preparatory program recommended. Required units include English 4, mathematics 3, social studies 2 and science 3.

2009-2010 Annual costs. Tuition/fees (projected): $23,490. Optional weekend meal plan available for $1,068. Room/board: $9,249. Books/supplies: $1,500. Personal expenses: $1,623.

2008-2009 Financial aid. **Need-based:** 377 full-time freshmen applied for aid; 295 were judged to have need; 295 of these received aid. Average need met was 66%. Average scholarship/grant was $7,226; average loan $3,260. 37% of total undergraduate aid awarded as scholarships/grants, 63% as loans/jobs. **Non-need-based:** Awarded to 1,089 full-time undergraduates, including 330 freshmen. Scholarships awarded for academics, alumni affiliation, job skills, leadership, state residency.

Application procedures. **Admission:** No deadline. No application fee. Admission notification on a rolling basis beginning on or about 11/1. Must reply by May 1 or within 2 week(s) if notified thereafter. **Financial aid:** No deadline. FAFSA required. Applicants notified on a rolling basis starting 3/1; must reply within 2 week(s) of notification.

Academics. Special study options: Accelerated study, cooperative education, dual enrollment of high school students, ESL, exchange student, honors, independent study, internships, study abroad. **Credit/placement by examination:** CLEP, institutional tests. **Support services:** Learning center, remedial instruction, study skills assistance, tutoring, writing center.

Majors. Business: Accounting, banking/financial services, business admin, entrepreneurial studies, hospitality admin, hotel/motel admin, international, investments/securities, marketing, public finance. **Family/consumer sciences:** Food/nutrition. **Parks/recreation:** Facilities management, sports admin. **Personal/culinary services:** Food service, restaurant/catering. **Protective services:** Law enforcement admin.

Most popular majors. Business/marketing 42%, family/consumer sciences 27%, parks/recreation 15%, personal/culinary services 12%.

Computing on campus. Dormitories wired for high-speed internet access and linked to campus network. Commuter students can connect to campus network. Online course registration, online library, helpline, repair service, wireless network available.

Student life. Freshman orientation: Mandatory, $250 fee. Preregistration for classes offered. **Housing:** Coed dorms available. $300 deposit. **Activities:** Drama, international student organizations, musical theater, student government, student newspaper.

Athletics. NAIA. **Intercollegiate:** Basketball, soccer, volleyball M. **Intramural:** Basketball, football (non-tackle), soccer, softball, volleyball. **Team name:** Wildcats.

Student services. Adult student services, alcohol/substance abuse counseling, career counseling, student employment services, financial aid counseling, health services, minority student services, personal counseling, placement for graduates. **Physically disabled:** Services for visually, speech, hearing impaired. **Learning disabled:** Comprehensive services available.

Contact. E-mail: admissions.den@jwu.edu
Phone: (303) 256-9300 Toll-free number: (877) 598-3368
Kim Ostrowski, Director of Admissions, Johnson & Wales University: Denver, 7150 Montview Boulevard, Denver, CO 80220

Jones International University
Centennial, Colorado
www.jiu.edu **CB code: 2785**

- For-profit 4-year virtual college
- Large city
- 60 full-time, degree-seeking undergraduates
- 1,300 graduate students

General. Regionally accredited. Asynchronous learning, 25 student class size limit, 24/7 technical support. **Degrees:** 54 bachelor's awarded; master's, doctoral offered. **Location:** 20 miles from Denver. **Calendar:** Continuous. **Full-time faculty:** 2 total. **Part-time faculty:** 120 total. **Special facilities:** Virtual library, online bookstore.

Basis for selection. Admissions based on students submitting requirements needed for each program and review by academic team for each program.

High school preparation. 16 units recommended. Recommended units include English 4, mathematics 4, social studies 1, history 1, science 3 (laboratory 3) and foreign language 2.

2009-2010 Annual costs. Tuition: $1,425 per course for bachelor's degrees. $65 technology fee per course. Books are approximately $170 per course. Books/supplies: $1,360.

Financial aid. Additional information: Loans available through Sallie Mae and PLATO. Most students have costs reimbursed by employers. GI Bill and VA benefits accepted.

Application procedures. Admission: No deadline. $60 fee. Application must be submitted online. Admission notification on a rolling basis. **Financial aid:** FAFSA required.

Academics. Special study options: Accelerated study, combined bachelor's/graduate degree, distance learning. **Credit/placement by examination:** CLEP, IB. 60 credit hours maximum toward bachelor's degree.

Majors. Business: General, business admin, communications, e-commerce, international, small business admin. **Communications:** General, digital media, journalism, organizational, public relations. **Communications technology:** General. **Computer sciences:** General, computer science, database management, programming, system admin, systems analysis. **Engineering:** Computer.

Computing on campus. PC or laptop required.

Student services. Career counseling, financial aid counseling.

Contact. E-mail: admissions@international.edu
Phone: (303) 784-8247 Toll-free number: (800) 811-5663 ext. 8247
Fax: (303) 799-0966
Joy Cadman, Director of Admissions and Records/Registrar, Jones International University, 9697 East Mineral Avenue, Centennial, CO 80112

Mesa State College
Grand Junction, Colorado
www.mesastate.edu **CB code: 4484**

- Public 4-year community and liberal arts college
- Commuter campus in small city
- 5,617 degree-seeking undergraduates: 23% part-time, 58% women, 2% African American, 3% Asian American, 10% Hispanic American, 2% Native American
- 94 degree-seeking graduate students
- 81% of applicants admitted
- SAT or ACT (ACT writing optional) required

General. Founded in 1925. Regionally accredited. **Degrees:** 527 bachelor's, 180 associate awarded; master's offered. **Location:** 250 miles from Denver, 300 miles from Salt Lake City. **Calendar:** Semester, limited summer session. **Full-time faculty:** 225 total. **Part-time faculty:** 248 total. **Class size:** 55% < 20, 35% 20-39, 4% 40-49, 5% 50-99, less than 1% >100. **Special facilities:** Electron microscope laboratory, herbarium, computer-aided drafting laboratory, technical training facility, environmental restoration laboratory.

Freshman class profile. 3,210 applied, 2,603 admitted, 1,251 enrolled.

Mid 50% test scores		**GPA 2.0-2.99:**	44%
SAT critical reading:	440-560	**Rank in top quarter:**	24%
SAT math:	430-570	**Rank in top tenth:**	7%
ACT composite:	17-23	**Return as sophomores:**	61%
GPA 3.75 or higher:	12%	**Out-of-state:**	11%
GPA 3.50-3.74:	11%	**Live on campus:**	53%
GPA 3.0-3.49:	29%		

Basis for selection. Admission based on GPA, ACT/SAT, class rank and satisfaction of HEAR requirements. Open admissions to most technical, associates and certificate programs. Audition required of music, music theater, theater majors. Interview recommended for nursing, allied health, teacher certification majors. **Homeschooled:** Statement describing homeschool structure and mission, transcript of courses and grades required.

High school preparation. College-preparatory program recommended. 15 units required. Required and recommended units include English 4, mathematics 3, social studies 3, history 2, science 3 (laboratory 2), foreign language 2 and academic electives 2.

2008-2009 Annual costs. Tuition/fees: $4,738; $13,512 out-of-state. Room/board: $7,355. Books/supplies: $1,698. Personal expenses: $1,942.

2007-2008 Financial aid. Need-based: 1,082 full-time freshmen applied for aid; 1,004 were judged to have need; 1,004 of these received aid. Average need met was 45%. Average scholarship/grant was $3,762; average loan $3,666. 46% of total undergraduate aid awarded as scholarships/grants, 54% as loans/jobs. **Non-need-based:** Awarded to 338 full-time undergraduates, including 365 freshmen. Scholarships awarded for academics, art, athletics, leadership, minority status, music/drama.

Application procedures. Admission: No deadline. $30 fee, may be waived for applicants with need. Admission notification on a rolling basis beginning on or about 9/1. **Financial aid:** Priority date 3/1; no closing date. FAFSA required. Applicants notified on a rolling basis starting 4/1; must reply within 5 week(s) of notification.

Academics. Special study options: Accelerated study, combined bachelor's/graduate degree, cooperative education, cross-registration, distance learning, double major, dual enrollment of high school students, ESL, exchange student, honors, independent study, internships, study abroad, teacher certification program. Area vocational school provides training in technical skills.

Credit/placement by examination: AP, CLEP, IB, SAT, ACT, institutional tests. 12 credit hours maximum toward associate degree, 20 toward bachelor's. **Support services:** Learning center, pre-admission summer program, reduced course load, remedial instruction, study skills assistance, tutoring, writing center.

Majors. **Biology:** General. **Business:** General, accounting, management information systems. **Communications:** Media studies. **Computer sciences:** General. **Conservation:** Environmental science. **Engineering technology:** Architectural. **Foreign languages:** Spanish. **Health:** Athletic training, nursing (RN). **History:** General. **Liberal arts:** Arts/sciences. **Math:** General. **Parks/recreation:** Exercise sciences, sports admin. **Physical sciences:** General. **Protective services:** Criminal justice. **Psychology:** General. **Public administration:** General. **Social sciences:** General, political science, sociology. **Visual/performing arts:** Art, dramatic, graphic design.

Most popular majors. Biology 7%, business/marketing 24%, health sciences 12%, parks/recreation 8%, psychology 7%, social sciences 6%, visual/performing arts 9%.

Computing on campus. 525 workstations in dormitories, library, computer center, student center. Dormitories wired for high-speed internet access and linked to campus network. Commuter students can connect to campus network. Online course registration, online library, helpline, student web hosting, wireless network available.

Student life. **Freshman orientation:** Available. Preregistration for classes offered. **Housing:** Coed dorms, special housing for disabled, apartments, wellness housing available. $150 partly refundable deposit. Suite style housing available for sophomores, juniors and seniors. **Activities:** Bands, choral groups, dance, drama, film society, literary magazine, music ensembles, musical theater, radio station, student government, student newspaper, symphony orchestra, TV station, African American college, La Raza, handicapped student organization, Newman Club, Christian fellowship, Latter-day Saints student association, Baptist student union, Circle-K, Native American council, Polynesian club.

Athletics. NCAA. **Intercollegiate:** Baseball M, basketball, cross-country W, football (tackle) M, golf W, soccer, softball W, swimming W, tennis, track and field W, volleyball W, wrestling M. **Intramural:** Badminton, basketball, football (non-tackle), handball, racquetball, skiing, soccer, softball, volleyball. **Team name:** Mavericks.

Student services. Adult student services, alcohol/substance abuse counseling, chaplain/spiritual director, career counseling, services for economically disadvantaged, student employment services, financial aid counseling, health services, minority student services, on-campus daycare, personal counseling, placement for graduates, veterans' counselor. **Physically disabled:** Services for visually, speech, hearing impaired.

Contact. E-mail: admissions@mesastate.edu
Phone: (970) 248-1875 Toll-free number: (800) 982-6372
Fax: (970) 248-1973
Jared Meier, Director of Admissions, Mesa State College, 1100 North Avenue, Grand Junction, CO 81501

Metropolitan State College of Denver

Denver, Colorado
www.mscd.edu **CB code: 4505**

- Public 4-year liberal arts college
- Commuter campus in very large city
- 20,662 degree-seeking undergraduates: 39% part-time, 55% women, 6% African American, 4% Asian American, 14% Hispanic American, 1% Native American, 1% international
- 64% of applicants admitted
- SAT or ACT (ACT writing optional) required

General. Founded in 1963. Regionally accredited. Library, student center, physical education facilities, child care center shared with Community College of Denver and University of Colorado at Denver. Degree completion programs offered at off-campus sites in North Glen and Englewood. **Degrees:** 2,479 bachelor's awarded. **ROTC:** Army, Air Force. **Location:** Downtown. **Calendar:** Semester, extensive summer session. **Full-time faculty:** 516 total; 21% minority, 46% women. **Part-time faculty:** 732 total; 13% minority, 55% women. **Class size:** 35% < 20, 55% 20-39, 7% 40-49, 3% 50-99. **Special facilities:** Art galleries, CAD/CAM laboratory, world indoor airport.

Freshman class profile. 6,726 applied, 4,318 admitted, 2,332 enrolled.

Mid 50% test scores		**GPA 3.0-3.49:**	28%
SAT critical reading:	450-550	**GPA 2.0-2.99:**	58%
SAT math:	420-550	**Rank in top quarter:**	8%
ACT composite:	18-22	**Rank in top tenth:**	5%
GPA 3.75 or higher:	5%	**Out-of-state:**	4%
GPA 3.50-3.74:	7%		

Basis for selection. ACT/SAT test results, GPA, and high school class rank important. ACT/SAT not required of those submitting GED. Open admission for applicants 20 years of age and older who are high school graduates, have GED, or have 30 transferable credits from another college.

High school preparation. College-preparatory program recommended. 15 units recommended. Recommended units include English 4, mathematics 3, social studies 2, history 1, science 3 and foreign language 2.

2008-2009 Annual costs. Tuition/fees: $3,241; $11,949 out-of-state.

2007-2008 Financial aid. **Need-based:** 34% of total undergraduate aid awarded as scholarships/grants, 66% as loans/jobs. **Non-need-based:** Scholarships awarded for academics, art, athletics, job skills, music/drama, state residency.

Application procedures. **Admission:** Closing date 8/25 (receipt date). $25 fee, may be waived for applicants with need. Admission notification on a rolling basis. **Financial aid:** Priority date 2/15; no closing date. FAFSA required. Applicants notified on a rolling basis starting 3/1.

Academics. **Special study options:** Accelerated study, cooperative education, cross-registration, distance learning, double major, dual enrollment of high school students, external degree, honors, independent study, internships, liberal arts/career combination, student-designed major, study abroad, teacher certification program, Washington semester. **Credit/placement by examination:** AP, CLEP, IB, SAT, ACT. 64 credit hours maximum toward bachelor's degree. **Support services:** Pre-admission summer program, study skills assistance, tutoring, writing center.

Majors. **Area/ethnic studies:** African-American, Hispanic-American/Latino/Chicano. **Biology:** General. **Business:** Accounting, business admin, finance, hospitality admin, hospitality/recreation, marketing, tourism promotion, tourism/travel. **Communications:** General, broadcast journalism, journalism. **Computer sciences:** General, computer science. **Conservation:** General, environmental studies, land use planning. **Education:** Art, music. **Engineering technology:** Civil, electrical, surveying. **Foreign languages:** General, Spanish. **Health:** Health care admin, nursing (RN). **History:** General. **Interdisciplinary:** Behavioral sciences. **Math:** General. **Parks/recreation:** General, exercise sciences. **Philosophy/religion:** Philosophy. **Physical sciences:** Atmospheric science, chemistry, physics. **Protective services:** Criminal justice, law enforcement admin. **Psychology:** General. **Public administration:** Human services, social work. **Social sciences:** Anthropology, economics, political science, sociology. **Transportation:** Air traffic control, aviation, aviation management. **Visual/performing arts:** Art, industrial design, music performance.

Most popular majors. Business/marketing 21%, English 8%, interdisciplinary studies 10%, psychology 7%, security/protective services 7%, visual/performing arts 6%.

Computing on campus. 700 workstations in library, computer center, student center. Commuter students can connect to campus network. Online course registration, online library, helpline, repair service, wireless network available.

Student life. **Freshman orientation:** Mandatory. Preregistration for classes offered. Several sessions held preceding each semester. **Housing:** Off-campus apartments in area. **Activities:** Bands, choral groups, dance, drama, international student organizations, literary magazine, music ensembles, musical theater, radio station, student government, student newspaper, TV station, Approximately 100 student organizations and clubs available.

Athletics. NCAA. **Intercollegiate:** Baseball M, basketball, cross-country, diving, soccer, swimming, tennis, volleyball W. **Intramural:** Basketball, handball, lacrosse M, racquetball, rugby M, skiing, softball W, tennis, volleyball. **Team name:** Roadrunners.

Student services. Adult student services, alcohol/substance abuse counseling, chaplain/spiritual director, career counseling, services for economically disadvantaged, student employment services, financial aid counseling, health services, legal services, on-campus daycare, personal counseling, placement for graduates, veterans' counselor, women's services. **Physically disabled:** Services for visually, speech, hearing impaired. **Learning disabled:** Comprehensive services available.

Contact. E-mail: askmetro@mscd.edu
Phone: (303) 556-3058 Fax: (303) 556-6345
Elena Sandoval-Lucero, Director of Admissions, Metropolitan State College of Denver, Campus Box 16, Denver, CO 80217

Naropa University

Boulder, Colorado **CB member**
www.naropa.edu **CB code: 0908**

- Private 4-year liberal arts college
- Commuter campus in small city
- 444 degree-seeking undergraduates: 7% part-time, 60% women, 2% African American, 3% Asian American, 3% Hispanic American, 2% Native American, 2% international
- 605 degree-seeking graduate students
- 79% of applicants admitted
- Application essay, interview required

General. Founded in 1974. Regionally accredited. Uses contemplative education, which is learning infused with the experience of awareness, insight and compassion for oneself and others, honed through the practice of sitting meditation and other contemplative disciplines. **Degrees:** 117 bachelor's awarded; master's, first professional offered. **Location:** 35 miles from Denver. **Calendar:** Semester, limited summer session. **Full-time faculty:** 73 total; 49% have terminal degrees, 15% minority, 60% women. **Part-time faculty:** 137 total; 23% have terminal degrees, 9% minority, 66% women. **Class size:** 56% < 20, 41% 20-39, 1% 40-49, 2% 50-99. **Special facilities:** Meditation halls, maitri rooms, consciousness laboratory, greenhouse, tea house, Chogyam Trungpa Rinpoche archives, performing arts center, dance studios, music studio, art studio, art exhibits, audio archives.

Freshman class profile. 170 applied, 135 admitted, 57 enrolled.

GPA 3.75 or higher:	15%	**End year in good standing:**	71%
GPA 3.50-3.74:	13%	**Return as sophomores:**	59%
GPA 3.0-3.49:	33%	**Out-of-state:**	85%
GPA 2.0-2.99:	38%	**Live on campus:**	83%

Basis for selection. Assessment of academic background, community service, mission, and readiness important. Determination based on fit with unique mission, as well as academic background and readiness. Supplemental applications and/or art samples required for applicants to performance, environmental studies, interdisciplinary studies, music, visual arts, and writing and literature programs. **Homeschooled:** Portfolio of work completed during high school required, including subjects studied and modes of learning for each subject; extracurricular/community activities; academic achievements that support academic preparedness for college, such as internship positions; parent or teacher narrative; self-evaluation of work and how it contributed to intellectual growth; and transcripts from mainstream high schools or colleges (if applicable).

High school preparation. College-preparatory program recommended. 23 units recommended. Recommended units include English 4, mathematics 3, social studies 3, history 3, science 3 (laboratory 2), foreign language 3 and academic electives 4. Art, dance, theatre and/or creative writing recommended.

2008-2009 Annual costs. Tuition/fees: $22,074. Room/board: $7,036. Books/supplies: $706. Personal expenses: $3,078.

2008-2009 Financial aid. All financial aid based on need. 38 full-time freshmen applied for aid; 34 were judged to have need; 34 of these received aid. Average need met was 88%. Average scholarship/grant was $14,474; average loan $4,344. 55% of total undergraduate aid awarded as scholarships/grants, 45% as loans/jobs.

Application procedures. Admission: Priority date 1/15; deadline 7/1 (postmark date). $50 fee, may be waived for applicants with need. Admission notification on a rolling basis. Must reply by May 1 or within 3 week(s) if notified thereafter. **Financial aid:** Priority date 1/15, closing date 7/1. FAFSA required. Applicants notified on a rolling basis starting 1/15; must reply within 4 week(s) of notification.

Academics. Special study options: Double major, dual enrollment of high school students, independent study, internships, student-designed major. Consortium agreement with University of Colorado allows degree-seeking students to take courses at University of Colorado at an in-state tuition rate. **Credit/placement by examination:** AP, CLEP, IB. 30 credit hours maximum toward bachelor's degree. **Support services:** Reduced course load, study skills assistance, tutoring, writing center.

Majors. Conservation: Environmental studies. **Education:** Early childhood. **Interdisciplinary:** Peace/conflict. **Philosophy/religion:** Religion. **Psychology:** General. **Visual/performing arts:** General, studio arts. **Other:** Interdisciplinary studies, Traditional Eastern arts.

Most popular majors. English 15%, interdisciplinary studies 19%, parks/recreation 9%, philosophy/religious studies 9%, psychology 28%, visual/performing arts 13%.

Computing on campus. 75 workstations in computer center. Online course registration, online library, wireless network available.

Student life. Freshman orientation: Mandatory. Preregistration for classes offered. Week-long session in August. One or 2-day orientations offered for parents and families. **Policies:** Code of Conduct enforced. **Housing:** Guaranteed on-campus for freshmen. Apartments, wellness housing available. $300 nonrefundable deposit, deadline 7/1. **Activities:** Jazz band, campus ministries, choral groups, dance, drama, international student organizations, literary magazine, music ensembles, musical theater, student government, Allies in Action, gender discussion group, students for peace and justice, healers, laughter club, Tibetan debate club, Reconnecting on Outer Terrain, Japanese tea ceremony club, international student club.

Student services. Alcohol/substance abuse counseling, chaplain/spiritual director, career counseling, financial aid counseling, minority student services, personal counseling. **Physically disabled:** Services for visually, hearing impaired.

Contact. E-mail: admissions@naropa.edu
Phone: (303) 546-3572 Toll-free number: (800) 772-6951
Fax: (303) 546-3583
Susan Boyle, Dean of Admissions, Naropa University, 2130 Arapahoe Avenue, Boulder, CO 80302-6697

National American University: Denver

Denver, Colorado
www.national.edu **CB code: 5354**

- For-profit 4-year university and branch campus college
- Commuter campus in very large city
- 185 degree-seeking undergraduates

General. Founded in 1941. Regionally accredited. **Degrees:** 21 bachelor's, 5 associate awarded. **Calendar:** Quarter, extensive summer session. **Part-time faculty:** 20 total. **Class size:** 92% < 20, 8% 20-39.

Basis for selection. Open admission, but selective for some programs. Selective admissions to nursing program.

2008-2009 Annual costs. Tuition/fees: $12,725. Books/supplies: $1,200.

Application procedures. Admission: No deadline. $25 fee. Admission notification on a rolling basis. **Financial aid:** No deadline. Applicants notified on a rolling basis.

Academics. Special study options: Accelerated study, cooperative education, distance learning, double major, ESL, external degree, independent study, internships, liberal arts/career combination, weekend college. **Credit/placement by examination:** AP, CLEP, institutional tests. 48 credit hours maximum toward bachelor's degree. **Support services:** Remedial instruction.

Majors. Business: Accounting, business admin, management information systems, management science. **Computer sciences:** Applications programming, information systems, LAN/WAN management, system admin. **Health:** Facilities admin, health care admin, health services, health services admin.

Computing on campus. Online library available.

Student life. Activities: Student government, Phi Beta Lamda (business club), data processing management association.

Athletics. Team name: Mavericks.

Student services. Career counseling, placement for graduates.

Contact. E-mail: kwalker@national.edu
Phone: (303) 876-7100 Fax: (303) 876-7105
Jacque McLaren, Director of Admissions, National American University: Denver, 1325 South Colorado Boulevard, Suite 100, Denver, CO 80222-3308

Nazarene Bible College
Colorado Springs, Colorado
www.nbc.edu **CB code: 0476**

- Private 4-year Bible college affiliated with Church of the Nazarene
- Commuter campus in very large city
- 975 degree-seeking undergraduates: 81% part-time, 39% women, 6% African American, 1% Asian American, 4% Hispanic American, 2% Native American
- Application essay required

General. Founded in 1964. Accredited by ABHE. **Degrees:** 65 bachelor's, 1 associate awarded. **Location:** 60 miles from Denver. **Calendar:** Trimester, limited summer session. **Full-time faculty:** 13 total. **Part-time faculty:** 89 total.

Freshman class profile.

End year in good standing:	100%	**Out-of-state:**	96%

Basis for selection. Open admission, but selective for some programs. Testimony, 2 recommendations required. **Homeschooled:** Transcript of courses and grades, letter of recommendation (nonparent) required.

2008-2009 Annual costs. Tuition/fees: $8,580. Books/supplies: $900.

2007-2008 Financial aid. **Non-need-based:** Scholarships awarded for religious affiliation. **Additional information:** Tuition waiver available to students serving as student body officers.

Application procedures. **Admission:** No deadline. No application fee. Admission notification on a rolling basis beginning on or about 5/1. **Financial aid:** Priority date 6/1; no closing date. FAFSA required. Applicants notified on a rolling basis starting 6/15; must reply within 2 week(s) of notification.

Academics. Full programs offered in evening classes, cater to adult students. Extensive online degree programs offered. Degree completion program offered online and on campus. **Special study options:** Accelerated study, distance learning, double major, internships. **Credit/placement by examination:** CLEP, institutional tests. 12 credit hours maximum toward associate degree, 24 toward bachelor's. **Support services:** Learning center, reduced course load, remedial instruction, tutoring.

Majors. **Theology:** Bible, pastoral counseling, religious ed, sacred music.

Computing on campus. 20 workstations in library, computer center. Online library, wireless network available.

Student life. **Freshman orientation:** Mandatory. Preregistration for classes offered. **Policies:** Religious observance required. **Activities:** Concert band, choral groups, music ensembles, student government, Missions in Action club, Wesley Theological Society.

Student services. Chaplain/spiritual director, career counseling, services for economically disadvantaged, student employment services, financial aid counseling, personal counseling, placement for graduates, women's services. **Physically disabled:** Services for visually, hearing impaired.

Contact. E-mail: admissions@nbc.edu
Phone: (719) 884-5000 ext. 5065 Toll-free number: (800) 873-3873 ext. 5065 Fax: (719) 884-5199
Jay Ott, Vice President for Campus Academic Services, Nazarene Bible College, 1111 Academy Park Loop, Colorado Springs, CO 80910-3704

Platt College: Aurora
Aurora, Colorado
www.plattcolorado.edu **CB code: 3012**

- For-profit 4-year visual arts and nursing college
- Commuter campus in very large city
- 160 degree-seeking undergraduates
- Application essay, interview required

General. Accredited by ACCSCT. **Degrees:** 31 bachelor's, 14 associate awarded. **Calendar:** Continuous. **Full-time faculty:** 10 total. **Part-time faculty:** 17 total.

Basis for selection. Entrance examination, interview, level of interest (assessed during interview) important. Background check, letter of recommendation required for nursing. Institutional entrance examination required. Wonderlic required for graphic arts students. Test of Essential Academic Skills (TEAS) required for nursing students. **Homeschooled:** State high school equivalency certificate required.

High school preparation. College-preparatory program recommended.

2008-2009 Annual costs. Visual and Performing Arts: associate program: $34,000; Bachelor's program: $50,107. Nursing program (RN): $68,000. Costs include tuition, registration fee, lab fees, supplies. Cost of books, art kit vary with program.

Financial aid. All financial aid based on need.

Application procedures. **Admission:** No deadline. $75 fee. Admission notification on a rolling basis. **Financial aid:** No deadline. FAFSA, institutional form required. Applicants notified on a rolling basis.

Academics. **Credit/placement by examination:** CLEP. **Support services:** Learning center, study skills assistance, writing center.

Majors. **Health:** Nursing (RN). **Visual/performing arts:** Commercial/advertising art.

Computing on campus. PC or laptop required.

Contact. E-mail: admissions@plattcolorado.edu
Phone: (303) 369-5151 Toll-free number: (877) 369-5151
Fax: (303) 745-1433
Joni Aaron-Horton, Senior Admissions Coordinator, Platt College: Aurora, 3100 South Parker Road, Aurora, CO 80014-3141

Regis University
Denver, Colorado **CB member**
www.regis.edu **CB code: 4656**

- Private 4-year university and liberal arts college affiliated with Roman Catholic Church
- Residential campus in very large city
- 1,277 degree-seeking undergraduates: 3% part-time, 57% women, 2% African American, 5% Asian American, 14% Hispanic American, 1% international
- 62 degree-seeking graduate students
- 74% of applicants admitted
- SAT or ACT (ACT writing optional), application essay required
- 61% graduate within 6 years

General. Founded in 1877. Regionally accredited. **Degrees:** 273 bachelor's awarded; master's, doctoral offered. **ROTC:** Army, Naval, Air Force. **Location:** 10 miles from downtown. **Calendar:** Semester, limited summer session. **Full-time faculty:** 86 total; 80% have terminal degrees, 13% minority, 45% women. **Part-time faculty:** 30 total; 7% have terminal degrees, 7% minority, 53% women. **Class size:** 66% < 20, 33% 20-39, less than 1% 40-49, less than 1% 50-99. **Special facilities:** Center for the study of war experience, Santos collection, recorder music center, arboretum.

Freshman class profile. 2,130 applied, 1,574 admitted, 418 enrolled.

Mid 50% test scores		**GPA 2.0-2.99:**	18%
SAT critical reading:	480-590	**Rank in top quarter:**	53%
SAT math:	460-570	**Rank in top tenth:**	29%
ACT composite:	20-26	**Return as sophomores:**	78%
GPA 3.75 or higher:	34%	**Out-of-state:**	43%
GPA 3.50-3.74:	18%	**Live on campus:**	80%
GPA 3.0-3.49:	30%		

Basis for selection. High school record, test scores, recommendations, essay, school and community activities most important. Interview, campus visit recommended. Audition recommended of music majors.

High school preparation. 15 units required. Required and recommended units include English 4, mathematics 2, social studies 3, history 2, science 2 (laboratory 1) and foreign language 2.

2008-2009 Annual costs. Tuition/fees: $28,700. Tuition-free for any student who does not graduate in 4 years while maintaining required amount of credit hours. Room/board: $8,982. Books/supplies: $1,698. Personal expenses: $1,161.

2007-2008 Financial aid. **Non-need-based:** Scholarships awarded for academics, athletics, leadership, minority status, religious affiliation, ROTC, state residency.

Application procedures. **Admission:** Priority date 3/1; deadline 8/1 (postmark date). $40 fee, may be waived for applicants with need, free for online applicants. Admission notification on a rolling basis beginning on or about 9/1. Must reply by May 1 or within 2 week(s) if notified thereafter. **Financial aid:** Priority date 3/1; no closing date. FAFSA required. Applicants notified on a rolling basis starting 3/15.

Academics. School of Professional Studies offers part-time undergraduate, graduate, certificate and corporate education programs to adult students on 6 campuses and online. **Special study options:** Combined bachelor's/graduate degree, cross-registration, double major, exchange student, honors, independent study, internships, student-designed major, study abroad, teacher certification program. **Credit/placement by examination:** AP, CLEP, IB, institutional tests. 30 credit hours maximum toward bachelor's degree. Regis, CLEP, DANTES, Challenge exams offered. **Support services:** Learning center, pre-admission summer program, reduced course load, remedial instruction, study skills assistance, tutoring, writing center.

Majors. Area/ethnic studies: Women's. **Biology:** General, biochemistry. **Business:** General, accounting, business admin. **Communications:** General. **Computer sciences:** General, computer science. **Education:** General, biology, chemistry, elementary, English, history, mathematics, middle, physical, science, secondary, special. **Foreign languages:** French, Spanish. **Health:** Medical records admin, predental, premedicine, preveterinary. **History:** General. **Interdisciplinary:** Neuroscience. **Legal studies:** Prelaw. **Liberal arts:** Arts/sciences. **Math:** General. **Philosophy/religion:** Philosophy, religion. **Physical sciences:** Chemistry. **Psychology:** General. **Social sciences:** Criminology, economics, political science, sociology. **Visual/performing arts:** General.

Most popular majors. Biology 10%, business/marketing 28%, communications/journalism 6%, English 6%, interdisciplinary studies 12%, mathematics 6%, social sciences 12%.

Computing on campus. 337 workstations in dormitories, library, computer center, student center. Dormitories wired for high-speed internet access and linked to campus network. Commuter students can connect to campus network. Online course registration, online library, helpline, wireless network available.

Student life. Freshman orientation: Mandatory, $75 fee. Preregistration for classes offered. Held weekend before classes begin. **Policies:** Freshmen required to live on campus unless residing with parent, guardian or spouse in Denver metropolitan area. **Housing:** Guaranteed on-campus for freshmen. Coed dorms, single-sex dorms, special housing for disabled, apartments, cooperative housing, wellness housing available. $150 nonrefundable deposit, deadline 5/1. **Activities:** Bands, campus ministries, choral groups, dance, drama, literary magazine, music ensembles, musical theater, radio station, student government, student newspaper, peer education, environmental action program, Christian Fellowship, Jewish student group, Asian awareness association, black student alliance, Mi Gente, multicultural awareness committee, Romero House, Young Democrats and Republicans.

Athletics. NCAA. **Intercollegiate:** Baseball M, basketball, cross-country, golf, lacrosse W, soccer, softball W, volleyball W. **Intramural:** Basketball, bowling, football (non-tackle), soccer, softball, tennis, volleyball. **Team name:** Rangers.

Student services. Adult student services, alcohol/substance abuse counseling, chaplain/spiritual director, career counseling, student employment services, financial aid counseling, health services, minority student services, personal counseling, placement for graduates, veterans' counselor. **Physically disabled:** Services for visually, speech, hearing impaired. **Learning disabled:** Comprehensive services available.

Contact. E-mail: regisadm@regis.edu
Phone: (303) 458-4900 Toll-free number: (800) 388-2366 ext. 4900
Fax: (303) 964-5534
Victor Davolt, Director of Admissions, Regis College, Regis University, 3333 Regis Boulevard, Mail Code B20, Denver, CO 80221-1099

Rocky Mountain College of Art & Design

Denver, Colorado
www.rmcad.edu **CB code: 1943**

- For-profit 4-year visual arts college
- Commuter campus in very large city
- 568 degree-seeking undergraduates: 15% part-time, 61% women, 1% African American, 3% Asian American, 10% Hispanic American, 1% Native American, 1% international
- 99% of applicants admitted
- SAT or ACT with writing, application essay, interview required
- 45% graduate within 6 years

General. Founded in 1963. Regionally accredited. **Degrees:** 87 bachelor's awarded. **Calendar:** Semester, extensive summer session. **Full-time faculty:** 26 total; 96% have terminal degrees, 4% minority, 46% women. **Part-time faculty:** 54 total; 80% have terminal degrees, 26% minority, 43% women. **Class size:** 89% < 20, 11% 20-39. **Special facilities:** Fine arts center exhibition space.

Freshman class profile. 410 applied, 405 admitted, 143 enrolled.

Mid 50% test scores		**GPA 3.0-3.49:**	29%
SAT critical reading:	470-590	**GPA 2.0-2.99:**	38%
SAT math:	450-590	**End year in good standing:**	81%
SAT writing:	440-580	**Return as sophomores:**	68%
ACT composite:	18-24	**Out-of-state:**	42%
GPA 3.75 or higher:	14%	**Live on campus:**	47%
GPA 3.50-3.74:	17%		

Basis for selection. Applicants must show desire to pursue art career. Portfolio, essay, and recommendations required. Test scores required for all degree candidates. Portfolio and essay required. Interview required of local applicants, recommended for others. **Homeschooled:** Statement describing homeschool structure and mission, transcript of courses and grades, state high school equivalency certificate required.

High school preparation. Art courses strongly recommended.

2009-2010 Annual costs. Tuition/fees (projected): $24,840. Flat fee of $12,420 per term for students taking 12 to 18 credits.

2008-2009 Financial aid. Need-based: 110 full-time freshmen applied for aid; 103 were judged to have need; 103 of these received aid. Average need met was 60%. Average scholarship/grant was $3,776; average loan $3,136. 33% of total undergraduate aid awarded as scholarships/grants, 67% as loans/jobs. **Non-need-based:** Awarded to 409 full-time undergraduates, including 127 freshmen. Scholarships awarded for academics, art, state residency.

Application procedures. Admission: No deadline. $50 fee, may be waived for applicants with need. Admission notification on a rolling basis. **Financial aid:** Priority date 3/15; no closing date. FAFSA, institutional form required. Applicants notified on a rolling basis starting 4/15; must reply within 2 week(s) of notification.

Academics. Special study options: Double major, dual enrollment of high school students, independent study, internships, teacher certification program. **Credit/placement by examination:** AP, CLEP, IB, SAT, ACT. 64 credit hours maximum toward bachelor's degree. **Support services:** Reduced course load, study skills assistance, tutoring, writing center.

Majors. Communications technology: Animation/special effects. **Education:** Art. **Visual/performing arts:** Design, graphic design, illustration, interior design, painting, photography, sculpture, studio arts. **Other:** Game art.

Most popular majors. Communication technologies 23%, education 7%, visual/performing arts 70%.

Computing on campus. 237 workstations in library, computer center. Commuter students can connect to campus network. Online course registration, online library, helpline, repair service, student web hosting, wireless network available.

Student life. Freshman orientation: Mandatory. 3-day program held before start of term. **Housing:** Coed dorms available. **Activities:** Student government, student newspaper.

Student services. Alcohol/substance abuse counseling, career counseling, student employment services, financial aid counseling, personal counseling, placement for graduates, veterans' counselor. **Physically disabled:** Services for visually, speech, hearing impaired.

Contact. E-mail: admissions@rmcad.edu
Phone: (303) 753-6046 Toll-free number: (800) 888-2787
Fax: (303) 759-4970
Angela Carlson, Director of Marketing and Admissions, Rocky Mountain College of Art & Design, 1600 Pierce Street, Denver, CO 80214

Teikyo Loretto Heights University

Denver, Colorado
www.tlhu.edu **CB code: 4878**

- Private 4-year business and liberal arts college
- Residential campus in very large city

General. Accredited by ACICS. **Calendar:** Semester.

Annual costs/financial aid. Tuition/fees (2008-2009): $14,970. Room/board: $7,300. Need-based financial aid available to full-time and part-time students.

Contact. Phone: (303) 937-4280
Admissions Coordinator, 3001 South Federal Boulevard, Denver, CO 80236

United States Air Force Academy

USAF Academy, Colorado — **CB member**
www.usafa.edu — **CB code: 4830**

- Public 4-year military college
- Residential campus in large city
- 4,537 degree-seeking undergraduates: 19% women, 5% African American, 8% Asian American, 7% Hispanic American, 2% Native American, 1% international
- 18% of applicants admitted
- SAT or ACT (ACT writing recommended), application essay, interview required
- 74% graduate within 6 years; 9% enter graduate study

General. Founded in 1954. Regionally accredited. **Degrees:** 1,024 bachelor's awarded. **Location:** 8 miles from Colorado Springs, 60 miles from Denver. **Calendar:** Semester, limited summer session. **Full-time faculty:** 519 total; 50% have terminal degrees, 8% minority, 21% women. **Part-time faculty:** 11 total; 46% have terminal degrees. **Class size:** 67% < 20, 33% 20-39, less than 1% 40-49. **Special facilities:** 2 airfields; tri-sonic wind tunnel; aeronautics, instrumentation, research and radio-frequency systems laboratories; consolidated educational training facility; meteorology lab; engineering mechanics lab; laser optics center.

Freshman class profile. 9,001 applied, 1,642 admitted, 1,336 enrolled.

Mid 50% test scores		**GPA 2.0-2.99:**	2%
SAT critical reading:	600-680	**Rank in top quarter:**	80%
SAT math:	620-700	**Rank in top tenth:**	52%
SAT writing:	560-660	**Return as sophomores:**	93%
ACT composite:	25-29	**Out-of-state:**	93%
GPA 3.75 or higher:	66%	**Live on campus:**	100%
GPA 3.50-3.74:	15%	**International:**	1%
GPA 3.0-3.49:	17%		

Basis for selection. Must be a citizen of the United States, unmarried with no dependents, between the ages of 17 and 23, and of good moral character. Legal nomination from member of Congress, US President or Vice President or other selected sources required. Secondary school record, test scores, leadership ability, extracurricular activities, character most important. Satisfactory completion of medical exam and fitness test, and personal interview required.

High school preparation. Recommended units include English 4, mathematics 4, social studies 3, history 3, science 4 (laboratory 4), foreign language 2 and computer science 1. English should include college preparatory composition and speech courses. Math should include algebra, geometry, trigonometry, calculus, and functional analysis (if available). Science should include biology, chemistry, physics, computers, and additional science courses. Foreign language instruction should be in a modern language.

2008-2009 Annual costs. Tuition, room, board, medical and dental care paid by U.S. Government. Each cadet receives monthly salary to pay for uniforms, supplies and personal expenses. A government loan is advanced to each member of the freshman class.

Application procedures. Admission: Closing date 1/31 (postmark date). No application fee. Admission notification on a rolling basis beginning on or about 11/15. Must reply by 5/1. Several stages of application process; begin junior year.

Academics. Special study options: Double major, ESL, exchange student, honors, independent study, student-designed major, study abroad. Academically at-risk, hospital instruction, extra instruction, and summer programs available. **Credit/placement by examination:** AP, CLEP, SAT, ACT, institutional tests. **Support services:** Study skills assistance, writing center.

Majors. Biology: General. **Business:** Management science. **Computer sciences:** Computer science. **Engineering:** General, aerospace, civil, computer, electrical, environmental, mechanical, mechanics, operations research, systems. **History:** General. **Interdisciplinary:** Behavioral sciences, math/computer science. **Legal studies:** General. **Liberal arts:** Humanities. **Physical sciences:** Atmospheric science, chemistry, physics. **Social sciences:** General, economics, geography, political science. **Other:** Foreign area studies, Space operations.

Most popular majors. Biology 7%, business/marketing 10%, engineering/engineering technologies 40%, interdisciplinary studies 9%, social sciences 15%.

Computing on campus. PC or laptop required. 200 workstations in library. Dormitories wired for high-speed internet access and linked to campus network. Online library, helpline, repair service, wireless network available.

Student life. Freshman orientation: Available. Three 2-day appointee orientation sessions held in April. **Housing:** Guaranteed on-campus for all undergraduates. Coed dorms available. **Activities:** Bands, campus ministries, choral groups, drama, Model UN, radio station.

Athletics. NCAA. **Intercollegiate:** Baseball M, basketball, boxing M, cheerleading, cross-country, diving, fencing, football (tackle) M, golf M, gymnastics, ice hockey M, lacrosse M, rifle, soccer, swimming, tennis, track and field, volleyball W, water polo M, wrestling M. **Intramural:** Basketball, boxing M, cross-country, football (non-tackle), racquetball, rugby, soccer, softball, tennis, volleyball. **Team name:** Falcons.

Student services. Alcohol/substance abuse counseling, chaplain/spiritual director, health services, legal services, personal counseling, women's services.

Contact. E-mail: rr_webmail@usafa.edu
Phone: (719) 333-2520 Toll-free number: (800) 443-9266
Fax: (719) 333-3647
Colonel. Chevalier Cleaves, Director of Admissions, United States Air Force Academy, HQ USAF/RRS, 2304 Cadet Drive, Suite 2300, USAF Academy, CO 80840

University of Colorado at Boulder

Boulder, Colorado — **CB member**
www.colorado.edu — **CB code: 4841**

- Public 4-year university
- Residential campus in small city
- 26,111 degree-seeking undergraduates: 7% part-time, 47% women, 2% African American, 6% Asian American, 6% Hispanic American, 1% Native American, 2% international
- 5,036 degree-seeking graduate students
- 78% of applicants admitted
- SAT or ACT (ACT writing optional), application essay required
- 67% graduate within 6 years; 21% enter graduate study

General. Founded in 1876. Regionally accredited. **Degrees:** 5,326 bachelor's awarded; master's, doctoral, first professional offered. **ROTC:** Army, Naval, Air Force. **Location:** 30 miles from Denver. **Calendar:** Semester, extensive summer session. **Full-time faculty:** 1,330 total; 89% have terminal degrees, 15% minority, 36% women. **Part-time faculty:** 602 total; 42% have terminal degrees, 12% minority, 47% women. **Class size:** 50% < 20, 30% 20-39, 6% 40-49, 8% 50-99, 6% >100. **Special facilities:** Natural history museum, art museum and galleries, heritage center, observatory, planetarium and science center, electron microscope, outdoor theater, video interactive foreign language laboratory, mountain research station, centrifuge, engineering lab, multipurpose conference center, concert hall, multidisciplinary IT center.

Freshman class profile. 23,004 applied, 17,933 admitted, 5,860 enrolled.

Mid 50% test scores		**Rank in top tenth:**	27%
SAT critical reading:	520-630	**End year in good standing:**	89%
SAT math:	550-650	**Return as sophomores:**	84%
ACT composite:	24-28	**Out-of-state:**	47%
GPA 3.75 or higher:	38%	**Live on campus:**	92%
GPA 3.50-3.74:	22%	**International:**	1%
GPA 3.0-3.49:	34%	**Fraternities:**	13%
GPA 2.0-2.99:	6%	**Sororities:**	12%
Rank in top quarter:	61%		

Basis for selection. Secondary school record (breadth and rigor of courses, grades, class rank) most important. Test scores and personal statement also very important. Recommendations and personal attributes and talents considered. Audition required of music majors.

High school preparation. College-preparatory program required. 17 units required. Required units include English 4, mathematics 4, social studies 2, history 1, science 3 (laboratory 2) and foreign language 3. Math must include 2 algebra, 1 geometry, and 1 college preparatory math such as trigonometry, analytic geometry, or elementary functions for College of Arts and Sciences. Physics or chemistry with lab, 1 geography, 3 single foreign language required for Colleges of Arts & Sciences and Business. 3 math required for Colleges of Music and Architecture & Planning. 4 math, 1 physics, 1 chemistry required for College of Engineering. 2 single foreign language required for Colleges of Music and Architecture & Planning.

2008-2009 Annual costs. Tuition/fees: $7,278; $26,756 out-of-state. One-time matriculation fee of $112. Room/board: $9,860. Books/supplies: $1,749. Personal expenses: $3,078.

2008-2009 Financial aid. **Need-based:** 4,170 full-time freshmen applied for aid; 1,928 were judged to have need; 1,924 of these received aid. Average need met was 93%. Average scholarship/grant was $7,460; average loan $5,000. 50% of total undergraduate aid awarded as scholarships/grants, 50% as loans/jobs. **Non-need-based:** Awarded to 5,996 full-time undergraduates, including 1,874 freshmen. Scholarships awarded for academics, alumni affiliation, art, athletics, leadership, music/drama, ROTC, state residency.

Application procedures. **Admission:** Closing date 2/15 (postmark date). $50 fee, may be waived for applicants with need. Admission notification 4/1. Must reply by May 1 or within 2 week(s) if notified thereafter. **Financial aid:** Priority date 4/1; no closing date. FAFSA required. Applicants notified on a rolling basis starting 2/1; must reply within 3 week(s) of notification.

Academics. Residential Academic Programs in leadership, natural or environmental sciences, humanities and service learning, the arts, honors, American West culture and society, international and global affairs, cultural diversity, business, or engineering available. **Special study options:** Accelerated study, combined bachelor's/graduate degree, cooperative education, cross-registration, distance learning, double major, dual enrollment of high school students, ESL, exchange student, honors, independent study, internships, liberal arts/career combination, semester at sea, student-designed major, study abroad, teacher certification program. Undergraduate research opportunities, concurrent bachelor's/master's programs, small group academic programs. **Credit/placement by examination:** AP, CLEP, IB, institutional tests. Policies vary by department. **Support services:** Learning center, pre-admission summer program, reduced course load, study skills assistance, tutoring, writing center.

Majors. **Architecture:** Environmental design. **Area/ethnic studies:** Asian, Russian/Slavic, women's. **Biology:** Biochemistry, cellular/molecular, ecology, physiology. **Business:** Accounting, business admin, finance, international, management information systems, marketing, real estate, small business admin. **Communications:** General, journalism. **Computer sciences:** Computer science. **Conservation:** Environmental studies. **Education:** Music. **Engineering:** Aerospace, architectural, chemical, civil, computer, electrical, environmental, mechanical, physics. **Foreign languages:** Chinese, classics, French, Germanic, Italian, Japanese, linguistics, Spanish. **Health:** Communication disorders. **History:** General. **Interdisciplinary:** Global studies. **Liberal arts:** Humanities. **Math:** General, applied. **Philosophy/religion:** Philosophy, religion. **Physical sciences:** Astronomy, chemistry, geology, physics. **Psychology:** General. **Social sciences:** Anthropology, economics, geography, political science, sociology. **Visual/performing arts:** Art history/conservation, dance, dramatic, film/cinema, music performance, studio arts. **Other:** Chemical and biological engineering, Ecology and evolutionary biology.

Most popular majors. Biology 11%, business/marketing 15%, communications/journalism 8%, engineering/engineering technologies 8%, psychology 9%, social sciences 15%, visual/performing arts 6%.

Computing on campus. 1,855 workstations in dormitories, library, computer center, student center. Dormitories wired for high-speed internet access and linked to campus network. Commuter students can connect to campus network. Online course registration, online library, helpline, repair service, student web hosting, wireless network available.

Student life. **Freshman orientation:** Mandatory. Preregistration for classes offered. 2-day programs for students and parents held throughout summer. **Policies:** Honor code, lifestyle code of conduct, and 2-strikes disciplinary policy regarding alcohol violations. **Housing:** Guaranteed on-campus for freshmen. Coed dorms, special housing for disabled, apartments, fraternity/sorority housing, wellness housing available. $300 nonrefundable deposit. Residential academic programs within specific dorms. **Activities:** Bands, campus ministries, choral groups, dance, drama, film society, international student organizations, literary magazine, music ensembles, Model UN, musical theater, opera, radio station, student government, student newspaper, symphony orchestra, TV station, student outreach and retention center for equity, multicultural affairs center, volunteer clearing house, victim assistance, disability services, gay lesbian bisexual transgender resource center, ethical and civic engagement institute, College Democrats, College Republicans.

Athletics. NCAA. **Intercollegiate:** Basketball, cross-country, football (tackle) M, golf, skiing, soccer W, tennis W, track and field, volleyball W. **Intramural:** Basketball, football (non-tackle), ice hockey, soccer, volleyball, water polo. **Team name:** Colorado Buffaloes.

Student services. Adult student services, alcohol/substance abuse counseling, chaplain/spiritual director, career counseling, services for economically disadvantaged, student employment services, financial aid counseling, health services, legal services, minority student services, on-campus daycare, personal counseling, placement for graduates, veterans' counselor, women's services. **Physically disabled:** Services for visually, speech, hearing impaired.

Contact. E-mail: apply@colorado.edu
Phone: (303) 492-6301 Fax: (303) 492-7115
Kevin McLennan, Director of Admissions, University of Colorado at Boulder, 552 UCB, Boulder, CO 80309-0552

University of Colorado at Colorado Springs

Colorado Springs, Colorado
www.uccs.edu **CB code: 4874**

- Public 4-year university
- Commuter campus in large city
- 6,495 degree-seeking undergraduates: 21% part-time, 57% women, 4% African American, 5% Asian American, 10% Hispanic American, 1% Native American
- 1,579 degree-seeking graduate students
- 69% of applicants admitted
- SAT or ACT (ACT writing optional) required
- 46% graduate within 6 years; 34% enter graduate study

General. Founded in 1965. Regionally accredited. **Degrees:** 1,166 bachelor's awarded; master's, doctoral offered. **ROTC:** Army. **Location:** 60 miles from Denver. **Calendar:** Semester, limited summer session. **Full-time faculty:** 305 total; 70% have terminal degrees, 12% minority, 51% women. **Part-time faculty:** 615 total; 38% have terminal degrees, 11% minority, 52% women. **Class size:** 38% < 20, 39% 20-39, 12% 40-49, 9% 50-99, 1% >100.

Freshman class profile. 4,374 applied, 3,006 admitted, 1,158 enrolled.

Mid 50% test scores		**GPA 2.0-2.99:**	26%
SAT critical reading:	470-600	**Rank in top quarter:**	37%
SAT math:	470-610	**Rank in top tenth:**	14%
SAT writing:	450-560	**End year in good standing:**	79%
ACT composite:	21-26	**Return as sophomores:**	73%
GPA 3.75 or higher:	23%	**Out-of-state:**	11%
GPA 3.50-3.74:	15%	**Live on campus:**	43%
GPA 3.0-3.49:	36%		

Basis for selection. Priority given to applicants who rank in top 40% of graduating class, scored 1080 SAT (exclusive of Writing) or 24 ACT, 2.8 GPA, and completed all high school course units as required. Test of Standard Written English required of liberal arts applicants. **Homeschooled:** Transcript of courses and grades, state high school equivalency certificate required.

High school preparation. College-preparatory program required. 15 units required; 16 recommended. Required and recommended units include English 4, mathematics 3-4, social studies 2, history 1, science 3 (laboratory 2-3), foreign language 2 and academic electives 1.

2008-2009 Annual costs. Tuition/fees: $5,770; $16,394 out-of-state. Tuition varies by program. One-time matriculation fee of $25 required. Room/board: $7,204.

2007-2008 Financial aid. **Need-based:** 574 full-time freshmen applied for aid; 306 were judged to have need; 287 of these received aid. Average need met was 54%. Average scholarship/grant was $5,537; average loan $2,523. 41% of total undergraduate aid awarded as scholarships/grants, 59% as loans/jobs. **Non-need-based:** Awarded to 424 full-time undergraduates, including 134 freshmen. Scholarships awarded for academics, alumni affiliation, athletics, state residency.

Application procedures. **Admission:** Priority date 4/1; deadline 7/1. $50 fee. Admission notification on a rolling basis. **Financial aid:** Priority date 4/1; no closing date. FAFSA required. Applicants notified on a rolling basis starting 4/15.

Academics. **Special study options:** Accelerated study, combined bachelor's/graduate degree, cooperative education, cross-registration, distance learning, double major, dual enrollment of high school students, ESL, exchange student, honors, independent study, internships, liberal arts/career combination, student-designed major, study abroad, teacher certification program. **Credit/placement by examination:** AP, CLEP, IB, institutional tests. 30 credit hours maximum toward bachelor's degree. **Support services:** Learning center, remedial instruction, study skills assistance, tutoring, writing center.

Majors. **Area/ethnic studies:** Women's. **Biology:** General. **Business:** Accounting, business admin, finance, human resources. **Communications:** General. **Computer sciences:** Computer graphics, computer science. **Education:** Special. **Engineering:** General, aerospace, civil, computer, electrical, mechanical. **Foreign languages:** Spanish. **Health:** Health services, nursing (RN). **History:** General. **Math:** General. **Philosophy/religion:** Philosophy. **Physical sciences:** Chemistry, physics. **Protective services:** Law enforcement admin. **Psychology:** General. **Public administration:** General. **Social sciences:** Anthropology, economics, geography, political science, sociology. **Visual/performing arts:** Studio arts.

Most popular majors. Biology 8%, business/marketing 20%, communications/journalism 10%, health sciences 13%, history 6%, psychology 10%, social sciences 15%.

Computing on campus. 250 workstations in dormitories, library, computer center. Dormitories wired for high-speed internet access and linked to campus network. Commuter students can connect to campus network. Online course registration, online library, helpline, repair service, wireless network available.

Student life. **Freshman orientation:** Mandatory, $45 fee. One-day sessions throughout summer. **Housing:** Coed dorms, single-sex dorms, special housing for disabled, apartments available. $150 partly refundable deposit. **Activities:** Jazz band, choral groups, dance, drama, film society, international student organizations, literary magazine, music ensembles, musical theater, radio station, student government, student newspaper, advocating woman's assistance resources education, counseling honor society, math club, chemistry honor society, black student union, Latino student union, Inter-Varsity Christian Fellowship.

Athletics. NCAA. **Intercollegiate:** Basketball, cross-country, golf M, soccer M, softball W, track and field, volleyball W. **Intramural:** Basketball, football (non-tackle), soccer, table tennis, volleyball. **Team name:** Mountain Lions.

Student services. Adult student services, career counseling, student employment services, financial aid counseling, health services, minority student services, on-campus daycare, personal counseling, veterans' counselor. **Physically disabled:** Services for visually, speech, hearing impaired.

Contact. E-mail: admrec@uccs.edu
Phone: (719) 255-3383 Toll-free number: (800) 990-8227 ext. 3383
Fax: (719) 255-3116
Steve Ellis, Director of Admissions, University of Colorado at Colorado Springs, PO Box 7150, Colorado Springs, CO 80933-7150

University of Colorado at Denver

Denver, Colorado — **CB member**
www.ucdenver.edu — **CB code: 4875**

- Public 4-year university
- Commuter campus in very large city
- 8,721 degree-seeking undergraduates: 26% part-time, 56% women, 5% African American, 10% Asian American, 12% Hispanic American, 1% Native American, 2% international
- 7,267 degree-seeking graduate students
- 63% of applicants admitted
- SAT or ACT (ACT writing optional), application essay required
- 55% graduate within 6 years

General. Founded in 1912. Regionally accredited. Library, student center, and classrooms shared with Metropolitan State College and Community College of Denver. **Degrees:** 1,718 bachelor's awarded; master's, doctoral, first professional offered. **ROTC:** Army, Air Force. **Calendar:** Semester, extensive summer session. **Full-time faculty:** 2,312 total; 70% have terminal degrees, 11% minority, 52% women. **Part-time faculty:** 715 total; 34% have terminal degrees, 10% minority, 56% women. **Class size:** 33% < 20, 46% 20-39, 13% 40-49, 7% 50-99, 2% >100. **Special facilities:** Computational math centers, applied psychology center, environmental science center, transportation research center, Fourth World center for study of indigenous law and politics.

Freshman class profile. 4,187 applied, 2,629 admitted, 1,073 enrolled.

Mid 50% test scores		**GPA 2.0-2.99:**	26%
SAT critical reading:	470-600	**Rank in top quarter:**	42%
SAT math:	480-590	**Rank in top tenth:**	20%
ACT composite:	20-25	**Return as sophomores:**	72%
GPA 3.75 or higher:	24%	**Out-of-state:**	6%
GPA 3.50-3.74:	15%	**International:**	4%
GPA 3.0-3.49:	35%		

Basis for selection. Previous academic performance including high school course work and GPA; evidence of academic ability and accomplishments as indicated by test scores; and evidence of maturity, motivation, potential for academic success most important. Audition required of music majors.

High school preparation. College-preparatory program recommended. 15 units required; 18 recommended. Required and recommended units include English 4, mathematics 3, social studies 2, history 1, science 3 (laboratory 2), foreign language 2 and academic electives 1. 4 math required for engineering and business students.

2008-2009 Annual costs. Tuition/fees: $6,279; $19,251 out-of-state. Tuition varies by program. One-time matriculation fee of $115 required. Books/supplies: $1,800. Personal expenses: $1,900.

2008-2009 Financial aid. **Need-based:** Average need met was 52%. Average scholarship/grant was $4,334; average loan $2,628. 38% of total undergraduate aid awarded as scholarships/grants, 62% as loans/jobs. **Non-need-based:** Scholarships awarded for academics, alumni affiliation, art, job skills, leadership, music/drama, ROTC, state residency.

Application procedures. **Admission:** Priority date 7/22; deadline 9/1. $50 fee, may be waived for applicants with need. Admission notification on a rolling basis. **Financial aid:** Priority date 4/1; no closing date. FAFSA, institutional form required. Applicants notified on a rolling basis starting 5/1.

Academics. Learning opportunities through center for internships and cooperative education. **Special study options:** Accelerated study, combined bachelor's/graduate degree, cooperative education, cross-registration, distance learning, double major, ESL, honors, independent study, internships, liberal arts/career combination, student-designed major, study abroad, teacher certification program, weekend college. **Credit/placement by examination:** AP, CLEP, IB, institutional tests. 30 credit hours maximum toward bachelor's degree. **Support services:** Learning center, study skills assistance, tutoring, writing center.

Majors. **Biology:** General, biomedical sciences. **Business:** General. **Communications:** General. **Computer sciences:** General. **Engineering:** Civil, electrical, mechanical. **Foreign languages:** French, Spanish. **Health:** Dental hygiene, nursing (RN). **History:** General. **Interdisciplinary:** Global studies. **Math:** General. **Philosophy/religion:** Philosophy. **Physical sciences:** Chemistry, physics. **Psychology:** General. **Social sciences:** Anthropology, economics, geography, political science, sociology. **Visual/performing arts:** Dramatic, studio arts.

Most popular majors. Biology 7%, business/marketing 21%, communications/journalism 7%, engineering/engineering technologies 6%, health sciences 15%, psychology 8%, social sciences 12%, visual/performing arts 10%.

Computing on campus. 205 workstations in library, computer center, student center. Dormitories wired for high-speed internet access. Commuter students can connect to campus network. Online course registration, online library, helpline, student web hosting, wireless network available.

Student life. **Freshman orientation:** Mandatory. **Housing:** Coed dorms, wellness housing available. **Activities:** Jazz band, choral groups, dance, drama, music ensembles, musical theater, student government, student newspaper, more than 60 groups available.

Athletics. **Intramural:** Basketball, racquetball, tennis, volleyball.

Student services. Alcohol/substance abuse counseling, career counseling, student employment services, financial aid counseling, health services, legal services, minority student services, on-campus daycare, personal counseling, placement for graduates, veterans' counselor, women's services. **Physically disabled:** Services for visually, speech, hearing impaired.

Contact. E-mail: admissions@ucdenver.edu
Phone: (303) 556-2704 Fax: (303) 556-4838
Barbara Edwards, Director of Admissions, University of Colorado at Denver, Box 173364, Campus Box 167, Denver, CO 80217-3364

University of Denver
Denver, Colorado CB member
www.du.edu CB code: 4842

- Private 4-year university affiliated with United Methodist Church
- Residential campus in very large city
- 5,305 degree-seeking undergraduates: 9% part-time, 56% women, 3% African American, 6% Asian American, 7% Hispanic American, 1% Native American, 5% international
- 5,750 degree-seeking graduate students
- 64% of applicants admitted
- SAT or ACT (ACT writing optional), application essay required
- 74% graduate within 6 years

General. Founded in 1864. Regionally accredited. **Degrees:** 1,101 bachelor's awarded; master's, doctoral, first professional offered. **ROTC:** Army, Air Force. **Location:** 8 miles from downtown. **Calendar:** Quarter, limited summer session. **Full-time faculty:** 586 total; 90% have terminal degrees, 15% minority, 43% women. **Part-time faculty:** 610 total; 4% have terminal degrees, 8% minority, 47% women. **Class size:** 65% < 20, 25% 20-39, 6% 40-49, 3% 50-99, less than 1% >100. **Special facilities:** Observatory, high-altitude research laboratory, mechanical engineering testing facility, centers for gifted children.

Freshman class profile. 7,144 applied, 4,600 admitted, 1,134 enrolled.

Mid 50% test scores		**Rank in top quarter:**	76%
SAT critical reading:	540-640	**Rank in top tenth:**	43%
SAT math:	540-660	**Return as sophomores:**	87%
ACT composite:	24-29	**Out-of-state:**	54%
GPA 3.75 or higher:	49%	**Live on campus:**	93%
GPA 3.50-3.74:	23%	**International:**	5%
GPA 3.0-3.49:	25%	**Fraternities:**	20%
GPA 2.0-2.99:	3%	**Sororities:**	23%

Basis for selection. GPA, test scores and strength of curriculum most important. Interview, academic maturity, contributions to school and community activities, leadership also important. Recommendations from teacher and counselor, and personal essay considered. Interview strongly encouraged. Audition required of music majors. Portfolio recommended of art majors. **Homeschooled:** Letter of recommendation (nonparent) required.

High school preparation. College-preparatory program recommended. Recommended units include English 4, mathematics 4, social studies 2, history 2, science 4 (laboratory 2) and foreign language 4.

2009-2010 Annual costs. Tuition/fees: $35,481. Room/board: $9,900. Books/supplies: $1,749. Personal expenses: $1,269.

2007-2008 Financial aid. Need-based: 646 full-time freshmen applied for aid; 489 were judged to have need; 488 of these received aid. Average need met was 77%. Average scholarship/grant was $18,908; average loan $3,252. 78% of total undergraduate aid awarded as scholarships/grants, 22% as loans/jobs. **Non-need-based:** Awarded to 2,073 full-time undergraduates, including 494 freshmen. Scholarships awarded for academics, art, athletics, leadership, music/drama, state residency.

Application procedures. Admission: Closing date 1/15 (postmark date). $50 fee, may be waived for applicants with need. Admission notification 3/15. Must reply by 5/1. **Financial aid:** Priority date 3/1; no closing date. FAFSA, CSS PROFILE required.

Academics. Special 3-week inter-term courses available for focused concentration. **Special study options:** Accelerated study, combined bachelor's/graduate degree, cooperative education, distance learning, double major, dual enrollment of high school students, ESL, honors, independent study, internships, semester at sea, student-designed major, study abroad, teacher certification program, Washington semester, weekend college. Learning disability services. **Credit/placement by examination:** AP, CLEP, IB, institutional tests. 45 credit hours maximum toward bachelor's degree. **Support services:** Reduced course load, study skills assistance, tutoring, writing center.

Majors. Agriculture: Animal sciences. **Area/ethnic studies:** Asian-American, women's. **Biology:** General, biochemistry, bioinformatics, ecology, molecular. **Business:** General, accounting, business admin, construction management, finance, hospitality admin, international, management information systems, managerial economics, marketing, organizational behavior, real estate, statistics. **Communications:** General, digital media, journalism. **Computer sciences:** Computer science, information technology, systems analysis. **Conservation:** Environmental science. **Engineering:** General, computer, electrical, mechanical. **Foreign languages:** French, German, Italian, Russian, Spanish. **History:** General. **Interdisciplinary:** Biological/physical sciences, global studies, science/society. **Legal studies:** General. **Liberal arts:** Arts/sciences. **Math:** General. **Philosophy/religion:** Philosophy, religion. **Physical sciences:** General, chemistry, physics. **Psychology:** General. **Public administration:** Policy analysis. **Social sciences:** General, anthropology, criminology, economics, geography, international relations, political science, sociology. **Visual/performing arts:** Art, art history/conservation, dramatic, graphic design, music performance, musicology. **Other:** Computer software and media applications, Ethnic, cultural, minority, gender studies.

Most popular majors. Biology 7%, business/marketing 48%, communications/journalism 8%, social sciences 14%, visual/performing arts 7%.

Computing on campus. PC or laptop required. 200 workstations in dormitories, library, computer center, student center. Dormitories wired for high-speed internet access and linked to campus network. Commuter students can connect to campus network. Online course registration, online library, helpline, repair service, student web hosting, wireless network available.

Student life. Freshman orientation: Mandatory. Preregistration for classes offered. Held the first week of September for 5 days. **Housing:** Guaranteed on-campus for freshmen. Coed dorms, apartments, fraternity/sorority housing, wellness housing available. $200 nonrefundable deposit, deadline 5/1. **Activities:** Bands, campus ministries, choral groups, dance, drama, film society, international student organizations, literary magazine, music ensembles, Model UN, musical theater, opera, radio station, student government, student newspaper, symphony orchestra.

Athletics. NCAA. **Intercollegiate:** Basketball, diving, golf, gymnastics W, ice hockey M, lacrosse, skiing, soccer, swimming, tennis, volleyball W. **Intramural:** Basketball, football (non-tackle), ice hockey M, soccer, softball. **Team name:** Pioneers.

Student services. Adult student services, alcohol/substance abuse counseling, chaplain/spiritual director, career counseling, student employment services, financial aid counseling, health services, minority student services, personal counseling, placement for graduates, women's services. **Physically disabled:** Services for visually, speech, hearing impaired. **Learning disabled:** Comprehensive services available.

Contact. E-mail: admission@du.edu
Phone: (303) 871-2036 Toll-free number: (800) 525-9495
Fax: (303) 871-3301
Thomas Willoughby, Vice Chancellor, Enrollment, University of Denver, 2197 South University Boulevard, Denver, CO 80208

University of Northern Colorado
Greeley, Colorado CB member
www.unco.edu CB code: 4074

- Public 4-year university
- Commuter campus in small city
- 9,690 degree-seeking undergraduates: 9% part-time, 61% women, 3% African American, 3% Asian American, 9% Hispanic American, 1% Native American, 1% international
- 1,759 degree-seeking graduate students
- 93% of applicants admitted
- SAT or ACT (ACT writing optional) required
- 48% graduate within 6 years; 3% enter graduate study

General. Founded in 1889. Regionally accredited. **Degrees:** 2,033 bachelor's awarded; master's, doctoral offered. **ROTC:** Army, Air Force. **Location:** 50 miles from Denver; 50 miles from Cheyenne, Wyoming. **Calendar:** Semester, limited summer session. **Full-time faculty:** 371 total; 9% minority, 49% women. **Part-time faculty:** 249 total; 6% minority, 58% women. **Class size:** 28% < 20, 56% 20-39, 3% 40-49, 12% 50-99, 2% >100. **Special facilities:** African-American cultural center, Hispanic cultural center, Native American and Asian Pacific cultural center.

Freshman class profile. 5,609 applied, 5,189 admitted, 2,083 enrolled.

Mid 50% test scores		**GPA 2.0-2.99:**	37%
SAT critical reading:	460-580	**Rank in top quarter:**	33%
SAT math:	470-590	**Rank in top tenth:**	12%
SAT writing:	460-560	**End year in good standing:**	77%
ACT composite:	20-25	**Return as sophomores:**	71%
GPA 3.75 or higher:	17%	**Out-of-state:**	14%
GPA 3.50-3.74:	14%	**Live on campus:**	92%
GPA 3.0-3.49:	32%	**International:**	1%

Basis for selection. Expected 2.9 GPA; 21 ACT or 970 SAT (exclusive of Writing). Higher ACT/SAT score can compensate for lower GPA and higher GPA can compensate for lower test score. Audition required of music majors.

High school preparation. 15 units required. Required and recommended units include English 4, mathematics 3, social studies 3, science 3 (laboratory 2), foreign language 2 and academic electives 2. Math should include 2 algebra, additional higher level math unit.

2008-2009 Annual costs. Tuition/fees: $4,680; $14,082 out-of-state. Costs reflect student share of tuition after the Colorado College Opportunity Fund. Room/board: $7,784. Books/supplies: $1,200. Personal expenses: $2,893.

2007-2008 Financial aid. Need-based: 1,684 full-time freshmen applied for aid; 995 were judged to have need; 932 of these received aid. Average need met was 100%. Average scholarship/grant was $4,405; average loan $3,788. 46% of total undergraduate aid awarded as scholarships/ grants, 54% as loans/jobs. **Non-need-based:** Awarded to 2,592 full-time undergraduates, including 898 freshmen. Scholarships awarded for academics, art, athletics, music/drama.

Application procedures. Admission: Priority date 8/1; no deadline. $45 fee, may be waived for applicants with need. Admission notification on a rolling basis. **Financial aid:** Priority date 3/1; no closing date. FAFSA required. Applicants notified on a rolling basis starting 4/15; must reply within 4 week(s) of notification.

Academics. Special study options: Cooperative education, cross-registration, distance learning, double major, ESL, exchange student, external degree, honors, independent study, internships, semester at sea, student-designed major, study abroad, teacher certification program. **Credit/ placement by examination:** AP, CLEP, IB, institutional tests. 30 credit hours maximum toward bachelor's degree. **Support services:** Learning center, reduced course load, remedial instruction, study skills assistance, tutoring, writing center.

Majors. Area/ethnic studies: African-American, Hispanic-American/Latino/ Chicano. **Biology:** General. **Business:** Business admin. **Communications:** General, journalism. **Education:** Music, special. **Family/consumer sciences:** Aging. **Foreign languages:** General, sign language interpretation, Spanish. **Health:** Audiology/hearing, audiology/speech pathology, dietetics, health care admin, health services, nursing (RN), public health ed, speech pathology, vocational rehab counseling. **History:** General. **Math:** General. **Parks/recreation:** Exercise sciences, facilities management. **Philosophy/ religion:** Philosophy. **Physical sciences:** Chemistry, geology, physics. **Protective services:** Criminal justice. **Psychology:** General. **Public administration:** Human services. **Social sciences:** General, anthropology, economics, geography, political science, sociology. **Visual/performing arts:** Dramatic, studio arts.

Most popular majors. Business/marketing 12%, communications/ journalism 8%, health sciences 12%, interdisciplinary studies 17%, parks/ recreation 7%, psychology 7%, social sciences 8%, visual/performing arts 8%.

Computing on campus. 1,169 workstations in dormitories, library, computer center, student center. Dormitories wired for high-speed internet access and linked to campus network. Commuter students can connect to campus network. Online course registration, online library, helpline, repair service, wireless network available.

Student life. Freshman orientation: Available. Preregistration for classes offered. **Housing:** Guaranteed on-campus for all undergraduates. Coed dorms, single-sex dorms, special housing for disabled, apartments, fraternity/ sorority housing, wellness housing available. $250 nonrefundable deposit. **Activities:** Bands, campus ministries, choral groups, dance, drama, film society, international student organizations, literary magazine, music ensembles, musical theater, opera, radio station, student government, student newspaper, symphony orchestra, TV station, African-American student union, Hispanic students organization, Native American student services, Asian/ Pacific American student services.

Athletics. NCAA. **Intercollegiate:** Baseball M, basketball, cross-country W, diving W, football (tackle) M, golf, soccer W, softball W, swimming W, tennis, track and field, volleyball W, wrestling M. **Intramural:** Basketball, football (non-tackle), golf, racquetball, soccer, softball, table tennis, tennis, volleyball, water polo. **Team name:** Bears.

Student services. Adult student services, alcohol/substance abuse counseling, chaplain/spiritual director, career counseling, student employment services, financial aid counseling, health services, legal services, minority student services, personal counseling, placement for graduates, veterans' counselor, women's services. **Physically disabled:** Services for visually, speech, hearing impaired.

Contact. E-mail: admissions.help@unco.edu
Phone: (970) 351-2881 Toll-free number: (888) 700-4862
Fax: (970) 351-2984
Director of Admissions, University of Northern Colorado, 1862 10th Avenue, Campus Box 10, Greeley, CO 80639

Western State College of Colorado
Gunnison, Colorado
www.western.edu **CB code: 4946**

- Public 4-year liberal arts college
- Residential campus in small town
- 1,875 full-time, degree-seeking undergraduates
- 91% of applicants admitted
- SAT or ACT (ACT writing optional) required

General. Founded in 1901. Regionally accredited. College-based mountain search and rescue team. **Degrees:** 439 bachelor's awarded. **Location:** 200 miles from Denver. **Calendar:** Semester, limited summer session. **Full-time faculty:** 118 total. **Part-time faculty:** 49 total. **Class size:** 49% < 20, 41% 20-39, 9% 40-49, 1% 50-99, less than 1% >100. **Special facilities:** Botanical gardens, archaeological site, dinosaur reconstruction lab.

Freshman class profile. 1,342 applied, 1,217 admitted, 566 enrolled.

Mid 50% test scores		**GPA 3.0-3.49:**	35%
SAT critical reading:	450-550	**GPA 2.0-2.99:**	48%
SAT math:	470-580	**Rank in top quarter:**	18%
ACT composite:	19-24	**Rank in top tenth:**	7%
GPA 3.75 or higher:	8%	**Out-of-state:**	35%
GPA 3.50-3.74:	8%	**Live on campus:**	94%

Basis for selection. School achievement record, test scores very important; recommendations considered. Essay recommended. Interview recommended for academically weak applicants.

High school preparation. Required and recommended units include English 4, mathematics 3-4, social studies 2, history 2, science 3 (laboratory 2) and foreign language 2.

2008-2009 Annual costs. Tuition/fees: $3,778; $12,754 out-of-state. Room/ board: $7,516. Books/supplies: $950. Personal expenses: $1,226.

2008-2009 Financial aid. Non-need-based: Scholarships awarded for academics, alumni affiliation, art, athletics, leadership, music/drama.

Application procedures. Admission: Priority date 3/15; deadline 6/1 (postmark date). $30 fee, may be waived for applicants with need. Admission notification on a rolling basis beginning on or about 11/1. Must reply by May 1 or within 2 week(s) if notified thereafter. **Financial aid:** Priority date 4/1; no closing date. FAFSA required. Applicants notified on a rolling basis starting 4/1; must reply within 4 week(s) of notification.

Academics. Special study options: Combined bachelor's/graduate degree, cooperative education, double major, dual enrollment of high school students, exchange student, honors, independent study, internships, liberal arts/career combination, semester at sea, study abroad, teacher certification program. **Credit/placement by examination:** AP, CLEP, IB, SAT, ACT, institutional tests. 30 credit hours maximum toward bachelor's degree. **Support services:** Study skills assistance, tutoring, writing center.

Majors. Biology: General. **Business:** Accounting, business admin, management information systems, resort management. **Communications:** General. **Conservation:** Environmental studies. **Education:** Art, elementary, English, foreign languages, mathematics, music, physical, science, social science, social studies, special. **Foreign languages:** Spanish. **History:** General. **Legal studies:** Prelaw. **Math:** General. **Parks/recreation:** Exercise sciences. **Physical sciences:** Chemistry, geology. **Protective services:** Criminal justice, police science. **Psychology:** General. **Social sciences:** Anthropology, economics, political science, sociology. **Visual/performing arts:** Art, music management, studio arts. **Other:** Outdoor leadership.

Computing on campus. 168 workstations in dormitories, library, student center. Dormitories linked to campus network. Commuter students can connect to campus network. Online course registration available.

Student life. Freshman orientation: Available, $65 fee. Preregistration for classes offered. Wilderness-based orientation available. **Housing:** Guaranteed on-campus for freshmen. Coed dorms, single-sex dorms, apartments available. $100 nonrefundable deposit. **Activities:** Bands, choral groups, dance, drama, literary magazine, music ensembles, radio station, student government, student newspaper, symphony orchestra, TV station, Hillel, black student alliance, Amigos, Campus Crusade, Hui-O-Ka-Aina, lesbian-gay-bisexual alliance, Newman club, Baptist student union, Christian athletes fellowship, women's action coalition.

Athletics. NCAA. **Intercollegiate:** Basketball, cross-country, football (tackle) M, skiing, track and field, volleyball W, wrestling M. **Intramural:** Baseball M, basketball, golf, ice hockey M, lacrosse, rugby, skiing, soccer, softball, swimming, tennis, track and field, volleyball, wrestling M. **Team name:** Mountaineers.

Student services. Adult student services, career counseling, health services, on-campus daycare, personal counseling, veterans' counselor. **Physically disabled:** Services for visually, hearing impaired. **Learning disabled:** Comprehensive services available.

Contact. E-mail: discover@western.edu
Phone: (970) 943-2119 Toll-free number: (800) 876-5309
Fax: (970) 943-2212
Tim Albers, Director of Admissions, Western State College of Colorado, 600 North Adams Street, Gunnison, CO 81231

Westwood College: Denver North

Denver, Colorado
www.westwood.edu **CB code: 3948**

- For-profit 4-year technical college
- Commuter campus in very large city
- 3,755 full-time, degree-seeking undergraduates
- 17 graduate students
- Interview required

General. Founded in 1953. Accredited by ACCSCT. **Degrees:** 448 bachelor's, 197 associate awarded; master's offered. **Location:** 5 miles from downtown. **Calendar:** 5 ten-week terms per year. Extensive summer session. **Full-time faculty:** 50 total. **Part-time faculty:** 80 total.

Basis for selection. Institutional test (ACCUPLACER) and interview most important. Developmental courses may be required for those who do not pass entrance examination. SAT or ACT recommended. Accuplacer waived for students with sufficient scores on SAT or ACT.

High school preparation. At least 1 algebra required for electronics, drafting and surveying programs. General math required for all other programs.

2008-2009 Annual costs. Full-time costs per 10-week term for most programs: $4,463 for tuition. Tuition and fees may vary. Books/supplies: $370. Personal expenses: $2,000.

Financial aid. Non-need-based: Scholarships awarded for academics, state residency.

Application procedures. Admission: No deadline. $25 fee. Admission notification on a rolling basis. **Financial aid:** No deadline. FAFSA, institutional form required. Applicants notified on a rolling basis starting 1/1; must reply within 2 week(s) of notification.

Academics. Instruction and emphasis on laboratory work and practical application. **Special study options:** Accelerated study, cooperative education, distance learning, independent study, internships, liberal arts/career combination. **Credit/placement by examination:** CLEP, institutional tests. 69 credit hours maximum toward associate degree, 140 toward bachelor's. **Support services:** Learning center, remedial instruction, study skills assistance, tutoring.

Majors. Architecture: Interior. **Business:** General, accounting, business admin, e-commerce, management information systems, marketing. **Communications:** General. **Communications technology:** Graphic/printing. **Computer sciences:** General, computer graphics, information systems, networking, security, web page design, webmaster. **Engineering:** Electrical. **Engineering technology:** Electrical. **Mechanic/repair:** Electronics/electrical. **Protective services:** Law enforcement admin. **Visual/performing arts:** Commercial/advertising art, design, graphic design.

Most popular majors. Business/marketing 20%, computer/information sciences 44%, engineering/engineering technologies 15%, visual/performing arts 21%.

Computing on campus. 50 workstations in library, computer center. Online library available.

Student life. Freshman orientation: Mandatory. Preregistration for classes offered. **Policies:** No-tolerance drug/alcohol policy.

Student services. Career counseling, student employment services, financial aid counseling, placement for graduates, veterans' counselor. **Physically disabled:** Services for visually impaired.

Contact. E-mail: rdejong@westwood.edu
Phone: (303) 650-5050 Fax: (303) 487-0214
Ron DeJong, Director of Admissions, Westwood College: Denver North, 7350 North Broadway, Denver, CO 80221

Westwood College: Denver South

Denver, Colorado
www.westwood.edu

- For-profit 4-year technical college
- Commuter campus in very large city
- 377 degree-seeking undergraduates
- 100% of applicants admitted
- Interview required

General. Accredited by ACCSCT. **Degrees:** 94 bachelor's, 23 associate awarded. **Calendar:** Continuous, extensive summer session. **Full-time faculty:** 9 total. **Part-time faculty:** 24 total.

Freshman class profile. 236 applied, 236 admitted, 197 enrolled.

Basis for selection. Admission based on scores from Accuplacer exam. Non-native English speakers must take ESL course. 475 TOEFL, high school diploma or GED, or proof of completion of accredited U.S. college program required. Accuplacer exam can be waived if student scores 17 ACT or SAT equivalent.

2009-2010 Annual costs. Tuition/fees (projected): $25,630. Tuition and fees may vary by program. Books/supplies: $1,250.

Application procedures. Admission: No deadline. $25 fee. Admission notification on a rolling basis. **Financial aid:** No deadline. FAFSA, institutional form required. Applicants notified on a rolling basis; must reply within 2 week(s) of notification.

Academics. Special study options: Accelerated study, distance learning, independent study, weekend college. **Credit/placement by examination:** CLEP, institutional tests. 67 credit hours maximum toward associate degree, 135 toward bachelor's. **Support services:** Reduced course load, remedial instruction, study skills assistance, tutoring, writing center.

Majors. Architecture: Interior. **Business:** E-commerce, fashion. **Communications technology:** Animation/special effects, desktop publishing, graphics. **Computer sciences:** Computer graphics, LAN/WAN management, networking, security, system admin, web page design, webmaster. **Protective services:** Law enforcement admin. **Visual/performing arts:** Commercial/advertising art, design, graphic design, interior design.

Computing on campus. 300 workstations in library, computer center, student center. Commuter students can connect to campus network. Online course registration, online library, wireless network available.

Student life. Freshman orientation: Mandatory. Preregistration for classes offered.

Student services. Adult student services, career counseling, student employment services, financial aid counseling, placement for graduates.

Contact. Phone: (303) 934-1122 Fax: (303) 934-2583
Michael Rushak, Director of Admissions, Westwood College: Denver South, 3150 South Sheridan Boulevard, Denver, CO 80227-5507

Yeshiva Toras Chaim Talmudical Seminary

Denver, Colorado
CB code: 7008

- Private 4-year rabbinical college for men affiliated with Jewish faith
- Very large city

General. Accredited by AARTS. **Calendar:** Trimester.

Contact. Phone: (303) 629-8200
1555 Stuart Street PO Box 40067, Denver, CO 80204

Connecticut

Albertus Magnus College

New Haven, Connecticut **CB member**
www.albertus.edu **CB code: 3001**

- Private 4-year liberal arts college affiliated with Roman Catholic Church
- Residential campus in small city
- 1,714 degree-seeking undergraduates: 8% part-time, 68% women, 28% African American, 1% Asian American, 11% Hispanic American
- 396 degree-seeking graduate students
- 83% of applicants admitted
- SAT or ACT (ACT writing optional) required
- 57% graduate within 6 years

General. Founded in 1925. Regionally accredited. Majority of students enrolled in adult education and graduate programs. Approximately 500 undergraduates are traditional age and are able to live on campus. **Degrees:** 393 bachelor's, 114 associate awarded; master's offered. **Location:** 90 miles from New York City. **Calendar:** Semester, limited summer session. **Full-time faculty:** 43 total; 81% have terminal degrees, 5% minority, 44% women. **Part-time faculty:** 26 total; 50% have terminal degrees, 12% minority, 65% women. **Class size:** 69% < 20, 31% 20-39.

Freshman class profile. 636 applied, 526 admitted, 185 enrolled.

Mid 50% test scores		**GPA 2.0-2.99:**	64%
SAT critical reading:	490-540	**Rank in top quarter:**	27%
SAT math:	470-520	**Rank in top tenth:**	11%
SAT writing:	400-500	**End year in good standing:**	92%
GPA 3.75 or higher:	1%	**Return as sophomores:**	78%
GPA 3.50-3.74:	8%	**Out-of-state:**	15%
GPA 3.0-3.49:	25%		

Basis for selection. School achievement record most important. Recommendations, test scores, interview, school and community activities also considered. **Homeschooled:** Letter of recommendation (nonparent) required. GED preferred.

High school preparation. 16 units required. Required and recommended units include English 4, mathematics 2-3, social studies 2-3, science 2-3 (laboratory 1) and foreign language 3.

2008-2009 Annual costs. Tuition/fees: $22,724. Room/board: $9,442. Books/supplies: $620. Personal expenses: $940.

2008-2009 Financial aid. Need-based: Average need met was 52%. Average scholarship/grant was $12,529; average loan $3,416. 43% of total undergraduate aid awarded as scholarships/grants, 57% as loans/jobs. **Non-need-based:** Scholarships awarded for academics, art, job skills, leadership, music/drama, religious affiliation, state residency.

Application procedures. Admission: No deadline. $35 fee, may be waived for applicants with need. Admission notification on a rolling basis beginning on or about 12/1. Must reply by May 1 or within 4 week(s) if notified thereafter. **Financial aid:** Closing date 2/28. FAFSA required. Applicants notified on a rolling basis starting 3/1; must reply within 2 week(s) of notification.

Academics. Special study options: Accelerated study, double major, honors, independent study, internships, liberal arts/career combination, student-designed major, teacher certification program. **Credit/placement by examination:** AP, CLEP, SAT, institutional tests. 21 credit hours maximum toward associate degree, 45 toward bachelor's. **Support services:** Learning center, reduced course load, study skills assistance, tutoring, writing center.

Majors. Biology: General. **Business:** Accounting, business admin, finance, international, management information systems, managerial economics. **Communications:** General, advertising, media studies. **Computer sciences:** Information systems. **Education:** General, art, biology, business, chemistry, English, history, mathematics, middle, science, secondary, social studies, Spanish. **Foreign languages:** Spanish. **Health:** Art therapy, premedicine. **History:** General. **Legal studies:** Prelaw. **Liberal arts:** Arts/sciences. **Math:** General. **Philosophy/religion:** Philosophy, religion. **Physical sciences:** Chemistry. **Protective services:** Criminal justice. **Psychology:** General. **Public administration:** Human services, social work. **Social sciences:** General, economics, political science, sociology. **Visual/performing arts:** General, art, art history/conservation, commercial/advertising art, dramatic, photography, studio arts. **Other:** Performance communications.

Most popular majors. Business/marketing 56%, English 6%, psychology 7%, social sciences 10%.

Computing on campus. 175 workstations in library, computer center, student center. Commuter students can connect to campus network. Repair service, wireless network available.

Student life. Freshman orientation: Mandatory. Preregistration for classes offered. **Housing:** Guaranteed on-campus for all undergraduates. Coed dorms, single-sex dorms, wellness housing available. $400 nonrefundable deposit, deadline 7/1. **Activities:** Campus ministries, choral groups, dance, drama, literary magazine, musical theater, student government, outspoken alliance, multi-cultural student union.

Athletics. NCAA. **Intercollegiate:** Baseball M, basketball, cross-country, soccer, softball W, tennis, volleyball W. **Team name:** Falcons.

Student services. Adult student services, chaplain/spiritual director, career counseling, student employment services, financial aid counseling, health services, personal counseling, placement for graduates, veterans' counselor.

Contact. E-mail: admissions@albertus.edu
Phone: (203) 773-8501 Toll-free number: (800) 578-9160
Fax: (203) 773-5248
Richard LoLatte, Dean of Admissions and Enrollment Management, Albertus Magnus College, 700 Prospect Street, New Haven, CT 06511-1189

Central Connecticut State University

New Britain, Connecticut **CB member**
www.ccsu.edu **CB code: 3898**

- Public 4-year university
- Commuter campus in small city
- 9,479 degree-seeking undergraduates: 18% part-time, 49% women, 8% African American, 3% Asian American, 6% Hispanic American, 1% international
- 2,032 degree-seeking graduate students
- 59% of applicants admitted
- SAT or ACT with writing, application essay required
- 46% graduate within 6 years

General. Founded in 1849. Regionally accredited. **Degrees:** 1,641 bachelor's awarded; master's, doctoral offered. **ROTC:** Army, Air Force. **Location:** 9 miles from Hartford. **Calendar:** Semester, extensive summer session. **Full-time faculty:** 434 total; 85% have terminal degrees, 16% minority, 42% women. **Part-time faculty:** 465 total; 10% have terminal degrees, 7% minority, 42% women. **Class size:** 41% < 20, 57% 20-39, 1% 40-49, 1% 50-99, less than 1% >100. **Special facilities:** Observatory, planetarium.

Freshman class profile. 6,090 applied, 3,619 admitted, 1,310 enrolled.

Mid 50% test scores		**End year in good standing:**	84%
SAT critical reading:	470-550	**Return as sophomores:**	79%
SAT math:	470-560	**Out-of-state:**	5%
SAT writing:	460-550	**Live on campus:**	56%
Rank in top quarter:	26%	**International:**	1%
Rank in top tenth:	7%		

Basis for selection. High school record, class rank, SAT scores most important. Letters of recommendation, optional student essay, and resume of activities to assess applicant's attitude toward future success considered. School of Business, social work program, communication program, and School of Education programs require acceptance into majors after admission to the university. Interview optional but would be considered. Audition required for music. **Homeschooled:** Statement describing homeschool structure and mission, transcript of courses and grades, state high school equivalency certificate required.

High school preparation. College-preparatory program recommended. 13 units required. Required and recommended units include English 4, mathematics 3, social studies 2, history 1, science 2 (laboratory 1) and foreign language 3. Social science should include US history; math should include algebra I and II and geometry.

2008-2009 Annual costs. Tuition/fees: $7,042; $16,179 out-of-state. Room/board: $8,838. Books/supplies: $1,010. Personal expenses: $1,920.

2007-2008 Financial aid. **Need-based:** 1,107 full-time freshmen applied for aid; 747 were judged to have need; 737 of these received aid. Average need met was 64%. Average scholarship/grant was $5,039; average loan $2,811. 45% of total undergraduate aid awarded as scholarships/grants, 55% as loans/jobs. **Non-need-based:** Awarded to 892 full-time undergraduates, including 233 freshmen. Scholarships awarded for academics, athletics, minority status.

Application procedures. **Admission:** Priority date 10/1; deadline 6/1 (receipt date). $50 fee, may be waived for applicants with need. Admission notification on a rolling basis beginning on or about 12/1. Must reply by May 1 or within 2 week(s) if notified thereafter. **Financial aid:** Priority date 3/1, closing date 9/15. FAFSA required. Applicants notified on a rolling basis starting 3/30; must reply within 2 week(s) of notification.

Academics. **Special study options:** Cooperative education, cross-registration, distance learning, double major, dual enrollment of high school students, ESL, exchange student, honors, independent study, internships, student-designed major, study abroad, teacher certification program. Undergraduates may take graduate classes. **Credit/placement by examination:** AP, CLEP, IB, SAT, institutional tests. 30 credit hours maximum toward bachelor's degree. **Support services:** Learning center, pre-admission summer program, reduced course load, remedial instruction, study skills assistance, tutoring, writing center.

Majors. **Biology:** General, biochemistry, molecular. **Business:** Accounting, business admin, finance, international, management information systems, marketing, organizational behavior, travel services. **Communications:** General. **Computer sciences:** General. **Construction:** General. **Education:** Art, elementary, music, secondary, technology/industrial arts. **Engineering:** Electrical, mechanical. **Engineering technology:** Civil, computer, industrial, manufacturing, mechanical. **Foreign languages:** French, German, Italian, Spanish. **Health:** Athletic training, nursing (RN). **History:** General. **Interdisciplinary:** Global studies. **Math:** General. **Philosophy/religion:** Philosophy. **Physical sciences:** Chemistry, geology, physics. **Psychology:** General. **Public administration:** Social work. **Social sciences:** General, anthropology, criminology, economics, geography, political science, sociology. **Visual/performing arts:** Art, design, dramatic.

Most popular majors. Business/marketing 29%, education 12%, engineering/engineering technologies 6%, psychology 9%, social sciences 13%.

Computing on campus. 875 workstations in dormitories, library, computer center, student center. Dormitories wired for high-speed internet access and linked to campus network. Commuter students can connect to campus network. Online course registration, online library, helpline, repair service, wireless network available.

Student life. **Freshman orientation:** Available, $65 fee. Preregistration for classes offered. One-day program in late June or early July. **Housing:** Coed dorms, single-sex dorms available. $250 nonrefundable deposit, deadline 5/1. **Activities:** Bands, campus ministries, choral groups, dance, drama, film society, international student organizations, literary magazine, music ensembles, musical theater, radio station, student government, student newspaper, TV station, Newman Club, Union of Jewish Students, Christian Fellowship, Christian Science Organization, Afro-American and African students, Latin American student association.

Athletics. NCAA. **Intercollegiate:** Baseball M, basketball, cross-country, diving W, football (tackle) M, golf, lacrosse W, soccer, softball W, swimming W, track and field, volleyball W. **Intramural:** Badminton, basketball, field hockey W, football (tackle) M, gymnastics W, lacrosse M, rugby, soccer, softball W, tennis, volleyball, water polo M. **Team name:** Blue Devils.

Student services. Adult student services, alcohol/substance abuse counseling, chaplain/spiritual director, career counseling, student employment services, financial aid counseling, health services, minority student services, on-campus daycare, personal counseling, placement for graduates, veterans' counselor, women's services. **Physically disabled:** Services for visually, speech, hearing impaired.

Contact. E-mail: admissions@ccsu.edu
Phone: (860) 832-2278 Fax: (860) 832-2295
Lawrence Hall, Director of Admissions, Central Connecticut State University, 1615 Stanley Street, New Britain, CT 06050

Charter Oak State College

New Britain, Connecticut — **CB member**
www.charteroak.edu — **CB code: 0870**

- Public 4-year virtual liberal arts college
- Commuter campus in small city
- 1,599 degree-seeking undergraduates: 92% part-time, 60% women, 14% African American, 2% Asian American, 7% Hispanic American, 1% Native American

General. Founded in 1973. Regionally accredited. **Degrees:** 429 bachelor's, 52 associate awarded. **Location:** 5 miles from Hartford. **Calendar:** Continuous, limited summer session. **Part-time faculty:** 97 total; 40% have terminal degrees, 9% minority, 50% women. **Class size:** 80% < 20, 19% 20-39, less than 1% 40-49.

Basis for selection. 9 college-level credits must be completed before enrolling. May be earned through college courses, testing, or ACE/PONSI recommendations for noncollege-sponsored instruction.

2008-2009 Annual costs. Academic Services Fee: In-state Bachelor's degree $1,015; In-state Associate's Degree $700; Out-of-state Bachelor's degree $1,335; Out-of-state Associate's degree $985. Books and supplies $1,000. Cost of education varies due to students having the option to take courses at other institutions.

2007-2008 Financial aid. All financial aid based on need.

Application procedures. **Admission:** No deadline. $75 fee, may be waived for applicants with need. Admission notification on a rolling basis. **Financial aid:** No deadline. FAFSA, institutional form required. Applicants notified on a rolling basis starting 8/23.

Academics. Tutoring and writing center available online free to students. **Special study options:** Accelerated study, distance learning, dual enrollment of high school students, external degree, independent study, liberal arts/career combination, student-designed major. Students can take courses at any regionally accredited institution. **Credit/placement by examination:** AP, CLEP, institutional tests. 60 credit hours maximum toward associate degree, 120 toward bachelor's. Unlimited number of hours of credit by examination may be counted toward degree. **Support services:** Tutoring, writing center.

Majors. **Liberal arts:** Arts/sciences.

Most popular majors. Liberal arts 16%.

Computing on campus. Online library, helpline, wireless network available.

Student life. **Activities:** Student government.

Student services. Adult student services, financial aid counseling, veterans' counselor.

Contact. E-mail: info@charteroak.edu
Phone: (860) 832-3800 Fax: (860) 832-3999
Lori Pendleton, Director of Admission, Charter Oak State College, 55 Paul Manafort Drive, New Britain, CT 06053-2150

Connecticut College

New London, Connecticut — **CB member**
www.conncoll.edu — **CB code: 3284**

- Private 4-year liberal arts college
- Residential campus in large town
- 1,741 degree-seeking undergraduates: 60% women, 4% African American, 5% Asian American, 6% Hispanic American, 4% international
- 7 degree-seeking graduate students
- 37% of applicants admitted
- Application essay required
- 88% graduate within 6 years

General. Founded in 1911. Regionally accredited. **Degrees:** 440 bachelor's awarded; master's offered. **Location:** 105 miles from Boston, 124 miles from New York City. **Calendar:** Semester, limited summer session. **Full-time faculty:** 169 total; 93% have terminal degrees, 14% minority, 46% women. **Part-time faculty:** 69 total; 17% have terminal degrees, 6% minority, 44% women. **Special facilities:** 750-acre arboretum, greenhouse, ion accelerator, refracting telescope and observatory, scanning and transmission electron microscopes, nuclear magnetic resonance spectrometer, tunable diode laser spectroscopy laboratory, center for electronic and digital sound, neuroscience and animal behavior laboratories, clinical and social psychology research observation suites.

Freshman class profile. 4,716 applied, 1,728 admitted, 493 enrolled.

Mid 50% test scores		Rank in top tenth:	60%
SAT critical reading:	600-700	Return as sophomores:	90%
SAT math:	600-690	Out-of-state:	85%
SAT writing:	620-710	Live on campus:	100%
ACT composite:	25-30	International:	5%
Rank in top quarter:	93%		

Basis for selection. School achievement record most important. Recommendations, personal qualities, personal essay, special talents, extracurricular activities also significant. Interview recommended. Audition recommended for dance or music majors. Portfolio recommended for art majors. **Homeschooled:** State high school equivalency certificate, letter of recommendation (nonparent) required. Extracurricular activities encouraged.

High school preparation. College-preparatory program recommended.

2009-2010 Annual costs. Tuition/fees: $42,335. Room/board: $8,780. Books/supplies: $1,000. Personal expenses: $500.

2008-2009 Financial aid. All financial aid based on need. 263 full-time freshmen applied for aid; 203 were judged to have need; 203 of these received aid. Average need met was 100%. Average scholarship/grant was $31,003; average loan $3,445. 85% of total undergraduate aid awarded as scholarships/grants, 15% as loans/jobs.

Application procedures. Admission: Closing date 1/1 (postmark date). $60 fee, may be waived for applicants with need. Admission notification 3/31. Must reply by 5/1. **Financial aid:** Closing date 2/1. FAFSA, CSS PROFILE required. Applicants notified by 4/1; must reply by 5/1.

Academics. 4 interdisciplinary centers through which students may earn a certificate to complement their major; competitive application process for acceptance. **Special study options:** Cross-registration, double major, dual enrollment of high school students, exchange student, independent study, internships, student-designed major, study abroad, teacher certification program, Washington semester. 12-college exchange, National Theater Institute, Mystic Seaport Program in American Maritime Studies, Institute for Architecture and Urban Studies, American Academy in Rome, Associated Kyoto Program, cross-registration with U.S. Coast Guard Academy, Trinity College and Wesleyan University, study away-teach away opportunities, specially funded student research opportunities. **Credit/placement by examination:** AP, CLEP, IB, institutional tests. 32 credit hours maximum toward bachelor's degree. Students may use AP credit to repair credit deficiencies that arise from voluntary course withdrawals or failing grades, or to accelerate. **Support services:** Pre-admission summer program, reduced course load, study skills assistance, tutoring, writing center.

Majors. Architecture: Architecture. **Area/ethnic studies:** African, American, East Asian, Hispanic-American/Latino/Chicano, Latin American, Slavic, women's. **Biology:** General, biochemistry, Biochemistry/biophysics and molecular biology, botany, cellular/molecular, molecular. **Computer sciences:** Computer science. **Conservation:** Environmental studies. **Engineering:** Physics. **Family/consumer sciences:** Family studies. **Foreign languages:** Chinese, classics, French, German, Italian, Japanese, Slavic, Spanish. **History:** General. **Interdisciplinary:** Medieval/Renaissance, neuroscience. **Math:** General. **Philosophy/religion:** Philosophy, religion. **Physical sciences:** Astrophysics, chemistry, physics. **Psychology:** General. **Social sciences:** Anthropology, economics, international relations, political science, sociology, urban studies. **Visual/performing arts:** Art history/conservation, dance, dramatic.

Most popular majors. Biology 10%, English 7%, foreign language 6%, social sciences 31%, visual/performing arts 11%.

Computing on campus. 500 workstations in library, computer center, student center. Dormitories wired for high-speed internet access and linked to campus network. Commuter students can connect to campus network. Online course registration, online library, helpline, student web hosting, wireless network available.

Student life. Freshman orientation: Mandatory. Preregistration for classes offered. Held week prior to start of classes. Optional outdoor orientation prior to full orientation (additional charge). **Policies:** Student-adjudicated social honor code in addition to academic honor code. **Housing:** Guaranteed on-campus for all undergraduates. Coed dorms, special housing for disabled, apartments, cooperative housing, wellness housing available. $500 nonrefundable deposit, deadline 5/1. Quiet housing, men's and women's floors, living-and-learning experience available. **Activities:** Bands, campus ministries, choral groups, dance, drama, film society, international student organizations, literary magazine, music ensembles, radio station, student government, student newspaper, symphony orchestra, College Democrats, College Republicans, Hillel, Intervarsity Christian Fellowship, multi-faith student council, Muslim student association, Asian/Asian American student association, Latino American student association, Sexual Orientations United for Liberation, African/African American student association.

Athletics. NCAA. **Intercollegiate:** Basketball, cross-country, diving, field hockey W, ice hockey, lacrosse, rowing (crew), sailing, soccer, squash, swimming, tennis, track and field, volleyball W, water polo. **Intramural:** Baseball M, basketball, football (non-tackle) M, racquetball, soccer, softball, squash, tennis, volleyball. **Team name:** Camels.

Student services. Adult student services, alcohol/substance abuse counseling, chaplain/spiritual director, career counseling, services for economically disadvantaged, student employment services, financial aid counseling, health services, minority student services, personal counseling, placement for graduates. **Physically disabled:** Services for visually, speech, hearing impaired. **Learning disabled:** Comprehensive services available.

Contact. E-mail: admission@conncoll.edu
Phone: (860) 439-2200 Fax: (860) 439-4301
Martha Merrill, Dean of Admission and Financial Aid, Connecticut College, 270 Mohegan Avenue, New London, CT 06320-4196

Eastern Connecticut State University

Willimantic, Connecticut — **CB member**
www.easternct.edu — **CB code: 3966**

- Public 4-year university and liberal arts college
- Residential campus in large town
- 4,896 degree-seeking undergraduates: 16% part-time, 55% women, 8% African American, 2% Asian American, 6% Hispanic American, 1% international
- 285 degree-seeking graduate students
- 63% of applicants admitted
- SAT or ACT (ACT writing optional) required
- 46% graduate within 6 years

General. Founded in 1889. Regionally accredited. **Degrees:** 989 bachelor's, 5 associate awarded; master's offered. **ROTC:** Army, Air Force. **Location:** 30 miles from Hartford. **Calendar:** Semester, extensive summer session. **Full-time faculty:** 202 total; 92% have terminal degrees, 26% minority, 43% women. **Part-time faculty:** 244 total; 23% have terminal degrees, 9% minority, 47% women. **Class size:** 44% < 20, 46% 20-39, 9% 40-49, less than 1% 50-99. **Special facilities:** Child and family development complex, sustainable energy institute, free enterprise institute, arboretum, planetarium, 2 electron microscopes, bell carillon.

Freshman class profile. 3,383 applied, 2,146 admitted, 1,020 enrolled.

Mid 50% test scores		Rank in top quarter:	26%
SAT critical reading:	460-540	Rank in top tenth:	5%
SAT math:	450-550	Return as sophomores:	74%
GPA 3.75 or higher:	5%	Out-of-state:	10%
GPA 3.50-3.74:	9%	Live on campus:	87%
GPA 3.0-3.49:	36%	International:	1%
GPA 2.0-2.99:	48%		

Basis for selection. Applicants should be in top half of class and recommended by high school. Quality of course work very important; 2.5 GPA in college preparatory program required. SAT score also important. Extracurricular activities considered. Interview and essay recommended.

High school preparation. Required units include English 4, mathematics 3, social studies 2, history 3, science 2 (laboratory 1) and foreign language 2.

2008-2009 Annual costs. Tuition/fees: $7,406; $16,543 out-of-state. Room/board: $8,855. Books/supplies: $1,284. Personal expenses: $2,900.

2007-2008 Financial aid. Need-based: 756 full-time freshmen applied for aid; 575 were judged to have need; 472 of these received aid. Average need met was 62%. Average scholarship/grant was $6,207; average loan $3,254. 36% of total undergraduate aid awarded as scholarships/grants, 64% as loans/jobs. **Non-need-based:** Awarded to 403 full-time undergraduates, including 207 freshmen. Scholarships awarded for academics. **Additional information:** Tuition waiver for veterans and members of National Guard.

Application procedures. Admission: Priority date 5/1; no deadline. $50 fee, may be waived for applicants with need. Admission notification on a rolling basis beginning on or about 12/1. Must reply by May 1 or within 2 week(s) if notified thereafter. **Financial aid:** Priority date 3/15; no closing date. FAFSA required. Applicants notified on a rolling basis starting 2/15; must reply within 2 week(s) of notification.

Academics. Life learning portfolio class available. **Special study options:** Accelerated study, cooperative education, cross-registration, distance learning, double major, dual enrollment of high school students, exchange student, honors, independent study, internships, student-designed major, study abroad, teacher certification program, weekend college. **Credit/placement by examination:** AP, CLEP, institutional tests. 30 credit hours maximum toward associate degree, 60 toward bachelor's. Institutional placement test required for all entering freshmen. **Support services:** Learning center, preadmission summer program, reduced course load, remedial instruction, study skills assistance, tutoring, writing center.

Majors. Biology: General, biochemistry. **Business:** Accounting, business admin, management information systems. **Communications:** General. **Computer sciences:** General. **Conservation:** Environmental science. **Education:** Early childhood, elementary, middle, physical, secondary. **Foreign languages:** Spanish. **History:** General. **Math:** General. **Parks/recreation:** Sports admin. **Psychology:** General. **Public administration:** Social work. **Social sciences:** Economics, political science, sociology. **Visual/performing arts:** General, studio arts.

Most popular majors. Business/marketing 15%, communications/journalism 8%, education 8%, English 8%, liberal arts 9%, psychology 10%, social sciences 15%.

Computing on campus. 637 workstations in dormitories, library, computer center. Dormitories wired for high-speed internet access and linked to campus network. Commuter students can connect to campus network. Online library, helpline, repair service, student web hosting, wireless network available.

Student life. Freshman orientation: Mandatory. Preregistration for classes offered. **Policies:** No alcohol permitted on campus; all halls are smoke-free; sign-in guest policy for all first-year halls from 7pm-12am. **Housing:** Coed dorms, apartments available. $250 nonrefundable deposit, deadline 5/1. **Activities:** Bands, choral groups, dance, drama, international student organizations, literary magazine, music ensembles, musical theater, radio station, student government, student newspaper, TV station, over 60 organizations.

Athletics. NCAA. **Intercollegiate:** Baseball M, basketball, cheerleading M, cross-country, field hockey W, lacrosse, soccer, softball W, swimming W, track and field, volleyball W. **Intramural:** Badminton, basketball, bowling, cross-country, football (tackle) M, gymnastics W, racquetball, rugby, skiing, soccer, softball, swimming, tennis, track and field, volleyball, water polo. **Team name:** Warriors.

Student services. Adult student services, alcohol/substance abuse counseling, chaplain/spiritual director, career counseling, services for economically disadvantaged, student employment services, financial aid counseling, health services, minority student services, on-campus daycare, personal counseling, placement for graduates, veterans' counselor, women's services. **Physically disabled:** Services for visually, speech, hearing impaired. **Learning disabled:** Comprehensive services available.

Contact. E-mail: admissions@easternct.edu
Phone: (860) 465-5286 Toll-free number: (877) 353-3278
Fax: (860) 465-5544
Kimberly Crone, Director of Admissions and Enrollment Planning, Eastern Connecticut State University, 83 Windham Street, Willimantic, CT 06226-2295

Fairfield University

Fairfield, Connecticut — **CB member**
www.fairfield.edu — **CB code: 3390**

- Private 4-year university affiliated with Roman Catholic Church
- Residential campus in small city
- 3,948 degree-seeking undergraduates: 13% part-time, 58% women
- 1,027 degree-seeking graduate students
- 59% of applicants admitted
- SAT or ACT (ACT writing optional), application essay required
- 79% graduate within 6 years; 22% enter graduate study

General. Founded in 1942. Regionally accredited. **Degrees:** 886 bachelor's, 3 associate awarded; master's offered. **ROTC:** Army, Air Force. **Location:** 50 miles from New York City. **Calendar:** Semester, limited summer session. **Full-time faculty:** 251 total; 93% have terminal degrees, 12% minority, 48% women. **Part-time faculty:** 259 total; 42% have terminal degrees, 5% minority, 42% women. **Class size:** 42% < 20, 57% 20-39, less than 1% 40-49, less than 1% 50-99, less than 1% >100. **Special facilities:** Fine arts center containing 2 theaters, campus ministry center, art galleries, Japanese meditation garden, business experimental, simulation and trading floor, nursing simulation lab.

Freshman class profile. 8,732 applied, 5,157 admitted, 899 enrolled.

Mid 50% test scores		**GPA 2.0-2.99:**	18%
SAT critical reading:	520-610	**Rank in top quarter:**	76%
SAT math:	540-630	**Rank in top tenth:**	38%
SAT writing:	540-630	**End year in good standing:**	98%
ACT composite:	23-27	**Return as sophomores:**	90%
GPA 3.75 or higher:	25%	**Out-of-state:**	76%
GPA 3.50-3.74:	20%	**Live on campus:**	94%
GPA 3.0-3.49:	37%	**International:**	1%

Basis for selection. GED not accepted. School achievement record, test scores, recommendations, school activities, personal statement important. Special consideration given to minority groups, children/siblings of alumni, and students with special talents and/or unique backgrounds. Interview recommended. Portfolio highly recommended for music majors, resume for theater majors. **Homeschooled:** Statement describing homeschool structure and mission, transcript of courses and grades required.

High school preparation. College-preparatory program required. 16 units required; 20 recommended. Required and recommended units include English 4, mathematics 3-4, social studies 2, history 2, science 2-3 (laboratory 2), foreign language 2-4 and academic electives 1. 1 additional math and 2 science recommended for math, business and science.

2008-2009 Annual costs. Tuition/fees: $36,075. Room/board: $10,850. Books/supplies: $900. Personal expenses: $900.

2008-2009 Financial aid. Need-based: 618 full-time freshmen applied for aid; 495 were judged to have need; 493 of these received aid. Average need met was 86%. Average scholarship/grant was $21,344; average loan $3,980. 75% of total undergraduate aid awarded as scholarships/grants, 25% as loans/jobs. **Non-need-based:** Awarded to 917 full-time undergraduates, including 286 freshmen. Scholarships awarded for academics, alumni affiliation, art, athletics, leadership, music/drama. **Additional information:** Free tuition to any eligible student from Bridgeport, CT with family income below $50,000. Enhanced financial aid available for veterans.

Application procedures. Admission: Closing date 1/15 (postmark date). $60 fee, may be waived for applicants with need. Admission notification 4/1. Must reply by 5/1. **Financial aid:** Closing date 2/15. FAFSA, CSS PROFILE required. Applicants notified by 4/1; must reply by 5/1.

Academics. Special study options: Combined bachelor's/graduate degree, cross-registration, distance learning, double major, exchange student, honors, independent study, internships, liberal arts/career combination, student-designed major, study abroad, teacher certification program, Washington semester. 3-2 engineering program with University of Connecticut, Rensselaer Polytechnic Institute, Columbia University, and Stevens Institute of Technology. **Credit/placement by examination:** AP, CLEP, IB, SAT, ACT, institutional tests. 15 credit hours maximum toward bachelor's degree. **Support services:** Reduced course load, study skills assistance, tutoring, writing center.

Majors. Area/ethnic studies: American. **Biology:** General, biochemistry. **Business:** Accounting, business admin, finance, international, management information systems, marketing. **Communications:** General. **Computer sciences:** General. **Engineering:** Computer, electrical, mechanical, software. **Foreign languages:** French, German, Italian, Spanish. **Health:** Nursing (RN). **History:** General. **Math:** General. **Philosophy/religion:** Philosophy, religion. **Physical sciences:** Chemistry, physics. **Psychology:** General. **Social sciences:** Economics, international relations, political science, sociology. **Visual/performing arts:** General, art history/conservation, dramatic, studio arts. **Other:** Individual design major, New media film/televison/radio.

Most popular majors. Business/marketing 33%, communications/journalism 10%, English 6%, health sciences 8%, psychology 7%, social sciences 15%.

Computing on campus. 220 workstations in dormitories, library, computer center, student center. Dormitories wired for high-speed internet access and linked to campus network. Commuter students can connect to campus network. Online course registration, online library, helpline, repair service, student web hosting, wireless network available.

Student life. Freshman orientation: Available, $230 fee. Preregistration for classes offered. Two-day program in late June/early July for students and parents. **Policies:** Juniors and seniors may enter lottery to move off-campus. **Housing:** Guaranteed on-campus for all undergraduates. Coed dorms, special housing for disabled, apartments, wellness housing available. $300 nonrefundable deposit, deadline 5/1. **Activities:** Bands, campus ministries, choral groups, dance, drama, film society, international student organizations, literary magazine, music ensembles, Model UN, radio station, student government, student newspaper, symphony orchestra, TV station, College Democrats, College Republicans, Circle K, Asian student association, Jewish cultural organization, Spanish and Latino student association, African-American & Caribbean student association, Colleges Against Cancer, student environmental association.

Athletics. NCAA. **Intercollegiate:** Baseball M, basketball, cross-country, diving, field hockey W, golf, lacrosse, rowing (crew), soccer, softball W, swimming, tennis, volleyball W. **Intramural:** Basketball, field hockey W, football (non-tackle) M, golf, lacrosse, racquetball, soccer, softball, table tennis, tennis, volleyball. **Team name:** Stags.

Student services. Adult student services, alcohol/substance abuse counseling, chaplain/spiritual director, career counseling, student employment services, financial aid counseling, health services, minority student services, on-campus daycare, personal counseling, placement for graduates. **Physically disabled:** Services for visually, hearing impaired.

Contact. E-mail: admis@mail.fairfield.edu
Phone: (203) 254-4100 Fax: (203) 254-4199
Karen Pellegrino, Director of Undergraduate Admission, Fairfield University, 1073 North Benson Road, Fairfield, CT 06824-5195

Holy Apostles College and Seminary

Cromwell, Connecticut
www.holyapostles.edu **CB code: 0921**

- Private 4-year liberal arts and seminary college affiliated with Roman Catholic Church
- Commuter campus in large town
- 39 degree-seeking undergraduates: 33% part-time, 31% women, 3% Asian American, 33% Hispanic American, 21% international
- 216 degree-seeking graduate students
- 100% of applicants admitted
- SAT, interview required

General. Founded in 1956. Regionally accredited. 75% of students are lay students, 25% are seminarians. **Degrees:** 13 bachelor's awarded; master's, first professional offered. **Location:** 13 miles from Hartford. **Calendar:** Semester, limited summer session. **Full-time faculty:** 16 total; 94% have terminal degrees, 6% minority, 25% women. **Part-time faculty:** 7 total; 86% have terminal degrees, 29% women.

Freshman class profile. 2 applied, 2 admitted, 2 enrolled.

End year in good standing:	80%	**Live on campus:**	100%
Return as sophomores:	80%	**International:**	50%
Out-of-state:	2%		

Basis for selection. Interview, level of interest and recommendations most important. 1050 SAT and B in high school core courses required. **Homeschooled:** State high school equivalency certificate, interview, letter of recommendation (nonparent) required.

2008-2009 Annual costs. Tuition/fees: $8,640. Books/supplies: $630. Personal expenses: $580.

2008-2009 Financial aid. All financial aid based on need. 2 full-time freshmen applied for aid; 2 were judged to have need; 2 of these received aid. Average need met was 70%. Average loan was $4,811. 6% of total undergraduate aid awarded as scholarships/grants, 94% as loans/jobs.

Application procedures. Admission: Priority date 8/15; no deadline. $25 fee, may be waived for applicants with need. Application must be submitted on paper. Admission notification on a rolling basis. Applications accepted up to one week before beginning of semester in which the applicant plans to enroll. **Financial aid:** Priority date 7/11; no closing date. FAFSA, institutional form required. Applicants notified on a rolling basis starting 8/25; must reply within 2 week(s) of notification.

Academics. 54-credit core curriculum required of all undergraduates. **Special study options:** Distance learning, ESL, independent study. **Credit/placement by examination:** AP, CLEP. 30 credit hours maximum toward bachelor's degree. **Support services:** Reduced course load, remedial instruction, tutoring.

Majors. Liberal arts: Humanities. **Philosophy/religion:** Philosophy, religion. **Social sciences:** General.

Most popular majors. Liberal arts 8%, philosophy/religious studies 92%.

Computing on campus. 10 workstations in library.

Student life. Freshman orientation: Available. Preregistration for classes offered. **Policies:** Men's dorms are for seminarians only; other students must commute. **Housing:** Single-sex dorms available. **Activities:** Choral groups, Life League, Toastmasters.

Student services. Chaplain/spiritual director, financial aid counseling, personal counseling.

Contact. E-mail: registrar@holyapostles.edu
Phone: (860) 632-3033 Toll-free number: (800) 330-7272
Fax: (860) 632-3075
Very Rev. Douglas Mosey, President-Rector, Holy Apostles College and Seminary, 33 Prospect Hill Road, Cromwell, CT 06416-2005

Lyme Academy College of Fine Arts

Old Lyme, Connecticut **CB member**
www.lymeacademy.edu **CB code: 1791**

- Private 4-year visual arts college
- Commuter campus in small town
- 96 degree-seeking undergraduates: 9% part-time, 57% women, 2% African American, 1% Asian American, 1% Hispanic American, 2% Native American
- 100% of applicants admitted
- Application essay, interview required

General. Founded in 1976. Regionally accredited. **Degrees:** 14 bachelor's awarded. **Location:** 40 miles from Hartford. **Calendar:** Semester, limited summer session. **Full-time faculty:** 7 total; 43% women. **Part-time faculty:** 19 total; 5% have terminal degrees, 32% women. **Class size:** 89% < 20, 11% 20-39. **Special facilities:** Art museum.

Freshman class profile. 30 applied, 30 admitted, 11 enrolled.

Mid 50% test scores		**GPA 3.0-3.49:**	37%
SAT critical reading:	520-620	**GPA 2.0-2.99:**	18%
SAT math:	450-590	**End year in good standing:**	82%
GPA 3.75 or higher:	18%	**Return as sophomores:**	82%
GPA 3.50-3.74:	27%	**Out-of-state:**	27%

Basis for selection. Admissions based on portfolio, interview, essay, GPA. SAT or ACT recommended. Portfolio, two letters of recommendation required. Campus visit highly recommended. **Homeschooled:** Statement describing homeschool structure and mission, transcript of courses and grades, state high school equivalency certificate, interview, letter of recommendation (nonparent) required.

2009-2010 Annual costs. Tuition/fees: $23,092. Books/supplies: $1,500. Personal expenses: $500.

2008-2009 Financial aid. Need-based: 11 full-time freshmen applied for aid; 11 were judged to have need; 11 of these received aid. 45% of total undergraduate aid awarded as scholarships/grants, 55% as loans/jobs. **Non-need-based:** Scholarships awarded for academics, art, leadership.

Application procedures. Admission: Priority date 2/15; no deadline. $55 fee. Admission notification on a rolling basis beginning on or about 2/15. Must reply by May 1 or within 2 week(s) if notified thereafter. **Financial aid:** Priority date 2/15, closing date 4/15. FAFSA required. Applicants notified on a rolling basis starting 3/1; must reply by 5/1 or within 2 week(s) of notification.

Academics. Special study options: Cross-registration, double major, independent study. **Credit/placement by examination:** CLEP. **Support services:** Pre-admission summer program, reduced course load, remedial instruction, study skills assistance.

Majors. Visual/performing arts: Drawing, illustration, painting, sculpture.

Computing on campus. 6 workstations in library. Online library available.

Student life. Freshman orientation: Mandatory. Preregistration for classes offered. Usually one day before start of Fall classes. **Activities:** Film society, literary magazine, student government.

Athletics. Intramural: Badminton, basketball, table tennis, volleyball. **Team name:** The Ticks.

Student services. Alcohol/substance abuse counseling, career counseling, financial aid counseling, personal counseling, veterans' counselor, women's services.

Contact. E-mail: csheridan@lymeacademy.edu
Phone: (860) 434-5232 ext. 119 Fax: (860) 434-8725
Cara Sheridan, Admissions Representative, Lyme Academy College of Fine Arts, 84 Lyme Street, Old Lyme, CT 06371

Mitchell College

New London, Connecticut — **CB member**
www.mitchell.edu — **CB code: 3528**

- Private 4-year liberal arts college
- Residential campus in small city
- 890 degree-seeking undergraduates: 12% part-time, 50% women
- 36% of applicants admitted
- Application essay, interview required

General. Founded in 1938. Regionally accredited. **Degrees:** 111 bachelor's, 66 associate awarded. **Location:** 100 miles from New York City and Boston. **Calendar:** Semester, limited summer session. **Full-time faculty:** 31 total; 36% have terminal degrees, 10% minority, 55% women. **Part-time faculty:** 53 total; 9% have terminal degrees, 8% minority, 47% women. **Special facilities:** Two beaches, dock with sailboat fleet, learning resource center for students with learning disabilities, hiking trails, nature preserve.

Freshman class profile. 1,500 applied, 540 admitted, 267 enrolled.

Out-of-state:	45%	**Live on campus:**	85%

Basis for selection. High school achievement, recommendations, motivation and interview very important. **Learning Disabled:** Students applying to Learning Resource Center should submit results of complete psychoeducational evaluation, testing accommodation recommendations made by professional who completed the evaluation, definitive diagnosis of learning disability or ADHD, and standardized achievement testing (reading, writing and math). All documentation should be less than 3 years old; testing must be administered by certified or licensed psychologist.

High school preparation. College-preparatory program recommended. Recommended units include English 4, mathematics 3, social studies 3, history 2, science 3, foreign language 1 and academic electives 4.

2008-2009 Annual costs. Tuition/fees: $24,358. Room/board: $10,977. Books/supplies: $900. Personal expenses: $1,050.

Financial aid. **Non-need-based:** Scholarships awarded for academics, alumni affiliation, leadership.

Application procedures. **Admission:** Priority date 4/1; no deadline. $30 fee, may be waived for applicants with need, free for online applicants. Admission notification on a rolling basis. Must reply by May 1 or within 2 week(s) if notified thereafter. **Financial aid:** Priority date 3/1; no closing date. FAFSA required. Applicants notified on a rolling basis starting 2/15; must reply within 2 week(s) of notification.

Academics. Free professional tutoring offered in most disciplines. **Special study options:** Dual enrollment of high school students, ESL, internships, student-designed major, study abroad, teacher certification program. **Credit/placement by examination:** AP, CLEP, institutional tests. 30 credit hours maximum toward associate degree. **Support services:** Learning center, pre-admission summer program, reduced course load, study skills assistance, tutoring, writing center.

Majors. **Biology:** Environmental. **Business:** Accounting/business management, business admin, hospitality admin, hotel/motel admin, restaurant/food services, small business admin, tourism/travel. **Communications:** Broadcast journalism, digital media, journalism, media studies, organizational, public relations, radio/tv. **Communications technology:** Graphics. **Conservation:** Environmental studies. **Education:** Early childhood, kindergarten/preschool. **Family/consumer sciences:** Child care, family studies. **Health:** Premedicine. **Interdisciplinary:** Behavioral sciences, global studies. **Legal studies:** General, prelaw. **Liberal arts:** Arts/sciences, humanities. **Parks/recreation:** Sports admin. **Protective services:** Criminal justice, emergency management/homeland security, juvenile corrections. **Psychology:** General, community, developmental. **Public administration:** Human services. **Social sciences:** Criminology, international economic development. **Visual/performing arts:** Graphic design.

Computing on campus. 155 workstations in dormitories, library, computer center, student center. Dormitories wired for high-speed internet access and linked to campus network. Commuter students can connect to campus network. Helpline, repair service available.

Student life. **Freshman orientation:** Available. Held in September prior to start of classes; concurrent program specific to parent issues. **Housing:** Guaranteed on-campus for all undergraduates. Coed dorms, single-sex dorms, special housing for disabled, wellness housing available. $300 nonrefundable deposit, deadline 5/1. **Activities:** Campus ministries, choral groups, dance, drama, international student organizations, student government, student newspaper, multicultural club, Hillel, spirituality club, African American alliance, communication club, improv club, Bible study club, peer educators, gay straight alliance.

Athletics. NCAA. **Intercollegiate:** Baseball M, basketball, cross-country, golf, lacrosse M, sailing, soccer, softball W, tennis, volleyball W. **Intramural:** Basketball, sailing, soccer, softball, tennis, volleyball. **Team name:** Mariners.

Student services. Adult student services, career counseling, services for economically disadvantaged, student employment services, financial aid counseling, health services, minority student services, on-campus daycare, personal counseling, placement for graduates, veterans' counselor. **Physically disabled:** Services for visually, speech, hearing impaired. **Learning disabled:** Comprehensive services available.

Contact. E-mail: admissions@mitchell.edu
Phone: (860) 701-5037 Toll-free number: (800) 443-2811
Fax: (860) 444-1209
Kimberly Hodges, Director of Admissions, Mitchell College, 437 Pequot Avenue, New London, CT 06320-4498

Paier College of Art

Hamden, Connecticut
www.paiercollegeofart.edu — **CB code: 3699**

- For-profit 4-year visual arts college
- Commuter campus in small city
- 207 degree-seeking undergraduates: 21% part-time, 69% women, 5% African American, 2% Asian American, 3% Hispanic American
- 73% of applicants admitted
- SAT or ACT, interview required
- 72% graduate within 6 years; 9% enter graduate study

General. Founded in 1946. Accredited by ACCSCT. **Degrees:** 43 bachelor's awarded. **Location:** 2 miles from New Haven. **Calendar:** Semester. **Full-time faculty:** 10 total; 40% have terminal degrees. **Part-time faculty:** 31 total; 45% have terminal degrees, 26% women. **Class size:** 89% < 20, 11% 20-39. **Special facilities:** Extensive image picture reference file.

Freshman class profile. 85 applied, 62 admitted, 31 enrolled.

Mid 50% test scores		**Rank in top quarter:**	17%
SAT critical reading:	410-510	**End year in good standing:**	90%
SAT math:	360-500	**Return as sophomores:**	80%

Basis for selection. Artistic ability, interest, and potential, as demonstrated in admission interview and portfolio review most important elements. Portfolio of 8 to 10 works of art required; essay recommended. **Homeschooled:** Statement describing homeschool structure and mission, transcript of courses and grades, interview, letter of recommendation (nonparent) required. Notification from school district required stating that student is being home-schooled.

High school preparation. Required units include English 4, mathematics 3, social studies 3, science 2, computer science 1 and visual/performing arts 4. Art classes recommended. All students must pass all state requirements.

2009-2010 Annual costs. Tuition/fees (projected): $12,365. Books/supplies: $1,000. Personal expenses: $600.

2007-2008 Financial aid. **Need-based:** 13 full-time freshmen applied for aid; 9 were judged to have need; 9 of these received aid. Average need met was 64%. Average scholarship/grant was $5,497; average loan $3,788. 57% of total undergraduate aid awarded as scholarships/grants, 43% as loans/jobs.

Application procedures. **Admission:** No deadline. $25 fee, may be waived for applicants with need. Application must be submitted on paper. Admission notification on a rolling basis beginning on or about 2/15. **Financial aid:** Priority date 4/15; no closing date. FAFSA required. Applicants notified on a rolling basis starting 6/1; must reply within 3 week(s) of notification.

Academics. Academics required for BFA degrees include: 4 art histories, English I and II, 1 requirement each in the humanities, math, physical and social sciences, and 1 academic elective. **Special study options:** Independent study. **Credit/placement by examination:** AP, CLEP, IB, SAT, ACT. 6 credit hours maximum toward associate degree, 12 toward bachelor's. **Support services:** Reduced course load, remedial instruction, study skills assistance, tutoring.

Majors. **Visual/performing arts:** Commercial photography, commercial/advertising art, design, graphic design, illustration, interior design, painting, photography, studio arts.

Computing on campus. 69 workstations in library, computer center. Wireless network available.

Student life. **Freshman orientation:** Available. Preregistration for classes offered. Open to incoming students and their parents/guardians. Separate 1-hour library orientation. **Activities:** Student government.

Student services. Career counseling, student employment services, financial aid counseling, personal counseling, placement for graduates, veterans' counselor.

Contact. E-mail: paier.admission@snet.net
Phone: (203) 287-3031 Fax: (203) 287-3021
Daniel Paier, Dean of Admissions, Paier College of Art, 20 Gorham Avenue, Hamden, CT 06514-3902

Post University

Waterbury, Connecticut — **CB member**
www.post.edu — **CB code: 3698**

- For-profit 4-year university and business college
- Residential campus in small city
- 1,320 degree-seeking undergraduates
- 178 graduate students
- 52% of applicants admitted
- SAT or ACT with writing required
- 36% graduate within 6 years

General. Founded in 1890. Regionally accredited. **Degrees:** 205 bachelor's, 25 associate awarded; master's offered. **Location:** 32 miles from Hartford, 80 miles from New York City. **Calendar:** Semester, limited summer session. **Full-time faculty:** 28 total; 46% have terminal degrees, 11% minority, 39% women.

Freshman class profile. 1,494 applied, 781 admitted, 221 enrolled.

Mid 50% test scores		**GPA 3.0-3.49:**	24%
SAT critical reading:	380-500	**GPA 2.0-2.99:**	70%
SAT math:	370-510	**Rank in top quarter:**	10%
SAT writing:	380-500	**Rank in top tenth:**	5%
ACT composite:	17-24	**Out-of-state:**	40%
GPA 3.75 or higher:	1%	**Live on campus:**	25%
GPA 3.50-3.74:	4%		

Basis for selection. Secondary school transcript, results of SAT/ACT most important. Guidance counselor's recommendation required. School and community activities and test scores also reviewed and considered. Interview recommended. **Homeschooled:** Statement describing homeschool structure and mission, transcript of courses and grades, interview, letter of recommendation (nonparent) required. **Learning Disabled:** Students must submit documentation once enrolled to receive services; documentation not used for admissions.

High school preparation. College-preparatory program recommended. 13 units required. Required and recommended units include English 4, mathematics 3, social studies 1, history 2, science 3 (laboratory 1) and foreign language 2.

2008-2009 Annual costs. Tuition/fees: $23,425. Room/board: $9,000. Books/supplies: $1,000. Personal expenses: $1,200.

2007-2008 Financial aid. **Need-based:** 96 full-time freshmen applied for aid; 90 were judged to have need; 90 of these received aid. Average need met was 73%. Average scholarship/grant was $5,000; average loan $2,600. 63% of total undergraduate aid awarded as scholarships/grants, 37% as loans/jobs. **Non-need-based:** Awarded to 530 full-time undergraduates, including 90 freshmen. **Additional information:** Academic merit scholarships available based on GPA and test scores. Renewable contingent upon maintaining specific GPA.

Application procedures. **Admission:** Priority date 3/1; no deadline. $40 fee, may be waived for applicants with need, free for online applicants. Admission notification on a rolling basis beginning on or about 11/15. Must reply by May 1 or within 2 week(s) if notified thereafter. **Financial aid:** Priority date 3/15; no closing date. FAFSA required. Applicants notified on a rolling basis starting 4/15; must reply by 5/1 or within 3 week(s) of notification.

Academics. **Special study options:** Accelerated study, cooperative education, cross-registration, distance learning, double major, dual enrollment of high school students, ESL, independent study, internships, liberal arts/career combination, student-designed major, study abroad, weekend college. **Credit/placement by examination:** AP, CLEP, IB, institutional tests. 15 credit hours maximum toward associate degree, 30 toward bachelor's. **Support services:** Learning center, pre-admission summer program, reduced course load, study skills assistance, tutoring, writing center.

Majors. **Agriculture:** Equestrian studies. **Biology:** General. **Business:** General, accounting, business admin, finance, marketing. **Computer sciences:** General. **Conservation:** General, environmental studies. **Legal studies:** Prelaw. **Protective services:** Law enforcement admin. **Psychology:** General. **Public administration:** Human services. **Social sciences:** Sociology.

Computing on campus. 94 workstations in library, computer center, student center. Dormitories wired for high-speed internet access and linked to campus network. Commuter students can connect to campus network. Online course registration, online library, helpline available.

Student life. **Freshman orientation:** Mandatory, $150 fee. Preregistration for classes offered. **Policies:** Student leadership opportunities encouraged and supported throughout student's experience. **Housing:** Guaranteed on-campus for all undergraduates. Coed dorms available. $150 fully refundable deposit, deadline 5/1. **Activities:** Dance, drama, international student organizations, literary magazine, musical theater, student government, Phi Theta Kappa, student ambassadors, peer advisors.

Athletics. NCAA. **Intercollegiate:** Baseball M, basketball, cross-country, golf, lacrosse W, soccer, softball W, swimming, tennis, volleyball W. **Intramural:** Basketball, lacrosse W, tennis. **Team name:** Eagles.

Student services. Adult student services, alcohol/substance abuse counseling, career counseling, student employment services, financial aid counseling, health services, minority student services, personal counseling, placement for graduates, veterans' counselor. **Physically disabled:** Services for visually impaired.

Contact. E-mail: admissions@post.edu
Phone: (203) 596-4520 Toll-free number: (800) 345-2562
Fax: (203) 756-5810
Jay Murray, Director of Admissions, Post University, 800 Country Club Road, Waterbury, CT 06723-2540

Quinnipiac University

Hamden, Connecticut — **CB member**
www.quinnipiac.edu — **CB code: 3712**

- Private 4-year university
- Residential campus in small city
- 5,747 degree-seeking undergraduates: 3% part-time, 61% women, 3% African American, 2% Asian American, 5% Hispanic American, 1% international
- 1,496 degree-seeking graduate students
- 45% of applicants admitted
- SAT or ACT (ACT writing optional), application essay required
- 72% graduate within 6 years; 38% enter graduate study

General. Founded in 1929. Regionally accredited. Additional campuses in York Hill, North Haven. **Degrees:** 1,327 bachelor's, 1 associate awarded; master's, doctoral, first professional offered. **ROTC:** Army, Air Force. **Location:** 8 miles from New Haven. **Calendar:** Semester, limited summer session. **Full-time faculty:** 304 total; 85% have terminal degrees, 12% minority, 48% women. **Part-time faculty:** 541 total; 7% minority, 52% women. **Class size:** 51% < 20, 48% 20-39, less than 1% 40-49. **Special facilities:** Financial technology center; polling institute; institute for community health education; critical care simulation laboratory; motion analysis lab; Irish Famine museum; fully-digital, high definition production studio; audio production studio; news technology center.

Freshman class profile. 14,994 applied, 6,721 admitted, 1,487 enrolled.

Mid 50% test scores		**Rank in top quarter:**	68%
SAT critical reading:	540-610	**Rank in top tenth:**	26%
SAT math:	560-630	**End year in good standing:**	93%
ACT composite:	23-27	**Return as sophomores:**	89%
GPA 3.75 or higher:	13%	**Out-of-state:**	75%
GPA 3.50-3.74:	31%	**Live on campus:**	95%
GPA 3.0-3.49:	48%	**International:**	1%
GPA 2.0-2.99:	8%		

Basis for selection. Primary emphasis placed on high school transcript, grades, grade pattern, level of difficulty. Test scores, essay and recommendation(s) also important. Interview recommended, extracurricular activities, evidence of leadership, and employment also considered. Must send official test scores for all SAT and/or ACT tests taken. Highest SAT (individual scores) or ACT (composite) scores used when reviewing applications for admission and for scholarships. Campus visit recommended. **Homeschooled:** Statement describing homeschool structure and mission, transcript of courses and grades, letter of recommendation (nonparent) required. Evaluation of completed education required.

High school preparation. College-preparatory program required. 16 units required. Required and recommended units include English 4, mathematics 3, social studies 2, science 3 (laboratory 2), foreign language 2-3 and academic electives 2. 4 lab science and 4 math required for students applying to physical therapy, occupational therapy, nursing and physician assistant programs. Physics highly recommended for physical therapy applicants.

2009-2010 Annual costs. Tuition/fees: $32,400. Room/board: $12,380. Books/supplies: $800. Personal expenses: $900.

2008-2009 Financial aid. **Need-based:** 1,111 full-time freshmen applied for aid; 835 were judged to have need; 834 of these received aid. Average need met was 69%. Average scholarship/grant was $13,813; average loan $3,567. 52% of total undergraduate aid awarded as scholarships/grants, 48% as loans/jobs. **Non-need-based:** Awarded to 2,194 full-time undergraduates, including 723 freshmen. Scholarships awarded for academics, athletics.

Application procedures. **Admission:** Priority date 11/30; deadline 2/1 (postmark date). $45 fee, may be waived for applicants with need. Admission notification on a rolling basis beginning on or about 12/15. Must reply by May 1 or within 2 week(s) if notified thereafter. Students encouraged to apply early in the fall of their senior year. Students applying for Nursing, BS/DPT in Physical Therapy or BS/MHS in Physician Assistant programs should apply by November 1. **Financial aid:** Priority date 3/1; no closing date. FAFSA required. Applicants notified on a rolling basis starting 2/15; must reply by 5/1 or within 2 week(s) of notification.

Academics. Incoming students must purchase a university recommended laptop computer. **Special study options:** Combined bachelor's/graduate degree, distance learning, double major, honors, independent study, internships, liberal arts/career combination, semester at sea, student-designed major, study abroad, teacher certification program, Washington semester. College of Professional Studies (online and hybrid program for degree completion). **Credit/placement by examination:** AP, CLEP, IB, institutional tests. 32 credit hours maximum toward bachelor's degree. **Support services:** Learning center, tutoring.

Majors. **Biology:** General, biochemistry, biomedical sciences, biotechnology. **Business:** General, accounting, business admin, communications, entrepreneurial studies, finance, human resources, international, international marketing, management information systems, management science, managerial economics, marketing, nonprofit/public, office management. **Communications:** General, advertising, broadcast journalism, digital media, journalism, public relations. **Computer sciences:** General, applications programming, computer graphics, computer science. **Education:** Biology, chemistry, elementary, English, foreign languages, history, mathematics, middle, multi-level teacher, science, secondary, social studies, Spanish. **Foreign languages:** Spanish. **Health:** Athletic training, health care admin, nursing (RN), physician assistant, predental, premedicine, preveterinary, radiologic technology/medical imaging. **History:** General. **Interdisciplinary:** Biopsychology, gerontology, math/computer science. **Legal studies:** General, paralegal, prelaw. **Math:** General. **Physical sciences:** Chemistry. **Protective services:** Criminal justice. **Psychology:** General. **Science technology:** Biological. **Social sciences:** General, criminology, economics, political science, sociology. **Visual/performing arts:** Dramatic. **Other:** Biomedical marketing.

Most popular majors. Business/marketing 22%, communications/journalism 17%, health sciences 25%, psychology 8%, social sciences 6%.

Computing on campus. PC or laptop required. 400 workstations in library, computer center. Dormitories wired for high-speed internet access and linked to campus network. Commuter students can connect to campus network. Online course registration, online library, helpline, repair service, student web hosting, wireless network available.

Student life. **Freshman orientation:** Mandatory. Preregistration for classes offered. Three Friday-Saturday weekend sessions offered in June; 2-day session offered prior to start of classes. **Policies:** Resident freshmen may not have cars on campus. **Housing:** Guaranteed on-campus for freshmen. Coed dorms, apartments, wellness housing available. $550 partly refundable deposit, deadline 5/1. **Activities:** Pep band, campus ministries, choral groups, dance, drama, international student organizations, literary magazine, radio station, student government, student newspaper, TV station, Hillel House, Hillel organization, Catholic services, black student union, Latino cultural society, Greenpeace, Amnesty International, SADD, women's center, Asian and Pacific Islander club, Christian Fellowship.

Athletics. NCAA. **Intercollegiate:** Baseball M, basketball, cheerleading M, cross-country, field hockey W, golf M, ice hockey, lacrosse, soccer, softball W, tennis, track and field, volleyball W. **Intramural:** Archery, badminton, baseball M, basketball, bowling, field hockey W, soccer, softball, table tennis, tennis, volleyball. **Team name:** Bobcats.

Student services. Adult student services, alcohol/substance abuse counseling, chaplain/spiritual director, career counseling, student employment services, financial aid counseling, health services, minority student services, personal counseling, placement for graduates.

Contact. E-mail: admissions@quinnipiac.edu
Phone: (203) 582-8600 Toll-free number: (800) 462-1944
Fax: (203) 582-8906
Carla Knowlton, Director of Admissions, Quinnipiac University, 275 Mount Carmel Avenue, Hamden, CT 06518-1908

Sacred Heart University

Fairfield, Connecticut — **CB member**
www.sacredheart.edu — **CB code: 3780**

- Private 4-year university and liberal arts college affiliated with Roman Catholic Church
- Residential campus in large town
- 4,239 degree-seeking undergraduates: 17% part-time, 61% women, 4% African American, 2% Asian American, 6% Hispanic American, 1% international
- 1,684 degree-seeking graduate students
- 65% of applicants admitted
- SAT or ACT (ACT writing optional), application essay required
- 62% graduate within 6 years; 50% enter graduate study

General. Founded in 1963. Regionally accredited. **Degrees:** 852 bachelor's, 25 associate awarded; master's, doctoral offered. **ROTC:** Army. **Location:** 55 miles from New York City. **Calendar:** Semester, extensive summer session. **Full-time faculty:** 212 total; 75% have terminal degrees, 12% minority, 49% women. **Part-time faculty:** 353 total; 29% have terminal degrees, 8% minority, 46% women. **Class size:** 50% < 20, 49% 20-39, less than 1% 40-49. **Special facilities:** Performing arts center, multipurpose communication studios, 36-hole golf course, rehabilitation clinics for occupational and physical therapies, contemporary art gallery.

Freshman class profile. 7,568 applied, 4,927 admitted, 980 enrolled.

Mid 50% test scores		**Rank in top tenth:**	16%
SAT critical reading:	490-560	**End year in good standing:**	95%
SAT math:	500-590	**Return as sophomores:**	81%
GPA 3.75 or higher:	20%	**Out-of-state:**	74%
GPA 3.50-3.74:	19%	**Live on campus:**	95%
GPA 3.0-3.49:	38%	**International:**	1%
GPA 2.0-2.99:	23%	**Fraternities:**	5%
Rank in top quarter:	52%	**Sororities:**	7%

Basis for selection. High school record and college preparatory curriculum most important. Interview required for early decision candidates, recommended for all others.

High school preparation. College-preparatory program required. 22 units required; 30 recommended. Required and recommended units include English 4, mathematics 3-4, social studies 3-4, history 3-4, science 3-4 (laboratory 1-2), foreign language 2-4 and academic electives 3-4.

2008-2009 Annual costs. Tuition/fees: $28,990. Room/board: $11,330. Books/supplies: $700. Personal expenses: $700.

2008-2009 Financial aid. **Need-based:** 880 full-time freshmen applied for aid; 671 were judged to have need; 671 of these received aid. Average need met was 66%. Average scholarship/grant was $14,220; average loan $3,660. 58% of total undergraduate aid awarded as scholarships/grants, 42% as loans/jobs. **Non-need-based:** Awarded to 971 full-time undergraduates, including 309 freshmen. Scholarships awarded for academics, alumni affiliation, art, athletics, leadership, minority status, music/drama. **Additional information:** Financial aid for first-year, full-time students from Fairfield County, CT who have family income at or below $50,000 will cover 100% tuition.

Application procedures. **Admission:** Priority date 2/1; no deadline. $50 fee, may be waived for applicants with need. Admission notification on a rolling basis beginning on or about 1/1. Must reply by May 1 or within 2 week(s) if notified thereafter. **Financial aid:** Priority date 2/15; no closing date. FAFSA, CSS PROFILE required. Applicants notified on a rolling basis starting 3/1; must reply within 2 week(s) of notification.

Academics. **Special study options:** Accelerated study, combined bachelor's/graduate degree, cooperative education, cross-registration, distance learning, double major, dual enrollment of high school students, ESL, honors, independent study, internships, liberal arts/career combination, student-designed major, study abroad, teacher certification program, United Nations semester, Washington semester, weekend college. Luxembourg semester, study abroad program in Ireland. **Credit/placement by examination:** AP, CLEP,

IB, SAT, ACT, institutional tests. 30 credit hours maximum toward bachelor's degree. **Support services:** Learning center, reduced course load, remedial instruction, study skills assistance, tutoring, writing center.

Honors college/program. Holistic review of applicant is conducted. Recommended eligibility requirements include: 3.4 GPA, 1250 SAT (exclusive of Writing) with 600 critical reading, rank in top 10% of high school class.

Majors. Biology: General, biochemistry. **Business:** General, accounting, finance, managerial economics, marketing. **Communications:** General, media studies. **Communications technology:** General. **Computer sciences:** General, computer science, information technology. **Conservation:** General. **Foreign languages:** Spanish. **Health:** Athletic training, kinesiotherapy, nursing (RN), preop/surgical nursing. **History:** General. **Liberal arts:** Arts/sciences. **Math:** General. **Parks/recreation:** Sports admin. **Philosophy/religion:** Philosophy, religion. **Physical sciences:** Chemistry. **Protective services:** Law enforcement admin. **Psychology:** General. **Public administration:** Social work. **Social sciences:** Economics, political science, sociology. **Visual/performing arts:** Art, commercial/advertising art, design.

Most popular majors. Business/marketing 32%, health sciences 14%, psychology 17%.

Computing on campus. PC or laptop required. 78 workstations in dormitories, library, computer center, student center. Dormitories wired for high-speed internet access and linked to campus network. Commuter students can connect to campus network. Online course registration, online library, helpline, repair service, student web hosting, wireless network available.

Student life. Freshman orientation: Mandatory. Preregistration for classes offered. Overnight 2-day program in late spring for both parents and students. **Housing:** Guaranteed on-campus for all undergraduates. Coed dorms, special housing for disabled, apartments, wellness housing available. $1,500 nonrefundable deposit, deadline 5/1. Living and learning communities available for specific academic programs, honors floors. **Activities:** Bands, campus ministries, choral groups, dance, drama, film society, international student organizations, literary magazine, music ensembles, musical theater, radio station, student government, student newspaper, TV station, campus challenge, La Hispanidad, Habitat for Humanity, Circle K, Best Buddies, Celtic club, Polish club, debate society.

Athletics. NCAA. **Intercollegiate:** Baseball M, basketball, bowling, cross-country, equestrian W, fencing, field hockey W, football (tackle) M, golf, ice hockey, lacrosse, rowing (crew) W, soccer, softball W, swimming W, tennis, track and field, volleyball, wrestling M. **Intramural:** Basketball, bowling, cheerleading W, field hockey W, football (non-tackle), golf, skiing, soccer, softball, table tennis, tennis, volleyball. **Team name:** Pioneers.

Student services. Adult student services, alcohol/substance abuse counseling, chaplain/spiritual director, career counseling, services for economically disadvantaged, student employment services, financial aid counseling, health services, minority student services, personal counseling, placement for graduates, women's services. **Physically disabled:** Services for visually, speech, hearing impaired.

Contact. E-mail: enroll@sacredheart.edu
Phone: (203) 371-7880 Fax: (203) 365-7607
Karen Guastelle, Dean of Undergraduate Admissions, Sacred Heart University, 5151 Park Avenue, Fairfield, CT 06825

St. Joseph College

West Hartford, Connecticut — **CB member**
www.sjc.edu — **CB code: 3754**

- Private 4-year liberal arts college for women affiliated with Roman Catholic Church
- Residential campus in small city
- 1,037 degree-seeking undergraduates: 21% part-time, 99% women, 10% African American, 3% Asian American, 10% Hispanic American
- 663 degree-seeking graduate students
- 82% of applicants admitted
- SAT or ACT (ACT writing optional) required
- 49% graduate within 6 years

General. Founded in 1932. Regionally accredited. Men admitted to adult undergraduate degree-completion program and graduate school. **Degrees:** 192 bachelor's awarded; master's offered. **Location:** 3 miles from Hartford. **Calendar:** Semester, limited summer session. **Full-time faculty:** 76 total; 71% women. **Part-time faculty:** 170 total. **Class size:** 78% < 20, 19% 20-39, 1% 40-49, 1% 50-99.

Freshman class profile. 1,268 applied, 1,043 admitted, 226 enrolled.

Mid 50% test scores		**GPA 2.0-2.99:**	41%
SAT critical reading:	440-530	**Rank in top quarter:**	39%
SAT math:	420-510	**Rank in top tenth:**	16%
GPA 3.75 or higher:	10%	**Return as sophomores:**	74%
GPA 3.50-3.74:	13%	**Out-of-state:**	9%
GPA 3.0-3.49:	35%	**Live on campus:**	73%

Basis for selection. Decisions based on application, transcripts, SAT/ACT scores. SAT recommended. **Homeschooled:** Statement describing homeschool structure and mission, letter of recommendation (nonparent) required.

High school preparation. College-preparatory program required. 16 units required. Required and recommended units include English 4, mathematics 3, social studies 3, science 3 and foreign language 3.

2009-2010 Annual costs. Tuition/fees: $27,202. Room/board: $12,437. Books/supplies: $1,000.

2008-2009 Financial aid. Non-need-based: Scholarships awarded for academics.

Application procedures. Admission: No deadline. $50 fee, may be waived for applicants with need, free for online applicants. Admission notification on a rolling basis. **Financial aid:** Priority date 2/15; no closing date. FAFSA required. Applicants notified on a rolling basis starting 3/1.

Academics. Special study options: Accelerated study, distance learning, double major, honors, independent study, internships, liberal arts/career combination, student-designed major, study abroad, teacher certification program, weekend college. **Credit/placement by examination:** CLEP, institutional tests. **Support services:** Learning center, pre-admission summer program, reduced course load, study skills assistance, tutoring, writing center.

Majors. Area/ethnic studies: American, women's. **Biology:** General, biochemistry. **Business:** Accounting, business admin. **Conservation:** Environmental studies. **Education:** Special. **Family/consumer sciences:** General, child development, food/nutrition. **Foreign languages:** Spanish. **Health:** Nursing (RN). **History:** General. **Interdisciplinary:** Global studies. **Liberal arts:** Arts/sciences. **Math:** General. **Philosophy/religion:** Philosophy, religion. **Physical sciences:** Chemistry. **Psychology:** General. **Public administration:** Social work. **Social sciences:** Economics, sociology. **Visual/performing arts:** Art history/conservation.

Most popular majors. English 7%, family/consumer sciences 14%, health sciences 26%, psychology 16%, public administration/social services 9%.

Computing on campus. Dormitories wired for high-speed internet access and linked to campus network. Online course registration, online library, helpline available.

Student life. Freshman orientation: Mandatory. **Housing:** Special housing for disabled, wellness housing available. $250 nonrefundable deposit, deadline 6/15. Single rooms available for nontraditional students. Medical singles with private bathrooms available on a limited basis. **Activities:** Campus ministries, choral groups, dance, drama, international student organizations, music ensembles, student government, student newspaper.

Athletics. NCAA. **Intercollegiate:** Basketball W, cross-country W, diving W, lacrosse W, soccer W, softball W, swimming W, tennis W, volleyball W. **Intramural:** Basketball W, soccer W, softball W, tennis W, track and field W, volleyball W. **Team name:** Blue Jays.

Student services. Adult student services, alcohol/substance abuse counseling, chaplain/spiritual director, career counseling, student employment services, financial aid counseling, health services, personal counseling, placement for graduates, women's services. **Physically disabled:** Services for visually, hearing impaired.

Contact. E-mail: admissions@sjc.edu
Phone: (860) 231-5216 Toll-free number: (866) 442-8752
Nance Wunderly, Director of Admissions, St. Joseph College, 1678 Asylum Avenue, West Hartford, CT 06117

Southern Connecticut State University

New Haven, Connecticut — **CB member**
www.southernct.edu — **CB code: 3662**

- Public 4-year university
- Residential campus in small city
- 8,496 degree-seeking undergraduates: 16% part-time, 63% women, 13% African American, 2% Asian American, 7% Hispanic American, 1% international

- 3,273 degree-seeking graduate students
- 63% of applicants admitted
- SAT or ACT with writing, application essay required
- 38% graduate within 6 years

General. Founded in 1893. Regionally accredited. **Degrees:** 1,426 bachelor's awarded; master's, doctoral offered. **ROTC:** Army, Air Force. **Location:** 75 miles from New York City. **Calendar:** Semester, extensive summer session. **Full-time faculty:** 449 total; 80% have terminal degrees, 15% minority, 48% women. **Part-time faculty:** 624 total; 31% have terminal degrees, 11% minority, 56% women. **Class size:** 39% < 20, 55% 20-39, 5% 40-49, less than 1% 50-99, less than 1% >100. **Special facilities:** Planetarium, photonics laboratory, geospatial technology laboratory.

Freshman class profile. 5,933 applied, 3,715 admitted, 1,296 enrolled.

Mid 50% test scores		**Return as sophomores:**	77%
SAT critical reading:	430-520	**Out-of-state:**	11%
SAT math:	430-530	**Live on campus:**	68%
Rank in top quarter:	24%	**Fraternities:**	1%
Rank in top tenth:	5%	**Sororities:**	1%

Basis for selection. School achievement record, test scores most important. Special consideration to culturally disadvantaged students. **Homeschooled:** Statement describing homeschool structure and mission, transcript of courses and grades, letter of recommendation (nonparent) required.

High school preparation. College-preparatory program recommended. 16 units required. Required and recommended units include English 4, mathematics 3-4, social studies 2, history 2, science 2 (laboratory 1) and foreign language 2-3. One unit of algebra II required.

2008-2009 Annual costs. Tuition/fees: $7,179; $15,038 out-of-state. Out-of-state students pay an additional $1,278 in fees. Room/board: $8,966. Books/supplies: $1,300. Personal expenses: $250.

Application procedures. Admission: Closing date 4/1 (postmark date). $50 fee, may be waived for applicants with need. Admission notification on a rolling basis beginning on or about 12/1. Must reply by May 1 or within 2 week(s) if notified thereafter. **Financial aid:** Priority date 3/6; no closing date. Must reply within 2 week(s) of notification.

Academics. Special study options: Accelerated study, cooperative education, cross-registration, distance learning, double major, dual enrollment of high school students, exchange student, external degree, honors, independent study, internships, liberal arts/career combination, student-designed major, study abroad, teacher certification program. **Credit/placement by examination:** AP, CLEP, institutional tests. 30 credit hours maximum toward associate degree, 30 toward bachelor's. **Support services:** Learning center, pre-admission summer program, reduced course load, remedial instruction, study skills assistance, tutoring, writing center.

Majors. Biology: General. **Business:** Accounting, business admin, finance, management science, managerial economics, marketing. **Communications:** General, journalism. **Computer sciences:** General. **Education:** General, art, biology, chemistry, elementary, English, history, mathematics, physical, physics, science, secondary, social science, social studies, Spanish. **Foreign languages:** General, French, German, Italian, Spanish. **Health:** Nursing (RN), predental, premedicine, prepharmacy, preveterinary. **History:** General. **Legal studies:** Prelaw. **Liberal arts:** Arts/sciences, library science. **Math:** General. **Parks/recreation:** General, exercise sciences. **Philosophy/religion:** Philosophy. **Physical sciences:** Chemistry, geology, physics. **Psychology:** General. **Public administration:** Social work. **Social sciences:** Geography, political science, sociology. **Visual/performing arts:** Art, art history/conservation, dramatic.

Most popular majors. Business/marketing 13%, communications/journalism 8%, education 12%, health sciences 9%, liberal arts 12%, psychology 13%, social sciences 8%.

Computing on campus. 750 workstations in dormitories, library, computer center, student center. Dormitories wired for high-speed internet access and linked to campus network. Commuter students can connect to campus network. Online course registration, online library, helpline, student web hosting, wireless network available.

Student life. Freshman orientation: Mandatory. Preregistration for classes offered. **Housing:** Guaranteed on-campus for all undergraduates. Coed dorms, special housing for disabled, apartments, wellness housing available. $250 nonrefundable deposit. Students must be 19 or older to live in upperclassmen apartments. **Activities:** Bands, campus ministries, choral groups, drama, literary magazine, music ensembles, radio station, student government, student newspaper, Christian Fellowship, Newman club, Latin American students organization, black student union, People to People, students for disability rights, veterans club.

Athletics. NCAA. **Intercollegiate:** Baseball M, basketball, cross-country, field hockey W, football (tackle) M, gymnastics W, lacrosse W, soccer, softball W, swimming, track and field, volleyball M. **Intramural:** Basketball, football (non-tackle), soccer, softball, tennis, volleyball. **Team name:** Owls.

Student services. Adult student services, alcohol/substance abuse counseling, chaplain/spiritual director, career counseling, student employment services, financial aid counseling, health services, personal counseling, placement for graduates, veterans' counselor, women's services. **Physically disabled:** Services for visually, speech, hearing impaired.

Contact. Phone: (203) 392-5644 Toll-free number: (888) 500-7278
Fax: (203) 392-5727
James Williams, Admissions and Enrollment Management, Southern Connecticut State University, 131 Farnham Avenue, New Haven, CT 06515-1202

Trinity College

Hartford, Connecticut **CB member**
www.trincoll.edu **CB code: 3899**

- Private 4-year liberal arts college
- Residential campus in large city
- 2,263 degree-seeking undergraduates: 2% part-time, 50% women, 6% African American, 6% Asian American, 6% Hispanic American, 4% international
- 129 degree-seeking graduate students
- 42% of applicants admitted
- SAT or ACT (ACT writing recommended), application essay required
- 86% graduate within 6 years; 18% enter graduate study

General. Founded in 1823. Regionally accredited. **Degrees:** 542 bachelor's awarded; master's offered. **ROTC:** Army. **Location:** 125 miles from New York City, 100 miles from Boston. **Calendar:** Semester, limited summer session. **Full-time faculty:** 183 total; 93% have terminal degrees, 20% minority, 40% women. **Part-time faculty:** 72 total; 67% have terminal degrees, 14% minority, 42% women. **Class size:** 63% < 20, 29% 20-39, 5% 40-49, 3% 50-99, less than 1% >100. **Special facilities:** Library collections on Native Americans, maritime history, early American texts; nuclear magnetic spectrometer, mass spectrometer, electronic microscope, plasma spectrometer, optical diagnostics and communications laboratory, natural science field station.

Freshman class profile. 5,136 applied, 2,141 admitted, 589 enrolled.

Mid 50% test scores		**Rank in top tenth:**	50%
SAT critical reading:	620-720	**End year in good standing:**	87%
SAT math:	620-710	**Return as sophomores:**	91%
SAT writing:	630-720	**Out-of-state:**	83%
ACT composite:	27-31	**Live on campus:**	99%
Rank in top quarter:	90%	**International:**	5%

Basis for selection. School record and recommendations most important. Test scores used for math and writing placement. SAT Subject Tests recommended. One of the following required: SAT, ACT, or 2 SAT Subject Tests. Interview recommended.

High school preparation. College-preparatory program recommended. 16 units required. Required units include English 4, mathematics 3, history 2, science 2 (laboratory 2) and foreign language 3.

2008-2009 Annual costs. Tuition/fees: $38,724. One-time $25 transcript fee for new students only. Room/board: $9,900. Books/supplies: $900. Personal expenses: $900.

2008-2009 Financial aid. Need-based: Average need met was 100%. Average scholarship/grant was $34,175; average loan $3,564. 88% of total undergraduate aid awarded as scholarships/grants, 12% as loans/jobs. **Non-need-based:** Scholarships awarded for academics, leadership.

Application procedures. Admission: Closing date 1/1 (postmark date). $60 fee, may be waived for applicants with need. Admission notification 4/1. Must reply by May 1 or within 2 week(s) if notified thereafter. **Financial aid:** Priority date 2/1, closing date 3/1. FAFSA, CSS PROFILE required. Applicants notified by 4/1; must reply by 5/1 or within 2 week(s) of notification.

Academics. Math center available. **Special study options:** Accelerated study, combined bachelor's/graduate degree, cross-registration, double major, exchange student, honors, independent study, internships, liberal arts/career combination, New York semester, semester at sea, student-designed major, study abroad, teacher certification program, United Nations semester, urban semester, Washington semester. Community Learning Initiative (courses with community-based components) available. **Credit/placement**

by examination: AP, CLEP, IB, SAT, ACT, institutional tests. **Support services:** Study skills assistance, tutoring, writing center.

Majors. **Area/ethnic studies:** African, African-American, American, Asian, gay/lesbian, Latin American, Near/Middle Eastern, Russian/Slavic, women's. **Biology:** General, biochemistry. **Computer sciences:** General, computer science. **Conservation:** Environmental science. **Education:** General. **Engineering:** General, biomedical, electrical, mechanical. **Foreign languages:** General, Chinese, classics, comparative lit, French, German, Italian, Japanese, Russian, Spanish. **Health:** Premedicine. **History:** General. **Interdisciplinary:** Neuroscience. **Legal studies:** Prelaw. **Math:** General. **Philosophy/religion:** Judaic, philosophy, religion. **Physical sciences:** Chemistry, physics. **Psychology:** General. **Public administration:** Policy analysis. **Social sciences:** General, anthropology, economics, international relations, political science, sociology, urban studies. **Visual/performing arts:** General, art, art history/conservation, dance, dramatic, film/cinema, studio arts.

Most popular majors. Area/ethnic studies 10%, English 6%, foreign language 7%, history 8%, interdisciplinary studies 6%, psychology 8%, social sciences 30%.

Computing on campus. 327 workstations in library, computer center. Dormitories wired for high-speed internet access and linked to campus network. Commuter students can connect to campus network. Online course registration, online library, helpline, student web hosting, wireless network available.

Student life. **Freshman orientation:** Available. Preregistration for classes offered. Four-day session beginning Thursday before Labor Day. Advising days held in June to begin registration process; optional outdoor challenge program in early August. **Policies:** All dorms are non-smoking. **Housing:** Guaranteed on-campus for freshmen. Coed dorms, special housing for disabled, apartments, fraternity/sorority housing, wellness housing available. Community service dorm, quiet dorm, alternative social programming dorm, cooking units available. **Activities:** Jazz band, campus ministries, choral groups, dance, drama, film society, international student organizations, literary magazine, Model UN, musical theater, radio station, student government, student newspaper, Asian-American student association, Intervarsity Christian Fellowship, Encouraging Respect Of Sexualities, Friends Active in Civic Engagement and Service, Hillel, Imani, La Voz Latina, Promoting Healthy Awareness of the Body, Promoting Respect for Inclusive Diversity in Education, black women's organization.

Athletics. NCAA. **Intercollegiate:** Baseball M, basketball, cross-country, diving, field hockey W, football (tackle) M, golf M, ice hockey, lacrosse, rowing (crew), soccer, softball W, squash, swimming, tennis, track and field, volleyball W, wrestling M. **Intramural:** Badminton, basketball, football (non-tackle), ice hockey, soccer, softball, squash, tennis. **Team name:** Bantams.

Student services. Adult student services, alcohol/substance abuse counseling, chaplain/spiritual director, career counseling, services for economically disadvantaged, student employment services, financial aid counseling, health services, minority student services, on-campus daycare, personal counseling, placement for graduates, women's services.

Contact. E-mail: admissions.office@trincoll.edu
Phone: (860) 297-2180 Fax: (860) 297-2287
Larry Dow, Dean of Admissions and Financial Aid, Trinity College, 300 Summit Street, Hartford, CT 06106

United States Coast Guard Academy

New London, Connecticut — **CB member**
www.uscga.edu — **CB code: 5807**

- Public 4-year engineering and maritime college
- Residential campus in small city
- 973 degree-seeking undergraduates: 27% women, 2% African American, 5% Asian American, 6% Hispanic American, 1% international
- 30% of applicants admitted
- SAT or ACT with writing, application essay required
- 72% graduate within 6 years

General. Founded in 1876. Regionally accredited. **Degrees:** 224 bachelor's awarded. **Location:** 120 miles from New York City, 130 miles from Boston. **Calendar:** Semester, limited summer session. **Full-time faculty:** 105 total; 57% have terminal degrees, 9% minority, 21% women. **Part-time faculty:** 20 total; 90% have terminal degrees, 25% women. **Class size:** 71% < 20, 29% 20-39. **Special facilities:** Museum, research and development center, 295-foot-tall ship, ship navigation simulation facilities with bridge simulator, 10,000 gallon circulating water channel, ship model towing tank, observatory with reflector telescope.

Freshman class profile. 1,388 applied, 412 admitted, 295 enrolled.

Mid 50% test scores		**Rank in top quarter:**	91%
SAT critical reading:	560-670	**Rank in top tenth:**	54%
SAT math:	600-680	**End year in good standing:**	95%
ACT composite:	25-29	**Return as sophomores:**	96%
GPA 3.75 or higher:	54%	**Out-of-state:**	96%
GPA 3.50-3.74:	29%	**Live on campus:**	100%
GPA 3.0-3.49:	14%	**International:**	1%
GPA 2.0-2.99:	3%		

Basis for selection. Test scores, high school class rank, recommendations, essay, leadership potential as demonstrated by extracurricular activities, athletics, community affairs, and part-time employment considered. Congressional nomination not required. Applicants required to pass medical and physical fitness exams. Interview recommended. **Homeschooled:** AP and SAT Subject Tests recommended. Application should include detailed account of curriculum and course content. Students advised to take courses in math and science at a local college and have professor submit a recommendation. Recommendations from other adults required. Essay should include reasons for undertaking homeschooling, benefits realized, and how experience prepared student to succeed in college.

High school preparation. College-preparatory program recommended. Required units include English 4, mathematics 4, science 3 (laboratory 3). Math units should include algebra, quadratics, plane or coordinate geometry, or equivalent. Calculus and pre-calculus recommended. Sciences should include chemistry and physics.

2009-2010 Annual costs. All tuition, room and board paid for by U.S. government. Students make one-time entrance deposit of $3,000 to help defray cost of uniforms, books, supplies and personal computer. All students paid monthly stipend of $734.

Application procedures. **Admission:** Closing date 2/1 (postmark date). No application fee. Application must be submitted online. Admission notification on a rolling basis beginning on or about 12/15. Must reply by May 1 or within 2 week(s) if notified thereafter. Application by 11/01 recommended to allow time to complete essays and supplemental forms, obtain teacher recommendations, and schedule required physical. **Financial aid:** No deadline.

Academics. Each student issued a laptop computer. Summers involve introductory and advanced Coast Guard/professional training including opportunities to sail aboard Eagle, fly Coast Guard aircraft, become small arms qualified (rifle and pistol), learn basic shipboard fire fighting and flooding control, and perform actual search and rescue coordination at Coast Guard units. Summer between junior and senior years typically involves piloting and navigation of Coast Guard Cutters and integration into all aspects of operational afloat Coast Guard missions. All graduates commissioned as officers in U.S Coast Guard with a 5-year obligatory military service after graduation. **Special study options:** Double major, exchange student, honors, independent study, internships. **Credit/placement by examination:** CLEP, institutional tests. **Support services:** Learning center, pre-admission summer program, reduced course load, remedial instruction, study skills assistance, tutoring, writing center.

Majors. **Business:** Business admin. **Engineering:** Civil, electrical, marine, mechanical. **Physical sciences:** Oceanography. **Social sciences:** Political science. **Other:** Operations research.

Most popular majors. Biology 14%, business/marketing 16%, engineering/engineering technologies 42%, mathematics 8%, social sciences 20%.

Computing on campus. PC or laptop required. 325 workstations in dormitories, library, computer center. Dormitories wired for high-speed internet access and linked to campus network. Online course registration, online library, helpline, repair service, student web hosting, wireless network available.

Student life. **Freshman orientation:** Mandatory. Seven-week "swab summer," including 1 week onboard the Coast Guard Cutter Eagle. **Policies:** Students part of corps of cadets. On-campus residence mandatory. **Housing:** Guaranteed on-campus for all undergraduates. Coed dorms, wellness housing available. **Activities:** Bands, choral groups, dance, drama, music ensembles, musical theater, student government, student newspaper, Officers Christian Fellowship, multicultural club, Fellowship of Christian Athletes, Big Brothers and Big Sisters, Boy Scouts, Genesis club.

Athletics. NCAA. **Intercollegiate:** Baseball M, basketball, cheerleading M, cross-country, diving, football (tackle) M, rifle, rowing (crew), sailing, soccer, softball W, swimming, tennis M, track and field, volleyball W, wrestling M. **Intramural:** Basketball, football (non-tackle), golf, racquetball, soccer, softball, tennis, volleyball. **Team name:** Bears.

Student services. Alcohol/substance abuse counseling, chaplain/spiritual director, career counseling, health services, legal services, minority student services, on-campus daycare, personal counseling, placement for graduates.

Contact. E-mail: admissions@uscga.edu
Phone: (860) 444-8500 Toll-free number: (800) 883-8724
Fax: (860) 701-6700
Capt. Susan Bibeau, Director of Admissions, United States Coast Guard Academy, 31 Mohegan Avenue, New London, CT 06320

University of Bridgeport

Bridgeport, Connecticut — **CB member**
www.bridgeport.edu — **CB code: 3914**

- Private 4-year university
- Residential campus in small city
- 2,028 degree-seeking undergraduates: 31% part-time, 69% women, 36% African American, 3% Asian American, 15% Hispanic American, 13% international
- 3,295 degree-seeking graduate students
- 62% of applicants admitted
- SAT or ACT (ACT writing optional), application essay required
- 43% graduate within 6 years; 50% enter graduate study

General. Founded in 1927. Regionally accredited. Off-campus facilities in Stamford and Waterbury. **Degrees:** 269 bachelor's, 41 associate awarded; master's, doctoral, first professional offered. **ROTC:** Army. **Location:** 60 miles from New York City. **Calendar:** Semester, extensive summer session. **Full-time faculty:** 117 total; 80% have terminal degrees, 21% minority, 35% women. **Part-time faculty:** 435 total; 16% minority, 43% women. **Class size:** 71% < 20, 27% 20-39, 1% 40-49, less than 1% 50-99. **Special facilities:** Theater, recital halls, studios, exhibit rooms.

Freshman class profile. 4,337 applied, 2,709 admitted, 453 enrolled.

Mid 50% test scores		**Rank in top quarter:**	36%
SAT critical reading:	400-490	**Rank in top tenth:**	11%
SAT math:	390-490	**End year in good standing:**	55%
SAT writing:	390-480	**Return as sophomores:**	49%
ACT composite:	16-22	**Out-of-state:**	59%
GPA 3.75 or higher:	7%	**Live on campus:**	84%
GPA 3.50-3.74:	8%	**International:**	11%
GPA 3.0-3.49:	27%	**Fraternities:**	1%
GPA 2.0-2.99:	54%	**Sororities:**	1%

Basis for selection. School achievement record most important, followed by test scores, activities, trend of grades and curriculum in high school. Audition required of music majors. Portfolio required of fine and applied arts majors. Interview recommended of dental hygiene, basic studies majors.

High school preparation. College-preparatory program recommended. 16 units required. Required units include English 4, mathematics 3, social studies 2, science 2 (laboratory 2) and academic electives 5. 4 math required for math, science, computer science and engineering applicants. Chemistry required for dental hygiene.

2008-2009 Annual costs. Tuition/fees: $24,470. Room/board: $10,600. Books/supplies: $1,500. Personal expenses: $2,897.

2007-2008 Financial aid. Need-based: 268 full-time freshmen applied for aid; 263 were judged to have need; 263 of these received aid. Average need met was 69%. Average scholarship/grant was $6,725; average loan $4,915. 67% of total undergraduate aid awarded as scholarships/grants, 33% as loans/jobs. **Non-need-based:** Awarded to 1,203 full-time undergraduates, including 296 freshmen. Scholarships awarded for academics, athletics, music/drama, state residency.

Application procedures. Admission: Priority date 4/1; no deadline. $25 fee, may be waived for applicants with need. Admission notification on a rolling basis. Must reply by May 1 or within 2 week(s) if notified thereafter. **Financial aid:** Priority date 4/1; no closing date. FAFSA required. Applicants notified on a rolling basis starting 4/1; must reply within 4 week(s) of notification.

Academics. Special study options: Accelerated study, combined bachelor's/graduate degree, cooperative education, cross-registration, distance learning, double major, dual enrollment of high school students, ESL, exchange student, honors, independent study, internships, liberal arts/career combination, New York semester, semester at sea, student-designed major, study abroad, teacher certification program, United Nations semester, Washington semester, weekend college. **Credit/placement by examination:** AP, CLEP, IB, SAT, ACT, institutional tests. 30 credit hours maximum toward associate degree, 30 toward bachelor's. **Support services:** Learning center, preadmission summer program, reduced course load, remedial instruction, study skills assistance, tutoring, writing center.

Majors. Area/ethnic studies: East Asian. **Biology:** General. **Business:** General, accounting, fashion, finance, international, labor relations, management information systems, marketing. **Communications:** General, advertising, journalism, media studies, public relations. **Computer sciences:** General. **Engineering:** Computer. **Health:** Dental hygiene. **Liberal arts:** Arts/sciences, humanities. **Math:** General. **Philosophy/religion:** Religion. **Physical sciences:** General. **Psychology:** General. **Public administration:** Community org/advocacy. **Social sciences:** General, international relations, political science, sociology. **Visual/performing arts:** Graphic design, illustration, industrial design, interior design.

Most popular majors. Business/marketing 21%, health sciences 13%, liberal arts 22%, psychology 8%, public administration/social services 11%, visual/performing arts 10%.

Computing on campus. 600 workstations in dormitories, library, computer center, student center. Dormitories wired for high-speed internet access and linked to campus network. Commuter students can connect to campus network. Online library, helpline, repair service, student web hosting, wireless network available.

Student life. Freshman orientation: Mandatory, $100 fee. Preregistration for classes offered. Placement listing, registration, and orientation held during the summer with final program just prior to class. **Policies:** Student and dormitory governments plan student life activities. **Housing:** Guaranteed on-campus for all undergraduates. Coed dorms, wellness housing available. $200 deposit, deadline 5/1. Dormitories have special facilities. **Activities:** Choral groups, film society, literary magazine, music ensembles, Model UN, student government, student newspaper, interfaith center, black student alliance, social service sorority, Newman Center, Hillel, Protestant fellowship, community service project.

Athletics. NCAA. **Intercollegiate:** Baseball M, basketball, cross-country, gymnastics W, soccer, softball W, swimming W, volleyball W. **Intramural:** Basketball, racquetball, soccer, softball, tennis, volleyball. **Team name:** Purple Knights.

Student services. Adult student services, alcohol/substance abuse counseling, chaplain/spiritual director, career counseling, student employment services, financial aid counseling, health services, minority student services, personal counseling, placement for graduates, veterans' counselor. **Physically disabled:** Services for visually, speech, hearing impaired.

Contact. E-mail: admit@bridgeport.edu
Phone: (203) 576-4552 Toll-free number: (800) 392-3582
Fax: (203) 576-4941
Barbara Maryak, Associate Vice President of Admissions, University of Bridgeport, 126 Park Avenue, Bridgeport, CT 06604

University of Connecticut

Storrs, Connecticut — **CB member**
www.uconn.edu — **CB code: 3915**

- Public 4-year university
- Residential campus in large town
- 16,459 degree-seeking undergraduates: 3% part-time, 50% women, 5% African American, 8% Asian American, 5% Hispanic American, 1% international
- 6,763 degree-seeking graduate students
- 54% of applicants admitted
- SAT or ACT with writing, application essay required
- 76% graduate within 6 years

General. Founded in 1881. Regionally accredited. Students may take courses at nonresidential campuses in Groton, Hartford, Stamford, Waterbury, and Torrington. **Degrees:** 4,591 bachelor's, 35 associate awarded; master's, doctoral, first professional offered. **ROTC:** Army, Air Force. **Location:** 26 miles from Hartford, 80 miles from Boston. **Calendar:** Semester, extensive summer session. **Full-time faculty:** 1,030 total; 93% have terminal degrees, 19% minority. **Part-time faculty:** 330 total; 22% have terminal degrees, 10% minority, 54% women. **Class size:** 45% < 20, 34% 20-39, 7% 40-49, 7% 50-99, 7% >100. **Special facilities:** Museum of natural history, research center, ice hockey/skating rink, dairy bar.

Freshman class profile. 21,058 applied, 11,474 admitted, 3,604 enrolled.

Mid 50% test scores		Return as sophomores:	93%
SAT critical reading:	540-630	Out-of-state:	33%
SAT math:	570-660	Live on campus:	97%
SAT writing:	550-640	International:	1%
ACT composite:	24-28	Fraternities:	6%
Rank in top quarter:	78%	Sororities:	8%
Rank in top tenth:	39%		

Basis for selection. Curriculum, grades, rank in class most important, followed by test scores. Particular consideration given to first generation college and/or socio-economically disadvantaged applicants and applicants with special talents. Audition required of music, acting, puppetry majors. Portfolio required for art major. Interview required for design/technical theater and theater studies majors. **Homeschooled:** Statement describing homeschool structure and mission, transcript of courses and grades required. **Learning Disabled:** Students may submit disability documentation to Center for Students with Disabilities upon admission.

High school preparation. College-preparatory program required. 16 units required. Required and recommended units include English 4, mathematics 3, social studies 2, science 2 (laboratory 2), foreign language 2-3 and academic electives 3. Some programs may require additional units.

2008-2009 Annual costs. Tuition/fees: $9,338; $24,050 out-of-state. Incoming out-of-state New England residents pay 175% of in-state tuition rate for programs of study not offered at their home state university. Room/board: $9,300. Books/supplies: $800. Personal expenses: $1,640.

2008-2009 Financial aid. Need-based: 2,866 full-time freshmen applied for aid; 1,812 were judged to have need; 1,754 of these received aid. Average need met was 72%. Average scholarship/grant was $7,389; average loan $3,835. 47% of total undergraduate aid awarded as scholarships/grants, 53% as loans/jobs. **Non-need-based:** Awarded to 5,450 full-time undergraduates, including 1,814 freshmen. Scholarships awarded for academics, art, athletics, leadership, minority status, music/drama. **Additional information:** Institution offers variety of need-based financial aid programs. Financial assistance packages may include grants, loans and work-study awards.

Application procedures. Admission: Closing date 2/1. $70 fee, may be waived for applicants with need. Admission notification on a rolling basis beginning on or about 1/1. Must reply by May 1 or within 2 week(s) if notified thereafter. **Financial aid:** Priority date 3/1; no closing date. FAFSA required. Applicants notified on a rolling basis starting 3/1; must reply within 4 week(s) of notification.

Academics. 5-year Eurotech Program program combining engineering and German language, including 6-month internship in Germany. **Special study options:** Accelerated study, combined bachelor's/graduate degree, cooperative education, distance learning, double major, dual enrollment of high school students, ESL, exchange student, honors, independent study, internships, liberal arts/career combination, New York semester, semester at sea, student-designed major, study abroad, teacher certification program, urban semester, Washington semester. Winter inter-session, summer session, urban semester. **Credit/placement by examination:** AP, CLEP, IB, SAT, institutional tests. 30 credit hours maximum toward bachelor's degree. **Support services:** Learning center, pre-admission summer program, study skills assistance, tutoring, writing center.

Majors. Agriculture: General, agronomy, animal sciences, economics, horticultural science. **Architecture:** Landscape. **Area/ethnic studies:** American, Latin American, Near/Middle Eastern, women's. **Biology:** General, animal physiology, biophysics, cellular/molecular, ecology, marine, pathology. **Business:** General, accounting, actuarial science, business admin, finance, insurance, management information systems, marketing, real estate. **Communications:** General, journalism. **Computer sciences:** Computer science. **Conservation:** General, environmental studies. **Education:** Agricultural, elementary, music, physical, special. **Engineering:** Biomedical, chemical, civil, computer, electrical, environmental, industrial, materials, materials science, mechanical, physics. **Family/consumer sciences:** Family studies. **Foreign languages:** Classics, French, German, Italian, linguistics, Spanish. **Health:** Clinical lab science, cytotechnology, dietetics, gene therapy, health care admin, health services, nursing (RN), prepharmacy. **History:** General. **Interdisciplinary:** Cognitive science, nutrition sciences. **Math:** General, applied, statistics. **Parks/recreation:** Facilities management. **Philosophy/religion:** Philosophy. **Physical sciences:** Chemistry, geology, physics. **Psychology:** General, cognitive. **Social sciences:** Anthropology, economics, geography, political science, sociology, urban studies. **Visual/performing arts:** Acting, art history/conservation, dramatic, studio arts, theater design. **Other:** Puppetry.

Most popular majors. Biology 7%, business/marketing 14%, communications/journalism 6%, engineering/engineering technologies 7%, health sciences 9%, liberal arts 8%, psychology 7%, social sciences 15%.

Computing on campus. 1,318 workstations in dormitories, library, computer center, student center. Dormitories wired for high-speed internet access and linked to campus network. Commuter students can connect to campus network. Online course registration, online library, helpline, repair service, wireless network available.

Student life. Freshman orientation: Available, $60 fee. Preregistration for classes offered. Twelve 2-day sessions extending from late May to early July. **Housing:** Coed dorms, single-sex dorms, special housing for disabled, apartments, fraternity/sorority housing available. $150 nonrefundable deposit, deadline 5/1. Special interests; honors; foreign languages; older-student housing; freshmen year experience housing; global house; women in math, science, and engineering; other learning communities. **Activities:** Bands, campus ministries, choral groups, dance, drama, film society, international student organizations, literary magazine, music ensembles, Model UN, musical theater, opera, radio station, student government, student newspaper, symphony orchestra, TV station, over 300 organizations available.

Athletics. NCAA. **Intercollegiate:** Baseball M, basketball, cross-country, diving, field hockey W, football (tackle) M, golf M, ice hockey, lacrosse W, rowing (crew) W, soccer, softball W, swimming, tennis, track and field, volleyball W. **Intramural:** Badminton, baseball M, basketball, bowling, cross-country, diving, equestrian, fencing, football (non-tackle), football (tackle) M, ice hockey, lacrosse, racquetball, rowing (crew), rugby, sailing, skiing, soccer, softball, squash, swimming, table tennis, tennis, track and field, volleyball, water polo, weight lifting M. **Team name:** Huskies.

Student services. Adult student services, alcohol/substance abuse counseling, chaplain/spiritual director, career counseling, student employment services, financial aid counseling, health services, minority student services, on-campus daycare, personal counseling, placement for graduates, veterans' counselor, women's services. **Physically disabled:** Services for visually, speech, hearing impaired.

Contact. E-mail: beahusky@uconn.edu
Phone: (860) 486-3137 Fax: (860) 486-1476
Lee Melvin, Director of Admission, University of Connecticut, 2131 Hillside Road, Unit 3088, Storrs, CT 06269-3088

University of Hartford

West Hartford, Connecticut — **CB member**
www.hartford.edu — **CB code: 3436**

- Private 4-year university
- Residential campus in small city
- 5,449 degree-seeking undergraduates: 12% part-time, 52% women, 12% African American, 3% Asian American, 6% Hispanic American, 3% international
- 1,578 degree-seeking graduate students
- 57% of applicants admitted
- SAT or ACT with writing required
- 58% graduate within 6 years

General. Founded in 1877. Regionally accredited. **Degrees:** 969 bachelor's, 176 associate awarded; master's, doctoral offered. **ROTC:** Army, Air Force. **Location:** 4 miles from downtown. **Calendar:** Semester, extensive summer session. **Full-time faculty:** 337 total; 72% have terminal degrees, 9% minority, 35% women. **Part-time faculty:** 591 total; 9% minority. **Class size:** 63% < 20, 35% 20-39, less than 1% 40-49, less than 1% 50-99, less than 1% >100. **Special facilities:** Engineering applications center, humanities center.

Freshman class profile. 11,627 applied, 6,574 admitted, 1,469 enrolled.

Mid 50% test scores		Return as sophomores:	75%
SAT critical reading:	470-570	Out-of-state:	74%
SAT math:	480-590	Live on campus:	95%
ACT composite:	20-25	International:	2%

Basis for selection. Quality of academic program, school achievement record, class rank important. Test scores secondary. Employment, extracurricular activities, and community service considered. Writing samples and interview also considered. Admission committee can offer admission to alternative program. Interview and essay recommended. Audition required of music, dance, acting majors. Portfolio required of art majors. **Homeschooled:** Statement describing homeschool structure and mission, transcript of courses and grades required.

High school preparation. 16 units required. Required and recommended units include English 4, mathematics 2-3, social studies 2, history 2, science 2-3, foreign language 2 and academic electives 4. Physics, chemistry, and 3.5 math (including trigonometry) recommended for engineering and science applicants.

2009-2010 Annual costs. Tuition/fees: $28,980. Room/board: $11,238. Books/supplies: $860. Personal expenses: $1,350.

2007-2008 Financial aid. Need-based: 1,198 full-time freshmen applied for aid; 1,043 were judged to have need; 1,042 of these received aid. Average need met was 81%. Average scholarship/grant was $15,135; average loan $3,014. 53% of total undergraduate aid awarded as scholarships/ grants, 47% as loans/jobs. **Non-need-based:** Awarded to 2,676 full-time undergraduates, including 724 freshmen. Scholarships awarded for academics, art, athletics, music/drama.

Application procedures. Admission: No deadline. $35 fee, may be waived for applicants with need. Admission notification on a rolling basis beginning on or about 10/1. Must reply by May 1 or within 2 week(s) if notified thereafter. **Financial aid:** Priority date 2/1; no closing date. FAFSA, institutional form required. Applicants notified on a rolling basis starting 3/1; must reply by 5/1.

Academics. Special study options: Combined bachelor's/graduate degree, cooperative education, cross-registration, distance learning, double major, dual enrollment of high school students, ESL, exchange student, honors, independent study, internships, liberal arts/career combination, student-designed major, study abroad, teacher certification program, Washington semester, weekend college. Saturday term. **Credit/placement by examination:** AP, CLEP, SAT, institutional tests. 30 credit hours maximum toward associate degree, 60 toward bachelor's. **Support services:** Learning center, reduced course load, tutoring, writing center.

Majors. Architecture: Architecture. **Area/ethnic studies:** Women's. **Biology:** General. **Business:** Accounting, business admin, entrepreneurial studies, finance, insurance, management information systems, marketing. **Communications:** General. **Computer sciences:** General, information systems. **Education:** Early childhood, elementary, music, secondary, special. **Engineering:** General, civil, computer, electrical, mechanical. **Engineering technology:** General, architectural, computer, electrical, environmental, mechanical. **Foreign languages:** General. **Health:** Clinical lab science, health services, medical radiologic technology/radiation therapy, respiratory therapy technology. **History:** General. **Legal studies:** General, paralegal. **Liberal arts:** Arts/sciences. **Math:** General. **Philosophy/religion:** Judaic, philosophy. **Physical sciences:** Chemistry, physics. **Protective services:** Police science. **Psychology:** General. **Public administration:** Community org/advocacy. **Social sciences:** Economics, international economics, political science, sociology. **Theology:** Sacred music. **Visual/performing arts:** General, acting, art history/ conservation, ceramics, cinematography, commercial/advertising art, dance, design, dramatic, drawing, film/cinema, jazz, music history, music management, music performance, music theory/composition, painting, photography, printmaking, sculpture. **Other:** Nursing RN to BSN completion.

Most popular majors. Business/marketing 15%, communications/ journalism 9%, education 7%, engineering/engineering technologies 15%, health sciences 10%, visual/performing arts 18%.

Computing on campus. 300 workstations in dormitories, library, computer center. Dormitories wired for high-speed internet access and linked to campus network. Commuter students can connect to campus network. Online course registration, online library, helpline, repair service, student web hosting, wireless network available.

Student life. Freshman orientation: Mandatory. **Housing:** Guaranteed on-campus for freshmen. Coed dorms, single-sex dorms, special housing for disabled, apartments available. $200 deposit, deadline 2/1. Dormitories with resident faculty members, international residential college, residential college for the arts available. **Activities:** Bands, choral groups, dance, drama, international student organizations, literary magazine, music ensembles, musical theater, opera, radio station, student government, student newspaper, symphony orchestra, TV station, Hillel foundation, Protestant student organization, Newman Club, African American students association, academic department clubs, prelaw and premedical societies, Brothers and Sisters United, Global Friends Association, Malaysian student association, Turkish student association.

Athletics. NCAA. **Intercollegiate:** Baseball M, basketball, cross-country, golf, lacrosse M, soccer, softball W, tennis, track and field, volleyball W. **Intramural:** Basketball, football (non-tackle), handball, racquetball, soccer, softball, tennis, volleyball, water polo. **Team name:** Hawks.

Student services. Chaplain/spiritual director, career counseling, student employment services, financial aid counseling, health services, minority student services, personal counseling, placement for graduates, veterans' counselor.

Contact. Phone: (860) 768-4296 Fax: (860) 768-4961
Richard Zeiser, Dean of Admission, University of Hartford, Bates House, West Hartford, CT 06117-1599

University of New Haven

West Haven, Connecticut — **CB member**
www.newhaven.edu — **CB code: 3663**

- Private 4-year university
- Residential campus in small city
- 3,494 degree-seeking undergraduates: 12% part-time, 50% women, 9% African American, 3% Asian American, 9% Hispanic American, 2% international
- 1,628 degree-seeking graduate students
- 68% of applicants admitted
- SAT or ACT (ACT writing optional), application essay required
- 45% graduate within 6 years

General. Founded in 1920. Regionally accredited. Experiential learning emphasized. **Degrees:** 569 bachelor's, 57 associate awarded; master's offered. **Location:** 3 miles from downtown New Haven, 75 miles from New York City. **Calendar:** 4-1-4, limited summer session. **Full-time faculty:** 183 total; 83% have terminal degrees, 16% minority, 30% women. **Part-time faculty:** 320 total; 11% minority, 37% women. **Class size:** 47% < 20, 49% 20-39, 3% 40-49, 2% 50-99. **Special facilities:** Theater, music and sound recording studio, shoreline environmental study preserve, institute of forensic science, learning center for finance and technology.

Freshman class profile. 5,623 applied, 3,824 admitted, 1,232 enrolled.

Mid 50% test scores		**GPA 2.0-2.99:**	36%
SAT critical reading:	450-550	**Rank in top quarter:**	20%
SAT math:	450-570	**Rank in top tenth:**	7%
SAT writing:	440-550	**Return as sophomores:**	76%
GPA 3.75 or higher:	9%	**Out-of-state:**	60%
GPA 3.50-3.74:	19%	**Live on campus:**	84%
GPA 3.0-3.49:	36%	**International:**	2%

Basis for selection. Academic record, recommendations, test scores, personal essay, advanced placement or honor courses, and extracurricular activities reviewed. **Learning Disabled:** Students required to meet with Disability Services Office to receive accommodations and/or services.

High school preparation. College-preparatory program recommended. Required units include English 4, mathematics 3, social studies 2, science 2 (laboratory 2), foreign language 2, computer science 1 and visual/ performing arts 1.

2008-2009 Annual costs. Tuition/fees: $28,190. Room/board: $11,566. Books/supplies: $800. Personal expenses: $1,000.

2008-2009 Financial aid. Need-based: 1,038 full-time freshmen applied for aid; 936 were judged to have need; 936 of these received aid. Average need met was 68%. Average scholarship/grant was $15,807; average loan $3,502. 77% of total undergraduate aid awarded as scholarships/ grants, 23% as loans/jobs. **Non-need-based:** Awarded to 573 full-time undergraduates, including 274 freshmen. Scholarships awarded for academics, alumni affiliation, athletics, leadership.

Application procedures. Admission: No deadline. $75 fee, may be waived for applicants with need. Admission notification on a rolling basis beginning on or about 12/1. Must reply by May 1 or within 2 week(s) if notified thereafter. **Financial aid:** Priority date 3/1; no closing date. FAFSA required. Applicants notified on a rolling basis starting 3/1; must reply by 5/1 or within 2 week(s) of notification.

Academics. Special study options: Accelerated study, combined bachelor's/ graduate degree, cooperative education, distance learning, double major, honors, independent study, internships, study abroad, teacher certification program, weekend college. **Credit/placement by examination:** AP, CLEP, IB, SAT, institutional tests. **Support services:** Learning center, reduced course load, remedial instruction, study skills assistance, tutoring, writing center.

Majors. Architecture: Interior. **Biology:** General, ecology, marine. **Business:** Accounting, business admin, finance, hospitality admin, hotel/motel admin, international, managerial economics, marketing. **Communications:** General. **Computer sciences:** General, information systems. **Conservation:** General. **Engineering:** General, chemical, civil, computer, electrical, mechanical. **Engineering technology:** Occupational safety. **Health:** Dental hygiene, dietetics. **History:** General. **Interdisciplinary:** Global studies, nutrition sciences. **Legal studies:** General. **Liberal arts:** Arts/sciences. **Math:** General, applied. **Parks/recreation:** Sports admin. **Physical sciences:** Chemistry. **Protective services:** Fire safety technology, firefighting, forensics, law enforcement admin. **Psychology:** General. **Public administration:** General. **Science technology:** Biological. **Social sciences:** Political science. **Visual/ performing arts:** Graphic design, interior design, music management, studio arts.

Most popular majors. Business/marketing 15%, engineering/ engineering technologies 6%, security/protective services 49%, visual/ performing arts 9%.

Computing on campus. Dormitories wired for high-speed internet access and linked to campus network. Online course registration, helpline, repair service, wireless network available.

Student life. Freshman orientation: Mandatory. **Housing:** Coed dorms, apartments available. $200 nonrefundable deposit, deadline 5/1. Living/ learning communities available for freshmen majoring in business, engineering, forensic science, or music. Some dorm rooms are handicapped accessible. **Activities:** Bands, campus ministries, choral groups, dance, drama, international student organizations, literary magazine, Model UN, radio station, student government, student newspaper.

Athletics. NCAA. **Intercollegiate:** Baseball M, basketball, cross-country, football (tackle), golf M, lacrosse W, soccer, softball W, tennis W, track and field, volleyball W. **Intramural:** Basketball, cricket, football (non-tackle), racquetball, soccer, softball, swimming, table tennis, volleyball. **Team name:** Chargers.

Student services. Career counseling, student employment services, financial aid counseling, health services, minority student services, personal counseling, placement for graduates, veterans' counselor, women's services. **Physically disabled:** Services for visually, speech, hearing impaired.

Contact. E-mail: adminfo@newhaven.edu
Phone: (203) 932-7319 Toll-free number: (800) 342-5864
Fax: (203) 931-6093
Kevin Phillips, Director of Undergraduate Admissions, University of New Haven, 300 Boston Post Road, West Haven, CT 06516

Wesleyan University

Middletown, Connecticut — **CB member**
www.wesleyan.edu — **CB code: 3959**

- Private 4-year university and liberal arts college
- Residential campus in large town
- 2,748 degree-seeking undergraduates: 49% women, 7% African American, 10% Asian American, 8% Hispanic American, 7% international
- 273 degree-seeking graduate students
- 27% of applicants admitted
- SAT and SAT Subject Tests or ACT (ACT writing recommended), application essay required
- 93% graduate within 6 years

General. Founded in 1831. Regionally accredited. **Degrees:** 732 bachelor's awarded; master's, doctoral offered. **ROTC:** Air Force. **Location:** 15 miles from Hartford, 25 miles from New Haven. **Calendar:** Semester, limited summer session. **Full-time faculty:** 325 total; 92% have terminal degrees, 15% minority, 40% women. **Part-time faculty:** 34 total; 41% have terminal degrees, 26% minority, 53% women. **Class size:** 63% < 20, 29% 20-39, 3% 40-49, 4% 50-99, less than 1% >100. **Special facilities:** 11-building arts center, observatory, science center with electron microscopes and nuclear magnetic resonance spectrometers, film studies center, center for humanities, East Asian studies center, African-American studies center.

Freshman class profile. 8,250 applied, 2,245 admitted, 715 enrolled.

Mid 50% test scores		**GPA 2.0-2.99:**	1%
SAT critical reading:	640-740	**Rank in top quarter:**	91%
SAT math:	660-740	**Rank in top tenth:**	65%
SAT writing:	650-740	**Return as sophomores:**	95%
ACT composite:	30-32	**Out-of-state:**	93%
GPA 3.75 or higher:	71%	**Live on campus:**	100%
GPA 3.50-3.74:	19%	**International:**	9%
GPA 3.0-3.49:	9%		

Basis for selection. High school transcript, class rank, test scores, extracurricular activities, 2 teacher evaluations, personal statement, and other evidence of outstanding accomplishments are considered. 2 SAT Subject Test scores required with SAT score. Interview recommended. **Homeschooled:** Campus interview, statement describing home school structure and mission, transcript of courses and grades, third-party recommendation, and home-school instructor recommendation strongly recommended. Financial aid applicants should be prepared to submit GED.

High school preparation. College-preparatory program recommended. 16 units required; 20 recommended. Required and recommended units include English 4, mathematics 4, social studies 3-4, science 4 (laboratory 3) and foreign language 3-4.

2008-2009 Annual costs. Tuition/fees: $38,934. Room/board: $10,636. Books/supplies: $1,155. Personal expenses: $1,155.

2007-2008 Financial aid. All financial aid based on need. 390 full-time freshmen applied for aid; 329 were judged to have need; 329 of these received aid. Average need met was 100%. Average scholarship/grant was $26,348; average loan $3,217. 78% of total undergraduate aid awarded as scholarships/grants, 22% as loans/jobs.

Application procedures. Admission: Closing date 1/1 (postmark date). $55 fee, may be waived for applicants with need. Admission notification 4/1. Must reply by May 1 or within 2 week(s) if notified thereafter. **Financial aid:** Closing date 2/15. FAFSA, CSS PROFILE required. Applicants notified by 4/1; must reply by 5/1.

Academics. Students expected to complete 3 classes in each of following areas before graduation: natural sciences and math, arts and humanities, social and behavioral sciences. **Special study options:** Combined bachelor's/ graduate degree, cross-registration, double major, dual enrollment of high school students, exchange student, honors, independent study, semester at sea, student-designed major, study abroad, urban semester, Washington semester. 12-college exchange, semester in environmental science at the Marine Biological Laboratory-Woods Hole, Wesleyan-Trinity-Connecticut College Consortium, 3-2 program in science and engineering, teaching apprentice program. **Credit/placement by examination:** AP, CLEP, IB, institutional tests. 2 credit hours maximum toward bachelor's degree. **Support services:** Reduced course load, tutoring, writing center.

Majors. Area/ethnic studies: African-American, American, Central/ Eastern European, East Asian, French, gay/lesbian, German, Latin American, Russian/Slavic. **Biology:** General, biochemistry, molecular, molecular biochemistry. **Computer sciences:** General. **Conservation:** Environmental science. **Foreign languages:** Chinese, classics, East Asian, French, German, Italian, Japanese, Romance, Russian, Spanish. **History:** General. **Interdisciplinary:** Ancient studies, medieval/Renaissance, neuroscience, science/ society. **Liberal arts:** Arts/sciences. **Math:** General. **Philosophy/religion:** Philosophy, religion. **Physical sciences:** Astronomy, chemistry, geology, physics, planetary. **Psychology:** General. **Social sciences:** Anthropology, archaeology, economics, political science, sociology. **Visual/performing arts:** Art history/conservation, dance, dramatic, film/cinema, studio arts.

Most popular majors. Area/ethnic studies 13%, English 11%, history 6%, psychology 12%, social sciences 25%, visual/performing arts 12%.

Computing on campus. 300 workstations in library, computer center, student center. Dormitories wired for high-speed internet access and linked to campus network. Commuter students can connect to campus network. Online course registration, online library, helpline, repair service, student web hosting, wireless network available.

Student life. Freshman orientation: Mandatory. Preregistration for classes offered. Begins 1 week before start of fall classes. **Housing:** Guaranteed on-campus for all undergraduates. Coed dorms, special housing for disabled, apartments, fraternity/sorority housing, wellness housing available. 17 residence halls, 25 program houses, 122 woodframe houses. **Activities:** Bands, campus ministries, choral groups, dance, drama, film society, international student organizations, literary magazine, music ensembles, musical theater, radio station, student government, student newspaper, symphony orchestra, more than 230 organizations.

Athletics. NCAA. **Intercollegiate:** Baseball M, basketball, cross-country, diving, field hockey W, football (tackle) M, golf M, ice hockey, lacrosse, rowing (crew), soccer, softball W, squash, swimming, tennis, track and field, volleyball W, wrestling M. **Intramural:** Basketball, ice hockey M, soccer, softball, squash, volleyball. **Team name:** Cardinals.

Student services. Adult student services, alcohol/substance abuse counseling, chaplain/spiritual director, career counseling, student employment services, financial aid counseling, health services, minority student services, on-campus daycare, personal counseling, placement for graduates, women's services. **Physically disabled:** Services for visually, speech, hearing impaired.

Contact. E-mail: admissions@wesleyan.edu
Phone: (860) 685-3000 Fax: (860) 685-3001
Nancy Meislahn, Dean of Admission and Financial Aid, Wesleyan University, 70 Wyllys Avenue, Middletown, CT 06459-0260

Western Connecticut State University

Danbury, Connecticut
www.wcsu.edu — **CB code: 3350**

- Public 4-year university
- Commuter campus in small city

- 5,348 degree-seeking undergraduates: 14% part-time, 54% women, 7% African American, 3% Asian American, 8% Hispanic American
- 584 degree-seeking graduate students
- 55% of applicants admitted
- SAT or ACT with writing required
- 40% graduate within 6 years

General. Founded in 1903. Regionally accredited. **Degrees:** 804 bachelor's, 10 associate awarded; master's, doctoral offered. **ROTC:** Army, Air Force. **Location:** 65 miles from New York City, 50 miles from Hartford. **Calendar:** Semester, extensive summer session. **Full-time faculty:** 221 total; 85% have terminal degrees, 13% minority, 46% women. **Part-time faculty:** 316 total; 5% minority, 44% women. **Class size:** 28% < 20, 69% 20-39, 3% 40-49, less than 1% 50-99, less than 1% >100. **Special facilities:** Weather station, observatory, nature preserve.

Freshman class profile. 4,221 applied, 2,315 admitted, 944 enrolled.

Mid 50% test scores			
SAT critical reading:	440-540	Rank in top quarter:	19%
SAT math:	440-550	Rank in top tenth:	6%
SAT writing:	440-530	Return as sophomores:	74%
GPA 3.75 or higher:	2%	Out-of-state:	10%
GPA 3.50-3.74:	19%	Live on campus:	55%
GPA 3.0-3.49:	30%	Fraternities:	4%
GPA 2.0-2.99:	49%	Sororities:	4%

Basis for selection. Limited freshman class spaces given to students with strongest academic and extracurricular backgrounds, including test results. Essay and interview recommended. Audition required of music majors. Portfolio recommended of graphic design majors. **Homeschooled:** Transcript of courses and grades required. **Learning Disabled:** To receive services or accommodations, students must provide appropriate documentation by contacting the coordinator of disability services.

High school preparation. College-preparatory program required. 13 units required. Required and recommended units include English 4, mathematics 3, social studies 1, history 1, science 2 (laboratory 2) and foreign language 2-3. Additional credits in fine arts and computer science recommended. Academic course work in computer science, visual arts, theater, music or dance may be substituted for one of the required areas.

2008-2009 Annual costs. Tuition/fees: $7,088; $16,225 out-of-state. Room/board: $9,158. Books/supplies: $1,200. Personal expenses: $2,218.

2007-2008 Financial aid. Need-based: 686 full-time freshmen applied for aid; 614 were judged to have need; 593 of these received aid. Average need met was 55%. Average scholarship/grant was $4,725; average loan $2,823. 40% of total undergraduate aid awarded as scholarships/grants, 60% as loans/jobs. **Non-need-based:** Awarded to 151 full-time undergraduates, including 38 freshmen. Scholarships awarded for academics.

Application procedures. Admission: Priority date 4/1; no deadline. $50 fee, may be waived for applicants with need. Admission notification on a rolling basis beginning on or about 12/1. Must reply by May 1 or within 2 week(s) if notified thereafter. **Financial aid:** Priority date 3/15, closing date 4/15. FAFSA, institutional form required. Applicants notified on a rolling basis starting 4/15; must reply by 5/1 or within 2 week(s) of notification.

Academics. Special study options: Cooperative education, cross-registration, distance learning, double major, dual enrollment of high school students, ESL, honors, independent study, internships, student-designed major, study abroad, teacher certification program. Honors Interdisciplinary Bachelor's Degree: honors contract major for the highly motivated student to pursue a specialized course of study that examines a single theme or idea from the perspective of two or more disciplines. **Credit/placement by examination:** AP, CLEP, IB, SAT, institutional tests. 30 credit hours maximum toward associate degree, 60 toward bachelor's. **Support services:** Learning center, pre-admission summer program, reduced course load, remedial instruction, study skills assistance, tutoring, writing center.

Majors. Area/ethnic studies: American. **Biology:** General. **Business:** Accounting, business admin, finance, management information systems, marketing. **Communications:** General. **Computer sciences:** General. **Education:** General, elementary, health, music, secondary. **Foreign languages:** Spanish. **Health:** Clinical lab science, community health services, nursing (RN). **History:** General. **Liberal arts:** Arts/sciences. **Math:** General. **Physical sciences:** Atmospheric science, chemistry, geology. **Protective services:** Police science. **Psychology:** General. **Public administration:** Social work. **Social sciences:** General, economics, political science, sociology. **Visual/performing arts:** Art, dramatic, music theory/composition.

Most popular majors. Business/marketing 26%, communications/journalism 7%, education 11%, health sciences 8%, history 6%, psychology 7%, security/protective services 13%, visual/performing arts 7%.

Computing on campus. 928 workstations in dormitories, library, computer center, student center. Dormitories wired for high-speed internet access and linked to campus network. Commuter students can connect to campus network. Online course registration, online library, student web hosting, wireless network available.

Student life. Freshman orientation: Available. Preregistration for classes offered. Two-day program for students and parents held the weekend before classes start. **Housing:** Guaranteed on-campus for all undergraduates. Coed dorms, single-sex dorms, apartments available. $250 nonrefundable deposit. **Activities:** Bands, campus ministries, choral groups, dance, drama, international student organizations, literary magazine, music ensembles, musical theater, opera, radio station, student government, student newspaper, symphony orchestra, black student alliance, nontraditional student, Habitat for Humanity, Latin American student organizations.

Athletics. NCAA. **Intercollegiate:** Baseball M, basketball, field hockey W, football (tackle) M, lacrosse, soccer, softball W, swimming W, tennis, volleyball W. **Intramural:** Basketball M, football (non-tackle) M. **Team name:** Colonials.

Student services. Adult student services, alcohol/substance abuse counseling, chaplain/spiritual director, career counseling, student employment services, financial aid counseling, health services, minority student services, on-campus daycare, personal counseling, placement for graduates, veterans' counselor. **Physically disabled:** Services for visually, speech, hearing impaired.

Contact. E-mail: admissions@wcsu.edu
Phone: (203) 837-9000 Toll-free number: (877) 837-9278
Fax: (203) 837-8338
William Hawkins, Enrollment Management Officer, Western Connecticut State University, 181 White Street, Danbury, CT 06810-6826

Yale University

New Haven, Connecticut — **CB member**
www.yale.edu — **CB code: 3987**

- Private 4-year university
- Residential campus in small city
- 5,256 degree-seeking undergraduates: 50% women, 9% African American, 14% Asian American, 9% Hispanic American, 1% Native American, 9% international
- 6,081 degree-seeking graduate students
- 9% of applicants admitted
- SAT and SAT Subject Tests or ACT with writing, application essay required
- 96% graduate within 6 years; 24% enter graduate study

General. Founded in 1701. Regionally accredited. **Degrees:** 1,319 bachelor's awarded; master's, doctoral, first professional offered. **ROTC:** Army, Air Force. **Location:** 75 miles from New York City. **Calendar:** Semester, limited summer session. **Full-time faculty:** 1,100 total; 91% have terminal degrees, 18% minority, 33% women. **Part-time faculty:** 477 total; 72% have terminal degrees, 10% minority, 40% women. **Class size:** 75% < 20, 15% 20-39, 2% 40-49, 4% 50-99, 3% >100. **Special facilities:** Natural history museum, clean room, wind tunnel, engine testing facility, graphic workstations, robotics labs, crystal growth, nuclear accelerators, nuclear magnetic resonance spectrometers, optical spectroscopy instruments, high-resolution mass spectrometer, x-ray diffraction instruments, electron microscopes, observatories, marine studies field station, Institute for Biospheric Studies, 10,000 acres of forest.

Freshman class profile. 22,817 applied, 1,952 admitted, 1,320 enrolled.

Mid 50% test scores			
SAT critical reading:	700-800	Rank in top tenth:	97%
SAT math:	700-780	Return as sophomores:	99%
SAT writing:	700-790	Out-of-state:	94%
ACT composite:	30-34	Live on campus:	100%
Rank in top quarter:	100%	International:	10%

Basis for selection. First criterion is evidence of ability to do successful academic work. Diversity of interests, background and special talents also sought. Successful candidates usually have done honors work at secondary level, have high SAT scores, and present high degree of accomplishment in one or more nonacademic areas. Interview recommended. **Homeschooled:** Require 2 recommendations from teachers of courses taken outside home, such as community college courses.

High school preparation. College-preparatory program recommended. Students recommended to take richest possible mix of demanding academic offerings.

2009-2010 Annual costs. Tuition/fees: $36,500. Room/board: $11,000. Books/supplies: $3,000. Personal expenses: $2,050.

2007-2008 Financial aid. All financial aid based on need. 750 full-time freshmen applied for aid; 611 were judged to have need; 611 of these received aid. Average need met was 100%. Average scholarship/grant was $32,138; average loan $2,921. 91% of total undergraduate aid awarded as scholarships/grants, 9% as loans/jobs. **Additional information:** All scholarships based on demonstrated need.

Application procedures. Admission: Closing date 12/31 (postmark date). $75 fee, may be waived for applicants with need. Admission notification 4/1. Must reply by 5/1. **Financial aid:** Closing date 3/1. FAFSA, CSS PROFILE required. Applicants notified by 4/1; must reply by 5/1 or within 1 week(s) of notification.

Academics. Special study options: Accelerated study, combined bachelor's/graduate degree, double major, ESL, honors, independent study, internships, liberal arts/career combination, student-designed major, study abroad, teacher certification program. **Credit/placement by examination:** AP, CLEP, IB, institutional tests. **Support services:** Study skills assistance, tutoring, writing center.

Majors. Architecture: Architecture. **Area/ethnic studies:** African, African-American, American, East Asian, European, Latin American, Russian/Slavic, women's. **Biology:** General, biochemistry, Biochemistry/biophysics and molecular biology, molecular. **Computer sciences:** General. **Conservation:** Environmental studies. **Engineering:** Biomedical, chemical, electrical, environmental, mechanical, physics, science. **Foreign languages:** Ancient Greek, Biblical, Chinese, classics, French, German, Italian, Japanese, Latin, linguistics, Portuguese, Russian, Spanish. **History:** General, science/technology. **Interdisciplinary:** Ancient studies, cognitive science, math/computer science, medieval/Renaissance. **Liberal arts:** Humanities. **Math:** General, applied. **Philosophy/religion:** Judaic, philosophy, religion. **Physical sciences:** Astronomy, astrophysics, chemistry, geology, physics. **Psychology:** General. **Social sciences:** Anthropology, archaeology, economics, political science, sociology. **Visual/performing arts:** Art, art history/conservation, dramatic, film/cinema.

Most popular majors. Area/ethnic studies 6%, biology 9%, English 7%, history 12%, interdisciplinary studies 10%, social sciences 25%, visual/performing arts 7%.

Computing on campus. 400 workstations in dormitories, library, computer center, student center. Dormitories wired for high-speed internet access and linked to campus network. Commuter students can connect to campus network. Online course registration, online library, helpline, student web hosting, wireless network available.

Student life. Freshman orientation: Mandatory. **Housing:** Guaranteed on-campus for freshmen. Coed dorms, special housing for disabled available. **Activities:** Bands, choral groups, dance, drama, film society, literary magazine, music ensembles, musical theater, opera, radio station, student government, student newspaper, symphony orchestra, TV station, over 135 organizations available.

Athletics. NCAA. **Intercollegiate:** Baseball M, basketball, cross-country, diving, fencing, field hockey W, football (tackle) M, golf, gymnastics W, ice hockey, lacrosse, rowing (crew), soccer, softball W, squash, swimming, tennis, track and field, volleyball W. **Intramural:** Baseball M, basketball, bowling, cross-country, field hockey W, football (tackle) M, golf, ice hockey, racquetball, rowing (crew), soccer, softball, squash, swimming, table tennis, tennis, volleyball, water polo, wrestling M. **Team name:** Bulldogs.

Student services. Alcohol/substance abuse counseling, chaplain/spiritual director, career counseling, student employment services, financial aid counseling, health services, minority student services, personal counseling, placement for graduates, women's services. **Physically disabled:** Services for visually, speech, hearing impaired.

Contact. E-mail: student.questions@yale.edu
Phone: (203) 432-9300 Fax: (203) 432-9392
Margit Dahl, Director of Undergraduate Admissions, Yale University, Box 208234, New Haven, CT 06520-8234

Four-Year Colleges

Delaware

Delaware State University

Dover, Delaware — **CB member**
www.desu.edu — **CB code: 5153**

- Public 4-year university
- Residential campus in large town
- 3,159 degree-seeking undergraduates: 9% part-time, 60% women, 76% African American, 1% Asian American, 2% Hispanic American
- 375 degree-seeking graduate students
- 39% of applicants admitted
- SAT or ACT (ACT writing optional) required
- 36% graduate within 6 years

General. Founded in 1891. Regionally accredited. University has its own fleet of planes. **Degrees:** 455 bachelor's awarded; master's, doctoral offered. **ROTC:** Army, Air Force. **Location:** 46 miles from Wilmington, 100 miles from Washington DC. **Calendar:** Semester, extensive summer session. **Full-time faculty:** 205 total; 91% have terminal degrees, 51% minority, 39% women. **Part-time faculty:** 134 total; 49% minority, 52% women. **Class size:** 55% < 20, 36% 20-39, 7% 40-49, 2% 50-99. **Special facilities:** Science center, observatory, herbarium.

Freshman class profile. 7,793 applied, 3,026 admitted, 730 enrolled.

Mid 50% test scores		**GPA 2.0-2.99:**	67%
SAT critical reading:	390-470	**Rank in top quarter:**	22%
SAT math:	390-480	**Rank in top tenth:**	7%
ACT composite:	15-20	**Return as sophomores:**	58%
GPA 3.75 or higher:	4%	**Out-of-state:**	70%
GPA 3.50-3.74:	6%	**Live on campus:**	88%
GPA 3.0-3.49:	21%		

Basis for selection. High school curriculum and GPA most important. Test scores only used in conjunction with GPA. Class rank considered. Interviews upon invitation; band students audition for scholarships.

High school preparation. 16 units required. Required units include English 4, mathematics 3, social studies 2, science 3 (laboratory 3) and academic electives 4. Math units must include 2 algebra and 1 geometry course.

2008-2009 Annual costs. Tuition/fees: $6,481; $13,742 out-of-state. Room/board: $9,112. Books/supplies: $1,500. Personal expenses: $1,600.

2007-2008 Financial aid. All financial aid based on need. 764 full-time freshmen applied for aid; 687 were judged to have need; 668 of these received aid. Average need met was 77%. Average scholarship/grant was $2,392; average loan $93. **Additional information:** Students must file FAFSA by March 17 every year.

Application procedures. Admission: Priority date 4/1; no deadline. $25 fee, may be waived for applicants with need. Admission notification on a rolling basis beginning on or about 9/1. May enroll in an Early Bird program. **Financial aid:** Priority date 3/1, closing date 7/1. FAFSA required. Applicants notified on a rolling basis starting 4/1; must reply by 8/20.

Academics. Special study options: Accelerated study, combined bachelor's/graduate degree, cooperative education, distance learning, double major, dual enrollment of high school students, ESL, exchange student, honors, independent study, internships, semester at sea, study abroad, teacher certification program, weekend college. **Credit/placement by examination:** AP, CLEP, SAT, ACT, institutional tests. 30 credit hours maximum toward bachelor's degree. **Support services:** Learning center, pre-admission summer program, reduced course load, remedial instruction, study skills assistance, tutoring, writing center.

Majors. Agriculture: General, business, food science, plant sciences, poultry, soil science. **Biology:** General. **Business:** Accounting, business admin, finance, hospitality admin, nonprofit/public. **Communications:** Broadcast journalism, journalism, media studies, radio/tv. **Computer sciences:** General, computer science, data processing, systems analysis. **Conservation:** Environmental science, fisheries, forestry, management/policy, wildlife. **Education:** General, art, biology, business, chemistry, early childhood, elementary, English, French, gifted/talented, health, mathematics, middle, music, physical, physics, science, Spanish, special, trade/industrial. **Engineering:** Aerospace, electrical, geotechnical. **Engineering technology:** Architectural, civil, drafting, electrical, electromechanical, industrial, mechanical. **Family/consumer sciences:** Clothing/textiles, consumer economics, food/nutrition. **Foreign languages:** French, German, Spanish. **Health:** Nursing (RN), prenursing, preveterinary. **History:** General. **Interdisciplinary:** Historic preservation, math/computer science. **Math:** General. **Parks/recreation:** Health/fitness, sports admin. **Philosophy/religion:** Philosophy. **Physical sciences:** Chemistry, forensic chemistry, physics. **Protective services:** Criminal justice, fire safety technology. **Psychology:** General. **Public administration:** Social work. **Science technology:** Biological. **Social sciences:** Criminology, political science, sociology, urban studies. **Transportation:** Aviation, aviation management. **Visual/performing arts:** General, arts management, studio arts. **Other:** Chemical lab technology, Engineering design, Fitness promotions, Natural resources technology, Physics pre-engineering, Political science business administration.

Most popular majors. Business/marketing 17%, communications/journalism 8%, health sciences 11%, parks/recreation 8%, psychology 10%, public administration/social services 9%, social sciences 11%.

Computing on campus. 400 workstations in library, computer center, student center. Dormitories wired for high-speed internet access and linked to campus network. Commuter students can connect to campus network. Online course registration, online library, helpline, wireless network available.

Student life. Freshman orientation: Mandatory, $125 fee. Two-day program during June, July and August. **Policies:** First-time, first-year freshmen must submit written request for parking permit. **Housing:** Guaranteed on-campus for freshmen. Coed dorms, single-sex dorms, special housing for disabled, apartments, wellness housing available. $200 nonrefundable deposit, deadline 4/15. Suite style accommodations available for upper class students and honor students; residence hall available for honors students. **Activities:** Bands, campus ministries, choral groups, dance, drama, international student organizations, music ensembles, musical theater, radio station, student government, student newspaper, TV station, Wesley Foundation, commuters club, NAACP, black studies club, honor societies, Greek letter organizations, student ambassadors.

Athletics. NCAA. **Intercollegiate:** Baseball M, basketball, bowling W, cross-country, equestrian W, football (tackle) M, soccer W, softball W, tennis, track and field, volleyball W, wrestling M. **Intramural:** Basketball, football (non-tackle), rugby, soccer, softball, swimming, table tennis, tennis, track and field, volleyball. **Team name:** Hornets.

Student services. Adult student services, alcohol/substance abuse counseling, chaplain/spiritual director, career counseling, health services, on-campus daycare, personal counseling, placement for graduates, veterans' counselor. **Physically disabled:** Services for visually, speech, hearing impaired.

Contact. E-mail: admissions@desu.edu
Phone: (302) 857-6351 Toll-free number: (800) 845-2544
Fax: (302) 857-6352
L Germaine Scott-Cheatham, Director of Admissions, Delaware State University, 1200 North DuPont Highway, Dover, DE 19901

Goldey-Beacom College

Wilmington, Delaware — **CB member**
www.gbc.edu — **CB code: 5255**

- Private 4-year business college
- Commuter campus in small city
- 998 degree-seeking undergraduates: 33% part-time, 53% women
- 692 degree-seeking graduate students
- SAT required

General. Founded in 1886. Regionally accredited. **Degrees:** 167 bachelor's, 27 associate awarded; master's offered. **ROTC:** Air Force. **Location:** 15 miles from Wilmington, 36 miles from Philadelphia. **Calendar:** Semester, extensive summer session. **Full-time faculty:** 20 total. **Part-time faculty:** 32 total. **Special facilities:** Non-denominational chapel, athletic facilities and fields, fitness center, computer lab.

Basis for selection. Bachelor degree candidates must submit SAT scores and official transcripts from high school(s) and or college(s) attended. High school performance is evaluated. When necessary, interviews are requested. Interview recommended. **Homeschooled:** Statement describing home-school structure and mission, transcript of courses and grades, state high school equivalency certificate, interview required. **Learning Disabled:** Evaluation of diability and submission of documentation regarding disability.

High school preparation. 16 units recommended. Recommended units include English 4, mathematics 3 and science 3. 3 math units required for bachelor's degree applicants.

2009-2010 Annual costs. Tuition/fees: $17,880. Room only: $4,982.

2008-2009 Financial aid. Need-based: 60% of total undergraduate aid awarded as scholarships/grants, 40% as loans/jobs. **Non-need-based:** Scholarships awarded for academics. **Additional information:** Essays required for scholarship applicants.

Application procedures. Admission: No deadline. Admission notification on a rolling basis. SAT not required but recommended for associate degree applicants for placement and counseling. **Financial aid:** Priority date 4/1; no closing date. FAFSA required. Applicants notified on a rolling basis starting 2/15; must reply within 2 week(s) of notification.

Academics. Special study options: Accelerated study, combined bachelor's/graduate degree, cross-registration, double major, honors, independent study, internships. **Credit/placement by examination:** AP, CLEP, SAT, ACT, institutional tests. **Support services:** Learning center, reduced course load, remedial instruction, study skills assistance, tutoring, writing center.

Majors. Business: General, accounting, business admin, international, management information systems, management science, marketing. **Computer sciences:** General.

Computing on campus. 150 workstations in library, computer center, student center. Dormitories linked to campus network. Commuter students can connect to campus network. Online library, wireless network available.

Student life. Freshman orientation: Mandatory. Preregistration for classes offered. **Housing:** Guaranteed on-campus for all undergraduates. Coed dorms, special housing for disabled, apartments, wellness housing available. $400 fully refundable deposit. Apartment-style residence halls. **Activities:** Student government, student newspaper.

Athletics. NCAA. **Intercollegiate:** Basketball, cross-country, golf M, soccer, softball W, tennis W, track and field, volleyball W. **Team name:** Lightning.

Student services. Career counseling, student employment services, financial aid counseling, placement for graduates. **Physically disabled:** Services for visually, speech, hearing impaired.

Contact. E-mail: admissions@gbc.edu
Phone: (302) 225-6248 Toll-free number: (800) 833-4877
Fax: (302) 996-5408
Larry Eby, Admissions Director, Goldey-Beacom College, 4701 Limestone Road, Wilmington, DE 19808

University of Delaware

Newark, Delaware — **CB member**
www.udel.edu — **CB code: 5811**

- Public 4-year university
- Residential campus in large town
- 15,407 degree-seeking undergraduates: 5% part-time, 58% women, 5% African American, 4% Asian American, 5% Hispanic American, 1% international
- 3,347 degree-seeking graduate students
- 56% of applicants admitted
- SAT or ACT with writing, application essay required
- 78% graduate within 6 years

General. Founded in 1743. Regionally accredited. **Degrees:** 3,500 bachelor's, 188 associate awarded; master's, doctoral offered. **ROTC:** Army, Air Force. **Location:** 12 miles from Wilmington, 30 miles from Philadelphia. **Calendar:** 4-1-4, limited summer session. **Full-time faculty:** 1,165 total; 85% have terminal degrees, 16% minority, 38% women. **Part-time faculty:** 259 total; 39% have terminal degrees, 14% minority, 47% women. **Class size:** 40% < 20, 42% 20-39, 6% 40-49, 9% 50-99, 4% >100. **Special facilities:** Science development center, human performance laboratory, greenhouse, preschool lab, nutrition clinic, engineering research centers, 400-acre agriculture research complex, center for composites manufacturing and research, apparel design laboratory, simulated hospital rooms for nursing, physical therapy clinic, applied coastal research, Delaware biotechnology institute.

Freshman class profile. 22,491 applied, 12,586 admitted, 3,526 enrolled.

Mid 50% test scores		**GPA 2.0-2.99:**	6%
SAT critical reading:	550-640	**Rank in top quarter:**	78%
SAT math:	570-660	**Rank in top tenth:**	42%
SAT writing:	560-650	**Return as sophomores:**	91%
ACT composite:	25-28	**Out-of-state:**	73%
GPA 3.75 or higher:	37%	**Live on campus:**	93%
GPA 3.50-3.74:	26%	**International:**	1%
GPA 3.0-3.49:	31%		

Basis for selection. High school record, program of study, test scores most important. References, essay, extracurricular accomplishments considered. SAT Subject Tests recommended. Recommended honors program applicants take SAT Subject Tests. Audition or portfolio required for music or art. **Homeschooled:** Transcript of courses and grades required. Students should provide reading lists for courses they have completed. Sample portfolio of work or sample research paper recommended. Applicants should submit at least 2 SAT Subject Tests of their choice. In lieu of SAT and SAT Subject Tests, students may submit ACT with Writing score.

High school preparation. 18 units required; 22 recommended. Required and recommended units include English 4, mathematics 3-4, social studies 2, history 2, science 3-4 (laboratory 2-3), foreign language 2-4 and academic electives 2. 4 math strongly recommended for engineering, business, science or math applicants. 4 laboratory science strongly recommended for science, nursing, and engineering applicants.

2008-2009 Annual costs. Tuition/fees: $8,646; $21,126 out-of-state. Room/board: $8,478. Books/supplies: $800. Personal expenses: $1,500.

2007-2008 Financial aid. All financial aid based on need. 2,901 full-time freshmen applied for aid; 1,484 were judged to have need; 1,444 of these received aid. Average need met was 73%. Average scholarship/grant was $5,892; average loan $5,634. 43% of total undergraduate aid awarded as scholarships/grants, 57% as loans/jobs. **Additional information:** December 15 application deadline to receive scholarship consideration. Sibling/parent tuition credit plan. Senior citizen tuition credit for state residents over 60.

Application procedures. Admission: Priority date 12/1; deadline 1/15 (postmark date). $70 fee, may be waived for applicants with need. Admission notification 3/15. Must reply by May 1 or within 3 week(s) if notified thereafter. **Financial aid:** Priority date 2/1, closing date 3/15. FAFSA required. Applicants notified on a rolling basis starting 3/15; must reply by 5/1 or within 3 week(s) of notification.

Academics. Special study options: Accelerated study, cooperative education, distance learning, double major, dual enrollment of high school students, ESL, honors, independent study, internships, liberal arts/career combination, student-designed major, study abroad, teacher certification program, Washington semester. Research program, minors in 68 disciplines, five-year engineering/liberal arts option. **Credit/placement by examination:** AP, CLEP, IB, SAT, institutional tests. For credit/placement to be awarded for International Baccalaureate, applicant must have taken higher level courses and have minimum score of 4 on exams. **Support services:** Pre-admission summer program, reduced course load, remedial instruction, study skills assistance, tutoring, writing center.

Honors college/program. Program emphasizes small classes, undergraduate research, honors housing, special scholarship opportunities. Special application required.

Majors. Agriculture: Agribusiness operations, agronomy, animal sciences, business, economics, food science, ornamental horticulture, plant sciences, soil science. **Area/ethnic studies:** Latin American, women's. **Biology:** General, biochemistry, biotechnology, entomology, plant pathology. **Business:** Accounting, business admin, fashion, finance, management information systems, operations. **Communications:** General, journalism. **Computer sciences:** General. **Conservation:** General, management/policy, wildlife. **Education:** General, agricultural, biology, chemistry, early childhood, elementary, English, ESL, family/consumer sciences, foreign languages, French, geography, German, health, history, mathematics, middle, music, physical, physics, psychology, science, secondary, social science, Spanish, special. **Engineering:** Aerospace, agricultural, biomedical, chemical, civil, computer, electrical, environmental, mechanical, operations research. **Family/consumer sciences:** General, child care, family studies, family/community services, food/nutrition. **Foreign languages:** General, Biblical, classics, comparative lit, French, German, Italian, Latin, Russian, Spanish. **Health:** Athletic training, clinical lab science, clinical lab technology, nursing (RN), predental, premedicine, prepharmacy, preveterinary. **History:** General. **Interdisciplinary:** Historic preservation, nutrition sciences. **Legal studies:** Prelaw. **Liberal arts:** Arts/sciences. **Math:** General, statistics. **Parks/recreation:** Exercise sciences, facilities management, health/fitness, sports admin. **Philosophy/religion:** Philosophy. **Physical sciences:** Astronomy, chemistry, geology, geophysics, physics, planetary. **Protective services:** Criminal justice. **Psychology:** General. **Social sciences:** Anthropology, economics, geography, international relations, political science, sociology. **Visual/performing arts:** Art, art history/conservation, commercial/advertising art, fashion design, music performance, music theory/composition, piano/organ, studio arts, theater design, theater history, voice/opera.

Most popular majors. Business/marketing 18%, education 10%, engineering/engineering technologies 8%, health sciences 8%, social sciences 12%.

Computing on campus. 900 workstations in dormitories, library, computer center. Dormitories wired for high-speed internet access and linked to campus network. Commuter students can connect to campus network. Online course registration, online library, helpline, repair service, student web hosting, wireless network available.

Student life. Freshman orientation: Mandatory, $65 fee. Preregistration for classes offered. One-day summer program, plus 3-day program before start of classes. **Housing:** Guaranteed on-campus for all undergraduates. Coed dorms, single-sex dorms, special housing for disabled, apartments, fraternity/sorority housing, wellness housing available. $200 partly refundable deposit, deadline 5/1. **Activities:** Bands, campus ministries, choral groups, dance, drama, film society, international student organizations, literary magazine, music ensembles, Model UN, musical theater, opera, radio station, student government, student newspaper, symphony orchestra, TV station, Black student union, Asian student association, Cosmopolitan Club, Hillel, Hispanic student association, Indian student association, lesbian/gay/ bisexual student union, returning adult student association.

Athletics. NCAA. **Intercollegiate:** Baseball M, basketball, cheerleading, cross-country, diving, field hockey W, football (tackle) M, golf M, lacrosse, rowing (crew) W, soccer, softball W, swimming, tennis, track and field, volleyball W. **Intramural:** Badminton, basketball, cross-country, fencing, field hockey W, golf, lacrosse, racquetball, soccer, softball, table tennis, tennis, volleyball, water polo M. **Team name:** Fightin' Blue Hens.

Student services. Adult student services, alcohol/substance abuse counseling, chaplain/spiritual director, career counseling, services for economically disadvantaged, student employment services, financial aid counseling, health services, minority student services, personal counseling, placement for graduates, veterans' counselor, women's services. **Physically disabled:** Services for visually, speech, hearing impaired.

Contact. E-mail: admissions@udel.edu
Phone: (302) 831-8123 Fax: (302) 831-6905
Lou Hirsh, Director of Admission, University of Delaware, 116 Hullihen Hall, Newark, DE 19716

Wesley College

Dover, Delaware — **CB member**
www.wesley.edu — **CB code: 5894**

- Private 4-year liberal arts college affiliated with United Methodist Church
- Residential campus in large town
- 1,869 degree-seeking undergraduates
- 198 graduate students
- SAT or ACT (ACT writing optional) required

General. Founded in 1873. Regionally accredited. **Degrees:** 260 bachelor's, 27 associate awarded; master's offered. **ROTC:** Army. **Location:** 75 miles from Philadelphia, 90 miles from Washington, DC. **Calendar:** Semester, limited summer session. **Full-time faculty:** 71 total. **Part-time faculty:** 91 total. **Class size:** 55% < 20, 43% 20-39, less than 1% 40-49, 1% 50-99.

Freshman class profile.

Mid 50% test scores		**GPA 2.0-2.99:**	58%
SAT critical reading:	400-490	**Rank in top quarter:**	56%
SAT math:	400-500	**Rank in top tenth:**	24%
SAT writing:	390-490	**Out-of-state:**	66%
GPA 3.75 or higher:	6%	**Live on campus:**	87%
GPA 3.50-3.74:	9%	**Sororities:**	6%
GPA 3.0-3.49:	27%		

Basis for selection. High school performance most important. Campus interview very important. Extracurricular activities important.

High school preparation. 20 units recommended. Recommended units include English 4, mathematics 4, social studies 2, history 2, science 4, foreign language 2 and academic electives 2.

2008-2009 Annual costs. Tuition/fees: $18,530. Room/board: $8,400. Books/supplies: $1,000. Personal expenses: $750.

2007-2008 Financial aid. All financial aid based on need.

Application procedures. Admission: Priority date 4/1; no deadline. $25 fee. Admission notification on a rolling basis. Must reply by May 1 or within 4 week(s) if notified thereafter. **Financial aid:** Priority date 2/1; no closing date. FAFSA, institutional form required. Applicants notified on a rolling basis starting 1/1; must reply within 2 week(s) of notification.

Academics. Credit requirement for bachelor's degree varies according to program. **Special study options:** Double major, ESL, exchange student, independent study, internships, liberal arts/career combination, study abroad, teacher certification program. **Credit/placement by examination:** AP, CLEP, institutional tests. 15 credit hours maximum toward associate degree, 33 toward bachelor's. **Support services:** Learning center, reduced course load, remedial instruction, study skills assistance, tutoring, writing center.

Majors. Area/ethnic studies: American. **Biology:** General. **Business:** Accounting, business admin, sales/distribution. **Communications:** General. **Conservation:** Environmental studies. **Education:** General, elementary, physical. **Health:** Clinical lab science, nursing (RN). **History:** General. **Legal studies:** Paralegal. **Liberal arts:** Arts/sciences. **Math:** General. **Parks/recreation:** Health/fitness. **Psychology:** General. **Social sciences:** Economics, political science. **Other:** Biology/chemistry.

Most popular majors. Business/marketing 30%, communications/journalism 7%, education 16%, parks/recreation 6%, psychology 16%, social sciences 8%.

Computing on campus. 225 workstations in library. Dormitories wired for high-speed internet access and linked to campus network. Commuter students can connect to campus network. Online course registration, online library, helpline, repair service available.

Student life. Freshman orientation: Mandatory. Preregistration for classes offered. **Housing:** Coed dorms, single-sex dorms, apartments, wellness housing available. $175 fully refundable deposit, deadline 5/1. Floors in coed dorms are single-sex. **Activities:** Jazz band, choral groups, drama, literary magazine, music ensembles, student government, student newspaper, TV station, community action, Christian student associations, student activity board, National Coed Community Service Organization, black student union.

Athletics. NCAA. **Intercollegiate:** Baseball M, basketball, cheerleading, cross-country, field hockey W, football (tackle) M, golf, lacrosse, soccer, softball W, tennis, volleyball W. **Intramural:** Basketball, cross-country, soccer M, volleyball. **Team name:** Wolverines.

Student services. Chaplain/spiritual director, career counseling, student employment services, financial aid counseling, health services, personal counseling, placement for graduates. **Physically disabled:** Services for speech impaired.

Contact. E-mail: admissions@wesley.edu
Phone: (302) 736-2400 Toll-free number: (800) 937-5398
Fax: (302) 736-2400
William Firman, Director of Admissions, Wesley College, 120 North State Street, Dover, DE 19901-3875

Wilmington University

New Castle, Delaware — **CB member**
www.wilmu.edu — **CB code: 5925**

- Private 4-year liberal arts college
- Commuter campus in large town
- 5,461 degree-seeking undergraduates: 49% part-time, 64% women
- 4,681 degree-seeking graduate students
- 38% graduate within 6 years

General. Founded in 1967. Regionally accredited. Two 7-week sessions within each trimester in addition to regular trimester sessions and weekend modules. **Degrees:** 642 bachelor's, 26 associate awarded; master's, doctoral offered. **ROTC:** Army, Air Force. **Location:** 7 miles from Wilmington. **Calendar:** Trimester, limited summer session. **Full-time faculty:** 94 total. **Part-time faculty:** 880 total. **Class size:** 76% < 20, 24% 20-39.

Freshman class profile.

End year in good standing:	68%	**Out-of-state:**	15%
Return as sophomores:	72%		

Basis for selection. Open admission. Math and English skills testing required of all freshmen. Interview recommended. **Homeschooled:** GED recommended for nonaccredited programs.

2008-2009 Annual costs. Tuition/fees: $8,760. Books/supplies: $1,000. Personal expenses: $165.

Financial aid. Non-need-based: Scholarships awarded for academics, athletics.

Application procedures. Admission: No deadline. $25 fee, may be waived for applicants with need. Admission notification on a rolling basis. **Financial aid:** Priority date 4/30; no closing date. FAFSA required. Applicants notified on a rolling basis starting 8/5; must reply within 2 week(s) of notification.

Academics. Mentoring program for all interested incoming freshmen. **Special study options:** Accelerated study, distance learning, double major, independent study, internships, liberal arts/career combination, teacher certification program, weekend college. **Credit/placement by examination:** AP, CLEP, institutional tests. 15 credit hours maximum toward associate degree, 15 toward bachelor's. **Support services:** Learning center, remedial instruction, tutoring, writing center.

Majors. Business: Accounting, finance, human resources, information resources management, marketing. **Computer sciences:** General, programming, web page design. **Education:** Early childhood, elementary. **Engineering technology:** Software. **Health:** Preop/surgical nursing. **Interdisciplinary:** Behavioral sciences. **Legal studies:** Prelaw. **Liberal arts:** Arts/sciences. **Protective services:** Criminal justice. **Psychology:** General. **Transportation:** Aviation, aviation management.

Most popular majors. Business/marketing 29%, computer/information sciences 12%, education 13%, liberal arts 18%, psychology 11%, social sciences 10%.

Computing on campus. 516 workstations in library, computer center.

Student life. Freshman orientation: Available. Videotaped orientation distributed to all new students. Two new student orientations offered in the fall. **Policies:** Adherence to student handbook expected. **Activities:** Student government, professional fraternities/organizations, Sigma Theta Tau Nursing Society, Business Professionals of America, Alpha Delta Chi, criminal justice club.

Athletics. NCAA. **Intercollegiate:** Baseball M, basketball, cross-country, golf M, lacrosse W, soccer, softball W, volleyball W. **Team name:** Wildcats.

Student services. Career counseling, student employment services, financial aid counseling, placement for graduates.

Contact. E-mail: inquire@wilmu.edu
Phone: (302) 356-4636 Toll-free number: (877) 967-5464
Fax: (302) 328-5902
Christopher Ferguson, Director of Admissions, Wilmington University, 320 Dupont Highway, New Castle, DE 19720

District of Columbia

American University
Washington, District of Columbia **CB member**
www.american.edu **CB code: 5007**

- Private 4-year university affiliated with United Methodist Church
- Residential campus in very large city
- 6,028 degree-seeking undergraduates: 3% part-time, 62% women, 4% African American, 5% Asian American, 4% Hispanic American, 6% international
- 5,230 degree-seeking graduate students
- 53% of applicants admitted
- SAT or ACT with writing, application essay required
- 76% graduate within 6 years

General. Founded in 1893. Regionally accredited. **Degrees:** 1,483 bachelor's awarded; master's, doctoral, first professional offered. **ROTC:** Army, Air Force. **Location:** 2 miles from downtown. **Calendar:** Semester, extensive summer session. **Full-time faculty:** 578 total; 94% have terminal degrees, 17% minority, 46% women. **Part-time faculty:** 500 total; 11% minority, 45% women. **Special facilities:** Arts center, museum, theater, spiritual life center.

Freshman class profile. 15,413 applied, 8,157 admitted, 1,577 enrolled.

Mid 50% test scores			
SAT critical reading:	580-700	GPA 2.0-2.99:	4%
SAT math:	570-670	Rank in top quarter:	79%
SAT writing:	580-680	Rank in top tenth:	46%
ACT composite:	25-30	Return as sophomores:	88%
GPA 3.75 or higher:	38%	Out-of-state:	80%
GPA 3.50-3.74:	27%	Live on campus:	97%
GPA 3.0-3.49:	31%	International:	6%

Basis for selection. High school record, GPA, test scores, writing sample, recommendations very important. Academic interests and demonstrated time commitments outside classroom of interest. Motivation and seriousness of purpose taken into consideration, often revealed in level and rigor of courses taken. Extracurricular activities, class rank, leadership roles considered. SAT Subject Tests recommended. Interview optional, nonevaluative and informational in scope. Audition/interview required of music and music theater majors. **Homeschooled:** Should submit at least 3 SAT Subject Test scores. **Learning Disabled:** Supplementary application, diagnostic reports, and high school transcript required for freshman learning services program.

High school preparation. 16 units required; 18 recommended. Required and recommended units include English 4, mathematics 3-4, social studies 2-4, science 3-4 (laboratory 2), foreign language 2-3 and academic electives 3-4.

2008-2009 Annual costs. Tuition/fees: $33,283. Room/board: $12,418.

2008-2009 Financial aid. All financial aid based on need. 1,076 full-time freshmen applied for aid; 759 were judged to have need; 756 of these received aid. Average need met was 93%. Average scholarship/grant was $11,448; average loan $3,918. 63% of total undergraduate aid awarded as scholarships/grants, 37% as loans/jobs. **Additional information:** Early decision applicants must submit estimated AU institutional financial aid application by 11/15 and a FASFA as soon as possible after Jan 1.

Application procedures. Admission: Closing date 1/15 (postmark date). $60 fee, may be waived for applicants with need, free for online applicants. Admission notification 4/1. Must reply by May 1 or within 4 week(s) if notified thereafter. **Financial aid:** Closing date 2/15. FAFSA, institutional form required. Applicants notified by 4/1; must reply by 5/1 or within 4 week(s) of notification.

Academics. Special study options: Accelerated study, combined bachelor's/graduate degree, cooperative education, cross-registration, double major, exchange student, honors, independent study, internships, student-designed major, study abroad, teacher certification program, Washington semester, weekend college. More than 100 study abroad programs in 33 geographic locations around the world. One-semester, full-year, alternative spring break and language-immersion options are available. **Credit/placement by examination:** AP, CLEP, IB, institutional tests. 30 credit hours maximum toward bachelor's degree. Credit awarded for some international high school learning programs such as British A Levels or German Arbitur; Advanced Placement, International Baccalaureate higher level tests only. **Support services:** Learning center, pre-admission summer program, reduced course load, study skills assistance, tutoring, writing center.

Majors. Area/ethnic studies: American, French, German, Latin American, Russian/Slavic, women's. **Biology:** General, biochemistry, environmental, marine. **Business:** Accounting, business admin, finance, management information systems. **Communications:** Journalism, media studies, public relations, radio/tv. **Communications technology:** Animation/special effects, recording arts. **Computer sciences:** General, computer graphics, computer science. **Conservation:** Environmental studies. **Education:** Elementary, secondary. **Foreign languages:** French, German, Russian, Spanish. **Health:** Predental, premedicine, prenursing, prepharmacy, preveterinary. **History:** General. **Interdisciplinary:** Biological/physical sciences, global studies. **Legal studies:** General, prelaw. **Liberal arts:** Arts/sciences. **Math:** General, applied, statistics. **Parks/recreation:** Health/fitness, sports admin. **Philosophy/religion:** Judaic, philosophy. **Physical sciences:** Acoustics, chemistry, physics. **Protective services:** Criminal justice, police science. **Psychology:** General. **Social sciences:** Anthropology, economics, international relations, political science, sociology. **Visual/performing arts:** General, art, art history/conservation, cinematography, design, dramatic, film/cinema, graphic design, multimedia, music history, music performance, music theory/composition, studio arts.

Most popular majors. Business/marketing 17%, communications/journalism 11%, social sciences 42%.

Computing on campus. 650 workstations in dormitories, library, computer center, student center. Dormitories wired for high-speed internet access and linked to campus network. Commuter students can connect to campus network. Online course registration, online library, helpline, repair service, student web hosting, wireless network available.

Student life. Freshman orientation: Available, $140 fee. Preregistration for classes offered. 2-day programs in late June and early July. Students take placement exams and meet advisors. Parents may attend. **Policies:** Academic integrity code. **Housing:** Guaranteed on-campus for freshmen. Coed dorms, special housing for disabled, wellness housing available. $200 nonrefundable deposit, deadline 5/1. Housing for handicapped students handled individually; community service floor available. Some single-sex floors in coed dorms. **Activities:** Bands, campus ministries, choral groups, dance, drama, film society, international student organizations, literary magazine, music ensembles, musical theater, opera, radio station, student government, student newspaper, symphony orchestra, TV station, NAACP, Kennedy Political Union, Amnesty International, Habitat for Humanity, Asian students association, concert choir, Hillel, Latin American student organization.

Athletics. NCAA. **Intercollegiate:** Basketball, cross-country, diving, field hockey W, lacrosse W, soccer, swimming, track and field, volleyball W, wrestling M. **Intramural:** Basketball, cheerleading W, football (non-tackle), soccer, softball, tennis, volleyball. **Team name:** Eagles.

Student services. Alcohol/substance abuse counseling, chaplain/spiritual director, career counseling, student employment services, financial aid counseling, health services, minority student services, on-campus daycare, personal counseling, placement for graduates, women's services. **Physically disabled:** Services for visually, speech, hearing impaired.

Contact. E-mail: admissions@american.edu
Phone: (202) 885-6000 Fax: (202) 885-6014
Greg Grauman, Director of Admissions, American University, 4400 Massachusetts Avenue NW, Washington, DC 20016-8001

Catholic University of America
Washington, District of Columbia **CB member**
www.cua.edu **CB code: 5104**

- Private 4-year university affiliated with Roman Catholic Church
- Residential campus in very large city
- 3,431 degree-seeking undergraduates: 7% part-time, 55% women, 5% African American, 3% Asian American, 7% Hispanic American, 3% international
- 3,114 degree-seeking graduate students
- 81% of applicants admitted
- SAT or ACT with writing, application essay required
- 75% graduate within 6 years; 66% enter graduate study

General. Founded in 1887. Regionally accredited. Strong orientation toward service-based activities; internship and study opportunities with Congress, federal agencies, and international embassies. **Degrees:** 599 bachelor's awarded; master's, doctoral, first professional offered. **ROTC:** Army,

Naval, Air Force. **Calendar:** Semester, limited summer session. **Full-time faculty:** 352 total; 98% have terminal degrees, 12% minority, 36% women. **Part-time faculty:** 342 total; 7% minority, 45% women. **Class size:** 53% < 20, 37% 20-39, 3% 40-49, 6% 50-99, less than 1% >100. **Special facilities:** Rare book collection, on-campus nuclear reactor, vitreous state laboratory.

Freshman class profile. 5,180 applied, 4,199 admitted, 908 enrolled.

Mid 50% test scores			
SAT critical reading:	510-610	Rank in top quarter:	50%
SAT math:	500-610	Rank in top tenth:	24%
ACT composite:	21-27	Return as sophomores:	80%
GPA 3.75 or higher:	20%	Out-of-state:	99%
GPA 3.50-3.74:	18%	Live on campus:	94%
GPA 3.0-3.49:	30%	International:	2%
GPA 2.0-2.99:	32%	Fraternities:	1%
		Sororities:	1%

Basis for selection. School achievement record, including strength of curriculum, ASSET/COMPASS scores may be submitted for placement in place of SAT or ACT scores. Minimum SAT, ACT, or ASSET scores required for allied health and nursing applicants. and test scores most important. Recommendations and extracurricular activities also important. SAT Subject Tests recommended. Students admitted to School of Arts and Sciences or School of Philosophy are asked to submit SAT Subject Test scores in foreign languages for placement purposes. Audition required for music. **Homeschooled:** Statement describing homeschool structure and mission, transcript of courses and grades, state high school equivalency certificate, letter of recommendation (nonparent) required. **Learning Disabled:** Matriculated students with learning disabilities asked to submit documentation to Office of Disability Support Services.

High school preparation. College-preparatory program recommended. 17 units recommended. Recommended units include English 4, mathematics 3, social studies 4, science 3 (laboratory 1) and foreign language 2. 1 fine arts or humanities recommended.

2008-2009 Annual costs. Tuition/fees: $30,670. Room/board: $11,320. Books/supplies: $1,000. Personal expenses: $1,000.

2008-2009 Financial aid. Need-based: 721 full-time freshmen applied for aid; 561 were judged to have need; 561 of these received aid. Average need met was 80%. Average scholarship/grant was $15,519; average loan $4,011. 56% of total undergraduate aid awarded as scholarships/grants, 44% as loans/jobs. **Non-need-based:** Awarded to 1,145 full-time undergraduates, including 279 freshmen. Scholarships awarded for academics, alumni affiliation, music/drama, religious affiliation.

Application procedures. Admission: Closing date 2/15 (postmark date). $55 fee, may be waived for applicants with need. Admission notification on a rolling basis beginning on or about 3/15. Must reply by 5/1. Must reply by May 1 or within 2 week(s) if notified thereafter. **Financial aid:** Priority date 2/15; no closing date. FAFSA required. Applicants notified on a rolling basis starting 4/1; must reply by 5/1 or within 2 week(s) of notification.

Academics. Special study options: Accelerated study, combined bachelor's/graduate degree, cross-registration, distance learning, double major, dual enrollment of high school students, ESL, honors, independent study, internships, study abroad, teacher certification program, Washington semester. **Credit/placement by examination:** AP, CLEP, IB, institutional tests. All credit-by-examination awarded on case-by-case basis. No credit by outside examination given to matriculated students. **Support services:** Learning center, pre-admission summer program, reduced course load, study skills assistance, tutoring, writing center.

Honors college/program. Applicants with a combined verbal and analytical SAT score of 1300 and a high school GPA of 3.5 or above are offered admission; students not meeting these requirements may petition for admission after their first semester. About 1 in 10 matriculated students belong to the University Honors Program.

Majors. Architecture: Architecture. **Biology:** General, biochemistry. **Business:** General, accounting, finance, human resources, international, international finance, management science. **Communications:** General. **Computer sciences:** General. **Education:** General, biology, chemistry, drama/dance, early childhood, elementary, English, ESL, French, history, mathematics, music, secondary, Spanish. **Engineering:** Biomedical, civil, electrical, mechanical. **Foreign languages:** Classics, French, German, Latin, Spanish. **Health:** Clinical lab science, nursing (RN). **History:** General. **Interdisciplinary:** Medieval/Renaissance. **Liberal arts:** Arts/sciences. **Math:** General. **Philosophy/religion:** Philosophy, religion. **Physical sciences:** Chemistry, physics. **Psychology:** General. **Public administration:** Social work. **Social sciences:** Anthropology, economics, political science, sociology. **Visual/performing arts:** Art, art history/conservation, dramatic, music history, music performance, music theory/composition, piano/organ, voice/opera.

Most popular majors. Architecture 14%, engineering/engineering technologies 6%, health sciences 11%, philosophy/religious studies 7%, social sciences 16%, visual/performing arts 10%.

Computing on campus. 500 workstations in dormitories, library, computer center, student center. Dormitories wired for high-speed internet access and linked to campus network. Commuter students can connect to campus network. Online course registration, online library, helpline, repair service, student web hosting, wireless network available.

Student life. Freshman orientation: Available. Preregistration for classes offered. Held Thursday-Sunday before start of fall semester. **Policies:** Code of Student Conduct is the guiding behavioral document; medical insurance is required for all full-time students and all full and part-time international students; immunization requirement for students under 26 years of age. **Housing:** Guaranteed on-campus for freshmen. Coed dorms, single-sex dorms, special housing for disabled, apartments, wellness housing available. **Activities:** Jazz band, campus ministries, choral groups, dance, drama, film society, international student organizations, literary magazine, music ensembles, musical theater, opera, radio station, student government, student newspaper, symphony orchestra, College Republicans, College Democrats, Filipino Organization of Catholic University Students, Alpha Phi Omega service fraternity, Habitat for Humanity, Latin Alliance.

Athletics. NCAA. **Intercollegiate:** Baseball M, basketball, cross-country, field hockey W, football (tackle) M, lacrosse, soccer, softball W, swimming, tennis, track and field, volleyball W. **Intramural:** Basketball, football (non-tackle), racquetball, soccer, softball, tennis, volleyball. **Team name:** Cardinals.

Student services. Adult student services, alcohol/substance abuse counseling, chaplain/spiritual director, career counseling, student employment services, financial aid counseling, health services, legal services, minority student services, personal counseling, placement for graduates, veterans' counselor. **Physically disabled:** Services for visually, speech, hearing impaired.

Contact. E-mail: cua-admissions@cua.edu
Phone: (202) 319-5305 Toll-free number: (800) 673-2772
Fax: (202) 319-6533
Christine Mica, Dean, University Admissions, Catholic University of America, 102 McMahon Hall, Washington, DC 20064

Corcoran College of Art and Design

Washington, District of Columbia — **CB member**
www.corcoran.edu — **CB code: 5705**

- Private 4-year visual arts college
- Commuter campus in very large city
- 320 degree-seeking undergraduates: 12% part-time, 65% women
- 201 degree-seeking graduate students
- 59% of applicants admitted
- SAT or ACT (ACT writing optional) required
- 67% graduate within 6 years; 20% enter graduate study

General. Founded in 1890. Regionally accredited. Member, Washington Consortium of Colleges. **Degrees:** 67 bachelor's, 7 associate awarded; master's offered. **Location:** Downtown. **Calendar:** Semester, limited summer session. **Full-time faculty:** 23 total; 70% have terminal degrees, 9% minority, 56% women. **Part-time faculty:** 133 total; 50% have terminal degrees, 56% women. **Class size:** 98% < 20, 2% 20-39. **Special facilities:** Full partnership to Corcoran Gallery of Art, Student Exhibition space within museum.

Freshman class profile. 273 applied, 161 admitted, 49 enrolled.

Mid 50% test scores			
SAT critical reading:	440-600	GPA 2.0-2.99:	40%
SAT math:	420-550	Rank in top quarter:	20%
SAT writing:	450-580	End year in good standing:	73%
ACT composite:	19-26	Return as sophomores:	70%
GPA 3.75 or higher:	15%	Out-of-state:	94%
GPA 3.50-3.74:	15%	Live on campus:	90%
GPA 3:0-3.49:	30%	International:	2%

Basis for selection. School achievement record, art portfolio, interview, and motivation important. Letters of recommendation and personal statement encouraged. School and community activities, test scores considered. Portfolio required (CD may replace original portfolio). Essay required. Interview required of applicants living within 200 miles of the school. **Homeschooled:** Statement describing homeschool structure and mission, transcript of courses and grades required.

High school preparation. College-preparatory program recommended. Recommended units include English 4, history 4 and visual/performing arts 4. Advanced art courses recommended.

2008-2009 Annual costs. Tuition/fees: $27,380. Room only: $9,694. Books/supplies: $2,500. Personal expenses: $1,334.

2007-2008 Financial aid. Need-based: 36 full-time freshmen applied for aid; 36 were judged to have need; 36 of these received aid. Average need met was 24%. Average scholarship/grant was $7,281; average loan $4,194. 30% of total undergraduate aid awarded as scholarships/grants, 70% as loans/jobs. **Non-need-based:** Awarded to 155 full-time undergraduates, including 41 freshmen. Scholarships awarded for academics, art.

Application procedures. Admission: Priority date 3/1; no deadline. $45 fee, may be waived for applicants with need. Admission notification on a rolling basis. Must reply by May 1 or within 2 week(s) if notified thereafter. **Financial aid:** Priority date 3/15; no closing date. FAFSA, institutional form required. Applicants notified on a rolling basis starting 4/15; must reply by 5/1 or within 2 week(s) of notification.

Academics. Special study options: Combined bachelor's/graduate degree, cross-registration, exchange student, independent study, internships, liberal arts/career combination, New York semester, study abroad, teacher certification program. Mobility programs with members of Association of Independent Art Colleges, Washington Consortium Member. **Credit/placement by examination:** AP, CLEP, IB. **Support services:** Reduced course load, study skills assistance, tutoring, writing center.

Majors. Education: Art. **Visual/performing arts:** General, art, graphic design, interior design, photography, studio arts.

Computing on campus. 110 workstations in library, computer center, student center. Dormitories wired for high-speed internet access. Commuter students can connect to campus network. Online library, helpline, student web hosting, wireless network available.

Student life. Freshman orientation: Mandatory. Preregistration for classes offered. Mandatory session introducing college, museum, faculty, majors, city. **Housing:** Guaranteed on-campus for freshmen. Coed dorms, apartments available. $400 fully refundable deposit, deadline 5/15.

Student services. Alcohol/substance abuse counseling, career counseling, student employment services, financial aid counseling, personal counseling, placement for graduates, veterans' counselor.

Contact. E-mail: admissions@corcoran.org
Phone: (202) 639-1814 Toll-free number: (888) 267-2672
Fax: (202) 639-1830
Elizabeth Paladino, Director of Admissions, Corcoran College of Art and Design, 500 17th Street, NW, Washington, DC 20006-4804

Gallaudet University

Washington, District of Columbia
www.gallaudet.edu **CB code: 5240**

- Private 4-year university and liberal arts college
- Residential campus in very large city
- 964 degree-seeking undergraduates: 4% part-time, 55% women, 10% African American, 5% Asian American, 8% Hispanic American, 2% Native American, 6% international
- 517 degree-seeking graduate students
- 64% of applicants admitted
- SAT or ACT (ACT writing recommended), application essay required

General. Founded in 1857. Regionally accredited. Only liberal arts university in the world designed exclusively for deaf and hard of hearing students. Bilingual (English/American Sign Language), multicultural environment, assistive devices (TTY's or campus phones, closed captioned television and campus films), specially-designed classrooms and dormitories available. **Degrees:** 198 bachelor's awarded; master's, doctoral offered. **Calendar:** Semester, limited summer session. **Full-time faculty:** 235 total. **Class size:** 92% < 20, 8% 20-39. **Special facilities:** Gallaudet Interpreting Services provides interpreters for university-related events.

Freshman class profile.

Mid 50% test scores		**GPA 2.0-2.99:**	13%
ACT composite:	15-20	**Out-of-state:**	99%
GPA 3.50-3.74:	23%	**International:**	5%
GPA 3.0-3.49:	64%		

Basis for selection. Applicants with hearing loss who show evidence of academic ability and motivation considered. Test scores, grades, class rank, essay, recommendation important. Interview recommended. **Learning Disabled:** Untimed tests, psychological evaluations confirming disabilities required.

High school preparation. College-preparatory program recommended. 16 units recommended. Recommended units include English 4, mathematics 4, social studies 4, history 4, science 4 (laboratory 2).

2008-2009 Annual costs. Tuition/fees: $11,226. Students from developing countries may apply for reduction in percentage of tuition surcharge. Room/board: $9,340. Books/supplies: $914. Personal expenses: $3,210.

2007-2008 Financial aid. Non-need-based: Scholarships awarded for academics. **Additional information:** Institution receives substantial aid from state vocational rehabilitation agencies, supplemented by institutional grants when needed.

Application procedures. Admission: No deadline. $50 fee, may be waived for applicants with need. Admission notification on a rolling basis. **Financial aid:** Priority date 7/1; no closing date. FAFSA, institutional form required. Applicants notified on a rolling basis starting 4/1; must reply within 4 week(s) of notification.

Academics. Undergraduate degree program open to deaf and hard of hearing students and a limited number of hearing students; visiting and exchange student programs available to any qualified student. **Special study options:** Accelerated study, combined bachelor's/graduate degree, cross-registration, distance learning, double major, ESL, honors, independent study, internships, study abroad, teacher certification program. Experiential programs off-campus including orientation program for employers of deaf students and paraprofessional jobs on campus, programs for interpreter-assisted mainstreaming of students into area colleges such as Georgetown University, George Mason University, Catholic University, Howard University. **Credit/placement by examination:** AP, CLEP, institutional tests. **Support services:** Learning center, pre-admission summer program, reduced course load, remedial instruction, study skills assistance, tutoring, writing center.

Majors. Biology: General. **Business:** General, accounting, business admin, entrepreneurial studies, management information systems. **Communications:** General, broadcast journalism. **Computer sciences:** General, computer science, information systems. **Education:** General, art, Deaf/hearing impaired, early childhood, elementary, family/consumer sciences, multiple handicapped, physical, secondary. **Family/consumer sciences:** General, child care, food/nutrition. **Foreign languages:** American Sign Language, French, Spanish. **Health:** Recreational therapy. **History:** General. **Math:** General. **Parks/recreation:** Facilities management. **Philosophy/religion:** Philosophy. **Physical sciences:** Chemistry, physics. **Psychology:** General. **Public administration:** Social work. **Social sciences:** Criminology, economics, political science, sociology. **Visual/performing arts:** General, art history/conservation, commercial/advertising art, dramatic, studio arts.

Computing on campus. 352 workstations in dormitories, library, computer center, student center. Dormitories wired for high-speed internet access and linked to campus network. Commuter students can connect to campus network. Online course registration, online library, helpline, repair service, student web hosting, wireless network available.

Student life. Freshman orientation: Mandatory. Preregistration for classes offered. Held 1 week before beginning of semester. **Policies:** No alcohol allowed in freshman dorms; no smoking in residence halls. Only full-time students may reside in dorms. All dormitories equipped for deaf and hard of hearing students. **Housing:** Guaranteed on-campus for freshmen. Coed dorms, special housing for disabled available. $150 fully refundable deposit, deadline 7/18. **Activities:** Campus ministries, dance, drama, international student organizations, literary magazine, student government, Asian Pacific association, black deaf student union, Hispanic student association, literary society.

Athletics. NCAA. **Intercollegiate:** Baseball M, basketball, cross-country, football (tackle) M, soccer, softball W, swimming, tennis, track and field, volleyball, wrestling M. **Intramural:** Basketball, football (non-tackle) M, softball, volleyball. **Team name:** Bisons.

Student services. Adult student services, alcohol/substance abuse counseling, chaplain/spiritual director, career counseling, student employment services, health services, minority student services, on-campus daycare, personal counseling, placement for graduates. **Physically disabled:** Services for visually, speech, hearing impaired.

Contact. E-mail: admissions@gallaudet.edu
Phone: (202) 651-5750 Toll-free number: (800) 995-0550
Fax: (202) 651-5774
Charity Reedy-Hines, Director of Admissions, Gallaudet University, 800 Florida Avenue, NE, Washington, DC 20002

George Washington University

Washington, District of Columbia **CB member**
www.gwu.edu **CB code: 5246**

- Private 4-year university
- Residential campus in very large city

- 10,291 degree-seeking undergraduates: 7% part-time, 56% women, 7% African American, 10% Asian American, 7% Hispanic American, 5% international
- 14,526 graduate students
- 37% of applicants admitted
- SAT or ACT (ACT writing recommended), application essay required
- 81% graduate within 6 years

General. Founded in 1821. Regionally accredited. **Degrees:** 2,485 bachelor's, 207 associate awarded; master's, doctoral, first professional offered. **ROTC:** Army, Naval, Air Force. **Calendar:** Semester, extensive summer session. **Full-time faculty:** 861 total; 91% have terminal degrees, 19% minority, 36% women. **Part-time faculty:** 1,219 total; 29% have terminal degrees, 15% minority, 43% women. **Class size:** 56% < 20, 27% 20-39, 6% 40-49, 7% 50-99, 4% >100. **Special facilities:** Observatory.

Freshman class profile. 19,430 applied, 7,261 admitted, 2,461 enrolled.

Mid 50% test scores			
SAT critical reading:	590-680	Rank in top tenth:	67%
SAT math:	600-690	Return as sophomores:	91%
SAT writing:	600-690	Out-of-state:	99%
ACT composite:	25-30	Live on campus:	98%
Rank in top quarter:	93%	International:	6%

Basis for selection. GED not accepted. Strong college-preparatory program, 3.0 GPA and class rank in top third important. Teacher and counselor recommendation and personal statement required. SAT Subject Tests recommended. SAT Subject Tests required for applicants to 7-year BA/MD and integrated engineering/MD programs (any math and any science); early admission applicants (any math, student's choice); and recommended for all for admission and placement. Interview recommended for all, required of early admission applicants. Audition required of bachelor of music applicants.

High school preparation. College-preparatory program required. Required and recommended units include English 4, mathematics 2-4, social studies 2-4, science 2-4 (laboratory 1) and foreign language 2-4. One physics, 1 chemistry, and additional 1 unit in math required for School of Engineering and Applied Science.

2008-2009 Annual costs. Tuition/fees: $40,437. Tuition stays fixed until student graduates, for a maximum of five years. Room/board: $9,920. Books/supplies: $1,000. Personal expenses: $1,350.

2007-2008 Financial aid. **Need-based:** 1,028 full-time freshmen applied for aid; 774 were judged to have need; 730 of these received aid. Average need met was 92%. Average scholarship/grant was $22,804; average loan $5,561. 71% of total undergraduate aid awarded as scholarships/grants, 29% as loans/jobs. **Non-need-based:** Awarded to 3,346 full-time undergraduates, including 476 freshmen. Scholarships awarded for academics, art, athletics, music/drama, ROTC. **Additional information:** Auditions required for performing arts scholarships.

Application procedures. **Admission:** Closing date 1/10. $65 fee, may be waived for applicants with need. Admission notification 4/1. Admission notification on a rolling basis. Must reply by May 1 or within 2 week(s) if notified thereafter. Applications received after 2/1 reviewed on space-available basis. Supplemental applications required for honors program, 7-year integrated engineering/law program, integrated engineering/MD program. **Financial aid:** Closing date 2/1. FAFSA, CSS PROFILE required. Applicants notified on a rolling basis starting 3/24; must reply by 5/1.

Academics. **Special study options:** Accelerated study, cooperative education, cross-registration, distance learning, double major, dual enrollment of high school students, honors, independent study, internships, liberal arts/career combination, student-designed major, study abroad. 7-year integrated BA/MD liberal arts program, 8-year integrated engineering/JD and engineering/MD programs. **Credit/placement by examination:** AP, CLEP, IB, institutional tests. 30 credit hours maximum toward bachelor's degree. **Support services:** Pre-admission summer program, reduced course load, tutoring.

Majors. **Area/ethnic studies:** American, European, Latin American, Near/Middle Eastern. **Biology:** General, biomedical sciences, biophysics, pharmacology. **Business:** Accounting, business admin, finance, international, management information systems, tourism promotion. **Communications:** General, journalism, political. **Computer sciences:** General, information systems. **Conservation:** General, environmental studies. **Education:** Physical. **Engineering:** General, biomedical, civil, computer, electrical, mechanical. **Foreign languages:** General, Arabic, Chinese, classics, French, German, Hebrew, Italian, Japanese, Latin, Portuguese, Romance, Russian, Spanish. **Health:** Audiology/speech pathology, clinical lab technology, cytotechnology, physician assistant, sonography. **History:** General. **Liberal arts:** Arts/sciences. **Math:** General, applied, statistics. **Parks/recreation:** Exercise sciences. **Philosophy/religion:** Judaic, philosophy, religion. **Physical sciences:** Chemistry, geology, physics. **Protective services:** Criminal justice, police science. **Psychology:** General. **Public administration:** Human services, policy analysis. **Social sciences:** Anthropology, archaeology, economics, geography, international relations, political science, sociology. **Visual/performing arts:** General, art history/conservation, dance, dramatic, interior design, studio arts, theater history.

Most popular majors. Business/marketing 16%, psychology 8%, social sciences 39%.

Computing on campus. 600 workstations in dormitories, library, computer center, student center. Dormitories linked to campus network. Commuter students can connect to campus network. Repair service available.

Student life. **Housing:** Guaranteed on-campus for freshmen. Coed dorms, apartments, fraternity/sorority housing, wellness housing available. $800 nonrefundable deposit, deadline 5/1. **Activities:** Bands, choral groups, dance, drama, film society, international student organizations, literary magazine, music ensembles, Model UN, musical theater, radio station, student government, student newspaper, TV station, religious groups, national political party organizations, ethnic, social action, public affairs groups.

Athletics. NCAA. **Intercollegiate:** Baseball M, basketball, cross-country, diving, golf M, gymnastics W, lacrosse W, rowing (crew), soccer, softball W, squash W, swimming, tennis, volleyball W, water polo. **Intramural:** Basketball, football (tackle) M, golf, racquetball, soccer, softball, table tennis, tennis, volleyball. **Team name:** Colonials.

Student services. Alcohol/substance abuse counseling, career counseling, student employment services, financial aid counseling, health services, on-campus daycare, personal counseling, placement for graduates, veterans' counselor. **Physically disabled:** Services for visually, speech, hearing impaired.

Contact. E-mail: gwadm@gwu.edu
Phone: (202) 994-6040 Toll-free number: (800) 447-3765
Fax: (202) 994-0325
Kathryn Napper, Executive Dean for Undergraduate Admissions, George Washington University, 2121 I Street NW, Suite 201, Washington, DC 20052

Georgetown University

Washington, District of Columbia **CB member**
www.georgetown.edu **CB code: 5244**

- Private 4-year university affiliated with Roman Catholic Church
- Residential campus in very large city
- 6,692 degree-seeking undergraduates: 2% part-time, 54% women, 7% African American, 10% Asian American, 7% Hispanic American, 5% international
- 8,076 degree-seeking graduate students
- 19% of applicants admitted
- SAT or ACT (ACT writing optional), application essay, interview required
- 93% graduate within 6 years; 20% enter graduate study

General. Founded in 1789. Regionally accredited. **Degrees:** 2,170 bachelor's awarded; master's, doctoral, first professional offered. **ROTC:** Army, Naval, Air Force. **Location:** 1.5 miles from downtown. **Calendar:** Semester, extensive summer session. **Full-time faculty:** 845 total; 88% have terminal degrees, 15% minority, 38% women. **Part-time faculty:** 744 total; 61% have terminal degrees, 8% minority, 36% women. **Special facilities:** Observatory, language learning technology lab with satellite link, library with special collections including archives, rare books, prints, manuscripts dealing with medieval and early modern periods, and American history.

Freshman class profile. 18,696 applied, 3,514 admitted, 1,571 enrolled.

Mid 50% test scores			
SAT critical reading:	650-740	Return as sophomores:	95%
SAT math:	660-750	Out-of-state:	97%
ACT composite:	26-33	Live on campus:	99%
End year in good standing:	100%	International:	5%

Basis for selection. School academic record most important, in addition to test scores, essays, extracurricular activities, interview, and recommendations. Special consideration given to qualified minorities, athletes, internationals, and alumni relatives. SAT Subject Tests recommended. Interview required unless not possible to assign based on geographic area; portfolio recommended for fine arts majors.

High school preparation. Required units include English 4, mathematics 2, social studies 2, history 2, science 1 and foreign language 2. Additional units in science, math, and foreign language recommended for some programs.

2008-2009 Annual costs. Tuition/fees: $37,947. Room/board: $12,753. Books/supplies: $1,060. Personal expenses: $1,620.

2008-2009 Financial aid. Non-need-based: Scholarships awarded for athletics.

Application procedures. Admission: Closing date 1/10 (receipt date). $65 fee, may be waived for applicants with need. Application must be submitted on paper. Admission notification 4/1. Must reply by May 1 or within 2 week(s) if notified thereafter. Early Action plan limits students from applying to binding Early Decision programs. **Financial aid:** Closing date 2/1. FAFSA, CSS PROFILE required. Applicants notified by 4/1; must reply by 5/1 or within 2 week(s) of notification.

Academics. Early assurance program to university's medical and law schools. **Special study options:** Combined bachelor's/graduate degree, cross-registration, double major, ESL, honors, independent study, internships, student-designed major, study abroad, Washington semester. **Credit/placement by examination:** AP, CLEP, IB, institutional tests. **Support services:** Learning center, pre-admission summer program, study skills assistance, tutoring, writing center.

Majors. Area/ethnic studies: American, women's. **Biology:** General, biochemistry, biomedical sciences, neurobiology/physiology. **Business:** Accounting, business admin, finance, international, marketing. **Computer sciences:** Computer science. **Foreign languages:** Arabic, Chinese, classics, comparative lit, French, German, Italian, Japanese, linguistics, Portuguese, Russian, Spanish. **Health:** Health care admin, international public health, nursing (RN). **History:** General. **Interdisciplinary:** Biological/physical sciences, medieval/Renaissance, peace/conflict, science/society. **Liberal arts:** Arts/sciences. **Math:** General. **Philosophy/religion:** Philosophy, religion. **Physical sciences:** Chemistry, physics. **Psychology:** General. **Social sciences:** Anthropology, economics, international relations, political science, sociology. **Visual/performing arts:** Art, art history/conservation, studio arts.

Most popular majors. Business/marketing 26%, English 8%, foreign language 7%, health sciences 6%, social sciences 32%.

Computing on campus. 400 workstations in dormitories, library, computer center. Dormitories wired for high-speed internet access and linked to campus network. Commuter students can connect to campus network. Online course registration, helpline, repair service, wireless network available.

Student life. Freshman orientation: Mandatory, $160 fee. Preregistration for classes offered. Student volunteer-led program. **Policies:** Freshmen and sophomores required to live on campus. Upperclass students obtain housing via lottery process. **Housing:** Guaranteed on-campus for freshmen. Coed dorms, special housing for disabled, apartments, wellness housing available. **Activities:** Bands, choral groups, dance, drama, film society, literary magazine, music ensembles, musical theater, radio station, student government, student newspaper, symphony orchestra, TV station, over 120 student organizations.

Athletics. NCAA. **Intercollegiate:** Baseball M, basketball, cross-country, diving, field hockey W, football (tackle) M, golf, lacrosse, rowing (crew), sailing, soccer, softball W, swimming, tennis, track and field, volleyball W. **Intramural:** Basketball, cross-country, football (non-tackle), golf, handball, racquetball, skiing, soccer, softball, squash, table tennis, tennis, volleyball. **Team name:** Hoyas.

Student services. Alcohol/substance abuse counseling, chaplain/spiritual director, career counseling, student employment services, financial aid counseling, health services, minority student services, on-campus daycare, personal counseling, placement for graduates, women's services. **Physically disabled:** Services for visually, hearing impaired.

Contact. E-mail: guadmiss@georgetown.edu
Phone: (202) 687-3600 Fax: (202) 687-5084
Charles Deacon, Dean of Admissions, Georgetown University, 103 White-Gravenor, Washington, DC 20057-1002

Howard University

Washington, District of Columbia — **CB member**
www.howard.edu — **CB code: 5297**

- Private 4-year university
- Residential campus in very large city
- 7,086 degree-seeking undergraduates: 6% part-time, 66% women, 49% African American, 1% Hispanic American, 4% international
- 3,175 degree-seeking graduate students
- 49% of applicants admitted
- SAT or ACT with writing required
- 65% graduate within 6 years; 20% enter graduate study

General. Founded in 1867. Regionally accredited. 5 campuses. 25 major research centers and several special programs. **Degrees:** 1,400 bachelor's awarded; master's, doctoral, first professional offered. **ROTC:** Army, Air Force. **Location:** 38 miles from Baltimore, 105 miles from Richmond, Virginia. **Calendar:** Semester, extensive summer session. **Full-time faculty:** 1,064 total; 91% have terminal degrees, 80% minority, 42% women. **Part-time faculty:** 456 total; 77% have terminal degrees, 81% minority, 45% women. **Class size:** 62% < 20, 29% 20-39, 5% 40-49, 3% 50-99, less than 1% >100. **Special facilities:** Research center, including museum and archives, with collections on Africa and persons of African descent; international affairs center.

Freshman class profile. 9,750 applied, 4,731 admitted, 1,464 enrolled.

Mid 50% test scores		**GPA 2.0-2.99:**	26%
SAT critical reading:	470-670	**Rank in top quarter:**	55%
SAT math:	460-680	**Rank in top tenth:**	26%
SAT writing:	430-670	**End year in good standing:**	85%
ACT composite:	19-29	**Return as sophomores:**	85%
GPA 3.75 or higher:	14%	**Out-of-state:**	98%
GPA 3.50-3.74:	18%	**Live on campus:**	92%
GPA 3.0-3.49:	42%	**International:**	3%

Basis for selection. High school achievement record, test scores most important. Requirements vary from college to college. SAT Subject Tests recommended. Dental Hygiene Aptitude Test required of dental hygiene applicants. Essay recommended; required of Early Action applicants. Audition required of music, drama majors. Portfolio required of art, architecture majors. Interview recommended for pharmacy and pharmaceutical programs, physician assistant majors. **Homeschooled:** Must have GED.

High school preparation. 16 units required; 21 recommended. Required and recommended units include English 4, mathematics 2-3, social studies 2, science 2, foreign language 2 and academic electives 4. 4 units of academic elective must be academic courses counted toward graduation.

2008-2009 Annual costs. Tuition/fees: $15,010. Room/board: $7,436. Books/supplies: $1,300. Personal expenses: $1,800.

2007-2008 Financial aid. Need-based: 1,396 full-time freshmen applied for aid; 1,270 were judged to have need; 1,210 of these received aid. Average scholarship/grant was $2,578; average loan $4,730. 28% of total undergraduate aid awarded as scholarships/grants, 72% as loans/jobs. **Non-need-based:** Awarded to 2,200 full-time undergraduates, including 473 freshmen. Scholarships awarded for academics, art, athletics, music/drama.

Application procedures. Admission: Priority date 11/1; deadline 2/15 (receipt date). $45 fee. Admission notification on a rolling basis beginning on or about 4/15. Must reply by 12/24. Must reply by May 1 or within 4 week(s) if notified thereafter. Fall term procedures for applicants does not differ from the spring, however spring term applicants stand a better chance of acceptance. **Financial aid:** Priority date 2/15, closing date 8/15. FAFSA, institutional form required. Applicants notified on a rolling basis starting 4/1; must reply by 8/1 or within 4 week(s) of notification.

Academics. Special study options: Accelerated study, combined bachelor's/graduate degree, cooperative education, cross-registration, distance learning, double major, dual enrollment of high school students, exchange student, honors, independent study, internships, student-designed major, study abroad, teacher certification program. **Credit/placement by examination:** AP, CLEP, IB, SAT, ACT, institutional tests. 60 credit hours maximum toward bachelor's degree. **Support services:** Learning center, pre-admission summer program, reduced course load, remedial instruction, study skills assistance, tutoring, writing center.

Majors. Architecture: Architecture. **Area/ethnic studies:** African, African-American. **Biology:** General. **Business:** Accounting, business admin, fashion, finance, hospitality admin, hospitality/recreation, insurance, international, management information systems, market research. **Communications:** General, broadcast journalism, journalism, radio/tv. **Computer sciences:** Information systems, systems analysis. **Education:** Art, English, health, music, physical. **Engineering:** Chemical, civil, computer, electrical, mechanical, systems. **Foreign languages:** Ancient Greek, classics, French, German, modern Greek, Russian, Spanish. **Health:** Clinical lab science, medical radiologic technology/radiation therapy, music therapy, physician assistant, recreational therapy. **History:** General. **Interdisciplinary:** Nutrition sciences. **Math:** General. **Parks/recreation:** General. **Philosophy/religion:** Philosophy. **Physical sciences:** Chemistry, physics. **Psychology:** General. **Social sciences:** Anthropology, economics, political science, sociology. **Visual/performing arts:** General, art, art history/conservation, arts management, conducting, dance, design, interior design, jazz, music history, music management, music theory/composition, piano/organ, theater arts management, theater design, theater history, voice/opera.

Most popular majors. Biology 7%, business/marketing 18%, communications/journalism 16%, health sciences 22%, psychology 6%, social sciences 6%.

Computing on campus. 7,006 workstations in dormitories, library, computer center, student center. Dormitories wired for high-speed internet access and linked to campus network. Commuter students can connect to campus network. Online course registration, online library, helpline, student web hosting, wireless network available.

Student life. Freshman orientation: Mandatory. Preregistration for classes offered. Held during the summer. **Housing:** Guaranteed on-campus for freshmen. Coed dorms, single-sex dorms, apartments, wellness housing available. $200 nonrefundable deposit, deadline 4/1. **Activities:** Bands, campus ministries, choral groups, dance, drama, film society, international student organizations, literary magazine, music ensembles, musical theater, opera, radio station, student government, student newspaper, symphony orchestra, TV station, Absalom Jones student association, Adventist committee, Baptist student union, Christian Science organization, Christian Fellowship-Igbimo Otito, Lutheran student organization, Muslim students, Wesley Foundation Methodist Fellowship, William J. Seymour Pentacostal Fellowship, academic honorary societies.

Athletics. NCAA. **Intercollegiate:** Baseball M, basketball, bowling, cross-country, diving, football (tackle) M, golf W, gymnastics, lacrosse W, soccer, softball W, swimming, tennis, track and field, volleyball W, wrestling M. **Intramural:** Badminton W, basketball, bowling, soccer W, softball, table tennis. **Team name:** Bison.

Student services. Alcohol/substance abuse counseling, chaplain/spiritual director, career counseling, student employment services, financial aid counseling, health services, on-campus daycare, personal counseling, placement for graduates, veterans' counselor, women's services. **Physically disabled:** Services for visually, speech impaired.

Contact. E-mail: admissions@howard.edu
Phone: (202) 806-2700 Toll-free number: (800) 469-2738
Fax: (202) 806-4467
Linda Saunders-Hawkins, Associate Director of Admissions, Howard University, 2400 Sixth Street NW, Washington, DC 20059

Potomac College
Washington, District of Columbia
www.potomac.edu **CB code: 3569**

- For-profit 3-year business college
- Commuter campus in very large city
- 450 degree-seeking undergraduates

General. Regionally accredited. Additional campus in Herndon, Va. **Degrees:** 64 bachelor's, 10 associate awarded. **Calendar:** Continuous, extensive summer session. **Full-time faculty:** 8 total. **Part-time faculty:** 30 total.

Basis for selection. Open admission.

2008-2009 Annual costs. Tuition/fees: $13,480. Books/supplies: $630.

Application procedures. Admission: No deadline. $15 fee. Admission notification on a rolling basis beginning on or about 3/31. **Financial aid:** No deadline. FAFSA, institutional form required. Applicants notified on a rolling basis; must reply within 4 week(s) of notification.

Academics. Credit earned for work-related research projects. **Special study options:** Accelerated study, independent study, weekend college. **Credit/placement by examination:** CLEP, institutional tests. 30 credit hours maximum toward bachelor's degree. **Support services:** Learning center.

Majors. BACHELOR'S. Business: Accounting, management science, purchasing. **Computer sciences:** General. **ASSOCIATE. Business:** Accounting, management science.

Computing on campus. 23 workstations in library, computer center. Online library available.

Student life. Freshman orientation: Mandatory. Preregistration for classes offered. **Activities:** Student government.

Student services. Adult student services.

Contact. E-mail: admissions@potomac.edu
Phone: (202) 686-0876 Fax: (202) 686-0818
Director of Admissions, Potomac College, 4000 Chesapeake Street NW, Washington, DC 20016

Southeastern University
Washington, District of Columbia
www.seu.edu **CB code: 5622**

- Private 4-year university and business college
- Commuter campus in very large city
- 467 degree-seeking undergraduates: 82% part-time, 74% women, 63% African American, 1% Asian American, 1% Hispanic American, 5% international
- 159 degree-seeking graduate students
- 67% of applicants admitted
- Application essay required

General. Founded in 1879. Regionally accredited. **Degrees:** 83 bachelor's, 46 associate awarded; master's offered. **Calendar:** Quarter, extensive summer session. **Full-time faculty:** 6 total. **Part-time faculty:** 111 total. **Class size:** 67% < 20, 32% 20-39, 1% 40-49.

Freshman class profile. 559 applied, 375 admitted, 167 enrolled.

Out-of-state:	3%	**International:**	6%

Basis for selection. GPA and accuplacer test considered. **Home-schooled:** Transcript of courses and grades, state high school equivalency certificate required.

High school preparation. Recommended units include English 4, mathematics 3, social studies 2 and foreign language 2.

2008-2009 Annual costs. Tuition/fees: $14,010. Books/supplies: $1,200. Personal expenses: $2,788.

2007-2008 Financial aid. Need-based: 20% of total undergraduate aid awarded as scholarships/grants, 80% as loans/jobs. **Non-need-based:** Scholarships awarded for academics, state residency.

Application procedures. Admission: No deadline. $50 fee, may be waived for applicants with need. Admission notification on a rolling basis. **Financial aid:** Closing date 8/15. FAFSA, institutional form required. Applicants notified on a rolling basis; must reply within 2 week(s) of notification.

Academics. Special study options: Cross-registration, double major, independent study, internships, weekend college. **Credit/placement by examination:** AP, CLEP, IB, institutional tests. 9 credit hours maximum toward associate degree, 9 toward bachelor's. **Support services:** Learning center, pre-admission summer program, reduced course load, remedial instruction, study skills assistance, tutoring, writing center.

Majors. Business: General, accounting, banking/financial services, business admin, management information systems, management science, market research, statistics, tourism/travel. **Computer sciences:** Programming, systems analysis. **Family/consumer sciences:** Child development. **Health:** Health care admin. **Liberal arts:** Arts/sciences. **Protective services:** Police science. **Public administration:** General. **Social sciences:** Economics.

Most popular majors. Business/marketing 47%, computer/information sciences 14%, liberal arts 29%, public administration/social services 10%.

Computing on campus. 137 workstations in library, computer center. Commuter students can connect to campus network. Online course registration, helpline available.

Student life. Freshman orientation: Mandatory, $75 fee. Preregistration for classes offered. **Activities:** Literary magazine, student government, student newspaper.

Student services. Career counseling, student employment services, financial aid counseling, personal counseling, placement for graduates, veterans' counselor. **Physically disabled:** Services for visually, hearing impaired.

Contact. E-mail: admissions@seu.edu
Phone: (202) 478-8210 ext. 210 Fax: (202) 488-3172
Dorothy Harris, Dean of Enrollment Management, Southeastern University, 501 I Street,SW, Washington, DC 20024

Strayer University

Washington, District of Columbia **CB member**
www.strayer.edu **CB code: 5632**

- For-profit 4-year university
- Commuter campus in very large city
- 28,992 degree-seeking undergraduates: 88% part-time, 68% women, 52% African American, 2% Asian American, 4% Hispanic American, 1% Native American, 2% international
- 12,166 degree-seeking graduate students

General. Founded in 1892. Regionally accredited. Additional campuses in 14 states. **Degrees:** 2,181 bachelor's, 637 associate awarded; master's offered. **Location:** Downtown. **Calendar:** Quarter, extensive summer session. **Full-time faculty:** 287 total. **Part-time faculty:** 1,635 total. **Class size:** 48% < 20, 51% 20-39, less than 1% 40-49.

Freshman class profile.

End year in good standing:	80%	**International:**	1%
Return as sophomores:	45%		

Basis for selection. Institutional placement tests required. Students with SAT scores of 400 or above in verbal and/or mathematics or who have prior college level mathematics/English credits, can waive placement tests. Interview recommended.

High school preparation. College-preparatory program required. 14 units recommended. Recommended units include English 3, mathematics 3, social studies 1, history 1, foreign language 2 and academic electives 4. 1 unit of sociology or psychology recommended; 3 units of art, music, or literature recommended.

2008-2009 Annual costs. Tuition/fees: $12,920. Tuition $1,435/course (3 or more courses), $1,510/course (less than 3 courses), $1,949/course (graduate courses). Application fee $50. Books/supplies: $1,200.

Application procedures. Admission: No deadline. $50 fee. Admission notification on a rolling basis. **Financial aid:** No deadline. FAFSA required. Applicants notified on a rolling basis; must reply within 2 week(s) of notification.

Academics. Special study options: Distance learning. **Credit/placement by examination:** AP, CLEP, IB, institutional tests. 63 credit hours maximum toward associate degree, 126 toward bachelor's. **Support services:** Learning center, remedial instruction, tutoring.

Majors. Business: Accounting, business admin, international. **Computer sciences:** Information technology. **Social sciences:** Economics.

Most popular majors. Business/marketing 75%, computer/information sciences 81%.

Computing on campus. 760 workstations in library, computer center. Online course registration, online library, helpline available.

Student life. Activities: Student newspaper, accounting club, international club, data processing management association, business administration club, marketing club, human resource management club, Alpha Chi National Honor Society, Alpha Sigma Lambda National Honor Society, Sigma Gamma Rho Sorority, Thai Student Association.

Student services. Adult student services, career counseling, student employment services, financial aid counseling, health services, placement for graduates, veterans' counselor. **Physically disabled:** Services for visually, hearing impaired.

Contact. E-mail: washington@strayer.edu
Phone: (202) 408-2400 Toll-free number: (888) 478-7293
Reginald Rainey, Vice President, Strayer University, 1133 15th Sreet NW, Washington, DC 20005

Trinity Washington University

Washington, District of Columbia **CB member**
www.trinitydc.edu **CB code: 5796**

- Private 4-year liberal arts college for women affiliated with Roman Catholic Church
- Residential campus in very large city
- 1,127 degree-seeking undergraduates
- 61% of applicants admitted
- Application essay required

General. Founded in 1897. Regionally accredited. **Degrees:** 142 bachelor's awarded; master's offered. **ROTC:** Army. **Calendar:** Semester, extensive summer session. **Full-time faculty:** 56 total. **Part-time faculty:** 138 total. **Class size:** 70% < 20, 30% 20-39.

Freshman class profile. 831 applied, 511 admitted, 230 enrolled.

Out-of-state:	50%	**Live on campus:**	53%

Basis for selection. School achievement record, essay, recommendations, interview, school and community activities important. 3.0 GPA preferred. Test scores considered. SAT and SAT Subject Tests or ACT recommended. Interview recommended. **Homeschooled:** Transcript of courses and grades required.

High school preparation. 16 units required. Required and recommended units include English 4, mathematics 3-4, social studies 3-4, history 2, science 2-3 (laboratory 1-2) and foreign language 2.

2008-2009 Annual costs. Tuition/fees: $18,960. Mandatory health insurance. Room/board: $8,450. Books/supplies: $1,000. Personal expenses: $1,500.

2008-2009 Financial aid. Need-based: 54% of total undergraduate aid awarded as scholarships/grants, 46% as loans/jobs. **Non-need-based:** Scholarships awarded for academics, alumni affiliation, leadership.

Application procedures. Admission: Priority date 2/1; deadline 9/1 (receipt date). $40 fee, may be waived for applicants with need, free for online applicants. Admission notification 9/1. Admission notification on a rolling basis beginning on or about 10/1. Must reply by May 1 or within 3 week(s) if notified thereafter. After August 1, must reply within 1 week. **Financial aid:** Priority date 3/1; no closing date. FAFSA required. Applicants notified on a rolling basis starting 2/1; must reply within 2 week(s) of notification.

Academics. Special study options: Accelerated study, cross-registration, distance learning, double major, dual enrollment of high school students, honors, independent study, internships, student-designed major, study abroad, teacher certification program, Washington semester, weekend college. **Credit/placement by examination:** AP, CLEP, institutional tests. **Support services:** Learning center, pre-admission summer program, reduced course load, remedial instruction, tutoring.

Majors. Biology: General, biochemistry. **Business:** Business admin. **Communications:** General. **Conservation:** Environmental science. **Foreign languages:** General. **History:** General. **Liberal arts:** Arts/sciences. **Math:** General. **Physical sciences:** General, chemistry. **Protective services:** Law enforcement admin. **Psychology:** General. **Public administration:** Human services. **Social sciences:** Economics, international relations, political science, sociology. **Visual/performing arts:** Art history/conservation. **Other:** Languages and cultural studies.

Most popular majors. Biology 7%, business/marketing 17%, communications/journalism 10%, English 6%, psychology 34%, social sciences 13%.

Computing on campus. 70 workstations in dormitories, library, computer center.

Student life. Freshman orientation: Available. Preregistration for classes offered. **Policies:** Student life mostly self-governed. Honor code exists. **Housing:** Guaranteed on-campus for all undergraduates. $100 fully refundable deposit. **Activities:** Choral groups, dance, drama, film society, international student organizations, literary magazine, student government, student newspaper, Young Democrats, Young Republicans, Black Student Alliance, Inter-American Club, peer ministry.

Athletics. NCAA. **Intercollegiate:** Basketball W, lacrosse W, soccer W, tennis W, volleyball W. **Team name:** Tigers.

Student services. Adult student services, alcohol/substance abuse counseling, chaplain/spiritual director, career counseling, student employment services, financial aid counseling, health services, on-campus daycare, personal counseling, placement for graduates, veterans' counselor. **Physically disabled:** Services for visually, speech, hearing impaired.

Contact. E-mail: admissions@trinitydc.edu
Phone: (202) 884-9400 Toll-free number: (800) 492-6882
Fax: (202) 884-9229
Kelly Gosnell, Director of Admissions, Trinity Washington University, 125 Michigan Avenue, NE, Washington, DC 20017

University of the District of Columbia

Washington, District of Columbia **CB member**
www.udc.edu **CB code: 5929**

- Public 4-year university and liberal arts college
- Commuter campus in very large city
- 5,121 degree-seeking undergraduates: 49% part-time, 57% women
- 93 degree-seeking graduate students

General. Founded in 1976. Regionally accredited. **Degrees:** 326 bachelor's, 157 associate awarded; master's offered. **ROTC:** Army, Naval, Air Force. **Calendar:** Semester, limited summer session. **Full-time faculty:** 247 total; 36% have terminal degrees, 43% women. **Part-time faculty:** 58 total.

Freshman class profile.

Out-of-state:	21%	**Sororities:**	2%
Fraternities:	1%		

Basis for selection. Open admission. Special requirements for nursing, art, and music programs. Interview recommended for nursing majors. Audition recommended for music majors. Portfolio recommended for art majors.

High school preparation. College-preparatory program required. Recommended units include English 4, mathematics 2, social studies 2, history 1, science 2, foreign language 2 and academic electives 3.

2008-2009 Annual costs. Tuition/fees: $3,770; $7,070 out-of-state. Books/supplies: $1,100. Personal expenses: $1,900.

Financial aid. All financial aid based on need.

Application procedures. Admission: Closing date 6/14 (postmark date). $75 fee ($100 out-of-state). Admission notification on a rolling basis. **Financial aid:** Priority date 3/15; no closing date. FAFSA required. Applicants notified on a rolling basis starting 5/1; must reply within 2 week(s) of notification.

Academics. Special study options: Cooperative education, cross-registration, double major, dual enrollment of high school students, ESL, honors, independent study, internships, teacher certification program, weekend college. **Credit/placement by examination:** AP, CLEP, IB, institutional tests. **Support services:** Learning center, pre-admission summer program, remedial instruction, tutoring.

Majors. Architecture: Architecture, urban/community planning. **Biology:** General. **Business:** Accounting, business admin, finance, office management. **Communications technology:** Graphic/printing. **Computer sciences:** General, computer science. **Conservation:** General. **Education:** Art, business, early childhood, elementary, health, physical. **Engineering:** Civil, electrical, mechanical. **Family/consumer sciences:** General, family studies, food/nutrition. **Foreign languages:** French, Spanish. **Health:** Nursing (RN), speech pathology. **History:** General. **Math:** General. **Parks/recreation:** General. **Philosophy/religion:** Philosophy. **Physical sciences:** Chemistry, physics. **Protective services:** Fire services admin. **Psychology:** General. **Public administration:** Social work. **Social sciences:** Anthropology, economics, geography, political science, sociology, urban studies. **Transportation:** Aviation. **Visual/performing arts:** Dramatic, studio arts.

Most popular majors. Business/marketing 19%, computer/information sciences 16%, education 6%, health sciences 9%, legal studies 12%, mathematics 14%, visual/performing arts 8%.

Computing on campus. 2 workstations in library, computer center. Helpline, repair service available.

Student life. Freshman orientation: Mandatory. Preregistration for classes offered. **Activities:** Bands, choral groups, dance, drama, student government, student newspaper, symphony orchestra, TV station.

Athletics. NCAA. **Intercollegiate:** Basketball, cross-country, soccer, tennis, track and field, volleyball W. **Intramural:** Basketball, softball, swimming, tennis, volleyball W. **Team name:** Firebirds.

Student services. Career counseling, student employment services, health services, personal counseling, placement for graduates, veterans' counselor. **Physically disabled:** Services for visually, speech, hearing impaired.

Contact. E-mail: www@udc.edu
Phone: (202) 274-6110 Fax: (202) 274-5552
LaVerne Hill-Flannigan, Director of Enrollment Services, University of the District of Columbia, 4200 Connecticut Avenue NW, Washington, DC 20008

Florida

Art Institute of Fort Lauderdale
Fort Lauderdale, Florida
www.aifl.edu **CB code: 5040**

- For-profit 4-year visual arts and technical college
- Commuter campus in large city
- 2,827 degree-seeking undergraduates: 42% part-time, 55% women, 19% African American, 2% Asian American, 36% Hispanic American
- Application essay, interview required
- 41% graduate within 6 years

General. Founded in 1968. Accredited by ACICS. **Degrees:** 382 bachelor's, 203 associate awarded. **Location:** 25 miles from Miami, 30 miles from West Palm Beach. **Calendar:** Quarter, extensive summer session. **Full-time faculty:** 84 total; 30% have terminal degrees, 99% minority, 51% women. **Part-time faculty:** 72 total; 33% have terminal degrees, 99% minority, 36% women. **Special facilities:** Broadcasting studio, silicon graphics lab, full culinary kitchens.

Freshman class profile.

Out-of-state:	20%	**Live on campus:**	10%

Basis for selection. Interview, essay important. Portfolio recommended. **Homeschooled:** State high school equivalency certificate required. **Learning Disabled:** Documentation must be submitted if student has special needs to be accommodated.

2009-2010 Annual costs. Tuition/fees (projected): $21,555. Books/supplies: $1,275. Personal expenses: $1,980.

2007-2008 Financial aid. All financial aid based on need. 75% of total undergraduate aid awarded as scholarships/grants, 25% as loans/jobs. **Additional information:** Internal scholarships available. Financial planning program allows personalized service to budget and meet college costs through individualized payment plans.

Application procedures. Admission: No deadline. $50 fee. Admission notification on a rolling basis. **Financial aid:** No deadline. FAFSA required.

Academics. Academic program designed to simulate working environment. After completion of associate degree students may continue to earn a bachelor of science. **Special study options:** Distance learning, ESL, honors, independent study, internships, study abroad. **Credit/placement by examination:** AP, CLEP, IB, SAT, ACT. SAT or ACT preferred for placement but ACCUPLACER accepted. **Support services:** Remedial instruction, tutoring, writing center.

Majors. Architecture: Interior. **Business:** Fashion. **Communications:** Advertising. **Computer sciences:** Computer graphics, programming, web page design. **Personal/culinary services:** Chef training. **Visual/performing arts:** Cinematography, commercial/advertising art, fashion design, illustration, industrial design, interior design.

Most popular majors. Architecture 19%, computer/information sciences 28%, visual/performing arts 42%.

Computing on campus. Dormitories wired for high-speed internet access and linked to campus network. Online course registration, online library, helpline, repair service, student web hosting, wireless network available.

Student life. Freshman orientation: Mandatory. Preregistration for classes offered. Held at the beginning of each quarter and midquarter. **Housing:** Guaranteed on-campus for all undergraduates. Coed dorms, apartments, wellness housing available. $275 deposit. **Activities:** Campus ministries, drama, film society, international student organizations, radio station, student government, Industrial Design Society of America, American Society of Interior Design, Gay Straight Alliance, fashion club, future video producers and broadcasters, Green club, Art Institute Ministries, Emerging Green Builders, Students for Democracy.

Student services. Adult student services, alcohol/substance abuse counseling, career counseling, services for economically disadvantaged, student employment services, financial aid counseling, personal counseling, placement for graduates. **Physically disabled:** Services for visually, speech, hearing impaired.

Contact. E-mail: kmoss@aii.edu
Phone: (954) 463-3000 ext. 2148 Toll-free number: (800) 275-7603 ext. 2148 Fax: (954) 728-8637
Kim Moss, Senior Director of Admissions, Art Institute of Fort Lauderdale, 1799 Southeast 17th Street, Fort Lauderdale, FL 33316

Ave Maria University
Ave Maria, Florida
www.avemaria.edu **CB code: 4249**

- Private 4-year university and liberal arts college affiliated with Roman Catholic Church
- Residential campus in small town
- 516 degree-seeking undergraduates
- 137 graduate students
- 56% of applicants admitted
- SAT or ACT (ACT writing optional), application essay required

General. Degrees: 85 bachelor's awarded; master's, doctoral offered. **Location:** 30 miles from Naples. **Calendar:** Semester, limited summer session. **Full-time faculty:** 54 total; 100% have terminal degrees, 9% minority. **Part-time faculty:** 10 total; 20% minority. **Class size:** 70% < 20, 29% 20-39, less than 1% 40-49.

Freshman class profile. 1,248 applied, 695 admitted, 293 enrolled.

Mid 50% test scores		**SAT writing:**	500-630
SAT critical reading:	510-640	**ACT composite:**	21-28
SAT math:	500-620	**Out-of-state:**	53%

Basis for selection. For regular admission, 2.8 GPA and 1580 SAT or 22 ACT required. Students who do not meet all requirements may attain admission by special recommendation of the Admissions Committee. **Homeschooled:** Transcript of courses and grades, letter of recommendation (nonparent) required.

High school preparation. College-preparatory program recommended. 15 units required; 17 recommended. Required and recommended units include English 3-4, mathematics 3-4, social studies 1, history 1-3, science 3 and foreign language 2.

2009-2010 Annual costs. Tuition/fees: $17,745. Room/board: $7,980.

2008-2009 Financial aid. Need-based: Average need met was 51%. Average scholarship/grant was $2,864; average loan $3,500. 61% of total undergraduate aid awarded as scholarships/grants, 39% as loans/jobs.

Application procedures. Admission: No deadline. No application fee. Admission notification on a rolling basis.

Academics. Special study options: Double major, dual enrollment of high school students, internships, study abroad. **Credit/placement by examination:** AP, CLEP, IB, SAT, ACT, institutional tests. **Support services:** Pre-admission summer program, reduced course load, study skills assistance, tutoring, writing center.

Majors. Biology: General. **Foreign languages:** Classics. **History:** General. **Math:** General. **Philosophy/religion:** Philosophy. **Social sciences:** Economics, political science. **Theology:** Sacred music, theology.

Computing on campus. 150 workstations in dormitories, library, computer center, student center. Dormitories wired for high-speed internet access and linked to campus network. Commuter students can connect to campus network. Online library, helpline, wireless network available.

Student life. Freshman orientation: Mandatory. Preregistration for classes offered. Three-day program held at beginning of semester. **Policies:** Policies and procedures aligned with Catholic moral teaching. Students required to live on campus unless living with a parent or legal guardian, are 23 years of age or older, or receive special permission in certain unusual cases. **Housing:** Guaranteed on-campus for all undergraduates. Single-sex dorms available. **Activities:** Campus ministries, choral groups, dance, drama, film society, international student organizations, music ensembles, Model UN, musical theater, student government, student newspaper.

Athletics. NAIA. **Intercollegiate:** Basketball, golf M, soccer, volleyball W. **Intramural:** Basketball, football (non-tackle), soccer, tennis, volleyball. **Team name:** Gyrene.

Student services. Alcohol/substance abuse counseling, chaplain/spiritual director, career counseling, student employment services, financial

aid counseling, health services, personal counseling. **Physically disabled:** Services for visually, hearing impaired.

Contact. E-mail: admissions@avemaria.edu
Phone: (239) 280-2556 Toll-free number: (877) 283-8648
Fax: (239) 280-2559
Brett Ormandy, Director of Admissions, Ave Maria University, 5050 Ave Maria Boulevard, Ave Maria, FL 34142-9505

Baptist College of Florida
Graceville, Florida
www.baptistcollege.edu **CB code: 7322**

- Private 4-year Bible and teachers college affiliated with Southern Baptist Convention
- Residential campus in small town
- 565 degree-seeking undergraduates: 27% part-time, 37% women, 3% African American, 1% Asian American, 3% Hispanic American
- 44% of applicants admitted
- SAT or ACT (ACT writing optional), application essay required

General. Founded in 1943. Regionally accredited. **Degrees:** 114 bachelor's, 7 associate awarded. **Location:** 90 miles from Tallahassee, 60 miles from Panama City. **Calendar:** Semester, limited summer session. **Full-time faculty:** 22 total; 68% have terminal degrees, 23% women. **Part-time faculty:** 43 total; 74% have terminal degrees, 21% women. **Class size:** 72% < 20, 22% 20-39, 2% 40-49, 4% 50-99.

Freshman class profile. 137 applied, 60 admitted, 60 enrolled.

Out-of-state:	21%	**Live on campus:**	90%

Basis for selection. Applicant must be member in good standing of church affiliated with Southern Baptist Convention or other evangelical body. Special program for non-high school graduates. Recommendations very important. Affirmation of faith required. Audition required of music applicants. Interview recommended. **Homeschooled:** Transcript of courses and grades required. Present ACT or SAT test scores no more than 5 years old. Minimum 2.5 GPA, evidence of having earned minimum of 20 units with at least 14 units from fields of English, math, social and natural sciences required.

High school preparation. Recommended units include English 4, mathematics 4, social studies 1, history 2 and science 3.

2008-2009 Annual costs. Tuition/fees: $8,150. Room/board: $3,886. Books/supplies: $900. Personal expenses: $400.

2007-2008 Financial aid. Need-based: 53 full-time freshmen applied for aid; 45 were judged to have need; 41 of these received aid. Average need met was 50%. Average scholarship/grant was $3,715; average loan $2,552. 57% of total undergraduate aid awarded as scholarships/grants, 43% as loans/jobs. **Non-need-based:** Awarded to 35 full-time undergraduates, including 9 freshmen. Scholarships awarded for academics, minority status, music/drama, religious affiliation.

Application procedures. Admission: Closing date 8/15 (receipt date). $20 fee, may be waived for applicants with need. Admission notification on a rolling basis. **Financial aid:** Priority date 4/1, closing date 4/15. FAFSA, institutional form required. Applicants notified on a rolling basis starting 6/15; must reply within 4 week(s) of notification.

Academics. Special study options: Distance learning, double major, independent study, internships, liberal arts/career combination, teacher certification program, weekend college. **Credit/placement by examination:** AP, CLEP, IB, SAT, ACT, institutional tests. 30 credit hours maximum toward bachelor's degree. **Support services:** Learning center, reduced course load, remedial instruction, study skills assistance, tutoring, writing center.

Majors. Education: Elementary, music. **Philosophy/religion:** Religion. **Theology:** Bible, pastoral counseling, religious ed, sacred music, theology.

Most popular majors. Education 6%, theological studies 94%.

Computing on campus. 25 workstations in library, computer center. Commuter students can connect to campus network. Online course registration, online library, wireless network available.

Student life. Freshman orientation: Mandatory. Preregistration for classes offered. Held week before classes begin for 1-2 days depending on major. **Policies:** Religious observance required. **Housing:** Single-sex dorms, apartments available. $100 fully refundable deposit. **Activities:** Bands, campus ministries, choral groups, drama, music ensembles, radio station, student government, Baptist collegiate ministry, Women of Worth.

Athletics. Intramural: Basketball, football (non-tackle), golf, soccer, softball, table tennis, volleyball.

Student services. Career counseling, student employment services, financial aid counseling, personal counseling, veterans' counselor. **Physically disabled:** Services for visually, speech, hearing impaired.

Contact. E-mail: admissions@baptistcollege.edu
Phone: (850) 263-3261 ext. 460 Toll-free number: (800) 328-2660 ext. 460
Fax: (850) 263-9026
Sandra Richards, Director of Marketing, Baptist College of Florida, 5400 College Drive, Graceville, FL 32440-3306

Barry University
Miami Shores, Florida **CB member**
www.barry.edu **CB code: 5053**

- Private 4-year university affiliated with Roman Catholic Church
- Residential campus in large town
- 4,963 degree-seeking undergraduates: 18% part-time, 69% women, 20% African American, 1% Asian American, 28% Hispanic American, 5% international
- 3,497 degree-seeking graduate students
- 62% of applicants admitted
- SAT or ACT (ACT writing optional) required
- 39% graduate within 6 years

General. Founded in 1940. Regionally accredited. 22 off-campus sites for adult and continuing education and some graduate degrees. Center for Dominican Studies. **Degrees:** 1,311 bachelor's awarded; master's, doctoral, first professional offered. **ROTC:** Army, Air Force. **Location:** 14 miles from Fort Lauderdale, 7 miles from Miami. **Calendar:** Semester, limited summer session. **Full-time faculty:** 325 total; 73% have terminal degrees, 28% minority, 54% women. **Part-time faculty:** 311 total; 29% minority, 49% women. **Class size:** 68% < 20, 31% 20-39, less than 1% 40-49, less than 1% 50-99, less than 1% >100. **Special facilities:** Human performance laboratory, athletic training room, cell biology/biotechnology lab, classroom of tomorrow, photography facilities, lighting studio, dark room, imaging lab, performing arts center, biomechanics lab.

Freshman class profile. 3,660 applied, 2,251 admitted, 586 enrolled.

Mid 50% test scores		**GPA 3.0-3.49:**	36%
SAT critical reading:	440-520	**GPA 2.0-2.99:**	38%
SAT math:	420-520	**Out-of-state:**	41%
ACT composite:	18-22	**Live on campus:**	63%
GPA 3.75 or higher:	12%	**International:**	7%
GPA 3.50-3.74:	14%		

Basis for selection. Test scores and school record important. Higher test score, GPA, and course requirements for certain majors. Interviews highly recommended. **Homeschooled:** Statement describing homeschool structure and mission, transcript of courses and grades, state high school equivalency certificate required. Academic portfolio or GED, copy of home school rules of the state which home school is chartered required. **Learning Disabled:** Students must apply directly to comprehensive service program.

High school preparation. 13 units required; 16 recommended. Required and recommended units include English 4, mathematics 3, social studies 3 and science 3. For nursing program, 1 chemistry, 1 biology, algebra II required. For biology and allied health programs, 2 laboratory science including biology and chemistry, 3.5 math required. For math program, 4 math including algebra, geometry, trigonometry, required. For chemistry program, 3 math, 1 chemistry with lab required.

2008-2009 Annual costs. Tuition/fees: $25,500. Room/board: $8,256. Books/supplies: $800. Personal expenses: $1,500.

2008-2009 Financial aid. Need-based: 503 full-time freshmen applied for aid; 457 were judged to have need; 456 of these received aid. Average need met was 74%. Average scholarship/grant was $7,985; average loan $3,507. 43% of total undergraduate aid awarded as scholarships/grants, 57% as loans/jobs. **Non-need-based:** Awarded to 3,586 full-time undergraduates, including 536 freshmen. Scholarships awarded for academics, art, athletics, music/drama.

Application procedures. Admission: No deadline. $30 fee. Admission notification on a rolling basis beginning on or about 9/8. Students are allowed to postpone enrollment after admissions for up to 1 year. **Financial aid:** No deadline. FAFSA required. Applicants notified on a rolling basis starting 1/25.

Academics. **Special study options:** Accelerated study, combined bachelor's/graduate degree, double major, ESL, honors, internships, study abroad, teacher certification program. **Credit/placement by examination:** AP, CLEP, IB, SAT, ACT, institutional tests. 30 credit hours maximum toward bachelor's degree. All credit by examination should be completed prior to junior status. **Support services:** Learning center, reduced course load, remedial instruction, study skills assistance, tutoring, writing center.

Majors. **Biology:** General. **Business:** Accounting, business admin, finance, international, marketing. **Communications:** General, advertising, public relations, radio/tv. **Computer sciences:** General, computer science, information technology. **Education:** Early childhood, elementary, physical, special. **Foreign languages:** French, Spanish. **Health:** Athletic training, cardiovascular technology, clinical lab science, cytotechnology, health care admin, nuclear medical technology, nursing (RN), predental, premedicine, prepharmacy, preveterinary, sonography. **History:** General. **Interdisciplinary:** Global studies. **Legal studies:** General, prelaw. **Liberal arts:** Arts/sciences. **Math:** General. **Parks/recreation:** Exercise sciences, health/fitness, sports admin. **Philosophy/religion:** Philosophy. **Physical sciences:** Chemistry. **Psychology:** General. **Public administration:** General, social work. **Social sciences:** Criminology, political science, sociology. **Theology:** Theology. **Visual/performing arts:** Art, dramatic, photography.

Most popular majors. Business/marketing 17%, computer/information sciences 9%, education 20%, health sciences 14%, liberal arts 14%, public administration/social services 9%.

Computing on campus. 165 workstations in dormitories, library, computer center. Dormitories wired for high-speed internet access and linked to campus network. Commuter students can connect to campus network. Online library, helpline, repair service, wireless network available.

Student life. **Freshman orientation:** Mandatory. Preregistration for classes offered. **Housing:** Coed dorms, single-sex dorms, special housing for disabled available. $200 nonrefundable deposit. **Activities:** Choral groups, dance, drama, literary magazine, music ensembles, musical theater, radio station, student government, student newspaper, TV station, Jamaican association, black student union, Habitat for Humanity, Caribbean student organization, Haitian intercultural association, Jewish/Christian/Muslim interfaith group, Latter-Day Saints student association, Best Buddies, Spanish club, Baptist dialogue group.

Athletics. NCAA. **Intercollegiate:** Baseball M, basketball, golf, rowing (crew) W, soccer, softball W, tennis, volleyball W. **Intramural:** Basketball, football (non-tackle), golf, skin diving, soccer, softball, volleyball. **Team name:** Buccaneers.

Student services. Adult student services, alcohol/substance abuse counseling, chaplain/spiritual director, career counseling, student employment services, financial aid counseling, health services, personal counseling, placement for graduates. **Physically disabled:** Services for visually, speech, hearing impaired. **Learning disabled:** Comprehensive services available.

Contact. E-mail: admissions@mail.barry.edu
Phone: (305) 899-3100 Toll-free number: (800) 695-2279
Fax: (305) 899-2971
Magda Castineyra, Director of Undergraduate Admissions, Barry University, 11300 Northeast Second Avenue, Miami Shores, FL 33161-6695

Beacon College

Leesburg, Florida
www.beaconcollege.edu **CB code: 3611**

- Private 4-year liberal arts college
- Residential campus in large town
- 122 degree-seeking undergraduates: 37% women
- 58% of applicants admitted
- Application essay required
- 79% graduate within 6 years; 33% enter graduate study

General. Regionally accredited. College solely for students with learning disabilities. **Degrees:** 25 bachelor's, 3 associate awarded. **Location:** 50 miles from Orlando. **Calendar:** Semester, limited summer session. **Full-time faculty:** 15 total; 67% have terminal degrees, 7% minority, 53% women. **Part-time faculty:** 4 total; 25% have terminal degrees, 50% women. **Class size:** 100% < 20.

Freshman class profile. 57 applied, 33 admitted, 30 enrolled.

GPA 3.0-3.49:	50%	**Live on campus:**	100%
GPA 2.0-2.99:	45%	**Fraternities:**	32%
Return as sophomores:	82%	**Sororities:**	27%
Out-of-state:	74%		

Basis for selection. Selective but noncompetitive process. Recommendations, interview, character, level of interest very important; followed by rigor of secondary school record, GPA, test scores, essay, extracurricular activities, ability, volunteer work. Class rank, work experience considered. SAT or ACT recommended. Scores used noncompetitively for informational purposes only. Interview may be required. **Homeschooled:** State high school equivalency certificate required. **Learning Disabled:** Students accepted by committee decision based on psychoeducational evaluation documenting learning disability, academic potential, evaluation of high school records, references, and campus interviews with assessments as part of admissions process. Students must provide current psychoeducational report (within 3 years) documenting learning disability as primary handicapping condition, including WAIS score.

High school preparation. College-preparatory program recommended. 12 units required. Required and recommended units include English 4, mathematics 1-2, social studies 1, history 2-3, science 1-2 and academic electives 3.

2008-2009 Annual costs. Tuition/fees: $26,150. Room/board: $8,000. Books/supplies: $800. Personal expenses: $2,565.

2007-2008 Financial aid. All financial aid based on need. 4 full-time freshmen applied for aid; 4 were judged to have need; 4 of these received aid. Average need met was 90%. Average scholarship/grant was $15,000. 50% of total undergraduate aid awarded as scholarships/grants, 50% as loans/jobs. **Additional information:** Work-study programs offered based on financial need.

Application procedures. **Admission:** Priority date 5/1; deadline 8/1 (receipt date). $50 fee. Application must be submitted on paper. Admission notification on a rolling basis. Must reply by May 1 or within 2 week(s) if notified thereafter. **Financial aid:** Priority date 4/1; no closing date. FAFSA, institutional form required. Applicants notified on a rolling basis starting 4/1; must reply within 2 week(s) of notification.

Academics. Provides remedial coursework in writing, reading, and math. **Special study options:** Double major, independent study, internships, liberal arts/career combination, study abroad. **Credit/placement by examination:** AP, CLEP, institutional tests. **Support services:** Learning center, reduced course load, remedial instruction, study skills assistance, tutoring, writing center.

Majors. **Computer sciences:** General. **Liberal arts:** Arts/sciences. **Public administration:** Human services.

Most popular majors. Computer/information sciences 20%, liberal arts 44%, public administration/social services 36%.

Computing on campus. 32 workstations in library, computer center, student center. Dormitories wired for high-speed internet access and linked to campus network. Commuter students can connect to campus network. Online library, helpline, repair service, student web hosting, wireless network available.

Student life. **Freshman orientation:** Mandatory. Preregistration for classes offered. **Housing:** Guaranteed on-campus for all undergraduates. Apartments, wellness housing available. $750 nonrefundable deposit, deadline 5/1. **Activities:** Dance, literary magazine, student government, student newspaper.

Athletics. **Team name:** Bull Dogs.

Student services. Career counseling, student employment services, financial aid counseling, personal counseling, placement for graduates. **Physically disabled:** Services for visually, speech, hearing impaired. **Learning disabled:** Comprehensive services available.

Contact. E-mail: admissions@beaconcollege.edu
Phone: (352) 787-7249 Fax: (352) 787-0721
Mary Bruck, Director of Admissions, Beacon College, 105 East Main Street, Leesburg, FL 34748

Bethune-Cookman University

Daytona Beach, Florida **CB member**
www.cookman.edu **CB code: 5061**

- Private 4-year liberal arts college affiliated with United Methodist Church
- Residential campus in small city

- 3,596 degree-seeking undergraduates: 3% part-time, 60% women, 92% African American, 2% Hispanic American, 3% international
- 35 degree-seeking graduate students
- 55% of applicants admitted
- SAT or ACT (ACT writing optional), application essay required
- 41% graduate within 6 years; 30% enter graduate study

General. Founded in 1904. Regionally accredited. **Degrees:** 398 bachelor's awarded; master's offered. **ROTC:** Army, Air Force. **Location:** 60 miles from Orlando. **Calendar:** Semester, limited summer session. **Full-time faculty:** 204 total; 49% have terminal degrees, 62% minority, 47% women. **Part-time faculty:** 59 total; 70% minority, 61% women. **Class size:** 47% < 20, 50% 20-39, 1% 40-49, 1% 50-99. **Special facilities:** Observatory.

Freshman class profile. 4,983 applied, 2,747 admitted, 1,194 enrolled.

Mid 50% test scores		**Rank in top quarter:**	15%
SAT critical reading:	360-460	**Rank in top tenth:**	5%
SAT math:	360-460	**End year in good standing:**	80%
ACT composite:	14-18	**Return as sophomores:**	63%
GPA 3.75 or higher:	3%	**Out-of-state:**	30%
GPA 3.50-3.74:	5%	**Live on campus:**	72%
GPA 3.0-3.49:	18%	**International:**	2%
GPA 2.0-2.99:	73%		

Basis for selection. School achievement record most important. Test scores and letters of recommendation important. Interview required of music majors.

High school preparation. 19 units required. Required and recommended units include English 4, mathematics 3, social studies 1, history 2, science 3 (laboratory 1), foreign language 2 and academic electives 6. 1 unit computer literacy.

2008-2009 Annual costs. Tuition/fees: $12,876. Room/board: $7,672. Books/supplies: $1,000. Personal expenses: $2,800.

2008-2009 Financial aid. All financial aid based on need.

Application procedures. Admission: Priority date 6/30; no deadline. $25 fee, may be waived for applicants with need. Application must be submitted on paper. Admission notification on a rolling basis. **Financial aid:** Priority date 4/1; no closing date. FAFSA required. Applicants notified on a rolling basis starting 4/1; must reply within 3 week(s) of notification.

Academics. Special study options: Accelerated study, combined bachelor's/graduate degree, cooperative education, distance learning, double major, honors, independent study, internships, study abroad, teacher certification program, weekend college. **Credit/placement by examination:** AP, CLEP, IB, SAT, ACT, institutional tests. 30 credit hours maximum toward bachelor's degree. **Support services:** Learning center, reduced course load, remedial instruction, study skills assistance, tutoring, writing center.

Majors. Biology: General. **Business:** Accounting, business admin, hotel/motel admin, international. **Communications:** Journalism. **Computer sciences:** Computer science, information systems. **Conservation:** Environmental science. **Education:** General, biology, business, chemistry, elementary, English, learning disabled, music, physical, physics, social studies. **Engineering:** Computer. **Health:** Nursing (RN). **History:** General. **Interdisciplinary:** Gerontology. **Math:** General. **Philosophy/religion:** Christian. **Physical sciences:** Chemistry, physics. **Protective services:** Law enforcement admin. **Psychology:** General. **Social sciences:** International relations, political science, sociology. **Visual/performing arts:** Music performance.

Computing on campus. 537 workstations in dormitories, library, computer center, student center. Dormitories wired for high-speed internet access and linked to campus network. Commuter students can connect to campus network. Online course registration, online library, helpline, wireless network available.

Student life. Freshman orientation: Mandatory. Preregistration for classes offered. One-week program in beginning of fall and spring semster. **Housing:** Guaranteed on-campus for freshmen. Single-sex dorms, wellness housing available. $200 nonrefundable deposit, deadline 8/15. Scholarship housing for honor students. **Activities:** Bands, choral groups, dance, drama, international student organizations, music ensembles, radio station, student government, student newspaper, YM/YWCA, Religious Life Fellowship, Pre-seminarian club, Greek letter organization, Gamma Sigma Sigma National Service sorority, Kappa Kappa Psi National Band fraternity, Alpha Chi honor sorority, Alpha Kappa Mu honor sorority.

Athletics. NCAA. **Intercollegiate:** Baseball M, basketball, bowling W, cross-country, football (tackle) M, golf, softball W, tennis, track and fieid, volleyball W. **Intramural:** Basketball, football (tackle) M. **Team name:** Wildcats.

Student services. Adult student services, chaplain/spiritual director, career counseling, student employment services, financial aid counseling, health services, personal counseling, placement for graduates, veterans' counselor.

Contact. E-mail: admissions@cookman.edu
Phone: (386) 481-2600 Toll-free number: (800) 448-0228
Fax: (386) 481-2601
Les Ferrier, Executive Director of Admissions, Bethune-Cookman University, Dr. Mary McLeod Bethune Boulevard, Daytona Beach, FL 32114-3099

Carlos Albizu University
Miami, Florida
www.albizu.edu **CB code: 2102**

- Private 4-year university
- Commuter campus in very large city
- 407 degree-seeking undergraduates
- Application essay, interview required

General. Founded in 1980. Regionally accredited. **Degrees:** 118 bachelor's awarded; master's, doctoral offered. **Calendar:** Semester, extensive summer session. **Full-time faculty:** 24 total. **Part-time faculty:** 94 total. **Class size:** 39% < 20, 61% 20-39.

Basis for selection. 2.0 GPA required. **Homeschooled:** State high school equivalency certificate required.

2008-2009 Annual costs. Tuition/fees: $14,269. Reported tuition, fees and per credit hour charge are for bachelor's degree program in business. Other programs individually priced. Books/supplies: $690. Personal expenses: $1,800.

Financial aid. All financial aid based on need.

Application procedures. Admission: No deadline. $25 fee, may be waived for applicants with need. Admission notification on a rolling basis. **Financial aid:** Priority date 6/1; no closing date. FAFSA, institutional form required. Applicants notified on a rolling basis starting 2/1.

Academics. Special study options: Accelerated study, cooperative education, cross-registration, distance learning, double major, dual enrollment of high school students, ESL, honors, independent study, internships, study abroad, teacher certification program, weekend college. **Credit/placement by examination:** CLEP, IB, institutional tests. 12 credit hours maximum toward bachelor's degree. 6 for foreign language, 6 for other foundation courses. **Support services:** Learning center, remedial instruction, study skills assistance, tutoring, writing center.

Majors. Business: General. **Education:** Elementary. **Psychology:** General.

Computing on campus. 50 workstations in library, computer center, student center. Commuter students can connect to campus network. Online course registration, online library, wireless network available.

Student life. Freshman orientation: Mandatory. Preregistration for classes offered. Two-hour program held before session. **Activities:** Student government, student newspaper.

Student services. Adult student services, career counseling, services for economically disadvantaged, student employment services, financial aid counseling, minority student services, placement for graduates.

Contact. E-mail: webmaster@albizu.edu
Phone: (305) 593-1223 ext. 137 Toll-free number: (888) 468-6228
Fax: (305) 593-1854
Carlos Alicea, Director of Recruitment and Outreach, Carlos Albizu University, 2173 NW 99th Avenue, Miami, FL 33172

Chipola College
Marianna, Florida
www.chipola.edu **CB code: 5106**

- Public 4-year community and junior college
- Commuter campus in small town
- 1,563 degree-seeking undergraduates: 37% part-time, 62% women

General. Founded in 1947. Regionally accredited. **Degrees:** 15 bachelor's, 316 associate awarded. **Location:** 70 miles from Tallahassee. **Calendar:** Semester, limited summer session. **Full-time faculty:** 47 total; 19% have terminal degrees, 4% minority, 40% women. **Part-time faculty:** 81 total; 16% minority, 28% women.

Basis for selection. Open admission, but selective for some programs.

High school preparation. Recommended units include English 4, mathematics 3, social studies 3 and science 3.

2008-2009 Annual costs. Tuition/fees: $2,250; $6,662 out-of-state. Books/supplies: $800. Personal expenses: $1,500.

2007-2008 Financial aid. Need-based: 91% of total undergraduate aid awarded as scholarships/grants, 9% as loans/jobs. **Non-need-based:** Scholarships awarded for academics, alumni affiliation, art, athletics, job skills, leadership, minority status, music/drama.

Application procedures. Admission: Priority date 8/1; no deadline. No application fee. Admission notification on a rolling basis. **Financial aid:** Priority date 5/1; no closing date. FAFSA, institutional form required. Applicants notified on a rolling basis starting 1/2; must reply within 2 week(s) of notification.

Academics. Special study options: Accelerated study, cooperative education, distance learning, dual enrollment of high school students, honors, independent study, internships, liberal arts/career combination, teacher certification program. **Credit/placement by examination:** AP, CLEP, IB. 45 credit hours maximum toward associate degree, 45 toward bachelor's. **Support services:** Remedial instruction, study skills assistance, tutoring, writing center.

Majors. Biology: General. **Business:** Business admin. **Education:** Elementary, mathematics, middle, science, secondary, special. **Health:** Nursing (RN). **Math:** General.

Computing on campus. 150 workstations in library. Dormitories linked to campus network. Online library available.

Student life. Freshman orientation: Mandatory. Preregistration for classes offered. **Housing:** Only men's and women's athletic dorms available. **Activities:** Jazz band, campus ministries, choral groups, dance, drama, musical theater, student government, student newspaper, Black Student Union, Baptist Campus Ministry, Fellowship of Christian Athletes.

Athletics. NJCAA. **Intercollegiate:** Baseball M, basketball, softball W. **Team name:** Indians.

Student services. Career counseling. **Physically disabled:** Services for visually, hearing impaired.

Contact. Phone: (850) 526-2761 Fax: (850) 718-2287
Jayne Roberts, Dean of Enrollment Services, Chipola College, 3094 Indian Circle, Marianna, FL 32446

City College: Fort Lauderdale
Fort Lauderdale, Florida
www.citycollege.edu **CB code: 3578**

- Private 4-year business and technical college
- Commuter campus in very large city
- 420 degree-seeking undergraduates
- Application essay, interview required

General. Accredited by ACICS. **Degrees:** 22 bachelor's, 141 associate awarded. **Calendar:** Quarter. **Full-time faculty:** 14 total. **Part-time faculty:** 46 total.

Basis for selection. Open admission, but selective for some programs. **Homeschooled:** Statement describing homeschool structure and mission, transcript of courses and grades required.

2008-2009 Annual costs. Tuition/fees: $12,340. Books/supplies: $1,044. Personal expenses: $2,931.

Application procedures. Admission: No deadline. $25 fee, may be waived for applicants with need. Admission notification on a rolling basis.

Academics. Special study options: Distance learning, independent study, internships. **Credit/placement by examination:** CLEP, IB, institutional tests. 15 credit hours maximum toward associate degree, 30 toward bachelor's. **Support services:** Remedial instruction, tutoring.

Majors. Business: Business admin.

Computing on campus. 70 workstations in library. Online library available.

Student life. Freshman orientation: Mandatory. Preregistration for classes offered.

Student services. Adult student services, alcohol/substance abuse counseling, career counseling, student employment services, financial aid counseling, personal counseling, placement for graduates.

Contact. Phone: (954) 492-5353 Fax: (954) 491-1965
Ron Lohrmann, Director of Admissions, City College: Fort Lauderdale, 2000 West Commercial Boulevard, Fort Lauderdale, FL 33309

Clearwater Christian College
Clearwater, Florida
www.clearwater.edu **CB code: 5142**

- Private 4-year liberal arts college affiliated with nondenominational tradition
- Residential campus in small city
- 586 degree-seeking undergraduates: 3% part-time, 51% women
- 3 degree-seeking graduate students
- 89% of applicants admitted
- SAT or ACT, application essay required

General. Founded in 1966. Regionally accredited. **Degrees:** 141 bachelor's, 4 associate awarded. **ROTC:** Army, Naval, Air Force. **Location:** 15 miles from Tampa, 15 miles from St. Petersburg. **Calendar:** Semester, limited summer session. **Full-time faculty:** 33 total. **Part-time faculty:** 17 total. **Class size:** 69% < 20, 23% 20-39, 6% 40-49, 3% 50-99.

Freshman class profile. 333 applied, 298 admitted, 151 enrolled.

Mid 50% test scores		Out-of-state:	52%
SAT critical reading:	470-600	Live on campus:	95%
SAT math:	450-560	Fraternities:	100%
ACT composite:	19-25	Sororities:	100%

Basis for selection. 2.0 GPA, 870 SAT (exclusive of Writing) or 18 ACT, recommendations, Christian testimony important. Interview recommended. Audition recommended for music majors. **Homeschooled:** Transcript of courses and grades required. GED required if transcript not available; liberal arts/college preparatory program recommended; academic placement testing may be administered.

High school preparation. Recommended units include English 4, mathematics 3, social studies 3, science 3 and foreign language 2. Math units should include geometry; English units should emphasize grammar and writing.

2008-2009 Annual costs. Tuition/fees: $14,040. Room/board: $5,900. Books/supplies: $900. Personal expenses: $2,050.

2008-2009 Financial aid. Non-need-based: Scholarships awarded for academics, alumni affiliation, leadership, music/drama, religious affiliation, ROTC. **Additional information:** Special consideration given to children of Christian service workers; need-based scholarships available to first-generation students; scholarships up to $3,000 available to dual-enrolled students.

Application procedures. Admission: Closing date 8/1 (receipt date). $35 fee, may be waived for applicants with need. Admission notification on a rolling basis. **Financial aid:** Priority date 3/15; no closing date. FAFSA, institutional form required. Applicants notified on a rolling basis starting 4/15; must reply within 2 week(s) of notification.

Academics. All students completing a bachelor's degree earn the equivalent of 20-credit minor in Bible. **Special study options:** Distance learning, double major, dual enrollment of high school students, honors, independent study, internships, liberal arts/career combination, student-designed major, study abroad, teacher certification program. **Credit/placement by examination:** AP, CLEP, IB, institutional tests. 24 credit hours maximum toward associate degree, 24 toward bachelor's. **Support services:** Reduced course load, remedial instruction, study skills assistance, tutoring.

Majors. Biology: General. **Business:** Accounting, business admin, office management. **Communications:** General. **Computer sciences:** Information systems. **Education:** Biology, elementary, English, mathematics, music, physical, social studies, special. **Health:** Premedicine. **History:** General. **Legal studies:** Prelaw. **Liberal arts:** Arts/sciences, humanities. **Math:** General. **Parks/recreation:** Exercise sciences, sports admin. **Psychology:** General.

Theology: Bible, pastoral counseling, sacred music. **Other:** Church ministries, Interdisciplinary studies.

Most popular majors. Biology 8%, business/marketing 11%, education 19%, interdisciplinary studies 10%, liberal arts 18%, theological studies 8%.

Computing on campus. 38 workstations in dormitories, library, computer center. Dormitories wired for high-speed internet access and linked to campus network. Commuter students can connect to campus network. Online library, helpline, repair service, wireless network available.

Student life. **Freshman orientation:** Mandatory. Preregistration for classes offered. 2-day program held prior to start of fall semester. **Policies:** Convocation and Christian Life Conference; chapel 4 days per week; evening Bible studies and prayer meetings required of students in the residence halls. Religious observance required. **Housing:** Guaranteed on-campus for all undergraduates. Single-sex dorms available. $100 deposit. **Activities:** Bands, campus ministries, choral groups, drama, film society, music ensembles, musical theater, student government, student newspaper, symphony orchestra, political club, College Republicans, Fellowship of Preministerial Students, student missionary fellowship, China team, music ministry team, joy club.

Athletics. NCCAA. **Intercollegiate:** Baseball M, basketball, golf, soccer, softball W, volleyball W. **Intramural:** Basketball, football (non-tackle) M, soccer, table tennis, tennis, volleyball. **Team name:** Cougars.

Student services. Chaplain/spiritual director, career counseling, student employment services, financial aid counseling, personal counseling, placement for graduates. **Physically disabled:** Services for speech impaired.

Contact. E-mail: admissions@clearwater.edu
Phone: (727) 726-1153 ext. 220 Toll-free number: (800) 348-4463
Fax: (727) 726-8597
Keith Hutchison, Director of Admissions and Advising, Clearwater Christian College, 3400 Gulf-to-Bay Boulevard, Clearwater, FL 33759-4595

DeVry University: Miramar

Miramar, Florida
www.devry.edu **CB code: 4134**

- For-profit 4-year university
- Commuter campus in large town
- 955 degree-seeking undergraduates: 52% part-time, 38% women, 33% African American, 1% Asian American, 41% Hispanic American, 10% international
- 144 degree-seeking graduate students
- Interview required

General. **Degrees:** 188 bachelor's, 24 associate awarded; master's offered. **Calendar:** Semester, extensive summer session. **Full-time faculty:** 20 total; 40% minority, 15% women. **Part-time faculty:** 76 total; 30% minority, 36% women.

Freshman class profile.

Out-of-state:	1%	International:	8%

Basis for selection. Applicants must have high school diploma or equivalent, or a degree from accredited postsecondary institution, demonstrate proficiency in basic college-level skills through SAT or ACT scores or institution-administered placement exams, and be at least 17 years of age. New students may enter at beginning of any semester. CPT also accepted.

2008-2009 Annual costs. Tuition/fees: $14,130. Books/supplies: $1,100. Personal expenses: $1,816.

2007-2008 Financial aid. All financial aid based on need.

Application procedures. **Admission:** No deadline. $50 fee. Admission notification on a rolling basis. **Financial aid:** No deadline. FAFSA required. Applicants notified on a rolling basis.

Academics. **Special study options:** Accelerated study, distance learning. **Credit/placement by examination:** CLEP. **Support services:** Learning center, remedial instruction, tutoring.

Majors. **Business:** Business admin. **Computer sciences:** Networking, systems analysis, web page design. **Engineering technology:** Biomedical, computer, electrical. **Other:** Technical management.

Most popular majors. Business/marketing 76%, computer/information sciences 14%, engineering/engineering technologies 10%.

Computing on campus. Online course registration, online library, helpline available.

Student life. **Activities:** Student government, student newspaper.

Student services. Career counseling, student employment services, financial aid counseling, placement for graduates, veterans' counselor. **Physically disabled:** Services for visually, hearing impaired.

Contact. E-mail: openhouse@mir.devry.edu
Phone: (954) 499-9700 Toll-free number: (866) 793-3879
Fax: (954) 499-9723
Aaron McCardell, Director of Admission, DeVry University: Miramar, 2300 Southwest 145th Avenue, Miramar, FL 33027

DeVry University: Orlando

Orlando, Florida
www.devry.edu **CB code: 2881**

- For-profit 4-year university
- Commuter campus in very large city
- 1,403 degree-seeking undergraduates: 51% part-time, 35% women, 24% African American, 3% Asian American, 24% Hispanic American, 1% international
- 169 degree-seeking graduate students
- Interview required

General. Regionally accredited. **Degrees:** 204 bachelor's, 18 associate awarded; master's offered. **Calendar:** Semester, extensive summer session. **Full-time faculty:** 23 total; 4% minority, 22% women. **Part-time faculty:** 172 total; 22% minority, 39% women.

Basis for selection. Applicants must have high school diploma or equivalent, or degree from an accredited postsecondary institution. New students may enter at the beginning of any semester. SAT or ACT or institution-administered placement examination used to determine proficiency in basic college-level skills.

High school preparation. Required units include mathematics 1. Math unit must be algebra or higher.

2008-2009 Annual costs. Tuition/fees: $14,130. Books/supplies: $1,300. Personal expenses: $3,152.

2007-2008 Financial aid. All financial aid based on need.

Application procedures. **Admission:** No deadline. $50 fee. Admission notification on a rolling basis. **Financial aid:** No deadline. FAFSA required. Applicants notified on a rolling basis.

Academics. **Special study options:** Accelerated study, distance learning. **Credit/placement by examination:** CLEP, institutional tests. **Support services:** Learning center, remedial instruction, tutoring.

Majors. **Business:** Business admin. **Computer sciences:** Networking, systems analysis, web page design. **Engineering:** Software. **Engineering technology:** Biomedical, computer, electrical. **Other:** Technical management.

Most popular majors. Business/marketing 70%, computer/information sciences 23%, engineering/engineering technologies 7%.

Computing on campus. 303 workstations in library, computer center. Online course registration, online library, helpline available.

Student life. **Freshman orientation:** Mandatory. **Activities:** Student newspaper, student activities council, National Society of Black Engineers, association for IT professionals, chess club, technology forum, Millennia Engineering Students Association.

Student services. Career counseling, student employment services, financial aid counseling, placement for graduates, veterans' counselor. **Physically disabled:** Services for visually, hearing impaired.

Contact. Phone: (407) 370-3131 Toll-free number: (866) 353-3879
Fax: (407) 370-3198
Jody Wasmer, Director of Admissions, DeVry University: Orlando, 4000 Millennia Boulevard, Orlando, FL 32839-2426

Eckerd College

St. Petersburg, Florida **CB member**
www.eckerd.edu **CB code: 5223**

- Private 4-year liberal arts college affiliated with Presbyterian Church (USA)
- Residential campus in large city

- 1,808 degree-seeking undergraduates: 1% part-time, 58% women, 3% African American, 2% Asian American, 5% Hispanic American, 3% international
- 66% of applicants admitted
- SAT or ACT (ACT writing optional), application essay required
- 64% graduate within 6 years

General. Founded in 1958. Regionally accredited. **Degrees:** 402 bachelor's awarded. **ROTC:** Army, Air Force. **Location:** 25 miles from Tampa. **Calendar:** 4-1-4, limited summer session. **Full-time faculty:** 112 total; 96% have terminal degrees, 11% minority, 41% women. **Part-time faculty:** 48 total; 35% have terminal degrees, 19% minority, 40% women. **Class size:** 42% < 20, 55% 20-39, 3% 40-49, less than 1% 50-99. **Special facilities:** Marine science laboratory, waterfront program.

Freshman class profile. 3,398 applied, 2,247 admitted, 489 enrolled.

Mid 50% test scores		**GPA 2.0-2.99:**	22%
SAT critical reading:	510-620	**Rank in top quarter:**	48%
SAT math:	500-610	**Rank in top tenth:**	16%
SAT writing:	500-600	**Return as sophomores:**	80%
ACT composite:	22-27	**Out-of-state:**	73%
GPA 3.75 or higher:	16%	**Live on campus:**	95%
GPA 3.50-3.74:	20%	**International:**	3%
GPA 3.0-3.49:	42%		

Basis for selection. School achievement record, school/community involvement, essay, student's character, test scores most important. Interview recommended. Audition tapes for music and theater majors accepted, portfolios accepted for art majors. **Homeschooled:** Statement describing homeschool structure and mission, transcript of courses and grades, state high school equivalency certificate, letter of recommendation (nonparent) required. **Learning Disabled:** Students should provide proper documentation for any disability they wish to inform the college about.

High school preparation. College-preparatory program required. 18 units required; 22 recommended. Required and recommended units include English 4, mathematics 3-4, social studies 2, history 1-2, science 3-4 (laboratory 2-3), foreign language 2-3 and academic electives 3.

2008-2009 Annual costs. Tuition/fees: $30,590. Room/board: $8,754. Books/supplies: $1,000. Personal expenses: $1,400.

2008-2009 Financial aid. Non-need-based: Scholarships awarded for academics, art, athletics, music/drama.

Application procedures. Admission: No deadline. $35 fee, may be waived for applicants with need. Admission notification on a rolling basis beginning on or about 10/1. Must reply by May 1 or within 2 week(s) if notified thereafter. **Financial aid:** Priority date 3/1; no closing date. FAFSA required. Applicants notified on a rolling basis starting 2/1.

Academics. Special study options: Accelerated study, combined bachelor's/graduate degree, double major, exchange student, honors, independent study, internships, liberal arts/career combination, semester at sea, student-designed major, study abroad, United Nations semester, Washington semester. Winter term exchange with other 4-1-4 colleges, 3-2 in engineering with Columbia University, Washington University (MO), University of Miami, and Auburn. **Credit/placement by examination:** AP, CLEP, IB, institutional tests. 63 credit hours maximum toward bachelor's degree. **Support services:** Reduced course load, tutoring, writing center.

Majors. Area/ethnic studies: American, East Asian, women's. **Biology:** General, biochemistry, environmental, marine. **Business:** Business admin, international, management science. **Communications:** General. **Computer sciences:** General. **Conservation:** Environmental studies. **Foreign languages:** General, classics, comparative lit, French, Spanish. **History:** General. **Interdisciplinary:** Global studies. **Liberal arts:** Humanities. **Math:** General. **Philosophy/religion:** Philosophy, religion. **Physical sciences:** Chemistry, physics. **Psychology:** General, developmental. **Social sciences:** Anthropology, economics, international relations, political science, sociology. **Visual/performing arts:** Art history/conservation, dramatic, studio arts.

Most popular majors. Biology 14%, business/marketing 22%, communications/journalism 6%, foreign language 6%, natural resources/environmental science 12%, psychology 8%, social sciences 13%.

Computing on campus. 300 workstations in dormitories, library. Dormitories wired for high-speed internet access and linked to campus network. Commuter students can connect to campus network. Online course registration, online library, helpline, repair service, student web hosting, wireless network available.

Student life. Freshman orientation: Mandatory. Preregistration for classes offered. Three-week session held in fall. **Housing:** Guaranteed on-campus for freshmen. Coed dorms, single-sex dorms, apartments, wellness housing available. Pets allowed in dorm rooms. **Activities:** Campus ministries, choral groups, drama, film society, international student organizations, literary magazine, music ensembles, Model UN, musical theater, radio station, student government, student newspaper, TV station, Phi Beta Kappa, Afro-American society, search and rescue team, Circle-K, honor societies, Earth society.

Athletics. NCAA. **Intercollegiate:** Baseball M, basketball, golf, sailing, soccer, softball W, tennis, volleyball W. **Intramural:** Baseball M, basketball, bowling, sailing, soccer, softball, swimming, table tennis, tennis, volleyball. **Team name:** Tritons.

Student services. Adult student services, alcohol/substance abuse counseling, career counseling, student employment services, financial aid counseling, health services, minority student services, personal counseling, placement for graduates, veterans' counselor, women's services.

Contact. E-mail: admissions@eckerd.edu
Phone: (727) 864-8331 Toll-free number: (800) 456-9009
Fax: (727) 866-2304
John Sullivan, Dean of Admissions and Financial Aid, Eckerd College, 4200 54th Avenue South, St. Petersburg, FL 33711-4700

Edison State College

Fort Myers, Florida — **CB member**
www.edison.edu — **CB code: 5191**

- Public 4-year liberal arts college
- Commuter campus in very large city
- 13,740 degree-seeking undergraduates

General. Founded in 1961. Regionally accredited. Additional campus sites: Charlotte, Hendry Glades, Collier. **Degrees:** 5 bachelor's, 1,269 associate awarded. **Location:** 35 miles from Naples, 120 miles from Tampa. **Calendar:** Semester, limited summer session. **Full-time faculty:** 156 total. **Part-time faculty:** 390 total. **Class size:** 31% < 20, 35% 20-39, 3% 40-49, 1% 50-99. **Special facilities:** Performing arts hall, observatory, 3-hole instructional golf course.

Basis for selection. Open admission, but selective for some programs. Special requirements for allied health programs. **Homeschooled:** Applicants must submit affidavit of completion.

High school preparation. 21 units required. Required units include English 4, mathematics 3, social studies 3 and science 3.

2008-2009 Annual costs. Tuition/fees: $2,348; $8,830 out-of-state. Books/supplies: $626. Personal expenses: $1,060.

Financial aid. Non-need-based: Scholarships awarded for art, music/drama.

Application procedures. Admission: Closing date 8/15 (receipt date). $25 fee, may be waived for applicants with need. Application must be submitted on paper. Admission notification on a rolling basis. **Financial aid:** Priority date 5/1; no closing date. FAFSA required. Applicants notified on a rolling basis starting 6/1; must reply within 2 week(s) of notification.

Academics. Special study options: Accelerated study, cooperative education, cross-registration, distance learning, double major, dual enrollment of high school students, ESL, honors, independent study, internships, liberal arts/career combination. **Credit/placement by examination:** AP, CLEP, IB, institutional tests. 45 credit hours maximum toward associate degree. Credit by exam not available. **Support services:** Learning center, reduced course load, remedial instruction, tutoring.

Majors. Protective services: Criminal justice.

Computing on campus. 80 workstations in library, computer center. Online course registration, online library, helpline available.

Student life. Freshman orientation: Mandatory. Preregistration for classes offered. **Activities:** Bands, choral groups, drama, music ensembles, student government, black student union, Intervarsity Christian Fellowship, Young Republicans, environmental club, foreign student club, Young Democrats, Rotaract, Latin American student association, student nurses association.

Student services. Career counseling, services for economically disadvantaged, student employment services, financial aid counseling, minority student services, on-campus daycare, placement for graduates, veterans' counselor. **Physically disabled:** Services for visually, speech, hearing impaired.

Contact. E-mail: registrar@edison.edu
Phone: (239) 489-9121 Toll-free number: (800) 749-2322
Fax: (239) 489-9094
Billee Silva, District Registrar, Edison State College, Box 60210, Fort Myers, FL 33906-6210

Edward Waters College

Jacksonville, Florida — **CB member**
www.ewc.edu — **CB code: 5182**

- Private 4-year liberal arts college affiliated with African Methodist Episcopal Church
- Commuter campus in very large city
- 847 degree-seeking undergraduates

General. Founded in 1866. Regionally accredited. **Degrees:** 126 bachelor's awarded. **Location:** 150 miles from Orlando; 90 miles from Savannah, Georgia. **Calendar:** Semester, extensive summer session. **Full-time faculty:** 48 total; 69% have terminal degrees, 85% minority, 27% women. **Part-time faculty:** 5 total; 100% minority, 60% women. **Class size:** 71% < 20, 29% 20-39. **Special facilities:** African art collection.

Freshman class profile.

GPA 3.75 or higher:	4%	**Return as sophomores:**	54%
GPA 3.50-3.74:	3%	**Out-of-state:**	22%
GPA 3.0-3.49:	17%	**Live on campus:**	82%
GPA 2.0-2.99:	72%		

Basis for selection. Open admission.

High school preparation. 13 units recommended. Recommended units include English 4, mathematics 3, social studies 3 and science 3.

2008-2009 Annual costs. Tuition/fees: $9,196. Room/board: $6,474. Books/supplies: $500. Personal expenses: $750.

Application procedures. Admission: Priority date 4/15; no deadline. $25 fee, may be waived for applicants with need. Admission notification on a rolling basis. Must reply by May 1 or within 4 week(s) if notified thereafter. **Financial aid:** Closing date 4/15. FAFSA required. Applicants notified on a rolling basis starting 5/1; must reply within 2 week(s) of notification.

Academics. Special study options: Accelerated study, combined bachelor's/graduate degree, cooperative education, cross-registration, double major, dual enrollment of high school students, independent study, internships, liberal arts/career combination, teacher certification program. **Credit/placement by examination:** AP, CLEP, institutional tests. 30 credit hours maximum toward bachelor's degree. **Support services:** Learning center, pre-admission summer program, remedial instruction, study skills assistance, tutoring.

Majors. Biology: General. **Business:** Business admin. **Communications:** General, journalism. **Computer sciences:** Computer science. **Education:** General, mathematics, mentally handicapped, physical, special. **History:** General. **Liberal arts:** Arts/sciences. **Math:** General. **Philosophy/religion:** Religion. **Protective services:** Law enforcement admin. **Psychology:** General. **Public administration:** Social work. **Social sciences:** Sociology.

Most popular majors. Business/marketing 52%, education 9%, psychology 9%, security/protective services 11%.

Computing on campus. 120 workstations in dormitories, library, computer center. Dormitories wired for high-speed internet access and linked to campus network. Repair service, wireless network available.

Student life. Freshman orientation: Mandatory. Preregistration for classes offered. **Policies:** Smoke-free campus. Religious observance required. **Housing:** Guaranteed on-campus for freshmen. Coed dorms, single-sex dorms, wellness housing available. $100 deposit, deadline 7/31. **Activities:** Bands, campus ministries, choral groups, dance, drama, international student organizations, music ensembles, student government, student newspaper, NAACP, college bowl team, ministerial alliance, debate club, Circle K.

Athletics. NAIA. **Intercollegiate:** Baseball M, basketball, cheerleading, cross-country M, football (tackle) M, golf, softball W, track and field M, volleyball W. **Intramural:** Table tennis, volleyball. **Team name:** Fighting Tigers.

Student services. Adult student services, career counseling, student employment services, financial aid counseling, health services, personal counseling, placement for graduates, veterans' counselor.

Contact. E-mail: admissions@ewc.edu
Phone: (904) 470-8000 Toll-free number: (888) 898-3191
Fax: (904) 470-8041
Lonnie Morris, Director of Admissions, Edward Waters College, 1658 Kings Road, Jacksonville, FL 32209

Embry-Riddle Aeronautical University

Daytona Beach, Florida
www.embryriddle.edu — **CB code: 5190**

- Private 4-year university
- Residential campus in small city
- 4,632 degree-seeking undergraduates: 6% part-time, 16% women, 7% African American, 6% Asian American, 8% Hispanic American, 11% international
- 403 degree-seeking graduate students
- 80% of applicants admitted
- SAT or ACT (ACT writing optional) required
- 60% graduate within 6 years; 4% enter graduate study

General. Founded in 1926. Regionally accredited. Over 130 teaching centers across United States and Europe. **Degrees:** 844 bachelor's awarded; master's offered. **ROTC:** Army, Naval, Air Force. **Location:** 50 miles from Orlando. **Calendar:** Semester, extensive summer session. **Full-time faculty:** 240 total; 66% have terminal degrees, 14% minority, 18% women. **Part-time faculty:** 82 total; 16% have terminal degrees, 16% minority, 44% women. **Class size:** 27% < 20, 68% 20-39, 4% 40-49, 2% 50-99. **Special facilities:** Airway science simulation lab.

Freshman class profile. 3,524 applied, 2,822 admitted, 1,064 enrolled.

Mid 50% test scores		**Rank in top quarter:**	48%
SAT critical reading:	450-580	**Rank in top tenth:**	21%
SAT math:	490-620	**Return as sophomores:**	74%
ACT composite:	21-27	**Out-of-state:**	74%
GPA 3.75 or higher:	19%	**Live on campus:**	95%
GPA 3.50-3.74:	17%	**International:**	8%
GPA 3.0-3.49:	35%	**Fraternities:**	11%
GPA 2.0-2.99:	28%	**Sororities:**	16%

Basis for selection. High school GPA, rank in class, and test scores important. Specific requirements vary by degree program. Interview and essay recommended.

High school preparation. 15 units required; 19 recommended. Required and recommended units include English 4, mathematics 3-4, social studies 2, history 1-2, science 2-3 (laboratory 2), foreign language 1 and academic electives 3.

2008-2009 Annual costs. Tuition/fees: $27,540. Room/board: $9,580. Books/supplies: $1,040. Personal expenses: $1,392.

2008-2009 Financial aid. Need-based: 876 full-time freshmen applied for aid; 738 were judged to have need; 738 of these received aid. Average scholarship/grant was $11,939; average loan $4,266. 50% of total undergraduate aid awarded as scholarships/grants, 50% as loans/jobs. **Non-need-based:** Awarded to 151 full-time undergraduates, including 27 freshmen. Scholarships awarded for academics, alumni affiliation, athletics, leadership, ROTC.

Application procedures. Admission: No deadline. $50 fee, may be waived for applicants with need. Admission notification on a rolling basis beginning on or about 11/1. Early application encouraged since available facilities limit enrollment in some programs. **Financial aid:** No deadline. FAFSA required. Applicants notified on a rolling basis starting 3/1; must reply within 4 week(s) of notification.

Academics. Special study options: Accelerated study, cooperative education, distance learning, double major, dual enrollment of high school students, ESL, honors, independent study, internships, student-designed major, study abroad. **Credit/placement by examination:** AP, CLEP, IB, SAT, ACT, institutional tests. 30 credit hours maximum toward bachelor's degree. **Support services:** Pre-admission summer program, remedial instruction, study skills assistance, tutoring.

Majors. Business: Business admin. **Communications:** General. **Computer sciences:** General, computer science. **Engineering:** General, aerospace, civil, computer, electrical, mechanical, physics, software. **Engineering technology:** Aerospace, electrical, occupational safety. **Mechanic/repair:** Aircraft powerplant. **Physical sciences:** Atmospheric science, physics. **Transportation:** Air traffic control, airline/commercial pilot, aviation, aviation management.

Four-Year Colleges

Most popular majors. Business/marketing 10%, engineering/engineering technologies 32%, trade and industry 50%.

Computing on campus. 1,013 workstations in library, computer center. Dormitories linked to campus network. Commuter students can connect to campus network. Helpline, student web hosting available.

Student life. Freshman orientation: Available. Preregistration for classes offered. **Housing:** Guaranteed on-campus for freshmen. Coed dorms available. $250 nonrefundable deposit, deadline 11/1. Special units available in regular coed dorms. **Activities:** Pep band, campus ministries, choral groups, dance, drama, international student organizations, music ensembles, Model UN, radio station, student government, student newspaper, more than 150 clubs and organizations available.

Athletics. NAIA. **Intercollegiate:** Baseball M, basketball M, cheerleading, cross-country, golf, soccer, tennis, track and field, volleyball W. **Intramural:** Badminton, basketball, bowling, football (non-tackle), golf, racquetball, soccer, table tennis, volleyball. **Team name:** Eagles.

Student services. Alcohol/substance abuse counseling, chaplain/spiritual director, career counseling, student employment services, financial aid counseling, health services, personal counseling, placement for graduates, veterans' counselor. **Physically disabled:** Services for visually, speech, hearing impaired.

Contact. E-mail: dbadmit@erau.edu
Phone: (386) 226-6100 Toll-free number: (800) 862-2416
Fax: (386) 226-7070
Robert Adams, Director of Admissions, Embry-Riddle Aeronautical University, 600 South Clyde Morris Boulevard, Daytona Beach, FL 32114-3900

Embry-Riddle Aeronautical University: Worldwide Campus

Daytona Beach, Florida
www.embryriddle.edu **CB code: 5036**

- Private 4-year university
- Commuter campus in small city
- 11,591 degree-seeking undergraduates: 83% part-time, 11% women, 9% African American, 4% Asian American, 9% Hispanic American, 1% Native American
- 4,066 degree-seeking graduate students

General. Regionally accredited. Campus is network of more than 130 centers and teaching sites in United States and Europe, with virtual presence via distance learning covering every continent. **Degrees:** 2,255 bachelor's, 626 associate awarded; master's offered. **Calendar:** Semester, extensive summer session. **Full-time faculty:** 127 total; 51% have terminal degrees, 8% minority, 20% women. **Part-time faculty:** 2,565 total; 16% have terminal degrees, 25% minority, 22% women.

Basis for selection. High school GPA, rank in class, and test scores important. Specific requirements vary by degree program.

2008-2009 Annual costs. Per credit hour charges range from $215 to $275.

2008-2009 Financial aid. Need-based: 7 full-time freshmen applied for aid; 7 were judged to have need; 7 of these received aid. Average scholarship/grant was $3,827; average loan $3,500. 21% of total undergraduate aid awarded as scholarships/grants, 79% as loans/jobs. **Non-need-based:** Scholarships awarded for academics.

Application procedures. Admission: No deadline. $50 fee, may be waived for applicants with need. **Financial aid:** Priority date 4/15; no closing date. FAFSA required. Applicants notified on a rolling basis starting 3/1; must reply within 4 week(s) of notification.

Academics. Special study options: Distance learning. **Credit/placement by examination:** AP, CLEP.

Majors. Business: Business admin. **Mechanic/repair:** Aircraft powerplant. **Transportation:** Aviation, aviation management.

Most popular majors. Business/marketing 13%, trade and industry 87%.

Contact. E-mail: ecinfo@erau.edu
Phone: (386) 225-6910 Toll-free number: (800) 522-6787
Fax: (386) 226-6984
Pamela Thomas, Director of Admissions, Embry-Riddle Aeronautical University: Worldwide Campus, 600 South Clyde Morris Boulevard, Daytona Beach, FL 32114-3900

Everest University: Brandon

Tampa, Florida
www.everest.edu **CB code: 3585**

- For-profit 4-year university and business college
- Commuter campus in very large city
- 1,165 degree-seeking undergraduates

General. Accredited by ACICS. **Degrees:** 178 bachelor's, 350 associate awarded; master's offered. **Calendar:** Quarter. **Full-time faculty:** 15 total. **Part-time faculty:** 66 total.

Basis for selection. Special requirements for nursing programs. CPAT required.

2008-2009 Annual costs. Tuition/fees: $15,750. Books/supplies: $1,200. Personal expenses: $1,799.

Financial aid. All financial aid based on need.

Application procedures. Admission: No deadline. $25 fee, may be waived for applicants with need. Admission notification on a rolling basis. **Financial aid:** No deadline. FAFSA, institutional form required. Applicants notified on a rolling basis; must reply within 2 week(s) of notification.

Academics. Special study options: Cooperative education, distance learning, ESL. **Credit/placement by examination:** AP, CLEP.

Majors. Business: Accounting, business admin, marketing. **Computer sciences:** Information systems. **Legal studies:** Paralegal. **Protective services:** Law enforcement admin.

Contact. E-mail: spointer@cci.edu
Phone: (813) 621-0041 Toll-free number: (877) 338-0068
Fax: (813) 628-0919
Shandretta Pointer, Director of Admissions, Everest University: Brandon, 3924 Coconut Palm Drive, Tampa, FL 33619

Everest University: Jacksonville

Jacksonville, Florida
www.fmu.edu **CB code: 3801**

- For-profit 4-year business college
- Commuter campus in large city

General. Accredited by ACICS. **Calendar:** Quarter.

Contact. Phone: (904) 731-4949
Director of Admissions, 8226 Phillips Highway, Jacksonville, FL 32256

Everest University: Lakeland

Lakeland, Florida
www.everest.edu **CB code: 3584**

- For-profit 4-year university and branch campus college
- Small city
- 700 degree-seeking undergraduates

General. Accredited by ACICS. **Degrees:** 32 bachelor's, 90 associate awarded; master's offered. **Calendar:** Quarter, extensive summer session. **Full-time faculty:** 15 total. **Part-time faculty:** 39 total.

Basis for selection. At least one of the following required: 15 ACT; 700 SAT (exclusive of Writing); passing grade on university-administered assessment examination.

2008-2009 Annual costs. Tuition/fees: $15,750. Tuition and fees may vary by program.

Financial aid. All financial aid based on need.

Application procedures. Admission: No deadline. $25 fee, may be waived for applicants with need. Admission notification on a rolling basis. **Financial aid:** No deadline.

Academics. Credit/placement by examination: CLEP.

Majors. Business: Accounting, business admin. **Computer sciences:** General. **Protective services:** Criminal justice.

Student life. Freshman orientation: Mandatory.

Contact. Phone: (863) 686-1444
Stephanie Andrews, Registrar, Everest University: Lakeland, 995 East Memorial Boulevard, Suite 110, Lakeland, FL 33801-1919

Everest University: Largo
Largo, Florida
www.everest.edu **CB code: 3583**

- For-profit 4-year university and business college
- Commuter campus in large city
- 536 degree-seeking undergraduates
- Interview required

General. Accredited by ACICS. **Degrees:** 55 bachelor's, 111 associate awarded; master's offered. **Location:** 15 miles from Tampa. **Calendar:** Quarter, extensive summer session. **Full-time faculty:** 5 total. **Part-time faculty:** 76 total. **Class size:** 64% < 20, 34% 20-39, 2% 40-49.

Basis for selection. Students without SAT, SAT Subject Test or ACT scores must pass CPAT entrance examination.

High school preparation. Required units include English 4, mathematics 4, social studies 4 and history 4.

2008-2009 Annual costs. Tuition/fees: $15,750. Tuition and fees may vary by program. Books/supplies: $500.

Application procedures. Admission: No deadline. No application fee. Admission notification on a rolling basis. **Financial aid:** No deadline. FAFSA, institutional form required. Applicants notified on a rolling basis.

Academics. Special study options: Cooperative education, distance learning, double major, ESL, independent study, internships. **Credit/placement by examination:** CLEP. 24 credit hours maximum toward associate degree, 48 toward bachelor's. **Support services:** Remedial instruction, study skills assistance, tutoring.

Majors. Business: Accounting, business admin, international, marketing. **Computer sciences:** General.

Most popular majors. Business/marketing 35%, computer/information sciences 10%, visual/performing arts 47%.

Computing on campus. 75 workstations in library, computer center. Online library available.

Student life. Freshman orientation: Mandatory. **Activities:** American Market Association, student human resource association, EXXTEND (service), criminal justice fraternity, Medical Assisting Drs.

Student services. Adult student services, alcohol/substance abuse counseling, career counseling, student employment services, financial aid counseling, personal counseling, placement for graduates, veterans' counselor.

Contact. Phone: (727) 725-2688 Toll-free number: (800) 353-3687
Fax: (727) 725-3827
Director of Admissions, Everest University: Largo, 1199 East Bay Drive Largo, Largo, FL 33770

Everest University: Melbourne
Melbourne, Florida
www.cci.edu **CB code: 3586**

- For-profit 4-year business college
- Commuter campus in small city

General. Accredited by ACICS. **Calendar:** Quarter.

Contact. Phone: (321) 253-2929
Director of Admission, 2401 North Harbor City Boulevard, Melbourne, FL 32935

Everest University: North Orlando
Orlando, Florida
www.everest.edu **CB code: 0742**

- For-profit 4-year business college
- Commuter campus in very large city
- 1,250 degree-seeking undergraduates
- Interview required

General. Founded in 1918. Accredited by ACICS. Additional campus south of downtown Orlando. **Degrees:** 63 bachelor's, 121 associate awarded; master's offered. **Location:** 2 miles from downtown. **Calendar:** Quarter, extensive summer session. **Full-time faculty:** 9 total. **Part-time faculty:** 69 total.

Basis for selection. CPAT exam, interview important. SAT or ACT may be substituted for CPAT.

2008-2009 Annual costs. Tuition/fees: $15,750. Tuition and fees may vary by program. Books/supplies: $700. Personal expenses: $1,764.

Application procedures. Admission: No deadline. No application fee. Admission notification on a rolling basis. **Financial aid:** No deadline. FAFSA required. Applicants notified on a rolling basis starting 6/1.

Academics. Special study options: Accelerated study, cooperative education, distance learning, independent study, internships. **Credit/placement by examination:** CLEP, institutional tests. 24 credit hours maximum toward associate degree, 48 toward bachelor's.

Majors. Business: General, accounting, business admin, marketing. **Computer sciences:** General.

Most popular majors. Business/marketing 72%, computer/information sciences 28%.

Computing on campus. 25 workstations in library, computer center.

Student life. Freshman orientation: Mandatory.

Student services. Placement for graduates.

Contact. E-mail: jdweber@cci.edu
Phone: (407) 628-5870 Fax: (407) 628-1344
Joann Derosa-Weber, Director of Admissions, Everest University: North Orlando, 5421 Diplomat Circle, Orlando, FL 32810

Everest University: Orange Park
Orange Park, Florida
www.fmu.edu

- For-profit 4-year business college
- Commuter campus in small city

General. Accredited by ACICS. **Calendar:** Quarter.

Contact. Phone: (904) 264-9122
805 Wells Road, Orange Park, FL 32073

Everest University: Pompano Beach
Pompano Beach, Florida
www.everest.edu **CB code: 5171**

- For-profit 4-year business college
- Small city

General. Founded in 1940. Accredited by ACICS. **Location:** 35 miles from Miami. **Calendar:** Quarter.

Annual costs/financial aid. Tuition/fees (2008-2009): $15,750. Tuition may vary by program. Books/supplies: $600. Personal expenses: $1,584. Need-based financial aid available to full-time and part-time students.

Contact. Phone: (954) 783-7339
Director of Admissions, 225 North Federal Highway, Pompano Beach, FL 33062

Everest University: South Orlando
Orlando, Florida
www.everest.edu **CB code: 3587**

- For-profit 4-year university and business college
- Very large city
- 1,860 degree-seeking undergraduates
- 77% of applicants admitted
- Interview required

Four-Year Colleges

General. Accredited by ACICS. **Degrees:** 87 bachelor's, 223 associate awarded; master's offered. **Calendar:** Quarter, extensive summer session. **Full-time faculty:** 40 total. **Part-time faculty:** 39 total.

Freshman class profile. 268 applied, 207 admitted, 171 enrolled.

Basis for selection. 15 ACT or 700 SAT (exclusive of Writing) or passing grade on university-administered assessment exam required. SAT or ACT recommended.

2008-2009 Annual costs. Tuition/fees: $15,750. Tuition and fees may vary by program. Books/supplies: $800. Personal expenses: $1,764.

Application procedures. Admission: No deadline. No application fee. **Financial aid:** No deadline.

Academics. Credit/placement by examination: CLEP.

Majors. Business: Business admin.

Contact. Phone: (407) 851-2525
Annette Cloin, Director of Admissions, Everest University: South Orlando, 9200 Southpark Center Loop, Orlando, FL 32819

Everest University: Tampa
Tampa, Florida
www.everest.edu **CB code: 0428**

- For-profit 4-year university and business college
- Commuter campus in large city
- 946 degree-seeking undergraduates

General. Founded in 1890. Accredited by ACICS. **Degrees:** 26 bachelor's, 80 associate awarded; master's offered. **Location:** 85 miles from Orlando. **Calendar:** Quarter, extensive summer session. **Full-time faculty:** 20 total. **Part-time faculty:** 61 total.

Basis for selection. SAT/ACT or university-administered assessment exam required.

2008-2009 Annual costs. Tuition/fees: $15,750. Cost of tuition may vary with program. Books/supplies: $540. Personal expenses: $1,710.

Financial aid. All financial aid based on need.

Application procedures. Admission: No deadline. No application fee. Admission notification on a rolling basis. **Financial aid:** No deadline. FAFSA required. Applicants notified on a rolling basis.

Academics. Special study options: Accelerated study, distance learning, double major, ESL, independent study, internships. **Credit/placement by examination:** CLEP, institutional tests. **Support services:** Tutoring.

Majors. Business: General, accounting, business admin, marketing. **Computer sciences:** General, information systems, programming. **Protective services:** Criminal justice.

Computing on campus. 50 workstations in library, computer center.

Student life. Freshman orientation: Mandatory. **Activities:** Student newspaper.

Student services. Career counseling, student employment services, personal counseling, placement for graduates, veterans' counselor.

Contact. Phone: (813) 879-6000 Fax: (813) 871-2483
Donald Broughton, Director of Admissions, Everest University: Tampa, 3319 West Hillsborough Avenue, Tampa, FL 33614

Everglades University: Boca Raton
Boca Raton, Florida
www.EvergladesUniversity.edu **CB code: 3191**

- Private 4-year university
- Commuter campus in small city

General. Accredited by ACCSCT. **Calendar:** Semester.

Annual costs/financial aid. Tuition/fees (2008-2009): $14,450. $1,600 education fee for online students. Books/supplies: $1,125. Need-based financial aid available for full-time students.

Contact. Phone: (561) 912-1211
Director of Admissions, 5002 T-REX Avenue, Suite 100, Boca Raton, FL 33431

Everglades University: Orlando
Altamonte Springs, Florida
www.evergladesuniversity.edu

- Private 4-year branch campus and liberal arts college
- Very large city
- 71 degree-seeking undergraduates

General. Regionally accredited; also accredited by ACCSCT. **Calendar:** Continuous. **Full-time faculty:** 6 total. **Part-time faculty:** 25 total.

Freshman class profile. 21 enrolled.

Academics. Credit/placement by examination: CLEP.

Majors. Business: Business admin, construction management, management science. **Mechanic/repair:** Avionics. **Transportation:** Aviation management. **Other:** Alternative medicine.

Contact. E-mail: admissions-orl@evergladesuniversity.edu
Phone: (407) 277-0311
Everglades University: Orlando, 887 East Altamonte Drive, Altamonte Springs, FL 32701

Flagler College
St. Augustine, Florida **CB member**
www.flagler.edu **CB code: 5235**

- Private 4-year liberal arts college
- Residential campus in large town
- 2,762 degree-seeking undergraduates: 3% part-time, 60% women, 2% African American, 1% Asian American, 4% Hispanic American, 1% international
- 45% of applicants admitted
- SAT or ACT (ACT writing optional), application essay required
- 61% graduate within 6 years; 6% enter graduate study

General. Founded in 1968. Regionally accredited. Historic St. Augustine Research Institute is a joint partnership of St. Augustine Foundation, Flagler College and the University of Florida. **Degrees:** 614 bachelor's awarded. **Location:** 35 miles from Jacksonville, 50 miles from Daytona Beach. **Calendar:** Semester, limited summer session. **Full-time faculty:** 91 total; 64% have terminal degrees, 8% minority, 46% women. **Part-time faculty:** 106 total; 24% have terminal degrees, 10% minority, 38% women. **Class size:** 36% < 20, 62% 20-39, 2% 40-49, less than 1% 50-99.

Freshman class profile. 2,358 applied, 1,065 admitted, 618 enrolled.

Mid 50% test scores		**GPA 2.0-2.99:**	20%
SAT critical reading:	520-580	**Rank in top quarter:**	49%
SAT math:	510-580	**Rank in top tenth:**	18%
SAT writing:	500-580	**End year in good standing:**	85%
ACT composite:	21-25	**Return as sophomores:**	78%
GPA 3.75 or higher:	12%	**Out-of-state:**	35%
GPA 3.50-3.74:	16%	**Live on campus:**	93%
GPA 3.0-3.49:	52%	**International:**	2%

Basis for selection. Academic record, including pattern of courses most important, followed by test scores. Extracurricular activities, recommendations, and intended major also considered. Education applicants must score at or above 45th percentile on SAT or ACT. Interview required for early admission applicants; recommended for all others.

High school preparation. College-preparatory program required. 16 units required; 24 recommended. Required and recommended units include English 4, mathematics 3-4, social studies 3, history 1-2, science 2-3 (laboratory 1-2), foreign language 2, computer science 1, visual/performing arts 1 and academic electives 2.

2008-2009 Annual costs. Tuition/fees: $12,520. Room/board: $6,900. Books/supplies: $1,100. Personal expenses: $2,400.

2008-2009 Financial aid. Need-based: Average need met was 90%. Average scholarship/grant was $4,494; average loan $3,586. 53% of total undergraduate aid awarded as scholarships/grants, 47% as loans/jobs. **Non-need-based:** Scholarships awarded for academics, art, athletics, job skills, leadership, minority status, music/drama, state residency.

Application procedures. Admission: Priority date 1/15; deadline 3/1 (postmark date). $40 fee, may be waived for applicants with need. Admission notification 3/30. Must reply by May 1 or within 3 week(s) if notified thereafter. **Financial aid:** Priority date 4/1; no closing date. FAFSA, institutional form required. Applicants notified on a rolling basis starting 4/1; must reply within 2 week(s) of notification.

Academics. Freshmen must earn at least 24 semester hours credit for good academic standing. **Special study options:** Double major, independent study, internships, liberal arts/career combination, study abroad, teacher certification program. Deaf education majors work directly with faculty and students at nearby Florida School for the Deaf and Blind. **Credit/placement by examination:** AP, CLEP, IB, SAT, ACT. 30 credit hours maximum toward bachelor's degree. **Support services:** Learning center, reduced course load, study skills assistance, tutoring, writing center.

Majors. Area/ethnic studies: Latin American. **Business:** Accounting, business admin. **Communications:** General. **Education:** Art, Deaf/hearing impaired, drama/dance, elementary, English, social science, social studies, special. **Foreign languages:** Spanish. **History:** General. **Liberal arts:** Arts/sciences. **Parks/recreation:** Sports admin. **Philosophy/religion:** Philosophy. **Psychology:** General. **Public administration:** General. **Social sciences:** Economics, political science, sociology. **Visual/performing arts:** General, dramatic, studio arts.

Most popular majors. Business/marketing 18%, communications/journalism 13%, education 12%, English 6%, psychology 8%, public administration/social services 7%, social sciences 8%, visual/performing arts 11%.

Computing on campus. 230 workstations in library, computer center. Dormitories wired for high-speed internet access and linked to campus network. Commuter students can connect to campus network. Online course registration, online library, helpline, student web hosting, wireless network available.

Student life. Freshman orientation: Mandatory. Preregistration for classes offered. 3-day program held each semester prior to classes. **Policies:** Male-female interdorm visitation not allowed in residence halls. Alcohol prohibited on campus. No smoking in buildings, including residence halls. **Housing:** Guaranteed on-campus for freshmen. Single-sex dorms available. $200 nonrefundable deposit, deadline 5/1. Freshman Learning Communities. **Activities:** Campus ministries, choral groups, drama, literary magazine, radio station, student government, student newspaper, TV station, Rotaract, Intervarsity Christian Fellowship, Catholic College Fellowship, Society for Advancement of Management, Students in Free Enterprises, deaf awareness club, sport management club, AIGA.

Athletics. NCAA. **Intercollegiate:** Baseball M, basketball, cross-country, golf, soccer, softball W, tennis, volleyball W. **Intramural:** Badminton, basketball, bowling, football (non-tackle), golf, soccer, softball, table tennis, tennis, volleyball, weight lifting. **Team name:** Saints.

Student services. Career counseling, student employment services, financial aid counseling, health services, personal counseling, veterans' counselor. **Physically disabled:** Services for visually, speech, hearing impaired.

Contact. E-mail: admiss@flagler.edu
Phone: (904) 829-6220 Toll-free number: (800) 304-4208
Fax: (904) 829-6838
Marc Williar, Director of Admissions, Flagler College, 74 King Street, St. Augustine, FL 32084

Florida Agricultural and Mechanical University

Tallahassee, Florida — **CB member**
www.famu.edu — **CB code: 5215**

- Public 4-year university
- Residential campus in small city
- 9,457 degree-seeking undergraduates: 9% part-time, 57% women, 94% African American, 1% Asian American, 1% Hispanic American, 1% international
- 2,233 degree-seeking graduate students
- 64% of applicants admitted
- SAT or ACT (ACT writing recommended) required

General. Founded in 1887. Regionally accredited. **Degrees:** 1,496 bachelor's, 98 associate awarded; master's, doctoral, first professional offered. **ROTC:** Army, Naval, Air Force. **Location:** 169 miles from Jacksonville. **Calendar:** Semester, extensive summer session. **Full-time faculty:** 617 total; 72% have terminal degrees, 73% minority, 44% women. **Part-time faculty:** 140 total; 36% have terminal degrees, 68% minority, 40% women. **Class size:** 44% < 20, 39% 20-39, 8% 40-49, 7% 50-99, 2% >100. **Special facilities:** African American archives research center and museum, observatory.

Freshman class profile. 6,283 applied, 4,023 admitted, 2,110 enrolled.

Mid 50% test scores		**GPA 2.0-2.99:**	48%
SAT critical reading:	410-500	**End year in good standing:**	95%
SAT math:	410-500	**Return as sophomores:**	91%
ACT composite:	17-21	**Out-of-state:**	24%
GPA 3.75 or higher:	8%	**Live on campus:**	96%
GPA 3.50-3.74:	8%	**International:**	1%
GPA 3.0-3.49:	36%		

Basis for selection. School achievement record and test scores most important. 2.5 GPA required. Essay required of borderline applicants. Interview recommended for nursing, physical therapy, architecture, pharmacy, engineering majors. Audition required of music majors. Portfolio required of architecture majors. **Homeschooled:** Applicant may be asked to complete GED.

High school preparation. 18 units required. Required units include English 4, mathematics 3, social studies 3, science 3 (laboratory 1), foreign language 2 and academic electives 3.

2008-2009 Annual costs. Tuition/fees: $3,572; $15,513 out-of-state. Room/board: $6,508. Books/supplies: $800. Personal expenses: $2,400.

2007-2008 Financial aid. Non-need-based: Scholarships awarded for academics, art, leadership.

Application procedures. Admission: Priority date 3/9; deadline 5/9. $25 fee. Admission notification on a rolling basis. **Financial aid:** Priority date 3/1, closing date 6/30. FAFSA required. Applicants notified on a rolling basis starting 3/1; must reply within 2 week(s) of notification.

Academics. Special study options: Accelerated study, combined bachelor's/graduate degree, cooperative education, distance learning, double major, dual enrollment of high school students, honors, independent study, internships, study abroad, teacher certification program, weekend college. **Credit/placement by examination:** AP, CLEP, IB. 30 credit hours maximum toward associate degree, 30 toward bachelor's. Student must have passing scores (determined by state) for AP and CLEP exams. **Support services:** Learning center, pre-admission summer program, reduced course load, remedial instruction, study skills assistance, tutoring, writing center.

Majors. Agriculture: Agribusiness operations, agronomy, animal sciences, food science, horticultural science, horticulture, landscaping, ornamental horticulture, plant protection. **Architecture:** Architecture. **Area/ethnic studies:** African-American. **Biology:** General. **Business:** Accounting, business admin, managerial economics. **Communications:** Broadcast journalism, journalism, public relations. **Computer sciences:** General. **Conservation:** Environmental science. **Education:** Art, business, early childhood, elementary, English, mathematics, music, physical, science, social studies, trade/industrial. **Engineering:** Agricultural, chemical, civil, electrical, mechanical. **Engineering technology:** Civil, construction, electrical. **Foreign languages:** French, Spanish. **Health:** Health care admin, medical records admin, nursing (RN), respiratory therapy technology. **History:** General. **Math:** General. **Philosophy/religion:** Philosophy, religion. **Physical sciences:** Chemistry, physics. **Protective services:** Criminal justice. **Psychology:** General. **Public administration:** Social work. **Social sciences:** Economics, political science, sociology. **Visual/performing arts:** General, commercial/advertising art, dramatic, music performance.

Most popular majors. Business/marketing 19%, communications/journalism 6%, education 9%, engineering/engineering technologies 6%, health sciences 14%, psychology 7%, security/protective services 10%, social sciences 10%.

Computing on campus. Dormitories wired for high-speed internet access and linked to campus network. Commuter students can connect to campus network. Online course registration, online library, helpline, repair service, wireless network available.

Student life. Freshman orientation: Mandatory, $15 fee. Preregistration for classes offered. Five-day session in fall. Cost contingent on whether student stays on campus. **Housing:** Coed dorms, single-sex dorms, apartments available. $350 partly refundable deposit, deadline 9/10. **Activities:** Bands, choral groups, dance, drama, music ensembles, radio station, student government, student newspaper, symphony orchestra, TV station, religious, honorary and scholastic organizations, marketing club, student social workers.

Athletics. NCAA. **Intercollegiate:** Baseball M, basketball, bowling W, cross-country, football (tackle) M, golf, softball W, swimming, tennis, track and field, volleyball W. **Intramural:** Badminton, basketball, bowling, football (tackle) M, gymnastics, racquetball, soccer, softball, table tennis, tennis, track and field, volleyball, weight lifting. **Team name:** Rattlers.

Student services. Alcohol/substance abuse counseling, career counseling, student employment services, financial aid counseling, health services, on-campus daycare, personal counseling, placement for graduates, veterans' counselor. **Physically disabled:** Services for visually, hearing impaired.

Contact. E-mail: ugrdadmissions@famu.edu
Phone: (850) 599-3796 Toll-free number: (866) 642-1198
Fax: (850) 599-3069
Barbara Cox, Admissions, Florida Agricultural and Mechanical University, FHAC, G-9, Tallahassee, FL 32307-3200

Florida Atlantic University

Boca Raton, Florida — **CB member**
www.fau.edu — **CB code: 5229**

- Public 4-year university
- Commuter campus in small city
- 20,946 degree-seeking undergraduates: 41% part-time, 58% women, 18% African American, 5% Asian American, 19% Hispanic American, 3% international
- 3,874 degree-seeking graduate students
- 49% of applicants admitted
- SAT or ACT (ACT writing optional), application essay required
- 38% graduate within 6 years

General. Founded in 1961. Regionally accredited. Courses and degree programs offered at additional sites in Palm Beach, Broward, and St. Lucie counties. **Degrees:** 4,481 bachelor's, 159 associate awarded; master's, doctoral offered. **ROTC:** Army, Air Force. **Location:** 17 miles from Fort Lauderdale. **Calendar:** Semester, extensive summer session. **Full-time faculty:** 799 total; 87% have terminal degrees, 21% minority, 40% women. **Part-time faculty:** 557 total; 14% minority, 52% women. **Class size:** 35% < 20, 48% 20-39, 5% 40-49, 7% 50-99, 4% >100. **Special facilities:** Environmental center, native fish research center, ocean engineering laboratory, marine research facility, robotics laboratory.

Freshman class profile. 13,150 applied, 6,388 admitted, 2,800 enrolled.

Mid 50% test scores			
SAT critical reading:	470-550	Rank in top quarter:	35%
SAT math:	480-570	Rank in top tenth:	9%
SAT writing:	450-540	End year in good standing:	79%
ACT composite:	20-23	Return as sophomores:	75%
GPA 3.75 or higher:	14%	Out-of-state:	9%
GPA 3.50-3.74:	12%	Live on campus:	64%
GPA 3.0-3.49:	42%	International:	1%
GPA 2.0-2.99:	32%	Fraternities:	1%
		Sororities:	1%

Basis for selection. Secondary school record, standardized test scores most important. Recommendation, talent, ability also important. Top 20% of state high school graduates guaranteed admission. Audition recommended for theater majors. Portfolio recommended for art majors. **Homeschooled:** State high school equivalency certificate required.

High school preparation. 18 units required; 19 recommended. Required and recommended units include English 4, mathematics 3-4, social studies 3, science 3 (laboratory 2), foreign language 2 and academic electives 3.

2008-2009 Annual costs. Tuition/fees: $3,782; $17,506 out-of-state. Room/board: $9,170. Books/supplies: $724. Personal expenses: $1,458.

2008-2009 Financial aid. Need-based: 2,113 full-time freshmen applied for aid; 1,135 were judged to have need; 1,111 of these received aid. Average need met was 97%. Average scholarship/grant was $7,338; average loan $3,165. 60% of total undergraduate aid awarded as scholarships/grants, 40% as loans/jobs. **Non-need-based:** Awarded to 618 full-time undergraduates, including 156 freshmen. Scholarships awarded for academics, athletics, music/drama, state residency.

Application procedures. Admission: Closing date 6/1 (receipt date). $30 fee, may be waived for applicants with need. Admission notification on a rolling basis beginning on or about 9/15. **Financial aid:** Priority date 3/1; no closing date. FAFSA required. Applicants notified on a rolling basis starting 4/1; must reply within 3 week(s) of notification.

Academics. Special study options: Accelerated study, combined bachelor's/graduate degree, cooperative education, cross-registration, distance learning, double major, dual enrollment of high school students, ESL, honors, independent study, internships, liberal arts/career combination, student-designed major, study abroad, teacher certification program, weekend college. **Credit/placement by examination:** AP, CLEP, IB. 45 credit hours maximum toward bachelor's degree. **Support services:** Learning center, pre-admission summer program, reduced course load, study skills assistance, tutoring, writing center.

Honors college/program. Most applicants will have 3.5 GPA, 1280 SAT (exclusive of Writing) or 29 on Enhanced ACT. Exceptional applicants who do not meet these criteria may be admitted on individual basis by Admissions Committee.

Majors. Architecture: Architecture, urban/community planning. **Biology:** General. **Business:** Accounting, business admin, finance, hospitality admin, human resources, international, management information systems, marketing, real estate. **Communications:** General, digital media. **Computer sciences:** General. **Education:** Elementary, English, mathematics, music, science, social science, special. **Engineering:** Civil, computer, electrical, mechanical, ocean, surveying. **Engineering technology:** Computer systems. **Foreign languages:** French, German, linguistics, Spanish. **Health:** Health care admin, health services, nursing (RN). **History:** General. **Liberal arts:** Arts/sciences. **Math:** General. **Parks/recreation:** Exercise sciences. **Philosophy/religion:** Judaic, philosophy. **Physical sciences:** Chemistry, geology, physics. **Protective services:** Criminal justice. **Psychology:** General, psychobiology, social. **Public administration:** General, social work. **Social sciences:** General, anthropology, economics, geography, political science, sociology. **Visual/performing arts:** Art, dramatic, music management.

Most popular majors. Business/marketing 25%, education 11%, health sciences 7%, psychology 6%, security/protective services 6%, social sciences 8%.

Computing on campus. 1,000 workstations in dormitories, library, computer center, student center. Dormitories wired for high-speed internet access and linked to campus network. Commuter students can connect to campus network. Online course registration, helpline, repair service, wireless network available.

Student life. Freshman orientation: Mandatory, $35 fee. Preregistration for classes offered. Held 2 different dates before semester starts. **Housing:** Guaranteed on-campus for freshmen. Coed dorms, single-sex dorms, apartments available. $200 partly refundable deposit, deadline 8/1. **Activities:** Bands, campus ministries, choral groups, dance, drama, film society, international student organizations, literary magazine, music ensembles, Model UN, musical theater, opera, radio station, student government, student newspaper, symphony orchestra, TV station, Circle K, College Democrats, College Republicans, B'nai B'rith Hillel, Neumann Club, Christian College Fellowship, Human Rights Organization, European Student Association, NAACP, Peace Finders.

Athletics. NCAA. **Intercollegiate:** Baseball M, basketball, cheerleading, cross-country, football (tackle) M, golf, soccer, softball W, swimming, tennis, track and field W, volleyball W. **Intramural:** Basketball, diving, football (non-tackle), rugby, soccer M, softball, table tennis, volleyball M. **Team name:** Owls.

Student services. Adult student services, alcohol/substance abuse counseling, chaplain/spiritual director, career counseling, student employment services, financial aid counseling, health services, minority student services, on-campus daycare, personal counseling, placement for graduates, veterans' counselor, women's services. **Physically disabled:** Services for visually, speech, hearing impaired. **Learning disabled:** Comprehensive services available.

Contact. E-mail: Admissions@fau.edu
Phone: (561) 297-3040 Toll-free number: (800) 299-4328
Fax: (561) 297-2758
Barbara Pletcher, Director of Admissions, Florida Atlantic University, 777 Glades Road, Boca Raton, FL 33431

Florida Career College: Lauderdale Lakes

Lauderdale Lakes, Florida
lauderdalelakes.college-info.com

- For-profit 4-year technical and career college
- Large town

General. Accredited by ACICS. **Calendar:** Quarter.

Annual costs/financial aid. Tuition varies by length of program and is $445 per credit hour; which leads to certificate, associate or bachelor degree.

Contact. Phone: (954) 535-8700
Director of Admissions, 3383 North State Road 7, Lauderdale Lakes, FL 33319

Florida Christian College

Kissimmee, Florida

www.fcc.edu **CB code: 2167**

- Private 4-year Bible and teachers college affiliated with Christian Churches and Churches of Christ
- Residential campus in small city
- 230 degree-seeking undergraduates: 26% part-time, 43% women, 10% African American, 12% Hispanic American
- 35% of applicants admitted
- SAT or ACT (ACT writing optional), application essay required
- 42% graduate within 6 years

General. Founded in 1975. Candidate for regional accreditation; also accredited by ABHE. **Degrees:** 54 bachelor's, 6 associate awarded. **Location:** 20 miles from Orlando. **Calendar:** Semester, limited summer session. **Full-time faculty:** 11 total; 100% have terminal degrees, 9% minority, 27% women. **Part-time faculty:** 18 total; 100% have terminal degrees, 6% minority. **Class size:** 79% < 20, 19% 20-39, 1% 40-49, 1% 50-99.

Freshman class profile. 154 applied, 54 admitted, 54 enrolled.

Return as sophomores:	19%	**Live on campus:**	84%
Out-of-state:	10%	**International:**	2%

Basis for selection. Autobiographical essays, personal recommendation, and church references required. **Homeschooled:** State high school equivalency certificate, letter of recommendation (nonparent) required.

2008-2009 Annual costs. Tuition/fees: $10,200. Room only: $2,400. Books/supplies: $850. Personal expenses: $895.

2007-2008 Financial aid. Non-need-based: Scholarships awarded for academics, alumni affiliation, leadership, music/drama, religious affiliation, state residency.

Application procedures. Admission: Priority date 7/15; deadline 8/1 (postmark date). $35 fee, may be waived for applicants with need. Admission notification on a rolling basis. **Financial aid:** Priority date 5/1, closing date 7/15. FAFSA, institutional form required. Applicants notified on a rolling basis starting 3/1.

Academics. Special study options: Accelerated study, distance learning, dual enrollment of high school students, independent study, internships, student-designed major, teacher certification program. **Credit/placement by examination:** AP, CLEP, IB. 15 credit hours maximum toward associate degree, 30 toward bachelor's. **Support services:** Reduced course load, study skills assistance, tutoring.

Majors. Education: Elementary. **Philosophy/religion:** Philosophy, religion. **Theology:** Bible, missionary, pastoral counseling, sacred music, theology.

Computing on campus. 8 workstations in library, student center. Dormitories wired for high-speed internet access and linked to campus network. Online course registration, online library, helpline, repair service, student web hosting, wireless network available.

Student life. Freshman orientation: Mandatory. **Policies:** Religious observance required. **Housing:** Special housing for disabled, apartments, wellness housing available. $100 fully refundable deposit, deadline 7/15. **Activities:** Choral groups, drama, music ensembles, student government, student newspaper, Christian service activities, mission group.

Athletics. NCCAA. **Intercollegiate:** Basketball M, volleyball W. **Intramural:** Football (non-tackle), soccer, softball, table tennis. **Team name:** Suns.

Student services. Career counseling, financial aid counseling, personal counseling, veterans' counselor. **Physically disabled:** Services for visually impaired.

Contact. E-mail: admissions@fcc.edu
Phone: (407) 569-1172 Toll-free number: (877) 468-6322
Fax: (321) 206-2007
Jake Deer, Director of Admission, Florida Christian College, 1011 Bill Beck Boulevard, Kissimmee, FL 34744-4402

Florida College

Temple Terrace, Florida

www.floridacollege.edu **CB code: 5216**

- Private 4-year liberal arts college
- Residential campus in large town
- 506 degree-seeking undergraduates: 4% part-time, 56% women, 3% African American, 1% Asian American, 4% Hispanic American, 1% Native American, 1% international
- 72% of applicants admitted
- SAT or ACT (ACT writing optional) required

General. Founded in 1944. Regionally accredited. **Degrees:** 27 bachelor's, 133 associate awarded. **ROTC:** Army, Air Force. **Location:** 2 miles from Tampa. **Calendar:** Semester, limited summer session. **Full-time faculty:** 35 total; 29% have terminal degrees, 3% minority, 23% women. **Part-time faculty:** 11 total; 36% have terminal degrees, 18% women. **Class size:** 67% < 20, 22% 20-39, 6% 40-49, 5% 50-99.

Freshman class profile. 298 applied, 214 admitted, 214 enrolled.

Mid 50% test scores			
SAT critical reading:	470-620	**GPA 3.75 or higher:**	38%
SAT math:	470-610	**GPA 3.50-3.74:**	15%
ACT composite:	18-26	**GPA 3.0-3.49:**	20%
		GPA 2.0-2.99:	26%

Basis for selection. 2 recommendations, 2.0 GPA required. Test scores, moral character important. Interview and essay recommended. Portfolio required for art majors. **Homeschooled:** Homeschool completion certification required. **Learning Disabled:** Provide voluntary declaration of disability form and documentation.

High school preparation. 16 units required. Required and recommended units include English 4, mathematics 3, social studies 2-3, science 2 (laboratory 2) and foreign language 2.

2008-2009 Annual costs. Tuition/fees: $12,060. Room/board: $6,300. Books/supplies: $1,300. Personal expenses: $2,500.

2008-2009 Financial aid. Need-based: Average need met was 47%. Average scholarship/grant was $1,121; average loan $1,743. 60% of total undergraduate aid awarded as scholarships/grants, 40% as loans/jobs. **Non-need-based:** Scholarships awarded for academics, athletics, music/drama, state residency.

Application procedures. Admission: Priority date 4/1; deadline 8/1 (postmark date). $30 fee, may be waived for applicants with need. Admission notification on a rolling basis. **Financial aid:** FAFSA, institutional form required. Applicants notified on a rolling basis starting 3/1; must reply within 2 week(s) of notification.

Academics. Special study options: Cross-registration, independent study, teacher certification program. **Credit/placement by examination:** AP, CLEP, IB, SAT, ACT, institutional tests. 30 credit hours maximum toward associate degree, 30 toward bachelor's. **Support services:** Reduced course load, remedial instruction, study skills assistance, tutoring, writing center.

Majors. Business: Business admin. **Education:** Elementary. **Liberal arts:** Arts/sciences. **Theology:** Bible.

Most popular majors. Education 19%, liberal arts 55%, philosophy/religious studies 15%, visual/performing arts 11%.

Computing on campus. 76 workstations in library, computer center. Dormitories wired for high-speed internet access and linked to campus network. Wireless network available.

Student life. Freshman orientation: Mandatory. **Policies:** All campus residents expected to attend Sunday worship services. **Housing:** Guaranteed on-campus for all undergraduates. Single-sex dorms, special housing for disabled, wellness housing available. $150 partly refundable deposit, deadline 8/1. **Activities:** Bands, choral groups, drama, literary magazine, music ensembles, musical theater, student government, honor society, social clubs.

Athletics. USCAA. **Intercollegiate:** Basketball M, cheerleading M, cross-country, soccer, volleyball W. **Intramural:** Basketball, football (non-tackle), soccer, softball, volleyball. **Team name:** Falcons.

Student services. Financial aid counseling, health services, personal counseling, veterans' counselor.

Contact. E-mail: admission@floridacollege.edu
Phone: (813) 899-6716 Toll-free number: (800) 326-7655
Fax: (813) 899-6772
Matthew Qualls, Director of Admissions, Florida College, 119 North Glen Arven Avenue, Temple Terrace, FL 33617

Florida Gulf Coast University

Ft. Myers, Florida — **CB member**
www.fgcu.edu — **CB code: 5221**

- Public 4-year university
- Residential campus in small city
- 8,645 degree-seeking undergraduates: 19% part-time, 58% women, 4% African American, 2% Asian American, 12% Hispanic American, 1% international
- 986 degree-seeking graduate students
- 65% of applicants admitted
- SAT or ACT required
- 35% graduate within 6 years

General. Regionally accredited. **Degrees:** 1,209 bachelor's, 184 associate awarded; master's, doctoral offered. **Location:** 100 miles from Tampa, 125 miles from Miami. **Calendar:** Semester, extensive summer session. **Full-time faculty:** 325 total; 79% have terminal degrees, 17% minority, 47% women. **Part-time faculty:** 202 total; 14% minority, 48% women. **Class size:** 23% < 20, 57% 20-39, 9% 40-49, 9% 50-99, 2% >100. **Special facilities:** Natural wetlands, observatory.

Freshman class profile. 6,939 applied, 4,541 admitted, 1,882 enrolled.

Mid 50% test scores		**Rank in top tenth:**	14%
SAT critical reading:	470-550	**End year in good standing:**	86%
SAT math:	470-570	**Return as sophomores:**	74%
ACT composite:	20-23	**Out-of-state:**	9%
GPA 3.75 or higher:	18%	**Live on campus:**	54%
GPA 3.50-3.74:	15%	**International:**	1%
GPA 3.0-3.49:	41%	**Fraternities:**	5%
GPA 2.0-2.99:	26%	**Sororities:**	10%
Rank in top quarter:	42%		

Basis for selection. Grades in academic units, test scores very important. **Homeschooled:** Transcript of courses and grades required. 1010 SAT (exclusive of Writing) or 21 ACT required.

High school preparation. 18 units required. Required units include English 4, mathematics 3, social studies 3, science 3 (laboratory 2), foreign language 2 and academic electives 3.

2008-2009 Annual costs. Tuition/fees: $3,969; $17,238 out-of-state. Room/board: $7,450. Books/supplies: $950. Personal expenses: $1,400.

2007-2008 Financial aid. **Need-based:** 1,491 full-time freshmen applied for aid; 619 were judged to have need; 619 of these received aid. Average need met was 65%. Average scholarship/grant was $4,012; average loan $3,308. 46% of total undergraduate aid awarded as scholarships/grants, 54% as loans/jobs. **Non-need-based:** Awarded to 2,470 full-time undergraduates, including 626 freshmen. Scholarships awarded for academics, alumni affiliation, athletics, leadership, minority status, music/drama, religious affiliation, state residency.

Application procedures. **Admission:** Priority date 2/15; deadline 6/2 (postmark date). $30 fee, may be waived for applicants with need. Admission notification on a rolling basis. **Financial aid:** Priority date 3/1, closing date 6/30. FAFSA required. Applicants notified on a rolling basis starting 2/15.

Academics. **Special study options:** Accelerated study, combined bachelor's/graduate degree, cross-registration, distance learning, double major, dual enrollment of high school students, honors, independent study, internships, student-designed major, study abroad, teacher certification program, Washington semester. **Credit/placement by examination:** AP, CLEP, IB, institutional tests. 45 credit hours maximum toward bachelor's degree. Credit received from one exam program may not be duplicated by another, nor duplicated through dual enrollment credit. **Support services:** Learning center, reduced course load, remedial instruction, study skills assistance, tutoring, writing center.

Majors. **Biology:** General, biotechnology. **Business:** Accounting, business admin, finance, management information systems, marketing, resort management. **Communications:** Media studies. **Computer sciences:** General. **Conservation:** Environmental studies, water/wetlands/marine. **Education:** General, early childhood, elementary, special. **Engineering:** General, biomedical, civil, environmental. **Foreign languages:** Spanish. **Health:** Athletic training, clinical lab science, community health, health care admin, health services, nursing (RN). **History:** General. **Legal studies:** Paralegal. **Liberal arts:** Arts/sciences. **Math:** General. **Parks/recreation:** Exercise sciences. **Philosophy/religion:** Philosophy. **Physical sciences:** Chemistry. **Protective services:** Criminal justice, criminalistics. **Psychology:** General. **Public administration:** Social work. **Social sciences:** Anthropology, political science, sociology. **Visual/performing arts:** Art, dramatic, music performance.

Most popular majors. Business/marketing 27%, education 12%, health sciences 14%, liberal arts 20%, security/protective services 8%.

Computing on campus. 302 workstations in dormitories, library, computer center. Dormitories wired for high-speed internet access and linked to campus network. Commuter students can connect to campus network. Online course registration, online library, helpline, student web hosting, wireless network available.

Student life. **Freshman orientation:** Mandatory, $35 fee. Preregistration for classes offered. Two-day summer program prior to fall semester; families invited. **Policies:** Student code of conduct in effect. **Housing:** Coed dorms, special housing for disabled, apartments, wellness housing available. **Activities:** Campus ministries, dance, drama, film society, international student organizations, literary magazine, Model UN, student government, student newspaper, College Republicans, College Democrats, Christian Campus Fellowship, Intervarsity Christian Fellowship, Navigators, Colleges Against Cancer, American Association of University Women Student Affiliates, human services student organization.

Athletics. NCAA. **Intercollegiate:** Baseball M, basketball, cross-country, golf, softball W, tennis, volleyball W. **Intramural:** Basketball, cross-country, football (non-tackle), soccer, softball, table tennis, tennis, volleyball, water polo. **Team name:** Eagles.

Student services. Adult student services, alcohol/substance abuse counseling, career counseling, student employment services, financial aid counseling, health services, minority student services, on-campus daycare, personal counseling, placement for graduates, veterans' counselor, women's services. **Physically disabled:** Services for visually, speech, hearing impaired.

Contact. E-mail: admissions@fgcu.edu
Phone: (239) 590-7878 Toll-free number: (888) 889-1095
Fax: (239) 590-7894
Marc Laviolette, Director of Admissions and Records, Florida Gulf Coast University, 10501 FGCU Boulevard South, Ft. Myers, FL 33965-6565

Florida Hospital College of Health Sciences

Orlando, Florida
www.FHCHS.edu — **CB code: 3614**

- Private 4-year health science and nursing college affiliated with Seventh-day Adventists
- Commuter campus in large city
- 2,369 degree-seeking undergraduates
- Application essay required

General. Regionally accredited. Affiliated with Florida Hospital. **Degrees:** 424 bachelor's, 206 associate awarded; master's offered. **Calendar:** Trimester, limited summer session. **Full-time faculty:** 53 total. **Part-time faculty:** 34 total. **Class size:** 57% < 20, 32% 20-39, 9% 40-49, 2% 50-99. **Special facilities:** Human patient simulators.

Freshman class profile.

GPA 3.75 or higher:	7%	**GPA 3.0-3.49:**	39%
GPA 3.50-3.74:	6%	**GPA 2.0-2.99:**	48%

Basis for selection. Standard high school diploma from regionally-accredited school required. 2.5 GPA, ACT/SAT and satisfactory recommendations required for general college admission. Professional program admission requirements vary and require essay explaining student's career choice. **Homeschooled:** Curriculums must be regionally accredited. Applicants who have completed non-regionally accredited home school programs may submit passing GED scores or complete 12 hours of credit from regionally accredited college with 2.5 GPA.

High school preparation. 21 units recommended. Recommended units include English 4, mathematics 3, social studies 3, history 3, science 3 (laboratory 3) and foreign language 2.

2008-2009 Annual costs. Tuition/fees: $8,540. Fees vary according to program. Room only: $3,360. Books/supplies: $1,950. Personal expenses: $1,296.

2007-2008 Financial aid. **Need-based:** 52% of total undergraduate aid awarded as scholarships/grants, 48% as loans/jobs. **Non-need-based:** Scholarships awarded for state residency.

Application procedures. **Admission:** Closing date 8/4 (postmark date). $20 fee, may be waived for applicants with need. Admission notification on a rolling basis. Students accepted to professional programs have reply dates in order to claim program seat. **Financial aid:** Priority date 4/12; no closing date. FAFSA, institutional form required. Applicants notified on a rolling basis starting 3/1.

Academics. **Special study options:** Distance learning, dual enrollment of high school students, independent study. **Credit/placement by examination:** CLEP, SAT, ACT, institutional tests. **Support services:** Learning center, pre-admission summer program, remedial instruction, study skills assistance, tutoring.

Majors. **Health:** Health services, nursing (RN), radiologic technology/medical imaging, sonography.

Computing on campus. 45 workstations in dormitories, library, computer center. Commuter students can connect to campus network. Online library, repair service, wireless network available.

Student life. **Freshman orientation:** Mandatory. One-day program. **Policies:** No-use policy for alcohol, drugs, smoking, and illegal substances. **Housing:** Apartments, wellness housing available. $200 fully refundable deposit, deadline 8/4. **Activities:** Campus ministries.

Athletics. **Intramural:** Basketball, football (non-tackle) M, soccer, volleyball.

Student services. Alcohol/substance abuse counseling, career counseling, student employment services, financial aid counseling, health services, personal counseling. **Physically disabled:** Services for visually, speech, hearing impaired.

Contact. E-mail: katie.shaw@fhchs.edu
Phone: (407) 303-7742 Toll-free number: (800) 500-7747
Fax: (407) 303-9408
Kaite Shaw, Director of Admissions, Florida Hospital College of Health Sciences, 671 Winyah Drive, Orlando, FL 32803

Florida Institute of Technology

Melbourne, Florida — **CB member**
www.fit.edu — **CB code: 5080**

- Private 4-year university
- Residential campus in small city
- 3,557 degree-seeking undergraduates: 17% part-time, 37% women, 8% African American, 3% Asian American, 6% Hispanic American, 1% Native American, 18% international
- 2,661 degree-seeking graduate students
- 82% of applicants admitted
- SAT or ACT (ACT writing optional) required
- 59% graduate within 6 years; 21% enter graduate study

General. Founded in 1958. Regionally accredited. **Degrees:** 429 bachelor's awarded; master's, doctoral offered. **ROTC:** Army. **Location:** 76 miles from Orlando. **Calendar:** Semester, limited summer session. **Full-time faculty:** 234 total; 89% have terminal degrees, 13% minority, 22% women. **Part-time faculty:** 250 total; 54% have terminal degrees, 7% minority, 25% women. **Class size:** 53% < 20, 40% 20-39, 4% 40-49, 3% 50-99. **Special facilities:** Telescope/observatory, botanical gardens, pantherium, medical genetics lab, wind and hurricane impact research lab, microelectronics lab, research vessel delphinus, infectious diseases lab, laser optics and instrumentation lab, robotics and spatial systems lab, synoptic meteorology lab, Vero Beach marine lab.

Freshman class profile. 3,168 applied, 2,591 admitted, 637 enrolled.

Mid 50% test scores			
SAT critical reading:	500-610	Rank in top tenth:	23%
SAT math:	540-640	End year in good standing:	76%
ACT composite:	22-28	Return as sophomores:	73%
GPA 3.75 or higher:	38%	Out-of-state:	52%
GPA 3.50-3.74:	16%	Live on campus:	89%
GPA 3.0-3.49:	32%	International:	16%
GPA 2.0-2.99:	14%	Fraternities:	6%
Rank in top quarter:	53%	Sororities:	10%

Basis for selection. Applications reviewed with reference to specific degree programs or for admission to first-year programs in engineering, science and general studies. High school curriculum, GPA, class rank, SAT/ACT, teachers' recommendations, experiential essay, special classes, clubs or teams that involve research projects/opportunities, and advanced problem-solving techniques important. Interview recommended. **Homeschooled:** Transcript of courses and grades required. Self-descriptive 1-page essay, proof of research project participation required. SAT Subject Test strongly recommended (English composition, Math Level II, any sciences related to desired area of study).

High school preparation. College-preparatory program recommended. 16 units required; 22 recommended. Required and recommended units include English 4, mathematics 3-4, social studies 2, history 2, science 3-4 (laboratory 3), foreign language 2, computer science 2 and academic electives 2.

2008-2009 Annual costs. Tuition/fees: $30,190. Tuition $27,280 for aeronautics, business, psychology, and humanities programs. Room/board: $10,250. Books/supplies: $1,200. Personal expenses: $1,500.

2008-2009 Financial aid. **Need-based:** 475 full-time freshmen applied for aid; 394 were judged to have need; 392 of these received aid. Average need met was 84%. Average scholarship/grant was $20,050; average loan $3,432. 60% of total undergraduate aid awarded as scholarships/grants, 40% as loans/jobs. **Non-need-based:** Scholarships awarded for academics, alumni affiliation, athletics, ROTC, state residency.

Application procedures. **Admission:** Priority date 1/15; no deadline. $50 fee, may be waived for applicants with need. Admission notification on a rolling basis beginning on or about 7/1. Must reply by May 1 or within 4 week(s) if notified thereafter. **Financial aid:** Priority date 3/1; no closing date. FAFSA required. Applicants notified on a rolling basis starting 2/15; must reply by 5/1 or within 4 week(s) of notification.

Academics. **Special study options:** Accelerated study, cooperative education, distance learning, double major, dual enrollment of high school students, ESL, independent study, internships, study abroad, teacher certification program. Dual degrees in computer engineering/electrical engineering, chemical engineering/chemistry, molecular/marine biology. **Credit/placement by examination:** AP, CLEP, IB, institutional tests. **Support services:** Learning center, pre-admission summer program, remedial instruction, study skills assistance, tutoring.

Majors. **Biology:** General, aquatic, biochemistry, biomedical sciences, ecology, marine, molecular. **Business:** Accounting, accounting/business management, business admin, e-commerce, information resources management, international, management information systems, marketing. **Communications:** General. **Computer sciences:** Computer science, information systems. **Conservation:** Environmental science. **Education:** Biology, chemistry, computer, mathematics, middle, physics, science. **Engineering:** General, aerospace, chemical, civil, computer, electrical, mechanical, ocean, software. **Engineering technology:** Construction. **Health:** Health care admin. **Interdisciplinary:** Biological/physical sciences. **Liberal arts:** Humanities. **Math:** General, applied. **Physical sciences:** Analytical chemistry, chemistry, hydrology, meteorology, oceanography, physics, planetary. **Protective services:** Law enforcement admin. **Psychology:** General, forensic. **Transportation:** Aviation, aviation management. **Other:** Aviation science, Military science, Preprofessional physics, Space systems management.

Most popular majors. Biology 13%, business/marketing 9%, engineering/engineering technologies 32%, physical sciences 11%, psychology 9%, trade and industry 15%.

Computing on campus. 400 workstations in library, computer center, student center. Dormitories wired for high-speed internet access and linked to campus network. Commuter students can connect to campus network. Online course registration, online library, helpline, repair service, student web hosting, wireless network available.

Student life. **Freshman orientation:** Mandatory. Preregistration for classes offered. Three-day program in late August. **Policies:** Function in accordance with written constitution and bylaws approved by Dean of Students. **Housing:** Guaranteed on-campus for freshmen. Coed dorms, apartments, wellness housing available. $200 fully refundable deposit. **Activities:** Pep band, campus ministries, choral groups, dance, drama, international student organizations, literary magazine, radio station, student government, student newspaper, TV station, Newman Club, InterVarsity Christian Fellowship, Taiwanese student association, Saudi student house, National Society of Black Engineers, Society of Women Engineers, Latin American student association, Caribbean students organization, College Republican, Muslim student association.

Athletics. NCAA. **Intercollegiate:** Baseball M, basketball, cross-country, golf, rowing (crew) W, soccer, softball W, tennis, volleyball W. **Intramural:** Badminton, basketball, bowling, cricket, football (non-tackle), racquetball, soccer, softball, tennis, volleyball, water polo. **Team name:** Panthers.

Student services. Alcohol/substance abuse counseling, career counseling, student employment services, financial aid counseling, health services, personal counseling, veterans' counselor. **Physically disabled:** Services for visually, speech, hearing impaired.

Contact. E-mail: admission@fit.edu
Phone: (321) 674-8030 Toll-free number: (800) 888-4348
Fax: (321) 674-8004
Michael Perry, Director, Undergraduate Admissions, Florida Institute of Technology, 150 West University Boulevard, Melbourne, FL 32901-6975

Florida International University

Miami, Florida — **CB member**
www.fiu.edu — **CB code: 5206**

- Public 4-year university
- Commuter campus in very large city
- 30,717 degree-seeking undergraduates: 38% part-time, 56% women, 12% African American, 4% Asian American, 64% Hispanic American, 4% international
- 6,496 degree-seeking graduate students
- 38% of applicants admitted
- SAT or ACT (ACT writing optional) required

General. Founded in 1965. Regionally accredited. **Degrees:** 5,811 bachelor's, 50 associate awarded; master's, doctoral, first professional offered. **ROTC:** Army, Air Force. **Location:** 10 miles from downtown. **Calendar:** Semester, extensive summer session. **Full-time faculty:** 854 total; 88% have terminal degrees, 34% minority, 37% women. **Part-time faculty:** 700 total; 37% have terminal degrees, 48% minority, 50% women. **Class size:** 26% < 20, 43% 20-39, 12% 40-49, 16% 50-99, 4% >100. **Special facilities:** Nature preserve, museum.

Freshman class profile. 14,627 applied, 5,581 admitted, 2,991 enrolled.

Mid 50% test scores		**GPA 2.0-2.99:**	11%
SAT critical reading:	500-580	**End year in good standing:**	89%
SAT math:	500-590	**Return as sophomores:**	81%
ACT composite:	21-24	**Out-of-state:**	4%
GPA 3.75 or higher:	40%	**Live on campus:**	23%
GPA 3.50-3.74:	21%	**International:**	2%
GPA 3.0-3.49:	28%		

Basis for selection. 3.0 GPA required. Lower GPA considered with higher test score. SAT Subject Tests recommended. Audition required of music performance, and theater majors. Portfolio required of art and architecture majors. Interview and essay recommended for academically marginal applicants. **Homeschooled:** State high school equivalency certificate required. GED required if equivalency certificate is not available.

High school preparation. College-preparatory program required. 18 units required. Required units include English 4, mathematics 3, social studies 3, science 3 (laboratory 2), foreign language 2 and academic electives 3.

2008-2009 Annual costs. Tuition/fees: $3,975; $16,374 out-of-state. Room/board: $11,120. Books/supplies: $980. Personal expenses: $2,216.

2008-2009 Financial aid. Non-need-based: Scholarships awarded for academics, art, athletics, minority status, music/drama, state residency.

Application procedures. Admission: Priority date 12/1; no deadline. $30 fee, may be waived for applicants with need. Admission notification on a rolling basis beginning on or about 12/1. Must reply by May 1 or within 2 week(s) if notified thereafter. **Financial aid:** Priority date 3/1, closing date 5/15. FAFSA required. Applicants notified on a rolling basis; must reply by 5/1 or within 4 week(s) of notification.

Academics. Special study options: Accelerated study, combined bachelor's/graduate degree, cooperative education, distance learning, double major, dual enrollment of high school students, ESL, exchange student, honors, independent study, internships, study abroad, teacher certification program, weekend college. **Credit/placement by examination:** AP, CLEP, IB, SAT, ACT, institutional tests. 45 credit hours maximum toward bachelor's degree. **Support services:** Learning center, pre-admission summer program, study skills assistance, tutoring.

Honors college/program. 3.5 GPA required. Students may pursue any major while completing honors curriculum.

Majors. Area/ethnic studies: Asian, women's. **Biology:** General, marine. **Business:** Accounting, business admin, finance, hospitality admin, human resources, international, management information systems, marketing, real estate. **Communications:** General. **Computer sciences:** General, information technology. **Conservation:** General. **Education:** Art, early childhood, elementary, foreign languages, physical, special. **Engineering:** Biomedical, civil, computer, electrical, environmental, mechanical. **Engineering technology:** Construction. **Foreign languages:** French, Portuguese, Spanish. **Health:** Health care admin, nursing (RN). **History:** General. **Liberal arts:** Arts/sciences. **Math:** General, applied, statistics. **Parks/recreation:** Facilities management. **Philosophy/religion:** Philosophy, religion. **Physical sciences:** Chemistry, geology, physics. **Protective services:** Criminal justice. **Psychology:** General. **Public administration:** General, social work. **Social sciences:** Economics, geography, international relations, political science, sociology. **Visual/performing arts:** Art history/conservation, dramatic, studio arts.

Most popular majors. Business/marketing 35%, education 8%, engineering/engineering technologies 6%, health sciences 8%, psychology 7%, social sciences 6%.

Computing on campus. 1,800 workstations in library, computer center, student center. Dormitories wired for high-speed internet access and linked to campus network. Commuter students can connect to campus network. Online course registration, online library, repair service; wireless network available.

Student life. Freshman orientation: Mandatory, $90 fee. **Housing:** Coed dorms, apartments, fraternity/sorority housing available. $100 nonrefundable deposit. **Activities:** Bands, choral groups, drama, film society, music ensembles, Model UN, opera, radio station, student government, student newspaper, symphony orchestra, over 120 student organizations.

Athletics. NCAA. **Intercollegiate:** Baseball M, basketball M, cross-country, football (tackle) M, golf W, soccer, softball W, swimming, tennis W, track and field, volleyball W. **Intramural:** Basketball W, cross-country, golf W, sailing, soccer, softball W, swimming, tennis W, volleyball W. **Team name:** Golden Panthers.

Student services. Adult student services, alcohol/substance abuse counseling, career counseling, student employment services, financial aid counseling, health services, minority student services, on-campus daycare, personal counseling, placement for graduates, veterans' counselor. **Physically disabled:** Services for visually, speech, hearing impaired.

Contact. E-mail: admiss@fiu.edu
Phone: (305) 348-2363 Fax: (305) 348-3648
Renee Peterson, Associate Director of Admissions, Florida International University, University Park Campus, PC 140, Miami, FL 33199

Florida Memorial University

Miami Gardens, Florida — **CB member**
www.fmuniv.edu — **CB code: 5217**

- Private 4-year liberal arts college affiliated with American Baptist Churches in the USA
- Residential campus in very large city
- 1,738 degree-seeking undergraduates: 8% part-time, 61% women
- 78 degree-seeking graduate students
- SAT or ACT with writing, application essay required

General. Founded in 1879. Regionally accredited. 4 branch campuses. **Degrees:** 184 bachelor's awarded; master's offered. **ROTC:** Army. **Location:** 15 miles from downtown Miami. **Calendar:** Semester, limited summer session. **Full-time faculty:** 94 total. **Part-time faculty:** 79 total. **Class size:** 70% < 20, 28% 20-39, 1% 40-49, less than 1% 50-99. **Special facilities:** Black archives, airway science building with simulator and air traffic control tower.

Freshman class profile.

GPA 3.75 or higher:	1%	**Return as sophomores:**	72%
GPA 3.50-3.74:	5%	**Out-of-state:**	20%
GPA 3.0-3.49:	15%	**Live on campus:**	80%
GPA 2.0-2.99:	71%	**International:**	10%
End year in good standing:	70%		

Basis for selection. High school GPA of 2.0 required. School achievement record, test scores, interview, recommendations, alumni affiliation considered. Interview recommended.

High school preparation. 15 units recommended. Recommended units include English 4, mathematics 4, social studies 2, science 3 and foreign language 2. College-preparatory program strongly recommended.

2008-2009 Annual costs. Tuition/fees: $12,254. Room/board: $5,340. Books/supplies: $1,200. Personal expenses: $3,500.

Financial aid. Additional information: Need-based financial aid available to part-time students taking 6 credits or more per semester.

Application procedures. **Admission:** No deadline. $15 fee, may be waived for applicants with need. Admission notification on a rolling basis. **Financial aid:** No deadline. Applicants notified on a rolling basis; must reply within 2 week(s) of notification.

Academics. **Special study options:** Combined bachelor's/graduate degree, cooperative education, double major, dual enrollment of high school students, honors, independent study, internships, liberal arts/career combination, study abroad, teacher certification program, weekend college. **Credit/placement by examination:** AP, CLEP, institutional tests. 30 credit hours maximum toward bachelor's degree. **Support services:** Learning center, pre-admission summer program, remedial instruction, study skills assistance, tutoring, writing center.

Majors. **Biology:** General. **Business:** Accounting, business admin, management information systems. **Computer sciences:** General, computer science. **Education:** Elementary, physical. **Health:** Clinical lab science. **Math:** General. **Psychology:** General. **Public administration:** General. **Social sciences:** Sociology. **Transportation:** Aviation.

Most popular majors. Biology 9%, business/marketing 17%, computer/information sciences 11%, education 21%, psychology 9%, social sciences 16%.

Computing on campus. 300 workstations in dormitories, library, computer center, student center. Dormitories wired for high-speed internet access and linked to campus network. Commuter students can connect to campus network. Online library, helpline, repair service, wireless network available.

Student life. **Freshman orientation:** Mandatory. Preregistration for classes offered. **Housing:** Guaranteed on-campus for freshmen. Single-sex dorms available. **Activities:** Jazz band, choral groups, international student organizations, music ensembles, musical theater, student government, student newspaper, TV station, Christian student union, broadcasting club, Junior NAACP, Toastmasters, Professional Women of Tomorrow.

Athletics. NAIA. **Intercollegiate:** Baseball M, basketball, track and field, volleyball W. **Intramural:** Baseball M, basketball, soccer M, softball W, swimming, tennis, volleyball. **Team name:** Figthing lions.

Student services. Chaplain/spiritual director, career counseling, student employment services, health services, minority student services, personal counseling, placement for graduates.

Contact. E-mail: admit@fmuniv.edu
Phone: (305) 626-3750 Fax: (305) 623-1462
Peggy Martin, Director of Admissions, Florida Memorial University, 15800 Northwest 42 Avenue, Miami Gardens, FL 33054

Florida Southern College

Lakeland, Florida — **CB member**
www.flsouthern.edu — **CB code: 5218**

- Private 4-year liberal arts college affiliated with United Methodist Church
- Residential campus in small city
- 1,736 degree-seeking undergraduates: 3% part-time, 59% women, 6% African American, 2% Asian American, 7% Hispanic American, 4% international
- 135 degree-seeking graduate students
- 67% of applicants admitted
- SAT or ACT (ACT writing optional), application essay required
- 52% graduate within 6 years; 27% enter graduate study

General. Founded in 1885. Regionally accredited. **Degrees:** 564 bachelor's awarded; master's offered. **ROTC:** Army, Air Force. **Location:** 30 miles from Tampa, 50 miles from Orlando. **Calendar:** Semester, limited summer session. **Full-time faculty:** 109 total; 87% have terminal degrees, 8% minority, 42% women. **Part-time faculty:** 87 total; 17% have terminal degrees, 2% minority, 42% women. **Class size:** 56% < 20, 41% 20-39, 3% 40-49. **Special facilities:** Planetarium, Frank Lloyd Wright visitor center, nuclear magnetic resonance spectrometer, boathouse, water dome.

Freshman class profile. 2,110 applied, 1,420 admitted, 497 enrolled.

Mid 50% test scores		**Rank in top quarter:**	53%
SAT critical reading:	470-580	**Rank in top tenth:**	25%
SAT math:	490-580	**End year in good standing:**	91%
SAT writing:	460-570	**Return as sophomores:**	75%
ACT composite:	20-25	**Out-of-state:**	27%
GPA 3.75 or higher:	28%	**Live on campus:**	88%
GPA 3.50-3.74:	14%	**International:**	3%
GPA 3.0-3.49:	34%	**Fraternities:**	31%
GPA 2.0-2.99:	24%	**Sororities:**	21%

Basis for selection. School achievement record most important, followed by test scores and recommendations. Character and motivation, demonstrated leadership and/or service, and extracurricular activities also are important. Interview recommended. Audition required for music; audition recommended (required for scholarship consideration) for theater majors. Portfolio recommended (required for scholarship consideration) for art majors. **Homeschooled:** Transcript of courses and grades required.

High school preparation. College-preparatory program required. 18 units required. Required and recommended units include English 4, mathematics 3, social studies 3, history 3, science 2 (laboratory 2), foreign language 2 and academic electives 2.

2008-2009 Annual costs. Tuition/fees: $22,145. Room/board: $7,850. Books/supplies: $1,150. Personal expenses: $1,050.

2008-2009 Financial aid. **Need-based:** 397 full-time freshmen applied for aid; 327 were judged to have need; 327 of these received aid. Average need met was 73%. Average scholarship/grant was $6,576; average loan $4,054. 82% of total undergraduate aid awarded as scholarships/grants, 18% as loans/jobs. **Non-need-based:** Awarded to 1,517 full-time undergraduates, including 465 freshmen. Scholarships awarded for academics, alumni affiliation, art, athletics, job skills, leadership, minority status, music/drama, religious affiliation, ROTC, state residency.

Application procedures. **Admission:** Priority date 3/1; no deadline. $30 fee, may be waived for applicants with need. Admission notification on a rolling basis beginning on or about 1/15. Must reply by May 1 or within 2 week(s) if notified thereafter. Housing deposit refundable only through May 1. **Financial aid:** Priority date 3/1, closing date 7/1. FAFSA, institutional form required. Applicants notified on a rolling basis starting 3/1; must reply within 3 week(s) of notification.

Academics. **Special study options:** Combined bachelor's/graduate degree, double major, dual enrollment of high school students, honors, independent study, internships, liberal arts/career combination, New York semester, student-designed major, study abroad, teacher certification program, United Nations semester, Washington semester. **Credit/placement by examination:** AP, CLEP, IB, SAT, ACT. 60 credit hours maximum toward bachelor's degree. **Support services:** Reduced course load, study skills assistance, tutoring, writing center.

Majors. **Agriculture:** Business, horticultural science, ornamental horticulture, turf management. **Biology:** General, Biochemistry/biophysics and molecular biology, environmental. **Business:** Accounting, business admin, finance, international, management information systems, marketing. **Communications:** Advertising, broadcast journalism, journalism, public relations. **Education:** General, art, elementary, music, physical. **Foreign languages:** Spanish. **Health:** Athletic training, nursing (RN), predental, premedicine, preveterinary. **History:** General. **Interdisciplinary:** Math/computer science. **Liberal arts:** Humanities. **Math:** General. **Parks/recreation:** Sports admin. **Philosophy/religion:** Philosophy, religion. **Physical sciences:** Chemistry. **Psychology:** General. **Social sciences:** General, criminology, economics, political science, sociology. **Visual/performing arts:** Art history/conservation, dramatic, graphic design, music management, music theory/composition, studio arts, theater design. **Other:** English: dramatic art.

Most popular majors. Biology 8%, business/marketing 22%, communications/journalism 10%, education 16%, psychology 9%, social sciences 12%.

Computing on campus. 376 workstations in dormitories, library, computer center. Dormitories wired for high-speed internet access and linked to campus network. Commuter students can connect to campus network. Online course registration, online library, helpline, wireless network available.

Student life. **Freshman orientation:** Mandatory, $100 fee. Preregistration for classes offered. 4-days prior to classes for fall semester. **Housing:** Guaranteed on-campus for all undergraduates. Coed dorms, single-sex dorms, special housing for disabled, apartments, fraternity/sorority housing, wellness housing available. $500 fully refundable deposit, deadline 5/1. **Activities:** Bands, campus ministries, choral groups, dance, drama, international student organizations, literary magazine, music ensembles, musical theater, opera, student government, student newspaper, symphony orchestra, Wesley

Fellowship, Fellowship of Christian Athletes, Upper Room Ministries, Antioch 2, Beyond Campus Ministries, Newman Club, TZeDeK - Social Justice Ministry; Jewish Student Opportunities, Sandwich Ministry to the homeless.

Athletics. NCAA. **Intercollegiate:** Baseball M, basketball, cross-country, golf, lacrosse M, soccer, softball W, swimming, tennis, track and field, volleyball W. **Intramural:** Basketball, bowling, football (non-tackle), golf, soccer, softball, swimming, tennis, volleyball. **Team name:** Moccasins.

Student services. Adult student services, alcohol/substance abuse counseling, chaplain/spiritual director, career counseling, student employment services, financial aid counseling, health services, minority student services, personal counseling, placement for graduates.

Contact. E-mail: fscadm@flsouthern.edu
Phone: (863) 680-4131 Toll-free number: (800) 274-4131
Fax: (863) 680-4120
Bill Langston, Director of Admission, Florida Southern College, 111 Lake Hollingsworth Drive, Lakeland, FL 33801-5698

Florida State University

Tallahassee, Florida — **CB member**
www.fsu.edu — **CB code: 5219**

- Public 4-year university
- Residential campus in small city
- 29,405 degree-seeking undergraduates: 11% part-time, 55% women, 10% African American, 3% Asian American, 12% Hispanic American, 1% Native American
- 8,364 degree-seeking graduate students
- 47% of applicants admitted
- SAT or ACT with writing, application essay required

General. Founded in 1851. Regionally accredited. **Degrees:** 7,615 bachelor's awarded; master's, doctoral, first professional offered. **ROTC:** Army, Naval, Air Force. **Location:** 191 miles from Pensacola, 163 miles from Jacksonville. **Calendar:** Semester, extensive summer session. **Full-time faculty:** 1,298 total; 92% have terminal degrees, 15% minority, 38% women. **Part-time faculty:** 368 total; 92% have terminal degrees, 8% minority, 55% women. **Class size:** 39% < 20, 43% 20-39, 6% 40-49, 8% 50-99, 4% >100. **Special facilities:** Marine laboratory/aquarium, institute of molecular biophysics, national high magnetic field laboratory, music research center, accelerator, oceanographic institute, planetarium, reservation, golf course, Middle East center, institute of science and public affairs, center for the advancement of human rights.

Freshman class profile. 25,485 applied, 11,901 admitted, 5,027 enrolled.

Mid 50% test scores		**GPA 2.0-2.99:**	2%
SAT critical reading:	550-640	**Rank in top quarter:**	71%
SAT math:	560-650	**Rank in top tenth:**	31%
ACT composite:	24-28	**Return as sophomores:**	89%
GPA 3.75 or higher:	47%	**Out-of-state:**	9%
GPA 3.50-3.74:	28%	**Live on campus:**	84%
GPA 3.0-3.49:	23%		

Basis for selection. Most Florida residents accepted have B+ average in academic subjects and 1100 SAT (exclusive of Writing) or 24 ACT. Out-of-state students must meet higher standards. Audition required of music, dance, BFA theater majors. Portfolio required of BFA art, interior design majors. Departmental application required for motion picture, television, and recording art programs. **Homeschooled:** Statement describing homeschool structure and mission, transcript of courses and grades required. Must provide detailed course syllabi with complete course description and names of textbooks used.

High school preparation. 19 units required; 23 recommended. Required and recommended units include English 4, mathematics 4, social studies 1-2, history 2, science 3-4 (laboratory 2), foreign language 2-4 and academic electives 3. Math courses must be algebra I and above; 2 units of same foreign language required; at least 3 units English with substantial writing requirements; social studies must include history. Additional consideration given for completion of higher level courses (AP, IB, honors, calculus and/or foreign language IV or V) and for completion of 4 or more senior academic courses.

2008-2009 Annual costs. Tuition/fees: $3,799; $18,243 out-of-state. Room/board: $8,178. Books/supplies: $1,000. Personal expenses: $3,462.

2008-2009 Financial aid. **Need-based:** 3,411 full-time freshmen applied for aid; 1,625 were judged to have need; 1,625 of these received aid. Average need met was 76%. Average scholarship/grant was $4,212; average loan $2,692. 55% of total undergraduate aid awarded as scholarships/grants, 45% as loans/jobs. **Non-need-based:** Scholarships awarded for academics, athletics, state residency.

Application procedures. **Admission:** Closing date 1/21 (receipt date). $30 fee. Application must be submitted online. Notification on 12/3 and 3/18. Must reply by May 1 or within 2 week(s) if notified thereafter. Students strongly encouraged to apply early. Those applying before 11/30 who are denied admission are given additional opportunities to improve application standing. **Financial aid:** No deadline. FAFSA required. Applicants notified on a rolling basis starting 3/15.

Academics. 2+2 distance learning available in cooperation with selected Florida community colleges includes programs in computer science, interdisciplinary social sciences, and nursing (RN to BSN). **Special study options:** Accelerated study, combined bachelor's/graduate degree, cooperative education, cross-registration, distance learning, double major, dual enrollment of high school students, ESL, honors, independent study, internships, study abroad, teacher certification program. Cooperative programs with Florida Agricultural and Mechanical University and Tallahassee Community College; degree in three years; International year abroad, year-round study abroad in England, Italy, Panama, Spain; summer study abroad in Australia, Brazil, China, Costa Rica, Croatia, Czech Republic, Ecuador, England, France, Ireland, Italy, Japan, Netherlands, Russia, Switzerland. **Credit/placement by examination:** AP, CLEP, IB, SAT, ACT, institutional tests. 30 credit hours maximum toward associate degree, 45 toward bachelor's. English AP credit not awarded for more than 1 exam. **Support services:** Learning center, reduced course load, study skills assistance, tutoring, writing center.

Majors. **Area/ethnic studies:** American, Asian, Caribbean, Central/Eastern European, Latin American, Russian/Slavic, women's. **Biology:** General, biochemistry, biophysics, marine, zoology. **Business:** Accounting, actuarial science, finance, hospitality admin, human resources, insurance, international, management information systems, marketing, operations, real estate. **Communications:** Advertising, media studies, public relations. **Computer sciences:** General, computer science, information technology. **Conservation:** Environmental science, environmental studies. **Education:** Art, bilingual, early childhood, elementary, emotionally handicapped, English, family/consumer sciences, foreign languages, health, learning disabled, mathematics, mentally handicapped, multicultural, music, physical, physics, science, social science, visually handicapped. **Engineering:** Chemical, civil, computer, electrical, environmental, industrial, materials, mechanical, software. **Family/consumer sciences:** General, child development, clothing/textiles, family studies, food/nutrition, merchandising. **Foreign languages:** Ancient Greek, Chinese, classics, French, German, Italian, Japanese, Latin, Russian, Spanish. **Health:** Athletic training, audiology/speech pathology, dietetics, music therapy, nursing (RN), predental, premedicine, prepharmacy, preveterinary, vocational rehab counseling. **History:** General. **Interdisciplinary:** Nutrition sciences. **Legal studies:** Prelaw. **Liberal arts:** Humanities. **Math:** General, applied, computational, statistics. **Parks/recreation:** Exercise sciences, facilities management, health/fitness, sports admin. **Philosophy/religion:** Philosophy, religion. **Physical sciences:** Atmospheric science, chemistry, geology, physics. **Psychology:** General. **Public administration:** Social work. **Social sciences:** General, anthropology, applied economics, criminology, economics, geography, international relations, political science, sociology. **Visual/performing arts:** Acting, art history/conservation, cinematography, dance, dramatic, interior design, jazz, music history, music performance, music theory/composition, piano/organ, stringed instruments, studio arts, theater design, voice/opera. **Other:** Computational Biology, Computer Criminology.

Most popular majors. Business/marketing 19%, education 7%, family/consumer sciences 6%, security/protective services 6%, social sciences 17%, visual/performing arts 6%.

Computing on campus. PC or laptop required. 2,958 workstations in dormitories, library, computer center, student center. Dormitories wired for high-speed internet access and linked to campus network. Commuter students can connect to campus network. Online course registration, online library, helpline, repair service, student web hosting, wireless network available.

Student life. **Freshman orientation:** Mandatory, $90 fee. Preregistration for classes offered. Held during Summer. **Housing:** Coed dorms, single-sex dorms, special housing for disabled, apartments, fraternity/sorority housing, wellness housing available. $225 partly refundable deposit. Honor residences and living and learning communities available. **Activities:** Bands, campus ministries, choral groups, dance, drama, film society, literary magazine, music ensembles, musical theater, opera, radio station, student government, student newspaper, symphony orchestra, TV station, Hillel, Christian student association, Catholic student union, Campus Crusade for Christ, College Democrats, College Republicans, black student union, Hispanic student union, American civil liberties union.

Athletics. NCAA. **Intercollegiate:** Baseball M, basketball, cheerleading, cross-country, diving, football (tackle) M, golf, soccer W, softball W, swimming, tennis, track and field, volleyball W. **Intramural:** Basketball, bowling, field hockey, football (non-tackle), golf, racquetball, soccer, softball, swimming, table tennis, tennis, volleyball, wrestling. **Team name:** Seminoles.

Student services. Adult student services, alcohol/substance abuse counseling, career counseling, student employment services, financial aid counseling, health services, legal services, minority student services, on-campus daycare, personal counseling, placement for graduates, veterans' counselor, women's services. **Physically disabled:** Services for visually, speech, hearing impaired.

Contact. E-mail: admissions@admin.fsu.edu
Phone: (850) 644-6200 Fax: (850) 644-0197
Janice Finney, Director of Admissions, Florida State University, PO Box 3062400, Tallahassee, FL 32306-2400

Hobe Sound Bible College

Hobe Sound, Florida
www.hsbc.edu **CB code: 5306**

- Private 4-year Bible college affiliated with interdenominational tradition
- Residential campus in small town
- 160 degree-seeking undergraduates
- SAT or ACT (ACT writing optional) required

General. Founded in 1960. Accredited by ABHE. **Degrees:** 15 bachelor's, 3 associate awarded. **Location:** 25 miles from West Palm Beach. **Calendar:** 4-1-4, limited summer session. **Full-time faculty:** 25 total. **Part-time faculty:** 10 total.

Freshman class profile.

Mid 50% test scores		SAT math:	430-570
SAT critical reading:	450-680	ACT composite:	14-23

Basis for selection. Recommendations, essay, religious commitment important. **Homeschooled:** Must submit official transcripts from reputable organizations documenting completion of all academic coursework required for high school diploma.

2008-2009 Annual costs. Tuition/fees: $4,850. Room/board: $4,400. Books/supplies: $450. Personal expenses: $2,000.

2008-2009 Financial aid. Non-need-based: Scholarships awarded for academics, leadership.

Application procedures. Admission: Closing date 8/25. $25 fee, may be waived for applicants with need. Admission notification on a rolling basis beginning on or about 3/1. **Financial aid:** Closing date 8/1. FAFSA required.

Academics. Double major required of all students in 4-year programs. All students complete major in Bible as well as major in Christian vocational field. **Special study options:** Distance learning, double major, dual enrollment of high school students, ESL, external degree, internships, teacher certification program. **Credit/placement by examination:** CLEP, institutional tests. **Support services:** Reduced course load, remedial instruction.

Majors. Education: Elementary, English, mathematics, music. **Philosophy/religion:** Religion. **Theology:** Bible, missionary, sacred music, theology. **Visual/performing arts:** Music performance, piano/organ. **Other:** Child Evangelism.

Computing on campus. 10 workstations in computer center.

Student life. Freshman orientation: Mandatory. **Policies:** Religious observance required. **Housing:** Guaranteed on-campus for all undergraduates. Single-sex dorms, apartments available. Unmarried students under 25 required to live in campus dormitories or with parents. **Activities:** Concert band, choral groups, music ensembles, student government, Christian service organizations.

Athletics. Intramural: Basketball, football (tackle) M, racquetball, soccer, softball, tennis, volleyball.

Student services. Health services, personal counseling.

Contact. E-mail: admissions@hsbc.edu
Phone: (772) 546-5534 ext. 1015 Toll-free number: (800) 881-5534
Fax: (772) 545-1422
Judy Fay, Director of Admissions, Hobe Sound Bible College, Box 1065, Hobe Sound, FL 33475

Hodges University

Naples, Florida
www.hodges.edu **CB code: 7113**

- Private 4-year university and business college
- Commuter campus in small city
- 1,658 degree-seeking undergraduates: 22% part-time, 70% women, 18% African American, 2% Asian American, 26% Hispanic American
- 229 degree-seeking graduate students
- 89% of applicants admitted

General. Founded in 1990. Regionally accredited. **Degrees:** 362 bachelor's, 135 associate awarded; master's offered. **Location:** 110 miles from Miami, 180 miles from Tampa. **Calendar:** Trimester, extensive summer session. **Full-time faculty:** 58 total; 69% have terminal degrees, 14% minority, 34% women. **Part-time faculty:** 58 total; 40% have terminal degrees, 9% minority, 53% women. **Class size:** 73% < 20, 24% 20-39, 1% 40-49, 1% 50-99.

Freshman class profile. 218 applied, 194 admitted, 188 enrolled.

Basis for selection. Essay and interview important; level of interest very important.

2008-2009 Annual costs. Tuition/fees: $13,880. Books/supplies: $1,000. Personal expenses: $530.

2008-2009 Financial aid. Need-based: 161 full-time freshmen applied for aid; 144 were judged to have need; 144 of these received aid. Average need met was 64%. Average scholarship/grant was $2,400; average loan $2,700. 31% of total undergraduate aid awarded as scholarships/grants, 69% as loans/jobs. **Non-need-based:** Awarded to 758 full-time undergraduates, including 86 freshmen. Scholarships awarded for academics.

Application procedures. Admission: No deadline. $20 fee. Admission notification on a rolling basis. **Financial aid:** Priority date 9/7; no closing date. FAFSA required. Applicants notified on a rolling basis starting 7/7.

Academics. Special study options: Accelerated study, combined bachelor's/graduate degree, cooperative education, distance learning, double major, ESL, independent study, internships, weekend college. **Credit/placement by examination:** AP, CLEP, IB, institutional tests. **Support services:** Remedial instruction, tutoring.

Majors. Business: Accounting, business admin. **Computer sciences:** Information technology. **Health:** Health care admin. **Legal studies:** Paralegal. **Protective services:** Criminal justice.

Most popular majors. Business/marketing 47%, health sciences 12%, interdisciplinary studies 25%, security/protective services 8%.

Computing on campus. 500 workstations in library, computer center. Wireless network available.

Student life. Freshman orientation: Mandatory. **Activities:** Literary magazine.

Student services. Career counseling, financial aid counseling, personal counseling, placement for graduates.

Contact. E-mail: admit@hodges.edu
Phone: (239) 513-1122 Toll-free number: (800) 466-8017
Fax: (239) 513-9071
Rita Lampus, Vice President of Student Enrollment Management, Hodges University, 2655 Northbrooke Drive, Naples, FL 34119

International Academy of Design and Technology: Orlando

Orlando, Florida
www.iadt.edu **CB code: 4366**

- For-profit 4-year career college
- Very large city
- 1,151 degree-seeking undergraduates

General. Accredited by ACICS. **Degrees:** 118 bachelor's, 18 associate awarded. **Location:** Downtown. **Calendar:** Quarter, extensive summer session. **Full-time faculty:** 19 total. **Part-time faculty:** 89 total.

Basis for selection. Open admission.

2007-2008 Financial aid. **Need-based:** 50% of total undergraduate aid awarded as scholarships/grants, 50% as loans/jobs.

Application procedures. **Admission:** No deadline. $50 fee. **Financial aid:** No deadline. FAFSA required.

Academics. **Special study options:** Accelerated study. **Credit/placement by examination:** AP, CLEP. **Support services:** Learning center, remedial instruction, tutoring.

Majors. **Business:** Fashion, marketing. **Computer sciences:** Computer graphics, webmaster. **Visual/performing arts:** Interior design.

Computing on campus. Online course registration, online library available.

Student life. **Freshman orientation:** Mandatory. Preregistration for classes offered.

Contact. Phone: (407) 857-2300
Dave Ritchie, Vice President Admissions and Marketing, International Academy of Design and Technology: Orlando, 5959 Lake Ellenor Drive, Orlando, FL 32809

International Academy of Design and Technology: Tampa

Tampa, Florida
www.academy.edu **CB code: 7114**

- For-profit 4-year visual arts and technical college
- Commuter campus in very large city
- 2,560 degree-seeking undergraduates
- Interview required

General. Accredited by ACICS. **Degrees:** 252 bachelor's, 211 associate awarded. **Calendar:** Quarter, extensive summer session. **Full-time faculty:** 19 total. **Part-time faculty:** 135 total.

Basis for selection. Open admission. Essay recommended. **Learning Disabled:** Submit Auxiliary Aid Application.

2008-2009 Annual costs. Tuition/fees: $18,780. Books/supplies: $1,800. Personal expenses: $2,015.

2007-2008 Financial aid. **Need-based:** 26% of total undergraduate aid awarded as scholarships/grants, 74% as loans/jobs. **Non-need-based:** Scholarships awarded for academics.

Application procedures. **Admission:** No deadline. $50 fee, may be waived for applicants with need. Admission notification on a rolling basis. **Financial aid:** No deadline. FAFSA required.

Academics. **Special study options:** Accelerated study, cooperative education, internships, study abroad. **Credit/placement by examination:** AP, CLEP, institutional tests. 67 credit hours maximum toward associate degree, 135 toward bachelor's. **Support services:** Learning center, study skills assistance, tutoring.

Majors. **Business:** Merchandising. **Communications technology:** Animation/special effects. **Computer sciences:** Web page design. **Visual/performing arts:** Fashion design, interior design. **Other:** Recording arts.

Computing on campus. Wireless network available.

Student life. **Freshman orientation:** Mandatory. Preregistration for classes offered.

Student services. Adult student services, student employment services, financial aid counseling, placement for graduates, veterans' counselor.

Contact. E-mail: admissions@academy.edu
Phone: (813) 881-0007 Toll-free number: (800) 222-3369
Fax: (813) 881-0008
Heidi Demello, Associate Vice President of Admissions and Marketing, International Academy of Design and Technology: Tampa, 5104 Eisenhower Boulevard, Tampa, FL 33634

ITT Technical Institute: Ft. Lauderdale

Ft. Lauderdale, Florida
www.itt-tech.edu **CB code: 2700**

- For-profit 4-year technical college
- Commuter campus in small city

General. Accredited by ACICS. **Calendar:** Quarter.

Contact. Phone: (954) 476-9300
Director of Recruitment, 3401 South University Drive, Ft. Lauderdale, FL 33328

ITT Technical Institute: Jacksonville

Jacksonville, Florida
www.itt-tech.edu **CB code: 2716**

- For-profit 4-year technical college
- Commuter campus in very large city

General. Accredited by ACICS. **Calendar:** Quarter.

Contact. Phone: (904) 573-9100
Director of Recruitment, 6600-10 Youngerman Circle, Jacksonville, FL 32244

ITT Technical Institute: Lake Mary

Lake Mary, Florida
www.itt-tech.edu

- For-profit 4-year technical college
- Commuter campus in large town

General. Accredited by ACICS. **Calendar:** Quarter.

Contact. Phone: (407) 660-2900
Director of Recruitment, 1400 International Parkway South, Lake Mary, FL 32746

ITT Technical Institute: Miami

Miami, Florida
www.itt-tech.edu **CB code: 2733**

- For-profit 4-year technical college
- Commuter campus in large city

General. Accredited by ACICS. **Calendar:** Quarter.

Contact. Phone: (305) 477-3080
Director of Recruitment, 7955 12th Street, Suite 119, Miami, FL 33126

ITT Technical Institute: Tampa

Tampa, Florida
www.itt-tech.edu **CB code: 2145**

- For-profit 4-year technical college
- Commuter campus in large city

General. Founded in 1981. Accredited by ACICS. **Calendar:** Quarter.

Contact. Phone: (813) 885-2244
Director of Recruitment, 4809 Memorial Highway, Tampa, FL 33634

Jacksonville University

Jacksonville, Florida **CB member**
www.ju.edu **CB code: 5331**

- Private 4-year university and liberal arts college
- Residential campus in very large city
- 2,950 degree-seeking undergraduates: 28% part-time, 60% women, 21% African American, 3% Asian American, 6% Hispanic American, 1% Native American, 3% international
- 387 degree-seeking graduate students
- 64% of applicants admitted
- SAT or ACT (ACT writing optional) required
- 38% graduate within 6 years

General. Founded in 1934. Regionally accredited. **Degrees:** 618 bachelor's awarded; master's offered. **ROTC:** Naval. **Calendar:** Semester, limited summer session. **Full-time faculty:** 158 total; 79% have terminal degrees, 11% minority, 48% women. **Part-time faculty:** 96 total; 38% have terminal degrees, 8% minority, 53% women. **Class size:** 60% < 20, 40%

20-39, less than 1% 40-49. **Special facilities:** Marine science research vessels, observatory, cybercafe.

Freshman class profile. 2,941 applied, 1,872 admitted, 540 enrolled.

Mid 50% test scores		**GPA 2.0-2.99:**	32%
SAT critical reading:	450-560	**Return as sophomores:**	60%
SAT math:	460-570	**Out-of-state:**	44%
ACT composite:	19-244	**Live on campus:**	77%
GPA 3.75 or higher:	19%	**International:**	3%
GPA 3.50-3.74:	16%	**Fraternities:**	21%
GPA 3.0-3.49:	33%	**Sororities:**	16%

Basis for selection. GPA and test scores very important, followed by rigor of secondary school record. Audition required of music, dance, theater majors. Portfolio required for art, computer art and design. **Homeschooled:** Transcript of courses and grades, interview, letter of recommendation (nonparent) required. Two letters of recommendation evaluating academic potential from qualified educator or evaluator outside of the homeschool environment, portfolio that includes 2 writing samples of not less than 100 words, bibliography of reading completed and texts used, and description of curriculum.

High school preparation. 13 units required; 16 recommended. Required and recommended units include English 4, mathematics 3-4, social studies 3, science 3 (laboratory 2) and foreign language 2. History units may be included for satisfaction of social studies requirement.

2008-2009 Annual costs. Tuition/fees: $23,900. $540 mandatory health insurance fee charged unless proof of other coverage is provided. Room/board: $8,760. Books/supplies: $600. Personal expenses: $600.

2008-2009 Financial aid. **Need-based:** Average need met was 52%. Average scholarship/grant was $15,971; average loan $3,906. 63% of total undergraduate aid awarded as scholarships/grants, 37% as loans/jobs. **Non-need-based:** Scholarships awarded for academics, art, athletics, job skills, leadership, music/drama, ROTC, state residency.

Application procedures. **Admission:** No deadline. $30 fee, may be waived for applicants with need. Admission notification on a rolling basis beginning on or about 10/1. Must reply by May 1 or within 2 week(s) if notified thereafter. **Financial aid:** Priority date 3/15; no closing date. FAFSA, institutional form required. Applicants notified on a rolling basis starting 2/15.

Academics. **Special study options:** Accelerated study, combined bachelor's/graduate degree, cooperative education, distance learning, double major, dual enrollment of high school students, honors, independent study, internships, liberal arts/career combination, semester at sea, student-designed major, study abroad, teacher certification program, Washington semester. **Credit/placement by examination:** AP, CLEP, IB, SAT, ACT, institutional tests. 30 credit hours maximum toward associate degree, 30 toward bachelor's. **Support services:** Learning center, remedial instruction, study skills assistance, tutoring, writing center.

Majors. **Biology:** General, marine. **Business:** General, accounting, business admin, finance, international, marketing. **Communications:** General. **Computer sciences:** General. **Education:** General, drama/dance, elementary, music, physical, secondary. **Engineering:** Electrical, mechanical, physics. **Foreign languages:** French, Spanish. **Health:** Nursing (RN), predental, premedicine, prenursing, preveterinary. **History:** General. **Legal studies:** Prelaw. **Liberal arts:** Arts/sciences, humanities. **Math:** General. **Parks/recreation:** Exercise sciences. **Philosophy/religion:** Philosophy. **Physical sciences:** Chemistry, physics. **Psychology:** General. **Social sciences:** Economics, geography, political science, sociology. **Theology:** Sacred music. **Transportation:** Airline/commercial pilot, aviation management. **Visual/performing arts:** Art, art history/conservation, dance, design, dramatic, music management, music performance, music theory/composition, studio arts, voice/opera.

Most popular majors. Business/marketing 18%, health sciences 42%, social sciences 9%, trade and industry 7%.

Computing on campus. 400 workstations in dormitories, library, computer center. Dormitories wired for high-speed internet access and linked to campus network. Commuter students can connect to campus network. Online course registration, online library, helpline, wireless network available.

Student life. **Freshman orientation:** Mandatory. Preregistration for classes offered. Spring program available for pre-registration; formal freshmen orientation occurs in the few days preceding first day of class. **Housing:** Guaranteed on-campus for freshmen. Coed dorms, single-sex dorms, special housing for disabled, apartments, fraternity/sorority housing available. $100 deposit, deadline 5/1. **Activities:** Bands, campus ministries, choral groups, dance, drama, international student organizations, literary magazine, music ensembles, musical theater, radio station, student government, student newspaper, symphony orchestra, TV station, political science society, black student union, Baptist campus ministry, Hillel, Circle-K, Rotaract, Caribbean student group, Dolphin Diversity.

Athletics. NCAA. **Intercollegiate:** Baseball M, basketball, cross-country, football (tackle) M, golf, rowing (crew) W, soccer, softball W, tennis, track and field W, volleyball W. **Intramural:** Basketball, bowling, football (non-tackle), soccer, softball, table tennis, tennis, volleyball. **Team name:** Dolphins.

Student services. Adult student services, alcohol/substance abuse counseling, career counseling, student employment services, financial aid counseling, health services, minority student services, personal counseling, placement for graduates. **Physically disabled:** Services for visually, speech, hearing impaired.

Contact. E-mail: admissions@ju.edu
Phone: (904) 256-7000 Toll-free number: (800) 225-2027
Fax: (904) 256-7012
Yvonne Martel, Director of First Year Admissions and Enrollment, Jacksonville University, 2800 University Boulevard North, Jacksonville, FL 32211-3394

Johnson & Wales University: North Miami

North Miami, Florida
www.jwu.edu **CB code: 3441**

- Private 4-year university
- Residential campus in large city
- 1,917 degree-seeking undergraduates: 3% part-time, 55% women, 25% African American, 1% Asian American, 17% Hispanic American, 9% international
- 79% of applicants admitted
- 49% graduate within 6 years

General. Regionally accredited. **Degrees:** 233 bachelor's, 369 associate awarded. **Calendar:** Quarter, extensive summer session. **Full-time faculty:** 59 total; 29% minority, 34% women. **Part-time faculty:** 33 total; 58% minority, 33% women. **Class size:** 51% < 20, 40% 20-39, 9% 40-49. **Special facilities:** University-operated hotel.

Freshman class profile. 4,844 applied, 3,849 admitted, 583 enrolled.

Mid 50% test scores		**GPA 3.0-3.49:**	32%
SAT critical reading:	400-500	**GPA 2.0-2.99:**	48%
SAT math:	380-500	**Out-of-state:**	43%
GPA 3.75 or higher:	7%	**Live on campus:**	73%
GPA 3.50-3.74:	13%	**International:**	3%

Basis for selection. Academic record, secondary school curriculum, GPA, class rank, test scores are important. It is recommended that students submit a personal statement, employment information, letters of recommendation. SAT and ACT required for admission to honors program.

High school preparation. College-preparatory program recommended. Required units include English 4, mathematics 3, social studies 2 and science 3.

2009-2010 Annual costs. Tuition/fees: $23,490. Room/board: $8,274. Books/supplies: $1,500.

2008-2009 Financial aid. **Need-based:** 563 full-time freshmen applied for aid; 493 were judged to have need; 491 of these received aid. Average need met was 66%. Average scholarship/grant was $8,864; average loan $3,393. 41% of total undergraduate aid awarded as scholarships/grants, 59% as loans/jobs. **Non-need-based:** Awarded to 1,256 full-time undergraduates, including 466 freshmen. Scholarships awarded for academics, alumni affiliation, job skills, leadership, state residency.

Application procedures. **Admission:** No deadline. No application fee. Admission notification on a rolling basis beginning on or about 10/1. Must reply by May 1 or within 2 week(s) if notified thereafter. **Financial aid:** No deadline. FAFSA required. Applicants notified on a rolling basis starting 3/1; must reply within 2 week(s) of notification.

Academics. **Special study options:** Accelerated study, cooperative education, dual enrollment of high school students, ESL, exchange student, honors, independent study, internships, study abroad. **Credit/placement by examination:** CLEP, SAT, ACT, institutional tests. **Support services:** Learning center, pre-admission summer program, reduced course load, remedial instruction, study skills assistance, tutoring, writing center.

Majors. **Business:** Accounting, business admin, hospitality admin, hotel/motel admin, marketing. **Family/consumer sciences:** Institutional food production. **Parks/recreation:** Facilities management, sports admin. **Personal/culinary services:** General, food service, restaurant/catering. **Protective services:** Law enforcement admin.

Most popular majors. Business/marketing 57%, family/consumer sciences 18%, parks/recreation 11%, personal/culinary services 7%, security/protective services 8%.

Computing on campus. 60 workstations in library, computer center, student center. Dormitories wired for high-speed internet access and linked to campus network. Commuter students can connect to campus network. Online course registration, online library, helpline, repair service, wireless network available.

Student life. **Freshman orientation:** Mandatory, $255 fee. Preregistration for classes offered. **Housing:** Guaranteed on-campus for freshmen. Coed dorms, wellness housing available. $300 nonrefundable deposit. All housing accessible for disabled students. **Activities:** Dance, drama, student government, student newspaper.

Athletics. NAIA. **Intramural:** Basketball M, bowling, football (non-tackle), soccer, softball, volleyball. **Team name:** Wildcats.

Student services. Adult student services, alcohol/substance abuse counseling, career counseling, student employment services, financial aid counseling, health services, personal counseling, placement for graduates, veterans' counselor. **Physically disabled:** Services for visually, speech, hearing impaired.

Contact. E-mail: admissions.mia@jwu.edu
Phone: (305) 892-7600 Toll-free number: (866) 598-3567
Fax: (305) 892-7020
Jeff Greenip, Director, Johnson & Wales University: North Miami, 1701 Northeast 127th Street, North Miami, FL 33181

Jones College

Jacksonville, Florida
www.jones.edu **CB code: 5343**

- Private 4-year business and teachers college
- Commuter campus in very large city
- 619 degree-seeking undergraduates: 64% part-time, 82% women
- Interview required

General. Founded in 1918. Accredited by ACICS. Branch campus in Miami. 2 campuses in Jacksonville. **Degrees:** 95 bachelor's, 26 associate awarded. **Calendar:** Trimester, extensive summer session. **Full-time faculty:** 10 total. **Part-time faculty:** 50 total. **Class size:** 91% < 20, 9% 20-39.

Basis for selection. Open admission. **Homeschooled:** State high school equivalency certificate required.

2008-2009 Annual costs. Tuition/fees: $8,340. Books/supplies: $1,500. Personal expenses: $1,312.

Financial aid. All financial aid based on need.

Application procedures. **Admission:** No deadline. No application fee. Admission notification on a rolling basis. **Financial aid:** No deadline. FAFSA required. Applicants notified on a rolling basis.

Academics. **Special study options:** Accelerated study, distance learning, double major, dual enrollment of high school students, independent study, internships, student-designed major, weekend college. **Credit/placement by examination:** AP, CLEP, institutional tests. 15 credit hours maximum toward associate degree, 15 toward bachelor's. Life experience: 21 hours if in bachelor's degree programs, 9 hours if in associate degree programs. **Support services:** Reduced course load, remedial instruction, study skills assistance, tutoring.

Majors. **Business:** Business admin. **Computer sciences:** General. **Education:** Elementary. **Health:** Medical assistant. **Legal studies:** Paralegal.

Most popular majors. Business/marketing 72%, computer/information sciences 11%, health sciences 8%, legal studies 8%.

Computing on campus. 166 workstations in library, computer center. Commuter students can connect to campus network. Online library, wireless network available.

Student life. **Freshman orientation:** Mandatory. Preregistration for classes offered. **Activities:** Radio station.

Student services. Career counseling, student employment services, financial aid counseling, personal counseling, placement for graduates, veterans' counselor.

Contact. E-mail: lvaughn@jones.edu
Phone: (904) 743-1122 ext. 112 Toll-free number: (800) 331-0176 ext. 112
Fax: (904) 743-4446
Linda Vaughn, Director of Admissions, Jones College, 5353 Arlington Expressway, Jacksonville, FL 32211

Jones College: Miami

Miami, Florida
www.jones.edu/ **CB code: 3444**

- Private 4-year branch campus and career college
- Very large city

General. Accredited by ACICS. **Calendar:** Trimester.

Basis for selection. All students required to take CPAT.

Academics. **Credit/placement by examination:** AP, CLEP.

Contact. Jones College: Miami

Lynn University

Boca Raton, Florida **CB member**
www.lynn.edu **CB code: 5437**

- Private 4-year university
- Residential campus in small city
- 1,972 degree-seeking undergraduates: 10% part-time, 49% women, 4% African American, 6% Hispanic American, 14% international
- 369 degree-seeking graduate students
- 62% of applicants admitted
- SAT or ACT (ACT writing recommended), application essay required
- 37% graduate within 6 years

General. Founded in 1962. Regionally accredited. **Degrees:** 453 bachelor's awarded; master's offered. **ROTC:** Air Force. **Location:** 20 miles from Fort Lauderdale, 20 miles from Palm Beach. **Calendar:** Semester, extensive summer session. **Full-time faculty:** 98 total; 69% have terminal degrees, 8% minority, 47% women. **Part-time faculty:** 59 total; 37% have terminal degrees, 20% minority, 44% women. **Class size:** 60% < 20, 39% 20-39, less than 1% 40-49. **Special facilities:** University club (private dining room that serves as laboratory for hotel and restaurant management students), flight simulator, conservatory of music.

Freshman class profile. 2,657 applied, 1,636 admitted, 375 enrolled.

Mid 50% test scores		**GPA 2.0-2.99:**	64%
SAT critical reading:	370-510	**Rank in top quarter:**	16%
SAT math:	410-520	**Rank in top tenth:**	7%
ACT composite:	17-21	**Return as sophomores:**	60%
GPA 3.75 or higher:	5%	**Out-of-state:**	70%
GPA 3.50-3.74:	5%	**Live on campus:**	88%
GPA 3.0-3.49:	22%	**International:**	14%

Basis for selection. School achievement record, high school counselor's recommendation, test scores important; class rank, school and community activities considered. Special consideration given to foreign and minority applicants. Interview and essay recommended. Portfolio recommended for art and graphic design majors. **Learning Disabled:** Submit psychological testing in addition to other admission documents.

High school preparation. 16 units required. Required units include English 4, mathematics 4, social studies 2, history 2 and science 4. Mathematics must include algebra I, algebra II, and either geometry, trigonometry, calculus, or analysis. Science must include biology and a physical science.

2008-2009 Annual costs. Tuition/fees: $29,300. Room/board: $10,900. Books/supplies: $1,000. Personal expenses: $1,100.

2008-2009 Financial aid. **Need-based:** 269 full-time freshmen applied for aid; 133 were judged to have need; 127 of these received aid. Average need met was 58%. Average scholarship/grant was $13,022; average loan $4,514. 51% of total undergraduate aid awarded as scholarships/grants, 49% as loans/jobs. **Non-need-based:** Awarded to 1,129 full-time undergraduates, including 271 freshmen. Scholarships awarded for academics, athletics, leadership, music/drama, religious affiliation, state residency.

Application procedures. **Admission:** No deadline. $35 fee, may be waived for applicants with need. Admission notification on a rolling basis beginning on or about 9/1. Must reply by May 1 or within 2 week(s) if notified thereafter. **Financial aid:** Priority date 3/1; no closing date. FAFSA, institutional form required. Applicants notified on a rolling basis starting 2/1; must reply within 2 week(s) of notification.

Academics. Special study options: Accelerated study, cooperative education, distance learning, double major, dual enrollment of high school students, ESL, honors, independent study, internships, liberal arts/career combination, study abroad, teacher certification program, Washington semester. **Credit/placement by examination:** AP, CLEP, IB, institutional tests. 30 credit hours maximum toward associate degree, 30 toward bachelor's. **Support services:** Learning center, reduced course load, tutoring, writing center.

Majors. Area/ethnic studies: American. **Biology:** General. **Business:** Business admin, hospitality admin, tourism promotion. **Communications:** Advertising, digital media, journalism, media studies, public relations. **Education:** Elementary. **Liberal arts:** Arts/sciences. **Protective services:** Law enforcement admin. **Psychology:** General. **Public administration:** Human services. **Social sciences:** International relations. **Visual/performing arts:** Arts management, dramatic, graphic design, music performance.

Most popular majors. Business/marketing 51%, communication technologies 13%, psychology 11%, security/protective services 10%.

Computing on campus. 220 workstations in dormitories, library, computer center. Dormitories wired for high-speed internet access and linked to campus network. Online library, helpline, repair service, wireless network available.

Student life. Freshman orientation: Mandatory. **Housing:** Guaranteed on-campus for all undergraduates. Coed dorms, single-sex dorms, special housing for disabled, wellness housing available. **Activities:** Campus ministries, choral groups, dance, drama, film society, international student organizations, literary magazine, music ensembles, radio station, student government, student newspaper, symphony orchestra, TV station, Black student union, debate team, gay-straight alliance, Hillel, honors colloquium, hospitality club, Knights of the Roundtable.

Athletics. NCAA. **Intercollegiate:** Baseball M, basketball, cross-country, golf, rowing (crew) M, soccer, softball W, tennis, volleyball W. **Intramural:** Basketball, bowling, cross-country, equestrian, golf, handball, ice hockey, lacrosse, rugby M, soccer, softball, swimming, table tennis, tennis, volleyball, water polo. **Team name:** Fighting Knights.

Student services. Adult student services, chaplain/spiritual director, career counseling, student employment services, health services, personal counseling, placement for graduates, veterans' counselor.

Contact. E-mail: admissions@lynn.edu
Phone: (561) 237-7900 Toll-free number: (800) 888-5966 ext. 1
Fax: (561) 237-7100
Juan Tamayo, Director of Admissions, Lynn University, 3601 North Military Trail, Boca Raton, FL 33431-5598

Miami International University of Art and Design

Miami, Florida
www.artinstitutes.edu/miami/ — **CB code: 5327**

- For-profit 3-year visual arts college
- Commuter campus in very large city
- 2,030 degree-seeking undergraduates: 20% part-time, 67% women, 4% African American, 18% Hispanic American, 2% international
- 57 graduate students
- Application essay, interview required

General. Founded in 1965. Regionally accredited. **Degrees:** 258 bachelor's, 76 associate awarded; master's offered. **Location:** 2 miles from downtown. **Calendar:** Quarter, extensive summer session. **Full-time faculty:** 81 total; 10% have terminal degrees, 22% minority, 40% women. **Part-time faculty:** 216 total; 4% have terminal degrees, 32% minority, 41% women. **Class size:** 41% < 20, 56% 20-39, 3% 40-49.

Freshman class profile.

Out-of-state:	74%	**International:**	2%
Live on campus:	33%		

Basis for selection. Keen interest in fashion, merchandising, art, interior design, or related areas. Secondary school record, recommendations, essay important. Portfolio recommended.

2008-2009 Annual costs. Tuition/fees: $21,020. Fees vary according to program. Room/board: $2,050. Books/supplies: $1,500. Personal expenses: $1,000.

Application procedures. Admission: No deadline. $50 fee. Admission notification on a rolling basis. **Financial aid:** Priority date 7/1; no closing date. FAFSA, CSS PROFILE required. Applicants notified on a rolling basis starting 8/1.

Academics. Special study options: Distance learning, ESL, internships, study abroad. **Credit/placement by examination:** AP, CLEP, IB, institutional tests. **Support services:** Learning center, reduced course load, remedial instruction, tutoring.

Majors. BACHELOR'S. Business: Fashion. **Communications:** Advertising. **Communications technology:** Animation/special effects, recording arts. **Computer sciences:** Web page design. **Visual/performing arts:** General, cinematography, commercial photography, fashion design, graphic design, interior design. **ASSOCIATE. Business:** Fashion. **Visual/performing arts:** Fashion design.

Computing on campus. 87 workstations in library, computer center. Online library, student web hosting, wireless network available.

Student life. Freshman orientation: Mandatory. Preregistration for classes offered. Held week before quarter starts for approximately 4 hours. Includes welcome, university policies, and break out sessions by major/program. **Housing:** Coed dorms available. **Activities:** Dance, international student organizations, student government, student newspaper.

Student services. Career counseling, student employment services, financial aid counseling, personal counseling, placement for graduates.

Contact. E-mail: admissions@aii.edu
Phone: (305) 428-5700 Toll-free number: (800) 225-9023
Fax: (305) 374-7946
Kevin Ryan, Senior Director of Admissions, Miami International University of Art and Design, 1501 Biscayne Boulevard, Suite 100, Miami, FL 33132-1418

New College of Florida

Sarasota, Florida — **CB member**
www.ncf.edu — **CB code: 5506**

- Public 4-year liberal arts college
- Residential campus in small city
- 785 degree-seeking undergraduates: 62% women, 2% African American, 3% Asian American, 10% Hispanic American, 1% Native American
- 58% of applicants admitted
- SAT or ACT (ACT writing optional), application essay required
- 63% graduate within 6 years; 57% enter graduate study

General. Founded in 1960. Regionally accredited. Legislatively-designated honors college for the liberal arts and sciences by state of Florida. **Degrees:** 168 bachelor's awarded. **Location:** 50 miles from Tampa. **Calendar:** 4-1-4. **Full-time faculty:** 73 total; 99% have terminal degrees, 15% minority, 47% women. **Part-time faculty:** 15 total; 87% have terminal degrees, 7% minority, 47% women. **Class size:** 66% < 20, 29% 20-39, 3% 40-49, 2% 50-99. **Special facilities:** High-field nuclear magnetic resonance spectrometer, hardware/software system for brain function analysis, scanning electron microscope, UV-visible and infrared spectrophotometer, inert atmosphere glove box, fine arts center, laboratories for environmental studies, anthropology, psychology, marine biology research facility and laboratories.

Freshman class profile. 1,221 applied, 705 admitted, 222 enrolled.

Mid 50% test scores		**GPA 3.0-3.49:**	16%
SAT critical reading:	630-730	**Rank in top quarter:**	79%
SAT math:	590-670	**Rank in top tenth:**	39%
SAT writing:	600-690	**End year in good standing:**	89%
ACT composite:	27-31	**Return as sophomores:**	82%
GPA 3.75 or higher:	67%	**Out-of-state:**	25%
GPA 3.50-3.74:	17%	**Live on campus:**	99%

Basis for selection. Challenging courses, strong grades, test scores, recommendations, and writing ability important. Class rank, extracurricular activities considered. Level of interest, and availability of limited guaranteed scholarship funds may be considered. Portfolios and interviews considered, but not required. **Homeschooled:** Transcript of courses and grades required. List of length and levels of study completed or planned for completion, textbook information and reading lists required. **Learning Disabled:** Documentaton of disability must be provided. Applicant should submit evidence that any unmet requirement is due to his or her disability, and would not constitute a fundamental alteration of the college's academic program.

High school preparation. College-preparatory program required. 18 units required; 20 recommended. Required and recommended units include English 4, mathematics 3-4, social studies 3-4, science 3-4 (laboratory 2), foreign language 2-4 and academic electives 3-5.

2008-2009 Annual costs. Tuition/fees: $4,128; $23,767 out-of-state. Room/board: $7,464. Books/supplies: $800. Personal expenses: $2,600.

2008-2009 Financial aid. Need-based: 155 full-time freshmen applied for aid; 93 were judged to have need; 93 of these received aid. Average need met was 93%. Average scholarship/grant was $9,010; average loan $2,908. 67% of total undergraduate aid awarded as scholarships/grants, 33% as loans/jobs. **Non-need-based:** Awarded to 495 full-time undergraduates, including 153 freshmen. Scholarships awarded for academics, state residency.

Application procedures. Admission: Priority date 2/15; deadline 4/15 (postmark date). $30 fee, may be waived for applicants with need. Admission notification 4/25. Must reply by 5/1. **Financial aid:** Priority date 2/15; no closing date. FAFSA required. Applicants notified on a rolling basis starting 10/1; must reply by 5/1 or within 4 week(s) of notification.

Academics. All students required to complete three 4-week independent study projects, senior thesis, and oral baccalaureate exam before committee of faculty. **Special study options:** Cross-registration, double major, exchange student, honors, independent study, internships, semester at sea, student-designed major, study abroad, Washington semester. Academic contract, January Interterm (independent study), narrative evaluation/pass-fail, senior thesis, tutorials, undergraduate research. **Credit/placement by examination:** AP, CLEP, institutional tests. AP exam scores, IB higher-level exam scores, and CLEP scores at certain levels may be used toward exemptions from Liberal Arts Curriculum requirements. **Support services:** Study skills assistance, tutoring, writing center.

Majors. Area/ethnic studies: European, French, German, Latin American, Spanish/Iberian. **Biology:** General, biochemistry, marine. **Conservation:** Environmental studies. **Foreign languages:** General, classics, French, German, Russian, Spanish. **History:** General. **Interdisciplinary:** Global studies, medieval/Renaissance, natural sciences. **Liberal arts:** Arts/sciences, humanities. **Math:** General, applied. **Philosophy/religion:** Philosophy, religion. **Physical sciences:** Chemistry, physics. **Psychology:** General. **Public administration:** Policy analysis. **Social sciences:** General, anthropology, economics, international relations, political science, sociology, urban studies. **Visual/performing arts:** Art history/conservation, studio arts.

Computing on campus. 41 workstations in library, computer center, student center. Dormitories wired for high-speed internet access and linked to campus network. Commuter students can connect to campus network. Online course registration, online library, helpline, student web hosting, wireless network available.

Student life. Freshman orientation: Mandatory, $125 fee. Seven-day program. **Policies:** First-year students required to live on campus unless granted waiver by housing department. **Housing:** Guaranteed on-campus for freshmen. Coed dorms, special housing for disabled, apartments available. Specialized housing options may be arranged in response to student interest. **Activities:** Campus ministries, choral groups, dance, drama, film society, literary magazine, music ensembles, musical theater, radio station, student government, student newspaper, Amnesty International, China club, climate justice, origami club, Jesus club, service club, Best Buddies, Africa club, Food not Bombs, Hillel.

Athletics. Intercollegiate: Sailing. **Intramural:** Basketball, fencing, football (non-tackle), lacrosse, racquetball, swimming, table tennis, tennis, volleyball, weight lifting, wrestling.

Student services. Alcohol/substance abuse counseling, chaplain/spiritual director, career counseling, student employment services, financial aid counseling, health services, minority student services, on-campus daycare, personal counseling, women's services. **Physically disabled:** Services for visually, hearing impaired.

Contact. E-mail: admissions@ncf.edu
Phone: (941) 487-5000 Fax: (941) 487-5010
Kathleen Killion, Dean of Admissions and Financial Aid, New College of Florida, 5800 Bay Shore Road, Sarasota, FL 34243-2109

Northwest Florida State College
Niceville, Florida
www.nwfstatecollege.edu **CB code: 5526**

- Public 4-year business and community college
- Commuter campus in large town
- 7,463 degree-seeking undergraduates

General. Founded in 1963. Regionally accredited. Additional teaching centers at Ft. Walton Beach, Eglin Air Force Base, Hurlburt Field, DeFuniak Springs and Crestview. **Degrees:** 51 bachelor's, 1,191 associate awarded. **ROTC:** Army. **Location:** 55 miles from Pensacola. **Calendar:** Semester, extensive summer session. **Full-time faculty:** 90 total. **Part-time faculty:** 180 total. **Class size:** 3% < 20, 97% 20-39. **Special facilities:** Fine and performing arts center with 2 theaters and 2 art galleries.

Basis for selection. Open admission. Applicants without high school diploma may be admitted to credit-bearing certificate programs.

High school preparation. Recommended units include English 4, mathematics 3, social studies 3 and science 3.

2008-2009 Annual costs. Tuition/fees: $2,003; $8,014 out-of-state. Books/supplies: $974.

2007-2008 Financial aid. Need-based: 93% of total undergraduate aid awarded as scholarships/grants, 7% as loans/jobs. **Non-need-based:** Scholarships awarded for academics, art, athletics, leadership, minority status, music/drama.

Application procedures. Admission: Priority date 7/25; no deadline. No application fee. Admission notification on a rolling basis. **Financial aid:** Priority date 4/1; no closing date. FAFSA, institutional form required. Applicants notified on a rolling basis starting 2/1; must reply within 2 week(s) of notification.

Academics. Special study options: Combined bachelor's/graduate degree, cooperative education, cross-registration, distance learning, dual enrollment of high school students, ESL, independent study, internships, student-designed major. **Credit/placement by examination:** AP, CLEP, institutional tests. 32 credit hours maximum toward associate degree. **Support services:** Learning center, remedial instruction, study skills assistance, tutoring.

Majors. Education: Elementary. **Health:** Nursing assistant. **Other:** Middle school math.

Computing on campus. 900 workstations in library, computer center. Commuter students can connect to campus network. Online course registration, online library, wireless network available.

Student life. Freshman orientation: Mandatory. Preregistration for classes offered. Orientation can be completed online. **Activities:** Bands, campus ministries, choral groups, dance, drama, literary magazine, music ensembles, musical theater, student government, symphony orchestra, Student Christian Fellowship, African American student association, Circle K, College Republicans, environmental club.

Athletics. NJCAA. **Intercollegiate:** Baseball M, basketball, softball W. **Intramural:** Softball, volleyball. **Team name:** Raiders.

Student services. Adult student services, career counseling, student employment services, on-campus daycare, personal counseling, placement for graduates, veterans' counselor. **Physically disabled:** Services for visually, speech, hearing impaired.

Contact. E-mail: registrar@nwfstatecollege.edu
Phone: (850) 729-5373 Fax: (850) 729-5215
Christine Bishop, Registrar, Northwest Florida State College, 100 College Boulevard, Niceville, FL 32578-1295

Northwood University: Florida
West Palm Beach, Florida
www.northwood.edu **CB code: 5162**

- Private 4-year university and business college
- Residential campus in small city
- 620 degree-seeking undergraduates: 2% part-time, 40% women, 10% African American, 2% Asian American, 11% Hispanic American, 34% international
- 61% of applicants admitted
- SAT or ACT (ACT writing optional), application essay required

General. Regionally accredited. Specialty university offering only business degrees in professional management; 3 residential campuses in Michigan, Florida, and Texas; 48 program centers; library center in Maine. **Degrees:** 193 bachelor's, 81 associate awarded. **Location:** 75 miles from Miami. **Calendar:** Quarter, limited summer session. **Full-time faculty:** 18 total; 28% have terminal degrees, 6% minority, 44% women. **Part-time faculty:** 26 total; 19% minority, 46% women. **Class size:** 54% < 20, 44% 20-39, 2% 40-49.

Freshman class profile. 778 applied, 472 admitted, 109 enrolled.

Mid 50% test scores		GPA 2.0-2.99:	51%
SAT critical reading:	390-500	Rank in top quarter:	20%
SAT math:	410-510	Rank in top tenth:	2%
SAT writing:	390-470	End year in good standing:	53%
ACT composite:	17-20	Return as sophomores:	55%
GPA 3.75 or higher:	9%	Out-of-state:	51%
GPA 3.50-3.74:	11%	Live on campus:	81%
GPA 3.0-3.49:	25%	International:	20%

Basis for selection. 2.0 GPA and strong interest in business or related field required. Test scores considered. Interview recommended. **Homeschooled:** Transcript of courses and grades required.

High school preparation. College-preparatory program recommended. 17 units recommended. Recommended units include English 4 and mathematics 3.

2008-2009 Annual costs. Tuition/fees: $17,544. Room/board: $8,404. Books/supplies: $1,482.

2008-2009 Financial aid. Need-based: 65 full-time freshmen applied for aid; 56 were judged to have need; 56 of these received aid. Average need met was 60%. Average scholarship/grant was $7,122; average loan $3,309. 53% of total undergraduate aid awarded as scholarships/grants, 47% as loans/jobs. **Non-need-based:** Awarded to 301 full-time undergraduates, including 60 freshmen. Scholarships awarded for academics, alumni affiliation, athletics, leadership, minority status, state residency.

Application procedures. Admission: No deadline. $25 fee, may be waived for applicants with need, free for online applicants. Admission notification on a rolling basis beginning on or about 10/1. **Financial aid:** No deadline. FAFSA required. Applicants notified on a rolling basis starting 3/1.

Academics. Writing, math and accounting labs available. **Special study options:** Accelerated study, combined bachelor's/graduate degree, distance learning, double major, dual enrollment of high school students, external degree, honors, independent study, internships, study abroad, weekend college. **Credit/placement by examination:** AP, CLEP, IB, SAT, ACT, institutional tests. 12 credit hours maximum toward associate degree, 12 toward bachelor's. **Support services:** Learning center, reduced course load, remedial instruction, study skills assistance, tutoring.

Majors. Business: Accounting, banking/financial services, business admin, hotel/motel admin, international, management information systems, marketing, vehicle parts marketing. **Communications:** Advertising. **Computer sciences:** General. **Parks/recreation:** Sports admin.

Most popular majors. Business/marketing 93%.

Computing on campus. 89 workstations in dormitories, library, computer center, student center. Dormitories wired for high-speed internet access and linked to campus network. Commuter students can connect to campus network. Online course registration, online library, helpline, student web hosting, wireless network available.

Student life. Freshman orientation: Mandatory, $125 fee. Preregistration for classes offered. 3-day program in early September. **Policies:** Adheres to all federal and state laws concerning alcohol and drugs. Freshmen and sophomores not living at home must live on campus. **Housing:** Guaranteed on-campus for freshmen. Single-sex dorms, wellness housing available. $100 nonrefundable deposit, deadline 5/1. **Activities:** International student organizations, student government, residence hall association, ambassador club.

Athletics. NAIA. **Intercollegiate:** Baseball M, basketball, golf, soccer, softball W, tennis, volleyball W. **Intramural:** Basketball, bowling, football (non-tackle), racquetball, tennis. **Team name:** Seahawks.

Student services. Adult student services, alcohol/substance abuse counseling, career counseling, student employment services, financial aid counseling, health services, personal counseling, placement for graduates. **Physically disabled:** Services for hearing impaired.

Contact. E-mail: fladmit@northwood.edu
Phone: (561) 478-5500 Toll-free number: (800) 458-8325
Fax: (561) 640-3328
Jack Letvintchuk, Director of Admissions, Northwood University: Florida, 2600 North Military Trail, West Palm Beach, FL 33409-2911

Nova Southeastern University

Fort Lauderdale, Florida — **CB member**
www.nova.edu — **CB code: 5514**

- Private 4-year university
- Commuter campus in small city
- 5,562 degree-seeking undergraduates: 34% part-time, 72% women, 26% African American, 6% Asian American, 27% Hispanic American, 4% international
- 22,382 degree-seeking graduate students
- 45% of applicants admitted
- SAT or ACT (ACT writing optional) required
- 46% graduate within 6 years

General. Founded in 1964. Regionally accredited. Field-based programs offered throughout the nation and at selected international sites. **Degrees:** 1,497 bachelor's, 8 associate awarded; master's, doctoral, first professional offered. **Location:** 10 miles from Fort Lauderdale. **Calendar:** Trimester, limited summer session. **Full-time faculty:** 678 total; 90% have terminal degrees, 24% minority, 46% women. **Part-time faculty:** 1,023 total; 79% have terminal degrees, 24% minority, 51% women. **Class size:** 72% < 20, 27% 20-39, less than 1% 40-49, less than 1% 50-99. **Special facilities:** Oceanographic center, university school (K-12).

Freshman class profile. 3,455 applied, 1,545 admitted, 504 enrolled.

Mid 50% test scores		GPA 2.0-2.99:	17%
SAT critical reading:	460-550	Rank in top quarter:	49%
SAT math:	450-560	Rank in top tenth:	15%
SAT writing:	440-530	Out-of-state:	23%
ACT composite:	19-24	Live on campus:	69%
GPA 3.75 or higher:	34%	International:	1%
GPA 3.50-3.74:	19%	Fraternities:	15%
GPA 3.0-3.49:	30%	Sororities:	13%

Basis for selection. Test scores, GPA important. Career Development Program (adult and evening/weekend) exempt from test score requirement and requires only high school diploma or GED. Interviews and essays recommended. **Homeschooled:** Information about home school program of study and GED score to demonstrate high school equivalence required.

High school preparation. College-preparatory program recommended. Recommended units include English 4, mathematics 3, social studies 1, history 2, science 3, foreign language 2, computer science 1 and visual/performing arts 1.

2008-2009 Annual costs. Tuition/fees: $20,350. Room/board: $8,360.

2007-2008 Financial aid. Need-based: 425 full-time freshmen applied for aid; 359 were judged to have need; 358 of these received aid. Average need met was 64%. Average scholarship/grant was $7,983; average loan $2,786. 55% of total undergraduate aid awarded as scholarships/grants, 45% as loans/jobs. **Non-need-based:** Awarded to 1,761 full-time undergraduates, including 398 freshmen. Scholarships awarded for academics, athletics, leadership, music/drama.

Application procedures. Admission: No deadline. $50 fee, may be waived for applicants with need. Admission notification on a rolling basis. **Financial aid:** Priority date 4/15; no closing date. FAFSA required. Applicants notified on a rolling basis starting 3/15.

Academics. 2 undergraduate programs: college of professional and liberal studies for traditional daytime students, college of career development for adult evening and weekend students. Core curriculum of liberal arts-based courses plus general education required. **Special study options:** Combined bachelor's/graduate degree, distance learning, double major, honors, independent study, internships, liberal arts/career combination, study abroad, teacher certification program. Dual admission with NSU graduate/professional programs. **Credit/placement by examination:** AP, CLEP, IB, SAT, ACT, institutional tests. 90 credit hours maximum toward bachelor's degree. **Support services:** Learning center, reduced course load, remedial instruction, study skills assistance, tutoring, writing center.

Majors. Area/ethnic studies: American. **Biology:** General, marine. **Business:** General, accounting, business admin, finance, marketing. **Communications:** General. **Computer sciences:** General, computer science. **Conservation:** Environmental science, environmental studies. **Education:** Early childhood, elementary, secondary, special. **Health:** Athletic training, health services, nursing (RN), premedicine, sonography. **History:** General. **Legal studies:** General, paralegal, prelaw. **Liberal arts:** Arts/sciences, humanities. **Parks/recreation:** Sports admin. **Protective services:** Criminal justice. **Psychology:** General. **Social sciences:** Economics, international relations, sociology. **Visual/performing arts:** Dance, theater arts management.

Most popular majors. Biology 13%, business/marketing 37%, education 13%, health sciences 16%, psychology 9%.

Computing on campus. 2,708 workstations in dormitories, library, computer center, student center. Dormitories wired for high-speed internet access and linked to campus network. Commuter students can connect to campus network. Online course registration, online library, helpline, student web hosting, wireless network available.

Student life. Freshman orientation: Mandatory. Preregistration for classes offered. Sessions offered 3 times in summer and last 2 days, 1 night. **Housing:** Guaranteed on-campus for freshmen. Coed dorms, special housing for disabled, apartments, fraternity/sorority housing, wellness housing available. $500 partly refundable deposit. **Activities:** Bands, choral groups, dance, drama, film society, international student organizations, literary magazine, music ensembles, musical theater, radio station, student government, student newspaper, symphony orchestra, black student association, psychology club, Hillel, pre-med society, Alpha Phi Omega, Salsa, Indian student association, international Muslim association.

Athletics. NCAA. **Intercollegiate:** Baseball M, basketball, cheerleading M, cross-country, golf, rowing (crew) W, soccer, softball W, tennis W, track and field, volleyball W. **Intramural:** Basketball, football (non-tackle), golf, racquetball, soccer, softball, volleyball. **Team name:** Sharks.

Student services. Adult student services, career counseling, student employment services, financial aid counseling, health services, personal counseling, veterans' counselor, women's services. **Physically disabled:** Services for visually, speech, hearing impaired.

Contact. E-mail: ncsinfo@nova.edu
Phone: (954) 262-8000 Toll-free number: (800) 338-4723 ext. 8000
Fax: (954) 262-3811
Maria Dillard, Director of Undergraduate Admissions, Nova Southeastern University, 3301 College Avenue, Fort Lauderdale, FL 33314

Palm Beach Atlantic University

West Palm Beach, Florida
www.pba.edu **CB code: 5553**

- Private 4-year university and liberal arts college affiliated with nondenominational tradition
- Residential campus in large city
- 2,393 degree-seeking undergraduates: 8% part-time, 64% women, 14% African American, 2% Asian American, 12% Hispanic American, 2% international
- 802 degree-seeking graduate students
- 49% of applicants admitted
- SAT or ACT (ACT writing optional), application essay, interview required
- 54% graduate within 6 years

General. Founded in 1968. Regionally accredited. Distinctly Christian university with emphasis on student community service. University offers mission trips around the world, weekly worship services, and student-led prayer groups. **Degrees:** 496 bachelor's, 12 associate awarded; master's, first professional offered. **Location:** 60 miles from Miami, 180 miles from Orlando. **Calendar:** Semester, limited summer session. **Full-time faculty:** 155 total; 77% have terminal degrees, 14% minority, 43% women. **Part-time faculty:** 146 total; 31% have terminal degrees, 19% minority, 47% women. **Class size:** 65% < 20, 33% 20-39, 2% 40-49, less than 1% 50-99, less than 1% >100.

Freshman class profile. 2,109 applied, 1,025 admitted, 424 enrolled.

Mid 50% test scores		**GPA 2.0-2.99:**	10%
SAT critical reading:	490-580	**Rank in top quarter:**	54%
SAT math:	480-570	**Rank in top tenth:**	25%
ACT composite:	21-25	**Return as sophomores:**	69%
GPA 3.75 or higher:	39%	**Out-of-state:**	38%
GPA 3.50-3.74:	22%	**Live on campus:**	86%
GPA 3.0-3.49:	29%	**International:**	2%

Basis for selection. Secondary school record, recommendations, test scores, interview, autobiographical essay important. Audition required of music, theater and dance majors.

High school preparation. 18 units recommended. Recommended units include English 4, mathematics 3, social studies 3 and science 3.

2008-2009 Annual costs. Tuition/fees: $21,550. Room/board: $8,108. Books/supplies: $1,200. Personal expenses: $1,500.

2007-2008 Financial aid. Need-based: 369 full-time freshmen applied for aid; 300 were judged to have need; 300 of these received aid. Average need met was 66%. Average scholarship/grant was $4,745; average loan $3,339. 41% of total undergraduate aid awarded as scholarships/grants, 59% as loans/jobs. **Non-need-based:** Awarded to 1,777 full-time undergraduates, including 390 freshmen. Scholarships awarded for academics, alumni affiliation, athletics, minority status, music/drama, state residency.

Application procedures. Admission: No deadline. $30 fee, may be waived for applicants with need. Admission notification on a rolling basis beginning on or about 9/1. **Financial aid:** Priority date 2/1; no closing date. FAFSA required. Applicants notified on a rolling basis starting 3/1; must reply within 3 week(s) of notification.

Academics. Special study options: Accelerated study, combined bachelor's/graduate degree, distance learning, double major, dual enrollment of high school students, honors, independent study, internships, student-designed major, study abroad, teacher certification program, Washington semester. **Credit/placement by examination:** AP, CLEP, IB, SAT, ACT. 32 credit hours maximum toward bachelor's degree. If enrolled in one of undergraduate evening adult programs, aggregate of credit by examinination or Professional Education Credit may not exceed 45 semester hours. **Support services:** Study skills assistance, tutoring, writing center.

Honors college/program. Students must rank in top 10 percent of the nation according to national test scores.

Majors. Biology: General. **Business:** Accounting/finance, business admin, entrepreneurial studies, international, marketing, nonprofit/public. **Communications:** General, broadcast journalism, journalism, organizational, radio/tv. **Education:** General, art, biology, drama/dance, English, history, mathematics, music, physical, social science. **Health:** Athletic training, nursing (RN). **History:** General. **Legal studies:** Prelaw. **Math:** General. **Philosophy/religion:** Philosophy, religion. **Psychology:** General. **Social sciences:** Political science. **Theology:** Bible, sacred music, theology. **Visual/performing arts:** General, acting, dance, dramatic, graphic design, music performance, music theory/composition, piano/organ, play/screenwriting, studio arts, voice/opera.

Most popular majors. Business/marketing 48%, communications/journalism 8%, education 6%, health sciences 6%, psychology 8%.

Computing on campus. 550 workstations in dormitories, library, computer center, student center. Dormitories wired for high-speed internet access and linked to campus network. Commuter students can connect to campus network. Online course registration, online library, helpline, wireless network available.

Student life. Freshman orientation: Mandatory, $40 fee. Preregistration for classes offered. **Policies:** Undergraduate students required to donate 45 hours of community service for each year of attendance. Religious observance required. **Housing:** Guaranteed on-campus for freshmen. Coed dorms, single-sex dorms, apartments available. $200 fully refundable deposit, deadline 5/1. **Activities:** Bands, campus ministries, choral groups, dance, drama, international student organizations, literary magazine, music ensembles, musical theater, radio station, student government, student newspaper, symphony orchestra, TV station, Students in Free Enterprise, Newman club, Kappa Delta Epsilon, Kappa Psi, Lambda Pi Eta, Theta Alpha Kappa, American Society of Health System Pharmacists, American Association of Christian Counselors, Alpha Psi Omega, campus programming association.

Athletics. NCAA, NCCAA. **Intercollegiate:** Baseball M, basketball, cheerleading, cross-country, golf, soccer, softball W, tennis, volleyball W. **Intramural:** Basketball, bowling, football (non-tackle), golf, racquetball, soccer, softball, table tennis, volleyball. **Team name:** Sailfish.

Student services. Career counseling, student employment services, financial aid counseling, health services, personal counseling, veterans' counselor.

Contact. E-mail: admit@pba.edu
Phone: (561) 803-2000 Toll-free number: (888) 468-6722
Fax: (561) 803-2115
Rod Sullivan, Director of Admission, Palm Beach Atlantic University, PO Box 24708, West Palm Beach, FL 33416-4708

Rasmussen College: Fort Myers

Fort Myers, Florida
www.rasmussen.edu

- For-profit 4-year technical college
- Small city
- 164 degree-seeking undergraduates

General. Regionally accredited. **Calendar:** Quarter. **Part-time faculty:** 16 total.

Basis for selection. Open admission, but selective for some programs.

2009-2010 Annual costs. Regular courses: $350/credit; designated allied health and technology courses and all 3000- and 4000- level courses: $395/credit.

Application procedures. Admission: No deadline. $20 fee. **Financial aid:** No deadline.

Academics. **Credit/placement by examination:** CLEP.

Majors. **Business:** Accounting, business admin. **Communications technology:** Animation/special effects. **Health:** Health care admin. **Protective services:** Police science.

Contact. Phone: (239) 477-2100
Carmen Cordisco, Director of Admissions, Rasmussen College: Fort Myers, 9160 Forum Corporate Parkway, Suite 100, Fort Myers, FL 33905-7805

Rasmussen College: Ocala

Ocala, Florida
www.rasmussen.edu **CB code: 3502**

- For-profit 4-year career college
- Commuter campus in small city
- 1,212 degree-seeking undergraduates
- 39% graduate within 6 years

General. Regionally accredited. **Degrees:** 18 bachelor's, 70 associate awarded. **Calendar:** Quarter, extensive summer session. **Full-time faculty:** 7 total. **Part-time faculty:** 18 total.

Basis for selection. Open admission, but selective for some programs. Some programs require entrance examinations and additional information. COMPASS used for placement.

2008-2009 Annual costs. Tuition/fees: $14,063. Tuition includes books and fees.

Application procedures. **Admission:** No deadline. $60 fee. Admission notification on a rolling basis. **Financial aid:** No deadline. FAFSA, institutional form required. Applicants notified on a rolling basis.

Academics. **Special study options:** Distance learning, double major, honors, independent study, internships. **Credit/placement by examination:** AP, CLEP, IB, institutional tests. 45 credit hours maximum toward associate degree, 90 toward bachelor's. Limited to specific programs, and to courses for which programs are available. **Support services:** Learning center, remedial instruction, study skills assistance, tutoring, writing center.

Majors. **Business:** Accounting, business admin. **Computer sciences:** Web page design. **Protective services:** Law enforcement admin.

Computing on campus. 100 workstations in library, computer center, student center. Online course registration, online library, helpline, wireless network available.

Student life. **Freshman orientation:** Mandatory.

Student services. Adult student services, career counseling, services for economically disadvantaged, student employment services, financial aid counseling, placement for graduates.

Contact. E-mail: miguel.ramos@rasmussen.edu
Phone: (352) 629-1941 Fax: (352) 629-0926
Miguel Ramos, Director of Admissions, Rasmussen College: Ocala, 2221 Southwest 19th Avenue Road, Ocala, FL 34471

Rasmussen College: Pasco County

Holiday, Florida
www.rasmussen.edu **CB code: 3503**

- For-profit 4-year career college
- Commuter campus in small city
- 568 degree-seeking undergraduates

General. Regionally accredited. **Degrees:** 133 bachelor's, 41 associate awarded. **Location:** 30 miles from Tampa. **Calendar:** Quarter, extensive summer session. **Full-time faculty:** 5 total. **Part-time faculty:** 14 total.

Basis for selection. Open admission, but selective for some programs. Some programs require entrance examinations and additional information. COMPASS used for placement.

2008-2009 Annual costs. Tuition/fees: $14,063.

Application procedures. **Admission:** No deadline. $20 fee. Admission notification on a rolling basis. **Financial aid:** No deadline. FAFSA, institutional form required. Applicants notified on a rolling basis.

Academics. **Special study options:** Distance learning, double major, honors, independent study, internships. **Credit/placement by examination:** AP, CLEP, IB, institutional tests. 45 credit hours maximum toward associate degree, 90 toward bachelor's. Limited to specific programs, and to courses. **Support services:** Learning center, remedial instruction, study skills assistance, tutoring, writing center.

Majors. **Business:** Accounting, business admin. **Computer sciences:** Web page design. **Health:** Health care admin. **Other:** Graphic technology.

Computing on campus. 100 workstations in library, computer center, student center. Online course registration, online library, helpline, wireless network available.

Student life. **Freshman orientation:** Mandatory.

Student services. Adult student services, career counseling, services for economically disadvantaged, student employment services, financial aid counseling, placement for graduates.

Contact. E-mail: staceyann.sinclair@rasmussen.edu
Phone: (727) 942-0069 Fax: (727) 938-5709
Staceyann Sinclair, Director of Admissions, Rasmussen College: Pasco County, 2127 Grand Boulevard, Holiday, FL 34690

Remington College: Largo

Largo, Florida
www.remingtoncollege.edu

- For-profit 4-year technical and career college
- Large city

General. Accredited by ACCSCT. **Calendar:** Differs by program. Monthly.

Annual costs/financial aid. Associate degree programs annual tuition $19,500 plus $50 fees. 8-month diploma program full tuition $13,900 plus $50 fees. Tuition includes textbooks and supplies.

Contact. Phone: (727) 532-1999
8550 Ulmerton Road, Unit 100, Largo, FL 33771

Remington College: Tampa

Tampa, Florida
www.remingtoncollege.edu **CB code: 0123**

- For-profit 4-year technical college
- Commuter campus in very large city
- 247 degree-seeking undergraduates
- Interview required

General. Founded in 1948. Accredited by ACCSCT. **Degrees:** 22 bachelor's, 112 associate awarded. **Calendar:** Quarter, extensive summer session. **Full-time faculty:** 11 total. **Part-time faculty:** 14 total.

Basis for selection. Recommendations considered; Wonderlic test used.

2008-2009 Annual costs. Personal expenses: $1,200.

Financial aid. All financial aid based on need.

Application procedures. **Admission:** No deadline. $50 fee. Admission notification on a rolling basis. **Financial aid:** No deadline. FAFSA, institutional form required.

Academics. **Special study options:** Accelerated study, combined bachelor's/graduate degree, distance learning. **Credit/placement by examination:** CLEP. **Support services:** Remedial instruction, tutoring.

Majors. **Protective services:** Law enforcement admin.

Computing on campus. 350 workstations in library, computer center. Online library, helpline, repair service, wireless network available.

Student life. **Freshman orientation:** Mandatory. Preregistration for classes offered.

Student services. Career counseling, student employment services, financial aid counseling, personal counseling, placement for graduates.

Contact. Phone: (813) 935-5700 Toll-free number: (800) 992-4850
Fax: (813) 935-7415
Gary Schwartz, Director of Recruiting, Remington College: Tampa, 2410 East Busch Boulevard, Tampa, FL 33612

Ringling College of Art and Design

Sarasota, Florida CB member
www.ringling.edu CB code: 5573

- Private 4-year visual arts college
- Residential campus in small city
- 1,229 degree-seeking undergraduates: 4% part-time, 57% women, 3% African American, 6% Asian American, 12% Hispanic American, 1% Native American, 5% international
- 70% of applicants admitted
- Application essay required
- 67% graduate within 6 years

General. Founded in 1931. Regionally accredited. **Degrees:** 241 bachelor's awarded. **Location:** 50 miles from Tampa. **Calendar:** Semester. **Full-time faculty:** 80 total; 64% have terminal degrees, 6% minority, 32% women. **Part-time faculty:** 64 total; 34% have terminal degrees, 3% minority, 42% women. **Class size:** 69% < 20, 30% 20-39, 1% 40-49, less than 1% 50-99. **Special facilities:** Art library, art center.

Freshman class profile. 1,326 applied, 925 admitted, 282 enrolled.

GPA 3.75 or higher:	13%	**Out-of-state:**	49%
GPA 3.50-3.74:	14%	**Live on campus:**	82%
GPA 3.0-3.49:	34%	**International:**	6%
GPA 2.0-2.99:	39%	**Fraternities:**	1%
End year in good standing:	79%	**Sororities:**	1%
Return as sophomores:	79%		

Basis for selection. Portfolio, school achievement record, statement of purpose, and recommendations important. Interview recommended. Portfolio required. **Learning Disabled:** Students seeking special accommodations for learning disabilities must provide documentation of disability.

2008-2009 Annual costs. Tuition/fees: $27,110. Required fees may vary according to program. Room/board: $10,750.

2008-2009 Financial aid. Need-based: 216 full-time freshmen applied for aid; 187 were judged to have need; 187 of these received aid. Average need met was 50%. Average scholarship/grant was $9,266; average loan $9,241. 32% of total undergraduate aid awarded as scholarships/grants, 68% as loans/jobs. **Non-need-based:** Awarded to 60 full-time undergraduates, including 24 freshmen. Scholarships awarded for academics, art.

Application procedures. Admission: Priority date 3/1; no deadline. $60 fee, may be waived for applicants with need. Admission notification on a rolling basis beginning on or about 9/1. **Financial aid:** Priority date 3/1; no closing date. FAFSA required. Applicants notified on a rolling basis starting 4/1; must reply within 2 week(s) of notification.

Academics. Special study options: Dual enrollment of high school students, exchange student, independent study, internships, New York semester, study abroad. **Credit/placement by examination:** AP, CLEP, IB. 30 credit hours maximum toward bachelor's degree. **Support services:** Learning center, pre-admission summer program, remedial instruction, study skills assistance, tutoring, writing center.

Majors. Communications technology: Animation/special effects. **Visual/performing arts:** Arts management, commercial/advertising art, graphic design, illustration, interior design, painting, photography, printmaking, sculpture, studio arts.

Most popular majors. Communication technologies 18%, visual/performing arts 82%.

Computing on campus. 650 workstations in dormitories, library, computer center, student center. Dormitories wired for high-speed internet access and linked to campus network. Commuter students can connect to campus network. Online course registration, helpline, repair service, student web hosting, wireless network available.

Student life. Freshman orientation: Mandatory. Held the week prior to classes, new students given pre-set schedules for their first semester. **Housing:** Single-sex dorms, special housing for disabled, apartments, wellness housing available. $100 fully refundable deposit. All housing accommodations are ADA compliant. **Activities:** Campus ministries, dance, student government.

Athletics. Intramural: Basketball, soccer, softball, table tennis, volleyball.

Student services. Career counseling, student employment services, financial aid counseling, health services, minority student services, personal counseling, placement for graduates, veterans' counselor, women's services. **Physically disabled:** Services for visually, hearing impaired.

Contact. E-mail: admissions@ringling.edu
Phone: (941) 351-5100 Toll-free number: (800) 255-7695
Fax: (941) 359-7517
James Dean, Dean of Admissions, Ringling College of Art and Design, 2700 North Tamiami Trail, Sarasota, FL 34234-5895

Rollins College

Winter Park, Florida CB member
www.rollins.edu CB code: 5572

- Private 4-year liberal arts college
- Residential campus in large town
- 1,785 degree-seeking undergraduates: 57% women, 4% African American, 4% Asian American, 10% Hispanic American, 1% Native American, 4% international
- 726 degree-seeking graduate students
- 53% of applicants admitted
- Application essay required
- 69% graduate within 6 years

General. Founded in 1885. Regionally accredited. **Degrees:** 378 bachelor's awarded; master's offered. **Location:** 5 miles from Orlando. **Calendar:** Semester, limited summer session. **Full-time faculty:** 194 total; 94% have terminal degrees, 11% minority, 39% women. **Part-time faculty:** 36 total; 42% have terminal degrees, 17% minority, 56% women. **Class size:** 67% < 20, 32% 20-39, less than 1% 40-49, less than 1% 50-99. **Special facilities:** 2 theaters, child development center, center for psychology, greenhouse, high tech classrooms.

Freshman class profile. 3,485 applied, 1,854 admitted, 464 enrolled.

Mid 50% test scores		**GPA 2.0-2.99:**	30%
SAT critical reading:	560-650	**Rank in top quarter:**	73%
SAT math:	560-650	**Rank in top tenth:**	43%
ACT composite:	24-29	**Return as sophomores:**	87%
GPA 3.75 or higher:	22%	**Out-of-state:**	55%
GPA 3.50-3.74:	13%	**Live on campus:**	94%
GPA 3.0-3.49:	35%	**International:**	6%

Basis for selection. School achievement record most important, followed by test scores, activities, essay, recommendations, interview. Audition recommended for music, theater arts majors.

High school preparation. College-preparatory program recommended. 17 units required; 24 recommended. Required and recommended units include English 4, mathematics 3-4, social studies 2-3, history 2-3, science 2-4, foreign language 2-3 and academic electives 2-3.

2008-2009 Annual costs. Tuition/fees: $34,520. Room/board: $10,780. Books/supplies: $700. Personal expenses: $2,210.

2008-2009 Financial aid. Need-based: 242 full-time freshmen applied for aid; 187 were judged to have need; 186 of these received aid. Average need met was 90%. Average scholarship/grant was $27,367; average loan $4,127. 86% of total undergraduate aid awarded as scholarships/grants, 14% as loans/jobs. **Non-need-based:** Awarded to 417 full-time undergraduates, including 109 freshmen. Scholarships awarded for academics, art, athletics, leadership, music/drama, state residency. **Additional information:** Audition required for theater arts and music scholarship applicants. Portfolio required for art scholarships.

Application procedures. Admission: Closing date 2/15 (postmark date). $40 fee, may be waived for applicants with need. Admission notification 4/1. Must reply by May 1 or within 3 week(s) if notified thereafter. **Financial aid:** Closing date 3/1. FAFSA, institutional form required. Applicants notified on a rolling basis starting 3/1.

Academics. International business major featuring language training, internships and study abroad available; pre-professional support services. **Special study options:** Accelerated study, combined bachelor's/graduate degree, cross-registration, double major, dual enrollment of high school students, exchange student, honors, independent study, internships, semester at sea, student-designed major, study abroad, teacher certification program, Washington semester. **Credit/placement by examination:** AP, CLEP, IB, institutional tests. 76 credit hours maximum toward bachelor's degree. **Support services:** Learning center, reduced course load, study skills assistance, tutoring, writing center.

Honors college/program. Top 10% of entering freshman class admitted.

Majors. **Area/ethnic studies:** Latin American. **Biology:** General, Biochemistry/biophysics and molecular biology, marine. **Business:** International. **Communications:** Media studies. **Computer sciences:** General. **Conservation:** Environmental studies. **Education:** General. **Foreign languages:** Classics, French, Spanish. **History:** General. **Math:** General. **Philosophy/religion:** Philosophy, religion. **Physical sciences:** Chemistry, physics. **Psychology:** General. **Social sciences:** Anthropology, economics, international relations, political science, sociology. **Visual/performing arts:** Art, art history/conservation, dramatic.

Most popular majors. Business/marketing 18%, English 10%, psychology 10%, social sciences 29%, visual/performing arts 12%.

Computing on campus. 205 workstations in dormitories, library, computer center, student center. Dormitories wired for high-speed internet access and linked to campus network. Commuter students can connect to campus network. Online course registration, online library, helpline, repair service, student web hosting, wireless network available.

Student life. **Freshman orientation:** Mandatory. Preregistration for classes offered. Held just prior to fall semester. **Housing:** Guaranteed on-campus for freshmen. Coed dorms, single-sex dorms, special housing for disabled, apartments, fraternity/sorority housing available. $500 nonrefundable deposit, deadline 5/15. **Activities:** Bands, campus ministries, choral groups, dance, drama, film society, international student organizations, literary magazine, music ensembles, musical theater, radio station, student government, student newspaper, symphony orchestra, TV station, ally alliance, Muslim student association, Hillel, Rollins, Habitat for Humanity, 5 Stones, cultural action committee, College Republicans, College Democrats, Black Student Union.

Athletics. NCAA. **Intercollegiate:** Baseball M, basketball, cross-country, golf, lacrosse, rowing (crew), sailing, skiing, soccer, softball W, swimming, tennis, volleyball W. **Intramural:** Basketball M, football (non-tackle), soccer, softball, table tennis, tennis, volleyball. **Team name:** Tars.

Student services. Alcohol/substance abuse counseling, chaplain/spiritual director, career counseling, student employment services, financial aid counseling, health services, personal counseling, placement for graduates, veterans' counselor. **Physically disabled:** Services for visually, speech, hearing impaired.

Contact. E-mail: admission@rollins.edu
Phone: (407) 646-2161 Fax: (407) 646-1502
Mike Lynch, Director of Admission, Rollins College, 1000 Holt Avenue, Winter Park, FL 32789

St. John Vianney College Seminary

Miami, Florida
www.sjvcs.edu **CB code: 5650**

- Private 4-year liberal arts and seminary college for men affiliated with Roman Catholic Church
- Residential campus in very large city
- 44 degree-seeking undergraduates
- 100% of applicants admitted
- Interview required

General. Founded in 1959. Regionally accredited. **Degrees:** 20 bachelor's awarded. **Location:** 12 miles from downtown. **Calendar:** Semester, limited summer session. **Full-time faculty:** 7 total; 71% have terminal degrees, 29% women. **Part-time faculty:** 12 total; 42% have terminal degrees, 25% women. **Class size:** 100% < 20.

Freshman class profile. 5 applied, 5 admitted, 5 enrolled.

Out-of-state:	2%	**Live on campus:**	100%

Basis for selection. Interview, academic record, recommendations required. Those to be formed for priesthood should present evidence of vocation for priesthood and submit psychological and physical evaluations. Applicants referred by home (church) Diocesan Offices of Vocations.

High school preparation. 20 units required. Required units include English 4, mathematics 2, social studies 2, history 2, science 2, foreign language 2 and academic electives 6.

2008-2009 Annual costs. Tuition/fees: $17,000. Room/board: $9,500. Books/supplies: $600.

Application procedures. **Admission:** Priority date 6/30; deadline 7/15 (receipt date). No application fee. Admission notification on a rolling basis. **Financial aid:** No deadline. FAFSA required. Applicants notified on a rolling basis.

Academics. Fluency in both English and Spanish must be achieved. Students required to take at least 1 course in alternate language each semester. **Special study options:** Cross-registration, ESL, independent study. **Credit/placement by examination:** AP, CLEP, institutional tests. **Support services:** Pre-admission summer program, reduced course load, remedial instruction, study skills assistance, tutoring.

Majors. **Philosophy/religion:** Philosophy.

Computing on campus. 12 workstations in library, computer center. Online library, wireless network available.

Student life. **Freshman orientation:** Mandatory, $2,000 fee. Preregistration for classes offered. 3 weeks during August. **Policies:** All sophomores and upperclassmen assigned weekly apostolic work at various locations. Religious observance required. **Housing:** Guaranteed on-campus for all undergraduates. **Activities:** Choral groups, drama, music ensembles, student government, student newspaper, apostolic works program.

Athletics. **Intramural:** Baseball M, basketball M, handball M, racquetball M, soccer M, softball M, swimming M, table tennis M, tennis M, volleyball M, weight lifting M.

Student services. Adult student services, career counseling, financial aid counseling, health services, personal counseling.

Contact. Phone: (305) 223-4561 Fax: (305) 223-0650
Ramon Santos, Academic Dean, St. John Vianney College Seminary, 2900 Southwest 87 Avenue, Miami, FL 33165-3244

St. Leo University

Saint Leo, Florida **CB member**
www.saintleo.edu **CB code: 5638**

- Private 4-year university affiliated with Roman Catholic Church
- Residential campus in rural community
- 1,699 degree-seeking undergraduates: 5% part-time, 53% women, 9% African American, 1% Asian American, 12% Hispanic American, 9% international
- 1,795 degree-seeking graduate students
- 73% of applicants admitted
- SAT or ACT (ACT writing optional), application essay required
- 42% graduate within 6 years

General. Founded in 1889. Regionally accredited. **Degrees:** 287 bachelor's, 5 associate awarded; master's offered. **ROTC:** Army, Air Force. **Location:** 25 miles from Tampa. **Calendar:** Semester, limited summer session. **Full-time faculty:** 98 total; 86% have terminal degrees, 11% minority, 36% women. **Part-time faculty:** 34 total; 24% have terminal degrees, 12% minority, 32% women. **Class size:** 42% < 20, 58% 20-39. **Special facilities:** Center for Catholic and Jewish studies.

Freshman class profile. 2,149 applied, 1,576 admitted, 500 enrolled.

Mid 50% test scores		**GPA 2.0-2.99:**	41%
SAT critical reading:	450-530	**Rank in top quarter:**	25%
SAT math:	450-540	**Rank in top tenth:**	8%
SAT writing:	440-510	**Return as sophomores:**	76%
ACT composite:	20-24	**Out-of-state:**	40%
GPA 3.75 or higher:	17%	**Live on campus:**	86%
GPA 3.50-3.74:	13%	**International:**	5%
GPA 3.0-3.49:	29%		

Basis for selection. Test scores, GPA, guidance counselor's recommendation, high school curriculum important. Interview recommended. **Homeschooled:** Transcript of courses and grades, interview, letter of recommendation (nonparent) required. Bibliography of all high school reading material, 2 letters of recommendation, portfolio of sample work required.

High school preparation. College-preparatory program required. 16 units recommended. Recommended units include English 4, mathematics 3, social studies 3, science 2, foreign language 2 and academic electives 2. Algebra I and II, geometry strongly recommended. Those planning to study science should complete courses in biology and chemistry.

2008-2009 Annual costs. Tuition/fees: $17,150. Room/board: $8,430. Books/supplies: $1,200. Personal expenses: $1,330.

2008-2009 Financial aid. **Need-based:** 454 full-time freshmen applied for aid; 361 were judged to have need; 361 of these received aid. Average need met was 84%. Average scholarship/grant was $11,991; average loan $4,143. 59% of total undergraduate aid awarded as scholarships/grants, 41% as loans/jobs. **Non-need-based:** Awarded to 226 full-time undergraduates, including 50 freshmen. Scholarships awarded for academics, alumni affiliation, athletics, leadership, minority status, music/drama, religious affiliation, state residency.

Application procedures. Admission: Priority date 3/1; deadline 8/15 (postmark date). $35 fee, may be waived for applicants with need. Admission notification on a rolling basis beginning on or about 10/15. Must reply by May 1 or within 2 week(s) if notified thereafter. **Financial aid:** Priority date 4/1; no closing date. FAFSA required. Applicants notified on a rolling basis starting 1/31.

Academics. Special study options: Combined bachelor's/graduate degree, distance learning, double major, honors, independent study, internships, liberal arts/career combination, study abroad, teacher certification program, weekend college. Opportunity to study abroad in Italy, Switzerland, France, Ecuador, Spain, United Kingdom, Ireland, Australia, Germany, and Scotland. **Credit/placement by examination:** AP, CLEP, IB, SAT, ACT, institutional tests. 40 credit hours maximum toward associate degree, 40 toward bachelor's. **Support services:** Learning center, pre-admission summer program, reduced course load, remedial instruction, study skills assistance, tutoring, writing center.

Honors college/program. 3.5 GPA and 1060 SAT (exclusive of Writing) or 23 ACT required. Full honors curriculum consists of integrated sequence of 6 courses plus 2 research courses.

Majors. Biology: General. **Business:** Accounting, business admin, entrepreneurial studies, hospitality admin, human resources, international, management science, marketing. **Communications:** Media studies. **Computer sciences:** General. **Conservation:** Environmental studies. **Education:** Elementary, middle. **Health:** Clinical lab science, facilities admin, health care admin. **History:** General. **Math:** General. **Parks/recreation:** Sports admin. **Philosophy/religion:** Religion. **Protective services:** Criminal justice. **Psychology:** General. **Public administration:** Community org/advocacy, social work. **Social sciences:** International relations, political science, sociology.

Most popular majors. Biology 8%, business/marketing 30%, education 12%, parks/recreation 7%, psychology 9%, security/protective services 13%.

Computing on campus. 1,243 workstations in dormitories, library, student center. Dormitories wired for high-speed internet access and linked to campus network. Commuter students can connect to campus network. Online course registration, online library, helpline, repair service, student web hosting, wireless network available.

Student life. Freshman orientation: Mandatory, $300 fee. Preregistration for classes offered. 4-day program in August includes team-building, personal responsibility activities. Advising, testing, introduction to student life in mid-July. **Policies:** Fish aquariums allowed in residence hall rooms. **Housing:** Guaranteed on-campus for all undergraduates. Coed dorms, single-sex dorms, special housing for disabled, apartments, wellness housing available. $150 nonrefundable deposit, deadline 8/15. Freshmen-only housing available. **Activities:** Concert band, campus ministries, choral groups, dance, drama, film society, literary magazine, music ensembles, musical theater, student government, student newspaper, TV station, Circle-K, Samaritans, intercultural student association, Saint Leo Ambassadors, Best Buddies, student chaplain program, Pi Sigma Alpha, Brothers and Sisters United, social work club, Latino club.

Athletics. NCAA. **Intercollegiate:** Baseball M, basketball, cross-country, golf, lacrosse M, soccer, softball W, swimming, tennis, volleyball W. **Intramural:** Basketball, football (non-tackle), racquetball, soccer, softball, table tennis, tennis, volleyball. **Team name:** Lions.

Student services. Adult student services, alcohol/substance abuse counseling, chaplain/spiritual director, career counseling, student employment services, financial aid counseling, health services, personal counseling. **Physically disabled:** Services for visually impaired.

Contact. E-mail: admission@saintleo.edu
Phone: (352) 588-8283 Toll-free number: (800) 334-5532
Fax: (352) 588-8257
Martin Smith, Assistant Vice President of Enrollment, St. Leo University, Office of Admission, Saint Leo, FL 33574-6665

Saint Thomas University

Miami Gardens, Florida

www.stu.edu **CB code: 5076**

- Private 4-year university affiliated with Roman Catholic Church
- Commuter campus in very large city
- 1,122 degree-seeking undergraduates: 7% part-time, 57% women, 25% African American, 1% Asian American, 49% Hispanic American, 9% international
- 1,332 degree-seeking graduate students
- 91% of applicants admitted
- SAT or ACT (ACT writing optional) required
- 37% graduate within 6 years

General. Founded in 1961. Regionally accredited. Multilocation institution. Affiliated with Archdiocese of Miami. **Degrees:** 320 bachelor's awarded; master's, doctoral, first professional offered. **Location:** 10 miles from Miami. **Calendar:** Semester, extensive summer session. **Full-time faculty:** 100 total; 89% have terminal degrees, 21% minority, 46% women. **Part-time faculty:** 144 total. **Class size:** 73% < 20, 27% 20-39, less than 1% 40-49.

Freshman class profile. 655 applied, 597 admitted, 213 enrolled.

Mid 50% test scores		**GPA 2.0-2.99:**	55%
SAT critical reading:	390-490	**Rank in top quarter:**	20%
SAT math:	380-490	**Rank in top tenth:**	6%
SAT writing:	400-490	**Return as sophomores:**	69%
ACT composite:	16-20	**Out-of-state:**	10%
GPA 3.75 or higher:	7%	**Live on campus:**	69%
GPA 3.50-3.74:	9%	**International:**	7%
GPA 3.0-3.49:	29%		

Basis for selection. High school grades, test scores primary factors. Class rank, interview, school, community activities, recommendations also considered. Interview recommended.

High school preparation. College-preparatory program recommended. 18 units required. Required units include English 4, mathematics 3, social studies 3, science 2 and academic electives 6.

2008-2009 Annual costs. Tuition/fees: $20,664. Room/board: $6,206. Books/supplies: $1,000. Personal expenses: $1,870.

2007-2008 Financial aid. Non-need-based: Scholarships awarded for academics, athletics, leadership, music/drama, religious affiliation, state residency.

Application procedures. Admission: No deadline. $40 fee, may be waived for applicants with need. Admission notification on a rolling basis. Must reply by May 1 or within 2 week(s) if notified thereafter. Applicants needing on-campus housing strongly encouraged to apply before May 15. **Financial aid:** Priority date 4/2; no closing date. FAFSA required. Applicants notified on a rolling basis starting 3/1.

Academics. Special study options: Combined bachelor's/graduate degree, distance learning, double major, dual enrollment of high school students, honors, independent study, internships, liberal arts/career combination, teacher certification program. **Credit/placement by examination:** AP, CLEP, SAT, ACT, institutional tests. 45 credit hours maximum toward bachelor's degree. **Support services:** Learning center, pre-admission summer program, reduced course load, remedial instruction, study skills assistance, tutoring, writing center.

Majors. Biology: General. **Business:** Accounting, business admin, finance, hospitality admin, international, organizational behavior, tourism/travel. **Communications:** General, media studies. **Computer sciences:** General, computer science. **Conservation:** Environmental studies. **Education:** Elementary, secondary, social studies. **Health:** Health care admin, premedicine, preveterinary. **History:** General. **Legal studies:** Prelaw. **Liberal arts:** Arts/sciences. **Parks/recreation:** Sports admin. **Philosophy/religion:** Religion. **Physical sciences:** Chemistry. **Protective services:** Criminal justice. **Psychology:** General. **Public administration:** Human services. **Social sciences:** Political science. **Theology:** Religious ed.

Most popular majors. Business/marketing 52%, education 6%, psychology 7%, security/protective services 10%.

Computing on campus. 123 workstations in library, computer center. Dormitories linked to campus network. Online course registration, helpline, wireless network available.

Student life. Freshman orientation: Mandatory. **Housing:** Single-sex dorms available. $225 fully refundable deposit. **Activities:** Campus ministries, choral groups, international student organizations, literary magazine, music ensembles, student government, TV station, political action club, Students for Global Preservation, prelaw society, premedicine club, accounting club.

Athletics. NAIA. **Intercollegiate:** Baseball M, cross-country, golf, soccer, softball W, tennis, volleyball W. **Intramural:** Golf, soccer M, softball, tennis, volleyball. **Team name:** Bobcats.

Student services. Adult student services, alcohol/substance abuse counseling, career counseling, student employment services, financial aid counseling, health services, personal counseling, placement for graduates. **Physically disabled:** Services for visually, hearing impaired.

Contact. E-mail: signup@stu.edu
Phone: (305) 628-6546 Toll-free number: (800) 367-9010
Fax: (305) 628-6591
Lydia Amy, Dean, Enrollment Services, Saint Thomas University, 16401 Northwest 37th Avenue, Miami Gardens, FL 33054-6459

Schiller International University
Largo, Florida
www.schiller.edu **CB code: 0601**

- For-profit 4-year university
- Residential campus in small city
- 191 degree-seeking undergraduates: 20% part-time, 40% women
- 481 degree-seeking graduate students

General. Founded in 1964. Accredited by ACICS. Campuses located in Florida, Paris, London, Madrid, Heidelberg, as well as Schiller Online. Students may transfer between campuses without loss of time or credit. **Degrees:** 81 bachelor's awarded; master's offered. **Location:** 20 miles from Tampa. **Calendar:** Semester, extensive summer session. **Full-time faculty:** 25 total. **Part-time faculty:** 168 total.

Basis for selection. Open admission. Interviews recommended.

2008-2009 Annual costs. Tuition/fees: $17,890. Room/board: $9,027. Books/supplies: $1,250. Personal expenses: $2,600.

2007-2008 Financial aid. Need-based: 9 full-time freshmen applied for aid; 9 were judged to have need; 9 of these received aid. 24% of total undergraduate aid awarded as scholarships/grants, 76% as loans/jobs. **Non-need-based:** Scholarships awarded for academics, alumni affiliation, leadership, minority status, state residency. **Additional information:** Special scholarship program for US students studying abroad at European campuses of Schiller. Work-study available to students taking 2 or more courses.

Application procedures. Admission: No deadline. $65 fee. Application must be submitted on paper. Admission notification on a rolling basis. **Financial aid:** Closing date 4/1. FAFSA, institutional form required. Applicants notified on a rolling basis starting 5/1; must reply within 3 week(s) of notification.

Academics. Completion of intermediate level of at least one foreign language required for most undergraduate degree programs. **Special study options:** Accelerated study, cooperative education, distance learning, double major, ESL, honors, independent study, internships, liberal arts/career combination, study abroad. **Credit/placement by examination:** AP, CLEP, IB, institutional tests. 16 credit hours maximum toward associate degree, 16 toward bachelor's. **Support services:** Learning center, reduced course load, study skills assistance, tutoring.

Majors. Business: General, banking/financial services, business admin, finance, hotel/motel admin, international, international marketing, management information systems, marketing, tourism/travel. **Computer sciences:** Information technology. **Foreign languages:** French, German. **Interdisciplinary:** Global studies. **Social sciences:** International economics, international relations.

Most popular majors. Business/marketing 77%.

Computing on campus. Online library, wireless network available.

Student life. Freshman orientation: Mandatory. **Housing:** Coed dorms available. **Activities:** Model UN, student government.

Student services. Adult student services, career counseling, services for economically disadvantaged, student employment services, financial aid counseling, minority student services, personal counseling, placement for graduates.

Contact. E-mail: admissions@schiller.edu
Phone: (727) 736-3920 Toll-free number: (877) 748-4338
Fax: (727) 738-6376
Marcus Leibrecht, Director of Admissions, Schiller International University, 300 East Bay Drive, Largo, FL 33770-3716

South University: Tampa
Tampa, Florida
www.southuniversity.edu

- For-profit 4-year business and health science college
- Large city

General. Regionally accredited. **Calendar:** Quarter.

Contact. Phone: (813) 393-3800
4401 North Himes Avenue, Tampa, FL 33614

South University: West Palm Beach
West Palm Beach, Florida
www.southuniversity.edu **CB code: 5321**

- For-profit 4-year university, business and health science college
- Commuter campus in large city
- 699 degree-seeking undergraduates: 31% part-time, 81% women
- 45 graduate students
- Application essay, interview required

General. Regionally accredited. **Degrees:** 73 bachelor's, 59 associate awarded; master's offered. **Location:** 3 miles from downtown, 29 miles from Fort Lauderdale. **Calendar:** Quarter, extensive summer session. **Full-time faculty:** 16 total. **Part-time faculty:** 82 total.

Basis for selection. Test scores most important. Satisfactory score on college-administered entrance exams (CPT), or 660 SAT (exclusive of Writing) or 14 ACT required. Some programs have higher requirements.

2008-2009 Annual costs. Tuition/fees: $13,035. Books/supplies: $900. Personal expenses: $1,476.

Financial aid. Non-need-based: Scholarships awarded for academics.

Application procedures. Admission: No deadline. $50 fee, may be waived for applicants with need. Admission notification on a rolling basis. **Financial aid:** No deadline. FAFSA, institutional form required. Applicants notified on a rolling basis; must reply within 2 week(s) of notification.

Academics. Special study options: Accelerated study, distance learning, double major, internships. **Credit/placement by examination:** CLEP, SAT, ACT, institutional tests. No more than 60% of any program requirements may be earned through credits by examinations. **Support services:** Remedial instruction, study skills assistance, tutoring.

Majors. Business: Business admin, finance. **Computer sciences:** Information systems. **Health:** Nursing (RN). **Legal studies:** Paralegal. **Psychology:** Counseling.

Computing on campus. 75 workstations in library, computer center. Online library available.

Student life. Freshman orientation: Mandatory. Preregistration for classes offered. **Activities:** Paralegal club, honor society.

Student services. Adult student services, career counseling, student employment services, personal counseling, placement for graduates, veterans' counselor.

Contact. E-mail: wpbadmis@southuniversity.edu
Phone: (561) 697-9200 Fax: (561) 697-9944
Gary Malisas, Director of Admissions, South University: West Palm Beach, 1760 North Congress Avenue, West Palm Beach, FL 33409-5178

Southeastern University
Lakeland, Florida
www.seuniversity.edu **CB code: 5621**

- Private 4-year liberal arts and teachers college affiliated with Assemblies of God
- Residential campus in small city
- 2,651 degree-seeking undergraduates: 7% part-time, 59% women, 8% African American, 1% Asian American, 12% Hispanic American
- 184 degree-seeking graduate students
- Application essay required
- 50% graduate within 6 years

General. Founded in 1935. Regionally accredited. **Degrees:** 492 bachelor's awarded; master's offered. **ROTC:** Army. **Location:** 40 miles from Tampa, 50 miles from Orlando. **Calendar:** Semester, limited summer session. **Full-time faculty:** 79 total; 56% have terminal degrees, 11% minority, 37% women. **Part-time faculty:** 85 total; 16% have terminal degrees, 14% minority, 42% women. **Class size:** 49% < 20, 35% 20-39, 8% 40-49, 6% 50-99, 1% >100.

Freshman class profile. 1,363 applied, 1,068 admitted, 532 enrolled.

Mid 50% test scores			
SAT critical reading:	440-560	GPA 3.50-3.74:	16%
SAT math:	430-570	GPA 3.0-3.49:	27%
SAT writing:	430-560	GPA 2.0-2.99:	24%
ACT composite:	18-24	Return as sophomores:	63%
GPA 3.75 or higher:	31%	Out-of-state:	44%
		Live on campus:	99%

Basis for selection. Open admission, but selective for some programs. SAT or ACT used for placement in Math, English; also used to determine scholarship eligibility. Accuplacer may be used in lieu of SAT/ACT. Interview recommended for academically weak applicants.

High school preparation. College-preparatory program recommended. Recommended units include English 4, mathematics 4, social studies 4, science 4 and foreign language 2.

2008-2009 Annual costs. Tuition/fees: $14,470. Room/board: $7,000. Books/supplies: $900. Personal expenses: $1,000.

2008-2009 Financial aid. Need-based: 49% of total undergraduate aid awarded as scholarships/grants, 51% as loans/jobs. **Non-need-based:** Scholarships awarded for academics, leadership, music/drama, ROTC.

Application procedures. Admission: Closing date 5/1 (postmark date). $40 fee, may be waived for applicants with need. Admission notification on a rolling basis. Must reply by 6/1. **Financial aid:** Priority date 4/15; no closing date. FAFSA, institutional form required. Applicants notified on a rolling basis starting 2/1; must reply within 4 week(s) of notification.

Academics. Special study options: Accelerated study, distance learning, double major, dual enrollment of high school students, independent study, internships, study abroad, teacher certification program. **Credit/placement by examination:** AP, CLEP, IB, institutional tests. 45 credit hours maximum toward bachelor's degree. **Support services:** Reduced course load, remedial instruction, study skills assistance, tutoring, writing center.

Majors. Biology: General. **Business:** General, accounting, finance, human resources, international, management information systems, marketing, office management. **Communications:** General, journalism, organizational, radio/tv. **Education:** General, biology, elementary, English, mathematics, middle, music, science, secondary, social science, special. **Health:** Premedicine. **History:** General. **Math:** General. **Parks/recreation:** Sports admin. **Protective services:** Law enforcement admin. **Psychology:** General. **Public administration:** Social work. **Theology:** Bible, missionary, preministerial, sacred music, youth ministry. **Visual/performing arts:** Dramatic, film/cinema, music performance, piano/organ, theater design, voice/opera. **Other:** Church leadership.

Most popular majors. Business/marketing 21%, communications/journalism 9%, education 10%, psychology 9%, public administration/social services 12%, theological studies 25%.

Computing on campus. 89 workstations in library, computer center, student center. Dormitories wired for high-speed internet access and linked to campus network. Commuter students can connect to campus network. Online course registration, online library, helpline, wireless network available.

Student life. Freshman orientation: Mandatory. Preregistration for classes offered. **Policies:** Religious observance required. **Housing:** Guaranteed on-campus for freshmen. Single-sex dorms, apartments, cooperative housing, wellness housing available. $200 fully refundable deposit, deadline 6/1. **Activities:** Bands, campus ministries, choral groups, drama, international student organizations, literary magazine, music ensembles, musical theater, opera, radio station, student government, student newspaper, symphony orchestra, TV station, College Republicans, Habitat for Humanity, International Justice Mission, Social Work Club, Christian Medical and Dental Association, Student Missions Organization.

Athletics. NAIA, NCCAA. **Intercollegiate:** Baseball M, basketball, cheerleading, golf M, soccer, tennis W, volleyball W. **Intramural:** Basketball, football (non-tackle), soccer, softball, tennis, volleyball. **Team name:** Fire.

Student services. Adult student services, chaplain/spiritual director, career counseling, student employment services, financial aid counseling, health services, personal counseling, placement for graduates.

Contact. E-mail: admission@seuniversity.edu
Phone: (863) 667-5018 Toll-free number: (800) 500-8760
Fax: (863) 667-5200
Kevin Jones, Director of Admission, Southeastern University, 1000 Longfellow Boulevard, Lakeland, FL 33801-6034

Stetson University

DeLand, Florida — CB member
www.stetson.edu — CB code: 5630

- Private 4-year university
- Residential campus in large town
- 2,186 degree-seeking undergraduates: 3% part-time, 57% women, 5% African American, 2% Asian American, 10% Hispanic American, 3% international
- 1,445 degree-seeking graduate students
- 54% of applicants admitted
- SAT or ACT (ACT writing optional), application essay required
- 67% graduate within 6 years; 59% enter graduate study

General. Founded in 1883. Regionally accredited. **Degrees:** 510 bachelor's awarded; master's, first professional offered. **ROTC:** Army. **Location:** 20 miles from Daytona Beach, 40 miles from Orlando. **Calendar:** Semester, limited summer session. **Full-time faculty:** 231 total; 93% have terminal degrees, 12% minority, 41% women. **Part-time faculty:** 130 total; 66% have terminal degrees, 7% minority, 39% women. **Class size:** 60% < 20, 39% 20-39, less than 1% 40-49. **Special facilities:** Geological museum, greenhouse with growth chambers, digital arts laboratory.

Freshman class profile. 4,110 applied, 2,215 admitted, 588 enrolled.

Mid 50% test scores		GPA 2.0-2.99:	10%
SAT critical reading:	500-610	End year in good standing:	83%
SAT math:	500-600	Return as sophomores:	77%
SAT writing:	480-580	Out-of-state:	18%
ACT composite:	21-26	Live on campus:	89%
GPA 3.75 or higher:	47%	International:	3%
GPA 3.50-3.74:	18%	Fraternities:	29%
GPA 3.0-3.49:	25%	Sororities:	27%

Basis for selection. High school record most important, followed by class rank, standardized test scores, and secondary school's recommendation. Extracurricular activities and particular talents or abilities also important. Interview recommended. Audition required of music majors. Portfolio recommended for art majors.

High school preparation. College-preparatory program required. 14 units required. Required units include English 4, mathematics 3, social studies 2, science 3 and foreign language 2.

2008-2009 Annual costs. Tuition/fees: $30,216. Room/board: $8,436. Books/supplies: $1,000. Personal expenses: $1,620.

2008-2009 Financial aid. Need-based: Average need met was 88%. Average scholarship/grant was $21,845; average loan $3,946. 74% of total undergraduate aid awarded as scholarships/grants, 26% as loans/jobs. **Non-need-based:** Scholarships awarded for academics, alumni affiliation, art, athletics, leadership, minority status, music/drama, religious affiliation, ROTC, state residency.

Application procedures. Admission: Priority date 3/15; no deadline. $40 fee, may be waived for applicants with need. Admission notification on a rolling basis beginning on or about 12/1. Must reply by May 1 or within 3 week(s) if notified thereafter. **Financial aid:** Priority date 3/15; no closing date. FAFSA, institutional form required. Applicants notified on a rolling basis starting 2/15.

Academics. Special study options: Accelerated study, combined bachelor's/graduate degree, double major, honors, independent study, internships, liberal arts/career combination, student-designed major, study abroad, teacher certification program, Washington semester, weekend college. **Credit/placement by examination:** AP, CLEP, IB, SAT, ACT, institutional tests. **Support services:** Reduced course load, study skills assistance, tutoring, writing center.

Majors. Area/ethnic studies: American, Latin American, Russian/Slavic. **Biology:** General, aquatic, biochemistry, molecular. **Business:** Accounting, business admin, entrepreneurial studies, finance, international, management information systems, management science, managerial economics, marketing. **Communications:** General. **Computer sciences:** General, computer science, web page design. **Conservation:** Environmental science. **Education:** Biology, elementary, English, foreign languages, French, German, mathematics, music, secondary, social science, Spanish. **Foreign languages:** French, German, Spanish. **Health:** Health services. **History:** General. **Liberal arts:** Humanities. **Math:** General. **Parks/recreation:** Exercise sciences, sports admin. **Philosophy/religion:** Philosophy, religion. **Physical sciences:** Chemistry, physics. **Psychology:** General. **Social sciences:** General, economics, geography, international relations, political science, sociology. **Visual/performing arts:** Art, dramatic, music performance, music theory/

composition, piano/organ, stringed instruments, studio arts, voice/opera. **Other:** Music technology, orchestral instrument.

Most popular majors. Biology 6%, business/marketing 38%, social sciences 9%, visual/performing arts 8%.

Computing on campus. 458 workstations in dormitories, library, computer center, student center. Dormitories wired for high-speed internet access and linked to campus network. Commuter students can connect to campus network. Online course registration, online library, helpline, repair service, student web hosting, wireless network available.

Student life. Freshman orientation: Mandatory, $100 fee. Preregistration for classes offered. Held 4 days prior to first day of classes. **Housing:** Guaranteed on-campus for all undergraduates. Coed dorms, single-sex dorms, apartments, fraternity/sorority housing, wellness housing available. $200 nonrefundable deposit. **Activities:** Bands, campus ministries, choral groups, dance, drama, film society, literary magazine, music ensembles, musical theater, opera, radio station, student government, student newspaper, symphony orchestra, Black student association, Caribbean club, Habitat for Humanity, Indian student association, Jewish Student Organization, Roots and Shoots, Multicultural student council, College Democrats, College Republicans.

Athletics. NCAA. **Intercollegiate:** Baseball M, basketball, cross-country, golf, rowing (crew), soccer, softball W, tennis, volleyball W. **Intramural:** Baseball, basketball, bowling, cross-country, football (non-tackle), golf, soccer, softball, swimming, table tennis, tennis, volleyball, water polo. **Team name:** Hatters.

Student services. Career counseling, student employment services, financial aid counseling, health services, minority student services, personal counseling, placement for graduates, women's services. **Physically disabled:** Services for visually, speech impaired.

Contact. E-mail: admissions@stetson.edu
Phone: (386) 822-7100 Toll-free number: (800) 688-0101
Fax: (386) 822-7112
Deborah Thompson, Vice President for Enrollment Management and Campus Life, Stetson University, Campus Box 8378, DeLand, FL 32723

Talmudic College of Florida
Miami Beach, Florida
www.talmudicu.edu **CB code: 0514**

- Private 4-year rabbinical college for men affiliated with Jewish faith
- Very large city
- 25 degree-seeking undergraduates
- 10 graduate students
- Interview required

General. Founded in 1974. Accredited by AARTS. **Degrees:** 5 bachelor's awarded; master's, doctoral, first professional offered. **Location:** 3 miles from downtown. **Calendar:** Semester, extensive summer session. **Full-time faculty:** 6 total. **Class size:** 100% < 20. **Special facilities:** Rabbinical studies research library.

Freshman class profile.

Out-of-state:	60%	**Live on campus:**	100%

Basis for selection. Recommendations and personal interview most important. Essay recommended.

High school preparation. Recommended units include foreign language 2. Two Bible and Talmud, 1 Jewish thought recommended.

2008-2009 Annual costs. Books/supplies: $900.

Financial aid. All financial aid based on need.

Application procedures. Admission: No deadline. $250 fee, may be waived for applicants with need. Admission notification on a rolling basis. **Financial aid:** No deadline. FAFSA, institutional form required. Applicants notified on a rolling basis.

Academics. Special study options: Cooperative education, distance learning, dual enrollment of high school students, honors, independent study, student-designed major, study abroad, weekend college. **Credit/placement by examination:** CLEP. **Support services:** Remedial instruction, study skills assistance, tutoring.

Majors. Philosophy/religion: Judaic. **Theology:** Religious ed.

Computing on campus. 8 workstations in library, computer center. Online library available.

Student life. Freshman orientation: Available. **Policies:** Students must be "Shomer Mitzvot". Religious observance required. **Housing:** Guaranteed on-campus for all undergraduates. Apartments available.

Student services. Adult student services, chaplain/spiritual director, career counseling, student employment services, financial aid counseling, health services, legal services, personal counseling.

Contact. Phone: (305) 534-0750 Toll-free number: (888) 825-6834
Fax: (305) 534-8444
Rabbi. Yeshaya Greenberg, Dean of Students, Talmudic College of Florida, 1910 Alton Road, Miami Beach, FL 33139

Trinity Baptist College
Jacksonville, Florida
www.tbc.edu

- Private 4-year Bible and teachers college
- Very large city
- 288 degree-seeking undergraduates

General. Regionally accredited. **Calendar:** Semester. **Full-time faculty:** 15 total. **Part-time faculty:** 40 total.

Freshman class profile. 70 enrolled.

2008-2009 Annual costs. Tuition/fees: $7,530.

Academics. Credit/placement by examination: CLEP.

Majors. Education: Elementary, secondary, special. **Theology:** Missionary, pastoral counseling. **Other:** Church ministries.

Contact. E-mail: admissions@tbc.edu
Phone: (800) 786-2206
Michael Nichols, Director of Enrollment Management, Trinity Baptist College, 800 Hammond Boulevard, Jacksonville, FL 32221

Trinity College of Florida
Trinity, Florida
www.trinitycollege.edu **CB code: 3975**

- Private 4-year Bible college affiliated with interdenominational tradition
- Commuter campus in small city
- 178 degree-seeking undergraduates: 12% part-time, 38% women
- 36% of applicants admitted
- SAT or ACT (ACT writing optional), application essay required
- 40% graduate within 6 years

General. Accredited by ABHE. **Degrees:** 31 bachelor's, 2 associate awarded. **Location:** 25 miles from Tampa. **Calendar:** Semester, limited summer session. **Full-time faculty:** 6 total; 83% have terminal degrees, 17% women. **Part-time faculty:** 20 total; 20% have terminal degrees, 30% women. **Class size:** 64% < 20, 30% 20-39, 6% 40-49.

Freshman class profile. 171 applied, 61 admitted, 35 enrolled.

Mid 50% test scores		**GPA 3.0-3.49:**	21%
SAT critical reading:	400-510	**GPA 2.0-2.99:**	59%
SAT math:	390-540	**End year in good standing:**	100%
ACT composite:	17-24	**Return as sophomores:**	61%
GPA 3.75 or higher:	4%	**Out-of-state:**	9%
GPA 3.50-3.74:	12%		

Basis for selection. Applicants must provide evidence of Christian character and witness, as well as academic ability largely based upon GPA and SAT/ACT scores. **Homeschooled:** GED may be required if student is not registered with local superintendent or umbrella school.

High school preparation. 18 units required. Required units include English 4, mathematics 4, social studies 2, history 2, science 4 and foreign language 2.

2009-2010 Annual costs. Tuition/fees: $11,200. Room/board: $6,534. Books/supplies: $1,150. Personal expenses: $2,538.

2007-2008 Financial aid. All financial aid based on need. 30 full-time freshmen applied for aid; 26 were judged to have need; 26 of these received aid. Average need met was 78%. Average scholarship/grant was $3,024;

average loan $1,750. 42% of total undergraduate aid awarded as scholarships/grants, 58% as loans/jobs.

Application procedures. Admission: Closing date 8/2 (receipt date). $25 fee, may be waived for applicants with need, free for online applicants. Admission notification on a rolling basis. **Financial aid:** Priority date 3/15, closing date 8/2. FAFSA, institutional form required. Applicants notified on a rolling basis.

Academics. Special study options: Accelerated study, double major, dual enrollment of high school students, honors, independent study, internships, weekend college. **Credit/placement by examination:** AP, CLEP, SAT, ACT, institutional tests. 24 credit hours maximum toward associate degree, 24 toward bachelor's. **Support services:** Reduced course load, tutoring, writing center.

Majors. Business: General. **Education:** Elementary. **Psychology:** Counseling. **Theology:** Missionary, pastoral counseling, preministerial, youth ministry. **Other:** Theological amd ministerial studies.

Most popular majors. Education 16%, theological studies 84%.

Computing on campus. 14 workstations in library, computer center. Dormitories wired for high-speed internet access and linked to campus network. Online library, repair service, wireless network available.

Student life. Freshman orientation: Mandatory. Preregistration for classes offered. Held 4 days before classes begin. Includes social gathering, vehicle registration, student IDs, and assessment testing. **Policies:** Religious observance required. **Housing:** Guaranteed on-campus for all undergraduates. Single-sex dorms, special housing for disabled, apartments, wellness housing available. $150 fully refundable deposit, deadline 7/1. **Activities:** Choral groups, drama, student government.

Athletics. NCCAA. **Intercollegiate:** Basketball, volleyball W. **Intramural:** Basketball M, softball M, volleyball. **Team name:** Tigers.

Student services. Chaplain/spiritual director, career counseling, financial aid counseling, personal counseling.

Contact. E-mail: admissions@trinitycollege.edu
Phone: (727) 569-1411 Toll-free number: (800) 388-0869
Fax: (727) 569-1410
Mark Sawyer, Director of Admissions, Trinity College of Florida, 2430 Welbilt Boulevard, Trinity, FL 34655-4401

Universidad FLET
Miami, Florida
www.flet.edu

- Private 4-year university and Bible college
- Large city
- 261 degree-seeking undergraduates

General. Accredited by DETC. **Degrees:** 28 bachelor's awarded; master's offered. **Calendar:** Continuous. **Full-time faculty:** 5 total. **Part-time faculty:** 15 total.

Basis for selection. Open admission. **Homeschooled:** Letter of recommendation (nonparent) required.

Application procedures. Admission: No deadline. $20 fee, may be waived for applicants with need. **Financial aid:** No deadline.

Academics. Special study options: Distance learning. **Credit/placement by examination:** CLEP.

Majors. Theology: Bible, theology.

Student life. Freshman orientation: Available. Preregistration for classes offered.

Contact. E-mail: admisiones@flet.edu
Phone: (305) 378-8700 Toll-free number: (888) 376-3538
Fax: (305) 232-5832
Janet Ramirez, Director of Admission, Universidad FLET, 14540 SW 136th Street, Suite 108, Miami, FL 33186

University of Central Florida
Orlando, Florida — **CB member**
www.ucf.edu — **CB code: 5233**

- Public 4-year university
- Residential campus in very large city
- 42,642 degree-seeking undergraduates: 25% part-time, 55% women, 9% African American, 5% Asian American, 14% Hispanic American, 1% international
- 6,593 degree-seeking graduate students
- 48% of applicants admitted
- SAT or ACT with writing required
- 63% graduate within 6 years

General. Founded in 1963. Regionally accredited. **Degrees:** 9,139 bachelor's, 250 associate awarded; master's, doctoral offered. **ROTC:** Army, Air Force. **Location:** 13 miles from downtown. **Calendar:** Semester, extensive summer session. **Full-time faculty:** 1,195 total; 77% have terminal degrees, 22% minority, 38% women. **Part-time faculty:** 464 total; 39% have terminal degrees, 15% minority, 54% women. **Class size:** 26% < 20, 40% 20-39, 10% 40-49, 18% 50-99, 7% >100. **Special facilities:** Solar energy center, simulation and training institute, research/education in optics and lasers center, space education and research center, biomolecular sciences center, forensic science center, arboretum, observatory.

Freshman class profile. 28,659 applied, 13,831 admitted, 6,344 enrolled.

Mid 50% test scores			
SAT critical reading:	530-630	**Rank in top quarter:**	77%
SAT math:	550-640	**Rank in top tenth:**	35%
SAT writing:	510-600	**End year in good standing:**	97%
ACT composite:	23-27	**Return as sophomores:**	86%
GPA 3.75 or higher:	41%	**Out-of-state:**	7%
GPA 3.50-3.74:	28%	**Live on campus:**	70%
GPA 3.0-3.49:	29%	**International:**	1%
GPA 2.0-2.99:	2%	**Fraternities:**	8%
		Sororities:	6%

Basis for selection. Two-thirds of admission offers made via review of GPA and standardized test scores. One-third made via review of factors such as grades, strength of coursework, essays, letters of recommendation, special talents. Essay recommended. Audition required of music majors. Portfolio recommended for art majors. **Homeschooled:** Provide detail about coursework and teaching process.

High school preparation. 18 units required. Required units include English 4, mathematics 3, social studies 3, science 3 (laboratory 2), foreign language 2 and academic electives 3.

2008-2009 Annual costs. Tuition/fees: $3,947; $18,689 out-of-state. Room/board: $8,574. Books/supplies: $924. Personal expenses: $2,276.

2007-2008 Financial aid. Need-based: 4,429 full-time freshmen applied for aid; 2,568 were judged to have need; 2,547 of these received aid. Average need met was 69%. Average scholarship/grant was $4,196; average loan $3,265. 48% of total undergraduate aid awarded as scholarships/grants, 52% as loans/jobs. **Non-need-based:** Awarded to 9,795 full-time undergraduates, including 3,131 freshmen. Scholarships awarded for academics, alumni affiliation, athletics, leadership, ROTC, state residency.

Application procedures. Admission: Priority date 1/1; deadline 5/1 (postmark date). $30 fee, may be waived for applicants with need. Admission notification on a rolling basis beginning on or about 10/1. Must reply by May 1 or within 3 week(s) if notified thereafter. **Financial aid:** Priority date 3/1, closing date 6/30. FAFSA required. Applicants notified on a rolling basis starting 3/15; must reply within 3 week(s) of notification.

Academics. Special study options: Accelerated study, combined bachelor's/graduate degree, cooperative education, distance learning, double major, dual enrollment of high school students, ESL, honors, independent study, internships, study abroad, teacher certification program. Lead Scholars program. **Credit/placement by examination:** AP, CLEP, IB, SAT, ACT, institutional tests. 45 credit hours maximum toward bachelor's degree. **Support services:** Learning center, pre-admission summer program, reduced course load, study skills assistance, tutoring, writing center.

Honors college/program. Requires separate application, admission based on GPA, test scores, and class rank. Small general and specialized honors courses, honors building, and residence hall available. Accepts approximately 700 freshmen in the fall.

Majors. Biology: General, bacteriology, biotechnology. **Business:** General, accounting, actuarial science, business admin, finance, hospitality admin, management information systems, managerial economics, marketing, real estate, restaurant/food services, tourism/travel. **Communications:** General, advertising, journalism, radio/tv. **Computer sciences:** General, information technology. **Education:** Art, early childhood, elementary, English, foreign languages, mathematics, music, physical, science, social science, special, trade/industrial. **Engineering:** Aerospace, civil, computer, electrical, environmental, industrial, mechanical. **Engineering technology:** General, computer systems, electrical. **Foreign languages:** General, French, Spanish. **Health:** Audiology/speech pathology, clinical lab science, health care admin, health services, medical radiologic technology/radiation therapy, medical records admin, nursing (RN), predental, premedicine, prepharmacy, preveterinary, respiratory therapy technology. **History:** General. **Interdisciplinary:** Global studies. **Legal studies:** Paralegal. **Liberal arts:** Arts/sciences, humanities. **Math:** General, statistics. **Philosophy/religion:** Philosophy, religion. **Physical sciences:** Chemistry, physics. **Protective services:** Criminal justice, forensics. **Psychology:** General. **Public administration:** General, social work. **Social sciences:** General, anthropology, economics, political science, sociology. **Visual/performing arts:** Art, cinematography, dramatic, multimedia, music performance, photography, studio arts.

Most popular majors. Business/marketing 26%, education 10%, engineering/engineering technologies 7%, health sciences 9%, liberal arts 7%, psychology 9%.

Computing on campus. 3,147 workstations in library, computer center, student center. Dormitories wired for high-speed internet access and linked to campus network. Commuter students can connect to campus network. Online course registration, online library, helpline, repair service, student web hosting, wireless network available.

Student life. Freshman orientation: Mandatory, $35 fee. Preregistration for classes offered. Ten sessions offered throughout spring and summer. 2-day event includes financial aid presentation, advising. **Housing:** Coed dorms, single-sex dorms, apartments, fraternity/sorority housing available. $250 nonrefundable deposit, deadline 3/1. Affiliated student residence housing. Students under guidance of university housing resident assistants considered part of on-campus housing. **Activities:** Bands, campus ministries, choral groups, drama, film society, international student organizations, literary magazine, music ensembles, Model UN, musical theater, radio station, student government, student newspaper, symphony orchestra, campus activities board, African American student union, orientation team, Hispanic American student association, Korean student association, Indian student association, Christian student association, Jewish student union.

Athletics. NCAA. **Intercollegiate:** Baseball M, basketball, cheerleading, cross-country, football (tackle) M, golf, rowing (crew) W, soccer, softball W, tennis, track and field W, volleyball W. **Intramural:** Badminton, baseball M, basketball, bowling, football (non-tackle), golf, racquetball, soccer, softball, tennis, volleyball, weight lifting, wrestling M. **Team name:** Golden Knights.

Student services. Adult student services, alcohol/substance abuse counseling, career counseling, student employment services, financial aid counseling, health services, legal services, minority student services, on-campus daycare, personal counseling, placement for graduates, veterans' counselor, women's services. **Physically disabled:** Services for visually, speech, hearing impaired.

Contact. E-mail: admission@mail.ucf.edu
Phone: (407) 823-3000 Fax: (407) 823-5625
Gordon Chavis, Assistant Vice President, University of Central Florida, Box 160111, Orlando, FL 32816-0111

University of Florida

Gainesville, Florida — **CB member**
www.ufl.edu — **CB code: 5812**

- Public 4-year university
- Residential campus in small city
- 34,094 degree-seeking undergraduates: 6% part-time, 54% women, 10% African American, 8% Asian American, 15% Hispanic American, 1% international
- 16,016 degree-seeking graduate students
- 39% of applicants admitted
- SAT or ACT with writing, application essay required

General. Founded in 1853. Regionally accredited. **Degrees:** 8,737 bachelor's awarded; master's, doctoral, first professional offered. **Location:** 70 miles from Jacksonville. **Calendar:** Semester, limited summer session. **Full-time faculty:** 1,937 total; 85% have terminal degrees, 20% minority, 31% women. **Part-time faculty:** 52 total; 77% have terminal degrees, 8% minority, 36% women. **Class size:** 40% < 20, 31% 20-39, 7% 40-49, 12% 50-99, 10% >100. **Special facilities:** Natural history museum, marine laboratory, wildlife sanctuary, citrus research center, bell carillon, pipe organ, center for performing arts, hyperbaric chamber, microkelvin laboratory, brain institute, art museum, nuclear reactor.

Freshman class profile. 27,612 applied, 10,897 admitted, 6,382 enrolled.

Mid 50% test scores		**Rank in top quarter:**	92%
SAT critical reading:	570-680	**Rank in top tenth:**	76%
SAT math:	590-700	**Return as sophomores:**	95%
ACT composite:	25-30	**Out-of-state:**	3%
GPA 3.75 or higher:	88%	**Live on campus:**	81%
GPA 3.50-3.74:	8%	**International:**	1%
GPA 3.0-3.49:	3%	**Fraternities:**	20%
GPA 2.0-2.99:	1%	**Sororities:**	21%

Basis for selection. High school grades, academic course selection, SAT/ACT scores, extracurricular activities, awards, honors, recognitions, special talents and recommendations considered. SAT subject tests used strictly for placement purposes except for applicants from non-regionally accredited schools. **Homeschooled:** Statement describing homeschool structure and mission, state high school equivalency certificate, letter of recommendation (nonparent) required. SAT subject test in math (level II-C), foreign language, science and social science required. Letter from principal or guidance counselor. **Learning Disabled:** Optional disclosure; students receive extra review by disability office.

High school preparation. 18 units required. Required units include English 4, mathematics 3, social studies 3, science 3 (laboratory 2) and foreign language 2. English must include substantial writing. Math must include algebra I and II, and geometry. Foreign language must be 2 units of same language.

2008-2009 Annual costs. Tuition/fees: $3,790; $20,640 out-of-state. Room/board: $7,150. Books/supplies: $940. Personal expenses: $3,220.

2007-2008 Financial aid. Need-based: 4,155 full-time freshmen applied for aid; 2,653 were judged to have need; 2,648 of these received aid. Average need met was 86%. Average scholarship/grant was $6,149; average loan $3,465. 60% of total undergraduate aid awarded as scholarships/grants, 40% as loans/jobs. **Non-need-based:** Awarded to 27,583 full-time undergraduates, including 6,218 freshmen. Scholarships awarded for academics, art, athletics, leadership, minority status, music/drama, ROTC, state residency.

Application procedures. Admission: Closing date 11/1 (postmark date). $30 fee, may be waived for applicants with need. Application must be submitted online. Admission notification on a rolling basis beginning on or about 2/15. Must reply by May 1 or within 3 week(s) if notified thereafter. $200 tuition deposit required by May 1. **Financial aid:** Priority date 3/15; no closing date. FAFSA required. Applicants notified on a rolling basis starting 4/1.

Academics. Special study options: Accelerated study, cooperative education, cross-registration, distance learning, double major, dual enrollment of high school students, ESL, exchange student, external degree, honors, independent study, internships, liberal arts/career combination, semester at sea, student-designed major, study abroad, teacher certification program, weekend college. **Credit/placement by examination:** AP, CLEP, IB, SAT, ACT, institutional tests. 45 credit hours maximum toward bachelor's degree. **Support services:** Learning center, reduced course load, study skills assistance, tutoring, writing center.

Majors. Agriculture: Agronomy, animal sciences, dairy, economics, food science, horticultural science, plant sciences, poultry, soil science. **Architecture:** Architecture, landscape. **Area/ethnic studies:** Asian. **Biology:** Bacteriology, botany, entomology, plant pathology, zoology. **Business:** General, accounting, finance, insurance, management science, marketing, real estate. **Communications:** Advertising, journalism, public relations. **Computer sciences:** General. **Conservation:** Forestry. **Education:** Agricultural, art, elementary, middle, music, special. **Engineering:** Aerospace, agricultural, chemical, civil, computer, electrical, environmental, materials, mechanical, nuclear, science, systems. **Engineering technology:** Construction, surveying. **Family/consumer sciences:** Family/community services. **Foreign languages:** Classics, French, German, linguistics, Portuguese, Russian, Spanish. **Health:** Audiology/speech pathology, health services, nursing (RN). **History:** General. **Math:** General, statistics. **Parks/recreation:** Exercise sciences, facilities management. **Philosophy/religion:** Judaic, philosophy, religion. **Physical sciences:** Astronomy, chemistry, geology, physics. **Protective services:** Criminalistics. **Psychology:** General. **Social sciences:** Anthropology, economics, geography, political science, sociology. **Visual/performing arts:** Art history/conservation, dance, dramatic, interior design, studio arts.

Most popular majors. Agriculture 6%, business/marketing 17%, engineering/engineering technologies 12%, health sciences 7%, psychology 6%, social sciences 14%.

Computing on campus. 1,000 workstations in library, student center. Dormitories wired for high-speed internet access and linked to campus network. Commuter students can connect to campus network. Online course registration, online library, helpline, student web hosting, wireless network available.

Student life. Freshman orientation: Mandatory, $106 fee. Two-day program held various dates in May, June and July. **Housing:** Coed dorms, special housing for disabled, apartments, fraternity/sorority housing available. $200 partly refundable deposit. Pets allowed in dorm rooms. Undergraduate honor halls, quiet/study floors, faculty-in-residence program, first-year experience program, wellness floor, no-visitation by opposite sex floor available. **Activities:** Bands, choral groups, dance, drama, film society, literary magazine, music ensembles, musical theater, radio station, student government, student newspaper, symphony orchestra, TV station, over 500 student groups on campus.

Athletics. NCAA. **Intercollegiate:** Baseball M, basketball, cheerleading, cross-country, diving, football (tackle) M, golf, gymnastics W, lacrosse W, soccer W, softball W, swimming, tennis, track and field, volleyball W. **Intramural:** Badminton, basketball, bowling, football (non-tackle), golf, racquetball, soccer, softball, swimming, table tennis, tennis, track and field, volleyball, weight lifting, wrestling M. **Team name:** Gators.

Student services. Adult student services, alcohol/substance abuse counseling, chaplain/spiritual director, career counseling, services for economically disadvantaged, student employment services, financial aid counseling, health services, legal services, minority student services, on-campus daycare, personal counseling, placement for graduates, veterans' counselor. **Physically disabled:** Services for visually, speech, hearing impaired.

Contact. Phone: (352) 392-1365
Zina Evans, Assistant Provost and Director of Admissions, University of Florida, 201 Criser Hall-PO Box 114000, Gainesville, FL 32611-4000

University of Miami

Coral Gables, Florida — **CB member**
www.miami.edu — **CB code: 5815**

- Private 4-year university
- Residential campus in small city
- 10,008 degree-seeking undergraduates: 5% part-time, 53% women, 8% African American, 5% Asian American, 23% Hispanic American, 7% international
- 4,785 degree-seeking graduate students
- 39% of applicants admitted
- SAT or ACT (ACT writing optional), application essay required
- 77% graduate within 6 years; 33% enter graduate study

General. Founded in 1925. Regionally accredited. **Degrees:** 2,445 bachelor's awarded; master's, doctoral, first professional offered. **ROTC:** Army, Air Force. **Location:** 7 miles from downtown. **Calendar:** Semester, extensive summer session. **Full-time faculty:** 947 total; 85% have terminal degrees, 28% minority, 35% women. **Part-time faculty:** 434 total; 62% have terminal degrees, 31% minority, 43% women. **Class size:** 52% < 20, 37% 20-39, 6% 40-49, 4% 50-99, 1% >100. **Special facilities:** Cinema, observatory, palmetum, marine science research vessels, broadcasting studios, concert hall, arboretum, performing arts theater, film studios, sound stage, museum.

Freshman class profile. 21,773 applied, 8,411 admitted, 2,010 enrolled.

Mid 50% test scores			
SAT critical reading:	580-680	Rank in top quarter:	90%
SAT math:	610-700	Rank in top tenth:	66%
SAT writing:	580-670	End year in good standing:	95%
ACT composite:	27-31	Return as sophomores:	90%
GPA 3.75 or higher:	76%	Out-of-state:	57%
GPA 3.50-3.74:	11%	Live on campus:	82%
GPA 3.0-3.49:	12%	International:	8%
GPA 2.0-2.99:	1%	Fraternities:	12%
		Sororities:	16%

Basis for selection. Secondary school record, test scores, recommendations, essay very important. Math and science SAT Subject Tests required for dual-degree honors programs in medicine. Auditions required for music and theater arts applicants. Portfolio required for art BFA program and architecture. **Homeschooled:** Interview required.

High school preparation. College-preparatory program recommended. 20 units recommended. Recommended units include English 4, mathematics 4, social studies 3, history 2, science 3 (laboratory 2), foreign language 2, computer science 1 and visual/performing arts 1.

2008-2009 Annual costs. Tuition/fees: $34,834. Room/board: $10,254.

2008-2009 Financial aid. Need-based: 1,234 full-time freshmen applied for aid; 907 were judged to have need; 907 of these received aid. Average need met was 88%. Average scholarship/grant was $22,661; average loan $4,554. 68% of total undergraduate aid awarded as scholarships/grants, 32% as loans/jobs. **Non-need-based:** Awarded to 3,620 full-time undergraduates, including 795 freshmen. Scholarships awarded for academics, athletics, music/drama, ROTC.

Application procedures. Admission: Priority date 11/1; deadline 1/15 (postmark date). $65 fee, may be waived for applicants with need. Admission notification 4/15. Must reply by May 1 or within 2 week(s) if notified thereafter. **Financial aid:** Priority date 2/1; no closing date. FAFSA required. Applicants notified on a rolling basis starting 3/1.

Academics. Special study options: Accelerated study, combined bachelor's/graduate degree, double major, dual enrollment of high school students, ESL, honors, independent study, internships, liberal arts/career combination, student-designed major, study abroad, teacher certification program, Washington semester, weekend college. Learning communities, International Exchange Students Program. **Credit/placement by examination:** AP, CLEP, IB, SAT, institutional tests. 60 credit hours maximum toward bachelor's degree. **Support services:** Learning center, pre-admission summer program, reduced course load, remedial instruction, study skills assistance, tutoring, writing center.

Majors. Architecture: Architecture. **Area/ethnic studies:** African-American, American, Latin American, women's. **Biology:** General, bacteriology, biochemistry, biophysics, marine. **Business:** Accounting, business admin, entrepreneurial studies, finance, human resources, international, management science, managerial economics, marketing. **Communications:** General, advertising, broadcast journalism, journalism, media studies, photojournalism, public relations, radio/tv. **Computer sciences:** Computer graphics, computer science, data processing, information systems, security. **Conservation:** Management/policy. **Education:** Elementary, music, secondary, special. **Engineering:** Aerospace, architectural, biomedical, civil, computer, electrical, environmental, industrial, mechanical, science. **Foreign languages:** Classics, French, German, Spanish. **Health:** Athletic training, health services, music therapy, nursing (RN). **History:** General. **Interdisciplinary:** Neuroscience. **Legal studies:** General. **Liberal arts:** Arts/sciences. **Math:** General, applied, probability. **Parks/recreation:** Exercise sciences, sports admin. **Philosophy/religion:** Judaic, philosophy, religion. **Physical sciences:** Chemistry, geology, meteorology, oceanography, physics. **Psychology:** General. **Social sciences:** Anthropology, criminology, economics, geography, international relations, political science, sociology. **Visual/performing arts:** Acting, art, art history/conservation, ceramics, cinematography, design, dramatic, film/cinema, graphic design, jazz, music performance, music theory/composition, painting, photography, piano/organ, printmaking, sculpture, studio arts, theater arts management, theater design, voice/opera. **Other:** Dramartic/Theatre Arts & Stagecraft.

Computing on campus. 1,800 workstations in dormitories, library, computer center, student center. Dormitories wired for high-speed internet access and linked to campus network. Commuter students can connect to campus network. Online course registration, online library, helpline, repair service, student web hosting, wireless network available.

Student life. Freshman orientation: Mandatory. Preregistration for classes offered. 3 day program in August. **Policies:** Student initiated and administered honor code. **Housing:** Guaranteed on-campus for freshmen. Coed dorms, special housing for disabled, apartments, fraternity/sorority housing available. $250 nonrefundable deposit, deadline 5/1. Students reside in one of 5 residential colleges along with live-in faculty members. Special interest floors available. **Activities:** Bands, campus ministries, choral groups, dance, drama, film society, international student organizations, literary magazine, music ensembles, Model UN, musical theater, opera, radio station, student government, student newspaper, symphony orchestra, TV station, 275 clubs and organizations.

Athletics. NCAA. **Intercollegiate:** Baseball M, basketball, cheerleading, cross-country, diving W, football (tackle) M, golf W, rowing (crew) W, soccer W, swimming W, tennis, track and field, volleyball W. **Intramural:** Basketball, football (non-tackle), golf, racquetball M, soccer, softball, table tennis, tennis, volleyball. **Team name:** Hurricanes.

Student services. Adult student services, alcohol/substance abuse counseling, career counseling, student employment services, financial aid counseling, health services, minority student services, on-campus daycare, personal counseling, placement for graduates, veterans' counselor, women's services. **Physically disabled:** Services for visually, speech, hearing impaired.

Contact. E-mail: admission@miami.edu
Phone: (305) 284-4323 Fax: (305) 284-2507
Edward Gillis, Assistant Vice President for Enrollment Management/Executive Director of Admissions, University of Miami, 132 Ashe Building, Coral Gables, FL 33124-4616

University of North Florida

Jacksonville, Florida **CB member**
www.unf.edu **CB code: 5490**

- Public 4-year university
- Residential campus in very large city
- 13,204 degree-seeking undergraduates: 27% part-time, 57% women, 10% African American, 6% Asian American, 7% Hispanic American, 1% international
- 1,781 degree-seeking graduate students
- 64% of applicants admitted
- SAT or ACT with writing required
- 46% graduate within 6 years

General. Founded in 1965. Regionally accredited. **Degrees:** 2,754 bachelor's, 410 associate awarded; master's, doctoral offered. **ROTC:** Naval. **Location:** 12 miles from downtown. **Calendar:** Semester, extensive summer session. **Full-time faculty:** 492 total; 78% have terminal degrees, 14% minority, 46% women. **Part-time faculty:** 232 total; 32% have terminal degrees, 10% minority, 53% women. **Class size:** 21% < 20, 52% 20-39, 15% 40-49, 7% 50-99, 4% >100. **Special facilities:** Nature trails, designated bird sanctuary, fine arts center.

Freshman class profile. 9,397 applied, 5,985 admitted, 1,856 enrolled.

Mid 50% test scores		**GPA 2.0-2.99:**	9%
SAT critical reading:	510-620	**Rank in top quarter:**	51%
SAT math:	510-620	**Rank in top tenth:**	20%
ACT composite:	21-24	**Return as sophomores:**	77%
GPA 3.75 or higher:	37%	**Out-of-state:**	4%
GPA 3.50-3.74:	18%	**International:**	1%
GPA 3.0-3.49:	36%		

Basis for selection. SAT or ACT score and high school GPA based on 19 academic units very important. High school academic courses (not including electives) used for calculating GPA. Summer program available for some students who do not meet fall admissions criteria; students admitted on probation. Audition required for music majors. **Homeschooled:** Required to pass all sections of GED. **Learning Disabled:** Register with Disability Resource Center.

High school preparation. College-preparatory program required. 19 units required. Required units include English 4, mathematics 3, social studies 3, science 3 (laboratory 1), foreign language 2 and academic electives 4.

2008-2009 Annual costs. Tuition/fees: $3,775; $15,417 out-of-state. Room/board: $7,366. Books/supplies: $600. Personal expenses: $819.

2008-2009 Financial aid. Need-based: Average need met was 90%. Average scholarship/grant was $975; average loan $1,717. 50% of total undergraduate aid awarded as scholarships/grants, 50% as loans/jobs. **Non-need-based:** Scholarships awarded for academics, athletics, leadership, minority status, music/drama, state residency.

Application procedures. Admission: Priority date 11/1; deadline 6/26 (receipt date). $30 fee, may be waived for applicants with need. Admission notification on a rolling basis beginning on or about 12/1. Must reply by 7/31. **Financial aid:** Priority date 4/1; no closing date. FAFSA required. Applicants notified on a rolling basis starting 3/15; must reply within 2 week(s) of notification.

Academics. Special study options: Accelerated study, combined bachelor's/graduate degree, cooperative education, distance learning, double major, dual enrollment of high school students, ESL, honors, independent study, internships, student-designed major, study abroad, teacher certification program, Washington semester, weekend college. Learning Communities. **Credit/placement by examination:** AP, CLEP, IB, SAT, ACT, institutional tests. 30 credit hours maximum toward bachelor's degree. **Support services:** Learning center, pre-admission summer program, reduced course load, study skills assistance, tutoring, writing center.

Honors college/program. Must be in top 10% of graduating class, have 3.75 GPA or higher, 1250 SAT (exclusive of Writing) or 28 ACT.

Majors. Area/ethnic studies: French. **Biology:** General. **Business:** Accounting, banking/financial services, business admin, finance, international, managerial economics, marketing, transportation. **Communications:** Media studies. **Computer sciences:** General. **Education:** Art, early childhood, elementary, mathematics, middle, music, physical, science, secondary, special, trade/industrial. **Engineering:** Civil, electrical, mechanical. **Engineering technology:** Construction. **Foreign languages:** Sign language interpretation, Spanish. **Health:** Athletic training, health services, nursing (RN). **History:** General. **Interdisciplinary:** Global studies. **Liberal arts:** Arts/sciences. **Math:** General, statistics. **Parks/recreation:** Sports admin. **Philosophy/religion:** Philosophy. **Physical sciences:** Chemistry, physics. **Protective services:** Criminal justice. **Psychology:** General. **Social sciences:** Anthropology, economics, political science, sociology. **Visual/performing arts:** Art, jazz, music performance, studio arts.

Most popular majors. Business/marketing 23%, communications/journalism 9%, education 12%, engineering/engineering technologies 6%, health sciences 13%, psychology 9%.

Computing on campus. 850 workstations in library, computer center, student center. Dormitories wired for high-speed internet access and linked to campus network. Commuter students can connect to campus network. Online course registration, online library, helpline, student web hosting, wireless network available.

Student life. Freshman orientation: Mandatory, $35 fee. Preregistration for classes offered. One-and-one-half day program held several times during summer. **Policies:** Students must abide by drug/alcohol policy, student code of conduct, model bill of rights and responsibilities. **Housing:** Coed dorms, special housing for disabled, apartments, fraternity/sorority housing available. $250 partly refundable deposit. Suite style housing available. **Activities:** Bands, campus ministries, choral groups, dance, drama, international student organizations, literary magazine, music ensembles, radio station, student government, student newspaper, TV station, African American student union, Jewish student union, InterVarsity Christian Fellowship, College Republicans, Jeffersonian Society, The New Left, Muslim student association, Filipino student association, Golden Key international honor society.

Athletics. NCAA. **Intercollegiate:** Baseball M, basketball, cross-country, diving W, golf M, soccer, softball W, swimming W, tennis, track and field, volleyball W. **Intramural:** Basketball, football (non-tackle), racquetball, soccer, softball, tennis, track and field, volleyball. **Team name:** Ospreys.

Student services. Adult student services, alcohol/substance abuse counseling, career counseling, student employment services, financial aid counseling, health services, minority student services, on-campus daycare, personal counseling, placement for graduates, veterans' counselor, women's services. **Physically disabled:** Services for visually, speech, hearing impaired.

Contact. E-mail: admissions@unf.edu
Phone: (904) 620-2624 Fax: (904) 620-2414
John Yancey, Director, University of North Florida, 1 UNF Drive, Jacksonville, FL 32224-7699

University of South Florida

Tampa, Florida **CB member**
www.usf.edu **CB code: 5828**

- Public 4-year university
- Commuter campus in very large city
- 35,104 degree-seeking undergraduates: 29% part-time, 58% women, 12% African American, 6% Asian American, 14% Hispanic American, 1% international
- 9,144 degree-seeking graduate students
- 46% of applicants admitted
- SAT or ACT (ACT writing optional) required
- 49% graduate within 6 years

General. Founded in 1956. Regionally accredited. Regional campuses in St. Petersburg, Sarasota/Manatee, and Lakeland Polytechnic. **Degrees:** 6,962 bachelor's, 253 associate awarded; master's, doctoral, first professional offered. **ROTC:** Army, Naval, Air Force. **Location:** 10 miles from downtown. **Calendar:** Semester, extensive summer session. **Full-time faculty:** 1,262 total; 79% have terminal degrees, 23% minority, 43% women. **Part-time faculty:** 132 total; 58% have terminal degrees, 17% minority, 52% women. **Class size:** 27% < 20, 51% 20-39, 8% 40-49, 11% 50-99, 3% >100. **Special facilities:** Art museum, weather station, botanical garden, anthropology museum.

Freshman class profile. 27,017 applied, 12,338 admitted, 3,738 enrolled.

Mid 50% test scores			
SAT critical reading:	510-610	Rank in top quarter:	60%
SAT math:	530-630	Rank in top tenth:	25%
SAT writing:	490-580	Return as sophomores:	85%
ACT composite:	23-28	Out-of-state:	4.85%
GPA 3.75 or higher:	47%	Live on campus:	56%
GPA 3.50-3.74:	24%	International:	1%
GPA 3.0-3.49:	27%	Fraternities:	7%
GPA 2.0-2.99:	2%	Sororities:	6%

Basis for selection. High school GPA and test scores most important. On sliding scale, higher grades compensate for lower test scores. Requirements higher for several degree programs. Audition required of music majors. Portfolio required of art majors.

High school preparation. College-preparatory program required. 20 units required. Required units include English 4, mathematics 3, social studies 3, science 3 (laboratory 2), foreign language 2 and academic electives 3. Foreign language units must be in 1 language.

2008-2009 Annual costs. Tuition/fees: $3,906; $16,623 out-of-state. Room/board: $8,080. Books/supplies: $1,500. Personal expenses: $4,100.

2007-2008 Financial aid. Need-based: 2,515 full-time freshmen applied for aid; 1,779 were judged to have need; 1,765 of these received aid. Average need met was 32%. Average scholarship/grant was $4,785; average loan $2,617. 46% of total undergraduate aid awarded as scholarships/grants, 54% as loans/jobs. **Non-need-based:** Awarded to 6,672 full-time undergraduates, including 1,653 freshmen. Scholarships awarded for academics, alumni affiliation, art, athletics, job skills, leadership, minority status, music/drama, religious affiliation, ROTC, state residency. **Additional information:** Deferred tuition payment plan available for late financial aid recipients.

Application procedures. Admission: Priority date 3/1; deadline 4/15 (postmark date). $30 fee, may be waived for applicants with need. Admission notification on a rolling basis beginning on or about 10/1. Must reply by May 1 or within 2 week(s) if notified thereafter. **Financial aid:** Priority date 3/1; no closing date. FAFSA required. Applicants notified on a rolling basis starting 3/15.

Academics. Special study options: Accelerated study, combined bachelor's/graduate degree, cooperative education, cross-registration, distance learning, double major, dual enrollment of high school students, exchange student, honors, internships, study abroad, teacher certification program, Washington semester, weekend college. **Credit/placement by examination:** AP, CLEP, IB, SAT, ACT, institutional tests. **Support services:** Learning center, pre-admission summer program, tutoring.

Majors. Area/ethnic studies: African-American, American, women's. **Biology:** General, bacteriology, biomedical sciences. **Business:** General, accounting, business admin, finance, hospitality admin, international, management information systems, managerial economics, marketing. **Communications:** General. **Computer sciences:** General, information systems, information technology. **Conservation:** General. **Education:** General, art, business, drama/dance, early childhood, elementary, emotionally handicapped, English, foreign languages, learning disabled, mathematics, mentally handicapped, music, physical, science, social science, special, trade/industrial. **Engineering:** General, chemical, civil, computer, electrical, manufacturing, mechanical. **Foreign languages:** Classics, French, German, Italian, Russian, Spanish. **Health:** Athletic training, audiology/speech pathology, clinical lab science, nursing (RN). **History:** General. **Interdisciplinary:** Biological/physical sciences, gerontology. **Liberal arts:** Arts/sciences, humanities. **Math:** General. **Philosophy/religion:** Philosophy, religion. **Physical sciences:** Chemistry, geology, physics. **Protective services:** Criminal justice. **Psychology:** General. **Public administration:** Social work. **Social sciences:** General, anthropology, criminology, economics, geography, international relations, political science, sociology. **Visual/performing arts:** Art, art history/conservation, dance, dramatic, music performance, studio arts.

Most popular majors. Biology 8%, business/marketing 21%, education 10%, English 7%, psychology 9%, social sciences 16%.

Computing on campus. 500 workstations in dormitories, library, computer center, student center. Dormitories wired for high-speed internet access and linked to campus network. Commuter students can connect to campus network. Online course registration, helpline, wireless network available.

Student life. Freshman orientation: Mandatory, $35 fee. Preregistration for classes offered. **Housing:** Coed dorms, single-sex dorms, special housing for disabled, apartments, cooperative housing, fraternity/sorority housing, wellness housing available. $225 partly refundable deposit, deadline 8/1. **Activities:** Bands, campus ministries, choral groups, dance, drama, film society, literary magazine, music ensembles, musical theater, opera, radio station, student government, student newspaper, symphony orchestra, TV station, approximately 300 student organizations available.

Athletics. NCAA. **Intercollegiate:** Baseball M, basketball, cross-country, football (tackle) M, golf, sailing, soccer, softball W, tennis, track and field, volleyball W. **Intramural:** Badminton, basketball, bowling, cross-country, fencing, football (tackle) M, golf, handball, ice hockey, lacrosse, racquetball, rugby, sailing, soccer, softball W, swimming, table tennis, tennis, track and field, volleyball, wrestling M. **Team name:** Bulls.

Student services. Adult student services, career counseling, student employment services, financial aid counseling, health services, legal services, on-campus daycare, personal counseling, placement for graduates, veterans' counselor. **Physically disabled:** Services for visually, speech, hearing impaired.

Contact. E-mail: admissions@admin.usf.edu
Phone: (813) 974-3350 Fax: (813) 974-9689
J. Robert Spatig, Director of Admissions, University of South Florida, 4202 East Fowler Avenue, SVC 1036, Tampa, FL 33620-9951

University of Tampa

Tampa, Florida — **CB member**
www.ut.edu — **CB code: 5819**

- Private 4-year university and liberal arts college
- Residential campus in large city
- 5,081 degree-seeking undergraduates: 7% part-time, 59% women, 6% African American, 2% Asian American, 10% Hispanic American, 9% international
- 661 degree-seeking graduate students
- 52% of applicants admitted
- SAT or ACT (ACT writing optional) required
- 58% graduate within 6 years; 24% enter graduate study

General. Founded in 1931. Regionally accredited. **Degrees:** 1,036 bachelor's, 1 associate awarded; master's offered. **ROTC:** Army, Naval, Air Force. **Location:** 20 miles from St. Petersburg, 70 miles from Orlando. **Calendar:** Semester, extensive summer session. **Full-time faculty:** 237 total; 89% have terminal degrees, 4% minority, 39% women. **Part-time faculty:** 247 total; 30% have terminal degrees, 9% minority, 57% women. **Class size:** 38% < 20, 59% 20-39, 2% 40-49, 1% 50-99. **Special facilities:** Art and furniture museum, dance studio, art studio, marine science research vessel, marine science research laboratory.

Freshman class profile. 8,408 applied, 4,414 admitted, 1,232 enrolled.

Mid 50% test scores			
SAT critical reading:	500-580	Rank in top quarter:	53%
SAT math:	500-590	Rank in top tenth:	17%
SAT writing:	490-580	End year in good standing:	84%
ACT composite:	21-25	Return as sophomores:	76%
GPA 3.75 or higher:	12%	Out-of-state:	66%
GPA 3.50-3.74:	19%	Live on campus:	88%
GPA 3.0-3.49:	47%	International:	8%
GPA 2.0-2.99:	22%	Fraternities:	6%
		Sororities:	12%

Basis for selection. Secondary school record, test scores most important. Recommendations, talent/ability, character/personal qualities considered. Interview recommended. Auditions required of music and performing arts majors. Portfolio recommended for art majors. **Learning Disabled:** Dean of Students coordinates assistance for students with disabilities. Student responsible for requesting accommodations each term. Documentation required.

High school preparation. College-preparatory program required. 18 units required. Required units include English 4, mathematics 3, social studies 3, science 3 (laboratory 2), foreign language 2 and academic electives 3.

2008-2009 Annual costs. Tuition/fees: $21,712. Room/board: $7,978. Books/supplies: $988. Personal expenses: $1,311.

2008-2009 Financial aid. Need-based: 845 full-time freshmen applied for aid; 628 were judged to have need; 628 of these received aid. Average need met was 77%. Average scholarship/grant was $7,031; average loan $4,230. 67% of total undergraduate aid awarded as scholarships/grants, 33% as loans/jobs. **Non-need-based:** Awarded to 2,334 full-time undergraduates, including 786 freshmen. Scholarships awarded for academics, alumni affiliation, art, athletics, leadership, music/drama, ROTC, state residency. **Additional information:** Early aid estimator service.

Application procedures. Admission: Priority date 11/15; no deadline. $40 fee, may be waived for applicants with need. Admission notification on a rolling basis beginning on or about 10/1. Must reply by May 1 or within 4 week(s) if notified thereafter. **Financial aid:** No deadline. FAFSA required. Applicants notified on a rolling basis starting 2/1; must reply within 3 week(s) of notification.

Academics. **Special study options:** Combined bachelor's/graduate degree, double major, dual enrollment of high school students, exchange student, honors, independent study, internships, liberal arts/career combination, study abroad, teacher certification program, Washington semester. Certificate of International Studies. **Credit/placement by examination:** AP, CLEP, IB, SAT, ACT, institutional tests. 30 credit hours maximum toward associate degree, 30 toward bachelor's. **Support services:** Learning center, reduced course load, study skills assistance, tutoring, writing center.

Majors. **Biology:** General, biochemistry, marine. **Business:** Accounting, business admin, entrepreneurial studies, finance, international, managerial economics, marketing. **Communications:** General, public relations. **Computer sciences:** General, computer graphics. **Conservation:** Environmental science. **Education:** General, art, biology, elementary, English, mathematics, music, physical, secondary. **Foreign languages:** Spanish. **Health:** Athletic training, nursing (RN), predental, premedicine, preveterinary. **History:** General. **Interdisciplinary:** Math/computer science. **Legal studies:** Prelaw. **Liberal arts:** Arts/sciences. **Math:** General. **Parks/recreation:** Exercise sciences, sports admin. **Physical sciences:** Chemistry, forensic chemistry. **Psychology:** General. **Social sciences:** General, criminology, economics, political science, sociology. **Visual/performing arts:** General, art, cinematography, commercial/advertising art, film/cinema, graphic design, music performance, music theory/composition. **Other:** Cultural studies, Electronic media, Financial and operations systems.

Most popular majors. Biology 8%, business/marketing 27%, communications/journalism 11%, parks/recreation 7%, psychology 6%, social sciences 14%, visual/performing arts 7%.

Computing on campus. 528 workstations in dormitories, library, computer center, student center. Dormitories wired for high-speed internet access and linked to campus network. Commuter students can connect to campus network. Online course registration, online library, helpline, student web hosting, wireless network available.

Student life. **Freshman orientation:** Mandatory, $65 fee. Preregistration for classes offered. **Housing:** Coed dorms, special housing for disabled, apartments available. $200 nonrefundable deposit, deadline 5/1. **Activities:** Bands, campus ministries, choral groups, dance, drama, film society, international student organizations, literary magazine, music ensembles, Model UN, musical theater, radio station, student government, student newspaper, symphony orchestra, TV station, over 120 student organizations.

Athletics. NCAA. **Intercollegiate:** Baseball M, basketball, cross-country, golf M, rowing (crew) W, soccer, softball W, swimming, tennis W, track and field, volleyball W. **Intramural:** Basketball, football (non-tackle) W, football (tackle) M, golf, soccer, softball, tennis, volleyball. **Team name:** Spartans.

Student services. Adult student services, career counseling, student employment services, financial aid counseling, health services, personal counseling, placement for graduates, veterans' counselor.

Contact. E-mail: admissions@ut.edu
Phone: (813) 253-6211 Toll-free number: (888) 646-2738
Fax: (813) 258-7398
Barbara Strickler, Vice President for Enrollment, University of Tampa, 401 West Kennedy Boulevard, Tampa, FL 33606-1490

University of West Florida

Pensacola, Florida — **CB member**
www.uwf.edu — **CB code: 5833**

- Public 4-year university
- Commuter campus in small city
- 8,412 degree-seeking undergraduates: 28% part-time, 60% women, 10% African American, 5% Asian American, 5% Hispanic American, 1% Native American, 1% international
- 1,393 degree-seeking graduate students
- 69% of applicants admitted
- SAT or ACT (ACT writing optional) required
- 48% graduate within 6 years

General. Founded in 1963. Regionally accredited. **Degrees:** 1,733 bachelor's, 139 associate awarded; master's, doctoral offered. **ROTC:** Army, Air Force. **Location:** 10 miles from downtown. **Calendar:** Semester, extensive summer session. **Full-time faculty:** 324 total; 81% have terminal degrees, 16% minority, 42% women. **Part-time faculty:** 76 total; 17% minority, 58% women. **Class size:** 31% < 20, 49% 20-39, 11% 40-49, 7% 50-99, 2% >100. **Special facilities:** Archaeology museum, nature preserve.

Freshman class profile. 4,149 applied, 2,863 admitted, 1,099 enrolled.

Mid 50% test scores		**GPA 3.0-3.49:**	29%
SAT critical reading:	500-600	**GPA 2.0-2.99:**	18%
SAT math:	480-590	**Rank in top quarter:**	44%
ACT composite:	21-25	**Rank in top tenth:**	16%
GPA 3.75 or higher:	36%	**Out-of-state:**	9%
GPA 3.50-3.74:	16%	**Live on campus:**	42%

Basis for selection. School achievement record, test scores, and school curriculum most important. **Homeschooled:** Transcript of courses and grades required. **Learning Disabled:** If requesting special consideration due to disability, student must provide documentation.

High school preparation. 19 units required. Required units include English 4, mathematics 3, social studies 3, science 3 (laboratory 2), foreign language 2 and academic electives 4. 4 academic electives includes courses chosen from list above. Social science includes history, economics, government, psychology, sociology and geography.

2008-2009 Annual costs. Tuition/fees: $3,655; $16,546 out-of-state. There is a $10 per course, per semester fee for online courses. Room/board: $7,256. Books/supplies: $1,200. Personal expenses: $2,200.

2007-2008 Financial aid. **Need-based:** 43% of total undergraduate aid awarded as scholarships/grants, 57% as loans/jobs. **Non-need-based:** Scholarships awarded for academics, alumni affiliation, art, athletics, minority status, music/drama, ROTC.

Application procedures. **Admission:** Closing date 6/30 (postmark date). $30 fee, may be waived for applicants with need. Admission notification on a rolling basis beginning on or about 10/1. Must apply by January 1 for scholarship consideration. **Financial aid:** Priority date 3/1; no closing date. FAFSA, institutional form required. Applicants notified on a rolling basis starting 2/1.

Academics. Weekend program in nursing (BSN) available. **Special study options:** Cooperative education, distance learning, double major, dual enrollment of high school students, exchange student, honors, independent study, internships, study abroad, teacher certification program. Joint electrical engineering and computer engineering with University of Florida. **Credit/placement by examination:** AP, CLEP, IB, institutional tests. 30 credit hours maximum toward associate degree, 30 toward bachelor's. Up to 60 hours can be accepted, but academic department determines how credit counts toward degree. **Support services:** Learning center, study skills assistance, tutoring, writing center.

Majors. **Biology:** General, marine. **Business:** Accounting, business admin, finance, hospitality admin, management information systems, managerial economics, marketing. **Communications:** Media studies. **Computer sciences:** General, information technology. **Conservation:** Environmental science. **Education:** Art, early childhood, elementary, English, mathematics, mentally handicapped, middle, special, trade/industrial. **Engineering:** Computer, electrical. **Engineering technology:** General. **Health:** Community health services, nursing (RN). **History:** General. **Interdisciplinary:** Biological/physical sciences. **Legal studies:** Paralegal. **Liberal arts:** Humanities. **Math:** General. **Parks/recreation:** Health/fitness. **Philosophy/religion:** Philosophy. **Physical sciences:** Chemistry, oceanography, physics. **Protective services:** Criminal justice. **Psychology:** General. **Public administration:** Social work. **Social sciences:** General, anthropology, international relations, political science, sociology. **Visual/performing arts:** Art, dramatic, music performance, studio arts.

Most popular majors. Business/marketing 17%, communications/journalism 8%, education 18%, psychology 6%, social sciences 7%.

Computing on campus. 200 workstations in dormitories, library, computer center, student center. Dormitories wired for high-speed internet access and linked to campus network. Commuter students can connect to campus network. Online course registration, online library, helpline, wireless network available.

Student life. **Freshman orientation:** Mandatory, $92 fee. Preregistration for classes offered. Two-day programs held throughout summer; includes parents. **Housing:** Coed dorms, apartments, fraternity/sorority housing, wellness housing available. $225 partly refundable deposit. **Activities:** Bands, campus ministries, choral groups, dance, drama, international student organizations, music ensembles, musical theater, radio station, student government, student newspaper, symphony orchestra, TV station, black student union, CLOVE, College Republicans.

Athletics. NCAA. **Intercollegiate:** Baseball M, basketball, cross-country, golf, soccer, softball W, tennis, track and field, volleyball W. **Intramural:** Badminton, bowling, fencing, football (non-tackle), handball, racquetball, soccer, swimming, table tennis, volleyball, water polo, weight lifting. **Team name:** Argonauts.

Student services. Alcohol/substance abuse counseling, career counseling, student employment services, financial aid counseling, health services, minority student services, on-campus daycare, personal counseling, placement for graduates, veterans' counselor. **Physically disabled:** Services for visually, speech, hearing impaired.

Contact. E-mail: admissions@uwf.edu
Phone: (850) 474-2230 Toll-free number: (800) 263-1074
Fax: (850) 474-3360
Kim Bryan, Director of Admissions, University of West Florida, 11000 University Parkway, Pensacola, FL 32514-5750

Warner University

Lake Wales, Florida
www.warner.edu **CB code: 5883**

- Private 4-year liberal arts college affiliated with Church of God
- Commuter campus in large town
- 1,003 degree-seeking undergraduates: 11% part-time, 59% women, 20% African American, 1% Asian American, 11% Hispanic American, 2% international
- 131 degree-seeking graduate students
- 54% of applicants admitted
- SAT or ACT (ACT writing optional), application essay required

General. Founded in 1968. Regionally accredited. Off-site locations including Lakeland Learning Center, Orlando Learning Center, Space Coast Learning Center in Melbourne, teaching sites in Arcadia and Titusville. **Degrees:** 322 bachelor's, 45 associate awarded; master's offered. **Location:** 60 miles from Tampa, 55 miles from Orlando. **Calendar:** Semester, limited summer session. **Full-time faculty:** 33 total; 64% have terminal degrees, 9% minority, 33% women. **Part-time faculty:** 106 total; 28% have terminal degrees, 58% women. **Class size:** 75% < 20, 25% 20-39. **Special facilities:** Natural scrub brush preserve.

Freshman class profile. 502 applied, 272 admitted, 143 enrolled.

Mid 50% test scores			
SAT critical reading:	350-550	Out-of-state:	18%
SAT math:	370-560	Live on campus:	79%
ACT composite:	15-23	International:	4%

Basis for selection. Two of the following required: 2.25 GPA, top 50% of class, or 18 ACT/870 SAT (exclusive of Writing). ACT Residual test administered to those without scores or with scores too low. Interview recommended. Audition required of music majors. **Homeschooled:** Statement describing homeschool structure and mission, transcript of courses and grades, interview, letter of recommendation (nonparent) required. GED or portfolio required of applicants without transcripts.

High school preparation. College-preparatory program recommended. Recommended units include English 4, mathematics 3, social studies 1, history 1, science 2, foreign language 2 and academic electives 2.

2008-2009 Annual costs. Tuition/fees: $14,690. One-time $50 security deposit for incoming freshmen living on campus. Room/board: $6,580. Books/supplies: $1,000. Personal expenses: $1,792.

2007-2008 Financial aid. Non-need-based: Scholarships awarded for academics, alumni affiliation, art, athletics, leadership, music/drama, religious affiliation, state residency.

Application procedures. Admission: No deadline. $20 fee, may be waived for applicants with need. Admission notification on a rolling basis beginning on or about 9/15. **Financial aid:** Priority date 5/1; no closing date. FAFSA required. Applicants notified on a rolling basis starting 3/15; must reply within 2 week(s) of notification.

Academics. Special study options: Accelerated study, combined bachelor's/graduate degree, distance learning, double major, dual enrollment of high school students, ESL, independent study, internships, study abroad, teacher certification program, Washington semester. Online distance learning opportunities available for those interested in Organizational Management or Church Ministry. **Credit/placement by examination:** AP, CLEP, IB, SAT, ACT, institutional tests. **Support services:** Learning center, remedial instruction, study skills assistance, tutoring.

Majors. Biology: General. **Business:** Business admin. **Communications:** General, journalism. **Education:** Elementary, English, music, physical, science, social science, special. **History:** General. **Parks/recreation:** Exercise sciences, sports admin. **Psychology:** General. **Public administration:** Social work. **Social sciences:** General. **Theology:** Bible, sacred music, theology.

Most popular majors. Business/marketing 63%, education 18%.

Computing on campus. 69 workstations in library, computer center, student center. Dormitories wired for high-speed internet access. Commuter students can connect to campus network. Online library, helpline, repair service, wireless network available.

Student life. Freshman orientation: Mandatory. Preregistration for classes offered. Three-day program at start of fall semester. **Policies:** Student lifestyle agreement keeping with the moral and spiritual nature of the institution required. Religious observance required. **Housing:** Guaranteed on-campus for all undergraduates. Single-sex dorms, wellness housing available. $50 nonrefundable deposit, deadline 8/15. **Activities:** Campus ministries, choral groups, drama, music ensembles, student government, student newspaper, star throwers, missions, Young Americans.

Athletics. NAIA. **Intercollegiate:** Baseball M, basketball, cheerleading, cross-country, golf, soccer, softball W, tennis, track and field, volleyball. **Intramural:** Basketball, football (non-tackle), soccer, volleyball W. **Team name:** Royals.

Student services. Alcohol/substance abuse counseling, career counseling, student employment services, financial aid counseling, health services, personal counseling, placement for graduates.

Contact. E-mail: admissions@warner.edu
Phone: (863) 638-7212 Toll-free number: (800) 309-9563
Fax: (863) 638-7290
Jason Roe, Director of Admissions, Warner University, 13895 Highway 27, Lake Wales, FL 33859

Webber International University

Babson Park, Florida
www.webber.edu **CB code: 5893**

- Private 4-year university and business college
- Residential campus in rural community
- 542 degree-seeking undergraduates: 9% part-time, 37% women
- 54 degree-seeking graduate students
- 53% of applicants admitted
- SAT or ACT (ACT writing recommended) required
- 52% graduate within 6 years

General. Founded in 1927. Regionally accredited. **Degrees:** 103 bachelor's, 10 associate awarded; master's offered. **Location:** 50 miles from Orlando, 60 miles from Tampa. **Calendar:** Semester, limited summer session. **Full-time faculty:** 20 total; 75% have terminal degrees, 10% minority, 45% women. **Part-time faculty:** 25 total; 4% have terminal degrees, 16% minority, 52% women. **Class size:** 54% < 20, 45% 20-39, less than 1% 50-99. **Special facilities:** Audubon Society nature preserve.

Freshman class profile. 513 applied, 273 admitted, 166 enrolled.

Mid 50% test scores		GPA 2.0-2.99:	45%
SAT critical reading:	380-500	Rank in top quarter:	12%
SAT math:	420-520	Rank in top tenth:	2%
ACT composite:	16-19	End year in good standing:	54%
GPA 3.75 or higher:	11%	Return as sophomores:	43%
GPA 3.50-3.74:	14%	Out-of-state:	5%
GPA 3.0-3.49:	30%	Live on campus:	87%

Basis for selection. GPA and standardized test scores very important, followed by school record. Interview recommended. **Homeschooled:** Transcript of courses and grades required. Proof of graduation with 2.0 GPA required. **Learning Disabled:** Documentation of disability required in order to adequately assist student in studies.

High school preparation. College-preparatory program recommended. 15 units recommended. Required and recommended units include English 4, mathematics 2-3, social studies 2, history 2, science 1-3, foreign language 1 and academic electives 4. 2 business courses recommended.

2009-2010 Annual costs. Tuition/fees (projected): $17,000. Room/board: $6,354. Books/supplies: $800. Personal expenses: $3,112.

2008-2009 Financial aid. Need-based: 126 full-time freshmen applied for aid; 100 were judged to have need; 100 of these received aid. Average

need met was 51%. Average scholarship/grant was $12,672; average loan $3,357. 56% of total undergraduate aid awarded as scholarships/grants, 44% as loans/jobs. **Non-need-based:** Awarded to 681 full-time undergraduates, including 194 freshmen. Scholarships awarded for academics, alumni affiliation, athletics, leadership, state residency.

Application procedures. Admission: Priority date 5/1; deadline 8/1 (postmark date). $35 fee, may be waived for applicants with need. Admission notification on a rolling basis beginning on or about 12/1. Must reply by May 1 or within 4 week(s) if notified thereafter. **Financial aid:** Priority date 5/1, closing date 8/1. FAFSA required. Applicants notified on a rolling basis starting 4/1; must reply within 4 week(s) of notification.

Academics. Special study options: Combined bachelor's/graduate degree, cooperative education, cross-registration, double major, dual enrollment of high school students, ESL, exchange student, internships, study abroad, weekend college. **Credit/placement by examination:** AP, CLEP, IB, institutional tests. 30 credit hours maximum toward associate degree, 30 toward bachelor's. No more than 6 semester hours credit awarded in each of 5 areas (English, humanities, science, social science, mathematics). **Support services:** Reduced course load, remedial instruction, study skills assistance, tutoring.

Majors. Business: General, accounting, business admin, finance, hospitality admin, marketing. **Communications:** General. **Computer sciences:** General. **Legal studies:** Prelaw. **Parks/recreation:** Facilities management. **Protective services:** Security management.

Most popular majors. Business/marketing 78%, parks/recreation 15%.

Computing on campus. 92 workstations in library, computer center. Dormitories wired for high-speed internet access. Commuter students can connect to campus network. Online library, helpline available.

Student life. Freshman orientation: Mandatory. Five-day program immediately preceding semester opening. **Housing:** Guaranteed on-campus for freshmen. Single-sex dorms available. $205 fully refundable deposit, deadline 8/28. **Activities:** Marching band, student government, student newspaper, service clubs, professional development organizations.

Athletics. NAIA. **Intercollegiate:** Baseball M, basketball, bowling, cross-country, football (tackle) M, golf, soccer, softball W, tennis, track and field, volleyball W. **Intramural:** Basketball, bowling, football (non-tackle), soccer, softball, table tennis, tennis. **Team name:** Warriors.

Student services. Adult student services, alcohol/substance abuse counseling, career counseling, student employment services, financial aid counseling, health services, personal counseling, placement for graduates, veterans' counselor, women's services.

Contact. E-mail: admissions@webber.edu
Phone: (863) 638-2910 Toll-free number: (800) 741-1844
Fax: (863) 638-1591
Julie Ragans, Director of Admission, Webber International University, 1201 North Scenic Highway, Babson Park, FL 33827-0096

Yeshiva Gedolah Rabbinical College
Miami Beach, Florida

- Private 4-year rabbinical college for men affiliated with Jewish faith
- Very large city

General. Accredited by AARTS. **Calendar:** Semester.

Contact. Phone: (305) 673-5664
1140 Alton Road, Miami Beach, FL 33139

Georgia

Agnes Scott College

Decatur, Georgia **CB member**
www.agnesscott.edu **CB code: 5002**

- Private 4-year liberal arts college for women affiliated with Presbyterian Church (USA)
- Residential campus in very large city
- 757 degree-seeking undergraduates: 2% part-time, 100% women, 21% African American, 4% Asian American, 3% Hispanic American, 4% international
- 17 degree-seeking graduate students
- 48% of applicants admitted
- SAT or ACT with writing, application essay required
- 71% graduate within 6 years; 26% enter graduate study

General. Founded in 1889. Regionally accredited. **Degrees:** 191 bachelor's awarded; master's offered. **ROTC:** Army, Air Force. **Location:** 6 miles from downtown Atlanta. **Calendar:** Semester, limited summer session. **Full-time faculty:** 84 total; 96% have terminal degrees, 20% minority, 61% women. **Part-time faculty:** 33 total; 70% have terminal degrees, 18% minority, 48% women. **Class size:** 80% < 20, 19% 20-39, less than 1% 40-49. **Special facilities:** Observatory, planetarium, art collection, electron microscope, 30-inch Beck telescope, center for writing and speaking, interactive learning center, multi-media classrooms.

Freshman class profile. 1,593 applied, 763 admitted, 179 enrolled.

Mid 50% test scores			
SAT critical reading:	520-680	GPA 2.0-2.99:	7%
SAT math:	500-610	Rank in top quarter:	68%
SAT writing:	520-660	Rank in top tenth:	34%
ACT composite:	22-28	End year in good standing:	93%
GPA 3.75 or higher:	46%	Return as sophomores:	82%
GPA 3.50-3.74:	20%	Out-of-state:	47%
GPA 3.0-3.49:	27%	Live on campus:	98%
		International:	3%

Basis for selection. High school record, class rank, test scores, counselor recommendation, personal qualities, and extracurricular activities considered. First-time, first-year applicants expected to have taken SAT or ACT test by December test date. Woodruff Scholars and transfer students must submit scores by May 1st. Interview recommended. Audition required for music scholarship. **Homeschooled:** Statement describing homeschool structure and mission, interview required. SAT Subject Test scores must be submitted.

High school preparation. College-preparatory program recommended. 16 units recommended. Recommended units include English 4, mathematics 3, social studies 2, history 2, science 2 (laboratory 2) and foreign language 2.

2009-2010 Annual costs. Tuition/fees (projected): $30,105. Room/board: $9,850. Books/supplies: $1,000. Personal expenses: $1,000.

2008-2009 Financial aid. Non-need-based: Scholarships awarded for academics, leadership, music/drama, religious affiliation, state residency. **Additional information:** Middle Income Assistance Grants available. Auditions required for music scholarship applicants.

Application procedures. Admission: Closing date 3/1 (postmark date). $35 fee, may be waived for applicants with need, free for online applicants. Admission notification on a rolling basis. Must reply by May 1 or within 2 week(s) if notified thereafter. Scholarship applicants must apply for regular admission by January 15. **Financial aid:** Priority date 2/15, closing date 5/1. FAFSA required. Applicants notified on a rolling basis starting 3/1; must reply by 5/1 or within 2 week(s) of notification.

Academics. Special study options: Accelerated study, combined bachelor's/graduate degree, cross-registration, double major, dual enrollment of high school students, exchange student, independent study, internships, semester at sea, student-designed major, study abroad, teacher certification program, United Nations semester, Washington semester. Global Awareness and Global Connections programs offer opportunities to visit other regions of the world. Internship opportunities guaranteed; over 250 internships and externships available in Atlanta and other cities. Atlanta Semester focuses on women, leadership and social change. Language Across the Curriculum links foreign languages to other disciplines. Opportunities to study at over 123 universities in 33 countries. **Credit/placement by examination:** AP, CLEP, IB, SAT, ACT, institutional tests. 32 credit hours maximum toward bachelor's degree. **Support services:** Learning center, reduced course load, study skills assistance, tutoring, writing center.

Majors. Area/ethnic studies: African, women's. **Biology:** General, biochemistry. **Foreign languages:** Classics, French, German, Spanish. **History:** General. **Math:** General. **Philosophy/religion:** Philosophy, religion. **Physical sciences:** Astrophysics, chemistry, physics. **Psychology:** General. **Social sciences:** Anthropology, applied economics, economics, international relations, political science, sociology. **Visual/performing arts:** Art, dance, dramatic, studio arts.

Most popular majors. Biology 9%, English 12%, foreign language 11%, history 8%, philosophy/religious studies 6%, psychology 12%, social sciences 20%, visual/performing arts 10%.

Computing on campus. 458 workstations in dormitories, library, computer center, student center. Dormitories wired for high-speed internet access and linked to campus network. Commuter students can connect to campus network. Online library, helpline, repair service, wireless network available.

Student life. Freshman orientation: Mandatory. Held five days prior to start of semester; includes signing of honor code, breakfast with college president, introduction to Big/Little Sister program. **Housing:** Guaranteed on-campus for all undergraduates. Apartments, wellness housing available. $350 nonrefundable deposit, deadline 5/1. College-owned houses for non-traditional students, CHOICE housing (Choosing Healthy Options in a Community Environment) available. **Activities:** Bands, campus ministries, choral groups, dance, drama, international student organizations, literary magazine, music ensembles, musical theater, student government, student newspaper, symphony orchestra, TV station, religious life council, conservative forum, College Democrats, green Earth organization, Circle-K, African American student group, Asian cultural awareness association, Amnesty International.

Athletics. NCAA. **Intercollegiate:** Basketball W, cross-country W, lacrosse W, soccer W, softball W, swimming W, tennis W, volleyball W. **Intramural:** Basketball W, cheerleading W, fencing W, field hockey W, football (non-tackle) W, soccer W, swimming W, tennis W, track and field W, volleyball W, weight lifting W. **Team name:** Scotties.

Student services. Adult student services, alcohol/substance abuse counseling, chaplain/spiritual director, career counseling, student employment services, financial aid counseling, health services, minority student services, personal counseling, placement for graduates, women's services. **Physically disabled:** Services for visually, speech, hearing impaired.

Contact. E-mail: admission@agnesscott.edu
Phone: (404) 471-6285 Toll-free number: (800) 868-8602
Fax: (404) 471-6414
Lee Ann Afton, Dean of Admission, Agnes Scott College, Office of Admissions, Decatur, GA 30030-3797

Albany State University

Albany, Georgia **CB member**
www.asurams.edu/ **CB code: 5004**

- Public 4-year university and liberal arts college
- Residential campus in small city
- 3,753 degree-seeking undergraduates: 16% part-time, 67% women, 92% African American, 1% international
- 423 degree-seeking graduate students
- 30% of applicants admitted
- SAT or ACT (ACT writing optional) required
- 41% graduate within 6 years

General. Founded in 1903. Regionally accredited. **Degrees:** 505 bachelor's awarded; master's offered. **ROTC:** Army. **Location:** 190 miles from Atlanta. **Calendar:** Semester, limited summer session. **Full-time faculty:** 142 total; 39% minority, 58% women. **Part-time faculty:** 108 total; 50% minority, 45% women. **Special facilities:** Health and physical education complex, early learning center.

Freshman class profile. 5,402 applied, 1,627 admitted, 625 enrolled.

Mid 50% test scores			
SAT critical reading:	410-480	GPA 3.0-3.49:	26%
SAT math:	400-470	GPA 2.0-2.99:	63%
SAT writing:	400-470	End year in good standing:	72%
GPA 3.75 or higher:	3%	Return as sophomores:	75%
GPA 3.50-3.74:	6%	Out-of-state:	4%
		International:	1%

Basis for selection. Academic record, GPA and test scores very important. **Homeschooled:** Statement describing homeschool structure and mission, transcript of courses and grades required. School must be accredited. **Learning Disabled:** Students with documented disabilities should register with the Office of Counseling, Testing, and Student Disabilities.

High school preparation. 16 units required. Required units include English 4, mathematics 4, social studies 1, history 2, science 3 (laboratory 2) and foreign language 2. 2 foreign language units must be same language.

2008-2009 Annual costs. Tuition/fees: $3,710; $13,002 out-of-state. Room/board: $4,990.

2007-2008 Financial aid. Non-need-based: Scholarships awarded for academics, alumni affiliation, art, athletics, music/drama, ROTC.

Application procedures. Admission: Priority date 5/1; deadline 7/1. $20 fee, may be waived for applicants with need. Admission notification on a rolling basis. **Financial aid:** Priority date 4/15, closing date 4/30. FAFSA required. Applicants notified on a rolling basis; must reply within 2 week(s) of notification.

Academics. Special study options: Cooperative education, cross-registration, distance learning, double major, dual enrollment of high school students, honors, independent study, internships, liberal arts/career combination, study abroad, teacher certification program, weekend college. 3+2 and 2+2 engineering program with Georgia Institute of Technology. **Credit/placement by examination:** CLEP, institutional tests. 45 credit hours maximum toward bachelor's degree. **Support services:** Learning center, remedial instruction, study skills assistance, tutoring, writing center.

Majors. Biology: General. **Business:** Accounting, business admin, management information systems, marketing. **Communications:** Journalism. **Computer sciences:** General, information systems. **Education:** Early childhood, elementary, mathematics, middle, music, physical, science, social science, special. **Foreign languages:** Spanish. **Health:** Nursing (RN). **History:** General. **Math:** General. **Parks/recreation:** Health/fitness. **Physical sciences:** Chemistry. **Protective services:** Criminal justice. **Psychology:** General. **Public administration:** Social work. **Social sciences:** Political science, sociology. **Visual/performing arts:** Drawing. **Other:** Technology management.

Computing on campus. 400 workstations in dormitories, library, computer center, student center. Dormitories wired for high-speed internet access and linked to campus network. Online course registration, online library, helpline available.

Student life. Freshman orientation: Mandatory, $120 fee. Preregistration for classes offered. Held in January, May, June and August. **Housing:** Coed dorms, single-sex dorms, special housing for disabled, apartments, wellness housing available. $150 partly refundable deposit. **Activities:** Bands, choral groups, dance, drama, music ensembles, musical theater, opera, radio station, student government, student newspaper, TV station, NAACP, Habitat for Humanity, history and political science club, HIV/AIDS peer educator, pre-alumni association, Florida Georgia Louis Stokes Alliance for Minority Participation, American Chemical Society, Kappa Kappa Psi band fraternity, Tau Beta Sigma band sorority.

Athletics. NCAA. **Intercollegiate:** Baseball M, basketball, cheerleading M, cross-country, football (tackle) M, softball W, tennis W, track and field, volleyball W. **Intramural:** Basketball M, football (tackle) M, track and field. **Team name:** Rams.

Student services. Career counseling, student employment services, financial aid counseling, health services, personal counseling, placement for graduates.

Contact. E-mail: admissions@asurams.edu
Phone: (229) 430-4646 Toll-free number: (800) 822-7267
Fax: (229) 430-3936
Albany State University, 504 College Drive, Albany, GA 31705-2796

American InterContinental University

Atlanta, Georgia — **CB member**
www.buckhead.aiuniv.edu/ — **CB code: 2486**

- For-profit 4-year virtual university
- Commuter campus in very large city
- 716 degree-seeking undergraduates
- Application essay, interview required

General. Founded in 1977. Regionally accredited. Additional campuses in Dunwoody, South Florida, Houston, London, Dubai, online. **Degrees:** 189 bachelor's, 30 associate awarded; master's offered. **Calendar:** Quarter, extensive summer session. **Full-time faculty:** 22 total. **Part-time faculty:** 26 total. **Special facilities:** Sewing laboratories, darkroom laboratories, interior design library, video production studios, learning center.

Basis for selection. Essay, results of personal interview, portfolio, high school GPA and references important. SAT or ACT recommended. Prefer that test scores be received prior to beginning of term since they are used for placement. **Homeschooled:** State high school equivalency certificate required.

2008-2009 Annual costs. Tuition/fees: $17,040. Costs vary by program. Room only: $5,400. Books/supplies: $1,500. Personal expenses: $960.

Application procedures. Admission: No deadline. $50 fee. Admission notification on a rolling basis. **Financial aid:** Priority date 6/1; no closing date. FAFSA, institutional form required. Applicants notified on a rolling basis.

Academics. Special study options: Accelerated study, distance learning, double major, independent study, internships, study abroad. **Credit/placement by examination:** CLEP, IB, SAT, ACT, institutional tests. **Support services:** Learning center, pre-admission summer program, reduced course load, remedial instruction, study skills assistance, tutoring, writing center.

Majors. Business: Business admin, e-commerce, fashion. **Computer sciences:** Information systems. **Visual/performing arts:** Cinematography, commercial/advertising art, fashion design, interior design.

Computing on campus. Online library, helpline available.

Student life. Freshman orientation: Mandatory. Preregistration for classes offered. **Housing:** Apartments available. **Activities:** Student government, student newspaper, American Society of Interior Designers, fashion association, marketing association, graphic arts association, dressers club, portfolio club, cultural club.

Student services. Career counseling, student employment services, health services, personal counseling, placement for graduates, veterans' counselor.

Contact. E-mail: info@aiuniv.edu
Phone: (404) 965-5700 Toll-free number: (800) 955-2120
Fax: (404) 965-5701
Tina Rowe, Senior Director of Admissions, American InterContinental University, 3330 Peachtree Road, NE, Atlanta, GA 30326-1016

Armstrong Atlantic State University

Savannah, Georgia — **CB member**
www.armstrong.edu — **CB code: 5012**

- Public 4-year university
- Commuter campus in small city
- 6,152 degree-seeking undergraduates: 32% part-time, 66% women, 21% African American, 2% Asian American, 3% Hispanic American, 4% international
- 851 degree-seeking graduate students
- 62% of applicants admitted
- SAT or ACT (ACT writing optional) required

General. Founded in 1935. Regionally accredited. Regional center for health professions. **Degrees:** 835 bachelor's, 77 associate awarded; master's offered. **ROTC:** Army, Naval. **Location:** 250 miles from Atlanta; 150 miles from Jacksonville, FL. **Calendar:** Semester, extensive summer session. **Full-time faculty:** 289 total; 53% women. **Part-time faculty:** 145 total; 56% women. **Class size:** 42% < 20, 46% 20-39, 8% 40-49, 4% 50-99, less than 1% >100.

Freshman class profile. 2,267 applied, 1,411 admitted, 902 enrolled.

Mid 50% test scores			
SAT critical reading:	460-560	GPA 2.0-2.99:	36%
SAT math:	450-550	Return as sophomores:	69%
ACT composite:	18-22	Out-of-state:	16%
GPA 3.75 or higher:	8%	Live on campus:	11%
GPA 3.50-3.74:	9%	International:	4%
GPA 3.0-3.49:	47%	Fraternities:	3%
		Sororities:	4%

Basis for selection. 430 SAT math, 460 SAT verbal and 2.0 GPA required for regular admissions. Conditional admission possible with 1.8 GPA and lower test scores. **Homeschooled:** Applicants who do not complete an accreditted program must pass SAT Subject Tests to satisfy college prep requirements.

High school preparation. College-preparatory program required. Required units include English 4, mathematics 4, social studies 3, science 3 (laboratory 2) and foreign language 2.

2008-2009 Annual costs. Tuition/fees: $3,876; $13,168 out-of-state. Room only: $5,048. Books/supplies: $1,000.

2007-2008 Financial aid. Non-need-based: Scholarships awarded for academics, alumni affiliation, art, athletics, leadership, minority status, music/drama, state residency.

Application procedures. Admission: Closing date 6/29. $25 fee, may be waived for applicants with need. Admission notification on a rolling basis beginning on or about 1/1. **Financial aid:** Priority date 3/15; no closing date. FAFSA required. Applicants notified on a rolling basis starting 2/1; must reply by 4/15 or within 2 week(s) of notification.

Academics. Special study options: Combined bachelor's/graduate degree, cooperative education, distance learning, double major, dual enrollment of high school students, honors, independent study, internships, study abroad, teacher certification program, weekend college. **Credit/placement by examination:** AP, CLEP, IB, SAT, ACT, institutional tests. 30 credit hours maximum toward associate degree, 30 toward bachelor's. **Support services:** Learning center, reduced course load, remedial instruction, study skills assistance, tutoring, writing center.

Majors. Biology: General. **Computer sciences:** General, information technology. **Education:** Art, business, early childhood, elementary, English, health, learning disabled, mathematics, middle, music, physical, science, secondary, social science, special, speech impaired. **Foreign languages:** Spanish. **Health:** Clinical lab science, communication disorders, dental hygiene, health services, medical radiologic technology/radiation therapy, nuclear medical technology, nursing (RN), respiratory therapy technology, sonography. **History:** General. **Math:** Applied. **Physical sciences:** Chemistry, physics. **Protective services:** Police science. **Psychology:** General. **Social sciences:** Economics, political science. **Visual/performing arts:** Art, dramatic.

Most popular majors. Education 18%, health sciences 33%, liberal arts 12%, social sciences 7%.

Computing on campus. Dormitories wired for high-speed internet access and linked to campus network. Commuter students can connect to campus network. Online course registration, online library, helpline, student web hosting, wireless network available.

Student life. Freshman orientation: Available, $45 fee. Preregistration for classes offered. One-day event prior to registration. **Housing:** Apartments available. $250 partly refundable deposit. **Activities:** Bands, choral groups, drama, international student organizations, literary magazine, music ensembles, Model UN, musical theater, student government, student newspaper, symphony orchestra, NAACP, Baptist student union, Hispanic outreach and leadership, Cercle Francais, Newman Club, Wesley Foundation, College Democrats, College Republicans.

Athletics. NCAA. **Intercollegiate:** Baseball M, basketball, golf, softball W, tennis, volleyball W. **Intramural:** Badminton, basketball, bowling, cheerleading, football (non-tackle), golf, racquetball, soccer, softball, swimming, table tennis, tennis, volleyball. **Team name:** Pirates.

Student services. Adult student services, alcohol/substance abuse counseling, career counseling, student employment services, financial aid counseling, health services, minority student services, personal counseling, placement for graduates, veterans' counselor. **Physically disabled:** Services for visually, hearing impaired.

Contact. E-mail: adm-info@armstrong.edu
Phone: (912) 344-2503 Toll-free number: (800) 633-2349
Fax: (912) 344-3470
Stephanie Whaley, Director of Admissions, Armstrong Atlantic State University, 11935 Abercorn Street, Savannah, GA 31419-1997

Art Institute of Atlanta

Atlanta, Georgia — **CB member**
www.aia.artinstitutes.edu — **CB code: 5429**

- For-profit 4-year visual arts college
- Commuter campus in very large city
- 3,400 degree-seeking undergraduates
- Application essay, interview required

General. Founded in 1949. Regionally accredited. **Degrees:** 255 bachelor's, 175 associate awarded. **Location:** 12 miles from city center. **Calendar:** Quarter, extensive summer session. **Full-time faculty:** 126 total. **Part-time faculty:** 116 total. **Class size:** 47% < 20, 53% 20-39. **Special facilities:** Art gallery, camera video studios, video editing suites, digital audio studio, professional photography studios, traditional darkroom, digital darkroom, digital image capture systems, color-calibrated monitors, scanners, and printers.

Freshman class profile.

Out-of-state:	32%	**Live on campus:**	23%

Basis for selection. GPA or GED transcript; ACT, SAT, ASSET or COMPASS test scores; essay most important. Applicants for associate degree should have 2.0 GPA; 2.5 GPA for bachelor's degree; Test scores or life experience may be considered if GPA not met. COMPASS test required but can be waived with 500 SAT math and verbal or 21 ACT. Portfolio required for national scholarship competition. **Learning Disabled:** Students with disabilities should submit current documentation of disability to disability services coordinator at least 6 weeks before accommodations will be needed.

2008-2009 Annual costs. Tuition/fees: $19,575. Students purchase starting kits for programs; costs vary depending on programs. Some programs require lab fees. Room only: $9,075. Books/supplies: $1,551.

2007-2008 Financial aid. Non-need-based: Scholarships awarded for academics, art, state residency.

Application procedures. Admission: No deadline. $50 fee. Admission notification on a rolling basis. **Financial aid:** No deadline. FAFSA required. Applicants notified on a rolling basis starting 3/15.

Academics. Special study options: Accelerated study, cross-registration, distance learning, dual enrollment of high school students, honors, independent study, internships, study abroad. Academic remediation. **Credit/placement by examination:** CLEP, IB, institutional tests. 24 credit hours maximum toward associate degree, 48 toward bachelor's. **Support services:** Learning center, pre-admission summer program, reduced course load, remedial instruction, study skills assistance, tutoring, writing center.

Majors. Communications: Advertising. **Communications technology:** Animation/special effects. **Computer sciences:** Web page design, webmaster. **Personal/culinary services:** Culinary arts, restaurant/catering. **Visual/performing arts:** Cinematography, commercial photography, commercial/advertising art, graphic design, interior design, multimedia.

Most popular majors. Visual/performing arts 76%.

Computing on campus. 382 workstations in dormitories, library, computer center, student center. Dormitories wired for high-speed internet access. Online course registration, online library, helpline, repair service, student web hosting available.

Student life. Freshman orientation: Mandatory. Preregistration for classes offered. Held for 1-2 days the week prior to class start. **Housing:** Guaranteed on-campus for freshmen. Coed dorms, special housing for disabled, apartments available. $250 deposit. Apartment & roommate referral service. **Activities:** Dance, student government, student newspaper, Student Ambassador Program, HAVEN, international student association, student government association.

Student services. Adult student services, career counseling, student employment services, financial aid counseling, personal counseling, placement for graduates, veterans' counselor. **Physically disabled:** Services for visually, hearing impaired.

Contact. E-mail: aiaadm@aii.edu
Phone: (770) 394-8300 Toll-free number: (800) 275-4242
Fax: (770) 394-0008
Donna Scott, Vice President, Admissions, Art Institute of Atlanta, 6600 Peachtree Dunwoody Road, Atlanta, GA 30328

Atlanta Christian College

East Point, Georgia
www.acc.edu — **CB code: 5029**

- Private 4-year Bible and liberal arts college affiliated with Christian Church
- Residential campus in small city
- 440 degree-seeking undergraduates: 7% part-time, 50% women, 37% African American, 1% Asian American, 3% Hispanic American

- 78% of applicants admitted
- SAT or ACT (ACT writing optional) required

General. Founded in 1937. Regionally accredited. **Degrees:** 61 bachelor's, 4 associate awarded. **Location:** 10 miles from Atlanta. **Calendar:** Semester, limited summer session. **Full-time faculty:** 24 total. **Part-time faculty:** 31 total.

Freshman class profile. 183 applied, 143 admitted, 87 enrolled.

Mid 50% test scores		SAT math:	350-470
SAT critical reading:	390-500	ACT composite:	15-20

Basis for selection. Recommendations, scholastic ability, and test scores most important. **Homeschooled:** Statement describing homeschool structure and mission, transcript of courses and grades, letter of recommendation (nonparent) required.

High school preparation. College-preparatory program recommended. 18 units required; 22 recommended. Required and recommended units include English 4, mathematics 3-4, history 3, science 3 (laboratory 3), foreign language 2 and academic electives 2.

2008-2009 Annual costs. Tuition/fees: $15,150. Room/board: $5,560. Books/supplies: $400. Personal expenses: $500.

2007-2008 Financial aid. **Need-based:** 45% of total undergraduate aid awarded as scholarships/grants, 55% as loans/jobs.

Application procedures. **Admission:** Priority date 7/1; deadline 8/1 (receipt date). $25 fee, may be waived for applicants with need, free for online applicants. Admission notification on a rolling basis. **Financial aid:** Priority date 6/1, closing date 8/1. FAFSA required. Applicants notified on a rolling basis starting 3/1; must reply within 3 week(s) of notification.

Academics. **Special study options:** Accelerated study, distance learning, double major, dual enrollment of high school students, independent study, internships, liberal arts/career combination, study abroad, teacher certification program. **Credit/placement by examination:** AP, CLEP, IB, SAT, ACT, institutional tests. 16 credit hours maximum toward associate degree, 32 toward bachelor's. **Support services:** Reduced course load, remedial instruction, study skills assistance, tutoring, writing center.

Majors. **Business:** General, business admin. **Education:** Business, early childhood, elementary. **Interdisciplinary:** Intercultural. **Liberal arts:** Arts/sciences. **Psychology:** General. **Theology:** Bible, theology.

Computing on campus. 30 workstations in library, computer center, student center. Dormitories wired for high-speed internet access and linked to campus network. Commuter students can connect to campus network. Online library, helpline, repair service, wireless network available.

Student life. **Freshman orientation:** Mandatory. Preregistration for classes offered. **Policies:** Religious observance required. **Housing:** Single-sex dorms, special housing for disabled, apartments, wellness housing available. $50 deposit. **Activities:** Choral groups, dance, drama, literary magazine, music ensembles, student government, student newspaper, religious organizations, Christian service clubs, service-oriented fraternities and sororities.

Athletics. NCCAA. **Intercollegiate:** Baseball M, basketball, golf M, soccer, track and field, volleyball W. **Intramural:** Basketball, football (non-tackle), volleyball. **Team name:** Chargers.

Student services. Alcohol/substance abuse counseling, chaplain/spiritual director, career counseling, financial aid counseling, health services, personal counseling, placement for graduates.

Contact. E-mail: admissions@acc.edu
Phone: (404) 669-3202 Toll-free number: (800) 776-1222
Fax: (404) 460-2451
Stacy Bartlett, Admissions Counselor, Atlanta Christian College, 2605 Ben Hill Road, East Point, GA 30344

Augusta State University

Augusta, Georgia — **CB member**
www.aug.edu — **CB code: 5336**

- Public 4-year liberal arts and teachers college
- Commuter campus in small city
- 5,394 degree-seeking undergraduates: 28% part-time, 64% women, 28% African American, 3% Asian American, 3% Hispanic American, 1% international
- 955 degree-seeking graduate students
- 57% of applicants admitted
- SAT or ACT (ACT writing optional) required

General. Founded in 1925. Regionally accredited. **Degrees:** 572 bachelor's, 71 associate awarded; master's offered. **ROTC:** Army. **Location:** 145 miles from Atlanta. **Calendar:** Semester, extensive summer session. **Full-time faculty:** 236 total; 64% have terminal degrees, 16% minority, 51% women. **Part-time faculty:** 166 total; 32% have terminal degrees, 16% minority, 57% women. **Class size:** 41% < 20, 55% 20-39, 4% 40-49, less than 1% 50-99. **Special facilities:** History walk and museum, 18-hole golf course.

Freshman class profile. 2,418 applied, 1,383 admitted, 941 enrolled.

Mid 50% test scores		GPA 2.0-2.99:	52%
SAT critical reading:	440-540	Return as sophomores:	69%
SAT math:	430-540	Out-of-state:	7%
ACT composite:	17-21	Live on campus:	16%
GPA 3.75 or higher:	7%	International:	1%
GPA 3.50-3.74:	11%	Fraternities:	1%
GPA 3.0-3.49:	28%	Sororities:	1%

Basis for selection. 430 SAT Verbal or 17 ACT English, and 400 SAT Math or 17 ACT Math required. SAT Subject Tests required of GED recipients or graduates of non-accredited high schools.

High school preparation. 18 units required. Required units include English 4, mathematics 4, social studies 3, science 3, foreign language 2 and academic electives 2.

2008-2009 Annual costs. Tuition/fees: $3,644; $12,936 out-of-state. Books/supplies: $1,000. Personal expenses: $1,980.

2007-2008 Financial aid. **Need-based:** 545 full-time freshmen applied for aid; 444 were judged to have need; 404 of these received aid. Average need met was 70%. Average scholarship/grant was $1,818; average loan $1,427. 33% of total undergraduate aid awarded as scholarships/grants, 67% as loans/jobs. **Non-need-based:** Awarded to 1,169 full-time undergraduates, including 142 freshmen. Scholarships awarded for academics, art, athletics, leadership, minority status, music/drama, ROTC, state residency.

Application procedures. **Admission:** Priority date 7/1; no deadline. $20 fee, may be waived for applicants with need. Application must be submitted on paper. Admission notification on a rolling basis. **Financial aid:** Closing date 6/1. FAFSA, institutional form required. Applicants notified on a rolling basis starting 3/1; must reply within 4 week(s) of notification.

Academics. **Special study options:** Cooperative education, cross-registration, distance learning, double major, dual enrollment of high school students, ESL, honors, independent study, internships, study abroad, teacher certification program. Paralegal certificate. **Credit/placement by examination:** AP, CLEP, institutional tests. 30 credit hours maximum toward associate degree, 30 toward bachelor's. **Support services:** Learning center, pre-admission summer program, reduced course load, remedial instruction, study skills assistance, tutoring, writing center.

Majors. **Biology:** General. **Business:** Accounting, business admin, finance, management information systems, marketing. **Communications:** General. **Computer sciences:** General. **Education:** Elementary, mentally handicapped, middle, music, physical, special. **Foreign languages:** French, Spanish. **Health:** Clinical lab science. **History:** General. **Math:** General. **Physical sciences:** Chemistry, physics. **Protective services:** Criminal justice. **Psychology:** General. **Public administration:** Social work. **Social sciences:** Political science, sociology. **Visual/performing arts:** Multimedia, music performance.

Most popular majors. Biology 6%, business/marketing 22%, education 24%, psychology 8%, social sciences 8%.

Computing on campus. 300 workstations in library, computer center, student center. Commuter students can connect to campus network. Online course registration, online library, helpline, student web hosting, wireless network available.

Student life. **Freshman orientation:** Available. Preregistration for classes offered. **Housing:** Apartments available. **Activities:** Bands, choral groups, drama, international student organizations, literary magazine, radio station, student government, student newspaper, black student union, Los Amigos Hispanos, Le Cercle Francais, Muslim student association, Circle K, chess club, anime club, College Conservatives, Baptist student union.

Athletics. NCAA. **Intercollegiate:** Baseball M, basketball, cross-country, golf, softball W, tennis, volleyball W. **Intramural:** Basketball M. **Team name:** Jaguars.

Student services. Adult student services, alcohol/substance abuse counseling, career counseling, student employment services, financial aid counseling, minority student services, personal counseling, placement for graduates, veterans' counselor. **Physically disabled:** Services for visually, hearing impaired.

Contact. E-mail: admissio@aug.edu
Phone: (706) 737-1632 Toll-free number: (800) 341-4373
Fax: (706) 667-4355
Katherine Sweeney, Registrar and Director of Admissions, Augusta State University, 2500 Walton Way, Augusta, GA 30904-2200

Bauder College

Atlanta, Georgia
www.bauder.edu **CB code: 5070**

- For-profit 4-year career college
- Commuter campus in very large city
- 1,078 degree-seeking undergraduates
- Application essay, interview required

General. Founded in 1964. Regionally accredited. Certified as a Pearson VUE Test Center. **Degrees:** 20 bachelor's, 264 associate awarded. **Location:** Downtown. **Calendar:** Quarter, extensive summer session. **Full-time faculty:** 28 total. **Part-time faculty:** 42 total.

Freshman class profile.

Out-of-state:	14%	**Live on campus:**	50%

Basis for selection. Open admission. Portfolio recommended for interior and fashion design majors. **Homeschooled:** GED recommended.

2008-2009 Annual costs. Tuition/fees: $13,639. Additional book fee of $1280. Books/supplies: $900. Personal expenses: $1,100.

Financial aid. All financial aid based on need.

Application procedures. Admission: No deadline. $100 fee. Application must be submitted on paper. Admission notification on a rolling basis. **Financial aid:** No deadline. FAFSA, institutional form required. Applicants notified on a rolling basis starting 7/15.

Academics. Special study options: Double major, internships. **Credit/placement by examination:** AP, CLEP. **Support services:** Reduced course load, remedial instruction, tutoring.

Majors. Business: Business admin. **Protective services:** Law enforcement admin.

Computing on campus. 38 workstations in library, computer center, student center. Online library, helpline, wireless network available.

Student life. Freshman orientation: Mandatory. Preregistration for classes offered. **Housing:** Cooperative housing available. **Activities:** Student government, student newspaper.

Student services. Alcohol/substance abuse counseling, career counseling, services for economically disadvantaged, student employment services, financial aid counseling, personal counseling, placement for graduates.

Contact. E-mail: admissions@bauder.edu
Phone: (404) 237-7573 Toll-free number: (800) 241-3797
Fax: (404) 237-1619
E. Trey McCray, Director of Admissions, Bauder College, 384 Northyards Boulevard NW, Ste 190, Atlanta, GA 30313

Berry College

Mount Berry, Georgia **CB member**
www.berry.edu **CB code: 5059**

- Private 4-year liberal arts college
- Residential campus in large town
- 1,681 degree-seeking undergraduates: 2% part-time, 68% women, 5% African American, 2% Asian American, 2% Hispanic American, 2% international
- 101 degree-seeking graduate students
- 70% of applicants admitted
- SAT or ACT (ACT writing optional), application essay required
- 60% graduate within 6 years

General. Founded in 1902. Regionally accredited. **Degrees:** 382 bachelor's awarded; master's offered. **Location:** 72 miles from Atlanta, 75 miles from Chattanooga, Tennessee. **Calendar:** Semester, limited summer session. **Full-time faculty:** 144 total; 90% have terminal degrees, 6% minority, 38% women. **Part-time faculty:** 56 total; 25% have terminal degrees, 5% minority, 41% women. **Class size:** 68% < 20, 30% 20-39, less than 1% 40-49, less than 1% 50-99. **Special facilities:** Museum, waterwheel, wildlife management area and refuge, equine center with boarding facilities, dairy and beef cattle research center, on-campus elementary and middle schools, child development center, science center with 60-foot Foucault pendulum, student campsites.

Freshman class profile. 2,121 applied, 1,493 admitted, 448 enrolled.

Mid 50% test scores		**GPA 2.0-2.99:**	10%
SAT critical reading:	520-620	**Rank in top quarter:**	65%
SAT math:	500-620	**Rank in top tenth:**	34%
SAT writing:	500-620	**End year in good standing:**	85%
ACT composite:	23-28	**Return as sophomores:**	78%
GPA 3.75 or higher:	41%	**Out-of-state:**	17%
GPA 3.50-3.74:	22%	**Live on campus:**	92%
GPA 3.0-3.49:	27%	**International:**	2%

Basis for selection. School achievement record and test scores most important. Class rank, recommendations and essays considered. Interview recommended; auditions required of music and theater majors; portfolio recommended for art majors. **Homeschooled:** Transcript of courses and grades, letter of recommendation (nonparent) required. Must meet or exceed academic profile of previous freshman class.

High school preparation. College-preparatory program required. 16 units required. Required units include English 4, mathematics 4, social studies 3, science 3 and foreign language 2. Algebra I, geometry or trigonometry, algebra II and fourth year higher than algebra II required.

2008-2009 Annual costs. Tuition/fees: $22,370. Room/board: $7,978. Books/supplies: $1,000. Personal expenses: $900.

2008-2009 Financial aid. Need-based: 371 full-time freshmen applied for aid; 275 were judged to have need; 275 of these received aid. Average need met was 84%. Average scholarship/grant was $15,269; average loan $3,044. 71% of total undergraduate aid awarded as scholarships/grants, 29% as loans/jobs. **Non-need-based:** Awarded to 935 full-time undergraduates, including 276 freshmen. Scholarships awarded for academics, art, athletics, leadership, minority status, music/drama, state residency. **Additional information:** Students are encouraged to work on-campus up to 20 hours per week.

Application procedures. Admission: Priority date 2/1; deadline 7/24 (receipt date). $50 fee, may be waived for applicants with need, free for online applicants. Admission notification on a rolling basis beginning on or about 11/1. Must reply by May 1 or within 4 week(s) if notified thereafter. **Financial aid:** Priority date 4/1; no closing date. Institutional form required. Applicants notified on a rolling basis starting 2/1.

Academics. Special study options: Combined bachelor's/graduate degree, cooperative education, cross-registration, double major, dual enrollment of high school students, honors, independent study, internships, student-designed major, study abroad, teacher certification program. 3-2 nursing with Emory University, 3-2 engineering with Georgia Institute of Technology. **Credit/placement by examination:** AP, CLEP, IB, SAT, ACT, institutional tests. No limit to credit by examination that may be applied to degree. **Support services:** Remedial instruction, study skills assistance, tutoring, writing center.

Majors. Agriculture: Animal sciences. **Biology:** General, exercise physiology. **Business:** Accounting, finance, marketing. **Communications:** General. **Computer sciences:** Computer science. **Conservation:** Environmental science. **Education:** Early childhood, mathematics, middle, music, physical. **Engineering technology:** General. **Foreign languages:** French, German, Spanish. **Health:** Nursing (RN). **History:** General. **Math:** General. **Philosophy/religion:** Religion. **Physical sciences:** Chemistry, physics. **Psychology:** General. **Social sciences:** General, economics, international relations, political science. **Visual/performing arts:** Art, music management, theater arts management.

Most popular majors. Biology 7%, business/marketing 20%, communications/journalism 10%, education 10%, foreign language 6%, psychology 8%, social sciences 11%.

Computing on campus. 140 workstations in library, computer center, student center. Dormitories wired for high-speed internet access and linked to campus network. Commuter students can connect to campus network. Online library, helpline, repair service, student web hosting, wireless network available.

Student life. Freshman orientation: Mandatory, $90 fee. Preregistration for classes offered. Sessions for students and parents in June based on date of prepayment. Additional orientation 4 days prior to start of classes. **Policies:** Limited visitation hours. Dry campus. **Housing:** Guaranteed on-campus for freshmen. Coed dorms, single-sex dorms, apartments, wellness housing available. $100 fully refundable deposit, deadline 5/1. Special-interest houses for women in math and science available. **Activities:** Bands, campus ministries, choral groups, dance, drama, international student organizations, literary magazine, music ensembles, Model UN, musical theater, student government, student newspaper, symphony orchestra, TV station, Amnesty International, Baptist Collegiate Ministries, Wesley Foundation, Catholic Student Association, Habitat for Humanity, Canterbury Club, Campus Outreach, Presbyterian Student Fellowship, Young Democrats, Republican Club.

Athletics. NAIA. **Intercollegiate:** Baseball M, basketball, cheerleading, cross-country, diving, equestrian W, golf, soccer, softball W, swimming, tennis, volleyball W. **Intramural:** Badminton, basketball, bowling, cross-country, football (non-tackle), golf, racquetball, soccer, softball, swimming, table tennis, tennis, volleyball, water polo, weight lifting. **Team name:** Vikings.

Student services. Alcohol/substance abuse counseling, career counseling, student employment services, financial aid counseling, health services, minority student services, on-campus daycare, personal counseling, placement for graduates, veterans' counselor, women's services. **Physically disabled:** Services for visually, hearing impaired.

Contact. E-mail: admissions@berry.edu
Phone: (706) 236-2215 Toll-free number: (800) 237-7942
Fax: (706) 290-2178
Brett Kennedy, Director of Admissions, Berry College, PO Box 490159, Mount Berry, GA 30149-0159

Beulah Heights University

Atlanta, Georgia
www.beulah.org **CB code: 5082**

- Private 5-year university and Bible college affiliated with International Pentecostal Church of Christ
- Commuter campus in very large city
- 598 degree-seeking undergraduates
- Application essay required

General. Accredited by ABHE. **Degrees:** 67 bachelor's, 35 associate awarded; master's offered. **Location:** Downtown Atlanta. **Calendar:** Semester, extensive summer session. **Full-time faculty:** 11 total. **Part-time faculty:** 46 total.

Basis for selection. Applicants must have accepted Christ, although personal denomination not considered. Pastoral and personal references required. Applicants pursuing GED may be accepted prior to completing GED, but must complete GED before college graduation.

2009-2010 Annual costs. Tuition/fees (projected): $7,180. Room only: $3,000.

Application procedures. Admission: No deadline. $35 fee. Admission notification on a rolling basis.

Academics. Special study options: Cross-registration, distance learning, double major, ESL, independent study, internships, weekend college. **Credit/placement by examination:** CLEP. **Support services:** Learning center, reduced course load, study skills assistance, tutoring, writing center.

Majors. Theology: Bible.

Computing on campus. Dormitories wired for high-speed internet access. Online course registration, online library, student web hosting, wireless network available.

Student life. Freshman orientation: Mandatory. **Policies:** Religious observance required. **Housing:** Single-sex dorms, apartments, wellness housing available. **Activities:** Campus ministries, choral groups, international student organizations, student government.

Student services. Adult student services, chaplain/spiritual director, career counseling, financial aid counseling, minority student services, personal counseling.

Contact. E-mail: admissions@beulah.org
Phone: (404) 627-2681 ext. 104 Toll-free number: (888) 777-2422
Fax: (404) 627-0702
John Dreher, Director of Admissions, Beulah Heights University, 892 Berne Street SE, Atlanta, GA 30316

Brenau University

Gainesville, Georgia **CB member**
www.brenau.edu **CB code: 5066**

- Private 4-year liberal arts college for women
- Residential campus in small city
- 805 degree-seeking undergraduates: 4% part-time, 100% women, 18% African American, 2% Asian American, 4% Hispanic American, 6% international
- 57 degree-seeking graduate students
- 42% of applicants admitted
- SAT or ACT (ACT writing optional) required
- 52% graduate within 6 years

General. Founded in 1878. Regionally accredited. Composed of 4 educational units: the Women's College (main campus), the Academy (women's secondary school), the Evening and Weekend College (coeducational), and the Online College. Performing arts and nursing daytime programs are coeducational. Male students may enroll in several Women's College programs through the Evening and Weekend College. **Degrees:** 189 bachelor's awarded; master's offered. **Location:** 45 miles from Atlanta. **Calendar:** Semester, limited summer session. **Full-time faculty:** 70 total; 73% have terminal degrees, 9% minority, 61% women. **Part-time faculty:** 44 total; 27% have terminal degrees, 9% minority, 68% women. **Class size:** 69% < 20, 29% 20-39, 2% 40-49, 1% 50-99. **Special facilities:** Visual arts center, performing arts center, regional history museum, vintage clothing museum.

Freshman class profile. 2,566 applied, 1,081 admitted, 173 enrolled.

Mid 50% test scores		**Out-of-state:**	12%
SAT critical reading:	460-560	**Live on campus:**	79%
SAT math:	450-520	**International:**	3%
ACT composite:	19-23	**Sororities:**	27%
Return as sophomores:	74%		

Basis for selection. Course selection most important, followed by GPA and standardized test scores. Admission policies for Evening/Weekend College differ from Women's College. SAT or ACT used for placement into math courses. Auditions required of performing arts majors. **Homeschooled:** Transcript of courses and grades, interview required. **Learning Disabled:** Learning disability must be professionally diagnosed.

High school preparation. College-preparatory program recommended.

2008-2009 Annual costs. Tuition/fees: $18,800. Room/board: $9,487. Books/supplies: $900. Personal expenses: $1,300.

2008-2009 Financial aid. Non-need-based: Scholarships awarded for academics, art, athletics, leadership, minority status, music/drama.

Application procedures. Admission: No deadline. $35 fee, may be waived for applicants with need. Admission notification on a rolling basis beginning on or about 10/1. **Financial aid:** Priority date 4/1; no closing date. FAFSA required. Applicants notified on a rolling basis starting 3/1.

Academics. Leadership curriculum available. **Special study options:** Combined bachelor's/graduate degree, cross-registration, distance learning, double major, dual enrollment of high school students, ESL, exchange student, honors, independent study, internships, student-designed major, study abroad, teacher certification program, weekend college. **Credit/placement by examination:** AP, CLEP, IB, SAT, ACT, institutional tests. 27 credit hours maximum toward bachelor's degree. Total of 27 hours for non-traditional students allowed. **Support services:** Learning center, pre-admission summer program, reduced course load, remedial instruction, study skills assistance, tutoring, writing center.

Majors. Biology: General. **Business:** Accounting, business admin, fashion, marketing, organizational behavior. **Communications:** Media studies. **Education:** Art, drama/dance, elementary, mentally handicapped, middle, music, special. **Health:** Health services, nursing (RN), physician assistant. **History:** General. **Legal studies:** General. **Liberal arts:** Arts/sciences. **Psychology:** General. **Social sciences:** International relations. **Visual/performing arts:** Arts management, dance, dramatic, fashion design, graphic design, interior design, music performance, studio arts.

Most popular majors. Biology 6%, business/marketing 8%, education 17%, health sciences 35%, psychology 6%, visual/performing arts 20%.

Computing on campus. 130 workstations in dormitories, library, computer center, student center. Dormitories wired for high-speed internet access and linked to campus network. Online course registration, online library, helpline, student web hosting, wireless network available.

Student life. **Freshman orientation:** Mandatory. Preregistration for classes offered. **Policies:** Single students under 22 years of age required to live on campus unless living with family or legal guardian; alcohol-free campus; required convocation attendance. **Housing:** Guaranteed on-campus for all undergraduates. Special housing for disabled, apartments, cooperative housing, fraternity/sorority housing available. $350 nonrefundable deposit. **Activities:** Campus ministries, choral groups, dance, drama, international student organizations, literary magazine, music ensembles, musical theater, radio station, student government, student newspaper, TV station, Brenau Fellowship Association, Eco-Friends, Fellowship of Christian Athletes, College Republicans, College Democrats, Silhouettes, volunteer center, student alumni council, Greek letter service organizations.

Athletics. NAIA. **Intercollegiate:** Basketball W, cross-country W, soccer W, softball W, swimming W, tennis W, volleyball W. **Team name:** Golden Tigers.

Student services. Alcohol/substance abuse counseling, career counseling, student employment services, financial aid counseling, health services, minority student services, personal counseling, placement for graduates, women's services. **Physically disabled:** Services for visually, speech, hearing impaired. **Learning disabled:** Comprehensive services available.

Contact. E-mail: wcadmissions@brenau.edu
Phone: (770) 534-6100 Toll-free number: (800) 252-5119
Fax: (770) 538-4701
Christina White, Associate Vice President of Enrollment Management, Brenau University, 500 Washington Street SE, Gainesville, GA 30501

Brewton-Parker College

Mount Vernon, Georgia — **CB member**
www.bpc.edu — **CB code: 5068**

- Private 4-year liberal arts college affiliated with Southern Baptist Convention
- Residential campus in small town
- 1,007 degree-seeking undergraduates: 27% part-time, 60% women, 23% African American, 2% Hispanic American, 2% international
- 96% of applicants admitted
- SAT or ACT (ACT writing optional) required

General. Founded in 1904. Regionally accredited. **Degrees:** 184 bachelor's, 20 associate awarded. **Location:** 90 miles from Macon and Savannah. **Calendar:** Semester, limited summer session. **Full-time faculty:** 57 total; 67% have terminal degrees, 12% minority, 40% women. **Part-time faculty:** 142 total. **Class size:** 84% < 20, 16% 20-39. **Special facilities:** Living history museum, recital hall, greenhouse, nature trail.

Freshman class profile. 383 applied, 369 admitted, 170 enrolled.

Mid 50% test scores			
SAT critical reading:	400-500	Return as sophomores:	42%
SAT math:	410-500	Out-of-state:	5%
SAT writing:	360-470	Live on campus:	44%
ACT composite:	16-20	International:	3%

Basis for selection. Students evaluated on SAT/ACT scores and high school performance. Audition and interview required of music and drama majors.

High school preparation. College-preparatory program recommended. 13 units required. Required units include English 4, mathematics 3, social studies 3 and science 3.

2008-2009 Annual costs. Tuition/fees: $14,730. $130 per-credit fee for applied music surcharge. Room/board: $6,240. Books/supplies: $1,200. Personal expenses: $1,700.

2007-2008 Financial aid. **Need-based:** Average scholarship/grant was $8,062; average loan $2,746. 58% of total undergraduate aid awarded as scholarships/grants, 42% as loans/jobs. **Non-need-based:** Scholarships awarded for academics, athletics, music/drama, religious affiliation, state residency.

Application procedures. **Admission:** No deadline. $25 fee. Admission notification on a rolling basis beginning on or about 9/1. **Financial aid:** Priority date 5/1; no closing date. FAFSA required. Applicants notified on a rolling basis starting 2/27; must reply within 2 week(s) of notification.

Academics. **Special study options:** Accelerated study, double major, dual enrollment of high school students, exchange student, external degree, honors, independent study, internships, teacher certification program. **Credit/placement by examination:** AP, CLEP, SAT, ACT. 30 credit hours maximum toward associate degree, 30 toward bachelor's. **Support services:** Learning center, reduced course load, remedial instruction, study skills assistance, tutoring, writing center.

Majors. **Biology:** General. **Business:** Accounting, business admin. **Communications:** General. **Computer sciences:** Information systems. **Education:** General, biology, early childhood, English, history, mathematics, middle, music, physical, science, secondary. **Foreign languages:** Spanish. **History:** General. **Legal studies:** Prelaw. **Math:** General. **Parks/recreation:** Health/fitness. **Philosophy/religion:** Religion. **Psychology:** General. **Social sciences:** General, political science, sociology. **Theology:** Theology. **Visual/performing arts:** Music performance.

Most popular majors. Business/marketing 25%, education 25%, liberal arts 10%, psychology 11%.

Computing on campus. 104 workstations in library, computer center. Dormitories wired for high-speed internet access. Online course registration, online library, helpline, wireless network available.

Student life. **Freshman orientation:** Available, $100 fee. Preregistration for classes offered. Held 4 days prior to start of classes. **Policies:** All day students required to live on campus except seniors, students residing with parents, students 22 or older. Religious observance required. **Housing:** Guaranteed on-campus for freshmen. Single-sex dorms available. $100 nonrefundable deposit. **Activities:** Bands, campus ministries, choral groups, drama, film society, literary magazine, music ensembles, musical theater, student government, student newspaper, ministerial association, Fellowship of Christian Athletes, Rotaract, Circle K, student activities council.

Athletics. NAIA. **Intercollegiate:** Baseball M, basketball, cheerleading, soccer, softball W, volleyball W. **Intramural:** Basketball, football (non-tackle), softball, table tennis, tennis, volleyball. **Team name:** Barons.

Student services. Alcohol/substance abuse counseling, chaplain/spiritual director, career counseling, student employment services, financial aid counseling, health services, personal counseling, placement for graduates, veterans' counselor. **Physically disabled:** Services for visually, speech, hearing impaired.

Contact. E-mail: admissions@bpc.edu
Phone: (912) 583-2241 ext. 265 Toll-free number: (800) 342-1087 ext. 265
Fax: (912) 583-3598
Kenneth Wuerzberger, Director of Admissions, Brewton-Parker College, Brewton-Parker College # 2011, Mount Vernon, GA 30445

Carver Bible College

Atlanta, Georgia
www.carver.edu

- Private 4-year Bible college
- Commuter campus in very large city
- 77 degree-seeking undergraduates

General. Accredited by ABHE. **Degrees:** 9 bachelor's, 2 associate awarded. **Calendar:** Semester, limited summer session. **Full-time faculty:** 3 total; 67% have terminal degrees. **Part-time faculty:** 12 total.

Basis for selection. Applicants assessed for admittance based on academic record, moral character and personal testimony of faith. Students who cannot meet the general entrance requirements may be given conditional admittance for probationary period.

2008-2009 Annual costs. Tuition/fees: $6,820.

Application procedures. **Admission:** No deadline.

Academics. **Special study options:** Distance learning, independent study. **Credit/placement by examination:** CLEP. **Support services:** Learning center.

Majors. **Theology:** Bible.

Computing on campus. Wireless network available.

Student life. **Freshman orientation:** Mandatory.

Contact. Phone: (404) 527-4520 Fax: (404) 527-4524
Patsy Singh, Director of Admissions, Carver Bible College, 3837 Cascade Road, SW, Atlanta, GA 30313

Clark Atlanta University

Atlanta, Georgia — **CB member**
www.cau.edu — **CB code: 5110**

- Private 4-year university affiliated with United Methodist Church
- Commuter campus in very large city
- 3,380 degree-seeking undergraduates: 4% part-time, 73% women, 89% African American, 1% international
- 688 degree-seeking graduate students
- 57% of applicants admitted
- SAT or ACT (ACT writing optional), application essay required
- 45% graduate within 6 years; 26% enter graduate study

General. Founded in 1869. Regionally accredited. Member of Atlanta University Center, a consortium of black private education institutions. **Degrees:** 573 bachelor's awarded; master's, doctoral offered. **ROTC:** Army, Naval. **Location:** 2 miles from downtown. **Calendar:** Semester, limited summer session. **Full-time faculty:** 230 total; 71% have terminal degrees, 89% minority, 36% women. **Part-time faculty:** 95 total; 30% have terminal degrees, 90% minority, 56% women. **Class size:** 38% < 20, 50% 20-39, 7% 40-49, 5% 50-99. **Special facilities:** Exhibition gallery, research center for science and technology.

Freshman class profile. 6,674 applied, 3,779 admitted, 823 enrolled.

Mid 50% test scores		**GPA 3.0-3.49:**	35%
SAT critical reading:	420-490	**GPA 2.0-2.99:**	52%
SAT math:	420-480	**End year in good standing:**	80%
ACT composite:	18-20	**Return as sophomores:**	73%
GPA 3.75 or higher:	5%	**Out-of-state:**	73%
GPA 3.50-3.74:	8%	**Live on campus:**	48%

Basis for selection. Secondary school record most important. Test scores, recommendations, essay also important. Audition recommended for music and drama majors. **Homeschooled:** Course work portfolio required.

High school preparation. College-preparatory program recommended. 18 units required. Required units include English 4, mathematics 3, social studies 3, science 3 (laboratory 1), foreign language 2 and academic electives 3.

2008-2009 Annual costs. Tuition/fees: $17,038. Room/board: $7,120. Books/supplies: $2,200. Personal expenses: $1,540.

2008-2009 Financial aid. Need-based: 789 full-time freshmen applied for aid; 762 were judged to have need; 762 of these received aid. Average need met was 12%. Average scholarship/grant was $5,500; average loan $3,500. 23% of total undergraduate aid awarded as scholarships/grants, 77% as loans/jobs. **Non-need-based:** Awarded to 915 full-time undergraduates, including 242 freshmen. Scholarships awarded for academics, art, athletics, leadership, minority status, music/drama, religious affiliation, ROTC, state residency.

Application procedures. Admission: Priority date 3/1; deadline 6/1 (postmark date). $35 fee, may be waived for applicants with need. Admission notification on a rolling basis beginning on or about 1/1. **Financial aid:** Priority date 3/1; no closing date. FAFSA required. Applicants notified on a rolling basis starting 4/1.

Academics. Special study options: Accelerated study, combined bachelor's/graduate degree, cooperative education, cross-registration, distance learning, double major, dual enrollment of high school students, exchange student, honors, independent study, internships, study abroad, teacher certification program, Washington semester, weekend college. **Credit/placement by examination:** AP, CLEP, IB, institutional tests. 45 credit hours maximum toward bachelor's degree. **Support services:** Learning center, pre-admission summer program, reduced course load, remedial instruction, study skills assistance, tutoring, writing center.

Majors. Biology: General. **Business:** Accounting, business admin, managerial economics. **Computer sciences:** General, computer science. **Education:** General, early childhood. **Foreign languages:** French, Spanish. **History:** General. **Math:** General. **Philosophy/religion:** Philosophy, religion. **Physical sciences:** Chemistry, physics. **Protective services:** Criminal justice. **Psychology:** General. **Public administration:** Social work. **Social sciences:** Political science, sociology. **Visual/performing arts:** Art, fashion design, theater history. **Other:** Radio, television, and digital communications.

Most popular majors. Biology 7%, business/marketing 24%, communications/journalism 22%, psychology 12%, security/protective services 6%, visual/performing arts 6%.

Computing on campus. 650 workstations in dormitories, library, computer center, student center. Dormitories wired for high-speed internet access and linked to campus network. Commuter students can connect to campus network. Online course registration, online library, helpline, repair service, wireless network available.

Student life. Freshman orientation: Mandatory, $150 fee. Preregistration for classes offered. **Policies:** Drug/alcohol policy, sanctions for violations, policies governing Greek and other student organizations. **Housing:** Guaranteed on-campus for freshmen. Coed dorms, single-sex dorms, special housing for disabled, apartments available. $325 partly refundable deposit, deadline 6/1. **Activities:** Bands, choral groups, dance, drama, film society, international student organizations, literary magazine, music ensembles, musical theater, opera, radio station, student government, student newspaper, symphony orchestra, TV station, NAACP, pan-Hellenic council, Anointed Students in Fellowship, Campus Crusade for Christ, Christian Fellowship, National Council of Negro Women, Forensic Society, Gamma Sigma Sigma, Caribbean-oriented student organization.

Athletics. NCAA. **Intercollegiate:** Baseball M, basketball, cross-country, football (tackle) M, softball W, tennis W, track and field, volleyball W. **Intramural:** Basketball, football (non-tackle), tennis W, track and field. **Team name:** Panthers.

Student services. Alcohol/substance abuse counseling, chaplain/spiritual director, career counseling, student employment services, financial aid counseling, health services, legal services, personal counseling, placement for graduates, veterans' counselor, women's services. **Physically disabled:** Services for visually, speech, hearing impaired.

Contact. E-mail: cauadmissions@cau.edu
Phone: (404) 880-8784 Toll-free number: (800) 688-3228
Fax: (404) 880-6174
Kevin Williams, Director of Admissions, Clark Atlanta University, 223 James P. Brawley Drive, SW, Atlanta, GA 30314-4391

Clayton State University

Morrow, Georgia — **CB member**
www.clayton.edu — **CB code: 5145**

- Public 4-year liberal arts and technical college
- Commuter campus in small city
- 5,773 degree-seeking undergraduates: 44% part-time, 70% women, 54% African American, 5% Asian American, 3% Hispanic American, 2% international
- 153 graduate students
- SAT or ACT (ACT writing optional) required

General. Founded in 1969. Regionally accredited. **Degrees:** 842 bachelor's, 126 associate awarded; master's offered. **ROTC:** Army, Naval, Air Force. **Location:** 12 miles from Atlanta. **Calendar:** Semester, extensive summer session. **Full-time faculty:** 208 total; 81% have terminal degrees, 31% minority, 51% women. **Part-time faculty:** 151 total; 27% have terminal degrees, 24% minority, 52% women. **Class size:** 42% < 20, 48% 20-39, 6% 40-49, 4% 50-99, less than 1% >100. **Special facilities:** Concert hall.

Freshman class profile.

Mid 50% test scores		**GPA 2.0-2.99:**	53%
SAT critical reading:	450-530	**Return as sophomores:**	59%
SAT math:	430-520	**Out-of-state:**	9%
ACT composite:	17-21	**Live on campus:**	30%
GPA 3.75 or higher:	5%	**International:**	2%
GPA 3.50-3.74:	9%	**Fraternities:**	8%
GPA 3.0-3.49:	33%	**Sororities:**	2%

Basis for selection. 17 ACT or 400 SAT math and 430 verbal required. Secondary school record also very important for health sciences, music, teacher education, and business programs. Auditions recommended for music majors. **Homeschooled:** Must validate the completion of a college prep curriculum. SAT tests may be used to do so.

High school preparation. 16 units required; 22 recommended. Required and recommended units include English 4, mathematics 4, social studies 3, history 2, science 3-4 (laboratory 3), foreign language 2-3 and academic electives 2. Students not meeting college-preparatory requirements must take remedial classes before entering any program.

2008-2009 Annual costs. Tuition/fees: $3,852; $13,144 out-of-state. Books/supplies: $1,000. Personal expenses: $3,440.

2008-2009 Financial aid. Non-need-based: Scholarships awarded for academics.

Application procedures. **Admission:** Priority date 2/1; no deadline. $40 fee, may be waived for applicants with need. Admission notification on a rolling basis beginning on or about 1/1. **Financial aid:** Priority date 7/18; no closing date. FAFSA required. Applicants notified on a rolling basis starting 3/12.

Academics. **Special study options:** Cooperative education, cross-registration, distance learning, double major, dual enrollment of high school students, exchange student, honors, independent study, internships, liberal arts/career combination, student-designed major, study abroad, teacher certification program. **Credit/placement by examination:** AP, CLEP, IB, institutional tests. **Support services:** Learning center, reduced course load, remedial instruction, study skills assistance, tutoring.

Majors. **Biology:** General. **Business:** General, accounting, business admin, marketing, office management, operations. **Communications:** General. **Computer sciences:** General, data processing, information systems, information technology, programming, systems analysis. **Education:** Middle. **Health:** Dental assistant, dental hygiene, facilities admin, health care admin, nursing (RN), nursing admin. **History:** General. **Liberal arts:** Arts/sciences. **Math:** General. **Parks/recreation:** Sports admin. **Protective services:** Criminal justice. **Psychology:** Community. **Social sciences:** Political science. **Visual/performing arts:** Dramatic, music performance, music theory/composition.

Most popular majors. Business/marketing 25%, health sciences 22%, liberal arts 13%, psychology 14%.

Computing on campus. PC or laptop required. Dormitories wired for high-speed internet access and linked to campus network. Online course registration, online library, helpline, repair service, student web hosting, wireless network available.

Student life. **Freshman orientation:** Mandatory, $40 fee. Preregistration for classes offered. **Housing:** Coed dorms, apartments available. **Activities:** Jazz band, choral groups, drama, literary magazine, music ensembles, musical theater, opera, student government, student newspaper, Approximately 20 student groups.

Athletics. NAIA, NCAA. **Intercollegiate:** Basketball, cross-country, golf M, soccer, tennis W, track and field. **Team name:** Lakers.

Student services. Adult student services, alcohol/substance abuse counseling, career counseling, student employment services, financial aid counseling, health services, minority student services, personal counseling, placement for graduates, veterans' counselor. **Physically disabled:** Services for visually, speech, hearing impaired.

Contact. E-mail: ccsu-info@mail.clayton.edu
Phone: (678) 466-4115 Fax: (678) 466-4149
Betty Momayezi, Director of Admissions, Clayton State University, 2000 Clayton State Boulevard, Morrow, GA 30260-0285

Columbus State University

Columbus, Georgia — **CB member**
www.colstate.edu — **CB code: 5123**

- Public 4-year university and liberal arts college
- Commuter campus in large city
- 6,668 degree-seeking undergraduates: 30% part-time, 60% women, 33% African American, 2% Asian American, 4% Hispanic American, 1% international
- 1,085 degree-seeking graduate students
- 66% of applicants admitted
- SAT or ACT (ACT writing optional) required

General. Founded in 1958. Regionally accredited. **Degrees:** 836 bachelor's, 27 associate awarded; master's offered. **ROTC:** Army. **Location:** 100 miles from Atlanta. **Calendar:** Semester, extensive summer session. **Full-time faculty:** 252 total; 78% have terminal degrees, 23% minority, 47% women. **Part-time faculty:** 177 total; 17% have terminal degrees, 14% minority, 49% women. **Class size:** 32% < 20, 55% 20-39, 7% 40-49, 5% 50-99, less than 1% >100. **Special facilities:** Environmental learning center, space science center, fine and performing arts center.

Freshman class profile. 3,090 applied, 2,050 admitted, 1,244 enrolled.

Mid 50% test scores		**GPA 2.0-2.99:**	47%
SAT critical reading:	440-550	**End year in good standing:**	75%
SAT math:	420-550	**Return as sophomores:**	69%
ACT composite:	17-22	**Out-of-state:**	12%
GPA 3.75 or higher:	10%	**Live on campus:**	32%
GPA 3.50-3.74:	9%	**Fraternities:**	1%
GPA 3.0-3.49:	34%	**Sororities:**	1%

Basis for selection. GED not accepted. 2.5 GPA, 460 SAT math/19 ACT math, and 490 SAT verbal/20 ACT English required. Students must be on track to graduate with college preparatory seal. Students with college prep deficiencies will be considered on individual basis. Interviews and auditions required of music majors. Portfolio recommended for art majors. **Homeschooled:** Statement describing homeschool structure and mission, transcript of courses and grades required. 1000 SAT (exclusive of Writing), Home School Credit Evaluation Table, letter from primary teacher certifying completion of high school and date of graduation and two letters of recommendation from non-family members required.

High school preparation. College-preparatory program required. 16 units required. Required units include English 4, mathematics 4, social studies 3, science 3 (laboratory 2) and foreign language 2. Social studies units required include U.S. history and world studies.

2008-2009 Annual costs. Tuition/fees: $3,772; $13,064 out-of-state. Room/board: $6,300. Books/supplies: $933. Personal expenses: $1,844.

2008-2009 Financial aid. **Need-based:** 927 full-time freshmen applied for aid; 590 were judged to have need; 572 of these received aid. Average need met was 66%. Average scholarship/grant was $3,146; average loan $2,899. 25% of total undergraduate aid awarded as scholarships/grants, 75% as loans/jobs. **Non-need-based:** Awarded to 4,000 full-time undergraduates, including 801 freshmen. Scholarships awarded for academics, alumni affiliation, art, athletics, job skills, leadership, minority status, music/drama, ROTC.

Application procedures. **Admission:** Priority date 5/1; deadline 7/1 (receipt date). $25 fee, may be waived for applicants with need. Admission notification on a rolling basis beginning on or about 9/1. **Financial aid:** Priority date 5/1; no closing date. FAFSA required. Applicants notified on a rolling basis starting 5/15; must reply within 4 week(s) of notification.

Academics. **Special study options:** Accelerated study, cooperative education, distance learning, double major, dual enrollment of high school students, honors, independent study, internships, liberal arts/career combination, study abroad, teacher certification program. **Credit/placement by examination:** AP, CLEP, IB, institutional tests. 30 credit hours maximum toward associate degree, 60 toward bachelor's. **Support services:** Learning center, reduced course load, remedial instruction, study skills assistance, tutoring, writing center.

Majors. **Biology:** General. **Business:** General, accounting, business admin, finance, management information systems, marketing. **Computer sciences:** General. **Education:** Art, drama/dance, early childhood, emotionally handicapped, English, learning disabled, mathematics, mentally handicapped, middle, music, physical, science, secondary, social science, social studies. **Foreign languages:** French, Spanish. **Health:** Health services, nursing (RN). **History:** General. **Math:** General. **Parks/recreation:** Exercise sciences. **Physical sciences:** Chemistry, geology. **Protective services:** Criminal justice. **Psychology:** General. **Social sciences:** Political science, sociology. **Visual/performing arts:** Art, dramatic, music performance.

Most popular majors. Business/marketing 27%, education 18%, English 8%, health sciences 10%, security/protective services 8%, social sciences 7%, visual/performing arts 6%.

Computing on campus. 966 workstations in dormitories, library, computer center, student center. Dormitories wired for high-speed internet access and linked to campus network. Commuter students can connect to campus network. Online course registration, online library, helpline, repair service, wireless network available.

Student life. **Freshman orientation:** Mandatory, $85 fee. Preregistration for classes offered. **Housing:** Coed dorms, single-sex dorms, special housing for disabled, apartments, fraternity/sorority housing, wellness housing available. $225 partly refundable deposit, deadline 5/1. Apartments take place of traditional dorms; weekday meals included in fee. **Activities:** Bands, choral groups, dance, drama, international student organizations, literary magazine, music ensembles, Model UN, musical theater, opera, student government, student newspaper, symphony orchestra, College Republicans, Islamic association, Freethought Society, Cougars for Christ, CSU Democrats, minority student union, student political awareness, Westminster Fellowship, Baptist student union.

Athletics. NCAA. **Intercollegiate:** Baseball M, basketball, cross-country, golf M, soccer W, softball W, tennis. **Intramural:** Badminton, basketball, football (tackle) M, skiing, soccer, softball, table tennis, tennis, volleyball. **Team name:** Cougars.

Student services. Adult student services, alcohol/substance abuse counseling, career counseling, student employment services, financial aid counseling, health services, minority student services, personal counseling, placement for graduates, veterans' counselor, women's services. **Physically disabled:** Services for visually, speech, hearing impaired.

Contact. E-mail: admissions@colstate.edu
Phone: (706) 568-2035 Toll-free number: (866) 264-2035
Fax: (706) 568-5091
Susan Lovell, Director of Admissions, Columbus State University, 4225 University Avenue, Columbus, GA 31907-5645

Covenant College
Lookout Mountain, Georgia
www.covenant.edu **CB code: 6124**

- Private 4-year liberal arts college affiliated with Presbyterian Church in America
- Residential campus in small city
- 983 degree-seeking undergraduates: 2% part-time, 56% women, 3% African American, 2% Asian American, 2% Hispanic American, 2% international
- 67 degree-seeking graduate students
- 64% of applicants admitted
- SAT or ACT with writing, application essay required
- 64% graduate within 6 years

General. Founded in 1955. Regionally accredited. **Degrees:** 170 bachelor's awarded; master's offered. **Location:** 120 miles from Atlanta, 5 miles from Chattanooga, Tennessee. **Calendar:** Semester, limited summer session. **Full-time faculty:** 63 total; 86% have terminal degrees, 6% minority, 18% women. **Part-time faculty:** 20 total; 45% have terminal degrees, 10% minority, 25% women. **Class size:** 62% < 20, 36% 20-39, 2% 40-49, less than 1% 50-99.

Freshman class profile. 996 applied, 639 admitted, 267 enrolled.

Mid 50% test scores		**GPA 2.0-2.99:**	11%
SAT critical reading:	520-650	**Rank in top quarter:**	50%
SAT math:	510-620	**Rank in top tenth:**	30%
SAT writing:	510-640	**Return as sophomores:**	75%
ACT composite:	22-28	**Out-of-state:**	71%
GPA 3.75 or higher:	51%	**Live on campus:**	98%
GPA 3.50-3.74:	14%	**International:**	1%
GPA 3.0-3.49:	24%		

Basis for selection. 1500 SAT (exclusive of Writing) or 21 ACT, 2.5 GPA, academic evaluation, church evaluation, and personal testimony of faith important. Students that do not meet minimum scores may be asked to provide additional information. Auditions required for music and voice majors. **Homeschooled:** Transcript of courses and grades, letter of recommendation (nonparent) required.

High school preparation. College-preparatory program recommended. 16 units required. Required and recommended units include English 4, mathematics 3, social studies 2, science 2, foreign language 2 and academic electives 3.

2008-2009 Annual costs. Tuition/fees: $24,320. Room/board: $6,900. Books/supplies: $1,000. Personal expenses: $650.

2007-2008 Financial aid. Need-based: 244 full-time freshmen applied for aid; 211 were judged to have need; 211 of these received aid. Average need met was 79%. Average scholarship/grant was $13,388; average loan $4,335. 71% of total undergraduate aid awarded as scholarships/grants, 29% as loans/jobs. **Non-need-based:** Awarded to 331 full-time undergraduates, including 96 freshmen. Scholarships awarded for academics, alumni affiliation, art, athletics, job skills, leadership, minority status, music/drama, religious affiliation, state residency.

Application procedures. Admission: Priority date 4/1; no deadline. $35 fee. Application must be submitted on paper. Admission notification on a rolling basis beginning on or about 8/1. Must reply by May 1 or within 3 week(s) if notified thereafter. **Financial aid:** No deadline. FAFSA required. Applicants notified on a rolling basis starting 2/1; must reply within 3 week(s) of notification.

Academics. Organizational management program for adult students with minimum 5 years work experience who have completed at least 2 years college. All classes held evenings, with degree completion in just over 1 year. **Special study options:** Double major, dual enrollment of high school students, exchange student, independent study, internships, student-designed major, study abroad, teacher certification program, Washington semester. Dual engineering degree with Georgia Tech, cooperative program with school of nursing at University of Tennessee at Chattanooga and Chattanooga State; bridge program leading to master of nursing science at Vanderbilt University. **Credit/placement by examination:** AP, CLEP, IB, SAT, ACT, institutional tests. 30 credit hours maximum toward associate degree, 30 toward bachelor's. **Support services:** Reduced course load, remedial instruction, study skills assistance, tutoring, writing center.

Majors. Biology: General. **Business:** General. **Computer sciences:** General. **Education:** Elementary, English, history, mathematics, science. **History:** General. **Interdisciplinary:** Biological/physical sciences. **Math:** General. **Philosophy/religion:** Philosophy. **Physical sciences:** General, chemistry, physics. **Psychology:** General. **Social sciences:** General, sociology. **Theology:** Bible. **Visual/performing arts:** Dramatic, music performance. **Other:** Multi-/interdisciplinary studies, Philosophy and religious studies.

Most popular majors. Business/marketing 9%, education 12%, English 9%, history 9%, interdisciplinary studies 14%, social sciences 15%, theological studies 7%, visual/performing arts 9%.

Computing on campus. 133 workstations in dormitories, library, computer center. Dormitories linked to campus network. Commuter students can connect to campus network. Online library, helpline, repair service, wireless network available.

Student life. Freshman orientation: Mandatory, $355 fee. Preregistration for classes offered. One week prior to beginning of classes. **Policies:** Smoking, alcoholic beverages, and drugs prohibited. Students are to use wisdom and Christ-like discretion in the application of Biblical principles to decisions regarding all areas of life. Religious observance required. **Housing:** Guaranteed on-campus for freshmen. Single-sex dorms, apartments available. $300 nonrefundable deposit. **Activities:** Concert band, campus ministries, choral groups, drama, literary magazine, music ensembles, radio station, student government, student newspaper, Rotaract, Young Life, pre-law club, Psi Chi, Reformed University Fellowship, Evangelism club.

Athletics. NAIA. **Intercollegiate:** Baseball M, basketball, cross-country, golf, soccer, softball W, tennis W, volleyball W. **Intramural:** Basketball, football (non-tackle), football (tackle) M, soccer, volleyball. **Team name:** Scots.

Student services. Adult student services, career counseling, student employment services, financial aid counseling, health services, personal counseling, placement for graduates.

Contact. E-mail: admissions@covenant.edu
Phone: (706) 419-1148 Toll-free number: (888) 451-2683
Fax: (706) 820-0893
Wallace Anderson, Vice President of Enrollment Management, Covenant College, 14049 Scenic Highway, Lookout Mountain, GA 30750

Dalton State College
Dalton, Georgia
www.daltonstate.edu **CB code: 5167**

- Public 4-year liberal arts and teachers college
- Commuter campus in large town
- 4,957 degree-seeking undergraduates: 46% part-time, 59% women
- 58% of applicants admitted

General. Founded in 1963. Regionally accredited. **Degrees:** 131 bachelor's, 291 associate awarded. **Location:** 90 miles from Atlanta. **Calendar:** Semester, limited summer session. **Full-time faculty:** 141 total; 60% have terminal degrees, 6% minority, 59% women. **Part-time faculty:** 73 total; 16% have terminal degrees, 6% minority, 56% women.

Freshman class profile. 3,052 applied, 1,755 admitted, 1,467 enrolled.

Basis for selection. 2.0 GPA in high school college preparatory curriculum and 2.2 GPA in Tech Prep curriculum required. **Homeschooled:** State high school equivalency certificate required.

High school preparation. 16 units required. Required units include English 4, mathematics 4, social studies 3, science 3 and foreign language 2.

2008-2009 Annual costs. Tuition/fees: $2,340; $8,322 out-of-state.

2007-2008 Financial aid. Non-need-based: Scholarships awarded for academics, leadership, minority status, state residency.

Application procedures. Admission: No deadline. $25 fee, may be waived for applicants with need. Admission notification on a rolling basis. **Financial aid:** Priority date 7/1; no closing date. FAFSA, institutional form required. Applicants notified on a rolling basis starting 7/1.

Academics. Special study options: Cooperative education, double major, dual enrollment of high school students, ESL, external degree, honors, independent study, internships, study abroad, weekend college. **Credit/placement by examination:** CLEP, institutional tests. Credit is awarded only to admitted students and recorded only for those who enroll for credit courses. Credit is awarded only for offered courses. **Support services:** Remedial instruction, study skills assistance, tutoring, writing center.

Honors college/program. For early admission, first-time freshmen and early enrollment students need 3.5 GPA, 1100 SAT (exclusive of Writing) with 580 verbal or 24 ACT. Honors essay, 2 letters of recommendation, and interview with honors program director and committee representatives required.

Majors. Biology: General. **Business:** Accounting, business admin, management information systems, management science, marketing, operations. **Computer sciences:** General. **Education:** Elementary. **Family/consumer sciences:** Work/family studies. **Math:** General. **Public administration:** Social work.

Computing on campus. 800 workstations in library, computer center, student center. Commuter students can connect to campus network. Online library, helpline available.

Student life. Freshman orientation: Mandatory. Preregistration for classes offered. **Activities:** International student organizations, literary magazine, student government, student newspaper, social work club, LPN, Baptist student union, Psychology, black student alliance, Phi The Kappa, Young Democrats, progressive student union.

Athletics. Intramural: Badminton, basketball, football (non-tackle) M, softball, table tennis, tennis, volleyball.

Student services. Adult student services, career counseling, student employment services, financial aid counseling, personal counseling, placement for graduates, veterans' counselor. **Physically disabled:** Services for hearing impaired.

Contact. Phone: (706) 272-4436 Toll-free number: (800) 829-4436
Fax: (706) 272-2530
Jodi Johnson, Vice President for Enrollment Services, Dalton State College, 650 College Drive, Dalton, GA 30720

DeVry University: Alpharetta

Alpharetta, Georgia
www.devry.edu **CB code: 0077**

- For-profit 4-year university
- Commuter campus in large town
- 708 degree-seeking undergraduates: 52% part-time, 44% women, 42% African American, 4% Asian American, 5% Hispanic American, 1% Native American, 1% international
- 147 degree-seeking graduate students
- Interview required

General. Regionally accredited. **Degrees:** 125 bachelor's, 20 associate awarded; master's offered. **Location:** 18 miles from Atlanta. **Calendar:** Semester, extensive summer session. **Full-time faculty:** 28 total; 39% minority, 46% women. **Part-time faculty:** 37 total; 30% minority, 32% women.

Basis for selection. Applicants must have high school diploma or equivalent, or degree from accredited postsecondary institution, demonstrate proficiency in basic college-level skills through ACT, SAT, or institution-administered placement examinations, and be at least 17 years of age. New students may enter at the beginning of any semester. DeVry-administered admissions test required for applicants without SAT/ACT.

2008-2009 Annual costs. Tuition/fees: $14,130. Books/supplies: $1,300. Personal expenses: $5,082.

2007-2008 Financial aid. All financial aid based on need.

Application procedures. Admission: No deadline. $50 fee. Admission notification on a rolling basis. **Financial aid:** No deadline. FAFSA required. Applicants notified on a rolling basis.

Academics. Special study options: Accelerated study, distance learning. **Credit/placement by examination:** CLEP, institutional tests. **Support services:** Learning center, remedial instruction, tutoring.

Majors. Business: Business admin, operations. **Communications technology:** General. **Computer sciences:** Information systems, networking, systems analysis. **Engineering:** Software. **Engineering technology:** Computer, electrical. **Other:** Technical management.

Most popular majors. Business/marketing 67%, computer/information sciences 30%.

Computing on campus. 218 workstations in library, computer center. Online course registration, online library, helpline available.

Student life. Freshman orientation: Mandatory. **Housing:** Private apartments, student-plan housing, private rooms available. **Activities:** Alpha Sigma Lambda, Toastmasters International, international student organization, National Society of Black Engineers, Alpha Beta Kappa, Delta Pi Chi, Epsilon Delta Pi, Tau Alpha Pi, Future Business Leaders of America.

Athletics. Intramural: Basketball, football (non-tackle), softball, volleyball.

Student services. Career counseling, student employment services, financial aid counseling, placement for graduates, veterans' counselor. **Physically disabled:** Services for visually, hearing impaired.

Contact. E-mail: admissions@devry.edu
Phone: (770) 664-9520 Toll-free number: (800) 346-5420
Fax: (770) 664-8824
Gerry Purcell, Director of Admissions, DeVry University: Alpharetta, 2555 Northwinds Parkway, Alpharetta, GA 30004

DeVry University: Decatur

Decatur, Georgia
www.devry.edu **CB code: 5715**

- For-profit 4-year university
- Commuter campus in large town
- 2,376 degree-seeking undergraduates: 48% part-time, 50% women, 71% African American, 2% Asian American, 3% Hispanic American, 1% international
- 337 degree-seeking graduate students
- Interview required

General. Founded in 1969. Regionally accredited. **Degrees:** 345 bachelor's, 56 associate awarded; master's offered. **Location:** 15 miles from Atlanta. **Calendar:** Semester, extensive summer session. **Full-time faculty:** 37 total; 38% minority, 40% women. **Part-time faculty:** 160 total; 51% minority, 46% women.

Freshman class profile.

Out-of-state:	9%	International:	1%

Basis for selection. Applicants must have high school diploma or equivalent, or degree from accredited post-secondary institution, demonstrate proficiency in basic college-level skills through SAT or ACT scores or institution-administered placement examinations, and be at least 17 years of age. New students may enter at beginning of any semester. Applicants may also take a DeVry administered admissions test.

2008-2009 Annual costs. Tuition/fees: $14,130. Books/supplies: $1,300. Personal expenses: $5,082.

2007-2008 Financial aid. All financial aid based on need.

Application procedures. Admission: No deadline. $50 fee. Admission notification on a rolling basis. **Financial aid:** No deadline. FAFSA required. Applicants notified on a rolling basis.

Academics. Special study options: Accelerated study, distance learning. **Credit/placement by examination:** CLEP, institutional tests. **Support services:** Learning center, remedial instruction, tutoring.

Majors. Business: Business admin, operations. **Computer sciences:** Information systems, networking, systems analysis. **Engineering:** Software. **Engineering technology:** Biomedical, computer, electrical. **Other:** Technical management.

Most popular majors. Business/marketing 70%, computer/information sciences 20%, engineering/engineering technologies 10%.

Computing on campus. 300 workstations in library, computer center. Online course registration, online library, helpline available.

Student life. Freshman orientation: Mandatory. **Housing:** Private apartments, student-plan housing, private rooms available. **Activities:** Toastmasters International, National Society of Black Engineers, International Student Organization, Delta Pi Chi, Tau Alpha Pi, Sigma Beta Delta, Alpha Beta Kappa.

Athletics. Intramural: Basketball, football (non-tackle), softball, volleyball.

Student services. Career counseling, student employment services, financial aid counseling, placement for graduates, veterans' counselor. **Physically disabled:** Services for visually, hearing impaired.

Contact. E-mail: dsilva@admin.atl.devry.edu
Phone: (404) 292-2645 Toll-free number: (800) 221-4771
Fax: (404) 292-7011
Barbara Silva, Director of Admissions, DeVry University: Decatur, 250 North Arcadia Avenue, Decatur, GA 30030-2198

Emmanuel College

Franklin Springs, Georgia
www.ec.edu
CB member
CB code: 5184

- Private 4-year liberal arts college affiliated with Pentecostal Holiness Church
- Residential campus in rural community
- 645 degree-seeking undergraduates: 5% part-time, 57% women, 17% African American, 1% Asian American, 4% Hispanic American, 1% international
- 56% of applicants admitted
- SAT or ACT (ACT writing optional) required
- 35% graduate within 6 years

General. Founded in 1919. Regionally accredited. **Degrees:** 105 bachelor's, 8 associate awarded. **Location:** 30 miles from Athens, 90 miles from Atlanta. **Calendar:** Semester, limited summer session. **Full-time faculty:** 42 total; 52% have terminal degrees, 2% minority, 45% women. **Part-time faculty:** 28 total; 14% have terminal degrees, 43% women. **Class size:** 61% < 20, 36% 20-39, 2% 40-49, less than 1% 50-99.

Freshman class profile. 1,176 applied, 664 admitted, 226 enrolled.

Return as sophomores:	66%	**Live on campus:**	50%
Out-of-state:	20%	**International:**	2%

Basis for selection. High school record and SAT/ACT scores important. Audition required and interview recommended for music majors. **Learning Disabled:** Must submit documentation of disability from professional.

2008-2009 Annual costs. Tuition/fees: $12,260. Room/board: $5,584. Books/supplies: $968. Personal expenses: $1,603.

2008-2009 Financial aid. Need-based: 120 full-time freshmen applied for aid; 103 were judged to have need; 103 of these received aid. Average need met was 81%. Average scholarship/grant was $8,481; average loan $3,304. 52% of total undergraduate aid awarded as scholarships/grants, 48% as loans/jobs. **Non-need-based:** Awarded to 196 full-time undergraduates, including 34 freshmen. Scholarships awarded for academics, art, athletics, leadership, music/drama, religious affiliation, state residency.

Application procedures. Admission: Closing date 8/1 (receipt date). $25 fee, may be waived for applicants with need, free for online applicants. Admission notification on a rolling basis beginning on or about 1/1. **Financial aid:** Priority date 5/1, closing date 7/1. FAFSA, institutional form required. Applicants notified on a rolling basis starting 3/1; must reply within 2 week(s) of notification.

Academics. Special study options: Dual enrollment of high school students, independent study, internships, teacher certification program. **Credit/placement by examination:** AP, CLEP, institutional tests. 24 credit hours maximum toward associate degree, 24 toward bachelor's. **Support services:** Remedial instruction, study skills assistance, tutoring, writing center.

Majors. Biology: General. **Business:** Business admin. **Communications:** General. **Education:** Business, elementary, English, history, mathematics, middle, music. **Health:** Premedicine. **History:** General. **Legal studies:** Prelaw. **Math:** General. **Parks/recreation:** Exercise sciences, sports admin. **Psychology:** General. **Theology:** Pastoral counseling, sacred music.

Most popular majors. Biology 6%, business/marketing 18%, communications/journalism 9%, education 21%, parks/recreation 7%, psychology 10%, theological studies 14%.

Computing on campus. 50 workstations in library, computer center. Dormitories wired for high-speed internet access and linked to campus network. Commuter students can connect to campus network. Online course registration, online library, repair service, wireless network available.

Student life. Freshman orientation: Mandatory. Preregistration for classes offered. Held first 2 days of semester. **Policies:** Chapel attendance required for all full-time students. Students not living at home must reside in college housing through junior year. Religious observance required. **Housing:** Guaranteed on-campus for all undergraduates. Single-sex dorms, apartments, wellness housing available. $150 fully refundable deposit, deadline 8/1. **Activities:** Concert band, choral groups, drama, literary magazine, music ensembles, musical theater, student government, student newspaper, ministerial fellowship, missions fellowship, Students in Free Enterprise.

Athletics. NAIA, NCCAA. **Intercollegiate:** Baseball M, basketball, soccer, softball W, tennis. **Intramural:** Basketball, soccer, softball, table tennis, tennis, track and field, volleyball. **Team name:** Lions.

Student services. Adult student services, chaplain/spiritual director, career counseling, financial aid counseling, personal counseling, veterans' counselor.

Contact. E-mail: admission@ec.edu
Phone: (706) 245-7226 Toll-free number: (800) 860-8800
Fax: (706) 245-4424
Wade Mawdesley, Director of Admissions, Emmanuel College, 181 Spring Street, Franklin Springs, GA 30639-0129

Emory University

Atlanta, Georgia
www.emory.edu
CB member
CB code: 5187

- Private 4-year university affiliated with United Methodist Church
- Residential campus in very large city
- 5,169 degree-seeking undergraduates: 1% part-time, 55% women
- 5,787 graduate students
- 27% of applicants admitted
- SAT or ACT with writing, application essay required
- 88% graduate within 6 years

General. Founded in 1836. Regionally accredited. **Degrees:** 1,513 bachelor's, 314 associate awarded; master's, doctoral, first professional offered. **ROTC:** Army, Naval, Air Force. **Location:** 5 miles from downtown. **Calendar:** Semester, limited summer session. **Full-time faculty:** 1,255 total; 99% have terminal degrees, 20% minority, 40% women. **Part-time faculty:** 192 total; 99% have terminal degrees, 14% minority, 47% women. **Class size:** 68% < 20, 22% 20-39, 3% 40-49, 6% 50-99, 1% >100. **Special facilities:** Art and archeology museum, biological field station, primate research center, 185-acre park, planetarium, healthcare facilities.

Freshman class profile. 17,446 applied, 4,644 admitted, 1,299 enrolled.

Mid 50% test scores		**Rank in top quarter:**	90%
SAT critical reading:	640-740	**Rank in top tenth:**	90%
SAT math:	670-760	**Return as sophomores:**	95%
SAT writing:	650-740	**Out-of-state:**	73%
ACT composite:	30-33	**Live on campus:**	99%
GPA 3.75 or higher:	72%	**Fraternities:**	36%
GPA 3.50-3.74:	22%	**Sororities:**	32%
GPA 3.0-3.49:	6%		

Basis for selection. GED not accepted. School achievement record, program content and rigor of coursework most important. Test scores, character and maturity important. Diversity of interests, background, and special talents sought. Campus visits or other indications of interest encouraged. **Homeschooled:** 3 SAT Subject Tests required (1 math and 2 of student's choice). Personal interview strongly recommended.

High school preparation. College-preparatory program required. 16 units required. Required and recommended units include English 4, mathematics 3-4, social studies 2, history 2, science 2-3 (laboratory 2), foreign language 2-3, visual/performing arts 1 and academic electives 2. At least 2 units required in either social studies or history, including history of a country/region other than the U.S. 4 units math and science, with at least 3 units laboratory science, recommended for students concentrating in science or math.

2008-2009 Annual costs. Tuition/fees: $36,336. Room/board: $10,572. Books/supplies: $1,000. Personal expenses: $1,000.

2008-2009 Financial aid. Need-based: 853 full-time freshmen applied for aid; 680 were judged to have need; 680 of these received aid. Average need met was 100%. Average scholarship/grant was $27,850; average loan $3,399. 85% of total undergraduate aid awarded as scholarships/grants, 15% as loans/jobs. **Non-need-based:** Awarded to 1,245 full-time undergraduates, including 257 freshmen. Scholarships awarded for academics, art, leadership, music/drama, state residency. **Additional information:** Loan replacement grant and loan cap program available to students from families with total annual incomes of $100,000 or less who demonstrate need for financial aid.

Application procedures. Admission: Closing date 1/15 (postmark date). $50 fee, may be waived for applicants with need. Admission notification 4/1. Must reply by 5/1. **Financial aid:** Priority date 2/15, closing date 3/1. FAFSA, CSS PROFILE required. Applicants notified by 4/1; must reply by 5/1 or within 4 week(s) of notification.

Academics. Special study options: Accelerated study, combined bachelor's/graduate degree, cooperative education, cross-registration, double major, dual enrollment of high school students, exchange student, honors, independent study, internships, liberal arts/career combination, study abroad, teacher certification program, Washington semester. 3-2 or 4-2 dual-degree program in engineering with Georgia Institute of Technology. **Credit/placement by examination:** AP, CLEP, IB, institutional tests. **Support services:** Learning center, pre-admission summer program, study skills assistance, tutoring, writing center.

Majors. Area/ethnic studies: African, African-American, Asian, Caribbean, Central/Eastern European, French, German, Italian, Latin American, Russian/Slavic, women's. **Biology:** General. **Business:** General, accounting, business admin, finance, management science, marketing. **Communications:** Journalism. **Computer sciences:** Computer science. **Conservation:** Environmental studies. **Education:** General. **Foreign languages:** Chinese, classics, comparative lit, French, German, Italian, Japanese, Latin, linguistics, Russian, Spanish. **History:** General. **Interdisciplinary:** Math/computer science, medieval/Renaissance. **Math:** General. **Philosophy/religion:** Judaic, philosophy, religion. **Physical sciences:** Astronomy, chemistry, physics. **Psychology:** General. **Social sciences:** Anthropology, economics, international relations, political science, sociology. **Visual/performing arts:** Art history/conservation, dance, dramatic, film/cinema.

Most popular majors. Biology 7%, business/marketing 17%, health sciences 8%, interdisciplinary studies 8%, psychology 10%, social sciences 23%.

Computing on campus. 700 workstations in dormitories, library, computer center, student center. Dormitories wired for high-speed internet access and linked to campus network. Commuter students can connect to campus network. Online course registration, online library, helpline, repair service, student web hosting, wireless network available.

Student life. Freshman orientation: Mandatory. Typically held over 5 days immediately prior to first day of classes. New students receive orientation information by mail in June. **Policies:** Two-year residency requirement. Guaranteed on-campus housing for freshmen and sophomores. **Housing:** Guaranteed on-campus for freshmen. Coed dorms, single-sex dorms, special housing for disabled, apartments, fraternity/sorority housing, wellness housing available. $100 nonrefundable deposit, deadline 5/1. **Activities:** Bands, campus ministries, choral groups, dance, drama, film society, international student organizations, literary magazine, music ensembles, Model UN, musical theater, radio station, student government, student newspaper, symphony orchestra, TV station, over 220 student clubs and organizations available.

Athletics. NCAA. **Intercollegiate:** Baseball M, basketball, cross-country, diving, golf M, soccer, softball W, swimming, tennis, track and field, volleyball W. **Intramural:** Badminton, basketball, diving, football (non-tackle), golf, handball, racquetball, soccer, softball, squash, swimming, table tennis, tennis, track and field, volleyball, wrestling. **Team name:** Eagles.

Student services. Alcohol/substance abuse counseling, career counseling, student employment services, financial aid counseling, health services, legal services, minority student services, on-campus daycare, personal counseling, placement for graduates, women's services. **Physically disabled:** Services for visually, speech, hearing impaired.

Contact. E-mail: admiss@emory.edu
Phone: (404) 727-6036 Toll-free number: (800) 727-6036
Fax: (404) 727-4303
Jean Jordan, Dean of Admission, Emory University, 200 Boisfeuillet Jones Center, Atlanta, GA 30322

Fort Valley State University

Fort Valley, Georgia — **CB member**
www.fvsu.edu — **CB code: 5220**

- Public 4-year liberal arts and teachers college
- Residential campus in small town
- 2,969 degree-seeking undergraduates: 7% part-time, 55% women, 96% African American, 1% Hispanic American, 1% international
- 131 degree-seeking graduate students
- 47% of applicants admitted
- SAT or ACT (ACT writing optional) required
- 30% graduate within 6 years

General. Founded in 1895. Regionally accredited. 1890 land-grant institution. **Degrees:** 268 bachelor's, 11 associate awarded; master's offered. **ROTC:** Army. **Location:** 30 miles from Macon. **Calendar:** Semester, limited summer session. **Full-time faculty:** 119 total; 75% have terminal degrees, 73% minority, 37% women. **Part-time faculty:** 43 total; 28% have terminal degrees, 74% minority, 56% women. **Class size:** 29% < 20, 34% 20-39, 15% 40-49, 18% 50-99, 4% >100.

Freshman class profile. 5,526 applied, 2,608 admitted, 1,195 enrolled.

Mid 50% test scores		**GPA 2.0-2.99:**	66%
SAT critical reading:	400-470	**Rank in top quarter:**	30%
SAT math:	410-470	**Rank in top tenth:**	10%
ACT composite:	16-19	**Return as sophomores:**	92%
GPA 3.75 or higher:	4%	**Out-of-state:**	7%
GPA 3.50-3.74:	6%	**Live on campus:**	93%
GPA 3.0-3.49:	22%		

Basis for selection. High school transcript, test scores, physical examination important. Audition recommended for music education majors.

High school preparation. College-preparatory program required. 16 units required. Required units include English 4, mathematics 4, social studies 1, history 2, science 3 and foreign language 2.

2008-2009 Annual costs. Tuition/fees: $4,018; $13,310 out-of-state. Room/board: $6,410. Books/supplies: $2,000. Personal expenses: $2,000.

2008-2009 Financial aid. Need-based: 1,045 full-time freshmen applied for aid; 1,038 were judged to have need; 1,035 of these received aid. Average need met was 96%. Average scholarship/grant was $2,140; average loan $2,300. 64% of total undergraduate aid awarded as scholarships/grants, 36% as loans/jobs. **Non-need-based:** Awarded to 617 full-time undergraduates, including 262 freshmen. Scholarships awarded for academics, job skills. **Additional information:** Loans decreased and grant aid offered to make institution more affordable.

Application procedures. Admission: Closing date 7/19. $30 fee. Admission notification on a rolling basis. **Financial aid:** Priority date 4/15, closing date 6/30. FAFSA required. Applicants notified on a rolling basis starting 7/1; must reply within 1 week(s) of notification.

Academics. Special study options: Cross-registration, distance learning, double major, honors, internships, teacher certification program. **Credit/placement by examination:** CLEP, SAT, ACT, institutional tests. 20 credit hours maximum toward associate degree, 45 toward bachelor's. **Support services:** Learning center, reduced course load, remedial instruction, tutoring, writing center.

Majors. Agriculture: Animal sciences, economics, farm/ranch, horticultural science, plant sciences. **Biology:** General. **Business:** General, accounting, business admin, marketing, office management. **Communications:** Journalism, public relations. **Computer sciences:** General, information systems. **Education:** Agricultural, elementary, English, family/consumer sciences, foreign languages, French, mathematics, middle, music, physical, secondary. **Engineering:** Agricultural. **Engineering technology:** Electrical. **Family/consumer sciences:** General, child care, child development, family studies, food/nutrition. **Health:** Medical assistant, veterinary technology/assistant. **Liberal arts:** Arts/sciences. **Math:** General. **Physical sciences:** Chemistry. **Psychology:** General. **Public administration:** Human services, social work. **Social sciences:** Economics, political science, sociology.

Most popular majors. Agriculture 7%, biology 12%, business/marketing 20%, computer/information sciences 6%, family/consumer sciences 9%, health sciences 6%, public administration/social services 7%, security/protective services 10%.

Computing on campus. Dormitories linked to campus network. Commuter students can connect to campus network. Helpline available.

Student life. Freshman orientation: Mandatory. Preregistration for classes offered. **Housing:** Coed dorms, single-sex dorms, apartments available. $200 fully refundable deposit, deadline 8/28. **Activities:** Bands, choral groups, drama, international student organizations, music ensembles, radio station, student government, student newspaper, TV station.

Athletics. NCAA. **Intercollegiate:** Basketball, cross-country, football (tackle) M, softball W, tennis, track and field, volleyball W. **Intramural:** Basketball, softball, swimming, tennis, track and field, volleyball. **Team name:** Wildcats.

Student services. Adult student services, career counseling, student employment services, health services, on-campus daycare, personal counseling, placement for graduates, veterans' counselor.

Contact. E-mail: admissap@fvsu.edu
Phone: (478) 825-6307 Toll-free number: (877) 462-3878
Fax: (478) 825-6394
Donovan Coley, Director of Admissions, Fort Valley State University, 1005 State University Drive, Fort Valley, GA 31030-4313

Georgia College and State University

Milledgeville, Georgia — **CB member**
www.gcsu.edu — **CB code: 5252**

- Public 4-year university and liberal arts college
- Residential campus in large town
- 5,464 degree-seeking undergraduates: 9% part-time, 59% women, 6% African American, 1% Asian American, 3% Hispanic American, 2% international
- 918 degree-seeking graduate students
- 59% of applicants admitted
- SAT or ACT with writing, application essay required
- 42% graduate within 6 years

General. Founded in 1889. Regionally accredited. Branch campuses in Macon and Warner Robins offering junior, senior, and graduate level options. **Degrees:** 915 bachelor's awarded; master's offered. **ROTC:** Army. **Location:** 95 miles from Atlanta, 30 miles from Macon. **Calendar:** Semester, limited summer session. **Full-time faculty:** 297 total; 75% have terminal degrees, 51% women. **Part-time faculty:** 115 total; 10% minority, 64% women. **Special facilities:** Art galleries, greenhouse, challenge/ropes course, former Governor's mansion, Flannery O'Connor collection, Georgia education museum and archives.

Freshman class profile. 3,906 applied, 2,314 admitted, 1,167 enrolled.

Mid 50% test scores		**GPA 2.0-2.99:**	13%
SAT critical reading:	520-600	**Rank in top quarter:**	59%
SAT math:	510-600	**Rank in top tenth:**	23%
SAT writing:	510-590	**Return as sophomores:**	84%
ACT composite:	22-25	**Out-of-state:**	1%
GPA 3.75 or higher:	17%	**Live on campus:**	99%
GPA 3.50-3.74:	22%	**International:**	1%
GPA 3.0-3.49:	48%	**Sororities:**	30%

Basis for selection. Admission decisions based on total student portfolio, demonstrated potential for contribution to the university and probability for success. Test scores used in academic advising for honors program consideration. Audition required of music and drama. **Homeschooled:** Transcript of courses and grades required. Admissions of home schooled students from non-accredited schools will be made based on students having SAT/ACT score equal to or above average score of previous year's entering freshmen class; other documentation may be required. **Learning Disabled:** Students must identify themselves as disabled during admissions process.

High school preparation. College-preparatory program required. 16 units required. Required and recommended units include English 4, mathematics 4, social studies 3, science 3 (laboratory 2-3) and foreign language 2-3. Additional courses from the following areas strongly recommended: trigonometry, fine arts and computer technology.

2008-2009 Annual costs. Tuition/fees: $5,476; $19,108 out-of-state. Room/board: $7,698. Books/supplies: $1,000. Personal expenses: $2,304.

2007-2008 Financial aid. Need-based: Average scholarship/grant was $2,932; average loan $3,005. 27% of total undergraduate aid awarded as scholarships/grants, 73% as loans/jobs. **Non-need-based:** Awarded to 1,846 full-time undergraduates, including 26 freshmen. Scholarships awarded for academics, alumni affiliation, art, athletics, job skills, leadership, minority status, music/drama, religious affiliation, ROTC, state residency.

Application procedures. Admission: Closing date 4/1 (postmark date). $40 fee. Admission notification on a rolling basis beginning on or about 1/1. Students encouraged to apply early to be considered for admission, university housing, scholarship funding, and financial aid. **Financial aid:** Priority date 3/1; no closing date. FAFSA, institutional form required. Applicants notified on a rolling basis starting 3/1; must reply within 2 week(s) of notification.

Academics. Special study options: Accelerated study, distance learning, double major, ESL, external degree, honors, independent study, internships, liberal arts/career combination, semester at sea, student-designed major, study abroad, teacher certification program, Washington semester. 3-2 engineering program with Georgia Institute of Technology. **Credit/placement by examination:** AP, CLEP, IB, SAT, ACT, institutional tests. 30 credit hours maximum toward bachelor's degree. **Support services:** Learning center, preadmission summer program, reduced course load, study skills assistance, tutoring, writing center.

Majors. Biology: General. **Business:** General, accounting, business admin, managerial economics, marketing. **Communications:** Journalism. **Computer sciences:** General. **Conservation:** Environmental science. **Education:** Early childhood, health, middle, music, special. **Foreign languages:** French, Spanish. **Health:** Music therapy, nursing (RN). **History:** General. **Liberal arts:** Arts/sciences. **Math:** General. **Parks/recreation:** General. **Philosophy/religion:** Philosophy. **Physical sciences:** Chemistry. **Protective services:** Law enforcement admin. **Psychology:** General. **Social sciences:** Political science, sociology. **Visual/performing arts:** Art, dramatic.

Most popular majors. Business/marketing 28%, communications/journalism 6%, education 18%, health sciences 9%, psychology 10%.

Computing on campus. 180 workstations in dormitories, library, computer center, student center. Dormitories wired for high-speed internet access and linked to campus network. Commuter students can connect to campus network. Online course registration, online library, helpline, wireless network available.

Student life. Freshman orientation: Available, $60 fee. Preregistration for classes offered. Several summer sessions with shorter programs held during the academic year; structured program allows students opportunity to establish link with faculty in intended major. **Policies:** Students who choose student housing must remain in dormitories for full academic year. Meal plan purchase required of all on-campus residents. Fish in 10 gallon or smaller tank allowed in dorm rooms. **Housing:** Guaranteed on-campus for freshmen. Coed dorms, apartments, wellness housing available. $235 partly refundable deposit, deadline 5/1. Living learning communities available. **Activities:** Bands, campus ministries, choral groups, dance, drama, international student organizations, literary magazine, music ensembles, musical theater, radio station, student government, student newspaper, TV station, Baptist Student Alliance, Student Political Movement, Young Democrats, ANGELS (AIDS Now Grasps Every Living Soul).

Athletics. NCAA. **Intercollegiate:** Baseball M, basketball, cheerleading, cross-country, golf M, soccer W, softball W, tennis. **Intramural:** Archery, basketball, bowling, football (non-tackle), golf, racquetball, soccer, softball, table tennis, tennis, volleyball. **Team name:** Bobcats.

Student services. Adult student services, career counseling, student employment services, financial aid counseling, health services, minority student services, personal counseling, placement for graduates, veterans' counselor, women's services. **Physically disabled:** Services for visually, hearing impaired.

Contact. E-mail: info@gcsu.edu
Phone: (478) 445-2774 Toll-free number: (800) 342-0471
Fax: (478) 445-1914
Mike Augustine, Director, Georgia College and State University, Campus Box 23, Milledgeville, GA 31061-0490

Georgia Institute of Technology

Atlanta, Georgia — **CB member**
www.gatech.edu — **CB code: 5248**

- Public 4-year university
- Residential campus in very large city
- 12,533 degree-seeking undergraduates: 5% part-time, 30% women, 7% African American, 17% Asian American, 5% Hispanic American, 5% international
- 6,379 degree-seeking graduate students
- 61% of applicants admitted
- SAT or ACT with writing, application essay required
- 77% graduate within 6 years; 30% enter graduate study

General. Founded in 1885. Regionally accredited. **Degrees:** 2,582 bachelor's awarded; master's, doctoral offered. **ROTC:** Army, Naval, Air Force. **Location:** Downtown Atlanta. **Calendar:** Semester, extensive summer session. **Full-time faculty:** 887 total; 98% have terminal degrees, 28% minority, 20% women. **Part-time faculty:** 9 total; 89% have terminal degrees, 22% minority, 22% women. **Class size:** 40% < 20, 31% 20-39, 8% 40-49, 15% 50-99, 7% >100. **Special facilities:** Nuclear magnetic resonance spectroscopy center, research institute, ovarian cancer institute, paper museum, mechanical properties research laboratory with scanning electron microscope, virtual factory laboratory, trading floor, advanced technology development center, advanced computing building, nanotechnology research center, wind tunnel.

Freshman class profile. 10,258 applied, 6,248 admitted, 2,640 enrolled.

Mid 50% test scores			
SAT critical reading:	600-690	Rank in top tenth:	58%
SAT math:	650-730	End year in good standing:	94%
SAT writing:	590-680	Return as sophomores:	93%
ACT composite:	27-31	Out-of-state:	31%
GPA 3.75 or higher:	60%	Live on campus:	97%
GPA 3.50-3.74:	25%	International:	7%
GPA 3.0-3.49:	15%	Fraternities:	25%
Rank in top quarter:	87%	Sororities:	31%

Basis for selection. School achievement record and SAT math score most important, followed by SAT verbal score. Activities, leadership, and personal statement required. Test scores accepted through November test dates for competition in President's Scholarship Program; accepted through December test date for admission consideration. **Homeschooled:** If home school not accredited by an approved Council for Higher Education accreditation organization, the following must be provided: official documentation of all subjects studied, credit earned per subject, time span of each unit, bibliography of all textbooks used, grades, verification of completion of college preparatory curriculum.

High school preparation. College-preparatory program required. 16 units required. Required units include English 4, mathematics 4, social studies 3, science 3 (laboratory 2) and foreign language 2.

2008-2009 Annual costs. Tuition/fees: $6,040; $25,182 out-of-state. Room/board: $7,694. Books/supplies: $2,500. Personal expenses: $1,500.

2008-2009 Financial aid. Need-based: 1,976 full-time freshmen applied for aid; 808 were judged to have need; 777 of these received aid. Average need met was 87%. Average scholarship/grant was $8,947; average loan $4,666. 55% of total undergraduate aid awarded as scholarships/grants, 45% as loans/jobs. **Non-need-based:** Awarded to 4,362 full-time undergraduates, including 1,322 freshmen. Scholarships awarded for academics, alumni affiliation, athletics, leadership, state residency. **Additional information:** Georgia Tech Promise Program offers a debt-free degree to qualified Georgia residents with family income less than $33,300.

Application procedures. Admission: Closing date 1/15 (postmark date). $50 fee, may be waived for applicants with need. Admission notification 3/15. Must reply by May 1 or within 2 week(s) if notified thereafter. Nonresident applicants advised to apply early. **Financial aid:** Closing date 3/1. FAFSA, institutional form required. Applicants notified on a rolling basis starting 4/1; must reply by 5/1.

Academics. Special study options: Accelerated study, combined bachelor's/graduate degree, cooperative education, cross-registration, distance learning, double major, dual enrollment of high school students, ESL, honors, independent study, internships, student-designed major, study abroad. Dual degree program (3-2); Regent's Engineering Transfer Program with 14 colleges in the University System of Georgia; Georgia Tech Regional Engineering Program offers undergraduate and graduate engineering degrees in collaboration with Armstrong Atlantic State University, Georgia Southern University, and Savannah State University. **Credit/placement by examination:** AP, CLEP, IB, SAT, ACT, institutional tests. **Support services:** Learning center, pre-admission summer program, reduced course load, remedial instruction, study skills assistance, tutoring, writing center.

Majors. Architecture: Architecture. **Biology:** General, biochemistry. **Business:** Business admin, managerial economics. **Communications:** Digital media. **Computer sciences:** General. **Engineering:** Aerospace, biomedical, chemical, civil, computer, electrical, environmental, industrial, materials, mechanical, nuclear, textile. **History:** Science/technology. **Interdisciplinary:** Global studies, science/society. **Math:** Applied. **Physical sciences:** Chemistry, geology, physics, polymer chemistry. **Psychology:** Industrial. **Public administration:** Policy analysis. **Social sciences:** International relations. **Visual/performing arts:** Industrial design. **Other:** Building construction, Discrete mathematics & algorithms, combinatorics, and optimization, Earth and atmospheric sciences, Global economics and modern languages/internationall affairs and modern language.

Most popular majors. Business/marketing 14%, computer/information sciences 6%, engineering/engineering technologies 56%.

Computing on campus. PC or laptop required. 2,018 workstations in dormitories, library, computer center, student center. Dormitories wired for high-speed internet access and linked to campus network. Commuter students can connect to campus network. Online course registration, online library, helpline, student web hosting, wireless network available.

Student life. Freshman orientation: Available, $150 fee. Preregistration for classes offered. Two-day program for new students, family and guests; 5 sessions offered throughout summer. **Policies:** First-time, first-year students not allowed to have car on campus during first semester. **Housing:** Guaranteed on-campus for freshmen. Coed dorms, single-sex dorms, special housing for disabled, apartments, fraternity/sorority housing, wellness housing available. $600 partly refundable deposit, deadline 5/1. **Activities:** Bands, campus ministries, choral groups, dance, drama, film society, international student organizations, literary magazine, music ensembles, Model UN, musical theater, radio station, student government, student newspaper, symphony orchestra, TV station, Campus Crusade for Christ, Christian Campus Fellowship, Muslim student association, African student association, Asian Christian Fellowship, College Democrats, College Republicans, Bahai campus association, Society of Hispanic Professional Engineers.

Athletics. NCAA. **Intercollegiate:** Baseball M, basketball, cheerleading, cross-country, diving, football (tackle) M, golf M, softball W, swimming, tennis, track and field, volleyball W. **Intramural:** Basketball, bowling, football (non-tackle), racquetball, soccer, softball, volleyball. **Team name:** Yellow Jackets.

Student services. Alcohol/substance abuse counseling, career counseling, student employment services, financial aid counseling, health services, legal services, minority student services, on-campus daycare, personal counseling, placement for graduates, women's services. **Physically disabled:** Services for visually, speech, hearing impaired. **Learning disabled:** Comprehensive services available.

Contact. E-mail: admission@gatech.edu
Phone: (404) 894-4154 Fax: (404) 894-9511
Rick Clark, Director of Undergraduate Admissions, Georgia Institute of Technology, Georgia Institute of Technology, Atlanta, GA 30332-0320

Georgia Southern University

Statesboro, Georgia — **CB member**
www.georgiasouthern.edu — **CB code: 5253**

- Public 4-year university
- Residential campus in large town
- 14,598 degree-seeking undergraduates: 6% part-time, 48% women, 22% African American, 1% Asian American, 2% Hispanic American, 1% international
- 2,148 degree-seeking graduate students
- 50% of applicants admitted
- SAT or ACT with writing required
- 45% graduate within 6 years; 50% enter graduate study

General. Founded in 1906. Regionally accredited. Carnegie Doctoral-Research university. **Degrees:** 2,384 bachelor's awarded; master's, doctoral offered. **ROTC:** Army. **Location:** 50 miles from Savannah, 200 miles from Atlanta. **Calendar:** Semester, extensive summer session. **Full-time faculty:** 711 total; 81% have terminal degrees, 16% minority, 46% women. **Part-time faculty:** 69 total; 33% have terminal degrees, 3% minority, 55% women. **Class size:** 26% < 20, 54% 20-39, 9% 40-49, 9% 50-99, 2% >100. **Special facilities:** Planetarium, electron microscope, woodland nature preserve, museum, eagle sanctuary, national tick collection, wildlife education center, raptor center, botanical garden, family life center, international studies center, institute for anthropology and parasitology, performing arts center, black box theater.

Freshman class profile. 8,620 applied, 4,335 admitted, 3,131 enrolled.

Mid 50% test scores			
SAT critical reading:	510-590	Rank in top tenth:	16%
SAT math:	510-600	End year in good standing:	75%
ACT composite:	21-24	Return as sophomores:	81%
GPA 3.75 or higher:	14%	Out-of-state:	4%
GPA 3.50-3.74:	13%	Live on campus:	68%
GPA 3.0-3.49:	40%	International:	1%
GPA 2.0-2.99:	33%	Fraternities:	8%
Rank in top quarter:	43%	Sororities:	12%

Basis for selection. GED not accepted. Test scores, high school GPA, and college preparatory curriculum considered. Students may be required to take placement exams. Audition required for music majors. **Homeschooled:** 1100 SAT (exclusive of Writing) or 24 ACT required. **Learning Disabled:** Admissions coordinated through student disability resource center.

High school preparation. College-preparatory program required. 16 units required. Required units include English 4, mathematics 4, social studies 3, science 3 (laboratory 2) and foreign language 2.

2008-2009 Annual costs. Tuition/fees: $4,348; $13,930 out-of-state. Room/board: $7,300. Books/supplies: $1,200. Personal expenses: $3,000.

2007-2008 Financial aid. Need-based: 2,750 full-time freshmen applied for aid; 1,538 were judged to have need; 1,488 of these received aid. Average need met was 60%. Average scholarship/grant was $5,619; average loan $3,230. 46% of total undergraduate aid awarded as scholarships/grants, 54% as loans/jobs. **Non-need-based:** Awarded to 941 full-time undergraduates, including 339 freshmen. Scholarships awarded for academics, alumni affiliation, art, athletics, leadership, minority status, music/drama, ROTC, state residency. **Additional information:** The majority of scholarships available are need-blind.

Application procedures. Admission: Closing date 5/1 (postmark date). $30 fee, may be waived for applicants with need. Admission notification on a rolling basis. **Financial aid:** Priority date 4/20; no closing date. FAFSA required. Applicants notified on a rolling basis starting 4/20.

Academics. Special study options: Accelerated study, combined bachelor's/graduate degree, cooperative education, distance learning, double major, ESL, honors, independent study, internships, student-designed major, study abroad, teacher certification program, Washington semester. **Credit/placement by examination:** AP, CLEP, IB, institutional tests. 30 credit hours maximum toward bachelor's degree. For AP exams, more credit hours will be awarded for higher-than-minimum scores. **Support services:** Learning center, pre-admission summer program, reduced course load, remedial instruction, study skills assistance, tutoring, writing center.

Majors. Biology: General, pharmacology. **Business:** Accounting, business admin, finance, hotel/motel admin, international, logistics, management information systems, managerial economics, marketing. **Communications:** General, journalism, public relations, radio/tv. **Communications technology:** Graphic/printing. **Computer sciences:** General, information systems. **Conservation:** Forestry. **Education:** Elementary, family/consumer sciences, middle, music, physical, special, technology/industrial arts. **Engineering:** General, civil, computer, electrical, mechanical. **Engineering technology:** Civil, construction, electrical, industrial management, mechanical, occupational safety. **Family/consumer sciences:** Clothing/textiles, family studies, food/nutrition. **Foreign languages:** French, German. **Health:** Cardiovascular technology, nursing (RN), predental, premedicine, prepharmacy, preveterinary, public health ed. **History:** General. **Math:** General. **Parks/recreation:** General, exercise sciences, health/fitness, sports admin. **Philosophy/religion:** Philosophy. **Physical sciences:** Chemistry, geology, physics. **Protective services:** Criminal justice. **Psychology:** General. **Social sciences:** Anthropology, economics, geography, international economic development, international relations, political science, sociology. **Visual/performing arts:** Art, dramatic, interior design, music performance, music theory/composition. **Other:** Modern languages, Sports medicine.

Most popular majors. Business/marketing 24%, education 13%, engineering/engineering technologies 7%, health sciences 6%, parks/recreation 6%.

Computing on campus. 2,385 workstations in dormitories, library, student center. Dormitories wired for high-speed internet access and linked to campus network. Commuter students can connect to campus network. Online course registration, online library, helpline, repair service, student web hosting, wireless network available.

Student life. Freshman orientation: Mandatory, $70 fee. Preregistration for classes offered. Freshman/parent program held for 2 days. **Policies:** Freshmen must live on campus. **Housing:** Coed dorms, special housing for disabled, apartments available. $200 partly refundable deposit. **Activities:** Bands, campus ministries, choral groups, dance, drama, film society, international student organizations, literary magazine, music ensembles, musical theater, radio station, student government, student newspaper, symphony orchestra, TV station.

Athletics. NCAA. **Intercollegiate:** Baseball M, basketball, cheerleading, cross-country W, diving W, football (tackle) M, golf M, soccer, softball W, swimming W, tennis, track and field W, volleyball W. **Intramural:** Basketball, bowling, football (non-tackle), golf, racquetball, soccer, softball, swimming, table tennis, tennis, volleyball, weight lifting. **Team name:** Eagles.

Student services. Adult student services, alcohol/substance abuse counseling, career counseling, services for economically disadvantaged, student employment services, financial aid counseling, health services, legal services, minority student services, on-campus daycare, personal counseling, veterans' counselor, women's services. **Physically disabled:** Services for visually, speech, hearing impaired. **Learning disabled:** Comprehensive services available.

Contact. E-mail: admissions@georgiasouthern.edu
Phone: (912) 478-5391 Fax: (912) 478-1156
Susan Davies, Director of Admission, Georgia Southern University, PO Box 8024, Statesboro, GA 30460

Georgia Southwestern State University

Americus, Georgia — **CB member**
www.gsw.edu — **CB code: 5250**

- Public 4-year university and liberal arts college
- Residential campus in large town
- 2,368 degree-seeking undergraduates: 26% part-time, 64% women, 32% African American, 1% Asian American, 1% Hispanic American, 2% international
- 284 degree-seeking graduate students
- 72% of applicants admitted
- SAT or ACT (ACT writing optional) required

General. Founded in 1906. Regionally accredited. **Degrees:** 362 bachelor's, 7 associate awarded; master's offered. **Location:** 135 miles from Atlanta. **Calendar:** Semester, limited summer session. **Full-time faculty:** 99 total; 69% have terminal degrees, 19% minority, 54% women. **Part-time faculty:** 56 total; 23% have terminal degrees, 16% minority, 64% women. **Class size:** 49% < 20, 44% 20-39, 5% 40-49, 2% 50-99. **Special facilities:** Observatory, glass blowing studio, golf course, indoor climbing wall.

Freshman class profile. 1,293 applied, 930 admitted, 478 enrolled.

Mid 50% test scores		**Rank in top quarter:**	42%
SAT critical reading:	450-550	**Rank in top tenth:**	19%
SAT math:	430-530	**Return as sophomores:**	76%
SAT writing:	430-520	**Out-of-state:**	4%
ACT composite:	17-20	**Live on campus:**	65%
GPA 3.75 or higher:	15%	**International:**	4%
GPA 3.50-3.74:	13%	**Fraternities:**	20%
GPA 3.0-3.49:	27%	**Sororities:**	16%
GPA 2.0-2.99:	44%		

Basis for selection. School achievement record, test scores most important. **Homeschooled:** Statement describing homeschool structure and mission, transcript of courses and grades, letter of recommendation (nonparent) required. Must complete home schooled application or submit SAT along with 7 SAT Subject tests or a portfolio outlining work in 5 critical college preparatory areas.

High school preparation. College-preparatory program required. 16 units required. Required and recommended units include English 4, mathematics 4, social studies 1, history 2, science 3 (laboratory 2), foreign language 2 and academic electives 2.

2008-2009 Annual costs. Tuition/fees: $3,836; $13,128 out-of-state. Room/board: $5,694. Books/supplies: $1,000.

2007-2008 Financial aid. Non-need-based: Scholarships awarded for academics, athletics, leadership.

Application procedures. Admission: Closing date 7/21 (postmark date). $25 fee, may be waived for applicants with need. Admission notification on a rolling basis. Must reply by May 1 or within 3 week(s) if notified thereafter. **Financial aid:** Priority date 4/1, closing date 6/1. FAFSA, institutional form required. Applicants notified on a rolling basis starting 3/1.

Academics. Special study options: Accelerated study, distance learning, double major, dual enrollment of high school students, ESL, honors, independent study, internships, study abroad, teacher certification program. 3+2 program in engineering with Georgia Institute of Technology. **Credit/placement by examination:** AP, CLEP, institutional tests. 45 credit hours maximum toward bachelor's degree. **Support services:** Learning center, reduced course load, remedial instruction, study skills assistance, tutoring, writing center.

Majors. Biology: General. **Business:** Accounting, business admin, human resources, marketing. **Computer sciences:** General, computer science. **Education:** Elementary, middle, physical, special. **Engineering technology:** Computer. **Health:** Nursing (RN). **History:** General. **Math:** General. **Parks/recreation:** Facilities management. **Physical sciences:** Chemistry, geology. **Psychology:** General. **Social sciences:** Political science, sociology. **Visual/performing arts:** Art, dramatic.

Most popular majors. Business/marketing 34%, education 24%, health sciences 8%, psychology 9%, social sciences 7%.

Computing on campus. 550 workstations in dormitories, library, computer center, student center. Dormitories wired for high-speed internet access and linked to campus network. Commuter students can connect to campus network. Online course registration, online library, wireless network available.

Student life. **Freshman orientation:** Mandatory, $70 fee. Preregistration for classes offered. Three sessions in summer; includes parents' program. **Housing:** Guaranteed on-campus for freshmen. Coed dorms, apartments, fraternity/sorority housing available. $250 deposit. **Activities:** Bands, campus ministries, choral groups, drama, international student organizations, literary magazine, music ensembles, musical theater, student government, student newspaper, TV station, Baptist Student Union, Wesley Foundation, Young Republicans, Young Democrats, SABU, Habitat for Humanity, campus activity board, ZEPHYR recruitment team, College Republicans.

Athletics. NCAA. **Intercollegiate:** Baseball M, basketball, cross-country W, golf, soccer, softball W, tennis. **Intramural:** Badminton, basketball, football (non-tackle), racquetball, soccer, table tennis, tennis, volleyball, weight lifting, wrestling M. **Team name:** Hurricanes.

Student services. Career counseling, services for economically disadvantaged, student employment services, financial aid counseling, health services, personal counseling, veterans' counselor. **Physically disabled:** Services for visually, speech, hearing impaired.

Contact. E-mail: gswapps@canes.gsw.edu
Phone: (229) 928-1273 Toll-free number: (800) 338-0082
Fax: (229) 931-2059
Gaye Hayes, Dean of Students & Admissions Services, Georgia Southwestern State University, 800 Georgia Southwestern State University Drive, Americus, GA 31709-9957

Georgia State University

Atlanta, Georgia — **CB member**
www.gsu.edu — **CB code: 5251**

- Public 4-year university
- Commuter campus in very large city
- 20,179 degree-seeking undergraduates: 24% part-time, 60% women, 29% African American, 10% Asian American, 5% Hispanic American, 3% international
- 6,903 degree-seeking graduate students
- 55% of applicants admitted
- SAT or ACT with writing required
- 43% graduate within 6 years

General. Founded in 1913. Regionally accredited. Courses offered at Alpharetta Center and Brookhaven Center. Distance learning and web courses available in College of Health and Human Sciences and College of Education. **Degrees:** 3,627 bachelor's awarded; master's, doctoral, first professional offered. **ROTC:** Army, Naval, Air Force. **Location:** Downtown. **Calendar:** Semester, extensive summer session. **Full-time faculty:** 1,120 total; 84% have terminal degrees, 22% minority, 48% women. **Part-time faculty:** 453 total. **Class size:** 18% < 20, 46% 20-39, 21% 40-49, 11% 50-99, 4% >100. **Special facilities:** Viral immunology center, writing studio, advanced biotechnology center, Asian studies center, multi-media instructional lab, child development center, performing arts center, language acquisition and research centers, military science leadership lab, music media center, learning disorders center, speech and language center, hearing center.

Freshman class profile. 10,301 applied, 5,684 admitted, 2,820 enrolled.

Mid 50% test scores			
SAT critical reading:	490-590	GPA 2.0-2.99:	15%
SAT math:	490-590	Return as sophomores:	83%
ACT composite:	21-25	Out-of-state:	4%
GPA 3.75 or higher:	10%	Live on campus:	48%
GPA 3.50-3.74:	19%	International:	2%
GPA 3.0-3.49:	56%	Fraternities:	4%
		Sororities:	5%

Basis for selection. GED not accepted. 430 SAT verbal and 400 SAT math or 17 ACT English and 17 ACT math required. Audition and interview required for music majors. Portfolio required for art majors. **Home-schooled:** Transcript of courses and grades required. 1090 SAT (exclusive of Writing) with 430 verbal and 400 math subscores or 24 ACT with 17 English and math subscores required. SAT Subject Test option available: 520 English Writing, 530 Literature, 500 Math IC or 570 Math IIC, 520 Biology, 540 Chemistry or 590 Physics, 560 American History and Social Studies, and 540 World History.

High school preparation. College-preparatory program required. 16 units required. Required units include English 4, mathematics 4, social studies 2, history 1, science 3 (laboratory 2) and foreign language 2. 1 life sciences lab, 1 physical sciences lab plus additional science unit; foreign language units must be same language; math units must be algebra I, geometry, algebra II, and higher.

2008-2009 Annual costs. Tuition/fees: $6,056; $20,624 out-of-state. Room only: $6,550. Books/supplies: $1,000. Personal expenses: $1,970.

2008-2009 Financial aid. All financial aid based on need. 2,342 full-time freshmen applied for aid; 1,783 were judged to have need; 1,713 of these received aid. Average need met was 27%. Average scholarship/grant was $2,684; average loan $2,994. 45% of total undergraduate aid awarded as scholarships/grants, 55% as loans/jobs.

Application procedures. **Admission:** Priority date 2/1; deadline 3/1 (postmark date). $50 fee, may be waived for applicants with need. Admission notification on a rolling basis beginning on or about 10/1. **Financial aid:** Priority date 4/1, closing date 11/1. FAFSA required. Applicants notified on a rolling basis starting 3/30; must reply within 2 week(s) of notification.

Academics. **Special study options:** Accelerated study, cooperative education, cross-registration, distance learning, double major, dual enrollment of high school students, ESL, honors, independent study, internships, student-designed major, study abroad, teacher certification program. Freshman learning communities available. **Credit/placement by examination:** AP, CLEP, IB, institutional tests. 30 credit hours maximum toward bachelor's degree. Some credit awarded for DANTES subject examinations. **Support services:** Learning center, pre-admission summer program, reduced course load, remedial instruction, study skills assistance, tutoring, writing center.

Honors college/program. 3.3 GPA and 1800 SAT or 26 ACT required.

Majors. **Area/ethnic studies:** African-American, Asian, regional, women's. **Biology:** General. **Business:** Accounting, actuarial science, business admin, finance, insurance, international, managerial economics, marketing, real estate. **Communications:** General, journalism. **Computer sciences:** General, computer science. **Education:** Art, early childhood, kindergarten/preschool. **Foreign languages:** General, classics, French, German, linguistics, Spanish. **Health:** Dietetics, nursing (RN), respiratory therapy technology. **History:** General. **Interdisciplinary:** Ancient studies, classical/archaeology, gerontology, global studies. **Math:** General. **Parks/recreation:** Exercise sciences, health/fitness. **Philosophy/religion:** Philosophy, religion. **Physical sciences:** Chemistry, geology, physics. **Protective services:** Criminal justice. **Psychology:** General. **Public administration:** Policy analysis, social work. **Social sciences:** Anthropology, economics, geography, international economics, political science, sociology, urban studies. **Visual/performing arts:** Art, art history/conservation, design, drawing, film/cinema, music management, music performance, theater history.

Most popular majors. Biology 6%, business/marketing 32%, education 6%, psychology 8%, social sciences 14%, visual/performing arts 6%.

Computing on campus. 1,000 workstations in library, computer center. Dormitories wired for high-speed internet access and linked to campus network. Commuter students can connect to campus network. Online course registration, online library, helpline, student web hosting, wireless network available.

Student life. **Freshman orientation:** Mandatory, $56 fee. Preregistration for classes offered. Various summer sessions offered. **Housing:** Coed dorms, special housing for disabled, apartments, wellness housing available. $525 nonrefundable deposit. **Activities:** Bands, campus ministries, choral groups, dance, drama, film society, literary magazine, music ensembles, radio station, student government, student newspaper, symphony orchestra, TV station, African students association, Amnesty International, Brazillian student association, Bridge Builders, Campus Civitan, Catholic student association, Chinese student union, College Republicans, Christian legal society.

Athletics. NCAA. **Intercollegiate:** Baseball M, basketball, cross-country, golf, soccer, softball W, tennis, track and field, volleyball. **Intramural:** Basketball, bowling, golf, racquetball, softball, table tennis, tennis. **Team name:** Panthers.

Student services. Career counseling, student employment services, financial aid counseling, health services, minority student services, on-campus daycare, personal counseling, placement for graduates, veterans' counselor. **Physically disabled:** Services for visually, speech, hearing impaired.

Contact. E-mail: admissions@gsu.edu
Phone: (404) 413-2500 Fax: (404) 413-2002
Scott Burke, Director of Admissions, Georgia State University, Box 4009, Atlanta, GA 30302-4009

Herzing College

Atlanta, Georgia
www.herzing.edu — **CB code: 2342**

- For-profit 3-year business and technical college
- Commuter campus in very large city

- 70% of applicants admitted
- Interview required

General. Founded in 1949. Regionally accredited. **Degrees:** 55 bachelor's, 35 associate awarded. **Location:** 120 miles from Birmingham, Alabama; 70 miles from Chattanooga, Tennessee. **Calendar:** Semester, extensive summer session. **Full-time faculty:** 6 total. **Part-time faculty:** 27 total. **Class size:** 84% < 20, 16% 20-39.

Freshman class profile. 443 applied, 311 admitted, 177 enrolled.

Basis for selection. Entrance test and evaluation for all applicants. SAT/ACT scores may be used for academic advising.

2008-2009 Annual costs. Tuition/fees: $11,640. Costs may vary by program.

Financial aid. **Non-need-based:** Scholarships awarded for academics.

Application procedures. **Admission:** No deadline. No application fee. Admission notification on a rolling basis. **Financial aid:** No deadline. FAFSA, institutional form required. Applicants notified on a rolling basis.

Academics. Students train on types of equipment used in the field. **Special study options:** Distance learning, independent study, internships, liberal arts/career combination. **Credit/placement by examination:** CLEP, IB, institutional tests. **Support services:** Learning center, study skills assistance, tutoring.

Majors. **BACHELOR'S. Business:** Business admin. **Computer sciences:** Information systems, programming. **ASSOCIATE. Business:** Business admin. **Computer sciences:** Information systems, programming. **Engineering technology:** Electrical.

Most popular majors. Business/marketing 31%, computer/information sciences 41%.

Computing on campus. 157 workstations in library, computer center. Online library available.

Student life. **Freshman orientation:** Mandatory, $25 fee. Preregistration for classes offered. Orientation held beginning of each term for 2 hours. **Activities:** Student government.

Student services. Career counseling, student employment services, financial aid counseling, personal counseling, placement for graduates, veterans' counselor.

Contact. E-mail: info@atl.herzing.edu
Phone: (404) 816-4533 Toll-free number: (800) 573-4533
Fax: (404) 816-5576
Jamey Kinard, Director of Admissions, Herzing College, 3393 Peachtree Road NE, Suite 1003, Atlanta, GA 30326

ITT Technical Institute: Duluth
Duluth, Georgia

- For-profit 4-year technical college
- Commuter campus in large town

General. Accredited by ACICS. **Calendar:** Quarter.

Contact. Phone: (866) 489-8818
Director of Recruitment, 10700 Abbotts Bridge Road, Duluth, GA 30097

Kennesaw State University
Kennesaw, Georgia — **CB member**
www.kennesaw.edu — **CB code: 5359**

- Public 4-year university
- Commuter campus in large town
- 19,113 degree-seeking undergraduates: 25% part-time, 60% women, 10% African American, 3% Asian American, 3% Hispanic American, 3% international
- 2,178 degree-seeking graduate students
- 63% of applicants admitted
- SAT or ACT (ACT writing optional) required
- 34% graduate within 6 years

General. Founded in 1963. Regionally accredited. **Degrees:** 2,854 bachelor's awarded; master's, doctoral offered. **ROTC:** Army, Air Force. **Location:** 20 miles from Atlanta. **Calendar:** Semester, limited summer session. **Full-time faculty:** 673 total; 76% have terminal degrees, 23% minority, 50% women. **Part-time faculty:** 493 total; 31% have terminal degrees, 17% minority, 60% women. **Class size:** 24% < 20, 53% 20-39, 11% 40-49, 11% 50-99, 1% >100. **Special facilities:** Educational technology center, presentation technology department, teacher resource and activity center, 2 art galleries.

Freshman class profile. 7,921 applied, 5,008 admitted, 2,799 enrolled.

Mid 50% test scores		**Rank in top quarter:**	53%
SAT critical reading:	500-570	**Rank in top tenth:**	21%
SAT math:	500-580	**End year in good standing:**	82%
SAT writing:	470-560	**Return as sophomores:**	75%
ACT composite:	20-24	**Out-of-state:**	2%
GPA 3.75 or higher:	9%	**Live on campus:**	45%
GPA 3.50-3.74:	13%	**International:**	1%
GPA 3.0-3.49:	44%	**Fraternities:**	1%
GPA 2.0-2.99:	34%	**Sororities:**	1%

Basis for selection. GED not accepted. 2.5 GPA in college prep courses and 490 SAT verbal/460 SAT math or 20 ACT English/19 ACT math required. Applicants with test scores below minimum must take institutional placement exams in appropriate subject areas. Audition required of music majors. Portfolio required of art majors. **Homeschooled:** Students considered based on portfolio, standardized tests scores, extra-curricular activities, and recommendations.

High school preparation. College-preparatory program required. 16 units required. Required units include English 4, mathematics 4, social studies 3, science 3 (laboratory 3) and foreign language 2.

2008-2009 Annual costs. Tuition/fees: $4,144; $13,726 out-of-state. Room only: $5,100. Books/supplies: $1,000. Personal expenses: $1,464.

2008-2009 Financial aid. **Need-based:** 48% of total undergraduate aid awarded as scholarships/grants, 52% as loans/jobs. **Non-need-based:** Scholarships awarded for academics, alumni affiliation, art, athletics, job skills, leadership, minority status, music/drama, ROTC, state residency.

Application procedures. **Admission:** Closing date 5/16 (receipt date). $40 fee, may be waived for applicants with need. Admission notification on a rolling basis beginning on or about 1/1. **Financial aid:** Priority date 4/1, closing date 7/1. FAFSA required. Applicants notified on a rolling basis starting 5/15.

Academics. **Special study options:** Cooperative education, cross-registration, distance learning, double major, ESL, honors, internships, study abroad, teacher certification program, weekend college. **Credit/placement by examination:** AP, CLEP, IB, institutional tests. 30 credit hours maximum toward bachelor's degree. **Support services:** Learning center, reduced course load, remedial instruction, study skills assistance, tutoring, writing center.

Honors college/program. 3.5 GPA and 1200 SAT (exclusive of Writing) required. Joint enrollment honors program for high school junior and seniors; requires 3.0 GPA, 1100 SAT with 530 SAT verbal and math subscores (exclusive of writing) or 25 ACT, with 24 English and 20 Math subscores.

Majors. **Area/ethnic studies:** African. **Biology:** General, biochemistry, biotechnology. **Business:** Accounting, business admin, finance, international, managerial economics, marketing, sales/distribution. **Communications:** General. **Computer sciences:** General, information systems, security. **Education:** Art, biology, elementary, English, mathematics, middle, music, physical, social studies. **Health:** Nursing (RN). **History:** General. **Math:** General. **Parks/recreation:** Exercise sciences, sports admin. **Physical sciences:** Chemistry. **Protective services:** Criminal justice. **Psychology:** General. **Public administration:** Human services. **Social sciences:** Anthropology, cartography, geography, international relations, political science, sociology. **Visual/performing arts:** Art, dramatic, music performance. **Other:** Modern language and culture.

Most popular majors. Business/marketing 28%, communications/journalism 7%, education 18%, health sciences 6%, psychology 6%, social sciences 6%.

Computing on campus. 1,400 workstations in library, computer center, student center. Dormitories wired for high-speed internet access. Commuter students can connect to campus network. Online course registration, online library, helpline, wireless network available.

Student life. **Freshman orientation:** Mandatory, $25 fee. Preregistration for classes offered. Held prior to semester. **Housing:** Apartments available. $350 nonrefundable deposit. **Activities:** Bands, campus ministries, choral groups, dance, drama, international student organizations, literary magazine, music ensembles, Model UN, musical theater, radio station, student government, student newspaper, symphony orchestra, Baptist student union, Student Nurses Association, College Ambassadors, volunteer club, American Marketing Association, African American student alliance, Circle K, Catholic student association.

Athletics. NCAA. **Intercollegiate:** Baseball M, basketball, cheerleading M, cross-country, golf, soccer W, softball W, tennis, track and field. **Intramural:** Basketball, bowling, football (non-tackle), soccer, softball, tennis, volleyball. **Team name:** Fighting Owls.

Student services. Adult student services, alcohol/substance abuse counseling, career counseling, student employment services, financial aid counseling, health services, minority student services, personal counseling, placement for graduates, veterans' counselor. **Physically disabled:** Services for visually, speech, hearing impaired.

Contact. E-mail: ksuadmit@kennesaw.edu
Phone: (770) 423-6300 Fax: (770) 423-6541
Angela Evans, Director of Admissions, Kennesaw State University, 1000 Chastain Road, Kennesaw, GA 30144-5591

LaGrange College

LaGrange, Georgia — **CB member**
www.lagrange.edu — **CB code: 5362**

- Private 4-year liberal arts college affiliated with United Methodist Church
- Residential campus in large town
- 834 degree-seeking undergraduates: 8% part-time, 57% women, 22% African American, 2% Asian American, 2% Hispanic American, 2% international
- 116 degree-seeking graduate students
- 54% of applicants admitted
- SAT or ACT (ACT writing optional), application essay required
- 54% graduate within 6 years

General. Founded in 1831. Regionally accredited. **Degrees:** 226 bachelor's, 1 associate awarded; master's offered. **Location:** 70 miles from Atlanta, 45 miles from Columbus. **Calendar:** 4-1-4, limited summer session. **Full-time faculty:** 67 total; 78% have terminal degrees, 4% minority, 45% women. **Part-time faculty:** 48 total; 25% have terminal degrees, 6% minority, 54% women. **Class size:** 80% < 20, 20% 20-39, less than 1% 50-99. **Special facilities:** Performing arts auditorium, natatorium, art center.

Freshman class profile. 1,310 applied, 703 admitted, 157 enrolled.

Mid 50% test scores			
SAT critical reading:	460-580	**Rank in top tenth:**	31%
SAT math:	470-590	**End year in good standing:**	98%
ACT composite:	19-24	**Return as sophomores:**	52%
GPA 3.75 or higher:	27%	**Out-of-state:**	16%
GPA 3.50-3.74:	20%	**Live on campus:**	82%
GPA 3.0-3.49:	47%	**International:**	2%
GPA 2.0-2.99:	6%	**Fraternities:**	10%
Rank in top quarter:	58%	**Sororities:**	20%

Basis for selection. School achievement record and test scores most important. Interview and recommendations considered. Separate application typically during sophomore year for nursing applicants. Students undergo a writing sample and math placement test prior to registration. **Homeschooled:** Bibliography of high school readings, including textbooks, letter of recommendation from outside the home required.

High school preparation. College-preparatory program recommended. 14 units required; 16 recommended. Required and recommended units include English 4, mathematics 4, social studies 3, science 3 and foreign language 2.

2008-2009 Annual costs. Tuition/fees: $19,900. Room/board: $8,168. Books/supplies: $1,000. Personal expenses: $1,975.

2007-2008 Financial aid. Need-based: 207 full-time freshmen applied for aid; 171 were judged to have need; 170 of these received aid. Average need met was 87%. Average scholarship/grant was $10,329; average loan $3,231. 65% of total undergraduate aid awarded as scholarships/grants, 35% as loans/jobs. **Non-need-based:** Awarded to 272 full-time undergraduates, including 77 freshmen. Scholarships awarded for academics, art, leadership, music/drama, religious affiliation, state residency.

Application procedures. Admission: Priority date 3/1; no deadline. $30 fee, may be waived for applicants with need, free for online applicants. Admission notification on a rolling basis beginning on or about 9/15. Early admission candidates must be highly recommended by counselors and parents. **Financial aid:** Priority date 3/1; no closing date. FAFSA required. Applicants notified on a rolling basis starting 3/15; must reply by 8/15 or within 2 week(s) of notification.

Academics. Special study options: Accelerated study, combined bachelor's/graduate degree, double major, dual enrollment of high school students, independent study, internships, liberal arts/career combination, student-designed major, study abroad, teacher certification program, Washington semester. **Credit/placement by examination:** AP, CLEP, IB, institutional tests. 6 credit hours maximum toward bachelor's degree. USAFI credit accepted. **Support services:** Study skills assistance, tutoring, writing center.

Majors. Biology: General, biochemistry. **Business:** Accounting, business admin, organizational behavior. **Computer sciences:** General, computer science. **Education:** Elementary. **Foreign languages:** Spanish. **Health:** Nursing (RN). **History:** General. **Math:** General. **Philosophy/religion:** Religion. **Physical sciences:** Chemistry. **Psychology:** General. **Public administration:** Social work. **Social sciences:** Political science, sociology. **Theology:** Religious ed. **Visual/performing arts:** General, dramatic.

Most popular majors. Biology 11%, business/marketing 27%, education 8%, health sciences 10%, public administration/social services 8%, social sciences 11%, visual/performing arts 9%.

Computing on campus. 141 workstations in dormitories, library, computer center. Dormitories wired for high-speed internet access and linked to campus network. Commuter students can connect to campus network. Online library, helpline, student web hosting, wireless network available.

Student life. Freshman orientation: Mandatory. Preregistration for classes offered. Three 2-day summer orientation sessions available. **Housing:** Guaranteed on-campus for freshmen. Coed dorms, single-sex dorms, apartments, fraternity/sorority housing available. $100 fully refundable deposit, deadline 4/9. **Activities:** Pep band, campus ministries, choral groups, drama, international student organizations, literary magazine, music ensembles, musical theater, student government, student newspaper, symphony orchestra, Wesley Fellowship, Baptist Student Union, Circle-K, Rotaract, Interfaith Council, volunteer corps, Habitat for Humanity, Catholic group.

Athletics. NCAA. **Intercollegiate:** Baseball M, basketball, cheerleading M, cross-country, football (tackle) M, golf M, lacrosse W, soccer, softball W, swimming, tennis, volleyball W. **Intramural:** Basketball, football (tackle) M, softball, tennis, volleyball. **Team name:** Panthers.

Student services. Adult student services, chaplain/spiritual director, career counseling, student employment services, financial aid counseling, health services, personal counseling, placement for graduates.

Contact. E-mail: admission@lagrange.edu
Phone: (706) 880-8005 Toll-free number: (800) 593-2885
Fax: (706) 880-8010
Dana Paul, Vice President for Enrollment Management, LaGrange College, 601 Broad Street, LaGrange, GA 30240-2999

Life University

Marietta, Georgia
www.life.edu — **CB code: 7006**

- Private 4-year university
- Very large city
- 597 degree-seeking undergraduates: 30% part-time, 47% women, 26% African American, 5% Asian American, 6% Hispanic American, 1% Native American
- 1,574 degree-seeking graduate students
- 28% of applicants admitted
- SAT or ACT with writing required

General. Regionally accredited. **Degrees:** 145 bachelor's, 5 associate awarded; master's, first professional offered. **Location:** 10 miles from downtown Atlanta. **Calendar:** Quarter, limited summer session. **Full-time faculty:** 99 total; 34% women. **Part-time faculty:** 34 total; 38% women. **Class size:** 74% < 20, 14% 20-39, 3% 40-49, 9% 50-99.

Freshman class profile. 359 applied, 101 admitted, 46 enrolled.

Mid 50% test scores		**GPA 3.50-3.74:**	9%
SAT critical reading:	390-490	**GPA 3.0-3.49:**	26%
SAT math:	360-460	**GPA 2.0-2.99:**	46%
ACT composite:	17-21	**Return as sophomores:**	70%
GPA 3.75 or higher:	15%	**Out-of-state:**	65%

Basis for selection. Standardized test scores and high school record most important. 2.0 GPA and 1430 SAT (including Writing) or 18 ACT important. **Homeschooled:** Transcript of courses and grades required. **Learning Disabled:** Letter from doctor required.

High school preparation. College-preparatory program recommended.

2008-2009 Annual costs. Tuition/fees: $7,830. Books/supplies: $1,650. Personal expenses: $2,187.

2008-2009 Financial aid. Need-based: 76 full-time freshmen applied for aid; 62 were judged to have need; 58 of these received aid. Average scholarship/grant was $2,000; average loan $3,000. 43% of total undergraduate aid awarded as scholarships/grants, 57% as loans/jobs. **Non-need-based:** Awarded to 149 full-time undergraduates, including 56 freshmen. Scholarships awarded for academics.

Application procedures. Admission: Closing date 9/1 (postmark date). $50 fee, may be waived for applicants with need. Admission notification on a rolling basis. **Financial aid:** No deadline. FAFSA required. Applicants notified on a rolling basis starting 5/1.

Academics. Special study options: Accelerated study, double major, ESL, independent study, internships. **Credit/placement by examination:** AP, CLEP, SAT, ACT. **Support services:** Learning center, reduced course load, remedial instruction, study skills assistance, tutoring, writing center.

Majors. Biology: General. **Business:** General, management information systems. **Health:** Dietetics. **Interdisciplinary:** Nutrition sciences. **Parks/recreation:** Exercise sciences.

Most popular majors. Biology 53%, business/marketing 28%, interdisciplinary studies 17%.

Computing on campus. Commuter students can connect to campus network. Online course registration, online library, wireless network available.

Student life. Freshman orientation: Mandatory. Two-day program usually held on Thursday and Friday before quarter begins. **Housing:** Apartments available. $250 partly refundable deposit. **Activities:** International student organizations, student newspaper.

Athletics. Intramural: Basketball, football (tackle), volleyball. **Team name:** Eagles.

Student services. Alcohol/substance abuse counseling, financial aid counseling, personal counseling.

Contact. E-mail: admissions@life.edu
Phone: (770) 426-2884 Toll-free number: (800) 543-3202
Fax: (770) 426-2895
Deborah Heairlston, Director of New Student Development, Life University, 1269 Barclay Circle, Marietta, GA 30060

Luther Rice University
Lithonia, Georgia
www.lru.edu

- Private 4-year Bible and seminary college
- Very large city
- 337 degree-seeking undergraduates

General. Regionally accredited. **Calendar:** Semester. **Full-time faculty:** 13 total. **Part-time faculty:** 23 total.

Freshman class profile. 51 enrolled.

Basis for selection. Open admission, but selective for some programs.

Application procedures. Financial aid: Closing date 8/18.

Academics. Credit/placement by examination: CLEP.

Majors. Other: Christian worldview/apologetics.

Contact. E-mail: admissions@lru.edu
Toll-free number: (800) 442-1577
Luther Rice University, 3038 Evans Mill Road, Lithonia, GA 30038

Macon State College
Macon, Georgia — **CB member**
www.maconstate.edu — **CB code: 5439**

- Public 4-year business and health science college
- Commuter campus in small city
- 6,303 degree-seeking undergraduates
- 55% of applicants admitted

General. Founded in 1968. Regionally accredited. **Degrees:** 353 bachelor's, 341 associate awarded. **Location:** 85 miles from Atlanta. **Calendar:** Semester, extensive summer session. **Full-time faculty:** 195 total. **Part-time faculty:** 111 total. **Special facilities:** Botanical gardens.

Freshman class profile. 4,242 applied, 2,327 admitted, 1,567 enrolled.

Basis for selection. 480 SAT verbal or 21 ACT English, 440 SAT math or 19 ACT math required for unconditional admission; early admission requires 1100 SAT (exclusive of Writing) with 530 SAT verbal or 24 ACT with 23 ACT English. College-preparatory requirements waived for students in career programs and adult applicants. SAT or ACT recommended. Interview required for respiratory therapy, health information technology, health information management, health services administration, and technology programs. Education and nursing may require interview. **Homeschooled:** Recent GED or home schooled applicants must submit SAT and provide portfolio indicating courses taken.

High school preparation. 16 units required. Required units include English 4, mathematics 4, social studies 1, history 2, science 3 (laboratory 2) and foreign language 2.

2008-2009 Annual costs. Tuition/fees: $2,182; $8,164 out-of-state. Books/supplies: $1,040. Personal expenses: $5,168.

2007-2008 Financial aid. All financial aid based on need.

Application procedures. Admission: Closing date 7/23 (receipt date). $20 fee, may be waived for applicants with need. Admission notification on a rolling basis. **Financial aid:** Priority date 4/1; no closing date. FAFSA required. Applicants notified on a rolling basis starting 4/15; must reply within 2 week(s) of notification.

Academics. Special study options: Distance learning, dual enrollment of high school students, honors, internships, liberal arts/career combination, study abroad, teacher certification program. **Credit/placement by examination:** AP, CLEP, IB, institutional tests. 40 credit hours maximum toward associate degree, 40 toward bachelor's. **Support services:** Learning center, pre-admission summer program, reduced course load, remedial instruction, study skills assistance, tutoring, writing center.

Majors. Business: General, accounting, business admin, marketing, operations. **Communications:** General. **Computer sciences:** Applications programming, information systems, programming. **Education:** Early childhood. **Health:** Health care admin, health services, medical records admin, nursing (RN). **Math:** General. **Public administration:** General, human services.

Computing on campus. 150 workstations in library, computer center, student center. Commuter students can connect to campus network. Online course registration, online library, helpline, wireless network available.

Student life. Freshman orientation: Mandatory, $25 fee. Preregistration for classes offered. **Activities:** Choral groups, drama, literary magazine, music ensembles, Model UN, musical theater, student government, student newspaper, TV station, black student unification, association of nursing students, Spanish club, Baptist student union, astronomy club, pre-med club, honors student association, Amnesty International, information technology club.

Athletics. Intramural: Basketball, bowling, golf, softball, swimming, table tennis, tennis, volleyball.

Student services. Career counseling, student employment services, financial aid counseling, health services, minority student services, personal counseling, veterans' counselor.

Contact. E-mail: admissions@maconstate.edu
Phone: (478) 471-2800 Toll-free number: (800) 272-7619
Fax: (478) 471-5343
Dee Minter, Associate Vice President for Enrollment Services, Macon State College, 100 College Station Drive, Macon, GA 31206-5145

Medical College of Georgia
Augusta, Georgia — **CB member**
www.mcg.edu — **CB code: 5406**

- Public two-year upper-division health science college
- Commuter campus in large city
- Test scores, application essay required

General. Founded in 1828. Regionally accredited. **Degrees:** 277 bachelor's awarded; master's, doctoral, first professional offered. **Location:** 157 miles from Atlanta. **Calendar:** Semester. **Full-time faculty:** 655 total; 88% have terminal degrees, 30% minority, 37% women. **Part-time faculty:** 148 total; 83% have terminal degrees, 18% minority, 46% women. **Special facilities:** 600-bed teaching hospital, over 80 clinics.

Student profile. 582 degree-seeking undergraduates, 1,873 degree-seeking graduate students.

Women:	86%	**Part-time:**	11%

Basis for selection. College transcript, application essay, standardized test scores required. Admission based on GPA, math and science test scores, 3 references, and statement of purpose. SAT or ACT and personal interview required. Minimum of 60 semester hours of transferable prescribed liberal arts courses required. Closing dates and score reports vary by program. Transfer accepted as juniors.

2008-2009 Annual costs. Tuition/fees: $5,568; $20,136 out-of-state. Declining balance account available for meals. Room only: $1,952.

Financial aid. Non-need-based: Scholarships awarded for academics, state residency. **Additional information:** State Hope scholarships only available to Georgia residents.

Application procedures. Admission: Rolling admission. $30 fee. **Financial aid:** Priority date 3/31, closing date 5/30. Applicants notified on a rolling basis; must reply within 2 weeks of notification. FAFSA, institutional form required.

Academics. Special study options: Combined bachelor's/graduate degree, distance learning, internships, liberal arts/career combination, study abroad. Cooperative program with Augusta State University. **Credit/placement by examination:** AP, CLEP.

Majors. Health: Clinical lab science, dental hygiene, medical radiologic technology/radiation therapy, medical records admin, nursing (RN), physician assistant, preop/surgical nursing, respiratory therapy technology, sonography.

Computing on campus. 323 workstations in library, student center. Commuter students can connect to campus network. Online library, wireless network available.

Student life. Housing: Coed dorms, apartments, wellness housing available. **Activities:** Student government, student newspaper, Christian Medical Society, Black Student Medical Alliance.

Athletics. Intramural: Badminton, basketball, football (non-tackle), golf, racquetball, soccer, softball, table tennis, volleyball, weight lifting.

Student services. Career counseling, student employment services, health services, minority student services, on-campus daycare, personal counseling.

Contact. E-mail: underadm@mcg.edu
Phone: (706) 721-2725 Toll-free number: (800) 519-3388
Fax: (706) 721-7279
Carol Nobles, Director of Student Recruitment and Admissions, Medical College of Georgia, Office of Academic Admissions, Room 170 Kelly Building, Augusta, GA 30912-7310

Mercer University

Macon, Georgia — **CB member**
www.mercer.edu — **CB code: 5409**

- Private 4-year university affiliated with Baptist faith
- Residential campus in small city
- 2,228 degree-seeking undergraduates: 3% part-time, 54% women, 17% African American, 6% Asian American, 3% Hispanic American, 3% international
- 3,115 degree-seeking graduate students
- 67% of applicants admitted
- SAT or ACT (ACT writing optional) required
- 58% graduate within 6 years; 20% enter graduate study

General. Founded in 1833. Regionally accredited. Evening and weekend continuing education programs available at 4 regional academic centers and transfer degree programs offered at Atlanta campus. **Degrees:** 476 bachelor's awarded; master's, doctoral, first professional offered. **ROTC:** Army. **Location:** 85 miles from Atlanta. **Calendar:** Semester, extensive summer session. **Full-time faculty:** 354 total; 88% have terminal degrees, 16% minority, 43% women. **Part-time faculty:** 252 total; 41% have terminal degrees, 21% minority, 51% women. **Class size:** 54% < 20, 42% 20-39, 2% 40-49, 2% 50-99.

Freshman class profile. 4,678 applied, 3,144 admitted, 594 enrolled.

Mid 50% test scores		**Rank in top quarter:**	75%
SAT critical reading:	530-640	**Rank in top tenth:**	42%
SAT math:	550-650	**End year in good standing:**	88%
SAT writing:	520-630	**Return as sophomores:**	78%
ACT composite:	23-29	**Out-of-state:**	18%
GPA 3.75 or higher:	54%	**Live on campus:**	94%
GPA 3.50-3.74:	21%	**International:**	2%
GPA 3.0-3.49:	20%	**Fraternities:**	20%
GPA 2.0-2.99:	5%	**Sororities:**	27%

Basis for selection. GED not accepted. Admissions based on academic merit. GPA, SAT scores and extracurricular activities important. Interview recommended. Audition recommended for music majors. **Homeschooled:** 1100 SAT (exclusive of Writing), certified transcript indicating college-preparatory curriculum including names and titles of textbooks used, interview required. SAT exams may be substituted for certified transcript. **Learning Disabled:** Documentation from licensed professional required.

High school preparation. College-preparatory program required. 16 units required. Required units include English 4, mathematics 4, social studies 1, history 2, science 3 and foreign language 2.

2008-2009 Annual costs. Tuition/fees: $28,700. Room/board: $8,450. Books/supplies: $1,200. Personal expenses: $1,201.

2008-2009 Financial aid. Need-based: 508 full-time freshmen applied for aid; 409 were judged to have need; 409 of these received aid. Average need met was 94%. Average scholarship/grant was $21,158; average loan $6,897. 75% of total undergraduate aid awarded as scholarships/grants, 25% as loans/jobs. **Non-need-based:** Awarded to 1,303 full-time undergraduates, including 374 freshmen. Scholarships awarded for academics, art, athletics, job skills, leadership, music/drama, religious affiliation, ROTC, state residency.

Application procedures. Admission: Priority date 4/1; deadline 7/1 (postmark date). $50 fee, may be waived for applicants with need, free for online applicants. Admission notification on a rolling basis beginning on or about 9/1. Must reply by May 1 or within 4 week(s) if notified thereafter. **Financial aid:** Priority date 4/1; no closing date. FAFSA, institutional form required. Applicants notified on a rolling basis starting 3/15; must reply within 2 week(s) of notification.

Academics. Special study options: Accelerated study, combined bachelor's/graduate degree, cooperative education, cross-registration, double major, dual enrollment of high school students, honors, independent study, internships, liberal arts/career combination, student-designed major, study abroad, teacher certification program. Students may satisfy general education requirements by completing either the Great Books Program or the Distributional Program. **Credit/placement by examination:** AP, CLEP, IB, SAT, ACT, institutional tests. 32 credit hours maximum toward bachelor's degree. **Support services:** Learning center, pre-admission summer program, reduced course load, study skills assistance, tutoring.

Majors. Area/ethnic studies: African-American, regional, women's. **Biology:** General, biochemistry. **Business:** General. **Communications:** Journalism, media studies. **Computer sciences:** Computer science, information systems. **Conservation:** Environmental science. **Education:** Elementary, middle, music. **Engineering:** General. **Foreign languages:** Classics, French, German, Latin, Spanish. **Health:** Nursing (RN), predental, premedicine. **History:** General. **Liberal arts:** Arts/sciences. **Math:** General. **Philosophy/religion:** Christian, philosophy. **Physical sciences:** Chemistry, physics. **Protective services:** Criminal justice. **Psychology:** General. **Public administration:** Community org/advocacy. **Social sciences:** Economics, international relations, political science, sociology. **Visual/performing arts:** Art, dramatic, music performance.

Most popular majors. Biology 10%, business/marketing 19%, communications/journalism 9%, engineering/engineering technologies 12%, English 6%, psychology 6%, social sciences 10%.

Computing on campus. 1,150 workstations in library, computer center, student center. Dormitories wired for high-speed internet access and linked to campus network. Commuter students can connect to campus network. Online course registration, online library, helpline, repair service, wireless network available.

Student life. Freshman orientation: Mandatory. Preregistration for classes offered. One-day summer orientation and 4-day program in fall before semester begins. **Policies:** Alcohol not permitted on campus. **Housing:** Guaranteed on-campus for freshmen. Coed dorms, single-sex dorms, special housing for disabled, apartments, fraternity/sorority housing available. **Activities:**

Bands, campus ministries, choral groups, dance, drama, film society, international student organizations, literary magazine, music ensembles, musical theater, opera, radio station, student government, student newspaper, TV station, Baptist student union, Reformed University Fellowship, Habitat for Humanity, black student organization, Catholic Newman center, College Republicans, College Democrats, Hispanic Latino student union, Islamic student organization.

Athletics. NCAA. **Intercollegiate:** Baseball M, basketball, cross-country, golf, rifle M, soccer, softball W, tennis, volleyball W. **Intramural:** Basketball, football (non-tackle), soccer, softball, swimming, tennis, volleyball, water polo. **Team name:** Bears.

Student services. Adult student services, alcohol/substance abuse counseling, career counseling, services for economically disadvantaged, student employment services, financial aid counseling, health services, minority student services, personal counseling, placement for graduates. **Physically disabled:** Services for visually, speech, hearing impaired.

Contact. E-mail: admissions@mercer.edu
Phone: (478) 301-2650 Toll-free number: (800) 840-8577
Fax: (478) 301-2828
Brian Dalton, Senior Vice President, Enrollment Services, Mercer University, 1400 Coleman Avenue, Macon, GA 31207-0001

Morehouse College

Atlanta, Georgia — **CB member**
www.morehouse.edu — **CB code: 5415**

- Private 4-year liberal arts college for men
- Residential campus in very large city
- 2,781 degree-seeking undergraduates: 6% part-time, 95% African American, 2% international
- 72% of applicants admitted
- SAT or ACT with writing, application essay required
- 66% graduate within 6 years

General. Founded in 1867. Regionally accredited. One of 4 members of Atlanta University Center sharing facilities including library. **Degrees:** 521 bachelor's awarded. **ROTC:** Army, Naval, Air Force. **Calendar:** Semester, limited summer session. **Full-time faculty:** 155 total; 81% minority, 35% women. **Part-time faculty:** 80 total; 90% minority, 42% women. **Special facilities:** Chapels, meditation room.

Freshman class profile. 2,279 applied, 1,645 admitted, 715 enrolled.

Mid 50% test scores			
SAT critical reading:	460-560	Rank in top quarter:	41%
SAT math:	450-570	Rank in top tenth:	14%
ACT composite:	18-24	International:	2%

Basis for selection. School academic record most important, followed by test scores, counselor recommendation, school and community activities, and student leadership. Interview recommended.

High school preparation. College-preparatory program required. 13 units required; 16 recommended. Required and recommended units include English 4, mathematics 3, social studies 2, science 2, foreign language 2 and academic electives 3.

2008-2009 Annual costs. Tuition/fees: $20,358. Room/board: $10,424. Books/supplies: $1,500. Personal expenses: $3,800.

2008-2009 Financial aid. **Need-based:** 653 full-time freshmen applied for aid; 653 were judged to have need; 653 of these received aid. Average need met was 25%. Average scholarship/grant was $9,250; average loan $3,500. 28% of total undergraduate aid awarded as scholarships/grants, 72% as loans/jobs. **Non-need-based:** Awarded to 560 full-time undergraduates, including 170 freshmen. Scholarships awarded for academics, alumni affiliation, art, athletics, leadership, music/drama, ROTC, state residency.

Application procedures. **Admission:** Priority date 11/1; deadline 2/15 (postmark date). $45 fee, may be waived for applicants with need. Application must be submitted on paper. Admission notification 4/1. Must reply by 5/1. **Financial aid:** Priority date 2/15, closing date 4/1. FAFSA, institutional form, CSS PROFILE required. Must reply by 5/1.

Academics. **Special study options:** Combined bachelor's/graduate degree, cooperative education, cross-registration, double major, dual enrollment of high school students, exchange student, honors, internships, liberal arts/career combination, semester at sea, study abroad. Dual degree program in engineering and architecture with other institutions. **Credit/placement by examination:** AP, CLEP, SAT, ACT, institutional tests. 30 credit hours maximum toward bachelor's degree. **Support services:** Learning center, pre-admission summer program, reduced course load, remedial instruction, study skills assistance, tutoring, writing center.

Majors. **Area/ethnic studies:** African-American. **Biology:** General. **Business:** Business admin. **Computer sciences:** General. **Education:** General. **Engineering:** General. **Foreign languages:** French, Spanish. **History:** General. **Math:** General. **Parks/recreation:** Health/fitness. **Philosophy/religion:** Philosophy, religion. **Physical sciences:** Chemistry, physics. **Psychology:** General. **Social sciences:** Economics, international relations, political science, sociology, urban studies. **Visual/performing arts:** Art, dramatic.

Most popular majors. Biology 6%, business/marketing 30%, English 6%, psychology 12%, social sciences 22%.

Computing on campus. 300 workstations in dormitories, library, computer center. Dormitories wired for high-speed internet access and linked to campus network. Commuter students can connect to campus network. Online course registration, online library, helpline, repair service, wireless network available.

Student life. **Freshman orientation:** Mandatory, $480 fee. Preregistration for classes offered. Held several days before class begins each fall. **Housing:** Guaranteed on-campus for freshmen. Apartments, wellness housing available. $500 nonrefundable deposit, deadline 6/24. **Activities:** Bands, choral groups, drama, international student organizations, literary magazine, music ensembles, student government, student newspaper, Martin Luther King International Chapel Assistants, mentoring program, Frederick Douglass Tutorial Program, political science club, New Life Inspirational Gospel Choir, NAACP, Eagle Scout Association.

Athletics. NCAA. **Intercollegiate:** Baseball M, basketball M, cross-country M, football (tackle) M, golf M, tennis M, track and field M. **Intramural:** Baseball M, basketball M, football (non-tackle) M, soccer M, softball M, swimming M, table tennis M, tennis M, weight lifting M. **Team name:** Maroon Tigers.

Student services. Alcohol/substance abuse counseling, chaplain/spiritual director, career counseling, student employment services, financial aid counseling, health services, personal counseling, placement for graduates, veterans' counselor. **Physically disabled:** Services for visually, speech, hearing impaired.

Contact. E-mail: admissions@morehouse.edu
Phone: (404) 681-2800 ext. 2632 Toll-free number: (800) 851-1254
Fax: (404) 524-5635
Terrance Dixon, Associate Dean of Admissions and Records, Morehouse College, 830 Westview Drive SW, Atlanta, GA 30314

North Georgia College & State University

Dahlonega, Georgia — **CB member**
www.ngcsu.edu — **CB code: 5497**

- Public 4-year university and military college
- Commuter campus in small town
- 4,719 degree-seeking undergraduates: 17% part-time, 59% women, 2% African American, 1% Asian American, 3% Hispanic American, 1% international
- 587 degree-seeking graduate students
- 57% of applicants admitted
- SAT or ACT (ACT writing optional) required
- 50% graduate within 6 years

General. Founded in 1873. Regionally accredited. **Degrees:** 763 bachelor's, 125 associate awarded; master's, doctoral offered. **ROTC:** Army. **Location:** 70 miles from Atlanta. **Calendar:** Semester, extensive summer session. **Full-time faculty:** 195 total; 64% have terminal degrees, 11% minority, 51% women. **Part-time faculty:** 123 total; 24% have terminal degrees, 10% minority, 60% women. **Class size:** 32% < 20, 62% 20-39, 5% 40-49, 2% 50-99. **Special facilities:** Observatory, rappeling tower, planetarium, nature preserve.

Freshman class profile. 2,777 applied, 1,582 admitted, 870 enrolled.

Mid 50% test scores		GPA 2.0-2.99:	21%
SAT critical reading:	500-580	Rank in top quarter:	53%
SAT math:	490-580	Rank in top tenth:	18%
SAT writing:	470-570	Return as sophomores:	80%
ACT composite:	20-24	Out-of-state:	6%
GPA 3.75 or higher:	19%	Live on campus:	64%
GPA 3.50-3.74:	19%	International:	1%
GPA 3.0-3.49:	41%		

Basis for selection. High school academic record, test scores important, disciplinary record considered. Students must provide certification of immunization against communicable diseases. Commuting students must apply for permission to commute. Audition recommended for music majors. Portfolio recommended for art majors. **Homeschooled:** SAT Subject Tests required.

High school preparation. College-preparatory program required. 17 units required. Required units include English 4, mathematics 4, social studies 3, science 3 (laboratory 1) and foreign language 2.

2008-2009 Annual costs. Tuition/fees: $4,070; $13,362 out-of-state. Room/board: $5,244. Books/supplies: $500. Personal expenses: $1,000.

2007-2008 Financial aid. Need-based: 40% of total undergraduate aid awarded as scholarships/grants, 60% as loans/jobs. **Non-need-based:** Scholarships awarded for academics, alumni affiliation, art, athletics, job skills, leadership, minority status, music/drama, religious affiliation, ROTC, state residency.

Application procedures. Admission: Closing date 7/1. $30 fee, may be waived for applicants with need. Admission notification on a rolling basis. **Financial aid:** Priority date 3/17; no closing date. FAFSA required. Applicants notified on a rolling basis starting 3/1; must reply within 3 week(s) of notification.

Academics. Consortium with Medical College of Georgia and Armstrong Atlantic State University to offer a Doctorate of Physical Therapy. Degree awarded from the Medical College of Georgia. **Special study options:** Combined bachelor's/graduate degree, cooperative education, distance learning, double major, dual enrollment of high school students, external degree, honors, independent study, internships, liberal arts/career combination, study abroad, teacher certification program. Dual degree program in engineering with Georgia Institute of Technology and Clemson University. **Credit/placement by examination:** AP, CLEP, SAT, ACT, institutional tests. 30 credit hours maximum toward associate degree, 30 toward bachelor's. **Support services:** Learning center, pre-admission summer program, reduced course load, remedial instruction, study skills assistance, tutoring, writing center.

Majors. Biology: General. **Business:** Accounting, business admin, finance, marketing. **Computer sciences:** General. **Education:** Art, early childhood, middle, music, physical, special. **Foreign languages:** French, German, Spanish. **Health:** Athletic training, nursing (RN). **History:** General. **Math:** General. **Parks/recreation:** Health/fitness. **Physical sciences:** Chemistry, physics. **Protective services:** Law enforcement admin. **Psychology:** General. **Social sciences:** International relations, political science, sociology.

Most popular majors. Biology 6%, business/marketing 23%, education 34%, security/protective services 9%, social sciences 9%.

Computing on campus. 470 workstations in dormitories, library, computer center, student center. Dormitories linked to campus network. Commuter students can connect to campus network. Online course registration, online library, helpline, repair service, student web hosting, wireless network available.

Student life. Freshman orientation: Available. Preregistration for classes offered. Two and 1/2-day program held 4 times during June, July, August; students stay in residence halls. **Policies:** All male residents must join Corps of Cadets; optional for female residents. **Housing:** Coed dorms, single-sex dorms, apartments available. $250 fully refundable deposit, deadline 5/1. **Activities:** Bands, campus ministries, choral groups, dance, drama, international student organizations, literary magazine, music ensembles, Model UN, student government, student newspaper, Students for Social Awareness, Baptist student union, commuter council, Muslim student association, Newman club, Habitat for Humanity.

Athletics. NCAA. **Intercollegiate:** Baseball M, basketball, cheerleading M, cross-country, rifle, soccer, softball W, tennis, track and field. **Intramural:** Basketball, football (non-tackle) W, football (tackle) M, golf, softball W, table tennis, volleyball, water polo. **Team name:** Saints.

Student services. Alcohol/substance abuse counseling, career counseling, student employment services, financial aid counseling, health services, minority student services, personal counseling, placement for graduates, veterans' counselor. **Physically disabled:** Services for visually, hearing impaired.

Contact. E-mail: admissions@ngcsu.edu
Phone: (706) 864-1800 Toll-free number: (800) 498-9581
Fax: (706) 864-1478
Jennifer Collins, Director of Admissions, North Georgia College & State University, 82 College Circle, Dahlonega, GA 30597

Oglethorpe University

Atlanta, Georgia — **CB member**
www.oglethorpe.edu — **CB code: 5521**

- Private 4-year liberal arts college
- Residential campus in very large city
- 958 degree-seeking undergraduates: 10% part-time, 60% women
- 11 degree-seeking graduate students
- 43% of applicants admitted
- SAT or ACT (ACT writing recommended) required
- 58% graduate within 6 years

General. Founded in 1835. Regionally accredited. Campus home to Georgia Shakespeare Festival. **Degrees:** 197 bachelor's awarded; master's offered. **ROTC:** Air Force. **Location:** 10 miles from downtown. **Calendar:** Semester, extensive summer session. **Full-time faculty:** 48 total; 96% have terminal degrees, 15% minority, 33% women. **Part-time faculty:** 47 total; 83% have terminal degrees, 11% minority, 49% women. **Class size:** 73% < 20, 27% 20-39. **Special facilities:** Art museum.

Freshman class profile. 4,150 applied, 1,773 admitted, 245 enrolled.

Mid 50% test scores		**GPA 2.0-2.99:**	14%
SAT critical reading:	540-640	**Rank in top quarter:**	54%
SAT math:	510-610	**Rank in top tenth:**	23%
SAT writing:	520-620	**Return as sophomores:**	80%
ACT composite:	22-27	**Out-of-state:**	27%
GPA 3.75 or higher:	35%	**Live on campus:**	87%
GPA 3.50-3.74:	22%	**International:**	3%
GPA 3.0-3.49:	29%		

Basis for selection. High school GPA and general academic record most important, followed by test scores. Recommendations required. Activities considered. Interview recommended.

High school preparation. College-preparatory program recommended. Required and recommended units include English 4, mathematics 3, social studies 3, science 2 and foreign language 2. Honors, AP, IB recommended where available.

2008-2009 Annual costs. Tuition/fees: $25,580. Room/board: $9,500. Books/supplies: $800. Personal expenses: $1,200.

2008-2009 Financial aid. Need-based: 206 full-time freshmen applied for aid; 179 were judged to have need; 179 of these received aid. Average need met was 75%. Average scholarship/grant was $20,488; average loan $4,747. 76% of total undergraduate aid awarded as scholarships/grants, 24% as loans/jobs. **Non-need-based:** Awarded to 419 full-time undergraduates, including 158 freshmen. Scholarships awarded for academics, music/drama.

Application procedures. Admission: No deadline. $35 fee, may be waived for applicants with need, free for online applicants. Admission notification on a rolling basis beginning on or about 12/1. Must reply by May 1 or within 3 week(s) if notified thereafter. **Financial aid:** Priority date 2/1; no closing date. FAFSA, institutional form required. Applicants notified on a rolling basis starting 3/1; must reply by 5/1 or within 3 week(s) of notification.

Academics. Special study options: Accelerated study, cooperative education, cross-registration, double major, dual enrollment of high school students, honors, independent study, internships, liberal arts/career combination, student-designed major, study abroad, Washington semester. Dual engineering degree program with Auburn University, Georgia Institute of Technology, University of Florida, and University of Southern California; dual art degree program with Atlanta College of Art; Urban Leadership Program. **Credit/placement by examination:** AP, CLEP, institutional tests. 30 credit hours maximum toward bachelor's degree. **Support services:** Learning center.

Majors. Area/ethnic studies: American. **Biology:** General. **Business:** Accounting, managerial economics, organizational behavior. **Communications:** General. **Health:** Clinical lab science, predental, premedicine, prepharmacy, preveterinary. **History:** General. **Interdisciplinary:** Math/computer science. **Legal studies:** Prelaw. **Liberal arts:** Arts/sciences. **Math:** General. **Philosophy/religion:** Philosophy. **Physical sciences:** Chemistry, physics. **Psychology:** General. **Public administration:** Social work. **Social sciences:** Economics, international relations, political science, sociology. **Visual/performing arts:** Art.

Most popular majors. Biology 6%, business/marketing 26%, English 20%, psychology 11%, social sciences 13%, visual/performing arts 9%.

Computing on campus. 57 workstations in library, computer center. Dormitories wired for high-speed internet access and linked to campus network. Commuter students can connect to campus network. Helpline, wireless network available.

Student life. **Housing:** Guaranteed on-campus for freshmen. Coed dorms, fraternity/sorority housing available. $200 fully refundable deposit, deadline 5/1. **Activities:** Campus ministries, choral groups, dance, drama, film society, international student organizations, literary magazine, musical theater, radio station, student government, student newspaper, Catholic student association, black student caucus, christian fellowship, environmentally concerned students, Jewish student union, Students Against Homophobia, APO service organization, Circle K.

Athletics. NCAA. **Intercollegiate:** Baseball M, basketball, cross-country, golf, soccer, tennis, track and field, volleyball W. **Intramural:** Badminton, basketball, softball, tennis, volleyball. **Team name:** Stormy Petrels.

Student services. Adult student services, career counseling, student employment services, health services, personal counseling, placement for graduates, veterans' counselor. **Physically disabled:** Services for visually impaired.

Contact. E-mail: admission@oglethorpe.edu
Phone: (404) 364-8307 Toll-free number: (800) 428-4484
Fax: (404) 364-8500
Dennis Matthews, Associate Dean for Enrollment Management, Oglethorpe University, 4484 Peachtree Road NE, Atlanta, GA 30319-2797

Paine College

Augusta, Georgia — **CB member**
www.paine.edu — **CB code: 5530**

- Private 4-year liberal arts college affiliated with Christian Methodist Episcopal Church and United Methodist Church
- Residential campus in large city
- 855 degree-seeking undergraduates: 4% part-time, 69% women, 95% African American
- 40% of applicants admitted
- SAT or ACT (ACT writing optional), application essay required
- 31% graduate within 6 years; 10% enter graduate study

General. Founded in 1882. Regionally accredited. **Degrees:** 100 bachelor's awarded. **ROTC:** Army. **Location:** 72 miles from Columbia, South Carolina; 150 miles from Atlanta. **Calendar:** Semester, limited summer session. **Full-time faculty:** 65 total; 52% have terminal degrees, 78% minority, 38% women. **Part-time faculty:** 15 total; 13% have terminal degrees, 93% minority, 67% women. **Class size:** 69% < 20, 31% 20-39, less than 1% 50-99.

Freshman class profile. 2,975 applied, 1,191 admitted, 244 enrolled.

Mid 50% test scores		**GPA 3.0-3.49:**	31%
SAT critical reading:	350-440	**GPA 2.0-2.99:**	48%
SAT math:	350-440	**Return as sophomores:**	54%
ACT composite:	14-18	**Out-of-state:**	34%
GPA 3.75 or higher:	3%	**Live on campus:**	85%
GPA 3.50-3.74:	8%		

Basis for selection. School achievement record, test scores, and recommendations considered. 2.0 GPA required. Interview recommended. Audition required of music majors if applying for scholarship.

High school preparation. College-preparatory program recommended. 16 units recommended. Recommended units include English 4, mathematics 3, social studies 2, history 1, science 3 (laboratory 2) and academic electives 3.

2008-2009 Annual costs. Tuition/fees: $11,224. Room/board: $5,476. Books/supplies: $800. Personal expenses: $1,940.

2008-2009 Financial aid. **Need-based:** Average need met was 53%. Average scholarship/grant was $5,732; average loan $3,303. 43% of total undergraduate aid awarded as scholarships/grants, 57% as loans/jobs. **Non-need-based:** Scholarships awarded for academics, alumni affiliation, athletics, music/drama, religious affiliation, ROTC.

Application procedures. **Admission:** Closing date 8/1 (receipt date). $20 fee, may be waived for applicants with need. Admission notification on a rolling basis. **Financial aid:** Priority date 3/1; no closing date. FAFSA required. Applicants notified on a rolling basis starting 5/1; must reply within 2 week(s) of notification.

Academics. **Special study options:** Combined bachelor's/graduate degree, cooperative education, cross-registration, distance learning, dual enrollment of high school students, honors, independent study, internships, liberal arts/career combination, study abroad, teacher certification program. Dual degree in engineering and mathematics with Florida A & M University, Tuskegee University, Tennessee State University. **Credit/placement by examination:** AP, CLEP, SAT, ACT, institutional tests. **Support services:** Learning center, pre-admission summer program, reduced course load, remedial instruction, study skills assistance, tutoring.

Majors. **Biology:** General. **Business:** Accounting, business admin, international, management information systems, marketing. **Communications:** Broadcast journalism, journalism, public relations. **Conservation:** Environmental science. **Education:** Biology, elementary, English, history, mathematics, middle. **History:** General. **Interdisciplinary:** Math/computer science. **Math:** General. **Philosophy/religion:** Philosophy, religion. **Physical sciences:** Chemistry. **Psychology:** General, counseling. **Social sciences:** Criminology, sociology. **Visual/performing arts:** Dramatic.

Most popular majors. Biology 10%, business/marketing 17%, communications/journalism 13%, education 11%, history 6%, psychology 20%, social sciences 16%.

Computing on campus. 150 workstations in dormitories, library, computer center, student center. Dormitories wired for high-speed internet access and linked to campus network. Commuter students can connect to campus network. Online course registration, online library, repair service, wireless network available.

Student life. **Freshman orientation:** Mandatory, $106 fee. Preregistration for classes offered. Pre-testing and orientation held in June and 1 week at beginning of semester. **Housing:** Single-sex dorms, wellness housing available. $75 nonrefundable deposit, deadline 8/1. **Activities:** Campus ministries, choral groups, dance, drama, international student organizations, literary magazine, music ensembles, student government, student newspaper, Baptist student union, Methodist student union, NAACP, pre-alumni club, National Pan Hellenic Council, Alpha Kappa Mu honor society.

Athletics. NCAA. **Intercollegiate:** Baseball M, basketball, cross-country, golf M, softball W, track and field, volleyball W. **Intramural:** Badminton, baseball M, basketball, cross-country, football (non-tackle) M, softball, table tennis, tennis, track and field, volleyball, weight lifting. **Team name:** Lions.

Student services. Alcohol/substance abuse counseling, chaplain/spiritual director, career counseling, student employment services, financial aid counseling, health services, personal counseling, placement for graduates, veterans' counselor.

Contact. E-mail: tinsleyj@mail.paine.edu
Phone: (706) 821-8320 Toll-free number: (800) 476-7703
Fax: (706) 821-8648
Joseph Tinsley, Director of Admissions, Paine College, 1235 15th Street, Augusta, GA 30901-3182

Piedmont College

Demorest, Georgia — **CB member**
www.piedmont.edu — **CB code: 5537**

- Private 4-year liberal arts and teachers college affiliated with United Church of Christ
- Commuter campus in rural community
- 1,135 degree-seeking undergraduates: 13% part-time, 69% women, 6% African American, 1% Asian American, 2% Hispanic American
- 1,505 degree-seeking graduate students
- 62% of applicants admitted
- SAT or ACT required
- 47% graduate within 6 years

General. Founded in 1897. Regionally accredited. **Degrees:** 226 bachelor's awarded; master's offered. **Location:** 30 miles from Gainesville, 75 miles from Atlanta. **Calendar:** Semester, limited summer session. **Full-time faculty:** 112 total; 81% have terminal degrees, 5% minority, 40% women. **Part-time faculty:** 110 total; 62% have terminal degrees, 11% minority, 48% women. **Class size:** 74% < 20, 26% 20-39, less than 1% 50-99. **Special facilities:** Performing arts and communication center, pipe organ, worship and music center, botanical center.

Freshman class profile. 1,438 applied, 891 admitted, 214 enrolled.

Mid 50% test scores			
SAT critical reading:	440-540	GPA 2.0-2.99:	15%
SAT math:	440-540	Rank in top quarter:	40%
ACT composite:	18-22	Rank in top tenth:	19%
GPA 3.75 or higher:	19%	Return as sophomores:	63%
GPA 3.50-3.74:	27%	Live on campus:	33%
GPA 3.0-3.49:	39%	International:	1%

Basis for selection. Test scores and GPA most important. Essay recommended. Interview recommended for academically weak. **Homeschooled:** Interview, letter of recommendation (nonparent) required. Transcript or portfolio detailing high school coursework completed, 2 letters of recommendation from sources outside home who have knowledge of student's academic/extracurricular achievements required. Interview with student and family may be required.

High school preparation. College-preparatory program recommended. 21 units recommended. Recommended units include English 4, mathematics 3, social studies 1, history 2, science 3 and foreign language 2.

2009-2010 Annual costs. Tuition/fees: $18,000. Room/board: $6,000. Books/supplies: $1,500. Personal expenses: $2,350.

2008-2009 Financial aid. Need-based: 161 full-time freshmen applied for aid; 120 were judged to have need; 109 of these received aid. Average need met was 61%. Average scholarship/grant was $1,155; average loan $3,415. 40% of total undergraduate aid awarded as scholarships/grants, 60% as loans/jobs. **Non-need-based:** Awarded to 624 full-time undergraduates, including 166 freshmen. Scholarships awarded for academics, art, leadership, music/drama, religious affiliation, state residency. **Additional information:** College meets 100% of unmet direct financial need for early applicants through grants, scholarships, and loan programs.

Application procedures. Admission: Closing date 7/1. No application fee. **Financial aid:** Priority date 5/1; no closing date. FAFSA, institutional form required. Applicants notified on a rolling basis; must reply within 2 week(s) of notification.

Academics. Experiential learning credit allows students to document work experience for college credit as appropriate. **Special study options:** Accelerated study, combined bachelor's/graduate degree, distance learning, double major, dual enrollment of high school students, honors, independent study, internships, student-designed major, study abroad, teacher certification program. **Credit/placement by examination:** AP, CLEP. 30 credit hours maximum toward bachelor's degree. **Support services:** Study skills assistance, tutoring.

Majors. Biology: General. **Business:** Business admin. **Communications:** Media studies. **Conservation:** Environmental science. **Education:** Biology, chemistry, drama/dance, early childhood, English, history, middle, secondary, special. **Foreign languages:** Spanish. **Health:** Nursing (RN). **History:** General. **Interdisciplinary:** Math/computer science. **Math:** General. **Philosophy/religion:** Philosophy, religion. **Physical sciences:** Chemistry. **Protective services:** Criminal justice. **Psychology:** General. **Social sciences:** General, political science, sociology. **Visual/performing arts:** Art, dramatic, studio arts.

Most popular majors. Business/marketing 25%, education 31%, social sciences 9%.

Computing on campus. 225 workstations in dormitories, library, computer center, student center. Dormitories wired for high-speed internet access and linked to campus network. Commuter students can connect to campus network. Online library available.

Student life. Freshman orientation: Mandatory. Preregistration for classes offered. Three-day weekend with activities for students, resident assistants, faculty and staff. **Policies:** Unmarried students under 21 must live in dormitories or with blood relatives. **Housing:** Guaranteed on-campus for all undergraduates. Coed dorms, single-sex dorms, special housing for disabled, apartments, wellness housing available. $100 deposit. **Activities:** Campus ministries, choral groups, drama, film society, literary magazine, music ensembles, radio station, student government, student newspaper, symphony orchestra, TV station, psychology club, Fellowhip of Christian Athletes, Green Giants, Student Association of Educators, literary society, science club, environmental club, Rotaract, history society.

Athletics. NCAA. **Intercollegiate:** Baseball M, basketball, cross-country, golf, soccer, softball W, tennis, volleyball W. **Intramural:** Basketball, football (non-tackle), soccer, softball, table tennis, volleyball. **Team name:** Lions.

Student services. Chaplain/spiritual director, career counseling, financial aid counseling, health services, personal counseling, placement for graduates, veterans' counselor.

Contact. E-mail: ugrad@piedmont.edu
Phone: (706) 776-0103 Toll-free number: (800) 277-7020
Fax: (706) 776-6635
Cynthia Peterson, Director of Admissions, Piedmont College, 165 Central Avenue, Demorest, GA 30535-0010

Reinhardt College

Waleska, Georgia — **CB member**
www.reinhardt.edu — **CB code: 5568**

- Private 4-year business and teachers college affiliated with United Methodist Church
- Commuter campus in rural community
- 994 degree-seeking undergraduates: 8% part-time, 60% women, 8% African American, 1% Asian American, 4% Hispanic American
- 26 degree-seeking graduate students
- 70% of applicants admitted
- SAT or ACT required
- 39% graduate within 6 years

General. Founded in 1883. Regionally accredited. Off-campus center in Alpharetta. **Degrees:** 158 bachelor's, 44 associate awarded; master's offered. **Location:** 50 miles from Atlanta. **Calendar:** Semester, extensive summer session. **Full-time faculty:** 53 total; 72% have terminal degrees, 13% minority, 49% women. **Part-time faculty:** 84 total; 4% minority, 46% women. **Class size:** 74% < 20, 26% 20-39. **Special facilities:** Indian history museum, visual arts center, performing arts center.

Freshman class profile. 1,111 applied, 776 admitted, 274 enrolled.

Mid 50% test scores			
SAT critical reading:	430-530	GPA 3.0-3.49:	35%
SAT math:	410-520	GPA 2.0-2.99:	54%
SAT writing:	410-520	Return as sophomores:	59%
GPA 3.75 or higher:	7%	Out-of-state:	3%
GPA 3.50-3.74:	3%	Live on campus:	44%

Basis for selection. School achievement record most important, followed by test scores, recommendations. Interview recommended. Audition required of music majors. Portfolio required of art majors. **Homeschooled:** Transcript of courses and grades, state high school equivalency certificate required. **Learning Disabled:** Recommend that students be counseled by Academic Support Office.

High school preparation. 14 units recommended. Recommended units include English 4, mathematics 4, social studies 3, science 3 and foreign language 2.

2008-2009 Annual costs. Tuition/fees: $16,070. Room/board: $7,950. Books/supplies: $1,100. Personal expenses: $900.

2008-2009 Financial aid. Non-need-based: Scholarships awarded for academics, art, athletics.

Application procedures. Admission: No deadline. $25 fee, may be waived for applicants with need. Admission notification on a rolling basis. **Financial aid:** Priority date 5/1; no closing date. Applicants notified on a rolling basis starting 3/15; must reply within 2 week(s) of notification.

Academics. Special study options: Accelerated study, combined bachelor's/graduate degree, double major, dual enrollment of high school students, external degree, honors, independent study, internships, study abroad, teacher certification program. **Credit/placement by examination:** AP, CLEP, institutional tests. 15 credit hours maximum toward associate degree, 30 toward bachelor's. **Support services:** Learning center, pre-admission summer program, reduced course load, remedial instruction, study skills assistance, tutoring, writing center.

Majors. Biology: General. **Business:** General, accounting, business admin. **Communications:** General. **Computer sciences:** Information systems. **Education:** Biology, early childhood, elementary, English, middle, music, physical. **History:** General. **Liberal arts:** Arts/sciences. **Parks/recreation:** Sports admin. **Philosophy/religion:** Religion. **Psychology:** General. **Social sciences:** Sociology. **Visual/performing arts:** Studio arts.

Most popular majors. Business/marketing 38%, communications/journalism 7%, education 29%, history 7%.

Computing on campus. 165 workstations in dormitories, library, computer center, student center. Dormitories wired for high-speed internet access and linked to campus network. Commuter students can connect to campus network. Online course registration, online library, helpline, student web hosting, wireless network available.

Student life. **Freshman orientation:** Mandatory, $35 fee. Preregistration for classes offered. One- or 2-day program. **Housing:** Guaranteed on-campus for freshmen. Coed dorms, single-sex dorms, apartments, wellness housing available. $200 fully refundable deposit, deadline 8/15. **Activities:** Bands, campus ministries, choral groups, drama, film society, international student organizations, music ensembles, student government, student newspaper, TV station, Baptist student union, Wesley Foundation, fellowship of Christian athletes, Reach Out Reinhardt, Phi Theta Kappa, Circle-K.

Athletics. NAIA. **Intercollegiate:** Baseball M, basketball, cheerleading, cross-country, golf M, soccer, softball W, tennis. **Intramural:** Basketball, football (non-tackle), soccer, softball, volleyball. **Team name:** Eagles.

Student services. Adult student services, alcohol/substance abuse counseling, chaplain/spiritual director, career counseling, student employment services, financial aid counseling, health services, personal counseling, placement for graduates, veterans' counselor. **Physically disabled:** Services for visually, speech, hearing impaired.

Contact. E-mail: admissions@mail.reinhardt.edu
Phone: (770) 720-5526 Toll-free number: (877) 343-4273
Fax: (770) 720-5602
Julie Fleming, Director of Admissions, Reinhardt College, 7300 Reinhardt College Circle, Waleska, GA 30183

Savannah College of Art and Design

Savannah, Georgia — **CB member**
www.scad.edu — **CB code: 5631**

- Private 4-year visual arts and performing arts college
- Commuter campus in small city
- 7,745 degree-seeking undergraduates: 10% part-time, 56% women, 4% African American, 3% Asian American, 3% Hispanic American, 4% international
- 1,476 degree-seeking graduate students
- 64% of applicants admitted
- SAT or ACT with writing required
- 69% graduate within 6 years

General. Founded in 1978. Regionally accredited. Additional location in Atlanta. eLearning program. Extensive study abroad program in France at Lacoste School of the Arts. **Degrees:** 1,362 bachelor's awarded; master's offered. **ROTC:** Army. **Location:** 250 miles from Atlanta; 150 miles from Jacksonville, Florida. **Calendar:** Quarter, limited summer session. **Full-time faculty:** 445 total; 74% have terminal degrees, 9% minority, 41% women. **Part-time faculty:** 123 total; 68% have terminal degrees, 6% minority, 37% women. **Class size:** 89% < 20, 11% 20-39. **Special facilities:** Art museums, 2 vintage diners, amphitheater, restored 1943 theater.

Freshman class profile. 7,194 applied, 4,626 admitted, 1,506 enrolled.

Mid 50% test scores			
SAT critical reading:	480-590	**GPA 3.0-3.49:**	34%
SAT math:	470-580	**GPA 2.0-2.99:**	27%
ACT composite:	21-25	**End year in good standing:**	87%
GPA 3.75 or higher:	21%	**Return as sophomores:**	81%
GPA 3.50-3.74:	18%	**Out-of-state:**	75%
		Live on campus:	92%

Basis for selection. Entrance test scores, 3 letters of recommendation, and high school transcript required. Interview, portfolio recommended. Essay recommended for historic preservation, art history, and architectural history programs only. Portfolio or audition required for scholarship consideration. **Homeschooled:** Statement describing homeschool structure and mission, transcript of courses and grades, state high school equivalency certificate required. **Learning Disabled:** Documentation of specific nature of disability required.

High school preparation. College-preparatory program recommended.

2009-2010 Annual costs. Tuition/fees: $27,765. A one-time matriculation fee of $500 is required of all students. Room/board: $11,710. Books/supplies: $1,560. Personal expenses: $1,560.

2008-2009 Financial aid. **Need-based:** 1,004 full-time freshmen applied for aid; 751 were judged to have need; 747 of these received aid. Average need met was 10%. Average scholarship/grant was $4,198; average loan $3,379. 93% of total undergraduate aid awarded as scholarships/grants, 7% as loans/jobs. **Non-need-based:** Awarded to 4,493 full-time undergraduates, including 905 freshmen. Scholarships awarded for academics, art, athletics, music/drama. **Additional information:** Degree-seeking students may be awarded maximum of one scholarship from college, but may receive additional scholarships from other sources, as well as additional forms of financial aid. Scholarships based on academic achievement are awarded through admission office.

Application procedures. **Admission:** Priority date 2/15; deadline 8/1 (receipt date). $50 fee. Admission notification on a rolling basis beginning on or about 9/1. Students encouraged to apply early to gain priority for housing. **Financial aid:** Priority date 2/15; no closing date. FAFSA, institutional form required. Applicants notified on a rolling basis starting 6/1.

Academics. Strong fine arts foundation along with strong liberal arts curriculum. **Special study options:** Distance learning, double major, dual enrollment of high school students, ESL, independent study, internships, New York semester, study abroad, teacher certification program, Washington semester. Off-campus programs in Europe and other art centers. Cross registration available at SCAD-Atlanta through membership in ARCHE. Teacher certification in art and drama available through MA in Teaching program. **Credit/placement by examination:** AP, CLEP, IB. 15 credit hours maximum toward bachelor's degree. **Support services:** Learning center, pre-admission summer program, reduced course load, study skills assistance, tutoring, writing center.

Majors. **Architecture:** Architecture, history/criticism. **Communications:** Digital media. **Communications technology:** Animation/special effects, recording arts. **Interdisciplinary:** Historic preservation. **Visual/performing arts:** Art history/conservation, cinematography, commercial/advertising art, dramatic, fashion design, fiber arts, graphic design, illustration, industrial design, interior design, metal/jewelry, painting, photography, printmaking, sculpture, theater design. **Other:** Furniture design.

Most popular majors. Architecture 7%, communication technologies 19%, visual/performing arts 68%.

Computing on campus. Dormitories wired for high-speed internet access and linked to campus network. Commuter students can connect to campus network. Online course registration, online library, helpline, repair service, student web hosting, wireless network available.

Student life. **Freshman orientation:** Available. Preregistration for classes offered. Two-day program, includes parents; summer options available. **Housing:** Coed dorms, single-sex dorms, apartments available. $250 nonrefundable deposit, deadline 6/1. Some apartment-style residence halls with full kitchen facilities available. Students with disabilities accommodated on individual basis. **Activities:** Campus ministries, choral groups, dance, drama, international student organizations, music ensembles, musical theater, radio station, student government, student newspaper, TV station, American Institute of Architecture Students, American Society of Interior Designers, united student forum, inter-club council, student activities council, intercultural student association, Society of Illustrators, art history society, Society for Collegiate Journalists.

Athletics. NAIA. **Intercollegiate:** Baseball M, basketball, cross-country, equestrian, golf, lacrosse, soccer, softball W, swimming, tennis, volleyball W. **Intramural:** Basketball, football (non-tackle), lacrosse, soccer, softball, tennis, volleyball. **Team name:** Bees.

Student services. Adult student services, alcohol/substance abuse counseling, career counseling, student employment services, financial aid counseling, health services, personal counseling, placement for graduates. **Physically disabled:** Services for visually, speech, hearing impaired.

Contact. E-mail: admission@scad.edu
Phone: (912) 525-5100 Toll-free number: (800) 869-7223
Fax: (912) 525-5986
Pamela Rhame, Vice President for Admission and Communication, Savannah College of Art and Design, PO Box 2072, Savannah, GA 31402-2072

Savannah State University

Savannah, Georgia — **CB member**
www.savstate.edu — **CB code: 5609**

- Public 4-year business and liberal arts college
- Commuter campus in small city
- 2,935 full-time, degree-seeking undergraduates
- SAT or ACT (ACT writing optional) required

General. Founded in 1890. Regionally accredited. **Degrees:** 300 bachelor's awarded; master's offered. **ROTC:** Army, Naval. **Location:** 250 miles from Atlanta; 120 miles from Jacksonville, Florida. **Calendar:** Semester, extensive summer session. **Full-time faculty:** 122 total. **Part-time faculty:** 38 total. **Special facilities:** Marine biology dock, college archives, natural estuary.

Freshman class profile.

Mid 50% test scores		GPA 3.0-3.49:	23%
SAT critical reading:	400-480	GPA 2.0-2.99:	69%
SAT math:	400-480	Out-of-state:	8%
GPA 3.75 or higher:	3%	Live on campus:	50%
GPA 3.50-3.74:	4%		

Basis for selection. Test scores and high school GPA very important.

High school preparation. 15 units required. Required units include English 4, mathematics 3, social studies 3, science 3 and foreign language 2. Students lacking complete college-preparatory requirements admitted on provisional basis.

2008-2009 Annual costs. Tuition/fees: $3,726; $13,018 out-of-state. Room/board: $5,644. Books/supplies: $750. Personal expenses: $800.

2008-2009 Financial aid. Non-need-based: Scholarships awarded for academics, alumni affiliation, music/drama.

Application procedures. Admission: Closing date 7/1. $20 fee, may be waived for applicants with need. Admission notification on a rolling basis beginning on or about 3/1. **Financial aid:** Closing date 4/1. FAFSA required. Applicants notified on a rolling basis starting 4/15; must reply within 2 week(s) of notification.

Academics. Special study options: Cooperative education, cross-registration, double major, dual enrollment of high school students, exchange student, honors, independent study, internships. **Credit/placement by examination:** AP, CLEP, institutional tests. 45 credit hours maximum toward associate degree, 45 toward bachelor's. **Support services:** Learning center, remedial instruction, tutoring.

Majors. Biology: General. **Business:** Accounting, hospitality/recreation, international, management science. **Communications:** General. **Computer sciences:** General, computer science, information systems. **Education:** Early childhood. **Engineering technology:** Civil, electrical. **Health:** Clinical lab science. **History:** General. **Math:** General. **Parks/recreation:** General. **Physical sciences:** Chemistry. **Public administration:** Social work. **Social sciences:** Political science, sociology. **Visual/performing arts:** Music performance.

Computing on campus. 300 workstations in library, computer center. Commuter students can connect to campus network.

Student life. Freshman orientation: Available. Preregistration for classes offered. Available during various times leading up to fall semester. Private appointments available upon request. **Housing:** Single-sex dorms, apartments available. $100 deposit. **Activities:** Bands, campus ministries, choral groups, dance, drama, literary magazine, music ensembles, radio station, student government, student newspaper.

Athletics. NCAA. **Intercollegiate:** Baseball M, basketball, bowling W, cross-country, football (tackle) M, golf, softball W, tennis W, track and field, volleyball W. **Intramural:** Baseball M, bowling, softball W, table tennis. **Team name:** Tigers.

Student services. Student employment services, health services, on-campus daycare, personal counseling, placement for graduates, veterans' counselor.

Contact. E-mail: ssvadms@savstate.edu
Phone: (912) 356-2181 Fax: (912) 356-2256
Gwendolyn Moore, Director of Admissions, Savannah State University, State College Branch, Savannah, GA 31404

Shorter College

Rome, Georgia — **CB member**
www.shorter.edu — **CB code: 5616**

- Private 4-year liberal arts college affiliated with Southern Baptist Convention
- Residential campus in large town
- 1,116 degree-seeking undergraduates: 2% part-time, 49% women, 15% African American, 1% Asian American, 3% Hispanic American, 5% international
- 61% of applicants admitted
- SAT or ACT (ACT writing optional), application essay required
- 49% graduate within 6 years; 51% enter graduate study

General. Founded in 1873. Regionally accredited. **Degrees:** 179 bachelor's awarded. **Location:** 70 miles from Atlanta, 65 miles from Chattanooga, Tennessee. **Calendar:** Semester, limited summer session. **Full-time faculty:** 76 total; 66% have terminal degrees, 8% minority, 41% women. **Part-time faculty:** 50 total; 24% have terminal degrees, 8% minority, 48% women. **Class size:** 60% < 20, 38% 20-39, 2% 40-49, less than 1% 50-99, less than 1% >100. **Special facilities:** Music collection, local history microfilm archive.

Freshman class profile. 1,543 applied, 942 admitted, 334 enrolled.

Mid 50% test scores		Rank in top quarter:	50%
SAT critical reading:	430-560	Rank in top tenth:	21%
SAT math:	430-550	End year in good standing:	81%
SAT writing:	420-550	Return as sophomores:	73%
ACT composite:	18-23	Out-of-state:	6%
GPA 3.75 or higher:	25%	Live on campus:	88%
GPA 3.50-3.74:	17%	International:	3%
GPA 3.0-3.49:	26%	Fraternities:	13%
GPA 2.0-2.99:	32%	Sororities:	29%

Basis for selection. High school achievement, curriculum most important. Test scores, essay, counselor recommendation considered. Auditions required of music and drama majors. Portfolios required of art majors. **Homeschooled:** Interview may be required.

High school preparation. College-preparatory program required. 16 units required. Required units include English 4, mathematics 4, history 3, science 3 and foreign language 2. Math units should include 2 algebra, 1 geometry.

2008-2009 Annual costs. Tuition/fees: $15,770. Room/board: $7,400. Books/supplies: $1,000. Personal expenses: $1,770.

2008-2009 Financial aid. Need-based: 283 full-time freshmen applied for aid; 235 were judged to have need; 235 of these received aid. Average need met was 75%. Average scholarship/grant was $11,934; average loan $3,013. 67% of total undergraduate aid awarded as scholarships/grants, 33% as loans/jobs. **Non-need-based:** Awarded to 502 full-time undergraduates, including 164 freshmen. Scholarships awarded for academics, art, athletics, music/drama, religious affiliation. **Additional information:** Cost is reduced for all in-state students by state tuition equalization grant program. College matches for out-of-state full-time students.

Application procedures. Admission: Priority date 3/15; no deadline. $25 fee, may be waived for applicants with need. Application must be submitted on paper. Admission notification on a rolling basis beginning on or about 11/1. Must reply by May 1 or within 2 week(s) if notified thereafter. **Financial aid:** Priority date 4/1; no closing date. FAFSA, institutional form required. Applicants notified on a rolling basis starting 4/1; must reply within 2 week(s) of notification.

Academics. Special study options: Cross-registration, double major, dual enrollment of high school students, honors, independent study, internships, student-designed major, study abroad, teacher certification program. Annual extended seacoast field trips in natural science. **Credit/placement by examination:** AP, CLEP, IB, SAT, institutional tests. 30 credit hours maximum toward bachelor's degree. **Support services:** Learning center, preadmission summer program, remedial instruction, study skills assistance, tutoring, writing center.

Majors. Biology: General. **Business:** Accounting, business admin, managerial economics. **Communications:** General, public relations. **Computer sciences:** General. **Conservation:** General, environmental studies. **Education:** Art, elementary, mathematics, middle, music. **Foreign languages:** French, Spanish. **History:** General. **Interdisciplinary:** Global studies. **Liberal arts:** Arts/sciences. **Math:** General. **Parks/recreation:** Sports admin. **Philosophy/religion:** Religion. **Physical sciences:** Chemistry. **Psychology:** General. **Social sciences:** General, sociology. **Theology:** Sacred music, theology. **Visual/performing arts:** Dramatic, piano/organ, studio arts, voice/opera.

Most popular majors. Biology 10%, business/marketing 30%, communications/journalism 7%, education 17%, visual/performing arts 12%.

Computing on campus. 50 workstations in library, computer center. Dormitories wired for high-speed internet access and linked to campus network. Online course registration, helpline, wireless network available.

Student life. Freshman orientation: Mandatory, $60 fee. Preregistration for classes offered. Several summer overnight sessions from June to August. Freshmen take placement exams. **Policies:** Religious observance required. **Housing:** Guaranteed on-campus for freshmen. Single-sex dorms, apartments available. $200 fully refundable deposit, deadline 8/20. **Activities:** Bands, campus ministries, choral groups, dance, drama, film society, international student organizations, literary magazine, music ensembles, Model UN, musical theater, opera, radio station, student government, student newspaper, TV station, Baptist student union, Shorter Relations Society, Fellowship of Christian Athletes.

Athletics. NAIA. **Intercollegiate:** Baseball M, basketball, cheerleading, cross-country, football (tackle) M, golf W, soccer, softball W, tennis, track and field, volleyball W. **Intramural:** Basketball, bowling, football (non-tackle), soccer, softball, table tennis, tennis, track and field, volleyball. **Team name:** Hawks.

Student services. Adult student services, alcohol/substance abuse counseling, career counseling, student employment services, financial aid counseling, health services, personal counseling, placement for graduates. **Physically disabled:** Services for visually, hearing impaired.

Contact. E-mail: admissions@shorter.edu
Phone: (706) 233-7319 Toll-free number: (800) 868-6980
Fax: (706) 233-7224
John Head, Vice President for Enrollment Management, Shorter College, 315 Shorter Avenue, Rome, GA 30165

South University: Savannah

Savannah, Georgia
www.southuniversity.edu **CB code: 5157**

- For-profit 4-year business and health science college
- Commuter campus in small city
- 7,384 degree-seeking undergraduates
- 921 graduate students
- SAT or ACT, interview required

General. Founded in 1899. Regionally accredited. **Degrees:** 26 bachelor's, 53 associate awarded; master's, doctoral, first professional offered. **Location:** 225 miles from Atlanta, 165 miles from Jacksonville, Florida. **Calendar:** Quarter, extensive summer session. **Full-time faculty:** 923 total; 18% minority, 84% women. **Part-time faculty:** 1,022 total; 26% minority, 93% women.

Basis for selection. Test scores and school achievement record considered. Physician assistant students must have completed 2 years of science-based curriculum. Computerized Placement Test may be submitted in place of test scores for admission. Essays required for master's level physician assistant and professional counseling programs. **Homeschooled:** Letter of recommendation (nonparent) required.

2008-2009 Annual costs. Books/supplies: $1,800. Personal expenses: $2,700.

Financial aid. **Non-need-based:** Scholarships awarded for state residency.

Application procedures. **Admission:** No deadline. $50 fee, may be waived for applicants with need. Admission notification on a rolling basis. **Financial aid:** No deadline. FAFSA required. Applicants notified on a rolling basis starting 9/1.

Academics. **Special study options:** Accelerated study, combined bachelor's/graduate degree, distance learning, double major, dual enrollment of high school students, independent study, internships, liberal arts/career combination. **Credit/placement by examination:** AP, CLEP, IB, SAT, ACT, institutional tests. 45 credit hours maximum toward associate degree, 90 toward bachelor's. 60% of total credits, 50% of major credits may be earned by examination. **Support services:** Learning center, reduced course load, remedial instruction, study skills assistance, tutoring.

Majors. **Business:** Accounting, business admin. **Computer sciences:** Information technology. **Health:** Health care admin, health services, nursing (RN), physician assistant. **Legal studies:** General. **Protective services:** Law enforcement admin. **Psychology:** General.

Most popular majors. Business/marketing 46%, health sciences 50%.

Computing on campus. 50 workstations in library, computer center. Commuter students can connect to campus network. Online library, helpline, repair service, wireless network available.

Student life. **Freshman orientation:** Mandatory. Preregistration for classes offered. **Housing:** Apartments available. $200 deposit.

Student services. Career counseling, student employment services, financial aid counseling, personal counseling, placement for graduates, veterans' counselor.

Contact. E-mail: mmills@southuniversity.edu
Phone: (912) 201-8100 Toll-free number: (866) 629-2901
Fax: (912) 201-8070
Matthew Mills, Director of Admissions, South University: Savannah, 709 Mall Boulevard, Savannah, GA 31406

Southern Polytechnic State University

Marietta, Georgia
www.spsu.edu **CB code: 5626**

- Public 4-year university and engineering college
- Commuter campus in small city
- 4,126 degree-seeking undergraduates: 28% part-time, 18% women, 20% African American, 6% Asian American, 4% Hispanic American, 5% international
- 567 graduate students
- 62% of applicants admitted
- SAT or ACT with writing required

General. Founded in 1948. Regionally accredited. **Degrees:** 550 bachelor's, 3 associate awarded; master's offered. **ROTC:** Army, Naval, Air Force. **Location:** 15 miles from Atlanta. **Calendar:** Semester, extensive summer session. **Full-time faculty:** 174 total; 68% have terminal degrees, 27% minority, 29% women. **Part-time faculty:** 91 total; 32% have terminal degrees, 25% minority, 34% women. **Class size:** 41% < 20, 54% 20-39, 3% 40-49, 1% 50-99, less than 1% >100.

Freshman class profile. 1,600 applied, 985 admitted, 600 enrolled.

Mid 50% test scores		**GPA 2.0-2.99:**	29%
SAT critical reading:	490-580	**Return as sophomores:**	79%
SAT math:	520-620	**Out-of-state:**	1%
ACT composite:	21-25	**Live on campus:**	51%
GPA 3.75 or higher:	15%	**International:**	1%
GPA 3.50-3.74:	16%	**Fraternities:**	8%
GPA 3.0-3.49:	40%	**Sororities:**	6%

Basis for selection. GED not accepted. Test scores, high school units, GPA important. **Homeschooled:** Portfolio and 1120 SAT (exclusive of Writing) with 500 verbal and math subscores required.

High school preparation. College-preparatory program required. 18 units required. Required units include English 4, mathematics 4, social studies 3, science 3 (laboratory 2), foreign language 2 and academic electives 2. 2 history (1 U.S., 1 World); 2 algebra, 1 geometry; foreign language must include 2 years same language.

2008-2009 Annual costs. Tuition/fees: $4,232; $14,728 out-of-state. Room/board: $5,870. Books/supplies: $1,700. Personal expenses: $1,700.

2007-2008 Financial aid. **Need-based:** 408 full-time freshmen applied for aid; 408 were judged to have need; 398 of these received aid. Average need met was 76%. Average scholarship/grant was $2,656; average loan $3,082. 36% of total undergraduate aid awarded as scholarships/grants, 64% as loans/jobs. **Non-need-based:** Awarded to 618 full-time undergraduates, including 289 freshmen. Scholarships awarded for academics, athletics.

Application procedures. **Admission:** Closing date 8/1 (postmark date). $20 fee, may be waived for applicants with need. Admission notification on a rolling basis. **Financial aid:** Priority date 4/1; no closing date. FAFSA required. Applicants notified on a rolling basis starting 6/1.

Academics. **Special study options:** Cooperative education, cross-registration, distance learning, double major, dual enrollment of high school students, honors, independent study, internships, liberal arts/career combination, study abroad. **Credit/placement by examination:** AP, CLEP, IB, institutional tests. 20 credit hours maximum toward associate degree, 30 toward bachelor's. **Support services:** Learning center, reduced course load, study skills assistance, tutoring.

Majors. **Architecture:** Architecture. **Biology:** General. **Business:** Construction management, entrepreneurial studies. **Computer sciences:** Computer science, information technology. **Engineering:** Construction, software, systems. **Engineering technology:** Architectural, civil, computer, electrical, industrial, mechanical, surveying, telecommunications. **Math:** General. **Physical sciences:** Chemistry, physics. **Psychology:** General. **Social sciences:** International relations. **Other:** Mechatronics engineering, Technical communication.

Most popular majors. Architecture 10%, business/marketing 18%, computer/information sciences 13%, engineering/engineering technologies 48%.

Computing on campus. 850 workstations in dormitories, library, computer center, student center. Dormitories wired for high-speed internet access and linked to campus network. Commuter students can connect to campus network. Online course registration, online library, helpline, student web hosting, wireless network available.

Student life. **Freshman orientation:** Mandatory, $80 fee. Preregistration for classes offered. One-and-a-half day program held twice prior to beginning of semester; includes 1 night in a dorm. One half-day session also available. **Housing:** Coed dorms, apartments available. $235 partly refundable deposit, deadline 8/1. **Activities:** Bands, choral groups, international student organizations, radio station, student government, student newspaper, campus activities board, National Society of Black Engineers, Baptist student union, African students association, Bahai club, Japanese Friendship Society, Muslim student association, Indian culture exchange, Chinese Friendship Association, Sexual Acceptance For Everyone, Caribbean student association.

Athletics. NAIA. **Intercollegiate:** Baseball M, basketball, soccer M. **Intramural:** Badminton, basketball, football (non-tackle), golf, racquetball, soccer, softball, table tennis, tennis, volleyball. **Team name:** Runnin' Hornets.

Student services. Alcohol/substance abuse counseling, career counseling, student employment services, financial aid counseling, health services, minority student services, personal counseling, placement for graduates, veterans' counselor. **Physically disabled:** Services for visually, speech, hearing impaired.

Contact. E-mail: admiss@spsu.edu
Phone: (678) 915-4188 Toll-free number: (800) 635-3204
Fax: (678) 915-7292
Gary Bush, Director of Admissions, Southern Polytechnic State University, 1100 South Marietta Parkway, Marietta, GA 30060-2896

Spelman College

Atlanta, Georgia — **CB member**
www.spelman.edu — **CB code: 5628**

- Private 4-year liberal arts college for women
- Residential campus in very large city
- 2,270 degree-seeking undergraduates: 5% part-time, 100% women
- 35% of applicants admitted
- SAT or ACT (ACT writing optional), application essay required
- 74% graduate within 6 years

General. Founded in 1881. Regionally accredited. One of 6 members of Atlanta University Center sharing facilities, resources, and activities. Students may take courses at the other undergraduate schools in the Atlanta University Consortium. **Degrees:** 483 bachelor's awarded. **ROTC:** Army, Naval, Air Force. **Location:** 2 miles from downtown. **Calendar:** Semester. **Full-time faculty:** 174 total; 82% have terminal degrees, 66% women. **Part-time faculty:** 75 total. **Special facilities:** Women's research and resource center, fine art museum.

Freshman class profile. 6,033 applied, 2,122 admitted, 550 enrolled.

Mid 50% test scores		**GPA 2.0-2.99:**	6%
SAT critical reading:	490-570	**Rank in top quarter:**	67%
SAT math:	470-550	**Rank in top tenth:**	29%
ACT composite:	20-24	**Return as sophomores:**	89%
GPA 3.75 or higher:	31%	**Out-of-state:**	73%
GPA 3.50-3.74:	29%	**Live on campus:**	98%
GPA 3.0-3.49:	34%	**International:**	7%

Basis for selection. School achievement record, letters of recommendation, test scores, leadership, activities, essay important.

High school preparation. 16 units required; 19 recommended. Required and recommended units include English 4, mathematics 3-4, social studies 3, science 3-4 (laboratory 2-3), foreign language 3-4 and academic electives 2. Mathematics units must include algebra and geometry. Must have 2 years of the same foreign language. Social studies units should include 2 years of history.

2008-2009 Annual costs. Tuition/fees: $20,281. Room/board: $9,734. Books/supplies: $1,150. Personal expenses: $2,100.

2007-2008 Financial aid. Need-based: 56% of total undergraduate aid awarded as scholarships/grants, 44% as loans/jobs. **Non-need-based:** Scholarships awarded for academics, alumni affiliation, leadership, music/drama, state residency.

Application procedures. Admission: Closing date 2/1 (postmark date). $35 fee, may be waived for applicants with need. Admission notification on a rolling basis beginning on or about 12/1. Must reply by 5/1. **Financial aid:** Priority date 3/1; no closing date. FAFSA, institutional form required. Applicants notified on a rolling basis starting 2/15; must reply within 2 week(s) of notification.

Academics. Special study options: Cross-registration, double major, dual enrollment of high school students, exchange student, honors, independent study, internships, New York semester, student-designed major, study abroad, teacher certification program, Washington semester. **Credit/placement by examination:** AP, CLEP, IB, institutional tests. 16 credit hours maximum toward bachelor's degree. **Support services:** Learning center, preadmission summer program, tutoring, writing center.

Majors. Area/ethnic studies: Women's. **Biology:** General, biochemistry. **Computer sciences:** General. **Conservation:** Environmental science. **Education:** Early childhood. **Engineering:** General. **Family/consumer sciences:** Child care. **Foreign languages:** French, Spanish. **History:** General. **Interdisciplinary:** Biological/physical sciences, global studies. **Math:** General. **Philosophy/religion:** Philosophy, religion. **Physical sciences:** Chemistry, physics. **Psychology:** General. **Public administration:** Human services. **Social sciences:** Economics, political science, sociology. **Visual/performing arts:** Dramatic, studio arts.

Most popular majors. Biology 11%, English 11%, psychology 20%, social sciences 35%.

Computing on campus. 102 workstations in dormitories, library, computer center, student center. Dormitories wired for high-speed internet access and linked to campus network. Commuter students can connect to campus network. Online library, helpline, repair service, wireless network available.

Student life. Freshman orientation: Mandatory. One-week program prior to registration. **Housing:** Guaranteed on-campus for freshmen. $100 deposit, deadline 5/1. **Activities:** Jazz band, choral groups, dance, drama, music ensembles, student government, student newspaper, subject-related clubs, community services office.

Athletics. NCAA. **Intercollegiate:** Basketball W, cross-country W, soccer W, softball W, tennis W, track and field W, volleyball W. **Intramural:** Basketball W, bowling W, golf W, soccer W, softball W, swimming W, tennis W, track and field W, volleyball W. **Team name:** Jaguars.

Student services. Adult student services, chaplain/spiritual director, career counseling, student employment services, health services, on-campus daycare, personal counseling, placement for graduates, women's services. **Physically disabled:** Services for visually, speech, hearing impaired.

Contact. E-mail: admiss@spelman.edu
Phone: (404) 270-5193 Toll-free number: (800) 982-2411
Fax: (404) 270-5201
Arlene Cash, Vice President, Enrollment Management, Spelman College, 350 Spelman Lane SW, Campus Box 277, Atlanta, GA 30314

Thomas University

Thomasville, Georgia
www.thomasu.edu — **CB code: 5072**

- Private 4-year university and liberal arts college
- Commuter campus in large town
- 748 degree-seeking undergraduates: 41% part-time, 68% women, 31% African American, 1% Asian American, 1% Hispanic American, 1% Native American
- 145 degree-seeking graduate students

General. Founded in 1950. Regionally accredited. **Degrees:** 108 bachelor's, 7 associate awarded; master's offered. **Location:** 60 miles from Albany, 35 miles from Tallahassee, Florida. **Calendar:** Semester, extensive summer session. **Full-time faculty:** 41 total; 46% have terminal degrees, 10% minority. **Part-time faculty:** 54 total; 17% have terminal degrees, 15% minority. **Class size:** 85% < 20, 14% 20-39, less than 1% 40-49.

Freshman class profile.

Out-of-state:	8%	**Live on campus:**	25%

Basis for selection. Open admission, but selective for some programs. Special requirements for nursing program. All students must take the Multiple Assessment Programs & Services examination and successfully complete remedial courses before enrolling in academic courses. **Homeschooled:** Transcript of courses and grades, state high school equivalency certificate required.

2008-2009 Annual costs. Tuition/fees: $11,664. Room only: $2,766. Books/supplies: $1,100. Personal expenses: $1,500.

2007-2008 Financial aid. Non-need-based: Scholarships awarded for academics, athletics, leadership, state residency.

Application procedures. Admission: No deadline. $25 fee. Admission notification on a rolling basis. **Financial aid:** Priority date 5/1; no closing date. FAFSA required. Applicants notified on a rolling basis.

Academics. Special study options: Accelerated study, distance learning, dual enrollment of high school students, internships, liberal arts/career combination, teacher certification program. **Credit/placement by examination:** AP, CLEP, institutional tests. 40 credit hours maximum toward associate degree, 40 toward bachelor's. Total of 40 hours applies to credit by examination and prior work/life experience credit combined. **Support services:** Learning center, reduced course load, remedial instruction, study skills assistance, tutoring, writing center.

Majors. Biology: General. **Business:** General, accounting, management information systems, marketing. **Education:** Early childhood, elementary, middle, music, secondary. **Health:** Nursing (RN), staff services technology. **History:** General. **Liberal arts:** Arts/sciences. **Protective services:** Criminal justice. **Psychology:** General. **Public administration:** Social work. **Social sciences:** General, anthropology.

Most popular majors. Business/marketing 12%, education 44%, health sciences 10%, legal studies 11%, social sciences 10%.

Computing on campus. 50 workstations in library, computer center. Dormitories wired for high-speed internet access and linked to campus network. Commuter students can connect to campus network. Online course registration, online library, wireless network available.

Student life. Freshman orientation: Available. Preregistration for classes offered. Half-day every semester. **Housing:** Guaranteed on-campus for freshmen. Coed dorms, apartments available. $250 deposit, deadline 8/1. **Activities:** Jazz band, choral groups, drama, literary magazine, music ensembles, student government, student newspaper.

Athletics. NAIA. **Intercollegiate:** Baseball M, golf, soccer, softball W. **Team name:** Night Hawks.

Student services. Adult student services, alcohol/substance abuse counseling, career counseling, student employment services, financial aid counseling, personal counseling, placement for graduates, veterans' counselor. **Physically disabled:** Services for visually, hearing impaired.

Contact. E-mail: admissions@thomasu.edu
Phone: (229) 226-1621 ext. 124 Toll-free number: (800) 538-9784 ext. 124
Fax: (229) 227-6919
Micky West, Executive Director for Enrollment Management and Student Affairs, Thomas University, 1501 Millpond Road, Thomasville, GA 31792-7499

Toccoa Falls College

Toccoa Falls, Georgia — **CB member**
www.tfc.edu — **CB code: 5799**

- Private 4-year Bible and liberal arts college affiliated with Christian and Missionary Alliance
- Residential campus in large town
- 877 degree-seeking undergraduates: 5% part-time, 55% women, 3% African American, 8% Asian American, 2% Hispanic American
- 45% of applicants admitted
- SAT or ACT (ACT writing recommended), application essay required
- 55% graduate within 6 years

General. Founded in 1907. Regionally accredited; also accredited by ABHE. **Degrees:** 132 bachelor's, 10 associate awarded. **Location:** 90 miles from Atlanta, 60 miles from Greenville, South Carolina. **Calendar:** 4-1-4, limited summer session. **Full-time faculty:** 49 total; 59% have terminal degrees, 6% minority, 20% women. **Part-time faculty:** 25 total; 8% have terminal degrees, 8% minority, 32% women. **Class size:** 68% < 20, 23% 20-39, 7% 40-49, 2% 50-99. **Special facilities:** 186-foot waterfall, 1898 hydroelectric generator, nature trails.

Freshman class profile. 1,137 applied, 507 admitted, 234 enrolled.

Mid 50% test scores			
SAT critical reading:	450-580	Return as sophomores:	60%
SAT math:	430-560	Out-of-state:	43%
ACT composite:	18-25	Live on campus:	83%

Basis for selection. Evidence of Christian commitment, character, capacity and desire to learn considered. Index score calculated by multiplying unweighted GPA by best total standardized test score. Students with score of 48 on GED also considered. Personal statement of Christian faith required.

High school preparation. 19 units recommended. Recommended units include English 4, mathematics 3, social studies 3, science 3 and academic electives 6.

2008-2009 Annual costs. Tuition/fees: $14,625. Room/board: $5,350. Books/supplies: $908. Personal expenses: $2,270.

2007-2008 Financial aid. Non-need-based: Scholarships awarded for academics, alumni affiliation, leadership, music/drama, religious affiliation, state residency.

Application procedures. Admission: Priority date 5/1; deadline 8/1 (postmark date). $20 fee, may be waived for applicants with need. Admission notification on a rolling basis beginning on or about 3/1. Must reply by May 1 or within 2 week(s) if notified thereafter. **Financial aid:** Priority date 5/1, closing date 8/1. FAFSA, institutional form required. Applicants notified on a rolling basis starting 3/1; must reply within 2 week(s) of notification.

Academics. All students complete at least 30 credit hours of Bible courses (18 credit hours for associate degrees). **Special study options:** Distance learning, double major, independent study, internships, teacher certification program. **Credit/placement by examination:** AP, CLEP, SAT, ACT, institutional tests. 30 credit hours maximum toward associate degree, 45 toward bachelor's. **Support services:** Learning center, reduced course load, study skills assistance, tutoring.

Majors. Biology: General. **Business:** Business admin. **Communications:** General, media studies. **Education:** Early childhood, English, history, middle, music. **History:** General. **Legal studies:** Prelaw. **Philosophy/religion:** Philosophy. **Psychology:** General. **Theology:** Bible, missionary, pastoral counseling, religious ed, sacred music, youth ministry. **Visual/performing arts:** Music performance.

Most popular majors. Business/marketing 7%, education 16%, psychology 22%, theological studies 35%.

Computing on campus. 60 workstations in library, computer center. Dormitories wired for high-speed internet access and linked to campus network. Commuter students can connect to campus network. Online course registration, online library, helpline, student web hosting, wireless network available.

Student life. Freshman orientation: Mandatory. Preregistration for classes offered. Held 1 week in fall and throughout spring semester. **Policies:** Students attend weekly church services and participate in student ministry field assignments. Religious observance required. **Housing:** Guaranteed on-campus for freshmen. Single-sex dorms, apartments, wellness housing available. $200 fully refundable deposit. Mobile homes available on campus lots for married students. **Activities:** Bands, campus ministries, choral groups, drama, international student organizations, music ensembles, radio station, student government, student newspaper, over 50 different ministry opportunities.

Athletics. NCCAA. **Intercollegiate:** Baseball M, basketball, cross-country, golf, soccer, volleyball W. **Intramural:** Basketball, football (non-tackle), soccer, softball, volleyball. **Team name:** Eagles.

Student services. Chaplain/spiritual director, career counseling, student employment services, financial aid counseling, health services, personal counseling. **Physically disabled:** Services for visually impaired.

Contact. E-mail: admissions@tfc.edu
Phone: (706) 886-6831 ext. 5380 Fax: (706) 282-6012
Debbie Moore, Director of Admissions, Toccoa Falls College, PO Box 800899, Toccoa Falls, GA 30598-0368

Truett-McConnell College

Cleveland, Georgia — **CB member**
www.truett.edu — **CB code: 5798**

- Private 4-year liberal arts college affiliated with Southern Baptist Convention
- Residential campus in small town
- 389 degree-seeking undergraduates
- SAT or ACT (ACT writing optional) required

General. Founded in 1946. Regionally accredited. Associated with Baptist Convention of the State of Georgia. **Degrees:** 25 bachelor's, 52 associate awarded. **Location:** 75 miles from Atlanta, 25 miles from Gainesville. **Calendar:** Semester, limited summer session. **Full-time faculty:** 22 total; 59% have terminal degrees. **Part-time faculty:** 32 total.

Four-Year Colleges

Freshman class profile. 177 enrolled.

Mid 50% test scores		SAT writing:	380-480
SAT critical reading:	390-500	ACT composite:	15-20
SAT math:	390-500		

Basis for selection. 2.0 GPA in core classes and 720 SAT (exclusive of Writing) or 15 ACT required. Students with lower scores may apply to academic enrichment program. Audition required of music majors. **Home-schooled:** Transcript of courses and grades required. Letter from local school board stating that student has completed home school program requirements and placement exams required. **Learning Disabled:** Students may request accommodations upon presentation of appropriate documentation of disability. Determination of reasonable accommodations made on individual basis.

High school preparation. College-preparatory program recommended. Recommended units include English 4, mathematics 3, social studies 3, science 3 and foreign language 2.

2008-2009 Annual costs. Tuition/fees: $14,000. Room/board: $5,240. Books/supplies: $1,000. Personal expenses: $3,500.

Financial aid. Non-need-based: Scholarships awarded for academics, athletics, music/drama, religious affiliation, state residency. **Additional information:** Installment plan available.

Application procedures. Admission: Closing date 8/1 (receipt date). $25 fee, may be waived for applicants with need. Admission notification on a rolling basis. Must reply by May 1 or within 1 week(s) if notified thereafter. **Financial aid:** Priority date 6/1; no closing date. FAFSA, institutional form required. Applicants notified on a rolling basis starting 4/1; must reply within 2 week(s) of notification.

Academics. Special study options: Double major, dual enrollment of high school students, independent study, teacher certification program. **Credit/placement by examination:** AP, CLEP, SAT, ACT, institutional tests. 30 credit hours maximum toward associate degree, 30 toward bachelor's. **Support services:** Remedial instruction, tutoring.

Majors. Education: Early childhood. **History:** General. **Liberal arts:** Humanities. **Philosophy/religion:** Christian.

Most popular majors. Education 46%, liberal arts 12%, philosophy/religious studies 19%, visual/performing arts 15%.

Computing on campus. 45 workstations in library, computer center, student center. Dormitories linked to campus network. Commuter students can connect to campus network. Online course registration, wireless network available.

Student life. Freshman orientation: Mandatory, $25 fee. Preregistration for classes offered. Several one-day sessions held during summer prior to fall classes beginning. **Policies:** Tobacco free campus. Religious observance required. **Housing:** Single-sex dorms, apartments, wellness housing available. $100 fully refundable deposit. **Activities:** Bands, choral groups, music ensembles, student government, Baptist Student Union, Phi Theta Kappa, Impact Teams and Majesty, Phi Beta Lambda, Ministerial Association, Student Professional Association of Georgia Educators, Fellowship of Christian Athletes.

Athletics. NJCAA. **Intercollegiate:** Baseball M, basketball, cross-country, golf M, soccer, softball W. **Intramural:** Basketball, football (non-tackle), soccer. **Team name:** Bears.

Student services. Chaplain/spiritual director, financial aid counseling, veterans' counselor. **Physically disabled:** Services for visually, speech, hearing impaired.

Contact. E-mail: admissions@truett.edu
Phone: (706) 865-2134 Toll-free number: (800) 226-8621
Fax: (706) 865-7615
Mike Davis, Dean of Admissions, Truett-McConnell College, 100 Alumni Drive, Cleveland, GA 30528

University of Georgia

Athens, Georgia — **CB member**
www.uga.edu — **CB code: 5813**

- Public 4-year university
- Commuter campus in small city
- 25,150 degree-seeking undergraduates: 6% part-time, 58% women, 7% African American, 7% Asian American, 2% Hispanic American, 1% international
- 8,097 degree-seeking graduate students
- 56% of applicants admitted
- SAT or ACT with writing, application essay required
- 80% graduate within 6 years

General. Founded in 1785. Regionally accredited. **Degrees:** 6,414 bachelor's awarded; master's, doctoral, first professional offered. **ROTC:** Army, Air Force. **Location:** 60 miles from of Atlanta. **Calendar:** Semester, extensive summer session. **Full-time faculty:** 1,761 total; 95% have terminal degrees, 16% minority, 34% women. **Part-time faculty:** 417 total; 64% have terminal degrees, 11% minority, 44% women. **Class size:** 37% < 20, 44% 20-39, 8% 40-49, 6% 50-99, 5% >100. **Special facilities:** Botanical garden, golf course.

Freshman class profile. 17,207 applied, 9,569 admitted, 4,834 enrolled.

Mid 50% test scores		GPA 2.0-2.99:	2%
SAT critical reading:	560-660	Return as sophomores:	93%
SAT math:	570-660	Out-of-state:	16%
SAT writing:	560-660	Live on campus:	98%
ACT composite:	24-29	International:	1%
GPA 3.75 or higher:	64%	Fraternities:	33%
GPA 3.50-3.74:	23%	Sororities:	28%
GPA 3.0-3.49:	11%		

Basis for selection. GPA in core academic courses, rigor of course selection, and best combination of SAT/ACT scores important. Applications reviewed for conduct issues, recommendations, and satisfactory completion of all courses including required college preparatory courses. Audition required of music majors.

High school preparation. College-preparatory program required. 16 units required; 18 recommended. Required and recommended units include English 4, mathematics 4, social studies 3, history 2, science 3 (laboratory 2), foreign language 2-3 and academic electives 1.

2008-2009 Annual costs. Tuition/fees: $6,031; $22,343 out-of-state. Room/board: $7,528. Books/supplies: $1,200. Personal expenses: $2,800.

2008-2009 Financial aid. Need-based: 3,068 full-time freshmen applied for aid; 1,439 were judged to have need; 1,433 of these received aid. Average need met was 81%. Average scholarship/grant was $8,153; average loan $2,900. 61% of total undergraduate aid awarded as scholarships/grants, 39% as loans/jobs. **Non-need-based:** Awarded to 3,049 full-time undergraduates, including 880 freshmen. Scholarships awarded for academics, athletics, ROTC, state residency.

Application procedures. Admission: Priority date 10/15; deadline 1/15 (postmark date). $50 fee, may be waived for applicants with need. Admission notification on a rolling basis beginning on or about 12/15. Must reply by 5/1. **Financial aid:** Priority date 3/1; no closing date. FAFSA required. Applicants notified on a rolling basis starting 5/15; must reply within 2 week(s) of notification.

Academics. Special study options: Accelerated study, combined bachelor's/graduate degree, cooperative education, cross-registration, distance learning, double major, dual enrollment of high school students, exchange student, external degree, honors, independent study, internships, liberal arts/career combination, student-designed major, study abroad, teacher certification program, Washington semester. **Credit/placement by examination:** AP, CLEP, IB, institutional tests. Unlimited number of hours of credit by examination may be counted toward bachelor's degree. **Support services:** Learning center, pre-admission summer program, reduced course load, remedial instruction, study skills assistance, tutoring, writing center.

Majors. Agriculture: General, agribusiness operations, animal sciences, communications, dairy, economics, food science, horticulture, poultry, turf management. **Architecture:** Landscape. **Area/ethnic studies:** African-American, Latin American, women's. **Biology:** General, biochemistry, biotechnology, botany, cell/histology, ecology, entomology, genetics, microbiology. **Business:** General, accounting, business admin, fashion, finance, insurance, international, management information systems, managerial economics, marketing, real estate. **Communications:** Advertising, broadcast journalism, journalism, public relations. **Communications technology:** Radio/tv. **Computer sciences:** Computer science. **Conservation:** General, environmental studies, fisheries, forestry, wildlife. **Education:** Agricultural, English, family/consumer sciences, foreign languages, health, kindergarten/preschool, mathematics, middle, music, physical, science, social studies, special, voc/tech. **Engineering:** General, agricultural, chemical, computer, environmental. **Family/consumer sciences:** Child development, communication, consumer economics, family resources, food/nutrition, housing. **Foreign languages:** Ancient Greek, Arabic, Chinese, classics, comparative lit, French, German, Italian, Japanese, Latin, linguistics, Romance, Russian, Spanish. **Health:** Communication disorders, dietetics, environmental health, music therapy, public health ed. **History:** General. **Interdisciplinary:** Biological/physical sciences, cognitive science. **Liberal arts:** Arts/sciences. **Math:** General, statistics. **Parks/recreation:** Sports admin. **Philosophy/religion:** Philosophy, religion. **Physical sciences:** Astronomy, chemistry, geology, physics. **Protective services:** Criminal justice. **Psychology:** General, educational. **Public administration:** Social work. **Social sciences:** Anthropology, economics, geography, international relations, political science, sociology. **Visual/performing arts:** Art, art history/conservation, dance, dramatic, film/cinema, music performance, music theory/composition, studio arts. **Other:** Environmental chemistry, Environmental resource science, Office information system.

Most popular majors. Biology 9%, business/marketing 21%, communications/journalism 6%, education 8%, family/consumer sciences 6%, psychology 6%, social sciences 11%.

Computing on campus. 2,600 workstations in dormitories, library, computer center, student center. Dormitories wired for high-speed internet access and linked to campus network. Commuter students can connect to campus network. Online course registration, online library, helpline, repair service, student web hosting, wireless network available.

Student life. **Freshman orientation:** Mandatory. Preregistration for classes offered. Two-day sessions offered during summer. **Housing:** Guaranteed on-campus for freshmen. Coed dorms, single-sex dorms, special housing for disabled, apartments, fraternity/sorority housing available. Honors and language focused housing available. **Activities:** Bands, campus ministries, choral groups, dance, drama, film society, international student organizations, literary magazine, music ensembles, Model UN, musical theater, opera, radio station, student government, student newspaper, symphony orchestra, TV station.

Athletics. NCAA. **Intercollegiate:** Baseball M, basketball, cross-country, diving, equestrian W, football (tackle) M, golf, gymnastics W, soccer W, softball W, swimming, tennis, track and field, volleyball W. **Intramural:** Basketball, cross-country, football (non-tackle), football (tackle) M, golf, racquetball, soccer, softball, squash, tennis, track and field, volleyball, wrestling M. **Team name:** Bulldogs.

Student services. Adult student services, alcohol/substance abuse counseling, career counseling, student employment services, financial aid counseling, health services, legal services, minority student services, on-campus daycare, personal counseling, placement for graduates, veterans' counselor, women's services. **Physically disabled:** Services for visually, speech, hearing impaired. **Learning disabled:** Comprehensive services available.

Contact. E-mail: undergrad@admissions.uga.edu
Phone: (706) 542-8776 Fax: (706) 542-1466
Nancy McDuff, Associate Vice President for Admissions and Enrollment Management, University of Georgia, Office of Undergraduate Admissions, Athens, GA 30602-1633

University of West Georgia

Carrollton, Georgia — **CB member**
www.westga.edu — **CB code: 5900**

- Public 4-year university
- Commuter campus in large town
- 9,230 degree-seeking undergraduates: 15% part-time, 60% women
- 2,022 graduate students
- 58% of applicants admitted
- SAT or ACT (ACT writing recommended) required

General. Founded in 1906. Regionally accredited. Off-campus sites in Newnan (undergraduate). Advanced Academy of Georgia for academically accelerated high school juniors and seniors. **Degrees:** 1,221 bachelor's awarded; master's, doctoral, first professional offered. **ROTC:** Army. **Location:** 50 miles from Atlanta. **Calendar:** Semester, extensive summer session. **Full-time faculty:** 428 total; 77% have terminal degrees, 16% minority, 52% women. **Part-time faculty:** 123 total; 43% have terminal degrees, 13% minority, 66% women. **Class size:** 41% < 20, 42% 20-39, 6% 40-49, 8% 50-99, 3% >100. **Special facilities:** Observatory, performing arts center, archaeological laboratory, technology enhanced learning center.

Freshman class profile. 6,159 applied, 3,589 admitted, 2,097 enrolled.

Mid 50% test scores			
SAT critical reading:	450-530	GPA 2.0-2.99:	48%
SAT math:	450-530	Return as sophomores:	75%
SAT writing:	430-510	Out-of-state:	2%
ACT composite:	18-21	Live on campus:	68%
GPA 3.75 or higher:	7%	International:	1%
GPA 3.50-3.74:	10%	Fraternities:	16%
GPA 3.0-3.49:	34%	Sororities:	15%

Basis for selection. GED not accepted. Freshman admission based on SAT/ACT, GPA in college preparatory subjects, and system-mandated college preparatory curriculum. **Homeschooled:** SAT scores equal to or greater than average score of previous fall freshman class required. 430 SAT verbal and 410 SAT math or 17 ACT English and math required. SAT and ACT cannot be mixed in determining admission eligibility. Must submit academic portfolio booklets detailing all 16 high school college prep courses.

High school preparation. College-preparatory program required. 16 units required. Required units include English 4, mathematics 4, social studies 1, history 2, science 3 (laboratory 2) and foreign language 2. 1 math higher than algebra II required.

2008-2009 Annual costs. Tuition/fees: $4,316; $13,898 out-of-state. Room/board: $5,714. Books/supplies: $1,000. Personal expenses: $645.

2008-2009 Financial aid. **Need-based:** 1,689 full-time freshmen applied for aid; 1,169 were judged to have need; 1,145 of these received aid. Average need met was 66%. Average scholarship/grant was $5,540; average loan $3,185. 64% of total undergraduate aid awarded as scholarships/grants, 36% as loans/jobs. **Non-need-based:** Awarded to 1,242 full-time undergraduates, including 458 freshmen. Scholarships awarded for academics, alumni affiliation, art, athletics, leadership, music/drama.

Application procedures. **Admission:** Priority date 5/1; deadline 6/1 (receipt date). $30 fee, may be waived for applicants with need. Admission notification on a rolling basis beginning on or about 9/1. **Financial aid:** Priority date 4/1, closing date 7/1. FAFSA required. Applicants notified on a rolling basis starting 5/15; must reply within 4 week(s) of notification.

Academics. **Special study options:** Accelerated study, cooperative education, distance learning, double major, dual enrollment of high school students, external degree, honors, independent study, internships, study abroad, teacher certification program. **Credit/placement by examination:** AP, CLEP, IB, institutional tests. 30 credit hours maximum toward bachelor's degree. **Support services:** Learning center, pre-admission summer program, reduced course load, remedial instruction, study skills assistance, tutoring, writing center.

Honors college/program. Open to entering freshmen who meet 2 of the following: 1200 SAT or 26 ACT; 610 SAT verbal or 27 ACT English; 3.5 GPA. Recommended entrance no later than beginning of sophomore year.

Majors. **Biology:** General. **Business:** Accounting, business admin, finance, management information systems, managerial economics, marketing, real estate. **Communications:** Journalism. **Computer sciences:** General. **Conservation:** Environmental science, environmental studies. **Education:** Biology, business, chemistry, elementary, kindergarten/preschool, middle, music, physical, physics, secondary, special. **Foreign languages:** French, German, Spanish. **Health:** Nursing (RN), speech pathology. **History:** General. **Math:** General. **Parks/recreation:** Facilities management. **Philosophy/religion:** Philosophy. **Physical sciences:** Chemistry, geology, physics. **Psychology:** General. **Social sciences:** Anthropology, criminology, economics, geography, international economics, international relations, political science, sociology. **Visual/performing arts:** Art, dramatic, music performance, music theory/composition.

Most popular majors. Biology 6%, business/marketing 23%, education 19%, health sciences 10%, psychology 6%, social sciences 11%.

Computing on campus. 1,000 workstations in dormitories, library, computer center, student center. Dormitories wired for high-speed internet access and linked to campus network. Online course registration, online library, helpline, repair service, student web hosting, wireless network available.

Student life. **Freshman orientation:** Mandatory, $25 fee. Preregistration for classes offered. **Policies:** All freshmen required to reside on-campus unless married or living with parents, relatives, or legal guardians. **Housing:** Guaranteed on-campus for freshmen. Coed dorms, single-sex dorms, special housing for disabled, apartments, cooperative housing, fraternity/sorority housing available. $250 partly refundable deposit, deadline 7/1. **Activities:** Bands, choral groups, dance, drama, international student organizations, literary magazine, music ensembles, musical theater, opera, radio station, student government, student newspaper, TV station, Baptist Student

Four-Year Colleges

Union, Catholic Student Life, Muslim student alliance, Latter-Day Saint student association, Jewish student group, Black Students Alliance, Democratic organization, Republican organization.

Athletics. NCAA. **Intercollegiate:** Baseball M, basketball, cheerleading, cross-country, football (tackle) M, golf, soccer W, softball W, volleyball W. **Intramural:** Basketball, football (non-tackle), golf, sailing, soccer, softball, table tennis, tennis, track and field, volleyball, weight lifting. **Team name:** Wolves.

Student services. Adult student services, career counseling, student employment services, financial aid counseling, health services, minority student services, on-campus daycare, personal counseling, placement for graduates, veterans' counselor. **Physically disabled:** Services for visually, speech, hearing impaired.

Contact. E-mail: admiss@westga.edu
Phone: (678) 839-4000 Fax: (678) 839-4747
Bobby Johnson, Director of Admissions, University of West Georgia, 1601 Maple Street, Carrollton, GA 30118

Valdosta State University

Valdosta, Georgia — **CB member**
www.valdosta.edu — **CB code: 5855**

- Public 4-year university
- Commuter campus in small city
- 9,654 degree-seeking undergraduates: 13% part-time, 59% women, 28% African American, 1% Asian American, 2% Hispanic American, 1% international
- 1,713 degree-seeking graduate students
- 62% of applicants admitted
- SAT or ACT (ACT writing optional) required
- 40% graduate within 6 years

General. Founded in 1906. Regionally accredited. **Degrees:** 1,421 bachelor's, 59 associate awarded; master's, doctoral offered. **ROTC:** Air Force. **Location:** 228 miles from Atlanta; 124 miles from Jacksonville, Florida. **Calendar:** Semester, extensive summer session. **Full-time faculty:** 469 total; 66% have terminal degrees, 10% minority, 48% women. **Part-time faculty:** 153 total; 20% have terminal degrees, 14% minority, 61% women. **Class size:** 37% < 20, 51% 20-39, 9% 40-49, 2% 50-99, less than 1% >100. **Special facilities:** Planetarium, herbarium, observatory, archives museum, pedestrian mall.

Freshman class profile. 7,025 applied, 4,360 admitted, 2,137 enrolled.

Mid 50% test scores		**GPA 2.0-2.99:**	46%
SAT critical reading:	480-560	**Return as sophomores:**	71%
SAT math:	460-560	**Out-of-state:**	3%
ACT composite:	20-23	**Live on campus:**	70%
GPA 3.75 or higher:	9%	**Fraternities:**	8%
GPA 3.50-3.74:	11%	**Sororities:**	10%
GPA 3.0-3.49:	34%		

Basis for selection. GED not accepted. 440 SAT Verbal, 410 SAT Math or 18 ACT English, 17 ACT Math required. Freshmen Index of 2040 required, based on academic GPA multiplied by 500 added to SAT verbal and math scores. **Homeschooled:** 1050 SAT (exclusive of Writing) or 23 ACT, declaration of intent to homeschool filed with Board of Education, portfolio that demonstrates satisfactory completion of college prep curriculum, letter from primary teacher certifying completion of high school and date of graduation, 2 letters of recommendation from non-family members, certificate of immunization required. **Learning Disabled:** Untimed SAT/ACT accepted.

High school preparation. College-preparatory program required. 16 units required. Required units include English 4, mathematics 4, social studies 3, science 3 (laboratory 2) and foreign language 2.

2008-2009 Annual costs. Tuition/fees: $4,456; $14,038 out-of-state. Room/board: $6,290. Books/supplies: $1,200. Personal expenses: $2,600.

2007-2008 Financial aid. Need-based: 1,622 full-time freshmen applied for aid; 1,170 were judged to have need; 1,160 of these received aid. Average need met was 89%. Average scholarship/grant was $5,309; average loan $4,559. 41% of total undergraduate aid awarded as scholarships/grants, 59% as loans/jobs. **Non-need-based:** Awarded to 448 full-time undergraduates, including 113 freshmen. Scholarships awarded for academics, alumni affiliation, art, athletics, minority status, music/drama, ROTC, state residency.

Application procedures. Admission: Closing date 6/15 (receipt date). $40 fee, may be waived for applicants with need. Admission notification on a rolling basis beginning on or about 9/1. **Financial aid:** Priority date 5/1; no closing date. FAFSA required. Applicants notified on a rolling basis starting 6/1.

Academics. Special study options: Cooperative education, distance learning, double major, dual enrollment of high school students, ESL, external degree, honors, independent study, internships, study abroad, teacher certification program, weekend college. **Credit/placement by examination:** AP, CLEP, IB, SAT, ACT. 30 credit hours maximum toward associate degree, 30 toward bachelor's. **Support services:** Study skills assistance, tutoring, writing center.

Majors. Biology: General. **Business:** Accounting, administrative services, business admin, finance, managerial economics, marketing. **Communications:** Media studies. **Computer sciences:** General, information systems. **Conservation:** Environmental science. **Education:** Art, business, early childhood, middle, music, physical, secondary, special, trade/industrial. **Foreign languages:** French, sign language interpretation, Spanish. **Health:** Athletic training, nursing (RN), speech pathology. **History:** General. **Legal studies:** Paralegal. **Liberal arts:** Arts/sciences. **Math:** General, applied. **Parks/recreation:** Exercise sciences. **Philosophy/religion:** Philosophy. **Physical sciences:** Astronomy, chemistry, physics. **Protective services:** Criminal justice. **Psychology:** General. **Social sciences:** Political science, sociology. **Visual/performing arts:** General, art, interior design, music performance.

Most popular majors. Business/marketing 20%, education 21%, English 7%, health sciences 9%, social sciences 6%.

Computing on campus. 1,600 workstations in dormitories, library. Dormitories wired for high-speed internet access and linked to campus network. Commuter students can connect to campus network. Online course registration, online library, helpline, repair service, student web hosting, wireless network available.

Student life. Freshman orientation: Available, $35 fee. Preregistration for classes offered. One-day programs held in June, July, and August. **Housing:** Coed dorms, special housing for disabled, apartments, wellness housing available. $300 fully refundable deposit, deadline 4/15. Honors floors available. **Activities:** Bands, campus ministries, choral groups, dance, drama, international student organizations, literary magazine, music ensembles, Model UN, radio station, student government, student newspaper, symphony orchestra, TV station, Black Student League, outdoor adventure club, Habitat for Humanity, other religious and social service organizations.

Athletics. NCAA. **Intercollegiate:** Baseball M, basketball, cross-country, football (tackle) M, golf M, softball W, tennis, volleyball W. **Intramural:** Badminton, basketball, bowling, football (non-tackle), golf, racquetball, soccer, softball, table tennis, tennis, volleyball, weight lifting. **Team name:** Blazers.

Student services. Alcohol/substance abuse counseling, career counseling, student employment services, financial aid counseling, health services, minority student services, personal counseling, placement for graduates, veterans' counselor. **Physically disabled:** Services for visually, speech, hearing impaired. **Learning disabled:** Comprehensive services available.

Contact. E-mail: admissions@valdosta.edu
Phone: (229) 333-5791 Toll-free number: (800) 618-1878
Fax: (229) 333-5482
Walter Peacock, Director of Admissions, Valdosta State University, 1500 North Patterson Street, Valdosta, GA 31698-0170

Wesleyan College

Macon, Georgia — **CB member**
www.wesleyancollege.edu — **CB code: 5895**

- Private 4-year liberal arts college for women affiliated with United Methodist Church
- Residential campus in small city
- 557 degree-seeking undergraduates: 32% part-time, 100% women, 33% African American, 3% Asian American, 2% Hispanic American, 14% international
- 93 degree-seeking graduate students
- 53% of applicants admitted
- SAT or ACT (ACT writing optional), application essay required

General. Founded in 1836. Regionally accredited. **Degrees:** 76 bachelor's awarded; master's offered. **Location:** 75 miles from Atlanta. **Calendar:** Semester, limited summer session. **Full-time faculty:** 47 total; 100% have terminal degrees, 8% minority, 55% women. **Part-time faculty:** 33 total; 21% have terminal degrees, 70% women. **Class size:** 91% < 20, 9% 20-39. **Special facilities:** Equestrian facilities, arboretum, lake.

Freshman class profile. 536 applied, 286 admitted, 100 enrolled.

Mid 50% test scores		Return as sophomores:	77%
SAT critical reading:	500-610	Out-of-state:	22%
SAT math:	460-600	Live on campus:	90%
SAT writing:	480-630	International:	11%
End year in good standing:	91%		

Basis for selection. Admission committee reviews applicants based on academic performance in college preparatory courses, standardized test scores, extra-curricular activities and recommendations. Interview recommended; required for scholarship competitions. Audition required of music or theater students interested in performance arts scholarship. Portfolio required of art majors. **Homeschooled:** Statement describing homeschool structure and mission, transcript of courses and grades, letter of recommendation (nonparent) required. Diplomas issued by parents are recognized. Student may provide biography of high school literature and essay to evaluate exposure and thinking skills. Extra-curricular activities, counselor interviews considered.

High school preparation. 15 units required; 22 recommended. Required and recommended units include English 4, mathematics 3-4, social studies 3-4, science 3-4 (laboratory 2-3), foreign language 2-4 and academic electives 2.

2009-2010 Annual costs. Tuition/fees: $17,500. Room/board: $8,000. Books/supplies: $1,000. Personal expenses: $1,000.

2008-2009 Financial aid. Need-based: 76 full-time freshmen applied for aid; 62 were judged to have need; 62 of these received aid. Average need met was 85%. Average scholarship/grant was $13,018; average loan $3,807. 63% of total undergraduate aid awarded as scholarships/grants, 37% as loans/jobs. **Non-need-based:** Awarded to 188 full-time undergraduates, including 46 freshmen. Scholarships awarded for academics, alumni affiliation, art, job skills, leadership, minority status, music/drama, religious affiliation, state residency.

Application procedures. Admission: Priority date 3/1; deadline 6/1 (postmark date). $30 fee, may be waived for applicants with need. Admission notification on a rolling basis beginning on or about 10/1. Must reply by 7/1. **Financial aid:** Priority date 2/15, closing date 6/3. FAFSA, institutional form required. Applicants notified on a rolling basis starting 3/1; must reply by 5/1 or within 3 week(s) of notification.

Academics. Special study options: Accelerated study, combined bachelor's/graduate degree, cross-registration, double major, dual enrollment of high school students, exchange student, honors, independent study, internships, liberal arts/career combination, student-designed major, study abroad, teacher certification program, weekend college. **Credit/placement by examination:** AP, CLEP, IB, institutional tests. 30 credit hours maximum toward bachelor's degree. **Support services:** Learning center, reduced course load, study skills assistance, tutoring, writing center.

Majors. Biology: General. **Business:** Business admin, international. **Communications:** General, advertising. **Computer sciences:** General. **Education:** Early childhood, middle. **Foreign languages:** French, Spanish. **History:** General. **Liberal arts:** Arts/sciences. **Math:** General. **Philosophy/religion:** Philosophy, religion. **Physical sciences:** Chemistry, physics. **Psychology:** General. **Social sciences:** General, economics, international relations. **Theology:** Preministerial. **Visual/performing arts:** Art history/conservation, dramatic, studio arts.

Most popular majors. Biology 10%, business/marketing 29%, communications/journalism 15%, psychology 20%, visual/performing arts 9%.

Computing on campus. PC or laptop required. 20 workstations in library, student center. Dormitories wired for high-speed internet access and linked to campus network. Commuter students can connect to campus network. Online course registration, online library, helpline, repair service, wireless network available.

Student life. Freshman orientation: Mandatory. Preregistration for classes offered. Summer orientation held in June; includes registration. Fall orientation held in August prior to start of classes. **Policies:** Students required to live on campus unless married or living with immediate family in the local area. Honor Code used. **Housing:** Guaranteed on-campus for all undergraduates. Special housing for disabled, apartments available. $150 deposit, deadline 7/1. **Activities:** Campus ministries, choral groups, dance, drama, international student organizations, literary magazine, music ensembles, Model UN, student government, student newspaper, honor council, Mortar board, Young Democrats, Circle K, College Republicans, Council on Religions Concerns, American Chemical Society, Wesleyan Disciples.

Athletics. NCAA. **Intercollegiate:** Basketball W, cross-country W, equestrian W, soccer W, softball W, tennis W. **Intramural:** Basketball W, cross-country W, soccer W, softball W, volleyball W. **Team name:** Pioneers.

Student services. Adult student services, alcohol/substance abuse counseling, chaplain/spiritual director, career counseling, student employment services, financial aid counseling, health services, minority student services, personal counseling, women's services.

Contact. E-mail: admission@wesleyancollege.edu
Phone: (478) 757-5206 Toll-free number: (800) 447-6610
Fax: (478) 757-4030
C. Stephen Farr, Vice President for Enrollment Services, Wesleyan College, 4760 Forsyth Road, Macon, GA 31210-4462

Westwood College: Atlanta Midtown
Atlanta, Georgia

- For-profit 3-year technical college
- Commuter campus in very large city

General. Accredited by ACICS. **Calendar:** Differs by program.

Contact. Phone: (404) 745-9096
Director of Admissions, 1100 Spring Street, Suite 200, Atlanta, GA 30309

Westwood College: Northlake
Atlanta, Georgia
www.westwood.edu

- For-profit 4-year visual arts and technical college
- Very large city

General. Accredited by ACICS. **Calendar:** Differs by program.

Contact. Phone: (404) 962-2998
2220 Parklake Drive, Suite 175, Atlanta, GA 30345

Hawaii

Brigham Young University-Hawaii

Laie, Hawaii — **CB member**
www.byuh.edu — **CB code: 4106**

- Private 4-year university and liberal arts college affiliated with Church of Jesus Christ of Latter-day Saints
- Residential campus in small town
- 2,309 degree-seeking undergraduates: 6% part-time, 55% women, 1% African American, 21% Asian American, 2% Hispanic American, 42% international
- 39% of applicants admitted
- Application essay, interview required
- 47% graduate within 6 years

General. Founded in 1955. Regionally accredited. Mission to educate students from Asia and Pacific Rim. **Degrees:** 535 bachelor's awarded. **ROTC:** Army, Naval, Air Force. **Location:** 38 miles from Honolulu. **Calendar:** Semester, limited summer session. **Full-time faculty:** 122 total; 80% have terminal degrees, 23% minority, 21% women. **Part-time faculty:** 116 total; 4% have terminal degrees, 47% minority, 64% women. **Class size:** 54% < 20, 40% 20-39, 4% 40-49, 2% 50-99, less than 1% >100. **Special facilities:** Center for Hawaiian language and cultural studies, museum of natural history, Polynesian cultural center, Pacific Islands collection housed in university archives, Pacific Islands research room.

Freshman class profile. 1,381 applied, 543 admitted, 300 enrolled.

Mid 50% test scores		**GPA 3.0-3.49:**	44%
SAT critical reading:	460-580	**GPA 2.0-2.99:**	15%
SAT math:	490-580	**Return as sophomores:**	58%
ACT composite:	21-26	**Out-of-state:**	76%
GPA 3.75 or higher:	21%	**Live on campus:**	90%
GPA 3.50-3.74:	20%	**International:**	27%

Basis for selection. GED not accepted. Interview, essay, recommendations very important. Test scores also important. 3.0 GPA required for domestic students. ACT recommended. Audition required for music majors. Portfolio required for art majors. Ecclesiastical interviews required for all students. Essays may make difference in admission.

High school preparation. Recommended units include English 4, mathematics 2, social studies 3, history 2 and science 2.

2008-2009 Annual costs. Tuition/fees: $3,600. 100% higher tuition and per-credit-hour charges for students who are not members of The Church of Jesus Christ of Latter-day Saints. Room/board: $5,568. Books/supplies: $800. Personal expenses: $1,600.

2007-2008 Financial aid. Non-need-based: Scholarships awarded for academics, art, athletics, leadership, music/drama, state residency.

Application procedures. Admission: Closing date 2/15 (receipt date). $30 fee. Admission notification on a rolling basis beginning on or about 4/1. Must reply by 8/25. **Financial aid:** Closing date 3/15. FAFSA required. Applicants notified by 5/1; must reply by 8/31.

Academics. Special study options: Cooperative education, double major, ESL, honors, independent study, internships, student-designed major, teacher certification program. **Credit/placement by examination:** AP, CLEP, IB, institutional tests. **Support services:** Learning center, remedial instruction, study skills assistance, tutoring, writing center.

Majors. Area/ethnic studies: Pacific. **Biology:** General, biochemistry. **Business:** Accounting, business admin. **Computer sciences:** Computer science, information systems, information technology. **Education:** Art, biology, business, chemistry, elementary, English, ESL, mathematics, music, physical, physics, science, secondary, social science, special. **History:** General. **Interdisciplinary:** Intercultural. **Math:** General. **Parks/recreation:** Exercise sciences, health/fitness. **Psychology:** General. **Public administration:** Social work. **Social sciences:** Political science. **Visual/performing arts:** Art, piano/organ, studio arts, voice/opera.

Most popular majors. Business/marketing 25%, computer/information sciences 7%, education 19%, interdisciplinary studies 13%, parks/recreation 6%, psychology 8%, public administration/social services 6%.

Computing on campus. 465 workstations in dormitories, library, computer center, student center. Dormitories wired for high-speed internet access and linked to campus network. Online course registration, online library, helpline, repair service, wireless network available.

Student life. Freshman orientation: Mandatory. Preregistration for classes offered. 2 weeks at the beginning of semester, includes luau, campus and island tour. **Policies:** Religious observance required. **Housing:** Guaranteed on-campus for freshmen. Single-sex dorms, apartments, wellness housing available. $50 deposit, deadline 4/30. All first-time, non-local freshmen required to live on campus until sophomore standing achieved. **Activities:** Bands, choral groups, dance, drama, film society, literary magazine, music ensembles, student government, student newspaper.

Athletics. NCAA. **Intercollegiate:** Basketball, cross-country, golf M, soccer, softball W, tennis, volleyball W. **Intramural:** Basketball, bowling, cross-country, golf, racquetball, rugby, soccer, softball, swimming, table tennis, tennis, volleyball, water polo M, weight lifting. **Team name:** Seasiders.

Student services. Chaplain/spiritual director, career counseling, student employment services, financial aid counseling, health services, personal counseling, placement for graduates, veterans' counselor, women's services. **Physically disabled:** Services for visually, speech, hearing impaired.

Contact. E-mail: admissions@byuh.edu
Phone: (808) 675-3738 Fax: (808) 675-3741
Arapata Meha, Dean of Admissions and Records, Brigham Young University-Hawaii, 55-220 Kulanui Street, #1973, Laie, HI 96762-1294

Chaminade University of Honolulu

Honolulu, Hawaii — **CB member**
www.chaminade.edu — **CB code: 4105**

- Private 4-year university affiliated with Roman Catholic Church
- Commuter campus in large city
- 1,046 degree-seeking undergraduates
- 93% of applicants admitted
- SAT or ACT (ACT writing optional), application essay required

General. Founded in 1955. Regionally accredited. Campus shared with St. Louis School. **Degrees:** 346 bachelor's, 126 associate awarded; master's offered. **ROTC:** Army, Air Force. **Location:** 2 miles from Waikiki. **Calendar:** Semester, limited summer session. **Full-time faculty:** 74 total. **Part-time faculty:** 51 total. **Class size:** 63% < 20, 36% 20-39, 1% 40-49. **Special facilities:** Montessori laboratory preschool, observatory, theater.

Freshman class profile. 861 applied, 803 admitted, 235 enrolled.

Mid 50% test scores		**ACT composite:**	17-23
SAT critical reading:	420-510	**Out-of-state:**	50%
SAT math:	410-520	**Live on campus:**	65%

Basis for selection. School achievement record, test scores, statement of purpose important. Interview recommended for marginal students.

High school preparation. Recommended units include English 4, mathematics 3, social studies 3, science 2 and academic electives 4.

2008-2009 Annual costs. Tuition/fees: $16,140. Room/board: $10,420. Books/supplies: $1,200. Personal expenses: $1,254.

2008-2009 Financial aid. Non-need-based: Scholarships awarded for academics, art, athletics, leadership, religious affiliation, ROTC, state residency. **Additional information:** For students whose eligibility for federal and institutional aid does not meet entire costs, alternative student loans may be secured for eligible applicants.

Application procedures. Admission: No deadline. $50 fee. Admission notification on a rolling basis. **Financial aid:** Priority date 2/15; no closing date. FAFSA required. Applicants notified on a rolling basis starting 2/15; must reply within 4 week(s) of notification.

Academics. Special study options: Accelerated study, distance learning, double major, exchange student, independent study, internships, semester at sea, student-designed major, teacher certification program. Accelerated sessions in evening division. **Credit/placement by examination:** AP, CLEP, IB, SAT, ACT, institutional tests. 30 credit hours maximum toward associate degree, 30 toward bachelor's. **Support services:** Learning center, preadmission summer program, remedial instruction, study skills assistance, tutoring.

Majors. Biology: General. **Business:** Accounting, business admin, marketing. **Communications:** General, broadcast journalism, media studies, public relations. **Computer sciences:** General, computer science. **Conservation:** Environmental studies. **Education:** Early childhood, elementary, secondary. **History:** General. **Interdisciplinary:** Behavioral sciences. **Liberal arts:** Arts/sciences. **Philosophy/religion:** Religion. **Protective services:** Criminalistics, forensics. **Psychology:** General. **Social sciences:** General, international relations, political science. **Visual/performing arts:** Interior design.

Computing on campus. 100 workstations in dormitories, library, computer center, student center. Dormitories wired for high-speed internet access and linked to campus network. Online library, helpline, repair service, wireless network available.

Student life. Freshman orientation: Mandatory, $140 fee. Preregistration for classes offered. **Housing:** Guaranteed on-campus for freshmen. Coed dorms, single-sex dorms, special housing for disabled, apartments, wellness housing available. $300 deposit, deadline 5/1. **Activities:** Choral groups, dance, drama, literary magazine, musical theater, student government, student newspaper, Samoan club, Hawaiian club, Rotaract club, accounting club, Black Student Union, Filipino club, CJ Sleuths, communications club.

Athletics. NCAA. **Intercollegiate:** Basketball M, cross-country, golf, softball W, tennis, volleyball W. **Intramural:** Cheerleading. **Team name:** Silverswords.

Student services. Adult student services, alcohol/substance abuse counseling, chaplain/spiritual director, career counseling, services for economically disadvantaged, student employment services, financial aid counseling, health services, personal counseling, placement for graduates. **Physically disabled:** Services for visually, speech, hearing impaired.

Contact. E-mail: admissions@chaminade.edu
Phone: (808) 735-4735 Toll-free number: (800) 735-3733
Fax: (808) 739-4647
Dan Yoshitake, Associate Director of Admissions, Chaminade University of Honolulu, 3140 Waialae Avenue, Honolulu, HI 96816

Hawaii Pacific University

Honolulu, Hawaii — **CB member**
www.hpu.edu — **CB code: 4352**

- Private 4-year university and liberal arts college
- Commuter campus in large city
- 6,505 degree-seeking undergraduates: 46% part-time, 60% women
- 1,123 degree-seeking graduate students
- 76% of applicants admitted
- SAT or ACT (ACT writing optional) required
- 40% graduate within 6 years

General. Founded in 1965. Regionally accredited. Three (3) main campuses connected by free shuttle service. Programs offered for military personnel and their dependents and for older students. Satellite campus on six (6) military installations on Oahu. Affiliated with the Oceanic Institute. **Degrees:** 1,088 bachelor's, 194 associate awarded; master's offered. **ROTC:** Army, Air Force. **Calendar:** Semester, extensive summer session. **Full-time faculty:** 274 total; 66% have terminal degrees, 25% minority, 44% women. **Part-time faculty:** 323 total; 32% have terminal degrees, 39% minority, 47% women. **Class size:** 58% < 20, 42% 20-39, less than 1% 40-49. **Special facilities:** Oceanic Institute, entrepreneurship center, research boat, theater.

Freshman class profile. 3,371 applied, 2,558 admitted, 622 enrolled.

Mid 50% test scores			
SAT critical reading:	420-550	GPA 2.0-2.99:	26%
SAT math:	430-560	Rank in top quarter:	50%
SAT writing:	410-540	Rank in top tenth:	21%
ACT composite:	18-24	End year in good standing:	99%
GPA 3.75 or higher:	21%	Return as sophomores:	70%
GPA 3.50-3.74:	20%	Out-of-state:	45%
GPA 3.0-3.49:	33%	Live on campus:	24%

Basis for selection. Academic record, test scores most important. Interview also important, recommendations considered. Essay recommended. **Homeschooled:** Interview, letter of recommendation (nonparent) required.

High school preparation. 14 units recommended. Recommended units include English 4, mathematics 4, social studies 3, history 2, science 2 (laboratory 1) and foreign language 2. Additional science and mathematics required for nursing and marine science.

2008-2009 Annual costs. Tuition/fees: $13,980. Room/board: $10,564. Books/supplies: $1,300. Personal expenses: $800.

2008-2009 Financial aid. Need-based: 501 full-time freshmen applied for aid; 283 were judged to have need; 275 of these received aid. Average need met was 83%. Average scholarship/grant was $4,428; average loan $6,003. 14% of total undergraduate aid awarded as scholarships/grants, 86% as loans/jobs. **Non-need-based:** Scholarships awarded for academics, alumni affiliation, athletics, job skills, leadership, music/drama, religious affiliation, ROTC.

Application procedures. Admission: Priority date 3/1; no deadline. $50 fee, may be waived for applicants with need. Admission notification on a rolling basis. Must reply by May 1 or within 4 week(s) if notified thereafter. **Financial aid:** Priority date 3/1; no closing date. FAFSA required. Applicants notified on a rolling basis starting 4/1; must reply within 3 week(s) of notification.

Academics. All students complete core requirements based on following themes: global systems, world cultures, communication skills, research/epistemology, values and choices. **Special study options:** Accelerated study, combined bachelor's/graduate degree, cooperative education, distance learning, double major, dual enrollment of high school students, ESL, honors, independent study, internships, liberal arts/career combination, student-designed major, study abroad, teacher certification program, weekend college. 3-2 engineering program with University of Southern California (CA), Washington University, St. Louis (MO). **Credit/placement by examination:** AP, CLEP, IB, SAT, ACT, institutional tests. 36 credit hours maximum toward associate degree, 36 toward bachelor's. **Support services:** Learning center, pre-admission summer program, reduced course load, remedial instruction, study skills assistance, tutoring.

Honors college/program. 3.5 minimum high school GPA, minimum 24 ACT or 1100 SAT (exclusive of Writing) required. 40-50 admitted and enrolled each fall.

Majors. Biology: General, marine. **Business:** General, accounting, banking/financial services, business admin, communications, finance, human resources, international, international finance, management information systems, managerial economics, marketing, tourism/travel. **Communications:** General, advertising, journalism, public relations. **Computer sciences:** General, computer science. **Conservation:** General, environmental science, environmental studies. **Education:** ESL. **Family/consumer sciences:** Family studies. **Foreign languages:** Comparative lit. **Health:** Nursing (RN), premedicine. **History:** General. **Interdisciplinary:** Behavioral sciences. **Liberal arts:** Arts/sciences. **Math:** Applied. **Physical sciences:** Oceanography. **Protective services:** Law enforcement admin. **Psychology:** General. **Public administration:** General, human services, social work. **Social sciences:** General, anthropology, economics, international relations, political science, sociology.

Most popular majors. Business/marketing 35%, communications/journalism 7%, health sciences 24%, psychology 6%, security/protective services 6%, social sciences 6%.

Computing on campus. 590 workstations in library, computer center, student center. Dormitories wired for high-speed internet access and linked to campus network. Commuter students can connect to campus network. Online course registration, online library, helpline, student web hosting, wireless network available.

Student life. Freshman orientation: Available, $10 fee. Preregistration for classes offered. Week of activities including on-campus sessions and off-campus activities. In fall, weekend (Friday, Saturday) including above. In spring, day activities that include on-campus sessions in summer. **Housing:** Coed dorms, apartments, wellness housing available. $500 nonrefundable deposit. **Activities:** Pep band, choral groups, dance, drama, film society, international student organizations, literary magazine, music ensembles, musical theater, student government, student newspaper, Rotaract, President's Hosts, Christian Fellowship, American marketing association, hiking club, honors societies, computing club, Students In Free Enterprise.

Athletics. NCAA. **Intercollegiate:** Baseball M, basketball, cheerleading, cross-country, golf M, soccer, softball W, tennis, volleyball W. **Intramural:** Basketball, football (tackle), soccer, softball, table tennis, volleyball. **Team name:** Sea Warriors.

Student services. Adult student services, alcohol/substance abuse counseling, chaplain/spiritual director, career counseling, student employment services, financial aid counseling, personal counseling, placement for graduates, veterans' counselor.

Contact. E-mail: admissions@hpu.edu
Phone: (808) 544-0238 Toll-free number: (866) 225-5478
Fax: (808) 544-1136
Sara Sato, Director of Admissions, Hawaii Pacific University, 1164 Bishop Street, Suite 200, Honolulu, HI 96813

University of Hawaii at Hilo

Hilo, Hawaii — **CB member**
www.uhh.hawaii.edu — **CB code: 4869**

- Public 4-year university
- Commuter campus in large town
- 3,208 degree-seeking undergraduates: 16% part-time, 55% women, 1% African American, 47% Asian American, 3% Hispanic American, 1% Native American, 6% international
- 381 degree-seeking graduate students
- SAT or ACT (ACT writing optional) required

General. Founded in 1970. Regionally accredited. **Degrees:** 522 bachelor's awarded; master's, doctoral, first professional offered. **Location:** 200 miles from Honolulu. **Calendar:** Semester, limited summer session. **Full-time faculty:** 262 total. **Part-time faculty:** 83 total. **Class size:** 47% < 20, 47% 20-39, 5% 40-49, 1% 50-99. **Special facilities:** Active volcanoes study center, space science center, small business development center, marine education center, 110-acre farm laboratory, fitness center/pool.

Freshman class profile.

Mid 50% test scores		**GPA 2.0-2.99:**	23%
SAT critical reading:	440-560	**Rank in top quarter:**	46%
SAT math:	440-600	**Rank in top tenth:**	22%
ACT composite:	17-24	**Out-of-state:**	27%
GPA 3.75 or higher:	20%	**Live on campus:**	64%
GPA 3.50-3.74:	17%	**International:**	2%
GPA 3.0-3.49:	40%		

Basis for selection. High school GPA in academic subjects, SAT/ACT test scores, class rank, and school recommendation considered.

High school preparation. 17 units required. Required and recommended units include English 4, mathematics 3, social studies 2, history 2, science 3, foreign language 2 and academic electives 7. 3 mathematics beyond pre-algebra, 7 academic electives not including physical education or ROTC. 4 math and 4 science recommended for science and business majors.

2008-2009 Annual costs. Tuition/fees: $4,360; $12,880 out-of-state. Room/board: $7,014. Books/supplies: $1,017. Personal expenses: $1,166.

2008-2009 Financial aid. **Additional information:** Hawaii student incentive grants and tuition waivers (merit and need-based) available to Hawaii residents at participating institutions.

Application procedures. **Admission:** Priority date 3/1; deadline 7/1 (postmark date). $50 fee, may be waived for applicants with need. Admission notification on a rolling basis beginning on or about 10/1. Must reply by May 1 or within 2 week(s) if notified thereafter. **Financial aid:** Priority date 3/1; no closing date. FAFSA required. Applicants notified on a rolling basis starting 4/15; must reply within 2 week(s) of notification.

Academics. **Special study options:** Cross-registration, distance learning, double major, dual enrollment of high school students, exchange student, honors, independent study, internships, student-designed major, study abroad, teacher certification program. Marine sciences and astronomy summer programs. **Credit/placement by examination:** CLEP, IB, institutional tests. 30 credit hours maximum toward bachelor's degree. **Support services:** Learning center, tutoring, writing center.

Majors. **Agriculture:** Agribusiness operations, agronomy, animal sciences, horticultural science, plant protection, soil science. **Area/ethnic studies:** Native American. **Biology:** General, marine. **Business:** General, accounting, business admin, finance, marketing. **Communications:** General. **Computer sciences:** General. **Foreign languages:** Japanese, linguistics. **Health:** Premedicine. **History:** General. **Interdisciplinary:** Natural sciences. **Liberal arts:** Arts/sciences. **Math:** General. **Parks/recreation:** Facilities management, health/fitness. **Philosophy/religion:** Philosophy, religion. **Physical sciences:** Astronomy, chemistry, geology, physics. **Psychology:** General. **Public administration:** General. **Social sciences:** Anthropology, economics, geography, political science, sociology. **Visual/performing arts:** Art.

Most popular majors. Business/marketing 10%, communication technologies 8%, interdisciplinary studies 7%, physical sciences 6%, psychology 15%, social sciences 17%.

Computing on campus. 600 workstations in dormitories, library, computer center, student center. Commuter students can connect to campus network. Online course registration, online library, helpline, repair service available.

Student life. **Freshman orientation:** Available, $25 fee. Preregistration for classes offered. 1-week program before start of classes. **Housing:** Coed dorms, special housing for disabled, apartments available. $20 deposit, deadline 7/15. Student housing units available for mobility-impaired students. **Activities:** Bands, choral groups, dance, drama, literary magazine, music ensembles, musical theater, student government, student newspaper, international student association, Samoan club, Delta Sigma Pi business fraternity, World Hope, Rotoract, Bayanihan club, Bahai Club, Chuukese Student Association, Earth Action, Nihon no kai.

Athletics. NCAA. **Intercollegiate:** Baseball M, basketball, cross-country, golf, soccer, softball W, tennis, volleyball W. **Intramural:** Archery, badminton, basketball, bowling, cross-country, golf, softball, table tennis, tennis, volleyball. **Team name:** Vulcans.

Student services. Career counseling, services for economically disadvantaged, student employment services, financial aid counseling, health services, minority student services, personal counseling, placement for graduates, women's services. **Physically disabled:** Services for visually, speech, hearing impaired.

Contact. E-mail: uhhadm@hawaii.edu
Phone: (808) 974-7414 Toll-free number: (800) 897-4456
Fax: (808) 933-0861
James Cromwell, Director of Admissions, University of Hawaii at Hilo, 200 West Kawili Street, Hilo, HI 96720-4091

University of Hawaii at Manoa

Honolulu, Hawaii — **CB member**
www.manoa.hawaii.edu — **CB code: 4867**

- Public 4-year university
- Commuter campus in very large city
- 13,438 degree-seeking undergraduates: 18% part-time, 54% women, 1% African American, 65% Asian American, 3% Hispanic American, 5% international
- 5,540 degree-seeking graduate students
- 67% of applicants admitted
- SAT or ACT with writing required
- 55% graduate within 6 years

General. Founded in 1907. Regionally accredited. **Degrees:** 2,994 bachelor's awarded; master's, doctoral, first professional offered. **ROTC:** Army, Air Force. **Location:** 3 miles from downtown. **Calendar:** Semester, extensive summer session. **Full-time faculty:** 1,222 total; 87% have terminal degrees, 34% minority, 41% women. **Part-time faculty:** 84 total; 70% have terminal degrees, 44% minority, 55% women. **Class size:** 51% < 20, 36% 20-39, 4% 40-49, 5% 50-99, 3% >100. **Special facilities:** Institute for astronomy, observatories, arboretum, East-West center, Japanese tea house and garden, Hawaiian studies center, Korean studies center.

Freshman class profile. 7,029 applied, 4,688 admitted, 1,866 enrolled.

Mid 50% test scores		**Rank in top quarter:**	58%
SAT critical reading:	480-570	**Rank in top tenth:**	25%
SAT math:	500-610	**Return as sophomores:**	78%
SAT writing:	470-560	**Out-of-state:**	30%
ACT composite:	21-25	**Live on campus:**	15%
GPA 3.75 or higher:	22%	**International:**	2%
GPA 3.50-3.74:	20%	**Fraternities:**	1%
GPA 3.0-3.49:	43%	**Sororities:**	1%
GPA 2.0-2.99:	15%		

Basis for selection. School achievement record, test scores, class rank important. **Homeschooled:** State high school equivalency certificate required. In absence of official transcript from accredited school, students must submit GED results in addition to other requirements.

High school preparation. College-preparatory program required. 22 units required. Required units include English 4, mathematics 3, social studies 3, science 3 and academic electives 5.

2008-2009 Annual costs. Tuition/fees: $6,259; $16,915 out-of-state. Room/board: $7,564. Books/supplies: $1,226. Personal expenses: $1,420.

2007-2008 Financial aid. **Need-based:** 1,220 full-time freshmen applied for aid; 589 were judged to have need; 514 of these received aid. Average need met was 59%. Average scholarship/grant was $5,119; average loan $3,088. 47% of total undergraduate aid awarded as scholarships/grants, 53% as loans/jobs. **Non-need-based:** Awarded to 2,883 full-time undergraduates, including 479 freshmen. Scholarships awarded for academics, alumni affiliation, art, athletics, job skills, leadership, minority status, music/drama, religious affiliation, ROTC, state residency. **Additional information:** Hawaii student incentive grants and tuition waivers (merit and need-based) available to Hawaii residents at participating institutions.

Application procedures. **Admission:** Priority date 1/2; deadline 5/1 (receipt date). $50 fee, may be waived for applicants with need. Admission notification on a rolling basis beginning on or about 12/1. Must reply by May 1 or within 2 week(s) if notified thereafter. **Financial aid:** Priority date 3/1; no closing date. FAFSA required. Applicants notified on a rolling basis starting 3/15; must reply within 4 week(s) of notification.

Academics. **Special study options:** Cooperative education, distance learning, double major, ESL, exchange student, honors, independent study, internships, semester at sea, student-designed major, study abroad, teacher certification program. **Credit/placement by examination:** AP, CLEP, IB, SAT, ACT, institutional tests. 30 credit hours maximum toward bachelor's degree. **Support services:** Learning center, pre-admission summer program, remedial instruction, study skills assistance, tutoring, writing center.

Majors. **Agriculture:** Animal sciences, plant protection. **Area/ethnic studies:** American, Asian, Native American. **Biology:** General, botany, marine, microbiology, zoology. **Business:** General, accounting, business admin, finance, human resources, international, management information systems, marketing, tourism/travel. **Communications:** General, journalism. **Computer sciences:** General, computer science. **Conservation:** Environmental science, management/policy. **Education:** Elementary, ESL, secondary. **Engineering:** Agricultural, civil, electrical, mechanical. **Family/consumer sciences:** General, clothing/textiles. **Foreign languages:** Chinese, classics, Filipino/Tagalog, French, German, Japanese, Korean, Russian, Spanish. **Health:** Audiology/speech pathology, clinical lab science, dental hygiene, nursing (RN). **History:** General. **Interdisciplinary:** Nutrition sciences. **Liberal arts:** Arts/sciences. **Math:** General. **Parks/recreation:** Exercise sciences. **Philosophy/religion:** Philosophy, religion. **Physical sciences:** Chemistry, geology, meteorology, physics. **Psychology:** General. **Public administration:** Social work. **Social sciences:** Anthropology, economics, geography, political science, sociology. **Visual/performing arts:** Art, dance, dramatic. **Other:** Ethnobotany, Plant and Environmental Biotechnology.

Most popular majors. Business/marketing 21%, education 8%, liberal arts 6%, psychology 7%, social sciences 11%.

Computing on campus. 1,400 workstations in dormitories, library, computer center, student center. Dormitories wired for high-speed internet access and linked to campus network. Commuter students can connect to campus network. Online course registration, online library, helpline, repair service, student web hosting, wireless network available.

Student life. **Freshman orientation:** Available, $80 fee. Preregistration for classes offered. 2-day program. **Housing:** Guaranteed on-campus for freshmen. Coed dorms, apartments, wellness housing available. $225 partly refundable deposit, deadline 5/1. **Activities:** Bands, campus ministries, choral groups, dance, drama, film society, international student organizations, literary magazine, music ensembles, musical theater, radio station, student government, student newspaper, symphony orchestra, TV station, over 150 registered organizations.

Athletics. NCAA. **Intercollegiate:** Baseball M, basketball, cheerleading, cross-country W, diving, football (tackle) M, golf, sailing, soccer W, softball W, swimming, tennis, track and field W, volleyball, water polo W. **Intramural:** Badminton, basketball, cross-country, golf, soccer, softball, table tennis, tennis, track and field W, volleyball, weight lifting. **Team name:** Warriors, Rainbow Warriors, Rainbows, Rainbow Wahine.

Student services. Adult student services, alcohol/substance abuse counseling, career counseling, services for economically disadvantaged, student employment services, financial aid counseling, health services, minority student services, on-campus daycare, personal counseling, placement for graduates, veterans' counselor, women's services. **Physically disabled:** Services for visually, speech, hearing impaired.

Contact. E-mail: ar-info@hawaii.edu
Phone: (808) 956-8975 Toll-free number: (800) 823-9771
Fax: (808) 956-4148
Jan Heu, Director of Admissions and Records, University of Hawaii at Manoa, 2600 Campus Road, QLC Rm 001, Honolulu, HI 96822

University of Hawaii: West Oahu

Pearl City, Hawaii — **CB member**
www.uhwo.hawaii.edu — **CB code: 1042**

- Public 4-year liberal arts and teachers college
- Commuter campus in large town
- 1,094 degree-seeking undergraduates: 64% part-time, 72% women, 2% African American, 77% Asian American, 2% Hispanic American, 1% international
- 55% of applicants admitted
- 53% graduate within 6 years

General. Founded in 1976. Regionally accredited. **Degrees:** 190 bachelor's awarded. **ROTC:** Army, Air Force. **Location:** 10 miles from Honolulu. **Calendar:** Semester, limited summer session. **Full-time faculty:** 46 total; 100% have terminal degrees, 70% minority, 46% women. **Part-time faculty:** 21 total; 29% minority, 24% women. **Class size:** 57% < 20, 39% 20-39, 4% 40-49.

Freshman class profile. 238 applied, 130 admitted, 74 enrolled.

Out-of-state:	1%	**International:**	1%

Basis for selection. Students with 2.7 high school GPA and 22 credits of required high school coursework will be automatically accepted. **Homeschooled:** State high school equivalency certificate required.

High school preparation. 22 units required. Required units include English 4, mathematics 3, social studies 3, science 3 and academic electives 5. Math credits must include Algebra II and Geometry. 4 credits of college prep coursework (language, fine arts, etc.) also required.

2008-2009 Annual costs. Tuition/fees: $3,706; $11,578 out-of-state. Foreign students pay out-of-state tuition rates. However, citizens of an eligible Pacific island district, commonwealth, territory or insular jurisdiction, state or nation which does not provide public institutions that grant baccalaureate degrees may be allowed to pay 150% of the resident tuition. Books/supplies: $1,123. Personal expenses: $1,265.

2007-2008 Financial aid. **Need-based:** 9 full-time freshmen applied for aid; 7 were judged to have need; 7 of these received aid. Average need met was 70%. Average scholarship/grant was $3,467; average loan $3,500. 63% of total undergraduate aid awarded as scholarships/grants, 37% as loans/jobs. **Non-need-based:** Awarded to 39 full-time undergraduates, including 19 freshmen. Scholarships awarded for academics, alumni affiliation, leadership, state residency.

Application procedures. **Admission:** Priority date 4/1; deadline 8/1 (postmark date). $50 fee. Application must be submitted on paper. Admission notification on a rolling basis. **Financial aid:** Priority date 4/1; no closing date. FAFSA required. Applicants notified on a rolling basis starting 4/1.

Academics. **Special study options:** Cross-registration, distance learning, double major, independent study, study abroad, teacher certification program. **Credit/placement by examination:** AP, CLEP, IB, SAT, ACT, institutional tests. 42 credit hours maximum toward bachelor's degree. 21 lower division and 21 upper division credits may be earned through examination. **Support services:** Study skills assistance, tutoring, writing center.

Majors. **Area/ethnic studies:** Pacific. **Business:** Accounting, business admin. **Computer sciences:** LAN/WAN management. **Education:** Early childhood, elementary. **History:** General. **Personal/culinary services:** Restaurant/catering. **Philosophy/religion:** Philosophy. **Protective services:** Law enforcement admin. **Psychology:** General. **Public administration:** General. **Social sciences:** General, anthropology, economics, political science, sociology.

Most popular majors. Business/marketing 30%, history 7%, psychology 27%, public administration/social services 18%, social sciences 18%.

Computing on campus. 18 workstations in computer center. Commuter students can connect to campus network. Online course registration, online library, helpline, student web hosting, wireless network available.

Student life. **Freshman orientation:** Available. Preregistration for classes offered. **Activities:** Student government, accounting club, anthropology/sociology club, business club, economics club, Hawaiian-Pacific Club, humanities club, political science club, psychology association, students in free enterprise.

Student services. Career counseling, student employment services, financial aid counseling, veterans' counselor. **Physically disabled:** Services for visually, hearing impaired.

Contact. E-mail: admissions@uhwo.hawaii.edu
Phone: (808) 454-4700 Fax: (808) 453-6075
Robyn Oshiro, Admissions Specialist, University of Hawaii: West Oahu, 96-129 Ala Ike, Pearl City, HI 96782

Idaho

Boise Bible College
Boise, Idaho
www.boisebible.edu **CB code: 0891**

- Private 4-year Bible college affiliated with nondenominational tradition
- Residential campus in small city
- 170 degree-seeking undergraduates
- 96% of applicants admitted
- SAT or ACT (ACT writing optional), application essay required

General. Founded in 1945. Accredited by ABHE. **Degrees:** 14 bachelor's, 14 associate awarded. **Location:** 4 miles from downtown. **Calendar:** Semester. **Full-time faculty:** 8 total. **Part-time faculty:** 8 total.

Freshman class profile. 73 applied, 70 admitted, 42 enrolled.

Mid 50% test scores			
SAT critical reading:	380-570	GPA 3.50-3.74:	11%
SAT math:	420-490	GPA 3.0-3.49:	39%
SAT writing:	350-490	GPA 2.0-2.99:	33%
ACT composite:	18-21	Rank in top quarter:	23%
GPA 3.75 or higher:	15%	Rank in top tenth:	3%

Basis for selection. Christian conduct or ethical code standards based on signed student statement, recommendation of home church minister, 1 employment/school reference, and 1 personal reference required. School achievement important. **Homeschooled:** Transcript of courses and grades required. GED or transcripts from homeschooling agency recommended. Applicants submitting home-prepared transcripts advised to consult admissions office.

High school preparation. Recommended units include English 4, mathematics 2, history 2 and foreign language 1.

2008-2009 Annual costs. Tuition/fees: $8,100. Room/board: $5,400. Books/supplies: $605. Personal expenses: $1,210.

Financial aid. Non-need-based: Scholarships awarded for academics, leadership, music/drama, religious affiliation.

Application procedures. Admission: Priority date 5/1; deadline 8/1 (receipt date). $25 fee. Application must be submitted on paper. Admission notification on a rolling basis. Must reply by June 1 or 3 weeks after acceptance date if accepted after June 1. **Financial aid:** Priority date 5/1; no closing date. FAFSA, institutional form required. Applicants notified on a rolling basis starting 5/2; must reply by 8/1 or within 2 week(s) of notification.

Academics. Special study options: Distance learning, double major, independent study, internships. **Credit/placement by examination:** AP, CLEP, IB, SAT, ACT, institutional tests. ABHE Bible Knowledge Test. **Support services:** Reduced course load, remedial instruction.

Majors. Theology: Bible, missionary, pastoral counseling, religious ed, sacred music, theology, youth ministry.

Computing on campus. 7 workstations in library, computer center.

Student life. Freshman orientation: Mandatory, $50 fee. Preregistration for classes offered. 2 days of training and testing, followed by whitewater boat trip. **Policies:** Religious observance required. **Housing:** Guaranteed on-campus for freshmen. Single-sex dorms available. $150 deposit, deadline 7/1. Trailer hookups for married students. **Activities:** Choral groups, music ensembles, student government, student newspaper, Christian service missions club.

Athletics. Intramural: Basketball, football (non-tackle) M, soccer, volleyball. **Team name:** Lions.

Student services. Adult student services, career counseling, student employment services, financial aid counseling, health services, personal counseling, placement for graduates, veterans' counselor.

Contact. E-mail: boisebible@boisebible.edu
Phone: (208) 376-7731 Toll-free number: (800) 893-7755
Fax: (208) 376-7743
Martin Flaherty, Admissions Director, Boise Bible College, 8695 West Marigold Street, Boise, ID 83714-1220

Boise State University
Boise, Idaho **CB member**
www.boisestate.edu **CB code: 4018**

- Public 4-year university
- Commuter campus in small city
- 16,485 degree-seeking undergraduates: 30% part-time, 54% women, 1% African American, 3% Asian American, 6% Hispanic American, 1% Native American, 1% international
- 1,696 degree-seeking graduate students
- 81% of applicants admitted
- SAT or ACT (ACT writing optional) required

General. Founded in 1932. Regionally accredited. **Degrees:** 1,940 bachelor's, 434 associate awarded; master's, doctoral offered. **ROTC:** Army. **Location:** Downtown. **Calendar:** Semester, limited summer session. **Full-time faculty:** 631 total; 82% have terminal degrees, 9% minority, 43% women. **Part-time faculty:** 497 total; 16% have terminal degrees, 9% minority, 50% women. **Class size:** 47% < 20, 41% 20-39, 5% 40-49, 5% 50-99, 2% >100. **Special facilities:** Performing arts center, technology center, natural area and world center for birds of prey research.

Freshman class profile. 4,102 applied, 3,323 admitted, 2,871 enrolled.

Mid 50% test scores			
SAT critical reading:	450-570	Rank in top tenth:	12%
SAT math:	460-580	End year in good standing:	95%
ACT composite:	19-24	Return as sophomores:	66%
GPA 3.75 or higher:	17%	Out-of-state:	9%
GPA 3.50-3.74:	20%	Live on campus:	30%
GPA 3.0-3.49:	41%	International:	1%
GPA 2.0-2.99:	22%	Fraternities:	1%
Rank in top quarter:	34%	Sororities:	1%

Basis for selection. Admission based on high school GPA and ACT or SAT score. Applicants without high school diploma or GED may petition for admission. Interview required for vocational-technical, nursing majors. **Homeschooled:** State high school equivalency certificate required.

High school preparation. College-preparatory program recommended. 15 units required. Required and recommended units include English 4, mathematics 3, social studies 3, science 3 and foreign language 1. One unit foreign language, humanities, or fine arts and 1.5 units other college preparatory also recommended.

2008-2009 Annual costs. Tuition/fees: $4,632; $13,208 out-of-state. Out-of-state students (undergraduate and graduate) taking less than 8 credit hours pay in-state rate. Room/board: $5,938. Books/supplies: $1,138. Personal expenses: $2,172.

2008-2009 Financial aid. Need-based: 1,626 full-time freshmen applied for aid; 1,623 were judged to have need; 1,623 of these received aid. Average need met was 21%. Average scholarship/grant was $3,300; average loan $4,333. 34% of total undergraduate aid awarded as scholarships/grants, 66% as loans/jobs. **Non-need-based:** Awarded to 1,146 full-time undergraduates, including 642 freshmen. Scholarships awarded for academics, athletics, music/drama, ROTC, state residency.

Application procedures. Admission: Closing date 7/12 (postmark date). $40 fee. Admission notification on a rolling basis beginning on or about 2/15. Strongly recommended that students apply January-March. **Financial aid:** Priority date 4/1; no closing date. FAFSA required. Applicants notified on a rolling basis starting 6/1; must reply within 2 week(s) of notification.

Academics. Basque studies program abroad. **Special study options:** Distance learning, double major, dual enrollment of high school students, exchange student, honors, independent study, internships, student-designed major, study abroad, teacher certification program, weekend college. **Credit/placement by examination:** AP, CLEP, SAT, ACT, institutional tests. 21 credit hours maximum toward associate degree, 42 toward bachelor's. **Support services:** Learning center, pre-admission summer program, reduced course load, remedial instruction, study skills assistance, tutoring, writing center.

Majors. **Biology:** General. **Business:** Accounting, construction management, finance, human resources, international, management information systems, managerial economics, market research, marketing, operations. **Communications:** General, journalism. **Computer sciences:** Computer science, information systems. **Education:** General, art, bilingual, biology, chemistry, elementary, French, German, history, music, physical, physics, science, social science, social studies, Spanish, special, speech. **Engineering:** Civil, electrical, materials science, mechanical. **Engineering technology:** Construction. **Foreign languages:** French, German, Spanish. **Health:** Athletic training, environmental health, medical radiologic technology/radiation therapy, medical records admin, nursing (RN), predental, premedicine, preveterinary, respiratory therapy technology. **History:** General. **Liberal arts:** Arts/sciences. **Math:** General, applied. **Parks/recreation:** Exercise sciences, health/fitness. **Philosophy/religion:** Philosophy. **Physical sciences:** Chemistry, geology, geophysics, physics, planetary. **Protective services:** Law enforcement admin. **Psychology:** General. **Public administration:** Social work. **Social sciences:** General, anthropology, economics, political science, sociology. **Visual/performing arts:** Art, commercial/advertising art, dramatic, music management, music performance, music theory/composition.

Most popular majors. Business/marketing 22%, communications/journalism 7%, education 10%, health sciences 10%, psychology 6%, social sciences 7%, visual/performing arts 6%.

Computing on campus. 900 workstations in dormitories, library, computer center. Dormitories wired for high-speed internet access and linked to campus network. Commuter students can connect to campus network. Online course registration, wireless network available.

Student life. **Freshman orientation:** Mandatory, $75 fee. Preregistration for classes offered. **Housing:** Coed dorms, single-sex dorms, special housing for disabled, apartments, fraternity/sorority housing, wellness housing available. $75 fully refundable deposit, deadline 7/12. **Activities:** Bands, choral groups, dance, drama, international student organizations, literary magazine, music ensembles, musical theater, radio station, student government, student newspaper, symphony orchestra, TV station, Black Student Union, Native American association, Organization de Estudiantes Latino-Americanos, Latter-day Saints student association, Alternative Mobility Adventure Seekers.

Athletics. NCAA. **Intercollegiate:** Basketball, cheerleading, cross-country, football (tackle) M, golf, gymnastics W, rodeo, soccer W, swimming W, tennis, track and field, volleyball W, wrestling M. **Intramural:** Baseball M, basketball, bowling, handball, racquetball, soccer M, softball, swimming, tennis, volleyball. **Team name:** Broncos.

Student services. Adult student services, alcohol/substance abuse counseling, career counseling, student employment services, financial aid counseling, health services, legal services, minority student services, on-campus daycare, personal counseling, placement for graduates, veterans' counselor, women's services. **Physically disabled:** Services for visually, speech, hearing impaired.

Contact. E-mail: bsuinfo@boisestate.edu
Phone: (208) 426-1156 Toll-free number: (800) 824-7017
Fax: (208) 426-3765
Jenny Cardenas, Director of Admissions, Boise State University, 1910 University Drive, Boise, ID 83725

Brigham Young University-Idaho

Rexburg, Idaho
www.byui.edu **CB code: 4657**

- Private 4-year university affiliated with Church of Jesus Christ of Latter-day Saints
- Residential campus in large town
- 13,759 degree-seeking undergraduates
- 96% of applicants admitted
- ACT (writing optional), application essay required

General. Founded in 1888. Regionally accredited. **Degrees:** 2,335 bachelor's, 875 associate awarded. **ROTC:** Army. **Location:** 30 miles from Idaho Falls, 240 miles from Salt Lake City. **Calendar:** Semester, extensive summer session. **Full-time faculty:** 470 total. **Part-time faculty:** 165 total. **Class size:** 28% < 20, 49% 20-39, 8% 40-49, 13% 50-99, 1% >100. **Special facilities:** Observatory, planetarium, livestock center, off-campus outdoor educational facility, leadership and service institute.

Freshman class profile. 10,797 applied, 10,322 admitted, 8,474 enrolled.

Mid 50% test scores		**GPA 3.50-3.74:**	30%
SAT critical reading:	480-600	**GPA 3.0-3.49:**	40%
SAT math:	490-610	**GPA 2.0-2.99:**	7%
ACT composite:	20-26	**Out-of-state:**	73%
GPA 3.75 or higher:	23%	**Live on campus:**	21%

Basis for selection. Religious affiliation, recommendations most important. High school record, test scores, personal essay, extracurricular activities also important. Interview with student's ecclesiastical leader required. Auditions required for music, dance, theater majors. **Homeschooled:** GED required; may be waived for homeschooled students with 24 ACT composite score.

2008-2009 Annual costs. Tuition/fees: $3,470. Tuition for students who are not members of The Church of Jesus Christ of Latter-day Saints is $6,340 for academic year. Room/board: $6,600. Books/supplies: $1,110. Personal expenses: $2,020.

Financial aid. **Non-need-based:** Scholarships awarded for academics, athletics, leadership. **Additional information:** Application deadline for merit scholarships 3/1.

Application procedures. **Admission:** Closing date 2/1 (receipt date). $25 fee. **Financial aid:** Priority date 5/1; no closing date. FAFSA required. Applicants notified on a rolling basis starting 2/1.

Academics. **Special study options:** Accelerated study, distance learning, double major, independent study, internships, student-designed major, study abroad, teacher certification program, urban semester. **Credit/placement by examination:** AP, CLEP, IB, institutional tests. **Support services:** Learning center, reduced course load, remedial instruction, study skills assistance, tutoring, writing center.

Majors. **Agriculture:** Agronomy, animal sciences, horticulture. **Biology:** General, zoology. **Business:** Accounting, business admin. **Communications:** General, advertising, broadcast journalism, journalism, public relations. **Computer sciences:** General, computer science. **Education:** Elementary. **Engineering:** Computer, mechanical. **Health:** Nursing (RN), predental, premedicine, prepharmacy, preveterinary. **History:** General. **Math:** General. **Parks/recreation:** General. **Physical sciences:** Geology, physics. **Psychology:** General. **Social sciences:** Economics, political science, sociology. **Visual/performing arts:** Art, interior design.

Most popular majors. Biology 6%, business/marketing 18%, communications/journalism 8%, education 18%, health sciences 9%, liberal arts 9%.

Computing on campus. 2,500 workstations in dormitories, library, computer center, student center. Dormitories wired for high-speed internet access and linked to campus network. Commuter students can connect to campus network. Online course registration, online library, helpline, student web hosting, wireless network available.

Student life. **Freshman orientation:** Available. **Policies:** Students encouraged to attend weekly devotional at which noted church leaders speak. Religious observance required. **Housing:** Single-sex dorms, apartments, wellness housing available. $175 deposit. **Activities:** Bands, choral groups, dance, drama, international student organizations, literary magazine, music ensembles, musical theater, radio station, student government, student newspaper, symphony orchestra, TV station, Lambda Delta Sigma, Sigma Gamma Chi, business club, married student association, outdoor club.

Athletics. **Intramural:** Archery, badminton, baseball, basketball, bowling, cheerleading, cross-country, diving, fencing, field hockey, football (non-tackle), football (tackle), golf, ice hockey, racquetball, skiing, skin diving, soccer, softball, swimming, table tennis, tennis, track and field, volleyball, water polo, wrestling M. **Team name:** Vikings.

Student services. Career counseling, student employment services, health services, personal counseling, placement for graduates, veterans' counselor. **Physically disabled:** Services for visually, hearing impaired.

Contact. E-mail: admissionser@byui.edu
Phone: (208) 496-1020 Fax: (208) 496-1185
Rob Garrett, Director of Admissions, Brigham Young University-Idaho, 120 Kimball Building, Rexburg, ID 83460-1615

College of Idaho

Caldwell, Idaho **CB member**
www.collegeofidaho.edu **CB code: 4060**

- Private 4-year liberal arts college
- Residential campus in large town

- 920 degree-seeking undergraduates: 3% part-time, 60% women, 1% African American, 2% Asian American, 8% Hispanic American, 6% international
- 16 degree-seeking graduate students
- 59% of applicants admitted
- SAT or ACT with writing, application essay required
- 67% graduate within 6 years

General. Founded in 1891. Regionally accredited. Founded by Presbyterian Church. **Degrees:** 167 bachelor's awarded; master's offered. **ROTC:** Army. **Location:** 30 miles from Boise. **Calendar:** 13-6-13. **Full-time faculty:** 65 total; 2% have terminal degrees, 3% minority, 42% women. **Part-time faculty:** 50 total; 2% have terminal degrees, 6% minority, 36% women. **Class size:** 81% < 20, 17% 20-39, 1% 40-49, less than 1% 50-99, less than 1% >100. **Special facilities:** Natural history museum, mineral and gem collection, planetarium, observatory, nuclear magnetic resonance spectrometer, performing and fine arts center.

Freshman class profile. 1,275 applied, 756 admitted, 277 enrolled.

Mid 50% test scores		**Rank in top quarter:**	68%
SAT critical reading:	470-620	**Rank in top tenth:**	29%
SAT math:	490-630	**End year in good standing:**	92%
SAT writing:	460-570	**Return as sophomores:**	80%
ACT composite:	22-27	**Live on campus:**	88%
GPA 3.75 or higher:	46%	**International:**	9%
GPA 3.50-3.74:	24%	**Fraternities:**	13%
GPA 3.0-3.49:	24%	**Sororities:**	10%
GPA 2.0-2.99:	6%		

Basis for selection. Academic record, test scores, extracurricular activities, essay, teacher recommendation important. Interview and essay recommended. Audition required of music, theater majors. Portfolio required of art majors. **Homeschooled:** Transcript of courses and grades, letter of recommendation (nonparent) required. Course descriptions. **Learning Disabled:** Student must submit a written request for accommodations, submit appropriate documentation of the diagnosed disability from a qualified treatment provider completed within the last 3 years; provide a signed release of information form with contact information to the Student Disability Services Office; and schedule an appointment with the Disability Services Coordinator.

High school preparation. College-preparatory program recommended. 15 units required; 20 recommended. Required and recommended units include English 4, mathematics 3-4, social studies 2, history 3, science 2-4, foreign language 4 and academic electives 3.

2009-2010 Annual costs. Tuition/fees: $20,070. Room/board: $7,478. Books/supplies: $900. Personal expenses: $700.

2008-2009 Financial aid. Need-based: 179 full-time freshmen applied for aid; 179 were judged to have need; 179 of these received aid. Average need met was 88%. Average scholarship/grant was $4,888; average loan $3,729. 59% of total undergraduate aid awarded as scholarships/grants, 41% as loans/jobs. **Non-need-based:** Awarded to 1,078 full-time undergraduates, including 328 freshmen. Scholarships awarded for academics, alumni affiliation, art, athletics, leadership, minority status, music/drama, religious affiliation, ROTC.

Application procedures. Admission: Priority date 6/1; deadline 8/1 (postmark date). No application fee. Admission notification on a rolling basis beginning on or about 10/15. Must reply by 5/1. **Financial aid:** Priority date 2/15; no closing date. FAFSA, institutional form required. Applicants notified on a rolling basis starting 2/1; must reply within 3 week(s) of notification.

Academics. All freshmen participate in first-year experience course and receive a book to read over summer as preparation. **Special study options:** Combined bachelor's/graduate degree, cross-registration, double major, dual enrollment of high school students, exchange student, honors, independent study, internships, liberal arts/career combination, semester at sea, student-designed major, study abroad, teacher certification program, Washington semester. Bachelor's/graduate program in law with University of Idaho, MBA with Gonzaga University (WA), Boise State University, bachelor's/master's degrees in accountancy with University of Idaho, management with Willamette University (OR), natural resources with University of Idaho, economics with University of Idaho, bachelor's in engineering with University of Idaho, Boise State University, Columbia University (NY), Washington University (MO), 5th-year teaching internship, cooperative nursing program with Idaho State University. **Credit/placement by examination:** AP, CLEP, IB, SAT, ACT, institutional tests. **Support services:** Learning center, reduced course load, remedial instruction, study skills assistance, tutoring, writing center.

Majors. Biology: General. **Business:** Accounting, business admin, international. **Conservation:** Environmental studies. **Education:** Physical. **Engineering:** General. **Foreign languages:** Spanish. **Health:** Prenursing. **History:** General. **Interdisciplinary:** Math/computer science. **Liberal arts:** Arts/sciences. **Math:** General, applied. **Parks/recreation:** Exercise sciences, health/fitness, sports admin. **Philosophy/religion:** Philosophy, religion. **Physical sciences:** Chemistry. **Psychology:** General. **Social sciences:** Anthropology, economics, international relations, political science, sociology. **Visual/performing arts:** Art, dramatic.

Most popular majors. Biology 14%, business/marketing 13%, history 8%, psychology 13%, social sciences 11%, visual/performing arts 6%.

Computing on campus. 276 workstations in dormitories, library, computer center, student center. Dormitories wired for high-speed internet access and linked to campus network. Commuter students can connect to campus network. Online library, helpline, repair service, student web hosting, wireless network available.

Student life. Freshman orientation: Mandatory. Preregistration for classes offered. Several 1-day sessions scheduled over the summer for registration, orientation, and tuition payment; 3-day fall orientation including an overnight stay in the nearby mountains before the start of fall semester. **Policies:** Freshman and sophomores under age 21 must live on campus unless living with parents or relatives. All buildings smoke-free. Honor's Code has been implemented for all students. Integrity is valued, expected, and practiced. **Housing:** Guaranteed on-campus for freshmen. Coed dorms, special housing for disabled, apartments, fraternity/sorority housing, wellness housing available. $300 fully refundable deposit, deadline 5/1. Pets allowed in dorm rooms. **Activities:** Bands, campus ministries, choral groups, dance, drama, international student organizations, literary magazine, music ensembles, Model UN, musical theater, opera, radio station, student government, student newspaper, symphony orchestra, over 75 activities or organizations.

Athletics. NAIA. **Intercollegiate:** Baseball M, basketball, cross-country, golf, skiing, soccer, softball W, swimming, tennis W, track and field, volleyball W. **Intramural:** Badminton, basketball, football (non-tackle), soccer, softball, swimming, table tennis, tennis, volleyball. **Team name:** Coyotes.

Student services. Alcohol/substance abuse counseling, chaplain/spiritual director, career counseling, student employment services, financial aid counseling, health services, minority student services, personal counseling, placement for graduates, women's services. **Physically disabled:** Services for visually, hearing impaired.

Contact. E-mail: admission@collegeofidaho.edu
Phone: (208) 459-5305 Toll-free number: (800) 224-3246
Fax: (208) 459-5757
John Klockentager, Vice President of Enrollment, College of Idaho, 2112 Cleveland Boulevard, Caldwell, ID 83605

Idaho State University

Pocatello, Idaho — **CB member**
www.isu.edu — **CB code: 4355**

- Public 4-year university
- Commuter campus in small city
- 9,249 degree-seeking undergraduates: 24% part-time, 55% women
- 1,830 degree-seeking graduate students
- 82% of applicants admitted

General. Founded in 1901. Regionally accredited. Designated by State Board of Education as institution specializing in health-related programs. **Degrees:** 1,045 bachelor's, 307 associate awarded; master's, doctoral, first professional offered. **ROTC:** Army. **Location:** 150 miles from Salt Lake City, 230 miles from Boise. **Calendar:** Semester, limited summer session. **Full-time faculty:** 619 total. **Part-time faculty:** 170 total. **Class size:** 63% < 20, 29% 20-39, 3% 40-49, 3% 50-99, less than 1% >100. **Special facilities:** Natural history museum, multi-purpose housing/classroom/meeting facility, accelerator center, geographical information systems center, performing arts center.

Freshman class profile. 2,836 applied, 2,331 admitted, 2,039 enrolled.

Mid 50% test scores		**Rank in top quarter:**	33%
SAT critical reading:	460-580	**Rank in top tenth:**	13%
SAT math:	450-570	**Return as sophomores:**	53%
SAT writing:	450-570	**Out-of-state:**	7%
ACT composite:	18-24	**Live on campus:**	21%
GPA 3.75 or higher:	21%	**International:**	1%
GPA 3.50-3.74:	14%	**Fraternities:**	1%
GPA 3.0-3.49:	29%	**Sororities:**	1%
GPA 2.0-2.99:	33%		

Basis for selection. For general admissions, predicted GPA of 2.0 (based on core GPA and test scores). Students not meeting those standards can be admitted through various levels and by petition. TOEFL, IELTS, Compass English, and SAT Critical Reading required for international students. US High School graduates with an "A" or "B" in English and students who completed ELS Language Centers level 112 are exempted. Students from countries where English is the official language can be exempted based on academic performance. SAT or ACT recommended. ACT preferred. Interview recommended. Audition recommended for music majors. Portfolio recommended for experiential credit-seeking applicants. **Homeschooled:** Students need to complete their GED along with taking the ACT or SAT test.

High school preparation. College-preparatory program required. 16 units required. Required and recommended units include English 4, mathematics 3-4, social studies 3, science 3 (laboratory 1) and foreign language 1. Humanities and health also required.

2008-2009 Annual costs. Tuition/fees: $4,664; $13,868 out-of-state. $1,046 refundable health insurance. Room/board: $5,270. Books/supplies: $900. Personal expenses: $2,030.

2007-2008 Financial aid. Need-based: 776 full-time freshmen applied for aid; 568 were judged to have need; 555 of these received aid. Average need met was 40%. Average scholarship/grant was $4,223; average loan $3,034. 35% of total undergraduate aid awarded as scholarships/grants, 65% as loans/jobs. **Non-need-based:** Awarded to 1,143 full-time undergraduates, including 353 freshmen. Scholarships awarded for academics, alumni affiliation, art, athletics, leadership, minority status, music/drama, ROTC, state residency.

Application procedures. Admission: No deadline. $40 fee, may be waived for applicants with need. Admission notification on a rolling basis beginning on or about 3/1. High school students who graduate early may petition admissions committee to enroll full time. **Financial aid:** Priority date 3/1; no closing date. FAFSA required. Applicants notified on a rolling basis starting 4/1.

Academics. Special study options: Accelerated study, combined bachelor's/graduate degree, cooperative education, cross-registration, distance learning, double major, dual enrollment of high school students, ESL, exchange student, honors, independent study, internships, liberal arts/career combination, student-designed major, study abroad, teacher certification program, weekend college. **Credit/placement by examination:** AP, CLEP, IB, institutional tests. 48 credit hours maximum toward bachelor's degree. A student is unable to receive credit by challenge exam for courses already taken, or for courses that are prerequisites to courses already completed. **Support services:** Learning center, remedial instruction, study skills assistance, tutoring, writing center.

Majors. Area/ethnic studies: American. **Biology:** General, biochemistry, botany, ecology, microbiology, zoology. **Business:** General, accounting, business admin, finance, human resources, marketing. **Communications:** General, media studies. **Computer sciences:** General, information systems. **Education:** Early childhood, elementary, health, music, physical, secondary, special. **Engineering:** General, civil, electrical, mechanical, nuclear. **Engineering technology:** Surveying. **Family/consumer sciences:** General. **Foreign languages:** French, German, sign language interpretation, Spanish. **Health:** Audiology/speech pathology, clinical lab science, dental hygiene, dietetics, health care admin, health services, medical radiologic technology/radiation therapy, nursing (RN). **History:** General. **Math:** General. **Philosophy/religion:** Philosophy. **Physical sciences:** Chemistry, geology, physics. **Psychology:** General. **Public administration:** Social work. **Social sciences:** Anthropology, economics, international relations, political science, sociology. **Visual/performing arts:** Art, dramatic, music performance. **Other:** Measurement & Control Engineering.

Most popular majors. Biology 8%, business/marketing 15%, education 17%, health sciences 21%, social sciences 9%.

Computing on campus. 507 workstations in dormitories, library, computer center, student center. Dormitories wired for high-speed internet access and linked to campus network. Commuter students can connect to campus network. Online course registration, online library, helpline, repair service, student web hosting, wireless network available.

Student life. Freshman orientation: Available, $35 fee. Preregistration for classes offered. **Housing:** Coed dorms, single-sex dorms, special housing for disabled, apartments, fraternity/sorority housing, wellness housing available. $150 partly refundable deposit, deadline 8/23. Housing modified for disabled available on request, subject to waiting list. Graduate house available. **Activities:** Bands, campus ministries, choral groups, dance, drama, international student organizations, literary magazine, musical theater, radio station, student government, student newspaper, symphony orchestra, TV station, Newman Center, Latter-day Saints Institute, student ambassadors, Young Democrats, Young Republicans, Campus Crusade for Christ, Associated Black Students, Native Americans United, Cooperative Wilderness Handicapped Outdoor Group.

Athletics. NCAA. **Intercollegiate:** Basketball, cheerleading, cross-country, football (tackle) M, golf, soccer W, softball W, tennis, track and field, volleyball W. **Intramural:** Badminton, basketball, bowling, fencing, judo, racquetball, soccer, softball, table tennis, tennis, volleyball. **Team name:** Bengals.

Student services. Adult student services, alcohol/substance abuse counseling, career counseling, student employment services, financial aid counseling, health services, legal services, minority student services, on-campus daycare, personal counseling, placement for graduates, veterans' counselor, women's services. **Physically disabled:** Services for visually, speech, hearing impaired.

Contact. E-mail: info@isu.edu
Phone: (208) 282-2475 Fax: (208) 282-4511
Laura McKenzie, Director, Idaho State University, 921 South 8th Stop 8270, Pocatello, ID 83209-8270

ITT Technical Institute: Boise

Boise, Idaho
www.itt-tech.edu **CB code: 3596**

- For-profit 4-year technical college
- Commuter campus in small city

General. Founded in 1906. Accredited by ACICS. **Calendar:** Quarter.

Contact. Phone: (208) 322-8844
Director of Recruitment, 12302 West Explorer Drive, Boise, ID 83713-1529

Lewis-Clark State College

Lewiston, Idaho
www.lcsc.edu **CB code: 4385**

- Public 4-year liberal arts and technical college
- Commuter campus in small city
- 3,027 degree-seeking undergraduates: 23% part-time, 61% women, 1% African American, 2% Asian American, 4% Hispanic American, 4% Native American, 5% international
- 59% of applicants admitted

General. Founded in 1893. Regionally accredited. Courses offered at outreach centers (Orofino, Grangeville, Coeur d'Alene, Kamiah, and Lapwai). **Degrees:** 387 bachelor's, 127 associate awarded. **ROTC:** Army, Naval, Air Force. **Location:** 300 miles from Boise, 100 miles from Spokane, Washington. **Calendar:** Semester, limited summer session. **Full-time faculty:** 159 total; 46% have terminal degrees, 4% minority, 53% women. **Part-time faculty:** 3 total; 100% women. **Class size:** 78% < 20, 21% 20-39, less than 1% 40-49, less than 1% 50-99, less than 1% >100. **Special facilities:** Biodiversity museum and collection, geographical information systems center, observatory.

Freshman class profile. 1,434 applied, 852 admitted, 630 enrolled.

Mid 50% test scores		**GPA 2.0-2.99:**	40%
SAT critical reading:	420-520	**Rank in top quarter:**	23%
SAT math:	440-550	**Rank in top tenth:**	7%
ACT composite:	17-23	**Return as sophomores:**	52%
GPA 3.75 or higher:	10%	**Out-of-state:**	17%
GPA 3.50-3.74:	12%	**International:**	6%
GPA 3.0-3.49:	33%		

Basis for selection. High school courses, GPA, test scores considered. Non-native speakers may be required to take ESL classes until they can pass TOEFL. ACT and SAT may be accepted for all students. Students may be asked to take COMPASS test under certain circumstances. **Homeschooled:** Must have predicted college GPA of 2.0 based on ACT or SAT. Must have acceptable performance on 2 testing indicators: GED score of

500 (50 if tested before 2002) or higher, or other standardized diagnostic test such as ACT, SAT, COMPASS, ASSET, or CPT.

High school preparation. 15 units required. Required units include English 4, mathematics 3, social studies 2, science 3 (laboratory 2) and academic electives 2. 1 fine arts.

2008-2009 Annual costs. Tuition/fees: $4,296; $11,920 out-of-state. Room/board: $5,400. Books/supplies: $1,500. Personal expenses: $5,400.

2007-2008 Financial aid. Need-based: 416 full-time freshmen applied for aid; 367 were judged to have need; 347 of these received aid. Average need met was 9%. Average scholarship/grant was $3,074; average loan $2,841. 42% of total undergraduate aid awarded as scholarships/grants, 58% as loans/jobs. **Non-need-based:** Awarded to 688 full-time undergraduates, including 279 freshmen. Scholarships awarded for academics, alumni affiliation, art, athletics, leadership, minority status, music/drama.

Application procedures. Admission: Priority date 3/1; no deadline. $35 fee. Admission notification on a rolling basis. **Financial aid:** Priority date 3/1; no closing date. FAFSA required. Applicants notified on a rolling basis starting 4/15; must reply within 2 week(s) of notification.

Academics. Communications/speech lab to help students prepare for speeches and presentations. **Special study options:** Accelerated study, cooperative education, distance learning, double major, dual enrollment of high school students, ESL, honors, independent study, internships, student-designed major, study abroad, teacher certification program, weekend college. **Credit/placement by examination:** AP, CLEP, IB, SAT, ACT, institutional tests. 16 credit hours maximum toward associate degree, 32 toward bachelor's. **Support services:** Learning center, reduced course load, remedial instruction, study skills assistance, tutoring, writing center.

Majors. Biology: General. **Business:** Accounting technology, administrative services, business admin, hospitality admin, small business admin. **Communications:** General. **Communications technology:** Graphic/printing. **Computer sciences:** General, computer science, webmaster. **Education:** Elementary, English, mathematics, physical, science, social science. **Engineering technology:** Drafting, manufacturing. **Family/consumer sciences:** Child development. **Health:** Management/clinical assistant, nursing (RN), office assistant. **Interdisciplinary:** Natural sciences. **Legal studies:** Legal secretary, paralegal. **Math:** General. **Mechanic/repair:** General, auto body, automotive, diesel, electronics/electrical, heating/ac/refrig, industrial electronics. **Parks/recreation:** Exercise sciences. **Physical sciences:** Chemistry. **Production:** Welding. **Protective services:** Corrections, criminal justice, firefighting. **Psychology:** General. **Public administration:** Social work. **Social sciences:** General.

Most popular majors. Business/marketing 28%, education 10%, health sciences 15%, interdisciplinary studies 9%, public administration/social services 9%.

Computing on campus. 455 workstations in dormitories, library, computer center, student center. Dormitories wired for high-speed internet access and linked to campus network. Commuter students can connect to campus network. Online course registration, helpline, student web hosting, wireless network available.

Student life. Freshman orientation: Available. Preregistration for classes offered. One-day session held in August. **Housing:** Coed dorms, apartments, wellness housing available. $200 partly refundable deposit. **Activities:** Jazz band, campus ministries, drama, international student organizations, literary magazine, radio station, student government, student newspaper, Native American Indian student organization, ambassadors' club, criminal justice society, Idaho student lobby, business students organization, Latter-day Saints student association, College Democrats, College Republicans.

Athletics. NAIA. **Intercollegiate:** Baseball M, basketball, cross-country, golf, tennis, track and field W, volleyball W. **Intramural:** Badminton, baseball, basketball, bowling, field hockey, football (non-tackle), golf, lacrosse, racquetball, rugby M, skiing, soccer, softball, table tennis, tennis, volleyball, weight lifting. **Team name:** Warriors.

Student services. Adult student services, alcohol/substance abuse counseling, career counseling, services for economically disadvantaged, student employment services, financial aid counseling, health services, minority student services, on-campus daycare, personal counseling, placement for graduates, veterans' counselor, women's services. **Physically disabled:** Services for visually, speech, hearing impaired.

Contact. E-mail: admissions@lcsc.edu
Phone: (208) 792-2210 Toll-free number: (800) 933-5272
Fax: (208) 792-2876
Diane Douglas, Registrar/Director of Admissions, Lewis-Clark State College, 500 Eighth Avenue, Lewiston, ID 83501-2698

New Saint Andrews College

Moscow, Idaho
www.nsa.edu **CB code: 3855**

- Private 4-year liberal arts college
- Residential campus in large town
- 168 degree-seeking undergraduates: 2% part-time, 52% women
- 16 degree-seeking graduate students
- 93% of applicants admitted
- SAT or ACT (ACT writing optional), application essay required

General. Regionally accredited. **Degrees:** 22 bachelor's, 11 associate awarded. **Calendar:** Quarter. **Full-time faculty:** 7 total. **Part-time faculty:** 7 total.

Freshman class profile. 85 applied, 79 admitted, 61 enrolled.

Mid 50% test scores			
SAT critical reading:	600-690	SAT writing:	540-660
SAT math:	500-600	ACT composite:	25-31

Basis for selection. Academic achievement and test scores very important.

2009-2010 Annual costs. Tuition/fees: $9,255. Books/supplies: $1,200.

Application procedures. Admission: Priority date 12/1; deadline 8/1 (postmark date). $40 fee. Admission notification on a rolling basis beginning on or about 12/10. **Financial aid:** Priority date 2/15; no closing date. Institutional form required.

Academics. Credit/placement by examination: CLEP.

Majors. Liberal arts: Arts/sciences.

Computing on campus. Online course registration, wireless network available.

Student life. Freshman orientation: Mandatory. **Housing:** Coed dorms available. **Activities:** Campus ministries, choral groups.

Contact. E-mail: admissions@nsa.edu
Phone: (208) 882-1566 Fax: (208) 882-4293
Brenda Schlect, Director of Admissions, New Saint Andrews College, PO Box 9025, Moscow, ID 83843

Northwest Nazarene University

Nampa, Idaho
www.nnu.edu **CB code: 4544**

- Private 4-year university affiliated with Church of the Nazarene
- Residential campus in small city
- 1,281 degree-seeking undergraduates: 5% part-time, 58% women, 1% African American, 2% Asian American, 3% Hispanic American, 1% Native American, 1% international
- 615 degree-seeking graduate students
- 66% of applicants admitted
- SAT or ACT (ACT writing optional), application essay required

General. Founded in 1913. Regionally accredited. **Degrees:** 251 bachelor's awarded; master's offered. **ROTC:** Army, Air Force. **Location:** 18 miles from Boise. **Calendar:** Semester, limited summer session. **Full-time faculty:** 98 total; 68% have terminal degrees, 7% minority, 41% women. **Part-time faculty:** 3 total; 67% have terminal degrees, 67% women. **Class size:** 46% < 20, 40% 20-39, 9% 40-49, 5% 50-99. **Special facilities:** Depository for federal government publications.

Freshman class profile. 1,042 applied, 692 admitted, 303 enrolled.

Mid 50% test scores			
SAT critical reading:	460-610	GPA 2.0-2.99:	17%
SAT math:	460-590	Rank in top quarter:	47%
ACT composite:	19-26	Rank in top tenth:	24%
GPA 3.75 or higher:	37%	Return as sophomores:	89.32%
GPA 3.50-3.74:	23%	Out-of-state:	54%
GPA 3.0-3.49:	23%	Live on campus:	89%
		International:	1%

Basis for selection. For unconditional admission 2 of following criteria must be met: minimum 2.5 high school GPA, class rank in top 50 percent, minimum ACT score of 18. Provisional admission available. Interview recommended for students with provisional admission.

High school preparation. College-preparatory program recommended. Recommended units include English 4, mathematics 3, history 3, science 3 and foreign language 2.

2009-2010 Annual costs. Tuition/fees (projected): $22,250. Room/board: $5,790. Books/supplies: $1,000. Personal expenses: $900.

2008-2009 Financial aid. **Non-need-based:** Scholarships awarded for academics, alumni affiliation, art, athletics, leadership, minority status, music/drama, religious affiliation, ROTC.

Application procedures. **Admission:** Priority date 3/1; deadline 8/15. $25 fee, may be waived for applicants with need. Admission notification on a rolling basis. **Financial aid:** Priority date 3/1; no closing date. FAFSA, institutional form required. Applicants notified on a rolling basis starting 3/1; must reply within 3 week(s) of notification.

Academics. **Special study options:** Accelerated study, combined bachelor's/graduate degree, cooperative education, cross-registration, distance learning, double major, exchange student, honors, independent study, internships, liberal arts/career combination, student-designed major, study abroad, teacher certification program. **Credit/placement by examination:** AP, CLEP, IB, SAT, ACT, institutional tests. 31 credit hours maximum toward bachelor's degree. **Support services:** Learning center, reduced course load, remedial instruction, study skills assistance, tutoring, writing center.

Majors. **Biology:** General, biochemistry, cellular/molecular, ecology. **Business:** Accounting, business admin. **Communications:** General, journalism, media studies. **Computer sciences:** Computer science. **Education:** Art, biology, chemistry, computer, elementary, English, health, history, mathematics, music, physical, physics, psychology, secondary, social science, Spanish. **Engineering:** Aerospace, chemical, civil, electrical, physics. **Foreign languages:** Spanish. **Health:** Nursing (RN), physician assistant, predental, premedicine, prepharmacy, preveterinary. **History:** General. **Legal studies:** Prelaw. **Liberal arts:** Arts/sciences. **Math:** General. **Parks/recreation:** General, exercise sciences, health/fitness, sports admin. **Philosophy/religion:** Philosophy, religion. **Physical sciences:** Chemistry, physics. **Psychology:** General, industrial. **Public administration:** Social work. **Social sciences:** General, international relations, political science. **Theology:** Bible, missionary, pastoral counseling, religious ed, sacred music, youth ministry. **Visual/performing arts:** Ceramics, drawing, graphic design, music performance, music theory/composition, painting, piano/organ, printmaking, sculpture, voice/opera. **Other:** Environmental chemistry.

Computing on campus. 275 workstations in dormitories, library, computer center, student center. Dormitories wired for high-speed internet access and linked to campus network. Commuter students can connect to campus network. Online library, helpline, repair service, student web hosting, wireless network available.

Student life. **Freshman orientation:** Mandatory. Preregistration for classes offered. **Policies:** All students required to live on campus until senior year or age 21. Religious observance required. **Housing:** Guaranteed on-campus for all undergraduates. Single-sex dorms, apartments available. $50 fully refundable deposit. Some rental units available. **Activities:** Bands, campus ministries, choral groups, drama, international student organizations, literary magazine, music ensembles, musical theater, opera, student government, student newspaper, symphony orchestra, summer ministries, Circle-K, urban ministries club, social work clubs, Angels Ministry, PALS ministry, AIDS ministry, Fellowship of Christian Athletes, multicultural affairs club.

Athletics. NCAA. **Intercollegiate:** Baseball M, basketball, cross-country, golf M, soccer W, softball W, track and field, volleyball W. **Intramural:** Basketball, cross-country, football (non-tackle), softball, volleyball. **Team name:** Crusaders.

Student services. Adult student services, alcohol/substance abuse counseling, chaplain/spiritual director, career counseling, student employment services, financial aid counseling, health services, minority student services, personal counseling, placement for graduates. **Physically disabled:** Services for visually, hearing impaired.

Contact. E-mail: admissions@nnu.edu
Phone: (208) 467-8496 Toll-free number: (877) 668-4968
Fax: (208) 467-8645
Stacey Berggren, Director of Admissions, Northwest Nazarene University, 623 Holly Street, Nampa, ID 83686-5897

University of Idaho

Moscow, Idaho — **CB member**
www.uidaho.edu — **CB code: 4843**

- Public 4-year university
- Residential campus in large town
- 8,542 degree-seeking undergraduates: 6% part-time, 46% women, 1% African American, 2% Asian American, 5% Hispanic American, 1% Native American, 2% international
- 2,268 degree-seeking graduate students
- 78% of applicants admitted
- SAT or ACT (ACT writing optional) required
- 57% graduate within 6 years

General. Founded in 1889. Regionally accredited. Residential land-grant university. **Degrees:** 1,849 bachelor's awarded; master's, doctoral, first professional offered. **ROTC:** Army, Naval, Air Force. **Location:** 85 miles from Spokane, Washington. **Calendar:** Semester, extensive summer session. **Full-time faculty:** 601 total; 75% have terminal degrees, 10% minority, 30% women. **Part-time faculty:** 94 total; 24% have terminal degrees, 4% minority, 49% women. **Class size:** 52% < 20, 35% 20-39, 5% 40-49, 6% 50-99, 1% >100. **Special facilities:** Arboretum, 18-hole golf course, indoor climbing facility.

Freshman class profile. 4,935 applied, 3,844 admitted, 1,709 enrolled.

Mid 50% test scores		**GPA 3.0-3.49:**	36%
SAT critical reading:	480-600	**GPA 2.0-2.99:**	22%
SAT math:	490-610	**Rank in top quarter:**	44%
SAT writing:	460-570	**Rank in top tenth:**	17%
ACT composite:	19-26	**Return as sophomores:**	77%
GPA 3.75 or higher:	22%	**Out-of-state:**	38%
GPA 3.50-3.74:	20%	**International:**	1%

Basis for selection. Applicants must have 3.0 high school GPA, or 2.2 to 3.0 high school GPA with high SAT/ACT scores. Recommendations, essay required of applicants with nonstandard high school diploma and adults long out of high school. **Homeschooled:** Letter of recommendation (nonparent) required. Copy of GED test results, three signed letters of recommendation from individuals who know of and can attest to applicant's academic ability, a written statement from applicant including goals, education and/or professional objective, and explanation of past academic performance.

High school preparation. 15 units required. Required units include English 4, mathematics 3, social studies 3, science 3 (laboratory 1), foreign language 1 and academic electives 2. Up to 1 unit of history, literature, philosophy, or fine arts may be substituted for foreign language requirement, but foreign language strongly recommended.

2008-2009 Annual costs. Tuition/fees: $4,632; $14,712 out-of-state. Room/board: $6,762. Books/supplies: $1,430. Personal expenses: $2,772.

2007-2008 Financial aid. **Need-based:** 1,300 full-time freshmen applied for aid; 947 were judged to have need; 931 of these received aid. Average need met was 78%. Average scholarship/grant was $3,469; average loan $4,066. 38% of total undergraduate aid awarded as scholarships/grants, 62% as loans/jobs. **Non-need-based:** Awarded to 5,341 full-time undergraduates, including 1,290 freshmen. Scholarships awarded for academics, alumni affiliation, art, athletics, leadership, minority status, music/drama, religious affiliation, ROTC, state residency.

Application procedures. **Admission:** Priority date 2/15; deadline 8/1 (receipt date). $40 fee. Admission notification on a rolling basis. **Financial aid:** Priority date 2/15; no closing date. FAFSA required. Applicants notified on a rolling basis starting 3/30; must reply within 4 week(s) of notification.

Academics. **Special study options:** Accelerated study, combined bachelor's/graduate degree, cooperative education, cross-registration, distance learning, double major, dual enrollment of high school students, ESL, exchange student, honors, independent study, internships, student-designed major, study abroad, teacher certification program. **Credit/placement by examination:** AP, CLEP, IB, SAT, ACT, institutional tests. 48 credit hours maximum toward bachelor's degree. **Support services:** Learning center, pre-admission summer program, reduced course load, remedial instruction, study skills assistance, tutoring, writing center.

Majors. **Agriculture:** Agronomy, animal sciences, business, dairy, economics, food science, horticultural science, livestock, plant protection, plant sciences, range science, soil science. **Architecture:** Architecture, landscape. **Area/ethnic studies:** American, Latin American. **Biology:** General, bacteriology, biochemistry, molecular. **Business:** Accounting, finance, human resources, management information systems, managerial economics, marketing, operations. **Communications:** General, journalism, public relations, radio/tv. **Computer sciences:** General. **Conservation:** General, environmental science, fisheries, forest resources, forestry, wildlife. **Education:** Agricultural, art, business, early childhood, elementary, English, health, music, physical, secondary, special, technology/industrial arts, trade/industrial, voc/tech. **Engineering:** Agricultural, chemical, civil, computer, electrical, materials science, mechanical, metallurgical. **Family/consumer sciences:** Clothing/

textiles, family studies, food/nutrition. **Foreign languages:** General, classics, French, German, Latin, Spanish. **Health:** Athletic training, premedicine. **History:** General. **Math:** General, applied. **Parks/recreation:** General. **Philosophy/religion:** Philosophy. **Physical sciences:** Chemistry, geology, physics. **Protective services:** Criminal justice. **Psychology:** General. **Social sciences:** Anthropology, economics, geography, international relations, political science, sociology. **Visual/performing arts:** Art, dance, design, dramatic, interior design, music history, music management, music performance, music theory/composition. **Other:** Applied music, Fire ecology and management, Naval science.

Most popular majors. Business/marketing 15%, communications/journalism 7%, education 9%, engineering/engineering technologies 8%, natural resources/environmental science 7%, psychology 6%, social sciences 6%.

Computing on campus. 492 workstations in dormitories, library, computer center, student center. Dormitories wired for high-speed internet access and linked to campus network. Commuter students can connect to campus network. Online course registration, online library, helpline, repair service, student web hosting, wireless network available.

Student life. **Freshman orientation:** Available. Preregistration for classes offered. **Housing:** Coed dorms, single-sex dorms, special housing for disabled, apartments, fraternity/sorority housing available. $250 partly refundable deposit. **Activities:** Bands, campus ministries, choral groups, dance, drama, film society, international student organizations, literary magazine, music ensembles, musical theater, opera, radio station, student government, student newspaper, symphony orchestra, TV station, Amnesty International, Women of Color Alliance, Environmental Club, War on Hunger, Intervarsity Christian Fellowship, Habitat for Humanity, Sabor de la Raza, Soil Stewards, Society of Professional Journalists.

Athletics. NCAA. **Intercollegiate:** Basketball, cross-country, football (tackle) M, golf, soccer W, swimming W, tennis, track and field, volleyball W. **Intramural:** Badminton, basketball, golf, racquetball, rifle, skiing, soccer, softball, table tennis, tennis, wrestling M. **Team name:** Vandals.

Student services. Adult student services, alcohol/substance abuse counseling, chaplain/spiritual director, career counseling, student employment services, financial aid counseling, health services, legal services, minority student services, on-campus daycare, personal counseling, placement for graduates, veterans' counselor, women's services. **Physically disabled:** Services for visually, speech, hearing impaired.

Contact. E-mail: admissions@uidaho.edu
Phone: (208) 885-6326 Toll-free number: (888) 884-3246
Fax: (208) 885-9119
Daniel Davenport, Director of Admissions and Student Financial Aid,
University of Idaho, PO Box 444264, Moscow, ID 83844-4264

Illinois

American Academy of Art
Chicago, Illinois
www.aaart.edu **CB code: 1013**

- For-profit 4-year visual arts college
- Commuter campus in very large city
- 383 degree-seeking undergraduates
- Interview required

General. Founded in 1923. Accredited by ACCSCT. **Degrees:** 59 bachelor's awarded; master's offered. **Location:** Downtown. **Calendar:** Semester, extensive summer session. **Full-time faculty:** 30 total. **Part-time faculty:** 2 total. **Class size:** 76% < 20, 24% 20-39. **Special facilities:** Art gallery.

Basis for selection. Open admission.

2008-2009 Annual costs. Tuition/fees: $22,780. Books/supplies: $800.

Financial aid. Non-need-based: Scholarships awarded for art.

Application procedures. Admission: No deadline. $25 fee, may be waived for applicants with need. Admission notification on a rolling basis. Essay explaining desire to enter art school used for counseling purposes. **Financial aid:** No deadline. FAFSA, institutional form required. Applicants notified on a rolling basis.

Academics. Special study options: Accelerated study, independent study, internships, study abroad. **Credit/placement by examination:** CLEP, institutional tests. **Support services:** Pre-admission summer program, tutoring.

Majors. Communications: Advertising. **Computer sciences:** Computer graphics. **Visual/performing arts:** General, commercial/advertising art, design, drawing, multimedia, painting, studio arts.

Computing on campus. 70 workstations in library, computer center.

Student life. Freshman orientation: Mandatory. Preregistration for classes offered. 1-day orientation held in week before classes start. **Activities:** Film society.

Student services. Career counseling, student employment services, personal counseling, placement for graduates, veterans' counselor.

Contact. E-mail: info@aaart.edu
Phone: (312) 461-0600 Toll-free number: (888) 461-0600
Fax: (312) 294-9570
Stuart Rosenbloom, Director of Admissions, American Academy of Art, 332 South Michigan Avenue, Suite 300, Chicago, IL 60604-4302

Argosy University
Chicago, Illinois
www.argosy.edu **CB code: 3922**

- For-profit 4-year university
- Very large city
- 99 degree-seeking undergraduates

General. Regionally accredited. Additional campuses in Northwest Chicago; Washington, D.C.; Atlanta; Seattle; Tampa; Minneapolis/St. Paul; San Francisco Bay area; Dallas; Honolulu; Nashville; Phoenix; Sarasota; and Orange County, CA. **Degrees:** 37 bachelor's awarded; master's, doctoral offered. **Calendar:** Continuous, extensive summer session. **Part-time faculty:** 7 total.

Basis for selection. 18 ACT, 850 SAT (exclusive of Writing) or passing score on institution's entrance exam required. Other requirements vary by program. SAT or ACT recommended.

2008-2009 Annual costs. Tuition/fees: $14,750. Costs vary by program.

Application procedures. Admission: No deadline. $50 fee.

Academics. Special study options: Distance learning. **Credit/placement by examination:** CLEP.

Majors. Psychology: General.

Computing on campus. Online library available.

Contact. Phone: (312) 201-0200 Toll-free number: (800) 626-4123
Micki Pyszkowski, Director of Admissions, Argosy University, 225 North Michigan Avenue, Suite 1300, Chicago, IL 60601

Augustana College
Rock Island, Illinois **CB member**
www.augustana.edu **CB code: 1025**

- Private 4-year liberal arts college affiliated with Evangelical Lutheran Church in America
- Residential campus in large city
- 2,530 degree-seeking undergraduates: 1% part-time, 57% women, 2% African American, 2% Asian American, 3% Hispanic American, 1% international
- 69% of applicants admitted
- 75% graduate within 6 years; 33% enter graduate study

General. Founded in 1860. Regionally accredited. **Degrees:** 520 bachelor's awarded. **Location:** 165 miles from Chicago. **Calendar:** Quarter, limited summer session. **Full-time faculty:** 181 total; 84% have terminal degrees, 8% minority, 42% women. **Part-time faculty:** 84 total; 21% have terminal degrees, 18% minority, 51% women. **Class size:** 55% < 20, 41% 20-39, 3% 40-49, less than 1% 50-99. **Special facilities:** Educational technology center, planetarium/observatory, map library, geology museum, Swedish immigration research center, research foundation, 500 acres of environmental laboratories, scanning electron microscope, high-field NMR, x-ray diffractometer, scanning tunneling microscope, HeliFlux station magnetometer.

Freshman class profile. 3,413 applied, 2,340 admitted, 639 enrolled.

Mid 50% test scores			
ACT composite:	23-29	Return as sophomores:	87%
Rank in top quarter:	54%	Out-of-state:	14%
Rank in top tenth:	32%	Live on campus:	95%
		International:	1%

Basis for selection. GPA, class rank, test scores, high school curriculum most important. Extracurricular activities and essay important. Academic honors and special qualifications also considered. Test optional for those who interview and submit a photocopy of a graded high school paper. Interview and essay required of freshman honors program applicants, recommended for all applicants. Essay required of academically marginal applicants and for certain departmental programs. Portfolio required of applicants to some art programs. Audition recommended for music and theater majors.

High school preparation. College-preparatory program recommended. 16 units recommended. Recommended units include English 4, mathematics 3, social studies 1, history 1, science 3 (laboratory 2), foreign language 2 and academic electives 4. Engineering, science, and math majors should have 3 units math (1.5 algebra, 1 plane geometry, .5 trigonometry).

2008-2009 Annual costs. Tuition/fees: $30,150. Room/board: $7,650. Books/supplies: $900. Personal expenses: $800.

2007-2008 Financial aid. Need-based: Average need met was 88%. Average scholarship/grant was $14,274; average loan $5,136. 41% of total undergraduate aid awarded as scholarships/grants, 59% as loans/jobs. **Non-need-based:** Awarded to 657 full-time undergraduates, including 203 freshmen. Scholarships awarded for academics, alumni affiliation, art, leadership, music/drama, religious affiliation.

Application procedures. Admission: Priority date 2/1; no deadline. $35 fee, may be waived for applicants with need. Admission notification on a rolling basis. **Financial aid:** Priority date 4/1; no closing date. FAFSA, institutional form required. Applicants notified on a rolling basis.

Academics. Term-abroad programs in Asia, Europe, and South America. Internship programs in cities throughout United States and in South America, Europe, Asia, Africa, and Australia. Exchange programs with universities in People's Republic of China, Peru, and Sweden. Summer language study programs in Sweden, France, Ecuador and Israel. Team-taught, interdisciplinary honors sequence available. June registration for classes. **Special study options:** Accelerated study, combined bachelor's/graduate degree, double major, honors, independent study, internships, liberal arts/career combination, student-designed major, study abroad, teacher certification program. 3-2 forestry and environmental management program with Duke University,

3-2 landscape architecture program with University of Illinois at Urbana-Champaign, 3-2 engineering program with Washington University (MO), Iowa State University, University of Illinois at Urbana-Champaign, and Purdue University, 3-2 occupational therapy program with Washington University, early selection programs in dentistry with University of Iowa, study abroad programs in Asia, Europe, and South America. **Credit/placement by examination:** AP, CLEP, IB, ACT, institutional tests. More than 18 hours of credit by examination must be approved by the Dean of the College. **Support services:** Learning center, pre-admission summer program, reduced course load, study skills assistance, tutoring, writing center.

Majors. Area/ethnic studies: Asian. **Biology:** General, biochemistry. **Business:** General, accounting, business admin, finance, international, management information systems, marketing. **Communications:** General. **Computer sciences:** Computer science. **Conservation:** General. **Education:** General, art, biology, chemistry, elementary, English, foreign languages, French, German, history, mathematics, middle, music, physical, physics, science, secondary, social science, Spanish, speech. **Engineering:** Physics. **Foreign languages:** Ancient Greek, classics, French, German, Latin, Scandinavian, Spanish. **Health:** Audiology/speech pathology, predental, premedicine. **History:** General. **Interdisciplinary:** Math/computer science. **Legal studies:** Prelaw. **Liberal arts:** Arts/sciences. **Math:** General. **Philosophy/religion:** Philosophy, religion. **Physical sciences:** Chemistry, geology, physics, planetary. **Psychology:** General. **Public administration:** General. **Social sciences:** Anthropology, economics, geography, political science, sociology. **Visual/performing arts:** Art, art history/conservation, dramatic, jazz, music performance, piano/organ, studio arts, voice/opera.

Most popular majors. Biology 15%, business/marketing 22%, education 6%, English 10%, health sciences 11%, psychology 6%, social sciences 8%.

Computing on campus. 500 workstations in dormitories, library, computer center, student center. Dormitories wired for high-speed internet access and linked to campus network. Commuter students can connect to campus network. Online course registration, online library, helpline, repair service, student web hosting, wireless network available.

Student life. Freshman orientation: Mandatory. Preregistration for classes offered. Three-day program held before start of fall classes. **Policies:** Students represented on all major faculty/administrative committees and act as observers at Board of Trustees meetings. Student life governed by Bill of Student Rights and code of social conduct. Campus judiciary process includes student participation. Lower-division students not living with parents required to live on campus unless released to live off-campus by student services office. **Housing:** Guaranteed on-campus for all undergraduates. Coed dorms, single-sex dorms, apartments, wellness housing available. **Activities:** Bands, campus ministries, choral groups, dance, drama, international student organizations, literary magazine, music ensembles, Model UN, musical theater, opera, radio station, student government, student newspaper, symphony orchestra, Black student union, Asian student organization, Latinos Unidos, Latin American council, multicultural programming board, feminist forum, Global Affect, Intervarsity Christian Fellowship, Catholic organization, Muslim student association, Viking Volunteers, College Republicans/Democrats, Habitat for Humanity, Amnesty International.

Athletics. NCAA. **Intercollegiate:** Baseball M, basketball, cross-country, diving, football (tackle) M, golf, soccer, softball W, swimming, tennis, track and field, volleyball W, wrestling M. **Intramural:** Badminton, basketball, bowling, cross-country, fencing, football (non-tackle), golf, handball, racquetball, rowing (crew), skiing, soccer, softball, swimming M, table tennis, tennis, track and field, volleyball, water polo, wrestling M. **Team name:** Vikings.

Student services. Alcohol/substance abuse counseling, chaplain/spiritual director, career counseling, student employment services, financial aid counseling, health services, minority student services, personal counseling, placement for graduates, women's services. **Physically disabled:** Services for visually, speech, hearing impaired.

Contact. E-mail: admissions@augustana.edu
Phone: (309) 794-7341 Toll-free number: (800) 798-8100
Fax: (309) 794-7422
W. Kent Barnds, Vice President of Enrollment, Augustana College, 639 38th Street, Rock Island, IL 61201-2296

Aurora University

Aurora, Illinois
www.aurora.edu **CB code: 1027**

- Private 4-year university
- Commuter campus in small city
- 2,181 degree-seeking undergraduates: 15% part-time, 68% women, 10% African American, 3% Asian American, 12% Hispanic American
- 1,925 degree-seeking graduate students
- 79% of applicants admitted
- SAT or ACT (ACT writing optional) required
- 47% graduate within 6 years

General. Founded in 1893. Regionally accredited. George Williams College of Aurora University is a branch campus located in Williams Bay, Wisconsin. **Degrees:** 497 bachelor's awarded; master's, doctoral offered. **ROTC:** Army. **Location:** 40 miles from Chicago. **Calendar:** Semester, limited summer session. **Full-time faculty:** 112 total; 81% have terminal degrees, 7% minority, 52% women. **Part-time faculty:** 281 total; 18% have terminal degrees, 12% minority, 52% women. **Class size:** 53% < 20, 47% 20-39, less than 1% 40-49. **Special facilities:** Museum of Native American history.

Freshman class profile. 1,443 applied, 1,141 admitted, 378 enrolled.

Mid 50% test scores		**GPA 2.0-2.99:**	31%
SAT critical reading:	440-570	**Rank in top quarter:**	41%
SAT math:	440-540	**Rank in top tenth:**	14%
ACT composite:	20-24	**End year in good standing:**	78%
GPA 3.75 or higher:	20%	**Return as sophomores:**	73%
GPA 3.50-3.74:	15%	**Out-of-state:**	10%
GPA 3.0-3.49:	34%	**Live on campus:**	64%

Basis for selection. School achievement record most important, followed by test scores. Recommendation considered. Interview and essay recommended. **Homeschooled:** State high school equivalency certificate, interview required. Writing sample (graded paper or personal statement) required.

High school preparation. College-preparatory program required. 16 units required. Required units include English 4, mathematics 3, social studies 3, science 3 and academic electives 3.

2009-2010 Annual costs. Tuition/fees: $18,100. Course laboratory fees in sciences, photography, nursing, physical education and student teaching. Tuition will vary for several adult degree completion programs. Room/board: $7,850. Books/supplies: $1,000. Personal expenses: $1,400.

2008-2009 Financial aid. Need-based: 352 full-time freshmen applied for aid; 301 were judged to have need; 301 of these received aid. Average need met was 88%. Average scholarship/grant was $6,851; average loan $3,238. 52% of total undergraduate aid awarded as scholarships/grants, 48% as loans/jobs. **Non-need-based:** Awarded to 1,753 full-time undergraduates, including 372 freshmen. Scholarships awarded for academics, alumni affiliation, art, music/drama, religious affiliation, ROTC, state residency.

Application procedures. Admission: Closing date 5/1 (receipt date). $25 fee, may be waived for applicants with need, free for online applicants. Admission notification on a rolling basis beginning on or about 9/1. Must reply by 6/20. Candidates may apply early and have until May 1 to have tuition and housing deposits refunded. **Financial aid:** Priority date 4/15; no closing date. FAFSA required. Applicants notified on a rolling basis starting 3/1; must reply by 5/1 or within 3 week(s) of notification.

Academics. Special study options: Accelerated study, cross-registration, double major, dual enrollment of high school students, honors, independent study, internships, liberal arts/career combination, student-designed major, study abroad, teacher certification program. **Credit/placement by examination:** AP, CLEP, SAT, ACT. 30 credit hours maximum toward bachelor's degree. **Support services:** Learning center, pre-admission summer program, reduced course load, remedial instruction, study skills assistance, tutoring, writing center.

Majors. Biology: General. **Business:** General, accounting, actuarial science, finance, management information systems, management science, marketing, operations. **Communications:** General. **Computer sciences:** General, computer science. **Education:** Elementary, physical, secondary, special. **Foreign languages:** Spanish. **Health:** Athletic training, clinical lab science, nursing (RN). **History:** General. **Legal studies:** Prelaw. **Liberal arts:** Arts/sciences. **Math:** General. **Parks/recreation:** General. **Philosophy/religion:** Religion. **Protective services:** Criminal justice. **Psychology:** General. **Public administration:** Social work. **Social sciences:** Political science, sociology. **Visual/performing arts:** Art, dramatic.

Most popular majors. Business/marketing 23%, education 20%, health sciences 17%, psychology 7%, public administration/social services 8%, security/protective services 6%.

Computing on campus. 90 workstations in library, computer center, student center. Dormitories wired for high-speed internet access and linked to campus network. Commuter students can connect to campus network. Online library, helpline, wireless network available.

Student life. Freshman orientation: Mandatory. Preregistration for classes offered. Day-long sessions held each May and June for admitted first-year students and their parents. **Housing:** Coed dorms, wellness housing available. $100 fully refundable deposit, deadline 5/1. **Activities:** Pep band, campus ministries, choral groups, drama, literary magazine, Model UN, radio station, student government, student newspaper, Black student association, Latin American student organization, Native American club, Students for Wellness, Fellowship of Christian Athletes, Circle K International, Intervarsity Christian Fellowship, political science club, Future Leaders of the World, games club.

Athletics. NCAA. **Intercollegiate:** Baseball M, basketball, cross-country, football (tackle) M, golf, soccer, softball W, tennis, track and field, volleyball W. **Intramural:** Basketball, football (non-tackle), volleyball. **Team name:** Spartans.

Student services. Adult student services, alcohol/substance abuse counseling, chaplain/spiritual director, career counseling, student employment services, financial aid counseling, health services, personal counseling, placement for graduates. **Physically disabled:** Services for visually, speech, hearing impaired.

Contact. E-mail: admission@aurora.edu
Phone: (630) 844-5533 Toll-free number: (800) 742-5281
Fax: (630) 844-5535
James Lancaster, Director of Freshman Admission, Aurora University, 347 South Gladstone Avenue, Aurora, IL 60506-4892

Benedictine University
Lisle, Illinois
www.ben.edu **CB code: 1707**

- Private 4-year university and liberal arts college affiliated with Roman Catholic Church
- Commuter campus in large town
- 3,185 degree-seeking undergraduates: 33% part-time, 57% women
- 1,791 degree-seeking graduate students
- 80% of applicants admitted
- SAT or ACT (ACT writing optional), application essay required
- 60% graduate within 6 years

General. Founded in 1887. Regionally accredited. **Degrees:** 596 bachelor's, 41 associate awarded; master's, doctoral offered. **ROTC:** Army. **Location:** 25 miles from Chicago. **Calendar:** Semester, extensive summer session. **Full-time faculty:** 102 total; 85% have terminal degrees, 16% minority, 45% women. **Part-time faculty:** 559 total; 22% have terminal degrees, 14% minority, 52% women. **Class size:** 57% < 20, 41% 20-39, 1% 40-49, less than 1% 50-99. **Special facilities:** Nature museum, Benedictine abbey, arboretum, Fermi nuclear accelerator laboratories, Argonne national laboratories.

Freshman class profile. 1,566 applied, 1,251 admitted, 449 enrolled.

GPA 3.75 or higher:	30%	**End year in good standing:**	84%
GPA 3.50-3.74:	13%	**Return as sophomores:**	78%
GPA 3.0-3.49:	28%	**Out-of-state:**	8%
GPA 2.0-2.99:	28%	**Live on campus:**	48%
Rank in top quarter:	42%	**International:**	3%
Rank in top tenth:	21%		

Basis for selection. Require rank in top half of class and 21 ACT. Candidates falling below these criteria reviewed by admissions committee. Audition required of musical instrument and voice majors.

High school preparation. 16 units required. Required and recommended units include English 4, mathematics 3-4, social studies 3, history 1, science 2-3 (laboratory 1-2) and foreign language 2.

2009-2010 Annual costs. Tuition/fees (projected): $22,310. Tuition freeze for all students 2009-2010 academic year. Room/board: $6,945. Books/supplies: $1,260. Personal expenses: $2,220.

2007-2008 Financial aid. Need-based: 326 full-time freshmen applied for aid; 273 were judged to have need; 273 of these received aid. Average scholarship/grant was $7,086; average loan $3,052. 50% of total undergraduate aid awarded as scholarships/grants, 50% as loans/jobs. **Non-need-based:** Awarded to 1,113 full-time undergraduates, including 323 freshmen. Scholarships awarded for academics, alumni affiliation, minority status, music/drama, ROTC, state residency.

Application procedures. Admission: Priority date 8/30; no deadline. $40 fee, may be waived for applicants with need. Admission notification on a rolling basis. Must reply by May 1 or within 2 week(s) if notified thereafter. **Financial aid:** Priority date 4/15; no closing date. FAFSA required. Applicants notified on a rolling basis starting 2/15; must reply within 2 week(s) of notification.

Academics. Special study options: Accelerated study, combined bachelor's/graduate degree, cross-registration, distance learning, double major, dual enrollment of high school students, ESL, honors, independent study, internships, liberal arts/career combination, study abroad, teacher certification program, weekend college. Engineering degree program with Illinois Institute of Technology. **Credit/placement by examination:** AP, CLEP, institutional tests. 30 credit hours maximum toward bachelor's degree. **Support services:** Learning center, reduced course load, remedial instruction, study skills assistance, tutoring, writing center.

Majors. Biology: General, biochemistry, molecular. **Business:** Accounting, finance, international, managerial economics, marketing, organizational behavior. **Communications:** General, publishing. **Computer sciences:** Computer science, information systems. **Conservation:** Environmental science. **Education:** Elementary, special. **Engineering:** Science. **Family/consumer sciences:** Food/nutrition. **Foreign languages:** Spanish. **Health:** Clinical lab science, health care admin, health services, nuclear medical technology, nursing (RN), sonography. **History:** General. **Interdisciplinary:** Global studies. **Math:** General. **Philosophy/religion:** Philosophy. **Physical sciences:** Chemistry, physics. **Psychology:** General. **Social sciences:** General, economics, international relations, political science, sociology. **Theology:** Theology. **Visual/performing arts:** Arts management, studio arts. **Other:** Bilingual journalism.

Most popular majors. Biology 9%, business/marketing 38%, education 8%, health sciences 16%, psychology 10%.

Computing on campus. 200 workstations in dormitories, library, computer center, student center. Dormitories wired for high-speed internet access and linked to campus network. Commuter students can connect to campus network. Online course registration, online library, helpline, wireless network available.

Student life. Freshman orientation: Mandatory, $75 fee. Preregistration for classes offered. Summer parent and student program. Student program 3 days prior to first day of classes. **Housing:** Coed dorms, single-sex dorms, apartments, wellness housing available. $125 deposit. **Activities:** Bands, campus ministries, choral groups, dance, drama, film society, international student organizations, literary magazine, music ensembles, Model UN, student government, student newspaper, symphony orchestra, TV station, Muslim student association, African-American student union, Knights of Columbus, Daughters of Isabella, Students for Life, Relay for Life, Best Buddies, South Asian student association, Democracy Matters, Hindu student association.

Athletics. NCAA. **Intercollegiate:** Baseball M, basketball, cross-country, football (tackle) M, golf, soccer, softball W, tennis W, track and field, volleyball W. **Intramural:** Basketball, bowling, football (non-tackle), softball, table tennis, volleyball. **Team name:** Eagles.

Student services. Adult student services, chaplain/spiritual director, career counseling, student employment services, financial aid counseling, health services, personal counseling, placement for graduates. **Physically disabled:** Services for visually, speech, hearing impaired. **Learning disabled:** Comprehensive services available.

Contact. E-mail: admissions@ben.edu
Phone: (630) 829-6300 Toll-free number: (888) 829-6363
Fax: (630) 829-6301
Kari Gibbons, Dean of Enrollment, Benedictine University, 5700 College Road, Lisle, IL 60532

Blackburn College
Carlinville, Illinois **CB member**
www.blackburn.edu **CB code: 1065**

- Private 4-year liberal arts college affiliated with Presbyterian Church (USA)
- Residential campus in small town
- 619 degree-seeking undergraduates
- 55% of applicants admitted
- SAT or ACT (ACT writing optional) required

General. Founded in 1837. Regionally accredited. **Degrees:** 101 bachelor's awarded. **Location:** 40 miles from Springfield, 60 miles from St. Louis. **Calendar:** Semester, limited summer session. **Full-time faculty:** 35 total. **Part-time faculty:** 40 total. **Class size:** 72% < 20, 25% 20-39, 2% 40-49, less than 1% 50-99.

Freshman class profile. 1,005 applied, 555 admitted, 173 enrolled.

Mid 50% test scores		GPA 2.0-2.99:	28%
ACT composite:	19-25	Rank in top quarter:	43%
GPA 3.75 or higher:	32%	Rank in top tenth:	15%
GPA 3.50-3.74:	15%	Out-of-state:	9%
GPA 3.0-3.49:	25%	Live on campus:	87%

Basis for selection. High school academic record, substantiated by test scores, most important. Interview recommended. Audition recommended for music majors. Portfolio recommended for art majors. **Homeschooled:** Statement describing homeschool structure and mission, transcript of courses and grades, state high school equivalency certificate required.

High school preparation. 16 units recommended. Recommended units include English 4, mathematics 3, social studies 2, history 2, science 3 and foreign language 2.

2008-2009 Annual costs. Tuition/fees: $13,610. All on-campus students participate in a work program which reduces net tuition costs. Room/board: $4,363. Books/supplies: $700. Personal expenses: $800.

2008-2009 Financial aid. Non-need-based: Scholarships awarded for academics, state residency. **Additional information:** Each resident student works 160 hours per semester.

Application procedures. Admission: No deadline. No application fee. Admission notification on a rolling basis beginning on or about 10/15. **Financial aid:** Priority date 4/1; no closing date. FAFSA required. Applicants notified on a rolling basis starting 3/1; must reply within 4 week(s) of notification.

Academics. Special study options: Accelerated study, cooperative education, double major, dual enrollment of high school students, independent study, internships, student-designed major, study abroad, teacher certification program, Washington semester. British studies semester, Mexico studies semester. **Credit/placement by examination:** AP, CLEP, SAT, ACT, institutional tests. 30 credit hours maximum toward bachelor's degree. **Support services:** Learning center, reduced course load, remedial instruction, study skills assistance, tutoring, writing center.

Majors. Area/ethnic studies: Latin American. **Biology:** General, biochemistry, environmental. **Business:** Accounting, marketing. **Communications:** General. **Computer sciences:** Computer science. **Education:** Art, biology, elementary, English, mathematics, physical, social science. **Foreign languages:** Spanish. **Health:** Clinical lab science. **History:** General. **Math:** General. **Parks/recreation:** Health/fitness. **Physical sciences:** Chemistry. **Protective services:** Criminal justice. **Psychology:** General. **Public administration:** General. **Social sciences:** Political science. **Visual/performing arts:** Art.

Most popular majors. Biology 9%, business/marketing 19%, communications/journalism 12%, education 24%, psychology 8%, security/protective services 7%.

Computing on campus. 75 workstations in library, computer center. Dormitories linked to campus network. Helpline available.

Student life. Freshman orientation: Mandatory. Preregistration for classes offered. One day summer orientation and two day orientation prior to beginning of fall semester. **Policies:** Participation in student-managed work program required for all resident students. Resident students work 160 hours per semester to reduce costs and gain valuable career skills. Alcohol allowed for students 21 and older. All residence halls are smoke-free. **Housing:** Guaranteed on-campus for all undergraduates. Coed dorms, single-sex dorms, wellness housing available. $150 fully refundable deposit, deadline 7/31. Quiet study housing available. **Activities:** Concert band, choral groups, drama, literary magazine, student government, student newspaper, Cultural Expressions, Habitat for Humanity chapter, Catacombs, Newman Club, Common Ground, Republican club, health and wellness club, fishing club, Beavers Against Destructive Decisions, psychology club.

Athletics. NCAA. **Intercollegiate:** Baseball M, basketball, cross-country, football (tackle) M, golf M, soccer, softball W, tennis W, volleyball W. **Intramural:** Badminton, basketball, racquetball, softball, swimming, table tennis, tennis, volleyball, water polo. **Team name:** Beavers.

Student services. Adult student services, alcohol/substance abuse counseling, career counseling, student employment services, financial aid counseling, minority student services, personal counseling, placement for graduates. **Physically disabled:** Services for visually, hearing impaired.

Contact. E-mail: jmali@blackburn.edu
Phone: (217) 854-3231 Toll-free number: (800) 233-3550
Fax: (217) 854-3713
John Malin, Dean of Enrollment Management, Blackburn College, 700 College Avenue, Carlinville, IL 62626

Blessing-Rieman College of Nursing

Quincy, Illinois
www.brcn.edu **CB code: 0139**

- Private 4-year nursing college
- Commuter campus in large town
- 201 degree-seeking undergraduates: 9% part-time, 91% women
- 8 degree-seeking graduate students
- SAT or ACT (ACT writing optional) required

General. Founded in 1891. Regionally accredited. Joint degree programs with Culver-Stockton College and Quincy University leading to Bachelor of Science in Nursing degree. General education classes held at partner campus, with nursing classes at B-RCN campus and regional medical center. **Degrees:** 40 bachelor's awarded; master's offered. **Location:** 120 miles from St. Louis, 100 miles from Springfield. **Calendar:** Semester, limited summer session. **Full-time faculty:** 20 total; 85% have terminal degrees, 100% women. **Part-time faculty:** 7 total; 100% women. **Class size:** 52% < 20, 48% 20-39.

Freshman class profile.

Mid 50% test scores		GPA 3.0-3.49:	34%
ACT composite:	21-29	GPA 2.0-2.99:	28%
GPA 3.75 or higher:	14%	Out-of-state:	39%
GPA 3.50-3.74:	20%	Live on campus:	82%

Basis for selection. 3.0 GPA and 22 ACT required.

High school preparation. Required units include English 4, mathematics 2, social studies 3, science 4 (laboratory 2). Biology, chemistry, algebra required.

2009-2010 Annual costs. Tuition/fees (projected): $22,050. Tuition and fees are average costs charged to freshman. Partnered with Quincy University and Culver-Stockton College. Freshmen and sophomores pay partnering school's tuition rate. Room/board: $7,145. Books/supplies: $1,000. Personal expenses: $1,775.

2008-2009 Financial aid. Additional information: Financial aid for freshmen and sophomores administered by Culver-Stockton College and Quincy University.

Application procedures. Admission: No deadline. No application fee. Admission notification on a rolling basis. **Financial aid:** No deadline. FAFSA required.

Academics. Special study options: Accelerated study, combined bachelor's/graduate degree, internships. **Credit/placement by examination:** CLEP, IB, SAT, ACT, institutional tests. **Support services:** Study skills assistance, tutoring.

Majors. Health: Nursing (RN).

Computing on campus. 25 workstations in dormitories, library, computer center. Dormitories linked to campus network. Online library available.

Student life. Policies: Immunization and background check required for sophomore level and up. **Housing:** Guaranteed on-campus for all undergraduates. Coed dorms, single-sex dorms, apartments, wellness housing available. Men's and women's dormitories available at Culver-Stockton College and Quincy University. **Activities:** Student government, student nurses organization.

Student services. Alcohol/substance abuse counseling, career counseling, student employment services, financial aid counseling, health services, on-campus daycare, personal counseling, placement for graduates.

Contact. E-mail: admissions@brcn.edu
Phone: (217) 228-5520 ext. 6949 Toll-free number: (800) 877-9140 ext. 6949 Fax: (217) 223-4661
Pam Brown, President, Blessing-Rieman College of Nursing, PO Box 7005, Quincy, IL 62305-7005

Bradley University

Peoria, Illinois **CB member**
www.bradley.edu **CB code: 1070**

- Private 4-year university
- Residential campus in large city

- 5,064 degree-seeking undergraduates: 6% part-time, 54% women, 7% African American, 4% Asian American, 3% Hispanic American, 1% international
- 680 degree-seeking graduate students
- 64% of applicants admitted
- SAT or ACT (ACT writing recommended), application essay required
- 76% graduate within 6 years; 16% enter graduate study

General. Founded in 1897. Regionally accredited. **Degrees:** 1,186 bachelor's awarded; master's, doctoral offered. **ROTC:** Army. **Location:** 157 miles from Chicago, 164 miles from St. Louis. **Calendar:** Semester, limited summer session. **Full-time faculty:** 337 total; 83% have terminal degrees, 14% minority, 36% women. **Part-time faculty:** 222 total; 4% minority, 47% women. **Class size:** 50% < 20, 43% 20-39, 3% 40-49, 2% 50-99, 1% >100. **Special facilities:** Global communications center, 2 art galleries, recreation center.

Freshman class profile. 5,932 applied, 3,817 admitted, 1,032 enrolled.

Mid 50% test scores		**Rank in top quarter:**	64%
SAT critical reading:	500-630	**Rank in top tenth:**	29%
SAT math:	520-650	**End year in good standing:**	95%
ACT composite:	22-27	**Return as sophomores:**	89%
GPA 3.75 or higher:	40%	**Out-of-state:**	14%
GPA 3.50-3.74:	20%	**Live on campus:**	92%
GPA 3.0-3.49:	31%	**Fraternities:**	44%
GPA 2.0-2.99:	9%	**Sororities:**	40%

Basis for selection. High school curriculum and achievement, test scores, special talents, co-curricular activities, letters of recommendation, personal statement, educational goals important. Student's academic interest, motivational level, and quality of secondary school education also considered. Interview recommended. Audition required of music majors, recommended for theater majors. Portfolio recommended for art majors. **Homeschooled:** Record of courses taken, grades earned, personal statement, letter of recommendation and record of activities or club memberships required. Interview may be required and highly recommended.

High school preparation. College-preparatory program recommended. 16 units required. Required and recommended units include English 4-5, mathematics 3-4, social studies 2-3, science 2-3 (laboratory 2-3) and foreign language 2. Additional requirements for business, science, engineering, music, nursing, and health science majors.

2008-2009 Annual costs. Tuition/fees: $22,814. Room/board: $7,350. Personal expenses: $1,500.

2007-2008 Financial aid. **Need-based:** 918 full-time freshmen applied for aid; 696 were judged to have need; 694 of these received aid. Average need met was 74%. Average scholarship/grant was $11,624; average loan $3,525. 66% of total undergraduate aid awarded as scholarships/grants, 34% as loans/jobs. **Non-need-based:** Awarded to 1,782 full-time undergraduates, including 347 freshmen. Scholarships awarded for academics, alumni affiliation, art, athletics, leadership, music/drama.

Application procedures. **Admission:** Priority date 3/1; deadline 8/1 (postmark date). $35 fee, may be waived for applicants with need, free for online applicants. Admission notification on a rolling basis beginning on or about 10/1. Must reply by May 1 or within 2 week(s) if notified thereafter. **Financial aid:** Priority date 3/1; no closing date. FAFSA required. Applicants notified on a rolling basis starting 2/15.

Academics. Academic Exploration Program assists undergraduates in choosing major. **Special study options:** Accelerated study, combined bachelor's/graduate degree, cooperative education, double major, honors, independent study, internships, liberal arts/career combination, student-designed major, study abroad, teacher certification program, Washington semester. **Credit/placement by examination:** AP, CLEP, IB, institutional tests. 60 credit hours maximum toward bachelor's degree. **Support services:** Learning center, study skills assistance, tutoring, writing center.

Majors. **Biology:** General, biochemistry, cellular/molecular. **Business:** Accounting, actuarial science, business admin, entrepreneurial studies, finance, human resources, insurance, international, management information systems, managerial economics, marketing, selling, small business admin. **Communications:** General, advertising, digital media, journalism, photojournalism, public relations, radio/tv. **Communications technology:** Animation/special effects. **Computer sciences:** Computer science, information systems. **Conservation:** Environmental science. **Education:** Art, biology, chemistry, drama/dance, early childhood, elementary, English, family/consumer sciences, French, German, history, learning disabled, mathematics, mentally handicapped, music, physics, psychology, science, social science, social studies, Spanish, speech. **Engineering:** Civil, computer, construction, electrical, industrial, manufacturing, mechanical, physics. **Engineering technology:** Manufacturing. **Family/consumer sciences:** General, merchandising. **Foreign languages:** French, German, Spanish. **Health:** Clinical lab science, dietetics, nursing (RN). **History:** General. **Liberal arts:** Arts/sciences, humanities. **Math:** General. **Philosophy/religion:** Philosophy, religion. **Physical sciences:** Chemistry, physics. **Protective services:** Law enforcement admin. **Psychology:** General. **Public administration:** Social work. **Social sciences:** Economics, international relations, political science, sociology. **Visual/performing arts:** Acting, art, art history/conservation, ceramics, directing/producing, dramatic, drawing, graphic design, music management, music performance, music theory/composition, painting, photography, printmaking, sculpture, studio arts. **Other:** 14.0899 Civil engineering, environmental, Legal studies in business.

Most popular majors. Business/marketing 22%, communications/journalism 11%, education 10%, engineering/engineering technologies 15%, health sciences 10%.

Computing on campus. 900 workstations in dormitories, library, computer center. Dormitories wired for high-speed internet access and linked to campus network. Commuter students can connect to campus network. Online course registration, helpline, student web hosting, wireless network available.

Student life. **Freshman orientation:** Mandatory, $115 fee. Preregistration for classes offered. 13 sessions throughout summer. **Housing:** Guaranteed on-campus for freshmen. Coed dorms, single-sex dorms, apartments, fraternity/sorority housing, wellness housing available. $100 partly refundable deposit, deadline 5/1. **Activities:** Bands, campus ministries, choral groups, dance, drama, film society, international student organizations, literary magazine, music ensembles, Model UN, musical theater, opera, radio station, student government, student newspaper, symphony orchestra, TV station, Alpha Phi Omega, center for student leadership and public services, Hillel, InterVarsity Christian Fellowship, mock trial, Amnesty International, Habitat for Humanity, Beyond Prejudice.

Athletics. NCAA. **Intercollegiate:** Baseball M, basketball, cross-country, golf, soccer M, softball W, tennis, track and field W, volleyball W. **Intramural:** Badminton, basketball, bowling, fencing, football (tackle) M, golf, handball, racquetball, soccer, softball, swimming, table tennis, tennis, volleyball, water polo, wrestling M. **Team name:** Braves.

Student services. Alcohol/substance abuse counseling, career counseling, student employment services, financial aid counseling, health services, minority student services, personal counseling, placement for graduates, veterans' counselor.

Contact. E-mail: admissions@bradley.edu
Phone: (309) 677-1000 Toll-free number: (800) 447-6460
Fax: (309) 677-2797
Rodney San Jose, Director of Admissions, Bradley University, 1501 West Bradley Avenue, Peoria, IL 61625

Chicago State University

Chicago, Illinois — **CB member**
www.csu.edu — **CB code: 1118**

- Public 4-year university
- Commuter campus in very large city
- 3,295 full-time, degree-seeking undergraduates
- ACT (writing optional) required

General. Founded in 1867. Regionally accredited. **Degrees:** 630 bachelor's awarded; master's offered. **ROTC:** Army. **Location:** 12 miles from downtown. **Calendar:** Semester, limited summer session. **Full-time faculty:** 304 total. **Part-time faculty:** 139 total. **Class size:** 48% < 20, 51% 20-39, less than 1% 40-49, less than 1% 50-99. **Special facilities:** Electron microscopy laboratory, video conference room, center of African heritage and culture.

Freshman class profile.

Mid 50% test scores		**Rank in top tenth:**	13%
ACT composite:	18-20	**Out-of-state:**	6%
Rank in top quarter:	35%	**Live on campus:**	23%

Basis for selection. High school GPA, standardized test scores, and subject/units completed important.

High school preparation. 15 units required. Required units include English 4, mathematics 3, social studies 3, science 3 and academic electives 2. 2 units foreign language, music, vocational education or art.

2008-2009 Annual costs. Tuition/fees: $8,878; $15,658 out-of-state. Rates guaranteed for 4 years. Room/board: $7,250. Books/supplies: $1,400. Personal expenses: $2,800.

2007-2008 Financial aid. **Non-need-based:** Scholarships awarded for academics, athletics, ROTC, state residency. **Additional information:** Freshmen of outstanding academic ability and talent eligible for Scholars Program full-tuition scholarship.

Application procedures. **Admission:** No deadline. $25 fee, may be waived for applicants with need. Admission notification on a rolling basis. **Financial aid:** Priority date 3/1; no closing date. FAFSA, institutional form required.

Academics. **Special study options:** Cooperative education, distance learning, double major, ESL, honors, independent study, internships, liberal arts/career combination, student-designed major, study abroad, teacher certification program. Programs for mature adults (University Without Walls, individualized curriculum, Board of Governors degree program). **Credit/placement by examination:** AP, CLEP, institutional tests. 60 credit hours maximum toward bachelor's degree. **Support services:** Learning center, remedial instruction, study skills assistance, tutoring, writing center.

Majors. **Area/ethnic studies:** African-American. **Biology:** General, bacteriology, biochemistry, environmental, molecular. **Business:** Accounting, business admin, fashion, finance, management information systems. **Communications:** Broadcast journalism. **Computer sciences:** General, data processing, information systems. **Education:** General, art, biology, business, chemistry, early childhood, elementary, English, health, history, mathematics, mentally handicapped, multi-level teacher, music, physical, secondary, technology/industrial arts. **Foreign languages:** Spanish. **Health:** Medical records admin, nursing (RN). **History:** General. **Math:** General. **Parks/recreation:** Health/fitness. **Physical sciences:** Chemistry, physics. **Psychology:** General. **Social sciences:** Anthropology, economics, geography, political science, sociology. **Visual/performing arts:** Art, commercial/advertising art.

Most popular majors. Business/marketing 14%, education 11%, health sciences 9%, liberal arts 30%, psychology 8%.

Computing on campus. 156 workstations in dormitories, library, computer center, student center. Dormitories wired for high-speed internet access. Commuter students can connect to campus network. Online course registration, online library available.

Student life. **Freshman orientation:** Mandatory. Preregistration for classes offered. One-day programs in July and August. **Housing:** Coed dorms available. $125 deposit, deadline 8/1. **Activities:** Bands, choral groups, dance, drama, literary magazine, music ensembles, radio station, student government, student newspaper, TV station, 47 clubs and organizations.

Athletics. NCAA. **Intercollegiate:** Baseball M, basketball, cross-country, golf, tennis, track and field, volleyball W. **Intramural:** Basketball, gymnastics, swimming, volleyball. **Team name:** Cougars.

Student services. Adult student services, alcohol/substance abuse counseling, chaplain/spiritual director, career counseling, student employment services, financial aid counseling, health services, minority student services, on-campus daycare, personal counseling, placement for graduates, veterans' counselor, women's services.

Contact. E-mail: ug-admissions@csu.edu
Phone: (773) 995-2513 Fax: (773) 995-3820
Addie Epps, Director of Admissions, Chicago State University, 9501 South King Drive, Chicago, IL 60628

Columbia College Chicago

Chicago, Illinois — **CB member**
www.colum.edu — **CB code: 1135**

- Private 4-year visual arts and liberal arts college
- Commuter campus in very large city
- 11,749 degree-seeking undergraduates: 10% part-time, 51% women, 14% African American, 4% Asian American, 10% Hispanic American, 1% Native American, 1% international
- 606 degree-seeking graduate students
- Application essay required
- 35% graduate within 6 years

General. Founded in 1890. Regionally accredited. **Degrees:** 3,226 bachelor's awarded; master's offered. **Location:** Downtown. **Calendar:** Semester, limited summer session. **Full-time faculty:** 321 total; 16% minority. **Part-time faculty:** 1,334 total; 13% minority. **Class size:** 74% < 20, 25% 20-39, 1% 40-49, less than 1% 50-99, less than 1% >100. **Special facilities:** Contemporary photography museum, photography studios, film/video sound stage, dance performance space, theater, audio technology center, psychoacoustic classroom, animation facilities, reverb chamber, book and paper arts center, black music research center, community media workshop, international Latino cultural center, community arts partnership center, concert hall.

Freshman class profile. 5,581 applied, 4,732 admitted, 2,387 enrolled.

Mid 50% test scores		**GPA 2.0-2.99:**	42%
SAT critical reading:	450-570	**Rank in top quarter:**	21%
SAT math:	430-540	**Rank in top tenth:**	6%
ACT composite:	18-25	**Return as sophomores:**	65%
GPA 3.75 or higher:	13%	**Out-of-state:**	28%
GPA 3.50-3.74:	12%	**Live on campus:**	59%
GPA 3.0-3.49:	27%	**International:**	1%

Basis for selection. Open admission, but selective for some programs. Proof of high school graduation (or earned GED), letter of recommendation, and essay required for placement/counseling. Students with less than 2.0 GPA may be required to attend special summer program. All freshmen take COMPASS placement test on campus. Interview recommended. **Homeschooled:** Transcript of courses and grades required. **Learning Disabled:** Student must have regular earned GED or HS diploma and may have to complete BRIDGE program.

High school preparation. College-preparatory program recommended.

2008-2009 Annual costs. Tuition/fees: $18,430. Room/board: $12,926. Books/supplies: $1,346. Personal expenses: $1,760.

2007-2008 Financial aid. **Need-based:** Average need met was 48%. Average scholarship/grant was $3,912; average loan $3,241. 19% of total undergraduate aid awarded as scholarships/grants, 81% as loans/jobs. **Non-need-based:** Scholarships awarded for academics, art, leadership, music/drama, state residency.

Application procedures. **Admission:** Priority date 5/1; no deadline. $35 fee, may be waived for applicants with need. Admission notification on a rolling basis beginning on or about 11/1. **Financial aid:** Priority date 5/1; no closing date. FAFSA, institutional form required. Applicants notified on a rolling basis.

Academics. **Special study options:** Cooperative education, distance learning, dual enrollment of high school students, ESL, independent study, internships, liberal arts/career combination, student-designed major, study abroad, teacher certification program. **Credit/placement by examination:** AP, CLEP, IB, institutional tests. 62 credit hours maximum toward bachelor's degree. **Support services:** Learning center, pre-admission summer program, reduced course load, remedial instruction, study skills assistance, tutoring, writing center.

Majors. **Architecture:** Interior. **Business:** Business admin, fashion, marketing. **Communications:** Advertising, broadcast journalism, journalism, public relations, radio/tv. **Communications technology:** Animation/special effects, recording arts. **Computer sciences:** Web page design. **Education:** Early childhood, kindergarten/preschool. **Foreign languages:** Sign language interpretation. **Liberal arts:** Arts/sciences. **Visual/performing arts:** General, acting, art, art history/conservation, arts management, cinematography, commercial/advertising art, dance, design, directing/producing, dramatic, fashion design, film/cinema, graphic design, illustration, industrial design, interior design, jazz, multimedia, music management, music performance, photography, play/screenwriting, studio arts, theater design, voice/opera. **Other:** Cultural studies, Interdisciplinary arts.

Most popular majors. Business/marketing 9%, communications/journalism 13%, communication technologies 6%, visual/performing arts 51%.

Computing on campus. 851 workstations in dormitories, library, computer center, student center. Dormitories wired for high-speed internet access and linked to campus network. Commuter students can connect to campus network. Online course registration, helpline, wireless network available.

Student life. **Freshman orientation:** Mandatory, $70 fee. Preregistration for classes offered. Parent orientation and parent weekend program available. **Housing:** Coed dorms, apartments available. $500 deposit. Student housing available at nearby colleges and universities. **Activities:** Bands, campus ministries, choral groups, dance, drama, film society, international student organizations, literary magazine, music ensembles, musical theater, radio station, student government, student newspaper, TV station, Association of Black Journalists, Umoja, Black Actor's Guild, Black Ink, Latino Alliance, environmental campus organization, Hillel, Not In Our Name.

Athletics. **Intramural:** Baseball, basketball, soccer.

Student services. Adult student services, alcohol/substance abuse counseling, career counseling, services for economically disadvantaged, student employment services, financial aid counseling, health services, minority student services, personal counseling, placement for graduates, veterans' counselor, women's services. **Physically disabled:** Services for visually, speech, hearing impaired.

Contact. E-mail: admissions@colum.edu
Phone: (312) 369-7130 Fax: (312) 369-8024
Murphy Monroe, Executive Director of Admissions, Columbia College Chicago, 600 South Michigan Avenue, Chicago, IL 60605-1996

Concordia University Chicago

River Forest, Illinois **CB member**
www.cuchicago.edu **CB code: 1140**

- Private 4-year university and teachers college affiliated with Lutheran Church - Missouri Synod
- Residential campus in large town
- 1,067 degree-seeking undergraduates: 4% part-time, 60% women
- 3,016 degree-seeking graduate students
- 83% of applicants admitted
- ACT (writing optional) required
- 48% graduate within 6 years

General. Founded in 1864. Regionally accredited. **Degrees:** 189 bachelor's awarded; master's, doctoral offered. **Location:** 10 miles from Chicago. **Calendar:** Semester, limited summer session. **Full-time faculty:** 110 total. **Part-time faculty:** 177 total. **Class size:** 69% < 20, 30% 20-39, less than 1% 40-49, less than 1% 50-99. **Special facilities:** Early childhood education laboratory school, curriculum center (teacher's resource), human performance laboratory.

Freshman class profile. 1,105 applied, 916 admitted, 253 enrolled.

Mid 50% test scores		**GPA 2.0-2.99:**	38%
SAT critical reading:	450-580	**Rank in top quarter:**	43%
SAT math:	450-580	**Rank in top tenth:**	20%
ACT composite:	19-25	**End year in good standing:**	75%
GPA 3.75 or higher:	14%	**Return as sophomores:**	71%
GPA 3.50-3.74:	18%	**Out-of-state:**	38%
GPA 3.0-3.49:	29%	**International:**	1%

Basis for selection. School achievement record, character reference most important. 2.0 GPA in college preparatory classes and rank in top half of class with 20 ACT or 930 SAT (exclusive of Writing) required. Interview recommended. Essay and interview required for students who do not meet academic admission requirements. **Homeschooled:** Statement describing homeschool structure and mission, transcript of courses and grades required. Syllabus for each course, personal statement or essay describing an important event or individual, certificate of completion from home school (if available), official transcripts of any college work completed required.

High school preparation. College-preparatory program required. 15 units required. Required and recommended units include English 4, mathematics 3, social studies 2, history 1, science 2-4 (laboratory 1) and foreign language 2.

2009-2010 Annual costs. Tuition/fees: $23,458. Room/board: $7,700. Books/supplies: $1,200. Personal expenses: $800.

2007-2008 Financial aid. Need-based: 207 full-time freshmen applied for aid; 173 were judged to have need; 173 of these received aid. Average need met was 79%. Average scholarship/grant was $11,675; average loan $4,271. 72% of total undergraduate aid awarded as scholarships/grants, 28% as loans/jobs. **Non-need-based:** Awarded to 322 full-time undergraduates, including 83 freshmen. Scholarships awarded for academics, alumni affiliation, music/drama, religious affiliation, state residency.

Application procedures. Admission: No deadline. No application fee. Admission notification on a rolling basis beginning on or about 9/4. **Financial aid:** Priority date 4/1; no closing date. FAFSA required. Applicants notified on a rolling basis starting 3/1; must reply within 4 week(s) of notification.

Academics. Special study options: Cross-registration, distance learning, double major, exchange student, honors, independent study, internships, study abroad, teacher certification program. Adult degree completion program. **Credit/placement by examination:** AP, CLEP, IB, institutional tests. 12 credit hours maximum toward bachelor's degree. **Support services:** Learning center, reduced course load, study skills assistance, tutoring, writing center.

Majors. Biology: General. **Business:** General, accounting, business admin, marketing. **Communications:** General, advertising. **Computer sciences:** General, computer science. **Education:** General, biology, chemistry, computer, early childhood, elementary, English, history, multi-level teacher, music, physical, science, secondary, social science, social studies. **Foreign languages:** Ancient Greek, Hebrew, Latin. **Health:** Prenursing. **History:** General. **Interdisciplinary:** Natural sciences. **Math:** General. **Parks/recreation:** Exercise sciences. **Philosophy/religion:** Philosophy. **Physical sciences:** Chemistry. **Protective services:** Criminal justice, law enforcement admin, police science. **Psychology:** General. **Public administration:** Social work. **Social sciences:** Geography, political science, sociology. **Theology:** Religious ed, sacred music, theology. **Visual/performing arts:** Art, music performance, music theory/composition.

Most popular majors. Business/marketing 16%, education 44%, psychology 9%, theological studies 8%.

Computing on campus. 85 workstations in library, computer center, student center. Dormitories wired for high-speed internet access and linked to campus network. Commuter students can connect to campus network. Online course registration, helpline, repair service, student web hosting, wireless network available.

Student life. Freshman orientation: Mandatory. Preregistration for classes offered. **Housing:** Guaranteed on-campus for freshmen. Coed dorms, single-sex dorms available. $200 deposit, deadline 7/1. **Activities:** Bands, campus ministries, choral groups, drama, literary magazine, music ensembles, musical theater, radio station, student government, student newspaper, TV station, minority student alliance, Ambassadors for Christ, sociology/social service club, Fellowship of Christian Athletes, environmental awareness club, Pace Jail Ministries, Latin student union.

Athletics. NCAA. **Intercollegiate:** Baseball M, basketball, cross-country, football (tackle) M, soccer, softball W, tennis, track and field, volleyball W. **Intramural:** Badminton, basketball, bowling, cross-country, softball, swimming, tennis, track and field, volleyball. **Team name:** Cougars.

Student services. Career counseling, student employment services, financial aid counseling, health services, on-campus daycare, personal counseling, placement for graduates.

Contact. E-mail: crfadmis@cuchicago.edu
Phone: (708) 209-3100 Toll-free number: (866) 462-2873
Fax: (708) 209-3473
Gwen Kanelos, Assistant Vice President for Enrollment, Concordia University Chicago, 7400 Augusta Street, River Forest, IL 60305-1499

DePaul University

Chicago, Illinois **CB member**
www.depaul.edu **CB code: 1165**

- Private 4-year university affiliated with Roman Catholic Church
- Residential campus in very large city
- 15,449 degree-seeking undergraduates: 18% part-time, 55% women, 8% African American, 8% Asian American, 12% Hispanic American, 2% international
- 8,389 degree-seeking graduate students
- 64% of applicants admitted
- SAT or ACT (ACT writing optional) required
- 64% graduate within 6 years

General. Founded in 1898. Regionally accredited. Largest Catholic university in the United States. **Degrees:** 2,917 bachelor's awarded; master's, doctoral, first professional offered. **ROTC:** Army. **Location:** Downtown. **Calendar:** Quarter, extensive summer session. **Full-time faculty:** 899 total; 88% have terminal degrees, 23% minority, 45% women. **Part-time faculty:** 943 total; 13% have terminal degrees, 16% minority, 46% women. **Class size:** 39% < 20, 50% 20-39, 10% 40-49, less than 1% 50-99, less than 1% >100.

Freshman class profile. 12,920 applied, 8,302 admitted, 2,555 enrolled.

Mid 50% test scores		**GPA 2.0-2.99:**	18%
SAT critical reading:	520-630	**Rank in top quarter:**	48%
SAT math:	510-620	**Rank in top tenth:**	22%
SAT writing:	530-630	**End year in good standing:**	93%
ACT composite:	22-27	**Return as sophomores:**	85%
GPA 3.75 or higher:	29%	**Out-of-state:**	34%
GPA 3.50-3.74:	19%	**Live on campus:**	72%
GPA 3.0-3.49:	34%	**International:**	1%

Basis for selection. Secondary school record most important; class rank, recommendations, test scores, essay, extracurricular activities, talent/ability, character, volunteer and work experience important. Interview, alumni/ae relation, geographical location, state residency, religious affiliation, racial or ethnic status considered. Interview required of acting, theater technologies, and recording sound technology majors. Auditions required of music and theater majors. Portfolios required of theater technology and design majors. **Homeschooled:** Transcript of courses and grades required. Official community college transcripts for any courses taken required. Listing of textbooks used, especially in math and science, recommended.

High school preparation. College-preparatory program required. 12 units required. Required and recommended units include English 4, mathematics 3, social studies 2, science 3 (laboratory 2) and foreign language 2.

2008-2009 Annual costs. Tuition/fees: $26,067. Room/board: $10,240. Books/supplies: $975. Personal expenses: $1,702.

2008-2009 Financial aid. Need-based: 2,195 full-time freshmen applied for aid; 1,674 were judged to have need; 1,637 of these received aid. Average need met was 65%. Average scholarship/grant was $14,229; average loan $3,739. 52% of total undergraduate aid awarded as scholarships/grants, 48% as loans/jobs. **Non-need-based:** Awarded to 3,339 full-time undergraduates, including 1,122 freshmen. Scholarships awarded for academics, art, athletics, leadership, music/drama, ROTC, state residency.

Application procedures. Admission: Priority date 11/15; deadline 2/1 (postmark date). $40 fee, may be waived for applicants with need. Admission notification 3/15. Must reply by May 1 or within 2 week(s) if notified thereafter. Early action applicants receive early financial aid estimates, priority registration, priority housing and priority advising. **Financial aid:** Priority date 3/1; no closing date. FAFSA required. Applicants notified on a rolling basis starting 3/15; must reply by 5/1 or within 4 week(s) of notification.

Academics. Honors programs offered in arts and sciences, business. Conservatory program in theater and music provides professional training. **Special study options:** Accelerated study, combined bachelor's/graduate degree, cooperative education, distance learning, double major, dual enrollment of high school students, ESL, honors, independent study, internships, student-designed major, study abroad, teacher certification program, weekend college. **Credit/placement by examination:** AP, CLEP, IB, SAT, ACT, institutional tests. Senior year residency requirement excludes CLEP, AP or IB credits. For transfer students, CLEP, IB or AP credits combined with transfer credits from 2-year institutions may total no more than 99 hours, and combined with transfer credits from 4-year institutions may total no more than 132 hours. **Support services:** Learning center, pre-admission summer program, reduced course load, remedial instruction, study skills assistance, tutoring, writing center.

Majors. Area/ethnic studies: African-American, American, East Asian, Latin American, women's. **Biology:** General. **Business:** General, accounting, banking/financial services, business admin, e-commerce, finance, human resources, management science, managerial economics, operations, organizational behavior, real estate. **Communications:** General. **Computer sciences:** General, applications programming, computer graphics, computer science, information systems, information technology, networking, programming, security, web page design. **Conservation:** Environmental science. **Education:** Art, biology, chemistry, computer, early childhood, elementary, English, French, geography, German, health, history, mathematics, music, physical, physics, secondary, social science, Spanish, special. **Foreign languages:** French, German, Italian, Spanish. **Health:** Art therapy, clinical lab science, nursing (RN). **History:** General. **Interdisciplinary:** Biological/physical sciences, math/computer science. **Liberal arts:** Humanities. **Math:** General. **Parks/recreation:** Health/fitness. **Philosophy/religion:** Islamic, Judaic, philosophy, religion. **Physical sciences:** Chemistry, physics. **Psychology:** General, educational. **Public administration:** Community org/advocacy, policy analysis. **Social sciences:** General, anthropology, economics, geography, international relations, political science, sociology, urban studies. **Visual/performing arts:** Acting, art, art history/conservation, arts management, dramatic, jazz, music management, music performance, music theory/composition, play/screenwriting, theater design, theater history. **Other:** Human computer interaction, Music - recording technology, Scientific data analysis/visualization.

Most popular majors. Business/marketing 32%, communications/journalism 10%, computer/information sciences 6%, education 7%, liberal arts 10%, psychology 8%, social sciences 10%.

Computing on campus. 1,117 workstations in dormitories, library, computer center, student center. Dormitories wired for high-speed internet access and linked to campus network. Commuter students can connect to campus network. Online course registration, online library, helpline, student web hosting, wireless network available.

Student life. Freshman orientation: Mandatory, $170 fee. Preregistration for classes offered. Two-day summer program for students and their families. **Housing:** Coed dorms, special housing for disabled, apartments available. $500 fully refundable deposit. **Activities:** Bands, campus ministries, choral groups, dance, drama, film society, international student organizations, literary magazine, music ensembles, Model UN, musical theater, opera, radio station, student government, student newspaper, symphony orchestra, over 70 clubs and organizations.

Athletics. NCAA. **Intercollegiate:** Basketball, cross-country, golf M, soccer, softball W, tennis, track and field, volleyball W. **Intramural:** Badminton, basketball, football (non-tackle), racquetball, soccer, softball, table tennis, tennis, volleyball, water polo. **Team name:** Blue Demons.

Student services. Adult student services, alcohol/substance abuse counseling, chaplain/spiritual director, career counseling, services for economically disadvantaged, student employment services, financial aid counseling, health services, legal services, minority student services, personal counseling, placement for graduates, veterans' counselor, women's services. **Physically disabled:** Services for visually, speech, hearing impaired.

Contact. E-mail: admission@depaul.edu
Phone: (312) 362-8300 Toll-free number: (800) 433-7285
Fax: (312) 362-5749
Carlene Klaas, Director of Undergraduate Admissions, DePaul University, One East Jackson Boulevard, Chicago, IL 60604-2287

DeVry University: Addison

Addison, Illinois
www.devry.edu **CB code: 3204**

- For-profit 4-year university
- Commuter campus in large town
- 1,397 degree-seeking undergraduates: 35% part-time, 27% women, 11% African American, 13% Asian American, 13% Hispanic American, 3% international
- Interview required

General. Founded in 1982. Regionally accredited. **Degrees:** 345 bachelor's, 43 associate awarded; master's offered. **Location:** 20 miles from Chicago. **Calendar:** Semester, extensive summer session. **Full-time faculty:** 43 total; 23% minority, 28% women. **Part-time faculty:** 78 total; 23% minority, 42% women.

Freshman class profile.

Out-of-state:	5%	**International:**	2%

Basis for selection. Applicants must have high school diploma or equivalent, or degree from an accredited postsecondary institution and demonstrate proficiency in basic college-level skills through test scores and/or institution-administered placement examinations, and be at least 17 years of age. New students may enter at the beginning of any semester. SAT/ACT or DeVry-administered admissions test required for all.

2008-2009 Annual costs. Tuition/fees: $14,130. Books/supplies: $1,300. Personal expenses: $5,082.

2007-2008 Financial aid. All financial aid based on need.

Application procedures. Admission: No deadline. $50 fee. Admission notification on a rolling basis. **Financial aid:** No deadline. FAFSA required. Applicants notified on a rolling basis.

Academics. Special study options: Accelerated study, distance learning. **Credit/placement by examination:** CLEP, institutional tests. **Support services:** Learning center, remedial instruction, tutoring.

Majors. Business: Business admin, e-commerce. **Computer sciences:** Information systems, information technology, networking, systems analysis, web page design. **Engineering:** Biomedical, electrical, software. **Engineering technology:** Biomedical, computer, electrical. **Other:** Technical management.

Most popular majors. Business/marketing 55%, computer/information sciences 33%, engineering/engineering technologies 13%.

Computing on campus. 548 workstations in library, computer center. Online course registration, online library, helpline available.

Student life. Freshman orientation: Mandatory. **Housing:** Private apartments, student-plan housing, private rooms available. **Activities:** International student organizations, literary magazine, student government, student newspaper, Muslim student association, Alpha Sigma Lambda, Christian Fellowship, Chi Pi Alpha, Epsilon Delta Pi, Phi Theta Kappa, Institute of Electrical and Electronics Engineers, computer users group.

Athletics. Intramural: Basketball, soccer M, softball, tennis.

Student services. Career counseling, student employment services, financial aid counseling, placement for graduates, veterans' counselor. **Physically disabled:** Services for visually, hearing impaired.

Contact. Phone: (630) 953-2000 Toll-free number: (800) 346-5420
Fax: (630) 953-1236
Sandra Stack, Director of Admissions, DeVry University: Addison, 1221 North Swift Road, Addison, IL 60101-6106

DeVry University: Chicago

Chicago, Illinois
www.devry.edu **CB code: 1171**

- For-profit 4-year university
- Commuter campus in very large city
- 1,882 degree-seeking undergraduates: 42% part-time, 43% women, 37% African American, 6% Asian American, 34% Hispanic American, 4% international
- Interview required

General. Founded in 1931. Regionally accredited. **Degrees:** 309 bachelor's, 163 associate awarded. **Location:** 6 miles from downtown. **Calendar:** Semester, extensive summer session. **Full-time faculty:** 39 total; 20% minority, 31% women. **Part-time faculty:** 120 total; 32% minority, 40% women.

Freshman class profile.

Out-of-state:	1%	**International:**	1%

Basis for selection. Applicants must have high school diploma or equivalent, or degree from an accredited postsecondary institution, demonstrate proficiency in basic college-level skills through ACT scores or institution-administered placement examinations, and be at least 17 years of age. New students may enter at beginning of any semester. SAT/ACT or DeVry-administered admissions test required for all.

2008-2009 Annual costs. Tuition/fees: $14,130. Books/supplies: $965. Personal expenses: $3,152.

2007-2008 Financial aid. All financial aid based on need.

Application procedures. Admission: No deadline. $50 fee. Admission notification on a rolling basis. **Financial aid:** No deadline. FAFSA required. Applicants notified on a rolling basis.

Academics. Special study options: Accelerated study, distance learning. **Credit/placement by examination:** CLEP, institutional tests. **Support services:** Learning center, remedial instruction, tutoring.

Majors. Business: Business admin. **Computer sciences:** Networking, systems analysis, web page design. **Engineering:** Biomedical, electrical. **Engineering technology:** Biomedical, computer, electrical. **Health:** Clinical lab science. **Other:** Technical management.

Most popular majors. Business/marketing 52%, computer/information sciences 27%, engineering/engineering technologies 22%.

Computing on campus. 600 workstations in library, computer center. Online course registration, online library, helpline available.

Student life. Freshman orientation: Mandatory. **Housing:** Private apartments, student-plan housing, private rooms available. **Activities:** Student government, student newspaper, Muslim student association, Alpha Beta Gamma, Alpha Chi, Bible club, National Society of Black Engineers, Tau Alpha Pi.

Student services. Career counseling, student employment services, financial aid counseling, placement for graduates, veterans' counselor. **Physically disabled:** Services for visually, hearing impaired.

Contact. E-mail: admissions2@devry.edu
Phone: (773) 929-6550 Toll-free number: (800) 383-3879
Fax: (773) 697-2710
Christine Hierl, Director of Admissions, DeVry University: Chicago, 3300 North Campbell Avenue, Chicago, IL 60618-5994

DeVry University: Online

Naperville, Illinois
www.devry.edu

- For-profit 4-year virtual college
- Small city
- 12,825 degree-seeking undergraduates: 72% part-time, 51% women, 26% African American, 2% Asian American, 7% Hispanic American, 1% Native American
- 4,114 degree-seeking graduate students

General. Regionally accredited. **Degrees:** 1,013 bachelor's, 134 associate awarded; master's offered. **Calendar:** Semester. **Part-time faculty:** 2,695 total; 6% have terminal degrees, 18% minority, 42% women.

Basis for selection. Applicants must have high school diploma or equivalent, or degree from accredited post-secondary institution, demonstrate proficiency in basic college-level skills through SAT or ACT scores or institution-administered placement examinations, and be at least 17 years of age.

2008-2009 Annual costs. Tuition/fees: $14,600. Books/supplies: $1,300. Personal expenses: $5,082.

2007-2008 Financial aid. Non-need-based: Scholarships awarded for academics.

Application procedures. Admission: No deadline. $50 fee. Admission notification on a rolling basis. **Financial aid:** No deadline. FAFSA required. Applicants notified on a rolling basis.

Academics. Special study options: Accelerated study, distance learning. **Credit/placement by examination:** CLEP.

Majors. Business: Accounting/finance, business admin, e-commerce. **Computer sciences:** Networking, systems analysis, web page design. **Engineering:** Software. **Engineering technology:** Computer, electrical. **Other:** Technical management.

Most popular majors. Business/marketing 91%, computer/information sciences 9%.

Contact. DeVry University: Online, One Tower Lane, Oakbrook Terrace, IL 60181

DeVry University: Tinley Park

Tinley Park, Illinois
www.devry.edu **CB code: 2818**

- For-profit 4-year university
- Commuter campus in large town
- 1,088 degree-seeking undergraduates: 40% part-time, 32% women, 36% African American, 2% Asian American, 8% Hispanic American, 1% Native American
- 309 degree-seeking graduate students
- Interview required

General. Regionally accredited. **Degrees:** 184 bachelor's, 22 associate awarded; master's offered. **Location:** 20 miles from Chicago. **Calendar:** Semester, extensive summer session. **Full-time faculty:** 35 total; 9% minority, 23% women. **Part-time faculty:** 40 total; 32% minority, 35% women.

Basis for selection. Applicants must have high school diploma or equivalent, or degree from an accredited postsecondary institution and demonstrate proficiency in basic college-level skills through test scores and/or institution-administered placement examinations, and be at least 17 years of age. New students may enter at the beginning of any semester. SAT/ACT or DeVry-administered admissions test required.

2008-2009 Annual costs. Tuition/fees: $14,130. Books/supplies: $1,300. Personal expenses: $5,082.

2007-2008 Financial aid. All financial aid based on need.

Application procedures. Admission: No deadline. $50 fee. Admission notification on a rolling basis. **Financial aid:** No deadline. FAFSA required. Applicants notified on a rolling basis.

Academics. Special study options: Accelerated study, distance learning. **Credit/placement by examination:** CLEP. **Support services:** Learning center, remedial instruction, tutoring.

Majors. Business: Business admin. **Communications technology:** General. **Computer sciences:** Information systems, networking, systems analysis, web page design. **Engineering:** Biomedical, computer, software. **Engineering technology:** Biomedical, computer, electrical. **Other:** Technical management.

Most popular majors. Business/marketing 54%, computer/information sciences 31%, engineering/engineering technologies 15%.

Computing on campus. 344 workstations in library, computer center. Online course registration, online library, helpline available.

Student life. Freshman orientation: Mandatory. **Housing:** Private apartments, student-plan housing, private rooms available. **Activities:** Student activities association, student leadership group, women in technology.

Student services. Career counseling, student employment services, financial aid counseling, placement for graduates, veterans' counselor. **Physically disabled:** Services for visually, hearing impaired.

Four-Year Colleges

Contact. Phone: (708) 342-3100 Toll-free number: (877) 305-8184
Fax: (708) 342-3505
Bruce Jones, Director of Admissions, DeVry University: Tinley Park, 18624 West Creek Drive, Tinley Park, IL 60477-6243

Dominican University

River Forest, Illinois — **CB member**
www.dom.edu — **CB code: 1667**

- Private 4-year university and liberal arts college affiliated with Roman Catholic Church
- Residential campus in large town
- 1,608 degree-seeking undergraduates: 8% part-time, 69% women, 7% African American, 3% Asian American, 25% Hispanic American, 2% international
- 1,379 degree-seeking graduate students
- 85% of applicants admitted
- SAT or ACT (ACT writing optional), application essay required
- 70% graduate within 6 years; 35% enter graduate study

General. Founded in 1901. Regionally accredited. **Degrees:** 339 bachelor's awarded; master's offered. **Location:** 10 miles from Chicago. **Calendar:** Semester, extensive summer session. **Full-time faculty:** 132 total; 86% have terminal degrees, 12% minority, 58% women. **Part-time faculty:** 275 total; 27% have terminal degrees, 61% women. **Class size:** 67% < 20, 32% 20-39, less than 1% 40-49. **Special facilities:** Food science laboratory.

Freshman class profile. 1,447 applied, 1,225 admitted, 417 enrolled.

Mid 50% test scores		**GPA 2.0-2.99:**	31%
SAT critical reading:	480-620	**Rank in top quarter:**	49%
SAT math:	460-590	**Rank in top tenth:**	20%
SAT writing:	480-610	**End year in good standing:**	86%
ACT composite:	20-25	**Return as sophomores:**	79%
GPA 3.75 or higher:	30%	**Out-of-state:**	8%
GPA 3.50-3.74:	12%	**Live on campus:**	58%
GPA 3.0-3.49:	27%	**International:**	1%

Basis for selection. Rank in upper half of class, 2.75 GPA, have ACT or SAT at or above national average, and 16 units of college prep work required. Interview recommended. **Homeschooled:** Transcript of courses and grades required.

High school preparation. 16 units required. Required and recommended units include English 4, mathematics 3, social studies 1, history 2, science 3 (laboratory 2) and foreign language 2. 14 credits must be in English, math, social science, laboratory science, and foreign languages.

2008-2009 Annual costs. Tuition/fees: $23,950. Room/board: $7,350. Books/supplies: $1,000. Personal expenses: $900.

2008-2009 Financial aid. Need-based: 382 full-time freshmen applied for aid; 350 were judged to have need; 350 of these received aid. Average need met was 85%. Average scholarship/grant was $15,411; average loan $3,289. 70% of total undergraduate aid awarded as scholarships/grants, 30% as loans/jobs. **Non-need-based:** Awarded to 129 full-time undergraduates, including 107 freshmen. Scholarships awarded for academics, alumni affiliation, leadership.

Application procedures. Admission: Priority date 6/1; no deadline. $25 fee, may be waived for applicants with need, free for online applicants. Admission notification on a rolling basis beginning on or about 10/1. Must reply by May 1 or within 2 week(s) if notified thereafter. **Financial aid:** Priority date 6/1; no closing date. FAFSA required. Applicants notified on a rolling basis starting 2/15; must reply within 2 week(s) of notification.

Academics. Special study options: Accelerated study, combined bachelor's/graduate degree, cross-registration, distance learning, double major, dual enrollment of high school students, ESL, honors, independent study, internships, liberal arts/career combination, study abroad, teacher certification program, Washington semester. 2+2 nursing with Rush University, 5-year BA/BS engineering program with Illinois Institute of Technology, license preparation in gerontology on-campus, 5 year program in occupational therapy with Rush University leading to master's degree. **Credit/placement by examination:** AP, CLEP, IB, institutional tests. 28 credit hours maximum toward bachelor's degree. **Support services:** Learning center, pre-admission summer program, reduced course load, remedial instruction, study skills assistance, tutoring, writing center.

Majors. Area/ethnic studies: African-American, American. **Biology:** General, biochemistry. **Business:** Accounting, business admin, communications, fashion, international, organizational behavior. **Communications:** General, journalism, public relations. **Computer sciences:** General, computer science, information systems. **Conservation:** Environmental science, environmental studies. **Education:** Early childhood. **Engineering:** Architectural, chemical, civil, computer, electrical, mechanical. **Family/consumer sciences:** Food/nutrition, institutional food production. **Foreign languages:** French, Italian, Spanish. **Health:** Dietetics, predental, premedicine, prenursing, prepharmacy, preveterinary, substance abuse counseling. **History:** General. **Interdisciplinary:** Gerontology, math/computer science, neuroscience, nutrition sciences. **Math:** General. **Philosophy/religion:** Philosophy. **Physical sciences:** Chemistry. **Psychology:** General. **Social sciences:** General, criminology, economics, international relations, political science, sociology. **Theology:** Pastoral counseling, theology. **Visual/performing arts:** Art, art history/conservation, commercial/advertising art, dramatic, fashion design, photography, studio arts.

Most popular majors. Business/marketing 26%, psychology 10%, social sciences 19%, visual/performing arts 10%.

Computing on campus. 309 workstations in dormitories, library, computer center, student center. Dormitories wired for high-speed internet access and linked to campus network. Commuter students can connect to campus network. Online course registration, online library, helpline, wireless network available.

Student life. Freshman orientation: Mandatory. Preregistration for classes offered. Two-day program with overnight on campus. **Housing:** Guaranteed on-campus for freshmen. Coed dorms, wellness housing available. $100 partly refundable deposit. **Activities:** Campus ministries, choral groups, dance, drama, international student organizations, literary magazine, musical theater, student government, student newspaper, Organization of Latino Americans, social service organization, business club, Italian club, black student union, psychology club, education club, gospel choir.

Athletics. NCAA. **Intercollegiate:** Baseball M, basketball, cross-country, soccer, softball W, tennis, volleyball W. **Intramural:** Basketball, bowling, cheerleading, racquetball, soccer, softball W, table tennis, volleyball, water polo. **Team name:** Stars.

Student services. Adult student services, alcohol/substance abuse counseling, career counseling, student employment services, financial aid counseling, health services, minority student services, on-campus daycare, personal counseling, placement for graduates, veterans' counselor. **Physically disabled:** Services for visually, hearing impaired.

Contact. E-mail: domadmis@dom.edu
Phone: (708) 524-6800 Toll-free number: (800) 828-8475
Fax: (708) 524-6864
Glenn Hamilton, Assistant Vice President for Enrollment Management, Dominican University, 7900 West Division Street, River Forest, IL 60305-1099

East-West University

Chicago, Illinois
www.eastwest.edu — **CB code: 0798**

- Private 4-year university
- Commuter campus in very large city
- 1,150 degree-seeking undergraduates
- Interview required

General. Founded in 1978. Regionally accredited. **Degrees:** 85 bachelor's, 48 associate awarded. **Calendar:** Quarter, limited summer session. **Full-time faculty:** 14 total; 100% have terminal degrees, 57% minority, 43% women. **Part-time faculty:** 93 total; 100% have terminal degrees, 56% minority, 46% women.

Basis for selection. Open admission.

2008-2009 Annual costs. Tuition/fees: $13,530. Books/supplies: $1,200. Personal expenses: $2,100.

Financial aid. Non-need-based: Scholarships awarded for academics. **Additional information:** Foreign students eligible for institutional scholarship.

Application procedures. Admission: No deadline. $30 fee, may be waived for applicants with need. Admission notification on a rolling basis. **Financial aid:** No deadline. FAFSA required. Applicants notified on a rolling basis starting 1/4; must reply within 4 week(s) of notification.

Academics. Special study options: Cooperative education, double major, ESL, honors, independent study, internships. **Credit/placement by examination:** CLEP, institutional tests. Interview recommended for placement. **Support services:** Tutoring.

Majors. **Business:** Business admin. **Communications:** General. **Computer sciences:** General. **Engineering technology:** Electrical. **Liberal arts:** Arts/sciences. **Math:** General.

Most popular majors. Business/marketing 32%, computer/information sciences 11%, engineering/engineering technologies 16%, liberal arts 40%.

Computing on campus. 10 workstations in computer center. Online library available.

Student life. **Freshman orientation:** Available. **Activities:** Drama, student government, student newspaper.

Athletics. **Team name:** Phantom.

Student services. Career counseling.

Contact. E-mail: seeyou@eastwest.edu
Phone: (312) 939-0111 Toll-free number: (877) 398-9376
Fax: (312) 939-0083
William Link, Director of Admissions, East-West University, 816 South Michigan Avenue, Chicago, IL 60605

Eastern Illinois University

Charleston, Illinois
www.eiu.edu **CB code: 1199**

- Public 4-year university and teachers college
- Residential campus in large town
- 10,065 degree-seeking undergraduates: 10% part-time, 57% women, 10% African American, 1% Asian American, 3% Hispanic American, 1% international
- 1,694 degree-seeking graduate students
- 69% of applicants admitted
- SAT or ACT (ACT writing optional) required
- 60% graduate within 6 years

General. Founded in 1895. Regionally accredited. Off-campus sites in Arlington Heights, Bridgeview, Carterville, Centralia, Champaign, Danville, Effingham, Olney, River Grove, Mattoon, Robinson and Vandalia. **Degrees:** 2,374 bachelor's awarded; master's offered. **ROTC:** Army. **Location:** 180 miles from Chicago, 125 miles from Indianapolis. **Calendar:** Semester, limited summer session. **Full-time faculty:** 650 total; 66% have terminal degrees, 10% minority, 47% women. **Part-time faculty:** 157 total; 7% have terminal degrees, 6% minority, 57% women. **Class size:** 36% < 20, 56% 20-39, 4% 40-49, 3% 50-99, 1% >100. **Special facilities:** Arts center, greenhouse, electron microscope, observatory.

Freshman class profile. 7,676 applied, 5,331 admitted, 1,780 enrolled.

Mid 50% test scores			
ACT composite:	19-24	Rank in top tenth:	7%
GPA 3.75 or higher:	10%	Return as sophomores:	81%
GPA 3.50-3.74:	11%	Out-of-state:	2%
GPA 3.0-3.49:	31%	Live on campus:	99%
GPA 2.0-2.99:	48%	International:	1%
Rank in top quarter:	22%	Fraternities:	21%
		Sororities:	18%

Basis for selection. Applicants must be in top quarter of class with 18 ACT, in top half of class with 19 ACT, or be in upper three-quarters of class with 22 ACT. Gateway admissions program for students with at least 14 ACT and 2.0 GPA. Audition required of music majors. **Homeschooled:** GED requirement may be waived with acceptable ACT score for students who present transcript of all courses completed with grades listed for each class.

High school preparation. College-preparatory program required. 15 units required. Required and recommended units include English 4, mathematics 3, social studies 3, science 3 (laboratory 3), foreign language 2 and academic electives 2. Significant science lab experience required.

2008-2009 Annual costs. Tuition/fees: $8,782; $21,862 out-of-state. New students have a guaranteed tuition rate for 4 years. Room/board: $7,588. Books/supplies: $120. Personal expenses: $1,500.

2008-2009 Financial aid. **Need-based:** 1,539 full-time freshmen applied for aid; 995 were judged to have need; 978 of these received aid. Average need met was 69%. Average scholarship/grant was $2,625; average loan $3,188. 41% of total undergraduate aid awarded as scholarships/grants, 59% as loans/jobs. **Non-need-based:** Awarded to 1,665 full-time undergraduates, including 382 freshmen. Scholarships awarded for academics, art, athletics, leadership, music/drama, ROTC.

Application procedures. **Admission:** No deadline. $30 fee, may be waived for applicants with need. Admission notification on a rolling basis. Consult university for possible early cut-off date. **Financial aid:** Priority date 3/1; no closing date. FAFSA required. Applicants notified on a rolling basis starting 2/1; must reply within 2 week(s) of notification.

Academics. **Special study options:** Distance learning, double major, dual enrollment of high school students, exchange student, honors, independent study, internships, study abroad, teacher certification program. Cooperative program in engineering with University of Illinois. **Credit/placement by examination:** AP, CLEP, ACT, institutional tests. **Support services:** Learning center, reduced course load, study skills assistance, tutoring, writing center.

Majors. **Area/ethnic studies:** African-American. **Biology:** General. **Business:** Accounting, business admin, finance, management science, marketing. **Communications:** Journalism. **Education:** Elementary, health, kindergarten/preschool, physical, science, social science, special, voc/tech. **Engineering:** General. **Engineering technology:** Industrial. **Family/consumer sciences:** General. **Foreign languages:** General. **Health:** Clinical lab science, communication disorders. **History:** General. **Interdisciplinary:** Math/computer science. **Liberal arts:** Arts/sciences. **Math:** General. **Parks/recreation:** Facilities management. **Philosophy/religion:** Philosophy. **Physical sciences:** Chemistry, geology, physics. **Psychology:** General. **Social sciences:** Economics, geography, political science, sociology. **Visual/performing arts:** Art, dramatic.

Most popular majors. Business/marketing 13%, education 28%, English 10%, family/consumer sciences 7%, liberal arts 8%, psychology 6%, social sciences 6%.

Computing on campus. 792 workstations in dormitories, library, computer center. Dormitories wired for high-speed internet access and linked to campus network. Commuter students can connect to campus network. Online course registration, helpline, student web hosting, wireless network available.

Student life. **Freshman orientation:** Mandatory. Preregistration for classes offered. All day sessions held on various dates from May-August. **Housing:** Guaranteed on-campus for freshmen. Coed dorms, single-sex dorms, special housing for disabled, apartments, fraternity/sorority housing available. $50 partly refundable deposit. Quiet study floors available. **Activities:** Bands, campus ministries, choral groups, dance, drama, international student organizations, literary magazine, music ensembles, musical theater, radio station, student government, student newspaper, symphony orchestra, TV station, College Democrats, Republicans, Christian Campus Fellowship, Newman Catholic center, Unity Gospel Choir, Black student union, Epsilon Sigma Alpha, Students United for World Change, Association of International Students, minority leaders group.

Athletics. NCAA. **Intercollegiate:** Baseball M, basketball, cross-country, diving, football (tackle) M, golf, rugby W, soccer, softball W, swimming, tennis, track and field, volleyball W. **Intramural:** Badminton, basketball, bowling, football (non-tackle), racquetball, soccer, softball, table tennis, tennis, volleyball, weight lifting. **Team name:** Panthers.

Student services. Adult student services, alcohol/substance abuse counseling, career counseling, services for economically disadvantaged, student employment services, financial aid counseling, health services, legal services, minority student services, personal counseling, placement for graduates, veterans' counselor, women's services. **Physically disabled:** Services for visually, speech, hearing impaired.

Contact. E-mail: admissions@eiu.edu
Phone: (217) 581-2223 Toll-free number: (877) 581-2348
Fax: (217) 581-7060
Brenda Major, Director of Admissions, Eastern Illinois University, 600 Lincoln Avenue, Charleston, IL 61920-3011

Elmhurst College

Elmhurst, Illinois **CB member**
www.elmhurst.edu **CB code: 1204**

- Private 4-year liberal arts college affiliated with United Church of Christ
- Commuter campus in large town
- 2,960 degree-seeking undergraduates: 7% part-time, 64% women
- 120 degree-seeking graduate students
- 69% of applicants admitted
- SAT or ACT (ACT writing optional) required

General. Founded in 1871. Regionally accredited. **Degrees:** 736 bachelor's awarded; master's offered. **ROTC:** Army, Air Force. **Location:** 15 miles from Chicago. **Calendar:** 4-1-4, limited summer session. **Full-time**

faculty: 125 total; 84% have terminal degrees, 10% minority, 52% women. **Part-time faculty:** 215 total; 18% have terminal degrees, 5% minority, 51% women. **Class size:** 59% < 20, 41% 20-39, less than 1% 40-49. **Special facilities:** 2 nuclear accelerators, 4 electron microscopes, collection of Impressionist art, computer science and technology center, media center, sound studio, greenhouse.

Freshman class profile. 2,779 applied, 1,917 admitted, 587 enrolled.

Mid 50% test scores		**Live on campus:**	61%
SAT critical reading:	490-630	**International:**	1%
SAT math:	490-590	**Fraternities:**	17%
ACT composite:	21-26	**Sororities:**	20%
Out-of-state:	12%		

Basis for selection. School achievement record, including grades and course levels, most important, followed by test scores. Applicants should rank in top half of class. Activities and counselor recommendations also important. Interview and essay recommended for all applicants, required of academically marginal applicants. Audition required of music majors. Portfolio recommended for art majors. **Homeschooled:** Interview strongly recommended.

High school preparation. College-preparatory program recommended. 16 units required; 21 recommended. Required and recommended units include English 4, mathematics 2-3, social studies 2-3, history 1-2, science 2-3 (laboratory 2-3), foreign language 1-2 and academic electives 4. Chemistry required for nursing applicants. 3 mathematics required for most business administration and computer-related specialties applicants.

2008-2009 Annual costs. Tuition/fees: $26,060. Room/board: $8,476. Books/supplies: $1,000. Personal expenses: $1,200.

2007-2008 Financial aid. Need-based: 420 full-time freshmen applied for aid; 384 were judged to have need; 384 of these received aid. Average need met was 91%. Average scholarship/grant was $14,576; average loan $3,957. 78% of total undergraduate aid awarded as scholarships/grants, 22% as loans/jobs. **Non-need-based:** Awarded to 944 full-time undergraduates, including 313 freshmen. Scholarships awarded for academics, alumni affiliation, art, minority status, music/drama, religious affiliation, state residency. **Additional information:** Must be admitted to the college by 1/15 to be considered for scholarships.

Application procedures. Admission: Priority date 4/15; no deadline. No application fee. Admission notification on a rolling basis beginning on or about 11/1. Must reply by May 1 or within 2 week(s) if notified thereafter. **Financial aid:** Priority date 4/15; no closing date. FAFSA required. Applicants notified on a rolling basis starting 2/21; must reply within 3 week(s) of notification.

Academics. Special study options: Accelerated study, cooperative education, double major, dual enrollment of high school students, honors, independent study, internships, liberal arts/career combination, study abroad, teacher certification program, Washington semester. 3+2 engineering with Illinois Institute of Technology, University of Illinois at Urbana-Champaign, and Washington University (MO). **Credit/placement by examination:** AP, CLEP, IB, institutional tests. 48 credit hours maximum toward bachelor's degree. **Support services:** Learning center, pre-admission summer program, reduced course load, study skills assistance, tutoring.

Majors. Area/ethnic studies: American. **Biology:** General. **Business:** Accounting, business admin, finance, international, logistics, marketing. **Communications:** General. **Computer sciences:** Computer science, information systems. **Conservation:** Management/policy. **Education:** General, agricultural, art, biology, chemistry, early childhood, elementary, English, French, German, history, kindergarten/preschool, mathematics, music, physical, physics, secondary, Spanish, special. **Foreign languages:** French, German, Spanish. **Health:** Nursing (RN), predental, premedicine, prepharmacy, preveterinary, speech pathology. **History:** General. **Legal studies:** Prelaw. **Liberal arts:** Arts/sciences. **Math:** General. **Parks/recreation:** Exercise sciences, health/fitness, sports admin. **Philosophy/religion:** Philosophy. **Physical sciences:** Chemistry, physics. **Protective services:** Criminal justice, law enforcement admin. **Psychology:** General. **Social sciences:** Criminology, economics, geography, political science, sociology, urban studies. **Theology:** Preministerial, theology. **Visual/performing arts:** Art, dramatic, music management.

Most popular majors. Business/marketing 20%, education 20%, health sciences 11%, psychology 9%.

Computing on campus. 440 workstations in library, computer center, student center. Dormitories wired for high-speed internet access and linked to campus network. Commuter students can connect to campus network. Online library, helpline, repair service, wireless network available.

Student life. Freshman orientation: Mandatory. Three-day program held immediately prior to term. **Policies:** Each residence hall is self-governing. **Housing:** Coed dorms, apartments available. $300 nonrefundable deposit, deadline 4/1. **Activities:** Bands, campus ministries, choral groups, drama, literary magazine, music ensembles, musical theater, radio station, student government, student newspaper, over 90 organizations.

Athletics. NCAA. **Intercollegiate:** Baseball M, basketball, bowling W, cross-country, football (tackle) M, golf, soccer, softball W, tennis, track and field, volleyball W, wrestling M. **Intramural:** Basketball, football (tackle) M, golf, racquetball, softball, volleyball. **Team name:** Blue Jays.

Student services. Adult student services, career counseling, student employment services, financial aid counseling, health services, minority student services, on-campus daycare, personal counseling, placement for graduates.

Contact. E-mail: admit@elmhurst.edu
Phone: (630) 617-3400 Toll-free number: (800) 697-1871
Fax: (630) 617-5501
Stephanie Levenson, Director of Admission, Elmhurst College, 190 South Prospect Avenue, Elmhurst, IL 60126-3296

Eureka College

Eureka, Illinois — **CB member**
www.eureka.edu — **CB code: 1206**

- Private 4-year liberal arts college affiliated with Christian Church (Disciples of Christ)
- Residential campus in small town
- 728 degree-seeking undergraduates
- 68% of applicants admitted
- SAT or ACT (ACT writing recommended) required

General. Founded in 1855. Regionally accredited. **Degrees:** 125 bachelor's awarded. **Location:** 140 miles from Chicago. **Calendar:** Semester, limited summer session. **Full-time faculty:** 44 total. **Part-time faculty:** 22 total. **Class size:** 64% < 20, 36% 20-39. **Special facilities:** Ronald Reagan Museum, peace garden, lilac arboretum, labyrinth, fitness center.

Freshman class profile. 1,225 applied, 837 admitted, 256 enrolled.

Mid 50% test scores		**Rank in top tenth:**	23%
ACT composite:	19-27	**Out-of-state:**	4%
Rank in top quarter:	56%	**Live on campus:**	90%

Basis for selection. Class rank, high school GPA, ACT scores, and high school curriculum most important. Recommendations and interviews also important. Audition required for music and drama scholarships. Portfolio required for art scholarship. **Homeschooled:** Interview required.

High school preparation. 14 units recommended. Recommended units include English 4, mathematics 3, social studies 3, science 2 and foreign language 2.

2008-2009 Annual costs. Tuition/fees: $16,255. Room/board: $7,130. Books/supplies: $1,000. Personal expenses: $510.

2008-2009 Financial aid. Non-need-based: Scholarships awarded for academics, alumni affiliation, art, leadership, music/drama, religious affiliation.

Application procedures. Admission: Priority date 5/1; deadline 8/10 (postmark date). No application fee. Admission notification on a rolling basis. Must reply by May 1 or within 3 week(s) if notified thereafter. **Financial aid:** Priority date 4/15; no closing date. FAFSA required. Applicants notified on a rolling basis starting 2/15; must reply by 5/1 or within 3 week(s) of notification.

Academics. Special study options: Cooperative education, double major, dual enrollment of high school students, honors, independent study, internships, liberal arts/career combination, student-designed major, study abroad, teacher certification program, Washington semester. Students who began as freshmen, have a record of leadership and service, and hold a 3.5 GPA at the end of their sophomore year qualify for a mentorship paid for by the college. **Credit/placement by examination:** AP, CLEP, institutional tests. **Support services:** Learning center, reduced course load, remedial instruction, study skills assistance, tutoring, writing center.

Honors college/program. Admitted by invitation, includes advanced and special classes, advanced general education requirements along with thesis preparation and presentation, honors seminars on special topics.

Majors. Biology: General, environmental. **Business:** General, accounting, business admin, finance, management information systems, marketing. **Communications:** General, media studies, public relations. **Computer sciences:**

General, computer science. **Education:** General, elementary, middle, multi-level teacher, secondary, special. **Engineering:** General. **Health:** Predental, premedicine, prenursing, preveterinary. **History:** General. **Interdisciplinary:** Math/computer science. **Legal studies:** Prelaw. **Liberal arts:** Arts/sciences. **Math:** General. **Philosophy/religion:** Philosophy, religion. **Physical sciences:** Chemistry. **Protective services:** Law enforcement admin. **Psychology:** General. **Social sciences:** Political science. **Visual/performing arts:** Art, arts management, dramatic, music performance. **Other:** Leadership.

Computing on campus. 50 workstations in dormitories, library, computer center, student center. Dormitories wired for high-speed internet access and linked to campus network. Commuter students can connect to campus network. Online library, helpline, repair service available.

Student life. Freshman orientation: Mandatory. Preregistration for classes offered. Orientation for new students held at start of school year. **Policies:** All single students under 24 not living with parents required to live on campus. **Housing:** Guaranteed on-campus for all undergraduates. Coed dorms, single-sex dorms, special housing for disabled, fraternity/sorority housing, wellness housing available. $150 fully refundable deposit, deadline 8/14. **Activities:** Bands, choral groups, dance, drama, film society, literary magazine, music ensembles, musical theater, student government, student newspaper, Disciples on Campus, PRIDE, Young Republicans, Campus Democrats, Catholic Salve Regina Newman Center, Campus Crusade for Christ, Black student union, Habitat for Humanity, Student Foundation, International Healthcare Development Program.

Athletics. NCAA. **Intercollegiate:** Baseball M, basketball, cross-country, diving, football (tackle) M, golf, soccer, softball W, swimming, tennis, track and field, volleyball W. **Intramural:** Badminton, basketball, bowling, football (non-tackle), golf, softball, swimming, table tennis, tennis, volleyball. **Team name:** Red Devils.

Student services. Adult student services, alcohol/substance abuse counseling, chaplain/spiritual director, career counseling, student employment services, financial aid counseling, health services, personal counseling, placement for graduates.

Contact. E-mail: admissions@eureka.edu
Phone: (309) 467-6350 Toll-free number: (888) 438-7352
Fax: (309) 467-6576
Kurt Krile, Dean of Admissions and Financial Aid, Eureka College, 300 East College Avenue, Eureka, IL 61530-1500

Governors State University

University Park, Illinois
www.govst.edu **CB code: 0807**

- Public two-year upper-division university
- Commuter campus in large town
- 85% of applicants admitted

General. Founded in 1969. Regionally accredited. **Degrees:** 908 bachelor's awarded; master's offered. **Articulation:** Agreements with Prairie State College, Joliet Junior College, Kankakee CC, Moraine Valley CC, South Suburban College of Cook County, College of DuPage, Morton College, City Colleges of Chicago, Waubonsee CC, Triton College, Parkland College, College of Lake County, Illinois Valley College, Ivy Tech State College (IN). **ROTC:** Army, Air Force. **Location:** 30 miles from Chicago. **Calendar:** Trimester, extensive summer session. **Full-time faculty:** 202 total. **Part-time faculty:** 201 total. **Special facilities:** 750-acre campus, nature trails, 6 lakes, sculpture park, prairie restoration.

Student profile. 2,583 degree-seeking undergraduates, 2,999 degree-seeking graduate students. 2,313 applied as first time-transfer students, 1,963 admitted, 1,168 enrolled. 63% transferred from two-year, 37% transferred from four-year institutions.

Women:	71%	**Out-of-state:**	5%
Part-time:	63%	**25 or older:**	61%

Basis for selection. College transcript required. 60 semester hours or associate degree required. Additional special criteria for selected undergraduate majors. Special admissions for applicants not meeting stated requirements available by petition. Institutional examinations required of nursing applicants. ACT/PEP required of nursing applicants from diploma program. Transfer accepted as juniors, seniors.

2008-2009 Annual costs. Tuition/fees: $7,542; $19,782 out-of-state. Books/supplies: $700. Personal expenses: $800.

Financial aid. Non-need-based: Scholarships awarded for academics, ROTC, state residency.

Application procedures. Admission: Priority date 5/15. $25 fee, may be waived for applicants with need. **Financial aid:** FAFSA required.

Academics. Special study options: Distance learning, dual enrollment of high school students, external degree, honors, independent study, internships, student-designed major, teacher certification program. Dual enrollment with several community colleges. **Credit/placement by examination:** AP, CLEP. 60 credit hours maximum toward bachelor's degree.

Majors. Biology: General. **Business:** Accounting, business admin, finance, human resources, international, international marketing, management information systems. **Communications:** General, broadcast journalism, journalism. **Computer sciences:** General, computer science. **Education:** Biology, chemistry, early childhood, elementary, English, mathematics. **Health:** Health care admin, preop/surgical nursing, speech pathology. **Liberal arts:** Arts/sciences. **Math:** General. **Physical sciences:** Chemistry. **Protective services:** Criminal justice. **Psychology:** General. **Public administration:** General, social work. **Social sciences:** General. **Visual/performing arts:** Art, art history/conservation.

Computing on campus. 280 workstations in library, computer center, student center. Commuter students can connect to campus network. Online library, helpline, wireless network available.

Student life. Activities: Choral groups, film society, international student organizations, literary magazine, student government, student newspaper, TV station, veterans organization, Union of African Peoples, naturalist club, 30-plus cocurricular professional service organizations.

Athletics. Intramural: Badminton, basketball, handball, racquetball, skiing, soccer, softball, table tennis, volleyball.

Student services. Career counseling, student employment services, financial aid counseling, minority student services, on-campus daycare, personal counseling, placement for graduates, veterans' counselor. **Physically disabled:** Services for visually, speech, hearing impaired.

Contact. Phone: (708) 534-4490 Fax: (708) 534-1640
Director of Admissions, Governors State University, One University Parkway, University Park, IL 60466

Greenville College

Greenville, Illinois
www.greenville.edu **CB code: 1256**

- Private 4-year liberal arts college affiliated with Free Methodist Church of North America
- Residential campus in small town
- 1,418 degree-seeking undergraduates: 2% part-time, 54% women, 7% African American, 1% Asian American, 2% Hispanic American, 1% international
- 179 degree-seeking graduate students
- 79% of applicants admitted
- SAT or ACT (ACT writing optional), application essay required
- 50% graduate within 6 years

General. Founded in 1892. Regionally accredited. Academic and Christian values emphasized. **Degrees:** 357 bachelor's awarded; master's offered. **Location:** 50 miles from St. Louis, 190 miles from Indianapolis. **Calendar:** 4-1-4, limited summer session. **Full-time faculty:** 58 total; 69% have terminal degrees, 7% minority, 40% women. **Part-time faculty:** 95 total; 48% women. **Class size:** 49% < 20, 37% 20-39, 8% 40-49, 5% 50-99, less than 1% >100. **Special facilities:** Sculpture collection, Frank Lloyd Wright architectural drawings, 140 acre field station and nature preserve, observatory, environmental education center.

Freshman class profile. 868 applied, 689 admitted, 305 enrolled.

Mid 50% test scores		**GPA 2.0-2.99:**	29%
SAT critical reading:	460-590	**Rank in top quarter:**	41%
SAT math:	440-560	**Rank in top tenth:**	18%
SAT writing:	450-560	**End year in good standing:**	73%
ACT composite:	19-26	**Return as sophomores:**	71%
GPA 3.75 or higher:	29%	**Out-of-state:**	36%
GPA 3.50-3.74:	13%	**Live on campus:**	94%
GPA 3.0-3.49:	29%	**International:**	1%

Basis for selection. Secondary school record, class rank, standardized test scores, essay, character/personal qualities, and religious affiliation or commitment all very important. Recommendations, extracurricular activities, talent/ability and alumni/ae relation considered. Interview required of academically weak applicants. Audition recommended for music majors. **Homeschooled:** Transcript of courses and grades required.

High school preparation. College-preparatory program recommended. 11 units recommended. Recommended units include English 4, mathematics 2, history 1, science 1 (laboratory 1) and foreign language 2. Math recommendation includes algebra and geometry.

2009-2010 Annual costs. Tuition/fees (projected): $20,216. Room/board: $6,878. Books/supplies: $900. Personal expenses: $1,572.

2007-2008 Financial aid. Need-based: 294 full-time freshmen applied for aid; 254 were judged to have need; 254 of these received aid. Average need met was 86%. Average scholarship/grant was $11,964; average loan $4,214. 63% of total undergraduate aid awarded as scholarships/grants, 37% as loans/jobs. **Non-need-based:** Awarded to 351 full-time undergraduates, including 89 freshmen. Scholarships awarded for academics, alumni affiliation, art, leadership, minority status, music/drama, religious affiliation, state residency.

Application procedures. Admission: Closing date 8/15. $25 fee, may be waived for applicants with need. Admission notification on a rolling basis beginning on or about 10/15. Housing deposit is not refundable after May 1st. **Financial aid:** Priority date 5/1; no closing date. FAFSA required. Applicants notified on a rolling basis starting 3/15; must reply within 3 week(s) of notification.

Academics. Special study options: Accelerated study, cooperative education, cross-registration, double major, external degree, honors, independent study, internships, liberal arts/career combination, semester at sea, student-designed major, study abroad, teacher certification program, urban semester, Washington semester. **Credit/placement by examination:** AP, CLEP, IB, SAT, ACT, institutional tests. 32 credit hours maximum toward bachelor's degree. **Support services:** Learning center, reduced course load, remedial instruction, study skills assistance, tutoring.

Majors. Biology: General, environmental. **Business:** Accounting, business admin, management information systems, marketing, organizational behavior. **Communications:** Media studies, public relations. **Computer sciences:** General. **Education:** Biology, chemistry, early childhood, elementary, English, history, mathematics, music, physical, physics, Spanish, special. **Foreign languages:** Spanish. **Health:** Predental, premedicine, prenursing, preveterinary. **History:** General. **Interdisciplinary:** Global studies. **Liberal arts:** Arts/sciences. **Math:** General. **Parks/recreation:** General, exercise sciences, sports admin. **Philosophy/religion:** Philosophy, religion. **Physical sciences:** Chemistry, physics. **Protective services:** Law enforcement admin. **Psychology:** General. **Public administration:** Social work. **Social sciences:** Sociology. **Theology:** Pastoral counseling, youth ministry. **Visual/performing arts:** Art, dramatic, music management.

Most popular majors. Business/marketing 32%, education 24%, visual/performing arts 8%.

Computing on campus. 95 workstations in library, computer center. Dormitories wired for high-speed internet access and linked to campus network. Commuter students can connect to campus network. Online library, helpline, repair service, wireless network available.

Student life. Freshman orientation: Mandatory. Preregistration for classes offered. Service project conducted over orientation weekend. **Policies:** Signed statements of Christian values and academic honesty requested. Required chapel. All single students not living at home must live in college housing. Religious observance required. **Housing:** Guaranteed on-campus for all undergraduates. Single-sex dorms, apartments, wellness housing available. $200 deposit. Upper division students may live in college-owned houses. **Activities:** Bands, campus ministries, choral groups, drama, music ensembles, musical theater, radio station, student government, student newspaper, Habitat for Humanity, Fellowship of Christian Athletes, Campus Activities Board, student outreach, Agape music festival, Circle K, E-cafe, Mosaic, Young Republicans, Big Brother/Big Sister.

Athletics. NCAA, NCCAA. **Intercollegiate:** Baseball M, basketball, cross-country, football (tackle) M, soccer, softball W, tennis, track and field, volleyball W. **Intramural:** Badminton, basketball, football (non-tackle), soccer, softball, table tennis, tennis, volleyball. **Team name:** Panthers.

Student services. Adult student services, career counseling, student employment services, financial aid counseling, personal counseling, placement for graduates.

Contact. E-mail: admissions@greenville.edu
Phone: (618) 664-7100 Toll-free number: (800) 345-4440
Fax: (618) 664-9841
Michael Ritter, Dean of Admissions, Greenville College, 315 East College Avenue, Greenville, IL 62246-0159

Harrington College of Design
Chicago, Illinois
www.harringtoncollege.com — **CB code: 0940**

- For-profit 4-year visual arts college
- Commuter campus in very large city
- 1,279 degree-seeking undergraduates
- Interview required

General. Founded in 1931. Accredited by ACICS. Accredited by Foundation for Interior Design Education Research and National Association of Schools of Art and Design. **Degrees:** 209 bachelor's, 127 associate awarded. **Location:** Downtown. **Calendar:** Semester, extensive summer session. **Full-time faculty:** 10 total. **Part-time faculty:** 115 total. **Class size:** 84% < 20, 16% 20-39. **Special facilities:** Access to Chicago Merchandise Mart's wholesale showroom.

Basis for selection. Personal interview, commitment to career, 2.0 GPA most important.

2008-2009 Annual costs. Tuition/fees: $16,565. Required fees vary depending on a program. Books/supplies: $850. Personal expenses: $2,500.

Financial aid. All financial aid based on need.

Application procedures. Admission: Priority date 6/1; no deadline. $60 fee, may be waived for applicants with need. Admission notification on a rolling basis. **Financial aid:** Closing date 7/15. FAFSA required. Applicants notified on a rolling basis; must reply within 2 week(s) of notification.

Academics. Exchange program with Interior Architecture Department, Rotterdam College of Art and Design, The Netherlands. **Special study options:** Cooperative education, internships, study abroad. **Credit/placement by examination:** CLEP. **Support services:** Tutoring, writing center.

Majors. Visual/performing arts: Graphic design, interior design.

Computing on campus. 35 workstations in library, computer center.

Student life. Freshman orientation: Mandatory. Preregistration for classes offered. One-day program held 1 or 2 weeks before classes begin. **Housing:** Students may reside at Crown Center Residence at nearby Roosevelt University. **Activities:** Student government, American Society of Interior Design student chapter.

Student services. Career counseling, financial aid counseling, personal counseling, placement for graduates, veterans' counselor.

Contact. E-mail: admissions@interiordesign.edu
Phone: (312) 939-4975 Toll-free number: (877) 939-4975
Fax: (312) 939-8005
Wendi Franczyk, Vice President of Admissions, Harrington College of Design, 200 West Madison Avenue, Chicago, IL 60606

Hebrew Theological College
Skokie, Illinois
www.htc.edu — **CB code: 0817**

- Private 4-year rabbinical college
- Residential campus in small city

General. Regionally accredited. **Calendar:** Semester.

Annual costs/financial aid. Tuition/fees (2008-2009): $16,935. Room/board: $8,035.

Contact. Phone: (847) 982-2500
7135 North Carpenter Road, Skokie, IL 60077

Illinois College
Jacksonville, Illinois — **CB member**
www.ic.edu — **CB code: 1315**

- Private 4-year liberal arts college affiliated with United Church of Christ and Presbyterian Church (USA)
- Residential campus in large town
- 870 degree-seeking undergraduates: 1% part-time, 52% women, 4% African American, 2% Hispanic American, 2% international
- 67% of applicants admitted

- SAT or ACT (ACT writing optional) required
- 63% graduate within 6 years

General. Founded in 1829. Regionally accredited. New England style quad and architecture. **Degrees:** 216 bachelor's awarded. **Location:** 30 miles from Springfield, 90 miles from St. Louis. **Calendar:** Semester, limited summer session. **Full-time faculty:** 73 total. **Part-time faculty:** 16 total. **Class size:** 71% < 20, 27% 20-39, less than 1% 40-49, 1% 50-99. **Special facilities:** Biology station, observatory.

Freshman class profile. 927 applied, 620 admitted, 166 enrolled.

Mid 50% test scores		**GPA 2.0-2.99:**	10%
SAT critical reading:	510-580	**Rank in top quarter:**	62%
SAT math:	490-640	**Rank in top tenth:**	33%
SAT writing:	460-630	**Return as sophomores:**	78%
ACT composite:	21-27	**Out-of-state:**	6%
GPA 3.75 or higher:	54%	**Live on campus:**	94%
GPA 3.50-3.74:	18%	**International:**	2%
GPA 3.0-3.49:	18%		

Basis for selection. Test scores, rank in top half of class, 1 letter of recommendation from teacher, 1 letter of recommendation from guidance counselor important. Interview recommended, essay considered. **Homeschooled:** Transcript of courses and grades, letter of recommendation (nonparent) required.

High school preparation. College-preparatory program recommended. 16 units required; 20 recommended. Required and recommended units include English 4, mathematics 3, social studies 1, history 1, science 2-3 (laboratory 2-3), foreign language 2 and academic electives 3.

2008-2009 Annual costs. Tuition/fees: $20,300. Room/board: $7,230. Books/supplies: $850. Personal expenses: $920.

2008-2009 Financial aid. Need-based: 160 full-time freshmen applied for aid; 147 were judged to have need; 147 of these received aid. Average need met was 91%. Average scholarship/grant was $9,813; average loan $4,650. 69% of total undergraduate aid awarded as scholarships/grants, 31% as loans/jobs. **Non-need-based:** Awarded to 633 full-time undergraduates, including 127 freshmen. Scholarships awarded for academics, art, minority status, music/drama.

Application procedures. Admission: Priority date 3/15; deadline 8/15 (postmark date). No application fee. Admission notification on a rolling basis beginning on or about 10/15. **Financial aid:** Priority date 3/1; no closing date. FAFSA required. Applicants notified on a rolling basis starting 3/1; must reply within 2 week(s) of notification.

Academics. Special study options: Combined bachelor's/graduate degree, cross-registration, double major, dual enrollment of high school students, independent study, internships, liberal arts/career combination, student-designed major, study abroad, teacher certification program, Washington semester. Intercultural exchange program with Ritsumeikan University, Japan. **Credit/placement by examination:** AP, CLEP, IB, SAT, ACT, institutional tests. 84 credit hours maximum toward bachelor's degree. **Support services:** Reduced course load, tutoring, writing center.

Majors. Biology: General. **Business:** General, accounting, finance, management information systems. **Computer sciences:** General. **Conservation:** Environmental science. **Education:** Early childhood, elementary, physical. **Engineering:** General. **Foreign languages:** French, German, Spanish. **Health:** Clinical lab science, cytotechnology. **History:** General. **Math:** General. **Parks/recreation:** Sports admin. **Philosophy/religion:** Philosophy, religion. **Physical sciences:** Chemistry, physics. **Psychology:** General. **Social sciences:** Economics, international relations, political science, sociology. **Visual/performing arts:** General, art.

Most popular majors. Biology 16%, business/marketing 13%, education 9%, English 10%, interdisciplinary studies 13%, psychology 6%, social sciences 13%.

Computing on campus. 125 workstations in library, computer center. Dormitories wired for high-speed internet access and linked to campus network. Commuter students can connect to campus network. Online course registration, online library, helpline, repair service, student web hosting, wireless network available.

Student life. Freshman orientation: Mandatory. Preregistration for classes offered. Overnight orientation program; four 2-day summer sessions available. **Policies:** Student representation on faculty committees. **Housing:** Guaranteed on-campus for all undergraduates. Coed dorms, single-sex dorms, apartments available. $200 fully refundable deposit, deadline 5/1. German, Spanish houses available. **Activities:** Concert band, campus ministries, choral groups, drama, international student organizations, music ensembles, Model UN, student government, student newspaper, Young Republicans, Young Democrats, Alpha Phi Omega, men's and women's literary societies, debate club, Action Jacksonville.

Athletics. NCAA. **Intercollegiate:** Baseball M, basketball, cheerleading, cross-country, football (tackle) M, golf, soccer, softball W, tennis, track and field, volleyball W. **Intramural:** Basketball, cricket, football (non-tackle) M, handball, racquetball, softball, volleyball. **Team name:** Blueboys, Lady Blues.

Student services. Alcohol/substance abuse counseling, chaplain/spiritual director, career counseling, student employment services, financial aid counseling, health services, personal counseling, placement for graduates. **Physically disabled:** Services for visually, hearing impaired.

Contact. E-mail: admissions@ic.edu
Phone: (217) 245-3030 Toll-free number: (866) 464-5265
Fax: (217) 245-3034
Barb Lundberg, Vice President for Enrollment, Illinois College, 1101 West College Avenue, Jacksonville, IL 62650

Illinois Institute of Art: Chicago

Chicago, Illinois
www.ilic.artinstitutes.edu **CB code: 2908**

- For-profit 4-year visual arts college
- Commuter campus in very large city
- 3,000 degree-seeking undergraduates
- Application essay required

General. Founded in 1916. Accredited by ACCSCT. Branch campus at Woodfield in Schaumburg. **Degrees:** 410 bachelor's, 87 associate awarded. **Calendar:** Semester. **Full-time faculty:** 66 total. **Part-time faculty:** 70 total. **Special facilities:** Computer graphics laboratories, exhibit galleries, incentive studio.

Freshman class profile.

Mid 50% test scores		**SAT writing:**	410-490
SAT critical reading:	410-490	**ACT composite:**	16-22
SAT math:	420-490	**Out-of-state:**	20%

Basis for selection. Secondary school record, interview, and personal statement most important. SAT or ACT recommended for placement and evaluation. Portfolio required for advertising design, illustration, photography, fashion design, fashion illustration majors.

High school preparation. Recommended units include English 4, mathematics 3, social studies 2, science 3 and foreign language 1. Recommend art, interior design, drafting, fashion.

2008-2009 Annual costs. Tuition/fees: $21,648. Room/board: $10,155. Books/supplies: $1,000.

Application procedures. Admission: No deadline. $150 fee. Admission notification on a rolling basis. **Financial aid:** Priority date 5/1; no closing date. FAFSA required. Applicants notified on a rolling basis.

Academics. Special study options: Accelerated study, cooperative education, internships. **Credit/placement by examination:** CLEP. **Support services:** Reduced course load.

Majors. Business: Fashion. **Communications:** Advertising. **Visual/performing arts:** Commercial/advertising art, fashion design, interior design.

Computing on campus. 25 workstations in computer center.

Student life. Activities: Student newspaper, Student Positive Action Committee.

Student services. Student employment services, placement for graduates, veterans' counselor.

Contact. E-mail: antonj@aii.edu
Phone: (312) 280-3500 Toll-free number: (800) 351-3450
Janice Anton, Senior Director of Admissions, Illinois Institute of Art: Chicago, 350 North Orleans Street, Chicago, IL 60654

Illinois Institute of Art: Schaumburg

Schaumburg, Illinois
www.artinstitutes.edu/schaumburg **CB code: 3043**

- For-profit 3-year visual arts college
- Commuter campus in small city

- 1,240 degree-seeking undergraduates
- Application essay, interview required

General. Accredited by ACCSCT. **Degrees:** 286 bachelor's, 3 associate awarded. **Location:** 26 miles from Chicago. **Calendar:** Continuous, extensive summer session. **Full-time faculty:** 37 total. **Part-time faculty:** 48 total. **Special facilities:** Gallery, motion capture studio, lighting lab, sound lab, green room.

Basis for selection. Open admission, but selective for some programs. SAT or ACT recommended. Portfolios required for some majors. **Homeschooled:** Transcript of courses and grades required.

2008-2009 Annual costs. Tuition/fees: $21,600. Room/board: $7,080. Books/supplies: $987. Personal expenses: $1,788.

Financial aid. Non-need-based: Scholarships awarded for academics, art.

Application procedures. Admission: No deadline. $50 fee. Admission notification on a rolling basis. **Financial aid:** Priority date 3/1; no closing date. FAFSA required.

Academics. Special study options: Accelerated study, internships, liberal arts/career combination. **Credit/placement by examination:** CLEP. **Support services:** Learning center, pre-admission summer program, reduced course load, remedial instruction, study skills assistance, tutoring.

Majors. BACHELOR'S. Business: Fashion, special products marketing. **Communications:** Advertising. **Communications technology:** Graphics, photo/film/video. **Computer sciences:** Webmaster. **Visual/performing arts:** General, art, commercial/advertising art, design, interior design, multimedia. **ASSOCIATE. Communications technology:** Graphics. **Computer sciences:** Webmaster. **Visual/performing arts:** Design.

Student life. Freshman orientation: Mandatory. Held the week before school begins. **Housing:** Single-sex dorms available. $200 deposit. Dormitory-style living in college-leased apartments. **Activities:** Jazz band, student government, student newspaper.

Student services. Adult student services, career counseling, student employment services, financial aid counseling, personal counseling, placement for graduates, veterans' counselor.

Contact. Phone: (847) 619-3450 Toll-free number: (800) 314-3450
Fax: (847) 619-3064
Jennifer Sorenson, Senior Director of Admissions, Illinois Institute of Art: Schaumburg, 1000 North Plaza Drive, Schaumburg, IL 60173

Illinois Institute of Technology

Chicago, Illinois — **CB member**
www.iit.edu — **CB code: 1318**

- Private 4-year university and engineering college
- Commuter campus in very large city
- 2,590 degree-seeking undergraduates: 7% part-time, 28% women, 4% African American, 13% Asian American, 7% Hispanic American, 1% Native American, 17% international
- 4,709 degree-seeking graduate students
- 57% of applicants admitted
- Application essay required
- 64% graduate within 6 years

General. Founded in 1890. Regionally accredited. **Degrees:** 465 bachelor's awarded; master's, doctoral, first professional offered. **ROTC:** Army, Naval, Air Force. **Location:** 3 miles from downtown. **Calendar:** Semester, extensive summer session. **Full-time faculty:** 369 total; 89% have terminal degrees, 15% minority, 20% women. **Part-time faculty:** 245 total; 53% have terminal degrees, 4% minority, 21% women. **Class size:** 60% < 20, 32% 20-39, 4% 40-49, 4% 50-99, less than 1% >100. **Special facilities:** Engineering, design, scientific, and medical research centers.

Freshman class profile. 3,092 applied, 1,768 admitted, 530 enrolled.

Mid 50% test scores			
SAT critical reading:	520-640	Rank in top quarter:	76%
SAT math:	610-700	Rank in top tenth:	42%
SAT writing:	520-630	End year in good standing:	96%
ACT composite:	25-30	Return as sophomores:	88%
GPA 3.75 or higher:	54%	Out-of-state:	37%
GPA 3.50-3.74:	23%	Live on campus:	76%
GPA 3.0-3.49:	20%	International:	16%
GPA 2.0-2.99:	3%	Fraternities:	15%
		Sororities:	15%

Basis for selection. Academic performance, strength of curriculum, test scores, counselor recommendations and essay most important. Class rank and interview, extracurricular activities, alumni relationship, volunteer and work experience also considered. Interview recommended. Portfolio optional for first-year freshmen entering the College of Architecture. **Homeschooled:** Statement describing homeschool structure and mission, letter of recommendation (nonparent) required.

High school preparation. College-preparatory program recommended. 17 units required; 21 recommended. Required and recommended units include English 4, mathematics 4, social studies 2, history 2, science 3 (laboratory 2), foreign language 2, computer science 1 and visual/performing arts 1.

2008-2009 Annual costs. Tuition/fees: $27,513. Tuition and fees cover unlimited number of courses during academic year and include library and computer usage fees. Room/board: $9,226.

2007-2008 Financial aid. Need-based: 380 full-time freshmen applied for aid; 333 were judged to have need; 331 of these received aid. Average need met was 89%. Average scholarship/grant was $18,002; average loan $4,403. 72% of total undergraduate aid awarded as scholarships/grants, 28% as loans/jobs. **Non-need-based:** Awarded to 1,225 full-time undergraduates, including 288 freshmen. Scholarships awarded for academics, alumni affiliation, athletics, leadership, ROTC.

Application procedures. Admission: Priority date 12/1; deadline 8/1. No application fee. Admission notification on a rolling basis beginning on or about 10/1. Must reply by May 1 or within 2 week(s) if notified thereafter. $300 enrollment deposit is required. **Financial aid:** Priority date 4/15; no closing date. FAFSA required. Applicants notified on a rolling basis starting 3/5.

Academics. Special study options: Combined bachelor's/graduate degree, cooperative education, cross-registration, distance learning, double major, ESL, independent study, liberal arts/career combination, study abroad, teacher certification program. Joint enrollment at 2 institutions for 2 degrees. **Credit/placement by examination:** AP, CLEP, IB, SAT, ACT, institutional tests. 18 credit hours maximum toward bachelor's degree. No limit for advanced placement credit. **Support services:** Learning center, study skills assistance, tutoring, writing center.

Majors. Architecture: Architecture. **Biology:** General, biochemistry, Biochemistry/biophysics and molecular biology. **Business:** Business admin. **Communications:** General, journalism. **Computer sciences:** General, computer science, information technology. **Engineering:** Aerospace, architectural, biomedical, chemical, civil, computer, electrical, materials, mechanical. **Engineering technology:** Industrial management. **Liberal arts:** Arts/sciences. **Math:** Applied. **Physical sciences:** Chemistry, physics. **Psychology:** General. **Social sciences:** Political science.

Most popular majors. Architecture 15%, biology 6%, computer/information sciences 10%, engineering/engineering technologies 53%.

Computing on campus. 500 workstations in dormitories, library, computer center, student center. Dormitories wired for high-speed internet access and linked to campus network. Online course registration, online library, helpline, student web hosting, wireless network available.

Student life. Freshman orientation: Mandatory, $150 fee. Preregistration for classes offered. Five summer sessions. Welcome Week held prior to start of classes. **Policies:** Student organizations register each semester, are nondiscriminatory and prohibit hazing. **Housing:** Coed dorms, single-sex dorms, special housing for disabled, apartments, fraternity/sorority housing available. **Activities:** Concert band, campus ministries, choral groups, dance, drama, film society, international student organizations, literary magazine, music ensembles, musical theater, radio station, student government, student newspaper, TV station, Red Cross club, Engineers Without Borders, greek council, Haiti Outreach, Intervarsity Christian Fellowship, Latinos Involved in Further Education, National Society of Black Engineers, Society of Women Engineers, union board.

Athletics. NAIA. **Intercollegiate:** Baseball M, basketball, cross-country, diving, soccer, swimming, volleyball W. **Intramural:** Badminton, basketball, football (non-tackle), racquetball, table tennis, volleyball. **Team name:** Scarlet Hawks.

Student services. Alcohol/substance abuse counseling, career counseling, student employment services, financial aid counseling, health services, legal services, minority student services, personal counseling, placement for graduates, women's services. **Physically disabled:** Services for visually, hearing impaired.

Contact. E-mail: admission@iit.edu
Phone: (312) 567-3025 Toll-free number: (800) 448-2329
Fax: (312) 567-6939
Gerald Doyle, Associate Vice President, Undergraduate Enrollment and Financial Aid, Illinois Institute of Technology, 10 West 33rd Street, Chicago, IL 60616

Illinois State University

Normal, Illinois — **CB member**
www.ilstu.edu — **CB code: 1319**

- Public 4-year university
- Residential campus in small city
- 17,997 degree-seeking undergraduates: 6% part-time, 57% women, 5% African American, 2% Asian American, 4% Hispanic American
- 2,381 degree-seeking graduate students
- 64% of applicants admitted
- SAT or ACT (ACT writing optional), application essay required
- 70% graduate within 6 years; 15% enter graduate study

General. Founded in 1857. Regionally accredited. **Degrees:** 4,186 bachelor's awarded; master's, doctoral offered. **ROTC:** Army. **Location:** 132 miles from Chicago, 168 miles from St. Louis. **Calendar:** Semester, limited summer session. **Full-time faculty:** 859 total; 83% have terminal degrees, 12% minority, 47% women. **Part-time faculty:** 324 total; 27% have terminal degrees, 7% minority, 57% women. **Class size:** 31% < 20, 54% 20-39, 3% 40-49, 7% 50-99, 4% >100. **Special facilities:** 310-acre farm, planetarium, museum of nations, laboratory school.

Freshman class profile. 13,549 applied, 8,699 admitted, 3,394 enrolled.

Mid 50% test scores		**End year in good standing:**	90%
ACT composite:	22-26	**Return as sophomores:**	83%
GPA 3.75 or higher:	20%	**Live on campus:**	97%
GPA 3.50-3.74:	18%	**Fraternities:**	15%
GPA 3.0-3.49:	44%	**Sororities:**	17%
GPA 2.0-2.99:	18%		

Basis for selection. School achievement record and test scores most important. Interview required of special admission applicants. Audition recommended for music majors. Portfolio recommended for art majors.

High school preparation. 15 units required. Required units include English 4, mathematics 3, social studies 2, science 2 (laboratory 2), foreign language 2 and academic electives 2. 2 units required in foreign language and/or fine arts, 2 units in social studies and/or history. Electives may include fundamentals of computing or vocational education courses.

2008-2009 Annual costs. Tuition/fees: $9,814; $16,444 out-of-state. Room/board: $7,860. Books/supplies: $933. Personal expenses: $2,314.

2008-2009 Financial aid. Need-based: 2,596 full-time freshmen applied for aid; 1,787 were judged to have need; 1,609 of these received aid. Average need met was 81%. Average scholarship/grant was $8,621; average loan $5,967. 66% of total undergraduate aid awarded as scholarships/grants, 34% as loans/jobs. **Non-need-based:** Awarded to 2,638 full-time undergraduates, including 761 freshmen. Scholarships awarded for academics, art, athletics, music/drama.

Application procedures. Admission: Priority date 11/15; deadline 3/1 (receipt date). $40 fee, may be waived for applicants with need. Admission notification on a rolling basis beginning on or about 9/1. **Financial aid:** Priority date 3/1; no closing date. FAFSA required. Applicants notified on a rolling basis starting 4/1; must reply within 2 week(s) of notification.

Academics. Special study options: Accelerated study, combined bachelor's/graduate degree, cooperative education, distance learning, double major, dual enrollment of high school students, ESL, exchange student, honors, independent study, internships, student-designed major, study abroad, teacher certification program, Washington semester. **Credit/placement by examination:** AP, CLEP, SAT, ACT, institutional tests. 26 credit hours maximum toward bachelor's degree. **Support services:** Learning center, preadmission summer program, tutoring.

Majors. Agriculture: Agribusiness operations. **Biology:** General, biochemistry. **Business:** Accounting, business admin, finance, insurance, international, management science, marketing. **Communications:** Journalism, public relations. **Computer sciences:** Computer science, information technology, networking. **Education:** Business, early childhood, elementary, health, middle, music, physical, social studies, special, technology/industrial arts. **Engineering technology:** Industrial. **Family/consumer sciences:** General. **Foreign languages:** General, French, German, Spanish. **Health:** Athletic training, audiology/speech pathology, clinical lab science, environmental health, medical records admin, nursing (RN), occupational health. **History:** General. **Liberal arts:** Arts/sciences. **Math:** General. **Parks/recreation:** Exercise sciences, facilities management. **Philosophy/religion:** Philosophy. **Physical sciences:** Chemistry, geology, physics. **Protective services:** Criminal justice. **Psychology:** General. **Public administration:** Social work. **Social sciences:** Anthropology, economics, geography, political science, sociology. **Visual/performing arts:** Art, dramatic, music history, music performance, studio arts.

Most popular majors. Business/marketing 17%, communications/journalism 6%, education 19%, health sciences 7%, social sciences 7%.

Computing on campus. PC or laptop required. 2,275 workstations in dormitories, library, computer center, student center. Dormitories wired for high-speed internet access and linked to campus network. Commuter students can connect to campus network. Online course registration, online library, helpline, repair service, student web hosting, wireless network available.

Student life. Freshman orientation: Mandatory, $50 fee. Preregistration for classes offered. Two-day sessions held each week from mid-June to end of July. Students meet with advisers, register, and take placement exams. **Housing:** Guaranteed on-campus for freshmen. Coed dorms, single-sex dorms, special housing for disabled, apartments, fraternity/sorority housing, wellness housing available. $150 deposit. **Activities:** Bands, campus ministries, choral groups, dance, drama, film society, international student organizations, literary magazine, music ensembles, Model UN, musical theater, radio station, student government, student newspaper, symphony orchestra, TV station, over 250 student organizations.

Athletics. NCAA. **Intercollegiate:** Baseball M, basketball, cross-country, diving W, football (tackle) M, golf, gymnastics W, soccer W, softball W, swimming W, tennis, track and field, volleyball W. **Intramural:** Badminton, basketball, football (tackle), golf, racquetball, soccer, softball, volleyball. **Team name:** Redbirds.

Student services. Adult student services, alcohol/substance abuse counseling, career counseling, student employment services, financial aid counseling, health services, legal services, minority student services, on-campus daycare, personal counseling, placement for graduates, veterans' counselor. **Physically disabled:** Services for visually, speech, hearing impaired.

Contact. E-mail: admissions@ilstu.edu
Phone: (309) 438-2181 Toll-free number: (800) 366-2478
Fax: (309) 438-3932
Molly Arnold, Director of Admissions, Illinois State University, Campus Box 2200, Normal, IL 61790-2200

Illinois Wesleyan University

Bloomington, Illinois — **CB member**
www.iwu.edu — **CB code: 1320**

- Private 4-year university and liberal arts college
- Residential campus in small city
- 2,115 degree-seeking undergraduates: 58% women, 6% African American, 4% Asian American, 3% Hispanic American, 4% international
- 52% of applicants admitted
- SAT or ACT (ACT writing optional), application essay required
- 83% graduate within 6 years; 35% enter graduate study

General. Founded in 1850. Regionally accredited. **Degrees:** 466 bachelor's awarded. **ROTC:** Army. **Location:** 125 miles from Chicago, 165 miles from St. Louis. **Calendar:** 4-4-1 (2 semesters plus May Term). **Full-time faculty:** 161 total; 94% have terminal degrees, 14% minority, 40% women. **Part-time faculty:** 72 total; 47% have terminal degrees, 8% minority, 58% women. **Class size:** 64% < 20, 33% 20-39, 2% 40-49, less than 1% 50-99, less than 1% >100. **Special facilities:** Observatory, natural sciences research labs, computerized music lab, social science research lab, visual anthropology lab, student-managed real-dollar investment portfolio program, nursing lab, lab theatre producing original works by undergraduates, Action Research Center (supporting community-based student research for academic credit).

Freshman class profile. 3,136 applied, 1,642 admitted, 562 enrolled.

Mid 50% test scores		**Return as sophomores:**	90%
SAT critical reading:	550-690	**Out-of-state:**	11%
SAT math:	590-710	**Live on campus:**	100%
ACT composite:	26-30	**International:**	6%
Rank in top quarter:	80%	**Fraternities:**	28%
Rank in top tenth:	45%	**Sororities:**	29%

Basis for selection. Test scores, class rank, high school record, and essay or personal statement most important. Interview strongly recommended. Audition required for bachelor of music or BFA in theater or music theater. Portfolio review required for BFA in art. **Homeschooled:** Transcript of courses and grades required. **Learning Disabled:** Students welcome to submit information on learning disabilities as part of application review process.

High school preparation. 15 units recommended. Recommended units include English 4, mathematics 3, social studies 2, science 3 (laboratory 2) and foreign language 3. Biology and chemistry are required for admission to nursing and biology.

2008-2009 Annual costs. Tuition/fees: $32,434. Room/board: $7,350. Books/supplies: $780. Personal expenses: $650.

2008-2009 Financial aid. Need-based: 421 full-time freshmen applied for aid; 360 were judged to have need; 360 of these received aid. Average need met was 95%. Average scholarship/grant was $18,287; average loan $4,627. 75% of total undergraduate aid awarded as scholarships/grants, 25% as loans/jobs. **Non-need-based:** Awarded to 848 full-time undergraduates, including 226 freshmen. Scholarships awarded for academics, art, music/drama.

Application procedures. Admission: Priority date 11/1; no deadline. No application fee. Admission notification on a rolling basis beginning on or about 12/15. Must reply by May 1 or within 3 week(s) if notified thereafter. **Financial aid:** Closing date 3/1. FAFSA, institutional form, CSS PROFILE required. Applicants notified on a rolling basis starting 2/15; must reply by 5/1 or within 3 week(s) of notification.

Academics. Optional 3-week May Term provides opportunities for students to pursue experimental courses, travel courses, interships, or independent research projects. Fall Term in London and Spring Term in Madrid led by Illinois Wesleyan faculty members where students may earn General Education credit during these terms. **Special study options:** Combined bachelor's/graduate degree, double major, exchange student, honors, independent study, internships, New York semester, student-designed major, study abroad, teacher certification program, United Nations semester, urban semester, Washington semester. 3-2 cooperative program in engineering with Washington University, Case Western Reserve University, and Northwestern University; 3-2 program in forestry and environmental management with Duke University; 3-2 program in occupational therapy with Washington University, 2-2 program in engineering with the University of Illinois, and a non-guaranteed cooperative program in engineering with Dartmouth College. **Credit/placement by examination:** AP, CLEP, IB, institutional tests. 32 credit hours maximum toward bachelor's degree. Limit of 16 hours (equivalent to four courses) may count toward general education credit. Up to 16 additional hours (equivalent to four courses) can be awarded as elective credit. **Support services:** Reduced course load, study skills assistance, tutoring, writing center.

Majors. Area/ethnic studies: African, American, Asian, Central/Eastern European, Latin American, Western European, women's. **Biology:** General. **Business:** Accounting, business admin, insurance, international. **Computer sciences:** General. **Conservation:** Environmental studies. **Education:** General, biology, chemistry, elementary, English, French, history, mathematics, music, physics, Spanish. **Foreign languages:** Classics, French, German, Spanish. **Health:** Nursing (RN). **History:** General. **Math:** General. **Philosophy/religion:** Philosophy, religion. **Physical sciences:** Chemistry, physics. **Psychology:** General. **Social sciences:** Anthropology, economics, political science, sociology. **Visual/performing arts:** Acting, art, dramatic, music performance, music theory/composition, piano/organ, stringed instruments, theater design, voice/opera.

Most popular majors. Biology 7%, business/marketing 19%, education 8%, English 7%, health sciences 6%, psychology 9%, social sciences 14%, visual/performing arts 10%.

Computing on campus. 400 workstations in dormitories, library, computer center, student center. Dormitories wired for high-speed internet access and linked to campus network. Commuter students can connect to campus network. Online course registration, online library, helpline, repair service, student web hosting, wireless network available.

Student life. Freshman orientation: Mandatory. Preregistration for classes offered. Orientation for parents held in June. New student orientation held 5-6 days prior to start of classes. **Policies:** No smoking permitted in residence halls. Beer and wine permitted in designated areas for students of legal age. **Housing:** Guaranteed on-campus for freshmen. Coed dorms, special housing for disabled, apartments, fraternity/sorority housing, wellness housing available. **Activities:** Bands, campus ministries, choral groups, dance, drama, film society, literary magazine, music ensembles, Model UN, musical theater, opera, radio station, student government, student newspaper, symphony orchestra, TV station, black student union, InterVarsity Christian Fellowship, Alpha Phi Omega, Council of Latin American Student Enrichment, Habitat for Humanity, several environmental concerns organizations, Amnesty International, Pan-Asian student association, College Democrats, College Republicans.

Athletics. NCAA. **Intercollegiate:** Baseball M, basketball, cross-country, diving, football (tackle) M, golf, soccer, softball W, swimming, tennis, track and field, volleyball W. **Intramural:** Badminton, basketball, football (non-tackle), golf, soccer, softball, tennis, volleyball. **Team name:** Titans.

Student services. Alcohol/substance abuse counseling, chaplain/spiritual director, career counseling, student employment services, financial aid counseling, health services, minority student services, personal counseling, placement for graduates. **Physically disabled:** Services for visually, speech, hearing impaired.

Contact. E-mail: iwuadmit@iwu.edu
Phone: (309) 556-3031 Toll-free number: (800) 332-2498
Fax: (309) 556-3820
Tony Bankston, Dean of Admissions, Illinois Wesleyan University, PO Box 2900, Bloomington, IL 61702-2900

International Academy of Design and Technology: Chicago

Chicago, Illinois
www.iadtchicago.edu **CB code: 3363**

- For-profit 4-year visual arts and technical college
- Commuter campus in very large city
- 1,736 degree-seeking undergraduates
- Interview required

General. Founded in 1977. Accredited by ACICS. **Degrees:** 363 bachelor's, 71 associate awarded. **Location:** Downtown. **Calendar:** Quarter, extensive summer session. **Full-time faculty:** 14 total. **Part-time faculty:** 119 total. **Class size:** 53% < 20, 44% 20-39, 3% 40-49.

Basis for selection. Open admission. **Homeschooled:** Transcript of courses and grades required. Should be registered with state or accrediting agency.

2008-2009 Annual costs. Tuition/fees: $17,730. Books/supplies: $1,800. Personal expenses: $1,596.

2007-2008 Financial aid. All financial aid based on need. 35% of total undergraduate aid awarded as scholarships/grants, 65% as loans/jobs. **Additional information:** College work study programs available to day and evening students.

Application procedures. Admission: No deadline. $50 fee. Admission notification on a rolling basis. **Financial aid:** No deadline. FAFSA required. Applicants notified on a rolling basis.

Academics. Special study options: Distance learning, independent study, internships, study abroad, weekend college. **Credit/placement by examination:** AP, CLEP, IB, institutional tests. 40 credit hours maximum toward associate degree, 100 toward bachelor's. **Support services:** Learning center, reduced course load, remedial instruction, study skills assistance, tutoring.

Majors. Business: Fashion. **Communications technology:** Animation/special effects. **Computer sciences:** Computer forensics, information technology. **Visual/performing arts:** Commercial/advertising art, fashion design, graphic design, interior design.

Most popular majors. Business/marketing 31%, communication technologies 14%, visual/performing arts 53%.

Computing on campus. 386 workstations in library, computer center, student center. Online course registration, online library, wireless network available.

Student life. Freshman orientation: Mandatory. **Activities:** Student newspaper, Fashion Council, merchandising management club, information technology club, video and animation club, Omega Pi Delta, International Interior Design Association, graphic design club, international club, chess club, movie club.

Student services. Adult student services, career counseling, student employment services, financial aid counseling, personal counseling, placement for graduates, veterans' counselor. **Physically disabled:** Services for visually impaired.

Contact. Phone: (312) 980-9200 Toll-free number: (877) 222-3369
Fax: (312) 541-3929
Ernest Cochran, Vice President of Admissions, International Academy of Design and Technology: Chicago, One North State Street, Suite 500, Chicago, IL 60602

International Academy of Design and Technology: Schaumburg
Schaumburg, Illinois
www.iadtschaumburg.com

- For-profit 4-year visual arts and technical college
- Commuter campus in small city
- 214 degree-seeking undergraduates

General. Accredited by ACICS. **Degrees:** 38 bachelor's, 4 associate awarded. **Calendar:** Quarter. **Full-time faculty:** 3 total. **Part-time faculty:** 25 total.

Basis for selection. Open admission.

2008-2009 Annual costs. Tuition/fees: $16,140. Bachelor's degree program is $63,360 plus books and fees. Books/supplies: $1,800.

2007-2008 Financial aid. Need-based: 21% of total undergraduate aid awarded as scholarships/grants, 79% as loans/jobs.

Academics. Credit/placement by examination: CLEP.

Majors. Communications technology: Animation/special effects. **Computer sciences:** Web page design. **Visual/performing arts:** Fashion design, interior design.

Contact. Phone: (847) 969-2800 Fax: (847) 969-0599
Kelly Stegmeyer, Director of Admissions, International Academy of Design and Technology: Schaumburg, 915 National Parkway, Schaumburg, IL 60173

ITT Technical Institute: Burr Ridge
Burr Ridge, Illinois
www.itt-tech.edu **CB code: 2698**

- For-profit 4-year technical college
- Commuter campus in small town

General. Accredited by ACICS. **Calendar:** Quarter.

Contact. Phone: (630) 455-6470
Director of Recruitment, 7040 High Grove Boulevard, Burr Ridge, IL 60527

ITT Technical Institute: Mount Prospect
Mount Prospect, Illinois
www.itt-tech.edu **CB code: 4271**

- For-profit 4-year technical college
- Commuter campus in small city

General. Founded in 1986. Accredited by ACICS. **Location:** 20 miles from Chicago. **Calendar:** Quarter.

Contact. Phone: (847) 375-8800
Director of Recruitment, 1401 Feehanville Drive, Mount Prospect, IL 60056

Judson University
Elgin, Illinois
www.judsonu.edu **CB code: 1351**

- Private 4-year university and liberal arts college affiliated with American Baptist Churches in the USA
- Residential campus in small city
- 926 full-time, degree-seeking undergraduates
- 147 graduate students
- 69% of applicants admitted
- SAT or ACT (ACT writing optional), application essay required
- 49% graduate within 6 years

General. Founded in 1963. Regionally accredited. **Degrees:** 316 bachelor's awarded; master's offered. **ROTC:** Army, Naval, Air Force. **Location:** 40 miles from Chicago. **Calendar:** Semester, limited summer session. **Full-time faculty:** 53 total; 74% have terminal degrees, 13% minority, 32% women. **Class size:** 78% < 20, 20% 20-39, less than 1% 40-49, less than 1% 50-99. **Special facilities:** Green academic center.

Freshman class profile. 621 applied, 431 admitted, 200 enrolled.

Mid 50% test scores		**GPA 3.50-3.74:**	15%
SAT critical reading:	440-560	**GPA 3.0-3.49:**	35%
SAT math:	440-640	**GPA 2.0-2.99:**	25%
ACT composite:	20-25	**Return as sophomores:**	60%
GPA 3.75 or higher:	23%		

Basis for selection. School achievement record and test scores important. Counselor's reference considered. Audition recommended for performing arts majors. Portfolio recommended for art majors. Essay required for architecture majors. **Homeschooled:** Transcript of courses and grades required.

High school preparation. Recommended units include English 4, mathematics 3, social studies 2, science 2 (laboratory 2).

2008-2009 Annual costs. Tuition/fees: $21,850. Room/board: $7,700. Books/supplies: $1,500. Personal expenses: $2,000.

2007-2008 Financial aid. Need-based: 116 full-time freshmen applied for aid; 99 were judged to have need; 99 of these received aid. Average scholarship/grant was $11,850. 44% of total undergraduate aid awarded as scholarships/grants, 56% as loans/jobs. **Non-need-based:** Awarded to 216 full-time undergraduates, including 39 freshmen. Scholarships awarded for academics, alumni affiliation, art, athletics, music/drama.

Application procedures. Admission: No deadline. $40 fee, may be waived for applicants with need. Admission notification on a rolling basis beginning on or about 7/1. **Financial aid:** Priority date 3/15, closing date 5/1. FAFSA required. Applicants notified on a rolling basis starting 3/1; must reply within 4 week(s) of notification.

Academics. Special study options: Accelerated study, combined bachelor's/graduate degree, distance learning, double major, honors, independent study, internships, student-designed major, study abroad, teacher certification program, urban semester, Washington semester. **Credit/placement by examination:** AP, CLEP, ACT, institutional tests. 30 credit hours maximum toward bachelor's degree. **Support services:** Learning center, reduced course load, remedial instruction, study skills assistance, tutoring.

Majors. Architecture: Architecture. **Biology:** General, biochemistry. **Business:** Accounting, business admin, human resources, management information systems. **Communications:** General, media studies. **Computer sciences:** Computer graphics, information technology, web page design, webmaster. **Conservation:** Environmental studies. **Education:** Art, early childhood, elementary, music, physical, secondary. **History:** General. **Math:** General. **Parks/recreation:** Sports admin. **Physical sciences:** Chemistry. **Protective services:** Criminal justice. **Psychology:** General. **Public administration:** Human services. **Social sciences:** Sociology. **Theology:** Bible, sacred music, youth ministry. **Visual/performing arts:** Art, graphic design, music performance, studio arts. **Other:** Management and leadership, Science/Mathematics general.

Most popular majors. Architecture 9%, business/marketing 34%, education 14%, psychology 6%, public administration/social services 16%, security/protective services 6%, theological studies 6%.

Computing on campus. 200 workstations in dormitories, library, computer center, student center. Dormitories wired for high-speed internet access and linked to campus network. Online course registration, online library, helpline, wireless network available.

Student life. Freshman orientation: Mandatory. Preregistration for classes offered. **Policies:** Chapel services held 3 mornings a week. **Housing:** Guaranteed on-campus for all undergraduates. Coed dorms, single-sex dorms, special housing for disabled, apartments, wellness housing available. $175 fully refundable deposit, deadline 5/1. **Activities:** Concert band, campus ministries, choral groups, drama, music ensembles, student government, student newspaper, symphony orchestra.

Athletics. NAIA, NCCAA. **Intercollegiate:** Baseball M, basketball, cross-country, soccer, softball W, volleyball W. **Intramural:** Badminton, basketball, racquetball, soccer, softball, volleyball. **Team name:** Eagles.

Student services. Adult student services, career counseling, student employment services, financial aid counseling, health services, personal counseling, placement for graduates.

Contact. E-mail: admissions@judsonu.edu
Phone: (847) 628-2510 Toll-free number: (800) 879-5376
Fax: (847) 628-2526
William Dean, Director of Admissions, Judson University, 1151 North State Street, Elgin, IL 60123-1404

Four-Year Colleges

Kendall College

Chicago, Illinois
www.kendall.edu **CB code: 1366**

- Private 4-year culinary school, business and teachers college affiliated with United Methodist Church
- Commuter campus in very large city
- 1,842 degree-seeking undergraduates: 34% part-time, 70% women, 15% African American, 4% Asian American, 12% Hispanic American, 5% international
- SAT or ACT (ACT writing optional), application essay, interview required
- 36% graduate within 6 years

General. Founded in 1934. Regionally accredited. Internships required in every major. **Degrees:** 110 bachelor's, 94 associate awarded. **Location:** Downtown. **Calendar:** Quarter, extensive summer session. **Full-time faculty:** 37 total; 14% minority, 38% women. **Part-time faculty:** 43 total; 30% minority, 54% women.

Freshman class profile.

Out-of-state:	20%	**International:**	4%

Basis for selection. High school record most important, followed by test scores, class rank, recommendations and interview. Placement test may be required.

High school preparation. Recommended units include English 4, mathematics 2, social studies 2, science 2 and foreign language 2. Specific academic units required for certain majors.

2008-2009 Annual costs. Tuition costs range from $7,200 to $21,450 per academic year. Required fees: $675. Room/board: $10,485. Books/supplies: $500.

2007-2008 Financial aid. Need-based: 33% of total undergraduate aid awarded as scholarships/grants, 67% as loans/jobs. **Non-need-based:** Scholarships awarded for academics.

Application procedures. Admission: No deadline. $50 fee, may be waived for applicants with need, free for online applicants. Admission notification on a rolling basis. Must reply by May 1 or within 4 week(s) if notified thereafter. **Financial aid:** Priority date 6/1; no closing date. FAFSA required. Applicants notified on a rolling basis starting 4/1; must reply within 2 week(s) of notification.

Academics. Special study options: Accelerated study, combined bachelor's/graduate degree, cooperative education, distance learning, independent study, internships, study abroad, teacher certification program, weekend college. **Credit/placement by examination:** AP, CLEP, IB, institutional tests. 24 credit hours maximum toward associate degree, 48 toward bachelor's. **Support services:** Learning center, reduced course load, remedial instruction, study skills assistance, tutoring, writing center.

Majors. Business: Business admin, entrepreneurial studies, hospitality admin, hotel/motel admin, nonprofit/public. **Education:** Early childhood. **Personal/culinary services:** Culinary arts.

Computing on campus. 100 workstations in library, computer center, student center. Dormitories wired for high-speed internet access and linked to campus network. Commuter students can connect to campus network. Online library, helpline, wireless network available.

Student life. Freshman orientation: Mandatory. Preregistration for classes offered. One-day event held 1 week before the start of the quarter. **Housing:** Coed dorms, wellness housing available. $350 nonrefundable deposit. **Activities:** Student government.

Student services. Adult student services, alcohol/substance abuse counseling, career counseling, student employment services, financial aid counseling, minority student services, personal counseling, placement for graduates.

Contact. E-mail: admissions@kendall.edu
Phone: (312) 752-2020 Toll-free number: (888) 653-6325
Fax: (312) 752-2021
Richard Kriofsky, Director of Admissions, Kendall College, 900 North Branch Street North, Chicago, IL 60642-4278

Knox College

Galesburg, Illinois **CB member**
www.knox.edu **CB code: 1372**

- Private 4-year liberal arts college
- Residential campus in large town
- 1,360 degree-seeking undergraduates: 58% women, 5% African American, 7% Asian American, 5% Hispanic American, 1% Native American, 7% international
- 66% of applicants admitted
- Application essay required
- 75% graduate within 6 years; 21% enter graduate study

General. Founded in 1837. Regionally accredited. **Degrees:** 289 bachelor's awarded. **Location:** 180 miles from Chicago, 200 miles from St. Louis. **Calendar:** Trimester. **Full-time faculty:** 98 total; 92% have terminal degrees, 13% minority, 39% women. **Part-time faculty:** 40 total; 42% have terminal degrees, 12% minority, 60% women. **Class size:** 58% < 20, 40% 20-39, 2% 40-49, less than 1% 50-99. **Special facilities:** Electron microscope, greenhouse, studio and large-scale production theaters, 760-acre biological field station, ceramics, sculpture, painting, and printmaking studios.

Freshman class profile. 2,750 applied, 1,804 admitted, 368 enrolled.

Mid 50% test scores		**Rank in top quarter:**	76%
SAT critical reading:	590-700	**Rank in top tenth:**	44%
SAT math:	580-660	**End year in good standing:**	90%
SAT writing:	560-670	**Return as sophomores:**	88%
ACT composite:	26-31	**Out-of-state:**	53%
GPA 3.75 or higher:	28%	**Live on campus:**	96%
GPA 3.50-3.74:	20%	**International:**	9%
GPA 3.0-3.49:	37%	**Fraternities:**	30%
GPA 2.0-2.99:	15%	**Sororities:**	17%

Basis for selection. Course of study, grades, essay, and recommendations most important. Class rank, extracurricular activities, special skills, talents and personal qualities, interview also considered. Preference given to students who have taken advantage of academic opportunities offered by high school (honors, Advanced Placement, International Baccalaureate and/or college level courses) if available. SAT or ACT submission optional for most applicants. Applicants from secondary schools that do not provide grades are asked to submit test scores. Interview strongly recommended. **Homeschooled:** Statement describing homeschool structure and mission, transcript of courses and grades, state high school equivalency certificate required. Applicants should provide detailed documentation of coursework completed, including course syllabi as appropriate. SAT/ACT scores required.

High school preparation. College-preparatory program required. 19 units recommended. Recommended units include English 4, mathematics 4, social studies 2, history 2, science 4 (laboratory 3) and foreign language 3.

2009-2010 Annual costs. Tuition/fees: $31,911. Room/board: $7,164. Books/supplies: $900. Personal expenses: $1,000.

2008-2009 Financial aid. Non-need-based: Scholarships awarded for academics, art, music/drama.

Application procedures. Admission: Priority date 12/1; deadline 2/1 (postmark date). $40 fee, may be waived for applicants with need. Admission notification 3/31. Must reply by May 1 or within 2 week(s) if notified thereafter. **Financial aid:** Priority date 2/1; no closing date. FAFSA, institutional form required. Applicants notified on a rolling basis starting 3/15; must reply by 5/1 or within 2 week(s) of notification.

Academics. Academic work conducted under honor system, placing primary responsibility for academic honesty on student. Examinations not proctored. **Special study options:** Combined bachelor's/graduate degree, double major, dual enrollment of high school students, honors, independent study, internships, liberal arts/career combination, student-designed major, study abroad, teacher certification program, urban semester, Washington semester. Extensive overseas study centers with more than 30 international and off-campus study programs. Significant independent research opportunities with funding for projects. Repertory theater, psychology, and Green Oaks (environmental) terms. **Credit/placement by examination:** AP, CLEP, IB, SAT, ACT, institutional tests. 9 credit hours maximum toward bachelor's degree. Up to 25% of 36 required Knox credits may be obtained through examination. **Support services:** Learning center, reduced course load, study skills assistance, tutoring, writing center.

Majors. Area/ethnic studies: African-American, American, Asian, women's. **Biology:** General, biochemistry. **Computer sciences:** Computer science. **Conservation:** Environmental studies. **Education:** General, social science. **Foreign languages:** General, classics, French, German, Spanish. **History:**

General. **Interdisciplinary:** Global studies, neuroscience. **Math:** General, applied. **Philosophy/religion:** Philosophy. **Physical sciences:** Chemistry, physics. **Psychology:** General. **Social sciences:** Anthropology, economics, international relations, political science, sociology. **Visual/performing arts:** Art history/conservation, dramatic, studio arts.

Most popular majors. Biology 10%, education 9%, English 15%, psychology 7%, social sciences 23%, visual/performing arts 9%.

Computing on campus. 335 workstations in library, computer center, student center. Dormitories wired for high-speed internet access and linked to campus network. Commuter students can connect to campus network. Online course registration, online library, helpline, student web hosting, wireless network available.

Student life. Freshman orientation: Mandatory. Preregistration for classes offered. 1 week before beginning of fall term. Additional orientation for international students. **Policies:** Students actively engaged in college governance. All students requred to live on campus. **Housing:** Coed dorms, single-sex dorms, special housing for disabled, apartments, fraternity/sorority housing, wellness housing available. $300 nonrefundable deposit, deadline 5/1. **Activities:** Jazz band, campus ministries, choral groups, dance, drama, international student organizations, literary magazine, music ensembles, Model UN, radio station, student government, student newspaper, symphony orchestra, InterVarsity Christian Fellowship, Amnesty International, Latin American Concerns, Allied Blacks for Liberty and Equality, Lo Nuestro, Habitat for Humanity, Common Ground.

Athletics. NCAA. **Intercollegiate:** Baseball M, basketball, cross-country, diving, football (tackle) M, golf, soccer, softball W, swimming, tennis, track and field, volleyball W, wrestling M. **Intramural:** Basketball, football (tackle), soccer, softball, volleyball. **Team name:** Prairie Fire.

Student services. Alcohol/substance abuse counseling, career counseling, services for economically disadvantaged, student employment services, financial aid counseling, health services, minority student services, personal counseling. **Physically disabled:** Services for visually, hearing impaired.

Contact. E-mail: admission@knox.edu
Phone: (309) 341-7100 Toll-free number: (800) 678-5669
Fax: (309) 341-7070
Paul Steenis, Dean of Admission, Knox College, Knox College - Campus Box 148, Galesburg, IL 61401-4999

Lake Forest College

Lake Forest, Illinois — **CB member**
www.lakeforest.edu — **CB code: 1392**

- Private 4-year liberal arts college affiliated with Presbyterian Church (USA)
- Residential campus in large town
- 1,350 degree-seeking undergraduates: 1% part-time, 58% women, 5% African American, 4% Asian American, 5% Hispanic American, 10% international
- 19 degree-seeking graduate students
- 59% of applicants admitted
- Application essay required
- 66% graduate within 6 years

General. Founded in 1857. Regionally accredited. **Degrees:** 340 bachelor's awarded; master's offered. **Location:** 30 miles from Chicago. **Calendar:** Semester, limited summer session. **Full-time faculty:** 94 total; 98% have terminal degrees, 12% minority, 43% women. **Part-time faculty:** 65 total; 48% have terminal degrees, 14% minority, 58% women. **Class size:** 66% < 20, 33% 20-39, less than 1% 40-49, less than 1% 50-99. **Special facilities:** Electron microscope, NMR spectrometer, neutron howitzer, multimedia language laboratory, electronic music studio.

Freshman class profile. 2,551 applied, 1,507 admitted, 379 enrolled.

Mid 50% test scores		**GPA 2.0-2.99:**	8%
SAT critical reading:	520-640	**Rank in top quarter:**	63%
SAT math:	530-630	**Rank in top tenth:**	36%
SAT writing:	530-630	**End year in good standing:**	93%
ACT composite:	23-28	**Return as sophomores:**	74%
GPA 3.75 or higher:	33%	**Out-of-state:**	65%
GPA 3.50-3.74:	21%	**Live on campus:**	91%
GPA 3.0-3.49:	38%	**International:**	12%

Basis for selection. Secondary school curriculum and record most important, followed by school and community activities, essay. Recommendations considered carefully. Copy of graded paper required. ACT/SAT optional except for applicants to the highest academic scholarships. Interview required for merit scholarships in leadership and science and for students who do not submit test scores, recommended for all. Audition required for theater and music scholarships. Portfolio required for art, foreign language and writing scholarships. **Homeschooled:** Statement describing home-school structure and mission, interview required. SAT/ACT required.

High school preparation. College-preparatory program required. 19 units required; 23 recommended. Required and recommended units include English 4, mathematics 3-4, social studies 2, history 2, science 3-4 (laboratory 3-4), foreign language 2-4 and academic electives 3.

2008-2009 Annual costs. Tuition/fees: $32,520. Room/board: $7,724. Books/supplies: $800. Personal expenses: $1,736.

2008-2009 Financial aid. Need-based: 311 full-time freshmen applied for aid; 284 were judged to have need; 284 of these received aid. Average need met was 92%. Average scholarship/grant was $22,988; average loan $4,674. 77% of total undergraduate aid awarded as scholarships/grants, 23% as loans/jobs. **Non-need-based:** Awarded to 402 full-time undergraduates, including 90 freshmen. Scholarships awarded for academics, alumni affiliation, art, leadership, music/drama, state residency.

Application procedures. Admission: Closing date 2/15 (postmark date). $40 fee, may be waived for applicants with need. Admission notification 3/20. Must reply by May 1 or within 3 week(s) if notified thereafter. **Financial aid:** Priority date 3/1; no closing date. FAFSA, institutional form required. Applicants notified on a rolling basis starting 3/15; must reply by 5/1 or within 3 week(s) of notification.

Academics. In freshman studies program, students select 1 of 4 fall courses from designated set with class size limit of 12 students. Faculty member teaching course serves as student's academic adviser. **Special study options:** Double major, honors, independent study, internships, liberal arts/career combination, semester at sea, student-designed major, study abroad, teacher certification program, urban semester, Washington semester. International internship program in Paris and Santiago, Chile; 3-2 engineering program with Washington University. **Credit/placement by examination:** AP, CLEP, IB, institutional tests. **Support services:** Learning center, study skills assistance, tutoring, writing center.

Majors. Area/ethnic studies: American, Asian, Latin American. **Biology:** General. **Business:** General. **Communications:** General. **Computer sciences:** Computer science. **Conservation:** Environmental studies. **Education:** General. **Foreign languages:** French, Spanish. **History:** General. **Math:** General. **Philosophy/religion:** Philosophy. **Physical sciences:** Chemistry, physics. **Psychology:** General. **Social sciences:** Anthropology, economics, international relations, political science, sociology. **Visual/performing arts:** Art, theater history.

Most popular majors. Business/marketing 10%, communications/journalism 11%, English 7%, foreign language 7%, psychology 8%, social sciences 24%, visual/performing arts 11%.

Computing on campus. 200 workstations in library, computer center, student center. Dormitories wired for high-speed internet access and linked to campus network. Commuter students can connect to campus network. Online library, helpline, repair service, student web hosting, wireless network available.

Student life. Freshman orientation: Mandatory, $100 fee. Preregistration for classes offered. **Housing:** Guaranteed on-campus for freshmen. Coed dorms, single-sex dorms, wellness housing available. $300 nonrefundable deposit, deadline 5/1. **Activities:** Bands, choral groups, dance, drama, film society, international student organizations, literary magazine, music ensembles, musical theater, radio station, student government, student newspaper, Christian Fellowship, Interfaith Council, Amnesty International, Habitat for Humanity, League for Environmental Awareness and Protection, United Black Association, Latinos Unidos, Asian Interest Group, Diversity Advocates (ALLY), Hillel.

Athletics. NCAA. **Intercollegiate:** Basketball, cross-country, diving, football (tackle) M, handball, ice hockey, soccer, softball W, swimming, tennis, volleyball W. **Intramural:** Basketball, football (non-tackle), racquetball, soccer, softball, tennis, volleyball. **Team name:** Foresters.

Student services. Adult student services, alcohol/substance abuse counseling, career counseling, student employment services, financial aid counseling, health services, minority student services, personal counseling, placement for graduates, women's services. **Physically disabled:** Services for visually, hearing impaired.

Contact. E-mail: admissions@lakeforest.edu
Phone: (847) 735-5000 Toll-free number: (800) 828-4751
Fax: (847) 735-6271
William Motzer, Vice President for Admissions and Career Services, Lake Forest College, 555 North Sheridan Road, Lake Forest, IL 60045-2338

Lakeview College of Nursing
Danville, Illinois
www.lakeviewcol.edu **CB code: 0149**

- Private two-year upper-division nursing college
- Commuter campus in large town
- 82% of applicants admitted
- Application essay required

General. Founded in 1894. Regionally accredited. **Degrees:** 120 bachelor's awarded. **Articulation:** Agreements with Danville Area Community College, Eastern Illinois University. **Location:** 35 miles from Urbana-Champaign, 130 miles from Chicago. **Calendar:** Semester, limited summer session. **Full-time faculty:** 20 total. **Part-time faculty:** 8 total. **Special facilities:** Free clinic, nature preserve.

Student profile. 283 degree-seeking undergraduates. 152 applied as first time-transfer students, 125 admitted, 96 enrolled.

Women:	84%	**Out-of-state:**	2%
Part-time:	20%	**25 or older:**	83%

Basis for selection. High school transcript, college transcript, application essay required. Based on interview, references, and transcripts. Applicant must have completed 33 credit hours of general course work with 2.5 GPA prior to admission. Transfer accepted as sophomores, juniors.

2008-2009 Annual costs. Tuition/fees: $11,715. Books/supplies: $582.

Financial aid. All financial aid based on need.

Application procedures. Admission: Rolling admission. $100 fee. Application must be submitted on paper. National League for Nursing examinations used to determine advanced placement for entering students who already have RN degree. **Financial aid:** Priority date 4/15, no deadline. FAFSA, institutional form required.

Academics. BS in nursing requires total of 125 credit hours. 95% of entering students complete degree in 5 years or less. **Special study options:** Distance learning, honors, independent study. **Credit/placement by examination:** CLEP. **Support services:** Reduced course load, study skills assistance, tutoring.

Majors. Health: Nursing (RN).

Computing on campus. 12 workstations in library, computer center.

Student life. Activities: Student government, student newspaper, Illinois Student Nurses Association, National Student Nurses Association.

Student services. Adult student services, career counseling, financial aid counseling, health services, personal counseling, veterans' counselor.

Contact. E-mail: admissions@lakeviewcol.edu
Phone: (217) 554-6899 Fax: (217) 477-2970
Connie Young, Director of Enrollment/Registrar, Lakeview College of Nursing, 903 North Logan Avenue, Danville, IL 61832

Lewis University
Romeoville, Illinois **CB member**
www.lewisu.edu **CB code: 1404**

- Private 4-year university affiliated with Roman Catholic Church
- Residential campus in large town
- 3,913 degree-seeking undergraduates: 21% part-time, 59% women, 10% African American, 4% Asian American, 11% Hispanic American, 3% international
- 467 degree-seeking graduate students
- 71% of applicants admitted
- SAT or ACT (ACT writing optional) required
- 58% graduate within 6 years

General. Founded in 1932. Regionally accredited. Sponsored by De La Salle Christian Brothers. **Degrees:** 856 bachelor's, 1 associate awarded; master's, doctoral offered. **ROTC:** Army, Air Force. **Location:** 30 miles from Chicago. **Calendar:** Semester, extensive summer session. **Full-time faculty:** 183 total; 67% have terminal degrees, 10% minority, 53% women. **Part-time faculty:** 380 total; 11% have terminal degrees, 14% minority, 50% women. **Class size:** 66% < 20, 33% 20-39, less than 1% 40-49, less than 1% 50-99. **Special facilities:** Campus airport, aeronautical training center, all digital radio station.

Freshman class profile. 2,644 applied, 1,865 admitted, 655 enrolled.

Mid 50% test scores		**GPA 2.0-2.99:**	36%
SAT critical reading:	420-530	**Rank in top quarter:**	35%
SAT math:	430-620	**Rank in top tenth:**	11%
ACT composite:	19-24	**Return as sophomores:**	78%
GPA 3.75 or higher:	17%	**Out-of-state:**	6%
GPA 3.50-3.74:	14%	**Live on campus:**	63%
GPA 3.0-3.49:	32%	**International:**	3%

Basis for selection. Applicants must graduate from approved high school with 2.0 GPA. Class rank and ACT/SAT scores must indicate strong likelihood of success in university studies. 20 ACT required for admission to nursing program. Interview recommended. **Homeschooled:** Statement describing homeschool structure and mission required.

High school preparation. College-preparatory program recommended. 18 units required. Required and recommended units include English 3-4, mathematics 3, social studies 2, history 1, science 2 (laboratory 1), foreign language 2 and academic electives 4. 1 year chemistry and 2 years math at 2.0 level or above strongly recommended for nursing applicants.

2008-2009 Annual costs. Tuition/fees: $21,990. Room/board: $8,000. Books/supplies: $1,000. Personal expenses: $1,320.

2008-2009 Financial aid. Need-based: Average need met was 79%. Average scholarship/grant was $8,718; average loan $3,391. 46% of total undergraduate aid awarded as scholarships/grants, 54% as loans/jobs. **Non-need-based:** Scholarships awarded for academics, alumni affiliation, art, athletics, leadership, music/drama, religious affiliation, ROTC.

Application procedures. Admission: Priority date 4/15; no deadline. $40 fee, may be waived for applicants with need. Admission notification on a rolling basis beginning on or about 10/1. Must reply by May 1 or within 2 week(s) if notified thereafter. **Financial aid:** Closing date 5/1. FAFSA required. Applicants notified on a rolling basis starting 2/1; must reply within 2 week(s) of notification.

Academics. Accelerated degree completion program available to students 24 years and older. **Special study options:** Accelerated study, combined bachelor's/graduate degree, distance learning, double major, dual enrollment of high school students, ESL, exchange student, honors, independent study, internships, liberal arts/career combination, student-designed major, study abroad, teacher certification program. **Credit/placement by examination:** AP, CLEP, institutional tests. 60 credit hours maximum toward bachelor's degree. **Support services:** Learning center, pre-admission summer program, reduced course load, remedial instruction, study skills assistance, tutoring, writing center.

Majors. Area/ethnic studies: American. **Biology:** General, biochemistry, environmental. **Business:** General, accounting, business admin, finance, human resources, international, management information systems, management science, managerial economics, marketing. **Communications:** General, broadcast journalism, digital media, journalism, public relations, radio/tv. **Communications technology:** General, radio/tv. **Computer sciences:** General, computer graphics, computer science, information systems. **Conservation:** General. **Education:** General, elementary, special. **Health:** Athletic training, chiropractic assistant, health care admin, health services, nursing (RN), pharmacy assistant, predental, premedicine, prenursing, prepharmacy, preveterinary. **History:** General. **Interdisciplinary:** Global studies. **Legal studies:** Prelaw. **Liberal arts:** Arts/sciences. **Math:** General. **Mechanic/repair:** Aircraft, avionics. **Parks/recreation:** Sports admin. **Philosophy/religion:** Philosophy, religion. **Physical sciences:** Chemistry, physics. **Protective services:** Correctional facilities, criminal justice, fire services admin, forensics, law enforcement admin, police science, security services. **Psychology:** General. **Public administration:** General, community org/advocacy, human services, social work. **Social sciences:** Economics, political science, sociology. **Transportation:** Air traffic control, airline/commercial pilot, aviation, aviation management. **Visual/performing arts:** Art, commercial/advertising art, dramatic, drawing, graphic design, illustration, music management, painting, studio arts, theater arts management. **Other:** Aviation security.

Most popular majors. Business/marketing 21%, education 9%, health sciences 20%, psychology 6%, security/protective services 13%, trade and industry 6%.

Computing on campus. 350 workstations in library, computer center. Dormitories wired for high-speed internet access and linked to campus network. Commuter students can connect to campus network. Online course registration, online library, helpline, wireless network available.

Student life. Freshman orientation: Mandatory, $80 fee. Preregistration for classes offered. Two-day program includes transition seminars, assessment, and academic advising. Summer/winter orientations (overnight optional) available, includes parent orientations and welcome weekend before first day of classes. **Housing:** Guaranteed on-campus for all undergraduates.

Coed dorms, special housing for disabled available. $100 nonrefundable deposit, deadline 5/1. Handicapped accessibility available in most residence halls. **Activities:** Jazz band, campus ministries, choral groups, dance, drama, international student organizations, literary magazine, music ensembles, musical theater, radio station, student government, student newspaper, TV station, Fellowship of Justice, Black student union, Latin American student organization, InterFraternity Council, National Panhellenic Council, American Association of Airport Executives, Coffey Aviation student organization, student nurses association, Teachers of Tomorrow.

Athletics. NCAA. **Intercollegiate:** Baseball M, basketball, cheerleading, cross-country, golf, soccer, softball W, swimming, tennis, track and field, volleyball. **Intramural:** Basketball, bowling, field hockey, football (non-tackle), golf, handball, racquetball, soccer, softball, table tennis, tennis, volleyball. **Team name:** Flyers.

Student services. Adult student services, alcohol/substance abuse counseling, career counseling, student employment services, financial aid counseling, health services, minority student services, personal counseling, placement for graduates, veterans' counselor.

Contact. E-mail: admissions@lewisu.edu
Phone: (815) 836-5250 Toll-free number: (800) 897-9000
Fax: (815) 836-5002
Andrew Sison, Dean of Admission, Lewis University, One University Parkway, Romeoville, IL 60446-2200

Lexington College
Chicago, Illinois
www.lexingtoncollege.edu **CB code: 3843**

- Private 4-year hospitality management college for women affiliated with Roman Catholic Church
- Commuter campus in very large city
- 60 degree-seeking undergraduates
- 55% of applicants admitted
- SAT or ACT, application essay required

General. Founded in 1977. Regionally accredited. **Degrees:** 5 bachelor's, 4 associate awarded. **Location:** Downtown. **Calendar:** Semester. **Full-time faculty:** 6 total. **Part-time faculty:** 15 total. **Class size:** 100% < 20. **Special facilities:** Culinary demonstration laboratory, computer laboratory.

Freshman class profile. 75 applied, 41 admitted, 24 enrolled.

Mid 50% test scores		**Out-of-state:**	8%
ACT composite:	19-25		

Basis for selection. School achievement record, essay, and interview most important. Work experience considered. **Homeschooled:** Letter of recommendation (nonparent) required. Must submit GED with scores.

High school preparation. 10 units recommended. Recommended units include English 4, mathematics 2, social studies 2 and science 2.

2008-2009 Annual costs. Tuition/fees: $22,800. Room/board: $8,000. Books/supplies: $750. Personal expenses: $400.

2008-2009 Financial aid. All financial aid based on need. **Additional information:** Work-study is available.

Application procedures. Admission: No deadline. $30 fee, may be waived for applicants with need. Admission notification on a rolling basis. **Financial aid:** Priority date 5/15; no closing date. FAFSA required. Applicants notified on a rolling basis starting 7/1; must reply within 2 week(s) of notification.

Academics. Special study options: Cooperative education, independent study, internships, study abroad. **Credit/placement by examination:** AP, CLEP, institutional tests. **Support services:** Remedial instruction, study skills assistance, tutoring.

Majors. Business: Business admin, hotel/motel admin, restaurant/food services. **Family/consumer sciences:** Institutional food production.

Computing on campus. 30 workstations in library, computer center. Online library, wireless network available.

Student life. Freshman orientation: Mandatory. Preregistration for classes offered. 2-day program before classes begin. **Activities:** Student government, student newspaper, campus ministry.

Student services. Chaplain/spiritual director, career counseling, student employment services, financial aid counseling, personal counseling, placement for graduates.

Contact. E-mail: admissions@lexingtoncollege.edu
Phone: (312) 226-6294 Toll-free number: (866) 647-3093
Fax: (312) 226-6405
Cynthia Selling, Director of Enrollment and Communication, Lexington College, 310 South Peoria Street, Suite 512, Chicago, IL 60607-3534

Lincoln Christian College and Seminary
Lincoln, Illinois
www.lccs.edu **CB code: 1405**

- Private 4-year Bible and seminary college affiliated with Church of Christ
- Residential campus in large town
- 672 degree-seeking undergraduates
- 339 graduate students
- SAT or ACT with writing, application essay required
- 48% graduate within 6 years

General. Founded in 1944. Regionally accredited; also accredited by ABHE, ATS. **Degrees:** 97 bachelor's, 8 associate awarded; master's, doctoral, first professional offered. **Location:** 30 miles from Springfield. **Calendar:** Semester, limited summer session. **Full-time faculty:** 44 total; 54% have terminal degrees, 7% minority, 20% women. **Part-time faculty:** 43 total; 9% have terminal degrees, 2% minority, 44% women. **Class size:** 77% < 20, 15% 20-39, 2% 40-49, 5% 50-99.

Freshman class profile. 193 enrolled.

Mid 50% test scores		**GPA 2.0-2.99:**	31%
ACT composite:	20-27	**Return as sophomores:**	67%
GPA 3.75 or higher:	19%	**Out-of-state:**	31%
GPA 3.50-3.74:	15%	**Live on campus:**	100%
GPA 3.0-3.49:	35%		

Basis for selection. Recommendation of applicant's church leaders as to suitability for church-related vocations very important. High school record (core courses) and ACT scores also considered. Subscores of writing and English, application essay also important. Interview recommended. Audition required of music majors. **Homeschooled:** Transcript of courses and grades, interview, letter of recommendation (nonparent) required. List of involvement outside of education/academics required. **Learning Disabled:** Students with learning disabilities usually recommended to academic resource center.

High school preparation. 17 units recommended. Recommended units include English 4, mathematics 3, social studies 3, history 3, science 2 and foreign language 2.

2009-2010 Annual costs. Tuition/fees (projected): $13,020. Room/board: $5,623. Books/supplies: $600. Personal expenses: $1,700.

Financial aid. Non-need-based: Scholarships awarded for academics.

Application procedures. Admission: No deadline. $25 fee, may be waived for applicants with need. Admission notification on a rolling basis. **Financial aid:** Priority date 8/10; no closing date. FAFSA, institutional form required. Applicants notified on a rolling basis starting 3/1; must reply within 2 week(s) of notification.

Academics. Special study options: Distance learning, double major, honors, independent study, internships, study abroad, teacher certification program, weekend college. Teacher preparatory program through University of Illinois at Springfield, Illinois State University, and Greenville College; study abroad opportunities include the CCCU-BestSemester program. **Credit/placement by examination:** AP, CLEP, ACT, institutional tests. **Support services:** Learning center, reduced course load, remedial instruction, study skills assistance, tutoring, writing center.

Majors. Business: Business admin. **Communications:** Media studies. **Education:** Early childhood, secondary. **Philosophy/religion:** Religion. **Psychology:** General. **Theology:** Bible, missionary, religious ed, sacred music, theology, youth ministry.

Most popular majors. Business/marketing 10%, education 7%, theological studies 78%.

Computing on campus. 51 workstations in library, computer center, student center. Dormitories wired for high-speed internet access and linked to campus network. Commuter students can connect to campus network.

Four-Year Colleges

Online course registration, online library, helpline, repair service, wireless network available.

Student life. **Freshman orientation:** Mandatory, $250 fee. Preregistration for classes offered. **Policies:** Religious observance required. **Housing:** Guaranteed on-campus for all undergraduates. Single-sex dorms, apartments, wellness housing available. $150 fully refundable deposit, deadline 8/10. **Activities:** Campus ministries, choral groups, drama, international student organizations, music ensembles, musical theater, student government, student newspaper, volunteer groups in local health care institutions, missions interest groups, Christian service and outreach groups.

Athletics. NCCAA. **Intercollegiate:** Baseball M, basketball, soccer M, softball W, volleyball W. **Intramural:** Badminton W, basketball M, football (non-tackle), soccer, volleyball. **Team name:** Preachers.

Student services. Adult student services, student employment services, financial aid counseling, health services, personal counseling. **Physically disabled:** Services for visually, hearing impaired. **Learning disabled:** Comprehensive services available.

Contact. E-mail: coladmis@lccs.edu
Phone: (217) 732-3168 ext. 2251 Toll-free number: (888) 522-5228
Fax: (217) 732-4199
Lynn Laughlin, Director of Admissions, Lincoln Christian College and Seminary, 100 Campus View Drive, Lincoln, IL 62656-2167

Loyola University Chicago

Chicago, Illinois — **CB member**
www.luc.edu — **CB code: 1412**

- Private 4-year university affiliated with Roman Catholic Church
- Residential campus in very large city
- 9,586 degree-seeking undergraduates: 5% part-time, 65% women, 4% African American, 12% Asian American, 10% Hispanic American, 1% international
- 5,429 degree-seeking graduate students
- 74% of applicants admitted
- SAT or ACT (ACT writing optional) required
- 66% graduate within 6 years

General. Founded in 1870. Regionally accredited. Extensive degree program for returning adults. Lake Shore and Water Tower campuses in Chicago, and Medical Center campus in suburbs. **Degrees:** 2,391 bachelor's awarded; master's, doctoral, first professional offered. **ROTC:** Army, Naval, Air Force. **Location:** Downtown. **Calendar:** Semester, extensive summer session. **Full-time faculty:** 597 total; 97% have terminal degrees, 10% minority, 47% women. **Part-time faculty:** 768 total; 13% minority, 54% women. **Class size:** 29% < 20, 38% 20-39, 20% 40-49, 12% 50-99, 2% >100. **Special facilities:** Gallery of medieval and renaissance art, job resource center for nursing, seismograph station, electron microscope, theater, art museum, language resource center.

Freshman class profile. 17,287 applied, 12,755 admitted, 2,176 enrolled.

Mid 50% test scores			
SAT critical reading:	540-650	Rank in top quarter:	70%
SAT math:	530-640	Rank in top tenth:	34%
SAT writing:	540-630	End year in good standing:	98%
ACT composite:	24-29	Return as sophomores:	84%
GPA 3.75 or higher:	31%	Out-of-state:	45%
GPA 3.50-3.74:	34%	Live on campus:	89%
GPA 3.0-3.49:	33%	International:	1%
GPA 2.0-2.99:	2%	Fraternities:	3%
		Sororities:	8%

Basis for selection. GPA, test scores, and rigor of high school curriculum important. Interview recommended. Essay required for honors program applicants.

High school preparation. College-preparatory program required. 15 units required; 20 recommended. Required and recommended units include English 4, mathematics 3-4, social studies 2, history 1-2, science 3, foreign language 2 and academic electives 3. Additional requirements for certain majors.

2008-2009 Annual costs. Tuition/fees: $29,486. Room/board: $10,490. Books/supplies: $1,200. Personal expenses: $1,600.

2007-2008 Financial aid. **Need-based:** 1,748 full-time freshmen applied for aid; 1,475 were judged to have need; 1,470 of these received aid. Average need met was 83%. Average scholarship/grant was $15,514; average loan $3,849. 60% of total undergraduate aid awarded as scholarships/grants, 40% as loans/jobs. **Non-need-based:** Awarded to 2,057 full-time undergraduates, including 537 freshmen. Scholarships awarded for academics, athletics, leadership, music/drama, religious affiliation.

Application procedures. **Admission:** Priority date 4/1; no deadline. $25 fee, may be waived for applicants with need, free for online applicants. Admission notification on a rolling basis beginning on or about 10/1. Must reply by May 1 or within 2 week(s) if notified thereafter. Honors program applicants must apply by March 1. **Financial aid:** Priority date 3/1; no closing date. FAFSA required. Applicants notified on a rolling basis starting 2/15; must reply within 3 week(s) of notification.

Academics. **Special study options:** Accelerated study, combined bachelor's/graduate degree, distance learning, double major, dual enrollment of high school students, exchange student, honors, independent study, internships, study abroad, teacher certification program, Washington semester. School of professional studies offers part-time evening programs leading to bachelor's degrees; cooperative programs with Erikson Institute for Early Education and St. Joseph's Seminary; study abroad in Italy and Mexico available. **Credit/placement by examination:** AP, CLEP, IB, SAT, ACT, institutional tests. 64 credit hours maximum toward bachelor's degree. **Support services:** Learning center, pre-admission summer program, reduced course load, study skills assistance, tutoring, writing center.

Majors. **Area/ethnic studies:** African-American, women's. **Biology:** General, biochemistry, bioinformatics. **Business:** Accounting, business admin, entrepreneurial studies, finance, human resources, international, management information systems, managerial economics, marketing, office management, operations, organizational behavior. **Communications:** General, journalism. **Computer sciences:** General, information technology, security. **Conservation:** Environmental science. **Education:** Bilingual, early childhood, elementary, mathematics, secondary, special. **Foreign languages:** Ancient Greek, classics, French, German, Italian, Latin, linguistics, Spanish. **Health:** Clinical lab science, clinical nutrition, health care admin, nursing (RN). **History:** General. **Interdisciplinary:** Behavioral sciences, math/computer science. **Math:** General, statistics. **Philosophy/religion:** Philosophy. **Physical sciences:** Chemistry, physics. **Protective services:** Criminal justice, forensics. **Psychology:** General. **Public administration:** General, human services, social work. **Social sciences:** Anthropology, international relations, political science, sociology. **Theology:** Religious ed, theology. **Visual/performing arts:** Art history/conservation, design, dramatic, studio arts. **Other:** International cinema and video.

Most popular majors. Biology 9%, business/marketing 21%, communications/journalism 7%, health sciences 12%, psychology 10%, social sciences 13%.

Computing on campus. 800 workstations in library, computer center, student center. Dormitories wired for high-speed internet access and linked to campus network. Commuter students can connect to campus network. Online course registration, online library, helpline, repair service, student web hosting, wireless network available.

Student life. **Freshman orientation:** Mandatory, $250 fee. Preregistration for classes offered. 2-day orientation program at Lake Shore campus. **Housing:** Guaranteed on-campus for freshmen. Coed dorms, special housing for disabled, apartments, wellness housing available. $250 nonrefundable deposit, deadline 5/1. 24-hour quiet facility available. **Activities:** Bands, campus ministries, choral groups, drama, film society, literary magazine, music ensembles, musical theater, radio station, student government, student newspaper, Agape Christian Fellowship, College Republicans, College Democrats, international club, student environmental alliance, Loyola Lutherans, Graduate Students of Color Alliance.

Athletics. NCAA. **Intercollegiate:** Basketball, cheerleading, cross-country, golf, soccer, softball W, track and field, volleyball. **Intramural:** Badminton, basketball, football (non-tackle), racquetball, soccer, table tennis, tennis, volleyball. **Team name:** Ramblers.

Student services. Adult student services, alcohol/substance abuse counseling, chaplain/spiritual director, career counseling, student employment services, financial aid counseling, health services, minority student services, on-campus daycare, personal counseling, placement for graduates, veterans' counselor. **Physically disabled:** Services for visually, speech, hearing impaired.

Contact. E-mail: admission@luc.edu
Phone: (312) 915-6500 Toll-free number: (800) 262-2373
Fax: (312) 915-7216
Lori Greene, Director of Admissions, Loyola University Chicago, 820 North Michigan Avenue, Chicago, IL 60611-9810

MacMurray College

Jacksonville, Illinois — **CB member**
www.mac.edu — **CB code: 1435**

- Private 4-year liberal arts college affiliated with United Methodist Church
- Residential campus in large town

- 581 degree-seeking undergraduates
- 50% of applicants admitted
- SAT or ACT (ACT writing optional) required

General. Founded in 1846. Regionally accredited. **Degrees:** 126 bachelor's, 5 associate awarded. **Location:** 30 miles from Springfield. **Calendar:** Semester, limited summer session. **Full-time faculty:** 31 total. **Part-time faculty:** 31 total. **Class size:** 59% < 20, 39% 20-39, 2% 40-49, 1% 50-99.

Freshman class profile. 860 applied, 429 admitted, 90 enrolled.

Mid 50% test scores		**GPA 2.0-2.99:**	49%
SAT critical reading:	370-470	**Rank in top quarter:**	18%
SAT math:	430-500	**Rank in top tenth:**	8%
SAT writing:	340-430	**Out-of-state:**	13%
ACT composite:	17-23	**Live on campus:**	86%
GPA 3.75 or higher:	10%	**Fraternities:**	5%
GPA 3.50-3.74:	7%	**Sororities:**	20%
GPA 3.0-3.49:	27%		

Basis for selection. 23 ACT, class ranking in top 25%, or 20 ACT and class ranking in top 50% important. Applicants with 20-22 ACT and in lower 50% of class, or 17-19 ACT (with no subtest score below 16) and 2.0 GPA reviewed by faculty admission committee. 20 ACT required for nursing applicants. SAT results (equivalent to ACT cutoffs) considered. Participation in school, community, and church activities, and recommendations important. Interview recommended for academically deficient applicants. Audition recommended for music scholarship. Portfolio recommended for art scholarship.

High school preparation. 17 units recommended. Recommended units include English 4, mathematics 3, social studies 2, history 3, science 3 (laboratory 2) and foreign language 2.

2008-2009 Annual costs. Tuition/fees: $17,450. Room/board: $6,995. Books/supplies: $1,000. Personal expenses: $900.

2008-2009 Financial aid. Need-based: 93% of total undergraduate aid awarded as scholarships/grants, 7% as loans/jobs. **Non-need-based:** Scholarships awarded for academics, alumni affiliation, art, leadership, music/drama, religious affiliation. **Additional information:** Merit scholarships for accepted, enrolled freshman based on academic record. Need-based program meets 100% of direct tuition charges after family contribution and financial aid.

Application procedures. Admission: Priority date 5/1; no deadline. No application fee. Admission notification on a rolling basis beginning on or about 9/1. **Financial aid:** Priority date 5/1; no closing date. FAFSA required. Applicants notified on a rolling basis starting 2/1; must reply within 2 week(s) of notification.

Academics. Special study options: Accelerated study, combined bachelor's/graduate degree, cooperative education, cross-registration, double major, dual enrollment of high school students, exchange student, independent study, internships, liberal arts/career combination, study abroad, teacher certification program, Washington semester. 3-2 programs in engineering with Washington University (MO) and Columbia University (NY). **Credit/placement by examination:** AP, CLEP, IB, institutional tests. 32 credit hours maximum toward bachelor's degree. **Support services:** Learning center, reduced course load, remedial instruction, study skills assistance, tutoring, writing center.

Majors. Biology: General. **Business:** Accounting, business admin, finance, management information systems. **Communications:** Journalism. **Computer sciences:** General, computer science. **Education:** Biology, Deaf/hearing impaired, elementary, emotionally handicapped, English, history, learning disabled, mathematics, music, physical, secondary, Spanish, special. **Engineering:** General. **Foreign languages:** French, sign language interpretation, Spanish. **Health:** Predental, premedicine, preveterinary. **History:** General. **Math:** General. **Parks/recreation:** Sports admin. **Philosophy/religion:** Philosophy, religion. **Physical sciences:** Chemistry, physics. **Psychology:** General. **Public administration:** Social work. **Social sciences:** International relations, political science. **Visual/performing arts:** Art, dramatic. **Other:** Student personnel services.

Most popular majors. Business/marketing 16%, education 22%, health sciences 11%, psychology 6%, security/protective services 9%.

Computing on campus. 75 workstations in dormitories, library, computer center. Dormitories wired for high-speed internet access and linked to campus network. Online library available.

Student life. Freshman orientation: Mandatory. Preregistration for classes offered. Two-day acclimation to campus life held prior to start of classes. **Housing:** Guaranteed on-campus for all undergraduates. Coed dorms, single-sex dorms, special housing for disabled, wellness housing available. $150 deposit. **Activities:** Choral groups, dance, drama, literary magazine, music ensembles, musical theater, student government, student newspaper, NAACP, Alpha Phi Omega, Circle-K, Holy Fools, Newman Club.

Athletics. NCAA. **Intercollegiate:** Baseball M, basketball, cross-country, football (tackle) M, golf, soccer, softball W, tennis, volleyball W, wrestling M. **Intramural:** Basketball, cheerleading, cross-country, soccer, table tennis, volleyball. **Team name:** Highlanders.

Student services. Alcohol/substance abuse counseling, chaplain/spiritual director, career counseling, student employment services, financial aid counseling, health services, personal counseling, placement for graduates. **Physically disabled:** Services for visually, hearing impaired.

Contact. E-mail: admissions@mac.edu
Phone: (217) 479-7056 Toll-free number: (800) 252-7485
Fax: (217) 291-0702
Robert LaVerriere, Director of Enrollment Services, MacMurray College, 447 East College Avenue, Jacksonville, IL 62650-2590

McKendree University

Lebanon, Illinois
www.mckendree.edu **CB code: 1456**

- Private 4-year university and liberal arts college affiliated with United Methodist Church
- Residential campus in small town
- 2,222 degree-seeking undergraduates: 27% part-time, 57% women, 13% African American, 1% Asian American, 2% Hispanic American, 2% international
- 866 degree-seeking graduate students
- 67% of applicants admitted
- SAT or ACT (ACT writing optional), application essay required
- 70% graduate within 6 years; 35% enter graduate study

General. Founded in 1828. Regionally accredited. **Degrees:** 587 bachelor's, 12 associate awarded; master's offered. **ROTC:** Army, Air Force. **Location:** 12 miles from Belleville, 23 miles from St. Louis. **Calendar:** Semester, limited summer session. **Full-time faculty:** 95 total; 77% have terminal degrees, 7% minority, 56% women. **Part-time faculty:** 243 total. **Class size:** 72% < 20, 28% 20-39. **Special facilities:** Networked faculty and classroom buildings, fine arts center with theatre.

Freshman class profile. 1,347 applied, 904 admitted, 309 enrolled.

Mid 50% test scores		**GPA 2.0-2.99:**	14%
SAT critical reading:	430-600	**Rank in top quarter:**	42%
SAT math:	410-620	**Rank in top tenth:**	18%
SAT writing:	430-550	**End year in good standing:**	85%
ACT composite:	20-28	**Return as sophomores:**	70%
GPA 3.75 or higher:	24%	**Out-of-state:**	11%
GPA 3.50-3.74:	21%	**Live on campus:**	82%
GPA 3.0-3.49:	41%	**International:**	3%

Basis for selection. Holistic approach to admissions; variety of criteria considered including GPA, rigor of secondary school record, standardized test scores, and interview, when possible. RN required of Nursing Completion Program applicants. Interviews recommended. Audition required of music majors and minors. Portfolio recommended for art majors. **Homeschooled:** Statement describing homeschool structure and mission, letter of recommendation (nonparent) required. Applicants must submit description of courses studied, 3 letters of recommendation (not including that of parents).

High school preparation. College-preparatory program recommended. 14 units recommended. Recommended units include English 4, mathematics 3, social studies 2, history 1, science 3 and foreign language 1.

2008-2009 Annual costs. Tuition/fees: $21,270. Room/board: $8,220. Books/supplies: $1,200. Personal expenses: $1,000.

2008-2009 Financial aid. Need-based: 295 full-time freshmen applied for aid; 269 were judged to have need; 267 of these received aid. Average need met was 87%. Average scholarship/grant was $16,620; average loan $3,502. 69% of total undergraduate aid awarded as scholarships/grants, 31% as loans/jobs. **Non-need-based:** Awarded to 544 full-time undergraduates, including 118 freshmen. Scholarships awarded for academics, alumni affiliation, art, athletics, leadership, minority status, music/drama, religious affiliation.

Application procedures. **Admission:** No deadline. $40 fee, may be waived for applicants with need, free for online applicants. Admission notification on a rolling basis beginning on or about 9/15. **Financial aid:** Priority date 5/31; no closing date. FAFSA required. Applicants notified on a rolling basis starting 3/1; must reply within 4 week(s) of notification.

Academics. **Special study options:** Accelerated study, combined bachelor's/graduate degree, cooperative education, distance learning, double major, external degree, honors, independent study, internships, liberal arts/career combination, student-designed major, study abroad, teacher certification program. 3-2 and 3-3 occupational therapy program with Washington University. **Credit/placement by examination:** AP, CLEP, IB, SAT, ACT, institutional tests. 36 credit hours maximum toward associate degree, 64 toward bachelor's. **Support services:** Learning center, reduced course load, remedial instruction, study skills assistance, tutoring, writing center.

Honors college/program. 3.6 GPA, 27 ACT, top 10% of class required; approximately 20 freshmen admitted.

Majors. **Biology:** General. **Business:** Accounting, business admin, management science, marketing. **Communications:** General. **Computer sciences:** General, computer science, information systems, information technology. **Education:** General, art, business, elementary, health, history, music, physical, science. **Health:** Athletic training, nursing (RN). **History:** General. **Liberal arts:** Arts/sciences. **Math:** General. **Philosophy/religion:** Philosophy, religion. **Physical sciences:** Chemistry. **Psychology:** General. **Social sciences:** General, economics, international relations, political science, sociology. **Visual/performing arts:** Studio arts.

Most popular majors. Business/marketing 37%, computer/information sciences 9%, education 11%, health sciences 11%, psychology 6%.

Computing on campus. 220 workstations in library, computer center, student center. Dormitories wired for high-speed internet access and linked to campus network. Commuter students can connect to campus network. Online course registration, online library, helpline, repair service, student web hosting, wireless network available.

Student life. **Freshman orientation:** Mandatory, $50 fee. Preregistration for classes offered. Three day program held weekend before start of classes. **Policies:** Students are required to live on campus unless 21 years of age, of senior class standing, married, commuting from the home of a parent or legal guardian, or a veteran with at least two years active military duty. **Housing:** Guaranteed on-campus for all undergraduates. Coed dorms, special housing for disabled, apartments, wellness housing available. $200 fully refundable deposit. **Activities:** Bands, campus ministries, choral groups, dance, drama, film society, international student organizations, literary magazine, music ensembles, Model UN, musical theater, radio station, student government, student newspaper, Campus Christian Fellowship, Students Against Social Injustice, black student organization, service organizations, resident hall association, Intergreek Council, Community Service Fellows.

Athletics. NAIA. **Intercollegiate:** Baseball M, basketball, bowling, cheerleading, cross-country, football (tackle) M, golf, ice hockey, soccer, softball W, tennis, track and field, volleyball W, wrestling M. **Intramural:** Basketball, football (non-tackle), softball, volleyball. **Team name:** Bearcats.

Student services. Adult student services, alcohol/substance abuse counseling, chaplain/spiritual director, career counseling, student employment services, financial aid counseling, health services, minority student services, personal counseling, placement for graduates, veterans' counselor. **Physically disabled:** Services for visually, speech, hearing impaired.

Contact. E-mail: inquiry@mckendree.edu
Phone: (618) 537-6831 Toll-free number: (800) 232-7228 ext. 6831
Fax: (618) 537-6496
Chris Hall, Vice President for Admission and Financial Aid, McKendree University, 701 College Road, Lebanon, IL 62254

Midstate College

Peoria, Illinois
www.midstate.edu **CB code: 3329**

- For-profit 4-year business college
- Commuter campus in small city
- 584 degree-seeking undergraduates: 54% part-time, 80% women, 22% African American, 2% Hispanic American
- 90% of applicants admitted
- Application essay, interview required

General. Founded in 1888. Regionally accredited. **Degrees:** 37 bachelor's, 79 associate awarded. **Location:** 165 miles from Chicago. **Calendar:** Quarter, extensive summer session. **Full-time faculty:** 25 total; 12% have terminal degrees, 8% minority, 64% women. **Part-time faculty:** 38 total; 8% minority, 55% women.

Freshman class profile. 42 applied, 38 admitted, 30 enrolled.

Basis for selection. Rigorous secondary school program and quality of application essay and interview important. Extracurricular acitivities, character and relationships to alumae considered. Entrance exam, including writing sample, and math placement tests administered to all applicants. Necessity for remedial support determined from results.

2009-2010 Annual costs. Tuition/fees (projected): $12,506. Fees vary according to program.

2008-2009 Financial aid. **Additional information:** Work-study program available.

Application procedures. **Admission:** No deadline. $25 fee. Admission notification on a rolling basis. **Financial aid:** No deadline. FAFSA, institutional form required. Applicants notified on a rolling basis; must reply within 4 week(s) of notification.

Academics. **Special study options:** Distance learning, double major, dual enrollment of high school students, internships. **Credit/placement by examination:** AP, CLEP, institutional tests. 24 credit hours maximum toward associate degree, 46 toward bachelor's. **Support services:** Learning center, reduced course load, remedial instruction, study skills assistance, tutoring.

Majors. **Business:** Accounting, business admin. **Computer sciences:** Information systems. **Health:** Medical records technology. **Legal studies:** Court reporting.

Computing on campus. 92 workstations in library, computer center. Commuter students can connect to campus network. Online library, helpline, repair service, wireless network available.

Student life. **Freshman orientation:** Mandatory. Preregistration for classes offered. Held first day of each quarter. **Activities:** Student government.

Student services. Career counseling, student employment services, financial aid counseling, personal counseling, placement for graduates, veterans' counselor.

Contact. E-mail: admissions@midstate.edu
Phone: (309) 692-4092 Toll-free number: (800) 251-4299
Fax: (309) 692-3893
Jessica Hancock, Director of Admissions, Midstate College, 411 West Northmoor Road, Peoria, IL 61614-3558

Millikin University

Decatur, Illinois **CB member**
www.millikin.edu **CB code: 1470**

- Private 4-year university affiliated with Presbyterian Church (USA)
- Residential campus in small city
- 2,238 degree-seeking undergraduates: 5% part-time, 62% women, 9% African American, 1% Asian American, 3% Hispanic American, 1% international
- 46 degree-seeking graduate students
- 89% of applicants admitted
- SAT or ACT (ACT writing optional) required
- 67% graduate within 6 years; 19% enter graduate study

General. Founded in 1901. Regionally accredited. **Degrees:** 544 bachelor's awarded; master's offered. **Location:** 180 miles from Chicago, 120 miles from St. Louis. **Calendar:** Semester, limited summer session. **Full-time faculty:** 158 total; 82% have terminal degrees, 10% minority, 49% women. **Part-time faculty:** 133 total; 20% have terminal degrees, 10% minority, 63% women. **Class size:** 67% < 20, 31% 20-39, less than 1% 40-49, 2% 50-99. **Special facilities:** Porcelain, glass and decorative arts museum, 32-track recording studio, computer imaging center, greenhouse, observatory, performance center, 24-hour computer labs, video-conferencing classroom, proscenium theater, science center, 3-D arts building, student-run art gallery, student-owned and operated publishing company, student-operated record label.

Freshman class profile. 2,820 applied, 2,522 admitted, 484 enrolled.

Mid 50% test scores			
SAT critical reading:	490-620	GPA 2.0-2.99:	27%
SAT math:	500-630	Rank in top quarter:	48%
SAT writing:	500-620	Rank in top tenth:	19%
ACT composite:	20-24	End year in good standing:	86%
GPA 3.75 or higher:	26%	Return as sophomores:	76%
GPA 3.50-3.74:	20%	Out-of-state:	14%
GPA 3.0-3.49:	27%	Live on campus:	87%
		International:	2%

Basis for selection. School achievement record most important. Class rank, GPA, recommendation, test scores important. Applicant should rank in top half of class. Character references considered. Interview recommended. Audition required of music, music/theater majors. Portfolio required of art majors.

High school preparation. College-preparatory program recommended. 16 units required. Required and recommended units include English 4, mathematics 3, social studies 2, history 2, science 3 and foreign language 2.

2008-2009 Annual costs. Tuition/fees: $25,295. Room/board: $7,485. Books/supplies: $1,000. Personal expenses: $1,250.

2007-2008 Financial aid. Need-based: 447 full-time freshmen applied for aid; 378 were judged to have need; 378 of these received aid. Average need met was 92%. Average scholarship/grant was $7,714; average loan $3,976. 62% of total undergraduate aid awarded as scholarships/grants, 38% as loans/jobs. **Non-need-based:** Awarded to 1,713 full-time undergraduates, including 447 freshmen. Scholarships awarded for academics, alumni affiliation, art, leadership, minority status, music/drama.

Application procedures. Admission: Priority date 5/1; no deadline. No application fee. Admission notification on a rolling basis beginning on or about 9/15. **Financial aid:** Priority date 3/15; no closing date. FAFSA required. Applicants notified on a rolling basis starting 3/15; must reply by 5/1 or within 4 week(s) of notification.

Academics. Small business consulting and accelerated adult education available. **Special study options:** Accelerated study, combined bachelor's/graduate degree, double major, exchange student, honors, independent study, internships, student-designed major, study abroad, teacher certification program, United Nations semester, urban semester, Washington semester. **Credit/placement by examination:** AP, CLEP, IB, ACT, institutional tests. 30 credit hours maximum toward bachelor's degree. To receive CLEP credit student must not have attended secondary school in the past 3 years; CLEP credit cannot count in the major and may not be used if the equivalent course has been attempted. **Support services:** Learning center, reduced course load, study skills assistance, tutoring, writing center.

Majors. Biology: General, molecular. **Business:** Accounting, business admin, entrepreneurial studies, finance, international, management information systems, marketing. **Communications:** General. **Education:** Art, biology, chemistry, early childhood, elementary, English, mathematics, music, physical, social science. **Foreign languages:** Spanish. **Health:** Art therapy, athletic training, nursing (RN), predental, premedicine, prepharmacy, preveterinary. **History:** General. **Legal studies:** Prelaw. **Math:** Applied. **Parks/recreation:** Sports admin. **Philosophy/religion:** Philosophy. **Physical sciences:** Chemistry, physics. **Protective services:** Law enforcement admin. **Psychology:** General. **Public administration:** Human services. **Social sciences:** International relations, political science, sociology. **Visual/performing arts:** Commercial/advertising art, dramatic, music performance, piano/organ, studio arts, theater design, voice/opera. **Other:** Management and organizational leadership, Multi-interdiscipinary studies.

Most popular majors. Business/marketing 21%, education 14%, health sciences 10%, visual/performing arts 18%.

Computing on campus. 198 workstations in dormitories, library, computer center, student center. Dormitories wired for high-speed internet access and linked to campus network. Commuter students can connect to campus network. Online course registration, online library, helpline, student web hosting, wireless network available.

Student life. Freshman orientation: Mandatory, $100 fee. Held 5 days before beginning of classes. **Housing:** Guaranteed on-campus for freshmen. Coed dorms, single-sex dorms, special housing for disabled, apartments, fraternity/sorority housing, wellness housing available. $150 fully refundable deposit, deadline 5/1. Learning communities available. **Activities:** Bands, choral groups, dance, drama, film society, international student organizations, literary magazine, music ensembles, Model UN, musical theater, opera, radio station, student government, student newspaper, symphony orchestra, Black student union, Latin American student organization, Amnesty International, Multicultural Voices of Praise, Multicultural Affairs Roundtable, Young Republicans, Inter-Varsity Christian Fellowship, Newman Catholic Community, pagan student association, Fellowship of Christian Athletes.

Athletics. NCAA. **Intercollegiate:** Baseball M, basketball, cheerleading, cross-country, football (tackle) M, golf, soccer, softball W, swimming, tennis W, track and field, volleyball W. **Intramural:** Basketball, bowling, football (non-tackle), soccer, softball, table tennis, volleyball. **Team name:** Big Blue.

Student services. Adult student services, alcohol/substance abuse counseling, career counseling, services for economically disadvantaged, student employment services, financial aid counseling, health services, minority student services, personal counseling, placement for graduates, women's services. **Physically disabled:** Services for visually, speech impaired.

Contact. E-mail: admis@millikin.edu
Phone: (217) 424-6210 Toll-free number: (800) 373-7733
Fax: (217) 425-4669
Stacey Hubbard, Dean of Admission and Financial Aid, Millikin University, 1184 West Main Street, Decatur, IL 62522-2084

Monmouth College

Monmouth, Illinois — **CB member**
www.monm.edu — **CB code: 1484**

- Private 4-year liberal arts college affiliated with Presbyterian Church (USA)
- Residential campus in large town
- 1,318 degree-seeking undergraduates: 52% women, 4% African American, 1% Asian American, 4% Hispanic American, 1% Native American, 1% international
- 74% of applicants admitted
- SAT or ACT (ACT writing optional) required
- 66% graduate within 6 years

General. Founded in 1853. Regionally accredited. **Degrees:** 261 bachelor's awarded. **ROTC:** Army. **Location:** 180 miles from Chicago, 60 miles from Peoria. **Calendar:** Semester. **Full-time faculty:** 80 total; 76% have terminal degrees, 11% minority, 42% women. **Part-time faculty:** 46 total; 22% have terminal degrees, 6% minority, 50% women. **Class size:** 53% < 20, 45% 20-39, less than 1% 40-49, less than 1% 50-99. **Special facilities:** Ecological field station, biology field station, nature preserve, art and antiquities collection, collection of letters by U.S. First Ladies, Federal government documents repository.

Freshman class profile. 1,919 applied, 1,421 admitted, 426 enrolled.

Mid 50% test scores			
ACT composite:	20-25	Rank in top tenth:	13%
GPA 3.75 or higher:	19%	Out-of-state:	10%
GPA 3.50-3.74:	16%	Live on campus:	93%
GPA 3.0-3.49:	31%	International:	1%
GPA 2.0-2.99:	34%	Fraternities:	18%
Rank in top quarter:	39%	Sororities:	17%

Basis for selection. School achievement record most important, followed by recommendations of counselor and teacher, test scores, and interview. Interview and essay recommended.

High school preparation. College-preparatory program required. 14 units required; 22 recommended. Required and recommended units include English 4, mathematics 3-4, social studies 2-3, history 1-2, science 2-3 (laboratory 1-2) and foreign language 2-3.

2009-2010 Annual costs. Tuition/fees (projected): $25,400. Room/board: $7,300. Books/supplies: $650. Personal expenses: $400.

2008-2009 Financial aid. Need-based: 372 full-time freshmen applied for aid; 310 were judged to have need; 310 of these received aid. Average need met was 91%. Average scholarship/grant was $16,780; average loan $3,775. 79% of total undergraduate aid awarded as scholarships/grants, 21% as loans/jobs. **Non-need-based:** Awarded to 417 full-time undergraduates, including 125 freshmen. Scholarships awarded for academics, art, music/drama, ROTC.

Application procedures. Admission: No deadline. No application fee. Admission notification on a rolling basis beginning on or about 9/15. **Financial aid:** Priority date 3/1; no closing date. FAFSA required. Applicants notified on a rolling basis starting 3/1.

Academics. Special study options: Combined bachelor's/graduate degree, double major, honors, independent study, internships, liberal arts/career combination, student-designed major, study abroad, teacher certification program, urban semester, Washington semester. Off-campus programs in cooperation with Associated Colleges of the Midwest, institutional off-campus programs. **Credit/placement by examination:** AP, CLEP, IB, SAT,

ACT, institutional tests. 5 credit hours maximum toward bachelor's degree. **Support services:** Learning center, study skills assistance, tutoring, writing center.

Majors. **Biology:** General, biochemistry. **Business:** Accounting, business admin, international, management information systems, managerial economics. **Communications:** General, public relations. **Computer sciences:** General, computer science. **Conservation:** General, environmental science. **Education:** General, art, elementary, history, multi-level teacher, music, physical, science, secondary, social studies. **Foreign languages:** Ancient Greek, classics, French, Latin, Spanish. **History:** General. **Interdisciplinary:** Biopsychology. **Liberal arts:** Arts/sciences. **Math:** General. **Philosophy/religion:** Philosophy, religion. **Physical sciences:** Chemistry, physics. **Psychology:** General. **Social sciences:** Economics, international relations, political science, sociology. **Visual/performing arts:** Art, studio arts.

Most popular majors. Biology 6%, business/marketing 26%, communications/journalism 13%, education 14%, parks/recreation 7%, psychology 6%.

Computing on campus. 300 workstations in dormitories, library, computer center, student center. Dormitories wired for high-speed internet access and linked to campus network. Online course registration, online library, helpline, student web hosting, wireless network available.

Student life. **Freshman orientation:** Mandatory, $110 fee. Preregistration for classes offered. **Housing:** Guaranteed on-campus for all undergraduates. Coed dorms, single-sex dorms, special housing for disabled, apartments, cooperative housing, fraternity/sorority housing, wellness housing available. $150 deposit, deadline 5/1. **Activities:** Bands, campus ministries, choral groups, dance, drama, film society, international student organizations, literary magazine, music ensembles, musical theater, radio station, student government, student newspaper, symphony orchestra, TV station, Coalition for Ethnic Awareness, Christian fellowship groups, interdenominational religious group, Students Organized for Service.

Athletics. NCAA. **Intercollegiate:** Baseball M, basketball, cheerleading, cross-country, football (tackle) M, golf, soccer, softball W, swimming, tennis, track and field, volleyball W. **Intramural:** Badminton, basketball, cross-country, golf, soccer, softball, swimming, tennis, track and field, volleyball, weight lifting. **Team name:** Fighting Scots.

Student services. Alcohol/substance abuse counseling, chaplain/spiritual director, career counseling, student employment services, financial aid counseling, health services, minority student services, personal counseling, placement for graduates.

Contact. E-mail: admit@monm.edu
Phone: (309) 457-2131 Toll-free number: (800) 747-2687
Fax: (309) 457-2141
Christine Johnston, Dean of Admission, Monmouth College, 700 East Broadway, Monmouth, IL 61462-1998

Moody Bible Institute
Chicago, Illinois
www.moody.edu **CB code: 1486**

- Private 4-year Bible college affiliated with interdenominational tradition
- Residential campus in very large city
- 1,821 full-time, degree-seeking undergraduates
- SAT or ACT with writing, application essay required

General. Founded in 1886. Regionally accredited; also accredited by ABHE. **Degrees:** 352 bachelor's, 3 associate awarded; master's, first professional offered. **Location:** Downtown. **Calendar:** Semester, limited summer session. **Full-time faculty:** 78 total. **Part-time faculty:** 80 total.

Freshman class profile.

Out-of-state:	81%	Live on campus:	98%

Basis for selection. Rank in top half of graduating class and/or high school GPA above 2.0. Applicants must have been Christians for at least 1 year. Membership in Evangelical Protestant Church and recommendation from church leadership required. Interview recommended. Audition required of music majors. **Homeschooled:** ACT plus GED or SAT required.

High school preparation. 12 units recommended.

2008-2009 Annual costs. Undergraduate students in the BA and BMus programs on main campus are not charged tuition. Undergraduate students taking courses through distance learning programs (ABS, BSBS) and in BSMAT (Bachelor of Science in Missionary Aviation) program pay tuition of $220 per credit hour. Students pay required fees of $1,569 and room/board of $8,040 per year. Books/supplies: $600. Personal expenses: $500.

Financial aid. All financial aid based on need. **Additional information:** Aid available to upperclassmen is based on private and not federal/state sources.

Application procedures. **Admission:** Priority date 12/1; deadline 3/1 (postmark date). $35 fee, may be waived for applicants with need. Admission notification 4/1. Must reply by May 1 or within 6 week(s) if notified thereafter. **Financial aid:** No deadline.

Academics. **Special study options:** Distance learning, double major, dual enrollment of high school students, external degree, independent study, internships, study abroad, teacher certification program. Exchange program with International Christian College, Scotland; European Bible Institute, France; Belfast Bible College, Ireland; Spanish Bible Institute, Barcelona, Spain. **Credit/placement by examination:** AP, CLEP, IB, institutional tests. 9 credit hours maximum toward associate degree, 12 toward bachelor's. **Support services:** Learning center, pre-admission summer program, reduced course load, study skills assistance, tutoring.

Majors. **Communications:** General. **Education:** General, ESL. **Foreign languages:** Ancient Greek, Hebrew, linguistics. **Mechanic/repair:** Aircraft. **Philosophy/religion:** Judaic, religion. **Theology:** Bible, missionary, religious ed, sacred music, theology. **Visual/performing arts:** Music performance, music theory/composition, piano/organ, voice/opera.

Computing on campus. 40 workstations in library, computer center. Dormitories linked to campus network. Commuter students can connect to campus network. Repair service available.

Student life. **Freshman orientation:** Mandatory. **Policies:** Religious observance required. **Housing:** Guaranteed on-campus for all undergraduates. Single-sex dorms, apartments available. $100 deposit, deadline 5/1. **Activities:** Concert band, choral groups, drama, music ensembles, radio station, student government, student newspaper, symphony orchestra, Student Missionary Fellowship, Gospel Teams, Afro Awareness Fellowship, International Student Fellowship, Big Brother/Big Sister Program, pre-aviation club, married students fellowship, residence activities council, Hispanic Student Fellowship.

Athletics. NCCAA. **Intercollegiate:** Basketball, soccer M, volleyball. **Intramural:** Badminton, basketball, cross-country, football (non-tackle) M, racquetball, soccer, swimming, table tennis, volleyball, water polo. **Team name:** Archers.

Student services. Career counseling, student employment services, health services, minority student services, on-campus daycare, personal counseling, placement for graduates, veterans' counselor. **Physically disabled:** Services for visually impaired. **Learning disabled:** Comprehensive services available.

Contact. E-mail: admissions@moody.edu
Phone: (312) 329-4400 Toll-free number: (800) 967-4624
Fax: (312) 329-8987
Charles Dresser, Dean of Enrollment Management, Moody Bible Institute, 820 North La Salle Boulevard, Chicago, IL 60610

National University of Health Sciences
Lombard, Illinois
www.nuhs.edu **CB code: 1567**

- Private 4-year university and health science college
- Commuter campus in large town
- 182 degree-seeking undergraduates
- 584 graduate students

General. Regionally accredited. **Degrees:** 49 bachelor's awarded; master's, first professional offered. **Location:** 20 miles from Chicago. **Calendar:** Trimester, extensive summer session. **Full-time faculty:** 41 total; 93% have terminal degrees, 22% women. **Part-time faculty:** 12 total; 100% have terminal degrees, 25% women. **Special facilities:** Learning resource center, medical library, onsite clinic.

Basis for selection. Associate degree and certificate programs require 2.0 GPA or GED; bachelor's completion program in biomedical science requires minimum of 60 semester hours of prerequisite courses. Must be 18 years of age and of good moral character. Applicants to BS degree completion program may be considered for conditional acceptance as a non-degree student for one semester to determine academic eligibility.

2008-2009 Annual costs. $17,997 represents average tuition cost for academic year 2008-2009 ($8,498 per trimester). Room only charge ranges from $2,974 to $6,522 for academic year.

Financial aid. Additional information: Massage Therapy certificate program is eligible for Title IV financial aid. Program is half-time and qualifies for half-time and less-than-half-time Pell grants, federal work-study, FSEOG, federal Perkins grants, and prorated federal Stafford loans.

Application procedures. Admission: Closing date 8/1. $55 fee.

Academics. College of Professional Studies offers doctor of chiropractic, with a doctor of naturopathy, and master's degrees in acupuncture and Oriental Medicine. Primary undergraduate enrollment is in certificate programs in massage therapy and chiropractic assistance. Accelerated prerequisite program available for students needing to complete science entrance requirements. Bachelor of science completion program available. **Special study options:** Distance learning, dual enrollment of high school students, internships. **Credit/placement by examination:** CLEP. **Support services:** Learning center, tutoring.

Majors. Biology: Biomedical sciences.

Computing on campus. 75 workstations in library, computer center. Online course registration, helpline, student web hosting, wireless network available.

Student life. Freshman orientation: Mandatory. Preregistration for classes offered. **Policies:** Must be 21 to live on campus. **Housing:** Coed dorms available. Pets allowed in dorm rooms. **Activities:** Student government, student newspaper, student chiropractic organizations, professional sororities and fraternities, christian chiropractic association.

Athletics. Intramural: Basketball, golf, soccer, softball, tennis, volleyball.

Student services. Financial aid counseling, health services.

Contact. E-mail: admissions@nuhs.edu
Phone: (630) 889-6566 Toll-free number: (800) 826-6285
Fax: (630) 889-6554
Victoria Sweeney, Director of Communications and Enrollment Services, National University of Health Sciences, 200 East Roosevelt Road, Lombard, IL 60148-4583

National-Louis University

Chicago, Illinois — **CB member**
www.nl.edu — **CB code: 1551**

- Private 4-year university and teachers college
- Commuter campus in small city
- 1,701 degree-seeking undergraduates: 28% part-time, 78% women, 36% African American, 2% Asian American, 14% Hispanic American
- 4,555 degree-seeking graduate students
- 81% of applicants admitted
- SAT or ACT required

General. Founded in 1886. Regionally accredited. Additional in-state locations in Evanston, Wheeling, Lisle and Elgin. Field programs available on and off campus. Out-of-state campuses located in Milwaukee/Beloit, McLean, Washington DC, and Tampa. **Degrees:** 644 bachelor's awarded; master's, doctoral offered. **Location:** 10 miles from Chicago. **Calendar:** Quarter, limited summer session. **Full-time faculty:** 222 total; 67% have terminal degrees. **Part-time faculty:** 408 total. **Class size:** 91% < 20, 8% 20-39, less than 1% 40-49. **Special facilities:** Elementary demonstration school for practice teaching and observation.

Freshman class profile. 16 applied, 13 admitted, 13 enrolled.

Basis for selection. Rank in top half of high school class, score 19 ACT, 750 SAT (exclusive of Writing) and 2 letters of recommendation from counselors or teachers. Interview and essay recommended.

High school preparation. Recommended units include English 4, mathematics 3, social studies 3, science 2 (laboratory 1) and foreign language 2. 1 unit U.S. government or U.S. history recommended.

2008-2009 Annual costs. Tuition/fees: $18,075. Books/supplies: $992. Personal expenses: $1,305.

2007-2008 Financial aid. Non-need-based: Scholarships awarded for academics.

Application procedures. Admission: No deadline. $40 fee, may be waived for applicants with need. Admission notification on a rolling basis. **Financial aid:** Priority date 4/15; no closing date. FAFSA, institutional form required. Applicants notified on a rolling basis starting 5/1; must reply within 2 week(s) of notification.

Academics. Degree-completion programs available in allied health leadership, management, and applied behavioral science. Field classes offered evenings/weekends. **Special study options:** Accelerated study, combined bachelor's/graduate degree, distance learning, double major, dual enrollment of high school students, ESL, honors, independent study, internships, liberal arts/career combination, teacher certification program. **Credit/placement by examination:** AP, CLEP. 132 credit hours maximum toward bachelor's degree. **Support services:** Learning center, pre-admission summer program, reduced course load, remedial instruction, study skills assistance, tutoring, writing center.

Majors. Biology: General. **Business:** Accounting, business admin. **Computer sciences:** Information systems. **Education:** Early childhood, elementary. **Health:** Clinical lab science, health care admin, medical radiologic technology/radiation therapy, respiratory therapy technology, substance abuse counseling. **Interdisciplinary:** Behavioral sciences, biological/physical sciences. **Liberal arts:** Arts/sciences. **Math:** General, applied. **Psychology:** General. **Public administration:** Human services. **Social sciences:** General, anthropology, economics. **Visual/performing arts:** Art, dramatic.

Computing on campus. 500 workstations in library, computer center. Commuter students can connect to campus network. Online course registration, online library, helpline, repair service available.

Student life. Freshman orientation: Available. **Housing:** Coed dorms available. $50 deposit, deadline 7/30. **Activities:** Drama, musical theater, student government, student newspaper, Chinese club, Polish club, educational club, social science club, school psychology club, drama club, educational honorary society.

Student services. Adult student services, career counseling, student employment services, health services, personal counseling, placement for graduates. **Physically disabled:** Services for visually, speech, hearing impaired.

Contact. E-mail: admissions@nl.edu
Phone: (847) 947-5718 Toll-free number: (800) 443-5522 ext. 5718
Fax: (847) 465-5730
Ken Gilson, Director of Admissions & Registrar, National-Louis University, 122 South Michigan Avenue, Chicago, IL 60603

North Central College

Naperville, Illinois — **CB member**
www.northcentralcollege.edu — **CB code: 1555**

- Private 4-year liberal arts college affiliated with United Methodist Church
- Residential campus in small city
- 2,302 degree-seeking undergraduates: 6% part-time, 55% women, 3% African American, 3% Asian American, 5% Hispanic American, 1% international
- 299 degree-seeking graduate students
- 69% of applicants admitted
- SAT or ACT (ACT writing optional) required
- 63% graduate within 6 years

General. Founded in 1861. Regionally accredited. **Degrees:** 550 bachelor's awarded; master's offered. **ROTC:** Army, Air Force. **Location:** 25 miles from Chicago. **Calendar:** Quarter, limited summer session. **Full-time faculty:** 119 total; 87% have terminal degrees, 13% minority, 46% women. **Part-time faculty:** 109 total; 37% have terminal degrees, 7% minority, 56% women. **Class size:** 36% < 20, 61% 20-39, 1% 40-49, less than 1% 50-99. **Special facilities:** Fermi accelerator laboratory, Argonne laboratory, arboretum.

Freshman class profile. 2,575 applied, 1,764 admitted, 529 enrolled.

Mid 50% test scores		**GPA 3.0-3.49:**	30%
SAT critical reading:	520-640	**GPA 2.0-2.99:**	19%
SAT math:	510-630	**End year in good standing:**	87%
SAT writing:	500-620	**Return as sophomores:**	79%
ACT composite:	22-27	**Out-of-state:**	10%
GPA 3.75 or higher:	34%	**Live on campus:**	80%
GPA 3.50-3.74:	17%	**International:**	1%

Basis for selection. Academic record, SAT or ACT scores, and personal character all considered important. Interview and essay recommended for marginal students. **Homeschooled:** Interview required. Review of the student's portfolio and curriculum, writing sample, interview with the Director of Freshman Admission, interview with a faculty member may be required. **Learning Disabled:** Students who self-identify are referred to the academic support center.

High school preparation. College-preparatory program required. 16 units required; 19 recommended. Required and recommended units include English 4, mathematics 3, social studies 2, history 1, science 3 (laboratory 1-3), foreign language 3 and academic electives 3.

2008-2009 Annual costs. Tuition/fees: $25,938. Room/board: $8,217. Books/supplies: $1,200. Personal expenses: $1,182.

2008-2009 Financial aid. Need-based: 462 full-time freshmen applied for aid; 398 were judged to have need; 395 of these received aid. Average need met was 82%. Average scholarship/grant was $15,907; average loan $3,306. 70% of total undergraduate aid awarded as scholarships/grants, 30% as loans/jobs. **Non-need-based:** Awarded to 662 full-time undergraduates, including 182 freshmen. Scholarships awarded for academics, art, leadership, minority status, music/drama, religious affiliation, ROTC, state residency.

Application procedures. Admission: Priority date 4/15; no deadline. $25 fee, may be waived for applicants with need, free for online applicants. Admission notification on a rolling basis beginning on or about 10/1. Must reply by May 1 or within 4 week(s) if notified thereafter. **Financial aid:** No deadline. FAFSA, institutional form required. Applicants notified on a rolling basis starting 3/1; must reply within 4 week(s) of notification.

Academics. Special study options: Accelerated study, combined bachelor's/graduate degree, cross-registration, double major, dual enrollment of high school students, ESL, exchange student, honors, independent study, internships, New York semester, student-designed major, study abroad, teacher certification program, United Nations semester, urban semester, Washington semester. Independent study project grants; 3-2 engineering program with Universities of Illiinois at Urbana-Champaign and Minnesota; 5-year bachelor's/master's degree programs. **Credit/placement by examination:** AP, CLEP, IB, SAT, ACT, institutional tests. 28 credit hours maximum toward bachelor's degree. Students must be tested or otherwise assessed in order for experiential credit to be awarded. **Support services:** Pre-admission summer program, reduced course load, remedial instruction, study skills assistance, tutoring, writing center.

Majors. Area/ethnic studies: East Asian. **Biology:** General, biochemistry. **Business:** Accounting, actuarial science, business admin, finance, human resources, international, management information systems, marketing, small business admin. **Communications:** General, journalism, organizational, radio/tv. **Communications technology:** Animation/special effects. **Computer sciences:** General. **Education:** General, art, elementary, music, physical. **Foreign languages:** Classics, French, German, Japanese, Spanish. **Health:** Athletic training, medical radiologic technology/radiation therapy, nuclear medical technology. **History:** General. **Interdisciplinary:** Global studies. **Liberal arts:** Arts/sciences. **Math:** General, applied. **Parks/recreation:** Exercise sciences, health/fitness, sports admin. **Philosophy/religion:** Philosophy, religion. **Physical sciences:** Chemistry, physics. **Psychology:** General. **Social sciences:** General, anthropology, economics, political science, sociology. **Visual/performing arts:** Art, dramatic, jazz. **Other:** Interactive media, Interactive media: graphic arts.

Most popular majors. Business/marketing 30%, communications/journalism 7%, education 14%, psychology 9%, social sciences 12%.

Computing on campus. 336 workstations in dormitories, library, computer center, student center. Dormitories wired for high-speed internet access and linked to campus network. Commuter students can connect to campus network. Online library, helpline, repair service, student web hosting, wireless network available.

Student life. Freshman orientation: Available, $125 fee. Three orientations held in June, one in August. Session also held the week before beginning of term. **Housing:** Guaranteed on-campus for all undergraduates. Coed dorms, single-sex dorms, special housing for disabled, wellness housing available. $100 nonrefundable deposit, deadline 5/1. **Activities:** Bands, campus ministries, choral groups, dance, drama, international student organizations, literary magazine, music ensembles, Model UN, musical theater, opera, radio station, student government, student newspaper, United Methodist Student Organization, Black student organization, Fellowship of Christian Athletes, Raza Unida, Cardinals in Action, Green Scene, commuter student organization, Students in Free Enterprise.

Athletics. NCAA. **Intercollegiate:** Baseball M, basketball, cross-country, football (tackle) M, golf, lacrosse W, soccer, softball W, swimming, tennis, track and field, volleyball W, wrestling M. **Intramural:** Basketball, bowling, cheerleading, football (tackle) M, golf, softball, table tennis, volleyball. **Team name:** Cardinals.

Student services. Adult student services, alcohol/substance abuse counseling, career counseling, student employment services, financial aid counseling, health services, minority student services, personal counseling, placement for graduates. **Physically disabled:** Services for visually, hearing impaired.

Contact. E-mail: admissions@noctrl.edu
Phone: (630) 637-5800 Toll-free number: (800) 411-1861
Fax: (630) 637-5819
Martin Sauer, Dean of Admissions and Financial Aid, North Central College, PO Box 3063, Naperville, IL 60566-7063

North Park University

Chicago, Illinois — **CB member**
www.northpark.edu — **CB code: 1556**

- Private 4-year university and liberal arts college affiliated with Evangelical Covenant Church
- Residential campus in very large city
- 2,188 degree-seeking undergraduates: 17% part-time, 63% women, 9% African American, 7% Asian American, 10% Hispanic American, 4% international
- 793 degree-seeking graduate students
- 71% of applicants admitted
- SAT or ACT (ACT writing recommended), application essay required
- 54% graduate within 6 years

General. Founded in 1891. Regionally accredited. Mid-sized Christian liberal arts institution. **Degrees:** 371 bachelor's awarded; master's, doctoral, first professional offered. **ROTC:** Army, Air Force. **Location:** 8 miles from downtown. **Calendar:** Semester, limited summer session. **Full-time faculty:** 125 total; 88% have terminal degrees, 17% minority, 50% women. **Part-time faculty:** 158 total; 16% minority, 49% women. **Class size:** 54% < 20, 41% 20-39, 3% 40-49, 2% 50-99, less than 1% >100.

Freshman class profile. 1,402 applied, 992 admitted, 415 enrolled.

Mid 50% test scores		**Rank in top quarter:**	35%
SAT critical reading:	470-580	**Rank in top tenth:**	11%
SAT math:	460-590	**End year in good standing:**	86%
ACT composite:	19-24	**Return as sophomores:**	71%
GPA 3.75 or higher:	13%	**Out-of-state:**	46%
GPA 3.50-3.74:	15%	**Live on campus:**	77%
GPA 3.0-3.49:	28%	**International:**	3%
GPA 2.0-2.99:	43%		

Basis for selection. Admission based on full review of student's record, and considers courses taken, GPA, class rank, test scores, recommendations, essay or writing sample, co-curricular involvements, and community service. Nursing has an early admission option available to high achieving students. An interview may be required for some applicants. All students who visit campus are interviewed by an admission counselor. **Homeschooled:** Transcript of courses and grades, letter of recommendation (nonparent) required.

High school preparation. College-preparatory program recommended. Recommended units include English 4, mathematics 3, social studies 1, history 1, science 3 and foreign language 2.

2009-2010 Annual costs. Tuition/fees (projected): $18,800. Room/board: $8,140. Books/supplies: $950. Personal expenses: $1,350.

2007-2008 Financial aid. Need-based: 361 full-time freshmen applied for aid; 289 were judged to have need; 289 of these received aid. Average need met was 69%. Average scholarship/grant was $4,793; average loan $3,700. 56% of total undergraduate aid awarded as scholarships/grants, 44% as loans/jobs. **Non-need-based:** Scholarships awarded for academics, art, music/drama, religious affiliation.

Application procedures. Admission: Priority date 4/1; deadline 7/1 (receipt date). $40 fee, may be waived for applicants with need. Admission notification on a rolling basis beginning on or about 9/15. Must reply by May 1 or within 4 week(s) if notified thereafter. **Financial aid:** Priority date 5/1, closing date 8/1. FAFSA required. Applicants notified on a rolling basis starting 10/1; must reply by 5/1 or within 4 week(s) of notification.

Academics. Special study options: Accelerated study, combined bachelor's/graduate degree, distance learning, double major, ESL, exchange student, honors, independent study, internships, liberal arts/career combination, student-designed major, study abroad, teacher certification program, Washington semester. **Credit/placement by examination:** AP, CLEP, IB, SAT, ACT, institutional tests. 60 credit hours maximum toward bachelor's degree. **Support services:** Learning center, pre-admission summer program, reduced course load, remedial instruction, study skills assistance, tutoring, writing center.

Majors. **Biology:** General. **Business:** General, business admin, organizational behavior. **Communications:** General, advertising. **Computer sciences:** General. **Education:** Early childhood, elementary, middle, multi-level teacher. **Foreign languages:** French, Scandinavian, Spanish. **Health:** Clinical lab science, nursing (RN). **History:** General. **Math:** General. **Philosophy/religion:** Philosophy. **Physical sciences:** Chemistry, physics. **Psychology:** General. **Social sciences:** Political science, sociology. **Theology:** Bible, theology, youth ministry. **Visual/performing arts:** Art, commercial/advertising art, music performance.

Most popular majors. Biology 7%, business/marketing 18%, communication technologies 8%, education 9%, health sciences 14%, psychology 6%, theological studies 7%.

Computing on campus. 100 workstations in dormitories, library, computer center, student center. Dormitories wired for high-speed internet access and linked to campus network. Commuter students can connect to campus network. Online course registration, online library, helpline, wireless network available.

Student life. **Freshman orientation:** Mandatory. Preregistration for classes offered. Begins 5 days before start of classes. **Policies:** Alcohol-free and smoke-free campus. Visiting hours in residence halls for persons of opposite sex. **Housing:** Guaranteed on-campus for all undergraduates. Single-sex dorms, apartments available. $250 nonrefundable deposit, deadline 5/1. **Activities:** Bands, campus ministries, choral groups, drama, literary magazine, music ensembles, musical theater, opera, student government, student newspaper, symphony orchestra, gospel teams, Black student association, Latino student organization, Korean student association, Catholic association, Middle Eastern student association, Scandinavian student association.

Athletics. NCAA. **Intercollegiate:** Baseball M, basketball, cross-country, football (tackle) M, golf, rowing (crew) W, soccer, softball W, track and field, volleyball W. **Intramural:** Basketball, cheerleading W, football (non-tackle), soccer, tennis, volleyball. **Team name:** Vikings.

Student services. Adult student services, alcohol/substance abuse counseling, chaplain/spiritual director, career counseling, services for economically disadvantaged, student employment services, financial aid counseling, health services, minority student services, personal counseling, placement for graduates.

Contact. E-mail: admission@northpark.edu
Phone: (773) 244-5500 Toll-free number: (800) 888-6728
Fax: (773) 244-5243
Shari Nordstrom, Director, Undergraduate Admission, North Park University, 3225 West Foster Avenue Box 19, Chicago, IL 60625-4895

Northeastern Illinois University

Chicago, Illinois — **CB member**
www.neiu.edu — **CB code: 1090**

- Public 4-year university
- Commuter campus in very large city
- 8,787 degree-seeking undergraduates: 44% part-time, 59% women, 10% African American, 11% Asian American, 31% Hispanic American, 1% international
- 1,844 degree-seeking graduate students
- 71% of applicants admitted
- SAT or ACT (ACT writing optional) required

General. Founded in 1961. Regionally accredited. Two extension centers serving Hispanic and African-American communities. **Degrees:** 1,503 bachelor's awarded; master's offered. **ROTC:** Army, Air Force. **Calendar:** Semester, limited summer session. **Full-time faculty:** 421 total; 71% have terminal degrees, 29% minority, 49% women. **Part-time faculty:** 276 total; 22% have terminal degrees, 33% minority, 47% women. **Class size:** 42% < 20, 51% 20-39, 5% 40-49, 2% 50-99, less than 1% >100.

Freshman class profile. 3,785 applied, 2,691 admitted, 1,017 enrolled.

Mid 50% test scores		Rank in top quarter:	17%
ACT composite:	16-21	Rank in top tenth:	7%
GPA 3.0-3.49:	40%	Return as sophomores:	64%
GPA 2.0-2.99:	52%	Out-of-state:	1%

Basis for selection. Rank in top half of graduating class or 19 ACT/equivalent SAT required. Audition recommended for dance and music majors. Portfolio recommended for art majors.

High school preparation. 15 units required. Required units include English 4, mathematics 3, social studies 3 and science 3. 2 additional units in fine arts, music, art, foreign languages, or vocational education. (Only 1 vocational education course accepted.).

2008-2009 Annual costs. Tuition/fees: $8,016; $14,616 out-of-state. Books/supplies: $1,650. Personal expenses: $3,798.

2008-2009 Financial aid. **Non-need-based:** Scholarships awarded for academics, art, leadership, music/drama.

Application procedures. **Admission:** Closing date 7/1 (receipt date). $25 fee, may be waived for applicants with need. Admission notification on a rolling basis beginning on or about 9/1. **Financial aid:** Priority date 2/28; no closing date. FAFSA, institutional form required. Applicants notified on a rolling basis starting 4/1; must reply within 3 week(s) of notification.

Academics. **Special study options:** Cooperative education, distance learning, double major, dual enrollment of high school students, exchange student, honors, independent study, student-designed major, study abroad, teacher certification program. **Credit/placement by examination:** AP, CLEP, IB, ACT, institutional tests. 30 credit hours maximum toward bachelor's degree. **Support services:** Learning center, pre-admission summer program, remedial instruction, study skills assistance, tutoring, writing center.

Majors. **Area/ethnic studies:** Women's. **Biology:** General. **Business:** General, accounting, business admin, finance, marketing. **Computer sciences:** Computer science. **Conservation:** Environmental studies. **Education:** Bilingual, early childhood, elementary, physical, special. **Foreign languages:** French, linguistics, Spanish. **Health:** Community health services. **History:** General. **Liberal arts:** Arts/sciences. **Math:** General. **Philosophy/religion:** Philosophy. **Physical sciences:** Chemistry, geology, physics. **Protective services:** Criminal justice. **Psychology:** General. **Public administration:** Social work. **Social sciences:** General, anthropology, economics, geography, political science, sociology. **Visual/performing arts:** Art.

Most popular majors. Business/marketing 19%, education 16%, English 9%, liberal arts 14%, security/protective services 10%, social sciences 8%.

Computing on campus. 315 workstations in library, computer center, student center. Commuter students can connect to campus network. Online course registration, helpline, wireless network available.

Student life. **Freshman orientation:** Available. **Activities:** Bands, choral groups, dance, drama, literary magazine, music ensembles, opera, radio station, student government, student newspaper, symphony orchestra, Muslim student association, black heritage club, politics club, Chimexla student union, Indian student association, university bible association, program board, Union of Puerto Rican Students, Hillel, outdoor adventure club.

Athletics. **Intramural:** Badminton, basketball, cross-country, racquetball, soccer, softball, table tennis, tennis, volleyball, weight lifting. **Team name:** Eagles.

Student services. Adult student services, career counseling, student employment services, financial aid counseling, health services, minority student services, on-campus daycare, personal counseling, placement for graduates, veterans' counselor, women's services. **Physically disabled:** Services for visually, speech impaired.

Contact. E-mail: admerc@neiu.edu
Phone: (773) 442-4000 Fax: (773) 442-4020
Janice Harring-Hendon, Director of Admissions and Records, Northeastern Illinois University, 5500 North St. Louis Avenue, Chicago, IL 60625

Northern Illinois University

DeKalb, Illinois — **CB member**
www.niu.edu — **CB code: 1559**

- Public 4-year university
- Residential campus in large town
- 18,398 degree-seeking undergraduates: 10% part-time, 51% women, 14% African American, 5% Asian American, 7% Hispanic American, 1% international
- 4,753 degree-seeking graduate students
- 58% of applicants admitted
- SAT or ACT required

General. Founded in 1895. Regionally accredited. Classes also held at Loredo Taft Field campus in Oregon. **Degrees:** 3,979 bachelor's awarded; master's, doctoral, first professional offered. **ROTC:** Army. **Location:** 65 miles from Chicago. **Calendar:** Semester, extensive summer session. **Full-time faculty:** 927 total; 83% have terminal degrees, 14% minority, 45% women. **Part-time faculty:** 272 total; 39% have terminal degrees, 7% minority, 53% women. **Class size:** 37% < 20, 47% 20-39, 4% 40-49, 9% 50-99, 3% >100.

Freshman class profile. 17,306 applied, 10,071 admitted, 2,881 enrolled.

Mid 50% test scores			
ACT composite:	19-24	Out-of-state:	3%
Rank in top quarter:	33%	Live on campus:	92%
Rank in top tenth:	9%	International:	1%

Basis for selection. 19 ACT required of applicants who rank in top half of class, 23 ACT required of applicants in top two-thirds of class or with high school equivalency certificate. Interview required of CHANCE program applicants. Audition required of music majors. Portfolio recommended for art majors.

High school preparation. 15 units required. Required and recommended units include English 4, mathematics 2-4, social studies 2-3, history 1, science 2-4 (laboratory 1-2) and foreign language 1-2. One unit of art, film, music, theater, or foreign language required. Mathematics must include algebra and/or geometry. Social sciences must include US history or a combination of US history and government.

2008-2009 Annual costs. Tuition/fees: $8,524; $15,244 out-of-state. Room/board: $8,970. Books/supplies: $700. Personal expenses: $1,584.

2007-2008 Financial aid. **Need-based:** 2,671 full-time freshmen applied for aid; 2,128 were judged to have need; 1,928 of these received aid. Average scholarship/grant was $8,288; average loan $3,386. 52% of total undergraduate aid awarded as scholarships/grants, 48% as loans/jobs. **Non-need-based:** Awarded to 3,655 full-time undergraduates, including 721 freshmen. Scholarships awarded for academics, athletics, ROTC.

Application procedures. **Admission:** Priority date 3/1; deadline 8/1. No application fee. Admission notification on a rolling basis. **Financial aid:** Priority date 3/1; no closing date. FAFSA, institutional form required. Applicants notified on a rolling basis starting 4/15.

Academics. **Special study options:** Cooperative education, distance learning, double major, dual enrollment of high school students, honors, independent study, internships, student-designed major, study abroad, teacher certification program. **Credit/placement by examination:** AP, CLEP, institutional tests. Credit by examination not awarded for courses that are prerequisites for courses for which the student already has credit or is currently enrolled. **Support services:** Tutoring.

Majors. **Biology:** General. **Business:** General, accounting, finance, marketing, operations. **Communications:** General, journalism. **Computer sciences:** General, computer science. **Education:** General, art, elementary, family/consumer sciences, health, physical, special. **Engineering:** Electrical, industrial, mechanical. **Engineering technology:** Industrial. **Family/consumer sciences:** Clothing/textiles, family studies, food/nutrition. **Foreign languages:** French, German, Russian, Spanish. **Health:** Clinical lab science, communication disorders, nursing (RN), public health nursing. **History:** General. **Liberal arts:** Arts/sciences. **Math:** General, applied, computational, probability. **Philosophy/religion:** Philosophy. **Physical sciences:** Atmospheric science, chemistry, geology, physics. **Psychology:** General. **Social sciences:** Anthropology, economics, geography, political science, sociology. **Visual/performing arts:** Art, art history/conservation, dramatic, studio arts.

Most popular majors. Business/marketing 20%, communications/journalism 8%, education 11%, engineering/engineering technologies 6%, health sciences 10%, social sciences 12%.

Computing on campus. 550 workstations in dormitories, library, computer center, student center. Commuter students can connect to campus network. Helpline available.

Student life. **Freshman orientation:** Mandatory, $60 fee. **Housing:** Guaranteed on-campus for freshmen. Coed dorms, special housing for disabled, apartments, fraternity/sorority housing available. $150 deposit. Quiet and alcohol-free lifestyle floors, 21 and over student floors, honors floors available. **Activities:** Bands, campus ministries, choral groups, dance, drama, film society, opera, radio station, student government, student newspaper, symphony orchestra, TV station, numerous organizations available.

Athletics. NCAA. **Intercollegiate:** Baseball M, basketball, cross-country W, football (tackle) M, golf, gymnastics W, soccer, softball W, swimming, tennis, track and field W, volleyball W, wrestling M. **Intramural:** Badminton, baseball M, basketball, football (tackle) M, golf, ice hockey M, racquetball, sailing, soccer, softball, table tennis, tennis, volleyball, wrestling M. **Team name:** Huskies.

Student services. Career counseling, student employment services, health services, legal services, minority student services, on-campus daycare, personal counseling, placement for graduates, veterans' counselor, women's services. **Physically disabled:** Services for visually, speech, hearing impaired.

Contact. E-mail: admission-info@niu.edu
Phone: (815) 753-0446 Toll-free number: (800) 892-3050
Fax: (815) 753-8312
Robert Burk, Director of Admissions, Northern Illinois University, DeKalb, IL 60115-2854

Northwestern University

Evanston, Illinois — **CB member**
www.northwestern.edu — **CB code: 1565**

- Private 4-year university
- Residential campus in small city
- 8,364 degree-seeking undergraduates: 1% part-time, 52% women, 5% African American, 18% Asian American, 7% Hispanic American, 5% international
- 9,866 degree-seeking graduate students
- 26% of applicants admitted
- SAT or ACT with writing, application essay required

General. Founded in 1851. Regionally accredited. **Degrees:** 2,037 bachelor's awarded; master's, doctoral, first professional offered. **ROTC:** Army, Naval, Air Force. **Location:** 12 miles from downtown Chicago. **Calendar:** Quarter, limited summer session. **Full-time faculty:** 1,027 total; 100% have terminal degrees, 17% minority, 29% women. **Part-time faculty:** 126 total; 100% have terminal degrees, 7% minority, 43% women. **Special facilities:** Fine-arts complex, dance center, observatory, engineering design center, tennis center.

Freshman class profile. 25,013 applied, 6,552 admitted, 2,078 enrolled.

Mid 50% test scores			
SAT critical reading:	670-750	Return as sophomores:	97%
SAT math:	690-780	Out-of-state:	80%
SAT writing:	670-750	Live on campus:	99%
ACT composite:	30-33	International:	6%
Rank in top quarter:	96%	Fraternities:	25%
Rank in top tenth:	85%	Sororities:	34%

Basis for selection. Academic record, essays, test scores, activity record, school recommendations important. SAT Subject Tests recommended. SAT Subject Tests in Math Level 2 and Chemistry required of all applicants for Honors Program in Medical Education. Applicants to Integrated Science Program must take SAT Subject Tests in Chemistry or Physics, Math Level 2, plus second science. Audition required for music majors. **Homeschooled:** 3 SAT Subject Tests required. Math Level 1 or 2 for students who plan to study sciences or engineering, Math Level 2 preferable, plus 2 other SAT Subject Tests of applicant's choice from different subject areas required.

High school preparation. College-preparatory program recommended. 16 units recommended. Recommended units include English 4, mathematics 3, social studies 2, science 2 (laboratory 2), foreign language 2 and academic electives 1. 4 units of mathematics recommended for engineering applicants. Applicants typically have 20 academic high school units.

2008-2009 Annual costs. Tuition/fees: $37,125. Room/board: $11,295. Books/supplies: $1,626. Personal expenses: $1,674.

2008-2009 Financial aid. **Need-based:** 1,095 full-time freshmen applied for aid; 841 were judged to have need; 841 of these received aid. Average need met was 100%. Average scholarship/grant was $26,100; average loan $3,651. 80% of total undergraduate aid awarded as scholarships/grants, 20% as loans/jobs. **Non-need-based:** Awarded to 755 full-time undergraduates, including 207 freshmen. Scholarships awarded for academics, athletics, music/drama, ROTC.

Application procedures. **Admission:** Closing date 1/1 (postmark date). $65 fee, may be waived for applicants with need. Admission notification 4/15. Must reply by May 1 or within 2 week(s) if notified thereafter. **Financial aid:** Closing date 2/15. FAFSA, CSS PROFILE required. Applicants notified by 4/15; must reply by 5/1 or within 2 week(s) of notification.

Academics. One unit of credit awarded for each course; 45-48 units required for graduation. **Special study options:** Accelerated study, combined bachelor's/graduate degree, cooperative education, double major, honors, independent study, internships, liberal arts/career combination, student-designed major, study abroad, teacher certification program. 3-year integrated science program; 4-year mathematical methods in social sciences bachelor's program; honors programs in undergraduate research engineering, engineering and management, medical education; 7-year BA/MD program resulting in both an undergraduate degree and MD. **Credit/placement**

by examination: AP, CLEP, IB, institutional tests. **Support services:** Study skills assistance, tutoring, writing center.

Majors. **Area/ethnic studies:** African-American, American, Asian, European, women's. **Biology:** General, ecology. **Business:** Organizational behavior. **Communications:** General, broadcast journalism, journalism, radio/tv. **Computer sciences:** General, computer science, information systems. **Conservation:** Environmental science, environmental studies. **Education:** General, learning disabled, mathematics, music, secondary. **Engineering:** General, biomedical, chemical, civil, computer, electrical, environmental, industrial, manufacturing, materials, materials science, mechanical, science. **Foreign languages:** Classics, comparative lit, East Asian, French, German, Italian, linguistics, Slavic, Spanish. **Health:** Communication disorders, premedicine. **History:** General. **Interdisciplinary:** Biological/physical sciences, neuroscience, science/society. **Legal studies:** General. **Liberal arts:** Arts/sciences. **Math:** General, applied, statistics. **Philosophy/religion:** Philosophy, religion. **Physical sciences:** Chemistry, geology, physics. **Psychology:** General, cognitive, community. **Public administration:** Community org/advocacy, policy analysis. **Social sciences:** Anthropology, economics, geography, international relations, political science, sociology, urban studies. **Visual/performing arts:** General, art, art history/conservation, dance, dramatic, jazz, music performance, music theory/composition, musicology, piano/organ, stringed instruments, theater history, voice/opera. **Other:** Area studies, Radio, television, and digital communication.

Most popular majors. Communications/journalism 20%, engineering/engineering technologies 15%, psychology 8%, social sciences 17%, visual/performing arts 10%.

Computing on campus. Dormitories wired for high-speed internet access and linked to campus network. Commuter students can connect to campus network. Online course registration, online library, helpline, repair service, student web hosting, wireless network available.

Student life. **Freshman orientation:** Mandatory. Held for 5 days prior to start of classes. **Housing:** Guaranteed on-campus for freshmen. Coed dorms, single-sex dorms, fraternity/sorority housing, wellness housing available. $200 nonrefundable deposit, deadline 5/25. Residential colleges available. **Activities:** Bands, campus ministries, choral groups, dance, drama, film society, international student organizations, literary magazine, music ensembles, musical theater, opera, radio station, student government, student newspaper, symphony orchestra, TV station, over 300 organizations.

Athletics. NCAA. **Intercollegiate:** Baseball M, basketball, cheerleading, cross-country W, diving, fencing W, field hockey W, football (tackle) M, golf, lacrosse W, soccer, softball W, swimming, tennis, volleyball W, wrestling M. **Intramural:** Basketball, football (non-tackle), ice hockey, soccer, softball, volleyball. **Team name:** Wildcats.

Student services. Adult student services, alcohol/substance abuse counseling, chaplain/spiritual director, career counseling, student employment services, financial aid counseling, health services, minority student services, personal counseling, placement for graduates, women's services. **Physically disabled:** Services for visually, speech, hearing impaired.

Contact. E-mail: ug-admission@northwestern.edu
Phone: (847) 491-7271
Christopher Watson, Dean of Undergraduate Admissions, Northwestern University, 1801 Hinman Avenue, Evanston, IL 60204-3060

Olivet Nazarene University

Bourbonnais, Illinois — CB member
www.olivet.edu — CB code: 1596

- Private 4-year university and liberal arts college affiliated with Church of the Nazarene
- Residential campus in small city
- 3,028 degree-seeking undergraduates: 19% part-time, 63% women, 11% African American, 1% Asian American, 4% Hispanic American, 1% international
- 1,410 degree-seeking graduate students
- 81% of applicants admitted
- ACT (writing optional) required
- 57% graduate within 6 years

General. Founded in 1907. Regionally accredited. Evangelical liberal arts institution emphasizing Christian values. **Degrees:** 628 bachelor's, 35 associate awarded; master's, doctoral offered. **ROTC:** Army. **Location:** 60 miles from Chicago. **Calendar:** Semester, extensive summer session. **Full-time faculty:** 118 total; 70% women. **Part-time faculty:** 350 total. **Class size:** 39% < 20, 46% 20-39, 5% 40-49, 9% 50-99, 1% >100. **Special facilities:** Planetarium, observatory, science museum, distance learning classroom.

Freshman class profile. 2,433 applied, 1,973 admitted, 601 enrolled.

Mid 50% test scores		**Out-of-state:**	52%
ACT composite:	19-26	**Live on campus:**	90%
Return as sophomores:	70%		

Basis for selection. 2.0 GPA in college-preparatory subjects, ranking in top three-quarters of class, 18 ACT, 2 recommendations required. Interview recommended. Audition required of music majors. Portfolios required for art scholarship applicants.

High school preparation. 15 units required. Required and recommended units include English 4, mathematics 3, social studies 4, history 2, science 3 and foreign language 2.

2009-2010 Annual costs. Tuition/fees: $23,590. Room/board: $6,400. Books/supplies: $1,000. Personal expenses: $400.

2007-2008 Financial aid. **Need-based:** 688 full-time freshmen applied for aid; 609 were judged to have need; 530 of these received aid. Average need met was 94%. Average scholarship/grant was $10,896; average loan $3,662. 36% of total undergraduate aid awarded as scholarships/grants, 64% as loans/jobs. **Non-need-based:** Awarded to 2,925 full-time undergraduates, including 770 freshmen. Scholarships awarded for academics, art, athletics, leadership, music/drama, religious affiliation, ROTC, state residency.

Application procedures. **Admission:** Closing date 5/15 (postmark date). $25 fee, may be waived for applicants with need, free for online applicants. Admission notification on a rolling basis. **Financial aid:** Priority date 3/1; no closing date. FAFSA, institutional form required. Applicants notified on a rolling basis starting 1/15; must reply within 2 week(s) of notification.

Academics. **Special study options:** Accelerated study, distance learning, double major, honors, independent study, internships, liberal arts/career combination, student-designed major, study abroad, teacher certification program, Washington semester. Council of Christian Colleges and Universities study programs, adult studies degree program. **Credit/placement by examination:** AP, CLEP, IB, ACT, institutional tests. **Support services:** Learning center, pre-admission summer program, reduced course load, remedial instruction, tutoring.

Majors. **Biology:** General, zoology. **Business:** General, accounting, business admin, fashion, finance, international, marketing. **Communications:** General, broadcast journalism, journalism. **Computer sciences:** General, computer science, information systems, programming. **Conservation:** Environmental studies. **Education:** Art, biology, chemistry, early childhood, elementary, English, family/consumer sciences, foreign languages, health, history, mathematics, music, physical, science, secondary, social science, social studies, Spanish. **Engineering:** General. **Family/consumer sciences:** General, family/community services, housing. **Foreign languages:** General, Spanish. **Health:** Athletic training. **History:** General. **Interdisciplinary:** Biological/physical sciences. **Liberal arts:** Arts/sciences. **Math:** General. **Parks/recreation:** Exercise sciences, sports admin. **Philosophy/religion:** Religion. **Physical sciences:** Chemistry, geology. **Protective services:** Criminal justice. **Psychology:** General. **Public administration:** Policy analysis, social work. **Social sciences:** General, economics, political science, sociology. **Theology:** Bible, religious ed, sacred music, theology. **Visual/performing arts:** Art, music performance, piano/organ, voice/opera.

Most popular majors. Business/marketing 20%, education 10%, health sciences 16%, social sciences 6%.

Computing on campus. 125 workstations in library, computer center, student center. Dormitories wired for high-speed internet access and linked to campus network. Commuter students can connect to campus network. Online library, helpline, repair service, student web hosting, wireless network available.

Student life. **Freshman orientation:** Mandatory. Preregistration for classes offered. Three-day program held on second and third weekends in June. Comprehensive for students and parents. **Policies:** Chapel convocations held twice weekly. Religious observance required. **Housing:** Guaranteed on-campus for all undergraduates. Single-sex dorms, special housing for disabled, apartments available. **Activities:** Bands, campus ministries, choral groups, drama, international student organizations, literary magazine, music ensembles, musical theater, radio station, student government, student newspaper, symphony orchestra, social service clubs, spiritual life groups.

Athletics. NAIA, NCCAA. **Intercollegiate:** Baseball M, basketball, cheerleading, cross-country, football (tackle) M, golf M, soccer, softball W, tennis, track and field, volleyball W. **Intramural:** Badminton, basketball, bowling, cross-country, football (non-tackle) W, golf, handball, racquetball, soccer, softball, table tennis, tennis, track and field, volleyball. **Team name:** Tigers.

Student services. Adult student services, alcohol/substance abuse counseling, chaplain/spiritual director, career counseling, services for economically disadvantaged, student employment services, financial aid counseling,

health services, personal counseling, placement for graduates, veterans' counselor.

Contact. E-mail: admissions@olivet.edu
Phone: (815) 939-5203 Toll-free number: (800) 648-1463
Fax: (815) 939-5069
Susan Wolff, Director of Admissions, Olivet Nazarene University, One University Avenue, Bourbonnais, IL 60914

Principia College

Elsah, Illinois — **CB member**
www.prin.edu — **CB code: 1630**

- Private 4-year liberal arts college affiliated with First Church of Christ, Scientist (Christian Science)
- Residential campus in rural community
- 514 degree-seeking undergraduates
- 84% of applicants admitted
- SAT or ACT with writing, application essay required

General. Founded in 1910. Regionally accredited. All faculty, staff, and students are Christian Scientists. **Degrees:** 111 bachelor's awarded. **Location:** 35 miles from St. Louis. **Calendar:** Quarter. **Full-time faculty:** 55 total. **Part-time faculty:** 11 total. **Class size:** 94% < 20, 6% 20-39. **Special facilities:** School of Nations museum, astronomical observatory telescope, media center, tropical aviary, on-site mammoth excavation, Christian Science practitioner's office, athletic center with natatorium, 3,069-pipe organ, 39 bronze bell carillon.

Freshman class profile. 243 applied, 204 admitted, 130 enrolled.

Mid 50% test scores		**GPA 3.0-3.49:**	17%
SAT critical reading:	510-640	**GPA 2.0-2.99:**	31%
SAT math:	490-630	**Rank in top quarter:**	63%
ACT composite:	22-29	**Rank in top tenth:**	38%
GPA 3.75 or higher:	41%	**Out-of-state:**	90%
GPA 3.50-3.74:	10%	**Live on campus:**	100%

Basis for selection. School achievement record and essay or personal statement most important. Applicant must be practicing Christian Scientist. Test scores important. Foreign language SAT Subject Test required for placement purposes. Interview recommended. Portfolio recommended for art majors. **Homeschooled:** Must submit curricula program from accredited high school or accepted agency, plus GED.

High school preparation. 16 units required; 20 recommended. Required and recommended units include English 4, mathematics 3, social studies 2, history 1-2, science 2-3 (laboratory 2), foreign language 2-3 and academic electives 2.

2009-2010 Annual costs. Tuition/fees: $22,950. Room/board: $8,730. Books/supplies: $900. Personal expenses: $750.

2008-2009 Financial aid. Need-based: Average need met was 100%. **Non-need-based:** Scholarships awarded for academics, alumni affiliation, leadership. **Additional information:** Need-based tuition reduction work plan combines job with grant.

Application procedures. Admission: Priority date 11/15; deadline 3/1 (postmark date). No application fee. Admission notification on a rolling basis beginning on or about 10/15. Must reply by May 1 or within 2 week(s) if notified thereafter. **Financial aid:** Closing date 3/1. Institutional form, CSS PROFILE required. Applicants notified by 4/1.

Academics. Special study options: Double major, independent study, internships, liberal arts/career combination, student-designed major, study abroad, teacher certification program. 3-2 engineering with Washington University, University of Southern California, Southern Illinois University at Edwardswille. **Credit/placement by examination:** AP, CLEP, IB, institutional tests. **Support services:** Learning center, study skills assistance, tutoring, writing center.

Majors. Biology: General. **Business:** Business admin. **Communications:** Media studies. **Computer sciences:** General, computer science. **Conservation:** General. **Education:** Elementary. **Engineering:** Science. **Foreign languages:** General, French, German, Spanish. **History:** General. **Interdisciplinary:** Global studies. **Liberal arts:** Arts/sciences, humanities. **Math:** General. **Parks/recreation:** Sports admin. **Philosophy/religion:** Philosophy, religion. **Physical sciences:** Chemistry, physics. **Social sciences:** General, anthropology, economics, political science, sociology. **Visual/performing arts:** Art history/conservation, dramatic, studio arts.

Computing on campus. 250 workstations in dormitories, library, computer center, student center. Dormitories wired for high-speed internet access and linked to campus network. Online course registration, online library, helpline, student web hosting, wireless network available.

Student life. Freshman orientation: Mandatory. Preregistration for classes offered. Pre-fall writing and orientation program immediately precedes start of classes. **Policies:** Students required to comply with standards of Christian Science. No alcoholic beverages, smoking, drugs. High moral standards and behavior expected. Standards maintained regarding abstinence from premarital sex or homosexual activity. Religious observance required. **Housing:** Guaranteed on-campus for all undergraduates. Single-sex dorms, apartments, wellness housing available. $100 deposit, deadline 5/1. Single-sex wings, 8 person cottages for non-traditional students available. **Activities:** Jazz band, choral groups, dance, drama, music ensembles, musical theater, radio station, student government, student newspaper, TV station, Christian Science Organization, black student union, Latin American student organization, student volunteer program, public affairs conference.

Athletics. NCAA. **Intercollegiate:** Baseball M, basketball, cross-country, diving, football (tackle) M, golf M, soccer, swimming, tennis, track and field, volleyball W. **Intramural:** Basketball, soccer, softball, volleyball W. **Team name:** Panthers.

Student services. Adult student services, career counseling, student employment services, financial aid counseling, health services, on-campus daycare, personal counseling.

Contact. E-mail: collegeadmissions@principia.edu
Phone: (618) 374-5181 Toll-free number: (800) 277-4648 ext. 2802
Fax: (618) 374-4000
Brian McCauley, Dean of Enrollment Management, Principia College, One Maybeck Place, Elsah, IL 62028-9799

Quincy University

Quincy, Illinois
www.quincy.edu — **CB code: 1645**

- Private 4-year university and liberal arts college affiliated with Roman Catholic Church
- Residential campus in large town
- 1,076 degree-seeking undergraduates: 5% part-time, 55% women, 10% African American, 1% Asian American, 3% Hispanic American
- 210 degree-seeking graduate students
- 90% of applicants admitted
- SAT or ACT (ACT writing optional), application essay required
- 52% graduate within 6 years; 26% enter graduate study

General. Founded in 1860. Regionally accredited. Service learning opportunities and trips offered throughout the year. **Degrees:** 215 bachelor's, 3 associate awarded; master's offered. **Location:** 300 miles from Chicago, 120 miles from St. Louis. **Calendar:** Semester, limited summer session. **Full-time faculty:** 49 total; 78% have terminal degrees, 12% minority, 31% women. **Part-time faculty:** 88 total; 20% have terminal degrees, 2% minority, 65% women. **Class size:** 73% < 20, 27% 20-39, less than 1% 40-49. **Special facilities:** College-operated national public radio station, 200-seat theater, multi-media and graphic design labs, environmental studies institute.

Freshman class profile. 978 applied, 885 admitted, 246 enrolled.

Mid 50% test scores		**Rank in top quarter:**	34%
SAT critical reading:	450-530	**Rank in top tenth:**	11%
SAT math:	440-580	**End year in good standing:**	81%
ACT composite:	19-25	**Return as sophomores:**	69%
GPA 3.75 or higher:	20%	**Out-of-state:**	27%
GPA 3.50-3.74:	16%	**Live on campus:**	89%
GPA 3.0-3.49:	27%	**Fraternities:**	2%
GPA 2.0-2.99:	35%	**Sororities:**	13%

Basis for selection. School achievement record and test scores most important. Applicants for BS in nursing must have 22 ACT and 3.0 GPA. All applicants must submit letter of recommendation and personal statement. Audition required of music majors. Portfolio recommended for art majors. **Homeschooled:** Transcript of courses and grades, letter of recommendation (nonparent) required. **Learning Disabled:** Must submit documentation of disability.

High school preparation. 16 units recommended. Required and recommended units include English 4, mathematics 3, social studies 3, science 3 and foreign language 2.

2008-2009 Annual costs. Tuition/fees: $20,790. Room/board: $7,900. Books/supplies: $1,250. Personal expenses: $1,500.

2008-2009 Financial aid. **Need-based:** 238 full-time freshmen applied for aid; 203 were judged to have need; 203 of these received aid. Average need met was 81%. Average scholarship/grant was $14,532; average loan $5,735. 68% of total undergraduate aid awarded as scholarships/grants, 32% as loans/jobs. **Non-need-based:** Awarded to 234 full-time undergraduates, including 52 freshmen. Scholarships awarded for academics, alumni affiliation, art, athletics, music/drama.

Application procedures. **Admission:** No deadline. $25 fee, may be waived for applicants with need, free for online applicants. Admission notification on a rolling basis. **Financial aid:** Priority date 3/15; no closing date. FAFSA required. Applicants notified on a rolling basis starting 2/15; must reply by 5/1 or within 2 week(s) of notification.

Academics. Associate degrees are offered in all majors by arrangement with institution. **Special study options:** Accelerated study, distance learning, double major, dual enrollment of high school students, ESL, honors, independent study, internships, liberal arts/career combination, student-designed major, study abroad, teacher certification program, Washington semester. 3-2 in engineering with Washington University; 3-1 in medical technology with various hospitals. **Credit/placement by examination:** AP, CLEP, IB, institutional tests. 40 credit hours maximum toward bachelor's degree. Combined total of 40 semester hours of credit from nontraditional sources accepted toward a bachelor's degree. **Support services:** Learning center, pre-admission summer program, reduced course load, remedial instruction, study skills assistance, tutoring, writing center.

Majors. **Biology:** General. **Business:** Accounting, business admin, finance, marketing. **Communications:** General, broadcast journalism, journalism, public relations. **Computer sciences:** Computer science, information systems. **Education:** Elementary, music, physical, special. **Foreign languages:** Translation. **Health:** Clinical lab science, nursing (RN). **History:** General. **Liberal arts:** Arts/sciences, humanities. **Math:** General. **Parks/recreation:** Sports admin. **Physical sciences:** Chemistry. **Protective services:** Criminal justice. **Psychology:** General. **Public administration:** Human services, social work. **Social sciences:** Political science. **Theology:** Theology. **Transportation:** Airline/commercial pilot, aviation management. **Visual/performing arts:** Art, graphic design. **Other:** Theology/philosophy.

Most popular majors. Business/marketing 31%, communications/journalism 7%, education 11%, health sciences 9%, psychology 6%.

Computing on campus. 190 workstations in dormitories, library, computer center. Dormitories wired for high-speed internet access and linked to campus network. Commuter students can connect to campus network. Online library, helpline, student web hosting, wireless network available.

Student life. **Freshman orientation:** Mandatory, $100 fee. Preregistration for classes offered. Academic year begins with 1-2 week registration and advisement program and 1-week social program. **Housing:** Guaranteed on-campus for all undergraduates. Coed dorms, single-sex dorms, apartments, fraternity/sorority housing available. $150 nonrefundable deposit. **Activities:** Bands, campus ministries, choral groups, dance, drama, literary magazine, music ensembles, musical theater, radio station, student government, student newspaper, symphony orchestra, Circle K International, environmental club, minority student association, Peers 2 Peers, student senate, student programming board.

Athletics. NAIA, NCAA. **Intercollegiate:** Baseball M, basketball, football (tackle) M, golf, soccer, softball W, tennis, volleyball. **Intramural:** Basketball, bowling, football (non-tackle), golf, racquetball, soccer, softball, table tennis, volleyball. **Team name:** Hawks.

Student services. Alcohol/substance abuse counseling, chaplain/spiritual director, career counseling, student employment services, financial aid counseling, health services, minority student services, personal counseling, placement for graduates. **Physically disabled:** Services for visually, hearing impaired.

Contact. E-mail: admissions@quincy.edu
Phone: (217) 228-5210 Toll-free number: (800) 688-4295
Fax: (217) 228-5479
Syndi Peck, Director of Admissions, Quincy University, 1800 College Avenue, Quincy, IL 62301-2699

Robert Morris College: Chicago

Chicago, Illinois — **CB member**
www.robertmorris.edu — **CB code: 1670**

- Private 4-year university
- Commuter campus in very large city
- 4,223 degree-seeking undergraduates: 6% part-time, 62% women, 33% African American, 3% Asian American, 23% Hispanic American, 1% international
- 350 degree-seeking graduate students
- 79% of applicants admitted
- 70% graduate within 6 years

General. Founded in 1913. Regionally accredited. Branch campuses in DuPage, Lake County, Bensenville, Orland Park, Peoria, Springfield, and Schaumburg. **Degrees:** 891 bachelor's, 1,053 associate awarded; master's offered. **ROTC:** Army. **Location:** Downtown. **Calendar:** 5 10-week sessions. Extensive summer session. **Full-time faculty:** 131 total; 21% have terminal degrees, 24% minority, 58% women. **Part-time faculty:** 186 total; 12% have terminal degrees, 19% minority, 48% women. **Class size:** 45% < 20, 49% 20-39, 5% 40-49, 1% 50-99, less than 1% >100.

Freshman class profile. 3,116 applied, 2,462 admitted, 1,005 enrolled.

GPA 3.75 or higher:	4%	**End year in good standing:**	64%
GPA 3.50-3.74:	5%	**Return as sophomores:**	55%
GPA 3.0-3.49:	18%	**Out-of-state:**	7%
GPA 2.0-2.99:	60%	**Live on campus:**	9%
Rank in top quarter:	20%	**International:**	1%
Rank in top tenth:	5%		

Basis for selection. Must submit high school transcript or GED for review. Secondary school record, class rank, GPA and interview most important. Extra curricular activities and level of interest considered. Meeting with admissions counselor and campus visit strongly recommended. **Homeschooled:** Transcript of courses and grades, state high school equivalency certificate required. Curriculum documentation, state certification, and standardized exam with acceptable achievement level required.

High school preparation. College-preparatory program recommended.

2009-2010 Annual costs. Tuition/fees: $19,200. Room/board: $9,900. Books/supplies: $1,500. Personal expenses: $2,277.

2007-2008 Financial aid. **Need-based:** 1,342 full-time freshmen applied for aid; 1,307 were judged to have need; 1,269 of these received aid. Average need met was 42%. Average scholarship/grant was $8,583; average loan $4,890. 47% of total undergraduate aid awarded as scholarships/grants, 53% as loans/jobs. **Non-need-based:** Awarded to 288 full-time undergraduates, including 62 freshmen. Scholarships awarded for academics, art, athletics, state residency.

Application procedures. **Admission:** No deadline. $30 fee, may be waived for applicants with need. Admission notification on a rolling basis. **Financial aid:** No deadline. FAFSA required. Applicants notified on a rolling basis.

Academics. **Special study options:** Accelerated study, combined bachelor's/graduate degree, distance learning, dual enrollment of high school students, honors, independent study, internships, study abroad. Master's Advantage. **Credit/placement by examination:** AP, CLEP, institutional tests. 44 credit hours maximum toward associate degree, 44 toward bachelor's. **Support services:** Learning center, study skills assistance, tutoring, writing center.

Majors. **Business:** Business admin. **Computer sciences:** Information technology. **Visual/performing arts:** Graphic design. **Other:** Professional studies.

Most popular majors. Business/marketing 83%, computer/information sciences 7%, visual/performing arts 10%.

Computing on campus. 1,702 workstations in library, computer center, student center. Dormitories wired for high-speed internet access. Wireless network available.

Student life. **Freshman orientation:** Mandatory. Held 1-4 weeks prior to commencement of classes. Students required to attend one 2 1/2-hour session. **Policies:** Students required to comply with college dress and attendance policies. **Housing:** Coed dorms, apartments available. $300 fully refundable deposit, deadline 5/1. **Activities:** Literary magazine, student newspaper.

Athletics. NAIA, USCAA. **Intercollegiate:** Baseball M, basketball, cross-country, diving W, golf, soccer, softball W, swimming W, tennis W, track and field W, volleyball W. **Team name:** Eagles.

Student services. Adult student services, alcohol/substance abuse counseling, career counseling, services for economically disadvantaged, student employment services, financial aid counseling, personal counseling, placement for graduates. **Physically disabled:** Services for visually, speech, hearing impaired.

Contact. E-mail: ais@robertmorris.edu
Phone: (312) 935-4400 Toll-free number: (800) 762-5960
Fax: (312) 935-4440
Catherine Lockwood, Vice President for Undergraduate Admissions, Robert Morris College: Chicago, 401South State Street, Chicago, IL 60605

Rockford College

Rockford, Illinois — **CB member**
www.rockford.edu — **CB code: 1665**

- Private 4-year liberal arts college
- Residential campus in small city
- 861 degree-seeking undergraduates: 13% part-time, 61% women, 8% African American, 2% Asian American, 6% Hispanic American, 1% international
- 288 degree-seeking graduate students
- 67% of applicants admitted
- SAT or ACT (ACT writing optional) required
- 34% graduate within 6 years

General. Founded in 1847. Regionally accredited. **Degrees:** 219 bachelor's awarded; master's offered. **Location:** 90 miles from Chicago. **Calendar:** Semester, limited summer session. **Full-time faculty:** 66 total; 76% have terminal degrees, 3% minority, 41% women. **Part-time faculty:** 78 total; 4% minority, 56% women. **Class size:** 75% < 20, 24% 20-39, less than 1% 40-49. **Special facilities:** Black box theater, nursing lab, center for civic engagement, prairie conservation area, center for ethics and entrepreneurship.

Freshman class profile. 606 applied, 406 admitted, 121 enrolled.

Mid 50% test scores			
ACT composite:	19-24	Rank in top quarter:	31%
GPA 3.75 or higher:	15%	Rank in top tenth:	14%
GPA 3.50-3.74:	13%	End year in good standing:	85%
GPA 3.0-3.49:	36%	Return as sophomores:	66%
GPA 2.0-2.99:	36%	Out-of-state:	22%
		Live on campus:	76%

Basis for selection. School achievement record and test scores are most important. Recommendations and activities also are considered. Auditions required of theater arts and musical theater performance majors. Personal statements required of students who fall below standard admission criteria.

High school preparation. College-preparatory program required. 15 units required. Required units include English 4, mathematics 3, social studies 3, science 3 (laboratory 3) and academic electives 2.

2009-2010 Annual costs. Tuition/fees (projected): $24,250. Room/board: $6,750. Books/supplies: $1,200. Personal expenses: $2,460.

2007-2008 Financial aid. Need-based: 104 full-time freshmen applied for aid; 94 were judged to have need; 94 of these received aid. Average need met was 73%. Average scholarship/grant was $14,972; average loan $3,256. 57% of total undergraduate aid awarded as scholarships/grants, 43% as loans/jobs. **Non-need-based:** Awarded to 188 full-time undergraduates, including 30 freshmen. Scholarships awarded for academics, alumni affiliation, leadership, minority status, music/drama, state residency.

Application procedures. Admission: No deadline. $35 fee, may be waived for applicants with need, free for online applicants. Admission notification on a rolling basis beginning on or about 9/15. **Financial aid:** Priority date 3/1; no closing date. FAFSA required. Applicants notified on a rolling basis starting 3/1; must reply within 4 week(s) of notification.

Academics. Community-based learning opportunities available. **Special study options:** Accelerated study, distance learning, double major, ESL, exchange student, honors, independent study, internships, study abroad, teacher certification program, United Nations semester, Washington semester. Tutorial classes, special studies courses. **Credit/placement by examination:** AP, CLEP, SAT, ACT, institutional tests. **Support services:** Learning center, reduced course load, remedial instruction, study skills assistance, tutoring, writing center.

Majors. Biology: General, biochemistry. **Business:** Accounting, business admin. **Computer sciences:** Computer science. **Education:** General, elementary, physical. **Foreign languages:** Classics, French, German, Latin, Romance, Spanish. **Health:** Nursing (RN). **History:** General. **Liberal arts:** Humanities. **Math:** General. **Philosophy/religion:** Philosophy. **Physical sciences:** Chemistry. **Psychology:** General. **Social sciences:** General, economics, international relations, political science. **Visual/performing arts:** Art, art history/conservation, dramatic. **Other:** Anthropology/sociology, Management studies, Science and mathematics.

Most popular majors. Biology 8%, business/marketing 21%, education 31%, health sciences 8%, psychology 11%, social sciences 6%.

Computing on campus. 75 workstations in library, computer center, student center. Dormitories wired for high-speed internet access and linked to campus network. Commuter students can connect to campus network. Helpline, repair service, wireless network available.

Student life. Freshman orientation: Mandatory. Preregistration for classes offered. Four-day program held the week prior to beginning of fall classes, includes introduction to college resources. **Policies:** Alcohol and guest policies, Academic Honor Code in place. **Housing:** Guaranteed on-campus for all undergraduates. Coed dorms, special housing for disabled, wellness housing available. $100 nonrefundable deposit. Special housing available for first-year students. **Activities:** Pep band, campus ministries, choral groups, dance, drama, international student organizations, literary magazine, music ensembles, musical theater, student government, Jane Adams Center for Civic Engagement, Intervarsity, multicultural club, Black student union, Democrats Encouraging and Motivating Students (DEMS), Rockford College Grand New Party, Rotoract.

Athletics. NCAA. **Intercollegiate:** Baseball M, basketball, cross-country, football (tackle) M, golf M, soccer, softball W, tennis, track and field, volleyball W. **Team name:** Regents.

Student services. Alcohol/substance abuse counseling, chaplain/spiritual director, career counseling, student employment services, financial aid counseling, health services, personal counseling, veterans' counselor. **Physically disabled:** Services for visually impaired.

Contact. E-mail: rcadmissions@rockford.edu
Phone: (815) 226-4050 Toll-free number: (800) 892-2984
Fax: (815) 226-2822
Jennifer Nordstrom, Associate Vice President for Undergraduate Admission and Strategic Marketing, Rockford College, 5050 East State Street, Rockford, IL 61108-2393

Roosevelt University

Chicago, Illinois — **CB member**
www.roosevelt.edu — **CB code: 1666**

- Private 4-year university
- Commuter campus in very large city
- 4,264 degree-seeking undergraduates: 36% part-time, 67% women, 22% African American, 5% Asian American, 11% Hispanic American, 2% international
- 3,269 degree-seeking graduate students
- 78% of applicants admitted
- SAT or ACT (ACT writing optional) required
- 41% graduate within 6 years

General. Founded in 1945. Regionally accredited. Additional campus in Schaumburg. **Degrees:** 958 bachelor's awarded; master's, doctoral offered. **Location:** Downtown. **Calendar:** Semester, extensive summer session. **Full-time faculty:** 219 total; 87% have terminal degrees, 17% minority, 41% women. **Part-time faculty:** 415 total; 46% women. **Class size:** 63% < 20, 34% 20-39, 2% 40-49, less than 1% 50-99, less than 1% >100.

Freshman class profile. 2,311 applied, 1,806 admitted, 502 enrolled.

Mid 50% test scores			
SAT critical reading:	510-640	Rank in top quarter:	12%
SAT math:	470-570	Rank in top tenth:	1%
ACT composite:	19-24	Return as sophomores:	70%
GPA 3.75 or higher:	16%	Out-of-state:	28%
GPA 3.50-3.74:	10%	Live on campus:	62%
GPA 3.0-3.49:	25%	International:	2%
GPA 2.0-2.99:	48%	Sororities:	2%

Basis for selection. Recent secondary school performance most crucial. Personal statement and recommended interview can be used to communicate special circumstances. Placement evaluation required for all admitted, degree-seeking undergraduate students. Interview recommended for early admission and borderline applicants. Audition required of music and theater majors. Portfolio recommended for art and theater majors. **Homeschooled:** Statement describing homeschool structure and mission, letter of recommendation (nonparent) required.

High school preparation. College-preparatory program required. 15 units required; 19 recommended. Required and recommended units include English 4, mathematics 3-4, social studies 2, history 1, science 3 (laboratory 2), foreign language 2 and academic electives 2. Extensive work in English, history, mathematics, foreign language, and science recommended.

2009-2010 Annual costs. Tuition/fees: $21,000. Tuition for Chicago College of the Performing Arts is $28,000 per year. Room/board: $11,100. Books/supplies: $1,200. Personal expenses: $2,300.

2007-2008 Financial aid. Non-need-based: Scholarships awarded for academics, alumni affiliation, leadership, minority status, music/drama, state residency.

Application procedures. Admission: Priority date 8/1; deadline 9/1 (receipt date). $25 fee, may be waived for applicants with need. Admission notification on a rolling basis beginning on or about 10/15. Must reply by May 1 or within 4 week(s) if notified thereafter. **Financial aid:** Priority date 4/1; no closing date. FAFSA, institutional form required. Applicants notified on a rolling basis starting 3/15; must reply within 2 week(s) of notification.

Academics. Special study options: Accelerated study, combined bachelor's/graduate degree, distance learning, double major, dual enrollment of high school students, ESL, honors, independent study, internships, study abroad, teacher certification program. **Credit/placement by examination:** AP, CLEP, SAT, ACT, institutional tests. 30 credit hours maximum toward bachelor's degree. **Support services:** Learning center, pre-admission summer program, reduced course load, remedial instruction, study skills assistance, tutoring, writing center.

Majors. Area/ethnic studies: African-American, women's. **Biology:** General, biotechnology. **Business:** General, accounting, actuarial science, communications, finance, financial planning, hospitality admin, human resources, insurance, management science, marketing, office management, organizational behavior. **Communications:** General, journalism, organizational. **Computer sciences:** Computer science, networking. **Education:** Early childhood, elementary, music, secondary, special. **Engineering technology:** Electrical. **Foreign languages:** General, comparative lit, Spanish. **Health:** Clinical lab science, medical radiologic technology/radiation therapy, nuclear medical technology. **History:** General. **Legal studies:** Paralegal. **Liberal arts:** Arts/sciences. **Math:** General. **Philosophy/religion:** Philosophy. **Physical sciences:** Chemistry. **Protective services:** Criminal justice. **Psychology:** General. **Social sciences:** Economics, international relations, political science, sociology. **Visual/performing arts:** Acting, art history/conservation, dramatic, jazz, music performance, music theory/composition, piano/organ, stringed instruments, voice/opera. **Other:** Allied health, Integrated communication.

Most popular majors. Business/marketing 34%, communications/journalism 6%, education 7%, personal/culinary services 8%, psychology 14%, social sciences 6%, visual/performing arts 8%.

Computing on campus. 250 workstations in dormitories, library, computer center, student center. Dormitories wired for high-speed internet access and linked to campus network. Commuter students can connect to campus network. Online course registration, online library, helpline, repair service available.

Student life. Freshman orientation: Mandatory. Preregistration for classes offered. Ongoing from mid-Spring through the summer; 1-2 days in duration, with coverage of academic and non-academic elements of student life. **Housing:** Guaranteed on-campus for all undergraduates. Coed dorms, apartments available. $500 fully refundable deposit, deadline 8/1. High-rise residence hall in cooperation with University Center of Chicago available. **Activities:** Dance, drama, international student organizations, literary magazine, musical theater, radio station, student government, student newspaper, Christian Bible groups, theater club, Black student union, Hispanic organization, residence hall council, Asociacion de Latinos Unidos.

Athletics. Intramural: Badminton, baseball M, basketball, table tennis.

Student services. Adult student services, alcohol/substance abuse counseling, career counseling, student employment services, financial aid counseling, personal counseling, placement for graduates, veterans' counselor. **Physically disabled:** Services for visually, hearing impaired.

Contact. E-mail: applyru@roosevelt.edu
Toll-free number: (877) 277-5978 Fax: (847) 619-8636
Elizabeth Gierach, Assistant Vice President for Admission, Roosevelt University, 430 South Michigan Avenue, Chicago, IL 60605-1394

Rosalind Franklin University of Medicine and Science

North Chicago, Illinois
www.rosalindfranklin.edu **CB code: 0768**

- Private two-year upper-division university and health science college
- Commuter campus in large town
- Application essay required

General. Founded in 1912. Regionally accredited. **Degrees:** 3 bachelor's awarded; master's, doctoral, first professional offered. **Location:** 40 miles from Chicago. **Calendar:** Quarter, limited summer session. **Full-time faculty:** 144 total. **Part-time faculty:** 51 total. **Special facilities:** 14 fully equipped patient examination rooms, anatomy lab.

Student profile. 5 degree-seeking undergraduates. 100% entered as juniors. 78% transferred from two-year, 22% transferred from four-year institutions.

Basis for selection. College transcript, application essay required. Undergraduate education must be completed in an accredited college or university, with at least a "C" in required courses. Proficiency in written and spoken English required. Transfer accepted as juniors.

2008-2009 Annual costs. Tuition/fees: $15,200. Full-time tuition rate is for bachelor's degree program in Medical Technology. Books/supplies: $300.

Financial aid. All financial aid based on need. **Additional information:** Financial aid application deadline 60 days prior to program start.

Application procedures. Admission: Deadline 7/1. $20 fee, may be waived for applicants with need. Application must be submitted on paper. **Financial aid:** FAFSA, institutional form required.

Academics. Special study options: Accelerated study, cooperative education, cross-registration, distance learning, double major, dual enrollment of high school students, internships. **Credit/placement by examination:** AP, CLEP, institutional tests. **Support services:** Learning center, reduced course load, study skills assistance, tutoring.

Majors. Health: Clinical lab technology.

Computing on campus. 106 workstations in library, computer center, student center. Dormitories wired for high-speed internet access and linked to campus network. Commuter students can connect to campus network. Helpline, repair service, wireless network available.

Student life. Housing: Apartments available. $500 deposit. Limited on-campus housing available. **Activities:** Choral groups, literary magazine, student government, student newspaper, Asian Pacific American medical student association, adolescent substance abuse prevention, Christian Medical Association, Hillel, internal health/medicine interest groups, lesbian/gay/bisexual and transgendered people in medicine, Middle Eastern medical student association, South Asian medical association, Salud Ofrecida A Latinos.

Student services. Alcohol/substance abuse counseling, career counseling, financial aid counseling, health services, minority student services, personal counseling, placement for graduates, veterans' counselor.

Contact. E-mail: grad.admissions@rosalindfranklin.edu
Phone: (847) 578-3209
Maryann DeCaire, Vice President for Enrollment Services, Rosalind Franklin University of Medicine and Science, 3333 Green Bay Road, North Chicago, IL 60064-3095

Rush University

Chicago, Illinois
www.rushu.rush.edu **CB code: 3262**

- Private two-year upper-division health science and nursing college
- Commuter campus in very large city
- Application essay required

General. Founded in 1971. Regionally accredited. Educational component of Rush University Medical Center. Students use clinical and laboratory facilities of the medical center, affiliated hospitals, and community health centers. Based on teacher-practitioner model. **Degrees:** 151 bachelor's awarded; master's, doctoral, first professional offered. **Articulation:** Agreements with College of DuPage, Triton College, Parkland College, Moraine Valley Community College, Oakton Community College, William Rainey Harper College, Kankakee Community College. **Location:** 2 miles from downtown. **Calendar:** Quarter, limited summer session. **Full-time faculty:** 450 total. **Part-time faculty:** 350 total. **Class size:** 37% < 20, 36% 20-39, 27% 50-99.

Student profile. 166 degree-seeking undergraduates. 100% entered as juniors.

Out-of-state:	15%	**25 or older:**	65%
Live on campus:	20%		

Basis for selection. College transcript, application essay required. Admission based on GPA and letters of recommendation. Application closing dates: nursing April 1, clinical lab sciences/medical technology June 1, perfusion technology, March 1. Transfer accepted as juniors.

2008-2009 Annual costs. Tuition/fees: $20,352. Tuition costs vary by program. Room only: $8,658. Books/supplies: $700. Personal expenses: $2,313.

Four-Year Colleges

Financial aid. Need-based: 281 applied for aid; 241 were judged to have need; 241 of these received aid. Average need met was 55%. 28% of total undergraduate aid awarded as scholarships/grants, 72% as loans/jobs.

Application procedures. Admission: Rolling admission. $50 fee, may be waived for applicants with need. **Financial aid:** Priority date 5/1, no deadline. Applicants notified on a rolling basis starting 4/1; must reply within 3 weeks of notification. FAFSA, institutional form required.

Academics. Special study options: Accelerated study, combined bachelor's/graduate degree, distance learning, liberal arts/career combination. Registered nurse completion program. **Credit/placement by examination:** AP, CLEP, institutional tests. 45 credit hours maximum toward bachelor's degree.

Majors. Health: Clinical lab science, nursing (RN), perfusion technology.

Computing on campus. 140 workstations in library, computer center, student center. Commuter students can connect to campus network. Online library, helpline, wireless network available.

Student life. Policies: Funds available for official student groups. **Housing:** Apartments available. $200 deposit. **Activities:** Student government, student newspaper, Christian Fellowship, rape victim advocate program, medical technicians club, National Student Nurses' Association chapter, Lesbian/Gay/Bisexual/Allies, Health Science Students for Choice.

Student services. Alcohol/substance abuse counseling, career counseling, student employment services, financial aid counseling, health services, on-campus daycare, personal counseling, veterans' counselor.

Contact. E-mail: rush_admissions@rush.edu
Phone: (312) 942-7100 Fax: (312) 942-2219
Hicela Woods, Director of College Admission Services, Rush University, College Admissions, Chicago, IL 60612

Saint Anthony College of Nursing

Rockford, Illinois
www.sacn.edu **CB code: 3923**

- Private two-year upper-division nursing college affiliated with Roman Catholic Church
- Commuter campus in small city
- Application essay, interview required

General. Regionally accredited. MSN in Nurse Educator, Clinical Nurse Specialist (Adult Health) and Clinical Nurse Leader offered. **Degrees:** 66 bachelor's awarded; master's offered. **Articulation:** Agreements with Rock Valley College, McHenry County College, Sauk Valley Community College, Kishwaukee College, Elgin Community College, Blackhawk Technical College, Highland Community College. **Location:** 90 miles from Chicago. **Calendar:** Semester, limited summer session. **Full-time faculty:** 11 total. **Part-time faculty:** 5 total. **Class size:** 18% < 20, 76% 20-39, 6% 40-49. **Special facilities:** Nursing labs, hospital facility.

Student profile. 151 degree-seeking undergraduates. 100% entered as juniors. 88% transferred from two-year, 12% transferred from four-year institutions.

Out-of-state:	6%	**25 or older:**	53%

Basis for selection. College transcript, application essay, interview required, 64 credits required in specific pre-nursing and general education courses. Transfer accepted as juniors.

2008-2009 Annual costs. Tuition/fees: $18,577. Required fees vary from $112-$262. Books/supplies: $1,500. Personal expenses: $1,785.

Financial aid. Non-need-based: Scholarships awarded for academics, leadership, state residency.

Application procedures. Admission: Deadline 8/15. $50 fee. Admission notification 9/30. Must reply by 10/31. **Financial aid:** No deadline. Applicants notified on a rolling basis starting 8/18. FAFSA required.

Academics. Special study options: Independent study, liberal arts/career combination. **Credit/placement by examination:** AP, CLEP.

Majors. Health: Adult health nursing.

Computing on campus. 21 workstations in library, computer center. Commuter students can connect to campus network. Online library available.

Student life. Activities: Student government.

Student services. Alcohol/substance abuse counseling, chaplain/spiritual director, career counseling, financial aid counseling, health services, legal services, personal counseling, women's services.

Contact. E-mail: admissions@sacn.edu
Phone: (815) 227-2141 Fax: (815) 227-2730
Nancy Sanders, Assistant Dean for Admissions and Student Affairs, Saint Anthony College of Nursing, 5658 East State Street, Rockford, IL 61108-2468

St. Augustine College

Chicago, Illinois
www.staugustinecollege.edu **CB code: 0697**

- Private 4-year liberal arts college affiliated with Episcopal Church
- Commuter campus in very large city
- 1,250 degree-seeking undergraduates

General. Founded in 1980. Regionally accredited. **Degrees:** 17 bachelor's, 221 associate awarded. **Calendar:** Semester, limited summer session. **Full-time faculty:** 24 total; 67% minority, 54% women. **Part-time faculty:** 118 total; 50% minority, 46% women.

Basis for selection. Open admission. Test scores considered for students over 17 years old who have not completed high school. High school diploma or GED required for students entering respiratory therapy technician program. Applicants without high school diploma or GED at time of enrollment must earn GED by end of first year of study. **Homeschooled:** Placement test in English, math, and Spanish required.

2008-2009 Annual costs. Tuition/fees: $9,600.

Application procedures. Admission: No deadline. No application fee. Application must be submitted on paper. Admission notification on a rolling basis. **Financial aid:** No deadline. FAFSA, institutional form required. Applicants notified on a rolling basis.

Academics. Curriculum offers several elective courses in English language primarily for Hispanic students. **Special study options:** Cooperative education, double major, ESL, independent study, internships, liberal arts/career combination. **Credit/placement by examination:** CLEP, IB, institutional tests. **Support services:** Learning center, pre-admission summer program, remedial instruction, tutoring.

Majors. Public administration: Social work.

Computing on campus. 100 workstations in library, computer center. Commuter students can connect to campus network. Online library available.

Student life. Freshman orientation: Mandatory. Preregistration for classes offered. **Activities:** Student government, student newspaper.

Athletics. Intercollegiate: Soccer M.

Student services. Adult student services, alcohol/substance abuse counseling, career counseling, financial aid counseling, minority student services, on-campus daycare, personal counseling, placement for graduates.

Contact. Phone: (773) 878-8756 Fax: (773) 878-9032
Soledad Ruiz, Assistant Dean of Admissions and Records, St. Augustine College, 1345 West Argyle, Chicago, IL 60640-3501

St. Francis Medical Center College of Nursing

Peoria, Illinois
www.sfmccon.edu **CB code: 1756**

- Private two-year upper-division nursing college affiliated with Roman Catholic Church
- Commuter campus in small city
- 46% of applicants admitted
- Application essay required

General. Founded in 1905. Regionally accredited. Located at large medical center. National League of Nursing accredited. NCA accredited. Offers experience at Tazewell County, Fulton County, Peoria City/County Health Departments, Human Service Center and various other community agencies. **Degrees:** 162 bachelor's awarded; master's offered. **Location:** 180 miles from Chicago, 160 miles from St. Louis. **Calendar:** Semester, limited summer session. **Full-time faculty:** 33 total; 33% have terminal degrees,

100% women. **Part-time faculty:** 15 total; 93% women. **Class size:** 7% < 20, 50% 20-39, 36% 40-49, 7% 50-99.

Student profile. 333 degree-seeking undergraduates, 119 degree-seeking graduate students. 321 applied as first time-transfer students, 148 admitted, 70 enrolled. 100% entered as juniors. 92% transferred from two-year, 8% transferred from four-year institutions.

Women:	90%	**Hispanic American:**	2%
African American:	5%	**Part-time:**	19%
Asian American:	3%	**25 or older:**	75%

Basis for selection. High school transcript, college transcript, application essay required. Enrollment depends on satisfactory completion of 62 semester hours of a specified prenursing curriculum. Applications may be submitted after satisfactory completion of 30 semester hours of required prenursing courses. Must include 8 semester hours of physical/life sciences. 2.5 GPA required. Transfer accepted as juniors.

2009-2010 Annual costs. Tuition/fees: $14,420. Room only: $2,400. Books/supplies: $1,230. Personal expenses: $2,700.

Financial aid. Need-based: 260 applied for aid; 210 were judged to have need; 210 of these received aid. Average need met was 64%. 48% of total undergraduate aid awarded as scholarships/grants, 52% as loans/jobs. **Non-need-based:** Awarded to 74 undergraduates. Scholarships awarded for academics, alumni affiliation. **Additional information:** OSF Saint Francis Medical Center Education student loan available to full-time students on a limited basis. Tuition waiver program for hospital employees available.

Application procedures. Admission: Deadline 9/1. $50 fee. Application must be submitted on paper. **Financial aid:** No deadline. Applicants notified on a rolling basis starting 5/15; must reply within 2 weeks of notification. FAFSA, institutional form required.

Academics. Special study options: Distance learning. **Credit/placement by examination:** CLEP.

Majors. Health: Nursing (RN).

Computing on campus. 31 workstations in library, computer center. Dormitories linked to campus network. Commuter students can connect to campus network. Online library, helpline, repair service available.

Student life. Housing: Guaranteed on-campus for all undergraduates. Coed dorms, wellness housing available. **Activities:** Student government, Christian fellowship, student nurses' association, minority association.

Student services. Adult student services, financial aid counseling, health services, personal counseling.

Contact. E-mail: janice.farquharson@osfhealthcare.org
Phone: (309) 655-2245 Fax: (309) 624-8973
Janice Farquharson, Director of Admissions and Recruitment, St. Francis Medical Center College of Nursing, 511 NE Greenleaf Street, Peoria, IL 61603-3783

St. John's College
Springfield, Illinois
www.st-johns.org/education/schools/nursing

- Private two-year upper-division nursing college affiliated with Roman Catholic Church
- Commuter campus in small city
- Test scores required

General. Degrees: 35 bachelor's awarded. **Location:** 220 miles from Chicago, 100 miles from St. Louis. **Calendar:** Semester. **Full-time faculty:** 11 total. **Part-time faculty:** 1 total.

Student profile. 71 degree-seeking undergraduates.

Women:	7%	**Part-time:**	1%
African American:	1%	**Out-of-state:**	2%
Asian American:	1%	**25 or older:**	30%

Basis for selection. High school transcript, college transcript, standardized test scores required. Transfer accepted as juniors.

2008-2009 Annual costs. Tuition/fees: $12,204. Books/supplies: $1,645. Personal expenses: $1,854.

Application procedures. Admission: $60 fee.

Academics. Credit/placement by examination: CLEP.

Majors. Health: Nursing (RN).

Computing on campus. Commuter students can connect to campus network. Online library, helpline, wireless network available.

Contact. E-mail: college@st-johns.org
Phone: (217) 525-5628 Fax: (217) 757-6870
Linda Quigley, Admissions Officer, St. John's College, 729 East Carpenter Street, Springfield, IL 62702

St. Xavier University
Chicago, Illinois — **CB member**
www.sxu.edu — **CB code: 1708**

- Private 4-year university affiliated with Roman Catholic Church
- Commuter campus in very large city
- 3,160 degree-seeking undergraduates: 18% part-time, 70% women, 18% African American, 3% Asian American, 14% Hispanic American
- 2,118 degree-seeking graduate students
- 71% of applicants admitted
- SAT or ACT (ACT writing optional) required

General. Founded in 1847. Regionally accredited. Affiliated with Sisters of Mercy. **Degrees:** 857 bachelor's awarded; master's offered. **ROTC:** Air Force. **Location:** 20 miles from downtown. **Calendar:** Semester, limited summer session. **Full-time faculty:** 176 total; 100% have terminal degrees, 14% minority, 56% women. **Part-time faculty:** 243 total; 23% have terminal degrees, 2% minority, 60% women. **Special facilities:** Music performance studio, reading clinic, speech clinic, learning disabilities clinic, mathematics laboratory.

Freshman class profile. 2,549 applied, 1,817 admitted, 554 enrolled.

Mid 50% test scores		**GPA 3.0-3.49:**	29%
SAT critical reading:	470-560	**GPA 2.0-2.99:**	32%
SAT math:	460-590	**Rank in top quarter:**	48%
SAT writing:	470-570	**Rank in top tenth:**	20%
ACT composite:	19-25	**Out-of-state:**	12%
GPA 3.75 or higher:	25%	**Live on campus:**	60%
GPA 3.50-3.74:	14%		

Basis for selection. GPA, test scores most important. Counselor recommendation, class rank considered. Interview recommended for borderline applicants. Audition required of music majors.

High school preparation. 16 units recommended. Recommended units include English 4, mathematics 3, foreign language 2 and academic electives 3. 4 units of science and social studies combined.

2008-2009 Annual costs. Tuition/fees: $22,926. Room/board: $8,007. Books/supplies: $900. Personal expenses: $986.

2007-2008 Financial aid. Need-based: 484 full-time freshmen applied for aid; 449 were judged to have need; 449 of these received aid. Average need met was 87%. Average scholarship/grant was $6,977; average loan $1,703. 56% of total undergraduate aid awarded as scholarships/grants, 44% as loans/jobs. **Non-need-based:** Awarded to 769 full-time undergraduates, including 138 freshmen. Scholarships awarded for academics, athletics, music/drama.

Application procedures. Admission: No deadline. $25 fee, may be waived for applicants with need, free for online applicants. Admission notification on a rolling basis. Must reply by May 1 or within 4 week(s) if notified thereafter. **Financial aid:** Priority date 3/1; no closing date. FAFSA required. Applicants notified on a rolling basis starting 2/1; must reply by 5/1 or within 2 week(s) of notification.

Academics. Special study options: Accelerated study, combined bachelor's/graduate degree, cooperative education, distance learning, dual enrollment of high school students, ESL, external degree, honors, independent study, internships, liberal arts/career combination, student-designed major, study abroad, teacher certification program. **Credit/placement by examination:** AP, CLEP, institutional tests. 27 credit hours maximum toward bachelor's degree. **Support services:** Learning center, pre-admission summer program, reduced course load, remedial instruction, study skills assistance, tutoring, writing center.

Majors. Biology: General, botany. **Business:** General, accounting, actuarial science, international. **Communications:** General. **Computer sciences:** General, computer science. **Education:** General, art, biology, history, mathematics, music, secondary, social science, Spanish. **Foreign languages:** Spanish. **Health:** Nursing (RN), premedicine, prepharmacy, preveterinary, speech pathology. **History:** General. **Interdisciplinary:** Biological/

physical sciences. **Legal studies:** Prelaw. **Liberal arts:** Arts/sciences. **Math:** General. **Philosophy/religion:** Philosophy, religion. **Physical sciences:** Chemistry. **Protective services:** Criminal justice. **Psychology:** General. **Social sciences:** General, international relations, political science, sociology. **Theology:** Theology. **Visual/performing arts:** Studio arts, voice/opera.

Most popular majors. Business/marketing 23%, education 19%, health sciences 19%, liberal arts 9%, psychology 6%.

Computing on campus. 306 workstations in dormitories, library, computer center, student center. Dormitories wired for high-speed internet access and linked to campus network. Commuter students can connect to campus network. Online course registration, helpline, student web hosting, wireless network available.

Student life. **Freshman orientation:** Mandatory. Preregistration for classes offered. Two-day overnight orientation held in summer. **Housing:** Coed dorms, apartments available. $100 nonrefundable deposit, deadline 5/1. **Activities:** Bands, campus ministries, choral groups, film society, international student organizations, literary magazine, music ensembles, radio station, student government, student newspaper, symphony orchestra, black student organization, Hispanic student organization, student activities board, student nurses association, Muslim student association, Celtic Connection, Fellowship of Christian Athletes, Xi Delta.

Athletics. NAIA. **Intercollegiate:** Baseball M, basketball, cross-country, football (tackle) M, soccer, softball W, volleyball W. **Intramural:** Basketball M, bowling, volleyball. **Team name:** Cougars.

Student services. Adult student services, alcohol/substance abuse counseling, chaplain/spiritual director, career counseling, services for economically disadvantaged, student employment services, financial aid counseling, health services, on-campus daycare, personal counseling, placement for graduates. **Physically disabled:** Services for speech impaired.

Contact. E-mail: admissions@sxu.edu
Phone: (773) 298-3050 Toll-free number: (800) 462-9288
Fax: (773) 298-3076
Kathleen Carlson, Vice President of Student Recruitment and Enrollment Planning, St. Xavier University, 3700 West 103rd Street, Chicago, IL 60655

School of the Art Institute of Chicago

Chicago, Illinois **CB member**
www.saic.edu **CB code: 1713**

- Private 4-year visual arts college
- Commuter campus in very large city
- 2,359 degree-seeking undergraduates: 6% part-time, 65% women, 3% African American, 12% Asian American, 9% Hispanic American, 1% Native American, 18% international
- 597 degree-seeking graduate students
- 81% of applicants admitted
- SAT or ACT (ACT writing optional), application essay required
- 62% graduate within 6 years

General. Founded in 1866. Regionally accredited. Interdisciplinary curriculum with 6 credit off-campus study requirement and "credit/no-credit" grading system. **Degrees:** 478 bachelor's awarded; master's offered. **Calendar:** Semester, extensive summer session. **Full-time faculty:** 140 total; 63% have terminal degrees, 20% minority. **Part-time faculty:** 524 total; 34% have terminal degrees, 13% minority. **Class size:** 86% <20, 11% 20-39, 1% 40-49, less than 1% 50-99, less than 1% >100. **Special facilities:** Film center, video data bank, poetry center, art galleries, fashion resource center, artists' book collection, Roger Brown study collection.

Freshman class profile. 2,075 applied, 1,683 admitted, 449 enrolled.

Return as sophomores:	74%	**Live on campus:**	85%
Out-of-state:	81%	**International:**	19%

Basis for selection. Portfolio very important, statement of purpose, 500 SAT Critical Reading or 20 ACT English, academic credentials, and recommendations also considered. Interview recommended. Portfolio required.

High school preparation. Advanced-level study of art recommended.

2009-2010 Annual costs. Tuition/fees (projected): $34,600. Students will be required to purchase a laptop through SAIC. Costs range from $2,000 to $2,200. Room only: $9,200. Books/supplies: $2,560. Personal expenses: $2,520.

2007-2008 Financial aid. **Need-based:** 299 full-time freshmen applied for aid; 260 were judged to have need; 259 of these received aid. Average need met was 76%. Average scholarship/grant was $12,783; average loan $3,668. 54% of total undergraduate aid awarded as scholarships/grants, 46% as loans/jobs. **Non-need-based:** Awarded to 640 full-time undergraduates, including 192 freshmen. Scholarships awarded for academics, art.

Application procedures. **Admission:** Priority date 2/15; deadline 6/1. $65 fee, may be waived for applicants with need. Application must be submitted online. Admission notification on a rolling basis beginning on or about 10/1. **Financial aid:** Priority date 3/15; no closing date. FAFSA required. Applicants notified on a rolling basis starting 3/1.

Academics. Interdisciplinary curriculum allows students to personalize education or concentrate on single discipline. **Special study options:** Cooperative education, cross-registration, double major, ESL, exchange student, independent study, internships, New York semester, student-designed major, study abroad, teacher certification program. **Credit/placement by examination:** AP, CLEP, IB. 18 credit hours maximum toward bachelor's degree. DANTES scores accepted. **Support services:** Learning center, preadmission summer program, reduced course load, remedial instruction, study skills assistance, tutoring.

Majors. **Architecture:** Interior. **Communications:** Digital media. **Communications technology:** Animation/special effects, desktop publishing, graphics, photo/film/video, recording arts. **Education:** Art. **Visual/performing arts:** General, art, art history/conservation, ceramics, cinematography, design, drawing, fashion design, fiber arts, graphic design, industrial design, interior design, multimedia, painting, photography, printmaking, sculpture, studio arts. **Other:** Designed objects, Visual and critical studies.

Computing on campus. PC or laptop required. 350 workstations in dormitories, library, computer center. Dormitories wired for high-speed internet access and linked to campus network. Commuter students can connect to campus network. Online library, helpline, repair service, student web hosting, wireless network available.

Student life. **Freshman orientation:** Mandatory, $75 fee. Preregistration for classes offered. Held 4 days prior to beginning of class. First day open to parents, family and friends. **Housing:** Coed dorms, special housing for disabled, wellness housing available. $550 nonrefundable deposit. **Activities:** Campus ministries, dance, drama, film society, international student organizations, literary magazine, radio station, student government, student newspaper, TV station, Agape, creative writing guild, Korean student association, Student Organization for the Advancement of Philosophy, Students for Sexual Diversity, Taiwanese student organization, Veggies Unite!, yoga group.

Student services. Alcohol/substance abuse counseling, career counseling, student employment services, financial aid counseling, health services, minority student services, personal counseling, veterans' counselor. **Physically disabled:** Services for visually, speech, hearing impaired.

Contact. E-mail: admiss@saic.edu
Phone: (312) 629-6100 Toll-free number: (800) 232-7242
Fax: (312) 629-6101
Scott Ramon, Director, Undergraduate Admissions, School of the Art Institute of Chicago, 36 South Wabash Avenue, Chicago, IL 60603

Shimer College

Chicago, Illinois
www.shimer.edu **CB code: 1717**

- Private 4-year liberal arts college
- Residential campus in very large city
- 91 degree-seeking undergraduates: 14% part-time, 51% women, 5% African American, 4% Asian American, 3% Hispanic American, 1% Native American, 2% international
- 90% of applicants admitted
- Application essay, interview required
- 61% graduate within 6 years; 30% enter graduate study

General. Founded in 1853. Regionally accredited. Located on campus of Illinois Institute of Technology. **Degrees:** 20 bachelor's awarded. **Location:** 3 miles from downtown. **Calendar:** Semester, limited summer session. **Full-time faculty:** 12 total; 92% have terminal degrees, 8% minority. **Part-time faculty:** 3 total; 33% have terminal degrees. **Class size:** 100% < 20.

Freshman class profile. 59 applied, 53 admitted, 27 enrolled.

GPA 3.75 or higher:	21%	**End year in good standing:**	94%
GPA 3.50-3.74:	21%	**Return as sophomores:**	73%
GPA 3.0-3.49:	37%	**Out-of-state:**	31%
GPA 2.0-2.99:	21%	**Live on campus:**	62%

Basis for selection. Essays and interviews most important. Test scores, GPA, recommendations, motivation, maturity considered. Demonstrated writing skills and interest in and enthusiasm about Great Books curriculum and discussion method important. Early entrants and other applicants who do not have high school diplomas may be required to submit GED; applicants without high school diplomas who are too young to take GED may be required to complete additional approved testing in order to comply with financial aid regulations.

High school preparation. 21 units recommended. Recommended units include English 4, mathematics 3, social studies 3, history 2, science 3 (laboratory 1), foreign language 3 and visual/performing arts 1.

2008-2009 Annual costs. Tuition/fees: $26,110. Required fees include cost of books. Room/board: $11,435. Books/supplies: $1,400. Personal expenses: $1,020.

2008-2009 Financial aid. Need-based: 23 full-time freshmen applied for aid; 18 were judged to have need; 18 of these received aid. Average need met was 62%. Average scholarship/grant was $9,000; average loan $5,400. 51% of total undergraduate aid awarded as scholarships/grants, 49% as loans/jobs. **Non-need-based:** Awarded to 73 full-time undergraduates, including 23 freshmen. Scholarships awarded for academics, alumni affiliation.

Application procedures. Admission: No deadline. $25 fee, may be waived for applicants with need. Admission notification on a rolling basis beginning on or about 9/15. Must reply by May 1 or within 3 week(s) if notified thereafter. **Financial aid:** Priority date 3/1; no closing date. FAFSA, institutional form required. Applicants notified on a rolling basis starting 4/1; must reply by 5/1 or within 3 week(s) of notification.

Academics. Curriculum is based on The Great Books of Western Culture. **Special study options:** Accelerated study, combined bachelor's/graduate degree, cross-registration, double major, independent study, internships, study abroad, weekend college. One-on-one tutorials with faculty member, accelerated BA to JD program, Shimer at Oxford program. **Credit/placement by examination:** CLEP, institutional tests. Shimer Institutional placement examinations may result in credit; no outside testing is accepted. **Support services:** Reduced course load, study skills assistance, tutoring, writing center.

Majors. Interdisciplinary: Natural sciences. **Liberal arts:** Arts/sciences, humanities. **Social sciences:** General.

Most popular majors. Biology 10%, liberal arts 15%, social sciences 30%.

Computing on campus. 25 workstations in dormitories, library, computer center, student center. Dormitories wired for high-speed internet access and linked to campus network. Commuter students can connect to campus network. Helpline, wireless network available.

Student life. Freshman orientation: Mandatory, $100 fee. Held 3-4 days prior to start of classes. Includes demonstration class, placement exams, orientation to residence hall and Chicago. **Housing:** Guaranteed on-campus for freshmen. Coed dorms, single-sex dorms, apartments, wellness housing available. $300 partly refundable deposit, deadline 5/1. **Activities:** Concert band, campus ministries, choral groups, drama, international student organizations, literary magazine, music ensembles, radio station, student government, student newspaper, American Red Cross, Catholic campus ministry, gays/lesbians/allies and more, Hillel, Hindu student council, gospel choir, Muslim students association, chess club.

Athletics. Intramural: Basketball, football (non-tackle), soccer, softball, track and field, volleyball. **Team name:** Flaming Smelts.

Student services. Adult student services, alcohol/substance abuse counseling, career counseling, student employment services, financial aid counseling, health services, personal counseling, placement for graduates.

Contact. E-mail: admission@shimer.edu
Phone: (312) 235-3506 Toll-free number: (800) 215-7173
Fax: (312) 235-3501
Elaine Vincent, Director of Enrollment Services, Shimer College, 3424 South State Street, Chicago, IL 60616

Southern Illinois University Carbondale

Carbondale, Illinois — **CB member**
www.siuc.edu — **CB code: 1726**

- Public 4-year university
- Residential campus in large town
- 15,921 degree-seeking undergraduates: 10% part-time, 43% women, 19% African American, 2% Asian American, 4% Hispanic American, 2% international
- 4,264 degree-seeking graduate students
- 69% of applicants admitted
- SAT or ACT (ACT writing optional) required

General. Founded in 1869. Regionally accredited. Active production schedule in several theaters includes contemporary works, musicals, operas, original plays by faculty and students, and world drama from major periods in theater history. **Degrees:** 4,262 bachelor's, 58 associate awarded; master's, doctoral, first professional offered. **ROTC:** Army, Air Force. **Location:** 100 miles from St. Louis. **Calendar:** Semester, extensive summer session. **Full-time faculty:** 931 total; 82% have terminal degrees, 17% minority, 36% women. **Part-time faculty:** 142 total; 58% have terminal degrees, 12% minority, 42% women. **Class size:** 51% < 20, 41% 20-39, 3% 40-49, 3% 50-99, 1% >100. **Special facilities:** University press, coal research center, materials technology center, outdoor education laboratory, university farms, center for study of crime, electron microscopy center, cooperative wildlife research laboratory, cooperative fisheries research laboratory, vivarium, airport training facility, laboratory theatre, child development laboratory, center for archaeological investigations, small business incubator, public policy institute, dental and medical clinics, environmental center.

Freshman class profile. 11,785 applied, 8,163 admitted, 2,686 enrolled.

Mid 50% test scores			
SAT critical reading:	420-570	**Rank in top quarter:**	29%
SAT math:	440-590	**Rank in top tenth:**	9%
SAT writing:	410-520	**Out-of-state:**	6%
ACT composite:	19-24	**Live on campus:**	70%
		International:	1%

Basis for selection. High school class rank and ACT scores most important.

High school preparation. 15 units required. Required units include English 4, mathematics 3, social studies 3, science 3 and academic electives 2.

2008-2009 Annual costs. Tuition/fees: $9,813; $20,276 out-of-state. Room/board: $7,137. Books/supplies: $900. Personal expenses: $1,218.

2008-2009 Financial aid. Need-based: 2,214 full-time freshmen applied for aid; 1,767 were judged to have need; 1,726 of these received aid. Average need met was 96%. Average scholarship/grant was $7,954; average loan $3,895. 48% of total undergraduate aid awarded as scholarships/grants, 52% as loans/jobs. **Non-need-based:** Awarded to 4,697 full-time undergraduates, including 1,094 freshmen. Scholarships awarded for academics, alumni affiliation, art, athletics, leadership, minority status, music/drama, ROTC. **Additional information:** Need-based financial aid available to part-time students enrolled in minimum of 6 semester hours.

Application procedures. Admission: Priority date 5/1; no deadline. $30 fee, may be waived for applicants with need. Admission notification on a rolling basis beginning on or about 9/1. Must reply by May 1 or within 6 week(s) if notified thereafter. **Financial aid:** Priority date 4/1; no closing date. FAFSA required. Applicants notified on a rolling basis starting 3/21; must reply within 3 week(s) of notification.

Academics. Special study options: Cooperative education, distance learning, double major, ESL, honors, independent study, internships, student-designed major, study abroad, teacher certification program, Washington semester. **Credit/placement by examination:** AP, CLEP, IB, ACT, institutional tests. 15 credit hours maximum toward associate degree, 30 toward bachelor's. Credit by proficiency exams available. **Support services:** Learning center, pre-admission summer program, remedial instruction, study skills assistance, tutoring, writing center.

Majors. Agriculture: General, animal sciences, economics, plant sciences. **Architecture:** Architecture. **Biology:** General, botany, microbiology, physiology, zoology. **Business:** Accounting, business admin, finance, hospitality admin, management science, managerial economics, marketing. **Communications:** Journalism, radio/tv. **Computer sciences:** Computer science, information systems. **Conservation:** Forestry. **Education:** Early childhood, elementary, health, physical, special, trade/industrial. **Engineering:** Civil, computer, electrical, mechanical, mining. **Engineering technology:** General, automotive, electrical, industrial. **Family/consumer sciences:** Clothing/textiles, food/nutrition. **Foreign languages:** Classics, French, German, linguistics, Spanish. **Health:** Athletic training, communication disorders, dental hygiene, health care admin, medical radiologic technology/radiation therapy, physician assistant. **History:** General. **Interdisciplinary:** Nutrition sciences. **Legal studies:** Paralegal. **Liberal arts:** Arts/sciences. **Math:** General. **Mechanic/repair:** Avionics. **Parks/recreation:** General, exercise sciences. **Personal/culinary services:** Mortuary science. **Philosophy/religion:** Philosophy. **Physical sciences:** Chemistry, geology, physics. **Protective services:** Fire services admin, law enforcement admin. **Psychology:** General.

Public administration: Social work. **Social sciences:** General, anthropology, economics, geography, political science, sociology. **Transportation:** Aviation management. **Visual/performing arts:** Art, cinematography, design, dramatic, interior design, studio arts. **Other:** 51.2399 Rehabilitation services, Electronics systems technologies, Foreign languages and international trade, Musical theater, Technical resource management.

Most popular majors. Business/marketing 10%, education 21%, engineering/engineering technologies 12%, health sciences 7%.

Computing on campus. 1,776 workstations in dormitories, library, computer center, student center. Dormitories wired for high-speed internet access and linked to campus network. Commuter students can connect to campus network. Online course registration, online library, helpline, student web hosting, wireless network available.

Student life. Freshman orientation: Mandatory, $75 fee. Preregistration for classes offered. Several 1-day seminars offered April through July. **Housing:** Guaranteed on-campus for freshmen. Coed dorms, single-sex dorms, special housing for disabled, apartments, fraternity/sorority housing available. $650 partly refundable deposit, deadline 6/1. Living/learning, residential college, freshman interest group housing available. **Activities:** Bands, campus ministries, choral groups, dance, drama, film society, international student organizations, literary magazine, music ensembles, musical theater, opera, radio station, student government, student newspaper, symphony orchestra, TV station, over 400 student organizations.

Athletics. NCAA. **Intercollegiate:** Baseball M, basketball, cheerleading, cross-country, diving, football (tackle) M, golf, softball W, swimming, tennis, track and field, volleyball W. **Intramural:** Badminton, basketball, cricket, cross-country, football (non-tackle), golf, handball, racquetball, soccer, softball, squash, swimming, table tennis, tennis, triathlon, volleyball, water polo, wrestling M. **Team name:** Salukis.

Student services. Adult student services, alcohol/substance abuse counseling, career counseling, services for economically disadvantaged, student employment services, financial aid counseling, health services, legal services, minority student services, on-campus daycare, personal counseling, placement for graduates, veterans' counselor, women's services. **Physically disabled:** Services for visually, speech, hearing impaired. **Learning disabled:** Comprehensive services available.

Contact. E-mail: admrec@siu.edu
Phone: (618) 453-4381 Fax: (618) 453-3250
Patsy Reynolds, Director, Admissions, Southern Illinois University Carbondale, Mailcode 4701, Carbondale, IL 62901-4701

Southern Illinois University Edwardsville

Edwardsville, Illinois — **CB member**
www.siue.edu — **CB code: 1759**

- Public 4-year university
- Commuter campus in very large city
- 10,892 degree-seeking undergraduates: 14% part-time, 54% women, 10% African American, 2% Asian American, 2% Hispanic American, 1% international
- 2,461 degree-seeking graduate students
- 89% of applicants admitted
- 45% graduate within 6 years

General. Founded in 1957. Regionally accredited. **Degrees:** 2,078 bachelor's awarded; master's, first professional offered. **ROTC:** Army, Air Force. **Location:** 18 miles from St. Louis. **Calendar:** Semester, extensive summer session. **Full-time faculty:** 592 total; 81% have terminal degrees, 12% minority, 46% women. **Part-time faculty:** 281 total; 12% minority, 43% women. **Class size:** 42% < 20, 38% 20-39, 10% 40-49, 9% 50-99, less than 1% >100. **Special facilities:** Museum collections, arboretum, greenhouse, engineering labs, clinical nursing facility, observatory, applied research and technology park, corn-to-ethanol research center, biotechnology laboratory incubator, pharmaceutical care lab.

Freshman class profile. 6,231 applied, 5,540 admitted, 1,922 enrolled.

Mid 50% test scores		**Return as sophomores:**	73%
ACT composite:	20-25	**Out-of-state:**	9%
Rank in top quarter:	43%	**Live on campus:**	68%
Rank in top tenth:	17%	**International:**	1%

Basis for selection. Students admitted with 2.5 GPA and 21 ACT (970-1000 SAT, exclusive of Writing), or with rank in top 25% of class. Applicants who do not meet requirements subject to additional review. SAT or ACT recommended. Audition recommended for music majors; portfolio recommended for art majors.

High school preparation. 15 units required. Required and recommended units include English 4, mathematics 3, social studies 3, science 3 (laboratory 3), foreign language 2 and academic electives 2. At least 2 years of history or government required; 2 years foreign language, music, dance, theater, art, or vocational education (1 year maximum) electives required; 2 years of 1 foreign language and 1 year music and/or art recommended; 1 year chemistry and 1 year biology required.

2008-2009 Annual costs. Tuition/fees: $7,831; $16,606 out-of-state. Required fees include book rental. Room/board: $7,071. Books/supplies: $696. Personal expenses: $1,506.

2007-2008 Financial aid. All financial aid based on need. 1,385 full-time freshmen applied for aid; 1,086 were judged to have need; 1,016 of these received aid. Average need met was 63%. Average scholarship/grant was $8,999; average loan $9,272. 39% of total undergraduate aid awarded as scholarships/grants, 61% as loans/jobs.

Application procedures. Admission: Priority date 12/1; deadline 5/1 (postmark date). $30 fee, may be waived for applicants with need. Admission notification on a rolling basis beginning on or about 9/1. Application and all official documents required to be on file 3 weeks before beginning of term. **Financial aid:** Priority date 3/1, closing date 6/1. FAFSA required. Applicants notified on a rolling basis starting 3/15; must reply within 4 week(s) of notification.

Academics. Senior project required. **Special study options:** Accelerated study, combined bachelor's/graduate degree, cooperative education, cross-registration, distance learning, double major, ESL, honors, independent study, internships, student-designed major, study abroad, teacher certification program. **Credit/placement by examination:** AP, CLEP, institutional tests. 32 credit hours maximum toward bachelor's degree. Placement tests required for some students in reading, writing and/or math; determination based on test scores and GPA. **Support services:** Learning center, pre-admission summer program, reduced course load, remedial instruction, study skills assistance, tutoring, writing center.

Majors. Biology: General, biotechnology. **Business:** Accounting, business admin, management information systems, managerial economics. **Communications:** Media studies. **Computer sciences:** General, computer science. **Education:** Early childhood, elementary, health, science, special. **Engineering:** Civil, computer, electrical, industrial, manufacturing, mechanical. **Engineering technology:** Construction. **Foreign languages:** General. **Health:** Audiology/speech pathology, nursing (RN). **History:** General. **Liberal arts:** Arts/sciences. **Math:** General. **Parks/recreation:** Exercise sciences, health/fitness. **Philosophy/religion:** Philosophy. **Physical sciences:** Chemistry, physics. **Protective services:** Criminal justice. **Psychology:** General. **Public administration:** Social work. **Social sciences:** Anthropology, economics, geography, political science, sociology. **Visual/performing arts:** Art, dramatic, studio arts.

Most popular majors. Biology 8%, business/marketing 19%, education 10%, engineering/engineering technologies 8%, health sciences 9%, psychology 8%, social sciences 8%.

Computing on campus. 600 workstations in dormitories, library, computer center, student center. Dormitories linked to campus network. Commuter students can connect to campus network. Online course registration, online library, helpline available.

Student life. Freshman orientation: Available. Preregistration for classes offered. Offer summer pre-entry advisement and registration program in addition to freshman orientation. **Housing:** Coed dorms, special housing for disabled, apartments, fraternity/sorority housing, wellness housing available. $300 deposit, deadline 5/1. Focused-interest communities. **Activities:** Bands, campus ministries, choral groups, dance, drama, literary magazine, music ensembles, musical theater, opera, radio station, student government, student newspaper, symphony orchestra, TV station, 170 organizations and honor societies available.

Athletics. NCAA. **Intercollegiate:** Baseball M, basketball, cross-country, golf, soccer, softball W, tennis, track and field, volleyball W, wrestling M. **Intramural:** Badminton, basketball, bowling, fencing, football (non-tackle), golf, racquetball, soccer, softball, table tennis, tennis, volleyball, water polo. **Team name:** Cougars.

Student services. Alcohol/substance abuse counseling, career counseling, services for economically disadvantaged, student employment services, financial aid counseling, health services, legal services, on-campus daycare, personal counseling, placement for graduates, veterans' counselor. **Physically disabled:** Services for visually, speech, hearing impaired. **Learning disabled:** Comprehensive services available.

Contact. E-mail: admissions@siue.edu
Phone: (618) 650-3705 Toll-free number: (800) 447-7483
Fax: (618) 650-5013
Todd Burrell, Director of Admissions, Southern Illinois University Edwardsville, Campus Box 1600, Rendleman Hall, Rm 2120, Edwardsville, IL 62026-1600

Telshe Yeshiva-Chicago

Chicago, Illinois

CB code: 7009

- Private 4-year rabbinical college for men affiliated with Jewish faith
- Very large city
- 71 degree-seeking undergraduates

General. Accredited by AARTS. **Degrees:** 2 bachelor's awarded; first professional offered. **Calendar:** Continuous. **Full-time faculty:** 5 total. **Part-time faculty:** 1 total.

2008-2009 Annual costs. Comprehensive fee: $11,000.

Application procedures. Admission: No deadline. No application fee.

Academics. Credit/placement by examination: CLEP.

Majors. Theology: Talmudic.

Contact. Phone: (773) 463-7738 Fax: (773) 463-2894
Director of Admissions, Telshe Yeshiva-Chicago, 3535 West Foster Avenue, Chicago, IL 60625

Trinity Christian College

Palos Heights, Illinois
www.trnty.edu

CB code: 1820

- Private 4-year liberal arts college affiliated with Reformed (unaffiliated)
- Residential campus in very large city
- 1,271 degree-seeking undergraduates: 17% part-time, 70% women, 8% African American, 2% Asian American, 6% Hispanic American, 2% international
- 94% of applicants admitted
- SAT or ACT (ACT writing optional), application essay, interview required
- 60% graduate within 6 years

General. Founded in 1959. Regionally accredited. **Degrees:** 307 bachelor's awarded. **Location:** 20 miles from Chicago. **Calendar:** Semester, limited summer session. **Full-time faculty:** 80 total; 65% have terminal degrees, 11% minority, 40% women. **Part-time faculty:** 74 total; 1% have terminal degrees, 7% minority, 49% women. **Class size:** 48% < 20, 48% 20-39, 3% 40-49, 1% 50-99. **Special facilities:** Dutch heritage center archives.

Freshman class profile. 589 applied, 553 admitted, 235 enrolled.

Mid 50% test scores		**Rank in top quarter:**	31%
SAT critical reading:	490-570	**Rank in top tenth:**	13%
SAT math:	490-580	**Return as sophomores:**	74%
ACT composite:	19-27	**Out-of-state:**	47%
GPA 3.50-3.74:	40%	**Live on campus:**	92%
GPA 3.0-3.49:	30%	**International:**	2%
GPA 2.0-2.99:	30%		

Basis for selection. 3.0 GPA with 2.0 GPA in English and math, and 22 ACT or 950 SAT (exclusive of Writing) required. ACT recommended. Statement of religious faith recommended.

High school preparation. College-preparatory program recommended. 16 units required; 18 recommended. Required and recommended units include English 3-4, mathematics 3-4, social studies 2-3, history 2, science 2-3 and foreign language 2. One 3-year major in mathematics, science, or social studies, and 2 2-year minors in mathematics, science, social studies, or foreign language recommended.

2008-2009 Annual costs. Tuition/fees: $20,256. Room/board: $7,420. Books/supplies: $1,100. Personal expenses: $2,015.

2008-2009 Financial aid. Need-based: 205 full-time freshmen applied for aid; 191 were judged to have need; 191 of these received aid. Average need met was 47%. Average scholarship/grant was $6,879; average loan $4,231. 52% of total undergraduate aid awarded as scholarships/grants, 48% as loans/jobs. **Non-need-based:** Awarded to 1,011 full-time undergraduates, including 247 freshmen. Scholarships awarded for academics, alumni affiliation, art, athletics, leadership, minority status, music/drama, religious affiliation. **Additional information:** High school transcripts and ACT or SAT scores required for merit scholarships.

Application procedures. Admission: No deadline. $20 fee, may be waived for applicants with need. Admission notification on a rolling basis beginning on or about 9/1. Must reply by May 1 or within 2 week(s) if notified thereafter. **Financial aid:** Priority date 2/15, closing date 4/15. FAFSA, institutional form required. Applicants notified on a rolling basis starting 4/1; must reply by 5/1 or within 2 week(s) of notification.

Academics. Special study options: Double major, ESL, honors, independent study, internships, liberal arts/career combination, study abroad, teacher certification program, urban semester, Washington semester. **Credit/placement by examination:** AP, CLEP, IB, SAT, ACT, institutional tests. 30 credit hours maximum toward bachelor's degree. **Support services:** Learning center, pre-admission summer program, reduced course load, remedial instruction, study skills assistance, tutoring, writing center.

Honors college/program. Must have 28 ACT, be in top 10% of high school class, and have 3.5 high school GPA. 13-19 semester hours of unique courses. Approximately 15 freshmen admitted each year.

Majors. Biology: General. **Business:** General, accounting, communications, management information systems. **Communications:** General. **Computer sciences:** Computer science, information systems. **Education:** General, art, biology, business, chemistry, elementary, English, history, mathematics, music, physical, science, Spanish, special. **Foreign languages:** Spanish. **Health:** Nursing (RN). **History:** General. **Math:** General. **Parks/recreation:** Exercise sciences, health/fitness. **Philosophy/religion:** Philosophy. **Physical sciences:** Chemistry. **Psychology:** General. **Public administration:** Social work. **Social sciences:** Political science, sociology. **Theology:** Theology. **Visual/performing arts:** Art, music performance, studio arts. **Other:** Church and ministry leadership, Sport and leisure studies.

Most popular majors. Business/marketing 16%, education 40%, health sciences 15%.

Computing on campus. 140 workstations in dormitories, library, computer center. Dormitories wired for high-speed internet access and linked to campus network. Commuter students can connect to campus network. Helpline, wireless network available.

Student life. Freshman orientation: Mandatory, $210 fee. Preregistration for classes offered. Two-day program in early July and two-week program in late August. **Housing:** Guaranteed on-campus for freshmen. Coed dorms, apartments available. $75 fully refundable deposit, deadline 9/1. **Activities:** Bands, campus ministries, choral groups, dance, drama, music ensembles, musical theater, student government, student newspaper, religious drama club, theology club, pro-life, Bread for the World, Inter-Varsity Fellowship, Big Brother/Big Sister, Association for Public Justice, PACE literacy program in Cook County jail.

Athletics. NAIA, NCCAA. **Intercollegiate:** Baseball M, basketball, cross-country, soccer, softball W, track and field, volleyball W. **Intramural:** Basketball, racquetball, soccer, volleyball. **Team name:** Trolls.

Student services. Adult student services, alcohol/substance abuse counseling, chaplain/spiritual director, career counseling, student employment services, financial aid counseling, health services, minority student services, personal counseling, placement for graduates, veterans' counselor. **Physically disabled:** Services for visually, speech, hearing impaired.

Contact. E-mail: admissions@trnty.edu
Phone: (708) 239-4708 Toll-free number: (866) 874-6463
Fax: (708) 239-4826
Jeremy Klyn, Director of Admissions, Trinity Christian College, 6601 West College Drive, Palos Heights, IL 60463

Trinity College of Nursing and Health Sciences

Rock Island, Illinois
www.trinitycollegeqc.edu

CB code: 2555

- Private 4-year nursing college
- Commuter campus in very large city
- 230 degree-seeking undergraduates
- SAT or ACT (ACT writing recommended) required

General. Affiliated with Trinity Medical Center and the Iowa Health System. **Degrees:** 16 bachelor's, 47 associate awarded. **Calendar:** Semester, limited summer session. **Full-time faculty:** 17 total; 94% women. **Part-time faculty:** 10 total; 90% women.

Freshman class profile.

GPA 3.75 or higher:	10%	**GPA 3.0-3.49:**	50%
GPA 3.50-3.74:	15%	**GPA 2.0-2.99:**	25%

Basis for selection. Requirements vary by program. **Homeschooled:** Transcript of courses and grades required.

High school preparation. Required units include English 4, mathematics 3, social studies 3, science 3 (laboratory 1).

2008-2009 Annual costs. Tuition/fees: $11,105. Students are required to have a uniform and other health equipment.

2007-2008 Financial aid. Need-based: 25% of total undergraduate aid awarded as scholarships/grants, 75% as loans/jobs.

Application procedures. Admission: Closing date 12/15 (postmark date). $50 fee, may be waived for applicants with need. Admission notification on a rolling basis beginning on or about 12/1.

Academics. Special study options: Accelerated study, combined bachelor's/graduate degree, cooperative education, distance learning. 15 month accelerated BSN program for students with a previous degree. **Credit/placement by examination:** CLEP, ACT. **Support services:** Study skills assistance, tutoring.

Majors. Health: Nursing (RN).

Computing on campus. 15 workstations in computer center. Wireless network available.

Student life. Freshman orientation: Mandatory, $10 fee. Preregistration for classes offered. **Activities:** Student government.

Student services. Career counseling, financial aid counseling, minority student services, on-campus daycare, personal counseling. **Learning disabled:** Comprehensive services available.

Contact. Phone: (309) 779-7814 Fax: (309) 779-7748
Cara Banks, Registrar, Trinity College of Nursing and Health Sciences, 2122 25th Avenue, Rock Island, IL 61201

Trinity International University

Deerfield, Illinois — **CB member**
www.tiu.edu — **CB code: 1810**

- Private 4-year university and liberal arts college affiliated with Evangelical Free Church of America
- Residential campus in large town
- 950 degree-seeking undergraduates: 11% part-time, 57% women, 17% African American, 5% Asian American, 4% Hispanic American, 1% international
- 1,429 degree-seeking graduate students
- 63% of applicants admitted
- SAT or ACT (ACT writing optional), application essay required
- 52% graduate within 6 years

General. Founded in 1897. Regionally accredited. Off-campus programs available through Christian College Consortium. **Degrees:** 205 bachelor's awarded; master's, doctoral, first professional offered. **Location:** 25 miles from Chicago. **Calendar:** Semester, limited summer session. **Full-time faculty:** 43 total; 84% have terminal degrees, 14% minority, 42% women. **Part-time faculty:** 39 total; 13% have terminal degrees, 8% minority, 51% women. **Class size:** 41% < 20, 39% 20-39, 16% 40-49, 5% 50-99. **Special facilities:** Seminary facilities.

Freshman class profile. 548 applied, 345 admitted, 134 enrolled.

Mid 50% test scores		**GPA 2.0-2.99:**	30%
SAT critical reading:	450-610	**Rank in top quarter:**	43%
SAT math:	440-600	**Rank in top tenth:**	37%
ACT composite:	19-26	**Return as sophomores:**	66%
GPA 3.75 or higher:	29%	**Out-of-state:**	51%
GPA 3.50-3.74:	14%	**Live on campus:**	93%
GPA 3.0-3.49:	27%		

Basis for selection. School achievement record, test scores, recommendations, evidence of Christian commitment, essays most important. Interview recommended for borderline applicants. **Homeschooled:** Transcript of courses and grades required.

High school preparation. College-preparatory program required. Required units include English 4, mathematics 2, social studies 2, history 2, science 2 (laboratory 1), foreign language 2 and visual/performing arts 2.

2008-2009 Annual costs. Tuition/fees: $21,930. Room/board: $7,270. Books/supplies: $1,080. Personal expenses: $1,130.

2008-2009 Financial aid. Non-need-based: Scholarships awarded for academics, alumni affiliation, athletics, minority status, music/drama, religious affiliation.

Application procedures. Admission: No deadline. $25 fee, may be waived for applicants with need. Admission notification on a rolling basis beginning on or about 9/1. **Financial aid:** Priority date 4/1; no closing date. FAFSA required. Applicants notified on a rolling basis starting 2/15; must reply within 4 week(s) of notification.

Academics. Special study options: Accelerated study, cooperative education, cross-registration, distance learning, double major, dual enrollment of high school students, exchange student, honors, independent study, internships, liberal arts/career combination, student-designed major, study abroad, teacher certification program, urban semester, Washington semester. REACH (for nontraditional students with previous college credit), graduate courses available to undergraduates with junior or senior standing. **Credit/placement by examination:** AP, CLEP, IB, SAT, ACT, institutional tests. Permission and approval by department chair required. May not be used to satisfy senior residency requirement. **Support services:** Learning center, remedial instruction, study skills assistance, tutoring, writing center.

Majors. Biology: General. **Business:** General, accounting, human resources, management science, marketing, nonprofit/public, organizational behavior, training/development. **Communications:** General. **Education:** Biology, elementary, English, history, mathematics, music, physical, secondary. **Health:** Athletic training, premedicine. **History:** General. **Legal studies:** Prelaw. **Liberal arts:** Humanities. **Math:** General. **Parks/recreation:** Health/fitness. **Philosophy/religion:** Philosophy. **Physical sciences:** Chemistry. **Psychology:** General. **Social sciences:** General. **Theology:** Bible, pastoral counseling, preministerial, religious ed, sacred music, theology, youth ministry. **Visual/performing arts:** Music pedagogy, music performance, music theory/composition, piano/organ, voice/opera.

Most popular majors. Business/marketing 22%, education 26%, health sciences 7%, liberal arts 6%, psychology 10%, theological studies 17%.

Computing on campus. 100 workstations in library, computer center, student center. Dormitories wired for high-speed internet access and linked to campus network. Commuter students can connect to campus network. Online course registration, online library, helpline, repair service, student web hosting, wireless network available.

Student life. Freshman orientation: Mandatory, $30 fee. Preregistration for classes offered. Orientation held the week before classes each fall and spring. Generally lasts entire week. **Policies:** Community expectations, general patterns of Christian lifestyle, policy on drug and alcohol abuse. Religious observance required. **Housing:** Guaranteed on-campus for freshmen. Single-sex dorms, special housing for disabled, apartments, wellness housing available. $50 partly refundable deposit, deadline 5/1. **Activities:** Bands, campus ministries, choral groups, dance, drama, music ensembles, musical theater, student government, student newspaper, symphony orchestra, Association of Believers for Black America, Global Christian Movement, Kappa Tau, Discipleship Cabinet, FAT Thursdays, Chapel Cabinet, Kids on Kampus, Wives Fellowship, Men's Ministry.

Athletics. NAIA, NCCAA. **Intercollegiate:** Baseball M, basketball, football (tackle) M, soccer, softball W, volleyball W. **Intramural:** Baseball M, basketball, bowling, football (non-tackle) M, racquetball, rugby M, soccer, softball, volleyball. **Team name:** Trojans.

Student services. Alcohol/substance abuse counseling, chaplain/spiritual director, career counseling, student employment services, financial aid counseling, health services, minority student services, on-campus daycare, personal counseling, placement for graduates. **Physically disabled:** Services for visually impaired.

Contact. E-mail: tcadmissions@tiu.edu
Phone: (847) 317-7000 Toll-free number: (800) 822-3225
Fax: (847) 317-8097
Aaron Mahl, Director of Admissions, Trinity International University, 2065 Half Day Road, Deerfield, IL 60015

University of Chicago

Chicago, Illinois — **CB member**
www.uchicago.edu — **CB code: 1832**

- Private 4-year university and liberal arts college
- Residential campus in very large city
- 5,027 degree-seeking undergraduates: 1% part-time, 50% women, 6% African American, 14% Asian American, 9% Hispanic American, 8% international
- 7,388 degree-seeking graduate students
- 28% of applicants admitted
- SAT or ACT (ACT writing optional), application essay required
- 92% graduate within 6 years

General. Founded in 1891. Regionally accredited. **Degrees:** 1,160 bachelor's awarded; master's, doctoral, first professional offered. **ROTC:** Army, Air Force. **Location:** 7 miles from Chicago. **Calendar:** Quarter, extensive summer session. **Full-time faculty:** 1,099 total; 100% have terminal degrees, 17% minority, 29% women. **Part-time faculty:** 618 total; 70% have terminal degrees, 12% minority, 33% women. **Class size:** 73% < 20, 20% 20-39, 2% 40-49, 3% 50-99, 1% >100. **Special facilities:** Oriental Institute, Argonne National Laboratory, library of sciences, Fermi National Accelerator Laboratory, film studies center, National Opinion Research Center, observatory.

Freshman class profile. 12,376 applied, 3,454 admitted, 1,306 enrolled.

Mid 50% test scores			
SAT critical reading:	660-770	Rank in top quarter:	96%
SAT math:	650-760	Rank in top tenth:	86%
ACT composite:	28-33	Return as sophomores:	98%
GPA 3.75 or higher:	89%	Out-of-state:	78%
GPA 3.50-3.74:	7%	Live on campus:	100%
GPA 3.0-3.49:	4%	International:	9%

Basis for selection. Secondary school record, recommendations, essay, talent/ability and character/personal qualities very important. Interview recommended.

High school preparation. Recommended units include English 4, mathematics 4, social studies 2, history 2, science 4 and foreign language 3.

2008-2009 Annual costs. Tuition/fees: $37,632. Room/board: $11,697. Books/supplies: $1,050. Personal expenses: $1,919.

2008-2009 Financial aid. Need-based: 890 full-time freshmen applied for aid; 636 were judged to have need; 636 of these received aid. Average need met was 100%. Average scholarship/grant was $33,838; average loan $4,264. 87% of total undergraduate aid awarded as scholarships/grants, 13% as loans/jobs. **Non-need-based:** Awarded to 602 full-time undergraduates, including 156 freshmen. Scholarships awarded for academics, leadership.

Application procedures. Admission: Closing date 1/2 (postmark date). $65 fee, may be waived for applicants with need. Admission notification 4/1. Must reply by 5/1. **Financial aid:** Closing date 2/1. FAFSA, institutional form, CSS PROFILE required. Applicants notified by 4/15; must reply by 5/1.

Academics. Special study options: Combined bachelor's/graduate degree, cross-registration, double major, dual enrollment of high school students, ESL, exchange student, independent study, internships, student-designed major, study abroad, teacher certification program, Washington semester. **Credit/placement by examination:** AP, CLEP, IB, institutional tests. **Support services:** Study skills assistance, tutoring.

Majors. Area/ethnic studies: African, African-American, German, Latin American, Near/Middle Eastern, Russian/Slavic, Slavic, South Asian. **Biology:** General, biochemistry. **Computer sciences:** General. **Conservation:** Environmental studies. **Foreign languages:** Ancient Greek, Arabic, Biblical, classics, comparative lit, East Asian, French, German, Hebrew, Italian, Latin, linguistics, Portuguese, Russian, Scandinavian, Slavic, South Asian, Spanish. **History:** General. **Liberal arts:** Arts/sciences. **Math:** General, applied, statistics. **Philosophy/religion:** Judaic, philosophy, religion. **Physical sciences:** Chemistry, geophysics, physics. **Psychology:** General. **Public administration:** Policy analysis. **Social sciences:** Anthropology, economics, geography, international relations, political science, sociology. **Visual/performing arts:** General, art history/conservation, film/cinema.

Most popular majors. Biology 11%, foreign language 8%, history 6%, mathematics 6%, physical sciences 8%, psychology 6%, social sciences 33%.

Computing on campus. 1,000 workstations in dormitories, library, computer center, student center. Dormitories wired for high-speed internet access and linked to campus network. Commuter students can connect to campus network. Online course registration, online library, helpline, repair service, student web hosting, wireless network available.

Student life. Freshman orientation: Mandatory, $536 fee. Held 10 days before classes begin in the fall. **Housing:** Guaranteed on-campus for all undergraduates. Coed dorms, apartments, fraternity/sorority housing available. **Activities:** Bands, campus ministries, choral groups, dance, drama, film society, international student organizations, literary magazine, music ensembles, Model UN, musical theater, radio station, student government, student newspaper, symphony orchestra, over 500 organizations.

Athletics. NCAA. **Intercollegiate:** Baseball M, basketball, cross-country, football (tackle) M, soccer, softball W, swimming, tennis, track and field, volleyball W, wrestling M. **Intramural:** Archery, badminton, basketball, cross-country, fencing, handball, racquetball, soccer, softball, swimming, table tennis, tennis, track and field, volleyball. **Team name:** Maroons.

Student services. Adult student services, alcohol/substance abuse counseling, chaplain/spiritual director, career counseling, services for economically disadvantaged, student employment services, financial aid counseling, health services, minority student services, personal counseling, placement for graduates, veterans' counselor, women's services. **Physically disabled:** Services for visually, hearing impaired.

Contact. E-mail: collegeadmissions@uchicago.edu
Phone: (773) 702-8650 Fax: (773) 702-4199
Theodore O'Neill, Dean of Admissions, University of Chicago, 1101 East 58th Street, Chicago, IL 60637

University of Illinois at Chicago

Chicago, Illinois — **CB member**
www.uic.edu — **CB code: 1851**

- Public 4-year university
- Commuter campus in very large city
- 15,576 degree-seeking undergraduates: 7% part-time, 53% women, 9% African American, 23% Asian American, 17% Hispanic American, 2% international
- 9,334 degree-seeking graduate students
- 60% of applicants admitted
- SAT or ACT (ACT writing recommended), application essay required
- 48% graduate within 6 years

General. Founded in 1946. Regionally accredited. Medical, dental, nursing and pharmacy colleges, and medical center within university complex. **Degrees:** 3,323 bachelor's awarded; master's, doctoral, first professional offered. **ROTC:** Army, Naval, Air Force. **Location:** One mile from downtown. **Calendar:** Semester, limited summer session. **Full-time faculty:** 1,201 total; 78% have terminal degrees, 24% minority, 44% women. **Part-time faculty:** 365 total; 55% have terminal degrees, 16% minority, 46% women. **Class size:** 36% < 20, 38% 20-39, 8% 40-49, 11% 50-99, 8% >100. **Special facilities:** Jane Addams' Hull House museum, prairie preserve, health sciences center, software technologies research facility.

Freshman class profile. 14,269 applied, 8,567 admitted, 2,964 enrolled.

Mid 50% test scores			
ACT composite:	21-26	Out-of-state:	2%
Rank in top quarter:	61%	Live on campus:	49%
Rank in top tenth:	25%	International:	1%
End year in good standing:	70%	Fraternities:	1%
Return as sophomores:	78%	Sororities:	1%

Basis for selection. Class rank, GPA, and test scores most important. High school course selection and personal statement strongly considered. Auditions required of music and theater majors. Portfolio required of art majors. **Homeschooled:** Transcript of courses and grades required. **Learning Disabled:** Students may add learning disability information to personal essay.

High school preparation. College-preparatory program required. 16 units required. Required and recommended units include English 4, mathematics 3-4, social studies 3, science 3 (laboratory 3), foreign language 2-4 and academic electives 1. Additional course requirements vary with college and program.

2008-2009 Annual costs. Tuition/fees: $11,710; $24,100 out-of-state. Room/board: $8,774. Books/supplies: $1,200. Personal expenses: $1,988.

2007-2008 Financial aid. **Need-based:** 2,577 full-time freshmen applied for aid; 2,112 were judged to have need; 1,992 of these received aid. Average need met was 75%. Average scholarship/grant was $10,580; average loan $3,941. 65% of total undergraduate aid awarded as scholarships/grants, 35% as loans/jobs. **Non-need-based:** Awarded to 1,250 full-time undergraduates, including 378 freshmen. Scholarships awarded for academics, art, athletics, music/drama, ROTC.

Application procedures. **Admission:** Closing date 1/31 (postmark date). $40 fee, may be waived for applicants with need. Admission notification on a rolling basis. Must reply by May 1 or within 2 week(s) if notified thereafter. **Financial aid:** Priority date 3/1; no closing date. FAFSA required. Applicants notified on a rolling basis starting 3/15; must reply by 5/1 or within 2 week(s) of notification.

Academics. **Special study options:** Accelerated study, combined bachelor's/graduate degree, cooperative education, distance learning, double major, dual enrollment of high school students, exchange student, honors, independent study, internships, student-designed major, study abroad, teacher certification program. Concurrent registration at another campus of University of Illinois. **Credit/placement by examination:** AP, CLEP, IB, ACT, institutional tests. 30 credit hours maximum toward bachelor's degree. **Support services:** Learning center, pre-admission summer program, remedial instruction, study skills assistance, tutoring, writing center.

Majors. **Area/ethnic studies:** African-American, German, Latin American. **Biology:** General, biochemistry. **Business:** Accounting, entrepreneurial studies, finance, management science, marketing. **Communications:** General. **Computer sciences:** Computer science, information systems. **Education:** Art, biology, chemistry, elementary, English, French, German, history, mathematics, physics, Spanish. **Engineering:** Biomedical, chemical, civil, computer, electrical, industrial, mechanical, physics. **Engineering technology:** Industrial management. **Foreign languages:** Classics, French, Italian, Polish, Russian, Spanish. **Health:** Dietetics, medical records admin, nursing (RN), predental. **History:** General. **Interdisciplinary:** Classical/archaeology, neuroscience. **Liberal arts:** Arts/sciences. **Math:** General, statistics. **Parks/recreation:** Exercise sciences. **Philosophy/religion:** Philosophy. **Physical sciences:** Chemistry, geology, physics. **Protective services:** Criminal justice. **Psychology:** General. **Social sciences:** Anthropology, economics, political science, sociology, urban studies. **Visual/performing arts:** Art history/conservation, cinematography, dramatic, graphic design, industrial design, photography, studio arts. **Other:** Gender and women's studies, Performance.

Most popular majors. Biology 11%, business/marketing 19%, engineering/engineering technologies 9%, health sciences 7%, psychology 12%, social sciences 9%.

Computing on campus. 1,100 workstations in dormitories, library, computer center, student center. Dormitories wired for high-speed internet access and linked to campus network. Commuter students can connect to campus network. Online course registration, online library, helpline, student web hosting, wireless network available.

Student life. **Freshman orientation:** Mandatory, $99 fee. Preregistration for classes offered. Two-day, overnight offered 12 times from early June to mid-August. **Housing:** Coed dorms, single-sex dorms, apartments available. $150 partly refundable deposit, deadline 4/1. Honors floors, Presidential Award House available. **Activities:** Bands, campus ministries, choral groups, drama, international student organizations, music ensembles, radio station, student government, student newspaper, over 200 student groups available.

Athletics. NCAA. **Intercollegiate:** Baseball M, basketball, cheerleading, cross-country, diving, gymnastics, soccer M, softball W, swimming, tennis, track and field, volleyball W. **Intramural:** Badminton, basketball, bowling, cross-country, football (non-tackle), racquetball, soccer, softball, table tennis, tennis, volleyball. **Team name:** Flames.

Student services. Adult student services, alcohol/substance abuse counseling, career counseling, services for economically disadvantaged, student employment services, financial aid counseling, health services, legal services, minority student services, on-campus daycare, personal counseling, placement for graduates, veterans' counselor, women's services. **Physically disabled:** Services for visually, speech, hearing impaired.

Contact. E-mail: uicadmit@uic.edu
Phone: (312) 996-4350 Fax: (312) 413-7628
Thomas Glenn, Executive Director Admissions and Records, University of Illinois at Chicago, PO Box 5220, Chicago, IL 60680-5220

University of Illinois at Urbana-Champaign

Champaign, Illinois — **CB member**
www.illinois.edu — **CB code: 1836**

- Public 4-year university
- Residential campus in small city
- 30,400 degree-seeking undergraduates
- 11,435 graduate students
- 69% of applicants admitted
- SAT or ACT with writing, application essay required
- 82% graduate within 6 years; 26% enter graduate study

General. Founded in 1867. Regionally accredited. **Degrees:** 249 bachelor's awarded; master's, doctoral, first professional offered. **ROTC:** Army, Naval, Air Force. **Location:** 130 miles from Chicago, 125 miles from Indianapolis. **Calendar:** Semester, extensive summer session. **Full-time faculty:** 2,722 total. **Part-time faculty:** 414 total. **Class size:** 38% < 20, 38% 20-39, 5% 40-49, 10% 50-99, 9% >100. **Special facilities:** Natural history museum, museum of world history and culture, performing and visual arts centers, 37 public libraries, institute of genomic biology, institute for advanced science and technology, computer science center, national center for supercomputing applications, arboretum, observatory, hiking trails, Japanese house and gardens, ice arena.

Freshman class profile. 23,240 applied, 16,035 admitted, 7,216 enrolled.

Mid 50% test scores			
SAT critical reading:	530-660	**ACT composite:**	26-31
SAT math:	650-750	**Return as sophomores:**	93%
		Out-of-state:	8%

Basis for selection. High school course work, personal essay, class rank, SAT/ACT test scores most important. Audition required of dance, music, theater (performance) majors. Professional interest statement required of all applicants. **Homeschooled:** Provide detailed information about home school environment/coursework; applicants should contact admissions office early in high school career with questions or concerns. **Learning Disabled:** Recommended that students address disability and any accommodations they receive in required personal statement section.

High school preparation. Required and recommended units include English 4, mathematics 3-4, social studies 2-4, science 2-4 (laboratory 2), foreign language 2-4 and academic electives 2. Specific subject requirements vary with college and program.

2008-2009 Annual costs. Tuition/fees: $12,240; $26,024 out-of-state. Freshman costs reflect guaranteed tuition plan figures; tuition rate is guaranteed for 4 years. Room/board: $8,764. Books/supplies: $1,200. Personal expenses: $2,510.

2007-2008 Financial aid. **Non-need-based:** Scholarships awarded for academics, alumni affiliation, art, athletics, leadership, music/drama, ROTC, state residency.

Application procedures. **Admission:** Priority date 11/1; deadline 1/2 (postmark date). $40 fee, may be waived for applicants with need. Notification by 12/14 and 2/15. Must reply by May 1 or within 2 week(s) if notified thereafter. **Financial aid:** Priority date 3/15; no closing date. FAFSA required.

Academics. Students generally declare a major upon enrollment. Students without a declared major may apply for the general curriculum option in the Division of General Studies. **Special study options:** Accelerated study, combined bachelor's/graduate degree, cooperative education, cross-registration, distance learning, double major, dual enrollment of high school students, ESL, exchange student, honors, independent study, internships, liberal arts/career combination, semester at sea, student-designed major, study abroad, teacher certification program, Washington semester. Honors programs, campus honors, Illinois Leadership & Entrepreneurial programs. **Credit/placement by examination:** AP, CLEP, IB, SAT, ACT, institutional tests. Unlimited credit hours may be counted toward a degree. **Support services:** Learning center, pre-admission summer program, reduced course load, remedial instruction, study skills assistance, tutoring, writing center.

Majors. **Agriculture:** Agronomy, animal husbandry, animal sciences, business, communications, economics, education services, food processing, food science, horticultural science, horticulture, international, mechanization, ornamental horticulture. **Architecture:** Architecture, landscape, urban/community planning. **Area/ethnic studies:** East Asian, Latin American, Russian/Slavic, women's. **Biology:** General, biochemistry, biophysics, biotechnology, botany, cell/histology, cellular/molecular, entomology, microbiology, physiology, plant molecular. **Business:** General, accounting, accounting/business management, actuarial science, auditing, banking/financial services, business admin, entrepreneurial studies, finance, financial planning, hospitality admin, human resources, insurance, logistics, management information systems, management science, market research, marketing, operations, organizational behavior, purchasing, real estate, sales/distribution. **Communications:** General, advertising, broadcast journalism, journalism, media studies, organizational. **Computer sciences:** General, computer science, programming, security. **Conservation:** General, environmental science, forest sciences, management/policy, urban forestry, wildlife. **Education:** Agricultural, art, biology, chemistry, early childhood, early childhood special, elementary, English, foreign languages, French, German, history, kindergarten/preschool, Latin, mathematics, multi-level teacher, multiple handicapped, music, physical, physics, science, secondary, social science, social studies, Spanish, special. **Engineering:** General, aerospace, agricultural, biomedical, ceramic, chemical, civil, computer, computer hardware, construction, electrical, environmental, geotechnical, industrial, manufacturing, materials, materials science, mechanical, mechanics, metallurgical, nuclear, operations research, physics, polymer, software, structural, transportation, water resource. **Family/consumer sciences:** Child development, consumer economics, family studies, human nutrition. **Foreign languages:** Classics, comparative lit, East Asian, French, German, Hebrew, Italian, linguistics, Portuguese, Russian, Spanish. **Health:** Athletic training, audiology/hearing, audiology/speech pathology, community health, dietetics, environmental health, health services admin, preveterinary, vocational rehab counseling. **History:** General. **Interdisciplinary:** Global studies, math/computer science, science/society. **Legal studies:** Prelaw. **Liberal arts:** Arts/sciences, humanities. **Math:** General, computational, statistics. **Parks/recreation:** General, exercise sciences, sports admin. **Philosophy/religion:** Philosophy, religion. **Physical sciences:** Astronomy, atmospheric science, chemistry, geology, physics. **Psychology:** General. **Social sciences:** Anthropology, economics, geography, political science, sociology. **Transportation:** Airline/commercial pilot, aviation management. **Visual/performing arts:** Acting, art history/conservation, crafts, dance, directing/producing, dramatic, film/cinema, graphic design, jazz, music history, music performance, music theory/composition, painting, photography, sculpture, studio arts, theater history, voice/opera. **Other:** Biological and biomedical sciences, Human sciences business services, Plant protection and integrated pest management.

Most popular majors. Biology 8%, business/marketing 15%, engineering/engineering technologies 14%, English 7%, psychology 7%, social sciences 10%.

Computing on campus. 4,420 workstations in dormitories, library, computer center, student center. Dormitories wired for high-speed internet access and linked to campus network. Commuter students can connect to campus network. Online course registration, online library, helpline, repair service, student web hosting, wireless network available.

Student life. **Freshman orientation:** Mandatory, $96 fee. Preregistration for classes offered. One-day program, held end of May through July. **Policies:** Freshmen required to live on campus unless over 21 years, married, or living with parents. **Housing:** Guaranteed on-campus for freshmen. Coed dorms, single-sex dorms, special housing for disabled, apartments, cooperative housing, fraternity/sorority housing, wellness housing available. $200 fully refundable deposit, deadline 5/1. Living/learning communities available. **Activities:** Bands, campus ministries, choral groups, dance, drama, film society, international student organizations, literary magazine, music ensembles, Model UN, musical theater, opera, radio station, student government, student newspaper, symphony orchestra, TV station, more than 1,000 registered student organizations.

Athletics. NCAA. **Intercollegiate:** Baseball M, basketball, cheerleading, cross-country, diving W, football (tackle) M, golf, gymnastics, soccer W, softball W, swimming W, tennis, track and field, volleyball W, wrestling M. **Intramural:** Badminton, basketball, cross-country, diving, football (non-tackle), football (tackle) M, golf, racquetball, soccer, softball W, tennis, volleyball, wrestling M. **Team name:** Illini.

Student services. Alcohol/substance abuse counseling, career counseling, services for economically disadvantaged, student employment services, financial aid counseling, health services, legal services, minority student services, on-campus daycare, personal counseling, placement for graduates, veterans' counselor, women's services. **Physically disabled:** Services for visually, speech, hearing impaired. **Learning disabled:** Comprehensive services available.

Contact. E-mail: admissions@illinois.edu
Phone: (217) 333-0302 Fax: (217) 244-4614
Stacey Kostell, Director of Undergraduate Admissions, University of Illinois at Urbana-Champaign, 901 West Illinois, Urbana, IL 61801-3028

University of Illinois: Springfield

Springfield, Illinois — **CB member**
www.uis.edu — **CB code: 0834**

- Public 4-year university and liberal arts college
- Commuter campus in small city
- 2,798 degree-seeking undergraduates: 37% part-time, 55% women, 12% African American, 3% Asian American, 3% Hispanic American, 1% Native American, 1% international
- 1,610 degree-seeking graduate students
- 78% of applicants admitted
- SAT or ACT (ACT writing recommended) required
- 57% graduate within 6 years

General. Founded in 1969. Regionally accredited. Third campus of University of Illinois system. **Degrees:** 684 bachelor's awarded; master's, doctoral offered. **Location:** 95 miles from St. Louis, 200 miles from Chicago. **Calendar:** Semester, extensive summer session. **Full-time faculty:** 209 total; 89% have terminal degrees, 15% minority, 42% women. **Part-time faculty:** 143 total; 21% have terminal degrees, 8% minority, 50% women. **Class size:** 51% < 20, 46% 20-39, 2% 40-49, less than 1% 50-99. **Special facilities:** Observatory, studio theater.

Freshman class profile. 872 applied, 681 admitted, 309 enrolled.

Mid 50% test scores		**Rank in top tenth:**	17%
ACT composite:	20-25	**End year in good standing:**	68%
GPA 3.75 or higher:	22%	**Return as sophomores:**	67%
GPA 3.50-3.74:	15%	**Out-of-state:**	3%
GPA 3.0-3.49:	31%	**Live on campus:**	86%
GPA 2.0-2.99:	31%	**International:**	1%
Rank in top quarter:	44%		

Basis for selection. GPA, rank, record, completion of college-prepatory program, recommendations, admission test scores, and formal demonstration of competencies all fully considered. Personal or telephone interview may be required.

High school preparation. College-preparatory program required. 15 units required. Required units include English 4, mathematics 3, science 3 (laboratory 3) and foreign language 2. Fine arts can be substituted for foreign language.

2008-2009 Annual costs. Tuition/fees: $8,605; $17,755 out-of-state. Freshman costs reflect guaranteed tuition plan figures; tuition rate guaranteed for 4 years. Room/board: $8,840.

2007-2008 Financial aid. **Need-based:** 215 full-time freshmen applied for aid; 159 were judged to have need; 156 of these received aid. Average need met was 74%. Average scholarship/grant was $7,722; average loan $2,943. 45% of total undergraduate aid awarded as scholarships/grants, 55% as loans/jobs. **Non-need-based:** Awarded to 427 full-time undergraduates, including 111 freshmen. Scholarships awarded for academics, alumni affiliation, art, athletics, job skills, leadership, minority status, music/drama, state residency.

Application procedures. **Admission:** Priority date 3/15; no deadline. $40 fee, may be waived for applicants with need. Admission notification on a rolling basis. It is requested that students reply as soon as possible after notification of admissions decision. **Financial aid:** Priority date 4/1, closing date 11/15. FAFSA required. Applicants notified on a rolling basis starting 1/1; must reply within 3 week(s) of notification.

Academics. **Special study options:** Distance learning, double major, ESL, honors, independent study, internships, study abroad, teacher certification program. **Credit/placement by examination:** AP, CLEP, IB, SAT, ACT, institutional tests. 30 credit hours maximum toward bachelor's degree. **Support services:** Learning center, reduced course load, study skills assistance, tutoring, writing center.

Majors. **Biology:** General. **Business:** Accounting, business admin. **Communications:** Media studies. **Computer sciences:** Computer science. **Health:** Clinical lab science. **History:** General. **Legal studies:** General. **Liberal arts:** Arts/sciences. **Math:** General. **Philosophy/religion:** Philosophy. **Physical sciences:** Chemistry. **Protective services:** Criminal justice. **Psychology:** General. **Public administration:** Social work. **Social sciences:** Economics, political science. **Visual/performing arts:** Studio arts.

Most popular majors. Business/marketing 29%, communications/journalism 7%, computer/information sciences 7%, liberal arts 6%, psychology 11%, security/protective services 9%.

Computing on campus. 475 workstations in dormitories, library, computer center, student center. Dormitories wired for high-speed internet access and linked to campus network. Commuter students can connect to campus network. Online course registration, online library, helpline, student web hosting, wireless network available.

Student life. **Freshman orientation:** Mandatory. **Housing:** Guaranteed on-campus for freshmen. Coed dorms, special housing for disabled, apartments, wellness housing available. $150 partly refundable deposit. Family housing available. **Activities:** Bands, campus ministries, choral groups, dance, drama, film society, international student organizations, music ensembles, Model UN, student government, student newspaper, Christian student fellowship, ACLU, Indian student organization, Habitat for Humanity, Living Word Bible Study, College Democrats, College Republicans, Queer Straight Alliance.

Athletics. NAIA. **Intercollegiate:** Basketball, cheerleading M, golf, soccer, softball W, tennis, volleyball W. **Intramural:** Badminton, basketball, bowling, football (non-tackle), golf, racquetball, skiing, soccer, softball, table tennis, volleyball. **Team name:** Prairie Stars.

Student services. Alcohol/substance abuse counseling, career counseling, student employment services, financial aid counseling, health services, minority student services, on-campus daycare, personal counseling, women's services. **Physically disabled:** Services for visually, speech, hearing impaired.

Contact. E-mail: admissions@uis.edu
Phone: (217) 206-4847 Toll-free number: (800) 977-4847
Fax: (217) 206-6620
Lori Giordano, Associate Director of Admissions, University of Illinois: Springfield, One University Plaza, MS UHB 1080, Springfield, IL 62703

University of St. Francis

Joliet, Illinois
www.stfrancis.edu **CB code: 1130**

- Private 4-year university and liberal arts college affiliated with Roman Catholic Church
- Commuter campus in small city
- 1,255 degree-seeking undergraduates: 3% part-time, 69% women, 7% African American, 5% Asian American, 9% Hispanic American, 1% international
- 824 degree-seeking graduate students
- 60% of applicants admitted
- SAT or ACT (ACT writing optional) required
- 54% graduate within 6 years; 17% enter graduate study

General. Founded in 1920. Regionally accredited. Affiliated with Argonne National Laboratories, Morton Arboretum, Will County Forest Preserve, Midewin Tallgrass Prairie, Shedd Aquarium. **Degrees:** 321 bachelor's awarded; master's offered. **Location:** 35 miles from Chicago. **Calendar:** Semester, extensive summer session. **Full-time faculty:** 84 total; 61% have terminal degrees, 10% minority, 60% women. **Part-time faculty:** 135 total; 22% have terminal degrees, 8% minority, 53% women. **Class size:** 70% < 20, 30% 20-39. **Special facilities:** Performing arts center, greenhouse, health and wellness center operated by nursing faculty and students, arthouse for visual arts majors.

Freshman class profile. 910 applied, 545 admitted, 203 enrolled.

Mid 50% test scores		**GPA 2.0-2.99:**	30%
ACT composite:	20-24	**End year in good standing:**	89%
GPA 3.75 or higher:	16%	**Return as sophomores:**	77%
GPA 3.50-3.74:	17%	**Out-of-state:**	6%
GPA 3.0-3.49:	37%	**Live on campus:**	68%

Basis for selection. High school GPA and rank, test scores important. Essay and letters of recommendation required and interview recommended for students who do not meet admissions requirements.

High school preparation. College-preparatory program required. 17 units required. Required units include English 4, mathematics 3, social studies 2, science 2 (laboratory 1) and academic electives 3. 3 units required from 2 areas: foreign language, music/art, or computer science.

2008-2009 Annual costs. Tuition/fees: $21,860. Room/board: $7,744.

2008-2009 Financial aid. Need-based: 192 full-time freshmen applied for aid; 163 were judged to have need; 163 of these received aid. Average need met was 82%. Average scholarship/grant was $8,129; average loan $3,866. 62% of total undergraduate aid awarded as scholarships/grants, 38% as loans/jobs. **Non-need-based:** Awarded to 1,195 full-time undergraduates, including 213 freshmen. Scholarships awarded for academics, alumni affiliation, art, athletics, leadership, music/drama, religious affiliation, state residency.

Application procedures. Admission: Priority date 5/1; deadline 8/1 (receipt date). $30 fee, may be waived for applicants with need. Admission notification on a rolling basis beginning on or about 9/15. **Financial aid:** Priority date 3/15; no closing date. FAFSA, institutional form required. Applicants notified on a rolling basis starting 2/15.

Academics. Special study options: Accelerated study, combined bachelor's/graduate degree, distance learning, double major, honors, independent study, internships, student-designed major, study abroad, teacher certification program, Washington semester. **Credit/placement by examination:** AP, CLEP, IB, SAT, ACT, institutional tests. 33 credit hours maximum toward bachelor's degree. **Support services:** Learning center, pre-admission summer program, reduced course load, remedial instruction, study skills assistance, tutoring, writing center.

Majors. Biology: General. **Business:** General, accounting, actuarial science, business admin, finance, human resources, management science, marketing, organizational behavior. **Communications:** Advertising, broadcast journalism, media studies, public relations, radio/tv. **Computer sciences:** Computer science, information technology, webmaster. **Conservation:** Environmental science. **Education:** Elementary, English, mathematics, music, science, social studies, special. **Health:** Clinical lab science, health care admin, medical radiologic technology/radiation therapy, nuclear medical technology, nursing (RN), predental, premedicine, preveterinary, radiologic technology/medical imaging, recreational therapy. **History:** General. **Interdisciplinary:** Math/computer science. **Liberal arts:** Arts/sciences. **Math:** General. **Parks/recreation:** Facilities management. **Protective services:** Law enforcement admin. **Psychology:** General. **Public administration:** Social work. **Social sciences:** Political science. **Theology:** Theology. **Visual/performing arts:** General, music performance.

Most popular majors. Biology 6%, business/marketing 8%, education 21%, health sciences 25%, public administration/social services 7%, social sciences 6%.

Computing on campus. 365 workstations in dormitories, library, computer center, student center. Dormitories wired for high-speed internet access and linked to campus network. Commuter students can connect to campus network. Online course registration, online library, helpline, wireless network available.

Student life. Freshman orientation: Mandatory, $120 fee. **Policies:** Visitation between 9am and 2am. Marian Hall is alcohol-free. All halls close during major breaks (fall break, winter break, spring break) unless special permission received to remain in hall. **Housing:** Guaranteed on-campus for freshmen. Coed dorms, apartments, wellness housing available. $50 fully refundable deposit, deadline 5/1. **Activities:** Campus ministries, choral groups, dance, drama, literary magazine, music ensembles, musical theater, radio station, student government, student newspaper, symphony orchestra, TV station, student activities board, black student association, student business association, Unidos Vamos a Alcanzar, student nurses organization, recreation club, council for environmental and scientific awareness, council for social activism, social work club, mock trial club.

Athletics. NAIA. **Intercollegiate:** Baseball M, basketball, cheerleading M, cross-country, football (tackle) M, golf, soccer, softball W, tennis, track and field, volleyball W. **Intramural:** Basketball, bowling, volleyball. **Team name:** Saints.

Student services. Adult student services, chaplain/spiritual director, career counseling, student employment services, financial aid counseling, health services, minority student services, personal counseling, placement for graduates. **Physically disabled:** Services for visually, speech, hearing impaired.

Contact. E-mail: admissions@stfrancis.edu
Phone: (815) 740-5037 Toll-free number: (800) 735-7500
Fax: (815) 740-5032
Julie Klinzing, Director Undergraduate Admissions, University of St. Francis, 500 Wilcox Street, Joliet, IL 60435

VanderCook College of Music

Chicago, Illinois
www.vandercook.edu **CB code: 1872**

- Private 4-year music and teachers college
- Residential campus in very large city
- 126 degree-seeking undergraduates
- 82% of applicants admitted
- Application essay, interview required

General. Founded in 1909. Regionally accredited. Access to student services at Illinois Institute of Technology. **Degrees:** 20 bachelor's awarded; master's offered. **Location:** Central Chicago. **Calendar:** Semester. **Full-time faculty:** 13 total; 46% have terminal degrees, 15% minority, 69% women. **Part-time faculty:** 17 total; 18% have terminal degrees, 6% minority, 29% women. **Class size:** 64% < 20, 30% 20-39, 1% 50-99, 4% >100. **Special facilities:** MIDI/electronic music laboratory, library with music education collection.

Freshman class profile. 57 applied, 47 admitted, 31 enrolled.

Mid 50% test scores		**Rank in top quarter:**	40%
SAT critical reading:	520-540	**Rank in top tenth:**	20%
SAT math:	390-550	**Out-of-state:**	12%
SAT writing:	430-670	**Live on campus:**	54%
ACT composite:	19-25		

Basis for selection. Academic credentials, SAT or ACT scores and recommendations are weighed along with student's musical audition and interview. Institutional test required. Audition required. **Homeschooled:** Should obtain experience performing with a concert band or chorus.

High school preparation. 15 units recommended. Recommended units include English 3, mathematics 2, social studies 3, science 2, foreign language 2 and academic electives 3. Art may be substituted for foreign language.

2008-2009 Annual costs. Tuition/fees: $20,140. Room/board: $9,451. Books/supplies: $1,620. Personal expenses: $2,000.

Financial aid. Non-need-based: Scholarships awarded for academics, alumni affiliation, leadership, minority status, music/drama, state residency. **Additional information:** Musical talent considered for partial tuition waiver.

Application procedures. Admission: Priority date 4/1; no deadline. $35 fee. Admission notification on a rolling basis. **Financial aid:** Priority date 3/1, closing date 4/30. FAFSA required. Applicants notified on a rolling basis starting 5/15; must reply within 2 week(s) of notification.

Academics. Special study options: Teacher certification program. **Credit/placement by examination:** AP, CLEP, SAT, ACT, institutional tests.

Majors. Education: Music.

Computing on campus. 10 workstations in dormitories, library, computer center, student center.

Student life. Freshman orientation: Mandatory. **Policies:** Student life focuses around musical activities at VanderCook and on the Illinois Institute of Technology campus. **Housing:** Guaranteed on-campus for all undergraduates. Coed dorms, apartments, fraternity/sorority housing available. $100 deposit. Apartments for single students 23 and older available. **Activities:** Bands, choral groups, music ensembles, musical theater.

Student services. Career counseling, student employment services, health services, personal counseling, placement for graduates.

Contact. E-mail: admissions@vandercook.edu
Phone: (312) 225-6288 ext. 230 Fax: (312) 225-5211
Amy Lenting, Director of Recruiting and Retention, VanderCook College of Music, 3140 South Federal Street, Chicago, IL 60616-3731

West Suburban College of Nursing

Oak Park, Illinois
www.wscn.edu **CB code: 1927**

- Private two-year upper-division nursing college affiliated with Roman Catholic Church
- Commuter campus in very large city
- Test scores, application essay required

General. Founded in 1982. Regionally accredited. Facilities located in West Suburban Medical Center. **Degrees:** 89 bachelor's awarded; master's offered. **Location:** 10 miles from downtown Chicago. **Calendar:** Semester, limited summer session. **Full-time faculty:** 19 total; 21% have terminal degrees, 5% minority, 95% women. **Part-time faculty:** 14 total; 21% minority, 93% women. **Class size:** 20% <20, 23% 20-39, 26% 40-49, 31% 50-99. **Special facilities:** In-hospital location, health sciences library, nursing clinical skills laboratory.

Student profile. 237 degree-seeking undergraduates, 25 degree-seeking graduate students.

Women:	83%	**Part-time:**	23%

Basis for selection. College transcript, application essay, standardized test scores required. Natural and behavioral science grades more heavily weighted. Recommendation and essay required. Must have 2.75 science GPA. Satisfactory score on TEAS required. Transfer accepted as juniors.

2008-2009 Annual costs. Tuition/fees: $20,910. Books/supplies: $1,400. Personal expenses: $2,116.

Financial aid. Need-based: 45% of total undergraduate aid awarded as scholarships/grants, 55% as loans/jobs. **Non-need-based:** Scholarships awarded for academics, alumni affiliation.

Application procedures. Admission: $30 fee. Application must be submitted online. **Financial aid:** Priority date 4/15, no deadline. Applicants notified on a rolling basis; must reply within 3 weeks of notification. FAFSA required.

Academics. Special study options: Accelerated study, independent study. Evening and weekend BS completion program for registered nurses. **Credit/placement by examination:** CLEP.

Majors. Health: Nursing (RN).

Computing on campus. 10 workstations in library, computer center. Online library, wireless network available.

Student life. Activities: Student government.

Student services. Career counseling, student employment services, health services, personal counseling.

Contact. E-mail: admissions@wscn.edu
Phone: (708) 763-6530 Fax: (708) 763-1531
Cindy Valdez, Director of Enrollment Management, West Suburban College of Nursing, Three Erie Court, Oak Park, IL 60302

Western Illinois University

Macomb, Illinois
www.wiu.edu **CB code: 1900**

- Public 4-year university
- Residential campus in large town
- 10,730 degree-seeking undergraduates: 9% part-time, 47% women, 8% African American, 1% Asian American, 5% Hispanic American, 1% Native American, 1% international
- 2,262 degree-seeking graduate students
- 68% of applicants admitted
- SAT or ACT (ACT writing optional) required

General. Founded in 1899. Regionally accredited. **Degrees:** 2,518 bachelor's awarded; master's, doctoral offered. **ROTC:** Army. **Location:** 83 miles from Rock Island, 78 miles from Peoria. **Calendar:** Semester, limited summer session. **Full-time faculty:** 679 total; 72% have terminal degrees, 14% minority, 43% women. **Part-time faculty:** 83 total; 18% have terminal degrees, 2% minority, 51% women. **Class size:** 34% <20, 51% 20-39, 8% 40-49, 5% 50-99, 2% >100. **Special facilities:** Geology museum.

Freshman class profile. 8,164 applied, 5,528 admitted, 1,816 enrolled.

Mid 50% test scores		**GPA 2.0-2.99:**	52%
ACT composite:	18-22	**Rank in top quarter:**	22%
GPA 3.75 or higher:	8%	**Rank in top tenth:**	6%
GPA 3.50-3.74:	10%	**Out-of-state:**	3%
GPA 3.0-3.49:	30%	**Live on campus:**	93%

Basis for selection. Standardized test scores, class rank very important. Audition required for music majors. **Homeschooled:** Transcript of courses and grades required.

High school preparation. 15 units recommended. Recommended units include English 4, mathematics 3, social studies 3, science 3 and academic electives 2. 2 units of art, film, foreign language, music, speech, theater, journalism, religion, philosophy or vocational education also recommended.

2008-2009 Annual costs. Tuition/fees: $8,828; $12,056 out-of-state. Residents of nearby counties in Iowa and Missouri pay in-state tuition during first year. Incoming freshmen guaranteed the first year tuition rate for their entire 4 years, provided they are continually enrolled. Room/board: $7,210.

2008-2009 Financial aid. Non-need-based: Scholarships awarded for academics, alumni affiliation, art, athletics, leadership, minority status, music/drama, ROTC.

Application procedures. Admission: Priority date 5/15; no deadline. $30 fee. Admission notification on a rolling basis. **Financial aid:** Priority date 2/15; no closing date. FAFSA required. Applicants notified on a rolling basis starting 1/15.

Academics. Special study options: Distance learning, double major, dual enrollment of high school students, ESL, external degree, honors, independent study, internships, student-designed major, study abroad, teacher certification program, weekend college. **Credit/placement by examination:** AP, CLEP, IB. 30 credit hours maximum toward bachelor's degree. **Support services:** Remedial instruction, study skills assistance, tutoring, writing center.

Honors college/program. 28 ACT or upper 10% of class and 24 ACT.

Majors. Agriculture: General. **Area/ethnic studies:** African-American, women's. **Biology:** General. **Business:** Accounting, business admin, construction management, finance, human resources, logistics, management information systems, managerial economics, marketing. **Communications:** General, journalism, radio/tv. **Communications technology:** Graphic/printing. **Computer sciences:** General, networking. **Education:** Bilingual, elementary, health, instructional media, special. **Engineering technology:** Industrial, manufacturing. **Family/consumer sciences:** General. **Foreign languages:** French, Spanish. **Health:** Clinical lab science, communication disorders, health care admin, nursing (RN). **History:** General. **Liberal arts:** Arts/sciences. **Math:** General. **Parks/recreation:** Exercise sciences, facilities management. **Philosophy/religion:** Philosophy, religion. **Physical sciences:** Chemistry, forensic chemistry, geology, meteorology, physics. **Protective services:** Emergency management/homeland security, law enforcement admin. **Psychology:** General. **Public administration:** Social work. **Social sciences:** Economics, geography, political science, sociology. **Visual/performing arts:** Art, dramatic, music performance, studio arts.

Most popular majors. Business/marketing 14%, communications/journalism 8%, education 9%, liberal arts 10%, parks/recreation 6%, security/protective services 15%.

Computing on campus. 1,000 workstations in dormitories, library, computer center. Dormitories wired for high-speed internet access and linked to campus network. Commuter students can connect to campus network. Online course registration, online library, helpline, wireless network available.

Student life. Freshman orientation: Mandatory. Preregistration for classes offered. Held week prior to beginning of classes. **Housing:** Guaranteed on-campus for all undergraduates. Coed dorms, single-sex dorms, apartments, fraternity/sorority housing, wellness housing available. $100 partly refundable deposit. **Activities:** Bands, choral groups, dance, drama, music ensembles, musical theater, radio station, student government, student newspaper, symphony orchestra, TV station, 67 special-interest organizations, 5 service organizations, 14 religious organizations, 32 national honorary and professional fraternities.

Athletics. NCAA. **Intercollegiate:** Baseball M, basketball, cheerleading, cross-country, diving, football (tackle) M, golf, soccer, softball W, swimming, tennis, track and field, volleyball W. **Intramural:** Badminton, basketball, bowling, cross-country, football (non-tackle), football (tackle) M, golf, handball, lacrosse M, racquetball, rugby, skin diving, soccer, softball, swimming, table tennis, tennis, volleyball, water polo. **Team name:** Leathernecks (M), Westerwinds (W).

Student services. Adult student services, alcohol/substance abuse counseling, career counseling, student employment services, financial aid counseling, health services, legal services, minority student services, on-campus daycare, personal counseling, placement for graduates, veterans' counselor, women's services. **Physically disabled:** Services for visually, speech, hearing impaired.

Contact. E-mail: wiuadm@wiu.edu
Phone: (309) 298-3157 Toll-free number: (877) 742-5948
Fax: (309) 298-3111
Eric Campbell, Director of Admissions, Western Illinois University, One University Circle, Macomb, IL 61455-1390

Western Illinois University: Quad Cities

Moline, Illinois
www.wiu.edu/qc

- Public two-year upper-division university and branch campus college
- Commuter campus in large city

General. Regionally accredited. **Degrees:** 2,518 bachelor's awarded; master's, doctoral offered. **Articulation:** Agreement with Illinois Articulation Initiative. **Calendar:** Semester, extensive summer session. **Full-time faculty:** 34 total. **Part-time faculty:** 25 total.

Student profile. 671 degree-seeking undergraduates. 77% transferred from two-year, 23% transferred from four-year institutions.

Out-of-state:	34%	25 or older:	85%

Basis for selection. College transcript required. Transfer accepted as sophomores, juniors, seniors.

2008-2009 Annual costs. Tuition/fees: $6,991; $10,219 out-of-state. Books/supplies: $1,150. Personal expenses: $1,676.

Financial aid. Non-need-based: Scholarships awarded for academics.

Application procedures. Admission: Rolling admission. $30 fee. **Financial aid:** Priority date 2/1, no deadline. Applicants notified on a rolling basis.

Academics. 9 upper-division undergraduate programs, 7 certificate programs, 16 graduate programs, education specialist and educational doctorate programs offered. **Special study options:** Distance learning, double major, independent study, internships, teacher certification program, weekend college. **Credit/placement by examination:** AP, CLEP, IB. 30 credit hours maximum toward bachelor's degree.

Majors. Business: Accounting, business admin, management information systems, marketing. **Education:** Elementary. **Engineering:** Manufacturing. **Liberal arts:** Arts/sciences. **Parks/recreation:** Facilities management. **Protective services:** Law enforcement admin.

Computing on campus. 71 workstations in library. Online library, wireless network available.

Contact. E-mail: wiu-qc@wiu.edu
Phone: (309) 762-9481 Fax: (309) 762-6989
Curtis Williams, Assistant Director of Admissions, Western Illinois University: Quad Cities, 3561 60th Street, Moline, IL 61265

Westwood College: Chicago Loop

Chicago, Illinois
www.westwood.edu

- For-profit 4-year technical college
- Commuter campus in very large city
- 623 degree-seeking undergraduates
- 62% of applicants admitted

General. Accredited by ACICS. **Degrees:** 79 bachelor's, 18 associate awarded. **Calendar:** Continuous. **Full-time faculty:** 15 total. **Part-time faculty:** 63 total.

Freshman class profile. 1,103 applied, 685 admitted, 623 enrolled.

Basis for selection. Admission based on interview, applicant's level of interest and test scores. SAT or ACT recommended.

High school preparation. 4 units required.

2008-2009 Annual costs. $4,251 per term; 5 terms per year.

Application procedures. Admission: Priority date 8/6; deadline 8/9. $25 fee. **Financial aid:** No deadline.

Academics. Special study options: Independent study, internships. **Credit/placement by examination:** CLEP, SAT, ACT, institutional tests.

Majors. Business: Marketing. **Communications technology:** Animation/special effects. **Computer sciences:** Security. **Protective services:** Police science. **Visual/performing arts:** Design.

Contact. Phone: (312) 739-0850 Fax: (312) 739-1004
Jeff Hill, Director of Admissions, Westwood College: Chicago Loop, 17 North State Street, Suite 300, Chicago, IL 60602

Westwood College: DuPage

Woodridge, Illinois
www.westwood.edu **CB code: 5096**

- For-profit 4-year technical college
- Commuter campus in large city
- 519 degree-seeking undergraduates: 18% part-time, 32% women
- Interview required

General. Accredited by ACICS. **Degrees:** 102 bachelor's, 11 associate awarded. **Location:** 20 miles from downtown Chicago. **Calendar:** Quarter. **Full-time faculty:** 5 total; 40% women. **Part-time faculty:** 41 total; 12% have terminal degrees, 20% minority, 29% women.

Basis for selection. Successful completion of Accuplacer test required prior to admission; SAT/ACT scores may be used in lieu of Accuplacer. SAT or ACT recommended.

2008-2009 Annual costs. Expenses vary by program; however, average cost for academic year is $14,867, which includes tuition, fees and books.

2007-2008 Financial aid. Need-based: 38% of total undergraduate aid awarded as scholarships/grants, 62% as loans/jobs.

Application procedures. Admission: No deadline. $100 fee.

Academics. **Special study options:** Accelerated study, independent study. **Credit/placement by examination:** CLEP, institutional tests.

Majors. **Business:** Business admin. **Computer sciences:** Security, webmaster. **Construction:** Site management. **Protective services:** Criminal justice. **Visual/performing arts:** Interior design.

Student life. **Activities:** Student government.

Contact. Phone: (630) 434-8244 Toll-free number: (866) 721-7646
Fax: (630) 743-0667
Scott Kawall, Director of Admissions, Westwood College: DuPage, 7155 Janes Avenue, Woodridge, IL 60517

Westwood College: O'Hare Airport
Chicago, Illinois
www.westwood.edu

- For-profit 4-year technical and career college
- Commuter campus in very large city
- 730 degree-seeking undergraduates: 17% part-time, 49% women
- Application essay, interview required

General. Accredited by ACICS. **Degrees:** 90 bachelor's, 10 associate awarded. **Location:** Downtown. **Calendar:** Continuous, extensive summer session. **Full-time faculty:** 7 total. **Part-time faculty:** 39 total. **Special facilities:** Graphic design finishing room, information systems security laboratory, interior design resource room, medical assisting laboratory, computer assisted drawing and design laboratory, game software design laboratory, animation and visual communication laboratory.

Basis for selection. Placement test and letter of intent required. Assessment given to all students; passing score required for admission to college programs.

2008-2009 Annual costs. Tuition/fees: $14,570. Books/supplies: $300. Personal expenses: $400.

Application procedures. **Admission:** No deadline. $25 fee. Application must be submitted on paper. **Financial aid:** Priority date 3/1, closing date 6/30. FAFSA, institutional form required.

Academics. **Special study options:** Accelerated study, cooperative education, distance learning, double major, independent study, internships, liberal arts/career combination, study abroad. **Credit/placement by examination:** AP, CLEP, institutional tests. **Support services:** Learning center, reduced course load, remedial instruction, study skills assistance, tutoring, writing center.

Majors. **Business:** Marketing. **Communications technology:** Animation/special effects. **Computer sciences:** Security. **Construction:** Site management. **Health:** Facilities admin, office admin. **Protective services:** Correctional facilities, corrections, criminal justice, criminalistics, forensics, juvenile corrections, law enforcement admin, police science, security management, security services. **Public administration:** General, community org/advocacy, human services, policy analysis. **Social sciences:** Criminology. **Visual/performing arts:** Design, graphic design, interior design.

Computing on campus. Commuter students can connect to campus network. Online library, wireless network available.

Student life. **Freshman orientation:** Mandatory. Preregistration for classes offered. **Housing:** Wellness housing available. **Activities:** Student government, student newspaper.

Student services. Adult student services, alcohol/substance abuse counseling, career counseling, student employment services, financial aid counseling, minority student services, personal counseling, placement for graduates, veterans' counselor, women's services. **Physically disabled:** Services for visually, hearing impaired.

Contact. E-mail: skasem@westwood.edu
Phone: (773) 380-6800 Toll-free number: (877) 877-8857
Fax: (773) 714-0828
Shahed Kasem, Director of Admissions, Westwood College: O'Hare Airport, 8501 West Higgins Road, Chicago, IL 60631

Westwood College: River Oaks
Calumet City, Illinois
www.westwood.edu

- For-profit 4-year career college
- Commuter campus in very large city

General. Accredited by ACICS. **Calendar:** Continuous.

Contact. Phone: (708) 832-1988
80 River Oaks Center, Suite D-49, Calumet City, IL 60409

Wheaton College
Wheaton, Illinois — **CB member**
www.wheaton.edu — **CB code: 1905**

- Private 4-year liberal arts college affiliated with nondenominational tradition
- Residential campus in small city
- 2,344 degree-seeking undergraduates: 3% part-time, 50% women, 3% African American, 8% Asian American, 4% Hispanic American, 1% international
- 470 degree-seeking graduate students
- 62% of applicants admitted
- SAT or ACT with writing, application essay required
- 86% graduate within 6 years; 34% enter graduate study

General. Founded in 1860. Regionally accredited. **Degrees:** 633 bachelor's awarded; master's, doctoral offered. **ROTC:** Army, Air Force. **Location:** 25 miles from Chicago. **Calendar:** Semester, limited summer session. **Full-time faculty:** 198 total; 94% have terminal degrees, 10% minority, 30% women. **Part-time faculty:** 102 total; 37% have terminal degrees, 11% minority, 49% women. **Class size:** 59% < 20, 32% 20-39, 5% 40-49, 3% 50-99, 1% >100. **Special facilities:** Billy Graham museum, science station, Christian residential camp, collection of books and papers of 7 British authors, center for applied Christian ethics.

Freshman class profile. 2,083 applied, 1,288 admitted, 581 enrolled.

Mid 50% test scores		**GPA 2.0-2.99:**	1%
SAT critical reading:	600-700	**Rank in top quarter:**	85%
SAT math:	610-690	**Rank in top tenth:**	59%
SAT writing:	600-710	**Return as sophomores:**	96%
ACT composite:	27-31	**Out-of-state:**	80%
GPA 3.75 or higher:	58%	**Live on campus:**	100%
GPA 3.50-3.74:	24%	**International:**	1%
GPA 3.0-3.49:	17%		

Basis for selection. Evidence of a vital Christian experience, moral character, personal integrity, social concern, academic ability, and desire for a liberal arts education as defined by the college are most important. Interview recommended. Audition required of music majors. **Homeschooled:** Statement describing homeschool structure and mission required. Applicants advised to take the ACT to satisfy the "Ability to Benefit" requirements. **Learning Disabled:** Personal interview required. Student must contact Registrar to request services or equipment and provide documentation/diagnosis of disability.

High school preparation. College-preparatory program required. 18 units required. Required and recommended units include English 4, mathematics 4, social studies 4, science 4 and foreign language 3.

2008-2009 Annual costs. Tuition/fees: $25,500. Room/board: $7,618. Books/supplies: $768. Personal expenses: $1,936.

2008-2009 Financial aid. **Need-based:** Average need met was 85%. Average scholarship/grant was $14,776; average loan $4,423. 72% of total undergraduate aid awarded as scholarships/grants, 28% as loans/jobs. **Non-need-based:** Scholarships awarded for academics, alumni affiliation, art, minority status, music/drama. **Additional information:** First $500 to $2,000 of need awarded as grant instead of loan.

Application procedures. **Admission:** Closing date 1/10 (receipt date). $50 fee, may be waived for applicants with need. Admission notification 4/1. Must reply by May 1 or within 3 week(s) if notified thereafter. **Financial aid:** Priority date 2/15; no closing date. FAFSA, institutional form required. Applicants notified on a rolling basis starting 3/1.

Academics. **Special study options:** Combined bachelor's/graduate degree, cross-registration, distance learning, exchange student, independent study, internships, liberal arts/career combination, student-designed major, study abroad, teacher certification program, urban semester, Washington semester. **Credit/placement by examination:** AP, CLEP, IB, SAT, ACT, institutional tests. 76 credit hours maximum toward bachelor's degree. **Support services:** Study skills assistance, writing center.

Majors. **Biology:** General. **Business:** Managerial economics. **Communications:** General. **Computer sciences:** Computer science. **Conservation:** Environmental studies. **Education:** Elementary, music, secondary. **Engineering:** General. **Foreign languages:** Classics, French, German, Spanish. **Health:**

Health services, nursing (RN). **History:** General. **Math:** General. **Philosophy/religion:** Philosophy. **Physical sciences:** Chemistry, geology, physics. **Psychology:** General. **Social sciences:** Anthropology, archaeology, economics, international relations, political science, sociology. **Theology:** Bible, religious ed. **Visual/performing arts:** Art, music history, music performance, music theory/composition.

Most popular majors. Business/marketing 9%, education 7%, English 9%, foreign language 6%, psychology 7%, social sciences 20%, theological studies 10%, visual/performing arts 7%.

Computing on campus. 125 workstations in dormitories, library, computer center, student center. Dormitories wired for high-speed internet access and linked to campus network. Commuter students can connect to campus network. Online library, helpline, wireless network available.

Student life. **Freshman orientation:** Mandatory. Preregistration for classes offered. Four-day program during the week before classes begin. **Policies:** All college and college-related functions are alcohol and tobacco free. Religious observance required. **Housing:** Guaranteed on-campus for freshmen. Single-sex dorms, special housing for disabled, apartments, cooperative housing available. **Activities:** Bands, campus ministries, choral groups, dance, drama, film society, international student organizations, literary magazine, music ensembles, Model UN, musical theater, opera, radio station, student government, student newspaper, symphony orchestra, TV station, Christian Service Council, Student Missionary Project, Youth Hostel Ministries, World Christian Fellowship, Students for Biblical Equality, Amnesty International, Earthkeepers, Jonathan Blanchard Society, Unidad Christiana, Koinonia.

Athletics. NCAA. **Intercollegiate:** Baseball M, basketball, cross-country, football (tackle) M, golf, soccer, softball W, swimming, tennis, track and field, volleyball W, water polo W, wrestling M. **Intramural:** Badminton, basketball, bowling, football (non-tackle) M, golf, soccer, softball M, tennis, volleyball, water polo. **Team name:** Thunder.

Student services. Career counseling, student employment services, financial aid counseling, health services, minority student services, personal counseling, placement for graduates, veterans' counselor. **Physically disabled:** Services for visually, speech, hearing impaired.

Contact. E-mail: admissions@wheaton.edu
Phone: (630) 752-5005 Toll-free number: (800) 222-2419
Fax: (630) 752-5285
Shawn Leftwich, Director of Undergraduate Admissions, Wheaton College, 501 College Avenue, Wheaton, IL 60187-5593

Indiana

Anderson University

Anderson, Indiana **CB member**
www.anderson.edu **CB code: 1016**

- Private 4-year liberal arts college affiliated with Church of God
- Residential campus in small city
- 2,147 degree-seeking undergraduates: 8% part-time, 57% women, 6% African American, 1% Asian American, 1% Hispanic American, 1% Native American, 2% international
- 575 degree-seeking graduate students
- 68% of applicants admitted
- SAT or ACT with writing required
- 54% graduate within 6 years

General. Founded in 1917. Regionally accredited. **Degrees:** 478 bachelor's awarded; master's, doctoral, first professional offered. **Location:** 45 miles from Indianapolis. **Calendar:** Semester, limited summer session. **Full-time faculty:** 134 total; 63% have terminal degrees, 3% minority, 42% women. **Part-time faculty:** 154 total; 6% have terminal degrees, 9% minority, 46% women. **Class size:** 57% < 20, 37% 20-39, 4% 40-49, 3% 50-99, less than 1% >100. **Special facilities:** Religious art collection, museum of Bible and Near Eastern studies, glass studio, wellness center.

Freshman class profile. 2,256 applied, 1,531 admitted, 544 enrolled.

Mid 50% test scores		**Rank in top quarter:**	47%
SAT critical reading:	460-570	**Rank in top tenth:**	24%
SAT math:	460-580	**End year in good standing:**	87%
ACT composite:	20-25	**Return as sophomores:**	76%
GPA 3.75 or higher:	30%	**Out-of-state:**	31%
GPA 3.50-3.74:	16%	**Live on campus:**	94%
GPA 3.0-3.49:	26%	**International:**	3%
GPA 2.0-2.99:	28%		

Basis for selection. GED not accepted. Rank in top half of class, test scores, reference important. School, church, and community activities also considered. Additional requirements for entry into nursing, athletic training, and educational programs. Essay recommended. Interview required of academically weak applicants. Audition required of music majors. Portfolio recommended for art majors. **Homeschooled:** Interview may be required.

High school preparation. 17 units required; 30 recommended. Required and recommended units include English 4, mathematics 3-4, social studies 1-2, history 1-2, science 3-4 (laboratory 3-4), foreign language 2-3, computer science 1, visual/performing arts 1 and academic electives 5.

2008-2009 Annual costs. Tuition/fees: $21,920. Room/board: $7,600. Books/supplies: $1,000. Personal expenses: $1,800.

Financial aid. Non-need-based: Scholarships awarded for academics, leadership, minority status, music/drama, state residency.

Application procedures. Admission: Priority date 1/15; deadline 7/1. $25 fee, may be waived for applicants with need, free for online applicants. Admission notification on a rolling basis beginning on or about 9/1. Must reply by May 1 or within 2 week(s) if notified thereafter. **Financial aid:** Priority date 3/1; no closing date. FAFSA required. Applicants notified on a rolling basis starting 3/1.

Academics. Special study options: Accelerated study, combined bachelor's/graduate degree, cross-registration, double major, honors, independent study, internships, student-designed major, study abroad, teacher certification program, urban semester. **Credit/placement by examination:** AP, CLEP, IB, SAT, ACT, institutional tests. 30 credit hours maximum toward bachelor's degree. **Support services:** Learning center, pre-admission summer program, reduced course load, tutoring.

Majors. Biology: General, biochemistry. **Business:** Accounting, business admin, entrepreneurial studies, finance, international, managerial economics, marketing, organizational behavior. **Communications:** Media studies. **Computer sciences:** Computer science, information systems. **Education:** General, art, biology, chemistry, drama/dance, elementary, English, French, mathematics, music, physical, physics, social studies, Spanish. **Family/consumer sciences:** Family systems. **Foreign languages:** French, Spanish. **Health:** Athletic training, nursing (RN). **History:** General. **Interdisciplinary:** Math/computer science. **Legal studies:** Prelaw. **Math:** General. **Parks/recreation:** Exercise sciences. **Philosophy/religion:** Philosophy, religion. **Physical sciences:** Chemistry, physics. **Protective services:** Criminal justice. **Psychology:** General. **Public administration:** Social work. **Social sciences:** Political science, sociology. **Theology:** Bible, sacred music, theology. **Visual/performing arts:** Design, dramatic, music management, music performance, studio arts, voice/opera.

Most popular majors. Business/marketing 23%, education 15%, health sciences 9%.

Computing on campus. 225 workstations in dormitories, library, computer center, student center. Dormitories linked to campus network. Commuter students can connect to campus network. Wireless network available.

Student life. Freshman orientation: Mandatory. Preregistration for classes offered. **Policies:** Religious observance required. **Housing:** Coed dorms, single-sex dorms, apartments, wellness housing available. $100 nonrefundable deposit, deadline 5/1. **Activities:** Bands, campus ministries, choral groups, dance, drama, international student organizations, literary magazine, music ensembles, Model UN, musical theater, opera, radio station, student government, student newspaper, symphony orchestra, multicultural student union, Religious Life Council, business club, women's clubs, men's clubs, international student association.

Athletics. NCAA. **Intercollegiate:** Baseball M, basketball, cross-country, football (tackle) M, golf, soccer, softball W, tennis, track and field, volleyball W. **Intramural:** Basketball, bowling, football (tackle), soccer, softball, swimming, tennis, volleyball, water polo. **Team name:** Ravens.

Student services. Adult student services, chaplain/spiritual director, career counseling, student employment services, financial aid counseling, health services, minority student services, personal counseling, placement for graduates, veterans' counselor. **Physically disabled:** Services for visually, speech impaired.

Contact. E-mail: info@anderson.edu
Phone: (765) 641-4080 Toll-free number: (800) 428-6414
Fax: (765) 641-4091
Jim King, Director of Admissions, Anderson University, 1100 East Fifth Street, Anderson, IN 46012-3495

Ball State University

Muncie, Indiana **CB member**
www.bsu.edu **CB code: 1051**

- Public 4-year university
- Residential campus in small city
- 16,575 degree-seeking undergraduates; 6% part-time, 52% women, 7% African American, 1% Asian American, 2% Hispanic American
- 3,082 degree-seeking graduate students
- 73% of applicants admitted
- 58% graduate within 6 years

General. Founded in 1918. Regionally accredited. **Degrees:** 3,321 bachelor's, 428 associate awarded; master's, doctoral offered. **ROTC:** Army. **Location:** 56 miles from Indianapolis. **Calendar:** Semester, extensive summer session. **Full-time faculty:** 925 total; 75% have terminal degrees, 14% minority, 43% women. **Part-time faculty:** 248 total; 22% have terminal degrees, 8% minority, 54% women. **Class size:** 36% < 20, 48% 20-39, 6% 40-49, 6% 50-99, 3% >100. **Special facilities:** Planetarium, nature preserves, wellness institute, art museum, media design center.

Freshman class profile. 13,773 applied, 10,109 admitted, 4,039 enrolled.

Mid 50% test scores		**Rank in top tenth:**	16%
SAT critical reading:	470-570	**Return as sophomores:**	78%
SAT math:	470-580	**Out-of-state:**	9%
SAT writing:	450-560	**Live on campus:**	91%
ACT composite:	19-23	**Fraternities:**	9%
Rank in top quarter:	44%	**Sororities:**	7%

Basis for selection. Curriculum, GPA, test scores most important. Credentials of non-traditional students (age 23 or older) evaluated for admission on individual basis. Personal statement required of all non-traditional students. Test for placement required for transfers and non-traditional freshmen. Interview and essay recommended; audition required of music and theater majors; portfolio recommended for art and architecture majors. **Homeschooled:** Statement describing homeschool structure and mission, transcript of courses and grades required.

High school preparation. College-preparatory program required. Required and recommended units include English 4, mathematics 3, social studies 3, science 3 (laboratory 2) and foreign language 3.

2008-2009 Annual costs. Tuition/fees: $7,500; $19,304 out-of-state. Room/board: $7,598. Books/supplies: $930. Personal expenses: $1,500.

2008-2009 Financial aid. **Need-based:** 3,501 full-time freshmen applied for aid; 2,479 were judged to have need; 2,433 of these received aid. Average need met was 63%. Average scholarship/grant was $5,692; average loan $3,501. 52% of total undergraduate aid awarded as scholarships/grants, 48% as loans/jobs. **Non-need-based:** Awarded to 4,629 full-time undergraduates, including 1,468 freshmen. Scholarships awarded for academics, athletics, leadership, minority status, music/drama, ROTC, state residency.

Application procedures. **Admission:** Priority date 3/1; deadline 8/15 (postmark date). $25 fee, may be waived for applicants with need. Admission notification on a rolling basis. Must reply by May 1 or within 2 week(s) if notified thereafter. **Financial aid:** Priority date 3/10; no closing date. FAFSA required. Applicants notified on a rolling basis starting 4/1.

Academics. Minimum credit hours in major for associate degree range from 30 to 45; for bachelor's, 45 to 65. All undergraduates must meet writing competency requirement. **Special study options:** Accelerated study, combined bachelor's/graduate degree, cooperative education, distance learning, double major, dual enrollment of high school students, ESL, exchange student, honors, independent study, internships, liberal arts/career combination, student-designed major, study abroad, teacher certification program, Washington semester, weekend college. **Credit/placement by examination:** AP, CLEP, IB, SAT, ACT, institutional tests. 15 credit hours maximum toward associate degree, 63 toward bachelor's. **Support services:** Learning center, pre-admission summer program, reduced course load, study skills assistance, tutoring, writing center.

Honors college/program. Separate curriculum, undergraduate research fellowships and study abroad programs; 280 freshmen students were admitted in Fall 2007.

Majors. **Architecture:** Architecture, environmental design, landscape, urban/community planning. **Area/ethnic studies:** Women's. **Biology:** General. **Business:** General, accounting, actuarial science, business admin, entrepreneurial studies, finance, human resources, management information systems, managerial economics, marketing, office management, operations. **Communications:** Journalism, radio/tv. **Computer sciences:** General. **Conservation:** General. **Education:** Business, elementary, health, kindergarten/preschool, multiple handicapped, physical, science, technology/industrial arts. **Engineering:** General. **Engineering technology:** Industrial. **Family/consumer sciences:** General. **Foreign languages:** Classics, French, German, Japanese, Latin, Spanish. **Health:** Audiology/speech pathology, clinical lab science, dietetics, nursing (RN), predental, premedicine, respiratory therapy technology. **History:** General. **Liberal arts:** Arts/sciences. **Math:** General. **Philosophy/religion:** Philosophy, religion. **Physical sciences:** Chemistry, geology, physics. **Protective services:** Criminal justice. **Psychology:** General. **Public administration:** Social work. **Social sciences:** General, anthropology, economics, geography, political science, sociology, urban studies. **Visual/performing arts:** Art, dance, dramatic. **Other:** Graphic arts management, Vocation, family, and consumer science.

Most popular majors. Business/marketing 14%, communications/journalism 10%, education 15%, health sciences 7%, liberal arts 11%, visual/performing arts 6%.

Computing on campus. PC or laptop required. 1,095 workstations in dormitories, library, computer center, student center. Dormitories wired for high-speed internet access and linked to campus network. Commuter students can connect to campus network. Online course registration, online library, helpline, repair service, student web hosting, wireless network available.

Student life. **Freshman orientation:** Mandatory. Preregistration for classes offered. Two-day program. **Policies:** Freshmen and sophomore transfer students required to live on campus unless living with parents or guardian, or 21 years of age or older. **Housing:** Guaranteed on-campus for freshmen. Coed dorms, single-sex dorms, special housing for disabled, apartments available. $125 fully refundable deposit. **Activities:** Bands, campus ministries, choral groups, dance, drama, film society, international student organizations, literary magazine, music ensembles, musical theater, radio station, student government, student newspaper, symphony orchestra, TV station, over 300 student organizations.

Athletics. NCAA. **Intercollegiate:** Baseball M, basketball, cheerleading, cross-country, diving, equestrian, field hockey W, football (tackle) M, golf, gymnastics W, soccer W, softball W, swimming, tennis, track and field, volleyball. **Intramural:** Badminton, baseball M, basketball, bowling, football (non-tackle), golf, racquetball, soccer, softball, swimming, tennis, track and field, volleyball. **Team name:** Cardinals.

Student services. Adult student services, alcohol/substance abuse counseling, career counseling, student employment services, financial aid counseling, health services, legal services, minority student services, on-campus daycare, personal counseling, placement for graduates, veterans' counselor, women's services. **Physically disabled:** Services for visually, speech, hearing impaired.

Contact. E-mail: askus@bsu.edu
Phone: (765) 285-8300 Toll-free number: (800) 482-4278
Fax: (765) 285-1632
Tom Taylor, Vice President of Enrollment, Marketing and Communications, Ball State University, 2000 University Avenue, Muncie, IN 47306-1022

Bethel College

Mishawaka, Indiana
www.bethelcollege.edu **CB code: 1079**

- Private 4-year liberal arts college affiliated with Missionary Church
- Commuter campus in large town
- 1,802 degree-seeking undergraduates
- 82% of applicants admitted
- SAT or ACT (ACT writing optional) required

General. Founded in 1947. Regionally accredited. **Degrees:** 352 bachelor's, 89 associate awarded; master's offered. **ROTC:** Army, Naval, Air Force. **Location:** 140 miles from Indianapolis, 90 miles from Chicago. **Calendar:** Semester, limited summer session. **Full-time faculty:** 94 total. **Part-time faculty:** 162 total. **Class size:** 75% < 20, 22% 20-39, 2% 40-49, 1% 50-99.

Freshman class profile. 691 applied, 564 admitted, 247 enrolled.

Mid 50% test scores		**GPA 3.0-3.49:**	26%
SAT critical reading:	470-570	**GPA 2.0-2.99:**	32%
SAT math:	460-580	**Rank in top quarter:**	56%
ACT composite:	20-26	**Rank in top tenth:**	30%
GPA 3.75 or higher:	27%	**Out-of-state:**	32%
GPA 3.50-3.74:	14%	**Live on campus:**	75%

Basis for selection. School achievement record, test scores, character recommendations, personal statement important. Interview recommended. Audition required of music majors and scholarship candidates. Portfolio recommended for returning adults, fine arts majors.

High school preparation. 17 units recommended. Recommended units include English 4, mathematics 3, social studies 1, history 2, science 1 (laboratory 1), foreign language 2 and academic electives 3.

2009-2010 Annual costs. Tuition/fees: $20,978. All first-time, full-time students must pay a one-time student activity and technology fee of $600. Room/board: $6,120. Books/supplies: $600. Personal expenses: $700.

2007-2008 Financial aid. **Need-based:** 43% of total undergraduate aid awarded as scholarships/grants, 57% as loans/jobs. **Non-need-based:** Scholarships awarded for academics, art, athletics, job skills, leadership, minority status, music/drama, religious affiliation, ROTC, state residency.

Application procedures. **Admission:** Priority date 12/1; deadline 8/15 (receipt date). $25 fee, may be waived for applicants with need. Admission notification on a rolling basis beginning on or about 10/1. Must reply by 5/1. **Financial aid:** Priority date 3/1, closing date 3/10. FAFSA required. Applicants notified by 4/15; must reply within 3 week(s) of notification.

Academics. **Special study options:** Accelerated study, cross-registration, double major, ESL, exchange student, independent study, internships, student-designed major, study abroad, teacher certification program, urban semester, Washington semester. **Credit/placement by examination:** AP, CLEP, IB, SAT, ACT, institutional tests. 20 credit hours maximum toward bachelor's degree. **Support services:** Learning center, reduced course load, remedial instruction, study skills assistance, tutoring.

Majors. **Biology:** General. **Business:** Accounting, business admin, human resources. **Communications:** General. **Computer sciences:** Information systems. **Conservation:** General. **Education:** Business, elementary, English, mathematics, music, physical, science, social studies. **Engineering:** General. **Foreign languages:** Sign language interpretation. **Health:** Nursing (RN), predental, premedicine. **History:** General. **Liberal arts:** Arts/sciences. **Math:** General. **Parks/recreation:** Facilities management. **Philosophy/religion:** Philosophy, religion. **Physical sciences:** Chemistry. **Psychology:** General. **Public administration:** Human services. **Social sciences:** General, international relations, sociology. **Theology:** Bible, sacred music, theology. **Visual/performing arts:** Art, design, dramatic.

Most popular majors. Business/marketing 31%, education 13%, health sciences 10%, liberal arts 10%, theological studies 12%.

Computing on campus. 215 workstations in dormitories, library, computer center.

Student life. **Freshman orientation:** Mandatory. **Policies:** Religious observance required. **Housing:** Single-sex dorms, special housing for disabled available. $200 fully refundable deposit, deadline 5/1. **Activities:** Bands, choral groups, drama, music ensembles, musical theater, opera, radio station, student government, student newspaper, symphony orchestra, Fellowship of Christian Athletes, ministerial association, interest clubs.

Athletics. NAIA, NCCAA. **Intercollegiate:** Baseball M, basketball, cross-country, golf M, soccer M, softball W, tennis, track and field, volleyball W. **Intramural:** Basketball M, football (tackle) M, soccer, table tennis, volleyball. **Team name:** Pilots.

Student services. Adult student services, chaplain/spiritual director, career counseling, student employment services, financial aid counseling, health services, minority student services, personal counseling, placement for graduates. **Physically disabled:** Services for hearing impaired.

Contact. E-mail: admissions@bethelcollege.edu
Phone: (574) 807-7350 Toll-free number: (800) 422-4101
Fax: (574) 257-3335
Krista Wong, Director of Admissions, Bethel College, 1001 Bethel Circle, Mishawaka, IN 46545

Butler University

Indianapolis, Indiana — **CB member**
www.butler.edu — **CB code: 1073**

- Private 4-year university
- Residential campus in very large city
- 3,607 degree-seeking undergraduates: 1% part-time, 61% women, 4% African American, 2% Asian American, 2% Hispanic American, 3% international
- 728 degree-seeking graduate students
- 72% of applicants admitted
- SAT or ACT with writing, application essay required
- 74% graduate within 6 years; 24% enter graduate study

General. Founded in 1855. Regionally accredited. **Degrees:** 693 bachelor's, 1 associate awarded; master's, first professional offered. **ROTC:** Army, Air Force. **Location:** 5 miles from downtown. **Calendar:** Semester, limited summer session. **Full-time faculty:** 306 total; 81% have terminal degrees, 12% minority, 44% women. **Part-time faculty:** 157 total; 22% have terminal degrees, 8% minority, 47% women. **Class size:** 56% < 20, 39% 20-39, 1% 40-49, 2% 50-99, 1% >100. **Special facilities:** Observatory, planetarium, herbarium, performing arts auditorium, canal, nature preserve.

Freshman class profile. 5,923 applied, 4,250 admitted, 934 enrolled.

Mid 50% test scores			
SAT critical reading:	530-640	GPA 2.0-2.99:	5%
SAT math:	550-650	Rank in top quarter:	79%
SAT writing:	520-620	Rank in top tenth:	51%
ACT composite:	25-29	End year in good standing:	93%
GPA 3.75 or higher:	56%	Return as sophomores:	89%
GPA 3.50-3.74:	18%	Out-of-state:	45%
GPA 3.0-3.49:	21%	Live on campus:	95%
		International:	2%

Basis for selection. Test scores, high school record most important. Recommendations, activities considered. Audition required of dance, drama, music, and media arts majors. **Homeschooled:** Statement describing homeschool structure and mission, transcript of courses and grades, letter of recommendation (nonparent) required.

High school preparation. College-preparatory program recommended. 16 units required. Required units include English 4, mathematics 3, history 2, science 3, foreign language 2 and academic electives 2. 4 math units required for business administration majors.

2008-2009 Annual costs. Tuition/fees: $28,266. Room/board: $9,410. Books/supplies: $800. Personal expenses: $1,450.

2008-2009 Financial aid. **Need-based:** 63% of total undergraduate aid awarded as scholarships/grants, 37% as loans/jobs. **Non-need-based:** Scholarships awarded for academics, athletics, music/drama.

Application procedures. **Admission:** Priority date 12/1; deadline 3/1 (postmark date). $35 fee, may be waived for applicants with need, free for online applicants. Admission notification on a rolling basis beginning on or about 12/20. Must reply by May 1 or within 2 week(s) if notified thereafter. **Financial aid:** Priority date 3/1; no closing date. FAFSA required. Applicants notified on a rolling basis starting 3/15; must reply within 3 week(s) of notification.

Academics. **Special study options:** Combined bachelor's/graduate degree, cross-registration, double major, dual enrollment of high school students, exchange student, honors, independent study, internships, student-designed major, study abroad, teacher certification program, Washington semester. Dual-degree engineering program with Purdue University; cooperative program in Business. **Credit/placement by examination:** AP, CLEP, IB, SAT, ACT, institutional tests. **Support services:** Learning center, reduced course load, study skills assistance, tutoring, writing center.

Majors. **Biology:** General. **Business:** Accounting, actuarial science, finance, international, marketing. **Communications:** General, journalism, radio/tv. **Communications technology:** Recording arts. **Computer sciences:** General, information systems. **Education:** Early childhood, elementary, kindergarten/preschool, middle, music, secondary. **Engineering:** Physics. **Foreign languages:** French, German, Latin, modern Greek, Spanish. **Health:** Communication disorders, pharmaceutical sciences, physician assistant. **History:** General. **Interdisciplinary:** Science/society. **Liberal arts:** Arts/sciences. **Math:** General. **Philosophy/religion:** Philosophy, religion. **Physical sciences:** Chemistry, physics. **Protective services:** Criminal justice. **Psychology:** General. **Social sciences:** Anthropology, criminology, economics, international relations, political science, sociology, urban studies. **Visual/performing arts:** Arts management, dance, dramatic, music management, music pedagogy, music performance, music theory/composition, piano/organ, stringed instruments, voice/opera.

Most popular majors. Business/marketing 15%, communications/journalism 8%, education 10%, health sciences 24%, social sciences 6%, visual/performing arts 8%.

Computing on campus. 430 workstations in dormitories, library, computer center, student center. Dormitories wired for high-speed internet access and linked to campus network. Commuter students can connect to campus network. Online course registration, helpline, wireless network available.

Student life. **Freshman orientation:** Mandatory, $100 fee. Preregistration for classes offered. Three-day program held in August. Early registration for Fall classes held March through June. **Housing:** Guaranteed on-campus for all undergraduates. Coed dorms, single-sex dorms, apartments, fraternity/sorority housing available. $100 fully refundable deposit, deadline 5/1. **Activities:** Bands, campus ministries, choral groups, dance, drama, international student organizations, literary magazine, music ensembles, Model UN, musical theater, opera, student government, student newspaper, symphony orchestra, TV station, volunteer center, black student union, Campus Crusade for Christ, YMCA, College Republicans, Mortar Board, academic honoraries, Alpha Phi Omega.

Athletics. NCAA. **Intercollegiate:** Baseball M, basketball, cross-country, football (tackle) M, golf, soccer, softball W, swimming W, tennis, track and field, volleyball W. **Intramural:** Badminton, baseball M, basketball, bowling, football (tackle) M, golf, soccer, softball, swimming, table tennis, tennis, track and field, volleyball, weight lifting. **Team name:** Bulldogs.

Student services. Alcohol/substance abuse counseling, career counseling, student employment services, financial aid counseling, health services, minority student services, on-campus daycare, personal counseling, placement for graduates. **Physically disabled:** Services for visually, speech impaired.

Contact. E-mail: admission@butler.edu
Phone: (317) 940-8100 Toll-free number: (888) 940-8100
Fax: (317) 940-8150
Scott Ham, Director of Admissions, Butler University, 4600 Sunset Avenue, Indianapolis, IN 46208

Calumet College of St. Joseph

Whiting, Indiana
www.ccsj.edu — **CB code: 1776**

- Private 4-year liberal arts college affiliated with Roman Catholic Church
- Commuter campus in small city
- 1,051 degree-seeking undergraduates: 53% part-time, 51% women
- 111 degree-seeking graduate students
- 60% of applicants admitted
- Application essay required

General. Founded in 1951. Regionally accredited. **Degrees:** 297 bachelor's, 16 associate awarded; master's offered. **Location:** 20 miles from Chicago. **Calendar:** Semester, limited summer session. **Full-time faculty:** 32 total; 62% have terminal degrees, 16% minority, 28% women. **Part-time**

faculty: 8 total; 12% have terminal degrees, 12% minority, 62% women. **Class size:** 68% < 20, 29% 20-39, 3% 40-49, less than 1% >100.

Freshman class profile. 372 applied, 224 admitted, 155 enrolled.

GPA 3.75 or higher:	6%	**GPA 2.0-2.99:**	50%
GPA 3.50-3.74:	4%	**Rank in top quarter:**	25%
GPA 3.0-3.49:	20%	**Rank in top tenth:**	8%

Basis for selection. High school record most important. ACT/COMPASS Assessment Test required for all applicants, top half of class, minimum 2.0 GPA. Compass testing used for placement. Essay used to place students in English courses as part of placement exam. SAT or ACT recommended. Interview recommended. **Homeschooled:** State high school equivalency certificate required.

High school preparation. 15 units recommended. Recommended units include English 4, mathematics 3, social studies 3, science 2 (laboratory 1) and foreign language 1.

2008-2009 Annual costs. Tuition/fees: $12,610. Books/supplies: $1,500. Personal expenses: $1,110.

2007-2008 Financial aid. Non-need-based: Scholarships awarded for academics, alumni affiliation, religious affiliation. **Additional information:** Immediate computerized estimate of financial aid eligibility available to students applying in person.

Application procedures. Admission: No deadline. No application fee. Admission notification on a rolling basis. **Financial aid:** Priority date 3/1; no closing date. FAFSA required. Applicants notified on a rolling basis; must reply within 2 week(s) of notification.

Academics. Special study options: Accelerated study, cooperative education, double major, dual enrollment of high school students, ESL, honors, independent study, internships, liberal arts/career combination, student-designed major, teacher certification program, weekend college. **Credit/placement by examination:** AP, CLEP, institutional tests. 30 credit hours maximum toward associate degree, 60 toward bachelor's. **Support services:** Learning center, reduced course load, remedial instruction, study skills assistance, tutoring, writing center.

Majors. Business: General, accounting, business admin, organizational behavior. **Communications:** General, media studies. **Computer sciences:** General. **Education:** General, elementary, science, secondary. **Health:** Health care admin. **Legal studies:** Paralegal. **Liberal arts:** Arts/sciences. **Philosophy/religion:** Religion. **Protective services:** Police science. **Psychology:** General. **Public administration:** Human services. **Social sciences:** General. **Visual/performing arts:** Studio arts.

Computing on campus. 72 workstations in library, computer center. Online library, wireless network available.

Student life. Freshman orientation: Mandatory, $70 fee. Preregistration for classes offered. Held 1 week before classes begin, followed up by mentoring program. **Activities:** Campus ministries, choral groups, dance, drama, literary magazine, student government, student newspaper, Los Amigos, black student organization, criminal justice club, media and fine arts club, creative writing club, paralegal studies club, booster club, human services club, educators club.

Athletics. NAIA. **Intercollegiate:** Baseball M, basketball, bowling, cross-country, golf, soccer, softball W, tennis, track and field, volleyball. **Team name:** Crimson Wave.

Student services. Chaplain/spiritual director, career counseling, student employment services, financial aid counseling, on-campus daycare, personal counseling, placement for graduates, veterans' counselor.

Contact. E-mail: admissions@ccsj.edu
Phone: (219) 473-4215 Toll-free number: (877) 700-9100
Fax: (219) 473-4259
Chuck Walz, Director of Admissions/Financial Aid, Calumet College of St. Joseph, 2400 New York Avenue, Whiting, IN 46394-2195

DePauw University

Greencastle, Indiana — **CB member**
www.depauw.edu — **CB code: 1166**

- Private 4-year liberal arts college affiliated with United Methodist Church
- Residential campus in small town
- 2,241 degree-seeking undergraduates: 57% women, 6% African American, 3% Asian American, 4% Hispanic American, 5% international
- 65% of applicants admitted
- SAT or ACT with writing, application essay required
- 85% graduate within 6 years

General. Founded in 1837. Regionally accredited. **Degrees:** 600 bachelor's awarded. **ROTC:** Army, Air Force. **Location:** 45 miles from Indianapolis. **Calendar:** 4-1-4. **Full-time faculty:** 230 total; 17% minority, 43% women. **Part-time faculty:** 64 total; 8% minority, 50% women. **Class size:** 70% < 20, 30% 20-39. **Special facilities:** Nature park and arboretum, ethnographic museums, closed circuit tv studio facilities, music instructional technology studio, digital media laboratory, visual resources library with digital image collection, digital video studio, observatory, 2 theaters, 2 music concert halls, concert pipe organ.

Freshman class profile. 4,064 applied, 2,625 admitted, 600 enrolled.

Mid 50% test scores		**Rank in top quarter:**	83%
SAT critical reading:	540-640	**Rank in top tenth:**	51%
SAT math:	570-670	**Return as sophomores:**	88%
SAT writing:	540-650	**Out-of-state:**	60%
ACT composite:	25-29	**Live on campus:**	100%
GPA 3.75 or higher:	35%	**International:**	11%
GPA 3.50-3.74:	26%	**Fraternities:**	64%
GPA 3.0-3.49:	35%	**Sororities:**	59%
GPA 2.0-2.99:	4%		

Basis for selection. Academic achievement and preparation, demonstrated verbal and quantitative skills, evidence of continuing commitment to learning most important. TOEFL recommended for international students. Interview strongly recommended. Audition required for School of Music candidates. **Homeschooled:** Transcript of courses and grades, interview required.

High school preparation. College-preparatory program recommended. 32 units recommended. Recommended units include English 4, mathematics 4, social studies 4, science 4 (laboratory 2), foreign language 4 and academic electives 10.

2008-2009 Annual costs. Tuition/fees: $31,825. Room/board: $8,400. Books/supplies: $700. Personal expenses: $1,000.

2008-2009 Financial aid. Non-need-based: Scholarships awarded for academics, alumni affiliation, leadership, minority status, music/drama, ROTC.

Application procedures. Admission: Closing date 2/1 (postmark date). $40 fee, may be waived for applicants with need, free for online applicants. Admission notification 4/1. Must reply by 5/1. **Financial aid:** Closing date 2/15. FAFSA, institutional form required. Applicants notified by 3/27; must reply by 5/1.

Academics. Demonstrated competence in writing, quantitative reasoning, and oral communication required of all students. Seminar, thesis, project, or comprehensive examination in major also required. More than 700 students participate in off-campus winter term programs; 40% study off-campus. **Special study options:** Combined bachelor's/graduate degree, double major, dual enrollment of high school students, exchange student, honors, independent study, internships, New York semester, student-designed major, study abroad, teacher certification program, urban semester, Washington semester. **Credit/placement by examination:** AP, CLEP, IB, SAT, ACT, institutional tests. 32 credit hours maximum toward bachelor's degree. **Support services:** Learning center, study skills assistance, tutoring, writing center.

Majors. Area/ethnic studies: African-American, East Asian, women's. **Biology:** General, biochemistry. **Communications:** Media studies. **Computer sciences:** Computer science. **Conservation:** Environmental science. **Education:** Elementary, music, physical. **Foreign languages:** Ancient Greek, classics, French, German, Latin, Romance, Spanish. **Health:** Athletic training. **History:** General. **Interdisciplinary:** Peace/conflict. **Math:** General. **Parks/recreation:** Exercise sciences. **Philosophy/religion:** Philosophy, religion. **Physical sciences:** Chemistry, geology, physics. **Psychology:** General. **Social sciences:** Anthropology, economics, political science, sociology. **Visual/performing arts:** Art history/conservation, dramatic, film/cinema, music management, music performance, music theory/composition, studio arts.

Most popular majors. Biology 12%, communications/journalism 9%, English 10%, foreign language 9%, social sciences 22%, visual/performing arts 6%.

Computing on campus. PC or laptop required. 413 workstations in dormitories, library, computer center, student center. Dormitories wired for high-speed internet access and linked to campus network. Commuter students can connect to campus network. Online course registration, online library, helpline, repair service, student web hosting, wireless network available.

Student life. Freshman orientation: Mandatory. Preregistration for classes offered. Four-day program in August. **Housing:** Guaranteed on-campus for all undergraduates. Coed dorms, apartments, fraternity/sorority housing, wellness housing available. $400 nonrefundable deposit, deadline 5/1. **Activities:** Bands, campus ministries, choral groups, dance, drama, film society, international student organizations, literary magazine, music ensembles, musical theater, opera, radio station, student government, student newspaper, symphony orchestra, TV station, Association of African American Students, international students association, Union Board, Coalition for Women's Concerns, College Republicans, College Democrats, Habitat for Humanity, JC Christian Fellowship, United DePauw, Committee for Latino Concerns.

Athletics. NCAA. **Intercollegiate:** Baseball M, basketball, cheerleading, cross-country, diving, field hockey W, football (tackle) M, golf, soccer, softball W, swimming, tennis, track and field, volleyball W. **Intramural:** Badminton, basketball, bowling, football (non-tackle), golf M, racquetball, soccer, softball, table tennis, tennis, volleyball. **Team name:** Tigers.

Student services. Alcohol/substance abuse counseling, chaplain/spiritual director, career counseling, student employment services, financial aid counseling, health services, minority student services, on-campus daycare, personal counseling, placement for graduates, women's services. **Physically disabled:** Services for visually, hearing impaired.

Contact. E-mail: admission@depauw.edu
Phone: (765) 658-4006 Toll-free number: (800) 447-2495
Fax: (765) 658-4007
Earl Macam, Director of Admission, DePauw University, 101 East Seminary Street, Greencastle, IN 46135-1611

DeVry University: Indianapolis

Indianapolis, Indiana
www.devry.edu

- For-profit 4-year university
- Commuter campus in very large city
- 184 degree-seeking undergraduates: 70% part-time, 53% women, 40% African American, 3% Asian American, 2% Hispanic American, 1% Native American, 1% international
- 118 degree-seeking graduate students
- 87% of applicants admitted

General. Degrees: 30 bachelor's awarded; master's offered. **Calendar:** Semester. **Part-time faculty:** 31 total; 23% minority, 36% women.

Freshman class profile. 89 applied, 77 admitted, 45 enrolled.

Basis for selection. Interview and GPA important; standardized test scores considered.

2008-2009 Annual costs. Tuition/fees: $13,930. Books/supplies: $1,300. Personal expenses: $5,082.

2007-2008 Financial aid. Non-need-based: Scholarships awarded for academics.

Application procedures. Admission: No deadline. $50 fee. Admission notification on a rolling basis. **Financial aid:** No deadline. FAFSA required. Applicants notified on a rolling basis.

Academics. Special study options: Accelerated study, distance learning. **Credit/placement by examination:** CLEP.

Majors. Business: Business admin. **Computer sciences:** Security.

Most popular majors. Business/marketing 93%, computer/information sciences 7%.

Student life. Housing: Private apartments, student-plan housing, private rooms.

Contact. Phone: (866) 513-3879
DeVry University: Indianapolis, 9100 Keystone Crossing, Suite 350, Indianapolis, IN 46240

Earlham College

Richmond, Indiana — **CB member**
www.earlham.edu — **CB code: 1195**

- Private 4-year liberal arts and seminary college affiliated with Society of Friends (Quaker)
- Residential campus in large town
- 1,146 degree-seeking undergraduates: 1% part-time, 55% women, 6% African American, 3% Asian American, 3% Hispanic American, 12% international
- 113 degree-seeking graduate students
- 75% of applicants admitted
- SAT or ACT with writing, application essay required
- 73% graduate within 6 years; 50% enter graduate study

General. Founded in 1847. Regionally accredited; also accredited by ATS. **Degrees:** 285 bachelor's awarded; master's, first professional offered. **Location:** 70 miles from Indianapolis; 45 miles from Dayton, Ohio. **Calendar:** Semester. **Full-time faculty:** 94 total; 96% have terminal degrees, 20% minority, 42% women. **Part-time faculty:** 10 total; 60% have terminal degrees, 10% minority, 60% women. **Class size:** 68% < 20, 25% 20-39, 3% 40-49, 3% 50-99. **Special facilities:** Natural history museum, observatory, planetarium, herbarium, working farm, biological field stations.

Freshman class profile. 1,825 applied, 1,376 admitted, 325 enrolled.

Mid 50% test scores		**GPA 2.0-2.99:**	15%
SAT critical reading:	570-690	**Rank in top quarter:**	70%
SAT math:	540-660	**Rank in top tenth:**	32%
SAT writing:	560-680	**End year in good standing:**	84%
ACT composite:	24-29	**Return as sophomores:**	85%
GPA 3.75 or higher:	39%	**Out-of-state:**	71%
GPA 3.50-3.74:	16%	**Live on campus:**	99%
GPA 3.0-3.49:	30%	**International:**	14%

Basis for selection. Combination of GPA, quality of high school program, SAT or ACT scores, recommendations, essay, and extracurricular activities important. Interview preferred. **Homeschooled:** Statement describing homeschool structure and mission, interview, letter of recommendation (nonparent) required. Portfolio or other evidence of learning, test scores, and essay.

High school preparation. College-preparatory program required. Required and recommended units include English 4, mathematics 3-4, social studies 4, history 2, science 3-4 (laboratory 2), foreign language 2-4 and visual/performing arts 1.

2008-2009 Annual costs. Tuition/fees: $34,030. Room/board: $6,814. Books/supplies: $850. Personal expenses: $1,000.

2007-2008 Financial aid. Need-based: 196 full-time freshmen applied for aid; 177 were judged to have need; 176 of these received aid. Average need met was 96%. Average scholarship/grant was $17,016; average loan $4,594. 73% of total undergraduate aid awarded as scholarships/grants, 27% as loans/jobs. **Non-need-based:** Awarded to 725 full-time undergraduates, including 153 freshmen. Scholarships awarded for academics, minority status.

Application procedures. Admission: Priority date 1/1; deadline 2/15 (postmark date). $30 fee, may be waived for applicants with need. Admission notification 3/15. Must reply by May 1 or within 3 week(s) if notified thereafter. **Financial aid:** Closing date 3/1. FAFSA, institutional form required. Applicants notified on a rolling basis starting 2/15; must reply by 5/1.

Academics. Special study options: Accelerated study, combined bachelor's/graduate degree, cross-registration, double major, dual enrollment of high school students, ESL, independent study, internships, New York semester, student-designed major, study abroad, urban semester. Teacher certification at Master's level only. **Credit/placement by examination:** AP, CLEP, IB, institutional tests. 18 credit hours maximum toward bachelor's degree. **Support services:** Learning center, pre-admission summer program, study skills assistance, tutoring, writing center.

Majors. Area/ethnic studies: African-American, Japanese, Latin American, women's. **Biology:** General, biochemistry. **Business:** Business admin. **Computer sciences:** General. **Conservation:** Environmental studies. **Foreign languages:** Classics, comparative lit, French, German, Spanish. **Health:** Premedicine. **History:** General. **Interdisciplinary:** Peace/conflict. **Math:** General. **Philosophy/religion:** Philosophy, religion. **Physical sciences:** Chemistry, physics. **Psychology:** General, psychobiology. **Social sciences:** Economics, political science, sociology. **Visual/performing arts:** Art, dramatic. **Other:** Geosciences, International studies.

Most popular majors. Area/ethnic studies 7%, biology 15%, English 7%, foreign language 9%, history 6%, interdisciplinary studies 10%, psychology 10%, social sciences 14%, visual/performing arts 10%.

Computing on campus. 175 workstations in library, computer center. Dormitories wired for high-speed internet access and linked to campus network. Commuter students can connect to campus network. Online course registration, online library, helpline, repair service, student web hosting, wireless network available.

Student life. **Freshman orientation:** Mandatory. Preregistration for classes offered. Five-day program held just prior to beginning of fall semester. **Policies:** Community and academic honor codes. **Housing:** Guaranteed on-campus for all undergraduates. Coed dorms, single-sex dorms, special housing for disabled, wellness housing available. 27 college-owned off-campus language and special interest houses (e.g. Japan House, German House, Peace House, Living/Learning House) available to upperclassmen. Single sex halls in some co-ed dorms. **Activities:** Bands, campus ministries, choral groups, dance, drama, film society, international student organizations, literary magazine, music ensembles, Model UN, musical theater, radio station, student government, student newspaper, symphony orchestra, Young Friends, Questing Catholics, Christian Fellowship, Jewish student union, Muslim student union, Bahai club, Amnesty International, Model UN, Coalition for Racial Justice, Fellowship of Christian Athletes.

Athletics. NCAA. **Intercollegiate:** Baseball M, basketball, cross-country, field hockey W, football (tackle) M, soccer, tennis, track and field, volleyball W. **Intramural:** Basketball, bowling, football (non-tackle) M, racquetball, soccer, triathlon. **Team name:** Quakers.

Student services. Chaplain/spiritual director, career counseling, student employment services, financial aid counseling, health services, minority student services, on-campus daycare, personal counseling, placement for graduates, women's services. **Physically disabled:** Services for visually, speech, hearing impaired.

Contact. E-mail: admission@earlham.edu
Phone: (765) 983-1600 Toll-free number: (800) 327-5426
Fax: (765) 983-1560
Jeff Rickey, Dean of Admissions and Financial Aid, Earlham College, 801 National Road West, Richmond, IN 47374-4095

Franklin College

Franklin, Indiana — **CB member**
www.franklincollege.edu — **CB code: 1228**

- Private 4-year liberal arts college affiliated with American Baptist Churches in the USA
- Residential campus in large town
- 1,153 degree-seeking undergraduates: 12% part-time, 50% women, 3% African American, 1% Asian American, 1% Hispanic American
- 66% of applicants admitted
- SAT or ACT with writing, application essay required
- 57% graduate within 6 years

General. Founded in 1834. Regionally accredited. **Degrees:** 200 bachelor's awarded. **ROTC:** Army. **Location:** 20 miles from Indianapolis. **Calendar:** 4-1-4, limited summer session. **Full-time faculty:** 65 total; 86% have terminal degrees, 5% minority, 38% women. **Part-time faculty:** 48 total; 19% have terminal degrees, 2% minority, 48% women. **Class size:** 67% < 20, 33% 20-39, less than 1% 40-49.

Freshman class profile. 1,457 applied, 968 admitted, 361 enrolled.

Mid 50% test scores		**GPA 2.0-2.99:**	28%
SAT critical reading:	430-550	**Rank in top quarter:**	31%
SAT math:	450-530	**Rank in top tenth:**	13%
SAT writing:	430-530	**Return as sophomores:**	63%
ACT composite:	18-23	**Live on campus:**	97%
GPA 3.75 or higher:	37%	**Fraternities:**	54%
GPA 3.50-3.74:	3%	**Sororities:**	66%
GPA 3.0-3.49:	31%		

Basis for selection. Class rank, test scores, essay and counselor recommendations important. Extracurricular activities considered. Interview recommended for all. **Homeschooled:** Transcript of courses and grades, interview, letter of recommendation (nonparent) required. Submit research paper(s), art work, community service projects, educational trip or programs, writing samples, other pertinent documents. Formal interview on campus required. **Learning Disabled:** Students with learning disabilities asked to schedule meeting with Director of Academic Support Services.

High school preparation. Required and recommended units include English 4, mathematics 4, social studies 3, science 2 and foreign language 2.

2008-2009 Annual costs. Tuition/fees: $22,445. Room/board: $6,640.

2007-2008 Financial aid. All financial aid based on need. 360 full-time freshmen applied for aid; 318 were judged to have need; 317 of these received aid. Average need met was 78%. Average scholarship/grant was $12,438; average loan $3,610. 73% of total undergraduate aid awarded as scholarships/grants, 27% as loans/jobs.

Application procedures. **Admission:** Priority date 1/15; no deadline. $30 fee, may be waived for applicants with need. Admission notification on a rolling basis beginning on or about 9/1. **Financial aid:** Closing date 3/1. FAFSA, institutional form required. Applicants notified by 4/1; must reply by 5/1 or within 4 week(s) of notification.

Academics. **Special study options:** Cross-registration, double major, dual enrollment of high school students, exchange student, independent study, internships, semester at sea, study abroad, teacher certification program, United Nations semester, Washington semester. **Credit/placement by examination:** AP, CLEP, SAT, ACT, institutional tests. 30 credit hours maximum toward bachelor's degree. **Support services:** Learning center, remedial instruction, study skills assistance, tutoring, writing center.

Majors. **Area/ethnic studies:** American, Canadian. **Biology:** General. **Business:** General, accounting, finance, marketing. **Communications:** Broadcast journalism, journalism. **Computer sciences:** General, computer science. **Education:** Biology, chemistry, elementary, English, French, mathematics, physical, Spanish. **Foreign languages:** French, Spanish. **Health:** Athletic training. **History:** General. **Math:** General. **Parks/recreation:** General. **Philosophy/religion:** Philosophy, religion. **Physical sciences:** Chemistry. **Psychology:** General. **Social sciences:** Economics, political science, sociology. **Visual/performing arts:** Dramatic.

Most popular majors. Biology 10%, business/marketing 9%, communications/journalism 15%, education 22%, public administration/social services 7%, social sciences 11%.

Computing on campus. 250 workstations in dormitories, library, student center. Dormitories wired for high-speed internet access and linked to campus network. Online course registration, online library, helpline, repair service, wireless network available.

Student life. **Freshman orientation:** Mandatory, $50 fee. Preregistration for classes offered. Orientation for all students held 4 days prior to start of classes. **Policies:** All students must live on campus until senior year unless living with family. **Housing:** Guaranteed on-campus for all undergraduates. Coed dorms, single-sex dorms, special housing for disabled, fraternity/sorority housing, wellness housing available. $100 deposit, deadline 5/1. **Activities:** Pep band, choral groups, dance, drama, literary magazine, musical theater, radio station, student government, student newspaper, student association for the support of multiculturalism, Habitat for Humanity, college mentors for kids, Fellowship of Christian Athletes, ODK Leadership, international club.

Athletics. NCAA. **Intercollegiate:** Baseball M, basketball, cheerleading M, cross-country, diving, football (tackle) M, golf, soccer, softball W, swimming, tennis, track and field, volleyball W. **Intramural:** Basketball, football (non-tackle), racquetball, softball, volleyball. **Team name:** Grizzlies.

Student services. Alcohol/substance abuse counseling, chaplain/spiritual director, career counseling, student employment services, financial aid counseling, health services, minority student services, personal counseling, placement for graduates, veterans' counselor, women's services.

Contact. E-mail: admissions@franklincollege.edu
Phone: (317) 738-8062 Toll-free number: (800) 852-0232
Fax: (317) 738-8274
Jacqueline Acosta, Director of Admissions, Franklin College, 101 Branigin Boulevard, Franklin, IN 46131-2623

Goshen College

Goshen, Indiana
www.goshen.edu — **CB code: 1251**

- Private 4-year liberal arts college affiliated with Mennonite Church
- Residential campus in large town
- 913 degree-seeking undergraduates: 6% part-time, 59% women, 4% African American, 2% Asian American, 6% Hispanic American, 5% international
- 28 degree-seeking graduate students
- 64% of applicants admitted
- SAT or ACT (ACT writing optional), application essay required
- 72% graduate within 6 years; 10% enter graduate study

General. Founded in 1894. Regionally accredited. 1150 acre environmental study facility located 30 miles from campus. **Degrees:** 237 bachelor's awarded; master's offered. **Location:** 25 miles from South Bend, 120 miles from Chicago. **Calendar:** Semester, limited summer session. **Full-time faculty:** 68 total; 66% have terminal degrees, 3% minority, 47% women. **Part-time faculty:** 46 total; 41% have terminal degrees, 9% minority, 61% women. **Class size:** 67% < 20, 27% 20-39, 4% 40-49, 2% 50-99. **Special facilities:**

Concert hall, X-ray precision laboratory, electron microscope, marine biology laboratory in Florida Keys, historical library and archives, laboratory kindergarten and child care center, media production studio, nature preserve, student-run coffee shop.

Freshman class profile. 604 applied, 384 admitted, 175 enrolled.

Mid 50% test scores		**GPA 2.0-2.99:**	16%
SAT critical reading:	480-650	**Rank in top quarter:**	55%
SAT math:	490-650	**Rank in top tenth:**	22%
SAT writing:	470-620	**End year in good standing:**	95%
ACT composite:	22-28	**Return as sophomores:**	84%
GPA 3.75 or higher:	38%	**Out-of-state:**	54%
GPA 3.50-3.74:	18%	**Live on campus:**	81%
GPA 3.0-3.49:	28%	**International:**	7%

Basis for selection. Admission review required for low GPA, class rank and/or test scores. Nursing and education programs require college GPA of 2.5 for entrance and continuation. Interview recommended. **Homeschooled:** Statement describing homeschool structure and mission, transcript of courses and grades required. **Learning Disabled:** Documentation of disability and special requirements dated within last 3 years required. Exit interview with high school special needs counselor, if working with one, required.

High school preparation. 12 units required; 16 recommended. Required and recommended units include English 4, mathematics 2-3, social studies 2, history 2, science 2-3 and foreign language 2.

2008-2009 Annual costs. Tuition/fees: $22,300. Room/board: $7,400. Books/supplies: $800. Personal expenses: $1,100.

2007-2008 Financial aid. Need-based: 69% of total undergraduate aid awarded as scholarships/grants, 31% as loans/jobs. **Non-need-based:** Scholarships awarded for academics, art, athletics, leadership, music/drama.

Application procedures. Admission: Priority date 2/1; deadline 8/1 (postmark date). $25 fee, may be waived for applicants with need. Admission notification on a rolling basis beginning on or about 9/15. Must reply by May 1 or within 2 week(s) if notified thereafter. **Financial aid:** Priority date 2/1; no closing date. FAFSA, institutional form required. Applicants notified by 3/1; must reply by 5/1 or within 2 week(s) of notification.

Academics. Practicum and senior seminar course required in all majors. International education through on-campus courses or study abroad required. Study abroad incorporates language study, academic and cultural learning and service. Students live in homes of country where studying for one semester. **Special study options:** Combined bachelor's/graduate degree, cross-registration, double major, dual enrollment of high school students, independent study, internships, liberal arts/career combination, student-designed major, study abroad, teacher certification program, urban semester, Washington semester. Adult degree completion program (one evening per week, concentrated study). **Credit/placement by examination:** AP, CLEP, IB, SAT, ACT, institutional tests. **Support services:** Learning center, reduced course load, remedial instruction, study skills assistance, tutoring, writing center.

Majors. Biology: General, molecular. **Business:** Accounting, business admin. **Communications:** General, broadcast journalism, journalism, public relations. **Computer sciences:** Computer science, information systems. **Conservation:** Environmental science. **Education:** General, art, biology, business, chemistry, elementary, English, ESL, mathematics, music, physical, physics, science, secondary, social studies, Spanish, special. **Foreign languages:** American Sign Language, sign language interpretation, Spanish. **Health:** Nursing (RN). **History:** General. **Interdisciplinary:** Peace/conflict. **Math:** General, applied. **Parks/recreation:** Health/fitness. **Physical sciences:** Chemistry, physics. **Psychology:** General. **Public administration:** Social work. **Social sciences:** Sociology. **Theology:** Youth ministry. **Visual/performing arts:** Art, dramatic. **Other:** Bible and religion, History and investigative skills, Journalism education.

Most popular majors. Business/marketing 16%, education 8%, health sciences 23%, interdisciplinary studies 7%, visual/performing arts 7%.

Computing on campus. 130 workstations in dormitories, library, computer center, student center. Dormitories wired for high-speed internet access and linked to campus network. Commuter students can connect to campus network. Online course registration, online library, helpline, student web hosting, wireless network available.

Student life. Freshman orientation: Mandatory. Preregistration for classes offered. 1 of 3 possible days during May, June and July, plus 3 days prior to fall semester in August. **Policies:** No smoking and no drinking alcoholic beverages on campus. **Housing:** Guaranteed on-campus for all undergraduates. Coed dorms, single-sex dorms, special housing for disabled, apartments, wellness housing available. $200 fully refundable deposit, deadline 5/1. **Activities:** Bands, campus ministries, choral groups, drama, film society, international student organizations, music ensembles, musical theater, opera, radio station, student government, student newspaper, symphony orchestra, black student union, Latino student union, women's association, Third Culture Support Group, Catholic student group, environmental concerns club, Peace (Pax) club, Fellowship of Christian Athletes.

Athletics. NAIA. **Intercollegiate:** Baseball M, basketball, cross-country, golf M, soccer, softball W, tennis, track and field, volleyball W. **Intramural:** Badminton, basketball, ice hockey M, racquetball, soccer, softball, table tennis, volleyball. **Team name:** Maple Leafs.

Student services. Adult student services, alcohol/substance abuse counseling, chaplain/spiritual director, career counseling, student employment services, financial aid counseling, health services, minority student services, on-campus daycare, personal counseling, placement for graduates, women's services. **Physically disabled:** Services for visually, speech, hearing impaired.

Contact. E-mail: admission@goshen.edu
Phone: (574) 535-7535 Toll-free number: (800) 348-7422
Fax: (574) 535-7609
Lynn Jackson, Executive Director of Enrollment Services, Goshen College, 1700 South Main Street, Goshen, IN 46526-4724

Grace College

Winona Lake, Indiana
www.grace.edu **CB code: 1252**

- Private 4-year liberal arts college affiliated with Brethren Church
- Residential campus in large town
- 1,265 degree-seeking undergraduates: 7% part-time, 49% women
- 155 degree-seeking graduate students
- 96% of applicants admitted
- SAT or ACT (ACT writing recommended) required

General. Founded in 1948. Regionally accredited. **Degrees:** 193 bachelor's, 60 associate awarded; master's, doctoral, first professional offered. **Location:** 40 miles from Fort Wayne. **Calendar:** Semester, limited summer session. **Full-time faculty:** 49 total; 65% have terminal degrees, 4% minority, 20% women. **Part-time faculty:** 80 total; 20% have terminal degrees, 2% minority, 35% women. **Class size:** 59% < 20, 32% 20-39, 5% 40-49, 5% 50-99, less than 1% >100. **Special facilities:** Creation science center, Winona history museum.

Freshman class profile. 1,074 applied, 1,028 admitted, 292 enrolled.

Mid 50% test scores		**GPA 3.0-3.49:**	25%
SAT critical reading:	460-490	**GPA 2.0-2.99:**	15%
SAT math:	460-590	**Rank in top quarter:**	59%
ACT composite:	21-28	**Rank in top tenth:**	29%
GPA 3.75 or higher:	43%	**Out-of-state:**	54%
GPA 3.50-3.74:	17%	**Live on campus:**	96%

Basis for selection. References, religious affiliation/commitment, high school class rank, test scores most important. Interview recommended for music and art majors. Audition recommended for music majors. Portfolio recommended for art majors.

High school preparation. Required and recommended units include English 3-4, mathematics 2-4, social studies 2-3, history 2-3, science 2-3 (laboratory 2-3) and foreign language 2-4.

2008-2009 Annual costs. Tuition/fees: $20,376. Room/board: $6,648. Books/supplies: $800. Personal expenses: $800.

2007-2008 Financial aid. Need-based: 71% of total undergraduate aid awarded as scholarships/grants, 29% as loans/jobs. **Non-need-based:** Scholarships awarded for academics, art, athletics, leadership, minority status, music/drama, religious affiliation.

Application procedures. Admission: Priority date 12/1; deadline 3/1 (postmark date). $20 fee, may be waived for applicants with need, free for online applicants. Admission notification on a rolling basis beginning on or about 9/15. Must reply by May 1 or within 2 week(s) if notified thereafter. **Financial aid:** Closing date 3/1. FAFSA required. Applicants notified on a rolling basis starting 3/1; must reply by 5/1.

Academics. Special study options: Cooperative education, cross-registration, distance learning, double major, dual enrollment of high school students, exchange student, honors, independent study, internships, liberal arts/career combination, study abroad, teacher certification program. **Credit/placement by examination:** AP, CLEP, IB, SAT, ACT, institutional tests. 30 credit hours maximum toward associate degree, 30 toward bachelor's.

Support services: Learning center, reduced course load, remedial instruction, study skills assistance, tutoring, writing center.

Majors. Biology: General. **Business:** General, accounting, administrative services, business admin, finance, international, management information systems, marketing. **Communications:** General, journalism. **Computer sciences:** Information technology. **Education:** Art, business, elementary, English, French, German, mathematics, music, physical, science, social studies, Spanish, special. **Foreign languages:** General, French, German, Spanish. **History:** General. **Math:** General, statistics. **Parks/recreation:** Health/fitness, sports admin. **Physical sciences:** General. **Protective services:** Criminal justice. **Psychology:** General. **Public administration:** Social work. **Social sciences:** Sociology. **Theology:** Bible, youth ministry. **Visual/performing arts:** Drawing, graphic design, illustration, music performance. **Other:** Journalism education, Social studies, non-teaching.

Most popular majors. Business/marketing 24%, education 10%, psychology 15%, theological studies 32%.

Computing on campus. 160 workstations in dormitories, library, computer center, student center. Dormitories wired for high-speed internet access and linked to campus network. Commuter students can connect to campus network. Online course registration, helpline, wireless network available.

Student life. Freshman orientation: Mandatory. Preregistration for classes offered. Weekend in the beginning of fall semester in late August. **Policies:** Students are to refrain from use of alcoholic beverages, illegal drugs, tobacco, sexual misconduct, coarse or obscene language or any other conduct inconsistent with the goals and traditions of the college. Further, students are to abstain from morally degrading media and literature. Religious observance required. **Housing:** Guaranteed on-campus for all undergraduates. Single-sex dorms, apartments, wellness housing available. $200 deposit, deadline 5/1. **Activities:** Bands, choral groups, drama, music ensembles, musical theater, opera, student government, student newspaper, symphony orchestra, 20 Christian clubs and organizations.

Athletics. NAIA, NCCAA. **Intercollegiate:** Baseball M, basketball, cross-country, golf M, soccer, softball W, tennis, track and field, volleyball W. **Intramural:** Badminton, basketball, soccer, volleyball. **Team name:** Lancers.

Student services. Chaplain/spiritual director, career counseling, student employment services, financial aid counseling, health services, personal counseling, placement for graduates, veterans' counselor. **Physically disabled:** Services for visually impaired.

Contact. E-mail: admissions@grace.edu
Phone: (574) 372-5100 ext. 6008 Toll-free
number: (800) 544-7223 ext. 6008 Fax: (574) 372-5120
Mark Weinstein, Dean of Enrollment and Marketing, Grace College, 200 Seminary Drive, Winona Lake, IN 46590

Hanover College

Hanover, Indiana — **CB member**
www.hanover.edu — **CB code: 1290**

- Private 4-year liberal arts college affiliated with Presbyterian Church (USA)
- Residential campus in rural community
- 921 degree-seeking undergraduates: 55% women, 1% African American, 2% Asian American, 1% Hispanic American, 1% Native American, 3% international
- 67% of applicants admitted
- SAT or ACT with writing, application essay required
- 59% graduate within 6 years; 27% enter graduate study

General. Founded in 1827. Regionally accredited. **Degrees:** 271 bachelor's awarded. **Calendar:** 4-1-4. 4-4-1. **Full-time faculty:** 91 total; 99% have terminal degrees, 9% minority, 36% women. **Part-time faculty:** 4 total; 75% have terminal degrees, 50% women. **Class size:** 85% < 20, 15% 20-39, less than 1% 40-49. **Special facilities:** Geology museum, observatory.

Freshman class profile. 2,180 applied, 1,463 admitted, 328 enrolled.

Mid 50% test scores		**GPA 2.0-2.99:**	9%
SAT critical reading:	500-630	**Rank in top quarter:**	66%
SAT math:	510-610	**Rank in top tenth:**	31%
SAT writing:	480-590	**End year in good standing:**	87%
ACT composite:	22-28	**Return as sophomores:**	83%
GPA 3.75 or higher:	41%	**Out-of-state:**	34%
GPA 3.50-3.74:	21%	**Live on campus:**	98%
GPA 3.0-3.49:	29%	**International:**	3%

Basis for selection. GED not accepted. Selection of and performance in academic courses most important. Interview recommended. **Homeschooled:** Transcript of courses and grades required.

High school preparation. College-preparatory program required. 18 units required; 25 recommended. Required and recommended units include English 4, mathematics 3-4, social studies 2-3, history 2-3, science 3-4 (laboratory 2-3), foreign language 2-4 and academic electives 2-3.

2008-2009 Annual costs. Tuition/fees: $25,220. Room/board: $7,500. Books/supplies: $900. Personal expenses: $900.

2007-2008 Financial aid. Need-based: 200 full-time freshmen applied for aid; 167 were judged to have need; 167 of these received aid. Average need met was 91%. Average scholarship/grant was $17,874; average loan $2,616. 82% of total undergraduate aid awarded as scholarships/grants, 18% as loans/jobs. **Non-need-based:** Awarded to 419 full-time undergraduates, including 96 freshmen. Scholarships awarded for academics, alumni affiliation, leadership, music/drama, religious affiliation, state residency. **Additional information:** Academic Honors Diploma Scholarship is a grant program committed to meeting 100% of Indiana student's demonstrated need. Available to Indiana students who graduate with an Academic Honors Diploma (AHD), have completed their application for admission by January 15, and file a complete and valid FAFSA by March 10.

Application procedures. Admission: Closing date 3/1 (postmark date). $40 fee, may be waived for applicants with need, free for online applicants. Admission notification on a rolling basis beginning on or about 9/1. Must reply by May 1 or within 2 week(s) if notified thereafter. **Financial aid:** Priority date 3/1; no closing date. FAFSA required. Applicants notified on a rolling basis starting 3/1; must reply by 5/1.

Academics. Students take only one course in the 4-week spring term. **Special study options:** Double major, dual enrollment of high school students, independent study, internships, student-designed major, study abroad, teacher certification program, Washington semester. Philadelphia Center, Washington Center internships, Center for Business Preparation. **Credit/placement by examination:** AP, CLEP, IB, institutional tests. **Support services:** Learning center, reduced course load, study skills assistance, tutoring, writing center.

Majors. Biology: General. **Communications:** General. **Computer sciences:** General. **Education:** Elementary. **Foreign languages:** Classics, French, German, Spanish. **History:** General. **Interdisciplinary:** Medieval/Renaissance. **Math:** General. **Parks/recreation:** Exercise sciences. **Philosophy/religion:** Philosophy. **Physical sciences:** Chemistry, geology, physics. **Psychology:** General. **Social sciences:** Anthropology, economics, political science, sociology. **Theology:** Theology. **Visual/performing arts:** Art history/conservation, dramatic, studio arts.

Most popular majors. Biology 8%, business/marketing 7%, communications/journalism 6%, English 6%, history 6%, physical sciences 7%, psychology 11%, social sciences 15%, visual/performing arts 9%.

Computing on campus. 195 workstations in library, computer center, student center. Dormitories wired for high-speed internet access and linked to campus network. Commuter students can connect to campus network. Online course registration, online library, helpline, student web hosting, wireless network available.

Student life. Freshman orientation: Available. Preregistration for classes offered. Eight 1-day orientation sessions in April, May, June, and August that include registering for fall courses. Additional orientation starts 1 week before classes begin. **Housing:** Guaranteed on-campus for freshmen. Coed dorms, single-sex dorms, apartments, fraternity/sorority housing, wellness housing available. $250 fully refundable deposit, deadline 5/1. **Activities:** Bands, campus ministries, choral groups, dance, drama, film society, international student organizations, literary magazine, music ensembles, musical theater, radio station, student government, student newspaper, symphony orchestra, TV station, Campus Fellowship, political and social service organizations, international club, academic clubs, Christian Life, Love Out Loud.

Athletics. NCAA. **Intercollegiate:** Baseball M, basketball, cross-country, football (tackle) M, golf, soccer, softball W, tennis, track and field, volleyball W. **Intramural:** Basketball, football (non-tackle) W, football (tackle)

M, racquetball, soccer, softball, table tennis, volleyball. **Team name:** Panthers.

Student services. Alcohol/substance abuse counseling, chaplain/spiritual director, career counseling, student employment services, financial aid counseling, health services, personal counseling, placement for graduates.

Contact. E-mail: admission@hanover.edu
Phone: (812) 866-7021 Toll-free number: (800) 213-2178
Fax: (812) 866-7098
William Preble, Dean of Admission and Financial Assistance, Hanover College, PO Box 108, Hanover, IN 47243-0108

Holy Cross College

Notre Dame, Indiana — **CB member**
www.hcc-nd.edu — **CB code: 1309**

- Private 4-year liberal arts college affiliated with Roman Catholic Church
- Residential campus in small city
- 510 degree-seeking undergraduates
- 82% of applicants admitted
- SAT or ACT (ACT writing optional), application essay required

General. Founded in 1966. Regionally accredited. **Degrees:** 30 bachelor's, 41 associate awarded. **ROTC:** Army, Air Force. **Location:** One mile from South Bend, 80 miles from Chicago. **Calendar:** Semester, limited summer session. **Full-time faculty:** 31 total. **Part-time faculty:** 28 total.

Freshman class profile. 515 applied, 420 admitted, 244 enrolled.

Mid 50% test scores		**Out-of-state:**	49%
SAT critical reading:	470-590	**Live on campus:**	49%
SAT math:	430-470		

Basis for selection. School achievement and student's perception of value of program for future plans most important. Interview recommended.

High school preparation. Required and recommended units include English 4, mathematics 3-4, social studies 2-4, science 2-4 and foreign language 2.

2008-2009 Annual costs. Tuition/fees: $17,900. Room/board: $8,500. Books/supplies: $1,000.

Financial aid. Non-need-based: Scholarships awarded for academics, leadership.

Application procedures. Admission: Priority date 7/1; deadline 8/15. $50 fee, may be waived for applicants with need, free for online applicants. Admission notification on a rolling basis. **Financial aid:** Closing date 3/1. FAFSA required. Applicants notified on a rolling basis starting 5/1; must reply within 2 week(s) of notification.

Academics. Special study options: Accelerated study, cross-registration, ESL, honors, study abroad. **Credit/placement by examination:** AP, CLEP, SAT, ACT, institutional tests. 30 credit hours maximum toward associate degree. **Support services:** Learning center, pre-admission summer program, reduced course load, remedial instruction, study skills assistance, tutoring, writing center.

Majors. Education: Elementary. **Liberal arts:** Arts/sciences. **Theology:** Theology.

Computing on campus. 32 workstations in computer center, student center. Dormitories wired for high-speed internet access and linked to campus network. Commuter students can connect to campus network. Online library, repair service, wireless network available.

Student life. Freshman orientation: Mandatory. Preregistration for classes offered. **Housing:** Coed dorms, single-sex dorms, special housing for disabled, apartments available. $500 deposit, deadline 8/15. **Activities:** Marching band, choral groups, drama, literary magazine, music ensembles, student government, student newspaper, campus ministry, student advisory committee, Flip Side.

Athletics. NAIA. **Intercollegiate:** Cross-country M. **Intramural:** Basketball, cheerleading, football (non-tackle), football (tackle) M, golf, lacrosse M, soccer, volleyball. **Team name:** Saints.

Student services. Alcohol/substance abuse counseling, chaplain/spiritual director, career counseling, financial aid counseling, health services, personal counseling.

Contact. E-mail: admissions@hcc-nd.edu
Phone: (574) 239-8400 Fax: (574) 239-8323
Vincent Duke, Director of Admissions, Holy Cross College, 54515 State Road 933N, Notre Dame, IN 46556-0308

Huntington University

Huntington, Indiana
www.huntington.edu — **CB code: 1304**

- Private 4-year university and liberal arts college affiliated with United Brethren in Christ
- Residential campus in large town
- 941 degree-seeking undergraduates: 2% part-time, 56% women, 1% African American, 1% Hispanic American, 3% international
- 233 degree-seeking graduate students
- 88% of applicants admitted
- SAT or ACT with writing, application essay required
- 59% graduate within 6 years; 10% enter graduate study

General. Founded in 1897. Regionally accredited. **Degrees:** 177 bachelor's, 10 associate awarded; master's offered. **Location:** 20 miles from Fort Wayne. **Calendar:** 4-1-4, limited summer session. **Full-time faculty:** 59 total; 80% have terminal degrees, 3% minority, 36% women. **Part-time faculty:** 33 total; 15% have terminal degrees, 6% minority, 46% women. **Class size:** 73% < 20, 24% 20-39, 4% 40-49. **Special facilities:** Nature preserve, greenhouse, disc golf course.

Freshman class profile. 850 applied, 745 admitted, 277 enrolled.

Mid 50% test scores		**Rank in top quarter:**	26%
SAT critical reading:	450-580	**End year in good standing:**	90%
SAT math:	450-590	**Return as sophomores:**	78%
ACT composite:	20-27	**Out-of-state:**	44%
GPA 3.75 or higher:	19%	**Live on campus:**	95%
GPA 3.50-3.74:	21%	**International:**	2%
GPA 3.0-3.49:	44%	**Sororities:**	1%
GPA 2.0-2.99:	16%		

Basis for selection. Class rank in top half, satisfactory test scores, 2.3 GPA most important. Selected students with 860 SAT (exclusive of Writing), 2.0 GPA, or rank in top 50% of class may be admitted on a minimum load. Interview recommended. Audition required of music majors. Portfolio required for art scholarships. Essay required for presidential scholarships. Test required for journalism scholarships. **Learning Disabled:** Documentation of learning disability required in some cases where both GPA and standardized test results are below minimum requirement for admission.

High school preparation. College-preparatory program required. Required and recommended units include English 4, mathematics 3, social studies 2, history 2, science 2 (laboratory 1), foreign language 2, computer science 1, visual/performing arts 2 and academic electives 2.

2008-2009 Annual costs. Tuition/fees: $20,300. Room/board: $6,940. Books/supplies: $900. Personal expenses: $460.

2008-2009 Financial aid. Need-based: 250 full-time freshmen applied for aid; 215 were judged to have need; 215 of these received aid. Average need met was 79%. Average scholarship/grant was $13,495; average loan $3,950. 60% of total undergraduate aid awarded as scholarships/grants, 40% as loans/jobs. **Non-need-based:** Scholarships awarded for academics, alumni affiliation, art, athletics, leadership, music/drama, religious affiliation.

Application procedures. Admission: Priority date 3/1; deadline 8/1 (receipt date). $20 fee, may be waived for applicants with need. Admission notification on a rolling basis beginning on or about 10/1. Education majors must apply separately to the Education Department before entering those major classes. Performance grants also require a separate application process for those majoring in music, theatre, art, and communication. **Financial aid:** Priority date 3/1; no closing date. FAFSA required. Applicants notified on a rolling basis starting 3/1; must reply by 5/1 or within 2 week(s) of notification.

Academics. Special study options: Cross-registration, double major, independent study, internships, study abroad, teacher certification program, Washington semester. **Credit/placement by examination:** AP, CLEP, SAT, ACT, institutional tests. 38 credit hours maximum toward bachelor's degree. **Support services:** Learning center, pre-admission summer program, reduced course load, remedial instruction, study skills assistance, tutoring, writing center.

Majors. Biology: General. **Business:** General, accounting, accounting/finance, business admin, entrepreneurial studies, managerial economics, nonprofit/public, small business admin. **Communications:** General, broadcast journalism, digital media, journalism, public relations, radio/tv. **Computer sciences:** General, computer science. **Education:** General, art, biology, business, chemistry, elementary, English, mathematics, music, physical, science, secondary, social studies, special. **Foreign languages:** Spanish. **Health:** Nursing (RN), premedicine. **History:** General. **Interdisciplinary:** Math/computer science. **Legal studies:** Prelaw. **Math:** General. **Parks/recreation:** Exercise sciences, facilities management, sports admin. **Philosophy/religion:** Philosophy, religion. **Physical sciences:** Chemistry. **Psychology:** General. **Public administration:** Social work. **Social sciences:** Sociology. **Theology:** Bible, missionary, religious ed, sacred music, youth ministry. **Visual/performing arts:** Art, dramatic, film/cinema, graphic design, music management, music performance, piano/organ, studio arts, theater design, voice/opera.

Most popular majors. Business/marketing 23%, communications/journalism 8%, education 20%, theological studies 14%.

Computing on campus. 164 workstations in dormitories, library, computer center, student center. Dormitories wired for high-speed internet access and linked to campus network. Commuter students can connect to campus network. Online library, helpline, student web hosting, wireless network available.

Student life. **Freshman orientation:** Mandatory. Three-day orientation held immediately before first semester. **Policies:** No social dancing. Chapel/convocation attendance required 2 out of 4 weekly programs. Use of alcohol, drugs, and tobacco prohibited. Religious observance required. **Housing:** Guaranteed on-campus for all undergraduates. Coed dorms, single-sex dorms, apartments available. $100 partly refundable deposit, deadline 8/15. College-owned houses available. Single-sex floors available. **Activities:** Bands, campus ministries, choral groups, drama, film society, international student organizations, literary magazine, music ensembles, musical theater, radio station, student government, student newspaper, symphony orchestra, TV station, Acting on AIDS, Alpha Gamma Pi Sorority, Global Vision, Habitat for Humanity, volunteer service center.

Athletics. NAIA, NCCAA. **Intercollegiate:** Baseball M, basketball, cross-country, golf M, soccer, softball W, tennis, track and field, volleyball W. **Intramural:** Basketball, football (non-tackle), racquetball, softball, volleyball. **Team name:** Foresters.

Student services. Adult student services, alcohol/substance abuse counseling, chaplain/spiritual director, career counseling, student employment services, financial aid counseling, health services, minority student services, on-campus daycare, personal counseling, placement for graduates, women's services. **Physically disabled:** Services for visually, speech, hearing impaired.

Contact. E-mail: admissions@huntington.edu
Phone: (260) 359-4000 Toll-free number: (800) 642-6493
Fax: (260) 358-3699
Jeffrey Berggren, Vice President of Enrollment Management & Marketing, Huntington University, 2303 College Avenue, Huntington, IN 46750-1237

Indiana Institute of Technology

Fort Wayne, Indiana — **CB member**
www.indianatech.edu — **CB code: 1323**

- Private 4-year business and engineering college
- Residential campus in large city
- 3,133 degree-seeking undergraduates: 38% part-time, 54% women, 21% African American, 1% Asian American, 2% Hispanic American, 1% international
- 329 degree-seeking graduate students
- 74% of applicants admitted
- SAT or ACT (ACT writing optional) required

General. Founded in 1930. Regionally accredited. ABET accreditation for electrical engineering and mechanical engineering. **Degrees:** 414 bachelor's, 144 associate awarded; master's offered. **Location:** 120 miles from Indianapolis. **Calendar:** Semester, limited summer session. **Full-time faculty:** 34 total; 35% have terminal degrees, 3% minority, 24% women. **Part-time faculty:** 261 total; 4% have terminal degrees, 11% minority, 40% women. **Class size:** 87% < 20, 13% 20-39. **Special facilities:** Computer-aided design center, amphitheater, movie theater.

Freshman class profile. 1,660 applied, 1,236 admitted, 303 enrolled.

Mid 50% test scores			
SAT critical reading:	400-530	Rank in top quarter:	30%
SAT math:	420-550	Rank in top tenth:	8%
ACT composite:	17-22	End year in good standing:	86%
GPA 3.75 or higher:	8%	Return as sophomores:	60%
GPA 3.50-3.74:	11%	Out-of-state:	36%
GPA 3.0-3.49:	26%	Live on campus:	66%
GPA 2.0-2.99:	47%	International:	2%
		Fraternities:	8%

Basis for selection. GPA and test scores most important. Interview recommended.

High school preparation. Required and recommended units include English 4, mathematics 2-4, science 2-3 and academic electives 7. Engineering and computer science majors require 13.5 units including 4 English; 3.5 math; 2 physical science; 4 history, social studies, or language.

2009-2010 Annual costs. Tuition/fees (projected): $21,400. Room/board: $8,040. Personal expenses: $3,000.

2008-2009 Financial aid. **Non-need-based:** Scholarships awarded for academics, alumni affiliation, athletics, leadership, minority status, music/drama, state residency.

Application procedures. **Admission:** No deadline. $50 fee, may be waived for applicants with need, free for online applicants. Admission notification on a rolling basis beginning on or about 10/15. **Financial aid:** Closing date 3/10. FAFSA, institutional form required. Applicants notified on a rolling basis starting 2/2; must reply within 2 week(s) of notification.

Academics. **Special study options:** Accelerated study, combined bachelor's/graduate degree, cross-registration, distance learning, double major, dual enrollment of high school students, external degree, independent study, internships, student-designed major. **Credit/placement by examination:** AP, CLEP, IB, SAT, ACT, institutional tests. 45 credit hours maximum toward associate degree, 90 toward bachelor's. **Support services:** Learning center, reduced course load, remedial instruction, study skills assistance, tutoring.

Majors. **Business:** General, accounting, business admin, human resources, management information systems, marketing, nonprofit/public, operations. **Communications:** General. **Computer sciences:** General, computer science, information systems, networking, security. **Education:** Elementary, physical. **Engineering:** Biomedical, computer, electrical, industrial, mechanical, software. **Health:** Recreational therapy. **Parks/recreation:** Facilities management, sports admin. **Protective services:** Criminal justice, law enforcement admin. **Psychology:** General. **Public administration:** Human services. **Other:** Energy engineering, Internet technologies.

Most popular majors. Business/marketing 87%, engineering/engineering technologies 6%.

Computing on campus. PC or laptop required. 270 workstations in library, computer center. Dormitories wired for high-speed internet access and linked to campus network. Commuter students can connect to campus network. Online library, helpline, repair service, student web hosting, wireless network available.

Student life. **Freshman orientation:** Mandatory. Preregistration for classes offered. One-day program. **Housing:** Guaranteed on-campus for freshmen. Coed dorms, apartments, fraternity/sorority housing available. $350 deposit. **Activities:** Bands, campus ministries, choral groups, dance, student government, student newspaper, student board, black student association, Nova Society, society for women engineers, American society of mechanical engineers, society for human resource management, society of automotive engineering, institute of electrical and electronics engineers, society for manufacturing engineers.

Athletics. NAIA. **Intercollegiate:** Baseball M, basketball, cross-country, golf, soccer, softball W, tennis, track and field, volleyball W. **Intramural:** Badminton, basketball, bowling, soccer, softball, volleyball. **Team name:** Warriors.

Student services. Adult student services, chaplain/spiritual director, career counseling, student employment services, financial aid counseling, personal counseling, placement for graduates, veterans' counselor.

Contact. E-mail: admissions@indianatech.edu
Phone: (260) 422-5561 ext. 2205 Toll-free number: (800) 937-2448 ext. 2205 Fax: (260) 422-7696
Allison Carnahan, Vice President of Enrollment Management, Indiana Institute of Technology, 1600 East Washington Boulevard, Fort Wayne, IN 46803-1297

Indiana State University

Terre Haute, Indiana **CB member**
www.indstate.edu **CB code: 1322**

- Public 4-year university
- Residential campus in small city
- 8,200 degree-seeking undergraduates: 12% part-time, 52% women, 13% African American, 1% Asian American, 1% Hispanic American, 2% international
- 2,004 degree-seeking graduate students
- 66% of applicants admitted
- SAT or ACT with writing required
- 41% graduate within 6 years

General. Founded in 1865. Regionally accredited. **Degrees:** 1,430 bachelor's, 132 associate awarded; master's, doctoral offered. **ROTC:** Army, Air Force. **Location:** 70 miles from Indianapolis. **Calendar:** Semester, extensive summer session. **Full-time faculty:** 436 total; 78% have terminal degrees, 13% minority, 40% women. **Part-time faculty:** 191 total; 18% have terminal degrees, 6% minority, 53% women. **Class size:** 50% < 20, 39% 20-39, 6% 40-49, 4% 50-99, 1% >100. **Special facilities:** Observatory, museum, flight simulator.

Freshman class profile. 7,575 applied, 5,024 admitted, 1,940 enrolled.

Mid 50% test scores		**Rank in top quarter:**	28%
SAT critical reading:	410-510	**Rank in top tenth:**	10%
SAT math:	410-530	**End year in good standing:**	69%
SAT writing:	400-500	**Return as sophomores:**	66%
ACT composite:	17-22	**Out-of-state:**	10%
GPA 3.75 or higher:	10%	**Live on campus:**	73%
GPA 3.50-3.74:	10%	**International:**	3%
GPA 3.0-3.49:	28%	**Fraternities:**	11%
GPA 2.0-2.99:	51%	**Sororities:**	10%

Basis for selection. Students who rank in top 50% of high school class usually admitted. High school curriculum, GPA, test scores, class rank, type of high school, and interview all considered. Interview required of some scholarship applicants, recommended for applicants below 50th percentile of high school graduating class. Essay recommended. Audition required of music majors. Portfolio recommended for art majors.

High school preparation. 20 units recommended. Recommended units include English 4, mathematics 3, social studies 2, history 1, science 3 (laboratory 3), foreign language 1 and academic electives 1. 3 or more units recommended in career area. 1 in health & safety/physical education recommended.

2008-2009 Annual costs. Tuition/fees: $7,148; $15,402 out-of-state. Room/board: $6,972. Books/supplies: $1,170. Personal expenses: $1,832.

2007-2008 Financial aid. All financial aid based on need. 1,607 full-time freshmen applied for aid; 1,296 were judged to have need; 1,291 of these received aid. Average scholarship/grant was $5,479; average loan $3,180. 53% of total undergraduate aid awarded as scholarships/grants, 47% as loans/jobs. **Additional information:** Financial aid application deadline March 1 for Indiana residents applying for state grant.

Application procedures. Admission: Priority date 7/1; deadline 8/15. $25 fee, may be waived for applicants with need. Admission notification on a rolling basis. Must reply by 5/1. **Financial aid:** Priority date 3/1; no closing date. FAFSA required. Applicants notified on a rolling basis starting 4/15.

Academics. Special study options: Accelerated study, cooperative education, distance learning, double major, dual enrollment of high school students, ESL, honors, independent study, internships, study abroad, teacher certification program. **Credit/placement by examination:** AP, CLEP, SAT, ACT, institutional tests. 31 credit hours maximum toward bachelor's degree. **Support services:** Learning center, pre-admission summer program, study skills assistance, tutoring, writing center.

Majors. Architecture: Interior. **Area/ethnic studies:** African-American. **Biology:** General. **Business:** Accounting, business admin, finance, human resources, insurance, management information systems, marketing, office management. **Communications:** General. **Computer sciences:** General, information technology. **Education:** Elementary, physical, science, special. **Engineering technology:** Architectural, automotive, computer, electrical, industrial, manufacturing, occupational safety, robotics. **Family/consumer sciences:** General, clothing/textiles, family studies, food/nutrition. **Health:** Athletic training, clinical lab science, community health services, nursing (RN). **History:** General. **Liberal arts:** Arts/sciences. **Math:** General. **Parks/recreation:** Facilities management. **Philosophy/religion:** Philosophy. **Physical sciences:** Chemistry, geology, physics. **Psychology:** General. **Public administration:** Social work. **Social sciences:** Anthropology, criminology, economics, geography, political science. **Transportation:** Airline/commercial pilot, aviation management. **Visual/performing arts:** Art, dramatic, music performance, studio arts. **Other:** Language studies, Mechanical engineering techology, Operations marketing and analysis.

Most popular majors. Business/marketing 18%, education 14%, engineering/engineering technologies 8%, health sciences 10%, social sciences 10%.

Computing on campus. PC or laptop required. 467 workstations in library, computer center, student center. Dormitories wired for high-speed internet access and linked to campus network. Commuter students can connect to campus network. Online course registration, online library, helpline, repair service, student web hosting, wireless network available.

Student life. Freshman orientation: Mandatory. Preregistration for classes offered. One-day program includes registration, question and answer sessions, placement testing, campus tour, and meeting with advisers. Parents encouraged to attend. **Housing:** Guaranteed on-campus for freshmen. Coed dorms, single-sex dorms, special housing for disabled, apartments, fraternity/sorority housing, wellness housing available. Apartments for students with dependent children and special housing for freshmen. **Activities:** Bands, campus ministries, choral groups, dance, drama, film society, international student organizations, literary magazine, music ensembles, musical theater, radio station, student government, student newspaper, symphony orchestra, over 170 student organizations available.

Athletics. NCAA. **Intercollegiate:** Baseball M, basketball, cross-country, football (tackle) M, golf W, soccer W, softball W, tennis, track and field, volleyball W. **Intramural:** Badminton, basketball, football (non-tackle), racquetball, soccer, softball, swimming, tennis, track and field, volleyball. **Team name:** Sycamores.

Student services. Adult student services, chaplain/spiritual director, career counseling, student employment services, financial aid counseling, health services, minority student services, on-campus daycare, personal counseling, placement for graduates, women's services. **Physically disabled:** Services for visually, speech, hearing impaired.

Contact. E-mail: admissions@indstate.edu
Phone: (812) 237-2121 Toll-free number: (800) 468-6478
Fax: (812) 237-8023
Richard Toomey, Director, Indiana State University, Office of Admissions, Erickson 114, Terre Haute, IN 47809-9989

Indiana University Bloomington

Bloomington, Indiana **CB member**
www.iub.edu **CB code: 1324**

- Public 4-year university
- Residential campus in small city
- 31,087 degree-seeking undergraduates: 3% part-time, 50% women, 5% African American, 4% Asian American, 2% Hispanic American, 5% international
- 8,272 degree-seeking graduate students
- 71% of applicants admitted
- SAT or ACT with writing required
- 73% graduate within 6 years

General. Founded in 1820. Regionally accredited. Big Ten research university. **Degrees:** 5,779 bachelor's, 45 associate awarded; master's, doctoral, first professional offered. **ROTC:** Army, Air Force. **Location:** 50 miles from Indianapolis. **Calendar:** Semester, extensive summer session. **Full-time faculty:** 2,007 total; 75% have terminal degrees, 16% minority, 38% women. **Part-time faculty:** 354 total; 27% have terminal degrees, 12% minority, 48% women. **Class size:** 34% < 20, 43% 20-39, 5% 40-49, 12% 50-99, 7% >100. **Special facilities:** Cyclotron; 2 observatories; museum of anthropology, history, and folklore; rare book library; outdoor educational center; center for excellence in education; garden and nature center; arboretum; automated virtual environment.

Freshman class profile. 31,160 applied, 22,030 admitted, 7,564 enrolled.

Mid 50% test scores			
SAT critical reading:	510-620	GPA 2.0-2.99:	5%
SAT math:	530-640	Rank in top quarter:	69%
ACT composite:	23-29	Rank in top tenth:	31%
GPA 3.75 or higher:	37%	Return as sophomores:	90%
GPA 3.50-3.74:	25%	Out-of-state:	37%
GPA 3.0-3.49:	33%	Live on campus:	98%
		International:	3%

Basis for selection. Strength of student's college preparatory program, senior year program, grade trends, class rank (if provided), and SAT or ACT test scores important. SAT Subject Tests recommended. Campus visit encouraged. Audition required for majority of music majors. **Learning Disabled:** Current and comprehensive documentation of disability required to receive services.

High school preparation. College-preparatory program required. 14 units required; 19 recommended. Required and recommended units include English 4, mathematics 3-4, social studies 2-3, science 1-3 (laboratory 1), foreign language 3 and academic electives 4. Indiana students expected to complete Core 40 state mandated requirements. Non-Indiana students expected to complete minimum of 32 semesters in required areas.

2008-2009 Annual costs. Tuition/fees: $8,231; $24,769 out-of-state. Room/board: $7,138. Books/supplies: $790. Personal expenses: $2,348.

2007-2008 Financial aid. **Need-based:** 4,671 full-time freshmen applied for aid; 2,940 were judged to have need; 2,848 of these received aid. Average need met was 93%. Average scholarship/grant was $8,207; average loan $4,032. 52% of total undergraduate aid awarded as scholarships/grants, 48% as loans/jobs. **Non-need-based:** Awarded to 7,269 full-time undergraduates, including 2,386 freshmen. Scholarships awarded for academics, art, athletics, leadership, minority status, music/drama, religious affiliation, ROTC. **Additional information:** Majority of institutional gift aid merit-based. Some need-based grants go to merit winners with financial need.

Application procedures. **Admission:** Priority date 4/1; no deadline. $50 fee, may be waived for applicants with need. Admission notification on a rolling basis. Must reply by May 1 or within 3 week(s) if notified thereafter. **Financial aid:** Priority date 3/1; no closing date. FAFSA required. Applicants notified on a rolling basis starting 4/1.

Academics. **Special study options:** Accelerated study, combined bachelor's/graduate degree, cooperative education, distance learning, double major, dual enrollment of high school students, ESL, external degree, honors, independent study, internships, liberal arts/career combination, semester at sea, student-designed major, study abroad, teacher certification program, United Nations semester, Washington semester. **Credit/placement by examination:** AP, CLEP, IB, SAT, ACT, institutional tests. **Support services:** Learning center, pre-admission summer program, reduced course load, remedial instruction, study skills assistance, tutoring, writing center.

Honors college/program. Top 5% of high school graduating class or 1350 SAT or 31 ACT required. Qualified students will receive application to Honors College Scholarship automatically. Completed applications reviewed by faculty panel. Honors College participants complete at least 3 approved honors courses during first 4 semesters on campus.

Majors. **Area/ethnic studies:** African-American, East Asian, women's. **Biology:** General, bacteriology, biochemistry. **Business:** General, accounting, business admin, finance, labor relations. **Communications:** General, digital media, journalism. **Communications technology:** Recording arts. **Computer sciences:** General. **Conservation:** General, environmental science. **Education:** General, art, biology, chemistry, early childhood, elementary, English, French, German, health, Latin, mathematics, multi-level teacher, music, physical, physics, science, secondary, social studies, Spanish, special, speech. **Family/consumer sciences:** Clothing/textiles. **Foreign languages:** General, African, ancient Greek, comparative lit, East Asian, French, German, Italian, Latin, linguistics, Portuguese, Slavic, Spanish. **Health:** Audiology/hearing, audiology/speech pathology, cytotechnology, dental hygiene, health care admin, medical radiologic technology/radiation therapy, medical records technology, nuclear medical technology, nursing (RN), respiratory therapy technology, sonography. **History:** General. **Interdisciplinary:** Science/society, systems science. **Liberal arts:** Arts/sciences. **Math:** General. **Parks/recreation:** General, facilities management. **Philosophy/religion:** Judaic, philosophy, religion. **Physical sciences:** Astronomy, astrophysics, chemistry, geology, physics. **Protective services:** Criminal justice. **Psychology:** General. **Public administration:** General. **Social sciences:** General, anthropology, economics, geography, political science, sociology. **Visual/performing arts:** General, art history/conservation, commercial/advertising art, conducting, dance, dramatic, interior design, jazz, music performance, music theory/composition, piano/organ, studio arts, voice/opera.

Most popular majors. Biology 6%, business/marketing 19%, communications/journalism 10%, education 17%, public administration/social services 6%, social sciences 6%.

Computing on campus. 2,262 workstations in dormitories, library, computer center, student center. Dormitories wired for high-speed internet access and linked to campus network. Commuter students can connect to campus network. Online course registration, helpline, repair service, student web hosting, wireless network available.

Student life. **Freshman orientation:** Mandatory, $112 fee. Preregistration for classes offered. Two-day program held between June 14 and July 20. **Housing:** Guaranteed on-campus for freshmen. Coed dorms, single-sex dorms, special housing for disabled, apartments, cooperative housing, fraternity/sorority housing, wellness housing available. $200 deposit. Residential language houses, living/learning centers, wellness center, African-American living/learning center, honors college floors, first-year academic interest group housing available. **Activities:** Bands, choral groups, dance, drama, literary magazine, music ensembles, musical theater, opera, radio station, student government, student newspaper, symphony orchestra, TV station, College Democrats, College Republicans, Young Americans for Freedom, black student union, Latinos Unidos, Asian-American association, Alpha Phi Omega, volunteers student bureau, College Mentors for Kids, Golden Key.

Athletics. NCAA. **Intercollegiate:** Baseball M, basketball, cross-country, diving, field hockey W, football (tackle) M, golf, rowing (crew) W, soccer, softball W, swimming, tennis, track and field, volleyball W, water polo W, wrestling M. **Intramural:** Archery, badminton, basketball, bowling, cross-country, diving, equestrian, fencing, field hockey W, gymnastics, handball, ice hockey M, lacrosse, racquetball, rifle, rowing (crew), rugby, sailing, skiing, skin diving, soccer, softball, squash, swimming, table tennis, tennis, track and field, volleyball, water polo, wrestling M. **Team name:** Hoosiers.

Student services. Adult student services, alcohol/substance abuse counseling, chaplain/spiritual director, career counseling, services for economically disadvantaged, student employment services, financial aid counseling, health services, legal services, minority student services, on-campus daycare, personal counseling, placement for graduates, veterans' counselor, women's services. **Physically disabled:** Services for visually, speech, hearing impaired.

Contact. E-mail: iuadmit@indiana.edu
Phone: (812) 855-0661 Fax: (812) 855-5102
Mary Ellen Anderson, Director of Undergraduate Admissions, Indiana University Bloomington, 300 North Jordan Avenue, Bloomington, IN 47405

Indiana University East

Richmond, Indiana
www.iue.edu **CB code: 1194**

- Public 4-year university and branch campus college
- Commuter campus in large town
- 2,081 degree-seeking undergraduates: 35% part-time, 69% women, 4% African American, 1% Asian American, 2% Hispanic American
- 25 degree-seeking graduate students

General. Founded in 1971. Regionally accredited. **Degrees:** 232 bachelor's, 82 associate awarded; master's offered. **Location:** 70 miles from Indianapolis. **Calendar:** Semester, extensive summer session. **Full-time faculty:** 81 total; 56% have terminal degrees, 12% minority, 60% women. **Part-time faculty:** 105 total; 23% have terminal degrees, 5% minority, 43% women. **Class size:** 63% < 20, 34% 20-39, 2% 40-49, 1% 50-99.

Freshman class profile. 682 applied, 547 admitted, 328 enrolled.

Mid 50% test scores			
SAT critical reading:	410-510	GPA 3.0-3.49:	26%
SAT math:	420-500	GPA 2.0-2.99:	50%
ACT composite:	17-21	Rank in top quarter:	26%
GPA 3.75 or higher:	7%	Rank in top tenth:	8%
GPA 3.50-3.74:	13%	Return as sophomores:	63%
		Out-of-state:	13%

Basis for selection. Open admission, but selective for some programs. Traditional students (3 years or less after high school graduation) required to take SAT or ACT for placement. May attend 1 semester while waiting to take test. Additional admission criteria for nursing program. Interview recommended. **Homeschooled:** Must graduate from national accredited home school program or take GED.

High school preparation. College-preparatory program recommended. 14 units required; 16 recommended. Required and recommended units include English 4, mathematics 3, social studies 2, science 1 (laboratory 1) and academic electives 4. 4 units in some combination of additional mathematics, laboratory science, social science, computer science, and other courses of college preparatory nature. Foreign language strongly recommended.

2008-2009 Annual costs. Tuition/fees: $5,556; $13,722 out-of-state. Books/supplies: $952. Personal expenses: $1,412.

2007-2008 Financial aid. **Need-based:** 236 full-time freshmen applied for aid; 187 were judged to have need; 180 of these received aid. Average need met was 94%. Average scholarship/grant was $4,849; average loan $2,953. 44% of total undergraduate aid awarded as scholarships/grants, 56% as loans/jobs. **Non-need-based:** Awarded to 79 full-time undergraduates, including 29 freshmen. Scholarships awarded for academics, alumni affiliation, leadership.

Application procedures. **Admission:** No deadline. $25 fee, may be waived for applicants with need. Admission notification on a rolling basis beginning on or about 9/1. **Financial aid:** Priority date 3/1; no closing date. FAFSA, institutional form required. Applicants notified on a rolling basis starting 5/1; must reply within 2 week(s) of notification.

Academics. **Special study options:** Cooperative education, cross-registration, distance learning, double major, dual enrollment of high school students, external degree, independent study, internships, teacher certification program, weekend college. State-wide technology program with Purdue University. **Credit/placement by examination:** AP, CLEP, institutional tests. **Support services:** Remedial instruction, study skills assistance, tutoring, writing center.

Majors. **Biology:** General. **Business:** Accounting, business admin, management information systems, marketing. **Communications:** General. **Education:** Elementary, secondary. **Health:** Nursing (RN). **Interdisciplinary:** Biological/physical sciences, natural sciences. **Liberal arts:** Humanities. **Protective services:** Criminal justice. **Psychology:** General. **Public administration:** Social work. **Social sciences:** Sociology.

Most popular majors. Business/marketing 40%, education 12%, health sciences 12%, liberal arts 10%, public administration/social services 6%, security/protective services 6%.

Computing on campus. 120 workstations in library, computer center.

Student life. **Freshman orientation:** Mandatory, $50 fee. Preregistration for classes offered. **Activities:** Drama, student government, student newspaper, TV station.

Athletics. **Intramural:** Basketball, softball, volleyball. **Team name:** Pioneers.

Student services. Adult student services, career counseling, student employment services, financial aid counseling, health services, on-campus daycare, personal counseling, placement for graduates. **Physically disabled:** Services for visually, speech, hearing impaired.

Contact. E-mail: eaadmit@indiana.edu
Phone: (765) 973-8208 Toll-free number: (800) 959-3278
Fax: (765) 973-8288
Molly Vanderpool, Director of Admissions, Indiana University East, 2325 Chester Boulevard, Richmond, IN 47374-1289

Indiana University Kokomo

Kokomo, Indiana
www.iuk.edu **CB code: 1337**

- Public 4-year university
- Commuter campus in large town
- 2,204 degree-seeking undergraduates: 41% part-time, 69% women, 5% African American, 1% Asian American, 2% Hispanic American, 1% Native American
- 91 degree-seeking graduate students
- 82% of applicants admitted
- SAT or ACT with writing required

General. Founded in 1945. Regionally accredited. **Degrees:** 291 bachelor's, 211 associate awarded; master's offered. **ROTC:** Army. **Location:** 50 miles from Indianapolis. **Calendar:** Semester, limited summer session. **Full-time faculty:** 90 total; 62% have terminal degrees, 13% minority, 56% women. **Part-time faculty:** 78 total; 5% have terminal degrees, 5% minority, 56% women. **Class size:** 52% < 20, 35% 20-39, 9% 40-49, 3% 50-99, less than 1% >100. **Special facilities:** Observatory.

Freshman class profile. 714 applied, 586 admitted, 401 enrolled.

Mid 50% test scores		**GPA 3.0-3.49:**	25%
SAT critical reading:	420-530	**GPA 2.0-2.99:**	52%
SAT math:	430-530	**Rank in top quarter:**	26%
ACT composite:	18-23	**Rank in top tenth:**	7%
GPA 3.75 or higher:	4%	**Return as sophomores:**	56%
GPA 3.50-3.74:	8%	**International:**	1%

Basis for selection. Test scores, class rank, course work important. In-state applicants should be in top half of graduating class (top third for out-of-state applicants).

High school preparation. College-preparatory program required. 14 units required. Required and recommended units include English 4, mathematics 3, social studies 2, history 2, science 1 and foreign language 2.

2008-2009 Annual costs. Tuition/fees: $5,591; $13,754 out-of-state. Books/supplies: $864. Personal expenses: $3,410.

2007-2008 Financial aid. **Need-based:** 302 full-time freshmen applied for aid; 215 were judged to have need; 195 of these received aid. Average need met was 92%. Average scholarship/grant was $5,140; average loan $2,741. 47% of total undergraduate aid awarded as scholarships/grants, 53% as loans/jobs. **Non-need-based:** Awarded to 118 full-time undergraduates, including 34 freshmen. Scholarships awarded for academics.

Application procedures. **Admission:** $30 fee, may be waived for applicants with need. Application must be submitted on paper. Admission notification on a rolling basis. **Financial aid:** Closing date 3/1. FAFSA, institutional form required. Applicants notified on a rolling basis starting 5/1; must reply within 4 week(s) of notification.

Academics. **Special study options:** Accelerated study, cross-registration, distance learning, double major, dual enrollment of high school students, external degree, honors, independent study, internships, liberal arts/career combination, study abroad, teacher certification program. **Credit/placement by examination:** AP, CLEP, SAT, ACT, institutional tests. **Support services:** Learning center, reduced course load, remedial instruction, tutoring.

Majors. **Biology:** General. **Business:** General, accounting, business admin, labor relations, marketing. **Communications:** General. **Computer sciences:** General. **Education:** Elementary. **Health:** Nursing (RN). **Interdisciplinary:** Behavioral sciences, biological/physical sciences, gerontology. **Liberal arts:** Humanities. **Math:** General. **Physical sciences:** Chemistry. **Protective services:** Criminal justice. **Psychology:** General. **Public administration:** General. **Social sciences:** General, sociology.

Most popular majors. Business/marketing 11%, education 13%, health sciences 32%, liberal arts 19%, security/protective services 7%.

Computing on campus. 100 workstations in library, computer center, student center. Online course registration, helpline available.

Student life. **Freshman orientation:** Available, $28 fee. Preregistration for classes offered. **Activities:** Choral groups, drama, music ensembles, student government, student newspaper.

Athletics. **Intramural:** Basketball M, soccer, softball, volleyball.

Student services. Adult student services, career counseling, student employment services, financial aid counseling, minority student services, on-campus daycare, personal counseling, placement for graduates, veterans' counselor. **Physically disabled:** Services for visually, hearing impaired.

Contact. E-mail: iuadmis@iuk.edu
Phone: (765) 455-9217 Toll-free number: (888) 875-4485
Fax: (765) 455-9537
Reeta Piirala-Skoglund, Assistant Director of Admissions, Indiana University Kokomo, Box 9003, KC 230A, Kokomo, IN 46904-9003

Indiana University Northwest

Gary, Indiana
www.iun.edu **CB code: 1338**

- Public 4-year university
- Commuter campus in small city
- 3,974 degree-seeking undergraduates: 36% part-time, 70% women, 20% African American, 2% Asian American, 13% Hispanic American, 1% Native American
- 458 degree-seeking graduate students
- 80% of applicants admitted
- SAT or ACT with writing required

General. Founded in 1948. Regionally accredited. **Degrees:** 380 bachelor's, 190 associate awarded; master's offered. **ROTC:** Army. **Location:** 35 miles from Chicago. **Calendar:** Semester, limited summer session. **Full-time faculty:** 186 total; 70% have terminal degrees, 23% minority, 50% women. **Part-time faculty:** 176 total; 21% have terminal degrees, 19% minority, 53% women. **Class size:** 45% < 20, 47% 20-39, 3% 40-49, 5% 50-99, less than 1% >100.

Four-Year Colleges

Freshman class profile. 1,433 applied, 1,150 admitted, 769 enrolled.

Mid 50% test scores			
SAT critical reading:	400-500	GPA 3.0-3.49:	19%
SAT math:	390-510	GPA 2.0-2.99:	48%
ACT composite:	16-22	Rank in top quarter:	24%
GPA 3.75 or higher:	6%	Rank in top tenth:	10%
GPA 3.50-3.74:	6%	Return as sophomores:	66%
		Out-of-state:	1%

Basis for selection. School achievement record and test scores most important. Applicants should be in top half of class and have 2.0 GPA.

High school preparation. College-preparatory program recommended. 16 units required. Required and recommended units include English 4, mathematics 3, social studies 2, science 1 (laboratory 1), foreign language 2 and academic electives 4.

2008-2009 Annual costs. Tuition/fees: $5,669. Books/supplies: $1,090. Personal expenses: $3,322.

2007-2008 Financial aid. Need-based: 424 full-time freshmen applied for aid; 326 were judged to have need; 302 of these received aid. Average need met was 91%. Average scholarship/grant was $5,160; average loan $2,902. 42% of total undergraduate aid awarded as scholarships/grants, 58% as loans/jobs. **Non-need-based:** Awarded to 147 full-time undergraduates, including 47 freshmen. Scholarships awarded for academics, athletics.

Application procedures. Admission: Priority date 8/1; no deadline. $25 fee, may be waived for applicants with need. Admission notification on a rolling basis. **Financial aid:** Priority date 3/1; no closing date. FAFSA, institutional form required. Applicants notified on a rolling basis starting 5/1; must reply within 2 week(s) of notification.

Academics. Special study options: Accelerated study, cooperative education, distance learning, double major, dual enrollment of high school students, external degree, independent study, internships, liberal arts/career combination, student-designed major, study abroad, teacher certification program, Washington semester, weekend college. **Credit/placement by examination:** AP, CLEP, institutional tests. **Support services:** Learning center, preadmission summer program, reduced course load, remedial instruction, tutoring.

Majors. Area/ethnic studies: African-American. **Biology:** General. **Business:** General, actuarial science, labor relations. **Communications:** General. **Computer sciences:** Data processing. **Education:** Elementary, English, mathematics, secondary, social studies, Spanish. **Foreign languages:** French, Spanish. **Health:** Health care admin, medical records admin, nursing (RN). **History:** General. **Math:** General. **Philosophy/religion:** Philosophy. **Physical sciences:** Chemistry, geology. **Protective services:** Criminal justice. **Psychology:** General. **Public administration:** General. **Social sciences:** Economics, political science, sociology. **Visual/performing arts:** Art, dramatic.

Most popular majors. Business/marketing 12%, education 9%, health sciences 26%, liberal arts 21%, security/protective services 10%.

Computing on campus. 170 workstations in library, computer center, student center. Commuter students can connect to campus network. Online course registration, helpline available.

Student life. Freshman orientation: Available. Preregistration for classes offered. **Activities:** Choral groups, drama, literary magazine, student government, student newspaper, Christian Student Fellowship, Young Republicans, Young Democrats, Women with a Challenge, student guide services, black student union.

Athletics. NAIA. **Intercollegiate:** Basketball, golf, volleyball W. **Intramural:** Baseball M, basketball M, bowling, cheerleading W, golf. **Team name:** Red Hawks.

Student services. Adult student services, career counseling, student employment services, financial aid counseling, on-campus daycare, personal counseling, placement for graduates, veterans' counselor, women's services. **Physically disabled:** Services for visually impaired.

Contact. E-mail: admit@iun.edu
Phone: (219) 980-6991 Toll-free number: (800) 968-7486
Fax: (219) 981-4219
Linda Templeton, Director of Admissions, Indiana University Northwest, 3400 Broadway, Gary, IN 46408

Indiana University South Bend

South Bend, Indiana
www.iusb.edu **CB code: 1339**

- Public 4-year university
- Commuter campus in small city
- 5,875 degree-seeking undergraduates: 34% part-time, 63% women, 7% African American, 1% Asian American, 5% Hispanic American, 2% international
- 783 degree-seeking graduate students
- 84% of applicants admitted
- SAT or ACT required

General. Founded in 1922. Regionally accredited. Off-campus course offerings in Elkhart, Warsaw, Plymouth. **Degrees:** 592 bachelor's, 206 associate awarded; master's offered. **ROTC:** Army, Naval, Air Force. **Location:** 90 miles from Chicago. **Calendar:** Semester, limited summer session. **Full-time faculty:** 283 total; 64% have terminal degrees, 20% minority, 50% women. **Part-time faculty:** 242 total; 19% have terminal degrees, 6% minority, 54% women. **Class size:** 43% < 20, 49% 20-39, 4% 40-49, 4% 50-99, less than 1% >100.

Freshman class profile. 2,083 applied, 1,754 admitted, 1,135 enrolled.

Mid 50% test scores			
SAT critical reading:	420-530	GPA 2.0-2.99:	53%
SAT math:	420-530	Rank in top quarter:	27%
ACT composite:	17-22	Rank in top tenth:	8%
GPA 3.75 or higher:	4%	Return as sophomores:	62%
GPA 3.50-3.74:	9%	Out-of-state:	2%
GPA 3.0-3.49:	30%	International:	2%

Basis for selection. Rank in top half of class important. Core 40 completion with 2.0 or higher. Interview recommended for academically weak applicants or those with unusual circumstances. Audition required of music majors. Portfolios required for some art majors. **Homeschooled:** Applicants to degree-seeking programs must meet institution's requirement for college-prep courses.

High school preparation. College-preparatory program required. 13 units required. Required and recommended units include English 4, mathematics 3, social studies 2, science 1 (laboratory 1) and foreign language 2. Strong preparation in math and sciences recommended.

2008-2009 Annual costs. Tuition/fees: $5,763; $14,880 out-of-state. Books/supplies: $1,116. Personal expenses: $1,604.

2007-2008 Financial aid. Need-based: 694 full-time freshmen applied for aid; 517 were judged to have need; 482 of these received aid. Average need met was 94%. Average scholarship/grant was $5,090; average loan $2,788. 48% of total undergraduate aid awarded as scholarships/grants, 52% as loans/jobs. **Non-need-based:** Awarded to 197 full-time undergraduates, including 54 freshmen. Scholarships awarded for academics, athletics.

Application procedures. Admission: Priority date 7/1; no deadline. $45 fee, may be waived for applicants with need. Admission notification on a rolling basis. **Financial aid:** Closing date 3/1. FAFSA, institutional form required. Applicants notified on a rolling basis starting 5/1.

Academics. Most allied health programs must be completed at Indianapolis campus. **Special study options:** Accelerated study, cross-registration, distance learning, double major, ESL, external degree, honors, internships, liberal arts/career combination, study abroad, teacher certification program, weekend college. Electrical, mechanical engineering, computer technology with Purdue University on Indiana University South Bend campus; Northern Indiana Consortium for Education (part of 6 member institutions sharing library resources, faculty expertise, and academic strengths). **Credit/placement by examination:** AP, CLEP, IB, institutional tests. 90 credit hours maximum toward bachelor's degree. **Support services:** Learning center, pre-admission summer program, reduced course load, remedial instruction, tutoring, writing center.

Majors. Area/ethnic studies: Women's. **Biology:** General. **Business:** General, actuarial science, business admin, finance, labor relations, labor studies, marketing. **Communications:** Media studies. **Computer sciences:** General. **Education:** Biology, chemistry, elementary, mathematics, music, physics, science, secondary, social studies, Spanish, special. **Foreign languages:** French, German, Spanish. **Health:** Health care admin, nursing (RN). **History:** General. **Math:** General, applied. **Philosophy/religion:** Philosophy. **Physical sciences:** Chemistry, physics. **Protective services:** Criminal justice. **Psychology:** General. **Public administration:** General. **Social sciences:** Economics, political science, sociology. **Visual/performing arts:** Art, dramatic, music performance, studio arts.

Most popular majors. Business/marketing 16%, education 13%, health sciences 13%, liberal arts 16%, psychology 6%, security/protective services 7%, social sciences 6%.

Computing on campus. 325 workstations in library, computer center. Commuter students can connect to campus network. Online library, helpline available.

Student life. **Freshman orientation:** Available, $35 fee. Preregistration for classes offered. Two and a half hour sessions held in May, June, July and August. **Housing:** Some housing for athletes and visiting scholars. **Activities:** Jazz band, campus ministries, choral groups, drama, film society, international student organizations, literary magazine, music ensembles, musical theater, opera, student government, student newspaper, symphony orchestra, student educational association, black student union, student council for exceptional children, Latino student union, Asian student union, women's student union, Habitat for Humanity, departmental clubs.

Athletics. NAIA. **Intercollegiate:** Basketball. **Intramural:** Badminton, basketball, bowling, football (tackle), racquetball, softball, table tennis, tennis, volleyball. **Team name:** Titans.

Student services. Adult student services, chaplain/spiritual director, career counseling, student employment services, on-campus daycare, personal counseling, placement for graduates, veterans' counselor. **Physically disabled:** Services for visually, speech, hearing impaired.

Contact. E-mail: admissio@iusb.edu
Phone: (574) 520-4480 Fax: (574) 520-4834
Jeff Johnston, Director Recruitment/Admissions, Indiana University South Bend, 1700 Mishawaka Avenue, South Bend, IN 46634-7111

Indiana University Southeast

New Albany, Indiana — **CB member**
www.ius.edu — **CB code: 1314**

- Public 4-year university
- Commuter campus in large town
- 5,352 degree-seeking undergraduates: 34% part-time, 61% women, 6% African American, 1% Asian American, 2% Hispanic American, 1% Native American
- 647 degree-seeking graduate students
- 87% of applicants admitted
- SAT or ACT with writing required

General. Founded in 1941. Regionally accredited. **Degrees:** 675 bachelor's, 105 associate awarded; master's offered. **ROTC:** Army, Air Force. **Location:** 10 miles from Louisville. **Calendar:** Semester, limited summer session. **Full-time faculty:** 201 total; 72% have terminal degrees, 14% minority, 47% women. **Part-time faculty:** 252 total; 16% have terminal degrees, 8% minority, 49% women. **Class size:** 37% < 20, 59% 20-39, 3% 40-49, 1% 50-99. **Special facilities:** Cultural and community center.

Freshman class profile. 1,870 applied, 1,624 admitted, 1,070 enrolled.

Mid 50% test scores		**GPA 3.0-3.49:**	30%
SAT critical reading:	420-520	**GPA 2.0-2.99:**	52%
SAT math:	420-520	**Rank in top quarter:**	28%
ACT composite:	18-22	**Rank in top tenth:**	6%
GPA 3.75 or higher:	7%	**Return as sophomores:**	63%
GPA 3.50-3.74:	8%	**Out-of-state:**	18%

Basis for selection. Rank in top half of class for in-state applicants. Interview recommended.

High school preparation. 14 units required; 19 recommended. Required and recommended units include English 4, mathematics 3-4, social studies 2, history 1, science 1-2 (laboratory 1-2), foreign language 2 and academic electives 4.

2008-2009 Annual costs. Tuition/fees: $5,644; $13,804 out-of-state. Room and board includes $600 meal plan. Meal plans can be purchased for $100, $300 or $600. Room/board: $6,240. Books/supplies: $880.

2007-2008 Financial aid. **Need-based:** 585 full-time freshmen applied for aid; 455 were judged to have need; 429 of these received aid. Average need met was 91%. Average scholarship/grant was $5,226; average loan $2,675. 46% of total undergraduate aid awarded as scholarships/grants, 54% as loans/jobs. **Non-need-based:** Awarded to 270 full-time undergraduates, including 85 freshmen. Scholarships awarded for academics, art, athletics, leadership, minority status, music/drama.

Application procedures. **Admission:** Priority date 7/15; no deadline. $30 fee, may be waived for applicants with need. Admission notification on a rolling basis. **Financial aid:** Priority date 3/1; no closing date. FAFSA required. Applicants notified on a rolling basis starting 5/1; must reply within 3 week(s) of notification.

Academics. **Special study options:** Accelerated study, cross-registration, double major, dual enrollment of high school students, external degree, independent study, internships, student-designed major, study abroad, teacher certification program, weekend college. Member of Metroversity consortium of institutions of higher education in Louisville area. **Credit/placement by examination:** AP, CLEP, IB, institutional tests. **Support services:** Reduced course load, remedial instruction, study skills assistance, tutoring, writing center.

Majors. **Biology:** General. **Business:** General, accounting, accounting technology, labor relations. **Communications:** General, journalism. **Computer sciences:** General. **Education:** General, biology, elementary, English, mathematics, science, secondary, social studies, special. **Foreign languages:** French, German, Spanish. **Health:** Clinical lab science, nursing (RN). **History:** General. **Math:** General. **Philosophy/religion:** Philosophy. **Physical sciences:** Chemistry, physics. **Psychology:** General. **Social sciences:** Economics, geography, international relations, political science, sociology. **Visual/performing arts:** Art, studio arts.

Most popular majors. Business/marketing 20%, communications/journalism 6%, education 17%, health sciences 10%, liberal arts 19%.

Computing on campus. 165 workstations in library, computer center, student center. Commuter students can connect to campus network. Online course registration, online library, helpline, student web hosting, wireless network available.

Student life. **Freshman orientation:** Mandatory, $50 fee. Preregistration for classes offered. One-day summer program. **Activities:** Concert band, choral groups, drama, literary magazine, music ensembles, student government, student newspaper, symphony orchestra, Christian fellowship, students for world peace, multicultural student union.

Athletics. NAIA. **Intercollegiate:** Baseball M, basketball, cross-country, tennis, volleyball W. **Intramural:** Basketball, bowling, softball, tennis, volleyball. **Team name:** Grenadier.

Student services. Adult student services, alcohol/substance abuse counseling, chaplain/spiritual director, career counseling, student employment services, financial aid counseling, minority student services, on-campus daycare, personal counseling, placement for graduates, veterans' counselor. **Physically disabled:** Services for visually, speech, hearing impaired.

Contact. E-mail: admissions@ius.edu
Phone: (812) 941-2212 Toll-free number: (800) 852-8835
Fax: (812) 941-2595
Anne Skuce, Assistant Vice Chancellor for Enrollment Management, Indiana University Southeast, 4201 Grant Line Road, New Albany, IN 47150-6405

Indiana University-Purdue University Fort Wayne

Fort Wayne, Indiana — **CB member**
www.ipfw.edu — **CB code: 1336**

- Public 4-year university and branch campus college
- Commuter campus in large city
- 10,787 degree-seeking undergraduates: 30% part-time, 56% women, 6% African American, 2% Asian American, 3% Hispanic American, 1% international
- 685 degree-seeking graduate students
- 96% of applicants admitted
- SAT or ACT (ACT writing optional) required

General. Founded in 1964. Regionally accredited. Degrees awarded through Indiana University or Purdue University, depending on course of study. **Degrees:** 999 bachelor's, 457 associate awarded; master's offered. **ROTC:** Army. **Location:** 110 miles from Indianapolis. **Calendar:** Semester, limited summer session. **Full-time faculty:** 399 total; 86% have terminal degrees, 18% minority, 41% women. **Part-time faculty:** 379 total; 11% have terminal degrees, 7% minority, 54% women. **Class size:** 46% < 20, 46% 20-39, 4% 40-49, 3% 50-99, less than 1% >100. **Special facilities:** Lake biological research station.

Freshman class profile. 3,277 applied, 3,158 admitted, 2,094 enrolled.

Mid 50% test scores		**GPA 2.0-2.99:**	46%
SAT critical reading:	420-530	**Rank in top quarter:**	30%
SAT math:	440-550	**Rank in top tenth:**	10%
SAT writing:	400-520	**End year in good standing:**	95%
ACT composite:	18-24	**Return as sophomores:**	62%
GPA 3.75 or higher:	11%	**Out-of-state:**	4%
GPA 3.50-3.74:	12%	**Live on campus:**	20%
GPA 3.0-3.49:	29%	**International:**	1%

Basis for selection. In-state applicants should rank in top half of high school class, out-of-state in top third. Test scores important. TOEFL or Michigan Test may be used to assess English proficiency. Audition required of music majors. Portfolio required of visual arts majors. **Homeschooled:** Transcript of courses and grades required.

High school preparation. College-preparatory program required. 20 units required. Required units include English 4, mathematics 3, social studies 3, science 3, foreign language 2 and academic electives 5. Additional requirements vary by program.

2008-2009 Annual costs. Tuition/fees: $6,596; $15,545 out-of-state. Room only: $5,400. Books/supplies: $1,300. Personal expenses: $1,680.

2007-2008 Financial aid. **Need-based:** 1,554 full-time freshmen applied for aid; 1,208 were judged to have need; 1,119 of these received aid. Average need met was 50%. Average scholarship/grant was $4,780; average loan $3,157. 35% of total undergraduate aid awarded as scholarships/grants, 65% as loans/jobs. **Non-need-based:** Awarded to 1,230 full-time undergraduates, including 438 freshmen. Scholarships awarded for academics, athletics, state residency.

Application procedures. **Admission:** Closing date 8/1. $30 fee, may be waived for applicants with need. Admission notification on a rolling basis beginning on or about 11/1. **Financial aid:** Priority date 3/10; no closing date. FAFSA required. Applicants notified on a rolling basis starting 5/15; must reply within 3 week(s) of notification.

Academics. **Special study options:** Accelerated study, cooperative education, distance learning, double major, ESL, exchange student, honors, independent study, internships, liberal arts/career combination, student-designed major, study abroad, teacher certification program, Washington semester, weekend college. **Credit/placement by examination:** AP, CLEP, IB, institutional tests. Hours of credit awarded by examination varies by program. **Support services:** Learning center, pre-admission summer program, remedial instruction, study skills assistance, tutoring, writing center.

Majors. **Area/ethnic studies:** Women's. **Biology:** General. **Business:** Accounting, business admin, finance, hospitality admin, labor studies, managerial economics, marketing, operations. **Communications:** General, media studies, organizational. **Computer sciences:** Computer science, information systems. **Education:** Art, biology, chemistry, elementary, English, French, German, history, mathematics, music, physics, science, secondary, social studies, Spanish, speech. **Engineering:** Civil, computer, electrical, mechanical. **Engineering technology:** Computer, construction, electrical, industrial, mechanical. **Foreign languages:** French, German, Spanish. **Health:** Audiology/hearing, clinical lab science, clinical lab technology, community health services, health care admin, health services admin, mental health services, music therapy, nursing (RN), predental, premedicine, preveterinary, substance abuse counseling. **History:** General. **Interdisciplinary:** Math/computer science. **Math:** General, computational, statistics. **Philosophy/religion:** Philosophy. **Physical sciences:** Chemistry, geology, physics. **Protective services:** Law enforcement admin. **Psychology:** General. **Public administration:** General, policy analysis. **Social sciences:** Anthropology, economics, political science, sociology. **Visual/performing arts:** Commercial/advertising art, crafts, dramatic, drawing, graphic design, interior design, painting, photography, piano/organ, printmaking, sculpture, studio arts, voice/opera.

Most popular majors. Business/marketing 19%, education 13%, engineering/engineering technologies 6%, liberal arts 17%.

Computing on campus. 472 workstations in dormitories, library, computer center, student center. Dormitories wired for high-speed internet access and linked to campus network. Commuter students can connect to campus network. Online course registration, online library, helpline, repair service, student web hosting, wireless network available.

Student life. **Freshman orientation:** Mandatory, $30 fee. Preregistration for classes offered. 8-hour program; 15 dates available between June and August; Freshmen Fest held 2 days in late August. **Housing:** Apartments available. $150 fully refundable deposit. **Activities:** Bands, campus ministries, choral groups, dance, drama, international student organizations, literary magazine, music ensembles, musical theater, opera, student government, student newspaper, symphony orchestra, TV station, Black Collegian Caucus, Hispanos Unidos, InterVarsity Christian Fellowship, Graduate Business Council.

Athletics. NCAA. **Intercollegiate:** Baseball M, basketball, cross-country, golf, soccer, softball W, tennis, track and field W, volleyball. **Intramural:** Badminton, basketball, bowling, football (non-tackle), football (tackle) M, golf, racquetball, soccer, tennis, volleyball. **Team name:** Mastodons.

Student services. Adult student services, alcohol/substance abuse counseling, chaplain/spiritual director, career counseling, student employment services, financial aid counseling, health services, minority student services, on-campus daycare, personal counseling, placement for graduates, veterans' counselor, women's services. **Physically disabled:** Services for visually, speech, hearing impaired.

Contact. E-mail: ask@ipfw.edu
Phone: (260) 481-6812 Toll-free number: (800) 324-4739
Fax: (260) 481-6880
Carol Isaacs, Director of Admissions, Indiana University-Purdue University Fort Wayne, 2101 East Coliseum Boulevard, Fort Wayne, IN 46805-1499

Indiana University-Purdue University Indianapolis

Indianapolis, Indiana — **CB member**
www.iupui.edu — **CB code: 1325**

- Public 4-year university
- Commuter campus in very large city
- 20,390 degree-seeking undergraduates: 28% part-time, 59% women, 10% African American, 3% Asian American, 3% Hispanic American, 3% international
- 8,174 degree-seeking graduate students
- 70% of applicants admitted
- SAT or ACT with writing required

General. Founded in 1969. Regionally accredited. **Degrees:** 2,933 bachelor's, 423 associate awarded; master's, doctoral, first professional offered. **ROTC:** Army, Naval, Air Force. **Calendar:** Semester, extensive summer session. **Full-time faculty:** 2,286 total; 81% have terminal degrees, 22% minority, 38% women. **Part-time faculty:** 966 total; 28% have terminal degrees, 11% minority, 52% women. **Class size:** 36% < 20, 47% 20-39, 7% 40-49, 8% 50-99, 1% >100.

Freshman class profile. 8,855 applied, 6,163 admitted, 3,040 enrolled.

Mid 50% test scores		**Rank in top quarter:**	46%
SAT critical reading:	440-550	**Rank in top tenth:**	17%
SAT math:	450-570	**Return as sophomores:**	68%
ACT composite:	19-24	**Out-of-state:**	4%
GPA 3.75 or higher:	15%	**Live on campus:**	14%
GPA 3.50-3.74:	14%	**International:**	3%
GPA 3.0-3.49:	38%	**Fraternities:**	1%
GPA 2.0-2.99:	32%	**Sororities:**	1%

Basis for selection. Course curriculum, grades, trend in grades, and test scores are the factors used. Portfolio recommended for some art applicants.

High school preparation. College-preparatory program required. 21 units required; 26 recommended. Required and recommended units include English 4, mathematics 3-4, social studies 2, history 2, science 3-4 (laboratory 3), foreign language 3 and academic electives 4. Additional math and science units required for science, engineering and nursing programs. 4 additional units required in some combination of foreign language, laboratory science, math, social science, or computer science. Courses that develop writing composition skills strongly recommended.

2008-2009 Annual costs. Tuition/fees: $7,191; $20,579 out-of-state. Room only: $3,140. Books/supplies: $672. Personal expenses: $2,600.

2007-2008 Financial aid. **Need-based:** 2,202 full-time freshmen applied for aid; 1,672 were judged to have need; 1,618 of these received aid. Average need met was 80%. Average scholarship/grant was $6,696; average loan $2,880. 43% of total undergraduate aid awarded as scholarships/grants, 57% as loans/jobs. **Non-need-based:** Awarded to 1,593 full-time undergraduates, including 472 freshmen. Scholarships awarded for academics, ROTC.

Application procedures. **Admission:** Closing date 5/1. $50 fee, may be waived for applicants with need. Admission notification on a rolling basis. Application deadlines for nursing and allied health programs range from October 15 to February 1. **Financial aid:** Priority date 3/1; no closing date. FAFSA required. Applicants notified on a rolling basis starting 4/1.

Academics. **Special study options:** Accelerated study, cooperative education, cross-registration, distance learning, double major, dual enrollment of high school students, ESL, exchange student, external degree, honors, independent study, internships, student-designed major, study abroad, teacher certification program, weekend college. **Credit/placement by examination:** AP, CLEP, IB, SAT, ACT, institutional tests. Policy varies by school. **Support services:** Learning center, reduced course load, remedial instruction, tutoring, writing center.

Majors. **Biology:** General. **Business:** General, accounting, finance, human resources, international, labor relations, labor studies, management information systems, market research, nonprofit/public, tourism/travel. **Communications:** General, advertising, journalism, public relations. **Computer sciences:** General, computer graphics, information systems, system admin, web page design, webmaster. **Conservation:** Environmental science. **Education:** Art, biology, chemistry, elementary, English, ESL, French, German, health occupations, mathematics, physical, physics, secondary, social studies, Spanish, speech. **Engineering:** General, biomedical, computer, electrical, mechanical. **Engineering technology:** Computer, computer hardware, computer systems, construction, electrical, mechanical, robotics, software. **Foreign languages:** American Sign Language, French, German, Spanish. **Health:** Clinical lab science, cytotechnology, dental hygiene, medical informatics, medical radiologic technology/radiation therapy, medical records admin, nuclear medical technology, nursing (RN), predental, premedicine, prenursing, prepharmacy, preveterinary, radiologic technology/medical imaging, respiratory therapy assistant. **History:** General. **Legal studies:** Prelaw. **Liberal arts:** Arts/sciences. **Math:** General. **Parks/recreation:** Exercise sciences. **Philosophy/religion:** Philosophy, religion. **Physical sciences:** Chemistry, geology, physics. **Protective services:** Criminal justice, forensics. **Psychology:** General. **Public administration:** General, social work. **Social sciences:** Anthropology, economics, geography, political science, sociology. **Visual/performing arts:** Art, art history/conservation, ceramics, design, interior design, painting, photography, printmaking, sculpture, studio arts.

Most popular majors. Business/marketing 16%, education 11%, engineering/engineering technologies 8%, health sciences 14%, liberal arts 15%.

Computing on campus. 750 workstations in library, computer center, student center. Dormitories wired for high-speed internet access and linked to campus network. Commuter students can connect to campus network. Online course registration, helpline, repair service, wireless network available.

Student life. **Freshman orientation:** Mandatory, $105 fee. Preregistration for classes offered. **Policies:** Smoking policy, code of conduct. **Housing:** Coed dorms, apartments available. $100 deposit. **Activities:** Bands, choral groups, dance, drama, literary magazine, music ensembles, student government, student newspaper, black student union, international affairs club.

Athletics. NCAA. **Intercollegiate:** Basketball, cheerleading, cross-country, diving, golf, soccer, softball W, swimming, tennis, volleyball W. **Intramural:** Basketball, football (non-tackle), golf, ice hockey, racquetball, soccer, softball, tennis, volleyball. **Team name:** Jaguars.

Student services. Adult student services, chaplain/spiritual director, career counseling, student employment services, financial aid counseling, health services, minority student services, on-campus daycare, personal counseling, placement for graduates, veterans' counselor, women's services. **Physically disabled:** Services for visually, speech, hearing impaired. **Learning disabled:** Comprehensive services available.

Contact. E-mail: apply@iupui.edu
Phone: (317) 274-4591 Fax: (317) 278-1862
Chris Foley, Director of Admissions, Indiana University-Purdue University Indianapolis, 420 North University Boulevard, Cavanaugh Hall R129, Indianapolis, IN 46202-5143

Indiana Wesleyan University
Marion, Indiana
www.indwes.edu **CB code: 1446**

- Private 4-year university and liberal arts college affiliated with Wesleyan Church
- Residential campus in large town
- 3,109 degree-seeking undergraduates: 3% part-time, 63% women, 1% African American, 1% Asian American, 1% Hispanic American
- 85% of applicants admitted
- SAT or ACT (ACT writing recommended), application essay required
- 66% graduate within 6 years

General. Founded in 1920. Regionally accredited. Education centers in Indianapolis, Fort Wayne, Columbus (IN), Kokomo, Merrillville, Shelbyville, Cleveland, Cincinnati, Lexington, Louisville and Dayton. **Degrees:** 583 bachelor's, 10 associate awarded; master's, doctoral offered. **ROTC:** Army. **Location:** 65 miles from Indianapolis. **Calendar:** Semester, limited summer session. **Full-time faculty:** 165 total; 54% have terminal degrees, 6% minority, 38% women. **Part-time faculty:** 144 total; 10% have terminal degrees, 4% minority, 44% women. **Class size:** 54% < 20, 35% 20-39, 4% 40-49, 6% 50-99, 1% >100. **Special facilities:** History museum, nature preserve, museum of European oil paintings, photograph collection.

Freshman class profile. 2,588 applied, 2,211 admitted, 894 enrolled.

Mid 50% test scores		**GPA 2.0-2.99:**	18%
SAT critical reading:	480-600	**Rank in top quarter:**	55%
SAT math:	480-600	**Rank in top tenth:**	28%
ACT composite:	21-27	**Return as sophomores:**	80%
GPA 3.75 or higher:	41%	**Out-of-state:**	52%
GPA 3.50-3.74:	17%	**Live on campus:**	96%
GPA 3.0-3.49:	24%		

Basis for selection. High school record, class rank, and test scores most important. Recommendations required. Standardized tests and insitutional tests used to assist students in selecting classes appropriate to their preparation; designated scores determine placement in Math and English. Audition recommended for music majors. Portfolio recommended for art majors. **Homeschooled:** Transcript of courses and grades, letter of recommendation (nonparent) required. Transcript must have GPA on 4.0 scale. Recommendation from pastor required.

High school preparation. College-preparatory program recommended. 20 units recommended. Recommended units include English 4, mathematics 3, social studies 3, science 3, foreign language 2 and academic electives 5.

2009-2010 Annual costs. Tuition/fees: $20,496. Required fees vary by program. Room/board: $6,770. Books/supplies: $800. Personal expenses: $800.

2008-2009 Financial aid. **Need-based:** 773 full-time freshmen applied for aid; 649 were judged to have need; 648 of these received aid. Average need met was 50%. Average scholarship/grant was $6,442; average loan $4,172. 54% of total undergraduate aid awarded as scholarships/grants, 46% as loans/jobs. **Non-need-based:** Awarded to 690 full-time undergraduates, including 217 freshmen. Scholarships awarded for academics, alumni affiliation, art, athletics, music/drama, ROTC.

Application procedures. **Admission:** Priority date 12/1; deadline 8/1 (receipt date). $25 fee, may be waived for applicants with need. Admission notification on a rolling basis beginning on or about 10/1. **Financial aid:** Closing date 3/1. FAFSA required. Applicants notified by 4/1.

Academics. **Special study options:** Accelerated study, cross-registration, distance learning, double major, dual enrollment of high school students, honors, independent study, internships, liberal arts/career combination, student-designed major, study abroad, teacher certification program. **Credit/placement by examination:** AP, CLEP, IB, SAT, ACT, institutional tests. Students must complete at least 30 hours in residence. **Support services:** Learning center, reduced course load, remedial instruction, study skills assistance, tutoring, writing center.

Honors college/program. 1250 SAT (exclusive of Writing) or 28 ACT, 3.6 GPA or class rank in the top 10%, and desire to participate in interdisciplinary community of committed learners required.

Majors. **Biology:** General, Biochemistry/biophysics and molecular biology. **Business:** Accounting, business admin, finance, management information systems, managerial economics, marketing. **Communications:** General, journalism, media studies, public relations. **Computer sciences:** General, applications programming, computer graphics, computer science, web page design, webmaster. **Education:** Art, business, elementary, English, mathematics, middle, music, physical, science, secondary, social studies. **Foreign languages:** Spanish. **Health:** Athletic training, nursing (RN), predental, premedicine, prepharmacy, preveterinary, substance abuse counseling. **History:** General. **Legal studies:** Prelaw. **Math:** General. **Parks/recreation:** Exercise sciences, facilities management, health/fitness, sports admin. **Philosophy/religion:** Philosophy, religion. **Physical sciences:** Chemistry. **Protective services:** Criminal justice. **Psychology:** General. **Public administration:** Social work. **Social sciences:** General, criminology, economics, international relations, political science, urban studies. **Theology:** Bible, religious ed, sacred music, theology. **Visual/performing arts:** Ceramics, dramatic, drawing, graphic design, illustration, interior design, music performance, music theory/composition, painting, photography, printmaking, studio arts.

Most popular majors. Business/marketing 13%, computer/information sciences 6%, education 17%, health sciences 17%, psychology 6%, theological studies 13%.

Computing on campus. 675 workstations in dormitories, library, computer center, student center. Dormitories wired for high-speed internet access and linked to campus network. Commuter students can connect to campus network. Online library, helpline, repair service, student web hosting, wireless network available.

Student life. **Freshman orientation:** Mandatory. Preregistration for classes offered. Held the weekend before school begins. **Policies:** No alcohol allowed on campus; students attend chapel services 3 times weekly. Religious observance required. **Housing:** Guaranteed on-campus for all undergraduates. Single-sex dorms, special housing for disabled, apartments, wellness housing available. $100 fully refundable deposit, deadline 8/15. **Activities:** Bands, campus ministries, choral groups, drama, film society, international student organizations, literary magazine, music ensembles, musical theater, opera, radio station, student government, student newspaper, symphony orchestra, TV station, World Christian Fellowship, Fellowship of Christian Athletes, Habitat for Humanity, Young Republicans, College Libertarians, IWU Democrats.

Athletics. NAIA, NCCAA. **Intercollegiate:** Baseball M, basketball, cross-country, golf M, soccer, softball W, tennis, track and field, volleyball W. **Intramural:** Badminton, basketball, bowling, football (non-tackle), golf, racquetball, soccer, softball, swimming, table tennis, tennis, volleyball, water polo, weight lifting. **Team name:** Wildcats.

Student services. Adult student services, alcohol/substance abuse counseling, chaplain/spiritual director, career counseling, services for economically disadvantaged, student employment services, financial aid counseling, health services, minority student services, personal counseling, placement for graduates. **Physically disabled:** Services for visually, speech, hearing impaired. **Learning disabled:** Comprehensive services available.

Contact. E-mail: admissions@indwes.edu
Phone: (765) 677-2138 Toll-free number: (800) 332-6901
Fax: (765) 677-2333
Daniel Solms, Director of Admissions, Indiana Wesleyan University, 4201 South Washington Street, Marion, IN 46953-4999

International Business College
Fort Wayne, Indiana
www.ibcfortwayne.edu — **CB code: 1330**

- For-profit 4-year business and community college
- Small city
- 639 degree-seeking undergraduates
- Interview required

General. Founded in 1889. Accredited by ACICS. Branch campus located in Indianapolis. **Degrees:** 79 bachelor's, 198 associate awarded. **Location:** 4 miles from downtown. **Calendar:** Semester, extensive summer session. **Full-time faculty:** 15 total. **Part-time faculty:** 40 total.

Freshman class profile.

Out-of-state:	30%	**Live on campus:**	40%

Basis for selection. Open admission, but selective for some programs.

2008-2009 Annual costs. Tuition varies by program. Medical assisting program $600 per semester. Books/supplies: $900.

Application procedures. Admission: No deadline. $50 fee. Admission notification on a rolling basis. **Financial aid:** Closing date 5/1. Applicants notified by 9/15.

Academics. Special study options: Independent study, internships. **Credit/placement by examination:** CLEP. **Support services:** Tutoring.

Majors. Business: General.

Computing on campus. 146 workstations in library, computer center.

Student life. Freshman orientation: Available. **Housing:** Coed dorms, single-sex dorms available. **Activities:** Student government, accounting club, secretarial club.

Student services. Career counseling, student employment services, personal counseling, placement for graduates.

Contact. Phone: (260) 459-4500 Toll-free number: (800) 589-6363
Fax: (260) 436-1896
Steve Kinzer, Director of Admissions, International Business College, 5699 Coventry Lane, Fort Wayne, IN 46804

ITT Technical Institute: Fort Wayne
Fort Wayne, Indiana
www.itt-tech.edu — **CB code: 0650**

- For-profit 4-year technical college
- Commuter campus in large city

General. Founded in 1967. Accredited by ACICS. **Location:** 122 miles from Indianapolis. **Calendar:** Quarter.

Contact. Phone: (260) 484-4107
Director of Recruitment, 2810 Dupont Commerce Court, Fort Wayne, IN 46825

ITT Technical Institute: Indianapolis
Indianapolis, Indiana
www.itt-tech.edu — **CB code: 0640**

- For-profit 4-year technical college
- Commuter campus in very large city

General. Founded in 1956. Accredited by ACICS. **Location:** 10 miles from downtown. **Calendar:** Quarter.

Contact. Phone: (317) 875-8640
Director of Recruitment, 9511 Angola Court, Indianapolis, IN 46268-1119

Manchester College
North Manchester, Indiana — **CB member**
www.manchester.edu — **CB code: 1440**

- Private 4-year liberal arts college affiliated with Church of the Brethren
- Residential campus in small town
- 1,120 degree-seeking undergraduates: 1% part-time, 51% women, 4% African American, 1% Asian American, 2% Hispanic American, 1% Native American, 3% international
- 79% of applicants admitted
- SAT or ACT with writing required

General. Founded in 1889. Regionally accredited. **Degrees:** 180 bachelor's, 1 associate awarded; master's offered. **Location:** 35 miles from Fort Wayne, 100 miles from Indianapolis. **Calendar:** 4-1-4, limited summer session. **Full-time faculty:** 67 total; 82% have terminal degrees, 8% minority. **Part-time faculty:** 22 total; 36% have terminal degrees. **Class size:** 56% < 20, 38% 20-39, 5% 40-49, less than 1% 50-99. **Special facilities:** Observatory, 100-acre environmental studies and retreat center.

Freshman class profile. 2,389 applied, 1,897 admitted, 389 enrolled.

Mid 50% test scores			
SAT critical reading:	440-550	**Rank in top quarter:**	49%
SAT math:	470-580	**Rank in top tenth:**	20%
SAT writing:	430-540	**Out-of-state:**	11%
ACT composite:	19-24	**Live on campus:**	95%
		International:	2%

Basis for selection. School achievement record most important, with emphasis on college-preparatory courses, followed by SAT or ACT scores, class rank, recommendations. Interview recommended. Essay recommended for academically borderline applicants. Audition recommended for music majors. **Homeschooled:** Provide full information in detailed cover letter with application. **Learning Disabled:** School reviews ability to meet student needs.

High school preparation. 14 units required; 17 recommended. Required and recommended units include English 4, mathematics 2-3, social studies 2, history 1-2, science 2-3 (laboratory 2-3), foreign language 2 and academic electives 1-2.

2008-2009 Annual costs. Tuition/fees: $22,700. Health insurance and other fees as required. Room/board: $8,100. Books/supplies: $1,000. Personal expenses: $900.

2008-2009 Financial aid. Need-based: 380 full-time freshmen applied for aid; 337 were judged to have need; 337 of these received aid. Average need met was 87%. Average scholarship/grant was $16,557; average loan $4,580. 73% of total undergraduate aid awarded as scholarships/grants, 27% as loans/jobs. **Non-need-based:** Awarded to 820 full-time undergraduates, including 297 freshmen. Scholarships awarded for academics, alumni affiliation, minority status, music/drama, religious affiliation. **Additional information:** Students are automatically considered for all scholarship programs.

Application procedures. Admission: Priority date 5/1; no deadline. $25 fee, may be waived for applicants with need, free for online applicants. Admission notification on a rolling basis beginning on or about 9/1. Must reply by May 1 or within 2 week(s) if notified thereafter. **Financial aid:** Priority date 3/1; no closing date. FAFSA required. Applicants notified on a rolling basis starting 2/15; must reply within 2 week(s) of notification.

Academics. Students required to earn 2 credits in Values, Ideas and the Arts. **Special study options:** Accelerated study, cross-registration, double major, dual enrollment of high school students, exchange student, honors, independent study, internships, liberal arts/career combination, student-designed major, study abroad, teacher certification program, urban semester. Medical technology programs with area hospitals, 3-2 engineering dual-degree program with Washington University (MO) and others, 2-2 nursing program with Goshen College. **Credit/placement by examination:** AP, CLEP, IB, SAT, ACT, institutional tests. First year students take college proficiency tests to place out of the first year of modern language. Unlimited credit hours by examination may be counted toward associate or bachelor's degree. **Support services:** Learning center, reduced course load, study skills assistance, tutoring, writing center.

Majors. Area/ethnic studies: Women's. **Biology:** General, biochemistry. **Business:** General, accounting, banking/financial services, business admin, marketing, nonprofit/public. **Communications:** General, broadcast journalism, journalism. **Computer sciences:** General, computer science. **Conservation:** General, environmental studies. **Education:** General, biology, chemistry, elementary, English, foreign languages, French, German, health, history, mathematics, mentally handicapped, middle, multi-level teacher, music, physical, physics, science, secondary, social science, social studies, Spanish, special. **Engineering:** Science. **Foreign languages:** General, French, German, Spanish. **Health:** Clinical lab science, predental, premedicine, prepharmacy, preveterinary. **History:** General. **Interdisciplinary:** Global studies, math/computer science, peace/conflict. **Legal studies:** Prelaw. **Liberal arts:** Arts/sciences. **Math:** General. **Philosophy/religion:** Philosophy, religion. **Physical sciences:** Chemistry, physics. **Psychology:** General. **Public administration:** Social work. **Social sciences:** General, economics, political science, sociology. **Theology:** Sacred music. **Visual/performing arts:** Art, music performance.

Most popular majors. Business/marketing 29%, education 16%, health sciences 8%, psychology 6%, social sciences 6%.

Computing on campus. 165 workstations in dormitories, library, computer center. Dormitories wired for high-speed internet access and linked to campus network. Helpline, student web hosting available.

Student life. Freshman orientation: Mandatory, $125 fee. Preregistration for classes offered. Held the 3 days prior to start of fall classes. **Policies:** Significant student involvement in governance, programming, activities, and administrative services such as security, health, and residence hall management. Students under 21 required to live on-campus unless living with family. **Housing:** Guaranteed on-campus for freshmen. Coed dorms, single-sex dorms, special housing for disabled, apartments, wellness housing available. **Activities:** Bands, campus ministries, choral groups, dance, drama, international student organizations, literary magazine, music ensembles, Model UN, radio station, student government, student newspaper, symphony orchestra, political clubs, black student union, Hispanos Unidos, Habitat for Humanity, volunteer corps, intercollegiate ministries, Amnesty International, environmental club.

Athletics. NCAA. **Intercollegiate:** Baseball M, basketball, cross-country, football (tackle) M, golf, soccer, softball W, tennis, track and field, volleyball W, wrestling M. **Intramural:** Badminton, basketball, bowling, cross-country, golf, racquetball, soccer, softball, swimming, table tennis, tennis, track and field, volleyball, wrestling M. **Team name:** Spartans.

Student services. Chaplain/spiritual director, career counseling, student employment services, financial aid counseling, health services, minority student services, personal counseling, placement for graduates, veterans' counselor. **Physically disabled:** Services for visually, hearing impaired.

Contact. E-mail: admitinfo@manchester.edu
Phone: (260) 982-5055 Toll-free number: (800) 852-3648
Fax: (260) 982-5239
Stuart Jones, Dean of Enrollment, Manchester College, 604 East College Avenue, North Manchester, IN 46962-0365

Marian College

Indianapolis, Indiana — **CB member**
www.marian.edu — **CB code: 1442**

- Private 4-year liberal arts college affiliated with Roman Catholic Church
- Residential campus in very large city
- 1,892 degree-seeking undergraduates: 25% part-time, 66% women, 17% African American, 1% Asian American, 3% Hispanic American
- 135 degree-seeking graduate students
- 54% of applicants admitted
- SAT or ACT with writing required
- 52% graduate within 6 years; 20% enter graduate study

General. Founded in 1851. Regionally accredited. **Degrees:** 313 bachelor's, 111 associate awarded; master's offered. **ROTC:** Army. **Location:** 4 miles from downtown. **Calendar:** Semester, limited summer session. **Full-time faculty:** 96 total; 45% have terminal degrees, 5% minority, 49% women. **Part-time faculty:** 103 total; 16% have terminal degrees, 3% minority, 59% women. **Class size:** 65% < 20, 31% 20-39, 2% 40-49, 3% 50-99. **Special facilities:** Archives (materials on development of education in Archdiocese), 35 acre wetlands biology/ecology laboratory, Allison and Wheeler-Stokely mansions, Japanese tea house and garden, undergraduate seminary.

Freshman class profile. 1,705 applied, 922 admitted, 338 enrolled.

Mid 50% test scores		**GPA 2.0-2.99:**	33%
SAT critical reading:	450-560	**Rank in top quarter:**	39%
SAT math:	470-570	**Rank in top tenth:**	12%
ACT composite:	19-24	**End year in good standing:**	87%
GPA 3.75 or higher:	21%	**Return as sophomores:**	70%
GPA 3.50-3.74:	14%	**Out-of-state:**	1%
GPA 3.0-3.49:	31%	**Live on campus:**	81%

Basis for selection. School achievement record, test scores, recommendations important. Interview recommended. Essay recommended for academically weak applicants. **Homeschooled:** Transcript of courses and grades required.

High school preparation. College-preparatory program recommended. 20 units required. Required and recommended units include English 4, mathematics 2-3, social studies 1, history 1, science 2-3 (laboratory 2), foreign language 1-2 and academic electives 9.

2008-2009 Annual costs. Tuition/fees: $22,400. Room/board: $7,228. Books/supplies: $1,200. Personal expenses: $900.

2008-2009 Financial aid. Need-based: 309 full-time freshmen applied for aid; 264 were judged to have need; 264 of these received aid. Average need met was 87%. Average scholarship/grant was $11,257; average loan $3,506. 65% of total undergraduate aid awarded as scholarships/grants, 35% as loans/jobs. **Non-need-based:** Scholarships awarded for academics, alumni affiliation, art, athletics, leadership, music/drama, religious affiliation.

Application procedures. Admission: Priority date 3/1; deadline 8/1. $20 fee, may be waived for applicants with need, free for online applicants. Admission notification on a rolling basis beginning on or about 9/1. Must reply by May 1 or within 2 week(s) if notified thereafter. **Financial aid:** Priority date 3/15; no closing date. FAFSA, institutional form required. Applicants notified on a rolling basis starting 3/15; must reply within 2 week(s) of notification.

Academics. Special study options: Accelerated study, cooperative education, cross-registration, double major, dual enrollment of high school students, honors, independent study, internships, liberal arts/career combination, study abroad, teacher certification program. **Credit/placement by examination:** AP, CLEP, IB, SAT, ACT, institutional tests. 30 credit hours maximum toward associate degree, 60 toward bachelor's. **Support services:** Learning center, reduced course load, remedial instruction, study skills assistance, tutoring, writing center.

Majors. Biology: General. **Business:** General, accounting, finance, management information systems, marketing. **Communications:** General. **Education:** Elementary, physical. **Foreign languages:** French, Spanish. **Health:** Nursing (RN). **History:** General. **Math:** General. **Parks/recreation:** Sports admin. **Philosophy/religion:** Philosophy. **Physical sciences:** Chemistry. **Psychology:** General. **Social sciences:** Economics, political science, sociology. **Theology:** Religious ed, theology. **Visual/performing arts:** Art, art history/conservation, commercial/advertising art.

Computing on campus. 225 workstations in dormitories, library, computer center, student center. Dormitories wired for high-speed internet access and linked to campus network. Online library, helpline, wireless network available.

Student life. Freshman orientation: Mandatory. Preregistration for classes offered. Held weekend prior to start of school. Community service project required. **Policies:** Drinking under the age of 21 on campus prohibited. **Housing:** Guaranteed on-campus for freshmen. Coed dorms, single-sex dorms, apartments, cooperative housing, wellness housing available. $125 fully refundable deposit, deadline 5/1. College-owned apartments for students 21 or older, voluntary spiritual living community, nonsmoking areas, suite-style rooms, singles available. **Activities:** Bands, campus ministries, choral groups, dance, drama, international student organizations, literary magazine, music ensembles, musical theater, student government, student newspaper, service organization, Campus America Life League, BACCHUS, Project Earth, community ministries, union for black identity, Fellowship of Christian Athletes, Campus Crusade for Christ.

Athletics. NAIA. **Intercollegiate:** Baseball M, basketball, cheerleading, cross-country, football (tackle) M, golf, soccer, softball W, tennis, track and field, volleyball W. **Intramural:** Basketball, football (non-tackle), racquetball, softball W, volleyball W. **Team name:** Knights.

Student services. Adult student services, alcohol/substance abuse counseling, chaplain/spiritual director, career counseling, student employment services, financial aid counseling, health services, personal counseling, placement for graduates. **Physically disabled:** Services for visually, hearing impaired.

Contact. E-mail: admissions@marian.edu
Phone: (317) 955-6300 Toll-free number: (800) 772-7264
Fax: (317) 955-6401
Luann Brames, Director of Enrollment, Marian College, 3200 Cold Spring Road, Indianapolis, IN 46222-1997

Martin University
Indianapolis, Indiana
www.martin.edu **CB code: 1379**

- Private 4-year university and liberal arts college
- Commuter campus in very large city
- 1,212 degree-seeking undergraduates: 72% part-time, 69% women
- 162 degree-seeking graduate students
- Interview required

General. Founded in 1977. Regionally accredited. **Degrees:** 75 bachelor's awarded; master's offered. **Calendar:** Semester, extensive summer session. **Full-time faculty:** 26 total; 85% have terminal degrees, 58% minority, 54% women. **Part-time faculty:** 17 total; 82% have terminal degrees, 82% minority, 24% women.

Freshman class profile. 318 applied, 309 admitted, 309 enrolled.

Basis for selection. Open admission.

2008-2009 Annual costs. Tuition/fees: $13,520. Books/supplies: $1,000. Personal expenses: $1,300.

Application procedures. Admission: Priority date 3/1; no deadline. $25 fee, may be waived for applicants with need. Application must be submitted on paper. Admission notification on a rolling basis. **Financial aid:** Priority date 5/1; no closing date. FAFSA required. Applicants notified on a rolling basis starting 6/1; must reply within 2 week(s) of notification.

Academics. Special study options: Accelerated study, cross-registration, double major, internships, liberal arts/career combination, student-designed major. **Credit/placement by examination:** CLEP. **Support services:** Learning center, remedial instruction, tutoring.

Majors. Biology: General. **Business:** General, accounting, insurance. **Conservation:** Environmental science. **Education:** Early childhood. **Health:** Substance abuse counseling. **Interdisciplinary:** Gerontology. **Liberal arts:** Arts/sciences. **Philosophy/religion:** Religion. **Physical sciences:** Chemistry. **Protective services:** Criminal justice. **Psychology:** General. **Social sciences:** Sociology.

Most popular majors. Biology 9%, business/marketing 18%, legal studies 9%, liberal arts 24%, philosophy/religious studies 9%, psychology 20%.

Computing on campus. 14 workstations in computer center.

Student life. Activities: Choral groups, dance, drama, music ensembles, opera, student government, student newspaper, GIFT of Brightwood.

Student services. Adult student services, career counseling, student employment services, health services, personal counseling, placement for graduates, veterans' counselor.

Contact. E-mail: bshaheed@martin.edu
Phone: (317) 917-3329 Fax: (317) 543-4790
Brenda Shaheed, Vice President for Student Affairs, Martin University, 2171 Avondale Place, Indianapolis, IN 46218

Oakland City University
Oakland City, Indiana
www.oak.edu **CB code: 1585**

- Private 4-year university and liberal arts college affiliated with Baptist General Conference
- Commuter campus in small town
- 1,529 degree-seeking undergraduates
- 223 graduate students
- SAT or ACT required

General. Founded in 1885. Regionally accredited. Branches in Bedford and at Branchville Training Center. Accelerated degrees offered at several off-campus sites (National Guard bases and civilian locations), Rockville Training Center, Madison Correctional Facility, NewCastle Correctional Facility, Miami Correctional Center, and Indiana Women's Prison. **Degrees:** 294 bachelor's, 185 associate awarded; master's, doctoral, first professional offered. **Location:** 30 miles from Evansville. **Calendar:** Semester, limited summer session. **Full-time faculty:** 65 total. **Part-time faculty:** 19 total. **Class size:** 81% < 20, 19% 20-39, less than 1% 40-49.

Freshman class profile. 402 applied, 331 admitted, 285 enrolled.

Mid 50% test scores		**GPA 3.50-3.74:**	14%
SAT critical reading:	400-510	**GPA 3.0-3.49:**	31%
SAT math:	420-530	**GPA 2.0-2.99:**	27%
SAT writing:	400-500	**Rank in top quarter:**	16%
ACT composite:	17-23	**Rank in top tenth:**	9%
GPA 3.75 or higher:	16%	**Out-of-state:**	10%

Basis for selection. Open admission, but selective for some programs. 2.5 high school GPA and SAT/ACT test scores most important. Recommendations considered. Interview and essay recommended. **Homeschooled:** Transcript of courses and grades required.

High school preparation. 12 units recommended. Recommended units include English 4, mathematics 3, social studies 2 and science 3.

2008-2009 Annual costs. Tuition/fees: $15,360. Room/board: $6,228. Books/supplies: $1,500. Personal expenses: $1,500.

2008-2009 Financial aid. Non-need-based: Scholarships awarded for academics, alumni affiliation, art, athletics, minority status, music/drama, religious affiliation.

Application procedures. Admission: Closing date 9/8 (receipt date). $35 fee, may be waived for applicants with need. Admission notification on a rolling basis. **Financial aid:** Closing date 3/1. FAFSA required. Applicants notified on a rolling basis starting 5/1.

Academics. Special study options: Accelerated study, combined bachelor's/graduate degree, cooperative education, distance learning, double major, dual enrollment of high school students, external degree, honors, independent study, internships, liberal arts/career combination, teacher certification program. Combined bachelor's/graduate degree: M.S. in Management. **Credit/placement by examination:** AP, CLEP, IB, institutional tests. 16 credit hours maximum toward associate degree, 32 toward bachelor's. **Support services:** Learning center, pre-admission summer program, reduced course load, remedial instruction, tutoring.

Majors. Biology: General. **Business:** General, accounting, business admin, human resources, management information systems, organizational behavior. **Computer sciences:** General. **Education:** Art, biology, business, early childhood, elementary, English, health, history, mathematics, music, physical, reading, science, social science, social studies, special, voc/tech. **History:** General. **Liberal arts:** Arts/sciences, humanities. **Math:** Applied. **Parks/recreation:** Health/fitness. **Philosophy/religion:** Religion. **Protective services:** Criminal justice. **Psychology:** General. **Social sciences:** General, sociology. **Visual/performing arts:** Art, graphic design, industrial design, music performance.

Most popular majors. Business/marketing 59%, education 15%, liberal arts 7%.

Computing on campus. 92 workstations in library, computer center, student center. Dormitories wired for high-speed internet access and linked to campus network. Commuter students can connect to campus network. Online library, wireless network available.

Student life. Freshman orientation: Mandatory, $75 fee. Preregistration for classes offered. One day immediately before each semester. **Housing:** Guaranteed on-campus for all undergraduates. Single-sex dorms, apartments, wellness housing available. $100 fully refundable deposit, deadline 7/22. **Activities:** Pep band, choral groups, drama, music ensembles, student government, student newspaper, mental health assistance group, Circle-K, Student Christian Association, Fellowship of Christian Athletes, Theologs, student education association.

Athletics. NCAA, NCCAA. **Intercollegiate:** Baseball M, basketball, cheerleading M, cross-country, golf, soccer, softball W, tennis, volleyball W. **Intramural:** Basketball, bowling, football (non-tackle), softball, table tennis, tennis, volleyball. **Team name:** Oaks.

Student services. Adult student services, chaplain/spiritual director, career counseling, services for economically disadvantaged, student employment services, financial aid counseling, personal counseling, placement for graduates, veterans' counselor.

Contact. E-mail: ocuadmit@oak.edu
Phone: (812) 749-4781 ext. 222 Toll-free number: (800) 737-5125
Fax: (812) 749-1433
Betty Burns, Director of Admissions, Oakland City University, 138 North Lucretia Street, Oakland City, IN 47660

Purdue University

West Lafayette, Indiana — **CB member**
www.purdue.edu — **CB code: 1631**

- Public 4-year university
- Residential campus in small city
- 31,491 degree-seeking undergraduates: 4% part-time, 42% women, 3% African American, 6% Asian American, 3% Hispanic American, 1% Native American, 7% international
- 8,052 degree-seeking graduate students
- 72% of applicants admitted
- SAT or ACT with writing, application essay required
- 72% graduate within 6 years

General. Founded in 1869. Regionally accredited. **Degrees:** 5,940 bachelor's, 458 associate awarded; master's, doctoral, first professional offered. **ROTC:** Army, Naval, Air Force. **Location:** 65 miles from Indianapolis. **Calendar:** Semester, limited summer session. **Full-time faculty:** 2,109 total; 84% have terminal degrees, 18% minority, 30% women. **Part-time faculty:** 315 total; 41% have terminal degrees, 7% minority, 54% women. **Class size:** 34% < 20, 40% 20-39, 6% 40-49, 11% 50-99, 9% >100. **Special facilities:** Linear accelerator, horticultural park, concert hall, 3 theaters, outdoor concert facility, 2 professional golf courses, on-campus airport.

Freshman class profile. 29,952 applied, 21,423 admitted, 7,063 enrolled.

Mid 50% test scores			
SAT critical reading:	490-610	GPA 2.0-2.99:	10%
SAT math:	530-660	Rank in top quarter:	65%
SAT writing:	490-600	Rank in top tenth:	30%
ACT composite:	23-28	End year in good standing:	91%
GPA 3.75 or higher:	35%	Return as sophomores:	86%
GPA 3.50-3.74:	23%	Out-of-state:	31%
GPA 3.0-3.49:	32%	International:	7%

Basis for selection. Rigor of high school curriculum, standardized test scores, GPA and information provided by both applicant and high school counselor considered. Interview required for veterinary medicine, veterinary technology and pharmacy applicants.

High school preparation. Required and recommended units include English 4, mathematics 3-4, social studies 3, science 2-3 (laboratory 2-3) and foreign language 2.

2008-2009 Annual costs. Tuition/fees: $7,750; $23,224 out-of-state. Engineering students pay additional $656 fee per year. Management students pay additional $1,022 fee per year. Room/board: $7,930. Books/supplies: $1,050. Personal expenses: $1,690.

2008-2009 Financial aid. Non-need-based: Scholarships awarded for academics, athletics, leadership, music/drama, ROTC, state residency. **Additional information:** Cooperative work for credit available in many programs.

Application procedures. Admission: Priority date 11/15; deadline 3/1 (receipt date). $30 fee, may be waived for applicants with need. Admission notification on a rolling basis beginning on or about 12/5. Must reply by May 1 or within 3 week(s) if notified thereafter. November 15 deadline for flight technology program, veterinary technology program, preferential deadline for pre-pharmacy, health sciences and nursing, and scholarships. **Financial aid:** Priority date 3/1; no closing date. FAFSA required. Applicants notified by 4/15.

Academics. Minimal number of courses outside major allowed on pass/fail basis, not to exceed 20% of total credit hours required. **Special study options:** Accelerated study, combined bachelor's/graduate degree, cooperative education, cross-registration, distance learning, double major, dual enrollment of high school students, exchange student, honors, independent study, internships, liberal arts/career combination, New York semester, study abroad, teacher certification program, weekend college. **Credit/placement by examination:** AP, CLEP, IB, SAT, ACT, institutional tests. **Support services:** Learning center, pre-admission summer program, reduced course load, remedial instruction, study skills assistance, tutoring, writing center.

Majors. Agriculture: General, agronomy, animal sciences, communications, economics, farm/ranch, food science, horticultural science, horticulture, mechanization, production, products processing. **Architecture:** Landscape. **Area/ethnic studies:** African-American, Asian, French, German, Japanese, women's. **Biology:** General, biochemistry, Biochemistry/biophysics and molecular biology, botany, cellular/molecular, entomology, microbiology, molecular, plant genetics, zoology. **Business:** Accounting, accounting/business management, accounting/finance, actuarial science, business admin, fashion, financial planning, hospitality admin, hotel/motel admin, human resources, marketing, operations, tourism/travel. **Communications:** General, advertising, broadcast journalism, journalism, public relations. **Computer sciences:** General, computer graphics, computer science, networking. **Conservation:** General, environmental science, fisheries, forestry, wildlife. **Education:** General, agricultural, art, biology, chemistry, early childhood, early childhood special, elementary, family/consumer sciences, foreign languages, French, German, health, kindergarten/preschool, mathematics, multi-level teacher, physical, physics, secondary, social studies, Spanish, technology/industrial arts. **Engineering:** Aerospace, agricultural, biomedical, chemical, civil, computer, construction, electrical, industrial, materials, mechanical, nuclear, surveying. **Engineering technology:** Aerospace, architectural, computer, construction, electrical, industrial, industrial management, manufacturing, mechanical, mechanical drafting, robotics, surveying. **Family/consumer sciences:** General, clothing/textiles, family studies, family/community services, food/nutrition. **Foreign languages:** General, classics, Japanese, Russian, Spanish. **Health:** Athletic training, audiology/hearing, audiology/speech pathology, clinical lab science, dietetic technician, health services, nursing (RN), occupational health, predental, premedicine, speech pathology, veterinary technology/assistant. **History:** General. **Interdisciplinary:** Biological/physical sciences, nutrition sciences. **Liberal arts:** Arts/sciences, humanities. **Math:** General, applied, statistics. **Parks/recreation:** Exercise sciences, health/fitness. **Philosophy/religion:** Philosophy, religion. **Physical sciences:** Atmospheric science, chemistry, geology, meteorology, physics. **Protective services:** Law enforcement admin. **Psychology:** General. **Public administration:** Social work. **Social sciences:** General, anthropology, political science, sociology. **Transportation:** Air traffic control, airline/commercial pilot, aviation, aviation management. **Visual/performing arts:** General, acting, art, art history/conservation, design, dramatic, fashion design, film/cinema, interior design, photography, studio arts.

Most popular majors. Business/marketing 15%, education 7%, engineering/engineering technologies 26%, family/consumer sciences 6%, health sciences 8%, social sciences 6%.

Computing on campus. 5,783 workstations in dormitories, library, computer center, student center. Dormitories wired for high-speed internet access and linked to campus network. Commuter students can connect to campus network. Online course registration, helpline, wireless network available.

Student life. Freshman orientation: Available, $320 fee. Preregistration for classes offered. Held the week before classes. **Policies:** Nondiscrimination, antiharassment, antihazing policies; bill of students' rights. **Housing:** Coed dorms, single-sex dorms, special housing for disabled, apartments, cooperative housing, fraternity/sorority housing, wellness housing available. $100 nonrefundable deposit, deadline 4/30. **Activities:** Bands, campus ministries, choral groups, dance, drama, international student organizations, literary magazine, music ensembles, radio station, student government, student newspaper, symphony orchestra, TV station, Over 850 religious, political, ethnic, academic, hobby and social service organizations.

Athletics. NCAA. **Intercollegiate:** Baseball M, basketball, cross-country, diving, football (tackle) M, golf, soccer W, softball W, swimming, tennis, track and field, volleyball W, wrestling M. **Intramural:** Badminton, basketball, cross-country, football (non-tackle), golf, racquetball, soccer, softball, swimming, table tennis, tennis, track and field, volleyball. **Team name:** Boilermakers.

Student services. Adult student services, alcohol/substance abuse counseling, career counseling, services for economically disadvantaged, student employment services, financial aid counseling, health services, legal services, minority student services, on-campus daycare, personal counseling, placement for graduates, veterans' counselor, women's services. **Physically disabled:** Services for visually, speech, hearing impaired.

Contact. E-mail: admissions@purdue.edu
Phone: (765) 494-1776 Fax: (765) 494-0544
Pamela Horne, Dean of Admissions, Purdue University, 475 Stadium Mall Drive, West Lafayette, IN 47907-2050

Purdue University Calumet

Hammond, Indiana — **CB member**
www.calumet.purdue.edu — **CB code: 1638**

- Public 4-year university and branch campus college
- Commuter campus in small city

- 8,053 degree-seeking undergraduates: 32% part-time, 56% women, 18% African American, 1% Asian American, 15% Hispanic American, 4% international
- 769 degree-seeking graduate students
- 74% of applicants admitted
- SAT or ACT with writing required

General. Founded in 1943. Regionally accredited. Experiential learning curricular components required by all undergraduate students. **Degrees:** 861 bachelor's, 251 associate awarded; master's offered. **ROTC:** Army. **Location:** 20 miles from Chicago. **Calendar:** Semester, extensive summer session. **Full-time faculty:** 264 total; 68% have terminal degrees, 24% minority, 45% women. **Part-time faculty:** 135 total; 14% have terminal degrees, 16% minority, 43% women. **Class size:** 26% < 20, 64% 20-39, 5% 40-49, 5% 50-99, less than 1% >100.

Freshman class profile. 3,208 applied, 2,380 admitted, 1,382 enrolled.

Mid 50% test scores		**Rank in top quarter:**	26%
SAT critical reading:	410-510	**Rank in top tenth:**	10%
SAT math:	400-520	**Return as sophomores:**	63%
GPA 3.75 or higher:	7%	**Out-of-state:**	15%
GPA 3.50-3.74:	7%	**Live on campus:**	9%
GPA 3.0-3.49:	21%	**International:**	7%
GPA 2.0-2.99:	53%		

Basis for selection. Class rank, grade average in subjects related to degree objectives, trends in achievement throughout high school, satisfactory high school subject matter requirements, strength of college preparatory program, and standardized test results most important. Graduation from high school with minimum of 15 units of credit required. **Homeschooled:** Transcript of courses and grades required.

High school preparation. College-preparatory program recommended. 14 units recommended. Recommended units include English 4, mathematics 2, social studies 1, history 1, science 2 and foreign language 2. Course requirements vary according to program.

2008-2009 Annual costs. Tuition/fees: $5,970; $13,279 out-of-state. Books/supplies: $1,050.

2007-2008 Financial aid. **Need-based:** 920 full-time freshmen applied for aid; 712 were judged to have need; 632 of these received aid. Average need met was 11%. Average scholarship/grant was $2,812; average loan $1,816. 37% of total undergraduate aid awarded as scholarships/grants, 63% as loans/jobs. **Non-need-based:** Awarded to 849 full-time undergraduates, including 243 freshmen. Scholarships awarded for academics, alumni affiliation, athletics, minority status, state residency.

Application procedures. **Admission:** No deadline. No application fee. Admission notification on a rolling basis. **Financial aid:** Priority date 3/10, closing date 6/30. FAFSA required. Applicants notified on a rolling basis starting 5/1; must reply within 2 week(s) of notification.

Academics. **Special study options:** Combined bachelor's/graduate degree, cooperative education, distance learning, double major, dual enrollment of high school students, ESL, honors, independent study, internships, study abroad, teacher certification program, weekend college. **Credit/placement by examination:** AP, CLEP, SAT, ACT, institutional tests. **Support services:** Learning center, reduced course load, remedial instruction, study skills assistance, tutoring, writing center.

Honors college/program. 3.5 GPA, 27 ACT/1200 SAT (exclusive of Writing) required. Must maintain 3.5. Additional factors include outstanding academic achievement, strength of academic program, demonstrated leadership, creativity, community involvement, essay, and letter(s) of recommendation.

Majors. **Biology:** General. **Business:** General, accounting, business admin, entrepreneurial studies, finance, human resources, retailing, small business admin. **Communications:** General, broadcast journalism, journalism, public relations. **Computer sciences:** General, computer graphics, computer science, database management, information systems, networking, programming. **Education:** General, biology, chemistry, early childhood, elementary, English, French, multi-level teacher, physics, science, secondary, social science, social studies, special. **Engineering:** General, computer, electrical, mechanical, mechanics, software. **Engineering technology:** Construction, electrical, industrial management. **Foreign languages:** General, French, Spanish. **Health:** Clinical lab science, nursing (RN), premedicine, preop/surgical nursing, prepharmacy, preveterinary. **History:** General. **Interdisciplinary:** Gerontology, math/computer science. **Legal studies:** Prelaw. **Math:** General, applied. **Philosophy/religion:** Philosophy. **Physical sciences:** Chemistry, physics. **Protective services:** Law enforcement admin. **Psychology:** General. **Social sciences:** Political science, sociology.

Most popular majors. Business/marketing 26%, communications/journalism 7%, education 8%, engineering/engineering technologies 16%, health sciences 7%, social sciences 9%.

Computing on campus. 1,500 workstations in library, computer center, student center. Dormitories wired for high-speed internet access and linked to campus network. Commuter students can connect to campus network. Online course registration, online library, helpline, wireless network available.

Student life. **Freshman orientation:** Mandatory. Preregistration for classes offered. **Housing:** Apartments, wellness housing available. **Activities:** Campus ministries, choral groups, dance, drama, international student organizations, literary magazine, musical theater, radio station, student government, student newspaper, TV station, black student union, Los Latinos, Society of Professional Hispanic Engineers, InterVarsity Christian Fellowship, Muslim student association, New Life Ministries, National Society of Black Engineers, Indian students association, Korean student organization, social justice club.

Athletics. NAIA. **Intercollegiate:** Basketball, cheerleading. **Intramural:** Basketball, bowling, golf, racquetball, sailing, soccer, softball, table tennis, volleyball, weight lifting. **Team name:** Peregrines.

Student services. Adult student services, career counseling, student employment services, financial aid counseling, health services, on-campus daycare, personal counseling, placement for graduates, veterans' counselor. **Physically disabled:** Services for visually, speech, hearing impaired.

Contact. E-mail: adms@calumet.purdue.edu
Phone: (219) 989-2213 Toll-free number: (800) 447-76383 ext. 2213
Fax: (219) 989-2775
Paul McGuinness, Director of Admissions, Purdue University Calumet, 2200 169th Street, Hammond, IN 46323-2094

Purdue University North Central

Westville, Indiana — **CB member**
www.pnc.edu — **CB code: 1640**

- Public 4-year branch campus college
- Commuter campus in rural community
- 3,762 degree-seeking undergraduates: 33% part-time, 58% women, 7% African American, 1% Asian American, 5% Hispanic American, 1% Native American
- 100 degree-seeking graduate students
- 84% of applicants admitted

General. Founded in 1943. Regionally accredited. **Degrees:** 321 bachelor's, 186 associate awarded; master's offered. **Location:** 10 miles from Michigan City, 13 miles from Laporte. **Calendar:** Semester, limited summer session. **Full-time faculty:** 119 total; 57% have terminal degrees, 17% minority, 43% women. **Part-time faculty:** 170 total; 16% have terminal degrees, 6% minority, 50% women. **Class size:** 55% < 20, 42% 20-39, 2% 40-49, 2% 50-99, less than 1% >100.

Freshman class profile. 1,508 applied, 1,273 admitted, 913 enrolled.

Mid 50% test scores		**GPA 3.0-3.49:**	26%
SAT critical reading:	410-520	**GPA 2.0-2.99:**	54%
SAT math:	420-530	**Rank in top quarter:**	19%
SAT writing:	390-510	**Rank in top tenth:**	6%
ACT composite:	17-22	**Return as sophomores:**	57%
GPA 3.75 or higher:	5%	**Out-of-state:**	2%
GPA 3.50-3.74:	7%		

Basis for selection. Class rank and test scores important. Admission requirements are reduced for community college division. SAT or ACT recommended. Interview recommended for academically weak applicants.

High school preparation. College-preparatory program recommended. 15 units recommended. Recommended units include English 4, mathematics 3, social studies 1, history 1, science 3 (laboratory 3).

2008-2009 Annual costs. Tuition/fees: $6,080; $14,205 out-of-state. Books/supplies: $1,749. Personal expenses: $1,616.

2008-2009 Financial aid. All financial aid based on need. 562 full-time freshmen applied for aid; 443 were judged to have need; 405 of these received aid. Average need met was 36%. Average scholarship/grant was $3,960; average loan $3,092. 51% of total undergraduate aid awarded as scholarships/grants, 49% as loans/jobs.

Application procedures. **Admission:** Priority date 8/1; no deadline. No application fee. Admission notification on a rolling basis. **Financial aid:**

Priority date 3/10, closing date 6/30. FAFSA required. Applicants notified on a rolling basis starting 5/31; must reply within 2 week(s) of notification.

Academics. **Special study options:** Combined bachelor's/graduate degree, distance learning, dual enrollment of high school students, independent study, internships, teacher certification program, weekend college. **Credit/placement by examination:** AP, CLEP, SAT, ACT, institutional tests. **Support services:** Learning center, reduced course load, remedial instruction, tutoring, writing center.

Majors. **Biology:** General. **Business:** General, accounting, human resources, labor relations, operations. **Communications:** General. **Computer sciences:** Applications programming, data processing. **Education:** Early childhood, elementary. **Engineering:** Mechanical. **Engineering technology:** General, electrical, mechanical. **Health:** Nursing (RN). **Liberal arts:** Arts/sciences.

Most popular majors. Business/marketing 28%, education 11%, engineering/engineering technologies 15%, interdisciplinary studies 9%, liberal arts 23%.

Computing on campus. 240 workstations in library, computer center. Commuter students can connect to campus network. Online course registration, online library, helpline, wireless network available.

Student life. **Freshman orientation:** Available. **Activities:** Campus ministries, drama, literary magazine, student government, student newspaper, Campus Crusade for Christ, computer club, photography club, accounting club, student cultural society, Students in Fall Enterprise.

Athletics. NAIA. **Intercollegiate:** Baseball M, basketball M, cross-country M, softball W, volleyball W. **Intramural:** Basketball, bowling, cross-country, football (tackle) M, golf, skiing, softball, table tennis, tennis, volleyball. **Team name:** Panthers.

Student services. Career counseling, student employment services, on-campus daycare, personal counseling, placement for graduates. **Physically disabled:** Services for visually, hearing impaired.

Contact. E-mail: admissions@pnc.edu
Phone: (219) 785-5505 Toll-free number: (800) 782-1231
Fax: (219) 785-5538
Anthony Cardenas, Director of Admissions, Purdue University North Central, 1401 South US Highway 421, Westville, IN 46391-9542

Rose-Hulman Institute of Technology

Terre Haute, Indiana — **CB member**
www.rose-hulman.edu — **CB code: 1668**

- Private 4-year engineering college
- Residential campus in small city
- 1,818 degree-seeking undergraduates: 20% women, 2% African American, 5% Asian American, 2% Hispanic American, 2% international
- 91 degree-seeking graduate students
- 70% of applicants admitted
- SAT or ACT (ACT writing optional) required
- 79% graduate within 6 years; 21% enter graduate study

General. Founded in 1874. Regionally accredited. **Degrees:** 417 bachelor's awarded; master's offered. **ROTC:** Army, Air Force. **Location:** 73 miles from Indianapolis. **Calendar:** Quarter, limited summer session. **Full-time faculty:** 164 total; 99% have terminal degrees, 10% minority, 23% women. **Part-time faculty:** 8 total; 88% have terminal degrees, 12% minority, 38% women. **Class size:** 39% < 20, 61% 20-39, less than 1% 40-49. **Special facilities:** Advanced learning center, observatory, center for technological research with industry.

Freshman class profile. 3,165 applied, 2,226 admitted, 482 enrolled.

Mid 50% test scores		**End year in good standing:**	83%
SAT critical reading:	550-660	**Return as sophomores:**	90%
SAT math:	620-720	**Out-of-state:**	57%
SAT writing:	530-640	**Live on campus:**	98%
ACT composite:	26-31	**International:**	2%
Rank in top quarter:	88%	**Fraternities:**	35%
Rank in top tenth:	57%	**Sororities:**	21%

Basis for selection. GED not accepted. Primary consideration given to school achievement record and subjects taken. Applicants must rank in top quarter of graduating class. Test scores also very important. Recommendations important. Extracurricular and leadership activities, alumni ties considered. Interviews, although not required, can be determining factor. **Homeschooled:** Statement describing homeschool structure and mission, transcript of courses and grades, letter of recommendation (nonparent) required. Lab courses must have been taken at high school or community college.

High school preparation. College-preparatory program required. 16 units required. Required and recommended units include English 4, mathematics 4-5, social studies 2, science 2-3 (laboratory 2) and academic electives 4.

2008-2009 Annual costs. Tuition/fees: $32,826. Purchase of laptop computer (approximately $2,500) required of freshmen. Room/board: $8,868. Books/supplies: $1,500. Personal expenses: $1,500.

2008-2009 Financial aid. **Need-based:** 419 full-time freshmen applied for aid; 351 were judged to have need; 351 of these received aid. Average need met was 85%. Average scholarship/grant was $20,042; average loan $12,642. 49% of total undergraduate aid awarded as scholarships/grants, 51% as loans/jobs. **Non-need-based:** Awarded to 539 full-time undergraduates, including 125 freshmen. Scholarships awarded for academics, minority status, ROTC.

Application procedures. **Admission:** Priority date 12/1; deadline 3/1 (postmark date). $40 fee, may be waived for applicants with need, free for online applicants. Admission notification on a rolling basis beginning on or about 10/1. Must reply by 5/1. **Financial aid:** Priority date 3/1; no closing date. FAFSA required. Applicants notified on a rolling basis starting 3/10.

Academics. Area minor programs in science, engineering, humanities and social sciences. Additional certificate and interdisciplinary programs available in imaging systems, technical translation, consulting engineering, semiconductor materials and devices, and management studies. **Special study options:** Accelerated study, cooperative education, cross-registration, double major, independent study, internships, study abroad. **Credit/placement by examination:** AP, CLEP, IB, institutional tests. **Support services:** Learning center, reduced course load, study skills assistance, tutoring, writing center.

Majors. **Biology:** General. **Computer sciences:** Computer science. **Engineering:** Biomedical, chemical, civil, computer, electrical, mechanical, physics, software. **Math:** General. **Physical sciences:** Chemistry, physics. **Social sciences:** Economics. **Other:** Optical Engineering.

Most popular majors. Computer/information sciences 10%, engineering/engineering technologies 78%.

Computing on campus. PC or laptop required. 14 workstations in library. Dormitories wired for high-speed internet access and linked to campus network. Commuter students can connect to campus network. Online course registration, online library, helpline, repair service, student web hosting, wireless network available.

Student life. **Freshman orientation:** Mandatory. **Housing:** Guaranteed on-campus for freshmen. Coed dorms, single-sex dorms, apartments, fraternity/sorority housing available. $75 fully refundable deposit, deadline 6/15. **Activities:** Bands, choral groups, dance, drama, international student organizations, literary magazine, music ensembles, musical theater, radio station, student government, student newspaper, Inter-Varsity Christian Fellowship, Circle K, National Society of Black Engineers, Spanish club, student activities board, Society of Woman Engineers, Alpha Phi Omega Service Fraternity, Catholic campus ministry.

Athletics. NCAA. **Intercollegiate:** Baseball M, basketball, cheerleading M, cross-country, diving, football (tackle) M, golf, rifle, soccer, softball W, swimming, tennis, track and field, volleyball W, wrestling M. **Intramural:** Basketball, cross-country, football (non-tackle), golf, racquetball, soccer, softball, swimming, table tennis, tennis, track and field, volleyball. **Team name:** Fightin' Engineers.

Student services. Alcohol/substance abuse counseling, career counseling, student employment services, financial aid counseling, health services, personal counseling, placement for graduates.

Contact. E-mail: admissions@rose-hulman.edu
Phone: (812) 877-8213 Toll-free number: (800) 248-7448
Fax: (812) 877-8941
James Goecker, Dean of Admissions and Financial Aid, Rose-Hulman Institute of Technology, Office of Admissions, Terre Haute, IN 47803-3999

Saint Joseph's College

Rensselaer, Indiana — **CB member**
www.saintjoe.edu — **CB code: 1697**

- Private 4-year liberal arts college affiliated with Roman Catholic Church
- Residential campus in small town
- 1,057 degree-seeking undergraduates: 4% part-time, 57% women, 9% African American, 1% Asian American, 4% Hispanic American, 1% international

- 74% of applicants admitted
- SAT or ACT (ACT writing optional) required
- 51% graduate within 6 years; 17% enter graduate study

General. Founded in 1889. Regionally accredited. **Degrees:** 194 bachelor's, 1 associate awarded; master's offered. **Location:** 80 miles from Chicago, 90 miles from Indianapolis. **Calendar:** Semester, limited summer session. **Full-time faculty:** 59 total; 86% have terminal degrees, 5% minority, 42% women. **Part-time faculty:** 48 total; 69% have terminal degrees, 2% minority, 69% women. **Class size:** 80% < 20, 17% 20-39, 1% 40-49, 1% 50-99.

Freshman class profile. 1,325 applied, 985 admitted, 274 enrolled.

Mid 50% test scores		**GPA 2.0-2.99:**	45%
SAT critical reading:	420-520	**Rank in top quarter:**	31%
SAT math:	420-540	**Rank in top tenth:**	11%
ACT composite:	18-24	**End year in good standing:**	88%
GPA 3.75 or higher:	10%	**Return as sophomores:**	60%
GPA 3.50-3.74:	11%	**Out-of-state:**	35%
GPA 3.0-3.49:	33%	**Live on campus:**	93%

Basis for selection. For applicants with requirement deficiencies, admissions decision may be deferred until additional requirements (which may include an interview, recommendations, further course work, or an essay) are evaluated. Limited number of these applicants will be admitted under the Freshman Academic Support Program. **Homeschooled:** Statement describing homeschool structure and mission, transcript of courses and grades required. **Learning Disabled:** Documentation of learning disability not considered in application process. After admission, documentation of learning disability must be submitted to Director of Counseling Services in order to receive academic accommodations.

High school preparation. College-preparatory program recommended. 15 units recommended. Recommended units include English 4, mathematics 3, social studies 3, science 3 (laboratory 2) and foreign language 2. 10 recommended units must be from English, foreign language, social studies, math, and natural science. 3 units distributed among social studies, history, and academic electives.

2008-2009 Annual costs. Tuition/fees: $23,180. Room/board: $7,170. Books/supplies: $800. Personal expenses: $670.

2007-2008 Financial aid. **Need-based:** 286 full-time freshmen applied for aid; 231 were judged to have need; 231 of these received aid. Average need met was 81%. Average scholarship/grant was $13,873; average loan $3,609. 67% of total undergraduate aid awarded as scholarships/grants, 33% as loans/jobs. **Non-need-based:** Awarded to 377 full-time undergraduates, including 140 freshmen. Scholarships awarded for academics, alumni affiliation, athletics, minority status, music/drama.

Application procedures. **Admission:** Priority date 12/1; no deadline. $25 fee, may be waived for applicants with need. Admission notification on a rolling basis beginning on or about 12/1. Must reply by May 1 or within 2 week(s) if notified thereafter. **Financial aid:** Priority date 3/1; no closing date. FAFSA required. Applicants notified on a rolling basis starting 3/1; must reply by 5/1 or within 2 week(s) of notification.

Academics. Core program is a sequence of 10 interdisciplinary courses and seeks to integrate Christian humanism with critical appraisal of human condition. **Special study options:** Accelerated study, cross-registration, double major, dual enrollment of high school students, honors, independent study, internships, liberal arts/career combination, student-designed major, study abroad, teacher certification program, Washington semester. **Credit/placement by examination:** AP, CLEP, institutional tests. **Support services:** Learning center, reduced course load, study skills assistance, tutoring.

Majors. **Biology:** General, biochemistry. **Business:** General, accounting, management information systems. **Communications:** Media studies. **Computer sciences:** General. **Education:** Art, elementary, physical, secondary. **Health:** Clinical lab science, nursing (RN), predental, premedicine, preveterinary. **History:** General. **Legal studies:** Prelaw. **Math:** General. **Parks/recreation:** Health/fitness, sports admin. **Philosophy/religion:** Philosophy. **Physical sciences:** Chemistry. **Protective services:** Criminal justice. **Psychology:** General. **Public administration:** Social work. **Social sciences:** Economics, international relations, political science, sociology. **Theology:** Pastoral counseling. **Visual/performing arts:** Directing/producing, music history, music management, studio arts. **Other:** Religion/philosophy.

Most popular majors. Biology 11%, business/marketing 18%, education 12%, health sciences 22%, visual/performing arts 6%.

Computing on campus. 69 workstations in library, computer center, student center. Dormitories wired for high-speed internet access and linked to campus network. Helpline, student web hosting, wireless network available.

Student life. **Freshman orientation:** Mandatory. Preregistration for classes offered. One-day optional early registrations in April, June and July; 4-day required orientation in August. **Housing:** Guaranteed on-campus for all undergraduates. Coed dorms, single-sex dorms, special housing for disabled, apartments, wellness housing available. $200 nonrefundable deposit, deadline 5/1. Special dormitories available for non-traditional full-time students. **Activities:** Bands, campus ministries, choral groups, dance, drama, film society, literary magazine, music ensembles, musical theater, radio station, student government, student newspaper, TV station, charitable society, Habitat for Humanity, Kairos Team, College Republicans, College Democrats, peer ministry, Right to Life, volunteer corps, diversity coalition, St. Thomas Aquinas Catholic society.

Athletics. NCAA. **Intercollegiate:** Baseball M, basketball, cross-country, football (tackle) M, golf, soccer, softball W, tennis, track and field, volleyball W. **Intramural:** Basketball, football (non-tackle), soccer, softball, volleyball. **Team name:** Pumas.

Student services. Chaplain/spiritual director, career counseling, financial aid counseling, health services, personal counseling, placement for graduates.

Contact. E-mail: admissions@saintjoe.edu
Phone: (219) 866-6170 Toll-free number: (800) 447-8781
Fax: (219) 866-6122
Karen Raftus, Director of Admissions, Saint Joseph's College, Box 890, Rensselaer, IN 47978

St. Mary-of-the-Woods College

St. Mary-of-the-Woods, Indiana — **CB member**
www.smwc.edu — **CB code: 1704**

- Private 4-year liberal arts college for women affiliated with Roman Catholic Church
- Residential campus in rural community
- 1,176 degree-seeking undergraduates: 58% part-time, 97% women
- 166 degree-seeking graduate students
- 70% of applicants admitted
- SAT or ACT with writing, application essay required
- 42% graduate within 6 years

General. Founded in 1840. Regionally accredited. The traditional campus program open to women only. External degree (distance education) undergraduate program and graduate programs open to men and women. **Degrees:** 166 bachelor's, 3 associate awarded; master's offered. **ROTC:** Army, Air Force. **Location:** 4 miles from Terre Haute, 70 miles from Indianapolis. **Calendar:** Semester, extensive summer session. **Full-time faculty:** 64 total. **Part-time faculty:** 2 total. **Class size:** 93% < 20, 7% 20-39. **Special facilities:** Equine indoor and outdoor arenas, wildlife habitat restoration areas.

Freshman class profile. 417 applied, 293 admitted, 129 enrolled.

Mid 50% test scores		**GPA 3.0-3.49:**	45%
SAT critical reading:	430-540	**GPA 2.0-2.99:**	27%
SAT math:	410-520	**End year in good standing:**	96%
SAT writing:	410-550	**Return as sophomores:**	77%
ACT composite:	18-25	**Out-of-state:**	25%
GPA 3.75 or higher:	20%	**Live on campus:**	70%
GPA 3.50-3.74:	8%		

Basis for selection. School achievement record, test scores most important. Recommendations, evaluation of potential for college success considered. Interview recommended. Audition required of music majors. Portfolio required of art and journalism majors. **Learning Disabled:** Meeting with Learning Resource Coordinator strongly recommended.

High school preparation. College-preparatory program required. 13 units required; 16 recommended. Required and recommended units include English 4, mathematics 3, social studies 3, science 3 (laboratory 3) and foreign language 2.

2008-2009 Annual costs. Tuition/fees: $21,550. Room/board: $7,890. Books/supplies: $1,500. Personal expenses: $1,000.

2007-2008 Financial aid. **Need-based:** 74 full-time freshmen applied for aid; 68 were judged to have need; 68 of these received aid. Average need met was 84%. Average scholarship/grant was $16,413; average loan $2,888. 49% of total undergraduate aid awarded as scholarships/grants, 51% as loans/jobs. **Non-need-based:** Awarded to 104 full-time undergraduates, including 53 freshmen. Scholarships awarded for academics, alumni affiliation, art, athletics, leadership, minority status, music/drama, state residency.

Additional information: Portfolio or audition required of applicants who wish to be considered for Creative Arts Scholarship.

Application procedures. Admission: Closing date 8/15 (receipt date). $30 fee, may be waived for applicants with need, free for online applicants. Admission notification on a rolling basis beginning on or about 10/1. Must reply by 5/1. **Financial aid:** Priority date 3/1; no closing date. FAFSA required. Applicants notified on a rolling basis starting 12/1; must reply within 6 week(s) of notification.

Academics. Distance education program available in over 20 majors. **Special study options:** Accelerated study, cross-registration, distance learning, double major, external degree, honors, independent study, internships, student-designed major, study abroad, teacher certification program, weekend college. Woods' External Degree Program: students throughout country visit campus 1 or 2 days twice a year and do course work at home. Exchange program with Providence University in Taiwan. Agreement with Regent's College, London. **Credit/placement by examination:** AP, CLEP, IB, SAT, ACT, institutional tests. 30 credit hours maximum toward associate degree, 60 toward bachelor's. We follow ACE guidelines for the awarding of credit by testing. **Support services:** Learning center, reduced course load, study skills assistance, tutoring, writing center.

Honors college/program. 1100 SAT, 24 ACT, 3.5 GPA, teacher recommendation and excellent writing skills required.

Majors. Agriculture: Animal husbandry, equestrian studies, equine science. **Biology:** General. **Business:** General, accounting, business admin, communications, e-commerce, human resources, marketing, nonprofit/public. **Communications:** Journalism, media studies, public relations. **Communications technology:** General, graphics. **Computer sciences:** General, web page design. **Education:** General, art, biology, early childhood, elementary, English, foreign languages, kindergarten/preschool, mathematics, music, science, secondary, social science, social studies, Spanish, special. **Health:** Music therapy, predental, premedicine, prepharmacy, preveterinary. **Interdisciplinary:** Biological/physical sciences. **Legal studies:** Paralegal, prelaw. **Liberal arts:** Arts/sciences, humanities. **Math:** General. **Psychology:** General. **Public administration:** Human services. **Social sciences:** General, criminology. **Theology:** Theology. **Visual/performing arts:** Art, design, dramatic, graphic design, music performance, photography. **Other:** Women and theatre.

Most popular majors. Agriculture 8%, business/marketing 17%, computer/information sciences 6%, education 31%, psychology 7%, visual/performing arts 6%.

Computing on campus. 90 workstations in dormitories, library, computer center, student center. Dormitories wired for high-speed internet access and linked to campus network. Commuter students can connect to campus network. Online library, helpline, wireless network available.

Student life. Freshman orientation: Mandatory. Preregistration for classes offered. Three-day program of before classes start; requires service component. **Policies:** All students whose families do not live in contiguous county must live on-campus all 4 years. **Housing:** Guaranteed on-campus for all undergraduates. Wellness housing available. $100 nonrefundable deposit, deadline 8/15. **Activities:** Bands, campus ministries, choral groups, dance, drama, international student organizations, literary magazine, music ensembles, musical theater, student government, student newspaper, symphony orchestra, Habitat for Humanity, literacy volunteers, environmentalist activities, peace and justice committee, arts and issues committee, Race-for-the-Cure, United Way.

Athletics. USCAA. **Intercollegiate:** Basketball W, equestrian W, soccer W, softball W. **Team name:** Pomeroys.

Student services. Adult student services, alcohol/substance abuse counseling, chaplain/spiritual director, career counseling, student employment services, financial aid counseling, health services, on-campus daycare, personal counseling, placement for graduates. **Physically disabled:** Services for visually, hearing impaired.

Contact. E-mail: smwcadms@smwc.edu
Phone: (812) 535-5106 Toll-free number: (800) 926-7692
Fax: (812) 535-5010
Jill Blunk, Director of Admission, St. Mary-of-the-Woods College, Guerin Hall, SMWC, St. Mary of the Woods, IN 47876

Saint Mary's College

Notre Dame, Indiana — **CB member**
www.saintmarys.edu — **CB code: 1702**

- Private 4-year liberal arts college for women affiliated with Roman Catholic Church
- Residential campus in small city
- 1,613 degree-seeking undergraduates: 1% African American, 2% Asian American, 6% Hispanic American
- 80% of applicants admitted
- SAT or ACT with writing, application essay required
- 76% graduate within 6 years; 30% enter graduate study

General. Founded in 1844. Regionally accredited. Campus in Rome, Italy and programs in Ireland, India, Spain, France and Australia. Summer European study tour. Co-exchange enrollment with the University of Notre Dame. Volunteer service opportunities in the United States and abroad. **Degrees:** 330 bachelor's awarded. **ROTC:** Army, Naval, Air Force. **Location:** One mile from South Bend. **Calendar:** Semester, limited summer session. **Full-time faculty:** 136 total; 90% have terminal degrees, 9% minority, 64% women. **Part-time faculty:** 67 total; 33% have terminal degrees, 6% minority, 76% women. **Class size:** 61% < 20, 36% 20-39, 1% 40-49, less than 1% 50-99, less than 1% >100. **Special facilities:** Nature trail, performing arts center, greenhouse, galleries.

Freshman class profile. 1,422 applied, 1,132 admitted, 455 enrolled.

Mid 50% test scores		**GPA 2.0-2.99:**	2%
SAT critical reading:	520-620	**Rank in top quarter:**	69%
SAT math:	520-620	**Rank in top tenth:**	35%
SAT writing:	530-630	**End year in good standing:**	93%
ACT composite:	23-27	**Return as sophomores:**	79%
GPA 3.75 or higher:	48%	**Out-of-state:**	72%
GPA 3.50-3.74:	22%	**Live on campus:**	99%
GPA 3.0-3.49:	28%	**International:**	1%

Basis for selection. School achievement record, high school transcript, GPA, class rank, test scores, and activities important. Essay and school recommendations considered. Students must submit at least one writing component; ACT with Writing required if applicant is not also taking SAT (with mandatory Writing); ACT with Writing recommended even if applicant is also taking SAT. Interview recommended. Audition recommended for music majors. Portfolio recommended for art majors. **Homeschooled:** Students are encouraged to apply. Candidate should contact the Admission Office for details.

High school preparation. College-preparatory program recommended. 16 units required; 20 recommended. Required and recommended units include English 4, mathematics 3-4, history 2, science 2-4 (laboratory 2), foreign language 2-4 and academic electives 4. Science and nursing programs require more science and math. All students must take an additional 4 units distributed among English, math, science, foreign language, and social studies.

2008-2009 Annual costs. Tuition/fees: $28,212. Room/board: $8,936. Books/supplies: $1,100. Personal expenses: $1,700.

2008-2009 Financial aid. Need-based: 442 full-time freshmen applied for aid; 288 were judged to have need; 287 of these received aid. Average need met was 84%. Average scholarship/grant was $17,804; average loan $3,702. 67% of total undergraduate aid awarded as scholarships/grants, 33% as loans/jobs. **Non-need-based:** Awarded to 1,153 full-time undergraduates, including 363 freshmen. Scholarships awarded for academics, art.

Application procedures. Admission: Priority date 2/15; no deadline. $30 fee, may be waived for applicants with need, free for online applicants. Admission notification on a rolling basis beginning on or about 12/15. $400 housing deposit refunded if letter sent in by May 1. Housing deposit nonrefundable for early decision. **Financial aid:** Priority date 3/1; no closing date. FAFSA, CSS PROFILE required. Applicants notified on a rolling basis starting 12/15; must reply by 5/1.

Academics. Department of Religious Studies coordinated with Department of Theology at University of Notre Dame. After first year, student can take courses in either department. **Special study options:** Accelerated study, cross-registration, double major, exchange student, independent study, internships, liberal arts/career combination, student-designed major, study abroad, teacher certification program, Washington semester. **Credit/placement by examination:** AP, CLEP, IB, institutional tests. 30 credit hours maximum toward bachelor's degree. **Support services:** Reduced course load, study skills assistance, tutoring, writing center.

Majors. Biology: General. **Business:** Accounting, business admin, management information systems. **Communications:** General. **Education:** Elementary. **Foreign languages:** French, Italian, Spanish. **Health:** Communication disorders, cytotechnology, nursing (RN). **History:** General. **Interdisciplinary:** Math/computer science. **Liberal arts:** Humanities. **Math:** General, applied, statistics. **Philosophy/religion:** Philosophy, religion. **Physical sciences:** Chemistry. **Psychology:** General. **Public administration:** Social work. **Social sciences:** Economics, political science, sociology. **Visual/performing arts:** Art, dramatic, studio arts.

Most popular majors. Biology 7%, business/marketing 12%, communications/journalism 10%, education 7%, English 8%, health sciences 9%, history 6%, psychology 6%, social sciences 10%.

Computing on campus. 236 workstations in dormitories, library, computer center, student center. Dormitories wired for high-speed internet access and linked to campus network. Commuter students can connect to campus network. Online course registration, online library, helpline, student web hosting, wireless network available.

Student life. Freshman orientation: Mandatory. Preregistration for classes offered. Held during weekend prior to beginning of fall semester. Preorientation sessions held for fall admits during summer months. **Policies:** Educational judicial system guaranteeing certain due process rights to all students involved in discipline situation; student judicial board provides opportunity for peer review system. **Housing:** Guaranteed on-campus for all undergraduates. Apartments available. $400 fully refundable deposit, deadline 5/1. **Activities:** Bands, campus ministries, choral groups, dance, drama, international student organizations, literary magazine, music ensembles, musical theater, opera, student government, student newspaper, TV station, neighborhood study help program, Community of International Lay Apostolate, Urban Plunge community program, Circle-K, World Hunger Coalition, Student Alliance for Women's Colleges, Right to Life, Women for the Environment, Sisters of Nefertiti, Fuerza y Union Entre las Razas.

Athletics. NCAA. **Intercollegiate:** Basketball W, cross-country W, diving W, golf W, soccer W, softball W, swimming W, tennis W, volleyball W. **Intramural:** Soccer W, softball W, tennis W, volleyball W. **Team name:** Belles.

Student services. Adult student services, chaplain/spiritual director, career counseling, student employment services, financial aid counseling, health services, minority student services, on-campus daycare, personal counseling, placement for graduates, women's services. **Physically disabled:** Services for visually, hearing impaired.

Contact. E-mail: admission@saintmarys.edu
Phone: (574) 284-4587 Toll-free number: (800) 551-7621
Fax: (574) 284-4841
Mona Bowe, Director of Admissions, Saint Mary's College, Notre Dame, IN 46556-5001

Taylor University

Upland, Indiana — **CB member**
www.taylor.edu — **CB code: 1802**

- Private 4-year university and liberal arts college affiliated with interdenominational tradition
- Residential campus in small town
- 1,841 degree-seeking undergraduates: 2% part-time, 55% women, 2% African American, 2% Asian American, 2% Hispanic American, 2% international
- 84% of applicants admitted
- SAT or ACT (ACT writing recommended), application essay required
- 78% graduate within 6 years; 18% enter graduate study

General. Founded in 1846. Regionally accredited. Christ-centered, covenant community committed to service. **Degrees:** 416 bachelor's, 3 associate awarded. **Location:** 20 miles from Muncie, 70 miles from Indianapolis. **Calendar:** 4-1-4, limited summer session. **Full-time faculty:** 126 total; 81% have terminal degrees, 7% minority, 25% women. **Part-time faculty:** 71 total; 21% have terminal degrees, 6% minority, 48% women. **Class size:** 61% < 20, 32% 20-39, 4% 40-49, 2% 50-99, 1% >100. **Special facilities:** Arboretum, environmental studies laboratory, NASA-approved clean room, particle accelerator, NASA project space research equipment, C.S. Lewis Collection of original manuscripts.

Freshman class profile. 1,557 applied, 1,308 admitted, 466 enrolled.

Mid 50% test scores			
SAT critical reading:	510-660	GPA 2.0-2.99:	14%
SAT math:	520-650	Rank in top quarter:	63%
SAT writing:	520-640	Rank in top tenth:	35%
ACT composite:	23-30	End year in good standing:	90%
GPA 3.75 or higher:	42%	Return as sophomores:	84%
GPA 3.50-3.74:	20%	Out-of-state:	71%
GPA 3.0-3.49:	24%	Live on campus:	97%
		International:	4%

Basis for selection. High school transcript, test scores important. Recommend rank in top 25% of graduating class with 3.3 GPA and 1000 SAT (exclusive of Writing). Recommendations from applicant's pastor and counselor required. Cocurricular activities considered. Audition required of music majors. Portfolio recommended for art majors. Interviews required for some financial and academic programs. **Homeschooled:** Letter of recommendation (nonparent) required.

High school preparation. College-preparatory program recommended. 15 units required. Required and recommended units include English 4, mathematics 3-4, social studies 2-3, science 3-4 (laboratory 3-4), foreign language 2 and academic electives 3.

2008-2009 Annual costs. Tuition/fees: $24,546. Room/board: $6,352. Books/supplies: $900.

2008-2009 Financial aid. Need-based: 339 full-time freshmen applied for aid; 266 were judged to have need; 266 of these received aid. Average need met was 76%. Average scholarship/grant was $13,352; average loan $4,421. 64% of total undergraduate aid awarded as scholarships/grants, 36% as loans/jobs. **Non-need-based:** Awarded to 648 full-time undergraduates, including 197 freshmen. Scholarships awarded for academics, alumni affiliation, art, athletics, leadership, minority status, music/drama, religious affiliation, state residency.

Application procedures. Admission: No deadline. $25 fee, may be waived for applicants with need. Admission notification on a rolling basis beginning on or about 10/1. Must reply by May 1 or within 2 week(s) if notified thereafter. **Financial aid:** Closing date 3/10. FAFSA required. Applicants notified on a rolling basis starting 3/1; must reply by 5/1.

Academics. Special study options: Combined bachelor's/graduate degree, cooperative education, distance learning, double major, dual enrollment of high school students, exchange student, honors, independent study, internships, semester at sea, student-designed major, study abroad, teacher certification program, urban semester, Washington semester. **Credit/placement by examination:** AP, CLEP, institutional tests. 30 credit hours maximum toward associate degree, 30 toward bachelor's. **Support services:** Learning center, remedial instruction, study skills assistance, tutoring, writing center.

Majors. Biology: General. **Business:** Accounting, business admin, finance, international, managerial economics, marketing. **Communications:** General, journalism, media studies. **Computer sciences:** General, computer graphics, computer science. **Conservation:** Environmental science. **Education:** Art, elementary, English, French, mathematics, music, physical, science, social studies, Spanish. **Engineering:** Computer, environmental, physics. **Foreign languages:** French, Spanish. **History:** General. **Interdisciplinary:** Biological/physical sciences, math/computer science. **Math:** General, applied. **Parks/recreation:** Exercise sciences, health/fitness, sports admin. **Philosophy/religion:** Philosophy. **Physical sciences:** General, chemistry, physics. **Psychology:** General. **Public administration:** Social work. **Social sciences:** General, economics, geography, international relations, political science, sociology. **Theology:** Bible, religious ed. **Visual/performing arts:** General, art, dramatic. **Other:** Computer science-new media, Mathematics-environmental science, Media communication, Visual arts-new media.

Most popular majors. Biology 6%, business/marketing 16%, communications/journalism 8%, education 17%, psychology 9%, social sciences 7%, theological studies 8%.

Computing on campus. 339 workstations in library, computer center. Dormitories wired for high-speed internet access and linked to campus network. Commuter students can connect to campus network. Online course registration, online library, helpline, repair service, student web hosting, wireless network available.

Student life. Freshman orientation: Available. Preregistration for classes offered. **Policies:** Students and faculty sign Life Together Covenant explaining expectations and responsibilities of living in Christian community where faith is integrated with academic progress. Religious observance required. **Housing:** Guaranteed on-campus for freshmen. Single-sex dorms, apartments, wellness housing available. $200 deposit, deadline 5/1. Some off-campus apartments available to upperclassmen with special permission. **Activities:** Bands, choral groups, drama, film society, literary magazine, music ensembles, musical theater, opera, radio station, student government, student newspaper, symphony orchestra, TV station, missions service program, multicultural society, missionary kids organizations, community outreach, Campus Life/Young Life, international student society, Habitat for Humanity, ReaLife Inner City Children's Ministry, high school youth conference, Acting on AIDS.

Athletics. NAIA, NCCAA. **Intercollegiate:** Baseball M, basketball, cross-country, football (tackle) M, golf M, soccer, softball W, tennis, track and field, volleyball W. **Intramural:** Badminton, basketball, football (non-tackle), golf, racquetball, soccer, softball, table tennis, tennis, volleyball. **Team name:** Trojans.

Student services. Chaplain/spiritual director, career counseling, student employment services, financial aid counseling, health services, minority student services, personal counseling, placement for graduates. **Physically disabled:** Services for visually, speech, hearing impaired.

Contact. E-mail: admissions@tayloru.edu
Phone: (765) 998-5511 Toll-free number: (800) 882-3456
Fax: (765) 998-4925
Stephen Mortland, Dean of Enrollment Management, Taylor University, 236 West Reade Avenue, Upland, IN 46989-1001

Trine University

Angola, Indiana — **CB member**
www.trine.edu — **CB code: 1811**

- Private 4-year university and engineering college
- Residential campus in small town
- 1,384 degree-seeking undergraduates: 6% part-time, 31% women, 3% African American, 1% Asian American, 2% Hispanic American, 2% international
- 10 graduate students
- 53% of applicants admitted
- SAT or ACT (ACT writing optional) required
- 50% graduate within 6 years; 35% enter graduate study

General. Founded in 1884. Regionally accredited. **Degrees:** 204 bachelor's, 26 associate awarded; master's offered. **ROTC:** Air Force. **Location:** 40 miles from Fort Wayne; 80 miles from Toledo, Ohio. **Calendar:** Semester, limited summer session. **Full-time faculty:** 69 total; 65% have terminal degrees, 4% minority, 25% women. **Part-time faculty:** 30 total; 17% have terminal degrees, 3% minority, 30% women. **Class size:** 56% < 20, 44% 20-39, less than 1% 40-49. **Special facilities:** Educational media resource center, 18 hole championship golf course, student-operated radio station.

Freshman class profile. 2,277 applied, 1,214 admitted, 427 enrolled.

Mid 50% test scores		**Rank in top quarter:**	48%
SAT critical reading:	440-570	**Rank in top tenth:**	22%
SAT math:	490-600	**Return as sophomores:**	69%
ACT composite:	20-25	**Out-of-state:**	38%
GPA 3.75 or higher:	23%	**Live on campus:**	90%
GPA 3.50-3.74:	14%	**International:**	1%
GPA 3.0-3.49:	35%	**Fraternities:**	5%
GPA 2.0-2.99:	27%	**Sororities:**	1%

Basis for selection. School achievement, class rank, test scores, school and community activities, and recommendations important. Interview and essay recommended. **Homeschooled:** Statement describing homeschool structure and mission, transcript of courses and grades required. **Learning Disabled:** Must submit clinical evaluation of learning disability (completed within last 5 years prior to enrollment).

High school preparation. College-preparatory program required. 18 units required. Required units include English 4, mathematics 3, social studies 3, science 3 (laboratory 2) and academic electives 3. 3 1/2 years of math, physics, and chemistry required for engineering, math and computer science majors.

2008-2009 Annual costs. Tuition/fees: $23,450. Room/board: $6,700. Books/supplies: $1,500. Personal expenses: $4,500.

2008-2009 Financial aid. Need-based: 420 full-time freshmen applied for aid; 288 were judged to have need; 288 of these received aid. Average need met was 93%. Average scholarship/grant was $5,127; average loan $3,350. 55% of total undergraduate aid awarded as scholarships/grants, 45% as loans/jobs. **Non-need-based:** Scholarships awarded for academics, alumni affiliation, minority status, music/drama, ROTC.

Application procedures. Admission: Priority date 6/1; deadline 8/1. No application fee. Application must be submitted online. Admission notification 8/1. Admission notification on a rolling basis beginning on or about 9/15. Must reply by 5/1. **Financial aid:** Priority date 3/10, closing date 3/10. FAFSA required. Applicants notified on a rolling basis starting 2/15; must reply by 5/1 or within 2 week(s) of notification.

Academics. Special study options: Combined bachelor's/graduate degree, cooperative education, distance learning, double major, dual enrollment of high school students, ESL, honors, internships, study abroad, teacher certification program. **Credit/placement by examination:** AP, CLEP, IB, institutional tests. **Support services:** Learning center, reduced course load, remedial instruction, study skills assistance, tutoring, writing center.

Majors. Biology: General. **Business:** Accounting, business admin, entrepreneurial studies, finance, management information systems, operations. **Communications:** General. **Computer sciences:** General, computer science. **Education:** Elementary, English, health, mathematics, middle, physical, science, social studies. **Engineering:** Chemical, civil, electrical, mechanical. **Engineering technology:** Drafting, industrial management. **Health:** Premedicine. **Math:** General. **Parks/recreation:** Health/fitness, sports admin. **Physical sciences:** Chemistry. **Protective services:** Criminal justice, forensics. **Psychology:** General. **Social sciences:** General.

Most popular majors. Business/marketing 23%, education 19%, engineering/engineering technologies 36%, parks/recreation 9%, security/protective services 10%.

Computing on campus. 150 workstations in dormitories, library, computer center, student center. Dormitories wired for high-speed internet access and linked to campus network. Commuter students can connect to campus network. Online library, helpline, wireless network available.

Student life. Freshman orientation: Mandatory. Preregistration for classes offered. Held 3 days at start of fall semester. **Housing:** Guaranteed on-campus for all undergraduates. Coed dorms, single-sex dorms, apartments available. $150 nonrefundable deposit, deadline 5/1. Honors housing; independent fraternity/sorority housing available. **Activities:** Bands, choral groups, dance, drama, international student organizations, music ensembles, radio station, student government, student newspaper, Circle K, Newman Fellowship, InterVarsity Christian Fellowship, international student association, multicultural student association, Students Against Destructive Decisions, Habitat for Humanity.

Athletics. NCAA. **Intercollegiate:** Baseball M, basketball, cross-country, football (tackle) M, golf, lacrosse, soccer, softball W, tennis, track and field, volleyball W, wrestling M. **Intramural:** Badminton, basketball, cheerleading, football (non-tackle) M, golf, handball, racquetball, softball, table tennis, volleyball. **Team name:** Thunder.

Student services. Alcohol/substance abuse counseling, chaplain/spiritual director, career counseling, student employment services, financial aid counseling, personal counseling, placement for graduates, veterans' counselor.

Contact. E-mail: admit@trine.edu
Phone: (260) 665-4100 Toll-free number: (800) 347-4878
Fax: (260) 665-4578
Scott Goplin, Dean of Admission, Trine University, One University Avenue, Angola, IN 46703

University of Evansville

Evansville, Indiana — **CB member**
www.evansville.edu — **CB code: 1208**

- Private 4-year university and liberal arts college affiliated with United Methodist Church
- Residential campus in small city
- 2,443 degree-seeking undergraduates: 4% part-time, 59% women, 3% African American, 1% Asian American, 2% Hispanic American, 7% international
- 156 degree-seeking graduate students
- 88% of applicants admitted
- SAT or ACT with writing required
- 63% graduate within 6 years; 28% enter graduate study

General. Founded in 1854. Regionally accredited. **Degrees:** 531 bachelor's, 9 associate awarded; master's, doctoral offered. **Location:** 170 miles from Indianapolis, 170 miles from St. Louis. **Calendar:** Semester, limited summer session. **Full-time faculty:** 176 total; 85% have terminal degrees, 7% minority, 35% women. **Part-time faculty:** 55 total; 31% have terminal degrees, 53% women. **Class size:** 47% < 20, 46% 20-39, 6% 40-49, 1% 50-99.

Freshman class profile. 2,887 applied, 2,532 admitted, 619 enrolled.

Mid 50% test scores		**Rank in top quarter:**	64%
SAT critical reading:	500-620	**Rank in top tenth:**	31%
SAT math:	510-610	**End year in good standing:**	93%
SAT writing:	480-590	**Return as sophomores:**	81%
ACT composite:	22-28	**Out-of-state:**	40%
GPA 3.75 or higher:	46%	**Live on campus:**	86%
GPA 3.50-3.74:	16%	**International:**	5%
GPA 3.0-3.49:	23%	**Fraternities:**	31%
GPA 2.0-2.99:	15%	**Sororities:**	20%

Basis for selection. Weighted GPA calculated using academic courses only. Extracurricular activities important. Interview recommended. Essay required for Physical Therapy applicants. Audition required of music and theater majors. **Homeschooled:** Letter of recommendation (nonparent) required. **Learning Disabled:** Students requesting accommodations must provide documentation of the disability and the significant impact of the disability on academic functioning.

High school preparation. College-preparatory program required. 11 units required; 15 recommended. Required and recommended units include English 4, mathematics 3-4, social studies 1, history 1, science 2-3 (laboratory 2) and foreign language 2. One or more years of physics, additional chemistry and math, and 2 or more years of a foreign language recommended for engineering programs.

2008-2009 Annual costs. Tuition/fees: $25,845. Room/board: $8,170.

2008-2009 Financial aid. Need-based: 520 full-time freshmen applied for aid; 452 were judged to have need; 452 of these received aid. Average need met was 92%. Average scholarship/grant was $20,695; average loan $4,040. 76% of total undergraduate aid awarded as scholarships/grants, 24% as loans/jobs. **Non-need-based:** Awarded to 1,987 full-time undergraduates, including 570 freshmen. Scholarships awarded for academics, alumni affiliation, art, athletics, leadership, minority status, music/drama, religious affiliation, state residency. **Additional information:** Early financial planning service allows prospective students to get free estimate of available aid.

Application procedures. Admission: Priority date 12/1; deadline 2/1 (postmark date). $35 fee, may be waived for applicants with need. Admission notification 2/15. Admission notification on a rolling basis. Must reply by 5/1. **Financial aid:** Priority date 3/10; no closing date. FAFSA required. Applicants notified on a rolling basis starting 3/25; must reply by 5/1.

Academics. Special study options: Accelerated study, cooperative education, double major, dual enrollment of high school students, ESL, external degree, honors, independent study, internships, semester at sea, student-designed major, study abroad, teacher certification program, Washington semester. British Campus at Harlaxton College, Italian archaeological excavation program, the Washington Center for Internships, US Pentagon internship, and undergraduate research. **Credit/placement by examination:** AP, CLEP, IB, SAT, ACT, institutional tests. 6 credit hours maximum toward associate degree, 6 toward bachelor's. **Support services:** Pre-admission summer program, study skills assistance, tutoring, writing center.

Majors. Biology: General, biochemistry. **Business:** Accounting, business admin, finance, international, management information systems, managerial economics, marketing. **Computer sciences:** General. **Conservation:** Environmental science, environmental studies. **Education:** General, art, biology, chemistry, drama/dance, elementary, English, French, German, mathematics, music, physical, physics, social science, social studies, Spanish, special. **Engineering:** Civil, computer, electrical, mechanical. **Foreign languages:** Classics, French, German, Spanish. **Health:** Athletic training, clinical lab science, health care admin, music therapy, nursing (RN), predental, premedicine, prepharmacy, preveterinary. **History:** General. **Interdisciplinary:** Cognitive science, neuroscience. **Liberal arts:** Arts/sciences. **Math:** General. **Parks/recreation:** Exercise sciences, sports admin. **Philosophy/religion:** Philosophy. **Physical sciences:** Chemistry, physics. **Psychology:** General. **Social sciences:** Archaeology, economics, international relations, political science, sociology. **Theology:** Bible, theology. **Visual/performing arts:** Art, art history/conservation, design, dramatic, graphic design, music management, music performance, theater arts management. **Other:** Communication and media studies, Legal professions.

Most popular majors. Business/marketing 10%, education 10%, engineering/engineering technologies 11%, health sciences 7%, parks/recreation 7%, psychology 6%, social sciences 8%, visual/performing arts 10%.

Computing on campus. 385 workstations in dormitories, library, computer center, student center. Dormitories wired for high-speed internet access and linked to campus network. Commuter students can connect to campus network. Online library, helpline, repair service, student web hosting, wireless network available.

Student life. Freshman orientation: Mandatory. Preregistration for classes offered. Two programs available: one in summer includes testing, advising, and registration; another 3 1/2 day program held prior to beginning of semester. **Housing:** Guaranteed on-campus for freshmen. Coed dorms, single-sex dorms, apartments, fraternity/sorority housing available. $100 partly refundable deposit, deadline 5/1. Honors program housing, global living and learning community. **Activities:** Bands, campus ministries, choral groups, dance, drama, film society, international student organizations, literary magazine, music ensembles, Model UN, musical theater, opera, radio station, student government, student newspaper, symphony orchestra, black student union, Hillel, Kappa Chi (service), Amnesty International, Habitat for Humanity, Circle K, College Democrats, College Republicans.

Athletics. NCAA. **Intercollegiate:** Baseball M, basketball, cross-country, diving, golf, soccer, softball W, swimming, tennis W, volleyball W. **Intramural:** Badminton, basketball, bowling, cross-country, diving, football (non-tackle), golf, racquetball, soccer, softball, swimming, table tennis, tennis, volleyball. **Team name:** Purple Aces.

Student services. Adult student services, alcohol/substance abuse counseling, chaplain/spiritual director, career counseling, student employment services, financial aid counseling, health services, minority student services, personal counseling, placement for graduates, veterans' counselor. **Physically disabled:** Services for visually, speech, hearing impaired.

Contact. E-mail: admission@evansville.edu
Phone: (812) 488-2468 Toll-free number: (800) 423-8633 ext. 2468
Fax: (812) 488-4076
Don Vos, Dean of Admissions, University of Evansville, 1800 Lincoln Avenue, Evansville, IN 47722

University of Indianapolis

Indianapolis, Indiana — **CB member**
www.uindy.edu — **CB code: 1321**

- Private 4-year university and liberal arts college affiliated with United Methodist Church
- Residential campus in very large city
- 3,548 degree-seeking undergraduates: 24% part-time, 66% women, 11% African American, 1% Asian American, 2% Hispanic American, 5% international
- 1,080 degree-seeking graduate students
- 79% of applicants admitted
- SAT or ACT (ACT writing optional) required
- 55% graduate within 6 years

General. Founded in 1902. Regionally accredited. **Degrees:** 569 bachelor's, 74 associate awarded; master's, doctoral offered. **ROTC:** Army. **Location:** 5 miles from downtown. **Calendar:** Semester, limited summer session. **Full-time faculty:** 199 total; 78% have terminal degrees, 6% minority, 52% women. **Part-time faculty:** 234 total; 36% have terminal degrees, 8% minority, 45% women. **Class size:** 62% < 20, 37% 20-39, 1% 40-49, less than 1% 50-99. **Special facilities:** Observatory, fine arts center.

Freshman class profile. 3,777 applied, 2,993 admitted, 746 enrolled.

Mid 50% test scores		**GPA 2.0-2.99:**	26%
SAT critical reading:	440-560	**Rank in top quarter:**	55%
SAT math:	450-580	**Rank in top tenth:**	26%
SAT writing:	420-550	**Return as sophomores:**	74%
ACT composite:	19-25	**Out-of-state:**	12%
GPA 3.75 or higher:	24%	**Live on campus:**	71%
GPA 3.50-3.74:	18%	**International:**	1%
GPA 3.0-3.49:	32%		

Basis for selection. Recommendations, GPA, SAT/ACT scores, class rank important. Involvement in extracurricular activities considered. Essay recommended. Interview recommended for borderline applicants. Audition required of music majors. Portfolio recommended for art majors. **Homeschooled:** Transcript of courses and grades required. **Learning Disabled:** Students with learning disabilities may apply to the BUILD program through separate application process.

High school preparation. 15 units required; 18 recommended. Required and recommended units include English 4, mathematics 3-4, social studies 1, history 1, science 2-3 (laboratory 1-2), foreign language 2 and academic electives 1-3.

2008-2009 Annual costs. Tuition/fees: $20,470. Room/board: $7,790. Books/supplies: $890. Personal expenses: $2,620.

2007-2008 Financial aid. Non-need-based: Scholarships awarded for academics, alumni affiliation, art, athletics, job skills, leadership, music/drama, religious affiliation, state residency.

Application procedures. Admission: No deadline. $25 fee, may be waived for applicants with need, free for online applicants. Admission notification on a rolling basis beginning on or about 9/1. Must reply by May 1 or within 2 week(s) if notified thereafter. **Financial aid:** Priority date 3/10; no closing date. FAFSA, institutional form required. Applicants notified on a rolling basis starting 3/1; must reply within 3 week(s) of notification.

Academics. Special study options: Accelerated study, combined bachelor's/graduate degree, cross-registration, double major, dual enrollment of high school students, ESL, honors, independent study, internships, liberal arts/career combination, student-designed major, study abroad, teacher certification program. Baccalaureate for University of Indianapolis Learning Disabled (BUILD). **Credit/placement by examination:** AP, CLEP, IB, SAT, ACT, institutional tests. 3-8 hours awarded for International Baccalaureate based on scores. **Support services:** Learning center, pre-admission summer program, reduced course load, remedial instruction, study skills assistance, tutoring, writing center.

Majors. **Biology:** General, cell/histology. **Business:** Accounting, business admin, international, management information systems, managerial economics, marketing, tourism/travel. **Communications:** General. **Computer sciences:** General, computer science, information systems. **Education:** General, art, biology, business, chemistry, elementary, English, foreign languages, French, history, mathematics, music, physical, physics, science, secondary, social studies, Spanish, speech. **Foreign languages:** French, German, Spanish. **Health:** Art therapy, athletic training, clinical lab technology, nursing (RN), respiratory therapy technology. **History:** General. **Math:** General. **Parks/recreation:** Exercise sciences, sports admin. **Philosophy/religion:** Philosophy, religion. **Physical sciences:** Chemistry, geology, physics. **Protective services:** Law enforcement admin. **Psychology:** General. **Public administration:** Social work. **Social sciences:** Anthropology, archaeology, economics, international relations, political science, sociology. **Visual/performing arts:** Art, commercial/advertising art, design, dramatic, music performance.

Most popular majors. Biology 6%, business/marketing 21%, education 13%, health sciences 15%, liberal arts 8%, psychology 10%.

Computing on campus. 222 workstations in library, computer center. Dormitories wired for high-speed internet access and linked to campus network. Commuter students can connect to campus network. Online library, helpline, wireless network available.

Student life. **Freshman orientation:** Mandatory, $40 fee. Preregistration for classes offered. Student attends one of 6 summer registration programs. **Housing:** Coed dorms, single-sex dorms, apartments, wellness housing available. $50 partly refundable deposit, deadline 5/1. **Activities:** Bands, campus ministries, choral groups, dance, drama, literary magazine, music ensembles, musical theater, opera, radio station, student government, student newspaper, TV station, Young Democrats, Young Republicans, Fellowship of Christian Athletes, Circle-K, social service, honorary societies.

Athletics. NCAA. **Intercollegiate:** Baseball M, basketball, cross-country, diving, football (tackle) M, golf, soccer, softball W, swimming, tennis, track and field, volleyball W, wrestling M. **Intramural:** Basketball, football (non-tackle) M, soccer, softball, volleyball. **Team name:** Greyhounds.

Student services. Adult student services, chaplain/spiritual director, career counseling, student employment services, health services, personal counseling, placement for graduates, veterans' counselor. **Physically disabled:** Services for visually, speech, hearing impaired. **Learning disabled:** Comprehensive services available.

Contact. E-mail: admissions@uindy.edu
Phone: (317) 788-3216 Toll-free number: (800) 232-8634
Fax: (317) 788-3300
Ron Wilks, Director of Admissions, University of Indianapolis, 1400 East Hanna Avenue, Indianapolis, IN 46227-3697

University of Notre Dame

Notre Dame, Indiana — **CB member**
www.nd.edu — **CB code: 1841**

- Private 4-year university affiliated with Roman Catholic Church
- Residential campus in small city
- 8,354 degree-seeking undergraduates: 47% women, 4% African American, 7% Asian American, 9% Hispanic American, 1% Native American, 3% international
- 3,192 degree-seeking graduate students
- 27% of applicants admitted
- SAT or ACT (ACT writing optional), application essay required
- 96% graduate within 6 years; 30% enter graduate study

General. Founded in 1842. Regionally accredited. Notre Dame Study Centers in Washington, DC; Dublin, Ireland; London, England; Rome, Italy; several other countries. **Degrees:** 2,087 bachelor's awarded; master's, doctoral, first professional offered. **ROTC:** Army, Naval, Air Force. **Location:** 90 miles from Chicago. **Calendar:** Semester, extensive summer session. **Special facilities:** Germ-free research facility, radiation laboratory, nature preserve for biological research, wind-tunnel research facility, art museum.

Freshman class profile. 13,945 applied, 3,727 admitted, 2,000 enrolled.

Mid 50% test scores		**Rank in top tenth:**	87%
SAT critical reading:	650-740	**Return as sophomores:**	97%
SAT math:	670-760	**Out-of-state:**	89%
ACT composite:	31-34	**Live on campus:**	100%
Rank in top quarter:	96%	**International:**	3%

Basis for selection. GED not accepted. Demonstrated academic achievement and test scores most important. Essay, teacher recommendations, extracurricular activities, and personal statement also important. Three SAT Subject Tests required for home schooled students. Audition recommended for music majors. Portfolio recommended for art majors.

High school preparation. College-preparatory program required. 16 units required; 20 recommended. Required and recommended units include English 4, mathematics 3-4, history 2-4, science 2-4 (laboratory 2), foreign language 2-4 and academic electives 3. Pre-calculus or calculus, chemistry and physics recommended for architecture, engineering and science programs. Social studies requirement should include history.

2009-2010 Annual costs. Tuition/fees: $38,477. Room/board: $10,368. Books/supplies: $850. Personal expenses: $900.

2008-2009 Financial aid. **Non-need-based:** Scholarships awarded for athletics, job skills, ROTC.

Application procedures. **Admission:** Closing date 12/31 (postmark date). $65 fee, may be waived for applicants with need. Admission notification 4/10. Must reply by May 1 or within 2 week(s) if notified thereafter. **Financial aid:** Closing date 2/15. FAFSA, CSS PROFILE required. Applicants notified by 4/1; must reply by 5/1.

Academics. **Special study options:** Accelerated study, cross-registration, distance learning, double major, honors, independent study, internships, liberal arts/career combination, student-designed major, study abroad, teacher certification program, Washington semester. Teacher certification available only through cross-registration with St. Mary's College; triple majors, quadruple majors, triple degrees, double majors within dual degrees. **Credit/placement by examination:** AP, CLEP, IB, institutional tests. Students with HL score of 6 or 7 eligible to receive credit in anthropology, biology, chemistry, English, French, German, Greek, American history, Latin, math, music, physics, psychology, and Spanish. **Support services:** Learning center, study skills assistance, tutoring, writing center.

Majors. **Architecture:** Architecture. **Area/ethnic studies:** African-American, American. **Biology:** General, biochemistry. **Business:** General, accounting, finance, management information systems, marketing. **Computer sciences:** General. **Conservation:** Environmental science. **Education:** Science. **Engineering:** Aerospace, chemical, computer, electrical, environmental, mechanical. **Foreign languages:** Ancient Greek, Arabic, Chinese, classics, French, German, Italian, Japanese, Romance, Russian, Spanish. **Health:** Premedicine. **History:** General. **Interdisciplinary:** Biological/physical sciences, medieval/Renaissance. **Liberal arts:** Arts/sciences. **Math:** General. **Philosophy/religion:** Philosophy. **Physical sciences:** Chemistry, physics. **Psychology:** General. **Social sciences:** Anthropology, economics, political science, sociology. **Theology:** Theology. **Visual/performing arts:** Art history/conservation, design, dramatic, studio arts.

Most popular majors. Biology 6%, business/marketing 19%, engineering/engineering technologies 9%, foreign language 6%, health sciences 7%, psychology 6%, social sciences 16%.

Computing on campus. 261 workstations in dormitories, library, computer center, student center. Dormitories linked to campus network. Commuter students can connect to campus network. Online course registration, helpline, repair service, wireless network available.

Student life. **Freshman orientation:** Mandatory. Preregistration for classes offered. **Housing:** Guaranteed on-campus for freshmen. Single-sex dorms available. $50 deposit, deadline 5/1. Requests for ground level housing or housing suitable for a disabled student will be honored. **Activities:** Bands, campus ministries, choral groups, dance, drama, film society, literary magazine, music ensembles, musical theater, opera, radio station, student government, student newspaper, symphony orchestra, More than 260 clubs and organizations available.

Athletics. NCAA. **Intercollegiate:** Baseball M, basketball, cross-country, diving, fencing, football (tackle) M, golf, ice hockey M, lacrosse, rowing (crew) W, soccer, softball W, swimming, tennis, track and field, volleyball W. **Intramural:** Badminton, baseball M, basketball, bowling, cross-country, football (non-tackle), football (tackle) M, golf, ice hockey, lacrosse, racquetball, soccer, softball, table tennis, tennis, volleyball, water polo. **Team name:** Fighting Irish.

Student services. Alcohol/substance abuse counseling, chaplain/spiritual director, career counseling, student employment services, health services, minority student services, on-campus daycare, personal counseling, placement for graduates, women's services. **Physically disabled:** Services for visually, hearing impaired.

Contact. E-mail: admissions@nd.edu
Phone: (574) 631-7505 Fax: (574) 631-8865
Daniel Saracino, Director of Admissions, University of Notre Dame, 220 Main Building, Notre Dame, IN 46556

University of St. Francis
Fort Wayne, Indiana
www.sf.edu **CB code: 1693**

- Private 4-year university and liberal arts college affiliated with Roman Catholic Church
- Commuter campus in small city
- 1,750 degree-seeking undergraduates: 17% part-time, 69% women, 5% African American, 1% Asian American, 2% Hispanic American
- 292 degree-seeking graduate students
- 47% of applicants admitted
- SAT or ACT (ACT writing optional) required
- 51% graduate within 6 years

General. Founded in 1890. Regionally accredited. **Degrees:** 217 bachelor's, 162 associate awarded; master's offered. **Location:** 120 miles from Indianapolis, 150 miles from Chicago. **Calendar:** Semester, limited summer session. **Full-time faculty:** 101 total; 44% have terminal degrees, 7% minority, 61% women. **Part-time faculty:** 122 total; 17% have terminal degrees, 5% minority, 61% women. **Class size:** 60% < 20, 37% 20-39, 2% 40-49, 2% 50-99. **Special facilities:** Planetarium, nature preserve.

Freshman class profile. 1,376 applied, 645 admitted, 325 enrolled.

Mid 50% test scores		**GPA 2.0-2.99:**	36%
SAT critical reading:	440-540	**Rank in top quarter:**	37%
SAT math:	440-550	**Rank in top tenth:**	12%
SAT writing:	410-530	**Return as sophomores:**	72%
ACT composite:	19-23	**Out-of-state:**	17%
GPA 3.75 or higher:	14%	**Live on campus:**	61%
GPA 3.50-3.74:	15%	**International:**	1%
GPA 3.0-3.49:	34%		

Basis for selection. School achievement record, rank in top half of class, and test scores most important. Additional requirements for health care majors, education majors. Admission procedures may vary among schools within the university. Essay and portfolio recommended. Interview recommended for underprepared applicants. **Homeschooled:** State high school equivalency certificate, letter of recommendation (nonparent) required. Bibliography of books read, extracurricular activities.

High school preparation. 20 units required; 26 recommended. Required and recommended units include English 4, mathematics 2-3, social studies 2-3, history 1, science 2-3 and academic electives 1-4.

2008-2009 Annual costs. Tuition/fees: $20,720. Room/board: $6,250. Books/supplies: $1,000. Personal expenses: $1,100.

2007-2008 Financial aid. Need-based: 289 full-time freshmen applied for aid; 260 were judged to have need; 259 of these received aid. Average need met was 80%. Average scholarship/grant was $11,729; average loan $3,031. 56% of total undergraduate aid awarded as scholarships/grants, 44% as loans/jobs. **Non-need-based:** Awarded to 390 full-time undergraduates, including 122 freshmen. Scholarships awarded for academics, alumni affiliation, art, athletics, music/drama.

Application procedures. Admission: Priority date 8/1; no deadline. $20 fee, may be waived for applicants with need, free for online applicants. Admission notification on a rolling basis beginning on or about 8/1. **Financial aid:** Priority date 3/10; no closing date. FAFSA required. Applicants notified on a rolling basis starting 3/1.

Academics. Special study options: Combined bachelor's/graduate degree, cross-registration, double major, dual enrollment of high school students, exchange student, honors, independent study, internships, liberal arts/career combination, teacher certification program. **Credit/placement by examination:** AP, CLEP, SAT, ACT, institutional tests. 16 credit hours maximum toward associate degree, 32 toward bachelor's. **Support services:** Learning center, reduced course load, remedial instruction, study skills assistance, tutoring, writing center.

Majors. Area/ethnic studies: American. **Business:** Accounting, business admin. **Communications:** General, public relations. **Conservation:** General, environmental studies. **Education:** Art, business, chemistry, elementary, English, health, science, social studies, special. **Health:** Clinical lab science, nursing (RN), physician assistant, predental, premedicine, prepharmacy. **History:** General. **Legal studies:** Prelaw. **Liberal arts:** Arts/sciences. **Math:** General. **Philosophy/religion:** Philosophy. **Physical sciences:** Chemistry. **Psychology:** General. **Public administration:** Social work. **Social sciences:** Political science, sociology. **Theology:** Theology. **Visual/performing arts:** Art, art history/conservation, commercial/advertising art, graphic design, studio arts.

Most popular majors. Business/marketing 14%, education 15%, health sciences 33%, interdisciplinary studies 6%, visual/performing arts 10%.

Computing on campus. 313 workstations in dormitories, library, computer center, student center. Dormitories wired for high-speed internet access and linked to campus network. Commuter students can connect to campus network. Online course registration, online library, helpline, repair service, wireless network available.

Student life. Freshman orientation: Mandatory, $32 fee. Three-day program held weekend prior to beginning of classes. **Policies:** No alcohol allowed in residence halls, no smoking in campus buildings. Full-time students under 21 not living at home or with adult relatives must live in residence halls. **Housing:** Guaranteed on-campus for freshmen. Coed dorms, apartments available. $200 deposit. **Activities:** Bands, campus ministries, choral groups, dance, drama, film society, student government, student newspaper, Educators in Action, student nursing association, peer ministers, Fellowship of Christian Athletes.

Athletics. NAIA. **Intercollegiate:** Baseball M, basketball, cheerleading, cross-country, football (tackle) M, golf, soccer, softball W, tennis W, track and field, volleyball W. **Intramural:** Basketball, bowling, volleyball. **Team name:** Cougars.

Student services. Adult student services, chaplain/spiritual director, career counseling, student employment services, financial aid counseling, health services, personal counseling, placement for graduates. **Physically disabled:** Services for visually, hearing impaired.

Contact. E-mail: admiss@sf.edu
Phone: (260) 399-8000 Toll-free number: (800) 729-4732
Fax: (260) 434-7590
Ron Schumacher, Vice President, Enrollment Management, University of St. Francis, 2701 Spring Street, Fort Wayne, IN 46808

University of Southern Indiana
Evansville, Indiana
www.usi.edu **CB code: 1335**

- Public 4-year university and liberal arts college
- Commuter campus in small city
- 9,137 degree-seeking undergraduates: 16% part-time, 59% women, 5% African American, 1% Asian American, 1% Hispanic American, 2% international
- 723 degree-seeking graduate students
- 88% of applicants admitted
- SAT or ACT (ACT writing recommended) required
- 35% graduate within 6 years

General. Founded in 1965. Regionally accredited. Credit courses offered at various off-campus sites in Evansville and surrounding areas. **Degrees:** 1,241 bachelor's, 123 associate awarded; master's, doctoral offered. **ROTC:** Army. **Location:** 150 miles from Indianapolis. **Calendar:** Semester, limited summer session. **Full-time faculty:** 323 total; 60% have terminal degrees, 6% minority, 53% women. **Part-time faculty:** 301 total; 21% have terminal degrees, 4% minority, 54% women. **Class size:** 36% < 20, 51% 20-39, 7% 40-49, 5% 50-99, 2% >100. **Special facilities:** Restored historic town managed by university.

Freshman class profile. 5,125 applied, 4,521 admitted, 2,104 enrolled.

Mid 50% test scores		**Rank in top quarter:**	27%
SAT critical reading:	420-530	**Rank in top tenth:**	9%
SAT math:	420-540	**Return as sophomores:**	66%
SAT writing:	410-510	**Out-of-state:**	7%
ACT composite:	18-23	**Live on campus:**	63%
GPA 3.75 or higher:	12%	**International:**	1%
GPA 3.50-3.74:	10%	**Fraternities:**	6%
GPA 3.0-3.49:	27%	**Sororities:**	4%
GPA 2.0-2.99:	46%		

Basis for selection. 2.0 GPA required for out-of-state applicants. 900 SAT (exclusive of Writing) required for applicants to health programs. Students accepted at 1 of 3 levels based on academic record and test scores. Placement test administered prior to registration. SAT/ACT used to place students at 1 of 3 levels within institution. **Homeschooled:** Transcript of courses and grades required.

High school preparation. College-preparatory program recommended. 18 units recommended. Recommended units include English 4, mathematics 4, social studies 2, history 2, science 2, foreign language 2 and academic electives 2. 2 units computer and/or art recommended.

2008-2009 Annual costs. Tuition/fees: $5,210; $12,140 out-of-state. Room/board: $6,570. Books/supplies: $1,000. Personal expenses: $2,474.

2008-2009 Financial aid. **Need-based:** 1,715 full-time freshmen applied for aid; 1,165 were judged to have need; 1,142 of these received aid. Average need met was 83%. Average scholarship/grant was $5,593; average loan $2,136. 42% of total undergraduate aid awarded as scholarships/grants, 58% as loans/jobs. **Non-need-based:** Awarded to 1,312 full-time undergraduates, including 439 freshmen. Scholarships awarded for academics, alumni affiliation, art, athletics, job skills, leadership, music/drama, state residency.

Application procedures. **Admission:** Closing date 8/15 (receipt date). $25 fee, may be waived for applicants with need. Admission notification on a rolling basis beginning on or about 7/1. Applicants accepted through first week of classes, but encouraged to apply by August 15 for fall and January 1 for spring. **Financial aid:** Closing date 3/1. FAFSA, institutional form required. Applicants notified on a rolling basis starting 4/1.

Academics. **Special study options:** Combined bachelor's/graduate degree, cooperative education, distance learning, double major, dual enrollment of high school students, ESL, honors, independent study, internships, study abroad, teacher certification program. **Credit/placement by examination:** AP, CLEP, SAT, ACT, institutional tests. 96 credit hours maximum toward bachelor's degree. **Support services:** Learning center, reduced course load, remedial instruction, study skills assistance, tutoring, writing center.

Majors. **Biology:** General, biophysics. **Business:** General, accounting, business admin, entrepreneurial studies, finance, marketing, office management. **Communications:** Advertising, journalism, media studies, radio/tv. **Computer sciences:** General, data processing. **Education:** Business, early childhood, elementary, physical. **Engineering:** General. **Foreign languages:** French, German, Spanish. **Health:** Dental hygiene, nursing (RN). **History:** General. **Interdisciplinary:** Biological/physical sciences, nutrition sciences. **Liberal arts:** Arts/sciences. **Math:** General. **Parks/recreation:** Exercise sciences. **Philosophy/religion:** Philosophy. **Physical sciences:** Chemistry, geology. **Psychology:** General. **Public administration:** Social work. **Social sciences:** General, economics, international relations, political science, sociology. **Visual/performing arts:** Art, dramatic.

Most popular majors. Business/marketing 21%, communications/journalism 9%, education 12%, health sciences 22%, social sciences 6%.

Computing on campus. 306 workstations in dormitories, library, computer center, student center. Dormitories linked to campus network. Commuter students can connect to campus network. Online course registration, online library, helpline, wireless network available.

Student life. **Freshman orientation:** Mandatory, $65 fee. Preregistration for classes offered. Two-day program, includes parent participation. **Housing:** Coed dorms, special housing for disabled, apartments, fraternity/sorority housing, wellness housing available. $200 partly refundable deposit, deadline 3/1. **Activities:** Jazz band, campus ministries, choral groups, dance, drama, international student organizations, literary magazine, Model UN, radio station, student government, student newspaper, Black Student Union, Habitat for Humanity, Kappa Chi (Christian Service Fraternity), Baptist Student Ministry, Newman Catholic Student Organization, Collegiate Democrats, Collegiate Republicans.

Athletics. NCAA. **Intercollegiate:** Baseball M, basketball, cheerleading, cross-country, golf, soccer, softball W, tennis, track and field, volleyball W. **Intramural:** Badminton, basketball, bowling, cross-country, football (non-tackle), golf, soccer, softball, swimming, table tennis, tennis, volleyball. **Team name:** Screaming Eagles.

Student services. Adult student services, chaplain/spiritual director, career counseling, student employment services, financial aid counseling, health services, minority student services, on-campus daycare, personal counseling, placement for graduates, veterans' counselor. **Physically disabled:** Services for visually, speech, hearing impaired.

Contact. E-mail: enroll@usi.edu
Phone: (812) 464-1765 Toll-free number: (800) 467-1965
Fax: (812) 465-7154
Eric Otto, Director of Admission, University of Southern Indiana, 8600 University Boulevard, Evansville, IN 47712

Valparaiso University

Valparaiso, Indiana — **CB member**
www.valpo.edu — **CB code: 1874**

- Private 4-year university affiliated with Lutheran Church
- Residential campus in large town
- 2,824 degree-seeking undergraduates: 4% part-time, 53% women, 5% African American, 2% Asian American, 4% Hispanic American, 3% international
- 1,053 degree-seeking graduate students
- 92% of applicants admitted
- SAT or ACT (ACT writing recommended), application essay required
- 75% graduate within 6 years; 25% enter graduate study

General. Founded in 1859. Regionally accredited. **Degrees:** 665 bachelor's, 21 associate awarded; master's, first professional offered. **ROTC:** Army, Air Force. **Location:** 55 miles from Chicago. **Calendar:** Semester, limited summer session. **Full-time faculty:** 257 total; 91% have terminal degrees, 9% minority, 35% women. **Part-time faculty:** 119 total; 34% have terminal degrees, 11% minority, 52% women. **Class size:** 49% < 20, 44% 20-39, 3% 40-49, 4% 50-99, less than 1% >100. **Special facilities:** Electron microscope, observatory, storm chasing equipment, weather station, Doppler Radar facility, planetarium, center for learning and information resources, virtual nursing learning center, scientific visualization laboratory.

Freshman class profile. 3,022 applied, 2,773 admitted, 657 enrolled.

Mid 50% test scores			
SAT critical reading:	490-600	Rank in top quarter:	61%
SAT math:	500-630	Rank in top tenth:	31%
SAT writing:	480-590	End year in good standing:	88%
ACT composite:	22-28	Return as sophomores:	85%
GPA 3.75 or higher:	28%	Out-of-state:	63%
GPA 3.50-3.74:	16%	Live on campus:	90%
GPA 3.0-3.49:	28%	International:	1%
GPA 2.0-2.99:	28%	Fraternities:	26%
		Sororities:	18%

Basis for selection. High school record most important. Test scores next in importance, followed by recommendations and activities. Nature of high school program considered. Interview recommended. Audition required of music majors. Portfolio recommended for art majors. **Homeschooled:** Transcript of courses and grades required. Must specify primary educator and provide course description list or reading list. **Learning Disabled:** Student should submit suitable documentation to the Disability Support Services Office following admission into the University in order to determine eligibility of services.

High school preparation. College-preparatory program recommended. 16 units required; 19 recommended. Required and recommended units include English 4, mathematics 3-4, social studies 1, history 2, science 2-3 (laboratory 2-3), foreign language 2 and academic electives 3.

2008-2009 Annual costs. Tuition/fees: $26,950. Room/board: $7,620. Books/supplies: $1,200. Personal expenses: $890.

2007-2008 Financial aid. **Need-based:** 657 full-time freshmen applied for aid; 545 were judged to have need; 545 of these received aid. Average need met was 86%. Average scholarship/grant was $16,375; average loan $5,243. 69% of total undergraduate aid awarded as scholarships/grants, 31% as loans/jobs. **Non-need-based:** Awarded to 968 full-time undergraduates, including 242 freshmen. Scholarships awarded for academics, alumni affiliation, art, athletics, leadership, music/drama, religious affiliation, ROTC. **Additional information:** Financial assistance based on need, academic record, talent available through university.

Application procedures. **Admission:** Priority date 1/15; deadline 8/15 (receipt date). $30 fee, may be waived for applicants with need, free for online applicants. Admission notification on a rolling basis beginning on or about 10/1. Must reply by May 1 or within 4 week(s) if notified thereafter. **Financial aid:** Priority date 3/1; no closing date. FAFSA required. Applicants notified on a rolling basis starting 3/1; must reply by 5/1.

Academics. **Special study options:** Accelerated study, combined bachelor's/graduate degree, cooperative education, cross-registration, distance learning, double major, ESL, exchange student, honors, independent study, internships, liberal arts/career combination, student-designed major, study abroad, teacher certification program, United Nations semester, urban semester, Washington semester. **Credit/placement by examination:** AP, CLEP, IB, institutional tests. **Support services:** Learning center, reduced course load, study skills assistance, tutoring, writing center.

Honors college/program. Approximately 80 students enroll per year in Christ College, the Honors College. Must demonstrate academic excellence in high school, intellectual curiosity, and leadership skills. Program integrates history, literature, philosophy, religion, and art.

Majors. **Area/ethnic studies:** American, East Asian. **Biology:** General, biochemistry. **Business:** Accounting, actuarial science, finance, international, management science, marketing. **Communications:** Journalism, media studies, organizational, public relations, radio/tv. **Computer sciences:** Computer science. **Conservation:** Environmental science. **Education:** Art, biology, chemistry, drama/dance, elementary, English, foreign languages, French, geography, German, history, mathematics, middle, music, physical, physics, psychology, science, secondary, social science, Spanish. **Engineering:** Civil, computer, electrical, mechanical. **Foreign languages:** Classics,

French, German, Spanish. **Health:** Nursing (RN). **History:** General. **Liberal arts:** Humanities. **Math:** General. **Parks/recreation:** Exercise sciences, health/fitness, sports admin. **Philosophy/religion:** Philosophy. **Physical sciences:** Atmospheric science, chemistry, geology, physics. **Psychology:** General. **Public administration:** Social work. **Social sciences:** General, criminology, economics, geography, international economics, international relations, political science, sociology. **Theology:** Theology. **Visual/performing arts:** Art, dramatic, music management, music performance, music theory/composition, piano/organ, voice/opera. **Other:** Church Music, Communication and Expressive Arts, Geoscience, Multi-/Interdisciplinary studies.

Most popular majors. Business/marketing 15%, communications/journalism 6%, education 8%, engineering/engineering technologies 9%, health sciences 8%, social sciences 12%.

Computing on campus. 901 workstations in dormitories, library, computer center, student center. Dormitories wired for high-speed internet access and linked to campus network. Commuter students can connect to campus network. Online course registration, helpline, student web hosting, wireless network available.

Student life. Freshman orientation: Available, $90 fee. Preregistration for classes offered. Overnight program held in June. **Housing:** Guaranteed on-campus for all undergraduates. Coed dorms, single-sex dorms, apartments, fraternity/sorority housing, wellness housing available. $100 fully refundable deposit, deadline 5/1. Residence hall for German language students. **Activities:** Bands, campus ministries, choral groups, dance, drama, film society, international student organizations, literary magazine, music ensembles, musical theater, radio station, student government, student newspaper, symphony orchestra, Alpha Phi Omega, InterVarsity Christian Fellowship, St. Teresa of Avila, Black Student Organization, Habitat for Humanity, Asian American Association, Latinos in Valparaiso for Excellence, College Democrats.

Athletics. NCAA. **Intercollegiate:** Baseball M, basketball, cross-country, diving, football (tackle) M, soccer, softball W, swimming, tennis, track and field, volleyball W. **Intramural:** Badminton, basketball, bowling, football (non-tackle), golf, racquetball, soccer, softball, swimming, table tennis, tennis, volleyball. **Team name:** Crusaders.

Student services. Adult student services, alcohol/substance abuse counseling, chaplain/spiritual director, career counseling, student employment services, financial aid counseling, health services, legal services, minority student services, personal counseling, placement for graduates. **Physically disabled:** Services for visually impaired.

Contact. E-mail: undergrad.admissions@valpo.edu
Phone: (219) 464-5011 Toll-free number: (888) 468-2576
Fax: (219) 464-6898
David Fevig, Director of Admission, Valparaiso University, Kretzmann Hall, 1700 Chapel Drive, Valparaiso, IN 46383-6493

Wabash College
Crawfordsville, Indiana — **CB member**
www.wabash.edu — **CB code: 1895**

- Private 4-year liberal arts college for men
- Residential campus in large town
- 903 degree-seeking undergraduates: 6% African American, 1% Asian American, 5% Hispanic American, 1% Native American, 5% international
- 48% of applicants admitted
- SAT or ACT (ACT writing optional), application essay required
- 70% graduate within 6 years; 27% enter graduate study

General. Founded in 1832. Regionally accredited. **Degrees:** 186 bachelor's awarded. **Location:** 45 miles from Indianapolis, 125 miles from Chicago. **Calendar:** Semester. **Full-time faculty:** 89 total; 97% have terminal degrees, 9% minority, 33% women. **Part-time faculty:** 2 total; 50% have terminal degrees, 50% women. **Class size:** 80% < 20, 17% 20-39, 2% 40-49, less than 1% 50-99. **Special facilities:** Biology field station, center for teaching and learning in theology and religion, center of inquiry in the liberal arts, qualitative and quantitative skills center, electron microscope, parallel computer, nature preserve, archival center.

Freshman class profile. 1,394 applied, 676 admitted, 256 enrolled.

Mid 50% test scores			
SAT critical reading:	500-620	Rank in top quarter:	65%
SAT math:	540-650	Rank in top tenth:	31%
SAT writing:	480-610	End year in good standing:	92%
ACT composite:	22-28	Return as sophomores:	86%
GPA 3.75 or higher:	35%	Out-of-state:	24%
GPA 3.50-3.74:	22%	Live on campus:	98%
GPA 3.0-3.49:	36%	International:	6%
GPA 2.0-2.99:	7%	Fraternities:	67%

Basis for selection. Class rank, school achievement, recommendation, essay and test scores important. Interview recommended. Character and personal qualities considered. **Learning Disabled:** All students considered on an individual basis.

High school preparation. College-preparatory program required. 17 units recommended. Recommended units include English 4, mathematics 4, social studies 2, science 2 (laboratory 2), foreign language 2 and academic electives 3.

2008-2009 Annual costs. Tuition/fees: $27,950. Room/board: $7,900. Books/supplies: $900. Personal expenses: $1,500.

2008-2009 Financial aid. Need-based: 239 full-time freshmen applied for aid; 222 were judged to have need; 222 of these received aid. Average need met was 100%. Average scholarship/grant was $19,159; average loan $4,597. 72% of total undergraduate aid awarded as scholarships/grants, 28% as loans/jobs. **Non-need-based:** Awarded to 328 full-time undergraduates, including 112 freshmen. Scholarships awarded for academics, art, leadership, music/drama, state residency.

Application procedures. Admission: Priority date 12/15; no deadline. $40 fee, may be waived for applicants with need. Admission notification on a rolling basis beginning on or about 12/15. Must reply by May 1 or within 2 week(s) if notified thereafter. **Financial aid:** Priority date 2/15, closing date 3/1. FAFSA, CSS PROFILE required. Applicants notified by 4/1; must reply by 5/1 or within 2 week(s) of notification.

Academics. Special study options: Combined bachelor's/graduate degree, double major, independent study, internships, liberal arts/career combination, New York semester, semester at sea, study abroad, teacher certification program, United Nations semester, urban semester, Washington semester. Cooperative law program with Columbia University, International and Domestic Study Program of Great Lakes Colleges Association, 3-2 engineering program with Columbia University and Washington University. **Credit/placement by examination:** AP, CLEP, SAT, institutional tests. AP credit based on AP exam scores and with in-house exams and subsequent coursework. **Support services:** Learning center, study skills assistance, tutoring, writing center.

Majors. Biology: General. **Foreign languages:** Ancient Greek, classics, French, German, Latin, Spanish. **History:** General. **Liberal arts:** Arts/sciences. **Math:** General. **Philosophy/religion:** Philosophy, religion. **Physical sciences:** Chemistry, physics. **Psychology:** General. **Social sciences:** Economics, political science. **Visual/performing arts:** Art, dramatic.

Most popular majors. Biology 11%, English 8%, foreign language 11%, history 13%, philosophy/religious studies 15%, psychology 13%, social sciences 17%.

Computing on campus. 360 workstations in dormitories, library, computer center, student center. Dormitories wired for high-speed internet access and linked to campus network. Commuter students can connect to campus network. Online library, helpline, repair service, student web hosting, wireless network available.

Student life. Freshman orientation: Mandatory. Preregistration for classes offered. Five-day program orients students to library and computer resources, the Gentleman's Rule, and includes all class members in community service projects. **Policies:** The Gentleman's Rule is the college's only rule. **Housing:** Guaranteed on-campus for all undergraduates. Apartments, cooperative housing, fraternity/sorority housing, wellness housing available. $150 nonrefundable deposit, deadline 6/25. Limited wheelchair accessibility available. **Activities:** Bands, campus ministries, choral groups, drama, film society, international student organizations, literary magazine, music ensembles, Model UN, musical theater, radio station, student government, student newspaper, symphony orchestra, political groups, Newman Center, Alpha Phi Omega, Fellowship of Christian Athletes, Muslim student association, Wabash Christian Fellowship, Model UN, pre-law society, moot court competition, Sphinx club, black studies association.

Athletics. NCAA. **Intercollegiate:** Baseball M, basketball M, cross-country M, diving M, football (tackle) M, golf M, soccer M, swimming M, tennis M, track and field M, wrestling M. **Intramural:** Badminton M, basketball M, bowling M, cross-country M, diving M, football (non-tackle) M, golf M, handball M, racquetball M, soccer M, softball M, swimming M, table tennis M, tennis M, track and field M, volleyball M, wrestling M. **Team name:** Little Giants.

Student services. Alcohol/substance abuse counseling, chaplain/spiritual director, career counseling, student employment services, financial aid counseling, health services, minority student services, personal counseling, placement for graduates. **Physically disabled:** Services for visually impaired.

Contact. E-mail: admissions@wabash.edu
Phone: (765) 361-6225 Toll-free number: (800) 345-5385
Fax: (765) 361-6437
Steven Klein, Dean of Admissions and Financial Aid, Wabash College, PO Box 352, Crawfordsville, IN 47933

Iowa

Allen College
Waterloo, Iowa
www.allencollege.edu **CB code: 3610**

- Private 4-year health science and nursing college
- Commuter campus in small city
- 308 degree-seeking undergraduates: 23% part-time, 95% women, 1% African American, 1% Hispanic American, 1% Native American
- 97 degree-seeking graduate students
- 43% of applicants admitted
- SAT or ACT, application essay required
- 56% graduate within 6 years; 5% enter graduate study

General. Regionally accredited. **Degrees:** 96 bachelor's, 14 associate awarded; master's offered. **ROTC:** Army. **Calendar:** Semester, limited summer session. **Full-time faculty:** 27 total; 22% have terminal degrees, 4% minority, 100% women. **Part-time faculty:** 5 total; 100% women. **Class size:** 70% < 20, 20% 20-39, 6% 40-49, 5% 50-99.

Freshman class profile. 14 applied, 6 admitted, 4 enrolled.

Mid 50% test scores		**Rank in top quarter:**	25%
ACT composite:	21-25	**End year in good standing:**	72%
GPA 3.50-3.74:	50%	**Return as sophomores:**	72%
GPA 3.0-3.49:	50%		

Basis for selection. College and secondary school record, class rank, test scores important; recommendations, essay considered. Pre-requisite courses required prior to admission to BSN and health science degree programs.

High school preparation. 4 units required. Required units include English 4, mathematics 3, social studies 3, science 3 (laboratory 2).

2008-2009 Annual costs. Tuition/fees: $14,895. Room/board: $6,178. Books/supplies: $891. Personal expenses: $2,724.

2007-2008 Financial aid. Non-need-based: Scholarships awarded for academics, leadership, minority status, ROTC.

Application procedures. Admission: Priority date 3/1; deadline 8/1 (receipt date). $50 fee, may be waived for applicants with need. Admission notification on a rolling basis. Must reply by May 1 or within 4 week(s) if notified thereafter. **Financial aid:** Priority date 6/1; no closing date. FAFSA, institutional form required. Applicants notified on a rolling basis starting 4/1; must reply within 2 week(s) of notification.

Academics. Special study options: Accelerated study, combined bachelor's/graduate degree, cooperative education, distance learning, external degree, honors, independent study, internships, liberal arts/career combination. **Credit/placement by examination:** AP, CLEP, IB. **Support services:** Learning center, study skills assistance, tutoring, writing center.

Majors. Health: Clinical lab science, nuclear medical technology, nursing (RN).

Computing on campus. 29 workstations in dormitories, library, computer center. Dormitories wired for high-speed internet access. Online library, helpline, wireless network available.

Student life. Freshman orientation: Mandatory. Includes registration, assessment testing, and completion of mandatory health career training. **Housing:** Coed dorms, single-sex dorms, special housing for disabled, apartments, cooperative housing, wellness housing available. $200 nonrefundable deposit. On-campus suite housing available and dorm-style housing offered at cooperating institutions. **Activities:** Choral groups, student government, student newspaper.

Student services. Alcohol/substance abuse counseling, chaplain/spiritual director, career counseling, financial aid counseling, health services, on-campus daycare, personal counseling, placement for graduates, women's services. **Physically disabled:** Services for visually, speech, hearing impaired.

Contact. E-mail: allencollegeadmissions@ihs.org
Phone: (319) 226-2000 Fax: (319) 226-2051
Michelle Koehn, Admissions Counselor, Allen College, 1825 Logan Avenue, Waterloo, IA 50703

Ashford University
Clinton, Iowa **CB member**
www.ashford.edu **CB code: 6418**

- For-profit 4-year university
- Commuter campus in large town
- 23,665 degree-seeking undergraduates: 75% women, 25% African American, 2% Asian American, 8% Hispanic American, 1% Native American
- 1,765 degree-seeking graduate students
- 39% graduate within 6 years

General. Founded in 1918. Regionally accredited. **Degrees:** 1,089 bachelor's, 5 associate awarded; master's offered. **Location:** 35 miles from Davenport, 138 miles from Chicago. **Calendar:** Semester, limited summer session. **Full-time faculty:** 50 total; 46% women. **Part-time faculty:** 1,251 total; 28% minority, 59% women. **Class size:** 15% < 20, 62% 20-39, 5% 40-49, 18% 50-99. **Special facilities:** Restored prairie land adjacent to campus.

Freshman class profile.

GPA 3.75 or higher:	9%	**GPA 2.0-2.99:**	53%
GPA 3.50-3.74:	8%	**Rank in top quarter:**	21%
GPA 3.0-3.49:	22%	**Rank in top tenth:**	5%

Basis for selection. High school record, GPA, class rank, test scores all considered. Applicants not meeting selection criteria may be admitted conditionally. Interview required for teacher education majors. Audition recommended for fine arts. Portfolio recommended for art majors. Essay recommended for academically weak applicants.

High school preparation. College-preparatory program recommended. 20 units recommended. Recommended units include English 4, mathematics 3, social studies 2, history 3, science 3, foreign language 2 and academic electives 3.

2008-2009 Annual costs. Tuition/fees: $15,890. Room/board: $5,800. Books/supplies: $1,000.

2008-2009 Financial aid. Need-based: 17% of total undergraduate aid awarded as scholarships/grants, 83% as loans/jobs. **Non-need-based:** Scholarships awarded for academics, art, athletics, music/drama.

Application procedures. Admission: No deadline. $20 fee, may be waived for applicants with need. Admission notification on a rolling basis beginning on or about 9/1. **Financial aid:** Priority date 3/1; no closing date. FAFSA, institutional form required. Applicants notified on a rolling basis starting 2/15; must reply within 2 week(s) of notification.

Academics. Special study options: Combined bachelor's/graduate degree, distance learning, double major, dual enrollment of high school students, ESL, external degree, honors, independent study, internships, student-designed major, study abroad, teacher certification program. **Credit/placement by examination:** AP, CLEP, institutional tests. 32 credit hours maximum toward associate degree, 32 toward bachelor's. Awards credit for CLEP exams in accordance with the American Council on Education (ACE) designated passing score and recommended credit. **Support services:** Learning center, reduced course load, remedial instruction, tutoring.

Majors. Biology: General. **Business:** General, accounting, business admin, communications, finance, human resources, marketing. **Communications:** General. **Computer sciences:** General. **Conservation:** Environmental studies. **Education:** Biology, chemistry, early childhood, elementary, English, history, mathematics, middle, music, reading, science, secondary, social science, social studies. **Health:** Cytotechnology, health care admin, premedicine. **Interdisciplinary:** Math/computer science. **Legal studies:** Prelaw. **Liberal arts:** Arts/sciences. **Psychology:** General. **Social sciences:** General. **Visual/performing arts:** Graphic design, studio arts.

Most popular majors. Business/marketing 57%, education 11%, psychology 29%.

Computing on campus. PC or laptop required. 109 workstations in dormitories, library, computer center. Dormitories wired for high-speed internet access and linked to campus network. Online library, helpline, repair service, wireless network available.

Student life. Freshman orientation: Mandatory. Preregistration for classes offered. Two-day program held in summer prior to beginning of fall classes.

Housing: Guaranteed on-campus for all undergraduates. Coed dorms available. $125 deposit. **Activities:** Choral groups, drama, music ensembles, student government, student newspaper, Christian Fellowship club, Hispanic American leadership organization, Circle K, black student union, Iowa Education Association.

Athletics. NAIA. **Intercollegiate:** Baseball M, basketball, cross-country, golf M, soccer, softball W, track and field, volleyball W. **Intramural:** Basketball, bowling, football (non-tackle), swimming, volleyball. **Team name:** Saints.

Student services. Adult student services, chaplain/spiritual director, career counseling, student employment services, financial aid counseling, minority student services, on-campus daycare, placement for graduates.

Contact. E-mail: admissions@ashford.edu
Phone: (563) 242-4153 Toll-free number: (800) 242-4153
Fax: (563) 243-6102
Jason Woods, Director of Enrollment, Ashford University, 400 North Bluff Boulevard, Clinton, IA 52733-2967

Briar Cliff University
Sioux City, Iowa
www.briarcliff.edu **CB code: 6046**

- Private 4-year liberal arts college affiliated with Roman Catholic Church
- Residential campus in small city
- 1,026 degree-seeking undergraduates: 12% part-time, 55% women, 5% African American, 2% Asian American, 6% Hispanic American, 1% Native American
- 82 degree-seeking graduate students
- 69% of applicants admitted
- ACT (writing optional) required
- 54% graduate within 6 years; 22% enter graduate study

General. Founded in 1930. Regionally accredited. **Degrees:** 236 bachelor's, 1 associate awarded; master's offered. **ROTC:** Army. **Location:** 90 miles from Omaha, Nebraska. **Calendar:** Trimester, limited summer session. **Full-time faculty:** 60 total; 68% have terminal degrees, 5% minority, 53% women. **Part-time faculty:** 48 total; 10% have terminal degrees, 60% women. **Class size:** 73% < 20, 24% 20-39, 2% 40-49, 2% 50-99. **Special facilities:** Prairie nature preserve, human anatomy/cadaver laboratory, integrated media lab, nursing simulation lab, entrepreneurship lab, music lab.

Freshman class profile. 1,402 applied, 965 admitted, 252 enrolled.

Mid 50% test scores		**GPA 2.0-2.99:**	34%
SAT critical reading:	410-510	**Rank in top quarter:**	29%
SAT math:	460-550	**Rank in top tenth:**	12%
ACT composite:	19-24	**End year in good standing:**	80%
GPA 3.75 or higher:	18%	**Return as sophomores:**	64%
GPA 3.50-3.74:	17%	**Out-of-state:**	46%
GPA 3.0-3.49:	29%	**Live on campus:**	90%

Basis for selection. 2.0 GPA and 18 ACT required for full acceptance. Students not meeting requirement may be accepted conditionally or may appeal admission decision if not accepted. Interview and essay recommended. **Homeschooled:** Transcript of high school work should be obtained from the school district where the student resides full time. **Learning Disabled:** Students should submit official documentation directly to Student Support Services office.

High school preparation. 16 units recommended. Recommended units include English 4, mathematics 3, social studies 3, science 3, foreign language 2 and academic electives 1.

2008-2009 Annual costs. Tuition/fees: $21,510. Room/board: $6,411. Books/supplies: $825. Personal expenses: $1,935.

2008-2009 Financial aid. Need-based: 246 full-time freshmen applied for aid; 184 were judged to have need; 184 of these received aid. Average need met was 90%. Average scholarship/grant was $6,500; average loan $3,900. 57% of total undergraduate aid awarded as scholarships/grants, 43% as loans/jobs. **Non-need-based:** Awarded to 1,014 full-time undergraduates, including 312 freshmen. Scholarships awarded for academics, alumni affiliation, art, athletics, leadership, music/drama, religious affiliation, state residency.

Application procedures. Admission: Priority date 4/1; no deadline. $20 fee, may be waived for applicants with need. Admission notification on a rolling basis beginning on or about 6/1. **Financial aid:** Priority date 3/15; no closing date. FAFSA required. Applicants notified on a rolling basis starting 3/15; must reply by 5/1 or within 2 week(s) of notification.

Academics. Special study options: Accelerated study, cross-registration, distance learning, double major, honors, independent study, internships, liberal arts/career combination, student-designed major, study abroad, teacher certification program, urban semester, weekend college. Radiologic technology 1-2-1 program, medical technology 3-1 program. **Credit/placement by examination:** AP, CLEP, IB, ACT, institutional tests. 45 credit hours maximum toward bachelor's degree. Examinations must be taken before student enters last 30 hours of study. **Support services:** Learning center, preadmission summer program, reduced course load, remedial instruction, study skills assistance, tutoring, writing center.

Majors. Biology: General. **Business:** Accounting, business admin, human resources, management information systems. **Communications:** Digital media, media studies. **Communications technology:** Graphics. **Computer sciences:** General, computer science. **Conservation:** Environmental science. **Education:** General, art, biology, chemistry, elementary, English, history, mathematics, music, physical, reading, science, secondary, social science. **Foreign languages:** Spanish. **Health:** Clinical lab science, medical radiologic technology/radiation therapy, nursing (RN). **History:** General. **Interdisciplinary:** Biological/physical sciences. **Math:** General. **Parks/recreation:** Exercise sciences, health/fitness, sports admin. **Physical sciences:** Chemistry. **Protective services:** Law enforcement admin. **Psychology:** General. **Public administration:** Social work. **Social sciences:** Political science, sociology. **Theology:** Theology. **Visual/performing arts:** Art, dramatic, film/cinema, graphic design.

Most popular majors. Business/marketing 26%, education 11%, health sciences 21%, parks/recreation 6%.

Computing on campus. 102 workstations in dormitories, library, computer center, student center. Dormitories wired for high-speed internet access and linked to campus network. Commuter students can connect to campus network. Online library, helpline, repair service, student web hosting, wireless network available.

Student life. Freshman orientation: Mandatory, $95 fee. Preregistration for classes offered. Orientation begins when students move onto campus, prior to beginning of classes. **Housing:** Guaranteed on-campus for freshmen. Coed dorms available. $150 fully refundable deposit. Quad suites available. **Activities:** Jazz band, campus ministries, choral groups, dance, drama, literary magazine, music ensembles, musical theater, opera, radio station, student government, student newspaper, Best Buddies, BCCares, Champions of Characters Council of Athletes, College Democrats, College Republicans, criminal justice club, departmental clubs, ethnic relations club, mentors in violence prevention.

Athletics. NAIA. **Intercollegiate:** Baseball M, basketball, cheerleading M, cross-country, football (tackle) M, golf, soccer, softball W, tennis, track and field, volleyball W, wrestling M. **Intramural:** Badminton, basketball, bowling, cross-country, football (non-tackle) M, golf, handball, racquetball, soccer, softball, table tennis, tennis, track and field, volleyball. **Team name:** Chargers.

Student services. Alcohol/substance abuse counseling, chaplain/spiritual director, career counseling, services for economically disadvantaged, student employment services, financial aid counseling, health services, personal counseling, placement for graduates. **Physically disabled:** Services for visually impaired.

Contact. E-mail: admissions@briarcliff.edu
Phone: (712) 279-5200 Toll-free number: (800) 662-3303 ext. 5200
Fax: (712) 279-1632
Sharisue Wilcoxon, Vice President for Enrollment Management, Briar Cliff University, 3303 Rebecca Street, Sioux City, IA 51104-0100

Buena Vista University
Storm Lake, Iowa
www.bvu.edu **CB code: 6047**

- Private 4-year liberal arts college affiliated with Presbyterian Church (USA)
- Residential campus in large town
- 957 degree-seeking undergraduates: 1% part-time, 50% women, 5% African American, 1% Asian American, 5% Hispanic American, 3% international
- 102 degree-seeking graduate students
- 75% of applicants admitted
- SAT or ACT (ACT writing optional) required
- 61% graduate within 6 years; 17% enter graduate study

General. Founded in 1891. Regionally accredited. 14 branch sites throughout Iowa and online programs provide educational opportunities for nontraditional students. **Degrees:** 768 bachelor's awarded; master's offered. **Location:** 150 miles from Des Moines, 80 miles from Sioux City. **Calendar:**

4-1-4, limited summer session. **Full-time faculty:** 82 total; 70% have terminal degrees, 4% minority, 43% women. **Part-time faculty:** 29 total; 10% have terminal degrees, 7% minority, 52% women. **Class size:** 70% < 20, 29% 20-39, less than 1% 40-49, less than 1% 50-99. **Special facilities:** Multimedia production facilities, underground buildings, information technology center, digitally-controlled acoustic music practice rooms.

Freshman class profile. 1,309 applied, 986 admitted, 274 enrolled.

Mid 50% test scores			
ACT composite:	19-25	Rank in top quarter:	38%
GPA 3.75 or higher:	23%	Rank in top tenth:	12%
GPA 3.50-3.74:	12%	Return as sophomores:	72%
GPA 3.0-3.49:	34%	Out-of-state:	30%
GPA 2.0-2.99:	31%	Live on campus:	98%
		International:	5%

Basis for selection. High school GPA and curriculum, rank in class, standardized test scores, interview, school and community activities important. Essay recommended.

High school preparation. College-preparatory program recommended. 15 units required. Required and recommended units include English 4, mathematics 4, social studies 2, history 2, science 2-4, foreign language 2 and computer science 1.

2008-2009 Annual costs. Tuition/fees: $24,796. Room/board: $7,014. Books/supplies: $1,000. Personal expenses: $1,500.

2008-2009 Financial aid. **Need-based:** 250 full-time freshmen applied for aid; 233 were judged to have need; 233 of these received aid. Average need met was 62%. Average scholarship/grant was $11,583; average loan $4,511. 66% of total undergraduate aid awarded as scholarships/grants, 34% as loans/jobs. **Non-need-based:** Awarded to 1,430 full-time undergraduates, including 225 freshmen. Scholarships awarded for academics, art, minority status, music/drama, religious affiliation. **Additional information:** Portfolio required of art scholarship applicants, audition required of music and drama scholarship applicants.

Application procedures. **Admission:** No deadline. No application fee. Admission notification on a rolling basis. **Financial aid:** Priority date 6/1; no closing date. FAFSA required. Applicants notified on a rolling basis starting 2/20.

Academics. Students must earn credit by attending the Academic and Cultural Events Series, featuring lectures by national and international leaders and performances by world-famous classical performing groups and artists. **Special study options:** Combined bachelor's/graduate degree, distance learning, double major, dual enrollment of high school students, ESL, external degree, honors, independent study, internships, student-designed major, study abroad, teacher certification program, Washington semester. Rollins Fellows (competitive international internships). **Credit/placement by examination:** AP, CLEP, IB, ACT, institutional tests. 20 credit hours maximum toward bachelor's degree. **Support services:** Learning center, reduced course load, remedial instruction, study skills assistance, tutoring, writing center.

Majors. **Biology:** General. **Business:** Accounting, banking/financial services, entrepreneurial studies, human resources, international, management information systems, managerial economics, marketing. **Communications:** General, media studies, organizational. **Computer sciences:** Computer science. **Conservation:** Environmental science. **Education:** Art, biology, business, chemistry, computer, elementary, English, history, mathematics, music, physical, physics, psychology, reading, science, social science, Spanish, special, speech. **Foreign languages:** Spanish. **Health:** Athletic training. **History:** General. **Interdisciplinary:** Biological/physical sciences. **Math:** General. **Parks/recreation:** Exercise sciences, sports admin. **Philosophy/religion:** Philosophy. **Physical sciences:** Chemistry, physics. **Protective services:** Criminal justice. **Psychology:** General. **Public administration:** General, social work. **Social sciences:** General, political science, sociology. **Visual/performing arts:** Art, arts management, commercial/advertising art, music performance, theater history.

Most popular majors. Business/marketing 28%, education 16%, interdisciplinary studies 15%, psychology 13%, security/protective services 7%.

Computing on campus. 400 workstations in dormitories, library, computer center, student center. Dormitories wired for high-speed internet access and linked to campus network. Commuter students can connect to campus network. Online course registration, online library, helpline, repair service, wireless network available.

Student life. **Freshman orientation:** Mandatory. Preregistration for classes offered. Two-day orientation offered during summer. **Housing:** Guaranteed on-campus for all undergraduates. Coed dorms, single-sex dorms, wellness housing available. $200 nonrefundable deposit. **Activities:** Bands, campus ministries, choral groups, drama, international student organizations, music ensembles, musical theater, radio station, student government, student newspaper, TV station, Circle-K, Students Concerned about Tomorrow's Environment, intervarsity multicultural club, Fellowship of Christian Athletes, College Democrats, College Republicans, Reshaping Our Campus Community.

Athletics. NCAA. **Intercollegiate:** Baseball M, basketball, cross-country, football (tackle) M, golf, soccer, softball W, tennis, track and field, volleyball W, wrestling M. **Intramural:** Basketball, football (non-tackle) M, racquetball, softball, table tennis, tennis, volleyball. **Team name:** Beavers.

Student services. Adult student services, alcohol/substance abuse counseling, chaplain/spiritual director, career counseling, student employment services, financial aid counseling, health services, minority student services, personal counseling, placement for graduates, veterans' counselor. **Physically disabled:** Services for visually, speech, hearing impaired.

Contact. E-mail: admissions@bvu.edu
Phone: (712) 749-2235 Toll-free number: (800) 383-9600
Fax: (712) 749-2037
Alan Coheley, Vice President, Enrollment Management, Buena Vista University, 610 West Fourth Street, Storm Lake, IA 50588

Central College

Pella, Iowa — **CB member**
www.central.edu — **CB code: 6087**

- Private 4-year liberal arts college affiliated with Reformed Church in America
- Residential campus in large town
- 1,445 degree-seeking undergraduates: 1% part-time, 52% women, 2% African American, 1% Asian American, 2% Hispanic American, 1% international
- 77% of applicants admitted
- SAT or ACT (ACT writing optional) required
- 68% graduate within 6 years

General. Founded in 1853. Regionally accredited. **Degrees:** 341 bachelor's awarded. **Location:** 45 miles from Des Moines. **Calendar:** Semester, limited summer session. **Full-time faculty:** 89 total; 91% have terminal degrees, 10% minority, 40% women. **Part-time faculty:** 67 total; 22% have terminal degrees, 3% minority, 40% women. **Class size:** 57% < 20, 37% 20-39, 6% 50-99. **Special facilities:** Glass-blowing studio, cross-cultural study center, center for communication and theater.

Freshman class profile. 2,072 applied, 1,602 admitted, 405 enrolled.

Mid 50% test scores			
SAT critical reading:	380-550	Rank in top quarter:	54%
SAT math:	420-630	Rank in top tenth:	25%
ACT composite:	19-29	Return as sophomores:	80%
GPA 3.75 or higher:	38%	Out-of-state:	20%
GPA 3.50-3.74:	19%	Live on campus:	100%
GPA 3.0-3.49:	26%	Fraternities:	1%
GPA 2.0-2.99:	17%	Sororities:	1%

Basis for selection. High school curriculum, GPA, class rank, test scores important. Recommendations, school and community activities, alumni affiliation also considered. Interview and essay recommended. Audition recommended for music and theater majors; required for scholarships. Portfolio recommended for art majors; required for scholarships. **Homeschooled:** Transcript of courses and grades required.

High school preparation. College-preparatory program recommended. 15 units recommended. Required and recommended units include English 4, mathematics 2-3, social studies 3, history 2, science 2-3 (laboratory 2) and foreign language 2.

2008-2009 Annual costs. Tuition/fees: $23,944. Costs provided are for main campus only. International location costs may vary by program location. Room/board: $8,006.

2008-2009 Financial aid. **Non-need-based:** Scholarships awarded for academics, alumni affiliation, art, leadership, minority status, music/drama, religious affiliation, state residency. **Additional information:** Institutional parent loan program and interest-earning, tuition prepayment savings account available.

Application procedures. **Admission:** No deadline. $25 fee, may be waived for applicants with need, free for online applicants. Admission notification on a rolling basis. **Financial aid:** Priority date 3/15; no closing date. FAFSA required. Applicants notified on a rolling basis starting 3/15; must reply by 5/1 or within 2 week(s) of notification.

Academics. Special study options: Combined bachelor's/graduate degree, cooperative education, cross-registration, double major, dual enrollment of high school students, ESL, honors, independent study, internships, liberal arts/career combination, student-designed major, study abroad, teacher certification program, urban semester, Washington semester. Chicago semester; study centers in France, Austria, Spain, England, Wales, Mexico, China, and the Netherlands. **Credit/placement by examination:** AP, CLEP, IB, SAT, ACT, institutional tests. **Support services:** Learning center, reduced course load, study skills assistance, tutoring, writing center.

Majors. Biology: General. **Business:** Accounting, business admin, international. **Communications:** General. **Computer sciences:** General, information systems. **Conservation:** Environmental studies. **Education:** Elementary, music. **Foreign languages:** French, German, linguistics, Spanish. **History:** General. **Interdisciplinary:** Global studies, math/computer science, natural sciences. **Math:** General. **Parks/recreation:** Exercise sciences. **Philosophy/religion:** Philosophy, religion. **Physical sciences:** Chemistry, physics. **Psychology:** General. **Social sciences:** General, anthropology, economics, political science, sociology. **Visual/performing arts:** Art, dramatic.

Most popular majors. Biology 9%, business/marketing 15%, communications/journalism 6%, education 11%, foreign language 9%, parks/recreation 11%, social sciences 11%.

Computing on campus. 256 workstations in dormitories, library, computer center, student center. Dormitories wired for high-speed internet access and linked to campus network. Commuter students can connect to campus network. Online library, helpline, repair service, student web hosting, wireless network available.

Student life. Freshman orientation: Mandatory. Preregistration for classes offered. Held weekends in June. **Housing:** Guaranteed on-campus for all undergraduates. Coed dorms, single-sex dorms, special housing for disabled, apartments, fraternity/sorority housing, wellness housing available. $200 fully refundable deposit, deadline 5/1. Townhouses for juniors and seniors, environmental stewardship house, foreign language houses available. **Activities:** Bands, campus ministries, choral groups, drama, international student organizations, literary magazine, music ensembles, musical theater, radio station, student government, student newspaper, symphony orchestra, Young Democrats, Young Republicans, Fellowship of Christian Athletes, Inter-Varsity Christian Fellowship, alcohol awareness committee, multicultural campus association, Circle-K, Amnesty International, Students Against Apartheid, students concerned about the environment.

Athletics. NCAA. **Intercollegiate:** Baseball M, basketball, cross-country, football (tackle) M, golf, soccer, softball W, tennis, track and field, volleyball W, wrestling M. **Intramural:** Basketball, racquetball, rugby, softball, volleyball. **Team name:** Dutch.

Student services. Alcohol/substance abuse counseling, chaplain/spiritual director, career counseling, services for economically disadvantaged, student employment services, financial aid counseling, health services, minority student services, personal counseling, placement for graduates, veterans' counselor. **Physically disabled:** Services for visually, speech, hearing impaired. **Learning disabled:** Comprehensive services available.

Contact. E-mail: admissions@central.edu
Phone: (641) 628-5286 Toll-free number: (877) 462-3687
Fax: (641) 628-5316
Carol Williamson, Dean of Admission, Central College, 812 University Street, Pella, IA 50219-1999

Clarke College
Dubuque, Iowa
www.clarke.edu **CB code: 6099**

- Private 4-year liberal arts college affiliated with Roman Catholic Church
- Residential campus in small city
- 940 degree-seeking undergraduates: 13% part-time, 69% women, 1% African American, 2% Hispanic American, 2% international
- 200 degree-seeking graduate students
- 62% of applicants admitted
- SAT or ACT (ACT writing optional) required
- 64% graduate within 6 years; 18% enter graduate study

General. Founded in 1843. Regionally accredited. **Degrees:** 246 bachelor's, 1 associate awarded; master's, doctoral offered. **ROTC:** Army. **Location:** 150 miles from Chicago. **Calendar:** Semester, limited summer session. **Full-time faculty:** 72 total; 64% have terminal degrees, 62% women. **Part-time faculty:** 58 total; 5% have terminal degrees, 57% women. **Class size:** 79% < 20, 21% 20-39, less than 1% 40-49, less than 1% 50-99. **Special facilities:** Planetarium, art and communications laboratory, writing center, art slide library, computerized mathematics laboratory, nursing laboratory, human gross anatomy laboratory with A.D.A.M. software.

Freshman class profile. 947 applied, 587 admitted, 139 enrolled.

Mid 50% test scores		**GPA 2.0-2.99:**	21%
SAT critical reading:	480-550	**Rank in top quarter:**	45%
SAT math:	460-640	**Rank in top tenth:**	17%
SAT writing:	510-560	**Return as sophomores:**	80%
ACT composite:	20-25	**Out-of-state:**	52%
GPA 3.75 or higher:	28%	**Live on campus:**	86%
GPA 3.50-3.74:	17%	**International:**	5%
GPA 3.0-3.49:	32%		

Basis for selection. High school record of primary importance. Particular attention paid to grades on college preparatory course work and test scores. Interview required of the academically weak. Auditions required of music and drama majors. Portfolio required of art majors.

High school preparation. 21 units required. Required and recommended units include English 4, mathematics 3-4, social studies 3, science 3-4 (laboratory 2), foreign language 2 and academic electives 4. 4 college preparatory math and science, including 3 lab, required for physical therapy program.

2008-2009 Annual costs. Tuition/fees: $22,378. Room/board: $6,574. Books/supplies: $700. Personal expenses: $700.

2008-2009 Financial aid. Need-based: 132 full-time freshmen applied for aid; 111 were judged to have need; 111 of these received aid. Average need met was 92%. Average scholarship/grant was $17,066; average loan $3,406. 69% of total undergraduate aid awarded as scholarships/grants, 31% as loans/jobs. **Non-need-based:** Awarded to 793 full-time undergraduates, including 198 freshmen. Scholarships awarded for academics, alumni affiliation, art, athletics, leadership, music/drama, religious affiliation, state residency. **Additional information:** Reduced tuition for family members of BVMs.

Application procedures. Admission: No deadline. $25 fee, may be waived for applicants with need, free for online applicants. Admission notification on a rolling basis beginning on or about 1/15. Must reply by May 1 or within 3 week(s) if notified thereafter. **Financial aid:** Priority date 4/15; no closing date. Applicants notified on a rolling basis starting 3/11; must reply by 5/1 or within 2 week(s) of notification.

Academics. Special study options: Accelerated study, cooperative education, cross-registration, distance learning, double major, ESL, honors, independent study, internships, liberal arts/career combination, student-designed major, study abroad, teacher certification program. **Credit/placement by examination:** AP, CLEP, IB, SAT, ACT, institutional tests. 15 credit hours maximum toward associate degree, 30 toward bachelor's. Students applying for prior learning assessment (PLA) credit must be 24 years of age or older. Maximum of 30 credits granted for PLA, CLEP or DANTES within 5-year period. If more than 15 PLA credits are awarded based on portfolio evaluation, additional credit up to 30 hours must be matched by regular college credit. PLA does not count toward the 30 hour residency requirement and is awarded only after 5 hours in degree program are completed. Guidelines may vary by department. **Support services:** Learning center, reduced course load, study skills assistance, tutoring, writing center.

Majors. Biology: General, biochemistry, bioinformatics. **Business:** Accounting, business admin. **Communications:** General. **Computer sciences:** General. **Education:** Elementary, music, physical. **Foreign languages:** Spanish. **Health:** Predental, premedicine, prepharmacy, preveterinary. **History:** General. **Math:** General. **Parks/recreation:** Sports admin. **Philosophy/religion:** Philosophy, religion. **Physical sciences:** Chemistry. **Psychology:** General. **Public administration:** Social work. **Visual/performing arts:** Art, art history/conservation, dramatic, studio arts.

Most popular majors. Biology 7%, business/marketing 16%, communications/journalism 6%, education 16%, health sciences 20%, psychology 6%, visual/performing arts 10%.

Computing on campus. 237 workstations in dormitories, library, computer center, student center. Dormitories wired for high-speed internet access and linked to campus network. Commuter students can connect to campus network. Online course registration, online library, wireless network available.

Student life. Freshman orientation: Available. Preregistration for classes offered. **Housing:** Guaranteed on-campus for freshmen. Coed dorms, single-sex dorms, apartments, wellness housing available. $100 fully refundable deposit, deadline 7/15. **Activities:** Jazz band, campus ministries, choral groups, drama, literary magazine, music ensembles, musical theater, radio station, student government, student newspaper, Amnesty International, peace and justice, peer ministry program, minority student organization, Walden Society (political discussion group).

Athletics. NAIA. **Intercollegiate:** Baseball M, basketball, cheerleading M, cross-country, golf, soccer, softball W, tennis, track and field, volleyball. **Intramural:** Basketball, bowling, football (non-tackle), softball, table tennis, tennis, volleyball. **Team name:** Crusaders.

Student services. Adult student services, alcohol/substance abuse counseling, chaplain/spiritual director, career counseling, student employment services, financial aid counseling, health services, minority student services, personal counseling. **Physically disabled:** Services for visually, hearing impaired.

Contact. E-mail: admissions@clarke.edu
Phone: (563) 588-6316 Toll-free number: (800) 383-2345
Fax: (563) 588-6789
Andy Schroeder, Director of Admission, Clarke College, 1550 Clarke Drive, Dubuque, IA 52001-3198

Coe College

Cedar Rapids, Iowa — **CB member**
www.coe.edu — **CB code: 6101**

- Private 4-year nursing and liberal arts college affiliated with Presbyterian Church (USA)
- Residential campus in small city
- 1,269 degree-seeking undergraduates: 2% part-time, 55% women
- 63% of applicants admitted
- SAT or ACT (ACT writing optional), application essay required
- 69% graduate within 6 years

General. Founded in 1851. Regionally accredited. **Degrees:** 287 bachelor's awarded; master's offered. **ROTC:** Army, Air Force. **Location:** 230 miles from Chicago, 300 miles from Minneapolis-St. Paul. **Calendar:** Semester, limited summer session. **Full-time faculty:** 88 total; 84% have terminal degrees, 9% minority, 35% women. **Part-time faculty:** 78 total; 14% have terminal degrees, 1% minority, 65% women. **Class size:** 68% < 20, 31% 20-39, less than 1% 40-49, less than 1% 50-99. **Special facilities:** Infrared spectrometer, analytical physiology units, music library, wilderness field station.

Freshman class profile. 1,943 applied, 1,224 admitted, 342 enrolled.

Mid 50% test scores			
SAT critical reading:	560-680	GPA 2.0-2.99:	2%
SAT math:	550-670	Rank in top quarter:	66%
SAT writing:	540-650	Rank in top tenth:	30%
ACT composite:	23-28	Return as sophomores:	80%
GPA 3.75 or higher:	47%	Live on campus:	97%
GPA 3.50-3.74:	21%	International:	4%
GPA 3.0-3.49:	30%	Fraternities:	17%

Basis for selection. School achievement record and test scores most important. Recommendations and school activities also important. Interview and community activities considered. **Homeschooled:** GED and portfolio required. **Learning Disabled:** Submission of disability assessment required.

High school preparation. College-preparatory program recommended. 18 units recommended. Recommended units include English 4, mathematics 3, social studies 3, science 3 (laboratory 1), foreign language 2 and academic electives 2.

2009-2010 Annual costs. Tuition/fees (projected): $29,270. Cost per course for part-time students (fewer than 3 course credits) is $3,620. Room/board: $7,150. Books/supplies: $1,000. Personal expenses: $1,600.

2008-2009 Financial aid. Need-based: 292 full-time freshmen applied for aid; 252 were judged to have need; 251 of these received aid. Average need met was 95%. Average scholarship/grant was $18,422; average loan $5,255. 71% of total undergraduate aid awarded as scholarships/grants, 29% as loans/jobs. **Non-need-based:** Awarded to 465 full-time undergraduates, including 155 freshmen. Scholarships awarded for academics, alumni affiliation, art, leadership, music/drama, ROTC.

Application procedures. Admission: Priority date 12/10; deadline 3/1 (postmark date). $30 fee, may be waived for applicants with need, free for online applicants. Admission notification on a rolling basis beginning on or about 10/1. Must reply by May 1 or within 2 week(s) if notified thereafter. **Financial aid:** Priority date 3/1; no closing date. FAFSA required. Applicants notified on a rolling basis starting 3/15; must reply by 5/1 or within 2 week(s) of notification.

Academics. Writing emphasis courses required. Semester practicum required for all students. **Special study options:** Accelerated study, combined bachelor's/graduate degree, cross-registration, double major, dual enrollment of high school students, ESL, exchange student, honors, independent study, internships, New York semester, student-designed major, study abroad, teacher certification program, urban semester, Washington semester. Oak Ridge science semester; research program at the Coe College wilderness field station- Minnesota Superior National Forest; tropical field research in Costa Rica; travel abroad to England, Hong Kong, India, Italy, Japan, Russia, Latin America, Czech Republic, Tanzania, Germany, Sweden, Spain, France, Korea, Thailand, Ireland. **Credit/placement by examination:** AP, CLEP, IB, SAT, ACT, institutional tests. **Support services:** Pre-admission summer program, reduced course load, study skills assistance, tutoring, writing center.

Majors. Area/ethnic studies: African-American, American, Asian, French, German, Spanish/Iberian. **Biology:** General, biochemistry, molecular. **Business:** Accounting, business admin. **Communications:** General, public relations. **Computer sciences:** Computer science. **Conservation:** Environmental science. **Education:** General, art, elementary, middle, music, physical, science, secondary. **Foreign languages:** Classics, French, German, Spanish. **Health:** Athletic training, nursing (RN), predental, premedicine, preveterinary. **History:** General. **Interdisciplinary:** Accounting/computer science, biological/physical sciences, math/computer science. **Legal studies:** Prelaw. **Math:** General. **Parks/recreation:** Health/fitness. **Philosophy/religion:** Philosophy, religion. **Physical sciences:** General, chemistry, physics. **Psychology:** General. **Social sciences:** Economics, political science, sociology. **Visual/performing arts:** Acting, art, ceramics, directing/producing, dramatic, music performance, music theory/composition, painting, photography, studio arts, theater design.

Most popular majors. Biology 6%, business/marketing 23%, communications/journalism 6%, health sciences 8%, parks/recreation 6%, psychology 8%, social sciences 10%, visual/performing arts 10%.

Computing on campus. Dormitories wired for high-speed internet access and linked to campus network. Commuter students can connect to campus network. Online course registration, online library, helpline, student web hosting, wireless network available.

Student life. Freshman orientation: Mandatory, $75 fee. Four- or five-day program. **Policies:** Students must live on campus unless residing with relatives or granted off-campus permission by Department of Residence Life. **Housing:** Guaranteed on-campus for all undergraduates. Coed dorms, single-sex dorms, apartments, fraternity/sorority housing, wellness housing available. $200 nonrefundable deposit, deadline 5/1. **Activities:** Bands, campus ministries, choral groups, dance, drama, international student organizations, literary magazine, music ensembles, musical theater, radio station, student government, student newspaper, symphony orchestra, TV station, black self-education organization, Friends club, Egalitarians Supporting the Advancement of Women, Christian Fellowship, College Republicans, Habitat for Humanity, green club, College Democrats, Fellowship of Christian Athletes.

Athletics. NCAA. **Intercollegiate:** Baseball M, basketball, cheerleading M, cross-country, diving, football (tackle) M, golf, soccer, softball W, swimming, tennis, track and field, volleyball W, wrestling M. **Intramural:** Badminton, basketball, football (non-tackle) M, racquetball, soccer, softball, squash, table tennis, tennis, volleyball, wrestling M. **Team name:** Kohawks.

Student services. Adult student services, alcohol/substance abuse counseling, career counseling, student employment services, financial aid counseling, health services, minority student services, personal counseling, placement for graduates.

Contact. E-mail: admission@coe.edu
Phone: (319) 399-8500 Toll-free number: (877) 225-5263
Fax: (319) 399-8816
John Grundig, Dean of Admission, Coe College, 1220 First Avenue NE, Cedar Rapids, IA 52402

Cornell College

Mount Vernon, Iowa — **CB member**
www.cornellcollege.edu — **CB code: 6119**

- Private 4-year liberal arts college affiliated with United Methodist Church
- Residential campus in small town
- 1,102 degree-seeking undergraduates: 4% African American, 3% Asian American, 4% Hispanic American, 1% Native American, 4% international
- 45% of applicants admitted
- SAT or ACT (ACT writing optional), application essay required
- 67% graduate within 6 years

General. Founded in 1853. Regionally accredited. Three distinct academic centers: Center for Teaching and Learning, Dimensions, Center for the Science and Culture of Healthcare, and Center for Economics, Business, and Public Policy. **Degrees:** 240 bachelor's awarded. **Location:** 15 miles from Cedar Rapids, 20 miles from Iowa City. **Calendar:** Nine terms of 3 and 1/2 weeks, one course per term. **Full-time faculty:** 81 total; 98% have terminal degrees, 7% minority, 49% women. **Part-time faculty:** 11 total; 82% have terminal degrees, 27% minority, 73% women. **Class size:** 67% < 20, 33% 20-39. **Special facilities:** Canadian/Minnesota border wilderness station, geology museum.

Freshman class profile. 2,659 applied, 1,209 admitted, 340 enrolled.

Mid 50% test scores		**Rank in top quarter:**	53%
SAT critical reading:	560-690	**Rank in top tenth:**	27%
SAT math:	540-660	**End year in good standing:**	85%
ACT composite:	24-30	**Return as sophomores:**	85%
GPA 3.75 or higher:	32%	**Out-of-state:**	78%
GPA 3.50-3.74:	25%	**Live on campus:**	99%
GPA 3.0-3.49:	30%	**International:**	5%
GPA 2.0-2.99:	13%		

Basis for selection. Academic record, essay, co-curricular involvement, evidence of character, standardized test score, letters of reference, and recommended optional interview important. Primary consideration given to academic performance in college preparatory courses. **Homeschooled:** Transcript of courses and grades, letter of recommendation (nonparent) required. Applicants asked to provide as many documents pertaining to their education as possible. **Learning Disabled:** Must have recent documentation of disability from official source if student requires special arrangements in academic setting.

High school preparation. College-preparatory program recommended. 15 units recommended. Recommended units include English 4, mathematics 3, social studies 3, science 3, foreign language 2 and academic electives 1. As many advanced, honors, and/or AP courses as possible recommended.

2009-2010 Annual costs. Tuition/fees: $29,580. Room/board: $7,350. Books/supplies: $720. Personal expenses: $540.

2007-2008 Financial aid. Need-based: 83% of total undergraduate aid awarded as scholarships/grants, 17% as loans/jobs. **Non-need-based:** Scholarships awarded for academics, art, leadership, minority status, music/drama, religious affiliation, state residency. **Additional information:** Portfolio required for art scholarship applicants. Audition required for music scholarship applicants.

Application procedures. Admission: Priority date 2/1; deadline 3/1 (postmark date). $30 fee, may be waived for applicants with need, free for online applicants. Must reply by May 1 or within 2 week(s) if notified thereafter. **Financial aid:** Closing date 3/1. FAFSA, institutional form required. Applicants notified on a rolling basis starting 3/1; must reply by 5/1 or within 2 week(s) of notification.

Academics. Special study options: Accelerated study, combined bachelor's/graduate degree, double major, ESL, exchange student, independent study, internships, liberal arts/career combination, semester at sea, student-designed major, study abroad, teacher certification program, urban semester, Washington semester. **Credit/placement by examination:** AP, CLEP, IB, institutional tests. **Support services:** Learning center, study skills assistance, tutoring, writing center.

Majors. Area/ethnic studies: Latin American, Russian/Slavic, women's. **Biology:** General, Biochemistry/biophysics and molecular biology. **Computer sciences:** Computer science. **Conservation:** Environmental studies. **Education:** General, art, biology, chemistry, elementary, English, French, German, history, mathematics, middle, music, physical, physics, science, secondary, social science, social studies, Spanish. **Foreign languages:** General, classics, French, German, Russian, Spanish. **History:** General. **Math:** General. **Parks/recreation:** Health/fitness. **Philosophy/religion:** Philosophy, religion. **Physical sciences:** Chemistry, geology, physics. **Psychology:** General. **Social sciences:** Economics, international relations, political science, sociology. **Visual/performing arts:** Art, dramatic, music performance. **Other:** Ethnic studies, Medieval and early modern studies, Sociology and anthropology.

Most popular majors. Biology 10%, education 7%, English 6%, interdisciplinary studies 6%, philosophy/religious studies 7%, psychology 9%, social sciences 18%, visual/performing arts 10%.

Computing on campus. 181 workstations in library, computer center, student center. Dormitories wired for high-speed internet access and linked to campus network. Commuter students can connect to campus network. Online library, helpline, repair service, student web hosting, wireless network available.

Student life. Freshman orientation: Mandatory. Five-day orientation held before fall classes begin. **Housing:** Guaranteed on-campus for freshmen. Coed dorms, single-sex dorms, apartments, wellness housing available. $300 partly refundable deposit, deadline 5/1. First-year halls/floors available. **Activities:** Bands, campus ministries, choral groups, dance, drama, international student organizations, literary magazine, music ensembles, musical theater, opera, radio station, student government, student newspaper, symphony orchestra, Alpha Phi Omega, alumni student association, fellowship of Christian athletes, black awareness cultural organization, women's action group, Young Democrats, College Republicans, Habitat for Humanity, women's social groups, men's social groups, lunch buddies/youth mentoring.

Athletics. NCAA. **Intercollegiate:** Baseball M, basketball, cross-country, football (tackle) M, golf, soccer, softball W, tennis, track and field, volleyball W, wrestling M. **Intramural:** Badminton, basketball, bowling, football (non-tackle), lacrosse, racquetball, soccer, softball, table tennis, track and field, volleyball. **Team name:** Rams.

Student services. Adult student services, alcohol/substance abuse counseling, career counseling, student employment services, financial aid counseling, health services, minority student services, personal counseling, women's services.

Contact. E-mail: admissions@cornellcollege.edu
Phone: (319) 895-4215 Toll-free number: (800) 747-1112
Fax: (319) 895-4451
Jonathan Stroud, Vice President for Enrollment/Dean of Admissions and Financial Aid, Cornell College, 600 First Street SW, Mount Vernon, IA 52314-1098

Divine Word College

Epworth, Iowa
www.dwci.edu **CB code: 6174**

- Private 4-year liberal arts and seminary college for men affiliated with Roman Catholic Church
- Rural community
- 33 degree-seeking undergraduates
- 75% of applicants admitted
- Application essay, interview required

General. Founded in 1912. Regionally accredited. **Degrees:** 4 bachelor's, 2 associate awarded. **Location:** 15 miles from Dubuque. **Calendar:** Semester. **Full-time faculty:** 22 total. **Part-time faculty:** 3 total.

Freshman class profile. 4 applied, 3 admitted, 3 enrolled.

Mid 50% test scores		**SAT math:**	520-570
SAT critical reading:	520-620		

Basis for selection. Interview and religious commitment most important. School achievement record, test scores, recommendations, and school and community activities also considered. Minnesota Multiphasic Personality Inventory (MMPI) used for admission and counseling. SAT or ACT writing component considered if submitted.

High school preparation. 16 units required. Required and recommended units include mathematics 3, social studies 3, science 3 and foreign language 2. 1 performing arts recommended.

2008-2009 Annual costs. Tuition/fees: $10,500. Room/board: $2,700. Books/supplies: $500.

Application procedures. Admission: Closing date 7/15. $25 fee, may be waived for applicants with need. Admission notification on a rolling basis beginning on or about 1/1. **Financial aid:** Priority date 8/31; no closing date. Applicants notified on a rolling basis starting 8/1.

Academics. Special study options: Double major, dual enrollment of high school students, independent study, study abroad. **Credit/placement by examination:** AP, CLEP, institutional tests. **Support services:** Reduced course load, remedial instruction, tutoring.

Majors. Interdisciplinary: Intercultural. **Philosophy/religion:** Philosophy.

Computing on campus. 26 workstations in computer center.

Student life. Policies: Religious observance required. **Housing:** All students live in dormitories on campus. **Activities:** Campus ministries, choral groups, student government, Vietnamese student organization, Sudanese student organization, social justice committee, Right to Life committee.

Athletics. **Intramural:** Basketball M, soccer M, swimming M, table tennis M, tennis M, volleyball M.

Student services. Career counseling, health services, personal counseling.

Contact. E-mail: svdvocations@dwci.edu
Phone: (563) 876-3332
Len Uhal, Vice President for Recruitment and Admissions, Divine Word College, 102 Jacoby Drive SW, Epworth, IA 52045

Dordt College
Sioux Center, Iowa
www.dordt.edu **CB code: 6171**

- Private 4-year liberal arts college affiliated with Christian Reformed Church
- Residential campus in small town
- 1,314 degree-seeking undergraduates: 4% part-time, 50% women, 1% Hispanic American, 17% international
- 87% of applicants admitted
- SAT or ACT (ACT writing optional) required
- 69% graduate within 6 years; 15% enter graduate study

General. Founded in 1955. Regionally accredited. **Degrees:** 242 bachelor's, 20 associate awarded; master's offered. **Location:** 45 miles from Sioux City; 55 miles from Sioux Falls, South Dakota. **Calendar:** Semester. **Full-time faculty:** 79 total; 62% have terminal degrees, 4% minority, 23% women. **Part-time faculty:** 27 total; 11% have terminal degrees, 59% women. **Class size:** 62% < 20, 30% 20-39, 5% 40-49, 3% 50-99, less than 1% >100. **Special facilities:** Farm, biotechnology research facility.

Freshman class profile. 988 applied, 855 admitted, 405 enrolled.

Mid 50% test scores		**GPA 2.0-2.99:**	16%
SAT critical reading:	480-600	**Rank in top quarter:**	52%
SAT math:	500-640	**Rank in top tenth:**	31%
SAT writing:	460-590	**End year in good standing:**	94%
ACT composite:	22-27	**Return as sophomores:**	75%
GPA 3.75 or higher:	33%	**Out-of-state:**	66%
GPA 3.50-3.74:	22%	**Live on campus:**	95%
GPA 3.0-3.49:	28%	**International:**	10%

Basis for selection. School achievement record, high school GPA, test scores, religious affiliation or commitment important. Applicants with less than 2.25 GPA considered on individual basis, may be admitted on probation. Interview recommended for academically borderline applicants. **Homeschooled:** Must submit certified GPA. **Learning Disabled:** Copies of prior testing and interview with learning disabilities advisor required.

High school preparation. 17 units required; 25 recommended. Required and recommended units include English 3-4, mathematics 2-3, social studies 1, history 2, science 2-4, foreign language 2-3 and academic electives 6. 10 units must be in social science, English, foreign language, natural science, or math. Math must include algebra, geometry.

2008-2009 Annual costs. Tuition/fees: $21,040. Room/board: $5,720. Books/supplies: $780. Personal expenses: $2,000.

2007-2008 Financial aid. **Need-based:** 362 full-time freshmen applied for aid; 303 were judged to have need; 303 of these received aid. Average need met was 91%. Average scholarship/grant was $11,295; average loan $5,399. 52% of total undergraduate aid awarded as scholarships/grants, 48% as loans/jobs. **Non-need-based:** Awarded to 330 full-time undergraduates, including 110 freshmen. Scholarships awarded for academics, alumni affiliation, art, athletics, job skills, leadership, minority status, music/drama, religious affiliation, state residency.

Application procedures. **Admission:** Closing date 7/31. $25 fee, may be waived for applicants with need. Admission notification on a rolling basis beginning on or about 10/1. Must reply by May 1 or within 1 week(s) if notified thereafter. **Financial aid:** Priority date 4/1; no closing date. FAFSA, institutional form required. Applicants notified on a rolling basis starting 3/15; must reply within 3 week(s) of notification.

Academics. **Special study options:** Combined bachelor's/graduate degree, double major, ESL, honors, independent study, internships, liberal arts/career combination, student-designed major, study abroad, teacher certification program, urban semester, Washington semester. Iowa Legislative Intern program; China, England, Costa Rica, Russia, Latin America, Netherlands, and Germany semesters; Los Angeles-Film Institute semester, Chicago Metro semester, American Studies semester. **Credit/placement by examination:** AP, CLEP, IB, SAT, ACT, institutional tests. Registrar makes determination on case-by-case basis. Some credit may be given for work experience. **Support services:** Learning center, reduced course load, remedial instruction, study skills assistance, tutoring.

Majors. **Agriculture:** Agribusiness operations, animal sciences, business, plant sciences. **Biology:** General. **Business:** General, accounting, accounting/business management, information resources management, marketing. **Communications:** General, broadcast journalism, digital media, journalism, media studies, public relations. **Communications technology:** General, graphics. **Computer sciences:** General, computer science, information systems, LAN/WAN management, system admin. **Conservation:** General, environmental studies. **Education:** General, art, biology, business, chemistry, drama/dance, elementary, English, foreign languages, health, history, mathematics, middle, music, physical, physics, reading, science, secondary, social science, social studies, Spanish, special, speech. **Engineering:** General, agricultural, biomedical, civil, computer, electrical, mechanical. **Engineering technology:** General. **Foreign languages:** Dutch/Flemish, Spanish. **Health:** Athletic training, clinical lab science, clinical lab technology, health services, nursing (RN), predental, premedicine, prepharmacy, preveterinary. **History:** General. **Legal studies:** Prelaw. **Liberal arts:** Arts/sciences. **Math:** General. **Parks/recreation:** General, exercise sciences, health/fitness, sports admin. **Philosophy/religion:** Philosophy, religion. **Physical sciences:** General, chemistry, physics. **Protective services:** Police science. **Psychology:** General. **Public administration:** General, social work. **Social sciences:** General, political science. **Theology:** Missionary, sacred music, theology, youth ministry. **Visual/performing arts:** Art, commercial/advertising art, design, dramatic, piano/organ, stringed instruments, voice/opera.

Most popular majors. Agriculture 6%, business/marketing 22%, communications/journalism 6%, education 16%, engineering/engineering technologies 8%, psychology 6%.

Computing on campus. 200 workstations in dormitories, library, computer center, student center. Dormitories wired for high-speed internet access and linked to campus network. Commuter students can connect to campus network. Online course registration, online library, helpline, wireless network available.

Student life. **Freshman orientation:** Mandatory. Preregistration for classes offered. Three-day program prior to beginning of classes. **Policies:** Religious observance required. **Housing:** Guaranteed on-campus for all undergraduates. Single-sex dorms, special housing for disabled, apartments, wellness housing available. $100 deposit, deadline 6/1. **Activities:** Bands, campus ministries, choral groups, dance, drama, film society, international student organizations, literary magazine, music ensembles, musical theater, opera, radio station, student government, student newspaper, symphony orchestra, 50 clubs and student organizations.

Athletics. NAIA. **Intercollegiate:** Baseball M, basketball, cross-country, football (tackle) M, golf M, ice hockey M, soccer, softball W, tennis, track and field, volleyball W. **Intramural:** Badminton, basketball, bowling, cross-country, field hockey W, golf, racquetball, soccer, softball, swimming, tennis, volleyball. **Team name:** Defenders.

Student services. Adult student services, alcohol/substance abuse counseling, chaplain/spiritual director, career counseling, student employment services, financial aid counseling, health services, minority student services, personal counseling, placement for graduates, veterans' counselor, women's services. **Physically disabled:** Services for visually, speech, hearing impaired. **Learning disabled:** Comprehensive services available.

Contact. E-mail: admission@dordt.edu
Phone: (712) 722-6080 Toll-free number: (800) 343-6738
Fax: (712) 722-6035
Quentin Van Essen, Executive Director of Admissions, Dordt College, 498 Fourth Avenue, NE, Sioux Center, IA 51250

Drake University
Des Moines, Iowa **CB member**
www.drake.edu **CB code: 6168**

- Private 4-year university
- Residential campus in large city
- 3,465 degree-seeking undergraduates: 5% part-time, 57% women, 3% African American, 4% Asian American, 2% Hispanic American, 7% international
- 2,063 degree-seeking graduate students
- 69% of applicants admitted
- SAT or ACT (ACT writing optional), application essay required
- 70% graduate within 6 years

General. Founded in 1881. Regionally accredited. **Degrees:** 736 bachelor's awarded; master's, doctoral, first professional offered. **ROTC:** Army.

Location: 150 miles from Omaha, Nebraska; 194 miles from Kansas City, Missouri. **Calendar:** Semester, extensive summer session. **Full-time faculty:** 270 total; 95% have terminal degrees, 14% minority, 46% women. **Part-time faculty:** 137 total. **Class size:** 47% < 20, 35% 20-39, 10% 40-49, 4% 50-99, 4% >100. **Special facilities:** Observatory, greenhouse.

Freshman class profile. 4,786 applied, 3,319 admitted, 902 enrolled.

Mid 50% test scores		**Rank in top quarter:**	73%
SAT critical reading:	520-640	**Rank in top tenth:**	41%
SAT math:	550-660	**Return as sophomores:**	86%
ACT composite:	24-29	**Out-of-state:**	70%
GPA 3.75 or higher:	55%	**Live on campus:**	92%
GPA 3.50-3.74:	17%	**International:**	2%
GPA 3.0-3.49:	21%	**Fraternities:**	15%
GPA 2.0-2.99:	7%	**Sororities:**	23%

Basis for selection. High school academic record, test scores, extracurricular activities, counselor recommendation, and essay important. Comprehensive review completed and each item in student's file considered. Interview recommended for all, required for some. Audition required of music and theater majors. Portfolio recommended for art majors.

High school preparation. College-preparatory program recommended. 16 units recommended. Recommended units include English 4, mathematics 3, social studies 4, science 2 (laboratory 1) and foreign language 2.

2008-2009 Annual costs. Tuition/fees: $24,872. Room/board: $7,410. Books/supplies: $900. Personal expenses: $1,500.

2008-2009 Financial aid. **Need-based:** 725 full-time freshmen applied for aid; 534 were judged to have need; 534 of these received aid. Average need met was 89%. Average scholarship/grant was $14,176; average loan $5,051. 60% of total undergraduate aid awarded as scholarships/grants, 40% as loans/jobs. **Non-need-based:** Awarded to 1,684 full-time undergraduates, including 478 freshmen. Scholarships awarded for academics, alumni affiliation, art, athletics, music/drama, ROTC, state residency.

Application procedures. **Admission:** Priority date 3/1; no deadline. $25 fee, may be waived for applicants with need, free for online applicants. Admission notification on a rolling basis beginning on or about 10/15. **Financial aid:** Priority date 3/1; no closing date. FAFSA required. Applicants notified on a rolling basis starting 3/1; must reply by 5/1 or within 3 week(s) of notification.

Academics. Peer support through academic departments and residence halls offered. **Special study options:** Accelerated study, combined bachelor's/graduate degree, cooperative education, distance learning, double major, dual enrollment of high school students, ESL, honors, independent study, internships, liberal arts/career combination, semester at sea, student-designed major, study abroad, teacher certification program, Washington semester. **Credit/placement by examination:** AP, CLEP, IB, institutional tests. 66 credit hours maximum toward bachelor's degree. **Support services:** Study skills assistance, tutoring, writing center.

Majors. **Biology:** General, biochemistry, cellular/molecular, pharmacology. **Business:** General, accounting, actuarial science, finance, international, management information systems, management science, managerial economics, marketing. **Communications:** General, advertising, broadcast journalism, journalism, media studies, public relations, radio/tv. **Computer sciences:** General, computer science, information technology. **Conservation:** Environmental science, management/policy. **Education:** Curriculum, elementary, mathematics, music, secondary. **Health:** Health services, pharmaceutical sciences. **History:** General. **Interdisciplinary:** Neuroscience. **Legal studies:** General. **Math:** General. **Philosophy/religion:** Ethics, philosophy, religion. **Physical sciences:** Astronomy, chemistry, physics. **Psychology:** General. **Social sciences:** General, anthropology, economics, international relations, political science, sociology. **Visual/performing arts:** Acting, art history/conservation, commercial/advertising art, directing/producing, dramatic, drawing, music management, music performance, painting, printmaking, sculpture, theater design.

Most popular majors. Biology 8%, business/marketing 31%, communications/journalism 13%, education 10%, social sciences 9%, visual/performing arts 7%.

Computing on campus. 4,900 workstations in dormitories, library, computer center, student center. Dormitories wired for high-speed internet access and linked to campus network. Commuter students can connect to campus network. Online course registration, online library, helpline, repair service, student web hosting, wireless network available.

Student life. **Freshman orientation:** Available, $90 fee. Preregistration for classes offered. Four 1-1/2 day sessions held in June; includes parents. **Policies:** Student leaders must maintain 2.0 GPA. Students must live on campus the first 2 years following high school. **Housing:** Guaranteed on-campus for freshmen. Coed dorms, special housing for disabled, apartments, fraternity/sorority housing, wellness housing available. $250 nonrefundable deposit, deadline 5/1. **Activities:** Bands, campus ministries, choral groups, drama, international student organizations, literary magazine, music ensembles, Model UN, musical theater, radio station, student government, student newspaper, symphony orchestra, Coalition of Black Students, Best Buddies, College Republicans, College Democrats, La Fuerza Latina, Alpha Phi Omega, South Asian student association, Rainbow Union, Drake Hillel.

Athletics. NCAA. **Intercollegiate:** Basketball, cheerleading, cross-country, football (tackle) M, golf, rowing (crew) W, soccer, softball W, tennis, track and field, volleyball W. **Intramural:** Badminton, basketball, football (non-tackle), football (tackle) M, golf, racquetball, soccer, swimming, tennis, volleyball. **Team name:** Bulldogs.

Student services. Career counseling, student employment services, financial aid counseling, health services, legal services, personal counseling, placement for graduates. **Physically disabled:** Services for visually, speech, hearing impaired.

Contact. E-mail: admission@drake.edu
Phone: (515) 271-3181 Toll-free number: (800) 443-7253
Fax: (515) 271-2831
Laura Linn, Director of Admission, Drake University, 2507 University Avenue, Des Moines, IA 50311-4505

Emmaus Bible College

Dubuque, Iowa
www.emmaus.edu **CB code: 1215**

- Private 4-year Bible college affiliated with Brethren Church
- Residential campus in small city
- 238 degree-seeking undergraduates: 7% part-time, 57% women
- 91% of applicants admitted
- SAT or ACT (ACT writing optional), application essay required
- 67% graduate within 6 years

General. Founded in 1942. Accredited by ABHE. **Degrees:** 38 bachelor's, 7 associate awarded. **Location:** 90 miles from Waterloo, 150 miles from Chicago. **Calendar:** Semester. **Full-time faculty:** 17 total. **Part-time faculty:** 12 total. **Class size:** 75% < 20, 14% 20-39, 4% 40-49, 7% 50-99.

Freshman class profile. 43 applied, 39 admitted, 30 enrolled.

Mid 50% test scores		**GPA 3.0-3.49:**	32%
SAT critical reading:	490-660	**GPA 2.0-2.99:**	27%
SAT math:	490-640	**Rank in top quarter:**	27%
SAT writing:	450-560	**Rank in top tenth:**	2%
ACT composite:	16-26	**Out-of-state:**	70%
GPA 3.75 or higher:	17%	**Live on campus:**	99%
GPA 3.50-3.74:	24%		

Basis for selection. Recommendations and essay most important. GPA also important. All high school students admitted, but some may be placed on academic probation. Interview recommended. **Homeschooled:** Transcript of courses and grades, letter of recommendation (nonparent) required.

2008-2009 Annual costs. Tuition/fees: $11,030. Room/board: $5,212. Books/supplies: $600. Personal expenses: $1,600.

Financial aid. **Non-need-based:** Scholarships awarded for academics, music/drama.

Application procedures. **Admission:** Priority date 7/9; no deadline. $25 fee. Admission notification on a rolling basis. Must reply by May 1 or within 2 week(s) if notified thereafter. **Financial aid:** Priority date 5/15, closing date 7/1. FAFSA, institutional form required. Applicants notified on a rolling basis starting 3/1; must reply within 2 week(s) of notification.

Academics. **Special study options:** Combined bachelor's/graduate degree, double major, dual enrollment of high school students, ESL, internships, teacher certification program. **Credit/placement by examination:** AP, CLEP, IB, SAT, ACT, institutional tests. 9 credit hours maximum toward associate degree, 18 toward bachelor's. **Support services:** Reduced course load, remedial instruction, study skills assistance, tutoring.

Majors. **Computer sciences:** General. **Education:** Elementary, music. **Theology:** Bible, missionary, theology, youth ministry.

Most popular majors. Computer/information sciences 13%, education 25%, theological studies 25%.

Computing on campus. 60 workstations in library, computer center, student center. Dormitories wired for high-speed internet access and linked to campus network. Online library, wireless network available.

Student life. Freshman orientation: Mandatory. Four days immediately preceding first day of class. **Policies:** No smoking, alcohol consumption, dancing. **Housing:** Guaranteed on-campus for all undergraduates. Single-sex dorms available. $170 nonrefundable deposit, deadline 7/9. **Activities:** Choral groups, drama, international student organizations, radio station, student government.

Athletics. NCCAA. **Intercollegiate:** Basketball. **Intramural:** Badminton, basketball, cross-country, football (non-tackle), golf, racquetball, soccer, softball, table tennis, tennis, volleyball. **Team name:** Eagles.

Student services. Chaplain/spiritual director, career counseling, student employment services, financial aid counseling, health services, personal counseling, veterans' counselor.

Contact. E-mail: info@emmaus.edu
Phone: (563) 588-8000 ext. 1310 Fax: (563) 588-1216
Steven Witter, Director of Admissions, Emmaus Bible College, 2570 Asbury Road, Dubuque, IA 52001

Faith Baptist Bible College and Theological Seminary

Ankeny, Iowa
www.faith.edu **CB code: 6214**

- Private 4-year Bible and seminary college affiliated with General Association of Regular Baptist Churches
- Residential campus in large town
- 310 degree-seeking undergraduates: 8% part-time, 54% women, 1% African American, 1% Asian American, 3% Hispanic American, 1% international
- 56 graduate students
- 87% of applicants admitted
- SAT or ACT (ACT writing optional), application essay required
- 37% graduate within 6 years

General. Founded in 1921. Regionally accredited; also accredited by ABHE. **Degrees:** 67 bachelor's, 17 associate awarded; master's, first professional offered. **Location:** 6 miles from Des Moines. **Calendar:** Semester, limited summer session. **Full-time faculty:** 21 total; 76% have terminal degrees, 10% minority, 14% women. **Part-time faculty:** 13 total; 31% have terminal degrees, 8% minority, 31% women. **Class size:** 68% < 20, 15% 20-39, 4% 40-49, 10% 50-99, 4% >100.

Freshman class profile. 149 applied, 129 admitted, 93 enrolled.

Mid 50% test scores		**GPA 3.0-3.49:**	30%
SAT critical reading:	380-560	**GPA 2.0-2.99:**	18%
SAT math:	430-520	**Rank in top quarter:**	44%
SAT writing:	370-570	**Rank in top tenth:**	8%
ACT composite:	19-25	**Return as sophomores:**	86%
GPA 3.75 or higher:	30%	**Out-of-state:**	53%
GPA 3.50-3.74:	22%	**Live on campus:**	95%

Basis for selection. Recommendations, church affiliation, character qualities important. Interview recommended for borderline applicants. **Homeschooled:** Transcript of courses and grades required. Validation by third-party testing recommended, such as SAT, ACT, GED. **Learning Disabled:** Request for accommodation must be submitted.

High school preparation. College-preparatory program required. Recommended units include English 4, mathematics 4, social studies 3, history 4, science 3 (laboratory 3), foreign language 2 and computer science 4.

2008-2009 Annual costs. Tuition/fees: $12,706. Room/board: $5,010.

2007-2008 Financial aid. Non-need-based: Scholarships awarded for academics, leadership, music/drama.

Application procedures. Admission: Priority date 6/1; deadline 8/1 (postmark date). $25 fee, may be waived for applicants with need. Application must be submitted on paper. Admission notification on a rolling basis. **Financial aid:** Priority date 4/1; no closing date. FAFSA required. Applicants notified on a rolling basis starting 3/15.

Academics. Special study options: Internships, liberal arts/career combination, study abroad, teacher certification program. **Credit/placement by examination:** AP, CLEP, institutional tests. 6 credit hours maximum toward associate degree, 12 toward bachelor's. **Support services:** Learning center, reduced course load, remedial instruction, study skills assistance, tutoring.

Majors. Education: Elementary, English, middle, music, secondary. **Theology:** Bible, missionary, religious ed, sacred music, theology.

Most popular majors. Education 27%, theological studies 73%.

Computing on campus. 46 workstations in dormitories, library, computer center. Dormitories wired for high-speed internet access and linked to campus network. Repair service, wireless network available.

Student life. Freshman orientation: Mandatory. Preregistration for classes offered. Held weekend before classes start in fall. **Policies:** All single students under the age of 26 and not living at home must live in the residence halls. Religious observance required. **Housing:** Guaranteed on-campus for freshmen. Single-sex dorms, special housing for disabled, apartments available. $200 deposit, deadline 6/1. **Activities:** Bands, choral groups, drama, music ensembles, student government, student missionary fellowship, missionary kids fellowship, missions ambassadors, student association, Future Christian Teachers Association, ladies fellowship.

Athletics. NCCAA. **Intercollegiate:** Basketball, soccer, volleyball W. **Intramural:** Basketball, football (tackle). **Team name:** Eagles.

Student services. Career counseling, financial aid counseling, health services, personal counseling, placement for graduates, veterans' counselor.

Contact. E-mail: admissions@faith.edu
Phone: (515) 964-0601 ext. 233 Toll-free number: (888) 324-8448
Fax: (515) 964-1638
Patrick Odle, Vice President Enrollment/Constituency Services, Faith Baptist Bible College and Theological Seminary, 1900 NW Fourth Street, Ankeny, IA 50023

Graceland University

Lamoni, Iowa
www.graceland.edu **CB code: 6249**

- Private 4-year university and liberal arts college affiliated with Community of Christ
- Residential campus in rural community
- 1,383 degree-seeking undergraduates: 15% part-time, 63% women, 9% African American, 2% Asian American, 3% Hispanic American, 10% international
- 740 degree-seeking graduate students
- 55% of applicants admitted
- SAT or ACT (ACT writing optional) required
- 49% graduate within 6 years; 11% enter graduate study

General. Founded in 1895. Regionally accredited. Additional campus in Independence, Missouri. Evening and weekend programs offered at Indian Hills Community College and North Central Missouri College. **Degrees:** 417 bachelor's awarded; master's offered. **Location:** 75 miles from Des Moines, 110 miles from Kansas City. **Calendar:** 4-1-4, limited summer session. **Full-time faculty:** 97 total; 70% have terminal degrees, 6% minority, 50% women. **Class size:** 63% < 20, 31% 20-39, 2% 40-49, 3% 50-99. **Special facilities:** Electron microscope, communications network, international health center, center for study of Korean War.

Freshman class profile. 837 applied, 461 admitted, 197 enrolled.

Mid 50% test scores		**Rank in top quarter:**	46%
SAT critical reading:	460-590	**Rank in top tenth:**	21%
SAT math:	430-600	**End year in good standing:**	94%
ACT composite:	21-25	**Return as sophomores:**	66%
GPA 3.75 or higher:	34%	**Out-of-state:**	35%
GPA 3.50-3.74:	14%	**Live on campus:**	97%
GPA 3.0-3.49:	34%	**International:**	13%
GPA 2.0-2.99:	18%		

Basis for selection. Rank in upper 50% of class, 2.5 GPA, 21 ACT or 960 SAT (exclusive of Writing) important. Applicants who do not meet admissions criteria may be considered individually. If accepted, they will be required to take developmental courses. Some applicants may be requested to test for Chance Program prior to being considered for acceptance. Interview required of applicants who do not meet admissions requirements, recommended for others. Portfolio recommended of art majors. Auditions required for music, theater and athletic performance areas. **Homeschooled:** Certificate of completion of home study program recognized by home state required.

High school preparation. College-preparatory program recommended. 16 units recommended. Recommended units include English 4, mathematics 2, social studies 2, science 2 and academic electives 6.

2009-2010 Annual costs. Tuition/fees (projected): $20,090. Room/board: $6,780. Books/supplies: $1,000. Personal expenses: $1,656.

2008-2009 Financial aid. **Need-based:** 169 full-time freshmen applied for aid; 151 were judged to have need; 147 of these received aid. Average need met was 89%. Average scholarship/grant was $15,109; average loan $5,202. 56% of total undergraduate aid awarded as scholarships/grants, 44% as loans/jobs. **Non-need-based:** Scholarships awarded for academics, alumni affiliation, art, athletics, job skills, leadership, music/drama, religious affiliation.

Application procedures. **Admission:** Priority date 5/1; no deadline. $50 fee, may be waived for applicants with need, free for online applicants. Admission notification on a rolling basis. **Financial aid:** No deadline. FAFSA required. Applicants notified on a rolling basis starting 3/1; must reply within 2 week(s) of notification.

Academics. Distance Learning programs delivered to online cohorts and at multiple off-campus locations. Nursing program delivered through online study and on-campus residency sessions, and available only to individuals licensed as registered nurses in the U.S. **Special study options:** Accelerated study, combined bachelor's/graduate degree, distance learning, double major, dual enrollment of high school students, ESL, honors, independent study, internships, liberal arts/career combination, student-designed major, study abroad, teacher certification program. Accelerated nursing program. **Credit/placement by examination:** AP, CLEP, IB, SAT, ACT, institutional tests. 30 credit hours maximum toward bachelor's degree. Credit by standardized examinations is awarded based on American Council on Education recommendations. **Support services:** Learning center, reduced course load, remedial instruction, study skills assistance, tutoring, writing center.

Majors. **Biology:** General. **Business:** Accounting, business admin, international. **Communications technology:** Desktop publishing. **Computer sciences:** General, computer science, information systems. **Education:** Elementary. **Family/consumer sciences:** Food/nutrition. **Foreign languages:** General, Spanish. **Health:** Athletic training, clinical lab science, nursing (RN). **History:** General. **Liberal arts:** Arts/sciences. **Math:** General. **Parks/recreation:** General, health/fitness, sports admin. **Philosophy/religion:** Religion. **Physical sciences:** Chemistry. **Psychology:** General. **Social sciences:** General, economics, sociology. **Visual/performing arts:** General, commercial/advertising art, dramatic, studio arts.

Most popular majors. Business/marketing 8%, education 27%, health sciences 36%, liberal arts 8%.

Computing on campus. 106 workstations in dormitories, library, computer center, student center. Dormitories wired for high-speed internet access and linked to campus network. Commuter students can connect to campus network. Online library, helpline, student web hosting, wireless network available.

Student life. **Freshman orientation:** Mandatory. Preregistration for classes offered. Early 1-day orientation sessions in spring and summer. Additional 2-3 day orientation at beginning of semester. **Policies:** No tobacco, alcohol, or drug use on campus. Students required to live on campus through sophomore year unless married or living with relatives. **Housing:** Guaranteed on-campus for all undergraduates. Single-sex dorms, special housing for disabled, apartments available. $200 fully refundable deposit, deadline 5/1. **Activities:** Bands, campus ministries, choral groups, dance, drama, film society, international student organizations, music ensembles, musical theater, radio station, student government, student newspaper, symphony orchestra, religious life program, social service projects, peace organization, Amnesty International, OASIS, Students for Free Enterprise, Habitat for Humanity, Young Republicans, Young Democrats.

Athletics. NAIA. **Intercollegiate:** Baseball M, basketball, cross-country, football (tackle) M, golf, soccer, softball W, tennis, track and field, volleyball. **Intramural:** Badminton, baseball M, basketball, cross-country, football (non-tackle), golf, handball, racquetball, soccer, softball, swimming, table tennis, tennis, track and field, volleyball. **Team name:** Yellowjackets.

Student services. Adult student services, alcohol/substance abuse counseling, chaplain/spiritual director, career counseling, student employment services, financial aid counseling, health services, minority student services, personal counseling, placement for graduates, veterans' counselor. **Physically disabled:** Services for visually impaired.

Contact. E-mail: admissions@graceland.edu
Phone: (641) 784-5196 Toll-free number: (866) 472-2352
Fax: (641) 784-5480
Greg Sutherland, Vice President for Enrollment and Dean of Admissions, Graceland University, One University Place, Lamoni, IA 50140

Grand View University

Des Moines, Iowa — **CB member**
www.grandview.edu — **CB code: 6251**

- Private 4-year liberal arts college affiliated with Evangelical Lutheran Church in America
- Commuter campus in large city
- 1,887 degree-seeking undergraduates: 18% part-time, 63% women, 6% African American, 2% Asian American, 3% Hispanic American, 1% international
- 95% of applicants admitted
- SAT or ACT (ACT writing recommended) required
- 47% graduate within 6 years

General. Founded in 1896. Regionally accredited. **Degrees:** 411 bachelor's, 1 associate awarded; master's offered. **ROTC:** Army, Air Force. **Location:** 200 miles from Kansas City, Missouri; 250 miles from Minneapolis-St. Paul. **Calendar:** Semester, extensive summer session. **Full-time faculty:** 87 total; 60% have terminal degrees, 7% minority, 62% women. **Part-time faculty:** 101 total; 31% have terminal degrees, 1% minority, 62% women. **Class size:** 70% < 20, 30% 20-39, less than 1% 40-49.

Freshman class profile. 790 applied, 753 admitted, 345 enrolled.

Return as sophomores:	72%	**Live on campus:**	82%
Out-of-state:	15%	**International:**	1%

Basis for selection. Admissions based on individualized evaluation of applicant's secondary school record and SAT or ACT score. **Homeschooled:** Transcript of courses and grades required.

High school preparation. College-preparatory program recommended. 15 units recommended. Recommended units include English 4, mathematics 3, social studies 3, science 3 and foreign language 2.

2008-2009 Annual costs. Tuition/fees: $18,554. Room/board: $6,164. Books/supplies: $900. Personal expenses: $2,150.

2008-2009 Financial aid. **Need-based:** 331 full-time freshmen applied for aid; 281 were judged to have need; 281 of these received aid. Average need met was 92%. Average scholarship/grant was $13,428; average loan $3,554. 55% of total undergraduate aid awarded as scholarships/grants, 45% as loans/jobs. **Non-need-based:** Awarded to 455 full-time undergraduates, including 140 freshmen. Scholarships awarded for academics, alumni affiliation, art, athletics, leadership, music/drama, religious affiliation.

Application procedures. **Admission:** Closing date 8/15 (receipt date). $35 fee, may be waived for applicants with need. Admission notification on a rolling basis beginning on or about 9/15. **Financial aid:** Priority date 3/1; no closing date. FAFSA required. Applicants notified on a rolling basis starting 3/1; must reply by 5/1 or within 4 week(s) of notification.

Academics. College emphasizes integration of liberal arts core with career-related majors. Internships are a primary focus in many majors. **Special study options:** Accelerated study, combined bachelor's/graduate degree, cooperative education, cross-registration, distance learning, double major, dual enrollment of high school students, honors, independent study, internships, liberal arts/career combination, student-designed major, study abroad, teacher certification program, Washington semester, weekend college. **Credit/placement by examination:** AP, CLEP, IB, SAT, ACT, institutional tests. 32 credit hours maximum toward bachelor's degree. ACT PEP credit accepted, DANTES accepted. **Support services:** Learning center, reduced course load, remedial instruction, study skills assistance, tutoring, writing center.

Majors. **Agriculture:** Business. **Biology:** General. **Business:** General, accounting, entrepreneurial studies, finance, hospitality admin, human resources, marketing, real estate. **Communications:** Broadcast journalism, journalism, media studies, public relations, radio/tv. **Communications technology:** Graphics. **Computer sciences:** General, information technology, programming. **Education:** Elementary, secondary. **Health:** Health services, nursing (RN), premedicine, prepharmacy. **History:** General. **Legal studies:** Paralegal, prelaw. **Liberal arts:** Arts/sciences. **Math:** Applied. **Parks/recreation:** Health/fitness, sports admin. **Philosophy/religion:** Religion. **Protective services:** Criminal justice. **Psychology:** General. **Public administration:** Human services. **Social sciences:** General, political science. **Visual/performing arts:** Dramatic, graphic design, studio arts.

Most popular majors. Business/marketing 17%, education 11%, health sciences 23%, liberal arts 7%, visual/performing arts 7%.

Computing on campus. Dormitories wired for high-speed internet access and linked to campus network. Commuter students can connect to campus network. Online library, helpline, student web hosting, wireless network available.

Student life. **Freshman orientation:** Mandatory. Preregistration for classes offered. Three-day program just before start of fall semester, includes low ropes course at nearby camp. **Housing:** Coed dorms, apartments available. College-owned on-campus houses available. **Activities:** Campus ministries, choral groups, dance, drama, international student organizations, literary magazine, music ensembles, radio station, student government, student newspaper, TV station, Concerned Black Students, student political awareness alliance, art club, Key Club, environmental club, human services club, education club, nursing club, Habitat for Humanity, College Republicans.

Athletics. NAIA. **Intercollegiate:** Baseball M, basketball, cross-country, football (tackle) M, golf, soccer, softball W, track and field, volleyball W, wrestling M. **Intramural:** Badminton, basketball, cheerleading W, football (non-tackle), soccer, softball, swimming, table tennis, tennis, track and field, volleyball. **Team name:** Vikings.

Student services. Adult student services, alcohol/substance abuse counseling, chaplain/spiritual director, career counseling, student employment services, financial aid counseling, health services, minority student services, personal counseling, placement for graduates, veterans' counselor. **Physically disabled:** Services for visually, speech, hearing impaired.

Contact. E-mail: admissions@GrandView.edu
Phone: (515) 263-2810 Toll-free number: (800) 444-6083
Fax: (515) 263-2974
Diane Johnson, Director of Admissions, Grand View University, 1200 Grandview Avenue, Des Moines, IA 50316-1599

Grinnell College

Grinnell, Iowa — **CB member**
www.grinnell.edu — **CB code: 6252**

- Private 4-year liberal arts college
- Residential campus in small town
- 1,639 degree-seeking undergraduates: 54% women, 5% African American, 8% Asian American, 6% Hispanic American, 11% international
- 43% of applicants admitted
- SAT or ACT (ACT writing optional), application essay required
- 86% graduate within 6 years; 60% enter graduate study

General. Founded in 1846. Regionally accredited. **Degrees:** 408 bachelor's awarded. **Location:** 55 miles from Des Moines. **Calendar:** Semester, limited summer session. **Full-time faculty:** 158 total; 95% have terminal degrees, 17% minority, 40% women. **Part-time faculty:** 49 total; 18% have terminal degrees, 8% minority, 51% women. **Class size:** 66% < 20, 34% 20-39. **Special facilities:** 365-acre environmental research area, observatory.

Freshman class profile. 3,217 applied, 1,383 admitted, 464 enrolled.

Mid 50% test scores		**End year in good standing:**	100%
SAT critical reading:	610-740	**Return as sophomores:**	94%
SAT math:	620-710	**Out-of-state:**	90%
ACT composite:	28-32	**Live on campus:**	100%
Rank in top quarter:	90%	**International:**	11%
Rank in top tenth:	64%		

Basis for selection. Scholastic ability plus extracurricular pursuits, accomplishments most important. Curiosity, motivation, and persistence are stressed. Interview recommended. **Homeschooled:** Statement describing homeschool structure and mission, transcript of courses and grades, interview, letter of recommendation (nonparent) required. Copy of curriculum, writing sample required. SAT Subject Tests strongly recommended.

High school preparation. College-preparatory program recommended. 20 units recommended. Recommended units include English 4, mathematics 4, social studies 4, science 4 (laboratory 3) and foreign language 4.

2008-2009 Annual costs. Tuition/fees: $35,428. Room/board: $8,272. Books/supplies: $900. Personal expenses: $1,100.

2008-2009 Financial aid. **Need-based:** 388 full-time freshmen applied for aid; 318 were judged to have need; 318 of these received aid. Average need met was 100%. Average scholarship/grant was $28,159; average loan $2,787. 89% of total undergraduate aid awarded as scholarships/grants, 11% as loans/jobs. **Non-need-based:** Awarded to 526 full-time undergraduates, including 141 freshmen. Scholarships awarded for academics. **Additional information:** Need-blind admission policy, meets 100% of demonstrated institutional need for all domestic students, with loan cap programs. Students may apply financial aid to off-campus study programs.

Application procedures. **Admission:** Closing date 1/2 (postmark date). $30 fee, may be waived for applicants with need, free for online applicants. Admission notification 4/1. Must reply by 5/1. **Financial aid:** Closing date 2/1. FAFSA, institutional form required. Applicants notified by 4/1; must reply by 5/1.

Academics. Internships available in public agencies, private organizations, and corporations. **Special study options:** Accelerated study, double major, independent study, internships, liberal arts/career combination, student-designed major, study abroad, teacher certification program, urban semester, Washington semester. Study abroad available in more than 30 countries. Other programs include study in Washington, 3-2 engineering, architecture, and law. **Credit/placement by examination:** AP, CLEP, IB, institutional tests. **Support services:** Reduced course load, study skills assistance, tutoring, writing center.

Majors. **Biology:** General, biochemistry. **Computer sciences:** Computer science. **Foreign languages:** Chinese, classics, French, German, Japanese, Russian, Spanish. **History:** General. **Interdisciplinary:** Biological/physical sciences. **Liberal arts:** Arts/sciences. **Math:** General. **Philosophy/religion:** Philosophy, religion. **Physical sciences:** Chemistry, physics. **Psychology:** General. **Social sciences:** Anthropology, economics, political science, sociology. **Visual/performing arts:** Art, dramatic.

Most popular majors. Biology 10%, English 7%, foreign language 12%, history 8%, mathematics 6%, philosophy/religious studies 6%, physical sciences 8%, psychology 6%, social sciences 25%, visual/performing arts 7%.

Computing on campus. 400 workstations in dormitories, library, computer center, student center. Dormitories wired for high-speed internet access and linked to campus network. Online library, helpline, student web hosting, wireless network available.

Student life. **Freshman orientation:** Mandatory. Held immediately prior to start of classes. **Policies:** All residence halls and college-owned off-campus houses are self-governing: residents decide how their individual hall will operate and share responsibility for budget, quiet hours, social policy, regulations. **Housing:** Guaranteed on-campus for freshmen. Coed dorms, special housing for disabled, cooperative housing, wellness housing available. $200 nonrefundable deposit, deadline 5/1. **Activities:** Bands, campus ministries, choral groups, dance, drama, film society, international student organizations, literary magazine, music ensembles, Model UN, musical theater, radio station, student government, student newspaper, symphony orchestra, Muslim prayer group, Chalutzim, Friends silent meeting, Concerned Black Students, Asian Students in Alliance, Student Organization of Latinas/Latinos, Campus Democrats, College Republicans, Alternative Break, Native American Student Alliance.

Athletics. NCAA. **Intercollegiate:** Baseball M, basketball, cross-country, diving, football (tackle) M, golf, soccer, softball W, swimming, tennis, track and field, volleyball W. **Intramural:** Badminton, basketball, football (non-tackle), racquetball, soccer, softball, tennis, volleyball. **Team name:** Pioneers.

Student services. Alcohol/substance abuse counseling, chaplain/spiritual director, career counseling, financial aid counseling, health services, minority student services, personal counseling, placement for graduates, veterans' counselor. **Physically disabled:** Services for visually, speech, hearing impaired.

Contact. E-mail: askgrin@grinnell.edu
Phone: (641) 269-3600 Toll-free number: (800) 247-0113
Fax: (641) 269-4800
Seth Allen, Dean of Admission and Financial Aid, Grinnell College, 1103 Park Street, Grinnell, IA 50112-1690

Hamilton Technical College

Davenport, Iowa
www.hamiltontechcollege.com — **CB code: 1588**

- For-profit 3-year technical college
- Commuter campus in small city
- 145 degree-seeking undergraduates
- Interview required

General. Founded in 1969. Accredited by ACCSCT. **Degrees:** 48 bachelor's, 69 associate awarded. **Location:** 190 miles from Des Moines, 175 miles from Chicago. **Calendar:** Semester. **Full-time faculty:** 15 total.

Basis for selection. Open admission. Pseudoisochromatic Color Plates and Wonderlic required for placement.

2009-2010 Annual costs. Medical assistant and medical/insurance coding specialist programs tuition: $11,250; associate of science in electronic engineering technology: $29,700; bachelor of science in electronic engineering technology: $39,600; includes all costs for entire degree program.

Application procedures. **Admission:** No deadline. No application fee. Admission notification on a rolling basis. **Financial aid:** No deadline. FAFSA, institutional form required. Applicants notified on a rolling basis.

Academics. **Credit/placement by examination:** CLEP. 35 credit hours maximum toward associate degree, 60 toward bachelor's. **Support services:** Tutoring.

Majors. **BACHELOR'S. Engineering technology:** Electrical. **ASSOCIATE. Engineering technology:** CAD/CADD, electrical.

Computing on campus. 125 workstations in library, computer center.

Student services. Career counseling, placement for graduates.

Contact. Phone: (563) 386-3570 Fax: (563) 386-6756
Scott Ervin, Admissions Director, Hamilton Technical College, 1011 East 53rd Street, Davenport, IA 52807

Iowa State University

Ames, Iowa — **CB member**
www.iastate.edu — **CB code: 6306**

- Public 4-year university
- Residential campus in small city
- 21,169 degree-seeking undergraduates: 5% part-time, 44% women, 3% African American, 3% Asian American, 3% Hispanic American, 4% international
- 4,884 degree-seeking graduate students
- 87% of applicants admitted
- SAT or ACT (ACT writing optional) required
- 67% graduate within 6 years; 17% enter graduate study

General. Founded in 1858. Regionally accredited. State's land-grant research university. **Degrees:** 4,404 bachelor's awarded; master's, doctoral, first professional offered. **ROTC:** Army, Naval, Air Force. **Location:** 30 miles from Des Moines. **Calendar:** Semester, extensive summer session. **Full-time faculty:** 1,411 total; 92% have terminal degrees, 20% minority, 31% women. **Part-time faculty:** 230 total; 70% have terminal degrees, 8% minority, 48% women. **Class size:** 34% < 20, 40% 20-39, 7% 40-49, 11% 50-99, 8% >100. **Special facilities:** Observatory, nature preserve, research park, molecular biology building, computation center, center for designing foods, Department of Energy laboratory, virtual reality applications center, crop utilization center, transportation research and education center, sustainable environmental technologies center, gardens, field-oriented lakeside research facility.

Freshman class profile. 12,549 applied, 10,953 admitted, 4,546 enrolled.

Mid 50% test scores		**Rank in top quarter:**	60%
SAT critical reading:	490-650	**Rank in top tenth:**	27%
SAT math:	550-680	**Return as sophomores:**	84%
ACT composite:	22-27	**Out-of-state:**	33%
GPA 3.75 or higher:	33%	**Live on campus:**	90%
GPA 3.50-3.74:	20%	**International:**	5%
GPA 3.0-3.49:	32%	**Fraternities:**	15%
GPA 2.0-2.99:	15%	**Sororities:**	16%

Basis for selection. Rank in top half of graduating class and completion of prescribed set of college-preparatory high school courses. Test scores considered as alternative criteria to class rank in some instances. Level of difficulty of courses also considered. **Homeschooled:** Emphasis placed on standardized examinations.

High school preparation. College-preparatory program required. 12 units required; 19 recommended. Required and recommended units include English 4, mathematics 3-4, social studies 2-4, science 3-4 (laboratory 2-3) and foreign language 2-3. 2 foreign language and 3 social studies required for the College of Liberal Arts & Sciences.

2008-2009 Annual costs. Tuition/fees: $6,360; $17,350 out-of-state. Additional tuition for junior and senior engineering students of $1,874 for residents and $1,836 for non-residents; additional tuition for junior and senior business students of $500. Increased fees of $216 for engineering and computer science programs, and of $40 for business students. Room/board: $6,884. Books/supplies: $1,000. Personal expenses: $2,814.

2008-2009 Financial aid. **Need-based:** 3,522 full-time freshmen applied for aid; 2,362 were judged to have need; 2,314 of these received aid. Average need met was 80%. Average scholarship/grant was $5,938; average loan $3,698. 42% of total undergraduate aid awarded as scholarships/grants, 58% as loans/jobs. **Non-need-based:** Awarded to 11,402 full-time undergraduates, including 2,601 freshmen. Scholarships awarded for academics, art, athletics, leadership, minority status, music/drama, ROTC, state residency. **Additional information:** Short-term loan program available to meet unplanned needs. Financial counseling clinic provides budget and credit education assistance.

Application procedures. **Admission:** Closing date 7/1. $30 fee. Admission notification on a rolling basis. Must reply by May 1 or within 2 week(s) if notified thereafter. **Financial aid:** Priority date 3/1; no closing date. FAFSA required. Applicants notified on a rolling basis starting 4/1.

Academics. Classes offered over the Internet, by videotape, at distant locations through the state's fiber-optic communication network, and at off-campus locations taught face-to-face by the university's professors. **Special study options:** Accelerated study, combined bachelor's/graduate degree, cooperative education, cross-registration, distance learning, double major, dual enrollment of high school students, ESL, exchange student, external degree, honors, independent study, internships, liberal arts/career combination, student-designed major, study abroad, teacher certification program, Washington semester, weekend college. National Collegiate Honors Council Honors Semester. Combined bachelor's/graduate programs include: landscape architecture, agriculture and biosystems engineering, biochemistry and biophysics, electrical and computer engineering, civil and construction engineering, chemical engineering, food science and human nutrition, material science engineering, zoology and genetics. **Credit/placement by examination:** AP, CLEP, IB, SAT, ACT, institutional tests. No limit on number of hours of credit by examination that may be counted toward degree. **Support services:** Learning center, pre-admission summer program, reduced course load, remedial instruction, study skills assistance, tutoring, writing center.

Majors. **Agriculture:** Agribusiness operations, agronomy, animal sciences, dairy, education services, farm/ranch, horticulture, international, mechanization, plant protection, plant sciences. **Architecture:** Architecture, landscape, urban/community planning. **Area/ethnic studies:** Women's. **Biology:** General, biochemistry, bioinformatics, biophysics, entomology, genetics, microbiology. **Business:** General, accounting, finance, hospitality admin, international, logistics, management information systems, managerial economics, marketing, operations, statistics. **Communications:** General, advertising, journalism. **Computer sciences:** General. **Conservation:** Environmental science, environmental studies, forestry. **Education:** General, agricultural, early childhood, elementary, family/consumer sciences, health, kindergarten/preschool, music, technology/industrial arts, trade/industrial. **Engineering:** General, aerospace, agricultural, chemical, civil, computer, construction, electrical, industrial, materials, materials science, mechanical, software. **Family/consumer sciences:** General, apparel marketing, clothing/textiles, family resources, family/community services, food/nutrition, housing, human nutrition, institutional food production, textile manufacture. **Foreign languages:** General, linguistics. **Health:** Dietetics, medical illustrating, premedicine, preveterinary. **History:** General. **Liberal arts:** Arts/sciences. **Math:** General, statistics. **Parks/recreation:** Exercise sciences. **Philosophy/religion:** Philosophy, religion. **Physical sciences:** Chemistry, geology, physics, planetary. **Psychology:** General. **Social sciences:** Anthropology, economics, international relations, political science, sociology. **Visual/performing arts:** General, art, commercial/advertising art, design, fashion design, graphic design, interior design. **Other:** Integrated studion arts.

Most popular majors. Agriculture 8%, business/marketing 21%, engineering/engineering technologies 17%, visual/performing arts 8%.

Computing on campus. 2,400 workstations in dormitories, library, computer center, student center. Dormitories wired for high-speed internet access and linked to campus network. Commuter students can connect to campus network. Online course registration, online library, helpline, repair service, wireless network available.

Student life. **Freshman orientation:** Available. Preregistration for classes offered. Two-day, overnight program. **Housing:** Guaranteed on-campus for all undergraduates. Coed dorms, single-sex dorms, special housing for disabled, apartments, cooperative housing, fraternity/sorority housing, wellness housing available. $135 partly refundable deposit, deadline 5/1. Learning communities, family, quiet, adult housing available. **Activities:** Bands, campus ministries, choral groups, dance, drama, film society, literary magazine, music ensembles, musical theater, opera, radio station, student government, student newspaper, symphony orchestra, TV station, more than 500 clubs and organizations.

Athletics. NCAA. **Intercollegiate:** Basketball, cross-country, football (tackle) M, golf, gymnastics W, soccer W, softball W, swimming W, tennis W, track and field, volleyball W, wrestling M. **Intramural:** Badminton, basketball, bowling, boxing M, cross-country, diving, golf, handball, ice hockey, racquetball, skiing, soccer, softball, squash, swimming, table tennis, tennis, volleyball, water polo, weight lifting, wrestling. **Team name:** Cyclones.

Student services. Adult student services, alcohol/substance abuse counseling, career counseling, student employment services, financial aid counseling, health services, legal services, minority student services, on-campus daycare, personal counseling, placement for graduates, veterans' counselor, women's services. **Physically disabled:** Services for visually, speech, hearing impaired. **Learning disabled:** Comprehensive services available.

Contact. E-mail: admissions@iastate.edu
Phone: (515) 294-5836 Toll-free number: (800) 262-3810
Fax: (515) 294-2592
Marc Harding, Director of Admissions, Iowa State University, 100 Enrollment Services Center, Ames, IA 50011-2011

Iowa Wesleyan College

Mount Pleasant, Iowa — **CB member**
www.iwc.edu — **CB code: 6308**

- Private 4-year liberal arts college affiliated with United Methodist Church
- Residential campus in small town
- 842 degree-seeking undergraduates: 25% part-time, 61% women, 12% African American, 1% Asian American, 6% Hispanic American, 6% international
- 67% of applicants admitted
- SAT or ACT (ACT writing optional) required

General. Founded in 1842. Regionally accredited. **Degrees:** 162 bachelor's awarded. **Location:** 47 miles from Iowa City, 25 miles from Burlington. **Calendar:** Semester, limited summer session. **Full-time faculty:** 50 total; 52% have terminal degrees, 6% minority, 42% women. **Part-time faculty:** 40 total; 8% have terminal degrees, 65% women. **Class size:** 86% < 20, 14% 20-39. **Special facilities:** Public interest institute, Harlan-Lincoln house museum.

Freshman class profile. 876 applied, 587 admitted, 150 enrolled.

Mid 50% test scores		**Out-of-state:**	67%
SAT critical reading:	410-520	**Live on campus:**	91%
SAT math:	420-520	**Fraternities:**	3%
ACT composite:	17-23	**Sororities:**	8%
Return as sophomores:	51%		

Basis for selection. Upper 50% class rank preferred. Automatic acceptance with 2.5 GPA and 19 ACT. Audition recommended for music majors. Portfolio recommended for art, creative programs majors. Essay recommended for applicants who do not meet regular admission requirements. **Homeschooled:** Transcript of courses and grades required. GED or portfolio may be substituted for high school transcript requirement.

High school preparation. College-preparatory program recommended. 16 units recommended. Recommended units include English 4, mathematics 3, social studies 3, science 2 (laboratory 2) and academic electives 4.

2008-2009 Annual costs. Tuition/fees: $20,000. Room/board: $6,240. Books/supplies: $800.

2007-2008 Financial aid. Need-based: 59% of total undergraduate aid awarded as scholarships/grants, 41% as loans/jobs. **Non-need-based:** Scholarships awarded for academics, art, athletics, music/drama.

Application procedures. Admission: Priority date 4/1; no deadline. $20 fee, may be waived for applicants with need, free for online applicants. Admission notification on a rolling basis beginning on or about 8/15. Must reply by May 1 or within 2 week(s) if notified thereafter. **Financial aid:** Priority date 4/1; no closing date. FAFSA required. Applicants notified on a rolling basis starting 1/1; must reply within 2 week(s) of notification.

Academics. Special study options: Combined bachelor's/graduate degree, cross-registration, distance learning, double major, dual enrollment of high school students, exchange student, independent study, internships, liberal arts/career combination, student-designed major, study abroad, teacher certification program, Washington semester. **Credit/placement by examination:** AP, CLEP, IB, institutional tests. 30 credit hours maximum toward bachelor's degree. **Support services:** Learning center, reduced course load, study skills assistance, tutoring, writing center.

Majors. Biology: General. **Business:** General, accounting, business admin, human resources. **Communications:** General. **Computer sciences:** General, computer science, web page design. **Conservation:** Forestry. **Education:** General, art, biology, chemistry, early childhood, elementary, English, health, history, mathematics, middle, music, physical, physics, secondary, social studies. **Engineering:** General. **Health:** Environmental health, nursing (RN), predental, premedicine, prepharmacy, preveterinary. **History:** General. **Legal studies:** Prelaw. **Liberal arts:** Library science. **Math:** General. **Parks/recreation:** Exercise sciences, health/fitness, sports admin. **Philosophy/religion:** Christian, philosophy, religion. **Physical sciences:** Chemistry. **Protective services:** Criminal justice. **Psychology:** General. **Public administration:** Human services. **Social sciences:** Sociology. **Visual/performing arts:** Design, studio arts. **Other:** Church leadership.

Most popular majors. Business/marketing 23%, education 32%, health sciences 10%, parks/recreation 6%, psychology 10%.

Computing on campus. 90 workstations in dormitories, library, computer center. Dormitories wired for high-speed internet access and linked to campus network. Commuter students can connect to campus network. Online library, repair service available.

Student life. Freshman orientation: Mandatory. Preregistration for classes offered. Three-day program held weekend before classes begin. **Policies:** All full-time, unmarried students under the age of 22 who do not live with parents required to live in college residential facilities. Exemptions may be made for seniors, students with dependent children and veterans. **Housing:** Guaranteed on-campus for all undergraduates. Coed dorms, single-sex dorms, wellness housing available. $100 deposit, deadline 8/20. **Activities:** Bands, campus ministries, choral groups, dance, drama, international student organizations, literary magazine, music ensembles, radio station, student government, student newspaper, symphony orchestra, black awareness organization, Fellowship of Christian Athletics, Bacchus, Unidad.

Athletics. NAIA. **Intercollegiate:** Baseball M, basketball, cross-country, football (tackle) M, golf, soccer, softball W, track and field, volleyball W. **Intramural:** Badminton, basketball, bowling, football (non-tackle), softball, table tennis, tennis, volleyball. **Team name:** Tigers.

Student services. Adult student services, alcohol/substance abuse counseling, chaplain/spiritual director, career counseling, student employment services, financial aid counseling, health services, personal counseling, placement for graduates.

Contact. E-mail: admit@iwc.edu
Phone: (319) 385-6231 Toll-free number: (800) 582-2383 ext. 6231
Fax: (319) 385-6240
Mark Petty, Dean of Admissions, Iowa Wesleyan College, 601 North Main Street, Mount Pleasant, IA 52641-1398

Kaplan University: Cedar Falls

Cedar Falls, Iowa
www.kucampus.edu

- For-profit 4-year university and branch campus college
- Commuter campus in small city
- 506 degree-seeking undergraduates: 32% part-time, 76% women
- Application essay, interview required

General. Degrees: 39 bachelor's, 131 associate awarded. **Location:** 120 miles from Des Moines. **Calendar:** Continuous, extensive summer session. **Full-time faculty:** 15 total; 7% minority, 73% women. **Part-time faculty:** 26 total; 15% have terminal degrees, 15% minority, 58% women. **Class size:** 64% < 20, 33% 20-39, 3% 40-49.

Basis for selection. Open admission, but selective for some programs. Entrance test required for most programs.

2008-2009 Annual costs. Tuition/fees: $14,070. Cost is for 3 terms of 12 hours each. Tuition includes books and supplies; may vary by program.

2007-2008 Financial aid. All financial aid based on need.

Application procedures. Admission: No deadline. $20 fee. Application must be submitted on paper. Admission notification on a rolling basis. **Financial aid:** No deadline. FAFSA, institutional form required. Applicants notified on a rolling basis.

Academics. Special study options: Cooperative education, distance learning. **Credit/placement by examination:** AP, CLEP, institutional tests. 32 credit hours maximum toward associate degree. **Support services:** Learning center, tutoring.

Majors. Business: Business admin.

Student life. Freshman orientation: Available. **Activities:** Student government, student newspaper.

Student services. Student employment services, financial aid counseling, personal counseling, placement for graduates.

Contact. Phone: (319) 277-0220 Toll-free number: (800) 728-1220
Fax: (319) 243-2961
Jill Lines, Director, Admissions, Kaplan University: Cedar Falls, 7009 Nordic Drive, Cedar Falls, IA 50613

Kaplan University: Davenport

Davenport, Iowa
www.kucampus.edu **CB code: 5848**

- For-profit 4-year university
- Residential campus in large city
- 35,797 degree-seeking undergraduates
- Interview required

General. Founded in 1937. Regionally accredited. **Degrees:** 1,704 bachelor's, 3,223 associate awarded; master's, first professional offered. **Location:** 165 miles from Des Moines, 180 miles from Chicago. **Calendar:** Quarter, extensive summer session. **Full-time faculty:** 64 total. **Part-time faculty:** 1,002 total.

Basis for selection. Open admission, but selective for some programs.

2008-2009 Annual costs. Tuition/fees: $14,120. Cost is for 3 terms of 12 hours each. Tuition includes books and supplies; may vary by program.

Financial aid. Non-need-based: Scholarships awarded for academics.

Application procedures. Admission: No deadline. $25 fee, may be waived for applicants with need. Admission notification on a rolling basis. **Financial aid:** No deadline. FAFSA, institutional form required. Applicants notified on a rolling basis starting 3/4; must reply by 6/15 or within 2 week(s) of notification.

Academics. Special study options: Distance learning, double major, honors, internships, teacher certification program. **Credit/placement by examination:** CLEP, institutional tests. 22 credit hours maximum toward associate degree, 45 toward bachelor's. Up to 25% of all credit in a particular program can be earned through examination. **Support services:** Learning center, reduced course load, remedial instruction, study skills assistance, tutoring, writing center.

Majors. Business: Business admin. **Communications:** General. **Computer sciences:** Information technology, networking. **Health:** Nursing (RN). **Legal studies:** General, paralegal. **Protective services:** Criminal justice. **Psychology:** General.

Most popular majors. Business/marketing 35%, computer/information sciences 12%, health sciences 7%, legal studies 19%, security/protective services 28%.

Computing on campus. 121 workstations in library, student center. Online course registration, online library, helpline, student web hosting, wireless network available.

Student life. Freshman orientation: Mandatory. **Activities:** Student government, student newspaper.

Student services. Career counseling, student employment services, financial aid counseling, personal counseling, placement for graduates.

Contact. E-mail: rhoffmann@kucampus.edu
Phone: (563) 355-3500 Toll-free number: (800) 747-1035
Fax: (563) 355-1320
Robert Hoffmann, Director of Admissions, Kaplan University: Davenport, 1801 East Kimberly Road, Suite 1, Davenport, IA 52807-2095

Kaplan University: Des Moines

Urbandale, Iowa
www.kucampus.edu **CB code: 3388**

- For-profit 4-year university
- Commuter campus in large city
- 767 degree-seeking undergraduates
- Interview required

General. Regionally accredited. **Degrees:** 75 bachelor's, 200 associate awarded. **Location:** 4 miles from Des Moines. **Calendar:** Continuous, extensive summer session. **Full-time faculty:** 20 total. **Part-time faculty:** 40 total.

Basis for selection. Open admission, but selective for some programs.

2008-2009 Annual costs. Tuition/fees: $14,070. Cost is for 3 terms of 12 hours each. Tuition includes books and supplies; may vary by program. Personal expenses: $1,500.

Financial aid. All financial aid based on need.

Application procedures. Admission: No deadline. $25 fee, may be waived for applicants with need. Application must be submitted on paper. Admission notification on a rolling basis. **Financial aid:** Priority date 6/30; no closing date. FAFSA, institutional form required.

Academics. Special study options: Accelerated study, distance learning, independent study, internships, liberal arts/career combination. **Credit/placement by examination:** AP, CLEP, institutional tests. 32 credit hours maximum toward associate degree, 32 toward bachelor's. **Support services:** Learning center, remedial instruction, study skills assistance, tutoring.

Majors. Business: Accounting, business admin. **Computer sciences:** Information technology. **Protective services:** Law enforcement admin.

Computing on campus. 195 workstations in library, computer center. Commuter students can connect to campus network. Online library, repair service available.

Student life. Freshman orientation: Mandatory. Preregistration for classes offered. **Activities:** Student government, student newspaper.

Student services. Adult student services, career counseling, student employment services, financial aid counseling, placement for graduates.

Contact. Phone: (515) 727-2100 Toll-free number: (800) 383-0253
Fax: (515) 727-2115
Bob Pilardi, Director of Admissions, Kaplan University: Des Moines, 4655 121st Street, Urbandale, IA 50323

Kaplan University: Mason City

Mason City, Iowa
www.kucampus.edu **CB code: 6289**

- For-profit 4-year branch campus college
- Commuter campus in large town
- 327 degree-seeking undergraduates: 35% part-time, 72% women
- Interview required

General. Regionally accredited; also accredited by ACICS. **Degrees:** 30 bachelor's, 100 associate awarded. **Location:** 127 miles from Des Moines. **Calendar:** Continuous, extensive summer session. **Full-time faculty:** 12 total; 75% women. **Part-time faculty:** 19 total; 21% have terminal degrees, 5% minority, 74% women. **Class size:** 92% < 20, 8% 20-39.

Basis for selection. Open admission. **Homeschooled:** Transcript of courses and grades, state high school equivalency certificate required. GED required.

2008-2009 Annual costs. Tuition/fees: $14,025. Cost is for 3 terms of 12 hours each. Tuition includes books and supplies; may vary by program. Personal expenses: $1,656.

2007-2008 Financial aid. Need-based: 41% of total undergraduate aid awarded as scholarships/grants, 59% as loans/jobs. **Non-need-based:** Scholarships awarded for academics.

Application procedures. Admission: No deadline. $20 fee. Application must be submitted on paper. Admission notification on a rolling basis. **Financial aid:** Closing date 6/1. FAFSA required. Applicants notified on a rolling basis.

Academics. Special study options: Accelerated study, combined bachelor's/graduate degree, distance learning, dual enrollment of high school students, independent study, internships, student-designed major, study abroad, teacher certification program. **Credit/placement by examination:** CLEP. **Support services:** Learning center, study skills assistance, tutoring.

Majors. Business: Accounting, business admin. **Computer sciences:** Information technology.

Computing on campus. 140 workstations in library, computer center. Commuter students can connect to campus network. Online library, helpline, repair service, wireless network available.

Student life. Freshman orientation: Mandatory. Preregistration for classes offered. **Activities:** Student government.

Student services. Adult student services, student employment services, financial aid counseling, placement for graduates. **Physically disabled:** Services for hearing impaired.

Contact. E-mail: mklacik@kaplan.edu
Phone: (641) 423-2530 Toll-free number: (800) 274-2530
Fax: (641) 423-7512
Michael Klacik, Director of Admissions, Kaplan University: Mason City, 2570 Fourth Street, SW, Mason City, IA 50401

Loras College

Dubuque, Iowa
www.loras.edu **CB code: 6370**

- Private 4-year liberal arts college affiliated with Roman Catholic Church
- Residential campus in small city
- 1,512 degree-seeking undergraduates
- 68% of applicants admitted
- SAT or ACT (ACT writing optional) required

General. Founded in 1839. Regionally accredited. **Degrees:** 386 bachelor's awarded; master's offered. **ROTC:** Army. **Location:** 180 miles from Chicago. **Calendar:** Semester, extensive summer session. **Full-time faculty:** 115 total. **Part-time faculty:** 46 total. **Class size:** 59% < 20, 41% 20-39, less than 1% 40-49. **Special facilities:** Planetarium, observatory, residential arts complex.

Freshman class profile. 1,858 applied, 1,266 admitted, 382 enrolled.

Mid 50% test scores		**GPA 2.0-2.99:**	25%
ACT composite:	19-26	**Rank in top quarter:**	30%
GPA 3.75 or higher:	20%	**Rank in top tenth:**	11%
GPA 3.50-3.74:	19%	**Out-of-state:**	50%
GPA 3.0-3.49:	36%	**Live on campus:**	96%

Basis for selection. High school academic record and test scores most important. Interview and essay recommended. **Homeschooled:** Considered by admissions committee on individual basis. **Learning Disabled:** All students applying for the enhanced learning disabilities program must have materials submitted by the required date. All files are reviewed by the learning disabilities program.

High school preparation. 16 units recommended. Recommended units include English 4, mathematics 3, social studies 3, history 3 and science 3.

2008-2009 Annual costs. Tuition/fees: $24,438. Room/board: $6,727. Books/supplies: $1,100.

2008-2009 Financial aid. Non-need-based: Scholarships awarded for academics, alumni affiliation, leadership, minority status, music/drama. **Additional information:** Audition or portfolio recommended for music and art financial aid applicants.

Application procedures. Admission: No deadline. $25 fee, may be waived for applicants with need. Admission notification on a rolling basis. Must reply by May 1 or within 2 week(s) if notified thereafter. **Financial aid:** Priority date 4/15; no closing date. FAFSA required. Applicants notified on a rolling basis starting 3/1; must reply within 3 week(s) of notification.

Academics. Special study options: Cooperative education, cross-registration, double major, dual enrollment of high school students, exchange student, honors, independent study, internships, student-designed major, study abroad, teacher certification program, urban semester, Washington semester. **Credit/placement by examination:** AP, CLEP, IB. **Support services:** Learning center, reduced course load, remedial instruction, study skills assistance, tutoring, writing center.

Majors. Biology: General, biochemistry. **Business:** General, accounting, business admin, finance, management information systems, marketing. **Communications:** Journalism, media studies, public relations. **Computer sciences:** Computer science. **Education:** General, art, early childhood, elementary, emotionally handicapped, mentally handicapped, multi-level teacher, physical, secondary, special. **Engineering:** Electrical, physics. **Foreign languages:** Spanish. **Health:** Athletic training. **History:** General. **Legal studies:** Prelaw. **Liberal arts:** Arts/sciences. **Math:** General. **Parks/recreation:** Exercise sciences. **Philosophy/religion:** Philosophy, religion. **Physical sciences:** General, chemistry. **Protective services:** Criminal justice. **Psychology:** General. **Public administration:** Social work. **Social sciences:** Economics, international relations, political science, sociology. **Visual/performing arts:** General.

Most popular majors. Business/marketing 24%, communications/journalism 6%, education 20%, English 7%, security/protective services 6%, social sciences 10%.

Computing on campus. PC or laptop required. 20 workstations in library, computer center, student center. Dormitories wired for high-speed internet access and linked to campus network. Commuter students can connect to campus network. Online course registration, online library, helpline, repair service, student web hosting, wireless network available.

Student life. Freshman orientation: Mandatory. Preregistration for classes offered. Held from early June through the start of fall term. **Housing:** Guaranteed on-campus for freshmen. Coed dorms, apartments available. $100 fully refundable deposit. **Activities:** Bands, choral groups, dance, drama, film society, international student organizations, literary magazine, music ensembles, musical theater, radio station, student government, student newspaper, TV station, peace and justice club, African/Hispanic/Asian/Native American club, Amnesty International, environmental action forum, fellowship of Christian athletes.

Athletics. NCAA. **Intercollegiate:** Baseball M, basketball, cross-country, diving, football (tackle) M, golf, soccer, softball W, swimming, tennis W, track and field, volleyball W, wrestling M. **Intramural:** Badminton, baseball M, basketball, bowling, cheerleading, cross-country, diving, football (non-tackle), golf, handball, racquetball, soccer, softball, swimming, table tennis, tennis, track and field, volleyball, water polo, weight lifting, wrestling M. **Team name:** Duhawks.

Student services. Adult student services, alcohol/substance abuse counseling, chaplain/spiritual director, career counseling, student employment services, financial aid counseling, health services, minority student services, personal counseling, placement for graduates, veterans' counselor. **Physically disabled:** Services for visually, speech, hearing impaired. **Learning disabled:** Comprehensive services available.

Contact. E-mail: adms@loras.edu
Phone: (563) 588-7236 Toll-free number: (800) 245-6727
Fax: (563) 588-7119
Sharon Lyons, Director of Admissions, Loras College, 1450 Alta Vista Street, Dubuque, IA 52004-0178

Luther College

Decorah, Iowa **CB member**
www.luther.edu **CB code: 6375**

- Private 4-year liberal arts college affiliated with Evangelical Lutheran Church in America
- Residential campus in small town
- 2,355 degree-seeking undergraduates: 58% women, 1% African American, 2% Asian American, 2% Hispanic American, 4% international
- 80% of applicants admitted
- SAT or ACT (ACT writing optional), application essay required
- 72% graduate within 6 years; 21% enter graduate study

General. Founded in 1861. Regionally accredited. **Degrees:** 549 bachelor's awarded. **Location:** 70 miles from Rochester, Minnesota; 50 miles from LaCrosse, Wisconsin. **Calendar:** 4-1-4, limited summer session. **Full-time faculty:** 178 total; 90% have terminal degrees, 3% minority, 39% women. **Part-time faculty:** 70 total; 29% have terminal degrees, 1% minority, 64% women. **Class size:** 57% < 20, 39% 20-39, 1% 40-49, 2% 50-99, less than 1% >100. **Special facilities:** Planetarium, Norwegian-American museum, extensive biology field study areas, cadaver laboratory.

Freshman class profile. 2,053 applied, 1,648 admitted, 630 enrolled.

Mid 50% test scores		**GPA 2.0-2.99:**	6%
SAT critical reading:	490-650	**Rank in top quarter:**	69%
SAT math:	510-670	**Rank in top tenth:**	39%
SAT writing:	500-630	**End year in good standing:**	92%
ACT composite:	23-29	**Return as sophomores:**	85%
GPA 3.75 or higher:	51%	**Out-of-state:**	65%
GPA 3.50-3.74:	20%	**Live on campus:**	100%
GPA 3.0-3.49:	23%	**International:**	4%

Basis for selection. Rigor of high school curriculum most important, followed by test scores and teacher recommendation(s). Applicants should rank in top half of high school class. Audition recommended for music scholarships. Portfolio recommended for art majors. Interview recommended for borderline students. **Homeschooled:** If graduate of non-diploma-granting organization, evidence of preparation for college required. Must provide at least 2 of the following: home school transcript listing all courses; detailed portfolio of high school work completed; bibliography of major books read, with brief essay on one of the selected works; additional reference letter completed by an educator assessing the applicant's academic preparation; scores from any AP exams and/or GED test results.

High school preparation. College-preparatory program recommended. 14 units recommended. Recommended units include English 4, mathematics 3, social studies 3, science 2 (laboratory 1) and foreign language 2.

2009-2010 Annual costs. Tuition/fees: $32,290. Room/board: $5,380. Books/supplies: $910. Personal expenses: $1,510.

2008-2009 Financial aid. **Need-based:** 541 full-time freshmen applied for aid; 428 were judged to have need; 428 of these received aid. Average need met was 92%. Average scholarship/grant was $17,526; average loan $5,376. 73% of total undergraduate aid awarded as scholarships/grants, 27% as loans/jobs. **Non-need-based:** Awarded to 509 full-time undergraduates, including 197 freshmen. Scholarships awarded for academics, alumni affiliation, art, minority status, music/drama.

Application procedures. **Admission:** No deadline. $25 fee, may be waived for applicants with need, free for online applicants. Admission notification on a rolling basis beginning on or about 11/1. Must reply by May 1 or within 4 week(s) if notified thereafter. **Financial aid:** Priority date 3/1; no closing date. FAFSA, institutional form required. Applicants notified on a rolling basis starting 3/15; must reply by 5/1 or within 4 week(s) of notification.

Academics. **Special study options:** Combined bachelor's/graduate degree, double major, dual enrollment of high school students, honors, independent study, internships, student-designed major, study abroad, teacher certification program, Washington semester. **Credit/placement by examination:** AP, CLEP, IB, institutional tests. No limit, but student must satisfy residency requirement. **Support services:** Learning center, reduced course load, remedial instruction, study skills assistance, tutoring, writing center.

Majors. **Area/ethnic studies:** African-American, Russian/Slavic, Scandinavian, women's. **Biology:** General. **Business:** Accounting, business admin, management information systems. **Communications:** Media studies. **Computer sciences:** Computer science. **Conservation:** Environmental studies. **Education:** Elementary, health, physical. **Foreign languages:** Ancient Greek, Biblical, classics, French, German, Latin, Spanish. **Health:** Nursing (RN). **History:** General. **Math:** General, statistics. **Parks/recreation:** Health/fitness, sports admin. **Philosophy/religion:** Philosophy, religion. **Physical sciences:** Chemistry, physics. **Psychology:** General. **Public administration:** Social work. **Social sciences:** Anthropology, economics, political science, sociology. **Visual/performing arts:** Art, dramatic.

Most popular majors. Biology 9%, business/marketing 13%, education 6%, psychology 7%, social sciences 11%, visual/performing arts 14%.

Computing on campus. 500 workstations in dormitories, library, computer center, student center. Dormitories wired for high-speed internet access and linked to campus network. Commuter students can connect to campus network. Online course registration, online library, helpline, student web hosting, wireless network available.

Student life. **Freshman orientation:** Mandatory. Preregistration for classes offered. Held prior to start of classes. **Housing:** Guaranteed on-campus for all undergraduates. Coed dorms, special housing for disabled, apartments, wellness housing available. Clusters, quiet floors, honors floor available. **Activities:** Bands, campus ministries, choral groups, dance, drama, international student organizations, literary magazine, music ensembles, Model UN, musical theater, radio station, student government, student newspaper, symphony orchestra, various religious and political clubs, black student union, Asian student association, Phi Beta Kappa, Amnesty International, Alpha Phi Omega.

Athletics. NCAA. **Intercollegiate:** Baseball M, basketball, cheerleading, cross-country, diving, football (tackle) M, golf, soccer, softball W, swimming, tennis, track and field, volleyball W, wrestling M. **Intramural:** Archery, badminton, basketball, football (non-tackle), handball, racquetball, soccer, softball, table tennis, tennis, track and field, volleyball. **Team name:** Norse.

Student services. Alcohol/substance abuse counseling, career counseling, student employment services, financial aid counseling, health services, minority student services, personal counseling, placement for graduates. **Physically disabled:** Services for visually, hearing impaired.

Contact. E-mail: admissions@luther.edu
Phone: (563) 387-1287 Toll-free number: (800) 458-8437
Fax: (563) 387-2159
Scot Schaeffer, Vice President for Enrollment Management, Luther College, 700 College Drive, Decorah, IA 52101-1042

Maharishi University of Management

Fairfield, Iowa
www.mum.edu **CB code: 4497**

- Private 4-year university and liberal arts college
- Residential campus in small town
- 236 degree-seeking undergraduates: 9% part-time, 41% women, 4% African American, 3% Asian American, 6% Hispanic American, 19% international
- 954 degree-seeking graduate students
- Application essay required
- 40% graduate within 6 years

General. Founded in 1971. Regionally accredited. Many campus buildings built according to Vedic system of natural architecture. **Degrees:** 59 bachelor's awarded; master's, doctoral offered. **Location:** 60 miles from Iowa City, 110 miles from Des Moines. **Calendar:** Semester. Modular block system: students study one subject per month, 10 subjects per year. Limited summer session. **Full-time faculty:** 52 total; 98% have terminal degrees, 14% minority, 21% women. **Special facilities:** Transcendental meditation domes, greenhouses, college prep-school, indoor rock-climbing wall, sustainable student center.

Freshman class profile. 50 enrolled.

Live on campus:	78%	**International:**	12%

Basis for selection. Academics, grades, academic test scores, recommendations, high school and college transcripts, advanced placement tests, extracurricular activities, work experience, interview with admissions officer, and essay important. SAT or ACT recommended. Students encouraged to visit campus for 4-day weekend. **Homeschooled:** Must supply detailed record of courses and objectives. Home school certification required.

High school preparation. College-preparatory program recommended. 15 units recommended. Recommended units include English 4, mathematics 3, social studies 3, science 3 and foreign language 2.

2008-2009 Annual costs. Tuition/fees: $24,430. Room/board: $6,000. Books/supplies: $800. Personal expenses: $1,500.

2007-2008 Financial aid. **Additional information:** Students may earn scholarships through volunteer staff program.

Application procedures. **Admission:** No deadline. $30 fee. Application must be submitted online. Admission notification on a rolling basis. **Financial aid:** Priority date 7/15, closing date 7/30. FAFSA required. Applicants notified on a rolling basis starting 3/1; must reply within 4 week(s) of notification.

Academics. Provides consciousness-based education and incorporates group practice of Maharishi Transcendental Meditation technique into traditional academic program. **Special study options:** Double major, exchange student, honors, independent study, internships, liberal arts/career combination, study abroad, teacher certification program. **Credit/placement by examination:** AP, CLEP, IB, institutional tests. 12 credit hours maximum toward bachelor's degree. **Support services:** Study skills assistance.

Majors. **Business:** Business admin. **Communications:** Media studies. **Computer sciences:** Computer science. **Education:** Elementary, secondary. **Health:** Premedicine. **Math:** General. **Visual/performing arts:** Studio arts. **Other:** Physiology and health, Sustainable living.

Most popular majors. Biology 6%, business/marketing 12%, computer/information sciences 6%, liberal arts 35%, mathematics 6%, natural resources/environmental science 18%, visual/performing arts 15%.

Computing on campus. 400 workstations in library, computer center, student center. Dormitories wired for high-speed internet access and linked to campus network. Commuter students can connect to campus network. Online library, helpline available.

Student life. **Freshman orientation:** Mandatory. One day, first day of class. **Policies:** Daily practice of Transcendental Meditation program by all students, faculty, and staff. Smoking, alcohol and drugs not permitted on campus. Organic, vegetarian food served in dining halls. **Housing:** Guaranteed on-campus for all undergraduates. Single-sex dorms, special housing for disabled, apartments, wellness housing available. $100 fully refundable deposit. Family housing, quiet dorms available. **Activities:** Choral groups, dance, drama, international student organizations, music ensembles, musical theater, radio station, student government, student newspaper, many clubs and activities available.

Athletics. **Team name:** Flyers.

Student services. Career counseling, financial aid counseling, health services, on-campus daycare, personal counseling, placement for graduates.

Contact. E-mail: admissions@mum.edu
Phone: (641) 472-1110 Toll-free number: (800) 369-6480
Fax: (641) 472-1179
Barbara Rainbow, Associate Dean of Admissions, Maharishi University of Management, Office of Admissions, Fairfield, IA 52557

Mercy College of Health Sciences

Des Moines, Iowa
www.mchs.edu **CB code: 2803**

- Private 4-year health science college affiliated with Roman Catholic Church
- Commuter campus in large city
- 669 degree-seeking undergraduates: 43% part-time, 89% women, 3% African American, 2% Asian American, 4% Hispanic American
- 72% of applicants admitted
- SAT or ACT (ACT writing optional) required

General. Regionally accredited. Clinical education components at local medical facilities. **Degrees:** 55 bachelor's, 149 associate awarded. **Calendar:** Semester, limited summer session. **Full-time faculty:** 43 total; 12% have terminal degrees, 7% minority, 81% women. **Part-time faculty:** 4 total; 100% women. **Class size:** 100% 50-99. **Special facilities:** Science and health care laboratory facilities.

Freshman class profile. 597 applied, 431 admitted, 227 enrolled.

Mid 50% test scores		**End year in good standing:**	55%
ACT composite:	20-23		

Basis for selection. Admission decisions based primarily on secondary school record and standardized test scores. Recommendations and interview also important. **Homeschooled:** State high school equivalency certificate required.

2008-2009 Annual costs. Tuition/fees: $13,000. Books/supplies: $1,200.

2007-2008 Financial aid. Need-based: 55 full-time freshmen applied for aid; 52 were judged to have need; 52 of these received aid. Average need met was 35%. Average scholarship/grant was $5,145; average loan $2,918. 51% of total undergraduate aid awarded as scholarships/grants, 49% as loans/jobs. **Non-need-based:** Awarded to 162 full-time undergraduates, including 32 freshmen. Scholarships awarded for academics.

Application procedures. Admission: Closing date 7/20 (postmark date). $25 fee, may be waived for applicants with need. Admission notification on a rolling basis. **Financial aid:** Closing date 7/1. FAFSA required. Applicants notified on a rolling basis; must reply by 1/1 or within 3 week(s) of notification.

Academics. Special study options: Accelerated study, combined bachelor's/graduate degree, distance learning, liberal arts/career combination. **Credit/placement by examination:** AP, CLEP, institutional tests. 24 credit hours maximum toward associate degree, 24 toward bachelor's. **Support services:** Study skills assistance, tutoring, writing center.

Majors. Health: Health care admin, nursing (RN), physical therapy assistant. **Other:** Allied health education/leadership.

Computing on campus. 49 workstations in library, computer center. Commuter students can connect to campus network. Online library, wireless network available.

Student life. Freshman orientation: Mandatory. Preregistration for classes offered. One-day orientation and registration sessions held at various times before beginning of term. **Activities:** Student government, student newspaper.

Student services. Alcohol/substance abuse counseling, career counseling, student employment services, financial aid counseling, minority student services, personal counseling.

Contact. E-mail: admissions@mchs.edu
Phone: (515) 643-6715 Toll-free number: (800) 637-2994 ext. 3-3180
Fax: (515) 643-6702
Kara Scholten, Admissions Counselor, Mercy College of Health Sciences, 921 Sixth Avenue, Des Moines, IA 50309

Morningside College

Sioux City, Iowa
www.morningside.edu **CB code: 6415**

- Private 4-year liberal arts college affiliated with United Methodist Church
- Residential campus in small city
- 1,180 degree-seeking undergraduates: 3% part-time, 54% women, 1% African American, 2% Asian American, 3% Hispanic American, 1% Native American, 1% international
- 404 degree-seeking graduate students
- 74% of applicants admitted
- SAT or ACT (ACT writing optional) required
- 44% graduate within 6 years; 11% enter graduate study

General. Founded in 1894. Regionally accredited. All full-time students receive notebook computers. **Degrees:** 217 bachelor's awarded; master's offered. **Location:** 90 miles from Omaha, Nebraska and Sioux Falls, South Dakota. **Calendar:** Semester, limited summer session. **Full-time faculty:** 69 total; 77% have terminal degrees, 3% minority, 45% women. **Part-time faculty:** 108 total; less than 1% minority, 75% women. **Class size:** 50% < 20, 47% 20-39, 2% 40-49, less than 1% 50-99. **Special facilities:** Biology research station.

Freshman class profile. 1,349 applied, 997 admitted, 302 enrolled.

Mid 50% test scores		**End year in good standing:**	89%
ACT composite:	20-25	**Return as sophomores:**	70%
GPA 3.75 or higher:	23%	**Out-of-state:**	34%
GPA 3.50-3.74:	18%	**Live on campus:**	94%
GPA 3.0-3.49:	41%	**International:**	1%
GPA 2.0-2.99:	18%	**Fraternities:**	3%
Rank in top quarter:	42%	**Sororities:**	3%
Rank in top tenth:	15%		

Basis for selection. 20 ACT/1410 SAT and either rank in top half of class or 2.5 GPA required. Interview recommended. Audition or audition tape recommended for music majors and theater applicants. Portfolio recommended for art majors. **Homeschooled:** Transcript or Home School Credit Evaluation form from Office of Admissions required. **Learning Disabled:** Separate admissions process required which includes application, materials and interview.

High school preparation. College-preparatory program recommended. 10 units recommended. Recommended units include English 3, mathematics 2, social studies 3 and science 2. 4 units math and science required of math or science majors.

2008-2009 Annual costs. Tuition/fees: $21,240. Room/board: $6,410. Books/supplies: $800. Personal expenses: $1,655.

2008-2009 Financial aid. Non-need-based: Scholarships awarded for academics, alumni affiliation, art, athletics, job skills, leadership, music/drama, religious affiliation, ROTC, state residency.

Application procedures. Admission: Priority date 8/15; no deadline. $25 fee, may be waived for applicants with need, free for online applicants. Admission notification on a rolling basis. **Financial aid:** Priority date 3/1; no closing date. FAFSA required. Applicants notified on a rolling basis starting 3/31.

Academics. Special study options: Distance learning, double major, dual enrollment of high school students, ESL, honors, independent study, internships, liberal arts/career combination, student-designed major, study abroad, teacher certification program, United Nations semester, Washington semester. **Credit/placement by examination:** AP, CLEP, IB, institutional tests. 32 credit hours maximum toward bachelor's degree. Maximum 12 hours may be used for general studies core requirements. **Support services:** Learning center, reduced course load, remedial instruction, study skills assistance, tutoring.

Majors. Biology: General. **Business:** Accounting, business admin, communications. **Communications:** Advertising, media studies. **Computer sciences:** Programming. **Education:** Art, biology, chemistry, elementary, English, history, mathematics, music, physics, science, Spanish, special. **Engineering:** Mechanics, physics. **Foreign languages:** Spanish. **Health:** Clinical lab science, nursing (RN). **History:** General, American. **Interdisciplinary:** Biopsychology. **Math:** General. **Philosophy/religion:** Philosophy, religion. **Physical sciences:** Chemistry, physics. **Psychology:** General, counseling, industrial. **Social sciences:** International relations, political science. **Visual/performing arts:** Dramatic, graphic design, music performance, photography, studio arts.

Most popular majors. Biology 9%, business/marketing 28%, education 21%, health sciences 9%, visual/performing arts 10%.

Computing on campus. PC or laptop required. Dormitories wired for high-speed internet access and linked to campus network. Commuter students can connect to campus network. Online library, helpline, repair service, student web hosting, wireless network available.

Student life. **Freshman orientation:** Mandatory. Preregistration for classes offered. Held 4 days before school begins. **Housing:** Guaranteed on-campus for freshmen. Coed dorms, apartments, fraternity/sorority housing available. $100 fully refundable deposit. Apartments for adult non-traditional students available. **Activities:** Bands, campus ministries, choral groups, dance, drama, international student organizations, literary magazine, music ensembles, musical theater, radio station, student government, student newspaper, TV station, civic union, Project Hope, Fellowship of Christian Athletes, peace and justice club, mission trips, Cross by Color, Spanish club.

Athletics. NAIA. **Intercollegiate:** Baseball M, basketball, cross-country, football (tackle) M, golf, soccer, softball W, swimming, tennis, track and field, volleyball W. **Intramural:** Basketball, bowling, football (non-tackle), golf, soccer, softball, swimming, tennis, track and field, volleyball. **Team name:** Mustangs.

Student services. Alcohol/substance abuse counseling, career counseling, student employment services, financial aid counseling, health services, minority student services, personal counseling, placement for graduates, veterans' counselor. **Physically disabled:** Services for visually, speech, hearing impaired. **Learning disabled:** Comprehensive services available.

Contact. E-mail: mscadm@morningside.edu
Phone: (712) 274-5000 ext. 5511 Toll-free
number: (800) 831-0806 ext. 5511 Fax: (712) 274-5101
Amy Williams, Co-Director of Admissions, Morningside College, 1501 Morningside Avenue, Sioux City, IA 51106

Mount Mercy College
Cedar Rapids, Iowa
www.mtmercy.edu **CB code: 6417**

- Private 4-year liberal arts college affiliated with Roman Catholic Church
- Commuter campus in small city
- 1,446 degree-seeking undergraduates: 38% part-time, 71% women, 2% African American, 1% Asian American, 2% Hispanic American, 2% international
- 81 degree-seeking graduate students
- 80% of applicants admitted
- SAT or ACT (ACT writing optional), application essay required
- 61% graduate within 6 years; 11% enter graduate study

General. Founded in 1928. Regionally accredited. **Degrees:** 429 bachelor's awarded; master's offered. **Location:** 220 miles from Chicago. **Calendar:** 4-1-4, limited summer session. **Full-time faculty:** 75 total; 49% have terminal degrees, 7% minority, 67% women. **Part-time faculty:** 75 total; 9% have terminal degrees, 56% women. **Class size:** 63% < 20, 34% 20-39, 2% 40-49, less than 1% 50-99. **Special facilities:** Campus buildings connected by tunnel system.

Freshman class profile. 402 applied, 323 admitted, 172 enrolled.

Mid 50% test scores			
ACT composite:	20-24	End year in good standing:	100%
GPA 3.75 or higher:	28%	Return as sophomores:	81%
GPA 3.50-3.74:	21%	Out-of-state:	9%
GPA 3.0-3.49:	35%	Live on campus:	84%
GPA 2.0-2.99:	16%	International:	4%

Basis for selection. 2.5 GPA, class rank in top half of class, 20 ACT required. **Homeschooled:** Transcript of courses and grades, letter of recommendation (nonparent) required. Submit records of studies or detailed account of subjects and materials.

High school preparation. Recommended units include English 4, mathematics 3, social studies 3, history 3, science 3 (laboratory 1) and foreign language 2.

2008-2009 Annual costs. Tuition/fees: $21,125. Room/board: $6,650. Books/supplies: $1,000. Personal expenses: $1,952.

2008-2009 Financial aid. **Need-based:** 158 full-time freshmen applied for aid; 114 were judged to have need; 114 of these received aid. Average need met was 72%. Average scholarship/grant was $17,274; average loan $5,491. 59% of total undergraduate aid awarded as scholarships/grants, 41% as loans/jobs. **Non-need-based:** Scholarships awarded for academics, alumni affiliation, art, athletics, leadership, music/drama, religious affiliation.

Application procedures. **Admission:** Closing date 8/15 (receipt date). $20 fee, may be waived for applicants with need, free for online applicants. Admission notification on a rolling basis. Must reply by May 1 or within 2 week(s) if notified thereafter. **Financial aid:** Priority date 3/1; no closing date. FAFSA required. Applicants notified on a rolling basis starting 3/15; must reply by 5/1 or within 3 week(s) of notification.

Academics. **Special study options:** Accelerated study, cross-registration, double major, dual enrollment of high school students, honors, independent study, internships, liberal arts/career combination, study abroad, teacher certification program. **Credit/placement by examination:** AP, CLEP, ACT, institutional tests. 60 credit hours maximum toward bachelor's degree. **Support services:** Learning center, remedial instruction, study skills assistance, tutoring, writing center.

Majors. **Biology:** General. **Business:** General, accounting, business admin, management information systems, marketing. **Communications:** General, digital media, journalism, public relations. **Computer sciences:** General, computer science. **Conservation:** General. **Education:** Elementary, secondary. **Health:** Clinical lab science, health care admin, nursing (RN). **History:** General. **Math:** General. **Philosophy/religion:** Philosophy, religion. **Protective services:** Law enforcement admin. **Psychology:** General. **Public administration:** Social work. **Social sciences:** International relations, political science, sociology, urban studies. **Visual/performing arts:** Art, graphic design. **Other:** Applied management, Health care systems, Multi/interdisciplinary studies.

Most popular majors. Business/marketing 42%, education 11%, health sciences 19%, security/protective services 7%.

Computing on campus. 135 workstations in dormitories, library, computer center. Dormitories wired for high-speed internet access and linked to campus network. Commuter students can connect to campus network. Online library, helpline, wireless network available.

Student life. **Freshman orientation:** Available. Preregistration for classes offered. Four-day orientation held prior to start of fall term; 3 one-day orientation/registration sessions in the spring and summer. **Housing:** Guaranteed on-campus for freshmen. Coed dorms, apartments, wellness housing available. $200 nonrefundable deposit, deadline 8/15. **Activities:** Choral groups, drama, literary magazine, musical theater, student government, student newspaper, Best Buddies, biology club, Circle K International, criminal justice association, English club, green club, history club, honors student association.

Athletics. NAIA. **Intercollegiate:** Baseball M, basketball, cheerleading M, cross-country, golf, soccer, softball W, track and field, volleyball W. **Intramural:** Basketball, football (non-tackle) M, racquetball, soccer, softball, table tennis, tennis, volleyball. **Team name:** Mustangs.

Student services. Adult student services, alcohol/substance abuse counseling, chaplain/spiritual director, career counseling, student employment services, financial aid counseling, health services, personal counseling, placement for graduates, veterans' counselor. **Physically disabled:** Services for visually, speech, hearing impaired.

Contact. E-mail: admission@mtmercy.edu
Phone: (319) 368-6460 Toll-free number: (800) 248-4504
Fax: (319) 363-5270
Sue Oatey, Vice President for Enrollment and Student Services, Mount Mercy College, 1330 Elmhurst Drive NE, Cedar Rapids, IA 52402-4797

Northwestern College
Orange City, Iowa
www.nwciowa.edu **CB code: 6490**

- Private 4-year liberal arts college affiliated with Reformed Church in America
- Residential campus in small town
- 1,201 degree-seeking undergraduates: 2% part-time, 60% women, 1% African American, 1% Asian American, 1% Hispanic American, 3% international
- 81% of applicants admitted
- SAT or ACT (ACT writing optional) required
- 58% graduate within 6 years

General. Founded in 1882. Regionally accredited. **Degrees:** 270 bachelor's awarded. **Location:** 40 miles from Sioux City, 75 miles from Sioux Falls, South Dakota. **Calendar:** Semester, limited summer session. **Full-time faculty:** 82 total; 77% have terminal degrees, 6% minority, 35% women.

Part-time faculty: 46 total; 4% have terminal degrees, 61% women. **Class size:** 66% < 20, 32% 20-39, 2% 40-49, less than 1% 50-99. **Special facilities:** Natural prairie restoration project.

Freshman class profile. 1,232 applied, 993 admitted, 293 enrolled.

Mid 50% test scores		**Return as sophomores:**	76%
ACT composite:	22-27	**Out-of-state:**	48%
Rank in top quarter:	49%	**Live on campus:**	97%
Rank in top tenth:	24%	**International:**	2%

Basis for selection. Top half of class and test scores above 50th percentile most important. Recommendations also important. Must have 2.0 GPA to be considered. Interview and essay recommended. Audition recommended for theater, music majors. Portfolio recommended for art majors. **Homeschooled:** Transcript of courses and grades required. **Learning Disabled:** Students provide documentation to the Director of Academic Support upon admittance.

High school preparation. 16 units recommended. Recommended units include English 4, mathematics 3, social studies 3, science 3 and foreign language 3.

2008-2009 Annual costs. Tuition/fees: $22,950. 1-4 credits, $445 per credit hour; 5-8 credits, $660 per credit hour; 9-11 credits, $870 per credit hour. Room/board: $6,580. Books/supplies: $900. Personal expenses: $2,026.

2007-2008 Financial aid. Need-based: 256 full-time freshmen applied for aid; 256 were judged to have need; 256 of these received aid. Average need met was 83%. Average scholarship/grant was $6,133; average loan $3,894. 57% of total undergraduate aid awarded as scholarships/grants, 43% as loans/jobs. **Non-need-based:** Awarded to 1,522 full-time undergraduates, including 409 freshmen. Scholarships awarded for academics, art, athletics, music/drama, religious affiliation, state residency.

Application procedures. Admission: Priority date 6/2; no deadline. $25 fee, may be waived for applicants with need. Admission notification on a rolling basis beginning on or about 10/1. Must reply by May 1 or within 3 week(s) if notified thereafter. **Financial aid:** Priority date 4/1, closing date 6/30. FAFSA required. Applicants notified on a rolling basis starting 3/15; must reply within 3 week(s) of notification.

Academics. Special study options: Double major, ESL, honors, independent study, internships, liberal arts/career combination, student-designed major, study abroad, teacher certification program, Washington semester. American Studies Program (Washington, D.C.), AuSable Institute of Environmental Studies Program (Michigan), Los Angeles Film Studies Semester, Chicago Metropolitan Studies Program, China Studies Program (Xiaman), Middle East Studies Program (Cairo), Oxford Summer Program (Oxford), Russian Studies Program, Contemporary Music Center (Martha's Vineyard, MA), Latin American Studies Program (Costa Rica), Oxford Honours Programme (England), Trinity Christian College: Semester in Spain, Creation Care Study Program, Summer Institute of Journalism (Washington, D.C.), Semester in Romania, Semester in Oman. **Credit/placement by examination:** AP, CLEP, IB, SAT, ACT, institutional tests. 24 credit hours maximum toward bachelor's degree. **Support services:** Learning center, reduced course load, remedial instruction, study skills assistance, tutoring, writing center.

Majors. Agriculture: Business. **Biology:** General. **Business:** Accounting, actuarial science, business admin, finance, human resources, managerial economics, marketing. **Communications:** Digital media, journalism, public relations. **Computer sciences:** General, computer science. **Conservation:** General. **Education:** General, elementary. **Foreign languages:** Spanish. **Health:** Athletic training, clinical lab technology, nursing (RN). **History:** General. **Liberal arts:** Arts/sciences. **Math:** General. **Parks/recreation:** Exercise sciences, health/fitness. **Philosophy/religion:** Philosophy, religion. **Physical sciences:** Chemistry. **Psychology:** General. **Public administration:** Social work. **Social sciences:** Economics, political science, sociology. **Theology:** Religious ed. **Visual/performing arts:** Art, dramatic.

Most popular majors. Biology 6%, business/marketing 20%, education 22%, history 6%, social sciences 7%, visual/performing arts 9%.

Computing on campus. 250 workstations in dormitories, library, computer center, student center. Dormitories linked to campus network. Commuter students can connect to campus network. Online course registration, online library, helpline, repair service, wireless network available.

Student life. Freshman orientation: Available. Preregistration for classes offered. One-day orientation program in late May. **Policies:** Use of alcohol prohibited on campus. Resident living required for all students unless granted commuting status or living with parents. Religious observance required. **Housing:** Guaranteed on-campus for all undergraduates. Single-sex dorms, special housing for disabled, apartments available. $100 fully refundable deposit, deadline 8/1. **Activities:** Bands, campus ministries, choral groups, dance, drama, international student organizations, literary magazine, music ensembles, student government, student newspaper, symphony orchestra, TV station, student activities council, Fellowship of Christian Athletes, College Republicans, Campus Democrats, Phi Beta Lambda, Sigma Tau, Spanish club, education club.

Athletics. NAIA. **Intercollegiate:** Baseball M, basketball, cross-country, football (tackle) M, golf, soccer, softball W, tennis, track and field, volleyball W, wrestling M. **Intramural:** Badminton, basketball, bowling, football (non-tackle), golf, racquetball, soccer, softball, table tennis, tennis, volleyball. **Team name:** Red Raiders.

Student services. Alcohol/substance abuse counseling, career counseling, student employment services, financial aid counseling, health services, personal counseling, placement for graduates, veterans' counselor. **Physically disabled:** Services for visually, speech, hearing impaired.

Contact. E-mail: admissions@nwciowa.edu
Phone: (712) 707-7130 Toll-free number: (800) 747-4757
Fax: (712) 707-7164
Mark Bloemendaal, Director of Admissions, Northwestern College, 101 Seventh Street, SW, Orange City, IA 51041

St. Ambrose University

Davenport, Iowa
www.sau.edu **CB code: 6617**

- Private 4-year university and liberal arts college affiliated with Roman Catholic Church
- Residential campus in small city
- 2,845 degree-seeking undergraduates: 15% part-time, 61% women, 2% African American, 1% Asian American, 4% Hispanic American, 1% Native American
- 848 degree-seeking graduate students
- 82% of applicants admitted
- SAT or ACT (ACT writing optional) required
- 53% graduate within 6 years

General. Founded in 1882. Regionally accredited. **Degrees:** 589 bachelor's awarded; master's, doctoral offered. **Location:** 180 miles from Des Moines, 175 miles from Chicago. **Calendar:** Semester, extensive summer session. **Full-time faculty:** 175 total; 77% have terminal degrees, 9% minority, 45% women. **Part-time faculty:** 203 total; 18% have terminal degrees, 6% minority, 49% women. **Class size:** 61% < 20, 39% 20-39, less than 1% 40-49. **Special facilities:** Transmission electron microscope, cable television channel, observatory, national prairie garden, radio station.

Freshman class profile. 2,150 applied, 1,760 admitted, 574 enrolled.

Mid 50% test scores		**Rank in top quarter:**	34%
ACT composite:	20-25	**Rank in top tenth:**	17%
GPA 3.75 or higher:	18%	**End year in good standing:**	78%
GPA 3.50-3.74:	12%	**Return as sophomores:**	76%
GPA 3.0-3.49:	30%	**Out-of-state:**	70%
GPA 2.0-2.99:	40%	**Live on campus:**	95%

Basis for selection. 2.5 GPA and 20 ACT/950 SAT (exclusive of Writing) or 18-19 ACT/870-950 SAT and rank in top half of class required. Interview recommended. Portfolio required for art majors. **Homeschooled:** Students who do not have high school diploma required to score 50 on GED with 18 ACT or 860 SAT (exclusive of Writing).

High school preparation. 18 units recommended. Recommended units include English 4, mathematics 3, social studies 1, history 1, science 2 (laboratory 2), foreign language 1 and academic electives 4.

2008-2009 Annual costs. Tuition/fees: $21,610. Room/board: $7,825.

2008-2009 Financial aid. Non-need-based: Scholarships awarded for academics, alumni affiliation, art, athletics, job skills, music/drama. **Additional information:** Iowa applicants must apply for financial aid by July 1. Audition required for music, drama scholarship applicants.

Application procedures. Admission: No deadline. $25 fee, may be waived for applicants with need, free for online applicants. Admission notification on a rolling basis beginning on or about 10/1. Must reply by May 1 or within 2 week(s) if notified thereafter. **Financial aid:** Priority date 3/15; no closing date. FAFSA required. Applicants notified on a rolling basis starting 2/1; must reply within 2 week(s) of notification.

Academics. Special study options: Accelerated study, combined bachelor's/graduate degree, cooperative education, distance learning, double major, independent study, internships, liberal arts/career combination, student-designed major, study abroad, teacher certification program. Service learning program in which students work as volunteers for community and earn 1-3 semester hours credit, license preparation for occupational therapy on campus, accounting majors volunteer to work on income tax forms for low income families on campus. **Credit/placement by examination:** AP, CLEP, IB, SAT, ACT, institutional tests. 60 credit hours maximum toward bachelor's degree. **Support services:** Learning center, pre-admission summer program, reduced course load, remedial instruction, study skills assistance, tutoring, writing center.

Majors. **Biology:** General. **Business:** General, accounting, business admin, finance, international, management science, marketing, organizational behavior. **Communications:** General, advertising, broadcast journalism, journalism, media studies, public relations, radio/tv. **Computer sciences:** General, computer science, information systems, LAN/WAN management, security, systems analysis. **Education:** General, art, biology, business, chemistry, early childhood, elementary, English, foreign languages, French, German, health, history, mathematics, music, physical, physics, psychology, science, secondary, social science, Spanish. **Engineering:** Industrial, physics. **Foreign languages:** French, German, Spanish. **Health:** Nursing (RN). **History:** General. **Interdisciplinary:** Biological/physical sciences, natural sciences, neuroscience. **Math:** General. **Parks/recreation:** Exercise sciences, health/fitness, sports admin. **Philosophy/religion:** Philosophy. **Physical sciences:** Chemistry, physics. **Protective services:** Criminal justice, criminalistics. **Psychology:** General, forensic. **Public administration:** General. **Social sciences:** Economics, political science, sociology. **Visual/performing arts:** Commercial/advertising art, dramatic, graphic design, multimedia, studio arts, theater arts management.

Most popular majors. Biology 7%, business/marketing 27%, communications/journalism 8%, education 12%, health sciences 10%, psychology 12%.

Computing on campus. 190 workstations in library, computer center, student center. Dormitories wired for high-speed internet access and linked to campus network. Commuter students can connect to campus network. Online course registration, online library, helpline, wireless network available.

Student life. **Freshman orientation:** Mandatory. Preregistration for classes offered. Held 2 days per month in April, June, August. **Policies:** All campus buildings smoke-free. **Housing:** Guaranteed on-campus for freshmen. Coed dorms, single-sex dorms, special housing for disabled, apartments, wellness housing available. $250 partly refundable deposit, deadline 5/1. Townhouses for seniors, houses for juniors and seniors available. **Activities:** Bands, campus ministries, choral groups, dance, drama, literary magazine, music ensembles, musical theater, opera, radio station, student government, student newspaper, symphony orchestra, TV station, Fellowship of Christian Athletes, black student union, philosophy club, Young Republicans, Young Democrats, veterans club, art club, music club, psychology club, multicultural club.

Athletics. NAIA. **Intercollegiate:** Baseball M, basketball, bowling, cheerleading, cross-country, football (tackle) M, golf, soccer, softball W, tennis, track and field, volleyball. **Intramural:** Badminton, basketball, bowling, football (non-tackle), golf, handball, racquetball, softball, tennis, triathlon, volleyball. **Team name:** Fighting Bees.

Student services. Adult student services, alcohol/substance abuse counseling, career counseling, student employment services, financial aid counseling, health services, minority student services, on-campus daycare, personal counseling, placement for graduates, veterans' counselor, women's services. **Physically disabled:** Services for visually, speech, hearing impaired.

Contact. E-mail: admit@sau.edu
Phone: (563) 333-6300 Toll-free number: (800) 383-2627
Fax: (563) 333-6243
Meg Halligan, Director of Admissions, St. Ambrose University, 518 West Locust Street, Davenport, IA 52803-2898

Simpson College

Indianola, Iowa — **CB member**
www.simpson.edu — **CB code: 6650**

- Private 4-year liberal arts college affiliated with United Methodist Church
- Residential campus in large town
- 1,929 degree-seeking undergraduates: 24% part-time, 59% women, 2% African American, 2% Asian American, 1% Hispanic American, 1% international
- 19 degree-seeking graduate students
- 88% of applicants admitted
- SAT or ACT (ACT writing optional) required
- 68% graduate within 6 years; 20% enter graduate study

General. Founded in 1860. Regionally accredited. **Degrees:** 396 bachelor's awarded; master's offered. **Location:** 12 miles from Des Moines. **Calendar:** 4-4-1. Extensive summer session. **Full-time faculty:** 101 total; 84% have terminal degrees, 4% minority, 46% women. **Part-time faculty:** 102 total; 41% have terminal degrees, 12% minority, 36% women. **Class size:** 64% < 20, 34% 20-39, less than 1% 40-49, 1% 50-99. **Special facilities:** Antebellum-era literature collection, cadaver laboratory, Iowa history center, urban studies institute, George Washington Carver research library, vocational and integrative learning center.

Freshman class profile. 1,259 applied, 1,112 admitted, 389 enrolled.

Mid 50% test scores		**Out-of-state:**	13%
ACT composite:	22-28	**Live on campus:**	96%
Rank in top quarter:	55%	**International:**	1%
Rank in top tenth:	28%	**Fraternities:**	23%
End year in good standing:	84%	**Sororities:**	27%
Return as sophomores:	79%		

Basis for selection. High school academic record, including college preparatory courses taken and grades received in those courses, class rank, and ACT/SAT scores most important. Recommendations also considered. Interview recommended. Audition recommended for music, drama majors. Portfolio recommended for art majors. Auditions and portfolios required for scholarships in music, theater, or art. **Homeschooled:** Letter of recommendation (nonparent) required. Must submit GED or high school diploma and transcripts with course content descriptions. **Learning Disabled:** Students should submit documentation of disability to ensure college can provide adequate facilities and programming.

High school preparation. College-preparatory program recommended. 16 units recommended. Recommended units include English 4, mathematics 3, social studies 3, science 3 (laboratory 3) and foreign language 3.

2008-2009 Annual costs. Tuition/fees: $24,771. Room/board: $6,988. Books/supplies: $900. Personal expenses: $1,300.

2008-2009 Financial aid. **Need-based:** 384 full-time freshmen applied for aid; 322 were judged to have need; 322 of these received aid. Average need met was 93%. Average scholarship/grant was $17,812; average loan $3,052. 71% of total undergraduate aid awarded as scholarships/grants, 29% as loans/jobs. **Non-need-based:** Awarded to 376 full-time undergraduates, including 123 freshmen. Scholarships awarded for academics, alumni affiliation, art, leadership, minority status, music/drama, religious affiliation, state residency. **Additional information:** Music and theater scholarships based on audition. Art scholarships based on portfolio.

Application procedures. **Admission:** Priority date 5/1; deadline 8/15. No application fee. Admission notification on a rolling basis. Must reply by May 1 or within 3 week(s) if notified thereafter. **Financial aid:** Priority date 4/1; no closing date. FAFSA required. Applicants notified on a rolling basis starting 3/12; must reply by 5/1 or within 3 week(s) of notification.

Academics. **Special study options:** Accelerated study, combined bachelor's/graduate degree, double major, honors, independent study, internships, liberal arts/career combination, New York semester, study abroad, teacher certification program, Washington semester. 3-2 and 4-2 engineering program with Washington University in St. Louis, Iowa State University, and Institute of Technology, University of Minnesota, Minneapolis. **Credit/placement by examination:** AP, CLEP, IB, ACT, institutional tests. 24 credit hours maximum toward bachelor's degree. **Support services:** Learning center, reduced course load, study skills assistance, tutoring, writing center.

Majors. **Biology:** General, biochemistry. **Business:** Accounting, business admin, international, managerial economics, marketing. **Communications:** Journalism, media studies. **Computer sciences:** Computer science, information systems. **Conservation:** Environmental science. **Education:** General, elementary, middle, music, physical. **Engineering:** General. **Foreign languages:** French, German, Spanish. **Health:** Athletic training, predental, premedicine, prepharmacy, preveterinary. **History:** General. **Legal studies:** Prelaw. **Liberal arts:** Arts/sciences. **Math:** General. **Parks/recreation:** Health/fitness, sports admin. **Philosophy/religion:** Philosophy, religion. **Physical sciences:** Chemistry, physics. **Protective services:** Criminal justice, forensics. **Psychology:** General. **Social sciences:** Economics, international relations, political science, sociology. **Theology:** Preministerial. **Visual/performing arts:** Art, dramatic, music performance.

Most popular majors. Biology 7%, business/marketing 29%, communications/journalism 9%, education 9%, social sciences 11%.

Computing on campus. 327 workstations in dormitories, library, computer center, student center. Dormitories wired for high-speed internet access and linked to campus network. Commuter students can connect to campus network. Online library, repair service, wireless network available.

Student life. **Freshman orientation:** Mandatory. Preregistration for classes offered. Four 1-day summer registration programs in June. Fall orientation held first week students are on campus. **Housing:** Guaranteed on-campus for all undergraduates. Coed dorms, apartments, fraternity/sorority housing, wellness housing available. $200 fully refundable deposit. Single sex rooms and floors in co-ed dorms available. **Activities:** Bands, campus ministries, choral groups, dance, drama, international student organizations, literary magazine, music ensembles, Model UN, musical theater, opera, radio station, student government, student newspaper, Religious Life Community, Interfaith Fellowship, Multicultural Student Alliance, Alpha Phi Omega Service Fraternity, College Democrats, College Republicans, Fellowship of Christian Athletes, Students Embracing Responsible Volunteer Experiences, Habitat for Humanity, Amnesty International.

Athletics. NCAA. **Intercollegiate:** Baseball M, basketball, cheerleading, cross-country, football (tackle) M, golf, soccer, softball W, swimming W, tennis, track and field, volleyball W, wrestling M. **Intramural:** Badminton, basketball, football (non-tackle), golf, racquetball, soccer, softball, swimming, table tennis, tennis, volleyball, weight lifting. **Team name:** Storm.

Student services. Adult student services, alcohol/substance abuse counseling, chaplain/spiritual director, career counseling, services for economically disadvantaged, student employment services, financial aid counseling, health services, minority student services, personal counseling, placement for graduates, women's services. **Physically disabled:** Services for visually, speech, hearing impaired.

Contact. E-mail: admiss@simpson.edu
Phone: (515) 961-1624 Toll-free number: (800) 362-2454 ext. 1624
Fax: (515) 961-1870
Deborah Tierney, Vice President for Enrollment, Simpson College, 701 North C Street, Indianola, IA 50125

University of Dubuque

Dubuque, Iowa — **CB member**
www.dbq.edu — **CB code: 6869**

- Private 4-year university and seminary college affiliated with Presbyterian Church (USA)
- Residential campus in small city
- 1,321 degree-seeking undergraduates: 3% part-time, 45% women, 13% African American, 2% Asian American, 4% Hispanic American, 1% Native American, 1% international
- 102 degree-seeking graduate students
- 70% of applicants admitted
- SAT or ACT (ACT writing optional), application essay required
- 54% graduate within 6 years; 23% enter graduate study

General. Founded in 1852. Regionally accredited. **Degrees:** 261 bachelor's awarded; master's, doctoral, first professional offered. **ROTC:** Army. **Location:** 180 miles from Chicago. **Calendar:** Semester, limited summer session. **Full-time faculty:** 83 total; 54% have terminal degrees, 7% minority, 36% women. **Part-time faculty:** 81 total; 51% women. **Class size:** 59% < 20, 40% 20-39, less than 1% 40-49, less than 1% 50-99. **Special facilities:** Floating laboratory on Mississippi River, curriculum laboratory for teachers, aviation operations center, studio laboratory for animation program, wetland area management, science center.

Freshman class profile. 1,152 applied, 811 admitted, 338 enrolled.

Mid 50% test scores		**Rank in top quarter:**	24%
SAT critical reading:	410-530	**Rank in top tenth:**	8%
SAT math:	400-520	**End year in good standing:**	90%
ACT composite:	18-23	**Return as sophomores:**	85%
GPA 3.75 or higher:	10%	**Out-of-state:**	60%
GPA 3.50-3.74:	10%	**Live on campus:**	71%
GPA 3.0-3.49:	30%	**Fraternities:**	18%
GPA 2.0-2.99:	50%	**Sororities:**	14%

Basis for selection. 18 ACT, 860 SAT (exclusive of Writing), rank in top half of class most important. 2.0 GPA in college preparatory classes also considered. Recommendations required. **Learning Disabled:** Students must request assistance.

High school preparation. College-preparatory program recommended. 10 units required; 15 recommended. Required and recommended units include English 4, mathematics 2-3, social studies 2-3, science 2-3 and foreign language 2.

2008-2009 Annual costs. Tuition/fees: $20,020. Room/board: $6,750. Books/supplies: $750.

2008-2009 Financial aid. Need-based: Average need met was 77%. Average scholarship/grant was $11,263; average loan $7,033. 53% of total undergraduate aid awarded as scholarships/grants, 47% as loans/jobs. **Non-need-based:** Scholarships awarded for academics, alumni affiliation, music/drama, ROTC.

Application procedures. Admission: No deadline. $25 fee, may be waived for applicants with need. Admission notification on a rolling basis beginning on or about 8/15. Must reply by May 1 or within 3 week(s) if notified thereafter. **Financial aid:** Priority date 4/1; no closing date. FAFSA required. Applicants notified on a rolling basis starting 3/1; must reply within 3 week(s) of notification.

Academics. Special study options: Combined bachelor's/graduate degree, cooperative education, cross-registration, double major, dual enrollment of high school students, independent study, internships, liberal arts/career combination, study abroad, teacher certification program, urban semester. Undergraduate students may take graduate courses. **Credit/placement by examination:** AP, CLEP, IB, SAT, ACT, institutional tests. 24 credit hours maximum toward associate degree, 24 toward bachelor's. **Support services:** Learning center, reduced course load, remedial instruction, study skills assistance, tutoring, writing center.

Majors. Biology: General, ecology. **Business:** Accounting, business admin. **Communications:** General. **Computer sciences:** General, computer graphics. **Conservation:** General, environmental studies. **Education:** General, elementary, physical. **Health:** Nursing (RN). **Parks/recreation:** General. **Philosophy/religion:** Philosophy, religion. **Physical sciences:** Planetary. **Protective services:** Criminal justice. **Psychology:** General. **Social sciences:** Sociology. **Transportation:** Aviation, aviation management, flight instructor. **Visual/performing arts:** Commercial/advertising art, graphic design.

Most popular majors. Business/marketing 20%, communication technologies 10%, education 11%, health sciences 9%, social sciences 10%.

Computing on campus. 200 workstations in dormitories, library, computer center, student center. Dormitories wired for high-speed internet access and linked to campus network. Commuter students can connect to campus network. Online course registration, online library, helpline, student web hosting available.

Student life. Freshman orientation: Mandatory, $100 fee. Preregistration for classes offered. Held 4 days prior to beginning of class. **Policies:** Students required to live on-campus through junior year, until they reach 21 years of age or unless living with parents within 50 miles of campus. **Housing:** Guaranteed on-campus for freshmen. Coed dorms, special housing for disabled, apartments, wellness housing available. $200 fully refundable deposit, deadline 6/1. Houses and townhouses available. **Activities:** Bands, campus ministries, choral groups, dance, drama, film society, international student organizations, music ensembles, student government, student newspaper, social service organizations, service fraternity, environmental group, student activities board, College Republicans, College Democrats.

Athletics. NCAA. **Intercollegiate:** Baseball M, basketball, cross-country, football (tackle) M, golf, soccer, softball W, tennis, track and field, volleyball W, wrestling M. **Intramural:** Archery, badminton, baseball M, basketball, bowling, cheerleading, football (non-tackle) M, golf, racquetball, soccer, softball, table tennis, tennis, volleyball. **Team name:** Spartans.

Student services. Alcohol/substance abuse counseling, chaplain/spiritual director, career counseling, student employment services, financial aid counseling, health services, minority student services, personal counseling, placement for graduates, veterans' counselor.

Contact. E-mail: admssns@dbq.edu
Phone: (563) 589-3200 Toll-free number: (800) 722-5583
Fax: (563) 589-3690
Jesse James, Dean of Admission, University of Dubuque, 2000 University Avenue, Dubuque, IA 52001-5099

University of Iowa

Iowa City, Iowa — **CB member**
www.uiowa.edu — **CB code: 6681**

- Public 4-year university
- Residential campus in small city
- 20,079 degree-seeking undergraduates: 8% part-time, 51% women
- 8,924 graduate students
- 82% of applicants admitted
- SAT or ACT (ACT writing optional) required
- 66% graduate within 6 years

General. Founded in 1847. Regionally accredited. **Degrees:** 4,482 bachelor's awarded; master's, doctoral, first professional offered. **ROTC:** Army, Air Force. **Location:** 20 miles from Cedar Rapids, 110 miles from Des

Moines. **Calendar:** Semester, extensive summer session. **Full-time faculty:** 1,588 total; 97% have terminal degrees, 17% minority, 29% women. **Part-time faculty:** 85 total; 94% have terminal degrees, 8% minority, 28% women. **Class size:** 51% < 20, 35% 20-39, 4% 40-49, 5% 50-99, 4% >100. **Special facilities:** Field campus, accelerator, observatory, natural history museum, driving simulator.

Freshman class profile. 15,582 applied, 12,827 admitted, 4,246 enrolled.

Mid 50% test scores		**GPA 2.0-2.99:**	6%
SAT critical reading:	510-660	**Rank in top quarter:**	55%
SAT math:	560-680	**Rank in top tenth:**	22%
ACT composite:	23-28	**Return as sophomores:**	83%
GPA 3.75 or higher:	34%	**Out-of-state:**	48%
GPA 3.50-3.74:	24%	**Live on campus:**	93%
GPA 3.0-3.49:	36%	**International:**	4%

Basis for selection. Regent Admission Index (RAI) computed based on ACT/SAT, high school rank, GPA and number of high school core courses. Iowa residents must successfully complete high school course requirements and have 245 RAI; nonresidents must have 255 RAI. College of Engineering applicants must demonstrate success (A's or B's) in math and science courses; have 25 ACT with 25 ACT math subscore or 1130 SAT (exclusive of Writing) with 630 SAT math subscore; and have 265 RAI. Audition required of music, dance majors. **Homeschooled:** Personal essay describing homeschool experience strongly recommended and required in certain circumstances.

High school preparation. College-preparatory program required. 15 units required. Required and recommended units include English 4, mathematics 3-4, social studies 3, science 3 and foreign language 2-4. Math units must include 2 algebra, 1 geometry; engineering majors require fourth unit of higher math. Science units must include 2 of the following: biology, chemistry, and physics. Engineering requires 1 unit chemistry and 1 unit physics. Engineering majors require only 2 units social studies.

2008-2009 Annual costs. Tuition/fees: $6,544; $20,658 out-of-state. Room/board: $7,079. Books/supplies: $1,090. Personal expenses: $2,630.

2007-2008 Financial aid. **Need-based:** 3,420 full-time freshmen applied for aid; 2,302 were judged to have need; 2,086 of these received aid. Average need met was 52%. Average scholarship/grant was $4,179; average loan $2,904. 41% of total undergraduate aid awarded as scholarships/grants, 59% as loans/jobs. **Non-need-based:** Awarded to 6,235 full-time undergraduates, including 2,100 freshmen. Scholarships awarded for academics, alumni affiliation, art, athletics, leadership, minority status, music/drama, ROTC.

Application procedures. **Admission:** Closing date 4/1 (postmark date). $40 fee, may be waived for applicants with need. Admission notification on a rolling basis beginning on or about 9/15. Must reply by May 1 or within 2 week(s) if notified thereafter. **Financial aid:** Priority date 1/1; no closing date. FAFSA, institutional form required. Applicants notified on a rolling basis starting 3/15.

Academics. Bachelor of Liberal Studies and Bachelor of Applied Studies may be earned with distance education course work. **Special study options:** Accelerated study, combined bachelor's/graduate degree, cooperative education, distance learning, double major, dual enrollment of high school students, ESL, exchange student, external degree, honors, independent study, internships, New York semester, semester at sea, student-designed major, study abroad, teacher certification program, Washington semester. **Credit/placement by examination:** AP, CLEP, IB, SAT, ACT, institutional tests. 30 credit hours maximum toward bachelor's degree. **Support services:** Learning center, pre-admission summer program, reduced course load, remedial instruction, study skills assistance, tutoring, writing center.

Majors. **Area/ethnic studies:** African, African-American, American, Asian, Russian/Slavic, women's. **Biology:** General, biochemistry, microbiology. **Business:** Accounting, actuarial science, business admin, finance, human resources, labor relations, management information systems, management science, managerial economics, marketing. **Communications:** General, journalism, media studies. **Computer sciences:** General, computer science. **Conservation:** Environmental science, environmental studies. **Education:** Elementary. **Engineering:** General, biomedical, chemical, civil, electrical, industrial, mechanical. **Foreign languages:** Ancient Greek, Chinese, classics, comparative lit, French, German, Italian, Japanese, Latin, linguistics, Portuguese, Russian, Sanskrit, Spanish. **Health:** Athletic training, audiology/hearing, clinical lab science, music therapy, nuclear medical technology, nursing (RN), predental, premedicine, prenursing, prepharmacy, preveterinary, radiologic technology/medical imaging, recreational therapy. **History:** General. **Interdisciplinary:** Ancient studies, global studies. **Legal studies:** Prelaw. **Liberal arts:** Arts/sciences. **Math:** General, applied, statistics. **Parks/recreation:** General, exercise sciences, facilities management, sports admin. **Philosophy/religion:** Philosophy, religion. **Physical sciences:** Astronomy, chemistry, geology, physics. **Psychology:** General. **Public administration:** Social work. **Social sciences:** Anthropology, economics, geography, political science, sociology. **Visual/performing arts:** Art, art history/conservation, arts management, ceramics, cinematography, dance, dramatic, drawing, film/cinema, jazz, metal/jewelry, music management, music performance, music theory/composition, painting, photography, piano/organ, printmaking, sculpture, stringed instruments, studio arts, voice/opera.

Most popular majors. Business/marketing 18%, communications/journalism 11%, health sciences 7%, psychology 8%, social sciences 10%, visual/performing arts 7%.

Computing on campus. 1,100 workstations in dormitories, library, computer center, student center. Dormitories wired for high-speed internet access and linked to campus network. Commuter students can connect to campus network. Online course registration, online library, helpline, repair service, student web hosting, wireless network available.

Student life. **Freshman orientation:** Mandatory, $235 fee. Preregistration for classes offered. Two-day summer program. **Policies:** Non-smoking campus. **Housing:** Coed dorms, special housing for disabled, apartments, fraternity/sorority housing, wellness housing available. $120 partly refundable deposit. International, freshman and transfer honors, leadership and service, quiet houses, some major specific housing also available. **Activities:** Bands, campus ministries, choral groups, dance, drama, film society, international student organizations, literary magazine, music ensembles, musical theater, opera, radio station, student government, student newspaper, symphony orchestra, College Republicans, University Democrats, American Indian student association, Hispanic Society, black student union, Amnesty International, gay/lesbian/bisexual/transgendered and allied union, honor societies, Habitat for Humanity, writer's club.

Athletics. NCAA. **Intercollegiate:** Baseball M, basketball, cheerleading, cross-country, diving, field hockey W, football (tackle) M, golf, gymnastics, rowing (crew) W, soccer W, softball W, swimming, tennis, track and field, volleyball W, wrestling M. **Intramural:** Badminton, basketball, bowling, football (non-tackle), golf, racquetball, soccer, softball, table tennis, tennis, volleyball, wrestling. **Team name:** Hawkeyes.

Student services. Adult student services, alcohol/substance abuse counseling, career counseling, services for economically disadvantaged, student employment services, financial aid counseling, health services, legal services, minority student services, on-campus daycare, personal counseling, placement for graduates, veterans' counselor, women's services. **Physically disabled:** Services for visually, speech, hearing impaired.

Contact. E-mail: admissions@uiowa.edu
Phone: (319) 335-3847 Toll-free number: (800) 553-4692
Fax: (319) 335-1535
Michael Barron, Assistant Provost for Enrollment Services, University of Iowa, 107 Calvin Hall, Iowa City, IA 52242-1396

University of Northern Iowa

Cedar Falls, Iowa
www.uni.edu **CB code: 6307**

- Public 4-year university
- Residential campus in small city
- 10,835 degree-seeking undergraduates: 8% part-time, 56% women, 3% African American, 1% Asian American, 2% Hispanic American, 2% international
- 1,447 degree-seeking graduate students
- 84% of applicants admitted
- SAT or ACT (ACT writing optional) required
- 63% graduate within 6 years

General. Founded in 1876. Regionally accredited. **Degrees:** 2,221 bachelor's awarded; master's, doctoral offered. **ROTC:** Army. **Location:** 63 miles from Cedar Rapids. **Calendar:** Semester, limited summer session. **Full-time faculty:** 639 total; 70% have terminal degrees, 12% minority, 45% women. **Part-time faculty:** 217 total; 27% have terminal degrees, 4% minority, 52% women. **Class size:** 34% < 20, 50% 20-39, 8% 40-49, 6% 50-99, 2% >100. **Special facilities:** Performing arts center, center for energy and environmental education, NASA teacher resource center, observatory, natural preserve, museum, wellness and recreation center.

Freshman class profile. 4,584 applied, 3,841 admitted, 2,015 enrolled.

Mid 50% test scores			
SAT critical reading:	460-580	Rank in top tenth:	19%
SAT math:	440-590	End year in good standing:	95%
ACT composite:	21-26	Return as sophomores:	84%
GPA 3.75 or higher:	29%	Out-of-state:	7%
GPA 3.50-3.74:	22%	Live on campus:	90%
GPA 3.0-3.49:	35%	International:	1%
GPA 2.0-2.99:	14%	Fraternities:	4%
Rank in top quarter:	48%	Sororities:	3%

Basis for selection. Rank in top half of class, completion of high school curriculum requirements most important factors for admission. In the absence of class rank, standardized test scores may carry greater weight in the admissions process. Audition required of music majors. Interview may be recommended for borderline applicants who do not meet admission requirements. **Homeschooled:** Statement describing homeschool structure and mission, transcript of courses and grades required.

High school preparation. 15 units required. Required and recommended units include English 4, mathematics 3, social studies 3, science 3 (laboratory 1), foreign language 2 and academic electives 2. English units must include 1 composition. Math units must include algebra, geometry and advanced algebra. 2 electives required in subjects listed above and/or fine arts.

2008-2009 Annual costs. Tuition/fees: $6,376; $14,596 out-of-state. Room/board: $6,810. Books/supplies: $1,002. Personal expenses: $2,644.

2008-2009 Financial aid. Need-based: 1,693 full-time freshmen applied for aid; 1,134 were judged to have need; 1,109 of these received aid. Average need met was 72%. Average scholarship/grant was $3,825; average loan $3,213. 35% of total undergraduate aid awarded as scholarships/grants, 65% as loans/jobs. **Non-need-based:** Awarded to 3,674 full-time undergraduates, including 1,367 freshmen. Scholarships awarded for academics, alumni affiliation, art, athletics, leadership, minority status, music/drama, ROTC, state residency.

Application procedures. Admission: Closing date 8/15 (postmark date). $40 fee. Admission notification on a rolling basis beginning on or about 9/1. **Financial aid:** No deadline. FAFSA required. Applicants notified on a rolling basis starting 3/1.

Academics. External undergraduate degree completion program available. **Special study options:** Accelerated study, combined bachelor's/graduate degree, cooperative education, distance learning, double major, dual enrollment of high school students, ESL, exchange student, external degree, honors, independent study, internships, liberal arts/career combination, student-designed major, study abroad, teacher certification program, Washington semester, weekend college. Combined bachelors/masters degree programs (BA/MA, BS/MS, BA/MS); undergraduate dual degree majors; Additional programs leading to combined bachelor's/graduate degree: biology, physics, and technology. **Credit/placement by examination:** AP, CLEP, IB, ACT, institutional tests. 32 credit hours maximum toward bachelor's degree. **Support services:** Learning center, pre-admission summer program, reduced course load, remedial instruction, study skills assistance, tutoring, writing center.

Majors. Area/ethnic studies: American, Asian, European, Latin American. **Biology:** General, biochemistry, bioinformatics, biomedical sciences, biotechnology, ecology, microbiology. **Business:** Accounting, actuarial science, business admin, construction management, finance, management information systems, marketing, real estate. **Communications:** General, digital media, organizational, public relations. **Communications technology:** Graphics. **Computer sciences:** General, computer science, networking. **Conservation:** Environmental science. **Education:** Business, elementary, ESL, foreign languages, health, kindergarten/preschool, middle, music, physical, reading, science, social science, speech, technology/industrial arts. **Engineering:** Physics. **Engineering technology:** Electromechanical, industrial, manufacturing. **Family/consumer sciences:** Clothing/textiles, family/community services. **Foreign languages:** General, French, German, Russian, Spanish. **Health:** Athletic training, speech pathology. **History:** General. **Interdisciplinary:** Biological/physical sciences, gerontology. **Liberal arts:** Arts/sciences, humanities. **Math:** General, applied. **Parks/recreation:** General, health/fitness. **Philosophy/religion:** Philosophy, religion. **Physical sciences:** Chemistry, geology, physics. **Psychology:** General. **Public administration:** General, social work. **Social sciences:** Anthropology, applied economics, criminology, econometrics, economics, geography, political science, sociology. **Visual/performing arts:** Acting, art, art history/conservation, dramatic, interior design, music performance, music theory/composition, studio arts, theater design.

Most popular majors. Business/marketing 22%, communications/journalism 6%, education 16%, social sciences 7%.

Computing on campus. 1,900 workstations in dormitories, library, computer center, student center. Dormitories wired for high-speed internet access and linked to campus network. Commuter students can connect to campus network. Online course registration, online library, helpline, student web hosting, wireless network available.

Student life. Freshman orientation: Available, $125 fee. Preregistration for classes offered. Ten 2-day sessions in summer and immediately preceding beginning of semesters. **Housing:** Guaranteed on-campus for freshmen. Coed dorms, single-sex dorms, special housing for disabled, apartments, fraternity/sorority housing, wellness housing available. $200 deposit. **Activities:** Bands, campus ministries, choral groups, dance, drama, international student organizations, literary magazine, music ensembles, Model UN, musical theater, opera, radio station, student government, student newspaper, symphony orchestra, Amnesty International, Asian American student union, black student union, Campus Crusade for Christ, Catholic student association, College Republicans, conservation club, Fellowship of Christian Athletes, Habitat for Humanity, Democrat club.

Athletics. NCAA. **Intercollegiate:** Baseball M, basketball, cross-country, diving W, football (tackle) M, golf, soccer W, softball W, swimming W, tennis W, track and field, volleyball W, wrestling M. **Intramural:** Badminton, basketball, bowling, cheerleading, cross-country, football (non-tackle), football (tackle) M, golf, racquetball, soccer, softball, swimming, table tennis, tennis, track and field, volleyball, weight lifting, wrestling M. **Team name:** Panthers.

Student services. Adult student services, alcohol/substance abuse counseling, career counseling, student employment services, financial aid counseling, health services, minority student services, on-campus daycare, personal counseling, placement for graduates, veterans' counselor. **Physically disabled:** Services for visually, speech, hearing impaired.

Contact. E-mail: admissions@uni.edu
Phone: (319) 273-2281 Toll-free number: (800) 772-2037
Fax: (319) 273-2885
Christie Kangas, Director of Admissions, University of Northern Iowa, 1227 West 27th Street, Cedar Falls, IA 50614-0018

Upper Iowa University

Fayette, Iowa
www.uiu.edu **CB code: 6885**

- Private 4-year university
- Residential campus in rural community
- 767 degree-seeking undergraduates
- 27 graduate students
- 62% of applicants admitted
- SAT or ACT (ACT writing recommended) required

General. Founded in 1857. Regionally accredited. **Degrees:** 1,002 bachelor's, 41 associate awarded; master's offered. **Location:** 50 miles from Waterloo, 70 miles from Cedar Rapids. **Calendar:** Semester, limited summer session. **Full-time faculty:** 50 total; 78% have terminal degrees, 6% minority, 42% women. **Part-time faculty:** 6 total; 100% have terminal degrees, 67% women. **Special facilities:** Electron microscope lab, greenhouse, television and media lab with computer animation suite.

Freshman class profile. 1,005 applied, 625 admitted, 162 enrolled.

Mid 50% test scores			
SAT critical reading:	400-460	ACT composite:	17-22
SAT math:	410-530	Return as sophomores:	60%
		Out-of-state:	45%

Basis for selection. 2.0 GPA, 16 ACT, 760 SAT (exclusive of Writing) important. Admission by individual review. Interview recommended for academically weak applicants. Portfolio recommended for art majors. **Homeschooled:** Letters of recommendation strongly encouraged. GED or proof of completed coursework required.

High school preparation. College-preparatory program recommended. 14 units recommended. Recommended units include English 4, mathematics 3, social studies 2, history 1, science 3 (laboratory 1).

2009-2010 Annual costs. Tuition/fees: $21,418. Room/board: $6,578. Books/supplies: $1,400. Personal expenses: $1,600.

2007-2008 Financial aid. Need-based: 42% of total undergraduate aid awarded as scholarships/grants, 58% as loans/jobs. **Non-need-based:** Scholarships awarded for academics.

Application procedures. Admission: No deadline. $15 fee, may be waived for applicants with need. Admission notification on a rolling basis.

Financial aid: Priority date 3/1; no closing date. FAFSA required. Applicants notified on a rolling basis starting 3/1.

Academics. 2 consecutive 8-week terms equal one semester. **Special study options:** Accelerated study, combined bachelor's/graduate degree, distance learning, double major, dual enrollment of high school students, exchange student, external degree, independent study, internships, liberal arts/career combination, student-designed major, study abroad, teacher certification program. **Credit/placement by examination:** AP, CLEP, IB. 30 credit hours maximum toward associate degree, 30 toward bachelor's. **Support services:** Learning center, tutoring.

Majors. Area/ethnic studies: American. **Biology:** General. **Business:** General, accounting, business admin, management information systems. **Communications:** General. **Conservation:** General, environmental science, forestry, management/policy. **Education:** General, biology, chemistry, early childhood, elementary, health, history, kindergarten/preschool, middle, physical, reading, science, secondary, social science, social studies, special. **Health:** Athletic training, facilities admin, health care admin, physical therapy assistant, predental, premedicine, prepharmacy, preveterinary. **Legal studies:** Prelaw. **Math:** General. **Parks/recreation:** Facilities management, health/fitness. **Personal/culinary services:** Mortuary science. **Physical sciences:** Chemistry. **Protective services:** Criminal justice. **Psychology:** General. **Public administration:** Human services. **Social sciences:** General, criminology, sociology. **Visual/performing arts:** Art, arts management, commercial/advertising art, studio arts.

Most popular majors. Business/marketing 44%, education 6%, psychology 7%, public administration/social services 22%, social sciences 7%.

Computing on campus. 4 workstations in dormitories, library, computer center, student center. Dormitories wired for high-speed internet access. Online course registration, online library, wireless network available.

Student life. Freshman orientation: Mandatory. Preregistration for classes offered. Held during summer, includes financial aid counseling. **Housing:** Guaranteed on-campus for all undergraduates. Coed dorms, single-sex dorms available. $100 deposit. **Activities:** Pep band, campus ministries, student government, student newspaper, various organizations available.

Athletics. NCAA. **Intercollegiate:** Baseball M, basketball, cheerleading, football (tackle) M, golf, soccer, softball W, tennis, volleyball W, wrestling M. **Intramural:** Badminton, basketball, bowling, football (tackle), softball, table tennis, volleyball. **Team name:** Peacocks.

Student services. Career counseling, student employment services, financial aid counseling, health services, personal counseling, placement for graduates.

Contact. E-mail: admission@uiu.edu
Phone: (563) 425-5281 Toll-free number: (800) 553-4150 ext. 2
Fax: (563) 425-5323
Linc Morris, Vice President of Enrollment Management, Upper Iowa University, Parker Fox Hall, Fayette, IA 52142

Waldorf College

Forest City, Iowa — **CB member**
www.waldorf.edu — **CB code: 6925**

- Private 4-year liberal arts college affiliated with Evangelical Lutheran Church in America
- Residential campus in small town
- 524 degree-seeking undergraduates: 3% part-time, 48% women, 8% African American, 1% Asian American, 5% Hispanic American, 1% Native American, 4% international
- 65% of applicants admitted
- SAT or ACT (ACT writing optional) required

General. Founded in 1903. Regionally accredited. **Degrees:** 127 bachelor's, 14 associate awarded. **Location:** 125 miles from Des Moines. **Calendar:** Semester, limited summer session. **Full-time faculty:** 40 total; 48% have terminal degrees, 42% women. **Part-time faculty:** 17 total. **Class size:** 63% < 20, 37% 20-39. **Special facilities:** Multimedia video lab, exercise physiology laboratory, GeoWall.

Freshman class profile. 655 applied, 424 admitted, 203 enrolled.

Mid 50% test scores		**Rank in top tenth:**	6%
ACT composite:	18-22	**End year in good standing:**	86%
GPA 3.75 or higher:	6%	**Return as sophomores:**	62%
GPA 3.50-3.74:	8%	**Out-of-state:**	42%
GPA 3.0-3.49:	27%	**Live on campus:**	90%
GPA 2.0-2.99:	52%	**International:**	3%
Rank in top quarter:	8%		

Basis for selection. School record and test scores most important, recommendations important, class rank and interview (when administered) considered. Interview recommended. Audition and portfolio recommended for music, theater majors. **Learning Disabled:** Interview during campus visit required.

High school preparation. College-preparatory program recommended. 16 units recommended. Recommended units include English 4, mathematics 3, social studies 4, science 3 and foreign language 2.

2008-2009 Annual costs. Tuition/fees: $20,054. Room/board: $5,810. Books/supplies: $935. Personal expenses: $1,655.

2007-2008 Financial aid. Need-based: 119 full-time freshmen applied for aid; 105 were judged to have need; 104 of these received aid. Average need met was 84%. Average scholarship/grant was $12,898; average loan $4,582. 59% of total undergraduate aid awarded as scholarships/grants, 41% as loans/jobs. **Non-need-based:** Awarded to 207 full-time undergraduates, including 102 freshmen. Scholarships awarded for academics, alumni affiliation, athletics, job skills, leadership, music/drama, religious affiliation, state residency.

Application procedures. Admission: No deadline. No application fee. Admission notification on a rolling basis beginning on or about 9/8. **Financial aid:** Priority date 3/1; no closing date. FAFSA, institutional form required. Applicants notified on a rolling basis starting 3/1; must reply within 2 week(s) of notification.

Academics. Internships required in all baccalaureate programs. **Special study options:** Accelerated study, combined bachelor's/graduate degree, double major, dual enrollment of high school students, ESL, honors, independent study, internships, liberal arts/career combination, student-designed major, study abroad, teacher certification program. **Credit/placement by examination:** AP, CLEP, IB, SAT, ACT, institutional tests. 8 credit hours maximum toward associate degree, 8 toward bachelor's. **Support services:** Learning center, reduced course load, remedial instruction, study skills assistance, tutoring, writing center.

Majors. Biology: General. **Business:** General, business admin, finance, marketing. **Communications:** Broadcast journalism, journalism, media studies, radio/tv. **Communications technology:** General. **Computer sciences:** General, information systems. **Education:** Drama/dance, elementary, English, history, middle, multi-level teacher, music, science, secondary, social studies. **Family/consumer sciences:** Food/nutrition. **History:** General. **Legal studies:** Prelaw. **Liberal arts:** Arts/sciences, humanities. **Psychology:** General. **Social sciences:** General, political science. **Visual/performing arts:** General, arts management, dramatic, music management, music performance, piano/organ, theater arts management, voice/opera.

Most popular majors. Business/marketing 25%, communications/journalism 15%, education 31%, health sciences 6%, psychology 6%.

Computing on campus. PC or laptop required. Dormitories wired for high-speed internet access and linked to campus network. Online library, helpline, repair service, wireless network available.

Student life. Freshman orientation: Mandatory. Preregistration for classes offered. Held 2 days prior to start of school. **Policies:** No alcohol on campus. **Housing:** Guaranteed on-campus for all undergraduates. Coed dorms, single-sex dorms, special housing for disabled, wellness housing available. $100 fully refundable deposit, deadline 9/8. Pets allowed in dorm rooms. **Activities:** Bands, campus ministries, choral groups, dance, drama, film society, international student organizations, literary magazine, music ensembles, musical theater, radio station, student government, student newspaper, TV station, Fellowship of Christian athletes, science club, student senate, global culture club, Amnesty International, awareness ambassadors, praise and worship groups, history club, Gay Straight Alliance, Campus Democrats/Republicans.

Athletics. NAIA. **Intercollegiate:** Baseball M, basketball, cheerleading M, football (tackle) M, golf, soccer, softball W, volleyball W, wrestling M. **Intramural:** Badminton, basketball, bowling, football (non-tackle), racquetball, rugby W, skiing, soccer, softball, table tennis, tennis, volleyball, weight lifting. **Team name:** Warriors.

Student services. Alcohol/substance abuse counseling, chaplain/spiritual director, career counseling, student employment services, financial

aid counseling, health services, personal counseling, placement for graduates. **Physically disabled:** Services for visually, hearing impaired. **Learning disabled:** Comprehensive services available.

Contact. E-mail: admissions@waldorf.edu
Phone: (641) 585-8112 Toll-free number: (800) 292-1903
Fax: (641) 585-8125
Dawn Johnson, Vice President of Admissions, Waldorf College, 106 South Sixth Street, Forest City, IA 50436-1713

Wartburg College

Waverly, Iowa
www.wartburg.edu **CB code: 6926**

- Private 4-year liberal arts college affiliated with Evangelical Lutheran Church in America
- Residential campus in small town
- 1,757 degree-seeking undergraduates: 2% part-time, 53% women, 4% African American, 2% Asian American, 1% Hispanic American, 5% international
- 74% of applicants admitted
- SAT or ACT (ACT writing optional) required
- 63% graduate within 6 years; 20% enter graduate study

General. Founded in 1852. Regionally accredited. **Degrees:** 350 bachelor's awarded. **Location:** 15 miles from Waterloo-Cedar Falls. **Calendar:** 4-4-1. Limited summer session. **Full-time faculty:** 110 total; 87% have terminal degrees, 4% minority, 49% women. **Part-time faculty:** 66 total; 11% have terminal degrees, 8% minority, 58% women. **Class size:** 42% < 20, 50% 20-39, 5% 40-49, 2% 50-99, less than 1% >100. **Special facilities:** Planetarium/observatory, prairie preserve, math simulation laboratory, institute for leadership education, international museum, music laboratory, science center, center for community engagement.

Freshman class profile. 2,209 applied, 1,632 admitted, 514 enrolled.

Mid 50% test scores			
SAT critical reading:	420-600	GPA 2.0-2.99:	14%
SAT math:	510-680	Rank in top quarter:	60%
SAT writing:	470-610	Rank in top tenth:	30%
ACT composite:	21-27	End year in good standing:	96%
GPA 3.75 or higher:	36%	Return as sophomores:	76%
GPA 3.50-3.74:	23%	Out-of-state:	25%
GPA 3.0-3.49:	27%	Live on campus:	98%
		International:	4%

Basis for selection. Class rank, GPA, courses taken, test scores, recommendations important. Students with 18 ACT or below or who rank in lower half of high school class are reviewed by admission and scholarship committee for final decision. Interview recommended. Audition recommended for music majors. Portfolio recommended for art majors. **Learning Disabled:** Documentation of disability required.

High school preparation. College-preparatory program required. 15 units recommended. Recommended units include English 4, mathematics 3, social studies 2, science 3, foreign language 2 and computer science 1.

2008-2009 Annual costs. Tuition/fees: $26,160. Room/board: $7,255. Books/supplies: $900.

2007-2008 Financial aid. Need-based: 504 full-time freshmen applied for aid; 418 were judged to have need; 418 of these received aid. Average need met was 90%. Average scholarship/grant was $15,882; average loan $5,324. 70% of total undergraduate aid awarded as scholarships/grants, 30% as loans/jobs. **Non-need-based:** Awarded to 577 full-time undergraduates, including 183 freshmen. Scholarships awarded for academics, alumni affiliation, leadership, music/drama.

Application procedures. Admission: Priority date 5/1; no deadline. No application fee. Admission notification on a rolling basis beginning on or about 9/1. **Financial aid:** Priority date 3/1; no closing date. FAFSA required. Applicants notified on a rolling basis starting 3/1; must reply within 2 week(s) of notification.

Academics. Special study options: Accelerated study, double major, dual enrollment of high school students, honors, independent study, internships, student-designed major, study abroad, teacher certification program, urban semester, Washington semester. Wartburg West urban academic internship experience in Denver, CO; Washington Center Academic Internship Program; cultural immersions in U.S. and around the world; Leadership Certificate Program; 3-2 engineering agreements; deferred admission program with the University of Iowa College of Dentistry, community-based learning courses and first-year seminars. **Credit/placement by examination:** AP, CLEP, SAT, ACT, institutional tests. **Support services:** Learning center, reduced course load, remedial instruction, study skills assistance, tutoring, writing center.

Majors. Biology: General, biochemistry. **Business:** Accounting, business admin, finance, international, marketing. **Communications:** General, broadcast journalism, journalism, public relations. **Computer sciences:** General, information systems. **Education:** Art, elementary, history, music, physical. **Engineering:** Science. **Foreign languages:** French, German, Spanish. **Health:** Clinical lab science, music therapy. **History:** General. **Math:** General. **Parks/recreation:** Sports admin. **Philosophy/religion:** Philosophy, religion. **Physical sciences:** Chemistry, physics. **Psychology:** General. **Public administration:** Social work. **Social sciences:** Economics, international relations, political science, sociology. **Theology:** Pastoral counseling, religious ed, sacred music. **Visual/performing arts:** Art, commercial/advertising art, dramatic, music performance, music theory/composition.

Most popular majors. Biology 15%, business/marketing 18%, communications/journalism 11%, education 11%.

Computing on campus. 275 workstations in dormitories, library, computer center, student center. Dormitories wired for high-speed internet access and linked to campus network. Commuter students can connect to campus network. Online course registration, online library, helpline, wireless network available.

Student life. Freshman orientation: Mandatory, $150 fee. Preregistration for classes offered. Two-day program in summer; continues in fall for 1 week. **Housing:** Guaranteed on-campus for freshmen. Coed dorms, single-sex dorms, apartments available. $100 deposit, deadline 5/1. Suite-style housing available. **Activities:** Bands, campus ministries, choral groups, dance, drama, film society, international student organizations, literary magazine, music ensembles, musical theater, opera, radio station, student government, student newspaper, symphony orchestra, TV station, campus ministry board, Democrat club, Republican club, Habitat for Humanity, students for peace and justice, Fellowship of Christian Athletes, volunteer action center, EARTH, Mosaico Latino, Faith Alive.

Athletics. NCAA. **Intercollegiate:** Baseball M, basketball, cross-country, football (tackle) M, golf, soccer, softball W, tennis, track and field, volleyball W, wrestling M. **Intramural:** Badminton, basketball, football (non-tackle), golf, racquetball, softball, tennis, volleyball. **Team name:** Knights.

Student services. Alcohol/substance abuse counseling, career counseling, student employment services, financial aid counseling, health services, minority student services, personal counseling.

Contact. E-mail: admissions@wartburg.edu
Phone: (319) 352-8264 Toll-free number: (800) 772-2085
Fax: (319) 352-8579
Todd Coleman, Assistant Vice President for Admissions and Alumni/Parent Programs, Wartburg College, 100 Wartburg Boulevard, PO Box 1003, Waverly, IA 50677-0903

William Penn University

Oskaloosa, Iowa
www.wmpenn.edu **CB code: 6943**

- Private 4-year liberal arts college affiliated with Society of Friends (Quaker)
- Residential campus in small town
- 1,697 degree-seeking undergraduates: 3% part-time, 55% women
- 80 degree-seeking graduate students
- 52% of applicants admitted
- SAT or ACT (ACT writing optional) required

General. Founded in 1873. Regionally accredited. Strong emphasis on leadership development. **Degrees:** 350 bachelor's, 121 associate awarded; master's offered. **Location:** 60 miles from Des Moines. **Calendar:** Differs by program, limited summer session. **Full-time faculty:** 45 total. **Part-time faculty:** 102 total. **Class size:** 62% < 20, 32% 20-39, 1% 40-49, 5% 50-99. **Special facilities:** Applied technology laboratories, multipurpose activity center, professional-level theater, Middle Eastern art collection, prairie wildlife preserve.

Freshman class profile. 730 applied, 382 admitted, 196 enrolled.

Mid 50% test scores			
SAT critical reading:	350-490	SAT writing:	380-480
SAT math:	410-510	ACT composite:	17-22
		Return as sophomores:	56%

Basis for selection. Class rank, test scores, high school GPA important. Extracurricular activities, alumni relationship, recommendation, personal essay considered. Interview and essay recommended for academically marginal applicants. Audition recommended for music grants.

High school preparation. College-preparatory program recommended. 15 units required. Required and recommended units include English 4, mathematics 2, social studies 2, history 2, science 2 and academic electives 3.

2008-2009 Annual costs. Tuition/fees: $18,034. Per-credit-hour charge of $215 for 1-7 credits, $425 for credits in excess of 18. Room/board: $5,132. Books/supplies: $950. Personal expenses: $2,062.

2007-2008 Financial aid. Need-based: 56% of total undergraduate aid awarded as scholarships/grants, 44% as loans/jobs. **Non-need-based:** Scholarships awarded for academics, alumni affiliation, athletics, leadership, music/drama, religious affiliation.

Application procedures. Admission: Priority date 7/1; no deadline. $20 fee, may be waived for applicants with need. Admission notification on a rolling basis beginning on or about 11/1. **Financial aid:** Priority date 4/15; no closing date. FAFSA required. Applicants notified on a rolling basis starting 1/1; must reply within 3 week(s) of notification.

Academics. College for Working Adults (CWA) degree program. Leadership core curriculum replaces general education requirements. **Special study options:** Accelerated study, distance learning, double major, dual enrollment of high school students, ESL, independent study, internships, liberal arts/career combination, study abroad, teacher certification program. 3-2 engineering program with Iowa State University. **Credit/placement by examination:** AP, CLEP, IB, SAT, ACT. 16 credit hours maximum toward associate degree, 32 toward bachelor's. **Support services:** Learning center, reduced course load, remedial instruction, study skills assistance, tutoring, writing center.

Majors. Biology: General. **Business:** Accounting, business admin. **Communications:** General. **Computer sciences:** General, information technology. **Education:** Elementary, secondary. **Engineering:** Mechanical. **Engineering technology:** Industrial. **History:** General. **Math:** General. **Parks/recreation:** Health/fitness. **Psychology:** General. **Public administration:** Human services. **Social sciences:** Sociology.

Most popular majors. Business/marketing 60%, education 10%, parks/recreation 12%.

Computing on campus. 125 workstations in dormitories, library, computer center, student center. Dormitories wired for high-speed internet access and linked to campus network. Commuter students can connect to campus network. Online library, helpline, repair service, wireless network available.

Student life. Freshman orientation: Mandatory. Preregistration for classes offered. Held the weekend prior to start of Fall classes; freshmen retreat hosted by faculty the weekend following first week of classes. **Policies:** Student Code of Conduct identifies academic conduct, conduct toward society, general conduct, and conduct toward others. **Housing:** Guaranteed on-campus for freshmen. Coed dorms, single-sex dorms, special housing for disabled, apartments, wellness housing available. $100 partly refundable deposit, deadline 8/1. **Activities:** Bands, campus ministries, choral groups, dance, drama, literary magazine, music ensembles, musical theater, radio station, student government, student newspaper, literary magazine, Students for Minority Interests, international student club, Presidents Diplomats, strength and conditioning club, Greek Council, honor societies, computer club.

Athletics. NAIA. **Intercollegiate:** Baseball M, basketball, cheerleading M, cross-country, football (tackle) M, golf M, soccer, softball W, track and field, volleyball W, wrestling M. **Intramural:** Basketball, bowling, football (non-tackle) M, softball, table tennis, tennis, volleyball. **Team name:** Lady Statesmen, Statesmen.

Student services. Adult student services, alcohol/substance abuse counseling, chaplain/spiritual director, career counseling, services for economically disadvantaged, student employment services, financial aid counseling, minority student services, personal counseling, placement for graduates, veterans' counselor. **Physically disabled:** Services for visually, hearing impaired.

Contact. E-mail: admissions@wmpenn.edu
Phone: (641) 673-1012 Toll-free number: (800) 779-7366
Fax: (641) 673-2113
John Ottosson, Vice President for Enrollment Management, William Penn University, 201 Trueblood Avenue, Oskaloosa, IA 52577

Kansas

Baker University
Baldwin City, Kansas
www.bakeru.edu
CB member
CB code: 6031

- Private 4-year liberal arts and teachers college affiliated with United Methodist Church
- Residential campus in small town
- 906 degree-seeking undergraduates: 1% part-time, 56% women, 9% African American, 1% Asian American, 2% Hispanic American, 1% Native American, 1% international
- 50% of applicants admitted
- SAT or ACT (ACT writing optional) required
- 58% graduate within 6 years

General. Founded in 1858. Regionally accredited. Additional campus locations include Overland Park, Topeka, Wichita, and Lee's Summit in Missouri. **Degrees:** 166 bachelor's awarded. **ROTC:** Army, Air Force. **Location:** 15 miles from Lawrence, 35 miles from Kansas City, Missouri. **Calendar:** 4-1-4, limited summer session. **Full-time faculty:** 64 total; 81% have terminal degrees, 5% minority, 44% women. **Part-time faculty:** 50 total; 28% have terminal degrees, 4% minority, 58% women. **Class size:** 74% < 20, 22% 20-39, 3% 40-49, less than 1% 50-99. **Special facilities:** Wetlands, museum, bible collections.

Freshman class profile. 1,276 applied, 638 admitted, 239 enrolled.

Mid 50% test scores		Rank in top quarter:	51%
SAT critical reading:	430-540	Rank in top tenth:	23%
SAT math:	460-560	Return as sophomores:	73%
ACT composite:	20-26	Out-of-state:	29%
GPA 3.75 or higher:	34%	Live on campus:	95%
GPA 3.50-3.74:	21%	Fraternities:	35%
GPA 3.0-3.49:	30%	Sororities:	40%
GPA 2.0-2.99:	15%		

Basis for selection. Strong core curriculum during high school very important. GPA, class rank, course selection, ACT or SAT, and recommendation from high school core teacher or guidance counselor important. Involvement in school, community and church activities considered. Interview and essay recommended. Audition recommended for music and theater majors. Portfolio recommended for art majors. **Homeschooled:** Letter of recommendation (nonparent) required.

High school preparation. 17 units recommended. Recommended units include English 4, mathematics 3, social studies 3, science 3 (laboratory 1) and foreign language 2. One fine arts and one computing course recommended.

2008-2009 Annual costs. Tuition/fees: $19,965. Room/board: $6,370. Books/supplies: $1,200. Personal expenses: $1,510.

2008-2009 Financial aid. Need-based: Average need met was 85%. Average scholarship/grant was $6,358; average loan $4,136. 49% of total undergraduate aid awarded as scholarships/grants, 51% as loans/jobs. **Non-need-based:** Scholarships awarded for academics, alumni affiliation, art, athletics, leadership, music/drama, religious affiliation, ROTC.

Application procedures. Admission: No deadline. No application fee. Admission notification on a rolling basis. **Financial aid:** Priority date 3/1; no closing date. FAFSA, institutional form required. Applicants notified on a rolling basis starting 3/1; must reply by 5/1 or within 6 week(s) of notification.

Academics. Liberal arts core consisting of nine hours stressing critical thinking skills, strong writing ability, and application of these skills to various academic disciplines required. **Special study options:** Accelerated study, double major, honors, independent study, internships, liberal arts/career combination, student-designed major, study abroad, teacher certification program. **Credit/placement by examination:** AP, CLEP, IB, SAT, ACT. **Support services:** Learning center, reduced course load, study skills assistance, tutoring, writing center.

Majors. Biology: General, molecular, wildlife. **Business:** General, accounting, international. **Communications:** General, media studies. **Computer sciences:** Computer science, information systems, web page design. **Education:** Art, elementary, middle, music, secondary. **Foreign languages:** French, German, Spanish. **History:** General. **Interdisciplinary:** Global studies. **Math:** General. **Parks/recreation:** Exercise sciences, health/fitness, sports admin. **Philosophy/religion:** Philosophy, religion. **Physical sciences:** Chemistry, physics. **Psychology:** General. **Social sciences:** Economics, political science, sociology. **Visual/performing arts:** Art history/conservation, dramatic, studio arts.

Most popular majors. Biology 9%, business/marketing 24%, communications/journalism 7%, education 11%, parks/recreation 9%, social sciences 7%.

Computing on campus. 222 workstations in dormitories, library, computer center. Dormitories wired for high-speed internet access and linked to campus network. Online library, helpline, repair service, student web hosting, wireless network available.

Student life. Freshman orientation: Available. Preregistration for classes offered. 2-day program in summer and 4-day program prior to start of fall term. **Policies:** Students required to live in campus or Greek housing unless granted permission to live off-campus. Freshmen not allowed to live in Greek housing. **Housing:** Guaranteed on-campus for freshmen. Coed dorms, single-sex dorms, special housing for disabled, apartments, fraternity/sorority housing available. $100 deposit. **Activities:** Bands, choral groups, dance, drama, international student organizations, literary magazine, music ensembles, radio station, student government, student newspaper, TV station, Mungano, Fellowship of Christian Athletes, Parmentors, Ambassadors, Earth We Are, College Republicans, Young Democrats, Bacchus.

Athletics. NAIA. **Intercollegiate:** Baseball M, basketball, cheerleading, cross-country, football (tackle) M, golf, soccer, softball W, tennis, track and field, volleyball W. **Intramural:** Basketball, football (non-tackle), softball, table tennis, volleyball. **Team name:** Wildcats.

Student services. Alcohol/substance abuse counseling, chaplain/spiritual director, career counseling, student employment services, financial aid counseling, health services, minority student services, personal counseling, placement for graduates, veterans' counselor, women's services. **Physically disabled:** Services for visually, hearing impaired.

Contact. E-mail: admissions@bakeru.edu
Phone: (785) 594-8307 Toll-free number: (800) 873-4282
Fax: (785) 594-8372
Daniel McKinney, Director of Admissions, Baker University, 618 Eighth Street, Baldwin City, KS 66006-0065

Barclay College
Haviland, Kansas
www.barclaycollege.edu
CB code: 6228

- Private 4-year Bible college affiliated with Evangelical Friends Alliance and Friends United Meeting
- Residential campus in rural community
- 138 degree-seeking undergraduates: 5% part-time, 51% women, 3% African American, 1% Asian American, 2% Hispanic American, 1% Native American, 2% international
- 100% of applicants admitted
- ACT (writing optional), application essay, interview required
- 30% graduate within 6 years; 10% enter graduate study

General. Founded in 1917. Accredited by ABHE. **Degrees:** 15 bachelor's, 2 associate awarded. **Location:** 100 miles from Wichita, 65 miles from Dodge City. **Calendar:** Semester, limited summer session. **Full-time faculty:** 7 total; 57% have terminal degrees, 14% minority, 14% women. **Part-time faculty:** 8 total; 50% women. **Class size:** 82% < 20, 17% 20-39, 2% 50-99.

Freshman class profile. 39 applied, 39 admitted, 34 enrolled.

Mid 50% test scores		Return as sophomores:	78%
ACT composite:	16-21	Out-of-state:	55%
End year in good standing:	86%	Live on campus:	100%

Basis for selection. Personal references and commitment to Christian vocation important. Committee reviews file and conducts phone interview. Audition recommended for music majors.

2008-2009 Annual costs. Tuition/fees: $13,000. Room/board: $6,300. Books/supplies: $1,000. Personal expenses: $1,300.

2008-2009 Financial aid. **Need-based:** 68% of total undergraduate aid awarded as scholarships/grants, 32% as loans/jobs. **Non-need-based:** Scholarships awarded for academics, alumni affiliation, leadership, music/drama, state residency.

Application procedures. **Admission:** Closing date 9/1. $25 fee, may be waived for applicants with need, free for online applicants. Admission notification on a rolling basis. **Financial aid:** Priority date 5/31, closing date 7/15. FAFSA, institutional form required. Applicants notified on a rolling basis starting 1/1; must reply within 4 week(s) of notification.

Academics. Each student has Bible major in addition to individually chosen major. Emphasis on practicums and internships. **Special study options:** Distance learning, double major, independent study, internships, liberal arts/career combination, teacher certification program. Cooperative classes with Pratt Community College. **Credit/placement by examination:** AP, CLEP, IB, SAT, ACT, institutional tests. 15 credit hours maximum toward associate degree, 30 toward bachelor's. **Support services:** Remedial instruction, study skills assistance, tutoring.

Majors. **Business:** General, business admin. **Education:** Elementary. **Philosophy/religion:** Religion. **Psychology:** General. **Theology:** Bible, missionary, pastoral counseling, sacred music, theology, youth ministry.

Most popular majors. Business/marketing 13%, education 13%, psychology 14%, theological studies 60%.

Computing on campus. 18 workstations in library, computer center. Dormitories wired for high-speed internet access and linked to campus network. Commuter students can connect to campus network. Online course registration, online library, repair service, wireless network available.

Student life. **Freshman orientation:** Mandatory. Preregistration for classes offered. **Policies:** Christian and social work required. Religious observance required. **Housing:** Guaranteed on-campus for freshmen. Single-sex dorms, wellness housing available. $50 deposit. **Activities:** Jazz band, choral groups, drama, music ensembles, student government.

Athletics. **Intercollegiate:** Basketball, cheerleading M, golf, soccer M, tennis, volleyball W. **Intramural:** Baseball, basketball, bowling, softball, volleyball. **Team name:** Bears.

Student services. Chaplain/spiritual director, career counseling, student employment services, financial aid counseling, health services, personal counseling, placement for graduates.

Contact. E-mail: admissions@barclaycollege.edu
Phone: (620) 862-5252 ext. 21 Toll-free number: (800) 862-0226
Fax: (620) 862-5242
Justin Kendall, Director of Admissions, Barclay College, 607 North Kingman, Haviland, KS 67059

Benedictine College

Atchison, Kansas — **CB member**
www.benedictine.edu — **CB code: 6056**

- Private 4-year liberal arts college affiliated with Roman Catholic Church
- Residential campus in large town
- 1,364 degree-seeking undergraduates: 1% part-time, 53% women, 4% African American, 1% Asian American, 5% Hispanic American, 1% Native American, 2% international
- 55 degree-seeking graduate students
- 20% of applicants admitted
- SAT or ACT (ACT writing optional) required
- 60% graduate within 6 years; 24% enter graduate study

General. Founded in 1858. Regionally accredited. Affiliated with Benedictine monastic order. Institution offers additional associate degree and bachelors degree programs in Hong Kong, Shanghai, Singapore and Kuala Lampur. **Degrees:** 225 bachelor's awarded; master's offered. **ROTC:** Army. **Location:** 45 miles from Kansas City, Missouri. **Calendar:** Semester, limited summer session. **Full-time faculty:** 76 total; 68% have terminal degrees, 7% minority, 26% women. **Part-time faculty:** 38 total; 40% have terminal degrees, 3% minority, 60% women. **Class size:** 63% < 20, 35% 20-39, 1% 40-49, less than 1% 50-99. **Special facilities:** Biological research area, high-tech classrooms, 2 performing arts theaters.

Freshman class profile. 2,192 applied, 433 admitted, 363 enrolled.

Mid 50% test scores		**Rank in top tenth:**	5%
ACT composite:	21-27	**End year in good standing:**	76%
GPA 3.75 or higher:	30%	**Return as sophomores:**	76%
GPA 3.50-3.74:	20%	**Out-of-state:**	73%
GPA 3.0-3.49:	26%	**Live on campus:**	98%
GPA 2.0-2.99:	24%	**International:**	1%
Rank in top quarter:	15%		

Basis for selection. Applicant must satisfy 2 of following requirements: GPA above 2.0, rank in top half of class, requisite ACT or SAT scores. Recommendations and interview considered. Interview recommended for academically weak applicants.

High school preparation. Required and recommended units include English 4, mathematics 3-4, social studies 2, history 2, science 2-4 and foreign language 2-4.

2008-2009 Annual costs. Tuition/fees: $18,800. Room/board: $6,400. Books/supplies: $2,400. Personal expenses: $2,800.

2008-2009 Financial aid. **Need-based:** 360 full-time freshmen applied for aid; 295 were judged to have need; 295 of these received aid. Average need met was 69%. Average scholarship/grant was $4,065; average loan $3,780. 54% of total undergraduate aid awarded as scholarships/grants, 46% as loans/jobs. **Non-need-based:** Awarded to 1,814 full-time undergraduates, including 533 freshmen. Scholarships awarded for academics, alumni affiliation, art, athletics, job skills, leadership, minority status, music/drama, religious affiliation, ROTC.

Application procedures. **Admission:** No deadline. $25 fee, may be waived for applicants with need. Admission notification on a rolling basis. Must reply by May 1 or within 4 week(s) if notified thereafter. **Financial aid:** Priority date 3/15; no closing date. FAFSA required. Applicants notified on a rolling basis starting 2/1; must reply within 2 week(s) of notification.

Academics. **Special study options:** Combined bachelor's/graduate degree, cooperative education, double major, dual enrollment of high school students, ESL, exchange student, independent study, internships, liberal arts/career combination, student-designed major, study abroad, teacher certification program. **Credit/placement by examination:** AP, CLEP, IB, ACT, institutional tests. 30 credit hours maximum toward associate degree, 30 toward bachelor's. **Support services:** Learning center, reduced course load, remedial instruction, study skills assistance, tutoring.

Majors. **Biology:** General, biochemistry. **Business:** Accounting, business admin, finance, international. **Communications:** Media studies. **Computer sciences:** Computer science. **Education:** Elementary, music, physical, special. **Foreign languages:** French, Spanish. **Health:** Athletic training. **History:** General. **Interdisciplinary:** Natural sciences. **Liberal arts:** Arts/sciences. **Math:** General. **Philosophy/religion:** Philosophy, religion. **Physical sciences:** Astronomy, chemistry, physics. **Psychology:** General. **Social sciences:** General, economics, political science, sociology. **Theology:** Youth ministry. **Visual/performing arts:** Dramatic, music management, theater arts management.

Most popular majors. Biology 6%, business/marketing 25%, communications/journalism 7%, education 18%, psychology 9%, theological studies 8%.

Computing on campus. 85 workstations in dormitories, library, computer center. Dormitories wired for high-speed internet access and linked to campus network. Online library, helpline, repair service, wireless network available.

Student life. **Freshman orientation:** Mandatory. Preregistration for classes offered. Weekend program before classes commence. **Housing:** Guaranteed on-campus for freshmen. Coed dorms, single-sex dorms available. $100 deposit. Off-campus college-owned housing available. **Activities:** Bands, campus ministries, choral groups, dance, drama, literary magazine, music ensembles, musical theater, student government, student newspaper, symphony orchestra, Ravens Respect Life, Young Democrats, Young Republicans, Knights of Columbus, hunger coalition, Fellowship of Catholic University Students, Students in Free Enterprise, Black Student Union, Amnesty International.

Athletics. NAIA. **Intercollegiate:** Baseball M, basketball, cheerleading, cross-country, football (tackle) M, golf, soccer, softball W, tennis, track and field, volleyball W. **Intramural:** Baseball M, basketball, handball, racquetball, soccer, softball, table tennis, tennis, volleyball. **Team name:** Ravens.

Student services. Alcohol/substance abuse counseling, chaplain/spiritual director, career counseling, student employment services, financial

aid counseling, health services, personal counseling, placement for graduates, veterans' counselor. **Physically disabled:** Services for visually, speech, hearing impaired.

Contact. E-mail: bcadmiss@benedictine.edu
Phone: (913) 360-7476 Toll-free number: (800) 467-5340
Fax: (913) 367-5462
Pete Helgesen, Dean of Enrollment Management, Benedictine College, 1020 North Second Street, Atchison, KS 66002-1499

Bethany College
Lindsborg, Kansas
www.bethanylb.edu **CB code: 6034**

- Private 4-year liberal arts college affiliated with Evangelical Lutheran Church in America
- Residential campus in small town
- 569 degree-seeking undergraduates: 3% part-time, 48% women, 11% African American, 1% Asian American, 7% Hispanic American, 1% Native American, 6% international
- 65% of applicants admitted
- SAT or ACT (ACT writing optional) required
- 40% graduate within 6 years; 17% enter graduate study

General. Founded in 1881. Regionally accredited. **Degrees:** 98 bachelor's awarded. **Location:** 20 miles from Salina, 60 miles from Wichita. **Calendar:** 4-1-4, limited summer session. **Full-time faculty:** 44 total; 57% have terminal degrees, 4% minority, 36% women. **Part-time faculty:** 43 total; 19% have terminal degrees, 51% women. **Class size:** 84% < 20, 15% 20-39, less than 1% 40-49, less than 1% 50-99.

Freshman class profile. 811 applied, 530 admitted, 178 enrolled.

Mid 50% test scores		**Rank in top quarter:**	42%
SAT critical reading:	370-500	**Rank in top tenth:**	15%
SAT math:	420-560	**End year in good standing:**	77%
SAT writing:	380-490	**Return as sophomores:**	61%
ACT composite:	19-24	**Out-of-state:**	63%
GPA 3.75 or higher:	29%	**Live on campus:**	95%
GPA 3.50-3.74:	17%	**International:**	6%
GPA 3.0-3.49:	33%	**Fraternities:**	2%
GPA 2.0-2.99:	20%	**Sororities:**	1%

Basis for selection. High school GPA, course selection, trends in grades, class rank, and standardized test scores very important. Interview, letters of recommendation, leadership, curriculum, and involvement considered. Interview and essay recommended for some. Audition required of music and theater majors. Portfolio required of art majors.

High school preparation. College-preparatory program recommended. Recommended units include English 4, mathematics 3, social studies 3, science 3 (laboratory 2) and foreign language 2.

2008-2009 Annual costs. Tuition/fees: $18,124. Room/board: $5,650. Books/supplies: $1,000. Personal expenses: $1,900.

2008-2009 Financial aid. Need-based: 175 full-time freshmen applied for aid; 145 were judged to have need; 145 of these received aid. Average need met was 89%. Average scholarship/grant was $7,254; average loan $4,304. 58% of total undergraduate aid awarded as scholarships/grants, 42% as loans/jobs. **Non-need-based:** Awarded to 207 full-time undergraduates, including 68 freshmen. Scholarships awarded for academics, alumni affiliation, art, athletics, leadership, music/drama, religious affiliation. **Additional information:** State financial aid deadline March 15.

Application procedures. Admission: Priority date 2/1; no deadline. $20 fee, may be waived for applicants with need, free for online applicants. Admission notification on a rolling basis. **Financial aid:** Priority date 3/15; no closing date. FAFSA required. Applicants notified on a rolling basis starting 2/1; must reply within 3 week(s) of notification.

Academics. Special study options: Accelerated study, combined bachelor's/graduate degree, cross-registration, double major, dual enrollment of high school students, exchange student, honors, independent study, internships, liberal arts/career combination, student-designed major, study abroad, teacher certification program, urban semester, Washington semester. Special education program with Associated Colleges of Central Kansas. **Credit/placement by examination:** AP, CLEP, IB. 32 credit hours maximum toward bachelor's degree. **Support services:** Learning center, reduced course load, study skills assistance, tutoring, writing center.

Majors. Biology: General. **Business:** Accounting, business admin, finance, managerial economics, marketing. **Communications:** General. **Education:** General, art, biology, business, chemistry, elementary, English, health, history, mathematics, music, physical, secondary, social science. **Health:** Art therapy, athletic training. **History:** General. **Liberal arts:** Arts/sciences. **Math:** General. **Parks/recreation:** Facilities management, sports admin. **Philosophy/religion:** Christian. **Physical sciences:** Chemistry. **Protective services:** Criminal justice, police science. **Psychology:** General. **Public administration:** Social work. **Social sciences:** General, economics, sociology. **Visual/performing arts:** Art, music performance.

Most popular majors. Biology 15%, business/marketing 15%, education 24%, parks/recreation 7%, psychology 8%, security/protective services 6%, visual/performing arts 7%.

Computing on campus. 40 workstations in library, computer center. Dormitories wired for high-speed internet access and linked to campus network. Commuter students can connect to campus network. Online library available.

Student life. Freshman orientation: Mandatory. Preregistration for classes offered. One week of activities prior to first day of classes; planned and organized by returning students. **Policies:** No alcohol allowed on campus. Full-time students required to live on campus until age 22 or special consideration given. **Housing:** Coed dorms, single-sex dorms, apartments, wellness housing available. $100 deposit, deadline 8/1. **Activities:** Bands, campus ministries, choral groups, dance, drama, international student organizations, music ensembles, musical theater, student government, student newspaper, symphony orchestra, SOAR, Blue Key, Gold Key, Alpha Omega, Bethany youth ministry program, Bread for the World, departmental organizations, honorary societies, Green Team.

Athletics. NAIA. **Intercollegiate:** Baseball M, basketball, cross-country, football (tackle) M, golf M, soccer, softball W, tennis, track and field, volleyball W. **Intramural:** Basketball, football (non-tackle), racquetball, soccer, softball, table tennis, volleyball, weight lifting. **Team name:** Swedes.

Student services. Alcohol/substance abuse counseling, chaplain/spiritual director, career counseling, student employment services, financial aid counseling, health services, minority student services, personal counseling, placement for graduates, veterans' counselor.

Contact. E-mail: admissions@bethanylb.edu
Phone: (785) 227-3380 ext. 8113 Toll-free number: (800) 826-2281
Fax: (785) 227-8993
Tricia Hawk, Dean of Admissions and Financial Aid, Bethany College, 335 East Swensson, Lindsborg, KS 67456-1897

Bethel College
North Newton, Kansas
www.bethelks.edu **CB code: 6037**

- Private 4-year liberal arts college affiliated with Mennonite Church
- Residential campus in large town
- 500 degree-seeking undergraduates: 5% part-time, 48% women, 5% African American, 1% Asian American, 5% Hispanic American, 1% Native American, 10% international
- 72% of applicants admitted
- SAT or ACT (ACT writing optional) required
- 61% graduate within 6 years

General. Founded in 1887. Regionally accredited. **Degrees:** 129 bachelor's awarded. **Location:** 25 miles from Wichita. **Calendar:** 4-1-4, limited summer session. **Full-time faculty:** 49 total; 55% have terminal degrees, 6% minority, 49% women. **Part-time faculty:** 34 total; 26% have terminal degrees, 9% minority, 41% women. **Class size:** 73% < 20, 22% 20-39, 2% 40-49, 2% 50-99, less than 1% >100. **Special facilities:** Natural history museum, 80-acre natural history field laboratory, institute for peace and conflict resolution, Mennonite library and archives, observatory, conservatory.

Freshman class profile. 404 applied, 292 admitted, 119 enrolled.

Mid 50% test scores		**Rank in top quarter:**	44%
SAT critical reading:	440-650	**Rank in top tenth:**	29%
SAT math:	500-670	**End year in good standing:**	85%
ACT composite:	20-27	**Return as sophomores:**	71%
GPA 3.75 or higher:	44%	**Out-of-state:**	27%
GPA 3.50-3.74:	12%	**Live on campus:**	97%
GPA 3.0-3.49:	23%	**International:**	5%
GPA 2.0-2.99:	21%		

Basis for selection. Automatic admission generally given to students with high school GPA of 2.5 and ACT score of at least 19 or SAT of at least

890 (exclusive of Writing). Essay recommended for academically weak applicants. Audition recommended for drama and music majors. Portfolio recommended for art majors. **Homeschooled:** Evaluative transcript or GED score. ACT or SAT score is also required.

High school preparation. College-preparatory program recommended. 18 units recommended. Recommended units include English 4, mathematics 4, social studies 3, history 1, science 3, foreign language 2 and computer science 1.

2008-2009 Annual costs. Tuition/fees: $18,900. Room/board: $6,650. Books/supplies: $800. Personal expenses: $2,050.

2007-2008 Financial aid. **Need-based:** 91 full-time freshmen applied for aid; 89 were judged to have need; 89 of these received aid. Average need met was 87%. Average scholarship/grant was $4,317; average loan $4,768. 33% of total undergraduate aid awarded as scholarships/grants, 67% as loans/jobs. **Non-need-based:** Awarded to 675 full-time undergraduates, including 153 freshmen. Scholarships awarded for academics, alumni affiliation, art, athletics, minority status, music/drama, religious affiliation, state residency.

Application procedures. **Admission:** No deadline. $20 fee, may be waived for applicants with need. Admission notification on a rolling basis beginning on or about 9/1. **Financial aid:** Priority date 4/1; no closing date. FAFSA required. Applicants notified on a rolling basis starting 2/1; must reply within 2 week(s) of notification.

Academics. Curriculum founded on general education program in liberal arts and sciences. Distinctive elements include peace, justice and conflict studies, collaborative inquiry seminary, convocation, and cross-cultural learning requirements and senior capstone course focusing on basic issues of faith and life. **Special study options:** Cross-registration, double major, dual enrollment of high school students, independent study, internships, liberal arts/career combination, study abroad, teacher certification program, urban semester, Washington semester. **Credit/placement by examination:** AP, CLEP, IB, SAT, ACT, institutional tests. **Support services:** Learning center, study skills assistance, tutoring.

Majors. **Biology:** General. **Business:** General. **Communications:** Media studies. **Computer sciences:** Computer science. **Education:** Elementary. **Foreign languages:** German, Spanish. **Health:** Athletic training, nursing (RN). **History:** General. **Interdisciplinary:** Natural sciences. **Math:** General. **Parks/recreation:** Health/fitness. **Philosophy/religion:** Religion. **Physical sciences:** Chemistry, physics. **Psychology:** General. **Public administration:** Social work. **Visual/performing arts:** Studio arts.

Most popular majors. Business/marketing 6%, communications/journalism 6%, education 6%, English 8%, health sciences 33%, visual/performing arts 8%.

Computing on campus. 56 workstations in library, computer center. Dormitories wired for high-speed internet access and linked to campus network. Commuter students can connect to campus network. Helpline, repair service, student web hosting, wireless network available.

Student life. **Freshman orientation:** Mandatory. Preregistration for classes offered. Held the Wednesday through Monday before classes begin. **Policies:** Chapel services voluntary. 2 weekly convocations required and credited as part of general education. **Housing:** Guaranteed on-campus for all undergraduates. Coed dorms, special housing for disabled, apartments, wellness housing available. **Activities:** Bands, campus ministries, choral groups, dance, drama, international student organizations, literary magazine, music ensembles, musical theater, opera, radio station, student government, student newspaper, symphony orchestra, TV station, Student Community Action Network for voluntary services, peace club, Bethel Christian Fellowship, service corps-disaster response, Fellowship of Christian Athletes, Amnesty International, environmental action club, Catholic student organization.

Athletics. NAIA. **Intercollegiate:** Basketball, cross-country, football (tackle) M, golf, soccer, tennis, track and field, volleyball W. **Intramural:** Badminton, basketball, bowling, football (non-tackle), golf, racquetball, softball, table tennis, tennis, volleyball. **Team name:** Threshers.

Student services. Alcohol/substance abuse counseling, chaplain/spiritual director, career counseling, student employment services, financial aid counseling, health services, minority student services, personal counseling. **Physically disabled:** Services for visually, hearing impaired.

Contact. E-mail: admissions@bethelks.edu
Phone: (316) 284-5230 Toll-free number: (800) 522-1887 ext. 230
Fax: (316) 284-5870
Allan Bartel, Director of Admissions and Enrollment, Bethel College, 300 East 27th Street, North Newton, KS 67117-0531

Central Christian College of Kansas

McPherson, Kansas
www.centralchristian.edu **CB code: 6088**

- Private 4-year liberal arts college affiliated with Free Methodist Church of North America
- Residential campus in large town
- 309 degree-seeking undergraduates: 47% women, 10% African American, 1% Asian American, 6% Hispanic American, 2% Native American, 2% international
- 71% of applicants admitted
- 33% graduate within 6 years; 20% enter graduate study

General. Founded in 1884. Regionally accredited. **Degrees:** 62 bachelor's, 20 associate awarded. **Location:** 55 miles from Wichita. **Calendar:** 4-1-4. **Full-time faculty:** 19 total; 10% have terminal degrees, 32% women. **Part-time faculty:** 18 total. **Class size:** 77% < 20, 18% 20-39, 4% 50-99, less than 1% >100.

Freshman class profile. 357 applied, 255 admitted, 125 enrolled.

Mid 50% test scores		**GPA 2.0-2.99:**	29%
SAT critical reading:	350-470	**Rank in top quarter:**	33%
SAT math:	360-450	**Rank in top tenth:**	13%
SAT writing:	310-420	**End year in good standing:**	92%
ACT composite:	18-24	**Return as sophomores:**	61%
GPA 3.75 or higher:	25%	**Out-of-state:**	56%
GPA 3.50-3.74:	19%	**Live on campus:**	99%
GPA 3.0-3.49:	25%		

Basis for selection. Secondary school record, recommendations very important; test scores important. SAT or ACT recommended. Interview and essay recommended. **Homeschooled:** Transcript of courses and grades, letter of recommendation (nonparent) required. Transcript required. **Learning Disabled:** Provide Individualized Education Program (IEP).

High school preparation. College-preparatory program recommended. 22 units required. Required units include English 4, mathematics 2, social studies 2, history 1, science 2 (laboratory 1). 1 computer technology recommended.

2009-2010 Annual costs. Tuition/fees (projected): $17,000. Room/board: $5,900. Books/supplies: $1,000. Personal expenses: $1,000.

2007-2008 Financial aid. **Need-based:** 90 full-time freshmen applied for aid; 87 were judged to have need; 87 of these received aid. Average need met was 72%. Average scholarship/grant was $4,847; average loan $4,749. 41% of total undergraduate aid awarded as scholarships/grants, 59% as loans/jobs. **Non-need-based:** Awarded to 340 full-time undergraduates, including 100 freshmen. Scholarships awarded for academics, alumni affiliation, athletics, leadership, music/drama, religious affiliation.

Application procedures. **Admission:** Closing date 7/1 (receipt date). $20 fee, may be waived for applicants with need. Admission notification on a rolling basis. **Financial aid:** Priority date 3/1; no closing date. FAFSA required. Applicants notified on a rolling basis starting 3/1; must reply within 4 week(s) of notification.

Academics. **Special study options:** Accelerated study, cooperative education, cross-registration, double major, dual enrollment of high school students, independent study, internships, liberal arts/career combination, student-designed major, teacher certification program, urban semester, Washington semester. **Credit/placement by examination:** AP, CLEP, IB, SAT, ACT. 30 credit hours maximum toward associate degree, 30 toward bachelor's. **Support services:** Learning center, reduced course load, remedial instruction, study skills assistance, tutoring.

Majors. **Biology:** General, exercise physiology. **Business:** General, accounting, accounting/business management, business admin, managerial economics, office management, small business admin. **Communications:** General, media studies. **Education:** Elementary, history, middle, physical, secondary. **Health:** Health services, preveterinary. **History:** General. **Interdisciplinary:** Accounting/computer science, natural sciences. **Legal studies:** Prelaw. **Liberal arts:** Arts/sciences. **Math:** General. **Parks/recreation:** Exercise sciences, facilities management, sports admin. **Philosophy/religion:** Religion. **Physical sciences:** Chemistry. **Protective services:** Law enforcement admin, police science, security management. **Psychology:** General. **Social sciences:** General. **Theology:** Bible, missionary, pastoral counseling, sacred music, theology, youth ministry. **Visual/performing arts:** General, dramatic, music performance, music theory/composition, piano/organ.

Most popular majors. Business/marketing 28%, liberal arts 18%, psychology 10%, theological studies 21%.

Computing on campus. 30 workstations in library, computer center, student center. Dormitories wired for high-speed internet access. Commuter students can connect to campus network. Online course registration, online library, helpline, repair service, wireless network available.

Student life. **Freshman orientation:** Mandatory. Preregistration for classes offered. Fall semester first seven weeks. Interterm and spring 1-2 days. **Policies:** Students must sign a life-style covenant. Alcohol, smoking, drugs not allowed on campus. **Housing:** Guaranteed on-campus for all undergraduates. Coed dorms, single-sex dorms, apartments, wellness housing available. $150 fully refundable deposit, deadline 8/1. Students 23 years of age or older can live off campus. **Activities:** Bands, campus ministries, choral groups, drama, literary magazine, music ensembles, musical theater, radio station, student government, student newspaper, symphony orchestra, Christian service organization, Flying Tigers, prison ministries, performing arts club, Share teams, C.O.L.O.R.S., PBL, student activities council.

Athletics. NAIA, NCCAA. **Intercollegiate:** Baseball M, basketball, cheerleading, cross-country, golf, soccer, softball W, tennis, volleyball W. **Intramural:** Badminton, basketball, bowling, football (non-tackle) M, golf, soccer, softball, table tennis, tennis, volleyball. **Team name:** Tigers.

Student services. Adult student services, chaplain/spiritual director, career counseling, student employment services, financial aid counseling, health services, personal counseling, placement for graduates. **Physically disabled:** Services for visually, speech impaired.

Contact. E-mail: admissions@centralchristian.edu
Phone: (620) 241-0723 ext. 337 Toll-free number: (800) 835-0078 ext. 337
Fax: (620) 241-6032
J. Ferrell, Dean of Enrollment, Central Christian College of Kansas, 1200 South Main, McPherson, KS 67460-5740

Emporia State University

Emporia, Kansas
www.emporia.edu **CB code: 6335**

- Public 4-year university
- Commuter campus in large town
- 4,148 degree-seeking undergraduates: 10% part-time, 59% women, 5% African American, 1% Asian American, 5% Hispanic American, 1% Native American, 6% international
- 1,821 degree-seeking graduate students
- 87% of applicants admitted
- SAT or ACT (ACT writing optional) required
- 47% graduate within 6 years; 20% enter graduate study

General. Founded in 1863. Regionally accredited. **Degrees:** 687 bachelor's awarded; master's, doctoral offered. **Location:** 50 miles from Topeka, 77 miles from Wichita. **Calendar:** Semester, extensive summer session. **Full-time faculty:** 258 total; 83% have terminal degrees, 9% minority, 43% women. **Part-time faculty:** 33 total; 3% minority, 61% women. **Class size:** 40% < 20, 43% 20-39, 10% 40-49, 7% 50-99, less than 1% >100. **Special facilities:** Planetarium, natural history reserve, natural history museum, National Teachers Hall of Fame, Great Plains study center.

Freshman class profile. 1,289 applied, 1,125 admitted, 681 enrolled.

Mid 50% test scores		**Rank in top tenth:**	10%
ACT composite:	19-25	**Return as sophomores:**	69%
GPA 3.75 or higher:	25%	**Out-of-state:**	10%
GPA 3.50-3.74:	16%	**Live on campus:**	94%
GPA 3.0-3.49:	29%	**International:**	4%
GPA 2.0-2.99:	29%	**Fraternities:**	16%
Rank in top quarter:	34%	**Sororities:**	10%

Basis for selection. Applicants must have one of following: minimum ACT score of 21, rank in top third of high school class, minimum 2.0 GPA in Kansas Core Curriculum for in-state students, or 2.5 GPA for out-of-state students. Limited number of students who do not meet qualifications may be admitted through 10% exceptions window. ACT scores must be received by end of first semester of study. **Homeschooled:** State high school equivalency certificate required. GED must be submitted.

High school preparation. College-preparatory program recommended. Required units include English 4, mathematics 3, social studies 3, science 3 and academic electives 1. 1 computer technology recommended. These units required for students who do not have minimum ACT score of 21, or in top 1/3 of high school class.

2008-2009 Annual costs. Tuition/fees: $4,136; $12,648 out-of-state. Room/board: $5,858. Books/supplies: $900. Personal expenses: $2,650.

2007-2008 Financial aid. **Need-based:** Average need met was 45%. Average scholarship/grant was $3,342; average loan $3,093. 37% of total undergraduate aid awarded as scholarships/grants, 63% as loans/jobs. **Non-need-based:** Scholarships awarded for academics, alumni affiliation, art, athletics, job skills, leadership, minority status, music/drama, religious affiliation, state residency. **Additional information:** Institution's own payment plan is available.

Application procedures. **Admission:** No deadline. $30 fee, may be waived for applicants with need. Admission notification on a rolling basis. Must reply by May 1 or within 2 week(s) if notified thereafter. **Financial aid:** Priority date 3/15; no closing date. FAFSA required. Applicants notified on a rolling basis starting 2/2; must reply within 2 week(s) of notification.

Academics. **Special study options:** Distance learning, double major, dual enrollment of high school students, ESL, honors, independent study, internships, student-designed major, study abroad, teacher certification program. Career development center and programs, continuing education courses, evening program, interdisciplinary or interdepartmental courses of study, learning assistance programs, pass-fail grading option, service members' opportunity college, summer sessions, tutorial program, trio programs. **Credit/placement by examination:** AP, CLEP, IB, ACT, institutional tests. 30 credit hours maximum toward bachelor's degree. **Support services:** Remedial instruction, writing center.

Majors. **Biology:** General, Biochemistry/biophysics and molecular biology. **Business:** Accounting, business admin, human resources, marketing. **Communications:** General. **Computer sciences:** General, information systems, security. **Education:** Elementary, music, secondary. **Foreign languages:** General. **Health:** Athletic training, nursing (RN), public health ed, vocational rehab counseling. **History:** General. **Liberal arts:** Arts/sciences. **Math:** General. **Parks/recreation:** General. **Physical sciences:** General, chemistry, geology, physics. **Psychology:** General. **Social sciences:** General, economics, political science, sociology. **Visual/performing arts:** Art, dramatic. **Other:** Crime and delinquencies studies, Information resources studies.

Most popular majors. Biology 6%, business/marketing 18%, education 25%, health sciences 9%, liberal arts 6%, social sciences 12%, visual/performing arts 6%.

Computing on campus. 410 workstations in dormitories, library, computer center, student center. Dormitories wired for high-speed internet access and linked to campus network. Commuter students can connect to campus network. Online course registration, online library, helpline, student web hosting, wireless network available.

Student life. **Freshman orientation:** Available, $35 fee. Preregistration for classes offered. One-day program for students and parents; held during summer and prior to start of classes. **Housing:** Guaranteed on-campus for freshmen. Coed dorms, single-sex dorms, special housing for disabled, apartments, cooperative housing, fraternity/sorority housing, wellness housing available. $145 partly refundable deposit, deadline 7/1. **Activities:** Bands, campus ministries, choral groups, dance, drama, film society, international student organizations, literary magazine, music ensembles, musical theater, opera, student government, student newspaper, symphony orchestra, Black Student Union, Hispanic American leadership organization, Catholic Campus Community, Christian student center, Black women's network, Muslim student association, Fellowship of Christian Athletes, Arabic language club, East Asian club, Campus Crusade for Christ.

Athletics. NCAA. **Intercollegiate:** Baseball M, basketball, cheerleading, cross-country, football (tackle) M, soccer W, softball W, tennis, track and field, volleyball W. **Intramural:** Badminton, basketball, football (non-tackle), softball, table tennis, tennis, volleyball. **Team name:** Hornets.

Student services. Adult student services, alcohol/substance abuse counseling, career counseling, services for economically disadvantaged, student employment services, financial aid counseling, health services, legal services, minority student services, on-campus daycare, personal counseling, placement for graduates, veterans' counselor, women's services. **Physically disabled:** Services for visually, speech, hearing impaired.

Contact. E-mail: go2esu@emporia.edu
Phone: (620) 341-5465 Toll-free number: (877) 468-6378
Fax: (620) 341-5599
Laura Eddy, Director of Admissions, Emporia State University, 1200 Commercial, Campus Box 4034, Emporia, KS 66801-5087

Fort Hays State University

Hays, Kansas **CB member**
www.fhsu.edu **CB code: 6218**

- Public 4-year university
- Commuter campus in large town

- 8,670 degree-seeking undergraduates
- SAT or ACT with writing required

General. Founded in 1902. Regionally accredited. **Degrees:** 1,646 bachelor's, 59 associate awarded; master's offered. **Location:** 170 miles from Wichita, 270 miles from Kansas City. **Calendar:** Semester, extensive summer session. **Full-time faculty:** 268 total; 67% have terminal degrees, 6% minority, 40% women. **Part-time faculty:** 135 total; 22% have terminal degrees, 2% minority, 57% women. **Class size:** 50% < 20, 41% 20-39, 5% 40-49, 3% 50-99, less than 1% >100. **Special facilities:** Observatory, paleontology, natural history, archeology, history, geology, botanical-zoological museums.

Freshman class profile.

Mid 50% test scores			
ACT composite:	18-24	Rank in top quarter:	31%
GPA 3.75 or higher:	23%	Rank in top tenth:	10%
GPA 3.50-3.74:	18%	Out-of-state:	15%
GPA 3.0-3.49:	31%	Live on campus:	69%
GPA 2.0-2.99:	26%	Fraternities:	4%
		Sororities:	3%

Basis for selection. One of following required: minimum ACT composite score of 21, rank in top third of high school class, or minimum 2.0 GPA on Kansas pre-college curriculum (2.5 GPA for out-of-state students). Audition recommended for music majors.

High school preparation. 14 units recommended. Recommended units include English 4, mathematics 3, social studies 2, history 1, science 3 and computer science 1.

2008-2009 Annual costs. Tuition/fees: $3,540; $11,125 out-of-state. Room/board: $6,252. Books/supplies: $800. Personal expenses: $2,082.

2007-2008 Financial aid. Need-based: 644 full-time freshmen applied for aid; 494 were judged to have need; 489 of these received aid. Average need met was 68%. Average scholarship/grant was $4,311; average loan $2,944. 34% of total undergraduate aid awarded as scholarships/grants, 66% as loans/jobs. **Non-need-based:** Scholarships awarded for academics, art, athletics, leadership, minority status, music/drama.

Application procedures. Admission: No deadline. $30 fee. Admission notification on a rolling basis. **Financial aid:** Priority date 3/15; no closing date. FAFSA required. Applicants notified on a rolling basis starting 3/15; must reply within 2 week(s) of notification.

Academics. Special study options: Combined bachelor's/graduate degree, distance learning, double major, dual enrollment of high school students, ESL, exchange student, external degree, honors, independent study, internships, liberal arts/career combination, student-designed major, study abroad, teacher certification program, United Nations semester. **Credit/placement by examination:** AP, CLEP, ACT, institutional tests. **Support services:** Learning center, pre-admission summer program, reduced course load, remedial instruction, study skills assistance, tutoring, writing center.

Majors. Agriculture: Business. **Biology:** General. **Business:** General, accounting, business admin, market research, marketing, office management. **Communications:** General. **Computer sciences:** General. **Education:** Business, elementary, music, physical, technology/industrial arts, trade/industrial. **Foreign languages:** General. **Health:** Physical therapy assistant, sonography. **History:** General. **Interdisciplinary:** Biological/physical sciences. **Math:** General. **Philosophy/religion:** Philosophy. **Physical sciences:** Chemistry, geology, physics. **Protective services:** Criminal justice. **Psychology:** General. **Public administration:** Social work. **Social sciences:** Economics, political science, sociology. **Visual/performing arts:** Art.

Most popular majors. Business/marketing 11%, education 13%, health sciences 7%, liberal arts 46%.

Computing on campus. 1,400 workstations in dormitories, library, computer center, student center. Dormitories linked to campus network. Commuter students can connect to campus network. Online course registration, helpline, wireless network available.

Student life. Freshman orientation: Mandatory, $25 fee. Preregistration for classes offered. 3-day program before start of classes; includes skills training. **Housing:** Guaranteed on-campus for freshmen. Coed dorms, single-sex dorms, apartments, fraternity/sorority housing available. $35 nonrefundable deposit. **Activities:** Bands, campus ministries, choral groups, dance, drama, international student organizations, literary magazine, music ensembles, musical theater, opera, radio station, student government, student newspaper, symphony orchestra, TV station, Campus Crusade for Christ, Disciples of the Catholic Campus Center, Black Student Union, Hispanic American leadership organization, Young Republicans, Young Democrats.

Athletics. NCAA. **Intercollegiate:** Baseball M, basketball, cross-country, football (tackle) M, golf, gymnastics W, rodeo, softball W, tennis, track and field, volleyball W, wrestling M. **Intramural:** Archery, badminton, baseball M, basketball, bowling, cross-country, diving, fencing, field hockey W, gymnastics W, racquetball, soccer, softball, swimming, table tennis, tennis, track and field, volleyball, water polo, wrestling M.

Student services. Adult student services, career counseling, student employment services, financial aid counseling, health services, on-campus daycare, personal counseling, placement for graduates, veterans' counselor. **Physically disabled:** Services for visually, speech, hearing impaired.

Contact. E-mail: tigers@fshu.edu
Phone: (785) 628-5666 Toll-free number: (800) 628-3478
Fax: (785) 432-0248
Roger Schieferecke, Director of Admissions Counseling, Fort Hays State University, 600 Park Street, Hays, KS 67601

Friends University
Wichita, Kansas
www.friends.edu **CB code: 6224**

- Private 4-year business and liberal arts college affiliated with nondenominational tradition
- Commuter campus in large city
- 1,183 full-time, degree-seeking undergraduates
- 70% of applicants admitted
- SAT or ACT (ACT writing optional) required

General. Founded in 1898. Regionally accredited. **Degrees:** 658 bachelor's, 37 associate awarded; master's offered. **Location:** 1 mile from downtown. **Calendar:** Semester, limited summer session. **Full-time faculty:** 80 total. **Part-time faculty:** 155 total. **Special facilities:** Art center, observatory, Quaker collection.

Freshman class profile. 623 applied, 435 admitted, 224 enrolled.

Mid 50% test scores			
SAT critical reading:	420-560	SAT math:	420-560
		ACT composite:	19-25

Basis for selection. ACT score multiplied by GPA must equal 45 or above for admission. Those with score between 20 and 29 admitted provisionally. Audition required of music majors. Portfolio recommended for art majors.

High school preparation. 11 units required. Required units include English 4, social studies 2 and science 2.

2008-2009 Annual costs. Tuition/fees: $18,320. Room/board: $5,450. Books/supplies: $1,000. Personal expenses: $1,642.

2008-2009 Financial aid. Non-need-based: Scholarships awarded for academics, alumni affiliation, art, athletics, leadership, music/drama. **Additional information:** Scholarships for clergy/family of clergy available.

Application procedures. Admission: No deadline. $45 fee, may be waived for applicants with need. Admission notification on a rolling basis. **Financial aid:** Priority date 3/15; no closing date. FAFSA, institutional form required. Applicants notified on a rolling basis; must reply within 3 week(s) of notification.

Academics. Special study options: Cross-registration, double major, dual enrollment of high school students, external degree, honors, independent study, liberal arts/career combination, student-designed major, study abroad, teacher certification program. Degree completion program for working adults. **Credit/placement by examination:** CLEP, IB. 60 credit hours maximum toward bachelor's degree. **Support services:** Reduced course load, study skills assistance, tutoring, writing center.

Majors. Biology: General. **Business:** Accounting, business admin, human resources, international, management information systems. **Communications:** General. **Computer sciences:** General. **Education:** Art, early childhood, elementary, English, mathematics, middle, music, physical, science, secondary, social science, Spanish. **Foreign languages:** Spanish. **Health:** Health care admin, medical radiologic technology/radiation therapy. **History:** General. **Liberal arts:** Arts/sciences. **Math:** General. **Parks/recreation:** Facilities management, health/fitness. **Physical sciences:** Chemistry. **Psychology:** General. **Social sciences:** Political science, sociology. **Theology:** Youth ministry. **Visual/performing arts:** Art, dance, dramatic, music performance.

Computing on campus. 142 workstations in dormitories, library, computer center. Dormitories linked to campus network. Commuter students can connect to campus network.

Student life. **Freshman orientation:** Mandatory. Preregistration for classes offered. **Housing:** Coed dorms, apartments available. $100 deposit. **Activities:** Bands, choral groups, dance, drama, literary magazine, music ensembles, musical theater, opera, student government, student newspaper, symphony orchestra.

Athletics. NAIA. **Intercollegiate:** Baseball M, basketball, cheerleading M, cross-country, football (tackle) M, golf M, soccer, softball W, tennis, track and field, volleyball W. **Intramural:** Basketball, bowling, racquetball, soccer, softball, table tennis, volleyball. **Team name:** Falcons.

Student services. Adult student services, career counseling, student employment services, health services, personal counseling, placement for graduates, veterans' counselor. **Physically disabled:** Services for visually, speech, hearing impaired.

Contact. E-mail: learn@friends.edu
Phone: (316) 295-5100 Toll-free number: (800) 577-2233
Fax: (316) 295-5101
Marla Sexson, Director of Undergraduate Admissions, Friends University, 2100 University, Wichita, KS 67213

Haskell Indian Nations University

Lawrence, Kansas
www.haskell.edu **CB code: 0919**

- Public 4-year university
- Residential campus in small city

General. Founded in 1884. Regionally accredited. **Location:** 38 miles from Kansas City, Missouri. **Calendar:** Semester.

Annual costs/financial aid. Haskell does not charge tuition. On-campus students pay $440 (includes room/board and required fees) for academic year; off-campus students pay $248 (required fees) for academic year. Books/supplies: $220. Need-based financial aid available to full-time and part-time students.

Contact. Phone: (785) 749-8454
Director of Admissions and Records, 155 Indian Avenue #5031, Lawrence, KS 66046-4800

Kansas State University

Manhattan, Kansas **CB member**
www.k-state.edu **CB code: 6334**

- Public 4-year university
- Commuter campus in large town
- 18,114 degree-seeking undergraduates: 11% part-time, 48% women, 4% African American, 1% Asian American, 3% Hispanic American, 1% Native American, 3% international
- 3,629 degree-seeking graduate students
- 84% of applicants admitted
- SAT or ACT (ACT writing optional) required
- 58% graduate within 6 years

General. Founded in 1863. Regionally accredited. Additional campus at Salina, Kansas. Off-campus site at Fort Riley army base. **Degrees:** 3,432 bachelor's, 63 associate awarded; master's, doctoral, first professional offered. **ROTC:** Army, Air Force. **Location:** 120 miles from Kansas City, Missouri. **Calendar:** Semester, extensive summer session. **Full-time faculty:** 940 total; 84% have terminal degrees, 19% minority, 34% women. **Part-time faculty:** 159 total; 54% have terminal degrees, 10% minority, 53% women. **Class size:** 45% < 20, 37% 20-39, 7% 40-49, 6% 50-99, 4% >100. **Special facilities:** Prairie for biological research, laser laboratory, cancer research center, nuclear reactor.

Freshman class profile. 9,453 applied, 7,980 admitted, 3,761 enrolled.

Mid 50% test scores		Return as sophomores:	78%
ACT composite:	21-28	Out-of-state:	17%
Rank in top quarter:	62%	International:	5%

Basis for selection. One of following required: minimum ACT score of 21, rank in top third of high school class, or minimum 2.0 GPA on Kansas pre-college curriculum (2.5 GPA for out-of-state students). Audition recommended for music and theater majors. Portfolio recommended for art and architecture majors.

High school preparation. 14 units recommended. Recommended units include English 4, mathematics 3, social studies 2, history 1.5 and science 3. One unit of technology recommended.

2008-2009 Annual costs. Tuition/fees: $6,627; $16,931 out-of-state. Room/board: $6,448. Books/supplies: $1,100. Personal expenses: $3,376.

2007-2008 Financial aid. **Need-based:** 2,715 full-time freshmen applied for aid; 1,892 were judged to have need; 1,851 of these received aid. Average need met was 67%. Average scholarship/grant was $3,889; average loan $3,297. 40% of total undergraduate aid awarded as scholarships/grants, 60% as loans/jobs. **Non-need-based:** Awarded to 4,998 full-time undergraduates, including 1,890 freshmen. Scholarships awarded for academics, alumni affiliation, art, athletics, leadership, music/drama, ROTC, state residency.

Application procedures. **Admission:** No deadline. $30 fee, may be waived for applicants with need. Admission notification on a rolling basis. **Financial aid:** Priority date 3/1; no closing date. FAFSA required. Applicants notified by 4/1; Applicants notified on a rolling basis starting 4/1; must reply within 2 week(s) of notification.

Academics. **Special study options:** Accelerated study, cooperative education, distance learning, double major, ESL, exchange student, honors, independent study, internships, study abroad, teacher certification program. **Credit/placement by examination:** AP, CLEP, IB, SAT, ACT. 10 credit hours maximum toward associate degree, 20 toward bachelor's. PEP, DANTES exams accepted for credit. **Support services:** Learning center, preadmission summer program, reduced course load, remedial instruction, study skills assistance, tutoring, writing center.

Majors. **Agriculture:** Agronomy, animal sciences, business, communications, economics, food science, horticultural science, mechanization. **Area/ethnic studies:** Women's. **Biology:** General, biochemistry, microbiology, wildlife. **Business:** General, accounting, business admin, finance. **Communications:** General, journalism, media studies. **Computer sciences:** General, information systems, networking. **Education:** Agricultural, art, elementary, family/consumer sciences, music, secondary. **Engineering:** Agricultural, architectural, chemical, civil, computer, electrical, industrial, mechanical. **Engineering technology:** General, electrical, industrial management. **Family/consumer sciences:** General, child development, clothing/textiles, family studies, human nutrition. **Foreign languages:** General. **Health:** Athletic training, communication disorders, dietetics, preveterinary. **History:** General. **Liberal arts:** Humanities. **Math:** General, statistics. **Mechanic/repair:** Aircraft. **Parks/recreation:** Exercise sciences, facilities management. **Philosophy/religion:** Philosophy. **Physical sciences:** General, chemistry, geology, physics. **Psychology:** General. **Public administration:** Social work. **Social sciences:** General, anthropology, economics, geography, political science, sociology. **Transportation:** Airline/commercial pilot. **Visual/performing arts:** Dramatic, interior design, music performance, studio arts.

Most popular majors. Agriculture 11%, business/marketing 18%, education 10%, engineering/engineering technologies 13%, family/consumer sciences 8%, social sciences 9%.

Computing on campus. 547 workstations in dormitories, library, computer center, student center. Dormitories wired for high-speed internet access and linked to campus network. Commuter students can connect to campus network. Online course registration, helpline, repair service, wireless network available.

Student life. **Freshman orientation:** Available, $25 fee. **Housing:** Coed dorms, single-sex dorms, apartments, cooperative housing, fraternity/sorority housing available. $25 deposit. **Activities:** Bands, campus ministries, choral groups, dance, drama, international student organizations, music ensembles, musical theater, radio station, student government, student newspaper, symphony orchestra, TV station, 340 religious, political, ethnic, and social service clubs and organizations available.

Athletics. NCAA. **Intercollegiate:** Baseball M, basketball, cross-country, equestrian W, football (tackle) M, golf, rowing (crew) W, tennis W, track and field, volleyball W. **Intramural:** Badminton, basketball, bowling, cross-country, golf, handball, soccer, softball, squash, swimming, table tennis, tennis, track and field, volleyball, water polo, wrestling M. **Team name:** Wildcats.

Student services. Adult student services, alcohol/substance abuse counseling, career counseling, student employment services, financial aid counseling, health services, legal services, minority student services, on-campus daycare, personal counseling, placement for graduates, veterans' counselor, women's services. **Physically disabled:** Services for visually, speech, hearing impaired.

Contact. E-mail: k-state@k-state.edu
Phone: (785) 532-6250 Toll-free number: (800) 432-8270
Fax: (785) 532-6393
Larry Moeder, Assistant Vice President for Student Financial Assistance and Admissions, Kansas State University, 119 Anderson Hall, Manhattan, KS 66506

Kansas Wesleyan University

Salina, Kansas
www.kwu.edu **CB code: 6337**

- Private 4-year liberal arts college affiliated with United Methodist Church
- Residential campus in large town
- 766 degree-seeking undergraduates
- 96 graduate students
- SAT or ACT (ACT writing optional) required

General. Founded in 1886. Regionally accredited. **Degrees:** 140 bachelor's, 1 associate awarded; master's offered. **Location:** 90 miles from Wichita, 180 miles from Kansas City. **Calendar:** Semester, limited summer session. **Full-time faculty:** 43 total. **Part-time faculty:** 25 total. **Class size:** 66% < 20, 26% 20-39, 6% 40-49, 1% 50-99, less than 1% >100. **Special facilities:** Observatory with 16-inch Cassegrain telescope.

Freshman class profile.

Mid 50% test scores			
SAT critical reading:	420-520	ACT composite:	20-24
SAT math:	500-590	Out-of-state:	32%
SAT writing:	420-520	Live on campus:	67%

Basis for selection. Applicant must have ACT composite score of 18 or SAT combined score of 850 (exclusive of Writing) and high school GPA of 2.5 or rank in top half of class. Interview recommended for academically weak applicants. Audition recommended for music majors. Portfolio recommended for art majors.

2008-2009 Annual costs. Tuition/fees: $18,200. $200 per-credit-hour charge for 1-5 credit hours; $1,800 per semester for 6-8 credit hours; $3,600 per semester for 9-11 credit hours. Room/board: $6,400. Books/supplies: $800. Personal expenses: $500.

Financial aid. Non-need-based: Scholarships awarded for academics, alumni affiliation, art, athletics, music/drama, state residency. **Additional information:** Awards available for residence hall students: minimum $7,000 for 3.0 GPA plus ACT score of 22 or SAT of 950 (exclusive of Writing); minimum $8,000 for 3.5 GPA plus ACT score of 22 or SAT score of 1030 (exclusive of Writing); minimum $9,000 for 3.75 GPA plus ACT score of 25 or SAT score of 1140 (exclusive of Writing). Application deadline March 15.

Application procedures. Admission: No deadline. $20 fee. Admission notification on a rolling basis. **Financial aid:** Closing date 3/15. FAFSA required. Applicants notified on a rolling basis starting 1/1; must reply by 8/1 or within 3 week(s) of notification.

Academics. Special study options: Accelerated study, cross-registration, double major, ESL, independent study, internships, liberal arts/career combination, student-designed major, teacher certification program. **Credit/ placement by examination:** AP, CLEP, institutional tests. 30 credit hours maximum toward bachelor's degree. **Support services:** Learning center, reduced course load, remedial instruction, tutoring, writing center.

Majors. Biology: General. **Business:** General, accounting. **Communications:** General, public relations. **Computer sciences:** General, computer science. **Education:** Art, elementary, English, secondary. **Foreign languages:** General, German, Spanish. **Health:** Preop/surgical nursing. **History:** General. **Math:** General. **Parks/recreation:** Health/fitness. **Philosophy/ religion:** Religion. **Physical sciences:** Chemistry, physics. **Protective services:** Criminal justice. **Psychology:** General. **Social sciences:** Sociology. **Theology:** Religious ed. **Visual/performing arts:** Arts management, dramatic, music performance, studio arts.

Most popular majors. Business/marketing 32%, education 9%, health sciences 9%, parks/recreation 7%, physical sciences 7%, social sciences 7%.

Computing on campus. 50 workstations in library, computer center. Dormitories wired for high-speed internet access and linked to campus network. Online library available.

Student life. Freshman orientation: Available. Preregistration for classes offered. **Housing:** Guaranteed on-campus for freshmen. Single-sex dorms, apartments available. $100 deposit. **Activities:** Jazz band, choral groups, dance, drama, literary magazine, music ensembles, musical theater, radio station, student government, student newspaper, Fellowship of Christian Athletes, Religious Life Committee.

Athletics. NAIA. **Intercollegiate:** Baseball M, basketball, cross-country, football (tackle) M, golf, soccer, softball W, tennis, track and field, volleyball W. **Intramural:** Basketball, softball, volleyball, weight lifting. **Team name:** Coyotes.

Student services. Adult student services, career counseling, student employment services, financial aid counseling, personal counseling, placement for graduates, veterans' counselor. **Physically disabled:** Services for visually impaired.

Contact. E-mail: admissions@kwu.edu
Phone: (785) 827-5541 ext. 1285 Toll-free number: (800) 874-1154
Fax: (785) 827-0927
Jim Allen, Director of Admissions, Kansas Wesleyan University, 100 East Claflin Avenue, Salina, KS 67401-6196

Manhattan Christian College

Manhattan, Kansas
www.mccks.edu **CB code: 6392**

- Private 4-year Bible college affiliated with Christian Church
- Residential campus in large town
- 380 degree-seeking undergraduates
- SAT or ACT (ACT writing optional), application essay required

General. Founded in 1927. Regionally accredited; also accredited by ABHE. Students have access to Kansas State University library and facilities at student rates. **Degrees:** 84 bachelor's, 5 associate awarded. **ROTC:** Army, Air Force. **Location:** 130 miles from Kansas City. **Calendar:** Semester, limited summer session. **Full-time faculty:** 12 total. **Part-time faculty:** 20 total.

Freshman class profile.

Out-of-state:	38%	Live on campus:	98%

Basis for selection. High school record, test scores, recommendations important. Character recommendations required. Interview recommended. Audition required for music majors.

High school preparation. Recommended units include English 4, mathematics 2 and science 2.

2008-2009 Annual costs. Tuition/fees: $10,932. Additional $6 required fee per-credit-hour, up to $72; $140 per-credit-hour charge for part-time, non-degree-seeking students. Part time non-degree and/or audit at $170 per-credit-hour. Room/board: $6,720. Books/supplies: $1,150. Personal expenses: $1,067.

2007-2008 Financial aid. Need-based: 38% of total undergraduate aid awarded as scholarships/grants, 62% as loans/jobs. **Non-need-based:** Scholarships awarded for academics, leadership.

Application procedures. Admission: Priority date 4/1; deadline 7/1. $25 fee, may be waived for applicants with need. Admission notification on a rolling basis beginning on or about 10/15. **Financial aid:** Priority date 4/1; no closing date. FAFSA required. Applicants notified on a rolling basis starting 5/1; must reply within 2 week(s) of notification.

Academics. Special study options: Combined bachelor's/graduate degree, double major, dual enrollment of high school students, internships, liberal arts/career combination. Dual degree program with Kansas State University. **Credit/placement by examination:** CLEP, institutional tests. 36 credit hours maximum toward bachelor's degree. **Support services:** Reduced course load, tutoring.

Majors. Business: Business admin. **Philosophy/religion:** Religion. **Theology:** Bible, missionary, pastoral counseling, religious ed, theology.

Computing on campus. 12 workstations in library, computer center.

Student life. Freshman orientation: Mandatory. Preregistration for classes offered. 3-day program held before start of classes. **Policies:** Religious observance required. **Housing:** Guaranteed on-campus for freshmen. Single-sex dorms, apartments available. $125 fully refundable deposit, deadline 6/1. **Activities:** Bands, choral groups, drama, music ensembles, student government, student newspaper.

Athletics. NCCAA. **Intercollegiate:** Basketball, soccer, volleyball W. **Intramural:** Softball M. **Team name:** Crusaders.

Student services. Career counseling, student employment services, health services, personal counseling, placement for graduates. **Physically disabled:** Services for speech impaired.

Contact. E-mail: admit@mccks.edu
Phone: (785) 539-3571 Toll-free number: (877) 246-4622
Fax: (785) 776-9251
Eric Ingmire, Director of Admissions, Manhattan Christian College, 1415 Anderson Avenue, Manhattan, KS 66502

McPherson College
McPherson, Kansas
www.mcpherson.edu **CB code: 6404**

- Private 4-year liberal arts college affiliated with Church of the Brethren
- Residential campus in large town
- 535 degree-seeking undergraduates
- 87% of applicants admitted
- SAT or ACT (ACT writing optional) required

General. Founded in 1887. Regionally accredited. **Degrees:** 132 bachelor's awarded. **Location:** 60 miles from Wichita. **Calendar:** 4-1-4, limited summer session. **Full-time faculty:** 39 total; 72% have terminal degrees, 8% minority, 28% women. **Part-time faculty:** 14 total; 50% have terminal degrees, 36% women. **Class size:** 70% < 20, 29% 20-39, less than 1% 40-49.

Freshman class profile. 423 applied, 367 admitted, 144 enrolled.

Mid 50% test scores		**GPA 3.0-3.49:**	30%
SAT critical reading:	450-570	**GPA 2.0-2.99:**	25%
SAT math:	420-560	**Rank in top quarter:**	38%
ACT composite:	19-24	**Rank in top tenth:**	14%
GPA 3.75 or higher:	21%	**Out-of-state:**	64%
GPA 3.50-3.74:	23%	**Live on campus:**	93%

Basis for selection. Satisfactory high school performance or completion of GED, corresponding standardized test scores, and appropriate personal qualities. Portfolio required for auto restoration program.

2008-2009 Annual costs. Tuition/fees: $17,200. Room/board: $6,500. Books/supplies: $1,100. Personal expenses: $1,850.

2008-2009 Financial aid. Non-need-based: Scholarships awarded for academics, alumni affiliation, art, athletics, music/drama, religious affiliation, state residency.

Application procedures. Admission: Priority date 3/1; no deadline. $25 fee, may be waived for applicants with need. Admission notification on a rolling basis. Must reply by May 1 or within 4 week(s) if notified thereafter. **Financial aid:** Priority date 3/1; no closing date. FAFSA required. Applicants notified on a rolling basis starting 3/1; must reply within 3 week(s) of notification.

Academics. Special study options: Combined bachelor's/graduate degree, cross-registration, double major, dual enrollment of high school students, ESL, independent study, internships, student-designed major, study abroad, teacher certification program, urban semester. Only degree program in antique auto restoration in United States. **Credit/placement by examination:** AP, CLEP, IB, institutional tests. **Support services:** Learning center, reduced course load, remedial instruction, study skills assistance, tutoring, writing center.

Majors. Biology: General. **Business:** Accounting, business admin, finance, international. **Communications:** General. **Conservation:** Environmental studies. **Education:** General, art, biology, business, chemistry, computer, early childhood, elementary, English, foreign languages, history, mathematics, middle, music, physical, science, social studies, Spanish, special, speech, technology/industrial arts. **Foreign languages:** General, Spanish. **Health:** Predental, premedicine, prepharmacy, preveterinary. **History:** General. **Legal studies:** Prelaw. **Liberal arts:** Arts/sciences. **Math:** General. **Mechanic/repair:** Automotive. **Parks/recreation:** Health/fitness. **Physical sciences:** Chemistry. **Psychology:** General. **Social sciences:** Sociology. **Visual/performing arts:** Art, dramatic, music performance.

Most popular majors. Biology 6%, business/marketing 22%, education 8%, engineering/engineering technologies 22%, parks/recreation 10%, psychology 6%, social sciences 6%, visual/performing arts 11%.

Computing on campus. 72 workstations in dormitories, library, computer center, student center. Dormitories wired for high-speed internet access and linked to campus network. Commuter students can connect to campus network. Online library, helpline, wireless network available.

Student life. Freshman orientation: Mandatory. Preregistration for classes offered. **Policies:** No alcohol permitted on campus. Unmarried students under 23 years old are required to live in residence halls. **Housing:** Guaranteed on-campus for all undergraduates. Coed dorms, single-sex dorms, special housing for disabled available. $150 nonrefundable deposit, deadline 5/1. **Activities:** Bands, choral groups, dance, drama, music ensembles, musical theater, student government, student newspaper, 28 clubs and organizations available.

Athletics. NAIA. **Intercollegiate:** Basketball, cheerleading, cross-country, football (tackle) M, softball W, track and field, volleyball W. **Intramural:** Badminton, basketball, football (non-tackle), football (tackle) M, handball, racquetball, soccer, softball, table tennis, volleyball. **Team name:** Bulldogs.

Student services. Adult student services, chaplain/spiritual director, career counseling, student employment services, financial aid counseling, health services, personal counseling, placement for graduates. **Physically disabled:** Services for hearing impaired.

Contact. E-mail: admiss@mcpherson.edu
Phone: (620) 241-0731 ext. 1270 Toll-free number: (800) 695-7402
Fax: (620) 241-8443
Dave Barrett, Director of Admission, McPherson College, 1600 East Euclid Street, McPherson, KS 67460-1402

MidAmerica Nazarene University
Olathe, Kansas
www.mnu.edu **CB code: 6437**

- Private 4-year university and liberal arts college affiliated with Church of the Nazarene
- Residential campus in small city
- 1,296 degree-seeking undergraduates: 13% part-time, 57% women
- 292 degree-seeking graduate students
- 73% of applicants admitted
- SAT or ACT (ACT writing optional) required
- 50% graduate within 6 years; 11% enter graduate study

General. Founded in 1966. Regionally accredited. **Degrees:** 346 bachelor's, 21 associate awarded; master's offered. **ROTC:** Army, Air Force. **Location:** 19 miles from Kansas City. **Calendar:** Semester, limited summer session. **Full-time faculty:** 87 total; 48% have terminal degrees, 8% minority, 38% women. **Part-time faculty:** 131 total; 16% have terminal degrees, 8% minority, 51% women. **Class size:** 66% < 20, 22% 20-39, 5% 40-49, 8% 50-99.

Freshman class profile. 548 applied, 399 admitted, 201 enrolled.

Mid 50% test scores		**GPA 2.0-2.99:**	21%
SAT critical reading:	480-610	**Rank in top quarter:**	39%
SAT math:	430-600	**Rank in top tenth:**	9%
ACT composite:	19-25	**End year in good standing:**	83%
GPA 3.75 or higher:	32%	**Return as sophomores:**	73%
GPA 3.50-3.74:	15%	**Out-of-state:**	46%
GPA 3.0-3.49:	31%	**Live on campus:**	91%

Basis for selection. Secondary school record, class rank, test scores, and moral principles important. Nursing, elementary education, and secondary education programs have higher standards for admission. Interview recommended for music, nursing, elementary and secondary education programs. Audition recommended for music majors. **Homeschooled:** Transcript of courses and grades, letter of recommendation (nonparent) required.

High school preparation. 14 units recommended. Recommended units include English 4, mathematics 3, social studies 3, science 3 and foreign language 1.

2009-2010 Annual costs. Tuition/fees (projected): $19,146. Room/board: $6,452. Books/supplies: $1,180. Personal expenses: $1,176.

2008-2009 Financial aid. Need-based: 176 full-time freshmen applied for aid; 143 were judged to have need; 143 of these received aid. Average need met was 71%. Average scholarship/grant was $10,410; average loan $4,821. 58% of total undergraduate aid awarded as scholarships/grants, 42% as loans/jobs. **Non-need-based:** Scholarships awarded for academics, athletics, leadership, music/drama, religious affiliation, ROTC.

Application procedures. Admission: Priority date 3/1; deadline 8/1 (postmark date). $25 fee. Admission notification on a rolling basis. **Financial aid:** Priority date 3/1; no closing date. FAFSA required. Applicants notified on a rolling basis starting 1/30; must reply within 2 week(s) of notification.

Academics. Adults 25 and older may earn bachelor's degree through evening division. **Special study options:** Accelerated study, cooperative education, cross-registration, distance learning, double major, dual enrollment of high school students, independent study, internships, student-designed major, study abroad, teacher certification program, Washington semester. Dual degree program in vocational agriculture with Kansas State University. **Credit/placement by examination:** AP, CLEP, IB, SAT, ACT, institutional tests. 34 credit hours maximum toward associate degree, 34 toward bachelor's. **Support services:** Learning center, reduced course load, remedial instruction, study skills assistance, tutoring.

Majors. **Biology:** General. **Business:** General, accounting, business admin, communications, human resources. **Communications:** General, media studies, public relations. **Computer sciences:** General, computer science, information systems. **Education:** Biology, business, elementary, English, foreign languages, health, mathematics, middle, music, physical, secondary, social studies, Spanish. **Foreign languages:** Spanish. **Health:** Athletic training, nursing (RN). **History:** General. **Math:** General. **Parks/recreation:** Exercise sciences, sports admin. **Philosophy/religion:** Religion. **Physical sciences:** Chemistry, physics. **Protective services:** Law enforcement admin. **Psychology:** General. **Social sciences:** General, sociology, urban studies. **Theology:** Missionary, religious ed, sacred music, youth ministry. **Visual/performing arts:** General, music performance, voice/opera.

Most popular majors. Business/marketing 56%, education 8%, health sciences 11%.

Computing on campus. 90 workstations in dormitories, library, computer center. Dormitories wired for high-speed internet access and linked to campus network. Commuter students can connect to campus network. Online course registration, online library, helpline, student web hosting, wireless network available.

Student life. **Freshman orientation:** Available, $44 fee. Preregistration for classes offered. Program concentrates on essential study skills, time management, value of liberal arts learning, career development aids, proficiency assessment. **Policies:** Religious observance required. **Housing:** Guaranteed on-campus for freshmen. Single-sex dorms, special housing for disabled, apartments, wellness housing available. $100 deposit, deadline 8/21. **Activities:** Bands, campus ministries, choral groups, drama, international student organizations, literary magazine, music ensembles, musical theater, radio station, student government, student newspaper, TV station, Circle K, College Republicans, gospel station, Fellowship of Christian Athletes, multicultural student asociation, BYTE, Psych Incorporated, medical careers club, covenant groups.

Athletics. NAIA. **Intercollegiate:** Baseball M, basketball, cheerleading, cross-country, football (tackle) M, soccer, softball W, track and field, volleyball W. **Intramural:** Basketball, bowling, football (non-tackle), football (tackle), golf, soccer, softball, table tennis, tennis, track and field, volleyball. **Team name:** Pioneers.

Student services. Adult student services, alcohol/substance abuse counseling, chaplain/spiritual director, career counseling, student employment services, financial aid counseling, health services, minority student services, personal counseling, placement for graduates, veterans' counselor. **Physically disabled:** Services for visually, speech, hearing impaired.

Contact. E-mail: admissions@mnu.edu
Phone: (913) 971-3380 Toll-free number: (800) 800-8887
Fax: (913) 971-3481
Brigit Mattox, Director of Admissions, MidAmerica Nazarene University, 2030 East College Way, Olathe, KS 66062-1899

Newman University
Wichita, Kansas
www.newmanu.edu **CB code: 6615**

- Private 4-year university and liberal arts college affiliated with Roman Catholic Church
- Commuter campus in large city
- 1,015 degree-seeking undergraduates: 16% part-time, 66% women, 5% African American, 4% Asian American, 9% Hispanic American, 2% Native American, 5% international
- 620 graduate students
- 44% of applicants admitted
- SAT and SAT Subject Tests or ACT (ACT writing optional) required
- 45% graduate within 6 years

General. Founded in 1933. Regionally accredited. The university is a sponsored ministry of the Adorers of the Blood of Christ. **Degrees:** 245 bachelor's, 63 associate awarded; master's, first professional offered. **Location:** 160 miles from Oklahoma City, 180 miles from Kansas City. **Calendar:** Semester, limited summer session. **Full-time faculty:** 80 total; 51% have terminal degrees, 52% women. **Part-time faculty:** 110 total; 59% women. **Class size:** 72% < 20, 26% 20-39, 2% 40-49, less than 1% 50-99. **Special facilities:** Photography laboratory, cadaver laboratory.

Freshman class profile. 1,576 applied, 688 admitted, 108 enrolled.

Mid 50% test scores			
SAT critical reading:	400-550	GPA 2.0-2.99:	19%
SAT math:	390-560	Rank in top quarter:	48%
SAT writing:	540-590	Rank in top tenth:	26%
ACT composite:	20-28	End year in good standing:	69%
GPA 3.75 or higher:	34%	Return as sophomores:	72%
GPA 3.50-3.74:	14%	Out-of-state:	23%
GPA 3.0-3.49:	33%	Live on campus:	71%
		International:	9%

Basis for selection. Minimum GPA 2.0, minimum ACT composite score of 18, or SAT score of 1290 (including Writing). Caliber of high school curriculum important. Portfolio recommended for art majors. **Learning Disabled:** Applicants should submit medical evaluation and recommendation.

High school preparation. College-preparatory program recommended. Recommended units include English 4, mathematics 3, social studies 3 and science 3.

2009-2010 Annual costs. Tuition/fees (projected): $19,650. Room/board: $6,500. Books/supplies: $959.

2008-2009 Financial aid. **Need-based:** Average need met was 77%. Average scholarship/grant was $5,306; average loan $2,943. 29% of total undergraduate aid awarded as scholarships/grants, 71% as loans/jobs. **Non-need-based:** Scholarships awarded for academics, alumni affiliation, art, athletics, leadership, music/drama.

Application procedures. **Admission:** No deadline. $20 fee, may be waived for applicants with need, free for online applicants. Admission notification on a rolling basis. **Financial aid:** Priority date 3/1; no closing date. FAFSA required. Applicants notified on a rolling basis starting 2/1.

Academics. **Special study options:** Accelerated study, cooperative education, cross-registration, distance learning, double major, dual enrollment of high school students, honors, independent study, internships, liberal arts/career combination, student-designed major, study abroad, teacher certification program. **Credit/placement by examination:** AP, CLEP, IB, institutional tests. 30 credit hours maximum toward bachelor's degree. **Support services:** Learning center, remedial instruction, study skills assistance, tutoring, writing center.

Majors. **Biology:** General. **Business:** Accounting, business admin, management information systems, marketing. **Communications:** Media studies. **Computer sciences:** Information systems. **Education:** General, elementary, middle, secondary. **Health:** Nursing (RN), sonography. **History:** General. **Liberal arts:** Arts/sciences. **Math:** General. **Philosophy/religion:** Philosophy. **Physical sciences:** Chemistry. **Protective services:** Law enforcement admin. **Psychology:** General. **Social sciences:** Sociology. **Theology:** Pastoral counseling, theology. **Visual/performing arts:** Art. **Other:** Counseling.

Most popular majors. Biology 9%, business/marketing 20%, education 24%, health sciences 19%, psychology 8%, theological studies 6%.

Computing on campus. 90 workstations in dormitories, library, computer center, student center. Dormitories wired for high-speed internet access and linked to campus network. Commuter students can connect to campus network. Online library, helpline, repair service, wireless network available.

Student life. **Freshman orientation:** Mandatory, $150 fee. Preregistration for classes offered. 4 days prior to first day of class. **Policies:** Freshmen required to live in college housing for first 2 years if not living with parents. **Housing:** Guaranteed on-campus for freshmen. Coed dorms, apartments, wellness housing available. $100 fully refundable deposit. **Activities:** Campus ministries, choral groups, international student organizations, literary magazine, student government, student newspaper, Koinonia, service scholars, Newman Club, Peer Educators, Kansas Catholic College Student Convention, peer ministers.

Athletics. NCAA. **Intercollegiate:** Baseball M, basketball, bowling, cheerleading, cross-country, golf, soccer, softball W, tennis, volleyball W, wrestling M. **Intramural:** Baseball M, basketball, bowling, football (tackle), golf, soccer, softball W, table tennis, volleyball, weight lifting. **Team name:** Jets.

Student services. Adult student services, chaplain/spiritual director, career counseling, student employment services, financial aid counseling, personal counseling, placement for graduates. **Physically disabled:** Services for visually, speech, hearing impaired.

Contact. E-mail: admissions@newmanu.edu
Phone: (316) 942-4291 ext. 2144 Toll-free number: (877) 639-6268
Fax: (316) 942-4483
John Clayton, Dean of Admissions, Newman University, 3100 McCormick, Wichita, KS 67213-2097

Ottawa University

Ottawa, Kansas **CB member**
www.ottawa.edu **CB code: 6547**

- Private 4-year liberal arts college affiliated with American Baptist Churches in the USA
- Residential campus in large town
- 541 degree-seeking undergraduates
- 67% of applicants admitted

General. Founded in 1865. Regionally accredited. Degree completion programs in Overland Park, KS; Phoenix, AZ; Milwaukee, WI; Jeffersonville, IN and Pacific Rim countries. Master's programs in Overland Park, KS, Phoenix, AZ, and Milwaukee, WI. **Degrees:** 80 bachelor's awarded. **Location:** 45 miles from Kansas City. **Calendar:** Semester, limited summer session. **Full-time faculty:** 25 total. **Part-time faculty:** 10 total. **Class size:** 63% < 20, 35% 20-39, 2% 40-49, less than 1% 50-99.

Freshman class profile. 928 applied, 626 admitted, 295 enrolled.

GPA 3.75 or higher:	25%	**Rank in top quarter:**	39%
GPA 3.50-3.74:	13%	**Rank in top tenth:**	17%
GPA 3.0-3.49:	37%	**Out-of-state:**	53%
GPA 2.0-2.99:	25%	**Live on campus:**	99%

Basis for selection. Rank in top half of class, 2.5 GPA, test scores important. Personal recommendation, school and community achievements, interview, special talents considered. SAT or ACT recommended. Audition recommended for music and drama majors. Portfolio recommended for art majors. **Homeschooled:** Transcript of courses and grades required. Must take ACT or SAT. Require a sample of most recent written work/portfolio.

High school preparation. Recommended units include English 4, mathematics 3, social studies 1, history 2, science 3 (laboratory 2) and foreign language 1.

2008-2009 Annual costs. Tuition/fees: $18,420. Room/board: $5,700. Books/supplies: $1,100. Personal expenses: $1,800.

2007-2008 Financial aid. Non-need-based: Scholarships awarded for academics, alumni affiliation, athletics, music/drama, religious affiliation.

Application procedures. Admission: Priority date 6/1; no deadline. $50 fee, may be waived for applicants with need. Admission notification on a rolling basis. **Financial aid:** Priority date 3/15; no closing date. FAFSA required. Applicants notified on a rolling basis starting 2/1; must reply within 4 week(s) of notification.

Academics. Special study options: Distance learning, double major, dual enrollment of high school students, internships, liberal arts/career combination, student-designed major, study abroad, teacher certification program. **Credit/placement by examination:** AP, CLEP, IB. **Support services:** Learning center, reduced course load, study skills assistance, tutoring.

Majors. Biology: General. **Business:** Accounting/business management, business admin, management information systems. **Communications:** General. **Computer sciences:** Information technology. **Education:** Art, elementary, English, mathematics, music, physical. **History:** General. **Math:** General. **Parks/recreation:** Health/fitness. **Philosophy/religion:** Religion. **Psychology:** General. **Public administration:** Human services. **Social sciences:** Political science, sociology. **Visual/performing arts:** Art, dramatic.

Most popular majors. Biology 10%, business/marketing 24%, communications/journalism 10%, education 11%, health sciences 10%, mathematics 6%, social sciences 14%.

Computing on campus. 71 workstations in dormitories, library, computer center. Dormitories wired for high-speed internet access and linked to campus network. Commuter students can connect to campus network. Online course registration, online library, helpline available.

Student life. Freshman orientation: Mandatory. Preregistration for classes offered. **Housing:** Guaranteed on-campus for freshmen. Coed dorms, single-sex dorms available. $150 fully refundable deposit, deadline 6/1. Pets allowed in dorm rooms. **Activities:** Jazz band, choral groups, drama, music ensembles, radio station, student government, student newspaper, symphony orchestra, Christian Faith in Action, voluntary service organization, Whole Earth club, Fellowship of Christian Athletes, student activities force, Cognoscenti (literary group), Amnesty International.

Athletics. NAIA. **Intercollegiate:** Baseball M, basketball, cross-country, football (tackle) M, golf M, soccer, softball W, track and field, volleyball W. **Intramural:** Badminton, basketball, bowling, golf, handball, racquetball, soccer, softball, table tennis, tennis, track and field, volleyball. **Team name:** Braves.

Student services. Alcohol/substance abuse counseling, chaplain/spiritual director, career counseling, student employment services, financial aid counseling, health services, personal counseling, placement for graduates.

Contact. E-mail: admiss@ottawa.edu
Phone: (785) 242-5200 ext. 5421 Toll-free number: (800) 755-5200 ext. 5421 Fax: (785) 242-1008
June Unrein, Dean of Enrollment Management, Ottawa University, 1001 South Cedar Street, #17, Ottawa, KS 66067-3399

Pittsburg State University

Pittsburg, Kansas
www.pittstate.edu **CB code: 6336**

- Public 4-year university
- Residential campus in large town
- 5,694 degree-seeking undergraduates: 6% part-time, 47% women, 2% African American, 1% Asian American, 3% Hispanic American, 2% Native American, 4% international
- 227 degree-seeking graduate students
- 88% of applicants admitted
- ACT (writing optional) required
- 50% graduate within 6 years

General. Founded in 1903. Regionally accredited. Centers in Kansas City and Wichita. **Degrees:** 1,074 bachelor's, 17 associate awarded; master's offered. **ROTC:** Army. **Location:** 120 miles from Kansas City. **Calendar:** Semester, limited summer session. **Full-time faculty:** 301 total; 70% have terminal degrees, 7% minority, 39% women. **Part-time faculty:** 107 total; 13% have terminal degrees, 6% minority, 54% women. **Class size:** 57% < 20, 34% 20-39, 5% 40-49, 5% 50-99, less than 1% >100. **Special facilities:** Planetarium, observatory, field biology reserve, nature reach, herbarium, technology center, gorilla village, mammal collection, greenhouse, polymer research lab, broadcasting lab, cadaver lab.

Freshman class profile. 1,821 applied, 1,605 admitted, 911 enrolled.

Mid 50% test scores		**Rank in top tenth:**	14%
ACT composite:	19-24	**Return as sophomores:**	74%
GPA 3.75 or higher:	25%	**Out-of-state:**	24%
GPA 3.50-3.74:	19%	**Live on campus:**	76%
GPA 3.0-3.49:	29%	**Fraternities:**	7%
GPA 2.0-2.99:	26%	**Sororities:**	8%
Rank in top quarter:	37%		

Basis for selection. Academics, school record, class rank and test scores most important. **Homeschooled:** GED, record of course content and completion required.

High school preparation. College-preparatory program recommended. 14 units recommended. Recommended units include English 4, mathematics 3, social studies 3, science 3 and computer science 1.

2008-2009 Annual costs. Tuition/fees: $4,322; $12,576 out-of-state. Room/board: $5,394. Books/supplies: $1,000. Personal expenses: $2,100.

2008-2009 Financial aid. Need-based: Average need met was 89%. Average scholarship/grant was $4,742; average loan $3,470. 46% of total undergraduate aid awarded as scholarships/grants, 54% as loans/jobs. **Non-need-based:** Scholarships awarded for academics, alumni affiliation, art, athletics, leadership, music/drama, ROTC.

Application procedures. Admission: No deadline. $30 fee. Admission notification on a rolling basis. **Financial aid:** Priority date 3/1; no closing date. FAFSA, institutional form required. Applicants notified on a rolling basis; must reply within 2 week(s) of notification.

Academics. Special study options: Accelerated study, combined bachelor's/graduate degree, cooperative education, distance learning, double major, dual enrollment of high school students, ESL, exchange student, external degree, honors, independent study, internships, liberal arts/career combination, student-designed major, study abroad, teacher certification program. **Credit/placement by examination:** AP, CLEP, IB, ACT, institutional tests. 24 credit hours maximum toward bachelor's degree. **Support services:** Learning center, tutoring, writing center.

Honors college/program. Separate application required. Criteria for selection include minimum 28 ACT score, minimum 3.5 GPA, recommendations, record of participation in academic and other extracurricular activities.

Majors. Biology: General, biochemistry, cellular/molecular, plant physiology. **Business:** Accounting, actuarial science, business admin, construction management, fashion, finance, international, managerial economics, marketing. **Communications:** General, advertising, journalism, photojournalism, public relations, radio/tv. **Computer sciences:** General, computer science. **Education:** Art, biology, chemistry, early childhood, elementary, English, family/consumer sciences, French, mathematics, music, physical, physics, psychology, Spanish, technology/industrial arts, voc/tech. **Engineering technology:** Construction, electrical, manufacturing, mechanical, plastics. **Family/consumer sciences:** General, child development. **Foreign languages:** French, Spanish. **Health:** Clinical lab science, nursing (RN), predental, premedicine, prepharmacy, preveterinary, recreational therapy. **History:** General. **Legal studies:** Prelaw. **Math:** General. **Mechanic/repair:** Automotive, diesel. **Parks/recreation:** General, facilities management. **Physical sciences:** Chemistry, physics, polymer chemistry. **Psychology:** General. **Public administration:** Social work. **Social sciences:** Geography, international relations, political science, sociology. **Visual/performing arts:** Art, ceramics, commercial/advertising art, graphic design, interior design, music performance, painting. **Other:** Automotive service management, Communication education, Community, corporate and hospital wellness, Environmental chemistry, Family and individual management, Graphics and imaging technologies, Information assurance and computer security, Justice studies, News editorial, Plant molecular biology, Pre-civil engineering, Pre-optometry, Technology management, Theater, Wood technology.

Most popular majors. Business/marketing 16%, education 15%, health sciences 8%, trade and industry 11%.

Computing on campus. 425 workstations in library, computer center, student center. Dormitories wired for high-speed internet access and linked to campus network. Commuter students can connect to campus network. Online course registration, online library, repair service, wireless network available.

Student life. Freshman orientation: Mandatory, $20 fee. Eight individual sessions are offered and last approximately eight hours each. **Housing:** Guaranteed on-campus for freshmen. Coed dorms, special housing for disabled, apartments, wellness housing available. $145 partly refundable deposit. **Activities:** Bands, campus ministries, choral groups, dance, drama, film society, international student organizations, literary magazine, music ensembles, musical theater, opera, radio station, student government, student newspaper, symphony orchestra, TV station, Over 160 clubs and organizations available.

Athletics. NCAA. **Intercollegiate:** Baseball M, basketball, cross-country, football (tackle) M, golf M, softball W, track and field, volleyball W. **Intramural:** Basketball, football (non-tackle), racquetball, softball, tennis, volleyball. **Team name:** Gorillas.

Student services. Alcohol/substance abuse counseling, chaplain/spiritual director, career counseling, student employment services, financial aid counseling, health services, legal services, minority student services, personal counseling, placement for graduates, veterans' counselor. **Physically disabled:** Services for visually, speech, hearing impaired.

Contact. E-mail: psuadmit@pittstate.edu
Phone: (620) 235-4251 Toll-free number: (800) 854-7488
Fax: (620) 235-6003
Melinda Roelfs, Director of Admission, Pittsburg State University, 1701 South Broadway, Pittsburg, KS 66762

Southwestern College

Winfield, Kansas
www.sckans.edu **CB code: 6670**

- Private 4-year liberal arts college affiliated with United Methodist Church
- Residential campus in large town
- 1,545 degree-seeking undergraduates: 64% part-time, 43% women, 9% African American, 2% Asian American, 5% Hispanic American, 1% Native American, 2% international
- 198 degree-seeking graduate students
- 90% of applicants admitted
- SAT or ACT (ACT writing optional), application essay required
- 49% graduate within 6 years

General. Founded in 1885. Regionally accredited. Laptop computers issued to all full-time students enrolled at main campus. **Degrees:** 502 bachelor's awarded; master's offered. **Location:** 40 miles from Wichita. **Calendar:** Semester, limited summer session. **Full-time faculty:** 49 total; 57% have terminal degrees, 6% minority, 33% women. **Part-time faculty:** 123 total; 5% have terminal degrees, 6% minority, 40% women. **Class size:** 81% < 20, 18% 20-39, less than 1% 40-49, less than 1% 50-99. **Special facilities:** Biological field station.

Freshman class profile. 328 applied, 296 admitted, 159 enrolled.

Mid 50% test scores			
SAT critical reading:	420-510	Rank in top quarter:	48%
SAT math:	430-530	Rank in top tenth:	21%
SAT writing:	400-480	End year in good standing:	84%
ACT composite:	19-25	Return as sophomores:	69%
GPA 3.75 or higher:	30%	Out-of-state:	41%
GPA 3.50-3.74:	17%	Live on campus:	99%
GPA 3.0-3.49:	32%	International:	6%
GPA 2.0-2.99:	21%	Fraternities:	2%
		Sororities:	4%

Basis for selection. School achievement record, test scores and personal essay statement most important. Portfolio required. Interview recommended for nursing majors. Audition required for music and drama majors.

High school preparation. 13.5 units required. Required units include English 4, mathematics 3, social studies 2.5, history 1, science 2 (laboratory 1). Computer or communication unit may be substituted for foreign language.

2009-2010 Annual costs. Tuition/fees (projected): $19,630. Room/board: $5,750. Books/supplies: $1,200. Personal expenses: $2,796.

2008-2009 Financial aid. Need-based: 138 full-time freshmen applied for aid; 114 were judged to have need; 114 of these received aid. Average need met was 90%. Average scholarship/grant was $14,299; average loan $3,306. 42% of total undergraduate aid awarded as scholarships/grants, 58% as loans/jobs. **Non-need-based:** Awarded to 490 full-time undergraduates, including 166 freshmen. Scholarships awarded for academics, alumni affiliation, athletics, leadership, minority status, music/drama, religious affiliation. **Additional information:** Academic and activity grants available.

Application procedures. Admission: Closing date 8/25 (receipt date). $25 fee, may be waived for applicants with need. Admission notification on a rolling basis beginning on or about 9/15. Must reply by May 1 or within 3 week(s) if notified thereafter. **Financial aid:** Priority date 4/1, closing date 8/15. FAFSA, institutional form required. Applicants notified on a rolling basis starting 2/1; must reply within 2 week(s) of notification.

Academics. Special study options: Accelerated study, distance learning, double major, honors, independent study, internships, student-designed major, study abroad, teacher certification program, urban semester, Washington semester. **Credit/placement by examination:** AP, CLEP, ACT, institutional tests. 30 credit hours maximum toward bachelor's degree. **Support services:** Learning center, reduced course load, remedial instruction, study skills assistance, tutoring, writing center.

Majors. Biology: General, biochemistry, marine. **Business:** Accounting, business admin, communications, entrepreneurial studies, finance, management information systems, management science, marketing, nonprofit/public, operations, training/development. **Communications:** General, digital media, radio/tv. **Computer sciences:** General, computer science, programming, web page design. **Education:** General, business, drama/dance, early childhood, elementary, English, foreign languages, mathematics, music, physical, science, secondary, speech. **Engineering:** Physics. **Engineering technology:** Computer systems, manufacturing. **Health:** Athletic training, nursing (RN). **History:** General. **Liberal arts:** Arts/sciences. **Math:** General. **Parks/recreation:** Health/fitness, sports admin. **Philosophy/religion:** Philosophy, religion. **Physical sciences:** Chemistry, physics. **Protective services:** Criminal justice, security services. **Psychology:** General. **Theology:** Pastoral counseling. **Visual/performing arts:** Dramatic, film/cinema.

Most popular majors. Business/marketing 47%, computer/information sciences 9%, education 9%, security/protective services 11%.

Computing on campus. PC or laptop required. 50 workstations in dormitories, library, computer center, student center. Dormitories wired for high-speed internet access and linked to campus network. Commuter students can connect to campus network. Online library, helpline, repair service, student web hosting, wireless network available.

Student life. Freshman orientation: Mandatory. Preregistration for classes offered. Three-day orientation held before upperclassmen arrive on campus. Includes laptop distribution and training, community service project. **Policies:** Drug and alcohol-free campus. **Housing:** Guaranteed on-campus for freshmen. Coed dorms, single-sex dorms, special housing for disabled, apartments available. $100 deposit. **Activities:** Bands, campus ministries, choral groups, dance, drama, international student organizations, literary magazine, music ensembles, musical theater, radio station, student government, student newspaper, symphony orchestra, TV station, Black Student Union, Campus Council on Ministries, Sharp Ambassadors, Student Foundation, Business Students Association, Fellowship of Christian Athletes, Discipleship Southwestern, Leadership Southwestern, outreach teams, SC Association of Nursing Students.

Athletics. NAIA. **Intercollegiate:** Basketball, cheerleading, cross-country, football (tackle) M, golf, soccer, softball W, tennis, track and field, volleyball W. **Intramural:** Basketball, bowling, softball, swimming, tennis, volleyball. **Team name:** Moundbuilders.

Student services. Adult student services, alcohol/substance abuse counseling, chaplain/spiritual director, career counseling, student employment services, financial aid counseling, health services, minority student services, on-campus daycare, personal counseling, placement for graduates. **Physically disabled:** Services for visually, hearing impaired.

Contact. E-mail: scadmit@sckans.edu
Phone: (620) 229-6236 Toll-free number: (800) 846-1543 ext. 6236
Fax: (620) 229-6344
Marla Sexson, Director of Admission, Southwestern College, 100 College Street, Winfield, KS 67156

Sterling College
Sterling, Kansas
www.sterling.edu **CB code: 6684**

- Private 4-year liberal arts college affiliated with Presbyterian Church (USA)
- Residential campus in rural community
- 611 degree-seeking undergraduates: 7% part-time, 48% women, 8% African American, 1% Asian American, 6% Hispanic American, 2% Native American, 1% international
- 53% of applicants admitted
- SAT or ACT (ACT writing optional), application essay required
- 50% graduate within 6 years

General. Founded in 1887. Regionally accredited. **Degrees:** 66 bachelor's awarded. **Location:** 20 miles from Hutchinson, 70 miles from Wichita. **Calendar:** 4-1-4, limited summer session. **Full-time faculty:** 40 total; 45% have terminal degrees, 8% minority, 28% women. **Part-time faculty:** 19 total; 21% have terminal degrees, 37% women. **Class size:** 74% < 20, 23% 20-39, 3% 40-49, less than 1% 50-99.

Freshman class profile. 971 applied, 519 admitted, 150 enrolled.

Mid 50% test scores		**GPA 3.0-3.49:**	26%
SAT critical reading:	430-530	**GPA 2.0-2.99:**	35%
SAT math:	440-590	**Rank in top quarter:**	25%
SAT writing:	420-510	**Rank in top tenth:**	7%
ACT composite:	18-23	**Return as sophomores:**	62%
GPA 3.75 or higher:	22%	**Out-of-state:**	59%
GPA 3.50-3.74:	15%	**Live on campus:**	97%

Basis for selection. High school record, test scores, recommendations from school counselor and pastor important; commitment to Christian values and service also important. Interview recommended. Audition required of performing arts majors. Portfolio recommended for art majors. **Homeschooled:** Transcript of courses and grades required. State certification strongly recommended for athletic eligibility. **Learning Disabled:** Must provide official documentation with recommended accommodations.

High school preparation. College-preparatory program recommended. 18 units recommended. Recommended units include English 4, mathematics 3, social studies 1, history 2, science 3 (laboratory 2), foreign language 2, computer science 1 and academic electives 1. Physical education recommended.

2008-2009 Annual costs. Tuition/fees: $16,700. $335 per credit hour charge for 1 to 6 credits. Room/board: $6,230. Books/supplies: $600. Personal expenses: $700.

2007-2008 Financial aid. Need-based: 86 full-time freshmen applied for aid; 76 were judged to have need; 76 of these received aid. Average need met was 73%. Average scholarship/grant was $6,367; average loan $2,233. 72% of total undergraduate aid awarded as scholarships/grants, 28% as loans/jobs. **Non-need-based:** Awarded to 80 full-time undergraduates, including 18 freshmen. Scholarships awarded for academics, athletics.

Application procedures. Admission: Priority date 3/1; no deadline. $25 fee, may be waived for applicants with need, free for online applicants. Admission notification on a rolling basis beginning on or about 9/15. **Financial aid:** Priority date 3/1; no closing date. FAFSA required. Applicants notified on a rolling basis starting 2/1; must reply within 3 week(s) of notification.

Academics. Special study options: Distance learning, double major, dual enrollment of high school students, honors, independent study, internships, liberal arts/career combination, student-designed major, study abroad, teacher certification program, Washington semester. **Credit/placement by examination:** AP, CLEP, SAT, ACT, institutional tests. **Support services:** Learning center, reduced course load, remedial instruction, study skills assistance, tutoring, writing center.

Majors. Biology: General. **Business:** Business admin. **Communications:** General. **Computer sciences:** General. **Education:** Elementary, mathematics, music. **Health:** Athletic training. **History:** General. **Math:** General. **Parks/recreation:** Health/fitness. **Physical sciences:** Chemistry. **Psychology:** General. **Theology:** Religious ed. **Visual/performing arts:** Art, dramatic.

Most popular majors. Business/marketing 16%, communications/journalism 8%, education 13%, English 7%, parks/recreation 8%, theological studies 8%, visual/performing arts 20%.

Computing on campus. 120 workstations in dormitories, library, computer center, student center. Dormitories wired for high-speed internet access and linked to campus network. Commuter students can connect to campus network. Online library, helpline, wireless network available.

Student life. Freshman orientation: Mandatory. Preregistration for classes offered. 3-day program prior to start of fall classes; includes service project. **Policies:** Prohibition of alcohol and tobacco products.All students under age 23 required to live in campus dormitories unless married or with dependents, living at home with parents, 5th-year senior, or by special circumstances. Religious observance required. **Housing:** Guaranteed on-campus for all undergraduates. Single-sex dorms, wellness housing available. $100 partly refundable deposit, deadline 8/1. **Activities:** Bands, campus ministries, choral groups, drama, literary magazine, music ensembles, musical theater, radio station, student government, student newspaper, TV station, Future Science Professionals Association, Alpha Phi Omega, Fellowship of Christian Athletes, behavioral science club, Habitat for Humanity, Chi Beta Sigma, PEACE club, Pi Kappa Delta, Catholic student association.

Athletics. NAIA. **Intercollegiate:** Baseball M, basketball, cross-country, football (tackle) M, golf, soccer, softball W, tennis, track and field, volleyball W. **Intramural:** Basketball, bowling, football (non-tackle), softball, table tennis, volleyball. **Team name:** Warriors.

Student services. Chaplain/spiritual director, career counseling, student employment services, financial aid counseling, health services, personal counseling.

Contact. E-mail: admissions@sterling.edu
Phone: (620) 278-4275 Toll-free number: (800) 346-1017
Fax: (620) 278-4416
Dennis Dutton, Vice President for Enrollment Services, Sterling College, 125 West Cooper, Sterling, KS 67579

Tabor College
Hillsboro, Kansas
www.tabor.edu **CB code: 6815**

- Private 4-year liberal arts college affiliated with Mennonite Brethren Church
- Residential campus in small town
- 583 degree-seeking undergraduates: 20% part-time, 48% women, 7% African American, 1% Asian American, 5% Hispanic American, 1% Native American, 2% international
- 11 degree-seeking graduate students
- 94% of applicants admitted
- SAT or ACT (ACT writing optional), application essay required
- 56% graduate within 6 years

General. Founded in 1908. Regionally accredited. Off-campus site in Wichita offers adult degree completion program and graduate studies. **Degrees:** 134 bachelor's awarded; master's offered. **Location:** 50 miles from Wichita. **Calendar:** 4-1-4, limited summer session. **Full-time faculty:** 33 total; 73% have terminal degrees, 6% minority, 39% women. **Part-time faculty:** 48 total; 15% have terminal degrees, 4% minority, 50% women. **Class size:** 71% < 20, 23% 20-39, 4% 40-49, 2% 50-99.

Freshman class profile. 405 applied, 379 admitted, 142 enrolled.

Mid 50% test scores		**GPA 2.0-2.99:**	29%
SAT critical reading:	410-500	**Rank in top quarter:**	34%
SAT math:	380-530	**Rank in top tenth:**	15%
ACT composite:	19-25	**Return as sophomores:**	64%
GPA 3.75 or higher:	28%	**Out-of-state:**	45%
GPA 3.50-3.74:	18%	**Live on campus:**	96%
GPA 3.0-3.49:	24%	**International:**	3%

Basis for selection. Life values and objectives, desire for Christian growth, and personal interviews important. Students must score a minimum of 18 on ACT and have ACT GPA (4.0 scale) product of 45 or above to be considered for admission. Audition recommended for music or drama. **Learning Disabled:** Must provide IEPs if special accommodations requested.

High school preparation. 17 units recommended. Recommended units include English 4, mathematics 3, social studies 2, history 2, science 3 and foreign language 1. 2 units of fine arts are also recommended.

2009-2010 Annual costs. Tuition/fees: $19,660. Room/board: $6,870. Books/supplies: $700. Personal expenses: $3,130.

2008-2009 Financial aid. Non-need-based: Scholarships awarded for academics, alumni affiliation, athletics, music/drama, religious affiliation, state residency.

Application procedures. Admission: Priority date 4/4; no deadline. $30 fee, may be waived for applicants with need. Admission notification on a rolling basis beginning on or about 9/1. **Financial aid:** Priority date 3/1, closing date 8/30. FAFSA required. Applicants notified on a rolling basis starting 3/15; must reply within 4 week(s) of notification.

Academics. Special study options: Accelerated study, combined bachelor's/graduate degree, cross-registration, distance learning, double major, dual enrollment of high school students, independent study, internships, student-designed major, study abroad, teacher certification program, Washington semester. **Credit/placement by examination:** AP, CLEP, IB, SAT, ACT. 30 credit hours maximum toward bachelor's degree. **Support services:** Learning center, reduced course load, remedial instruction, study skills assistance, tutoring, writing center.

Majors. Biology: General, biochemistry. **Business:** Accounting/business management, administrative services, business admin, marketing, office management. **Communications:** General, journalism, organizational, public relations. **Computer sciences:** Computer science, system admin. **Conservation:** Environmental studies. **Education:** General, biology, business, chemistry, developmentally delayed, elementary, emotionally handicapped, English, health, history, kindergarten/preschool, learning disabled, mathematics, mentally handicapped, middle, multi-level teacher, multiple handicapped, music, physical, science, secondary, social science, social studies, special. **Health:** Athletic training, clinical lab technology, predental, premedicine, preop/surgical nursing, prepharmacy, preveterinary. **History:** General. **Interdisciplinary:** Biological/physical sciences, math/computer science, natural sciences. **Legal studies:** Prelaw. **Liberal arts:** Humanities. **Math:** General. **Parks/recreation:** General, health/fitness, sports admin. **Philosophy/religion:** Philosophy, religion. **Physical sciences:** Chemistry. **Psychology:** General. **Social sciences:** General, sociology. **Theology:** Bible, theology, youth ministry. **Visual/performing arts:** Commercial/advertising art. **Other:** Social Welfare.

Most popular majors. Business/marketing 21%, education 15%, health sciences 14%, parks/recreation 6%, social sciences 8%, theological studies 10%.

Computing on campus. 58 workstations in library, computer center, student center. Dormitories wired for high-speed internet access and linked to campus network. Commuter students can connect to campus network. Online library, wireless network available.

Student life. Freshman orientation: Mandatory. Preregistration for classes offered. 3-day program prior to fall semester; includes service day. **Policies:** Sudents required to live on campus until age 23. Religious observance required. **Housing:** Guaranteed on-campus for freshmen. Single-sex dorms, special housing for disabled, wellness housing available. $125 fully refundable deposit, deadline 8/1. **Activities:** Bands, campus ministries, choral groups, drama, music ensembles, musical theater, student government, student newspaper, science club, student music association, Christian student organizations, multicultural student union, international student union, English society, student education association, Fellowship of Christian Athletes.

Athletics. NAIA. **Intercollegiate:** Baseball M, basketball, cheerleading, cross-country, football (tackle) M, soccer, softball W, tennis, track and field, volleyball W. **Intramural:** Basketball, football (non-tackle), racquetball, soccer, table tennis, tennis, track and field, volleyball. **Team name:** Blue Jays.

Student services. Chaplain/spiritual director, career counseling, student employment services, financial aid counseling, minority student services, personal counseling, placement for graduates. **Physically disabled:** Services for visually, hearing impaired.

Contact. E-mail: admissions@tabor.edu
Phone: (620) 947-3121 ext. 1723 Toll-free number: (800) 822-6799
Fax: (620) 947-6276
Rusty Allen, Vice President of Enrollment Management, Tabor College, 400 South Jefferson, Hillsboro, KS 67063-1799

University of Kansas

Lawrence, Kansas — **CB member**
www.ku.edu — **CB code: 6871**

- Public 4-year university
- Commuter campus in small city
- 20,555 degree-seeking undergraduates: 9% part-time, 49% women, 4% African American, 4% Asian American, 4% Hispanic American, 1% Native American, 3% international
- 6,188 graduate students
- 92% of applicants admitted
- SAT or ACT (ACT writing optional) required
- 60% graduate within 6 years

General. Founded in 1866. Regionally accredited. **Degrees:** 3,750 bachelor's awarded; master's, doctoral, first professional offered. **ROTC:** Army, Naval, Air Force. **Location:** 40 miles from Kansas City. **Calendar:** Semester, extensive summer session. **Full-time faculty:** 1,011 total; 99% have terminal degrees, 17% minority, 32% women. **Part-time faculty:** 61 total; 90% have terminal degrees, 7% minority, 25% women. **Class size:** 38% < 20, 45% 20-39, 5% 40-49, 6% 50-99, 6% >100. **Special facilities:** 12 libraries including art and architecture, engineering, science, music, government documents and maps, rare books, manuscripts, and regional collections; art and natural history museums, space technology center, Institute for Life Span Studies, Lied Performing Arts Center and Bales Organ Recital Hall, Kansas Ecological Reserves, design lab, flight research lab, radar systems and remote sensing lab, film studio, Center for the Humanities, Sabatini Multicultural Resource Center, Dole Institute of Politics.

Freshman class profile. 10,902 applied, 10,003 admitted, 4,483 enrolled.

Mid 50% test scores		**Rank in top quarter:**	60%
ACT composite:	22-27	**Rank in top tenth:**	27%
GPA 3.75 or higher:	31%	**Return as sophomores:**	80%
GPA 3.50-3.74:	19%	**Out-of-state:**	29%
GPA 3.0-3.49:	31%	**Live on campus:**	58%
GPA 2.0-2.99:	19%	**International:**	3%

Basis for selection. Admission to College of Liberal Arts and Sciences requires one of following for in-state students: minimum ACT score of 21 or SAT score of 980 (exclusive of Writing), rank in top third of high school class, or completion of required college preparatory curriculum with 2.0 GPA. For out-of-state students: minimum test scores are 24 on ACT or 1090 on SAT (exclusive of Writing); minimum GPA 2.5 on college preparatory curriculum; rank in top third of high school class. Admission policies for other colleges within university may vary. Audition required for music performance, music education, music therapy majors. **Homeschooled:** Admission based on test scores.

High school preparation. College-preparatory program required. 14 units required; 17 recommended. Required and recommended units include English 4, mathematics 3-4, social studies 3, science 3, foreign language 2 and computer science 1. 1 science unit must be chemistry or physics. 4 units mathematics recommended for mathematics, engineering and architecture majors. Social studies units include history.

2008-2009 Annual costs. Tuition/fees: $7,725; $18,909 out-of-state. Room/board: $6,474. Books/supplies: $800. Personal expenses: $2,272.

2007-2008 Financial aid. Need-based: 3,173 full-time freshmen applied for aid; 1,584 were judged to have need; 1,512 of these received aid. Average need met was 58%. Average scholarship/grant was $4,550; average loan $2,873. 42% of total undergraduate aid awarded as scholarships/grants, 58% as loans/jobs. **Non-need-based:** Awarded to 4,387 full-time undergraduates, including 1,580 freshmen. Scholarships awarded for academics, alumni affiliation, art, athletics, leadership, minority status, music/drama, ROTC, state residency. **Additional information:** Students awarded federal work study are responsible for securing their own jobs on campus. There are positions on campus with a variety of schedules beyond 8-5.

Application procedures. Admission: Priority date 12/1; deadline 4/1 (receipt date). $30 fee. Admission notification on a rolling basis beginning on or about 9/1. Must reply by May 1 or within 2 week(s) if notified thereafter. **Financial aid:** Priority date 3/1; no closing date. FAFSA required. Applicants notified on a rolling basis starting 4/1; must reply within 2 week(s) of notification.

Academics. Special study options: Accelerated study, combined bachelor's/graduate degree, cooperative education, distance learning, double major, dual enrollment of high school students, ESL, honors, independent study, internships, liberal arts/career combination, study abroad, teacher certification program, Washington semester. **Credit/placement by examination:** AP, CLEP,

IB, SAT, ACT, institutional tests. **Support services:** Learning center, remedial instruction, study skills assistance, tutoring, writing center.

Honors college/program. Students should have an ACT composite score of 30 or higher, a rigorous college preparatory curriculum, an un-weighted GPA of 3.75 or higher, participation in activities that supplement academic work and/or demonstrate community involvement and a sense of social responsibility, and an essay that reveals intellectual curiosity and academic rigor. Admission is competitive.

Majors. **Architecture:** History/criticism. **Area/ethnic studies:** African, American, European, Latin American, Russian/Slavic, women's. **Biology:** General, biochemistry, microbiology, molecular. **Business:** General, accounting, business admin, finance, logistics, management information systems, marketing. **Communications:** Journalism. **Computer sciences:** General. **Conservation:** Environmental studies. **Education:** Art, biology, chemistry, early childhood, elementary, English, foreign languages, history, mathematics, middle, music, physical, physics, science, secondary, social studies. **Engineering:** Aerospace, architectural, chemical, civil, computer, electrical, mechanical, petroleum, physics. **Foreign languages:** Classics, East Asian, French, Germanic, linguistics, Slavic, Spanish. **Health:** Athletic training, communication disorders, community health services, music therapy. **History:** General. **Interdisciplinary:** Ancient studies, behavioral sciences. **Liberal arts:** Arts/sciences, humanities. **Math:** General. **Parks/recreation:** Health/fitness. **Philosophy/religion:** Philosophy, religion. **Physical sciences:** Astronomy, atmospheric science, chemistry, geology, physics. **Psychology:** General, developmental. **Public administration:** General, social work. **Social sciences:** Anthropology, economics, geography, international relations, political science, sociology. **Visual/performing arts:** Art history/conservation, ceramics, commercial/advertising art, dance, design, dramatic, fiber arts, graphic design, illustration, industrial design, interior design, metal/jewelry, music performance, music theory/composition, musicology, painting, piano/organ, printmaking, sculpture, stringed instruments, studio arts, theater design, voice/opera.

Most popular majors. Biology 7%, business/marketing 13%, communications/journalism 7%, engineering/engineering technologies 6%, English 8%, health sciences 6%, psychology 8%, social sciences 11%, visual/performing arts 9%.

Computing on campus. 1,500 workstations in dormitories, library, computer center, student center. Dormitories wired for high-speed internet access and linked to campus network. Commuter students can connect to campus network. Online course registration, online library, helpline, student web hosting, wireless network available.

Student life. **Freshman orientation:** Available, $55 fee. Preregistration for classes offered. One-day program throughout summer; several 2 day programs available. Additional charges for parent participation and 2 day program. **Policies:** No alcohol permitted on campus, no smoking in any buildings. Parking by permit only. **Housing:** Coed dorms, single-sex dorms, apartments, cooperative housing, fraternity/sorority housing, wellness housing available. $335 partly refundable deposit. Scholarship halls available to students with high scholastic achievement and financial need. **Activities:** Bands, choral groups, dance, drama, international student organizations, literary magazine, music ensembles, musical theater, opera, radio station, student government, student newspaper, symphony orchestra, TV station, over 500 student organizations and activities.

Athletics. NCAA. **Intercollegiate:** Baseball M, basketball, cross-country, football (tackle) M, golf, rowing (crew) W, soccer W, softball W, swimming W, tennis W, track and field, volleyball W. **Intramural:** Basketball, bowling, football (non-tackle), golf, racquetball, soccer, softball, table tennis, tennis, volleyball. **Team name:** Jayhawks.

Student services. Adult student services, alcohol/substance abuse counseling, career counseling, services for economically disadvantaged, student employment services, financial aid counseling, health services, legal services, minority student services, on-campus daycare, personal counseling, placement for graduates, veterans' counselor, women's services. **Physically disabled:** Services for visually, speech, hearing impaired.

Contact. E-mail: adm@ku.edu
Phone: (785) 864-3911 Fax: (785) 864-5017
Lisa Pinamonti Kress, Director of Admissions and Scholarships, University of Kansas, 1502 Iowa Street, Lawrence, KS 66045-7576

University of Kansas Medical Center

Kansas City, Kansas
www.kumc.edu **CB code: 0414**

- Public two-year upper-division university and health science college
- Commuter campus in small city

General. Founded in 1905. Regionally accredited. **Degrees:** 247 bachelor's awarded; master's, doctoral, first professional offered. **Location:** Downtown. **Calendar:** Semester, limited summer session. **Full-time faculty:** 267 total; 77% have terminal degrees, 20% minority, 57% women. **Part-time faculty:** 38 total; 60% have terminal degrees, 3% minority, 68% women. **Class size:** 76% < 20, 16% 20-39, 4% 50-99, 4% >100.

Student profile. 490 degree-seeking undergraduates, 2,521 degree-seeking graduate students. 127 applied as first time-transfer students.

Women:	87%	**International:**	1%
African American:	5%	**Part-time:**	21%
Asian American:	5%	**Out-of-state:**	16%
Hispanic American:	4%	**25 or older:**	37%
Native American:	1%		

Basis for selection. College transcript required. Admissions regulations, policies and application closing dates vary by degree program. Transfer accepted as juniors, seniors.

2008-2009 Annual costs. Tuition/fees: $6,554; $16,631 out-of-state. Books/supplies: $1,440. Personal expenses: $6,120.

Financial aid. **Need-based:** 346 applied for aid; 318 were judged to have need; 305 of these received aid. Average need met was 57%. 24% of total undergraduate aid awarded as scholarships/grants, 76% as loans/jobs. **Non-need-based:** Awarded to 79 undergraduates. Scholarships awarded for academics, leadership, state residency.

Application procedures. **Admission:** $60 fee. Admissions deadlines vary by school and program. **Financial aid:** Priority date 2/14, no deadline. Applicants notified on a rolling basis starting 4/1.

Academics. Assessment and reading skills screened. Assistance offered in reviewing APA-style papers. **Special study options:** Combined bachelor's/graduate degree, distance learning, ESL, honors, independent study, internships, study abroad. **Credit/placement by examination:** CLEP.

Majors. **Health:** Clinical lab science, cytotechnology, nursing (RN), respiratory therapy technology.

Computing on campus. 157 workstations in library, computer center, student center. Commuter students can connect to campus network. Online library, helpline, student web hosting, wireless network available.

Student life. **Activities:** International student organizations, literary magazine, student government, allied health student senate, graduate student council, medical student assembly, association of undergraduate nurses, Latino Midwest medical student association, American medical women's association, Students for Women's Wellness, Lifewatch Bible Study, Students Educating and Advocating for Diversity.

Athletics. **Intramural:** Basketball, racquetball, soccer, softball, swimming, volleyball.

Student services. Chaplain/spiritual director, career counseling, financial aid counseling, health services, legal services, personal counseling. **Physically disabled:** Services for visually, speech, hearing impaired.

Contact. E-mail: kumcregistrar@kumc.edu
Phone: (913) 588-7055 Fax: (913) 588-4697
University of Kansas Medical Center, 3901 Rainbow Boulevard, Kansas City, KS 66160-7116

University of St. Mary

Leavenworth, Kansas
www.stmary.edu **CB code: 6630**

- Private 4-year university affiliated with Roman Catholic Church
- Residential campus in large town
- 575 degree-seeking undergraduates: 18% part-time, 61% women, 12% African American, 1% Asian American, 8% Hispanic American, 1% Native American
- 298 degree-seeking graduate students
- 69% of applicants admitted
- SAT or ACT (ACT writing optional) required
- 44% graduate within 6 years

General. Founded in 1923. Regionally accredited. **Degrees:** 115 bachelor's, 1 associate awarded; master's offered. **ROTC:** Army, Air Force. **Location:** 26 miles from Kansas City. **Calendar:** Semester, limited summer session. **Full-time faculty:** 40 total; 58% have terminal degrees, 5% minority, 58% women. **Part-time faculty:** 62 total; 19% have terminal degrees,

8% minority, 64% women. **Class size:** 74% < 20, 25% 20-39, less than 1% 40-49, less than 1% >100. **Special facilities:** Sacred Scripture and History of the Catholic Church in Kansas collections in library.

Freshman class profile. 535 applied, 368 admitted, 115 enrolled.

Mid 50% test scores		**GPA 2.0-2.99:**	39%
SAT critical reading:	420-500	**Rank in top quarter:**	42%
SAT math:	420-510	**Rank in top tenth:**	13%
ACT composite:	18-22	**End year in good standing:**	79%
GPA 3.75 or higher:	7%	**Return as sophomores:**	71%
GPA 3.50-3.74:	12%	**Out-of-state:**	55%
GPA 3.0-3.49:	42%	**Live on campus:**	79%

Basis for selection. 2.5 GPA, 18 ACT, 870 SAT (exclusive of Writing) required. Applicants below required GPA or ACT/SAT may be considered for admission. Portfolio recommended for fine and applied arts majors.

High school preparation. 12 units required; 24 recommended. Required and recommended units include English 4, mathematics 2-4, social studies 2, history 2-4, science 2-4 (laboratory 2), foreign language 2 and academic electives 2. 1-2 computer programming recommended.

2008-2009 Annual costs. Tuition/fees: $18,090. Room/board: $6,050. Books/supplies: $1,000. Personal expenses: $1,820.

2008-2009 Financial aid. **Need-based:** 103 full-time freshmen applied for aid; 86 were judged to have need; 86 of these received aid. Average need met was 76%. Average scholarship/grant was $10,927; average loan $3,741. 53% of total undergraduate aid awarded as scholarships/grants, 47% as loans/jobs. **Non-need-based:** Awarded to 91 full-time undergraduates, including 34 freshmen. Scholarships awarded for academics, art, athletics, leadership, music/drama.

Application procedures. **Admission:** No deadline. $25 fee, may be waived for applicants with need. Admission notification on a rolling basis. Must reply by May 1 or within 4 week(s) if notified thereafter. **Financial aid:** Priority date 4/1; no closing date. FAFSA required. Applicants notified on a rolling basis starting 2/8; must reply within 2 week(s) of notification.

Academics. **Special study options:** Accelerated study, distance learning, double major, dual enrollment of high school students, exchange student, honors, independent study, internships, student-designed major, study abroad, teacher certification program. Degree completion programs. **Credit/placement by examination:** AP, CLEP, IB, SAT, ACT, institutional tests. 30 credit hours maximum toward bachelor's degree. **Support services:** Learning center, remedial instruction, study skills assistance, tutoring.

Majors. **Biology:** General. **Business:** General, accounting, business admin, international. **Communications:** General. **Computer sciences:** Information technology. **Education:** Elementary. **Family/consumer sciences:** Child development. **Health:** Nursing (RN). **History:** General. **Liberal arts:** Arts/sciences. **Math:** General. **Parks/recreation:** Sports admin. **Physical sciences:** Chemistry. **Psychology:** General. **Social sciences:** Criminology, political science. **Theology:** Pastoral counseling, theology. **Visual/performing arts:** Art, dramatic.

Most popular majors. Business/marketing 15%, education 12%, health sciences 26%, parks/recreation 7%, psychology 16%, social sciences 6%.

Computing on campus. 95 workstations in dormitories, library, computer center. Dormitories wired for high-speed internet access and linked to campus network. Helpline, student web hosting, wireless network available.

Student life. **Freshman orientation:** Mandatory. Preregistration for classes offered. Three-day program at beginning of fall semester. **Housing:** Guaranteed on-campus for freshmen. Coed dorms available. $100 nonrefundable deposit. **Activities:** Bands, campus ministries, choral groups, drama, international student organizations, literary magazine, music ensembles, musical theater, opera, student government, student newspaper, Bacchus, Aristotle Club, Amnesty International, Students in Free Enterprise, Young Democrats, Campus Republicans.

Athletics. NAIA. **Intercollegiate:** Baseball M, basketball, football (tackle) M, soccer, softball W, volleyball W. **Intramural:** Basketball, bowling, racquetball, softball, table tennis, volleyball. **Team name:** Spires.

Student services. Adult student services, alcohol/substance abuse counseling, chaplain/spiritual director, career counseling, student employment services, financial aid counseling, health services, on-campus daycare, personal counseling, placement for graduates, veterans' counselor.

Contact. E-mail: admiss@stmary.edu
Phone: (913) 758-6118 Toll-free number: (800) 752-7043
Fax: (913) 758-6140
Brandon Johnson, Director of Admissions, University of St. Mary, 4100 South Fourth Street Trafficway, Leavenworth, KS 66048

Washburn University

Topeka, Kansas
www.washburn.edu **CB code: 6928**

- Public 4-year university
- Commuter campus in small city
- 5,396 degree-seeking undergraduates: 29% part-time, 61% women
- 843 degree-seeking graduate students
- 47% graduate within 6 years

General. Founded in 1865. Regionally accredited. **Degrees:** 816 bachelor's, 143 associate awarded; master's, first professional offered. **ROTC:** Army, Naval, Air Force. **Location:** 60 miles from Kansas City. **Calendar:** Semester, extensive summer session. **Full-time faculty:** 265 total; 83% have terminal degrees, 11% minority, 50% women. **Part-time faculty:** 259 total; 42% have terminal degrees, 8% minority, 49% women. **Class size:** 43% < 20, 50% 20-39, 6% 40-49, 2% 50-99. **Special facilities:** Concert hall, observatory, planetarium, 30-acre natural study and research area.

Freshman class profile. 1,573 applied, 1,573 admitted, 830 enrolled.

Mid 50% test scores		**Rank in top tenth:**	12%
ACT composite:	19-25	**End year in good standing:**	63%
GPA 3.75 or higher:	22%	**Return as sophomores:**	63%
GPA 3.50-3.74:	15%	**Out-of-state:**	9%
GPA 3.0-3.49:	29%	**Live on campus:**	60%
GPA 2.0-2.99:	31%	**Fraternities:**	10%
Rank in top quarter:	32%	**Sororities:**	8%

Basis for selection. Open admission, but selective for some programs. Special requirements for health science programs, nursing, school of business, and education. ACT or ASSET required of all students for placement purposes.

High school preparation. College-preparatory program recommended. Recommended units include English 4, mathematics 3, social studies 3, history 1, science 3, foreign language 2 and computer science 1.

2008-2009 Annual costs. Tuition/fees: $5,996; $13,496 out-of-state. Room/board: $5,602. Books/supplies: $1,400. Personal expenses: $2,486.

2008-2009 Financial aid. **Need-based:** 632 full-time freshmen applied for aid; 443 were judged to have need; 441 of these received aid. Average need met was 43%. Average scholarship/grant was $4,296; average loan $3,338. 32% of total undergraduate aid awarded as scholarships/grants, 68% as loans/jobs. **Non-need-based:** Awarded to 1,772 full-time undergraduates, including 345 freshmen. Scholarships awarded for academics, alumni affiliation, art, athletics, job skills, leadership, minority status, music/drama, religious affiliation, ROTC, state residency.

Application procedures. **Admission:** Priority date 7/1; deadline 8/1. $20 fee. Admission notification on a rolling basis beginning on or about 9/1. **Financial aid:** Priority date 2/15; no closing date. FAFSA required. Applicants notified on a rolling basis starting 3/15; must reply within 4 week(s) of notification.

Academics. **Special study options:** Cooperative education, cross-registration, distance learning, double major, dual enrollment of high school students, ESL, honors, independent study, internships, liberal arts/career combination, student-designed major, study abroad, teacher certification program. **Credit/placement by examination:** AP, CLEP, institutional tests. 40 credit hours maximum toward bachelor's degree. **Support services:** Learning center, remedial instruction, study skills assistance, tutoring, writing center.

Majors. **Biology:** General, biochemistry. **Business:** General, accounting, business admin, finance, managerial economics, marketing. **Communications:** General, media studies. **Computer sciences:** General, systems analysis. **Education:** General, art, biology, chemistry, early childhood, elementary, English, French, German, history, mathematics, music, physical, science, secondary, Spanish. **Foreign languages:** French, German, Spanish. **Health:** Athletic training, clinical lab technology, health services, nursing (RN), predental, premedicine, prepharmacy, preveterinary, sonography, substance abuse counseling. **History:** General. **Interdisciplinary:** Gerontology. **Legal studies:** Paralegal, prelaw. **Liberal arts:** Arts/sciences. **Math:** General. **Parks/recreation:** Exercise sciences, health/fitness, sports admin. **Philosophy/religion:** Philosophy, religion. **Physical sciences:** General, chemistry, physics. **Protective services:** Corrections, criminal justice, forensics, law enforcement admin, police science, security services. **Psychology:** General. **Public administration:** General, social work. **Social sciences:** Anthropology, economics, political science, sociology. **Visual/performing arts:** General, art, art history/conservation, dramatic, music performance, studio arts. **Other:** Design and applied arts.

Most popular majors. Business/marketing 24%, communications/journalism 6%, education 8%, health sciences 22%, security/protective services 9%.

Computing on campus. 1,200 workstations in dormitories, library, computer center, student center. Dormitories wired for high-speed internet access and linked to campus network. Commuter students can connect to campus network. Online course registration, online library, helpline, student web hosting, wireless network available.

Student life. Freshman orientation: Available. Preregistration for classes offered. Half-day session in summer for pre-registration; 3-day session prior to start of classes. **Housing:** Coed dorms, apartments, fraternity/sorority housing, wellness housing available. $200 partly refundable deposit. Special interest housing available. **Activities:** Bands, campus ministries, choral groups, dance, drama, film society, international student organizations, literary magazine, music ensembles, Model UN, musical theater, student government, student newspaper, symphony orchestra, TV station, College Republicans, Young Democrats, Learning in the Community, Campus Crusade for Christ, Circle K, Project Equal, Fellowship of Christian Athletes, Hispanic American Leadership Organization, Black Men and Women of Today.

Athletics. NCAA. **Intercollegiate:** Baseball M, basketball, cheerleading, football (tackle) M, golf M, soccer W, softball W, tennis, volleyball W. **Intramural:** Badminton, basketball, football (non-tackle), golf, soccer, softball, swimming, table tennis, tennis, volleyball. **Team name:** Ichabods.

Student services. Adult student services, alcohol/substance abuse counseling, career counseling, services for economically disadvantaged, student employment services, financial aid counseling, health services, minority student services, personal counseling, placement for graduates, veterans' counselor. **Physically disabled:** Services for visually, hearing impaired.

Contact. E-mail: admissions@washburn.edu
Phone: (785) 670-1030 Toll-free number: (800) 332-0291 ext. 1030
Fax: (785) 670-1113
Kirk Haskins, Director of Admissions, Washburn University, 1700 SW College Avenue, Morgan 114, Topeka, KS 66621

Wichita State University

Wichita, Kansas
www.wichita.edu **CB code: 6884**

- Public 4-year university
- Commuter campus in large city
- 10,590 degree-seeking undergraduates: 27% part-time, 55% women, 6% African American, 6% Asian American, 6% Hispanic American, 1% Native American, 6% international
- 2,649 degree-seeking graduate students
- 86% of applicants admitted
- 39% graduate within 6 years

General. Founded in 1895. Regionally accredited. **Degrees:** 1,839 bachelor's, 80 associate awarded; master's, doctoral offered. **Calendar:** Semester, extensive summer session. **Full-time faculty:** 472 total; 78% have terminal degrees, 16% minority, 40% women. **Part-time faculty:** 44 total; 50% have terminal degrees, 7% minority, 52% women. **Class size:** 46% < 20, 37% 20-39, 6% 40-49, 10% 50-99, 2% >100. **Special facilities:** Sculpture garden, wind tunnels, Marcusson pipe organ, flow-visualization water tunnel, National Aviation Research Institute, observatory, anthropology museum, rock climbing wall, bowling alley.

Freshman class profile. 3,064 applied, 2,634 admitted, 1,420 enrolled.

Mid 50% test scores		**Rank in top tenth:**	20%
SAT critical reading:	470-620	**End year in good standing:**	75%
SAT math:	500-650	**Return as sophomores:**	72%
ACT composite:	21-26	**Out-of-state:**	6%
GPA 3.75 or higher:	25%	**Live on campus:**	32%
GPA 3.50-3.74:	18%	**International:**	4%
GPA 3.0-3.49:	34%	**Fraternities:**	12%
GPA 2.0-2.99:	22%	**Sororities:**	2%
Rank in top quarter:	45%		

Basis for selection. In-state criteria: 21 ACT or greater, rank in top 1/3 of high school class, or minimum 2.00 GPA in pre-college curriculum. Some academic colleges within WSU require a higher GPA for admission. Out-of-state criteria: varies by college. **Homeschooled:** State high school equivalency certificate required. ACT required.

High school preparation. College-preparatory program recommended. 14 units required. Required units include English 4, mathematics 3, social studies 3, science 3 and computer science 1.

2008-2009 Annual costs. Tuition/fees: $5,084; $12,761 out-of-state. Room/board: $5,860. Books/supplies: $945. Personal expenses: $1,661.

2008-2009 Financial aid. Need-based: 1,157 full-time freshmen applied for aid; 578 were judged to have need; 565 of these received aid. Average need met was 48%. Average scholarship/grant was $3,661; average loan $2,933. 30% of total undergraduate aid awarded as scholarships/grants, 70% as loans/jobs. **Non-need-based:** Awarded to 2,221 full-time undergraduates, including 745 freshmen. Scholarships awarded for academics, alumni affiliation, art, athletics, leadership, music/drama. **Additional information:** Top freshman applicants admitted by October 1 invited to university scholarship competition.

Application procedures. Admission: No deadline. $30 fee. Admission notification on a rolling basis. **Financial aid:** Priority date 3/1; no closing date. FAFSA required. Applicants notified on a rolling basis starting 3/1; must reply within 2 week(s) of notification.

Academics. 24-hour study room with Internet access. All library databases and other software maintained for student use. **Special study options:** Accelerated study, cooperative education, distance learning, double major, dual enrollment of high school students, ESL, exchange student, honors, independent study, internships, liberal arts/career combination, study abroad, teacher certification program, Washington semester. Peace Corps Returnee Program. **Credit/placement by examination:** AP, CLEP, IB, SAT, ACT, institutional tests. 30 credit hours maximum toward associate degree, 60 toward bachelor's. **Support services:** Learning center, pre-admission summer program, reduced course load, remedial instruction, study skills assistance, tutoring, writing center.

Majors. Area/ethnic studies: Women's. **Biology:** General. **Business:** Accounting, business admin, finance, human resources, international, management information systems, marketing. **Communications:** General. **Computer sciences:** General, computer science. **Education:** Art, early childhood, elementary, music, physical, secondary. **Engineering:** Aerospace, computer, electrical, industrial, manufacturing, mechanical. **Foreign languages:** French, Latin, Spanish. **Health:** Athletic training, communication disorders, dental hygiene, health care admin, physician assistant, staff services technology. **History:** General. **Interdisciplinary:** Classical/archaeology, gerontology. **Legal studies:** Prelaw. **Liberal arts:** Arts/sciences. **Math:** General. **Parks/recreation:** Exercise sciences, sports admin. **Philosophy/religion:** Philosophy. **Physical sciences:** Chemistry, geology, physics. **Protective services:** Criminal justice. **Psychology:** General. **Public administration:** Social work. **Social sciences:** Anthropology, economics, political science, sociology. **Visual/performing arts:** General, art, art history/conservation, commercial/advertising art, dramatic, music performance, music theory/composition, studio arts, voice/opera. **Other:** Athletic training, Biochemistry, International studies.

Most popular majors. Business/marketing 24%, education 9%, engineering/engineering technologies 8%, health sciences 11%, psychology 7%.

Computing on campus. 1,500 workstations in dormitories, library, computer center, student center. Dormitories wired for high-speed internet access and linked to campus network. Commuter students can connect to campus network. Online course registration, online library, helpline, wireless network available.

Student life. Freshman orientation: Mandatory. Preregistration for classes offered. Held prior to fall semester and spring semester. **Policies:** Freshmen are required to live on campus, however, exceptions are made for freshmen who are 21 or older, married, living with a parent, legal gaurdian, grandparent, aunt or uncle in the greater Sedgwick County area, are taking fewer than 9 credit hours, or living in official Greek housing. **Housing:** Guaranteed on-campus for freshmen. Coed dorms, special housing for disabled, apartments, fraternity/sorority housing available. **Activities:** Bands, campus ministries, choral groups, dance, drama, film society, international student organizations, literary magazine, music ensembles, Model UN, musical theater, opera, radio station, student government, student newspaper, symphony orchestra, TV station, Campus Crusade for Christ, College Republicans, Chinese Student Friendship Association, Black Student Union, Hispanic American Leadership Association, Students in Free Enterprise, Association of Hindu Students, Muslim Student Association, That Gay Group, Emory Lindquist Honor Society.

Athletics. NCAA. **Intercollegiate:** Baseball M, basketball, cheerleading, cross-country, golf, softball W, tennis, track and field, volleyball W. **Intramural:** Badminton, basketball, football (non-tackle), golf, racquetball, rowing (crew), soccer, softball, swimming, table tennis, tennis, volleyball. **Team name:** Shockers.

Student services. Adult student services, alcohol/substance abuse counseling, chaplain/spiritual director, career counseling, services for economically disadvantaged, student employment services, financial aid counseling, health services, minority student services, on-campus daycare, personal counseling, placement for graduates, veterans' counselor, women's services. **Physically disabled:** Services for visually, speech, hearing impaired.

Contact. E-mail: admissions@wichita.edu
Phone: (316) 978-3085 Toll-free number: (800) 362-2594
Fax: (316) 978-3174
Bobby Gandu, Director of Admissions, Wichita State University, 1845 Fairmount Box 124, Wichita, KS 67260-0124

Kentucky

Alice Lloyd College

Pippa Passes, Kentucky
www.alc.edu **CB code: 1098**

- Private 4-year liberal arts college
- Residential campus in rural community
- 615 degree-seeking undergraduates
- 41% of applicants admitted
- SAT or ACT (ACT writing optional) required

General. Founded in 1923. Regionally accredited. **Degrees:** 110 bachelor's awarded. **Location:** 150 miles from Lexington, 100 miles from Huntington, West Virginia. **Calendar:** Semester. **Full-time faculty:** 30 total. **Part-time faculty:** 15 total. **Class size:** 41% < 20, 54% 20-39, 5% 40-49. **Special facilities:** Appalachian history collection, photographic archives.

Freshman class profile. 1,659 applied, 680 admitted, 187 enrolled.

Mid 50% test scores		**GPA 3.0-3.49:**	33%
SAT critical reading:	440-590	**GPA 2.0-2.99:**	23%
SAT math:	480-570	**Rank in top quarter:**	58%
SAT writing:	430-530	**Rank in top tenth:**	21%
ACT composite:	17-23	**Out-of-state:**	21%
GPA 3.75 or higher:	21%	**Live on campus:**	91%
GPA 3.50-3.74:	21%		

Basis for selection. High school record and test scores important. Essay and interview recommended. **Homeschooled:** Transcript of courses and grades, letter of recommendation (nonparent) required. Interview highly recommended.

High school preparation. 12 units required. Required units include English 4, mathematics 3, social studies 2 and science 3.

2008-2009 Annual costs. Tuition/fees: $7,300. Guaranteed tuition for students from 108-county central Appalachian service area in Kentucky, West Virginia, Virginia, Tennessee, and Ohio. Room/board: $5,450. Books/supplies: $850. Personal expenses: $1,300.

2007-2008 Financial aid. Non-need-based: Scholarships awarded for athletics, minority status, state residency. **Additional information:** All students receive financial aid through student work program. No student denied admission because of inability to pay. All full-time students required to work minimum of 10 hours per week.

Application procedures. Admission: Priority date 5/1; no deadline. No application fee. Admission notification on a rolling basis beginning on or about 9/1. **Financial aid:** Priority date 3/15; no closing date. FAFSA required. Applicants notified on a rolling basis starting 4/1; must reply within 6 week(s) of notification.

Academics. Scholarships for graduate work following graduation. **Special study options:** Double major, independent study, internships, liberal arts/career combination, student-designed major, study abroad, teacher certification program, Washington semester. **Credit/placement by examination:** AP, CLEP, IB, SAT, ACT, institutional tests. 30 credit hours maximum toward bachelor's degree. Limited number of hours of credit by examination may be counted toward degree, decided on individual basis. **Support services:** Reduced course load, remedial instruction, study skills assistance, tutoring, writing center.

Majors. Biology: General. **Business:** Business admin. **Education:** Biology, elementary, English, mathematics, middle, physical, science, secondary, social studies. **History:** General. **Interdisciplinary:** Biological/physical sciences. **Parks/recreation:** General. **Social sciences:** General.

Most popular majors. Biology 26%, business/marketing 18%, education 23%, English 6%, history 10%, social sciences 11%.

Computing on campus. 80 workstations in library, computer center. Dormitories wired for high-speed internet access and linked to campus network. Online library, helpline, repair service, wireless network available.

Student life. Freshman orientation: Mandatory. Preregistration for classes offered. Held 3 days before start of first semester. **Policies:** Zero tolerance of on-campus alcohol and/or drug usage or possession. **Housing:** Guaranteed on-campus for all undergraduates. Single-sex dorms available. $50 deposit, deadline 5/15. **Activities:** Choral groups, drama, radio station, student government, student newspaper, Students for Christ, Baptist student union, cultural diversity club, children's outreach club, community service volunteers, Circle K.

Athletics. NAIA. **Intercollegiate:** Baseball M, basketball, cheerleading M, cross-country, softball W. **Intramural:** Basketball, bowling, football (non-tackle), golf, racquetball, soccer, softball, swimming, table tennis, tennis, volleyball, weight lifting. **Team name:** Eagles.

Student services. Alcohol/substance abuse counseling, career counseling, student employment services, financial aid counseling, health services, on-campus daycare, personal counseling, placement for graduates, veterans' counselor.

Contact. E-mail: admissions@alc.edu
Phone: (606) 368-6036 Toll-free number: (888) 280-4252
Fax: (606) 368-6215
Bryan Swafford, Director of Admissions, Alice Lloyd College, 100 Purpose Road, Pippa Passes, KY 41844

Asbury College

Wilmore, Kentucky **CB member**
www.asbury.edu **CB code: 1019**

- Private 4-year liberal arts college affiliated with interdenominational tradition
- Residential campus in small town
- 1,216 degree-seeking undergraduates: 2% part-time, 60% women, 1% African American, 2% Asian American, 2% Hispanic American, 1% international
- 100 degree-seeking graduate students
- 56% of applicants admitted
- SAT or ACT (ACT writing optional), application essay required
- 71% graduate within 6 years

General. Founded in 1890. Regionally accredited. **Degrees:** 251 bachelor's awarded; master's offered. **ROTC:** Army, Air Force. **Location:** 20 miles from Lexington. **Calendar:** Semester, limited summer session. **Full-time faculty:** 80 total; 72% have terminal degrees, 2% minority, 31% women. **Part-time faculty:** 61 total; 26% have terminal degrees, 12% minority, 48% women. **Class size:** 57% < 20, 38% 20-39, 6% 40-49.

Freshman class profile. 1,563 applied, 872 admitted, 313 enrolled.

Mid 50% test scores		**GPA 2.0-2.99:**	13%
SAT critical reading:	520-660	**Rank in top quarter:**	61%
SAT math:	500-620	**Rank in top tenth:**	31%
ACT composite:	21-27	**Return as sophomores:**	79%
GPA 3.75 or higher:	47%	**Out-of-state:**	58%
GPA 3.50-3.74:	18%	**Live on campus:**	94%
GPA 3.0-3.49:	22%	**International:**	1%

Basis for selection. Careful consideration given to academic records, test scores, application essays, references, and ability to benefit. Probationary acceptance possible if GPA below 2.5. ACT required prior to admission to education department; both ACT and SAT required for presidential level scholarships. Interview recommended for music majors, academically weak applicants, scholarship applicants. Audition required for music majors. Portfolio recommended for art majors. **Homeschooled:** Transcript of courses and grades, state high school equivalency certificate required.

High school preparation. College-preparatory program recommended. 15 units recommended. Recommended units include English 4, mathematics 3, social studies 1, history 1, science 2 (laboratory 2) and foreign language 2.

2009-2010 Annual costs. Tuition/fees: $23,748. Room/board: $5,620. Books/supplies: $815. Personal expenses: $1,240.

Financial aid. Non-need-based: Scholarships awarded for academics, alumni affiliation, art, athletics, leadership, minority status, music/drama, religious affiliation, ROTC.

Application procedures. Admission: Priority date 5/1; no deadline. $30 fee, may be waived for applicants with need, free for online applicants. Admission notification on a rolling basis. Confirmation of intention to enroll requires $200 pre-tuition deposit within 30 days of admission notification. **Financial aid:** Priority date 3/1; no closing date. Institutional form required. Applicants notified on a rolling basis starting 1/31; must reply within 4 week(s) of notification.

Academics. **Special study options:** Double major, ESL, internships, study abroad, teacher certification program, urban semester, Washington semester. Exchange program with colleges in Christian College Consortium, 3-2 programs in engineering with the University of Kentucky. **Credit/placement by examination:** AP, CLEP, IB, SAT, ACT, institutional tests. **Support services:** Remedial instruction, study skills assistance, tutoring, writing center.

Majors. **Agriculture:** Equestrian studies. **Biology:** General, biochemistry. **Business:** General, accounting. **Communications:** Journalism. **Communications technology:** Radio/tv. **Education:** Art, elementary, middle, music, physical. **Foreign languages:** Biblical, classics, French, Spanish. **Health:** Health services. **History:** General. **Math:** General, computational. **Parks/recreation:** Facilities management, health/fitness, sports admin. **Philosophy/religion:** Philosophy. **Physical sciences:** General, chemistry. **Psychology:** General. **Public administration:** Social work. **Social sciences:** General, political science, sociology. **Theology:** Bible, missionary, religious ed, sacred music, youth ministry. **Visual/performing arts:** Dramatic, studio arts. **Other:** Mathematics, financial, Pre-physical therapy.

Most popular majors. Business/marketing 13%, communication technologies 16%, education 8%, English 8%, foreign language 6%, history 6%, psychology 7%, theological studies 10%.

Computing on campus. 200 workstations in dormitories, library, computer center, student center. Dormitories wired for high-speed internet access and linked to campus network. Commuter students can connect to campus network. Online course registration, online library, helpline, repair service available.

Student life. **Freshman orientation:** Mandatory. Preregistration for classes offered. Held weekend before fall semester begins. **Policies:** Christian values stressed. Religious observance required. **Housing:** Guaranteed on-campus for freshmen. Single-sex dorms, apartments available. **Activities:** Bands, campus ministries, choral groups, drama, literary magazine, music ensembles, musical theater, opera, radio station, student government, student newspaper, symphony orchestra, TV station, Christian service association, student fellowships, Impact, Asburians for Life, ministerial association, outdoors club.

Athletics. NAIA, NCCAA. **Intercollegiate:** Baseball M, basketball, cross-country, diving, soccer, softball W, swimming, tennis, volleyball W. **Intramural:** Basketball, football (non-tackle), golf, racquetball, soccer, softball, volleyball. **Team name:** Eagles.

Student services. Chaplain/spiritual director, career counseling, student employment services, financial aid counseling, health services, minority student services, personal counseling.

Contact. E-mail: admissions@asbury.edu
Phone: (859) 858-3511 ext. 2142 Toll-free number: (800) 888-1818
Fax: (859) 858-3921
Lisa Harper, Director of Admissions, Asbury College, One Macklem Drive, Wilmore, KY 40390-1198

Beckfield College

Florence, Kentucky
www.beckfield.edu **CB code: 3404**

- For-profit 4-year business, health science and nursing college
- Commuter campus in large town
- 600 degree-seeking undergraduates
- Interview required

General. Accredited by ACICS. **Degrees:** 8 bachelor's, 129 associate awarded. **Location:** 10 miles from Cincinnati. **Calendar:** Quarter, extensive summer session. **Full-time faculty:** 20 total. **Part-time faculty:** 30 total. **Class size:** 100% < 20.

Basis for selection. Open admission, but selective for some programs. Nursing program requires qualifying ACT or SAT scores. **Homeschooled:** Transcript of courses and grades required. Accredited home study course will be considered for admission.

2008-2009 Annual costs. Tuition/fees: $12,927. Fees vary by program. Books/supplies: $1,200.

2007-2008 Financial aid. All financial aid based on need. **Additional information:** Deadline for filing of financial aid forms is end of first week of classes.

Application procedures. **Admission:** No deadline. $150 fee. Application must be submitted on paper. Admission notification on a rolling basis. **Financial aid:** FAFSA required. Applicants notified on a rolling basis.

Academics. **Special study options:** Combined bachelor's/graduate degree, independent study, internships. **Credit/placement by examination:** CLEP, IB, institutional tests. **Support services:** Reduced course load, remedial instruction, study skills assistance, tutoring.

Majors. **Business:** Business admin. **Health:** Nursing (RN). **Legal studies:** Paralegal. **Protective services:** Law enforcement admin.

Computing on campus. 90 workstations in library, computer center. Online library, wireless network available.

Student life. **Freshman orientation:** Mandatory. Preregistration for classes offered. Held for half day 3 days before beginning of quarter.

Student services. Alcohol/substance abuse counseling, career counseling, student employment services, financial aid counseling, personal counseling, placement for graduates, veterans' counselor.

Contact. E-mail: lboerger@beckfield.edu
Phone: (859) 371-9393 Fax: (859) 371-5096
Leah Boerger, Director of Admissions, Beckfield College, 16 Spiral Drive, Florence, KY 41042

Bellarmine University

Louisville, Kentucky **CB member**
www.bellarmine.edu **CB code: 1056**

- Private 4-year university and liberal arts college affiliated with Roman Catholic Church
- Commuter campus in very large city
- 2,068 degree-seeking undergraduates: 7% part-time, 64% women, 3% African American, 3% Asian American, 2% Hispanic American, 2% international
- 682 degree-seeking graduate students
- 58% of applicants admitted
- SAT or ACT (ACT writing optional), application essay required
- 60% graduate within 6 years; 23% enter graduate study

General. Founded in 1950. Regionally accredited. **Degrees:** 521 bachelor's awarded; master's, doctoral offered. **ROTC:** Army, Air Force. **Location:** 7 miles from downtown, 100 miles from Cincinnati. **Calendar:** Semester, extensive summer session. **Full-time faculty:** 150 total; 78% have terminal degrees, 6% minority, 48% women. **Part-time faculty:** 175 total; 30% have terminal degrees, 9% minority, 51% women. **Class size:** 59% < 20, 37% 20-39, 3% 40-49, less than 1% 50-99.

Freshman class profile. 4,336 applied, 2,534 admitted, 572 enrolled.

Mid 50% test scores		**Rank in top tenth:**	22%
SAT critical reading:	500-600	**End year in good standing:**	94%
SAT math:	500-600	**Return as sophomores:**	80%
ACT composite:	22-26	**Out-of-state:**	41%
GPA 3.75 or higher:	31%	**Live on campus:**	73%
GPA 3.50-3.74:	25%	**International:**	2%
GPA 3.0-3.49:	29%	**Fraternities:**	1%
GPA 2.0-2.99:	15%	**Sororities:**	1%
Rank in top quarter:	55%		

Basis for selection. Minimum 2.5 GPA, college preparatory curriculum, 21 ACT or 1000 SAT (exclusive of Writing), strong high school recommendation, submission of acceptable essay (if requested). Applicants not meeting requirements may be admitted on strength of each criterion. School activities also considered. Interview recommended. Audition required of music majors. Portfolio recommended for art majors.

High school preparation. 20 units required; 26 recommended. Required and recommended units include English 4, mathematics 3-4, social studies 2-3, history 1-2, science 3-4 (laboratory 2), foreign language 2 and academic electives 5-7.

2009-2010 Annual costs. Tuition/fees: $28,900. Room and board based on 10 meal per week plan. Room/board: $8,400.

2008-2009 Financial aid. **Need-based:** 500 full-time freshmen applied for aid; 428 were judged to have need; 428 of these received aid. Average need met was 74%. Average scholarship/grant was $19,981; average loan $3,586. 76% of total undergraduate aid awarded as scholarships/grants, 24% as loans/jobs. **Non-need-based:** Awarded to 1,239 full-time undergraduates, including 358 freshmen. Scholarships awarded for academics, alumni affiliation, art, athletics, leadership, minority status, music/drama, religious affiliation, ROTC, state residency.

Application procedures. Admission: Priority date 2/1; no deadline. $25 fee, may be waived for applicants with need, free for online applicants. Admission notification on a rolling basis beginning on or about 9/1. Must reply by May 1 or within 3 week(s) if notified thereafter. **Financial aid:** Priority date 3/1; no closing date. FAFSA required. Applicants notified on a rolling basis starting 3/15; must reply by 5/1 or within 3 week(s) of notification.

Academics. Special study options: Accelerated study, combined bachelor's/graduate degree, cross-registration, double major, dual enrollment of high school students, honors, independent study, internships, liberal arts/career combination, semester at sea, student-designed major, study abroad, teacher certification program, Washington semester. **Credit/placement by examination:** AP, CLEP, IB, institutional tests. **Support services:** Learning center, reduced course load, study skills assistance, tutoring.

Majors. Biology: General, biochemistry. **Business:** Accounting, actuarial science, business admin. **Communications:** General. **Computer sciences:** General, computer science. **Education:** Elementary, middle, special. **Engineering:** Computer. **Health:** Clinical lab science, nursing (RN), respiratory therapy technology. **History:** General. **Liberal arts:** Arts/sciences. **Math:** General. **Philosophy/religion:** Philosophy. **Physical sciences:** Chemistry. **Protective services:** Law enforcement admin. **Psychology:** General. **Social sciences:** Economics, political science, sociology. **Theology:** Theology. **Visual/performing arts:** Art, arts management. **Other:** Foreign languages and international studies.

Most popular majors. Business/marketing 14%, communications/journalism 6%, health sciences 31%, psychology 10%, social sciences 7%.

Computing on campus. 600 workstations in dormitories, library, computer center, student center. Dormitories wired for high-speed internet access and linked to campus network. Commuter students can connect to campus network. Online course registration, helpline, repair service, wireless network available.

Student life. Freshman orientation: Mandatory, $300 fee. Preregistration for classes offered. Off-campus 3-day session held in August before classes begin. **Housing:** Guaranteed on-campus for freshmen. Coed dorms, single-sex dorms, special housing for disabled, wellness housing available. $200 fully refundable deposit, deadline 5/1. Pets allowed in dorm rooms. Suites available to upperclassmen. **Activities:** Bands, campus ministries, choral groups, dance, drama, literary magazine, music ensembles, musical theater, opera, radio station, student government, student newspaper, symphony orchestra, Catholic students association, Fellowship of Christian Athletes, Hillel, Highland community ministries, Habitat for Humanity.

Athletics. NCAA. **Intercollegiate:** Baseball M, basketball, bowling, cross-country, field hockey W, golf, lacrosse M, soccer, softball W, tennis, track and field, volleyball W. **Intramural:** Basketball, cheerleading, football (non-tackle) M, golf, soccer, softball, swimming, tennis, volleyball. **Team name:** Knights.

Student services. Adult student services, chaplain/spiritual director, career counseling, student employment services, financial aid counseling, health services, personal counseling, placement for graduates. **Physically disabled:** Services for visually, hearing impaired.

Contact. E-mail: admissions@bellarmine.edu
Phone: (502) 452-8131 Toll-free number: (800) 274-4723 ext. 8131
Fax: (502) 452-8002
Timothy Sturgeon, Dean of Admissions, Bellarmine University, 2001 Newburg Road, Louisville, KY 40205

Berea College

Berea, Kentucky — **CB member**
www.berea.edu — **CB code: 1060**

- Private 4-year liberal arts college
- Residential campus in small town
- 1,491 degree-seeking undergraduates: 60% women, 17% African American, 1% Asian American, 2% Hispanic American, 1% Native American, 7% international
- 22% of applicants admitted
- SAT or ACT (ACT writing optional), application essay, interview required
- 64% graduate within 6 years

General. Founded in 1855. Regionally accredited. **Degrees:** 332 bachelor's awarded. **Location:** 40 miles from Lexington, 100 miles from Louisville. **Calendar:** 4-1-4, limited summer session. **Full-time faculty:** 131 total; 88% have terminal degrees, 13% minority, 42% women. **Part-time faculty:** 52 total; 4% minority, 56% women. **Class size:** 61% < 20, 38% 20-39, less than 1% 40-49. **Special facilities:** Geology museum, planetarium with observatory, Ecovillage, Appalachian artifacts and exhibit studio.

Freshman class profile. 2,468 applied, 531 admitted, 413 enrolled.

Mid 50% test scores		**GPA 2.0-2.99:**	15%
SAT critical reading:	490-620	**Rank in top quarter:**	64%
SAT math:	480-590	**Rank in top tenth:**	25%
SAT writing:	480-610	**Return as sophomores:**	78%
ACT composite:	21-25	**Out-of-state:**	56%
GPA 3.75 or higher:	37%	**Live on campus:**	98%
GPA 3.50-3.74:	16%	**International:**	6%
GPA 3.0-3.49:	32%		

Basis for selection. Rank in top half of class, recommendations, essays, interviews, test scores, involvement in community and school activities important. Financial need absolute prerequisite for admission. **Homeschooled:** If transcript not available, list of home schooled courses and titles of textbooks used required.

High school preparation. College-preparatory program required. 13 units recommended. Recommended units include English 4, mathematics 3, social studies 1, history 1, science 2 (laboratory 2) and foreign language 2.

2008-2009 Annual costs. Books/supplies: $750. Personal expenses: $1,350.

2008-2009 Financial aid. All financial aid based on need. 413 full-time freshmen applied for aid; 413 were judged to have need; 413 of these received aid. Average need met was 94%. Average scholarship/grant was $31,200; average loan $927. 93% of total undergraduate aid awarded as scholarships/grants, 7% as loans/jobs.

Application procedures. Admission: Closing date 4/30. No application fee. Admission notification on a rolling basis beginning on or about 12/20. Must reply by 5/1. **Financial aid:** Priority date 3/15; no closing date. FAFSA required. Applicants notified on a rolling basis starting 4/15.

Academics. All students are provided with a laptop computer that becomes their property upon graduation. **Special study options:** Combined bachelor's/graduate degree, double major, ESL, exchange student, honors, independent study, internships, student-designed major, study abroad, teacher certification program. 3-2 engineering program with Washington University (MO) and University of Kentucky. **Credit/placement by examination:** AP, CLEP, SAT, ACT, institutional tests. Unlimited number of credit hours may be counted toward degree. **Support services:** Learning center, remedial instruction, study skills assistance, tutoring, writing center.

Majors. Agriculture: General. **Area/ethnic studies:** African-American, Asian, women's. **Biology:** General, neuroanatomy. **Business:** General, accounting, finance, marketing. **Communications:** Media studies. **Computer sciences:** General. **Education:** General, art, elementary, family/consumer sciences, kindergarten/preschool, middle, music, secondary, technology/industrial arts. **Engineering technology:** Manufacturing. **Family/consumer sciences:** General. **Foreign languages:** French, German, Latin, Spanish. **Health:** Nursing (RN). **History:** General. **Math:** General. **Parks/recreation:** Exercise sciences, health/fitness. **Philosophy/religion:** Philosophy, religion. **Physical sciences:** Chemistry, physics. **Psychology:** General. **Social sciences:** Economics, political science, sociology. **Visual/performing arts:** Art, art history/conservation, dramatic, music performance, studio arts, voice/opera. **Other:** Applied science in mathematics.

Most popular majors. Biology 7%, business/marketing 12%, education 6%, family/consumer sciences 7%, health sciences 6%, social sciences 8%, visual/performing arts 8%.

Computing on campus. Dormitories wired for high-speed internet access and linked to campus network. Online course registration, online library, helpline, repair service, wireless network available.

Student life. Freshman orientation: Mandatory. Preregistration for classes offered. Held during the summer for a long weekend; week-long session before classes begin. **Housing:** Guaranteed on-campus for all undergraduates. Single-sex dorms, apartments, wellness housing available. Apartments for single parent students; 9 small houses which hold 9-12 upperclassmen; Ecovillage. **Activities:** Bands, campus ministries, choral groups, dance, drama, international student organizations, literary magazine, music ensembles, student government, student newspaper, religious organizations, People Who Care, Students for Appalachia, Habitat for Humanity, Cosmopolitan Club.

Athletics. NAIA. **Intercollegiate:** Baseball M, basketball, cross-country, diving, golf M, soccer, softball W, swimming, tennis, track and field, volleyball W. **Intramural:** Basketball, football (non-tackle), racquetball, soccer, softball, volleyball. **Team name:** Mountaineers.

Student services. Adult student services, alcohol/substance abuse counseling, chaplain/spiritual director, career counseling, services for economically disadvantaged, student employment services, financial aid counseling,

health services, minority student services, on-campus daycare, personal counseling, placement for graduates, veterans' counselor, women's services. **Physically disabled:** Services for visually, speech, hearing impaired.

Contact. E-mail: admissions@berea.edu
Phone: (859) 985-3500 Toll-free number: (800) 326-5948
Fax: (859) 985-3512
Joe Bagnoli, Director of Admissions, Berea College, CPO 2220, Berea, KY 40404

Brescia University

Owensboro, Kentucky
www.brescia.edu **CB code: 1071**

- Private 4-year university and liberal arts college affiliated with Roman Catholic Church
- Residential campus in small city
- 462 degree-seeking undergraduates: 10% part-time, 60% women
- 44 degree-seeking graduate students
- 73% of applicants admitted
- SAT or ACT (ACT writing optional), application essay required
- 56% graduate within 6 years

General. Founded in 1950. Regionally accredited. Weekend college for nontraditional students. Lay ministry formation program nationally accredited. **Degrees:** 91 bachelor's, 5 associate awarded; master's offered. **Location:** 120 miles from Louisville; 120 miles from Nashville, Tennessee. **Calendar:** Semester, limited summer session. **Full-time faculty:** 43 total; 58% have terminal degrees, 16% minority, 51% women. **Part-time faculty:** 19 total; 10% have terminal degrees, 10% minority, 47% women. **Class size:** 84% < 20, 16% 20-39. **Special facilities:** Observatory, greenhouse.

Freshman class profile. 577 applied, 423 admitted, 109 enrolled.

Mid 50% test scores			
SAT critical reading:	380-450	GPA 3.0-3.49:	36%
SAT math:	410-540	GPA 2.0-2.99:	36%
ACT composite:	18-23	Return as sophomores:	83%
GPA 3.75 or higher:	19%	Out-of-state:	21%
GPA 3.50-3.74:	9%	Live on campus:	73%

Basis for selection. Students admitted based on high school grades and ACT/SAT scores. **Homeschooled:** Transcript of courses and grades required.

High school preparation. College-preparatory program recommended. 17 units recommended. Recommended units include English 4, mathematics 3, social studies 2, history 2, science 2, foreign language 2 and academic electives 2. 2 units in fine arts, 2 units in computer science also recommended.

2008-2009 Annual costs. Tuition/fees: $15,440. Room/board: $7,000. Books/supplies: $1,000. Personal expenses: $1,800.

2008-2009 Financial aid. Non-need-based: Scholarships awarded for academics, alumni affiliation, art, athletics, minority status, music/drama, religious affiliation, state residency.

Application procedures. Admission: No deadline. $25 fee, may be waived for applicants with need, free for online applicants. Admission notification on a rolling basis beginning on or about 9/1. **Financial aid:** Priority date 8/1, closing date 8/23. FAFSA required. Applicants notified on a rolling basis starting 3/1; must reply within 3 week(s) of notification.

Academics. Special study options: Combined bachelor's/graduate degree, cross-registration, distance learning, double major, ESL, exchange student, honors. **Credit/placement by examination:** AP, CLEP, IB, SAT, ACT, institutional tests. 18 credit hours maximum toward associate degree, 36 toward bachelor's. **Support services:** Reduced course load, remedial instruction, study skills assistance, tutoring.

Majors. Biology: General. **Business:** General, accounting, business admin. **Computer sciences:** General. **Education:** Art, elementary, middle, secondary, social studies, Spanish, special. **Foreign languages:** Spanish. **Health:** Audiology/speech pathology, clinical lab science, health care admin. **History:** General. **Interdisciplinary:** Biological/physical sciences, math/computer science. **Liberal arts:** Arts/sciences. **Math:** Applied. **Philosophy/religion:** Religion. **Physical sciences:** Chemistry. **Psychology:** General. **Public administration:** Social work. **Social sciences:** General, political science, sociology. **Theology:** Pastoral counseling, theology. **Visual/performing arts:** Art, commercial/advertising art.

Most popular majors. Business/marketing 24%, education 13%, health sciences 8%, liberal arts 14%, psychology 9%, public administration/social services 13%.

Computing on campus. 67 workstations in library, computer center, student center. Dormitories wired for high-speed internet access and linked to campus network. Commuter students can connect to campus network. Online library available.

Student life. Freshman orientation: Available, $100 fee. Preregistration for classes offered. Activities begin on Sunday prior to classes through Tuesday. **Housing:** Guaranteed on-campus for freshmen. Coed dorms, single-sex dorms, special housing for disabled, apartments available. $100 fully refundable deposit, deadline 8/23. Shared apartment houses available. **Activities:** Campus ministries, choral groups, drama, international student organizations, literary magazine, student government, student newspaper, Fellowship of Christian Athletes, social work association, Council for Exceptional Children, Christian Life Experience, Grave Robbers, Alternative Spring Break.

Athletics. NAIA. **Intercollegiate:** Baseball M, basketball, golf, soccer, softball W, tennis W, volleyball W. **Intramural:** Basketball, racquetball, table tennis, volleyball. **Team name:** Bearcats.

Student services. Adult student services, alcohol/substance abuse counseling, chaplain/spiritual director, career counseling, services for economically disadvantaged, student employment services, financial aid counseling, personal counseling, placement for graduates, veterans' counselor, women's services. **Physically disabled:** Services for visually, speech impaired.

Contact. E-mail: admissions@brescia.edu
Phone: (270) 686-4241 Toll-free number: (877) 273-7242
Fax: (270) 686-4314
Chris Houk, Dean of Enrollment, Brescia University, 717 Frederica Street, Owensboro, KY 42301-3023

Campbellsville University

Campbellsville, Kentucky **CB member**
www.campbellsville.edu **CB code: 1097**

- Private 4-year university affiliated with Baptist faith
- Residential campus in large town
- 1,714 degree-seeking undergraduates: 9% part-time, 52% women, 11% African American, 1% Asian American, 1% Hispanic American, 7% international
- 390 degree-seeking graduate students
- 70% of applicants admitted
- SAT or ACT (ACT writing optional) required
- 39% graduate within 6 years

General. Founded in 1906. Regionally accredited. Affiliated with Kentucky Baptist Convention. **Degrees:** 220 bachelor's, 35 associate awarded; master's offered. **ROTC:** Army. **Location:** 80 miles from Louisville, 140 miles from Nashville, Tennessee. **Calendar:** Semester, extensive summer session. **Full-time faculty:** 105 total; 67% have terminal degrees, 8% minority, 49% women. **Part-time faculty:** 173 total; 8% minority, 60% women. **Class size:** 75% < 20, 24% 20-39, less than 1% 40-49, less than 1% 50-99. **Special facilities:** Educational and research woodland, American Civil War institute, fine arts center with computer-enhanced practice room with acoustical adjustment system.

Freshman class profile. 1,760 applied, 1,228 admitted, 449 enrolled.

Mid 50% test scores		Rank in top quarter:	38%
SAT critical reading:	410-540	Rank in top tenth:	17%
SAT math:	420-560	End year in good standing:	86%
ACT composite:	18-23	Return as sophomores:	71%
GPA 3.75 or higher:	22%	Out-of-state:	15%
GPA 3.50-3.74:	10%	Live on campus:	68%
GPA 3.0-3.49:	29%	International:	9%
GPA 2.0-2.99:	38%		

Basis for selection. Achievement in strong high school program and satisfactory ACT or SAT scores most important. Special consideration for entry to basic skills program may be given to other highly motivated and potentially successful applicants. Interview and essay recommended. **Homeschooled:** State high school equivalency certificate required.

High school preparation. College-preparatory program recommended. 21 units recommended. Recommended units include English 4, mathematics 3, social studies 2, history 2, science 3 (laboratory 1), foreign language 1 and academic electives 6. At least 2 units in the arts recommended for academic elective.

2008-2009 Annual costs. Tuition/fees: $18,100. Room/board: $6,410. Books/supplies: $1,000. Personal expenses: $1,900.

2007-2008 Financial aid. **Additional information:** Matching scholarships available for students whose church contributes $200 annually. Performance grants available to members of marching band.

Application procedures. **Admission:** Priority date 4/15; no deadline. $20 fee, may be waived for applicants with need, free for online applicants. Admission notification on a rolling basis beginning on or about 1/2. **Financial aid:** Priority date 4/1; no closing date. FAFSA required. Applicants notified on a rolling basis starting 5/15.

Academics. **Special study options:** Cooperative education, distance learning, double major, dual enrollment of high school students, ESL, exchange student, honors, independent study, internships, study abroad, teacher certification program, Washington semester. London semester. **Credit/placement by examination:** AP, CLEP, institutional tests. 32 credit hours maximum toward bachelor's degree. Institutional/departmental examinations given in some areas. **Support services:** Learning center, preadmission summer program, reduced course load, remedial instruction, study skills assistance, tutoring, writing center.

Majors. **Biology:** General. **Business:** General, accounting, business admin, marketing, office management. **Communications:** General, broadcast journalism, journalism, public relations. **Computer sciences:** General. **Education:** General, art, biology, chemistry, early childhood, elementary, English, health, history, mathematics, middle, music, physical, physics, reading, science, secondary, social science, social studies. **Health:** Athletic training, predental, premedicine, prepharmacy, preveterinary. **History:** General. **Legal studies:** Prelaw. **Math:** General. **Parks/recreation:** General, exercise sciences, health/fitness. **Philosophy/religion:** Religion. **Physical sciences:** Chemistry, physics. **Protective services:** Law enforcement admin. **Psychology:** General. **Public administration:** Social work. **Social sciences:** General, economics, political science, sociology. **Theology:** Bible, religious ed, sacred music. **Visual/performing arts:** Art, conducting, dramatic, music performance, music theory/composition, piano/organ, studio arts, voice/opera.

Most popular majors. Business/marketing 21%, education 16%, psychology 9%, public administration/social services 9%, security/protective services 7%, theological studies 11%.

Computing on campus. 200 workstations in dormitories, library, computer center, student center. Dormitories wired for high-speed internet access and linked to campus network. Online course registration, online library available.

Student life. **Freshman orientation:** Mandatory. Preregistration for classes offered. Held in June and July. **Policies:** Religious observance required. **Housing:** Guaranteed on-campus for all undergraduates. Single-sex dorms, apartments, wellness housing available. $100 deposit, deadline 7/1. **Activities:** Bands, campus ministries, choral groups, dance, drama, literary magazine, music ensembles, musical theater, opera, radio station, student government, student newspaper, symphony orchestra, TV station, Baptist student union, Young Republicans, Young Democrats, Student Foundation, Fellowship of Christian Athletes, student ambassadors, African American leadership league, world community club.

Athletics. NAIA. **Intercollegiate:** Baseball M, basketball, bowling, cross-country, football (tackle) M, golf, soccer, softball W, swimming W, tennis, track and field, volleyball W, wrestling M. **Intramural:** Basketball, racquetball, soccer, softball, table tennis, tennis, volleyball. **Team name:** Tigers.

Student services. Adult student services, alcohol/substance abuse counseling, chaplain/spiritual director, career counseling, student employment services, financial aid counseling, health services, personal counseling, placement for graduates, veterans' counselor.

Contact. E-mail: admissions@campbellsville.edu
Phone: (270) 789-5220 Toll-free number: (800) 264-6014
Fax: (270) 789-5071
David Walters, Vice President for Admissions, Campbellsville University, 1 University Drive, Campbellsville, KY 42718-2799

Centre College

Danville, Kentucky — **CB member**
www.centre.edu — **CB code: 1109**

- Private 4-year liberal arts college affiliated with Presbyterian Church (USA)
- Residential campus in large town
- 1,193 degree-seeking undergraduates: 54% women, 4% African American, 2% Asian American, 2% Hispanic American, 2% international
- 63% of applicants admitted
- SAT or ACT (ACT writing optional), application essay required
- 83% graduate within 6 years

General. Founded in 1819. Regionally accredited. **Degrees:** 281 bachelor's awarded. **ROTC:** Army, Air Force. **Location:** 35 miles from Lexington, 85 miles from Louisville. **Calendar:** 4-1-4. **Full-time faculty:** 101 total; 95% have terminal degrees, 4% minority, 41% women. **Part-time faculty:** 21 total; 43% have terminal degrees, 5% minority, 48% women. **Class size:** 56% < 20, 44% 20-39. **Special facilities:** Regional performing arts center, hot glass studio.

Freshman class profile. 2,176 applied, 1,367 admitted, 337 enrolled.

Mid 50% test scores		**GPA 2.0-2.99:**	12%
SAT critical reading:	560-700	**Rank in top quarter:**	81%
SAT math:	570-670	**Rank in top tenth:**	53%
SAT writing:	550-680	**Return as sophomores:**	91%
ACT composite:	26-30	**Out-of-state:**	37%
GPA 3.75 or higher:	40%	**Live on campus:**	99%
GPA 3.50-3.74:	22%	**International:**	2%
GPA 3.0-3.49:	26%		

Basis for selection. Achievement and quality of high school program most important. Recommendations, test scores, academic and nonacademic interests, experiences considered. Interview recommended.

High school preparation. College-preparatory program required. 14 units required; 24 recommended. Required and recommended units include English 4, mathematics 4, social studies 2, history 2, science 2-4 (laboratory 2-3), foreign language 2-4 and visual/performing arts 1.

2008-2009 Annual costs. Comprehensive fee: $37,000. Reduced comprehensive fee may be available if student is approved to live off-campus by dean of students. Books/supplies: $900. Personal expenses: $800.

2008-2009 Financial aid. **Need-based:** 266 full-time freshmen applied for aid; 203 were judged to have need; 203 of these received aid. Average need met was 88%. Average scholarship/grant was $21,160; average loan $3,488. 84% of total undergraduate aid awarded as scholarships/grants, 16% as loans/jobs. **Non-need-based:** Awarded to 450 full-time undergraduates, including 122 freshmen. Scholarships awarded for academics, alumni affiliation, music/drama, ROTC.

Application procedures. **Admission:** Closing date 2/1 (postmark date). $40 fee, may be waived for applicants with need, free for online applicants. Admission notification 3/15. Must reply by May 1 or within 2 week(s) if notified thereafter. **Financial aid:** Closing date 3/1. FAFSA, institutional form required. Applicants notified by 3/25; must reply by 5/1 or within 2 week(s) of notification.

Academics. Unusual courses and off-campus study options offered during 3-week winter term. Long-term study abroad sites in England, France, Mexico, Japan, and Ireland. Winter-term international locations vary. **Special study options:** Double major, honors, independent study, internships, liberal arts/career combination, student-designed major, study abroad, teacher certification program, Washington semester. Science semester at Oak Ridge National Laboratories, Tennessee, and 5 other national science laboratories, 3-2 engineering program with Columbia University (NY), Washington University (MO), Vanderbilt University (TN), and University of Kentucky. **Credit/placement by examination:** AP, CLEP, IB, SAT, ACT, institutional tests. **Support services:** Study skills assistance, tutoring, writing center.

Majors. **Biology:** General, biochemistry, molecular. **Computer sciences:** Computer science. **Education:** Elementary. **Foreign languages:** Classics, French, German, Spanish. **History:** General. **Math:** General. **Philosophy/religion:** Philosophy, religion. **Physical sciences:** Chemical physics, chemistry, physics. **Psychology:** General. **Social sciences:** Anthropology, economics, international relations, political science, sociology. **Visual/performing arts:** Art, dramatic.

Most popular majors. Biology 11%, English 11%, foreign language 10%, history 9%, philosophy/religious studies 6%, psychology 7%, social sciences 25%, visual/performing arts 7%.

Computing on campus. 170 workstations in dormitories, library, computer center, student center. Dormitories wired for high-speed internet access and linked to campus network. Commuter students can connect to campus network. Online course registration, helpline, repair service, student web hosting, wireless network available.

Student life. **Freshman orientation:** Mandatory. Preregistration for classes offered. Held at beginning of fall term. **Housing:** Guaranteed on-campus for all undergraduates. Coed dorms, single-sex dorms, special housing for disabled, apartments, fraternity/sorority housing, wellness housing available. Fraternity/sorority housing for officers. **Activities:** Bands, campus ministries, choral groups, dance, drama, film society, international student organizations, literary magazine, music ensembles, student government, student newspaper, symphony orchestra, TV station, student government association, student activities council, Centre Action Reaches Everyone (volunteer services), diversity student union, Centre Christian Fellowship, Campus Democrats and Republicans, CentreFaith (ecumenical organization), CentrePeace, student environmental organization, Muslim student association.

Athletics. NCAA. **Intercollegiate:** Baseball M, basketball, cross-country, diving, field hockey W, football (tackle) M, golf, soccer, softball W, swimming, tennis, track and field, volleyball W. **Intramural:** Badminton, basketball, bowling, cross-country, fencing, field hockey W, football (tackle), golf, racquetball, rugby M, soccer, softball, swimming, table tennis, tennis, track and field, volleyball, wrestling M. **Team name:** Colonels.

Student services. Alcohol/substance abuse counseling, chaplain/spiritual director, career counseling, student employment services, financial aid counseling, health services, minority student services, personal counseling, placement for graduates. **Physically disabled:** Services for visually, hearing impaired.

Contact. E-mail: admission@centre.edu
Phone: (859) 238-5350 Toll-free number: (800) 423-6236
Fax: (859) 238-5373
Bob Nesmith, Director of Admission, Centre College, 600 West Walnut Street, Danville, KY 40422-1394

Clear Creek Baptist Bible College

Pineville, Kentucky
www.ccbbc.edu **CB code: 5975**

- Private 4-year Bible college affiliated with Southern Baptist Convention
- Residential campus in small town
- 145 degree-seeking undergraduates: 20% part-time, 17% women, 1% African American, 1% Hispanic American, 1% Native American
- Application essay, interview required
- 46% graduate within 6 years; 30% enter graduate study

General. Founded in 1926. Regionally accredited; also accredited by ABHE. Adult family Bible college affiliated with Kentucky Baptist Convention that trains individuals for ministry in local church. Prefer students to be at least 21 years of age. **Degrees:** 30 bachelor's, 7 associate awarded. **Location:** 110 miles from Lexington; 76 miles from Knoxville, Tennessee. **Calendar:** Semester, limited summer session. **Full-time faculty:** 6 total; 83% have terminal degrees. **Part-time faculty:** 17 total; 35% have terminal degrees, 24% women. **Class size:** 79% < 20, 21% 20-39. **Special facilities:** Family life center, hiking/walking trails, campus thrift store.

Freshman class profile. 17 applied, 17 admitted, 16 enrolled.

End year in good standing:	100%	**Out-of-state:**	54%
Return as sophomores:	76%		

Basis for selection. Open admission. Applicants must demonstrate a clear call to the gospel ministry. Recommendations by church required. **Homeschooled:** Transcript of courses and grades required.

2008-2009 Annual costs. Tuition/fees: $5,322. Room/board: $3,750. Books/supplies: $800. Personal expenses: $1,600.

2007-2008 Financial aid. **Need-based:** 21 full-time freshmen applied for aid; 17 were judged to have need; 17 of these received aid. Average need met was 49%. Average scholarship/grant was $3,411. 95% of total undergraduate aid awarded as scholarships/grants, 5% as loans/jobs. **Non-need-based:** Awarded to 67 full-time undergraduates, including 18 freshmen. Scholarships awarded for academics.

Application procedures. **Admission:** Priority date 7/15; deadline 8/2 (receipt date). $40 fee. Admission notification on a rolling basis. **Financial aid:** Priority date 6/30; no closing date. FAFSA, institutional form required. Applicants notified on a rolling basis; must reply by 8/1.

Academics. **Special study options:** Cross-registration, distance learning, double major, dual enrollment of high school students, independent study. **Credit/placement by examination:** CLEP, institutional tests. **Support services:** Reduced course load, remedial instruction, study skills assistance, tutoring.

Majors. **Theology:** Bible.

Computing on campus. 12 workstations in library, computer center. Dormitories wired for high-speed internet access and linked to campus network. Online course registration, online library, wireless network available.

Student life. **Freshman orientation:** Available. Preregistration for classes offered. Four-day program held week of registration. **Policies:** Dress code; no tobacco, alcohol, or drugs on campus. Religious observance required. **Housing:** Single-sex dorms, apartments, wellness housing available. $50 nonrefundable deposit, deadline 7/25. Cottages, family housing available. **Activities:** Campus ministries, choral groups, drama, music ensembles, radio station, student government, student newspaper, women's missionary union, Brotherhood, Young Disciples, Acteens, Royal Ambassadors, Girls in Action, Mission Friends.

Athletics. **Intramural:** Basketball, football (non-tackle) M, softball, swimming, table tennis, tennis, volleyball.

Student services. Chaplain/spiritual director, career counseling, student employment services, financial aid counseling, health services, on-campus daycare, personal counseling, placement for graduates, veterans' counselor.

Contact. E-mail: ccbbc@ccbbc.edu
Phone: (606) 337-3196 Toll-free number: (866) 340-3196
Fax: (606) 337-2372
Billy Howell, Director of Admissions, Clear Creek Baptist Bible College, 300 Clear Creek Road, Pineville, KY 40977-9754

Eastern Kentucky University

Richmond, Kentucky **CB member**
www.eku.edu **CB code: 1200**

- Public 4-year university
- Residential campus in large town
- 12,710 degree-seeking undergraduates
- 72% of applicants admitted
- SAT or ACT (ACT writing optional) required

General. Founded in 1906. Regionally accredited. Courses offered at additional sites in Corbin, Danville, Manchester, Lancaster, London, Somerset and Barbourville. **Degrees:** 2,030 bachelor's, 189 associate awarded; master's offered. **ROTC:** Army. **Location:** 28 miles from Lexington, 110 miles from Cincinnati. **Calendar:** Semester, extensive summer session. **Full-time faculty:** 658 total. **Part-time faculty:** 411 total. **Class size:** 48% < 20, 44% 20-39, 4% 40-49, 3% 50-99, 1% >100. **Special facilities:** Planetarium, nature preserves, law enforcement facilities, music library.

Freshman class profile. 7,213 applied, 5,213 admitted, 2,495 enrolled.

Mid 50% test scores		**Live on campus:**	69%
SAT math:	440-550	**Fraternities:**	13%
ACT composite:	18-24	**Sororities:**	8%
Out-of-state:	17%		

Basis for selection. Out-of-state applicants must rank in top half of graduating class or have 21 ACT or 890 SAT (exclusive of Writing). Resident applicants must have completed specified high school curriculum. Applicants without college preparatory courses subject to remediation. ACT only required for placement for in-state applicants. Interview recommended. Audition recommended for music majors. Portfolio recommended for art and graphic art majors. **Homeschooled:** Transcript of courses and grades required.

High school preparation. 25 units required. Required units include English 4, mathematics 3, social studies 3, science 3 (laboratory 1), foreign language 2 and academic electives 7. Art, drama, music, and computer science also recommended.

2008-2009 Annual costs. Tuition/fees: $6,080; $16,612 out-of-state. Targeted out-of-state tuition: $9,596. Room/board: $6,360. Books/supplies: $1,000. Personal expenses: $1,500.

2008-2009 Financial aid. **Need-based:** 2,119 full-time freshmen applied for aid; 1,580 were judged to have need; 1,558 of these received aid. Average need met was 87%. Average scholarship/grant was $5,704; average loan $2,506. 34% of total undergraduate aid awarded as scholarships/grants, 66% as loans/jobs. **Non-need-based:** Awarded to 4,890 full-time undergraduates, including 1,645 freshmen. Scholarships awarded for academics, alumni affiliation, art, athletics, job skills, leadership, minority status, music/drama, ROTC.

Application procedures. **Admission:** Closing date 8/1. $30 fee, may be waived for applicants with need. Admission notification on a rolling basis beginning on or about 8/1. **Financial aid:** Priority date 3/15; no closing date. FAFSA required. Applicants notified on a rolling basis starting 4/1.

Academics. **Special study options:** Cooperative education, distance learning, double major, ESL, honors, independent study, internships, liberal arts/career combination, student-designed major, study abroad, teacher certification program. **Credit/placement by examination:** AP, CLEP, SAT, ACT, institutional tests. 30 credit hours maximum toward associate degree, 65 toward bachelor's. **Support services:** Learning center, pre-admission summer program, reduced course load, remedial instruction, study skills assistance, tutoring, writing center.

Majors. **Agriculture:** Ornamental horticulture, turf management. **Area/ethnic studies:** Canadian. **Biology:** General, bacteriology, ecology. **Business:** General, accounting, business admin, fashion, finance, insurance, management information systems, managerial economics, marketing, office management. **Communications:** General, broadcast journalism, journalism, public relations. **Computer sciences:** General, computer science. **Conservation:** Management/policy, wildlife. **Education:** Art, biology, business, Deaf/hearing impaired, elementary, family/consumer sciences, geography, mathematics, middle, music, physical, science, Spanish, special, speech impaired, technology/industrial arts, trade/industrial. **Engineering:** Science. **Engineering technology:** Architectural, manufacturing, water quality. **Family/consumer sciences:** Family studies, food/nutrition, housing. **Foreign languages:** General, French, German, sign language interpretation, Spanish. **Health:** Clinical lab assistant, clinical lab science, clinical lab technology, EMT paramedic, health care admin, medical assistant, medical records admin, medical records technology, nursing (RN), predental, premedicine, preop/surgical nursing, prepharmacy. **History:** General. **Legal studies:** Paralegal. **Liberal arts:** Arts/sciences. **Math:** General, statistics. **Parks/recreation:** General, facilities management. **Philosophy/religion:** Philosophy. **Physical sciences:** Chemistry, geology, physics. **Protective services:** Corrections, fire safety technology, forensics, police science, security services. **Psychology:** General. **Public administration:** Social work. **Social sciences:** Anthropology, economics, geography, political science, sociology. **Transportation:** Aviation. **Visual/performing arts:** Art, ceramics, dramatic, drawing, interior design, painting, printmaking, sculpture, studio arts.

Most popular majors. Business/marketing 11%, education 13%, health sciences 15%, security/protective services 15%.

Computing on campus. 250 workstations in dormitories, library, computer center, student center. Dormitories wired for high-speed internet access and linked to campus network. Commuter students can connect to campus network. Online course registration, online library, helpline, wireless network available.

Student life. **Freshman orientation:** Mandatory. Preregistration for classes offered. Registration and campus tour. **Policies:** Students required to live on campus until age 21 unless living with parent or guardian. **Housing:** Guaranteed on-campus for freshmen. Coed dorms, single-sex dorms, apartments, fraternity/sorority housing available. $100 fully refundable deposit. **Activities:** Bands, choral groups, dance, drama, literary magazine, music ensembles, musical theater, radio station, student government, student newspaper, symphony orchestra, 160 religious, political, ethnic, social service, and special interest organizations.

Athletics. NCAA. **Intercollegiate:** Baseball M, basketball, cheerleading, cross-country, football (tackle) M, golf, soccer W, softball W, swimming, tennis, track and field, volleyball W. **Intramural:** Basketball, football (tackle) M, golf, racquetball, softball, tennis, volleyball. **Team name:** Colonels.

Student services. Alcohol/substance abuse counseling, chaplain/spiritual director, career counseling, student employment services, financial aid counseling, health services, personal counseling, placement for graduates, veterans' counselor. **Physically disabled:** Services for visually, speech, hearing impaired.

Contact. E-mail: admissions@eku.edu
Phone: (859) 622-2106 Toll-free number: (800) 465-9191
Fax: (859) 622-8024
Steve Byrn, Director of Admissions, Eastern Kentucky University, SSB CPO 54, 521 Lancaster Avenue, Richmond, KY 40475-3102

Georgetown College

Georgetown, Kentucky
www.georgetowncollege.edu **CB code: 1249**

- Private 4-year liberal arts college affiliated with Southern Baptist Convention
- Residential campus in large town
- 1,321 degree-seeking undergraduates: 1% part-time, 57% women, 7% African American, 1% Hispanic American, 1% international
- 500 degree-seeking graduate students
- 84% of applicants admitted
- SAT or ACT (ACT writing optional) required
- 57% graduate within 6 years; 66% enter graduate study

General. Founded in 1829. Regionally accredited. **Degrees:** 261 bachelor's awarded; master's offered. **ROTC:** Army, Air Force. **Location:** 12 miles from Lexington, 60 miles from Louisville. **Calendar:** Semester, limited summer session. **Full-time faculty:** 111 total; 93% have terminal degrees, 6% minority, 42% women. **Part-time faculty:** 38 total; 3% minority, 55% women. **Class size:** 63% < 20, 37% 20-39. **Special facilities:** Planetarium, Foucault pendulum, arboretum, fine arts building.

Freshman class profile. 1,376 applied, 1,154 admitted, 379 enrolled.

Mid 50% test scores		**Rank in top quarter:**	66%
SAT critical reading:	450-580	**Rank in top tenth:**	39%
SAT math:	440-580	**Return as sophomores:**	79%
ACT composite:	21-27	**Out-of-state:**	19%
GPA 3.75 or higher:	36%	**Live on campus:**	98%
GPA 3.50-3.74:	19%	**International:**	1%
GPA 3.0-3.49:	28%	**Fraternities:**	26%
GPA 2.0-2.99:	17%	**Sororities:**	37%

Basis for selection. School achievement record, test scores, and rank in top half of class most important. Interview recommended for academically weak or special needs applicants. Audition recommended for music and communication arts majors. Portfolio recommended for art majors. **Homeschooled:** Transcript of courses and grades required. ACT or SAT and essay required.

High school preparation. College-preparatory program recommended. 20 units recommended. Recommended units include English 4, mathematics 3, social studies 2, science 3 and foreign language 2.

2008-2009 Annual costs. Tuition/fees: $24,150. Room/board: $6,700. Books/supplies: $1,250. Personal expenses: $1,580.

2008-2009 Financial aid. **Need-based:** 324 full-time freshmen applied for aid; 283 were judged to have need; 283 of these received aid. Average need met was 92%. Average scholarship/grant was $21,085; average loan $3,686. 82% of total undergraduate aid awarded as scholarships/grants, 18% as loans/jobs. **Non-need-based:** Awarded to 604 full-time undergraduates, including 172 freshmen. Scholarships awarded for academics, alumni affiliation, art, athletics, leadership, minority status, music/drama, religious affiliation, ROTC, state residency.

Application procedures. **Admission:** Priority date 5/1; deadline 8/1 (postmark date). $30 fee, may be waived for applicants with need. Admission notification on a rolling basis beginning on or about 10/1. Must reply by May 1 or within 4 week(s) if notified thereafter. **Financial aid:** Priority date 2/15, closing date 8/1. FAFSA, institutional form required. Applicants notified on a rolling basis starting 3/1; must reply by 5/1.

Academics. **Special study options:** Accelerated study, cooperative education, double major, dual enrollment of high school students, honors, independent study, internships, liberal arts/career combination, student-designed major, study abroad, teacher certification program. 3-2 programs in Nursing and in Engineering with the University of Kentucky. **Credit/placement by examination:** AP, CLEP, IB, SAT, ACT, institutional tests. **Support services:** Study skills assistance, tutoring, writing center.

Majors. **Area/ethnic studies:** American, European. **Biology:** General, ecology. **Business:** General, accounting. **Communications:** Media studies. **Computer sciences:** General. **Conservation:** Environmental science. **Education:** Elementary, middle, music, special. **Foreign languages:** French, German, Spanish. **Health:** Athletic training, predental, prenursing, prepharmacy, preveterinary. **History:** General. **Liberal arts:** Arts/sciences. **Math:** General. **Parks/recreation:** Exercise sciences, health/fitness. **Philosophy/religion:** Philosophy, religion. **Physical sciences:** Chemistry, physics. **Psychology:** General. **Social sciences:** Economics, political science, sociology. **Visual/performing arts:** Dramatic, studio arts. **Other:** Security studies.

Most popular majors. Biology 7%, business/marketing 16%, communications/journalism 13%, education 9%, history 7%, parks/recreation 8%, psychology 13%, social sciences 6%.

Computing on campus. 115 workstations in library, computer center, student center. Dormitories wired for high-speed internet access and linked to campus network. Commuter students can connect to campus network. Online course registration, online library, helpline, repair service, wireless network available.

Student life. **Freshman orientation:** Mandatory, $100 fee. Preregistration for classes offered. Five-day orientation held prior to beginning of fall semester. **Policies:** Academic honor code enforced. **Housing:** Single-sex dorms, fraternity/sorority housing available. $200 deposit, deadline 5/1. Most students housed in minidorms of fewer than 80 students each. New apartments available for seniors. **Activities:** Bands, campus ministries, choral groups, dance, drama, literary magazine, music ensembles, Model UN, musical theater, radio station, student government, student newspaper, Baptist Student Union, Fellowship of Christian Athletes, Union of Black Leaders.

Athletics. NAIA. **Intercollegiate:** Baseball M, basketball, cheerleading M, cross-country, football (tackle) M, golf, soccer, softball W, tennis, track and field, volleyball W. **Intramural:** Basketball, equestrian, football (non-tackle), golf, racquetball, soccer, softball, table tennis, tennis, volleyball. **Team name:** Tigers.

Student services. Alcohol/substance abuse counseling, chaplain/spiritual director, career counseling, student employment services, financial aid counseling, health services, minority student services, personal counseling, placement for graduates.

Contact. E-mail: admissions@georgetowncollege.edu
Phone: (502) 863-8009 Toll-free number: (800) 788-9985
Fax: (502) 868-7733
Johnnie Johnson, Director of Admissions, Georgetown College, 400 East College Street, Georgetown, KY 40324

ITT Technical Institute: Louisville

Louisville, Kentucky
www.itt-tech.edu **CB code: 2728**

- For-profit 4-year technical college
- Large city

General. Accredited by ACICS. **Calendar:** Quarter.

Contact. Phone: (502) 327-7424
Director of Recruitment, 10509 Timberwood Circle, Louisville, KY 40223

Kentucky Christian University

Grayson, Kentucky
www.kcu.edu **CB code: 1377**

- Private 4-year Bible and liberal arts college affiliated with Independent Christian Church/Church of Christ
- Residential campus in small town
- 599 degree-seeking undergraduates: 5% part-time, 50% women, 7% African American, 1% Hispanic American, 1% Native American, 6% international
- 33 degree-seeking graduate students
- 71% of applicants admitted
- SAT or ACT (ACT writing optional), application essay required
- 39% graduate within 6 years

General. Founded in 1919. Regionally accredited. **Degrees:** 108 bachelor's awarded; master's offered. **ROTC:** Army. **Location:** 25 miles from Ashland, 100 miles from Lexington. **Calendar:** Semester, limited summer session. **Full-time faculty:** 34 total; 71% have terminal degrees, 26% women. **Part-time faculty:** 25 total; 8% have terminal degrees, 40% women. **Class size:** 78% < 20, 15% 20-39, 4% 40-49, 3% 50-99.

Freshman class profile. 485 applied, 345 admitted, 191 enrolled.

Mid 50% test scores			
SAT critical reading:	370-520	**Return as sophomores:**	70%
SAT math:	390-510	**Out-of-state:**	44%
ACT composite:	15-24	**Live on campus:**	91%
		International:	7%

Basis for selection. High school grades, rank in class, ACT or SAT test scores, personal references, and religious commitment given equal weight. Interview recommended for academically weak. **Learning Disabled:** Students with special needs should contact Director of Campus Counseling to make arrangements for special accommodations.

2008-2009 Annual costs. Tuition/fees: $12,120. Room/board: $5,298.

2008-2009 Financial aid. Non-need-based: Scholarships awarded for academics, alumni affiliation, leadership, minority status, music/drama, religious affiliation.

Application procedures. Admission: No deadline. $30 fee. Admission notification on a rolling basis. **Financial aid:** Priority date 3/1; no closing date. FAFSA required. Applicants notified on a rolling basis starting 3/15; must reply within 2 week(s) of notification.

Academics. All students required to major in Bible as a second degree. **Special study options:** Distance learning, double major, dual enrollment of high school students, independent study, internships, liberal arts/career combination, study abroad, teacher certification program. **Credit/placement by examination:** AP, CLEP, IB, ACT. **Support services:** Learning center, reduced course load, remedial instruction, study skills assistance, tutoring, writing center.

Majors. Business: Business admin. **Education:** Elementary, English, middle, music, secondary, social studies. **Health:** Nursing (RN). **History:** General. **Liberal arts:** Humanities. **Psychology:** Counseling. **Public administration:** Social work. **Theology:** Bible, pastoral counseling, sacred music. **Visual/performing arts:** Music management, music performance. **Other:** University studies.

Most popular majors. Business/marketing 12%, education 24%, health sciences 14%, interdisciplinary studies 8%, liberal arts 6%, social sciences 10%, theological studies 23%.

Computing on campus. 50 workstations in library, computer center, student center. Dormitories wired for high-speed internet access and linked to campus network. Commuter students can connect to campus network. Online library, helpline, repair service, wireless network available.

Student life. Freshman orientation: Mandatory. Preregistration for classes offered. **Policies:** All students under 26 not living with parents must live in on-campus housing. Religious observance required. **Housing:** Guaranteed on-campus for all undergraduates. Single-sex dorms, special housing for disabled, apartments available. $100 nonrefundable deposit. **Activities:** Bands, campus ministries, choral groups, drama, international student organizations, music ensembles, student government, Global Mission Awareness, Pi Chi Delta, Collegiate Music Educators National Conference, Herodotus Society, Laos Protos, American Association of Christian Counselors, Students in Free Enterprise.

Athletics. NAIA, NCCAA. **Intercollegiate:** Basketball, cheerleading M, cross-country, football (tackle) M, soccer, volleyball W. **Intramural:** Basketball, football (non-tackle) M, soccer, softball, table tennis, volleyball. **Team name:** Knights.

Student services. Chaplain/spiritual director, career counseling, financial aid counseling, health services, minority student services, personal counseling, women's services. **Physically disabled:** Services for visually, hearing impaired.

Contact. E-mail: knights@kcu.edu
Phone: (606) 474-3266 Toll-free number: (800) 522-3181
Fax: (606) 474-3155
Sandra Deakins, Vice President of Enrollment Management, Kentucky Christian University, 100 Academic Parkway, Grayson, KY 41143-2205

Kentucky Mountain Bible College

Vancleve, Kentucky
www.kmbc.edu **CB code: 1384**

- Private 4-year Bible college affiliated with Kentucky Mountain Holiness Association
- Residential campus in rural community
- 59 degree-seeking undergraduates: 15% part-time, 54% women, 3% African American, 2% Hispanic American, 3% international
- ACT (writing optional), application essay required

General. Founded in 1931. Accredited by ABHE. **Degrees:** 8 bachelor's, 6 associate awarded. **Location:** 75 miles from Lexington. **Calendar:** Semester. **Full-time faculty:** 3 total; 33% women. **Part-time faculty:** 13 total; 23% have terminal degrees, 23% women. **Class size:** 79% < 20, 21% 20-39.

Freshman class profile. 51 applied, 30 admitted, 23 enrolled.

Mid 50% test scores		**Rank in top quarter:**	11%
ACT composite:	15-21	**Rank in top tenth:**	11%
GPA 3.75 or higher:	7%	**End year in good standing:**	1%
GPA 3.50-3.74:	29%	**Return as sophomores:**	88%
GPA 3.0-3.49:	14%	**Out-of-state:**	66%
GPA 2.0-2.99:	50%	**Live on campus:**	100%

Basis for selection. Open admission, but selective for some programs and for out-of-state students. All students must have C average or above and provide 2 recommendations. 15 ACT required. Provisional admission granted. Interview recommended.

High school preparation. 18 units required. Required and recommended units include English 4, mathematics 2, history 2 and science 2. A total of 10 units in English, math, science or language required out of 18 units.

2008-2009 Annual costs. Tuition/fees: $5,940. Room/board: $3,700. Books/supplies: $400. Personal expenses: $250.

2007-2008 Financial aid. Need-based: 8 full-time freshmen applied for aid; 8 were judged to have need; 8 of these received aid. 65% of total undergraduate aid awarded as scholarships/grants, 35% as loans/jobs. **Non-need-based:** Scholarships awarded for academics, job skills, leadership, music/drama.

Application procedures. Admission: Priority date 6/1; no deadline. $25 fee, may be waived for applicants with need. Admission notification on a rolling basis. **Financial aid:** Priority date 4/1, closing date 6/30. FAFSA, institutional form required. Applicants notified on a rolling basis starting 3/15; must reply by 7/1.

Academics. Special study options: Independent study, internships, teacher certification program. **Credit/placement by examination:** AP, CLEP, ACT. **Support services:** Reduced course load, remedial instruction, study skills assistance, tutoring.

Majors. Communications: General. **Education:** Elementary. **Theology:** Missionary, religious ed, sacred music, theology.

Computing on campus. 12 workstations in library, computer center. Wireless network available.

Student life. Freshman orientation: Mandatory. Preregistration for classes offered. Two-day program immediately before the semester, includes Bible-knowledge testing. **Policies:** Religious observance required. **Housing:** Guaranteed on-campus for all undergraduates. Single-sex dorms, apartments, wellness housing available. **Activities:** Campus ministries, choral groups, drama, radio station, student government, student newspaper, missionary student involvement group, student council, class organizations.

Athletics. Intramural: Basketball M, volleyball W.

Student services. Chaplain/spiritual director, financial aid counseling, personal counseling.

Contact. E-mail: kmbc@kmbc.edu
Phone: (606) 693-5000 ext. 130 Toll-free number: (800) 879-5622 ext. 130
Fax: (606) 693-4884
David Lorimer, Chief Admissions Counselor, Kentucky Mountain Bible College, Box 10, Vancleve, KY 41385-0010

Kentucky State University

Frankfort, Kentucky — **CB member**
www.kysu.edu — **CB code: 1368**

- Public 4-year university and liberal arts college
- Residential campus in large town
- 2,209 degree-seeking undergraduates: 15% part-time, 56% women, 66% African American, 1% international
- 157 degree-seeking graduate students
- 31% of applicants admitted
- SAT or ACT (ACT writing optional) required

General. Founded in 1886. Regionally accredited. **Degrees:** 231 bachelor's, 37 associate awarded; master's offered. **ROTC:** Army, Air Force. **Location:** 50 miles from Louisville, 25 miles from Lexington. **Calendar:** Semester, limited summer session. **Full-time faculty:** 131 total; 70% have terminal degrees, 35% minority, 41% women. **Part-time faculty:** 53 total; 24% have terminal degrees, 23% minority, 66% women. **Class size:** 59% < 20, 39% 20-39, 1% 40-49, less than 1% >100. **Special facilities:** Center of Excellence for the Study of Kentucky African Americans, land grant institution.

Freshman class profile. 7,770 applied, 2,401 admitted, 687 enrolled.

Mid 50% test scores		**GPA 3.50-3.74:**	6%
SAT critical reading:	360-460	**GPA 3.0-3.49:**	19%
SAT math:	360-460	**GPA 2.0-2.99:**	61%
SAT writing:	350-450	**Return as sophomores:**	48%
ACT composite:	15-19	**Out-of-state:**	72%
GPA 3.75 or higher:	3%	**Live on campus:**	72%

Basis for selection. Unconditional admission for graduates of accredited high schools meeting Pre-College Curriculum (PCC) requirements established by Kentucky Council on Higher Education and having admission index of 430. Interview recommended for nursing majors and applicants to College of Leadership Studies. Audition recommended for music majors. Portfolio recommended for art majors. Essay required of applicants to College of Leadership Studies. **Homeschooled:** Transcript of courses and grades required. A notarized statement from the home school teacher detailing the content and duration of the student's home school curriculum required.

High school preparation. 22 units required. Required units include English 4, mathematics 3, social studies 3, history 1, science 3, foreign language 2, computer science 1 and academic electives 7.

2008-2009 Annual costs. Tuition/fees: $5,692; $13,490 out-of-state. Room/board: $6,392. Books/supplies: $1,200. Personal expenses: $2,200.

2008-2009 Financial aid. Need-based: Average scholarship/grant was $2,746; average loan $1,781. 48% of total undergraduate aid awarded as scholarships/grants, 52% as loans/jobs. **Non-need-based:** Awarded to 156 full-time undergraduates, including 35 freshmen. Scholarships awarded for academics, alumni affiliation, art, athletics, minority status, music/drama.

Application procedures. Admission: No deadline. $30 fee, may be waived for applicants with need. Admission notification on a rolling basis. **Financial aid:** Closing date 4/15. FAFSA required.

Academics. Special study options: Combined bachelor's/graduate degree, cooperative education, distance learning, double major, ESL, honors, independent study, internships, liberal arts/career combination, student-designed major, study abroad, teacher certification program. **Credit/placement by examination:** AP, CLEP, SAT, ACT, institutional tests. **Support services:** Learning center, pre-admission summer program, reduced course load, remedial instruction, study skills assistance, tutoring, writing center.

Majors. Biology: General. **Business:** General. **Communications:** Media studies. **Computer sciences:** General, webmaster. **Education:** Elementary, physical. **Family/consumer sciences:** Family studies. **Health:** Nursing (RN). **Liberal arts:** Arts/sciences. **Math:** General. **Physical sciences:** Chemistry. **Protective services:** Criminal justice. **Psychology:** General. **Public administration:** General, social work. **Social sciences:** General, political science. **Visual/performing arts:** Studio arts.

Most popular majors. Biology 7%, business/marketing 21%, education 12%, health sciences 6%, liberal arts 6%, psychology 9%, public administration/social services 11%, security/protective services 8%, social sciences 6%.

Computing on campus. 306 workstations in dormitories, library, student center. Dormitories wired for high-speed internet access and linked to campus network. Commuter students can connect to campus network. Online library, helpline, repair service, wireless network available.

Student life. Freshman orientation: Available. **Housing:** Guaranteed on-campus for freshmen. Coed dorms, single-sex dorms available. $300 nonrefundable deposit. **Activities:** Bands, campus ministries, choral groups, dance, drama, international student organizations, music ensembles, musical theater, opera, student government, student newspaper, Alpha Kappa Mu National Honor Society, MANNRS (Minorities in Agriculture, National Resources & Related Sciences), Students in Free Enterprises (SIFE), Student National Education Association (SNEA), Baptist Student Union, Chi Alpha Christian Fellowship, The NAACP (National Association for the Advancement of Black People), Wesley Foundation, Alpha Kappa Alpha Sorority, Kappa Alpha Psi Fraternity.

Athletics. NCAA. **Intercollegiate:** Baseball M, basketball, cross-country, football (tackle) M, golf, softball W, track and field, volleyball W. **Team name:** Thorobreds.

Student services. Adult student services, career counseling, student employment services, financial aid counseling, health services, personal counseling, placement for graduates, veterans' counselor. **Physically disabled:** Services for visually, hearing impaired.

Contact. E-mail: admissions@kysu.edu
Phone: (502) 597-6813 Toll-free number: (877) 367-5978
Fax: (502) 597-5814
James Burrell, Director of Admissions, Kentucky State University, 400 East Main Street, ASB 312, Frankfort, KY 40601

Kentucky Wesleyan College

Owensboro, Kentucky — **CB member**
www.kwc.edu — **CB code: 1369**

- Private 4-year liberal arts college affiliated with United Methodist Church
- Residential campus in small city
- 893 degree-seeking undergraduates: 3% part-time, 47% women, 10% African American, 1% Hispanic American, 1% international
- 70% of applicants admitted
- SAT or ACT (ACT writing optional) required
- 41% graduate within 6 years; 30% enter graduate study

General. Founded in 1858. Regionally accredited. **Degrees:** 144 bachelor's awarded. **ROTC:** Army. **Location:** 116 miles from Louisville, 120 miles from Nashville, Tennessee. **Calendar:** Semester, limited summer session. **Full-time faculty:** 47 total; 77% have terminal degrees, 4% minority, 36% women. **Part-time faculty:** 49 total; 49% women. **Class size:** 67%

< 20, 31% 20-39, 1% 40-49, less than 1% 50-99. **Special facilities:** Center for the sciences, center for the arts, fully computerized writing workshop, center for business studies.

Freshman class profile. 1,485 applied, 1,040 admitted, 219 enrolled.

Mid 50% test scores			
SAT critical reading:	440-560	Rank in top quarter:	29%
SAT math:	460-560	Rank in top tenth:	19%
SAT writing:	410-580	End year in good standing:	85%
ACT composite:	19-25	Return as sophomores:	61%
GPA 3.75 or higher:	26%	Out-of-state:	24%
GPA 3.50-3.74:	15%	Live on campus:	76%
GPA 3.0-3.49:	31%	International:	1%
GPA 2.0-2.99:	27%	Fraternities:	14%
		Sororities:	23%

Basis for selection. Secondary school record very important. Test scores, GPA, class rank, and school activities important.

High school preparation. College-preparatory program recommended. 13 units required. Required and recommended units include English 4, mathematics 3, social studies 3, science 3 and foreign language 2.

2008-2009 Annual costs. Tuition/fees: $15,625. Room/board: $6,160. Books/supplies: $1,250. Personal expenses: $2,000.

2007-2008 Financial aid. **Need-based:** 273 full-time freshmen applied for aid; 247 were judged to have need; 242 of these received aid. Average need met was 70%. Average scholarship/grant was $11,157; average loan $3,052. 60% of total undergraduate aid awarded as scholarships/grants, 40% as loans/jobs. **Non-need-based:** Awarded to 234 full-time undergraduates, including 54 freshmen. Scholarships awarded for academics, alumni affiliation, art, athletics, leadership, music/drama, religious affiliation, state residency.

Application procedures. **Admission:** No deadline. No application fee. Admission notification on a rolling basis beginning on or about 9/1. **Financial aid:** Closing date 3/15. FAFSA required. Applicants notified on a rolling basis starting 2/15; must reply within 2 week(s) of notification.

Academics. Co-curricular leadership program available. **Special study options:** Double major, independent study, internships, liberal arts/career combination, student-designed major, study abroad, teacher certification program, Washington semester. **Credit/placement by examination:** AP, CLEP, IB, SAT, ACT, institutional tests. 42 credit hours maximum toward bachelor's degree. International Baccalaureate Diploma credit will be awarded for advanced course scores of 6 or 7, with up to 10 hours of credit awarded. **Support services:** Learning center, reduced course load, remedial instruction, study skills assistance, tutoring, writing center.

Majors. **Biology:** General, zoology. **Business:** General, accounting, business admin. **Communications:** General. **Computer sciences:** General. **Education:** Art, biology, chemistry, elementary, English, mathematics, middle, physical, social studies, Spanish. **Foreign languages:** Spanish. **History:** General. **Math:** General. **Parks/recreation:** Sports admin. **Philosophy/religion:** Religion. **Physical sciences:** Chemistry, physics. **Protective services:** Criminal justice. **Psychology:** General. **Public administration:** Human services. **Social sciences:** Political science, sociology. **Visual/performing arts:** Art, studio arts.

Most popular majors. Biology 14%, business/marketing 16%, communications/journalism 7%, education 13%, physical sciences 7%, psychology 11%, security/protective services 6%.

Computing on campus. 100 workstations in dormitories, library, computer center, student center. Dormitories wired for high-speed internet access and linked to campus network. Commuter students can connect to campus network. Online course registration, online library, helpline, repair service, wireless network available.

Student life. **Freshman orientation:** Mandatory, $125 fee. Preregistration for classes offered. **Housing:** Guaranteed on-campus for freshmen. Coed dorms, single-sex dorms, special housing for disabled, fraternity/sorority housing, wellness housing available. $100 fully refundable deposit, deadline 5/1. **Activities:** Bands, campus ministries, choral groups, dance, drama, literary magazine, music ensembles, radio station, student government, student newspaper, student activities programming board, Baptist Student Union, United Methodist Student Fellowship, Brothers and Sisters in Christ, criminal justice association, Kentucky Wesleyan Singers, College Republicans, Young Democrats.

Athletics. NCAA. **Intercollegiate:** Baseball M, basketball, cheerleading, cross-country, football (tackle) M, golf, soccer, softball W, tennis W, volleyball W. **Intramural:** Basketball, bowling, football (non-tackle), soccer, softball, table tennis, tennis, volleyball. **Team name:** Panthers.

Student services. Alcohol/substance abuse counseling, chaplain/spiritual director, career counseling, student employment services, financial aid counseling, health services, personal counseling, placement for graduates. **Physically disabled:** Services for visually impaired.

Contact. E-mail: admitme@kwc.edu
Phone: (270) 852-3120 Toll-free number: (800) 999-0592
Fax: (270) 852-3133
Clayton Daniels, Dean of Admissions and Financial Aid, Kentucky Wesleyan College, 3000 Frederica Street, Owensboro, KY 42301

Lindsey Wilson College

Columbia, Kentucky
www.lindsey.edu **CB code: 1409**

- Private 4-year liberal arts college affiliated with United Methodist Church
- Residential campus in small town
- 1,615 degree-seeking undergraduates

General. Founded in 1903. Regionally accredited. **Degrees:** 271 bachelor's, 28 associate awarded; master's offered. **Location:** 100 miles from Louisville. **Calendar:** Semester, limited summer session. **Full-time faculty:** 70 total; 83% have terminal degrees, 3% minority, 47% women. **Part-time faculty:** 45 total.

Freshman class profile.

GPA 3.75 or higher:	15%	GPA 2.0-2.99:	42%
GPA 3.50-3.74:	13%	Out-of-state:	5%
GPA 3.0-3.49:	25%	Live on campus:	69%

Basis for selection. Open admission, but selective for some programs. Special requirements for education and human services programs. ACCUPLACER or ACT required for placement. Interview recommended.

2008-2009 Annual costs. Tuition/fees: $16,670. Room/board: $6,925. Books/supplies: $900. Personal expenses: $1,200.

2007-2008 Financial aid. All financial aid based on need.

Application procedures. **Admission:** Priority date 6/1; no deadline. No application fee. Admission notification on a rolling basis beginning on or about 1/1. **Financial aid:** Priority date 4/15; no closing date. FAFSA, institutional form required. Applicants notified on a rolling basis starting 5/1; must reply within 2 week(s) of notification.

Academics. **Special study options:** Dual enrollment of high school students, independent study, internships, student-designed major, study abroad, teacher certification program, weekend college. On-campus and extension evening program for associate degree in business management and computer science, weekend extension program in human services. **Credit/placement by examination:** AP, CLEP. 16 credit hours maximum toward associate degree, 32 toward bachelor's. **Support services:** Learning center, reduced course load, remedial instruction, study skills assistance, tutoring, writing center.

Majors. **Area/ethnic studies:** American. **Biology:** General. **Business:** Business admin. **Communications:** General, journalism. **Education:** Art, biology, elementary, English, mathematics, middle, physical, secondary, social science. **History:** General. **Legal studies:** Prelaw. **Liberal arts:** Humanities. **Math:** General. **Parks/recreation:** Health/fitness. **Philosophy/religion:** Christian. **Protective services:** Criminal justice. **Psychology:** General. **Social sciences:** General. **Visual/performing arts:** Studio arts.

Most popular majors. Biology 6%, business/marketing 13%, communications/journalism 7%, education 7%, public administration/social services 47%.

Computing on campus. 100 workstations in library, computer center. Dormitories wired for high-speed internet access and linked to campus network. Commuter students can connect to campus network. Online course registration, online library, wireless network available.

Student life. **Freshman orientation:** Available. Preregistration for classes offered. **Policies:** All students not living with family must live in campus housing. **Housing:** Single-sex dorms, apartments, wellness housing available. $40 deposit. **Activities:** Pep band, choral groups, drama, literary magazine, music ensembles, student government, student newspaper, Christian student organizations, Student Ambassadors, black student union, Students in Free Enterprise, Raider Republicans, international student association.

Athletics. NAIA. **Intercollegiate:** Baseball M, basketball, bowling, cross-country, golf, soccer, softball W, tennis, track and field, volleyball W. **Intramural:** Basketball, football (tackle), softball, table tennis, tennis, volleyball. **Team name:** Blue Raiders.

Student services. Alcohol/substance abuse counseling, chaplain/spiritual director, career counseling, student employment services, financial aid counseling, health services, personal counseling, placement for graduates. **Physically disabled:** Services for visually impaired.

Contact. E-mail: admissions@lindsey.edu
Phone: (270) 384-8100 Toll-free number: (800) 264-0138
Fax: (270) 384-8591
Traci Pooler, Dean of Admissions, Lindsey Wilson College, 210 Lindsey Wilson Street, Columbia, KY 42728

Mid-Continent University
Mayfield, Kentucky
www.midcontinent.edu **CB code: 0254**

- Private 4-year Bible and liberal arts college affiliated with Southern Baptist Convention
- Commuter campus in large town
- 1,634 degree-seeking undergraduates: 14% part-time, 64% women, 11% African American, 1% Hispanic American, 3% international
- 56% of applicants admitted
- SAT or ACT (ACT writing optional), application essay required

General. Founded in 1949. Regionally accredited. **Degrees:** 301 bachelor's, 110 associate awarded. **Location:** 20 miles from Paducah, 125 miles from Nashville, Tennessee. **Calendar:** Semester, limited summer session. **Full-time faculty:** 27 total; 44% have terminal degrees, 22% minority, 11% women. **Part-time faculty:** 88 total; 10% have terminal degrees, 3% minority, 40% women. **Class size:** 74% < 20, 25% 20-39, 1% 40-49.

Freshman class profile. 372 applied, 210 admitted, 191 enrolled.

Mid 50% test scores		**GPA 3.0-3.49:**	25%
SAT critical reading:	420-450	**GPA 2.0-2.99:**	46%
SAT math:	390-450	**Rank in top quarter:**	19%
SAT writing:	440-440	**Rank in top tenth:**	9%
ACT composite:	17-21	**Out-of-state:**	14%
GPA 3.75 or higher:	5%	**Live on campus:**	61%
GPA 3.50-3.74:	18%	**International:**	7%

Basis for selection. Secondary school record and standardized test scores most important. Entering students tested in mathematics and English. **Homeschooled:** Statement describing homeschool structure and mission, transcript of courses and grades, letter of recommendation (nonparent) required.

High school preparation. College-preparatory program recommended. Required units include English 4, mathematics 2, social studies 2, science 2 and foreign language 1.

2008-2009 Annual costs. Tuition/fees: $13,100. Room/board: $6,300. Books/supplies: $1,100. Personal expenses: $1,500.

2007-2008 Financial aid. Need-based: 122 full-time freshmen applied for aid; 112 were judged to have need; 111 of these received aid. Average need met was 43%. Average scholarship/grant was $6,160; average loan $2,609. 47% of total undergraduate aid awarded as scholarships/grants, 53% as loans/jobs. **Non-need-based:** Scholarships awarded for academics.

Application procedures. Admission: Priority date 8/1; no deadline. $20 fee ($20 out-of-state), may be waived for applicants with need. Admission notification on a rolling basis. **Financial aid:** Priority date 3/15, closing date 5/30. FAFSA, institutional form required. Applicants notified on a rolling basis starting 4/1; must reply within 2 week(s) of notification.

Academics. Bachelor of Ministry degree awarded after 36 hours above earned baccalaureate degree from regionally accredited institution. Accelerated programs in Business Management for adult learners available. **Special study options:** Accelerated study, combined bachelor's/graduate degree, double major, dual enrollment of high school students, independent study, study abroad, teacher certification program. **Credit/placement by examination:** AP, CLEP, SAT, ACT, institutional tests. 30 credit hours maximum toward bachelor's degree. **Support services:** Remedial instruction, tutoring.

Majors. Business: Business admin, organizational behavior. **Education:** Elementary. **Math:** General. **Philosophy/religion:** Christian. **Psychology:** General, counseling. **Social sciences:** General. **Theology:** Bible, missionary, religious ed.

Most popular majors. Business/marketing 90%.

Computing on campus. 43 workstations in library, computer center, student center. Dormitories wired for high-speed internet access. Online library available.

Student life. Freshman orientation: Mandatory. Preregistration for classes offered. 2-3 day orientation process at beginning of academic year. **Policies:** Religious observance required. **Housing:** Single-sex dorms available. $200 fully refundable deposit, deadline 8/1. **Activities:** Student government, student newspaper, Baptist Student Union, Fellowship of Christian Athletes, psychology club, international student association.

Athletics. NAIA, NCCAA. **Intercollegiate:** Baseball M, basketball, soccer M, softball W. **Team name:** Lady Cougars, Cougars.

Student services. Chaplain/spiritual director, career counseling, financial aid counseling, personal counseling, veterans' counselor. **Physically disabled:** Services for visually, hearing impaired.

Contact. E-mail: admissions@midcontinent.edu
Phone: (270) 247-8521 ext. 238 Toll-free number: (866) 894-8878
Fax: (270) 247-3115
Debbie Smith, Director of Admissions, Mid-Continent University, 99 Powell Road East, Mayfield, KY 42066-0357

Midway College
Midway, Kentucky **CB member**
www.midway.edu **CB code: 1467**

- Private 4-year liberal arts college for women affiliated with Christian Church (Disciples of Christ)
- Commuter campus in small town
- 1,284 degree-seeking undergraduates: 29% part-time, 84% women, 7% African American, 1% Hispanic American, 1% Native American
- 11 degree-seeking graduate students
- SAT or ACT required

General. Founded in 1847. Regionally accredited. Men admitted to evening and weekend programs; degree areas include nursing, business administration, organizational administration, computer information systems, healthcare management, homeland security, human resource management, sport management. **Degrees:** 271 bachelor's, 70 associate awarded; master's offered. **ROTC:** Army. **Location:** 12 miles from Lexington, 60 miles from Louisville. **Calendar:** Semester, limited summer session. **Full-time faculty:** 52 total; 38% have terminal degrees, 6% minority, 56% women. **Part-time faculty:** 61 total; 26% have terminal degrees, 10% minority, 46% women. **Class size:** 80% < 20, 19% 20-39, 1% 40-49. **Special facilities:** Equine science center, riding arena, campus farm.

Freshman class profile. 391 applied, 277 admitted, 166 enrolled.

Mid 50% test scores		**GPA 3.0-3.49:**	34%
SAT critical reading:	430-570	**GPA 2.0-2.99:**	26%
SAT math:	410-560	**Rank in top quarter:**	38%
ACT composite:	19-23	**Rank in top tenth:**	14%
GPA 3.75 or higher:	14%	**Out-of-state:**	9%
GPA 3.50-3.74:	24%	**Live on campus:**	45%

Basis for selection. Open admission, but selective for some programs. High school record and test scores important. Essay and letters of recommendation encouraged. More competitive requirements established for certain programs such as biology, education, nursing. Interview required for majors in nursing; also required of academically weak. Essay recommended for students who are conditionally admitted.

High school preparation. 15 units required. Required and recommended units include English 4, mathematics 3, social studies 1, history 1 and science 2. Specific college-preparatory program required for some majors.

2008-2009 Annual costs. Tuition/fees: $17,100. Room/board: $6,600. Books/supplies: $1,200. Personal expenses: $1,000.

Financial aid. Non-need-based: Scholarships awarded for academics, alumni affiliation, art, athletics, leadership, minority status, religious affiliation. **Additional information:** Audition required of applicants for music scholarships. Portfolio required for art scholarships.

Application procedures. Admission: Priority date 4/1; no deadline. $25 fee, may be waived for applicants with need. Admission notification on a rolling basis. Must reply by May 1 or within 4 week(s) if notified thereafter. **Financial aid:** Priority date 4/1, closing date 8/1. FAFSA, institutional form required. Applicants notified on a rolling basis; must reply within 4 week(s) of notification.

Academics. Special study options: Accelerated study, cooperative education, distance learning, double major, dual enrollment of high school students, independent study, internships, liberal arts/career combination, study abroad, teacher certification program. Evening programs in business, nursing and teacher certification. **Credit/placement by examination:** AP, CLEP, IB, institutional tests. 12 credit hours maximum toward associate degree, 12 toward bachelor's. **Support services:** Learning center, reduced course load, remedial instruction, tutoring, writing center.

Majors. **Agriculture:** Equestrian studies. **Biology:** General. **Business:** General, human resources, organizational behavior. **Computer sciences:** General. **Conservation:** Environmental science. **Education:** Elementary, middle, multi-level teacher, secondary, special. **Health:** Health care admin, nursing (RN). **Interdisciplinary:** Intercultural. **Liberal arts:** Arts/sciences. **Math:** General. **Parks/recreation:** Sports admin. **Protective services:** Emergency management/homeland security. **Psychology:** General.

Most popular majors. Agriculture 8%, business/marketing 31%, education 48%.

Computing on campus. 60 workstations in dormitories, library, computer center, student center. Dormitories wired for high-speed internet access and linked to campus network. Commuter students can connect to campus network. Online course registration, online library, helpline available.

Student life. **Freshman orientation:** Mandatory. Preregistration for classes offered. 2-3 day orientation prior to start of term. **Policies:** All students under 21, unmarried, and not living at home required to live in campus housing. **Housing:** Guaranteed on-campus for all undergraduates. Special housing for disabled, wellness housing available. $100 nonrefundable deposit, deadline 5/1. **Activities:** Campus ministries, choral groups, international student organizations, student government, commuters committee, Fellowship of Christian Athletes, Disciples on Campus, Ruth Slack Roach Scholars.

Athletics. NAIA. **Intercollegiate:** Basketball W, cross-country W, equestrian W, soccer W, softball W, tennis W, track and field W, volleyball W. **Team name:** Eagles.

Student services. Adult student services, chaplain/spiritual director, career counseling, student employment services, financial aid counseling, health services, personal counseling, placement for graduates.

Contact. E-mail: admissions@midway.edu
Phone: (859) 846-5347 Toll-free number: (800) 755-0031
Fax: (859) 846-5787
Jim Wombles, Chief Enrollment Officer, Midway College, 512 East Stephens Street, Midway, KY 40347-1120

Morehead State University
Morehead, Kentucky
www.moreheadstate.edu **CB code: 1487**

- Public 4-year university
- Residential campus in small town
- 6,773 degree-seeking undergraduates: 17% part-time, 61% women, 3% African American, 1% Hispanic American
- 1,250 degree-seeking graduate students
- 55% of applicants admitted
- SAT or ACT (ACT writing optional) required
- 41% graduate within 6 years

General. Founded in 1922. Regionally accredited. **Degrees:** 992 bachelor's, 149 associate awarded; master's offered. **ROTC:** Army. **Location:** 65 miles from Lexington; 70 miles from Huntington, West Virginia. **Calendar:** Semester, extensive summer session. **Full-time faculty:** 369 total; 69% have terminal degrees, 12% minority, 47% women. **Part-time faculty:** 104 total; 3% minority, 57% women. **Class size:** 60% < 20, 32% 20-39, 6% 40-49, 3% 50-99, less than 1% >100. **Special facilities:** Planetarium, agriculture complex, outdoor learning center at Cave Run, Kentucky folk art center, space science center, space tracking radio telescope, Center for Traditional Music.

Freshman class profile. 5,720 applied, 3,118 admitted, 1,338 enrolled.

Mid 50% test scores			
SAT critical reading:	420-560	Rank in top quarter:	52%
SAT math:	430-590	Rank in top tenth:	22%
ACT composite:	19-24	Return as sophomores:	66%
GPA 3.75 or higher:	27%	Out-of-state:	15%
GPA 3.50-3.74:	17%	Live on campus:	72%
GPA 3.0-3.49:	28%	International:	1%
GPA 2.0-2.99:	26%	Fraternities:	10%
		Sororities:	9%

Basis for selection. Test scores and GPA used to calculate index to determine admission. Status and review of pre-college curriculum important. Interview recommended for applicants to specialized allied health programs. Audition recommended for music majors. Students not meeting academic requirements may request an interview and submit additional documentation in order to be admitted with conditions. **Homeschooled:** Statement describing homeschool structure and mission, transcript of courses and grades required.

High school preparation. College-preparatory program required. 22 units required. Required units include English 4, mathematics 3, social studies 3, history 0.5, science 3 (laboratory 1), foreign language 2, computer science 1, visual/performing arts .5 and academic electives 7. 1 unit history and appreciation of fine arts required.

2008-2009 Annual costs. Tuition/fees: $5,670; $14,742 out-of-state. Tuition is based on enrollment of 15 credit hours. Room/board: $5,852. Books/supplies: $900. Personal expenses: $1,200.

2007-2008 Financial aid. **Need-based:** 1,226 full-time freshmen applied for aid; 957 were judged to have need; 947 of these received aid. Average need met was 71%. Average scholarship/grant was $4,416; average loan $2,896. 52% of total undergraduate aid awarded as scholarships/grants, 48% as loans/jobs. **Non-need-based:** Awarded to 2,752 full-time undergraduates, including 983 freshmen. Scholarships awarded for academics, alumni affiliation, art, athletics, leadership, minority status, music/drama, ROTC, state residency.

Application procedures. **Admission:** No deadline. $30 fee. Admission notification on a rolling basis. **Financial aid:** Priority date 3/15; no closing date. FAFSA, institutional form required. Applicants notified on a rolling basis.

Academics. 2-year transfer programs in prechiropractic, predentistry, preengineering, preforestry, prelaw, premedicine, preoptometry, prepharmacy, prephysical therapy, preveterinary medicine, and others offered. **Special study options:** Accelerated study, cooperative education, cross-registration, distance learning, double major, dual enrollment of high school students, exchange student, honors, independent study, internships, student-designed major, study abroad, teacher certification program, Washington semester, weekend college. **Credit/placement by examination:** AP, CLEP, SAT, ACT, institutional tests. 16 credit hours maximum toward associate degree, 32 toward bachelor's. **Support services:** Learning center, pre-admission summer program, remedial instruction, study skills assistance, tutoring, writing center.

Majors. **Agriculture:** General. **Biology:** General. **Business:** Accounting, business admin, finance, management information systems, managerial economics, marketing, real estate. **Communications:** General. **Computer sciences:** General. **Education:** Business, early childhood, elementary, health, middle, physical, special. **Engineering technology:** Manufacturing. **Foreign languages:** French, Spanish. **Health:** Medical radiologic technology/radiation therapy, nursing (RN). **History:** General. **Legal studies:** Paralegal. **Math:** General. **Parks/recreation:** Exercise sciences. **Philosophy/religion:** Philosophy. **Physical sciences:** Chemistry, geology, physics. **Psychology:** General. **Public administration:** Social work. **Social sciences:** General, geography, political science, sociology. **Visual/performing arts:** Dramatic, studio arts.

Most popular majors. Business/marketing 13%, communications/journalism 6%, education 16%, health sciences 6%, liberal arts 15%, public administration/social services 8%, social sciences 7%.

Computing on campus. 2,075 workstations in dormitories, library, computer center, student center. Dormitories wired for high-speed internet access and linked to campus network. Commuter students can connect to campus network. Online course registration, online library, helpline, repair service, student web hosting, wireless network available.

Student life. **Freshman orientation:** Available. Preregistration for classes offered. Offered several times in June and July. **Housing:** Coed dorms, single-sex dorms, special housing for disabled, apartments, fraternity/sorority housing, wellness housing available. $100 fully refundable deposit. Limited housing available at agriculture complex for agriculture science students. Housing for handicapped students and private rooms available. **Activities:** Bands, choral groups, dance, drama, literary magazine, music ensembles, musical theater, opera, radio station, student government, student newspaper, symphony orchestra, TV station, seven religious organizations, Young Democrats, Young Republicans, several service organizations.

Athletics. NCAA. **Intercollegiate:** Baseball M, basketball, cheerleading, cross-country, football (tackle) M, golf M, rifle, soccer W, softball W, tennis, track and field, volleyball W. **Intramural:** Archery, badminton, basketball, bowling, football (non-tackle) M, golf, racquetball, soccer M, softball, swimming, table tennis, tennis, track and field, volleyball. **Team name:** Eagles.

Student services. Adult student services, alcohol/substance abuse counseling, career counseling, services for economically disadvantaged, student employment services, financial aid counseling, health services, minority student services, on-campus daycare, personal counseling, placement for graduates, veterans' counselor. **Physically disabled:** Services for visually, hearing impaired.

Contact. E-mail: admissions@moreheadstate.edu
Phone: (606) 783-2000 Toll-free number: (800) 585-6781
Fax: (606) 783-5038
Jeffrey Liles, Assistant Vice President of Enrollment Services, Morehead State University, 100 Admissions Center, Morehead, KY 40351

Murray State University

Murray, Kentucky CB member
www.murraystate.edu CB code: 1494

- Public 4-year university
- Residential campus in large town
- 7,630 degree-seeking undergraduates: 10% part-time, 58% women, 6% African American, 1% Asian American, 1% Hispanic American, 2% international
- 1,631 degree-seeking graduate students
- 88% of applicants admitted
- ACT (writing recommended) required
- 49% graduate within 6 years

General. Founded in 1922. Regionally accredited. **Degrees:** 1,550 bachelor's, 19 associate awarded; master's offered. **ROTC:** Army. **Location:** 115 miles from Nashville, Tennessee. **Calendar:** Semester, limited summer session. **Full-time faculty:** 398 total; 79% have terminal degrees, 12% minority, 39% women. **Part-time faculty:** 164 total; 29% have terminal degrees, 6% minority, 56% women. **Class size:** 50% < 20, 40% 20-39, 6% 40-49, 4% 50-99, less than 1% >100. **Special facilities:** Biological research station, aquatic wildlife area, veterinary diagnostic research center, center of excellence for reservoir research, NASA-related technology transfer station, 2 farms, archaeological research and excavation site, West Kentucky regional museum, state center of excellence for telecommunication systems management.

Freshman class profile. 2,972 applied, 2,629 admitted, 1,311 enrolled.

Mid 50% test scores		**End year in good standing:**	87%
ACT composite:	19-25	**Return as sophomores:**	72%
GPA 3.75 or higher:	38%	**Out-of-state:**	31%
GPA 3.50-3.74:	22%	**Live on campus:**	82%
GPA 3.0-3.49:	33%	**International:**	2%
GPA 2.0-2.99:	7%	**Fraternities:**	12%
Rank in top quarter:	64%	**Sororities:**	10%
Rank in top tenth:	27%		

Basis for selection. Selective admission to nursing, business and social work programs. Students must rank in the top half of graduating class or have cumulative GPA of 3.0 or above, ACT score of 18 or above and complete precollege curriculum. Interview recommended for art, music, nursing majors. Auditions recommended for music majors. Portfolio recommended for art majors. **Homeschooled:** Transcript of courses and grades required. Students may be asked to verify lab experience and provide GED if ACT score is less than average. **Learning Disabled:** Contact office for students with learning disabilities.

High school preparation. College-preparatory program required. 22 units required. Required and recommended units include English 4, mathematics 3-4, social studies 3, science 3-4 (laboratory 1), foreign language 2 and academic electives 5. 1 art appreciation required. Social sciences must include U.S. history and world civilization. 1 arts and 1 computer science recommended. Math must include 3 algebra I and above. Sciences must include biology and chemistry or physics.

2008-2009 Annual costs. Tuition/fees: $5,748; $8,242 out-of-district; $15,612 out-of-state. Room/board: $6,004. Books/supplies: $990. Personal expenses: $1,500.

2008-2009 Financial aid. Need-based: 1,161 full-time freshmen applied for aid; 697 were judged to have need; 655 of these received aid. Average need met was 92%. Average scholarship/grant was $2,610; average loan $1,857. 47% of total undergraduate aid awarded as scholarships/grants, 53% as loans/jobs. **Non-need-based:** Awarded to 3,957 full-time undergraduates, including 912 freshmen. Scholarships awarded for academics, alumni affiliation, art, athletics, job skills, leadership, minority status, music/drama, ROTC, state residency. **Additional information:** Tuition discount for children and grandchildren of out-of-state alumni. Regional tuition for students from certain counties in Illinois, Tennessee, Missouri, and Indiana.

Application procedures. Admission: Closing date 8/1 (postmark date). $30 fee, may be waived for applicants with need. Admission notification on a rolling basis. **Financial aid:** Priority date 4/1; no closing date. FAFSA, institutional form required. Applicants notified on a rolling basis starting 4/15.

Academics. Special study options: Combined bachelor's/graduate degree, cooperative education, cross-registration, distance learning, double major, dual enrollment of high school students, ESL, exchange student, external degree, honors, independent study, internships, liberal arts/career combination, semester at sea, study abroad, teacher certification program, weekend college. Cooperative center for study in Britain, Kentucky Institute for International Studies, national and international student exchange. **Credit/placement by examination:** AP, CLEP, ACT, institutional tests. 96 credit hours maximum toward bachelor's degree. **Support services:** Learning center, pre-admission summer program, reduced course load, remedial instruction, study skills assistance, tutoring, writing center.

Honors college/program. Based on standardized test scores, GPA, evidence of creative and leadership abilities as displayed in extracurricular interests and activities, and faculty recommendation.

Majors. Agriculture: General. **Biology:** General. **Business:** General, accounting, business admin, finance, international, management information systems, marketing. **Communications:** Advertising, journalism, organizational, public relations, radio/tv. **Communications technology:** Desktop publishing, printing management. **Computer sciences:** General, information systems. **Conservation:** Wildlife. **Education:** Art, early childhood, elementary, health, middle, music, special. **Engineering:** Electrical, physics. **Engineering technology:** Civil, drafting, electromechanical, manufacturing, occupational safety, water quality. **Family/consumer sciences:** Food/nutrition. **Foreign languages:** French, German, Spanish. **Health:** Audiology/speech pathology, nursing (RN), veterinary technology/assistant. **History:** General. **Liberal arts:** Arts/sciences. **Math:** General. **Parks/recreation:** Exercise sciences, facilities management, health/fitness. **Philosophy/religion:** Philosophy. **Physical sciences:** Chemistry, geology, physics. **Protective services:** Criminal justice. **Psychology:** General. **Public administration:** Social work. **Social sciences:** Economics, international relations, political science, sociology. **Visual/performing arts:** Dramatic, studio arts. **Other:** Music business.

Most popular majors. Business/marketing 14%, communications/journalism 9%, education 17%, engineering/engineering technologies 7%, health sciences 10%, liberal arts 7%.

Computing on campus. 1,800 workstations in dormitories, library, computer center, student center. Dormitories wired for high-speed internet access and linked to campus network. Commuter students can connect to campus network. Online course registration, online library, helpline, repair service, student web hosting, wireless network available.

Student life. Freshman orientation: Available, $125 fee. Preregistration for classes offered. Fee covers entire family for two-day orientation; $75 for family attending one-day orientation. **Housing:** Guaranteed on-campus for freshmen. Coed dorms, single-sex dorms, special housing for disabled, apartments, fraternity/sorority housing, wellness housing available. $75 deposit, deadline 3/1. **Activities:** Bands, campus ministries, choral groups, dance, drama, film society, international student organizations, literary magazine, music ensembles, musical theater, opera, radio station, student government, student newspaper, symphony orchestra, TV station, Rotaract, Young Democrats, Young Republicans, Black Student council, Newman center, Baptist Student Center, Chi Alpha, Christian Fellowship, Wesley Foundation.

Athletics. NCAA. **Intercollegiate:** Baseball M, basketball, bowling M, cheerleading, cross-country, equestrian, football (tackle) M, golf, rifle, rodeo, rowing (crew) W, soccer W, tennis, track and field W, volleyball W. **Intramural:** Basketball, football (non-tackle), golf, racquetball, soccer, softball, tennis, volleyball. **Team name:** Racers.

Student services. Adult student services, alcohol/substance abuse counseling, chaplain/spiritual director, career counseling, services for economically disadvantaged, student employment services, financial aid counseling, health services, legal services, minority student services, on-campus daycare, personal counseling, placement for graduates, veterans' counselor, women's services. **Physically disabled:** Services for visually, hearing impaired. **Learning disabled:** Comprehensive services available.

Contact. E-mail: admissions@murraystate.edu
Phone: (270) 809-3741 Toll-free number: (800) 272-4678
Fax: (270) 809-3780
Lesa Harris, Director of Admission Services, Murray State University, 113 Sparks Hall, Murray, KY 42071

Northern Kentucky University

Highland Heights, Kentucky — **CB member**
www.nku.edu — **CB code: 1574**

- Public 4-year university
- Commuter campus in large city
- 12,296 degree-seeking undergraduates: 23% part-time, 57% women, 6% African American, 1% Asian American, 1% Hispanic American, 1% international
- 1,909 degree-seeking graduate students
- 32% graduate within 6 years

General. Founded in 1968. Regionally accredited. **Degrees:** 1,706 bachelor's, 226 associate awarded; master's, doctoral, first professional offered. **ROTC:** Army, Air Force. **Location:** 7 miles from Cincinnati. **Calendar:** Semester, extensive summer session. **Full-time faculty:** 538 total; 12% minority, 50% women. **Part-time faculty:** 534 total; 7% minority, 57% women. **Class size:** 39% < 20, 51% 20-39, 8% 40-49, 2% 50-99, less than 1% >100. **Special facilities:** Planetarium, anthropology museum, biology museum, geology exhibit, wildlife exhibit, cadaver lab.

Freshman class profile. 5,330 applied, 4,146 admitted, 2,183 enrolled.

Mid 50% test scores			
SAT critical reading:	440-550	Rank in top quarter:	29%
SAT math:	430-560	Rank in top tenth:	9%
ACT composite:	19-24	Return as sophomores:	67%
GPA 3.75 or higher:	17%	Out-of-state:	32%
GPA 3.50-3.74:	12%	Live on campus:	23%
GPA 3.0-3.49:	30%	International:	1%
GPA 2.0-2.99:	37%	Fraternities:	8%
		Sororities:	7%

Basis for selection. Open admission, but selective for some programs. Requirements vary by program. SAT/ACT scores required for admission to selective programs. General college preparatory programs required for placement, recommended for admission. **Homeschooled:** Transcript of courses and grades required.

High school preparation. College-preparatory program required. 22 units required. Required units include English 4, mathematics 3, social studies 3, history 1, science 3 (laboratory 1), foreign language 2, computer science 1, visual/performing arts 1 and academic electives 5.

2008-2009 Annual costs. Tuition/fees: $6,528; $11,952 out-of-state. Room/board: $6,082. Books/supplies: $800. Personal expenses: $3,279.

2007-2008 Financial aid. **Need-based:** 1,441 full-time freshmen applied for aid; 1,035 were judged to have need; 1,024 of these received aid. Average need met was 62%. Average scholarship/grant was $5,134; average loan $2,940. 38% of total undergraduate aid awarded as scholarships/grants, 62% as loans/jobs. **Non-need-based:** Awarded to 2,821 full-time undergraduates, including 917 freshmen. Scholarships awarded for academics, alumni affiliation, art, athletics, leadership, music/drama, state residency.

Application procedures. **Admission:** Priority date 5/1; deadline 8/1 (postmark date). $40 fee, may be waived for applicants with need. Admission notification on a rolling basis beginning on or about 9/15. Must reply by May 1 or within 2 week(s) if notified thereafter. **Financial aid:** Priority date 3/1; no closing date. FAFSA required. Applicants notified on a rolling basis starting 4/1.

Academics. **Special study options:** Accelerated study, cooperative education, cross-registration, distance learning, double major, dual enrollment of high school students, exchange student, honors, independent study, internships, liberal arts/career combination, study abroad, teacher certification program, weekend college. Introductory-level courses and some graduate-level courses and business seminars available at University College Campus in Covington; Summer NKU Academy gives remediation for denied students. **Credit/placement by examination:** AP, CLEP, IB, institutional tests. 24 credit hours maximum toward associate degree, 45 toward bachelor's. Credit awarded for CLEP, military, vocational, and National Occupational Competency Testing Institute exams. **Support services:** Learning center, preadmission summer program, reduced course load, remedial instruction, study skills assistance, tutoring, writing center.

Honors college/program. Admission requirements for honors program include 26 ACT composite or SAT score of 1760 or above, 3.5 high school GPA, and rank in top 10% of high school class. Students can take courses towards an honors minor. Courses vary in topic on a semester basis and most classes have 15 students or less. There are 550 total students in the honors program.

Majors. **Biology:** General. **Business:** General, accounting, business admin, entrepreneurial studies, finance, management information systems, managerial economics, marketing, organizational behavior. **Communications:** Broadcast journalism, journalism, public relations. **Computer sciences:** General, information systems, information technology. **Conservation:** Environmental science. **Education:** Business, elementary, kindergarten/preschool, middle, physical, trade/industrial. **Engineering technology:** Architectural, electrical, industrial. **Foreign languages:** French, German, Spanish. **Health:** Athletic training, health services, mental health services, nursing (RN). **History:** General. **Liberal arts:** Arts/sciences. **Math:** General. **Parks/recreation:** Sports admin. **Philosophy/religion:** Philosophy. **Physical sciences:** Chemistry, geology, physics. **Protective services:** Criminal justice. **Psychology:** General. **Public administration:** Social work. **Social sciences:** General, anthropology, geography, international relations, political science, sociology. **Visual/performing arts:** Commercial/advertising art, dramatic, studio arts. **Other:** Human Resource Management.

Most popular majors. Business/marketing 28%, communications/journalism 7%, education 11%, health sciences 11%, social sciences 6%, visual/performing arts 6%.

Computing on campus. 1,500 workstations in dormitories, library, computer center, student center. Dormitories wired for high-speed internet access and linked to campus network. Commuter students can connect to campus network. Online course registration, online library, helpline, repair service, student web hosting, wireless network available.

Student life. **Freshman orientation:** Mandatory, $45 fee. Preregistration for classes offered. Two day summer orientation program for new traditional-aged first-time students coming in the fall semester. One day program for new students entering in the spring semester. Half-day transfer student/nontraditional student orientation offered 3 times in the summer for new students coming in the fall. Half-day program in January for new students coming in the spring. **Policies:** Student organizations required to register annually and attend student organization orientation session annually. **Housing:** Coed dorms, single-sex dorms, special housing for disabled, apartments, fraternity/sorority housing, wellness housing available. $200 nonrefundable deposit, deadline 5/1. **Activities:** Bands, campus ministries, choral groups, dance, drama, international student organizations, literary magazine, music ensembles, musical theater, radio station, student government, student newspaper, TV station, Baptist Student Union, Newman Center, Schools for Schools, Up til Dawn, Black United Students, Common Ground, College Republicans, Campus Democrats, Latino Student Union.

Athletics. NCAA. **Intercollegiate:** Baseball M, basketball, cheerleading, cross-country, golf, soccer, softball W, tennis, track and field, volleyball W. **Intramural:** Basketball, bowling, football (non-tackle), racquetball, soccer, volleyball. **Team name:** Norse.

Student services. Alcohol/substance abuse counseling, career counseling, services for economically disadvantaged, student employment services, financial aid counseling, health services, legal services, minority student services, on-campus daycare, personal counseling, placement for graduates. **Physically disabled:** Services for visually, speech, hearing impaired.

Contact. E-mail: admitnku@nku.edu
Phone: (859) 572-5220 Toll-free number: (800) 637-9948
Fax: (859) 572-6665
Melissa Gorbandt, Director of Admissions - Outreach, Northern Kentucky University, Administrative Center 401, Northern Kentucky University, Highland Heights, KY 41099

Pikeville College

Pikeville, Kentucky — **CB member**
www.pc.edu — **CB code: 1625**

- Private 4-year liberal arts college affiliated with Presbyterian Church (USA)
- Residential campus in small town
- 755 degree-seeking undergraduates: 9% part-time, 55% women, 7% African American, 1% Asian American, 1% Hispanic American, 1% international
- 306 graduate students
- 34% graduate within 6 years; 32% enter graduate study

General. Founded in 1889. Regionally accredited. **Degrees:** 115 bachelor's, 19 associate awarded; first professional offered. **Location:** 150 miles from Lexington, 140 miles from Charleston, West Virginia. **Calendar:** Semester, limited summer session. **Full-time faculty:** 57 total; 51% have terminal degrees, 54% women. **Part-time faculty:** 15 total; 13% have terminal degrees, 53% women. **Class size:** 64% < 20, 35% 20-39, less than 1% 40-49.

Freshman class profile. 696 applied, 696 admitted, 183 enrolled.

Mid 50% test scores		GPA 2.0-2.99:	31%
ACT composite:	17-23	End year in good standing:	71%
GPA 3.75 or higher:	29%	Return as sophomores:	51%
GPA 3.50-3.74:	17%	Out-of-state:	31%
GPA 3.0-3.49:	22%	Live on campus:	60%

Basis for selection. Open admission, but selective for some programs. 19 ACT required for nursing, 21 ACT required for education majors.

High school preparation. College-preparatory program recommended. 13 units recommended. Recommended units include English 4, mathematics 3, social studies 2, history 1 and science 3.

2008-2009 Annual costs. Tuition/fees: $14,250. Room/board: $6,000. Books/supplies: $2,000. Personal expenses: $2,000.

2008-2009 Financial aid. All financial aid based on need. 180 full-time freshmen applied for aid; 179 were judged to have need; 179 of these received aid. Average need met was 93%. Average scholarship/grant was $12,971; average loan $4,573. 63% of total undergraduate aid awarded as scholarships/grants, 37% as loans/jobs.

Application procedures. Admission: Priority date 3/15; deadline 8/15 (receipt date). No application fee. Admission notification on a rolling basis beginning on or about 9/15. **Financial aid:** Priority date 3/15; no closing date. FAFSA, institutional form required. Applicants notified on a rolling basis starting 1/15; must reply by 5/1 or within 2 week(s) of notification.

Academics. Special study options: Double major, independent study, internships, liberal arts/career combination, student-designed major, study abroad, teacher certification program, Washington semester. **Credit/placement by examination:** AP, CLEP. 15 credit hours maximum toward associate degree, 15 toward bachelor's. **Support services:** Reduced course load, remedial instruction, study skills assistance, tutoring, writing center.

Majors. Biology: General. **Business:** Business admin. **Communications:** General. **Computer sciences:** General. **Education:** Elementary, middle. **History:** General. **Math:** General. **Philosophy/religion:** Religion. **Physical sciences:** Chemistry. **Protective services:** Criminal justice. **Psychology:** General. **Public administration:** Social work. **Social sciences:** Sociology. **Visual/performing arts:** Art.

Most popular majors. Biology 10%, business/marketing 22%, communications/journalism 11%, education 20%, history 7%, psychology 11%.

Computing on campus. 162 workstations in library, computer center. Dormitories wired for high-speed internet access and linked to campus network. Commuter students can connect to campus network. Online library, student web hosting, wireless network available.

Student life. Freshman orientation: Mandatory. Preregistration for classes offered. Held first 3 days before start of classes. **Policies:** No alcohol allowed on campus. **Housing:** Guaranteed on-campus for freshmen. Coed dorms, single-sex dorms available. $50 nonrefundable deposit, deadline 5/30. **Activities:** Pep band, choral groups, dance, literary magazine, student government, student newspaper, academic team, Appalachian Association for Justice, Baptist student union, Blessed Unity of God, Fellowship of Christian Athletes, Lambda Sigma society, Phi Beta Lambda, Psi Chi, Sigma Tau Delta, Young Republicans club.

Athletics. NAIA. **Intercollegiate:** Baseball M, basketball, bowling, cheerleading, cross-country, football (tackle) M, golf, soccer, softball W, tennis, track and field, volleyball W. **Intramural:** Basketball, bowling, football (non-tackle), softball, tennis, volleyball. **Team name:** Bears.

Student services. Chaplain/spiritual director, career counseling, student employment services, financial aid counseling, health services, personal counseling, veterans' counselor.

Contact. E-mail: wewantyou@pc.edu
Phone: (606) 218-5251 Toll-free number: (866) 232-7700
Fax: (606) 218-5255
Melinda Lynch, Dean, Enrollment Management, Pikeville College, 147 Sycamore Street, Pikeville, KY 41501-1194

St. Catharine College

St. Catharine, Kentucky
www.sccky.edu **CB code: 1690**

- Private 4-year health science and liberal arts college affiliated with Roman Catholic Church
- Commuter campus in small town
- 552 full-time, degree-seeking undergraduates

General. Founded in 1931. Regionally accredited. **Degrees:** 13 bachelor's, 84 associate awarded. **Location:** 50 miles from Louisville and Lexington. **Calendar:** Semester, limited summer session. **Full-time faculty:** 44 total; 7% minority, 50% women. **Part-time faculty:** 24 total; 79% women.

Basis for selection. Open admission. Assessment tests in mathematics, English and reading administered upon admission for course placement or remediation.

2008-2009 Annual costs. Tuition/fees: $13,600. Higher tuition applies for health science program. Room/board: $6,740. Books/supplies: $700. Personal expenses: $1,080.

Financial aid. All financial aid based on need.

Application procedures. Admission: No deadline. $15 fee, may be waived for applicants with need. Application must be submitted on paper. Admission notification on a rolling basis. **Financial aid:** Priority date 3/15; no closing date. FAFSA, institutional form required. Applicants notified on a rolling basis; must reply by 8/15.

Academics. Special study options: Distance learning, dual enrollment of high school students, independent study, internships, liberal arts/career combination, teacher certification program, weekend college. **Credit/placement by examination:** AP, CLEP, institutional tests. 35 credit hours maximum toward associate degree, 35 toward bachelor's. **Support services:** Learning center, reduced course load, remedial instruction, study skills assistance, tutoring.

Majors. Business: Business admin. **Education:** Elementary, middle. **Health:** Health services, sonography. **Liberal arts:** Arts/sciences. **Psychology:** General. **Other:** Criminal Justic/Law Enforcement Administration.

Most popular majors. Business/marketing 55%, education 36%, psychology 9%.

Computing on campus. 33 workstations in library, computer center. Dormitories wired for high-speed internet access. Online library available.

Student life. Freshman orientation: Mandatory. Preregistration for classes offered. Three-day program before start of classes. Optional semester-long orientation course. **Housing:** Single-sex dorms available. $25 deposit, deadline 8/15. **Activities:** Pep band, campus ministries, choral groups, literary magazine, student government, Phi Theta Kappa, Christian athletics club, African American club, art club, Students Above Traditional Age, student ambassadors, Students in Free Enterprise.

Athletics. NAIA, NCCAA. **Intercollegiate:** Baseball M, basketball, golf, soccer, softball W, volleyball W. **Team name:** Patriots.

Student services. Chaplain/spiritual director, career counseling, student employment services, financial aid counseling, on-campus daycare, personal counseling, veterans' counselor.

Contact. E-mail: twiley@sccky.edu
Phone: (859) 336-5082 ext. 1259 Toll-free
number: (800) 599-2000 ext. 1259 Fax: (859) 336-9381
Toni Wiley, Director of Admissions, St. Catharine College, 2735 Bardstown Road, St. Catharine, KY 40061

Spalding University

Louisville, Kentucky **CB member**
www.spalding.edu **CB code: 1552**

- Private 4-year university affiliated with Roman Catholic Church
- Commuter campus in large city
- 1,057 degree-seeking undergraduates: 32% part-time, 76% women, 26% African American, 1% Asian American, 1% Hispanic American, 1% international
- 647 degree-seeking graduate students
- 43% of applicants admitted
- SAT or ACT (ACT writing recommended) required
- 20% graduate within 6 years

General. Founded in 1814. Regionally accredited. **Degrees:** 209 bachelor's, 7 associate awarded; master's, doctoral offered. **ROTC:** Army, Air Force. **Location:** One mile from downtown. **Calendar:** Continuous, extensive summer session. **Full-time faculty:** 73 total; 84% have terminal degrees, 18% minority, 66% women. **Part-time faculty:** 89 total; 67% have terminal degrees, 17% minority, 57% women. **Class size:** 68% < 20, 30% 20-39, 1% 40-49. **Special facilities:** Historical collection of Edith Stein works.

Freshman class profile. 639 applied, 276 admitted, 131 enrolled.

Mid 50% test scores			
SAT critical reading:	440-570	GPA 3.0-3.49:	26%
SAT math:	470-520	GPA 2.0-2.99:	48%
SAT writing:	430-470	Return as sophomores:	69%
ACT composite:	16-20	Out-of-state:	1%
GPA 3.75 or higher:	5%	Live on campus:	3%
GPA 3.50-3.74:	15%	International:	2%

Basis for selection. Class rank (top half), academic preparation, and SAT or ACT test scores important. Interview and recommendations recommended.

High school preparation. College-preparatory program recommended. 16 units recommended. Recommended units include English 4, mathematics 3, social studies 2, science 2 and foreign language 2. 2 units of social science recommended.

2008-2009 Annual costs. Tuition/fees: $17,700. Room/board: $4,560. Books/supplies: $1,620. Personal expenses: $2,700.

2007-2008 Financial aid. Need-based: 18% of total undergraduate aid awarded as scholarships/grants, 82% as loans/jobs. **Non-need-based:** Scholarships awarded for academics, religious affiliation.

Application procedures. Admission: No deadline. $20 fee, may be waived for applicants with need. Admission notification on a rolling basis. **Financial aid:** Priority date 3/1; no closing date. FAFSA required. Applicants notified on a rolling basis starting 3/31; must reply within 2 week(s) of notification.

Academics. Special study options: Accelerated study, cross-registration, distance learning, double major, independent study, internships, study abroad, teacher certification program, weekend college. **Credit/placement by examination:** AP, CLEP, institutional tests. 32 credit hours maximum toward associate degree, 32 toward bachelor's. **Support services:** Learning center, reduced course load, remedial instruction, study skills assistance, tutoring, writing center.

Majors. Business: General, accounting. **Communications:** General. **Education:** General, elementary, middle, special. **Health:** Nursing (RN), occupational therapy assistant. **Interdisciplinary:** Natural sciences. **Liberal arts:** Humanities. **Psychology:** General. **Public administration:** Social work. **Social sciences:** General.

Most popular majors. Business/marketing 19%, education 9%, health sciences 40%, psychology 12%, public administration/social services 7%.

Computing on campus. 130 workstations in library, student center. Online course registration, online library, helpline, wireless network available.

Student life. Freshman orientation: Available. Preregistration for classes offered. **Housing:** Guaranteed on-campus for freshmen. Coed dorms available. $100 deposit. **Activities:** Campus ministries, student government, student newspaper, International club, Campus Crusade for Christ, Fellowship of Christian Athletes, Black student association, Advocates for Campus Accessibility.

Athletics. NAIA. **Intercollegiate:** Baseball M, basketball, cross-country, golf M, soccer, softball W, volleyball W. **Intramural:** Basketball, bowling, soccer, softball W, table tennis, tennis, volleyball, weight lifting. **Team name:** Golden Eagles.

Student services. Adult student services, alcohol/substance abuse counseling, chaplain/spiritual director, career counseling, services for economically disadvantaged, student employment services, financial aid counseling, minority student services, personal counseling. **Physically disabled:** Services for visually impaired.

Contact. E-mail: admissions@spalding.edu
Phone: (502) 585-7111 Toll-free number: (800) 896-8941 ext. 2111
Fax: (502) 585-7128
Chris Hart, Director of Admissions, Spalding University, 845 S. Third Street, Louisville, KY 40203

Sullivan University

Louisville, Kentucky
www.sullivan.edu **CB code: 0811**

- For-profit 4-year university
- Commuter campus in large city
- 4,338 undergraduates
- 440 graduate students
- Interview required

General. Founded in 1962. Regionally accredited. **Degrees:** 392 bachelor's, 420 associate awarded; master's, doctoral offered. **Location:** 110 miles from Indianapolis, 110 miles from Cincinnati. **Calendar:** Quarter, extensive summer session. **Full-time faculty:** 109 total; 32% have terminal degrees. **Part-time faculty:** 122 total; 34% have terminal degrees. **Special facilities:** University-operated fine dining restaurant.

Freshman class profile.

Out-of-state:	17%	Live on campus:	19%

Basis for selection. Test scores, interview, high school record important. CPAT required for placement if no ACT or SAT scores are available.

2008-2009 Annual costs. Room only: $4,680. Books/supplies: $1,800. Personal expenses: $1,200.

Financial aid. All financial aid based on need.

Application procedures. Admission: No deadline. $100 fee. Admission notification on a rolling basis. **Financial aid:** No deadline. FAFSA required. Applicants notified on a rolling basis starting 1/2.

Academics. Day classes meet Monday to Thursday; special program on Friday for additional help. Night/Weekend classes meet Monday through Sunday; many graduate and undergraduate classes are offered online. **Special study options:** Accelerated study, distance learning, double major, independent study, internships, weekend college. **Credit/placement by examination:** CLEP, IB, SAT, ACT, institutional tests. **Support services:** Reduced course load, remedial instruction, study skills assistance, tutoring.

Majors. Business: Accounting, business admin, tourism promotion. **Computer sciences:** General, applications programming. **Legal studies:** Paralegal. **Personal/culinary services:** Culinary arts.

Computing on campus. 252 workstations in library, computer center. Commuter students can connect to campus network. Online course registration, online library, helpline available.

Student life. Freshman orientation: Mandatory. One and two day orientations held at the beginning of each quarter. **Housing:** Apartments, wellness housing available. $95 nonrefundable deposit, deadline 9/30. Housing for freshmen under 21 who live outside a 75-mile radius from Louisville. **Activities:** Student newspaper, student activities committee, travel club, Culinary Salon Competition Team, Student Paralegal Association, International Association of Administrative Professionals, Rotarac.

Athletics. Intramural: Basketball, bowling, softball, volleyball.

Student services. Career counseling, student employment services, financial aid counseling, personal counseling, placement for graduates, veterans' counselor.

Contact. E-mail: admissions@sullivan.edu
Phone: (502) 456-6505 Toll-free number: (800) 844-1354
Fax: (502) 456-0040
Terri Thomas, Director of Admissions, Sullivan University, 3101 Bardstown Road, Louisville, KY 40205

Thomas More College

Crestview Hills, Kentucky **CB member**
www.thomasmore.edu **CB code: 1876**

- Private 4-year liberal arts college affiliated with Roman Catholic Church
- Commuter campus in small town
- 1,397 degree-seeking undergraduates
- 1,894 degree-seeking graduate students
- 80% of applicants admitted
- SAT or ACT (ACT writing optional) required
- 42% graduate within 6 years

General. Founded in 1921. Regionally accredited. **Degrees:** 271 bachelor's, 73 associate awarded; master's offered. **ROTC:** Army, Air Force. **Location:** 8 miles from Cincinnati. **Calendar:** Semester, limited summer session. **Full-time faculty:** 71 total; 68% have terminal degrees, 6% minority, 42% women. **Part-time faculty:** 67 total. **Class size:** 74% < 20, 25% 20-39, less than 1% 40-49. **Special facilities:** Biology field station, observatory.

Freshman class profile. 1,055 applied, 843 admitted, 275 enrolled.

Mid 50% test scores			
SAT critical reading:	440-570	**GPA 2.0-2.99:**	28%
SAT math:	460-570	**Rank in top quarter:**	32%
ACT composite:	19-25	**Rank in top tenth:**	14%
GPA 3.75 or higher:	21%	**Return as sophomores:**	73%
GPA 3.50-3.74:	18%	**Out-of-state:**	49%
GPA 3.0-3.49:	32%	**Live on campus:**	56%

Basis for selection. Rank in top half of graduating class, 2.0 GPA (college-preparatory curriculum), and 20 ACT with at least 20 English score, or 1010 SAT (exclusive of writing) with at least 530 verbal score important. Test scores required prior to registration. Interview recommended. Essay recommended for special admissions. **Learning Disabled:** Need to submit legal documentation of disabilities.

High school preparation. 15 units required. Required and recommended units include English 4, mathematics 3, social studies 3, science 3 (laboratory 1), foreign language 2 and academic electives 2. Art appreciation and computer literacy recommended.

2008-2009 Annual costs. Tuition/fees: $22,220. All full-time freshmen are guaranteed a maximum of 3% increase in tuition per year. Room/board: $5,870. Books/supplies: $1,000. Personal expenses: $2,300.

2007-2008 Financial aid. Non-need-based: Scholarships awarded for academics, alumni affiliation, art, job skills, leadership, minority status, music/drama, religious affiliation, ROTC, state residency.

Application procedures. Admission: Priority date 3/15; deadline 8/15 (postmark date). $25 fee, may be waived for applicants with need, free for online applicants. Admission notification on a rolling basis. Housing discount for those who finalize registration for classes by May 15th. **Financial aid:** Priority date 3/15; no closing date. FAFSA, institutional form required. Applicants notified on a rolling basis; must reply by 5/1.

Academics. Special study options: Accelerated study, cooperative education, cross-registration, double major, dual enrollment of high school students, honors, independent study, internships, liberal arts/career combination, student-designed major, study abroad, teacher certification program, weekend college. **Credit/placement by examination:** AP, CLEP, IB, SAT, ACT, institutional tests. 30 credit hours maximum toward associate degree, 60 toward bachelor's. **Support services:** Learning center, pre-admission summer program, reduced course load, remedial instruction, study skills assistance, tutoring, writing center.

Majors. Area/ethnic studies: Latin American. **Biology:** General. **Business:** General, accounting. **Communications:** General. **Computer sciences:** General. **Conservation:** Environmental science. **Education:** General, art, biology, business, chemistry, computer, elementary, English, mathematics, middle, physics, science, secondary, social studies. **Foreign languages:** General. **Health:** Clinical lab science, nursing (RN), predental, premedicine, prepharmacy, preveterinary. **History:** General. **Liberal arts:** Arts/sciences, humanities. **Math:** General. **Parks/recreation:** Sports admin. **Philosophy/religion:** Philosophy, religion. **Physical sciences:** Chemistry, physics. **Protective services:** Forensics, law enforcement admin. **Psychology:** General. **Social sciences:** Economics, international relations, political science, sociology. **Visual/performing arts:** General, dramatic, studio arts.

Most popular majors. Business/marketing 49%, communications/journalism 12%, education 8%, health sciences 6%.

Computing on campus. 163 workstations in dormitories, library, computer center, student center. Dormitories wired for high-speed internet access and linked to campus network. Commuter students can connect to campus network. Online course registration, online library, helpline, repair service, student web hosting, wireless network available.

Student life. Freshman orientation: Mandatory, $125 fee. Preregistration for classes offered. Two-day program held at beginning of fall semester in August. **Housing:** Guaranteed on-campus for all undergraduates. Coed dorms, single-sex dorms available. $200 partly refundable deposit, deadline 8/15. **Activities:** Campus ministries, choral groups, drama, international student organizations, literary magazine, student government, student activities board, residence hall government association, African American Society, deans council, service learning, Habitat for Humanity, business society, social issues commune.

Athletics. NCAA. **Intercollegiate:** Baseball M, basketball, cross-country, football (tackle) M, golf, soccer, softball W, tennis, volleyball W. **Intramural:** Basketball, football (non-tackle), golf, racquetball, softball, volleyball. **Team name:** Saints.

Student services. Adult student services, alcohol/substance abuse counseling, chaplain/spiritual director, career counseling, student employment services, financial aid counseling, health services, minority student services, personal counseling, placement for graduates, veterans' counselor. **Physically disabled:** Services for visually, speech, hearing impaired.

Contact. E-mail: admissions@thomasmore.edu
Phone: (859) 344-3332 Toll-free number: (800) 825-4557
Fax: (859) 344-3444
Matthew Webster, Vice President for Student Services, Thomas More College, 333 Thomas More Parkway, Crestview Hills, KY 41017-3495

Transylvania University

Lexington, Kentucky — **CB member**
www.transy.edu — **CB code: 1808**

- Private 4-year liberal arts college affiliated with Christian Church (Disciples of Christ)
- Residential campus in large city
- 1,154 degree-seeking undergraduates: 1% part-time, 60% women, 3% African American, 2% Asian American, 1% Hispanic American
- 80% of applicants admitted
- SAT or ACT (ACT writing optional), application essay required
- 69% graduate within 6 years; 41% enter graduate study

General. Founded in 1780. Regionally accredited. **Degrees:** 261 bachelor's awarded. **ROTC:** Army, Air Force. **Location:** 80 miles from Louisville, 80 miles from Cincinnati. **Calendar:** 4-1-4. 4-4-1. Limited summer session. **Full-time faculty:** 85 total; 92% have terminal degrees, 7% minority, 39% women. **Part-time faculty:** 24 total; 21% have terminal degrees, 12% minority, 29% women. **Class size:** 61% < 20, 39% 20-39. **Special facilities:** Museum of early scientific apparatus, special library collections of early medical and scientific works and Kentucky books.

Freshman class profile. 1,334 applied, 1,063 admitted, 317 enrolled.

Mid 50% test scores			
SAT critical reading:	530-640	**GPA 2.0-2.99:**	7%
SAT math:	530-640	**Rank in top quarter:**	66%
SAT writing:	510-640	**Rank in top tenth:**	40%
ACT composite:	24-29	**Return as sophomores:**	84%
GPA 3.75 or higher:	54%	**Out-of-state:**	18%
GPA 3.50-3.74:	19%	**Live on campus:**	96%
GPA 3.0-3.49:	20%	**Fraternities:**	55%
		Sororities:	55%

Basis for selection. Rigor of high school curriculum, high school grade point average, and standardized test scores are most important. Recommendations, essay, and extracurricular activities are important as are excellence of character and high personal goals. Interview recommended. Audition required for music scholarship applicants. Portfolio required for art scholarship applicants. **Learning Disabled:** Meet with coordinator of disability services.

High school preparation. 12 units required; 16 recommended. Required and recommended units include English 4, mathematics 3-4, social studies 2, history 1, science 3-4 (laboratory 2), foreign language 2 and academic electives 1. Broad high school curriculum important to allow full participation in required liberal arts course work. Solid background in English highly recommended.

2008-2009 Annual costs. Tuition/fees: $23,810. Room/board: $7,450. Books/supplies: $750. Personal expenses: $1,250.

2008-2009 Financial aid. Need-based: 272 full-time freshmen applied for aid; 217 were judged to have need; 217 of these received aid. Average need met was 86%. Average scholarship/grant was $15,690; average loan $4,250. 74% of total undergraduate aid awarded as scholarships/grants, 26% as loans/jobs. **Non-need-based:** Awarded to 487 full-time undergraduates, including 133 freshmen. Scholarships awarded for academics, art, leadership, minority status, music/drama, religious affiliation, ROTC, state residency. **Additional information:** Auditions and portfolios required for music and art scholarships respectively. Essays required for other scholarship programs. Applications for William T. Young scholarships must be received by December 1.

Application procedures. Admission: Priority date 12/1; deadline 2/1 (postmark date). $30 fee, may be waived for applicants with need, free for online applicants. Admission notification 3/1. Must reply by 5/1. **Financial aid:** Priority date 3/1; no closing date. FAFSA required. Applicants notified on a rolling basis starting 3/15; must reply by 5/1 or within 2 week(s) of notification.

Academics. Special study options: Combined bachelor's/graduate degree, double major, independent study, internships, liberal arts/career combination, student-designed major, study abroad, teacher certification program, Washington semester. **Credit/placement by examination:** AP, CLEP,

IB, ACT, institutional tests. No limit to credit for AP or IB. **Support services:** Learning center, study skills assistance, tutoring, writing center.

Majors. **Biology:** General. **Business:** General, accounting. **Computer sciences:** General. **Education:** Elementary, middle, music, physical. **Foreign languages:** Classics, French, Spanish. **History:** General. **Liberal arts:** Arts/sciences. **Math:** General. **Parks/recreation:** Exercise sciences. **Philosophy/religion:** Philosophy, religion. **Physical sciences:** Chemistry, physics. **Psychology:** General. **Social sciences:** Anthropology, economics, political science, sociology. **Visual/performing arts:** Dramatic, music performance, studio arts.

Most popular majors. Biology 8%, business/marketing 12%, foreign language 10%, interdisciplinary studies 7%, parks/recreation 6%, psychology 10%, social sciences 14%, visual/performing arts 6%.

Computing on campus. 250 workstations in dormitories, library, computer center, student center. Dormitories wired for high-speed internet access and linked to campus network. Commuter students can connect to campus network. Online library, helpline, student web hosting, wireless network available.

Student life. **Freshman orientation:** Mandatory. Preregistration for classes offered. One-day summer event; 4-day program before classes begin. **Housing:** Guaranteed on-campus for freshmen. Coed dorms, single-sex dorms, special housing for disabled, apartments, wellness housing available. $200 nonrefundable deposit, deadline 5/1. Efficiency apartment option for upperclassmen; two units with facilities for disabled students available. **Activities:** Bands, choral groups, dance, drama, literary magazine, music ensembles, musical theater, opera, radio station, student government, student newspaper, Diversity Action Council, College Democrats, College Republicans, Alternative Spring Break, Campus Crusade, student government association, student activities board, student alumni association, Transylvania Environmental Rights and Responsibilities Alliance.

Athletics. NCAA. **Intercollegiate:** Baseball M, basketball, cross-country, diving, field hockey W, golf, soccer, softball W, swimming, tennis, track and field, volleyball W. **Intramural:** Badminton, basketball, bowling, cross-country, football (non-tackle), football (tackle), golf, handball, racquetball, soccer, softball, swimming, table tennis, tennis, volleyball. **Team name:** Pioneers.

Student services. Alcohol/substance abuse counseling, chaplain/spiritual director, career counseling, student employment services, financial aid counseling, health services, minority student services, personal counseling, veterans' counselor. **Physically disabled:** Services for visually, hearing impaired.

Contact. E-mail: admissions@transy.edu
Phone: (859) 233-8242 Toll-free number: (800) 872-6798
Fax: (859) 281-3649
Brad Goan, Director of Admissions, Transylvania University, 300 North Broadway, Lexington, KY 40508-1797

Union College
Barbourville, Kentucky
www.unionky.edu **CB code: 1825**

- Private 4-year liberal arts and teachers college affiliated with United Methodist Church
- Residential campus in small town
- 804 degree-seeking undergraduates: 5% part-time, 45% women, 9% African American, 2% Hispanic American, 4% international
- SAT or ACT (ACT writing recommended) required
- 33% graduate within 6 years

General. Founded in 1879. Regionally accredited. **Degrees:** 121 bachelor's awarded; master's offered. **ROTC:** Army. **Location:** 107 miles from Lexington, 107 miles from Knoxville, TN. **Calendar:** Semester, limited summer session. **Full-time faculty:** 57 total; 70% have terminal degrees, 9% minority, 42% women. **Part-time faculty:** 33 total; 46% have terminal degrees, 3% minority, 52% women. **Class size:** 78% < 20, 22% 20-39.

Freshman class profile. 1,410 applied, 1,069 admitted, 245 enrolled.

Mid 50% test scores		**GPA 3.0-3.49:**	27%
SAT critical reading:	380-460	**GPA 2.0-2.99:**	53%
SAT math:	410-490	**Out-of-state:**	32%
ACT composite:	17-21	**Live on campus:**	79%
GPA 3.75 or higher:	6%	**International:**	2%
GPA 3.50-3.74:	11%		

Basis for selection. Open admission, but selective for some programs. School achievement record, course work, class rank, SAT or ACT scores important. ACT preferred for all, required for teacher education program. Interview recommended. **Homeschooled:** Statement describing homeschool structure and mission, transcript of courses and grades, letter of recommendation (nonparent) required. Academic calender with attendance required. Submission of a writing sample, a summary of travel related or work experience may be requested. **Learning Disabled:** Students must provide documentation to coordinator of special program to receive necessary accommodations.

High school preparation. College-preparatory program recommended. Recommended units include English 4, mathematics 3, science 2 (laboratory 2) and foreign language 1.

2009-2010 Annual costs. Tuition/fees (projected): $17,894. Room/board: $3,300. Books/supplies: $1,300. Personal expenses: $1,400.

2007-2008 Financial aid. **Need-based:** 231 full-time freshmen applied for aid; 215 were judged to have need; 215 of these received aid. Average need met was 82%. Average scholarship/grant was $11,460; average loan $6,118. 58% of total undergraduate aid awarded as scholarships/grants, 42% as loans/jobs. **Non-need-based:** Awarded to 148 full-time undergraduates, including 58 freshmen. Scholarships awarded for academics, athletics, leadership, minority status, music/drama, religious affiliation, state residency.

Application procedures. **Admission:** No deadline. $10 fee, may be waived for applicants with need. Admission notification on a rolling basis. **Financial aid:** Priority date 3/15; no closing date. FAFSA required. Applicants notified on a rolling basis starting 3/1; must reply within 2 week(s) of notification.

Academics. **Special study options:** Combined bachelor's/graduate degree, distance learning, double major, honors, independent study, internships, student-designed major, study abroad, teacher certification program. **Credit/placement by examination:** AP, CLEP, ACT, institutional tests. 30 credit hours maximum toward bachelor's degree. **Support services:** Learning center, remedial instruction, study skills assistance, tutoring, writing center.

Majors. **Biology:** General. **Business:** Accounting, business admin. **Communications:** General. **Education:** Elementary, health, middle, physical, science, social studies, special. **History:** General. **Math:** General. **Parks/recreation:** Facilities management, sports admin. **Philosophy/religion:** Religion. **Physical sciences:** Chemistry. **Protective services:** Law enforcement admin. **Psychology:** General. **Social sciences:** Sociology. **Theology:** Religious ed.

Most popular majors. Business/marketing 29%, education 33%, history 7%, psychology 7%, security/protective services 7%.

Computing on campus. 230 workstations in dormitories, library, computer center, student center. Dormitories wired for high-speed internet access and linked to campus network. Commuter students can connect to campus network. Online course registration, online library, wireless network available.

Student life. **Freshman orientation:** Mandatory. Preregistration for classes offered. One day session offered in May, June, and July. **Housing:** Guaranteed on-campus for freshmen. Single-sex dorms, apartments, wellness housing available. $50 fully refundable deposit. Private rooms occasionally available to upperclassmen. **Activities:** Pep band, choral groups, drama, literary magazine, student government, student newspaper, Fellowship of Christian Athletes, Appalachian wilderness club, Baptist student union, Methodist student organizations, Newman club, student ambassadors, science society, philosophy society.

Athletics. NAIA. **Intercollegiate:** Baseball M, basketball, bowling, cross-country, football (tackle) M, golf, soccer, softball W, swimming, tennis, volleyball W. **Intramural:** Basketball, football (non-tackle), soccer, softball, table tennis, tennis, volleyball. **Team name:** Bulldogs.

Student services. Alcohol/substance abuse counseling, chaplain/spiritual director, career counseling, services for economically disadvantaged, financial aid counseling, health services, personal counseling, placement for graduates. **Physically disabled:** Services for visually, hearing impaired.

Contact. E-mail: enrollme@unionky.edu
Phone: (606) 546-1229 Toll-free number: (800) 489-8646
Fax: (606) 546-1667
Jerry Jackson, Dean of Enrollment Management, Union College, 310 College Street, Box 005, Barbourville, KY 40906

University of Kentucky

Lexington, Kentucky **CB member**
www.uky.edu **CB code: 1837**

- Public 4-year university
- Commuter campus in large city
- 18,591 degree-seeking undergraduates: 7% part-time, 50% women, 7% African American, 2% Asian American, 1% Hispanic American, 1% international
- 6,704 degree-seeking graduate students
- 79% of applicants admitted
- SAT or ACT (ACT writing optional) required
- 61% graduate within 6 years

General. Founded in 1865. Regionally accredited. **Degrees:** 3,775 bachelor's awarded; master's, doctoral, first professional offered. **ROTC:** Army, Air Force. **Location:** 80 miles from Louisville, 90 miles from Cincinnati. **Calendar:** Semester, limited summer session. **Full-time faculty:** 1,250 total. **Part-time faculty:** 440 total. **Class size:** 23% < 20, 53% 20-39, 6% 40-49, 11% 50-99, 7% >100. **Special facilities:** Center for the arts, Van de Graaff accelerator, equine research center, center for the humanities.

Freshman class profile. 11,120 applied, 8,757 admitted, 4,110 enrolled.

Mid 50% test scores		**GPA 2.0-2.99:**	14%
SAT critical reading:	500-620	**Rank in top quarter:**	50%
SAT math:	500-630	**Rank in top tenth:**	23%
ACT composite:	22-27	**Return as sophomores:**	81%
GPA 3.75 or higher:	46%	**Out-of-state:**	20%
GPA 3.50-3.74:	16%	**International:**	1%
GPA 3.0-3.49:	24%		

Basis for selection. Test scores and GPA should indicate potential for academic success. Required course work and extracurricular activities also considered. Students out of high school 2 years or more with no college credit admitted on probationary basis. Audition required of music majors. **Homeschooled:** List of textbooks, attendance record and 2 letters of recommendation from persons outside family required.

High school preparation. 22 units required. Required and recommended units include English 4, mathematics 3-4, social studies 3, science 3-4, foreign language 2 and academic electives 5. 1 fine or performing arts, .5 health, .5 physical education required.

2008-2009 Annual costs. Tuition/fees: $7,736; $15,884 out-of-state. Tuition charges include fees. Upper division tuition $7,302, in-state; $15,094, out-of-state. Room/board: $5,887. Books/supplies: $800. Personal expenses: $1,452.

2008-2009 Financial aid. Non-need-based: Scholarships awarded for academics, alumni affiliation, art, athletics, job skills, leadership, minority status, music/drama, ROTC, state residency.

Application procedures. Admission: Closing date 2/15 (postmark date). $40 fee, may be waived for applicants with need. Admission notification on a rolling basis beginning on or about 10/1. Reply by 05/01 preferred. **Financial aid:** Priority date 2/15; no closing date. FAFSA required. Applicants notified on a rolling basis starting 4/1; must reply within 3 week(s) of notification.

Academics. Special study options: Accelerated study, combined bachelor's/graduate degree, cooperative education, distance learning, double major, ESL, exchange student, honors, independent study, internships, study abroad, teacher certification program, weekend college. **Credit/placement by examination:** AP, CLEP, IB, SAT, ACT, institutional tests. Students who receive Advanced Placement credit for a course may apply this credit the same way credit earned by passing a course is applied. **Support services:** Learning center, reduced course load, remedial instruction, tutoring, writing center.

Majors. Agriculture: Agronomy, animal sciences, economics, food science. **Architecture:** Architecture, landscape. **Area/ethnic studies:** Latin American. **Biology:** General. **Business:** General, accounting, finance, hospitality admin, management science, managerial economics, marketing. **Communications:** General, advertising, journalism, radio/tv. **Computer sciences:** General. **Conservation:** General, forest sciences. **Education:** Art, early childhood, elementary, health, mathematics, middle, music, physical, science, special. **Engineering:** Agricultural, chemical, civil, electrical, materials, mechanical, mining. **Family/consumer sciences:** General, food/nutrition. **Foreign languages:** Classics, French, German, linguistics, Russian, Spanish. **Health:** Audiology/speech pathology, clinical lab science, health care admin. **History:** General. **Math:** General. **Philosophy/religion:** Philosophy. **Physical sciences:** Chemistry, geology, physics. **Psychology:** General. **Public administration:** Social work. **Social sciences:** General, anthropology, economics, geography, political science, sociology. **Visual/performing arts:** Art history/conservation, arts management, dramatic, interior design, music history, music performance.

Most popular majors. Biology 6%, business/marketing 18%, communications/journalism 10%, education 8%, engineering/engineering technologies 7%, psychology 6%, social sciences 9%.

Computing on campus. 810 workstations in dormitories, library, computer center, student center. Dormitories wired for high-speed internet access and linked to campus network. Commuter students can connect to campus network. Online course registration, online library, helpline, wireless network available.

Student life. Freshman orientation: Mandatory, $40 fee. Preregistration for classes offered. $20 additional charge per guest. **Housing:** Coed dorms, single-sex dorms, special housing for disabled, apartments, fraternity/sorority housing available. $300 deposit, deadline 6/1. **Activities:** Bands, choral groups, dance, drama, literary magazine, music ensembles, musical theater, opera, radio station, student government, student newspaper, symphony orchestra, More than 300 organizations.

Athletics. NCAA. **Intercollegiate:** Baseball M, basketball, cross-country, diving, football (tackle) M, golf, gymnastics W, rifle, soccer, softball W, swimming, tennis, track and field, volleyball W. **Intramural:** Archery, badminton, basketball, bowling, cross-country, fencing, field hockey W, football (non-tackle), golf, handball, ice hockey M, lacrosse, racquetball, rugby M, skiing, soccer, softball, squash, swimming, table tennis, tennis, track and field, volleyball, wrestling M. **Team name:** Wildcats.

Student services. Adult student services, career counseling, student employment services, health services, on-campus daycare, personal counseling, placement for graduates, veterans' counselor. **Physically disabled:** Services for visually, speech, hearing impaired.

Contact. E-mail: admisso@uky.edu
Phone: (859) 257-2000 Toll-free number: (800) 432-0967
Fax: (859) 257-3823
Don Witt, Assistant Provost for Enrollment Management, University of Kentucky, 100 W.D. Funkhouser Building, Lexington, KY 40506-0054

University of Louisville

Louisville, Kentucky **CB member**
www.louisville.edu **CB code: 1838**

- Public 4-year university
- Commuter campus in very large city
- 14,524 degree-seeking undergraduates: 20% part-time, 51% women, 12% African American, 3% Asian American, 2% Hispanic American, 1% international
- 5,203 degree-seeking graduate students
- 70% of applicants admitted
- SAT or ACT (ACT writing optional) required
- 46% graduate within 6 years

General. Founded in 1798. Regionally accredited. **Degrees:** 2,298 bachelor's, 19 associate awarded; master's, doctoral, first professional offered. **ROTC:** Army, Air Force. **Location:** 3 miles from downtown, 92 miles from Cincinnati, OH. **Calendar:** Semester, extensive summer session. **Full-time faculty:** 862 total; 90% have terminal degrees, 20% minority, 40% women. **Part-time faculty:** 492 total; 43% have terminal degrees, 11% minority, 52% women. **Class size:** 26% < 20, 54% 20-39, 8% 40-49, 9% 50-99, 4% >100. **Special facilities:** Planetarium, computer-aided engineering building with robotics laboratory, rapid prototype facility with Sinterstation 2000 system.

Freshman class profile. 7,861 applied, 5,473 admitted, 2,610 enrolled.

Mid 50% test scores		**Rank in top quarter:**	56%
SAT critical reading:	500-620	**Rank in top tenth:**	28%
SAT math:	510-640	**Return as sophomores:**	78%
ACT composite:	21-27	**Out-of-state:**	15%
GPA 3.75 or higher:	33%	**Live on campus:**	62%
GPA 3.50-3.74:	20%	**International:**	1%
GPA 3.0-3.49:	30%	**Fraternities:**	24%
GPA 2.0-2.99:	17%	**Sororities:**	13%

Basis for selection. High school grades, curriculum, class rank and test scores very important. Rank in top half of graduating class. Partnership with local community college for those not meeting unit admission requirements. Diagnostic testing/interview option for those failing to meet minimum. Freshmen must have completed state precollege curriculum. SAT/ACT score reports must be received by registration before the first day of class. **Homeschooled:** Transcript of courses and grades required.

High school preparation. Required and recommended units include English 4, mathematics 3-4, social studies 3, science 3-4 (laboratory 1), foreign language 2-3, visual/performing arts 1 and academic electives 5. History requirement included in social studies, 5 electives must be rigorous.

2008-2009 Annual costs. Tuition/fees: $7,564; $18,354 out-of-state. Room/board: $6,288. Books/supplies: $1,000. Personal expenses: $4,086.

2008-2009 Financial aid. **Non-need-based:** Scholarships awarded for academics, art, athletics, leadership, minority status, music/drama, ROTC.

Application procedures. **Admission:** Priority date 2/15; deadline 8/25 (receipt date). $40 fee, may be waived for applicants with need. Admission notification on a rolling basis. Must reply by 5/1. **Financial aid:** Priority date 3/15; no closing date. FAFSA required. Applicants notified on a rolling basis starting 4/1; must reply by 5/1.

Academics. **Special study options:** Accelerated study, combined bachelor's/graduate degree, cooperative education, cross-registration, distance learning, double major, dual enrollment of high school students, ESL, honors, independent study, internships, student-designed major, study abroad, teacher certification program. **Credit/placement by examination:** AP, CLEP, IB, SAT, ACT, institutional tests. 24 credit hours maximum toward bachelor's degree. Candidates for the nursing program may apply no more than 37 semester hours of CLEP credit toward the bachelor's degree. **Support services:** Learning center, pre-admission summer program, reduced course load, remedial instruction, tutoring.

Majors. **Area/ethnic studies:** African-American, women's. **Biology:** General. **Business:** Accounting, business admin, finance, management information systems, managerial economics, marketing. **Communications:** General. **Education:** Elementary, music, trade/industrial. **Engineering:** General, biomedical, chemical, civil, computer, electrical, industrial, mechanical. **Foreign languages:** French, Spanish. **Health:** Dental hygiene, music therapy, nursing (RN). **History:** General. **Liberal arts:** Arts/sciences, humanities. **Math:** General. **Parks/recreation:** Health/fitness, sports admin. **Philosophy/religion:** Philosophy. **Physical sciences:** Chemistry, physics. **Protective services:** Law enforcement admin. **Psychology:** General. **Social sciences:** Anthropology, economics, geography, political science, sociology. **Visual/performing arts:** Art history/conservation, dramatic, studio arts. **Other:** Equine Business, Science - Medical and Dental.

Most popular majors. Business/marketing 22%, communications/journalism 7%, engineering/engineering technologies 8%, health sciences 8%, parks/recreation 7%, psychology 8%, social sciences 10%.

Computing on campus. 327 workstations in dormitories, library, computer center, student center. Dormitories wired for high-speed internet access and linked to campus network. Commuter students can connect to campus network. Online course registration, online library, helpline, repair service, student web hosting, wireless network available.

Student life. **Freshman orientation:** Mandatory, $125 fee. Preregistration for classes offered. **Housing:** Coed dorms, special housing for disabled, apartments, fraternity/sorority housing available. $200 fully refundable deposit. Special residence hall floors with in-house computer facilities for honors students, coed suites available. **Activities:** Bands, campus ministries, choral groups, dance, drama, international student organizations, literary magazine, music ensembles, musical theater, opera, radio station, student government, student newspaper, symphony orchestra, Alpha Phi Omega, College Democrats, College Republicans, UNICEF, Common Ground, L-Raisers, Baptist Student Union, Debate Society, Rho Lambda Honor Society, The Redshirt Company.

Athletics. NCAA. **Intercollegiate:** Baseball M, basketball, cross-country, diving, field hockey W, football (tackle) M, golf, soccer, softball W, swimming, tennis, track and field, volleyball W. **Intramural:** Badminton, basketball, bowling, cheerleading, football (non-tackle) M, golf, racquetball, soccer, swimming, table tennis, tennis, track and field, volleyball. **Team name:** Cardinals.

Student services. Alcohol/substance abuse counseling, chaplain/spiritual director, career counseling, student employment services, financial aid counseling, health services, legal services, minority student services, personal counseling, placement for graduates, women's services. **Physically disabled:** Services for visually, speech, hearing impaired.

Contact. E-mail: admitme@gwise.louisville.edu
Phone: (502) 852-6531 Toll-free number: (800) 334-8635 ext. 6531
Fax: (502) 852-4776
Jenny Sawyer, Director of Admissions, University of Louisville, 2211 South Brook Street, Louisville, KY 40292

University of the Cumberlands

Williamsburg, Kentucky — **CB member**
www.ucumberlands.edu — **CB code: 1145**

- Private 4-year university and liberal arts college affiliated with Baptist faith
- Residential campus in small town
- 1,429 degree-seeking undergraduates: 3% part-time, 49% women, 9% African American, 1% Asian American, 3% Hispanic American, 3% international
- 536 degree-seeking graduate students
- 76% of applicants admitted
- SAT or ACT (ACT writing optional) required
- 41% graduate within 6 years; 30% enter graduate study

General. Founded in 1889. Regionally accredited. **Degrees:** 234 bachelor's awarded; master's, doctoral offered. **ROTC:** Army. **Location:** 100 miles from Lexington, 65 miles from Knoxville, Tennessee. **Calendar:** Semester, limited summer session. **Full-time faculty:** 95 total; 68% have terminal degrees, 5% minority, 40% women. **Part-time faculty:** 48 total; 50% have terminal degrees, 54% women. **Class size:** 59% < 20, 33% 20-39, 6% 40-49, 1% 50-99, less than 1% >100. **Special facilities:** Life science museum, greenhouse, conference center and inn.

Freshman class profile. 1,272 applied, 970 admitted, 432 enrolled.

Mid 50% test scores		**GPA 2.0-2.99:**	33%
SAT critical reading:	400-510	**Rank in top quarter:**	42%
SAT math:	400-500	**Rank in top tenth:**	14%
ACT composite:	18-23	**End year in good standing:**	85%
GPA 3.75 or higher:	21%	**Return as sophomores:**	62%
GPA 3.50-3.74:	17%	**Out-of-state:**	43%
GPA 3.0-3.49:	29%	**Live on campus:**	86%

Basis for selection. School achievement and activities, test scores important. **Homeschooled:** Must have GED or high school transcript.

High school preparation. College-preparatory program recommended. Required and recommended units include English 4, mathematics 3, social studies 1-2 and science 2-3.

2008-2009 Annual costs. Tuition/fees: $14,658. Room/board: $6,626. Books/supplies: $1,000. Personal expenses: $1,800.

2008-2009 Financial aid. **Need-based:** 420 full-time freshmen applied for aid; 386 were judged to have need; 386 of these received aid. Average need met was 86%. Average scholarship/grant was $11,734; average loan $3,478. 70% of total undergraduate aid awarded as scholarships/grants, 30% as loans/jobs. **Non-need-based:** Awarded to 1,480 full-time undergraduates, including 453 freshmen. Scholarships awarded for academics, alumni affiliation, art, athletics, leadership, music/drama, religious affiliation, ROTC, state residency.

Application procedures. **Admission:** Priority date 3/1; deadline 8/15 (receipt date). $30 fee, may be waived for applicants with need. Admission notification 8/15. Admission notification on a rolling basis beginning on or about 9/1. Must reply by May 1 or within 2 week(s) if notified thereafter. **Financial aid:** Priority date 3/1; no closing date. FAFSA required. Applicants notified on a rolling basis starting 4/1; must reply within 2 week(s) of notification.

Academics. All students encouraged to take advantage of individualized or computerized tutoring assistance. **Special study options:** Distance learning, double major, honors, independent study, internships, liberal arts/career combination, student-designed major, study abroad, teacher certification program. **Credit/placement by examination:** AP, CLEP, IB, SAT, ACT, institutional tests. 30 credit hours maximum toward bachelor's degree. **Support services:** Learning center, reduced course load, remedial instruction, study skills assistance, tutoring, writing center.

Majors. **Biology:** General. **Business:** General, accounting, management information systems. **Communications:** General. **Education:** Art, computer, elementary, health, middle, music, physical, social studies, special. **Foreign languages:** Spanish. **Health:** Community health services. **History:** General. **Math:** General. **Parks/recreation:** Health/fitness, sports admin. **Philosophy/religion:** Religion. **Physical sciences:** Chemistry, physics. **Psychology:** General. **Public administration:** Human services. **Social sciences:** Political science. **Theology:** Religious ed. **Visual/performing arts:** Dramatic, studio arts. **Other:** Applied science - engineering transfer, History & government, Philosophy & religion.

Most popular majors. Biology 8%, business/marketing 25%, communications/journalism 7%, education 11%, health sciences 10%, parks/recreation 6%, psychology 7%.

Computing on campus. 300 workstations in dormitories, library, computer center, student center. Dormitories wired for high-speed internet access and linked to campus network. Commuter students can connect to campus network. Online library, helpline, wireless network available.

Student life. Freshman orientation: Mandatory. Preregistration for classes offered. One-day session in summer. **Policies:** All students required to complete 40-hour community service project. Religious observance required. **Housing:** Guaranteed on-campus for all undergraduates. Single-sex dorms available. $125 partly refundable deposit, deadline 8/15. **Activities:** Bands, campus ministries, choral groups, dance, drama, music ensembles, musical theater, radio station, student government, student newspaper, TV station, Baptist Student Union, Fellowship of Christian Athletes, Appalachian Ministries, Mountain Outreach.

Athletics. NAIA. **Intercollegiate:** Baseball M, basketball, cheerleading, cross-country, football (non-tackle) M, football (tackle) M, golf, soccer, softball W, swimming, tennis, track and field, volleyball W, wrestling. **Intramural:** Archery, badminton, basketball, football (non-tackle), golf, soccer, softball, table tennis, volleyball. **Team name:** Patriots.

Student services. Alcohol/substance abuse counseling, chaplain/spiritual director, career counseling, student employment services, financial aid counseling, health services, personal counseling, placement for graduates, veterans' counselor, women's services. **Physically disabled:** Services for visually, speech, hearing impaired.

Contact. E-mail: admiss@ucumberlands.edu
Phone: (606) 539-4241 Toll-free number: (800) 343-1609
Fax: (606) 539-4303
Erica Harris, Director of Admissions, University of the Cumberlands, 6178 College Station Drive, Williamsburg, KY 40769

Western Kentucky University

Bowling Green, Kentucky
www.wku.edu **CB code: 1901**

- Public 4-year university
- Commuter campus in small city
- 15,731 degree-seeking undergraduates: 15% part-time, 58% women, 11% African American, 1% Asian American, 2% Hispanic American, 2% international
- 2,215 degree-seeking graduate students
- 49% graduate within 6 years

General. Founded in 1906. Regionally accredited. Branch campus located in Glasgow offering general education, nursing, and elementary education programs. Upper division and graduate courses also offered at branch campuses in Owensboro and Fort Knox/Elizabethtown area. **Degrees:** 2,391 bachelor's, 240 associate awarded; master's, doctoral offered. **ROTC:** Army, Air Force. **Location:** 110 miles from Louisville; 65 miles from Nashville, Tennessee. **Calendar:** Semester, limited summer session. **Full-time faculty:** 722 total; 70% have terminal degrees, 12% minority, 46% women. **Part-time faculty:** 395 total; 16% have terminal degrees, 5% minority, 52% women. **Class size:** 41% < 20, 45% 20-39, 8% 40-49, 5% 50-99, less than 1% >100. **Special facilities:** University farm, planetarium, observatory,.

Freshman class profile. 7,409 applied, 6,994 admitted, 3,307 enrolled.

Mid 50% test scores			
SAT critical reading:	430-550	Rank in top quarter:	40%
SAT math:	440-560	Rank in top tenth:	18%
ACT composite:	18-24	Return as sophomores:	72%
GPA 3.75 or higher:	20%	Out-of-state:	17%
GPA 3.50-3.74:	15%	Live on campus:	74%
GPA 3.0-3.49:	30%	International:	1%
GPA 2.0-2.99:	31%	Fraternities:	12%
		Sororities:	11%

Basis for selection. Open admission, but selective for some programs.

High school preparation. College-preparatory program required. 22 units required. Required units include English 4, mathematics 3, social studies 3, science 3 (laboratory 1), foreign language 2, visual/performing arts .5. 0.5 credits required in health, physical education, history, performing arts.

2008-2009 Annual costs. Tuition/fees: $6,930; $17,088 out-of-state. Room/board: $6,248. Books/supplies: $800. Personal expenses: $1,600.

2007-2008 Financial aid. Need-based: 2,433 full-time freshmen applied for aid; 1,833 were judged to have need; 1,815 of these received aid. Average need met was 35%. Average scholarship/grant was $4,730; average loan $2,962. 48% of total undergraduate aid awarded as scholarships/grants, 52% as loans/jobs. **Non-need-based:** Awarded to 5,940 full-time undergraduates, including 1,977 freshmen. Scholarships awarded for academics, alumni affiliation, art, athletics, job skills, leadership, minority status, music/drama, religious affiliation, ROTC, state residency.

Application procedures. Admission: Closing date 8/1 (postmark date). $40 fee, may be waived for applicants with need. Admission notification on a rolling basis. **Financial aid:** Priority date 4/1; no closing date. FAFSA required. Applicants notified on a rolling basis starting 3/1.

Academics. Special study options: Cooperative education, distance learning, double major, dual enrollment of high school students, ESL, exchange student, external degree, honors, independent study, internships, New York semester, student-designed major, study abroad, teacher certification program, Washington semester. **Credit/placement by examination:** AP, CLEP, IB, institutional tests. Unlimited number of hours of credit by examination may be counted toward degree. **Support services:** Learning center, preadmission summer program, reduced course load, remedial instruction, study skills assistance, tutoring, writing center.

Honors college/program. Students must have 27 ACT composite or combined verbal and math SAT of 1210, 3.8 unweighted high school GPA and be in top 15 percent of graduating high school class for admission to honors program.

Majors. Agriculture: General. **Architecture:** Technology. **Biology:** General, biochemistry. **Business:** Accounting, business admin, entrepreneurial studies, finance, hospitality admin, management information systems, managerial economics, marketing. **Communications:** General, advertising, journalism, organizational, photojournalism, public relations, radio/tv. **Computer sciences:** General, information technology. **Education:** Business, early childhood, elementary, family/consumer sciences, middle, physical, special, trade/industrial. **Engineering:** Civil, electrical, mechanical. **Engineering technology:** Construction, industrial, manufacturing. **Family/consumer sciences:** Clothing/textiles. **Foreign languages:** French, German, Spanish. **Health:** Clinical lab science, communication disorders, community health, dental hygiene, environmental health, health care admin, health services, nursing (RN). **History:** General. **Math:** General. **Parks/recreation:** Exercise sciences, facilities management, sports admin. **Philosophy/religion:** Philosophy, religion. **Physical sciences:** Chemistry, geology, meteorology, physics. **Psychology:** General. **Public administration:** Social work. **Social sciences:** General, anthropology, cartography, economics, geography, political science, sociology. **Visual/performing arts:** General, dance, dramatic, studio arts.

Most popular majors. Business/marketing 16%, communications/journalism 10%, education 15%, health sciences 9%, liberal arts 9%, social sciences 9%.

Computing on campus. 1,350 workstations in dormitories, library, computer center, student center. Dormitories wired for high-speed internet access and linked to campus network. Commuter students can connect to campus network. Online course registration, online library, helpline, student web hosting, wireless network available.

Student life. Freshman orientation: Mandatory, $45 fee. Preregistration for classes offered. **Housing:** Guaranteed on-campus for freshmen. Coed dorms, single-sex dorms, special housing for disabled, fraternity/sorority housing, wellness housing available. $150 partly refundable deposit, deadline 3/31. Learning communities, diversity housing, honors community available. **Activities:** Bands, campus ministries, choral groups, dance, drama, film society, international student organizations, literary magazine, music ensembles, Model UN, musical theater, opera, radio station, student government, student newspaper, symphony orchestra, TV station, American Democracy Project, Amnesty International, Habitat for Humanity, College Republicans, College Democrats, Campus Crusade, Women in Transition, NAACP, Black Student Alliance, Green Party, Mock Trial Club, ONE Campaign Challenge.

Athletics. NCAA. **Intercollegiate:** Baseball M, basketball, cross-country, diving, football (tackle) M, golf, rifle, soccer, softball W, swimming, tennis, track and field, volleyball W. **Intramural:** Archery, badminton, basketball, bowling, equestrian, football (non-tackle), golf, handball, racquetball, soccer, softball, swimming, table tennis, triathlon, volleyball, water polo, wrestling M. **Team name:** Hilltoppers.

Student services. Adult student services, alcohol/substance abuse counseling, chaplain/spiritual director, career counseling, services for economically disadvantaged, student employment services, financial aid counseling, health services, minority student services, on-campus daycare, personal counseling, placement for graduates, veterans' counselor, women's services. **Physically disabled:** Services for visually, speech, hearing impaired.

Contact. E-mail: admission@wku.edu
Phone: (270) 745-2551 Toll-free number: (800) 495-8463
Fax: (270) 745-6133
Scott Gordon, Director of Admission and Academic Services, Western Kentucky University, 1906 College Heights Boulevard, Bowling Green, KY 42101

Louisiana

Centenary College of Louisiana
Shreveport, Louisiana **CB member**
www.centenary.edu **CB code: 6082**

- Private 4-year liberal arts college affiliated with United Methodist Church
- Residential campus in small city
- 816 full-time, degree-seeking undergraduates
- 69% of applicants admitted
- SAT or ACT (ACT writing optional) required

General. Founded in 1825. Regionally accredited. **Degrees:** 195 bachelor's awarded; master's offered. **Location:** 325 miles from New Orleans, 189 miles from Dallas. **Calendar:** Semester, extensive summer session. **Full-time faculty:** 70 total. **Part-time faculty:** 51 total. **Class size:** 67% < 20, 32% 20-39, less than 1% 40-49. **Special facilities:** Amphitheater, playhouse, music library, archives, Jack London collection.

Freshman class profile. 1,076 applied, 740 admitted, 246 enrolled.

Mid 50% test scores			
SAT critical reading:	480-610	ACT composite:	22-27
SAT math:	500-610	Rank in top quarter:	67%
SAT writing:	480-590	Rank in top tenth:	37%
		Out-of-state:	45%

Basis for selection. Academic achievement record, high school GPA, test scores, essay, letters of recommendation, interview recommended. Extracurricular activities and leadership ability considered. Audition required of music, theater, dance majors. Portfolio recommended for art majors. **Homeschooled:** Transcript of courses and grades required.

High school preparation. 15 units recommended. Recommended units include English 4, mathematics 3, social studies 3, science 3 (laboratory 2) and foreign language 2.

2008-2009 Annual costs. Tuition/fees: $21,630. Room/board: $7,360. Books/supplies: $1,120. Personal expenses: $1,600.

2007-2008 Financial aid. Non-need-based: Scholarships awarded for academics, art, athletics, leadership, music/drama, religious affiliation, state residency.

Application procedures. Admission: Priority date 2/15; deadline 8/1 (postmark date). $30 fee, may be waived for applicants with need. Admission notification on a rolling basis beginning on or about 11/15. Must reply by May 1 or within 3 week(s) if notified thereafter. **Financial aid:** Priority date 2/15; no closing date. FAFSA, institutional form required. Applicants notified on a rolling basis starting 2/15.

Academics. Special study options: Combined bachelor's/graduate degree, cross-registration, double major, dual enrollment of high school students, exchange student, honors, independent study, internships, liberal arts/career combination, student-designed major, study abroad, teacher certification program, Washington semester. Oak Ridge National Laboratory semester, 3-2 engineering program, 3-2 communication disorders program. **Credit/placement by examination:** AP, CLEP, IB, institutional tests. 40 credit hours maximum toward bachelor's degree. Credit awarded only when the student has not already attempted to earn credit in a college classroom at or below the level of the subject covered by the exam. **Support services:** Learning center, reduced course load, study skills assistance, tutoring, writing center.

Majors. Biology: General, biochemistry, biophysics. **Business:** Accounting, accounting/business management, accounting/finance, business admin, finance, managerial economics. **Communications:** General, digital media, media studies. **Conservation:** Environmental science. **Education:** Art, biology, chemistry, drama/dance, elementary, English, foreign languages, French, German, health, history, mathematics, middle, multi-level teacher, music, physical, psychology, science, secondary, social studies, Spanish. **Foreign languages:** General, classics, French, German, Latin, Spanish. **Health:** Predental, premedicine, prepharmacy, preveterinary, speech pathology. **History:** General. **Interdisciplinary:** Neuroscience. **Legal studies:** Prelaw. **Liberal arts:** Arts/sciences. **Math:** General. **Parks/recreation:** Exercise sciences, health/fitness. **Philosophy/religion:** Philosophy, religion. **Physical sciences:** Chemistry, geology, physics. **Psychology:** General. **Social sciences:** Applied economics, economics, political science, sociology. **Theology:** Sacred music. **Visual/performing arts:** General, art, cinematography, dance, dramatic, music performance, music theory/composition, painting, piano/organ, sculpture, studio arts, theater design, voice/opera.

Most popular majors. Biology 18%, business/marketing 23%, communications/journalism 12%, psychology 6%, social sciences 10%, visual/performing arts 6%.

Computing on campus. 250 workstations in dormitories, library, computer center. Dormitories linked to campus network. Commuter students can connect to campus network. Online course registration, student web hosting, wireless network available.

Student life. Freshman orientation: Mandatory, $100 fee. Held 4 days prior to beginning of fall classes. **Policies:** Students participate on enrollment management committee, academic affairs committee, student/faculty discipline and other college-wide committees. All students 21 years of age or younger who are not local residents required to live in college housing. **Housing:** Guaranteed on-campus for all undergraduates. Coed dorms, single-sex dorms, fraternity/sorority housing available. $200 partly refundable deposit, deadline 7/1. **Activities:** Bands, choral groups, dance, drama, film society, music ensembles, musical theater, opera, radio station, student government, student newspaper, symphony orchestra, Church Careers Institute, United Methodist Student Movement, Baptist Collegiate Ministry, Canterbury House, Fellowship of Christian Athletes, Student Government Association, Young Democrats, Young Republicans, Students for Diversity, Tutoring Service.

Athletics. NCAA. **Intercollegiate:** Baseball M, basketball, cross-country, golf, gymnastics W, soccer, softball W, swimming, tennis, volleyball W. **Intramural:** Archery, badminton, basketball, bowling, football (non-tackle), golf, lacrosse M, racquetball, rowing (crew), soccer, softball, table tennis, tennis, volleyball. **Team name:** Gents/Ladies.

Student services. Alcohol/substance abuse counseling, chaplain/spiritual director, career counseling, financial aid counseling, health services, personal counseling, veterans' counselor. **Physically disabled:** Services for visually impaired.

Contact. E-mail: tcrowley@centenary.edu
Phone: (318) 869-5131 Toll-free number: (800) 234-4448
Fax: (318) 869-5005
Tim Crowley, Director of Admissions, Centenary College of Louisiana, Box 41188, Shreveport, LA 71134-1188

Dillard University
New Orleans, Louisiana **CB member**
www.dillard.edu **CB code: 6164**

- Private 4-year university and liberal arts college affiliated with United Church of Christ and United Methodist Church
- Residential campus in very large city
- 781 full-time, degree-seeking undergraduates
- 35% of applicants admitted
- SAT or ACT with writing, application essay required

General. Founded in 1869. Regionally accredited. **Degrees:** 176 bachelor's awarded. **ROTC:** Army, Naval, Air Force. **Calendar:** Semester, limited summer session. **Full-time faculty:** 101 total. **Part-time faculty:** 31 total. **Class size:** 60% < 20, 34% 20-39, 5% 40-49, 1% 50-99, less than 1% >100.

Freshman class profile. 1,974 applied, 685 admitted, 173 enrolled.

Mid 50% test scores			
SAT critical reading:	310-560	Rank in top quarter:	44%
SAT math:	400-560	Rank in top tenth:	2%
ACT composite:	15-20	Out-of-state:	46%

Basis for selection. Preference to applicants in top 25% of class with 2.5 GPA. Test scores, class rank, participation in extracurricular activities and community projects considered. Interview recommended. **Homeschooled:** Recommended that student apply for state diploma.

High school preparation. 19 units required. Required and recommended units include English 4, mathematics 3, social studies 3, science 3, foreign language 2 and academic electives 6.

2008-2009 Annual costs. Tuition/fees: $13,540. Room/board: $8,210. Books/supplies: $1,000. Personal expenses: $1,533.

Financial aid. All financial aid based on need.

Application procedures. **Admission:** Priority date 12/1; deadline 7/1 (postmark date). $30 fee, may be waived for applicants with need. Admission notification on a rolling basis. Must reply by May 1 or within 2 week(s) if notified thereafter. **Financial aid:** Priority date 12/1, closing date 5/1. FAFSA, institutional form required. Applicants notified on a rolling basis starting 3/1; must reply by 5/1 or within 2 week(s) of notification.

Academics. **Special study options:** Combined bachelor's/graduate degree, double major, dual enrollment of high school students, honors, independent study, internships, liberal arts/career combination, study abroad, teacher certification program. **Credit/placement by examination:** AP, CLEP, IB, institutional tests. 20 credit hours maximum toward bachelor's degree. **Support services:** Learning center, pre-admission summer program, reduced course load, remedial instruction, tutoring.

Majors. **Area/ethnic studies:** African, Japanese. **Biology:** General. **Business:** Accounting, business admin, finance. **Communications:** General. **Computer sciences:** Computer science. **Education:** Brain injured, early childhood, early childhood special, elementary, physical, secondary, special. **Foreign languages:** General, French, German, Japanese, Spanish. **Health:** Nursing (RN), premedicine, public health ed. **History:** General. **Math:** General. **Physical sciences:** Chemistry, physics. **Psychology:** General. **Public administration:** Social work. **Social sciences:** Criminology, economics, political science, sociology, urban studies. **Visual/performing arts:** Art, arts management, dramatic, music management.

Computing on campus. 400 workstations in dormitories, library, computer center. Dormitories wired for high-speed internet access and linked to campus network. Commuter students can connect to campus network. Online library, helpline, repair service available.

Student life. **Freshman orientation:** Mandatory, $200 fee. Preregistration for classes offered. **Housing:** Guaranteed on-campus for freshmen. Coed dorms, single-sex dorms, special housing for disabled, apartments, wellness housing available. $300 deposit, deadline 5/1. **Activities:** Jazz band, choral groups, dance, drama, music ensembles, musical theater, radio station, student government, student newspaper, service sororities and fraternities, honor societies, religious groups, NAACP, Santa Filomena, Young Republicans, Baptist student union.

Athletics. NAIA. **Intercollegiate:** Basketball, cross-country, tennis, volleyball W. **Intramural:** Basketball, football (non-tackle), football (tackle) M, soccer, softball, swimming, table tennis, tennis, track and field, volleyball. **Team name:** Blue Devils.

Student services. Chaplain/spiritual director, career counseling, student employment services, financial aid counseling, health services, personal counseling, placement for graduates.

Contact. E-mail: admission@dillard.edu
Phone: (504) 816-4670 Toll-free number: (800) 216-6637
Fax: (504) 816-4895
Meredith Reed, Director of Admissions, Dillard University, 2601 Gentilly Boulevard, New Orleans, LA 70122-3097

Grambling State University

Grambling, Louisiana
www.gram.edu **CB code: 6250**

- Public 4-year university
- Residential campus in small town
- 4,799 degree-seeking undergraduates: 6% part-time, 58% women, 87% African American, 10% international
- 449 degree-seeking graduate students
- 76% of applicants admitted
- SAT or ACT required
- 35% graduate within 6 years

General. Founded in 1901. Regionally accredited. **Degrees:** 537 bachelor's, 36 associate awarded; master's, doctoral offered. **ROTC:** Army. **Location:** 35 miles from Monroe, 65 miles from Shreveport. **Calendar:** Semester, limited summer session. **Full-time faculty:** 258 total; 54% have terminal degrees, 78% minority, 48% women. **Part-time faculty:** 33 total; 64% minority, 67% women. **Class size:** 38% < 20, 51% 20-39, 6% 40-49, 4% 50-99, less than 1% >100.

Freshman class profile. 2,619 applied, 1,996 admitted, 1,215 enrolled.

Mid 50% test scores		**GPA 2.0-2.99:**	69%
SAT critical reading:	380-460	**Rank in top quarter:**	18%
SAT math:	370-470	**Rank in top tenth:**	6%
ACT composite:	15-19	**End year in good standing:**	74%
GPA 3.75 or higher:	3%	**Return as sophomores:**	59%
GPA 3.50-3.74:	4%	**Out-of-state:**	46%
GPA 3.0-3.49:	20%	**International:**	11%

Basis for selection. GED not accepted. 2.0 GPA or 20 ACT and completion of 17.5 high school core units required for in-state applicants. Graduates of non-Louisiana high schools must complete the required units plus have either a 2.0 GPA and 20 ACT or have a 23 ACT. Neither group can require more than 1 developmental course. **Homeschooled:** State high school equivalency certificate required.

High school preparation. College-preparatory program recommended. 17.5 units required. Required units include English 4, mathematics 3, history 3, science 3, foreign language 2, computer science .5 and visual/performing arts 1. One additional unit of advanced math (geometry or above) or advanced science required (biology II, chemistry II, physics, or above). Foreign language units must be of the same language.

2008-2009 Annual costs. Tuition/fees: $3,804; $9,154 out-of-state. Room/board: $5,202. Books/supplies: $1,200. Personal expenses: $2,514.

2008-2009 Financial aid. **Need-based:** Average scholarship/grant was $1,506; average loan $1,731. 48% of total undergraduate aid awarded as scholarships/grants, 52% as loans/jobs. **Non-need-based:** Awarded to 460 full-time undergraduates, including 97 freshmen. Scholarships awarded for academics, alumni affiliation, art, athletics, job skills, leadership, minority status, music/drama, religious affiliation, ROTC, state residency.

Application procedures. **Admission:** Priority date 4/1; deadline 6/1 (receipt date). $20 fee, may be waived for applicants with need. Admission notification on a rolling basis. **Financial aid:** Priority date 4/1, closing date 6/1. FAFSA required. Applicants notified on a rolling basis starting 3/1; must reply within 2 week(s) of notification.

Academics. **Special study options:** Cooperative education, cross-registration, distance learning, double major, exchange student, honors, independent study, internships, study abroad, teacher certification program. **Credit/placement by examination:** AP, CLEP, institutional tests. 30 credit hours maximum toward associate degree, 30 toward bachelor's. **Support services:** Learning center, reduced course load, remedial instruction, study skills assistance, tutoring, writing center.

Honors college/program. 25 ACT/SAT equivalent and 3.5 GPA required.

Majors. **Biology:** General. **Business:** Accounting, business admin, hotel/motel admin, managerial economics, marketing. **Communications:** Media studies. **Computer sciences:** Computer science, information systems. **Education:** Art, biology, business, early childhood, elementary, English, French, mathematics, middle, music, physical, physics, social studies, special. **Engineering technology:** Drafting, electrical. **Foreign languages:** French, Spanish. **Health:** Nursing (RN). **History:** General. **Legal studies:** Paralegal, prelaw. **Math:** General. **Parks/recreation:** General. **Physical sciences:** Chemistry, physics. **Protective services:** Criminal justice. **Psychology:** General. **Public administration:** Social work. **Social sciences:** Political science, sociology. **Visual/performing arts:** Art, dramatic, music performance.

Most popular majors. Biology 6%, business/marketing 16%, communications/journalism 7%, computer/information sciences 9%, education 9%, health sciences 12%, security/protective services 11%.

Computing on campus. 200 workstations in library, computer center, student center. Dormitories wired for high-speed internet access and linked to campus network. Commuter students can connect to campus network. Online course registration, online library, helpline, wireless network available.

Student life. **Freshman orientation:** Mandatory. Preregistration for classes offered. **Housing:** Single-sex dorms, apartments, wellness housing available. $50 fully refundable deposit, deadline 7/15. **Activities:** Bands, choral groups, dance, drama, music ensembles, opera, radio station, student government, student newspaper, symphony orchestra, Bayou Boyz social organization, Favrot student union, College Democrats, Ladies of Essence, NAACP, Bayou Girlz.

Athletics. NCAA. **Intercollegiate:** Baseball M, basketball, bowling W, cross-country, football (tackle) M, golf, soccer W, softball W, tennis, track and field, volleyball W. **Intramural:** Badminton, baseball M, basketball, bowling, cross-country, golf, gymnastics M, softball W, swimming, tennis, track and field, volleyball. **Team name:** Tigers.

Student services. Career counseling, student employment services, financial aid counseling, health services, personal counseling, placement for graduates, veterans' counselor. **Physically disabled:** Services for visually, speech, hearing impaired.

Contact. E-mail: admissions@gram.edu
Phone: (318) 274-6183 Toll-free number: (888) 863-3655
Fax: (318) 274-3292
Annie Moss, Director of Admissions and Recruitment, Grambling State University, 403 Main Street, GSU Box 4200, Grambling, LA 71245

Herzing College
Kenner, Louisiana
www.herzing.edu **CB code: 3430**

- For-profit 4-year branch campus and technical college
- Commuter campus in very large city
- 90 full-time, degree-seeking undergraduates
- Interview required

General. Regionally accredited. **Degrees:** 16 bachelor's, 21 associate awarded. **Location:** 10 miles from downtown New Orleans. **Calendar:** Semester, extensive summer session. **Full-time faculty:** 4 total. **Part-time faculty:** 20 total. **Class size:** 16% < 20, 84% 20-39.

Basis for selection. Wonderlic entrance test required.

2008-2009 Annual costs. Tuition costs vary by program, $315-$375 per credit hour.

Application procedures. Admission: No deadline. No application fee.

Academics. Special study options: Combined bachelor's/graduate degree, distance learning, liberal arts/career combination, weekend college. **Credit/placement by examination:** CLEP, IB, institutional tests. **Support services:** Learning center, reduced course load, study skills assistance, tutoring.

Majors. Business: Accounting, business admin, management information systems. **Computer sciences:** Information technology, LAN/WAN management, programming.

Computing on campus. 115 workstations in library, computer center, student center. Online library, helpline, repair service available.

Student life. Freshman orientation: Mandatory. **Activities:** Student government.

Student services. Career counseling, student employment services, financial aid counseling, placement for graduates. **Physically disabled:** Services for visually, hearing impaired.

Contact. E-mail: info@nor.herzing.edu
Phone: (504) 733-0074 Fax: (504) 733-0020
Director of Admissions, Herzing College, 2400 Veterans Boulevard, Suite 410, Kenner, LA 70062

ITT Technical Institute: St. Rose
St. Rose, Louisiana
www.itt-tech.edu **CB code: 2766**

- For-profit 4-year technical college
- Commuter campus in small town

General. Accredited by ACICS. **Calendar:** Quarter.

Contact. Phone: (504) 463-0338
Director of Recruitment, 140 James Drive East, St. Rose, LA 70087

Louisiana College
Pineville, Louisiana
www.lacollege.edu **CB code: 6371**

- Private 4-year liberal arts college affiliated with Southern Baptist Convention
- Residential campus in small city
- 858 degree-seeking undergraduates: 5% part-time, 49% women
- 199 degree-seeking graduate students
- 59% of applicants admitted
- SAT or ACT (ACT writing optional) required
- 46% graduate within 6 years

General. Founded in 1906. Regionally accredited. **Degrees:** 130 bachelor's awarded; master's offered. **ROTC:** Army. **Calendar:** Semester, limited summer session. **Full-time faculty:** 67 total; 61% have terminal degrees, 3% minority, 46% women. **Part-time faculty:** 34 total; 12% have terminal degrees, 44% women. **Class size:** 70% < 20, 26% 20-39, 3% 40-49, less than 1% 50-99.

Freshman class profile. 699 applied, 413 admitted, 230 enrolled.

Mid 50% test scores			
SAT critical reading:	430-600	SAT writing:	400-600
SAT math:	420-600	ACT composite:	17-24

Basis for selection. 20 ACT (930 SAT) and 2.0 GPA or 17 ACT (810 SAT) and 2.0 GPA and rank in the upper 50% of graduating class required. Interview required of nursing, respiratory care majors. Portfolio recommended for art majors.

High school preparation. 17 units required. Required units include English 4, mathematics 3, social studies 3, science 3 (laboratory 2) and academic electives 4.

2008-2009 Annual costs. Tuition/fees: $12,030. Room/board: $4,316. Books/supplies: $535. Personal expenses: $1,040.

Financial aid. Non-need-based: Scholarships awarded for academics, art, leadership, music/drama, ROTC.

Application procedures. Admission: Closing date 8/15. $25 fee, may be waived for applicants with need. Admission notification on a rolling basis. Must reply by May 1 or within 2 week(s) if notified thereafter. **Financial aid:** Priority date 3/31; no closing date. FAFSA, institutional form required. Applicants notified on a rolling basis starting 3/1; must reply by 5/1 or within 2 week(s) of notification.

Academics. Special study options: Double major, dual enrollment of high school students, independent study, internships, liberal arts/career combination, student-designed major, study abroad, teacher certification program. **Credit/placement by examination:** AP, CLEP, institutional tests. 30 credit hours maximum toward bachelor's degree. **Support services:** Preadmission summer program, reduced course load, remedial instruction, tutoring.

Majors. Biology: General. **Business:** General, accounting, business admin, finance, marketing. **Communications:** General, journalism, media studies. **Computer sciences:** Webmaster. **Education:** General, art, business, elementary, English, foreign languages, French, health, mathematics, middle, music, physical, physically handicapped, science, secondary, social studies, Spanish. **Foreign languages:** General, French. **Health:** Athletic training, clinical lab technology, nursing (RN), predental, premedicine, prepharmacy, preveterinary. **History:** General. **Interdisciplinary:** Biological/physical sciences. **Legal studies:** Prelaw. **Math:** General. **Parks/recreation:** Health/fitness. **Philosophy/religion:** Religion. **Physical sciences:** Chemistry. **Protective services:** Law enforcement admin. **Psychology:** General. **Public administration:** General, social work. **Social sciences:** General, economics, political science, sociology. **Theology:** Religious ed, sacred music. **Visual/performing arts:** Commercial/advertising art, dramatic, music pedagogy, music performance, piano/organ, studio arts, voice/opera.

Most popular majors. Biology 10%, business/marketing 7%, communications/journalism 6%, education 11%, health sciences 15%, history 8%, public administration/social services 7%, social sciences 9%, visual/performing arts 7%.

Computing on campus. 242 workstations in library, computer center, student center. Dormitories linked to campus network.

Student life. Freshman orientation: Mandatory. Preregistration for classes offered. **Policies:** Religious observance required. **Housing:** Guaranteed on-campus for all undergraduates. Single-sex dorms, apartments, wellness housing available. $75 deposit, deadline 8/1. **Activities:** Bands, campus ministries, choral groups, drama, international student organizations, literary magazine, music ensembles, musical theater, opera, radio station, student government, student newspaper, Lamda Chi Beta, Delta Xi Omega, Sigma Theta, Kappa Tau Beta, Union Board, church vocation fellowship, Fellowship of Christian Athletes, Jacob's Society.

Athletics. NCAA, NCCAA. **Intercollegiate:** Baseball M, basketball, cheerleading, cross-country, football (tackle) M, golf M, soccer, softball W, tennis W. **Intramural:** Badminton, basketball, bowling, golf, softball, swimming, table tennis, tennis, volleyball. **Team name:** Wildcats.

Student services. Chaplain/spiritual director, career counseling, student employment services, financial aid counseling, health services, personal counseling, placement for graduates. **Physically disabled:** Services for visually impaired.

Contact. E-mail: admissions@lacollege.edu
Phone: (318) 487-7259 Toll-free number: (800) 487-1906
Fax: (318) 487-7550
Byron McGee, Director of Enrollment Management and Admissions, Louisiana College, LC Box 566, Pineville, LA 71359

Louisiana State University and Agricultural and Mechanical College

Baton Rouge, Louisiana — **CB member**
www.lsu.edu — **CB code: 6373**

- Public 4-year university and agricultural college
- Commuter campus in large city
- 23,057 degree-seeking undergraduates: 6% part-time, 51% women, 9% African American, 3% Asian American, 3% Hispanic American, 1% international
- 5,185 degree-seeking graduate students
- 73% of applicants admitted
- SAT or ACT with writing required
- 61% graduate within 6 years

General. Founded in 1860. Regionally accredited. **Degrees:** 4,600 bachelor's awarded; master's, doctoral, first professional offered. **ROTC:** Army, Naval, Air Force. **Location:** 80 miles from New Orleans. **Calendar:** Semester, extensive summer session. **Full-time faculty:** 1,324 total; 87% have terminal degrees, 14% minority, 34% women. **Part-time faculty:** 179 total; 59% have terminal degrees, 10% minority, 38% women. **Class size:** 34% < 20, 40% 20-39, 7% 40-49, 12% 50-99, 8% >100. **Special facilities:** Mycological herbarium, lichenological herbarium, natural science museum, geoscience museum, rural life museum, Anglo-American art museum, Civil War center, biomedical research center, coastal ecology center, center for advanced microstructures and devices.

Freshman class profile. 15,093 applied, 11,092 admitted, 5,141 enrolled.

Mid 50% test scores		**GPA 2.0-2.99:**	8%
SAT critical reading:	520-630	**Rank in top quarter:**	53%
SAT math:	550-650	**Rank in top tenth:**	26%
SAT writing:	490-600	**End year in good standing:**	88%
ACT composite:	23-28	**Return as sophomores:**	85%
GPA 3.75 or higher:	28%	**Out-of-state:**	21%
GPA 3.50-3.74:	24%	**Live on campus:**	66%
GPA 3.0-3.49:	40%	**International:**	1%

Basis for selection. Sliding scale admissions criteria include number of academic units earned, GPA on those units, ACT or SAT scores. Students must also meet minimum Board of Regents Master Plan requirements. Applicants not meeting course units and/or grades or test score requirements may be considered by admissions committee. Out-of-state students must have 17 ACT or 830 SAT (exclusive of Writing). ACT/SAT writing component required for scholarship and honors college consideration. Audition required for MDA majors. Portfolio required for Art and Landscape Architecture majors. **Homeschooled:** Statement describing homeschool structure and mission, transcript of courses and grades required. Students with ACT score below 26 will be reviewed by admission committee. **Learning Disabled:** Students with learning disabilities who do not meet regular admission requirements may appeal to admission committee and submit documentation explaining positions.

High school preparation. College-preparatory program required. 18 units required. Required and recommended units include English 4, mathematics 3-4, social studies 1, history 2, science 3, foreign language 2, academic electives 2.5. Computer literacy (.5 units) also required. Specific courses required in some subject areas.

2008-2009 Annual costs. Tuition/fees: $5,086; $13,800 out-of-state. Room/board: $7,238. Books/supplies: $1,500. Personal expenses: $1,726.

2007-2008 Financial aid. **Need-based:** 2,752 full-time freshmen applied for aid; 1,573 were judged to have need; 1,573 of these received aid. Average need met was 75%. Average scholarship/grant was $8,083; average loan $3,324. 53% of total undergraduate aid awarded as scholarships/grants, 47% as loans/jobs. **Non-need-based:** Awarded to 4,116 full-time undergraduates, including 1,477 freshmen. Scholarships awarded for academics, alumni affiliation, art, athletics, leadership, music/drama, ROTC, state residency.

Application procedures. **Admission:** Priority date 11/15; deadline 4/15 (receipt date). $40 fee, may be waived for applicants with need. Application must be submitted online. Admission notification on a rolling basis. **Financial aid:** No deadline. FAFSA, institutional form required. Applicants notified on a rolling basis starting 3/1; must reply within 3 week(s) of notification.

Academics. **Special study options:** Accelerated study, cooperative education, cross-registration, distance learning, double major, dual enrollment of high school students, ESL, exchange student, honors, independent study, internships, student-designed major, study abroad, teacher certification program. **Credit/placement by examination:** AP, CLEP, IB, SAT, ACT, institutional tests. 30 credit hours maximum toward bachelor's degree. **Support services:** Learning center, study skills assistance, tutoring, writing center.

Honors college/program. 30 ACT with 30 English, or 29 ACT with 31 English, or 1320 SAT (exclusive of Writing) with 660 Verbal. 3.5 GPA and essay required.

Majors. **Agriculture:** Animal sciences, business, food science, plant sciences. **Architecture:** Architecture, interior, landscape. **Area/ethnic studies:** Women's. **Biology:** General, biochemistry, microbiology. **Business:** Accounting, business admin, construction management, fashion, finance, international, management science, managerial economics, marketing. **Communications:** Media studies. **Computer sciences:** Computer science. **Conservation:** Environmental science, forest management, management/policy. **Education:** Adult/continuing, early childhood, elementary, music, physical, secondary. **Engineering:** Biomedical, chemical, civil, computer, electrical, environmental, industrial, mechanical, petroleum. **Family/consumer sciences:** General. **Foreign languages:** French, German, Latin, Spanish. **Health:** Audiology/speech pathology, dietetics. **History:** General. **Interdisciplinary:** Global studies. **Liberal arts:** Arts/sciences. **Math:** General. **Philosophy/religion:** Philosophy. **Physical sciences:** Chemistry, geology, oceanography, physics. **Psychology:** General. **Social sciences:** Anthropology, economics, geography, political science, sociology. **Visual/performing arts:** Dramatic, music performance, studio arts.

Most popular majors. Biology 8%, business/marketing 20%, communications/journalism 6%, education 10%, engineering/engineering technologies 8%, English 6%, liberal arts 8%, social sciences 8%.

Computing on campus. 1,500 workstations in dormitories, library, student center. Dormitories wired for high-speed internet access and linked to campus network. Commuter students can connect to campus network. Online course registration, online library, helpline, student web hosting, wireless network available.

Student life. **Freshman orientation:** Mandatory, $76 fee. Preregistration for classes offered. Held in June, July, and August; testing held in spring. **Housing:** Coed dorms, single-sex dorms, special housing for disabled, apartments, fraternity/sorority housing available. $150 partly refundable deposit. **Activities:** Bands, campus ministries, choral groups, dance, drama, film society, international student organizations, literary magazine, music ensembles, musical theater, opera, radio station, student government, student newspaper, symphony orchestra, TV station, various religious, professional, honorary, political, service, and special interest organizations.

Athletics. NCAA. **Intercollegiate:** Baseball M, basketball, cross-country, football (tackle) M, golf, gymnastics W, soccer W, softball W, swimming, tennis, track and field, volleyball W. **Intramural:** Badminton, basketball, football (non-tackle), racquetball, soccer, softball, table tennis, tennis, volleyball. **Team name:** Tigers.

Student services. Adult student services, alcohol/substance abuse counseling, career counseling, student employment services, financial aid counseling, health services, minority student services, on-campus daycare, personal counseling, placement for graduates, veterans' counselor, women's services. **Physically disabled:** Services for visually, speech, hearing impaired.

Contact. E-mail: admissions@lsu.edu
Phone: (225) 578-1175 Fax: (225) 578-4433
Mary Parker, Executive Director of Undergraduate Admissions & Student Aid, Louisiana State University and Agricultural and Mechanical College, 1146 Pleasant Halll, Baton Rouge, LA 70803-2750

Louisiana State University at Alexandria

Alexandria, Louisiana
www.lsua.edu — **CB code: 1632**

- Public 4-year university
- Commuter campus in small city
- 2,950 undergraduates
- 31 graduate students
- 78% of applicants admitted
- ACT required

General. Founded in 1959. Regionally accredited. **Degrees:** 131 bachelor's, 156 associate awarded. **ROTC:** Army. **Location:** 10 miles from downtown. **Calendar:** Semester, extensive summer session. **Full-time faculty:** 111 total. **Part-time faculty:** 65 total. **Class size:** 42% < 20, 50% 20-39, 4% 40-49, 3% 50-99.

Freshman class profile. 548 applied, 427 admitted, 332 enrolled.

Mid 50% test scores		**Out-of-state:**	1%
ACT composite:	18-23		

Basis for selection. Admissibility based on high school curriculum, GPA, class rank, ACT, and the need, if any, for developmental course work. Completion of Regents high school core curriculum required, along with one of the following: 2.0 GPA or rank in top 50% of class or 20 ACT. Students must also need no more than one developmental course by having one of the following: 18 ACT English or 19 ACT math. **Homeschooled:** Applicants must submit transcript of high school level work with graduation date.

High school preparation. 17.5 units required. Required units include English 4, mathematics 3, social studies 3, science 3 and foreign language 2. 1 additional unit in math or science, .5 units in computer studies and 1 unit in fine arts survey required. Foreign language units must be in same language.

2008-2009 Annual costs. Tuition/fees: $3,381; $5,963 out-of-state. On-campus housing (double-occupancy) $510 per month; meal plan $608 per 160 meals. Books/supplies: $1,200. Personal expenses: $1,726.

Financial aid. Non-need-based: Scholarships awarded for academics, state residency.

Application procedures. Admission: Priority date 8/1; no deadline. $20 fee. Admission notification on a rolling basis. **Financial aid:** Priority date 4/1; no closing date. FAFSA, institutional form required. Applicants notified on a rolling basis starting 4/20; must reply within 3 week(s) of notification.

Academics. Special study options: Distance learning, dual enrollment of high school students. **Credit/placement by examination:** AP, CLEP, institutional tests. Credit by examination limited to one-fourth number of hours required for degree. **Support services:** Learning center, pre-admission summer program, remedial instruction, study skills assistance, tutoring, writing center.

Majors. Biology: General. **Business:** Business admin. **Education:** General, elementary. **Health:** Nursing (RN). **History:** General. **Liberal arts:** Arts/sciences. **Math:** General. **Protective services:** Criminal justice. **Psychology:** General.

Most popular majors. Education 24%, liberal arts 74%.

Computing on campus. 163 workstations in library, computer center, student center. Commuter students can connect to campus network.

Student life. Freshman orientation: Mandatory. Preregistration for classes offered. **Housing:** Apartments available. **Activities:** Choral groups, drama, literary magazine, student government, student newspaper, Baptist ministry, Catholic student organization, Apostolic student fellowship, Canterbury club, College Republicans, College Democrats, international student organization, nontraditional student organization, Identity, Circle K.

Athletics. Intramural: Basketball, cross-country, football (non-tackle) M, soccer, softball, tennis, volleyball. **Team name:** Generals.

Student services. Adult student services, chaplain/spiritual director, career counseling, student employment services, financial aid counseling, minority student services, on-campus daycare, personal counseling, placement for graduates, veterans' counselor.

Contact. E-mail: generalinfo@lsua.edu
Phone: (318) 473-6417 Toll-free number: (888) 473-6417
Fax: (318) 473-6418
Teresa Seymour, Registrar, Louisiana State University at Alexandria, 8100 Highway 71 South, Alexandria, LA 71302-9121

Louisiana State University Health Sciences Center

New Orleans, Louisiana
www.lsuhsc.edu **CB code: 1192**

- Public two-year upper-division health science and nursing college
- Commuter campus in large city
- Interview required

General. Founded in 1931. Regionally accredited. **Degrees:** 244 bachelor's, 5 associate awarded; master's, doctoral, first professional offered. **Articulation:** Agreement with University of New Orleans. **Calendar:** Differs by program, limited summer session. **Part-time faculty:** 9 total.

Student profile. 747 undergraduates, 1,685 graduate students.

Out-of-state:	1%	**25 or older:**	28%
Live on campus:	20%		

Basis for selection. College transcript, interview required. Application closing, notification, and response dates vary by program. Transfer accepted as sophomores, juniors, seniors.

2008-2009 Annual costs. Tuition/fees: $3,978; $7,110 out-of-state. Room only: $2,210.

Financial aid. Non-need-based: Scholarships awarded for academics.

Application procedures. Admission: $50 fee. **Financial aid:** FAFSA, institutional form required.

Academics. Special study options: Cross-registration, double major, honors, independent study, internships. **Credit/placement by examination:** CLEP.

Majors. Health: Cardiovascular technology, clinical lab science, dental hygiene, dental lab technology, nursing (RN), vocational rehab counseling.

Computing on campus. 227 workstations in dormitories, library, computer center, student center. Dormitories wired for high-speed internet access and linked to campus network. Commuter students can connect to campus network. Online library, helpline, repair service, wireless network available.

Student life. Housing: Coed dorms, apartments, wellness housing available. **Activities:** Choral groups, student government.

Student services. Alcohol/substance abuse counseling, career counseling, financial aid counseling, health services, personal counseling. **Physically disabled:** Services for visually, speech, hearing impaired.

Contact. Phone: (504) 568-4808
Louisiana State University Health Sciences Center, 433 Bolivar Street, New Orleans, LA 70112-2223

Louisiana State University in Shreveport

Shreveport, Louisiana
www.lsus.edu **CB code: 6355**

- Public 4-year university
- Commuter campus in large city
- 3,108 degree-seeking undergraduates
- 388 graduate students
- 76% of applicants admitted
- ACT (writing optional) required

General. Founded in 1965. Regionally accredited. **Degrees:** 521 bachelor's awarded; master's offered. **ROTC:** Army. **Location:** 180 miles from Dallas. **Calendar:** Semester, extensive summer session. **Full-time faculty:** 161 total. **Part-time faculty:** 110 total. **Class size:** 39% < 20, 45% 20-39, 8% 40-49, 8% 50-99. **Special facilities:** Life science museum, pioneer heritage center.

Freshman class profile. 732 applied, 553 admitted, 438 enrolled.

Mid 50% test scores		**GPA 3.0-3.49:**	29%
SAT critical reading:	480-570	**GPA 2.0-2.99:**	37%
SAT math:	420-530	**End year in good standing:**	81%
ACT composite:	20-24	**Return as sophomores:**	59%
GPA 3.75 or higher:	13%	**Out-of-state:**	4%
GPA 3.50-3.74:	20%		

Basis for selection. Completion of Regents high school core curriculum of 16.5 course units and one of the following required: 2.0 GPA, high school rank in top 50% of class, or 20 ACT. For early admission, principal's recommendation, 29 ACT, 15 specific high school units, 3.0 GPA required. Regardless of age, students who have accumulated at least 12 term hours of non-developmental college credit may transfer if all transfer requirements met. **Homeschooled:** GED required.

High school preparation. Recommended units include English 4, mathematics 3, social studies 3, science 3, foreign language 2, computer science 1 and visual/performing arts 1.

2008-2009 Annual costs. Tuition/fees: $3,687; $8,230 out-of-state. Books/supplies: $702. Personal expenses: $1,365.

Application procedures. **Admission:** Closing date 7/15. $10 fee. Application must be submitted on paper. Admission notification on a rolling basis. **Financial aid:** No deadline. Applicants notified on a rolling basis.

Academics. **Special study options:** Combined bachelor's/graduate degree, cooperative education, distance learning, double major, dual enrollment of high school students, independent study, internships, student-designed major, study abroad, teacher certification program, Washington semester. Cooperative education program with Southern University at Shreveport. **Credit/placement by examination:** AP, CLEP, ACT, institutional tests. 62 credit hours maximum toward bachelor's degree. **Support services:** Learning center, remedial instruction, study skills assistance, tutoring, writing center.

Majors. **Biology:** General, biochemistry. **Business:** Accounting, banking/financial services, business admin, financial planning, managerial economics, marketing. **Communications:** General, media studies. **Computer sciences:** Computer science, information systems. **Conservation:** Environmental science. **Education:** Art, biology, chemistry, early childhood, elementary, English, mathematics, physical, physics, science, social studies. **Foreign languages:** French, Spanish. **History:** General. **Liberal arts:** Arts/sciences. **Math:** General. **Parks/recreation:** Health/fitness. **Physical sciences:** Chemistry, physics. **Protective services:** Criminal justice. **Psychology:** General. **Social sciences:** Geography, political science, sociology. **Visual/performing arts:** Art.

Most popular majors. Biology 10%, business/marketing 25%, education 13%, liberal arts 20%, psychology 11%.

Computing on campus. 250 workstations in library, computer center, student center. Commuter students can connect to campus network. Online course registration, online library, helpline, student web hosting, wireless network available.

Student life. **Freshman orientation:** Mandatory. Preregistration for classes offered. **Housing:** Guaranteed on-campus for all undergraduates. Apartments available. Pets allowed in dorm rooms. **Activities:** Jazz band, dance, literary magazine, radio station, student government, student newspaper, Baptist student union, College Republicans, government and law society, Catholic student union, Rotaract, foreign language club, psychology club, black student association.

Athletics. NAIA. **Intercollegiate:** Baseball M. **Intramural:** Badminton, basketball, football (non-tackle), golf, racquetball, soccer, softball, swimming, table tennis, tennis, track and field, volleyball. **Team name:** Pilots.

Student services. Career counseling, student employment services, financial aid counseling, minority student services, personal counseling, placement for graduates, veterans' counselor. **Physically disabled:** Services for visually, speech, hearing impaired.

Contact. E-mail: admissions@pilot.lsus.edu
Phone: (318) 797-5061 Toll-free number: (800) 229-5957
Fax: (318) 797-5286
Mickey Diez, Dean of Enrollment Services & Registrar, Louisiana State University in Shreveport, One University Place, Shreveport, LA 71115-2399

Louisiana Tech University

Ruston, Louisiana — **CB member**
www.latech.edu — **CB code: 6372**

- Public 4-year university
- Commuter campus in large town
- 6,560 full-time, degree-seeking undergraduates
- 2,299 graduate students
- 65% of applicants admitted
- SAT or ACT (ACT writing optional) required

General. Founded in 1894. Regionally accredited. **Degrees:** 1,382 bachelor's, 90 associate awarded; master's, doctoral offered. **ROTC:** Army, Naval. **Location:** 70 miles from Shreveport, 30 miles from Monroe. **Calendar:** Quarter, extensive summer session. **Full-time faculty:** 395 total. **Part-time faculty:** 109 total. **Class size:** 37% < 20, 42% 20-39, 11% 40-49, 8% 50-99, 2% >100. **Special facilities:** Natural history museum, on-campus lab school, arboretum, planetarium, rehabilitation science and biomedical engineering center, micromanufacturing institute, water resource center.

Freshman class profile. 4,354 applied, 2,817 admitted, 1,558 enrolled.

Mid 50% test scores			
SAT critical reading:	440-550	Out-of-state:	14%
SAT math:	460-590	Fraternities:	9%
ACT composite:	20-26	Sororities:	17%

Basis for selection. High school record, test scores most important. Special talents, school and community activities, recommendations considered. To be admitted, applicant must need no more than one remedial course. Admission deadline for scholarship consideration is January 2 for the following fall term. **Homeschooled:** Applicants must have 2.5 GPA, 23 ACT/1060 SAT (exclusive of Writing).

High school preparation. Required units include English 4, mathematics 3, social studies 3, science 3, academic electives 4.5. 2 algebra required. Social studies must include 1 U.S. history. 4.5 units of electives from foreign language, sciences, math, social studies, speech, advanced fine arts, or computer literacy required. Prefer English courses that emphasize grammar, composition, and literature.

2008-2009 Annual costs. Tuition/fees: $4,628; $11,006 out-of-state. Room/board: $4,770. Books/supplies: $1,800. Personal expenses: $1,500.

2007-2008 Financial aid. **Non-need-based:** Scholarships awarded for academics, art, athletics, leadership, music/drama, ROTC.

Application procedures. **Admission:** Priority date 8/1; no deadline. $20 fee, may be waived for applicants with need. Admission notification on a rolling basis beginning on or about 6/1. **Financial aid:** Priority date 4/15; no closing date. FAFSA, institutional form required. Applicants notified on a rolling basis starting 3/18; must reply within 4 week(s) of notification.

Academics. **Special study options:** Combined bachelor's/graduate degree, cooperative education, cross-registration, distance learning, double major, dual enrollment of high school students, ESL, honors, independent study, internships, liberal arts/career combination, study abroad, teacher certification program. Cooperative programs with Grambling State University. **Credit/placement by examination:** AP, CLEP, institutional tests. 30 credit hours maximum toward associate degree, 30 toward bachelor's. **Support services:** Remedial instruction, study skills assistance, tutoring.

Majors. **Agriculture:** Animal sciences, business. **Architecture:** Architecture, interior. **Biology:** General. **Business:** Accounting, business admin, finance, human resources, management information systems, management science, managerial economics, marketing. **Communications:** Journalism. **Computer sciences:** Computer science. **Conservation:** General, forest resources, forestry. **Education:** Art, early childhood, elementary, French, music, physical, secondary, special, speech impaired. **Engineering:** Biomedical, chemical, civil, electrical, mechanical. **Engineering technology:** Civil, electrical. **Family/consumer sciences:** Family studies. **Foreign languages:** French, Spanish. **Health:** Audiology/speech pathology, clinical lab science, medical records admin. **History:** General. **Liberal arts:** Arts/sciences. **Math:** General. **Parks/recreation:** Health/fitness. **Physical sciences:** Chemistry, geology, physics. **Psychology:** General. **Social sciences:** Geography, political science, sociology. **Transportation:** Aviation, aviation management. **Visual/performing arts:** Art, commercial/advertising art, music performance, photography. **Other:** Nanosystems engineering.

Computing on campus. 1,800 workstations in dormitories, library, computer center. Dormitories linked to campus network.

Student life. **Freshman orientation:** Available, $55 fee. Preregistration for classes offered. Four sessions offered during summer. **Housing:** Guaranteed on-campus for freshmen. Single-sex dorms, special housing for disabled, apartments available. $50 deposit, deadline 7/15. **Activities:** Bands, choral groups, dance, drama, music ensembles, musical theater, radio station, student government, student newspaper, Wesley Foundation, Baptist student union, Union Board, College Republicans, Campus Crusade for Christ, international student association, NAACP, Circle K, Angel Flight.

Athletics. NCAA. **Intercollegiate:** Baseball M, basketball, bowling W, cross-country, football (tackle) M, golf M, soccer W, softball W, tennis W, track and field, volleyball W. **Intramural:** Badminton, basketball, bowling, golf M, racquetball, soccer, softball, tennis, volleyball. **Team name:** Bulldogs (M), Lady Techsters (W).

Student services. Chaplain/spiritual director, career counseling, student employment services, financial aid counseling, health services, legal services, minority student services, personal counseling, placement for graduates, veterans' counselor, women's services. **Physically disabled:** Services for speech impaired.

Contact. E-mail: bulldog@latech.edu
Phone: (318) 257-3036 Toll-free number: (800) 528-3241
Fax: (318) 257-2499
Jan Albritton, Director of Admissions, College of Basic and Career Studies, Louisiana Tech University, Box 3178, Ruston, LA 71272

Loyola University New Orleans

New Orleans, Louisiana — **CB member**
www.loyno.edu — **CB code: 6374**

- Private 4-year university and liberal arts college affiliated with Roman Catholic Church
- Residential campus in large city
- 2,600 degree-seeking undergraduates: 11% part-time, 57% women, 13% African American, 4% Asian American, 11% Hispanic American, 1% Native American, 3% international
- 1,776 degree-seeking graduate students
- 63% of applicants admitted
- SAT or ACT (ACT writing optional), application essay required
- 68% graduate within 6 years; 63% enter graduate study

General. Founded in 1912. Regionally accredited. **Degrees:** 653 bachelor's awarded; master's, first professional offered. **ROTC:** Army, Naval, Air Force. **Location:** Uptown. **Calendar:** Semester, limited summer session. **Full-time faculty:** 255 total; 91% have terminal degrees, 13% minority, 42% women. **Part-time faculty:** 144 total; 41% have terminal degrees, 11% minority, 48% women. **Class size:** 59% < 20, 39% 20-39, 1% 40-49, 1% 50-99, less than 1% >100. **Special facilities:** Humanities lab with Perseus Project and TLG TV, multimedia classrooms, 24-hour microcomputer labs, computer science lab, graphics lab, visual arts lab, ad club/communications lab, RATHE business computer lab, multi-media training center, non-profit communications center, chemistry wing, television broadcast studio, multimedia studio, audio recording studio, editing studio, library learning commons, multimedia exhibit room, performance area, international education center, suspended pool, career development center, Jesuit social research institute, learning communities.

Freshman class profile. 3,651 applied, 2,306 admitted, 709 enrolled.

Mid 50% test scores		**Rank in top tenth:**	30%
SAT critical reading:	560-660	**End year in good standing:**	87%
SAT math:	520-630	**Return as sophomores:**	73%
ACT composite:	23-28	**Out-of-state:**	45%
GPA 3.75 or higher:	48%	**Live on campus:**	73%
GPA 3.50-3.74:	19%	**International:**	3%
GPA 3.0-3.49:	26%	**Fraternities:**	15%
GPA 2.0-2.99:	7%	**Sororities:**	21%
Rank in top quarter:	60%		

Basis for selection. High school performance, test scores, counselor/teacher evaluation, personal essay, extracurricular activity, community involvement and work experience all considered. Interview recommended. Audition required for music, theater arts and dance majors. Portfolio required for visual arts program applicants. **Homeschooled:** Require proof of high school graduation or its equivalent.

High school preparation. College-preparatory program recommended. 17 units required; 22 recommended. Required and recommended units include English 4, mathematics 2-3, social studies 2, science 2-3 (laboratory 1) and foreign language 2.

2009-2010 Annual costs. Tuition/fees: $29,706. Room/board: $9,826. Books/supplies: $1,000. Personal expenses: $1,500.

2008-2009 Financial aid. Need-based: 533 full-time freshmen applied for aid; 409 were judged to have need; 409 of these received aid. Average need met was 92%. Average scholarship/grant was $16,505; average loan $3,565. 82% of total undergraduate aid awarded as scholarships/grants, 18% as loans/jobs. **Non-need-based:** Awarded to 2,084 full-time undergraduates, including 631 freshmen. Scholarships awarded for academics, alumni affiliation, art, leadership, ROTC.

Application procedures. Admission: Priority date 12/1; no deadline. $20 fee, may be waived for applicants with need, free for online applicants. Admission notification on a rolling basis beginning on or about 10/20. Must reply by May 1 or within 2 week(s) if notified thereafter. Students recommended by high school principals and considered ready for college work by the Committee on Admissions may be admitted immediately following completion of junior year of high school. Program intended to serve applicants of unusual promise who will benefit from beginning college careers a year early. **Financial aid:** Priority date 2/15, closing date 6/1. FAFSA required. Applicants notified on a rolling basis starting 3/1; must reply by 5/1 or within 2 week(s) of notification.

Academics. Jesuit tradition of contributing to the liberal education of the whole person emphasized. **Special study options:** Accelerated study, combined bachelor's/graduate degree, cross-registration, distance learning, double major, dual enrollment of high school students, exchange student, honors, independent study, internships, liberal arts/career combination, student-designed major, study abroad, teacher certification program, Washington semester, weekend college. Evening courses; Internet-based program in nursing. **Credit/placement by examination:** AP, CLEP, IB, SAT, ACT, institutional tests. 30 credit hours maximum toward bachelor's degree. At least 25% of semester credit hours required for degree must be earned through instruction offered by Loyola. Unless special permission granted by the dean for the student to pursue coursework elsewhere, last 30 credit hours must be completed at Loyola. **Support services:** Learning center, pre-admission summer program, reduced course load, remedial instruction, study skills assistance, tutoring, writing center.

Majors. Biology: General. **Business:** Accounting, finance, international, managerial economics, marketing. **Communications:** General. **Education:** Music. **Foreign languages:** Ancient Greek, French, German, Spanish. **Health:** Music therapy, nursing (RN), predental, premedicine, preveterinary. **History:** General. **Liberal arts:** Arts/sciences. **Math:** General. **Philosophy/religion:** Philosophy, religion. **Physical sciences:** Chemistry, physics. **Protective services:** Criminal justice, forensics. **Psychology:** General. **Social sciences:** General, political science, sociology. **Visual/performing arts:** General, art, commercial/advertising art, dramatic, jazz, music management, music performance, music theory/composition, studio arts. **Other:** Jazz, music business.

Most popular majors. Business/marketing 21%, communications/journalism 14%, health sciences 7%, psychology 10%, social sciences 14%, visual/performing arts 10%.

Computing on campus. 525 workstations in dormitories, library, computer center, student center. Dormitories wired for high-speed internet access and linked to campus network. Commuter students can connect to campus network. Online course registration, online library, helpline, repair service, student web hosting, wireless network available.

Student life. Freshman orientation: Mandatory, $150 fee. Preregistration for classes offered. **Housing:** Guaranteed on-campus for freshmen. Coed dorms, special housing for disabled, apartments, wellness housing available. $100 nonrefundable deposit, deadline 5/1. Honors floors available. Counselors live in each hall to provide spiritual/counseling assistance. **Activities:** Bands, campus ministries, choral groups, dance, drama, film society, international student organizations, literary magazine, music ensembles, musical theater, opera, radio station, student government, student newspaper, symphony orchestra, student government association, black student union, community action program, international student association, Muslim student association, Asian student organization, gay/lesbian outreach, university programming board, Big Brothers/Big Sisters, society for civic engagement.

Athletics. NAIA. **Intercollegiate:** Baseball M, basketball, cross-country, track and field, volleyball W. **Intramural:** Basketball, golf, racquetball, soccer, softball, swimming, volleyball, weight lifting. **Team name:** Wolfpack.

Student services. Adult student services, alcohol/substance abuse counseling, chaplain/spiritual director, career counseling, student employment services, financial aid counseling, health services, on-campus daycare, personal counseling, placement for graduates, women's services. **Physically disabled:** Services for visually, speech, hearing impaired.

Contact. E-mail: admit@loyno.edu
Phone: (504) 865-3240 Toll-free number: (800) 456-9652
Fax: (504) 865-3383
Salvadore Liberto, Vice President for Enrollment Management, Loyola University New Orleans, 6363 St. Charles Avenue, New Orleans, LA 70118-6195

McNeese State University

Lake Charles, Louisiana
www.mcneese.edu — **CB code: 6403**

- Public 4-year university
- Commuter campus in small city
- 7,256 degree-seeking undergraduates: 19% part-time, 61% women
- 782 degree-seeking graduate students
- 75% of applicants admitted
- SAT or ACT (ACT writing optional) required

General. Founded in 1939. Regionally accredited. **Degrees:** 1,055 bachelor's, 148 associate awarded; master's offered. **Location:** 193 miles from New Orleans, 124 miles from Houston. **Calendar:** Semester, extensive summer session. **Full-time faculty:** 325 total; 65% have terminal degrees, 15%

minority, 46% women. **Part-time faculty:** 109 total; 19% have terminal degrees, 7% minority, 63% women. **Class size:** 44% < 20, 39% 20-39, 10% 40-49, 7% 50-99, less than 1% >100. **Special facilities:** Environmental research center, planetarium, vertebrate museum, farm, community health care clinic.

Freshman class profile. 2,700 applied, 2,031 admitted, 1,332 enrolled.

GPA 3.75 or higher:	18%	**Rank in top tenth:**	15%
GPA 3.50-3.74:	13%	**Return as sophomores:**	68%
GPA 3.0-3.49:	30%	**Out-of-state:**	7%
GPA 2.0-2.99:	37%	**International:**	2%
Rank in top quarter:	37%		

Basis for selection. Applicants must complete Louisiana Board of Regents high school core curriculum and have 18 ACT English or math score (450 SAT Verbal or 430 Math). Applicants also must have either 2.0 GPA, 20 ACT, or rank in top 50% of graduating class. Audition required of music majors. Essay and interview required for Honors College. **Homeschooled:** 23 ACT/1060 SAT required.

High school preparation. 16.5 units recommended. Recommended units include English 4, mathematics 3, social studies 3, science 3 and foreign language 2. 1 fine arts, 0.5 computer science, computer literacy or business computer applications.

2008-2009 Annual costs. Tuition/fees: $3,246; $9,312 out-of-state. Room/board: $5,436. Books/supplies: $1,200. Personal expenses: $2,250.

Financial aid. Non-need-based: Scholarships awarded for academics, alumni affiliation, art, athletics, leadership, minority status, music/drama, state residency. **Additional information:** Books may be charged and paid in 2 installments during semester.

Application procedures. Admission: Priority date 7/15; no deadline. $20 fee. Admission notification on a rolling basis beginning on or about 3/15. **Financial aid:** Priority date 5/1; no closing date. FAFSA, institutional form required. Applicants notified on a rolling basis starting 4/15; must reply within 2 week(s) of notification.

Academics. Special study options: Accelerated study, cooperative education, distance learning, double major, dual enrollment of high school students, ESL, honors, independent study, internships, study abroad, teacher certification program. **Credit/placement by examination:** AP, CLEP, ACT, institutional tests. 24 credit hours maximum toward associate degree, 45 toward bachelor's. **Support services:** Learning center, remedial instruction, tutoring, writing center.

Honors college/program. 25 freshmen admitted. Requirements include 27 ACT, 3.4 GPA, essay, interview, and 3 recommendations.

Majors. Agriculture: General. **Biology:** General. **Business:** Accounting, business admin, finance, marketing. **Communications:** Media studies. **Computer sciences:** Computer science. **Conservation:** Environmental science, wildlife. **Education:** Agricultural, art, biology, business, chemistry, early childhood, elementary, English, family/consumer sciences, foreign languages, mathematics, music, physical, social studies, special, speech. **Engineering:** General. **Engineering technology:** General. **Family/consumer sciences:** General. **Foreign languages:** French, Spanish. **Health:** Clinical lab science, nursing (RN), radiologic technology/medical imaging. **History:** General. **Liberal arts:** Arts/sciences. **Math:** General. **Parks/recreation:** Exercise sciences. **Physical sciences:** Chemistry, physics. **Protective services:** Criminal justice. **Psychology:** General. **Social sciences:** Political science, sociology. **Visual/performing arts:** Art, dramatic, music performance.

Most popular majors. Business/marketing 16%, education 12%, health sciences 15%, liberal arts 21%.

Computing on campus. 450 workstations in dormitories, library, computer center, student center. Dormitories wired for high-speed internet access and linked to campus network. Commuter students can connect to campus network. Online course registration, online library, helpline, student web hosting, wireless network available.

Student life. Freshman orientation: Mandatory, $10 fee. Preregistration for classes offered. Four 2-day programs offered in late May, June and mid-July. **Housing:** Coed dorms, apartments, fraternity/sorority housing available. $175 deposit. **Activities:** Bands, choral groups, dance, drama, literary magazine, music ensembles, musical theater, opera, student government, student newspaper, symphony orchestra, 93 organizations available.

Athletics. NCAA. **Intercollegiate:** Baseball M, basketball, cheerleading, cross-country, football (tackle) M, golf, rodeo, soccer W, softball W, tennis W, track and field, volleyball W. **Intramural:** Badminton, basketball, bowling, football (non-tackle), golf, handball, racquetball, softball, table tennis, tennis, volleyball, water polo. **Team name:** Cowboys.

Student services. Adult student services, alcohol/substance abuse counseling, chaplain/spiritual director, career counseling, student employment services, financial aid counseling, health services, minority student services, personal counseling, placement for graduates, veterans' counselor. **Physically disabled:** Services for visually, speech, hearing impaired.

Contact. E-mail: info@mcneese.edu
Phone: (337) 475-5356 Toll-free number: (800) 622-3352 ext. 5356
Fax: (337) 475-5151
Kara Smith, Director of Admissions and Recruiting, McNeese State University, Box 91740 MSU, Lake Charles, LA 70609-1740

New Orleans Baptist Theological Seminary: Leavell College

New Orleans, Louisiana
www.nobts.edu **CB code: 5034**

- Private 4-year Bible and seminary college affiliated with Southern Baptist Convention
- Very large city
- 1,126 degree-seeking undergraduates
- 100% of applicants admitted
- Application essay, interview required

General. Regionally accredited. **Degrees:** 53 bachelor's, 14 associate awarded; master's, doctoral, first professional offered. **Calendar:** Semester, limited summer session. **Full-time faculty:** 16 total. **Part-time faculty:** 132 total. **Special facilities:** Learning extension centers in Baton Rouge, Lake Charles, and Shreveport. Other centers in Mississippi, Alabama, Florida, and Georgia.

Freshman class profile. 257 applied, 256 admitted, 227 enrolled.

Basis for selection. Must be at least 18 years old and a Christian for at least one year.

2008-2009 Annual costs. Tuition/fees: $4,200. Tuition reported for Southern Baptist students. Other Baptist and non-Baptist students pay tuition at a slightly higher rate. Room only: $2,340. Books/supplies: $500.

Application procedures. Admission: No deadline. $25 fee, may be waived for applicants with need. Admission notification on a rolling basis. **Financial aid:** Closing date 6/1. Applicants notified by 8/1.

Academics. Credit/placement by examination: CLEP. 30 credit hours maximum toward bachelor's degree.

Majors. Theology: Bible, religious ed.

Student life. Freshman orientation: Mandatory. **Housing:** Single-sex dorms, apartments available.

Contact. E-mail: leavelladmission@nobts.edu
Phone: (504) 282-4455
Paul Gregoire, Registrar and Dean of Admissions, New Orleans Baptist Theological Seminary: Leavell College, 3939 Gentilly Boulevard, New Orleans, LA 70126-4858

Nicholls State University

Thibodaux, Louisiana
www.nicholls.edu **CB code: 6221**

- Public 4-year university
- Commuter campus in large town
- 6,246 degree-seeking undergraduates: 18% part-time, 61% women, 18% African American, 1% Asian American, 1% Hispanic American, 2% Native American, 2% international
- 215 degree-seeking graduate students
- 82% of applicants admitted
- SAT or ACT (ACT writing optional) required

General. Founded in 1948. Regionally accredited. **Degrees:** 738 bachelor's, 146 associate awarded; master's offered. **Location:** 60 miles from New Orleans, 75 miles from Baton Rouge. **Calendar:** Semester, extensive summer session. **Full-time faculty:** 295 total; 54% have terminal degrees, 11% minority, 51% women. **Part-time faculty:** 6 total; 33% have terminal degrees, 33% women. **Class size:** 38% < 20, 43% 20-39, 9% 40-49, 9% 50-99, 1% >100. **Special facilities:** Marine research facility, culinary institute, center for women and government, marine biology laboratory, center for study of dyslexia, center for economic education, small business development center, center for traditional boat building, economic council.

Freshman class profile. 2,420 applied, 1,993 admitted, 1,263 enrolled.

Mid 50% test scores		End year in good standing:	62%
ACT composite:	20-24	Return as sophomores:	65%
GPA 3.75 or higher:	15%	Out-of-state:	4%
GPA 3.50-3.74:	14%	Live on campus:	46%
GPA 3.0-3.49:	35%	International:	3%
GPA 2.0-2.99:	35%	Fraternities:	13%
Rank in top quarter:	43%	Sororities:	10%
Rank in top tenth:	18%		

Basis for selection. Must meet the Board of Regents Core (TOPS Core) requirement, have a 2.0 GPA, and meet at least one of the following: 20 ACT or rank in the top half of graduating class.

High school preparation. 16.5 units required. Required units include English 4, mathematics 3, social studies 1, history 2, science 3, foreign language 2, academic electives 1.5.

2008-2009 Annual costs. Tuition/fees: $3,651; $9,099 out-of-state. Room/board: $6,798. Books/supplies: $1,200. Personal expenses: $1,692.

2007-2008 Financial aid. Need-based: 1,068 full-time freshmen applied for aid; 548 were judged to have need; 535 of these received aid. Average need met was 94%. Average scholarship/grant was $4,060; average loan $2,598. 63% of total undergraduate aid awarded as scholarships/grants, 37% as loans/jobs. **Non-need-based:** Awarded to 1,130 full-time undergraduates, including 479 freshmen. Scholarships awarded for academics, athletics, state residency.

Application procedures. Admission: Priority date 8/15; no deadline. $20 fee ($30 out-of-state). Admission notification on a rolling basis beginning on or about 9/1. **Financial aid:** Priority date 4/17; no closing date. FAFSA, institutional form required. Applicants notified on a rolling basis; must reply within 2 week(s) of notification.

Academics. Special study options: Cooperative education, cross-registration, distance learning, dual enrollment of high school students, exchange student, honors, independent study, internships, study abroad, teacher certification program. **Credit/placement by examination:** AP, CLEP, SAT, ACT, institutional tests. 15 credit hours maximum toward associate degree, 30 toward bachelor's. **Support services:** Learning center, pre-admission summer program, reduced course load, remedial instruction, study skills assistance, tutoring, writing center.

Majors. Agriculture: Business. **Biology:** General. **Business:** Accounting, business admin, finance, management information systems, marketing. **Communications:** Media studies. **Computer sciences:** Computer science. **Education:** Art, business, early childhood, elementary, English, French, mathematics, middle, music, physical, science, social studies. **Engineering technology:** Mechanical, petroleum, surveying. **Family/consumer sciences:** General. **Foreign languages:** French. **Health:** Audiology/speech pathology, dietetics, health services, nursing (RN). **History:** General. **Math:** General. **Personal/culinary services:** Chef training. **Physical sciences:** Chemistry. **Psychology:** General. **Social sciences:** Political science, sociology. **Visual/performing arts:** Art.

Most popular majors. Business/marketing 23%, education 7%, family/consumer sciences 7%, health sciences 18%, liberal arts 12%, social sciences 6%.

Computing on campus. 285 workstations in dormitories, library, computer center. Dormitories wired for high-speed internet access and linked to campus network. Commuter students can connect to campus network. Online course registration, online library, wireless network available.

Student life. Freshman orientation: Mandatory, $50 fee. Preregistration for classes offered. **Housing:** Guaranteed on-campus for all undergraduates. Coed dorms, single-sex dorms, special housing for disabled, apartments, wellness housing available. $200 partly refundable deposit, deadline 8/15. **Activities:** Bands, choral groups, dance, drama, film society, international student organizations, literary magazine, music ensembles, musical theater, radio station, student government, student newspaper, TV station, Baptist student union, Circle K, Young Democrats, Support for Older and Returning Students, Order of Athena, Young Republicans, UNITE, Newman club, Muslim student association.

Athletics. NCAA. **Intercollegiate:** Baseball M, basketball, cross-country, football (tackle) M, golf, soccer W, softball W, tennis, track and field W, volleyball W. **Intramural:** Basketball, football (non-tackle), softball, volleyball. **Team name:** Colonels.

Student services. Adult student services, alcohol/substance abuse counseling, chaplain/spiritual director, career counseling, services for economically disadvantaged, student employment services, financial aid counseling, health services, legal services, minority student services, personal counseling, placement for graduates, veterans' counselor, women's services. **Physically disabled:** Services for visually, speech, hearing impaired. **Learning disabled:** Comprehensive services available.

Contact. E-mail: nicholls@nicholls.edu
Phone: (985) 448-4507 Toll-free number: (877) 642-4655
Fax: (985) 448-4929
Becky Durocher, Director of Admissions, Nicholls State University, PO Box 2004-NSU, Thibodaux, LA 70310

Northwestern State University

Natchitoches, Louisiana
www.nsula.edu **CB code: 6492**

- Public 4-year university
- Commuter campus in large town
- 7,440 degree-seeking undergraduates: 27% part-time, 68% women, 30% African American, 1% Asian American, 2% Hispanic American, 2% Native American, 1% international
- 881 degree-seeking graduate students
- 83% of applicants admitted
- SAT or ACT (ACT writing optional) required

General. Founded in 1884. Regionally accredited. Additional campuses in Shreveport, Leesville, Alexandria, and off-campus sites. **Degrees:** 1,098 bachelor's, 238 associate awarded; master's offered. **ROTC:** Army, Air Force. **Location:** 75 miles from Shreveport, 57 miles from Alexandria. **Calendar:** Semester, extensive summer session. **Full-time faculty:** 334 total; 59% have terminal degrees, 8% minority, 53% women. **Part-time faculty:** 289 total; 29% have terminal degrees, 15% minority, 59% women. **Class size:** 53% < 20, 32% 20-39, 6% 40-49, 9% 50-99, less than 1% >100. **Special facilities:** Regional folklife center, Creole heritage center, Southern studies institute, heritage resources laboratory, preservation technology and training center.

Freshman class profile. 2,674 applied, 2,211 admitted, 1,233 enrolled.

Mid 50% test scores		Rank in top quarter:	38%
SAT critical reading:	420-530	Rank in top tenth:	14%
SAT math:	440-550	End year in good standing:	88%
ACT composite:	18-23	Return as sophomores:	69%
GPA 3.75 or higher:	14%	Out-of-state:	12%
GPA 3.50-3.74:	15%	Live on campus:	61%
GPA 3.0-3.49:	33%	Fraternities:	12%
GPA 2.0-2.99:	37%	Sororities:	8%

Basis for selection. Applicants must have completed the 17.5 unit college preparatory program, need no more than one developmental class, and must have one of the following: 20 ACT (or SAT equivalent), 2.0 GPA, or be in top 50% of graduating class. Out-of-state and homeschooled students admitted based on ACT/SAT scores. Students 21 and older and Louisiana Scholars' College have own admission criteria. Exceptions on case-by-case basis. The COMPASS test can be used for admission/placement for some students.

High school preparation. College-preparatory program required. 17.5 units required. Required units include English 4, mathematics 3, social studies 1, history 2, science 3 (laboratory 3), foreign language 2, computer science .5 and visual/performing arts 1. Additional unit of math or science.

2008-2009 Annual costs. Tuition/fees: $3,598; $9,676 out-of-state. Room/board: $6,272. Books/supplies: $1,200. Personal expenses: $1,726.

2007-2008 Financial aid. Need-based: 994 full-time freshmen applied for aid; 849 were judged to have need; 817 of these received aid. Average need met was 51%. Average scholarship/grant was $3,821; average loan $4,390. 43% of total undergraduate aid awarded as scholarships/grants, 57% as loans/jobs. **Non-need-based:** Awarded to 2,841 full-time undergraduates, including 849 freshmen. Scholarships awarded for academics, alumni affiliation, art, athletics, job skills, leadership, minority status, music/drama, religious affiliation, ROTC, state residency.

Application procedures. Admission: Closing date 7/6 (receipt date). $20 fee. Admission notification on a rolling basis. Applications may be submitted after fall deadline but consideration is not guaranteed. **Financial aid:** Priority date 5/1; no closing date. FAFSA, institutional form required. Applicants notified on a rolling basis starting 5/1; must reply within 4 week(s) of notification.

Academics. Special study options: Cooperative education, distance learning, double major, dual enrollment of high school students, honors, independent study, internships, study abroad, teacher certification program. **Credit/placement by examination:** AP, CLEP, SAT, ACT, institutional tests. 30

credit hours maximum toward associate degree, 62 toward bachelor's. Maximum semester hours of credit by examination may not exceed half the number of credits required for degree. **Support services:** Learning center, preadmission summer program, reduced course load, remedial instruction, study skills assistance, tutoring, writing center.

Honors college/program. Student must have 25 ACT, or 1130 SAT (exclusive of Writing); must score 20 on each ACT subscore or 480 on SAT verbal and math; must have 3.0 high school GPA in the Louisiana core curriculum or 3.0 college GPA.

Majors. Biology: General. **Business:** Accounting, business admin, hospitality admin. **Communications:** Journalism. **Computer sciences:** Information systems. **Education:** Biology, business, chemistry, early childhood, elementary, English, family/consumer sciences, mathematics, middle, music, physical, physics, social studies, speech. **Engineering technology:** Electrical, industrial. **Family/consumer sciences:** General. **Health:** Nursing (RN), radiologic technology/medical imaging, substance abuse counseling. **History:** General. **Interdisciplinary:** Cultural resource management. **Liberal arts:** Arts/sciences. **Math:** General. **Parks/recreation:** Health/fitness. **Physical sciences:** Chemistry, physics. **Protective services:** Criminal justice. **Psychology:** General. **Public administration:** Social work. **Social sciences:** Anthropology, political science, sociology. **Visual/performing arts:** Dramatic, music performance, studio arts. **Other:** Unified public safety administration.

Most popular majors. Business/marketing 13%, education 7%, health sciences 22%, liberal arts 12%, psychology 11%.

Computing on campus. Dormitories linked to campus network. Commuter students can connect to campus network. Online course registration, online library, helpline, student web hosting, wireless network available.

Student life. Freshman orientation: Available, $80 fee. Preregistration for classes offered. One- to 2-day program held 5 times during the summer; includes program for parents. **Housing:** Coed dorms, special housing for disabled, apartments, fraternity/sorority housing available. $75 nonrefundable deposit, deadline 3/5. **Activities:** Bands, campus ministries, choral groups, dance, drama, international student organizations, literary magazine, music ensembles, musical theater, opera, radio station, student government, student newspaper, symphony orchestra, TV station, Catholic student organization, Fellowship of Christian Athletes, Wesley Westminster Ministry, Latter-day Saints Institute, honor society, Purple Jackets, College Republicans, College Democrats, African-American caucus.

Athletics. NCAA. **Intercollegiate:** Baseball M, basketball, cross-country, football (tackle) M, soccer W, softball W, tennis W, track and field, volleyball W. **Intramural:** Badminton, baseball, basketball, bowling, football (non-tackle), golf, racquetball, soccer, softball, table tennis, tennis, volleyball, water polo. **Team name:** Demons.

Student services. Adult student services, alcohol/substance abuse counseling, chaplain/spiritual director, career counseling, services for economically disadvantaged, student employment services, financial aid counseling, health services, minority student services, personal counseling, placement for graduates, veterans' counselor. **Physically disabled:** Services for visually, speech, hearing impaired. **Learning disabled:** Comprehensive services available.

Contact. E-mail: admissions@nsula.edu
Phone: (318) 357-4078 Toll-free number: (800) 767-8115
Fax: (318) 357-4660
Andrea Maley, Director of Admissions, Northwestern State University, Roy Hall, Room 209, Natchitoches, LA 71497

Our Lady of Holy Cross College

New Orleans, Louisiana
www.olhcc.edu **CB code: 6002**

- Private 4-year liberal arts college affiliated with Roman Catholic Church
- Commuter campus in very large city
- 610 full-time, degree-seeking undergraduates
- 170 graduate students
- ACT required

General. Founded in 1916. Regionally accredited. Campus offerings available for senior citizens. **Degrees:** 170 bachelor's, 5 associate awarded; master's offered. **ROTC:** Army, Naval, Air Force. **Location:** 3 miles from downtown. **Calendar:** Semester, limited summer session. **Full-time faculty:** 45 total. **Part-time faculty:** 85 total. **Class size:** 51% < 20, 43% 20-39, 3% 40-49, 2% 50-99. **Special facilities:** Training and counseling center.

Freshman class profile.

Mid 50% test scores		Out-of-state:	1%
ACT composite:	17-21		

Basis for selection. Those with 2.0 GPA and 20 ACT unconditionally accepted. Students with less than 2.0 GPA and 17 ACT will be denied. Students entering directly from high school required to submit ACT, while others must take institutional test. English and math proficiency tests required.

High school preparation. 17.5 units recommended. Recommended units include English 4, mathematics 2, social studies 3, science 4 and foreign language 2. .5 unit of computer literacy recommended.

2009-2010 Annual costs. Tuition/fees (projected): $10,320. Books/supplies: $1,200. Personal expenses: $1,819.

2008-2009 Financial aid. Non-need-based: Scholarships awarded for academics, state residency.

Application procedures. Admission: Priority date 12/1; no deadline. $25 fee. Admission notification on a rolling basis. **Financial aid:** Priority date 7/1; no closing date. FAFSA required. Applicants notified on a rolling basis starting 5/15; must reply within 4 week(s) of notification.

Academics. Special study options: Cross-registration, distance learning, dual enrollment of high school students, exchange student, independent study, internships, study abroad, teacher certification program. **Credit/placement by examination:** AP, CLEP, institutional tests. 60 credit hours maximum toward bachelor's degree. **Support services:** Learning center, preadmission summer program, reduced course load, remedial instruction, tutoring.

Majors. Biology: General. **Business:** Accounting, business admin. **Education:** Business, elementary, English, mathematics, secondary, social studies, special. **Health:** Medical radiologic technology/radiation therapy, respiratory therapy technology. **History:** General. **Interdisciplinary:** Biological/physical sciences. **Liberal arts:** Arts/sciences. **Social sciences:** General.

Computing on campus. 68 workstations in library, computer center. Commuter students can connect to campus network. Online library, wireless network available.

Student life. Freshman orientation: Mandatory. Preregistration for classes offered. **Activities:** Campus ministries, choral groups, drama, international student organizations, literary magazine, student government, student newspaper, Rotaract Club, various honor societies.

Athletics. Intramural: Bowling, soccer M, softball, volleyball. **Team name:** Hurricanes.

Student services. Adult student services, chaplain/spiritual director, career counseling, student employment services, financial aid counseling, health services, personal counseling, placement for graduates, veterans' counselor.

Contact. E-mail: admissions@olhcc.edu
Phone: (504) 394-7744 ext. 175 Toll-free number: (800) 259-7744
Fax: (504) 394-1182
Kristine Hatfield, Vice President for Enrollment Services, Our Lady of Holy Cross College, 4123 Woodland Drive, New Orleans, LA 70131-7399

Our Lady of the Lake College

Baton Rouge, Louisiana
www.ololcollege.edu **CB code: 3928**

- Private 4-year health science and nursing college affiliated with Roman Catholic Church
- Commuter campus in large city
- 1,570 degree-seeking undergraduates: 65% part-time, 84% women, 22% African American, 4% Asian American, 2% Hispanic American, 1% Native American
- 153 degree-seeking graduate students
- ACT (writing optional) required

General. Regionally accredited. **Degrees:** 99 bachelor's, 330 associate awarded; master's offered. **ROTC:** Air Force. **Calendar:** Semester, extensive summer session. **Full-time faculty:** 99 total; 26% minority, 78% women. **Part-time faculty:** 161 total; 20% minority, 52% women. **Class size:** 54% < 20, 42% 20-39, 4% 40-49, less than 1% 50-99.

Freshman class profile. 79 enrolled.

Mid 50% test scores		**GPA 3.0-3.49:**	50%
ACT composite:	19-22	**GPA 2.0-2.99:**	30%
GPA 3.75 or higher:	5%	**Out-of-state:**	4%
GPA 3.50-3.74:	15%		

Basis for selection. Open admission, but selective for some programs. High school record and test scores important. **Homeschooled:** State high school equivalency certificate required.

High school preparation. Required and recommended units include English 4, mathematics 3, social studies 3, science 3 (laboratory 3), foreign language 2 and academic electives 2.

2009-2010 Annual costs. Tuition/fees (projected): $9,217. Books/supplies: $1,500. Personal expenses: $1,710.

2007-2008 Financial aid. Need-based: 96% of total undergraduate aid awarded as scholarships/grants, 4% as loans/jobs.

Application procedures. Admission: Priority date 2/1; deadline 7/1 (receipt date). $35 fee. Admission notification on a rolling basis. **Financial aid:** Closing date 3/1. FAFSA, institutional form required.

Academics. Special study options: Accelerated study, combined bachelor's/graduate degree, cross-registration, distance learning, liberal arts/career combination. **Credit/placement by examination:** CLEP, ACT, institutional tests. 15 credit hours maximum toward associate degree, 30 toward bachelor's. **Support services:** Learning center, reduced course load, study skills assistance, tutoring.

Majors. Biology: General, biomedical sciences. **Health:** Clinical lab science, facilities admin, health care admin, health services, health services admin, nursing (RN), premedicine. **Liberal arts:** Humanities. **Psychology:** General.

Most popular majors. Health sciences 98%.

Computing on campus. 150 workstations in library. Commuter students can connect to campus network. Online library, helpline, wireless network available.

Student life. Freshman orientation: Mandatory. Preregistration for classes offered. One-day program held the week before classes begin. **Policies:** Smoke-free campus. **Activities:** Student government, student newspaper, American College of Healthcare Executives, Beta Epsilon Fraternity of Radiologic Technology Students, Beta Sigma Mu (human medicine), Christian student fellowship, clinical laboratory scientist association, cultural arts association, Epsilon Mu Theta, math and science association, Phi Theta Alpha.

Student services. Adult student services, chaplain/spiritual director, career counseling, financial aid counseling.

Contact. E-mail: admission@ololcollege.edu
Phone: (225) 768-1700 Toll-free number: (877) 242-3509
Fax: (225) 768-1726
Rebecca Cannon, Director of Admissions, Our Lady of the Lake College, 7434 Perkins Road, Baton Rouge, LA 70808

St. Joseph Seminary College

St. Benedict, Louisiana
www.sjasc.edu **CB code: 6689**

- Private 4-year liberal arts and seminary college for men affiliated with Roman Catholic Church
- Residential campus in rural community
- 76 degree-seeking undergraduates: 4% African American, 7% Asian American, 22% Hispanic American, 1% Native American
- ACT (writing optional) required

General. Founded in 1891. Regionally accredited. Non-seminarian, non-degree-seeking students may attend part-time. **Degrees:** 9 bachelor's awarded. **Location:** 40 miles from New Orleans. **Calendar:** Semester. **Full-time faculty:** 10 total; 30% have terminal degrees, 50% women. **Part-time faculty:** 17 total; 35% have terminal degrees, 29% women. **Class size:** 90% < 20, 10% 20-39. **Special facilities:** 1,200 acres of forest, Romanesque abbey church.

Freshman class profile. 6 applied, 6 admitted, 6 enrolled.

End year in good standing:	6%	**Out-of-state:**	50%
Return as sophomores:	12%	**Live on campus:**	100%

Basis for selection. Open admission, but selective for some programs. Recommendation by diocesan bishop, academic standing, and test scores required. Michigan test used for placement and proficiency. Interview recommended. **Homeschooled:** State high school equivalency certificate required.

High school preparation. 17 units recommended. Recommended units include English 4, mathematics 3, social studies 1, history 1, science 2, foreign language 2 and academic electives 7. Second foreign language recommended.

2008-2009 Annual costs. Tuition/fees: $12,769. Room/board: $10,784. Books/supplies: $1,000. Personal expenses: $1,387.

Financial aid. Non-need-based: Scholarships awarded for academics, leadership.

Application procedures. Admission: No deadline. No application fee. Admission notification on a rolling basis. **Financial aid:** Priority date 3/15; no closing date. FAFSA required. Applicants notified on a rolling basis starting 7/1; must reply within 4 week(s) of notification.

Academics. Special study options: ESL. **Credit/placement by examination:** AP, CLEP, IB. 24 credit hours maximum toward bachelor's degree. **Support services:** Reduced course load, remedial instruction, tutoring, writing center.

Majors. Liberal arts: Arts/sciences.

Computing on campus. 14 workstations in library, computer center. Repair service available.

Student life. Freshman orientation: Mandatory. Preregistration for classes offered. **Housing:** Guaranteed on-campus for all undergraduates. All students live on campus. **Activities:** Choral groups, student government, community, religious, social service activities.

Athletics. Team name: Ravens.

Student services. Career counseling, health services, personal counseling, veterans' counselor.

Contact. E-mail: acdean@sjasc.edu
Phone: (985) 867-2248 ext. 2248 Fax: (985) 867-2270
George Binder, Registrar, St. Joseph Seminary College, 75376 River Road, St. Benedict, LA 70457-9990

School of Urban Missions: New Orleans

New Orleans, Louisiana
www.sum.edu

- Private 4-year Bible college affiliated with Assemblies of God, Church of God in Christ
- Commuter campus in very large city
- 37 degree-seeking undergraduates: 46% part-time, 43% women
- 100% of applicants admitted
- Application essay, interview required
- 75% graduate within 6 years; 10% enter graduate study

General. Accredited by ABHE. Additional campus in Oakland, California. All face-to-face classes taught as streaming video with interactive audio. **Location:** 2 miles from New Orleans. **Calendar:** Trimester, limited summer session. **Full-time faculty:** 1 total; 100% have terminal degrees. **Part-time faculty:** 4 total; 25% minority, 25% women. **Class size:** 92% < 20, 8% 20-39.

Freshman class profile. 5 applied, 5 admitted, 4 enrolled.

End year in good standing:	85%	**Return as sophomores:**	67%

Basis for selection. Phone interview and personal written testimony of call to ministry and salvation required. SAT or ACT recommended. **Homeschooled:** State high school equivalency certificate required.

High school preparation. College-preparatory program recommended.

2009-2010 Annual costs. Tuition/fees (projected): $7,155. Room only: $2,400. Books/supplies: $1,500. Personal expenses: $4,675.

2007-2008 Financial aid. Need-based: 72% of total undergraduate aid awarded as scholarships/grants, 28% as loans/jobs. **Non-need-based:** Scholarships awarded for academics, leadership, religious affiliation.

Application procedures. Admission: Closing date 7/31 (postmark date). $20 fee. Admission notification 8/15. Admission notification on a rolling basis beginning on or about 1/1. **Financial aid:** No deadline. FAFSA, institutional form required.

Academics. Each trimester, students do 80 hours of ministry. **Special study options:** Accelerated study, distance learning, internships. Cohort system at various locations for non-traditional students. **Credit/placement by examination:** AP, CLEP, SAT, ACT. **Support services:** Remedial instruction, tutoring.

Majors. Theology: Missionary. **Other:** Church planting.

Computing on campus. 20 workstations in library, computer center. Dormitories wired for high-speed internet access and linked to campus network. Online course registration, online library, wireless network available.

Student life. Freshman orientation: Mandatory. Preregistration for classes offered. Occurs during the first chapel. **Policies:** Morning devotions and chapel attendance required; full-time students required to participate in practicum ministries. Religious observance required. **Housing:** Guaranteed on-campus for all undergraduates. Single-sex dorms, wellness housing available. $100 nonrefundable deposit, deadline 8/1. **Activities:** Campus ministries, student government, Assemblies of God, Church of God in Christ, Full Gospel Baptist.

Student services. Adult student services, chaplain/spiritual director, career counseling, financial aid counseling, health services, personal counseling, placement for graduates, veterans' counselor.

Contact. E-mail: sum@sum.edu
Phone: (504) 362-6364 Toll-free number: (800) 385-6364
Fax: (504) 362-4895
Rev. Dwight Davis, Admissions Director, School of Urban Missions: New Orleans, 511 Westbank Expressway, Gretna, LA 70053-3677

Southeastern Louisiana University

Hammond, Louisiana
www.selu.edu **CB code: 6656**

- Public 4-year university
- Commuter campus in large town
- 12,921 degree-seeking undergraduates: 14% part-time, 62% women, 18% African American, 1% Asian American, 2% Hispanic American, 1% international
- 989 degree-seeking graduate students
- 93% of applicants admitted
- SAT or ACT (ACT writing optional) required

General. Founded in 1925. Regionally accredited. **Degrees:** 1,765 bachelor's, 76 associate awarded; master's, doctoral offered. **ROTC:** Army. **Location:** 55 miles from New Orleans, 40 miles from Baton Rouge. **Calendar:** Semester, extensive summer session. **Full-time faculty:** 537 total; 63% have terminal degrees, 12% minority, 57% women. **Part-time faculty:** 155 total; 30% have terminal degrees, 10% minority, 63% women. **Class size:** 30% < 20, 56% 20-39, 6% 40-49, 7% 50-99, less than 1% >100. **Special facilities:** Environmental research station, social science research center, maritime museum, contemporary art gallery, performing arts theatre.

Freshman class profile. 3,617 applied, 3,360 admitted, 2,761 enrolled.

Mid 50% test scores		**Rank in top quarter:**	27%
ACT composite:	19-23	**Rank in top tenth:**	9%
GPA 3.75 or higher:	10%	**End year in good standing:**	65%
GPA 3.50-3.74:	11%	**Return as sophomores:**	64%
GPA 3.0-3.49:	31%	**Out-of-state:**	2%
GPA 2.0-2.99:	47%	**Live on campus:**	45%

Basis for selection. In-state students: completion of Regents high school core curriculum; 20 ACT, or rank in upper 50% of graduating class, or 2.0 GPA; have no more than 1 developmental course requirement. Out-of-state students must meet same criteria as in-state students, or score 23 ACT, or meet all of following criteria: 20 ACT, rank in upper 50% of class, 2.0 GPA. Audition recommended for music majors. **Homeschooled:** Must have GED and 23 ACT, and have no more than one developmental course requirement. **Learning Disabled:** No special requirements or procedures.

High school preparation. College-preparatory program required. 17.5 units required. Required units include English 4, mathematics 3, social studies 3, science 3, foreign language 2, computer science .5 and visual/performing arts 1. 1 additional math or science required.

2008-2009 Annual costs. Tuition/fees: $3,721; $9,721 out-of-state. Room/board: $6,220. Books/supplies: $1,200. Personal expenses: $1,726.

2007-2008 Financial aid. Need-based: 2,110 full-time freshmen applied for aid; 1,297 were judged to have need; 1,151 of these received aid. Average scholarship/grant was $4,307; average loan $2,698. 46% of total undergraduate aid awarded as scholarships/grants, 54% as loans/jobs. **Non-need-based:** Awarded to 3,091 full-time undergraduates, including 808 freshmen. Scholarships awarded for academics, athletics, job skills, leadership, music/drama, state residency.

Application procedures. Admission: Closing date 8/1 (postmark date). $20 fee. Admission notification on a rolling basis beginning on or about 9/1. **Financial aid:** Priority date 5/1; no closing date. FAFSA, institutional form required. Applicants notified on a rolling basis starting 3/1; must reply within 2 week(s) of notification.

Academics. Special study options: Accelerated study, cross-registration, distance learning, double major, ESL, honors, independent study, internships, liberal arts/career combination, study abroad, teacher certification program. **Credit/placement by examination:** AP, CLEP, SAT, ACT, institutional tests. 30 credit hours maximum toward bachelor's degree. Maximum of 60 hours through all types of nontraditional educational experiences, i.e., advanced placement credit, correspondence courses, and military service credits. **Support services:** Learning center, remedial instruction, study skills assistance, tutoring, writing center.

Majors. Agriculture: Horticultural science. **Biology:** General. **Business:** Accounting, business admin, finance, marketing. **Communications:** General. **Computer sciences:** Computer science. **Education:** Art, computer, early childhood, elementary, English, family/consumer sciences, French, mathematics, middle, music, physical, science, social studies, Spanish, special, speech. **Engineering technology:** General, industrial, occupational safety. **Family/consumer sciences:** General. **Foreign languages:** French, Spanish. **Health:** Athletic training, audiology/speech pathology, nursing (RN), public health ed. **History:** General. **Liberal arts:** Arts/sciences. **Math:** General. **Parks/recreation:** Sports admin. **Physical sciences:** Chemistry, physics. **Protective services:** Criminal justice. **Psychology:** General. **Public administration:** Social work. **Social sciences:** Political science, sociology. **Visual/performing arts:** Art, arts management, music performance.

Most popular majors. Business/marketing 31%, education 11%, health sciences 11%, liberal arts 15%.

Computing on campus. 833 workstations in library, computer center, student center. Dormitories wired for high-speed internet access and linked to campus network. Commuter students can connect to campus network. Online course registration, online library, helpline, repair service, student web hosting, wireless network available.

Student life. Freshman orientation: Mandatory, $75 fee. Preregistration for classes offered. Students may take orientation either during summer or at beginning of first semester. Must pay room and board for summer session. **Policies:** Freshmen and sophomores must live on campus. **Housing:** Coed dorms, single-sex dorms, apartments, fraternity/sorority housing available. $150 nonrefundable deposit, deadline 6/15. **Activities:** Bands, campus ministries, choral groups, dance, drama, film society, international student organizations, literary magazine, music ensembles, musical theater, opera, radio station, student government, student newspaper, symphony orchestra, TV station, gospel choir, Baptist collegiate ministries, student government association, international student organization, Wesley Foundation, campus activities board, black student union, campus outreach, Circle K International, Best Buddies.

Athletics. NCAA. **Intercollegiate:** Baseball M, basketball, cross-country, football (tackle) M, golf M, soccer W, softball W, tennis, track and field, volleyball W. **Intramural:** Basketball, football (non-tackle), racquetball, soccer, softball, volleyball, weight lifting. **Team name:** Lions, Lady Lions.

Student services. Adult student services, alcohol/substance abuse counseling, career counseling, services for economically disadvantaged, student employment services, financial aid counseling, health services, minority student services, personal counseling, placement for graduates, veterans' counselor. **Physically disabled:** Services for visually, speech, hearing impaired.

Contact. E-mail: admissions@selu.edu
Phone: (985) 549-2066 Toll-free number: (800) 222-7358
Fax: (985) 549-5632
Jeff Rhodes, Dean of Enrollment Management, Southeastern Louisiana University, SLU 10752, Hammond, LA 70402

Southern University and Agricultural and Mechanical College

Baton Rouge, Louisiana
www.subr.edu **CB code: 6663**

- Public 4-year university
- Commuter campus in large city

- 6,382 degree-seeking undergraduates: 10% part-time, 62% women, 96% African American, 1% international
- 1,132 degree-seeking graduate students
- 57% of applicants admitted
- SAT or ACT (ACT writing optional) required

General. Founded in 1880. Regionally accredited. **Degrees:** 904 bachelor's, 4 associate awarded; master's, doctoral offered. **ROTC:** Army, Naval, Air Force. **Location:** 80 miles from New Orleans. **Calendar:** Semester, extensive summer session. **Full-time faculty:** 405 total; 66% have terminal degrees, 85% minority, 47% women. **Part-time faculty:** 141 total; 43% have terminal degrees, 86% minority, 57% women. **Class size:** 16% < 20, 57% 20-39, 27% 40-49, less than 1% 50-99, less than 1% >100. **Special facilities:** Experimental (laboratory) farm, outdoor learning resource center (nature trail), meat processing plant, Black heritage museum.

Freshman class profile. 2,943 applied, 1,667 admitted, 1,045 enrolled.

Mid 50% test scores		**Rank in top quarter:**	9%
SAT math:	380-510	**Rank in top tenth:**	3%
ACT composite:	17-20	**End year in good standing:**	56%
GPA 3.75 or higher:	4%	**Return as sophomores:**	68%
GPA 3.50-3.74:	8%	**Out-of-state:**	24%
GPA 3.0-3.49:	31%	**Live on campus:**	53%
GPA 2.0-2.99:	56%	**International:**	1%

Basis for selection. 20 ACT (940 SAT) or 2.0 GPA or rank in top 50% of class and require no more than 1 remedial course by having 18 ACT English and Math (450 SAT Verbal or 430 Math) as well as 16.5-unit core class requirements. Auditions required for music program.

High school preparation. College-preparatory program required. 16.5 units required. Required units include English 4, mathematics 3, social studies 2, history 1, science 3 and foreign language 2. .5 computer literacy, 1 fine arts required.

2008-2009 Annual costs. Tuition/fees: $3,906; $9,698 out-of-state. Room/board: $5,558. Books/supplies: $1,200. Personal expenses: $1,726.

2007-2008 Financial aid. **Non-need-based:** Scholarships awarded for academics, athletics, ROTC, state residency.

Application procedures. **Admission:** Closing date 7/1 (postmark date). $20 fee. Admission notification on a rolling basis. Admission can be deferred for 2 semesters. High school students admitted early must be in good academic standing and have approval from their high school. **Financial aid:** Priority date 1/31, closing date 3/30. FAFSA required. Applicants notified on a rolling basis starting 5/1; must reply within 3 week(s) of notification.

Academics. **Special study options:** Combined bachelor's/graduate degree, cooperative education, cross-registration, distance learning, double major, dual enrollment of high school students, exchange student, honors, independent study, internships, liberal arts/career combination, study abroad, teacher certification program, weekend college. **Credit/placement by examination:** AP, CLEP, SAT, ACT, institutional tests. 30 credit hours maximum toward bachelor's degree. **Support services:** Learning center, preadmission summer program, reduced course load, remedial instruction, study skills assistance, tutoring, writing center.

Honors college/program. Must have 23 ACT (1070 SAT, exclusive of Writing) and 3.0 GPA.

Majors. **Agriculture:** Animal sciences, economics. **Architecture:** Architecture. **Biology:** General. **Business:** Accounting, business admin, e-commerce, finance, managerial economics, marketing. **Communications:** Media studies. **Computer sciences:** Computer science. **Conservation:** Urban forestry. **Education:** Agricultural, art, biology, chemistry, computer, early childhood, elementary, English, French, mathematics, middle, music, physical, physics, science, secondary, social studies, Spanish, special. **Engineering:** Civil, electrical, mechanical. **Engineering technology:** Electrical. **Family/consumer sciences:** General. **Foreign languages:** French, Spanish. **Health:** Audiology/speech pathology, nursing (RN), recreational therapy, vocational rehab counseling. **History:** General. **Math:** General. **Physical sciences:** Chemistry, physics. **Protective services:** Criminal justice. **Psychology:** General. **Public administration:** Social work. **Social sciences:** Political science, sociology. **Visual/performing arts:** Dramatic, music performance, studio arts.

Most popular majors. Business/marketing 17%, family/consumer sciences 7%, health sciences 20%, psychology 7%, security/protective services 8%.

Computing on campus. 1,500 workstations in library, computer center. Dormitories wired for high-speed internet access and linked to campus network. Commuter students can connect to campus network. Online course registration, online library, helpline, wireless network available.

Student life. **Freshman orientation:** Mandatory. Preregistration for classes offered. Two-day program held during registration. **Housing:** Guaranteed on-campus for freshmen. Single-sex dorms, special housing for disabled, wellness housing available. $50 fully refundable deposit, deadline 12/30. **Activities:** Bands, campus ministries, choral groups, dance, drama, literary magazine, music ensembles, musical theater, student government, student newspaper, Catholic student club, Committed to Christ student organization, Love Alive Christian Fellowship, Muslim student organization, Nation of Islam student organization, Sigma Omega Delta social service organization, College Democrats, College Republicans, Collegiate 100 Black Men.

Athletics. NCAA. **Intercollegiate:** Baseball M, basketball, bowling W, cross-country, football (non-tackle) M, football (tackle) M, golf, soccer W, softball W, tennis, track and field, volleyball W. **Intramural:** Football (non-tackle), golf, swimming, volleyball, weight lifting. **Team name:** Jaguars.

Student services. Career counseling, student employment services, financial aid counseling, health services, personal counseling, placement for graduates, veterans' counselor. **Physically disabled:** Services for visually, speech, hearing impaired.

Contact. E-mail: admit@subr.edu
Phone: (225) 771-2430 Toll-free number: (800) 256-1531
Fax: (225) 771-2500
Velva Thomas, Director, Southern University and Agricultural and Mechanical College, T.H. Harris Hall, Baton Rouge, LA 70813

Southern University at New Orleans

New Orleans, Louisiana
www.suno.edu **CB code: 1647**

- Public 4-year university
- Commuter campus in large city
- 2,603 degree-seeking undergraduates

General. Founded in 1959. Regionally accredited. Part of Southern University System. **Degrees:** 229 bachelor's, 16 associate awarded; master's offered. **ROTC:** Army, Naval, Air Force. **Location:** Downtown. **Calendar:** Semester, limited summer session. **Full-time faculty:** 99 total. **Part-time faculty:** 2 total. **Class size:** 49% < 20, 47% 20-39, 3% 40-49, less than 1% 50-99, less than 1% >100.

Basis for selection. Open admission. ACT required by state law for placement.

High school preparation. 16 units recommended. Recommended units include English 4, mathematics 3, social studies 3, science 3 (laboratory 2) and foreign language 1.

2008-2009 Annual costs. Tuition/fees: $3,002; $6,742 out-of-state. Books/supplies: $1,000. Personal expenses: $6,000.

Financial aid. All financial aid based on need.

Application procedures. **Admission:** Closing date 7/1. $5 fee ($15 out-of-state). Admission notification on a rolling basis. **Financial aid:** Closing date 4/1. FAFSA required. Applicants notified by 5/15; must reply within 1 week(s) of notification.

Academics. **Special study options:** Combined bachelor's/graduate degree, cooperative education, cross-registration, distance learning, double major, dual enrollment of high school students, internships, teacher certification program, weekend college. **Credit/placement by examination:** CLEP. 30 credit hours maximum toward bachelor's degree. **Support services:** Reduced course load, remedial instruction, study skills assistance, tutoring, writing center.

Majors. **Biology:** General. **Business:** Entrepreneurial studies, management information systems. **Education:** Early childhood, elementary. **Family/consumer sciences:** Family studies. **Health:** Medical records admin, substance abuse counseling. **Physical sciences:** Physics. **Protective services:** Criminal justice. **Psychology:** General. **Public administration:** General, social work. **Social sciences:** Sociology.

Most popular majors. Biology 6%, business/marketing 18%, computer/information sciences 9%, liberal arts 15%, psychology 13%, public administration/social services 9%, security/protective services 13%.

Computing on campus. 60 workstations in library, computer center. Online library, helpline, wireless network available.

Student life. **Freshman orientation:** Available. Preregistration for classes offered. **Housing:** Wellness housing available. **Activities:** Student government.

Athletics. NAIA. **Intercollegiate:** Basketball, cross-country. **Team name:** Knights.

Student services. Chaplain/spiritual director, career counseling, student employment services, financial aid counseling, health services, personal counseling, placement for graduates. **Physically disabled:** Services for visually, speech, hearing impaired.

Contact. Phone: (504) 286-5000 ext. 5314 Fax: (504) 284-5481
Rene Gill Pratt, Director of Recruitment, Admissions, & Retention, Southern University at New Orleans, 6801 Press Drive, New Orleans, LA 70126

Southwest University
Kenner, Louisiana
www.southwest.edu

- For-profit 4-year virtual university
- Very large city
- 520 degree-seeking undergraduates

General. Accredited by DETC. **Degrees:** 35 bachelor's awarded; master's offered. **Calendar:** Continuous. **Full-time faculty:** 6 total. **Part-time faculty:** 40 total.

Basis for selection. Open admission.

2008-2009 Annual costs. Tuition/fees: $5,500. Graduate tuition $250 per credit hour.

Application procedures. Admission: No deadline. $50 fee. Admission notification on a rolling basis.

Academics. Special study options: Accelerated study, distance learning, double major, independent study. **Credit/placement by examination:** CLEP.

Majors. Business: Business admin, management science. **Protective services:** Law enforcement admin.

Computing on campus. Online library available.

Student services. Adult student services, veterans' counselor.

Contact. E-mail: admissions@southwest.edu
Phone: (504) 468-2900 Toll-free number: (800) 433-5923
Fax: (504) 468-3213
Lydia Ocmand, Director of Admissions, Southwest University, 2200 Veterans Memorial Boulevard, Kenner, LA 70062-4005

Tulane University
New Orleans, Louisiana **CB member**
www.tulane.edu **CB code: 6832**

- Private 4-year university
- Residential campus in very large city
- 6,692 degree-seeking undergraduates: 22% part-time, 54% women, 9% African American, 5% Asian American, 4% Hispanic American, 2% Native American, 3% international
- 4,408 degree-seeking graduate students
- 27% of applicants admitted
- SAT or ACT with writing, application essay required
- 74% graduate within 6 years

General. Founded in 1834. Regionally accredited. **Degrees:** 1,483 bachelor's, 29 associate awarded; master's, doctoral, first professional offered. **ROTC:** Army, Naval, Air Force. **Location:** 4 miles from downtown. **Calendar:** Semester, limited summer session. **Full-time faculty:** 897 total; 92% have terminal degrees, 23% minority, 34% women. **Part-time faculty:** 660 total; 53% have terminal degrees, 14% minority, 41% women. **Class size:** 65% < 20, 25% 20-39, 4% 40-49, 4% 50-99, 1% >100. **Special facilities:** Jazz archive, Louisiana collection of historical materials, Southeastern architecture archive, center for research on women, political economy institute, center for Latin American studies, middle American research institute, center for bioenvironmental research, performing arts center, Amistad research center.

Freshman class profile. 34,125 applied, 9,206 admitted, 1,560 enrolled.

Mid 50% test scores		**GPA 2.0-2.99:**	9%
SAT critical reading:	630-720	**Rank in top quarter:**	88%
SAT math:	620-700	**Rank in top tenth:**	59%
SAT writing:	640-720	**Return as sophomores:**	87%
ACT composite:	29-32	**Out-of-state:**	84%
GPA 3.75 or higher:	29%	**Live on campus:**	98%
GPA 3.50-3.74:	24%	**International:**	4%
GPA 3.0-3.49:	37%		

Basis for selection. High school achievement record most important, followed by test scores, recommendation, personal qualities; special consideration for children of alumni and minority applicants. Candidates should be in top third of graduating class with 3.5 GPA. Audition recommended for music majors. Portfolio recommended for architecture, art majors. **Homeschooled:** State high school equivalency certificate, letter of recommendation (nonparent) required. SAT Subject Tests required.

High school preparation. Recommended units include English 4, mathematics 4, social studies 3, science 4 (laboratory 4), foreign language 3 and academic electives 3. Chemistry and physics recommended for science or engineering majors.

2009-2010 Annual costs. Tuition/fees (projected): $38,664. Room/board: $9,296. Books/supplies: $1,200. Personal expenses: $936.

2007-2008 Financial aid. Need-based: 801 full-time freshmen applied for aid; 584 were judged to have need; 582 of these received aid. Average need met was 95%. Average scholarship/grant was $22,465; average loan $5,630. 76% of total undergraduate aid awarded as scholarships/grants, 24% as loans/jobs. **Non-need-based:** Awarded to 2,431 full-time undergraduates, including 681 freshmen. Scholarships awarded for academics, athletics, leadership, music/drama, state residency. **Additional information:** Application deadline for merit scholarships December 1.

Application procedures. Admission: Priority date 11/1; deadline 1/15 (postmark date). No application fee. Admission notification 4/1. Admission notification on a rolling basis. Must reply by May 1 or within 2 week(s) if notified thereafter. **Financial aid:** Priority date 2/1; no closing date. FAFSA, CSS PROFILE required. Applicants notified on a rolling basis starting 2/1; must reply by 5/1 or within 2 week(s) of notification.

Academics. Special study options: Accelerated study, combined bachelor's/graduate degree, cross-registration, distance learning, double major, ESL, exchange student, honors, independent study, internships, liberal arts/career combination, student-designed major, study abroad, teacher certification program, Washington semester. **Credit/placement by examination:** AP, CLEP, IB, institutional tests. **Support services:** Learning center, study skills assistance, tutoring, writing center.

Majors. Architecture: Architecture. **Area/ethnic studies:** African, American, Asian, German, Latin American, Russian/Slavic, women's. **Biology:** General, biochemistry, cell/histology, ecology, evolutionary, molecular. **Business:** General, accounting, business admin, finance, management information systems, marketing. **Communications:** Media studies. **Conservation:** Environmental science, environmental studies. **Engineering:** Biomedical, chemical. **Foreign languages:** Classics, French, German, Italian, linguistics, modern Greek, Portuguese, Russian, Spanish. **History:** General. **Interdisciplinary:** Medieval/Renaissance, neuroscience. **Legal studies:** General. **Math:** General. **Philosophy/religion:** Judaic, philosophy. **Physical sciences:** Chemistry, geology, physics. **Psychology:** General. **Social sciences:** Anthropology, economics, international economics, political science, sociology, urban studies. **Visual/performing arts:** Art, art history/conservation, dance, dramatic, multimedia, music performance, music theory/composition, studio arts, theater history. **Other:** Earth sciences, Legal studies in business, Mathematical economics, Social policy and practice.

Most popular majors. Business/marketing 21%, psychology 7%, social sciences 18%.

Computing on campus. 556 workstations in dormitories, library, computer center, student center. Dormitories wired for high-speed internet access and linked to campus network. Commuter students can connect to campus network. Online course registration, online library, helpline, repair service, student web hosting, wireless network available.

Student life. Freshman orientation: Mandatory, $400 fee. Preregistration for classes offered. **Policies:** Alcohol and sexual harrassment policies in place. **Housing:** Guaranteed on-campus for freshmen. Coed dorms, single-sex dorms, special housing for disabled, apartments, wellness housing available. $150 nonrefundable deposit, deadline 5/1. Honors program residence hall, language floors, women in science, healthy lifestyle, engineering and technology, performing and creative arts, pre-med and pre-law special living floors, quiet-study floors, and international living floors available. **Activities:** Bands, choral groups, dance, drama, film society, international student organizations, literary magazine, music ensembles, musical theater, radio station, student government, student newspaper, symphony orchestra, TV station, Hillel, Episcopal center, Inter-Varsity Christian Fellowship, Catholic center, Baptist student union, African-American Congress, Latin American students association, Amnesty International.

Athletics. NCAA. **Intercollegiate:** Baseball M, basketball, cross-country, diving W, field hockey, football (tackle) M, golf, soccer W, swimming W, tennis, track and field, volleyball W. **Intramural:** Badminton, basketball, bowling, cross-country M, football (tackle) M, golf, handball M, racquetball, soccer, softball, swimming, table tennis M, tennis, track and field M, volleyball, wrestling M. **Team name:** Green Wave.

Student services. Alcohol/substance abuse counseling, chaplain/spiritual director, career counseling, student employment services, financial aid counseling, health services, legal services, minority student services, personal counseling, women's services. **Physically disabled:** Services for visually, speech, hearing impaired.

Contact. E-mail: undergrad.admission@tulane.edu
Phone: (504) 865-5731 Toll-free number: (800) 873-9283
Fax: (504) 862-8715
Earl Retif, Vice President for Enrollment Management and University Registrar, Tulane University, 6823 St. Charles Avenue, New Orleans, LA 70118-5680

University of Louisiana at Lafayette

Lafayette, Louisiana — **CB member**
www.louisiana.edu — **CB code: 6672**

- Public 4-year university
- Commuter campus in small city
- 14,240 degree-seeking undergraduates: 14% part-time, 58% women, 19% African American, 2% Asian American, 2% Hispanic American, 2% international
- 1,404 degree-seeking graduate students
- 68% of applicants admitted
- SAT or ACT (ACT writing optional) required
- 40% graduate within 6 years

General. Founded in 1898. Regionally accredited. **Degrees:** 2,142 bachelor's, 2 associate awarded; master's, doctoral offered. **ROTC:** Army. **Location:** 130 miles from New Orleans, 200 miles from Houston. **Calendar:** Semester, extensive summer session. **Full-time faculty:** 591 total; 74% have terminal degrees, 15% minority, 42% women. **Part-time faculty:** 156 total; 20% have terminal degrees, 8% minority, 53% women. **Class size:** 30% < 20, 50% 20-39, 13% 40-49, 5% 50-99, 2% >100. **Special facilities:** 2 nuclear accelerators, 2 electron microscopes, CAD/CAM laboratory, Acadiana folklore archives, confocal microscope, atomic force microscope, Louisiana Emersive Technology Center, on campus restaurant and hotel (which include instructional facilities), nursery school laboratory, 600-acre sustainable farm, television production studio, marine research facility.

Freshman class profile. 7,634 applied, 5,227 admitted, 2,630 enrolled.

Mid 50% test scores		**End year in good standing:**	84%
ACT composite:	20-24	**Return as sophomores:**	74%
GPA 3.75 or higher:	16%	**Out-of-state:**	4%
GPA 3.50-3.74:	16%	**Live on campus:**	26%
GPA 3.0-3.49:	37%	**International:**	1%
GPA 2.0-2.99:	31%	**Fraternities:**	6%
Rank in top quarter:	39%	**Sororities:**	8%
Rank in top tenth:	15%		

Basis for selection. Guaranteed admissions for students who complete Louisiana Board of Regents' high school core curriculum with 19 ACT math (460 SAT math) or 18 ACT English (450 SAT verbal) and one of the following: 2.5 unweighted GPA or 23 ACT composite (1050 SAT math and verbal) with 2.0 GPA or rank in the top 25% of class with 2.0 GPA. Audition required of music majors. Portfolio required of art, architecture majors. Essays required for some applicants.

High school preparation. Required units include English 4, mathematics 4, social studies 2, history 1, science 3, academic electives 4.5. Suggested electives: .5 unit computer science, 1 unit fine arts, 1 unit speech.

2008-2009 Annual costs. Tuition/fees: $3,604; $9,784 out-of-state. Room/board: $4,200. Books/supplies: $1,200. Personal expenses: $1,726.

2007-2008 Financial aid. All financial aid based on need. 2,393 full-time freshmen applied for aid; 1,380 were judged to have need; 1,344 of these received aid. Average need met was 68%. Average scholarship/grant was $5,285; average loan $3,081. 49% of total undergraduate aid awarded as scholarships/grants, 51% as loans/jobs.

Application procedures. Admission: Priority date 7/15; no deadline. $25 fee. Admission notification on a rolling basis. **Financial aid:** Priority date 5/1; no closing date. FAFSA, institutional form required. Applicants notified on a rolling basis starting 4/1; must reply within 2 week(s) of notification.

Academics. Special study options: Accelerated study, cooperative education, cross-registration, distance learning, double major, dual enrollment of high school students, ESL, exchange student, honors, independent study, internships, student-designed major, study abroad, teacher certification program, Washington semester. **Credit/placement by examination:** AP, CLEP, SAT, ACT, institutional tests. 30 credit hours maximum toward bachelor's degree. **Support services:** Learning center, reduced course load, remedial instruction, study skills assistance, tutoring, writing center.

Majors. Agriculture: General. **Architecture:** Architecture, interior. **Biology:** General, conservation, microbiology. **Business:** Accounting, business admin, fashion, finance, hospitality admin, insurance, management information systems, managerial economics, marketing. **Communications:** General, media studies, public relations. **Computer sciences:** Computer science. **Conservation:** Land use planning, management/policy. **Education:** Agricultural, art, biology, business, chemistry, early childhood, early childhood special, elementary, English, family/consumer sciences, French, German, mathematics, middle, music, physical, physics, science, secondary, social studies, Spanish, special, speech, technology/industrial arts. **Engineering:** Chemical, civil, computer, electrical, mechanical, petroleum. **Engineering technology:** Industrial. **Family/consumer sciences:** Family studies. **Foreign languages:** General. **Health:** Athletic training, audiology/speech pathology, dental hygiene, dietetics, medical records admin, nursing (RN). **History:** General. **Math:** General. **Philosophy/religion:** Philosophy. **Physical sciences:** Chemistry, geology, physics. **Protective services:** Criminal justice. **Psychology:** General. **Social sciences:** Anthropology, political science, sociology. **Visual/performing arts:** General, art, industrial design, music performance. **Other:** Earth science education grades 6-12.

Most popular majors. Business/marketing 23%, education 13%, engineering/engineering technologies 7%, health sciences 9%, liberal arts 16%.

Computing on campus. 2,000 workstations in dormitories, library, computer center, student center. Commuter students can connect to campus network. Online course registration, online library, helpline, wireless network available.

Student life. Freshman orientation: Mandatory, $75 fee. Preregistration for classes offered. **Housing:** Single-sex dorms, special housing for disabled, apartments, fraternity/sorority housing, wellness housing available. $50 deposit, deadline 6/15. **Activities:** Bands, campus ministries, choral groups, dance, drama, film society, international student organizations, literary magazine, music ensembles, musical theater, opera, radio station, student government, student newspaper, Young Republicans, Young Democrats, Omega Phi Alpha, Afro-American student groups.

Athletics. NCAA. **Intercollegiate:** Baseball M, basketball, cheerleading, cross-country, football (tackle) M, golf M, soccer W, softball W, tennis, track and field, volleyball W. **Intramural:** Basketball, football (non-tackle), racquetball, soccer, softball, tennis, volleyball, water polo. **Team name:** Ragin' Cajuns.

Student services. Adult student services, career counseling, student employment services, financial aid counseling, health services, minority student services, on-campus daycare, personal counseling, placement for graduates, veterans' counselor. **Physically disabled:** Services for visually, speech, hearing impaired.

Contact. E-mail: enroll@louisiana.edu
Phone: (337) 482-6553 Toll-free number: (800) 752-6553
Fax: (337) 482-1112
Leroy Broussard, Director of Admissions, University of Louisiana at Lafayette, Box 41210, Lafayette, LA 70504-1210

University of Louisiana at Monroe

Monroe, Louisiana
www.ulm.edu — **CB code: 6482**

- Public 4-year university
- Commuter campus in small city
- 7,424 degree-seeking undergraduates: 23% part-time, 63% women, 27% African American, 2% Asian American, 1% Hispanic American, 1% international
- 1,075 degree-seeking graduate students
- 77% of applicants admitted
- SAT or ACT (ACT writing optional) required

General. Founded in 1931. Regionally accredited. **Degrees:** 931 bachelor's, 50 associate awarded; master's, doctoral, first professional offered. **ROTC:** Army. **Location:** 90 miles from Shreveport, 120 miles from Jackson, Mississippi. **Calendar:** Semester, extensive summer session. **Full-time faculty:** 365 total; 12% minority, 49% women. **Part-time faculty:** 69 total; 9% minority, 61% women. **Class size:** 35% < 20, 45% 20-39, 8% 40-49, 10% 50-99, 2% >100. **Special facilities:** National Public Radio station, Louisiana state cancer tumor registry archives, regional small business development center, weather research center, museum of natural history, flight simulator.

Freshman class profile. 2,523 applied, 1,931 admitted, 1,227 enrolled.

Mid 50% test scores		**GPA 2.0-2.99:**	30%
SAT critical reading:	420-520	**Rank in top quarter:**	45%
SAT math:	410-530	**Rank in top tenth:**	20%
ACT composite:	19-23	**Return as sophomores:**	66%
GPA 3.75 or higher:	17%	**Out-of-state:**	8%
GPA 3.50-3.74:	16%	**Live on campus:**	51%
GPA 3.0-3.49:	33%		

Basis for selection. Students who do not meet defined criteria evaluated on other evidence of academic promise for admittance by exception. Only limited number of students will be granted admittance by exception. **Homeschooled:** Transcript of courses and grades required. Must submit official transcript of grades and official proof of graduation or original diploma to admissions office.

High school preparation. College-preparatory program required. 17.5 units required. Required units include English 4, mathematics 4, social studies 1, history 2, science 3, foreign language 2, computer science .5. 1 fine arts, 0.5 free enterprise, 0.5 civics required.

2008-2009 Annual costs. Tuition/fees: $3,791; $8,734 out-of-state. Room/board: $4,350. Books/supplies: $1,200.

Financial aid. Non-need-based: Scholarships awarded for academics, alumni affiliation, art, athletics, job skills, leadership, minority status, music/drama, religious affiliation, ROTC, state residency.

Application procedures. Admission: Priority date 4/1; no deadline. $20 fee, may be waived for applicants with need. Admission notification on a rolling basis. **Financial aid:** Priority date 4/1; no closing date. FAFSA required. Applicants notified on a rolling basis starting 6/1; must reply within 2 week(s) of notification.

Academics. Credit hours toward graduation may be earned through examination, military service, correspondence and extension courses taken through accredited extension divisions of other colleges and universities. **Special study options:** Accelerated study, combined bachelor's/graduate degree, cooperative education, distance learning, double major, dual enrollment of high school students, ESL, honors, independent study, internships, study abroad, teacher certification program. Evening college. **Credit/placement by examination:** AP, CLEP, SAT, ACT, institutional tests. 22 credit hours maximum toward associate degree, 43 toward bachelor's. Maximum of one-third of credits required for degree may be earned through examination, military experience, and correspondence courses. **Support services:** Learning center, reduced course load, remedial instruction, study skills assistance, tutoring, writing center.

Majors. Agriculture: Business. **Biology:** General, toxicology. **Business:** Accounting, business admin, entrepreneurial studies, finance, insurance, management information systems, managerial economics, marketing. **Communications:** Media studies. **Computer sciences:** Computer science. **Education:** Art, biology, chemistry, elementary, English, family/consumer sciences, French, mathematics, music, physical, social studies, Spanish, speech. **Engineering technology:** Construction. **Family/consumer sciences:** General. **Foreign languages:** French, Spanish. **Health:** Audiology/speech pathology, clinical lab science, dental hygiene, health care admin, health services, nursing (RN), radiologic technology/medical imaging. **History:** General. **Math:** General. **Parks/recreation:** Exercise sciences. **Physical sciences:** Atmospheric science, chemistry. **Protective services:** Criminal justice. **Psychology:** General, educational. **Public administration:** Social work. **Social sciences:** Political science, sociology. **Transportation:** Airline/commercial pilot. **Visual/performing arts:** Music performance, studio arts.

Most popular majors. Business/marketing 19%, education 7%, health sciences 18%, liberal arts 17%.

Computing on campus. Dormitories wired for high-speed internet access and linked to campus network. Commuter students can connect to campus network. Online course registration, online library, helpline, repair service, student web hosting, wireless network available.

Student life. Freshman orientation: Mandatory. Preregistration for classes offered. Five regular sessions plus one computer PREP session available. **Housing:** Coed dorms, single-sex dorms, apartments, fraternity/sorority housing, wellness housing available. $50 partly refundable deposit, deadline 7/1. **Activities:** Bands, campus ministries, choral groups, dance, drama, international student organizations, literary magazine, music ensembles, musical theater, opera, radio station, student government, student newspaper, symphony orchestra.

Athletics. NCAA. **Intercollegiate:** Baseball M, basketball, cheerleading, cross-country, football (tackle) M, golf, soccer W, softball W, swimming, track and field, volleyball W. **Intramural:** Basketball, cross-country, football (non-tackle), golf, racquetball, soccer, softball, swimming, tennis, track and field, volleyball, weight lifting. **Team name:** Warhawks.

Student services. Adult student services, alcohol/substance abuse counseling, chaplain/spiritual director, career counseling, student employment services, financial aid counseling, health services, on-campus daycare, personal counseling, placement for graduates, veterans' counselor. **Physically disabled:** Services for visually, speech, hearing impaired.

Contact. E-mail: self@ulm.edu
Phone: (318) 342-5430 Toll-free number: (800) 372-5127
Fax: (318) 342-1915
Susan Duggins, Executive Director of Recruitment and Admissions, University of Louisiana at Monroe, 700 University Avenue, Monroe, LA 71209-1160

University of New Orleans

New Orleans, Louisiana — **CB member**
www.uno.edu — **CB code: 6379**

- Public 4-year university
- Commuter campus in very large city
- 8,628 degree-seeking undergraduates: 24% part-time, 52% women, 18% African American, 6% Asian American, 7% Hispanic American, 1% Native American, 4% international
- 2,800 degree-seeking graduate students
- 55% of applicants admitted
- SAT or ACT (ACT writing optional) required

General. Founded in 1956. Regionally accredited. **Degrees:** 1,260 bachelor's awarded; master's, doctoral offered. **ROTC:** Army, Naval, Air Force. **Calendar:** Semester, extensive summer session. **Full-time faculty:** 449 total; 68% have terminal degrees, 14% minority, 41% women. **Part-time faculty:** 155 total; 39% have terminal degrees, 12% minority, 44% women. **Class size:** 44% < 20, 40% 20-39, 5% 40-49, 7% 50-99, 3% >100.

Freshman class profile. 3,615 applied, 1,998 admitted, 1,267 enrolled.

Mid 50% test scores		**Rank in top quarter:**	35%
SAT critical reading:	470-600	**Rank in top tenth:**	16%
SAT math:	490-650	**Return as sophomores:**	69%
SAT writing:	460-580	**Out-of-state:**	7%
ACT composite:	20-24	**Live on campus:**	16%
GPA 3.75 or higher:	11%	**International:**	7%
GPA 3.50-3.74:	14%	**Fraternities:**	2%
GPA 3.0-3.49:	33%	**Sororities:**	6%
GPA 2.0-2.99:	41%		

Basis for selection. Students who graduate from state-approved high schools must complete Louisiana Board of Regents core curriculum, require no more than 1 developmental/remedial course and satisfy one of the following: 23 ACT (or SAT equivalent), 2.5 GPA with 18 ACT English and/or Math subscores (or SAT equivalent), or rank in top 25% of class. Students who do not meet core curriculum must satisfy all of the following: 23 ACT (SAT equivalent), 2.5 GPA and rank in top 25% of class. If these are not met, student must have 26 ACT (SAT equivalent) and require no more than 1 remedial/developmental course. Audition required of music majors. Portfolio required of fine arts/studio majors.

High school preparation. College-preparatory program required. 17.5 units required. Required units include English 4, mathematics 3, social studies 1, history 2, science 3, foreign language 2, computer science .5 and visual/performing arts 1. 1 additional math or science required.

2008-2009 Annual costs. Tuition/fees: $4,306; $11,702 out-of-state. Room/board: $6,130. Books/supplies: $1,200. Personal expenses: $1,726.

2008-2009 Financial aid. Need-based: 838 full-time freshmen applied for aid; 744 were judged to have need; 670 of these received aid. Average need met was 74%. Average scholarship/grant was $6,690; average loan $3,212. 60% of total undergraduate aid awarded as scholarships/grants, 40%

as loans/jobs. **Non-need-based:** Awarded to 2,055 full-time undergraduates, including 707 freshmen. Scholarships awarded for academics, athletics. **Additional information:** Students in good academic and financial standing eligible to participate in Extended Payment Plan option.

Application procedures. Admission: Priority date 7/1; deadline 8/20 (receipt date). $40 fee. Admission notification on a rolling basis beginning on or about 10/1. **Financial aid:** Priority date 5/15; no closing date. FAFSA required. Applicants notified on a rolling basis starting 4/20; must reply within 4 week(s) of notification.

Academics. Special study options: Cooperative education, cross-registration, distance learning, double major, dual enrollment of high school students, ESL, exchange student, honors, independent study, internships, student-designed major, study abroad, teacher certification program, Washington semester, weekend college. **Credit/placement by examination:** AP, CLEP, IB, SAT, ACT, institutional tests. 30 credit hours maximum toward bachelor's degree. **Support services:** Learning center, remedial instruction, tutoring, writing center.

Majors. Area/ethnic studies: Women's. **Biology:** General. **Business:** Accounting, business admin, entrepreneurial studies, finance, hospitality admin, management information systems, managerial economics, marketing. **Communications:** General. **Computer sciences:** Computer science. **Conservation:** Environmental studies. **Education:** Biology, chemistry, early childhood, elementary, English, mathematics, music, secondary, social studies. **Engineering:** Civil, electrical, marine, mechanical. **Foreign languages:** French, Spanish. **History:** General. **Interdisciplinary:** Global studies. **Math:** General. **Parks/recreation:** Health/fitness. **Philosophy/religion:** Philosophy. **Physical sciences:** Chemistry, geology, physics. **Psychology:** General. **Social sciences:** Anthropology, geography, political science, sociology, urban studies. **Visual/performing arts:** Art history/conservation, studio arts. **Other:** Earth science education.

Most popular majors. Biology 6%, business/marketing 39%, communications/journalism 6%, engineering/engineering technologies 7%, liberal arts 10%, psychology 7%, social sciences 6%.

Computing on campus. Dormitories wired for high-speed internet access and linked to campus network. Commuter students can connect to campus network. Online course registration, online library, helpline, wireless network available.

Student life. Freshman orientation: Mandatory, $100 fee. Preregistration for classes offered. **Housing:** Coed dorms, special housing for disabled, apartments available. Apartment referral and roommate locator services available. **Activities:** Bands, campus ministries, choral groups, dance, drama, film society, international student organizations, literary magazine, music ensembles, musical theater, opera, radio station, student government, student newspaper, African students organization, Chinese students and scholars association, international student organization, InterVarsity Christian Fellowship, Latin American student association, Muslim student association, Pakistan students association, College Republicans, Taiwanese students association, Vietnamese American student association.

Athletics. NCAA. **Intercollegiate:** Baseball M, basketball, diving, golf M, swimming, tennis, volleyball W. **Intramural:** Basketball, football (non-tackle), racquetball, soccer, softball, swimming, table tennis, tennis, volleyball. **Team name:** Privateers.

Student services. Adult student services, alcohol/substance abuse counseling, chaplain/spiritual director, career counseling, student employment services, financial aid counseling, health services, legal services, minority student services, on-campus daycare, personal counseling, placement for graduates, veterans' counselor, women's services. **Physically disabled:** Services for visually, speech, hearing impaired.

Contact. E-mail: admissions@uno.edu
Phone: (504) 280-6595 Toll-free number: (800) 256-5866
Fax: (504) 280-5522
Andy Benoit, Director of Admissions Office, University of New Orleans, Administration Building Room 103, New Orleans, LA 70148

Xavier University of Louisiana

New Orleans, Louisiana — **CB member**
www.xula.edu — **CB code: 6975**

- Private 4-year university affiliated with Roman Catholic Church
- Commuter campus in very large city
- 2,435 degree-seeking undergraduates: 4% part-time, 72% women, 75% African American, 8% Asian American, 1% Hispanic American, 2% international
- 782 degree-seeking graduate students
- 66% of applicants admitted
- SAT or ACT (ACT writing optional) required
- 46% graduate within 6 years

General. Founded in 1915. Regionally accredited. **Degrees:** 344 bachelor's awarded; master's, first professional offered. **ROTC:** Army, Naval, Air Force. **Location:** One mile from downtown. **Calendar:** Semester, limited summer session. **Full-time faculty:** 212 total; 84% have terminal degrees, 52% minority, 48% women. **Part-time faculty:** 28 total; 46% minority, 43% women. **Class size:** 42% < 20, 47% 20-39, 4% 40-49, 4% 50-99, 3% >100.

Freshman class profile. 3,516 applied, 2,307 admitted, 778 enrolled.

Mid 50% test scores		**GPA 2.0-2.99:**	38%
SAT critical reading:	410-530	**Rank in top quarter:**	49%
SAT math:	400-520	**Rank in top tenth:**	25%
SAT writing:	410-520	**Return as sophomores:**	73%
ACT composite:	18-23	**Out-of-state:**	47%
GPA 3.75 or higher:	21%	**Live on campus:**	56%
GPA 3.50-3.74:	14%	**International:**	2%
GPA 3.0-3.49:	25%		

Basis for selection. High school record or GED scores, standardized test results, and recommendation from counselor important. Interview recommended for academically weak. Audition required for music majors. Portfolio required for art majors.

High school preparation. College-preparatory program recommended. 16 units required. Required and recommended units include English 4, mathematics 2-4, social studies 1, history 1, science 1-3, foreign language 1 and academic electives 8. Math must include 1 algebra.

2008-2009 Annual costs. Tuition/fees: $15,000. Room/board: $6,800. Books/supplies: $1,200.

2007-2008 Financial aid. Need-based: 639 full-time freshmen applied for aid; 584 were judged to have need; 578 of these received aid. Average need met was 86%. Average scholarship/grant was $5,578; average loan $3,645. 47% of total undergraduate aid awarded as scholarships/grants, 53% as loans/jobs. **Non-need-based:** Awarded to 1,247 full-time undergraduates, including 456 freshmen. Scholarships awarded for music/drama.

Application procedures. Admission: Priority date 3/1; deadline 7/1 (postmark date). $25 fee, may be waived for applicants with need. Must reply by May 1 or within 2 week(s) if notified thereafter. **Financial aid:** Priority date 1/1; no closing date. FAFSA required. Applicants notified on a rolling basis starting 4/1; must reply within 2 week(s) of notification.

Academics. Special study options: Accelerated study, combined bachelor's/graduate degree, cooperative education, cross-registration, double major, dual enrollment of high school students, exchange student, honors, independent study, internships, study abroad. **Credit/placement by examination:** AP, CLEP, SAT, ACT, institutional tests. 30 credit hours maximum toward bachelor's degree. **Support services:** Learning center, pre-admission summer program, reduced course load, remedial instruction, study skills assistance, tutoring, writing center.

Majors. Biology: General, biochemistry, microbiology. **Business:** Accounting, business admin, finance, management science, marketing. **Communications:** Media studies. **Computer sciences:** General, computer science. **Education:** General, art, biology, chemistry, early childhood, elementary, English, foreign languages, French, history, mathematics, multi-level teacher, music, physical, science, social studies, Spanish, special. **Engineering:** Computer. **Foreign languages:** French, Spanish. **Health:** Predental, premedicine, prepharmacy, preveterinary, speech pathology. **History:** General. **Legal studies:** Prelaw. **Math:** General, statistics. **Parks/recreation:** Health/fitness. **Philosophy/religion:** Philosophy. **Physical sciences:** Chemistry, physics. **Psychology:** General. **Social sciences:** Political science, sociology. **Theology:** Theology. **Visual/performing arts:** Art, music performance, piano/organ, stringed instruments, voice/opera.

Most popular majors. Biology 40%, business/marketing 8%, physical sciences 15%, psychology 14%, social sciences 7%.

Computing on campus. 350 workstations in dormitories, library, computer center. Dormitories wired for high-speed internet access and linked to campus network. Commuter students can connect to campus network. Online course registration, online library, helpline available.

Student life. Freshman orientation: Mandatory. Preregistration for classes offered. One-week program. **Policies:** All recognized student organizations must perform 2 community service activities per semester. **Housing:** Coed dorms, single-sex dorms, special housing for disabled available. $300 partly refundable deposit, deadline 4/9. **Activities:** Bands, campus ministries, choral groups, dance, drama, international student organizations, literary magazine, music ensembles, opera, student government, student newspaper, symphony orchestra, TV station, over 30 organizations.

Athletics. NAIA. **Intercollegiate:** Basketball, cross-country, tennis, volleyball W. **Intramural:** Basketball, cheerleading, football (non-tackle), softball, swimming, table tennis, tennis, track and field, volleyball. **Team name:** Gold Rush.

Student services. Adult student services, alcohol/substance abuse counseling, chaplain/spiritual director, career counseling, student employment services, financial aid counseling, health services, personal counseling, placement for graduates, veterans' counselor, women's services. **Physically disabled:** Services for visually, speech, hearing impaired.

Contact. E-mail: apply@xula.edu
Phone: (504) 520-7388 Toll-free number: (877) 928-4378
Fax: (504) 520-7941
Winston Brown, Dean of Admissions, Xavier University of Louisiana, 1 Drexel Drive, New Orleans, LA 70125-1098

Maine

Bates College

Lewiston, Maine
www.bates.edu

CB member
CB code: 3076

- Private 4-year liberal arts college
- Residential campus in large town
- 1,776 degree-seeking undergraduates: 54% women, 4% African American, 6% Asian American, 4% Hispanic American, 5% international
- 29% of applicants admitted
- Application essay required
- 89% graduate within 6 years

General. Founded in 1855. Regionally accredited. **Degrees:** 440 bachelor's awarded. **Location:** 35 miles from Portland. **Calendar:** 4-4-1 semester system. **Full-time faculty:** 166 total; 90% have terminal degrees, 14% minority, 46% women. **Part-time faculty:** 27 total; 67% have terminal degrees, 11% minority, 63% women. **Class size:** 67% < 20, 24% 20-39, 5% 40-49, 4% 50-99. **Special facilities:** Mountain seacoast conservation area, Edmund S. Muskie Archives, art museum, observatory.

Freshman class profile. 5,098 applied, 1,487 admitted, 521 enrolled.

Mid 50% test scores			
SAT critical reading:	630-720	Rank in top tenth:	53%
SAT math:	630-710	Return as sophomores:	96%
SAT writing:	630-720	Out-of-state:	89%
Rank in top quarter:	88%	Live on campus:	100%
		International:	6%

Basis for selection. GED not accepted. School achievement record, recommendations, special talents, leadership, essay, interview all important. Submission of standardized test scores is optional for admission. Interviews are strongly recommended.

High school preparation. College-preparatory program required. 17 units required; 23 recommended. Required and recommended units include English 4, mathematics 3-4, social studies 3-4, science 3-4 (laboratory 2-3) and foreign language 2-4. History included in social studies requirement.

2008-2009 Annual costs. Comprehensive fee: $49,350. Books/supplies: $1,150.

2008-2009 Financial aid. All financial aid based on need. 287 full-time freshmen applied for aid; 238 were judged to have need; 227 of these received aid. Average need met was 100%. Average scholarship/grant was $31,175; average loan $3,786. 88% of total undergraduate aid awarded as scholarships/grants, 12% as loans/jobs. **Additional information:** Priority date for filing required financial aid forms for early decision students is 11/15.

Application procedures. Admission: Closing date 1/1 (postmark date). $60 fee, may be waived for applicants with need. Admission notification 3/31. Must reply by 5/1. **Financial aid:** Closing date 2/1. FAFSA, CSS PROFILE required. Applicants notified by 4/1; must reply by 5/1.

Academics. Special study options: Accelerated study, combined bachelor's/graduate degree, cooperative education, double major, honors, independent study, internships, liberal arts/career combination, semester at sea, student-designed major, study abroad, teacher certification program, urban semester, Washington semester. Marine studies program at Mystic Seaport, liberal arts-engineering dual degree program with 5 universities. **Credit/placement by examination:** AP, CLEP, IB, institutional tests. **Support services:** Reduced course load, study skills assistance, tutoring, writing center.

Majors. Area/ethnic studies: African-American, American, East Asian, women's. **Biology:** General, biochemistry. **Conservation:** Environmental studies. **Engineering:** General. **Foreign languages:** Chinese, French, German, Japanese, Russian, Spanish. **History:** General. **Interdisciplinary:** Ancient studies, neuroscience. **Math:** General. **Philosophy/religion:** Philosophy, religion. **Physical sciences:** Chemistry, geology, physics. **Psychology:** General. **Social sciences:** Anthropology, economics, political science, sociology. **Visual/performing arts:** Art, dramatic.

Most popular majors. Biology 8%, English 11%, foreign language 6%, history 8%, psychology 11%, social sciences 30%.

Computing on campus. 415 workstations in dormitories, library, computer center. Dormitories wired for high-speed internet access and linked to campus network. Commuter students can connect to campus network. Online course registration, helpline, repair service, student web hosting, wireless network available.

Student life. Freshman orientation: Mandatory. Preregistration for classes offered. Held 5 days prior to start of classes. **Housing:** Guaranteed on-campus for all undergraduates. Coed dorms, single-sex dorms, wellness housing available. $300 nonrefundable deposit, deadline 5/1. **Activities:** Pep band, campus ministries, choral groups, dance, drama, film society, international student organizations, literary magazine, music ensembles, radio station, student government, student newspaper, symphony orchestra, Amandla!, Bates Christian Fellowship, Bates Democrats, Bates Hindu Awareness Group, College Republicans, Feminist Action Coalition, Hillel, Latinos Unidos, Mushahada Club, OUTFront.

Athletics. NCAA. **Intercollegiate:** Baseball M, basketball, cross-country, diving, field hockey W, football (tackle) M, golf, lacrosse, rowing (crew), skiing, soccer, softball W, squash, swimming, tennis, track and field, volleyball W. **Intramural:** Badminton, baseball M, basketball, football (tackle), golf, handball, ice hockey, lacrosse, racquetball, rugby, sailing, soccer, softball, squash, table tennis, tennis, volleyball. **Team name:** Bobcats.

Student services. Alcohol/substance abuse counseling, chaplain/spiritual director, career counseling, student employment services, financial aid counseling, health services, minority student services, personal counseling, placement for graduates, women's services. **Physically disabled:** Services for visually, hearing impaired.

Contact. E-mail: admissions@bates.edu
Phone: (207) 786-6000 Fax: (207) 786-6025
Wylie Mitchell, Dean of Admissions, Bates College, 23 Campus Avenue, Lindholm House, Lewiston, ME 04240-9917

Bowdoin College

Brunswick, Maine
www.bowdoin.edu

CB member
CB code: 3089

- Private 4-year liberal arts college
- Residential campus in large town
- 1,716 degree-seeking undergraduates: 51% women, 6% African American, 12% Asian American, 9% Hispanic American, 1% Native American, 3% international
- 19% of applicants admitted
- Application essay required
- 91% graduate within 6 years; 15% enter graduate study

General. Founded in 1794. Regionally accredited. **Degrees:** 450 bachelor's awarded. **Location:** 25 miles from Portland, 120 miles from Boston. **Calendar:** Semester. **Full-time faculty:** 174 total; 98% have terminal degrees, 16% minority, 48% women. **Part-time faculty:** 32 total; 81% have terminal degrees, 19% minority, 41% women. **Class size:** 64% < 20, 28% 20-39, 4% 40-49, 4% 50-99. **Special facilities:** Arctic museum, arctic studies center, coastal marine biology and ornithology research facility, scientific station, farm, center for learning and teaching, 2 theaters, visual arts center, hall of music, environmental studies center, outdoor leadership center, community service resource center, African-American center, women's resource center, educational research and development program, career planning center, boathouse, electronic classroom, recital hall, nature trails, language media center, recording studio, crafts center, ceramic studio and photography darkroom.

Freshman class profile. 6,033 applied, 1,119 admitted, 489 enrolled.

Mid 50% test scores			
SAT critical reading:	650-760	Rank in top tenth:	82%
SAT math:	650-750	Return as sophomores:	97%
SAT writing:	660-750	Out-of-state:	87%
ACT composite:	29-33	Live on campus:	100%
Rank in top quarter:	98%	International:	3%

Basis for selection. GED not accepted. Academic record, level of challenge represented in the candidate's course work, counselor/teacher recommendations, interview, quality of application and essay, character and personal qualities, extracurricular activities, talents and abilities, and overall academic potential most important. Test scores considered, but not required. Motivation of candidate also considered. Interview recommended. Candidates with unusual talent in music, theater or visual arts encouraged to complete Arts Supplement when applying for admission. Audition recommended for music majors. Portfolio recommended for art majors.

Homeschooled: Applicants applying from systems providing written evaluations rather than grades are required to submit either SAT or ACT-plus-SAT-Subject Test results. SAT Subject Tests should include Math Level 1 or Math Level 2 and one science. Personal interview strongly recommended.

High school preparation. College-preparatory program required. 20 units recommended. Recommended units include English 4, mathematics 4, social studies 4, science 4 (laboratory 3) and foreign language 4. Arts, music and computer science or computer literacy recommended.

2008-2009 Annual costs. Tuition/fees: $38,190. Room/board: $10,380. Books/supplies: $800. Personal expenses: $1,200.

2007-2008 Financial aid. Need-based: 268 full-time freshmen applied for aid; 198 were judged to have need; 198 of these received aid. Average need met was 100%. Average scholarship/grant was $28,359; average loan $3,622. 84% of total undergraduate aid awarded as scholarships/grants, 16% as loans/jobs. **Non-need-based:** Awarded to 74 full-time undergraduates, including 19 freshmen. Scholarships awarded for academics, leadership. **Additional information:** Regardless of financial circumstances, students admitted will receive money they need to attend. International students for regular admission must submit their financial aid applications by January 1st.

Application procedures. Admission: Closing date 1/1 (receipt date). $60 fee, may be waived for applicants with need. Admission notification on a rolling basis beginning on or about 4/5. Must reply by May 1 or within 1 week(s) if notified thereafter. **Financial aid:** Closing date 2/15. FAFSA, CSS PROFILE required. Applicants notified by 4/5; must reply by 5/1 or within 1 week(s) of notification.

Academics. Most students pursue independent scholarly research, working closely with a faculty advisor, through an independent study or honors project. About half of the student body studies abroad for one or 2 semesters, usually during the junior year. First-year seminars are limited to 16 first-year students and emphasize college-level reading and writing. Interdisciplinary and self-designed majors are available. **Special study options:** Accelerated study, combined bachelor's/graduate degree, double major, exchange student, independent study, liberal arts/career combination, semester at sea, student-designed major, study abroad, teacher certification program, Washington semester. 3-2 or 4-2 engineering degree programs with California Institute of Technology, Dartmouth College, Columbia University or University of Maine, Orono, 3-3 legal studies program with Columbia University Law School, first-year seminars, summer research fellowships, service-learning courses, The Writing Project, Quantitative Skills Program, Legal Studies Advisory Group, Health Professions Advising, ESL Writing Tutor. **Credit/placement by examination:** AP, CLEP, IB, institutional tests. **Support services:** Learning center, reduced course load, study skills assistance, tutoring, writing center.

Majors. Area/ethnic studies: African, Asian, Central/Eastern European, Latin American, women's. **Biology:** General, biochemistry. **Computer sciences:** Computer science. **Conservation:** Environmental studies. **Foreign languages:** Classics, French, German, Romance, Russian, Spanish. **History:** General. **Interdisciplinary:** Ancient studies, classical/archaeology, math/computer science, neuroscience. **Math:** General. **Philosophy/religion:** Philosophy, religion. **Physical sciences:** Chemical physics, chemistry, geochemistry, geology, geophysics, physics. **Psychology:** General. **Social sciences:** Anthropology, archaeology, econometrics, economics, political science, sociology. **Visual/performing arts:** Art history/conservation, studio arts, theater history.

Most popular majors. Area/ethnic studies 7%, biology 8%, English 7%, foreign language 10%, history 7%, social sciences 29%, visual/performing arts 7%.

Computing on campus. 450 workstations in dormitories, library, computer center, student center. Dormitories wired for high-speed internet access and linked to campus network. Commuter students can connect to campus network. Online library, helpline, repair service, student web hosting, wireless network available.

Student life. Freshman orientation: Mandatory. 4-5 day program at the end of August, just before the start of classes. Pre-orientation outing trips offered over 4 nights prior to formal orientation; separate charge depending on the trip. **Policies:** Honor code, social code, judicial authority, drug and alcohol policies, policies on sexual misconduct, smoking, illegal drugs, discrimination, information technology use, residential life. **Housing:** Guaranteed on-campus for freshmen. Coed dorms, special housing for disabled, apartments, wellness housing available. Three small college houses and 8 college system houses available. **Activities:** Bands, choral groups, dance, drama, film society, international student organizations, literary magazine, music ensembles, musical theater, radio station, student government, student newspaper, symphony orchestra, TV station, African-American society, Asian student organization, Latin American student organization, Hillel, Catholic student union, Christian fellowship, community service council, Evergreens, Democrats, Republicans.

Athletics. NCAA. **Intercollegiate:** Baseball M, basketball, cross-country, diving, field hockey W, football (tackle) M, golf, ice hockey, lacrosse, rugby W, sailing, skiing, soccer, softball W, squash, swimming, tennis, track and field, volleyball W. **Intramural:** Badminton, basketball, cricket, cross-country, field hockey, football (non-tackle), ice hockey, rugby, soccer, softball, squash, tennis, volleyball, water polo. **Team name:** Polar Bears.

Student services. Alcohol/substance abuse counseling, career counseling, student employment services, health services, minority student services, on-campus daycare, personal counseling, placement for graduates, women's services. **Physically disabled:** Services for visually, speech, hearing impaired.

Contact. E-mail: admissions@bowdoin.edu
Phone: (207) 725-3100 Fax: (207) 725-3101
Scott Meiklejohn, Dean of Admissions and Student Aid, Bowdoin College, 5000 College Station, Brunswick, ME 04011-8441

Colby College

Waterville, Maine — **CB member**
www.colby.edu — **CB code: 3280**

- Private 4-year liberal arts college
- Residential campus in large town
- 1,846 degree-seeking undergraduates: 54% women, 2% African American, 8% Asian American, 3% Hispanic American, 5% international
- 31% of applicants admitted
- Application essay required
- 90% graduate within 6 years; 19% enter graduate study

General. Founded in 1813. Regionally accredited. Off-campus facilities available for teaching and research in biology, ecology, geology. **Degrees:** 521 bachelor's awarded. **ROTC:** Army. **Location:** 180 miles from Boston, 75 miles from Portland. **Calendar:** 4-1-4. **Full-time faculty:** 159 total; 96% have terminal degrees, 13% minority, 45% women. **Part-time faculty:** 69 total; 55% have terminal degrees, 6% minority, 49% women. **Class size:** 60% < 20, 33% 20-39, 4% 40-49, 3% 50-99. **Special facilities:** Public art museum, astronomical observatory, arboretum, research greenhouses, kettle-hole research bog, professional blacksmith's forge, woodworking shop, crew rowing center, technical climbing wall, Nordic ski trails, synthetic turf field, community radio station, scanning and transmission electron microscopes, laser flash photolysis, 400 MHz NMR, x-ray diffractometer, spectrophotometers, chromatographs, electrophoresis, microcalorimeters, piezometers (groundwater monitoring wells).

Freshman class profile. 4,835 applied, 1,492 admitted, 482 enrolled.

Mid 50% test scores		**Rank in top tenth:**	61%
SAT critical reading:	640-720	**Return as sophomores:**	96%
SAT math:	640-710	**Out-of-state:**	84%
SAT writing:	630-710	**Live on campus:**	100%
ACT composite:	28-31	**International:**	4%
Rank in top quarter:	90%		

Basis for selection. School record and personal qualities very important. Test scores, recommendations, potential contribution to college life, essay, and interview important. Social, economic, racial, and geographic diversity considered. SAT/ACT or three Subject Tests of the student's choice.

High school preparation. 16 units recommended. Recommended units include English 4, mathematics 3, social studies 2, science 2 (laboratory 2), foreign language 3 and academic electives 2. Social studies units recommended could include history courses.

2008-2009 Annual costs. Comprehensive fee: $48,520. Books/supplies: $700. Personal expenses: $900.

2008-2009 Financial aid. All financial aid based on need. 263 full-time freshmen applied for aid; 191 were judged to have need; 191 of these received aid. Average need met was 100%. Average scholarship/grant was $30,303; average loan $512. 98% of total undergraduate aid awarded as scholarships/grants, 2% as loans/jobs. **Additional information:** Institutional loans have been replaced with institutional grants.

Application procedures. Admission: Closing date 1/1 (postmark date). $65 fee, may be waived for applicants with need, free for online applicants. Admission notification 4/1. Must reply by 5/1. **Financial aid:** Closing date 2/1. FAFSA, CSS PROFILE required. Applicants notified by 4/1; must reply by 5/1.

Academics. Special study options: Combined bachelor's/graduate degree, cross-registration, double major, exchange student, honors, independent study, internships, semester at sea, student-designed major, study abroad, teacher certification program, Washington semester. Numerous research, service learning, and intership opportunities through the Goldfarb Center for Public Affairs; summer research assistantships; course exchange programs with Bowdoin College, Bates College, Thomas College; stipends to enable student internships; coordinated 3-2 engineering program with Dartmouth; Idea Network of Biomedical Research Excellence (partnerships with Jackson Labs, Mt. Desert Island Biological Labs, and other colleges). **Credit/placement by examination:** AP, CLEP, IB, institutional tests. 12 credit hours maximum toward bachelor's degree. When appropriate, distribution requirements, as well as certain requirements for the major, may be absolved by examination without course enrollment at the discretion of the department concerned. Matriculated students may earn credit by examination in 100- or 200-level courses to a maximum of 12 hours. Departmental examinations or external examinations approved by the department may be used, with credit given for the equivalent of at least C-level work. The cost of each examination is paid by the student. The college will exempt students from the language requirement for attaining before entrance a score of 64 in a SAT Subject Test in a foreign language or for attaining a score of 64 in Colby's placement test during first-year orientation; in either case, no academic credit will be granted. **Support services:** Tutoring, writing center.

Majors. **Area/ethnic studies:** African-American, American, East Asian, Latin American, Russian/Slavic, women's. **Biology:** General, biochemistry, cell/histology, environmental, molecular, molecular biochemistry, neurobiology/physiology. **Business:** Business admin. **Computer sciences:** Computer science. **Conservation:** Environmental science, environmental studies. **Foreign languages:** Classics, French, German, Spanish. **History:** General. **Interdisciplinary:** Biological/physical sciences, classical/archaeology, global studies, math/computer science, neuroscience, science/society. **Math:** General. **Philosophy/religion:** Philosophy, religion. **Physical sciences:** Chemistry, geology, physics. **Psychology:** General. **Social sciences:** Anthropology, econometrics, economics, international relations, political science, sociology. **Visual/performing arts:** Art, art history/conservation, dramatic, studio arts. **Other:** Classical civilization: English.

Most popular majors. Area/ethnic studies 11%, biology 11%, English 8%, foreign language 7%, history 8%, interdisciplinary studies 6%, physical sciences 7%, social sciences 22%.

Computing on campus. 350 workstations in library, computer center, student center. Dormitories wired for high-speed internet access and linked to campus network. Commuter students can connect to campus network. Online course registration, online library, helpline, repair service, student web hosting, wireless network available.

Student life. **Freshman orientation:** Mandatory. Preregistration for classes offered. 4-day optional outdoor component ($175); 3-day on-campus component follows, both held the week before classes begin. **Policies:** Students participate in forming policies and governing social and community activities through student government and serving on official college committees up to and including the Board of Trustees. **Housing:** Guaranteed on-campus for all undergraduates. Coed dorms, wellness housing available. Senior apartments. **Activities:** Bands, choral groups, dance, drama, film society, international student organizations, literary magazine, music ensembles, musical theater, radio station, student government, student newspaper, symphony orchestra, Black and Hispanic student group, environmental coalition, social service and political organizations, volunteer center, five a capella groups, Amnesty International, women's group, outing club, Habitat for Humanity.

Athletics. NCAA. **Intercollegiate:** Baseball M, basketball, cross-country, diving, field hockey W, football (tackle) M, golf, ice hockey, lacrosse, rowing (crew), skiing, soccer, softball W, squash, swimming, tennis, track and field, volleyball W. **Intramural:** Basketball, field hockey, football (non-tackle), soccer, softball. **Team name:** White Mules.

Student services. Alcohol/substance abuse counseling, chaplain/spiritual director, career counseling, student employment services, financial aid counseling, health services, minority student services, personal counseling, placement for graduates, women's services. **Physically disabled:** Services for visually, hearing impaired.

Contact. E-mail: admissions@colby.edu
Phone: (800) 723-3032 Toll-free number: (800) 723-3032
Fax: (207) 859-4828
Parker Beverage, Dean of Admissions and Financial Aid, Colby College, 4800 Mayflower Hill, Waterville, ME 04901-8848

College of the Atlantic

Bar Harbor, Maine
www.coa.edu **CB code: 3305**

- Private 4-year liberal arts college
- Residential campus in small town
- 312 degree-seeking undergraduates: 4% part-time, 63% women, 1% Asian American, 1% Hispanic American, 13% international
- 3 degree-seeking graduate students
- 69% of applicants admitted
- Application essay required
- 62% graduate within 6 years; 15% enter graduate study

General. Founded in 1969. Regionally accredited. **Degrees:** 68 bachelor's awarded; master's offered. **Location:** 300 miles from Boston, 50 miles from Bangor. **Calendar:** Three 10-week terms. Limited summer session. **Full-time faculty:** 24 total; 79% have terminal degrees, 4% minority, 29% women. **Part-time faculty:** 14 total; 36% have terminal degrees, 57% women. **Class size:** 85% < 20, 15% 20-39. **Special facilities:** Natural history museum, herbarium, greenhouse, pier, research boat, organic farm, island research stations.

Freshman class profile. 314 applied, 217 admitted, 71 enrolled.

Mid 50% test scores		**GPA 2.0-2.99:**	2.5%
SAT critical reading:	600-690	**Rank in top quarter:**	62%
SAT math:	500-650	**Rank in top tenth:**	31%
SAT writing:	550-680	**End year in good standing:**	95%
ACT composite:	25-29	**Return as sophomores:**	82%
GPA 3.75 or higher:	30%	**Out-of-state:**	82%
GPA 3.50-3.74:	35%	**Live on campus:**	97%
GPA 3.0-3.49:	30%	**International:**	20%

Basis for selection. Academic ability, motivation, intellectual enthusiasm, independence, creativity, and commitment to ecological concerns and to goals and philosophies of college as demonstrated by high school record, recommendations, and interview important. **Homeschooled:** Thorough outline of topics covered, books read, homework completed, the evaluation process used in assessing work and the progress made over the years required. Standardized test scores recommended. **Learning Disabled:** Meeting with dean of academic services recommended.

High school preparation. College-preparatory program recommended. 15 units required; 19 recommended. Required and recommended units include English 4, mathematics 3-4, social studies 2, history 2, science 2-3 (laboratory 2), foreign language 2 and academic electives 1.

2008-2009 Annual costs. Tuition/fees: $31,470. Room/board: $8,490. Books/supplies: $600. Personal expenses: $630.

2008-2009 Financial aid. All financial aid based on need. 58 full-time freshmen applied for aid; 55 were judged to have need; 55 of these received aid. Average need met was 96%. Average scholarship/grant was $28,949; average loan $4,031. 80% of total undergraduate aid awarded as scholarships/grants, 20% as loans/jobs.

Application procedures. **Admission:** Closing date 2/15 (postmark date). $45 fee, may be waived for applicants with need. Admission notification 4/1. Must reply by May 1 or within 2 week(s) if notified thereafter. **Financial aid:** Closing date 2/15. FAFSA, institutional form required. Applicants notified by 4/1; must reply by 5/1.

Academics. Interdisciplinary curriculum consists of problem-solving course work, seminars, independent study, tutorials, specialized skill courses, and supervised internships away from college. **Special study options:** Independent study, internships, semester at sea, student-designed major, study abroad, teacher certification program. Winter Term program in Yucatan, Mexico. Consortium agreement (Eco-League) with four other colleges for student exchanges (Alaska Pacific University, Green Mountain College, Northland College, Prescott College); as well as academic partnerships with Olin College of Engineering, SALT Institute for Documentary Studies, National Outdoor Leadership School, The Landing School of Boat Design, and Sea Education Association. **Credit/placement by examination:** AP, CLEP, IB. 30 credit hours maximum toward bachelor's degree. **Support services:** Reduced course load, remedial instruction, study skills assistance, tutoring, writing center.

Majors. **Biology:** Ecology.

Computing on campus. 50 workstations in library, computer center. Dormitories wired for high-speed internet access and linked to campus network. Online library, helpline, student web hosting, wireless network available.

Student life. **Freshman orientation:** Mandatory, $120 fee. Preregistration for classes offered. 4 days on campus with optional 6-day outdoor adventure trips available. **Policies:** Students participate in developing college policy and operate student activities fund. **Housing:** Guaranteed on-campus for freshmen. Coed dorms, special housing for disabled, wellness housing available. $150 nonrefundable deposit, deadline 5/1. **Activities:** Choral groups, dance, drama, international student organizations, literary magazine, music ensembles, student government, student newspaper, SustainUs, outdoor experience program, life-drawing club, student democrats, international culture and issue group, GLBTQ group.

Athletics. **Intramural:** Badminton, cricket, ice hockey, sailing, soccer, softball, table tennis, volleyball, water polo.

Student services. Alcohol/substance abuse counseling, career counseling, student employment services, financial aid counseling, health services, minority student services, personal counseling, placement for graduates. **Physically disabled:** Services for visually, hearing impaired.

Contact. E-mail: inquiry@coa.edu
Phone: (207) 288-5015 ext. 230 Toll-free number: (800) 528-0025
Fax: (207) 288-4126
Sarah Baker, Dean of Admission, College of the Atlantic, 105 Eden Street, Bar Harbor, ME 04609

Husson University

Bangor, Maine — **CB member**
www.husson.edu — **CB code: 3440**

- Private 4-year business and health science college
- Residential campus in large town
- 2,196 degree-seeking undergraduates: 17% part-time, 58% women, 4% African American, 1% Asian American, 1% Hispanic American, 1% international
- 268 degree-seeking graduate students
- 86% of applicants admitted
- SAT or ACT with writing, application essay required
- 42% graduate within 6 years; 6% enter graduate study

General. Founded in 1898. Regionally accredited. **Degrees:** 416 bachelor's, 37 associate awarded; master's, doctoral offered. **ROTC:** Army, Naval. **Location:** 125 miles from Portland. **Calendar:** Semester, extensive summer session. **Full-time faculty:** 84 total; 64% have terminal degrees, 4% minority, 46% women. **Part-time faculty:** 4 total; 100% women. **Class size:** 54% < 20, 41% 20-39, 3% 40-49, 1% 50-99. **Special facilities:** Center for family business.

Freshman class profile. 1,203 applied, 1,034 admitted, 471 enrolled.

Mid 50% test scores			
SAT critical reading:	390-490	GPA 3.0-3.49:	30%
SAT math:	400-520	GPA 2.0-2.99:	41%
SAT writing:	390-500	Rank in top quarter:	28%
ACT composite:	16-21	Rank in top tenth:	10%
GPA 3.75 or higher:	10%	End year in good standing:	69%
GPA 3.50-3.74:	19%	Out-of-state:	20%
		Live on campus:	60%

Basis for selection. Class rank and school achievement record most important. Counselor recommendations considered. Test scores important for nursing applicants and occupational and physical therapy applicants. Test scores are used only for placement purposes for business and humanities school applicants. SAT recommended but not required for 2-year program and undeclared majors. Interview recommended. **Homeschooled:** GED required for financial aid to be awarded. **Learning Disabled:** School must be apprised of special accommodation needs at time of payment of tuition deposit.

High school preparation. College-preparatory program recommended. Recommended units include English 4, mathematics 3, social studies 1, history 1, science 3 (laboratory 2).

2009-2010 Annual costs. Tuition/fees: $12,990. Room/board: $6,994. Books/supplies: $970. Personal expenses: $1,070.

2008-2009 Financial aid. **Need-based:** Average need met was 77%. Average scholarship/grant was $8,801; average loan $3,265. 50% of total undergraduate aid awarded as scholarships/grants, 50% as loans/jobs. **Non-need-based:** Scholarships awarded for academics, leadership.

Application procedures. **Admission:** Priority date 3/1; deadline 9/1 (postmark date). $25 fee, may be waived for applicants with need. Admission notification on a rolling basis beginning on or about 12/1. Must reply by May 1 or within 2 week(s) if notified thereafter. **Financial aid:** Priority date 4/15; no closing date. FAFSA required. Applicants notified on a rolling basis starting 4/1; must reply by 5/1 or within 2 week(s) of notification.

Academics. Strong liberal arts core within business programs. **Special study options:** Combined bachelor's/graduate degree, cooperative education, double major, independent study, internships, liberal arts/career combination, student-designed major, teacher certification program, weekend college. **Credit/placement by examination:** AP, CLEP, IB, institutional tests. 30 credit hours maximum toward bachelor's degree. **Support services:** Learning center, pre-admission summer program, reduced course load, remedial instruction, study skills assistance, tutoring, writing center.

Majors. **Biology:** General. **Business:** General, accounting, accounting/business management, banking/financial services, business admin, entrepreneurial studies, finance, hospitality admin, hospitality/recreation, hotel/motel admin, international, international marketing, management information systems, managerial economics, market research, marketing, public finance, sales/distribution, small business admin. **Computer sciences:** Applications programming, programming, systems analysis. **Education:** Biology, elementary, English, physical, secondary. **Health:** Nursing (RN), prepharmacy. **Legal studies:** Paralegal. **Liberal arts:** Arts/sciences. **Parks/recreation:** Facilities management, health/fitness, sports admin. **Physical sciences:** Chemistry. **Protective services:** Criminal justice, law enforcement admin. **Psychology:** General, clinical. **Social sciences:** Criminology.

Most popular majors. Business/marketing 40%, education 8%, health sciences 27%, legal studies 12%, psychology 7%.

Computing on campus. 115 workstations in library, computer center, student center. Dormitories wired for high-speed internet access and linked to campus network. Commuter students can connect to campus network. Online course registration, online library, helpline, student web hosting, wireless network available.

Student life. **Freshman orientation:** Mandatory, $75 fee. Preregistration for classes offered. 2 days of meetings with faculty, staff, administration; departmental orientation and activities for students and parents. **Housing:** Guaranteed on-campus for all undergraduates. Coed dorms, fraternity/sorority housing, wellness housing available. **Activities:** Bands, campus ministries, drama, international student organizations, literary magazine, radio station, student government, student newspaper, campus crusade for Christ, Chi Alpha, political clubs.

Athletics. NCAA. **Intercollegiate:** Baseball M, basketball, field hockey W, football (tackle) M, golf M, lacrosse, soccer, softball W, swimming W, volleyball W. **Intramural:** Basketball, football (non-tackle) M, ice hockey, lacrosse, soccer, swimming W, tennis, volleyball. **Team name:** Eagles.

Student services. Adult student services, alcohol/substance abuse counseling, chaplain/spiritual director, career counseling, student employment services, financial aid counseling, health services, personal counseling, placement for graduates, veterans' counselor.

Contact. E-mail: admit@husson.edu
Phone: (207) 941-7100 Toll-free number: (800) 448-7766
Fax: (207) 941-7935
Carlena Bean, Director of Admissions, Husson University, One College Circle, Bangor, ME 04401-2999

Maine College of Art

Portland, Maine — **CB member**
www.meca.edu — **CB code: 3701**

- Private 4-year visual arts college
- Commuter campus in small city
- 341 degree-seeking undergraduates: 5% part-time, 66% women, 1% African American, 1% Asian American, 1% Hispanic American, 1% Native American
- 28 degree-seeking graduate students
- 80% of applicants admitted
- SAT or ACT (ACT writing optional), application essay required
- 45% graduate within 6 years

General. Founded in 1882. Regionally accredited. Personal studio space for all juniors and seniors. **Degrees:** 79 bachelor's awarded; master's offered. **Location:** 100 miles from Boston. **Calendar:** Semester. **Full-time faculty:** 21 total; 90% have terminal degrees, 10% minority, 43% women. **Part-time faculty:** 30 total; 70% have terminal degrees, 3% minority, 53% women. **Class size:** 71% < 20, 29% 20-39. **Special facilities:** 2 art galleries, visual arts library.

Freshman class profile. 381 applied, 304 admitted, 103 enrolled.

Mid 50% test scores			
SAT critical reading:	480-600	GPA 3.0-3.49:	37%
SAT math:	450-580	GPA 2.0-2.99:	41%
SAT writing:	460-580	Rank in top quarter:	31%
ACT composite:	20-28	Rank in top tenth:	10%
GPA 3.75 or higher:	10%	End year in good standing:	93%
GPA 3.50-3.74:	12%	Return as sophomores:	69%
		Out-of-state:	72%

Basis for selection. Decision based on interview and portfolio in conjunction with high school achievement record; essay, recommendations important, test scores considered. Interview recommended. Portfolio required. **Homeschooled:** Transcript of courses and grades required. Show evidence through the State Certification of Completion of high school program or

GED. **Learning Disabled:** Submit proper documentation to Director of Student Affairs (once admitted) and request specific accommodations.

High school preparation. 27 units recommended. Recommended units include English 4, mathematics 3, social studies 4, history 4, science 3, foreign language 2 and academic electives 3. 4 units of art strongly recommended.

2008-2009 Annual costs. Tuition/fees: $27,215. Studio fees vary per class. Room/board: $9,400. Books/supplies: $2,100. Personal expenses: $1,200.

2008-2009 Financial aid. Non-need-based: Scholarships awarded for academics, art.

Application procedures. Admission: Priority date 2/1; no deadline. $40 fee, may be waived for applicants with need. Admission notification on a rolling basis beginning on or about 1/2. Students strongly encouraged to reply by May 1 or within 3 weeks if notified thereafter. **Financial aid:** Priority date 3/1; no closing date. FAFSA required. Applicants notified on a rolling basis starting 2/15; must reply within 2 week(s) of notification.

Academics. 1- to 2-year foundation program in drawing, color, and 2- and 3-dimensional design, followed by transitional year, and final 2 years in major. **Special study options:** Combined bachelor's/graduate degree, cross-registration, double major, exchange student, independent study, internships, liberal arts/career combination, student-designed major, study abroad, teacher certification program. Mobility program with 36 AICAD (Associated Independent Colleges of Art and Design) across the country and in Canada, cross-registration program with 4 other colleges and universities in the greater Portland area; special exchange program with Hanoi Fine Arts College, Vietnam; BFA credit available through Provincetown, MA Fine Arts Work Center. **Credit/placement by examination:** AP, CLEP. **Support services:** Learning center, study skills assistance, tutoring, writing center.

Majors. Visual/performing arts: Art, art history/conservation, ceramics, graphic design, illustration, metal/jewelry, painting, photography, printmaking, sculpture, studio arts.

Computing on campus. 57 workstations in library, computer center, student center. Dormitories wired for high-speed internet access. Online library, helpline, student web hosting, wireless network available.

Student life. Freshman orientation: Mandatory. Preregistration for classes offered. Held the week before the start of classes. **Housing:** Coed dorms, wellness housing available. $500 partly refundable deposit. **Activities:** Film society, student government, student newspaper, student representative association, movie club, peer mentor scholarships.

Student services. Adult student services, alcohol/substance abuse counseling, career counseling, student employment services, financial aid counseling, health services, minority student services, personal counseling.

Contact. E-mail: admissions@meca.edu
Phone: (207) 699-5026 Toll-free number: (800) 699-1509
Fax: (207) 699-5080
Karen Townsend, Director of Admissions, Maine College of Art, 522 Congress Street, Portland, ME 04101

Maine Maritime Academy

Castine, Maine
www.mainemaritime.edu **CB code: 3505**

- Public 4-year maritime college
- Residential campus in rural community
- 868 degree-seeking undergraduates
- 67% of applicants admitted
- SAT or ACT with writing required

General. Founded in 1941. Regionally accredited. **Degrees:** 166 bachelor's, 4 associate awarded; master's offered. **ROTC:** Army, Naval. **Location:** 38 miles from Bangor. **Calendar:** Semester, limited summer session. **Full-time faculty:** 69 total; 33% have terminal degrees, 4% minority, 26% women. **Part-time faculty:** 21 total; 52% women. **Special facilities:** 500-foot training ship, 40-foot marine research vessel, 80-foot ocean going tugboat and barge, two-masted arctic schooner, steam and diesel engine laboratories, power plant simulators, bridge simulator, planetarium, ocean classrooms.

Freshman class profile. 578 applied, 388 admitted, 182 enrolled.

Mid 50% test scores			
SAT critical reading:	450-560	ACT composite:	18-25
SAT math:	480-570	Out-of-state:	31%
SAT writing:	430-550	Live on campus:	95%

Basis for selection. High school academic record followed by SAT/ACT test scores the most important. Interview, school and community activities, work ethic, and recommendations also considered. Interview and personal statement are highly recommended. **Homeschooled:** Transcript of courses and grades, letter of recommendation (nonparent) required. ACT/SAT scores and possibly have transcripts/course records evaluated by Maine Department of Education.

High school preparation. College-preparatory program required. Required and recommended units include English 4, mathematics 4, science 2-3 (laboratory 2) and foreign language 2. 1 unit computer literacy recommended.

2008-2009 Annual costs. Tuition/fees: $9,600; $13,350 out-of-district; $16,900 out-of-state. Fee of $3,000 for U.S. Coast Guard licensing programs. Room/board: $8,000. Books/supplies: $1,000. Personal expenses: $800.

Financial aid. Non-need-based: Scholarships awarded for academics, leadership, ROTC, state residency.

Application procedures. Admission: Priority date 5/31; deadline 7/1 (receipt date). $15 fee, may be waived for applicants with need, free for online applicants. Admission notification on a rolling basis beginning on or about 1/1. Must reply by 5/1. **Financial aid:** Priority date 4/15; no closing date. FAFSA, institutional form required. Applicants notified on a rolling basis starting 3/1; must reply within 4 week(s) of notification.

Academics. Special study options: Cooperative education, internships, liberal arts/career combination, semester at sea, student-designed major, study abroad, teacher certification program. 2-month training cruise for USCG unlimited license majors. **Credit/placement by examination:** AP, CLEP, institutional tests. **Support services:** Study skills assistance, tutoring, writing center.

Majors. Biology: Marine. **Business:** General, business admin, entrepreneurial studies, international, logistics. **Engineering:** Marine, systems. **Engineering technology:** General. **Physical sciences:** Oceanography. **Transportation:** Maritime/Merchant Marine.

Most popular majors. Biology 8%, business/marketing 8%, engineering/engineering technologies 64%, trade and industry 20%.

Computing on campus. PC or laptop required. 40 workstations in dormitories, library. Dormitories wired for high-speed internet access and linked to campus network. Commuter students can connect to campus network. Online library, helpline, repair service, wireless network available.

Student life. Freshman orientation: Mandatory. Preregistration for classes offered. 2.5 days available through 4 different sessions in August. **Policies:** Regimental lifestyle optional for the 2-year program and those majoring in power engineering, ocean studies, international business, and small vessel operations. Regiment is mandatory for United States Coast Guard unlimited license programs (marine transportation and marine engineering). No military obligation. Students required to live on-campus unless married, over age 23, or have completed 2 or more years of active military service or 6 semesters of study. **Housing:** Guaranteed on-campus for all undergraduates. Coed dorms, apartments, wellness housing available. $200 nonrefundable deposit, deadline 8/15. **Activities:** Bands, choral groups, drama, music ensembles, student government, student newspaper, Alpha Phi Omega, other service organizations.

Athletics. NCAA. **Intercollegiate:** Basketball, cross-country, football (tackle) M, golf M, lacrosse M, sailing, soccer, softball W, volleyball W. **Intramural:** Basketball, golf, handball, ice hockey M, racquetball, rifle, rugby M, sailing, skiing, soccer, softball, squash, tennis, volleyball, water polo. **Team name:** Mariners.

Student services. Alcohol/substance abuse counseling, career counseling, student employment services, financial aid counseling, health services, personal counseling, placement for graduates, veterans' counselor, women's services.

Contact. E-mail: admissions@mma.edu
Phone: (207) 326-2206 Toll-free number: (800) 227-8465
Fax: (207) 326-2515
Jeffrey Wright, Director of Admissions, Maine Maritime Academy, 66 Pleasant Street, Castine, ME 04420

New England School of Communications
Bangor, Maine
www.nescom.edu **CB code: 3101**

- Private 4-year college of communications
- Residential campus in small city
- 440 degree-seeking undergraduates
- 65% of applicants admitted
- Application essay, interview required

General. Accredited by ACCSCT. **Degrees:** 48 bachelor's, 22 associate awarded. **ROTC:** Army. **Location:** 250 miles from Boston. **Calendar:** Semester, limited summer session. **Full-time faculty:** 11 total; 36% have terminal degrees, 9% women. **Part-time faculty:** 46 total; 24% have terminal degrees, 2% minority, 30% women. **Class size:** 40% < 20, 52% 20-39, 3% 40-49, 5% 50-99. **Special facilities:** Sound recording studio, digital photography lab, mobile production studio.

Freshman class profile. 454 applied, 294 admitted, 188 enrolled.

Out-of-state:	23%	**Sororities:**	2%
Live on campus:	69%		

Basis for selection. Interview and Placement Test most important. High school record and essay also important. SAT or ACT recommended. Timed scholastic placement exam, audio reading required for on-air candidates. **Homeschooled:** Transcript of courses and grades, state high school equivalency certificate, interview, letter of recommendation (nonparent) required. Require GED score if homeschooling is not through an accredited curriculum-based program. **Learning Disabled:** Students requiring additional placement test time must provide professional evaluation documentation requesting extra time prior to interview date.

High school preparation. College-preparatory program recommended. Recommended units include English 4, mathematics 2, social studies 1, history 2, science 2, foreign language 2, computer science 1 and visual/performing arts 1. Recommend additional computer, public speaking, creative arts coursework.

2008-2009 Annual costs. Tuition/fees: $10,690. Additional cost of $160 for FireWire hard drive. Room/board: $6,790. Books/supplies: $1,300. Personal expenses: $1,000.

2007-2008 Financial aid. Need-based: 29% of total undergraduate aid awarded as scholarships/grants, 71% as loans/jobs. **Non-need-based:** Scholarships awarded for academics, leadership.

Application procedures. Admission: Priority date 4/1; no deadline. $15 fee, may be waived for applicants with need. Admission notification on a rolling basis. **Financial aid:** Priority date 4/15; no closing date. FAFSA, institutional form required. Applicants notified on a rolling basis starting 2/1; must reply by 8/15.

Academics. Special study options: Cross-registration, double major, internships, liberal arts/career combination, student-designed major. **Credit/placement by examination:** AP, CLEP, institutional tests. 6 credit hours maximum toward associate degree, 15 toward bachelor's. **Support services:** Reduced course load, study skills assistance, tutoring, writing center.

Majors. Communications: Advertising, broadcast journalism, digital media, photojournalism, public relations, radio/tv. **Communications technology:** General, photo/film/video, radio/tv, recording arts. **Computer sciences:** Web page design. **Visual/performing arts:** Acting, cinematography, directing/producing, theater design.

Computing on campus. 195 workstations in dormitories, library, computer center, student center. Dormitories wired for high-speed internet access and linked to campus network. Commuter students can connect to campus network. Online library, helpline, wireless network available.

Student life. Freshman orientation: Mandatory. Preregistration for classes offered. 3 days before start of fall session. Spring orientation held the Monday before classes start. **Housing:** Guaranteed on-campus for freshmen. Coed dorms, fraternity/sorority housing, wellness housing available. **Activities:** Pep band, campus ministries, choral groups, drama, international student organizations, literary magazine, music ensembles, musical theater, radio station, student government, student newspaper, TV station, Crusade for Christ, Diversity Club, Habitat for Humanity.

Athletics. Intramural: Baseball, basketball, cheerleading, diving, field hockey, football (non-tackle), skiing, soccer, softball, swimming, table tennis, tennis, volleyball, water polo.

Student services. Adult student services, alcohol/substance abuse counseling, chaplain/spiritual director, career counseling, student employment services, financial aid counseling, health services, personal counseling, placement for graduates, veterans' counselor.

Contact. E-mail: info@nescom.edu
Phone: (207) 941-7176 Toll-free number: (888) 877-1876 ext. 1093
Fax: (207) 947-3987
Louise Grant, Director of Admissions, New England School of Communications, One College Circle, Bangor, ME 04401

St. Joseph's College
Standish, Maine **CB member**
www.sjcme.edu **CB code: 3755**

- Private 4-year liberal arts college affiliated with Roman Catholic Church
- Residential campus in small town
- 1,066 degree-seeking undergraduates
- 78% of applicants admitted
- SAT or ACT (ACT writing recommended), application essay required

General. Founded in 1912. Regionally accredited. **Degrees:** 302 bachelor's awarded; master's offered. **ROTC:** Army. **Location:** 18 miles from Portland, 120 miles from Boston. **Calendar:** Semester, limited summer session. **Full-time faculty:** 68 total; 85% have terminal degrees, 2% minority, 52% women. **Part-time faculty:** 73 total. **Class size:** 60% < 20, 36% 20-39, 2% 40-49, 1% 50-99. **Special facilities:** Telescope, observatory.

Freshman class profile. 1,256 applied, 976 admitted, 322 enrolled.

Mid 50% test scores		**SAT writing:**	440-540
SAT critical reading:	440-530	**Out-of-state:**	44%
SAT math:	440-540	**Live on campus:**	93%

Basis for selection. School record, class rank, test scores, recommendations, essays, extracurricular activities all considered. Interview optional, but recommended.

High school preparation. 16 units recommended. Recommended units include English 4, mathematics 3, social studies 2, history 2, science 2 (laboratory 2) and foreign language 2. Laboratory biology and laboratory chemistry required of nursing and science applicants. For any intended major, transcripts from candidates for admission should include 16 or more college-preparatory courses.

2008-2009 Annual costs. Tuition/fees: $25,049. Room/board: $9,950. Books/supplies: $900. Personal expenses: $1,200.

2008-2009 Financial aid. Non-need-based: Scholarships awarded for academics, leadership.

Application procedures. Admission: Priority date 3/1; no deadline. $50 fee, may be waived for applicants with need, free for online applicants. Admission notification on a rolling basis beginning on or about 12/15. Must reply by May 1 or within 3 week(s) if notified thereafter. **Financial aid:** Priority date 3/1; no closing date. FAFSA, institutional form required. Applicants notified on a rolling basis starting 3/1; must reply within 3 week(s) of notification.

Academics. College belongs to Greater Portland Alliance, a 5-college consortium with cross registration. **Special study options:** Combined bachelor's/graduate degree, cooperative education, cross-registration, distance learning, double major, honors, independent study, internships, liberal arts/career combination, semester at sea, student-designed major, study abroad, teacher certification program, Washington semester. **Credit/placement by examination:** AP, CLEP, SAT, ACT, institutional tests. 30 credit hours maximum toward bachelor's degree. **Support services:** Study skills assistance, tutoring, writing center.

Majors. Biology: General. **Business:** Accounting, business admin, finance, human resources, international, marketing. **Communications:** Digital media, journalism, public relations. **Conservation:** Environmental science, environmental studies. **Education:** Biology, elementary, English, history, mathematics, physical. **Health:** Medical radiologic technology/radiation therapy, nursing (RN). **History:** General. **Math:** General. **Parks/recreation:** Exercise sciences, sports admin. **Philosophy/religion:** Philosophy. **Physical sciences:** Chemistry. **Protective services:** Criminal justice. **Psychology:** General. **Social sciences:** General, political science, sociology. **Theology:** Theology.

Most popular majors. Biology 6%, business/marketing 20%, communications/journalism 8%, education 13%, health sciences 21%, parks/recreation 6%, social sciences 6%.

Computing on campus. 102 workstations in library, computer center, student center. Dormitories wired for high-speed internet access and linked to campus network. Commuter students can connect to campus network. Helpline, repair service, wireless network available.

Student life. Freshman orientation: Available, $50 fee. Preregistration for classes offered. Two-day session in June or July. **Policies:** Mass available daily on campus. **Housing:** Guaranteed on-campus for all undergraduates. Coed dorms, single-sex dorms, wellness housing available. $100 deposit, deadline 5/1. **Activities:** Choral groups, dance, drama, literary magazine, radio station, student government, student newspaper, Habitat for Humanity, High Adventure, Superkids, business club, campus ministry, culture and heritage club, interhall council, student nurses association.

Athletics. NCAA. **Intercollegiate:** Baseball M, basketball, cross-country, field hockey W, golf M, lacrosse, soccer, softball W, swimming, volleyball W. **Intramural:** Basketball, football (non-tackle), soccer, softball, swimming, volleyball. **Team name:** Monks.

Student services. Alcohol/substance abuse counseling, chaplain/spiritual director, career counseling, student employment services, financial aid counseling, health services, personal counseling, placement for graduates, veterans' counselor. **Physically disabled:** Services for visually, speech, hearing impaired. **Learning disabled:** Comprehensive services available.

Contact. E-mail: admission@sjcme.edu
Phone: (207) 893-7746 Toll-free number: (800) 338-7057
Fax: (207) 893-7862
Jennifer Gronros, Dean of Admission, St. Joseph's College, 278 Whites Bridge Road, Standish, ME 04084-5263

Thomas College

Waterville, Maine
www.thomas.edu
CB member
CB code: 3903

- Private 4-year business and liberal arts college
- Residential campus in large town
- 737 degree-seeking undergraduates: 14% part-time, 48% women, 2% African American, 1% Asian American, 1% Hispanic American, 1% Native American
- 149 degree-seeking graduate students
- 82% of applicants admitted
- SAT or ACT (ACT writing optional), application essay required
- 47% graduate within 6 years

General. Founded in 1894. Regionally accredited. Evening division (undergraduate and graduate) on trimester system. **Degrees:** 98 bachelor's, 7 associate awarded; master's offered. **Location:** 75 miles from Portland. **Calendar:** Semester, limited summer session. **Full-time faculty:** 23 total; 48% have terminal degrees, 39% women. **Part-time faculty:** 53 total; 15% have terminal degrees, 43% women. **Class size:** 55% < 20, 45% 20-39.

Freshman class profile. 649 applied, 531 admitted, 217 enrolled.

Mid 50% test scores		**GPA 2.0-2.99:**	43%
SAT critical reading:	380-540	**Rank in top quarter:**	32%
SAT math:	380-570	**Rank in top tenth:**	16%
SAT writing:	360-540	**End year in good standing:**	94%
ACT composite:	15-19	**Return as sophomores:**	56%
GPA 3.75 or higher:	4%	**Out-of-state:**	21%
GPA 3.50-3.74:	8%	**Live on campus:**	88%
GPA 3.0-3.49:	37%		

Basis for selection. Academic transcripts most important. Letters of recommendation, SAT, ACT and/or TOEFL Exam scores also important. Recommend minimum 2.0 overall GPA, rank in top half of class. Test scores required of bachelor's degree candidates, not required for associate degree candidates. Interview recommended. **Homeschooled:** Transcript of courses and grades, state high school equivalency certificate, letter of recommendation (nonparent) required.

High school preparation. College-preparatory program recommended. 16 units recommended. Recommended units include English 4, mathematics 3, social studies 2, history 2, science 3 and foreign language 2.

2008-2009 Annual costs. Tuition/fees: $19,750. Room/board: $8,170. Books/supplies: $800. Personal expenses: $1,000.

2008-2009 Financial aid. Need-based: 204 full-time freshmen applied for aid; 198 were judged to have need; 198 of these received aid. Average need met was 85%. Average scholarship/grant was $13,240; average loan $4,189. 71% of total undergraduate aid awarded as scholarships/grants, 29% as loans/jobs. **Non-need-based:** Awarded to 167 full-time undergraduates, including 89 freshmen. Scholarships awarded for academics, leadership, state residency.

Application procedures. Admission: No deadline. $50 fee, may be waived for applicants with need. Admission notification on a rolling basis beginning on or about 12/1. Must reply by May 1 or within 4 week(s) if notified thereafter. **Financial aid:** Priority date 2/15; no closing date. FAFSA required. Applicants notified on a rolling basis starting 3/15; must reply within 2 week(s) of notification.

Academics. Special study options: Combined bachelor's/graduate degree, cross-registration, double major, dual enrollment of high school students, independent study, internships, study abroad, teacher certification program, Washington semester. **Credit/placement by examination:** AP, CLEP. 15 credit hours maximum toward associate degree, 15 toward bachelor's. **Support services:** Learning center, reduced course load, study skills assistance, tutoring.

Majors. Business: Accounting, business admin, finance, hospitality admin, human resources, international, management information systems, marketing. **Communications:** General. **Computer sciences:** General, computer science, information systems, webmaster. **Education:** Early childhood, elementary. **Legal studies:** Prelaw. **Parks/recreation:** Sports admin. **Protective services:** Criminal justice, law enforcement admin. **Psychology:** General, forensic. **Social sciences:** Political science.

Most popular majors. Business/marketing 43%, computer/information sciences 6%, education 9%, parks/recreation 7%, psychology 10%, security/protective services 22%.

Computing on campus. 120 workstations in dormitories, library, computer center, student center. Dormitories wired for high-speed internet access and linked to campus network. Commuter students can connect to campus network. Online course registration, online library, helpline, repair service, student web hosting, wireless network available.

Student life. Freshman orientation: Mandatory. Preregistration for classes offered. 3-day program held at the end of August; extended programs during fall semester. **Housing:** Guaranteed on-campus for freshmen. Coed dorms, wellness housing available. $200 nonrefundable deposit, deadline 5/1. **Activities:** Choral groups, dance, drama, student government, student newspaper, Diversity Coalition, Fellowship Group, Habitat for Humanity, environmental club.

Athletics. NCAA. **Intercollegiate:** Baseball M, basketball, cross-country, field hockey W, golf M, lacrosse, soccer, softball W, tennis, volleyball W. **Intramural:** Basketball, bowling, football (non-tackle), soccer, softball, table tennis, tennis, volleyball, weight lifting. **Team name:** Terriers.

Student services. Alcohol/substance abuse counseling, chaplain/spiritual director, career counseling, student employment services, financial aid counseling, health services, personal counseling, placement for graduates, veterans' counselor.

Contact. E-mail: admiss@thomas.edu
Phone: (207) 859-1101 Toll-free number: (800) 339-7001
Fax: (207) 859-1114
Wendy Martin, Associate Dean for Undergraduate Admissions, Thomas College, 180 West River Road, Waterville, ME 04901

Unity College

Unity, Maine
www.unity.edu
CB code: 3925

- Private 4-year liberal arts college
- Residential campus in rural community
- 544 degree-seeking undergraduates: 2% part-time, 43% women, 1% African American, 1% Asian American, 1% Hispanic American
- 72% of applicants admitted
- Application essay required
- 42% graduate within 6 years; 10% enter graduate study

General. Founded in 1965. Regionally accredited. **Degrees:** 124 bachelor's, 4 associate awarded. **ROTC:** Army. **Location:** 20 miles from Waterville. **Calendar:** Semester, limited summer session. **Full-time faculty:** 37 total; 89% have terminal degrees, 5% minority, 35% women. **Part-time faculty:** 25 total; 72% have terminal degrees, 4% minority, 76% women. **Class size:** 62% < 20, 36% 20-39, 2% 40-49, less than 1% 50-99. **Special facilities:** Wetlands research area.

Freshman class profile. 613 applied, 444 admitted, 166 enrolled.

End year in good standing:	90%	**Out-of-state:**	80%
Return as sophomores:	67%	**Live on campus:**	98%

Basis for selection. High school transcripts, interviews, recommendations and essay most important. Test scores not required but highly recommended. SAT or ACT recommended. **Homeschooled:** Informative portfolio.

High school preparation. 18 units recommended. Required and recommended units include English 4, mathematics 4, social studies 3, history 3, science 3 (laboratory 3) and foreign language 2.

2008-2009 Annual costs. Tuition/fees: $20,750. Room/board: $7,680. Books/supplies: $450. Personal expenses: $800.

2008-2009 Financial aid. Need-based: 154 full-time freshmen applied for aid; 128 were judged to have need; 128 of these received aid. Average need met was 77%. Average scholarship/grant was $11,047; average loan $4,878. 54% of total undergraduate aid awarded as scholarships/grants, 46% as loans/jobs. **Non-need-based:** Awarded to 101 full-time undergraduates, including 36 freshmen. Scholarships awarded for academics, leadership, minority status.

Application procedures. Admission: Priority date 7/1; no deadline. $25 fee, may be waived for applicants with need, free for online applicants. Admission notification on a rolling basis. **Financial aid:** Priority date 3/1; no closing date. FAFSA required. Applicants notified on a rolling basis starting 3/10; must reply within 2 week(s) of notification.

Academics. Special study options: Accelerated study, combined bachelor's/graduate degree, cooperative education, double major, independent study, internships, semester at sea, student-designed major, study abroad, teacher certification program, Washington semester. **Credit/placement by examination:** AP, CLEP, IB, institutional tests. 15 credit hours maximum toward associate degree, 15 toward bachelor's. **Support services:** Learning center, reduced course load, remedial instruction, study skills assistance, tutoring, writing center.

Majors. Agriculture: Aquaculture, ornamental horticulture. **Biology:** Ecology, environmental, marine, wildlife. **Conservation:** Environmental science, environmental studies, forestry, management/policy, wildlife. **Health:** Recreational therapy. **Liberal arts:** Arts/sciences. **Parks/recreation:** General, facilities management. **Social sciences:** General.

Most popular majors. Agriculture 10%, biology 28%, English 7%, natural resources/environmental science 30%, parks/recreation 19%.

Computing on campus. 80 workstations in dormitories, library, computer center, student center. Dormitories wired for high-speed internet access and linked to campus network. Commuter students can connect to campus network. Online library, wireless network available.

Student life. Freshman orientation: Mandatory, $100 fee. Preregistration for classes offered. A 5-day outdoor wilderness-based program. **Housing:** Guaranteed on-campus for all undergraduates. Coed dorms, single-sex dorms, cooperative housing available. **Activities:** Drama, radio station, student government, student newspaper, search and rescue crew, photography club, Environmental Awareness, recycling, community service.

Athletics. USCAA. **Intercollegiate:** Basketball, cross-country, soccer, volleyball W. **Intramural:** Baseball M, basketball, cross-country, lacrosse M, soccer, softball, volleyball. **Team name:** Rams.

Student services. Alcohol/substance abuse counseling, chaplain/spiritual director, career counseling, student employment services, financial aid counseling, health services, personal counseling, placement for graduates, veterans' counselor.

Contact. E-mail: admissions@unity.edu
Phone: (207) 948-3131 ext. 231 Toll-free number: (800) 624-1024
Fax: (207) 948-2928
Kay Fiedler, Director of Admission, Unity College, P.O. 532, Unity, ME 04988-0532

University of Maine

Orono, Maine — **CB member**
www.umaine.edu — **CB code: 3916**

- Public 4-year university
- Residential campus in large town
- 8,868 degree-seeking undergraduates: 9% part-time, 49% women, 1% African American, 1% Asian American, 1% Hispanic American, 1% Native American, 2% international
- 2,151 degree-seeking graduate students
- 77% of applicants admitted
- SAT or ACT (ACT writing optional), application essay required
- 59% graduate within 6 years

General. Founded in 1865. Regionally accredited. **Degrees:** 1,641 bachelor's awarded; master's, doctoral offered. **ROTC:** Army, Naval. **Location:** 12 miles from Bangor. **Calendar:** Semester, extensive summer session. **Full-time faculty:** 506 total; 84% have terminal degrees, 7% minority, 33% women. **Part-time faculty:** 305 total; 30% have terminal degrees, 4% minority, 53% women. **Class size:** 43% < 20, 36% 20-39, 7% 40-49, 9% 50-99, 4% >100. **Special facilities:** Advanced manufacturing center, machine tool lab, laboratory for surface science and technology, planetarium, anthropology museum, woodland preserve, botanical garden, art museum, observatory, environmental research facility, performing arts hall, Canadian-American center, Franco-American center, digital media lab, farm museum, marine lab, aquatic production facility, climbing wall, center for undergraduate research, student innovation center.

Freshman class profile. 7,407 applied, 5,721 admitted, 2,075 enrolled.

Mid 50% test scores			
SAT critical reading:	480-580	GPA 2.0-2.99:	21%
SAT math:	480-600	Rank in top quarter:	52%
SAT writing:	470-570	Rank in top tenth:	21%
ACT composite:	19-25	End year in good standing:	78%
GPA 3.75 or higher:	19%	Return as sophomores:	77%
GPA 3.50-3.74:	10%	Out-of-state:	22%
GPA 3.0-3.49:	50%	Live on campus:	86%
		International:	2%

Basis for selection. Strong emphasis on grades earned, GPA, class rank (if available) and standardized test scores. Academic requirements for admission may vary by program. Interviews available. Audition required of music majors. Portfolio recommended for art majors. **Homeschooled:** Statement describing homeschool structure and mission, transcript of courses and grades, state high school equivalency certificate, letter of recommendation (nonparent) required. GED requirement may be waived if thorough records submitted.

High school preparation. College-preparatory program required. 17 units required; 21 recommended. Required and recommended units include English 4, mathematics 3-4, social studies 2, history 1, science 2-4 (laboratory 2-3), foreign language 2 and academic electives 4. 1 unit physical education required of all College of Education candidates.

2008-2009 Annual costs. Tuition/fees: $9,100; $22,510 out-of-state. Room/board: $8,008. Books/supplies: $700. Personal expenses: $1,100.

2008-2009 Financial aid. Non-need-based: Scholarships awarded for academics, alumni affiliation, art, athletics, job skills, leadership, minority status, music/drama, religious affiliation, ROTC, state residency. **Additional information:** Financial aid is available for students entering in the spring.

Application procedures. Admission: Priority date 3/1; no deadline. $40 fee, may be waived for applicants with need. Admission notification on a rolling basis beginning on or about 2/1. Must reply by May 1 or within 2 week(s) if notified thereafter. **Financial aid:** Priority date 3/1; no closing date. FAFSA required. Applicants notified on a rolling basis starting 3/15; must reply by 5/1 or within 2 week(s) of notification.

Academics. Special study options: Accelerated study, combined bachelor's/graduate degree, cooperative education, distance learning, double major, dual enrollment of high school students, ESL, exchange student, honors, independent study, internships, liberal arts/career combination, semester at sea, study abroad, teacher certification program. **Credit/placement by examination:** AP, CLEP, IB, institutional tests. Duplicate credit may not be granted. Each department may develop or adopt examinations other than CLEP examinations for the purpose of granting credit for specific courses. **Support services:** Reduced course load, remedial instruction, study skills assistance, tutoring, writing center.

Honors college/program. Admission for first-time and transfer students based on test scores and high school record.

Majors. Agriculture: Animal sciences, business, economics, food science, greenhouse operations, horticultural science, landscaping, nursery operations, ornamental horticulture, plant sciences, soil science, turf management. **Area/ethnic studies:** Women's. **Biology:** General, bacteriology, biochemistry, biomedical sciences, botany, cell/histology, ecology, entomology, marine, molecular, pathology, zoology. **Business:** General, accounting, business admin, finance, labor relations, management information systems, managerial economics. **Communications:** General, journalism. **Computer sciences:** General. **Conservation:** General, environmental studies, forest management, forest resources, forestry, management/policy, wildlife, wood science. **Education:** General, art, biology, chemistry, elementary, English, foreign languages, French, history, mathematics, music, physical, science, secondary, social studies, Spanish. **Engineering:** General, agricultural, chemical, civil, computer, electrical, forest, mechanical, physics, systems. **Engineering technology:** Civil, electrical, surveying. **Family/consumer sciences:** Family/community services, food/nutrition. **Foreign languages:** General,

French, German, Latin, Spanish. **Health:** Audiology/speech pathology, clinical lab science, communication disorders, nursing (RN). **History:** General. **Interdisciplinary:** Biological/physical sciences, natural sciences. **Liberal arts:** Arts/sciences. **Math:** General. **Parks/recreation:** Facilities management. **Philosophy/religion:** Philosophy. **Physical sciences:** Chemistry, geology, oceanography, physics. **Psychology:** General. **Public administration:** General, social work. **Social sciences:** Anthropology, economics, international relations, political science, sociology. **Visual/performing arts:** Art history/conservation, dramatic, music performance, studio arts.

Most popular majors. Biology 6%, business/marketing 11%, communications/journalism 7%, education 12%, engineering/engineering technologies 14%, health sciences 8%, social sciences 8%.

Computing on campus. 500 workstations in library, computer center, student center. Dormitories wired for high-speed internet access and linked to campus network. Commuter students can connect to campus network. Online course registration, online library, helpline, repair service, student web hosting, wireless network available.

Student life. **Freshman orientation:** Available. Preregistration for classes offered. 2-day events in June, parents invited; 4-day welcome program in fall; additional adventure orientations available. **Housing:** Guaranteed on-campus for freshmen. Coed dorms, special housing for disabled, apartments, fraternity/sorority housing, wellness housing available. Academic grouping wings, men-only sections, women-only sections available. **Activities:** Bands, campus ministries, choral groups, dance, drama, film society, international student organizations, literary magazine, music ensembles, Model UN, musical theater, opera, radio station, student government, student newspaper, symphony orchestra, TV station, InterVarsity Christian Fellowship, Campus Crusade for Christ, Catholic Student Association, Hillel, Maine Christian Association, Muslim student organization, Newman Center.

Athletics. NCAA. **Intercollegiate:** Baseball M, basketball, cheerleading, cross-country, diving, field hockey W, football (tackle) M, ice hockey, soccer, softball, swimming, track and field, volleyball W. **Intramural:** Badminton, basketball, cross-country, diving, field hockey W, football (non-tackle) M, golf, racquetball, skiing, soccer, softball, squash, swimming, table tennis, tennis, track and field, triathlon, volleyball, water polo. **Team name:** Black Bears.

Student services. Adult student services, alcohol/substance abuse counseling, chaplain/spiritual director, career counseling, services for economically disadvantaged, student employment services, financial aid counseling, health services, legal services, minority student services, on-campus daycare, personal counseling, placement for graduates, veterans' counselor, women's services. **Physically disabled:** Services for visually, speech, hearing impaired.

Contact. E-mail: um-admit@maine.edu
Phone: (207) 581-1561 Toll-free number: (877) 486-2364
Fax: (207) 581-1213
Sharon Oliver, Director of Admissions, University of Maine, 5713 Chadbourne Hall, Orono, ME 04469-5713

University of Maine at Augusta

Augusta, Maine — **CB member**
www.uma.edu — **CB code: 3929**

- Public 4-year university
- Commuter campus in large town
- 4,369 degree-seeking undergraduates: 62% part-time, 74% women, 1% African American, 1% Asian American, 1% Hispanic American, 3% Native American

General. Founded in 1965. Regionally accredited. Additional centers in Rockland, Brunswick, Rumford, Saco, Sanford, Ellsworth, East Millinocket; additional campuses in Bangor. **Degrees:** 313 bachelor's, 263 associate awarded. **ROTC:** Army, Naval, Air Force. **Location:** 65 miles from Portland, 75 miles from Bangor. **Calendar:** Semester, extensive summer session. **Full-time faculty:** 103 total; 43% have terminal degrees, 54% women. **Part-time faculty:** 177 total; 54% women. **Class size:** 64% < 20, 34% 20-39, less than 1% 40-49, 1% 50-99. **Special facilities:** Holocaust center, human rights center.

Freshman class profile. 1,213 applied, 933 admitted, 517 enrolled.

Basis for selection. Open admission, but selective for some programs. High school achievement record and test scores considered for admission to allied health and bachelor's degree programs. Talent/ability assessed for admission to music programs. TOEFL is requested of non-native English speakers. Interviews required of dental hygiene and medical laboratory technology majors. Audition required of music majors. **Homeschooled:** Transcript of courses and grades required. Documentation of high school completion required of all.

High school preparation. Recommended units include English 4, mathematics 2, social studies 2, history 2, science 2 (laboratory 2). Applicants to health science programs must have biology, chemistry, and Algebra II. Business administration and public administration applicants must have Algebra II and geometry.

2008-2009 Annual costs. Tuition/fees: $6,495; $14,595 out-of-state. New England Regional Student Program tuition is $8,580. Books/supplies: $1,040. Personal expenses: $1,800.

2008-2009 Financial aid. **Need-based:** 288 full-time freshmen applied for aid; 253 were judged to have need; 245 of these received aid. Average need met was 63%. Average scholarship/grant was $4,491; average loan $2,941. 29% of total undergraduate aid awarded as scholarships/grants, 71% as loans/jobs. **Non-need-based:** Awarded to 167 full-time undergraduates, including 32 freshmen. Scholarships awarded for academics, athletics, leadership, music/drama, state residency.

Application procedures. **Admission:** Priority date 6/15; deadline 8/30 (receipt date). $40 fee, may be waived for applicants with need. Admission notification on a rolling basis. Must reply by May 1 or within 2 week(s) if notified thereafter. **Financial aid:** Priority date 3/1; no closing date. FAFSA required. Applicants notified on a rolling basis starting 3/15; must reply within 2 week(s) of notification.

Academics. **Special study options:** Combined bachelor's/graduate degree, cross-registration, distance learning, double major, dual enrollment of high school students, honors, independent study, internships, liberal arts/career combination, student-designed major, study abroad. **Credit/placement by examination:** AP, CLEP, institutional tests. 45 credit hours maximum toward associate degree, 90 toward bachelor's. **Support services:** Reduced course load, remedial instruction, study skills assistance, tutoring.

Majors. **Architecture:** Technology. **Biology:** General. **Business:** Accounting, business admin, financial planning. **Computer sciences:** General. **Health:** Dental hygiene, nursing (RN). **Liberal arts:** Library science. **Protective services:** Law enforcement admin. **Public administration:** General. **Social sciences:** General. **Visual/performing arts:** Studio arts.

Most popular majors. Business/marketing 21%, health sciences 31%, liberal arts 12%, library sciences 8%, visual/performing arts 6%.

Computing on campus. 191 workstations in library, computer center. Commuter students can connect to campus network. Online course registration, online library, wireless network available.

Student life. **Freshman orientation:** Available. Preregistration for classes offered. One-day program held 1 week prior to start of each semester and mid-summer. **Activities:** Bands, drama, international student organizations, music ensembles, student government, student newspaper, art and architectural student association, Gay Lesbian Bisexual Transgender friends and associates, honors English program, english society, student nursing association, Pi Alpha Alpha, college republicans, mental health and human services club, campus crusade.

Athletics. USCAA. **Intercollegiate:** Basketball, golf, soccer W. **Intramural:** Basketball, racquetball, soccer, volleyball. **Team name:** Moose.

Student services. Alcohol/substance abuse counseling, career counseling, services for economically disadvantaged, financial aid counseling, personal counseling. **Physically disabled:** Services for visually, hearing impaired.

Contact. E-mail: umaadm@maine.edu
Phone: (207) 621-3465 Toll-free number: (877) 862-1234
Fax: (207) 621-3333
Jonathan Henry, Director of Admissions and Dean of Enrollment, University of Maine at Augusta, 46 University Drive, Augusta, ME 04330

University of Maine at Farmington

Farmington, Maine — **CB member**
www.farmington.edu — **CB code: 3506**

- Public 4-year liberal arts and teachers college
- Residential campus in small town
- 2,145 degree-seeking undergraduates: 5% part-time, 64% women
- 37 degree-seeking graduate students
- 68% of applicants admitted
- Application essay required
- 62% graduate within 6 years

General. Founded in 1863. Regionally accredited. **Degrees:** 430 bachelor's awarded. **Location:** 38 miles from Augusta, 80 miles from Portland.

Calendar: Semester, extensive summer session. **Full-time faculty:** 139 total; 81% have terminal degrees, 5% minority, 53% women. **Part-time faculty:** 45 total; 31% have terminal degrees, 60% women. **Class size:** 69% < 20, 30% 20-39, less than 1% 40-49, 1% 50-99. **Special facilities:** Archaeology research center, campus-wide wireless laptop network, 24/7 computer center, on-site nursery school, day care center teaching labs, multi-media graphics lab, observatory.

Freshman class profile. 1,902 applied, 1,293 admitted, 525 enrolled.

Mid 50% test scores		**GPA 2.0-2.99:**	15%
SAT critical reading:	440-560	**Rank in top quarter:**	27%
SAT math:	440-550	**Rank in top tenth:**	13%
SAT writing:	450-560	**Return as sophomores:**	73%
GPA 3.75 or higher:	1%	**Out-of-state:**	20%
GPA 3.50-3.74:	3%	**Live on campus:**	90%
GPA 3.0-3.49:	81%		

Basis for selection. School achievement record and recommendation most important. School and community activities, interviews and personal essay also important. On campus placement tests required for those below SAT 490 Verbal, 450 Math. Interview recommended. 13-15 page writing sample required for Creative Writing BFA. **Homeschooled:** Transcript of courses and grades, state high school equivalency certificate required. **Learning Disabled:** Students may submit disclosure of learning disability to learning center after admission.

High school preparation. 19 units recommended. Required and recommended units include English 4, mathematics 3-4, social studies 2-3, science 2-3 (laboratory 2-3), foreign language 2-3 and academic electives 3. Algebra I and II and geometry required. Two years of same foreign language required. General college preparatory program required for all except those admitted to Liberal Studies Bridge.

2008-2009 Annual costs. Tuition/fees: $7,976; $15,752 out-of-state. New England Regional Student Program tuition and fees: $10,677. Room/board: $7,158. Books/supplies: $560. Personal expenses: $2,122.

2007-2008 Financial aid. Need-based: 425 full-time freshmen applied for aid; 379 were judged to have need; 360 of these received aid. Average need met was 72%. Average scholarship/grant was $4,935; average loan $3,536. 44% of total undergraduate aid awarded as scholarships/grants, 56% as loans/jobs. **Non-need-based:** Awarded to 585 full-time undergraduates, including 252 freshmen. Scholarships awarded for academics, leadership, minority status, state residency. **Additional information:** FAFSA must arrive at Federal processor by 3/1.

Application procedures. Admission: No deadline. $40 fee, may be waived for applicants with need. Admission notification on a rolling basis beginning on or about 12/15. Must reply by May 1 or within 3 week(s) if notified thereafter. **Financial aid:** Priority date 3/1; no closing date. FAFSA required. Applicants notified on a rolling basis starting 3/15; must reply within 2 week(s) of notification.

Academics. Interdisciplinary first year seminar. **Special study options:** Accelerated study, cross-registration, distance learning, double major, dual enrollment of high school students, exchange student, honors, independent study, internships, liberal arts/career combination, semester at sea, student-designed major, study abroad, teacher certification program. **Credit/placement by examination:** AP, CLEP, IB, SAT, institutional tests. **Support services:** Learning center, pre-admission summer program, reduced course load, remedial instruction, study skills assistance, tutoring, writing center.

Majors. Area/ethnic studies: Women's. **Biology:** General. **Business:** Managerial economics. **Computer sciences:** Computer science. **Conservation:** Environmental science, land use planning. **Education:** Biology, early childhood, early childhood special, elementary, English, health, kindergarten/preschool, mathematics, science, secondary, social science, special. **Health:** Community health, public health ed. **History:** General. **Interdisciplinary:** Global studies. **Math:** General. **Physical sciences:** Geochemistry, geology. **Psychology:** General. **Social sciences:** Anthropology, geography, political science. **Visual/performing arts:** Art, arts management, dramatic, music management, theater arts management. **Other:** Interdisciplinary studies, Philosophy and religious studies, Rehabilitation Administration and Rehabilitation services.

Most popular majors. Business/marketing 6%, education 42%, English 6%, health sciences 12%, interdisciplinary studies 9%, psychology 11%.

Computing on campus. 180 workstations in library, computer center, student center. Dormitories wired for high-speed internet access and linked to campus network. Commuter students can connect to campus network. Online course registration, online library, helpline, wireless network available.

Student life. Freshman orientation: Available, $175 fee. Preregistration for classes offered. Held immmediately before classes; includes outdoor activities and community service. **Housing:** Guaranteed on-campus for freshmen. Coed dorms, single-sex dorms, special housing for disabled, wellness housing available. Housing for students maintaining certain GPA, medical single rooms, quiet floors, wellness community, independent living environment housing available. **Activities:** Concert band, choral groups, dance, drama, literary magazine, music ensembles, radio station, student government, student newspaper, symphony orchestra, Justice Uniting Students Together, student environmental and political awareness club, Amnesty International, Inter-Varsity Christian Fellowship, student alcohol educators, student admissions club, Alpha Phi Omega, literary guild, Newman Club, student-run entertainment board.

Athletics. NCAA. **Intercollegiate:** Baseball M, basketball, cross-country, field hockey W, golf, soccer, softball W, volleyball W. **Intramural:** Basketball, football (non-tackle), soccer, softball, swimming, tennis, volleyball. **Team name:** Beavers.

Student services. Alcohol/substance abuse counseling, career counseling, services for economically disadvantaged, student employment services, financial aid counseling, health services, on-campus daycare, personal counseling, placement for graduates, veterans' counselor, women's services. **Physically disabled:** Services for visually, hearing impaired.

Contact. E-mail: umfadmit@maine.edu
Phone: (207) 778-7050 Fax: (207) 778-8182
Brandon Lagana, Director of Admission, University of Maine at Farmington, 246 Main Street, Farmington, ME 04938

University of Maine at Fort Kent

Fort Kent, Maine — **CB member**
www.umfk.maine.edu — **CB code: 3393**

- Public 4-year university
- Commuter campus in small town
- 784 degree-seeking undergraduates: 22% part-time, 64% women, 1% African American, 1% Hispanic American, 2% Native American, 25% international
- 76% of applicants admitted
- Application essay required
- 45% graduate within 6 years

General. Founded in 1878. Regionally accredited. Bilingual Franco-American region. **Degrees:** 256 bachelor's, 33 associate awarded. **Location:** 200 miles from Bangor, 21 miles from Edmundston, Canada. **Calendar:** Semester, limited summer session. **Full-time faculty:** 41 total; 78% have terminal degrees, 2% minority, 42% women. **Part-time faculty:** 29 total; 7% have terminal degrees, 66% women. **Class size:** 65% < 20, 32% 20-39, 2% 40-49, 2% 50-99. **Special facilities:** 16-acre biological park, Acadian Archives, interactive television site, Northern Maine Center for Rural Health Science, Center for Sustainable Rural Development.

Freshman class profile. 348 applied, 265 admitted, 113 enrolled.

GPA 3.75 or higher:	2%	**Rank in top quarter:**	20%
GPA 3.50-3.74:	4%	**Rank in top tenth:**	5%
GPA 3.0-3.49:	29%	**Return as sophomores:**	63%
GPA 2.0-2.99:	57%	**International:**	9%

Basis for selection. High school courses and achievement record most important. Recommendations considered. SAT, ACT scores, or on-campus placement exams required. Interview recommended.

High school preparation. 16 units required. Required and recommended units include English 4, mathematics 2, social studies 2, science 2 and foreign language 2. Biology and chemistry required for nursing and environmental studies.

2008-2009 Annual costs. Tuition/fees: $6,413; $15,023 out-of-state. New England Regional tuition is 150% of public in-district tuition. Room/board: $6,940. Books/supplies: $1,000. Personal expenses: $1,000.

2007-2008 Financial aid. Need-based: 143 full-time freshmen applied for aid; 122 were judged to have need; 122 of these received aid. Average need met was 84%. Average scholarship/grant was $5,291; average loan $3,155. 70% of total undergraduate aid awarded as scholarships/grants, 30% as loans/jobs. **Non-need-based:** Awarded to 50 full-time undergraduates, including 12 freshmen. Scholarships awarded for academics, leadership, state residency.

Application procedures. Admission: No deadline. $40 fee, may be waived for applicants with need. Admission notification on a rolling basis. Must reply by May 1 or within 4 week(s) if notified thereafter. **Financial**

aid: Priority date 3/1, closing date 2/1. FAFSA, institutional form required. Applicants notified on a rolling basis starting 3/15; must reply within 2 week(s) of notification.

Academics. **Special study options:** Accelerated study, cross-registration, distance learning, double major, dual enrollment of high school students, honors, independent study, internships, liberal arts/career combination, student-designed major, study abroad, teacher certification program. **Credit/placement by examination:** AP, CLEP, IB, institutional tests. 30 credit hours maximum toward associate degree, 90 toward bachelor's. **Support services:** Learning center, pre-admission summer program, reduced course load, remedial instruction, tutoring, writing center.

Majors. **Biology:** General. **Business:** General, business admin, e-commerce, management information systems. **Computer sciences:** General, information technology. **Conservation:** Environmental science, management/policy. **Education:** General, business, elementary, English, multi-level teacher, music, science, secondary, social studies. **Foreign languages:** General, comparative lit, French. **Health:** Nursing (RN). **Interdisciplinary:** Math/computer science. **Liberal arts:** Arts/sciences. **Psychology:** General. **Public administration:** Social work. **Social sciences:** General. **Other:** Public Safety Administration.

Most popular majors. Business/marketing 7%, education 61%, health sciences 20%.

Computing on campus. 100 workstations in dormitories, library, computer center, student center. Dormitories wired for high-speed internet access and linked to campus network. Commuter students can connect to campus network. Online course registration, repair service, student web hosting, wireless network available.

Student life. **Freshman orientation:** Mandatory. Preregistration for classes offered. 3-day social and educational orientation; includes workshops. **Housing:** Coed dorms available. $100 deposit, deadline 8/15. **Activities:** Jazz band, choral groups, dance, drama, music ensembles, musical theater, student government, Christian Fellowship, Newman Club.

Athletics. NAIA. **Intercollegiate:** Basketball, skiing, soccer. **Intramural:** Baseball M, basketball, cross-country, golf, ice hockey M, racquetball, skiing, soccer, softball, table tennis, tennis, volleyball, weight lifting. **Team name:** Bengals.

Student services. Adult student services, career counseling, financial aid counseling, health services, personal counseling, placement for graduates, veterans' counselor.

Contact. E-mail: umfkadm@maine.edu
Phone: (207) 834-7600 Toll-free number: (888) 879-8635
Fax: (207) 834-7609
Jill Cairns, Director of Admissions, University of Maine at Fort Kent, 23 University Drive, Fort Kent, ME 04743

University of Maine at Machias

Machias, Maine — **CB member**
www.umm.maine.edu — **CB code: 3956**

- Public 4-year university and liberal arts college
- Commuter campus in rural community
- 565 degree-seeking undergraduates
- 83% of applicants admitted
- SAT or ACT (ACT writing optional), application essay required

General. Founded in 1909. Regionally accredited. **Degrees:** 77 bachelor's, 4 associate awarded. **Location:** 85 miles from Bangor, 65 miles from Bar Harbor. **Calendar:** Semester, limited summer session. **Full-time faculty:** 40 total. **Part-time faculty:** 60 total. **Class size:** 70% < 20, 30% 20-39. **Special facilities:** Institute for applied marine research and education, mariculture student research facility, greenhouse, GIS lab, early childhood center, field station, international park, sail loft.

Freshman class profile. 363 applied, 302 admitted, 116 enrolled.

Mid 50% test scores		**GPA 3.0-3.49:**	48%
SAT critical reading:	420-580	**GPA 2.0-2.99:**	36%
SAT math:	410-540	**Rank in top quarter:**	24%
SAT writing:	400-530	**Rank in top tenth:**	13%
ACT composite:	16-25	**Out-of-state:**	25%
GPA 3.75 or higher:	9%	**Live on campus:**	67%
GPA 3.50-3.74:	7%		

Basis for selection. Applicants should rank in top half of class and have a B average. Recommendations and test scores important. Essay and outstanding nonacademic achievement (extracurricular, community, military, life, or work) considered. SAT/ACT not required of applicants for associate of science degree. Test score for fall-term admission must be received before first day of classes. Interview recommended. **Homeschooled:** Statement describing homeschool structure and mission, transcript of courses and grades required. Records of all completed coursework plus documentation verifying proficiency in coursework (such as examples of writing, math skills). Portfolio beneficial for some coursework. Standardized test scores required; campus visit with interview important. **Learning Disabled:** Students evaluated on results of required college preparatory work. Documentation of disability important if seeking assistance from Student Resource Center.

High school preparation. 11 units required. Required and recommended units include English 4, mathematics 3, social studies 2, science 2 (laboratory 2), foreign language 2 and academic electives 3. Social studies may include history. Computer applications, fine arts also recommended.

2008-2009 Annual costs. Tuition/fees: $6,410; $16,550 out-of-state. New England Regional Student Program tuition is 150% of public in-district tuition. Room/board: $6,574. Books/supplies: $800. Personal expenses: $1,600.

Financial aid. **Non-need-based:** Scholarships awarded for academics, alumni affiliation, art, job skills, leadership, minority status, music/drama, state residency.

Application procedures. **Admission:** Closing date 8/15 (receipt date). $40 fee, may be waived for applicants with need. Admission notification on a rolling basis. Must reply by May 1 or within 2 week(s) if notified thereafter. **Financial aid:** Priority date 3/1; no closing date. FAFSA required. Applicants notified on a rolling basis starting 2/15; must reply within 2 week(s) of notification.

Academics. Internships and/or cooperative education program available in business studies, recreation management, biology, environmental studies, and behavioral science. **Special study options:** Cooperative education, distance learning, double major, dual enrollment of high school students, honors, independent study, internships, student-designed major, study abroad, teacher certification program. **Credit/placement by examination:** AP, CLEP, SAT, ACT, institutional tests. **Support services:** Learning center, reduced course load, remedial instruction, study skills assistance, tutoring, writing center.

Majors. **Biology:** General, ecology, marine. **Business:** General, accounting, business admin, hospitality admin, hospitality/recreation, marketing, office management, office/clerical, tourism promotion, tourism/travel. **Conservation:** General, environmental studies. **Education:** Business, elementary, middle, secondary. **Health:** Mental health services. **History:** General. **Interdisciplinary:** Behavioral sciences. **Liberal arts:** Arts/sciences. **Parks/recreation:** General, facilities management. **Psychology:** General. **Public administration:** Human services. **Visual/performing arts:** General.

Most popular majors. Biology 8%, business/marketing 17%, education 14%, English 7%, interdisciplinary studies 18%, liberal arts 7%, natural resources/environmental science 8%, parks/recreation 14%.

Computing on campus. 117 workstations in dormitories, library, computer center. Dormitories wired for high-speed internet access and linked to campus network. Commuter students can connect to campus network. Online course registration, online library, helpline, repair service, wireless network available.

Student life. **Freshman orientation:** Available. Preregistration for classes offered. Orientation in June, August, and January. **Policies:** Students over 21 may drink in their rooms. Firearms must be stored in safe in Resident Director's office. **Housing:** Guaranteed on-campus for all undergraduates. Coed dorms, wellness housing available. $100 deposit. Pets allowed in dorm rooms. **Activities:** Concert band, choral groups, dance, drama, literary magazine, music ensembles, musical theater, radio station, student government, Newman Club, Students of Service.

Athletics. NAIA. **Intercollegiate:** Basketball, cross-country, soccer, volleyball W. **Intramural:** Basketball, cheerleading W, fencing, football (non-tackle), soccer, softball W, water polo. **Team name:** Clippers.

Student services. Career counseling, student employment services, financial aid counseling, health services, on-campus daycare, personal counseling, placement for graduates, veterans' counselor.

Contact. E-mail: ummadmissions@maine.edu
Phone: (207) 255-1318 Toll-free number: (888) 468-6866
Fax: (207) 255-1363
Stewart Bennett, Director of Admissions, University of Maine at Machias, 9 O'Brien Avenue, Machias, ME 04654

University of Maine at Presque Isle

Presque Isle, Maine **CB member**
www.umpi.edu **CB code: 3008**

- Public 4-year university
- Commuter campus in small town
- 1,567 degree-seeking undergraduates: 39% part-time, 64% women, 1% African American, 1% Hispanic American, 3% Native American, 30% international
- Application essay required

General. Founded in 1903. Regionally accredited. **Degrees:** 335 bachelor's, 14 associate awarded. **Location:** 165 miles from Bangor. **Calendar:** Semester, limited summer session. **Full-time faculty:** 55 total. **Part-time faculty:** 65 total. **Class size:** 63% < 20, 37% 20-39. **Special facilities:** Small business institute, kinesiology laboratory, local history center, human services laboratory, museum of natural science.

Freshman class profile.

Mid 50% test scores		**Rank in top quarter:**	23%
SAT critical reading:	390-530	**Rank in top tenth:**	8%
SAT math:	390-500	**Return as sophomores:**	85%
GPA 3.75 or higher:	12%	**Out-of-state:**	4%
GPA 3.50-3.74:	9%	**Live on campus:**	38%
GPA 3.0-3.49:	38%	**International:**	10%
GPA 2.0-2.99:	40%		

Basis for selection. Admissions based on secondary school record, class rank, recommendations, and essay. Interview also important. Interview recommended for academically borderline. Portfolio required of bachelor of fine arts applicants.

High school preparation. 16 units required. Required units include English 4, mathematics 3, social studies 3, science 2 (laboratory 2), foreign language 2 and academic electives 2. Medical laboratory technology and nursing programs: 4 English, 1 biology w/lab, 1 chemistry w/lab, 2 math, 1 social studies, 6 electives, totaling 15.

2008-2009 Annual costs. Tuition/fees: $6,340; $14,950 out-of-state. Room/board: $6,192. Books/supplies: $800. Personal expenses: $1,100.

2008-2009 Financial aid. Non-need-based: Scholarships awarded for academics, alumni affiliation, art, job skills, leadership, minority status, music/drama, state residency.

Application procedures. Admission: No deadline. $40 fee, may be waived for applicants with need. Admission notification on a rolling basis. **Financial aid:** Priority date 4/1; no closing date. FAFSA required. Applicants notified on a rolling basis starting 3/1; must reply within 2 week(s) of notification.

Academics. Special study options: Accelerated study, combined bachelor's/graduate degree, cooperative education, cross-registration, distance learning, double major, exchange student, honors, independent study, internships, student-designed major, study abroad, teacher certification program. **Credit/placement by examination:** AP, CLEP, IB, SAT, ACT, institutional tests. 30 credit hours maximum toward associate degree, 60 toward bachelor's. Scores of 3, 4, and 5 acceptable on AP tests; hours awarded decided on case-by-case basis. **Support services:** Learning center, reduced course load, remedial instruction, study skills assistance, tutoring, writing center.

Majors. Biology: General. **Business:** Accounting, business admin, communications. **Conservation:** Environmental studies. **Education:** General, art, elementary, health, physical, secondary. **Health:** Athletic training. **Interdisciplinary:** Behavioral sciences. **Liberal arts:** Arts/sciences. **Parks/recreation:** General. **Physical sciences:** Geology. **Protective services:** Law enforcement admin. **Psychology:** General. **Public administration:** Social work. **Social sciences:** International relations, political science, sociology. **Visual/performing arts:** Art, studio arts.

Most popular majors. Business/marketing 9%, education 17%, liberal arts 46%.

Computing on campus. 120 workstations in library, computer center. Dormitories wired for high-speed internet access and linked to campus network. Commuter students can connect to campus network. Helpline available.

Student life. Freshman orientation: Mandatory, $35 fee. Preregistration for classes offered. Held during the spring, summer, and in January. **Housing:** Guaranteed on-campus for freshmen. Coed dorms, apartments available. $100 deposit, deadline 8/1. **Activities:** Drama, radio station, student government, student newspaper, Geo-ecology club, honors club, Campus Crusade for Christ, outdoor adventure program, physical education majors club, games club, Big Brothers and Big Sisters, accounting/business/MIS club.

Athletics. Intercollegiate: Baseball M, basketball, cross-country, golf M, skiing, soccer, softball W, volleyball W. **Team name:** Owls.

Student services. Adult student services, chaplain/spiritual director, career counseling, student employment services, financial aid counseling, health services, on-campus daycare, personal counseling, placement for graduates, veterans' counselor. **Physically disabled:** Services for visually, hearing impaired.

Contact. E-mail: erin.benson@umpi.edu
Phone: (207) 768-9532 Fax: (207) 768-9777
Erin Benson, Director of Admissions, University of Maine at Presque Isle, 181 Main Street, Presque Isle, ME 04769

University of New England

Biddeford, Maine **CB member**
www.une.edu **CB code: 3751**

- Private 4-year university
- Residential campus in small city
- 2,113 degree-seeking undergraduates: 5% part-time, 71% women, 1% African American, 2% Asian American, 1% Hispanic American, 1% international
- 1,872 graduate students
- 78% of applicants admitted
- SAT or ACT (ACT writing optional) required
- 49% graduate within 6 years

General. Founded in 1831. Regionally accredited. **Degrees:** 293 bachelor's, 99 associate awarded; master's, first professional offered. **ROTC:** Army. **Location:** 15 miles from Portland. **Calendar:** Semester, limited summer session. **Full-time faculty:** 180 total; 49% women. **Part-time faculty:** 140 total; 54% women. **Class size:** 45% < 20, 47% 20-39, 4% 40-49, 4% 50-99, less than 1% >100. **Special facilities:** Maine Women Writers collection, osteopathic center, performance enhancement and evaluation center, marine science education and research center.

Freshman class profile. 3,149 applied, 2,449 admitted, 565 enrolled.

Mid 50% test scores		**Out-of-state:**	63%
SAT critical reading:	480-570	**Live on campus:**	90%
SAT math:	470-590	**International:**	1%
Return as sophomores:	77%		

Basis for selection. School achievement record most important. Test scores, school, community activities considered. Exposure to health careers recommended if seeking admission to health science majors. Rigor of curriculum considered. Essay recommended. Interview required for nursing program, recommended for all, strongly recommended for academically weaker students. **Homeschooled:** Statement describing homeschool structure and mission, transcript of courses and grades required.

High school preparation. College-preparatory program recommended. 16 units required; 20 recommended. Required and recommended units include English 4, mathematics 3-4, social studies 1-2, history 1-2, science 2-3 (laboratory 2-3), foreign language 2 and academic electives 2-4.

2009-2010 Annual costs. Tuition/fees (projected): $27,920. Room/board: $10,870. Books/supplies: $1,350. Personal expenses: $1,400.

2007-2008 Financial aid. Non-need-based: Scholarships awarded for academics, alumni affiliation, leadership.

Application procedures. Admission: Priority date 12/1; deadline 2/15 (postmark date). $40 fee, may be waived for applicants with need. Admission notification on a rolling basis beginning on or about 12/15. Must reply by May 1 or within 4 week(s) if notified thereafter. **Financial aid:** Priority date 5/1; no closing date. FAFSA required. Applicants notified on a rolling basis starting 2/1.

Academics. Special study options: Combined bachelor's/graduate degree, cooperative education, cross-registration, distance learning, double major, dual enrollment of high school students, honors, independent study, internships, liberal arts/career combination, student-designed major, study abroad, teacher certification program. **Credit/placement by examination:** AP, CLEP, IB, SAT, ACT, institutional tests. **Support services:** Learning center, reduced course load, remedial instruction, study skills assistance, tutoring, writing center.

Majors. **Agriculture:** Aquaculture. **Biology:** General, biochemistry, marine. **Business:** Business admin. **Conservation:** Environmental science, environmental studies. **Education:** General, art, elementary. **Health:** Athletic training, clinical lab technology, dental hygiene, health services admin, nursing (RN). **History:** General. **Liberal arts:** Arts/sciences. **Math:** General. **Parks/recreation:** Exercise sciences, sports admin. **Physical sciences:** Chemistry. **Psychology:** General, psychobiology, social. **Social sciences:** Political science, sociology.

Most popular majors. Biology 25%, education 7%, health sciences 30%, parks/recreation 11%, psychology 14%.

Computing on campus. 170 workstations in dormitories, library, computer center, student center. Dormitories wired for high-speed internet access and linked to campus network. Commuter students can connect to campus network. Online course registration, online library, helpline, student web hosting, wireless network available.

Student life. **Freshman orientation:** Mandatory. Preregistration for classes offered. **Housing:** Guaranteed on-campus for freshmen. Coed dorms, single-sex dorms, wellness housing available. $200 partly refundable deposit, deadline 5/1. **Activities:** Literary magazine, student government, Earth's ECO, Rotoract, Marine Animal Stranding Helpline, Make A Wish, EMS, campus diversity club, Intervarsity Christian Fellowship, Cross Seekers, Habitat for Humanity, College Democrats.

Athletics. NCAA. **Intercollegiate:** Basketball, cross-country, field hockey W, golf M, lacrosse, soccer, softball W, swimming W, volleyball W. **Intramural:** Basketball, gymnastics, racquetball, soccer, softball, table tennis, volleyball W, water polo. **Team name:** Nor-easters.

Student services. Adult student services, alcohol/substance abuse counseling, chaplain/spiritual director, career counseling, student employment services, financial aid counseling, health services, minority student services, personal counseling, veterans' counselor.

Contact. E-mail: admissions@une.edu
Phone: (207) 283-0170 ext. 2297 Toll-free number: (800) 477-4863
Fax: (207) 602-5900
Robert Pecchia, Associate Dean of Admissions, University of New England, Hills Beach Road, Biddeford, ME 04005

University of Southern Maine

Gorham, Maine — **CB member**
www.usm.maine.edu — **CB code: 3691**

- Public 4-year university and liberal arts college
- Commuter campus in small city
- 6,483 degree-seeking undergraduates: 30% part-time, 58% women, 2% African American, 2% Asian American, 1% Hispanic American, 1% Native American
- 1,565 degree-seeking graduate students
- 81% of applicants admitted
- SAT or ACT with writing, application essay required

General. Founded in 1878. Regionally accredited. **Degrees:** 1,208 bachelor's, 12 associate awarded; master's, doctoral, first professional offered. **ROTC:** Army, Air Force. **Location:** 110 miles from Boston. **Calendar:** Semester, extensive summer session. **Full-time faculty:** 408 total; 5% minority, 43% women. **Part-time faculty:** 302 total; 1% minority, 53% women. **Class size:** 45% < 20, 47% 20-39, 4% 40-49, 3% 50-99, less than 1% >100. **Special facilities:** Planetarium, cartographic collection, olympic-sized ice arena.

Freshman class profile. 4,252 applied, 3,455 admitted, 1,051 enrolled.

Mid 50% test scores			
SAT critical reading:	450-560	GPA 3.0-3.49:	31%
SAT math:	450-560	GPA 2.0-2.99:	48%
SAT writing:	440-540	Rank in top quarter:	28%
ACT composite:	18-24	Rank in top tenth:	9%
GPA 3.75 or higher:	10%	Return as sophomores:	67%
GPA 3.50-3.74:	8%	Out-of-state:	22%
		Live on campus:	64%

Basis for selection. Level and content of academic program with performance or achievement record, class rank, and standardized test scores most important. Counselor recommendation, essay, and experience outside classroom also important. Interview recommended for all. Audition required of music majors. **Homeschooled:** Transcript of courses and grades, letter of recommendation (nonparent) required. SAT or ACT, annual assessment of courses, and GED required for financial aid purposes. **Learning Disabled:** Must be otherwise qualified to be admitted, may be asked to provide documentation.

High school preparation. 16 units required. Required and recommended units include English 4, mathematics 3-4, social studies 2-3, history 2-3, science 2-3 (laboratory 2-3) and foreign language 2-3. 3 lab sciences for science majors. Math, business and electrical engineering majors require 4 years of math.

2008-2009 Annual costs. Tuition/fees: $7,364; $18,884 out-of-state. New England Regional Student Program tuition is 150% of public in-district tuition. Room/board: $8,334. Books/supplies: $900. Personal expenses: $2,000.

2008-2009 Financial aid. **Need-based:** Average need met was 62%. Average scholarship/grant was $4,894; average loan $3,592. 40% of total undergraduate aid awarded as scholarships/grants, 60% as loans/jobs. **Non-need-based:** Scholarships awarded for academics, music/drama.

Application procedures. **Admission:** Priority date 2/15; no deadline. $40 fee, may be waived for applicants with need. Admission notification on a rolling basis beginning on or about 1/1. Must reply by May 1 or within 2 week(s) if notified thereafter. **Financial aid:** Priority date 2/15; no closing date. FAFSA required. Applicants notified on a rolling basis starting 3/15; must reply by 5/1 or within 2 week(s) of notification.

Academics. **Special study options:** Accelerated study, combined bachelor's/graduate degree, cooperative education, cross-registration, distance learning, double major, ESL, exchange student, honors, independent study, internships, liberal arts/career combination, semester at sea, student-designed major, study abroad, teacher certification program, Washington semester, weekend college. Preengineering program with University of Maine at Orono, living/learning scholars program, Greater Portland Alliance - cross registration with University of New England, St. Joseph's (Maine), Southern Maine Technical College, and Maine College of Art. **Credit/placement by examination:** AP, CLEP, IB, institutional tests. No numerical limit. Students must meet all course requirements and 30 credit residency for BA/BS and 15 credit residency for AA/AS degrees. **Support services:** Learning center, reduced course load, remedial instruction, study skills assistance, tutoring, writing center.

Honors college/program. Honors application required. Several course options available. Interdisciplinary curriculum with small seminar classes.

Majors. **Area/ethnic studies:** French, German, Hispanic-American/Latino/Chicano, Russian/Slavic, women's. **Biology:** General, biotechnology. **Business:** General, accounting, accounting/finance, business admin, finance, management information systems, marketing, organizational behavior. **Communications:** General, media studies. **Computer sciences:** General, applications programming, computer science, programming. **Conservation:** Environmental science, environmental studies. **Construction:** Site management. **Education:** Art, elementary, mathematics, music, technology/industrial arts, voc/tech. **Engineering:** Electrical, mechanical. **Engineering technology:** Electrical, manufacturing. **Foreign languages:** General, classics, French, linguistics. **Health:** Athletic training, environmental health, medical radiologic technology/radiation therapy, nursing (RN), pediatric nursing, predental, premedicine, preop/surgical nursing, preveterinary, psychiatric nursing, recreational therapy. **History:** General. **Interdisciplinary:** Behavioral sciences, global studies, math/computer science, natural sciences. **Legal studies:** Prelaw. **Liberal arts:** Arts/sciences, humanities. **Math:** General. **Parks/recreation:** General, exercise sciences. **Philosophy/religion:** Philosophy. **Physical sciences:** Chemistry, geology, physics. **Psychology:** General. **Public administration:** Social work. **Social sciences:** General, anthropology, criminology, economics, geography, international relations, political science, sociology. **Visual/performing arts:** General, acting, art, art history/conservation, arts management, directing/producing, dramatic, drawing, jazz, music performance, painting, piano/organ, sculpture, stringed instruments, studio arts, theater arts management, voice/opera. **Other:** Environmental Saftey and Health.

Most popular majors. Business/marketing 17%, communications/journalism 8%, health sciences 17%, social sciences 18%, visual/performing arts 6%.

Computing on campus. 410 workstations in dormitories, library, computer center, student center. Dormitories wired for high-speed internet access and linked to campus network. Commuter students can connect to campus network. Online course registration, helpline, repair service, wireless network available.

Student life. **Freshman orientation:** Mandatory, $150 fee. Preregistration for classes offered. Sessions in summer and autumn. **Policies:** Smoking is not allowed within 50 feet of any dormitory. **Housing:** Coed dorms, special housing for disabled, apartments, fraternity/sorority housing, wellness housing available. $75 deposit, deadline 5/1. **Activities:** Bands, choral groups, dance, drama, international student organizations, literary magazine, music ensembles, musical theater, opera, radio station, student government, student newspaper, symphony orchestra, TV station, Amnesty International, American Indian student association, Environmental Coalition, College Republicans, Alliance of Sexual Diversity, Women's Forum, Bahai Association, ethnic student association.

Athletics. NCAA. **Intercollegiate:** Baseball M, basketball, cheerleading, cross-country, field hockey W, golf, ice hockey, lacrosse, soccer, softball W, tennis, track and field, volleyball W, wrestling M. **Intramural:** Basketball, cheerleading W, football (non-tackle), football (tackle) M, ice hockey, lacrosse, racquetball, rugby, sailing, skiing, soccer, softball, squash, table tennis, tennis, volleyball, weight lifting. **Team name:** Huskies.

Student services. Adult student services, alcohol/substance abuse counseling, chaplain/spiritual director, career counseling, services for economically disadvantaged, student employment services, financial aid counseling, health services, legal services, minority student services, on-campus daycare, personal counseling, placement for graduates, veterans' counselor, women's services. **Physically disabled:** Services for visually, speech, hearing impaired.

Contact. E-mail: usmadm@usm.maine.edu
Phone: (207) 780-5670 Toll-free number: (800) 800-4876 ext. 5670
Fax: (207) 780-5640
Scott Steinberg, Director of Undergraduate Admission, University of Southern Maine, 37 College Avenue, Gorham, ME 04038

Maryland

Baltimore Hebrew University
Baltimore, Maryland
www.bhu.edu **CB code: 2165**

- Private 4-year university and teachers college
- Commuter campus in very large city
- 4 degree-seeking undergraduates
- Application essay, interview required

General. Founded in 1919. Regionally accredited. Easy access to regional Jewish community. University population consists primarily of graduate students. **Degrees:** 1 bachelor's awarded; master's, doctoral offered. **Calendar:** Semester, extensive summer session. **Full-time faculty:** 8 total. **Part-time faculty:** 4 total.

Basis for selection. Dean reviews high school record, Jewish communal activity and conducts personal interview. Students must have completed 60 hours of undergraduate credit at an accredited insitution before applying.

2008-2009 Annual costs. Tuition/fees: $11,350. Books/supplies: $400. Personal expenses: $1,300.

2007-2008 Financial aid. Need-based: 34% of total undergraduate aid awarded as scholarships/grants, 66% as loans/jobs. **Non-need-based:** Scholarships awarded for academics.

Application procedures. Admission: Closing date 6/1. $50 fee. Admission notification on a rolling basis beginning on or about 5/1. **Financial aid:** Priority date 4/15, closing date 6/1. FAFSA required. Applicants notified on a rolling basis starting 7/15; must reply by 9/9.

Academics. University-operated Judaic/Hebraic library. **Special study options:** Cross-registration, dual enrollment of high school students. **Credit/placement by examination:** CLEP, IB, institutional tests. 12 credit hours maximum toward bachelor's degree.

Majors. Foreign languages: Hebrew. **Other:** Jewish studies.

Computing on campus. 12 workstations in library, computer center.

Student services. Career counseling, financial aid counseling, veterans' counselor. **Physically disabled:** Services for hearing impaired.

Contact. E-mail: lkott@bhu.edu
Phone: (410) 578-6970 Toll-free number: (888) 248-7420
Fax: (410) 578-6940
Laurie Kott, Director of Admissions and Recruitment, Baltimore Hebrew University, 5800 Park Heights Avenue, Baltimore, MD 21215

Baltimore International College
Baltimore, Maryland
www.bic.edu **CB code: 5086**

- Private 4-year culinary school and business college
- Commuter campus in very large city
- 478 degree-seeking undergraduates
- 72% of applicants admitted

General. Founded in 1972. Regionally accredited. **Degrees:** 24 bachelor's, 95 associate awarded; master's offered. **Location:** Downtown. **Calendar:** Semester, limited summer session. **Full-time faculty:** 15 total. **Part-time faculty:** 20 total. **Class size:** 46% < 20, 52% 20-39, 2% 40-49. **Special facilities:** Culinary arts center.

Freshman class profile. 284 applied, 205 admitted, 183 enrolled.

Out-of-state:	18%	**Live on campus:**	23%

Basis for selection. Institutional placement evaluation most important. School achievement record, interview, test scores, and recommendations also important. SAT or ACT recommended. Interview recommended. **Homeschooled:** Must be an accredited home school program or approved by the local school district.

2008-2009 Annual costs. Tuition/fees: $17,436. Fees shown are for culinary school and include use of computer, culinary supplies, upgrading and maintenance of kitchen equipment and facilities. Day students provided one full meal daily. Business program students pay lower fees. ($8764). Room/board: $9,828. Books/supplies: $1,500.

2007-2008 Financial aid. Non-need-based: Scholarships awarded for academics, alumni affiliation, job skills, leadership, state residency.

Application procedures. Admission: Closing date 8/14. $50 fee. Admission notification on a rolling basis. **Financial aid:** Priority date 3/1; no closing date. FAFSA, institutional form required. Applicants notified on a rolling basis; must reply within 2 week(s) of notification.

Academics. Special study options: Accelerated study, cooperative education, double major, honors, internships, liberal arts/career combination, study abroad. Honors program available at the Virginia Park campus in Ireland. **Credit/placement by examination:** AP, CLEP, institutional tests. 15 credit hours maximum toward associate degree, 15 toward bachelor's. **Support services:** Remedial instruction, study skills assistance, tutoring.

Majors. Personal/culinary services: Restaurant/catering.

Computing on campus. 45 workstations in dormitories, library, computer center.

Student life. Freshman orientation: Mandatory. Preregistration for classes offered. One-day program held approximately a week before first day of classes. **Policies:** Freshmen under 21, single, with permanent residence more than 50 miles from campus required to live on campus. **Housing:** Guaranteed on-campus for freshmen. Coed dorms, wellness housing available. $100 deposit. **Activities:** Student government, American Culinary Federation.

Athletics. Team name: Wolfhounds.

Student services. Alcohol/substance abuse counseling, career counseling, services for economically disadvantaged, student employment services, financial aid counseling, health services, minority student services, personal counseling, placement for graduates, veterans' counselor, women's services.

Contact. E-mail: admissions@bic.edu
Phone: (410) 752-4710 ext. 120 Toll-free number: (800) 624-9926 ext. 120
Fax: (410) 752-3730
Michael Eddy, Director of Admissions, Baltimore International College, 17 Commerce Street, Baltimore, MD 21202-3230

Bowie State University
Bowie, Maryland **CB member**
www.bowiestate.edu **CB code: 5401**

- Public 4-year university
- Commuter campus in small city
- 4,340 degree-seeking undergraduates
- 1,144 graduate students
- 41% of applicants admitted
- SAT or ACT (ACT writing optional) required

General. Founded in 1865. Regionally accredited. Limited courses offered at off-site locations. **Degrees:** 616 bachelor's awarded; master's, doctoral offered. **ROTC:** Army, Air Force. **Location:** 25 miles from Baltimore, 20 miles from Washington, DC. **Calendar:** Semester, limited summer session. **Full-time faculty:** 219 total; 71% have terminal degrees, 85% minority, 49% women. **Part-time faculty:** 163 total; 39% have terminal degrees, 80% minority, 53% women. **Special facilities:** NASA operations and control center, art gallery, green house, super computer center(limited access).

Freshman class profile. 5,253 applied, 2,168 admitted, 781 enrolled.

Basis for selection. School achievement record in college-preparatory curriculum, test scores, minimum GPA of 2.0, counselor/school recommendation important. Audition required for music program. Portfolio required for art program. Praxis I required for education program. **Homeschooled:** Statement describing homeschool structure and mission required.

High school preparation. Required units include English 4, mathematics 3, social studies 1, history 2, science 3 and foreign language 2.

2008-2009 Annual costs. Tuition/fees: $5,939; $15,629 out-of-state. Room/board: $6,879. Books/supplies: $1,338. Personal expenses: $1,804.

2008-2009 Financial aid. Non-need-based: Scholarships awarded for academics, alumni affiliation, art, athletics, leadership, music/drama, ROTC, state residency.

Application procedures. **Admission:** No deadline. $40 fee, may be waived for applicants with need. Admission notification on a rolling basis. **Financial aid:** Closing date 3/1. FAFSA required. Applicants notified on a rolling basis starting 4/1; must reply within 2 week(s) of notification.

Academics. For more information please contact Monica Turner at (301) 860-3296. **Special study options:** Combined bachelor's/graduate degree, cooperative education, cross-registration, distance learning, double major, dual enrollment of high school students, exchange student, honors, independent study, internships, liberal arts/career combination, study abroad, teacher certification program. Dual degree programs in engineering and dentistry with cooperating universities. **Credit/placement by examination:** AP, CLEP, institutional tests. 60 credit hours maximum toward bachelor's degree. **Support services:** Learning center, pre-admission summer program, reduced course load, remedial instruction, tutoring, writing center.

Majors. **Biology:** General. **Business:** Business admin. **Communications technology:** Radio/tv. **Computer sciences:** Computer science. **Education:** Elementary, kindergarten/preschool, science. **Family/consumer sciences:** Child development. **Health:** Nursing (RN). **History:** General. **Math:** General. **Psychology:** General. **Public administration:** Social work. **Social sciences:** Sociology. **Visual/performing arts:** Art, dramatic. **Other:** Technology.

Most popular majors. Business/marketing 18%, communication technologies 13%, computer/information sciences 7%, education 7%, health sciences 8%, psychology 11%, social sciences 23%.

Computing on campus. 150 workstations in dormitories, library, computer center. Dormitories wired for high-speed internet access and linked to campus network. Commuter students can connect to campus network. Online course registration, online library, helpline, repair service, wireless network available.

Student life. **Freshman orientation:** Mandatory, $75 fee. Preregistration for classes offered. One-day session in the 2nd or 3rd week of August. **Policies:** Zero tolerance policy for illegal substance use and violence. **Housing:** Coed dorms, single-sex dorms, apartments, wellness housing available. $150 fully refundable deposit. **Activities:** Bands, campus ministries, choral groups, dance, drama, international student organizations, music ensembles, musical theater, radio station, student government, student newspaper, TV station, NAACP, greater Washington urban league chapter, commuter senate.

Athletics. NCAA. **Intercollegiate:** Basketball, bowling W, cross-country, football (tackle) M, softball W, tennis W, track and field, volleyball W. **Intramural:** Basketball, football (non-tackle), golf, gymnastics, racquetball, soccer, softball, swimming, table tennis, tennis, volleyball, weight lifting. **Team name:** Bulldogs.

Student services. Adult student services, alcohol/substance abuse counseling, chaplain/spiritual director, career counseling, student employment services, financial aid counseling, health services, personal counseling, placement for graduates, veterans' counselor. **Physically disabled:** Services for visually, hearing impaired.

Contact. E-mail: dkiah@bowiestate.edu
Phone: (301) 860-3415 Fax: (301) 860-3438
Don Kiah, Assistant Vice President, Enrollment Management, Bowie State University, 14000 Jericho Park Road, Bowie, MD 20715

Capitol College

Laurel, Maryland
www.capitol-college.edu **CB code: 5101**

- Private 4-year business and engineering college
- Commuter campus in large town
- 360 degree-seeking undergraduates
- 80% of applicants admitted
- SAT or ACT (ACT writing optional), application essay required

General. Founded in 1964. Regionally accredited. **Degrees:** 51 bachelor's, 1 associate awarded; master's offered. **ROTC:** Army. **Location:** 19 miles from Washington, DC, 22 miles from Baltimore. **Calendar:** Semester, limited summer session. **Full-time faculty:** 20 total. **Part-time faculty:** 60 total. **Special facilities:** Video lab, interactive computer classrooms, two engineering labs, telecommunications lab.

Freshman class profile. 500 applied, 400 admitted, 85 enrolled.

Mid 50% test scores		**ACT composite:**	12-20
SAT critical reading:	380-510	**Live on campus:**	20%
SAT math:	430-540		

Basis for selection. Academic preparation, school record and test scores most important. Mathematics foundation necessary for successful completion of programs. Interview and essay recommended.

High school preparation. 20 units required. Required and recommended units include English 4, mathematics 3-4, social studies 2, history 2, science 1-3 (laboratory 1-2) and academic electives 2-3. Mathematic units include algebra I, geometry, algebra II/trigonometry. Calculus recommended for advanced standing.

2008-2009 Annual costs. Tuition/fees: $19,404. Room only: $4,514. Books/supplies: $800. Personal expenses: $1,900.

2008-2009 Financial aid. **Non-need-based:** Scholarships awarded for academics, alumni affiliation, leadership, minority status.

Application procedures. **Admission:** Priority date 5/1; no deadline. $25 fee, may be waived for applicants with need, free for online applicants. Admission notification on a rolling basis beginning on or about 3/1. Must reply by May 1 or within 3 week(s) if notified thereafter. **Financial aid:** Priority date 2/1; no closing date. FAFSA, institutional form required. Applicants notified on a rolling basis starting 6/3; must reply by 5/1 or within 3 week(s) of notification.

Academics. **Special study options:** Combined bachelor's/graduate degree, cooperative education, distance learning, double major, independent study, liberal arts/career combination, weekend college. **Credit/placement by examination:** AP, CLEP, institutional tests. **Support services:** Learning center, pre-admission summer program, reduced course load, remedial instruction, tutoring.

Majors. **Business:** Business admin. **Computer sciences:** Computer science. **Engineering:** Computer, electrical, software. **Engineering technology:** Aerospace, electrical, telecommunications. **Other:** Information assurance.

Most popular majors. Business/marketing 12%, computer/information sciences 29%, engineering/engineering technologies 59%.

Computing on campus. 60 workstations in library, computer center. Dormitories wired for high-speed internet access and linked to campus network. Helpline, wireless network available.

Student life. **Freshman orientation:** Mandatory. **Housing:** Coed dorms available. $200 deposit, deadline 5/1. **Activities:** Drama, literary magazine, radio station, student government, student newspaper, computer club, chess club, robotics club, music club, Society of Black Engineers, Society of Women Engineers.

Athletics. **Intramural:** Basketball M, boxing M, fencing M, golf M, soccer M, softball M, table tennis, tennis, track and field, volleyball, water polo.

Student services. Adult student services, career counseling, student employment services, personal counseling, placement for graduates, veterans' counselor.

Contact. E-mail: admissions@capitol-college.edu
Phone: (301) 369-2800 Toll-free number: (800) 950-1992
Fax: (301) 953-1442
Tony Miller, Director of Admissions, Capitol College, 11301 Springfield Road, Laurel, MD 20708

College of Notre Dame of Maryland

Baltimore, Maryland **CB member**
www.ndm.edu **CB code: 5114**

- Private 4-year liberal arts college for women affiliated with Roman Catholic Church
- Residential campus in very large city
- 1,338 degree-seeking undergraduates
- 71% of applicants admitted
- SAT or ACT (ACT writing recommended), application essay required

General. Founded in 1873. Regionally accredited. Men admitted only to undergraduate and graduate weekend college programs. **Degrees:** 437 bachelor's awarded; master's, doctoral, first professional offered. **ROTC:** Army. **Location:** 5 miles from Baltimore, 37 miles from Washington, DC. **Calendar:** Semester, limited summer session. **Full-time faculty:** 77 total. **Part-time faculty:** 10 total. **Class size:** 78% < 20, 22% 20-39. **Special facilities:** Planetarium, photography laboratories.

Freshman class profile. 387 applied, 276 admitted, 105 enrolled.

Mid 50% test scores		Rank in top tenth:	15%
SAT critical reading:	470-570	Out-of-state:	14%
SAT math:	440-550	Live on campus:	66%
Rank in top quarter:	46%		

Basis for selection. Careful evaluation of academic record, high school curriculum, test scores, recommendations, personal abilities/talents and goals, intellectual potential and eagerness to learn and be challenged. Students should take SAT by January of senior year. Interview and campus visit highly recommended; visits required for scholarship consideration. Audition recommended for music majors. Portfolio recommended for art, writing majors. **Homeschooled:** Transcript or GED required. **Learning Disabled:** Students with learning disabilities should self-report during admissions process.

High school preparation. College-preparatory program required. 18 units required. Required units include English 4, mathematics 3, social studies 2, science 2 (laboratory 2), foreign language 3 and academic electives 4.

2008-2009 Annual costs. Tuition/fees: $25,750. Room/board: $8,900. Books/supplies: $800. Personal expenses: $800.

2008-2009 Financial aid. Non-need-based: Scholarships awarded for academics, alumni affiliation, art, leadership, music/drama, ROTC. **Additional information:** Maximum consideration for financial aid if application received by February 15. Auditions and portfolios in areas of art, music and writing considered for scholarships.

Application procedures. Admission: Priority date 2/15; no deadline. $45 fee, may be waived for applicants with need. Admission notification on a rolling basis beginning on or about 10/1. Must reply by May 1 or within 2 week(s) if notified thereafter. **Financial aid:** Priority date 2/15; no closing date. FAFSA required. Applicants notified on a rolling basis starting 3/15; must reply by 5/1 or within 2 week(s) of notification.

Academics. Special study options: Accelerated study, combined bachelor's/graduate degree, cross-registration, double major, dual enrollment of high school students, ESL, honors, independent study, internships, liberal arts/career combination, student-designed major, study abroad, teacher certification program, weekend college. 3-2 programs in engineering and nursing with Johns Hopkins University; academic consortium with seven local colleges and universities. **Credit/placement by examination:** AP, CLEP, IB, institutional tests. 30 credit hours maximum toward bachelor's degree. AP, CLEP and IB credits are posted upon admissions to college. Students should send testing information with their admissions application or prior to start of their first semester. **Support services:** Learning center, reduced course load, study skills assistance, tutoring, writing center.

Majors. Biology: General. **Business:** General, finance, international, nonprofit/public. **Communications:** General. **Computer sciences:** General, computer science. **Education:** Early childhood, elementary, secondary, special. **Engineering:** General. **Foreign languages:** General, classics, French, Spanish. **Health:** Medical radiologic technology/radiation therapy. **History:** General. **Interdisciplinary:** Biopsychology. **Legal studies:** Prelaw. **Liberal arts:** Arts/sciences. **Math:** General. **Philosophy/religion:** Philosophy, religion. **Physical sciences:** Chemistry, physics. **Psychology:** General. **Public administration:** Community org/advocacy. **Social sciences:** Criminology, economics, international relations, political science. **Visual/performing arts:** Art, art history/conservation, photography, studio arts.

Most popular majors. Biology 7%, business/marketing 21%, communications/journalism 8%, education 14%, health sciences 7%, interdisciplinary studies 6%, liberal arts 11%.

Computing on campus. 80 workstations in dormitories, library, computer center, student center. Dormitories wired for high-speed internet access and linked to campus network. Commuter students can connect to campus network. Online course registration, online library, helpline, repair service, wireless network available.

Student life. Freshman orientation: Mandatory. Preregistration for classes offered. 2-day program in June; 4-day program prior to start of school in late August/early September. **Policies:** Must abide by honor code. **Housing:** Guaranteed on-campus for all undergraduates. Wellness housing available. $200 nonrefundable deposit, deadline 5/1. **Activities:** Campus ministries, choral groups, dance, drama, film society, international student organizations, literary magazine, music ensembles, musical theater, radio station, student government, student newspaper, TV station, community service organization, Hispanic society, black student organization, inter-organizational council.

Athletics. NCAA. **Intercollegiate:** Basketball W, field hockey W, lacrosse W, soccer W, softball W, swimming W, tennis W, volleyball W. **Intramural:** Basketball W, cross-country W, lacrosse W, soccer W, softball W. **Team name:** Gators.

Student services. Adult student services, alcohol/substance abuse counseling, chaplain/spiritual director, career counseling, student employment services, financial aid counseling, health services, personal counseling, placement for graduates, veterans' counselor.

Contact. E-mail: admiss@ndm.edu
Phone: (410) 532-5330 Toll-free number: (800) 435-0200
Fax: (410) 532-6287
Director of Admissions, College of Notre Dame of Maryland, 4701 North Charles Street, Baltimore, MD 21210

Columbia Union College

Takoma Park, Maryland
www.cuc.edu **CB code: 5890**

- Private 4-year liberal arts college affiliated with Seventh-day Adventists
- Residential campus in large town
- 859 degree-seeking undergraduates
- 53 graduate students
- SAT or ACT with writing required

General. Founded in 1904. Regionally accredited. **Degrees:** 176 bachelor's, 8 associate awarded; master's offered. **Location:** 1 mile from Washington, DC. **Calendar:** Semester, limited summer session. **Full-time faculty:** 51 total. **Part-time faculty:** 2 total.

Basis for selection. High school GPA of 2.5, school achievement record, test scores very important; recommendations considered. Audition required of music majors. **Homeschooled:** Transcript of courses and grades required. Recognized high school diploma or GED required. **Learning Disabled:** Students must provide written documentation of disabilities and submit written request for all needed services for review by the Disabilities Coordinator three months before registration. All forms may be obtained from Center for Learning Resources.

High school preparation. 16 units required. Required units include English 4, mathematics 2, history 2, science 2 (laboratory 2) and academic electives 4. One unit of computer science also recommended.

2009-2010 Annual costs. Tuition/fees (projected): $19,430. Room/board: $6,887.

2007-2008 Financial aid. Non-need-based: Scholarships awarded for academics, athletics, leadership, music/drama, state residency.

Application procedures. Admission: Closing date 8/1 (postmark date). $25 fee, may be waived for applicants with need, free for online applicants. Admission notification on a rolling basis. Must reply by 8/15. **Financial aid:** Closing date 3/31. FAFSA required. Applicants notified on a rolling basis starting 5/31; must reply within 4 week(s) of notification.

Academics. Special study options: Accelerated study, combined bachelor's/graduate degree, cooperative education, cross-registration, distance learning, double major, ESL, external degree, honors, independent study, internships, liberal arts/career combination, student-designed major, study abroad, teacher certification program, Washington semester. Adult evening program. **Credit/placement by examination:** AP, CLEP, SAT, ACT, institutional tests. 12 credit hours maximum toward associate degree, 24 toward bachelor's. CLEP business exams not accepted for traditional business majors. **Support services:** Learning center, reduced course load, remedial instruction, study skills assistance, tutoring, writing center.

Majors. Biology: General, biochemistry. **Business:** Accounting, business admin, marketing, organizational behavior. **Communications:** General, broadcast journalism, journalism. **Computer sciences:** General, computer science, information systems. **Education:** General, elementary, English, mathematics, music, physical, science, secondary. **Health:** Health care admin, nursing (RN), predental, premedicine, prepharmacy, preveterinary. **History:** General. **Legal studies:** Prelaw. **Liberal arts:** Arts/sciences. **Math:** General. **Parks/recreation:** Health/fitness, sports admin. **Philosophy/religion:** Religion. **Physical sciences:** Chemistry. **Psychology:** General, counseling. **Social sciences:** Political science. **Theology:** Religious ed, theology. **Visual/performing arts:** Music performance. **Other:** Health/fitness management, Philosophy and religion.

Computing on campus. Dormitories wired for high-speed internet access and linked to campus network. Commuter students can connect to campus network. Online library, wireless network available.

Student life. Freshman orientation: Mandatory, $150 fee. Preregistration for classes offered. **Policies:** Attendance required at weekly chapel service. Resident students required to attend dormitory worships. Religious observance required. **Housing:** Guaranteed on-campus for freshmen. Single-sex dorms, apartments, wellness housing available. $200 fully refundable deposit, deadline 8/15. **Activities:** Bands, campus ministries, choral groups, international student organizations, literary magazine, music ensembles, musical theater, opera, radio station, student government, student newspaper, symphony orchestra, Humanitas, Loaves and Fishes, Shepherd's Hands (puppet ministry), Teach-a-Kid, Youth-to-Youth (drug prevention), student mission club.

Athletics. NCAA. **Intercollegiate:** Baseball M, basketball, cross-country, soccer, softball W, track and field. **Intramural:** Basketball M, soccer M, volleyball. **Team name:** Pioneers.

Student services. Adult student services, chaplain/spiritual director, career counseling, student employment services, financial aid counseling, health services, personal counseling, placement for graduates, veterans' counselor.

Contact. E-mail: admissions@cuc.edu
Phone: (301) 891-4080 Toll-free number: (800) 835-4212
Fax: (301) 891-4230
Elaine Oliver, Vice President of Enrollment Management, Columbia Union College, 7600 Flower Avenue, Takoma Park, MD 20912

Coppin State University

Baltimore, Maryland — **CB member**
www.coppin.edu — **CB code: 5122**

- Public 4-year liberal arts college
- Commuter campus in very large city
- 3,201 degree-seeking undergraduates: 21% part-time, 78% women, 87% African American, 4% international
- 331 degree-seeking graduate students
- 43% of applicants admitted
- SAT or ACT (ACT writing optional) required

General. Founded in 1900. Regionally accredited. Manages Rosemont Elementary School; educational corridor between Coppin and selected elementary, middle, and high schools; mentorship program with elementary students. **Degrees:** 293 bachelor's awarded; master's offered. **ROTC:** Army. **Location:** 50 miles from Washington, DC. **Calendar:** Semester, extensive summer session. **Full-time faculty:** 162 total; 59% have terminal degrees, 56% women. **Part-time faculty:** 139 total; 20% have terminal degrees, 56% women.

Freshman class profile. 5,138 applied, 2,197 admitted, 675 enrolled.

Mid 50% test scores		Return as sophomores:	58%
SAT critical reading:	400-470	Out-of-state:	16%
SAT math:	380-460	International:	2%

Basis for selection. Minimum GPA of 2.5 and predictive index based on test scores and school achievement record. Essay recommended. Interview recommended for nursing majors. Portfolio recommended for art majors. **Homeschooled:** Location must be certified by Maryland Department of Education.

High school preparation. 16 units required. Required units include English 4, mathematics 3, social studies 3, science 2 (laboratory 2) and foreign language 2. 2 years of advanced tech program courses can be substituted for foreign language requirement.

2008-2009 Annual costs. Tuition/fees: $5,140; $13,365 out-of-state. Room/board: $7,139. Books/supplies: $700. Personal expenses: $3,085.

2008-2009 Financial aid. Non-need-based: Scholarships awarded for academics, alumni affiliation, athletics, ROTC, state residency. **Additional information:** Funds allocated by State of Maryland for minority students enrolled for at least 6 credits who are Maryland residents and U.S. citizens (Other Race Grant).

Application procedures. Admission: Closing date 7/15. $35 fee, may be waived for applicants with need. Admission notification on a rolling basis beginning on or about 3/15. **Financial aid:** Priority date 3/1; no closing date. FAFSA required. Applicants notified on a rolling basis starting 4/15; must reply within 2 week(s) of notification.

Academics. Special study options: Accelerated study, combined bachelor's/graduate degree, cooperative education, distance learning, double major, dual enrollment of high school students, external degree, honors, independent study, internships, liberal arts/career combination, study abroad, teacher certification program, weekend college. 3-2 programs in engineering, pharmacy, dentistry, physical therapy. **Credit/placement by examination:** AP, CLEP, IB, SAT, institutional tests. 30 credit hours maximum toward bachelor's degree. **Support services:** Learning center, pre-admission summer program, remedial instruction, study skills assistance, tutoring, writing center.

Majors. Biology: General. **Business:** Management science. **Computer sciences:** Computer science. **Education:** Biology, chemistry, early childhood, elementary, mathematics, secondary, special. **Health:** Medical records admin, nursing (RN). **History:** General. **Liberal arts:** Arts/sciences. **Math:** General. **Parks/recreation:** Sports admin. **Physical sciences:** Chemistry. **Protective services:** Criminal justice. **Psychology:** General. **Public administration:** Social work. **Social sciences:** General, political science, sociology. **Visual/performing arts:** Art. **Other:** Rehabilitation and Therapeutic Professions.

Computing on campus. 371 workstations in dormitories, library, computer center, student center. Dormitories wired for high-speed internet access and linked to campus network. Commuter students can connect to campus network. Online course registration, online library, helpline, repair service, student web hosting, wireless network available.

Student life. Freshman orientation: Mandatory. Preregistration for classes offered. **Housing:** Coed dorms, special housing for disabled, wellness housing available. $150 deposit. **Activities:** Campus ministries, choral groups, dance, drama, film society, international student organizations, music ensembles, radio station, student government, student newspaper, TV station, criminal justice club, gospel choir, history club, psychology club, Thurgood Marshall Club, social work association.

Athletics. NCAA. **Intercollegiate:** Baseball M, basketball, bowling W, cheerleading M, cross-country, golf W, softball W, tennis, track and field, volleyball W. **Intramural:** Basketball, football (non-tackle), softball, tennis, volleyball. **Team name:** Eagles.

Student services. Adult student services, alcohol/substance abuse counseling, career counseling, services for economically disadvantaged, student employment services, financial aid counseling, health services, minority student services, personal counseling, placement for graduates, veterans' counselor, women's services. **Physically disabled:** Services for visually, hearing impaired.

Contact. E-mail: admissions@coppin.edu
Phone: (410) 951-3600 Toll-free number: (800) 635-3674
Fax: (410) 523-7351
Michelle Gross, Director of Admissions, Coppin State University, 2500 West North Avenue, Baltimore, MD 21216

DeVry University: Bethesda

Bethesda, Maryland
www.devry.edu

- For-profit 4-year university
- Commuter campus in small city
- 44 degree-seeking undergraduates: 64% part-time, 45% women, 45% African American, 2% Asian American, 30% Hispanic American
- 51 degree-seeking graduate students

General. Degrees: 3 bachelor's awarded; master's offered. **Calendar:** Semester. **Full-time faculty:** 1 total. **Part-time faculty:** 15 total; 53% minority, 20% women.

Basis for selection. Interview important.

2008-2009 Annual costs. Tuition/fees: $14,600. Books/supplies: $1,300. Personal expenses: $5,082.

2007-2008 Financial aid. Non-need-based: Scholarships awarded for academics.

Application procedures. Admission: No deadline. $50 fee. Admission notification on a rolling basis. **Financial aid:** No deadline. FAFSA required. Applicants notified on a rolling basis.

Academics. Special study options: Accelerated study, distance learning. **Credit/placement by examination:** CLEP.

Majors. Business: Business admin. **Computer sciences:** General. **Other:** Technical management.

Contact. Phone: (301) 652-8477 Fax: (301) 652-8577
DeVry University: Bethesda, 4550 Montgomery Avenue, Suite 100 N, Bethesda, MD 20814

Four-Year Colleges

Frostburg State University

Frostburg, Maryland **CB member**
www.frostburg.edu **CB code: 5402**

- Public 4-year university and teachers college
- Residential campus in small town
- 4,470 degree-seeking undergraduates: 5% part-time, 49% women, 22% African American, 2% Asian American, 2% Hispanic American
- 585 degree-seeking graduate students
- 60% of applicants admitted
- SAT or ACT (ACT writing optional) required
- 48% graduate within 6 years

General. Founded in 1898. Regionally accredited. Center in Hagerstown offers upper-division undergraduate and graduate courses. **Degrees:** 790 bachelor's awarded; master's offered. **Location:** 150 miles from Baltimore. **Calendar:** Semester, limited summer session. **Full-time faculty:** 233 total; 85% have terminal degrees, 12% minority, 37% women. **Part-time faculty:** 111 total; 15% have terminal degrees, 4% minority, 52% women. **Class size:** 54% < 20, 41% 20-39, 2% 40-49, 3% 50-99. **Special facilities:** Planetarium, arboretum, electron microscope, exploratorium.

Freshman class profile. 4,497 applied, 2,687 admitted, 1,031 enrolled.

Mid 50% test scores		**GPA 3.50-3.74:**	11%
SAT critical reading:	430-530	**GPA 3.0-3.49:**	33%
SAT math:	430-540	**GPA 2.0-2.99:**	45%
SAT writing:	430-520	**Out-of-state:**	7%
ACT composite:	17-20	**Live on campus:**	78%
GPA 3.75 or higher:	11%		

Basis for selection. High school record and SAT scores most important. Interview recommended. Audition required of music majors. Portfolio required of art majors.

High school preparation. 15 units required. Required units include English 4, mathematics 3, social studies 3, science 3 (laboratory 2) and foreign language 2.

2008-2009 Annual costs. Tuition/fees: $6,614; $16,810 out-of-state. Room/board: $7,016. Books/supplies: $750. Personal expenses: $900.

2008-2009 Financial aid. Need-based: Average need met was 71%. Average scholarship/grant was $5,585; average loan $3,055. 54% of total undergraduate aid awarded as scholarships/grants, 46% as loans/jobs. **Non-need-based:** Scholarships awarded for academics, leadership, minority status.

Application procedures. Admission: No deadline. $30 fee, may be waived for applicants with need. Admission notification on a rolling basis beginning on or about 11/1. Must reply by May 1 or within 4 week(s) if notified thereafter. **Financial aid:** Priority date 3/1; no closing date. FAFSA required. Applicants notified on a rolling basis starting 3/15; must reply within 3 week(s) of notification.

Academics. Special study options: Combined bachelor's/graduate degree, distance learning, double major, dual enrollment of high school students, honors, independent study, internships, study abroad, teacher certification program. International student exchange program, dual degree program, combined bachelor's program. **Credit/placement by examination:** AP, CLEP, IB, institutional tests. 30 credit hours maximum toward bachelor's degree. **Support services:** Learning center, reduced course load, remedial instruction, tutoring, writing center.

Majors. Architecture: Urban/community planning. **Biology:** General. **Business:** Accounting, business admin. **Communications:** General. **Computer sciences:** General. **Conservation:** General, environmental studies, fisheries, wildlife. **Education:** Early childhood, elementary, English, mathematics, music, physical, social science. **Foreign languages:** General. **Health:** Predental, premedicine, prenursing, prepharmacy, preveterinary. **History:** General. **Liberal arts:** Arts/sciences. **Math:** General. **Parks/recreation:** General, exercise sciences, health/fitness, sports admin. **Philosophy/religion:** Philosophy. **Physical sciences:** Chemistry, physics. **Protective services:** Law enforcement admin, police science. **Psychology:** General. **Public administration:** Social work. **Social sciences:** General, economics, geography, international relations, political science, sociology. **Visual/performing arts:** General, commercial/advertising art, dramatic, studio arts. **Other:** Ethnobotany.

Most popular majors. Business/marketing 17%, education 12%, liberal arts 7%, parks/recreation 7%, psychology 8%, social sciences 11%, visual/performing arts 6%.

Computing on campus. 668 workstations in dormitories, library, computer center, student center. Dormitories wired for high-speed internet access and linked to campus network. Commuter students can connect to campus network. Online course registration, online library, helpline, wireless network available.

Student life. Freshman orientation: Mandatory. **Housing:** Coed dorms, single-sex dorms, special housing for disabled, wellness housing available. $100 deposit. **Activities:** Bands, campus ministries, choral groups, dance, drama, literary magazine, music ensembles, Model UN, radio station, student government, student newspaper, TV station, social, religious, political, and ethnic organizations.

Athletics. NCAA. **Intercollegiate:** Baseball M, basketball, cross-country, diving, field hockey W, football (tackle) M, golf, lacrosse W, soccer, softball W, swimming, tennis, track and field, volleyball W. **Intramural:** Basketball, field hockey, football (tackle), golf, lacrosse, racquetball, rugby M, soccer, softball, table tennis, tennis, volleyball, weight lifting, wrestling M. **Team name:** Bobcats.

Student services. Chaplain/spiritual director, career counseling, student employment services, health services, minority student services, on-campus daycare, personal counseling, placement for graduates, veterans' counselor. **Physically disabled:** Services for visually, speech, hearing impaired.

Contact. E-mail: fsuadmissions@frostburg.edu
Phone: (301) 687-4201 Fax: (301) 687-7074
Trish Gregory, Director of Admissions, Frostburg State University, 101 Braddock Road, Frostburg, MD 21532-1099

Goucher College

Baltimore, Maryland **CB member**
www.goucher.edu **CB code: 5257**

- Private 4-year liberal arts college
- Residential campus in small city
- 1,434 degree-seeking undergraduates: 1% part-time, 68% women, 6% African American, 3% Asian American, 4% Hispanic American, 1% international
- 525 degree-seeking graduate students
- 64% of applicants admitted
- Application essay required
- 64% graduate within 6 years; 31% enter graduate study

General. Founded in 1885. Regionally accredited. Students are required to study abroad and are given a voucher of at least $1,200 to help offset travel expenses. **Degrees:** 318 bachelor's awarded; master's offered. **ROTC:** Army. **Location:** 8 miles from Baltimore. **Calendar:** Semester. **Full-time faculty:** 130 total; 89% have terminal degrees, 15% minority, 62% women. **Part-time faculty:** 79 total; 46% have terminal degrees, 10% minority, 60% women. **Class size:** 74% < 20, 23% 20-39, 1% 40-49, less than 1% 50-99, less than 1% >100.

Freshman class profile. 4,077 applied, 2,591 admitted, 360 enrolled.

Mid 50% test scores		**GPA 2.0-2.99:**	38%
SAT critical reading:	530-660	**End year in good standing:**	88%
SAT math:	490-620	**Return as sophomores:**	83%
SAT writing:	530-650	**Out-of-state:**	76%
GPA 3.75 or higher:	12%	**Live on campus:**	96%
GPA 3.50-3.74:	12%	**International:**	2%
GPA 3.0-3.49:	37%		

Basis for selection. Record in traditional college-preparatory program, secondary school record, and recommendations most important. Interview recommended. **Homeschooled:** Statement describing homeschool structure and mission, transcript of courses and grades, state high school equivalency certificate, letter of recommendation (nonparent) required.

High school preparation. College-preparatory program required. 16 units required; 20 recommended. Required and recommended units include English 4-4, mathematics 3-4, social studies 3-3, science 2-3, foreign language 2-4 and academic electives 2-2.

2009-2010 Annual costs. Tuition/fees (projected): $33,786. Room/board: $10,008. Books/supplies: $800. Personal expenses: $800.

2008-2009 Financial aid. Need-based: 242 full-time freshmen applied for aid; 192 were judged to have need; 190 of these received aid. Average need met was 81%. Average scholarship/grant was $22,609; average loan $3,394. 80% of total undergraduate aid awarded as scholarships/grants, 20% as loans/jobs. **Non-need-based:** Awarded to 388 full-time undergraduates,

including 83 freshmen. Scholarships awarded for academics, art, leadership, music/drama.

Application procedures. Admission: Closing date 2/1 (postmark date). $55 fee, may be waived for applicants with need. Admission notification 4/1. Must reply by 5/1. **Financial aid:** Closing date 2/1. FAFSA, CSS PROFILE required. Applicants notified on a rolling basis starting 4/1; must reply by 5/1 or within 2 week(s) of notification.

Academics. Special study options: Combined bachelor's/graduate degree, cross-registration, distance learning, double major, dual enrollment of high school students, independent study, internships, student-designed major, study abroad, teacher certification program, Washington semester. Community service, service learning. **Credit/placement by examination:** AP, CLEP, IB, SAT, ACT, institutional tests. 30 credit hours maximum toward bachelor's degree. **Support services:** Learning center, reduced course load, study skills assistance, tutoring, writing center.

Majors. Area/ethnic studies: American, women's. **Biology:** General. **Business:** Business admin. **Communications:** Media studies. **Computer sciences:** Computer science. **Education:** Elementary, special. **Foreign languages:** French, Russian, Spanish. **History:** General. **Interdisciplinary:** Peace/conflict. **Math:** General. **Philosophy/religion:** Philosophy, religion. **Physical sciences:** Chemistry, physics. **Psychology:** General. **Social sciences:** Economics, international relations, political science, sociology. **Visual/performing arts:** Art, dance, dramatic, studio arts. **Other:** Multi-interdisciplinary studies.

Most popular majors. Business/marketing 7%, communications/journalism 12%, English 11%, psychology 13%, social sciences 15%, visual/performing arts 13%.

Computing on campus. 150 workstations in library, computer center, student center. Dormitories wired for high-speed internet access and linked to campus network. Commuter students can connect to campus network. Online course registration, online library, helpline, repair service, student web hosting, wireless network available.

Student life. Freshman orientation: Mandatory. Preregistration for classes offered. **Housing:** Guaranteed on-campus for freshmen. Coed dorms, single-sex dorms, special housing for disabled, apartments, wellness housing available. $100 fully refundable deposit, deadline 5/1. **Activities:** Jazz band, campus ministries, choral groups, dance, drama, film society, international student organizations, literary magazine, music ensembles, Model UN, musical theater, opera, radio station, student government, student newspaper, symphony orchestra, TV station, African alliance, community action program, Prism, Hillel, Christian fellowship, Amnesty International, environmental organization, Jubilate Deo, Concern for International Children.

Athletics. NCAA. **Intercollegiate:** Basketball, cross-country, equestrian, field hockey W, lacrosse, soccer, swimming, tennis, track and field, volleyball W. **Intramural:** Football (tackle), racquetball, soccer, softball, tennis, volleyball, water polo, weight lifting. **Team name:** Gophers.

Student services. Adult student services, alcohol/substance abuse counseling, chaplain/spiritual director, career counseling, services for economically disadvantaged, student employment services, financial aid counseling, health services, minority student services, personal counseling, placement for graduates, veterans' counselor, women's services. **Physically disabled:** Services for visually, hearing impaired.

Contact. E-mail: admissions@goucher.edu
Phone: (410) 337-6100 Toll-free number: (800) 468-2437
Fax: (410) 337-6354
Carlton Surbeck, Director of Admissions, Goucher College, 1021 Dulaney Valley Road, Baltimore, MD 21204-2753

Griggs University
Silver Spring, Maryland
www.griggs.edu

- Private 4-year virtual Bible college affiliated with Seventh-day Adventists
- Small city
- 750 degree-seeking undergraduates
- Application essay required

General. Accredited by DETC. **Degrees:** 25 bachelor's, 13 associate awarded; master's offered. **Location:** 30 miles from Washington, DC. **Calendar:** Semester. **Part-time faculty:** 60 total.

Basis for selection. Minimum secondary school grade average of 2.00 required. SAT or ACT recommended. **Homeschooled:** Statement describing homeschool structure and mission required.

High school preparation. 21 units required; 24 recommended. Required and recommended units include English 4, mathematics 3-4, social studies 1-2, history 2, science 3-4 (laboratory 2-3), foreign language 2, computer science 1, visual/performing arts 1 and academic electives 2-3.

2008-2009 Annual costs. Tuition/fees: $8,990.

Application procedures. Admission: No deadline. $50 fee, may be waived for applicants with need. Admission notification on a rolling basis. **Financial aid:** No deadline. Institutional form required.

Academics. Special study options: Cross-registration, distance learning, dual enrollment of high school students, independent study, student-designed major, study abroad. **Credit/placement by examination:** AP, CLEP, IB, SAT, ACT, institutional tests. 12 credit hours maximum toward associate degree, 24 toward bachelor's. **Support services:** Reduced course load, remedial instruction, tutoring.

Majors. Business: Business admin. **Philosophy/religion:** Religion. **Theology:** Bible, religious ed.

Computing on campus. PC or laptop required.

Contact. Phone: (301) 680-6570
Marietta Fowler, Registrar Assistant, Griggs University, 12501 Old Columbia Pike, Silver Spring, MD 20904-6600

Hood College
Frederick, Maryland — **CB member**
www.hood.edu — **CB code: 5296**

- Private 4-year liberal arts college
- Residential campus in small city
- 1,385 degree-seeking undergraduates: 9% part-time, 69% women, 10% African American, 3% Asian American, 3% Hispanic American, 2% international
- 928 degree-seeking graduate students
- 78% of applicants admitted
- SAT or ACT (ACT writing optional) required
- 65% graduate within 6 years; 50% enter graduate study

General. Founded in 1893. Regionally accredited. **Degrees:** 345 bachelor's awarded; master's offered. **ROTC:** Army. **Location:** 52 miles from Baltimore, 52 miles from Washington, DC. **Calendar:** Semester, limited summer session. **Full-time faculty:** 80 total; 90% have terminal degrees, 9% minority, 56% women. **Part-time faculty:** 179 total; 42% have terminal degrees, 4% minority, 55% women. **Class size:** 65% < 20, 34% 20-39, less than 1% 50-99. **Special facilities:** Psychology and preschool laboratories, observatory.

Freshman class profile. 1,570 applied, 1,227 admitted, 308 enrolled.

Mid 50% test scores		**GPA 2.0-2.99:**	20%
SAT critical reading:	470-600	**Rank in top quarter:**	53%
SAT math:	480-580	**Rank in top tenth:**	22%
SAT writing:	480-590	**End year in good standing:**	86%
ACT composite:	18-25	**Return as sophomores:**	79%
GPA 3.75 or higher:	37%	**Out-of-state:**	27%
GPA 3.50-3.74:	12%	**Live on campus:**	83%
GPA 3.0-3.49:	31%	**International:**	4%

Basis for selection. High school record, class rank, test scores important. Recommendations, contributions to school, family and community, essay considered. Interview recommended; essay required of some. **Homeschooled:** Must interview and present bibliography of all reading materials used; two recommendations; partial portfolio of work.

High school preparation. College-preparatory program required. 16 units required. Required units include English 4, mathematics 3, social studies 1, history 2, science 3 (laboratory 2), foreign language 2 and academic electives 1.

2008-2009 Annual costs. Tuition/fees: $26,580. Room/board: $8,980. Books/supplies: $800. Personal expenses: $700.

2008-2009 Financial aid. Need-based: 278 full-time freshmen applied for aid; 230 were judged to have need; 228 of these received aid. Average need met was 83%. Average scholarship/grant was $18,092; average loan $3,703. 77% of total undergraduate aid awarded as scholarships/grants, 23% as loans/jobs. **Non-need-based:** Awarded to 463 full-time undergraduates, including 121 freshmen. Scholarships awarded for academics, alumni affiliation, music/drama, ROTC.

Application procedures. Admission: Priority date 2/15; no deadline. $35 fee, may be waived for applicants with need, free for online applicants. Admission notification on a rolling basis beginning on or about 10/1. Must reply by May 1 or within 2 week(s) if notified thereafter. Early Action closing dates of 10/1, 11/1 and 12/1. Applications received after February 1 considered on a space available basis. **Financial aid:** Priority date 2/15; no closing date. FAFSA required. Applicants notified on a rolling basis starting 3/1; must reply by 5/1 or within 3 week(s) of notification.

Academics. Students in all fields may earn academic credits for internships. Opportunities available for students to earn degree in 3 years, 2 degrees in 4 years, or bachelor's and master's in 5 years. **Special study options:** Accelerated study, combined bachelor's/graduate degree, double major, dual enrollment of high school students, honors, independent study, internships, liberal arts/career combination, student-designed major, study abroad, teacher certification program, Washington semester. **Credit/placement by examination:** AP, CLEP, IB, SAT, institutional tests. 30 credit hours maximum toward bachelor's degree. **Support services:** Learning center, reduced course load, remedial instruction, study skills assistance, tutoring.

Majors. Area/ethnic studies: Latin American. **Biology:** General, biochemistry. **Business:** Business admin. **Communications:** General. **Computer sciences:** Computer science. **Conservation:** Environmental science. **Education:** Early childhood, special. **Foreign languages:** French, German, Spanish. **History:** General. **Legal studies:** General. **Math:** General. **Philosophy/religion:** Philosophy, religion. **Physical sciences:** Chemistry. **Psychology:** General. **Public administration:** Social work. **Social sciences:** Economics, political science, sociology. **Visual/performing arts:** Art. **Other:** Art and archaeology, French/German.

Most popular majors. Biology 10%, business/marketing 11%, education 14%, English 6%, history 6%, psychology 12%, social sciences 7%.

Computing on campus. 252 workstations in dormitories, library, computer center, student center. Dormitories wired for high-speed internet access and linked to campus network. Commuter students can connect to campus network. Online course registration, online library, helpline, wireless network available.

Student life. Freshman orientation: Mandatory. Preregistration for classes offered. Choice of 3 programs held on weekends in June for preregistration with the final program 4 days prior to start of classes. **Policies:** Students responsible for governing themselves through honor code. **Housing:** Guaranteed on-campus for all undergraduates. Coed dorms, single-sex dorms available. $300 nonrefundable deposit, deadline 5/1. **Activities:** Jazz band, campus ministries, choral groups, dance, drama, film society, international student organizations, literary magazine, music ensembles, Model UN, musical theater, radio station, student government, student newspaper, Black student union, Circle K, La Union Latina, Best Buddies, intervarsity christian fellowship, College Democrats, Jewish student union, College Republicans, For Goodness Sake.

Athletics. NCAA. **Intercollegiate:** Basketball, cross-country, field hockey W, golf, lacrosse, soccer, softball W, swimming, tennis, track and field, volleyball W. **Intramural:** Basketball, football (tackle) M, soccer, table tennis, volleyball W. **Team name:** Blazers.

Student services. Adult student services, alcohol/substance abuse counseling, chaplain/spiritual director, career counseling, student employment services, financial aid counseling, health services, minority student services, personal counseling, placement for graduates, veterans' counselor, women's services. **Physically disabled:** Services for speech, hearing impaired.

Contact. E-mail: admissions@hood.edu
Phone: (301) 696-3400 Toll-free number: (800) 922-1599
Fax: (301) 696-3819
David Adams, Director of Admissions, Hood College, 401 Rosemont Avenue, Frederick, MD 21701-8575

ITT Technical Institute: Owings Mill

Owings Mills, Maryland

- For-profit 4-year business and technical college
- Large town

General. Accredited by ACICS. **Calendar:** Quarter.

Contact. 11301 Red Run Boulevard, Owings Mills, MD 21117

Johns Hopkins University

Baltimore, Maryland CB member
www.jhu.edu CB code: 5332

- Private 4-year university
- Residential campus in very large city
- 4,725 degree-seeking undergraduates: 48% women, 7% African American, 24% Asian American, 7% Hispanic American, 1% Native American, 6% international
- 1,648 degree-seeking graduate students
- 25% of applicants admitted
- SAT or ACT with writing, application essay required
- 91% graduate within 6 years; 43% enter graduate study

General. Founded in 1876. Regionally accredited. Centers in Bologna and Florence, Italy, and Nanjing, China. **Degrees:** 1,548 bachelor's awarded; master's, doctoral, first professional offered. **ROTC:** Army, Air Force. **Location:** 4 miles from downtown. **Calendar:** 4-1-4, limited summer session. **Full-time faculty:** 451 total; 94% have terminal degrees, 12% minority, 25% women. **Part-time faculty:** 74 total; 8% minority, 31% women. **Class size:** 65% < 20, 20% 20-39, 4% 40-49, 6% 50-99, 5% >100. **Special facilities:** Space telescope science institute.

Freshman class profile. 16,011 applied, 4,062 admitted, 1,236 enrolled.

Mid 50% test scores			
SAT critical reading:	630-740	**Rank in top quarter:**	98%
SAT math:	660-770	**Rank in top tenth:**	84%
SAT writing:	640-740	**End year in good standing:**	98%
ACT composite:	29-33	**Return as sophomores:**	98%
GPA 3.75 or higher:	53%	**Out-of-state:**	87%
GPA 3.50-3.74:	27%	**Live on campus:**	99%
GPA 3.0-3.49:	18%	**International:**	8%
GPA 2.0-2.99:	2%	**Fraternities:**	26%
		Sororities:	27%

Basis for selection. School achievement record most important, with emphasis on course grades related to applicant's major field of academic interest. Test scores important. Intellectual interests and accomplishments, recommendations, personal character, extracurricular activities also significant. Students wishing to enroll in the biomedical engineering major (BME) must indicate BME as their first-choice major. Students are admitted specifically into the BME major based on evaluation of credentials and space availability. SAT Subject Tests recommended. Early Decision applicants should have test scores in by November 1. Recommend 3 SAT Subject Tests. SAT Math Level 2 recommended for students applying to school of engineering. Interview recommended. Audition required of applicants to dual-degree program with Peabody Institute. **Homeschooled:** Statement describing homeschool structure and mission, transcript of courses and grades, letter of recommendation (nonparent) required. Secondary school report must include summary of program, complete transcript with course descriptions, bibliography of textbooks, description of evaluation methods, and actual grades or evaluations.

High school preparation. College-preparatory program recommended. Recommended units include English 4, mathematics 4, social studies 2, history 2, science 4 and foreign language 4. 4 combined units recommended for social studies and history.

2008-2009 Annual costs. Tuition/fees: $38,200. Room/board: $11,578. Books/supplies: $1,000. Personal expenses: $1,000.

2008-2009 Financial aid. Non-need-based: Scholarships awarded for academics, athletics, leadership, ROTC, state residency. **Additional information:** Selected students receive aid packages without loan expectation, grants to full need. Private merit aid does not reduce Hopkins grant.

Application procedures. Admission: Closing date 1/1 (postmark date). $70 fee, may be waived for applicants with need. Admission notification 4/1. Must reply by May 1 or within 2 week(s) if notified thereafter. **Financial aid:** Closing date 3/1. FAFSA, CSS PROFILE required. Applicants notified by 4/1; must reply by 5/1 or within 2 week(s) of notification.

Academics. Special study options: Combined bachelor's/graduate degree, cross-registration, double major, dual enrollment of high school students, independent study, internships, student-designed major, study abroad, Washington semester. Combined bachelor's/master's programs. **Credit/placement by examination:** AP, CLEP, IB, institutional tests. **Support services:** Pre-admission summer program, reduced course load, study skills assistance, tutoring, writing center.

Majors. Area/ethnic studies: African-American, East Asian, Latin American, Near/Middle Eastern. **Biology:** General, biophysics, cell/histology, molecular. **Computer sciences:** General. **Engineering:** General, biomedical, chemical, civil, computer, electrical, environmental, materials, materials science, mechanical, mechanics. **Foreign languages:** Classics, French, German, Italian, Spanish. **History:** General, science/technology. **Interdisciplinary:** Behavioral sciences, cognitive science, neuroscience. **Liberal arts:** Arts/sciences. **Math:** General, statistics. **Philosophy/religion:** Philosophy. **Physical sciences:** Astronomy, chemistry, geology, physics. **Psychology:** General. **Public administration:** Policy analysis. **Social sciences:** General, anthropology, economics, geography, international relations, political science, sociology. **Visual/performing arts:** Art history/conservation, film/cinema. **Other:** Film and media studies.

Most popular majors. Biology 14%, engineering/engineering technologies 15%, health sciences 25%, social sciences 15%.

Computing on campus. 140 workstations in dormitories, library, computer center. Dormitories wired for high-speed internet access and linked to campus network. Commuter students can connect to campus network. Online course registration, online library, helpline, repair service, student web hosting, wireless network available.

Student life. Freshman orientation: Mandatory. Preregistration for classes offered. 5-day extensive program held 1 week prior to start of fall semester. **Policies:** Freshmen and sophomores required to live on campus unless they live with a parent or legal guardian within commuting distance. **Housing:** Guaranteed on-campus for freshmen. Coed dorms, single-sex dorms, special housing for disabled, apartments, fraternity/sorority housing, wellness housing available. $200 nonrefundable deposit, deadline 5/30. Substance-free and vacation housing floors available. Specific spaces accessible or modified for disabled students. **Activities:** Bands, campus ministries, choral groups, dance, drama, film society, international student organizations, literary magazine, music ensembles, Model UN, musical theater, radio station, student government, student newspaper, symphony orchestra, Jewish Student Association, Catholic Community, Christian Fellowship, Black Student Union, Organizacion Latina Estudiantil, Chinese Student Association, emergency response organization, senior citizens community outreach program, College Democrats, College Republicans.

Athletics. NCAA. **Intercollegiate:** Baseball M, basketball, cross-country, diving, fencing, field hockey W, football (tackle) M, lacrosse, rowing (crew), soccer, swimming, tennis, track and field, volleyball W, water polo M, wrestling M. **Intramural:** Basketball, football (non-tackle), soccer, volleyball. **Team name:** Blue Jays.

Student services. Alcohol/substance abuse counseling, chaplain/spiritual director, career counseling, student employment services, financial aid counseling, health services, minority student services, personal counseling, placement for graduates. **Physically disabled:** Services for visually, speech, hearing impaired.

Contact. E-mail: gotojhu@jhu.edu
Phone: (410) 516-8171 Fax: (410) 516-6025
John Latting, Dean of Undergraduate Admissions, Johns Hopkins University, 3400 North Charles Street, Mason Hall, Baltimore, MD 21218

Johns Hopkins University: Peabody Conservatory of Music

Baltimore, Maryland
www.peabody.jhu.edu **CB code: 5532**

- Private 4-year music college
- Residential campus in very large city
- 329 degree-seeking undergraduates: 3% part-time, 48% women, 4% African American, 14% Asian American, 5% Hispanic American, 17% international
- 328 degree-seeking graduate students
- 46% of applicants admitted
- SAT or ACT required
- 62% graduate within 6 years

General. Founded in 1857. Regionally accredited. **Degrees:** 87 bachelor's awarded; master's, doctoral offered. **Location:** 36 miles from Washington, DC. **Calendar:** Semester. **Full-time faculty:** 70 total. **Part-time faculty:** 80 total. **Special facilities:** Concert halls.

Freshman class profile. 685 applied, 316 admitted, 83 enrolled.

End year in good standing:	90%	**Live on campus:**	100%
Return as sophomores:	87%	**International:**	16%

Basis for selection. Audition most important; secondary school record, test scores also important. Interview recommended. Audition required.

2008-2009 Annual costs. Tuition/fees: $34,060. Room/board: $10,200. Books/supplies: $625. Personal expenses: $1,000.

Financial aid. Non-need-based: Scholarships awarded for academics, music/drama.

Application procedures. Admission: Priority date 11/15; deadline 4/1 (postmark date). $100 fee, may be waived for applicants with need. Admission notification 4/1. Must reply by 5/1. Must apply by December 15 for guarantee of scholarship consideration. **Financial aid:** Closing date 2/1. FAFSA, institutional form required. Applicants notified by 4/7; must reply by 5/1 or within 2 week(s) of notification.

Academics. Special study options: Cross-registration, double major, internships, teacher certification program. **Credit/placement by examination:** AP, CLEP, IB, institutional tests. 8 credit hours maximum toward bachelor's degree. **Support services:** Remedial instruction, tutoring.

Majors. Communications technology: Recording arts. **Education:** Music. **Visual/performing arts:** Music performance, music theory/composition, piano/organ, voice/opera.

Most popular majors. Education 7%.

Computing on campus. 28 workstations in dormitories, library, computer center. Dormitories linked to campus network. Commuter students can connect to campus network. Online library, helpline, repair service, wireless network available.

Student life. Freshman orientation: Available. **Housing:** Guaranteed on-campus for freshmen. Coed dorms, single-sex dorms available. $250 partly refundable deposit, deadline 1/7. **Activities:** Bands, choral groups, music ensembles, opera, student government, symphony orchestra.

Student services. Alcohol/substance abuse counseling, career counseling, student employment services, financial aid counseling, health services, personal counseling, placement for graduates. **Physically disabled:** Services for visually, speech, hearing impaired.

Contact. Phone: (410) 659-8110 Toll-free number: (800) 368-2521
David Lane, Director of Admissions, Johns Hopkins University: Peabody Conservatory of Music, One East Mount Vernon Place, Baltimore, MD 21202

Loyola College in Maryland

Baltimore, Maryland **CB member**
www.loyola.edu **CB code: 5370**

- Private 4-year business and liberal arts college affiliated with Roman Catholic Church
- Residential campus in very large city
- 3,716 degree-seeking undergraduates: 1% part-time, 58% women, 4% African American, 3% Asian American, 4% Hispanic American, 1% international
- 2,364 degree-seeking graduate students
- 69% of applicants admitted
- SAT or ACT (ACT writing optional) required
- 86% graduate within 6 years

General. Founded in 1852. Regionally accredited. **Degrees:** 819 bachelor's awarded; master's, doctoral offered. **ROTC:** Army, Air Force. **Location:** 38 miles from Washington, DC, 103 miles from Philadelphia. **Calendar:** Semester, extensive summer session. **Full-time faculty:** 332 total; 80% have terminal degrees, 10% minority, 47% women. **Part-time faculty:** 225 total; 9% have terminal degrees, 7% minority, 48% women. **Class size:** 55% < 20, 44% 20-39, less than 1% 40-49, less than 1% 50-99, less than 1% >100.

Freshman class profile. 7,623 applied, 5,232 admitted, 1,068 enrolled.

Mid 50% test scores		**GPA 2.0-2.99:**	5%
SAT critical reading:	540-630	**Rank in top quarter:**	71%
SAT math:	560-650	**Rank in top tenth:**	30%
SAT writing:	550-650	**Return as sophomores:**	91%
ACT composite:	24-28	**Out-of-state:**	82%
GPA 3.75 or higher:	23%	**Live on campus:**	98%
GPA 3.50-3.74:	30%	**International:**	1%
GPA 3.0-3.49:	42%		

Basis for selection. Test scores, school record, academic qualifications most important. Extracurricular activities, recommendations, personal background, class rank also considered. Mid-year senior grades and additional SAT scores required for borderline applicants. Interview and essay recommended.

High school preparation. College-preparatory program recommended. 16 units required; 19 recommended. Required and recommended units include English 4, mathematics 4, social studies 4, history 4, science 4 and foreign language 4.

2008-2009 Annual costs. Tuition/fees: $36,240. Room/board: $9,740. Books/supplies: $1,010. Personal expenses: $1,060.

2008-2009 Financial aid. **Need-based:** 768 full-time freshmen applied for aid; 576 were judged to have need; 576 of these received aid. Average need met was 100%. Average scholarship/grant was $19,530; average loan $5,235. 79% of total undergraduate aid awarded as scholarships/grants, 21% as loans/jobs. **Non-need-based:** Awarded to 1,177 full-time undergraduates, including 355 freshmen. Scholarships awarded for academics, athletics, ROTC.

Application procedures. **Admission:** Priority date 11/15; deadline 1/15. $50 fee, may be waived for applicants with need. Admission notification 4/1. Must reply by 5/1. **Financial aid:** Closing date 2/1. FAFSA, CSS PROFILE required. Applicants notified by 4/1; must reply by 5/1.

Academics. Service learning courses available. **Special study options:** Cooperative education, cross-registration, double major, honors, independent study, internships, liberal arts/career combination, study abroad, teacher certification program, weekend college. **Credit/placement by examination:** AP, CLEP, IB, institutional tests. 30 credit hours maximum toward bachelor's degree. **Support services:** Learning center, remedial instruction, study skills assistance, tutoring.

Majors. **Biology:** General. **Business:** General, accounting. **Communications:** General. **Computer sciences:** General. **Education:** Elementary. **Engineering:** General, electrical. **Foreign languages:** Classics, French, German, Latin, Spanish. **Health:** Speech pathology. **History:** General. **Math:** Applied. **Philosophy/religion:** Philosophy, religion. **Physical sciences:** Chemistry, physics. **Psychology:** General. **Social sciences:** Economics, political science, sociology. **Visual/performing arts:** Art.

Most popular majors. Biology 6%, business/marketing 32%, communications/journalism 13%, foreign language 9%, psychology 8%, social sciences 9%.

Computing on campus. 292 workstations in dormitories, library, computer center, student center. Dormitories wired for high-speed internet access and linked to campus network. Commuter students can connect to campus network. Helpline, student web hosting available.

Student life. **Freshman orientation:** Mandatory, $125 fee. Preregistration for classes offered. Must attend 1 of 4 programs offered in summer; parents invited to attend. **Housing:** Guaranteed on-campus for freshmen. Coed dorms, apartments, wellness housing available. $500 partly refundable deposit, deadline 5/1. **Activities:** Bands, campus ministries, choral groups, dance, drama, international student organizations, literary magazine, music ensembles, musical theater, radio station, student government, student newspaper, TV station, black student association, College Republicans, Korean students association, Circle K, Amnesty International, Jewish students association, College Democrats, Evergreens for Life.

Athletics. NCAA. **Intercollegiate:** Basketball, cross-country, diving, golf M, lacrosse, rowing (crew), soccer, swimming, tennis, track and field, volleyball W. **Intramural:** Baseball M, basketball, football (non-tackle), lacrosse, racquetball, rifle, soccer M, softball, squash, tennis, volleyball. **Team name:** Greyhounds.

Student services. Alcohol/substance abuse counseling, chaplain/spiritual director, career counseling, student employment services, financial aid counseling, health services, minority student services, personal counseling, placement for graduates. **Physically disabled:** Services for visually, speech, hearing impaired.

Contact. E-mail: admissions@loyola.edu
Phone: (410) 617-5012 Toll-free number: (800) 221-9107
Fax: (410) 617-2176
Elena Hicks, Director of Undergraduate Admission, Loyola College in Maryland, 4501 North Charles Street, Baltimore, MD 21210-2699

Maryland Institute College of Art

Baltimore, Maryland — **CB member**
www.mica.edu — **CB code: 5399**

- Private 4-year visual arts college
- Residential campus in very large city
- 1,631 degree-seeking undergraduates: 1% part-time, 67% women, 4% African American, 11% Asian American, 4% Hispanic American, 4% international
- 214 degree-seeking graduate students
- 52% of applicants admitted
- SAT or ACT (ACT writing optional), application essay required
- 72% graduate within 6 years; 23% enter graduate study

General. Founded in 1826. Regionally accredited. **Degrees:** 383 bachelor's awarded; master's offered. **ROTC:** Army. **Location:** 180 miles from New York City, 50 miles from Washington, DC. **Calendar:** Semester, extensive summer session. **Full-time faculty:** 133 total; 82% have terminal degrees, 14% minority, 50% women. **Part-time faculty:** 171 total; 82% have terminal degrees, 14% minority, 50% women. **Class size:** 80% < 20, 19% 20-39, less than 1% 40-49, less than 1% 50-99. **Special facilities:** Nature library, slide library with over 250,000 slides, graphics laboratory, independent studios, art galleries, digital print studio.

Freshman class profile. 2,278 applied, 1,177 admitted, 429 enrolled.

Mid 50% test scores			
SAT critical reading:	540-660	Return as sophomores:	86%
SAT math:	500-620	Out-of-state:	84%
SAT writing:	530-650	Live on campus:	88%
End year in good standing:	98%	International:	4%

Basis for selection. Emphasis placed on artistic ability as demonstrated in the portfolio, academic achievement, test scores, GPA, and level of coursework. Essays, recommendations, interview, and extra-curricular activities also considered. Portfolio of 12-20 pieces of artwork must be submitted with application. Interview recommended. **Learning Disabled:** Students with documented learning disabilities not required to submit SAT or ACT test scores.

High school preparation. College-preparatory program required. 24 units required. Required and recommended units include English 4, mathematics 2-3, social studies 4, history 3-4, science 2-3 (laboratory 1) and academic electives 6. 2 studio art required, 4 studio art recommended, 1 art history recommended.

2008-2009 Annual costs. Tuition/fees: $32,680. Room/board: $9,000. Books/supplies: $1,400. Personal expenses: $650.

Financial aid. **Non-need-based:** Scholarships awarded for academics, art.

Application procedures. **Admission:** Closing date 2/13 (receipt date). $60 fee, may be waived for applicants with need. Application must be submitted on paper. Admission notification 3/13. Must reply by 5/1. **Financial aid:** Closing date 3/1. FAFSA, institutional form required. Applicants notified by 4/10; must reply by 5/1.

Academics. One-third of course work in liberal arts and two-thirds in studio art required for graduation. Minors available in academic subjects. Independent studio and study requirement sometimes met by job internships. Foundation program required in the first year. **Special study options:** Accelerated study, combined bachelor's/graduate degree, cross-registration, distance learning, double major, dual enrollment of high school students, exchange student, independent study, internships, New York semester, student-designed major, study abroad, teacher certification program. Cooperative exchange programs with Johns Hopkins University, Goucher College, Peabody Conservatory of Music, University of Baltimore, Loyola College, Notre Dame College, University of Maryland Baltimore County, Morgan State University, Baltimore Hebrew College and Towson University; 5-year BFA/MA; 5-year BFA/MAT. **Credit/placement by examination:** AP, CLEP, IB, institutional tests. 15 credit hours maximum toward bachelor's degree. **Support services:** Learning center, reduced course load, remedial instruction, study skills assistance, tutoring, writing center.

Majors. **Education:** Art. **Visual/performing arts:** Art history/conservation, ceramics, drawing, fiber arts, graphic design, illustration, interior design, multimedia, painting, photography, printmaking, sculpture. **Other:** Video.

Most popular majors. Education 6%, visual/performing arts 94%.

Computing on campus. 440 workstations in dormitories, library, computer center, student center. Dormitories wired for high-speed internet access and linked to campus network. Commuter students can connect to campus network. Helpline, student web hosting, wireless network available.

Student life. **Freshman orientation:** Mandatory, $130 fee. Preregistration for classes offered. **Housing:** Guaranteed on-campus for freshmen. Coed dorms, special housing for disabled, apartments available. $650 partly refundable deposit, deadline 5/1. **Activities:** Jazz band, choral groups, dance, drama, film society, international student organizations, literary magazine, student government, Asian student alliance, Black student union, Chinese student associaton, Koinonia Christian Fellowship, Korean student association, MICA Baha'i association, Mission in Christian Artists, OY! Jewish student organization, Student Voice Association.

Student services. Career counseling, student employment services, financial aid counseling, health services, minority student services, personal counseling, placement for graduates.

Contact. E-mail: admissions@mica.edu
Phone: (410) 225-2222 Fax: (410) 225-2337
Theresa Bedoya, Vice President and Dean of Admission and Financial Aid, Maryland Institute College of Art, 1300 Mount Royal Avenue, Baltimore, MD 21217-4134

McDaniel College

Westminster, Maryland **CB member**
www.mcdaniel.edu **CB code: 5898**

- Private 4-year liberal arts college
- Residential campus in large town
- 1,739 degree-seeking undergraduates: 3% part-time, 55% women, 5% African American, 3% Asian American, 2% Hispanic American, 1% Native American
- 1,662 degree-seeking graduate students
- 77% of applicants admitted
- SAT or ACT (ACT writing optional), application essay required
- 73% graduate within 6 years; 97% enter graduate study

General. Founded in 1867. Regionally accredited. **Degrees:** 395 bachelor's awarded; master's offered. **ROTC:** Army. **Location:** 30 miles from Baltimore, 60 miles from Washington, DC. **Calendar:** 4-1-4, limited summer session. **Full-time faculty:** 135 total; 88% have terminal degrees, 11% minority, 53% women. **Part-time faculty:** 244 total; 34% have terminal degrees, 7% minority, 54% women. **Class size:** 68% < 20, 31% 20-39, less than 1% 40-49, less than 1% 50-99. **Special facilities:** 9-hole golf course, film/video production laboratory, photography studio, audiology laboratory, human performance laboratory, graphics laboratory, physics observatory.

Freshman class profile. 2,651 applied, 2,050 admitted, 429 enrolled.

Mid 50% test scores			
SAT critical reading:	500-620	GPA 2.0-2.99:	20%
SAT math:	510-610	Rank in top quarter:	57%
ACT composite:	21-26	Rank in top tenth:	28%
GPA 3.75 or higher:	36%	End year in good standing:	91%
GPA 3.50-3.74:	16%	Return as sophomores:	87%
GPA 3.0-3.49:	28%	Out-of-state:	41%
		Live on campus:	95%

Basis for selection. Rigor of course work completed and academic performance test scores, writing skills, personal and academic accomplishments, recommendations by counselors and teachers, leadership and participation in non-academic activities. Academic recommendations required. Interview recommended. **Homeschooled:** Statement describing homeschool structure and mission, transcript of courses and grades, letter of recommendation (nonparent) required. Must submit documentation used to satisfy your state graduation requirement.

High school preparation. College-preparatory program recommended. 16 units required; 19 recommended. Required and recommended units include English 4, mathematics 3-4, social studies 3, science 3-4 (laboratory 3) and foreign language 3-4.

2008-2009 Annual costs. Tuition/fees: $30,780. Room/board: $6,150. Books/supplies: $1,200.

2008-2009 Financial aid. Need-based: 340 full-time freshmen applied for aid; 285 were judged to have need; 285 of these received aid. Average need met was 93%. Average scholarship/grant was $12,559; average loan $4,680. 83% of total undergraduate aid awarded as scholarships/grants, 17% as loans/jobs. **Non-need-based:** Awarded to 572 full-time undergraduates, including 135 freshmen. Scholarships awarded for academics, ROTC, state residency.

Application procedures. Admission: Closing date 2/1 (postmark date). $50 fee, may be waived for applicants with need. Admission notification 1/1. Must reply by May 1 or within 2 week(s) if notified thereafter. **Financial aid:** Priority date 3/1; no closing date. FAFSA, institutional form required. Applicants notified on a rolling basis starting 2/15; must reply by 5/1 or within 2 week(s) of notification.

Academics. January term offered as a two-credit period of concentrated study. May include travel, classroom study or independent study. **Special study options:** Cross-registration, double major, dual enrollment of high school students, honors, independent study, internships, New York semester, semester at sea, student-designed major, study abroad, teacher certification program, United Nations semester, Washington semester. 3-2 program in engineering with University of Maryland. **Credit/placement by examination:** AP, CLEP, IB, SAT, ACT, institutional tests. 32 credit hours maximum toward bachelor's degree. **Support services:** Learning center, reduced course load, remedial instruction, study skills assistance, tutoring, writing center.

Majors. Biology: General, biochemistry, environmental. **Business:** Business admin. **Communications:** General. **Computer sciences:** General. **Conservation:** Environmental science. **Foreign languages:** French, German, Spanish. **History:** General. **Math:** General. **Parks/recreation:** Exercise sciences. **Philosophy/religion:** Philosophy, religion. **Physical sciences:** Chemistry, physics. **Psychology:** General. **Public administration:** Social work. **Social sciences:** Economics, political science, sociology. **Visual/performing arts:** Art, art history/conservation, dramatic.

Most popular majors. Biology 7%, business/marketing 11%, communications/journalism 10%, English 7%, parks/recreation 7%, psychology 13%, social sciences 15%, visual/performing arts 12%.

Computing on campus. 175 workstations in library, computer center. Dormitories wired for high-speed internet access and linked to campus network. Commuter students can connect to campus network. Online course registration, helpline, wireless network available.

Student life. Freshman orientation: Mandatory. Preregistration for classes offered. 5-day program. **Housing:** Guaranteed on-campus for freshmen. Coed dorms, single-sex dorms, apartments, fraternity/sorority housing, wellness housing available. Single-family homes available. **Activities:** Bands, campus ministries, choral groups, dance, drama, international student organizations, literary magazine, music ensembles, Model UN, musical theater, radio station, student government, student newspaper, TV station, Jewish student union, Christian fellowship, Circle K, ecology club, Black student union, multicultural student association, German club, French club, Spanish club.

Athletics. NCAA. **Intercollegiate:** Baseball M, basketball, cross-country, field hockey W, football (tackle) M, golf, lacrosse, soccer, softball W, swimming, tennis, track and field, volleyball W, wrestling M. **Intramural:** Badminton, basketball, football (non-tackle) M, golf, soccer, softball, swimming, tennis, volleyball. **Team name:** The Green Terror.

Student services. Career counseling, student employment services, financial aid counseling, health services, minority student services, personal counseling. **Physically disabled:** Services for visually, hearing impaired. **Learning disabled:** Comprehensive services available.

Contact. E-mail: admissions@mcdaniel.edu
Phone: (410) 857-2230 Toll-free number: (800) 638-5005
Fax: (410) 857-2757
Florence Hines, Vice President for Enrollment Management and Dean of Admissions, McDaniel College, Two College Hill, Westminster, MD 21157-4390

Morgan State University

Baltimore, Maryland **CB member**
www.morgan.edu **CB code: 5416**

- Public 4-year university and liberal arts college
- Commuter campus in large city
- 6,114 degree-seeking undergraduates: 92% African American, 1% Asian American, 1% Hispanic American, 4% international
- 44% of applicants admitted
- 33% graduate within 6 years

General. Founded in 1867. Regionally accredited. **Degrees:** 813 bachelor's awarded; master's, doctoral offered. **ROTC:** Army. **Location:** 45 miles from Washington, DC, 100 miles from Philadelphia. **Calendar:** Semester, limited summer session. **Full-time faculty:** 436 total; 69% have terminal degrees, 76% minority, 39% women. **Part-time faculty:** 122 total; 30% have terminal degrees, 80% minority, 41% women. **Special facilities:** Historical and government documents collections, special collections of African American history, super computer, engineering complex.

Freshman class profile. 9,483 applied, 4,132 admitted, 1,449 enrolled.

Mid 50% test scores			
SAT critical reading:	400-490	Return as sophomores:	68%
SAT math:	400-500	International:	1%

Basis for selection. School achievement record and test scores most important. 820 SAT (exclusive of Writing) with 2.5 high school GPA or 900 SAT (exclusive of Writing) with 2.0 high school GPA, principal's recommendation, and parents' consent form (for minors) required. Interview and essay recommended. Audition recommended for music majors. **Homeschooled:** State high school equivalency certificate required. State-recognized diploma. **Learning Disabled:** Students with learning disability must provide documentation and take untimed SAT with assistance from counseling center.

High school preparation. College-preparatory program recommended. 13 units recommended. Recommended units include English 4, mathematics 3, social studies 2, history 3, science 3 and foreign language 1. History can be substituted for social studies; computer science can be used in place of foreign language.

2008-2009 Annual costs. Tuition/fees: $6,438; $14,928 out-of-state. Room/board: $8,030. Books/supplies: $721. Personal expenses: $2,369.

Application procedures. Admission: Priority date 2/15; deadline 4/15. $35 fee, may be waived for applicants with need. Admission notification on a rolling basis beginning on or about 11/15. Must reply by 5/15. Must reply by May 1 or within 2 week(s) if notified thereafter. **Financial aid:** Priority date 4/1; no closing date. FAFSA required. Applicants notified on a rolling basis starting 6/1; must reply within 2 week(s) of notification.

Academics. Special study options: Cooperative education, cross-registration, distance learning, double major, dual enrollment of high school students, honors, independent study, internships, liberal arts/career combination, teacher certification program, weekend college. Fulbright Program. **Credit/placement by examination:** AP, CLEP, institutional tests. 46 credit hours maximum toward bachelor's degree. Proficiency tests in general education requirements. **Support services:** Learning center, pre-admission summer program, reduced course load, remedial instruction, study skills assistance, tutoring, writing center.

Majors. Architecture: Architecture, environmental design. **Area/ethnic studies:** African-American. **Biology:** General. **Business:** Accounting, business admin, finance, hospitality admin, marketing. **Computer sciences:** Computer science, information systems, networking. **Education:** Elementary, health, physical, science. **Engineering:** General, civil, electrical, industrial, physics. **Family/consumer sciences:** Food/nutrition. **Health:** Staff services technology. **History:** General. **Math:** General. **Physical sciences:** Chemistry, physics. **Psychology:** General. **Social sciences:** Economics, political science, sociology. **Visual/performing arts:** Dramatic, studio arts.

Most popular majors. Business/marketing 27%, education 6%, engineering/engineering technologies 10%, psychology 7%.

Computing on campus. Dormitories wired for high-speed internet access and linked to campus network. Commuter students can connect to campus network. Online course registration, online library, helpline, repair service, student web hosting, wireless network available.

Student life. Freshman orientation: Mandatory. Preregistration for classes offered. Held twice during summer for 5 days. **Housing:** Coed dorms, single-sex dorms, special housing for disabled, apartments, wellness housing available. $200 nonrefundable deposit, deadline 5/1. **Activities:** Bands, choral groups, dance, drama, film society, international student organizations, music ensembles, musical theater, radio station, student government, student newspaper, TV station, Council on Religious Life.

Athletics. NCAA. **Intercollegiate:** Basketball, bowling W, cheerleading M, cross-country, football (tackle) M, softball W, tennis, track and field, volleyball W. **Intramural:** Basketball, cross-country, handball, racquetball, rifle, soccer, softball, swimming, table tennis, tennis, track and field, volleyball. **Team name:** Bears.

Student services. Alcohol/substance abuse counseling, career counseling, student employment services, health services, on-campus daycare, personal counseling, placement for graduates, veterans' counselor. **Physically disabled:** Services for visually, speech, hearing impaired.

Contact. E-mail: admissions@morgan.edu
Phone: (443) 885-3000 Toll-free number: (800) 332-6674
Fax: (443) 885-8260
Shonda Gray, Director of Admissions/ Recruitment, Morgan State University, 1700 East Cold Spring Lane, Baltimore, MD 21251

Mount St. Mary's University

Emmitsburg, Maryland — **CB member**
www.msmary.edu — **CB code: 5421**

- Private 4-year university and liberal arts college affiliated with Roman Catholic Church
- Residential campus in rural community
- 1,632 degree-seeking undergraduates: 6% part-time, 58% women, 7% African American, 3% Asian American, 5% Hispanic American, 1% international
- 429 degree-seeking graduate students
- 78% of applicants admitted
- SAT or ACT (ACT writing optional) required
- 62% graduate within 6 years; 38% enter graduate study

General. Founded in 1808. Regionally accredited. **Degrees:** 358 bachelor's awarded; master's, first professional offered. **ROTC:** Army. **Location:** 65 miles from Washington, DC, 50 miles from Baltimore. **Calendar:** Semester, limited summer session. **Full-time faculty:** 117 total; 88% have terminal degrees, 4% minority, 40% women. **Part-time faculty:** 68 total; 24% have terminal degrees, 3% minority, 44% women. **Class size:** 49% < 20, 49% 20-39, less than 1% 40-49, less than 1% 50-99. **Special facilities:** 300 acre recreation area.

Freshman class profile. 2,716 applied, 2,115 admitted, 410 enrolled.

Mid 50% test scores		**Rank in top quarter:**	45%
SAT critical reading:	480-580	**Rank in top tenth:**	19%
SAT math:	480-590	**End year in good standing:**	91%
GPA 3.75 or higher:	14%	**Return as sophomores:**	79%
GPA 3.50-3.74:	13%	**Out-of-state:**	45%
GPA 3.0-3.49:	32%	**Live on campus:**	96%
GPA 2.0-2.99:	41%	**International:**	1%

Basis for selection. High school record most important followed by standardized test scores, character, extracurricular activities. Interview and essay recommended. Auditions and/or portfolios are recommended for VPA majors, but not required. **Homeschooled:** Statement describing homeschool structure and mission, letter of recommendation (nonparent) required.

High school preparation. College-preparatory program required. 16 units required. Required units include English 4, mathematics 3, social studies 3, science 3 (laboratory 2), foreign language 2 and academic electives 1.

2009-2010 Annual costs. Tuition/fees: $29,020. Room/board: $9,878. Books/supplies: $1,000. Personal expenses: $500.

2008-2009 Financial aid. Need-based: 342 full-time freshmen applied for aid; 268 were judged to have need; 266 of these received aid. Average need met was 72%. Average scholarship/grant was $14,983; average loan $3,968. 68% of total undergraduate aid awarded as scholarships/grants, 32% as loans/jobs. **Non-need-based:** Awarded to 854 full-time undergraduates, including 223 freshmen. Scholarships awarded for academics, art, athletics, leadership, minority status, ROTC.

Application procedures. Admission: No deadline. $35 fee, may be waived for applicants with need. Admission notification on a rolling basis beginning on or about 12/1. Must reply by May 1 or within 2 week(s) if notified thereafter. **Financial aid:** Closing date 3/1. FAFSA, institutional form required. Applicants notified on a rolling basis starting 2/1; must reply by 5/1.

Academics. Liberal arts core curriculum integrated over 4 years includes: western civilization (clustered with literature and art courses), American experience, philosophy, theology, ethics, non-western cultures, mathematical science, foreign language, social science, written and oral communication. Undergraduate professional studies programs in business and criminal justice in an accelerated format offered off-campus; open to adult students only. **Special study options:** Accelerated study, combined bachelor's/graduate degree, cross-registration, double major, dual enrollment of high school students, honors, independent study, internships, liberal arts/career combination, student-designed major, study abroad, teacher certification program, Washington semester, weekend college. 3-2 with Johns Hopkins University (BS Biology, BS Nursing), 3-3 with Sacred Heart University (BS in Biology, Ph.D in Physical Therapy), 4-2 with Sacred Heart University (BS in Biology, MS in Occupational Therapy). **Credit/placement by examination:** AP, CLEP, IB, SAT, ACT, institutional tests. 30 credit hours maximum toward bachelor's degree. **Support services:** Learning center, reduced course load, remedial instruction, study skills assistance, tutoring, writing center.

Majors. Biology: General, biochemistry. **Business:** General, accounting, information resources management. **Communications:** General. **Computer sciences:** General. **Conservation:** Environmental studies. **Education:** Elementary. **Foreign languages:** French, German, Spanish. **History:** General. **Math:** General. **Parks/recreation:** Sports admin. **Philosophy/religion:** Philosophy. **Physical sciences:** Chemistry. **Protective services:** Criminal justice. **Psychology:** General. **Social sciences:** General, economics, international relations, political science, sociology. **Theology:** Theology. **Visual/performing arts:** General.

Most popular majors. Biology 6%, business/marketing 32%, communications/journalism 7%, education 10%, social sciences 12%.

Computing on campus. 125 workstations in library, computer center. Dormitories wired for high-speed internet access and linked to campus network. Commuter students can connect to campus network. Online course registration, helpline, repair service, student web hosting, wireless network available.

Student life. Freshman orientation: Mandatory. Preregistration for classes offered. 3-day weekend in August and choice of 1 of 2 weekends in June for pre-registration. **Housing:** Guaranteed on-campus for all undergraduates.

Coed dorms, special housing for disabled, apartments, wellness housing available. **Activities:** Bands, campus ministries, choral groups, dance, drama, international student organizations, literary magazine, music ensembles, musical theater, radio station, student government, student newspaper, TV station, College Democrats, College Republicans, Amnesty International, Circle K, Heritage, commuter student association, Habitat for Humanity, students for life.

Athletics. NCAA. **Intercollegiate:** Baseball M, basketball, cross-country, golf, lacrosse, soccer, softball W, swimming W, tennis, track and field. **Intramural:** Basketball, field hockey W, football (non-tackle) M, racquetball, skiing, soccer, softball, swimming, tennis, volleyball. **Team name:** Mountaineers.

Student services. Adult student services, alcohol/substance abuse counseling, chaplain/spiritual director, career counseling, student employment services, financial aid counseling, health services, minority student services, personal counseling, placement for graduates. **Physically disabled:** Services for visually, hearing impaired.

Contact. E-mail: admissions@msmary.edu
Phone: (301) 447-5214 Toll-free number: (800) 448-4347
Fax: (301) 447-5860
Michael Post, Dean of Admissions and Enrollment Management, Mount St. Mary's University, 16300 Old Emmitsburg Road, Emmitsburg, MD 21727

National Labor College

Silver Spring, Maryland
www.georgemeany.org **CB code: 3930**

- Private 4-year liberal arts and career college
- Commuter campus in small city
- 280 degree-seeking undergraduates

General. Regionally accredited. **Degrees:** 80 bachelor's awarded. **Calendar:** Trimester, limited summer session. **Full-time faculty:** 12 total. **Part-time faculty:** 6 total.

Basis for selection. Open admission. **Homeschooled:** Transcript of courses and grades required.

2008-2009 Annual costs. $158 per-credit-hour for union members affiliated with the AFL-CIO. $210 per-credit-hour for union members not affiliated with the AFL-CIO. $1031 per-credit-hour for non-union members.

Application procedures. Admission: No deadline. $60 fee. Admission notification on a rolling basis.

Academics. Credit/placement by examination: CLEP. **Support services:** Reduced course load, study skills assistance, tutoring, writing center.

Majors. Business: Labor relations, labor studies. **Health:** Occupational health. **Other:** Union leadership and administration.

Computing on campus. 30 workstations in computer center. Dormitories wired for high-speed internet access. Commuter students can connect to campus network. Online course registration, online library, wireless network available.

Student life. Freshman orientation: Mandatory.

Student services. Personal counseling.

Contact. Phone: (301) 431-6400 Fax: (301) 431-5411
Karen Banks, Director of Admissions, National Labor College, 10000 New Hampshire Avenue, Silver Spring, MD 20904

Ner Israel Rabbinical College

Baltimore, Maryland
CB code: 0839

- Private 4-year rabbinical college for men affiliated with Jewish faith
- Very large city

General. Accredited by AARTS. **Calendar:** Semester.

Annual costs/financial aid. Tuition/fees (2008-2009): $8,500. Room/board: $6,500.

Contact. Phone: (410) 484-7200
Admissions Director, 400 Mount Wilson Lane, Baltimore, MD 21208

St. John's College

Annapolis, Maryland **CB member**
www.stjohnscollege.edu **CB code: 5598**

- Private 4-year liberal arts college
- Residential campus in large town
- 488 degree-seeking undergraduates: 47% women
- 71 degree-seeking graduate students
- 81% of applicants admitted
- Application essay required
- 73% graduate within 6 years; 9% enter graduate study

General. Founded in 1784. Regionally accredited. Second campus in Santa Fe, New Mexico. Students may transfer between campuses. **Degrees:** 106 bachelor's awarded; master's offered. **Location:** 35 miles from Washington, DC, 30 miles from Baltimore. **Calendar:** Semester. **Full-time faculty:** 71 total; 83% have terminal degrees, 6% minority, 22% women. **Part-time faculty:** 8 total; 38% have terminal degrees, 25% women. **Class size:** 94% < 20, 5% 20-39, less than 1% >100. **Special facilities:** Planetarium, boathouse, observatory.

Freshman class profile. 460 applied, 374 admitted, 156 enrolled.

Mid 50% test scores		**End year in good standing:**	89%
SAT critical reading:	640-740	**Return as sophomores:**	78%
SAT math:	590-680	**Out-of-state:**	82%
Rank in top quarter:	63%	**Live on campus:**	100%
Rank in top tenth:	34%		

Basis for selection. One optional and 3 required essays most important. School achievement record and teacher recommendations important. 2-day campus visit and interview recommended. Standardized tests required for homeschooled and international students. **Homeschooled:** Statement describing homeschool structure and mission, letter of recommendation (nonparent) required. Must submit results of PSAT, SAT, or ACT if high school diploma will not be earned.

High school preparation. College-preparatory program recommended. 5 units required. Required and recommended units include English 4, mathematics 3-4, social studies 2, history 2, science 3 (laboratory 3) and foreign language 2-4.

2008-2009 Annual costs. Tuition/fees: $39,154. Room/board: $9,284. Books/supplies: $280. Personal expenses: $750.

2008-2009 Financial aid. All financial aid based on need. 122 full-time freshmen applied for aid; 95 were judged to have need; 95 of these received aid. Average need met was 82%. Average scholarship/grant was $26,542; average loan $4,325. 75% of total undergraduate aid awarded as scholarships/grants, 25% as loans/jobs.

Application procedures. Admission: Priority date 3/1; no deadline. No application fee. Admission notification on a rolling basis. Must reply by May 1 or within 2 week(s) if notified thereafter. Early application encouraged as class generally fills by first week in May. **Financial aid:** Priority date 2/15; no closing date. FAFSA, CSS PROFILE required. Applicants notified on a rolling basis starting 1/15; must reply by 5/1.

Academics. Special study options: Internships. **Credit/placement by examination:** CLEP. **Support services:** Tutoring, writing center.

Majors. Area/ethnic studies: Western European. **Liberal arts:** Arts/sciences, humanities.

Computing on campus. 20 workstations in library, computer center. Dormitories wired for high-speed internet access and linked to campus network. Commuter students can connect to campus network.

Student life. Freshman orientation: Mandatory. 2-day program, after registration and prior to start of classes. **Policies:** Freshmen required to live in dormitories. **Housing:** Guaranteed on-campus for freshmen. Coed dorms, wellness housing available. **Activities:** Choral groups, dance, drama, film society, international student organizations, literary magazine, music ensembles, musical theater, student government, student newspaper, Political Forum, Project Politae (campus community service organization), Pink Triangle Society, Christian Fellowship, Jewish Students Society, Student Committee on Instruction, Environmental Club, Amnesty International, Delegate Council.

Athletics. Intramural: Badminton, basketball, boxing M, fencing, football (non-tackle) M, handball, rowing (crew), sailing, soccer, softball, table tennis, tennis, track and field, volleyball.

Student services. Alcohol/substance abuse counseling, career counseling, student employment services, financial aid counseling, health services, personal counseling, placement for graduates, women's services.

Contact. E-mail: admissions@sjca.edu
Phone: (410) 626-2522 Toll-free number: (800) 727-9238
Fax: (410) 269-7916
John Christensen, Director of Admissions, St. John's College, PO Box 2800, Annapolis, MD 21404

St. Mary's College of Maryland

St. Mary's City, Maryland — **CB member**
www.smcm.edu — **CB code: 5601**

- Public 4-year liberal arts college
- Residential campus in large town
- 1,988 degree-seeking undergraduates: 2% part-time, 58% women
- 30 degree-seeking graduate students
- 52% of applicants admitted
- SAT or ACT (ACT writing optional), application essay required
- 75% graduate within 6 years; 35% enter graduate study

General. Founded in 1840. Regionally accredited. Opportunities for participating in colonial and archaeological research. Designated a public honors college. **Degrees:** 426 bachelor's awarded; master's offered. **Location:** 70 miles from Washington, DC. **Calendar:** Semester, limited summer session. **Full-time faculty:** 144 total; 98% have terminal degrees, 15% minority, 46% women. **Part-time faculty:** 87 total; 45% have terminal degrees, 6% minority, 45% women. **Class size:** 64% < 20, 33% 20-39, less than 1% 40-49, 2% 50-99. **Special facilities:** Archaeological site of Historic St. Mary's City, electron microscope, marine research vessel, fresh and salt water research facilities.

Freshman class profile. 2,723 applied, 1,411 admitted, 456 enrolled.

Mid 50% test scores		**GPA 2.0-2.99:**	7%
SAT critical reading:	580-680	**Rank in top quarter:**	78%
SAT math:	570-660	**Rank in top tenth:**	47%
SAT writing:	570-680	**Return as sophomores:**	90%
GPA 3.75 or higher:	39%	**Out-of-state:**	21%
GPA 3.50-3.74:	27%	**Live on campus:**	95%
GPA 3.0-3.49:	27%	**International:**	1%

Basis for selection. High school record, SAT or ACT scores, recommendations by counselors/teachers, co-curricular resume, and essay most important. Interview recommended for admissions. **Homeschooled:** Transcript of courses and grades, state high school equivalency certificate required.

High school preparation. College-preparatory program recommended. 20 units required; 24 recommended. Required and recommended units include English 4, mathematics 3-4, social studies 2, history 1-2, science 3 (laboratory 2), foreign language 2-4 and academic electives 3.

2008-2009 Annual costs. Tuition/fees: $12,604; $23,454 out-of-state. Room/board: $9,225. Books/supplies: $1,000. Personal expenses: $1,800.

2007-2008 Financial aid. Need-based: 345 full-time freshmen applied for aid; 221 were judged to have need; 221 of these received aid. Average need met was 59%. Average scholarship/grant was $3,500; average loan $2,625. 69% of total undergraduate aid awarded as scholarships/grants, 31% as loans/jobs. **Non-need-based:** Awarded to 802 full-time undergraduates, including 252 freshmen. Scholarships awarded for academics, alumni affiliation.

Application procedures. Admission: Closing date 1/1 (postmark date). $50 fee, may be waived for applicants with need. Admission notification 4/1. Must reply by May 1 or within 2 week(s) if notified thereafter. **Financial aid:** Priority date 2/15, closing date 3/1. FAFSA required. Applicants notified by 4/1; must reply by 5/1.

Academics. Special study options: Double major, dual enrollment of high school students, exchange student, honors, independent study, internships, student-designed major, study abroad, teacher certification program, Washington semester. International study programs in China, England, France, Germany, the Gambia, Japan, Italy, Thailand, Costa Rica and Argentina; pre-engineering 3-2 program with University of Maryland School of Engineering. **Credit/placement by examination:** AP, CLEP, IB, SAT, institutional tests. 45 credit hours maximum toward bachelor's degree. **Support services:** Reduced course load, study skills assistance, tutoring, writing center.

Majors. Biology: General, biochemistry. **Computer sciences:** General. **Foreign languages:** General. **History:** General. **Interdisciplinary:** Biological/physical sciences. **Math:** General. **Philosophy/religion:** Philosophy, religion. **Physical sciences:** Chemistry, physics. **Psychology:** General. **Public administration:** Policy analysis. **Social sciences:** Anthropology, economics, political science, sociology. **Visual/performing arts:** Art, dramatic.

Most popular majors. Biology 10%, English 14%, history 7%, psychology 15%, social sciences 25%, visual/performing arts 7%.

Computing on campus. 387 workstations in dormitories, library, computer center, student center. Dormitories wired for high-speed internet access and linked to campus network. Commuter students can connect to campus network. Online course registration, online library, helpline, student web hosting, wireless network available.

Student life. Freshman orientation: Mandatory, $100 fee. Preregistration for classes offered. Offered in July; additional program in August. **Housing:** Guaranteed on-campus for all undergraduates. Coed dorms, single-sex dorms, special housing for disabled, apartments, wellness housing available. $500 nonrefundable deposit, deadline 5/1. Pets allowed in dorm rooms. Townhouses available. **Activities:** Jazz band, campus ministries, choral groups, dance, drama, international student organizations, literary magazine, music ensembles, musical theater, radio station, student government, student newspaper, symphony orchestra, TV station, Black student union, College Republicans, College Democrats, Amnesty International, For Goodness Sake, Hillel, Habitat for Humanity, Student Environmental Action Coalition, Intervarsity Christian Fellowship, St. Mary's Triangle and Rainbow Society.

Athletics. NCAA. **Intercollegiate:** Baseball M, basketball, field hockey W, lacrosse, sailing, soccer, swimming, tennis, volleyball W. **Intramural:** Basketball, cross-country, football (non-tackle), soccer, softball. **Team name:** Seahawks.

Student services. Alcohol/substance abuse counseling, career counseling, student employment services, financial aid counseling, health services, minority student services, personal counseling, placement for graduates, veterans' counselor, women's services. **Physically disabled:** Services for visually, hearing impaired.

Contact. E-mail: admissions@smcm.edu
Phone: (240) 895-5000 Toll-free number: (800) 492-7181
Fax: (240) 895-5001
Richard Edgar, Director of Admissions, St. Mary's College of Maryland, 18952 East Fisher Road, St. Mary's City, MD 20686-3001

Salisbury University

Salisbury, Maryland — **CB member**
www.salisbury.edu — **CB code: 5403**

- Public 4-year university and liberal arts college
- Residential campus in large town
- 7,025 degree-seeking undergraduates: 5% part-time, 55% women, 11% African American, 3% Asian American, 3% Hispanic American, 1% international
- 494 degree-seeking graduate students
- 53% of applicants admitted
- 68% graduate within 6 years; 27% enter graduate study

General. Founded in 1925. Regionally accredited. **Degrees:** 1,553 bachelor's awarded; master's offered. **ROTC:** Army, Air Force. **Location:** 110 miles from Baltimore and Washington, DC. **Calendar:** 4-1-4, extensive summer session. **Full-time faculty:** 379 total; 82% have terminal degrees, 11% minority, 45% women. **Part-time faculty:** 276 total; 6% have terminal degrees, 5% minority, 66% women. **Class size:** 29% < 20, 65% 20-39, 4% 40-49, 2% 50-99, less than 1% >100. **Special facilities:** Arboretum, galleries, history and culture research center, center for conflict resolution, small business development center, museum of wildfowl art.

Freshman class profile. 7,275 applied, 3,856 admitted, 1,199 enrolled.

Mid 50% test scores		**GPA 2.0-2.99:**	10%
SAT critical reading:	520-600	**Rank in top quarter:**	55%
SAT math:	520-610	**Rank in top tenth:**	17%
SAT writing:	510-590	**End year in good standing:**	81%
ACT composite:	22-23	**Return as sophomores:**	83%
GPA 3.75 or higher:	30%	**Out-of-state:**	18%
GPA 3.50-3.74:	28%	**Live on campus:**	83%
GPA 3.0-3.49:	32%		

Basis for selection. Rigor of secondary school record, including level of courses, depth of subjects, GPA, most important. Activities, leadership roles, artistic or athletic talents, ability to contribute to a culturally diverse community also important. SAT/ACT scores optional for applicants with high school GPA of 3.5 or higher. Auditions required for music and fine art programs. Essays recommended.

High school preparation. College-preparatory program recommended. 15 units required; 21 recommended. Required and recommended units include English 4, mathematics 3-4, social studies 3, science 3-4 (laboratory 2-3), foreign language 2-3 and academic electives 3.

2008-2009 Annual costs. Tuition/fees: $6,492; $14,794 out-of-state. Room/board: $7,798. Books/supplies: $1,200. Personal expenses: $1,450.

2007-2008 Financial aid. Need-based: 874 full-time freshmen applied for aid; 498 were judged to have need; 473 of these received aid. Average need met was 61%. Average scholarship/grant was $6,467; average loan $3,034. 44% of total undergraduate aid awarded as scholarships/grants, 56% as loans/jobs. **Non-need-based:** Awarded to 1,027 full-time undergraduates, including 224 freshmen. Scholarships awarded for academics, alumni affiliation, art, leadership, music/drama, state residency. **Additional information:** Job opportunities provided for almost 17% of full-time undergraduate students. Students can expect to earn between $1,200 and $2,000 per academic year by working 10 to 15 hours per week.

Application procedures. Admission: Closing date 1/15. $45 fee, may be waived for applicants with need. Application must be submitted online. Admission notification 3/15. Must reply by 5/1. **Financial aid:** Closing date 3/1. FAFSA required. Applicants notified by 3/15; Applicants notified on a rolling basis starting 3/15; must reply by 5/1 or within 2 week(s) of notification.

Academics. Special study options: Accelerated study, combined bachelor's/graduate degree, cooperative education, cross-registration, distance learning, double major, dual enrollment of high school students, ESL, exchange student, external degree, honors, independent study, internships, liberal arts/career combination, student-designed major, study abroad, teacher certification program, Washington semester. **Credit/placement by examination:** AP, CLEP, IB, institutional tests. 60 credit hours maximum toward bachelor's degree. **Support services:** Learning center, study skills assistance, tutoring, writing center.

Majors. Biology: General. **Business:** Accounting, business admin, finance, marketing. **Communications:** General. **Computer sciences:** General, information systems. **Conservation:** Environmental science. **Education:** Early childhood, elementary, ESL, health, physical. **Foreign languages:** French, Spanish. **Health:** Athletic training, clinical lab science, environmental health, nursing (RN), respiratory therapy technology. **History:** General. **Interdisciplinary:** Global studies, peace/conflict. **Math:** General. **Parks/recreation:** Exercise sciences. **Philosophy/religion:** Philosophy. **Physical sciences:** Chemistry, physics. **Psychology:** General. **Public administration:** Social work. **Social sciences:** Economics, geography, political science, sociology. **Visual/performing arts:** Art, dramatic, studio arts. **Other:** Interdisciplinary studies.

Most popular majors. Biology 6%, business/marketing 19%, communications/journalism 10%, education 11%, health sciences 7%, psychology 7%.

Computing on campus. 423 workstations in library, computer center, student center. Dormitories wired for high-speed internet access and linked to campus network. Commuter students can connect to campus network. Online course registration, online library, helpline, repair service, student web hosting, wireless network available.

Student life. Freshman orientation: Mandatory. Preregistration for classes offered. Orientation fee varies per program. **Policies:** Class attendance policies vary by instructor. Hazing and smoking is prohibited. **Housing:** Coed dorms, single-sex dorms, apartments, wellness housing available. $300 nonrefundable deposit. Affiliated off-campus apartments. **Activities:** Bands, campus ministries, choral groups, dance, drama, film society, international student organizations, literary magazine, music ensembles, musical theater, radio station, student government, student newspaper, symphony orchestra, TV station, Campus Crusade for Christ, Christian fellowship, reformed university fellowship, Muslim student organization, junior gospel choir, Union of African-Americans, NAACP, African American historical & philosophical society.

Athletics. NCAA. **Intercollegiate:** Baseball M, basketball, cross-country, field hockey W, football (tackle) M, lacrosse, soccer, softball W, swimming, tennis, track and field, volleyball W. **Intramural:** Basketball, football (non-tackle), golf, racquetball, soccer, softball, tennis, volleyball, water polo. **Team name:** Seagulls.

Student services. Alcohol/substance abuse counseling, career counseling, student employment services, financial aid counseling, health services, minority student services, personal counseling, veterans' counselor. **Physically disabled:** Services for visually, speech, hearing impaired.

Contact. E-mail: admissions@salisbury.edu
Phone: (410) 543-6161 Toll-free number: (888) 543-0148
Fax: (410) 546-6016
Aaron Basko, Director of Admissions, Salisbury University, 1200 Camden Avenue, Salisbury, MD 21801-6862

Sojourner-Douglass College

Baltimore, Maryland
www.sdc.edu **CB code: 0504**

- Private 4-year liberal arts college
- Very large city
- 1,246 degree-seeking undergraduates
- Interview required

General. Founded in 1980. Regionally accredited. Campus in the Bahamas. **Degrees:** 141 bachelor's awarded; master's offered. **Location:** Downtown. **Calendar:** Semester. **Full-time faculty:** 60 total. **Part-time faculty:** 150 total. **Special facilities:** Learning resource center, writing lab.

Basis for selection. Open admission. Institutional placement tests used for all programs.

2008-2009 Annual costs. Tuition/fees: $7,478. Books/supplies: $800. Personal expenses: $2,800.

Application procedures. Admission: No deadline. $25 fee, may be waived for applicants with need. Admission notification on a rolling basis. **Financial aid:** Priority date 3/1; no closing date. FAFSA, institutional form required. Applicants notified on a rolling basis; must reply within 2 week(s) of notification.

Academics. Special study options: Accelerated study, cooperative education, honors, independent study, internships. **Credit/placement by examination:** CLEP. **Support services:** Learning center, remedial instruction, tutoring.

Majors. Business: Business admin, hospitality admin, management information systems. **Health:** Health care admin. **Interdisciplinary:** Gerontology. **Public administration:** Social work. **Social sciences:** General.

Most popular majors. Business/marketing 26%, education 11%, psychology 19%, public administration/social services 45%.

Computing on campus. 100 workstations in computer center.

Student life. Freshman orientation: Available. Held the Saturday before classes start in the fall. **Activities:** Student government, student newspaper, Phi Beta Sigma, Zeta Phi Beta, Sigma Beta Delta honor society, student government association, Association for the Study of African American Life and History.

Student services. Career counseling, on-campus daycare, personal counseling.

Contact. Phone: (410) 276-0306 ext. 248 Fax: (410) 675-1811
Diana Samuels, Coordinator of Admissions, Sojourner-Douglass College, 500 North Caroline Street, Baltimore, MD 21205

Stevenson University

Stevenson, Maryland **CB member**
www.stevenson.edu **CB code: 5856**

- Private 4-year university and career college
- Residential campus in very large city
- 3,118 degree-seeking undergraduates: 17% part-time, 71% women, 15% African American, 3% Asian American, 1% Hispanic American, 1% Native American
- 258 degree-seeking graduate students
- 62% of applicants admitted
- SAT or ACT (ACT writing optional), application essay required
- 66% graduate within 6 years

General. Founded in 1947. Regionally accredited. **Degrees:** 605 bachelor's awarded; master's offered. **ROTC:** Army. **Location:** 8 miles from Baltimore. **Calendar:** Semester, limited summer session. **Full-time faculty:** 111 total; 66% have terminal degrees, 10% minority, 59% women. **Part-time faculty:** 241 total; 45% have terminal degrees, 8% minority, 44% women. **Class size:** 67% < 20, 33% 20-39. **Special facilities:** Theater.

Freshman class profile. 3,687 applied, 2,286 admitted, 631 enrolled.

Mid 50% test scores			
SAT critical reading:	460-560	GPA 3.0-3.49:	31%
SAT math:	460-570	GPA 2.0-2.99:	20%
SAT writing:	460-560	Rank in top quarter:	49%
ACT composite:	19-24	Rank in top tenth:	23%
GPA 3.75 or higher:	33%	Return as sophomores:	74%
GPA 3.50-3.74:	16%	Out-of-state:	10%
		Live on campus:	73%

Basis for selection. High school record and test scores most important. Optional interview, recommendations, essay, extracurricular activities also important. Admissions after March 1st priority deadline on space available basis. Interviews are recommended but not required.

High school preparation. College-preparatory program recommended. 17 units required. Required and recommended units include English 4, mathematics 3, social studies 2, history 1, science 3 (laboratory 2), foreign language 2 and academic electives 4.

2008-2009 Annual costs. Tuition/fees: $19,200. Room/board: $9,506. Books/supplies: $1,500. Personal expenses: $2,070.

2007-2008 Financial aid. Need-based: 504 full-time freshmen applied for aid; 402 were judged to have need; 402 of these received aid. Average need met was 69%. Average scholarship/grant was $10,005; average loan $3,287. 66% of total undergraduate aid awarded as scholarships/grants, 34% as loans/jobs. **Non-need-based:** Awarded to 841 full-time undergraduates, including 174 freshmen. Scholarships awarded for academics, art, leadership, music/drama, ROTC. **Additional information:** Cooperative Education Program allows students to work in their field of study with area corporations.

Application procedures. Admission: Priority date 3/1; no deadline. $40 fee, may be waived for applicants with need, free for online applicants. Admission notification on a rolling basis beginning on or about 12/1. Must reply by May 1 or within 2 week(s) if notified thereafter. **Financial aid:** Priority date 2/15; no closing date. FAFSA required. Applicants notified on a rolling basis starting 3/15; must reply by 5/1 or within 2 week(s) of notification.

Academics. Advanced technology programs, forensic science program and forensic studies programs offered. Cooperative education program available to third- and fourth-year students. Career Architecture, a program for personal and professional development, is integrated into all programs. **Special study options:** Accelerated study, cooperative education, cross-registration, distance learning, double major, dual enrollment of high school students, honors, independent study, internships, liberal arts/career combination, student-designed major, study abroad, teacher certification program, Washington semester, weekend college. **Credit/placement by examination:** AP, CLEP, IB, SAT, ACT, institutional tests. 15 credit hours maximum toward associate degree, 30 toward bachelor's. **Support services:** Learning center, pre-admission summer program, reduced course load, remedial instruction, study skills assistance, tutoring, writing center.

Majors. Biology: General, biotechnology. **Business:** Accounting, business admin, communications, management information systems. **Computer sciences:** Programming. **Education:** Elementary, kindergarten/preschool, middle. **Family/consumer sciences:** Family/community services. **Health:** Clinical lab science, nursing (RN). **History:** Public archives. **Legal studies:** Paralegal. **Math:** Applied. **Physical sciences:** Chemistry. **Psychology:** General. **Visual/performing arts:** Design, film/cinema. **Other:** Interdisciplinary studies.

Most popular majors. Business/marketing 25%, computer/information sciences 9%, education 7%, health sciences 18%, interdisciplinary studies 7%, legal studies 7%, visual/performing arts 10%.

Computing on campus. 575 workstations in library, computer center, student center. Dormitories wired for high-speed internet access and linked to campus network. Commuter students can connect to campus network. Online course registration, online library, helpline, repair service, wireless network available.

Student life. Freshman orientation: Mandatory. Preregistration for classes offered. Full-day program, conducted by major, normally held during June. Freshmen also attend second orientation in August, prior to start of fall semester. **Housing:** Special housing for disabled, apartments available. Suite style housing (2 bedrooms, share bath). **Activities:** Bands, campus ministries, choral groups, dance, drama, international student organizations, literary magazine, music ensembles, student government, student newspaper, symphony orchestra, Black Student Union, Service Corps, Campus Crusade for Christ, Extreme Acts, Reformed University Fellowship, Angus Dei.

Athletics. NCAA. **Intercollegiate:** Baseball M, basketball, cheerleading, cross-country, field hockey W, golf, lacrosse, soccer, softball W, tennis, track and field, volleyball. **Intramural:** Badminton, basketball, fencing, football (tackle) M, sailing, skiing, soccer, table tennis, tennis, track and field, volleyball. **Team name:** Mustangs.

Student services. Adult student services, alcohol/substance abuse counseling, career counseling, student employment services, financial aid counseling, health services, personal counseling, placement for graduates, veterans' counselor.

Contact. E-mail: admissions@stevenson.edu
Phone: (410) 486-7001 Toll-free number: (877) 468-6852
Fax: (443) 352-4440
Mark Hergan, Vice President for Enrollment Management, Stevenson University, 1525 Greenspring Valley Road, Stevenson, MD 21153-0641

Towson University

Towson, Maryland — **CB member**
www.towson.edu — **CB code: 5404**

- Public 4-year university
- Commuter campus in large city
- 16,628 degree-seeking undergraduates: 10% part-time, 60% women, 12% African American, 4% Asian American, 3% Hispanic American, 3% international
- 3,063 degree-seeking graduate students
- 61% of applicants admitted
- SAT or ACT with writing required
- 66% graduate within 6 years

General. Founded in 1866. Regionally accredited. **Degrees:** 3,204 bachelor's awarded; master's, doctoral offered. **ROTC:** Army, Air Force. **Location:** 1.5 miles from Baltimore. **Calendar:** Semester, extensive summer session. **Full-time faculty:** 788 total; 74% have terminal degrees, 16% minority, 52% women. **Part-time faculty:** 704 total; 28% have terminal degrees, 10% minority, 56% women. **Class size:** 35% < 20, 60% 20-39, 4% 40-49, 1% 50-99, less than 1% >100. **Special facilities:** Planetarium, Asian art collection, concert hall, greenhouse, herbarium, observatory, animal museum.

Freshman class profile. 15,699 applied, 9,609 admitted, 2,832 enrolled.

Mid 50% test scores			
SAT critical reading:	480-570	Rank in top quarter:	53%
SAT math:	490-590	Rank in top tenth:	21%
SAT writing:	500-590	Return as sophomores:	82%
ACT composite:	20-24	Out-of-state:	29%
GPA 3.75 or higher:	21%	Live on campus:	87%
GPA 3.50-3.74:	25%	International:	1%
GPA 3.0-3.49:	51%	Fraternities:	9%
GPA 2.0-2.99:	3%	Sororities:	10%

Basis for selection. High school record, test scores important; class rank, recommendations, essay considered. Interview and essay recommended. Audition required of music, dance majors. **Homeschooled:** Writing samples, 3 letters of recommendation, course-work summary required.

High school preparation. College-preparatory program recommended. 23 units required. Required and recommended units include English 4, mathematics 3, social studies 3, science 3 (laboratory 2-3), foreign language 2-4 and academic electives 6.

2008-2009 Annual costs. Tuition/fees: $7,314; $17,860 out-of-state. Room/board: $8,306.

2008-2009 Financial aid. Need-based: 2,149 full-time freshmen applied for aid; 1,342 were judged to have need; 1,267 of these received aid. Average need met was 69%. Average scholarship/grant was $8,416; average loan $3,177. 59% of total undergraduate aid awarded as scholarships/grants, 41% as loans/jobs. **Non-need-based:** Awarded to 3,290 full-time undergraduates, including 864 freshmen. Scholarships awarded for academics, alumni affiliation, art, athletics, leadership, minority status, music/drama.

Application procedures. Admission: Priority date 12/1; deadline 2/15 (postmark date). $45 fee, may be waived for applicants with need. Admission notification on a rolling basis beginning on or about 10/1. Must reply by May 1 or within 2 week(s) if notified thereafter. **Financial aid:** Closing date 2/10. FAFSA required. Applicants notified on a rolling basis starting 3/21; must reply within 2 week(s) of notification.

Academics. Special study options: Combined bachelor's/graduate degree, cooperative education, cross-registration, distance learning, double major, dual enrollment of high school students, ESL, exchange student, honors, independent study, internships, liberal arts/career combination, student-designed major, study abroad, teacher certification program. 3-2 engineering with University of Maryland, College Park. **Credit/placement by examination:** AP, CLEP, IB, SAT, ACT, institutional tests. 45 credit hours maximum toward bachelor's degree. Portfolio reviews, oral exams, demonstrations or written reports/papers considered for credit. **Support services:** Learning center, remedial instruction, study skills assistance, tutoring, writing center.

Honors college/program. Guaranteed admission with unweighted GPA of 3.60 on 4.00 scale and score of 1800 on SAT. If either criterion lacking, admission based on comprehensive review of course selection, HS curriculum, and skills.

Majors. **Area/ethnic studies:** American, women's. **Biology:** General, Biochemistry/biophysics and molecular biology, ecology. **Business:** Accounting, business admin. **Communications:** General, journalism, media studies. **Communications technology:** Radio/tv. **Computer sciences:** General, computer science, information technology. **Conservation:** Environmental studies. **Education:** Art, early childhood, elementary, music, physical, special. **Family/consumer sciences:** Family systems. **Foreign languages:** General. **Health:** Athletic training, audiology/speech pathology, health care admin, health services, nursing (RN), substance abuse counseling. **History:** General. **Interdisciplinary:** Biological/physical sciences, gerontology. **Legal studies:** General. **Math:** General. **Parks/recreation:** Exercise sciences, sports admin. **Philosophy/religion:** Philosophy, religion. **Physical sciences:** Chemistry, geology, physics, planetary. **Protective services:** Forensics. **Psychology:** General. **Social sciences:** General, economics, geography, international relations, political science, sociology, urban studies. **Visual/performing arts:** Art, dance, dramatic, studio arts.

Most popular majors. Business/marketing 18%, communications/journalism 9%, education 12%, health sciences 10%, psychology 8%, social sciences 11%, visual/performing arts 6%.

Computing on campus. 1,200 workstations in dormitories, library, computer center, student center. Dormitories wired for high-speed internet access and linked to campus network. Commuter students can connect to campus network. Online course registration, online library, helpline, student web hosting, wireless network available.

Student life. **Freshman orientation:** Mandatory. Preregistration for classes offered. **Policies:** Students play active role in university governance. **Housing:** Guaranteed on-campus for freshmen. Coed dorms, special housing for disabled, apartments, wellness housing available. $350 nonrefundable deposit, deadline 5/1. Honors hall, alcohol free floors, academic emphasis floors, non-traditional age area, non-smoking floors, leadership floor, special quiet floors available. **Activities:** Bands, campus ministries, choral groups, dance, drama, international student organizations, literary magazine, music ensembles, musical theater, radio station, student government, student newspaper, symphony orchestra, TV station, Black student union, Jewish student association, Circle K, student ambassadors, Newman Club, Campus Crusades, Hillel, sisterhood.

Athletics. NCAA. **Intercollegiate:** Baseball M, basketball, cheerleading, cross-country, diving, field hockey W, football (tackle) M, golf M, gymnastics W, lacrosse, soccer, softball W, swimming, tennis, track and field, volleyball W. **Intramural:** Basketball, cross-country, football (non-tackle), lacrosse, racquetball, soccer, softball, tennis, triathlon, volleyball. **Team name:** Tigers.

Student services. Adult student services, alcohol/substance abuse counseling, chaplain/spiritual director, career counseling, student employment services, financial aid counseling, health services, minority student services, on-campus daycare, personal counseling, placement for graduates, veterans' counselor, women's services. **Physically disabled:** Services for visually, speech, hearing impaired.

Contact. E-mail: admissions@towson.edu
Phone: (410) 704-2113 Toll-free number: (888) 486-9766
Fax: (410) 704-3030
Louise Shulack, Director of Undergraduate Admissions, Towson University, 8000 York Road, Towson, MD 21252-0001

United States Naval Academy

Annapolis, Maryland — **CB member**
www.usna.edu — **CB code: 5809**

- Public 4-year military college
- Residential campus in large town
- 4,489 degree-seeking undergraduates: 20% women, 4% African American, 3% Asian American, 10% Hispanic American, 1% Native American, 1% international
- 14% of applicants admitted
- SAT or ACT (ACT writing optional), application essay, interview required
- 86% graduate within 6 years; 2% enter graduate study

General. Founded in 1845. Regionally accredited. Military environment and organization under student leadership with military officer supervision. Professional training at US bases and with units of fleet during summer months. Graduates receive B.S. degree with a major in one of 22 disciplines, plus commission as Ensign in US Navy or Second Lieutenant in US Marine Corps. **Degrees:** 1,047 bachelor's awarded. **Location:** 30 miles from Baltimore, 35 miles from Washington, DC. **Calendar:** Semester, limited summer session. **Full-time faculty:** 525 total; 64% have terminal degrees, 9% minority, 22% women. **Class size:** 61% < 20, 39% 20-39. **Special facilities:** Observatory, planetarium, satellite dish, oceanographic research vessel, weather station, towing tanks, propulsion laboratory, transsonic and hypersonic sound tunnels, museum.

Freshman class profile. 10,960 applied, 1,525 admitted, 1,261 enrolled.

Mid 50% test scores		End year in good standing:	96%
SAT critical reading:	560-670	Return as sophomores:	96%
SAT math:	600-700	Out-of-state:	95%
Rank in top quarter:	81%	Live on campus:	100%
Rank in top tenth:	56%	International:	1%

Basis for selection. Test scores, school achievement record, interview, recommendations of school officials, participation in sports, school, and community activities important. Rank in top 40% of class usually required. Successful candidate must be qualified medically, pass a candidate physical fitness assessment, and be nominated by an official source.

High school preparation. College-preparatory program recommended. Recommended units include English 4, mathematics 4, history 2, science 2 (laboratory 2) and foreign language 2. Familiarity with the use of personal computers, including the Windows operating system, word processing, spreadsheets, and the Internet required.

2009-2010 Annual costs. First-year students pay one-time fee of $2,500 upon entering the Naval Academy for initial outfitting of uniforms and other supplies. Tuition, room and board, and medical and dental care provided by United States government. Each midshipman receives monthly salary of about $895 to cover costs of books, supplies, uniforms, laundry, and equipment, including microcomputer. Books/supplies: $1,000.

Application procedures. **Admission:** Closing date 1/31 (receipt date). No application fee. Application must be submitted online. Admission notification on a rolling basis beginning on or about 9/1. Must reply by May 1 or within 2 week(s) if notified thereafter. Nomination essential prior to consideration for appointment. Nominating authorities include President, Vice President, Secretary of Navy, members of Congress, delegates to Congress, governors of United States Territories, and resident commissioner of Puerto Rico. Applicants for presidential appointments limited by law to sons and daughters of career military personnel, active or retired. Applicants encouraged to apply to the Academy and nominating authority by May one year prior to desired admission.

Academics. **Special study options:** Double major, honors, independent study, study abroad. Qualified students have opportunities to begin work in senior year towards a Master's degree at local graduate schools. Selected midshipmen can also engage in research with thesis, or work towards honors in their majors. **Credit/placement by examination:** AP, CLEP, SAT, ACT, institutional tests. Midshipmen take local examinations after admission for placement. AP Exam scores also used for validation of some courses. **Support services:** Learning center, remedial instruction, study skills assistance, tutoring, writing center.

Majors. **Computer sciences:** General, information technology. **Engineering:** General, aerospace, computer hardware, electrical, marine, mechanical, ocean, systems. **Foreign languages:** Arabic, Chinese. **History:** General. **Math:** General. **Physical sciences:** General, chemistry, oceanography, physics. **Social sciences:** Econometrics, economics, political science.

Most popular majors. Engineering/engineering technologies 36%, English 6%, history 10%, physical sciences 12%, social sciences 26%.

Computing on campus. PC or laptop required. Dormitories wired for high-speed internet access and linked to campus network. Online course registration, helpline, repair service available.

Student life. **Freshman orientation:** Mandatory. All freshmen (plebes) report in late June/early July for approximately 6 weeks of military indoctrination. **Policies:** The Naval Academy has an Honor Concept administered by the Brigade of Midshipmen. **Housing:** Guaranteed on-campus for all undergraduates. Coed dorms, wellness housing available. Midshipmen must live in dormitory on campus all four years. **Activities:** Bands, choral groups, drama, film society, literary magazine, music ensembles, musical theater, radio station, student newspaper, Fellowship of Christian Athletes, Black Studies Club, Midshipmen Action Group, Officers' Christian Fellowship, Foreign Affairs Conference, Women's Professional Association.

Athletics. NCAA. **Intercollegiate:** Baseball M, basketball, cross-country, diving, football (tackle) M, golf M, gymnastics M, lacrosse, rifle, rowing (crew), sailing, soccer, squash M, swimming, tennis M, track and field, volleyball W, water polo M, wrestling M. **Intramural:** Basketball, boxing, cross-country, football (non-tackle), golf, handball, judo, racquetball, sailing, soccer, softball, swimming, volleyball, weight lifting, wrestling. **Team name:** Midshipmen.

Student services. Alcohol/substance abuse counseling, chaplain/spiritual director, career counseling, health services, legal services, minority student services, personal counseling, placement for graduates, women's services.

Contact. E-mail: webmail@usna.edu
Phone: (410) 293-4361 Toll-free number: (888) 249-7707
Fax: (410) 293-1815
Dean of Admissions, United States Naval Academy, 117 Decatur Road, Annapolis, MD 21402-5018

University of Baltimore

Baltimore, Maryland — **CB member**
www.ubalt.edu — **CB code: 5810**

- Public 4-year business and liberal arts college
- Commuter campus in very large city
- 2,710 degree-seeking undergraduates: 45% part-time, 56% women, 35% African American, 4% Asian American, 3% Hispanic American, 1% international
- 3,974 degree-seeking graduate students
- 51% of applicants admitted
- SAT or ACT (ACT writing optional), application essay required

General. Founded in 1925. Regionally accredited. Active career center, off-campus housing support. **Degrees:** 517 bachelor's awarded; master's, doctoral, first professional offered. **ROTC:** Army. **Location:** Midtown Baltimore. **Calendar:** Semester, limited summer session. **Full-time faculty:** 166 total. **Part-time faculty:** 186 total. **Special facilities:** Graphics laboratory, business center, interactive video network.

Freshman class profile. 757 applied, 385 admitted, 172 enrolled.

Mid 50% test scores		**GPA 3.50-3.74:**	9%
SAT critical reading:	480-570	**GPA 3.0-3.49:**	32%
SAT math:	460-570	**GPA 2.0-2.99:**	47%
SAT writing:	470-550	**Out-of-state:**	2%
GPA 3.75 or higher:	11%	**International:**	1%

Basis for selection. Application, high school transcript, standardized test scores (ACT/SAT) and personal essay.

High school preparation. 22 units required; 24 recommended. Required and recommended units include English 4, mathematics 3, social studies 3, history 3, science 3, foreign language 1-2, computer science 1-2 and academic electives 4.

2008-2009 Annual costs. Tuition/fees: $7,051; $20,557 out-of-state. Books/supplies: $730.

Application procedures. Admission: No deadline. $30 fee, may be waived for applicants with need. Admission notification on a rolling basis beginning on or about 9/15. Must reply by 5/1. **Financial aid:** No deadline. FAFSA, institutional form required. Applicants notified on a rolling basis.

Academics. All undergraduate students take 9 hours in an upper-level core curriculum in a general humanities-based general education. **Special study options:** Accelerated study, combined bachelor's/graduate degree, cooperative education, cross-registration, distance learning, dual enrollment of high school students, exchange student, honors, independent study, internships, student-designed major, study abroad, weekend college. **Credit/placement by examination:** AP, CLEP, IB, institutional tests. 30 credit hours maximum toward bachelor's degree. **Support services:** Learning center, reduced course load, remedial instruction, study skills assistance, tutoring, writing center.

Majors. Business: General, accounting, business admin, communications, entrepreneurial studies, finance, human resources, international, management information systems, managerial economics, marketing, real estate. **Communications:** Public relations. **Computer sciences:** General. **Health:** Health care admin. **History:** General. **Legal studies:** Prelaw. **Liberal arts:** Arts/sciences. **Protective services:** Criminal justice, forensics. **Psychology:** General. **Public administration:** Human services. **Social sciences:** Political science.

Most popular majors. Business/marketing 47%, communications/journalism 6%, health sciences 9%, legal studies 6%, liberal arts 8%, social sciences 17%.

Computing on campus. 155 workstations in library, computer center, student center. Commuter students can connect to campus network. Online library, helpline, wireless network available.

Student life. Freshman orientation: Available. **Activities:** International student organizations, literary magazine, student government, student newspaper, 60 student organizations.

Athletics. Intramural: Badminton, basketball, golf, judo, racquetball, rowing (crew), skiing, soccer W, table tennis, tennis, volleyball.

Student services. Career counseling, student employment services, health services, personal counseling, placement for graduates, veterans' counselor. **Physically disabled:** Services for visually, speech, hearing impaired.

Contact. E-mail: admissions@ubalt.edu
Phone: (410) 837-4777 Toll-free number: (877) 277-5982
Fax: (410) 837-4793
Laura Bristow, Director of Freshman Admissions, University of Baltimore, 1420 North Charles Street, Baltimore, MD 21201-5779

University of Maryland: Baltimore

Baltimore, Maryland
www.umaryland.edu — **CB code: 0527**

- Public two-year upper-division university and health science college
- Commuter campus in very large city
- 52% of applicants admitted

General. Founded in 1807. Regionally accredited. **Degrees:** 350 bachelor's awarded; master's, doctoral, first professional offered. **Articulation:** Agreements with all Maryland community colleges. **Calendar:** 4-1-4, limited summer session. **Full-time faculty:** 380 total; 70% have terminal degrees, 23% minority, 58% women. **Part-time faculty:** 94 total; 69% have terminal degrees, 16% minority, 40% women. **Special facilities:** Dental, medical, pharmacy and nursing museums; law library, health sciences library, center for health policy and health services research, center for research on aging, center for vaccine development, biotechnology institute, center for health and homeland security.

Student profile. 851 degree-seeking undergraduates, 5,189 degree-seeking graduate students. 833 applied as first time-transfer students, 436 admitted, 319 enrolled. 65% transferred from two-year, 35% transferred from four-year institutions.

Women:	85%	**International:**	6%
African American:	26%	**Part-time:**	37%
Asian American:	12%	**Out-of-state:**	11%
Hispanic American:	3%	**25 or older:**	67%

Basis for selection. College transcript required. Undergraduate deadlines range from February 1 to August 15 (nursing, dental hygiene, medical technology). Transfer accepted as juniors, seniors.

2008-2009 Annual costs. Tuition/fees: $7,803; $21,542 out-of-state. Books/supplies: $1,955. Personal expenses: $2,765.

Financial aid. Need-based: 36% of total undergraduate aid awarded as scholarships/grants, 64% as loans/jobs. **Additional information:** Maryland state deadline 3/1.

Application procedures. Admission: $50 fee. Admission process, fees, and dates differ among undergraduate programs (nursing, dental hygiene, medical technology). **Financial aid:** FAFSA required.

Academics. Special study options: Distance learning, double major. **Credit/placement by examination:** CLEP, institutional tests. 30 credit hours maximum toward bachelor's degree.

Majors. Health: Clinical lab science, dental hygiene, nursing (RN).

Computing on campus. 100 workstations in library, computer center, student center. Dormitories wired for high-speed internet access and linked to campus network. Commuter students can connect to campus network. Online library, helpline, wireless network available.

Student life. Housing: Apartments available. **Activities:** International student organizations, student government, Newman Center, African-American student association, Community Volunteer Program.

Athletics. Intramural: Badminton, basketball, football (non-tackle), golf, racquetball, soccer, softball, squash, tennis, volleyball.

Student services. Alcohol/substance abuse counseling, career counseling, services for economically disadvantaged, student employment services, financial aid counseling, health services, minority student services, on-campus daycare, personal counseling, placement for graduates, women's services. **Physically disabled:** Services for visually, speech, hearing impaired.

Contact. E-mail: gradinfo@umaryland.edu
Phone: (410) 706-7480 Fax: (410) 706-4053
Thomas Day, Director of Records and Registration, University of Maryland: Baltimore, 620 West Lexington Street, Baltimore, MD 21201

University of Maryland: Baltimore County

Baltimore, Maryland — **CB member**
www.umbc.edu — **CB code: 5835**

- Public 4-year university
- Residential campus in large city
- 9,468 degree-seeking undergraduates: 13% part-time, 45% women, 17% African American, 22% Asian American, 4% Hispanic American, 4% international
- 2,430 degree-seeking graduate students
- 72% of applicants admitted
- SAT or ACT (ACT writing optional), application essay required
- 61% graduate within 6 years

General. Founded in 1963. Regionally accredited. **Degrees:** 1,844 bachelor's awarded; master's, doctoral offered. **ROTC:** Army, Air Force. **Location:** 5 miles from Baltimore, 35 miles from Washington, DC. **Calendar:** 4-1-4, extensive summer session. **Full-time faculty:** 483 total; 87% have terminal degrees, 16% minority, 43% women. **Part-time faculty:** 275 total; 33% have terminal degrees, 19% minority, 46% women. **Class size:** 41% < 20, 39% 20-39, 8% 40-49, 9% 50-99, 4% >100. **Special facilities:** Research telescope, greenhouse, research spectrometers, nuclear magnetic resonance machines, electron microscope facility, imaging/digital art laboratory, healthcare informatics laboratory, two galleries - contemporary art and photography, conservation and environmental research area.

Freshman class profile. 5,820 applied, 4,175 admitted, 1,569 enrolled.

Mid 50% test scores		**GPA 2.0-2.99:**	13%
SAT critical reading:	520-630	**Rank in top quarter:**	55%
SAT math:	560-670	**Rank in top tenth:**	26%
SAT writing:	520-630	**End year in good standing:**	79%
ACT composite:	22-27	**Return as sophomores:**	87%
GPA 3.75 or higher:	38%	**Out-of-state:**	10%
GPA 3.50-3.74:	19%	**Live on campus:**	28%
GPA 3.0-3.49:	30%	**International:**	4%

Basis for selection. High school record, test scores important. Audition required for music, dance, theater majors. Portfolio required for visual arts majors.

High school preparation. College-preparatory program recommended. Required and recommended units include English 4, mathematics 3, social studies 3, science 3-4 and foreign language 2. Algebra I and II, and geometry required. History combined with Social Studies.

2008-2009 Annual costs. Tuition/fees: $8,780; $17,512 out-of-state. Room/board: $8,960. Books/supplies: $1,100. Personal expenses: $1,450.

2007-2008 Financial aid. Need-based: 981 full-time freshmen applied for aid; 657 were judged to have need; 657 of these received aid. Average need met was 86%. Average scholarship/grant was $10,287; average loan $3,622. 64% of total undergraduate aid awarded as scholarships/grants, 36% as loans/jobs. **Non-need-based:** Awarded to 1,585 full-time undergraduates, including 625 freshmen. Scholarships awarded for academics, alumni affiliation, art, athletics, music/drama.

Application procedures. Admission: Priority date 11/1; deadline 2/1 (postmark date). $50 fee, may be waived for applicants with need. Admission notification on a rolling basis beginning on or about 12/15. Must reply by May 1 or within 2 week(s) if notified thereafter. **Financial aid:** Priority date 2/14; no closing date. FAFSA required. Applicants notified by 3/15; Applicants notified on a rolling basis starting 4/1; must reply within 2 week(s) of notification.

Academics. Special study options: Accelerated study, combined bachelor's/graduate degree, cooperative education, cross-registration, distance learning, double major, dual enrollment of high school students, ESL, honors, independent study, internships, liberal arts/career combination, semester at sea, student-designed major, study abroad, teacher certification program. **Credit/placement by examination:** AP, CLEP, IB, institutional tests. 60 credit hours maximum toward bachelor's degree. **Support services:** Learning center, remedial instruction, study skills assistance, tutoring, writing center.

Honors college/program. Minimum 1300 SAT (exclusive of Writing) and 3.5 GPA required. Approximately 140 students accepted each year, with average SAT of 1300 (exclusive of Writing) and 3.81 GPA. Each semester 40-50 courses offered along with non-curricular activities.

Majors. Area/ethnic studies: African-American, American. **Biology:** General, Biochemistry/biophysics and molecular biology, bioinformatics. **Communications:** Media studies. **Computer sciences:** General, information systems. **Conservation:** Environmental science, environmental studies. **Education:** Physics. **Engineering:** General, chemical, computer, mechanical. **Foreign languages:** General, linguistics. **Health:** EMT paramedic, health services. **History:** General. **Interdisciplinary:** Ancient studies. **Math:** General, statistics. **Philosophy/religion:** Philosophy. **Physical sciences:** Chemistry, physics. **Psychology:** General. **Public administration:** Social work. **Social sciences:** Anthropology, economics, geography, political science, sociology. **Visual/performing arts:** General, acting, dance, dramatic. **Other:** Gender Studies, Physics Education.

Most popular majors. Biology 13%, communication technologies 16%, engineering/engineering technologies 7%, psychology 13%, social sciences 16%, visual/performing arts 7%.

Computing on campus. 1,100 workstations in dormitories, library, computer center, student center. Dormitories wired for high-speed internet access and linked to campus network. Commuter students can connect to campus network. Online course registration, online library, helpline, repair service, student web hosting, wireless network available.

Student life. Freshman orientation: Mandatory, $125 fee. Preregistration for classes offered. Held June and July. Separate program for honors college students. **Housing:** Guaranteed on-campus for freshmen. Coed dorms, special housing for disabled, apartments, wellness housing available. $200 nonrefundable deposit, deadline 5/1. **Activities:** Bands, campus ministries, choral groups, dance, drama, film society, international student organizations, literary magazine, music ensembles, Model UN, musical theater, opera, radio station, student government, student newspaper, symphony orchestra, TV station, Black student union, Chinese student association, Jewish student association, Korean club, gay and lesbian organization, progressive action committee, Christian Fellowship, women's union.

Athletics. NCAA. **Intercollegiate:** Baseball M, basketball, cheerleading, cross-country, diving, lacrosse, soccer, softball W, swimming, tennis, track and field, volleyball W. **Intramural:** Basketball, football (non-tackle), handball, lacrosse, soccer, softball, tennis, volleyball, weight lifting. **Team name:** Retrievers.

Student services. Adult student services, alcohol/substance abuse counseling, chaplain/spiritual director, career counseling, services for economically disadvantaged, student employment services, financial aid counseling, health services, minority student services, on-campus daycare, personal counseling, placement for graduates, veterans' counselor, women's services. **Physically disabled:** Services for visually, hearing impaired.

Contact. E-mail: admissions@umbc.edu
Phone: (410) 455-2291 Toll-free number: (800) 862-2482
Fax: (410) 455-1094
Dale Bittinger, Director of Admissions, University of Maryland: Baltimore County, 1000 Hilltop Circle, Baltimore, MD 21250

University of Maryland: College Park

College Park, Maryland — **CB member**
www.maryland.edu — **CB code: 5814**

- Public 4-year university
- Commuter campus in large town
- 25,852 degree-seeking undergraduates: 6% part-time, 48% women, 13% African American, 15% Asian American, 6% Hispanic American, 2% international
- 9,920 degree-seeking graduate students
- 39% of applicants admitted
- SAT or ACT with writing, application essay required
- 82% graduate within 6 years

General. Founded in 1856. Regionally accredited. Research and internship opportunities at Smithsonian Institution, National Institutes for Health, NASA, US Capitol, White House, FBI, Department of Agriculture, other federal agencies. **Degrees:** 6,307 bachelor's awarded; master's, doctoral, first professional offered. **ROTC:** Army, Naval, Air Force. **Location:** 30 miles from Baltimore, 3 miles from Washington, DC. **Calendar:** Semester, extensive summer session. **Full-time faculty:** 1,644 total; 92% have terminal degrees, 20% minority, 34% women. **Part-time faculty:** 629 total; 49% have terminal degrees, 12% minority, 44% women. **Class size:** 35% < 20, 44% 20-39, 7% 40-49, 7% 50-99, 7% >100. **Special facilities:** National Archives II, astronomy observatory, engineering wind tunnel, space systems lab, nuclear reactor, performing arts center, center for young children, agricultural biotechnology, superconductivity research, institute for systems research, fire and rescue institute.

Freshman class profile. 28,054 applied, 10,885 admitted, 3,912 enrolled.

Mid 50% test scores		**Rank in top quarter:**	91%
SAT critical reading:	570-680	**Rank in top tenth:**	73%
SAT math:	600-700	**Return as sophomores:**	94%
GPA 3.75 or higher:	65%	**Out-of-state:**	30%
GPA 3.50-3.74:	17%	**Live on campus:**	92%
GPA 3.0-3.49:	15%	**International:**	2%
GPA 2.0-2.99:	3%		

Basis for selection. Academic record, rigor of the high school academic program, standardized admission test scores, class rank (if available), essay, extracurricular activities, counselor recommendation, and other letters of recommendation reviewed. Test scores submitted after 2/01 will be considered based on space-availability. ACT with or without Writing component accepted when SAT Writing has been submitted. Audition required of music majors. Portfolio recommended for architecture majors. **Homeschooled:** Statement describing homeschool structure and mission, transcript of courses and grades required. Transcript should include description of course work, books used, method of evaluation and actual grades or evaluation. Letter of recommendation required and must be from academic professional.

High school preparation. College-preparatory program recommended. 17 units required; 18 recommended. Required and recommended units include English 4, mathematics 3-4, social studies 3, science 3 (laboratory 2) and foreign language 2. Algebra I and II, plane geometry required. Social studies units should include history.

2008-2009 Annual costs. Tuition/fees: $8,005; $23,076 out-of-state. Room/board: $9,109. Books/supplies: $1,025. Personal expenses: $2,268.

2007-2008 Financial aid. **Non-need-based:** Scholarships awarded for academics, art, athletics, music/drama. **Additional information:** Prepaid tuition plans available through state.

Application procedures. **Admission:** Priority date 12/1; deadline 1/20 (receipt date). $55 fee, may be waived for applicants with need. Admission notification 4/1. Must reply by 5/1. Must reply by May 1 or within 4 week(s) if notified thereafter. **Financial aid:** Priority date 2/15; no closing date. FAFSA required. Applicants notified on a rolling basis starting 4/1.

Academics. **Special study options:** Accelerated study, combined bachelor's/graduate degree, cooperative education, cross-registration, distance learning, double major, dual enrollment of high school students, ESL, exchange student, external degree, honors, independent study, internships, semester at sea, student-designed major, study abroad, teacher certification program. Living/learning programs. **Credit/placement by examination:** AP, CLEP, IB, SAT, ACT, institutional tests. 60 credit hours maximum toward bachelor's degree. **Support services:** Learning center, pre-admission summer program, reduced course load, remedial instruction, study skills assistance, tutoring, writing center.

Majors. **Agriculture:** General, animal sciences, economics, food science. **Architecture:** Architecture, landscape. **Area/ethnic studies:** African-American, American, Russian/Slavic, women's. **Biology:** General, biochemistry, ecology, microbiology. **Business:** General, accounting, finance, international, logistics, management science, marketing. **Communications:** General, journalism. **Computer sciences:** General, information systems. **Conservation:** General, environmental science. **Education:** Art, elementary, English, foreign languages, health, kindergarten/preschool, mathematics, music, physical, science, social studies, special. **Engineering:** General, aerospace, agricultural, chemical, civil, computer, electrical, materials, mechanical. **Family/consumer sciences:** Family/community services, food/nutrition. **Foreign languages:** Arabic, Chinese, classics, French, German, Italian, Japanese, linguistics, Romance, Russian, Spanish. **Health:** Communication disorders, dietetics, predental, preveterinary. **History:** General. **Legal studies:** Prelaw. **Math:** General. **Parks/recreation:** Exercise sciences. **Philosophy/religion:** Judaic, philosophy. **Physical sciences:** General, astronomy, chemistry, geology, physics. **Psychology:** General. **Social sciences:** Anthropology, criminology, economics, geography, political science, sociology. **Visual/performing arts:** Art history/conservation, dance, dramatic, music performance, studio arts.

Most popular majors. Biology 8%, business/marketing 16%, communications/journalism 6%, engineering/engineering technologies 9%, social sciences 22%.

Computing on campus. 11,637 workstations in dormitories, library, computer center, student center. Dormitories wired for high-speed internet access and linked to campus network. Commuter students can connect to campus network. Online course registration, online library, helpline, student web hosting, wireless network available.

Student life. **Freshman orientation:** Mandatory, $145 fee. Preregistration for classes offered. 2-day program. **Housing:** Guaranteed on-campus for freshmen. Coed dorms, single-sex dorms, special housing for disabled, apartments, cooperative housing, fraternity/sorority housing, wellness housing available. **Activities:** Bands, campus ministries, choral groups, dance, drama, film society, international student organizations, literary magazine, music ensembles, musical theater, opera, radio station, student government, student newspaper, symphony orchestra, TV station, Black student union, Asian American student union, Latino student union, Native American student union, Alpha Phi Omega, Habitat for Humanity.

Athletics. NCAA. **Intercollegiate:** Baseball M, basketball, cheerleading M, cross-country, equestrian, field hockey W, football (tackle) M, golf, gymnastics W, lacrosse, soccer, softball W, swimming, tennis, track and field, volleyball W, water polo W, wrestling M. **Intramural:** Badminton, basketball, football (non-tackle), golf, ice hockey W, racquetball, soccer, softball, table tennis, tennis, track and field, volleyball, wrestling M. **Team name:** Terrapins.

Student services. Adult student services, alcohol/substance abuse counseling, chaplain/spiritual director, career counseling, services for economically disadvantaged, student employment services, financial aid counseling, health services, legal services, minority student services, on-campus daycare, personal counseling, placement for graduates, veterans' counselor, women's services. **Physically disabled:** Services for visually, speech, hearing impaired.

Contact. E-mail: um-admit@uga.umd.edu
Phone: (301) 314-8385 Toll-free number: (800) 422-5867
Fax: (301) 314-9693
Barbara Gill, Director of Undergraduate Admissions, University of Maryland: College Park, Mitchell Building, College Park, MD 20742-5235

University of Maryland: Eastern Shore

Princess Anne, Maryland — **CB member**
www.umes.edu — **CB code: 5400**

- Public 4-year university
- Residential campus in rural community
- 3,716 degree-seeking undergraduates: 5% part-time, 60% women
- 437 degree-seeking graduate students
- 63% of applicants admitted
- SAT or ACT (ACT writing optional), application essay required
- 38% graduate within 6 years

General. Founded in 1886. Regionally accredited. **Degrees:** 448 bachelor's awarded; master's, doctoral offered. **Location:** 12 miles from Salisbury. **Calendar:** Semester, extensive summer session. **Full-time faculty:** 173 total; 66% have terminal degrees, 58% minority, 43% women. **Part-time faculty:** 122 total; 17% have terminal degrees, 42% minority, 57% women. **Class size:** 53% < 20, 41% 20-39, 3% 40-49, 3% 50-99, less than 1% >100. **Special facilities:** Arts and technology center, performing arts center, hydroponic greenhouse, education center.

Freshman class profile. 4,267 applied, 2,670 admitted, 1,086 enrolled.

Mid 50% test scores		**GPA 3.50-3.74:**	6%
SAT critical reading:	370-460	**GPA 3.0-3.49:**	23%
SAT math:	360-450	**GPA 2.0-2.99:**	66%
SAT writing:	380-460	**Return as sophomores:**	66%
ACT composite:	14-17	**Out-of-state:**	29%
GPA 3.75 or higher:	5%	**Live on campus:**	83%

Basis for selection. School record, class rank, and test scores most important. Interview recommended for honors program and physical therapy applicants. Audition required for music majors.

High school preparation. 20 units required. Required units include English 4, mathematics 3, social studies 3, science 2, foreign language 2 and academic electives 6.

2008-2009 Annual costs. Tuition/fees: $6,042; $12,830 out-of-state. Room/board: $6,880. Books/supplies: $1,800. Personal expenses: $1,800.

2007-2008 Financial aid. **Need-based:** 74% of total undergraduate aid awarded as scholarships/grants, 26% as loans/jobs. **Non-need-based:** Scholarships awarded for academics, alumni affiliation, art, athletics, leadership, music/drama, ROTC, state residency.

Application procedures. **Admission:** Priority date 3/1; deadline 7/15. $25 fee, may be waived for applicants with need. Admission notification on a rolling basis. **Financial aid:** Priority date 3/1, closing date 4/1. FAFSA required. Applicants notified on a rolling basis starting 4/15.

Academics. The doctoral program in organizational leadership is a weekend program to meet scheduling needs of its students who are mostly full-time employees. The Library opens in the evenings. **Special study options:** Accelerated study, cooperative education, cross-registration, distance learning, double major, dual enrollment of high school students, exchange student, honors, independent study, internships, liberal arts/career combination, New York semester, study abroad, teacher certification program. **Credit/placement by examination:** AP, CLEP, IB, institutional tests. 60 credit hours maximum toward bachelor's degree. **Support services:** Learning center, pre-admission summer program, reduced course load, remedial instruction, study skills assistance, tutoring, writing center.

Majors. **Agriculture:** General, business, poultry. **Architecture:** Architecture. **Area/ethnic studies:** African-American. **Biology:** General, ecology. **Business:** General, accounting, business admin, hospitality admin, hotel/motel admin. **Computer sciences:** General. **Conservation:** Forestry. **Construction:** General. **Education:** General, agricultural, art, business, English, family/consumer sciences, mathematics, music, physical, science, social studies, special, technology/industrial arts. **Engineering:** General. **Engineering technology:** General, civil. **Family/consumer sciences:** General. **Health:** Physician assistant. **History:** General. **Liberal arts:** Arts/sciences. **Math:** General. **Parks/recreation:** Exercise sciences. **Physical sciences:** Chemistry. **Protective services:** Police science. **Social sciences:** Sociology. **Transportation:** Aviation. **Visual/performing arts:** Commercial/advertising art. **Other:** Rehabilitation services.

Most popular majors. Biology 9%, business/marketing 22%, family/consumer sciences 9%, health sciences 11%, security/protective services 16%, social sciences 8%.

Computing on campus. 739 workstations in dormitories, library, computer center. Dormitories wired for high-speed internet access and linked to campus network. Commuter students can connect to campus network. Online library, helpline, wireless network available.

Student life. **Freshman orientation:** Mandatory, $100 fee. Preregistration for classes offered. 2 day program in the Fall. **Housing:** Coed dorms, single-sex dorms, apartments, wellness housing available. $300 partly refundable deposit, deadline 5/1. **Activities:** Bands, campus ministries, choral groups, dance, drama, international student organizations, music ensembles, radio station, student government, student newspaper, NAACP, Students for Progressive Action, Phenomenal Women, Rotaract club, College Democrats of America, Students in Free Enterprise, For Sisters Only, National Student Business League.

Athletics. NCAA. **Intercollegiate:** Baseball M, basketball, bowling W, cheerleading M, cross-country, golf M, softball W, tennis, track and field, volleyball W. **Intramural:** Basketball, bowling, football (non-tackle) M, soccer, softball W, swimming, table tennis, volleyball. **Team name:** Hawks.

Student services. Adult student services, career counseling, student employment services, financial aid counseling, health services, on-campus daycare, personal counseling, placement for graduates, veterans' counselor. **Physically disabled:** Services for speech, hearing impaired.

Contact. E-mail: umesadmissions@umes.edu
Phone: (410) 651-6410 Fax: (410) 651-7922
Tyrone Young, Director of Admissions and Recruitment, University of Maryland: Eastern Shore, Bird Hall, Princess Anne, MD 21853

University of Maryland: University College

Adelphi, Maryland
www.umuc.edu **CB code: 0551**

- Public 4-year university
- Commuter campus in large town
- 21,061 degree-seeking undergraduates: 86% part-time, 57% women, 30% African American, 4% Asian American, 6% Hispanic American, 1% Native American, 2% international
- 11,413 degree-seeking graduate students

General. Founded in 1947. Regionally accredited. Courses held at over 20 locations throughout Maryland, Virginia and Washington, D.C. Associate degree programs available only to active military personnel. Offers BA/BS program with 12 other universities through National University Degree Consortium. Courses offered at more than 120 locations in Europe and Asia. **Degrees:** 2,793 bachelor's, 191 associate awarded; master's, doctoral offered. **Location:** 9 miles from Washington, DC. **Calendar:** Semester, extensive summer session. **Full-time faculty:** 233 total; 70% have terminal degrees, 14% minority, 48% women. **Part-time faculty:** 1,523 total; 67% have terminal degrees, 14% minority, 40% women. **Class size:** 61% < 20, 37% 20-39, 1% 40-49.

Freshman class profile. 3,972 applied, 3,972 admitted, 862 enrolled.

Out-of-state:	35%	**International:**	2%

Basis for selection. Open admission.

2008-2009 Annual costs. Tuition/fees: $5,820; $12,060 out-of-state. Books/supplies: $1,360. Personal expenses: $4,250.

2007-2008 Financial aid. **Need-based:** 72 full-time freshmen applied for aid; 70 were judged to have need; 54 of these received aid. Average need met was 18%. Average scholarship/grant was $3,624; average loan $2,799. 28% of total undergraduate aid awarded as scholarships/grants, 72% as loans/jobs. **Non-need-based:** Awarded to 280 full-time undergraduates, including 1 freshmen. Scholarships awarded for academics, leadership.

Application procedures. **Admission:** No deadline. $50 fee. Admission notification on a rolling basis. **Financial aid:** Priority date 6/1; no closing date. FAFSA, institutional form required. Applicants notified on a rolling basis starting 5/1; must reply within 2 week(s) of notification.

Academics. Degree programs offered primarily for adults attending part-time. No traditional freshman class. **Special study options:** Accelerated study, cooperative education, cross-registration, distance learning, double major, dual enrollment of high school students, external degree, teacher certification program, weekend college. **Credit/placement by examination:** AP, CLEP, IB, institutional tests. 30 credit hours maximum toward associate degree, 60 toward bachelor's. **Support services:** Tutoring, writing center.

Majors. **Area/ethnic studies:** Asian. **Business:** Accounting, business admin, human resources, marketing. **Communications:** General. **Computer sciences:** General, computer science, information systems. **Conservation:** General. **History:** General. **Liberal arts:** Arts/sciences. **Psychology:** General. **Social sciences:** General, criminology.

Most popular majors. Business/marketing 38%, computer/information sciences 21%, interdisciplinary studies 9%, psychology 9%.

Computing on campus. Commuter students can connect to campus network. Online course registration, online library, helpline, student web hosting, wireless network available.

Student life. **Freshman orientation:** Available.

Student services. Adult student services, career counseling, veterans' counselor. **Physically disabled:** Services for visually, hearing impaired.

Contact. E-mail: admissions@umuc.edu
Phone: (301) 985-7000 Toll-free number: (800) 888-8682
Fax: (301) 985-7364
Jessica Sadaka, Director of Admissions, University of Maryland: University College, 3501 University Boulevard East, Adelphi, MD 20783-8010

Washington Bible College

Lanham, Maryland
www.bible.edu **CB code: 5884**

- Private 4-year Bible and seminary college affiliated with nondenominational tradition
- Commuter campus in large town
- 253 degree-seeking undergraduates
- 315 graduate students
- SAT or ACT (ACT writing optional), application essay required

General. Founded in 1938. Regionally accredited; also accredited by ABHE. Main Campus in Lanham, MD. Branch sites in Annapolis, MD and in Springfield, VA. **Degrees:** 32 bachelor's, 1 associate awarded; master's offered. **Location:** 10 miles from Washington, DC. **Calendar:** Semester, limited summer session. **Full-time faculty:** 9 total. **Part-time faculty:** 16 total.

Freshman class profile.

Mid 50% test scores		Out-of-state:	31%
SAT critical reading:	420-580	Live on campus:	68%
SAT math:	410-550		

Basis for selection. Student's spiritual qualifications most important, followed by academic achievement, test scores, essay, recommendations. 2 references required. Interview recommended. Audition required of music majors.

High school preparation. 15 units recommended. Recommended units include English 4, mathematics 2, social studies 2, science 2 and academic electives 5. Typing recommended.

2008-2009 Annual costs. Tuition/fees: $13,050. Room/board: $6,770. Books/supplies: $500. Personal expenses: $1,300.

2007-2008 Financial aid. **Non-need-based:** Scholarships awarded for academics, leadership, music/drama, state residency.

Application procedures. **Admission:** Closing date 8/1 (receipt date). $35 fee, may be waived for applicants with need, free for online applicants. Admission notification on a rolling basis. Campus visit suggested. Deadline for housing deposit 30 days after acceptance. **Financial aid:** Closing date 3/1. FAFSA, institutional form required. Applicants notified on a rolling basis starting 7/1; must reply within 2 week(s) of notification.

Academics. All students major in Bible; other areas may be studied for concentrations. **Special study options:** Accelerated study, double major, ESL, independent study, internships, study abroad, teacher certification program. **Credit/placement by examination:** AP, CLEP, SAT, ACT, institutional tests. 15 credit hours maximum toward bachelor's degree. **Support services:** Reduced course load, tutoring, writing center.

Majors. **Education:** General, early childhood, elementary, multi-level teacher, music, physical, school counseling. **Family/consumer sciences:** Work/family studies. **Psychology:** Counseling. **Theology:** Bible, missionary, pastoral counseling, preministerial, religious ed, sacred music, theology, youth ministry. **Visual/performing arts:** Music performance, piano/organ, voice/opera.

Computing on campus. 10 workstations in library, student center. Dormitories wired for high-speed internet access and linked to campus network. Commuter students can connect to campus network. Online library, helpline, wireless network available.

Student life. **Freshman orientation:** Mandatory. 2-day spring and summer programs. **Policies:** Religious observance required. **Housing:** Guaranteed on-campus for freshmen. Single-sex dorms, apartments, wellness housing available. $100 nonrefundable deposit, deadline 6/1. **Activities:** Choral groups, drama, music ensembles, student government, student newspaper, Student Missions Fellowship, Fellowship of Christian Athletes.

Athletics. NCCAA. **Intercollegiate:** Basketball M, volleyball W. **Intramural:** Basketball, cheerleading, football (tackle) M, racquetball, soccer, table tennis, volleyball, weight lifting. **Team name:** Cougars.

Student services. Chaplain/spiritual director, career counseling, student employment services, financial aid counseling, health services, personal counseling, placement for graduates, veterans' counselor. **Physically disabled:** Services for visually, hearing impaired.

Contact. E-mail: iadmissions@bible.edu
Phone: (301) 552-1400 ext. 1212 Toll-free
number: (877) 793-7227 ext. 1212 Fax: (301) 552-2775
Mark Johnson, Director of Admission, Washington Bible College, 6511 Princess Garden Parkway, Lanham, MD 20706-3599

Washington College

Chestertown, Maryland — **CB member**
www.washcoll.edu — **CB code: 5888**

- Private 4-year liberal arts college
- Residential campus in small town
- 1,275 degree-seeking undergraduates: 59% women, 5% African American, 1% Asian American, 1% Hispanic American, 2% international
- 56 degree-seeking graduate students
- 69% of applicants admitted
- SAT or ACT (ACT writing optional), application essay required
- 80% graduate within 6 years

General. Founded in 1782. Regionally accredited. **Degrees:** 243 bachelor's awarded; master's offered. **Location:** 70 miles from Baltimore, 75 miles from Washington, DC. **Calendar:** Semester, limited summer session. **Full-time faculty:** 97 total; 91% have terminal degrees, 11% minority, 39% women. **Part-time faculty:** 52 total; 40% have terminal degrees, 8% minority, 44% women. **Class size:** 66% < 20, 30% 20-39, 2% 40-49, 2% 50-99. **Special facilities:** Center for the study of the American experience, center for the environment and society.

Freshman class profile. 3,413 applied, 2,355 admitted, 415 enrolled.

Mid 50% test scores		Rank in top quarter:	65%
SAT critical reading:	530-630	Rank in top tenth:	29%
SAT math:	510-610	Return as sophomores:	82%
SAT writing:	520-620	Out-of-state:	53%
ACT composite:	22-26	Live on campus:	98%
GPA 3.75 or higher:	27%	International:	1%
GPA 3.50-3.74:	20%	Fraternities:	8%
GPA 3.0-3.49:	30%	Sororities:	14%
GPA 2.0-2.99:	23%		

Basis for selection. High school program and grades, class rank, test scores, recommendations important, extracurricular activities considered. Interview recommended. **Homeschooled:** Interview required.

High school preparation. College-preparatory program required. 16 units required; 20 recommended. Required and recommended units include English 4, mathematics 3-4, social studies 2-4, history 2, science 3-4 (laboratory 2-3) and foreign language 2-4.

2008-2009 Annual costs. Tuition/fees: $34,005. Room/board: $7,180. Books/supplies: $1,250. Personal expenses: $1,500.

2008-2009 Financial aid. **Need-based:** 297 full-time freshmen applied for aid; 209 were judged to have need; 209 of these received aid. Average need met was 82%. Average scholarship/grant was $19,757; average loan $2,380. 76% of total undergraduate aid awarded as scholarships/grants, 24% as loans/jobs. **Non-need-based:** Awarded to 452 full-time undergraduates, including 139 freshmen. Scholarships awarded for academics.

Application procedures. **Admission:** Priority date 2/15; deadline 3/1 (postmark date). $50 fee, may be waived for applicants with need. Admission notification on a rolling basis beginning on or about 1/15. Must reply by May 1 or within 2 week(s) if notified thereafter. Applicants applying after February 15 may be wait-listed. **Financial aid:** Priority date 2/15; no closing date. FAFSA, institutional form required. Applicants notified on a rolling basis starting 2/15; must reply by 5/1.

Academics. **Special study options:** Combined bachelor's/graduate degree, cross-registration, double major, dual enrollment of high school students, exchange student, honors, independent study, internships, liberal arts/career combination, student-designed major, study abroad, teacher certification program, Washington semester. **Credit/placement by examination:** AP, CLEP, IB, institutional tests. **Support services:** Learning center, reduced course load, study skills assistance, tutoring, writing center.

Majors. **Area/ethnic studies:** American. **Biology:** General. **Business:** General. **Computer sciences:** Computer science. **Conservation:** Environmental studies. **Education:** General. **Foreign languages:** French, German, Spanish. **History:** General. **Interdisciplinary:** Math/computer science, neuroscience. **Liberal arts:** Arts/sciences, humanities. **Philosophy/religion:** Philosophy. **Physical sciences:** Chemistry, physics. **Psychology:** General. **Social sciences:** Anthropology, economics, international relations, political science, sociology. **Visual/performing arts:** Art, dramatic. **Other:** Interdisciplinary studies.

Most popular majors. Biology 8%, business/marketing 17%, English 9%, psychology 12%, social sciences 21%, visual/performing arts 6%.

Computing on campus. 200 workstations in dormitories, library, computer center, student center. Dormitories wired for high-speed internet access and linked to campus network. Commuter students can connect to campus network. Online course registration, online library, helpline, repair service, student web hosting, wireless network available.

Student life. **Freshman orientation:** Mandatory. Preregistration for classes offered. **Housing:** Guaranteed on-campus for freshmen. Coed dorms, single-sex dorms, special housing for disabled, fraternity/sorority housing, wellness housing available. $200 nonrefundable deposit, deadline 6/1. **Activities:** Bands, choral groups, dance, drama, international student organizations, literary magazine, music ensembles, Model UN, student government, student newspaper, College Republicans, Christian Fellowship, Amnesty International, International Relations Club, Hillel, Black Student Alliance, Cleopatra's Daughters, College Democrats, Best Buddies, EROS, Newman Club, Canterbury Club.

Athletics. NCAA. **Intercollegiate:** Baseball M, basketball, field hockey W, lacrosse, rowing (crew), sailing, soccer, softball W, swimming, tennis, volleyball W. **Intramural:** Basketball, fencing, golf M, ice hockey M, racquetball, rugby, sailing, soccer, softball, squash, tennis, volleyball. **Team name:** Shoremen/Shorewomen.

Student services. Adult student services, alcohol/substance abuse counseling, career counseling, student employment services, financial aid counseling, health services, minority student services, personal counseling, placement for graduates, veterans' counselor. **Physically disabled:** Services for hearing impaired.

Contact. E-mail: adm.off@washcoll.edu
Phone: (410) 778-7700 Toll-free number: (800) 442-1782
Fax: (410) 778-7287
Kevin Coveney, Vice President for Admissions, Washington College, 300 Washington Avenue, Chestertown, MD 21620-1197

Yeshiva College of the Nations Capital
Silver Spring, Maryland

- Private 4-year rabbinical college for men affiliated with Jewish faith
- Residential campus in small city

General. Accredited by AARTS. **Calendar:** Continuous.

Annual costs/financial aid. Tuition/fees (2008-2009): $9,200. Room/board: $8,200.

Contact. Phone: (301) 593-2534
Academic Dean, 1216 Arcola Avenue, Silver Spring, MD 20902

Massachusetts

American International College
Springfield, Massachusetts **CB member**
www.aic.edu **CB code: 3002**

- Private 4-year liberal arts college
- Residential campus in small city
- 1,717 degree-seeking undergraduates: 11% part-time, 59% women, 26% African American, 3% Asian American, 10% Hispanic American, 1% Native American, 3% international
- 1,437 graduate students
- 78% of applicants admitted
- SAT or ACT (ACT writing recommended) required
- 50% graduate within 6 years; 12% enter graduate study

General. Founded in 1885. Regionally accredited. **Degrees:** 264 bachelor's, 2 associate awarded; master's, doctoral offered. **ROTC:** Army, Air Force. **Location:** 90 miles from Boston; 27 miles from Hartford, Connecticut. **Calendar:** Semester, extensive summer session. **Full-time faculty:** 78 total; 47% have terminal degrees, 8% minority, 56% women. **Part-time faculty:** 177 total; 31% have terminal degrees, 8% minority. **Class size:** 49% < 20, 45% 20-39, 3% 40-49, 3% 50-99. **Special facilities:** Cultural arts center, performing arts center, anatomical laboratory, communications media laboratory.

Freshman class profile. 1,713 applied, 1,330 admitted, 382 enrolled.

Mid 50% test scores		**GPA 2.0-2.99:**	46%
SAT critical reading:	420-510	**Rank in top quarter:**	27%
SAT math:	420-520	**Rank in top tenth:**	10%
SAT writing:	420-500	**End year in good standing:**	87%
ACT composite:	17-23	**Return as sophomores:**	73%
GPA 3.75 or higher:	4%	**Out-of-state:**	51%
GPA 3.50-3.74:	8%	**Live on campus:**	79%
GPA 3.0-3.49:	38%	**International:**	6%

Basis for selection. Must have satisfied school's graduation requirements except for one course in English and one course in Social Studies. Must have unqualified approval of school counselor or principal and must possess strong academic skills and maturity necessary for success in college. Essay or personal statement recommended. **Homeschooled:** Statement describing homeschool structure and mission, transcript of courses and grades, interview, letter of recommendation (nonparent) required. **Learning Disabled:** Wechsler Adult Intelligence Scale, interview, diagnostic documentation recommended.

High school preparation. College-preparatory program recommended. 16 units required. Required and recommended units include English 4, mathematics 3-4, social studies 1-2, history 2, science 2-3 (laboratory 2), foreign language 1-2 and academic electives 4.

2008-2009 Annual costs. Tuition/fees: $24,100. Room/board: $10,150. Books/supplies: $1,000. Personal expenses: $1,000.

2008-2009 Financial aid. Need-based: 333 full-time freshmen applied for aid; 316 were judged to have need; 316 of these received aid. Average need met was 75%. Average scholarship/grant was $17,778; average loan $3,305. 61% of total undergraduate aid awarded as scholarships/grants, 39% as loans/jobs. **Non-need-based:** Scholarships awarded for academics, alumni affiliation, athletics, leadership.

Application procedures. Admission: Priority date 7/1; no deadline. $25 fee, may be waived for applicants with need. Admission notification on a rolling basis beginning on or about 12/1. Must reply by May 1 or within 2 week(s) if notified thereafter. **Financial aid:** Priority date 5/1; no closing date. FAFSA required. Applicants notified on a rolling basis starting 3/15; must reply by 5/1 or within 2 week(s) of notification.

Academics. Special study options: Accelerated study, combined bachelor's/graduate degree, cross-registration, distance learning, double major, dual enrollment of high school students, ESL, honors, independent study, internships, liberal arts/career combination, study abroad, teacher certification program, Washington semester, weekend college. **Credit/placement by examination:** AP, CLEP, IB, institutional tests. 30 credit hours maximum toward bachelor's degree. **Support services:** Learning center, reduced course load, remedial instruction, study skills assistance, tutoring, writing center.

Majors. Area/ethnic studies: American. **Biology:** General, biochemistry. **Business:** General, accounting, business admin, finance, international, management science, managerial economics, marketing. **Communications:** Advertising, broadcast journalism, journalism, media studies, public relations, radio/tv. **Computer sciences:** Computer science, information systems. **Education:** Early childhood, elementary, middle, secondary, special. **Health:** Nursing (RN), predental, premedicine, preveterinary. **History:** General. **Interdisciplinary:** Accounting/computer science, biological/physical sciences, math/computer science. **Legal studies:** Prelaw. **Liberal arts:** Arts/sciences. **Math:** General. **Parks/recreation:** General, sports admin. **Physical sciences:** Chemistry. **Protective services:** Criminal justice, law enforcement admin, police science. **Psychology:** General. **Social sciences:** Criminology, economics, international relations, political science, sociology.

Most popular majors. Business/marketing 31%, health sciences 21%, interdisciplinary studies 8%, liberal arts 7%, psychology 10%, security/protective services 11%.

Computing on campus. 100 workstations in dormitories, library, computer center, student center. Dormitories wired for high-speed internet access and linked to campus network. Commuter students can connect to campus network. Online course registration, online library, helpline, wireless network available.

Student life. Freshman orientation: Available. Preregistration for classes offered. Three-day program in early September prior to start of Fall term. **Housing:** Guaranteed on-campus for all undergraduates. Coed dorms, single-sex dorms, apartments, wellness housing available. $100 fully refundable deposit, deadline 8/1. **Activities:** Pep band, campus ministries, choral groups, dance, drama, international student organizations, literary magazine, musical theater, radio station, student government, student newspaper, Model Congress, minority student organizations, Partners, Best Buddies, Intervarsity Christian Fellowship, Young Professionals for International Cooperation.

Athletics. NCAA. **Intercollegiate:** Baseball M, basketball, cheerleading, cross-country, field hockey W, football (tackle) M, golf M, ice hockey M, lacrosse, soccer, softball W, tennis, track and field, volleyball W, wrestling M. **Intramural:** Basketball, football (non-tackle) M, skiing, soccer, softball, swimming, volleyball. **Team name:** Yellow Jackets.

Student services. Adult student services, alcohol/substance abuse counseling, chaplain/spiritual director, career counseling, services for economically disadvantaged, student employment services, financial aid counseling, health services, minority student services, personal counseling, placement for graduates, veterans' counselor, women's services. **Physically disabled:** Services for visually impaired. **Learning disabled:** Comprehensive services available.

Contact. E-mail: inquiry@aic.edu
Phone: (413) 205-3201 Toll-free number: (800) 242-3142
Fax: (413) 205-3051
Peter Miller, Vice President for Admission Services, American International College, 1000 State Street, Springfield, MA 01109

Amherst College
Amherst, Massachusetts **CB member**
www.amherst.edu **CB code: 3003**

- Private 4-year liberal arts college
- Residential campus in large town
- 1,697 degree-seeking undergraduates: 51% women
- 15% of applicants admitted
- SAT and SAT Subject Tests or ACT (ACT writing recommended), application essay required

General. Founded in 1821. Regionally accredited. **Degrees:** 445 bachelor's awarded. **ROTC:** Air Force. **Location:** 90 miles from Boston, 150 miles from New York City. **Calendar:** Semester. **Full-time faculty:** 195 total; 93% have terminal degrees, 19% minority, 38% women. **Part-time faculty:** 17 total; 59% have terminal degrees, 18% minority, 41% women. **Class size:** 75% < 20, 19% 20-39, 3% 40-49, 3% 50-99, less than 1% >100. **Special facilities:** Recital hall, observatory, planetarium, center for Russian culture, Dickinson homestead, natural history museum, fine arts museum, center for community engagement.

Freshman class profile. 7,745 applied, 1,144 admitted, 439 enrolled.

Mid 50% test scores			
SAT critical reading:	670-770	Rank in top quarter:	95%
SAT math:	660-760	Rank in top tenth:	85%
SAT writing:	670-760	Out-of-state:	90%
ACT composite:	29-34	Live on campus:	100%

Basis for selection. Grades, test scores, essays, recommendations, independent work, quality of individual's secondary school program, achievements outside of classroom most important.

High school preparation. Recommended units include English 4, mathematics 4, social studies 2, history 2, science 3 (laboratory 1) and foreign language 4.

2008-2009 Annual costs. Tuition/fees: $37,622. Health Insurance (waivable): $950. Room/board: $9,790. Books/supplies: $1,000. Personal expenses: $1,700.

2008-2009 Financial aid. All financial aid based on need. 249 full-time freshmen applied for aid; 224 were judged to have need; 224 of these received aid. Average need met was 100%. Average scholarship/grant was $36,075; average loan $2,375. 95% of total undergraduate aid awarded as scholarships/grants, 5% as loans/jobs.

Application procedures. Admission: Closing date 1/1 (postmark date). $60 fee, may be waived for applicants with need. Admission notification 4/1. Must reply by 5/1. **Financial aid:** Priority date 2/15; no closing date. FAFSA, CSS PROFILE required. Applicants notified by 4/1; must reply by 5/1.

Academics. First-year students must choose 1 seminar from range of 20 special topics, often interdisciplinary. No core curriculum, no distribution requirements. Students select major at end of sophomore year. **Special study options:** Cross-registration, double major, exchange student, honors, independent study, internships, student-designed major, study abroad, teacher certification program. Member of 5-college consortium. **Credit/placement by examination:** AP, CLEP, IB, institutional tests. **Support services:** Study skills assistance, tutoring, writing center.

Majors. Area/ethnic studies: African, African-American, American, Asian, Central/Eastern European, European, Western European, women's. **Biology:** General. **Computer sciences:** Computer science. **Foreign languages:** Ancient Greek, classics, French, German, Latin, Russian, Spanish. **History:** General. **Interdisciplinary:** Math/computer science, neuroscience. **Legal studies:** General. **Math:** General. **Philosophy/religion:** Philosophy, religion. **Physical sciences:** Astronomy, chemistry, geology, physics. **Psychology:** General. **Social sciences:** Anthropology, economics, political science, sociology. **Visual/performing arts:** Dance, dramatic, studio arts.

Most popular majors. Area/ethnic studies 8%, English 9%, foreign language 13%, psychology 10%, social sciences 22%, visual/performing arts 9%.

Computing on campus. 230 workstations in library, computer center, student center. Dormitories wired for high-speed internet access and linked to campus network. Commuter students can connect to campus network. Helpline, repair service, wireless network available.

Student life. Freshman orientation: Mandatory. Eight-day orientation with events planned by student groups and cultural organizations. **Housing:** Guaranteed on-campus for all undergraduates. Coed dorms, cooperative housing, wellness housing available. Language and other theme houses available including French/Spanish, Russian/German, Latino, African American, health and wellness house, and arts house. Men's and women's floors available to all students. **Activities:** Jazz band, choral groups, dance, drama, film society, international student organizations, literary magazine, music ensembles, Model UN, musical theater, opera, radio station, student government, student newspaper, symphony orchestra, Hillel, service organization, Christian association, Newman club, black student union, Asian student association, Cambodian family tutoring, LaCausa, Christian Fellowship, Korean American students association.

Athletics. NCAA. **Intercollegiate:** Baseball M, basketball, cross-country, diving, field hockey W, football (tackle) M, golf, ice hockey, lacrosse, soccer, softball W, squash, swimming, tennis, track and field, volleyball W. **Intramural:** Badminton, basketball, football (non-tackle), golf, ice hockey, soccer, softball, squash, table tennis, tennis, volleyball. **Team name:** Lord Jeffs.

Student services. Alcohol/substance abuse counseling, chaplain/spiritual director, career counseling, services for economically disadvantaged, student employment services, financial aid counseling, health services, minority student services, personal counseling, placement for graduates, women's services. **Physically disabled:** Services for visually, speech, hearing impaired.

Contact. E-mail: admission@amherst.edu
Phone: (413) 542-2328 Fax: (413) 542-2040
Katie Fretwell, Director of Admission, Amherst College, PO Box 5000, Amherst, MA 01002-5000

Anna Maria College

Paxton, Massachusetts — **CB member**
www.annamaria.edu — **CB code: 3005**

- Private 4-year liberal arts college affiliated with Roman Catholic Church
- Residential campus in small town
- 978 degree-seeking undergraduates: 20% part-time, 56% women, 6% African American, 1% Asian American, 5% Hispanic American, 1% international
- 268 degree-seeking graduate students
- 89% of applicants admitted
- SAT or ACT (ACT writing optional) required
- 59% graduate within 6 years

General. Founded in 1946. Regionally accredited. **Degrees:** 145 bachelor's, 8 associate awarded; master's offered. **ROTC:** Air Force. **Location:** 8 miles from Worcester, 40 miles from Boston. **Calendar:** Semester, limited summer session. **Full-time faculty:** 50 total; 72% have terminal degrees, 66% women. **Part-time faculty:** 129 total; 30% have terminal degrees, 36% women. **Class size:** 72% < 20, 27% 20-39, less than 1% 40-49. **Special facilities:** Nature trail, arts building.

Freshman class profile. 935 applied, 832 admitted, 253 enrolled.

Mid 50% test scores			
SAT critical reading:	380-490	GPA 2.0-2.99:	71%
SAT math:	380-480	Rank in top quarter:	13%
ACT composite:	18-21	Rank in top tenth:	2%
GPA 3.75 or higher:	2%	Return as sophomores:	70%
GPA 3.50-3.74:	7%	Out-of-state:	12%
GPA 3.0-3.49:	15%	Live on campus:	73%

Basis for selection. High school record most important, followed by test scores, recommendations, school and community activities, interview. Audition required of music majors; portfolio required of art majors, essays required of nursing and transfer students.

High school preparation. College-preparatory program recommended. 21 units required. Required units include English 4, mathematics 3, social studies 2, history 2, science 3 (laboratory 1), foreign language 2 and academic electives 4.

2008-2009 Annual costs. Tuition/fees: $25,850. Annual tuition for music program: $26,800. Room/board: $9,350. Books/supplies: $800. Personal expenses: $1,200.

2008-2009 Financial aid. Need-based: 225 full-time freshmen applied for aid; 199 were judged to have need; 199 of these received aid. Average need met was 66%. Average scholarship/grant was $13,617; average loan $4,443. 56% of total undergraduate aid awarded as scholarships/grants, 44% as loans/jobs. **Non-need-based:** Awarded to 732 full-time undergraduates, including 241 freshmen. Scholarships awarded for academics, alumni affiliation, music/drama, religious affiliation, state residency.

Application procedures. Admission: Priority date 3/1; no deadline. $40 fee, may be waived for applicants with need. Admission notification on a rolling basis beginning on or about 12/1. Must reply by May 1 or within 2 week(s) if notified thereafter. Nursing track students required to submit recommendation, essay, work experience and TEAS testing. **Financial aid:** Priority date 3/1; no closing date. FAFSA required. Applicants notified on a rolling basis starting 4/1; must reply within 4 week(s) of notification.

Academics. Special study options: Accelerated study, combined bachelor's/graduate degree, cooperative education, cross-registration, double major, honors, independent study, internships, liberal arts/career combination, student-designed major, study abroad, teacher certification program, Washington semester. Member of 13-college Worcester Consortium. **Credit/placement by examination:** AP, CLEP, institutional tests. 30 credit hours maximum toward bachelor's degree. **Support services:** Learning center, reduced course load, remedial instruction, study skills assistance, tutoring, writing center.

Majors. Business: Business admin, management information systems. **Communications:** Media studies. **Computer sciences:** General. **Conservation:** Environmental science. **Education:** Art, elementary, English, history, kindergarten/preschool, music. **Foreign languages:** Spanish. **Health:** Art therapy, health services, music therapy, nursing (RN). **History:** General. **Legal studies:** Paralegal. **Liberal arts:** Arts/sciences. **Parks/recreation:** Sports admin. **Protective services:** Criminal justice, firefighting. **Psychology:** General. **Public administration:** Human services, policy analysis, social work. **Social sciences:** Political science, sociology. **Theology:** Theology. **Visual/performing arts:** Art, graphic design, music performance. **Other:** Related humanities.

Most popular majors. Business/marketing 11%, education 6%, health sciences 14%, public administration/social services 11%, security/protective services 44%.

Computing on campus. 94 workstations in dormitories, library, computer center, student center. Dormitories wired for high-speed internet access and linked to campus network. Online library, wireless network available.

Student life. **Freshman orientation:** Mandatory. Preregistration for classes offered. **Housing:** Guaranteed on-campus for freshmen. Coed dorms, special housing for disabled, wellness housing available. $300 fully refundable deposit, deadline 5/1. **Activities:** Bands, campus ministries, choral groups, dance, drama, music ensembles, musical theater, student government, student newspaper.

Athletics. NCAA. **Intercollegiate:** Baseball M, basketball, cross-country, field hockey W, football (tackle) M, golf, lacrosse, soccer, softball W, tennis, volleyball W. **Intramural:** Baseball, basketball, football (non-tackle) M, volleyball, weight lifting. **Team name:** Amcats.

Student services. Alcohol/substance abuse counseling, chaplain/spiritual director, career counseling, student employment services, financial aid counseling, health services, minority student services, personal counseling, placement for graduates. **Physically disabled:** Services for visually, speech, hearing impaired.

Contact. E-mail: admission@annamaria.edu
Phone: (508) 849-3360 Toll-free number: (800) 344-4586 ext. 360
Fax: (508) 849-3362
Paula Green, Director of Admission, Anna Maria College, 50 Sunset Lane, Box O, Paxton, MA 01612-1198

Art Institute of Boston at Lesley University

Boston, Massachusetts
www.aiboston.edu **CB code: 3777**

- Private 4-year visual arts college
- Residential campus in very large city

General. Regionally accredited. **Location:** Downtown. **Calendar:** Semester.

Annual costs/financial aid. Tuition/fees (projected): $26,530. Room/board: $12,400. Books/supplies: $1,575. Personal expenses: $1,580. Need-based financial aid available to full-time and part-time students.

Contact. Phone: (617) 585-6710
Director of Operations, 700 Beacon Street, Boston, MA 02215-2598

Assumption College

Worcester, Massachusetts **CB member**
www.assumption.edu **CB code: 3009**

- Private 4-year liberal arts college affiliated with Roman Catholic Church
- Residential campus in small city
- 2,163 degree-seeking undergraduates: 59% women, 2% African American, 2% Asian American, 3% Hispanic American, 1% international
- 418 degree-seeking graduate students
- 71% of applicants admitted
- SAT or ACT (ACT writing optional), application essay required
- 75% graduate within 6 years; 23% enter graduate study

General. Founded in 1904. Regionally accredited. Students may register for courses at 11 area colleges. Volunteer programs available: comprehensive 2-week programs in Mexico and Puerto Rico, 1-week spring break programs in various locations. **Degrees:** 502 bachelor's awarded; master's offered. **ROTC:** Army, Air Force. **Location:** 45 miles from Boston. **Calendar:** Semester, limited summer session. **Full-time faculty:** 155 total; 92% have terminal degrees, 6% minority, 41% women. **Part-time faculty:** 69 total; 56% have terminal degrees, 12% minority, 49% women. **Class size:** 45% < 20, 54% 20-39, less than 1% 40-49, less than 1% 50-99. **Special facilities:** French institute (academic research center for study of Francophone questions).

Freshman class profile. 3,889 applied, 2,776 admitted, 607 enrolled.

Mid 50% test scores		**Rank in top quarter:**	43%
SAT critical reading:	470-580	**Rank in top tenth:**	14%
SAT math:	480-580	**End year in good standing:**	81%
ACT composite:	20-25	**Return as sophomores:**	85%
GPA 3.75 or higher:	5%	**Out-of-state:**	35%
GPA 3.50-3.74:	29%	**Live on campus:**	95%
GPA 3.0-3.49:	66%	**International:**	1%

Basis for selection. School achievement most important, followed by class rank in top 40%, test scores, extracurricular activities, interview, recommendations. **Homeschooled:** Statement describing homeschool structure and mission, letter of recommendation (nonparent) required.

High school preparation. College-preparatory program required. 18 units required. Required units include English 4, mathematics 3, history 2, science 2, foreign language 2 and academic electives 5.

2008-2009 Annual costs. Tuition/fees: $28,851. Room/board: $9,776. Books/supplies: $850. Personal expenses: $1,000.

2008-2009 Financial aid. **Need-based:** 542 full-time freshmen applied for aid; 450 were judged to have need; 450 of these received aid. Average need met was 74%. Average scholarship/grant was $14,950; average loan $3,756. 68% of total undergraduate aid awarded as scholarships/grants, 32% as loans/jobs. **Non-need-based:** Awarded to 676 full-time undergraduates, including 225 freshmen. Scholarships awarded for academics, athletics.

Application procedures. **Admission:** Closing date 2/15 (postmark date). $50 fee, may be waived for applicants with need. Admission notification 5/1. Admission notification on a rolling basis. Must reply by May 1 or within 2 week(s) if notified thereafter. **Financial aid:** Closing date 2/1. FAFSA required. Applicants notified on a rolling basis starting 2/16; must reply by 5/1.

Academics. **Special study options:** Combined bachelor's/graduate degree, cross-registration, double major, honors, independent study, internships, semester at sea, student-designed major, study abroad, teacher certification program, Washington semester. Worcester Consortium gerontology studies program; 3-2 engineering program (BA/BS) with Worcester Polytechnic Institute. **Credit/placement by examination:** AP, CLEP, IB, SAT, institutional tests. **Support services:** Learning center, study skills assistance, tutoring, writing center.

Majors. **Area/ethnic studies:** Latin American. **Biology:** General. **Business:** Accounting, business admin, international, marketing. **Communications:** Organizational. **Computer sciences:** General. **Conservation:** Environmental science. **Foreign languages:** General, classics, French, Italian, Spanish. **History:** General. **Interdisciplinary:** Global studies. **Math:** General. **Philosophy/religion:** Philosophy. **Physical sciences:** Chemistry. **Psychology:** General. **Social sciences:** Economics, political science, sociology. **Theology:** Theology. **Visual/performing arts:** General. **Other:** Human services and rehabilitation studies.

Most popular majors. Biology 8%, business/marketing 28%, communications/journalism 9%, English 6%, health sciences 6%, history 10%, psychology 10%, social sciences 8%.

Computing on campus. 300 workstations in dormitories, library, computer center, student center. Dormitories wired for high-speed internet access and linked to campus network. Commuter students can connect to campus network. Online course registration, online library, helpline, repair service, student web hosting, wireless network available.

Student life. **Freshman orientation:** Mandatory, $265 fee. Preregistration for classes offered. Two-day program in June includes choosing rooms, testing, scheduling fall courses, meeting faculty, workshops. **Housing:** Guaranteed on-campus for all undergraduates. Coed dorms, single-sex dorms, special housing for disabled, wellness housing available. Freshman dorms, substance-free dorms, living/learning center available. **Activities:** Bands, campus ministries, choral groups, drama, film society, literary magazine, musical theater, student government, student newspaper, TV station, ALANA network, College Democrats, College Republicans, student volunteer organization, students advocating change, student health network, service program, Omicron Delta Kappa leadership circle, retreat programs.

Athletics. NCAA. **Intercollegiate:** Baseball M, basketball, cross-country, field hockey W, football (tackle) M, golf M, ice hockey M, lacrosse, rowing (crew) W, soccer, softball W, swimming W, tennis, track and field, volleyball W. **Intramural:** Basketball, football (non-tackle) M, golf, ice hockey, racquetball, soccer, softball, volleyball. **Team name:** Greyhounds.

Student services. Alcohol/substance abuse counseling, chaplain/spiritual director, career counseling, student employment services, financial aid counseling, health services, minority student services, personal counseling, placement for graduates. **Physically disabled:** Services for visually, speech, hearing impaired.

Contact. E-mail: admiss@assumption.edu
Phone: (508) 767-7285 Toll-free number: (866) 477-7776
Fax: (508) 799-4412
Evan Lipp, Vice President for Enrollment Management, Assumption College, 500 Salisbury Street, Worcester, MA 01609-1296

Atlantic Union College
South Lancaster, Massachusetts
www.auc.edu **CB code: 3010**

- Private 4-year liberal arts college affiliated with Seventh-day Adventists
- Residential campus in small town
- 362 degree-seeking undergraduates: 15% part-time, 61% women, 49% African American, 3% Asian American, 19% Hispanic American
- 2 degree-seeking graduate students
- 37% of applicants admitted
- SAT or ACT with writing required

General. Founded in 1882. Regionally accredited. **Degrees:** 86 bachelor's, 35 associate awarded; master's offered. **Location:** 45 miles from Boston. **Calendar:** Semester, limited summer session. **Full-time faculty:** 26 total; 62% have terminal degrees, 50% women. **Part-time faculty:** 41 total; 42% women. **Class size:** 88% < 20, 10% 20-39, 2% 40-49. **Special facilities:** Music conservatory.

Freshman class profile. 284 applied, 104 admitted, 36 enrolled.

Mid 50% test scores			
SAT math:	350-450	GPA 3.50-3.74:	10%
ACT composite:	16-21	GPA 3.0-3.49:	27%
GPA 3.75 or higher:	7%	GPA 2.0-2.99:	56%

Basis for selection. School achievement record, interview, recommendations, test scores important. Interview recommended for non-Seventh-day Adventists. Audition required of music majors. Portfolio recommended for art majors. **Homeschooled:** Transcript of courses and grades required. GED test score accepted in lieu of transcript.

High school preparation. 14 units required. Required and recommended units include English 4, mathematics 3, social studies 2, science 2 (laboratory 1), foreign language 2 and computer science 1.

2008-2009 Annual costs. Tuition/fees: $16,570. Additional fees for nursing program. Room/board: $5,000. Books/supplies: $1,000. Personal expenses: $2,300.

2008-2009 Financial aid. Need-based: Average need met was 35%. Average scholarship/grant was $4,617; average loan $3,318. 38% of total undergraduate aid awarded as scholarships/grants, 62% as loans/jobs. **Non-need-based:** Scholarships awarded for academics, alumni affiliation, art, leadership.

Application procedures. Admission: Closing date 8/1. $25 fee, may be waived for applicants with need. Admission notification on a rolling basis. **Financial aid:** Priority date 3/1, closing date 9/16. FAFSA, institutional form required. Applicants notified on a rolling basis starting 3/1; must reply by 9/12 or within 2 week(s) of notification.

Academics. External degree program of directed independent study for those 25 and over. Master of education program available summer session only. **Special study options:** Accelerated study, combined bachelor's/graduate degree, cooperative education, cross-registration, distance learning, double major, dual enrollment of high school students, ESL, external degree, honors, independent study, internships, liberal arts/career combination, study abroad, teacher certification program. **Credit/placement by examination:** AP, CLEP, IB, institutional tests. 32 credit hours maximum toward bachelor's degree. **Support services:** Learning center, reduced course load, remedial instruction, study skills assistance, tutoring, writing center.

Majors. Biology: General. **Business:** Accounting, business admin. **Education:** Early childhood, elementary, secondary. **Health:** Nursing (RN). **Liberal arts:** Arts/sciences. **Philosophy/religion:** Religion. **Psychology:** General. **Theology:** Theology. **Visual/performing arts:** Interior design, studio arts.

Computing on campus. 64 workstations in dormitories, library, computer center. Dormitories linked to campus network. Commuter students can connect to campus network.

Student life. Freshman orientation: Mandatory, $150 fee. Preregistration for classes offered. Program held one week before official registration. **Policies:** Religious observance required. **Housing:** Single-sex dorms, apartments available. $350 deposit, deadline 8/1. **Activities:** Concert band, choral groups, drama, music ensembles, student government, student newspaper, symphony orchestra, campus community outreach, Big Brother, Adopt-A-Grandparent.

Athletics. Intramural: Cross-country, golf, gymnastics, racquetball, sailing, skiing, skin diving, softball, swimming, tennis, track and field, volleyball.

Student services. Chaplain/spiritual director, career counseling, student employment services, financial aid counseling, health services, personal counseling, placement for graduates.

Contact. E-mail: rosita.lashley@auc.edu
Phone: (978) 368-2235 Toll-free number: (800) 282-2030
Fax: (978) 368-2015
Rosita Lashley, Director of Admissions, Atlantic Union College, Main Street, South Lancaster, MA 01561

Babson College
Babson Park, Massachusetts **CB member**
www.babson.edu **CB code: 3075**

- Private 4-year business college
- Residential campus in large town
- 1,851 degree-seeking undergraduates: 42% women, 4% African American, 13% Asian American, 9% Hispanic American, 20% international
- 1,565 degree-seeking graduate students
- 35% of applicants admitted
- SAT or ACT with writing, application essay required
- 88% graduate within 6 years

General. Founded in 1919. Regionally accredited. **Degrees:** 457 bachelor's awarded; master's offered. **ROTC:** Army, Naval, Air Force. **Location:** 14 miles from Boston. **Calendar:** Semester, limited summer session. **Full-time faculty:** 157 total; 89% have terminal degrees, 14% minority, 32% women. **Part-time faculty:** 90 total; 37% have terminal degrees, 7% minority, 30% women. **Class size:** 22% < 20, 51% 20-39, 24% 40-49, 3% 50-99. **Special facilities:** Entrepreneurship center, woman's leadership center, social entrepreneurship institute.

Freshman class profile. 4,318 applied, 1,513 admitted, 470 enrolled.

Mid 50% test scores		Return as sophomores:	97%
SAT critical reading:	560-650	Out-of-state:	58%
SAT math:	610-690	Live on campus:	99%
SAT writing:	580-660	International:	27%
ACT composite:	25-29	Fraternities:	17%
Rank in top quarter:	82%	Sororities:	18%
Rank in top tenth:	44%		

Basis for selection. Academic performance and level of course work (college preparation, honors, Advanced Placement) most important; followed by academic motivation, including interest in learning and willingness to challenge oneself; test scores; writing ability; involvement in cocurricular activities and/or work experience; leadership, creativity, enthusiasm. SAT Subject Tests recommended. **Homeschooled:** Statement describing homeschool structure and mission, transcript of courses and grades, state high school equivalency certificate, letter of recommendation (nonparent) required. Provide information about completed courses, schooling, testing, and diploma requirements.

High school preparation. 20 units required. Required and recommended units include English 4, mathematics 4, social studies 2, history 2, science 4 (laboratory 3) and foreign language 4. Pre-calculus strongly recommended.

2008-2009 Annual costs. Tuition/fees: $36,096. Room/board: $12,020. Books/supplies: $1,000. Personal expenses: $900.

2008-2009 Financial aid. All financial aid based on need. Average need met was 97%. Average scholarship/grant was $26,223; average loan $2,684. 85% of total undergraduate aid awarded as scholarships/grants, 15% as loans/jobs.

Application procedures. Admission: Priority date 11/1; deadline 1/15 (postmark date). $65 fee, may be waived for applicants with need. Admission notification 4/1. Must reply by 5/1. **Financial aid:** Closing date 2/15. FAFSA, CSS PROFILE required. Applicants notified by 4/1; must reply by 5/1.

Academics. Special study options: Accelerated study, combined bachelor's/graduate degree, cross-registration, exchange student, honors, independent study, internships, liberal arts/career combination, semester at sea, student-designed major, study abroad. **Credit/placement by examination:** AP, CLEP, IB, institutional tests. 64 credit hours maximum toward bachelor's degree. **Support services:** Reduced course load, study skills assistance, tutoring, writing center.

Majors. Business: General, accounting, accounting/business management, accounting/finance, auditing, business admin, communications, entrepreneurial studies, finance, international, international finance, international marketing, investments/securities, management information systems, management science, managerial economics, marketing, office management, operations, sales/distribution, small business admin, statistics. **Communications:** Advertising. **Computer sciences:** General, information systems. **Legal studies:** Prelaw.

Computing on campus. PC or laptop required. 290 workstations in dormitories, library, computer center, student center. Dormitories wired for high-speed internet access and linked to campus network. Commuter students can connect to campus network. Online course registration, online library, helpline, repair service, wireless network available.

Student life. Freshman orientation: Mandatory. Preregistration for classes offered. Three-day program preceding start of classes. **Policies:** First-year students required to live on campus unless commuting from home (must live within 25-mile radius of campus). **Housing:** Guaranteed on-campus for all undergraduates. Coed dorms, single-sex dorms, special housing for disabled, fraternity/sorority housing, wellness housing available. $500 partly refundable deposit, deadline 5/1. Cultural, nontraditional, suite style, single-sex floors, wings for women available. **Activities:** Jazz band, campus ministries, choral groups, dance, drama, film society, international student organizations, literary magazine, music ensembles, musical theater, radio station, student government, student newspaper, symphony orchestra, 60 student-run organizations.

Athletics. NCAA. **Intercollegiate:** Baseball M, basketball, cross-country, diving, field hockey W, golf M, ice hockey M, lacrosse, skiing, soccer, softball W, swimming, tennis, track and field, volleyball W. **Intramural:** Basketball, football (non-tackle), ice hockey, racquetball, soccer, softball, squash, tennis, volleyball, water polo. **Team name:** Beavers.

Student services. Alcohol/substance abuse counseling, chaplain/spiritual director, career counseling, student employment services, financial aid counseling, health services, minority student services, personal counseling, placement for graduates, women's services. **Physically disabled:** Services for visually, speech, hearing impaired.

Contact. E-mail: ugradadmission@babson.edu
Phone: (781) 239-5522 Toll-free number: (800) 488-3696
Fax: (781) 239-4135
Grant Gosselin, Dean of Undergraduate Admission, Babson College, 231 Forest Street, Babson Park, MA 02457-0310

Bard College at Simon's Rock

Great Barrington, Massachusetts — **CB member**
www.simons-rock.edu — **CB code: 3795**

- Private 4-year liberal arts college
- Residential campus in small town
- 427 degree-seeking undergraduates: 60% women
- Application essay, interview required
- 96% graduate within 6 years

General. Founded in 1964. Regionally accredited. Provides students with the opportunity to begin college in a residential environment after completing the 10th or 11th grade. **Degrees:** 47 bachelor's, 98 associate awarded. **Location:** 135 miles from Boston, 132 miles from New York. **Calendar:** Semester. **Full-time faculty:** 48 total; 90% have terminal degrees, 19% minority, 38% women. **Part-time faculty:** 30 total; 60% have terminal degrees, 10% minority, 60% women. **Class size:** 98% < 20, 2% 20-39. **Special facilities:** Visual and performing arts center, environmental research center.

Freshman class profile. 333 applied, 267 admitted, 178 enrolled.

Mid 50% test scores			
SAT critical reading:	560-690	GPA 2.0-2.99:	27%
SAT math:	530-680	Rank in top quarter:	82%
ACT composite:	25-30	Rank in top tenth:	60%
GPA 3.75 or higher:	31%	Return as sophomores:	76%
GPA 3.50-3.74:	24%	Out-of-state:	79%
GPA 3.0-3.49:	18%	Live on campus:	100%
		International:	3%

Basis for selection. School achievement record, essays, recommendations (counselor and teacher), interview most important. Institutional testing used for math and foreign language placement. SAT or ACT recommended. Standardized tests are optional for most students but will be considered if submitted. Students in home school or ungraded academic settings should submit test scores. **Homeschooled:** Statement describing homeschool structure and mission, transcript of courses and grades, interview required.

High school preparation. 15 units recommended. Recommended units include English 2, mathematics 2, social studies 2, history 2, science 2 (laboratory 1), foreign language 2 and academic electives 2. Applicants who have completed 10th or 11th grade should have 2 or 3 years college-preparatory curriculum respectively.

2008-2009 Annual costs. Tuition/fees: $37,860. Annual health services fee of $640. Student activity fee $150. Room/board: $10,600. Books/supplies: $1,000. Personal expenses: $640.

2007-2008 Financial aid. Need-based: 168 full-time freshmen applied for aid; 110 were judged to have need; 110 of these received aid. Average need met was 68%. Average scholarship/grant was $15,500; average loan $4,425. 96% of total undergraduate aid awarded as scholarships/grants, 4% as loans/jobs. **Non-need-based:** Awarded to 243 full-time undergraduates, including 35 freshmen. Scholarships awarded for academics, alumni affiliation, leadership, state residency.

Application procedures. Admission: Priority date 4/15; deadline 5/31 (postmark date). $50 fee, may be waived for applicants with need. Application must be submitted on paper. Admission notification on a rolling basis beginning on or about 1/15. Must reply by May 1 or within 2 week(s) if notified thereafter. **Financial aid:** Priority date 4/15; no closing date. FAFSA, CSS PROFILE required. Applicants notified on a rolling basis starting 4/15; must reply within 2 week(s) of notification.

Academics. Upper-class students may take courses at Bard College. **Special study options:** Cooperative education, cross-registration, double major, dual enrollment of high school students, exchange student, independent study, internships, liberal arts/career combination, student-designed major, study abroad. Globalization and International Affairs, undergraduate summer research fellows program with Rockefeller University, International Human Rights Exchange, 3/2 engineering program with Columbia University. **Credit/placement by examination:** AP, CLEP, institutional tests. 10 credit hours maximum toward associate degree, 10 toward bachelor's. Credit for Advanced Placement determined by individual divisions. **Support services:** Learning center, reduced course load, study skills assistance, tutoring, writing center.

Majors. Area/ethnic studies: African, African-American, American, Asian, Central/Eastern European, Chinese, East Asian, European, French, gay/lesbian, German, Latin American, regional, Russian/Slavic, South Asian, Southeast Asian, Spanish/Iberian, Western European, women's. **Biology:** General, ecology. **Communications technology:** Photo/film/video. **Computer sciences:** Computer science. **Conservation:** Environmental science, environmental studies. **Engineering:** General. **Foreign languages:** General, Arabic, Chinese, comparative lit, French, German, Germanic, Latin, linguistics, Spanish. **History:** American. **Interdisciplinary:** Math/computer science. **Liberal arts:** Arts/sciences. **Math:** General. **Philosophy/religion:** Philosophy. **Physical sciences:** Chemistry, physics. **Psychology:** General. **Social sciences:** General, anthropology, political science, sociology. **Visual/performing arts:** General, acting, art history/conservation, ceramics, cinematography, dance, dramatic, drawing, music history, music performance, music theory/composition, painting, photography, play/screenwriting, printmaking, sculpture, studio arts, theater history.

Most popular majors. Area/ethnic studies 10%, biology 8%, English 8%, interdisciplinary studies 8%, legal studies 8%, visual/performing arts 27%.

Computing on campus. 72 workstations in dormitories, library, student center. Dormitories wired for high-speed internet access and linked to campus network. Commuter students can connect to campus network. Online library, helpline, repair service, student web hosting, wireless network available.

Student life. Freshman orientation: Mandatory, $500 fee. Preregistration for classes offered. One-week writing and thinking workshop held prior to start of semester. **Policies:** No alcohol, illegal drugs or weapons allowed on campus. **Housing:** Guaranteed on-campus for freshmen. Coed dorms, single-sex dorms, special housing for disabled, apartments, wellness housing available. **Activities:** Bands, choral groups, dance, drama, film society, international student organizations, literary magazine, music ensembles, musical theater, opera, radio station, student government, student newspaper, symphony orchestra, TV station, black student union, Latino student union, international students club, Amnesty International, Bible study group, QueerSA, women's center.

Athletics. Intercollegiate: Basketball, cricket, cross-country, fencing, field hockey W, racquetball, soccer, softball, swimming. **Intramural:** Archery, basketball, cricket, cross-country, diving, fencing, field hockey W, handball, racquetball, skiing, soccer, softball, squash, swimming. **Team name:** Llamas.

Student services. Alcohol/substance abuse counseling, chaplain/spiritual director, career counseling, student employment services, financial aid counseling, health services, minority student services, personal counseling, placement for graduates, women's services.

Contact. E-mail: admit@simons-rock.edu
Phone: (413) 528-7312 Toll-free number: (800) 235-7186
Fax: (413) 541-0081
Mary Davidson, Dean of Admission and Student Affairs, Bard College at Simon's Rock, Office of Admission, Great Barrington, MA 01230-1990

Bay Path College

Longmeadow, Massachusetts
www.baypath.edu **CB code: 3078**

- Private 4-year business college for women
- Residential campus in large town
- 1,409 degree-seeking undergraduates: 22% part-time, 100% women, 11% African American, 2% Asian American, 12% Hispanic American, 1% international
- 375 degree-seeking graduate students
- 83% of applicants admitted
- SAT or ACT (ACT writing recommended) required
- 52% graduate within 6 years

General. Founded in 1897. Regionally accredited. Member of 8-college consortium. **Degrees:** 264 bachelor's, 49 associate awarded; master's offered. **ROTC:** Army, Air Force. **Location:** 5 miles from Springfield; 23 miles from Hartford, Connecticut. **Calendar:** Semester, limited summer session. **Full-time faculty:** 44 total; 52% have terminal degrees, 7% minority, 70% women. **Part-time faculty:** 179 total; 34% have terminal degrees, 9% minority, 59% women. **Class size:** 75% < 20, 25% 20-39. **Special facilities:** Academic development center, on-campus preschool, occupational therapy laboratory, business hall, career development center.

Freshman class profile. 635 applied, 526 admitted, 152 enrolled.

Mid 50% test scores		**GPA 2.0-2.99:**	43%
SAT critical reading:	430-540	**Rank in top quarter:**	47%
SAT math:	420-530	**Rank in top tenth:**	16%
SAT writing:	420-540	**End year in good standing:**	73%
ACT composite:	17-21	**Return as sophomores:**	73%
GPA 3.75 or higher:	18%	**Out-of-state:**	50%
GPA 3.50-3.74:	11%	**Live on campus:**	82%
GPA 3.0-3.49:	28%		

Basis for selection. High school transcript and performance, class rank, GPA, SAT or ACT, letters of recommendation, and essay. Interview and essay or personal statement recommended. **Homeschooled:** Statement describing homeschool structure and mission, transcript of courses and grades, state high school equivalency certificate, letter of recommendation (nonparent) required.

High school preparation. College-preparatory program recommended. 15 units required; 20 recommended. Required and recommended units include English 4, mathematics 3-4, social studies 2, history 1-2, science 2-3 (laboratory 2) and foreign language 2.

2009-2010 Annual costs. Tuition/fees (projected): $23,840. Room/board: $9,750. Books/supplies: $1,200. Personal expenses: $900.

2008-2009 Financial aid. Need-based: 169 full-time freshmen applied for aid; 155 were judged to have need; 154 of these received aid. Average need met was 77%. Average scholarship/grant was $13,941; average loan $4,483. 70% of total undergraduate aid awarded as scholarships/grants, 30% as loans/jobs. **Non-need-based:** Awarded to 203 full-time undergraduates, including 33 freshmen. Scholarships awarded for academics, state residency. **Additional information:** Opportunity Grant program for students whose family may be facing financial difficulties paying tuition resulting from economic conditions. Additional funding available in an endowment program to assist students who qualify.

Application procedures. Admission: Priority date 12/15; no deadline. $25 fee, may be waived for applicants with need, free for online applicants. Admission notification on a rolling basis beginning on or about 9/15. Must reply by May 1 or within 2 week(s) if notified thereafter. **Financial aid:** Priority date 3/15; no closing date. FAFSA required. Applicants notified on a rolling basis starting 3/1; must reply within 2 week(s) of notification.

Academics. Special study options: Accelerated study, combined bachelor's/graduate degree, cooperative education, cross-registration, distance learning, double major, ESL, exchange student, honors, independent study, internships, student-designed major, study abroad, teacher certification program, Washington semester, weekend college. **Credit/placement by examination:** AP, CLEP, IB, institutional tests. **Support services:** Learning center, study skills assistance, tutoring, writing center.

Majors. Biology: General, biotechnology. **Business:** General, business admin, marketing. **Communications:** Organizational. **Education:** Early childhood, elementary. **Legal studies:** General, prelaw. **Liberal arts:** Arts/sciences. **Protective services:** Criminal justice. **Psychology:** General, child, forensic.

Most popular majors. Business/marketing 24%, liberal arts 36%, psychology 19%, security/protective services 12%.

Computing on campus. 214 workstations in dormitories, library, computer center, student center. Dormitories wired for high-speed internet access and linked to campus network. Commuter students can connect to campus network. Online course registration, online library, helpline, wireless network available.

Student life. Freshman orientation: Mandatory. Preregistration for classes offered. **Policies:** No smoking or alcohol in dormitories. **Housing:** Guaranteed on-campus for all undergraduates. Wellness housing available. $100 nonrefundable deposit, deadline 5/1. **Activities:** Choral groups, dance, drama, international student organizations, literary magazine, Model UN, musical theater, student government, student newspaper, interfaith council, Habitat for Humanity, women in technology, women of culture, Alliance, Phi Beta Lambda.

Athletics. NCAA. **Intercollegiate:** Basketball W, cross-country W, field hockey W, soccer W, softball W, tennis W, volleyball W. **Intramural:** Lacrosse W, track and field W. **Team name:** Wildcats.

Student services. Adult student services, career counseling, student employment services, financial aid counseling, health services, minority student services, personal counseling, placement for graduates, women's services.

Contact. E-mail: admiss@baypath.edu
Phone: (413) 565-1000 ext. 1331 Toll-free number: (800) 782-7284 ext. 1331 Fax: (413) 565-1105
Julie Richardson, Dean of Enrollment Management, Traditional Programs, Bay Path College, 588 Longmeadow Street, Longmeadow, MA 01106

Becker College

Worcester, Massachusetts **CB member**
www.becker.edu **CB code: 3079**

- Private 4-year liberal arts college
- Residential campus in small city
- 1,728 degree-seeking undergraduates: 22% part-time, 67% women
- 72% of applicants admitted
- SAT or ACT with writing required

General. Founded in 1887. Regionally accredited. Campuses in Worcester and Leicester. Member of Colleges of the Worcester Consortium. **Degrees:** 150 bachelor's, 132 associate awarded. **ROTC:** Army, Naval, Air Force. **Location:** 49 miles from Boston; 39 miles from Providence, Rhode Island. **Calendar:** Semester, limited summer session. **Full-time faculty:** 49 total; 69% women. **Part-time faculty:** 82 total; 62% women. **Class size:** 68% < 20, 31% 20-39, less than 1% 40-49, less than 1% 50-99. **Special facilities:** Veterinary clinic, on-site preschool and day-care facility, 96-acre off-campus stable for equine programs.

Freshman class profile. 2,692 applied, 1,937 admitted, 335 enrolled.

Mid 50% test scores		Rank in top tenth:	8%
SAT critical reading:	450-540	End year in good standing:	84%
SAT math:	370-420	Return as sophomores:	62%
ACT composite:	12-20	Out-of-state:	34%
Rank in top quarter:	40%		

Basis for selection. High school record, GPA, extracurricular activities important. Recommendations, interview considered. Additional prerequisites for nursing, veterinary technology, and veterinary science programs. Essay recommended. **Homeschooled:** Statement describing homeschool structure and mission, letter of recommendation (nonparent) required. Official transcript required from high school with which student is affiliated.

High school preparation. Required and recommended units include English 4, mathematics 3, social studies 1, history 2 and science 2. 2 math including 1 algebra, 1 chemistry with lab, 1 biology with lab required for nursing, veterinary technician, veterinary science, pre-vet programs.

2008-2009 Annual costs. Tuition/fees: $24,780. Additional one-time charge of $285 for nursing program. Room/board: $9,760. Books/supplies: $1,000. Personal expenses: $1,170.

2007-2008 Financial aid. Non-need-based: Scholarships awarded for academics.

Application procedures. Admission: No deadline. $30 fee, may be waived for applicants with need. Admission notification on a rolling basis. Must reply by May 1 or within 4 week(s) if notified thereafter. **Financial aid:** Priority date 3/1; no closing date. FAFSA required. Applicants notified on a rolling basis starting 2/1; must reply within 2 week(s) of notification.

Academics. Special study options: Accelerated study, cross-registration, distance learning, independent study, internships, liberal arts/career combination, teacher certification program. Member of 15-school Colleges of Worcester consortium. **Credit/placement by examination:** AP, CLEP, IB, institutional tests. 30 credit hours maximum toward associate degree, 60 toward bachelor's. **Support services:** Learning center, reduced course load, remedial instruction, study skills assistance, tutoring, writing center.

Majors. Biology: General. **Business:** Accounting, business admin, hospitality admin, human resources, marketing, tourism/travel. **Communications technology:** General. **Computer sciences:** Networking. **Education:** Early childhood, elementary. **Health:** Nursing (RN), preveterinary, veterinary technology/assistant. **Legal studies:** General, prelaw. **Liberal arts:** Arts/sciences. **Parks/recreation:** Health/fitness, sports admin. **Protective services:** Criminal justice. **Psychology:** General. **Public administration:** Human services. **Visual/performing arts:** Commercial/advertising art, interior design.

Most popular majors. Business/marketing 58%, health sciences 7%, psychology 6%, visual/performing arts 18%.

Computing on campus. 155 workstations in dormitories, library, computer center. Dormitories wired for high-speed internet access and linked to campus network. Commuter students can connect to campus network. Online library, helpline, wireless network available.

Student life. Freshman orientation: Mandatory. Preregistration for classes offered. **Housing:** Guaranteed on-campus for freshmen. Coed dorms, single-sex dorms, apartments, wellness housing available. $300 deposit. Substance-free dormitory and over-21 housing available. **Activities:** Choral groups, dance, drama, student government, student newspaper, campus community service club, international club, animal health club, business club, commuter club, early childhood education club, outdoors club, travel club, nursing club.

Athletics. NCAA. **Intercollegiate:** Baseball M, basketball, cross-country, equestrian, field hockey W, football (tackle) M, golf M, ice hockey M, lacrosse, soccer, softball W, tennis, volleyball W. **Intramural:** Badminton, basketball, soccer, table tennis, volleyball. **Team name:** Hawks.

Student services. Adult student services, alcohol/substance abuse counseling, career counseling, student employment services, financial aid counseling, health services, on-campus daycare, personal counseling, placement for graduates. **Physically disabled:** Services for visually, speech, hearing impaired.

Contact. E-mail: admissions@beckercollege.edu
Phone: (508) 373-9400 Toll-free number: (877) 523-2537
Fax: (508) 890-1500
Michael Perron, Director of Admissions, Becker College, 61 Sever Street, Worcester, MA 01609

Bentley University

Waltham, Massachusetts — **CB member**
www.bentley.edu — **CB code: 3096**

- Private 4-year business college
- Residential campus in small city
- 4,187 degree-seeking undergraduates: 5% part-time, 40% women, 3% African American, 8% Asian American, 5% Hispanic American, 8% international
- 1,404 degree-seeking graduate students
- 38% of applicants admitted
- SAT or ACT with writing, application essay required
- 83% graduate within 6 years; 16% enter graduate study

General. Founded in 1917. Regionally accredited. **Degrees:** 1,065 bachelor's, 4 associate awarded; master's, doctoral offered. **ROTC:** Army, Air Force. **Location:** 10 miles from Boston. **Calendar:** Semester, extensive summer session. **Full-time faculty:** 285 total; 82% have terminal degrees, 13% minority, 39% women. **Part-time faculty:** 199 total; 40% have terminal degrees, 6% minority, 39% women. **Class size:** 31% < 20, 69% 20-39, less than 1% 40-49. **Special facilities:** Academic technology center; alliance for ethics and social responsibility; business ethics center; international students and scholars center; languages and international collaboration center; marketing technology center; quantitative analysis center; international center; cyber law center; design and usability center; financial services center; library, media and culture labs and studio; service-learning center; trading room; arts and sciences center; accounting center; women?s leadership institute.

Freshman class profile. 7,238 applied, 2,718 admitted, 974 enrolled.

Mid 50% test scores		Return as sophomores:	93%
SAT critical reading:	550-630	Out-of-state:	56%
SAT math:	610-680	Live on campus:	98%
SAT writing:	550-650	International:	9%
ACT composite:	25-29	Fraternities:	10%
Rank in top quarter:	85%	Sororities:	10%
Rank in top tenth:	45%		

Basis for selection. Decisions based on application with essay, secondary school transcript(s), standardized test scores, recommendations. Any supplemental information submitted by applicant will also be considered. Interviews recommended. **Homeschooled:** Statement describing homeschool structure and mission, transcript of courses and grades, letter of recommendation (nonparent) required. Interview strongly recommended.

High school preparation. College-preparatory program required. 19 units recommended. Recommended units include English 4, mathematics 4, science 3 (laboratory 3) and foreign language 3. 2 additional units English, math, social or lab science, or foreign language recommended.

2008-2009 Annual costs. Tuition/fees: $34,488. Room/board: $11,320. Books/supplies: $1,030. Personal expenses: $1,120.

2007-2008 Financial aid. Need-based: 687 full-time freshmen applied for aid; 448 were judged to have need; 444 of these received aid. Average need met was 95%. Average scholarship/grant was $19,436; average loan $4,402. 72% of total undergraduate aid awarded as scholarships/grants, 28% as loans/jobs. **Non-need-based:** Awarded to 908 full-time undergraduates, including 391 freshmen. Scholarships awarded for academics, athletics, leadership, minority status. **Additional information:** Deadlines for receipt of CSS PROFILE: early decision 12/1, early action and regular decision 2/1.

Application procedures. Admission: Closing date 1/15 (postmark date). $50 fee, may be waived for applicants with need. Admission notification 4/1. Must reply by 5/1. **Financial aid:** Closing date 2/1. FAFSA required. CSS PROFILE required if student is applying for institutional grants. Applicants notified on a rolling basis starting 3/25.

Academics. Special study options: Accelerated study, combined bachelor's/graduate degree, cross-registration, double major, honors, independent study, internships, liberal arts/career combination, semester at sea, student-designed major, study abroad, Washington semester. 5-year bachelor's/master's programs in business administration, accountancy, finance, marketing analytics, information technology, financial planning, taxation. **Credit/placement by examination:** AP, CLEP, IB, SAT, ACT, institutional tests. 30 credit hours maximum toward bachelor's degree. CLEP credit for French, German, Spanish not available to native speakers. Language exams require oral test with department. **Support services:** Learning center, reduced course load, study skills assistance, tutoring, writing center.

Majors. Business: General, accounting, business admin, communications, finance, managerial economics, marketing. **Computer sciences:** General.

History: General. **Liberal arts:** Arts/sciences. **Math:** General. **Philosophy/religion:** Philosophy. **Public administration:** Policy analysis.

Most popular majors. Business/marketing 95%.

Computing on campus. PC or laptop required. 4,789 workstations in library, computer center. Dormitories wired for high-speed internet access and linked to campus network. Commuter students can connect to campus network. Online course registration, online library, helpline, repair service, student web hosting, wireless network available.

Student life. **Freshman orientation:** Available. Preregistration for classes offered. Three-day program, usually held in June; family members invited on last day. **Policies:** Academic honesty system, minimum GPA for student leaders. **Housing:** Guaranteed on-campus for all undergraduates. Coed dorms, special housing for disabled, apartments, wellness housing available. Global living floors available. **Activities:** Bands, campus ministries, choral groups, dance, drama, film society, international student organizations, music ensembles, Model UN, radio station, student government, student newspaper, TV station, black united body, South Asian student association, La Cultura Latina, People Respecting Individuality and Diversity through Education, University Democrats, University Republicans, green society, Muslim students' association, Circle K, Habitat For Humanity.

Athletics. NCAA. **Intercollegiate:** Baseball M, basketball, cross-country, diving, field hockey W, football (tackle) M, golf M, ice hockey M, lacrosse, soccer, softball W, swimming, tennis, track and field, volleyball W. **Intramural:** Basketball, football (non-tackle) M, soccer, softball, volleyball. **Team name:** Falcons.

Student services. Adult student services, alcohol/substance abuse counseling, chaplain/spiritual director, career counseling, student employment services, financial aid counseling, health services, minority student services, personal counseling, placement for graduates, veterans' counselor, women's services. **Physically disabled:** Services for visually, speech, hearing impaired. **Learning disabled:** Comprehensive services available.

Contact. E-mail: ugadmission@bentley.edu
Phone: (781) 891-2244 Toll-free number: (800) 523-2354
Fax: (781) 891-3414
Erika Vardaro, Director of Admissions, Bentley University, 175 Forest Street, Waltham, MA 02452-4705

Berklee College of Music

Boston, Massachusetts — **CB member**
www.berklee.edu — **CB code: 3107**

- Private 4-year music college
- Commuter campus in very large city
- 4,054 degree-seeking undergraduates: 8% part-time, 28% women, 8% African American, 3% Asian American, 7% Hispanic American, 1% Native American, 23% international
- 44% of applicants admitted
- Application essay, interview required
- 53% graduate within 6 years

General. Founded in 1945. Regionally accredited. **Degrees:** 732 bachelor's awarded. **Calendar:** Semester, extensive summer session. **Full-time faculty:** 238 total; 100% have terminal degrees, 16% minority, 21% women. **Part-time faculty:** 291 total; 100% have terminal degrees, 21% minority, 28% women. **Class size:** 93% < 20, 7% 20-39, less than 1% 40-49, less than 1% 50-99. **Special facilities:** Performance center, student-run music venue and coffee house, music technology facilities and practice spaces, synthesizer laboratories, recording studios, film scoring laboratories, technology labs, media center.

Freshman class profile. 2,959 applied, 1,289 admitted, 622 enrolled.

Return as sophomores:	81%	**International:**	13%

Basis for selection. Musical training and experience, recommendations, academic record, test scores, extracurricular music activities, interview important. Auditions required. **Homeschooled:** Statement describing homeschool structure and mission, state high school equivalency certificate required. **Learning Disabled:** Students with disabilities should contact Special Services Coordinator.

High school preparation. Recommended units include English 4, mathematics 1, history 1, science 1 (laboratory 1) and academic electives 6. Minimum 2 years recent formal musical study on principal instrument covering standard methods/materials and/or significant practical performance experience plus knowledge of written-music fundamentals normally required of all applicants.

2009-2010 Annual costs. Tuition/fees (projected): $33,653. $2,950 one-time charge for purchase of laptop, which all freshmen must purchase. Room/board: $15,080. Books/supplies: $464. Personal expenses: $2,354.

2008-2009 Financial aid. **Need-based:** 402 full-time freshmen applied for aid; 343 were judged to have need; 341 of these received aid. Average need met was 26%. Average scholarship/grant was $6,826; average loan $4,068. 43% of total undergraduate aid awarded as scholarships/grants, 57% as loans/jobs.

Application procedures. **Admission:** Priority date 11/1; deadline 1/15 (postmark date). $150 fee, may be waived for applicants with need. Application must be submitted online. Admission notification 3/31. Must reply by May 1 or within 4 week(s) if notified thereafter. Applicants should submit completed application materials well in advance of deadline to ensure placement in desired entry class. **Financial aid:** Closing date 5/1. FAFSA required. Applicants notified on a rolling basis starting 3/7; must reply within 2 week(s) of notification.

Academics. Bachelor's degree program includes 30 credits general education courses. Four-year professional diploma available (not including general education). **Special study options:** Cross-registration, double major, ESL, internships, student-designed major, study abroad, teacher certification program. ProArts Consortium with Boston Architectural Center, Boston Conservatory, Emerson College, Massachusetts College of Art, School of the Museum of Fine Arts. **Credit/placement by examination:** CLEP, institutional tests. 60 credit hours maximum toward bachelor's degree. **Support services:** Learning center, pre-admission summer program, tutoring, writing center.

Majors. **Health:** Music therapy. **Visual/performing arts:** Jazz, music management, music performance, music theory/composition, piano/organ, voice/opera. **Other:** Music business/management, Music synthesis.

Computing on campus. PC or laptop required. 50 workstations in dormitories, library, computer center. Dormitories wired for high-speed internet access and linked to campus network. Online library, helpline, repair service, student web hosting, wireless network available.

Student life. **Freshman orientation:** Available. Series of events before and during registration week. **Housing:** Coed dorms available. $300 nonrefundable deposit. Residence space limited. **Activities:** Bands, campus ministries, choral groups, dance, drama, international student organizations, literary magazine, music ensembles, musical theater, radio station, student government, student newspaper, symphony orchestra, black student union, Christian Fellowship, Berklee Cares, women musicians' network, Latinos association, GLBT Allies at Berklee, Korean student association, Amnesty International.

Athletics. **Intramural:** Basketball, football (non-tackle), ice hockey, soccer. **Team name:** IceCats.

Student services. Career counseling, student employment services, minority student services, personal counseling, veterans' counselor. **Physically disabled:** Services for visually impaired.

Contact. E-mail: admissions@berklee.edu
Phone: (617) 747-2221 Toll-free number: (800) 237-5533
Fax: (617) 747-2047
Damien Bracken, Director of Admissions/OSSE, Berklee College of Music, 1140 Boylston Street, Boston, MA 02215

Boston Architectural College

Boston, Massachusetts
www.the-bac.edu — **CB code: 1168**

- Private 6-year architecture and design college
- Commuter campus in very large city
- 624 degree-seeking undergraduates: 2% part-time, 33% women
- 1,686 degree-seeking graduate students

General. Founded in 1889. Regionally accredited. Program offers practice-based learning with simultaneous employment in field and academic study. **Degrees:** 45 bachelor's awarded; master's, first professional offered. **Location:** Downtown. **Calendar:** Semester, limited summer session. **Full-time faculty:** 11 total; 27% women. **Part-time faculty:** 352 total; 37% women. **Class size:** 96% < 20, less than 1% 20-39, 2% 40-49, less than 1% 50-99, less than 1% >100. **Special facilities:** On-campus gallery featuring exhibits of architectural and interior design interest, CAD lab, photography studio.

Freshman class profile.

Mid 50% test scores		GPA 2.0-2.99:	46%
ACT composite:	21-28	Rank in top quarter:	34%
GPA 3.75 or higher:	3%	Rank in top tenth:	11%
GPA 3.50-3.74:	14%	Out-of-state:	40%
GPA 3.0-3.49:	28%		

Basis for selection. Open admission. Portfolio required for transfer credits for design courses.

2008-2009 Annual costs. Tuition/fees: $10,620. Academic Only program tuition is $14,200 plus $20 required fees. Books/supplies: $1,476. Personal expenses: $3,006.

2007-2008 Financial aid. **Need-based:** 64 full-time freshmen applied for aid; 44 were judged to have need; 28 of these received aid. Average need met was 33%. Average scholarship/grant was $5,960; average loan $3,918. 20% of total undergraduate aid awarded as scholarships/grants, 80% as loans/jobs. **Non-need-based:** Awarded to 36 full-time undergraduates, including 7 freshmen. Scholarships awarded for academics, art, leadership.

Application procedures. **Admission:** Priority date 5/15; deadline 8/31 (receipt date). $50 fee, may be waived for applicants with need. Admission notification on a rolling basis beginning on or about 1/26. Must reply by May 1 or within 2 week(s) if notified thereafter. **Financial aid:** Priority date 4/15; no closing date. FAFSA required. Applicants notified on a rolling basis starting 3/1; must reply within 2 week(s) of notification.

Academics. Bachelor of architecture or interior design awarded after 6-year program of concurrent work and academic curriculum. Students usually transfer into program during second or third years. **Special study options:** Cross-registration, distance learning, independent study, internships, liberal arts/career combination. Member Professional Arts Consortium. **Credit/placement by examination:** AP, CLEP, institutional tests. **Support services:** Learning center, tutoring, writing center.

Majors. **Architecture:** Architecture, environmental design, interior, landscape.

Computing on campus. 175 workstations in library, computer center. Online library, helpline, wireless network available.

Student life. **Freshman orientation:** Mandatory. Preregistration for classes offered. Several dates; includes writing test. **Policies:** Campus code of conduct. **Housing:** Dormitory space, when available, at ProArts Consortium schools. **Activities:** Student government.

Student services. Adult student services, career counseling, student employment services, financial aid counseling, minority student services, veterans' counselor. **Physically disabled:** Services for visually, speech, hearing impaired.

Contact. E-mail: admissions@the-bac.edu
Phone: (617) 585-0123 Toll-free number: (877) 585-0100
Fax: (617) 585-0121
Richard Moyer, Director of Admissions, Boston Architectural College, 320 Newbury Street, Boston, MA 02115-2795

Boston Baptist College
Boston, Massachusetts
www.boston.edu/

- Private 4-year Bible college
- Very large city

General. Regionally accredited. **Calendar:** Semester.

Annual costs/financial aid. Tuition/fees: $11,674.

Contact. Phone: (617) 364-3510 ext. 217
Director of Admissions, 950 Metropolitan Avenue, Boston, MA 02136

Boston College
Chestnut Hill, Massachusetts — **CB member**
www.bc.edu — **CB code: 3083**

- Private 4-year university affiliated with Roman Catholic Church
- Residential campus in small city
- 9,060 degree-seeking undergraduates: 52% women, 6% African American, 9% Asian American, 8% Hispanic American, 3% international
- 4,843 graduate students
- 26% of applicants admitted
- SAT and SAT Subject Tests or ACT with writing, application essay required
- 91% graduate within 6 years; 27% enter graduate study

General. Founded in 1863. Regionally accredited. **Degrees:** 2,319 bachelor's awarded; master's, doctoral, first professional offered. **ROTC:** Army, Naval, Air Force. **Location:** 6 miles from downtown Boston. **Calendar:** Semester, extensive summer session. **Full-time faculty:** 679 total; 98% have terminal degrees, 17% minority, 38% women. **Part-time faculty:** 647 total. **Class size:** 48% < 20, 38% 20-39, 7% 40-49, 5% 50-99, 2% >100. **Special facilities:** Observatory, theatre arts center, chemistry center, recreation complex.

Freshman class profile. 30,845 applied, 8,093 admitted, 2,167 enrolled.

Mid 50% test scores		Rank in top tenth:	80%
SAT critical reading:	610-700	Return as sophomores:	96%
SAT math:	640-730	Out-of-state:	74%
SAT writing:	620-710	Live on campus:	99%
ACT composite:	28-32	International:	5%
Rank in top quarter:	96%		

Basis for selection. Evidence of academic ability, intellectual curiosity, strength of character, motivation, creativity, energy, and promise for personal growth and development very important. Recommendations by counselors and teachers, required personal statement and extracurricular activities important. 2 SAT Subject Tests of student's choice required if SAT is submitted. Portfolio recommended for studio art majors. **Learning Disabled:** May provide documentation of disability at option of applicant.

High school preparation. College-preparatory program recommended. 20 units recommended. Recommended units include English 4, mathematics 4, social studies 4, science 4 (laboratory 4) and foreign language 4. 4 combined social studies and history recommended. 2 laboratory science (including 1 chemistry) required of nursing applicants.

2008-2009 Annual costs. Tuition/fees: $37,950. Room/board: $11,610. Books/supplies: $750. Personal expenses: $1,000.

2007-2008 Financial aid. **Need-based:** 1,214 full-time freshmen applied for aid; 939 were judged to have need; 939 of these received aid. Average need met was 100%. Average scholarship/grant was $24,075; average loan $3,513. 78% of total undergraduate aid awarded as scholarships/grants, 22% as loans/jobs. **Non-need-based:** Awarded to 470 full-time undergraduates, including 110 freshmen. Scholarships awarded for academics, athletics, leadership, ROTC.

Application procedures. **Admission:** Closing date 1/1 (postmark date). $70 fee, may be waived for applicants with need. Admission notification 4/15. Must reply by 5/1. **Financial aid:** Priority date 2/1; no closing date. FAFSA, CSS PROFILE required. Applicants notified by 4/1; must reply by 5/1.

Academics. **Special study options:** Accelerated study, combined bachelor's/graduate degree, cross-registration, double major, ESL, exchange student, honors, independent study, internships, liberal arts/career combination, student-designed major, study abroad, teacher certification program, Washington semester. 3-2 program in engineering with Boston University; Tufts Medical School Early Acceptance Program. **Credit/placement by examination:** AP, CLEP, IB. 24 credit hours maximum toward bachelor's degree. **Support services:** Learning center, pre-admission summer program, reduced course load, study skills assistance, tutoring, writing center.

Majors. **Area/ethnic studies:** Hispanic-American/Latino/Chicano. **Biology:** General, biochemistry. **Business:** Accounting, business admin, finance, human resources, management information systems, managerial economics, operations. **Communications:** General. **Computer sciences:** General, computer science, information systems. **Education:** Early childhood, elementary, secondary. **Foreign languages:** Ancient Greek, classics, French, German, Italian, Latin, linguistics, Russian, Spanish. **Health:** Nursing (RN). **History:** General. **Math:** General. **Philosophy/religion:** Philosophy. **Physical sciences:** Chemistry, geology, geophysics, physics. **Psychology:** General. **Social sciences:** Economics, political science, sociology. **Visual/performing arts:** Art history/conservation, dramatic, film/cinema, studio arts.

Most popular majors. Biology 6%, business/marketing 24%, communications/journalism 9%, English 8%, history 7%, psychology 9%, social sciences 15%.

Computing on campus. 1,000 workstations in library, computer center, student center. Dormitories wired for high-speed internet access and linked to campus network. Commuter students can connect to campus network. Online course registration, online library, helpline, repair service, student web hosting, wireless network available.

Student life. **Freshman orientation:** Mandatory, $400 fee. Preregistration for classes offered. Three-day, 2-night program; 4-6 scheduled options offered during summer. **Policies:** Alcohol prohibited for students under 21, smoking prohibited in all residence halls. Halogen lights, space heaters, egg crate style foam mattress pads, and candles prohibited in dorm rooms. **Housing:** Guaranteed on-campus for freshmen. Coed dorms, single-sex dorms, special housing for disabled, wellness housing available. $250 partly refundable deposit, deadline 5/1. Honors house, multicultural floor, 24-hour quiet living floor, social justice floor available. Apartment-style housing and townhouse-style housing available for upperclassmen. **Activities:** Bands, campus ministries, choral groups, dance, drama, film society, international student organizations, literary magazine, music ensembles, musical theater, radio station, student government, student newspaper, symphony orchestra, TV station, 4Boston, Amnesty International, Appalachia Volunteers, Asian Caucus, Black Student Forum, Buddhist club, Hillel, Ignatian Society, Puerto Rican Association, Muslim students association.

Athletics. NCAA. **Intercollegiate:** Baseball M, basketball, cross-country, diving, fencing, field hockey W, football (tackle) M, golf, ice hockey, lacrosse W, rowing (crew) W, sailing, skiing, soccer, softball W, swimming, tennis, track and field, volleyball W. **Intramural:** Basketball, football (non-tackle), golf, ice hockey, racquetball, soccer, softball, squash, tennis, volleyball. **Team name:** Eagles.

Student services. Alcohol/substance abuse counseling, chaplain/spiritual director, career counseling, services for economically disadvantaged, student employment services, financial aid counseling, health services, minority student services, on-campus daycare, personal counseling, placement for graduates, women's services. **Physically disabled:** Services for visually, speech, hearing impaired.

Contact. Phone: (617) 552-3100 Toll-free number: (800) 360-2522
Fax: (617) 552-0798
John Mahoney, Director of Undergraduate Admission, Boston College, 140 Commonwealth Avenue, Devlin Hall 208, Chestnut Hill, MA 02467-3809

Boston Conservatory

Boston, Massachusetts — **CB member**
www.bostonconservatory.edu — **CB code: 3084**

- Private 4-year music and performing arts college
- Residential campus in very large city
- 482 degree-seeking undergraduates
- 33% of applicants admitted
- SAT or ACT (ACT writing optional), application essay required

General. Founded in 1867. Regionally accredited. **Degrees:** 68 bachelor's awarded; master's offered. **Location:** Downtown. **Calendar:** Semester, limited summer session. **Full-time faculty:** 74 total. **Part-time faculty:** 115 total. **Class size:** 89% < 20, 9% 20-39, less than 1% 40-49, less than 1% 50-99. **Special facilities:** College operated theater.

Freshman class profile. 1,136 applied, 370 admitted, 150 enrolled.

Out-of-state:	75%	**Sororities:**	5%
Live on campus:	98%		

Basis for selection. Audition carries most weight. Academic record and artistic background strongly considered. Test scores, recommendations, personal essay, school and community activities, interview important. Audition required. Interview required of music education, composition majors.

High school preparation. Required units include English 4, mathematics 3, social studies 2, history 2, science 2 and foreign language 2.

2008-2009 Annual costs. Tuition/fees: $32,350. Room/board: $15,670. Books/supplies: $750. Personal expenses: $1,705.

2008-2009 Financial aid. **Need-based:** 48% of total undergraduate aid awarded as scholarships/grants, 52% as loans/jobs. **Non-need-based:** Scholarships awarded for music/drama.

Application procedures. **Admission:** Closing date 12/1 (postmark date). $105 fee. Admission notification 4/1. Must reply by 5/1. **Financial aid:** Priority date 3/1; no closing date. FAFSA, institutional form required.

Academics. **Special study options:** Cross-registration, double major, ESL, independent study, teacher certification program. **Credit/placement by examination:** CLEP, institutional tests. 75 credit hours maximum toward bachelor's degree. **Support services:** Pre-admission summer program, study skills assistance, tutoring, writing center.

Majors. **Education:** Music. **Visual/performing arts:** Dance, music performance, music theory/composition, piano/organ, voice/opera.

Computing on campus. 20 workstations in dormitories, library, student center. Dormitories linked to campus network. Online library available.

Student life. **Freshman orientation:** Mandatory, $320 fee. Held the week prior to registration includes college life seminar, advising, parent luncheon, school tours, city-wide tours, placements, auditions. Fee for music education students is $95. **Housing:** Coed dorms, single-sex dorms available. $250 deposit, deadline 5/1. **Activities:** International student organizations, literary magazine, student government, student newspaper, African American artists' association, community services association, Christian Fellowship, environmental awareness group, peer support aides, Taiwan Chinese student association, gay and lesbian artists' association, Organizacion De Artistas Hispanos, Korean society.

Student services. Career counseling, health services, personal counseling.

Contact. E-mail: admissions@bostonconservatory.edu
Phone: (617) 912-9153 Fax: (617) 536-3176
Kristy Errera-Solomon, Dean of Enrollment Services, Boston Conservatory, 8 The Fenway, Boston, MA 02215

Boston University

Boston, Massachusetts — **CB member**
www.bu.edu — **CB code: 3087**

- Private 4-year university
- Residential campus in very large city
- 16,474 degree-seeking undergraduates: 3% part-time, 60% women, 3% African American, 14% Asian American, 7% Hispanic American, 7% international
- 12,626 degree-seeking graduate students
- 54% of applicants admitted
- SAT or ACT with writing, SAT Subject Tests, application essay required
- 80% graduate within 6 years; 28% enter graduate study

General. Founded in 1839. Regionally accredited. **Degrees:** 4,177 bachelor's awarded; master's, doctoral, first professional offered. **ROTC:** Army, Naval, Air Force. **Location:** Downtown. **Calendar:** Semester, extensive summer session. **Full-time faculty:** 1,502 total; 78% have terminal degrees, 11% minority, 35% women. **Part-time faculty:** 997 total; 4% minority, 41% women. **Class size:** 56% < 20, 30% 20-39, 4% 40-49, 6% 50-99, 4% >100. **Special facilities:** Biodiversity station in Ecuador, dedicated management library, planetarium, National Public Radio station, 20th century archives, professional theater/theater company, center for remote sensing, speech, language and hearing clinic, culinary center, communication multimedia lab.

Freshman class profile. 38,010 applied, 20,640 admitted, 4,131 enrolled.

Mid 50% test scores		**Rank in top quarter:**	87%
SAT critical reading:	580-670	**Rank in top tenth:**	55%
SAT math:	600-690	**Return as sophomores:**	91%
SAT writing:	590-680	**Out-of-state:**	80%
ACT composite:	25-30	**Live on campus:**	99%
GPA 3.75 or higher:	26%	**International:**	10%
GPA 3.50-3.74:	30%	**Fraternities:**	1%
GPA 3.0-3.49:	40%	**Sororities:**	1%
GPA 2.0-2.99:	4%		

Basis for selection. Evidence of strong academic performance in challenging college-prep curriculum most important. SAT Subject Tests in Chemistry and Math (level 2) required for accelerated medical and dental programs. Others required to submit 2 subject tests in subject areas of their choice. Interview required for accelerated medical/dental programs, all non-performance theater arts majors. Audition required for music, theater performance programs. Portfolio required of visual arts, stage management, theatrical design majors. Portfolio or audition required for College of Fine Arts. **Homeschooled:** Students should contact Office of Admissions prior to application.

High school preparation. College-preparatory program required. 15 units required; 20 recommended. Required and recommended units include English 4, mathematics 3-4, social studies 3-4, science 3-4 (laboratory 3-4) and foreign language 2-4. Pre-calculus required. Social studies should include history.

2008-2009 Annual costs. Tuition/fees: $37,050. Room/board: $11,418. Books/supplies: $860. Personal expenses: $1,226.

2008-2009 Financial aid. **Need-based:** 2,427 full-time freshmen applied for aid; 1,954 were judged to have need; 1,952 of these received aid. Average need met was 90%. Average scholarship/grant was $21,485; average loan $4,960. 74% of total undergraduate aid awarded as scholarships/grants, 26% as loans/jobs. **Non-need-based:** Awarded to 3,543 full-time undergraduates, including 1,054 freshmen. Scholarships awarded for academics, alumni affiliation, art, athletics, leadership, music/drama, religious affiliation, ROTC, state residency. **Additional information:** Financial aid deadline for early decision applicants: 11/01; notification date: 2/15. Graduates of Boston's public high schools who complete financial aid application and demonstrate need will be awarded financial aid packages which contain no loans and meet their full demonstrated need.

Application procedures. **Admission:** Closing date 1/1 (receipt date). $75 fee, may be waived for applicants with need. Admission notification 4/15. Must reply by 5/1. Application deadline December 1 for accelerated medical and dental combined degree and trustee, Boston high school, Cardinal Medeiros Scholar programs. **Financial aid:** Closing date 2/15. FAFSA, CSS PROFILE required. Applicants notified on a rolling basis starting 3/15; must reply by 5/1 or within 2 week(s) of notification.

Academics. **Special study options:** Accelerated study, combined bachelor's/graduate degree, cooperative education, cross-registration, distance learning, double major, dual enrollment of high school students, ESL, honors, independent study, internships, liberal arts/career combination, semester at sea, student-designed major, study abroad, teacher certification program, Washington semester, weekend college. Extensive opportunities for study abroad as well as internships available in South and Central America, Europe, Africa, China, Pacific Rim, Russia. Field study in marine science at Woods Hole Institute, in environmental/ecological science in Ecuador, and at Photonics Center, combined bachelor's/master's degrees, 6-year physical therapy (BS/DPT) program, 5-year occupational therapy (BS/MS) program; 7-year accelerated MD, DMD programs. **Credit/placement by examination:** AP, CLEP, IB, SAT, ACT, institutional tests. 32 credit hours maximum toward bachelor's degree. Credits assigned vary by school and college. Scores higher than minimums may result in additional credit depending on department. **Support services:** Learning center, study skills assistance, tutoring, writing center.

Majors. **Area/ethnic studies:** American, East Asian, Italian, Latin American, Russian/Slavic. **Biology:** General, biochemistry, ecology, marine, molecular. **Business:** Accounting, business admin, entrepreneurial studies, finance, hospitality admin, international, international finance, management information systems, market research, marketing, operations, organizational behavior. **Communications:** General, advertising, broadcast journalism, journalism, public relations. **Computer sciences:** General. **Conservation:** General, environmental science, environmental studies, management/policy. **Education:** General, art, bilingual, chemistry, Deaf/hearing impaired, drama/dance, early childhood, elementary, English, mathematics, music, physical, science, social studies, special. **Engineering:** General, aerospace, biomedical, computer, electrical, mechanical. **Foreign languages:** General, ancient Greek, classics, French, German, Italian, Latin, linguistics, modern Greek, Russian, Spanish. **Health:** Athletic training, communication disorders, dental lab technology. **History:** General. **Interdisciplinary:** Math/computer science, neuroscience, nutrition sciences. **Legal studies:** Legal secretary, paralegal. **Math:** General. **Parks/recreation:** Exercise sciences. **Philosophy/religion:** Philosophy, religion. **Physical sciences:** Astronomy, astrophysics, chemistry, geology, geophysics, physics, planetary. **Psychology:** General. **Social sciences:** Anthropology, archaeology, economics, geography, international relations, political science, sociology, urban studies. **Visual/performing arts:** General, acting, art history/conservation, cinematography, commercial/advertising art, directing/producing, drawing, music history, music performance, music theory/composition, painting, piano/organ, sculpture, theater design, theater history, voice/opera.

Most popular majors. Biology 6%, business/marketing 18%, communications/journalism 17%, engineering/engineering technologies 6%, health sciences 6%, psychology 7%, social sciences 18%.

Computing on campus. 750 workstations in dormitories, library, computer center, student center. Dormitories wired for high-speed internet access and linked to campus network. Commuter students can connect to campus network. Online course registration, online library, helpline, repair service, student web hosting, wireless network available.

Student life. **Freshman orientation:** Mandatory, $135 fee. Preregistration for classes offered. Summer program. **Policies:** Campus residents must abide by guest/visitor policy. **Housing:** Guaranteed on-campus for all undergraduates. Coed dorms, single-sex dorms, special housing for disabled, apartments, cooperative housing, wellness housing available. $650 nonrefundable deposit, deadline 5/1. Specialty halls/floors available for groups of students with common interest or academic major. **Activities:** Bands, campus ministries, choral groups, dance, drama, film society, international student organizations, literary magazine, music ensembles, Model UN, musical theater, opera, radio station, student government, student newspaper, symphony orchestra, TV station, 468 student organizations available.

Athletics. NCAA. **Intercollegiate:** Basketball, cross-country, diving, field hockey W, golf, ice hockey, lacrosse W, rowing (crew), soccer, softball W, swimming, tennis, track and field, wrestling M. **Intramural:** Basketball, football (non-tackle), ice hockey W, soccer, softball, swimming, tennis, volleyball, water polo. **Team name:** Terriers.

Student services. Adult student services, chaplain/spiritual director, career counseling, student employment services, financial aid counseling, health services, minority student services, personal counseling, placement for graduates, veterans' counselor. **Physically disabled:** Services for visually, speech, hearing impaired. **Learning disabled:** Comprehensive services available.

Contact. E-mail: admissions@bu.edu
Phone: (617) 353-2300 Fax: (617) 353-9695
Kelly Walter, Director, Office of Undergraduate Admissions, Boston University, 121 Bay State Road, Boston, MA 02215

Brandeis University

Waltham, Massachusetts — **CB member**
www.brandeis.edu — **CB code: 3092**

- Private 4-year university
- Residential campus in small city
- 3,169 degree-seeking undergraduates: 56% women, 4% African American, 10% Asian American, 5% Hispanic American, 8% international
- 1,653 degree-seeking graduate students
- 33% of applicants admitted
- SAT and SAT Subject Tests or ACT with writing, application essay required
- 90% graduate within 6 years

General. Founded in 1948. Regionally accredited. **Degrees:** 1,180 bachelor's awarded; master's, doctoral offered. **ROTC:** Army, Air Force. **Location:** 10 miles from Boston. **Calendar:** Semester, limited summer session. **Full-time faculty:** 350 total. **Part-time faculty:** 120 total. **Class size:** 69% < 20, 19% 20-39, 6% 40-49, 5% 50-99, 2% >100. **Special facilities:** Basic medical sciences research center, spatial orientation laboratory, center for complex systems, astronomical observatory.

Freshman class profile. 7,724 applied, 2,511 admitted, 759 enrolled.

Mid 50% test scores		**GPA 2.0-2.99:**	1%
SAT critical reading:	640-720	**Rank in top quarter:**	94%
SAT math:	650-730	**Rank in top tenth:**	82%
SAT writing:	640-730	**Return as sophomores:**	93%
ACT composite:	29-32	**Out-of-state:**	74%
GPA 3.75 or higher:	61%	**Live on campus:**	99%
GPA 3.50-3.74:	24%	**International:**	7%
GPA 3.0-3.49:	14%		

Basis for selection. Evidence of accomplishment and development most important. School and teacher statements, test scores also important. Students taking SAT must take 2 SAT Subject Tests from 2 subject areas. Interview recommended.

High school preparation. College-preparatory program required. 16 units recommended. Recommended units include English 4, mathematics 3, history 1, science 1 (laboratory 1), foreign language 3 and academic electives 4.

2008-2009 Annual costs. Tuition/fees: $37,294. Room/board: $10,354. Books/supplies: $700. Personal expenses: $1,000.

2008-2009 Financial aid. **Need-based:** 546 full-time freshmen applied for aid; 405 were judged to have need; 403 of these received aid. Average need met was 86%. Average scholarship/grant was $26,874; average loan $3,990. 78% of total undergraduate aid awarded as scholarships/grants, 22% as loans/jobs. **Non-need-based:** Awarded to 786 full-time undergraduates, including 190 freshmen. Scholarships awarded for academics.

Application procedures. **Admission:** Closing date 1/15 (receipt date). $55 fee, may be waived for applicants with need. Admission notification

4/1. Must reply by May 1 or within 2 week(s) if notified thereafter. **Financial aid:** Priority date 2/1; no closing date. FAFSA, CSS PROFILE required. Applicants notified on a rolling basis starting 4/1.

Academics. Special study options: Cross-registration, double major, independent study, internships, student-designed major, study abroad. BA/MA in physics, history; seminars at Boston Museum of Fine Arts and seminars available through Massachusetts Bay Marine Studies Consortium, early admission to Mt. Sinai Medical School and Tufts Medical School. **Credit/placement by examination:** AP, CLEP, IB, institutional tests. **Support services:** Reduced course load, remedial instruction, study skills assistance, tutoring, writing center.

Majors. Area/ethnic studies: African-American, American, East Asian, European, Italian, Latin American, women's. **Biology:** General, biochemistry, biophysics. **Computer sciences:** Computer science. **Conservation:** Environmental studies. **Education:** General. **Foreign languages:** Classics, comparative lit, French, German, Hebrew, linguistics, Russian, Spanish. **Health:** Health care admin. **History:** General. **Interdisciplinary:** Global studies, neuroscience. **Math:** General. **Philosophy/religion:** Philosophy. **Physical sciences:** Chemistry, physics. **Psychology:** General. **Social sciences:** Anthropology, economics, sociology, U.S. government. **Visual/performing arts:** Art history/conservation, dramatic, film/cinema, studio arts.

Most popular majors. Area/ethnic studies 11%, biology 11%, history 8%, interdisciplinary studies 11%, psychology 8%, social sciences 24%, visual/performing arts 6%.

Computing on campus. 104 workstations in library, computer center, student center. Dormitories wired for high-speed internet access and linked to campus network. Commuter students can connect to campus network. Online course registration, helpline, repair service, student web hosting, wireless network available.

Student life. Freshman orientation: Mandatory, $183 fee. Preregistration for classes offered. Five-day program begins weekend before Labor Day weekend. **Housing:** Guaranteed on-campus for freshmen. Coed dorms, single-sex dorms, special housing for disabled, apartments available. Thematic learning communities available. **Activities:** Bands, campus ministries, choral groups, dance, drama, film society, international student organizations, literary magazine, music ensembles, musical theater, radio station, student government, student newspaper, symphony orchestra, TV station, 246 recognized clubs and organizations.

Athletics. NCAA. **Intercollegiate:** Baseball M, basketball, cross-country, diving, fencing, golf M, sailing, soccer, softball W, swimming, tennis, track and field, volleyball W. **Intramural:** Basketball, equestrian, football (non-tackle) M, golf, ice hockey M, softball, squash, table tennis, tennis, volleyball, water polo, weight lifting. **Team name:** Judges.

Student services. Alcohol/substance abuse counseling, chaplain/spiritual director, career counseling, student employment services, financial aid counseling, health services, minority student services, on-campus daycare, personal counseling, placement for graduates, veterans' counselor, women's services. **Physically disabled:** Services for visually, speech, hearing impaired.

Contact. E-mail: admissions@brandeis.edu
Phone: (781) 736-3500 Toll-free number: (800) 622-0622
Fax: (781) 736-3536
Gil Villanueva, Dean of Admissions, Brandeis University, Box 549110, Waltham, MA 02454-9110

Bridgewater State College

Bridgewater, Massachusetts — **CB member**
www.bridgew.edu — **CB code: 3517**

- Public 4-year liberal arts and teachers college
- Commuter campus in large town
- 8,310 degree-seeking undergraduates: 15% part-time, 60% women, 6% African American, 2% Asian American, 2% Hispanic American, 1% international
- 1,238 degree-seeking graduate students
- 62% of applicants admitted
- SAT or ACT (ACT writing optional) required
- 51% graduate within 6 years

General. Founded in 1840. Regionally accredited. **Degrees:** 1,413 bachelor's awarded; master's offered. **ROTC:** Army, Air Force. **Location:** 30 miles from Boston; 35 miles from Providence, Rhode Island. **Calendar:** Semester, extensive summer session. **Full-time faculty:** 306 total; 90% have terminal degrees, 11% minority, 48% women. **Part-time faculty:** 366 total; 5% minority, 50% women. **Class size:** 42% < 20, 56% 20-39, 1% 40-49, less than 1% 50-99.

Freshman class profile. 7,226 applied, 4,503 admitted, 1,502 enrolled.

Mid 50% test scores		**GPA 2.0-2.99:**	40%
SAT critical reading:	460-560	**Rank in top quarter:**	32%
SAT math:	470-560	**Rank in top tenth:**	8%
ACT composite:	19-23	**Return as sophomores:**	80%
GPA 3.75 or higher:	9%	**Out-of-state:**	4%
GPA 3.50-3.74:	10%	**Live on campus:**	59%
GPA 3.0-3.49:	41%		

Basis for selection. High school achievement most important, including weighted high school GPA and completion of 16 college preparatory courses. Test scores, essay, extracurricular activities also important. Class rank, recommendations considered. Essay recommended. **Learning Disabled:** Exemption from admissions standardized testing upon documentation of diagnostic test results. Must complete 16 required academic courses with 3.0 GPA or present evidence of potential for academic success.

High school preparation. 16 units required. Required units include English 4, mathematics 3, social studies 1, history 1, science 3 (laboratory 2), foreign language 2 and academic electives 2.

2008-2009 Annual costs. Tuition/fees: $6,107; $12,247 out-of-state. Room/board: $8,405. Books/supplies: $1,000. Personal expenses: $1,800.

2007-2008 Financial aid. Need-based: 1,369 full-time freshmen applied for aid; 975 were judged to have need; 967 of these received aid. Average need met was 75%. Average scholarship/grant was $3,632; average loan $3,400. 40% of total undergraduate aid awarded as scholarships/grants, 60% as loans/jobs. **Non-need-based:** Awarded to 75 full-time undergraduates, including 255 freshmen. Scholarships awarded for academics, leadership, minority status, state residency.

Application procedures. Admission: Priority date 2/15; no deadline. $25 fee, may be waived for applicants with need. Admission notification on a rolling basis beginning on or about 12/15. **Financial aid:** Priority date 3/1; no closing date. FAFSA required. Applicants notified on a rolling basis starting 4/1.

Academics. Special study options: Accelerated study, combined bachelor's/graduate degree, cross-registration, distance learning, double major, dual enrollment of high school students, ESL, exchange student, honors, independent study, internships, study abroad, teacher certification program, Washington semester. **Credit/placement by examination:** AP, CLEP, IB, institutional tests. **Support services:** Learning center, pre-admission summer program, reduced course load, remedial instruction, study skills assistance, tutoring, writing center.

Majors. Architecture: Urban/community planning. **Biology:** General, biochemistry, biomedical sciences, cellular/molecular, environmental. **Business:** Accounting, business admin, finance, international, management information systems, marketing, transportation. **Communications:** General. **Computer sciences:** Computer science. **Education:** Art, biology, drama/dance, early childhood, elementary, English, health, health occupations, kindergarten/preschool, music, physical, special. **Foreign languages:** Spanish. **Health:** Athletic training, communication disorders, kinesiotherapy. **History:** General. **Legal studies:** General. **Math:** General. **Parks/recreation:** General, exercise sciences, sports admin. **Philosophy/religion:** Ethics, philosophy. **Physical sciences:** Chemistry, geochemistry, geology, physics. **Protective services:** Criminal justice. **Psychology:** General. **Public administration:** Social work. **Social sciences:** Anthropology, archaeology, economics, geography, international relations, political science, sociology, U.S. government, urban studies. **Transportation:** Airline/commercial pilot, aviation management. **Visual/performing arts:** Art history/conservation, crafts, dramatic, graphic design, photography, studio arts.

Most popular majors. Business/marketing 14%, communications/journalism 7%, education 13%, psychology 14%, security/protective services 10%, social sciences 6%.

Computing on campus. PC or laptop required. 780 workstations in library, computer center, student center. Dormitories wired for high-speed internet access and linked to campus network. Commuter students can connect to campus network. Online course registration, online library, helpline, repair service, wireless network available.

Student life. Freshman orientation: Mandatory, $160 fee. Preregistration for classes offered. **Housing:** Coed dorms, single-sex dorms, apartments, wellness housing available. $150 fully refundable deposit, deadline 5/1. Quiet floor, nonsmoking floor available in residence hall. Housing available over breaks for athletes, student teachers, international students. **Activities:** Bands, campus ministries, choral groups, dance, drama, literary magazine, music ensembles, musical theater, radio station, student government, student newspaper, Christian Fellowship, College Democrats, Afro-American society, international club, La Sociedad Latina, Amnesty International, Big Brothers/Big Sisters, Habitat for Humanity.

Athletics. NCAA. **Intercollegiate:** Baseball M, basketball, cross-country, diving, field hockey W, football (tackle) M, lacrosse W, soccer, softball W, swimming, tennis, track and field, volleyball W, wrestling M. **Intramural:** Basketball, football (tackle) M, lacrosse M, soccer, softball, tennis, volleyball, water polo. **Team name:** Bears.

Student services. Adult student services, chaplain/spiritual director, career counseling, student employment services, financial aid counseling, health services, minority student services, on-campus daycare, personal counseling, placement for graduates, veterans' counselor, women's services. **Physically disabled:** Services for visually, speech, hearing impaired.

Contact. E-mail: admission@bridgew.edu
Phone: (508) 531-1237 Fax: (508) 531-1746
Gregg Meyer, Director of Admissions, Bridgewater State College, Gates House, Bridgewater, MA 02325

Cambridge College
Cambridge, Massachusetts
www.cambridgecollege.edu **CB code: 3612**

- Private 4-year liberal arts and teachers college
- Commuter campus in very large city
- 1,130 degree-seeking undergraduates: 69% part-time, 72% women
- 3,763 degree-seeking graduate students

General. Regionally accredited. Cambridge College serves mostly working adults. **Degrees:** 136 bachelor's awarded; master's, doctoral offered. **Calendar:** Continuous, extensive summer session. **Full-time faculty:** 28 total; 68% have terminal degrees, 29% minority, 54% women. **Part-time faculty:** 1,065 total; 37% have terminal degrees, 30% minority, 60% women.

Basis for selection. Open admission. 3 years work experience after high school recommended, including employment, volunteer work, training, community involvement. Placement testing may be used if applicant does not have high school degree or GED.

2008-2009 Annual costs. Tuition/fees: $10,350.

2007-2008 Financial aid. All financial aid based on need.

Application procedures. Admission: No deadline. $30 fee. Admission notification on a rolling basis. **Financial aid:** No deadline. FAFSA, institutional form required. Applicants notified on a rolling basis starting 5/1.

Academics. Special study options: Accelerated study, cooperative education, distance learning, independent study, liberal arts/career combination, teacher certification program, weekend college. **Credit/placement by examination:** CLEP. **Support services:** Reduced course load, tutoring, writing center.

Majors. Business: Management science. **Psychology:** General, counseling, family. **Public administration:** Human services.

Most popular majors. Business/marketing 24%, liberal arts 44%, psychology 23%, public administration/social services 9%.

Computing on campus. Online course registration, online library, helpline, wireless network available.

Student life. Freshman orientation: Available.

Student services. Adult student services, services for economically disadvantaged, financial aid counseling. **Learning disabled:** Comprehensive services available.

Contact. E-mail: admit@cambridgecollege.edu
Phone: (888) 800-4723 Toll-free number: (800) 877-4723
Farah Ravanbakhsh, Senior Director, Admissions and Enrollment, Cambridge College, 1000 Massachusetts Avenue, Cambridge, MA 02138-5304

Clark University
Worcester, Massachusetts **CB member**
www.clarku.edu **CB code: 3279**

- Private 4-year university and liberal arts college
- Residential campus in small city
- 2,293 degree-seeking undergraduates: 2% part-time, 60% women, 2% African American, 4% Asian American, 2% Hispanic American, 8% international
- 921 degree-seeking graduate students
- 56% of applicants admitted
- SAT or ACT (ACT writing optional), application essay required
- 76% graduate within 6 years; 36% enter graduate study

General. Founded in 1887. Regionally accredited. **Degrees:** 493 bachelor's awarded; master's, doctoral offered. **ROTC:** Army, Naval, Air Force. **Location:** 50 miles from Boston. **Calendar:** Semester, limited summer session. **Full-time faculty:** 184 total; 97% have terminal degrees, 16% minority, 42% women. **Part-time faculty:** 115 total; 42% women. **Class size:** 59% < 20, 31% 20-39, 5% 40-49, 4% 50-99, less than 1% >100. **Special facilities:** Robert Goddard exhibition, map library, rare book room, NMR research facility, observatory, electronic music facility, arboretum, crafts studio, 2 theaters, environmental education laboratory, student-run recycling center, pulsed magnetic field laboratory, Holocaust studies center.

Freshman class profile. 5,299 applied, 2,988 admitted, 591 enrolled.

Mid 50% test scores			
SAT critical reading:	550-660	GPA 2.0-2.99:	13%
SAT math:	540-650	Rank in top quarter:	76%
SAT writing:	550-660	Rank in top tenth:	39%
ACT composite:	24-28	End year in good standing:	90%
GPA 3.75 or higher:	27%	Return as sophomores:	91%
GPA 3.50-3.74:	25%	Out-of-state:	63%
GPA 3.0-3.49:	35%	Live on campus:	99%
		International:	9%

Basis for selection. School achievement record and courses, recommendations, test scores most important. Special talents, accomplishments, motivation, and individual circumstances, including outside activities and jobs, also important. Interview recommended. Portfolio recommended for art majors.

High school preparation. College-preparatory program required. 16 units recommended. Recommended units include English 4, mathematics 3, social studies 2, history 2, science 3 (laboratory 2) and foreign language 2.

2008-2009 Annual costs. Tuition/fees: $34,220. New student contingency fee: $50. Fifth-year tuition waived for eligible undergraduates admitted to accelerated bachelor's/master's programs. Room/board: $6,650. Books/supplies: $800. Personal expenses: $700.

2008-2009 Financial aid. Need-based: 418 full-time freshmen applied for aid; 312 were judged to have need; 302 of these received aid. Average need met was 95%. Average scholarship/grant was $21,932; average loan $4,731. 74% of total undergraduate aid awarded as scholarships/grants, 26% as loans/jobs. **Non-need-based:** Awarded to 1,343 full-time undergraduates, including 352 freshmen. Scholarships awarded for academics, leadership.

Application procedures. Admission: Closing date 1/15 (postmark date). $55 fee, may be waived for applicants with need. Admission notification 4/1. Must reply by May 1 or within 2 week(s) if notified thereafter. **Financial aid:** Closing date 1/15. FAFSA, CSS PROFILE required. Applicants notified by 3/31; must reply by 5/1 or within 2 week(s) of notification.

Academics. Interdisciplinary majors, special programs, and accelerated bachelor's/master's program with fifth-year tuition-free available. **Special study options:** Combined bachelor's/graduate degree, cross-registration, double major, ESL, independent study, internships, liberal arts/career combination, student-designed major, study abroad, teacher certification program, Washington semester. Courses at Bermuda Biological Station, May term at Clark European Center in Luxembourg, semester-long environmental science program at marine biological laboratory at Woods Hole Oceanographic Institute. 3-2 engineering programs with Columbia University, Worcester Polytechnic Institute, Washington University. **Credit/placement by examination:** AP, CLEP, IB, SAT, institutional tests. 16 credit hours maximum toward bachelor's degree. **Support services:** Reduced course load, study skills assistance, writing center.

Majors. Area/ethnic studies: Women's. **Biology:** General, biochemistry, bioinformatics, molecular. **Business:** General, business admin. **Communications:** General. **Computer sciences:** General, computer science. **Conservation:** Environmental science, environmental studies. **Foreign languages:** General, classics, comparative lit, French, Spanish. **History:** General. **Interdisciplinary:** Global studies, math/computer science, science/society. **Liberal arts:** Arts/sciences. **Math:** General. **Philosophy/religion:** Philosophy. **Physical sciences:** Chemistry, physics. **Psychology:** General. **Public administration:** General. **Social sciences:** Economics, geography, international relations, political science, sociology. **Visual/performing arts:** General, art, art history/conservation, dramatic, film/cinema, studio arts.

Most popular majors. Biology 9%, business/marketing 6%, communications/journalism 7%, English 6%, psychology 18%, social sciences 29%, visual/performing arts 8%.

Computing on campus. 79 workstations in dormitories, library, computer center, student center. Dormitories wired for high-speed internet access and linked to campus network. Commuter students can connect to campus network. Online course registration, online library, helpline, student web hosting, wireless network available.

Student life. **Freshman orientation:** Mandatory, $200 fee. Preregistration for classes offered. Program held during week prior to fall semester; includes course selection and registration. **Housing:** Guaranteed on-campus for freshmen. Coed dorms, single-sex dorms, special housing for disabled, apartments, wellness housing available. $100 nonrefundable deposit, deadline 5/1. Some university-owned off-campus housing available. Year-round house, quiet house, other special interest houses available. All residence halls nonsmoking. **Activities:** Bands, campus ministries, choral groups, dance, drama, film society, international student organizations, literary magazine, music ensembles, Model UN, musical theater, radio station, student government, student newspaper, symphony orchestra, TV station, Approximately 95 student clubs and organizations.

Athletics. NCAA. **Intercollegiate:** Baseball M, basketball, cross-country, diving, field hockey W, lacrosse M, rowing (crew), soccer, softball W, swimming, tennis, volleyball W. **Intramural:** Badminton, basketball, racquetball, soccer, softball, squash, volleyball, water polo. **Team name:** Cougars.

Student services. Adult student services, alcohol/substance abuse counseling, chaplain/spiritual director, career counseling, services for economically disadvantaged, student employment services, financial aid counseling, health services, minority student services, personal counseling, placement for graduates, women's services. **Physically disabled:** Services for visually, speech, hearing impaired.

Contact. E-mail: admissions@clarku.edu
Phone: (508) 793-7431 Toll-free number: (800) 462-5275
Fax: (508) 793-8821
Harold Wingood, Dean of Admissions, Clark University, 950 Main Street, Worcester, MA 01610-1477

College of the Holy Cross

Worcester, Massachusetts — **CB member**
www.holycross.edu — **CB code: 3282**

- Private 4-year liberal arts college affiliated with Roman Catholic Church
- Residential campus in small city
- 2,866 degree-seeking undergraduates: 56% women, 4% African American, 6% Asian American, 6% Hispanic American, 1% international
- 34% of applicants admitted
- Application essay required
- 94% graduate within 6 years; 25% enter graduate study

General. Founded in 1843. Regionally accredited. **Degrees:** 670 bachelor's awarded. **ROTC:** Army, Naval, Air Force. **Location:** 45 miles from Boston. **Calendar:** Semester. **Full-time faculty:** 259 total; 92% have terminal degrees, 12% minority, 46% women. **Part-time faculty:** 59 total; 12% minority, 42% women. **Class size:** 55% < 20, 43% 20-39, 2% 40-49, less than 1% 50-99. **Special facilities:** Greenhouse, facilities for aquatic research, research-level scientific equipment.

Freshman class profile. 7,227 applied, 2,441 admitted, 738 enrolled.

Mid 50% test scores		**Return as sophomores:**	95%
SAT critical reading:	580-670	**Out-of-state:**	67%
SAT math:	600-680	**Live on campus:**	100%
Rank in top quarter:	90%	**International:**	2%
Rank in top tenth:	61%		

Basis for selection. Academic record, recommendations, interview, essay, extracurricular activities important. Evidence of superior achievement in analytical reading and writing of particular importance. Advanced placement and honors courses recommended. Standardized test scores are optional. Students may submit scores if they believe the results present a fuller picture of their achievements and potential. Students who do not submit scores will not be at any disadvantage in admissions decisions. Personal interview optional but highly recommended. **Homeschooled:** On-campus interview highly encouraged. Applicants should submit course work samples, personal statement, and college transcripts if applicable. If homeschooling associated with particular organization or program, submit description.

High school preparation. College-preparatory program recommended. 20 units recommended. Recommended units include English 4, mathematics 4, social studies 2, history 2, science 4, foreign language 3 and academic electives 1.

2009-2010 Annual costs. Tuition/fees: $38,722. Room/board: $10,620. Books/supplies: $700. Personal expenses: $900.

2008-2009 Financial aid. **Need-based:** 517 full-time freshmen applied for aid; 401 were judged to have need; 397 of these received aid. Average need met was 100%. Average scholarship/grant was $26,693; average loan $4,673. 77% of total undergraduate aid awarded as scholarships/grants, 23% as loans/jobs. **Non-need-based:** Awarded to 192 full-time undergraduates, including 37 freshmen. Scholarships awarded for academics, athletics, ROTC. **Additional information:** Cost of tuition waived above the amount of the Pell Grant award for Worcester residents whose families earn less than $50,000.

Application procedures. **Admission:** Closing date 1/15 (receipt date). $60 fee, may be waived for applicants with need. Admission notification 4/1. Must reply by 5/1. **Financial aid:** Closing date 2/1. FAFSA required. CSS PROFILE required of all students applying for institutional aid. Applicants notified by 3/30; must reply by 5/1.

Academics. Students encouraged to participate in Oxford-style tutorials. 32 courses of 1 or more units required for graduation. 10 to 14 courses of 1 or more units required in major. **Special study options:** Accelerated study, cross-registration, double major, dual enrollment of high school students, exchange student, honors, independent study, internships, liberal arts/career combination, semester at sea, student-designed major, study abroad, teacher certification program, Washington semester. First-year living and learning academic enrichment program. **Credit/placement by examination:** AP, CLEP, IB. **Support services:** Tutoring, writing center.

Majors. **Area/ethnic studies:** Asian, German, Russian/Slavic. **Biology:** General. **Business:** Accounting. **Computer sciences:** General. **Conservation:** Environmental studies. **Foreign languages:** Classics, comparative lit, French, German, Italian, Russian, Spanish. **History:** General. **Interdisciplinary:** Medieval/Renaissance. **Math:** General. **Philosophy/religion:** Philosophy, religion. **Physical sciences:** Chemistry, physics. **Psychology:** General. **Social sciences:** Anthropology, economics, political science, sociology. **Visual/performing arts:** Art history/conservation, dramatic, studio arts.

Most popular majors. English 13%, foreign language 9%, history 10%, mathematics 6%, psychology 10%, social sciences 32%.

Computing on campus. 485 workstations in dormitories, library, computer center, student center. Dormitories wired for high-speed internet access and linked to campus network. Commuter students can connect to campus network. Online library, helpline, repair service, student web hosting, wireless network available.

Student life. **Freshman orientation:** Available, $210 fee. Two-day programs available in mid-June combined with a 3-day orientation prior to fall registration. **Policies:** Responsible drinking policy for students 21 and older. Initiation hazing prohibited. **Housing:** Guaranteed on-campus for all undergraduates. Coed dorms, special housing for disabled, apartments, wellness housing available. $500 nonrefundable deposit, deadline 5/1. **Activities:** Bands, choral groups, dance, drama, literary magazine, music ensembles, musical theater, radio station, student government, student newspaper, black student union, Purple Key Society, student program for urban development, women's forum, Latin American student organization, Asian student society, Muslim student association, Appalachia service project, Habitat for Humanity, association of bisexuals, gays and lesbians.

Athletics. NCAA. **Intercollegiate:** Baseball M, basketball, cross-country, diving, field hockey W, football (tackle) M, golf, ice hockey, lacrosse, rowing (crew), soccer, softball W, swimming, tennis, track and field, volleyball W. **Intramural:** Basketball, football (non-tackle), softball, tennis, volleyball. **Team name:** Crusaders.

Student services. Alcohol/substance abuse counseling, chaplain/spiritual director, career counseling, student employment services, financial aid counseling, health services, minority student services, personal counseling, placement for graduates, women's services. **Physically disabled:** Services for visually, hearing impaired.

Contact. E-mail: admissions@holycross.edu
Phone: (508) 793-2443 Toll-free number: (800) 442-2421
Fax: (508) 793-3888
Ann McDermott, Director of Admissions, College of the Holy Cross, One College Street, Worcester, MA 01610-2395

Curry College

Milton, Massachusetts — **CB member**
www.curry.edu — **CB code: 3285**

- Private 4-year nursing and liberal arts college
- Residential campus in large town

- 2,598 degree-seeking undergraduates: 22% part-time, 58% women, 7% African American, 1% Asian American, 3% Hispanic American, 1% international
- 259 degree-seeking graduate students
- 67% of applicants admitted
- Application essay required
- 47% graduate within 6 years

General. Founded in 1879. Regionally accredited. **Degrees:** 591 bachelor's awarded; master's offered. **ROTC:** Army, Air Force. **Location:** Seven miles from downtown Boston. **Calendar:** Semester, limited summer session. **Full-time faculty:** 118 total; 67% have terminal degrees, 10% minority, 64% women. **Part-time faculty:** 345 total; 17% minority, 56% women. **Class size:** 59% < 20, 40% 20-39, less than 1% 40-49.

Freshman class profile. 3,944 applied, 2,655 admitted, 587 enrolled.

Mid 50% test scores		**GPA 2.0-2.99:**	57%
SAT critical reading:	470-590	**Return as sophomores:**	67%
SAT math:	470-550	**Out-of-state:**	37%
GPA 3.75 or higher:	8%	**Live on campus:**	90%
GPA 3.50-3.74:	8%	**International:**	1%
GPA 3.0-3.49:	27%		

Basis for selection. High school record, recommendations, extracurricular activities most important. Test scores also important. Interviews strongly recommended. **Homeschooled:** Statement describing homeschool structure and mission, transcript of courses and grades, state high school equivalency certificate required. **Learning Disabled:** Wechsler Adult Intelligence Scale required of learning disabled applicants for admission. This replaces SAT requirement but SAT or ACT still recommended.

High school preparation. 16 units required. Required and recommended units include English 4, mathematics 3, social studies 2, science 2-3 (laboratory 2) and foreign language 2. 3 math through algebra II, 1 chemistry, and 1 biology required for nursing applicants.

2008-2009 Annual costs. Tuition/fees: $27,540. PAL (Program for Advancement of Learning) students pay additional program participation fee of up to $5,700. Room/board: $11,080. Books/supplies: $800. Personal expenses: $1,000.

2007-2008 Financial aid. Need-based: 445 full-time freshmen applied for aid; 445 were judged to have need; 445 of these received aid. Average need met was 63%. Average scholarship/grant was $11,372; average loan $3,447. 70% of total undergraduate aid awarded as scholarships/grants, 30% as loans/jobs. **Non-need-based:** Awarded to 97 full-time undergraduates, including 38 freshmen. Scholarships awarded for academics, leadership.

Application procedures. Admission: Closing date 4/1 (postmark date). $50 fee, may be waived for applicants with need. Admission notification on a rolling basis beginning on or about 12/1. Must reply by May 1 or within 2 week(s) if notified thereafter. **Financial aid:** Priority date 3/1; no closing date. FAFSA required. Applicants notified on a rolling basis starting 3/1; must reply by 5/1 or within 2 week(s) of notification.

Academics. Special study options: Accelerated study, double major, honors, independent study, internships, liberal arts/career combination, New York semester, semester at sea, student-designed major, study abroad, teacher certification program. **Credit/placement by examination:** AP, CLEP, IB, SAT, institutional tests. 60 credit hours maximum toward bachelor's degree. **Support services:** Learning center, pre-admission summer program, reduced course load, remedial instruction, study skills assistance, tutoring, writing center.

Majors. Biology: General. **Business:** Business admin. **Communications:** General. **Computer sciences:** General. **Conservation:** Environmental science. **Education:** General, early childhood, elementary, special. **Health:** Health services, nursing (RN). **Liberal arts:** Arts/sciences. **Philosophy/religion:** Philosophy. **Protective services:** Criminal justice. **Psychology:** General. **Social sciences:** Sociology. **Visual/performing arts:** Graphic design, studio arts. **Other:** Politics and history.

Most popular majors. Business/marketing 16%, communications/journalism 13%, health sciences 25%, psychology 10%, security/protective services 23%.

Computing on campus. 100 workstations in dormitories, library, computer center. Dormitories wired for high-speed internet access and linked to campus network. Commuter students can connect to campus network. Helpline, student web hosting available.

Student life. Freshman orientation: Available, $150 fee. Preregistration for classes offered. Three summer 2-day programs and follow-up 2-day August program available. **Housing:** Coed dorms, single-sex dorms, wellness housing available. $300 nonrefundable deposit, deadline 5/1. Wellness, honors housing available. **Activities:** Campus ministries, choral groups, dance, drama, international student organizations, literary magazine, music ensembles, musical theater, radio station, student government, student newspaper, TV station, nursing association, student activities board, community service organization, Hillel, One Curry, Newman club.

Athletics. NCAA. **Intercollegiate:** Baseball M, basketball, cross-country W, football (tackle) M, ice hockey M, lacrosse, soccer, softball W, tennis. **Intramural:** Basketball, cheerleading W, football (non-tackle), golf, rugby M, softball, tennis, volleyball. **Team name:** Colonels.

Student services. Adult student services, alcohol/substance abuse counseling, chaplain/spiritual director, career counseling, student employment services, financial aid counseling, health services, minority student services, on-campus daycare, personal counseling, placement for graduates, veterans' counselor, women's services. **Learning disabled:** Comprehensive services available.

Contact. E-mail: curryadm@curry.edu
Phone: (617) 333-2210 Toll-free number: (800) 669-0686
Fax: (617) 333-2114
Jane Fidler, Dean of Admissions, Curry College, 1071 Blue Hill Avenue, Milton, MA 02186-9984

Eastern Nazarene College

Quincy, Massachusetts — **CB member**
www.enc.edu — **CB code: 3365**

- Private 4-year liberal arts college affiliated with Church of the Nazarene
- Residential campus in small city

General. Founded in 1900. Regionally accredited. **Location:** 6 miles from Boston. **Calendar:** 4-1-4.

Annual costs/financial aid. Tuition/fees (2008-2009): $22,014. Room/board: $7,913. Books/supplies: $1,000. Personal expenses: $2,000. Need-based financial aid available to full-time and part-time students.

Contact. Phone: (617) 745-3711
Director of Admissions, 23 East Elm Avenue, Quincy, MA 02170-2999

Elms College

Chicopee, Massachusetts — **CB member**
www.elms.edu — **CB code: 3283**

- Private 4-year liberal arts college affiliated with Roman Catholic Church
- Residential campus in small city
- 991 degree-seeking undergraduates: 20% part-time, 77% women
- 220 degree-seeking graduate students
- 82% of applicants admitted
- SAT or ACT with writing, application essay required

General. Founded in 1928. Regionally accredited. **Degrees:** 190 bachelor's, 6 associate awarded; master's offered. **ROTC:** Army, Air Force. **Location:** 2 miles from Springfield; 30 miles from Hartford, Connecticut. **Calendar:** Semester, extensive summer session. **Full-time faculty:** 62 total. **Part-time faculty:** 7 total. **Class size:** 79% < 20, 21% 20-39. **Special facilities:** Rare book collection, Federal Depository, Irish cultural center, Polish center for discovery and learning.

Freshman class profile. 617 applied, 506 admitted, 198 enrolled.

Mid 50% test scores		**GPA 3.0-3.49:**	36%
SAT critical reading:	420-530	**GPA 2.0-2.99:**	40%
SAT math:	420-530	**Rank in top quarter:**	35%
SAT writing:	440-540	**Rank in top tenth:**	10%
ACT composite:	18-23	**Out-of-state:**	23%
GPA 3.75 or higher:	10%	**Live on campus:**	64%
GPA 3.50-3.74:	13%		

Basis for selection. Students should rank in top half of high school class. 2.5 GPA, 1000 SAT (exclusive of Writing) recommended. Interview recommended. **Homeschooled:** Transcript of courses and grades, letter of recommendation (nonparent) required.

High school preparation. 12 units required; 20 recommended. Required and recommended units include English 4, mathematics 2-4, social studies 1-2, history 1-2, science 2-4 (laboratory 2) and foreign language 2-4. Biology, chemistry required for nursing applicants.

2008-2009 Annual costs. Tuition/fees: $24,942. Room/board: $9,260. Books/supplies: $1,000. Personal expenses: $1,000.

2007-2008 Financial aid. Non-need-based: Scholarships awarded for academics, alumni affiliation, leadership, religious affiliation, state residency.

Application procedures. Admission: No deadline. $30 fee, may be waived for applicants with need. Admission notification on a rolling basis beginning on or about 12/15. Must reply by May 1 or within 2 week(s) if notified thereafter. **Financial aid:** Priority date 3/1; no closing date. FAFSA, institutional form required. Applicants notified on a rolling basis starting 3/10; must reply by 5/1 or within 2 week(s) of notification.

Academics. Tutor training certified by College Reading and Learning Association. **Special study options:** Cross-registration, distance learning, double major, dual enrollment of high school students, ESL, exchange student, honors, independent study, internships, liberal arts/career combination, study abroad, teacher certification program, Washington semester, weekend college. **Credit/placement by examination:** AP, CLEP, IB, SAT, ACT, institutional tests. 6 credit hours maximum toward bachelor's degree. **Support services:** Learning center, reduced course load, study skills assistance, tutoring, writing center.

Majors. Area/ethnic studies: American, Spanish/Iberian. **Biology:** General. **Business:** Accounting, accounting/business management, business admin, international, marketing. **Communications:** General. **Computer sciences:** General. **Education:** General, bilingual, Deaf/hearing impaired, early childhood, elementary, English, ESL, secondary, special. **Foreign languages:** Spanish. **Health:** Audiology/hearing, audiology/speech pathology, communication disorders, facilities admin, health care admin, health services admin, nursing (RN), pediatric nursing, predental, premedicine, preop/surgical nursing, preveterinary, public health nursing, speech pathology, speech-language pathology assistant. **History:** General, American, European. **Interdisciplinary:** Biological/physical sciences, natural sciences. **Legal studies:** General, paralegal, prelaw. **Liberal arts:** Arts/sciences. **Math:** General. **Parks/recreation:** Sports admin. **Philosophy/religion:** Religion. **Physical sciences:** Chemistry. **Psychology:** General. **Public administration:** Social work. **Social sciences:** International relations, sociology. **Visual/performing arts:** Studio arts.

Most popular majors. Business/marketing 14%, health sciences 43%, legal studies 6%, social sciences 12%.

Computing on campus. 70 workstations in dormitories, library, computer center, student center. Dormitories wired for high-speed internet access and linked to campus network. Commuter students can connect to campus network. Helpline, wireless network available.

Student life. Freshman orientation: Mandatory. Preregistration for classes offered. One-day programs held in June and August. **Housing:** Guaranteed on-campus for all undergraduates. Coed dorms available. **Activities:** Campus ministries, choral groups, dance, drama, international student organizations, literary magazine, music ensembles, radio station, student government, student newspaper, student government association, social work club, foreign language club, speech pathology and audiology club, Student Ambassadors organization, affirmative action committee, student nurse association.

Athletics. NCAA. **Intercollegiate:** Baseball M, basketball, cross-country, field hockey W, golf M, lacrosse W, soccer, softball W, swimming, volleyball. **Intramural:** Baseball M, basketball, cross-country, field hockey W, football (non-tackle), golf M, lacrosse W, soccer, softball W, swimming, volleyball. **Team name:** Blazers.

Student services. Adult student services, alcohol/substance abuse counseling, chaplain/spiritual director, career counseling, student employment services, financial aid counseling, health services, minority student services, personal counseling, placement for graduates. **Physically disabled:** Services for visually, speech, hearing impaired.

Contact. E-mail: admissions@elms.edu
Phone: (413) 592-3189 Toll-free number: (800) 255-3567
Fax: (413) 594-2781
Joseph Wagner, Director of Admission, Elms College, 291 Springfield Street, Chicopee, MA 01013

Emerson College

Boston, Massachusetts — **CB member**
www.emerson.edu — **CB code: 3367**

- Private 4-year college of communication and the arts
- Residential campus in very large city
- 3,418 degree-seeking undergraduates: 2% part-time, 57% women, 3% African American, 5% Asian American, 7% Hispanic American, 1% Native American, 3% international
- 892 degree-seeking graduate students
- 37% of applicants admitted
- SAT or ACT with writing, application essay required
- 76% graduate within 6 years; 12% enter graduate study

General. Founded in 1880. Regionally accredited. Residential study and internship program in Los Angeles; off-campus study in Washington, DC; study abroad programs in the Netherlands, Czech Republic, Taiwan. **Degrees:** 840 bachelor's awarded; master's, doctoral offered. **Calendar:** Semester, limited summer session. **Full-time faculty:** 162 total; 72% have terminal degrees, 15% minority, 57% women. **Part-time faculty:** 242 total; 34% have terminal degrees, 8% minority, 49% women. **Class size:** 62% < 20, 28% 20-39, 8% 40-49, 2% 50-99. **Special facilities:** Theaters, sound treated television studios, integrated digital newsroom, clinics/programs to observe speech and hearing therapy, media center, marketing research suite, film production facilities, performance and production center.

Freshman class profile. 6,944 applied, 2,571 admitted, 774 enrolled.

Mid 50% test scores		**GPA 2.0-2.99:**	4%
SAT critical reading:	580-680	**Rank in top quarter:**	81%
SAT math:	550-640	**Rank in top tenth:**	39%
SAT writing:	580-670	**Return as sophomores:**	90%
ACT composite:	25-29	**Out-of-state:**	82%
GPA 3.75 or higher:	36%	**Live on campus:**	99%
GPA 3.50-3.74:	33%	**International:**	4%
GPA 3.0-3.49:	27%		

Basis for selection. Secondary school record, recommendations, writing competency, and personal qualities as seen in extracurricular activities, community involvement, demonstrated leadership important. Applicants for programs in the performing arts must submit a theatrical resume and either audition or interview, or submit portfolio or essay. Candidates for film program must either submit a script (5-10 pages) or video sample of creative work. **Homeschooled:** Common Application Home School Supplement required.

High school preparation. 16 units required; 20 recommended. Required and recommended units include English 4, mathematics 3, social studies 3, science 3, foreign language 3 and academic electives 4.

2008-2009 Annual costs. Tuition/fees: $28,884. Room/board: $11,868. Books/supplies: $720. Personal expenses: $1,431.

2007-2008 Financial aid. Need-based: 625 full-time freshmen applied for aid; 468 were judged to have need; 468 of these received aid. Average need met was 86%. Average scholarship/grant was $12,792; average loan $3,698. 55% of total undergraduate aid awarded as scholarships/grants, 45% as loans/jobs. **Non-need-based:** Awarded to 625 full-time undergraduates, including 216 freshmen. Scholarships awarded for academics, music/drama, state residency. **Additional information:** Massachusetts Loan Plan available for parents of dependent undergraduates.

Application procedures. Admission: Closing date 1/5 (postmark date). $65 fee, may be waived for applicants with need. Admission notification 4/1. Must reply by May 1 or within 2 week(s) if notified thereafter. **Financial aid:** Priority date 3/1; no closing date. FAFSA, CSS PROFILE required. Applicants notified by 4/1; must reply by 5/1 or within 3 week(s) of notification.

Academics. Special study options: Cross-registration, double major, honors, independent study, internships, liberal arts/career combination, student-designed major, study abroad, teacher certification program, Washington semester. Los Angeles Center study and internship program. Course cross-registration available with Suffolk University and Boston ProArts Consortium (Berklee College of Music, Boston Architectural Center, Boston Conservatory, Massachusetts College of Art, School of the Museum of Fine Arts). **Credit/placement by examination:** AP, CLEP, IB, SAT, ACT, institutional tests. 32 credit hours maximum toward bachelor's degree. Math requirement waived with 550 SAT Math or 24 ACT math. Writing requirement waived with 700 SAT Critical Reading. **Support services:** Learning center, reduced course load, study skills assistance, tutoring, writing center.

Majors. Business: Communications, marketing. **Communications:** General, advertising, broadcast journalism, journalism, media studies, political, public relations, publishing. **Education:** Autistic, Deaf/hearing impaired, drama/dance, speech, speech impaired. **Health:** Audiology/hearing, audiology/speech pathology, communication disorders, speech pathology. **Visual/performing arts:** General, acting, cinematography, directing/producing, dramatic, film/cinema, play/screenwriting, theater arts management, theater design.

Most popular majors. Business/marketing 13%, communications/journalism 34%, English 18%, visual/performing arts 32%.

Computing on campus. 480 workstations in dormitories, library, computer center, student center. Dormitories wired for high-speed internet access and linked to campus network. Commuter students can connect to campus network. Online course registration, online library, helpline, repair service, wireless network available.

Student life. **Freshman orientation:** Mandatory, $140 fee. Preregistration for classes offered. Multi-day event preceding first day of classes; includes computer workshops, library tours, social activities, field trips around Boston. **Housing:** Coed dorms, wellness housing available. $300 nonrefundable deposit, deadline 5/1. **Activities:** Campus ministries, choral groups, dance, drama, film society, international student organizations, literary magazine, music ensembles, musical theater, radio station, student government, student newspaper, TV station, Hillel, Newman Club, Goodnews Fellowship, Islamic community, Alliance of Gays and Lesbians and Everyone, Latino student organization, international club, Earth Emerson, Asian Students for Intercultural Awareness, Amnesty International.

Athletics. NCAA. **Intercollegiate:** Baseball M, basketball, cross-country, golf, lacrosse, soccer, softball W, tennis, track and field, volleyball W. **Team name:** Lions.

Student services. Adult student services, chaplain/spiritual director, career counseling, student employment services, financial aid counseling, health services, minority student services, personal counseling, placement for graduates. **Physically disabled:** Services for visually, speech, hearing impaired.

Contact. E-mail: admission@emerson.edu
Phone: (617) 824-8600 Fax: (617) 824-8609
Sara Ramirez, Director of Undergraduate Admission, Emerson College, 120 Boylston Street, Boston, MA 02116-4624

Emmanuel College

Boston, Massachusetts — **CB member**
www.emmanuel.edu — **CB code: 3368**

- Private 4-year liberal arts college affiliated with Roman Catholic Church
- Residential campus in very large city
- 1,682 degree-seeking undergraduates: 1% part-time, 72% women, 5% African American, 3% Asian American, 5% Hispanic American, 1% international
- 206 degree-seeking graduate students
- 56% of applicants admitted
- SAT or ACT (ACT writing optional), application essay required
- 62% graduate within 6 years

General. Founded in 1919. Regionally accredited. Member of the Colleges of the Fenway consortium, which enables cross-registration with Massachusetts College of Pharmacy & Health Services, Wentworth Institute of Technology, Simmons College, Massachusetts College of Art, and Wheelock College. **Degrees:** 348 bachelor's awarded; master's offered. **ROTC:** Army. **Calendar:** Semester, limited summer session. **Full-time faculty:** 92 total; 75% have terminal degrees, 15% minority, 63% women. **Part-time faculty:** 143 total; 34% have terminal degrees, 13% minority, 46% women. **Class size:** 61% < 20, 39% 20-39, less than 1% 50-99.

Freshman class profile. 4,931 applied, 2,761 admitted, 480 enrolled.

Mid 50% test scores		**GPA 2.0-2.99:**	21%
SAT critical reading:	490-590	**Rank in top quarter:**	41%
SAT math:	480-580	**Rank in top tenth:**	12%
ACT composite:	20-24	**Return as sophomores:**	76%
GPA 3.75 or higher:	28%	**Out-of-state:**	44%
GPA 3.50-3.74:	18%	**Live on campus:**	98%
GPA 3.0-3.49:	33%	**International:**	1%

Basis for selection. High school curriculum and record most important, followed by recommendations, test scores, essay, creativity, initiative. Interview recommended. **Homeschooled:** Portfolio, on-campus interview recommended.

High school preparation. College-preparatory program required. 16 units required. Required units include English 4, mathematics 3, social studies 2, science 2 (laboratory 2) and foreign language 2.

2008-2009 Annual costs. Tuition/fees: $28,350. Room/board: $11,800. Books/supplies: $880. Personal expenses: $1,935.

2008-2009 Financial aid. **Need-based:** 426 full-time freshmen applied for aid; 387 were judged to have need; 387 of these received aid. Average need met was 71%. Average scholarship/grant was $16,954; average loan $3,552. 53% of total undergraduate aid awarded as scholarships/grants, 47% as loans/jobs. **Non-need-based:** Awarded to 627 full-time undergraduates, including 312 freshmen. Scholarships awarded for academics, alumni affiliation, leadership.

Application procedures. **Admission:** Priority date 12/1; deadline 3/1 (postmark date). $40 fee, may be waived for applicants with need, free for online applicants. Admission notification on a rolling basis beginning on or about 12/1. Must reply by May 1 or within 2 week(s) if notified thereafter. **Financial aid:** Priority date 4/1; no closing date. FAFSA, institutional form required. Applicants notified on a rolling basis starting 3/15.

Academics. Interdepartmental program allows students to concentrate in 2 departments. Internship offerings available in all areas of study. **Special study options:** Accelerated study, cross-registration, double major, exchange student, honors, independent study, internships, liberal arts/career combination, student-designed major, study abroad, teacher certification program, Washington semester. Degree completion opportunities at corporate sites for non-traditional students. **Credit/placement by examination:** AP, CLEP, IB, SAT, ACT, institutional tests. 32 credit hours maximum toward bachelor's degree. **Support services:** Learning center, pre-admission summer program, remedial instruction, study skills assistance, tutoring, writing center.

Majors. **Area/ethnic studies:** American. **Biology:** General, biochemistry, biostatistics. **Business:** Business admin. **Communications:** General. **Conservation:** Environmental studies. **Education:** Elementary, secondary. **Foreign languages:** Spanish. **Health:** Art therapy, nursing (RN). **History:** General. **Interdisciplinary:** Global studies, neuroscience. **Liberal arts:** Arts/sciences. **Math:** General. **Physical sciences:** Chemistry. **Psychology:** General, counseling, developmental. **Social sciences:** Political science, sociology. **Visual/performing arts:** Graphic design, studio arts.

Most popular majors. Biology 6%, business/marketing 11%, communications/journalism 15%, education 8%, history 6%, liberal arts 7%, psychology 14%, social sciences 7%.

Computing on campus. 145 workstations in dormitories, library, computer center, student center. Dormitories wired for high-speed internet access and linked to campus network. Commuter students can connect to campus network. Online course registration, online library, helpline, student web hosting, wireless network available.

Student life. **Freshman orientation:** Mandatory, $100 fee. Preregistration for classes offered. Summer and fall program. **Policies:** No alcohol permitted on campus. **Housing:** Guaranteed on-campus for all undergraduates. Coed dorms, special housing for disabled, apartments available. $200 nonrefundable deposit, deadline 5/1. **Activities:** Pep band, campus ministries, choral groups, dance, drama, international student organizations, literary magazine, musical theater, radio station, student government, student newspaper, symphony orchestra, black student union, College Democrats, political forum, feminist coalition, Helping Unite Emmanuel Latinos to Lead & Achieve Success, peace and justice club, Republican club, social awareness club.

Athletics. NCAA. **Intercollegiate:** Basketball, cross-country, soccer, softball W, tennis W, track and field, volleyball. **Team name:** Saints.

Student services. Adult student services, alcohol/substance abuse counseling, chaplain/spiritual director, career counseling, student employment services, financial aid counseling, health services, minority student services, personal counseling, placement for graduates. **Physically disabled:** Services for visually, speech, hearing impaired.

Contact. E-mail: enroll@emmanuel.edu
Phone: (617) 735-9715 Fax: (617) 735-9801
Sandra Robbins, Dean of Enrollment Management, Emmanuel College, 400 The Fenway, Boston, MA 02115

Endicott College

Beverly, Massachusetts — **CB member**
www.endicott.edu — **CB code: 3369**

- Private 4-year liberal arts college
- Residential campus in large town
- 2,296 degree-seeking undergraduates: 8% part-time, 56% women, 1% African American, 1% Asian American, 1% Hispanic American, 3% international
- 424 degree-seeking graduate students
- 49% of applicants admitted
- SAT or ACT with writing, application essay required
- 67% graduate within 6 years; 15% enter graduate study

General. Founded in 1939. Regionally accredited. **Degrees:** 376 bachelor's, 5 associate awarded; master's offered. **ROTC:** Army, Air Force. **Location:** 24 miles from Boston. **Calendar:** 4-1-4, limited summer session. **Full-time faculty:** 76 total; 59% have terminal degrees, 24% minority. **Part-time faculty:** 97 total; 29% have terminal degrees, 4% minority, 64% women. **Class size:** 49% < 20, 51% 20-39. **Special facilities:** Student-run restaurant/classroom, archives museum.

Freshman class profile. 4,032 applied, 1,958 admitted, 587 enrolled.

Mid 50% test scores		**Rank in top tenth:**	10%
SAT critical reading:	500-570	**Return as sophomores:**	81%
SAT math:	500-590	**Out-of-state:**	58%
SAT writing:	500-580	**Live on campus:**	97%
ACT composite:	20-25	**International:**	2%
Rank in top quarter:	38%		

Basis for selection. School achievement record and SAT/ACT scores most important. Class rank, essay, volunteer work, extracurricular activities, leadership also important. Teacher, counselor recommendations considered. Interview recommended. **Homeschooled:** Verification that curriculum has been certified by local school system or state, or GED.

High school preparation. College-preparatory program recommended. 16 units recommended. Recommended units include English 4, mathematics 3, social studies 2, history 1, science 2 and academic electives 4. One chemistry with laboratory and algebra required for nursing and athletic training programs.

2008-2009 Annual costs. Tuition/fees: $24,530. Room/board: $11,380. Books/supplies: $1,000. Personal expenses: $1,000.

2008-2009 Financial aid. Need-based: 405 full-time freshmen applied for aid; 283 were judged to have need; 279 of these received aid. Average need met was 58%. Average scholarship/grant was $7,651; average loan $3,762. 64% of total undergraduate aid awarded as scholarships/grants, 36% as loans/jobs. **Non-need-based:** Awarded to 1,061 full-time undergraduates, including 262 freshmen. Scholarships awarded for academics, alumni affiliation, art, leadership, religious affiliation, ROTC, state residency.

Application procedures. Admission: Closing date 2/15. $40 fee, may be waived for applicants with need. Admission notification on a rolling basis beginning on or about 11/1. Must reply by May 1 or within 1 week(s) if notified thereafter. **Financial aid:** Priority date 3/15; no closing date. FAFSA, institutional form required. Applicants notified on a rolling basis starting 3/15; must reply within 2 week(s) of notification.

Academics. Three Internships required of all traditional undergraduates. **Special study options:** Accelerated study, combined bachelor's/graduate degree, cross-registration, distance learning, exchange student, honors, independent study, internships, liberal arts/career combination, student-designed major, study abroad, teacher certification program. **Credit/placement by examination:** AP, CLEP, IB, SAT, institutional tests. 32 credit hours maximum toward bachelor's degree. **Support services:** Learning center, study skills assistance, tutoring, writing center.

Majors. Biology: Biotechnology. **Business:** Accounting, business admin, hospitality admin. **Communications:** Media studies. **Computer sciences:** Computer science. **Conservation:** Environmental studies. **Education:** Early childhood, elementary, physical. **Foreign languages:** Spanish. **Health:** Athletic training, nursing (RN). **History:** General. **Interdisciplinary:** Global studies. **Liberal arts:** Arts/sciences. **Parks/recreation:** Sports admin. **Protective services:** Criminal justice. **Psychology:** General. **Public administration:** Human services. **Visual/performing arts:** Design, interior design, studio arts.

Most popular majors. Business/marketing 27%, communications/journalism 11%, education 7%, health sciences 7%, parks/recreation 13%, psychology 7%, visual/performing arts 12%.

Computing on campus. 186 workstations in library, computer center. Dormitories wired for high-speed internet access and linked to campus network. Commuter students can connect to campus network. Online course registration, online library, helpline, repair service, wireless network available.

Student life. Freshman orientation: Available. Preregistration for classes offered. Sessions held in July and September; includes placement testing and preparation for fall course assignment. **Housing:** Guaranteed on-campus for freshmen. Coed dorms, single-sex dorms, special housing for disabled, apartments, wellness housing available. $500 deposit, deadline 5/1. Single-parent housing, suite-type, modular housing available. **Activities:** Bands, campus ministries, choral groups, dance, drama, film society, international student organizations, literary magazine, music ensembles, Model UN, musical theater, radio station, student government, student newspaper, TV station, intercultural club, Phi Theta Kappa, ALANA, Christian fellowship, political debate society, Rotaract service club.

Athletics. NCAA. **Intercollegiate:** Baseball M, basketball, cross-country, equestrian, field hockey W, football (tackle) M, golf, lacrosse, rowing (crew), sailing, soccer, softball W, tennis, volleyball. **Intramural:** Basketball, football (non-tackle), racquetball, soccer, softball, volleyball. **Team name:** Gulls.

Student services. Alcohol/substance abuse counseling, chaplain/spiritual director, career counseling, financial aid counseling, health services, personal counseling.

Contact. E-mail: admission@endicott.edu
Phone: (978) 921-1000 Toll-free number: (800) 325-1114
Fax: (978) 232-2520
Thomas Redman, Vice President for Admissions and Financial Aid, Endicott College, 376 Hale Street, Beverly, MA 01915-9985

Fitchburg State College

Fitchburg, Massachusetts — **CB member**
www.fsc.edu — **CB code: 3518**

- Public 4-year liberal arts and teachers college
- Residential campus in small city
- 3,762 degree-seeking undergraduates: 13% part-time, 54% women, 4% African American, 2% Asian American, 3% Hispanic American
- 1,008 degree-seeking graduate students
- 64% of applicants admitted
- SAT or ACT (ACT writing optional), application essay required
- 51% graduate within 6 years

General. Founded in 1894. Regionally accredited. **Degrees:** 628 bachelor's awarded; master's offered. **ROTC:** Army. **Location:** 50 miles from Boston, 25 miles from Worcester. **Calendar:** Semester, limited summer session. **Full-time faculty:** 184 total; 93% have terminal degrees, 12% minority, 48% women. **Part-time faculty:** 86 total; 22% have terminal degrees, 5% minority, 48% women. **Class size:** 44% < 20, 55% 20-39, less than 1% 40-49. **Special facilities:** Teacher education laboratory school, 120-acre conservation area.

Freshman class profile. 3,651 applied, 2,354 admitted, 775 enrolled.

Mid 50% test scores		**GPA 3.0-3.49:**	32%
SAT critical reading:	440-550	**GPA 2.0-2.99:**	49%
SAT math:	460-560	**Out-of-state:**	11%
SAT writing:	450-540	**Live on campus:**	72%
ACT composite:	18-23	**Fraternities:**	3%
GPA 3.75 or higher:	10%	**Sororities:**	8%
GPA 3.50-3.74:	9%		

Basis for selection. Secondary school record, test scores, essay important. Recommendations considered. Interview recommended for nursing, undeclared major, computer science, business administration, communications/media majors. **Learning Disabled:** Students with professionally diagnosed learning disabilities exempt from standardized test requirements.

High school preparation. College-preparatory program required. 16 units required. Required units include English 4, mathematics 3, social studies 1, history 1, science 3 (laboratory 2), foreign language 2 and academic electives 2. Additional units of math and science preferred for nursing, medical technology, computer science, business applicants.

2008-2009 Annual costs. Tuition/fees: $6,400; $12,480 out-of-state. Room/board: $7,148. Books/supplies: $600. Personal expenses: $1,500.

Financial aid. Non-need-based: Scholarships awarded for academics, alumni affiliation, leadership, state residency.

Application procedures. Admission: Priority date 1/1; no deadline. $10 fee ($40 out-of-state), may be waived for applicants with need. Admission notification on a rolling basis beginning on or about 12/1. Must reply by May 1 or within 2 week(s) if notified thereafter. **Financial aid:** Priority date 2/1; no closing date. FAFSA required. Applicants notified on a rolling basis starting 3/15; must reply within 2 week(s) of notification.

Academics. Many major programs include internship, practicum, or clinical experience. All degree programs require completion of 48 credits in liberal arts and sciences. **Special study options:** Cross-registration, distance learning, double major, dual enrollment of high school students, honors, independent study, internships, liberal arts/career combination, student-designed major, study abroad, teacher certification program. **Credit/placement by examination:** AP, CLEP, institutional tests. 60 credit hours maximum toward bachelor's degree. **Support services:** Learning center, pre-admission summer program, reduced course load, remedial instruction, study skills assistance, tutoring, writing center.

Honors college/program. Selected freshmen students invited to join Leadership Academy based on high school preparation, test scores, and leadership potential. Students complete integrated sequence of courses over 4-year period. Students expected to demonstrate leadership through extracurricular activities, volunteer positions, and service learning placements. 25 new students accepted into program annually and 3.3 GPA required to continue.

Majors. Architecture: Technology. **Biology:** General, biotechnology, environmental, exercise physiology. **Business:** Accounting, business admin, finance, international, management science, marketing. **Communications:** General, digital media. **Computer sciences:** General, computer science. **Education:** General, biology, early childhood, elementary, English, geography, history, mathematics, middle, secondary, special, technology/industrial arts, trade/industrial. **Engineering technology:** Architectural, construction, electrical, energy systems, industrial, manufacturing. **Health:** Nursing (RN). **History:** General. **Liberal arts:** Arts/sciences. **Math:** General. **Parks/recreation:** Exercise sciences, sports admin. **Protective services:** Criminal justice. **Psychology:** General, developmental, industrial. **Public administration:** Human services. **Social sciences:** Economics, geography, international economics, political science, sociology. **Visual/performing arts:** Cinematography, dramatic, graphic design, photography, theater design.

Most popular majors. Business/marketing 12%, education 12%, health sciences 6%, liberal arts 18%, security/protective services 7%, visual/performing arts 12%.

Computing on campus. PC or laptop required. 150 workstations in dormitories, library, computer center, student center. Dormitories wired for high-speed internet access and linked to campus network. Commuter students can connect to campus network. Online course registration, online library, helpline, wireless network available.

Student life. Freshman orientation: Mandatory. Preregistration for classes offered. Testing, academic advising, registration for classes key components of program. **Housing:** Coed dorms, special housing for disabled, apartments, wellness housing available. $150 nonrefundable deposit, deadline 5/1. Quiet halls available. **Activities:** Bands, choral groups, dance, drama, literary magazine, Model UN, radio station, student government, student newspaper, student government association, Christian Fellowship, black student union, Habitat for Humanity, Latin American student organization, MASSPIRG, peer educators, First Responders, Chavarium.

Athletics. NCAA. **Intercollegiate:** Baseball M, basketball, cross-country, field hockey W, football (tackle) M, ice hockey M, lacrosse W, soccer, softball W, track and field. **Intramural:** Basketball, bowling, football (non-tackle), racquetball, soccer, softball, volleyball. **Team name:** Falcons.

Student services. Alcohol/substance abuse counseling, career counseling, services for economically disadvantaged, student employment services, financial aid counseling, health services, minority student services, on-campus daycare, personal counseling. **Physically disabled:** Services for visually, speech, hearing impaired. **Learning disabled:** Comprehensive services available.

Contact. E-mail: admissions@fsc.edu
Phone: (978) 665-3144 Toll-free number: (800) 705-9692
Fax: (978) 665-4540
Pamela McCafferty, Dean of Enrollment Management, Fitchburg State College, 160 Pearl Street, Fitchburg, MA 01420-2697

Framingham State College

Framingham, Massachusetts — **CB member**
www.framingham.edu — **CB code: 3519**

- Public 4-year liberal arts and teachers college
- Residential campus in small city
- 3,448 degree-seeking undergraduates: 12% part-time, 65% women, 5% African American, 2% Asian American, 4% Hispanic American, 1% Native American, 1% international
- 856 degree-seeking graduate students
- 61% of applicants admitted
- SAT or ACT with writing, application essay required
- 49% graduate within 6 years

General. Founded in 1839. Regionally accredited. **Degrees:** 631 bachelor's awarded; master's offered. **ROTC:** Army. **Location:** 20 miles from Boston. **Calendar:** Semester, extensive summer session. **Full-time faculty:** 168 total; 83% have terminal degrees, 6% minority, 56% women. **Part-time faculty:** 98 total; 45% have terminal degrees, 2% minority, 48% women. **Class size:** 43% < 20, 56% 20-39, 1% 50-99. **Special facilities:** Global education center, social research center, learning center, economic research center, STEM pipeline center, food and nutrition institute, greenhouse, early childhood demonstration lab, education curriculum library.

Freshman class profile. 3,964 applied, 2,416 admitted, 650 enrolled.

Mid 50% test scores		**GPA 2.0-2.99:**	42%
SAT critical reading:	460-560	**Rank in top quarter:**	34%
SAT math:	470-560	**Rank in top tenth:**	9%
GPA 3.75 or higher:	10%	**Return as sophomores:**	73%
GPA 3.50-3.74:	14%	**Out-of-state:**	5%
GPA 3.0-3.49:	34%	**Live on campus:**	82%

Basis for selection. Strength of high school curriculum, weighted high school GPA, class rank, test scores most important. Some attention given to organized and volunteer activities, recommendations and special talents. Consideration given to students whose educational opportunities have been limited due to economic disadvantage. Admission standards policy of Massachusetts Board of Higher Education requires minimum of 16 college-preparatory courses with weighted GPA of 3.0. Students with lower GPA may qualify based on sliding scale combining SAT scores with GPA. Portfolio required of studio art majors. **Homeschooled:** Students may be required to submit results of additional nationally normed tests, such as SAT Subject Tests. **Learning Disabled:** Students with diagnosed learning disability must submit individualized educational plan/504 plan along with all psychoeducational testing current within last 3 years.

High school preparation. College-preparatory program required. 16 units required; 21 recommended. Required and recommended units include English 4, mathematics 3-4, social studies 1, history 1-2, science 3-4 (laboratory 2-3), foreign language 2-4 and academic electives 2. Math must include algebra I, algebra II, and geometry. Additional unit of math strongly recommended for computer science, math, pre-engineering, and science majors. Additional units of biology, chemistry, physics recommended for science majors. Foreign language must be 2 units of same language. All units must be college-preparatory level.

2008-2009 Annual costs. Tuition/fees: $6,141; $12,221 out-of-state. Fees include mandatory laptop purchase by new students. New England Regional tuition rate $1,455. Room/board: $7,625. Books/supplies: $800. Personal expenses: $1,200.

2007-2008 Financial aid. Non-need-based: Scholarships awarded for academics.

Application procedures. Admission: Priority date 2/15; no deadline. $35 fee, may be waived for applicants with need. Admission notification on a rolling basis beginning on or about 1/15. Must reply by May 1 or within 2 week(s) if notified thereafter. Contact admissions office after priority date of 2/15 to determine if applications are still being accepted. Some majors and on-campus housing may be filled by priority date. Application fee waiver available to in-state students who submit College Board fee waiver. **Financial aid:** Priority date 3/1; no closing date. FAFSA required. Applicants notified on a rolling basis starting 4/15; must reply by 5/1 or within 2 week(s) of notification.

Academics. Special study options: Cross-registration, distance learning, double major, honors, independent study, internships, liberal arts/career combination, study abroad, teacher certification program, Washington semester. Pre-engineering program in conjunction with University of Massachusetts at Amherst, University of Massachusetts at Dartmouth, University of Massachusetts at Lowell. **Credit/placement by examination:** AP, CLEP, IB, institutional tests. 64 credit hours maximum toward bachelor's degree. **Support services:** Learning center, reduced course load, study skills assistance, tutoring, writing center.

Majors. Agriculture: Food science. **Biology:** General. **Business:** General, knowledge management. **Computer sciences:** General. **Education:** Early childhood, elementary. **Family/consumer sciences:** General, clothing/textiles, food/nutrition. **Foreign languages:** General. **Health:** Nursing (RN). **History:** General. **Liberal arts:** Arts/sciences. **Math:** General. **Physical sciences:** Chemistry. **Psychology:** General. **Social sciences:** Economics, geography, political science, sociology. **Visual/performing arts:** Art.

Most popular majors. Business/marketing 18%, communication technologies 6%, education 8%, English 6%, family/consumer sciences 12%, liberal arts 8%, psychology 11%, social sciences 14%.

Computing on campus. PC or laptop required. 232 workstations in dormitories, library, computer center, student center. Dormitories wired for high-speed internet access and linked to campus network. Commuter students can connect to campus network. Online course registration, online library, helpline, wireless network available.

Student life. Freshman orientation: Mandatory. Preregistration for classes offered. One-day orientation offered in June, followed up by additional day in late August or early September. **Housing:** Coed dorms, single-sex dorms, wellness housing available. $150 nonrefundable deposit, deadline 5/1. **Activities:** Choral groups, dance, drama, literary magazine, musical theater, radio station, student government, student newspaper, active sociologists, Hispanic student club, black student union, Christian Fellowship, Hillel,

Newman Association, student union activities board, MASSPIRG, international student union.

Athletics. NCAA. **Intercollegiate:** Baseball M, basketball, cross-country, field hockey W, football (tackle) M, ice hockey M, lacrosse W, soccer, softball W, volleyball W. **Intramural:** Basketball, football (non-tackle), golf, lacrosse, soccer, softball, tennis, volleyball, weight lifting. **Team name:** Rams.

Student services. Adult student services, alcohol/substance abuse counseling, chaplain/spiritual director, career counseling, services for economically disadvantaged, student employment services, financial aid counseling, health services, minority student services, on-campus daycare, personal counseling, placement for graduates, veterans' counselor, women's services. **Physically disabled:** Services for visually, hearing impaired.

Contact. E-mail: admissions@framingham.edu
Phone: (508) 626-4500 Fax: (508) 626-4017
Nick Figueroa, Dean of Admissions, Framingham State College, PO Box 9101, Framingham, MA 01701-9101

Franklin W. Olin College of Engineering

Needham, Massachusetts — **CB member**
www.olin.edu — **CB code: 2824**

- Private 4-year engineering college
- Residential campus in large town
- 301 degree-seeking undergraduates: 40% women, 1% African American, 11% Asian American, 4% Hispanic American, 3% international
- 14% of applicants admitted
- SAT or ACT (ACT writing optional), SAT Subject Tests, application essay required
- 92% graduate within 6 years; 29% enter graduate study

General. Regionally accredited. **Degrees:** 66 bachelor's awarded. **Location:** 14 miles from Boston. **Calendar:** Semester. **Full-time faculty:** 33 total; 94% have terminal degrees, 15% minority, 39% women. **Part-time faculty:** 5 total; 40% have terminal degrees. **Class size:** 56% < 20, 40% 20-39, 3% 40-49, 1% 50-99.

Freshman class profile. 969 applied, 131 admitted, 80 enrolled.

Mid 50% test scores		**GPA 3.0-3.49:**	3%
SAT critical reading:	700-790	**End year in good standing:**	99%
SAT math:	740-800	**Return as sophomores:**	97%
SAT writing:	670-770	**Out-of-state:**	91%
ACT composite:	32-35	**Live on campus:**	100%
GPA 3.75 or higher:	88%	**International:**	5%
GPA 3.50-3.74:	9%		

Basis for selection. Secondary school achievement, course rigor, test scores, personal character most important; creativity and entrepreneurial spirit also very important. Cultural, economic, geographic diversity encouraged. Candidates for admission selected from all applicants. Candidates required to attend 1 of 2 weekends on campus to participate in design project, individual interviews, and team exercises. Incoming class selected from this group. 2 SAT Subject Tests required: Math (Level 2 preferred, Level 1 accepted) and any science subject. **Homeschooled:** Statement describing homeschool structure and mission, transcript of courses and grades, letter of recommendation (nonparent) required.

High school preparation. College-preparatory program required. Required units include English 4, mathematics 4, social studies 2, history 2, science 3 (laboratory 3) and foreign language 2. 1 calculus unit and 1 physics unit required.

2008-2009 Annual costs. Tuition/fees: $35,375. Each admitted student receives 4-year full-tuition-plus-fees scholarship. Room and Board not included in scholarship. Additional $1,000 enrollment confirmation deposit required; $2,500 charge for laptop and software. Room/board: $12,400. Books/supplies: $750.

2008-2009 Financial aid. Need-based: 90% of total undergraduate aid awarded as scholarships/grants, 10% as loans/jobs. **Non-need-based:** Scholarships awarded for academics, leadership. **Additional information:** All students receive full tuition scholarships. No financial aid forms necessary.

Application procedures. Admission: Closing date 12/1 (postmark date). $70 fee, may be waived for applicants with need. Application must be submitted online. Admission notification 3/21. Must reply by 5/1. **Financial aid:** Priority date 2/15; no closing date. FAFSA required. Applicants notified on a rolling basis starting 3/31; must reply by 5/1.

Academics. Special study options: Combined bachelor's/graduate degree, cross-registration, exchange student, independent study, internships, liberal arts/career combination, student-designed major, study abroad. **Credit/placement by examination:** AP, CLEP, institutional tests. **Support services:** Tutoring, writing center.

Majors. Engineering: General, electrical, mechanical.

Computing on campus. PC or laptop required. Dormitories wired for high-speed internet access and linked to campus network. Commuter students can connect to campus network. Online course registration, online library, helpline, repair service, student web hosting, wireless network available.

Student life. Freshman orientation: Available. **Policies:** All students sign honor code that addresses personal and academic integrity. **Housing:** Guaranteed on-campus for all undergraduates. Coed dorms available. **Activities:** Jazz band, choral groups, dance, drama, film society, music ensembles, musical theater, student government, symphony orchestra, Christian club, Support, Encourage and Recognize Volunteerism, international club, Korean club, political caucus, martial arts club.

Athletics. Intramural: Basketball, football (non-tackle), ice hockey, racquetball, soccer, softball, squash, tennis, volleyball.

Student services. Alcohol/substance abuse counseling, chaplain/spiritual director, career counseling, financial aid counseling, health services, personal counseling, placement for graduates, women's services.

Contact. E-mail: info@olin.edu
Phone: (781) 292-2222 Fax: (781) 292-2210
Charles Nolan, Dean of Admission, Franklin W. Olin College of Engineering, Olin Way, Needham, MA 02492-1245

Gordon College

Wenham, Massachusetts — **CB member**
www.gordon.edu — **CB code: 3417**

- Private 4-year liberal arts college affiliated with nondenominational tradition
- Residential campus in small town
- 1,585 degree-seeking undergraduates: 3% part-time, 63% women, 2% African American, 2% Asian American, 3% Hispanic American, 3% international
- 123 degree-seeking graduate students
- 71% of applicants admitted
- SAT or ACT with writing, application essay, interview required
- 75% graduate within 6 years

General. Founded in 1889. Regionally accredited. Full ropes course. **Degrees:** 325 bachelor's awarded; master's offered. **ROTC:** Army, Air Force. **Location:** 25 miles from Boston. **Calendar:** Semester, limited summer session. **Full-time faculty:** 98 total; 4% minority, 36% women. **Part-time faculty:** 80 total; 6% minority, 56% women. **Class size:** 65% < 20, 25% 20-39, 4% 40-49, 4% 50-99, 1% >100. **Special facilities:** Christian studies center, international office for Christians in the Visual Arts, electron microscope, gene sequencing machine, Shakespearean folios, center for balance and mobility.

Freshman class profile. 1,570 applied, 1,116 admitted, 421 enrolled.

Mid 50% test scores		**Rank in top tenth:**	33%
SAT critical reading:	530-650	**End year in good standing:**	99%
SAT math:	520-620	**Return as sophomores:**	85%
SAT writing:	530-650	**Out-of-state:**	77%
ACT composite:	23-29	**Live on campus:**	99%
Rank in top quarter:	65%	**International:**	4%

Basis for selection. High school course selection and grades, rank in class, essay of Christian commitment, test scores, references, interview important. School and community activities considered. SAT Subject Tests not required but may be used for placement. Audition required of music majors. Portfolio required of visual art majors. **Homeschooled:** Statement describing homeschool structure and mission, transcript of courses and grades, letter of recommendation (nonparent) required. Information regarding course of study, including description of curriculum and reading list, required. **Learning Disabled:** Students with diagnosed learning disability may submit documentation with application, as well as any learning plans used through high school.

High school preparation. College-preparatory program required. 20 units required; 25 recommended. Required and recommended units include English 4, mathematics 2-3, social studies 2-3, science 2-3 (laboratory 1-3), foreign language 2-4 and academic electives 5. Academic profile should include AP, honors, or accelerated courses.

2008-2009 Annual costs. Tuition/fees: $27,294. Room/board: $7,424. Books/supplies: $800. Personal expenses: $1,000.

2008-2009 Financial aid. Need-based: 337 full-time freshmen applied for aid; 275 were judged to have need; 275 of these received aid. Average need met was 69%. Average scholarship/grant was $12,993; average loan $3,648. 59% of total undergraduate aid awarded as scholarships/grants, 41% as loans/jobs. **Non-need-based:** Awarded to 474 full-time undergraduates, including 172 freshmen. Scholarships awarded for academics, alumni affiliation, art, leadership, minority status, music/drama, religious affiliation.

Application procedures. Admission: Priority date 3/1; no deadline. $50 fee, may be waived for applicants with need. Admission notification on a rolling basis beginning on or about 12/15. Must reply by May 1 or within 2 week(s) if notified thereafter. **Financial aid:** Closing date 3/1. FAFSA, institutional form required. Applicants notified on a rolling basis starting 4/15; must reply by 5/1 or within 2 week(s) of notification.

Academics. Study abroad in England, France, Israel, Italy, Egypt, Russia, China, Canada, Belize, Latin America, Uganda. Extensive domestic programs include marine biology, film studies in Hollywood. Great Books Honors Program in Jerusalem and Athens. Outdoor education immersion semester in urban Boston, South Africa. **Special study options:** Cooperative education, cross-registration, double major, honors, independent study, internships, liberal arts/career combination, student-designed major, study abroad, teacher certification program, urban semester, Washington semester. Programs in Boston; Aix-en-Provence, France; Orvieto, Italy. Outdoor Education Immersion Semester; Kinesiology Semester; Public History Semester; Oregon Extension; co-op programs in arts, business, computer science, education, engineering, health professions, humanities, natural science, social/behavioral science. **Credit/placement by examination:** AP, CLEP, IB, SAT, institutional tests. **Support services:** Learning center, reduced course load, remedial instruction, study skills assistance, tutoring, writing center.

Majors. Biology: General, exercise physiology. **Business:** Accounting, business admin, finance. **Communications:** General. **Computer sciences:** Computer science. **Education:** Early childhood, elementary, middle, music, secondary, special. **Engineering:** Physics. **Foreign languages:** General, French, German, Spanish. **History:** General. **Math:** General. **Parks/recreation:** General. **Philosophy/religion:** Christian, philosophy. **Physical sciences:** Chemistry, physics. **Psychology:** General. **Public administration:** Social work. **Social sciences:** Economics, international relations, political science, sociology. **Theology:** Youth ministry. **Visual/performing arts:** Art, dramatic, music performance.

Most popular majors. Biology 6%, business/marketing 9%, communications/journalism 9%, education 11%, English 11%, philosophy/religious studies 8%, psychology 6%, social sciences 10%, visual/performing arts 8%.

Computing on campus. 125 workstations in dormitories, library, computer center, student center. Dormitories wired for high-speed internet access and linked to campus network. Commuter students can connect to campus network. Online library, helpline, repair service, wireless network available.

Student life. Freshman orientation: Mandatory, $100 fee. Preregistration for classes offered. Five-day program prior to fall semester; includes program for parents. **Policies:** No alcohol or smoking allowed on campus or at college-sponsored events. Religious observance required. **Housing:** Guaranteed on-campus for freshmen. Coed dorms, single-sex dorms, special housing for disabled, apartments, wellness housing available. $250 nonrefundable deposit. **Activities:** Bands, campus ministries, choral groups, dance, drama, film society, international student organizations, literary magazine, music ensembles, musical theater, student government, student newspaper, symphony orchestra, Society for New Politics, Advocates for Cultural Diversity, Christians for Social Action, fellowship group for children of missionaries, ministry to deaf persons, outreach service, short-term mission trips, Amnesty International, ALANA.

Athletics. NCAA. **Intercollegiate:** Baseball M, basketball, cross-country, field hockey W, golf, lacrosse, soccer, softball W, swimming, tennis, track and field, volleyball W. **Intramural:** Basketball, football (non-tackle), racquetball, soccer, softball, table tennis, volleyball. **Team name:** Fighting Scots.

Student services. Alcohol/substance abuse counseling, chaplain/spiritual director, career counseling, student employment services, financial aid counseling, health services, minority student services, personal counseling, placement for graduates. **Physically disabled:** Services for visually, speech, hearing impaired.

Contact. E-mail: admissions@gordon.edu
Phone: (978) 867-4218 Toll-free number: (866) 464-6736
Fax: (978) 867-4682
Silvio Vazquez, Vice President of Enrollment, Gordon College, 255 Grapevine Road, Wenham, MA 01984

Hampshire College

Amherst, Massachusetts — **CB member**
www.hampshire.edu — **CB code: 3447**

- Private 4-year liberal arts college
- Residential campus in large town
- 1,402 degree-seeking undergraduates: 58% women, 4% African American, 4% Asian American, 6% Hispanic American, 1% Native American, 4% international
- 46% of applicants admitted
- Application essay required
- 67% graduate within 6 years; 10% enter graduate study

General. Founded in 1965. Regionally accredited. All students work closely with faculty advisors to design individual academic programs and complete capstone project. **Degrees:** 289 bachelor's awarded. **ROTC:** Army. **Location:** 90 miles from Boston, 20 miles from Springfield. **Calendar:** 4-1-4. **Full-time faculty:** 103 total; 85% have terminal degrees, 16% minority, 55% women. **Part-time faculty:** 60 total; 78% have terminal degrees, 18% minority, 50% women. **Class size:** 66% < 20, 32% 20-39, 1% 40-49. **Special facilities:** Bioshelter (integrated greenhouse/aquaculture facility), farm center, electronic music production studio, extensive film and photography facilities, fabrication center, national Yiddish book center, picturebook art museum.

Freshman class profile. 3,289 applied, 1,508 admitted, 404 enrolled.

Mid 50% test scores		**GPA 2.0-2.99:**	15%
SAT critical reading:	610-700	**Rank in top quarter:**	56%
SAT math:	540-660	**Rank in top tenth:**	25%
SAT writing:	590-700	**Return as sophomores:**	79%
ACT composite:	26-29	**Out-of-state:**	81%
GPA 3.75 or higher:	26%	**Live on campus:**	100%
GPA 3.50-3.74:	20%	**International:**	5%
GPA 3.0-3.49:	39%		

Basis for selection. Criteria include desire to do rigorous independent work, school record, academic writing samples, recommendations, school and community activities. Interview recommended.

High school preparation. 16 units required; 20 recommended. Required and recommended units include English 4, mathematics 3-4, history 3-4, science 3-4 (laboratory 2) and foreign language 3-4.

2008-2009 Annual costs. Tuition/fees: $38,649. Room/board: $10,080. Books/supplies: $700. Personal expenses: $700.

2008-2009 Financial aid. Need-based: 249 full-time freshmen applied for aid; 218 were judged to have need; 218 of these received aid. Average need met was 98%. Average scholarship/grant was $26,785; average loan $3,500. 81% of total undergraduate aid awarded as scholarships/grants, 19% as loans/jobs. **Non-need-based:** Awarded to 679 full-time undergraduates, including 217 freshmen. Scholarships awarded for academics, leadership.

Application procedures. Admission: Priority date 11/15; deadline 1/15 (receipt date). $55 fee, may be waived for applicants with need. Admission notification 4/1. Must reply by May 1 or within 2 week(s) if notified thereafter. **Financial aid:** Priority date 2/1; no closing date. FAFSA, CSS PROFILE required. Applicants notified by 4/1; must reply by 5/1.

Academics. All students pursue individualized program of study. Requirements for graduation not based on credit, but on completion of division one courses in all 5 schools, an independent concentration consisting of combination of courses, independent project work, year-long thesis. **Special study options:** Exchange student, independent study, internships, student-designed major, study abroad, teacher certification program. Member 5-college consortium; may take classes at other member institutions. **Credit/placement by examination:** AP, CLEP. **Support services:** Study skills assistance, writing center.

Majors. Agriculture: Animal sciences, plant sciences, soil science. **Architecture:** Environmental design. **Area/ethnic studies:** African-American, American, Asian, Asian-American, gay/lesbian, Hispanic-American/Latino/Chicano, Latin American, Native American, women's. **Biology:** General, biochemistry, botany, ecology, environmental, evolutionary, zoology. **Business:** General, international, labor studies. **Communications:** General, digital media, media studies. **Communications technology:** Animation/special effects. **Computer sciences:** General, a.i./robotics, computer graphics, computer science. **Conservation:** General, environmental science, environmental studies. **Education:** General, early childhood, elementary, foundations, multicultural, secondary. **Family/consumer sciences:** Child development, family studies, food/nutrition. **Foreign languages:** Comparative lit, East Asian, Germanic, linguistics, Romance, sign language linguistics. **Health:**

International public health, predental, premedicine, prenursing, prepharmacy, preveterinary, public health ed. **History:** General, American, Asian, European, science/technology. **Interdisciplinary:** Behavioral sciences, biological/physical sciences, biopsychology, cognitive science, cultural resource management, global studies, holocaust studies, intercultural, math/computer science, natural sciences, neuroscience, nutrition sciences, peace/conflict, science/society. **Legal studies:** General, prelaw. **Liberal arts:** Arts/sciences, humanities. **Math:** General. **Philosophy/religion:** Ethics, Judaic, philosophy, religion. **Physical sciences:** General, chemistry, geology, inorganic chemistry, organic chemistry, physics. **Psychology:** General, cognitive, developmental, experimental. **Public administration:** Community org/advocacy. **Social sciences:** General, anthropology, demography, economics, international economic development, international economics, international relations, political science, sociology, U.S. government, urban studies. **Visual/performing arts:** General, acting, art, art history/conservation, cinematography, crafts, dance, design, directing/producing, dramatic, drawing, film/cinema, graphic design, illustration, multimedia, music performance, musicology, painting, photography, play/screenwriting, sculpture, studio arts, theater history.

Most popular majors. Area/ethnic studies 7%, biology 6%, English 10%, social sciences 15%, visual/performing arts 34%.

Computing on campus. 215 workstations in library, computer center, student center. Dormitories wired for high-speed internet access and linked to campus network. Commuter students can connect to campus network. Online course registration, online library, helpline, repair service, student web hosting, wireless network available.

Student life. **Freshman orientation:** Mandatory, $175 fee. Preregistration for classes offered. Program held during week immediately before matriculation. **Policies:** Students design individual concentrations of study, test theory with off-campus study and community service, and complete original research and projects. **Housing:** Guaranteed on-campus for freshmen. Coed dorms, special housing for disabled, apartments, wellness housing available. $200 nonrefundable deposit, deadline 5/1. **Activities:** Jazz band, choral groups, dance, drama, film society, international student organizations, music ensembles, radio station, student government, student newspaper, Jewish student union, Amnesty International, Pan Asian student association, Counselor Advocates, Blacksmiths Collective, outing club.

Student services. Alcohol/substance abuse counseling, chaplain/spiritual director, career counseling, financial aid counseling, health services, minority student services, on-campus daycare, personal counseling, women's services. **Physically disabled:** Services for visually, speech, hearing impaired. **Learning disabled:** Comprehensive services available.

Contact. E-mail: admissions@hampshire.edu
Phone: (413) 559-5471 Toll-free number: (877) 937-4267
Fax: (413) 559-5631
Karen Parker, Director of Admissions, Hampshire College, 893 West Street, Amherst, MA 01002-9988

Harvard College

Cambridge, Massachusetts
www.college.harvard.edu **CB code: 3434**

- Private 4-year university and liberal arts college
- Residential campus in large city
- 6,678 degree-seeking undergraduates: 50% women, 8% African American, 17% Asian American, 7% Hispanic American, 1% Native American, 10% international
- 12,235 degree-seeking graduate students
- 8% of applicants admitted
- SAT or ACT with writing, SAT Subject Tests, application essay, interview required
- 98% graduate within 6 years

General. Founded in 1636. Regionally accredited. Harvard College is the undergraduate program within Harvard University, part of the faculty of arts and sciences, and offers programs in liberal arts. **Degrees:** 1,723 bachelor's awarded; master's, doctoral, first professional offered. **ROTC:** Army, Naval, Air Force. **Location:** 3 miles from Boston. **Calendar:** Semester, extensive summer session. **Full-time faculty:** 1,833 total; 99% have terminal degrees, 14% minority, 32% women. **Part-time faculty:** 432 total; 99% have terminal degrees, 12% minority, 37% women. **Class size:** 75% < 20, 14% 20-39, 3% 40-49, 5% 50-99, 4% >100. **Special facilities:** Museum of Scandinavian and Germanic art; experimental forest in New York state; center for study of Italian Renaissance in Florence, Italy; center for Byzantine studies in Washington, DC; Smithsonian astrophysical observatory.

Freshman class profile. 27,462 applied, 2,175 admitted, 1,648 enrolled.

Mid 50% test scores			
SAT critical reading:	690-800	Rank in top quarter:	100%
SAT math:	700-780	Rank in top tenth:	95%
SAT writing:	690-790	Return as sophomores:	97%
ACT composite:	31-35	Out-of-state:	85%
		International:	10%

Basis for selection. Secondary school record most important; character, creative ability in some discipline or activity, leadership, liveliness of mind, demonstrated stamina and ability to carry out demanding college program, and strong sense of social responsibility important. Any 3 SAT Subject Tests required. Interview with alumnus/alumna required of all applicants if possible; documentation of special talents encouraged.

High school preparation. Recommended units include English 4, mathematics 4, social studies 3, history 2, science 4 and foreign language 4. Applicants encouraged to take rigorous courses and make the most of any opportunities for enrichment.

2008-2009 Annual costs. Tuition/fees: $36,173. Room/board: $11,042. Books/supplies: $1,000. Personal expenses: $2,035.

2008-2009 Financial aid. All financial aid based on need. 1,146 full-time freshmen applied for aid; 999 were judged to have need; 999 of these received aid. Average need met was 100%. Average scholarship/grant was $39,164; average loan $2,510. 94% of total undergraduate aid awarded as scholarships/grants, 6% as loans/jobs. **Additional information:** Institution meets full need of all admitted students. Aid includes no loans; home equity and retirement excluded from need analysis; families with incomes below $60,000 have zero parent contribution; $60,000 to $180,000 and standard assets have parent contributions from 0-10% of income.

Application procedures. **Admission:** Priority date 12/1; deadline 1/1 (postmark date). $65 fee, may be waived for applicants with need. Admission notification 4/1. Must reply by 5/1. **Financial aid:** Closing date 2/1. FAFSA required. CSS PROFILE required of all US citizens and US permanent residents plus all Canadians. Applicants notified by 4/1; must reply by 5/1 or within 2 week(s) of notification.

Academics. Require 12 one-term courses for completion of major and 32 one-term courses for graduation. **Special study options:** Accelerated study, cross-registration, double major, exchange student, honors, independent study, internships, student-designed major, study abroad, teacher certification program. **Credit/placement by examination:** AP, CLEP, IB, institutional tests. SAT Subject Test policy varies depending on subject matter and score. Sophomore standing available on basis of 4 AP exams with qualifying scores, or on basis of IB scores. Students with fewer than 4 AP qualifying scores eligible for placement in more challenging courses. **Support services:** Learning center, study skills assistance, tutoring, writing center.

Majors. **Area/ethnic studies:** African-American, East Asian, Near/Middle Eastern, women's. **Biology:** General, biochemistry, evolutionary, neurobiology/physiology. **Computer sciences:** Computer science. **Conservation:** Environmental studies. **Engineering:** Science. **Foreign languages:** Ancient Greek, classics, comparative lit, German, Latin, linguistics, Romance, Sanskrit, Slavic. **History:** General, science/technology. **Interdisciplinary:** Classical/archaeology. **Liberal arts:** Arts/sciences. **Math:** General, applied, statistics. **Philosophy/religion:** Philosophy, religion. **Physical sciences:** Chemistry, geology, molecular physics, physics. **Psychology:** General. **Social sciences:** General, anthropology, economics, political science, sociology. **Visual/performing arts:** General, art history/conservation.

Most popular majors. Biology 13%, history 8%, psychology 7%, social sciences 41%.

Computing on campus. 605 workstations in dormitories, library, computer center. Dormitories wired for high-speed internet access and linked to campus network. Commuter students can connect to campus network. Online course registration, online library, helpline, repair service, student web hosting, wireless network available.

Student life. **Freshman orientation:** Mandatory. Week-long program in early September. **Housing:** Guaranteed on-campus for all undergraduates. Coed dorms, special housing for disabled, apartments, cooperative housing available. All freshmen live together. Other students and some faculty members reside in 13 on-campus houses, self-contained communities offering seminars and tutorials. **Activities:** Bands, campus ministries, choral groups, dance, drama, film society, international student organizations, literary magazine, music ensembles, Model UN, musical theater, opera, radio station, student government, student newspaper, symphony orchestra, TV station, Over 320 official clubs available.

Athletics. NCAA. **Intercollegiate:** Baseball M, basketball, cross-country, diving, fencing, field hockey, football (tackle) M, golf, ice hockey, lacrosse, rowing (crew), sailing, skiing, soccer, softball W, squash, swimming, tennis, track and field, volleyball, water polo, wrestling M. **Intramural:** Basketball, cross-country, fencing, football (non-tackle), ice hockey, rowing (crew), soccer, softball, squash, swimming, table tennis, tennis, volleyball. **Team name:** Crimson.

Student services. Alcohol/substance abuse counseling, chaplain/spiritual director, career counseling, services for economically disadvantaged, student employment services, financial aid counseling, health services, on-campus daycare, personal counseling, placement for graduates, women's services. **Physically disabled:** Services for visually, speech, hearing impaired.

Contact. E-mail: college@fas.harvard.edu
Phone: (617) 495-1551 Fax: (617) 495-8821
William Fitzsimmons, Dean of Admissions, Harvard College, 86 Brattle Street, Cambridge, MA 02138

Hellenic College/Holy Cross

Brookline, Massachusetts — **CB member**
www.hchc.edu — **CB code: 3449**

- Private 4-year liberal arts and seminary college affiliated with Eastern Orthodox Church
- Residential campus in large town
- 69 degree-seeking undergraduates: 36% women
- 132 degree-seeking graduate students
- SAT or ACT (ACT writing optional), application essay, interview required

General. Founded in 1937. Regionally accredited. **Degrees:** 37 bachelor's awarded; master's, first professional offered. **Location:** 5 miles from downtown Boston. **Calendar:** Semester, limited summer session. **Full-time faculty:** 14 total; 79% have terminal degrees, 50% women. **Part-time faculty:** 19 total; 47% have terminal degrees, 21% women. **Class size:** 49% < 20, 51% 20-39.

Freshman class profile.

Mid 50% test scores			
SAT critical reading:	480-620	GPA 3.75 or higher:	10%
SAT math:	460-520	GPA 3.0-3.49:	60%
SAT writing:	430-610	GPA 2.0-2.99:	30%
ACT composite:	21-27	Out-of-state:	90%
		Live on campus:	95%

Basis for selection. High school achievement, GPA, 2 recommendations from instructors, test scores very important, school and community activities also important. For religious studies majors, 2 letters from clergy important if members of Orthodox Christian Church. **Homeschooled:** Transcript of courses and grades, state high school equivalency certificate required.

High school preparation. 15 units required. Required units include English 4, mathematics 2, social studies 2, history 2, science 3 and foreign language 2.

2008-2009 Annual costs. Tuition/fees: $18,245. Room/board: $11,430. Books/supplies: $1,000. Personal expenses: $1,500.

2007-2008 Financial aid. All financial aid based on need.

Application procedures. Admission: Priority date 5/1; deadline 8/15 (receipt date). $50 fee, may be waived for applicants with need. Admission notification on a rolling basis. Students who apply by December 1 eligible to have application fee waived and receive priority consideration for scholarships; early applications encouraged. **Financial aid:** Closing date 4/1. FAFSA, institutional form required. Applicants notified on a rolling basis starting 10/1; must reply within 2 week(s) of notification.

Academics. Special study options: Cross-registration, exchange student, honors, independent study, internships, liberal arts/career combination, study abroad. **Credit/placement by examination:** AP, CLEP, IB, institutional tests. Credit granted varies by degree program. **Support services:** Tutoring.

Majors. Education: Elementary. **Family/consumer sciences:** Family studies. **Foreign languages:** Classics. **Liberal arts:** Arts/sciences. **Psychology:** General. **Theology:** Theology.

Computing on campus. Online library, wireless network available.

Student life. Freshman orientation: Available. **Policies:** Religious observance required for some students. **Housing:** Guaranteed on-campus for freshmen. Single-sex dorms, apartments available. $300 nonrefundable deposit. **Activities:** Campus ministries, choral groups, dance, drama, music ensembles, student government, several Orthodox groups, prison ministry, missions group.

Athletics. Intramural: Basketball, soccer M, table tennis, tennis, volleyball.

Student services. Chaplain/spiritual director, career counseling, student employment services, financial aid counseling, health services, personal counseling, placement for graduates.

Contact. E-mail: admissions@hchc.edu
Phone: (617) 850-1260 Toll-free number: (866) 424-2338
Fax: (617) 850-1460
Gregory Floor, Director of Admissions and Records, Hellenic College/Holy Cross, 50 Goddard Avenue, Brookline, MA 02445

Lasell College

Newton, Massachusetts — **CB member**
www.lasell.edu — **CB code: 3481**

- Private 4-year liberal arts college
- Residential campus in small city
- 1,374 degree-seeking undergraduates: 1% part-time, 69% women, 5% African American, 3% Asian American, 4% Hispanic American, 3% international
- 92 degree-seeking graduate students
- 61% of applicants admitted
- SAT or ACT (ACT writing optional), application essay required
- 46% graduate within 6 years; 32% enter graduate study

General. Founded in 1851. Regionally accredited. **Degrees:** 272 bachelor's awarded; master's offered. **Location:** 8 miles from Boston. **Calendar:** Semester. **Full-time faculty:** 67 total; 91% have terminal degrees, 13% minority, 64% women. **Part-time faculty:** 112 total; 6% minority, 59% women. **Class size:** 73% < 20, 27% 20-39. **Special facilities:** Community-based learning center, art and cultural center with antique clothing collection, center for research on aging and intergenerational studies, institute for values and public life, technology for learning center, 2 child study centers.

Freshman class profile. 3,222 applied, 1,977 admitted, 487 enrolled.

Mid 50% test scores			
SAT critical reading:	450-530	GPA 2.0-2.99:	59%
SAT math:	460-540	Rank in top quarter:	15%
ACT composite:	19-23	Rank in top tenth:	4%
GPA 3.75 or higher:	6%	Return as sophomores:	70%
GPA 3.50-3.74:	8%	Out-of-state:	53%
GPA 3.0-3.49:	26%	Live on campus:	93%
		International:	2%

Basis for selection. GPA, curriculum, class rank, interview, recommendations, extracurricular activities, personal essay, and standardized test scores considered. Interview recommended.

High school preparation. College-preparatory program required. 15 units required; 21 recommended. Required and recommended units include English 4, mathematics 3-4, social studies 2-3, history 2-3, science 2-3 (laboratory 2) and foreign language 2.

2009-2010 Annual costs. Tuition/fees: $25,300. Room/board: $10,500. Books/supplies: $1,000. Personal expenses: $2,000.

2008-2009 Financial aid. Non-need-based: Scholarships awarded for academics, alumni affiliation.

Application procedures. Admission: Priority date 3/15; no deadline. $40 fee, may be waived for applicants with need, free for online applicants. Admission notification on a rolling basis beginning on or about 12/15. Must reply by May 1 or within 2 week(s) if notified thereafter. **Financial aid:** Priority date 3/1; no closing date. FAFSA, institutional form required. Applicants notified on a rolling basis starting 2/15; must reply by 5/1 or within 2 week(s) of notification.

Academics. Free tutoring available in many academic subjects. **Special study options:** Double major, honors, independent study, internships, liberal arts/career combination, student-designed major, study abroad, teacher certification program. Fifth-year master of science programs in management and communication. **Credit/placement by examination:** AP, CLEP, IB, SAT, ACT, institutional tests. **Support services:** Learning center, reduced course load, study skills assistance, tutoring.

Majors. Business: Accounting, accounting/business management, accounting/finance, business admin, entrepreneurial studies, fashion, finance, hospitality admin, hotel/motel admin, international, marketing, tourism/travel. **Communications:** General, advertising, digital media, journalism, media studies, public relations, radio/tv. **Conservation:** Environmental studies. **Education:** Early childhood, elementary, English, history, mathematics, secondary. **Family/consumer sciences:** Fashion consultant. **Health:** Athletic training. **History:** General. **Legal studies:** General, prelaw. **Liberal arts:** Humanities. **Parks/recreation:** Exercise sciences, sports admin. **Protective services:** Law enforcement admin. **Psychology:** General. **Public administration:** Human services. **Social sciences:** General, sociology. **Visual/ performing arts:** Fashion design, graphic design.

Most popular majors. Business/marketing 59%, communications/ journalism 6%, health sciences 6%, legal studies 8%.

Computing on campus. 175 workstations in dormitories, library, computer center, student center. Dormitories wired for high-speed internet access and linked to campus network. Commuter students can connect to campus network. Online course registration, online library, helpline, wireless network available.

Student life. Freshman orientation: Mandatory, $40 fee. Preregistration for classes offered. **Housing:** Guaranteed on-campus for all undergraduates. Coed dorms, single-sex dorms, wellness housing available. $200 nonrefundable deposit, deadline 5/1. Community service, special interest housing available. **Activities:** Jazz band, campus ministries, choral groups, dance, drama, literary magazine, music ensembles, musical theater, radio station, student government, student newspaper.

Athletics. NCAA. **Intercollegiate:** Baseball M, basketball, cross-country, field hockey W, lacrosse, soccer, softball W, track and field, volleyball. **Intramural:** Basketball, football (non-tackle), soccer, softball, volleyball. **Team name:** Lasers.

Student services. Alcohol/substance abuse counseling, chaplain/ spiritual director, career counseling, student employment services, financial aid counseling, health services, personal counseling, placement for graduates.

Contact. E-mail: info@lasell.edu
Phone: (617) 243-2225 Toll-free number: (888) 527-3554
Fax: (617) 243-2380
James Tweed, Director of Undergraduate Admission, Lasell College, 1844 Commonwealth Avenue, Newton, MA 02466-2709

Lesley University

Cambridge, Massachusetts — **CB member**
www.lesley.edu/lc — **CB code: 3483**

- Private 4-year liberal arts and teachers college
- Residential campus in very large city
- 1,261 degree-seeking undergraduates: 5% part-time, 75% women, 4% African American, 3% Asian American, 5% Hispanic American, 3% international
- 4,921 degree-seeking graduate students
- 65% of applicants admitted
- SAT or ACT with writing, application essay, interview required
- 49% graduate within 6 years

General. Founded in 1909. Regionally accredited. Lesley University includes 2 undergraduate colleges, Lesley College and The Art Institute of Boston. Main campus in Cambridge. **Degrees:** 362 bachelor's, 1 associate awarded; master's, doctoral offered. **Calendar:** Semester, limited summer session. **Full-time faculty:** 73 total; 68% have terminal degrees, 12% minority, 55% women. **Part-time faculty:** 152 total; 30% have terminal degrees, 56% women. **Class size:** 77% < 20, 22% 20-39, less than 1% 40-49, less than 1% 50-99. **Special facilities:** Center for teaching resources, media production facility, fine arts studios.

Freshman class profile. 2,523 applied, 1,639 admitted, 328 enrolled.

Mid 50% test scores		**GPA 3.0-3.49:**	35%
SAT critical reading:	490-600	**GPA 2.0-2.99:**	45%
SAT math:	460-560	**Rank in top quarter:**	38%
SAT writing:	490-590	**Rank in top tenth:**	12%
ACT composite:	19-26	**Return as sophomores:**	66%
GPA 3.75 or higher:	4%	**Out-of-state:**	52%
GPA 3.50-3.74:	14%	**International:**	2%

Basis for selection. Primary focus given to academic record, both grades and challenging courses. Test scores, recommendations, interview, community service, leadership experience also considered.

High school preparation. College-preparatory program required. 18 units required; 20 recommended. Required and recommended units include English 4, mathematics 3-4, social studies 1-2, history 1-2, science 3-4 (laboratory 2), foreign language 2 and academic electives 4. 2 units visual/ performing arts recommended for some programs in art or expressive therapies.

2009-2010 Annual costs. Tuition/fees (projected): $28,460. Room/ board: $12,400. Books/supplies: $700. Personal expenses: $1,580.

2008-2009 Financial aid. Need-based: Average need met was 70%. Average scholarship/grant was $15,024; average loan $4,057. 58% of total undergraduate aid awarded as scholarships/grants, 42% as loans/jobs. **Non-need-based:** Awarded to 234 full-time undergraduates, including 59 freshmen. Scholarships awarded for academics, art, leadership, minority status, state residency.

Application procedures. Admission: Priority date 2/15; no deadline. $50 fee, may be waived for applicants with need, free for online applicants. Admission notification on a rolling basis beginning on or about 1/15. Must reply by May 1 or within 2 week(s) if notified thereafter. **Financial aid:** Priority date 2/15; no closing date. FAFSA required. Applicants notified on a rolling basis starting 2/15.

Academics. Students complete between 450 and 650 hours of significant internship experience that begins freshman year. **Special study options:** Accelerated study, combined bachelor's/graduate degree, cross-registration, distance learning, double major, dual enrollment of high school students, exchange student, honors, independent study, internships, liberal arts/career combination, New York semester, student-designed major, study abroad, teacher certification program, Washington semester. Studio courses. **Credit/ placement by examination:** AP, CLEP, IB, SAT, ACT, institutional tests. 16 credit hours maximum toward bachelor's degree. **Support services:** Learning center, pre-admission summer program, reduced course load, study skills assistance, tutoring, writing center.

Majors. Area/ethnic studies: American. **Biology:** General. **Business:** Business admin. **Communications technology:** General. **Conservation:** Environmental studies. **Education:** General, art, early childhood, early childhood special, elementary, English, kindergarten/preschool, mathematics, middle, science, secondary, social studies, special. **Family/consumer sciences:** Child development, family studies. **Health:** Art therapy, health services. **Interdisciplinary:** Global studies, natural sciences. **Liberal arts:** Arts/sciences. **Math:** General. **Social sciences:** General. **Visual/performing arts:** Art, studio arts.

Most popular majors. Business/marketing 6%, education 7%, liberal arts 31%, psychology 13%, visual/performing arts 27%.

Computing on campus. 195 workstations in dormitories, library, computer center, student center. Dormitories wired for high-speed internet access and linked to campus network. Commuter students can connect to campus network. Online course registration, online library, helpline, wireless network available.

Student life. Freshman orientation: Mandatory. Begins 1 week prior to start of classes. **Housing:** Guaranteed on-campus for all undergraduates. Coed dorms, single-sex dorms, wellness housing available. $300 nonrefundable deposit, deadline 5/1. **Activities:** Campus ministries, choral groups, dance, drama, film society, international student organizations, literary magazine, musical theater, student government, student newspaper, women for social justice, Hillel, Third Wave women's group, Prism, students for a free Tibet, ALANA, Christian fellowship.

Athletics. NCAA. **Intercollegiate:** Basketball, rowing (crew), soccer, softball W, volleyball. **Team name:** Lynx.

Student services. Adult student services, alcohol/substance abuse counseling, chaplain/spiritual director, career counseling, student employment services, financial aid counseling, health services, minority student services, personal counseling, placement for graduates. **Physically disabled:** Services for visually, speech, hearing impaired. **Learning disabled:** Comprehensive services available.

Contact. E-mail: lcadmissions@lesley.edu
Phone: (617) 349-8800 Toll-free number: (800) 999-1959 ext. 8800
Fax: (617) 349-8810
Deb Kocar, Director of Admissions, Lesley University, 29 Everett Street, Cambridge, MA 02138-2790

Massachusetts College of Art and Design

Boston, Massachusetts — **CB member**
www.massart.edu — **CB code: 3516**

- Public 4-year visual arts college
- Residential campus in very large city
- 1,692 degree-seeking undergraduates: 11% part-time, 68% women, 4% African American, 6% Asian American, 6% Hispanic American, 1% Native American, 2% international
- 147 degree-seeking graduate students
- 51% of applicants admitted

- SAT or ACT with writing, application essay required
- 63% graduate within 6 years

General. Founded in 1873. Regionally accredited. **Degrees:** 274 bachelor's awarded; master's offered. **Calendar:** Semester, extensive summer session. **Full-time faculty:** 98 total; 80% have terminal degrees, 12% minority, 48% women. **Part-time faculty:** 161 total. **Class size:** 86% < 20, 14% 20-39, less than 1% 40-49. **Special facilities:** 7 art galleries, foundry, glass furnaces, ceramic kilns, video and film studios, performance and studio spaces, Polaroid 20X24 camera.

Freshman class profile. 1,499 applied, 771 admitted, 276 enrolled.

Mid 50% test scores		**GPA 2.0-2.99:**	17%
SAT critical reading:	520-630	**Rank in top quarter:**	53%
SAT math:	490-610	**Rank in top tenth:**	18%
SAT writing:	510-610	**Return as sophomores:**	87%
GPA 3.75 or higher:	15%	**Out-of-state:**	34%
GPA 3.50-3.74:	19%	**Live on campus:**	87%
GPA 3.0-3.49:	49%	**International:**	2%

Basis for selection. Emphasis on portfolio, academic record, essay, test scores, recommendations. 3.0 GPA recommended. For GPA between 2.0 and 2.9, SAT/ACT scores considered in combination with GPA on sliding scale. Applicants must meet Massachusetts public college admission standards. Portfolio of at least 15 pieces of artwork required, presented as 35 mm 2x2 slides. Work may also be submitted on VHS videotape or digital media. **Homeschooled:** General college preparatory program required for degree-seeking students. **Learning Disabled:** Testing may be waived for applicants with professionally certified learning disabilities.

High school preparation. 17 units required. Required units include English 4, mathematics 2, social studies 2, science 2 (laboratory 2), foreign language 2 and academic electives 2. At least 2 additional academic units of computer science, humanities, or visual and performing arts required. Additional math or science required. Social Studies requirement must include 1 U.S. history course. Foreign Language units must be in one language.

2008-2009 Annual costs. Tuition/fees: $7,900; $23,000 out-of-state. Tuition for New England resident students $14,000. Room/board: $10,170. Books/supplies: $2,000. Personal expenses: $1,350.

2008-2009 Financial aid. Non-need-based: Scholarships awarded for academics, art, leadership, state residency. **Additional information:** Tuition waiver available to Vietnam veterans.

Application procedures. Admission: Closing date 2/1. $30 fee ($65 out-of-state), may be waived for applicants with need. Admission notification on a rolling basis. Must reply by May 1 or within 3 week(s) if notified thereafter. **Financial aid:** Priority date 3/1; no closing date. FAFSA required. Applicants notified on a rolling basis starting 3/15; must reply within 3 week(s) of notification.

Academics. Three-year certificates available. **Special study options:** Cross-registration, double major, exchange student, independent study, internships, liberal arts/career combination, student-designed major, study abroad. Member of American Independent Colleges of Art and Design (AICAD), College Academic Program Sharing (CAPS), Colleges of the Fenway, and Pro Arts Consortium. Exchange programs available in Holland, England, Germany, Ireland, Italy, France. Study abroad available in Spain, Greece, China, Mexico. **Credit/placement by examination:** CLEP, IB, institutional tests. **Support services:** Pre-admission summer program, reduced course load, remedial instruction, study skills assistance, tutoring.

Majors. Architecture: Environmental design. **Education:** Art. **Visual/performing arts:** Art history/conservation, ceramics, cinematography, design, fashion design, fiber arts, film/cinema, graphic design, industrial design, metal/jewelry, multimedia, painting, photography, printmaking, sculpture, studio arts.

Most popular majors. Education 7%, visual/performing arts 93%.

Computing on campus. 370 workstations in library, computer center. Dormitories wired for high-speed internet access and linked to campus network. Commuter students can connect to campus network. Online library, helpline, wireless network available.

Student life. Freshman orientation: Mandatory. **Policies:** Intercollegiate sports program available through Emerson College. **Housing:** Coed dorms available. $240 nonrefundable deposit, deadline 5/1. Additional housing available in Simmons College dorm. **Activities:** Dance, drama, film society, music ensembles, radio station, student government, student newspaper, TV station, minority student organization, gay/lesbian organization, student-run design firm, international student organization, nontraditional student organization.

Athletics. Intramural: Basketball, cross-country, field hockey, football (non-tackle), ice hockey, soccer, softball W, table tennis, tennis, volleyball.

Student services. Adult student services, career counseling, student employment services, health services, personal counseling, placement for graduates, veterans' counselor. **Physically disabled:** Services for visually, hearing impaired.

Contact. E-mail: admissions@massart.edu
Phone: (617) 879-7222 Fax: (617) 879-7250
Kathleen Keenan, Associate Vice President for Planning and Enrollment, Massachusetts College of Art and Design, 621 Huntington Avenue, Boston, MA 02115-5882

Massachusetts College of Liberal Arts

North Adams, Massachusetts — **CB member**
www.mcla.edu — **CB code: 3521**

- Public 4-year liberal arts college
- Residential campus in large town
- 1,531 degree-seeking undergraduates: 12% part-time, 60% women, 5% African American, 1% Asian American, 4% Hispanic American
- 269 degree-seeking graduate students
- 78% of applicants admitted
- SAT or ACT (ACT writing optional), application essay required
- 57% graduate within 6 years

General. Founded in 1894. Regionally accredited. **Degrees:** 299 bachelor's awarded; master's offered. **Location:** 60 miles from Springfield, 120 miles from Boston. **Calendar:** Semester, limited summer session. **Full-time faculty:** 90 total; 79% have terminal degrees, 6% minority, 43% women. **Part-time faculty:** 81 total; 24% have terminal degrees, 1% minority, 44% women. **Class size:** 67% < 20, 32% 20-39, less than 1% 40-49, less than 1% 50-99.

Freshman class profile. 1,232 applied, 961 admitted, 332 enrolled.

Mid 50% test scores		**GPA 3.0-3.49:**	33%
SAT critical reading:	450-570	**GPA 2.0-2.99:**	53%
SAT math:	430-550	**End year in good standing:**	89%
ACT composite:	18-22	**Return as sophomores:**	76%
GPA 3.75 or higher:	7%	**Out-of-state:**	26%
GPA 3.50-3.74:	7%	**Live on campus:**	85%

Basis for selection. Secondary school record most important; test scores, essay also important; recommendations, extracurricular activities considered. Interview recommended. **Homeschooled:** State high school equivalency certificate required. **Learning Disabled:** Massachusetts law prohibits requiring standardized test scores from students with documented learning disabilities.

High school preparation. College-preparatory program required. 16 units required. Required units include English 4, mathematics 3, science 3 (laboratory 2), foreign language 2 and academic electives 2.

2008-2009 Annual costs. Tuition/fees: $6,565; $15,510 out-of-state. Room/board: $7,754.

2008-2009 Financial aid. Need-based: 301 full-time freshmen applied for aid; 217 were judged to have need; 216 of these received aid. Average scholarship/grant was $5,125. 34% of total undergraduate aid awarded as scholarships/grants, 66% as loans/jobs. **Non-need-based:** Awarded to 459 full-time undergraduates, including 156 freshmen. Scholarships awarded for academics, alumni affiliation, art, leadership, minority status, music/drama.

Application procedures. Admission: Priority date 3/1; no deadline. $25 fee, may be waived for applicants with need. Admission notification on a rolling basis beginning on or about 12/15. Must reply by May 1 or within 2 week(s) if notified thereafter. **Financial aid:** Priority date 3/1; no closing date. FAFSA, institutional form required. Applicants notified on a rolling basis starting 3/1; must reply by 5/1 or within 2 week(s) of notification.

Academics. Special study options: Accelerated study, cross-registration, distance learning, double major, dual enrollment of high school students, exchange student, honors, independent study, internships, liberal arts/career combination, student-designed major, study abroad, teacher certification program, Washington semester. **Credit/placement by examination:** AP, CLEP, IB, institutional tests. **Support services:** Learning center, pre-admission summer program, reduced course load, remedial instruction, tutoring, writing center.

Majors. Biology: General. **Business:** Business admin. **Computer sciences:** General. **Conservation:** Environmental studies. **Education:** General. **History:** General. **Math:** General. **Philosophy/religion:** Philosophy.

Physical sciences: Physics. **Psychology:** General. **Social sciences:** Political science, sociology. **Visual/performing arts:** General, art, arts management.

Most popular majors. Business/marketing 16%, English 23%, history 10%, interdisciplinary studies 8%, psychology 8%, social sciences 13%, visual/performing arts 10%.

Computing on campus. PC or laptop required. 125 workstations in dormitories, library, computer center, student center. Dormitories wired for high-speed internet access and linked to campus network. Commuter students can connect to campus network. Online course registration, helpline, wireless network available.

Student life. Freshman orientation: Mandatory, $75 fee. **Housing:** Guaranteed on-campus for all undergraduates. Coed dorms, special housing for disabled, apartments available. $100 nonrefundable deposit. **Activities:** Bands, choral groups, dance, drama, international student organizations, literary magazine, music ensembles, radio station, student government, student newspaper, TV station, interfaith association, Campus Christian Fellowship, Jewish student organization, Newman club, gay and lesbian student society, multicultural society.

Athletics. NCAA. **Intercollegiate:** Baseball M, basketball, cross-country, golf M, soccer, softball W, tennis W, volleyball W. **Intramural:** Basketball, bowling, equestrian, football (non-tackle), soccer, softball, swimming, tennis, volleyball, water polo M. **Team name:** Trailblazers.

Student services. Adult student services, career counseling, student employment services, financial aid counseling, health services, minority student services, personal counseling, placement for graduates, veterans' counselor, women's services. **Physically disabled:** Services for visually, hearing impaired.

Contact. E-mail: admissions@mcla.edu
Phone: (413) 662-5410 Toll-free number: (800) 969-6252
Fax: (413) 662-5179
Steve King, Assistant Dean, Director of Admission and Student Records, Massachusetts College of Liberal Arts, 375 Church Street, North Adams, MA 01247

Massachusetts College of Pharmacy and Health Sciences

Boston, Massachusetts — **CB member**
www.mcphs.edu — **CB code: 3512**

- Private 4-year health science and pharmacy college
- Commuter campus in very large city
- 2,708 degree-seeking undergraduates: 3% part-time, 70% women
- 1,163 graduate students
- 69% of applicants admitted
- SAT or ACT (ACT writing optional), application essay required
- 65% graduate within 6 years

General. Founded in 1823. Regionally accredited. Member of Fenway College Consortium, 14-college library consortium, Worcester Consortium, and Manchester Area College Consortium. Students have access to Harvard Medical School library. Accelerated PharmD program available at Worcester campus and Manchester campus; physician assistant program and nursing also offered at Boston and Manchester campuses. **Degrees:** 217 bachelor's awarded; master's, doctoral, first professional offered. **ROTC:** Army, Naval, Air Force. **Calendar:** Semester, limited summer session. **Full-time faculty:** 195 total; 86% have terminal degrees, 66% women. **Part-time faculty:** 4 total; 75% have terminal degrees, 75% women. **Class size:** 17% < 20, 50% 20-39, 10% 40-49, 7% 50-99, 15% >100. **Special facilities:** Pharmacy practice lab, dental hygiene clinic, patient assessment lab, nursing skills and technology lab.

Freshman class profile. 2,768 applied, 1,900 admitted, 604 enrolled.

Mid 50% test scores		**GPA 2.0-2.99:**	13%
SAT critical reading:	490-580	**Rank in top quarter:**	61%
SAT math:	520-620	**Rank in top tenth:**	26%
SAT writing:	500-590	**Return as sophomores:**	85%
ACT composite:	21-25	**Out-of-state:**	42%
GPA 3.75 or higher:	31%	**Live on campus:**	82%
GPA 3.50-3.74:	22%	**International:**	1%
GPA 3.0-3.49:	34%		

Basis for selection. School academic record most important, with emphasis on math and science courses. Student's interest, aptitude for pharmacy and allied health fields considered. **Homeschooled:** Require documentation of curriculum and program of study; equivalency exam. **Learning Disabled:** Must submit documents to Academic Support Services.

High school preparation. 18 units recommended. Recommended units include English 4, mathematics 3, social studies 1, history 1, science 2 (laboratory 2) and academic electives 5. Additional units of advanced math and science (especially chemistry) strongly recommended.

2008-2009 Annual costs. Tuition/fees: $23,620. Room/board: $11,790. Books/supplies: $840. Personal expenses: $2,120.

2008-2009 Financial aid. Non-need-based: Scholarships awarded for academics.

Application procedures. Admission: $70 fee, may be waived for applicants with need. Admission notification on a rolling basis beginning on or about 12/19. Must reply by May 1 or within 2 week(s) if notified thereafter. Varies by program. **Financial aid:** Priority date 3/15; no closing date. FAFSA required. Applicants notified on a rolling basis.

Academics. Academic success seminars/workshops, peer mentors. **Special study options:** Accelerated study, combined bachelor's/graduate degree, cross-registration, distance learning, double major, dual enrollment of high school students, independent study, internships, liberal arts/career combination, study abroad. **Credit/placement by examination:** AP, CLEP, IB, SAT, ACT, institutional tests. 6 credit hours maximum toward bachelor's degree. CLEP exams must be taken before student's first semester of enrollment in order for credit to be granted. **Support services:** Learning center, reduced course load, study skills assistance, tutoring, writing center.

Majors. Health: Dental hygiene, health services, medical radiologic technology/radiation therapy, nuclear medical technology, nursing (RN), premedicine, radiologic technology/medical imaging. **Physical sciences:** Chemistry. **Psychology:** Medical. **Other:** Pharmaceutical sciences/pharmaceutical marketing and management.

Computing on campus. 500 workstations in dormitories, library, computer center, student center. Dormitories wired for high-speed internet access and linked to campus network. Commuter students can connect to campus network. Online library, helpline, wireless network available.

Student life. Freshman orientation: Mandatory, $100 fee. Preregistration for classes offered. Two-day overnight program in summer; 1-day freshman parent orientation. **Policies:** Identification must be worn and displayed while on campus. Academic honesty policy, alcohol and drug abuse policies; electronic communications policy; good neighbor policy; hazing policy; smoke-free policy; sexual harassment policy. **Housing:** Guaranteed on-campus for freshmen. Coed dorms, single-sex dorms, wellness housing available. $250 fully refundable deposit, deadline 5/1. **Activities:** Concert band, choral groups, dance, drama, international student organizations, literary magazine, music ensembles, student government, student newspaper, symphony orchestra, Academy of Student Pharmacists, Kappa Psi fraternity, Vietnamese student association, student American dental hygienist association, black student union, physician assistant society, Academy of Students of Health Systems Pharmacy, campus activities board, student government association, Indian student organization.

Athletics. Intramural: Baseball, basketball, bowling, cross-country, field hockey W, football (non-tackle), golf, racquetball, soccer, softball, squash, table tennis, tennis, volleyball, water polo. **Team name:** Cardinals.

Student services. Adult student services, alcohol/substance abuse counseling, career counseling, student employment services, financial aid counseling, health services, minority student services, personal counseling, placement for graduates, veterans' counselor, women's services. **Physically disabled:** Services for visually, speech, hearing impaired.

Contact. E-mail: admissions@mcphs.edu
Phone: (617) 732-2850 Toll-free number: (800) 225-5506
Fax: (617) 732-2118
Kathleen Ryan, Executive Director of Admission, Massachusetts College of Pharmacy and Health Sciences, 179 Longwood Avenue, Boston, MA 02115-5896

Massachusetts Institute of Technology

Cambridge, Massachusetts — **CB member**
web.mit.edu — **CB code: 3514**

- Private 4-year university
- Residential campus in small city
- 4,138 degree-seeking undergraduates: 1% part-time, 45% women, 8% African American, 25% Asian American, 12% Hispanic American, 1% Native American, 9% international
- 6,010 degree-seeking graduate students
- 12% of applicants admitted

- SAT or ACT with writing, SAT Subject Tests, application essay required
- 94% graduate within 6 years; 47% enter graduate study

General. Founded in 1861. Regionally accredited. **Degrees:** 1,217 bachelor's awarded; master's, doctoral offered. **ROTC:** Army, Naval, Air Force. **Location:** One mile from Boston. **Calendar:** 4-1-4, limited summer session. **Full-time faculty:** 1,365 total; 88% have terminal degrees, 14% minority, 21% women. **Part-time faculty:** 470 total; 73% have terminal degrees, 7% minority, 24% women. **Class size:** 65% < 20, 19% 20-39, 3% 40-49, 9% 50-99, 3% >100. **Special facilities:** Museum, visual arts center, computer science and artificial intelligence laboratory, institute for soldier nanotechnologies, institute for learning and memory.

Freshman class profile. 13,396 applied, 1,589 admitted, 1,048 enrolled.

Mid 50% test scores		**End year in good standing:**	98%
SAT critical reading:	660-760	**Return as sophomores:**	98%
SAT math:	720-800	**Out-of-state:**	92%
SAT writing:	660-750	**Live on campus:**	100%
ACT composite:	31-34	**International:**	9%
Rank in top quarter:	100%	**Fraternities:**	50%
Rank in top tenth:	97%	**Sororities:**	27%

Basis for selection. Holistic review of application. Important factors include character, creativity, grades, leadership, love of learning, personal accomplishments, quality of academic program, recommendations, resiliency, test scores. 2 SAT Subject Tests required (one each in math and science). Interviews strongly recommended.

High school preparation. College-preparatory program recommended. Recommended units include English 4, mathematics 4, social studies 2, science 4 and foreign language 2.

2009-2010 Annual costs. Tuition/fees: $37,782. Room/board: $11,360. Books/supplies: $1,150. Personal expenses: $1,708.

2007-2008 Financial aid. All financial aid based on need. 853 full-time freshmen applied for aid; 667 were judged to have need; 667 of these received aid. Average need met was 100%. Average scholarship/grant was $30,232; average loan $1,978. 91% of total undergraduate aid awarded as scholarships/grants, 9% as loans/jobs. **Additional information:** Filing deadline 2/15 for CSS PROFILE.

Application procedures. Admission: Closing date 1/1 (postmark date). $75 fee, may be waived for applicants with need. Admission notification 3/20. Must reply by May 1 or within 2 week(s) if notified thereafter. **Financial aid:** Closing date 2/15. FAFSA, CSS PROFILE required. Applicants notified by 4/1; must reply by 5/1.

Academics. Special study options: Combined bachelor's/graduate degree, cooperative education, cross-registration, double major, internships, semester at sea, study abroad, teacher certification program, Washington semester. Undergraduate research opportunities program, independent activities period, alternative freshman programs. **Credit/placement by examination:** AP, CLEP, IB, institutional tests. **Support services:** Learning center, pre-admission summer program, study skills assistance, tutoring, writing center.

Majors. Architecture: Architecture, urban/community planning. **Biology:** General. **Business:** General. **Communications:** Media studies. **Computer sciences:** Computer science. **Engineering:** Aerospace, biomedical, chemical, civil, electrical, environmental, materials, mechanical, nuclear. **Foreign languages:** General, linguistics. **History:** General. **Interdisciplinary:** Cognitive science, math/computer science, neuroscience, science/society. **Liberal arts:** Arts/sciences. **Math:** General. **Philosophy/religion:** Philosophy. **Physical sciences:** Chemistry, geology, physics. **Social sciences:** Anthropology, economics, political science.

Most popular majors. Biology 8%, business/marketing 9%, computer/information sciences 14%, engineering/engineering technologies 38%, mathematics 8%, physical sciences 11%.

Computing on campus. 1,100 workstations in dormitories, library, computer center, student center. Dormitories wired for high-speed internet access and linked to campus network. Commuter students can connect to campus network. Online course registration, online library, helpline, repair service, student web hosting, wireless network available.

Student life. Freshman orientation: Mandatory. Held last 2 weeks of August. Includes programs for parents and international students. Additional 20 optional pre-orientation programs held week prior to orientation. **Policies:** Many undergraduate buildings designated smoke-free. **Housing:** Guaranteed on-campus for freshmen. Coed dorms, single-sex dorms, special housing for disabled, apartments, cooperative housing, fraternity/sorority housing, wellness housing available. Independent living group housing, housing for students with children, cultural theme housing, living learning communities available. **Activities:** Bands, campus ministries, choral groups, dance, drama, film society, international student organizations, literary magazine, music ensembles, Model UN, musical theater, radio station, student government, student newspaper, symphony orchestra, TV station, numerous recognized organizations available.

Athletics. NCAA. **Intercollegiate:** Baseball M, basketball, cross-country, diving, fencing, field hockey W, football (tackle) M, golf M, gymnastics, ice hockey W, lacrosse, rifle, rowing (crew), sailing, skiing, soccer, softball W, squash M, swimming, tennis, track and field, volleyball, water polo M, wrestling M. **Intramural:** Badminton, basketball, bowling, cross-country, football (non-tackle), ice hockey, rugby, soccer, softball, squash, table tennis, tennis, triathlon W, volleyball, water polo. **Team name:** Engineers.

Student services. Alcohol/substance abuse counseling, chaplain/spiritual director, career counseling, student employment services, financial aid counseling, health services, on-campus daycare, personal counseling, placement for graduates. **Physically disabled:** Services for visually, speech, hearing impaired.

Contact. E-mail: admissions@mit.edu
Phone: (617) 253-3400 Fax: (617) 258-8304
Stuart Schmill, Dean of Admissions, Massachusetts Institute of Technology, 77 Massachusetts Avenue, Rm 3-108, Cambridge, MA 02139-4307

Massachusetts Maritime Academy

Buzzards Bay, Massachusetts — **CB member**
www.maritime.edu — **CB code: 3515**

- Public 4-year military and maritime college
- Residential campus in large town
- 1,050 degree-seeking undergraduates
- 60 graduate students
- 55% of applicants admitted
- SAT or ACT (ACT writing optional), application essay required

General. Founded in 1891. Regionally accredited. **Degrees:** 190 bachelor's awarded; master's offered. **ROTC:** Army, Naval, Air Force. **Location:** 55 miles from Boston; 50 miles from Providence, Rhode Island. **Calendar:** 2 semesters and 8-week winter sea term. Limited summer session. **Full-time faculty:** 60 total. **Part-time faculty:** 20 total. **Class size:** 43% < 20, 57% 20-39, less than 1% 40-49. **Special facilities:** 540' training ship enterprise, slow-speed diesel simulator, video full-function bridge navigation simulator, commercial fishing simulator, spill management simulator, cargo handling simulator, hands-on aquaculture center, emergency management simulator.

Freshman class profile. 1,027 applied, 567 admitted, 304 enrolled.

Mid 50% test scores		**ACT composite:**	17-23
SAT critical reading:	440-560	**Live on campus:**	100%
SAT math:	480-580		

Basis for selection. School achievement record, test scores, extracurricular accomplishments most important. Character and personality emphasized, leadership potential desirable. Interview recommended.

High school preparation. 18 units required. Required units include English 4, mathematics 3, social studies 2, history 2, science 3 (laboratory 2) and foreign language 2. Math units must include 2 algebra, 1 plane geometry. Science units must include 1 chemistry, or two courses with a lab. Physics recommended.

2008-2009 Annual costs. Tuition/fees: $5,827; $17,864 out-of-state. Semester at Sea cost: $3,218. Room/board: $8,607. Books/supplies: $800. Personal expenses: $1,200.

2007-2008 Financial aid. Non-need-based: Scholarships awarded for academics, leadership, music/drama.

Application procedures. Admission: No deadline. $50 fee, may be waived for applicants with need, free for online applicants. Admission notification on a rolling basis beginning on or about 11/15. Must reply by May 1 or within 1 week(s) if notified thereafter. **Financial aid:** Priority date 4/30; no closing date. FAFSA, institutional form required. Applicants notified on a rolling basis starting 3/1.

Academics. Technical and practical training for third assistant engineer and third mate licenses. Graduates may apply for commissions in U.S. Navy, Coast Guard, Marine Reserve, Army, or Air Force. **Special study options:** Combined bachelor's/graduate degree, cooperative education, double major, internships, liberal arts/career combination, semester at sea. **Credit/**

placement by examination: AP, CLEP, IB, institutional tests. 6 credit hours maximum toward bachelor's degree. **Support services:** Learning center, pre-admission summer program, reduced course load, study skills assistance, tutoring.

Majors. Business: Transportation. **Engineering:** General. **Engineering technology:** Industrial management. **Protective services:** Security management. **Transportation:** Maritime/Merchant Marine.

Most popular majors. Engineering/engineering technologies 50%, natural resources/environmental science 15%, security/protective services 15%, trade and industry 20%.

Computing on campus. PC or laptop required. 70 workstations in dormitories, library, computer center. Dormitories wired for high-speed internet access and linked to campus network. Commuter students can connect to campus network. Helpline, wireless network available.

Student life. Freshman orientation: Mandatory, $400 fee. Preregistration for classes offered. Held last 2 weeks of August, paramilitary style orientation. **Policies:** No mandatory military obligation. **Housing:** Guaranteed on-campus for all undergraduates. Coed dorms, wellness housing available. All majors required to live on campus. **Activities:** Bands, drama, literary magazine, music ensembles, student government, student newspaper, Newman Club, marine careers group, Association of Industrial Plant Engineers.

Athletics. NCAA. **Intercollegiate:** Baseball M, cross-country, football (tackle) M, lacrosse M, rifle, rowing (crew), sailing, soccer M, softball W, track and field W, volleyball W. **Intramural:** Basketball, boxing M, football (tackle) M, ice hockey, racquetball, rifle, sailing, soccer, softball, swimming, table tennis, tennis, track and field W, volleyball, water polo, wrestling M. **Team name:** Buccaneers.

Student services. Adult student services, alcohol/substance abuse counseling, chaplain/spiritual director, career counseling, student employment services, financial aid counseling, health services, personal counseling, placement for graduates, veterans' counselor, women's services. **Learning disabled:** Comprehensive services available.

Contact. E-mail: admissions@maritime.edu
Phone: (508) 830-5000 ext. 1102 Toll-free number: (800) 544-3411
Fax: (508) 830-5077
Roy Fulgueras, Director of Admissions, Massachusetts Maritime Academy, 101 Academy Drive, Buzzards Bay, MA 02532-1803

Merrimack College

North Andover, Massachusetts — **CB member**
www.merrimack.edu — **CB code: 3525**

- Private 4-year business and liberal arts college affiliated with Roman Catholic Church
- Residential campus in large town
- 2,057 degree-seeking undergraduates: 8% part-time, 50% women, 2% African American, 2% Asian American, 3% Hispanic American, 2% international
- 36 degree-seeking graduate students
- 79% of applicants admitted
- Application essay required
- 64% graduate within 6 years; 8% enter graduate study

General. Founded in 1947. Regionally accredited. Associated with Augustinian Friars. **Degrees:** 430 bachelor's, 2 associate awarded; master's offered. **ROTC:** Air Force. **Location:** 25 miles from Boston. **Calendar:** Semester, limited summer session. **Full-time faculty:** 126 total; 84% have terminal degrees, 7% minority, 41% women. **Part-time faculty:** 91 total; 38% have terminal degrees, 12% minority, 50% women. **Class size:** 64% < 20, 35% 20-39, less than 1% 40-49, less than 1% 50-99, less than 1% >100. **Special facilities:** Astronomy dome and telescope, arts center.

Freshman class profile. 3,915 applied, 3,080 admitted, 621 enrolled.

GPA 3.75 or higher:	8%	**Rank in top tenth:**	18%
GPA 3.50-3.74:	16%	**End year in good standing:**	90%
GPA 3.0-3.49:	58%	**Return as sophomores:**	71%
GPA 2.0-2.99:	18%	**Live on campus:**	90%
Rank in top quarter:	24%	**International:**	1%

Basis for selection. School achievement record, course selection, class rank, essay, recommendations important. Interview recommended. **Homeschooled:** State certificate of completion, list of coursework, interview required.

High school preparation. 20 units required; 26 recommended. Required and recommended units include English 4, mathematics 3-4, social studies 1-2, history 1-2, science 3-4 (laboratory 3-4), foreign language 2-3 and academic electives 3. Math must include algebra I and II and plane geometry. 1 additional math and 3 science, including physics, required of math, science, engineering, and computer science applicants.

2008-2009 Annual costs. Tuition/fees: $29,810. Room/board: $10,190. Books/supplies: $800. Personal expenses: $2,750.

2007-2008 Financial aid. Need-based: 485 full-time freshmen applied for aid; 481 were judged to have need; 481 of these received aid. Average need met was 70%. Average scholarship/grant was $13,107; average loan $3,337. 57% of total undergraduate aid awarded as scholarships/grants, 43% as loans/jobs. **Non-need-based:** Awarded to 894 full-time undergraduates, including 252 freshmen. Scholarships awarded for academics, athletics, leadership, minority status, religious affiliation. **Additional information:** Accept the Challenge program provides tuition for students from Lawrence who meet program criteria.

Application procedures. Admission: Closing date 2/1 (postmark date). $60 fee, may be waived for applicants with need. Admission notification 4/1. Admission notification on a rolling basis. Must reply by May 1 or within 2 week(s) if notified thereafter. **Financial aid:** Closing date 2/1. FAFSA required. Applicants notified by 3/15; must reply by 5/1 or within 2 week(s) of notification.

Academics. Writing intensive courses available in all areas. Associate degree and M.Ed programs offered through continuing education division only. **Special study options:** Accelerated study, combined bachelor's/graduate degree, cooperative education, cross-registration, double major, dual enrollment of high school students, ESL, independent study, internships, liberal arts/career combination, student-designed major, study abroad, teacher certification program, Washington semester. 5-year combined BA/BS program. **Credit/placement by examination:** AP, CLEP, IB, institutional tests. **Support services:** Learning center, reduced course load, remedial instruction, study skills assistance, tutoring, writing center.

Majors. Biology: General, biochemistry. **Business:** Business admin. **Communications:** General. **Computer sciences:** Computer science. **Engineering:** General, civil, computer, electrical. **Foreign languages:** French, Romance, Spanish. **Health:** Athletic training, health services. **History:** General. **Liberal arts:** Arts/sciences. **Math:** General. **Philosophy/religion:** Philosophy, religion. **Physical sciences:** Chemistry, physics. **Psychology:** General. **Public administration:** Human services. **Social sciences:** Economics, political science, sociology. **Visual/performing arts:** Studio arts.

Most popular majors. Biology 6%, business/marketing 32%, engineering/engineering technologies 7%, health sciences 6%, psychology 9%, social sciences 10%.

Computing on campus. 250 workstations in dormitories, library, computer center, student center. Dormitories wired for high-speed internet access and linked to campus network. Commuter students can connect to campus network. Online course registration, online library, helpline, repair service, wireless network available.

Student life. Freshman orientation: Mandatory, $150 fee. Preregistration for classes offered. Two-day June sessions and 3-day August pre-class orientation. **Policies:** All residence halls are drug-free. **Housing:** Guaranteed on-campus for freshmen. Coed dorms, special housing for disabled, apartments, cooperative housing, wellness housing available. $300 fully refundable deposit, deadline 5/1. Townhouses for upperclassmen. Applications accepted from groups of students for theme housing in townhouses. Austin Scholars residential program available to selected students. **Activities:** Bands, campus ministries, choral groups, dance, drama, film society, international student organizations, music ensembles, Model UN, musical theater, student government, student newspaper, TV station, student tutoring group, community service organizations, College Democrats, College Republicans, Society Organized Against Racism, Latinos Organization.

Athletics. NCAA. **Intercollegiate:** Baseball M, basketball, cross-country, field hockey W, football (tackle) M, ice hockey M, lacrosse, soccer, softball W, tennis, volleyball W. **Intramural:** Basketball, ice hockey M, soccer, softball, volleyball. **Team name:** Warriors.

Student services. Adult student services, alcohol/substance abuse counseling, chaplain/spiritual director, career counseling, student employment services, financial aid counseling, health services, minority student services, personal counseling, placement for graduates.

Contact. E-mail: admission@merrimack.edu
Phone: (978) 837-5000 ext. 5100 Fax: (978) 837-5133
Jorge Hernandez, Director of Freshman Admission, Merrimack College, 315 Turnpike Street, North Andover, MA 01845

Montserrat College of Art
Beverly, Massachusetts **CB member**
www.montserrat.edu **CB code: 9101**

- Private 4-year visual arts college
- Residential campus in large town
- 281 degree-seeking undergraduates: 4% part-time, 72% women
- 74% of applicants admitted
- Application essay required

General. Founded in 1970. Regionally accredited. **Degrees:** 67 bachelor's awarded. **Location:** 18 miles from Boston. **Calendar:** Semester, limited summer session. **Full-time faculty:** 18 total; 83% have terminal degrees, 6% minority, 56% women. **Part-time faculty:** 45 total; 84% have terminal degrees, 7% minority, 44% women. **Class size:** 84% < 20, 16% 20-39. **Special facilities:** Computer design laboratory, photography, printmaking and sculpture facilities, college-operated galleries, student-operated gallery.

Freshman class profile. 406 applied, 302 admitted, 80 enrolled.

Mid 50% test scores			
SAT critical reading:	480-550	GPA 3.50-3.74:	1%
SAT math:	420-540	GPA 3.0-3.49:	18%
SAT writing:	430-540	GPA 2.0-2.99:	65%
GPA 3.75 or higher:	1%	Out-of-state:	43%
		Live on campus:	86%

Basis for selection. Visual art portfolio most important. High school record, interview, artist statement, and letters of recommendation required of BFA applicants. If personal visit is impractical, portfolio in digital or slide form may be sent; follow-up telephone interview will be conducted. SAT or ACT scores required for applicants with GED. Interview recommended. **Homeschooled:** Statement describing homeschool structure and mission, transcript of courses and grades, state high school equivalency certificate, letter of recommendation (nonparent) required. Must take SAT/ACT and successfully pass GED. **Learning Disabled:** Official documentation of disability required if accommodation requested.

High school preparation. Recommended units include English 4, social studies 2 and history 2. Visual arts courses including drawing recommended.

2008-2009 Annual costs. Tuition/fees: $23,320. Room/board: $6,000. Books/supplies: $1,275. Personal expenses: $2,300.

2008-2009 Financial aid. Need-based: 73 full-time freshmen applied for aid; 66 were judged to have need; 66 of these received aid. Average need met was 48%. Average scholarship/grant was $9,172; average loan $3,862. 45% of total undergraduate aid awarded as scholarships/grants, 55% as loans/jobs. **Non-need-based:** Awarded to 39 full-time undergraduates, including 12 freshmen. Scholarships awarded for academics, art.

Application procedures. Admission: Priority date 2/15; no deadline. $50 fee, may be waived for applicants with need. Admission notification on a rolling basis beginning on or about 12/20. Must reply by May 1 or within 3 week(s) if notified thereafter. If completed admissions application and financial aid application is received by 1/2, admissions decision and estimated financial aid package will be sent by 1/15. **Financial aid:** Closing date 3/1. FAFSA, institutional form required. Applicants notified on a rolling basis starting 12/20; must reply within 2 week(s) of notification.

Academics. In addition to frequent class critiques, students' work reviewed by faculty panel in semester-end evaluations. **Special study options:** Cross-registration, double major, dual enrollment of high school students, exchange student, independent study, internships, New York semester, student-designed major, study abroad, teacher certification program. Summer study abroad opportunities in Italy and Japan; winter study abroad opportunities in Africa and Puerto Rico; on-campus summer and winter session classes available. **Credit/placement by examination:** AP, CLEP, IB. **Support services:** Learning center, pre-admission summer program, reduced course load, remedial instruction, study skills assistance, tutoring, writing center.

Majors. Visual/performing arts: Art, design, drawing, graphic design, illustration, painting, photography, printmaking, sculpture, studio arts.

Computing on campus. 158 workstations in dormitories, library, computer center, student center. Dormitories wired for high-speed internet access. Online library, helpline, wireless network available.

Student life. Freshman orientation: Mandatory, $100 fee. Preregistration for classes offered. **Housing:** Coed dorms, single-sex dorms, wellness housing available. $275 nonrefundable deposit, deadline 5/1. **Activities:** Literary magazine, music ensembles, radio station, student government, student newspaper, Cooking Outside the Lines.

Athletics. Intramural: Basketball, bowling, football (tackle).

Student services. Adult student services, alcohol/substance abuse counseling, career counseling, student employment services, financial aid counseling, personal counseling, placement for graduates. **Physically disabled:** Services for visually, speech, hearing impaired.

Contact. E-mail: admiss@montserrat.edu
Phone: (978) 921-4242 ext. 1153 Toll-free
number: (800) 836-0487 ext. 1153 Fax: (978) 921-4241
Jessica Sarin-Perry, Dean of Admissions and Enrollment Management, Montserrat College of Art, 23 Essex Street, Beverly, MA 01915

Mount Holyoke College
South Hadley, Massachusetts **CB member**
www.mtholyoke.edu **CB code: 3529**

- Private 4-year liberal arts college for women
- Residential campus in large town
- 2,182 degree-seeking undergraduates: 1% part-time, 100% women, 5% African American, 12% Asian American, 5% Hispanic American, 17% international
- 1 degree-seeking graduate students
- 53% of applicants admitted
- Application essay required
- 82% graduate within 6 years; 20% enter graduate study

General. Founded in 1837. Regionally accredited. Member of 5-college consortium with Amherst College, Hampshire College, Smith College, and University of Massachusetts at Amherst. **Degrees:** 548 bachelor's awarded; master's offered. **ROTC:** Army, Air Force. **Location:** 10 miles from Springfield, 90 miles from Boston. **Calendar:** Semester. **Full-time faculty:** 208 total; 94% have terminal degrees, 27% minority, 53% women. **Part-time faculty:** 32 total; 59% have terminal degrees, 22% minority, 59% women. **Class size:** 64% < 20, 29% 20-39, 4% 40-49, 3% 50-99, less than 1% >100. **Special facilities:** Nuclear accelerator, nuclear magnetic resonance equipment, electron microscope, bronze-casting foundry, solar greenhouse, Japanese meditation garden and tea house, equestrian center, language learning center with satellite communication and interactive video, child study center, environmental literacy center, greenhouse and botanical garden, conference center, leadership center, global initiatives center.

Freshman class profile. 3,127 applied, 1,645 admitted, 527 enrolled.

Mid 50% test scores			
SAT critical reading:	620-720	GPA 2.0-2.99:	7%
SAT math:	590-700	Rank in top quarter:	91%
SAT writing:	630-700	Rank in top tenth:	62%
ACT composite:	27-31	Return as sophomores:	92%
GPA 3.75 or higher:	41%	Out-of-state:	80%
GPA 3.50-3.74:	27%	Live on campus:	100%
GPA 3.0-3.49:	25%	International:	19%

Basis for selection. School record most important, followed by special talents, particular goals, evidence of determination. Test scores optional. Personal interview on campus recommended if candidate lives within 200 miles of college, or with alumna admissions representative if applicant resides outside of area. **Homeschooled:** Detailed outline of study and 5 SAT Subject Tests recommended.

High school preparation. College-preparatory program recommended. Recommended units include English 4, mathematics 3, history 3, science 3 (laboratory 3), foreign language 3 and academic electives 1. History requirement includes U.S. and world history. Either 4 units of one foreign language, or 2 units of one and 3 units of a second foreign language recommended.

2009-2010 Annual costs. Tuition/fees: $39,126. Room/board: $11,450. Books/supplies: $1,900.

2008-2009 Financial aid. Need-based: 387 full-time freshmen applied for aid; 315 were judged to have need; 315 of these received aid. Average need met was 100%. Average scholarship/grant was $29,044; average loan $3,008. 79% of total undergraduate aid awarded as scholarships/grants, 21% as loans/jobs. **Non-need-based:** Scholarships awarded for academics, leadership. **Additional information:** Parent loan plans include MASSPLAN, Achievers and PLUS. 10-month payment plan offered.

Application procedures. Admission: Closing date 1/15 (postmark date). $60 fee, may be waived for applicants with need, free for online applicants. Admission notification 4/1. Must reply by 5/1. **Financial aid:** Priority date 2/15, closing date 3/1. FAFSA, CSS PROFILE required. Applicants notified by 4/1; must reply by 5/1.

Academics. Honor system and self-scheduled examinations practiced. All students must complete minor. **Special study options:** Combined bachelor's/graduate degree, cooperative education, cross-registration, double major, exchange student, independent study, internships, liberal arts/career combination, semester at sea, student-designed major, study abroad, teacher certification program, Washington semester. Community-based learning courses. **Credit/placement by examination:** AP, CLEP, IB, institutional tests. 32 credit hours maximum toward bachelor's degree. **Support services:** Reduced course load, study skills assistance, tutoring, writing center.

Majors. Architecture: Architecture. **Area/ethnic studies:** African-American, American, Asian, European, German, Latin American, Russian/Slavic. **Biology:** General, biochemistry. **Computer sciences:** Computer science. **Conservation:** Environmental studies. **Education:** General. **Foreign languages:** Ancient Greek, classics, French, Italian, Latin, Romance, Spanish. **History:** General. **Interdisciplinary:** Ancient studies, medieval/Renaissance, neuroscience. **Math:** General, statistics. **Philosophy/religion:** Philosophy, religion. **Physical sciences:** Astronomy, chemistry, geology, physics. **Psychology:** General. **Social sciences:** Anthropology, economics, geography, international relations, political science, sociology. **Visual/performing arts:** Art history/conservation, dance, dramatic, film/cinema, studio arts. **Other:** Complex organizations, Self-designed studies.

Most popular majors. Biology 11%, English 9%, interdisciplinary studies 6%, psychology 7%, social sciences 28%, visual/performing arts 8%.

Computing on campus. 577 workstations in dormitories, library, computer center, student center. Dormitories wired for high-speed internet access and linked to campus network. Commuter students can connect to campus network. Online course registration, online library, helpline, repair service, student web hosting, wireless network available.

Student life. Freshman orientation: Available. Preregistration for classes offered. Program held week before start of classes. Specific orientation programs for international students, women of color. **Policies:** Smoke-free campus. **Housing:** Guaranteed on-campus for all undergraduates. Special housing for disabled, apartments available. $200 nonrefundable deposit, deadline 5/15. Kosher/halal kitchen available; special accommodations by need. **Activities:** Jazz band, campus ministries, choral groups, dance, drama, film society, international student organizations, literary magazine, music ensembles, Model UN, musical theater, radio station, student government, student newspaper, symphony orchestra.

Athletics. NCAA. **Intercollegiate:** Basketball W, cross-country W, diving W, equestrian W, field hockey W, golf W, lacrosse W, rowing (crew) W, soccer W, squash W, swimming W, tennis W, track and field W, volleyball W. **Team name:** Lyons.

Student services. Adult student services, alcohol/substance abuse counseling, chaplain/spiritual director, career counseling, student employment services, financial aid counseling, health services, minority student services, personal counseling, placement for graduates, women's services. **Physically disabled:** Services for visually, speech, hearing impaired.

Contact. E-mail: admission@mtholyoke.edu
Phone: (413) 538-2023 Fax: (413) 538-2409
Diane Anci, Dean of Admission, Mount Holyoke College, Newhall Center, South Hadley, MA 01075-1488

Mount Ida College

Newton, Massachusetts — **CB member**
www.mountida.edu — **CB code: 3530**

- Private 4-year business and liberal arts college
- Residential campus in small city
- 1,445 degree-seeking undergraduates: 4% part-time, 67% women, 10% African American, 2% Asian American, 6% Hispanic American, 5% international
- 74% of applicants admitted
- SAT or ACT (ACT writing recommended) required
- 54% graduate within 6 years

General. Founded in 1899. Regionally accredited. **Degrees:** 181 bachelor's, 37 associate awarded. **Location:** 8 miles from downtown Boston. **Calendar:** Semester, limited summer session. **Full-time faculty:** 63 total; 57% have terminal degrees, 8% minority, 60% women. **Part-time faculty:** 111 total; 32% have terminal degrees, 7% minority, 58% women. **Class size:** 66% < 20, 33% 20-39, less than 1% 40-49, less than 1% 50-99. **Special facilities:** Darkroom, blueprint making facility, veterinary kennel and operating facility, dental laboratory, design labs.

Freshman class profile. 2,222 applied, 1,648 admitted, 411 enrolled.

Mid 50% test scores		**GPA 3.0-3.49:**	18%
SAT critical reading:	390-490	**GPA 2.0-2.99:**	66%
SAT math:	380-490	**Return as sophomores:**	57%
SAT writing:	400-500	**Out-of-state:**	43%
ACT composite:	15-20	**Live on campus:**	88%
GPA 3.75 or higher:	1%	**International:**	3%
GPA 3.50-3.74:	3%		

Basis for selection. Special requirements for science applicants and students interested in Learning Opportunities Program. 2.0 GPA required for admission to all bachelor's degree programs, except interior design, which requires 2.5 GPA. Veterinary science students must have some science background. Prefer art students to have art background. Portfolio recommended for art, interior design, fashion illustration majors. Essay or personal statement, interview and campus visit strongly recommended and may be required for certain programs.

High school preparation. 14 units recommended. Recommended units include English 4, mathematics 3, social studies 2, science 3 (laboratory 3) and foreign language 2. 4 math, 2 physical science strongly recommended for science majors.

2008-2009 Annual costs. Tuition/fees: $22,500. Room/board: $11,100. Books/supplies: $1,000. Personal expenses: $1,200.

2008-2009 Financial aid. Need-based: Average need met was 55%. Average scholarship/grant was $11,015; average loan $3,462. 50% of total undergraduate aid awarded as scholarships/grants, 50% as loans/jobs.

Application procedures. Admission: No deadline. $45 fee, may be waived for applicants with need, free for online applicants. Admission notification on a rolling basis beginning on or about 10/1. **Financial aid:** Priority date 5/1; no closing date. FAFSA, institutional form required. Applicants notified on a rolling basis starting 3/1; must reply within 3 week(s) of notification.

Academics. Professionally intensive courses of study coupled with liberal arts requirements. **Special study options:** Distance learning, ESL, independent study, internships, semester at sea, student-designed major, study abroad, teacher certification program. Affiliation with Tufts Veterinary School and Tufts University School of Dental Medicine. **Credit/placement by examination:** AP, CLEP, IB, institutional tests. 9 credit hours maximum toward bachelor's degree. **Support services:** Learning center, reduced course load, remedial instruction, study skills assistance, tutoring, writing center.

Majors. Agriculture: Equestrian studies. **Biology:** General. **Business:** Business admin, fashion, hospitality admin, tourism/travel. **Education:** Early childhood. **Health:** Veterinary technology/assistant. **History:** American. **Legal studies:** General. **Liberal arts:** Arts/sciences. **Parks/recreation:** Sports admin. **Personal/culinary services:** Mortuary science. **Protective services:** Criminal justice. **Psychology:** General. **Public administration:** Human services. **Visual/performing arts:** Fashion design, graphic design, interior design.

Most popular majors. Business/marketing 37%, health sciences 14%, security/protective services 6%, visual/performing arts 26%.

Computing on campus. 122 workstations in library, computer center. Dormitories wired for high-speed internet access and linked to campus network. Online library, wireless network available.

Student life. Freshman orientation: Mandatory. Preregistration for classes offered. Held in July. Students able to make housing selections. Orientation activities also held prior to first day of class in late August. **Housing:** Guaranteed on-campus for freshmen. Coed dorms, single-sex dorms, special housing for disabled, wellness housing available. $300 fully refundable deposit. **Activities:** Choral groups, dance, drama, international student organizations, literary magazine, radio station, student government, student newspaper, black student achievement coalition, gay and lesbian association, Jewish society, student association for Latino and Spanish Americans.

Athletics. NCAA. **Intercollegiate:** Basketball, cheerleading, cross-country W, equestrian W, football (tackle) M, lacrosse M, soccer, softball W, volleyball. **Intramural:** Badminton, basketball, handball, ice hockey, soccer, volleyball. **Team name:** Mustangs.

Student services. Adult student services, alcohol/substance abuse counseling, chaplain/spiritual director, career counseling, services for economically disadvantaged, student employment services, financial aid counseling, health services, minority student services, personal counseling, placement for graduates.

Contact. E-mail: admissions@mountida.edu
Phone: (617) 928-4553 Fax: (617) 928-4507
Jay Titus, Dean of Admissions, Mount Ida College, 777 Dedham Street, Newton, MA 02459

New England Conservatory of Music
Boston, Massachusetts **CB member**
www.newenglandconservatory.edu **CB code: 3659**

- Private 4-year music college
- Commuter campus in very large city
- 351 degree-seeking undergraduates: 7% part-time, 45% women, 4% African American, 8% Asian American, 6% Hispanic American, 23% international
- 305 degree-seeking graduate students
- 31% of applicants admitted
- Application essay required
- 72% graduate within 6 years

General. Founded in 1867. Regionally accredited. In close proximity to Symphony Hall. Faculty includes members of Boston Symphony Orchestra. **Degrees:** 101 bachelor's awarded; master's, doctoral offered. **Location:** 2 miles from downtown. **Calendar:** Semester, limited summer session. **Full-time faculty:** 89 total; 18% have terminal degrees, 7% minority, 34% women. **Part-time faculty:** 114 total; 5% have terminal degrees, 10% minority, 31% women. **Class size:** 79% < 20, 20% 20-39, 2% 40-49. **Special facilities:** Listening library.

Freshman class profile. 1,080 applied, 334 admitted, 85 enrolled.

End year in good standing:	96%	**Live on campus:**	94%
Return as sophomores:	92%	**International:**	31%
Out-of-state:	95%		

Basis for selection. Audition most important, followed by recommendations, essay, high school record. Accepted students permitted to postpone admission one-half year. Live or taped auditions required. **Homeschooled:** Must provide curriculum overview.

2008-2009 Annual costs. Tuition/fees: $33,325. On-campus residents and all incoming students pay $440 health center fee. Room/board: $11,600. Books/supplies: $700. Personal expenses: $2,386.

2008-2009 Financial aid. Need-based: Average need met was 68%. Average scholarship/grant was $14,079; average loan $5,323. 61% of total undergraduate aid awarded as scholarships/grants, 39% as loans/jobs. **Non-need-based:** Scholarships awarded for academics, music/drama.

Application procedures. Admission: Priority date 12/1; no deadline. $100 fee. Admission notification on a rolling basis beginning on or about 4/1. Must reply by May 1 or within 4 week(s) if notified thereafter. **Financial aid:** Closing date 12/1. FAFSA, institutional form required. Applicants notified by 4/1; must reply by 5/1 or within 2 week(s) of notification.

Academics. Undergraduate diploma available in lieu of bachelor's degree (performance-oriented, with fewer academic requirements). Artist's diploma (professional degree) available for particularly gifted performers. Graduate diploma also available. **Special study options:** Cross-registration, dual enrollment of high school students, ESL, independent study, internships, study abroad. 5-year double degree program with Tufts University; 5-year AB/MM program with Harvard University. **Credit/placement by examination:** CLEP, IB, institutional tests. 12 credit hours maximum toward bachelor's degree. **Support services:** Tutoring, writing center.

Majors. Visual/performing arts: Jazz, music history, music performance, music theory/composition, piano/organ, stringed instruments, voice/opera.

Computing on campus. 48 workstations in dormitories, library, computer center, student center. Online library, wireless network available.

Student life. Freshman orientation: Mandatory. Preregistration for classes offered. Held 5 days before start of classes. **Housing:** Guaranteed on-campus for freshmen. Coed dorms available. $500 fully refundable deposit, deadline 5/1. **Activities:** Bands, choral groups, music ensembles, opera, student government, student newspaper, symphony orchestra, Christian Fellowship, feminist and minority student organizations.

Athletics. Team name: Penguins.

Student services. Career counseling, student employment services, health services, personal counseling, placement for graduates. **Physically disabled:** Services for visually impaired.

Contact. E-mail: admissions@newenglandconservatory.edu
Phone: (617) 585-1101 Fax: (617) 585-1115
Christina Daly, Director of Admissions, New England Conservatory of Music, 290 Huntington Avenue, Boston, MA 02115

New England Institute of Art
Brookline, Massachusetts
www.artinstitutes.edu/boston **CB code: 3636**

- For-profit 4-year visual arts and technical college
- Commuter campus in very large city
- 1,687 degree-seeking undergraduates
- 44% of applicants admitted
- Application essay, interview required

General. Regionally accredited. **Degrees:** 286 bachelor's, 26 associate awarded. **Calendar:** Semester, extensive summer session. **Full-time faculty:** 30 total. **Part-time faculty:** 50 total. **Class size:** 79% < 20, 19% 20-39, 2% 40-49. **Special facilities:** Radio, TV, and audio production studios; drafting rooms.

Freshman class profile. 1,293 applied, 570 admitted, 570 enrolled.

Basis for selection. Essay and interview most important, followed by secondary school record. Class rank, recommendations, test scores considered. Second interview required for audio programs. Portfolio required for Media Arts and Animation program.

2008-2009 Annual costs. Tuition/fees: $23,288.

Financial aid. Non-need-based: Scholarships awarded for academics.

Application procedures. Admission: No deadline. $150 fee. Admission notification on a rolling basis. **Financial aid:** Priority date 5/1; no closing date. FAFSA, institutional form required. Applicants notified on a rolling basis starting 3/1.

Academics. Bachelor's degrees offered in graphic design and multimedia/web design. Non-collegiate certificates offered in web site development and digital graphic design. **Special study options:** Internships. **Credit/placement by examination:** AP, CLEP, institutional tests. **Support services:** Learning center, remedial instruction, study skills assistance, tutoring.

Majors. Business: Fashion. **Communications:** Digital media. **Communications technology:** Graphics, photo/film/video, recording arts. **Computer sciences:** Web page design. **Visual/performing arts:** Commercial/advertising art, fashion design, graphic design, illustration, multimedia.

Computing on campus. Dormitories wired for high-speed internet access. Student web hosting available.

Student life. Freshman orientation: Mandatory. Half-day program held prior to start of semester. **Policies:** Student code of conduct. **Housing:** Coed dorms, apartments available. $400 nonrefundable deposit. **Activities:** Drama, film society, literary magazine, radio station, student government.

Student services. Adult student services, alcohol/substance abuse counseling, career counseling, student employment services, financial aid counseling, personal counseling, placement for graduates.

Contact. E-mail: neiaadm@aii.edu
Phone: (617) 739-1700 Toll-free number: (800) 903-4425
Fax: (617) 582-0974
Ken Post, Vice President/Senior Director of Admissions, New England Institute of Art, 10 Brookline Place West, Brookline, MA 02445-7295

Newbury College
Brookline, Massachusetts **CB member**
www.newbury.edu **CB code: 3639**

- Private 4-year business and liberal arts college
- Commuter campus in large city
- 1,200 degree-seeking undergraduates
- 68% of applicants admitted
- Application essay required

General. Founded in 1962. Regionally accredited. **Degrees:** 170 bachelor's, 27 associate awarded. **Location:** 3 miles from Boston. **Calendar:**

Semester, limited summer session. **Full-time faculty:** 30 total. **Special facilities:** 7 culinary arts production kitchens, on-campus restaurant open to the public.

Freshman class profile. 2,200 applied, 1,500 admitted, 310 enrolled.

Mid 50% test scores			
SAT critical reading:	380-490	SAT writing:	370-480
SAT math:	370-510	Out-of-state:	25%
		Live on campus:	35%

Basis for selection. Holistic approach includes application, essay, high school transcript, extra-curricular activities and 2 letters of recommendation. SAT or ACT recommended. SAT or ACT scores required for scholarship consideration. Interviews recommended. **Learning Disabled:** Students with a learning disability should submit copy of IEP with application.

High school preparation. College-preparatory program recommended. Recommended units include English 3, mathematics 3, social studies 3, history 3, science 2, foreign language 2 and computer science 1.

2008-2009 Annual costs. Tuition/fees: $22,000. Room/board: $10,750. Books/supplies: $750. Personal expenses: $1,000.

Financial aid. All financial aid based on need.

Application procedures. Admission: Priority date 3/1; no deadline. $50 fee, may be waived for applicants with need. Admission notification on a rolling basis beginning on or about 11/1. Must reply by May 1 or within 4 week(s) if notified thereafter. **Financial aid:** Closing date 5/1. FAFSA required. Applicants notified on a rolling basis starting 3/1; must reply within 2 week(s) of notification.

Academics. Academic enrichment program available for students entering who demonstrate need for academic support. **Special study options:** Combined bachelor's/graduate degree, cross-registration, double major, honors, independent study, internships, liberal arts/career combination, study abroad, weekend college. **Credit/placement by examination:** CLEP, IB, institutional tests. 30 credit hours maximum toward associate degree, 60 toward bachelor's. **Support services:** Learning center, remedial instruction, study skills assistance, tutoring.

Majors. Architecture: Interior. **Business:** Accounting, business admin, finance, hospitality admin, hospitality/recreation, international, international marketing, marketing. **Communications:** General. **Computer sciences:** General, computer graphics, computer science. **Health:** Facilities admin, health care admin. **Legal studies:** General, paralegal, prelaw. **Personal/culinary services:** Chef training, culinary arts, restaurant/catering. **Protective services:** Law enforcement admin. **Psychology:** General. **Visual/performing arts:** Commercial/advertising art, graphic design, interior design.

Most popular majors. Business/marketing 66%, computer/information sciences 10%, legal studies 15%.

Computing on campus. 65 workstations in dormitories, library, computer center, student center. Dormitories wired for high-speed internet access and linked to campus network. Online library, helpline available.

Student life. Freshman orientation: Mandatory, $150 fee. Preregistration for classes offered. Information sessions and activities held a few days before each semester. **Housing:** Guaranteed on-campus for freshmen. Coed dorms, single-sex dorms available. $250 nonrefundable deposit, deadline 5/1. Summer housing available. **Activities:** Jazz band, dance, drama, radio station, student government, TV station, international student organization, black student union, Latino student association, Habitat for Humanity, innkeepers club, chef society, business club, radio club, programming board.

Athletics. NCAA. **Intercollegiate:** Basketball, cross-country, golf, soccer M, softball W, tennis, volleyball. **Intramural:** Basketball, softball W, volleyball, weight lifting. **Team name:** Nighthawks.

Student services. Alcohol/substance abuse counseling, chaplain/spiritual director, career counseling, student employment services, financial aid counseling, personal counseling, placement for graduates.

Contact. E-mail: info@newbury.edu
Phone: (617) 730-7007 Toll-free number: (800) 639-2879
Fax: (617) 731-9618
Joseph Chillo, Vice President for Enrollment Management, Newbury College, 129 Fisher Avenue, Brookline, MA 02445

Nichols College

Dudley, Massachusetts — **CB member**
www.nichols.edu — **CB code: 3666**

- Private 4-year business and liberal arts college
- Residential campus in small town
- 1,285 degree-seeking undergraduates: 14% part-time, 42% women, 5% African American, 2% Asian American, 4% Hispanic American, 1% international
- 203 degree-seeking graduate students
- 65% of applicants admitted
- SAT or ACT (ACT writing recommended), application essay required
- 38% graduate within 6 years

General. Founded in 1815. Regionally accredited. **Degrees:** 192 bachelor's, 7 associate awarded; master's offered. **ROTC:** Army. **Location:** 20 miles from Worcester, 50 miles from Boston. **Calendar:** Semester, limited summer session. **Full-time faculty:** 37 total; 57% have terminal degrees, 5% minority, 32% women. **Part-time faculty:** 32 total; 19% have terminal degrees, 3% minority, 44% women. **Class size:** 39% < 20, 61% 20-39, less than 1% 50-99. **Special facilities:** Policy and cultural institute, observatory.

Freshman class profile. 2,307 applied, 1,501 admitted, 389 enrolled.

Mid 50% test scores			
SAT critical reading:	410-500	GPA 3.0-3.49:	23%
SAT math:	420-520	GPA 2.0-2.99:	69%
SAT writing:	420-500	Return as sophomores:	66%
ACT composite:	16-20	Out-of-state:	41%
GPA 3.75 or higher:	1%	Live on campus:	93%
GPA 3.50-3.74:	6%	International:	1%

Basis for selection. Secondary school record most important; test scores important, followed by recommendations, essay and interview. Interview recommended. **Homeschooled:** Statement describing homeschool structure and mission, state high school equivalency certificate, interview, letter of recommendation (nonparent) required.

High school preparation. College-preparatory program recommended. 16 units required. Required and recommended units include English 4, mathematics 3-4, social studies 2, science 2-3 (laboratory 2-3), foreign language 2 and academic electives 5. 2 foreign language recommended for liberal arts majors.

2008-2009 Annual costs. Tuition/fees: $26,970. Room/board: $9,100. Books/supplies: $1,050. Personal expenses: $1,200.

2008-2009 Financial aid. Need-based: 379 full-time freshmen applied for aid; 366 were judged to have need; 366 of these received aid. Average need met was 76%. Average scholarship/grant was $14,123; average loan $3,668. 55% of total undergraduate aid awarded as scholarships/grants, 45% as loans/jobs. **Non-need-based:** Awarded to 1,017 full-time undergraduates, including 70 freshmen. Scholarships awarded for academics, alumni affiliation, ROTC.

Application procedures. Admission: Priority date 3/1; no deadline. $25 fee, may be waived for applicants with need, free for online applicants. Admission notification on a rolling basis beginning on or about 10/1. Must reply by May 1 or within 2 week(s) if notified thereafter. **Financial aid:** Priority date 3/1, closing date 6/1. FAFSA required. Applicants notified on a rolling basis starting 2/26; must reply within 4 week(s) of notification.

Academics. Special study options: Combined bachelor's/graduate degree, cooperative education, distance learning, double major, honors, independent study, internships, liberal arts/career combination, semester at sea, study abroad, teacher certification program, Washington semester. **Credit/placement by examination:** AP, CLEP. 30 credit hours maximum toward bachelor's degree. **Support services:** Learning center, reduced course load, remedial instruction, study skills assistance, tutoring, writing center.

Majors. Business: Accounting, business admin, communications, finance, human resources, international, management information systems, managerial economics, marketing, training/development. **Education:** Secondary. **History:** General. **Legal studies:** General. **Math:** General. **Parks/recreation:** Sports admin. **Protective services:** Criminal justice. **Psychology:** General. **Social sciences:** Economics. **Other:** Arts and entertainment management.

Most popular majors. Business/marketing 88%, psychology 6%.

Computing on campus. 69 workstations in library, computer center, student center. Dormitories wired for high-speed internet access and linked to campus network. Commuter students can connect to campus network. Online course registration, online library, helpline, repair service, wireless network available.

Student life. Freshman orientation: Mandatory. Preregistration for classes offered. Overnight pre-college summer programs for students and parents. **Housing:** Guaranteed on-campus for all undergraduates. Coed dorms, single-sex dorms, special housing for disabled, apartments, wellness housing available. $250 deposit, deadline 5/1. **Activities:** Campus ministries, drama, literary magazine, radio station, student government, student newspaper, TV station, Institute for American Values, Republican club, Young Democrats, Umoja.

Athletics. NCAA. **Intercollegiate:** Baseball M, basketball, field hockey W, football (tackle) M, golf M, ice hockey, lacrosse, soccer, softball W, tennis. **Intramural:** Basketball, football (non-tackle), racquetball, rugby, softball M, volleyball. **Team name:** Bison.

Student services. Alcohol/substance abuse counseling, chaplain/spiritual director, career counseling, student employment services, financial aid counseling, health services, personal counseling, placement for graduates.

Contact. E-mail: admissions@nichols.edu
Phone: (508) 213-2203 Toll-free number: (800) 470-3379
Fax: (508) 943-9885
Diane Gillespie, Director of Admissions, Nichols College, PO Box 5000, Dudley, MA 01571-5000

Northeastern University

Boston, Massachusetts
www.northeastern.edu
CB member
CB code: 3667

- Private 4-year university
- Residential campus in very large city
- 15,521 degree-seeking undergraduates: 50% women, 5% African American, 8% Asian American, 5% Hispanic American, 6% international
- 5,803 graduate students
- 35% of applicants admitted
- SAT or ACT with writing, application essay required
- 70% graduate within 6 years; 19% enter graduate study

General. Founded in 1898. Regionally accredited. Several additional suburban campuses. **Degrees:** 2,926 bachelor's awarded; master's, doctoral, first professional offered. **ROTC:** Army, Naval, Air Force. **Calendar:** Semester, extensive summer session. **Full-time faculty:** 967 total; 15% minority, 38% women. **Part-time faculty:** 411 total; 12% minority, 52% women. **Class size:** 49% < 20, 32% 20-39, 9% 40-49, 7% 50-99, 2% >100. **Special facilities:** African-American institute, science engineering research center, health sciences center, marine science center, center for subsurfacing and imaging systems, institute of chemical and biological analysis, research vessel.

Freshman class profile. 35,948 applied, 12,592 admitted, 2,923 enrolled.

Mid 50% test scores			
SAT critical reading:	570-660	Rank in top tenth:	42%
SAT math:	600-680	Return as sophomores:	93%
ACT composite:	25-29	Out-of-state:	67%
Rank in top quarter:	77%	Live on campus:	96%
		International:	6%

Basis for selection. Academic achievement as measured by grades, quality of classes, test scores, class rank most important. Recommendations, personal statement, school and community activities also important. Portfolios/auditions required for art and design, music technology programs. **Homeschooled:** Transcript of courses and grades required. Students should submit comprehensive outline of academic curriculum, list of textbooks, special projects and activities.

High school preparation. 17 units required. Required and recommended units include English 4, mathematics 3-4, social studies 2, history 2, science 3-4 (laboratory 2-4) and foreign language 2-4. Each department and college of university may have more specific recommendations for additional preparation.

2008-2009 Annual costs. Tuition/fees: $33,721. Room/board: $11,940. Books/supplies: $900. Personal expenses: $900.

2008-2009 Financial aid. Need-based: 54% of total undergraduate aid awarded as scholarships/grants, 46% as loans/jobs. **Non-need-based:** Scholarships awarded for academics, athletics, minority status.

Application procedures. Admission: Closing date 1/15 (postmark date). $75 fee, may be waived for applicants with need. Admission notification 4/1. Must reply by May 1 or within 4 week(s) if notified thereafter. **Financial aid:** Closing date 2/15. FAFSA, CSS PROFILE required. Applicants notified on a rolling basis starting 2/15; must reply by 5/1.

Academics. Special study options: Accelerated study, combined bachelor's/graduate degree, cooperative education, cross-registration, distance learning, double major, ESL, exchange student, honors, independent study, internships, liberal arts/career combination, semester at sea, student-designed major, study abroad, teacher certification program, Washington semester. International cooperative experience. **Credit/placement by examination:** AP, CLEP, IB, institutional tests. **Support services:** Learning center, preadmission summer program, reduced course load, remedial instruction, study skills assistance, tutoring, writing center.

Majors. Architecture: Architecture. **Biology:** General, biochemistry, marine. **Business:** General, accounting, entrepreneurial studies, finance, human resources, international, logistics, management information systems, management science, marketing, operations. **Communications:** General, broadcast journalism, journalism, public relations. **Computer sciences:** General, computer science. **Conservation:** Environmental studies. **Education:** General, art, biology, chemistry, elementary, English, foreign languages, history, mathematics, music, social studies. **Engineering:** General, chemical, civil, computer, electrical, mechanical. **Engineering technology:** Computer, electrical, mechanical. **Health:** Athletic training, audiology/speech pathology, clinical lab science, clinical lab technology, medical records admin, nursing (RN), recreational therapy, speech pathology. **History:** General. **Interdisciplinary:** Global studies, neuroscience. **Liberal arts:** Arts/sciences. **Math:** General. **Parks/recreation:** Health/fitness. **Philosophy/religion:** Philosophy. **Physical sciences:** Chemistry, geology, physics. **Protective services:** Criminal justice, police science, security services. **Psychology:** General. **Social sciences:** General, anthropology, economics, international relations, political science, sociology. **Visual/performing arts:** General, art, art history/conservation, commercial/advertising art, design, dramatic, music history, music management, music performance, studio arts.

Most popular majors. Business/marketing 25%, communications/journalism 7%, engineering/engineering technologies 14%, health sciences 9%, security/protective services 8%, social sciences 10%, visual/performing arts 7%.

Computing on campus. 1,993 workstations in dormitories, library, computer center, student center. Dormitories wired for high-speed internet access and linked to campus network. Commuter students can connect to campus network. Online course registration, online library, helpline, student web hosting, wireless network available.

Student life. Freshman orientation: Mandatory, $100 fee. Preregistration for classes offered. **Housing:** Guaranteed on-campus for freshmen. Coed dorms, special housing for disabled, apartments, fraternity/sorority housing, wellness housing available. $400 deposit, deadline 5/1. Honors, wellness, quiet, living and learning, international, multicultural, leadership, college/program housing, and other academic themes available. **Activities:** Bands, choral groups, dance, drama, international student organizations, literary magazine, music ensembles, musical theater, radio station, student government, student newspaper, symphony orchestra, TV station, Over 250 student organizations available.

Athletics. NCAA. **Intercollegiate:** Baseball M, basketball, cross-country, diving W, field hockey W, football (tackle) M, ice hockey, rowing (crew), soccer, swimming W, track and field, volleyball W. **Intramural:** Basketball, ice hockey, racquetball, soccer, softball, squash, tennis, volleyball, water polo. **Team name:** Huskies.

Student services. Alcohol/substance abuse counseling, chaplain/spiritual director, career counseling, services for economically disadvantaged, student employment services, financial aid counseling, health services, legal services, minority student services, personal counseling, placement for graduates, women's services. **Physically disabled:** Services for visually, speech, hearing impaired. **Learning disabled:** Comprehensive services available.

Contact. E-mail: admissions@neu.edu
Phone: (617) 373-2200 Fax: (617) 373-8780
Ronne Turner, Dean of Undergraduate Admissions, Northeastern University, 360 Huntington Avenue, 150 Richards Hall, Boston, MA 02115-9959

Pine Manor College

Chestnut Hill, Massachusetts
www.pmc.edu
CB member
CB code: 3689

- Private 4-year liberal arts college for women
- Residential campus in very large city
- 163 degree-seeking undergraduates: 1% part-time, 100% women, 45% African American, 6% Asian American, 20% Hispanic American, 1% Native American, 6% international
- 33 degree-seeking graduate students
- 70% of applicants admitted
- SAT or ACT, application essay required
- 55% graduate within 6 years

General. Founded in 1911. Regionally accredited. **Degrees:** 51 bachelor's, 1 associate awarded; master's offered. **ROTC:** Army, Air Force. **Location:** 5 miles from Boston. **Calendar:** Semester, limited summer session. **Full-time faculty:** 32 total; 75% have terminal degrees, 12% minority, 75% women. **Part-time faculty:** 44 total; 57% have terminal degrees, 14% minority, 75% women. **Class size:** 83% < 20, 17% 20-39. **Special facilities:** Center for inclusive leadership and social responsibility, child study center.

Freshman class profile. 635 applied, 443 admitted, 163 enrolled.

Mid 50% test scores			
SAT critical reading:	340-450	ACT composite:	15-17
SAT math:	340-460	Out-of-state:	26%
		Live on campus:	93%

Basis for selection. School achievement record, test scores, GPA, and recommendations important. Rolling deadline for SAT/ACT score submission. Interview recommended. **Learning Disabled:** Students may be required to submit learning disability documentation.

High school preparation. Required units include English 4, mathematics 3, social studies 2, science 3 and foreign language 2.

2008-2009 Annual costs. Tuition/fees: $18,957. Room/board: $11,115. Books/supplies: $800. Personal expenses: $1,000.

2007-2008 Financial aid. Non-need-based: Scholarships awarded for academics, alumni affiliation, leadership.

Application procedures. Admission: No deadline. $25 fee, may be waived for applicants with need, free for online applicants. Admission notification on a rolling basis. Must reply by May 1 or within 2 week(s) if notified thereafter. **Financial aid:** Priority date 5/1; no closing date. FAFSA required. Applicants notified on a rolling basis starting 3/1; must reply by 5/1 or within 2 week(s) of notification.

Academics. All students required to participate in internship program. All students receive comprehensive advising. **Special study options:** Cross-registration, double major, honors, independent study, internships, liberal arts/career combination, semester at sea, student-designed major, study abroad, teacher certification program, Washington semester. Students with sophomore status or higher eligible to take courses offered by Marine Studies Consortium. **Credit/placement by examination:** AP, CLEP, IB, institutional tests. 24 credit hours maximum toward bachelor's degree. **Support services:** Learning center, reduced course load, study skills assistance, tutoring, writing center.

Majors. Biology: General. **Business:** Business admin. **Communications:** Media studies. **History:** General. **Liberal arts:** Arts/sciences. **Psychology:** General. **Social sciences:** Political science. **Visual/performing arts:** General.

Most popular majors. Biology 18%, business/marketing 19%, psychology 26%, visual/performing arts 11%.

Computing on campus. 108 workstations in dormitories, library, computer center, student center. Dormitories wired for high-speed internet access and linked to campus network. Commuter students can connect to campus network. Online course registration, helpline, repair service available.

Student life. Freshman orientation: Mandatory, $150 fee. Preregistration for classes offered. Held in June and September. **Housing:** Guaranteed on-campus for freshmen. Wellness housing available. $250 nonrefundable deposit. Quiet residence halls available. **Activities:** Choral groups, dance, drama, literary magazine, radio station, student government, Ladies of Various Ebony Shades, African American/Latina/Asian/Native American and All club, Alianza Latina, bisexuals/gays/lesbians and allies in diversity club, Cape Verdean student alliance, dance ensemble, student government association, student health advisory board, Imani Christian club, Camerata singers.

Athletics. NCAA. **Intercollegiate:** Basketball W, cross-country W, lacrosse W, soccer W, softball W, tennis W, volleyball W. **Team name:** Gators.

Student services. Alcohol/substance abuse counseling, career counseling, services for economically disadvantaged, student employment services, financial aid counseling, health services, minority student services, personal counseling, placement for graduates, women's services.

Contact. E-mail: admission@pmc.edu
Phone: (617) 731-7104 Toll-free number: (800) 762-1357
Fax: (617) 731-7102
Robin Engel, Dean of Admissions and Financial Aid, Pine Manor College, 400 Heath Street, Chestnut Hill, MA 02467

Regis College

Weston, Massachusetts — **CB member**
www.regiscollege.edu — **CB code: 3723**

- Private 4-year nursing and liberal arts college affiliated with Roman Catholic Church
- Residential campus in large town
- 991 degree-seeking undergraduates: 22% part-time, 86% women, 20% African American, 6% Asian American, 11% Hispanic American, 2% international
- 599 degree-seeking graduate students
- 75% of applicants admitted
- SAT or ACT (ACT writing optional), application essay required
- 60% graduate within 6 years; 30% enter graduate study

General. Founded in 1927. Regionally accredited. College founded by Sisters of St. Joseph. **Degrees:** 180 bachelor's, 139 associate awarded; master's, doctoral offered. **ROTC:** Army. **Location:** 12 miles from Boston. **Calendar:** Semester, limited summer session. **Full-time faculty:** 64 total; 72% have terminal degrees, 6% minority, 78% women. **Part-time faculty:** 65 total; 35% have terminal degrees, 6% minority, 85% women. **Class size:** 63% < 20, 35% 20-39, 2% 40-49, less than 1% 50-99. **Special facilities:** Philatelic museum, fine arts center, 2 digital imaging studios, music laboratory with electronic keyboards and computers.

Freshman class profile. 1,549 applied, 1,157 admitted, 237 enrolled.

Mid 50% test scores		GPA 2.0-2.99:	60%
SAT critical reading:	390-490	Rank in top quarter:	43%
SAT math:	400-500	Rank in top tenth:	15%
SAT writing:	400-500	End year in good standing:	75%
ACT composite:	16-21	Return as sophomores:	77%
GPA 3.75 or higher:	6%	Out-of-state:	6%
GPA 3.50-3.74:	3%	Live on campus:	77%
GPA 3.0-3.49:	28%	International:	3%

Basis for selection. All credentials within student's file reviewed. At times, interview or additional grades requested or guidance counselors called. Interview highly recommended. Portfolio recommended for art majors. **Homeschooled:** Statement describing homeschool structure and mission, transcript of courses and grades, letter of recommendation (nonparent) required. **Learning Disabled:** Should apprise Director of Student Disabilities of disability status and document condition to receive appropriate accommodations.

High school preparation. 16 units required. Required units include English 4, mathematics 3, social studies 2, science 2 (laboratory 1), foreign language 2 and academic electives 3.

2008-2009 Annual costs. Tuition/fees: $27,800. Room/board: $11,950. Books/supplies: $1,000. Personal expenses: $1,520.

2008-2009 Financial aid. Need-based: 228 full-time freshmen applied for aid; 212 were judged to have need; 210 of these received aid. Average need met was 62%. Average scholarship/grant was $14,351; average loan $4,267. 66% of total undergraduate aid awarded as scholarships/grants, 34% as loans/jobs. **Non-need-based:** Scholarships awarded for academics, alumni affiliation, leadership, ROTC. **Additional information:** Family tuition discount scholarship; offered during any semester in which 2 or more unmarried, dependent siblings attend full-time.

Application procedures. Admission: No deadline. $50 fee, may be waived for applicants with need. Admission notification on a rolling basis beginning on or about 12/1. Must reply by May 1 or within 2 week(s) if notified thereafter. Students encouraged to apply by January 1. **Financial aid:** Priority date 2/15; no closing date. FAFSA, institutional form required. Applicants notified on a rolling basis starting 3/15; must reply by 5/1 or within 2 week(s) of notification.

Academics. Online tutoring assistance, professional math and writing tutor, and academic skills workshops available. **Special study options:** Accelerated study, combined bachelor's/graduate degree, cross-registration, double major, ESL, exchange student, honors, independent study, internships, liberal arts/career combination, student-designed major, study abroad, teacher certification program, Washington semester. **Credit/placement by examination:** AP, CLEP, IB, SAT, institutional tests. 24 credit hours maximum toward bachelor's degree. **Support services:** Learning center, reduced course load, remedial instruction, study skills assistance, tutoring, writing center.

Majors. Biology: General, biochemistry. **Business:** General. **Communications:** General, public relations. **Computer sciences:** General, computer science. **Education:** Mathematics. **Foreign languages:** Spanish. **Health:** Nursing (RN). **History:** General. **Interdisciplinary:** Museum. **Liberal arts:** Arts/sciences. **Physical sciences:** Chemistry. **Psychology:** General. **Public**

administration: Social work. **Social sciences:** International relations, political science, sociology. **Visual/performing arts:** Dramatic, graphic design. **Other:** Human computer interaction, Law and government.

Most popular majors. Biology 7%, communications/journalism 7%, health sciences 52%, social sciences 10%.

Computing on campus. 196 workstations in library, computer center, student center. Dormitories wired for high-speed internet access and linked to campus network. Commuter students can connect to campus network. Online course registration, online library, helpline, wireless network available.

Student life. Freshman orientation: Mandatory, $195 fee. Preregistration for classes offered. Three 2-day programs in June, July, and August. 2-day program for entire class in September. **Policies:** Must complete series of effective decision-making courses in order to obtain guest privileges. All residences smoke-free. **Housing:** Guaranteed on-campus for all undergraduates. Coed dorms, single-sex dorms, special housing for disabled, wellness housing available. $450 nonrefundable deposit, deadline 5/1. Quiet floors available. **Activities:** Campus ministries, choral groups, dance, drama, international student organizations, literary magazine, music ensembles, Model UN, musical theater, radio station, student government, Asian American, African American, Hispanic, Asian, and Native American organizations; student organization for Latino culture; campus activities board; student government association; student athletic advisory committee.

Athletics. NCAA. **Intercollegiate:** Basketball, diving, field hockey W, lacrosse W, soccer, softball W, swimming, tennis W, track and field W, volleyball W. **Intramural:** Basketball, soccer, softball. **Team name:** Regis Pride.

Student services. Adult student services, alcohol/substance abuse counseling, chaplain/spiritual director, career counseling, services for economically disadvantaged, student employment services, financial aid counseling, health services, minority student services, on-campus daycare, personal counseling, placement for graduates, veterans' counselor. **Physically disabled:** Services for visually, hearing impaired.

Contact. E-mail: admission@regiscollege.edu
Phone: (781) 768-7100 Toll-free number: (866) 438-7344
Fax: (781) 768-7071
Emily Keily, Director of Admission, Regis College, 235 Wellesley Street, Weston, MA 02493-1571

Rhodec International
Quincy, Massachusetts
www.rhodec.edu/us

- For-profit 4-year virtual visual arts college
- Small city
- 154 degree-seeking undergraduates: 100% part-time, 94% women

General. Accredited by DETC. **Degrees:** 5 bachelor's, 22 associate awarded. **Calendar:** Continuous. **Part-time faculty:** 10 total.

Basis for selection. Open admission, but selective for some programs.

2008-2009 Annual costs. $541 to $1,358 per course, depending on number of credits.

Application procedures. Admission: No deadline. No application fee.

Academics. Special study options: Accelerated study, distance learning. **Credit/placement by examination:** CLEP.

Majors. Visual/performing arts: Interior design.

Contact. E-mail: uscontact@rhodec.edu
Phone: (617) 472-4942 Toll-free number: (877) 274-6332
Rhodec International, 59 Coddington Street, Suite 104, Quincy, MA 02169

Salem State College
Salem, Massachusetts **CB member**
www.salemstate.edu **CB code: 3522**

- Public 4-year university
- Commuter campus in large town
- 7,082 degree-seeking undergraduates: 19% part-time, 63% women, 8% African American, 3% Asian American, 7% Hispanic American, 4% international
- 1,457 degree-seeking graduate students
- 55% of applicants admitted
- SAT or ACT (ACT writing optional) required
- 43% graduate within 6 years

General. Founded in 1854. Regionally accredited. **Degrees:** 1,213 bachelor's awarded; master's offered. **ROTC:** Army, Air Force. **Location:** 20 miles from Boston. **Calendar:** Semester, extensive summer session. **Full-time faculty:** 338 total; 9% minority, 51% women. **Part-time faculty:** 433 total; 4% minority, 56% women. **Class size:** 58% < 20, 40% 20-39, 2% 40-49, less than 1% 50-99. **Special facilities:** Media facility, center for creative and performing arts, observatories, glass blowing studio.

Freshman class profile. 6,676 applied, 3,656 admitted, 1,151 enrolled.

Mid 50% test scores		**GPA 2.0-2.99:**	60%
SAT critical reading:	430-540	**Return as sophomores:**	71%
SAT math:	430-540	**Out-of-state:**	4%
GPA 3.75 or higher:	6%	**Live on campus:**	60%
GPA 3.50-3.74:	7%	**International:**	1%
GPA 3.0-3.49:	27%		

Basis for selection. Students with 3.0 GPA and college prep curriculum admitted. Students with less than 3.0 GPA admitted with balancing SAT/ACT scores. Special consideration possible. Some majors require higher GPA. Recommendations considered. Interview recommended. Portfolio required for art applicants. **Homeschooled:** Transcript of courses and grades, state high school equivalency certificate required.

High school preparation. College-preparatory program required. 16 units required; 18 recommended. Required and recommended units include English 4, mathematics 3, social studies 2-3, history 1-2, science 3 (laboratory 2), foreign language 2, computer science 1 and visual/performing arts 1. Additional requirements for some programs.

2008-2009 Annual costs. Tuition/fees: $6,460; $12,600 out-of-state. Room/board: $8,628. Books/supplies: $900. Personal expenses: $1,010.

Application procedures. Admission: No deadline. $25 fee ($40 out-of-state), may be waived for applicants with need. Admission notification on a rolling basis beginning on or about 12/1. Must reply within 30 days. **Financial aid:** Priority date 4/1; no closing date. FAFSA required. Applicants notified on a rolling basis starting 4/1; must reply within 2 week(s) of notification.

Academics. Special study options: Distance learning, double major, ESL, honors, independent study, internships, study abroad, teacher certification program. **Credit/placement by examination:** AP, CLEP, institutional tests. **Support services:** Learning center, pre-admission summer program, reduced course load, remedial instruction, tutoring, writing center.

Majors. Biology: General, biochemistry, ecology, marine. **Business:** Accounting, business admin, entrepreneurial studies, finance, human resources, international, management information systems, managerial economics, marketing. **Communications:** General, advertising, journalism, media studies, public relations. **Computer sciences:** General. **Education:** General, early childhood, elementary, middle, physical, secondary. **Foreign languages:** Comparative lit, Spanish, translation. **Health:** Athletic training, clinical lab science, nuclear medical technology, nursing (RN). **History:** General, American, European, public archives. **Interdisciplinary:** Math/computer science. **Liberal arts:** Arts/sciences. **Math:** General. **Parks/recreation:** General, exercise sciences, health/fitness, sports admin. **Physical sciences:** Chemistry, geology. **Protective services:** Fire services admin, law enforcement admin. **Psychology:** General. **Public administration:** Social work. **Social sciences:** Cartography, economics, geography, political science, sociology. **Visual/performing arts:** Acting, art, art history/conservation, commercial/advertising art, dramatic, drawing, photography, printmaking, sculpture, theater design, theater history.

Most popular majors. Business/marketing 24%, education 12%, health sciences 16%, psychology 6%, security/protective services 8%.

Computing on campus. PC or laptop required. 84 workstations in library, computer center, student center. Dormitories wired for high-speed internet access and linked to campus network. Commuter students can connect to campus network. Online course registration, online library, helpline, repair service, student web hosting, wireless network available.

Student life. Freshman orientation: Mandatory, $85 fee. Preregistration for classes offered. Sessions held prior to start of semester. **Housing:** Coed dorms, wellness housing available. $225 nonrefundable deposit, deadline 6/1. **Activities:** Bands, choral groups, dance, drama, literary magazine, music ensembles, musical theater, radio station, student government, student newspaper, Hillel, women's center, international student association, political science academy, Catholic student community, African American student association, Hispanic American society, student nurses association, criminal justice academy, MASSPIRG.

Athletics. NCAA. **Intercollegiate:** Baseball M, basketball, cross-country, field hockey W, golf M, ice hockey M, lacrosse M, soccer, softball W, tennis, track and field, volleyball W. **Intramural:** Baseball M, basketball, cheerleading W, football (non-tackle), ice hockey, softball W, volleyball. **Team name:** Vikings.

Student services. Adult student services, alcohol/substance abuse counseling, chaplain/spiritual director, career counseling, services for economically disadvantaged, student employment services, financial aid counseling, health services, legal services, minority student services, on-campus daycare, personal counseling, placement for graduates, veterans' counselor, women's services. **Physically disabled:** Services for visually, speech, hearing impaired. **Learning disabled:** Comprehensive services available.

Contact. E-mail: admissions@salemstate.edu
Phone: (978) 542-6200 Fax: (978) 542-6893
Nate Bryant, Assistant Dean of Student Development, Salem State College, 352 Lafayette Street, Salem, MA 01970-5353

School of the Museum of Fine Arts

Boston, Massachusetts
www.smfa.edu **CB code: 3794**

- Private 4-year visual arts college
- Commuter campus in very large city
- 576 degree-seeking undergraduates: 5% part-time, 66% women, 2% African American, 5% Asian American, 6% Hispanic American, 8% international
- 94 degree-seeking graduate students
- 82% of applicants admitted
- Application essay required
- 48% graduate within 6 years

General. Founded in 1876. All degree programs offered in affiliation with Tufts University, and all degree students may join sporting, musical, and other extracurricular activities offered at Tufts. Students may also cross-register at other schools in Boston's ProArts Consortium, including Emerson College, Berklee College of Music, Boston Conservatory, and Boston Architectural Center. Affiliated with the Museum of Fine Arts, Boston. **Degrees:** 157 bachelor's awarded; master's offered. **Location:** One mile from downtown. **Calendar:** Semester, limited summer session. **Full-time faculty:** 52 total; 65% have terminal degrees, 4% minority, 54% women. **Part-time faculty:** 62 total; 56% have terminal degrees, 58% women. **Class size:** 93% < 20, 7% 20-39.

Freshman class profile. 862 applied, 707 admitted, 129 enrolled.

Mid 50% test scores			
SAT critical reading:	510-610	End year in good standing:	84%
SAT math:	460-580	Return as sophomores:	84%
SAT writing:	490-600	Out-of-state:	65%
ACT composite:	20-25	Live on campus:	49%
		International:	5%

Basis for selection. Portfolio, previous schooling, and quality and content of essays important; grades and test scores important for BFA applicants, considered for Studio Diploma applicants. Combined Degree program applicants must apply to the Museum School and Tufts University simultaneously. Scores accepted on a rolling basis after February 1. Test scores not required for Studio Diploma applicants. Portfolio required. Interview available by appointment. **Homeschooled:** Transcript of courses and grades required. Must have graduation date indicating successful completion of program; must be signed and dated by recognized record keeper, which may include outside testing agency, homeschool representative, or parent.

2008-2009 Annual costs. Tuition/fees: $29,612. Room only: $12,500. Books/supplies: $1,500. Personal expenses: $2,000.

2008-2009 Financial aid. Need-based: 92 full-time freshmen applied for aid; 86 were judged to have need; 85 of these received aid. Average need met was 42%. Average scholarship/grant was $10,941; average loan $3,392. 57% of total undergraduate aid awarded as scholarships/grants, 43% as loans/jobs. **Non-need-based:** Awarded to 98 full-time undergraduates, including 23 freshmen. Scholarships awarded for art.

Application procedures. Admission: Priority date 2/1; no deadline. $65 fee, may be waived for applicants with need. Admission notification on a rolling basis beginning on or about 3/15. Must reply by May 1 or within 2 week(s) if notified thereafter. Students may apply early and request early notification of admission. **Financial aid:** Closing date 3/15. FAFSA, institutional form required. Applicants notified by 4/1; must reply by 5/1 or within 2 week(s) of notification.

Academics. Special study options: Combined bachelor's/graduate degree, cross-registration, double major, ESL, exchange student, independent study, internships, liberal arts/career combination, New York semester, student-designed major, study abroad, teacher certification program. 5-year BFA/BA with Tufts University, studio art elective diploma program, optional fifth-year certificate program for Diploma recipients. **Credit/placement by examination:** AP, CLEP. **Support services:** Pre-admission summer program, study skills assistance, writing center.

Majors. Communications technology: Animation/special effects. **Education:** Art. **Visual/performing arts:** Art, ceramics, cinematography, drawing, illustration, metal/jewelry, multimedia, painting, photography, printmaking, sculpture, studio arts. **Other:** Stained glass.

Most popular majors. Visual/performing arts 96%.

Computing on campus. 170 workstations in library, computer center, student center. Dormitories wired for high-speed internet access. Online course registration, wireless network available.

Student life. Freshman orientation: Mandatory, $125 fee. Preregistration for classes offered. Typically held during last week in August, right before beginning of semester. **Housing:** Coed dorms available. $450 nonrefundable deposit, deadline 5/1. **Activities:** Film society, student government, alternative spring break in New Orleans, queer social club, recycling club, voting rally, open studios.

Student services. Adult student services, career counseling, student employment services, financial aid counseling, personal counseling, placement for graduates. **Physically disabled:** Services for hearing impaired.

Contact. E-mail: admissions@smfa.edu
Phone: (617) 369-3626 Toll-free number: (800) 643-6078
Fax: (617) 369-4264
Susan Clain, Dean of Admissions, School of the Museum of Fine Arts, 230 The Fenway, Boston, MA 02115

Simmons College

Boston, Massachusetts **CB member**
www.simmons.edu **CB code: 3761**

- Private 4-year liberal arts college for women
- Residential campus in very large city
- 2,023 degree-seeking undergraduates: 9% part-time, 100% women, 6% African American, 7% Asian American, 4% Hispanic American, 3% international
- 2,873 graduate students
- 55% of applicants admitted
- SAT or ACT (ACT writing optional), application essay required
- 73% graduate within 6 years

General. Founded in 1899. Regionally accredited. **Degrees:** 483 bachelor's awarded; master's, doctoral offered. **ROTC:** Army. **Location:** 2 miles from downtown. **Calendar:** Semester, extensive summer session. **Full-time faculty:** 250 total; 22% minority, 70% women. **Part-time faculty:** 227 total; 10% minority, 73% women. **Class size:** 66% < 20, 26% 20-39, 3% 40-49, 5% 50-99, less than 1% >100. **Special facilities:** Art gallery, technology resource center.

Freshman class profile. 3,222 applied, 1,756 admitted, 391 enrolled.

Mid 50% test scores			
SAT critical reading:	510-600	GPA 2.0-2.99:	33%
SAT math:	500-590	Rank in top quarter:	55%
SAT writing:	520-620	Rank in top tenth:	20%
ACT composite:	22-26	Return as sophomores:	83%
GPA 3.75 or higher:	8%	Out-of-state:	43%
GPA 3.50-3.74:	17%	Live on campus:	90%
GPA 3.0-3.49:	42%	International:	2%

Basis for selection. School achievement record most important. Test scores, 2 recommendations, essay, interview (if available), personal qualities also important. Interests, accomplishments considered. **Homeschooled:** Statement describing homeschool structure and mission, transcript of courses and grades, letter of recommendation (nonparent) required.

High school preparation. College-preparatory program required. 19 units required; 22 recommended. Required and recommended units include English 4, mathematics 3-4, social studies 3-4, history 3, science 3 and foreign language 3-4.

2008-2009 Annual costs. Tuition/fees: $30,000. Room/board: $11,500. Books/supplies: $800. Personal expenses: $1,250.

2008-2009 Financial aid. Need-based: 321 full-time freshmen applied for aid; 277 were judged to have need; 277 of these received aid. Average need met was 63%. Average scholarship/grant was $13,369; average loan $3,863. 67% of total undergraduate aid awarded as scholarships/grants, 33% as loans/jobs. **Non-need-based:** Awarded to 420 full-time undergraduates, including 105 freshmen. Scholarships awarded for academics, alumni affiliation, leadership, minority status.

Application procedures. Admission: Closing date 2/1 (postmark date). $55 fee, may be waived for applicants with need, free for online applicants. Admission notification 4/15. Must reply by May 1 or within 2 week(s) if notified thereafter. **Financial aid:** Priority date 2/15, closing date 3/1. FAFSA required. Applicants notified on a rolling basis starting 3/15; must reply by 5/1 or within 4 week(s) of notification.

Academics. Special study options: Accelerated study, combined bachelor's/graduate degree, cross-registration, double major, dual enrollment of high school students, ESL, exchange student, honors, independent study, internships, liberal arts/career combination, semester at sea, student-designed major, study abroad, teacher certification program, Washington semester. Exchange programs with Mills College, Spelman College, Fisk University, American University, Colleges of the Fenway; double degree programs with Massachusetts College of Pharmacy and Health Sciences and Hebrew College. **Credit/placement by examination:** AP, CLEP, IB, institutional tests. 32 credit hours maximum toward bachelor's degree. **Support services:** Learning center, reduced course load, study skills assistance, tutoring, writing center.

Majors. Area/ethnic studies: African-American, East Asian, women's. **Biology:** General, biochemistry. **Business:** Business admin, finance, management information systems, sales/distribution. **Communications:** General, public relations. **Computer sciences:** General. **Conservation:** General, environmental science. **Education:** General, early childhood, elementary, ESL, middle, secondary, social studies, special. **Foreign languages:** Comparative lit, French, Spanish. **Health:** Nursing (RN), predental, premedicine, prepharmacy. **History:** General. **Interdisciplinary:** Biopsychology, nutrition sciences. **Math:** General. **Philosophy/religion:** Philosophy. **Physical sciences:** Chemistry, physics. **Psychology:** General. **Public administration:** Policy analysis. **Social sciences:** Economics, international relations, political science, sociology. **Visual/performing arts:** Art history/conservation, arts management, commercial/advertising art, graphic design, music history, music performance.

Most popular majors. Business/marketing 9%, communications/journalism 8%, health sciences 30%, psychology 9%, social sciences 15%.

Computing on campus. 350 workstations in dormitories, library, computer center, student center. Dormitories wired for high-speed internet access and linked to campus network. Commuter students can connect to campus network. Online course registration, online library, helpline, wireless network available.

Student life. Freshman orientation: Mandatory. Preregistration for classes offered. **Housing:** Special housing for disabled, wellness housing available. $250 fully refundable deposit, deadline 5/1. Special interest housing available. **Activities:** Choral groups, dance, drama, film society, literary magazine, radio station, student government, student newspaper, Asian student association, black students organization, Organizacion Latino Americana, international multicultural student association, Caribbean culture association, Hillel, Amnesty International, Feminist Union, The Alliance, Students Take Action Now-Darfur (STAND).

Athletics. NCAA. **Intercollegiate:** Basketball W, diving W, field hockey W, lacrosse W, rowing (crew) W, soccer W, softball W, swimming W, tennis W, volleyball W. **Intramural:** Basketball W, diving W, softball W, tennis W, volleyball W. **Team name:** Sharks.

Student services. Adult student services, alcohol/substance abuse counseling, chaplain/spiritual director, career counseling, student employment services, financial aid counseling, health services, personal counseling, placement for graduates, veterans' counselor, women's services. **Physically disabled:** Services for visually, speech, hearing impaired.

Contact. E-mail: ugadm@simmons.edu
Phone: (617) 521-2051 Toll-free number: (800) 345-8468
Fax: (617) 521-3190
Catherine Capolupo, Director of Undergraduate Admissions, Simmons College, 300 The Fenway, Boston, MA 02115-5898

Smith College

Northampton, Massachusetts — **CB member**
www.smith.edu — **CB code: 3762**

- Private 4-year liberal arts college for women
- Residential campus in large town
- 2,610 degree-seeking undergraduates: 1% part-time, 100% women, 7% African American, 13% Asian American, 7% Hispanic American, 1% Native American, 7% international
- 489 degree-seeking graduate students
- 48% of applicants admitted
- Application essay required
- 88% graduate within 6 years

General. Founded in 1871. Regionally accredited. **Degrees:** 708 bachelor's awarded; master's, doctoral offered. **ROTC:** Army, Air Force. **Location:** 35 miles from Hartford, Connecticut; 90 miles from Boston. **Calendar:** Semester. **Full-time faculty:** 278 total; 98% have terminal degrees, 16% minority, 54% women. **Part-time faculty:** 27 total; 89% have terminal degrees, 7% minority, 48% women. **Class size:** 69% < 20, 24% 20-39, 3% 40-49, 4% 50-99, less than 1% >100. **Special facilities:** Physiology and horticultural laboratories, printmaking studio, darkroom and sculpture (including bronze casting studio) facilities, dance, theater and television studios, electronic music studio, recital hall, digital design studio, animal care facilities, electron microscopes, on-campus elementary school, multimedia language lab, greenhouses, astronomy observatories.

Freshman class profile. 3,771 applied, 1,800 admitted, 643 enrolled.

Mid 50% test scores			
SAT critical reading:	600-710	Rank in top quarter:	91%
SAT math:	570-680	Rank in top tenth:	64%
SAT writing:	590-700	End year in good standing:	94%
ACT composite:	25-31	Return as sophomores:	90%
GPA 3.75 or higher:	56%	Out-of-state:	83%
GPA 3.50-3.74:	32%	Live on campus:	100%
GPA 3.0-3.49:	12%	International:	7%

Basis for selection. Secondary school record, including GPA and difficulty of courses, recommendations most important. Class rank, essay, school and community activities and test scores also important. Interview strongly recommended, may be conducted off-campus by alumna. **Homeschooled:** Statement describing homeschool structure and mission, transcript of courses and grades, letter of recommendation (nonparent) required. Submit portfolio and evaluation of coursework and sample of short research or analytical paper with evaluator's remarks.

High school preparation. College-preparatory program recommended. 16 units recommended. Recommended units include English 4, mathematics 3, history 2, science 3 (laboratory 3) and foreign language 3. 3 units of 1 foreign language or 2 each of 2 languages recommended.

2009-2010 Annual costs. Tuition/fees (projected): $37,848. Room/board: $12,652. Books/supplies: $800. Personal expenses: $1,550.

2007-2008 Financial aid. Need-based: 496 full-time freshmen applied for aid; 396 were judged to have need; 396 of these received aid. Average need met was 100%. Average scholarship/grant was $26,530; average loan $3,538. 81% of total undergraduate aid awarded as scholarships/grants, 19% as loans/jobs. **Non-need-based:** Awarded to 171 full-time undergraduates, including 32 freshmen. Scholarships awarded for academics, state residency. **Additional information:** Financial aid policy guarantees to meet full financial need, as calculated by college, of all admitted students.

Application procedures. Admission: Closing date 1/15 (postmark date). $60 fee, may be waived for applicants with need, free for online applicants. Notification by early April. Must reply by May 1 or within 2 week(s) if notified thereafter. **Financial aid:** Closing date 2/15. FAFSA, CSS PROFILE required. Applicants notified by 4/1; must reply by 5/1.

Academics. Academic honor code; writing course required in first year. **Special study options:** Accelerated study, cross-registration, double major, exchange student, honors, independent study, internships, semester at sea, student-designed major, study abroad, teacher certification program, Washington semester. Member of Five College Consortium, program in engineering and technology, engineering science program within liberal arts curriculum leading to BS degree, post-baccalaureate certificate in American studies (available to international students). **Credit/placement by examination:** AP, CLEP, IB, institutional tests. 32 credit hours maximum toward bachelor's degree. **Support services:** Learning center, study skills assistance, tutoring, writing center.

Majors. Area/ethnic studies: African-American, American, Asian, Latin American, women's. **Biology:** General, biochemistry. **Computer sciences:** Computer science. **Education:** General. **Engineering:** General, biomedical, chemical, civil, computer, electrical, environmental, mechanical, mechanics, science. **Foreign languages:** Ancient Greek, classics, comparative lit, East Asian, French, German, Italian, Latin, Portuguese, Russian, Spanish. **History:** General. **Interdisciplinary:** Ancient studies, medieval/

Renaissance, neuroscience. **Math:** General. **Philosophy/religion:** Philosophy, religion. **Physical sciences:** Astronomy, astrophysics, chemistry, geology, physics. **Psychology:** General. **Social sciences:** Anthropology, economics, political science, sociology. **Visual/performing arts:** Art, art history/conservation, dance, dramatic, film/cinema, studio arts.

Most popular majors. Area/ethnic studies 9%, English 6%, foreign language 13%, psychology 9%, social sciences 23%, visual/performing arts 11%.

Computing on campus. 624 workstations in dormitories, library, computer center, student center. Dormitories wired for high-speed internet access and linked to campus network. Commuter students can connect to campus network. Online course registration, online library, helpline, repair service, student web hosting, wireless network available.

Student life. Freshman orientation: Mandatory. Program held 4-5 days prior to beginning of classes; includes parent day. **Policies:** Each residence self-governed within framework of college regulations. Residents determine house responsibilities. **Housing:** Guaranteed on-campus for all undergraduates. Cooperative housing available. $200 nonrefundable deposit, deadline 5/1. French-speaking house, senior house, nontraditional age house, apartment complexes for juniors and seniors available. **Activities:** Bands, campus ministries, choral groups, dance, drama, international student organizations, literary magazine, music ensembles, Model UN, musical theater, radio station, student government, student newspaper, TV station, service organizations, women's resource center, black student alliance, Asian student association, Hillel, Newman Club, Christian council, international relations club, Latina organization, Native American organization.

Athletics. NCAA. **Intercollegiate:** Basketball W, cross-country W, diving W, equestrian W, field hockey W, lacrosse W, rowing (crew) W, skiing W, soccer W, softball W, squash W, swimming W, tennis W, track and field W, volleyball W. **Intramural:** Basketball W, soccer W. **Team name:** Pioneers.

Student services. Adult student services, alcohol/substance abuse counseling, chaplain/spiritual director, career counseling, services for economically disadvantaged, student employment services, financial aid counseling, health services, minority student services, on-campus daycare, personal counseling, placement for graduates, women's services. **Physically disabled:** Services for visually, speech, hearing impaired.

Contact. E-mail: admission@smith.edu
Phone: (413) 585-2500 Fax: (413) 585-2527
Debra Shaver, Director of Admission, Smith College, 7 College Lane, Northampton, MA 01063

Springfield College

Springfield, Massachusetts — **CB member**
www.springfieldcollege.edu — **CB code: 3763**

- Private 4-year health science and liberal arts college
- Residential campus in small city
- 2,216 degree-seeking undergraduates: 1% part-time, 47% women, 4% African American, 1% Asian American, 2% Hispanic American
- 75% of applicants admitted
- SAT or ACT with writing, application essay required
- 65% graduate within 6 years; 30% enter graduate study

General. Founded in 1885. Regionally accredited. Adult weekend programs at 11 sites across the country. **Degrees:** 969 bachelor's awarded; master's, doctoral offered. **ROTC:** Army, Air Force. **Location:** 90 miles from Boston; 26 miles from Hartford, Connecticut. **Calendar:** Semester, limited summer session. **Full-time faculty:** 176 total; 81% have terminal degrees, 10% minority, 44% women. **Part-time faculty:** 159 total; 9% minority, 50% women. **Class size:** 46% < 20, 52% 20-39, less than 1% 40-49, less than 1% 50-99, less than 1% >100. **Special facilities:** 57-acre campground and outdoor adventure area.

Freshman class profile. 2,105 applied, 1,573 admitted, 618 enrolled.

Mid 50% test scores		**End year in good standing:**	95%
SAT critical reading:	450-540	**Return as sophomores:**	82%
SAT math:	460-570	**Out-of-state:**	72%
Rank in top quarter:	38%	**Live on campus:**	98%
Rank in top tenth:	13%		

Basis for selection. School achievement record, essay, extracurricular activities, personal references, and test scores important. Portfolio required of art majors. **Homeschooled:** Statement describing homeschool structure and mission, transcript of courses and grades, letter of recommendation (nonparent) required.

High school preparation. College-preparatory program required. 16 units required. Required and recommended units include English 4, mathematics 3, social studies 2, history 1, science 3 (laboratory 2) and foreign language 3. Emphasis on science for majors in allied health fields.

2008-2009 Annual costs. Tuition/fees: $25,520. Room/board: $9,820. Books/supplies: $900. Personal expenses: $1,200.

2007-2008 Financial aid. Additional information: Co-operative education program available to students after freshman year.

Application procedures. Admission: Priority date 3/1; deadline 4/1 (postmark date). $50 fee, may be waived for applicants with need. Admission notification on a rolling basis beginning on or about 12/1. Must reply by May 1 or within 2 week(s) if notified thereafter. Application closing date for athletic training, physical therapy majors 12/1; closing date for physician assistant and occupational therapy majors 1/15. **Financial aid:** Priority date 3/15; no closing date. FAFSA, institutional form, CSS PROFILE required. Applicants notified on a rolling basis starting 3/15; must reply by 5/1 or within 2 week(s) of notification.

Academics. Emphasis on practical fieldwork experiences to supplement classroom learning. **Special study options:** Combined bachelor's/graduate degree, cooperative education, cross-registration, double major, ESL, independent study, internships, liberal arts/career combination, study abroad, teacher certification program, weekend college. **Credit/placement by examination:** AP, CLEP, IB, SAT, ACT, institutional tests. 30 credit hours maximum toward bachelor's degree. **Support services:** Learning center, reduced course load, study skills assistance, tutoring, writing center.

Majors. Biology: General. **Business:** Business admin. **Computer sciences:** General, computer graphics, information systems. **Conservation:** General, environmental studies. **Education:** Art, early childhood, elementary, health, physical, secondary, special. **Health:** Art therapy, athletic training, clinical lab science, clinical lab technology, EMT paramedic, health care admin, medical records admin, physician assistant, predental, recreational therapy. **History:** General. **Interdisciplinary:** Biological/physical sciences. **Legal studies:** Prelaw. **Liberal arts:** Arts/sciences. **Math:** General. **Parks/recreation:** Exercise sciences, facilities management, health/fitness, sports admin. **Protective services:** Law enforcement admin. **Psychology:** General. **Public administration:** Community org/advocacy, human services. **Social sciences:** Political science, sociology. **Visual/performing arts:** Art, dance.

Computing on campus. 235 workstations in dormitories, library, computer center, student center. Dormitories wired for high-speed internet access and linked to campus network. Commuter students can connect to campus network. Online course registration, helpline, wireless network available.

Student life. Freshman orientation: Mandatory, $110 fee. Four-day program immediately preceding fall semester. **Housing:** Guaranteed on-campus for all undergraduates. Coed dorms, single-sex dorms, special housing for disabled, apartments, wellness housing available. **Activities:** Jazz band, campus ministries, choral groups, dance, drama, international student organizations, literary magazine, music ensembles, musical theater, radio station, student government, student newspaper, environmental club, Fellowship of Christian Athletes, Habitat for Humanity, Hillel, Newman community, outreach committee, student society for cultural diversity, students against violence everywhere, international student organization.

Athletics. NCAA. **Intercollegiate:** Baseball M, basketball, cross-country, diving, field hockey W, football (tackle) M, golf, gymnastics, lacrosse, soccer, softball W, swimming, tennis, track and field, volleyball, wrestling M. **Intramural:** Basketball, bowling, field hockey, football (non-tackle), golf, handball, lacrosse, racquetball, soccer, softball, swimming, tennis, track and field, volleyball, wrestling M. **Team name:** Pride.

Student services. Adult student services, alcohol/substance abuse counseling, chaplain/spiritual director, career counseling, student employment services, financial aid counseling, health services, minority student services, on-campus daycare, personal counseling, placement for graduates, veterans' counselor, women's services. **Physically disabled:** Services for visually, speech, hearing impaired.

Contact. E-mail: admissions@spfldcol.edu
Phone: (413) 748-3136 Toll-free number: (800) 343-1257
Fax: (413) 748-3694
Richard Veres, Director of Admissions, Springfield College, 263 Alden Street, Springfield, MA 01109

Stonehill College

Easton, Massachusetts — **CB member**
www.stonehill.edu — **CB code: 3770**

- Private 4-year liberal arts college affiliated with Roman Catholic Church
- Residential campus in large town

- 2,408 degree-seeking undergraduates: 2% part-time, 60% women, 2% African American, 1% Asian American, 4% Hispanic American
- 45% of applicants admitted
- Application essay required
- 82% graduate within 6 years; 33% enter graduate study

General. Founded in 1948. Regionally accredited. **Degrees:** 588 bachelor's awarded. **ROTC:** Army. **Location:** 19 miles from Boston, 25 miles from Providence. **Calendar:** Semester, limited summer session. **Full-time faculty:** 148 total; 84% have terminal degrees, 7% minority, 40% women. **Part-time faculty:** 94 total; 40% have terminal degrees, 6% minority, 38% women. **Class size:** 43% < 20, 56% 20-39, less than 1% 40-49, less than 1% 50-99. **Special facilities:** Observatory, shovel museum.

Freshman class profile. 6,838 applied, 3,080 admitted, 634 enrolled.

Mid 50% test scores		**GPA 2.0-2.99:**	11%
SAT critical reading:	550-640	**Rank in top quarter:**	93%
SAT math:	550-650	**Rank in top tenth:**	57%
ACT composite:	24-28	**End year in good standing:**	94%
GPA 3.75 or higher:	22%	**Return as sophomores:**	89%
GPA 3.50-3.74:	31%	**Out-of-state:**	52%
GPA 3.0-3.49:	36%	**Live on campus:**	97%

Basis for selection. Competitive high school course profile, grades, weighted GPA, class rank, high school profile, counselor recommendation important. **Homeschooled:** Statement describing homeschool structure and mission, transcript of courses and grades required. Common Application Home Schooled Supplement form required.

High school preparation. College-preparatory program required. 16 units required; 20 recommended. Required and recommended units include English 4, mathematics 3-4, history 3, science 1-3 (laboratory 1-2), foreign language 2-3 and academic electives 3. Foreign language units should be in same language. 3 combined units in history, political science, social science required. Math units should consist of algegra I, algebra II, and geometry. Additional units in science and math recommended for science applicants. Additional math units recommended for business applicants.

2008-2009 Annual costs. Tuition/fees: $30,150. Room/board: $11,830.

2008-2009 Financial aid. Need-based: 541 full-time freshmen applied for aid; 427 were judged to have need; 427 of these received aid. Average need met was 80%. Average scholarship/grant was $18,275; average loan $3,755. 68% of total undergraduate aid awarded as scholarships/grants, 32% as loans/jobs. **Non-need-based:** Awarded to 711 full-time undergraduates, including 227 freshmen. Scholarships awarded for academics, athletics, ROTC.

Application procedures. Admission: Closing date 1/15 (postmark date). $60 fee, may be waived for applicants with need. Admission notification 4/1. Admission notification on a rolling basis. Must reply by 5/1. **Financial aid:** Priority date 2/1; no closing date. FAFSA, CSS PROFILE required. Applicants notified by 4/1; must reply by 5/1.

Academics. Special study options: Cross-registration, double major, dual enrollment of high school students, honors, independent study, internships, liberal arts/career combination, New York semester, student-designed major, study abroad, teacher certification program, Washington semester. Full-semester international internship sites in Dublin, Geneva, London, Madrid, and Paris; 3-2 computer engineering BA/BS program with University of Notre Dame, Indiana; Stonehill Undergraduate Research Experience (SURE) program. **Credit/placement by examination:** AP, CLEP, IB, SAT, ACT, institutional tests. **Support services:** Learning center, pre-admission summer program, reduced course load, study skills assistance, tutoring, writing center.

Majors. Area/ethnic studies: American, women's. **Biology:** General, biochemistry. **Business:** Accounting, business admin, finance, international, marketing. **Communications:** General. **Computer sciences:** Computer science. **Conservation:** Environmental studies. **Education:** Early childhood, elementary. **Foreign languages:** General. **Health:** Health care admin. **History:** General. **Interdisciplinary:** Neuroscience. **Math:** General. **Philosophy/religion:** Philosophy, religion. **Physical sciences:** Chemistry, physics. **Psychology:** General. **Public administration:** General. **Social sciences:** Criminology, economics, international relations, political science, sociology. **Visual/performing arts:** Studio arts.

Most popular majors. Biology 6%, business/marketing 22%, communications/journalism 9%, education 7%, English 7%, psychology 11%, social sciences 15%.

Computing on campus. 346 workstations in library, computer center, student center. Dormitories wired for high-speed internet access and linked to campus network. Commuter students can connect to campus network. Online course registration, online library, helpline, repair service, student web hosting, wireless network available.

Student life. Freshman orientation: Mandatory. Preregistration for classes offered. Two-day program in June. **Housing:** Guaranteed on-campus for all undergraduates. Coed dorms, single-sex dorms, special housing for disabled, wellness housing available. $500 nonrefundable deposit, deadline 5/1. Special interest housing proposals considered for groups. **Activities:** Pep band, campus ministries, choral groups, dance, drama, film society, literary magazine, music ensembles, musical theater, radio station, student government, student newspaper, College Republicans, College Democrats, PRIDE, BACCHUS, cultural committee, Habitat for Humanity, Circle K, politics society, environmental club, free thought alliance club.

Athletics. NCAA. **Intercollegiate:** Baseball M, basketball, cross-country, equestrian W, field hockey W, football (tackle) M, ice hockey M, lacrosse W, soccer, softball W, tennis, track and field, volleyball W. **Intramural:** Basketball, field hockey, football (non-tackle), handball, racquetball, soccer, softball, tennis, volleyball. **Team name:** Skyhawks.

Student services. Adult student services, alcohol/substance abuse counseling, chaplain/spiritual director, career counseling, services for economically disadvantaged, student employment services, financial aid counseling, health services, minority student services, on-campus daycare, personal counseling, placement for graduates, women's services. **Physically disabled:** Services for visually, speech, hearing impaired.

Contact. E-mail: admissions@stonehill.edu
Phone: (508) 565-1373 Fax: (508) 565-1545
Brian Murphy, Dean of Admissions and Enrollment, Stonehill College, 320 Washington Street, Easton, MA 02357-0100

Suffolk University

Boston, Massachusetts — **CB member**
www.suffolk.edu — **CB code: 3771**

- Private 4-year university
- Commuter campus in very large city
- 5,639 degree-seeking undergraduates: 8% part-time, 56% women, 3% African American, 6% Asian American, 6% Hispanic American, 10% international
- 3,502 degree-seeking graduate students
- 82% of applicants admitted
- SAT or ACT with writing required
- 55% graduate within 6 years; 23% enter graduate study

General. Founded in 1906. Regionally accredited. Campuses in Spain and Senegal. Branch campuses in Cape Cod, Merrimack, and Franklin. **Degrees:** 1,041 bachelor's, 3 associate awarded; master's, doctoral, first professional offered. **ROTC:** Army. **Location:** Downtown. **Calendar:** Semester, extensive summer session. **Full-time faculty:** 430 total; 91% have terminal degrees, 12% minority, 38% women. **Part-time faculty:** 607 total; 24% have terminal degrees, 10% minority, 42% women. **Class size:** 50% < 20, 48% 20-39, less than 1% 40-49, less than 1% 50-99, less than 1% >100. **Special facilities:** Marine biology station, poetry center, energy research lab, political research center, television studio.

Freshman class profile. 9,171 applied, 7,513 admitted, 1,572 enrolled.

Mid 50% test scores		**GPA 2.0-2.99:**	48%
SAT critical reading:	450-550	**Rank in top quarter:**	32%
SAT math:	450-560	**Rank in top tenth:**	11%
SAT writing:	450-560	**End year in good standing:**	85%
ACT composite:	20-24	**Return as sophomores:**	72%
GPA 3.75 or higher:	7%	**Out-of-state:**	39%
GPA 3.50-3.74:	10%	**Live on campus:**	62%
GPA 3.0-3.49:	35%	**International:**	8%

Basis for selection. High school record including courses taken, level of study, class rank, test scores, essay important. Counselor recommendation considered. Interview recommended. Portfolio required for BFA program applicants. **Homeschooled:** Transcript of courses and grades, state high school equivalency certificate, letter of recommendation (nonparent) required. Admission interview highly recommended. Transcript/Record of courses and grades or written evaluation of work required.

High school preparation. College-preparatory program recommended. 17 units required; 22 recommended. Required and recommended units include English 4, mathematics 3-4, history 1-4, science 2-4 (laboratory 1), foreign language 2-3 and academic electives 4.

2008-2009 Annual costs. Tuition/fees: $25,954. Room/board: $13,970. Books/supplies: $1,000. Personal expenses: $2,400.

2008-2009 Financial aid. Need-based: 1,121 full-time freshmen applied for aid; 911 were judged to have need; 905 of these received aid. Average need met was 62%. Average scholarship/grant was $9,755; average loan $3,996. 55% of total undergraduate aid awarded as scholarships/grants, 45% as loans/jobs. **Non-need-based:** Awarded to 1,372 full-time undergraduates, including 393 freshmen. Scholarships awarded for academics, alumni affiliation. **Additional information:** Foreign students may apply for institutional employment awards.

Application procedures. **Admission:** Closing date 3/1. $50 fee, may be waived for applicants with need. Admission notification on a rolling basis beginning on or about 2/5. Must reply by May 1 or within 2 week(s) if notified thereafter. Strongly suggest housing deposit before March 15. Housing awarded on a first-come first-serve basis by date of the admission deposit. Housing deposit refundable in full until May 1. **Financial aid:** Closing date 3/1. FAFSA, institutional form required. Applicants notified on a rolling basis starting 2/5.

Academics. **Special study options:** Accelerated study, combined bachelor's/graduate degree, cooperative education, cross-registration, distance learning, double major, ESL, exchange student, honors, independent study, internships, liberal arts/career combination, study abroad, Washington semester. **Credit/placement by examination:** AP, CLEP, IB, SAT, ACT, institutional tests. 30 credit hours maximum toward associate degree, 30 toward bachelor's. **Support services:** Learning center, pre-admission summer program, reduced course load, remedial instruction, study skills assistance, tutoring, writing center.

Honors college/program. Separate application required. Class rank, GPA, personal essay, interview, and quality of secondary school curriculum, including advanced placement, honors, and other types of accelerated courses, and any other relevant information considered. Applicants from the College of Arts and Sciences and Sawyer Business School will normally meet at least 2 of the following criteria: 3.7 GPA, class rank within upper 10% (if class rank is available), 1300 SAT (exclusive of Writing), or 29 ACT.

Majors. **Area/ethnic studies:** African-American, French, German, women's. **Biology:** General, biochemistry, biomedical sciences, biophysics, environmental, marine, radiobiology. **Business:** General, accounting, business admin, entrepreneurial studies, finance, international, management information systems, marketing, office technology. **Communications:** General, advertising, broadcast journalism, journalism, media studies, organizational, political, public relations. **Communications technology:** General, radio/tv. **Computer sciences:** General, computer science, information systems. **Conservation:** Environmental science. **Education:** General. **Engineering:** Computer, electrical, environmental. **Engineering technology:** Biomedical. **Foreign languages:** General, French, German, Spanish. **History:** General, American, European. **Legal studies:** Paralegal, prelaw. **Liberal arts:** Arts/sciences, humanities. **Math:** General. **Philosophy/religion:** Philosophy. **Physical sciences:** General, chemistry, physics. **Protective services:** Law enforcement admin. **Psychology:** General. **Public administration:** General, policy analysis. **Social sciences:** General, criminology, economics, international economics, international relations, political science, sociology, U.S. government. **Visual/performing arts:** General, acting, art, art history/conservation, arts management, commercial/advertising art, dramatic, film/cinema, interior design, studio arts, theater history.

Most popular majors. Business/marketing 40%, communications/journalism 12%, social sciences 17%, visual/performing arts 6%.

Computing on campus. 539 workstations in dormitories, library, computer center, student center. Dormitories wired for high-speed internet access and linked to campus network. Commuter students can connect to campus network. Online course registration, online library, helpline, wireless network available.

Student life. **Freshman orientation:** Mandatory, $85 fee. Preregistration for classes offered. Three-day orientation held in June and August. **Housing:** Coed dorms, apartments, wellness housing available. $600 fully refundable deposit, deadline 5/1. **Activities:** Jazz band, campus ministries, choral groups, dance, drama, literary magazine, music ensembles, musical theater, radio station, student government, student newspaper, TV station, Islamic cultural society, Newman club, Jewish society, finance committee, student government association, student judiciary review board, Jumpstart Inc., S.O.U.L.S., Best Buddies, Up 'Til Dawn.

Athletics. NCAA. **Intercollegiate:** Baseball M, basketball, cross-country, golf M, ice hockey M, soccer M, softball W, tennis, volleyball W. **Intramural:** Basketball, football (non-tackle), soccer W, table tennis, volleyball. **Team name:** Rams.

Student services. Adult student services, alcohol/substance abuse counseling, chaplain/spiritual director, career counseling, student employment services, financial aid counseling, health services, minority student services, personal counseling, placement for graduates, veterans' counselor, women's services. **Physically disabled:** Services for visually, speech, hearing impaired.

Contact. E-mail: admission@suffolk.edu
Phone: (617) 573-8460 Toll-free number: (800) 678-3365
Fax: (617) 742-4291
John Hamel, Director of Admissions, Suffolk University, 8 Ashburton Place, Boston, MA 02108

Tufts University

Medford, Massachusetts — **CB member**
www.tufts.edu — **CB code: 3901**

- Private 4-year university
- Residential campus in small city
- 5,029 degree-seeking undergraduates: 51% women, 6% African American, 13% Asian American, 6% Hispanic American, 6% international
- 4,604 degree-seeking graduate students
- 26% of applicants admitted
- SAT and SAT Subject Tests or ACT with writing, application essay required
- 92% graduate within 6 years

General. Founded in 1852. Regionally accredited. **Degrees:** 1,407 bachelor's awarded; master's, doctoral, first professional offered. **ROTC:** Army, Naval, Air Force. **Location:** 5 miles from Boston. **Calendar:** Semester, limited summer session. **Full-time faculty:** 640 total; 94% have terminal degrees, 21% minority, 40% women. **Part-time faculty:** 304 total; 46% have terminal degrees, 12% minority, 55% women. **Class size:** 69% < 20, 22% 20-39, 3% 40-49, 4% 50-99, 2% >100. **Special facilities:** Computer-aided design laboratory, arts center, theater in the round, engineering project design center.

Freshman class profile. 15,619 applied, 3,986 admitted, 1,300 enrolled.

Mid 50% test scores			
SAT critical reading:	670-750	Return as sophomores:	97%
SAT math:	670-750	Out-of-state:	77%
SAT writing:	670-760	Live on campus:	100%
ACT composite:	30-33	International:	6%

Basis for selection. School achievement record most important. School recommendation, test scores, character, personality, extracurricular participation, special talents also important. Geographical distribution, alumni relationship, minority status, socioeconomic status all considered. For applicants who submit SAT scores: 2 SAT Subject Tests required of liberal arts applicants; Math 1 or 2 and either physics or chemistry required of engineering applicants. Interview optional but recommended. **Homeschooled:** Transcript of courses and grades required.

High school preparation. Recommended units include English 4, mathematics 4, history 4, science 4 and foreign language 4. 4 math, 2 laboratory science recommended for engineering, math, and science majors.

2008-2009 Annual costs. Tuition/fees: $38,840. Room/board: $10,518.

2008-2009 Financial aid. All financial aid based on need.

Application procedures. **Admission:** Closing date 1/1 (postmark date). $70 fee, may be waived for applicants with need. Admission notification 4/1. Must reply by 5/1. **Financial aid:** Closing date 2/15. FAFSA, CSS PROFILE required. Applicants notified by 4/1; must reply by 5/1.

Academics. **Special study options:** Combined bachelor's/graduate degree, cross-registration, double major, exchange student, independent study, internships, liberal arts/career combination, semester at sea, student-designed major, study abroad, teacher certification program, Washington semester. Experimental college, semester exchange with Lincoln University and Swarthmore College, 3-2 programs with New England Conservatory of Music (BA/BM), School of the Museum of Fine Arts (BA/BFA) European Center in Talloires, France. **Credit/placement by examination:** AP, CLEP, IB, institutional tests. Limit 1 year of credit by acceleration. **Support services:** Learning center, study skills assistance, tutoring.

Majors. **Area/ethnic studies:** African, African-American, American, Asian, Central/Eastern European, East Asian, European, Latin American, Near/Middle Eastern, Russian/Slavic, Western European, women's. **Biology:** General, ecology. **Computer sciences:** General, computer science, information systems, programming. **Education:** Early childhood. **Engineering:** General, architectural, biomedical, chemical, civil, computer, electrical, environmental, mechanical, physics, science. **Foreign languages:** General, ancient Greek, Chinese, classics, comparative lit, French, German, Italian, Japanese, Latin, Russian, Spanish. **History:** General. **Interdisciplinary:** Math/

computer science, peace/conflict. **Liberal arts:** Arts/sciences. **Math:** General, applied. **Philosophy/religion:** Philosophy, religion. **Physical sciences:** Astronomy, chemistry, geology, physics. **Psychology:** General. **Social sciences:** Anthropology, archaeology, economics, international relations, political science, sociology. **Visual/performing arts:** Art history/conservation, music history, music theory/composition, musicology, studio arts, theater history.

Most popular majors. Engineering/engineering technologies 12%, foreign language 7%, psychology 7%, social sciences 29%, visual/performing arts 10%.

Computing on campus. 500 workstations in library, computer center. Dormitories wired for high-speed internet access and linked to campus network. Commuter students can connect to campus network. Online course registration, online library, helpline, repair service, wireless network available.

Student life. Freshman orientation: Mandatory. Preregistration for classes offered. Three-day program prior to beginning of fall semester. **Housing:** Guaranteed on-campus for freshmen. Coed dorms, single-sex dorms, special housing for disabled, cooperative housing, fraternity/sorority housing, wellness housing available. Culture, special interest, language houses available. **Activities:** Bands, campus ministries, choral groups, dance, drama, film society, international student organizations, literary magazine, music ensembles, musical theater, opera, radio station, student government, student newspaper, symphony orchestra, TV station, over 200 student organizations.

Athletics. NCAA. **Intercollegiate:** Baseball M, basketball, cross-country, diving, fencing W, field hockey W, football (tackle) M, golf M, ice hockey M, lacrosse, rowing (crew), rugby, sailing, soccer, softball W, squash, swimming, tennis, track and field, volleyball W. **Intramural:** Basketball, fencing M, handball, racquetball, softball, squash, tennis, volleyball. **Team name:** Jumbos.

Student services. Adult student services, alcohol/substance abuse counseling, chaplain/spiritual director, career counseling, services for economically disadvantaged, student employment services, financial aid counseling, health services, legal services, minority student services, on-campus daycare, personal counseling, placement for graduates, women's services. **Physically disabled:** Services for visually, speech, hearing impaired.

Contact. E-mail: admissions.inquiry@ase.tufts.edu
Phone: (617) 627-3170 Fax: (617) 627-3860
Lee Coffin, Dean of Undergraduate Admissions and Enrollment Management, Tufts University, Bendetson Hall, Medford, MA 02155

University of Massachusetts Amherst

Amherst, Massachusetts — **CB member**
www.umass.edu — **CB code: 3917**

- Public 4-year university
- Residential campus in large town
- 19,964 degree-seeking undergraduates: 6% part-time, 50% women, 5% African American, 8% Asian American, 4% Hispanic American, 1% international
- 5,150 degree-seeking graduate students
- 64% of applicants admitted
- SAT or ACT (ACT writing recommended), application essay required
- 69% graduate within 6 years

General. Founded in 1863. Regionally accredited. **Degrees:** 4,431 bachelor's, 73 associate awarded; master's, doctoral offered. **ROTC:** Army, Air Force. **Location:** 90 miles from Boston, 30 miles from Springfield. **Calendar:** Semester, limited summer session. **Full-time faculty:** 1,154 total; 93% have terminal degrees, 19% minority, 37% women. **Part-time faculty:** 202 total; 55% have terminal degrees, 6% minority, 53% women. **Class size:** 36% < 20, 41% 20-39, 6% 40-49, 8% 50-99, 9% >100. **Special facilities:** Observatory, botanical gardens, sports arena with ice rink.

Freshman class profile. 28,931 applied, 18,610 admitted, 4,144 enrolled.

Mid 50% test scores		**Rank in top tenth:**	25%
SAT critical reading:	510-620	**Return as sophomores:**	86%
SAT math:	540-640	**Out-of-state:**	22%
GPA 3.75 or higher:	30%	**Live on campus:**	98%
GPA 3.50-3.74:	26%	**International:**	1%
GPA 3.0-3.49:	40%	**Fraternities:**	4%
GPA 2.0-2.99:	4%	**Sororities:**	3%
Rank in top quarter:	65%		

Basis for selection. High school grades most important, followed by test scores, extracurricular activities, essay and recommendations. Audition required of music and dance majors. Portfolio required of art and design majors. **Homeschooled:** Detailed transcript required. **Learning Disabled:** Applicants must submit diagnostic data and/or individualized educational plan. Massachusetts residents with documented learning disabilities not required to submit standardized test scores for admissions consideration.

High school preparation. College-preparatory program required. 16 units required. Required units include English 4, mathematics 3, social studies 2, science 3 (laboratory 2), foreign language 2 and academic electives 2.

2008-2009 Annual costs. Tuition/fees: $10,232; $21,729 out-of-state. Room/board: $8,114. Books/supplies: $1,000. Personal expenses: $1,000.

2007-2008 Financial aid. Need-based: 3,701 full-time freshmen applied for aid; 2,266 were judged to have need; 2,206 of these received aid. Average need met was 83%. Average scholarship/grant was $7,865; average loan $3,577. 50% of total undergraduate aid awarded as scholarships/grants, 50% as loans/jobs. **Non-need-based:** Awarded to 1,789 full-time undergraduates, including 645 freshmen. Scholarships awarded for academics, art, athletics, music/drama, ROTC, state residency.

Application procedures. Admission: Closing date 1/15 (postmark date). $70 fee, may be waived for applicants with need. Admission notification on a rolling basis beginning on or about 3/7. Must reply by 5/1. **Financial aid:** Priority date 2/14; no closing date. FAFSA required. Applicants notified on a rolling basis starting 3/1.

Academics. Students may take courses at Amherst, Hampshire, Mt. Holyoke and Smith Colleges at no extra charge. **Special study options:** Accelerated study, cooperative education, cross-registration, distance learning, double major, dual enrollment of high school students, ESL, exchange student, honors, independent study, internships, liberal arts/career combination, student-designed major, study abroad, teacher certification program, Washington semester. University Without Walls program offers individualized degrees to working adults; residential academic programs allow first-year students to live and take classes together. **Credit/placement by examination:** AP, CLEP, IB, institutional tests. 30 credit hours maximum toward bachelor's degree. Credit awarded for International Baccalaureate scores of 4-7. **Support services:** Learning center, study skills assistance, tutoring, writing center.

Honors college/program. First-year students admitted by invitation, approximately 600 freshmen admitted. Interdisciplinary seminars, enriched honors courses, colloquia, independent study, service learning offered; honors thesis, project, or activity required.

Majors. Agriculture: Animal sciences, economics, food science, plant sciences. **Architecture:** Environmental design, interior, landscape. **Area/ethnic studies:** African-American, Near/Middle Eastern, Russian/Slavic, women's. **Biology:** General, Biochemistry/biophysics and molecular biology, exercise physiology, microbiology. **Business:** Accounting, apparel, business admin, finance, hospitality admin, marketing. **Communications:** General, journalism. **Computer sciences:** Computer science. **Conservation:** Environmental science, forestry, management/policy, wildlife, wood science. **Engineering:** Chemical, civil, computer, electrical, industrial, mechanical. **Family/consumer sciences:** Family resources, human nutrition. **Foreign languages:** Chinese, classics, comparative lit, French, German, Italian, Japanese, linguistics, Portuguese, Spanish. **Health:** Communication disorders, nursing (RN), predental, premedicine, preveterinary. **History:** General. **Interdisciplinary:** Biological/physical sciences. **Legal studies:** General. **Math:** General. **Parks/recreation:** Sports admin. **Philosophy/religion:** Judaic, philosophy. **Physical sciences:** Astronomy, chemistry, geology, physics. **Psychology:** General. **Social sciences:** Anthropology, economics, geography, political science, sociology. **Visual/performing arts:** Art history/conservation, dance, dramatic, music performance, studio arts. **Other:** Individual concentration, Social thought and political economy.

Most popular majors. Biology 7%, business/marketing 17%, communications/journalism 8%, health sciences 6%, psychology 8%, social sciences 12%.

Computing on campus. Dormitories wired for high-speed internet access and linked to campus network. Commuter students can connect to campus network. Online course registration, online library, helpline, repair service, student web hosting, wireless network available.

Student life. Freshman orientation: Mandatory. Preregistration for classes offered. Two-and-a-half-day sessions in June or July, with a make-up orientation at end of August. **Policies:** Students required to live on-campus through sophomore year unless eligible for housing exemption (parents of dependent children, veterans, commuting students). **Housing:** Guaranteed on-campus for freshmen. Coed dorms, single-sex dorms, special housing for disabled, apartments, fraternity/sorority housing, wellness housing available. Special interest housing; residential academic programs for first-year students. Gradual penalty for cancellation of housing up to $300. **Activities:** Bands, campus ministries, choral groups, dance, drama, film society, international student organizations, literary magazine, music ensembles, Model UN, musical theater, opera, radio station, student government, student newspaper, symphony orchestra, TV station, Over 280 student organizations.

Athletics. NCAA. **Intercollegiate:** Baseball M, basketball, cheerleading, cross-country, diving, field hockey W, football (tackle) M, ice hockey M, lacrosse, rowing (crew) W, skiing, soccer, softball W, swimming, tennis W, track and field. **Intramural:** Basketball, field hockey W, football (non-tackle), ice hockey, lacrosse W, soccer, softball, tennis, volleyball. **Team name:** Minutemen, Minutewomen.

Student services. Adult student services, alcohol/substance abuse counseling, chaplain/spiritual director, career counseling, student employment services, financial aid counseling, health services, legal services, minority student services, on-campus daycare, personal counseling, placement for graduates, veterans' counselor, women's services. **Physically disabled:** Services for visually, speech, hearing impaired. **Learning disabled:** Comprehensive services available.

Contact. E-mail: mail@admissions.umass.edu
Phone: (413) 545-0222 Fax: (413) 545-4312
Kevin Kelly, Director of Admissions, University of Massachusetts Amherst, University Admissions Center, Amherst, MA 01003-9291

University of Massachusetts Boston

Boston, Massachusetts — **CB member**
www.umb.edu — **CB code: 3924**

- Public 4-year university
- Commuter campus in very large city
- 9,564 degree-seeking undergraduates: 27% part-time, 58% women, 16% African American, 14% Asian American, 9% Hispanic American, 3% international
- 2,989 degree-seeking graduate students
- 63% of applicants admitted
- SAT or ACT (ACT writing optional), application essay required

General. Founded in 1964. Regionally accredited. **Degrees:** 1,505 bachelor's awarded; master's, doctoral offered. **ROTC:** Army, Naval, Air Force. **Location:** 3 miles from downtown. **Calendar:** Semester, extensive summer session. **Full-time faculty:** 462 total; 93% have terminal degrees, 23% minority, 48% women. **Part-time faculty:** 451 total; 30% have terminal degrees, 11% minority, 58% women. **Class size:** 36% < 20, 56% 20-39, 3% 40-49, 4% 50-99, 1% >100. **Special facilities:** Tropical greenhouse, observatory, adaptive computer laboratory.

Freshman class profile. 4,576 applied, 2,884 admitted, 1,020 enrolled.

Mid 50% test scores		**GPA 3.0-3.49:**	34%
SAT critical reading:	470-570	**GPA 2.0-2.99:**	46%
SAT math:	480-580	**Return as sophomores:**	75%
GPA 3.75 or higher:	10%	**Out-of-state:**	8%
GPA 3.50-3.74:	10%	**International:**	5%

Basis for selection. School achievement record, range of test scores, GPA most important. Recommendations, essay also important. Extracurricular activities considered. Grades for college preparatory background should be B- or better. Interview recommended for nontraditional students.

High school preparation. College-preparatory program required. 16 units required. Required units include English 4, mathematics 3, social studies 1, history 1, science 3 (laboratory 2), foreign language 2 and academic electives 2.

2008-2009 Annual costs. Tuition/fees: $9,111; $21,297 out-of-state. Books/supplies: $800. Personal expenses: $1,170.

2007-2008 Financial aid. Need-based: 737 full-time freshmen applied for aid; 616 were judged to have need; 616 of these received aid. Average need met was 90%. Average scholarship/grant was $6,757; average loan $3,730. 47% of total undergraduate aid awarded as scholarships/grants, 53% as loans/jobs. **Non-need-based:** Awarded to 268 full-time undergraduates, including 109 freshmen. Scholarships awarded for academics, leadership, state residency. **Additional information:** Some Massachusetts state employees and Massachusetts Vietnam veterans eligible for tuition waiver. Some waivers available based on talent and academic excellence.

Application procedures. Admission: Priority date 3/1; deadline 6/1. $40 fee ($60 out-of-state), may be waived for applicants with need. Admission notification on a rolling basis. Must reply by May 1 or within 3 week(s) if notified thereafter. **Financial aid:** Priority date 3/1; no closing date. FAFSA required. Applicants notified on a rolling basis starting 3/21.

Academics. Certificates available in many areas, including communication studies, computer and information sciences, technical and business writing, international relations, accounting, geographic information systems, alcohol/substance abuse, Spanish translation, management information systems. **Special study options:** Combined bachelor's/graduate degree, cooperative education, cross-registration, distance learning, double major, dual enrollment of high school students, ESL, exchange student, honors, independent study, internships, liberal arts/career combination, student-designed major, study abroad, teacher certification program. 2-2 programs in engineering with area institutions. **Credit/placement by examination:** AP, CLEP, SAT, ACT, institutional tests. 90 credit hours maximum toward bachelor's degree. **Support services:** Learning center, pre-admission summer program, reduced course load, remedial instruction, study skills assistance, tutoring, writing center.

Majors. Area/ethnic studies: African-American, American, women's. **Biology:** General, biochemistry, biotechnology. **Business:** Business admin. **Computer sciences:** General, information technology. **Engineering:** Physics. **Foreign languages:** Classics, French, Italian, Spanish. **Health:** Nursing (RN). **History:** General. **Interdisciplinary:** Gerontology. **Legal studies:** General. **Math:** General. **Parks/recreation:** Health/fitness. **Philosophy/religion:** Philosophy. **Physical sciences:** Chemistry, geology, physics. **Protective services:** Criminal justice. **Psychology:** General. **Public administration:** General, community org/advocacy, human services. **Social sciences:** General, anthropology, economics, political science, sociology. **Visual/performing arts:** Art, dramatic. **Other:** Individual major.

Most popular majors. Biology 6%, business/marketing 20%, English 7%, health sciences 12%, psychology 12%, public administration/social services 7%, security/protective services 7%, social sciences 14%.

Computing on campus. 350 workstations in library, computer center, student center. Commuter students can connect to campus network. Online course registration, online library, helpline, repair service, wireless network available.

Student life. Freshman orientation: Mandatory, $25 fee. Preregistration for classes offered. **Housing:** Housing referral services available. **Activities:** Bands, campus ministries, choral groups, dance, drama, film society, international student organizations, literary magazine, music ensembles, Model UN, radio station, student government, student newspaper, symphony orchestra.

Athletics. NCAA. **Intercollegiate:** Baseball M, basketball, cross-country, ice hockey M, lacrosse M, soccer, softball W, tennis, track and field, volleyball W. **Intramural:** Basketball, ice hockey M, racquetball, sailing, soccer, softball, squash, tennis, volleyball. **Team name:** Beacons.

Student services. Adult student services, alcohol/substance abuse counseling, chaplain/spiritual director, career counseling, student employment services, health services, legal services, minority student services, on-campus daycare, personal counseling, placement for graduates, veterans' counselor, women's services. **Physically disabled:** Services for visually, speech, hearing impaired.

Contact. E-mail: enrollment.info@umb.edu
Phone: (617) 287-6000 Fax: (617) 287-5999
Liliana Mickle, Director of Admissions, University of Massachusetts Boston, 100 Morrissey Boulevard, Boston, MA 02125-3393

University of Massachusetts Dartmouth

North Dartmouth, Massachusetts — **CB member**
www.umassd.edu — **CB code: 3786**

- Public 4-year university
- Residential campus in large town
- 7,738 degree-seeking undergraduates: 10% part-time, 48% women, 7% African American, 3% Asian American, 3% Hispanic American, 1% Native American
- 940 degree-seeking graduate students
- 65% of applicants admitted
- SAT or ACT, application essay required
- 47% graduate within 6 years

General. Founded in 1895. Regionally accredited. **Degrees:** 1,140 bachelor's awarded; master's, doctoral offered. **ROTC:** Army. **Location:** 60 miles from Boston; 30 miles from Providence, Rhode Island. **Calendar:** Semester, extensive summer session. **Full-time faculty:** 368 total; 79% have terminal degrees, 21% minority, 39% women. **Part-time faculty:** 243 total; 12% minority, 47% women. **Class size:** 39% < 20, 44% 20-39, 10% 40-49, 6% 50-99, 2% >100. **Special facilities:** Observatory, marine research vessel, coastal marine laboratory, full art studios, Jewish culture and Portuguese studies centers, Robert F. Kennedy assassination archive.

Freshman class profile. 7,633 applied, 4,930 admitted, 1,556 enrolled.

Mid 50% test scores		**GPA 3.0-3.49:**	31%
SAT critical reading:	470-560	**GPA 2.0-2.99:**	48%
SAT math:	490-590	**Rank in top quarter:**	36%
ACT composite:	20-24	**Rank in top tenth:**	11%
GPA 3.75 or higher:	11%	**Out-of-state:**	4%
GPA 3.50-3.74:	10%	**Live on campus:**	80%

Basis for selection. High school record, test scores most important; class rank, essay, recommendations considered. Minimum 2.0 GPA required. 3.0 GPA recommended. Audition required for music majors; portfolio required for design majors. **Homeschooled:** State high school equivalency certificate required. Must get certification or equivalency from local high school. **Learning Disabled:** SAT scores may be waived for Massachusetts students with documented disability.

High school preparation. College-preparatory program required. 16 units required. Required units include English 4, mathematics 3, social studies 1, history 1, science 3 (laboratory 2), foreign language 2 and academic electives 2. 1 U.S. history required. Programs in science, engineering and business require additional math. Science and engineering require physical science. 2 foreign language must be same language.

2008-2009 Annual costs. Tuition/fees: $8,861; $18,561 out-of-state. Room/board: $9,457. Books/supplies: $800. Personal expenses: $1,320.

2007-2008 Financial aid. Need-based: 1,580 full-time freshmen applied for aid; 1,155 were judged to have need; 1,155 of these received aid. Average need met was 91%. Average scholarship/grant was $6,433; average loan $4,841. 40% of total undergraduate aid awarded as scholarships/grants, 60% as loans/jobs. **Non-need-based:** Awarded to 495 full-time undergraduates, including 222 freshmen. Scholarships awarded for academics, minority status, ROTC, state residency.

Application procedures. Admission: No deadline. $40 fee ($60 out-of-state), may be waived for applicants with need. Admission notification on a rolling basis beginning on or about 1/1. Must reply by May 1 or within 2 week(s) if notified thereafter. Competitive programs may be filled by March 1. Nursing closes by late January. Freshman applicants advised to apply before end of December and not later than March. **Financial aid:** Priority date 3/1; no closing date. FAFSA required. Applicants notified on a rolling basis starting 3/25; must reply within 3 week(s) of notification.

Academics. Alternative admissions program for academically disadvantaged Massachusetts residents; program offers special freshman curriculum and counseling support. **Special study options:** Combined bachelor's/graduate degree, cooperative education, cross-registration, distance learning, double major, dual enrollment of high school students, honors, independent study, internships, student-designed major, study abroad, teacher certification program, Washington semester. **Credit/placement by examination:** AP, CLEP, IB, SAT, ACT, institutional tests. 30 credit hours maximum toward bachelor's degree. **Support services:** Learning center, reduced course load, remedial instruction, study skills assistance, tutoring, writing center.

Majors. Area/ethnic studies: Women's. **Biology:** General. **Business:** Accounting, business admin, finance, management information systems, marketing. **Computer sciences:** General. **Education:** Art. **Engineering:** Civil, computer, electrical, mechanical, textile. **Foreign languages:** French, Portuguese, Spanish. **Health:** Clinical lab science, nursing (RN). **History:** General. **Liberal arts:** Arts/sciences. **Math:** General. **Philosophy/religion:** Philosophy. **Physical sciences:** Chemistry, physics. **Psychology:** General. **Social sciences:** Criminology, economics, political science, sociology. **Visual/performing arts:** General, art history/conservation, ceramics, commercial/advertising art, design, fiber arts, metal/jewelry, multimedia, painting, photography, sculpture, studio arts.

Most popular majors. Business/marketing 29%, engineering/engineering technologies 6%, health sciences 12%, psychology 8%, social sciences 11%, visual/performing arts 9%.

Computing on campus. 650 workstations in dormitories, library, computer center, student center. Dormitories wired for high-speed internet access and linked to campus network. Commuter students can connect to campus network. Helpline, repair service, wireless network available.

Student life. Freshman orientation: Mandatory, $200 fee. Preregistration for classes offered. Three-day, 2-night program in June and July. **Housing:** Coed dorms, special housing for disabled, apartments, wellness housing available. $200 nonrefundable deposit, deadline 5/1. Quiet substance-free, smoke-free housing, program-dedicated suites available. **Activities:** Bands, choral groups, dance, drama, international student organizations, literary magazine, music ensembles, musical theater, radio station, student government, student newspaper, symphony orchestra, women's center, Portuguese center, Unity House, Indian student organization, Arab student organization, Luso-American student organization, Taiwanese student organization, MASSPIRG.

Athletics. NCAA. **Intercollegiate:** Baseball M, basketball, cheerleading M, cross-country, diving, equestrian W, field hockey W, football (tackle) M, golf M, ice hockey M, lacrosse, soccer, softball W, swimming, tennis, track and field, volleyball W. **Intramural:** Badminton, basketball, cross-country, football (non-tackle), sailing, soccer, softball, swimming, table tennis, tennis, volleyball. **Team name:** Corsairs.

Student services. Adult student services, alcohol/substance abuse counseling, chaplain/spiritual director, career counseling, student employment services, financial aid counseling, health services, minority student services, on-campus daycare, personal counseling, placement for graduates, veterans' counselor, women's services. **Physically disabled:** Services for visually, speech, hearing impaired.

Contact. E-mail: admissions@umassd.edu
Phone: (508) 999-8605 Fax: (508) 999-8755
Carnell Jones, Director of Admissions, University of Massachusetts Dartmouth, 285 Old Westport Road, North Dartmouth, MA 02747-2300

University of Massachusetts Lowell

Lowell, Massachusetts — **CB member**
www.uml.edu — **CB code: 3911**

- Public 4-year university
- Commuter campus in small city
- 7,151 degree-seeking undergraduates: 9% part-time, 39% women, 5% African American, 8% Asian American, 6% Hispanic American, 1% international
- 2,751 degree-seeking graduate students
- 75% of applicants admitted
- SAT or ACT (ACT writing optional), application essay required
- 46% graduate within 6 years

General. Founded in 1894. Regionally accredited. **Degrees:** 1,362 bachelor's, 23 associate awarded; master's, doctoral offered. **ROTC:** Air Force. **Location:** 25 miles from Boston, 45 miles from Worcester. **Calendar:** Semester, extensive summer session. **Full-time faculty:** 414 total; 94% have terminal degrees, 21% minority, 34% women. **Part-time faculty:** 276 total; 4% minority, 45% women. **Class size:** 49% < 20, 36% 20-39, 10% 40-49, 3% 50-99, 2% >100. **Special facilities:** Tsongas Industrial History center, teaching and research laboratories in sound recording technology, digital imaging, wellness resource room.

Freshman class profile. 5,549 applied, 4,174 admitted, 1,528 enrolled.

Mid 50% test scores		**Rank in top quarter:**	40%
SAT critical reading:	470-570	**Rank in top tenth:**	14%
SAT math:	490-600	**Return as sophomores:**	80%
GPA 3.75 or higher:	14%	**Out-of-state:**	11%
GPA 3.50-3.74:	12%	**Live on campus:**	54%
GPA 3.0-3.49:	36%	**International:**	1%
GPA 2.0-2.99:	38%		

Basis for selection. School record, test scores, recommendations most important. Interview recommended. Audition required of music majors. **Homeschooled:** Statement describing homeschool structure and mission, transcript of courses and grades, state high school equivalency certificate, letter of recommendation (nonparent) required. **Learning Disabled:** Students with documented learning differences do not have to submit SAT or ACT.

High school preparation. 16 units required. Required and recommended units include English 4, mathematics 3-4, social studies 2, science 3-4 (laboratory 2), foreign language 2 and academic electives 2.

2008-2009 Annual costs. Tuition/fees: $9,147; $21,167 out-of-state. Room/board: $7,519. Books/supplies: $800. Personal expenses: $850.

2008-2009 Financial aid. Need-based: 1,281 full-time freshmen applied for aid; 853 were judged to have need; 853 of these received aid. Average need met was 95%. Average scholarship/grant was $6,287; average loan $4,461. 38% of total undergraduate aid awarded as scholarships/grants, 62% as loans/jobs. **Non-need-based:** Awarded to 891 full-time undergraduates, including 335 freshmen. Scholarships awarded for academics, alumni affiliation, art, athletics, job skills, leadership, minority status, music/drama, ROTC, state residency.

Application procedures. Admission: Priority date 7/1; no deadline. $60 fee, may be waived for applicants with need. Admission notification on a rolling basis beginning on or about 4/1. Must reply by May 1 or within 2 week(s) if notified thereafter. **Financial aid:** Priority date 3/1; no closing date. FAFSA required. Applicants notified on a rolling basis starting 3/20.

Academics. Special focus on applied science and technology; coursework emphasizes context and implications of each discipline. Funded research initiatives available in nanotechnology, bioinformatics, advanced materials, photonics. **Special study options:** Accelerated study, combined bachelor's/graduate degree, cooperative education, cross-registration, distance learning, double major, dual enrollment of high school students, honors, internships, liberal arts/career combination, study abroad, teacher certification program. **Credit/placement by examination:** AP, CLEP, SAT, ACT, institutional tests. 30 credit hours maximum toward bachelor's degree. **Support services:** Learning center, pre-admission summer program, reduced course load, study skills assistance, tutoring, writing center.

Majors. **Area/ethnic studies:** American. **Biology:** General. **Business:** Business admin, entrepreneurial studies. **Computer sciences:** Computer science, information systems. **Education:** Health, music. **Engineering:** Chemical, civil, electrical, mechanical, polymer. **Engineering technology:** Civil, electrical, industrial. **Foreign languages:** General. **Health:** Clinical lab science, nursing (RN). **History:** General. **Liberal arts:** Arts/sciences. **Math:** General, applied. **Philosophy/religion:** Philosophy. **Physical sciences:** Chemistry, physics. **Protective services:** Law enforcement admin. **Psychology:** General. **Social sciences:** Economics, political science, sociology. **Visual/performing arts:** General, graphic design, music performance, studio arts.

Most popular majors. Business/marketing 21%, computer/information sciences 9%, engineering/engineering technologies 14%, health sciences 10%, liberal arts 6%, psychology 7%, security/protective services 13%, visual/performing arts 7%.

Computing on campus. 4,000 workstations in dormitories, library, computer center, student center. Dormitories linked to campus network. Commuter students can connect to campus network. Online course registration, online library, helpline available.

Student life. **Freshman orientation:** Mandatory. Preregistration for classes offered. **Housing:** Coed dorms, single-sex dorms, special housing for disabled, apartments, cooperative housing available. $200 nonrefundable deposit. **Activities:** Bands, choral groups, dance, drama, film society, literary magazine, music ensembles, radio station, student government, student newspaper, symphony orchestra, Abundant Life Christian Fellowship, Chi Alpha, Latter-day Saints student association, association of students of African origin, Cambodian student association, Latin American student association, community service organization, College Democrats, College Republicans.

Athletics. NCAA. **Intercollegiate:** Baseball M, basketball, cross-country, field hockey W, golf M, ice hockey M, rowing (crew), soccer, softball W, track and field, volleyball W. **Intramural:** Badminton, basketball, bowling, diving, equestrian W, ice hockey, racquetball, rowing (crew), soccer, softball, squash, swimming, table tennis, tennis M, volleyball. **Team name:** River Hawks.

Student services. Adult student services, alcohol/substance abuse counseling, chaplain/spiritual director, career counseling, financial aid counseling, health services, personal counseling, placement for graduates, veterans' counselor. **Physically disabled:** Services for visually, speech, hearing impaired.

Contact. E-mail: admissions@uml.edu
Phone: (978) 934-3931 Toll-free number: (800) 410-4607
Fax: (978) 934-3086
Kerri Mead, Director Undergraduate Admissions, University of Massachusetts Lowell, 883 Broadway Street, Room 110, Lowell, MA 01854-5104

Wellesley College

Wellesley, Massachusetts — **CB member**
www.wellesley.edu — **CB code: 3957**

- Private 4-year liberal arts college for women
- Residential campus in large town
- 2,212 degree-seeking undergraduates: 1% part-time, 100% women, 7% African American, 27% Asian American, 7% Hispanic American, 1% Native American, 8% international
- 36% of applicants admitted
- SAT and SAT Subject Tests or ACT with writing, application essay required
- 91% graduate within 6 years

General. Founded in 1870. Regionally accredited. **Degrees:** 604 bachelor's awarded. **ROTC:** Army, Air Force. **Location:** 12 miles from Boston. **Calendar:** Semester, limited summer session. **Full-time faculty:** 251 total; 96% have terminal degrees, 24% minority, 56% women. **Part-time faculty:** 75 total; 79% have terminal degrees, 27% minority, 68% women. **Class size:** 69% < 20, 30% 20-39, less than 1% 40-49, less than 1% 50-99. **Special facilities:** Science center with X-ray diffractometer, nuclear magnetic resonance, spectrometers (NMR and microMRI), electron microscopes, argon and dye lasers, observatory with three telescopes (6-, 12-, and 24-inch), cultural center, greenhouses, botanic gardens, arboretum, media and technology center with linear editing room for video, digital-based video editing suite, plotter, film recorder, slide scanner.

Freshman class profile. 4,001 applied, 1,442 admitted, 596 enrolled.

Mid 50% test scores		**Rank in top tenth:**	76%
SAT critical reading:	640-740	**Return as sophomores:**	94%
SAT math:	630-730	**Out-of-state:**	86%
SAT writing:	650-740	**Live on campus:**	100%
ACT composite:	28-32	**International:**	8%
Rank in top quarter:	97%		

Basis for selection. Evidence in student's record, both in and out of the classroom, of ability to meet rigorous academic standards and willingness to engage in the community important. Candidates should have taken advantage of the opportunities available at high school. If SAT submitted, 2 SAT Subject Tests required, at least one of which should be quantitative. Interview recommended. **Homeschooled:** Statement describing homeschool structure and mission, transcript of courses and grades, letter of recommendation (nonparent) required. Applicants must meet home schooling requirements of their own state.

High school preparation. College-preparatory program recommended. Recommended units include English 4, mathematics 4, social studies 4, history 4, science 3 (laboratory 2) and foreign language 4.

2008-2009 Annual costs. Tuition/fees: $36,640. Room/board: $11,336. Books/supplies: $800. Personal expenses: $1,200.

2008-2009 Financial aid. All financial aid based on need. 423 full-time freshmen applied for aid; 344 were judged to have need; 344 of these received aid. Average need met was 100%. Average scholarship/grant was $34,528; average loan $2,417. 92% of total undergraduate aid awarded as scholarships/grants, 8% as loans/jobs. **Additional information:** Wellesley has increased scholarships and eliminated or reduced student loans for nearly all students.

Application procedures. **Admission:** Closing date 1/15 (postmark date). $50 fee, may be waived for applicants with need, free for online applicants. Admission notification 4/1. Must reply by 5/1. **Financial aid:** Closing date 1/15. FAFSA, institutional form, CSS PROFILE required. Applicants notified by 4/1; must reply by 5/1.

Academics. **Special study options:** Cross-registration, double major, dual enrollment of high school students, exchange student, honors, independent study, internships, semester at sea, student-designed major, study abroad, teacher certification program, Washington semester. **Credit/placement by examination:** AP, CLEP, IB, institutional tests. **Support services:** Learning center, reduced course load, study skills assistance, tutoring, writing center.

Majors. **Architecture:** Architecture. **Area/ethnic studies:** African, African-American, American, Asian, Central/Eastern European, East Asian, European, Latin American, Russian/Slavic, South Asian, women's. **Biology:** General, biochemistry. **Computer sciences:** General, computer science. **Conservation:** Environmental studies. **Engineering:** General. **Foreign languages:** General, ancient Greek, Chinese, classics, comparative lit, French, German, Italian, Japanese, Latin, linguistics, Russian, Spanish. **History:** General. **Interdisciplinary:** Biological/physical sciences, classical/archaeology, medieval/Renaissance, neuroscience, peace/conflict, science/society. **Math:** General. **Philosophy/religion:** Judaic, philosophy, religion. **Physical sciences:** Astronomy, chemistry, geology, physics. **Psychology:** General. **Social sciences:** Anthropology, archaeology, economics, international relations, political science, sociology. **Visual/performing arts:** Art history/conservation, dramatic, music history, studio arts.

Most popular majors. Area/ethnic studies 9%, biology 7%, English 7%, foreign language 11%, interdisciplinary studies 7%, psychology 7%, social sciences 28%, visual/performing arts 8%.

Computing on campus. 481 workstations in dormitories, library, computer center, student center. Dormitories wired for high-speed internet access and linked to campus network. Commuter students can connect to campus network. Online course registration, online library, helpline, repair service, student web hosting, wireless network available.

Student life. **Freshman orientation:** Mandatory. Preregistration for classes offered. Multiday program held in late August. **Housing:** Guaranteed on-campus for all undergraduates. Apartments, cooperative housing, wellness housing available. Pets allowed in dorm rooms. French and Spanish language houses available. **Activities:** Jazz band, campus ministries, choral groups, dance, drama, film society, international student organizations, literary magazine, music ensembles, Model UN, radio station, student government, student newspaper, black student club, Latina student club, Asian student union, Hillel, Al-Muslimat, Intervarsity Christian Fellowship, political and legislative action organization, Best Buddies, Habitat for Humanity.

Athletics. NCAA. **Intercollegiate:** Basketball W, cross-country W, diving W, fencing W, field hockey W, golf W, lacrosse W, rowing (crew) W, soccer W, softball W, swimming W, tennis W, track and field W, volleyball W. **Intramural:** Basketball W, ice hockey W, racquetball W, rowing (crew) W, rugby W, sailing W, soccer W, table tennis W. **Team name:** Wellesley Blue.

Student services. Adult student services, alcohol/substance abuse counseling, chaplain/spiritual director, career counseling, services for economically disadvantaged, student employment services, financial aid counseling, health services, minority student services, on-campus daycare, personal counseling, placement for graduates, women's services. **Physically disabled:** Services for visually, hearing impaired.

Contact. E-mail: admission@wellesley.edu
Phone: (781) 283-2270 Fax: (781) 283-3678
Jennifer Desjarlais, Dean of Admission, Wellesley College, 106 Central Street, Wellesley, MA 02481-8203

Wentworth Institute of Technology

Boston, Massachusetts — **CB member**
www.wit.edu — **CB code: 3958**

- Private 4-year engineering and technical college
- Residential campus in very large city
- 3,764 degree-seeking undergraduates: 10% part-time, 20% women, 4% African American, 5% Asian American, 4% Hispanic American, 3% international
- 63% of applicants admitted
- SAT or ACT (ACT writing optional), application essay required
- 49% graduate within 6 years; 2% enter graduate study

General. Founded in 1904. Regionally accredited. Mandatory Cooperative education program. Member of Colleges of the Fenway. **Degrees:** 603 bachelor's, 52 associate awarded. **ROTC:** Army, Air Force. **Location:** 2 miles from downtown. **Calendar:** Semester, limited summer session. **Full-time faculty:** 144 total; 51% have terminal degrees, 12% minority, 22% women. **Part-time faculty:** 151 total; 8% minority, 24% women. **Class size:** 43% < 20, 54% 20-39, less than 1% 40-49, 1% 50-99, less than 1% >100.

Freshman class profile. 3,601 applied, 2,261 admitted, 813 enrolled.

Mid 50% test scores		**GPA 3.0-3.49:**	38%
SAT critical reading:	470-560	**GPA 2.0-2.99:**	47%
SAT math:	510-610	**Return as sophomores:**	79%
SAT writing:	460-560	**Out-of-state:**	42%
ACT composite:	20-25	**Live on campus:**	82%
GPA 3.75 or higher:	3%	**International:**	3%
GPA 3.50-3.74:	10%		

Basis for selection. School achievement record most important, followed by test scores. **Homeschooled:** Transcript of courses and grades, letter of recommendation (nonparent) required. Course content description may be requested.

High school preparation. College-preparatory program recommended. Required units include English 4, mathematics 4, social studies 1, science 2 (laboratory 1). 4 college-preparatory math, 1 physics recommended for many programs. Architecture program requires drafting.

2009-2010 Annual costs. Tuition/fees: $21,800. Tuition includes cost of laptop computer; students in architecture and design programs pay $2,000 in required fees for academic year. Room/board: $10,500. Books/supplies: $1,500. Personal expenses: $1,000.

2008-2009 Financial aid. **Need-based:** 813 full-time freshmen applied for aid; 571 were judged to have need; 571 of these received aid. Average need met was 38%. Average scholarship/grant was $2,800; average loan $3,300. 43% of total undergraduate aid awarded as scholarships/grants, 57% as loans/jobs. **Non-need-based:** Scholarships awarded for academics, leadership, ROTC, state residency.

Application procedures. **Admission:** Priority date 5/1; no deadline. $30 fee, may be waived for applicants with need. Admission notification on a rolling basis beginning on or about 10/30. Must reply by May 1 or within 2 week(s) if notified thereafter. **Financial aid:** Priority date 3/1; no closing date. FAFSA required. Applicants notified on a rolling basis starting 3/15; must reply within 2 week(s) of notification.

Academics. Some bachelor's programs require 5 years. All bachelor's candidates required to complete 2 semesters full-time co-op. Architecture students enter 2-year core curriculum, must petition to enter junior year. **Special study options:** Cooperative education, cross-registration, distance learning, study abroad. Cross-registration with Simmons College, Emmanuel College, Wheelock College, Massachusetts College of Pharmacy and Health Sciences, Massachusetts College of Art (Colleges of the Fenway). **Credit/placement by examination:** AP, CLEP, IB, institutional tests. 32 credit hours maximum toward associate degree, 64 toward bachelor's. Students may only receive maximum of one half of total credit requirement from credit by examination. **Support services:** Learning center, reduced course load, study skills assistance, tutoring, writing center.

Majors. **Architecture:** Architecture. **Business:** Business admin, construction management, operations. **Computer sciences:** General, computer science. **Engineering technology:** General, civil, computer, electrical, mechanical. **Visual/performing arts:** Industrial design, interior design. **Other:** Electromechanical Engineering.

Most popular majors. Architecture 7%, computer/information sciences 10%, engineering/engineering technologies 55%, visual/performing arts 7%.

Computing on campus. PC or laptop required. 370 workstations in dormitories, library, computer center. Dormitories wired for high-speed internet access and linked to campus network. Commuter students can connect to campus network. Online course registration, online library, helpline, repair service, wireless network available.

Student life. **Freshman orientation:** Mandatory. Preregistration for classes offered. Week-long session held week before classes begin. **Housing:** Coed dorms, apartments available. $500 fully refundable deposit, deadline 5/1. Apartments available for upperclassmen. **Activities:** Choral groups, drama, film society, international student organizations, music ensembles, musical theater, radio station, student government, student newspaper, honor society, society of women engineers, student association of interior design, solar-powered vehicle club, National Society of Black Engineers, Asian student association, architecture club.

Athletics. NCAA. **Intercollegiate:** Baseball M, basketball, golf M, ice hockey M, lacrosse M, rifle, soccer, softball W, tennis, volleyball. **Intramural:** Basketball, football (non-tackle), sailing, softball, volleyball. **Team name:** Leopards.

Student services. Alcohol/substance abuse counseling, career counseling, student employment services, financial aid counseling, health services, minority student services, personal counseling, placement for graduates, veterans' counselor, women's services.

Contact. E-mail: admissions@wit.edu
Phone: (617) 989-4000 Toll-free number: (800) 556-0610
Fax: (617) 989-4010
Maureen Dischino, Director of Admissions, Wentworth Institute of Technology, 550 Huntington Avenue, Boston, MA 02115

Western New England College

Springfield, Massachusetts — **CB member**
www.wnec.edu — **CB code: 3962**

- Private 4-year university
- Residential campus in small city
- 2,768 degree-seeking undergraduates: 10% part-time, 39% women, 3% African American, 2% Asian American, 3% Hispanic American
- 924 degree-seeking graduate students
- 73% of applicants admitted
- SAT or ACT (ACT writing optional) required
- 58% graduate within 6 years

General. Founded in 1919. Regionally accredited. **Degrees:** 652 bachelor's, 1 associate awarded; master's, doctoral, first professional offered. **ROTC:** Army, Air Force. **Location:** 95 miles from Boston, 20 miles from Hartford. **Calendar:** Semester, limited summer session. **Full-time faculty:** 180 total; 88% have terminal degrees, 10% minority, 37% women. **Part-time faculty:** 125 total; 4% minority, 31% women. **Class size:** 43% < 20, 57% 20-39.

Freshman class profile. 4,809 applied, 3,526 admitted, 736 enrolled.

Mid 50% test scores		**GPA 2.0-2.99:**	47%
SAT critical reading:	470-550	**Rank in top quarter:**	36%
SAT math:	490-600	**Rank in top tenth:**	14%
ACT composite:	19-25	**Return as sophomores:**	75%
GPA 3.75 or higher:	18%	**Out-of-state:**	62%
GPA 3.50-3.74:	10%	**Live on campus:**	92%
GPA 3.0-3.49:	25%		

Four-Year Colleges

Basis for selection. School achievement record, test scores, recommendation most important. Interview, class rank, extracurricular activities also considered. Interview and essay recommended.

High school preparation. College-preparatory program required. 10 units required; 18 recommended. Required and recommended units include English 4, mathematics 2-4, social studies 1-2, history 1-2, science 1-2 (laboratory 1-2) and foreign language 2. 1 American history required. Additional science and math required for certain programs.

2008-2009 Annual costs. Tuition/fees: $27,470. Room/board: $10,554. Books/supplies: $1,050. Personal expenses: $1,335.

2008-2009 Financial aid. Need-based: 687 full-time freshmen applied for aid; 558 were judged to have need; 558 of these received aid. Average need met was 74%. Average scholarship/grant was $15,099; average loan $4,027. 68% of total undergraduate aid awarded as scholarships/grants, 32% as loans/jobs. **Non-need-based:** Awarded to 381 full-time undergraduates, including 134 freshmen. Scholarships awarded for academics, music/drama, ROTC.

Application procedures. Admission: Priority date 2/15; no deadline. $50 fee, may be waived for applicants with need. Admission notification on a rolling basis beginning on or about 12/1. Must reply by May 1 or within 2 week(s) if notified thereafter. **Financial aid:** Priority date 4/15, closing date 5/1. FAFSA required. Applicants notified on a rolling basis starting 3/15; must reply by 5/1 or within 2 week(s) of notification.

Academics. Special study options: Accelerated study, combined bachelor's/graduate degree, cross-registration, distance learning, double major, dual enrollment of high school students, honors, independent study, internships, liberal arts/career combination, student-designed major, study abroad, teacher certification program, Washington semester. 3+3 law program. Accelerated part-time degree completion. 3+2 programs for completion of MBA or MSA for a variety of majors. **Credit/placement by examination:** AP, CLEP, IB, SAT, ACT, institutional tests. **Support services:** Pre-admission summer program, reduced course load, study skills assistance, tutoring, writing center.

Majors. Biology: General, molecular. **Business:** General, accounting, business admin, finance, management information systems, marketing. **Communications:** General, advertising, journalism, media studies, public relations. **Computer sciences:** Computer science, information systems. **Education:** Elementary, secondary. **Engineering:** Biomedical, electrical, industrial, mechanical. **Health:** Prepharmacy. **History:** General. **Interdisciplinary:** Global studies. **Legal studies:** General. **Liberal arts:** Arts/sciences. **Math:** General. **Parks/recreation:** Sports admin. **Philosophy/religion:** Philosophy. **Physical sciences:** Chemistry. **Protective services:** Criminal justice. **Psychology:** General. **Public administration:** Social work. **Social sciences:** Economics, political science, sociology.

Most popular majors. Business/marketing 31%, engineering/engineering technologies 11%, parks/recreation 6%, psychology 11%, security/protective services 19%.

Computing on campus. 400 workstations in dormitories, library, computer center, student center. Dormitories wired for high-speed internet access and linked to campus network. Commuter students can connect to campus network. Online library, helpline, repair service, wireless network available.

Student life. Freshman orientation: Available. Preregistration for classes offered. Two-day program held over summer for students and parents. Parents assessed meals and materials fee. **Housing:** Guaranteed on-campus for freshmen. Coed dorms, special housing for disabled, apartments available. $300 nonrefundable deposit, deadline 5/1. **Activities:** Bands, campus ministries, choral groups, dance, drama, international student organizations, literary magazine, music ensembles, radio station, student government, student newspaper, United and Mutually Equal, Helping Hands Society.

Athletics. NCAA. **Intercollegiate:** Baseball M, basketball, bowling, cross-country, field hockey W, football (tackle) M, golf M, ice hockey M, lacrosse, soccer, softball W, swimming W, tennis, volleyball W, wrestling M. **Intramural:** Badminton, basketball, football (non-tackle), handball, soccer, softball, table tennis, volleyball, water polo. **Team name:** Golden Bears.

Student services. Adult student services, alcohol/substance abuse counseling, chaplain/spiritual director, career counseling, student employment services, financial aid counseling, health services, minority student services, personal counseling, veterans' counselor. **Physically disabled:** Services for visually, hearing impaired.

Contact. E-mail: ugradmis@wnec.edu
Phone: (413) 782-1321 Toll-free number: (800) 325-1122 ext. 1321
Fax: (413) 782-1777
Charles Pollock, Vice President for Enrollment Management, Western New England College, 1215 Wilbraham Road, Springfield, MA 01119-2684

Westfield State College

Westfield, Massachusetts — **CB member**
www.wsc.ma.edu — **CB code: 3523**

- Public 4-year liberal arts and teachers college
- Residential campus in large town
- 4,739 degree-seeking undergraduates: 7% part-time, 53% women, 4% African American, 1% Asian American, 3% Hispanic American
- 448 degree-seeking graduate students
- 62% of applicants admitted
- SAT or ACT (ACT writing optional) required
- 59% graduate within 6 years

General. Founded in 1838. Regionally accredited. **Degrees:** 918 bachelor's awarded; master's offered. **ROTC:** Army, Air Force. **Location:** 10 miles from Springfield, 100 miles from Boston. **Calendar:** Semester, limited summer session. **Full-time faculty:** 198 total; 84% have terminal degrees, 12% minority, 46% women. **Part-time faculty:** 190 total; 44% women. **Class size:** 38% < 20, 59% 20-39, 1% 40-49, 2% 50-99, less than 1% >100. **Special facilities:** Electron microscope, natural history museum/collections, art gallery, television production studio.

Freshman class profile. 5,188 applied, 3,210 admitted, 1,126 enrolled.

Mid 50% test scores		**GPA 2.0-2.99:**	52%
SAT critical reading:	450-540	**Rank in top quarter:**	29%
SAT math:	470-560	**Rank in top tenth:**	9%
ACT composite:	18-22	**Return as sophomores:**	75%
GPA 3.75 or higher:	8%	**Out-of-state:**	92%
GPA 3.50-3.74:	8%	**Live on campus:**	88%
GPA 3.0-3.49:	32%		

Basis for selection. School achievement record, test scores most important; school and community activities also important; recommendations considered. Essay recommended. Audition required of music majors. Portfolio required of art majors. **Homeschooled:** Requirements based on AACROA standards. **Learning Disabled:** SAT/ACT test score requirement waived for students with documented learning disability. Interview required.

High school preparation. College-preparatory program required. 16 units required. Required units include English 4, mathematics 3, social studies 1, history 1, science 3 (laboratory 2), foreign language 2 and academic electives 2.

2008-2009 Annual costs. Tuition/fees: $6,515; $12,595 out-of-state. New England Regional tuition and fees per year: $7,000. Room/board: $7,204. Books/supplies: $950. Personal expenses: $1,200.

2007-2008 Financial aid. Need-based: 821 full-time freshmen applied for aid; 471 were judged to have need; 460 of these received aid. Average need met was 78%. Average scholarship/grant was $5,121; average loan $3,318. 45% of total undergraduate aid awarded as scholarships/grants, 55% as loans/jobs. **Non-need-based:** Awarded to 332 full-time undergraduates, including 141 freshmen.

Application procedures. Admission: Closing date 2/1 (postmark date). $35 fee ($50 out-of-state), may be waived for applicants with need. Admission notification 4/15. Admission notification on a rolling basis beginning on or about 1/1. Must reply by May 1 or within 2 week(s) if notified thereafter. **Financial aid:** Priority date 3/1; no closing date. FAFSA required. Applicants notified on a rolling basis starting 4/1.

Academics. Special study options: Cooperative education, cross-registration, distance learning, double major, dual enrollment of high school students, exchange student, honors, independent study, internships, semester at sea, student-designed major, study abroad, teacher certification program, Washington semester. **Credit/placement by examination:** AP, CLEP, institutional tests. 60 credit hours maximum toward bachelor's degree. Maximum of 3 credits awarded for AP tests in English. Students taking CLEP tests in English Composition with Essay or Freshman Composition must also submit writing portfolio; portfolio evaluated before credit can be awarded. Maximum of 3 credits awarded for composition. **Support services:** Learning center, pre-admission summer program, reduced course load, study skills assistance, tutoring, writing center.

Majors. Architecture: Urban/community planning. **Biology:** General. **Business:** General. **Communications:** General. **Computer sciences:** Computer science, information systems. **Conservation:** Environmental science. **Education:** Art, biology, business, elementary, English, history, kindergarten/preschool, mathematics, music, physical, science, special, technology/industrial arts. **History:** General. **Liberal arts:** Arts/sciences. **Math:** General. **Parks/recreation:** Health/fitness. **Physical sciences:** General. **Protective services:** Criminal justice. **Psychology:** General. **Public administration:**

Social work. **Social sciences:** Economics, political science, sociology. **Visual/performing arts:** Art, dramatic.

Most popular majors. Business/marketing 13%, communications/journalism 7%, education 10%, liberal arts 16%, psychology 9%, security/protective services 17%.

Computing on campus. 275 workstations in dormitories, library, computer center, student center. Dormitories wired for high-speed internet access and linked to campus network. Commuter students can connect to campus network. Online course registration, online library, helpline, student web hosting, wireless network available.

Student life. Freshman orientation: Available. **Housing:** Guaranteed on-campus for freshmen. Coed dorms, special housing for disabled, apartments available. $100 nonrefundable deposit, deadline 5/1. Living/learning unit (academic intensive), quiet living section, all women section, designated smoking section (other housing smoke-free), movement science student section available. **Activities:** Bands, campus ministries, choral groups, dance, drama, literary magazine, music ensembles, musical theater, radio station, student government, student newspaper, TV station, third world group, public interest research group, Campus Crusade, Circle K, Habitat for Humanity, international relations club, Latino association for empowerment, gay straight alliance, peace and justice club, Republican club.

Athletics. NCAA. **Intercollegiate:** Baseball M, basketball, cheerleading M, cross-country, diving W, field hockey W, football (tackle) M, golf, ice hockey M, lacrosse W, soccer, softball W, swimming W, track and field, volleyball W. **Intramural:** Badminton, basketball, bowling, football (tackle), racquetball, soccer, softball, table tennis, tennis, volleyball. **Team name:** Owls.

Student services. Adult student services, alcohol/substance abuse counseling, career counseling, services for economically disadvantaged, student employment services, financial aid counseling, health services, minority student services, personal counseling, placement for graduates, veterans' counselor. **Physically disabled:** Services for visually, speech, hearing impaired. **Learning disabled:** Comprehensive services available.

Contact. E-mail: admission@wsc.ma.edu
Phone: (413) 572-5218 Toll-free number: (800) 322-8401
Fax: (413) 572-0520
Emily Gibbings, Director, Admissions, Westfield State College, 577 Western Avenue, Westfield, MA 01086-1630

Wheaton College

Norton, Massachusetts — **CB member**
www.wheatoncollege.edu — **CB code: 3963**

- Private 4-year liberal arts college
- Residential campus in large town
- 1,655 degree-seeking undergraduates: 62% women, 5% African American, 3% Asian American, 3% Hispanic American, 4% international
- 43% of applicants admitted
- Application essay required
- 82% graduate within 6 years; 38% enter graduate study

General. Founded in 1834. Regionally accredited. **Degrees:** 403 bachelor's awarded. **ROTC:** Army. **Location:** 35 miles from Boston; 15 miles from Providence, Rhode Island. **Calendar:** Semester. **Full-time faculty:** 141 total; 92% have terminal degrees, 21% minority, 48% women. **Part-time faculty:** 40 total; 42% have terminal degrees, 15% minority, 62% women. **Class size:** 68% < 20, 26% 20-39, 4% 40-49, 2% 50-99. **Special facilities:** Observatory, language laboratory receiving international broadcasts via satellite.

Freshman class profile. 3,832 applied, 1,653 admitted, 420 enrolled.

Mid 50% test scores			
SAT critical reading:	580-680	Rank in top quarter:	72%
SAT math:	580-670	Rank in top tenth:	56%
ACT composite:	26-29	End year in good standing:	95%
GPA 3.75 or higher:	21%	Return as sophomores:	83%
GPA 3.50-3.74:	22%	Out-of-state:	71%
GPA 3.0-3.49:	38%	Live on campus:	100%
GPA 2.0-2.99:	19%	International:	5%

Basis for selection. School record, essay/writing sample, personal academic portfolio, extracurricular activities, recommendations, interview important. Standardized testing optional. Interviews strongly recommended. **Homeschooled:** Statement describing homeschool structure and mission, transcript of courses and grades required. **Learning Disabled:** Students who have diagnosed learning difference encouraged to submit supporting testing for review.

High school preparation. College-preparatory program recommended. 20 units recommended. Recommended units include English 4, mathematics 4, social studies 3, history 2, science 3 (laboratory 2) and foreign language 4. English should emphasize composition skills.

2008-2009 Annual costs. Tuition/fees: $38,980. Freshmen pay one-time $50 general fee (non-refundable). Room/board: $9,150. Books/supplies: $940. Personal expenses: $760.

2008-2009 Financial aid. Need-based: 279 full-time freshmen applied for aid; 237 were judged to have need; 237 of these received aid. Average need met was 97%. Average scholarship/grant was $26,139; average loan $4,237. 79% of total undergraduate aid awarded as scholarships/grants, 21% as loans/jobs. **Non-need-based:** Awarded to 239 full-time undergraduates, including 60 freshmen. Scholarships awarded for academics.

Application procedures. Admission: Closing date 1/15 (postmark date). $55 fee, may be waived for applicants with need, free for online applicants. Admission notification 4/1. Must reply by 5/1. **Financial aid:** Closing date 2/1. FAFSA, CSS PROFILE required. Applicants notified by 4/1; must reply by 5/1.

Academics. Special study options: Accelerated study, combined bachelor's/graduate degree, cross-registration, double major, dual enrollment of high school students, exchange student, honors, independent study, internships, liberal arts/career combination, student-designed major, study abroad, teacher certification program, Washington semester. BS in engineering with George Washington University and Dartmouth College; MA in Intergrated Marketing Communications with Emerson College; MBA in management with University of Rochester; BFA in studio art with School of the Museum of Fine Arts; MA in religion with Andover Newton Theological School; Doctor of Optometry with New England School of Optometry. **Credit/placement by examination:** AP, CLEP, IB, institutional tests. 8 credit hours maximum toward bachelor's degree. **Support services:** Learning center, reduced course load, study skills assistance, tutoring, writing center.

Majors. Area/ethnic studies: American, Asian, French, German, Italian, Latin American, Russian/Slavic, women's. **Biology:** General, biochemistry, bioinformatics. **Computer sciences:** General, computer science. **Conservation:** Environmental science. **Foreign languages:** Classics, French, German, Italian, Latin, modern Greek, Russian, Spanish. **History:** General. **Interdisciplinary:** Biological/physical sciences, math/computer science. **Liberal arts:** Arts/sciences. **Math:** General. **Philosophy/religion:** Philosophy, religion. **Physical sciences:** Astronomy, chemistry, physics. **Psychology:** General, psychobiology. **Social sciences:** Anthropology, economics, international relations, political science, sociology. **Visual/performing arts:** Art history/conservation, studio arts. **Other:** Ancient studies, Classical civilization, Mathematics and economics, Religion and history, Theatre and English dramatic literature.

Most popular majors. Area/ethnic studies 10%, biology 6%, English 9%, history 10%, psychology 15%, social sciences 27%, visual/performing arts 10%.

Computing on campus. 348 workstations in library, computer center, student center. Dormitories wired for high-speed internet access and linked to campus network. Commuter students can connect to campus network. Online course registration, online library, helpline, repair service, student web hosting, wireless network available.

Student life. Freshman orientation: Mandatory. Preregistration for classes offered. Held 2-3 days prior to start of classes. **Housing:** Guaranteed on-campus for all undergraduates. Coed dorms, single-sex dorms, special housing for disabled, wellness housing available. Quiet housing available. **Activities:** Bands, choral groups, dance, drama, film society, international student organizations, literary magazine, music ensembles, musical theater, radio station, student government, student newspaper, symphony orchestra, Amnesty International, student art league, black students association, Latino students association, Asian and Southeast students association.

Athletics. NCAA. **Intercollegiate:** Baseball M, basketball, cross-country, diving, field hockey W, lacrosse, soccer, softball W, swimming, synchronized swimming W, tennis, track and field, volleyball W. **Intramural:** Badminton, basketball, football (non-tackle), soccer, softball, tennis, volleyball. **Team name:** Lyons.

Student services. Career counseling, student employment services, financial aid counseling, health services, minority student services, personal counseling, placement for graduates, women's services. **Physically disabled:** Services for visually, hearing impaired.

Contact. E-mail: admission@wheatoncollege.edu
Phone: (508) 286-8251 Toll-free number: (800) 394-6003
Fax: (508) 286-8271
Gail Berson, Vice President for Enrollment and Dean of Admission and Student Aid, Wheaton College, 26 East Main Street, Norton, MA 02766

Wheelock College

Boston, Massachusetts — **CB member**
www.wheelock.edu — **CB code: 3964**

- Private 4-year liberal arts and teachers college
- Residential campus in very large city
- 818 degree-seeking undergraduates: 3% part-time, 92% women, 9% African American, 3% Asian American, 7% Hispanic American, 1% international
- 260 degree-seeking graduate students
- 74% of applicants admitted
- SAT or ACT (ACT writing optional), application essay required
- 58% graduate within 6 years

General. Founded in 1888. Regionally accredited. Member of the Colleges of the Fenway. **Degrees:** 160 bachelor's awarded; master's offered. **Location:** 2 miles from downtown. **Calendar:** Semester. **Full-time faculty:** 63 total; 87% have terminal degrees, 24% minority, 78% women. **Part-time faculty:** 80 total; 26% have terminal degrees, 25% minority, 78% women. **Class size:** 71% < 20, 29% 20-39, less than 1% 40-49.

Freshman class profile. 1,096 applied, 808 admitted, 237 enrolled.

Mid 50% test scores		**GPA 3.0-3.49:**	30%
SAT critical reading:	440-520	**GPA 2.0-2.99:**	48%
SAT math:	420-530	**Rank in top quarter:**	30%
SAT writing:	430-540	**Rank in top tenth:**	11%
ACT composite:	18-23	**Out-of-state:**	56%
GPA 3.75 or higher:	11%	**Live on campus:**	91%
GPA 3.50-3.74:	11%	**International:**	2%

Basis for selection. School achievement record most important. Test scores, school and community activities considered. Interview recommended.

High school preparation. College-preparatory program recommended. 16 units required. Required units include English 4, mathematics 3, social studies 2, science 2 (laboratory 1). Child development course recommended.

2008-2009 Annual costs. Tuition/fees: $27,205. Room/board: $10,825. Books/supplies: $880. Personal expenses: $1,050.

2008-2009 Financial aid. **Need-based:** 209 full-time freshmen applied for aid; 178 were judged to have need; 178 of these received aid. Average need met was 74%. Average scholarship/grant was $15,734; average loan $3,916. 61% of total undergraduate aid awarded as scholarships/grants, 39% as loans/jobs. **Non-need-based:** Awarded to 178 full-time undergraduates, including 81 freshmen. Scholarships awarded for academics, job skills, leadership.

Application procedures. **Admission:** Priority date 3/1; no deadline. $35 fee, may be waived for applicants with need, free for online applicants. Application must be submitted on paper. Admission notification on a rolling basis beginning on or about 1/1. Must reply by May 1 or within 2 week(s) if notified thereafter. **Financial aid:** Priority date 2/15; no closing date. FAFSA required. Applicants notified on a rolling basis starting 3/1; must reply by 5/1.

Academics. Fieldwork throughout all 4 years supplements classwork in day care, infant and toddler behavior, museum teaching, children in health care settings, elementary education, special education, social work programs. Students choose major and professional studies concentration in early childhood care and education, elementary school education, juvenile justice, social work, or child life. **Special study options:** Combined bachelor's/graduate degree, cross-registration, double major, independent study, internships, liberal arts/career combination, study abroad, teacher certification program. **Credit/placement by examination:** AP, CLEP, institutional tests. 32 credit hours maximum toward bachelor's degree. **Support services:** Learning center, pre-admission summer program, reduced course load, remedial instruction, study skills assistance, tutoring, writing center.

Majors. **Education:** Early childhood, elementary, special. **Family/consumer sciences:** Child care, child development. **Liberal arts:** Arts/sciences. **Public administration:** Social work. **Visual/performing arts:** General.

Computing on campus. 120 workstations in dormitories, library, computer center, student center. Dormitories wired for high-speed internet access and linked to campus network. Commuter students can connect to campus network. Online course registration, online library, helpline, repair service, wireless network available.

Student life. **Freshman orientation:** Mandatory, $200 fee. Preregistration for classes offered. Two-day program held in summer; students have choice of 2 sessions. **Housing:** Guaranteed on-campus for freshmen. Coed dorms, single-sex dorms, special housing for disabled, cooperative housing, wellness housing available. $100 nonrefundable deposit, deadline 5/1. Smoke-free areas, wellness floor available. **Activities:** Choral groups, dance, drama, musical theater, student government, social work club, women's center, Boston Association for the Education of Young Children, child life council, sign language club, Bible study, juvenile justice and youth advocacy council.

Athletics. NCAA. **Intercollegiate:** Basketball, diving W, field hockey W, soccer W, softball W, swimming W, tennis M. **Intramural:** Basketball, racquetball, soccer, softball, squash, volleyball. **Team name:** Wildcats.

Student services. Alcohol/substance abuse counseling, career counseling, student employment services, financial aid counseling, health services, personal counseling, placement for graduates, women's services. **Physically disabled:** Services for visually, speech, hearing impaired.

Contact. E-mail: undergrad@wheelock.edu
Phone: (617) 879-2206 Toll-free number: (800) 734-5212
Fax: (617) 879-2449
Lisa Slavin, Dean of Enrollment and Financial Aid, Wheelock College, 200 The Riverway, Boston, MA 02215-4176

Williams College

Williamstown, Massachusetts — **CB member**
www.williams.edu — **CB code: 3965**

- Private 4-year liberal arts college affiliated with United Church of Christ
- Residential campus in small town
- 1,970 degree-seeking undergraduates: 50% women, 10% African American, 11% Asian American, 9% Hispanic American, 1% Native American, 7% international
- 48 degree-seeking graduate students
- 17% of applicants admitted
- SAT or ACT with writing, SAT Subject Tests, application essay required
- 96% graduate within 6 years

General. Founded in 1793. Regionally accredited. **Degrees:** 510 bachelor's awarded; master's offered. **ROTC:** Air Force. **Location:** 35 miles from Albany, New York; 150 miles from Boston. **Calendar:** 4-1-4. **Full-time faculty:** 257 total; 97% have terminal degrees, 18% minority, 41% women. **Part-time faculty:** 48 total; 73% have terminal degrees, 15% minority, 40% women. **Class size:** 75% < 20, 19% 20-39, 3% 40-49, 2% 50-99, less than 1% >100. **Special facilities:** Performing arts center, experimental forest, environmental studies center, observatory, electron-scanning microscope, transmission microscopes, studio art center, nuclear magnetic resonance imager, college museum.

Freshman class profile. 7,552 applied, 1,281 admitted, 539 enrolled.

Mid 50% test scores		**Rank in top tenth:**	87%
SAT critical reading:	660-760	**Return as sophomores:**	97%
SAT math:	660-760	**Out-of-state:**	87%
ACT composite:	29-33	**Live on campus:**	100%
Rank in top quarter:	99%	**International:**	9%

Basis for selection. School achievement record, character and personal promise, test scores, essay important. College seeks diversity of social, economic, and geographic backgrounds. Leadership and accomplishment in extracurricular activities also considered.

High school preparation. College-preparatory program required. Recommended units include English 4, mathematics 4, social studies 3, science 3 (laboratory 3) and foreign language 4. Writing skills stressed. Course work should be at highest level available.

2008-2009 Annual costs. Tuition/fees: $37,640. Room/board: $9,890. Books/supplies: $800. Personal expenses: $1,200.

2008-2009 Financial aid. All financial aid based on need. 334 full-time freshmen applied for aid; 269 were judged to have need; 269 of these received aid. Average need met was 100%. Average scholarship/grant was $38,410. 96% of total undergraduate aid awarded as scholarships/grants, 4% as loans/jobs.

Application procedures. Admission: Closing date 1/1 (postmark date). $60 fee, may be waived for applicants with need. Admission notification 4/1. Must reply by May 1 or within 2 week(s) if notified thereafter. **Financial aid:** Closing date 2/1. FAFSA, CSS PROFILE required. Applicants notified by 4/1; must reply by 5/1.

Academics. Special study options: Combined bachelor's/graduate degree, cross-registration, double major, independent study, internships, New York semester, student-designed major, study abroad. Summer science research program, Williams in Oxford, Mystic maritime studies program, tutorials, 3-2 engineering program with Columbia University and Washington University. **Credit/placement by examination:** AP, CLEP, IB, institutional tests. **Support services:** Pre-admission summer program, study skills assistance, tutoring, writing center.

Majors. Area/ethnic studies: American, Asian. **Biology:** General. **Computer sciences:** Computer science. **Foreign languages:** Chinese, classics, comparative lit, French, German, Japanese, Russian, Spanish. **History:** General. **Math:** General. **Philosophy/religion:** Philosophy, religion. **Physical sciences:** Astronomy, astrophysics, chemistry, geology, physics. **Psychology:** General. **Social sciences:** Anthropology, economics, political science, sociology. **Visual/performing arts:** Art history/conservation, dramatic, studio arts.

Most popular majors. Biology 9%, English 10%, history 7%, mathematics 7%, physical sciences 8%, psychology 8%, social sciences 25%, visual/performing arts 12%.

Computing on campus. 247 workstations in library, computer center, student center. Dormitories wired for high-speed internet access and linked to campus network. Commuter students can connect to campus network. Online course registration, helpline, repair service, student web hosting, wireless network available.

Student life. Freshman orientation: Mandatory. **Housing:** Guaranteed on-campus for all undergraduates. Coed dorms, cooperative housing available. $200 nonrefundable deposit, deadline 5/1. **Activities:** Pep band, choral groups, dance, drama, film society, international student organizations, literary magazine, music ensembles, radio station, student government, student newspaper, symphony orchestra, black student union, Purple Key, Asian Link, VISTA (Hispanic students), Korean club, minority coalition, nonviolent alternatives committee, women's club, Hillel.

Athletics. NCAA. **Intercollegiate:** Baseball M, basketball, cross-country, diving, field hockey W, football (tackle) M, golf, ice hockey, lacrosse, rowing (crew), skiing, soccer, softball W, squash, swimming, tennis, track and field, volleyball W, wrestling M. **Intramural:** Badminton, basketball, ice hockey M, skiing, soccer, softball, volleyball. **Team name:** Ephs.

Student services. Alcohol/substance abuse counseling, chaplain/spiritual director, career counseling, services for economically disadvantaged, student employment services, financial aid counseling, health services, minority student services, personal counseling, placement for graduates. **Physically disabled:** Services for visually, hearing impaired.

Contact. E-mail: admission@williams.edu
Phone: (413) 597-2211 Fax: (413) 597-4052
Richard Nesbitt, Director of Admissions, Williams College, 33 Stetson Court, Williamstown, MA 01267

Worcester Polytechnic Institute

Worcester, Massachusetts — **CB member**
www.wpi.edu — **CB code: 3969**

- Private 4-year university
- Residential campus in small city
- 3,160 degree-seeking undergraduates: 3% part-time, 26% women, 3% African American, 6% Asian American, 5% Hispanic American, 8% international
- 988 degree-seeking graduate students
- 67% of applicants admitted
- Application essay required
- 80% graduate within 6 years; 26% enter graduate study

General. Founded in 1865. Regionally accredited. Participation by most students in overseas or off-campus projects; over 20 project centers located throughout North America, Central America, Africa, Australia, Asia and Europe. **Degrees:** 676 bachelor's awarded; master's, doctoral offered. **ROTC:** Army, Naval, Air Force. **Location:** 35 miles from Boston. **Calendar:** Quarter, limited summer session. **Full-time faculty:** 251 total; 94% have terminal degrees, 16% minority, 24% women. **Part-time faculty:** 63 total; 59% have terminal degrees, 5% minority, 30% women. **Class size:** 69% < 20, 18% 20-39, 4% 40-49, 7% 50-99, 2% >100. **Special facilities:** Centers for life sciences and bioengineering, biomaterials, bioprocessing, comparative neuroimaging, molecular sensors, nanoscience and technology, untethered healthcare, water research, computer-controlled machining, holographic studies and laser technology, wireless information network studies, fuel cell, industrial math and statistics, fire science laboratory, pavement research laboratory, atomic force microscopy laboratory.

Freshman class profile. 5,706 applied, 3,819 admitted, 907 enrolled.

Mid 50% test scores		**Rank in top quarter:**	88%
SAT critical reading:	550-660	**Rank in top tenth:**	53%
SAT math:	630-720	**End year in good standing:**	92%
SAT writing:	550-650	**Return as sophomores:**	92%
ACT composite:	25-30	**Out-of-state:**	46%
GPA 3.75 or higher:	59%	**Live on campus:**	90%
GPA 3.50-3.74:	21%	**International:**	11%
GPA 3.0-3.49:	18%	**Fraternities:**	33%
GPA 2.0-2.99:	2%	**Sororities:**	29%

Basis for selection. High school record including academic rigor most important. Extracurricular activities, recommendations, motivation, creativity, initiative important. In lieu of test scores, students may submit alternative documentation of potential for academic success. SAT/ACT scores or alternative materials that will better reflect the applicant's potential for success (Flex Path) required. Students who choose the Flex Path encouraged to submit examples of academic work or extracurricular projects that reflect a high level of organization, motivation, creativity and problem-solving ability. Interviews offered, but not required. **Homeschooled:** Statement describing homeschool structure and mission, transcript of courses and grades, interview, letter of recommendation (nonparent) required. Submit as much relevant support material as possible and outside recommendations. Detailed course descriptions recommended.

High school preparation. College-preparatory program required. 10 units required. Required and recommended units include English 4, mathematics 4, social studies 2, history 1, science 2-4 (laboratory 2), foreign language 2 and computer science 1. Math requirement includes algebra, geometry, trigonometry and pre-calculus. Science should include physics, chemistry, or biology.

2009-2010 Annual costs. Tuition/fees (projected): $37,845. Room/board: $11,315. Books/supplies: $1,000. Personal expenses: $1,200.

2007-2008 Financial aid. Need-based: 696 full-time freshmen applied for aid; 599 were judged to have need; 596 of these received aid. Average need met was 65%. Average scholarship/grant was $16,584; average loan $5,806. 75% of total undergraduate aid awarded as scholarships/grants, 25% as loans/jobs. **Non-need-based:** Awarded to 1,156 full-time undergraduates, including 327 freshmen. Scholarships awarded for academics, leadership, minority status, ROTC.

Application procedures. Admission: Closing date 2/1 (postmark date). $60 fee, may be waived for applicants with need. Admission notification 4/1. Must reply by May 1 or within 2 week(s) if notified thereafter. Second early action closing date January 1; notification date February 1. **Financial aid:** Closing date 2/1. FAFSA, CSS PROFILE required. Applicants notified by 4/1; must reply by 5/1.

Academics. Programs student-designed, stress projects and individualized study combining classroom and professional experience. **Special study options:** Accelerated study, combined bachelor's/graduate degree, cooperative education, cross-registration, distance learning, double major, dual enrollment of high school students, ESL, honors, independent study, liberal arts/career combination, student-designed major, study abroad, teacher certification program, Washington semester. Completion of degree-required projects at off-campus locations (international and domestic) supervised by WPI faculty. **Credit/placement by examination:** AP, CLEP, IB, institutional tests. **Support services:** Reduced course load, study skills assistance, tutoring, writing center.

Majors. Biology: General, biochemistry, biotechnology. **Business:** Business admin, management information systems, management science, operations. **Computer sciences:** Computer science, web page design. **Conservation:** Environmental studies. **Engineering:** Aerospace, biomedical, chemical, civil, electrical, environmental, industrial, mechanical, physics, systems. **Engineering technology:** Industrial management. **Health:** Predental, premedicine, preveterinary. **Interdisciplinary:** Biological/physical sciences, global studies, science/society. **Legal studies:** Prelaw. **Liberal arts:** Humanities. **Math:** General, applied. **Physical sciences:** Chemistry, physics. **Social sciences:** General, economics. **Other:** Robotics engineering.

Most popular majors. Biology 11%, computer/information sciences 7%, engineering/engineering technologies 66%.

Computing on campus. 1,000 workstations in dormitories, library, computer center, student center. Dormitories wired for high-speed internet access and linked to campus network. Commuter students can connect to campus network. Online course registration, online library, helpline, repair service, student web hosting, wireless network available.

Student life. **Freshman orientation:** Available, $200 fee. Preregistration for classes offered. Program held in late August. **Housing:** Guaranteed on-campus for freshmen. Coed dorms, special housing for disabled, apartments, fraternity/sorority housing, wellness housing available. Special interest housing available. **Activities:** Bands, campus ministries, choral groups, dance, drama, film society, international student organizations, literary magazine, music ensembles, musical theater, radio station, student government, student newspaper, symphony orchestra, African American cultural society, volunteer tutoring group, Big Brother/Big Sister, World House, European student association, Asian society, Hispanic student association, women's awareness group, students for social awareness, Amnesty International.

Athletics. NCAA. **Intercollegiate:** Baseball M, basketball, cross-country, field hockey W, football (tackle) M, rowing (crew), soccer, softball W, swimming, track and field, volleyball W, wrestling M. **Intramural:** Basketball, bowling, cross-country, fencing, football (non-tackle) M, racquetball, soccer, softball, swimming, table tennis, volleyball, water polo M, wrestling M. **Team name:** Engineers.

Student services. Adult student services, alcohol/substance abuse counseling, chaplain/spiritual director, career counseling, student employment services, financial aid counseling, health services, minority student services, personal counseling, placement for graduates, veterans' counselor, women's services. **Physically disabled:** Services for visually, speech, hearing impaired.

Contact. E-mail: admissions@wpi.edu
Phone: (508) 831-5286 Fax: (508) 831-5875
Edward Connor, Director of Admission, Worcester Polytechnic Institute, 100 Institute Road, Worcester, MA 01609-2280

Worcester State College

Worcester, Massachusetts — **CB member**
www.worcester.edu — **CB code: 3524**

- Public 4-year liberal arts and teachers college
- Commuter campus in small city
- 4,077 degree-seeking undergraduates: 18% part-time, 59% women, 5% African American, 4% Asian American, 5% Hispanic American, 1% international
- 437 degree-seeking graduate students
- 54% of applicants admitted
- SAT or ACT (ACT writing optional) required
- 47% graduate within 6 years

General. Founded in 1874. Regionally accredited. **Degrees:** 762 bachelor's awarded; master's offered. **ROTC:** Army, Naval, Air Force. **Location:** 45 miles from Boston; 65 miles from Hartford, Connecticut. **Calendar:** Semester, extensive summer session. **Full-time faculty:** 185 total; 77% have terminal degrees, 18% minority, 52% women. **Part-time faculty:** 201 total; 6% minority, 53% women. **Class size:** 51% < 20, 49% 20-39. **Special facilities:** Photographic labs; multimedia classrooms with satellite connectivity; speech, language and hearing clinic.

Freshman class profile. 3,736 applied, 2,025 admitted, 682 enrolled.

Mid 50% test scores		**GPA 3.0-3.49:**	31%
SAT critical reading:	450-540	**GPA 2.0-2.99:**	48%
SAT math:	450-560	**Return as sophomores:**	76%
ACT composite:	18-23	**Out-of-state:**	3%
GPA 3.75 or higher:	12%	**Live on campus:**	55%
GPA 3.50-3.74:	9%		

Basis for selection. Secondary school record most important; test scores important; extracurricular activities considered. Interview and personal essay recommended for academically weak. **Homeschooled:** Student must submit documentation that home school plan meets district curriculum standards. **Learning Disabled:** SAT waiver available for students with learning disabilties with IEP plan.

High school preparation. College-preparatory program required. 16 units required. Required units include English 4, mathematics 3, social studies 1, history 1, science 3 (laboratory 1), foreign language 2 and academic electives 2. History unit must be US history.

2008-2009 Annual costs. Tuition/fees: $6,170; $12,250 out-of-state. Room/board: $8,527.

2007-2008 Financial aid. **Need-based:** 601 full-time freshmen applied for aid; 382 were judged to have need; 372 of these received aid. Average need met was 81%. Average scholarship/grant was $4,252; average loan $2,059. 59% of total undergraduate aid awarded as scholarships/grants, 41% as loans/jobs. **Non-need-based:** Awarded to 499 full-time undergraduates, including 162 freshmen. Scholarships awarded for academics, ROTC. **Additional information:** Veterans, Native Americans and those certified by Massachusetts Rehabilitation Commission and Massachusetts Commission for the Blind considered for tuition waivers while funds available. Tuition also waived for needy Massachusetts residents and in-state National Guard members.

Application procedures. **Admission:** Priority date 3/15; deadline 6/1 (receipt date). $20 fee, may be waived for applicants with need. Admission notification on a rolling basis beginning on or about 12/1. Must reply by May 1 or within 4 week(s) if notified thereafter. **Financial aid:** Priority date 3/1, closing date 5/1. FAFSA required. Applicants notified on a rolling basis starting 3/1; must reply within 2 week(s) of notification.

Academics. **Special study options:** Combined bachelor's/graduate degree, cross-registration, distance learning, double major, ESL, exchange student, honors, independent study, internships, liberal arts/career combination, study abroad, teacher certification program, Washington semester. Foreign exchange student program. **Credit/placement by examination:** AP, CLEP, IB, institutional tests. 30 credit hours maximum toward bachelor's degree. **Support services:** Learning center, pre-admission summer program, reduced course load, remedial instruction, study skills assistance, tutoring, writing center.

Majors. **Biology:** General, biotechnology. **Business:** Business admin. **Communications:** General, media studies. **Communications technology:** Radio/tv. **Computer sciences:** General. **Education:** Early childhood, elementary. **Foreign languages:** Spanish. **Health:** Adult health nursing, communication disorders, community health services, nursing (RN). **History:** General. **Math:** General. **Physical sciences:** General, chemistry. **Protective services:** Criminal justice. **Psychology:** General. **Social sciences:** Economics, geography, sociology, urban studies.

Most popular majors. Biology 6%, business/marketing 20%, communications/journalism 6%, health sciences 11%, psychology 10%, security/protective services 8%.

Computing on campus. PC or laptop required. 102 workstations in dormitories, library, computer center, student center. Dormitories wired for high-speed internet access and linked to campus network. Commuter students can connect to campus network. Online course registration, online library, helpline, repair service, student web hosting, wireless network available.

Student life. **Freshman orientation:** Mandatory, $75 fee. Preregistration for classes offered. Four-hour parent orientation in Spring; 4.5-day session for students last week in August. **Housing:** Coed dorms, single-sex dorms, special housing for disabled, wellness housing available. $150 nonrefundable deposit, deadline 2/15. **Activities:** Bands, campus ministries, choral groups, dance, drama, international student organizations, music ensembles, radio station, student government, student newspaper, TV station, student events committee, Third World alliance, campus ambassadors, gay-straight alliance.

Athletics. NCAA. **Intercollegiate:** Baseball M, basketball, cheerleading, cross-country, field hockey W, football (tackle) M, golf M, ice hockey M, lacrosse W, soccer, softball W, tennis W, track and field, volleyball. **Intramural:** Baseball M, basketball, cheerleading, cross-country, field hockey W, football (tackle) M, golf M, ice hockey M, lacrosse W, rowing (crew), soccer, softball W, tennis W, track and field, volleyball. **Team name:** Lancers.

Student services. Alcohol/substance abuse counseling, chaplain/spiritual director, career counseling, student employment services, financial aid counseling, health services, personal counseling, placement for graduates, veterans' counselor, women's services. **Physically disabled:** Services for visually, speech, hearing impaired.

Contact. E-mail: admissions@worcester.edu
Phone: (508) 929-8040 Toll-free number: (866) 972-2255
Fax: (508) 929-8183
Beth Axelson, Admissions Director, Worcester State College, 486 Chandler Street, Worcester, MA 01602-2597

Zion Bible College

Haverhill, Massachusetts
www.zbc.edu — **CB code: 3942**

- Private 4-year Bible college affiliated with Assemblies of God
- Residential campus in small city
- 250 degree-seeking undergraduates: 18% part-time, 49% women
- Application essay required

General. Accredited by ABHE. **Degrees:** 46 bachelor's awarded. **ROTC:** Army. **Location:** 40 miles north of Boston. **Calendar:** Semester, limited summer session. **Full-time faculty:** 9 total; 22% have terminal degrees. **Part-time faculty:** 20 total; 10% have terminal degrees, 5% minority, 50% women. **Class size:** 63% < 20, 26% 20-39, 8% 40-49, 3% 50-99.

Freshman class profile. 86 applied, 86 admitted, 41 enrolled.

Mid 50% test scores			
SAT critical reading:	380-610	SAT writing:	380-580
SAT math:	390-590	Out-of-state:	68%
		Live on campus:	93%

Basis for selection. Open admission. Three references are required for admission, including a pastoral recommendation; high school transcript, immunizations, health certificate, and test scores also required. **Homeschooled:** Transcript of courses and grades required. Applicants must produce diploma and transcript that verify graduation by the state department of education, local school district or accrediting association. Students who cannot produce this must submit a GED.

2008-2009 Annual costs. Tuition/fees: $7,640. Room/board: $5,700. Books/supplies: $600.

2008-2009 Financial aid. Need-based: 36 full-time freshmen applied for aid; 32 were judged to have need; 31 of these received aid. Average need met was 28%. Average scholarship/grant was $3,530; average loan $1,715. **Non-need-based:** Awarded to 62 full-time undergraduates, including 19 freshmen. Scholarships awarded for academics, leadership, minority status, state residency.

Application procedures. Admission: No deadline. $35 fee. Admission notification on a rolling basis. Must reply by May 1 or within 4 week(s) if notified thereafter. Letter of Intent with deposit (tuition and board) required one month after notification. **Financial aid:** Priority date 6/1; no closing date. FAFSA required. Applicants notified on a rolling basis; must reply within 4 week(s) of notification.

Academics. Special study options: Independent study, internships, weekend college. **Credit/placement by examination:** AP, CLEP. **Support services:** Learning center, reduced course load, study skills assistance.

Majors. Theology: Bible.

Computing on campus. 15 workstations in library, computer center. Dormitories wired for high-speed internet access. Online library, wireless network available.

Student life. Freshman orientation: Mandatory. **Policies:** Nightly curfew of 10:30, except for Fridays (11:00 or midnight for seniors). Chapel attendance required Tuesday through Friday. No alcohol, drugs, or smoking permitted on or off-campus. Full-time students assigned to assist in an area church. Religious observance required. **Housing:** Guaranteed on-campus for all undergraduates. Single-sex dorms available. $100 fully refundable deposit. **Activities:** Campus ministries, choral groups, music ensembles, student government.

Student services. Chaplain/spiritual director, financial aid counseling.

Contact. E-mail: admissions@zbc.edu
Phone: (978) 478-3400 ext. 3431 Toll-free number: (800) 356-4014
Fax: (978) 478-3406
David Hodge, Director of Admissions and Records, Zion Bible College, 320 South Main Street, Haverhill, MA 01835

Michigan

Adrian College

Adrian, Michigan **CB member**
www.adrian.edu **CB code: 1001**

- Private 4-year liberal arts college affiliated with United Methodist Church
- Residential campus in large town
- 1,469 degree-seeking undergraduates: 3% part-time, 47% women, 4% African American, 2% Hispanic American, 4% international
- 58% of applicants admitted
- SAT or ACT (ACT writing optional) required
- 50% graduate within 6 years

General. Founded in 1859. Regionally accredited. **Degrees:** 221 bachelor's awarded. **Location:** 75 miles from Detroit, 30 miles from Toledo, Ohio. **Calendar:** Semester, limited summer session. **Full-time faculty:** 82 total; 80% have terminal degrees, 13% minority, 39% women. **Class size:** 66% < 20, 33% 20-39, less than 1% 40-49, 1% 50-99. **Special facilities:** Observatory, planetarium, arboretum, solar greenhouse, human anatomy laboratory, writing laboratory, educational curriculum center.

Freshman class profile. 3,944 applied, 2,285 admitted, 500 enrolled.

Mid 50% test scores		**Rank in top quarter:**	51%
ACT composite:	20-25	**Rank in top tenth:**	24%
GPA 3.75 or higher:	25%	**Return as sophomores:**	74%
GPA 3.50-3.74:	16%	**Out-of-state:**	23%
GPA 3.0-3.49:	57%	**Live on campus:**	93%
GPA 2.0-2.99:	2%	**International:**	3%

Basis for selection. School achievement most important, followed by test scores. Applicants should rank in top half of high school class. School recommendations and extracurricular activities considered. ACT preferred. **Homeschooled:** Must have transcript approved by school district.

High school preparation. College-preparatory program recommended. 15 units recommended. Recommended units include English 4, mathematics 3, social studies 1, history 1, science 2 (laboratory 1), foreign language 2 and academic electives 2.

2008-2009 Annual costs. Tuition/fees: $23,390. Room/board: $7,600. Books/supplies: $400. Personal expenses: $928.

2007-2008 Financial aid. Need-based: 420 full-time freshmen applied for aid; 420 were judged to have need; 420 of these received aid. Average need met was 100%. Average scholarship/grant was $9,159; average loan $4,483. 70% of total undergraduate aid awarded as scholarships/grants, 30% as loans/jobs. **Non-need-based:** Awarded to 1,100 full-time undergraduates, including 431 freshmen. Scholarships awarded for academics, alumni affiliation, art, leadership, music/drama, religious affiliation, state residency.

Application procedures. Admission: No deadline. No application fee. Admission notification on a rolling basis beginning on or about 9/1. **Financial aid:** Priority date 3/1; no closing date. FAFSA required. Applicants notified on a rolling basis starting 3/15; must reply by 5/1 or within 2 week(s) of notification.

Academics. Special study options: Combined bachelor's/graduate degree, double major, dual enrollment of high school students, honors, independent study, internships, student-designed major, study abroad, teacher certification program, Washington semester. **Credit/placement by examination:** AP, CLEP, IB, institutional tests. 15 credit hours maximum toward associate degree, 30 toward bachelor's. **Support services:** Learning center, pre-admission summer program, reduced course load, remedial instruction, study skills assistance, tutoring, writing center.

Majors. Area/ethnic studies: Japanese. **Biology:** General. **Business:** Accounting, business admin, international, international marketing, management science, marketing. **Communications:** General, journalism, media studies. **Conservation:** Environmental science, environmental studies. **Education:** General, art, elementary, health, multi-level teacher, music, physical, secondary, social science. **Foreign languages:** French, German, Spanish. **Health:** Athletic training, prededical, premedicine, prepharmacy, preveterinary. **History:** General. **Interdisciplinary:** Global studies. **Legal studies:** Prelaw. **Math:** General. **Parks/recreation:** Exercise sciences, health/fitness. **Philosophy/religion:** Philosophy, religion. **Physical sciences:** Chemistry, geology, physics. **Protective services:** Criminal justice. **Psychology:** General. **Public administration:** Social work. **Social sciences:** Economics, political science, sociology. **Theology:** Preministerial. **Visual/performing arts:** Art, arts management, dramatic, interior design.

Most popular majors. Business/marketing 10%, education 8%, parks/recreation 9%, visual/performing arts 17%.

Computing on campus. 170 workstations in library, computer center, student center. Dormitories wired for high-speed internet access and linked to campus network. Commuter students can connect to campus network. Online course registration, online library, helpline, student web hosting, wireless network available.

Student life. Freshman orientation: Mandatory. Preregistration for classes offered. Week-long program in August. Students take placement exams and take a first-year trip. **Policies:** Freshmen, sophomores, and juniors required to live on campus unless living with family. **Housing:** Guaranteed on-campus for all undergraduates. Coed dorms, single-sex dorms, apartments, fraternity/sorority housing available. $100 deposit, deadline 7/1. **Activities:** Bands, campus ministries, choral groups, dance, drama, international student organizations, literary magazine, music ensembles, Model UN, musical theater, radio station, student government, student newspaper, symphony orchestra, Wesley Fellowship, Circle K, Religious Life Council, Habitat for Humanity, African-American Leaders Promoting Higher Achievement, Leaders in College Service, Catholic student organization.

Athletics. NCAA. **Intercollegiate:** Baseball M, basketball, cross-country, football (tackle) M, golf, ice hockey, lacrosse, soccer, softball W, tennis, track and field, volleyball W. **Intramural:** Basketball, bowling, football (non-tackle), lacrosse, racquetball, soccer, softball, tennis, volleyball. **Team name:** Bulldogs.

Student services. Adult student services, alcohol/substance abuse counseling, chaplain/spiritual director, career counseling, student employment services, financial aid counseling, health services, minority student services, personal counseling, placement for graduates. **Physically disabled:** Services for visually, speech, hearing impaired.

Contact. E-mail: admissions@adrian.edu
Phone: (517) 265-5161 ext. 4326 Toll-free number: (800) 877-2246
Fax: (517) 264-3878
Carolyn Quinlan, Director of Admissions, Adrian College, 110 South Madison Street, Adrian, MI 49221-2575

Albion College

Albion, Michigan **CB member**
www.albion.edu **CB code: 1007**

- Private 4-year liberal arts college affiliated with United Methodist Church
- Residential campus in small town
- 1,845 degree-seeking undergraduates: 54% women, 3% African American, 2% Asian American, 1% Hispanic American, 1% international
- 83% of applicants admitted
- SAT or ACT (ACT writing optional), application essay required
- 73% graduate within 6 years

General. Founded in 1835. Regionally accredited. **Degrees:** 442 bachelor's awarded. **Location:** 55 miles from Lansing, 55 miles from Ann Arbor. **Calendar:** Semester, limited summer session. **Full-time faculty:** 136 total; 90% have terminal degrees, 10% minority, 42% women. **Part-time faculty:** 31 total; 23% have terminal degrees, 3% minority, 55% women. **Class size:** 66% < 20, 32% 20-39, 2% 40-49, less than 1% 50-99. **Special facilities:** Science complex, 144-acre nature center, observatory, equestrian center, institutes for public service, professional management, environmental studies, K-12 education, pre-medical and health care studies, honors studies, foundation for undergraduate research, scholarship, and creative activity.

Freshman class profile. 1,958 applied, 1,630 admitted, 484 enrolled.

Mid 50% test scores		**GPA 2.0-2.99:**	7%
SAT critical reading:	560-630	**Rank in top quarter:**	61%
SAT math:	500-650	**Rank in top tenth:**	27%
SAT writing:	500-630	**Return as sophomores:**	86%
ACT composite:	23-27	**Out-of-state:**	6%
GPA 3.75 or higher:	34%	**Live on campus:**	99%
GPA 3.50-3.74:	26%	**Fraternities:**	45%
GPA 3.0-3.49:	33%	**Sororities:**	28%

Basis for selection. Admission based on school achievement record, ACT/SAT test scores, recommendations from counselor or principal. Interview recommended. Audition recommended for music and theater majors.

High school preparation. College-preparatory program required. 15 units required; 19 recommended. Required and recommended units include English 4, mathematics 3-4, social studies 3-4, science 3-4 (laboratory 2) and foreign language 2-3.

2008-2009 Annual costs. Tuition/fees: $28,880. Room/board: $8,190. Books/supplies: $650. Personal expenses: $350.

2008-2009 Financial aid. **Need-based:** 384 full-time freshmen applied for aid; 318 were judged to have need; 318 of these received aid. Average need met was 91%. Average scholarship/grant was $20,133; average loan $3,908. 80% of total undergraduate aid awarded as scholarships/grants, 20% as loans/jobs. **Non-need-based:** Awarded to 1,726 full-time undergraduates, including 468 freshmen. Scholarships awarded for academics, alumni affiliation, art, music/drama, state residency.

Application procedures. **Admission:** Priority date 12/1; deadline 5/1 (postmark date). $20 fee, may be waived for applicants with need, free for online applicants. Admission notification on a rolling basis beginning on or about 1/1. Must reply by 5/1. **Financial aid:** Priority date 3/1; no closing date. FAFSA required. Applicants notified on a rolling basis starting 3/15; must reply by 5/1 or within 2 week(s) of notification.

Academics. **Special study options:** Combined bachelor's/graduate degree, double major, dual enrollment of high school students, honors, independent study, internships, liberal arts/career combination, New York semester, semester at sea, student-designed major, study abroad, teacher certification program, urban semester, Washington semester. Environmental institute, public service institute, liberal arts program in professional management. **Credit/placement by examination:** AP, CLEP, IB, institutional tests. **Support services:** Learning center, reduced course load, study skills assistance, tutoring, writing center.

Majors. **Area/ethnic studies:** American. **Biology:** General, biochemistry. **Business:** Business admin. **Communications:** General. **Computer sciences:** General, computer science. **Conservation:** Environmental science, environmental studies. **Education:** Art, biology, chemistry, English, foreign languages, French, German, history, mathematics, music, physical, physics, science, social studies, Spanish. **Foreign languages:** French, German, Spanish. **History:** General. **Interdisciplinary:** Behavioral sciences, biological/physical sciences, math/computer science, natural sciences, neuroscience. **Math:** General. **Philosophy/religion:** Philosophy, religion. **Physical sciences:** Chemistry, geology, physics. **Psychology:** General. **Public administration:** Policy analysis. **Social sciences:** Anthropology, economics, international relations, political science, sociology. **Visual/performing arts:** General, art, art history/conservation, dramatic, music performance, studio arts.

Most popular majors. Biology 12%, business/marketing 7%, communications/journalism 7%, education 7%, English 8%, foreign language 6%, physical sciences 6%, psychology 9%, social sciences 20%.

Computing on campus. 435 workstations in dormitories, library, computer center, student center. Dormitories wired for high-speed internet access and linked to campus network. Commuter students can connect to campus network. Online course registration, online library, helpline, repair service, wireless network available.

Student life. **Freshman orientation:** Mandatory. Preregistration for classes offered. **Housing:** Guaranteed on-campus for all undergraduates. Coed dorms, single-sex dorms, special housing for disabled, apartments, cooperative housing, fraternity/sorority housing available. Special interest annexes available. **Activities:** Bands, campus ministries, choral groups, dance, drama, international student organizations, literary magazine, music ensembles, Model UN, musical theater, radio station, student government, student newspaper, symphony orchestra, 110 campus organizations.

Athletics. NCAA. **Intercollegiate:** Baseball M, basketball, cheerleading, cross-country, diving, equestrian, football (tackle) M, golf, soccer, softball W, swimming, tennis, track and field, volleyball W. **Intramural:** Badminton, basketball, diving, football (non-tackle), football (tackle) M, racquetball, rugby, soccer, softball, swimming, tennis, volleyball. **Team name:** Britons.

Student services. Alcohol/substance abuse counseling, chaplain/spiritual director, career counseling, services for economically disadvantaged, student employment services, financial aid counseling, health services, minority student services, personal counseling, placement for graduates, women's services. **Physically disabled:** Services for visually, hearing impaired.

Contact. E-mail: admissions@albion.edu
Phone: (517) 629-0321 Toll-free number: (800) 858-6770
Fax: (517) 629-0569
Kevin Kropf, Director of Admission, Albion College, 611 East Porter Street, Albion, MI 49224-1831

Alma College

Alma, Michigan — **CB member**
www.alma.edu — **CB code: 1010**

- Private 4-year liberal arts college affiliated with Presbyterian Church (USA)
- Residential campus in small town
- 1,350 degree-seeking undergraduates: 1% part-time, 55% women, 2% African American, 1% Asian American, 2% Hispanic American, 1% Native American
- 73% of applicants admitted
- SAT or ACT (ACT writing optional) required
- 70% graduate within 6 years

General. Founded in 1886. Regionally accredited. Scottish heritage honored through marching band clad in kilts, Scottish dance troupe, student pipers, tartan, Alma Highland Festival and Games. **Degrees:** 230 bachelor's awarded. **ROTC:** Army. **Location:** 50 miles from Lansing, 45 miles from Saginaw. **Calendar:** 4-4-1 semester system. Limited summer session. **Full-time faculty:** 86 total; 87% have terminal degrees, 8% minority, 42% women. **Part-time faculty:** 52 total; 29% have terminal degrees, 8% minority, 44% women. **Class size:** 56% < 20, 39% 20-39, 2% 40-49, 3% 50-99. **Special facilities:** Planetarium, performing arts center, climbing wall, ecological station.

Freshman class profile. 1,854 applied, 1,354 admitted, 429 enrolled.

Mid 50% test scores		**GPA 2.0-2.99:**	16%
SAT critical reading:	520-680	**Rank in top quarter:**	60%
SAT math:	530-680	**Rank in top tenth:**	27%
ACT composite:	21-26	**End year in good standing:**	91%
GPA 3.75 or higher:	36%	**Return as sophomores:**	76%
GPA 3.50-3.74:	20%	**Out-of-state:**	4%
GPA 3.0-3.49:	28%	**Live on campus:**	97%

Basis for selection. Applicant should be in top half of class, have 3.0 high school GPA or 22 ACT or 1030 SAT (exclusive of Writing). Cocurricular activities considered. Portfolio recommended for art majors. Interview recommended for all, strongly recommended for academically weak and those whose grades and test scores show discrepancies.

High school preparation. College-preparatory program required. 16 units required. Required and recommended units include English 4, mathematics 3, social studies 3, science 3 and foreign language 2.

2008-2009 Annual costs. Tuition/fees: $24,850. Room/board: $8,120. Books/supplies: $800. Personal expenses: $700.

2008-2009 Financial aid. **Need-based:** 420 full-time freshmen applied for aid; 348 were judged to have need; 348 of these received aid. Average need met was 95%. Average scholarship/grant was $18,287; average loan $3,767. 74% of total undergraduate aid awarded as scholarships/grants, 26% as loans/jobs. **Non-need-based:** Awarded to 443 full-time undergraduates, including 167 freshmen. Scholarships awarded for academics, alumni affiliation, art, minority status, music/drama. **Additional information:** Auditions required for music, drama, dance scholarship candidates. Portfolios required for art scholarship candidates.

Application procedures. **Admission:** No deadline. $25 fee, may be waived for applicants with need, free for online applicants. Admission notification on a rolling basis beginning on or about 9/1. Must reply by May 1 or within 3 week(s) if notified thereafter. **Financial aid:** Priority date 3/1; no closing date. FAFSA required. Applicants notified on a rolling basis starting 3/1; must reply within 3 week(s) of notification.

Academics. One-month spring term provides special opportunities for study in United States or overseas. Students required to complete 2 spring terms. **Special study options:** Combined bachelor's/graduate degree, double major, dual enrollment of high school students, exchange student, honors, independent study, internships, New York semester, student-designed major, study abroad, teacher certification program, urban semester, Washington semester. Pre-engineering 3-2 programs with University of Michigan, Michigan Technological University; pre-occupational therapy 3-2 program with Washington University (MO). **Credit/placement by examination:** AP, CLEP, IB, SAT, ACT, institutional tests. 32 credit hours maximum toward bachelor's degree. **Support services:** Pre-admission summer program, reduced course load, remedial instruction, study skills assistance, tutoring, writing center.

Majors. **Biology:** General, biochemistry. **Business:** Accounting, business admin, finance, international, marketing. **Communications:** Media studies. **Computer sciences:** Computer science. **Education:** General, elementary, secondary. **Foreign languages:** French, German, Spanish. **Health:** Medical illustrating, predental, premedicine, preveterinary. **History:** General. **Interdisciplinary:** Biological/physical sciences, gerontology. **Legal studies:** Prelaw. **Liberal arts:** Arts/sciences, humanities. **Math:** General. **Parks/recreation:** Exercise sciences. **Philosophy/religion:** Philosophy, religion. **Physical sciences:** Chemistry, physics. **Psychology:** General. **Social sciences:** Anthropology, economics, political science, sociology. **Theology:** Preministerial. **Visual/performing arts:** General, art, art history/conservation, dance, design, dramatic, graphic design, music performance, studio arts.

Most popular majors. Biology 13%, business/marketing 15%, communications/journalism 6%, education 7%, health sciences 13%, psychology 6%, social sciences 9%, visual/performing arts 10%.

Computing on campus. 291 workstations in dormitories, library, computer center, student center. Dormitories wired for high-speed internet access and linked to campus network. Commuter students can connect to campus network. Online course registration, online library, helpline, student web hosting, wireless network available.

Student life. **Freshman orientation:** Mandatory, $330 fee. Preregistration for classes offered. One-week session begins last weekend of August and runs to Labor Day weekend. **Housing:** Guaranteed on-campus for all undergraduates. Coed dorms, single-sex dorms, fraternity/sorority housing available. $200 nonrefundable deposit, deadline 5/1. **Activities:** Bands, campus ministries, choral groups, dance, drama, international student organizations, literary magazine, music ensembles, Model UN, musical theater, opera, radio station, student government, student newspaper, symphony orchestra, College Republicans/College Democrats, Amnesty International, Big Brothers/Big Sisters, Catholic student organization, Habitat for Humanity, multicultural black student union, Students Offering Service.

Athletics. NCAA. **Intercollegiate:** Baseball M, basketball, cross-country, diving, football (tackle) M, golf, soccer, softball W, swimming, tennis, track and field, volleyball W. **Intramural:** Basketball, football (non-tackle), ice hockey, racquetball, soccer, softball, tennis, volleyball. **Team name:** Scots.

Student services. Alcohol/substance abuse counseling, chaplain/spiritual director, career counseling, student employment services, financial aid counseling, health services, personal counseling. **Physically disabled:** Services for visually, hearing impaired.

Contact. E-mail: admissions@alma.edu
Phone: (989) 463-7139 Toll-free number: (800) 321-2562
Fax: (989) 463-7057
Evan Montague, Director of Admissions, Alma College, 614 West Superior Street, Alma, MI 48801-1599

Freshman class profile. 1,687 applied, 949 admitted, 396 enrolled.

Mid 50% test scores			
SAT critical reading:	470-610	GPA 2.0-2.99:	25%
SAT math:	460-590	Rank in top quarter:	42%
SAT writing:	440-580	Rank in top tenth:	19%
ACT composite:	20-26	Return as sophomores:	78%
GPA 3.75 or higher:	31%	Out-of-state:	67%
GPA 3.50-3.74:	14%	Live on campus:	84%
GPA 3.0-3.49:	28%	International:	12%

Basis for selection. School achievement record, test scores, recommendations important. Interview recommended. Audition recommended for music majors. Portfolios recommended for architecture, art majors. **Homeschooled:** Portfolio required. **Learning Disabled:** Must advise student services of learning disability prior to admission interview and testing.

High school preparation. 13 units required; 15 recommended. Required and recommended units include English 3-4, mathematics 2-3, social studies 1, history 2, science 2 and academic electives 3. Additional 1 unit chemistry, 1 unit physics, 1 unit computer recommended.

2009-2010 Annual costs. Tuition/fees (projected): $21,170. Room/board: $6,360. Books/supplies: $1,050. Personal expenses: $800.

2007-2008 Financial aid. **Non-need-based:** Scholarships awarded for academics, alumni affiliation, leadership, music/drama, religious affiliation.

Application procedures. **Admission:** No deadline. $30 fee. Application must be submitted on paper. Admission notification on a rolling basis beginning on or about 1/1. **Financial aid:** Priority date 3/31; no closing date. FAFSA, institutional form required. Applicants notified on a rolling basis starting 3/15.

Academics. **Special study options:** Accelerated study, combined bachelor's/graduate degree, cooperative education, distance learning, double major, dual enrollment of high school students, ESL, honors, internships, student-designed major, study abroad, teacher certification program. **Credit/placement by examination:** AP, CLEP, IB, institutional tests. 32 credit hours maximum toward associate degree, 32 toward bachelor's. DANTES (for nontraditional students). **Support services:** Learning center, preadmission summer program, reduced course load, remedial instruction, study skills assistance, tutoring, writing center.

Majors. **Agriculture:** Animal sciences, business, horticulture. **Architecture:** Architecture. **Biology:** General, biochemistry, biophysics, botany, molecular, zoology. **Business:** Accounting, business admin, entrepreneurial studies, finance, managerial economics, nonprofit/public, training/development. **Communications:** General, journalism, public relations. **Communications technology:** General. **Computer sciences:** General, information systems. **Conservation:** Environmental science. **Education:** Elementary, mathematics, secondary, social science, social studies. **Engineering:** General, electrical, industrial, mechanical. **Family/consumer sciences:** Family studies, food/nutrition. **Foreign languages:** French, Spanish. **Health:** Audiology/speech pathology, clinical lab science, dietetics, nursing (RN). **History:** General. **Interdisciplinary:** Biological/physical sciences, neuroscience. **Math:** General. **Mechanic/repair:** Aircraft. **Philosophy/religion:** Religion. **Physical sciences:** Chemistry, physics. **Psychology:** General. **Public administration:** Social work. **Social sciences:** General, anthropology, economics, international economic development, political science, sociology. **Theology:** Religious ed, sacred music, theology, youth ministry. **Transportation:** Aviation. **Visual/performing arts:** General, art, art history/conservation, ceramics, commercial/advertising art, design, graphic design, multimedia, music performance, painting, photography, printmaking, studio arts.

Most popular majors. Architecture 7%, biology 8%, business/marketing 9%, education 6%, foreign language 10%, health sciences 17%, visual/performing arts 8%.

Computing on campus. 130 workstations in dormitories, library, computer center. Dormitories wired for high-speed internet access and linked to campus network. Commuter students can connect to campus network. Online course registration, online library, helpline, repair service, student web hosting, wireless network available.

Student life. **Freshman orientation:** Mandatory. Preregistration for classes offered. Held week before fall registration. **Policies:** Students expected to abide by ethical and moral standards of the university, which are mission-driven as published in official documents. Resident students required to stay in dorm until age 22. Religious observance required. **Housing:** Guaranteed on-campus for all undergraduates. Single-sex dorms, apartments, wellness housing available. $150 deposit. **Activities:** Concert band, choral groups, drama, international student organizations, music ensembles, musical theater, radio station, student government, student newspaper, symphony orchestra, Christian Youth Action.

Andrews University

Berrien Springs, Michigan
www.andrews.edu **CB code: 1030**

- Private 4-year university affiliated with Seventh-day Adventists
- Residential campus in small town
- 1,760 degree-seeking undergraduates: 7% part-time, 55% women, 24% African American, 10% Asian American, 12% Hispanic American, 12% international
- 1,478 degree-seeking graduate students
- 56% of applicants admitted
- SAT or ACT (ACT writing optional), application essay required
- 59% graduate within 6 years

General. Founded in 1874. Regionally accredited. **Degrees:** 330 bachelor's, 1 associate awarded; master's, doctoral, first professional offered. **Location:** 10 miles from St. Joseph-Benton Harbor, 25 miles from South Bend, Indiana. **Calendar:** Semester, limited summer session. **Full-time faculty:** 216 total; 74% have terminal degrees, 26% minority, 34% women. **Part-time faculty:** 82 total; 38% have terminal degrees, 18% minority, 55% women. **Class size:** 61% < 20, 28% 20-39, 4% 40-49, 6% 50-99, 1% >100. **Special facilities:** Natural history museum, archaeology museum, performing arts center, arboretum.

Athletics. **Intramural:** Badminton, basketball, field hockey, football (non-tackle), soccer, softball, triathlon, volleyball.

Student services. Chaplain/spiritual director, career counseling, student employment services, financial aid counseling, health services, on-campus daycare, personal counseling, placement for graduates, veterans' counselor. **Physically disabled:** Services for visually, speech, hearing impaired.

Contact. E-mail: enroll@andrews.edu
Phone: (800) 253-2874 Toll-free number: (800) 253-2874
Fax: (269) 471-3228
Stephen Payne, Vice President for Enrollment Management, Andrews University, 100 US Highway 31, Berrien Springs, MI 49104

Aquinas College
Grand Rapids, Michigan
www.aquinas.edu **CB code: 1018**

- Private 4-year liberal arts college affiliated with Roman Catholic Church
- Residential campus in small city
- 1,872 degree-seeking undergraduates: 14% part-time, 63% women, 4% African American, 2% Asian American, 4% Hispanic American, 1% Native American
- 287 degree-seeking graduate students
- 82% of applicants admitted
- SAT or ACT (ACT writing optional) required
- 49% graduate within 6 years; 20% enter graduate study

General. Founded in 1886. Regionally accredited. **Degrees:** 311 bachelor's, 5 associate awarded; master's offered. **Location:** 140 miles from Detroit, 180 miles from Chicago. **Calendar:** Semester, extensive summer session. **Full-time faculty:** 94 total; 80% have terminal degrees, 7% minority, 48% women. **Part-time faculty:** 168 total; 36% have terminal degrees, 5% minority, 48% women. **Class size:** 55% < 20, 44% 20-39, less than 1% 40-49, less than 1% 50-99. **Special facilities:** Greenhouse, astronomy tower, nature trails, community theater.

Freshman class profile. 2,079 applied, 1,715 admitted, 456 enrolled.

Mid 50% test scores		**Rank in top quarter:**	42%
ACT composite:	20-26	**Rank in top tenth:**	15%
GPA 3.75 or higher:	25%	**Return as sophomores:**	76%
GPA 3.50-3.74:	20%	**Out-of-state:**	9%
GPA 3.0-3.49:	30%	**Live on campus:**	84%
GPA 2.0-2.99:	25%		

Basis for selection. GED not accepted. 2.5 high school GPA in academic subjects. Test scores important. Interview required for applicants with above average test scores but less than 2.5 high school GPA in academic subjects, recommended for others. Audition recommended for music majors. Portfolio recommended for art majors. **Homeschooled:** Transcript of courses and grades required. Greater emphasis placed upon results of ACT or SAT. Students may be required to complete Ability to Benefit test. **Learning Disabled:** Make appointment with Academic Achievement Center to express needed accommodations prior to enrollment.

High school preparation. College-preparatory program recommended. 15 units required. Required units include English 4, mathematics 4, social studies 4 and science 3.

2008-2009 Annual costs. Tuition/fees: $21,150. Room/board: $6,678. Books/supplies: $767. Personal expenses: $757.

2008-2009 Financial aid. **Need-based:** 436 full-time freshmen applied for aid; 379 were judged to have need; 379 of these received aid. Average need met was 90%. Average scholarship/grant was $17,500; average loan $3,500. 81% of total undergraduate aid awarded as scholarships/grants, 19% as loans/jobs. **Non-need-based:** Scholarships awarded for academics, alumni affiliation, art, athletics, leadership, music/drama.

Application procedures. **Admission:** No deadline. No application fee. Admission notification on a rolling basis beginning on or about 8/1. **Financial aid:** Priority date 3/1; no closing date. FAFSA required. Applicants notified on a rolling basis starting 2/15; must reply within 2 week(s) of notification.

Academics. **Special study options:** Accelerated study, cooperative education, cross-registration, distance learning, double major, dual enrollment of high school students, exchange student, honors, independent study, internships, liberal arts/career combination, student-designed major, study abroad, teacher certification program. **Credit/placement by examination:** AP, CLEP, institutional tests. 30 credit hours maximum toward bachelor's degree. **Support services:** Learning center, remedial instruction, study skills assistance, tutoring, writing center.

Majors. **Biology:** General. **Business:** Accounting, business admin, communications, international, management information systems. **Communications:** General. **Computer sciences:** General. **Conservation:** Environmental science, environmental studies. **Education:** General, English, learning disabled, music, physical, science, social science, social studies, special. **Foreign languages:** French, German, Japanese, Spanish. **Health:** Athletic training. **History:** General. **Liberal arts:** Arts/sciences. **Math:** General. **Parks/recreation:** General, health/fitness, sports admin. **Philosophy/religion:** Philosophy, religion. **Physical sciences:** Chemistry. **Protective services:** Fire safety technology. **Psychology:** General. **Public administration:** Community org/advocacy. **Social sciences:** General, economics, geography, international relations, political science, sociology. **Theology:** Sacred music. **Visual/performing arts:** Art, art history/conservation, arts management, theater arts management. **Other:** Sustainable business.

Most popular majors. Business/marketing 20%, communications/journalism 6%, education 19%, parks/recreation 6%, social sciences 9%.

Computing on campus. 162 workstations in dormitories, library, computer center, student center. Dormitories wired for high-speed internet access and linked to campus network. Commuter students can connect to campus network. Online library, helpline, wireless network available.

Student life. **Freshman orientation:** Mandatory, $100 fee. Preregistration for classes offered. 3 days during week before fall classes begin. Includes start of common freshman class. **Policies:** Students serve on administrative and faculty committees. **Housing:** Guaranteed on-campus for freshmen. Coed dorms, single-sex dorms, apartments, wellness housing available. $100 deposit, deadline 8/15. **Activities:** Jazz band, campus ministries, choral groups, dance, drama, international student organizations, literary magazine, music ensembles, radio station, student government, student newspaper, community action volunteers, social action commission, community senate, Bible Study, College Democrats, College Republicans, Catholic studies club, Habitat for Humanity.

Athletics. NAIA. **Intercollegiate:** Baseball M, basketball, cross-country, golf, soccer, softball W, tennis, track and field, volleyball W. **Intramural:** Basketball, bowling, fencing M, golf, ice hockey M, lacrosse, skiing, soccer, softball, tennis, volleyball. **Team name:** Saints.

Student services. Adult student services, alcohol/substance abuse counseling, chaplain/spiritual director, career counseling, student employment services, financial aid counseling, health services, minority student services, personal counseling, placement for graduates, veterans' counselor, women's services. **Physically disabled:** Services for visually, speech, hearing impaired.

Contact. E-mail: admissions@aquinas.edu
Phone: (616) 632-2900 Toll-free number: (800) 678-9593
Fax: (616) 732-4469
Angela Schlosser-Bacon, Director of Admissions, Aquinas College, 1607 Robinson Road Southeast, Grand Rapids, MI 49506-1799

Art Institute of Michigan
Novi, Michigan
www.artinstitutes.edu/detroit

- Private 4-year branch campus and visual arts college
- Large city
- 285 degree-seeking undergraduates
- Application essay, interview required

General. Regionally accredited; also accredited by ACCSCT. **Calendar:** Quarter. **Full-time faculty:** 3 total. **Part-time faculty:** 27 total.

Basis for selection. Academic record and interview very important. SAT or ACT recommended. **Homeschooled:** Transcript of courses and grades, state high school equivalency certificate required.

2008-2009 Annual costs. Tuition/fees: $26,630.

Application procedures. **Admission:** Closing date 10/12 (receipt date). $50 fee, may be waived for applicants with need. Admission notification on a rolling basis. **Financial aid:** Closing date 10/12.

Academics. **Credit/placement by examination:** CLEP, SAT, ACT.

Majors. **Business:** Fashion. **Communications:** Advertising. **Personal/culinary services:** Restaurant/catering. **Visual/performing arts:** Interior design. **Other:** Interactive media design, Visual communications.

Contact. Phone: (248) 675-3800
Assistant Director of Admissions, Art Institute of Michigan, 28125 Cabot Drive, Suite 120, Novi, MI 48377

Baker College of Allen Park
Allen Park, Michigan
www.baker.edu

- Private 4-year business and health science college
- Commuter campus in large city
- 2,551 degree-seeking undergraduates

General. Regionally accredited. **Degrees:** 34 bachelor's, 141 associate awarded. **Location:** 10 miles from Detroit. **Calendar:** Quarter, limited summer session. **Full-time faculty:** 5 total. **Part-time faculty:** 100 total.

Freshman class profile. 1,056 applied, 1,056 admitted, 825 enrolled.

Basis for selection. Open admission, but selective for some programs. **Homeschooled:** Transcript of courses and grades required.

2008-2009 Annual costs. Tuition/fees: $8,550.

Application procedures. Admission: No deadline. $20 fee, may be waived for applicants with need. Admission notification on a rolling basis.

Academics. Special study options: Combined bachelor's/graduate degree, cooperative education, distance learning, double major, dual enrollment of high school students, independent study, internships, teacher certification program. **Credit/placement by examination:** CLEP. **Support services:** Learning center, remedial instruction, study skills assistance, tutoring.

Majors. Business: Human resources. **Computer sciences:** Information technology. **Education:** Elementary, middle, secondary. **Health:** Health services. **Public administration:** Human services.

Computing on campus. 208 workstations in library, computer center, student center. Online library, helpline, wireless network available.

Student life. Freshman orientation: Mandatory.

Contact. Phone: (313) 425-3700
Steve Peterson, Vice President for Admissions, Baker College of Allen Park, 4500 Enterprise Drive, Allen Park, MI 48101

Baker College of Auburn Hills
Auburn Hills, Michigan
www.baker.edu **CB code: 1457**

- Private 4-year business and technical college
- Commuter campus in small city
- 3,824 degree-seeking undergraduates

General. Founded in 1990. Regionally accredited. Part of multi-campus system specializing in career education. **Degrees:** 146 bachelor's, 294 associate awarded. **Location:** 30 miles from Detroit. **Calendar:** Quarter, limited summer session. **Full-time faculty:** 10 total. **Part-time faculty:** 150 total. **Class size:** 45% < 20, 55% 20-39.

Freshman class profile. 1,619 applied, 1,619 admitted, 1,096 enrolled.

Basis for selection. Open admission. Specific entrance requirements for allied health programs and bachelor of business leadership degree program. Interview recommended.

2008-2009 Annual costs. Tuition/fees: $8,550. Books/supplies: $1,000.

Financial aid. Non-need-based: Scholarships awarded for academics, alumni affiliation.

Application procedures. Admission: No deadline. $20 fee, may be waived for applicants with need. Admission notification on a rolling basis. **Financial aid:** Priority date 2/21, closing date 9/1. FAFSA, institutional form required. Applicants notified on a rolling basis starting 4/1.

Academics. 2+2 system allows students to begin required courses in major while completing associate degree. **Special study options:** Accelerated study, combined bachelor's/graduate degree, distance learning, double major, dual enrollment of high school students, independent study, internships, liberal arts/career combination, teacher certification program. **Credit/placement by examination:** AP, CLEP, IB, institutional tests. 48 credit hours maximum toward associate degree, 96 toward bachelor's. **Support services:** Learning center, reduced course load, remedial instruction, study skills assistance, tutoring, writing center.

Majors. Business: General, accounting, business admin, management science. **Education:** General, elementary, middle, multi-level teacher, secondary.

Computing on campus. 131 workstations in library, computer center, student center. Commuter students can connect to campus network. Helpline available.

Student life. Freshman orientation: Mandatory. **Activities:** Accounting club, management club, interior design society, society of automotive engineers, marketing club.

Student services. Career counseling, student employment services, financial aid counseling, personal counseling, placement for graduates, veterans' counselor. **Physically disabled:** Services for visually, hearing impaired.

Contact. Phone: (248) 340-0600 Toll-free number: (888) 429-0410
Fax: (248) 340-0600
Jan Bohlen, Vice President for Admissions, Baker College of Auburn Hills, 1500 University Drive, Auburn Hills, MI 48326

Baker College of Cadillac
Cadillac, Michigan
www.baker.edu **CB code: 1381**

- Private 4-year business and health science college
- Commuter campus in large town
- 1,952 degree-seeking undergraduates

General. Founded in 1911. Regionally accredited. Part of multicampus system specializing in career education. **Degrees:** 26 bachelor's, 145 associate awarded. **Location:** 90 miles from Grand Rapids, 45 miles from Traverse City. **Calendar:** Quarter, limited summer session. **Full-time faculty:** 5 total. **Part-time faculty:** 100 total. **Class size:** 68% < 20, 31% 20-39, 1% 40-49. **Special facilities:** Mock operating room, massage therapy room.

Freshman class profile. 603 applied, 603 admitted, 457 enrolled.

Basis for selection. Open admission. Some allied health programs require health appraisal. Interview recommended.

2008-2009 Annual costs. Tuition/fees: $8,550. Books/supplies: $1,000.

Financial aid. Non-need-based: Scholarships awarded for academics.

Application procedures. Admission: No deadline. $20 fee, may be waived for applicants with need. Admission notification on a rolling basis beginning on or about 10/1. **Financial aid:** Priority date 2/21; no closing date. FAFSA, institutional form required. Applicants notified on a rolling basis starting 5/1.

Academics. Special study options: Accelerated study, combined bachelor's/graduate degree, cooperative education, distance learning, double major, dual enrollment of high school students, external degree, independent study, internships, liberal arts/career combination, weekend college. 2+2 bachelor's degree and bachelor of business leadership degree. **Credit/placement by examination:** AP, CLEP, IB, institutional tests. 48 credit hours maximum toward associate degree, 96 toward bachelor's. **Support services:** Learning center, reduced course load, remedial instruction, study skills assistance, tutoring, writing center.

Majors. Business: Accounting, business admin, human resources, office management. **Computer sciences:** Computer science. **Public administration:** Human services.

Computing on campus. 154 workstations in library, computer center. Commuter students can connect to campus network. Online library, helpline, repair service available.

Student life. Freshman orientation: Mandatory. Preregistration for classes offered. **Activities:** Student activities group, professional student organizations.

Student services. Career counseling, student employment services, financial aid counseling, personal counseling, placement for graduates, veterans' counselor. **Physically disabled:** Services for visually, hearing impaired.

Contact. E-mail: mike.tisdale@baker.edu
Phone: (231) 876-3100 Toll-free number: (888) 313-3463
Fax: (231) 775-8505
Mike Tisdale, Director of Admissions, Baker College of Cadillac, 9600 East 13th Street, Cadillac, MI 49601

Baker College of Clinton Township

Clinton Township, Michigan
www.baker.edu **CB code: 1386**

- Private 4-year business and technical college
- Commuter campus in very large city
- 5,637 degree-seeking undergraduates

General. Founded in 1911. Regionally accredited. Part of multicampus system specializing in career education. **Degrees:** 205 bachelor's, 407 associate awarded. **Location:** 15 miles from Detroit. **Calendar:** Quarter, limited summer session. **Full-time faculty:** 20 total. **Part-time faculty:** 195 total. **Class size:** 25% < 20, 74% 20-39, less than 1% 40-49.

Freshman class profile. 2,685 applied, 2,685 admitted, 1,755 enrolled.

Basis for selection. Open admission, but selective for some programs. Physical exam may be required for some programs. Interview recommended. **Learning Disabled:** Students must complete special needs intake form signed by professional.

High school preparation. Recommended units include English 4, mathematics 4, social studies 2, science 3 and foreign language 4.

2008-2009 Annual costs. Tuition/fees: $8,550. Books/supplies: $1,000. Personal expenses: $2,000.

Financial aid. Non-need-based: Scholarships awarded for academics, minority status.

Application procedures. Admission: Priority date 9/1; no deadline. $20 fee, may be waived for applicants with need. Admission notification on a rolling basis. **Financial aid:** Priority date 2/21, closing date 9/1. FAFSA, institutional form required. Applicants notified on a rolling basis starting 4/1.

Academics. 2+2 system allows students to begin required courses in major while completing associate degree. **Special study options:** Accelerated study, combined bachelor's/graduate degree, cooperative education, distance learning, double major, dual enrollment of high school students, external degree, independent study, internships, teacher certification program. **Credit/placement by examination:** AP, CLEP, IB, institutional tests. 48 credit hours maximum toward associate degree, 96 toward bachelor's. **Support services:** Learning center, reduced course load, remedial instruction, study skills assistance, tutoring, writing center.

Majors. Business: Accounting, administrative services, business admin, human resources, management science, office management. **Computer sciences:** General, computer science. **Education:** Elementary, middle, multi-level teacher, secondary. **Health:** Health care admin, nursing (RN), office admin. **Public administration:** Human services.

Computing on campus. 120 workstations in library, computer center. Commuter students can connect to campus network. Helpline available.

Student life. Freshman orientation: Mandatory. Preregistration for classes offered.

Student services. Adult student services, career counseling, student employment services, financial aid counseling, personal counseling, placement for graduates, veterans' counselor. **Physically disabled:** Services for visually, hearing impaired.

Contact. E-mail: adm_mc@baker.edu
Phone: (586) 791-3000 Toll-free number: (888) 272-2842
Fax: (586) 791-6610
Annette Looser, Director of Admissions, Baker College of Clinton Township, 34950 Little Mack Avenue, Clinton Township, MI 48035

Baker College of Flint

Flint, Michigan
www.baker.edu **CB code: 0806**

- Private 4-year business and technical college
- Commuter campus in large city
- 5,820 degree-seeking undergraduates

General. Founded in 1911. Regionally accredited. Corporate services division offers degree-granting programs on campus and/or at work site, coordinated with corporate training and professional development programs. Part of multicampus system specializing in career education. **Degrees:** 166 bachelor's, 472 associate awarded; master's offered. **Location:** 10 miles from downtown, 60 miles from Detroit. **Calendar:** Quarter, limited summer session. **Full-time faculty:** 40 total. **Part-time faculty:** 300 total. **Special facilities:** Polysommnography sleep lab, orthotic/prosthetic lab.

Freshman class profile. 2,470 applied, 2,470 admitted, 1,709 enrolled.

Out-of-state:	2%	**Live on campus:**	5%

Basis for selection. Open admission, but selective for some programs. Health applicants must have health appraisal. Occupational therapy applicants must present minimum of 1 year biology, 1 year chemistry/physics, 2 years math including algebra or equivalent. All health programs require 2.0 GPA for entrance to professional classes. Class size may be limited. Trucking programs require drug screening prior to enrollment acceptance. Interview recommended.

2008-2009 Annual costs. Tuition/fees: $8,550. Additional fees vary with program. Room only: $2,600. Books/supplies: $900.

Financial aid. Non-need-based: Scholarships awarded for academics, minority status.

Application procedures. Admission: Priority date 9/1; no deadline. $20 fee, may be waived for applicants with need. Admission notification on a rolling basis. **Financial aid:** Priority date 2/21, closing date 9/1. FAFSA, institutional form required. Applicants notified on a rolling basis starting 4/1.

Academics. 2+2 system allows students to begin required courses in major while completing associate degree. Calendar based on 10-week quarters. **Special study options:** Accelerated study, combined bachelor's/graduate degree, cooperative education, distance learning, double major, dual enrollment of high school students, external degree, independent study, internships. **Credit/placement by examination:** AP, CLEP, IB, institutional tests. 48 credit hours maximum toward associate degree, 96 toward bachelor's. **Support services:** Learning center, reduced course load, remedial instruction, study skills assistance, tutoring, writing center.

Majors. Business: Accounting, business admin, management information systems, office management, operations. **Computer sciences:** General. **Education:** Elementary, middle, multi-level teacher, secondary. **Engineering:** Mechanical. **Engineering technology:** Electrical. **Health:** Health care admin, medical records admin, nursing (RN). **Transportation:** Aviation management. **Visual/performing arts:** Commercial/advertising art, interior design.

Most popular majors. Business/marketing 65%, health sciences 25%.

Computing on campus. 300 workstations in library, computer center. Commuter students can connect to campus network. Helpline available.

Student life. Freshman orientation: Mandatory. Preregistration for classes offered. **Housing:** Guaranteed on-campus for freshmen. Coed dorms, wellness housing available. $50 deposit, deadline 9/20. **Activities:** Literary magazine, National Association of Accountants, American Marketing Association, Interior Design Society, travel club, environmental club, physical therapy assistant club, medical assistants student organization, Health Information Management Association, graphic communications club, Society of Manufacturing Engineers student chapter.

Athletics. Intramural: Basketball, volleyball.

Student services. Career counseling, student employment services, on-campus daycare, personal counseling, placement for graduates, veterans' counselor. **Physically disabled:** Services for visually, hearing impaired.

Contact. E-mail: adm-fl@baker.edu
Phone: (810) 766-4000 Toll-free number: (800) 964-4299
Fax: (810) 766-4293
Jodi Cuneaz, Director of Admissions, Baker College of Flint, 1050 West Bristol Road, Flint, MI 48507

Baker College of Jackson

Jackson, Michigan
www.baker.edu **CB code: 1887**

- Private 4-year business and technical college
- Commuter campus in small city
- 1,830 degree-seeking undergraduates

General. Founded in 1994. Regionally accredited. Part of multicampus system specializing in career education. **Degrees:** 64 bachelor's, 153 associate awarded. **Location:** 40 miles from Lansing, 40 miles from Ann Arbor. **Calendar:** Quarter, limited summer session. **Full-time faculty:** 5 total. **Part-time faculty:** 95 total.

Freshman class profile. 669 applied, 669 admitted, 554 enrolled.

Basis for selection. Open admission, but selective for some programs. Physical exam may be required for allied health programs. All health programs require specific GPA. Interview recommended.

2008-2009 Annual costs. Tuition/fees: $8,550. Books/supplies: $975.

Financial aid. Non-need-based: Scholarships awarded for academics, minority status.

Application procedures. Admission: No deadline. $20 fee, may be waived for applicants with need. Admission notification on a rolling basis. **Financial aid:** Priority date 2/21, closing date 9/1. FAFSA, institutional form required. Applicants notified on a rolling basis starting 4/1.

Academics. 2+2 system allows students to begin required courses in major while completing associate degree. **Special study options:** Accelerated study, combined bachelor's/graduate degree, cooperative education, distance learning, double major, dual enrollment of high school students, external degree, independent study, internships. **Credit/placement by examination:** AP, CLEP, IB, institutional tests. 48 credit hours maximum toward associate degree, 96 toward bachelor's. **Support services:** Learning center, reduced course load, remedial instruction, study skills assistance, tutoring, writing center.

Majors. Business: General, accounting. **Education:** Elementary, middle, multi-level teacher, secondary.

Computing on campus. 114 workstations in library, computer center. Commuter students can connect to campus network. Helpline available.

Student life. Freshman orientation: Mandatory. Preregistration for classes offered. **Activities:** Student government.

Student services. Career counseling, student employment services, personal counseling, placement for graduates, veterans' counselor. **Physically disabled:** Services for visually, hearing impaired.

Contact. E-mail: adm-jk@baker.edu
Phone: (517) 788-7800 Toll-free number: (888) 343-3683
Fax: (517) 789-7331
Kelli Stepka, Director of Admissions, Baker College of Jackson, 2800 Springport Road, Jackson, MI 49202

Baker College of Muskegon

Muskegon, Michigan
www.baker.edu **CB code: 1527**

- Private 4-year business and technical college
- Commuter campus in small city
- 5,232 degree-seeking undergraduates

General. Founded in 1888. Regionally accredited. Part of multicampus system specializing in career education. All associate degree programs include internship, co-op or clinical affiliation experience. **Degrees:** 158 bachelor's, 468 associate awarded. **Location:** 40 miles from Grand Rapids. **Calendar:** Quarter, limited summer session. **Full-time faculty:** 20 total. **Part-time faculty:** 170 total. **Class size:** 38% < 20, 57% 20-39, 3% 40-49, 2% 50-99. **Special facilities:** Restaurant run by culinary and food and beverage management students.

Freshman class profile. 2,319 applied, 2,319 admitted, 1,700 enrolled.

Basis for selection. Open admission, but selective for some programs. 2.75 GPA required for admission to occupational therapy assisting, physical therapist assisting, veterinary technician, surgical technology, teacher preparation. Class size may be limited in some programs. Physical examination, background check required for some programs. Interview recommended. **Homeschooled:** Basic skills placement assessments in math, language arts, and reading part of orientation/registration process. **Learning Disabled:** Learning disability must be documented and presented to counseling staff before registering for classes.

2008-2009 Annual costs. Tuition/fees: $8,550. Room only: $2,865. Books/supplies: $975. Personal expenses: $2,000.

Financial aid. Non-need-based: Scholarships awarded for academics, minority status.

Application procedures. Admission: Priority date 9/1; no deadline. $20 fee, may be waived for applicants with need. Admission notification on a rolling basis. **Financial aid:** Priority date 2/21; no closing date. FAFSA, institutional form required. Applicants notified on a rolling basis starting 4/1.

Academics. 2-2 system allows students to begin required courses in major while completing associate degree. Maximum number of credits awarded for prior work and/or life experiences, 48 for associate and 144 for bachelor. **Special study options:** Accelerated study, combined bachelor's/graduate degree, cooperative education, distance learning, double major, dual enrollment of high school students, external degree, independent study, internships, liberal arts/career combination, teacher certification program. Accelerated bachelor of business administration offered in weekend delivery format. **Credit/placement by examination:** AP, CLEP, IB, institutional tests. 48 credit hours maximum toward associate degree, 144 toward bachelor's. **Support services:** Learning center, reduced course load, remedial instruction, study skills assistance, tutoring.

Majors. Business: Accounting, accounting/business management, administrative services, business admin, human resources, management science, marketing, office management, restaurant/food services. **Computer sciences:** General, computer science, information systems, systems analysis. **Education:** Elementary, kindergarten/preschool, middle, multi-level teacher, secondary. **Engineering technology:** Industrial management. **Health:** Health care admin. **Personal/culinary services:** General, culinary arts, restaurant/catering. **Public administration:** Human services. **Transportation:** Aviation management.

Computing on campus. 180 workstations in dormitories, library, computer center. Dormitories wired for high-speed internet access and linked to campus network. Commuter students can connect to campus network. Online course registration, online library, helpline, wireless network available.

Student life. Freshman orientation: Mandatory. Preregistration for classes offered. 3-4 hour session prior to start of quarter; includes COMPASS testing, registration, academic advising. **Policies:** No drug or alcohol use permitted anywhere on campus or in residence halls. **Housing:** Coed dorms, special housing for disabled, apartments, wellness housing available. $50 deposit, deadline 9/1. **Activities:** Student government, travel club, rehab club, residence hall association, culinary arts club, human resource management club.

Athletics. Intramural: Bowling.

Student services. Adult student services, career counseling, student employment services, financial aid counseling, personal counseling, placement for graduates, veterans' counselor. **Physically disabled:** Services for visually, hearing impaired.

Contact. E-mail: kathy.jacobson@baker.edu
Phone: (231) 777-5200 Toll-free number: (800) 937-0337
Fax: (231) 777-5201
Kathy Jacobson, Vice President and Director of Admissions, Baker College of Muskegon, 1903 Marquette Avenue, Muskegon, MI 49442

Baker College of Owosso

Owosso, Michigan
www.baker.edu **CB code: 5270**

- Private 4-year business and technical college
- Commuter campus in large town
- 2,996 degree-seeking undergraduates

General. Founded in 1911. Regionally accredited. Part of multicampus system, with affiliated graduate school, specializing in career education. Master's degree available at Flint campus. **Degrees:** 91 bachelor's, 284 associate awarded. **Location:** 30 miles from Lansing, 300 miles from Flint. **Calendar:** Quarter, limited summer session. **Full-time faculty:** 10 total. **Part-time faculty:** 150 total. **Special facilities:** Diesel technology center.

Freshman class profile. 1,335 applied, 1,335 admitted, 9[illegible]8 enrolled.

Out-of-state:	3%	**Live on campus:**	30%

Basis for selection. Open admission. Limited enrollment for medical programs.

2008-2009 Annual costs. Tuition/fees: $8,550. Room only: $2,700. Books/supplies: $1,000.

Financial aid. Non-need-based: Scholarships awarded for academics, minority status.

Application procedures. Admission: Priority date 9/1; no deadline. $20 fee, may be waived for applicants with need. Admission notification on a rolling basis. **Financial aid:** Priority date 2/21, closing date 9/1. FAFSA, institutional form required. Applicants notified on a rolling basis starting 4/1.

Academics. 2+2 system allows students to begin required courses in major while completing associate degree. **Special study options:** Accelerated study, combined bachelor's/graduate degree, cooperative education, distance learning, double major, dual enrollment of high school students, external degree, independent study, internships. **Credit/placement by examination:** AP, CLEP, IB, institutional tests. 48 credit hours maximum toward associate degree, 96 toward bachelor's. **Support services:** Learning center, reduced course load, remedial instruction, study skills assistance, tutoring, writing center.

Majors. Business: Accounting, administrative services, business admin, human resources, management information systems, marketing, office management. **Communications technology:** Graphics. **Computer sciences:** General, computer graphics, computer science. **Education:** Elementary, middle, multi-level teacher, secondary. **Health:** Health care admin. **Public administration:** Human services.

Computing on campus. 226 workstations in dormitories, library, computer center. Dormitories wired for high-speed internet access. Commuter students can connect to campus network. Online library, helpline available.

Student life. Freshman orientation: Mandatory. Preregistration for classes offered. **Housing:** Guaranteed on-campus for freshmen. Coed dorms, wellness housing available. $50 deposit. **Activities:** Student newspaper, accounting club, MLT club, interior design club, radiology club, graphics club.

Athletics. Intramural: Basketball, volleyball.

Student services. Adult student services, career counseling, services for economically disadvantaged, student employment services, financial aid counseling, on-campus daycare, personal counseling, placement for graduates, veterans' counselor. **Physically disabled:** Services for visually, speech, hearing impaired.

Contact. E-mail: michael.konopacke@baker.edu
Phone: (989) 729-3350 Toll-free number: (800) 879-3797
Fax: (989) 729-3359
Michael Konopacke, Vice President of Admissions, Baker College of Owosso, 1020 South Washington Street, Owosso, MI 48867

Baker College of Port Huron

Port Huron, Michigan
www.baker.edu **CB code: 1413**

- Private 4-year business and technical college
- Commuter campus in large town
- 1,716 degree-seeking undergraduates

General. Founded in 1911. Regionally accredited. Part of multicampus system specializing in career education. **Degrees:** 69 bachelor's, 171 associate awarded; master's offered. **Location:** 60 miles from Detroit. **Calendar:** Quarter, limited summer session. **Full-time faculty:** 10 total. **Part-time faculty:** 115 total. **Class size:** 58% < 20, 37% 20-39, 1% 40-49, 4% 50-99. **Special facilities:** Dental hygiene clinic.

Freshman class profile. 619 admitted, 481 enrolled.

Basis for selection. Open admission, but selective for some programs. Specific entrance requirements for health and human services programs. Waiting list for Dental Hygiene. Interview recommended.

2008-2009 Annual costs. Tuition/fees: $8,550. Books/supplies: $1,000. Personal expenses: $2,000.

Financial aid. All financial aid based on need.

Application procedures. Admission: Priority date 9/1; no deadline. $20 fee, may be waived for applicants with need. Admission notification on a rolling basis. **Financial aid:** Priority date 2/21; no closing date. FAFSA, institutional form required. Applicants notified on a rolling basis starting 4/1.

Academics. 2+2 system allows students to begin required courses in major while completing associate degree. Accelerated BBA available. **Special study options:** Accelerated study, combined bachelor's/graduate degree, cooperative education, distance learning, double major, dual enrollment of high school students, external degree, independent study, internships, liberal arts/career combination. **Credit/placement by examination:** AP, CLEP, IB, institutional tests. 48 credit hours maximum toward associate degree, 96 toward bachelor's. **Support services:** Learning center, reduced course load, remedial instruction, study skills assistance, tutoring, writing center.

Majors. Business: General, accounting, administrative services, business admin, human resources, international, management information systems, marketing, office management. **Computer sciences:** General, computer science, information systems. **Health:** Health care admin.

Computing on campus. 229 workstations in library, computer center. Commuter students can connect to campus network. Online course registration, helpline available.

Student life. Freshman orientation: Mandatory. Preregistration for classes offered. **Activities:** Dental hygiene society.

Student services. Adult student services, career counseling, student employment services, personal counseling, placement for graduates, veterans' counselor. **Physically disabled:** Services for visually, hearing impaired.

Contact. E-mail: daniel.kenny@baker.edu
Phone: (810) 985-7000 Toll-free number: (888) 262-2442
Fax: (810) 985-7066
Dan Kenny, Vice President of Admissions, Baker College of Port Huron, 3403 Lapeer Road, Port Huron, MI 48060-2597

Calvin College

Grand Rapids, Michigan **CB member**
www.calvin.edu **CB code: 1095**

- Private 4-year liberal arts college affiliated with Christian Reformed Church
- Residential campus in large city
- 4,021 degree-seeking undergraduates: 2% part-time, 54% women, 2% African American, 3% Asian American, 1% Hispanic American, 7% international
- 30 degree-seeking graduate students
- 94% of applicants admitted
- SAT or ACT (ACT writing optional), application essay required
- 76% graduate within 6 years; 37% enter graduate study

General. Founded in 1876. Regionally accredited. **Degrees:** 823 bachelor's awarded; master's offered. **ROTC:** Army. **Location:** 150 miles from Detroit and Chicago. **Calendar:** 4-1-4, limited summer session. **Full-time faculty:** 320 total; 81% have terminal degrees, 9% minority, 32% women. **Part-time faculty:** 98 total; 20% have terminal degrees, 7% minority, 51% women. **Class size:** 37% < 20, 60% 20-39, 2% 40-49, 1% 50-99. **Special facilities:** Ecosystem preserve and interpretive center, electron microscope, rhetoric center, observatory.

Freshman class profile. 2,169 applied, 2,039 admitted, 936 enrolled.

Mid 50% test scores		**Rank in top quarter:**	53%
SAT critical reading:	530-660	**Rank in top tenth:**	27%
SAT math:	550-670	**End year in good standing:**	96%
ACT composite:	23-28	**Return as sophomores:**	86%
GPA 3.75 or higher:	43%	**Out-of-state:**	43%
GPA 3.50-3.74:	19%	**Live on campus:**	97%
GPA 3.0-3.49:	25%	**International:**	8%
GPA 2.0-2.99:	13%		

Basis for selection. Genuine interest in Christian goals of college and 2.5 GPA required. Recommendation, personal statement important. Minimum 20 ACT or 470 SAT Verbal and 470 SAT Math recommended. GED accepted only for those age 19 years or over. SAT Subject Tests recommended. **Homeschooled:** Must provide some form of transcript with grades.

High school preparation. College-preparatory program recommended. 12 units required; 17 recommended. Required and recommended units include English 3-4, mathematics 3, social studies 2-3, science 2 (laboratory 1), foreign language 2 and academic electives 3. Math must include algebra and geometry.

2009-2010 Annual costs. Tuition/fees: $24,035. Room/board: $8,275. Books/supplies: $860. Personal expenses: $1,070.

2008-2009 Financial aid. Need-based: 773 full-time freshmen applied for aid; 596 were judged to have need; 596 of these received aid. Average need met was 87%. Average scholarship/grant was $11,443; average loan $4,670. 60% of total undergraduate aid awarded as scholarships/grants, 40% as loans/jobs. **Non-need-based:** Scholarships awarded for academics, alumni affiliation, art, leadership, minority status, music/drama, religious affiliation, state residency.

Application procedures. Admission: Closing date 8/15 (postmark date). $35 fee, may be waived for applicants with need. Admission notification on a rolling basis beginning on or about 11/1. Must reply by May 1 or within 4 week(s) if notified thereafter. **Financial aid:** Priority date 2/15; no closing date. FAFSA required. Applicants notified on a rolling basis starting 3/15.

Academics. Importance of faith perspective in all disciplines and co-curricular activities emphasized. **Special study options:** Accelerated study, combined bachelor's/graduate degree, double major, dual enrollment of high school students, honors, independent study, internships, student-designed major, study abroad, teacher certification program, urban semester, Washington semester. Overseas programs with Central College, January interim exchange with other colleges, academically-based service-learning. **Credit/placement by examination:** AP, CLEP, IB, institutional tests. **Support services:** Learning center, reduced course load, remedial instruction, study skills assistance, tutoring, writing center.

Majors. Area/ethnic studies: Asian. **Biology:** General, biochemistry, biotechnology. **Business:** General, accounting, business admin, communications, management information systems. **Communications:** General, digital media, media studies. **Computer sciences:** General, computer science, information systems, networking, programming. **Conservation:** Environmental science. **Education:** General, art, bilingual, biology, chemistry, Deaf/hearing impaired, early childhood, elementary, English, French, German, history, mathematics, mentally handicapped, middle, music, physical, physics, reading, secondary, social studies, Spanish, special, speech impaired. **Engineering:** General, chemical, civil, electrical, mechanical. **Foreign languages:** Ancient Greek, Biblical, classics, Dutch/Flemish, French, German, Latin, modern Greek, Spanish. **Health:** Athletic training, audiology/speech pathology, communication disorders, predental, premedicine, preop/surgical nursing, prepharmacy, preveterinary, recreational therapy, speech pathology. **History:** General, American, European. **Interdisciplinary:** Biological/physical sciences, classical/archaeology, natural sciences. **Legal studies:** Prelaw. **Liberal arts:** Arts/sciences. **Math:** General. **Parks/recreation:** General, exercise sciences, health/fitness. **Philosophy/religion:** Philosophy, religion. **Physical sciences:** Chemistry, geology, physics. **Psychology:** General. **Public administration:** General, social work. **Social sciences:** General, economics, geography, international economic development, international relations, political science, sociology. **Theology:** Bible, sacred music. **Visual/performing arts:** General, art, art history/conservation, cinematography, conducting, dramatic, film/cinema, music history, music performance, music theory/composition, piano/organ, studio arts, voice/opera.

Most popular majors. Biology 7%, business/marketing 14%, education 9%, engineering/engineering technologies 7%, foreign language 7%, health sciences 9%, social sciences 9%, visual/performing arts 6%.

Computing on campus. 900 workstations in dormitories, library, computer center. Dormitories wired for high-speed internet access and linked to campus network. Commuter students can connect to campus network. Online course registration, online library, helpline, student web hosting, wireless network available.

Student life. Freshman orientation: Mandatory, $75 fee. Two-day program held in summer. **Policies:** Strong emphasis on student leadership and service. Religious observance strongly expected and encouraged. First- and second-year students (under 21) not living at home required to live in residence halls. **Housing:** Guaranteed on-campus for freshmen. Single-sex dorms, apartments available. $50 deposit, deadline 5/1. Project Neighborhood houses available. **Activities:** Bands, choral groups, dance, drama, film society, international student organizations, literary magazine, music ensembles, Model UN, musical theater, student government, student newspaper, symphony orchestra, Amnesty International, Campus Crusade for Christ, Environmental Stewardship, Republicans club, InterVarsity Christian Fellowship, Liberals and Democrats, Young Life, Social Justice, Korean Christian Fellowship.

Athletics. NCAA. **Intercollegiate:** Baseball M, basketball, cross-country, diving, golf, soccer, softball W, swimming, tennis, track and field, volleyball W. **Intramural:** Badminton, basketball, football (non-tackle), golf, racquetball, soccer, softball, swimming, table tennis, tennis, track and field, volleyball, water polo. **Team name:** Knights.

Student services. Adult student services, alcohol/substance abuse counseling, chaplain/spiritual director, career counseling, student employment services, financial aid counseling, health services, minority student services, personal counseling, placement for graduates. **Physically disabled:** Services for visually, speech, hearing impaired.

Contact. E-mail: admissions@calvin.edu
Phone: (616) 526-6106 Toll-free number: (800) 688-0122
Fax: (616) 526-6777
Dale Kuiper, Director of Admissions and Financial Aid, Calvin College, 3201 Burton Street Southeast, Grand Rapids, MI 49546

Central Michigan University

Mount Pleasant, Michigan — **CB member**
www.cmich.edu — **CB code: 1106**

- Public 4-year university
- Commuter campus in large town
- 20,022 degree-seeking undergraduates: 11% part-time, 55% women, 6% African American, 1% Asian American, 2% Hispanic American, 1% Native American, 1% international
- 6,275 degree-seeking graduate students
- 70% of applicants admitted
- ACT (writing recommended) required
- 57% graduate within 6 years

General. Founded in 1892. Regionally accredited. 60 off-campus locations in the United States and surrounding countries. **Degrees:** 3,493 bachelor's awarded; master's, doctoral offered. **ROTC:** Army. **Location:** 70 miles from Lansing. **Calendar:** Semester, limited summer session. **Full-time faculty:** 742 total; 82% have terminal degrees, 17% minority, 39% women. **Part-time faculty:** 448 total; 27% have terminal degrees, 10% minority, 50% women. **Class size:** 33% < 20, 45% 20-39, 12% 40-49, 7% 50-99, 3% >100. **Special facilities:** Center for clinical care and education, English language institute, center for applied research and rural studies, Michigan services for children and young adults who are deaf-blind, psychological training and consultation center, language learning center, biological station, conservation genetics lab, water research center, museum of cultural and natural history, historical library, 255-acre natural woodland.

Freshman class profile. 17,021 applied, 11,921 admitted, 3,864 enrolled.

Mid 50% test scores		Rank in top tenth:	13%
SAT critical reading:	470-580	End year in good standing:	80%
SAT math:	480-600	Return as sophomores:	78%
ACT composite:	20-24	Out-of-state:	2%
GPA 3.75 or higher:	18%	Live on campus:	94%
GPA 3.50-3.74:	19%	International:	1%
GPA 3.0-3.49:	41%	Fraternities:	4%
GPA 2.0-2.99:	22%	Sororities:	5%
Rank in top quarter:	36%		

Basis for selection. School achievement record, test scores, recommendations important. Transfer students with over 30 credits are not required to take the ACT. Interview and essay recommended. Audition required for music majors. **Learning Disabled:** Students urged to register with Student Disability Services.

High school preparation. College-preparatory program recommended. 20 units recommended. Recommended units include English 4, mathematics 4, social studies 2, history 2, science 4 (laboratory 1), foreign language 2, computer science 1 and visual/performing arts 1.

2008-2009 Annual costs. Tuition/fees: $9,720; $22,590 out-of-state. Room/board: $7,667. Books/supplies: $1,000. Personal expenses: $1,665.

2007-2008 Financial aid. Need-based: 3,003 full-time freshmen applied for aid; 2,128 were judged to have need; 2,087 of these received aid. Average need met was 78%. Average scholarship/grant was $5,113; average loan $4,747. 36% of total undergraduate aid awarded as scholarships/grants, 64% as loans/jobs. **Non-need-based:** Awarded to 2,425 full-time undergraduates, including 746 freshmen. Scholarships awarded for academics, alumni affiliation, art, athletics, leadership, minority status, music/drama, ROTC, state residency. **Additional information:** Tuition waiver for Native American students qualifying under state program criteria.

Application procedures. Admission: Priority date 10/1; deadline 7/1 (receipt date). $35 fee, may be waived for applicants with need. Admission notification on a rolling basis beginning on or about 9/1. Must reply by May 1 or within 2 week(s) if notified thereafter. **Financial aid:** Priority date 3/1; no closing date. FAFSA required. Applicants notified on a rolling basis starting 4/1.

Academics. Special study options: Accelerated study, combined bachelor's/graduate degree, distance learning, double major, dual enrollment of high school students, ESL, honors, independent study, internships, semester at sea, student-designed major, study abroad, teacher certification program, Washington semester. Leadership Institute, Pre-professional studies. **Credit/placement by examination:** AP, CLEP, IB, ACT, institutional tests. 40 credit hours maximum toward bachelor's degree. Credit by examination may not be used to repeat any course previously taken. **Support services:** Learning center, pre-admission summer program, reduced course load, remedial instruction, study skills assistance, tutoring, writing center.

Honors college/program. Applicants must have 3.75 GPA or 3.6 GPA and 25 ACT.

Majors. Architecture: Interior. **Area/ethnic studies:** European, women's. **Biology:** General, biochemistry, biomedical sciences. **Business:** Accounting, actuarial science, business admin, entrepreneurial studies, fashion, finance, financial planning, hospitality admin, hotel/motel admin, human resources, international, logistics, management information systems, marketing, operations, purchasing, real estate, retailing. **Communications:** General, advertising, journalism, organizational, photojournalism, public relations. **Computer sciences:** Computer science, information technology. **Conservation:** General, environmental science, environmental studies. **Education:** Art, biology, business, chemistry, early childhood, elementary, emotionally handicapped, English, family/consumer sciences, French, geography, German, health, history, mathematics, mentally handicapped, music, physical, physics, science, Spanish, speech, technology/industrial arts. **Engineering:** Electrical, manufacturing, mechanical. **Engineering technology:** Automotive, computer systems, construction, electrical, manufacturing, mechanical. **Family/consumer sciences:** Child development, family systems, institutional food production. **Foreign languages:** French, German, Spanish. **Health:** Athletic training, clinical lab science, communication disorders, dietetics, health care admin, public health ed, recreational therapy. **History:** General. **Interdisciplinary:** Cognitive science, math/computer science, neuroscience. **Legal studies:** General. **Liberal arts:** Arts/sciences. **Math:** General, statistics. **Parks/recreation:** General, exercise sciences, facilities management, health/fitness, sports admin. **Philosophy/religion:** Philosophy, religion. **Physical sciences:** Astronomy, chemistry, geology, meteorology, oceanography, physics. **Psychology:** General. **Public administration:** Community org/advocacy, social work. **Social sciences:** General, anthropology, economics, geography, international relations, political science, sociology. **Visual/performing arts:** Acting, art, dramatic, graphic design, music theory/composition, studio arts, theater design.

Most popular majors. Business/marketing 25%, communications/journalism 8%, education 15%, parks/recreation 9%, social sciences 7%.

Computing on campus. 3,000 workstations in dormitories, library, computer center, student center. Dormitories wired for high-speed internet access and linked to campus network. Commuter students can connect to campus network. Online course registration, online library, helpline, repair service, student web hosting, wireless network available.

Student life. Freshman orientation: Mandatory, $175 fee. Preregistration for classes offered. One-day sessions; morning refreshments and lunch provided. **Housing:** Guaranteed on-campus for freshmen. Coed dorms, single-sex dorms, special housing for disabled, apartments, fraternity/sorority housing, wellness housing available. $800 partly refundable deposit, deadline 5/1. **Activities:** Bands, choral groups, dance, drama, film society, literary magazine, music ensembles, musical theater, radio station, student government, student newspaper, TV station, Asian cultural organization, Hispanic student organization, North American Indian student organization, organization for black unity, gay/lesbian/bisexual club, College Republicans, University Democrats, Baha'i club, Campus Crusade for Christ, Fellowship of Christian Athletes.

Athletics. NCAA. **Intercollegiate:** Baseball M, basketball, cross-country, field hockey W, football (tackle) M, gymnastics W, soccer W, softball W, track and field, volleyball W, wrestling M. **Intramural:** Basketball, football (non-tackle), golf, racquetball, soccer, softball, table tennis, tennis, volleyball, wrestling M. **Team name:** Chippewas.

Student services. Alcohol/substance abuse counseling, career counseling, student employment services, financial aid counseling, health services, minority student services, personal counseling, placement for graduates, veterans' counselor. **Physically disabled:** Services for visually, speech, hearing impaired.

Contact. E-mail: cmuadmit@cmich.edu
Phone: (989) 774-3076 Toll-free number: (888) 292-5366
Fax: (989) 774-7267
Betty Wagner, Director of Admissions, Central Michigan University, Admissions Office, Mount Pleasant, MI 48859

Cleary University
Howell, Michigan
www.cleary.edu **CB code: 1123**

- Private 4-year university and business college
- Commuter campus in small city
- 694 degree-seeking undergraduates: 40% part-time, 54% women, 8% African American, 1% Asian American, 1% Hispanic American
- 116 graduate students

General. Founded in 1883. Regionally accredited. Campuses in Howell and Ann Arbor; extension sites throughout Southeastern Michigan. **Degrees:** 189 bachelor's, 66 associate awarded; master's offered. **Location:** 55 miles from Detroit, 27 miles from Ann Arbor. **Calendar:** Quarter, limited summer session. **Full-time faculty:** 6 total; 33% have terminal degrees, 17% minority, 67% women. **Part-time faculty:** 159 total; 14% have terminal degrees, 20% minority, 46% women. **Class size:** 89% < 20, 11% 20-39. **Special facilities:** Nature trails.

Freshman class profile. 55 applied, 44 admitted, 30 enrolled.

Basis for selection. Open admission, but selective for some programs. 2.0 GPA, high school record or GED most important. 20 ACT or 1000 SAT (exclusive of Writing) recommended. Regular, special, guest, dual, provisional, transfer, and international admissions available. Applicants with below 2.0 GPA may be accepted if probable success in chosen program indicated.

High school preparation. 24 units recommended. Recommended units include English 4, mathematics 2, social studies 2, history 2, science 2 and academic electives 12.

2008-2009 Annual costs. Tuition/fees: $14,880. Tuition prices guaranteed if student enrolled continuously. Tuition includes all books and fees.

2007-2008 Financial aid. Need-based: 66 full-time freshmen applied for aid; 66 were judged to have need; 66 of these received aid. Average need met was 43%. Average scholarship/grant was $1,028; average loan $1,295. 29% of total undergraduate aid awarded as scholarships/grants, 71% as loans/jobs. **Non-need-based:** Awarded to 81 full-time undergraduates, including 23 freshmen. Scholarships awarded for academics. **Additional information:** Filing electronically preferred; paper applications available. Tuition guarantee based on continuous enrollment. Essay and recommendations required for scholarship consideration.

Application procedures. Admission: Closing date 8/15. $25 fee, may be waived for applicants with need. Admission notification on a rolling basis. **Financial aid:** Priority date 3/15, closing date 8/15. FAFSA required. Applicants notified on a rolling basis; must reply within 2 week(s) of notification.

Academics. Compressed academic calendar reduces time to degree completion. First-time college students can complete bachelor's degree in 3.5 years and adults with previous college experience can complete degree in just over 1 year. **Special study options:** Accelerated study, combined bachelor's/graduate degree, cooperative education, distance learning, double major, dual enrollment of high school students, independent study, internships. **Credit/placement by examination:** AP, CLEP, institutional tests. 36 credit hours maximum toward bachelor's degree. **Support services:** Pre-admission summer program, reduced course load, remedial instruction, study skills assistance, tutoring.

Majors. Business: Accounting, business admin, e-commerce, entrepreneurial studies, financial planning, human resources, management information systems, marketing, nonprofit/public, public finance. **Computer sciences:** Security.

Computing on campus. 60 workstations in computer center, student center. Commuter students can connect to campus network. Online library, helpline, wireless network available.

Student life. Freshman orientation: Mandatory. Preregistration for classes offered. **Activities:** DECA, Rotaract, Automation Alley, Michigan Quality Council, Livingston Economic Club, Washtenaw Economic Club.

Athletics. Intramural: Basketball. **Team name:** Cougars.

Student services. Adult student services, career counseling, student employment services, financial aid counseling, placement for graduates.

Contact. E-mail: admissions@cleary.edu
Phone: (800) 686-1883 ext. 2249 Toll-free number: (800) 686-1883 ext. 2249 Fax: (517) 552-7805
Carrie Bonofiglio, Director of Admissions, Cleary University, 3750 Cleary Drive, Howell, MI 48843

College for Creative Studies
Detroit, Michigan **CB member**
www.collegeforcreativestudies.edu **CB code: 1035**

- Private 4-year visual arts college
- Commuter campus in very large city
- 1,354 degree-seeking undergraduates: 14% part-time, 43% women, 7% African American, 4% Asian American, 5% Hispanic American, 6% international

- 4 graduate students
- 37% of applicants admitted
- SAT or ACT (ACT writing optional) required
- 57% graduate within 6 years

General. Founded in 1926. Regionally accredited. **Degrees:** 227 bachelor's awarded. **Location:** 4 miles from downtown. **Calendar:** Semester, limited summer session. **Full-time faculty:** 58 total; 60% have terminal degrees, 16% minority, 31% women. **Part-time faculty:** 190 total; 42% women. **Special facilities:** Extensive studio space, art gallery for student exhibitions, foundry, computer studios, wood shop, metals shop, glassblowing studio, ceramic studio, fiber studio.

Freshman class profile. 1,533 applied, 561 admitted, 241 enrolled.

Mid 50% test scores		**GPA 2.0-2.99:**	40%
ACT composite:	18-23	**Return as sophomores:**	77%
GPA 3.75 or higher:	10%	**Out-of-state:**	21%
GPA 3.50-3.74:	11%	**Live on campus:**	64%
GPA 3.0-3.49:	39%	**International:**	5%

Basis for selection. Art portfolio, test scores, and high school record important. Minimum 2.5 high school GPA for applicants. ACT/SAT scores required. Portfolio required. **Homeschooled:** Transcript of courses and grades required.

High school preparation. 13 units recommended. Recommended units include English 4, mathematics 3, social studies 2, science 2 and foreign language 2. College-preparatory program recommended, art courses highly recommended.

2008-2009 Annual costs. Tuition/fees: $28,275. Books/supplies: $2,500. Personal expenses: $1,500.

2007-2008 Financial aid. Need-based: 52% of total undergraduate aid awarded as scholarships/grants, 48% as loans/jobs. **Non-need-based:** Scholarships awarded for academics, art.

Application procedures. Admission: Priority date 3/1; deadline 8/1 (postmark date). $35 fee, may be waived for applicants with need, free for online applicants. Admission notification on a rolling basis beginning on or about 9/15. Must reply by May 1 or within 3 week(s) if notified thereafter. **Financial aid:** Priority date 7/1; no closing date. FAFSA required. Applicants notified on a rolling basis starting 3/15; must reply within 3 week(s) of notification.

Academics. Special study options: Cooperative education, cross-registration, double major, dual enrollment of high school students, exchange student, independent study, internships, New York semester, study abroad, teacher certification program. Advanced students may petition for 1 semester in New York studio space. **Credit/placement by examination:** AP, CLEP, IB, institutional tests. 6 credit hours maximum toward bachelor's degree. **Support services:** Learning center, pre-admission summer program, reduced course load, remedial instruction, study skills assistance, tutoring, writing center.

Majors. Business: Transportation. **Communications:** Digital media. **Communications technology:** Animation/special effects. **Production:** Furniture. **Visual/performing arts:** Ceramics, cinematography, commercial photography, commercial/advertising art, crafts, design, drawing, fiber arts, graphic design, illustration, industrial design, interior design, metal/jewelry, multimedia, painting, photography, printmaking, sculpture, studio arts.

Computing on campus. 400 workstations in dormitories, library, computer center. Dormitories wired for high-speed internet access and linked to campus network. Commuter students can connect to campus network. Online library, student web hosting, wireless network available.

Student life. Freshman orientation: Mandatory. Preregistration for classes offered. **Housing:** Apartments available. $200 fully refundable deposit, deadline 5/1. Furnished, college-owned apartments available. **Activities:** Student government, black student club, women artists club, industrial design students club.

Student services. Alcohol/substance abuse counseling, career counseling, student employment services, financial aid counseling, minority student services, personal counseling, placement for graduates. **Physically disabled:** Services for hearing impaired.

Contact. E-mail: admissions@collegeforcreativestudies.edu
Phone: (313) 664-7425 Toll-free number: (800) 952-2787
Fax: (313) 872-2739
Lori Watson, Director of Admissions, College for Creative Studies, 201 East Kirby, Detroit, MI 48202-4034

Concordia University

Ann Arbor, Michigan
www.cuaa.edu **CB code: 1094**

- Private 4-year liberal arts and teachers college affiliated with Lutheran Church - Missouri Synod
- Residential campus in small city
- 459 degree-seeking undergraduates
- 64% of applicants admitted
- SAT or ACT (ACT writing optional) required

General. Founded in 1962. Regionally accredited. **Degrees:** 139 bachelor's, 1 associate awarded; master's offered. **ROTC:** Army, Air Force. **Location:** 40 miles from Detroit. **Calendar:** Semester, limited summer session. **Full-time faculty:** 32 total. **Part-time faculty:** 61 total. **Class size:** 85% < 20, 14% 20-39, less than 1% 40-49. **Special facilities:** Earhart Manor (certified Michigan Historical Landmark).

Freshman class profile. 428 applied, 275 admitted, 107 enrolled.

Mid 50% test scores		**GPA 3.50-3.74:**	16%
SAT critical reading:	520-600	**GPA 3.0-3.49:**	30%
SAT math:	510-600	**GPA 2.0-2.99:**	35%
SAT writing:	500-570	**Out-of-state:**	22%
ACT composite:	20-26	**Live on campus:**	95%
GPA 3.75 or higher:	19%		

Basis for selection. School achievement record most important. Test scores and rank in top half of class also important. Interview and essay recommended. Audition recommended for music majors. Portfolio recommended for art majors. **Homeschooled:** Letter of recommendation (nonparent) required. 300-500 word personal statement and resume or extracurricular activities sheet required. **Learning Disabled:** Require an explanation of the disability and written recommended accommodations from an appropriate professional.

High school preparation. 20 units recommended. Recommended units include English 4, mathematics 3, social studies 2, science 2 (laboratory 2), foreign language 2 and academic electives 5. Math should include two units of algebra and one unit of geometry.

2008-2009 Annual costs. Tuition/fees: $19,770. Additional one-time fees for all undergraduates include: $125 pre-enrollment deposit, $100 matriculation fee. Room/board: $7,350. Books/supplies: $600. Personal expenses: $1,200.

2007-2008 Financial aid. Need-based: 68% of total undergraduate aid awarded as scholarships/grants, 32% as loans/jobs. **Non-need-based:** Scholarships awarded for academics, alumni affiliation, art, athletics, leadership, music/drama, religious affiliation.

Application procedures. Admission: Closing date 8/15. $25 fee, may be waived for applicants with need, free for online applicants. Admission notification on a rolling basis. **Financial aid:** Closing date 3/1. FAFSA, institutional form required. Applicants notified on a rolling basis starting 3/1; must reply within 3 week(s) of notification.

Academics. Special study options: Accelerated study, cross-registration, double major, dual enrollment of high school students, exchange student, independent study, internships, liberal arts/career combination, student-designed major, study abroad, teacher certification program, weekend college. Accelerated degree program for mature students. **Credit/placement by examination:** AP, CLEP, IB, institutional tests. No limit on credit by examination. **Support services:** Reduced course load, remedial instruction, study skills assistance, tutoring, writing center.

Majors. Biology: General. **Business:** Business admin, hospitality admin. **Communications:** General, journalism. **Education:** Art, biology, chemistry, early childhood, elementary, English, health, history, mathematics, music, physical, psychology, science, secondary, social studies, Spanish, speech. **Family/consumer sciences:** Family studies. **Foreign languages:** Ancient Greek, Biblical, Spanish. **Health:** Premedicine. **History:** General. **Interdisciplinary:** Biological/physical sciences. **Legal studies:** Prelaw. **Math:** General. **Parks/recreation:** Health/fitness. **Philosophy/religion:** Philosophy, religion. **Physical sciences:** Chemistry, physics. **Protective services:** Law enforcement admin. **Psychology:** General. **Social sciences:** General, sociology. **Theology:** Preministerial, religious ed, sacred music. **Visual/performing arts:** Art, theater arts management. **Other:** Pre-engineering, Public safety.

Most popular majors. Business/marketing 18%, communications/journalism 9%, education 24%, security/protective services 7%, theological studies 9%.

Computing on campus. 80 workstations in library, computer center, student center. Dormitories wired for high-speed internet access and linked to campus network. Commuter students can connect to campus network. Online library, helpline, repair service, student web hosting, wireless network available.

Student life. **Freshman orientation:** Mandatory, $125 fee. Preregistration for classes offered. 3-day program includes academic, social, and orientation events. **Policies:** Students must live on campus (or with family member) until attaining junior status or 21 years of age. **Housing:** Guaranteed on-campus for all undergraduates. Single-sex dorms, apartments, wellness housing available. $100 nonrefundable deposit, deadline 8/15. **Activities:** Bands, campus ministries, choral groups, dance, drama, music ensembles, musical theater, student government, student newspaper, several religious and community service groups.

Athletics. NAIA. **Intercollegiate:** Baseball M, basketball, cross-country, golf M, soccer, softball W, volleyball W. **Intramural:** Badminton, basketball, football (non-tackle), soccer, softball, table tennis, volleyball. **Team name:** Cardinals.

Student services. Adult student services, alcohol/substance abuse counseling, chaplain/spiritual director, career counseling, student employment services, financial aid counseling, health services, personal counseling, placement for graduates, women's services. **Physically disabled:** Services for visually, speech, hearing impaired.

Contact. E-mail: admissions@cuaa.edu
Phone: (734) 995-7322 Toll-free number: (800) 253-0680
Fax: (734) 995-4610
Amy Becher, Executive Director of Enrollment Services, Concordia University, 4090 Geddes Road, Ann Arbor, MI 48105

Cornerstone University
Grand Rapids, Michigan
www.cornerstone.edu **CB code: 1253**

- Private 4-year university and liberal arts college affiliated with interdenominational tradition
- Residential campus in small city
- 1,741 degree-seeking undergraduates: 24% part-time, 59% women, 11% African American, 1% Asian American, 4% Hispanic American, 1% international
- 643 graduate students
- 75% of applicants admitted
- SAT or ACT (ACT writing recommended), application essay required
- 41% graduate within 6 years; 10% enter graduate study

General. Founded in 1941. Regionally accredited. **Degrees:** 366 bachelor's, 45 associate awarded; master's, doctoral, first professional offered. **Location:** 4 miles from downtown. **Calendar:** Semester, limited summer session. **Full-time faculty:** 62 total; 50% have terminal degrees, 5% minority, 32% women. **Part-time faculty:** 65 total; 6% have terminal degrees, 8% minority, 48% women. **Class size:** 63% < 20, 33% 20-39, 2% 40-49, 3% 50-99.

Freshman class profile. 939 applied, 704 admitted, 220 enrolled.

Mid 50% test scores		**End year in good standing:**	90%
ACT composite:	20-25	**Return as sophomores:**	69%
GPA 3.75 or higher:	33%	**Out-of-state:**	21%
GPA 3.50-3.74:	20%	**Live on campus:**	87%
GPA 3.0-3.49:	28%	**International:**	1%
GPA 2.0-2.99:	18%		

Basis for selection. Statement of Christian commitment, pastoral reference, 2.5 high school GPA, and ACT score of 19. Students with lower scores and GPA may be admitted conditionally. Interview recommended. Audition required for music majors. **Homeschooled:** Statement describing homeschool structure and mission, transcript of courses and grades, letter of recommendation (nonparent) required.

High school preparation. College-preparatory program recommended. 18 units recommended. Recommended units include English 4, mathematics 3, social studies 2, history 1, science 2 (laboratory 1), foreign language 2 and academic electives 4.

2008-2009 Annual costs. Tuition/fees: $19,530. Tuition includes laptop computer. Room/board: $6,500. Books/supplies: $1,000. Personal expenses: $1,234.

2008-2009 Financial aid. **Need-based:** 185 full-time freshmen applied for aid; 166 were judged to have need; 166 of these received aid. Average need met was 88%. Average scholarship/grant was $13,016; average loan $3,725. 53% of total undergraduate aid awarded as scholarships/grants, 47% as loans/jobs. **Non-need-based:** Scholarships awarded for academics, athletics, leadership, music/drama, state residency. **Additional information:** Audition required for music scholarship applicants.

Application procedures. **Admission:** No deadline. $25 fee, may be waived for applicants with need, free for online applicants. Admission notification on a rolling basis. **Financial aid:** Priority date 3/1; no closing date. FAFSA required. Applicants notified on a rolling basis starting 3/15; must reply within 2 week(s) of notification.

Academics. All students must complete internship in major field. Core curriculum. **Special study options:** Accelerated study, cross-registration, distance learning, double major, dual enrollment of high school students, ESL, honors, independent study, internships, liberal arts/career combination, study abroad, teacher certification program, urban semester, Washington semester, weekend college. **Credit/placement by examination:** AP, CLEP, IB, ACT, institutional tests. 15 credit hours maximum toward associate degree, 30 toward bachelor's. **Support services:** Learning center, reduced course load, remedial instruction, study skills assistance, tutoring, writing center.

Honors college/program. Requires 28 ACT; 12-15 admitted annually.

Majors. **Biology:** General, environmental. **Business:** Accounting, business admin, financial planning, international, management information systems, management science, marketing. **Communications:** General, digital media, media studies. **Education:** Biology, early childhood, elementary, English, history, mathematics, music, physical, science, secondary, social science, social studies, voc/tech. **Family/consumer sciences:** Family systems, work/family studies. **Foreign languages:** Spanish. **Health:** Health services, predental, premedicine, preveterinary. **History:** General. **Math:** General. **Parks/recreation:** Exercise sciences, sports admin. **Psychology:** General, family. **Public administration:** Social work. **Social sciences:** General. **Theology:** Bible, youth ministry. **Visual/performing arts:** Music performance, music theory/composition.

Most popular majors. Business/marketing 43%, education 21%, theological studies 11%.

Computing on campus. PC or laptop required. 117 workstations in dormitories, library, computer center, student center. Dormitories wired for high-speed internet access and linked to campus network. Commuter students can connect to campus network. Online course registration, online library, helpline, repair service, wireless network available.

Student life. **Freshman orientation:** Mandatory. Preregistration for classes offered. 4-day program held prior to start of Fall classes. **Policies:** Dry campus; chapel attendance required. Students under 21 with fewer than 63 credit hours must live on campus unless living with immediate family. Religious observance required. **Housing:** Guaranteed on-campus for all undergraduates. Single-sex dorms, special housing for disabled, apartments available. $150 fully refundable deposit, deadline 5/29. **Activities:** Bands, campus ministries, choral groups, dance, drama, film society, international student organizations, literary magazine, music ensembles, musical theater, opera, radio station, student government, student newspaper, student outreach committee, Young Republicans, cross-cultural ministries, social committee, fine arts committee, literature club, diversity club, right-to-life campus organization.

Athletics. NAIA. **Intercollegiate:** Basketball, cross-country, golf, soccer, softball W, track and field, volleyball W. **Intramural:** Basketball, football (non-tackle), ice hockey M, racquetball, soccer, softball, volleyball. **Team name:** Golden Eagles.

Student services. Adult student services, alcohol/substance abuse counseling, chaplain/spiritual director, career counseling, student employment services, financial aid counseling, health services, personal counseling, placement for graduates, veterans' counselor. **Physically disabled:** Services for visually, hearing impaired.

Contact. E-mail: admissions@cornerstone.edu
Phone: (616) 222-1426 Toll-free number: (800) 787-9778
Fax: (616) 222-1418
Tim Johnston, Vice-President of Enrollment Management and Marketing, Cornerstone University, 1001 East Beltline NE, Grand Rapids, MI 49525-5897

Davenport University
Grand Rapids, Michigan
www.davenport.edu **CB code: 1183**

- Private 4-year university and business college
- Commuter campus in small city

- 9,673 degree-seeking undergraduates: 68% part-time, 70% women, 18% African American, 2% Asian American, 3% Hispanic American
- 959 degree-seeking graduate students

General. Founded in 1866. Regionally accredited. Locations in Alma, Battle Creek, Caro, Flint, Gaylord, Holland, Kalamazoo, Lansing, Livonia, Midland, Saginaw, Traverse City, Warren, Merrillville (Indiana), South Bend (Indiana). **Degrees:** 1,033 bachelor's, 664 associate awarded; master's offered. **Location:** 10 miles from Grand Rapids. **Calendar:** Semester, extensive summer session. **Full-time faculty:** 157 total; 22% have terminal degrees, 8% minority, 59% women. **Part-time faculty:** 932 total; 18% minority, 51% women. **Class size:** 87% < 20, 13% 20-39, less than 1% 40-49.

Freshman class profile. 1,102 admitted, 925 enrolled.

Out-of-state:	3%	**Live on campus:**	5%

Basis for selection. GPA and test scores important; prospective students without ACT or SAT scores may take standard COMPASS assessment as arranged by a Davenport representative. SAT or ACT recommended. Interview recommended.

High school preparation. Recommended units include English 6.

2008-2009 Annual costs. Tuition/fees: $13,250. Books/supplies: $1,600. Personal expenses: $1,200.

2007-2008 Financial aid. **Non-need-based:** Scholarships awarded for academics, alumni affiliation, athletics, leadership.

Application procedures. **Admission:** No deadline. $25 fee. Admission notification on a rolling basis beginning on or about 9/1. **Financial aid:** Priority date 3/1; no closing date. FAFSA required. Applicants notified on a rolling basis starting 3/1; must reply within 2 week(s) of notification.

Academics. **Special study options:** Accelerated study, distance learning, dual enrollment of high school students, ESL, honors, independent study, internships, study abroad. **Credit/placement by examination:** AP, CLEP, IB, ACT, institutional tests. **Support services:** Learning center, remedial instruction, tutoring, writing center.

Majors. **Biology:** Bioinformatics. **Business:** General, accounting, business admin, finance, human resources, international, marketing. **Communications technology:** Animation/special effects. **Computer sciences:** General, networking, security. **Health:** Health care admin, management/clinical assistant, medical records admin, nursing (RN). **Legal studies:** Paralegal. **Parks/recreation:** Sports admin. **Protective services:** Security management. **Other:** Service management and marketing.

Most popular majors. Business/marketing 78%, computer/information sciences 15%, health sciences 7%.

Computing on campus. 3,224 workstations in dormitories, library, computer center, student center. Dormitories wired for high-speed internet access and linked to campus network. Commuter students can connect to campus network. Online course registration, online library, wireless network available.

Student life. **Freshman orientation:** Mandatory. Preregistration for classes offered. **Housing:** Coed dorms, wellness housing available. **Activities:** Minority student association, Alternative Spring Break, Business Professionals of America, Delta Epsilon Chi, Global Student Organization, Health Information Management Student Association, legal assistants club, residence hall community council, Society of Human Resource Management, student activites committee.

Athletics. NAIA. **Intercollegiate:** Basketball, cross-country, golf, ice hockey M, lacrosse, soccer, track and field, volleyball. **Team name:** Panthers.

Student services. Career counseling, student employment services, financial aid counseling, placement for graduates.

Contact. E-mail: gradmiss@davenport.edu
Phone: (616) 698-7111 Toll-free number: (866) 925-3884
Daryl Kingrey, Executive Director of Admissions, Davenport University, 6191 Kraft Avenue SE, Grand Rapids, MI 49512-5926

Eastern Michigan University

Ypsilanti, Michigan — **CB member**
www.emich.edu — **CB code: 1201**

- Public 4-year university
- Residential campus in small city
- 16,902 degree-seeking undergraduates: 29% part-time, 58% women, 20% African American, 3% Asian American, 3% Hispanic American, 1% Native American, 1% international
- 3,873 degree-seeking graduate students
- 73% of applicants admitted
- SAT or ACT (ACT writing optional) required
- 36% graduate within 6 years

General. Founded in 1849. Regionally accredited. **Degrees:** 2,964 bachelor's awarded; master's, doctoral offered. **ROTC:** Army, Naval, Air Force. **Location:** 7 miles from Ann Arbor, 35 miles from Detroit. **Calendar:** Semester, limited summer session. **Full-time faculty:** 738 total; 81% have terminal degrees, 17% minority, 48% women. **Part-time faculty:** 498 total; 15% minority, 60% women. **Class size:** 37% < 20, 52% 20-39, 6% 40-49, 5% 50-99, less than 1% >100. **Special facilities:** Corporate education center, observatory, laser laboratory, textiles research and training institute.

Freshman class profile. 9,754 applied, 7,083 admitted, 2,212 enrolled.

Mid 50% test scores		**GPA 2.0-2.99:**	50%
SAT critical reading:	450-570	**Rank in top quarter:**	34%
SAT math:	450-580	**Rank in top tenth:**	12%
SAT writing:	440-570	**End year in good standing:**	75%
ACT composite:	18-23	**Return as sophomores:**	79%
GPA 3.75 or higher:	8%	**Out-of-state:**	12%
GPA 3.50-3.74:	10%	**Live on campus:**	68%
GPA 3.0-3.49:	32%		

Basis for selection. School achievement record and test scores important. Grades and test results combined to predict academic success. Michigan English Language Assessment Battery accepted in place of TOEFL with minimum score 72 for unconditional acceptance. Essay recommended. Audition required of music majors. Portfolio required of art majors.

High school preparation. College-preparatory program recommended. 21 units recommended. Recommended units include English 4, mathematics 4, social studies 2, history 1, science 4 (laboratory 1), foreign language 2 and academic electives 4. 2 units fine arts and 1 computer literacy also recommended.

2008-2009 Annual costs. Tuition/fees: $8,069; $21,464 out-of-state. Room/board: $7,352. Books/supplies: $900. Personal expenses: $1,150.

2007-2008 Financial aid. **Need-based:** 1,940 full-time freshmen applied for aid; 1,514 were judged to have need; 1,469 of these received aid. Average need met was 66%. Average scholarship/grant was $3,657; average loan $3,824. 35% of total undergraduate aid awarded as scholarships/grants, 65% as loans/jobs. **Non-need-based:** Awarded to 3,050 full-time undergraduates, including 1,842 freshmen. Scholarships awarded for academics, alumni affiliation, art, athletics, leadership, minority status, music/drama, ROTC, state residency.

Application procedures. **Admission:** Priority date 2/15; no deadline. $30 fee, may be waived for applicants with need. Admission notification on a rolling basis beginning on or about 10/1. **Financial aid:** Priority date 3/15; no closing date. FAFSA required. Applicants notified on a rolling basis starting 3/1.

Academics. **Special study options:** Accelerated study, combined bachelor's/graduate degree, cooperative education, distance learning, double major, dual enrollment of high school students, ESL, external degree, honors, independent study, internships, student-designed major, study abroad, teacher certification program, Washington semester, weekend college. Dual enrollment program requires students to apply for admission to EMU. **Credit/placement by examination:** AP, CLEP, IB, SAT, ACT, institutional tests. 30 credit hours maximum toward bachelor's degree. **Support services:** Learning center, reduced course load, remedial instruction, tutoring, writing center.

Honors college/program. Admission based on high school GPA, test scores, letters of recommendation. Approximately 250 freshmen per year admitted; reduced class size emphasizing student-professor interaction.

Majors. **Architecture:** Architecture, urban/community planning. **Area/ethnic studies:** African-American, women's. **Biology:** General, biochemistry, toxicology. **Business:** General, accounting, actuarial science, business admin, construction management, entrepreneurial studies, fashion, finance, hospitality admin, international, labor studies, logistics, management information systems, managerial economics, marketing, office management. **Communications:** General, journalism, public relations. **Communications technology:** General, radio/tv. **Computer sciences:** General, computer science. **Education:** Art, biology, business, chemistry, computer, Deaf/hearing impaired, elementary, emotionally handicapped, English, foreign languages, French, German, history, mathematics, mentally handicapped, music, physical, physically handicapped, physics, reading, sales/marketing, science, secondary, social science, social studies, Spanish, special, speech impaired, technology/industrial arts, visually handicapped. **Engineering:** Physics. **Engineering technology:** CAD/CADD, computer, electrical, industrial, industrial management, manufacturing, mechanical, mechanical drafting, plastics. **Family/consumer sciences:** Facilities/event planning. **Foreign languages:** French, German, Germanic, Japanese, linguistics, Spanish. **Health:** Athletic training, clinical lab science, dietetics, health care admin, music therapy, nursing (RN), predental, premedicine, prepharmacy, preveterinary, recreational therapy, speech pathology. **History:** General. **Interdisciplinary:** Biological/physical sciences, science/society. **Legal studies:** Paralegal, prelaw. **Math:** General, statistics. **Parks/recreation:** Facilities management, health/fitness. **Personal/culinary services:** Mortuary science. **Philosophy/religion:** Philosophy. **Physical sciences:** Chemistry, geology, geophysics, physics. **Psychology:** General. **Public administration:** General, social work. **Social sciences:** General, anthropology, criminology, economics, geography, political science, sociology. **Transportation:** Airline/commercial pilot, aviation management. **Visual/performing arts:** Art, art history/conservation, arts management, dance, dramatic, film/cinema, interior design, music performance.

Most popular majors. Business/marketing 20%, communications/journalism 6%, education 24%, health sciences 8%, social sciences 8%, visual/performing arts 8%.

Computing on campus. 1,500 workstations in dormitories, library, computer center, student center. Dormitories wired for high-speed internet access and linked to campus network. Commuter students can connect to campus network. Helpline, student web hosting, wireless network available.

Student life. **Freshman orientation:** Mandatory, $150 fee. Preregistration for classes offered. 4-day orientation held Saturday through Tuesday. **Housing:** Coed dorms, special housing for disabled, apartments, fraternity/sorority housing, wellness housing available. $200 partly refundable deposit, deadline 5/1. **Activities:** Bands, campus ministries, choral groups, dance, drama, film society, international student organizations, literary magazine, music ensembles, musical theater, opera, radio station, student government, student newspaper, symphony orchestra, TV station, 10 honor societies, over 140 student organizations.

Athletics. NCAA. **Intercollegiate:** Baseball M, basketball, cross-country, diving, football (tackle), golf, gymnastics W, rowing (crew) W, soccer W, softball W, swimming, tennis W, track and field, volleyball W, wrestling M. **Intramural:** Badminton, basketball, bowling, cross-country, football (non-tackle), golf, racquetball, soccer, softball, swimming, table tennis, tennis, track and field, volleyball, weight lifting. **Team name:** Eagles.

Student services. Adult student services, alcohol/substance abuse counseling, chaplain/spiritual director, career counseling, student employment services, health services, minority student services, on-campus daycare, personal counseling, placement for graduates, veterans' counselor, women's services. **Physically disabled:** Services for visually, speech, hearing impaired.

Contact. E-mail: admissions@emich.edu
Phone: (734) 487-3060 Toll-free number: (800) 468-6368
Fax: (734) 487-6559
Kathryn Orscheln, Director, Admissions, Eastern Michigan University, 400 Pierce Hall, Ypsilanti, MI 48197

Ferris State University

Big Rapids, Michigan — **CB member**
www.ferris.edu — **CB code: 1222**

- Public 4-year university
- Residential campus in large town
- 11,863 degree-seeking undergraduates: 23% part-time, 48% women, 6% African American, 2% Asian American, 2% Hispanic American, 1% Native American, 1% international
- 1,238 degree-seeking graduate students
- SAT or ACT (ACT writing optional) required
- 46% graduate within 6 years

General. Founded in 1884. Regionally accredited. **Degrees:** 1,901 bachelor's, 873 associate awarded; master's, first professional offered. **ROTC:** Army. **Location:** 55 miles from Grand Rapids. **Calendar:** Semester, limited summer session. **Full-time faculty:** 533 total; 38% women. **Part-time faculty:** 324 total; 47% women. **Special facilities:** Observatory, wildlife museum, Jim Crow museum, art walk, greenhouse.

Freshman class profile.

GPA 3.75 or higher:	16%	**Out-of-state:**	4%
GPA 3.50-3.74:	13%	**Live on campus:**	77%
GPA 3.0-3.49:	30%	**International:**	1%
GPA 2.0-2.99:	41%		

Basis for selection. School achievement record most important. General admission requirements: 2.5 GPA (509 GED) or 17 ACT/1210 SAT. Specific program requirements vary. ACT and SAT scores used for admissions purposes for marginal applicants. Interview recommended. Portfolio recommended of visual communication majors. **Learning Disabled:** Students with learning disabilities should submit documentation from professional psychologist or social worker to Disabilities Services Office in the Educational and Career Services Counseling Center.

High school preparation. College-preparatory program recommended. 24 units recommended. Recommended units include English 4, mathematics 4, social studies 2, history 2, science 4 (laboratory 2), foreign language 3 and academic electives 3. 2 units in fine arts and 1 unit in computer literacy recommended.

2008-2009 Annual costs. Tuition/fees: $9,162; $16,062 out-of-state. Midwest Compact states of Illinois, Indiana, Kansas, Minnesota, Missouri, Nebraska, Ohio, and Wisconsin tuition is $13,500. Room/board: $7,944. Books/supplies: $1,100. Personal expenses: $797.

2008-2009 Financial aid. **Need-based:** Average need met was 84%. Average scholarship/grant was $1,487; average loan $3,224. 34% of total undergraduate aid awarded as scholarships/grants, 66% as loans/jobs. **Non-need-based:** Scholarships awarded for academics, alumni affiliation, art, athletics, leadership, minority status, music/drama, religious affiliation, ROTC.

Application procedures. **Admission:** Closing date 8/1 (postmark date). $30 fee, may be waived for applicants with need, free for online applicants. Admission notification on a rolling basis beginning on or about 7/1. **Financial aid:** Priority date 3/1; no closing date. FAFSA required. Applicants notified on a rolling basis starting 3/1; must reply within 3 week(s) of notification.

Academics. **Special study options:** Accelerated study, cooperative education, cross-registration, distance learning, double major, dual enrollment of high school students, exchange student, external degree, honors, independent study, internships, liberal arts/career combination, study abroad, teacher certification program. **Credit/placement by examination:** AP, CLEP, SAT, ACT, institutional tests. **Support services:** Learning center, remedial instruction, study skills assistance, tutoring, writing center.

Majors. **Architecture:** Interior. **Biology:** General, biochemistry, biotechnology, environmental. **Business:** Accounting, accounting technology, accounting/finance, business admin, construction management, e-commerce, entrepreneurial studies, finance, hospitality admin, hospitality/recreation, hotel/motel admin, human resources, international, marketing, operations. **Communications:** General, advertising, public relations. **Communications technology:** Animation/special effects, graphic/printing, printing management, radio/tv. **Education:** Art, biology, business, chemistry, elementary, English, family/consumer sciences, health, history, mathematics, secondary, social science, social studies, voc/tech. **Engineering technology:** Automotive, electrical, energy systems, environmental, industrial, manufacturing, mechanical, plastics, quality control, surveying, telecommunications. **Family/consumer sciences:** Child care. **Health:** Clinical lab science, health care admin, medical records admin, nuclear medical technology, nursing (RN). **History:** General. **Math:** General, applied, statistics. **Mechanic/repair:** Heavy equipment. **Parks/recreation:** Facilities management. **Physical sciences:** Chemistry. **Protective services:** Police science. **Psychology:** General. **Public administration:** General, social work. **Social sciences:** Sociology. **Visual/performing arts:** Art history/conservation, commercial/advertising art, design, graphic design, industrial design, interior design, metal/jewelry, music management, painting, photography, sculpture, studio arts. **Other:** Business administration/leadership-organizational development, Furniture design, Rubber technology.

Most popular majors. Business/marketing 25%, education 8%, engineering/engineering technologies 16%, health sciences 8%, security/protective services 11%, visual/performing arts 8%.

Computing on campus. 2,373 workstations in dormitories, library, computer center, student center. Dormitories wired for high-speed internet access and linked to campus network. Commuter students can connect to campus network. Online course registration, online library, helpline, repair service, wireless network available.

Student life. **Freshman orientation:** Mandatory, $75 fee. Preregistration for classes offered. **Policies:** All students sign ethics statement during orientation. **Housing:** Guaranteed on-campus for all undergraduates. Coed dorms, special housing for disabled, apartments, wellness housing available. $200 nonrefundable deposit, deadline 5/31. **Activities:** Bands, choral groups, dance, drama, international student organizations, music ensembles, radio station, student government, student newspaper, symphony orchestra, TV station, Alpha Omega Co-ed Christian Fraternity, Circle K, Diverse Sexuality and Gender Alliance, gospel choir, Habitat for Humanity, Indian students association, Muslim student organization, National Organization for Women, Red Cross student chapter.

Athletics. NCAA. **Intercollegiate:** Basketball, cheerleading, cross-country, football (tackle) M, golf, ice hockey M, soccer W, softball W, tennis, track and field, volleyball W. **Intramural:** Badminton, basketball, football (non-tackle), golf, handball, ice hockey M, racquetball, softball, swimming, table tennis, tennis, volleyball, water polo M. **Team name:** Bulldogs.

Student services. Adult student services, alcohol/substance abuse counseling, chaplain/spiritual director, career counseling, student employment services, financial aid counseling, health services, minority student services, on-campus daycare, personal counseling, placement for graduates, veterans' counselor. **Physically disabled:** Services for visually, speech, hearing impaired.

Contact. E-mail: admissions@ferris.edu
Phone: (231) 591-2100 Toll-free number: (800) 433-7747
Fax: (231) 591-3944
Kristen Salomonson, Dean of Enrollment Services, Ferris State University, 1201 South State Street, CSS 201, Big Rapids, MI 49307-2714

Finlandia University
Hancock, Michigan
www.finlandia.edu **CB code: 1743**

- Private 4-year university and liberal arts college affiliated with Evangelical Lutheran Church in America
- Commuter campus in small town
- 507 degree-seeking undergraduates: 8% part-time, 64% women, 3% African American, 2% Asian American, 2% Hispanic American, 1% Native American
- 89% of applicants admitted
- Application essay required
- 53% graduate within 6 years

General. Founded in 1896. Regionally accredited. **Degrees:** 86 bachelor's, 29 associate awarded. **ROTC:** Army, Naval, Air Force. **Location:** 100 miles from Marquette, 220 miles from Green Bay, Wisconsin. **Calendar:** Semester, limited summer session. **Full-time faculty:** 32 total; 22% have terminal degrees, 72% women. **Part-time faculty:** 36 total; 14% have terminal degrees, 67% women. **Class size:** 70% < 20, 28% 20-39, 3% 40-49. **Special facilities:** Finnish-American historical archive.

Freshman class profile. 550 applied, 492 admitted, 115 enrolled.

GPA 3.75 or higher:	4%	**End year in good standing:**	75%
GPA 3.50-3.74:	3%	**Return as sophomores:**	63%
GPA 3.0-3.49:	33%	**Out-of-state:**	19%
GPA 2.0-2.99:	59%	**Live on campus:**	28%

Basis for selection. One unit of algebra and chemistry with grade of 3.0 and 2.5 cumulative GPA required for nursing. 1 unit of algebra and biology with grade of 3.0 and 3.0 cumulative GPA required for physical therapist assistant. GPA of 2.0 required of all other programs. If GPA below 2.0, special consideration given in determining admission. Student may obtain admission into academic warning program based on placement test results. Nursing applicants should apply by March 15, physical therapy assistant applicants by April 15. SAT or ACT recommended. **Homeschooled:** Transcript of courses and grades required. Placement tests required. **Learning Disabled:** Evaluation results and/or IEP that specifically states the disability is required for eligibility for accommodations, but not for admission to the university.

High school preparation. College-preparatory program recommended. Recommended units include English 4, mathematics 2, science 2 (laboratory 2).

2009-2010 Annual costs. Tuition/fees (projected): $18,014. Room/board: $5,800. Books/supplies: $1,300. Personal expenses: $100.

2008-2009 Financial aid. Need-based: Average scholarship/grant was $2,000; average loan $3,500. 52% of total undergraduate aid awarded as scholarships/grants, 48% as loans/jobs. **Non-need-based:** Scholarships awarded for academics, leadership, religious affiliation, state residency. **Additional information:** Work/study program; up to $2,800 per year.

Application procedures. Admission: Priority date 8/1; deadline 8/25 (postmark date). $30 fee, may be waived for applicants with need, free for online applicants. Admission notification on a rolling basis. **Financial aid:** Priority date 3/1; no closing date. FAFSA, institutional form required. Applicants notified on a rolling basis starting 3/1; must reply within 2 week(s) of notification.

Academics. Special study options: Double major, dual enrollment of high school students, ESL, exchange student, honors, independent study, internships, liberal arts/career combination, student-designed major, study abroad, teacher certification program. **Credit/placement by examination:** AP, CLEP, IB, SAT, ACT, institutional tests. 18 credit hours maximum toward associate degree, 30 toward bachelor's. **Support services:** Learning center, remedial instruction, study skills assistance, tutoring, writing center.

Majors. Business: Accounting, business admin, international, marketing. **Education:** Elementary. **Health:** Nursing (RN). **Liberal arts:** Arts/sciences. **Psychology:** General. **Public administration:** Human services. **Social sciences:** General. **Visual/performing arts:** Art, ceramics, commercial/advertising art, design, drawing, fashion design, fiber arts, graphic design, illustration, interior design, painting, studio arts.

Most popular majors. Business/marketing 24%, education 14%, health sciences 20%, liberal arts 7%, public administration/social services 14%, visual/performing arts 21%.

Computing on campus. 80 workstations in dormitories, library, computer center. Dormitories wired for high-speed internet access and linked to campus network. Online library, helpline, wireless network available.

Student life. Freshman orientation: Mandatory. Preregistration for classes offered. 3-day program includes testing, workshops, and special speakers. **Housing:** Guaranteed on-campus for all undergraduates. Coed dorms available. $100 nonrefundable deposit, deadline 8/25. **Activities:** Pep band, campus ministries, choral groups, dance, drama, music ensembles, musical theater, student government, student newspaper, servant leadership program, local agency volunteer programs.

Athletics. NCAA. **Intercollegiate:** Baseball M, basketball, cross-country, golf, ice hockey, soccer, softball W, volleyball W. **Intramural:** Bowling, football (non-tackle), softball, swimming, table tennis, volleyball. **Team name:** Lions.

Student services. Chaplain/spiritual director, career counseling, student employment services, financial aid counseling, personal counseling, placement for graduates. **Learning disabled:** Comprehensive services available.

Contact. E-mail: admissions@finlandia.edu
Phone: (906) 487-7274 Toll-free number: (877) 202-5491
Fax: (906) 487-7383
Martin Kinard, Director of Admissions, Finlandia University, 601 Quincy Street, Hancock, MI 49930-1882

Grace Bible College
Grand Rapids, Michigan
www.gbcol.edu **CB code: 0809**

- Private 4-year Bible and liberal arts college affiliated with Grace Gospel Fellowship
- Residential campus in small city
- 177 degree-seeking undergraduates: 5% part-time, 45% women, 3% African American, 1% Asian American
- 65% of applicants admitted
- SAT or ACT (ACT writing optional) required
- 56% graduate within 6 years

General. Founded in 1945. Regionally accredited; also accredited by ABHE. **Degrees:** 20 bachelor's, 13 associate awarded. **ROTC:** Army. **Location:** 50 miles from Kalamazoo. **Calendar:** Semester. **Full-time faculty:** 8 total; 12% have terminal degrees, 38% women. **Part-time faculty:** 13 total; 23% have terminal degrees, 23% women. **Class size:** 73% < 20, 23% 20-39, 5% 50-99. **Special facilities:** College-operated recording studio.

Freshman class profile. 159 applied, 104 admitted, 53 enrolled.

Mid 50% test scores		**GPA 2.0-2.99:**	28%
SAT critical reading:	460-540	**Rank in top quarter:**	39%
SAT math:	400-560	**Rank in top tenth:**	17%
SAT writing:	400-460	**End year in good standing:**	80%
ACT composite:	18-23	**Return as sophomores:**	61%
GPA 3.75 or higher:	19%	**Out-of-state:**	17%
GPA 3.50-3.74:	21%	**Live on campus:**	60%
GPA 3.0-3.49:	28%		

Basis for selection. Evidence of personal salvation through Jesus Christ important. 2.5 GPA, 20 ACT, and rank in top half of class for regular admission. Probationary admission for those in third quarter of class. Interview may be recommended.

High school preparation. Recommended units include English 4, mathematics 3, social studies 3, science 3 and foreign language 1.

2008-2009 Annual costs. Tuition/fees: $13,320. Room/board: $6,700. Books/supplies: $548. Personal expenses: $976.

2007-2008 Financial aid. **Need-based:** 48 full-time freshmen applied for aid; 41 were judged to have need; 41 of these received aid. Average need met was 78%. Average scholarship/grant was $3,875; average loan $2,864. 46% of total undergraduate aid awarded as scholarships/grants, 54% as loans/jobs. **Non-need-based:** Awarded to 121 full-time undergraduates, including 48 freshmen. Scholarships awarded for academics, music/drama, religious affiliation.

Application procedures. **Admission:** Closing date 6/1 (receipt date). No application fee. Admission notification on a rolling basis. Must reply by May 1 or within 4 week(s) if notified thereafter. **Financial aid:** Priority date 3/1; no closing date. FAFSA required. Applicants notified on a rolling basis starting 5/15; must reply within 2 week(s) of notification.

Academics. All students major in Bible and theology in addition to degree major. **Special study options:** Combined bachelor's/graduate degree, cross-registration, double major, dual enrollment of high school students, independent study, internships, liberal arts/career combination. **Credit/placement by examination:** AP, CLEP, institutional tests. **Support services:** Reduced course load, remedial instruction, tutoring, writing center.

Majors. **Business:** General, accounting, business admin, international, management science, marketing. **Communications technology:** Photo/film/video, recording arts. **Computer sciences:** General, information technology, web page design. **Education:** Early childhood, elementary, music, secondary. **Liberal arts:** Arts/sciences. **Public administration:** Human services. **Theology:** Bible, missionary, pastoral counseling, religious ed, sacred music, theology, youth ministry.

Most popular majors. Business/marketing 10%, education 45%, interdisciplinary studies 10%, public administration/social services 10%, theological studies 10%, visual/performing arts 10%.

Computing on campus. 25 workstations in library, computer center. Dormitories wired for high-speed internet access and linked to campus network. Helpline, wireless network available.

Student life. **Freshman orientation:** Mandatory. Preregistration for classes offered. Freshmen meet for 5 days prior to start of fall semester. **Policies:** Religious observance required. **Housing:** Guaranteed on-campus for freshmen. Single-sex dorms, apartments, wellness housing available. $100 deposit, deadline 5/1. **Activities:** Jazz band, campus ministries, choral groups, drama, music ensembles, student government.

Athletics. NCCAA. **Intercollegiate:** Basketball, cross-country, soccer M, volleyball W. **Intramural:** Basketball M, bowling, golf, handball, racquetball, skiing, soccer, table tennis, tennis, volleyball. **Team name:** Tigers.

Student services. Chaplain/spiritual director, career counseling, student employment services, financial aid counseling, health services, personal counseling, placement for graduates.

Contact. E-mail: gbc@gbcol.edu
Phone: (616) 538-2330 Toll-free number: (800) 968-1887
Fax: (616) 538-0599
Kevin Gilliam, Enrollment Director, Grace Bible College, 1011 Aldon Street SW, PO Box 910, Grand Rapids, MI 49509

Grand Valley State University

Allendale, Michigan — **CB member**
www.gvsu.edu — **CB code: 1258**

- Public 4-year university
- Residential campus in large town
- 20,285 degree-seeking undergraduates: 11% part-time, 60% women, 5% African American, 3% Asian American, 3% Hispanic American, 1% Native American, 1% international
- 3,029 degree-seeking graduate students
- 78% of applicants admitted
- SAT or ACT (ACT writing recommended) required
- 52% graduate within 6 years; 24% enter graduate study

General. Founded in 1960. Regionally accredited. **Degrees:** 3,541 bachelor's awarded; master's, doctoral offered. **Location:** 12 miles from Grand Rapids. **Calendar:** Semester, extensive summer session. **Full-time faculty:** 993 total; 59% have terminal degrees, 16% minority, 45% women. **Part-time faculty:** 536 total; 7% have terminal degrees, 6% minority, 53% women. **Class size:** 23% < 20, 58% 20-39, 12% 40-49, 5% 50-99, 2% >100. **Special facilities:** Cross-country fitness trail, recital hall, two Great Lakes research vessels, water resources research institute, center for presidential studies.

Freshman class profile. 12,855 applied, 10,009 admitted, 3,890 enrolled.

Mid 50% test scores		**GPA 2.0-2.99:**	3%
SAT critical reading:	480-600	**Rank in top quarter:**	60%
SAT math:	510-630	**Rank in top tenth:**	24%
SAT writing:	480-600	**End year in good standing:**	92%
ACT composite:	21-26	**Return as sophomores:**	86%
GPA 3.75 or higher:	33%	**Out-of-state:**	4%
GPA 3.50-3.74:	27%	**Live on campus:**	84%
GPA 3.0-3.49:	37%		

Basis for selection. Admission based on secondary school grades, courses, personal and academic data, ACT/SAT results.

High school preparation. College-preparatory program recommended. Required units include English 4, mathematics 3, social studies 3, science 3 (laboratory 1) and foreign language 2.

2008-2009 Annual costs. Tuition/fees: $8,196; $12,510 out-of-state. Room/board: $7,224. Books/supplies: $900. Personal expenses: $1,000.

2008-2009 Financial aid. **Need-based:** 3,279 full-time freshmen applied for aid; 2,097 were judged to have need; 2,087 of these received aid. Average need met was 83%. Average scholarship/grant was $5,721; average loan $4,169. 47% of total undergraduate aid awarded as scholarships/grants, 53% as loans/jobs. **Non-need-based:** Awarded to 2,460 full-time undergraduates, including 681 freshmen. Scholarships awarded for academics, alumni affiliation, art, athletics, minority status, music/drama.

Application procedures. **Admission:** $30 fee, may be waived for applicants with need. Admission notification on a rolling basis. Application closing date December 31 for scholarships. **Financial aid:** Priority date 3/1; no closing date. FAFSA required. Applicants notified on a rolling basis starting 4/1; must reply within 3 week(s) of notification.

Academics. **Special study options:** Combined bachelor's/graduate degree, double major, dual enrollment of high school students, ESL, honors, independent study, internships, student-designed major, study abroad, teacher certification program, Washington semester. Undergraduates may take graduate level classes as seniors; co-op programs in education, engineering, health professions. **Credit/placement by examination:** AP, CLEP, IB, SAT, ACT, institutional tests. 32 credit hours maximum toward bachelor's degree. **Support services:** Learning center, pre-admission summer program, remedial instruction, study skills assistance, tutoring, writing center.

Honors college/program. 3.5 GPA and 28 ACT required.

Majors. **Architecture:** Urban/community planning. **Area/ethnic studies:** Chinese, Russian/Slavic. **Biology:** General, biochemistry, cellular/molecular. **Business:** Accounting, business admin, finance, human resources, international, management science, managerial economics, marketing, tourism promotion, tourism/travel. **Communications:** General, advertising, broadcast journalism, journalism, public relations. **Computer sciences:** General, computer science, information systems, programming. **Conservation:** Management/policy. **Education:** Music, physical, science, special. **Engineering:** Electrical, manufacturing, mechanical. **Engineering technology:** Occupational safety. **Foreign languages:** Ancient Greek, classics, French, German, Latin, Spanish. **Health:** Athletic training, clinical lab science, medical radiologic technology/radiation therapy, nursing (RN), occupational health, predental, premedicine, prepharmacy, preveterinary. **History:** General. **Interdisciplinary:** Behavioral sciences, biological/physical sciences, biopsychology. **Legal studies:** General, paralegal. **Liberal arts:** Arts/sciences. **Math:** General, statistics. **Parks/recreation:** General, health/fitness. **Philosophy/religion:** Philosophy. **Physical sciences:** Chemistry, geochemistry, geology, physics. **Protective services:** Law enforcement admin, security services. **Psychology:** General, social. **Public administration:** General, social work. **Social sciences:** General, anthropology, economics, geography, international relations, political science, sociology. **Visual/performing arts:** Art, art history/conservation, ceramics, commercial/advertising art, dance, dramatic, film/cinema, metal/jewelry, painting, photography, printmaking, sculpture, studio arts.

Most popular majors. Biology 9%, business/marketing 20%, communications/journalism 7%, English 6%, health sciences 9%, psychology 9%, social sciences 9%, visual/performing arts 6%.

Computing on campus. 1,270 workstations in dormitories, library, computer center, student center. Dormitories wired for high-speed internet access and linked to campus network. Commuter students can connect to campus network. Online course registration, helpline, repair service, student web hosting, wireless network available.

Student life. **Freshman orientation:** Mandatory, $75 fee. Preregistration for classes offered. One day long and held for small groups on 50 possible dates through May, June, July, and August. Students register for classes for full year. **Housing:** Guaranteed on-campus for freshmen. Coed dorms, apartments, fraternity/sorority housing, wellness housing available. $150 deposit, deadline 3/1. **Activities:** Bands, campus ministries, choral groups, dance, drama, international student organizations, music ensembles, musical theater, radio station, student government, student newspaper, symphony orchestra, TV station, 143 registered organizations.

Athletics. NCAA. **Intercollegiate:** Baseball M, basketball, cheerleading, cross-country, diving, football (tackle) M, golf, soccer W, softball W, swimming, tennis, track and field, volleyball W. **Intramural:** Archery, badminton, basketball, bowling, cross-country, diving, fencing, field hockey, football (tackle) M, golf, gymnastics, racquetball, rowing (crew), skiing, skin diving, soccer, softball, squash, swimming, table tennis, tennis, volleyball, wrestling M. **Team name:** Lakers.

Student services. Adult student services, alcohol/substance abuse counseling, chaplain/spiritual director, career counseling, services for economically disadvantaged, student employment services, financial aid counseling, health services, minority student services, on-campus daycare, personal counseling, placement for graduates, women's services. **Physically disabled:** Services for visually, speech, hearing impaired.

Contact. E-mail: go2gvsu@gvsu.edu
Phone: (616) 331-2025 Toll-free number: (800) 748-0246
Fax: (616) 331-2000
Jodi Chycinski, Director of Admissions, Grand Valley State University, 1 Campus Drive, Allendale, MI 49401-9403

Great Lakes Christian College

Lansing, Michigan
www.glcc.edu **CB code: 7320**

- Private 4-year Bible college affiliated with Church of Christ / Christian Church
- Residential campus in small city
- 258 degree-seeking undergraduates
- 92% of applicants admitted
- SAT or ACT (ACT writing optional) required

General. Founded in 1949. Accredited by ABHE. **Degrees:** 22 bachelor's, 2 associate awarded. **Location:** 90 miles from Detroit, 65 miles from Grand Rapids. **Calendar:** Semester, limited summer session. **Full-time faculty:** 10 total. **Part-time faculty:** 11 total.

Freshman class profile. 102 applied, 94 admitted, 60 enrolled.

Basis for selection. Recommendations of character from applicant's minister and church leaders required. Students with GPA below 2.25 or ACT below 16 or SAT below 820 (exclusive of Writing) admitted on probation. **Homeschooled:** Transcript of courses and grades, letter of recommendation (nonparent) required.

2009-2010 Annual costs. Tuition/fees: $11,980. Room/board: $7,000. Books/supplies: $950. Personal expenses: $1,700.

2008-2009 Financial aid. **Non-need-based:** Scholarships awarded for academics, alumni affiliation, music/drama.

Application procedures. **Admission:** Closing date 8/1 (receipt date). $30 fee, may be waived for applicants with need. Admission notification on a rolling basis. **Financial aid:** Priority date 8/1; no closing date. FAFSA, institutional form required. Applicants notified on a rolling basis starting 5/1; must reply within 3 week(s) of notification.

Academics. **Special study options:** Double major, dual enrollment of high school students, internships. **Credit/placement by examination:** CLEP. **Support services:** Remedial instruction, study skills assistance, tutoring.

Majors. **History:** General. **Theology:** Bible, religious ed, sacred music.

Computing on campus. 23 workstations in library, computer center, student center. Dormitories wired for high-speed internet access and linked to campus network. Commuter students can connect to campus network. Online library, helpline, repair service, wireless network available.

Student life. **Freshman orientation:** Mandatory. Preregistration for classes offered. **Policies:** Regular Christian service participation required of all graduates. Religious observance required. **Housing:** Single-sex dorms, apartments, wellness housing available. $200 fully refundable deposit, deadline 6/1. **Activities:** Campus ministries, choral groups, drama, music ensembles, musical theater, student government, student newspaper.

Athletics. NCCAA. **Intercollegiate:** Basketball M, soccer M, volleyball W. **Intramural:** Baseball M, volleyball M. **Team name:** Crusaders.

Student services. Chaplain/spiritual director, financial aid counseling, personal counseling. **Physically disabled:** Services for visually, hearing impaired.

Contact. E-mail: admissions@glcc.edu
Phone: (517) 321-0242 ext. 221 Toll-free number: (800) 937-4522
Fax: (517) 321-5902
Lloyd Scharer, Director of Admissions & College Relations, Great Lakes Christian College, 6211 West Willow Highway, Lansing, MI 48917-1299

Hillsdale College

Hillsdale, Michigan **CB member**
www.hillsdale.edu **CB code: 1295**

- Private 4-year liberal arts college
- Residential campus in large town
- 1,378 degree-seeking undergraduates
- 64% of applicants admitted
- SAT or ACT (ACT writing optional), application essay required

General. Founded in 1844. Regionally accredited. **Degrees:** 273 bachelor's awarded. **Location:** 120 miles from Detroit, 75 miles from Ann Arbor. **Calendar:** Semester, limited summer session. **Full-time faculty:** 117 total. **Part-time faculty:** 37 total. **Class size:** 77% < 20, 22% 20-39, less than 1% 40-49, less than 1% 50-99. **Special facilities:** Arboretum, preschool, K-12 private academy, economics library, special collections library for first editions, 685-acre lake biological station, Kirby Center for Constitutional Studies and Citizenship.

Freshman class profile. 1,502 applied, 965 admitted, 385 enrolled.

Mid 50% test scores		**GPA 2.0-2.99:**	3%
SAT critical reading:	640-720	**Rank in top quarter:**	75%
SAT math:	570-660	**Rank in top tenth:**	47%
SAT writing:	610-690	**Out-of-state:**	63%
ACT composite:	25-30	**Live on campus:**	99%
GPA 3.75 or higher:	60%	**Fraternities:**	30%
GPA 3.50-3.74:	22%	**Sororities:**	40%
GPA 3.0-3.49:	15%		

Basis for selection. Minimum 3.3 GPA, class rank in top third preferred. Test scores, recommendations, interview, personal essay important. SAT Subject Tests recommended. Portfolio recommended for art majors. Audition required for music scholarship applicants. **Homeschooled:** Transcript of courses and grades required.

High school preparation. 16 units recommended. Recommended units include English 4, mathematics 4, social studies 1, history 2, science 3 (laboratory 1) and foreign language 2.

2008-2009 Annual costs. Tuition/fees: $19,920. Room/board: $7,570. Books/supplies: $900. Personal expenses: $500.

2008-2009 Financial aid. **Need-based:** 53% of total undergraduate aid awarded as scholarships/grants, 47% as loans/jobs. **Non-need-based:** Scholarships awarded for academics, alumni affiliation, art, athletics, leadership, music/drama, state residency. **Additional information:** Campus employment available.

Application procedures. **Admission:** Priority date 11/15; deadline 2/15 (postmark date). $35 fee. Admission notification on a rolling basis beginning on or about 12/1. Must reply by 5/1. **Financial aid:** Priority date 3/1, closing date 3/15. Institutional form required. CSS PROFILE required for returning students only. Applicants notified on a rolling basis starting 2/1; must reply by 5/1 or within 4 week(s) of notification.

Academics. Highly qualified students may study at Oxford University, England for semester or summer. Summer business program at Regents College, London, England as well as study abroad programs in France, Germany and Spain. **Special study options:** Accelerated study, double major, dual enrollment of high school students, honors, independent study, internships, study abroad, teacher certification program, Washington semester. **Credit/placement by examination:** AP, CLEP, IB, SAT, ACT, institutional tests.

Support services: Reduced course load, study skills assistance, tutoring, writing center.

Majors. Area/ethnic studies: American, European. **Biology:** General. **Business:** General, accounting, business admin, finance, international marketing, marketing. **Communications:** General, journalism. **Computer sciences:** Computer science. **Education:** General, early childhood, elementary, multi-level teacher, physical, secondary. **Foreign languages:** Classics, comparative lit, French, German, Spanish. **Health:** Predental, premedicine, prenursing, prepharmacy, preveterinary. **History:** General. **Interdisciplinary:** Math/computer science. **Legal studies:** Prelaw. **Liberal arts:** Arts/sciences. **Math:** General, computational. **Philosophy/religion:** Christian, philosophy, religion. **Physical sciences:** Chemistry, physics. **Psychology:** General. **Social sciences:** Economics, political science, sociology. **Theology:** Preministerial. **Visual/performing arts:** Art, dramatic.

Most popular majors. Biology 7%, business/marketing 15%, education 12%, English 11%, history 14%, social sciences 13%, visual/performing arts 7%.

Computing on campus. 200 workstations in library, computer center, student center. Dormitories wired for high-speed internet access and linked to campus network. Commuter students can connect to campus network. Online library, helpline, repair service, wireless network available.

Student life. Freshman orientation: Mandatory. Preregistration for classes offered. 3-day program in the fall. **Housing:** Guaranteed on-campus for all undergraduates. Single-sex dorms, apartments, fraternity/sorority housing, wellness housing available. $200 nonrefundable deposit, deadline 5/1. **Activities:** Bands, choral groups, dance, drama, international student organizations, literary magazine, music ensembles, musical theater, student government, student newspaper, symphony orchestra, Catholic student council, Varsity H-Club, student federation, enterprising leaders, Intervarsity Christian Fellowship, Fellowship of Christian Athletes, College Republicans, Young Life, Praxis, Charis.

Athletics. NCAA. **Intercollegiate:** Baseball M, basketball, cross-country, diving W, equestrian W, football (tackle) M, softball W, swimming W, track and field, volleyball W. **Intramural:** Basketball, football (non-tackle), handball, racquetball, soccer, softball, swimming, table tennis, tennis, track and field, volleyball. **Team name:** Chargers.

Student services. Chaplain/spiritual director, career counseling, student employment services, financial aid counseling, health services, personal counseling, placement for graduates. **Physically disabled:** Services for visually impaired.

Contact. E-mail: admissions@hillsdale.edu
Phone: (517) 607-2327 Fax: (517) 607-2223
Jeffrey Lantis, Director of Admissions, Hillsdale College, 33 East College Street, Hillsdale, MI 49242

Hope College

Holland, Michigan — **CB member**
www.hope.edu — **CB code: 1301**

- Private 4-year liberal arts college affiliated with Reformed Church in America
- Residential campus in small city
- 3,153 degree-seeking undergraduates: 2% part-time, 60% women, 2% African American, 2% Asian American, 3% Hispanic American, 1% international
- 82% of applicants admitted
- SAT or ACT (ACT writing optional), application essay required
- 73% graduate within 6 years; 28% enter graduate study

General. Founded in 1862. Regionally accredited. **Degrees:** 699 bachelor's awarded. **ROTC:** Army. **Location:** 30 miles from Grand Rapids, 160 miles from Chicago. **Calendar:** Semester, limited summer session. **Full-time faculty:** 217 total; 82% have terminal degrees, 9% minority, 59% women. **Class size:** 54% < 20, 43% 20-39, 1% 40-49, 2% 50-99. **Special facilities:** Museum, Pelletron particle accelerator, biological field station, electron microscopes, laser research, cadaver lab.

Freshman class profile. 2,846 applied, 2,342 admitted, 808 enrolled.

Mid 50% test scores			
SAT critical reading:	530-650	**End year in good standing:**	96%
SAT math:	530-660	**Return as sophomores:**	90%
ACT composite:	23-29	**Out-of-state:**	32%
Rank in top quarter:	72%	**Live on campus:**	99%
Rank in top tenth:	38%	**International:**	2%

Basis for selection. Strength of curriculum, achievement, test scores, perceived ability to succeed important. Interviews recommended. **Homeschooled:** Transcript of courses and grades, letter of recommendation (nonparent) required. Paper of at least 3 pages from final 2 years of homeschooling, list of non-textbooks read in last 2 years of homeschooling required. **Learning Disabled:** Students should consult the director of the academic support program to ensure available resources and personnel to accommodate the disability.

High school preparation. College-preparatory program recommended. 18 units recommended. Recommended units include English 4, mathematics 3, science 2 (laboratory 2), foreign language 2 and academic electives 5.

2008-2009 Annual costs. Tuition/fees: $24,920. Room/board: $7,650. Books/supplies: $772. Personal expenses: $1,200.

2008-2009 Financial aid. Need-based: 650 full-time freshmen applied for aid; 488 were judged to have need; 488 of these received aid. Average need met was 87%. Average scholarship/grant was $16,696; average loan $4,699. 73% of total undergraduate aid awarded as scholarships/grants, 27% as loans/jobs. **Non-need-based:** Awarded to 2,190 full-time undergraduates, including 670 freshmen. Scholarships awarded for academics, art, minority status, music/drama, religious affiliation.

Application procedures. Admission: Priority date 3/1; no deadline. $50 fee, may be waived for applicants with need. Admission notification on a rolling basis beginning on or about 12/15. Must reply by May 1 or within 2 week(s) if notified thereafter. **Financial aid:** Priority date 3/1; no closing date. FAFSA, institutional form required. Applicants notified on a rolling basis starting 3/15.

Academics. Extensive undergraduate scientific research opportunities available. All fine arts divisions nationally accredited. **Special study options:** Distance learning, double major, ESL, independent study, internships, New York semester, student-designed major, study abroad, teacher certification program, urban semester, Washington semester. Internships in Chicago, New York City, Washington DC, Philadelphia. **Credit/placement by examination:** AP, CLEP, IB, institutional tests. 32 credit hours maximum toward bachelor's degree. **Support services:** Reduced course load, study skills assistance, tutoring, writing center.

Majors. Area/ethnic studies: Japanese, women's. **Biology:** General. **Business:** Accounting, business admin, managerial economics. **Communications:** General. **Computer sciences:** General. **Conservation:** Environmental science. **Education:** Art, biology, chemistry, drama/dance, emotionally handicapped, English, French, German, history, Latin, learning disabled, mathematics, music, physical, physics, science, social studies, Spanish. **Engineering:** General, physics. **Foreign languages:** Biblical, classics, French, German, Latin, Spanish. **Health:** Athletic training, nursing (RN). **History:** General. **Interdisciplinary:** Global studies. **Math:** General. **Parks/recreation:** Exercise sciences. **Philosophy/religion:** Philosophy, religion. **Physical sciences:** Chemistry, geochemistry, geology, geophysics, physics. **Psychology:** General. **Public administration:** Social work. **Social sciences:** Economics, political science, sociology. **Visual/performing arts:** Art history/conservation, dance, dramatic, jazz, music performance, piano/organ, stringed instruments, studio arts, voice/opera.

Most popular majors. Biology 6%, business/marketing 12%, communications/journalism 7%, education 15%, foreign language 6%, psychology 7%, social sciences 7%.

Computing on campus. 350 workstations in dormitories, library, computer center, student center. Dormitories wired for high-speed internet access and linked to campus network. Commuter students can connect to campus network. Online library, helpline, repair service, student web hosting, wireless network available.

Student life. Freshman orientation: Mandatory. Preregistration for classes offered. 3-day orientation for students and parents begins Friday before school starts. **Policies:** Visitors of opposite gender not allowed after 12 a.m. on weekdays and 2 a.m. on weekends. No alcohol allowed on campus. **Housing:** Guaranteed on-campus for all undergraduates. Coed dorms, single-sex dorms, special housing for disabled, apartments, fraternity/sorority housing, wellness housing available. $300 nonrefundable deposit, deadline 5/1. Cottages (houses on or near campus). **Activities:** Bands, campus ministries, choral groups, dance, drama, international student organizations, literary magazine, music ensembles, Model UN, musical theater, radio station, student government, student newspaper, symphony orchestra, Fellowship of Christian Athletes, Inter-Varsity Christian Fellowship, Fellowship of Christian Students, College Republicans and Democrats, Higher Horizons, black student union, Hispanic students organization, Catholic student union.

Athletics. NCAA. **Intercollegiate:** Baseball M, basketball, cheerleading, cross-country, diving, football (tackle) M, golf, soccer, softball W, swimming, tennis, track and field, volleyball W. **Intramural:** Basketball, bowling, football (non-tackle), racquetball, soccer, softball, tennis, volleyball, water polo. **Team name:** Flying Dutchmen, Flying Dutch.

Student services. Adult student services, alcohol/substance abuse counseling, chaplain/spiritual director, career counseling, student employment services, financial aid counseling, health services, minority student services, personal counseling, placement for graduates, women's services. **Physically disabled:** Services for visually, hearing impaired.

Contact. E-mail: admissions@hope.edu
Phone: (616) 395-7850 Toll-free number: (800) 968-7850
Fax: (616) 395-7130
William Vanderbilt, Vice President for Admissions, Hope College, 69 East 10th Street, Holland, MI 49422-9000

International Academy of Design and Technology: Detroit

Troy, Michigan
www.iadtdetroit.com/

- For-profit 4-year visual arts and technical college
- Small city
- 951 degree-seeking undergraduates

General. Accredited by ACICS. **Degrees:** 57 bachelor's, 39 associate awarded. **Calendar:** Semester. **Full-time faculty:** 15 total. **Part-time faculty:** 59 total.

Basis for selection. Open admission.

2008-2009 Annual costs. Tuition/fees: $16,620.

2007-2008 Financial aid. Need-based: 34% of total undergraduate aid awarded as scholarships/grants, 66% as loans/jobs.

Application procedures. Admission: No deadline. $50 fee. Admission notification on a rolling basis. **Financial aid:** No deadline.

Academics. Special study options: Distance learning. **Credit/placement by examination:** CLEP.

Majors. Communications technology: Desktop publishing, graphics. **Visual/performing arts:** Fashion design, graphic design, interior design.

Contact. Phone: (248) 457-2700
Richard Reed, Senior Director of Admissions, International Academy of Design and Technology: Detroit, 1850 Research Drive, Troy, MI 48083

Kalamazoo College

Kalamazoo, Michigan — **CB member**
www.kzoo.edu — **CB code: 1365**

- Private 4-year liberal arts college
- Residential campus in small city
- 1,361 degree-seeking undergraduates: 56% women, 4% African American, 6% Asian American, 3% Hispanic American, 2% international
- 70% of applicants admitted
- SAT or ACT with writing, application essay required
- 76% graduate within 6 years

General. Founded in 1833. Regionally accredited. Study abroad centers in Kenya, Senegal, Ecuador, Spain, France, Germany, Mexico, and China. **Degrees:** 290 bachelor's awarded. **ROTC:** Army. **Location:** 140 miles from Detroit, 140 miles from Chicago. **Calendar:** Quarter. **Full-time faculty:** 93 total; 86% have terminal degrees, 18% minority, 48% women. **Part-time faculty:** 18 total; 50% have terminal degrees, 22% minority, 61% women. **Class size:** 61% < 20, 36% 20-39, 3% 40-49, less than 1% 50-99. **Special facilities:** 3 theaters, rare books collection, science center, 100 acre arboretum.

Freshman class profile. 2,059 applied, 1,447 admitted, 364 enrolled.

Mid 50% test scores		**GPA 2.0-2.99:**	3%
SAT critical reading:	600-710	**Rank in top quarter:**	78%
SAT math:	590-670	**Rank in top tenth:**	42%
SAT writing:	580-680	**Return as sophomores:**	92%
ACT composite:	26-30	**Out-of-state:**	32%
GPA 3.75 or higher:	43%	**Live on campus:**	100%
GPA 3.50-3.74:	29%	**International:**	3%
GPA 3.0-3.49:	25%		

Basis for selection. Curriculum, grades, essay, recommendations, and special accomplishments influence decision. Interview recommended. **Homeschooled:** Statement describing homeschool structure and mission, transcript of courses and grades, interview, letter of recommendation (nonparent) required.

High school preparation. 17 units required. Required and recommended units include English 4, mathematics 3-4, social studies 2, history 2, science 3-4 and foreign language 2-3.

2008-2009 Annual costs. Tuition/fees: $30,823. Room/board: $7,443. Books/supplies: $750. Personal expenses: $828.

2008-2009 Financial aid. Need-based: 267 full-time freshmen applied for aid; 190 were judged to have need; 190 of these received aid. Average scholarship/grant was $18,260; average loan $4,225. 80% of total undergraduate aid awarded as scholarships/grants, 20% as loans/jobs. **Non-need-based:** Awarded to 1,003 full-time undergraduates, including 355 freshmen. Scholarships awarded for academics, alumni affiliation. **Additional information:** Paid career development internship and senior project experiences available on campus.

Application procedures. Admission: Priority date 12/1; deadline 2/1 (postmark date). $35 fee, may be waived for applicants with need. Application must be submitted online. Admission notification 4/1. Must reply by 5/1. **Financial aid:** Priority date 2/15; no closing date. FAFSA, institutional form required. CSS PROFILE required for Early Decision applicants requesting need-based financial aid. Applicants notified on a rolling basis starting 3/21; must reply by 5/1.

Academics. Most students participate in career internships and study abroad. College subsidizes most study abroad expenses. Students complete a senior individualized project as part of graduation requirements. **Special study options:** Combined bachelor's/graduate degree, cross-registration, double major, dual enrollment of high school students, exchange student, independent study, internships, New York semester, study abroad, urban semester. **Credit/placement by examination:** AP, CLEP, IB, institutional tests. 18 credit hours maximum toward bachelor's degree. **Support services:** Learning center, reduced course load, study skills assistance, tutoring, writing center.

Majors. Biology: General. **Computer sciences:** General. **Family/consumer sciences:** Family studies. **Foreign languages:** Classics, French, German, Spanish. **Health:** Predental, premedicine, preveterinary. **History:** General. **Legal studies:** Prelaw. **Math:** General. **Philosophy/religion:** Philosophy, religion. **Physical sciences:** Chemistry, physics. **Psychology:** General. **Social sciences:** Anthropology, economics, political science, sociology. **Visual/performing arts:** Art, art history/conservation, dramatic.

Most popular majors. Biology 12%, English 7%, foreign language 9%, history 7%, physical sciences 7%, psychology 10%, social sciences 24%, visual/performing arts 8%.

Computing on campus. 130 workstations in library, computer center, student center. Dormitories wired for high-speed internet access and linked to campus network. Commuter students can connect to campus network. Online course registration, online library, helpline, student web hosting, wireless network available.

Student life. Freshman orientation: Mandatory. Preregistration for classes offered. Held the week before fall classes begin. **Housing:** Guaranteed on-campus for all undergraduates. Coed dorms, wellness housing available. **Activities:** Bands, campus ministries, choral groups, dance, drama, international student organizations, literary magazine, music ensembles, Model UN, musical theater, radio station, student government, student newspaper, symphony orchestra, African American student organization, women's equity coalition, volunteer bureau, environmental organization, film society, Habitat for Humanity, Amnesty International, coalition on racial diversity.

Athletics. NCAA. **Intercollegiate:** Baseball M, basketball, cross-country, diving, football (tackle) M, golf, soccer, softball W, swimming, tennis, volleyball W. **Intramural:** Basketball, cheerleading W, golf, gymnastics W, racquetball, rugby, skiing, soccer, softball, squash, table tennis, tennis, volleyball, water polo. **Team name:** Hornets.

Student services. Alcohol/substance abuse counseling, career counseling, student employment services, health services, personal counseling, placement for graduates, women's services.

Contact. E-mail: admission@kzoo.edu
Phone: (269) 337-7166 Toll-free number: (800) 253-3602
Fax: (269) 337-7390
Eric Staab, Dean of Admission, Kalamazoo College, Kalamazoo College Office of Admission, Kalamazoo, MI 49006-3295

Kendall College of Art and Design of Ferris State University

Grand Rapids, Michigan
www.kcad.edu **CB code: 1376**

- Public 4-year visual arts college
- Commuter campus in large city
- 1,303 undergraduates
- 49 graduate students
- 65% of applicants admitted
- SAT or ACT (ACT writing optional), application essay required

General. Founded in 1928. Regionally accredited. **Degrees:** 150 bachelor's awarded; master's offered. **Location:** 175 miles from Detroit, 160 miles from Chicago. **Calendar:** Semester, extensive summer session. **Full-time faculty:** 50 total. **Part-time faculty:** 95 total.

Freshman class profile. 544 applied, 355 admitted, 313 enrolled.

Basis for selection. High school GPA, statement of purpose/essay, ACT or SAT test scores, and portfolio considered in admission process. Portfolio not required for the following 3 programs: Art History, Furniture Design, Interior Design. Applicants for Interior Design are required to complete an Observation Exercise. **Homeschooled:** Transcript of courses and grades required. **Learning Disabled:** Highly recommended that students with learning disabilities meet college counselor to discuss education needs/assistance to help achieve learning success.

2008-2009 Annual costs. Tuition/fees: $14,412; $21,390 out-of-state. Studio art courses: $582 per credit hour in-state and $873 out-of-state. General education courses: $300 per credit hour in-state and $450 out-of-state. Books/supplies: $4,480. Personal expenses: $902.

2008-2009 Financial aid. All financial aid based on need.

Application procedures. Admission: Priority date 6/1; no deadline. $30 fee, may be waived for applicants with need. Admission notification on a rolling basis. **Financial aid:** Priority date 2/15; no closing date. FAFSA required. Applicants notified on a rolling basis starting 4/15.

Academics. For bachelor's degree, 42-54 credits in major required, depending on specified major. **Special study options:** Combined bachelor's/graduate degree, double major, dual enrollment of high school students, independent study, internships, liberal arts/career combination, New York semester, study abroad, teacher certification program. **Credit/placement by examination:** AP, CLEP, institutional tests. **Support services:** Reduced course load, study skills assistance, tutoring, writing center.

Majors. Education: Art. **Production:** Furniture. **Visual/performing arts:** Art history/conservation, commercial/advertising art, design, drawing, graphic design, illustration, industrial design, interior design, metal/jewelry, multimedia, painting, photography, printmaking, sculpture, studio arts.

Most popular majors. Visual/performing arts 99%.

Computing on campus. PC or laptop required. Commuter students can connect to campus network. Online course registration, online library, wireless network available.

Student life. Freshman orientation: Available. Preregistration for classes offered. **Housing:** Apartments available.

Student services. Adult student services, career counseling, student employment services, financial aid counseling, personal counseling, placement for graduates, veterans' counselor. **Physically disabled:** Services for hearing impaired.

Contact. E-mail: brittons@ferris.edu
Phone: (616) 451-2787 Toll-free number: (800) 676-2787
Fax: (616) 831-9689
Sandra Britton, Director of Enrollment Management, Kendall College of Art and Design of Ferris State University, 17 Fountain Street NW, Grand Rapids, MI 49503-3002

Kettering University

Flint, Michigan **CB member**
www.kettering.edu **CB code: 1246**

- Private 4-year university and engineering college
- Residential campus in small city
- 2,134 degree-seeking undergraduates: 17% women, 5% African American, 4% Asian American, 3% Hispanic American, 1% international
- 466 degree-seeking graduate students
- 67% of applicants admitted
- SAT or ACT (ACT writing optional) required
- 61% graduate within 6 years

General. Founded in 1919. Regionally accredited. Formerly GMI Engineering and Management Institute. **Degrees:** 402 bachelor's awarded; master's offered. **Location:** 70 miles from Detroit. **Calendar:** Semester, extensive summer session. **Full-time faculty:** 123 total; 85% have terminal degrees, 10% minority, 18% women. **Part-time faculty:** 17 total; 35% women. **Class size:** 42% < 20, 49% 20-39, 7% 40-49, 2% 50-99. **Special facilities:** Computer-integrated manufacturing laboratory, GM-PACE e-design and e-manufacturing studio, acoustics laboratory, polymer optimization center, engine test center, SAE vehicle development laboratory, mechatronics laboratory, biomedical laboratories on campus and at nearby medical center, Ford design simulation studio, crash study lab, fuel cell research center.

Freshman class profile. 2,529 applied, 1,702 admitted, 442 enrolled.

Mid 50% test scores		**GPA 2.0-2.99:**	2%
SAT critical reading:	530-630	**Rank in top quarter:**	68%
SAT math:	590-670	**Rank in top tenth:**	33%
ACT composite:	24-29	**Return as sophomores:**	94%
GPA 3.75 or higher:	33%	**Out-of-state:**	34%
GPA 3.50-3.74:	30%	**Live on campus:**	100%
GPA 3.0-3.49:	35%		

Basis for selection. GED not accepted. Strength of preparation, performance in school, test scores, nonscholastic activities and achievements most important. Accepted students encouraged to confirm enrollment plans early so co-op employment search process can begin. SAT Subject Tests (especially math level II, chemistry, and physics), while not required, helpful when presented. Interview recommended. **Homeschooled:** Laboratory science experience very important and may need to be documented.

High school preparation. College-preparatory program required. 10.5 units required; 21 recommended. Required and recommended units include English 3-4, mathematics 3.5-4, social studies 2, history 2, science 2-3 (laboratory 2-3), foreign language 2 and computer science 1. At least 1 unit of either chemistry or physics with laboratory required. Both chemistry and physics strongly recommended. Algebra I and II, geometry and trigonometry required. Drafting or CAD recommended, especially for those considering engineering.

2008-2009 Annual costs. Tuition/fees: $26,936. Room/board: $6,182. Books/supplies: $1,099. Personal expenses: $2,924.

2008-2009 Financial aid. Need-based: 413 full-time freshmen applied for aid; 370 were judged to have need; 370 of these received aid. Average scholarship/grant was $15,782; average loan $3,935. 69% of total undergraduate aid awarded as scholarships/grants, 31% as loans/jobs. **Non-need-based:** Awarded to 613 full-time undergraduates, including 147 freshmen. Scholarships awarded for academics, alumni affiliation, leadership, state residency.

Application procedures. Admission: No deadline. $35 fee, may be waived for applicants with need, free for online applicants. Admission notification on a rolling basis beginning on or about 10/15. Must reply by May 1 or within 3 week(s) if notified thereafter. **Financial aid:** Priority date 2/14; no closing date. FAFSA required. Applicants notified on a rolling basis starting 1/15; must reply within 2 week(s) of notification.

Academics. All students required to participate in paid professional cooperative work experiences typically beginning freshman year. Students alternate 11-week terms of full-time study on campus with 12-week terms of full-time work experience with their co-op employer, generally located near home. **Special study options:** Accelerated study, combined bachelor's/graduate degree, cooperative education, distance learning, double major, dual enrollment of high school students, independent study, study abroad. Paid professional co-op experience in industry required of all undergraduates. Co-op typically begins in first year. Each 24-week semester divided into 11 weeks of classes and 12 weeks of co-op. **Credit/placement by examination:** AP, CLEP, IB, institutional tests. **Support services:** Learning center, study skills assistance, tutoring, writing center.

Majors. Biology: Biochemistry. **Business:** Business admin. **Computer sciences:** Computer science. **Engineering:** Computer, electrical, industrial, mechanical. **Math:** Applied. **Physical sciences:** Applied physics, chemistry. **Other:** Engineering physics.

Most popular majors. Engineering/engineering technologies 93%.

Computing on campus. 450 workstations in dormitories, library, computer center, student center. Dormitories wired for high-speed internet access and linked to campus network. Commuter students can connect to campus network. Online library, helpline, wireless network available.

Student life. **Freshman orientation:** Mandatory, $150 fee. Four-day program begins Thursday before start of classes. **Policies:** Grade requirement to be eligible to join or maintain active membership in Greek letter organizations. **Housing:** Guaranteed on-campus for freshmen. Coed dorms, apartments, fraternity/sorority housing, wellness housing available. $100 fully refundable deposit, deadline 6/1. **Activities:** Jazz band, drama, international student organizations, music ensembles, radio station, student government, student newspaper, Campus Crusade, Muslim student association, Real Service, Engineers Without Borders, Society of Automotive Engineers, Society of Women Engineers, National Society of Black Engineers, National Society of Hispanic Engineers, Asian American association.

Athletics. **Intramural:** Basketball, bowling, cross-country, football (non-tackle), golf, handball, ice hockey, lacrosse, racquetball, rifle, rugby, skiing, skin diving, soccer, softball, squash, swimming, table tennis, tennis, volleyball, water polo, weight lifting. **Team name:** Bulldogs.

Student services. Alcohol/substance abuse counseling, career counseling, student employment services, financial aid counseling, health services, minority student services, personal counseling, placement for graduates, women's services. **Physically disabled:** Services for visually, speech, hearing impaired.

Contact. E-mail: admissions@kettering.edu
Phone: (810) 762-7865 Toll-free number: (800) 955-4464 ext. 7865
Fax: (810) 762-9837
Barbara Sosin, Director of Admissions, Kettering University, 1700 West University Avenue, Flint, MI 48504-4898

Kuyper College
Grand Rapids, Michigan
www.kuyper.edu **CB code: 1672**

- Private 4-year Bible college affiliated with Reformed
- Residential campus in large city
- 308 degree-seeking undergraduates: 14% part-time, 50% women, 4% African American, 2% Asian American, 3% Hispanic American, 1% Native American, 9% international
- 4 degree-seeking graduate students
- 86% of applicants admitted
- SAT or ACT (ACT writing optional), application essay required
- 52% graduate within 6 years

General. Founded in 1939. Regionally accredited; also accredited by ABHE. **Degrees:** 47 bachelor's, 7 associate awarded. **ROTC:** Army. **Location:** 7 miles from downtown, 180 miles from Chicago. **Calendar:** Semester. **Full-time faculty:** 14 total; 50% have terminal degrees, 14% minority, 50% women. **Part-time faculty:** 19 total; 16% have terminal degrees, 10% minority, 53% women. **Class size:** 64% < 20, 36% 20-39.

Freshman class profile. 138 applied, 118 admitted, 70 enrolled.

Mid 50% test scores		**GPA 3.0-3.49:**	32%
SAT critical reading:	440-500	**GPA 2.0-2.99:**	25%
SAT math:	440-500	**Return as sophomores:**	57%
SAT writing:	380-490	**Out-of-state:**	11%
ACT composite:	21-25	**Live on campus:**	77%
GPA 3.75 or higher:	27%	**International:**	9%
GPA 3.50-3.74:	14%		

Basis for selection. Secondary school record, test scores important. Applicants with 2.0-2.5 GPA evaluated individually and possibly admitted on conditional acceptance. Interview required for borderline applicants. **Home-schooled:** Transcript of courses and grades required.

2008-2009 Annual costs. Tuition/fees: $13,869. Room/board: $6,100. Books/supplies: $649. Personal expenses: $815.

2008-2009 Financial aid. **Need-based:** 63 full-time freshmen applied for aid; 56 were judged to have need; 56 of these received aid. Average need met was 78%. Average scholarship/grant was $7,316; average loan $4,047. 59% of total undergraduate aid awarded as scholarships/grants, 41% as loans/jobs. **Non-need-based:** Awarded to 49 full-time undergraduates, including 14 freshmen. Scholarships awarded for academics, leadership, minority status.

Application procedures. **Admission:** Priority date 8/15; no deadline. $25 fee, may be waived for applicants with need, free for online applicants. Admission notification on a rolling basis. **Financial aid:** Priority date 3/1; no closing date. FAFSA, institutional form required. Applicants notified on a rolling basis starting 3/15; must reply within 2 week(s) of notification.

Academics. **Special study options:** Combined bachelor's/graduate degree, double major, dual enrollment of high school students, ESL, independent study, internships, study abroad, teacher certification program. **Credit/placement by examination:** AP, CLEP, SAT, ACT, institutional tests. **Support services:** Learning center, pre-admission summer program, reduced course load, remedial instruction, study skills assistance, tutoring, writing center.

Majors. **Business:** Accounting, business admin, international, office management. **Communications:** General, journalism, public relations. **Computer sciences:** General. **Education:** Elementary, secondary. **Family/consumer sciences:** Child development. **Health:** Prenursing. **Interdisciplinary:** Accounting/computer science. **Parks/recreation:** Exercise sciences. **Philosophy/religion:** Religion. **Public administration:** Social work. **Theology:** Bible, missionary, preministerial, theology, youth ministry. **Visual/performing arts:** Dramatic, film/cinema. **Other:** Music and worship.

Most popular majors. Business/marketing 13%, education 11%, public administration/social services 17%, theological studies 55%.

Computing on campus. 54 workstations in dormitories, library, computer center. Dormitories linked to campus network. Commuter students can connect to campus network. Online library, helpline, student web hosting, wireless network available.

Student life. **Freshman orientation:** Available. Preregistration for classes offered. Held first week of fall semester. **Policies:** Smoke-free campus, alcohol and drug-free campus, standards of conduct and housing policies in accordance with school's moral values. **Housing:** Guaranteed on-campus for freshmen. Coed dorms, special housing for disabled, apartments, wellness housing available. $100 nonrefundable deposit. **Activities:** Choral groups, drama, international student organizations, music ensembles, student government, Bible studies, Student Activities Committee, Spiritual Life Committee, Social Work organization, Intramurals Committee, Street Team.

Athletics. NCCAA. **Intercollegiate:** Basketball. **Intramural:** Baseball, basketball, field hockey, football (non-tackle), soccer, softball, table tennis, volleyball. **Team name:** Cougars.

Student services. Alcohol/substance abuse counseling, chaplain/spiritual director, career counseling, student employment services, financial aid counseling, health services, minority student services, personal counseling, placement for graduates, veterans' counselor. **Physically disabled:** Services for visually impaired. **Learning disabled:** Comprehensive services available.

Contact. E-mail: admissions@kuyper.edu
Phone: (616) 988-3621 Toll-free number: (800) 511-3749
Fax: (616) 988-3608
Ryan Struck-VanderHaak, Vice President for Enrollment, Kuyper College, 3333 East Beltline Avenue Northeast, Grand Rapids, MI 49525-9749

Lake Superior State University
Sault Ste. Marie, Michigan **CB member**
www.lssu.edu **CB code: 1421**

- Public 4-year university
- Residential campus in small city
- 2,460 degree-seeking undergraduates
- 10 graduate students
- 75% of applicants admitted
- SAT or ACT (ACT writing recommended) required
- 44% graduate within 6 years

General. Founded in 1946. Regionally accredited. **Degrees:** 10 bachelor's, 517 associate awarded; master's offered. **Calendar:** Semester, limited summer session. **Full-time faculty:** 105 total. **Part-time faculty:** 100 total. **Class size:** 40% < 20, 42% 20-39, 7% 40-49, 10% 50-99, less than 1% >100. **Special facilities:** Aquatic research laboratory with fish hatchery and toxicology lab, planetarium, natural science museum, 200-acre biology station, robotics laboratory, indoor rifle range, indoor ice arena.

Freshman class profile. 1,831 applied, 1,382 admitted, 539 enrolled.

Mid 50% test scores		**Return as sophomores:**	68%
ACT composite:	18-24	**Out-of-state:**	1%
Rank in top quarter:	35%	**Live on campus:**	63%
Rank in top tenth:	13%		

Basis for selection. Cumulative GPA, high school course curriculum, and ACT or SAT most important. **Learning Disabled:** Students with learning disabilities referred to coordinator for Resource Center for Students with Disabilities.

High school preparation. College-preparatory program recommended. 18 units recommended. Recommended units include English 4, mathematics 3, social studies 2, history 1, science 3 (laboratory 3) and foreign language 2. Specific academic units required vary by college program.

2008-2009 Annual costs. Tuition/fees: $7,964; $15,788 out-of-state. Residents of Ontario pay in-state tuition. Residents of Kansas, Minnesota, Missouri, Nebraska, and North Dakota eligible for Midwest Consortium agreement rate of $489 per credit. Room/board: $7,567. Books/supplies: $900. Personal expenses: $1,397.

2007-2008 Financial aid. **Non-need-based:** Scholarships awarded for academics, alumni affiliation, athletics, state residency.

Application procedures. **Admission:** No deadline. $35 fee, may be waived for applicants with need. Admission notification on a rolling basis beginning on or about 9/15. **Financial aid:** Priority date 3/1; no closing date. FAFSA required. Applicants notified on a rolling basis starting 11/1; must reply within 3 week(s) of notification.

Academics. **Special study options:** Combined bachelor's/graduate degree, cooperative education, cross-registration, distance learning, double major, dual enrollment of high school students, honors, independent study, internships, student-designed major, study abroad, teacher certification program, weekend college. **Credit/placement by examination:** AP, CLEP, IB, SAT, ACT, institutional tests. **Support services:** Learning center, reduced course load, remedial instruction, study skills assistance, tutoring, writing center.

Majors. **Biology:** General. **Business:** General, accounting, business admin, managerial economics. **Communications:** General. **Computer sciences:** General. **Conservation:** General, environmental science, fisheries, management/policy, wildlife. **Education:** Early childhood, elementary, multi-level teacher, secondary. **Engineering:** Computer, electrical, mechanical. **Engineering technology:** Electrical, industrial management, manufacturing. **Foreign languages:** French, Spanish. **Health:** Clinical lab science, nursing (RN), recreational therapy. **History:** General. **Interdisciplinary:** Math/computer science. **Legal studies:** Paralegal. **Liberal arts:** Arts/sciences. **Math:** General. **Parks/recreation:** Exercise sciences, facilities management. **Physical sciences:** Chemistry, forensic chemistry, geology. **Protective services:** Fire safety technology, law enforcement admin. **Psychology:** General. **Social sciences:** General, political science, sociology. **Visual/performing arts:** Studio arts.

Most popular majors. Business/marketing 19%, education 9%, engineering/engineering technologies 8%, health sciences 7%, security/protective services 21%, social sciences 8%.

Computing on campus. 450 workstations in library, computer center, student center. Dormitories wired for high-speed internet access and linked to campus network. Commuter students can connect to campus network. Online course registration, online library, helpline, wireless network available.

Student life. **Freshman orientation:** Mandatory, $125 fee. Preregistration for classes offered. One-day program held during the summer; 5 dates available. **Housing:** Guaranteed on-campus for freshmen. Coed dorms, single-sex dorms, apartments, fraternity/sorority housing, wellness housing available. $300 partly refundable deposit, deadline 6/1. **Activities:** Bands, campus ministries, choral groups, dance, drama, literary magazine, music ensembles, musical theater, radio station, student government, student newspaper, symphony orchestra, Campus Crusade for Christ, Christian fellowship, Newman Center, Native American students' council, political science club, environmental awareness club, professional organizations.

Athletics. NCAA. **Intercollegiate:** Basketball, cross-country, golf, ice hockey M, softball W, tennis, track and field, volleyball W. **Intramural:** Badminton, basketball, football (non-tackle) M, handball, ice hockey, racquetball, soccer, softball, tennis, track and field, volleyball, water polo, wrestling M. **Team name:** Lakers.

Student services. Adult student services, alcohol/substance abuse counseling, chaplain/spiritual director, career counseling, services for economically disadvantaged, student employment services, financial aid counseling, health services, minority student services, on-campus daycare, personal counseling, placement for graduates, veterans' counselor. **Physically disabled:** Services for visually, speech, hearing impaired.

Contact. E-mail: admissions@lssu.edu
Phone: (906) 635-2231 Toll-free number: (888) 800-5778
Fax: (906) 635-6696
Susan Camp, Director of Admissions, Lake Superior State University, 650 West Easterday Avenue, Sault Ste. Marie, MI 49783-1699

Lawrence Technological University

Southfield, Michigan — **CB member**
www.ltu.edu — **CB code: 1399**

- Private 4-year university
- Commuter campus in small city
- 2,278 degree-seeking undergraduates: 29% part-time, 23% women, 11% African American, 3% Asian American, 2% Hispanic American, 8% international
- 1,389 degree-seeking graduate students
- 51% of applicants admitted
- SAT or ACT (ACT writing optional), application essay required

General. Founded in 1932. Regionally accredited. **Degrees:** 425 bachelor's, 38 associate awarded; master's, doctoral offered. **ROTC:** Army, Naval, Air Force. **Location:** 20 miles from Detroit. **Calendar:** Semester, extensive summer session. **Full-time faculty:** 125 total; 72% have terminal degrees, 10% minority, 30% women. **Part-time faculty:** 298 total; 36% have terminal degrees, 9% minority, 22% women. **Class size:** 75% < 20, 24% 20-39, less than 1% 40-49, less than 1% 50-99. **Special facilities:** Frank Lloyd Wright-designed residence for academic study.

Freshman class profile. 1,498 applied, 760 admitted, 278 enrolled.

Mid 50% test scores		**End year in good standing:**	81%
ACT composite:	20-27	**Return as sophomores:**	72%
GPA 3.75 or higher:	26%	**Out-of-state:**	4%
GPA 3.50-3.74:	12%	**Live on campus:**	50%
GPA 3.0-3.49:	28%	**International:**	4%
GPA 2.0-2.99:	31%	**Fraternities:**	18%
Rank in top quarter:	43%	**Sororities:**	13%
Rank in top tenth:	20%		

Basis for selection. Minimum 2.50 GPA required; Architecture/Transportation Design program requires 2.75. **Homeschooled:** Transcript of courses and grades, letter of recommendation (nonparent) required.

High school preparation. 12 units required. Required and recommended units include English 4, mathematics 3-4, social studies 3, history 2, science 2-4 (laboratory 2).

2008-2009 Annual costs. Tuition/fees: $21,979. Room/board: $8,071. Books/supplies: $1,270. Personal expenses: $2,000.

2007-2008 Financial aid. **Need-based:** 274 full-time freshmen applied for aid; 217 were judged to have need; 215 of these received aid. Average need met was 77%. Average scholarship/grant was $8,761; average loan $3,791. 49% of total undergraduate aid awarded as scholarships/grants, 51% as loans/jobs. **Non-need-based:** Awarded to 864 full-time undergraduates, including 209 freshmen. Scholarships awarded for academics, alumni affiliation, art, job skills, leadership, minority status, ROTC, state residency. **Additional information:** March 1 state deadline for Michigan Competitive Scholarship and Michigan Tuition Grant.

Application procedures. **Admission:** No deadline. $30 fee, may be waived for applicants with need. Admission notification on a rolling basis. **Financial aid:** Priority date 4/1; no closing date. FAFSA required. Applicants notified on a rolling basis starting 3/1; must reply within 2 week(s) of notification.

Academics. **Special study options:** Cooperative education, cross-registration, distance learning, double major, dual enrollment of high school students, ESL, honors, independent study, internships, liberal arts/career combination, study abroad, weekend college. **Credit/placement by examination:** AP, CLEP, IB, institutional tests. **Support services:** Learning center, pre-admission summer program, reduced course load, remedial instruction, study skills assistance, tutoring, writing center.

Majors. **Architecture:** Architecture, environmental design, interior. **Biology:** Biochemistry, molecular. **Business:** Business admin, construction management, international. **Communications:** General. **Communications technology:** General. **Computer sciences:** Computer science, information technology. **Engineering:** Biomedical, civil, computer, electrical, industrial, mechanical. **Engineering technology:** General, industrial. **Interdisciplinary:** Math/computer science. **Liberal arts:** Humanities. **Math:** General. **Physical sciences:** Chemistry, physics. **Psychology:** General. **Visual/performing arts:** Design, illustration.

Most popular majors. Architecture 30%, business/marketing 7%, computer/information sciences 12%, engineering/engineering technologies 46%.

Computing on campus. PC or laptop required. 100 workstations in dormitories, library, computer center, student center. Dormitories wired for

high-speed internet access and linked to campus network. Commuter students can connect to campus network. Online course registration, online library, helpline, repair service, student web hosting, wireless network available.

Student life. Freshman orientation: Mandatory. Preregistration for classes offered. **Housing:** Special housing for disabled, apartments, wellness housing available. $200 nonrefundable deposit, deadline 6/30. **Activities:** Literary magazine, music ensembles, student government, student newspaper, Campus Crusade for Christ, Alpha Kappa Alpha Sorority, Phi Beta Sigma Fraternity, National Society of Black Engineers, Young Republicans, Alpha Phi Omega.

Athletics. Intramural: Badminton, basketball, bowling, football (non-tackle) M, golf, racquetball, skiing, soccer, softball, table tennis, tennis, volleyball. **Team name:** Blue Devils.

Student services. Alcohol/substance abuse counseling, career counseling, services for economically disadvantaged, student employment services, financial aid counseling, minority student services, personal counseling, placement for graduates, veterans' counselor. **Physically disabled:** Services for visually, speech, hearing impaired.

Contact. E-mail: admissions@ltu.edu
Phone: (248) 204-3160 Toll-free number: (800) 225-5588
Fax: (248) 204-3188
Jane Rohrback, Director of Admissions, Lawrence Technological University, 21000 West Ten Mile Road, Southfield, MI 48075-1058

Madonna University

Livonia, Michigan
www.madonna.edu **CB code: 1437**

- Private 4-year university and liberal arts college affiliated with Roman Catholic Church
- Commuter campus in small city
- 2,851 degree-seeking undergraduates: 42% part-time, 76% women, 14% African American, 2% Asian American, 3% Hispanic American, 7% international
- 1,067 graduate students
- 76% of applicants admitted
- SAT or ACT (ACT writing optional), application essay required
- 45% graduate within 6 years

General. Founded in 1947. Regionally accredited. **Degrees:** 594 bachelor's, 22 associate awarded; master's, doctoral offered. **Location:** 18 miles from Detroit, 20 miles from Ann Arbor. **Calendar:** Semester, limited summer session. **Full-time faculty:** 113 total; 98% have terminal degrees, 7% minority, 59% women. **Part-time faculty:** 194 total; 92% have terminal degrees, 11% minority, 59% women. **Class size:** 66% < 20, 30% 20-39, 2% 40-49, 1% 50-99.

Freshman class profile. 700 applied, 534 admitted, 212 enrolled.

Mid 50% test scores		**End year in good standing:**	94%
ACT composite:	19-23	**Return as sophomores:**	94%
GPA 3.75 or higher:	20%	**Out-of-state:**	2%
GPA 3.50-3.74:	31%	**Live on campus:**	32%
GPA 3.0-3.49:	27%	**International:**	9%
GPA 2.0-2.99:	21%		

Basis for selection. GPA and curriculum most important. Majors in sciences, allied health and nursing, and math require specific high school subjects. ACT test results important. Some majors require letters of recommendation. ACT preferred. Interview recommended.

High school preparation. College-preparatory program recommended. 19 units required. Required and recommended units include English 3-4, mathematics 2-4, social studies 3-4, history 4, science 3-4 (laboratory 1) and foreign language 2. 1 biology, 1 chemistry, 1 algebra required for nursing applicants; biology, 1 chemistry, 2 algebra required for medical and radiologic technology program applicants.

2008-2009 Annual costs. Tuition/fees: $12,430. Nursing students pay $466 per credit hour. Nonresident aliens pay $2,500 deposit. Room/board: $6,440. Books/supplies: $944. Personal expenses: $1,036.

2007-2008 Financial aid. Need-based: 112 full-time freshmen applied for aid; 81 were judged to have need; 81 of these received aid. Average need met was 52%. Average scholarship/grant was $4,958; average loan $2,591. 35% of total undergraduate aid awarded as scholarships/grants, 65% as loans/jobs. **Non-need-based:** Awarded to 222 full-time undergraduates, including 79 freshmen. Scholarships awarded for academics, alumni affiliation, art, athletics, leadership, minority status, music/drama, religious affiliation, state residency.

Application procedures. Admission: Priority date 9/1; no deadline. $25 fee, may be waived for applicants with need. Admission notification on a rolling basis. **Financial aid:** Priority date 2/21; no closing date. FAFSA required. Applicants notified on a rolling basis starting 4/1; must reply by 9/1 or within 2 week(s) of notification.

Academics. Special study options: Combined bachelor's/graduate degree, cooperative education, cross-registration, distance learning, double major, dual enrollment of high school students, ESL, independent study, internships, liberal arts/career combination, student-designed major, study abroad, teacher certification program. **Credit/placement by examination:** AP, CLEP, IB, ACT, institutional tests. 30 credit hours maximum toward associate degree, 60 toward bachelor's. **Support services:** Learning center, reduced course load, remedial instruction, study skills assistance, tutoring, writing center.

Majors. Biology: General, biochemistry. **Business:** Accounting, business admin, hospitality admin, human resources, international, management information systems, management science, marketing. **Communications:** General, journalism. **Computer sciences:** Computer science. **Conservation:** Environmental science. **Education:** Early childhood, mathematics, physical, science, social studies. **Engineering technology:** Occupational safety. **Family/consumer sciences:** General, aging, child development, food/nutrition, merchandising. **Foreign languages:** American Sign Language, Spanish. **Health:** Clinical lab science, clinical lab technology, health care admin, nursing (RN), predental, premedicine, prenursing, prepharmacy, preveterinary. **History:** General. **Interdisciplinary:** Gerontology, natural sciences. **Legal studies:** Paralegal, prelaw. **Liberal arts:** Humanities. **Math:** General. **Parks/recreation:** Sports admin. **Philosophy/religion:** Philosophy, religion. **Physical sciences:** Chemistry, physics. **Protective services:** Criminal justice, firefighting, forensics. **Psychology:** General, industrial. **Public administration:** Social work. **Social sciences:** Political science, sociology. **Theology:** Pastoral counseling, sacred music, theology. **Visual/performing arts:** Art history/conservation, graphic design, music performance, studio arts. **Other:** Applied science, Engineering, pre-engineering, Health/medical preparatory programs, Occupational safety and health/fire science, Psychological trauma research, Security and protective services, Television and video communications.

Most popular majors. Business/marketing 13%, family/consumer sciences 8%, health sciences 22%, psychology 6%, public administration/social services 8%, security/protective services 10%.

Computing on campus. 146 workstations in dormitories, library, computer center. Dormitories wired for high-speed internet access and linked to campus network. Commuter students can connect to campus network. Online course registration, online library, helpline, wireless network available.

Student life. Freshman orientation: Mandatory. Preregistration for classes offered. All day orientation held in May, June, and July; evening orientation held in January, June, and July; Saturday orientation held in August and December. **Policies:** Use of alcohol or drugs prohibited on campus; all buildings smoke-free; sexual assault, harassment policies in place. **Housing:** Single-sex dorms, wellness housing available. $75 deposit, deadline 9/1. **Activities:** Campus ministries, choral groups, international student organizations, music ensembles, musical theater, radio station, student government, student newspaper, TV station, social work student association, gerontology association, student-faculty academic clubs, athletic club, nursing student association, business professional association, student teacher association.

Athletics. NAIA. **Intercollegiate:** Baseball M, basketball, cross-country, golf, soccer, softball W, volleyball W. **Team name:** Crusaders.

Student services. Adult student services, alcohol/substance abuse counseling, chaplain/spiritual director, career counseling, services for economically disadvantaged, student employment services, financial aid counseling, health services, minority student services, personal counseling, placement for graduates, women's services. **Physically disabled:** Services for visually, speech, hearing impaired.

Contact. E-mail: muinfo@madonna.edu
Phone: (734) 432-5339 Toll-free number: (800) 852-4951
Fax: (734) 432-5424
Michael Quattro, Director of Undergraduate Admission, Madonna University, 36600 Schoolcraft Road, Livonia, MI 48150-1176

Marygrove College

Detroit, Michigan
www.marygrove.edu **CB code: 1452**

- Private 4-year liberal arts college affiliated with Roman Catholic Church
- Commuter campus in very large city

- 771 degree-seeking undergraduates
- 2,095 graduate students
- 43% of applicants admitted
- Application essay required

General. Founded in 1905. Regionally accredited. **Degrees:** 78 bachelor's, 5 associate awarded; master's offered. **Location:** 6 miles from downtown. **Calendar:** Semester, limited summer session. **Full-time faculty:** 57 total; 63% have terminal degrees, 42% minority, 58% women. **Part-time faculty:** 7 total; 29% have terminal degrees, 29% minority, 86% women.

Freshman class profile. 1,287 applied, 559 admitted, 128 enrolled.

Mid 50% test scores	ACT composite:	15-19

Basis for selection. School achievement record and test scores most important. ACT recommended. Audition required of music, theater, dance majors. Portfolio required of art majors. Interview required of older applicants and academically weak applicants.

High school preparation. College-preparatory program recommended. 17 units recommended. Recommended units include English 4, mathematics 2, social studies 2, history 2, science 3 (laboratory 1), foreign language 2 and computer science 1.

2008-2009 Annual costs. Tuition/fees: $15,520. Room/board: $6,800. Books/supplies: $1,040. Personal expenses: $2,200.

2008-2009 Financial aid. All financial aid based on need.

Application procedures. Admission: Priority date 12/1; deadline 3/15 (postmark date). $25 fee, may be waived for applicants with need. Admission notification on a rolling basis. Must reply by 5/1. **Financial aid:** Priority date 3/15; no closing date. FAFSA, institutional form required. Applicants notified on a rolling basis starting 5/15; must reply within 2 week(s) of notification.

Academics. Special study options: Cooperative education, cross-registration, distance learning, double major, dual enrollment of high school students, honors, independent study, internships, student-designed major, study abroad, teacher certification program. **Credit/placement by examination:** AP, CLEP, ACT, institutional tests. 16 credit hours maximum toward associate degree, 32 toward bachelor's. Credit awarded for score of 3 or higher on AP exam. Credit hours awarded determined by faculty. **Support services:** Learning center, pre-admission summer program, reduced course load, remedial instruction, study skills assistance, tutoring, writing center.

Majors. Biology: General. **Business:** General, accounting, business admin, international. **Computer sciences:** General. **Conservation:** Environmental science. **Education:** General, early childhood, special. **Health:** Art therapy. **History:** General. **Interdisciplinary:** Natural sciences. **Math:** General. **Philosophy/religion:** Religion. **Physical sciences:** Chemistry. **Psychology:** General. **Public administration:** Social work. **Social sciences:** General, political science. **Visual/performing arts:** Art, dance, music performance, music theory/composition, studio arts.

Computing on campus. 50 workstations in dormitories, library, computer center, student center. Dormitories wired for high-speed internet access and linked to campus network. Commuter students can connect to campus network. Online course registration, online library, helpline, wireless network available.

Student life. Freshman orientation: Mandatory. Preregistration for classes offered. 2-day weekday program; students spend night in dorms. **Housing:** Coed dorms available. $250 deposit, deadline 8/1. **Activities:** Campus ministries, choral groups, dance, international student organizations, music ensembles, student government, student newspaper, debate teams (political & philosophical), Black social worker club, Ensemble gospel choir, art club, diversity club, optimist club, criminal justice, math & science club, English Honors Society, Hype Squad.

Athletics. NAIA. **Intercollegiate:** Basketball, cross-country, soccer, volleyball W. **Intramural:** Badminton, basketball, bowling, football (non-tackle), golf, soccer, softball, table tennis, track and field, volleyball. **Team name:** Mustangs.

Student services. Alcohol/substance abuse counseling, chaplain/spiritual director, career counseling, services for economically disadvantaged, student employment services, financial aid counseling, health services, on-campus daycare, personal counseling, placement for graduates, women's services.

Contact. E-mail: info@marygrove.edu
Phone: (313) 927-1240 Toll-free number: (866) 313-1927
Fax: (313) 927-1345
Carl Badynee, Associate Director of Undergraduate Admissions, Marygrove College, 8425 West McNichols Road, Detroit, MI 48221

Michigan Jewish Institute

Oak Park, Michigan
www.mji.edu **CB code: 1505**

- Private 4-year business and liberal arts college affiliated with Jewish faith
- Commuter campus in very large city
- 72 degree-seeking undergraduates

General. Accredited by ACICS. **Degrees:** 5 bachelor's awarded. **Calendar:** Semester, limited summer session. **Full-time faculty:** 3 total. **Part-time faculty:** 15 total. **Special facilities:** Synagogue available on West Bloomfield campus.

Freshman class profile. 51 applied, 51 admitted, 51 enrolled.

Basis for selection. Open admission, but selective for some programs. 2.0 GPA required; applicants with less than 2.0 GPA or with GED may be accepted under provisional status. **Homeschooled:** Statement describing homeschool structure and mission, transcript of courses and grades, interview, letter of recommendation (nonparent) required.

High school preparation. Recommended units include English 3, mathematics 3, social studies 1, history 2, science 3 (laboratory 1), foreign language 2 and computer science 1.

2008-2009 Annual costs. Tuition/fees: $10,500. Books/supplies: $1,215. Personal expenses: $1,060.

Financial aid. Non-need-based: Scholarships awarded for academics.

Application procedures. Admission: No deadline. $50 fee. Admission notification on a rolling basis. High school students may enroll in dual studies program to earn high school and college credits for the same courses. Students may also be admitted into the college for up to 6 months before high school graduation. Should an admitted student not complete high school within the 6 months, they will not be able to continue until proof of high school graduation or GED is provided.

Academics. Special study options: Accelerated study, cooperative education, distance learning, double major, dual enrollment of high school students, ESL, independent study, internships, liberal arts/career combination, study abroad, weekend college. **Credit/placement by examination:** AP, CLEP, IB, institutional tests. **Support services:** Learning center, reduced course load, remedial instruction, study skills assistance, tutoring.

Majors. Business: Business admin. **Computer sciences:** General. **Philosophy/religion:** Judaic. **Other:** Judaic education, Judaic organizational leadership.

Most popular majors. Area/ethnic studies 10%, business/marketing 30%, computer/information sciences 20%, education 10%, philosophy/religious studies 20%, theological studies 10%.

Computing on campus. PC or laptop required. 16 workstations in library, computer center, student center. Online library, helpline, wireless network available.

Student life. Freshman orientation: Available. Preregistration for classes offered. Scheduled onsite sessions and online tutorials available.

Student services. Adult student services, alcohol/substance abuse counseling, chaplain/spiritual director, career counseling, student employment services, financial aid counseling, personal counseling.

Contact. E-mail: info@mji.edu
Phone: (248) 414-6900 ext. 102 Fax: (248) 414-6907
Fran Herman, Registrar, Michigan Jewish Institute, 25401 Coolidge Highway, Oak Park, MI 48237

Michigan State University

East Lansing, Michigan **CB member**
www.msu.edu **CB code: 1465**

- Public 4-year university
- Residential campus in small city
- 35,986 degree-seeking undergraduates: 8% part-time, 53% women, 8% African American, 5% Asian American, 3% Hispanic American, 1% Native American, 5% international
- 8,955 degree-seeking graduate students
- 70% of applicants admitted

- SAT or ACT with writing, application essay required
- 74% graduate within 6 years; 25% enter graduate study

General. Founded in 1855. Regionally accredited. **Degrees:** 7,941 bachelor's awarded; master's, doctoral, first professional offered. **ROTC:** Army, Air Force. **Location:** 3 miles from Lansing, 80 miles from Detroit. **Calendar:** Semester, extensive summer session. **Full-time faculty:** 2,616 total; 93% have terminal degrees, 22% minority, 36% women. **Part-time faculty:** 381 total; 54% have terminal degrees, 15% minority, 55% women. **Class size:** 24% < 20, 47% 20-39, 8% 40-49, 9% 50-99, 12% >100. **Special facilities:** Planetarium, observatory, botanical garden, center for environmental toxicology, superconducting cyclotron laboratory, pesticide research center, experimental farms, 2 museums, center for performing arts, 2 golf courses, agricultural and livestock pavilion, children's garden.

Freshman class profile. 25,589 applied, 17,919 admitted, 7,555 enrolled.

Mid 50% test scores		**GPA 2.0-2.99:**	5%
SAT critical reading:	480-620	**Rank in top quarter:**	72%
SAT math:	540-660	**Rank in top tenth:**	31%
SAT writing:	480-610	**Return as sophomores:**	91%
ACT composite:	23-27	**Out-of-state:**	12%
GPA 3.75 or higher:	37%	**Live on campus:**	95%
GPA 3.50-3.74:	32%	**International:**	8%
GPA 3.0-3.49:	26%		

Basis for selection. Freshman admission based upon academic performance in high school, strength and quality of curriculum, recent trends in academic performance, class rank, test scores, leadership, talents, conduct and diversity of experience. Recommended that test scores be received no later than April. Audition required of music majors. **Homeschooled:** Submit grades, even if from parent. List or provide information on curriculum and be prepared to answer questions. Test scores have stronger emphasis; transcript required.

High school preparation. College-preparatory program recommended. Required and recommended units include English 4, mathematics 3, social studies 2, history 1-2, science 2 (laboratory 2) and foreign language 2.

2008-2009 Annual costs. Tuition/fees: $10,214; $25,672 out-of-state. Room/board: $7,026. Books/supplies: $944. Personal expenses: $1,696.

2008-2009 Financial aid. All financial aid based on need. 5,286 full-time freshmen applied for aid; 3,376 were judged to have need; 3,348 of these received aid. Average need met was 74%. Average scholarship/grant was $8,212; average loan $3,392. 50% of total undergraduate aid awarded as scholarships/grants, 50% as loans/jobs.

Application procedures. Admission: No deadline. $35 fee, may be waived for applicants with need. Admission notification on a rolling basis. Must reply by May 1 or within 4 week(s) if notified thereafter. Although Common Application accepted, use of internal application preferred. Early Action by invitation only. Test scores should be submitted by April. **Financial aid:** No deadline. FAFSA required. Applicants notified on a rolling basis starting 3/15; must reply within 4 week(s) of notification.

Academics. Special study options: Accelerated study, cooperative education, distance learning, double major, dual enrollment of high school students, ESL, exchange student, honors, independent study, internships, liberal arts/career combination, student-designed major, study abroad, teacher certification program, weekend college. **Credit/placement by examination:** AP, CLEP, IB, SAT, ACT, institutional tests. 60 credit hours maximum toward bachelor's degree. **Support services:** Learning center, preadmission summer program, reduced course load, remedial instruction, study skills assistance, tutoring, writing center.

Honors college/program. Selection criteria include test scores and class rank. Number admitted varies.

Majors. Agriculture: Animal sciences, business, communications, economics, food science, horticultural science, soil science. **Architecture:** Interior, landscape, urban/community planning. **Area/ethnic studies:** African-American, American, Asian, Central/Eastern European, Native American, Russian/Slavic, women's. **Biology:** General, biochemistry, Biochemistry/biophysics and molecular biology, botany, entomology, environmental, microbiology, molecular, molecular genetics, physiology, plant pathology, zoology. **Business:** Accounting, apparel, business admin, construction management, fashion, finance, hospitality admin, human resources, information resources management, logistics, management information systems, marketing, operations. **Communications:** General, advertising, journalism, public relations, radio/tv. **Computer sciences:** General, information systems. **Conservation:** Economics, environmental science, environmental studies, fisheries, forestry, wildlife. **Education:** General, art, biology, chemistry, computer, Deaf/hearing impaired, early childhood, elementary, family/consumer sciences, French, geography, German, health, history, kindergarten/preschool, learning disabled, mathematics, middle, music, physical, physics, reading, science, secondary, social science, social studies, Spanish, special. **Engineering:** General, agricultural, biomedical, chemical, civil, computer, electrical, materials, materials science, mechanical. **Family/consumer sciences:** General, apparel marketing, child development, clothing/textiles, family/community services, textile manufacture, textile science. **Foreign languages:** Chinese, classics, East Asian, French, German, Japanese, linguistics, Russian, Spanish. **Health:** Audiology/speech pathology, clinical lab science, communication disorders, community health services, dietetics, marriage/family therapy, music therapy, nurse practitioner, nursing (RN), premedicine, veterinary technology/assistant. **History:** General. **Interdisciplinary:** Biological/physical sciences, global studies, nutrition sciences, science/society. **Legal studies:** Prelaw. **Liberal arts:** Humanities. **Math:** General, computational, statistics. **Parks/recreation:** General, exercise sciences, facilities management. **Philosophy/religion:** Philosophy, religion. **Physical sciences:** General, astrophysics, chemical physics, chemistry, geology, geophysics, physics. **Protective services:** Criminal justice, law enforcement admin. **Psychology:** General. **Public administration:** General, policy analysis, social work. **Social sciences:** General, anthropology, economics, geography, international relations, political science, sociology. **Visual/performing arts:** Acting, art, art history/conservation, design, dramatic, fashion design, interior design, jazz, music pedagogy, music performance, music theory/composition, theater arts management. **Other:** Packaging.

Most popular majors. Biology 8%, business/marketing 18%, communications/journalism 12%, engineering/engineering technologies 8%, health sciences 7%, social sciences 10%.

Computing on campus. PC or laptop required. 2,000 workstations in dormitories, library, computer center, student center. Dormitories wired for high-speed internet access and linked to campus network. Commuter students can connect to campus network. Online course registration, helpline, repair service, student web hosting, wireless network available.

Student life. Freshman orientation: Mandatory, $175 fee. Preregistration for classes offered. Freshmen attend day-and-a-half session in summer; includes placement tests. **Housing:** Guaranteed on-campus for freshmen. Coed dorms, single-sex dorms, special housing for disabled, apartments, cooperative housing, fraternity/sorority housing, wellness housing available. $250 fully refundable deposit, deadline 5/1. **Activities:** Bands, campus ministries, choral groups, dance, drama, film society, international student organizations, literary magazine, music ensembles, Model UN, musical theater, opera, radio station, student government, student newspaper, symphony orchestra, TV station, over 500 organizations.

Athletics. NCAA. **Intercollegiate:** Baseball M, basketball, cheerleading, cross-country, diving, field hockey W, football (tackle) M, golf, gymnastics W, ice hockey M, rowing (crew) W, soccer, softball W, swimming, tennis, track and field, volleyball W, wrestling M. **Intramural:** Archery, baseball M, basketball, cross-country, fencing, football (non-tackle) M, golf, gymnastics, ice hockey, lacrosse M, racquetball, rowing (crew) M, rugby, sailing, skiing, soccer, softball, squash, swimming, tennis, track and field, volleyball, water polo, wrestling M. **Team name:** Spartans.

Student services. Adult student services, alcohol/substance abuse counseling, career counseling, services for economically disadvantaged, student employment services, financial aid counseling, health services, legal services, minority student services, on-campus daycare, personal counseling, placement for graduates, veterans' counselor, women's services. **Physically disabled:** Services for visually, speech, hearing impaired. **Learning disabled:** Comprehensive services available.

Contact. E-mail: admis@msu.edu
Phone: (517) 355-8332 Fax: (517) 353-1647
James Cotter, Director of Admissions, Michigan State University, 250 Administration Building, East Lansing, MI 48824

Michigan Technological University

Houghton, Michigan — **CB member**
www.mtu.edu — **CB code: 1464**

- Public 4-year university
- Residential campus in small town
- 5,923 degree-seeking undergraduates: 6% part-time, 23% women, 2% African American, 1% Asian American, 1% Hispanic American, 1% Native American, 7% international
- 916 degree-seeking graduate students
- 75% of applicants admitted
- SAT or ACT (ACT writing optional) required
- 65% graduate within 6 years; 17% enter graduate study

General. Founded in 1885. Regionally accredited. **Degrees:** 1,146 bachelor's, 20 associate awarded; master's, doctoral offered. **ROTC:** Army, Air

Force. **Location:** 210 miles from Green Bay, Wisconsin, 325 miles from Milwaukee. **Calendar:** Semester, limited summer session. **Full-time faculty:** 362 total; 86% have terminal degrees, 14% minority, 27% women. **Part-time faculty:** 66 total; 50% have terminal degrees, 8% minority, 39% women. **Class size:** 43% < 20, 36% 20-39, 8% 40-49, 10% 50-99, 3% >100. **Special facilities:** Anechoic chamber, mineral museum, performing arts center, forestry center and research forest, cosmic ray observatory, X-ray fluorescence spectrometer, process simulation and control center, remote sensing institute, computer-aided engineering lab, microfabrication lab, subsurface visualization lab.

Freshman class profile. 5,049 applied, 3,781 admitted, 1,365 enrolled.

Mid 50% test scores		**Rank in top quarter:**	57%
SAT critical reading:	530-650	**Rank in top tenth:**	28%
SAT math:	570-700	**End year in good standing:**	75%
SAT writing:	490-620	**Return as sophomores:**	82%
ACT composite:	23-28	**Out-of-state:**	22%
GPA 3.75 or higher:	35%	**Live on campus:**	91%
GPA 3.50-3.74:	22%	**International:**	4%
GPA 3.0-3.49:	30%	**Fraternities:**	5%
GPA 2.0-2.99:	13%	**Sororities:**	7%

Basis for selection. Academic record, ACT or SAT scores, and class rank (if available) are very important. SAT or ACT scores are required to make an admission decision. Scores should be received as soon as possible to process the application and for the student to be considered for merit-based scholorships. Students applying for programs within the visual and performing arts department are required to submit additional admission materials including essay response and a portfolio of creative work or performance audition. **Homeschooled:** Transcript of courses and grades required. ACT or SAT required.

High school preparation. College-preparatory program recommended. 8 units required; 20 recommended. Required and recommended units include English 3-4, mathematics 3-4, social studies 3, history 1, science 2-3, foreign language 2, computer science 1 and academic electives 2.

2008-2009 Annual costs. Tuition/fees: $10,762; $22,522 out-of-state. Room/board: $7,738. Books/supplies: $1,000. Personal expenses: $1,244.

2008-2009 Financial aid. Need-based: 1,167 full-time freshmen applied for aid; 835 were judged to have need; 832 of these received aid. Average need met was 72%. Average scholarship/grant was $5,359; average loan $3,210. 44% of total undergraduate aid awarded as scholarships/grants, 56% as loans/jobs. **Non-need-based:** Awarded to 3,852 full-time undergraduates, including 1,199 freshmen. Scholarships awarded for academics, alumni affiliation, art, athletics, job skills, leadership, music/drama, ROTC, state residency.

Application procedures. Admission: Priority date 1/15; no deadline. No application fee. Admission notification on a rolling basis beginning on or about 9/15. Must reply by May 1 or within 2 week(s) if notified thereafter. Students applying by 1/15 for fall term admission receive priority consideration for admission and scholarships. **Financial aid:** Priority date 2/16; no closing date. FAFSA required. Applicants notified on a rolling basis starting 5/1.

Academics. Special study options: Cooperative education, distance learning, double major, dual enrollment of high school students, ESL, exchange student, honors, independent study, internships, semester at sea, study abroad, teacher certification program. Dual Degrees with Northwestern Michigan College, Adrian College, Albion College, Augsburg College (MN), College of St. Scholastica (MN), Mount Senario College, Olivet College, Northland College, University of Wisconsin-Superior. **Credit/placement by examination:** AP, CLEP, IB, SAT, ACT, institutional tests. **Support services:** Learning center, reduced course load, study skills assistance, tutoring, writing center.

Majors. Biology: General, Biochemistry/biophysics and molecular biology, bioinformatics. **Business:** Business admin, construction management. **Communications:** General. **Communications technology:** Recording arts. **Computer sciences:** General, networking, system admin. **Conservation:** Environmental science, forestry, wildlife. **Engineering:** General, biomedical, chemical, civil, computer, electrical, environmental, geological, materials, mechanical, software, surveying. **Engineering technology:** Electrical, industrial, mechanical. **Health:** Clinical lab science. **History:** General. **Liberal arts:** Arts/sciences. **Math:** General. **Parks/recreation:** Exercise sciences, health/fitness. **Physical sciences:** Chemistry, geology, geophysics, physics. **Psychology:** General. **Social sciences:** General, anthropology, economics. **Visual/performing arts:** General, theater design. **Other:** Chemistry, Communication, journalism, and related programs.

Most popular majors. Business/marketing 11%, computer/information sciences 6%, engineering/engineering technologies 63%.

Computing on campus. 1,300 workstations in dormitories, library, computer center, student center. Dormitories wired for high-speed internet access and linked to campus network. Commuter students can connect to campus network. Online course registration, online library, helpline, student web hosting, wireless network available.

Student life. Freshman orientation: Mandatory, $250 fee. Preregistration for classes offered. Week-long program before start of classes. **Housing:** Guaranteed on-campus for freshmen. Coed dorms, special housing for disabled, apartments, fraternity/sorority housing, wellness housing available. **Activities:** Bands, campus ministries, choral groups, dance, drama, film society, international student organizations, literary magazine, music ensembles, musical theater, opera, radio station, student government, student newspaper, symphony orchestra.

Athletics. NCAA. **Intercollegiate:** Basketball, cross-country, football (tackle) M, ice hockey M, skiing, tennis, track and field, volleyball W. **Intramural:** Archery, badminton, basketball, bowling, cross-country, football (non-tackle), golf, ice hockey, racquetball, rifle, soccer, softball, squash, swimming, table tennis, tennis, volleyball, water polo, wrestling. **Team name:** Huskies.

Student services. Adult student services, alcohol/substance abuse counseling, chaplain/spiritual director, career counseling, services for economically disadvantaged, student employment services, financial aid counseling, health services, minority student services, on-campus daycare, personal counseling, placement for graduates, veterans' counselor, women's services. **Physically disabled:** Services for visually, speech, hearing impaired.

Contact. E-mail: mtu4u@mtu.edu
Phone: (906) 487-2335 Toll-free number: (888) 688-1885
Fax: (906) 487-2125
Allison Carter, Director of Admissions, Michigan Technological University, 1400 Townsend Drive, Houghton, MI 49931-1295

Michigan Theological Seminary

Plymouth, Michigan
www.mts.edu

- Private 4-year seminary college
- Small town

General. Regionally accredited. **Calendar:** Semester.

Annual costs/financial aid. Tuition/fees (2008-2009): $11,660.

Contact. Phone: (734) 207-9581
Registrar, 41550 East Ann Arbor Trail, Plymouth, MI 48170-1622

Northern Michigan University

Marquette, Michigan — **CB member**
www.nmu.edu — **CB code: 1560**

- Public 4-year university
- Residential campus in large town
- 8,240 degree-seeking undergraduates: 7% part-time, 53% women, 1% African American, 1% Asian American, 1% Hispanic American, 2% Native American, 1% international
- 541 degree-seeking graduate students
- 78% of applicants admitted
- SAT or ACT (ACT writing optional) required
- 50% graduate within 6 years

General. Founded in 1899. Regionally accredited. Every full-time student receives a ThinkPad or MacBook notebook computer as part of tuition and fees, which are replaced every 2 years. **Degrees:** 1,206 bachelor's, 122 associate awarded; master's offered. **ROTC:** Army. **Location:** 300 miles from Milwaukee, 380 miles from Chicago. **Calendar:** Semester, limited summer session. **Full-time faculty:** 328 total; 78% have terminal degrees, 6% minority, 40% women. **Part-time faculty:** 129 total; less than 1% have terminal degrees, 9% minority, 45% women. **Class size:** 28% < 20, 57% 20-39, 4% 40-49, 9% 50-99, 1% >100. **Special facilities:** Education center, center for teaching and learning science and math, art and design studios, observatory with 12.5 F:6 Newtonian telescope, 120-acre nature preserve.

Freshman class profile. 5,608 applied, 4,367 admitted, 1,816 enrolled.

Mid 50% test scores		**GPA 2.0-2.99:**	38%
ACT composite:	19-24	**End year in good standing:**	79%
GPA 3.75 or higher:	19%	**Return as sophomores:**	74%
GPA 3.50-3.74:	12%	**Out-of-state:**	26%
GPA 3.0-3.49:	26%	**Live on campus:**	76%

Basis for selection. High school record, test scores most important. Recommendations considered. Students who do not fulfill normal requirements for admission may be conditionally admitted for freshman probation and college transition programs. Applicants may re-take exams and submit new scores any time prior to the first day of fall classes. Some certificate, diploma and associate degree programs do not require test scores. Audition recommended for music, drama majors. Portfolio recommended for art majors. Interview, extracurricular activities, talent/ability considered for borderline students. **Homeschooled:** Transcript of courses and grades required.

High school preparation. College-preparatory program recommended. 19 units recommended. Recommended units include English 4, mathematics 4, social studies 4, science 4 and foreign language 3.

2008-2009 Annual costs. Tuition/fees: $7,078; $11,230 out-of-state. Excludes one-time $200 athletic fee for first time freshmen. All full-time students provided with ThinkPad or MacBook computer as part of tuition and fees. Room/board: $7,442. Books/supplies: $800. Personal expenses: $1,070.

2007-2008 Financial aid. **Need-based:** 1,644 full-time freshmen applied for aid; 1,109 were judged to have need; 1,077 of these received aid. Average need met was 65%. Average scholarship/grant was $3,940; average loan $2,931. 39% of total undergraduate aid awarded as scholarships/grants, 61% as loans/jobs. **Non-need-based:** Awarded to 2,211 full-time undergraduates, including 761 freshmen. Scholarships awarded for academics, art, athletics, leadership, minority status, music/drama, religious affiliation, ROTC, state residency. **Additional information:** Audition or portfolio required for music, drama, and art scholarship applicants. Alumni Dependent Tuition Program gives resident tuition rates to nonresident dependents of NMU alumni who received master's, baccalaureate, or associate degree; renewable.

Application procedures. **Admission:** No deadline. $30 fee, may be waived for applicants with need. Admission notification on a rolling basis. Students may defer enrollment for one year. After one year, they must reapply. **Financial aid:** Priority date 3/1; no closing date. FAFSA required. Applicants notified on a rolling basis starting 4/1; must reply within 2 week(s) of notification.

Academics. **Special study options:** Combined bachelor's/graduate degree, distance learning, double major, dual enrollment of high school students, ESL, honors, independent study, internships, liberal arts/career combination, student-designed major, study abroad, teacher certification program, Washington semester, weekend college. **Credit/placement by examination:** AP, CLEP, IB, SAT, ACT, institutional tests. 11 credit hours maximum toward associate degree, 32 toward bachelor's. 8 credits may be counted toward certificate. **Support services:** Learning center, pre-admission summer program, reduced course load, remedial instruction, study skills assistance, tutoring, writing center.

Honors college/program. Limited to 50 students; requires 3.5 GPA and 27 ACT or equivalent.

Majors. **Architecture:** Urban/community planning. **Biology:** General, biochemistry, botany, ecology, microbiology, physiology, zoology. **Business:** Accounting, accounting/finance, business admin, entrepreneurial studies, finance, financial planning, hospitality admin, management information systems, marketing, small business admin. **Communications:** General, digital media, media studies, public relations. **Computer sciences:** General, networking. **Conservation:** General, environmental science. **Education:** Art, biology, chemistry, elementary, English, French, geography, German, health, history, mathematics, mentally handicapped, music, physical, physics, science, secondary, social studies, Spanish, technology/industrial arts. **Engineering technology:** Construction, electrical, industrial, manufacturing, mechanical. **Family/consumer sciences:** Child development, family studies. **Foreign languages:** French, Spanish. **Health:** Athletic training, clinical lab science, community health services, cytogenetics, cytotechnology, histologic technology, nursing (RN), predental, premedicine, prepharmacy, preveterinary, speech pathology. **History:** General. **Interdisciplinary:** Behavioral sciences. **Legal studies:** Prelaw. **Liberal arts:** Arts/sciences. **Math:** General. **Parks/recreation:** General, health/fitness, sports admin. **Philosophy/religion:** Philosophy. **Physical sciences:** Geology, physics. **Protective services:** Criminal justice, security services. **Psychology:** General, developmental, experimental. **Public administration:** General, social work. **Social sciences:** General, cartography, economics, geography, international relations, political science, sociology. **Visual/performing arts:** Art, ceramics, cinematography, design, dramatic, drawing, graphic design, illustration, industrial design, metal/jewelry, painting, photography, printmaking, sculpture. **Other:** Chemistry, ACS Certified, Digital cinema, Earth science teacher education, Entertainment/sports promotion, Forensic biochemistry, Pre-architecture, Pre-engineering, Pre-optometry.

Most popular majors. Business/marketing 17%, education 12%, health sciences 11%, security/protective services 6%, social sciences 8%, visual/performing arts 7%.

Computing on campus. PC or laptop required. 9,900 workstations in library. Dormitories wired for high-speed internet access and linked to campus network. Commuter students can connect to campus network. Online course registration, online library, helpline, repair service, student web hosting, wireless network available.

Student life. **Freshman orientation:** Mandatory, $75 fee. Preregistration for classes offered. 3-day sessions held throughout the summer prior to start of classes. **Housing:** Guaranteed on-campus for all undergraduates. Coed dorms, special housing for disabled, apartments, wellness housing available. $125 partly refundable deposit. **Activities:** Bands, campus ministries, choral groups, dance, drama, film society, international student organizations, literary magazine, music ensembles, Model UN, musical theater, opera, radio station, student government, student newspaper, symphony orchestra, TV station, Room at the Inn Student Chapter, Catholic Campus Ministry, Presque Isle Zen Community, Amnesty International, Political Review, Native American Student Association, All Nations Club, International Dancers, Superior Edge citizen-leader program, Student Leader Fellowship Program.

Athletics. NCAA. **Intercollegiate:** Basketball, cheerleading, cross-country W, diving W, football (tackle) M, golf M, ice hockey M, skiing, soccer W, swimming W, track and field W, volleyball W. **Intramural:** Basketball, football (non-tackle), ice hockey, lacrosse M, racquetball, soccer, softball, table tennis, volleyball. **Team name:** Wildcats.

Student services. Adult student services, chaplain/spiritual director, career counseling, student employment services, financial aid counseling, health services, minority student services, personal counseling, placement for graduates, veterans' counselor. **Physically disabled:** Services for visually, speech, hearing impaired.

Contact. E-mail: admiss@nmu.edu
Phone: (906) 227-2650 Toll-free number: (800) 682-9797
Fax: (906) 227-1747
Gerri Daniels, Director of Admissions, Northern Michigan University, 1401 Presque Isle Avenue, Marquette, MI 49855

Northwood University: Michigan

Midland, Michigan
www.northwood.edu **CB code: 1568**

- Private 4-year university and business college
- Residential campus in large town
- 1,946 degree-seeking undergraduates: 3% part-time, 38% women, 12% African American, 1% Asian American, 2% Hispanic American, 8% international
- 319 degree-seeking graduate students
- 74% of applicants admitted
- SAT or ACT (ACT writing optional), application essay required
- 46% graduate within 6 years; 10% enter graduate study

General. Founded in 1959. Regionally accredited. Specialty university offering only business degrees in professional management; 3 residential campuses in Michigan, Florida, and Texas; 40 program centers; library center in Maine. **Degrees:** 479 bachelor's, 317 associate awarded; master's offered. **Location:** 125 miles from Detroit, 25 miles from Saginaw. **Calendar:** Quarter, extensive summer session. **Full-time faculty:** 55 total; 26% have terminal degrees, 11% minority, 34% women. **Part-time faculty:** 39 total. **Class size:** 40% < 20, 49% 20-39, 9% 40-49, 1% 50-99. **Special facilities:** Creativity center, university-operated hotel.

Freshman class profile. 1,750 applied, 1,295 admitted, 441 enrolled.

Mid 50% test scores		**Rank in top tenth:**	10%
SAT critical reading:	420-530	**End year in good standing:**	83%
SAT math:	440-560	**Return as sophomores:**	74%
ACT composite:	19-23	**Out-of-state:**	9%
GPA 3.75 or higher:	11%	**Live on campus:**	89%
GPA 3.50-3.74:	12%	**International:**	3%
GPA 3.0-3.49:	31%	**Fraternities:**	6%
GPA 2.0-2.99:	44%	**Sororities:**	9%
Rank in top quarter:	28%		

Basis for selection. Minimum 2.0 GPA and strong interest in business or related field important. Test scores considered. Students with lower GPA possibly admitted on probation. Interview recommended. **Homeschooled:** State high school equivalency certificate required.

High school preparation. College-preparatory program recommended. 17 units recommended. Recommended units include English 4, mathematics 3, social studies 3, science 3 (laboratory 2), foreign language 1 and computer science 1.

2008-2009 Annual costs. Tuition/fees: $17,544. Room/board: $7,548. Books/supplies: $1,404. Personal expenses: $1,203.

2008-2009 Financial aid. **Need-based:** Average need met was 55%. Average scholarship/grant was $6,457; average loan $3,196. 55% of total undergraduate aid awarded as scholarships/grants, 45% as loans/jobs. **Non-need-based:** Scholarships awarded for academics, alumni affiliation, athletics, leadership, minority status, ROTC.

Application procedures. **Admission:** No deadline. $25 fee, may be waived for applicants with need, free for online applicants. Admission notification on a rolling basis beginning on or about 9/1. **Financial aid:** No deadline. FAFSA required. Applicants notified on a rolling basis starting 3/1.

Academics. **Special study options:** Accelerated study, combined bachelor's/graduate degree, double major, dual enrollment of high school students, ESL, external degree, honors, independent study, internships, study abroad. **Credit/placement by examination:** AP, CLEP, IB, SAT, ACT, institutional tests. 12 credit hours maximum toward associate degree, 12 toward bachelor's. **Support services:** Learning center, reduced course load, remedial instruction, study skills assistance, tutoring.

Majors. **Business:** Accounting, banking/financial services, business admin, entrepreneurial studies, fashion, hotel/motel admin, international, management information systems, managerial economics, marketing, vehicle parts marketing. **Communications:** Advertising. **Computer sciences:** General. **Parks/recreation:** Sports admin.

Most popular majors. Business/marketing 89%, parks/recreation 6%.

Computing on campus. 215 workstations in dormitories, library, computer center. Dormitories wired for high-speed internet access and linked to campus network. Commuter students can connect to campus network. Online course registration, online library, helpline, student web hosting, wireless network available.

Student life. **Freshman orientation:** Mandatory. Preregistration for classes offered. Two-day programs held in early August and early September. **Housing:** Guaranteed on-campus for freshmen. Single-sex dorms, apartments, wellness housing available. $100 fully refundable deposit, deadline 8/1. **Activities:** Jazz band, choral groups, dance, drama, student government, student newspaper, Business Professionals of America, American Marketing Association, ambassador club, Rotaract, law club, International Business Association, Minority Business Women, American Advertising Federation, The Church Reloaded, diversity club.

Athletics. NCAA. **Intercollegiate:** Baseball M, basketball, cheerleading, cross-country, football (tackle) M, golf, soccer, softball W, tennis, track and field, volleyball W. **Intramural:** Badminton, basketball, field hockey, football (non-tackle) M, soccer, tennis, volleyball. **Team name:** Timberwolves.

Student services. Adult student services, alcohol/substance abuse counseling, career counseling, student employment services, financial aid counseling, health services, minority student services, personal counseling, placement for graduates, veterans' counselor. **Physically disabled:** Services for visually, speech, hearing impaired.

Contact. E-mail: miadmit@northwood.edu
Phone: (989) 837-4273 Toll-free number: (800) 457-7878
Fax: (989) 837-4490
Daniel Toland, Dean of Admissions, Northwood University: Michigan, 4000 Whiting Drive, Midland, MI 48640

Oakland University

Rochester, Michigan — **CB member**
www.oakland.edu — **CB code: 1497**

- Public 4-year university
- Commuter campus in small city
- 13,991 degree-seeking undergraduates: 24% part-time, 61% women, 8% African American, 4% Asian American, 2% Hispanic American, 1% international
- 3,588 degree-seeking graduate students
- 78% of applicants admitted
- 44% graduate within 6 years; 20% enter graduate study

General. Founded in 1957. Regionally accredited. **Degrees:** 2,241 bachelor's awarded; master's, doctoral offered. **ROTC:** Air Force. **Location:** 30 miles from Detroit. **Calendar:** Semester, limited summer session. **Full-time faculty:** 496 total; 87% have terminal degrees, 25% minority, 45% women. **Class size:** 41% < 20, 39% 20-39, 7% 40-49, 11% 50-99, 2% >100. **Special facilities:** Music pavilion, engineering and science research laboratories, robotics laboratory, product development and manufacturing center.

Freshman class profile. 7,695 applied, 6,022 admitted, 2,350 enrolled.

Mid 50% test scores		End year in good standing:	83%
ACT composite:	19-25	Return as sophomores:	72%
GPA 3.75 or higher:	16%	Out-of-state:	1%
GPA 3.50-3.74:	15%	Live on campus:	34%
GPA 3.0-3.49:	41%	International:	1%
GPA 2.0-2.99:	28%	Fraternities:	3%
Rank in top quarter:	42%	Sororities:	3%

Basis for selection. Admission based on 2.5 GPA in academic subjects, school and community activities, recommendations. Applicants with minimum 2.0 GPA may be admitted to summer program. Engineering, business, education, nursing, and physical therapy programs require higher GPA. SAT or ACT recommended. Except for home schooled students, ACT scores used only for placement and scholarship purposes. Audition required of music majors. **Homeschooled:** ACT composite score of 25 or above.

High school preparation. College-preparatory program recommended. Required and recommended units include English 4, mathematics 3, social studies 3, science 3 and foreign language 2.

2008-2009 Annual costs. Tuition/fees: $8,055; $18,803 out-of-state. Room/board: $7,105. Books/supplies: $1,320. Personal expenses: $1,790.

2007-2008 Financial aid. **Non-need-based:** Scholarships awarded for academics, art, athletics, leadership, music/drama, state residency.

Application procedures. **Admission:** No deadline. No application fee. Admission notification on a rolling basis. **Financial aid:** Priority date 2/15; no closing date. FAFSA required. Applicants notified on a rolling basis starting 3/15.

Academics. **Special study options:** Accelerated study, cooperative education, distance learning, double major, ESL, honors, independent study, internships, student-designed major, study abroad, teacher certification program. **Credit/placement by examination:** AP, CLEP, IB, ACT, institutional tests. 60 credit hours maximum toward bachelor's degree. **Support services:** Learning center, pre-admission summer program, reduced course load, remedial instruction, study skills assistance, tutoring, writing center.

Majors. **Area/ethnic studies:** African, East Asian, Latin American, Slavic, South Asian, women's. **Biology:** General, biochemistry, biophysics. **Business:** General, accounting, finance, human resources, management information systems, managerial economics, marketing, operations, training/development. **Communications:** General, journalism. **Computer sciences:** General, information technology. **Education:** Elementary, music. **Engineering:** Computer, electrical, industrial, mechanical, physics. **Foreign languages:** General, French, German, Japanese, linguistics, Spanish. **Health:** Clinical lab science, cytotechnology, environmental health, health services, histologic technology, medical radiologic technology/radiation therapy, nuclear medical technology, nursing (RN), occupational health, radiologic technology/medical imaging. **History:** General. **Liberal arts:** Arts/sciences. **Math:** General, statistics. **Philosophy/religion:** Philosophy. **Physical sciences:** Chemistry, physics. **Psychology:** General. **Public administration:** General, social work. **Social sciences:** Anthropology, economics, international relations, political science, sociology. **Visual/performing arts:** Acting, art history/conservation, dance, dramatic, drawing, music performance, music theory/composition, painting, photography, piano/organ, studio arts, theater design, voice/opera. **Other:** Engineering chemistry, engineering biology, Musical theatre, Wellness health promotion/ injury prevention.

Most popular majors. Business/marketing 19%, communications/journalism 12%, education 10%, health sciences 17%, social sciences 7%.

Computing on campus. Dormitories linked to campus network. Commuter students can connect to campus network. Online course registration, online library, helpline, student web hosting, wireless network available.

Student life. **Freshman orientation:** Mandatory. Preregistration for classes offered. Held on weekdays from end of June through mid-July. 1.5-day program requires overnight stay in residence halls. Condensed 1-day orientation available. **Policies:** Freshmen must live on campus unless living with family. **Housing:** Guaranteed on-campus for freshmen. Coed dorms, special housing for disabled, apartments, cooperative housing, fraternity/sorority housing, wellness housing available. $100 nonrefundable deposit, deadline 9/1. Pets allowed in dorm rooms. Residence halls easily accessible to handicapped persons. **Activities:** Bands, campus ministries, choral groups, dance, drama, film society, international student organizations, literary magazine, music ensembles, musical theater, radio station, student government, student newspaper, symphony orchestra, TV station, association of black students, Indian students association, Arab American association, College Democrats, College Republicans, Inter varsity Christian Fellowship, Hillel, Muslim student association, Chinese friendship association, gay/straight alliance.

Athletics. NCAA. **Intercollegiate:** Baseball M, basketball, cross-country, diving, golf, soccer, softball W, swimming, tennis W, track and field, volleyball W. **Intramural:** Basketball, football (non-tackle), soccer, softball, volleyball. **Team name:** Golden Grizzlies.

Student services. Alcohol/substance abuse counseling, chaplain/spiritual director, career counseling, student employment services, financial aid counseling, health services, minority student services, on-campus daycare, personal counseling, placement for graduates. **Physically disabled:** Services for visually, speech, hearing impaired.

Contact. E-mail: ouinfo@oakland.edu
Phone: (248) 370-3360 Toll-free number: (800) 625-8648
Fax: (248) 370-4462
Eleanor Reynolds, Assistant Vice President Student Affairs, Oakland University, 101 North Foundation Hall, Rochester, MI 48309-4401

Olivet College

Olivet, Michigan — **CB member**
www.olivetcollege.edu — **CB code: 1595**

- Private 4-year liberal arts college affiliated with Congregational Christian Churches and United Church of Christ
- Residential campus in rural community
- 990 degree-seeking undergraduates
- 48 graduate students
- 60% of applicants admitted
- ACT (writing recommended) required

General. Founded in 1844. Regionally accredited. **Degrees:** 173 bachelor's awarded; master's offered. **Location:** 30 miles from Lansing, 120 miles from Detroit. **Calendar:** Semester, limited summer session. **Full-time faculty:** 41 total. **Part-time faculty:** 52 total. **Class size:** 65% < 20, 33% 20-39, less than 1% 40-49, less than 1% 50-99, less than 1% >100. **Special facilities:** Observatory/planetarium, dynamic ecology laboratory, character education resource center, women's resource center, biological preserve.

Freshman class profile. 1,451 applied, 876 admitted, 293 enrolled.

Mid 50% test scores		**Out-of-state:**	8%
ACT composite:	17-21	**Live on campus:**	82%
Rank in top quarter:	38%	**Fraternities:**	10%
Rank in top tenth:	25%	**Sororities:**	10%

Basis for selection. Minimum 2.6 GPA most important. Test scores, school achievement record, recommendations for those below 2.6 GPA important. Interview recommended. Portfolio recommended for art majors. **Homeschooled:** Transcript of courses and grades required.

High school preparation. 14 units required; 19 recommended. Required and recommended units include English 4, mathematics 3-4, social studies 2-3, science 3-4 (laboratory 1-2) and foreign language 2.

2008-2009 Annual costs. Tuition/fees: $19,888. Room/board: $6,472. Books/supplies: $900. Personal expenses: $1,000.

2007-2008 Financial aid. All financial aid based on need.

Application procedures. Admission: No deadline. $25 fee, may be waived for applicants with need, free for online applicants. Admission notification on a rolling basis beginning on or about 11/1. **Financial aid:** No deadline. FAFSA required. Applicants notified on a rolling basis starting 2/1; must reply within 3 week(s) of notification.

Academics. Olivet Plan degree program includes service learning experience, portfolio assessment measuring 6 essential competencies, senior experience, professional mentoring, and 3 1/2 week intensive learning term. **Special study options:** Cooperative education, double major, dual enrollment of high school students, honors, independent study, internships, liberal arts/career combination, student-designed major, teacher certification program. **Credit/placement by examination:** AP, CLEP, ACT, institutional tests. **Support services:** Learning center, pre-admission summer program, remedial instruction, tutoring, writing center.

Majors. Biology: General, biochemistry. **Business:** Business admin, financial planning, insurance, managerial economics, marketing. **Communications:** General, journalism, media studies. **Computer sciences:** Computer science. **Conservation:** Environmental science. **Education:** General, art, biology, chemistry, emotionally handicapped, English, health, history, mathematics, music, science, social studies, speech. **Health:** Athletic training. **History:** General. **Interdisciplinary:** Biological/physical sciences. **Liberal arts:** Arts/sciences. **Math:** General. **Parks/recreation:** Health/fitness, sports admin. **Physical sciences:** Chemistry. **Protective services:** Criminal justice. **Psychology:** General. **Social sciences:** General, sociology. **Visual/performing arts:** Art, dramatic.

Most popular majors. Biology 12%, business/marketing 24%, English 7%, parks/recreation 14%, security/protective services 7%, social sciences 6%.

Computing on campus. 60 workstations in dormitories, library, computer center, student center. Dormitories wired for high-speed internet access and linked to campus network. Commuter students can connect to campus network. Online course registration, helpline, repair service, student web hosting, wireless network available.

Student life. Freshman orientation: Mandatory, $75 fee. Preregistration for classes offered. Held approximately 3 times during the summer. **Housing:** Guaranteed on-campus for all undergraduates. Coed dorms, single-sex dorms, apartments, fraternity/sorority housing, wellness housing available. African American house, honors house, wellness floor available. **Activities:** Bands, choral groups, drama, international student organizations, literary magazine, music ensembles, musical theater, radio station, student government, student newspaper, symphony orchestra, Phi Kappa Delta, Psi Chi, Earth Bound, black student union, NOW, campus media board, Students Organizing Community Service.

Athletics. NCAA. **Intercollegiate:** Baseball M, basketball, cross-country, diving, football (tackle) M, golf, soccer, softball W, swimming, tennis W, track and field, volleyball W, wrestling M. **Intramural:** Basketball, cheerleading, football (non-tackle) M, weight lifting M. **Team name:** Comets.

Student services. Adult student services, alcohol/substance abuse counseling, chaplain/spiritual director, career counseling, services for economically disadvantaged, student employment services, financial aid counseling, health services, minority student services, personal counseling, placement for graduates, women's services. **Physically disabled:** Services for visually, speech, hearing impaired.

Contact. E-mail: admissions@olivetcollege.edu
Phone: (269) 749-7635 Toll-free number: (800) 456-7189
Fax: (269) 749-6617
Larry Vallar, Vice President for Enrollment Management, Olivet College, Admissions Office, Olivet, MI 49076

Rochester College

Rochester Hills, Michigan
www.rc.edu — **CB code: 1516**

- Private 4-year liberal arts college affiliated with Church of Christ
- Residential campus in small city
- 895 degree-seeking undergraduates
- 83% of applicants admitted
- ACT (writing optional), application essay required

General. Founded in 1959. Regionally accredited. **Degrees:** 263 bachelor's, 14 associate awarded; master's offered. **Location:** 25 miles from Detroit. **Calendar:** Semester, limited summer session. **Full-time faculty:** 50 total. **Part-time faculty:** 115 total. **Class size:** 86% < 20, 14% 20-39, less than 1% 40-49.

Freshman class profile. 236 applied, 196 admitted, 109 enrolled.

Mid 50% test scores		**GPA 3.50-3.74:**	15%
SAT critical reading:	420-520	**GPA 3.0-3.49:**	26%
SAT math:	390-480	**GPA 2.0-2.99:**	38%
ACT composite:	19-24	**Rank in top quarter:**	28%
GPA 3.75 or higher:	18%	**Rank in top tenth:**	14%

Basis for selection. ACT score and high school GPA most important. Recommendations and interview considered. **Homeschooled:** Transcript of courses and grades required.

2008-2009 Annual costs. Tuition/fees: $16,610. Room/board: $7,020. Books/supplies: $600. Personal expenses: $750.

Financial aid. Non-need-based: Scholarships awarded for academics, alumni affiliation, athletics, leadership, music/drama, state residency.

Application procedures. Admission: No deadline. $25 fee. Admission notification on a rolling basis. **Financial aid:** Priority date 8/1; no closing date. FAFSA required. Applicants notified on a rolling basis starting 6/1; must reply within 2 week(s) of notification.

Academics. Special study options: Accelerated study, combined bachelor's/graduate degree, cross-registration, double major, dual enrollment of high school students, honors, independent study, internships, liberal arts/career combination, study abroad, teacher certification program, weekend college. **Credit/placement by examination:** AP, CLEP, IB, institutional tests. 32 credit hours maximum toward associate degree, 64 toward bachelor's. Credit awarded for successful completion of selected DANTES Subject Standardized Testing Program. **Support services:** Learning center, reduced course load, remedial instruction, study skills assistance, tutoring, writing center.

Majors. Business: Accounting, business admin, management information systems, marketing. **Communications:** General. **Computer sciences:** General. **Education:** General, early childhood, elementary, English, history, mathematics, middle, music, science, secondary. **History:** General. **Philosophy/religion:** Religion. **Psychology:** General. **Public administration:** Social work. **Theology:** Bible, theology. **Visual/performing arts:** Music performance.

Most popular majors. Business/marketing 35%, communications/journalism 6%, education 22%, psychology 20%.

Computing on campus. 34 workstations in dormitories, library, computer center. Dormitories wired for high-speed internet access and linked to campus network. Online library, helpline, student web hosting, wireless network available.

Student life. Freshman orientation: Mandatory, $100 fee. Preregistration for classes offered. **Housing:** Guaranteed on-campus for freshmen. Single-sex dorms, apartments available. $180 deposit, deadline 5/1. **Activities:** Bands, choral groups, drama, music ensembles, musical theater, opera, student government, student newspaper, service and mission organizations, social clubs, departmental organizations, honor societies.

Athletics. NCCAA. **Intercollegiate:** Baseball M, basketball, soccer, softball W, volleyball W. **Intramural:** Basketball, football (non-tackle), softball, volleyball. **Team name:** Warriors.

Student services. Adult student services, alcohol/substance abuse counseling, chaplain/spiritual director, career counseling, student employment services, financial aid counseling, minority student services, personal counseling, placement for graduates, veterans' counselor. **Physically disabled:** Services for visually, speech, hearing impaired.

Contact. E-mail: admissions@rc.edu
Phone: (248) 218-2031 Toll-free number: (800) 521-6010
Fax: (248) 218-2035
Larry Norman, Vice President for Enrollment Management, Rochester College, 800 West Avon Road, Rochester Hills, MI 48307

Sacred Heart Major Seminary

Detroit, Michigan
www.shms.org **CB code: 1686**

- Private 4-year seminary college affiliated with Roman Catholic Church
- Commuter campus in very large city
- 70 degree-seeking undergraduates: 47% part-time, 40% women
- 169 degree-seeking graduate students
- 100% of applicants admitted
- SAT or ACT (ACT writing optional), application essay, interview required

General. Founded in 1919. Regionally accredited. **Degrees:** 18 bachelor's, 2 associate awarded; master's, first professional offered. **Calendar:** Semester, limited summer session. **Full-time faculty:** 35 total; 71% have terminal degrees, 20% women. **Part-time faculty:** 24 total; 58% have terminal degrees, 21% women.

Freshman class profile. 3 applied, 3 admitted, 3 enrolled.

GPA 3.75 or higher:	50%	**GPA 2.0-2.99:**	50%

Basis for selection. Recommendations of parish pastor, high school principal, and college counselor vital. School, community, and church-related activities viewed as important formative experiences. Religious commitment very important. Interview required for priesthood candidates. **Homeschooled:** Transcript of courses and grades, interview, letter of recommendation (nonparent) required. **Learning Disabled:** Once admitted, students should contact the Office of the Dean of Studies for accommodations.

High school preparation. College-preparatory program recommended. Recommended units include English 4, mathematics 2, social studies 2, history 2, science 2 (laboratory 1), foreign language 2 and academic electives 3.

2008-2009 Annual costs. Tuition/fees: $13,580. Room/board: $7,400. Books/supplies: $1,366. Personal expenses: $3,150.

2007-2008 Financial aid. Non-need-based: Scholarships awarded for academics, religious affiliation.

Application procedures. Admission: Closing date 8/1 (postmark date). $30 fee. Application must be submitted online. Admission notification on a rolling basis. **Financial aid:** No deadline. FAFSA, institutional form required. Applicants notified on a rolling basis.

Academics. 30 to 40% of undergraduate course work taken at other consortium colleges. **Special study options:** Cross-registration. **Credit/placement by examination:** AP, CLEP, institutional tests. 6 credit hours maximum toward associate degree, 12 toward bachelor's. Must accumulate 15 hours at SHMS before credit is recorded. **Support services:** Learning center, reduced course load, study skills assistance, tutoring.

Majors. Liberal arts: Arts/sciences. **Philosophy/religion:** Philosophy.

Most popular majors. Liberal arts 16%, philosophy/religious studies 82%.

Computing on campus. 12 workstations in library, computer center. Online library available.

Student life. Freshman orientation: Mandatory. 3 days for seminarians, 1 day for commuters at beginning of fall term. **Policies:** On-campus housing available and guaranteed to seminarians only. Religious observance required. **Housing:** Wellness housing available. On-campus housing available and guaranteed to seminarians only. **Activities:** Campus ministries, choral groups, student newspaper.

Student services. Chaplain/spiritual director, financial aid counseling.

Contact. E-mail: IFM@shms.edu
Phone: (313) 883-8520 Fax: (313) 883-8530
Janet Diaz, Director of Admissions and Enrollment Management, Sacred Heart Major Seminary, 2701 Chicago Boulevard, Detroit, MI 48206-1799

Saginaw Valley State University

University Center, Michigan
www.svsu.edu **CB code: 1766**

- Public 4-year university
- Commuter campus in small city
- 8,018 degree-seeking undergraduates: 17% part-time, 59% women, 7% African American, 1% Asian American, 2% Hispanic American, 1% Native American, 3% international
- 1,647 degree-seeking graduate students
- 88% of applicants admitted
- ACT (writing optional) required
- 38% graduate within 6 years

General. Founded in 1963. Regionally accredited. **Degrees:** 1,158 bachelor's awarded; master's offered. **Location:** 10 miles from Bay City and Saginaw. **Calendar:** Semester, limited summer session. **Full-time faculty:** 294 total; 75% have terminal degrees. **Part-time faculty:** 300 total. **Class size:** 27% < 20, 63% 20-39, 4% 40-49, 5% 50-99. **Special facilities:** Fine arts center, sculpture museum, observatory.

Freshman class profile. 5,467 applied, 4,804 admitted, 1,661 enrolled.

Mid 50% test scores		**Rank in top tenth:**	18%
ACT composite:	18-24	**End year in good standing:**	81%
GPA 3.75 or higher:	20%	**Return as sophomores:**	69%
GPA 3.50-3.74:	17%	**Out-of-state:**	1%
GPA 3.0-3.49:	28%	**Live on campus:**	73%
GPA 2.0-2.99:	35%	**International:**	2%
Rank in top quarter:	41%		

Basis for selection. Minimum high school GPA of 2.5 preferred. **Homeschooled:** Interview required.

High school preparation. Required and recommended units include English 4, mathematics 3-4, social studies 3-4, science 2-4 and foreign language 2. One unit of communications recommended.

2008-2009 Annual costs. Tuition/fees: $6,492; $14,890 out-of-state. Room/board: $6,830. Books/supplies: $900. Personal expenses: $968.

2007-2008 Financial aid. Need-based: 1,500 full-time freshmen applied for aid; 1,004 were judged to have need; 986 of these received aid. Average need met was 68%. Average scholarship/grant was $3,368; average loan $2,976. 37% of total undergraduate aid awarded as scholarships/grants, 63% as loans/jobs. **Non-need-based:** Awarded to 4,121 full-time undergraduates, including 1,062 freshmen. Scholarships awarded for academics, art, athletics, leadership, minority status, music/drama.

Application procedures. Admission: No deadline. $25 fee, may be waived for applicants with need. Admission notification on a rolling basis. **Financial aid:** Priority date 2/14; no closing date. FAFSA required. Applicants notified on a rolling basis starting 3/20; must reply within 10 week(s) of notification.

Academics. **Special study options:** Accelerated study, combined bachelor's/graduate degree, cooperative education, distance learning, double major, dual enrollment of high school students, ESL, honors, independent study, internships, student-designed major, study abroad, teacher certification program. **Credit/placement by examination:** AP, CLEP, IB, ACT, institutional tests. 62 credit hours maximum toward bachelor's degree. **Support services:** Learning center, reduced course load, remedial instruction, study skills assistance, tutoring, writing center.

Majors. **Biology:** General, biochemistry. **Business:** General, accounting, business admin, finance, international, managerial economics, marketing, operations. **Communications:** General. **Computer sciences:** General, systems analysis. **Education:** Elementary, physical, special. **Engineering:** Electrical, mechanical. **Engineering technology:** General. **Foreign languages:** French, Spanish. **Health:** Athletic training, clinical lab science, health services, nursing (RN). **History:** General. **Interdisciplinary:** Global studies. **Math:** General, applied. **Parks/recreation:** Exercise sciences. **Physical sciences:** Chemical physics, chemistry, optics, physics. **Protective services:** Criminal justice. **Psychology:** General. **Public administration:** General, social work. **Social sciences:** Economics, political science, sociology. **Visual/performing arts:** Art, dramatic, graphic design, studio arts. **Other:** Applied studies, Business chemistry.

Most popular majors. Business/marketing 14%, education 19%, health sciences 9%, history 7%, public administration/social services 9%, security/protective services 6%.

Computing on campus. 1,100 workstations in library, computer center, student center. Dormitories linked to campus network. Commuter students can connect to campus network. Online course registration, online library, helpline, student web hosting, wireless network available.

Student life. **Freshman orientation:** Mandatory, $55 fee. Preregistration for classes offered. Day-long sessions before each semester include university placement testing, advising, and registration. **Housing:** Coed dorms, special housing for disabled, apartments, wellness housing available. $200 partly refundable deposit. **Activities:** Bands, campus ministries, choral groups, dance, drama, film society, international student organizations, literary magazine, music ensembles, Model UN, musical theater, student government, student newspaper, Over 110 student clubs and organizations.

Athletics. NCAA. **Intercollegiate:** Baseball M, basketball, bowling M, cheerleading, cross-country, football (tackle) M, golf M, soccer, softball W, tennis W, track and field, volleyball W. **Intramural:** Badminton, basketball, football (non-tackle), golf, lacrosse, racquetball, soccer, softball, squash, table tennis, tennis, volleyball. **Team name:** Cardinals.

Student services. Adult student services, alcohol/substance abuse counseling, career counseling, services for economically disadvantaged, student employment services, financial aid counseling, health services, legal services, minority student services, personal counseling, placement for graduates, veterans' counselor, women's services. **Physically disabled:** Services for visually, hearing impaired.

Contact. E-mail: admissions@svsu.edu
Phone: (989) 964-4200 Toll-free number: (800) 968-9500
Fax: (989) 790-0180
Jennifer Pahl, Director of Admissions, Saginaw Valley State University, 7400 Bay Road, University Center, MI 48710

Siena Heights University

Adrian, Michigan — **CB member**
www.sienaheights.edu — **CB code: 1719**

- Private 4-year university and liberal arts college affiliated with Roman Catholic Church
- Residential campus in large town
- 1,850 degree-seeking undergraduates
- 353 graduate students
- 75% of applicants admitted
- SAT or ACT (ACT writing recommended) required

General. Founded in 1919. Regionally accredited. Branch campuses in Benton Harbor, Battle Creek, Kalamazoo, Lansing, Southfield, Monroe, and Jackson. Monroe County Community College, Lake Michigan College, and Southfield Community Center provide off-campus upper-division degree completion. **Degrees:** 668 bachelor's, 7 associate awarded; master's offered. **Location:** 30 miles from Toledo, Ohio; 60 miles from Detroit. **Calendar:** Semester, limited summer session. **Full-time faculty:** 66 total. **Part-time faculty:** 152 total. **Special facilities:** Montessori children's house on campus.

Freshman class profile. 751 applied, 567 admitted, 217 enrolled.

Mid 50% test scores		Out-of-state:	15%
ACT composite:	17-21	Live on campus:	70%

Basis for selection. School achievement record, test scores, self-motivation, and ability to benefit from available resources most important. Interview required for art, theater, and music majors; audition required for music majors; portfolio required for art majors. Essay recommended for marginally qualified applicants. **Homeschooled:** Must complete GED for state or federal assistance.

High school preparation. College-preparatory program recommended. Recommended units include English 4, mathematics 3, social studies 3, history 3, science 3, foreign language 2, computer science 1 and visual/performing arts 1.

2008-2009 Annual costs. Tuition/fees: $18,494. Room/board: $6,600. Books/supplies: $800. Personal expenses: $900.

2007-2008 Financial aid. **Non-need-based:** Scholarships awarded for academics, art, athletics, music/drama, religious affiliation.

Application procedures. **Admission:** No deadline. $25 fee, may be waived for applicants with need, free for online applicants. Admission notification on a rolling basis. **Financial aid:** Priority date 3/15, closing date 8/15. FAFSA, institutional form, CSS PROFILE required. Applicants notified on a rolling basis starting 2/15.

Academics. **Special study options:** Combined bachelor's/graduate degree, cooperative education, distance learning, double major, dual enrollment of high school students, ESL, exchange student, external degree, internships, liberal arts/career combination, student-designed major, study abroad, teacher certification program, weekend college. **Credit/placement by examination:** AP, CLEP, ACT, institutional tests. 36 credit hours maximum toward bachelor's degree. **Support services:** Learning center, preadmission summer program, reduced course load, remedial instruction, study skills assistance, tutoring, writing center.

Majors. **Area/ethnic studies:** American. **Biology:** General. **Business:** General, accounting, hospitality/recreation. **Communications:** General. **Computer sciences:** General. **Education:** Business, elementary, secondary. **Foreign languages:** Spanish. **Health:** Predental, premedicine, prepharmacy. **History:** General. **Interdisciplinary:** Natural sciences. **Legal studies:** Prelaw. **Liberal arts:** Arts/sciences. **Math:** General. **Parks/recreation:** Sports admin. **Philosophy/religion:** Philosophy, religion. **Physical sciences:** Chemistry. **Protective services:** Criminal justice. **Psychology:** General. **Public administration:** Social work. **Social sciences:** General. **Visual/performing arts:** Art, ceramics, commercial/advertising art, dramatic, drawing, metal/jewelry, painting, photography, sculpture, studio arts.

Computing on campus. 80 workstations in dormitories, library, computer center. Dormitories linked to campus network. Commuter students can connect to campus network. Online course registration, online library, helpline, repair service, wireless network available.

Student life. **Freshman orientation:** Mandatory. Preregistration for classes offered. One-day program offered in April, May, June, July, and August. **Policies:** Religious observance required. **Housing:** Guaranteed on-campus for all undergraduates. Coed dorms, single-sex dorms, apartments available. $100 partly refundable deposit. **Activities:** Jazz band, campus ministries, choral groups, dance, drama, film society, international student organizations, literary magazine, music ensembles, musical theater, student government, student newspaper, Siena Heights African American Knowledge Association, student programming association, Greek council, Students Against Violent Environments.

Athletics. NAIA. **Intercollegiate:** Baseball M, basketball, cross-country, golf, lacrosse M, soccer, softball W, track and field, volleyball. **Intramural:** Basketball, softball, volleyball. **Team name:** Saints.

Student services. Adult student services, career counseling, student employment services, financial aid counseling, health services, personal counseling, placement for graduates, veterans' counselor.

Contact. E-mail: admissions@sienaheights.edu
Phone: (517) 264-7180 Toll-free number: (800) 521-0009 ext. 7180
Fax: (517) 264-7745
Sara Johnson, Director of Admissions, Siena Heights University, 1247 East Siena Heights Drive, Adrian, MI 49221-1796

Spring Arbor University

Spring Arbor, Michigan
www.arbor.edu — **CB code: 1732**

- Private 4-year university and liberal arts college affiliated with Free Methodist Church of North America
- Residential campus in rural community

- 2,615 degree-seeking undergraduates: 25% part-time, 67% women
- 1,184 degree-seeking graduate students
- 78% of applicants admitted
- 58% graduate within 6 years; 27% enter graduate study

General. Founded in 1873. Regionally accredited. School of Professional Studies offers degree completion with courses and majors available at 14 regional sites. **Degrees:** 686 bachelor's, 1 associate awarded; master's offered. **ROTC:** Army, Air Force. **Location:** 8 miles from Jackson, 40 miles from Lansing. **Calendar:** Semester, limited summer session. **Full-time faculty:** 83 total; 61% have terminal degrees, 8% minority, 32% women. **Part-time faculty:** 46 total; 26% have terminal degrees, 6% minority, 54% women. **Class size:** 60% < 20, 33% 20-39, 5% 40-49, 2% 50-99. **Special facilities:** Trading center.

Freshman class profile. 1,791 applied, 1,401 admitted, 381 enrolled.

Mid 50% test scores			
SAT critical reading:	460-660	GPA 2.0-2.99:	20%
SAT math:	440-600	Rank in top quarter:	49%
SAT writing:	450-580	Rank in top tenth:	25%
ACT composite:	20-25	Return as sophomores:	77%
GPA 3.75 or higher:	31%	Out-of-state:	17%
GPA 3.50-3.74:	18%	Live on campus:	98%
GPA 3.0-3.49:	30%	International:	1%

Basis for selection. 20 ACT/930 SAT and 2.6 GPA recommended. Applicants whose scores are below recommendations may be admitted conditionally. ACT recommended. Interview recommended for borderline applicants. **Homeschooled:** Letter of recommendation from the parent/teacher and a 2-3 page paper regarding applicant's home school experience required.

High school preparation. College-preparatory program required. 12 units required. Required and recommended units include English 4, mathematics 3, history 2, science 2 (laboratory 2), foreign language 2 and computer science 1. Physical education or other health-related course is also required.

2008-2009 Annual costs. Tuition/fees: $19,240. Room/board: $6,650. Books/supplies: $685. Personal expenses: $839.

2008-2009 Financial aid. Need-based: 361 full-time freshmen applied for aid; 311 were judged to have need; 311 of these received aid. Average need met was 97%. Average scholarship/grant was $11,613; average loan $3,822. 63% of total undergraduate aid awarded as scholarships/grants, 37% as loans/jobs. **Non-need-based:** Scholarships awarded for academics, art, athletics, minority status, music/drama, religious affiliation.

Application procedures. Admission: Priority date 2/15; deadline 8/1 (receipt date). $30 fee, may be waived for applicants with need, free for online applicants. Admission notification on a rolling basis beginning on or about 9/1. **Financial aid:** Priority date 3/1; no closing date. FAFSA required. Applicants notified on a rolling basis starting 3/1; must reply within 2 week(s) of notification.

Academics. Special study options: Accelerated study, combined bachelor's/graduate degree, cross-registration, distance learning, double major, dual enrollment of high school students, ESL, honors, independent study, internships, student-designed major, study abroad, teacher certification program, Washington semester, weekend college. Environmental study semester offered at AuSable Trails Institute in northern Michigan; cross-cultural program with several destinations. **Credit/placement by examination:** AP, CLEP, IB, SAT, ACT, institutional tests. 10 credit hours maximum toward associate degree, 60 toward bachelor's. No more than 1/3 of credits for a major can be earned through credit by examination. **Support services:** Learning center, pre-admission summer program, reduced course load, remedial instruction, study skills assistance, tutoring.

Majors. Biology: General, biochemistry. **Business:** Accounting, actuarial science, business admin, finance, management information systems, managerial economics, operations. **Communications:** General, advertising, broadcast journalism, public relations. **Computer sciences:** Computer science. **Education:** Art, elementary, secondary, special. **Engineering technology:** General. **Family/consumer sciences:** Family studies. **Foreign languages:** Spanish. **Health:** Health care admin, nursing (RN). **History:** General. **Interdisciplinary:** Global studies. **Math:** General. **Parks/recreation:** General, health/fitness. **Philosophy/religion:** Christian, philosophy, religion. **Physical sciences:** Chemistry, theoretical physics. **Psychology:** General. **Public administration:** Social work. **Social sciences:** General, political science, sociology, urban studies. **Theology:** Bible, missionary, pastoral counseling, sacred music, theology, youth ministry. **Visual/performing arts:** Art, design, film/cinema, graphic design. **Other:** Biology health careers.

Most popular majors. Business/marketing 30%, education 15%, family/consumer sciences 18%, health sciences 8%, philosophy/religious studies 6%.

Computing on campus. 368 workstations in dormitories, library, computer center, student center. Dormitories wired for high-speed internet access and linked to campus network. Commuter students can connect to campus network. Online course registration, helpline, repair service, student web hosting, wireless network available.

Student life. Freshman orientation: Mandatory. Preregistration for classes offered. 3-day session held at the beginning of September; parents are encouraged to attend the first day. **Policies:** Emphasis placed on an active commitment to Jesus Christ and his teachings. Chapel attendance is required twice a week. Religious observance required. **Housing:** Guaranteed on-campus for freshmen. Single-sex dorms, special housing for disabled, apartments, wellness housing available. $200 fully refundable deposit, deadline 5/1. Community homes on campus. **Activities:** Bands, campus ministries, choral groups, drama, film society, international student organizations, literary magazine, music ensembles, musical theater, radio station, student government, student newspaper, symphony orchestra, TV station, interfaith shelter, Action Jackson, Habitat for Humanity.

Athletics. NAIA, NCCAA. **Intercollegiate:** Baseball M, basketball, cross-country, golf M, soccer, softball W, tennis, track and field, volleyball W. **Intramural:** Basketball, field hockey M, football (non-tackle) M, golf M, soccer, softball, table tennis, tennis, volleyball. **Team name:** Cougars.

Student services. Adult student services, chaplain/spiritual director, career counseling, student employment services, financial aid counseling, health services, minority student services, personal counseling, placement for graduates, veterans' counselor. **Physically disabled:** Services for visually, speech, hearing impaired.

Contact. E-mail: admissions@arbor.edu
Phone: (517) 750-6468 Toll-free number: (800) 968-0011
Fax: (517) 750-6620
Randy Comfort, Executive Director of Admissions, Spring Arbor University, 106 East Main Street, Spring Arbor, MI 49283-9799

University of Detroit Mercy

Detroit, Michigan — **CB member**
www.udmercy.edu — **CB code: 1835**

- Private 4-year university affiliated with Roman Catholic Church
- Commuter campus in very large city
- 2,995 degree-seeking undergraduates
- 64% of applicants admitted
- SAT or ACT (ACT writing optional) required

General. Founded in 1991. Regionally accredited. **Degrees:** 602 bachelor's awarded; master's, doctoral, first professional offered. **Calendar:** Semester, extensive summer session. **Full-time faculty:** 250 total. **Part-time faculty:** 321 total. **Class size:** 61% < 20, 35% 20-39, 3% 40-49, 2% 50-99.

Freshman class profile. 3,173 applied, 2,021 admitted, 608 enrolled.

Mid 50% test scores			
SAT critical reading:	470-630	Rank in top quarter:	63%
SAT math:	450-600	Rank in top tenth:	31%
ACT composite:	20-26	Out-of-state:	4%
		Live on campus:	45%

Basis for selection. High school GPA in college-preparatory work, test scores, counselor's recommendation considered. Interview required for University College applicants, recommended for all others.

High school preparation. 16 units required. Required and recommended units include English 4, mathematics 3-4, social studies 2, history 2, science 2-3 (laboratory 1) and academic electives 4. Units in speech, foreign language, music, art recommended.

2008-2009 Annual costs. Tuition/fees: $27,319. Engineering and architecture students pay slightly higher tuition. Room/board: $8,250. Books/supplies: $1,420. Personal expenses: $2,567.

Financial aid. Non-need-based: Scholarships awarded for academics, alumni affiliation, athletics, leadership, minority status, music/drama, religious affiliation.

Application procedures. Admission: Closing date 7/1. $25 fee, may be waived for applicants with need. Admission notification on a rolling basis beginning on or about 9/1. Must reply by May 1 or within 3 week(s) if notified thereafter. **Financial aid:** Priority date 3/1; no closing date. FAFSA required. Applicants notified on a rolling basis starting 3/1; must reply within 3 week(s) of notification.

Academics. Special study options: Combined bachelor's/graduate degree, cooperative education, distance learning, double major, dual enrollment of high school students, ESL, honors, independent study, internships, liberal arts/career combination, study abroad, teacher certification program, Washington semester, weekend college. Bachelor's degree completion program for registered nurses, 5-year program leading to master's degree in architecture. **Credit/placement by examination:** AP, CLEP, institutional tests. 30 credit hours maximum toward bachelor's degree. **Support services:** Learning center, reduced course load, remedial instruction, study skills assistance, tutoring, writing center.

Majors. **Architecture:** Architecture. **Biology:** General, biochemistry. **Business:** General, accounting, business admin, marketing. **Communications:** General, broadcast journalism, journalism, public relations. **Computer sciences:** General, computer science, systems analysis. **Education:** General, biology, chemistry, elementary, emotionally handicapped, history, mathematics, mentally handicapped, middle, reading, science, secondary, social science, social studies, special. **Engineering:** General, civil, computer, electrical, manufacturing, mechanical. **Health:** Dental hygiene, nursing (RN), predental, premedicine, substance abuse counseling. **History:** General. **Legal studies:** Paralegal, prelaw. **Liberal arts:** Arts/sciences. **Math:** General, applied. **Philosophy/religion:** Philosophy, religion. **Physical sciences:** Chemistry. **Protective services:** Criminal justice, law enforcement admin, police science. **Psychology:** General. **Public administration:** Social work. **Social sciences:** Economics, political science, sociology. **Visual/performing arts:** Dramatic.

Most popular majors. Biology 8%, business/marketing 12%, engineering/engineering technologies 13%, health sciences 36%.

Computing on campus. 250 workstations in dormitories, library, computer center, student center. Dormitories wired for high-speed internet access and linked to campus network. Commuter students can connect to campus network. Online library, helpline, repair service, student web hosting, wireless network available.

Student life. **Freshman orientation:** Available, $200 fee. Preregistration for classes offered. **Housing:** Coed dorms available. $100 deposit. **Activities:** Pep band, dance, drama, international student organizations, literary magazine, radio station, student government, student newspaper, American Institute of Architecture students, College Democrats, College Republicans, minority student association, NAACP, philosophy club, chemistry club, engineering societies, poet and writers forum, student environmental club.

Athletics. NCAA. **Intercollegiate:** Basketball, cheerleading, cross-country, fencing, golf, lacrosse, soccer, softball W, tennis W, track and field. **Intramural:** Baseball M, basketball, racquetball, soccer M, softball, table tennis, tennis, volleyball. **Team name:** Detroit Titans.

Student services. Adult student services, alcohol/substance abuse counseling, chaplain/spiritual director, career counseling, student employment services, financial aid counseling, health services, on-campus daycare, personal counseling, placement for graduates, veterans' counselor.

Contact. E-mail: admissions@udmercy.edu
Phone: (313) 993-1245 Toll-free number: (800) 635-5020
Fax: (313) 993-3326
Denise Williams, Director of Admissions, University of Detroit Mercy, 4001 West McNichols Road, Detroit, MI 48221-3038

University of Michigan

Ann Arbor, Michigan — **CB member**
www.umich.edu — **CB code: 1839**

- Public 4-year university
- Residential campus in small city
- 25,865 degree-seeking undergraduates: 3% part-time, 50% women, 6% African American, 12% Asian American, 4% Hispanic American, 1% Native American, 5% international
- 13,411 degree-seeking graduate students
- 42% of applicants admitted
- SAT or ACT with writing, application essay required
- 88% graduate within 6 years

General. Founded in 1817. Regionally accredited. Over 150 first-year seminars and several thousand undergraduate research opportunities. **Degrees:** 6,258 bachelor's awarded; master's, doctoral, first professional offered. **ROTC:** Army, Naval, Air Force. **Location:** 50 miles from Detroit. **Calendar:** Trimester, limited summer session. **Full-time faculty:** 2,420 total; 91% have terminal degrees, 23% minority, 37% women. **Part-time faculty:** 585 total; 76% have terminal degrees, 15% minority, 50% women. **Class size:** 45% < 20, 34% 20-39, 4% 40-49, 11% 50-99, 7% >100. **Special facilities:** Botanical garden, biological station in northern Michigan, arboretum, planetarium, laboratories, observatory, field station in the greater Yellowstone ecosystem, exhibit museum, art museum, herbarium, galleries.

Freshman class profile. 29,814 applied, 12,567 admitted, 5,827 enrolled.

Mid 50% test scores		**Rank in top quarter:**	99%
SAT critical reading:	580-690	**Rank in top tenth:**	92%
SAT math:	640-740	**Return as sophomores:**	96%
SAT writing:	590-700	**Out-of-state:**	28%
ACT composite:	27-31	**Live on campus:**	97%
GPA 3.75 or higher:	63%	**International:**	4%
GPA 3.50-3.74:	25%	**Fraternities:**	15%
GPA 3.0-3.49:	10%	**Sororities:**	21%
GPA 2.0-2.99:	2%		

Basis for selection. Admissions based on school achievement record, including quality of school and courses elected, and test scores. Talents and extracurricular activities considered. Special consideration to educationally disadvantaged applicants. Audition required for music majors; portfolio required for art majors. **Homeschooled:** Homeschooled students must submit 3-4 SAT Subject Tests or other proficiency results depending on school/college of application.

High school preparation. College-preparatory program recommended. 16 units required; 20 recommended. Required and recommended units include English 4, mathematics 3-4, social studies 3, history 3, science 3-4 (laboratory 1), foreign language 2-4, computer science 1, visual/performing arts 2 and academic electives 1.

2008-2009 Annual costs. Tuition/fees: $11,037; $33,069 out-of-state. Room/board: $8,590. Books/supplies: $1,048. Personal expenses: $2,054.

2007-2008 Financial aid. **Need-based:** 3,514 full-time freshmen applied for aid; 2,853 were judged to have need; 2,853 of these received aid. Average need met was 90%. Average scholarship/grant was $7,737; average loan $6,623. 48% of total undergraduate aid awarded as scholarships/grants, 52% as loans/jobs. **Non-need-based:** Awarded to 15,308 full-time undergraduates, including 5,175 freshmen. Scholarships awarded for academics, alumni affiliation, art, athletics, leadership, music/drama, religious affiliation, ROTC, state residency.

Application procedures. **Admission:** Closing date 2/1 (postmark date). $40 fee, may be waived for applicants with need. Admission notification on a rolling basis beginning on or about 9/1. Must reply by 5/1. Students should apply early in the fall of senior year. Applications may be considered after 2/1 for School of Art and Design, School of Music, Theatre and Dance, School of Natural Resources and Environment, and School of Nursing programs on space availability basis. **Financial aid:** Priority date 4/30, closing date 5/30. FAFSA, CSS PROFILE required. Applicants notified on a rolling basis starting 3/15.

Academics. Small-scale, interdisciplinary instruction programs in residence halls; freshman and sophomore seminars, undergraduate research, and mentoring opportunities available. The School of Public Health's "On Job/On Campus" students attend classes one four-day weekend per month for 18-25 months for a master's degree. The Community Health Nursing Program involves staying on-campus from Friday through Sunday once a month for 47-credit master's degree. **Special study options:** Accelerated study, combined bachelor's/graduate degree, cooperative education, cross-registration, distance learning, double major, dual enrollment of high school students, ESL, exchange student, external degree, honors, independent study, internships, liberal arts/career combination, semester at sea, student-designed major, study abroad, teacher certification program, Washington semester, weekend college. **Credit/placement by examination:** AP, CLEP, IB, institutional tests. 60 credit hours maximum toward bachelor's degree. Policies on credit by examination varies by exam. **Support services:** Learning center, reduced course load, study skills assistance, tutoring, writing center.

Honors college/program. 10 percent of each incoming freshman class admitted; grades, test scores, recommendations, and essay used in decision process.

Majors. **Architecture:** Architecture. **Area/ethnic studies:** African-American, American, Asian, Hispanic-American/Latino/Chicano, Latin American, Near/Middle Eastern, Russian/Slavic, women's. **Biology:** General, biochemistry, biophysics, botany, cellular/molecular, ecology, microbiology. **Business:** Business admin, organizational behavior. **Communications:** General. **Computer sciences:** General. **Conservation:** Environmental studies. **Education:** Elementary, music, physical. **Engineering:** General, aerospace, biomedical, chemical, civil, computer, electrical, geological, industrial, marine, materials science, mechanical, nuclear, physics, science. **Foreign languages:** Ancient Greek, Arabic, classics, comparative lit, French, German, Hebrew, Italian, Latin, linguistics, modern Greek, Russian, Spanish, Turkish. **Health:** Athletic training, dental hygiene, nursing (RN), pharmaceutical sciences. **History:** General. **Interdisciplinary:** Ancient studies, classical/archaeology, global studies, medieval/Renaissance, neuroscience. **Liberal arts:** Humanities. **Math:** General, statistics. **Parks/recreation:** Exercise sciences, sports admin. **Philosophy/religion:** Judaic, philosophy, religion. **Physical sciences:** Astronomy, atmospheric science, chemistry, geology, oceanography, physics. **Psychology:** General, cognitive. **Public administration:**

Policy analysis. **Social sciences:** General, anthropology, economics, political science, sociology. **Visual/performing arts:** General, art, art history/conservation, ceramics, dance, dramatic, drawing, fiber arts, film/cinema, graphic design, illustration, industrial design, jazz, metal/jewelry, music history, music performance, music theory/composition, photography, printmaking, sculpture, theater design. **Other:** Anthropology-zoology, Environmental geosciences, Sound engineering.

Most popular majors. Biology 6%, business/marketing 6%, engineering/engineering technologies 15%, English 6%, psychology 11%, social sciences 18%, visual/performing arts 6%.

Computing on campus. 2,254 workstations in dormitories, library, computer center, student center. Dormitories wired for high-speed internet access and linked to campus network. Commuter students can connect to campus network. Online course registration, online library, helpline, repair service, student web hosting, wireless network available.

Student life. **Freshman orientation:** Mandatory, $242 fee. Preregistration for classes offered. Students must attend 1 of several 3-day summer programs. **Housing:** Guaranteed on-campus for freshmen. Coed dorms, single-sex dorms, special housing for disabled, apartments, cooperative housing, fraternity/sorority housing, wellness housing available. **Activities:** Bands, campus ministries, choral groups, dance, drama, film society, international student organizations, literary magazine, music ensembles, Model UN, musical theater, opera, radio station, student government, student newspaper, symphony orchestra, TV station, over 1,000 student organizations.

Athletics. NCAA. **Intercollegiate:** Baseball M, basketball, cross-country, diving, field hockey W, football (tackle) M, golf, gymnastics, ice hockey M, rowing (crew) W, soccer, softball W, swimming, tennis, track and field, volleyball W, water polo, wrestling M. **Intramural:** Badminton, basketball, cross-country, diving, football (non-tackle), golf, racquetball, soccer, softball, swimming, table tennis, tennis, track and field, volleyball, water polo, wrestling. **Team name:** Wolverines.

Student services. Adult student services, alcohol/substance abuse counseling, chaplain/spiritual director, career counseling, student employment services, financial aid counseling, health services, legal services, minority student services, on-campus daycare, personal counseling, placement for graduates, women's services. **Physically disabled:** Services for visually, speech, hearing impaired.

Contact. Phone: (734) 764-7433 Fax: (734) 936-0740
Theodore Spencer, Associate Vice Provost and Executive Director, Undergraduate Admissions, University of Michigan, 1220 Student Activities Building, Ann Arbor, MI 48109-1316

University of Michigan: Dearborn

Dearborn, Michigan — **CB member**
www.umd.umich.edu — **CB code: 1861**

- Public 4-year university
- Commuter campus in small city
- 6,346 degree-seeking undergraduates: 31% part-time, 52% women
- 1,656 degree-seeking graduate students
- 61% of applicants admitted
- SAT or ACT (ACT writing optional) required
- 53% graduate within 6 years

General. Founded in 1959. Regionally accredited. **Degrees:** 1,147 bachelor's awarded; master's offered. **ROTC:** Army, Naval, Air Force. **Location:** 10 miles from Detroit. **Calendar:** Semester, limited summer session. **Full-time faculty:** 294 total; 100% have terminal degrees, 29% minority, 35% women. **Part-time faculty:** 191 total; 100% have terminal degrees, 8% minority, 39% women. **Class size:** 33% < 20, 45% 20-39, 14% 40-49, 6% 50-99, less than 1% >100. **Special facilities:** Henry Ford's Fair Lane estate, environmental study area, extensive rotating art collection, engineering CAD-CAM robotics laboratory, Armenian research center.

Freshman class profile. 3,864 applied, 2,338 admitted, 953 enrolled.

Mid 50% test scores		**GPA 2.0-2.99:**	15%
SAT math:	520-640	**Rank in top quarter:**	60%
SAT writing:	470-580	**Rank in top tenth:**	23%
ACT composite:	21-26	**Return as sophomores:**	81%
GPA 3.75 or higher:	29%	**Out-of-state:**	1%
GPA 3.50-3.74:	19%	**Fraternities:**	2%
GPA 3.0-3.49:	37%	**Sororities:**	2%

Basis for selection. Minimum 3.0 GPA with 500 SAT verbal and math or 22 ACT preferred; class rank considered. Interview recommended for applicants with less than 3.0 GPA or 20 ACT or 1000 SAT (exclusive of Writing). Essay recommended for all.

High school preparation. 15 units required; 20 recommended. Required and recommended units include English 4, mathematics 4, social studies 4, history 4, science 3 (laboratory 1) and foreign language 3. 1 unit information technology and 1 unit fine and performing arts recommended.

2008-2009 Annual costs. Tuition/fees: $8,506; $18,612 out-of-state. Books/supplies: $960. Personal expenses: $3,200.

2007-2008 Financial aid. **Need-based:** 550 full-time freshmen applied for aid; 347 were judged to have need; 347 of these received aid. Average need met was 41%. Average scholarship/grant was $3,832; average loan $2,771. 42% of total undergraduate aid awarded as scholarships/grants, 58% as loans/jobs. **Non-need-based:** Awarded to 2,914 full-time undergraduates, including 806 freshmen. Scholarships awarded for academics, alumni affiliation, athletics, job skills, leadership, minority status, ROTC.

Application procedures. **Admission:** Priority date 5/1; no deadline. $30 fee, may be waived for applicants with need. Admission notification on a rolling basis beginning on or about 9/1. Must reply by May 1 or within 4 week(s) if notified thereafter. **Financial aid:** Priority date 2/15; no closing date. FAFSA required. Applicants notified on a rolling basis starting 3/10; must reply within 3 week(s) of notification.

Academics. **Special study options:** Accelerated study, cooperative education, cross-registration, distance learning, double major, dual enrollment of high school students, honors, independent study, internships, liberal arts/career combination, student-designed major, study abroad, teacher certification program, Washington semester. Professional development courses in education, engineering, liberal arts, and management. **Credit/placement by examination:** AP, CLEP, institutional tests. 30 credit hours maximum toward bachelor's degree. **Support services:** Learning center, pre-admission summer program, tutoring.

Majors. **Area/ethnic studies:** American. **Biology:** General, bacteriology, biochemistry, ecology. **Business:** Business admin, management science. **Communications:** General. **Computer sciences:** General, programming. **Conservation:** General, environmental studies. **Education:** General, art, business, chemistry, early childhood, foreign languages, mathematics, science, secondary, social studies. **Engineering:** General, computer, electrical, manufacturing, mechanical. **Foreign languages:** French, Spanish. **Health:** Health care admin. **History:** General. **Interdisciplinary:** Behavioral sciences. **Liberal arts:** Arts/sciences. **Math:** General. **Philosophy/religion:** Philosophy. **Physical sciences:** Chemistry, physics. **Psychology:** General. **Public administration:** General. **Social sciences:** Anthropology, economics, political science, sociology. **Visual/performing arts:** Painting.

Most popular majors. Biology 7%, business/marketing 19%, education 19%, engineering/engineering technologies 13%, psychology 9%, social sciences 8%.

Computing on campus. 140 workstations in library, computer center, student center. Commuter students can connect to campus network. Online course registration, helpline, wireless network available.

Student life. **Freshman orientation:** Mandatory, $50 fee. **Activities:** Choral groups, drama, film society, literary magazine, radio station, student government, student newspaper, TV station, Arab student union, African American association, campus engineers, Asian American association, student activities board, professional accounting society, Muslim student association.

Athletics. NAIA. **Intercollegiate:** Basketball, ice hockey M, volleyball W. **Intramural:** Basketball, ice hockey, softball, table tennis, tennis, volleyball. **Team name:** Wolves.

Student services. Adult student services, alcohol/substance abuse counseling, career counseling, student employment services, financial aid counseling, health services, on-campus daycare, personal counseling, placement for graduates, veterans' counselor, women's services. **Physically disabled:** Services for visually, speech, hearing impaired.

Contact. E-mail: admissions@umd.umich.edu
Phone: (313) 593-5100 Fax: (313) 436- 9167
Christopher Tremblay, Director of Admissions, University of Michigan: Dearborn, 4901 Evergreen Road, 1145 UC, Dearborn, MI 48128-1491

University of Michigan: Flint

Flint, Michigan — **CB member**
www.umflint.edu — **CB code: 1853**

- Public 4-year university and branch campus college
- Commuter campus in small city
- 5,868 degree-seeking undergraduates: 35% part-time, 62% women, 13% African American, 2% Asian American, 3% Hispanic American, 1% Native American, 1% international

- 1,074 degree-seeking graduate students
- 87% of applicants admitted
- SAT or ACT (ACT writing optional) required
- 36% graduate within 6 years

General. Founded in 1956. Regionally accredited. Institution shares many resources of entire University of Michigan system. **Degrees:** 915 bachelor's awarded; master's, doctoral offered. **Location:** 60 miles from Detroit. **Calendar:** Semester, limited summer session. **Full-time faculty:** 245 total; 64% have terminal degrees, 18% minority, 52% women. **Part-time faculty:** 224 total; 18% have terminal degrees, 13% minority, 60% women. **Class size:** 41% < 20, 49% 20-39, 6% 40-49, 4% 50-99. **Special facilities:** Green Arts Project House.

Freshman class profile. 2,486 applied, 2,160 admitted, 909 enrolled.

Mid 50% test scores		**Rank in top quarter:**	38%
SAT critical reading:	380-560	**Rank in top tenth:**	16%
SAT math:	460-590	**Return as sophomores:**	72%
SAT writing:	450-490	**Out-of-state:**	1%
ACT composite:	18-23	**Live on campus:**	34%
GPA 3.75 or higher:	14%	**International:**	1%
GPA 3.50-3.74:	14%	**Fraternities:**	2%
GPA 3.0-3.49:	36%	**Sororities:**	3%
GPA 2.0-2.99:	34%		

Basis for selection. GPA of 2.7 or higher and test scores equaling national average automatically admitted. Essay and interview recommended. Audition required for art and music majors. **Homeschooled:** Transcript of courses and grades required.

High school preparation. College-preparatory program recommended. 9 units required; 22 recommended. Required and recommended units include English 4, mathematics 3-4, social studies 3, history 3, science 2-4 (laboratory 2) and foreign language 2. Fine arts and computer science courses recommended.

2008-2009 Annual costs. Tuition/fees: $7,376; $14,384 out-of-state. Room/board: $6,800. Books/supplies: $1,000. Personal expenses: $1,380.

2007-2008 Financial aid. Need-based: 460 full-time freshmen applied for aid; 311 were judged to have need; 301 of these received aid. Average need met was 68%. Average scholarship/grant was $4,365; average loan $3,161. 32% of total undergraduate aid awarded as scholarships/grants, 68% as loans/jobs. **Non-need-based:** Awarded to 1,249 full-time undergraduates, including 244 freshmen. Scholarships awarded for academics, art, leadership, minority status, music/drama. **Additional information:** SAT/ACT scores must be submitted for scholarship consideration.

Application procedures. Admission: No deadline. $30 fee, may be waived for applicants with need. Admission notification on a rolling basis beginning on or about 12/1. Must reply by May 1 or within 2 week(s) if notified thereafter. **Financial aid:** Priority date 3/1; no closing date. FAFSA required. Applicants notified on a rolling basis starting 3/15.

Academics. Special study options: Combined bachelor's/graduate degree, cooperative education, distance learning, double major, dual enrollment of high school students, ESL, honors, independent study, internships, student-designed major, study abroad, teacher certification program. **Credit/placement by examination:** AP, CLEP, SAT, ACT, institutional tests. 9 credit hours maximum toward bachelor's degree. Maximum of 3 courses may be passed by examination in Arts & Sciences, School of Management and Nursing. **Support services:** Learning center, reduced course load, remedial instruction, study skills assistance, tutoring, writing center.

Majors. Area/ethnic studies: African-American. **Biology:** General, Biochemistry/biophysics and molecular biology, biomedical sciences, ecology, molecular, wildlife. **Business:** Accounting, actuarial science, business admin, finance, international, marketing, operations, organizational behavior. **Communications:** General, journalism, media studies, organizational. **Computer sciences:** General, computer science, information systems. **Conservation:** Environmental science. **Education:** General, art, biology, chemistry, elementary, English, foreign languages, French, history, mathematics, music, physics, science, secondary, social studies, Spanish. **Engineering:** Mechanical, science. **Foreign languages:** French, Spanish. **Health:** Clinical lab science, health care admin, health services, medical radiologic technology/radiation therapy, nursing (RN), public health ed. **History:** General. **Liberal arts:** Arts/sciences. **Math:** General. **Philosophy/religion:** Ethics, philosophy. **Physical sciences:** Chemistry, physics. **Protective services:** Law enforcement admin. **Psychology:** General, clinical. **Public administration:** General, social work. **Social sciences:** General, anthropology, economics, political science, sociology. **Visual/performing arts:** Acting, ceramics, dramatic, graphic design, music performance, painting, photography, printmaking, sculpture, studio arts, theater design, theater history.

Most popular majors. Business/marketing 17%, education 21%, health sciences 17%.

Computing on campus. 205 workstations in library, computer center, student center. Dormitories wired for high-speed internet access and linked to campus network. Commuter students can connect to campus network. Online course registration, online library, helpline, repair service, student web hosting, wireless network available.

Student life. Freshman orientation: Mandatory, $80 fee. Preregistration for classes offered. One-day program for students and parents before start of fall semester. **Housing:** Coed dorms available. **Activities:** Bands, choral groups, dance, drama, literary magazine, music ensembles, musical theater, student government, student newspaper, TV station, College Democrats, College Republicans, College Libertarians, Intervarsity Christian Fellowship, Muslim student association, Students Moving the UCEN Forward, Voices for Women on Campus, chess club, Michigan Poetry Society.

Athletics. Intramural: Basketball, football (non-tackle), golf, racquetball, soccer, table tennis, volleyball.

Student services. Adult student services, alcohol/substance abuse counseling, career counseling, student employment services, financial aid counseling, health services, minority student services, on-campus daycare, personal counseling, veterans' counselor, women's services. **Physically disabled:** Services for visually, speech, hearing impaired.

Contact. E-mail: admissions@umflint.edu
Phone: (810) 762-3300 Fax: (810) 762-3272
Kimberley Buster-Williams, Director of Admissions, University of Michigan: Flint, 303 East Kearsley Street, Flint, MI 48502-1950

Walsh College of Accountancy and Business Administration

Troy, Michigan
www.walshcollege.edu **CB code: 0372**

- Private two-year upper-division business college
- Commuter campus in large city
- 71% of applicants admitted

General. Founded in 1922. Regionally accredited. **Degrees:** 398 bachelor's awarded; master's, doctoral offered. **Articulation:** Agreements with Henry Ford CC, Oakland CC, Macomb CC, Mott CC, Schoolcraft College, Washtenaw CC, St. Clair County CC, Wayne County CC, Kellogg CC, Jackson CC, Lansing CC. **Location:** 17 miles from Detroit. **Calendar:** Semester, extensive summer session. **Full-time faculty:** 18 total; 72% have terminal degrees, 6% minority, 44% women. **Part-time faculty:** 160 total; 28% have terminal degrees, 8% minority, 29% women. **Class size:** 25% < 20, 70% 20-39, 5% 40-49.

Student profile. 984 degree-seeking undergraduates, 2,072 degree-seeking graduate students. 403 applied as first time-transfer students, 285 admitted, 244 enrolled. 100% entered as juniors.

Women:	55%	**International:**	4%
African American:	5%	**Part-time:**	85%
Asian American:	3%	**Out-of-state:**	2%
Hispanic American:	1%	**25 or older:**	64%

Basis for selection. Open admission. College transcript required. 30 transferred credits must be in liberal arts, including course in English composition or written communication. Transfer accepted as juniors.

2008-2009 Annual costs. Tuition/fees: $9,070. Books/supplies: $2,016.

Financial aid. Need-based: 141 applied for aid; 129 were judged to have need; 129 of these received aid. Average need met was 46%. 22% of total undergraduate aid awarded as scholarships/grants, 78% as loans/jobs. **Non-need-based:** Awarded to 46 undergraduates. Scholarships awarded for academics.

Application procedures. Admission: Rolling admission. $25 fee, may be waived for applicants with need. **Financial aid:** Priority date 3/1, no deadline. Applicants notified on a rolling basis. FAFSA required.

Academics. Special study options: Accelerated study, combined bachelor's/graduate degree, distance learning, double major, internships. Joint partnerships with area community colleges to offer 150-hour honors program in which students complete associate, bachelor and MBA degrees in 5 years. **Credit/placement by examination:** CLEP, IB.

Majors. Business: General, accounting, business admin, finance. **Computer sciences:** General, information technology.

Most popular majors. Business/marketing 75%.

Computing on campus. 200 workstations in library, computer center. Commuter students can connect to campus network. Online course registration, online library, helpline, wireless network available.

Student life. Activities: International student organizations, student government, American Marketing Association, finance/economics club, National Association of Black Accountants, accounting club, Association of Information Technology Professionals, international club.

Student services. Career counseling, student employment services, financial aid counseling, placement for graduates. **Physically disabled:** Services for visually, hearing impaired.

Contact. E-mail: admissions@walshcollege.edu
Phone: (248) 823-1610 Toll-free number: (800) 925-7401
Fax: (248) 823-1662
Jeremy Guc, Director of Admissions and Academic Advising, Walsh College of Accountancy and Business Administration, PO Box 7006, Troy, MI 48007-7006

Wayne State University

Detroit, Michigan — **CB member**
www.wayne.edu — **CB code: 1898**

- Public 4-year university
- Commuter campus in very large city
- 19,007 degree-seeking undergraduates: 36% part-time, 58% women, 31% African American, 7% Asian American, 3% Hispanic American, 3% international
- 10,539 degree-seeking graduate students
- 79% of applicants admitted
- SAT or ACT (ACT writing optional) required
- 34% graduate within 6 years

General. Founded in 1868. Regionally accredited. 4 off-campus locations and 2 University Centers at local community colleges. **Degrees:** 2,783 bachelor's awarded; master's, doctoral, first professional offered. **ROTC:** Army, Air Force. **Location:** 3 miles from downtown. **Calendar:** Semester, extensive summer session. **Full-time faculty:** 1,021 total; 66% have terminal degrees, 26% minority, 41% women. **Part-time faculty:** 950 total; 18% have terminal degrees, 26% minority, 52% women. **Class size:** 52% < 20, 37% 20-39, 4% 40-49, 5% 50-99, 2% >100. **Special facilities:** 3 theaters.

Freshman class profile. 9,743 applied, 7,690 admitted, 2,917 enrolled.

Mid 50% test scores		**Return as sophomores:**	70%
ACT composite:	17-23	**Out-of-state:**	2%
GPA 3.75 or higher:	17%	**Live on campus:**	23%
GPA 3.50-3.74:	14%	**International:**	3%
GPA 3.0-3.49:	29%	**Fraternities:**	1%
GPA 2.0-2.99:	39%	**Sororities:**	1%
End year in good standing:	68%		

Basis for selection. High school record and test scores are important. Minimum 2.75 GPA or 2.0 GPA combined with 21 ACT is acceptable for admission. Audition required of music applicants, recommended for dance and theater applicants; portfolio required for art applicants.

High school preparation. College-preparatory program recommended. 18 units recommended. Recommended units include English 4, mathematics 4, social studies 3, science 3, foreign language 2 and visual/performing arts 2. Computer literacy.

2008-2009 Annual costs. Tuition/fees: $8,109; $17,379 out-of-state. Room/board: $6,932. Books/supplies: $950. Personal expenses: $1,800.

2007-2008 Financial aid. Need-based: 2,291 full-time freshmen applied for aid; 1,904 were judged to have need; 1,890 of these received aid. Average need met was 68%. Average scholarship/grant was $4,473; average loan $3,404. 31% of total undergraduate aid awarded as scholarships/grants, 69% as loans/jobs. **Non-need-based:** Awarded to 3,941 full-time undergraduates, including 1,292 freshmen. Scholarships awarded for academics, art, athletics, leadership, music/drama.

Application procedures. Admission: No deadline. $30 fee, may be waived for applicants with need. Admission notification on a rolling basis beginning on or about 9/15. **Financial aid:** Priority date 2/15, closing date 4/30. FAFSA required. Applicants notified on a rolling basis starting 3/1; must reply within 2 week(s) of notification.

Academics. Special study options: Accelerated study, combined bachelor's/graduate degree, cooperative education, cross-registration, distance learning, double major, dual enrollment of high school students, ESL, exchange student, honors, independent study, internships, liberal arts/career combination, study abroad, teacher certification program, weekend college. Off-campus courses for credit, city-wide adult education program. **Credit/placement by examination:** AP, CLEP, IB, institutional tests. 32 credit hours maximum toward bachelor's degree. **Support services:** Learning center, pre-admission summer program, reduced course load, remedial instruction, study skills assistance, tutoring, writing center.

Honors college/program. Selected incoming freshmen are invited into the program each year through Scholars Day and are awarded at least $6,000 in a tuition scholarship for four years. All other incoming freshmen may take honors courses if they have a minimum 3.50 high school grade point average or comparable ACT or SAT scores. Current Wayne State students must have 3.30 grade point average for 24 consecutive college credits before taking honors courses or applying to the program.

Majors. Area/ethnic studies: African-American, American, East Asian. **Biology:** General. **Business:** Accounting, finance, international, labor studies, management information systems, marketing, organizational behavior. **Communications:** General, journalism, public relations, radio/tv. **Computer sciences:** General, information systems. **Conservation:** Environmental science. **Education:** Art, elementary, English, health, mathematics, physical, science, social studies, special, speech impaired, voc/tech. **Engineering:** Chemical, civil, electrical, industrial, mechanical. **Engineering technology:** Computer systems, electrical, electromechanical, industrial, manufacturing, mechanical. **Family/consumer sciences:** Apparel marketing, food/nutrition. **Foreign languages:** General, classics, German, linguistics, Slavic. **Health:** Clinical lab science, communication disorders, dietetics, medical radiologic technology/radiation therapy, nursing (RN), pathology assistant. **History:** General. **Math:** General. **Personal/culinary services:** Mortuary science. **Philosophy/religion:** Philosophy. **Physical sciences:** Chemistry, geology, physics. **Protective services:** Criminal justice. **Psychology:** General. **Public administration:** General, social work. **Social sciences:** Anthropology, economics, geography, political science, sociology, urban studies. **Visual/performing arts:** Art, art history/conservation, cinematography, dance, dramatic, film/cinema. **Other:** Biomedical physics, Elementary language arts, Molecular biotechnology, Near eastern languages, Near eastern studies, Product design engineering technology, Technical and interdisciplinary studies.

Most popular majors. Biology 7%, business/marketing 16%, education 13%, engineering/engineering technologies 7%, health sciences 9%, psychology 8%, social sciences 6%, visual/performing arts 8%.

Computing on campus. 1,020 workstations in library. Dormitories wired for high-speed internet access and linked to campus network. Commuter students can connect to campus network. Online course registration, online library, helpline, repair service, wireless network available.

Student life. Freshman orientation: Mandatory, $75 fee. Preregistration for classes offered. **Housing:** Coed dorms, special housing for disabled, apartments, fraternity/sorority housing, wellness housing available. $150 nonrefundable deposit. **Activities:** Bands, campus ministries, choral groups, dance, drama, international student organizations, literary magazine, music ensembles, Model UN, musical theater, opera, radio station, student government, student newspaper, symphony orchestra, Indian Student Association, Golden Key Honor Society, Campus Crusade for Christ, Friendship Association of Chinese Students.

Athletics. NCAA. **Intercollegiate:** Baseball M, basketball, cross-country, diving, fencing, football (tackle) M, golf M, ice hockey W, softball W, swimming, tennis, volleyball W. **Intramural:** Badminton, basketball, bowling, cheerleading, football (non-tackle), racquetball, soccer, softball, tennis, volleyball. **Team name:** Warriors.

Student services. Adult student services, alcohol/substance abuse counseling, chaplain/spiritual director, career counseling, services for economically disadvantaged, student employment services, financial aid counseling, health services, legal services, minority student services, on-campus daycare, personal counseling, placement for graduates, veterans' counselor, women's services. **Physically disabled:** Services for visually, speech, hearing impaired.

Contact. E-mail: admissions@wayne.edu
Phone: (313) 577-3577 Toll-free number: (877) 978-4636
Fax: (313) 577-7536
Susan Zwieg, Director of University Admissions, Wayne State University, 42 West Warren, Detroit, MI 48202

Western Michigan University

Kalamazoo, Michigan — **CB member**
www.wmich.edu — **CB code: 1902**

- Public 4-year university
- Residential campus in small city

- 19,715 degree-seeking undergraduates: 11% part-time, 50% women, 7% African American, 2% Asian American, 3% Hispanic American, 1% Native American, 3% international
- 4,447 degree-seeking graduate students
- 85% of applicants admitted
- SAT or ACT (ACT writing optional) required
- 54% graduate within 6 years

General. Founded in 1903. Regionally accredited. **Degrees:** 4,046 bachelor's awarded; master's, doctoral offered. **ROTC:** Army. **Location:** 140 miles from Detroit, 140 miles from Chicago. **Calendar:** Semester, extensive summer session. **Full-time faculty:** 935 total; 80% have terminal degrees, 14% minority, 40% women. **Part-time faculty:** 501 total; 55% women. **Class size:** 38% < 20, 41% 20-39, 10% 40-49, 7% 50-99, 4% >100. **Special facilities:** Van de Graaff particle accelerator, pilot plant for manufacturing and printing of paper and fiber recovery, aviation flight simulators, business technology park.

Freshman class profile. 12,884 applied, 10,938 admitted, 3,828 enrolled.

Mid 50% test scores		**Rank in top tenth:**	10%
ACT composite:	20-25	**End year in good standing:**	69%
GPA 3.75 or higher:	16%	**Return as sophomores:**	73%
GPA 3.50-3.74:	13%	**Out-of-state:**	9%
GPA 3.0-3.49:	37%	**Live on campus:**	88%
GPA 2.0-2.99:	34%	**International:**	2%
Rank in top quarter:	29%		

Basis for selection. School achievement record, test scores most important. Trend of grades and number of solid high school academic subjects completed considered; students not meeting college-preparatory program requirements may be admitted conditionally if they meet other admission requirements. Interview recommended. Audition required for dance, music, and theater applicants. Portfolio required for some art applicants. **Homeschooled:** State high school equivalency certificate, letter of recommendation (nonparent) required.

High school preparation. College-preparatory program recommended. 15 units required; 18 recommended. Required and recommended units include English 4, mathematics 3, social studies 2-3, history 1, science 2 (laboratory 1), foreign language 2 and academic electives 2.

2008-2009 Annual costs. Tuition/fees: $7,928; $18,420 out-of-state. Room/board: $7,565.

2008-2009 Financial aid. Non-need-based: Scholarships awarded for academics, alumni affiliation, art, athletics, minority status, music/drama, ROTC, state residency.

Application procedures. Admission: Priority date 2/1; deadline 8/1. $35 fee, may be waived for applicants with need. Admission notification on a rolling basis beginning on or about 9/15. **Financial aid:** Priority date 3/15; no closing date. FAFSA required. Applicants notified on a rolling basis starting 3/15.

Academics. Special study options: Accelerated study, combined bachelor's/graduate degree, cross-registration, distance learning, double major, dual enrollment of high school students, ESL, exchange student, honors, independent study, internships, student-designed major, study abroad, teacher certification program. **Credit/placement by examination:** AP, CLEP, IB, SAT, ACT, institutional tests. Maximum semester hours of credit by examination which may be counted toward degree varies by department. Credit by examination may not be used to satisfy minimum residency requirement of 30 semester hours. **Support services:** Learning center, pre-admission summer program, reduced course load, remedial instruction, study skills assistance, tutoring, writing center.

Honors college/program. ACT composite score of at least 26 and a GPA of 3.6 or can demonstrate a rank within the top 10% of their high school class; must provide two letters of reference from teachers, instructors, professors, and/or counselors who can describe their academic ability along with application.

Majors. Area/ethnic studies: African, African-American, American, women's. **Biology:** General, biochemistry, biomedical sciences. **Business:** General, accounting, e-commerce, finance, financial planning, information resources management, logistics, management science, marketing, travel services. **Communications:** General, advertising, journalism, organizational, public relations. **Computer sciences:** General, computer science. **Conservation:** Environmental studies. **Education:** Art, biology, business, chemistry, college student counseling, drama/dance, early childhood, elementary, emotionally handicapped, English, family/consumer sciences, French, geography, German, health, history, Latin, mathematics, mentally handicapped, music, physical, physics, sales/marketing, science, social science, Spanish, technology/industrial arts, voc/tech. **Engineering:** Aerospace, chemical, civil, computer, electrical, environmental, industrial, manufacturing, mechanical, structural. **Engineering technology:** Construction, industrial management. **Family/consumer sciences:** Child development, clothing/textiles, family systems, institutional food production. **Foreign languages:** French, German, Latin, Spanish. **Health:** Athletic training, audiology/speech pathology, dietetics, health services, music therapy, nursing (RN). **History:** General, public archives. **Interdisciplinary:** Global studies. **Math:** General, applied, statistics. **Mechanic/repair:** Avionics. **Parks/recreation:** General, exercise sciences. **Philosophy/religion:** Philosophy, religion. **Physical sciences:** Chemistry, geochemistry, geology, geophysics, hydrology, physics. **Protective services:** Criminal justice. **Psychology:** General. **Public administration:** General, social work. **Social sciences:** Anthropology, economics, geography, political science, sociology. **Transportation:** Airline/commercial pilot, aviation management. **Visual/performing arts:** Acting, art, art history/conservation, cinematography, dance, dramatic, graphic design, industrial design, interior design, jazz, music performance, music theory/composition, studio arts, theater design, theater history. **Other:** Business-oriented chemistry, Paper science and engineering, imaging, Student-planned major.

Most popular majors. Business/marketing 24%, communications/journalism 6%, education 17%, engineering/engineering technologies 7%, health sciences 6%, visual/performing arts 6%.

Computing on campus. 2,000 workstations in dormitories, library, computer center, student center. Dormitories wired for high-speed internet access and linked to campus network. Commuter students can connect to campus network. Online course registration, helpline, repair service, student web hosting, wireless network available.

Student life. Freshman orientation: Mandatory, $175 fee. Preregistration for classes offered. 2-day program in June; includes session for parents. **Policies:** Student code. **Housing:** Guaranteed on-campus for freshmen. Coed dorms, single-sex dorms, special housing for disabled, apartments, fraternity/sorority housing, wellness housing available. $500 partly refundable deposit. **Activities:** Bands, campus ministries, choral groups, dance, drama, film society, international student organizations, literary magazine, music ensembles, musical theater, opera, radio station, student government, student newspaper, symphony orchestra, Over 275 organizations available.

Athletics. NCAA. **Intercollegiate:** Baseball M, basketball, cross-country W, football (tackle) M, golf W, gymnastics W, ice hockey M, soccer, softball W, tennis, track and field W, volleyball W. **Intramural:** Badminton, basketball, bowling, equestrian, fencing, football (tackle), golf M, ice hockey, lacrosse, racquetball, rugby, sailing, skiing, soccer, softball, swimming, table tennis, tennis, volleyball. **Team name:** Broncos.

Student services. Adult student services, alcohol/substance abuse counseling, chaplain/spiritual director, career counseling, student employment services, financial aid counseling, health services, minority student services, on-campus daycare, personal counseling, placement for graduates, veterans' counselor, women's services. **Physically disabled:** Services for visually, speech, hearing impaired.

Contact. E-mail: www.ask-wmu@wmich.edu
Phone: (269) 387-2000 Toll-free number: (800) 400-4968
Fax: (269) 387-2096
Penny Bundy, Director of Admissions, Western Michigan University, 1903 West Michigan Avenue, Kalamazoo, MI 49008-5211

Yeshiva Beth Yehuda-Yeshiva Gedolah of Greater Detroit

Oak Park, Michigan

CB code: 7010

- Private 5-year rabbinical college for men affiliated with Jewish faith
- Residential campus in large town

General. Accredited by AARTS. **Calendar:** Semester.

Annual costs/financial aid. Books/supplies: $500. Personal expenses: $200.

Contact. Phone: (248) 968-3360
24600 Greenfield Road, Oak Park, MI 48237

Minnesota

Art Institutes International Minnesota

Minneapolis, Minnesota
www.artinstitutes.edu/minneapolis **CB code: 2332**

- For-profit 4-year culinary school and visual arts college
- Commuter campus in large city
- 1,872 degree-seeking undergraduates: 27% part-time, 61% women
- Application essay, interview required

General. Accredited by ACICS. **Degrees:** 207 bachelor's, 107 associate awarded. **Calendar:** Quarter, extensive summer session. **Full-time faculty:** 56 total; 36% women. **Part-time faculty:** 63 total; 44% women. **Special facilities:** Student-run dining lab, wireless internet.

Basis for selection. Open admission. School tour required prior to admission. **Homeschooled:** Transcript of courses and grades, interview required. **Learning Disabled:** Notify Dean of Student Affairs.

2008-2009 Annual costs. Tuition/fees: $21,552. Typical full-time credit load 16 credits/quarter. Starter kits for most programs $600 to $1200. Books/supplies: $1,649. Personal expenses: $2,880.

Application procedures. Admission: No deadline. $50 fee. Admission notification on a rolling basis. **Financial aid:** FAFSA required.

Academics. Special study options: Cooperative education, distance learning, honors, independent study, internships, study abroad, weekend college. **Credit/placement by examination:** AP, CLEP, institutional tests. **Support services:** Learning center, remedial instruction, study skills assistance, tutoring.

Majors. Business: Customer service, hospitality admin, hospitality/recreation, hotel/motel admin, marketing, merchandising, resort management, restaurant/food services, retailing, selling. **Communications:** Advertising, digital media, photojournalism. **Communications technology:** Animation/special effects, graphics. **Computer sciences:** Computer graphics, webmaster. **Personal/culinary services:** Restaurant/catering. **Visual/performing arts:** Commercial photography, commercial/advertising art, design, graphic design, interior design, multimedia, photography. **Other:** Hospitality management.

Computing on campus. 320 workstations in library, computer center, student center. Dormitories wired for high-speed internet access. Online library, student web hosting, wireless network available.

Student life. Freshman orientation: Mandatory. Preregistration for classes offered. **Housing:** Apartments, wellness housing available. $250 deposit. **Activities:** Campus ministries, film society, student government, student newspaper.

Student services. Alcohol/substance abuse counseling, career counseling, student employment services, financial aid counseling, personal counseling, placement for graduates. **Physically disabled:** Services for hearing impaired.

Contact. E-mail: aimadm@aii.edu
Phone: (612) 332-3361 Toll-free number: (800) 777-3643
Fax: (612) 332-3934
Mary Strand, Senior Director of Admissions, Art Institutes International Minnesota, 15 South Ninth Street, Minneapolis, MN 55402

Augsburg College

Minneapolis, Minnesota **CB member**
www.augsburg.edu **CB code: 6014**

- Private 4-year liberal arts college affiliated with Evangelical Lutheran Church in America
- Residential campus in large city
- 2,919 degree-seeking undergraduates: 17% part-time, 55% women
- 842 degree-seeking graduate students
- 56% of applicants admitted
- Application essay required
- 58% graduate within 6 years; 24% enter graduate study

General. Founded in 1869. Regionally accredited. **Degrees:** 589 bachelor's awarded; master's offered. **ROTC:** Army, Naval, Air Force. **Location:** 5 miles from downtown. **Calendar:** Differs by program, extensive summer session. **Full-time faculty:** 188 total; 97% have terminal degrees, 8% minority, 49% women. **Part-time faculty:** 230 total; 25% have terminal degrees, 2% minority, 65% women. **Class size:** 62% < 20, 36% 20-39, less than 1% 40-49, less than 1% 50-99. **Special facilities:** Center for atmospheric research.

Freshman class profile. 1,924 applied, 1,076 admitted, 455 enrolled.

Mid 50% test scores		**GPA 2.0-2.99:**	33%
SAT critical reading:	510-640	**Rank in top quarter:**	34%
SAT math:	500-640	**Rank in top tenth:**	16%
SAT writing:	480-600	**End year in good standing:**	91%
ACT composite:	20-25	**Return as sophomores:**	80%
GPA 3.75 or higher:	21%	**Out-of-state:**	15%
GPA 3.50-3.74:	11%	**Live on campus:**	90%
GPA 3.0-3.49:	34%	**International:**	2%

Basis for selection. School achievement record, class rank in top half, test scores, essays and recommendations very important; extracurricular activities important. SAT or ACT recommended. Interview recommended.

High school preparation. College-preparatory program recommended. 15 units required. Required and recommended units include English 4, mathematics 3, social studies 2-4, history 2, science 3 and foreign language 2.

2008-2009 Annual costs. Tuition/fees: $26,103. Room/board: $7,161. Books/supplies: $1,000. Personal expenses: $1,670.

2007-2008 Financial aid. Non-need-based: Scholarships awarded for academics, alumni affiliation, leadership, minority status, music/drama, religious affiliation.

Application procedures. Admission: Priority date 5/1; deadline 8/1 (receipt date). $25 fee, may be waived for applicants with need, free for online applicants. Admission notification on a rolling basis beginning on or about 11/1. Must reply by 5/1. Must reply by May 1 or within 2 week(s) if notified thereafter. **Financial aid:** Priority date 4/15, closing date 8/1. FAFSA required. Applicants notified on a rolling basis starting 3/1; must reply within 3 week(s) of notification.

Academics. Special study options: Combined bachelor's/graduate degree, cooperative education, cross-registration, double major, dual enrollment of high school students, ESL, honors, independent study, internships, liberal arts/career combination, student-designed major, study abroad, teacher certification program, urban semester, weekend college. Metro-urban studies internship program; global education program in Central America, Mexico, Namibia and Norway. **Credit/placement by examination:** AP, CLEP, IB, institutional tests. 1 credit hours maximum toward bachelor's degree. **Support services:** Learning center, pre-admission summer program, reduced course load, remedial instruction, study skills assistance, tutoring, writing center.

Majors. Area/ethnic studies: Central/Eastern European, East Asian, Native American, Scandinavian, women's. **Biology:** General. **Business:** Accounting, accounting/business management, business admin, finance, international, management information systems, marketing. **Communications:** General, media studies, organizational. **Computer sciences:** Computer science. **Education:** General, biology, early childhood, elementary, emotionally handicapped, health, music, physical, secondary. **Engineering:** General. **Foreign languages:** French, German, Scandinavian, Spanish. **Health:** Clinical lab science, music therapy, nursing (RN), public health nursing. **History:** General. **Interdisciplinary:** Medieval/Renaissance. **Liberal arts:** Arts/sciences. **Math:** General. **Philosophy/religion:** Philosophy, religion. **Physical sciences:** Chemistry, physics. **Psychology:** General. **Public administration:** Social work. **Social sciences:** General, applied economics, economics, international relations, political science, sociology, urban studies. **Theology:** Youth ministry. **Visual/performing arts:** Art history/conservation, dramatic, film/cinema, music management, music performance, studio arts, theater history.

Computing on campus. 260 workstations in dormitories, library, computer center, student center. Dormitories wired for high-speed internet access and linked to campus network. Commuter students can connect to campus network. Online course registration, online library, helpline, student web hosting, wireless network available.

Student life. Freshman orientation: Available, $100 fee. Preregistration for classes offered. Students attend in June or July; lasts Friday through Saturday morning. **Housing:** Guaranteed on-campus for freshmen. Coed dorms, special housing for disabled, apartments, wellness housing available. $350 partly refundable deposit, deadline 6/1. **Activities:** Bands, campus ministries, choral groups, drama, international student organizations, literary magazine, music ensembles, radio station, student government, student newspaper, symphony orchestra, Auggie Ultimate Frisbee, art club, chemistry society, Spanish club, Muslim student association, Fellowship of Christian Athletes, Tri-Beta Biology honor society, cycling club, KAUG radio.

Athletics. NCAA. **Intercollegiate:** Baseball M, basketball, cross-country, football (tackle) M, golf, ice hockey, soccer, softball W, swimming W, tennis, track and field, volleyball W, wrestling M. **Intramural:** Basketball, softball, tennis, volleyball. **Team name:** Auggies.

Student services. Adult student services, alcohol/substance abuse counseling, chaplain/spiritual director, career counseling, student employment services, financial aid counseling, health services, minority student services, personal counseling, placement for graduates. **Physically disabled:** Services for visually, speech, hearing impaired.

Contact. E-mail: admissions@augsburg.edu
Phone: (612) 330-1001 Toll-free number: (800) 788-5678
Fax: (612) 330-1590
Carrie Carroll, Director of Admissions, Augsburg College, 2211 Riverside Avenue, Minneapolis, MN 55454

Bemidji State University

Bemidji, Minnesota
www.bemidjistate.edu **CB code: 6676**

- Public 4-year university
- Residential campus in large town
- 4,362 degree-seeking undergraduates: 24% part-time, 52% women
- 509 degree-seeking graduate students
- 83% of applicants admitted
- ACT (writing optional) required
- 49% graduate within 6 years; 15% enter graduate study

General. Founded in 1919. Regionally accredited. Arrowhead University Center located on Minnesota's Mesabi Iron Range offers several degree programs. **Degrees:** 804 bachelor's, 54 associate awarded; master's offered. **Location:** 150 miles from Duluth, 230 miles from Minneapolis-St. Paul. **Calendar:** Semester, extensive summer session. **Full-time faculty:** 192 total; 60% have terminal degrees, 6% minority, 40% women. **Part-time faculty:** 62 total; 3% have terminal degrees, 52% women. **Class size:** 57% < 20, 36% 20-39, 4% 40-49, 2% 50-99, 1% >100. **Special facilities:** Freshwater aquatics laboratory, research center, forest and nature preserve.

Freshman class profile. 2,062 applied, 1,706 admitted, 774 enrolled.

Mid 50% test scores		**Rank in top quarter:**	27%
ACT composite:	19-24	**Rank in top tenth:**	4%
GPA 3.75 or higher:	15%	**Return as sophomores:**	69%
GPA 3.50-3.74:	14%	**Out-of-state:**	2%
GPA 3.0-3.49:	35%	**Live on campus:**	75%
GPA 2.0-2.99:	33%		

Basis for selection. Rank in top half of class or test scores above 50th percentile preferred. ACT scores considered for applicants in bottom half of class. Composite score of 21 or higher preferred. Interview recommended. Audition recommended for music applicants; portfolio recommended for art applicants. **Learning Disabled:** Students encouraged to identify themselves to Office of Disabilities to be apprised of services available.

High school preparation. 16 units required. Required and recommended units include English 4, mathematics 3, social studies 3, history 1, science 3 (laboratory 1), foreign language 2 and academic electives 1. 1 unit of art, music, world culture required.

2008-2009 Annual costs. Tuition/fees: $6,996; $6,996 out-of-state. Out-of-state students pay the same rate as in-state students. Room/board: $6,024. Books/supplies: $800. Personal expenses: $1,245.

2008-2009 Financial aid. Need-based: 593 full-time freshmen applied for aid; 427 were judged to have need; 421 of these received aid. Average need met was 77%. Average scholarship/grant was $5,448; average loan $3,420. 49% of total undergraduate aid awarded as scholarships/grants, 51% as loans/jobs. **Non-need-based:** Awarded to 2,059 full-time undergraduates, including 560 freshmen. Scholarships awarded for academics, alumni affiliation, art, athletics, music/drama.

Application procedures. Admission: Priority date 8/15; no deadline. $20 fee, may be waived for applicants with need. Admission notification on a rolling basis. **Financial aid:** Priority date 5/15; no closing date. FAFSA, institutional form required. Applicants notified on a rolling basis starting 5/15.

Academics. Special study options: Accelerated study, combined bachelor's/graduate degree, cooperative education, distance learning, double major, dual enrollment of high school students, ESL, external degree, honors, independent study, internships, liberal arts/career combination, study abroad, teacher certification program. Exchange program with other Minnesota state universities, Euro-spring semester, Sino-summer semester. **Credit/placement by examination:** AP, CLEP, institutional tests. Department defined number of hours of credit by examination may be counted towards degree. **Support services:** Learning center, pre-admission summer program, reduced course load, remedial instruction, study skills assistance, tutoring, writing center.

Majors. Area/ethnic studies: Native American. **Biology:** General, marine. **Business:** Accounting, business admin. **Communications:** Journalism. **Computer sciences:** General, computer science. **Conservation:** General. **Education:** General, elementary, voc/tech. **Engineering:** Physics. **Foreign languages:** German, Spanish. **Health:** Clinical lab science, preop/surgical nursing. **History:** General. **Liberal arts:** Arts/sciences. **Math:** General. **Parks/recreation:** Health/fitness. **Philosophy/religion:** Philosophy. **Physical sciences:** Chemistry, geology, physics. **Protective services:** Criminal justice. **Psychology:** General. **Public administration:** Community org/advocacy, social work. **Social sciences:** General, economics, geography, political science, sociology. **Visual/performing arts:** Art, commercial/advertising art, dramatic.

Most popular majors. Business/marketing 19%, education 18%, engineering/engineering technologies 9%, psychology 8%, security/protective services 6%, social sciences 9%, visual/performing arts 6%.

Computing on campus. 1,600 workstations in dormitories, library, computer center, student center. Dormitories wired for high-speed internet access and linked to campus network. Commuter students can connect to campus network. Online course registration, online library, helpline, repair service, student web hosting, wireless network available.

Student life. Freshman orientation: Available, $25 fee. Preregistration for classes offered. One-day orientation for students and parents. **Policies:** Zero tolerance for discrimination, racism, sexual violence, illegal activities including drug use. **Housing:** Coed dorms, single-sex dorms, wellness housing available. $100 partly refundable deposit. Single parents hall (includes child care facilities), quiet floors, hall/dorm for students older than average age. **Activities:** Bands, campus ministries, choral groups, dance, drama, film society, international student organizations, literary magazine, music ensembles, musical theater, opera, radio station, student government, student newspaper, symphony orchestra, TV station, Newman Center, Lutheran center, Young Republicans, Young Democrats, social service organization, veterans club, Council of Indian Students, Black Student Coalition.

Athletics. NCAA. **Intercollegiate:** Baseball M, basketball, cross-country, football (tackle) M, golf, ice hockey, soccer W, softball W, tennis W, track and field, volleyball W. **Intramural:** Badminton, baseball, basketball, field hockey, football (non-tackle), golf, ice hockey, racquetball, skiing, soccer, softball, table tennis, tennis, triathlon, volleyball, weight lifting M, wrestling M. **Team name:** Beavers.

Student services. Adult student services, alcohol/substance abuse counseling, chaplain/spiritual director, career counseling, services for economically disadvantaged, student employment services, financial aid counseling, health services, minority student services, on-campus daycare, personal counseling, placement for graduates, veterans' counselor, women's services. **Physically disabled:** Services for visually, speech, hearing impaired.

Contact. E-mail: admissions@bemidjistate.edu
Phone: (218) 755-2040 Toll-free number: (800) 475-2001
Fax: (218) 755-2074
Russ Kreager, Director of Admissions, Bemidji State University, 1500 Birchmont Drive NE, D-102, Bemidji, MN 56601

Bethany Lutheran College

Mankato, Minnesota
www.blc.edu **CB code: 6035**

- Private 4-year liberal arts college affiliated with Evangelical Lutheran Synod
- Residential campus in large town
- 610 degree-seeking undergraduates: 57% women, 2% African American, 4% Asian American, 1% Hispanic American
- 83% of applicants admitted
- SAT or ACT (ACT writing recommended), application essay required
- 75% graduate within 6 years

General. Founded in 1927. Regionally accredited. **Degrees:** 97 bachelor's awarded. **ROTC:** Army. **Location:** 80 miles from Minneapolis-St. Paul. **Calendar:** Semester. **Full-time faculty:** 42 total; 43% have terminal degrees, 21% women. **Part-time faculty:** 24 total; 42% women. **Class size:** 70% < 20, 28% 20-39, less than 1% 40-49, less than 1% 50-99.

Freshman class profile. 467 applied, 387 admitted, 181 enrolled.

Mid 50% test scores		**GPA 2.0-2.99:**	20%
ACT composite:	20-26	**Rank in top quarter:**	32%
GPA 3.75 or higher:	27%	**Rank in top tenth:**	11%
GPA 3.50-3.74:	19%	**Out-of-state:**	26%
GPA 3.0-3.49:	34%	**Live on campus:**	97%

Basis for selection. College-prep GPA, overall GPA, test scores most important. **Learning Disabled:** Students with learning disabilities must meet with head of tutorial program.

High school preparation. College-preparatory program recommended. Recommended units include English 4, mathematics 3, social studies 3, history 3, science 3 (laboratory 1) and foreign language 2.

2008-2009 Annual costs. Tuition/fees: $18,710. Room/board: $5,800. Books/supplies: $800. Personal expenses: $1,500.

2007-2008 Financial aid. Need-based: 160 full-time freshmen applied for aid; 145 were judged to have need; 145 of these received aid. Average need met was 90%. Average scholarship/grant was $11,520; average loan $3,819. 67% of total undergraduate aid awarded as scholarships/grants, 33% as loans/jobs. **Non-need-based:** Awarded to 141 full-time undergraduates, including 40 freshmen. Scholarships awarded for academics, art, music/drama.

Application procedures. Admission: Closing date 7/1 (postmark date). No application fee. Admission notification on a rolling basis beginning on or about 9/15. **Financial aid:** Priority date 4/15; no closing date. FAFSA, institutional form required. Applicants notified on a rolling basis starting 3/1; must reply within 2 week(s) of notification.

Academics. Special study options: Combined bachelor's/graduate degree, cross-registration, double major, dual enrollment of high school students, independent study, internships, student-designed major, study abroad, teacher certification program. **Credit/placement by examination:** AP, CLEP, IB, SAT, ACT, institutional tests. 15 credit hours maximum toward associate degree, 15 toward bachelor's. **Support services:** Learning center, reduced course load, remedial instruction, tutoring.

Majors. Biology: Biomedical sciences. **Business:** Business admin. **Communications:** General. **Education:** Elementary. **History:** General. **Liberal arts:** Arts/sciences. **Physical sciences:** General, chemistry. **Psychology:** General. **Social sciences:** General, sociology. **Theology:** Sacred music. **Visual/performing arts:** Dramatic, studio arts.

Most popular majors. Biology 10%, business/marketing 14%, communications/journalism 16%, education 11%, English 6%, liberal arts 9%, psychology 12%, social sciences 7%, visual/performing arts 9%.

Computing on campus. 100 workstations in dormitories, library, computer center, student center. Dormitories wired for high-speed internet access and linked to campus network. Commuter students can connect to campus network. Helpline, repair service, student web hosting, wireless network available.

Student life. Freshman orientation: Mandatory. Preregistration for classes offered. **Policies:** Freshmen and sophomores not living with family required to live on campus. **Housing:** Guaranteed on-campus for all undergraduates. Single-sex dorms, apartments, wellness housing available. **Activities:** Bands, choral groups, drama, literary magazine, music ensembles, musical theater, student government, student newspaper, TV station, spiritual life committee, Lutherans for Life, student senate, Lambda Pi Eta, scholastic leadership society.

Athletics. NCAA, NCCAA. **Intercollegiate:** Baseball M, basketball, golf, soccer, softball W, tennis, volleyball W. **Intramural:** Baseball M, basketball, football (non-tackle), soccer, softball, table tennis, tennis, volleyball. **Team name:** Vikings.

Student services. Chaplain/spiritual director, career counseling, financial aid counseling, minority student services, personal counseling.

Contact. E-mail: admissions@blc.edu
Phone: (507) 344-7331 Toll-free number: (800) 944-3066
Fax: (507) 344-7376
Don Westphal, Dean of Admissions, Bethany Lutheran College, 700 Luther Drive, Mankato, MN 56001-4490

Bethel University

Saint Paul, Minnesota — **CB member**
www.bethel.edu — **CB code: 6038**

- Private 4-year university and liberal arts college affiliated with Baptist General Conference
- Residential campus in large city
- 3,302 degree-seeking undergraduates: 18% part-time, 62% women, 4% African American, 2% Asian American, 2% Hispanic American
- 1,967 degree-seeking graduate students
- 81% of applicants admitted
- SAT or ACT (ACT writing optional), application essay required
- 76% graduate within 6 years

General. Founded in 1871. Regionally accredited. **Degrees:** 769 bachelor's, 10 associate awarded; master's, doctoral offered. **ROTC:** Army, Air Force. **Location:** 10 miles from Minneapolis-St. Paul. **Calendar:** Differs by program, limited summer session. **Full-time faculty:** 174 total; 83% have terminal degrees, 14% minority, 40% women. **Part-time faculty:** 149 total; 27% have terminal degrees, 7% minority, 58% women. **Class size:** 53% < 20, 39% 20-39, 4% 40-49, 3% 50-99, less than 1% >100.

Freshman class profile. 1,945 applied, 1,583 admitted, 664 enrolled.

Mid 50% test scores		**GPA 2.0-2.99:**	13%
SAT critical reading:	510-660	**Rank in top quarter:**	59%
SAT math:	530-630	**Rank in top tenth:**	32%
SAT writing:	470-610	**End year in good standing:**	90%
ACT composite:	22-28	**Return as sophomores:**	85%
GPA 3.75 or higher:	40%	**Out-of-state:**	24%
GPA 3.50-3.74:	22%	**Live on campus:**	95%
GPA 3.0-3.49:	25%	**International:**	1%

Basis for selection. Rank in top half of class, 92 PSAT, 21 ACT, or 920 SAT (exclusive of Writing). Applicant must make personal statement regarding Christian commitment and agree to live in accordance with college's lifestyle. Interview recommended for art, drama, and music applicants; audition recommended for music applicants; portfolio recommended for art applicants.

High school preparation. College-preparatory program required. Required and recommended units include English 4, mathematics 3, social studies 4, history 2, science 3 (laboratory 2), foreign language 2, computer science 1, visual/performing arts 3 and academic electives 4.

2008-2009 Annual costs. Tuition/fees: $25,860. 2008-2009 housing for first-time students $4,540. Rate frozen as long as student continues to reside in campus housing. Room/board: $7,620. Books/supplies: $950. Personal expenses: $1,610.

2007-2008 Financial aid. Need-based: 460 full-time freshmen applied for aid; 387 were judged to have need; 387 of these received aid. Average need met was 75%. Average scholarship/grant was $12,159; average loan $4,020. 59% of total undergraduate aid awarded as scholarships/grants, 41% as loans/jobs. **Non-need-based:** Awarded to 749 full-time undergraduates, including 188 freshmen. Scholarships awarded for academics, alumni affiliation, art, leadership, music/drama, state residency.

Application procedures. Admission: Priority date 11/1; no deadline. No application fee. Admission notification on a rolling basis beginning on or about 11/1. Must reply by May 1 or within 3 week(s) if notified thereafter. **Financial aid:** Priority date 4/15; no closing date. FAFSA, institutional form required. Applicants notified on a rolling basis starting 3/1; must reply by 5/1 or within 3 week(s) of notification.

Academics. Special study options: Combined bachelor's/graduate degree, distance learning, double major, exchange student, honors, independent study, internships, liberal arts/career combination, New York semester, semester at sea, student-designed major, study abroad, teacher certification program, urban semester, Washington semester. Dual degree program for engineering science with the University of Minnesota and Washington University. Terms in South Africa, Guatemala, Spain, Australia, England, Thailand; New York Center for Art and Media Studies (NYCAMS). **Credit/placement by examination:** AP, CLEP, IB, institutional tests. 30 credit hours maximum toward associate degree, 30 toward bachelor's. **Support services:** Learning center, reduced course load, study skills assistance, tutoring, writing center.

Majors. Biology: General. **Business:** Accounting/finance, business admin, human resources, organizational behavior. **Communications:** General, journalism, media studies. **Computer sciences:** General. **Conservation:** Environmental science, environmental studies. **Education:** General, art, biology, business, chemistry, elementary, English, ESL, French, health, mathematics, music, physical, physics, social studies, Spanish. **Engineering:** Science. **Foreign languages:** French, Spanish. **Health:** Athletic training, community health services, nursing (RN). **History:** General. **Interdisciplinary:** Peace/conflict. **Math:** General. **Parks/recreation:** Exercise sciences, health/fitness. **Philosophy/religion:** Philosophy. **Physical sciences:** Chemistry, physics. **Psychology:** General. **Public administration:** Social work. **Social sciences:** General, economics, international relations, political science. **Theology:** Bible, sacred music, youth ministry. **Visual/performing arts:** Art, art history/conservation, dramatic, music performance, studio arts. **Other:** Biochemistry and molecular biology, Christian ministries, Third World studies.

Most popular majors. Biology 6%, business/marketing 15%, communications/journalism 8%, education 16%, health sciences 11%, psychology 6%.

Computing on campus. 400 workstations in dormitories, library, computer center. Dormitories wired for high-speed internet access and linked to campus network. Commuter students can connect to campus network. Online course registration, online library, helpline, student web hosting, wireless network available.

Student life. **Freshman orientation:** Mandatory. Preregistration for classes offered. 2 days prior to the start of classes. **Policies:** High moral standards stressed. Use of tobacco and alcohol prohibited. **Housing:** Guaranteed on-campus for freshmen. Coed dorms, special housing for disabled, apartments available. $150 fully refundable deposit. All campus housing is alcohol/drug/smoke free. **Activities:** Bands, campus ministries, choral groups, dance, drama, film society, international student organizations, literary magazine, music ensembles, musical theater, radio station, student government, student newspaper, symphony orchestra, United Cultures of Bethel, administrative fellowship groups, College Republicans, Habitat for Humanity, dormitory discipleship programs.

Athletics. NCAA. **Intercollegiate:** Baseball M, basketball, cross-country, football (tackle) M, golf, ice hockey, soccer, softball W, tennis, track and field, volleyball W. **Intramural:** Badminton, basketball, football (non-tackle) M, ice hockey, softball, volleyball. **Team name:** Royals.

Student services. Adult student services, alcohol/substance abuse counseling, chaplain/spiritual director, career counseling, student employment services, financial aid counseling, health services, minority student services, on-campus daycare, personal counseling, placement for graduates, women's services. **Physically disabled:** Services for visually, speech, hearing impaired.

Contact. E-mail: buadmissions-cas@bethel.edu
Phone: (651) 638-6242 Toll-free number: (800) 255-8706 ext. 6242
Fax: (651) 635-1490
Jay Fedje, Director of Admissions, Bethel University, 3900 Bethel Drive, Saint Paul, MN 55112

Brown College
Mendota Heights, Minnesota
www.browncollege.edu **CB code: 1210**

- For-profit 4-year business and liberal arts college
- Commuter campus in small city
- 1,250 degree-seeking undergraduates
- Interview required

General. Founded in 1946. Accredited by ACCSCT. **Degrees:** 116 bachelor's, 230 associate awarded. **Location:** 14 miles from Minneapolis-St. Paul. **Calendar:** Quarter, extensive summer session. **Full-time faculty:** 70 total. **Part-time faculty:** 156 total.

Basis for selection. Open admission. ACCUPLACER Test required in lieu of other tests. **Learning Disabled:** IEP's and/or other requests for ADA-level accomodations accepted. Eligible students must complete brief Application for Auxiliary Aid and return with any supporting documentation available well in advance of enrollment.

High school preparation. Recommended units include English 4, mathematics 2 and science 1.

2008-2009 Annual costs. Tuition/fees: $16,835. Books/supplies: $2,000. Personal expenses: $1,600.

Financial aid. **Non-need-based:** Scholarships awarded for academics.

Application procedures. **Admission:** No deadline. $50 fee. Admission notification on a rolling basis beginning on or about 1/1. **Financial aid:** Priority date 7/1; no closing date. FAFSA, institutional form required. Applicants notified on a rolling basis starting 1/1; must reply within 2 week(s) of notification.

Academics. **Special study options:** Cooperative education, internships, liberal arts/career combination. **Credit/placement by examination:** AP, CLEP, institutional tests. **Support services:** Learning center, reduced course load, remedial instruction, study skills assistance, tutoring, writing center.

Majors. **Business:** General. **Communications:** General. **Communications technology:** Graphics. **Computer sciences:** Information systems, information technology. **Protective services:** Criminal justice. **Visual/performing arts:** Design.

Computing on campus. PC or laptop required. 231 workstations in library, computer center. Commuter students can connect to campus network. Online course registration, online library, helpline, repair service, wireless network available.

Student life. **Freshman orientation:** Mandatory. **Housing:** Apartments available. **Activities:** Radio station, student government, student senate, Campus Crusade for Christ, minority students club.

Athletics. **Intramural:** Football (non-tackle) M.

Student services. Adult student services, career counseling, student employment services, financial aid counseling, placement for graduates.

Contact. E-mail: info@browncollege.edu
Phone: (651) 905-3240 Toll-free number: (800) 627-6966 ext. 240
Fax: (651) 905-3540
William Cowan, Admissions Director, Brown College, 1440 Northland Drive, Mendota Heights, MN 55120

Capella University
Minneapolis, Minnesota
www.capella.edu **CB code: 3829**

- For-profit 4-year virtual university
- Very large city
- 4,103 degree-seeking undergraduates: 78% part-time, 55% women, 15% African American, 2% Asian American, 4% Hispanic American, 1% Native American, 1% international
- 20,868 degree-seeking graduate students

General. Regionally accredited. **Degrees:** 466 bachelor's awarded; master's, doctoral offered. **Calendar:** Quarter, extensive summer session.

Basis for selection. Open admission, but selective for some programs. Applicants must be at least 24 years of age unless in military or unless they enter with 90 college level credits from previous institution. Bachelor's programs are completion programs for students who have associate's degree or at least 90 quarter credits of undergraduate coursework completed.

2008-2009 Annual costs. Tuition/fees: $13,950.

Application procedures. **Admission:** No deadline. $75 fee. Admission notification on a rolling basis.

Academics. 16 degree programs, 82 specializations, 16 certificate programs. **Special study options:** Combined bachelor's/graduate degree. **Credit/placement by examination:** AP, CLEP, IB. **Support services:** Learning center.

Majors. **Business:** Accounting, finance, human resources, marketing. **Computer sciences:** Computer graphics, information technology, LAN/WAN management, security, web page design.

Most popular majors. Business/marketing 39%, computer/information sciences 61%.

Computing on campus. PC or laptop required.

Student life. **Freshman orientation:** Available. Preregistration for classes offered. Online seminar that provides students with knowledge, skills, and advice needed to be successful in Capella's online environment.

Student services. Adult student services, career counseling, financial aid counseling. **Physically disabled:** Services for visually, hearing impaired.

Contact. E-mail: info@capella.edu
Phone: (888) 227-2736
Capella University, 225 South Sixth Street, 9th Floor, Minneapolis, MN 55402

Carleton College
Northfield, Minnesota **CB member**
www.carleton.edu **CB code: 6081**

- Private 4-year liberal arts college
- Residential campus in large town
- 1,975 degree-seeking undergraduates: 52% women, 5% African American, 10% Asian American, 5% Hispanic American, 1% Native American, 6% international
- 27% of applicants admitted
- SAT or ACT with writing, application essay required
- 93% graduate within 6 years; 23% enter graduate study

General. Founded in 1866. Regionally accredited. Interest in sustainability initiatives - green roofs, eco-building class, eco house built by students, 1.65 megawatt wind turbine. **Degrees:** 461 bachelor's awarded. **Location:** 35 miles from Minneapolis-St. Paul. **Calendar:** Trimester. **Full-time faculty:** 215 total; 96% have terminal degrees, 21% minority, 45% women. **Part-time faculty:** 17 total; 65% have terminal degrees, 6% minority, 47% women. **Class size:** 66% < 20, 31% 20-39, 3% 40-49, less than 1% 50-99. **Special facilities:** 955 acre arboretum, 35 acre virgin prairie, greenhouse, observatory, scanning and transmission electron microscope, refractor and reflector telescopes, nuclear magnet resonance spectrometer.

Freshman class profile. 4,956 applied, 1,361 admitted, 490 enrolled.

Mid 50% test scores			
SAT critical reading:	650-750	Rank in top tenth:	74%
SAT math:	660-740	Return as sophomores:	95%
SAT writing:	650-730	Out-of-state:	77%
ACT composite:	29-33	Live on campus:	100%
Rank in top quarter:	96%	International:	7%

Basis for selection. School achievement record and recommendations most important. Test scores, extracurricular school and community activities also important. SAT Subject Tests recommended. Interview recommended. **Learning Disabled:** Untimed standardized tests and GED accepted.

High school preparation. College-preparatory program recommended. Recommended units include English 4, mathematics 3, social studies 3, science 3 (laboratory 1) and foreign language 3. 3 units distributed between history and social sciences recommended.

2008-2009 Annual costs. Tuition/fees: $38,046. Room/board: $9,993.

2007-2008 Financial aid. Need-based: 378 full-time freshmen applied for aid; 264 were judged to have need; 264 of these received aid. Average need met was 100%. Average scholarship/grant was $29,064; average loan $3,896. 76% of total undergraduate aid awarded as scholarships/grants, 24% as loans/jobs. **Non-need-based:** Awarded to 362 full-time undergraduates, including 81 freshmen. Scholarships awarded for academics. **Additional information:** Full financial need of all admitted applicants met through combination of work, loans, grants. Carleton Access Scholarship reduces loans for incoming students whose family income is below $75,000.

Application procedures. Admission: Closing date 1/15 (postmark date). $30 fee, may be waived for applicants with need, free for online applicants. Admission notification 4/15. Must reply by May 1 or within 2 week(s) if notified thereafter. **Financial aid:** Priority date 2/15, closing date 2/15. FAFSA, CSS PROFILE required. Applicants notified by 4/1; must reply by 5/1 or within 2 week(s) of notification.

Academics. 15-20 freshman seminars offered, enrollment limited to 15 students each. **Special study options:** Accelerated study, cross-registration, double major, dual enrollment of high school students, independent study, internships, student-designed major, study abroad, teacher certification program, urban semester. **Credit/placement by examination:** AP, CLEP, IB, institutional tests. 36 credit hours maximum toward bachelor's degree. **Support services:** Learning center, tutoring, writing center.

Majors. Area/ethnic studies: African, African-American, American, Asian, Latin American, Russian/Slavic, women's. **Biology:** General. **Computer sciences:** Computer science. **Foreign languages:** Ancient Greek, classics, French, German, Hebrew, Latin, Romance, Russian, Spanish. **History:** General. **Interdisciplinary:** Math/computer science. **Math:** General. **Philosophy/religion:** Philosophy, religion. **Physical sciences:** Chemistry, geology, physics. **Psychology:** General. **Social sciences:** Anthropology, economics, international relations, political science, sociology. **Visual/performing arts:** Art history/conservation, studio arts.

Most popular majors. Biology 12%, English 7%, history 8%, physical sciences 13%, psychology 8%, social sciences 27%, visual/performing arts 7%.

Computing on campus. 300 workstations in library, computer center, student center. Dormitories wired for high-speed internet access and linked to campus network. Online course registration, online library, helpline, repair service, student web hosting, wireless network available.

Student life. Freshman orientation: Mandatory. Preregistration for classes offered. 4 days prior to start of fall classes. **Housing:** Guaranteed on-campus for all undergraduates. Coed dorms, special housing for disabled, apartments, wellness housing available. 25 college-owned houses within 2 blocks of campus, some coeducational, with varying board options. Several for special interest groups. **Activities:** Bands, campus ministries, choral groups, dance, drama, film society, international student organizations, literary magazine, music ensembles, Model UN, musical theater, radio station, student government, student newspaper, symphony orchestra, 132 registered student organizations.

Athletics. NCAA. **Intercollegiate:** Baseball M, basketball, cross-country, diving, football (tackle) M, golf, soccer, softball W, swimming, synchronized swimming W, tennis, track and field, volleyball W, wrestling M. **Intramural:** Basketball, ice hockey, racquetball, soccer, softball, table tennis, tennis, triathlon, volleyball. **Team name:** Knights.

Student services. Alcohol/substance abuse counseling, chaplain/spiritual director, career counseling, student employment services, financial aid counseling, health services, minority student services, personal counseling, placement for graduates, women's services. **Physically disabled:** Services for visually, hearing impaired.

Contact. E-mail: admissions@carleton.edu
Phone: (507) 222-4190 Toll-free number: (800) 995-2275
Fax: (507) 222-4526
Paul Thiboutot, Dean of Admissions, Carleton College, 100 South College Street, Northfield, MN 55057

College of St. Benedict
St. Joseph, Minnesota **CB member**
www.csbsju.edu **CB code: 6104**

- Private 4-year liberal arts college for women affiliated with Roman Catholic Church
- Residential campus in small town
- 2,068 degree-seeking undergraduates: 100% women, 1% African American, 3% Asian American, 2% Hispanic American, 6% international
- 75% of applicants admitted
- SAT or ACT (ACT writing optional), application essay required
- 84% graduate within 6 years; 38% enter graduate study

General. Founded in 1887. Regionally accredited. CSB located six miles from St. John's University; students enrolled on both campuses have access to classes, activities held by the two institutions. **Degrees:** 434 bachelor's awarded. **ROTC:** Army. **Location:** 10 miles from St. Cloud, 70 miles from Minneapolis-St. Paul. **Calendar:** Semester, limited summer session. **Full-time faculty:** 156 total; 85% have terminal degrees, 8% minority, 48% women. **Part-time faculty:** 35 total; 31% have terminal degrees, 6% minority, 37% women. **Class size:** 49% < 20, 51% 20-39, less than 1% 40-49, less than 1% 50-99. **Special facilities:** Observatory, ecumenical center, museum and manuscript library, liturgical press, nature preserve, arboretum, natural history museum, pottery kiln.

Freshman class profile. 1,737 applied, 1,305 admitted, 519 enrolled.

Mid 50% test scores			
SAT critical reading:	510-660	Rank in top quarter:	76%
SAT math:	520-670	Rank in top tenth:	64%
ACT composite:	23-28	End year in good standing:	99%
GPA 3.75 or higher:	58%	Return as sophomores:	90%
GPA 3.50-3.74:	26%	Out-of-state:	13%
GPA 3.0-3.49:	15%	Live on campus:	100%
GPA 2.0-2.99:	1%	International:	6%

Basis for selection. Course selection, scholastic achievement, GPA, test scores and essay are most important. Extracurricular involvement, high school rank, and recommendation are also important. Students who have completed the application process by 11/15 will receive notification of their scholarship award on 12/20. Those that complete the application process by 12/15 will recieve notification of their scholarship award on 2/1. Interview recommended for conditionally accepted/academically weak applicants. **Homeschooled:** Applicants are not required to have a high school diploma but are required to provide appropriate documentation of college preparatory curriculum.

High school preparation. College-preparatory program required. 15 units required. Required and recommended units include English 4, mathematics 3, social studies 2, science 2 (laboratory 2), foreign language 2 and academic electives 4.

2008-2009 Annual costs. Tuition/fees: $28,668. Room/board: $7,959. Books/supplies: $800. Personal expenses: $700.

2008-2009 Financial aid. Need-based: 419 full-time freshmen applied for aid; 340 were judged to have need; 340 of these received aid. Average need met was 93%. Average scholarship/grant was $17,550; average loan $4,540. 59% of total undergraduate aid awarded as scholarships/grants, 41% as loans/jobs. **Non-need-based:** Awarded to 1,908 full-time undergraduates, including 478 freshmen. Scholarships awarded for academics, art, leadership, music/drama, ROTC.

Application procedures. Admission: Priority date 11/15; no deadline. No application fee. Admission notification on a rolling basis. A nonrefundable enrollment deposit of $300 is due by May 1. **Financial aid:** Priority date 3/15; no closing date. FAFSA, institutional form required. Applicants notified on a rolling basis starting 3/15; must reply by 5/1.

Academics. Special study options: Combined bachelor's/graduate degree, cross-registration, double major, dual enrollment of high school students, ESL, exchange student, honors, independent study, internships, student-designed major, study abroad, teacher certification program, United Nations semester. 3-2 program in engineering with University of Minnesota, 3-1 program in dentistry with University of Minnesota, cross registration with St. Cloud State University. **Credit/placement by examination:** AP, CLEP, IB, institutional tests. **Support services:** Study skills assistance, tutoring, writing center.

Majors. Area/ethnic studies: Women's. **Biology:** General, biochemistry. **Business:** Accounting, business admin. **Computer sciences:** Computer science. **Conservation:** Environmental studies. **Education:** General, elementary. **Foreign languages:** Classics, French, German, Spanish. **Health:** Dietetics, nursing (RN), predental, premedicine, prepharmacy, preveterinary. **History:** General. **Interdisciplinary:** Biological/physical sciences, math/computer science, natural sciences, nutrition sciences, peace/conflict. **Legal studies:** Prelaw. **Liberal arts:** Arts/sciences, humanities. **Math:** General. **Philosophy/religion:** Philosophy. **Physical sciences:** Chemistry, physics. **Psychology:** General. **Public administration:** Social work. **Social sciences:** General, economics, political science, sociology. **Theology:** Theology. **Visual/performing arts:** Art, dramatic.

Most popular majors. Biology 9%, business/marketing 11%, education 6%, English 19%, foreign language 8%, health sciences 11%, psychology 12%, social sciences 6%.

Computing on campus. 791 workstations in dormitories, library, computer center, student center. Dormitories wired for high-speed internet access and linked to campus network. Commuter students can connect to campus network. Online course registration, helpline, repair service, student web hosting, wireless network available.

Student life. Freshman orientation: Mandatory. Preregistration for classes offered. Fall orientation begins the evening of move-in day and concludes with convocation the first day of classes. **Policies:** Freshmen and sophomores are required to live on campus. **Housing:** Guaranteed on-campus for freshmen. Special housing for disabled, apartments, wellness housing available. Global initiative group house available. **Activities:** Bands, campus ministries, choral groups, dance, drama, international student organizations, literary magazine, music ensembles, Model UN, musical theater, opera, radio station, student government, student newspaper, symphony orchestra, Volunteers in Service to Others, College Republicans, College Democrats, Joints Events Council, Asia Club, Student Coalition for Global Solidarity, Students in Free Enterprise, Magis, Cultural Fusion Club, Outdoor Leadership Center.

Athletics. NCAA. **Intercollegiate:** Basketball W, cross-country W, diving W, golf W, ice hockey W, skiing W, soccer W, softball W, swimming W, tennis W, track and field W, volleyball W. **Intramural:** Badminton W, basketball W, racquetball W, soccer W, softball W, table tennis W, tennis W, volleyball W. **Team name:** Blazers.

Student services. Alcohol/substance abuse counseling, chaplain/spiritual director, career counseling, student employment services, financial aid counseling, health services, minority student services, personal counseling, placement for graduates, women's services. **Physically disabled:** Services for hearing impaired.

Contact. E-mail: admissions@csbsju.edu
Phone: (320) 363-2196 Toll-free number: (800) 544-1489
Fax: (320) 363-2750
Jon McGee, Vice President of Enrollment, Planning & Public Affairs, College of St. Benedict, PO Box 7155, Collegeville, MN 56321-7155

College of St. Catherine

St. Paul, Minnesota — **CB member**
www.stkate.edu — **CB code: 6105**

- Private 4-year health science and liberal arts college for women affiliated with Roman Catholic Church
- Commuter campus in large city
- 3,636 degree-seeking undergraduates: 34% part-time, 97% women, 11% African American, 8% Asian American, 3% Hispanic American, 1% Native American, 1% international
- 1,417 degree-seeking graduate students
- 77% of applicants admitted
- SAT or ACT (ACT writing optional) required
- 59% graduate within 6 years

General. Founded in 1905. Regionally accredited. Men may attend classes through cross-registration. Traditional day, weekend and graduate programs offered on St. Paul campus. 2-year associate's program in various health professions at Minneapolis campus. **Degrees:** 518 bachelor's, 191 associate awarded; master's, doctoral offered. **ROTC:** Army, Air Force. **Location:** 6 miles from downtown. **Calendar:** 4-1-4, extensive summer session. **Full-time faculty:** 271 total; 80% women. **Part-time faculty:** 29 total. **Class size:** 61% < 20, 34% 20-39, 2% 40-49, 3% 50-99. **Special facilities:** Center for women's research, observatory.

Freshman class profile. 1,528 applied, 1,177 admitted, 362 enrolled.

Mid 50% test scores		**Rank in top quarter:**	60%
ACT composite:	22-26	**Rank in top tenth:**	33%
GPA 3.75 or higher:	40%	**Return as sophomores:**	76%
GPA 3.50-3.74:	22%	**Out-of-state:**	10%
GPA 3.0-3.49:	29%	**Live on campus:**	81%
GPA 2.0-2.99:	9%	**International:**	2%

Basis for selection. School achievement record with rank in top half of class and test scores important. Extracurricular and community involvement also considered. Recommendations important. Interview recommended for all applicants, required for marginal students. Audition recommended for music students; portfolio recommended for art students. Essay recommended for marginal students.

High school preparation. College-preparatory program recommended. 15 units recommended. Recommended units include English 4, mathematics 3, social studies 2, science 2 and foreign language 4.

2008-2009 Annual costs. Tuition/fees: $25,803. Room/board: $7,090. Books/supplies: $625. Personal expenses: $400.

2007-2008 Financial aid. Non-need-based: Scholarships awarded for academics, alumni affiliation, leadership. **Additional information:** Audition required for music scholarships.

Application procedures. Admission: No deadline. No application fee. Admission notification on a rolling basis. Students must be accepted by 02/01 to be eligible to compete in merit scholarship competition. **Financial aid:** Priority date 4/15; no closing date. FAFSA, institutional form required. Applicants notified on a rolling basis starting 3/30; must reply within 2 week(s) of notification.

Academics. Special study options: Combined bachelor's/graduate degree, cross-registration, double major, dual enrollment of high school students, exchange student, honors, independent study, internships, student-designed major, study abroad, urban semester, Washington semester, weekend college. Cooperative program in fashion merchandising with Fashion Institute of Technology in New York City and Fashion Institute of Design in Los Angeles, academic year of study in New York City, exchange program with other Carondolet Colleges, internship program includes over 500 sites in Twin Cities area. **Credit/placement by examination:** AP, CLEP, IB, institutional tests. 32 credit hours maximum toward bachelor's degree. **Support services:** Learning center, reduced course load, study skills assistance, tutoring, writing center.

Majors. Area/ethnic studies: Women's. **Biology:** General, biochemistry. **Business:** Accounting, business admin, fashion, international, management information systems, sales/distribution. **Communications:** General. **Computer sciences:** General, information systems. **Education:** General, art, business, early childhood, elementary, English, family/consumer sciences, foreign languages, mathematics, middle, music, physical, secondary. **Family/consumer sciences:** General, food/nutrition. **Foreign languages:** American Sign Language, French, sign language interpretation, Spanish. **Health:** Dietetics, medical records admin, nursing (RN), predental, premedicine, prepharmacy, preveterinary, respiratory therapy technology. **History:** General. **Interdisciplinary:** Intercultural. **Legal studies:** Prelaw. **Math:** General. **Parks/recreation:** Exercise sciences. **Philosophy/religion:** Philosophy. **Physical**

sciences: Chemistry, physics. **Psychology:** General. **Public administration:** Social work. **Social sciences:** General, economics, international relations, political science, sociology. **Theology:** Theology. **Visual/performing arts:** Art history/conservation, dramatic, fashion design, music performance, studio arts.

Most popular majors. Business/marketing 14%, education 7%, English 7%, health sciences 26%, public administration/social services 6%, social sciences 7%.

Computing on campus. 350 workstations in dormitories, library, computer center, student center. Dormitories wired for high-speed internet access and linked to campus network. Commuter students can connect to campus network. Online course registration, online library, helpline available.

Student life. **Freshman orientation:** Mandatory. **Housing:** Guaranteed on-campus for freshmen. Apartments available. $100 deposit. Apartments for student-parents available. **Activities:** Campus ministries, choral groups, drama, literary magazine, music ensembles, musical theater, student government, student newspaper, Volunteers in Action, League of Women Voters, Minnesota Public Interest Research Group, Women of Color, clubs for majors, women's issues groups.

Athletics. NCAA. **Intercollegiate:** Basketball W, cross-country W, diving W, ice hockey W, soccer W, softball W, swimming W, tennis W, track and field W, volleyball W. **Intramural:** Basketball W, cheerleading W, football (non-tackle) W, golf W, lacrosse W, racquetball W, soccer W, softball W, tennis W, volleyball W. **Team name:** Wildcats.

Student services. Adult student services, chaplain/spiritual director, career counseling, student employment services, financial aid counseling, health services, minority student services, on-campus daycare, personal counseling, placement for graduates, women's services. **Physically disabled:** Services for visually, speech, hearing impaired.

Contact. E-mail: admissions@stkate.edu
Phone: (651) 690-8850 Toll-free number: (800) 945-4599
Fax: (651) 690-8824
Brian Bruess, Vice President of Enrollment Management and Dean of Students, College of St. Catherine, 2004 Randolph Avenue #4-02, St. Paul, MN 55105

College of St. Scholastica

Duluth, Minnesota — **CB member**
www.css.edu — **CB code: 6107**

- Private 4-year liberal arts college affiliated with Roman Catholic Church
- Residential campus in small city
- 2,138 degree-seeking undergraduates: 2% part-time, 68% women, 2% African American, 2% Asian American, 1% Hispanic American, 3% Native American, 4% international
- 800 degree-seeking graduate students
- 83% of applicants admitted
- SAT or ACT (ACT writing optional) required
- 66% graduate within 6 years; 27% enter graduate study

General. Founded in 1912. Regionally accredited. **Degrees:** 680 bachelor's awarded; master's, doctoral offered. **ROTC:** Air Force. **Location:** 2 miles from downtown, 150 miles from Minneapolis-St. Paul. **Calendar:** Semester, limited summer session. **Full-time faculty:** 161 total; 58% have terminal degrees, 8% minority, 59% women. **Part-time faculty:** 120 total; 22% have terminal degrees, 6% minority, 68% women. **Class size:** 49% < 20, 45% 20-39, 3% 40-49, 2% 50-99, 1% >100. **Special facilities:** Wellness center with climbing wall.

Freshman class profile. 1,899 applied, 1,584 admitted, 571 enrolled.

Mid 50% test scores		**GPA 2.0-2.99:**	15%
SAT critical reading:	460-580	**Rank in top quarter:**	51%
SAT math:	500-620	**Rank in top tenth:**	22%
SAT writing:	460-580	**End year in good standing:**	91%
ACT composite:	20-25	**Return as sophomores:**	83%
GPA 3.75 or higher:	32%	**Out-of-state:**	16%
GPA 3.50-3.74:	21%	**Live on campus:**	81%
GPA 3.0-3.49:	32%	**International:**	4%

Basis for selection. School achievement record and test scores most important. Interview recommended.

High school preparation. College-preparatory program recommended. Recommended units include English 4, mathematics 2, social studies 3, history 3, science 3 and foreign language 3.

2008-2009 Annual costs. Tuition/fees: $26,489. Room/board: $6,972. Books/supplies: $1,000. Personal expenses: $1,054.

2008-2009 Financial aid. **Need-based:** Average need met was 78%. Average scholarship/grant was $6,458; average loan $3,122. 56% of total undergraduate aid awarded as scholarships/grants, 44% as loans/jobs. **Non-need-based:** Scholarships awarded for academics, alumni affiliation, ROTC.

Application procedures. **Admission:** No deadline. $25 fee, may be waived for applicants with need, free for online applicants. Admission notification on a rolling basis beginning on or about 9/1. Must reply by May 1 or within 2 week(s) if notified thereafter. **Financial aid:** Priority date 3/15; no closing date. FAFSA required. Applicants notified on a rolling basis starting 3/1; must reply by 5/1 or within 2 week(s) of notification.

Academics. **Special study options:** Accelerated study, combined bachelor's/graduate degree, cross-registration, distance learning, double major, dual enrollment of high school students, external degree, honors, independent study, internships, liberal arts/career combination, student-designed major, study abroad, teacher certification program, Washington semester. **Credit/placement by examination:** AP, CLEP, IB, ACT, institutional tests. 96 credit hours maximum toward bachelor's degree. All external credit meeting score expectations will be accepted; last 32 semester hours must be completed in residence. **Support services:** Pre-admission summer program, reduced course load, study skills assistance, tutoring, writing center.

Honors college/program. Should meet 2 of the following: top 15% of high school class, 26 ACT or 1100 (exclusive of Writing) SAT, GPA of 3.5; others may apply by contacting the honors director. Students must complete 20 honors credits, at least 8 of which are upper-level credits.

Majors. **Biology:** General, biochemistry, exercise physiology. **Business:** Accounting, business admin, finance, marketing, organizational behavior. **Communications:** General, advertising, journalism. **Computer sciences:** General. **Education:** Elementary, multi-level teacher, school librarian, social science. **Foreign languages:** Spanish. **Health:** Health services, medical records admin, nursing (RN). **History:** General. **Interdisciplinary:** Global studies. **Liberal arts:** Humanities. **Math:** General. **Philosophy/religion:** Christian, religion. **Physical sciences:** Chemistry. **Psychology:** General. **Public administration:** Social work. **Social sciences:** General, applied economics. **Visual/performing arts:** Art, music performance.

Most popular majors. Biology 8%, business/marketing 31%, computer/information sciences 6%, health sciences 32%, social sciences 6%.

Computing on campus. 222 workstations in dormitories, library, computer center, student center. Dormitories wired for high-speed internet access and linked to campus network. Commuter students can connect to campus network. Online course registration, online library, helpline, student web hosting, wireless network available.

Student life. **Freshman orientation:** Mandatory. Preregistration for classes offered. **Housing:** Guaranteed on-campus for freshmen. Coed dorms, special housing for disabled, apartments, wellness housing available. $150 fully refundable deposit, deadline 5/1. Quiet or study wing; apartments for students with dependent children. **Activities:** Bands, campus ministries, choral groups, dance, drama, international student organizations, literary magazine, music ensembles, student government, student newspaper, TV station, Circle-K, InterVarsity Christian Fellowship, Indigenous Students' Association, Benedictine Friends,Volunteers Involved Through Action, Amnesty International, Kaleidoscope Multicultural Club, Habitat for Humanity, United for Africa, Earth Action.

Athletics. NCAA. **Intercollegiate:** Baseball M, basketball, cross-country, football (tackle) M, ice hockey M, skiing, soccer, softball W, tennis, track and field, volleyball W. **Intramural:** Badminton, basketball, bowling, football (non-tackle), tennis, volleyball. **Team name:** Saints.

Student services. Adult student services, alcohol/substance abuse counseling, chaplain/spiritual director, career counseling, student employment services, financial aid counseling, health services, minority student services, personal counseling, placement for graduates, veterans' counselor, women's services. **Physically disabled:** Services for visually, hearing impaired.

Contact. E-mail: admissions@css.edu
Phone: (218) 723-6046 Toll-free number: (800) 249-6412
Fax: (218) 723-5991
Eric Berg, Vice President for Enrollment Management, College of St. Scholastica, 1200 Kenwood Avenue, Duluth, MN 55811-4199

College of Visual Arts

Saint Paul, Minnesota
www.cva.edu — **CB code: 6147**

- Private 4-year visual arts college
- Commuter campus in large city

- 186 degree-seeking undergraduates: 3% part-time, 62% women
- 72% of applicants admitted
- SAT or ACT (ACT writing optional), application essay required
- 40% graduate within 6 years

General. Founded in 1924. Regionally accredited. **Degrees:** 32 bachelor's awarded. **Calendar:** Semester, limited summer session. **Full-time faculty:** 7 total; 29% have terminal degrees, 71% women. **Part-time faculty:** 43 total; 12% have terminal degrees, 2% minority, 44% women. **Class size:** 92% < 20, 8% 20-39. **Special facilities:** Exhibition gallery, photography facilities, sculpture studio, printmaking studio, drawing studio, painting studio.

Freshman class profile. 160 applied, 115 admitted, 64 enrolled.

Mid 50% test scores		**Return as sophomores:**	61%
ACT composite:	19-25	**Out-of-state:**	11%
End year in good standing:	80%		

Basis for selection. Statement of interest, test scores, transcript and portfolio very important. Students with 30+ college credits are not required to submit ACT/SAT scores. Review of portfolio required. **Homeschooled:** Transcript of courses and grades required. List of classes, textbooks used. **Learning Disabled:** Documentation of disabilities required.

High school preparation. Recommended units include English 4, mathematics 4, social studies 4, science 4 and foreign language 2. Progression of classes in art preferred.

2008-2009 Annual costs. Tuition/fees: $22,426. Books/supplies: $2,334.

2008-2009 Financial aid. **Need-based:** Average scholarship/grant was $8,468; average loan $3,420. 41% of total undergraduate aid awarded as scholarships/grants, 59% as loans/jobs. **Non-need-based:** Scholarships awarded for academics, art.

Application procedures. **Admission:** Priority date 3/9; no deadline. $40 fee, may be waived for applicants with need. Admission notification on a rolling basis. Must reply by May 1 or within 2 week(s) if notified thereafter. **Financial aid:** Priority date 3/1; no closing date. FAFSA, institutional form required. Applicants notified on a rolling basis starting 2/15; must reply within 2 week(s) of notification.

Academics. **Special study options:** Honors, independent study, internships, study abroad. **Credit/placement by examination:** AP, CLEP. **Support services:** Learning center, study skills assistance, tutoring, writing center.

Majors. **Visual/performing arts:** Commercial/advertising art, design, drawing, illustration, painting, photography, printmaking, sculpture, studio arts.

Computing on campus. 50 workstations in library, computer center. Online library, helpline available.

Student life. **Freshman orientation:** Mandatory. Preregistration for classes offered. **Housing:** Housing coordinator and roommate matching services. **Activities:** Student government.

Student services. Alcohol/substance abuse counseling, career counseling, services for economically disadvantaged, student employment services, financial aid counseling, minority student services, personal counseling, placement for graduates.

Contact. E-mail: admissions@cva.edu
Phone: (651) 757-4040 Toll-free number: (800) 224-1536
Fax: (651) 757-4010
Susan Ant, Executive Director of Enrollment, College of Visual Arts, 344 Summit Avenue, Saint Paul, MN 55102-2199

Concordia College: Moorhead

Moorhead, Minnesota — **CB member**
www.concordiacollege.edu — **CB code: 6113**

- Private 4-year liberal arts college affiliated with Evangelical Lutheran Church in America
- Residential campus in small city
- 2,745 degree-seeking undergraduates: 1% part-time, 61% women, 1% African American, 2% Asian American, 1% Hispanic American, 4% international
- 13 degree-seeking graduate students
- 78% of applicants admitted
- SAT or ACT (ACT writing optional) required
- 65% graduate within 6 years

General. Founded in 1891. Regionally accredited. **Degrees:** 611 bachelor's awarded; master's offered. **ROTC:** Army, Air Force. **Location:** 234 miles from Minneapolis-St. Paul, 1 mile from Fargo, North Dakota. **Calendar:** Semester, limited summer session. **Full-time faculty:** 190 total; 77% have terminal degrees, 7% minority, 42% women. **Part-time faculty:** 76 total; 7% have terminal degrees, 57% women. **Class size:** 45% < 20, 51% 20-39, 3% 40-49, 2% 50-99. **Special facilities:** Observatory, microparticle accelerator, language villages, television production studio, biology research facility, nursing lab.

Freshman class profile. 2,885 applied, 2,262 admitted, 776 enrolled.

Mid 50% test scores		**GPA 2.0-2.99:**	9%
SAT critical reading:	520-640	**Rank in top quarter:**	63%
SAT math:	540-660	**Rank in top tenth:**	33%
SAT writing:	490-630	**Return as sophomores:**	83%
ACT composite:	22-28	**Out-of-state:**	30%
GPA 3.75 or higher:	45%	**Live on campus:**	97%
GPA 3.50-3.74:	21%	**International:**	3%
GPA 3.0-3.49:	25%		

Basis for selection. Academic record (types of courses and grades) most important, followed by test scores and recommendations. Interview recommended.

High school preparation. College-preparatory program recommended. Recommended units include English 4, mathematics 3, social studies 3, science 3 and foreign language 2. Computer science and exposure to fine arts recommended.

2008-2009 Annual costs. Tuition/fees: $24,120. Room/board: $6,160. Books/supplies: $740. Personal expenses: $1,170.

2007-2008 Financial aid. All financial aid based on need. 721 full-time freshmen applied for aid; 567 were judged to have need; 567 of these received aid. Average need met was 91%. Average scholarship/grant was $13,156; average loan $4,046. 63% of total undergraduate aid awarded as scholarships/grants, 37% as loans/jobs. **Additional information:** Students in ACCORD program (age 25 and older) may apply for tuition reductions for first 4 courses.

Application procedures. **Admission:** No deadline. $20 fee, may be waived for applicants with need, free for online applicants. Admission notification on a rolling basis beginning on or about 6/15. **Financial aid:** Priority date 4/15; no closing date. FAFSA, institutional form required. Applicants notified on a rolling basis starting 3/1.

Academics. **Special study options:** Cooperative education, cross-registration, distance learning, double major, exchange student, honors, independent study, internships, semester at sea, study abroad, teacher certification program, urban semester, Washington semester. Urban studies program in Chicago, Lutheran Consortium with Dar es Salaam University in Tanzania; master of science in nursing offered through consortium with Minnesota State University Moorhead and North Dakota State University. **Credit/placement by examination:** AP, CLEP, IB, SAT, ACT, institutional tests. 20 credit hours maximum toward bachelor's degree. **Support services:** Learning center, reduced course load, study skills assistance, tutoring, writing center.

Majors. **Area/ethnic studies:** French, German, Russian/Slavic, Scandinavian, Spanish/Iberian. **Biology:** General. **Business:** General, accounting, business admin, international, office management. **Communications:** General, advertising, broadcast journalism, journalism, media studies, public relations. **Computer sciences:** Computer science. **Conservation:** Environmental studies. **Education:** General, art, biology, business, chemistry, elementary, English, French, German, health, history, Latin, mathematics, music, physical, physics, science, secondary, social science, social studies, Spanish, speech. **Family/consumer sciences:** General, clothing/textiles, family studies, food/nutrition. **Foreign languages:** Classics, French, German, Latin, Russian, Scandinavian, Spanish. **Health:** Clinical lab science, facilities admin, health care admin, nursing (RN), predental, premedicine, prepharmacy, preveterinary. **History:** General. **Interdisciplinary:** Math/computer science. **Legal studies:** Prelaw. **Liberal arts:** Arts/sciences. **Math:** General, applied. **Parks/recreation:** Exercise sciences, health/fitness. **Philosophy/religion:** Philosophy, religion. **Physical sciences:** Chemistry, physics. **Psychology:** General. **Public administration:** Social work. **Social sciences:** Economics, international relations, political science, sociology. **Theology:** Theology. **Visual/performing arts:** Art, art history/conservation, conducting, dramatic, music performance, piano/organ, studio arts, voice/opera.

Most popular majors. Biology 8%, business/marketing 11%, communications/journalism 11%, education 13%, foreign language 9%, psychology 6%, social sciences 7%, visual/performing arts 6%.

Computing on campus. 453 workstations in dormitories, library, computer center, student center. Dormitories wired for high-speed internet access and linked to campus network. Commuter students can connect to campus network. Online library, repair service, student web hosting, wireless network available.

Student life. **Freshman orientation:** Mandatory. Preregistration for classes offered. 4-day program one week prior to fall semester. **Housing:** Guaranteed on-campus for freshmen. Coed dorms, single-sex dorms, apartments, wellness housing available. $200 fully refundable deposit, deadline 8/1. Students studying Spanish, French, or German have opportunity to live with native speakers in campus apartments. **Activities:** Bands, choral groups, dance, drama, literary magazine, music ensembles, musical theater, radio station, student government, student newspaper, TV station, Over 100 clubs and organizations.

Athletics. NCAA. **Intercollegiate:** Baseball M, basketball, cross-country, diving W, football (tackle) M, golf, ice hockey, soccer, softball W, swimming W, tennis, track and field, volleyball W, wrestling M. **Intramural:** Badminton, baseball M, basketball, bowling, cross-country, football (non-tackle), golf, ice hockey, racquetball, rugby, skiing, soccer, softball, swimming, table tennis, tennis, track and field, volleyball, weight lifting. **Team name:** Cobbers.

Student services. Adult student services, alcohol/substance abuse counseling, chaplain/spiritual director, career counseling, student employment services, financial aid counseling, health services, minority student services, on-campus daycare, personal counseling, placement for graduates. **Physically disabled:** Services for visually, speech, hearing impaired.

Contact. E-mail: admissions@cord.edu
Phone: (218) 299-3004 Toll-free number: (800) 699-9897
Fax: (218) 299-4720
Scott Ellingson, Admissions Director, Concordia College: Moorhead, 901 Eighth Street South, Moorhead, MN 56562-9981

Concordia University: St. Paul

St. Paul, Minnesota — **CB member**
www.csp.edu — **CB code: 6114**

- Private 4-year university affiliated with Lutheran Church - Missouri Synod
- Residential campus in large city
- 1,420 degree-seeking undergraduates: 8% part-time, 60% women, 10% African American, 7% Asian American, 1% Hispanic American
- 953 degree-seeking graduate students
- 59% of applicants admitted
- SAT or ACT (ACT writing optional) required
- 50% graduate within 6 years

General. Founded in 1893. Regionally accredited. **Degrees:** 459 bachelor's, 2 associate awarded; master's offered. **ROTC:** Army, Naval, Air Force. **Calendar:** Semester, limited summer session. **Full-time faculty:** 78 total; 68% have terminal degrees, 4% minority, 50% women. **Part-time faculty:** 184 total; 3% minority, 50% women. **Class size:** 75% < 20, 24% 20-39, 1% 40-49.

Freshman class profile. 1,073 applied, 634 admitted, 211 enrolled.

Mid 50% test scores		**Rank in top quarter:**	37%
ACT composite:	18-25	**Rank in top tenth:**	16%
GPA 3.75 or higher:	18%	**End year in good standing:**	75%
GPA 3.50-3.74:	16%	**Return as sophomores:**	72%
GPA 3.0-3.49:	28%	**Out-of-state:**	19%
GPA 2.0-2.99:	36%	**Live on campus:**	78%

Basis for selection. School record, test scores, recommendations important. ACT preferred. Interview recommended.

High school preparation. College-preparatory program recommended. 15 units required; 16 recommended. Required and recommended units include English 4, mathematics 2, social studies 1, history 1, science 2 (laboratory 2) and foreign language 1. 2 units of fine arts, 1 unit of health/physical education.

2009-2010 Annual costs. Tuition/fees (projected): $26,400. Adult learners in degree completion programs have discounted tuition rates based on cost per credit. Rates vary by program. Room/board: $7,250. Books/supplies: $700. Personal expenses: $900.

2008-2009 Financial aid. **Need-based:** 209 full-time freshmen applied for aid; 175 were judged to have need; 175 of these received aid. Average need met was 79%. Average scholarship/grant was $15,085; average loan $4,408. 48% of total undergraduate aid awarded as scholarships/grants, 52% as loans/jobs. **Non-need-based:** Awarded to 153 full-time undergraduates, including 43 freshmen. Scholarships awarded for academics, art, athletics, minority status, music/drama, religious affiliation. **Additional information:** Church districts and local congregations are major sources of aid for church-vocation students.

Application procedures. **Admission:** Priority date 5/1; deadline 8/1 (receipt date). $30 fee, may be waived for applicants with need. Admission notification on a rolling basis. **Financial aid:** Priority date 5/1; no closing date. FAFSA, institutional form required. Applicants notified on a rolling basis starting 3/1; must reply within 3 week(s) of notification.

Academics. We have a variety of non-traditional undergraduate degree completion programs designed for working adults in both face-to-face and distance education formats. Approximately 37% of our undergraduates fall into this non-traditional category. **Special study options:** Accelerated study, cross-registration, distance learning, double major, dual enrollment of high school students, exchange student, honors, independent study, internships, student-designed major, study abroad, teacher certification program. **Credit/placement by examination:** AP, CLEP, IB, ACT, institutional tests. **Support services:** Learning center, reduced course load, study skills assistance, tutoring, writing center.

Majors. **Biology:** General. **Business:** Accounting, business admin, finance, management information systems, marketing. **Communications:** Media studies. **Education:** Art, bilingual, biology, chemistry, early childhood, elementary, English, ESL, health, history, kindergarten/preschool, mathematics, middle, music, physical, science, secondary, social studies. **Family/consumer sciences:** Child development, family studies. **History:** General. **Math:** General. **Parks/recreation:** Exercise sciences, health/fitness. **Protective services:** Criminal justice, law enforcement admin. **Psychology:** General. **Public administration:** Human services. **Social sciences:** Sociology. **Theology:** Missionary, religious ed, sacred music, theology. **Visual/performing arts:** Art, dramatic, studio arts.

Most popular majors. Business/marketing 48%, computer/information sciences 6%, education 10%, family/consumer sciences 9%, security/protective services 6%.

Computing on campus. Dormitories wired for high-speed internet access and linked to campus network. Commuter students can connect to campus network. Helpline, repair service, wireless network available.

Student life. **Freshman orientation:** Mandatory. Preregistration for classes offered. 3-day program prior to start of fall semester provides information about student life, support services, social programs, employment opportunities, and technology training. **Housing:** Guaranteed on-campus for freshmen. Coed dorms, single-sex dorms, special housing for disabled, apartments, wellness housing available. $125 deposit. **Activities:** Bands, campus ministries, choral groups, dance, drama, music ensembles, musical theater, student government, student newspaper, TV station, Fellowship of Christian Athletes, Southeast Asian student association, United Minds of Joint Action, student senate, mission society.

Athletics. NCAA. **Intercollegiate:** Baseball M, basketball, cross-country, football (tackle) M, golf, soccer W, softball W, track and field, volleyball W. **Intramural:** Basketball, bowling, football (non-tackle), racquetball, skiing, soccer, softball, table tennis, volleyball. **Team name:** Golden Bears.

Student services. Adult student services, alcohol/substance abuse counseling, chaplain/spiritual director, career counseling, services for economically disadvantaged, student employment services, financial aid counseling, health services, minority student services, on-campus daycare, personal counseling, placement for graduates. **Physically disabled:** Services for visually, speech, hearing impaired.

Contact. E-mail: admission@csp.edu
Phone: (651) 641-8230 Toll-free number: (800) 333-4705
Fax: (651) 603-6320
Kristin Schoon, Director of Undergraduate Admission, Concordia University: St. Paul, 275 Syndicate Street North, St. Paul, MN 55104-5494

Crossroads College

Rochester, Minnesota
www.crossroadscollege.edu — **CB code: 6412**

- Private 4-year Bible college affiliated with Christian Church
- Residential campus in small city
- 148 degree-seeking undergraduates: 14% part-time, 46% women
- 68% of applicants admitted
- SAT or ACT (ACT writing recommended), application essay required

General. Founded in 1913. Accredited by ABHE. **Degrees:** 31 bachelor's, 12 associate awarded. **Location:** 85 miles from Minneapolis-St. Paul. **Calendar:** Semester, limited summer session. **Full-time faculty:** 10 total; 50% have terminal degrees, 10% minority, 20% women. **Part-time faculty:** 20 total; 5% have terminal degrees, 5% minority, 30% women. **Class size:** 79% < 20, 16% 20-39, 2% 40-49, 4% 50-99. **Special facilities:** 38-acre wooded area with nature trails, pond.

Freshman class profile. 44 applied, 30 admitted, 22 enrolled.

Mid 50% test scores		**Rank in top quarter:**	58%
SAT critical reading:	470-540	**Out-of-state:**	28%
SAT math:	640-660	**Live on campus:**	86%
ACT composite:	17-23		

Basis for selection. High school rank, experience, aptitude for Christian ministry, character references, and personal statement of goals considered. High school GPA, rank and ACT/SAT scores determine number of credit hours a student may take during first semester if accepted. Interview recommended. **Learning Disabled:** Provide Vice President of Student Development with verification of learning disability.

2008-2009 Annual costs. Tuition/fees: $13,210. Room only: $3,900. Books/supplies: $700. Personal expenses: $1,500.

2008-2009 Financial aid. Non-need-based: Scholarships awarded for academics, leadership, music/drama, religious affiliation.

Application procedures. Admission: Closing date 8/15 (receipt date). $30 fee. Admission notification on a rolling basis. **Financial aid:** Priority date 4/1; no closing date. FAFSA, institutional form required. Applicants notified on a rolling basis starting 2/1; must reply within 4 week(s) of notification.

Academics. Minors in religious music, counseling psychology, biblical and classical languages, missions, youth ministries. **Special study options:** Double major, independent study, internships, liberal arts/career combination, student-designed major. **Credit/placement by examination:** AP, CLEP, SAT, ACT, institutional tests. 30 credit hours maximum toward bachelor's degree. **Support services:** Reduced course load, remedial instruction, study skills assistance, tutoring, writing center.

Majors. Business: Business admin, nonprofit/public. **Psychology:** Counseling. **Theology:** Missionary, religious ed, sacred music, theology, youth ministry.

Computing on campus. 17 workstations in library, computer center. Dormitories wired for high-speed internet access. Wireless network available.

Student life. Freshman orientation: Mandatory. Preregistration for classes offered. 2-day session with some placement testing in August; one-day session in January. **Policies:** Attendance required at weekly Chapel and Spiritual Formation Group meetings; Field Service participation required. Religious observance required. **Housing:** Guaranteed on-campus for freshmen. Single-sex dorms, special housing for disabled, apartments, wellness housing available. **Activities:** Choral groups, drama, music ensembles, student government, student newspaper, Christians outdoors, ambassadors group, international students fellowship.

Athletics. Intercollegiate: Baseball M, basketball, golf M, soccer M, softball W, tennis, volleyball W. **Intramural:** Bowling, golf, ice hockey, racquetball, skiing, soccer W, swimming, table tennis, tennis, volleyball. **Team name:** Knights.

Student services. Adult student services, chaplain/spiritual director, career counseling, student employment services, financial aid counseling, personal counseling, placement for graduates, veterans' counselor.

Contact. E-mail: admissions@crossroads.edu
Phone: (507) 288-4563 ext. 313 Toll-free number: (800) 456-7651
Fax: (507) 288-9046
Scott Klaehn, Director of Admissions, Crossroads College, 920 Mayowood Road, SW, Rochester, MN 55902

Crown College

St. Bonifacius, Minnesota
www.crown.edu **CB code: 6639**

- Private 4-year Bible and liberal arts college affiliated with Christian and Missionary Alliance
- Residential campus in small town
- 955 degree-seeking undergraduates
- 123 degree-seeking graduate students
- SAT or ACT (ACT writing optional), application essay required
- 58% graduate within 6 years

General. Founded in 1916. Regionally accredited; also accredited by ABHE. **Degrees:** 208 bachelor's, 31 associate awarded; master's offered. **Location:** 25 miles from Minneapolis-St. Paul. **Calendar:** Semester, limited summer session. **Full-time faculty:** 30 total. **Part-time faculty:** 155 total. **Class size:** 66% < 20, 29% 20-39, 4% 40-49, 1% 50-99. **Special facilities:** Nursing lab.

Freshman class profile.

Mid 50% test scores		**GPA 2.0-2.99:**	21%
SAT critical reading:	480-620	**Rank in top quarter:**	41%
SAT math:	470-600	**Rank in top tenth:**	18%
ACT composite:	19-25	**End year in good standing:**	88%
GPA 3.75 or higher:	30%	**Return as sophomores:**	70%
GPA 3.50-3.74:	22%	**Out-of-state:**	39%
GPA 3.0-3.49:	24%	**Live on campus:**	93%

Basis for selection. Applicants must profess personal faith in Jesus Christ. Pastor's and general recommendations very important, academic records and test scores important. **Learning Disabled:** Applicant should meet with director of academic support.

High school preparation. College-preparatory program recommended. Recommended units include English 4, mathematics 3, social studies 3, science 3 and foreign language 2.

2009-2010 Annual costs. Tuition/fees: $19,870. Room/board: $6,986. Books/supplies: $1,600. Personal expenses: $2,340.

2008-2009 Financial aid. Need-based: Average need met was 67%. Average scholarship/grant was $5,799; average loan $3,871. 47% of total undergraduate aid awarded as scholarships/grants, 53% as loans/jobs. **Non-need-based:** Scholarships awarded for academics, alumni affiliation, leadership, minority status, music/drama, religious affiliation.

Application procedures. Admission: Closing date 8/18 (postmark date). $35 fee, may be waived for applicants with need. Admission notification on a rolling basis. **Financial aid:** Priority date 4/1, closing date 8/1. FAFSA, institutional form required. Applicants notified on a rolling basis starting 4/1; must reply within 3 week(s) of notification.

Academics. Special study options: Accelerated study, combined bachelor's/graduate degree, distance learning, double major, dual enrollment of high school students, ESL, exchange student, honors, independent study, internships, liberal arts/career combination, study abroad, teacher certification program, urban semester, weekend college. 2-2 with non-accredited Bible colleges. **Credit/placement by examination:** AP, CLEP, IB, ACT, institutional tests. 30 credit hours maximum toward associate degree, 30 toward bachelor's. **Support services:** Learning center, reduced course load, remedial instruction, study skills assistance, tutoring, writing center.

Majors. Biology: General. **Business:** General, business admin. **Communications:** General, digital media. **Computer sciences:** General, information systems, information technology. **Education:** Early childhood, elementary, English, history, music, secondary, social studies. **Foreign languages:** Linguistics. **Health:** Nursing (RN), public health nursing. **History:** General. **Liberal arts:** Arts/sciences. **Parks/recreation:** Sports admin. **Physical sciences:** General. **Psychology:** General. **Public administration:** Youth services. **Theology:** Bible, missionary, pastoral counseling, religious ed, theology, youth ministry. **Visual/performing arts:** Music performance. **Other:** Social entrepreneurship.

Most popular majors. Business/marketing 18%, communications/journalism 7%, education 17%, psychology 10%, theological studies 37%.

Computing on campus. 105 workstations in library, computer center. Dormitories wired for high-speed internet access and linked to campus network. Commuter students can connect to campus network. Online library, helpline, wireless network available.

Student life. Freshman orientation: Available. Preregistration for classes offered. 2-day orientation program at the beginning of the spring semester, 4 days prior to fall semester. **Policies:** Religious observance required. **Housing:** Guaranteed on-campus for all undergraduates. Single-sex dorms, special housing for disabled, apartments, wellness housing available. $50 deposit. **Activities:** Jazz band, campus ministries, choral groups, dance, drama, film society, international student organizations, literary magazine, music ensembles, musical theater, student government, student newspaper, Christian service groups, mission support groups, Student Missionary Society, ethnic clubs, activity planning group, student family association, Intercultural Experiences, College Conservatives, Missionary Cabinet, Hmong Student Fellowship.

Athletics. NCAA. **Intercollegiate:** Baseball M, basketball, cross-country, football (tackle) M, golf, soccer, softball W, volleyball W. **Intramural:** Basketball, football (non-tackle) M, soccer, track and field, volleyball. **Team name:** The Storm.

Student services. Adult student services, chaplain/spiritual director, career counseling, student employment services, financial aid counseling, health services, personal counseling. **Physically disabled:** Services for visually, hearing impaired.

Contact. E-mail: info@crown.edu
Phone: (952) 446-4142 Toll-free number: (800) 682-7696
Fax: (952) 446-4149
Jill Pautz, Director of Admissions, Crown College, 8700 College View Drive, St. Bonifacius, MN 55375-9001

DeVry University: Edina
Edina, Minnesota
www.devry.edu

- For-profit 4-year university
- Commuter campus in large town
- 188 degree-seeking undergraduates: 65% part-time, 42% women, 8% African American, 5% Asian American, 2% Hispanic American, 2% Native American
- 60 degree-seeking graduate students

General. **Degrees:** 26 bachelor's awarded; master's offered. **Calendar:** Semester. **Part-time faculty:** 12 total; 33% women.

Basis for selection. Interview and GPA important, test scores and class rank considered.

2008-2009 Annual costs. Tuition/fees: $13,930. Books/supplies: $1,300. Personal expenses: $5,082.

2007-2008 Financial aid. **Non-need-based:** Scholarships awarded for academics.

Application procedures. **Admission:** No deadline. $50 fee. Admission notification on a rolling basis. **Financial aid:** No deadline. FAFSA required. Applicants notified on a rolling basis.

Academics. **Special study options:** Accelerated study, distance learning. **Credit/placement by examination:** CLEP.

Majors. **Business:** Business admin. **Computer sciences:** Networking, security, systems analysis, web page design. **Engineering:** Software.

Most popular majors. Business/marketing 94%, computer/information sciences 6%.

Student life. **Housing:** Private apartments, student-plan housing, private rooms available.

Contact. Phone: (877) 733-3879
DeVry University: Edina, 7700 France Avenue South, Suite 575, Edina, MN 55435

Globe University
Woodbury, Minnesota
www.globeuniversity.edu **CB code: 2296**

- For-profit 4-year business and health science college
- Commuter campus in small city
- 769 degree-seeking undergraduates
- Interview required

General. Accredited by ACICS. **Degrees:** 25 bachelor's, 152 associate awarded; master's offered. **Location:** 8 miles from Minneapolis-St. Paul. **Calendar:** Quarter, extensive summer session. **Full-time faculty:** 16 total. **Part-time faculty:** 42 total. **Class size:** 87% < 20, 13% 20-39.

Freshman class profile. 121 applied, 99 admitted, 99 enrolled.

Basis for selection. Open admission. **Learning Disabled:** Interview with Dean of Students.

2008-2009 Annual costs. Tuition/fees: $17,550. Books/supplies: $900.

Application procedures. **Admission:** No deadline. $50 fee. Admission notification on a rolling basis. **Financial aid:** No deadline. FAFSA, institutional form required. Applicants notified on a rolling basis starting 5/1.

Academics. **Special study options:** Distance learning, independent study, internships, liberal arts/career combination. **Credit/placement by examination:** AP, CLEP, institutional tests. **Support services:** Learning center, reduced course load, study skills assistance, tutoring, writing center.

Majors. **Agriculture:** Animal sciences. **Business:** Accounting, business admin. **Computer sciences:** General, information technology, LAN/WAN management, security, system admin, web page design. **Engineering:** Software. **Engineering technology:** Computer, computer hardware, computer systems, software. **Health:** Office admin. **Legal studies:** Paralegal. **Parks/recreation:** Exercise sciences.

Computing on campus. 173 workstations in library, computer center. Commuter students can connect to campus network. Online library, helpline, repair service, wireless network available.

Student life. **Freshman orientation:** Mandatory. 4-hour orientation held prior to each quarter. **Activities:** Student government, student newspaper.

Student services. Career counseling, services for economically disadvantaged, student employment services, financial aid counseling, placement for graduates. **Physically disabled:** Services for hearing impaired.

Contact. E-mail: admissions@globeuniversity.edu
Phone: (651) 730-5100 Toll-free number: (800) 231-0660
Fax: (651) 730-5151
Stacy Severson, Director of Admissions, Globe University, 8089 Globe Drive, Woodbury, MN 55125

Gustavus Adolphus College
St. Peter, Minnesota **CB member**
www.gustavus.edu **CB code: 6253**

- Private 4-year liberal arts college affiliated with Evangelical Lutheran Church in America
- Residential campus in small town
- 2,515 degree-seeking undergraduates: 57% women
- 75% of applicants admitted
- Application essay required
- 81% graduate within 6 years; 19% enter graduate study

General. Founded in 1862. Regionally accredited. **Degrees:** 588 bachelor's awarded. **ROTC:** Army. **Location:** 65 miles from Minneapolis-St. Paul. **Calendar:** 4-1-4, limited summer session. **Full-time faculty:** 200 total; 84% have terminal degrees, 13% minority, 46% women. **Part-time faculty:** 51 total; 35% have terminal degrees, 2% minority, 49% women. **Class size:** 51% < 20, 40% 20-39, 6% 40-49, 3% 50-99, less than 1% >100. **Special facilities:** Arboretum with walking and skiing paths, theme gardens, native woods and prairies, art museum, interpretive center.

Freshman class profile. 3,128 applied, 2,343 admitted, 635 enrolled.

Mid 50% test scores		**Rank in top quarter:**	69%
SAT math:	580-690	**Rank in top tenth:**	34%
ACT composite:	24-29	**End year in good standing:**	91%
GPA 3.75 or higher:	46%	**Return as sophomores:**	91%
GPA 3.50-3.74:	24%	**Out-of-state:**	18%
GPA 3.0-3.49:	26%	**Live on campus:**	99%
GPA 2.0-2.99:	4%	**International:**	1%

Basis for selection. School achievement record, test scores, recommendations, interview, essay or personal statement, school and community activities most important. Special consideration given to children of alumni and minority applicants. SAT or ACT recommended. **Homeschooled:** Statement describing homeschool structure and mission, interview, letter of recommendation (nonparent) required.

High school preparation. College-preparatory program recommended. 17 units required; 22 recommended. Required and recommended units include English 4, mathematics 3-4, social studies 2, history 2, science 2-3 (laboratory 2-3), foreign language 2-3 and academic electives 2.

2009-2010 Annual costs. Tuition/fees (projected): $32,080. Room/board: $7,910. Books/supplies: $750. Personal expenses: $1,210.

2008-2009 Financial aid. **Need-based:** 526 full-time freshmen applied for aid; 441 were judged to have need; 441 of these received aid. Average need met was 94%. Average scholarship/grant was $9,815; average loan $3,352. 72% of total undergraduate aid awarded as scholarships/grants, 28% as loans/jobs. **Non-need-based:** Awarded to 811 full-time undergraduates, including 415 freshmen. Scholarships awarded for academics, alumni affiliation, art, music/drama, religious affiliation, ROTC.

Application procedures. **Admission:** Closing date 4/1. No application fee. Admission notification 4/15. Admission notification on a rolling basis beginning on or about 11/20. Must reply by May 1 or within 2 week(s) if notified thereafter. **Financial aid:** Priority date 2/15, closing date 4/15. FAFSA required. CSS PROFILE required of students applying for need-based assistance. Applicants notified on a rolling basis starting 12/20; must reply by 5/1 or within 2 week(s) of notification.

Academics. **Special study options:** Cooperative education, cross-registration, double major, dual enrollment of high school students, exchange student, honors, independent study, internships, liberal arts/career combination, student-designed major, study abroad, teacher certification program, Washington semester. **Credit/placement by examination:** AP, CLEP, IB, institutional tests. **Support services:** Reduced course load, study skills assistance, tutoring, writing center.

Majors. **Area/ethnic studies:** Japanese, Russian/Slavic, Scandinavian, women's. **Biology:** General, biochemistry. **Business:** General, accounting, international. **Communications:** General. **Computer sciences:** General, computer science. **Conservation:** General, environmental studies. **Education:** General, elementary, secondary. **Foreign languages:** Classics, French, German, Japanese, Russian, Scandinavian, Spanish. **Health:** Athletic training, nursing (RN), predental, premedicine, preveterinary. **History:** General. **Legal studies:** Prelaw. **Math:** General. **Parks/recreation:** Health/fitness. **Philosophy/religion:** Philosophy, religion. **Physical sciences:** Chemistry, geology, physics. **Protective services:** Criminal justice. **Psychology:** General. **Social sciences:** Anthropology, economics, geography, political science, sociology. **Theology:** Sacred music. **Visual/performing arts:** Art, art history/conservation, dance, dramatic, music performance.

Most popular majors. Biology 9%, business/marketing 15%, communications/journalism 6%, education 9%, physical sciences 6%, psychology 10%, social sciences 16%.

Computing on campus. 440 workstations in dormitories, library, computer center, student center. Dormitories wired for high-speed internet access and linked to campus network. Commuter students can connect to campus network. Online course registration, online library, helpline, repair service, student web hosting, wireless network available.

Student life. **Freshman orientation:** Mandatory, $100 fee. Preregistration for classes offered. On-campus registration and pre-orientation sessions take place in June for students and families. Orientation program begins for first-year students four days prior to the beginning of classes. **Housing:** Guaranteed on-campus for all undergraduates. Coed dorms, special housing for disabled, apartments, wellness housing available. $300 nonrefundable deposit, deadline 5/1. **Activities:** Bands, choral groups, dance, drama, literary magazine, music ensembles, musical theater, radio station, student government, student newspaper, symphony orchestra, TV station, over 100 religious, political, ethnic, and social service organizations.

Athletics. NCAA. **Intercollegiate:** Baseball M, basketball, cross-country, diving, football (tackle) M, golf, gymnastics W, ice hockey, skiing, soccer, softball W, swimming, tennis, track and field, volleyball W. **Intramural:** Badminton, basketball, football (non-tackle) M, golf, handball, ice hockey, lacrosse M, racquetball, rugby, skiing, soccer, softball, swimming, table tennis, tennis, volleyball. **Team name:** Gusties.

Student services. Alcohol/substance abuse counseling, chaplain/spiritual director, career counseling, student employment services, financial aid counseling, health services, minority student services, personal counseling, placement for graduates, women's services. **Physically disabled:** Services for visually, hearing impaired.

Contact. E-mail: admission@gustavus.edu
Phone: (507) 933-7676 Toll-free number: (800) 487-8288
Fax: (507) 933-7474
Mark Anderson, Vice-President for Enrollment Management, Gustavus Adolphus College, 800 West College Avenue, St. Peter, MN 56082

Hamline University

St. Paul, Minnesota — **CB member**
www.hamline.edu — **CB code: 6265**

- Private 4-year university and liberal arts college affiliated with United Methodist Church
- Residential campus in very large city
- 1,957 degree-seeking undergraduates: 2% part-time, 55% women, 6% African American, 5% Asian American, 3% Hispanic American, 1% Native American, 3% international
- 2,300 degree-seeking graduate students
- 80% of applicants admitted
- SAT or ACT (ACT writing optional), application essay required
- 72% graduate within 6 years; 26% enter graduate study

General. Founded in 1854. Regionally accredited. **Degrees:** 454 bachelor's awarded; master's, doctoral, first professional offered. **ROTC:** Air Force. **Location:** 5 miles from downtown. **Calendar:** 4-1-4, extensive summer session. **Full-time faculty:** 193 total; 90% have terminal degrees, 15% minority, 52% women. **Part-time faculty:** 358 total; 31% have terminal degrees, 5% minority, 60% women. **Class size:** 58% < 20, 33% 20-39, 5% 40-49, 4% 50-99. **Special facilities:** Music hall.

Freshman class profile. 2,234 applied, 1,784 admitted, 452 enrolled.

Mid 50% test scores			
SAT critical reading:	480-630	GPA 2.0-2.99:	25%
SAT math:	500-610	Rank in top quarter:	43%
SAT writing:	460-620	Rank in top tenth:	16%
ACT composite:	21-27	End year in good standing:	86%
GPA 3.75 or higher:	24%	Return as sophomores:	80%
GPA 3.50-3.74:	20%	Out-of-state:	15%
GPA 3.0-3.49:	30%	Live on campus:	83%
		International:	3%

Basis for selection. Class rank, high school GPA, and selection of college-preparatory courses of primary importance. Test scores, extracurricular activities, recommendations of teacher and guidance counselor also emphasized. ACT writing exam preferred but not required. Interview recommended.

High school preparation. College-preparatory program recommended. 20 units recommended. Recommended units include English 4, mathematics 3, social studies 4, science 3 (laboratory 3), foreign language 2 and academic electives 4.

2008-2009 Annual costs. Tuition/fees: $28,143. All new students must pay $30 transcript fee. Room/board: $7,784. Books/supplies: $1,200.

2007-2008 Financial aid. **Need-based:** 406 full-time freshmen applied for aid; 337 were judged to have need; 336 of these received aid. Average need met was 83%. Average scholarship/grant was $14,096; average loan $4,459. 71% of total undergraduate aid awarded as scholarships/grants, 29% as loans/jobs. **Non-need-based:** Awarded to 122 full-time undergraduates, including 36 freshmen. Scholarships awarded for academics, alumni affiliation, art, job skills, leadership, minority status, music/drama, religious affiliation, state residency.

Application procedures. **Admission:** Priority date 5/1; no deadline. No application fee. Admission notification on a rolling basis beginning on or about 10/1. Must reply by May 1 or within 2 week(s) if notified thereafter. **Financial aid:** Priority date 3/1; no closing date. FAFSA required. Applicants notified on a rolling basis starting 3/1; must reply within 2 week(s) of notification.

Academics. Intensive fall semester course for conditionally-admitted students. **Special study options:** Combined bachelor's/graduate degree, cross-registration, double major, dual enrollment of high school students, ESL, exchange student, honors, independent study, internships, student-designed major, study abroad, teacher certification program, urban semester, Washington semester. **Credit/placement by examination:** AP, CLEP, IB. **Support services:** Learning center, study skills assistance, tutoring, writing center.

Majors. **Area/ethnic studies:** East Asian, Latin American, women's. **Biology:** General, biochemistry. **Business:** Business admin, international. **Communications:** General. **Conservation:** Environmental studies. **Education:** General, art, elementary, ESL, health, music, physical, science, secondary. **Foreign languages:** French, German, Spanish. **Health:** Athletic training, predental, premedicine, preveterinary. **History:** General. **Interdisciplinary:** Peace/conflict. **Legal studies:** General, paralegal. **Math:** General. **Parks/recreation:** Exercise sciences, health/fitness. **Philosophy/religion:** Philosophy, religion. **Physical sciences:** Chemistry, physics. **Protective services:** Criminal justice. **Psychology:** General. **Social sciences:** General, anthropology, criminology, economics, international relations, political science, sociology, urban studies. **Visual/performing arts:** Art history/conservation, dramatic, music performance, music theory/composition, studio arts.

Most popular majors. Biology 8%, business/marketing 10%, English 6%, legal studies 7%, psychology 10%, security/protective services 6%, social sciences 23%.

Computing on campus. 200 workstations in dormitories, library, computer center. Dormitories wired for high-speed internet access and linked to campus network. Commuter students can connect to campus network. Online course registration, online library, helpline, repair service, wireless network available.

Student life. **Freshman orientation:** Mandatory, $220 fee. 3 days immediately before classes begin. **Housing:** Guaranteed on-campus for all undergraduates. Coed dorms, special housing for disabled, apartments, fraternity/sorority housing, wellness housing available. $50 deposit, deadline 5/1. Black Student Alliance House, Hmong Student Association House, Spanish Language House, residence halls organized around area of interest such as arts, weekends on campus, GLBT, social justice. **Activities:** Bands, choral groups, dance, drama, literary magazine, music ensembles, musical theater, radio station, student government, student newspaper, symphony orchestra, TV station, PRIDE Black Student Alliance, MPIRG, Intervarsity Christian Fellowship, Habitat for Humanity, Asian student association, Spectrum GLBT organization, Hand in Hand mentoring program, MAMADADA Art League, Native American Student Association, Anthropological Society.

Athletics. NCAA. **Intercollegiate:** Baseball M, basketball, cross-country, diving, football (tackle) M, gymnastics W, ice hockey, soccer, softball W, swimming, tennis, track and field, volleyball W. **Intramural:** Basketball, bowling, football (non-tackle), volleyball. **Team name:** Pipers.

Student services. Alcohol/substance abuse counseling, chaplain/spiritual director, career counseling, student employment services, financial aid counseling, health services, minority student services, personal counseling, placement for graduates, women's services. **Physically disabled:** Services for visually, speech, hearing impaired.

Contact. E-mail: cla-admis@hamline.edu
Phone: (651) 523-2207 Toll-free number: (800) 753-9753
Fax: (651) 523-2458
Brian Peterson, Associate Dean of Admission, Hamline University, 1536 Hewitt Avenue, St. Paul, MN 55104-1284

Macalester College

St. Paul, Minnesota — **CB member**
www.macalester.edu — **CB code: 6390**

- Private 4-year liberal arts college affiliated with Presbyterian Church (USA)
- Residential campus in large city
- 1,871 degree-seeking undergraduates: 1% part-time, 58% women, 4% African American, 9% Asian American, 4% Hispanic American, 1% Native American, 11% international
- 41% of applicants admitted
- SAT or ACT (ACT writing optional), application essay required
- 87% graduate within 6 years; 20% enter graduate study

General. Founded in 1874. Regionally accredited. **Degrees:** 446 bachelor's awarded. **ROTC:** Army, Naval, Air Force. **Location:** 5 miles from Minneapolis-St. Paul. **Calendar:** Semester. **Full-time faculty:** 164 total; 92% have terminal degrees, 20% minority, 48% women. **Part-time faculty:** 61 total; 62% have terminal degrees, 20% minority, 51% women. **Class size:** 69% < 20, 29% 20-39, less than 1% 40-49, less than 1% 50-99. **Special facilities:** Observatory with DT-M 16 inch F/8 cassegrain telescope, 250-acre nature preserve, nuclear accelerator, computer modeling facilities, laser spectroscopy laboratory, x-ray diffractometer and a nuclear magnetic spectrometer, fully equipped animal operant chamber, international research center, econometrics lab, ethnographic lab, geographic information systems (GIS) lab.

Freshman class profile. 5,041 applied, 2,074 admitted, 479 enrolled.

Mid 50% test scores		**Rank in top tenth:**	66%
SAT critical reading:	640-740	**End year in good standing:**	93%
SAT math:	630-710	**Return as sophomores:**	92%
SAT writing:	630-730	**Out-of-state:**	79%
ACT composite:	28-32	**Live on campus:**	100%
Rank in top quarter:	96%	**International:**	10%

Basis for selection. Test scores and curriculum most important. Leadership potential and extracurricular involvements also important, with special attention given to service to others. Students whose native language is not English must also submit the results of English as a Foreign Language (TOEFL) or the English Language Proficiency Test (ELPT). SAT Reading is not required of these students. Interview recommended. **Homeschooled:** Transcript of courses and grades, letter of recommendation (nonparent) required.

High school preparation. College-preparatory program recommended. Recommended units include English 4, mathematics 3, social studies 3, science 3 (laboratory 3) and foreign language 3. Honors, AP, or IB level courses recommended.

2008-2009 Annual costs. Tuition/fees: $36,504. Room/board: $8,472. Books/supplies: $924. Personal expenses: $830.

2008-2009 Financial aid. **Need-based:** 359 full-time freshmen applied for aid; 305 were judged to have need; 305 of these received aid. Average need met was 100%. Average scholarship/grant was $26,361; average loan $2,276. 81% of total undergraduate aid awarded as scholarships/grants, 19% as loans/jobs. **Non-need-based:** Awarded to 88 full-time undergraduates, including 20 freshmen. Scholarships awarded for academics, minority status. **Additional information:** College meets full need for all admitted students. Minnesota Self Loan available to qualified students.

Application procedures. **Admission:** Closing date 1/15 (postmark date). $40 fee, may be waived for applicants with need. Admission notification 3/30. Must reply by 5/1. **Financial aid:** Priority date 2/8, closing date 3/1. FAFSA, CSS PROFILE required. Applicants notified by 4/1; must reply by 5/1 or within 1 week(s) of notification.

Academics. **Special study options:** Cross-registration, double major, honors, independent study, internships, student-designed major, study abroad, urban semester, Washington semester. BA/masters in architecture with Washington University of St. Louis, BA/BS in engineering with Washington University of St. Louis and with the University of Minnesota. **Credit/placement by examination:** AP, CLEP, IB, institutional tests. **Support services:** Learning center, remedial instruction, study skills assistance, tutoring, writing center.

Majors. **Area/ethnic studies:** Asian, Latin American, women's. **Biology:** General. **Computer sciences:** General. **Conservation:** Environmental studies. **Foreign languages:** Classics, French, German, Japanese, linguistics, Russian, Spanish. **History:** General. **Interdisciplinary:** Global studies, intercultural, neuroscience. **Liberal arts:** Humanities. **Math:** General. **Philosophy/religion:** Philosophy, religion. **Physical sciences:** Chemistry, geology, physics. **Psychology:** General. **Social sciences:** Anthropology, economics, geography, political science, sociology. **Visual/performing arts:** Art history/conservation, dramatic, studio arts.

Most popular majors. Biology 7%, English 6%, foreign language 11%, interdisciplinary studies 9%, physical sciences 6%, psychology 6%, social sciences 29%, visual/performing arts 6%.

Computing on campus. 400 workstations in dormitories, library, computer center, student center. Dormitories wired for high-speed internet access and linked to campus network. Commuter students can connect to campus network. Online library, helpline, repair service, student web hosting, wireless network available.

Student life. **Freshman orientation:** Mandatory. Preregistration for classes offered. 5 days prior to classes in September. **Housing:** Guaranteed on-campus for freshmen. Coed dorms, apartments available. $300 nonrefundable deposit, deadline 5/1. 6 language houses (French, German, Russian, Spanish, Japanese, Chinese), Jewish cultural house, vegetarian co-op housing available. 2-year residency requirement for first-year students, single-sex floors within coed dorms. **Activities:** Bands, campus ministries, choral groups, dance, drama, international student organizations, literary magazine, music ensembles, Model UN, radio station, student government, student newspaper, Voices of Tamani, production studio, theater club, Asian Student Alliance, GOP club, Habitat for Humanity, Model United Nations, Amnesty International, council for religious understanding, Young Dems.

Athletics. NCAA. **Intercollegiate:** Baseball M, basketball, cross-country, diving, football (tackle) M, golf, soccer, softball W, swimming, tennis, track and field, volleyball W, water polo W. **Intramural:** Badminton, basketball, bowling, football (non-tackle), racquetball, soccer, softball, table tennis, tennis, volleyball, water polo. **Team name:** Fighting Scots.

Student services. Alcohol/substance abuse counseling, chaplain/spiritual director, career counseling, student employment services, financial aid counseling, health services, minority student services, personal counseling, placement for graduates. **Physically disabled:** Services for visually, speech, hearing impaired.

Contact. E-mail: admissions@macalester.edu
Phone: (651) 696-6357 Toll-free number: (800) 231-7974
Fax: (651) 696-6724
Lorne Robinson, Dean of Admissions and Financial Aid, Macalester College, 1600 Grand Avenue, St. Paul, MN 55105-1899

Martin Luther College

New Ulm, Minnesota
www.mlc-wels.edu — **CB code: 6435**

- Private 4-year college of theology and education affiliated with Wisconsin Evangelical Lutheran Synod
- Residential campus in large town
- 770 degree-seeking undergraduates: 8% part-time, 50% women, 1% African American, 1% Hispanic American, 2% international

- 62 degree-seeking graduate students
- ACT (writing optional) required
- 67% graduate within 6 years

General. Founded in 1995. Regionally accredited. Offers programs of study in early childhood education and staff ministry. **Degrees:** 151 bachelor's awarded; master's offered. **Location:** 90 miles from Minneapolis-St. Paul. **Calendar:** Semester, limited summer session. **Full-time faculty:** 51 total; 47% have terminal degrees. **Part-time faculty:** 28 total; 29% have terminal degrees. **Class size:** 49% < 20, 48% 20-39, less than 1% 40-49, 2% 50-99, less than 1% >100.

Freshman class profile.

Mid 50% test scores		**Rank in top quarter:**	42%
ACT composite:	22-27	**Rank in top tenth:**	16%
GPA 3.75 or higher:	41%	**Return as sophomores:**	91%
GPA 3.50-3.74:	22%	**Out-of-state:**	85%
GPA 3.0-3.49:	25%	**Live on campus:**	99%
GPA 2.0-2.99:	11%		

Basis for selection. Primarily pastor's letter of recommendation, high school transcript, and test scores required. Rating provided by student's high school considered.

High school preparation. 14 units required. Required units include English 4, mathematics 3, social studies 2, science 3 (laboratory 2), foreign language 2 and academic electives 2. 5 units in foreign language required for pastoral program.

2009-2010 Annual costs. Tuition/fees (projected): $10,660. Room/board: $4,140. Books/supplies: $800. Personal expenses: $2,000.

2007-2008 Financial aid. Need-based: 168 full-time freshmen applied for aid; 134 were judged to have need; 134 of these received aid. Average need met was 60%. Average scholarship/grant was $4,034; average loan $3,748. 62% of total undergraduate aid awarded as scholarships/grants, 38% as loans/jobs. **Non-need-based:** Awarded to 390 full-time undergraduates, including 106 freshmen. Scholarships awarded for academics, music/drama, religious affiliation.

Application procedures. Admission: Closing date 4/15 (postmark date). $25 fee, may be waived for applicants with need. Admission notification on a rolling basis beginning on or about 9/15. Must reply by May 1 or within 2 week(s) if notified thereafter. **Financial aid:** Priority date 4/15, closing date 9/30. FAFSA, institutional form required. Applicants notified by 3/1.

Academics. Special study options: Distance learning, double major, teacher certification program. **Credit/placement by examination:** AP, CLEP, ACT, institutional tests. **Support services:** Learning center, reduced course load, remedial instruction, study skills assistance, tutoring.

Majors. Education: Early childhood, elementary, multi-level teacher. **Theology:** Theology.

Computing on campus. 129 workstations in dormitories, library, computer center. Dormitories linked to campus network. Helpline, repair service available.

Student life. Freshman orientation: Mandatory, $20 fee. **Policies:** Religious observance required. **Housing:** Guaranteed on-campus for freshmen. Single-sex dorms available. $100 nonrefundable deposit, deadline 5/1. **Activities:** Bands, campus ministries, choral groups, dance, drama, literary magazine, music ensembles, musical theater, student government, symphony orchestra.

Athletics. NAIA, NCAA. **Intercollegiate:** Baseball M, basketball, cross-country, football (tackle) M, golf M, soccer, softball W, tennis, track and field, volleyball W. **Intramural:** Badminton, basketball, bowling, football (tackle) M, soccer, softball, tennis, volleyball. **Team name:** Knights.

Student services. Chaplain/spiritual director, student employment services, financial aid counseling, health services, personal counseling.

Contact. E-mail: mlcadmit@mlc-wels.edu
Phone: (507) 354-8221 Fax: (507) 354-8225
Ronald Brutlag, Director of Admissions, Martin Luther College, 1995 Luther Court, New Ulm, MN 56073-3965

Metropolitan State University

St. Paul, Minnesota
www.metrostate.edu **CB code: 1245**

- Public 4-year university
- Commuter campus in very large city
- 5,880 degree-seeking undergraduates: 63% part-time, 59% women, 14% African American, 10% Asian American, 2% Hispanic American, 1% Native American, 1% international
- 516 degree-seeking graduate students

General. Founded in 1971. Regionally accredited. **Degrees:** 1,319 bachelor's awarded; master's, doctoral offered. **Calendar:** Semester, extensive summer session. **Full-time faculty:** 123 total; 81% have terminal degrees, 17% minority, 51% women. **Part-time faculty:** 358 total; 24% have terminal degrees, 14% minority, 45% women. **Class size:** 34% < 20, 64% 20-39, less than 1% 40-49, less than 1% 50-99.

Freshman class profile.

Mid 50% test scores		**Rank in top tenth:**	8%
ACT composite:	16-24	**Out-of-state:**	2%
Rank in top quarter:	24%		

Basis for selection. School achievement record and test scores most important. ACT or SAT at or above national median or high school rank in upper half of class. Interview and essays only used as part of the appeals process if admission was denied.

High school preparation. 16 units required. Required units include English 4, mathematics 3, social studies 3, science 3 (laboratory 1) and academic electives 3. 3 years of electives from language, world culture, or arts.

2008-2009 Annual costs. Tuition/fees: $5,473; $10,633 out-of-state. Books/supplies: $1,500. Personal expenses: $1,976.

2008-2009 Financial aid. Non-need-based: Scholarships awarded for academics, leadership, minority status, state residency.

Application procedures. Admission: Closing date 6/15. $20 fee, may be waived for applicants with need. Admission notification on a rolling basis. **Financial aid:** Priority date 5/1; no closing date. FAFSA required. Applicants notified on a rolling basis starting 5/1; must reply within 2 week(s) of notification.

Academics. Special study options: Cross-registration, distance learning, double major, dual enrollment of high school students, external degree, independent study, internships, liberal arts/career combination, student-designed major, teacher certification program, weekend college. **Credit/placement by examination:** AP, CLEP, IB, institutional tests. 90 credit hours maximum toward bachelor's degree. **Support services:** Learning center, reduced course load, study skills assistance, tutoring, writing center.

Majors. Area/ethnic studies: Women's. **Biology:** General. **Business:** Accounting, business admin, finance, hospitality admin, human resources, information resources management, international, management information systems, marketing, operations, sales/distribution. **Communications:** General, advertising. **Computer sciences:** Computer science, information systems, security. **Education:** Biology, elementary, English, kindergarten/preschool, mathematics, social studies. **Health:** Dental assistant, dental hygiene, nursing (RN), substance abuse counseling. **History:** General. **Liberal arts:** Arts/sciences. **Math:** Applied. **Philosophy/religion:** Philosophy. **Protective services:** Criminal justice, police science. **Psychology:** General, developmental. **Public administration:** Human services, social work. **Social sciences:** General, economics. **Visual/performing arts:** Dramatic, play/screenwriting.

Most popular majors. Business/marketing 35%, health sciences 7%, liberal arts 17%, psychology 7%, public administration/social services 6%, security/protective services 8%.

Computing on campus. 550 workstations in library, computer center. Commuter students can connect to campus network. Online course registration, helpline, wireless network available.

Student life. Freshman orientation: Mandatory, $10 fee. Preregistration for classes offered. Orientation sessions of 3-1/2 hours are held several times each semester. **Policies:** Annual registration required of all student organizations. **Activities:** Drama, international student organizations, literary magazine, student government, student newspaper, Asian student organization, Lavender Bridge, African-American student association, graduate student advisory committee, Voice of Indian Council for Educational Success, social work student association, psychology club, Muslim student association, Urban Teachers Student Program Organization.

Student services. Adult student services, career counseling, minority student services, personal counseling, women's services. **Physically disabled:** Services for visually, speech, hearing impaired.

Contact. E-mail: admission.metro@metrostate.edu
Phone: (651) 793-1300 Fax: (651) 793-1310
Monir Johnson, Admissions Director, Metropolitan State University, 700 East Seventh Street, St. Paul, MN 55106-5000

Minneapolis College of Art and Design
Minneapolis, Minnesota — **CB member**
www.mcad.edu — **CB code: 6411**

- Private 4-year visual arts college
- Residential campus in very large city
- 678 degree-seeking undergraduates: 4% part-time, 55% women
- 33 degree-seeking graduate students
- 56% of applicants admitted
- SAT or ACT (ACT writing optional), application essay required
- 70% graduate within 6 years

General. Founded in 1886. Regionally accredited. **Degrees:** 148 bachelor's awarded; master's offered. **Calendar:** Semester, limited summer session. **Full-time faculty:** 43 total; 100% have terminal degrees, 35% women. **Part-time faculty:** 85 total; 85% have terminal degrees, 47% women. **Class size:** 84% < 20, 16% 20-39. **Special facilities:** Art and design galleries, personal on-campus studio space, 3-D furniture/sculpture studios, animation studios, drawing studios, film studios, print/paper/book studios, painting studios, photo studios.

Freshman class profile. 506 applied, 281 admitted, 103 enrolled.

Mid 50% test scores			
SAT critical reading:	540-670	GPA 3.50-3.74:	19%
SAT math:	470-590	GPA 3.0-3.49:	43%
SAT writing:	480-600	GPA 2.0-2.99:	10%
ACT composite:	21-27	Return as sophomores:	80%
GPA 3.75 or higher:	28%	Out-of-state:	58%
		Live on campus:	81%

Basis for selection. Bachelor of Fine Arts applicants required to submit a portfolio of creative work. For all students (BFA & BS), academic record and test scores reviewed. Level of interest and motivation determined through personal statement of interest, letter of recommendation and essay requirement. Tests not required for transfer applicants who have completed 12 or more satisfactory credits (C or better) at the college level. Interview recommended. Personal statement required on specific topic. Visual arts portfolio required for all BFA applications; essay on specific topic required for all BS applications.

High school preparation. College-preparatory program recommended. Recommended units include English 4, social studies 4, history 4 and visual/performing arts 6.

2008-2009 Annual costs. Tuition/fees: $29,300. Housing costs vary; figure quoted is for double-occupancy (furnished) one-bedroom apartment. Required fees include $900 laptop computer that freshmen must purchase. Room only: $4,160. Books/supplies: $2,200. Personal expenses: $1,000.

2008-2009 Financial aid. **Non-need-based:** Scholarships awarded for academics, alumni affiliation, art.

Application procedures. **Admission:** Priority date 2/15; deadline 5/1 (receipt date). $50 fee, may be waived for applicants with need. Admission notification on a rolling basis. **Financial aid:** Priority date 3/15, closing date 3/15. FAFSA required. Applicants notified by 4/1; Applicants notified on a rolling basis starting 4/1; must reply by 5/1 or within 2 week(s) of notification.

Academics. **Special study options:** Combined bachelor's/graduate degree, cooperative education, cross-registration, distance learning, exchange student, independent study, internships, New York semester, study abroad. **Credit/placement by examination:** AP, CLEP, IB. **Support services:** Learning center, reduced course load, study skills assistance, tutoring, writing center.

Majors. **Communications:** Advertising, public relations. **Communications technology:** Animation/special effects. **Production:** Furniture. **Visual/performing arts:** Drawing, graphic design, illustration, painting, photography, printmaking, sculpture, studio arts. **Other:** Comic art, Print and web communications, Project management.

Computing on campus. PC or laptop required. 160 workstations in library, computer center, student center. Dormitories wired for high-speed internet access and linked to campus network. Commuter students can connect to campus network. Online library, helpline, repair service, student web hosting, wireless network available.

Student life. **Freshman orientation:** Mandatory. Preregistration for classes offered. 3 days prior to first day of fall semester classes; includes 1 day for parent/guardian orientation. **Housing:** Guaranteed on-campus for freshmen. Coed dorms, apartments available. $175 fully refundable deposit, deadline 5/1. **Activities:** Film society, international student organizations, student government, animation club, anime club, bike club, Comic Heads, film club, Madcad musicians club, MCAD design club, MCAD green club, OH NO HOMO, recess club.

Student services. Alcohol/substance abuse counseling, career counseling, student employment services, financial aid counseling, personal counseling.

Contact. E-mail: admissions@mcad.edu
Phone: (612) 874-3760 Toll-free number: (800) 874-6223
Fax: (612) 874-3701
William Mullen, Vice President, Enrollment Management, Minneapolis College of Art and Design, 2501 Stevens Avenue, Minneapolis, MN 55404

Minnesota School of Business
Minneapolis, Minnesota
www.msbcollege.edu — **CB code: 3313**

- For-profit 4-year business and technical college
- Commuter campus in very large city
- 444 full-time, degree-seeking undergraduates
- Interview required

General. Accredited by ACICS. **Degrees:** 34 bachelor's, 130 associate awarded; master's offered. **Calendar:** Quarter, extensive summer session. **Full-time faculty:** 12 total; 33% have terminal degrees, 33% women. **Part-time faculty:** 63 total; 8% have terminal degrees, 8% minority, 44% women. **Class size:** 97% < 20, 3% 20-39.

Basis for selection. Standardized test scores most important. Interview also important. Scores are used to exempt applicants from entrance exam. **Learning Disabled:** Students with learning disabilities are allowed 90 minutes for exams while all other students are allowed 60 minutes.

2008-2009 Annual costs. Tuition/fees: $18,770. Books/supplies: $1,500. Personal expenses: $2,178.

Application procedures. **Admission:** No deadline. $50 fee. Application must be submitted online. Admission notification on a rolling basis. **Financial aid:** No deadline. FAFSA, institutional form required. Applicants notified on a rolling basis starting 7/1; must reply within 2 week(s) of notification.

Academics. **Special study options:** Combined bachelor's/graduate degree, distance learning, liberal arts/career combination. **Credit/placement by examination:** CLEP. **Support services:** Study skills assistance, tutoring, writing center.

Majors. **Business:** Accounting, business admin. **Computer sciences:** Information technology. **Health:** Nursing (RN). **Legal studies:** Paralegal.

Computing on campus. 12 workstations in library, computer center. Online library, helpline, wireless network available.

Student life. **Freshman orientation:** Mandatory.

Student services. Student employment services, financial aid counseling, placement for graduates.

Contact. E-mail: pmurray@msbcollege.edu
Phone: (612) 861-2000 Toll-free number: (800) 752-4223
Fax: (612) 861-5548
Patricia Murray, Director of Admissions, Minnesota School of Business, 1401 West 76 Street, Suite 500, Richfield, MN 55423

Minnesota School of Business: Blaine
Blaine, Minnesota
www.msbcollege.edu

- For-profit 4-year branch campus and business college
- Very large city

General. Regionally accredited. **Calendar:** Quarter.

Annual costs/financial aid. Tuition/fees (2008-2009): $17,550.

Contact. 3680 Pheasant Ridge Dr. NE, Blaine, MN 55449

Minnesota School of Business: Plymouth
Plymouth, Minnesota
www.msbcollege.edu

- For-profit 4-year business and technical college
- Small city
- 492 degree-seeking undergraduates

General. Accredited by ACICS. **Degrees:** 29 bachelor's, 89 associate awarded. **Calendar:** Quarter. **Full-time faculty:** 13 total. **Part-time faculty:** 74 total.

Basis for selection. Admissions based on results of Accuplacer entrance exam.

2008-2009 Annual costs. Tuition/fees: $18,770.

Application procedures. Admission: Closing date 10/1.

Academics. Special study options: Distance learning, independent study, internships, liberal arts/career combination. **Credit/placement by examination:** CLEP.

Majors. Business: Accounting, business admin. **Computer sciences:** Information technology. **Health:** Health care admin. **Other:** Health fitness specialist.

Contact. Phone: (866) 476-2121
Stacy Severson, Director of Admissions, Minnesota School of Business: Plymouth, 1455 County Road 101 North, Plymouth, MN 55447

Minnesota School of Business: Rochester
Rochester, Minnesota
www.msbcollege.edu

- For-profit 4-year career college
- Small city
- 367 full-time, degree-seeking undergraduates

General. Accredited by ACICS. **Degrees:** 16 bachelor's, 72 associate awarded. **Calendar:** Quarter. **Full-time faculty:** 11 total. **Part-time faculty:** 42 total.

Basis for selection. Admissions based on results of Accuplacer entrance exam.

2009-2010 Annual costs. Tuition/fees (projected): $20,045. Books/supplies: $1,200.

Application procedures. Admission: Closing date 10/1. $50 fee. Application must be submitted online. Admission notification on a rolling basis.

Academics. Special study options: Distance learning. **Credit/placement by examination:** CLEP. **Support services:** Learning center, remedial instruction, study skills assistance, tutoring, writing center.

Majors. Business: Accounting, business admin.

Computing on campus. 14 workstations in library, student center. Online library, helpline, wireless network available.

Contact. Phone: (507) 536-9500
Angie Helm, Director of Admissions, Minnesota School of Business: Rochester, 2521 Pennington Drive NW, Rochester, MN 55901

Minnesota School of Business: St. Cloud
Waite Park, Minnesota
www.msbcollege.edu

- For-profit 4-year virtual university
- Small city
- 953 degree-seeking undergraduates
- 100% of applicants admitted

General. Accredited by ACICS. **Degrees:** 16 bachelor's, 163 associate awarded; master's offered. **Calendar:** Quarter, extensive summer session. **Full-time faculty:** 12 total. **Part-time faculty:** 52 total.

Freshman class profile. 173 applied, 173 admitted, 173 enrolled.

Basis for selection. Applicants to all diploma, associate, and bachelor degree programs must achieve minimum scores on the Accuplacer test administered at the college: 35 (reading comprehension), 35 (sentence skills), 21 (arithmetic). Alternatively, applicants to these programs must provide documentation of a bachelor's degree, minimum composite score of 21 on the ACT, or SAT score of 1485 (unless SAT was taken prior to March 2006, in which case composite score must be at least 990). Finally, if an applicant has already taken the CPAt exam through MSB/GC, entrance scores will be honored according to the requirements listed in the catalog at the time of past enrollment (though students may be required to take the Accuplacer exam for placement purposes). **Homeschooled:** State high school equivalency certificate required.

2008-2009 Annual costs. Tuition/fees: $18,770.

Application procedures. Admission: No deadline. $50 fee. Application must be submitted online. Admission notification on a rolling basis.

Academics. Special study options: Combined bachelor's/graduate degree, distance learning, internships. **Credit/placement by examination:** CLEP. **Support services:** Remedial instruction, study skills assistance, tutoring, writing center.

Majors. Business: Accounting, business admin. **Computer sciences:** Information technology. **Health:** Health care admin. **Other:** Health fitness specialist, Paralegal.

Computing on campus. Online course registration, helpline, wireless network available.

Contact. E-mail: info@msbcollege.edu
Phone: (866) 403-3333
Candi Janssen, Director of Admissions, Minnesota School of Business: St. Cloud, 1201 Second Street South, Waite Park, MN 55387

Minnesota School of Business: Shakopee
Shakopee, Minnesota
www.msbcollege.edu

- For-profit 4-year business and technical college
- Commuter campus in large town
- 409 degree-seeking undergraduates: 2% African American, 2% Asian American, 2% Hispanic American, 1% Native American
- Interview required

General. Accredited by ACICS. **Degrees:** 19 bachelor's, 194 associate awarded; master's offered. **Calendar:** Quarter. **Full-time faculty:** 10 total; 30% have terminal degrees, 60% women. **Part-time faculty:** 31 total; 13% have terminal degrees, 3% minority, 45% women. **Class size:** 97% < 20, 3% 20-39.

Freshman class profile. 51 enrolled.

Basis for selection. Interview with admissions and SAT, ACT, or entrance exam (Accuplacer) important.

2009-2010 Annual costs. Tuition/fees (projected): $19,970.

2008-2009 Financial aid. Non-need-based: Scholarships awarded for academics.

Application procedures. Admission: No deadline. $50 fee. Admission notification on a rolling basis. **Financial aid:** No deadline. FAFSA, institutional form required. Applicants notified on a rolling basis.

Academics. Special study options: Combined bachelor's/graduate degree, distance learning, liberal arts/career combination. **Credit/placement by examination:** CLEP, SAT, ACT, institutional tests. 75 credit hours maximum toward associate degree, 75 toward bachelor's. **Support services:** Learning center, remedial instruction, study skills assistance, tutoring, writing center.

Majors. Business: Business admin.

Computing on campus. 50 workstations in computer center. Online course registration, online library, helpline, wireless network available.

Student life. Freshman orientation: Mandatory.

Contact. Phone: (866) 776-1200
Gretchen Seifert, Director of Admissions, Minnesota School of Business: Shakopee, 1200 Shakopee Town Square, Shakopee, MN 55379

Minnesota State University: Mankato

Mankato, Minnesota **CB member**
www.mnsu.edu **CB code: 6677**

- Public 4-year university
- Commuter campus in large town
- 12,251 degree-seeking undergraduates: 7% part-time, 51% women, 4% African American, 2% Asian American, 1% Hispanic American, 3% international
- 1,700 graduate students
- 73% of applicants admitted
- SAT or ACT (ACT writing optional) required
- 50% graduate within 6 years

General. Founded in 1867. Regionally accredited. **Degrees:** 2,123 bachelor's, 46 associate awarded; master's, doctoral offered. **ROTC:** Army. **Location:** 85 miles from Minneapolis-St. Paul. **Calendar:** Semester, extensive summer session. **Full-time faculty:** 504 total; 81% have terminal degrees, 8% minority, 43% women. **Part-time faculty:** 259 total; 10% have terminal degrees, 2% minority, 58% women. **Class size:** 35% < 20, 49% 20-39, 8% 40-49, 6% 50-99, 3% >100. **Special facilities:** 2 observatories, ropes course.

Freshman class profile. 6,115 applied, 4,477 admitted, 2,360 enrolled.

Mid 50% test scores		**Return as sophomores:**	80%
ACT composite:	20-24	**Out-of-state:**	13%
Rank in top quarter:	25%	**Live on campus:**	84%
Rank in top tenth:	7%	**International:**	1%

Basis for selection. Students must rank in top 50 percent of high school class or score 21 or better on the ACT. College preparatory courses also reviewed. ACT used only when admission cannot be achieved using high school rank and college preparatory courses. Essays and/or recommendations used only for contract/admission review by faculty committees. **Homeschooled:** Must submit standardized test results in lieu of rank/record.

High school preparation. 16 units required. Required units include English 4, mathematics 3, social studies 2, history 1, science 3 (laboratory 3) and foreign language 2. One year world culture course or arts course.

2008-2009 Annual costs. Tuition/fees: $6,263; $12,508 out-of-state. Room/board: $5,665. Books/supplies: $820. Personal expenses: $2,600.

2007-2008 Financial aid. Need-based: 1,922 full-time freshmen applied for aid; 1,215 were judged to have need; 1,215 of these received aid. Average need met was 71%. Average scholarship/grant was $4,506; average loan $3,020. 42% of total undergraduate aid awarded as scholarships/grants, 58% as loans/jobs. **Non-need-based:** Awarded to 1,978 full-time undergraduates, including 761 freshmen. Scholarships awarded for academics, art, athletics, leadership, minority status, music/drama.

Application procedures. Admission: $20 fee, may be waived for applicants with need. Admission notification on a rolling basis. **Financial aid:** Priority date 3/15; no closing date. FAFSA required. Applicants notified on a rolling basis starting 3/30; must reply within 2 week(s) of notification.

Academics. Special study options: Combined bachelor's/graduate degree, cross-registration, distance learning, double major, dual enrollment of high school students, ESL, exchange student, external degree, honors, independent study, internships, semester at sea, student-designed major, study abroad, teacher certification program. **Credit/placement by examination:** AP, CLEP, IB, institutional tests. **Support services:** Learning center, reduced course load, remedial instruction, study skills assistance, tutoring, writing center.

Majors. Agriculture: Food science, plant sciences. **Architecture:** Urban/community planning. **Area/ethnic studies:** French, German, Scandinavian, women's. **Biology:** General, anatomy, bacteriology, biochemistry, biotechnology, botany, ecology, genetics, toxicology, zoology. **Business:** General, accounting, banking/financial services, business admin, finance, financial planning, human resources, international, management information systems, management science, operations. **Communications:** General, journalism, media studies, public relations. **Computer sciences:** General, computer science. **Conservation:** General, environmental studies. **Construction:** Maintenance. **Education:** General, art, biology, business, chemistry, computer, curriculum, drama/dance, early childhood, elementary, English, family/consumer sciences, foreign languages, French, German, health, health occupations, history, mathematics, middle, music, physical, physics, science, secondary, social science, social studies, Spanish, speech, technology/industrial arts, voc/tech. **Engineering:** General, civil, computer, electrical, mechanical. **Engineering technology:** Automotive, computer, electrical, manufacturing, mechanical. **Family/consumer sciences:** General, clothing/textiles, family studies, family/community services, food/nutrition, housing. **Foreign languages:** French, German, Spanish. **Health:** Athletic training, communication disorders, cytotechnology, dental hygiene, health care admin, nursing (RN), predental, premedicine, preop/surgical nursing, prepharmacy, preveterinary, public health ed, recreational therapy. **History:** General. **Interdisciplinary:** Biological/physical sciences, gerontology, math/computer science. **Legal studies:** Prelaw. **Math:** General. **Mechanic/repair:** Automotive. **Parks/recreation:** General, exercise sciences, facilities management, health/fitness, sports admin. **Philosophy/religion:** Philosophy. **Physical sciences:** Astronomy, chemistry, physics. **Protective services:** Corrections, law enforcement admin, police science. **Psychology:** General. **Public administration:** General, human services, social work. **Social sciences:** Anthropology, economics, geography, international relations, political science, sociology, urban studies. **Transportation:** Aviation management. **Visual/performing arts:** General, art, art history/conservation, ceramics, commercial/advertising art, dramatic, drawing, fiber arts, music management, music performance, painting, sculpture, studio arts, theater design.

Most popular majors. Business/marketing 24%, education 13%, health sciences 10%, security/protective services 6%, social sciences 6%, visual/performing arts 6%.

Computing on campus. 900 workstations in dormitories, library, computer center, student center. Dormitories wired for high-speed internet access and linked to campus network. Commuter students can connect to campus network. Online course registration, online library, helpline, repair service, student web hosting, wireless network available.

Student life. Freshman orientation: Mandatory, $65 fee. Preregistration for classes offered. Includes overnight stay. **Housing:** Coed dorms, special housing for disabled available. $250 partly refundable deposit. **Activities:** Bands, campus ministries, choral groups, dance, drama, international student organizations, music ensembles, musical theater, radio station, student government, student newspaper, symphony orchestra, Hmong student association, American Indian student association, Chicano Latino AM student association, Fellowship of Christian Athletes, InterVarsity, MSU Pagan Organization.

Athletics. NCAA. **Intercollegiate:** Baseball M, basketball, bowling W, cheerleading, cross-country, diving, football (tackle) M, golf, ice hockey, soccer W, softball W, swimming, tennis, track and field, volleyball W, wrestling M. **Intramural:** Archery, basketball, bowling, football (non-tackle), golf, ice hockey, racquetball, rugby, soccer, softball, swimming, tennis, track and field, triathlon, volleyball, wrestling M. **Team name:** Mavericks.

Student services. Adult student services, alcohol/substance abuse counseling, chaplain/spiritual director, career counseling, services for economically disadvantaged, student employment services, financial aid counseling, health services, legal services, minority student services, on-campus daycare, personal counseling, placement for graduates, veterans' counselor, women's services. **Physically disabled:** Services for visually, speech, hearing impaired.

Contact. E-mail: admissions@mnsu.edu
Phone: (507) 389-1822 Toll-free number: (800) 722-0544
Fax: (507) 389-1511
Walt Wolff, Director of Admissions, Minnesota State University: Mankato, 122 Taylor Center, Mankato, MN 56001

Minnesota State University: Moorhead

Moorhead, Minnesota
www.mnstate.edu **CB code: 6678**

- Public 4-year university
- Residential campus in small city
- 6,730 degree-seeking undergraduates
- 80% of applicants admitted
- SAT or ACT (ACT writing recommended) required

General. Founded in 1885. Regionally accredited. **Degrees:** 1,345 bachelor's, 43 associate awarded; master's offered. **ROTC:** Army, Air Force. **Location:** 240 miles from Minneapolis-St. Paul. **Calendar:** Semester, limited summer session. **Full-time faculty:** 307 total. **Part-time faculty:** 185 total. **Special facilities:** Planetarium, biology museum.

Freshman class profile. 3,125 applied, 2,490 admitted, 1,219 enrolled.

Mid 50% test scores		**ACT composite:**	19-24
SAT critical reading:	420-570	**Rank in top quarter:**	31%
SAT math:	430-530	**Rank in top tenth:**	10%

Basis for selection. Applicants must rank in top half of class or have minimum ACT composite score of 21 or equivalent scores on SAT or PSAT/NMSQT. Some applicants not meeting requirements will be admitted to transitional college program. Applicants must also fulfill minimum requirements of secondary course work. Students not meeting automatic admission standards may apply through alternative admissions program, New Center. **Learning Disabled:** Contact Office of Disability Services to make sure appropriate accommodations can be provided.

High school preparation. 16 units required. Required units include English 4, mathematics 3, social studies 3, science 3 (laboratory 1) and academic electives 3. One unit fine arts, .5 computer science recommended.

2008-2009 Annual costs. Tuition/fees: $6,142. Out-of-state students pay same rate as in-state. Room/board: $5,936. Books/supplies: $800. Personal expenses: $2,206.

2008-2009 Financial aid. **Non-need-based:** Scholarships awarded for academics, art, athletics, leadership, music/drama, state residency.

Application procedures. **Admission:** Closing date 8/1 (postmark date). $20 fee. Admission notification on a rolling basis. **Financial aid:** Priority date 2/15; no closing date. FAFSA required. Applicants notified on a rolling basis starting 6/1; must reply within 2 week(s) of notification.

Academics. **Special study options:** Cross-registration, distance learning, double major, dual enrollment of high school students, exchange student, external degree, honors, independent study, internships, student-designed major, study abroad, teacher certification program. Reciprocal bachelor's degree programs with North Dakota State University. **Credit/placement by examination:** AP, CLEP, institutional tests. 12 credit hours maximum toward bachelor's degree. **Support services:** Pre-admission summer program, reduced course load, remedial instruction, study skills assistance, tutoring, writing center.

Majors. **Area/ethnic studies:** American, East Asian. **Biology:** General. **Business:** Accounting, business admin, finance, international, management information systems, marketing. **Communications:** Media studies. **Computer sciences:** General, computer science. **Education:** Art, biology, chemistry, elementary, English, health, kindergarten/preschool, mathematics, music, physical, physics, science, social studies, Spanish, special, speech. **Engineering technology:** Construction, industrial. **Foreign languages:** Spanish. **Health:** Athletic training, audiology/speech pathology, clinical lab science, community health services, health care admin, nurse practitioner, predental, premedicine, prepharmacy, preveterinary. **History:** General. **Interdisciplinary:** Gerontology. **Legal studies:** General, paralegal. **Math:** General. **Parks/recreation:** Exercise sciences, health/fitness. **Philosophy/religion:** Philosophy. **Physical sciences:** Chemistry, physics. **Protective services:** Criminal justice. **Psychology:** General. **Public administration:** Social work. **Social sciences:** Anthropology, economics, political science, sociology. **Visual/performing arts:** Art, commercial/advertising art, dramatic, music management, music performance.

Computing on campus. 791 workstations in dormitories, library, computer center. Dormitories linked to campus network. Commuter students can connect to campus network. Online course registration, online library, helpline, repair service, student web hosting, wireless network available.

Student life. **Freshman orientation:** Available, $50 fee. Preregistration for classes offered. **Housing:** Coed dorms, single-sex dorms, special housing for disabled, apartments, fraternity/sorority housing available. $350 deposit. **Activities:** Bands, choral groups, dance, drama, literary magazine, music ensembles, musical theater, radio station, student government, student newspaper, symphony orchestra, TV station, 125 student clubs, including Spurs, Circle-K, Newman Club, United Campus Ministry, Spanish Club, Habitat for Humanity, Amnesty International, Model United Nations, Volunteer Visions.

Athletics. NCAA. **Intercollegiate:** Basketball, cross-country, diving W, football (tackle) M, golf W, soccer W, softball W, swimming W, tennis W, track and field, volleyball W, wrestling M. **Intramural:** Badminton, basketball, golf, ice hockey M, lacrosse M, racquetball, rugby, soccer, softball, swimming, tennis, track and field, volleyball, water polo, wrestling M. **Team name:** Dragons.

Student services. Adult student services, alcohol/substance abuse counseling, career counseling, student employment services, financial aid counseling, health services, minority student services, on-campus daycare, personal counseling, placement for graduates, veterans' counselor, women's services. **Physically disabled:** Services for visually, speech, hearing impaired.

Contact. E-mail: dragon@mnstate.edu
Phone: (218) 477-2161 Toll-free number: (800) 593-7246
Fax: (218) 477-4374
Gina Monson, Director of Admissions, Minnesota State University: Moorhead, Owens Hall, Moorhead, MN 56563

National American University: Roseville

Roseville, Minnesota
www.national.edu

- For-profit 4-year university and branch campus college
- Very large city
- 350 degree-seeking undergraduates

General. Regionally accredited. **Degrees:** 20 bachelor's, 25 associate awarded. **Calendar:** Quarter. **Part-time faculty:** 39 total.

Freshman class profile. 100 applied, 100 admitted, 100 enrolled.

Basis for selection. Open admission.

Application procedures. **Admission:** $25 fee. **Financial aid:** Closing date 8/25.

Academics. **Credit/placement by examination:** CLEP.

Majors. **Business:** Business admin. **Computer sciences:** General.

Contact. Nicole Ryan, Director of Admissions, National American University: Roseville, 1550 West Highway 36, Roseville, MN 55431

National American University: St. Paul

Bloomington, Minnesota
www.national.edu **CB code: 5358**

- For-profit 4-year branch campus and business college
- Commuter campus in very large city
- 350 degree-seeking undergraduates

General. Founded in 1974. Regionally accredited. Campuses in Bloomington/Mall of America, Brooklyn Center and Roseville. **Degrees:** 40 bachelor's, 30 associate awarded; master's offered. **Calendar:** Quarter, extensive summer session. **Full-time faculty:** 5 total. **Part-time faculty:** 65 total. **Class size:** 95% < 20, 5% 20-39.

Freshman class profile. 100 applied, 100 admitted, 80 enrolled.

Basis for selection. Open admission.

2008-2009 Annual costs. Books/supplies: $1,000.

Financial aid. **Non-need-based:** Scholarships awarded for academics.

Application procedures. **Admission:** No deadline. $25 fee. Admission notification on a rolling basis. **Financial aid:** Priority date 8/21; no closing date. FAFSA required. Applicants notified on a rolling basis.

Academics. **Special study options:** Accelerated study, distance learning, double major, independent study, internships. **Credit/placement by examination:** AP, CLEP, IB, institutional tests. **Support services:** Reduced course load, tutoring.

Majors. **Business:** General, accounting, business admin, hospitality admin, international, management information systems, marketing. **Computer sciences:** General, programming.

Computing on campus. 112 workstations in library, computer center. Online library available.

Student life. **Freshman orientation:** Mandatory. Preregistration for classes offered. **Activities:** Student government, student business club, Southeast Asian student organization, student government, international student organizations.

Athletics. **Team name:** Mavericks.

Student services. Career counseling, student employment services, placement for graduates.

Contact. E-mail: mmottl@national.edu
Phone: (952) 883-0439 Toll-free number: (866) 628-6387
Fax: (952) 883-0439
Michael Curtis, Director of Admissions, National American University: St. Paul, Mall of America West 112 West Market, Bloomington, MN 55425

North Central University

Minneapolis, Minnesota
www.northcentral.edu **CB code: 0051**

- Private 4-year university and Bible college affiliated with Assemblies of God
- Residential campus in large city

General. Founded in 1930. Regionally accredited. **Location:** One mile from downtown. **Calendar:** Semester.

Annual costs/financial aid. Tuition/fees (2008-2009): $14,586. Room/board: $5,330. Books/supplies: $600. Need-based financial aid available to full-time and part-time students.

Contact. Phone: (612) 343-4460
Director of Admissions, 910 Elliot Avenue, Minneapolis, MN 55404

Northwestern College

Saint Paul, Minnesota
www.nwc.edu **CB code: 6489**

- Private 4-year Bible and liberal arts college affiliated with nondenominational tradition
- Residential campus in very large city
- 1,842 degree-seeking undergraduates: 3% part-time, 59% women, 2% African American, 4% Asian American, 2% Hispanic American
- 93 degree-seeking graduate students
- 95% of applicants admitted
- SAT or ACT (ACT writing optional), application essay required
- 57% graduate within 6 years; 7% enter graduate study

General. Founded in 1902. Regionally accredited. **Degrees:** 348 bachelor's, 5 associate awarded; master's offered. **ROTC:** Army, Air Force. **Location:** 9 miles from Minneapolis-St. Paul. **Calendar:** Semester, limited summer session. **Full-time faculty:** 100 total; 61% have terminal degrees, 7% minority, 36% women. **Part-time faculty:** 81 total; 31% have terminal degrees, 9% minority, 51% women. **Class size:** 54% < 20, 40% 20-39, 3% 40-49, 2% 50-99, less than 1% >100.

Freshman class profile. 1,022 applied, 967 admitted, 437 enrolled.

Mid 50% test scores		**GPA 2.0-2.99:**	11%
SAT critical reading:	530-680	**Rank in top quarter:**	55%
SAT math:	510-640	**Rank in top tenth:**	28%
ACT composite:	21-27	**End year in good standing:**	90%
GPA 3.75 or higher:	41%	**Return as sophomores:**	79%
GPA 3.50-3.74:	22%	**Out-of-state:**	29%
GPA 3.0-3.49:	25%	**Live on campus:**	95%

Basis for selection. Evidence that student will benefit from the education and contribute to the community important. School record, recommendations, test scores, essay, character, and religious affiliation very important. Audition required for music students. Portfolio recommended for art students. Interview recommended for borderline students.

High school preparation. 16 units recommended. Recommended units include English 4, mathematics 3, social studies 3, science 3, foreign language 2 and academic electives 1.

2009-2010 Annual costs. Tuition/fees: $22,990. Computer technology fee of $190. Room/board: $7,426. Books/supplies: $610. Personal expenses: $1,610.

2007-2008 Financial aid. Need-based: 464 full-time freshmen applied for aid; 421 were judged to have need; 421 of these received aid. Average need met was 69%. Average scholarship/grant was $11,022; average loan $3,895. 63% of total undergraduate aid awarded as scholarships/grants, 37% as loans/jobs. **Non-need-based:** Awarded to 365 full-time undergraduates, including 117 freshmen. Scholarships awarded for academics, alumni affiliation, leadership, music/drama. **Additional information:** Students enrolled at least half-time in the FOCUS or Distance Education degree programs may apply for financial aid from the same Federal and state sources as traditional undergraduates. However, their expense budgets and aid are less due to lower tuition: FOCUS, $345/credit; Center for Distance Education, $260/credit.

Application procedures. Admission: Priority date 5/1; deadline 8/1 (receipt date). $30 fee, may be waived for applicants with need. Admission notification on a rolling basis beginning on or about 10/1. **Financial aid:** Priority date 3/1, closing date 6/1. FAFSA, institutional form required. Applicants notified on a rolling basis starting 3/1; must reply within 2 week(s) of notification.

Academics. Core currilum built around a biblical worldview theme thoroughly integrates general education and biblical studies (64-68 credits). Transfer students meet core curriculum requirements on a proportional basis. **Special study options:** Combined bachelor's/graduate degree, distance learning, double major, exchange student, honors, independent study, internships, liberal arts/career combination, student-designed major, study abroad, teacher certification program, Washington semester. **Credit/placement by examination:** AP, CLEP, IB, SAT, ACT, institutional tests. 32 credit hours maximum toward associate degree, 32 toward bachelor's. **Support services:** Learning center, reduced course load, remedial instruction, study skills assistance, tutoring.

Majors. Biology: General. **Business:** Accounting, business admin, finance, international, management information systems, marketing. **Communications:** General, journalism, public relations, radio/tv. **Communications technology:** Animation/special effects. **Education:** Art, early childhood, elementary, English, ESL, mathematics, music, physical, social studies. **Foreign languages:** Spanish. **History:** General. **Math:** General. **Parks/recreation:** Exercise sciences, health/fitness. **Protective services:** Criminal justice. **Psychology:** General. **Theology:** Bible, missionary, preministerial, youth ministry. **Visual/performing arts:** Dramatic, graphic design, music performance, music theory/composition, piano/organ, stringed instruments, studio arts, voice/opera. **Other:** Adult and family ministry, Multi/interdisciplinary studies, Urban studies.

Most popular majors. Business/marketing 14%, communications/journalism 13%, education 16%, psychology 12%, theological studies 20%, visual/performing arts 8%.

Computing on campus. PC or laptop required. 100 workstations in library, computer center, student center. Dormitories wired for high-speed internet access and linked to campus network. Commuter students can connect to campus network. Online course registration, online library, helpline, wireless network available.

Student life. Freshman orientation: Mandatory. Preregistration for classes offered. 6 one-day events during summer. General orientation: 4 days prior to start of classes. Multicultural orientation: 4 days prior to general orientation. **Policies:** Religious observance required. **Housing:** Guaranteed on-campus for freshmen. Single-sex dorms, special housing for disabled, apartments, wellness housing available. **Activities:** Bands, choral groups, drama, literary magazine, music ensembles, musical theater, opera, radio station, student government, student newspaper, symphony orchestra, Student Missions Fellowship, The Gathering, transfer student organization, Guardian Angels, Mu Kappa, organization for students of color, Young Republicans.

Athletics. NCAA, NCCAA. **Intercollegiate:** Baseball M, basketball, cross-country, football (tackle) M, golf M, soccer, softball W, tennis, track and field, volleyball W. **Intramural:** Basketball, football (non-tackle), softball, tennis, volleyball. **Team name:** Eagles.

Student services. Adult student services, chaplain/spiritual director, career counseling, student employment services, financial aid counseling, health services, minority student services, personal counseling, placement for graduates.

Contact. E-mail: admissions@nwc.edu
Phone: (651) 631-5111 Toll-free number: (800) 827-6827
Fax: (651) 631-5680
Kenneth Faffler, Director of Admissions, Northwestern College, 3003 Snelling Avenue North, Saint Paul, MN 55113-1598

Northwestern Health Sciences University

Bloomington, Minnesota
www.nwhealth.edu

- Private two-year upper-division university and health science college
- Very large city

General. Regionally accredited. **Degrees:** 49 bachelor's awarded; master's, first professional offered. **Calendar:** Trimester, limited summer session. **Full-time faculty:** 80 total. **Part-time faculty:** 38 total.

Student profile. 70 degree-seeking undergraduates, 808 graduate students.

2008-2009 Annual costs. Tuition/fees: $12,155. Reported costs are for undergraduate massage therapy certificate for 2 trimesters. Books/supplies: $972. Personal expenses: $2,400.

Application procedures. Admission: $50 fee.

Academics. **Credit/placement by examination:** CLEP.

Majors. **Other:** Human biology.

Computing on campus. Wireless network available.

Contact. E-mail: admit@nwhealth.edu
Phone: (952) 888-4777 ext. 409
Bill Kuehl, Director of Admissions, Northwestern Health Sciences University, 2501 West 84th Street, Bloomington, MN 55431

Oak Hills Christian College
Bemidji, Minnesota
www.oakhills.edu **CB code: 7247**

- Private 4-year Bible college affiliated with interdenominational tradition
- Residential campus in large town
- 144 degree-seeking undergraduates: 15% part-time, 51% women, 1% African American, 2% Asian American, 1% Hispanic American, 1% Native American
- 91% of applicants admitted
- ACT (writing optional), application essay required
- 33% graduate within 6 years

General. Founded in 1946. Accredited by ABHE. **Degrees:** 21 bachelor's, 11 associate awarded. **Location:** 4 miles from Bemidji, 230 miles from Minneapolis-St. Paul. **Calendar:** Semester. **Full-time faculty:** 6 total; 67% have terminal degrees. **Part-time faculty:** 14 total; 29% have terminal degrees, 29% women. **Class size:** 64% < 20, 28% 20-39, 3% 40-49, 5% 50-99. **Special facilities:** American Indian resource center.

Freshman class profile. 45 applied, 41 admitted, 26 enrolled.

Mid 50% test scores		**Rank in top quarter:**	40%
ACT composite:	26-26	**Rank in top tenth:**	20%
GPA 3.75 or higher:	22%	**Return as sophomores:**	59%
GPA 3.50-3.74:	6%	**Out-of-state:**	30%
GPA 3.0-3.49:	17%	**Live on campus:**	96%
GPA 2.0-2.99:	55%		

Basis for selection. Applicants must have high school GPA of 2.0 or above and/or ACT score of 18 or above to be eligible for consideration. Applicants not meeting minimum requirements considered on individual basis. SAT/ACT scores must be received at latest 4 weeks after first day of classes. Not required if student has 1 year of college credit or if 2 years out of high school. An essay or personal statement may generate an interview. **Homeschooled:** Transcript of courses and grades, letter of recommendation (nonparent) required. Proof of graduation from high school. **Learning Disabled:** All special education or diagnostic (IEP) records required. Interview may be requested.

2009-2010 Annual costs. Tuition/fees (projected): $13,480. Room/board: $4,840. Books/supplies: $750. Personal expenses: $2,975.

2007-2008 Financial aid. **Need-based:** 21 full-time freshmen applied for aid; 20 were judged to have need; 20 of these received aid. Average need met was 55%. Average scholarship/grant was $5,140; average loan $3,116. 65% of total undergraduate aid awarded as scholarships/grants, 35% as loans/jobs. **Non-need-based:** Awarded to 10 full-time undergraduates, including 1 freshmen. Scholarships awarded for academics, alumni affiliation.

Application procedures. **Admission:** No deadline. $25 fee, may be waived for applicants with need. Admission notification on a rolling basis beginning on or about 9/1. **Financial aid:** No deadline. FAFSA, institutional form required. Applicants notified on a rolling basis starting 3/1.

Academics. **Special study options:** Combined bachelor's/graduate degree, cooperative education, double major, independent study, internships. **Credit/placement by examination:** AP, CLEP, ACT, institutional tests. **Support services:** Reduced course load, remedial instruction, study skills assistance, tutoring.

Majors. **Psychology:** General. **Theology:** Bible, missionary, sacred music.

Most popular majors. Liberal arts 38%, theological studies 63%.

Computing on campus. 12 workstations in library. Dormitories wired for high-speed internet access and linked to campus network. Online course registration, online library, wireless network available.

Student life. **Freshman orientation:** Mandatory. Preregistration for classes offered. Held first weekend prior to start of fall classes. **Policies:** Mandatory chapel, no alcohol, illegal drugs, gambling, or smoking on campus. Religious observance required. **Housing:** Guaranteed on-campus for freshmen. Single-sex dorms, special housing for disabled, apartments, wellness housing available. $100 fully refundable deposit. Apartments for students with dependent children. **Activities:** Campus ministries, choral groups, music ensembles, student government, married students group, students older than average group, women's group, engaged couples group, many outreach programs, single student cell groups.

Athletics. **Intercollegiate:** Basketball, volleyball W. **Intramural:** Basketball, football (non-tackle), golf, racquetball, soccer, softball, table tennis, volleyball. **Team name:** Wolfpack.

Student services. Adult student services, chaplain/spiritual director, career counseling, student employment services, financial aid counseling, health services, personal counseling, placement for graduates. **Physically disabled:** Services for visually, speech, hearing impaired. **Learning disabled:** Comprehensive services available.

Contact. E-mail: admissions@oakhills.edu
Phone: (218) 751-8671 ext. 1285 Toll-free
number: (888) 751-8670 ext. 1285 Fax: (218) 751-8825
Dan Hovestol, Admissions Director, Oak Hills Christian College, 1600 Oak Hills Road SW, Bemidji, MN 56601-8826

Rasmussen College: Lake Elmo/Woodbury
Lake Elmo, Minnesota
www.rasmussen.edu

- For-profit 4-year technical college
- Small city
- 534 degree-seeking undergraduates

General. Regionally accredited. **Degrees:** 2 associate awarded. **Calendar:** Quarter. **Full-time faculty:** 6 total. **Part-time faculty:** 9 total.

Basis for selection. Open admission, but selective for some programs.

2009-2010 Annual costs. Regular courses: $405/credit; networking courses: $515/credit; child care courses: $280/credit.

Application procedures. **Admission:** $60 fee.

Academics. **Credit/placement by examination:** CLEP.

Majors. **Business:** Business admin.

Contact. Phone: (651) 259-6600
David Tan, Director of Admissions, Rasmussen College: Lake Elmo/Woodbury, 8565 Eagle Point Circle, Lake Elmo, MN 55042-8637

Saint Cloud State University
St. Cloud, Minnesota
www.stcloudstate.edu **CB code: 6679**

- Public 4-year university
- Commuter campus in small city
- 13,501 degree-seeking undergraduates: 12% part-time, 51% women, 4% African American, 3% Asian American, 1% Hispanic American, 1% Native American, 6% international
- 1,472 degree-seeking graduate students
- 86% of applicants admitted
- SAT or ACT (ACT writing optional) required
- 48% graduate within 6 years

General. Founded in 1869. Regionally accredited. **Degrees:** 2,508 bachelor's, 100 associate awarded; master's, doctoral offered. **ROTC:** Army. **Location:** 80 miles from Minneapolis-St. Paul. **Calendar:** Semester, limited summer session. **Full-time faculty:** 645 total; 71% have terminal degrees, 17% minority, 44% women. **Part-time faculty:** 300 total; 10% have terminal degrees, 7% minority, 52% women. **Class size:** 35% < 20, 53% 20-39, 7% 40-49, 4% 50-99, 2% >100. **Special facilities:** Planetarium, greenhouse, nature preserve, observatory, GIS cartographic center, aviation facilities, weather labs, National Hockey Center, AVID editing equipment.

Freshman class profile. 6,104 applied, 5,245 admitted, 2,403 enrolled.

Mid 50% test scores		Rank in top quarter:	23%
ACT composite:	19-24	Rank in top tenth:	6%
GPA 3.75 or higher:	10%	Return as sophomores:	73%
GPA 3.50-3.74:	16%	Out-of-state:	9%
GPA 3.0-3.49:	41%	Live on campus:	71%
GPA 2.0-2.99:	32%	International:	5%

Basis for selection. Each application individually reviewed and evaluated using a combination of high school rank, GPA, curriculum, test scores, and other indicators of academic performance and potential.

High school preparation. College-preparatory program required. 16 units required. Required units include English 4, mathematics 3, social studies 2, history 1, science 3 (laboratory 1), foreign language 2 and visual/performing arts 1.

2008-2009 Annual costs. Tuition/fees: $6,147; $12,474 out-of-state. Room/board: $5,770.

2008-2009 Financial aid. **Need-based:** 1,790 full-time freshmen applied for aid; 1,249 were judged to have need; 1,249 of these received aid. Average need met was 66%. Average scholarship/grant was $5,094; average loan $4,563. 33% of total undergraduate aid awarded as scholarships/grants, 67% as loans/jobs. **Non-need-based:** Awarded to 549 full-time undergraduates, including 159 freshmen. Scholarships awarded for academics, art, athletics, leadership, music/drama.

Application procedures. **Admission:** Priority date 5/1; deadline 6/1 (receipt date). $20 fee, may be waived for applicants with need. Admission notification on a rolling basis beginning on or about 9/15. Early application recommended for those who want to live on-campus. **Financial aid:** No deadline. FAFSA, institutional form required. Applicants notified on a rolling basis starting 6/15.

Academics. **Special study options:** Accelerated study, cooperative education, cross-registration, distance learning, double major, dual enrollment of high school students, ESL, honors, independent study, internships, student-designed major, study abroad, teacher certification program, weekend college. **Credit/placement by examination:** AP, CLEP, IB, institutional tests. 32 credit hours maximum toward bachelor's degree. **Support services:** Learning center, pre-admission summer program, remedial instruction, study skills assistance, tutoring, writing center.

Majors. **Area/ethnic studies:** Latin American, women's. **Biology:** General, aquatic, biochemistry, biotechnology, cellular/anatomical, ecology, marine. **Business:** General, accounting, business admin, entrepreneurial studies, finance, human resources, insurance, international, management information systems, marketing, real estate, tourism/travel. **Communications:** General, advertising, broadcast journalism, journalism, media studies, public relations, radio/tv. **Computer sciences:** General, computer science, networking, security. **Conservation:** Environmental science, environmental studies. **Education:** Art, biology, chemistry, drama/dance, driver/safety, early childhood, elementary, English, foreign languages, French, German, health, history, instructional media, kindergarten/preschool, mathematics, multi-level teacher, music, physical, physics, psychology, reading, science, secondary, social science, social studies, Spanish, special, speech, technology/industrial arts. **Engineering:** Computer, electrical, manufacturing, mechanical. **Engineering technology:** Surveying. **Foreign languages:** French, German, linguistics, Spanish. **Health:** Audiology/speech pathology, clinical lab science, communication disorders, community health services, medical radiologic technology/radiation therapy, nuclear medical technology, nursing (RN), predental, premedicine, prepharmacy, preveterinary, public health ed, recreational therapy, substance abuse counseling. **History:** General. **Interdisciplinary:** Gerontology, global studies, natural sciences. **Legal studies:** Prelaw. **Liberal arts:** Arts/sciences, library science. **Math:** General, statistics. **Parks/recreation:** General, health/fitness. **Philosophy/religion:** Philosophy. **Physical sciences:** General, atmospheric science, chemistry, geology, hydrology, meteorology, physics, planetary. **Protective services:** Criminal justice. **Psychology:** General, community. **Public administration:** General, social work. **Social sciences:** General, anthropology, econometrics, economics, geography, international relations, political science, sociology, urban studies. **Transportation:** Air traffic control, airline/commercial pilot, aviation management, flight instructor. **Visual/performing arts:** Acting, art, art history/conservation, ceramics, dramatic, drawing, film/cinema, jazz, music history, music performance, painting, piano/organ, printmaking, sculpture, stringed instruments, studio arts, voice/opera. **Other:** Business economics, Communication studies, Earth science.

Most popular majors. Business/marketing 27%, communications/journalism 9%, education 12%, psychology 6%, social sciences 8%.

Computing on campus. 1,489 workstations in dormitories, library, computer center, student center. Dormitories wired for high-speed internet access and linked to campus network. Commuter students can connect to campus network. Online course registration, online library, helpline, repair service, student web hosting, wireless network available.

Student life. **Freshman orientation:** Mandatory. Preregistration for classes offered. Includes assistance with fall term registration. **Housing:** Coed dorms, single-sex dorms, special housing for disabled, apartments available. $100 fully refundable deposit, deadline 3/31. **Activities:** Bands, campus ministries, choral groups, dance, drama, film society, international student organizations, literary magazine, music ensembles, Model UN, musical theater, opera, radio station, student government, student newspaper, symphony orchestra, TV station, more than 240 clubs and departmental organizations.

Athletics. NCAA. **Intercollegiate:** Baseball M, basketball, cross-country, diving, football (tackle) M, golf, ice hockey, skiing W, soccer W, softball W, swimming, tennis, track and field, volleyball W, wrestling M. **Intramural:** Badminton, basketball, football (non-tackle), golf, ice hockey, racquetball, soccer, softball, tennis, volleyball, water polo. **Team name:** Huskies.

Student services. Adult student services, alcohol/substance abuse counseling, career counseling, student employment services, financial aid counseling, health services, legal services, minority student services, on-campus daycare, personal counseling, placement for graduates, veterans' counselor, women's services. **Physically disabled:** Services for visually, speech, hearing impaired.

Contact. E-mail: scsu4u@stcloudstate.edu
Phone: (320) 308-2244 Toll-free number: (877) 654-7278
Fax: (320) 308-2243
Richard Shearer, Director of Admissions, Saint Cloud State University, 720 Fourth Avenue South, St. Cloud, MN 56301

St. John's University

Collegeville, Minnesota — **CB member**
www.csbsju.edu — **CB code: 6624**

- Private 4-year university and liberal arts college for men affiliated with Roman Catholic Church
- Residential campus in rural community
- 1,897 degree-seeking undergraduates: 1% African American, 2% Asian American, 1% Hispanic American, 6% international
- 125 graduate students
- 74% of applicants admitted
- SAT or ACT (ACT writing optional), application essay required
- 83% graduate within 6 years; 19% enter graduate study

General. Founded in 1857. Regionally accredited. SJU located six miles from the College of Saint Benedict; students enrolled on both campuses have access to classes, activities held by the two institutions. **Degrees:** 469 bachelor's awarded; master's, first professional offered. **ROTC:** Army. **Location:** 70 miles from Minneapolis-St. Paul, 15 miles from St. Cloud. **Calendar:** Semester, limited summer session. **Full-time faculty:** 144 total; 85% have terminal degrees, 8% minority, 48% women. **Part-time faculty:** 32 total; 34% have terminal degrees, 3% minority, 38% women. **Class size:** 49% < 20, 51% 20-39, less than 1% 40-49, less than 1% 50-99. **Special facilities:** Observatory, ecumenical center, museum and manuscript library, liturgical press, nature preserve, arboretum, natural history museum, pottery kiln.

Freshman class profile. 1,557 applied, 1,152 admitted, 461 enrolled.

Mid 50% test scores		Rank in top quarter:	64%
SAT critical reading:	480-650	Rank in top tenth:	51%
SAT math:	540-650	End year in good standing:	93%
ACT composite:	23-28	Return as sophomores:	90%
GPA 3.75 or higher:	37%	Out-of-state:	16%
GPA 3.50-3.74:	23%	Live on campus:	100%
GPA 3.0-3.49:	35%	International:	6%
GPA 2.0-2.99:	5%		

Basis for selection. Course selection, scholastic achievement, GPA, test scores and essay are most important. Extracurricular involvement, high school rank, and recommendation are also important. Students who have completed the application process by 11/15 will receive notification of their scholarship award on 12/20. Those that complete by 12/15 will receive notification of their scholarship award on 2/1. Interview recommended for academically weak/conditionally accepted students. **Homeschooled:** Applicants are not required to have a high school diploma, but are required to provide appropriate documentation of college preparatory curriculum.

High school preparation. College-preparatory program required. 15 units required. Required and recommended units include English 4, mathematics 3, social studies 2, science 2 (laboratory 2), foreign language 2 and academic electives 4.

2008-2009 Annual costs. Tuition/fees: $28,668. Room/board: $7,248. Books/supplies: $800. Personal expenses: $700.

2008-2009 Financial aid. **Need-based:** 356 full-time freshmen applied for aid; 280 were judged to have need; 280 of these received aid. Average need met was 95%. Average scholarship/grant was $17,934; average loan $4,635. 59% of total undergraduate aid awarded as scholarships/grants, 41% as loans/jobs. **Non-need-based:** Awarded to 1,673 full-time undergraduates, including 409 freshmen. Scholarships awarded for academics, art, leadership, music/drama, ROTC.

Application procedures. **Admission:** Priority date 11/15; no deadline. No application fee. Admission notification on a rolling basis. A nonrefundable enrollment deposit of $300 is due by May 1. **Financial aid:** Closing date 3/15. FAFSA, institutional form required. Applicants notified on a rolling basis starting 3/15; must reply by 5/1.

Academics. **Special study options:** Combined bachelor's/graduate degree, cross-registration, double major, dual enrollment of high school students, ESL, exchange student, honors, independent study, internships, student-designed major, study abroad, teacher certification program, United Nations semester. 3-2 program in engineering with University of Minnesota, 3-1 program in dentistry with University of Minnesota, cross registration with St. Cloud State University. **Credit/placement by examination:** AP, CLEP, IB, institutional tests. **Support services:** Study skills assistance, tutoring, writing center.

Majors. **Area/ethnic studies:** Women's. **Biology:** General, biochemistry. **Business:** Accounting, business admin. **Computer sciences:** Computer science. **Conservation:** Environmental science. **Education:** General, elementary. **Foreign languages:** Classics, French, German, Spanish. **Health:** Dietetics, nursing (RN), predental, premedicine, prepharmacy, preveterinary. **History:** General. **Interdisciplinary:** Biological/physical sciences, math/computer science, natural sciences, nutrition sciences, peace/conflict. **Legal studies:** Prelaw. **Liberal arts:** Arts/sciences, humanities. **Math:** General. **Philosophy/religion:** Philosophy. **Physical sciences:** Chemistry, physics. **Psychology:** General. **Public administration:** Social work. **Social sciences:** General, economics, political science, sociology. **Theology:** Preministerial, theology. **Visual/performing arts:** Art, dramatic.

Most popular majors. Biology 8%, business/marketing 28%, English 10%, social sciences 12%.

Computing on campus. 791 workstations in dormitories, library, computer center, student center. Dormitories wired for high-speed internet access and linked to campus network. Commuter students can connect to campus network. Online course registration, helpline, repair service, student web hosting, wireless network available.

Student life. **Freshman orientation:** Mandatory. Preregistration for classes offered. Fall orientation begins the evening of move-in day and concludes with convocation the first day of classes. **Policies:** Freshmen and sophomores are required to live on campus. **Housing:** Guaranteed on-campus for freshmen. Special housing for disabled, apartments, wellness housing available. Earth-sheltered, solar-heated apartments available to upperclassmen; ROTC housing. **Activities:** Bands, campus ministries, choral groups, dance, drama, international student organizations, literary magazine, music ensembles, Model UN, musical theater, opera, radio station, student government, student newspaper, symphony orchestra, Volunteers in Service to Others, College Republicans, College Democrats, Joints Events Council, Asia club, Student Coalition for Global Solidarity, Students in Free Enterprise, Magis, Cultural Fusion Club, Outdoor Leadership center.

Athletics. NCAA. **Intercollegiate:** Baseball M, basketball M, cross-country M, diving M, football (tackle) M, golf M, ice hockey M, skiing M, soccer M, swimming M, tennis M, track and field M, wrestling M. **Intramural:** Basketball M, football (tackle) M, ice hockey M, racquetball M, soccer M, softball M, table tennis M, tennis M, volleyball M, water polo M. **Team name:** Johnnies.

Student services. Alcohol/substance abuse counseling, chaplain/spiritual director, career counseling, student employment services, financial aid counseling, health services, minority student services, personal counseling, placement for graduates. **Physically disabled:** Services for hearing impaired.

Contact. E-mail: admissions@csbsju.edu
Phone: (320) 363-2196 Toll-free number: (800) 544-1489
Fax: (320) 363-2750
Jon McGee, VP Enrollment, Planning & Public Affairs, St. John's University, PO Box 7155, Collegeville, MN 56321-7155

St. Mary's University of Minnesota

Winona, Minnesota — **CB member**
www.smumn.edu — **CB code: 6632**

- Private 4-year university affiliated with Roman Catholic Church
- Residential campus in large town
- 1,999 degree-seeking undergraduates: 28% part-time, 53% women, 4% African American, 2% Asian American, 3% Hispanic American, 4% international
- 3,305 degree-seeking graduate students
- 74% of applicants admitted
- SAT or ACT (ACT writing optional), application essay required
- 57% graduate within 6 years; 23% enter graduate study

General. Founded in 1912. Regionally accredited. **Degrees:** 427 bachelor's awarded; master's, doctoral offered. **ROTC:** Army. **Location:** 110 miles from Minneapolis-St. Paul, 45 miles from Rochester. **Calendar:** Semester, limited summer session. **Full-time faculty:** 110 total; 82% have terminal degrees, 3% minority, 38% women. **Part-time faculty:** 466 total; 37% have terminal degrees, 6% minority, 50% women. **Class size:** 61% < 20, 39% 20-39, less than 1% 40-49. **Special facilities:** Woodland and stream, nature preserve, observatory.

Freshman class profile. 1,556 applied, 1,158 admitted, 404 enrolled.

Mid 50% test scores		**Rank in top quarter:**	44%
SAT critical reading:	450-630	**Rank in top tenth:**	18%
SAT math:	440-590	**End year in good standing:**	86%
ACT composite:	20-26	**Return as sophomores:**	70%
GPA 3.75 or higher:	25%	**Out-of-state:**	33%
GPA 3.50-3.74:	14%	**Live on campus:**	97%
GPA 3.0-3.49:	28%	**International:**	1%
GPA 2.0-2.99:	32%		

Basis for selection. Minimum 2.5 GPA, upper half of class, 50th percentile on standardized tests, essay, college prep coursework required. Recommendations, interview, school and community activities considered. Interview recommended for academically marginal students. **Homeschooled:** Statement describing homeschool structure and mission, transcript of courses and grades required.

High school preparation. College-preparatory program required. 18 units required. Required and recommended units include English 4, mathematics 3, social studies 2, science 3 (laboratory 2), foreign language 2 and academic electives 6.

2009-2010 Annual costs. Tuition/fees: $25,570. Room/board: $6,760. Books/supplies: $1,220. Personal expenses: $850.

2008-2009 Financial aid. **Need-based:** 320 full-time freshmen applied for aid; 273 were judged to have need; 271 of these received aid. Average need met was 84%. Average scholarship/grant was $15,305; average loan $4,237. 60% of total undergraduate aid awarded as scholarships/grants, 40% as loans/jobs. **Non-need-based:** Awarded to 367 full-time undergraduates, including 129 freshmen. Scholarships awarded for academics, alumni affiliation, art, leadership, minority status, music/drama.

Application procedures. **Admission:** Priority date 4/1; deadline 5/1 (postmark date). $25 fee, may be waived for applicants with need, free for online applicants. Admission notification 5/1. Admission notification on a rolling basis. Must reply by May 1 or within 2 week(s) if notified thereafter. **Financial aid:** Priority date 3/15; no closing date. FAFSA required. Applicants notified on a rolling basis starting 2/1; must reply within 3 week(s) of notification.

Academics. **Special study options:** Cooperative education, cross-registration, double major, dual enrollment of high school students, ESL, honors, independent study, internships, student-designed major, study abroad, teacher certification program, urban semester, Washington semester. **Credit/placement by examination:** AP, CLEP, IB, SAT, ACT, institutional tests. 15 credit hours maximum toward bachelor's degree. **Support services:** Learning center, reduced course load, remedial instruction, study skills assistance, tutoring, writing center.

Majors. **Biology:** General, biochemistry, biophysics, environmental. **Business:** General, accounting, business admin, human resources, international, marketing, sales/distribution. **Communications:** Journalism, public relations, publishing. **Communications technology:** General. **Computer sciences:** General, computer science, information systems. **Education:** Biology, chemistry, elementary, English, foreign languages, French, mathematics, music, physics, social science, Spanish. **Engineering:** Computer, physics. **Engineering technology:** Industrial. **Foreign languages:** French, Spanish. **Health:** Clinical lab science, cytogenetics, cytotechnology, nuclear medical technology, nursing (RN). **History:** General. **Interdisciplinary:** Global studies, math/computer science. **Math:** General. **Philosophy/religion:** Philosophy. **Physical sciences:** Chemistry. **Protective services:** Corrections, criminal justice, law enforcement admin, police science, security management. **Psychology:** General. **Public administration:** Human services. **Social sciences:** General, political science, sociology. **Theology:** Preministerial, religious ed, theology, youth ministry. **Visual/performing arts:** Dramatic, graphic design, music management, music performance, studio arts.

Most popular majors. Business/marketing 39%, computer/information sciences 7%, security/protective services 9%, visual/performing arts 6%.

Computing on campus. 365 workstations in dormitories, library, computer center, student center. Dormitories wired for high-speed internet access and linked to campus network. Commuter students can connect to campus network. Online course registration, online library, helpline, student web hosting, wireless network available.

Student life. Freshman orientation: Mandatory. Preregistration for classes offered. Held during summer prior to fall enrollment. **Housing:** Guaranteed on-campus for all undergraduates. Coed dorms, single-sex dorms, special housing for disabled, apartments, wellness housing available. **Activities:** Bands, campus ministries, choral groups, dance, drama, international student organizations, literary magazine, music ensembles, musical theater, radio station, student government, student newspaper, Big and Little Pals, College Democrats, College Republicans, Serving Others United in Love, Intercultural Awareness Association, liturgical ministers, BUDDIES, Habitat for Humanity, Colleges Against Cancer.

Athletics. NCAA. **Intercollegiate:** Baseball M, basketball, cross-country, diving, golf, ice hockey, soccer, softball W, swimming, tennis, track and field, volleyball W. **Intramural:** Basketball, football (non-tackle), ice hockey M, racquetball, soccer, softball, tennis, volleyball. **Team name:** Cardinals.

Student services. Alcohol/substance abuse counseling, chaplain/spiritual director, career counseling, financial aid counseling, health services, personal counseling. **Physically disabled:** Services for visually, hearing impaired.

Contact. E-mail: admission@smumn.edu
Phone: (507) 457-1700 Toll-free number: (800) 635-5987
Fax: (507) 457-1722
Anthony Piscitiello, Vice President for Admission, St. Mary's University of Minnesota, 700 Terrace Heights #2, Winona, MN 55987-1399

St. Olaf College

Northfield, Minnesota — **CB member**
www.stolaf.edu — **CB code: 6638**

- Private 4-year liberal arts college affiliated with Evangelical Lutheran Church in America
- Residential campus in large town
- 3,014 degree-seeking undergraduates: 55% women, 1% African American, 5% Asian American, 2% Hispanic American, 1% international
- 59% of applicants admitted
- SAT or ACT (ACT writing optional), application essay required
- 87% graduate within 6 years; 30% enter graduate study

General. Founded in 1874. Regionally accredited. **Degrees:** 722 bachelor's awarded. **Location:** 35 miles from Minneapolis-St. Paul. **Calendar:** 4-1-4, limited summer session. **Full-time faculty:** 194 total; 91% have terminal degrees, 9% minority, 42% women. **Part-time faculty:** 129 total; 59% have terminal degrees, 5% minority, 47% women. **Class size:** 61% < 20, 33% 20-39, 2% 40-49, 3% 50-99, less than 1% >100. **Special facilities:** Norwegian-American Historical Society Archives; Kierkegaard Library, natural habitat includes 5 wetland areas, 45-acre native prairie grasses and bluebird trail of 70 houses.

Freshman class profile. 3,964 applied, 2,336 admitted, 813 enrolled.

Mid 50% test scores		**GPA 2.0-2.99:**	9%
SAT critical reading:	590-700	**Rank in top quarter:**	85%
SAT math:	590-710	**Rank in top tenth:**	59%
SAT writing:	580-680	**End year in good standing:**	95%
ACT composite:	27-31	**Return as sophomores:**	92%
GPA 3.75 or higher:	53%	**Out-of-state:**	50%
GPA 3.50-3.74:	22%	**Live on campus:**	100%
GPA 3.0-3.49:	16%	**International:**	3%

Basis for selection. Academic achievement most important, with academic aptitude and personal qualifications, as well as leadership and significant involvement in school and community, strongly considered. Interview recommended. Audition required for music students. **Learning Disabled:** Personal interview recommended. Untimed standardized tests accepted.

High school preparation. College-preparatory program recommended. 14 units required; 24 recommended. Required and recommended units include English 4, mathematics 2-4, social studies 1-2, history 1-2, science 2-4 (laboratory 1-2), foreign language 2-4 and academic electives 2-4.

2009-2010 Annual costs. Tuition/fees: $35,500. Room/board: $8,200. Books/supplies: $1,000. Personal expenses: $900.

2008-2009 Financial aid. Need-based: 690 full-time freshmen applied for aid; 519 were judged to have need; 519 of these received aid. Average need met was 100%. Average scholarship/grant was $21,424; average loan $4,589. 68% of total undergraduate aid awarded as scholarships/grants, 32% as loans/jobs. **Non-need-based:** Awarded to 1,832 full-time undergraduates, including 445 freshmen. Scholarships awarded for academics, leadership, music/drama. **Additional information:** Limited number of music lesson fee waivers available for music majors, awarded on audition basis only.

Application procedures. Admission: Priority date 1/15; deadline 1/15. No application fee. Admission notification 3/20. Admission notification on a rolling basis. **Financial aid:** Priority date 1/15, closing date 2/1. FAFSA, CSS PROFILE required. Applicants notified on a rolling basis starting 3/1; must reply by 5/1 or within 2 week(s) of notification.

Academics. Students may propose self-designed integrative majors. **Special study options:** Combined bachelor's/graduate degree, cross-registration, double major, dual enrollment of high school students, independent study, internships, student-designed major, study abroad, teacher certification program, urban semester, Washington semester. Great Conversation: 5-semester program emphasizing reading, writing, and outside-of-the-classroom discussion available to 70 incoming students each year; BA/BS in engineering with Washington University (MO), University of Minnesota, Minneapolis; center for experiential learning; center for integrative studies; joint law degree with Columbia University; undergraduate research in the sciences, Center for Integrative Studies study-travel programs in 38 different countries; includes Global semester, Term in Asia, Environmental Studies in Australia, ACM and HECUA program, 30-40 different interims, both domestic and abroad, all with a St. Olaf College faculty member as leader/instructor. **Credit/placement by examination:** AP, CLEP, IB, institutional tests. 5 credit hours maximum toward bachelor's degree. **Support services:** Learning center, pre-admission summer program, reduced course load, study skills assistance, tutoring, writing center.

Majors. Area/ethnic studies: American, Asian, Latin American, Russian/Slavic, women's. **Biology:** General. **Computer sciences:** Computer science. **Conservation:** Environmental studies. **Education:** Music, social studies. **Foreign languages:** Ancient Greek, classics, French, German, Latin, Norwegian, Russian, Spanish. **Health:** Nursing (RN). **History:** General. **Interdisciplinary:** Ancient studies, medieval/Renaissance. **Liberal arts:** Arts/sciences. **Math:** General. **Parks/recreation:** Exercise sciences. **Philosophy/religion:** Philosophy, religion. **Physical sciences:** Chemistry, physics. **Psychology:** General. **Public administration:** Social work. **Social sciences:** Economics, political science, sociology. **Theology:** Sacred music. **Visual/performing arts:** Art, art history/conservation, dance, dramatic, music performance, music theory/composition. **Other:** American racial and multicultural studies.

Most popular majors. Area/ethnic studies 7%, biology 13%, English 8%, mathematics 7%, physical sciences 6%, psychology 6%, social sciences 13%, visual/performing arts 13%.

Computing on campus. 969 workstations in dormitories, library, computer center, student center. Dormitories wired for high-speed internet access and linked to campus network. Commuter students can connect to campus network. Helpline, wireless network available.

Student life. Freshman orientation: Mandatory. Preregistration for classes offered. Held 5 days before start of fall classes. **Policies:** Alcohol not permitted on campus. **Housing:** Guaranteed on-campus for all undergraduates. Coed dorms, special housing for disabled, wellness housing available. $600 nonrefundable deposit, deadline 5/1. Honor houses, language houses, quiet halls, first-year only dorms. **Activities:** Bands, campus ministries, choral groups, dance, drama, film society, international student organizations, literary magazine, music ensembles, Model UN, musical theater, opera, radio station, student government, student newspaper, symphony orchestra, TV station, 137 registered student organizations.

Athletics. NCAA. **Intercollegiate:** Baseball M, basketball, cross-country, diving, football (tackle) M, golf, ice hockey, skiing, soccer, softball W, swimming, tennis, track and field, volleyball W, wrestling M. **Intramural:** Basketball, football (non-tackle), golf, soccer, softball, tennis, triathlon, volleyball. **Team name:** Oles.

Student services. Alcohol/substance abuse counseling, chaplain/spiritual director, career counseling, services for economically disadvantaged, student employment services, financial aid counseling, health services, minority student services, personal counseling. **Physically disabled:** Services for visually, hearing impaired.

Contact. E-mail: admissions@stolaf.edu
Phone: (507) 786-3025 Toll-free number: (800) 800-3025
Fax: (507) 786-3832
Derek Gueldenzoph, Dean of Admissions, St. Olaf College, 1520 St. Olaf Avenue, Northfield, MN 55057

Southwest Minnesota State University

Marshall, Minnesota
www.smsu.edu **CB code: 6703**

- Public 4-year university and liberal arts college
- Residential campus in large town
- 2,600 degree-seeking undergraduates: 15% part-time, 55% women, 4% African American, 2% Asian American, 2% Hispanic American, 1% Native American, 10% international
- 364 degree-seeking graduate students
- 72% of applicants admitted
- SAT or ACT (ACT writing optional) required
- 43% graduate within 6 years; 8% enter graduate study

General. Founded in 1963. Regionally accredited. **Degrees:** 505 bachelor's, 4 associate awarded; master's offered. **Location:** 150 miles from Minneapolis-St. Paul. **Calendar:** Semester, limited summer session. **Full-time faculty:** 127 total; 76% have terminal degrees, 14% minority, 45% women. **Part-time faculty:** 88 total; 28% have terminal degrees, 7% minority, 54% women. **Class size:** 49% < 20, 44% 20-39, 5% 40-49, 1% 50-99, less than 1% >100. **Special facilities:** Natural history museum, anthropology museum, planetarium, wildlife area.

Freshman class profile. 1,804 applied, 1,293 admitted, 506 enrolled.

Mid 50% test scores		**Rank in top tenth:**	9%
ACT composite:	19-25	**End year in good standing:**	91%
GPA 3.75 or higher:	17%	**Return as sophomores:**	69%
GPA 3.50-3.74:	15%	**Out-of-state:**	22%
GPA 3.0-3.49:	32%	**Live on campus:**	84%
GPA 2.0-2.99:	35%	**International:**	14%
Rank in top quarter:	30%		

Basis for selection. Class rank in top half of class or SAT combined score of 970 (exclusive of Writing) or ACT composite score of 21. Provisional admission may be granted to students who rank in top two-thirds of class or have ACT composite score of 19 or SAT combined score of 890. GED students must submit ACT. ACT recommended. PSAT/NMSQT may be submitted in place of SAT or ACT. Interview recommended for academically weak students; audition recommended for music students.

High school preparation. College-preparatory program required. 15 units required. Required units include English 4, mathematics 3, social studies 3, history 1, science 3 and foreign language 2. Social studies units must include American history and geography.

2008-2009 Annual costs. Tuition/fees: $6,696. Room/board: $5,984. Books/supplies: $1,000. Personal expenses: $1,800.

2008-2009 Financial aid. **Need-based:** 391 full-time freshmen applied for aid; 296 were judged to have need; 294 of these received aid. Average need met was 59%. Average scholarship/grant was $5,047; average loan $3,309. 43% of total undergraduate aid awarded as scholarships/grants, 57% as loans/jobs. **Non-need-based:** Awarded to 1,208 full-time undergraduates, including 348 freshmen. Scholarships awarded for academics, alumni affiliation, art, athletics, leadership, minority status, music/drama, state residency.

Application procedures. **Admission:** Priority date 8/15; deadline 9/1 (receipt date). $20 fee. Admission notification on a rolling basis. **Financial aid:** Priority date 3/1; no closing date. FAFSA, institutional form required. Applicants notified on a rolling basis starting 5/15.

Academics. **Special study options:** Accelerated study, combined bachelor's/graduate degree, cooperative education, cross-registration, distance learning, double major, dual enrollment of high school students, ESL, external degree, honors, independent study, internships, student-designed major, study abroad, teacher certification program. 2+2 bachelor's programs with Ridgewater College, St. Cloud Technical College, Minnesota West, South Central (Mankato) and Riverland College. Visiting Exchange Student Program. **Credit/placement by examination:** AP, CLEP, ACT, institutional tests. 36 credit hours maximum toward associate degree, 36 toward bachelor's. **Support services:** Learning center, reduced course load, remedial instruction, study skills assistance, tutoring, writing center.

Majors. **Agriculture:** Agribusiness operations, food science, soil science. **Biology:** General, cell/histology, ecology. **Business:** Accounting, business admin, finance, hospitality admin, marketing, nonprofit/public, restaurant/food services. **Communications:** General, broadcast journalism, public relations, radio/tv. **Computer sciences:** General, information technology. **Conservation:** Environmental science. **Education:** Art, biology, chemistry, drama/dance, early childhood, elementary, health, mathematics, music, physical, science, speech. **Foreign languages:** Spanish. **History:** General. **Liberal arts:** Arts/sciences. **Math:** General. **Parks/recreation:** Health/fitness. **Philosophy/religion:** Philosophy. **Physical sciences:** Chemistry. **Protective services:** Criminal justice, fire services admin, law enforcement admin. **Psychology:** General. **Public administration:** General, social work. **Social sciences:** Political science, sociology. **Visual/performing arts:** Art, dramatic, music management.

Most popular majors. Business/marketing 34%, education 17%, parks/recreation 6%.

Computing on campus. 300 workstations in dormitories, library, computer center, student center. Dormitories wired for high-speed internet access and linked to campus network. Commuter students can connect to campus network. Online course registration, online library, helpline, repair service, student web hosting, wireless network available.

Student life. **Freshman orientation:** Available, $45 fee. Preregistration for classes offered. **Housing:** Coed dorms, single-sex dorms, special housing for disabled, apartments, wellness housing available. $100 fully refundable deposit. **Activities:** Bands, campus ministries, choral groups, dance, drama, film society, international student organizations, literary magazine, music ensembles, musical theater, radio station, student government, student newspaper, symphony orchestra, TV station, Black Student Union, InterVarsity Christian Fellowship, Lutheran Student Commission, student activities committee, Republican Speakers Club, Young DFL, non-traditional students organization.

Athletics. NAIA. **Intercollegiate:** Baseball M, basketball, football (tackle) M, golf W, soccer W, softball W, tennis W, volleyball W, wrestling M. **Intramural:** Basketball, ice hockey M, racquetball, skiing, softball, tennis, track and field, volleyball, wrestling M. **Team name:** Mustangs.

Student services. Adult student services, alcohol/substance abuse counseling, chaplain/spiritual director, career counseling, student employment services, financial aid counseling, health services, minority student services, on-campus daycare, personal counseling, placement for graduates, veterans' counselor, women's services. **Physically disabled:** Services for visually, speech, hearing impaired.

Contact. E-mail: thooft@southwestmsu.edu
Phone: (507) 537-6286 Toll-free number: (800) 642-0684
Fax: (507) 537-7154
LeAnn Thooft, Director of Admissions, Southwest Minnesota State University, 1501 State Street, Marshall, MN 56258-1598

University of Minnesota: Crookston

Crookston, Minnesota
www.UMCrookston.edu **CB code: 6893**

- Public 4-year branch campus college
- Commuter campus in small town
- 1,207 degree-seeking undergraduates: 16% part-time, 41% women, 4% African American, 1% Asian American, 1% Hispanic American, 1% Native American, 8% international
- 75% of applicants admitted
- SAT or ACT (ACT writing optional) required
- 36% graduate within 6 years

General. Founded in 1965. Regionally accredited. Each student and faculty member issued laptop computer. **Degrees:** 209 bachelor's, 20 associate awarded. **ROTC:** Air Force. **Location:** 25 miles from Grand Forks, North Dakota, 170 miles from Winnipeg, Canada. **Calendar:** Semester, limited summer session. **Full-time faculty:** 53 total; 47% have terminal degrees, 11% minority, 34% women. **Part-time faculty:** 55 total; 31% have terminal degrees, 7% minority, 49% women. **Class size:** 55% < 20, 36% 20-39, 6% 40-49, 3% 50-99. **Special facilities:** 85-acre Red River Valley natural history area with prairie, marshes and forests.

Freshman class profile. 776 applied, 583 admitted, 276 enrolled.

Mid 50% test scores		**Rank in top quarter:**	33%
SAT critical reading:	420-520	**Rank in top tenth:**	10%
SAT math:	430-530	**Return as sophomores:**	68%
SAT writing:	480-560	**Out-of-state:**	33%
ACT composite:	19-24	**Live on campus:**	81%
GPA 3.75 or higher:	17%	**International:**	6%
GPA 3.50-3.74:	14%	**Fraternities:**	3%
GPA 3.0-3.49:	27%	**Sororities:**	1%
GPA 2.0-2.99:	41%		

Basis for selection. High school class rank and ACT test scores most important. ACT recommended. **Learning Disabled:** Students encouraged to contact Disability Services early in the admissions process to insure availability of appropriate services.

High school preparation. College-preparatory program recommended. 13 units required. Required and recommended units include English 4, mathematics 3, social studies 3, science 3 (laboratory 2) and foreign language 2.

2008-2009 Annual costs. Tuition/fees: $9,381; $9,381 out-of-state. Room/board: $5,950. Books/supplies: $800. Personal expenses: $1,000.

2008-2009 Financial aid. **Need-based:** 230 full-time freshmen applied for aid; 177 were judged to have need; 177 of these received aid. Average need met was 79%. Average scholarship/grant was $7,248; average loan $4,929. **Non-need-based:** Awarded to 251 full-time undergraduates, including 105 freshmen. Scholarships awarded for academics, athletics, leadership, minority status, ROTC. **Additional information:** Tuition guarantee plan available to all students who apply for it.

Application procedures. **Admission:** Priority date 2/1; no deadline. $30 fee, may be waived for applicants with need. Admission notification on a rolling basis beginning on or about 9/1. **Financial aid:** Priority date 2/15; no closing date. FAFSA required. Applicants notified on a rolling basis starting 3/15.

Academics. 10-week applied internship for all programs. **Special study options:** Cross-registration, distance learning, double major, dual enrollment of high school students, ESL, honors, independent study, internships, student-designed major, study abroad, teacher certification program. **Credit/placement by examination:** AP, CLEP, IB, ACT. Proficiency examinations are administered by appropriate academic department, require no fee, and yield no credit or grade but may fulfill prerequisites for advanced courses or satisfy requirements. Special Examinations for Credit have fee of $50 per credit. Credits earned by examination do not count as residence credits. Exams given at discretion of appropriate academic department. **Support services:** Learning center, pre-admission summer program, reduced course load, remedial instruction, study skills assistance, tutoring, writing center.

Majors. **Agriculture:** Agribusiness operations, agronomy, animal sciences, business, equestrian studies, horticultural science, turf management. **Biology:** General. **Business:** Accounting, business admin, hospitality admin, management information systems. **Communications:** General. **Conservation:** General. **Education:** Agricultural, kindergarten/preschool. **Engineering:** Industrial. **Engineering technology:** Software. **Health:** Health care admin, health services. **Parks/recreation:** Sports admin. **Psychology:** Industrial. **Transportation:** Aviation.

Computing on campus. PC or laptop required. 1,250 workstations in dormitories, library, computer center, student center. Dormitories wired for high-speed internet access and linked to campus network. Commuter students can connect to campus network. Online course registration, online library, helpline, repair service, student web hosting, wireless network available.

Student life. **Freshman orientation:** Mandatory, $75 fee. Preregistration for classes offered. The new student orientation program for the fall term begins three days before the first day of class. **Housing:** Coed dorms, special housing for disabled, apartments available. $100 partly refundable deposit, deadline 9/1. **Activities:** Concert band, campus ministries, choral groups, drama, international student organizations, radio station, student government, campus ministry club, multicultural club, UMC Ambassadors, Students in Free Enterprise, Wildlife Society Chapter, Collegiate FFA, flying club, Habitat for Humanity, Rodeo Association, Student Athletic Advisory Committee.

Athletics. NCAA. **Intercollegiate:** Baseball M, basketball, cheerleading, equestrian W, football (tackle) M, golf, ice hockey M, soccer W, softball W, tennis W, volleyball W. **Intramural:** Basketball, bowling, racquetball, table tennis, tennis, volleyball. **Team name:** Golden Eagles.

Student services. Adult student services, alcohol/substance abuse counseling, chaplain/spiritual director, career counseling, services for economically disadvantaged, student employment services, financial aid counseling, health services, minority student services, on-campus daycare, personal counseling, placement for graduates, women's services. **Physically disabled:** Services for visually, hearing impaired.

Contact. E-mail: info@umn.edu
Phone: (218) 281-8569 Toll-free number: (800) 862-6466
Fax: (218) 281-8575 ext. 369
Amber Evans-Dailey, Director of Admissions, University of Minnesota: Crookston, 2900 University Avenue, Crookston, MN 56716-5001

University of Minnesota: Duluth

Duluth, Minnesota
www.d.umn.edu **CB code: 6873**

- Public 4-year university
- Residential campus in small city
- 9,324 degree-seeking undergraduates
- 1,070 graduate students
- 66% of applicants admitted
- SAT or ACT with writing required

General. Founded in 1947. Regionally accredited. All buildings at UMD are connected by a unique skyway and concourse system. **Degrees:** 1,545 bachelor's awarded; master's, doctoral offered. **ROTC:** Air Force. **Location:** 130 miles from Minneapolis-St. Paul. **Calendar:** Semester, extensive summer session. **Full-time faculty:** 438 total. **Part-time faculty:** 90 total. **Class size:** 37% < 20, 48% 20-39, 6% 40-49, 5% 50-99, 5% >100. **Special facilities:** Planetarium, visual imaging laboratory, Tweed Museum of Art.

Freshman class profile. 8,606 applied, 5,657 admitted, 2,251 enrolled.

Mid 50% test scores		**GPA 2.0-2.99:**	25%
ACT composite:	21-26	**Rank in top quarter:**	41%
GPA 3.75 or higher:	16%	**Rank in top tenth:**	15%
GPA 3.50-3.74:	17%	**Out-of-state:**	13%
GPA 3.0-3.49:	42%	**Live on campus:**	90%

Basis for selection. 65th percentile of high school class or above typically admitted. Test scores are required. Students ranking between the 40th and 64th percentile are selectively admitted based on test scores and academic preparation. Essays or personal statements considered in an admissions decision appeals process. Audition required for music students. **Learning Disabled:** Students must meet our general admission policy.

High school preparation. 15 units required. Required units include English 4, mathematics 3, social studies 2, history 1, science 3 and foreign language 2. One year of physical and biological science required; mathematics sequence includes algebra, geometry, and higher algebra. Visual and performing arts courses and computer skills courses strongly recommended.

2008-2009 Annual costs. Tuition/fees: $10,261; $12,261 out-of-state. Room/board: $6,078. Books/supplies: $1,100. Personal expenses: $1,600.

2008-2009 Financial aid. **Non-need-based:** Scholarships awarded for academics, athletics, ROTC.

Application procedures. **Admission:** Priority date 2/1; deadline 8/1 (receipt date). $35 fee. Admission notification on a rolling basis beginning on or about 9/15. Must reply by May 1 or within 4 week(s) if notified thereafter. Applications are accepted on a space available basis after 2/01. **Financial aid:** Priority date 3/1; no closing date. FAFSA required. Applicants notified on a rolling basis starting 3/1; must reply within 2 week(s) of notification.

Academics. **Special study options:** Cross-registration, distance learning, double major, dual enrollment of high school students, honors, independent study, internships, student-designed major, study abroad, teacher certification program. **Credit/placement by examination:** AP, CLEP, IB, ACT, institutional tests. **Support services:** Learning center, reduced course load, remedial instruction, study skills assistance, tutoring.

Majors. **Area/ethnic studies:** German, Native American, women's. **Biology:** General, biochemistry, cell/histology, molecular. **Business:** Accounting, actuarial science, business admin, finance, human resources, management information systems. **Communications:** General. **Computer sciences:** General, computer science, information systems. **Conservation:** Environmental science, environmental studies. **Education:** Art, biology, chemistry, early childhood, elementary, English, French, German, health, mathematics, middle, music, physical, physics, science, secondary, social studies, Spanish. **Engineering:** Chemical, civil, computer, electrical, mechanical. **Foreign languages:** French, German, Spanish. **Health:** Athletic training, communication disorders, health care admin, predental, premedicine, prepharmacy, preveterinary. **History:** General. **Legal studies:** Prelaw. **Math:** General, statistics. **Parks/recreation:** General, exercise sciences. **Philosophy/religion:** Philosophy. **Physical sciences:** Chemistry, geology, physics. **Psychology:** General. **Social sciences:** Anthropology, criminology, economics, geography, political science, sociology, urban studies. **Visual/performing arts:** Acting, art, art history/conservation, dramatic, graphic design, jazz, music pedagogy, music performance, studio arts, theater design.

Most popular majors. Biology 7%, business/marketing 20%, education 14%, engineering/engineering technologies 7%, psychology 8%, social sciences 12%, visual/performing arts 6%.

Computing on campus. PC or laptop required. 465 workstations in library, computer center. Dormitories wired for high-speed internet access and linked to campus network. Commuter students can connect to campus network. Online course registration, online library, helpline, repair service, student web hosting, wireless network available.

Student life. **Freshman orientation:** Mandatory, $40 fee. Preregistration for classes offered. Academic advisement and registration (orientation) is held in March and April of student's senior year of high school. **Policies:** Smoke and alcohol free campus. **Housing:** Coed dorms, single-sex dorms, apartments, wellness housing available. $200 partly refundable deposit, deadline 5/1. Housing facilities are fully accessible to persons with physical disabilities. All facilities are smoke free. **Activities:** Bands, campus ministries, choral groups, dance, drama, film society, international student organizations, literary magazine, music ensembles, musical theater, opera, radio station, student government, student newspaper, symphony orchestra, Intervarsity Christian Fellowship, Minnesota Public Interest Research Group, Anishinabe club, Black student association, Queer and Allied Students Union, Hispanic organization, Southeast Asian association, Students Engaged in Rewarding Volunteer Experiences.

Athletics. NCAA. **Intercollegiate:** Baseball M, basketball, cross-country, football (tackle) M, ice hockey, soccer W, softball W, tennis W, track and field, volleyball W. **Intramural:** Badminton, basketball, bowling, football (non-tackle), golf, ice hockey, sailing, skiing, soccer, softball, table tennis, tennis, track and field, volleyball, water polo. **Team name:** Bulldogs.

Student services. Chaplain/spiritual director, career counseling, student employment services, financial aid counseling, health services, minority student services, on-campus daycare, personal counseling, placement for graduates, veterans' counselor, women's services. **Physically disabled:** Services for visually, speech, hearing impaired.

Contact. E-mail: umdadmis@d.umn.edu
Phone: (218) 726-7171 Toll-free number: (800) 232-1339
Fax: (218) 726-7040
Beth Esselstrom, Director of Admissions, University of Minnesota: Duluth, 25 Solon Campus Center, Duluth, MN 55812-3000

University of Minnesota: Morris

Morris, Minnesota
www.morris.umn.edu **CB code: 6890**

- Public 4-year university and liberal arts college
- Residential campus in small town
- 1,510 degree-seeking undergraduates
- 71% of applicants admitted
- SAT or ACT with writing required

General. Founded in 1959. Regionally accredited. **Degrees:** 360 bachelor's awarded. **Location:** 150 miles from Minneapolis-St. Paul; 100 miles from Fargo, North Dakota. **Calendar:** Semester, limited summer session. **Full-time faculty:** 109 total. **Part-time faculty:** 57 total. **Class size:** 69% < 20, 25% 20-39, 3% 40-49, 3% 50-99. **Special facilities:** Tropical conservatory, prairie gate press, historical center, experiment station, USDA soil laboratory, center for small towns, observatory.

Freshman class profile. 1,506 applied, 1,068 admitted, 374 enrolled.

Mid 50% test scores			
SAT critical reading:	520-700	Rank in top quarter:	60%
SAT math:	560-680	Rank in top tenth:	32%
SAT writing:	520-650	Out-of-state:	13%
ACT composite:	21-27	Live on campus:	98%

Basis for selection. Admission based on four primary factors: high school performance, ACT/SAT scores, extra-curricular involvement/leadership experience/honors. Interview recommended. Audition required for music students receiving scholarships. **Homeschooled:** Submit portfolio of works studied.

High school preparation. 17 units recommended. Recommended units include English 4, mathematics 3, social studies 4, history 4, science 3 (laboratory 2) and foreign language 2. Science units must include 1 biological science and 1 physical science.

2008-2009 Annual costs. Tuition/fees: $9,996; $9,996 out-of-state. Room/board: $6,710. Books/supplies: $600. Personal expenses: $1,200.

2007-2008 Financial aid. Non-need-based: Scholarships awarded for academics, alumni affiliation, leadership, minority status, music/drama. **Additional information:** Land-grant program waiving tuition for Native Americans.

Application procedures. Admission: Priority date 12/15; deadline 3/15 (postmark date). $35 fee, may be waived for applicants with need. Admission notification on a rolling basis beginning on or about 9/1. Must reply by May 1 or within 2 week(s) if notified thereafter. **Financial aid:** Priority date 3/1; no closing date. FAFSA required. Applicants notified on a rolling basis starting 3/1; must reply within 3 week(s) of notification.

Academics. Academic opportunities that allow students to assist faculty in research or teaching endeavors and receive a stipend or expense allowances include: The Undergraduate Research Opportunities Program, The Morris Academic Partnership, The Minority Mentorship Program, The Morris Administrative Internship, and The Student Internship Program. **Special study options:** Combined bachelor's/graduate degree, cooperative education, cross-registration, distance learning, double major, exchange student, honors, independent study, internships, liberal arts/career combination, New York semester, semester at sea, student-designed major, study abroad, teacher certification program, United Nations semester, urban semester, Washington semester. **Credit/placement by examination:** AP, CLEP, IB, ACT, institutional tests. No limit for credit by exam, but the credit awarded does not count as resident credit; must have 30 resident credits. **Support services:** Learning center, pre-admission summer program, reduced course load, study skills assistance, tutoring, writing center.

Majors. Area/ethnic studies: European, Latin American, Native American, women's. **Biology:** General. **Business:** Management science. **Communications:** General. **Computer sciences:** Computer science. **Conservation:** Environmental studies. **Education:** Elementary. **Foreign languages:** French, German, Spanish. **History:** General. **Liberal arts:** Humanities. **Math:** General, statistics. **Philosophy/religion:** Philosophy. **Physical sciences:** Chemistry, geology, physics. **Psychology:** General. **Public administration:** Social work. **Social sciences:** Anthropology, economics, political science, sociology. **Visual/performing arts:** Art history/conservation, dramatic, music performance, studio arts.

Computing on campus. 220 workstations in dormitories, library, computer center, student center. Dormitories wired for high-speed internet access and linked to campus network. Commuter students can connect to campus network. Online course registration, online library, helpline, repair service, wireless network available.

Student life. Freshman orientation: Mandatory. Preregistration for classes offered. Held 4 days prior to fall semester. **Housing:** Guaranteed on-campus for all undergraduates. Coed dorms, special housing for disabled, wellness housing available. $200 deposit, deadline 8/1. **Activities:** Bands, choral groups, dance, drama, film society, literary magazine, music ensembles, musical theater, radio station, student government, student newspaper, symphony orchestra, TV station, Amnesty International, Big Friend/Little Friend, Campus Aglow Outreach, E-Quality, Habitat for Humanity, Intervarsity Christian Fellowship, Minnesota Public Interest Research Group (MPIRG), Morris Campus Student Association (MCSA), Positive Spirituality, Women of Color Association.

Athletics. NCAA. **Intercollegiate:** Baseball M, basketball, cross-country, diving W, football (tackle) M, golf, soccer, softball W, swimming W, tennis, track and field, volleyball W. **Intramural:** Baseball, basketball, bowling, field hockey, football (non-tackle), ice hockey, softball, triathlon, volleyball. **Team name:** Cougars.

Student services. Alcohol/substance abuse counseling, career counseling, student employment services, financial aid counseling, health services, minority student services, personal counseling, placement for graduates, veterans' counselor, women's services. **Physically disabled:** Services for visually, speech, hearing impaired. **Learning disabled:** Comprehensive services available.

Contact. E-mail: admissions@morris.umn.edu
Phone: (320) 589-6035 Toll-free number: (888) 866-3382
Fax: (320) 589-1673
Nancy Helsper, Director of Institutional Research, University of Minnesota: Morris, 600 East 4th Street, Morris, MN 56267

University of Minnesota: Twin Cities

Minneapolis, Minnesota **CB member**
www.umn.edu/tc **CB code: 6874**

- Public 4-year university
- Residential campus in very large city
- 28,505 degree-seeking undergraduates: 8% part-time, 53% women, 5% African American, 10% Asian American, 2% Hispanic American, 1% Native American, 3% international
- 17,874 degree-seeking graduate students
- 53% of applicants admitted
- SAT or ACT with writing required
- 64% graduate within 6 years

General. Founded in 1851. Regionally accredited. Campuses in Minneapolis and St. Paul. **Degrees:** 6,650 bachelor's awarded; master's, doctoral, first professional offered. **ROTC:** Army, Naval, Air Force. **Calendar:** Semester, extensive summer session. **Full-time faculty:** 1,933 total; 81% have terminal degrees, 15% minority, 39% women. **Part-time faculty:** 959 total; 43%

have terminal degrees, 8% minority, 40% women. **Class size:** 43% < 20, 36% 20-39, 5% 40-49, 10% 50-99, 6% >100. **Special facilities:** West bank arts quarter, natural history museum, showboat, rehabilitation museum, arboretum, concert hall.

Freshman class profile. 29,159 applied, 15,322 admitted, 5,106 enrolled.

Mid 50% test scores		**Rank in top tenth:**	45%
SAT critical reading:	530-670	**Return as sophomores:**	88%
SAT math:	580-710	**Out-of-state:**	31%
ACT composite:	24-29	**Live on campus:**	82%
Rank in top quarter:	83%	**International:**	5%

Basis for selection. Successful completion of a college preparatory curriculum, high school rank percentile, grade point average, ACT or SAT scores, and strength of curriculum very important. Writing tests required. Results considered as secondary admission factor.

High school preparation. College-preparatory program required. 16 units required. Required units include English 4, mathematics 3, social studies 3, history 1, science 3 and foreign language 2. 1 year of visual and/or performing arts also required. Management, biological sciences, and technology applicants require a fourth year of mathematics and 3 years of science including 1 year each of biological science, chemistry, and physics.

2008-2009 Annual costs. Tuition/fees: $10,634; $14,634 out-of-state. Room/board: $7,280. Books/supplies: $976. Personal expenses: $2,132.

2008-2009 Financial aid. All financial aid based on need. 3,970 full-time freshmen applied for aid; 2,599 were judged to have need; 2,586 of these received aid. Average need met was 86%. Average scholarship/grant was $7,809; average loan $6,273. 46% of total undergraduate aid awarded as scholarships/grants, 54% as loans/jobs.

Application procedures. Admission: Priority date 12/15; no deadline. $45 fee, may be waived for applicants with need. Admission notification on a rolling basis. Must reply by May 1 or within 2 week(s) if notified thereafter. **Financial aid:** Priority date 3/1; no closing date. FAFSA, institutional form required. Applicants notified on a rolling basis starting 2/15.

Academics. Four year graduation guarantee offered. **Special study options:** Accelerated study, combined bachelor's/graduate degree, cooperative education, cross-registration, distance learning, double major, dual enrollment of high school students, ESL, exchange student, external degree, honors, independent study, internships, liberal arts/career combination, student-designed major, study abroad, teacher certification program. Qualified undergraduates may take graduate-level classes. **Credit/placement by examination:** AP, CLEP, IB, SAT, ACT, institutional tests. **Support services:** Learning center, pre-admission summer program, reduced course load, remedial instruction, study skills assistance, tutoring, writing center.

Majors. Agriculture: Animal sciences, business, economics, food science. **Architecture:** Architecture, environmental design, landscape. **Area/ethnic studies:** African, African-American, American, East Asian, European, Hispanic-American/Latino/Chicano, Latin American, Native American, Near/Middle Eastern, Russian/Slavic, women's. **Biology:** General, bacteriology, biochemistry, biostatistics, cell/histology, ecology. **Business:** Accounting, actuarial science, business admin, human resources, insurance, international, labor relations, logistics, management information systems, marketing, sales/distribution. **Communications:** Journalism. **Computer sciences:** Computer science, networking. **Conservation:** General, fisheries, forest resources, forestry, wildlife. **Construction:** Maintenance. **Education:** Agricultural, art, business, early childhood, elementary, foundations, mathematics, music, physical, sales/marketing, technology/industrial arts. **Engineering:** Aerospace, agricultural, chemical, civil, computer, electrical, geological, materials, materials science, mechanical. **Family/consumer sciences:** General, clothing/textiles, family studies, food/nutrition, housing. **Foreign languages:** General, ancient Greek, Chinese, classics, comparative lit, French, German, Hebrew, Italian, Japanese, Latin, linguistics, Portuguese, Russian, Scandinavian, Spanish. **Health:** Audiology/speech pathology, dental hygiene, music therapy, nurse anesthetist, nursing (RN), predental, premedicine, prepharmacy, preveterinary. **History:** General. **Interdisciplinary:** Biological/physical sciences, nutrition sciences. **Legal studies:** Prelaw. **Liberal arts:** Arts/sciences. **Math:** General, statistics. **Parks/recreation:** General. **Personal/culinary services:** Mortuary science. **Philosophy/religion:** Judaic, philosophy, religion. **Physical sciences:** Astronomy, astrophysics, chemistry, geology, geophysics, physics. **Psychology:** General. **Social sciences:** Anthropology, applied economics, criminology, econometrics, economics, geography, international relations, political science, sociology, urban studies. **Visual/performing arts:** Art history/conservation, commercial/advertising art, dance, design, dramatic, fashion design, film/cinema, interior design, music performance. **Other:** Bio-based products engineering.

Most popular majors. Biology 8%, business/marketing 9%, engineering/engineering technologies 11%, English 6%, psychology 8%, social sciences 12%, visual/performing arts 6%.

Computing on campus. Dormitories wired for high-speed internet access and linked to campus network. Commuter students can connect to campus network. Online course registration, online library, helpline, repair service, student web hosting, wireless network available.

Student life. Freshman orientation: Mandatory. **Housing:** Guaranteed on-campus for freshmen. Coed dorms, special housing for disabled, apartments, cooperative housing, fraternity/sorority housing, wellness housing available. $100 fully refundable deposit, deadline 5/1. Honors housing available. 24 living and learning communities. **Activities:** Bands, choral groups, dance, drama, film society, international student organizations, literary magazine, music ensembles, musical theater, opera, radio station, student government, student newspaper, symphony orchestra, TV station, 600 student-run organizations.

Athletics. NCAA. **Intercollegiate:** Baseball, basketball, cheerleading, cross-country, diving, football (tackle), golf, gymnastics, ice hockey, rowing (crew) W, soccer W, softball W, swimming, tennis, track and field, volleyball W, wrestling M. **Intramural:** Badminton, baseball, basketball, bowling, fencing, football (tackle) M, golf, gymnastics, handball, ice hockey, judo, lacrosse, racquetball, rugby, sailing, skiing, soccer, softball, squash, swimming, synchronized swimming, tennis, volleyball, water polo, wrestling M. **Team name:** Gophers.

Student services. Adult student services, alcohol/substance abuse counseling, chaplain/spiritual director, career counseling, services for economically disadvantaged, student employment services, financial aid counseling, health services, legal services, minority student services, on-campus daycare, personal counseling, placement for graduates, veterans' counselor, women's services. **Physically disabled:** Services for visually, speech, hearing impaired.

Contact. Phone: (612) 625-2008 Toll-free number: (800) 752-1000
Fax: (612) 626-1693
Wayne Sigler, Director of Admissions, University of Minnesota: Twin Cities, 240 Williamson Hall, 231 Pillsbury Drive SE, Minneapolis, MN 55455-0115

University of St. Thomas

Saint Paul, Minnesota — **CB member**
www.stthomas.edu — **CB code: 6110**

- Private 4-year university and liberal arts college affiliated with Roman Catholic Church
- Commuter campus in very large city
- 6,017 degree-seeking undergraduates: 4% part-time, 48% women, 3% African American, 5% Asian American, 3% Hispanic American, 1% international
- 4,464 degree-seeking graduate students
- 81% of applicants admitted
- SAT or ACT (ACT writing optional), application essay required
- 72% graduate within 6 years

General. Founded in 1885. Regionally accredited. **Degrees:** 1,492 bachelor's awarded; master's, doctoral, first professional offered. **ROTC:** Army, Naval, Air Force. **Location:** 5 miles from downtown. **Calendar:** 4-1-4, limited summer session. **Class size:** 38% < 20, 59% 20-39, 2% 40-49, 1% 50-99, less than 1% >100.

Freshman class profile. 5,055 applied, 4,094 admitted, 1,322 enrolled.

Mid 50% test scores		**GPA 2.0-2.99:**	7%
SAT critical reading:	530-620	**Rank in top quarter:**	51%
SAT math:	540-650	**Rank in top tenth:**	20%
ACT composite:	23-27	**Return as sophomores:**	88%
GPA 3.75 or higher:	32%	**Out-of-state:**	19%
GPA 3.50-3.74:	26%	**Live on campus:**	94%
GPA 3.0-3.49:	35%	**International:**	1%

Basis for selection. Admissions decision by formula using a combination of high school rank and standardized test scores. Applicants who don't meet these conditions are given individual review. Interview recommended. **Homeschooled:** Submit course descriptions.

High school preparation. Required and recommended units include English 4, mathematics 3-4, social studies 2, science 2 and foreign language 4. Some departments may require 3 units social studies (includes 1 geography), 1 US history, 1 unit visual or performing arts.

2008-2009 Annual costs. Tuition/fees: $27,822. Room/board: $7,612.

2008-2009 Financial aid. Need-based: 1,004 full-time freshmen applied for aid; 750 were judged to have need; 749 of these received aid.

Average need met was 87%. Average scholarship/grant was $14,344; average loan $6,555. 64% of total undergraduate aid awarded as scholarships/grants, 36% as loans/jobs. **Non-need-based:** Awarded to 2,414 full-time undergraduates, including 697 freshmen. Scholarships awarded for academics, music/drama, ROTC.

Application procedures. Admission: No deadline. No application fee. Admission notification on a rolling basis. Applications accepted until class is full; reviewed starting 10/01. **Financial aid:** Priority date 4/1; no closing date. FAFSA required. Applicants notified on a rolling basis starting 3/1; must reply within 3 week(s) of notification.

Academics. Special study options: Cross-registration, double major, exchange student, honors, independent study, internships, semester at sea, student-designed major, study abroad, teacher certification program, urban semester, Washington semester. Renaissance Program in which students major in a liberal arts area, take career-oriented classes as a minor, and after graduation can take additional undergraduate business courses free of charge. **Credit/placement by examination:** AP, CLEP, IB, institutional tests. Typically credit by exam can be used for only 1/8 of a student's courses. CLEP credit awarded if student scores at 50th percentile or above for those examinations that have been approved by the department in which the subject is usually taught. **Support services:** Learning center, reduced course load, study skills assistance, tutoring, writing center.

Majors. Area/ethnic studies: Women's. **Biology:** General, biochemistry. **Business:** Accounting, actuarial science, business admin, entrepreneurial studies, finance, human resources, international, marketing, operations, real estate. **Communications:** General, journalism. **Computer sciences:** Computer science, information systems, information technology, security. **Conservation:** Environmental science, environmental studies. **Education:** Chemistry, elementary, English, French, German, health, mathematics, middle, multi-level teacher, music, physical, physics, science, social studies, Spanish. **Engineering:** General, electrical, mechanical. **Foreign languages:** Classics, comparative lit, French, German, Latin, Spanish. **Health:** Predental, preveterinary, public health ed. **History:** General. **Interdisciplinary:** Classical/archaeology, neuroscience, peace/conflict. **Legal studies:** Prelaw. **Liberal arts:** Arts/sciences. **Math:** General, statistics. **Philosophy/religion:** Philosophy, religion. **Physical sciences:** Chemistry, geology, physics. **Psychology:** General. **Public administration:** Social work. **Social sciences:** General, criminology, econometrics, economics, geography, international economics, international relations, political science, sociology. **Theology:** Preministerial, theology. **Visual/performing arts:** Art history/conservation, music performance.

Most popular majors. Business/marketing 41%, communications/journalism 8%, philosophy/religious studies 8%, social sciences 9%.

Computing on campus. Dormitories wired for high-speed internet access and linked to campus network. Commuter students can connect to campus network. Online course registration, online library, helpline, student web hosting, wireless network available.

Student life. Freshman orientation: Mandatory. Preregistration for classes offered. Held 2 days over summer; students and parents can stay overnight in the dorms. Separate programs for students and parents. **Housing:** Single-sex dorms, apartments available. $200 fully refundable deposit, deadline 5/1. Chemical-free lifestyle, women in science house, first year experience houses, Catholic women's and Catholic men's communities. **Activities:** Bands, choral groups, dance, drama, literary magazine, music ensembles, radio station, student government, student newspaper, Globally Minded Student Association, campus ministry, Volunteers in Action, HANA, Student Coalition for Social Justice, African Nations Students Association, Fellowship of Christian Athletes, St. Paul's Outreach student organization, theology club, Black Empowerment Student Alliance.

Athletics. NCAA. **Intercollegiate:** Baseball M, basketball, cross-country, football (tackle) M, golf, ice hockey, soccer, softball W, swimming, tennis, track and field, volleyball W. **Intramural:** Basketball, football (non-tackle), racquetball, soccer, softball, tennis, volleyball. **Team name:** Tommies.

Student services. Adult student services, alcohol/substance abuse counseling, chaplain/spiritual director, career counseling, student employment services, financial aid counseling, health services, minority student services, on-campus daycare, personal counseling, veterans' counselor, women's services. **Physically disabled:** Services for visually, speech, hearing impaired. **Learning disabled:** Comprehensive services available.

Contact. E-mail: admissions@stthomas.edu
Phone: (651) 962-6150 Toll-free number: (800) 328-6819 ext. 26150
Fax: (651) 962-6160
Marla Friederichs, Associate Vice President for Enrollment Management, University of St. Thomas, 2115 Summit Avenue, 32F, St. Paul, MN 55105-1096

Walden University
Minneapolis, Minnesota
www.waldenu.edu

- For-profit 4-year virtual university
- Large city
- 2,466 degree-seeking undergraduates: 93% part-time, 65% women, 20% African American, 1% Asian American, 4% Hispanic American, 1% Native American, 35% international
- 31,935 degree-seeking graduate students
- Application essay required

General. Walden University is a fully online institution offering programs in a variety of disciplines and degree levels, from undergraduate to doctorate. **Degrees:** 199 bachelor's awarded; master's, doctoral offered. **Calendar:** Differs by program, extensive summer session. **Full-time faculty:** 770 total. **Part-time faculty:** 512 total.

Basis for selection. Admission decisions based on transcript and years of work experience in profession.

2008-2009 Annual costs. Tuition/fees: $11,700.

2007-2008 Financial aid. All financial aid based on need.

Application procedures. Admission: No deadline. $50 fee. Application must be submitted online. Admission notification on a rolling basis. Offer remains in effect for 12 months. **Financial aid:** No deadline. FAFSA required. Applicants notified on a rolling basis.

Academics. Special study options: Distance learning, internships, student-designed major, teacher certification program. **Credit/placement by examination:** AP, CLEP, IB. 30 credit hours maximum toward bachelor's degree. **Support services:** Tutoring, writing center.

Majors. Business: Business admin, finance, human resources, management information systems, marketing. **Computer sciences:** General, security. **Family/consumer sciences:** Child care, child development. **Health:** Medical informatics. **Psychology:** General. **Other:** Educational computing, Interdisciplinary studies, Online work and communities.

Most popular majors. Business/marketing 73%, family/consumer sciences 10%, psychology 14%.

Computing on campus. PC or laptop required. Commuter students can connect to campus network. Online course registration, online library, helpline available.

Student life. Activities: Student newspaper.

Student services. Career counseling, financial aid counseling, personal counseling, veterans' counselor. **Physically disabled:** Services for visually, speech, hearing impaired. **Learning disabled:** Comprehensive services available.

Contact. E-mail: admissions@waldenu.edu
Phone: (866) 492-5336 Toll-free number: (866) 492-5336
Dawn Wolff, Director of Admissions, Walden University, 650 South Exeter Street, 8th Floor, Baltimore, MD 21202

Winona State University
Winona, Minnesota
www.winona.edu **CB code: 6680**

- Public 4-year university
- Residential campus in large town
- 7,641 degree-seeking undergraduates: 6% part-time, 61% women, 2% African American, 2% Asian American, 1% Hispanic American, 2% international
- 409 degree-seeking graduate students
- 74% of applicants admitted
- SAT and SAT Subject Tests or ACT (ACT writing optional) required
- 57% graduate within 6 years

General. Founded in 1858. Regionally accredited. **Degrees:** 1,387 bachelor's, 33 associate awarded; master's, doctoral offered. **ROTC:** Army. **Location:** 90 miles from Minneapolis-St. Paul. **Calendar:** Semester, extensive summer session. **Full-time faculty:** 340 total; 15% minority, 44% women. **Part-time faculty:** 136 total; 2% minority, 67% women. **Class size:** 30% < 20, 56% 20-39, 7% 40-49, 5% 50-99, 2% >100.

Freshman class profile. 6,157 applied, 4,527 admitted, 1,877 enrolled.

Mid 50% test scores		**GPA 2.0-2.99:**	25%
SAT critical reading:	440-580	**Rank in top quarter:**	34%
SAT math:	490-610	**Rank in top tenth:**	10%
ACT composite:	21-24	**Return as sophomores:**	72%
GPA 3.75 or higher:	16%	**Out-of-state:**	37%
GPA 3.50-3.74:	21%	**Live on campus:**	89%
GPA 3.0-3.49:	37%		

Basis for selection. 16 units of college prep high school courses and rank in top half of class or SAT combined score of 1000 (exclusive of Writing) or ACT composite score of 21 required for regular admission. Interview required for academically marginal students.

High school preparation. College-preparatory program required. 16 units required. Required units include English 4, mathematics 3, social studies 2, history 1, science 3 (laboratory 3), foreign language 2 and academic electives 1. One English unit may be speech.

2008-2009 Annual costs. Tuition/fees: $6,661; $11,257 out-of-state. Fees include mandatory laptop lease for full-time students. Room/board: $6,432. Books/supplies: $1,160. Personal expenses: $2,050.

2007-2008 Financial aid. **Non-need-based:** Scholarships awarded for academics, alumni affiliation, art, athletics, leadership, minority status, music/drama, ROTC, state residency.

Application procedures. **Admission:** Priority date 3/1; deadline 7/30 (postmark date). $20 fee, may be waived for applicants with need. Admission notification on a rolling basis beginning on or about 8/15. **Financial aid:** Priority date 3/1; no closing date. FAFSA required. Applicants notified on a rolling basis starting 5/1; must reply within 3 week(s) of notification.

Academics. **Special study options:** Accelerated study, cross-registration, distance learning, double major, dual enrollment of high school students, external degree, independent study, internships, student-designed major, study abroad, teacher certification program. **Credit/placement by examination:** AP, CLEP, IB, ACT, institutional tests. **Support services:** Learning center, reduced course load, study skills assistance, tutoring, writing center.

Majors. **Biology:** General, cell/histology, molecular. **Business:** General, accounting, administrative services, business admin, finance, human resources, management information systems, management science, managerial economics, market research, office/clerical, operations. **Communications:** General, advertising, broadcast journalism, journalism, media studies, photojournalism, public relations. **Communications technology:** General. **Computer sciences:** General, applications programming, computer science, information technology, programming. **Conservation:** General, environmental studies. **Education:** General, art, bilingual, biology, business, chemistry, curriculum, drama/dance, early childhood, elementary, emotionally handicapped, English, foreign languages, French, German, health, health occupations, history, learning disabled, mathematics, mentally handicapped, middle, multi-level teacher, multiple handicapped, music, physical, physically handicapped, physics, reading, science, secondary, social science, social studies, Spanish, special, speech. **Engineering:** Materials, materials science, polymer. **Foreign languages:** General, French, German, Spanish. **Health:** Athletic training, clinical lab technology, cytotechnology, health care admin, nursing (RN), predental, premedicine, preop/surgical nursing, prepharmacy, preveterinary, public health ed, recreational therapy. **History:** General. **Interdisciplinary:** Biological/physical sciences. **Legal studies:** Paralegal, prelaw. **Liberal arts:** Arts/sciences. **Math:** General, applied, statistics. **Parks/recreation:** General, exercise sciences, facilities management, health/fitness, sports admin. **Physical sciences:** Chemistry, geology, physics, planetary, polymer chemistry. **Protective services:** Corrections, criminal justice, law enforcement admin, police science, security services. **Psychology:** General. **Public administration:** General, social work. **Social sciences:** General, economics, political science, sociology, urban studies. **Visual/performing arts:** General, art, commercial/advertising art, design, dramatic, music management, music performance, studio arts.

Most popular majors. Biology 6%, business/marketing 21%, communications/journalism 6%, education 18%, health sciences 12%.

Computing on campus. PC or laptop required. 1,600 workstations in dormitories, library, computer center, student center. Dormitories wired for high-speed internet access and linked to campus network. Commuter students can connect to campus network. Online course registration, helpline, repair service, student web hosting, wireless network available.

Student life. **Freshman orientation:** Available, $25 fee. Preregistration for classes offered. **Housing:** Guaranteed on-campus for freshmen. Coed dorms, single-sex dorms, special housing for disabled, apartments available. $175 partly refundable deposit, deadline 3/1. Residence hall with classrooms and faculty offices. **Activities:** Bands, choral groups, dance, drama, film society, international student organizations, literary magazine, music ensembles, musical theater, radio station, student government, student newspaper, symphony orchestra, TV station, over 130 organizations.

Athletics. NCAA. **Intercollegiate:** Baseball M, basketball, cross-country, football (tackle) M, golf, gymnastics W, soccer W, softball W, tennis, track and field W, volleyball W. **Intramural:** Archery, badminton, baseball M, basketball, bowling, cross-country, diving, equestrian, fencing, field hockey, golf, gymnastics W, handball, ice hockey, racquetball, rifle, rugby, skiing, soccer, softball, swimming, table tennis, tennis, track and field, volleyball, wrestling M. **Team name:** Warriors.

Student services. Adult student services, alcohol/substance abuse counseling, chaplain/spiritual director, career counseling, services for economically disadvantaged, student employment services, financial aid counseling, health services, legal services, minority student services, on-campus daycare, personal counseling, placement for graduates, veterans' counselor, women's services. **Physically disabled:** Services for visually, speech, hearing impaired.

Contact. E-mail: admissions@winona.edu
Phone: (507) 457-5100 Toll-free number: (800) 342-5978
Fax: (507) 457-5620
Carl Stange, Director of Admissions, Winona State University, Office of Admissions, Winona, MN 55987

Mississippi

Alcorn State University

Alcorn State, Mississippi **CB member**
www.alcorn.edu **CB code: 1008**

- Public 4-year university and agricultural college
- Residential campus in rural community
- 2,626 degree-seeking undergraduates: 9% part-time, 67% women, 92% African American, 1% Hispanic American, 1% international
- 626 degree-seeking graduate students
- 85% of applicants admitted
- SAT or ACT (ACT writing optional), application essay, interview required
- 39% graduate within 6 years; 34% enter graduate study

General. Founded in 1871. Regionally accredited. School of Nursing is located in Natchez. **Degrees:** 444 bachelor's, 40 associate awarded; master's offered. **ROTC:** Army. **Location:** 40 miles from Natchez, 45 miles from Vicksburg. **Calendar:** Semester, limited summer session. **Full-time faculty:** 176 total; 66% have terminal degrees, 77% minority, 44% women. **Part-time faculty:** 41 total; 61% have terminal degrees, 80% minority, 66% women. **Special facilities:** Nature trails, lakes.

Freshman class profile. 3,065 applied, 2,619 admitted, 401 enrolled.

Mid 50% test scores		**GPA 3.0-3.49:**	24%
SAT critical reading:	370-440	**GPA 2.0-2.99:**	45%
SAT math:	360-480	**Return as sophomores:**	59%
ACT composite:	16-20	**Out-of-state:**	20%
GPA 3.75 or higher:	9%	**Live on campus:**	92%
GPA 3.50-3.74:	15%	**International:**	2%

Basis for selection. Test scores, school achievement record important; specific academic units considered. Test score requirements depend upon high school GPA. Audition required for music majors. **Homeschooled:** Transcript of courses and grades, state high school equivalency certificate required.

High school preparation. 15.5 units required. Required and recommended units include English 4, mathematics 3, social studies 3, science 3 (laboratory 2), foreign language 1, computer science .5 and academic electives 2. One advanced elective must be in foreign language or world geography.

2008-2009 Annual costs. Tuition/fees: $4,448; $10,692 out-of-state. 2008-09 Public institution tuition - $4498 Room and board (on-campus) - $5128 Undergraduate per credit hour charge - Public instiutions - $250 Out-of-State - $594. Room/board: $5,168. Books/supplies: $1,392. Personal expenses: $2,320.

2008-2009 Financial aid. Need-based: 396 full-time freshmen applied for aid; 368 were judged to have need; 368 of these received aid. Average need met was 82%. Average scholarship/grant was $3,977; average loan $3,352. 55% of total undergraduate aid awarded as scholarships/grants, 45% as loans/jobs. **Non-need-based:** Awarded to 968 full-time undergraduates, including 276 freshmen. Scholarships awarded for academics, athletics, ROTC.

Application procedures. Admission: No deadline. No application fee. Application must be submitted on paper. Admission notification on a rolling basis. **Financial aid:** Priority date 4/1; no closing date. FAFSA, institutional form required. Applicants notified on a rolling basis starting 4/1; must reply within 4 week(s) of notification.

Academics. Special study options: Accelerated study, cooperative education, distance learning, double major, honors, independent study, internships, liberal arts/career combination, teacher certification program. **Credit/placement by examination:** AP, CLEP, SAT, ACT, institutional tests. 15 credit hours maximum toward associate degree, 30 toward bachelor's. Student must earn 12 hours at Alcorn State University before credit by examination may be recorded on the student's transcript. **Support services:** Learning center, pre-admission summer program, reduced course load, remedial instruction, tutoring.

Majors. Agriculture: General, business, economics. **Biology:** General. **Business:** Accounting, business admin. **Communications:** Media studies. **Computer sciences:** General, LAN/WAN management. **Education:** Elementary, special. **Engineering technology:** Robotics. **Family/consumer sciences:** Child development, food/nutrition. **Health:** Athletic training, nursing (RN). **History:** General. **Liberal arts:** Arts/sciences. **Math:** General. **Parks/recreation:** General. **Physical sciences:** Chemistry. **Protective services:** Criminal justice. **Psychology:** General, educational. **Social sciences:** Economics, political science, sociology. **Visual/performing arts:** Music performance.

Most popular majors. Biology 13%, business/marketing 8%, education 8%, health sciences 11%, liberal arts 22%, social sciences 7%.

Computing on campus. 500 workstations in library, computer center, student center. Dormitories wired for high-speed internet access and linked to campus network. Commuter students can connect to campus network. Online course registration, helpline available.

Student life. Freshman orientation: Mandatory. Preregistration for classes offered. Entrance and placement exams given. **Housing:** Guaranteed on-campus for all undergraduates. Single-sex dorms available. $75 fully refundable deposit. **Activities:** Bands, choral groups, dance, drama, music ensembles, radio station, student government, student newspaper, TV station, Baptist Student Union, Wesley Foundation, NAACP, Black History Month Society, Young Women's Christian Association, Adventist Youth Society.

Athletics. NCAA. **Intercollegiate:** Baseball M, basketball, cross-country, football (tackle) M, golf, soccer W, softball W, tennis, track and field, volleyball W. **Intramural:** Basketball. **Team name:** Braves.

Student services. Career counseling, student employment services, health services, on-campus daycare, personal counseling, placement for graduates, veterans' counselor.

Contact. E-mail: ebarnes@alcorn.edu
Phone: (601) 877-6147 Toll-free number: (800) 222-6790
Fax: (601) 877-6347
Emanuel Barnes, Director of Admissions and Recruiting, Alcorn State University, 1000 ASU Drive #300, Alcorn State, MS 39096-7500

Belhaven College

Jackson, Mississippi
www.belhaven.edu **CB code: 1055**

- Private 4-year liberal arts college affiliated with Presbyterian Church (USA)
- Commuter campus in large city
- 2,152 degree-seeking undergraduates: 6% part-time, 67% women
- 378 degree-seeking graduate students
- 63% of applicants admitted
- SAT or ACT (ACT writing optional), application essay required
- 40% graduate within 6 years; 24% enter graduate study

General. Founded in 1883. Regionally accredited. Christian liberal arts college. **Degrees:** 174 bachelor's awarded; master's offered. **ROTC:** Army, Air Force. **Location:** 188 miles from New Orleans, 200 miles from Memphis, Tennessee. **Calendar:** Semester, extensive summer session. **Full-time faculty:** 63 total; 71% have terminal degrees, 35% women. **Part-time faculty:** 57 total; 32% have terminal degrees, 53% women. **Class size:** 59% < 20, 34% 20-39, 6% 40-49, less than 1% 50-99, less than 1% >100. **Special facilities:** Museum, heritage room.

Freshman class profile. 1,094 applied, 685 admitted, 192 enrolled.

Mid 50% test scores		**GPA 2.0-2.99:**	29%
SAT critical reading:	490-650	**Rank in top quarter:**	30%
SAT math:	460-600	**Rank in top tenth:**	5%
ACT composite:	19-25	**End year in good standing:**	73%
GPA 3.75 or higher:	22%	**Return as sophomores:**	64%
GPA 3.50-3.74:	12%	**Out-of-state:**	68%
GPA 3.0-3.49:	35%	**Live on campus:**	93%

Basis for selection. Test scores, school record, recommendations, and character important. Interview recommended for art, dance, music, and theater majors; portfolio recommended for art majors. Audition required for dance, music, and theater majors.

High school preparation. 16 units required. Required units include English 4, mathematics 2, social studies 1, science 1, computer science 1 and academic electives 8.

2009-2010 Annual costs. Tuition/fees: $16,780. Room/board: $6,120. Books/supplies: $1,400.

2008-2009 Financial aid. Need-based: 165 full-time freshmen applied for aid; 145 were judged to have need; 145 of these received aid. Average need met was 63%. Average scholarship/grant was $10,677; average loan

$2,965. 53% of total undergraduate aid awarded as scholarships/grants, 47% as loans/jobs. **Non-need-based:** Scholarships awarded for academics, alumni affiliation, art, athletics, music/drama.

Application procedures. Admission: No deadline. $25 fee, may be waived for applicants with need. Admission notification on a rolling basis. Accepted applicants must reply within 30 days after acceptance. **Financial aid:** Priority date 3/1; no closing date. FAFSA required. Applicants notified on a rolling basis starting 2/1.

Academics. Special study options: Accelerated study, combined bachelor's/graduate degree, distance learning, double major, dual enrollment of high school students, ESL, honors, independent study, internships, student-designed major, study abroad, teacher certification program, weekend college. **Credit/placement by examination:** AP, CLEP, IB, SAT, ACT, institutional tests. 30 credit hours maximum toward bachelor's degree. **Support services:** Learning center, reduced course load, remedial instruction, study skills assistance, tutoring, writing center.

Majors. Biology: General. **Business:** Accounting, business admin. **Communications:** General. **Computer sciences:** General, computer science. **Education:** Elementary. **Health:** Health care admin. **History:** General. **Interdisciplinary:** Global studies. **Liberal arts:** Humanities. **Math:** General. **Parks/recreation:** Exercise sciences, sports admin. **Philosophy/religion:** Philosophy. **Physical sciences:** Chemistry. **Psychology:** General. **Social sciences:** General, political science. **Theology:** Bible. **Visual/performing arts:** Art, arts management, dance, dramatic. **Other:** Sports ministry.

Most popular majors. Business/marketing 17%, communications/journalism 6%, education 9%, parks/recreation 18%, psychology 9%, visual/performing arts 17%.

Computing on campus. 40 workstations in library, computer center. Dormitories wired for high-speed internet access and linked to campus network. Commuter students can connect to campus network. Online course registration, online library, wireless network available.

Student life. Freshman orientation: Mandatory. Preregistration for classes offered. Held 5 days before fall classes begin. **Policies:** Religious observance required. **Housing:** Guaranteed on-campus for all undergraduates. Single-sex dorms, wellness housing available. $100 fully refundable deposit, deadline 6/1. **Activities:** Bands, campus ministries, choral groups, dance, drama, international student organizations, literary magazine, music ensembles, student government, student newspaper, Baptist Student Union, College Republicans, Fellowship of Christian Athletes, Praise & Worship Fellowship, Reformed University Fellowship, Student Missions Fellowship.

Athletics. NAIA. **Intercollegiate:** Baseball M, basketball, cross-country, football (tackle) M, golf, soccer, softball W, tennis, volleyball W. **Intramural:** Basketball, football (non-tackle), soccer W, softball, volleyball, weight lifting W. **Team name:** Blazers.

Student services. Adult student services, chaplain/spiritual director, career counseling, student employment services, financial aid counseling, health services, personal counseling.

Contact. E-mail: admission@belhaven.edu
Phone: (601) 968-5940 Toll-free number: (800) 960-5940
Fax: (601) 968-8946
Suzanne Sullivan, Director of Admission, Belhaven College, 1500 Peachtree Street, Jackson, MS 39202

Blue Mountain College

Blue Mountain, Mississippi
www.bmc.edu — **CB code: 1066**

- Private 4-year liberal arts college affiliated with Southern Baptist Convention
- Commuter campus in rural community
- 442 degree-seeking undergraduates: 12% part-time, 64% women, 12% African American, 1% Hispanic American
- 14 degree-seeking graduate students
- 56% of applicants admitted
- SAT or ACT (ACT writing optional) required
- 58% graduate within 6 years

General. Founded in 1873. Regionally accredited. **Degrees:** 84 bachelor's awarded; master's offered. **Location:** 69 miles from Memphis, Tennessee. **Calendar:** Semester, limited summer session. **Full-time faculty:** 26 total; 69% have terminal degrees, 4% minority, 58% women. **Part-time faculty:** 20 total; 30% have terminal degrees, 50% women. **Class size:** 72% < 20, 22% 20-39, 1% 40-49, 4% 50-99.

Freshman class profile. 226 applied, 126 admitted, 79 enrolled.

Mid 50% test scores		**Rank in top quarter:**	45%
ACT composite:	17-24	**Rank in top tenth:**	9%
GPA 3.75 or higher:	23%	**End year in good standing:**	80%
GPA 3.50-3.74:	14%	**Return as sophomores:**	72%
GPA 3.0-3.49:	27%	**Out-of-state:**	23%
GPA 2.0-2.99:	29%	**Live on campus:**	85%

Basis for selection. High school record, test scores, and individual motivation considered.

High school preparation. College-preparatory program recommended. 15 units recommended. Recommended units include English 4, mathematics 3, social studies 1, history 2, science 3 (laboratory 2) and foreign language 2.

2009-2010 Annual costs. Tuition/fees (projected): $8,880. Room/board: $3,800. Books/supplies: $750. Personal expenses: $500.

2007-2008 Financial aid. Need-based: Average need met was 81%. Average scholarship/grant was $2,495; average loan $5,080. 46% of total undergraduate aid awarded as scholarships/grants, 54% as loans/jobs. **Non-need-based:** Scholarships awarded for academics, alumni affiliation, art, athletics, leadership, music/drama, religious affiliation, state residency.

Application procedures. Admission: No deadline. $10 fee, may be waived for applicants with need, free for online applicants. Admission notification on a rolling basis beginning on or about 10/1. **Financial aid:** Priority date 3/1, closing date 7/31. FAFSA, institutional form required. Applicants notified on a rolling basis starting 4/1; must reply within 2 week(s) of notification.

Academics. Special study options: Accelerated study, combined bachelor's/graduate degree, double major, dual enrollment of high school students, honors, internships, teacher certification program. **Credit/placement by examination:** AP, CLEP, IB, SAT, ACT, institutional tests. 30 credit hours maximum toward bachelor's degree. **Support services:** Learning center, reduced course load, remedial instruction.

Majors. Biology: General. **Business:** Business admin. **Education:** Biology, elementary, English, mathematics, music, physical, science, social science, Spanish. **Foreign languages:** Spanish. **Health:** Clinical lab science. **History:** General. **Interdisciplinary:** Natural sciences. **Math:** General. **Parks/recreation:** Health/fitness. **Psychology:** General. **Social sciences:** General. **Theology:** Bible, sacred music.

Most popular majors. Biology 7%, business/marketing 6%, education 49%, philosophy/religious studies 19%, psychology 12%.

Computing on campus. 69 workstations in dormitories, library, computer center. Dormitories wired for high-speed internet access. Online library, helpline, wireless network available.

Student life. Freshman orientation: Mandatory, $50 fee. Preregistration for classes offered. Held the week prior to the opening of the fall semester; designed to provide opportunities for learning methods that support college success. **Policies:** Smoking and alcoholic beverages forbidden. Chapel attendance is required of all full-time students. Unmarried full-time students under the age of 21 are required to live on campus unless they are independent students, are living at home with their parents or immediate family members and commuting to school. **Housing:** Single-sex dorms, wellness housing available. $50 fully refundable deposit. **Activities:** Choral groups, drama, literary magazine, music ensembles, musical theater, student government, Alpha Psi Omega, Baptist Student Union, Cap and Gown Honor Society, Mississippi Association of Educators student chapter, psychology club, Society of Mathematicians and Scientists, Vivace club, Ministerial Association, Koinonia.

Athletics. NAIA. **Intercollegiate:** Basketball, cross-country. **Intramural:** Basketball, cross-country, football (non-tackle) M, golf M, softball, swimming, table tennis, tennis W, volleyball W. **Team name:** Toppers.

Student services. Health services, personal counseling, placement for graduates. **Physically disabled:** Services for visually, hearing impaired.

Contact. E-mail: admissions@bmc.edu
Phone: (662) 685-4771 ext. 166 Toll-free number: (800) 235-0136
Fax: (662) 685-4776
Maria Teel, Director of Admissions, Blue Mountain College, 201 West Main Street, PO Box 160, Blue Mountain, MS 38610-0160

Delta State University

Cleveland, Mississippi — **CB member**
www.deltastate.edu — **CB code: 1163**

- Public 4-year university
- Commuter campus in large town

- 3,212 degree-seeking undergraduates: 35% African American, 1% Asian American, 9% international
- 852 graduate students
- 31% of applicants admitted
- ACT (writing optional) required
- 37% graduate within 6 years

General. Founded in 1924. Regionally accredited. **Degrees:** 635 bachelor's awarded; master's, doctoral offered. **ROTC:** Army. **Location:** 40 miles from Greenville, 110 miles from Memphis, Tennessee. **Calendar:** Semester, extensive summer session. **Full-time faculty:** 191 total; 66% have terminal degrees, 13% minority, 50% women. **Part-time faculty:** 67 total; 43% have terminal degrees, 10% minority, 57% women. **Class size:** 62% < 20, 36% 20-39, 2% 40-49, less than 1% 50-99. **Special facilities:** Planetarium, airport, archives & museum.

Freshman class profile. 1,964 applied, 605 admitted, 398 enrolled.

Mid 50% test scores		**Return as sophomores:**	64%
ACT composite:	17-20	**Out-of-state:**	3%
GPA 3.75 or higher:	13%	**Live on campus:**	37%
GPA 3.50-3.74:	10%	**International:**	14%
GPA 3.0-3.49:	39%	**Fraternities:**	40%
GPA 2.0-2.99:	33%	**Sororities:**	30%
Rank in top quarter:	46%		

Basis for selection. Combination of college preparatory curriculum, test scores, class rank. Mississippi residents must take ACT for admission. Interview required for art, music majors. Audition recommended for music majors; portfolio recommended for art majors.

High school preparation. College-preparatory program required. 15.5 units required. Required units include English 4, mathematics 3, social studies 3, science 3 (laboratory 2), computer science .5 and academic electives 2.

2008-2009 Annual costs. Tuition/fees: $4,449; $11,182 out-of-state. Room/board: $5,341. Books/supplies: $800.

2007-2008 Financial aid. Need-based: 35% of total undergraduate aid awarded as scholarships/grants, 65% as loans/jobs. **Non-need-based:** Scholarships awarded for academics, alumni affiliation, art, athletics, leadership, music/drama, state residency.

Application procedures. Admission: No deadline. $25 fee. Admission notification on a rolling basis. **Financial aid:** No deadline. FAFSA, institutional form required. Applicants notified on a rolling basis starting 5/1.

Academics. Special study options: Accelerated study, distance learning, double major, dual enrollment of high school students, ESL, honors, independent study, internships, study abroad, teacher certification program. **Credit/placement by examination:** AP, CLEP, SAT, ACT, institutional tests. 30 credit hours maximum toward bachelor's degree. **Support services:** Learning center, pre-admission summer program, remedial instruction, study skills assistance, tutoring, writing center.

Majors. Biology: General. **Business:** General, accounting, business admin, finance, hospitality admin, insurance, management information systems, marketing, office management. **Communications:** Journalism. **Education:** Elementary, English, mathematics, music, physical, social science. **Family/consumer sciences:** General. **Foreign languages:** General. **Health:** Athletic training, audiology/speech pathology, nursing (RN). **History:** General. **Math:** General. **Physical sciences:** Chemistry. **Protective services:** Criminal justice. **Psychology:** General. **Public administration:** Social work. **Social sciences:** General, political science. **Transportation:** Airline/commercial pilot, aviation. **Visual/performing arts:** General.

Most popular majors. Biology 8%, business/marketing 23%, education 18%, family/consumer sciences 7%, health sciences 12%, social sciences 6%.

Computing on campus. 293 workstations in library, computer center. Dormitories wired for high-speed internet access and linked to campus network. Commuter students can connect to campus network. Online course registration, student web hosting available.

Student life. Freshman orientation: Available, $35 fee. Preregistration for classes offered. Orientation provides opportunity for academic advisement and pre-registration. **Housing:** Guaranteed on-campus for all undergraduates. Single-sex dorms, apartments, fraternity/sorority housing available. $50 fully refundable deposit. **Activities:** Bands, campus ministries, choral groups, dance, drama, international student organizations, literary magazine, music ensembles, musical theater, opera, student government, student newspaper, several religious, ethnic, social, political organizations available on campus.

Athletics. NCAA. **Intercollegiate:** Baseball M, basketball, cross-country W, diving, football (tackle) M, golf M, soccer, softball W, swimming, tennis. **Intramural:** Archery, badminton, basketball, bowling, cross-country, diving, football (non-tackle), golf, racquetball, rifle, soccer, softball, swimming, table tennis, tennis, triathlon, volleyball. **Team name:** Statesmen; Lady Statesmen.

Student services. Career counseling, student employment services, health services, on-campus daycare, personal counseling, placement for graduates. **Physically disabled:** Services for speech, hearing impaired.

Contact. E-mail: admissions@deltastate.edu
Phone: (662) 846-4655 Toll-free number: (800) 468-6378
Fax: (662) 846-4684
Debbie Heslep, Dean of Enrollment Management, Delta State University, 117 Kent Wyatt Hall, Cleveland, MS 38733

Jackson State University

Jackson, Mississippi — CB member
www.jsums.edu — CB code: 1341

- Public 4-year university
- Commuter campus in small city
- 6,501 degree-seeking undergraduates: 15% part-time, 63% women, 96% African American
- 1,815 degree-seeking graduate students
- 52% of applicants admitted
- SAT or ACT required

General. Founded in 1877. Regionally accredited. **Degrees:** 915 bachelor's awarded; master's, doctoral offered. **ROTC:** Army, Air Force. **Location:** 210 miles from Memphis, Tennessee, 190 miles from New Orleans. **Calendar:** Semester, extensive summer session. **Full-time faculty:** 345 total; 78% have terminal degrees, 38% minority, 44% women. **Part-time faculty:** 104 total; 42% have terminal degrees, 19% minority, 52% women. **Special facilities:** National research center, science observatory, academic research and computing center.

Freshman class profile. 8,962 applied, 4,661 admitted, 965 enrolled.

Mid 50% test scores		**Rank in top quarter:**	33%
ACT composite:	17-20	**End year in good standing:**	84%
GPA 3.75 or higher:	7%	**Return as sophomores:**	74%
GPA 3.50-3.74:	8%	**Out-of-state:**	34%
GPA 3.0-3.49:	26%	**Live on campus:**	75%
GPA 2.0-2.99:	51%		

Basis for selection. Test scores and high school transcript important. Audition recommended for music majors.

High school preparation. 15 units required. Required units include English 4, mathematics 3, social studies 3, science 3, foreign language 2 and academic electives 2.

2008-2009 Annual costs. Tuition/fees: $4,634; $10,978 out-of-state. Room/board: $5,720. Books/supplies: $800. Personal expenses: $2,250.

2007-2008 Financial aid. All financial aid based on need.

Application procedures. Admission: Priority date 8/1; no deadline. No application fee. Admission notification on a rolling basis beginning on or about 1/1. **Financial aid:** Priority date 4/1, closing date 5/1. FAFSA required. Applicants notified on a rolling basis starting 5/1.

Academics. Special study options: Distance learning, double major, dual enrollment of high school students, exchange student, honors, independent study, internships, study abroad, teacher certification program, weekend college. **Credit/placement by examination:** AP, CLEP, SAT, ACT. 30 credit hours maximum toward bachelor's degree. **Support services:** Learning center, pre-admission summer program, reduced course load, remedial instruction, study skills assistance, tutoring, writing center.

Majors. Biology: General. **Business:** Accounting, business admin, finance, marketing. **Communications:** Media studies. **Computer sciences:** General. **Education:** Elementary, instructional media, music, physical, social science, special. **Engineering:** Civil, computer, electrical. **Engineering technology:** Industrial. **Foreign languages:** General. **Health:** Communication disorders, health care admin, predental. **History:** General. **Math:** General. **Physical sciences:** Atmospheric science, chemistry, geology, physics. **Protective services:** Criminal justice. **Psychology:** General. **Public administration:** Social work. **Social sciences:** General, political science, sociology, urban studies. **Visual/performing arts:** General, music performance. **Other:** Childcare and family education, Professional interdisciplinary studies.

Most popular majors. Biology 8%, business/marketing 24%, education 17%, engineering/engineering technologies 7%, interdisciplinary studies 6%, security/protective services 6%.

Computing on campus. Dormitories wired for high-speed internet access and linked to campus network. Commuter students can connect to campus network. Online course registration, helpline, wireless network available.

Student life. Freshman orientation: Mandatory. Preregistration for classes offered. **Housing:** Single-sex dorms available. $50 nonrefundable deposit. **Activities:** Bands, choral groups, dance, drama, film society, literary magazine, music ensembles, opera, radio station, student government, student newspaper, symphony orchestra, TV station, Pierre Toussaint Catholic Student Union, Bapstis Student Union, Church of God in Christ (COGIC) club, NAACP, Alpha Phi Omega,.

Athletics. NCAA. **Intercollegiate:** Baseball M, basketball, bowling, cross-country, football (tackle) M, golf, rifle, soccer W, softball W, tennis, track and field, volleyball W. **Intramural:** Basketball, rifle, swimming, tennis, volleyball. **Team name:** JSU Tigers.

Student services. Adult student services, career counseling, student employment services, financial aid counseling, health services, on-campus daycare, personal counseling, placement for graduates, veterans' counselor. **Physically disabled:** Services for visually, speech, hearing impaired.

Contact. E-mail: admappl@jsums.edu
Phone: (601) 979-2100 Toll-free number: (800) 848-6917
Fax: (601) 979-2237
Stephanie Chatman, Director of Admissions and Financial Aid, Jackson State University, 1400 JR Lynch Street, Jackson, MS 39217

Magnolia Bible College

Kosciusko, Mississippi
www.magnolia.edu **CB code: 0162**

- Private 4-year Bible college affiliated with Church of Christ
- Commuter campus in small town
- 19 degree-seeking undergraduates: 26% African American

General. Founded in 1976. Regionally accredited. **Degrees:** 9 bachelor's awarded. **Location:** 70 miles from Jackson. **Calendar:** Semester, limited summer session. **Full-time faculty:** 2 total; 50% have terminal degrees. **Part-time faculty:** 9 total; 33% have terminal degrees, 11% minority, 33% women. **Class size:** 100% < 20. **Special facilities:** Restoration artifacts collection, preaching laboratory.

Freshman class profile. 3 applied, 1 admitted, 1 enrolled.

End year in good standing:	50%	**Live on campus:**	100%
Return as sophomores:	50%		

Basis for selection. Open admission, but selective for some programs. Recommendations, religious commitment, and personal character very important. Students encouraged to take ACT by end of first semester. Audition and portfolio recommended. **Homeschooled:** Complete junior year of high school with B average and score of 20 on ACT. Need transcript and letter of readiness from group leader or official.

2008-2009 Annual costs. Tuition/fees: $7,290. Reduced tuition for Attala County residents: $1,950 full-time, $65 per credit hour, $90 required fees. Room only: $1,520. Books/supplies: $500. Personal expenses: $1,935.

2008-2009 Financial aid. Non-need-based: Scholarships awarded for academics, leadership, religious affiliation.

Application procedures. Admission: No deadline. No application fee. Application must be submitted on paper. Admission notification on a rolling basis. **Financial aid:** Priority date 8/1; no closing date. FAFSA, institutional form required. Applicants notified on a rolling basis starting 4/15; must reply within 4 week(s) of notification.

Academics. Credit/placement by examination: AP, CLEP, institutional tests. 30 credit hours maximum toward bachelor's degree. **Support services:** Remedial instruction, writing center.

Majors. Theology: Bible, missionary, pastoral counseling, religious ed, sacred music, theology.

Computing on campus. 3 workstations in dormitories, library, computer center. Dormitories wired for high-speed internet access. Online library, wireless network available.

Student life. Freshman orientation: Mandatory. **Policies:** Religious observance required. **Housing:** Single-sex dorms, apartments available. $100 deposit, deadline 8/1. Women students housed with families in area. **Activities:** Student government.

Student services. Personal counseling, placement for graduates.

Contact. E-mail: tbrown@magnolia.edu
Phone: (662) 289-2896 ext. 109 Toll-free number: (800) 748-8655
Fax: (662) 289-1850
Travis Brown, Director of Admissions, Magnolia Bible College, PO Box 1109, Kosciusko, MS 39090

Millsaps College

Jackson, Mississippi
www.millsaps.edu **CB code: 1471**

- Private 4-year business and liberal arts college affiliated with United Methodist Church
- Residential campus in large city
- 999 degree-seeking undergraduates: 1% part-time, 51% women, 11% African American, 4% Asian American, 2% Hispanic American, 1% international
- 105 degree-seeking graduate students
- 77% of applicants admitted
- SAT or ACT (ACT writing optional), application essay required
- 68% graduate within 6 years; 49% enter graduate study

General. Founded in 1890. Regionally accredited. 4,000-acre biocultural reserve and learning center in Yucatan, Mexico. **Degrees:** 248 bachelor's awarded; master's offered. **ROTC:** Army. **Location:** 190 miles from New Orleans, 210 miles from Memphis, Tennessee. **Calendar:** Semester, limited summer session. **Full-time faculty:** 97 total; 94% have terminal degrees, 10% minority, 43% women. **Part-time faculty:** 17 total; 41% have terminal degrees, 6% minority, 47% women. **Class size:** 71% < 20, 29% 20-39, less than 1% 40-49, less than 1% >100. **Special facilities:** Molecular biology/functional genomics research laboratory, fluorescence microscopy suite and imaging facility, GIS workstation, automated 24-hour food monitoring system for rats, animal microsurgical lab, hydro geologic monitoring stations, computational modeling lab, spectrometers, chromatographs, electrophoresis instruments, inert atmosphere reaction chamber, storm water and oil spill remediation research laboratory.

Freshman class profile. 1,266 applied, 970 admitted, 271 enrolled.

Mid 50% test scores		**End year in good standing:**	90%
SAT critical reading:	540-670	**Return as sophomores:**	79%
SAT math:	540-650	**Out-of-state:**	64%
ACT composite:	23-29	**Live on campus:**	98%
GPA 3.75 or higher:	31%	**International:**	2%
GPA 3.50-3.74:	21%	**Fraternities:**	47%
GPA 3.0-3.49:	36%	**Sororities:**	48%
GPA 2.0-2.99:	12%		

Basis for selection. Test scores, GPA in academic courses, recommendations, essays, and school and community activities are important. Advanced credit is awarded for A-Levels, International Baccalaureate, and some other systems. Auditions and portfolios are recommended. **Homeschooled:** Statement describing homeschool structure and mission, transcript of courses and grades, letter of recommendation (nonparent) required. **Learning Disabled:** If accommodations are needed, form must be completed by student's healthcare provider.

High school preparation. 14 units required; 20 recommended. Required and recommended units include English 4, mathematics 3-4, social studies 2, history 2, science 3-4 (laboratory 1), foreign language 2 and computer science 2.

2008-2009 Annual costs. Tuition/fees: $24,754. Room/board: $8,800. Books/supplies: $1,000. Personal expenses: $1,000.

2008-2009 Financial aid. Need-based: 229 full-time freshmen applied for aid; 175 were judged to have need; 175 of these received aid. Average need met was 88%. Average scholarship/grant was $18,510; average loan $3,692. 75% of total undergraduate aid awarded as scholarships/grants, 25% as loans/jobs. **Non-need-based:** Awarded to 531 full-time undergraduates, including 159 freshmen. Scholarships awarded for academics, art, leadership, music/drama, religious affiliation.

Application procedures. Admission: No deadline. No application fee. Admission notification on a rolling basis beginning on or about 10/1. Must reply by May 1 or within 2 week(s) if notified thereafter. Early action priority deadline is 01/08, with notification 2 weeks after applying. **Financial**

aid: Priority date 3/1; no closing date. FAFSA required. Applicants notified on a rolling basis starting 3/15; must reply by 5/1 or within 2 week(s) of notification.

Academics. Special study options: Accelerated study, combined bachelor's/graduate degree, double major, honors, independent study, internships, liberal arts/career combination, New York semester, semester at sea, student-designed major, study abroad, teacher certification program, United Nations semester, urban semester, Washington semester. Faith & Work Initiative; direct exchange programs with Kansai Gaida University (Osaka, Japan) and with Queens University, the University of Ulster, and the Belfast Institute for Further and Higher Education (Belfast, Northern Ireland); McNair Fund mission work in Honduras, India, Malawi, Rwanda and Zimbabwe, Bolivia, Romania, South Africa and the West Bank; dual degrees in engineering, applied science and nursing through Auburn University, Columbia University, Vanderbilt University, Washington University, and the University of Mississippi Medical Center. **Credit/placement by examination:** AP, CLEP, IB, institutional tests. 28 credit hours maximum toward bachelor's degree. Limited to two courses in any discipline and seven courses overall. **Support services:** Pre-admission summer program, reduced course load, study skills assistance, tutoring, writing center.

Majors. Area/ethnic studies: European. **Biology:** General, biochemistry. **Business:** Accounting, business admin. **Communications:** General. **Computer sciences:** Computer science. **Education:** Elementary. **Foreign languages:** Classics, French, Spanish. **History:** General. **Math:** General, applied. **Philosophy/religion:** Philosophy, religion. **Physical sciences:** Chemistry, geology, physics. **Psychology:** General. **Public administration:** General. **Social sciences:** Anthropology, economics, political science, sociology. **Visual/performing arts:** Art history/conservation, dramatic, studio arts. **Other:** Self-designed major.

Most popular majors. Biology 9%, business/marketing 22%, English 9%, foreign language 6%, history 8%, physical sciences 6%, psychology 12%, social sciences 13%.

Computing on campus. 150 workstations in dormitories, library, computer center, student center. Dormitories wired for high-speed internet access and linked to campus network. Commuter students can connect to campus network. Online course registration, online library, helpline, student web hosting, wireless network available.

Student life. Freshman orientation: Mandatory. Preregistration for classes offered. 3 days before classes start, emphasizes wellness education, interpersonal skills development, and college mission. Includes initial 8 days of educational and social activities and 8-week Foundations program held once weekly to explore student issues and involvement in campus activities. **Policies:** Students required to live on campus through sophomore year. Students with family in the area may be exempted from the policy. **Housing:** Guaranteed on-campus for freshmen. Coed dorms, single-sex dorms, fraternity/sorority housing, wellness housing available. Community service dormitory available. **Activities:** Campus ministries, choral groups, dance, drama, film society, international student organizations, literary magazine, music ensembles, Model UN, musical theater, student government, student newspaper, Circle K, Millsaps Christian Fellowship, Black student association, Habitat for Humanity, Catholic student association, Fellowship of Christian Athletes, College Republicans, Young Democrats, Multicultural Affairs Diversity Group, E.A.R.T.H. (environmental service club), Jewish cultural organization.

Athletics. NCAA. **Intercollegiate:** Baseball M, basketball, cheerleading, cross-country, football (tackle) M, golf, soccer, softball W, tennis, volleyball W. **Intramural:** Basketball, bowling, football (non-tackle), golf, racquetball, soccer, softball, table tennis, tennis, volleyball, weight lifting. **Team name:** Millsaps Majors, Lady Majors.

Student services. Adult student services, alcohol/substance abuse counseling, chaplain/spiritual director, career counseling, student employment services, financial aid counseling, health services, minority student services, personal counseling, placement for graduates, women's services.

Contact. E-mail: admissions@millsaps.edu
Phone: (601) 974-1050 Toll-free number: (800) 352-1050
Fax: (601) 974-1059
Mathew Cox, Dean of Enrollment Management, Millsaps College, 1701 North State Street, Jackson, MS 39210-0001

Mississippi College

Clinton, Mississippi
www.mc.edu **CB code: 1477**

- Private 4-year university affiliated with Southern Baptist Convention
- Residential campus in large city
- 3,032 degree-seeking undergraduates: 12% part-time, 62% women, 25% African American, 1% Asian American, 1% Hispanic American, 3% international
- 1,659 degree-seeking graduate students
- 62% of applicants admitted
- SAT or ACT (ACT writing optional) required
- 59% graduate within 6 years; 36% enter graduate study

General. Founded in 1826. Regionally accredited. **Degrees:** 547 bachelor's awarded; master's, doctoral, first professional offered. **ROTC:** Army. **Location:** 10 miles from Jackson. **Calendar:** Semester, limited summer session. **Full-time faculty:** 172 total; 80% have terminal degrees, 4% minority, 48% women. **Part-time faculty:** 230 total; 12% minority, 48% women. **Class size:** 48% < 20, 39% 20-39, 11% 40-49, 3% 50-99. **Special facilities:** Baptist healthplex, Choctaw trails.

Freshman class profile. 1,728 applied, 1,071 admitted, 533 enrolled.

Mid 50% test scores		**GPA 2.0-2.99:**	24%
SAT critical reading:	460-610	**Rank in top quarter:**	53%
SAT math:	470-600	**Rank in top tenth:**	27%
ACT composite:	20-26	**End year in good standing:**	84%
GPA 3.75 or higher:	32%	**Return as sophomores:**	69%
GPA 3.50-3.74:	16%	**Out-of-state:**	37%
GPA 3.0-3.49:	27%	**Live on campus:**	95%

Basis for selection. ACT/SAT scores most important, followed by high school record. Recommendations considered in marginal cases. For placement purposes, provisional admission if ACT score is less than 18. Admission and advising affects course load and course selection. Audition recommended for music majors; portfolio recommended for art majors. **Homeschooled:** Transcript of courses and grades required.

High school preparation. College-preparatory program recommended. 22 units recommended. Recommended units include English 4, mathematics 4, social studies 2, history 2, science 4 (laboratory 2), foreign language 1, computer science .5, visual/performing arts 1, academic electives 3.5. 2 units of advanced electives recommended.

2009-2010 Annual costs. Tuition/fees: $13,290. Room/board: $6,020. Books/supplies: $1,000. Personal expenses: $1,775.

2008-2009 Financial aid. Need-based: 524 full-time freshmen applied for aid; 290 were judged to have need; 290 of these received aid. Average need met was 78%. Average scholarship/grant was $10,952; average loan $4,802. 48% of total undergraduate aid awarded as scholarships/grants, 52% as loans/jobs. **Non-need-based:** Awarded to 1,316 full-time undergraduates, including 318 freshmen. Scholarships awarded for academics, alumni affiliation, art, leadership, music/drama, religious affiliation. **Additional information:** Student reply date for institutional scholarships: May 1.

Application procedures. Admission: No deadline. No application fee. Admission notification on a rolling basis. Either SAT or ACT may be substituted for TOEFL scores for foreign students. **Financial aid:** Priority date 3/1; no closing date. FAFSA required. Applicants notified on a rolling basis starting 3/1; must reply by 5/1.

Academics. Special study options: Accelerated study, combined bachelor's/graduate degree, distance learning, double major, dual enrollment of high school students, ESL, honors, independent study, internships, study abroad, teacher certification program. **Credit/placement by examination:** AP, CLEP, IB, institutional tests. 30 credit hours maximum toward bachelor's degree. **Support services:** Reduced course load, remedial instruction, study skills assistance, tutoring, writing center.

Majors. Biology: General, biochemistry. **Business:** Accounting, business admin, marketing. **Communications:** General, journalism, media studies, public relations. **Computer sciences:** General, computer science. **Education:** Art, biology, business, chemistry, elementary, English, French, mathematics, music, physical, secondary, social studies, Spanish, special. **Engineering:** Physics. **Foreign languages:** French, Spanish, translation. **Health:** Nursing (RN), premedicine. **History:** General. **Interdisciplinary:** Global studies. **Legal studies:** Paralegal, prelaw. **Math:** General. **Parks/recreation:** Exercise sciences, sports admin. **Philosophy/religion:** Christian. **Physical sciences:** Chemistry, physics. **Protective services:** Law enforcement admin. **Psychology:** General. **Public administration:** Social work. **Social sciences:** Political science, sociology. **Theology:** Sacred music. **Visual/performing arts:** Art, graphic design, interior design, music performance, music theory/composition, piano/organ, studio arts, voice/opera. **Other:** French and German.

Most popular majors. Biology 9%, business/marketing 24%, communications/journalism 6%, education 13%, health sciences 13%.

Computing on campus. 207 workstations in dormitories, library, computer center. Dormitories wired for high-speed internet access and linked to campus network. Commuter students can connect to campus network. Online course registration, helpline, student web hosting, wireless network available.

Student life. **Freshman orientation:** Available, $65 fee. Preregistration for classes offered. Held on a Thursday, Friday, and Saturday in July. **Policies:** No alcohol allowed, no smoking in front of buildings. **Housing:** Single-sex dorms, special housing for disabled, apartments, wellness housing available. $100 nonrefundable deposit, deadline 7/15. **Activities:** Bands, campus ministries, choral groups, dance, drama, international student organizations, literary magazine, music ensembles, musical theater, opera, radio station, student government, student newspaper, Baptist Student Union, Civitan, Circle-K, Rotoract, Young Democrats, Young Republicans, Black Student Association, 5 women's social/service clubs, Reformed University Fellowship, Habitat for Humanity.

Athletics. NCAA. **Intercollegiate:** Baseball M, basketball, cheerleading, cross-country, equestrian W, football (tackle) M, golf, soccer, softball W, table tennis, tennis, track and field, volleyball W. **Intramural:** Badminton, basketball, field hockey, football (non-tackle), soccer, softball, table tennis, tennis, volleyball. **Team name:** Choctaws.

Student services. Adult student services, chaplain/spiritual director, career counseling, student employment services, financial aid counseling, health services, personal counseling, placement for graduates. **Physically disabled:** Services for visually, speech, hearing impaired.

Contact. E-mail: enrollment-services@mc.edu
Phone: (601) 925-3800 Toll-free number: (800) 738-1236
Fax: (601) 925-3950
Chad Phillips, Director of Admissions, Mississippi College, PO Box 4026, Clinton, MS 39058

Mississippi State University

Mississippi State, Mississippi — **CB member**
www.msstate.edu — **CB code: 1480**

- Public 4-year university
- Commuter campus in large town
- 13,204 degree-seeking undergraduates: 9% part-time, 48% women, 21% African American, 1% Asian American, 1% Hispanic American, 1% Native American, 1% international
- 3,481 degree-seeking graduate students
- 65% of applicants admitted
- SAT or ACT (ACT writing optional) required
- 58% graduate within 6 years

General. Founded in 1878. Regionally accredited. MSU has a branch campus located in Meridian. Branch stations and research units located throughout the state. **Degrees:** 2,554 bachelor's awarded; master's, doctoral, first professional offered. **ROTC:** Army, Air Force. **Location:** 125 miles from Jackson. **Calendar:** Semester, extensive summer session. **Full-time faculty:** 881 total; 76% have terminal degrees, 13% minority, 35% women. **Part-time faculty:** 172 total; 34% have terminal degrees, 8% minority, 57% women. **Class size:** 37% < 20, 42% 20-39, 8% 40-49, 10% 50-99, 4% >100. **Special facilities:** Clock museum, art gallery, observatory, entomological museum, historic costumes and textiles collection, museum of anthropology.

Freshman class profile. 7,429 applied, 4,864 admitted, 2,489 enrolled.

Mid 50% test scores		**Rank in top quarter:**	58%
SAT critical reading:	490-630	**Rank in top tenth:**	30%
SAT math:	480-640	**Return as sophomores:**	84%
ACT composite:	20-27	**Out-of-state:**	25%
GPA 3.75 or higher:	20%	**Live on campus:**	90%
GPA 3.50-3.74:	13%	**International:**	1%
GPA 3.0-3.49:	28%	**Fraternities:**	29%
GPA 2.0-2.99:	37%	**Sororities:**	37%

Basis for selection. Admission based on standardized test scores, GPA, class rank. Students with academic deficiencies may be admitted after additional review. Requirements may vary by department; student should contact department to ensure that requirements are met. Successful completion of summer developmental program results in admission for fall term with mandatory participation in academic support program freshmen year. Audition, portfolio required. Interview recommended for architecture, professional golf management, and veterinary medicine students. **Homeschooled:** Transcript of courses and grades required.

High school preparation. College-preparatory program recommended. 15.5 units required; 20.5 recommended. Required and recommended units include English 4, mathematics 3-4, social studies 1-2, history 2, science 3-4 (laboratory 2), foreign language 1, computer science .5 and academic electives 2. One of the two academic electives must be a foreign language or world geography. Additional unit recommended.

2008-2009 Annual costs. Tuition/fees: $5,151; $12,503 out-of-state. Room/board: $7,333. Books/supplies: $1,000. Personal expenses: $1,883.

2007-2008 Financial aid. **Need-based:** 1,565 full-time freshmen applied for aid; 1,564 were judged to have need; 1,521 of these received aid. Average need met was 64%. Average scholarship/grant was $3,708; average loan $3,542. 37% of total undergraduate aid awarded as scholarships/grants, 63% as loans/jobs. **Non-need-based:** Awarded to 4,093 full-time undergraduates, including 1,240 freshmen. Scholarships awarded for academics, alumni affiliation, art, athletics, job skills, leadership, minority status, music/drama, ROTC, state residency. **Additional information:** No institutional closing date for FAFSA.

Application procedures. **Admission:** No deadline. $35 fee, may be waived for applicants with need. Admission notification on a rolling basis beginning on or about 9/1. **Financial aid:** Priority date 4/1; no closing date. FAFSA required. Applicants notified on a rolling basis starting 12/1; must reply by 5/1.

Academics. **Special study options:** Cooperative education, distance learning, double major, dual enrollment of high school students, ESL, exchange student, external degree, honors, independent study, internships, liberal arts/career combination, student-designed major, study abroad, teacher certification program, weekend college. **Credit/placement by examination:** AP, CLEP, IB, SAT, ACT, institutional tests. Maximum of 25% of any curriculum may be earned by examination. **Support services:** Learning center, pre-admission summer program, reduced course load, remedial instruction, study skills assistance, tutoring, writing center.

Honors college/program. ACT composite score of 27 or above (SAT 1230) and a 3.75 high school core GPA.

Majors. **Agriculture:** General, agribusiness operations, agronomy, animal sciences, economics, food science, horticultural science, landscaping, plant protection, poultry. **Architecture:** Architecture, interior, landscape. **Biology:** General, bacteriology, biochemistry. **Business:** Accounting, business admin, construction management, finance, insurance, management information systems, managerial economics, marketing, real estate. **Communications:** General. **Computer sciences:** General. **Conservation:** Forestry, wildlife. **Education:** Agricultural, business, elementary, music, physical, secondary, special, voc/tech. **Engineering:** Aerospace, biomedical, chemical, civil, computer, electrical, industrial, mechanical. **Engineering technology:** Industrial. **Family/consumer sciences:** General. **Foreign languages:** General. **Health:** Clinical lab science. **History:** General. **Interdisciplinary:** Biological/physical sciences. **Liberal arts:** Arts/sciences. **Math:** General. **Philosophy/religion:** Philosophy. **Physical sciences:** Chemistry, geology, physics. **Psychology:** General, educational. **Public administration:** Social work. **Social sciences:** Anthropology, economics, political science, sociology. **Visual/performing arts:** General. **Other:** Agricultural engineering technology and business, Computational engineering, Instructional technology, Veterinary medical science.

Most popular majors. Agriculture 6%, business/marketing 23%, education 20%, engineering/engineering technologies 12%.

Computing on campus. 1,000 workstations in dormitories, library, computer center, student center. Dormitories wired for high-speed internet access and linked to campus network. Commuter students can connect to campus network. Online course registration, online library, helpline, student web hosting, wireless network available.

Student life. **Freshman orientation:** Available, $95 fee. Preregistration for classes offered. 2-day program for freshmen; 1-day program for transfer students. Held three times during the summer and prior to the beginning of each semester. Orientation fees and parents' fees vary for freshman and transfer students. **Housing:** Guaranteed on-campus for freshmen. Single-sex dorms, apartments available. $50 nonrefundable deposit. Co-residential housing available. Residence halls are ADA accessible. **Activities:** Bands, campus ministries, choral groups, dance, drama, international student organizations, literary magazine, music ensembles, Model UN, musical theater, radio station, student government, student newspaper, symphony orchestra, TV station, more than 300 organizations on campus.

Athletics. NCAA. **Intercollegiate:** Baseball M, basketball, cross-country, football (tackle) M, golf, soccer W, softball W, tennis, track and field, volleyball W. **Intramural:** Badminton, basketball, bowling, football (non-tackle), golf, racquetball, soccer, softball, table tennis, tennis, volleyball, water polo, weight lifting. **Team name:** Bulldogs.

Student services. Adult student services, alcohol/substance abuse counseling, chaplain/spiritual director, career counseling, services for economically disadvantaged, student employment services, financial aid counseling, health services, minority student services, on-campus daycare, personal counseling, placement for graduates, veterans' counselor. **Physically disabled:** Services for visually, speech, hearing impaired.

Contact. E-mail: admit@msstate.edu
Phone: (662) 325-2224 Fax: (662) 325-1678
Phil Bonfanti, Director of Admissions and Scholarships, Mississippi State University, Box 6334, Mississippi State, MS 39762

Mississippi University for Women

Columbus, Mississippi — **CB member**
www.muw.edu — **CB code: 1481**

- Public 4-year university and liberal arts college
- Commuter campus in large town
- 1,999 degree-seeking undergraduates: 17% part-time, 86% women
- 172 graduate students
- 49% of applicants admitted
- 42% graduate within 6 years

General. Founded in 1884. Regionally accredited. **Degrees:** 356 bachelor's, 40 associate awarded; master's offered. **ROTC:** Army, Air Force. **Location:** 120 miles from Birmingham, Alabama, 160 miles from Memphis, Tennessee. **Calendar:** Semester, limited summer session. **Full-time faculty:** 135 total; 56% have terminal degrees, 8% minority, 64% women. **Part-time faculty:** 59 total; 27% have terminal degrees, 5% minority, 56% women. **Class size:** 60% < 20, 33% 20-39, 4% 40-49, 2% 50-99, 2% >100. **Special facilities:** Environmental education center.

Freshman class profile. 1,223 applied, 594 admitted, 258 enrolled.

Mid 50% test scores		**Rank in top quarter:**	57%
SAT critical reading:	420-570	**Rank in top tenth:**	24%
SAT math:	500-650	**Return as sophomores:**	68%
ACT composite:	18-24	**Out-of-state:**	10%
GPA 3.75 or higher:	20%	**Live on campus:**	66%
GPA 3.50-3.74:	20%	**Fraternities:**	42%
GPA 3.0-3.49:	33%	**Sororities:**	43%
GPA 2.0-2.99:	26%		

Basis for selection. Test scores, high school GPA, academic achievement considered in that order. SAT or ACT recommended. Students with a 3.2 GPA or higher not required to provide test scores. Interview recommended.

High school preparation. 16 units required; 20 recommended. Required and recommended units include English 4, mathematics 3-4, social studies 3, science 3-4 (laboratory 2), foreign language 1, computer science .5 and academic electives 2. One elective of foreign language or world geography required; other elective must be in foreign language, world geography, 4th year mathematics, or 4th year laboratory based science.

2008-2009 Annual costs. Tuition/fees: $4,423; $11,688 out-of-state. Room/board: $5,066. Books/supplies: $800. Personal expenses: $1,200.

2007-2008 Financial aid. Non-need-based: Scholarships awarded for academics, alumni affiliation, leadership, minority status, music/drama, ROTC, state residency.

Application procedures. Admission: Priority date 5/1; no deadline. No application fee. Admission notification on a rolling basis. **Financial aid:** Priority date 3/1; no closing date. FAFSA required. Applicants notified on a rolling basis starting 3/15; must reply within 2 week(s) of notification.

Academics. Special study options: Cross-registration, distance learning, double major, dual enrollment of high school students, honors, independent study, internships, study abroad, teacher certification program, weekend college. **Credit/placement by examination:** AP, CLEP, SAT, ACT, institutional tests. 60 credit hours maximum toward bachelor's degree. **Support services:** Learning center, pre-admission summer program, remedial instruction, tutoring.

Majors. Biology: General, bacteriology. **Business:** Accounting, business admin. **Communications:** General. **Education:** Art, elementary, music. **Family/consumer sciences:** Family systems. **Foreign languages:** Spanish. **Health:** Music therapy, nursing (RN), speech pathology. **History:** General. **Legal studies:** Paralegal. **Liberal arts:** Arts/sciences. **Math:** General. **Parks/recreation:** Health/fitness. **Personal/culinary services:** Culinary arts. **Physical sciences:** General, chemistry. **Psychology:** General. **Social sciences:** General, political science. **Visual/performing arts:** General.

Most popular majors. Biology 6%, business/marketing 11%, education 13%, family/consumer sciences 7%, health sciences 30%, psychology 8%.

Computing on campus. 500 workstations in dormitories, library, computer center. Dormitories wired for high-speed internet access and linked to campus network. Commuter students can connect to campus network. Online course registration, online library, helpline, student web hosting available.

Student life. Freshman orientation: Available, $50 fee. Preregistration for classes offered. **Housing:** Guaranteed on-campus for all undergraduates. Single-sex dorms, apartments, wellness housing available. $25 deposit, deadline 7/1. **Activities:** Jazz band, choral groups, drama, international student organizations, literary magazine, music ensembles, radio station, student government, student newspaper, Methodist, Presbyterian, Episcopal, Baptist, Catholic, Student Interfaith Association, Black student organizations, College Republicans, Young Democrats.

Athletics. Intramural: Badminton, basketball, football (non-tackle), golf, racquetball, soccer, softball, table tennis, tennis, volleyball.

Student services. Adult student services, alcohol/substance abuse counseling, career counseling, student employment services, financial aid counseling, health services, on-campus daycare, personal counseling, placement for graduates, veterans' counselor. **Physically disabled:** Services for visually, speech, hearing impaired.

Contact. E-mail: admissions@muw.edu
Phone: (662) 329-7106 Toll-free number: (877) 462-8439
Fax: (662) 241-7481
Cassie Derden, Director of Admissions, Mississippi University for Women, 1100 College St. MUW-1613, Columbus, MS 39701

Mississippi Valley State University

Itta Bena, Mississippi — **CB member**
www.mvsu.edu — **CB code: 1482**

- Public 4-year university and liberal arts college
- Commuter campus in small town
- 2,513 degree-seeking undergraduates
- 25% of applicants admitted
- SAT or ACT (ACT writing optional) required

General. Founded in 1946. Regionally accredited. **ROTC:** Army. **Location:** 100 miles from Jackson, 130 miles from Memphis, Tennessee. **Calendar:** Semester, extensive summer session. **Full-time faculty:** 130 total. **Part-time faculty:** 47 total. **Class size:** 62% < 20, 32% 20-39, 2% 40-49, 3% 50-99, less than 1% >100.

Freshman class profile. 5,157 applied, 1,274 admitted, 452 enrolled.

Mid 50% test scores		**GPA 3.0-3.49:**	22%
ACT composite:	15-18	**GPA 2.0-2.99:**	55%
GPA 3.75 or higher:	5%	**Rank in top quarter:**	27%
GPA 3.50-3.74:	5%		

Basis for selection. High school curriculum and test scores very important. Audition required for music education majors. Interview required of some students, but recommended for all students.

High school preparation. 16 units required; 18 recommended. Required and recommended units include English 4, mathematics 3, social studies 3, science 3 (laboratory 2), foreign language 1 and academic electives 2. Mathematics requirement includes algebra I and II and geometry. Social sciences must include US government and US history. Sciences must be chosen from introductory and advanced biology, physics, and chemistry. Advanced science or mathematics may be substituted for a foreign language.

2008-2009 Annual costs. Tuition/fees: $4,575; $11,116 out-of-state. Room/board: $4,748.

Financial aid. Non-need-based: Scholarships awarded for academics, athletics, minority status, ROTC.

Application procedures. Admission: Priority date 8/1; deadline 8/17 (receipt date). No application fee. Admission notification on a rolling basis. **Financial aid:** Priority date 3/1, closing date 5/1. FAFSA, institutional form required. Applicants notified on a rolling basis starting 4/1; must reply within 2 week(s) of notification.

Academics. Special study options: Cooperative education, double major, dual enrollment of high school students, honors, independent study, internships, teacher certification program. **Credit/placement by examination:** AP, CLEP, ACT. 30 credit hours maximum toward bachelor's degree. **Support services:** Learning center, pre-admission summer program, reduced course load, remedial instruction, study skills assistance, tutoring, writing center.

Majors. **Biology:** General. **Business:** Accounting, business admin, office management. **Communications:** General. **Computer sciences:** General. **Education:** Biology, early childhood, elementary, English, mathematics, music, physical, social science. **Engineering technology:** Industrial. **Health:** Environmental health. **History:** General. **Math:** General. **Physical sciences:** Chemistry. **Protective services:** Criminal justice. **Public administration:** General, social work. **Social sciences:** Political science, sociology. **Visual/performing arts:** Music management, studio arts.

Most popular majors. Business/marketing 12%, education 33%, English 6%, history 10%, public administration/social services 15%, security/protective services 6%.

Computing on campus. 600 workstations in dormitories, library, computer center. Dormitories wired for high-speed internet access and linked to campus network. Commuter students can connect to campus network. Online course registration, online library, wireless network available.

Student life. **Freshman orientation:** Mandatory, $75 fee. Preregistration for classes offered. **Housing:** Single-sex dorms, apartments available. $50 deposit, deadline 7/31. **Activities:** Bands, choral groups, dance, drama, music ensembles, radio station, student government, student newspaper, TV station, numerous honor societies, political, social, religious organizations, prelaw club.

Athletics. NCAA. **Intercollegiate:** Baseball M, basketball, bowling, cross-country, football (tackle) M, golf, soccer W, softball W, tennis, track and field, volleyball W. **Intramural:** Baseball M, basketball, bowling, cross-country, softball W, swimming, tennis, volleyball. **Team name:** Delta Devils (M), Devilettes (W).

Student services. Adult student services, career counseling, student employment services, financial aid counseling, health services, on-campus daycare, personal counseling, placement for graduates, veterans' counselor.

Contact. E-mail: nbtaylor@mvsu.edu
Phone: (662) 254-3347 Fax: (662) 254-3759
Nora Taylor, Director of Admissions and Recruitment, Mississippi Valley State University, 14000 Highway 82 West, Itta Bena, MS 38941-1400

Rust College

Holly Springs, Mississippi
www.rustcollege.edu **CB code: 1669**

- Private 4-year liberal arts college affiliated with United Methodist Church
- Residential campus in small town
- 967 degree-seeking undergraduates
- 40% of applicants admitted
- ACT (writing optional) required

General. Founded in 1866. Regionally accredited. **Degrees:** 119 bachelor's, 5 associate awarded. **Location:** 35 miles from Memphis, Tennessee. **Calendar:** Semester, limited summer session. **Full-time faculty:** 46 total. **Part-time faculty:** 4 total. **Class size:** 59% < 20, 19% 20-39, 4% 40-49, 12% 50-99, 5% >100. **Special facilities:** Histories, religious, poetry, speech writing books for ministers and ministerial students, Inuit and African art collections, international artifacts collection.

Freshman class profile. 5,000 applied, 2,000 admitted, 340 enrolled.

Mid 50% test scores		**GPA 3.0-3.49:**	17%
ACT composite:	14-17	**GPA 2.0-2.99:**	71%
GPA 3.75 or higher:	6%	**Out-of-state:**	52%
GPA 3.50-3.74:	6%		

Basis for selection. School achievement record and recommendations most important. Test scores also important. **Homeschooled:** State high school equivalency certificate, letter of recommendation (nonparent) required.

High school preparation. 19 units required. Required units include English 4, mathematics 3, social studies 3, science 3 and academic electives 6.

2008-2009 Annual costs. Tuition/fees: $7,000. Room/board: $3,120. Books/supplies: $500. Personal expenses: $1,450.

Financial aid. **Non-need-based:** Scholarships awarded for academics, leadership, music/drama, religious affiliation, state residency.

Application procedures. **Admission:** Priority date 5/5; no deadline. $10 fee, may be waived for applicants with need. Admission notification on a rolling basis. Must reply by May 1 or within 2 week(s) if notified thereafter. **Financial aid:** Closing date 5/1. FAFSA, institutional form required. Applicants notified on a rolling basis starting 5/1; must reply within 2 week(s) of notification.

Academics. **Special study options:** Double major, honors, independent study, internships, liberal arts/career combination, study abroad, teacher certification program. Nursing and medical technology cooperative program with other institutions. **Credit/placement by examination:** CLEP, ACT, institutional tests. 12 credit hours maximum toward associate degree, 12 toward bachelor's. **Support services:** Learning center, pre-admission summer program, reduced course load, remedial instruction, study skills assistance, tutoring, writing center.

Majors. **Biology:** General. **Business:** Business admin. **Communications:** Broadcast journalism, journalism. **Computer sciences:** Computer science. **Education:** Biology, business, elementary, English, mathematics, social science. **Family/consumer sciences:** Child care. **Math:** General. **Physical sciences:** Chemistry. **Public administration:** Social work. **Social sciences:** General, political science, sociology.

Most popular majors. Biology 27%, business/marketing 14%, computer/information sciences 12%, English 7%, family/consumer sciences 12%, public administration/social services 8%, social sciences 9%.

Computing on campus. 220 workstations in dormitories, library, computer center. Dormitories wired for high-speed internet access and linked to campus network. Commuter students can connect to campus network. Online library, helpline, wireless network available.

Student life. **Freshman orientation:** Mandatory. Orientation and assessment program begins 1 week prior to registration. **Housing:** Guaranteed on-campus for all undergraduates. Single-sex dorms, apartments available. $50 deposit. **Activities:** Bands, choral groups, dance, drama, music ensembles, radio station, student government, student newspaper, TV station, Methodist Student Movement, Baptist Student Union, Catholic Student Association, pre-law club, NAACP, social work club, Sunday School Association, international student association, All Saints Student Movement.

Athletics. NCAA. **Intercollegiate:** Baseball M, basketball, cheerleading, cross-country, soccer M, softball W, tennis, track and field, volleyball. **Intramural:** Badminton, baseball, basketball, bowling, cheerleading, cross-country, football (non-tackle), soccer, softball, swimming, table tennis, tennis, track and field, volleyball, weight lifting. **Team name:** Bearcats.

Student services. Adult student services, career counseling, student employment services, health services, minority student services, on-campus daycare, personal counseling, placement for graduates, veterans' counselor.

Contact. E-mail: jbmcdonald@rustcollege.edu
Phone: (662) 252-8000 ext. 4059 Toll-free number: (888) 886-8492 ext. 4059 Fax: (662) 252-8895
Johnny McDonald, Director of Enrollment Services, Rust College, 150 Rust Avenue, Holly Springs, MS 38635-2328

Southeastern Baptist College

Laurel, Mississippi
www.southeasternbaptist.edu **CB code: 1781**

- Private 4-year Bible college affiliated with Baptist faith
- Commuter campus in large town

General. Founded in 1949. Accredited by ABHE. **Location:** 90 miles from Jackson. **Calendar:** Semester.

Annual costs/financial aid. Tuition/fees (2008-2009): $5,350. Room: $800. Books/supplies: $300. Personal expenses: $350.

Contact. Phone: (601) 426-6346
Academic Dean, 4229 Highway 15 North, Laurel, MS 39440

Tougaloo College

Tougaloo, Mississippi **CB member**
www.tougaloo.edu **CB code: 1807**

- Private 4-year liberal arts college affiliated with United Christian Mission Society and United Church of Christ
- Residential campus in large city
- 862 degree-seeking undergraduates: 4% part-time, 67% women, 100% African American
- 96% of applicants admitted
- SAT or ACT (ACT writing optional) required
- 42% graduate within 6 years

General. Founded in 1869. Regionally accredited. Cooperative program with Brown University provides exchange of financial resources and students. Exchange opportunities available between New York and Boston universities in pre-med and other areas. **Degrees:** 129 bachelor's, 2 associate awarded. **ROTC:** Army, Naval. **Calendar:** Semester, limited summer session. **Full-time faculty:** 74 total; 35% minority, 55% women. **Part-time faculty:** 22 total; 4% minority, 82% women. **Class size:** 68% < 20, 30% 20-39, 2% 40-49, less than 1% 50-99. **Special facilities:** Civil rights documents and prints, East and West African art and artifacts.

Freshman class profile. 1,222 applied, 1,172 admitted, 237 enrolled.

Mid 50% test scores			
SAT critical reading:	410-560	End year in good standing:	99%
SAT math:	370-530	Return as sophomores:	74%
ACT composite:	25-29	Out-of-state:	26%
		Live on campus:	90%

Basis for selection. Transcript, test scores important. Minimum 3.0 GPA and ACT composite score of 18 required of applicants in junior year of high school. Audition required for music majors. Portfolio recommended for art majors.

High school preparation. College-preparatory program recommended. 16 units required. Required and recommended units include English 3, mathematics 2, social studies 2, science 2, foreign language 2 and academic electives 9.

2009-2010 Annual costs. Tuition/fees (projected): $9,710. Room/board: $6,572. Books/supplies: $500. Personal expenses: $800.

2008-2009 Financial aid. **Non-need-based:** Scholarships awarded for academics, athletics, ROTC.

Application procedures. **Admission:** Priority date 4/15; no deadline. $25 fee, may be waived for applicants with need. Admission notification on a rolling basis. **Financial aid:** Priority date 4/15; no closing date. FAFSA, institutional form required. Applicants notified on a rolling basis starting 5/1; must reply within 2 week(s) of notification.

Academics. **Special study options:** Accelerated study, cooperative education, cross-registration, double major, exchange student, honors, independent study, internships, liberal arts/career combination, New York semester, student-designed major, study abroad, teacher certification program, Washington semester, weekend college. 3-2 program in pre-engineering and physical sciences with Brown University, Georgia Institute of Technology, University of Mississippi, University of Wisconsin Madison, Tuskegee Institute, Washington University St. Louis, Howard University, University of Memphis, Florida A&M. **Credit/placement by examination:** CLEP, IB, SAT, ACT, institutional tests. 12 credit hours maximum toward bachelor's degree. **Support services:** Learning center, pre-admission summer program, reduced course load, remedial instruction, study skills assistance, tutoring, writing center.

Majors. **Biology:** General. **Communications:** Media studies. **Education:** General, elementary, health, secondary. **History:** General. **Interdisciplinary:** Math/computer science. **Liberal arts:** Arts/sciences. **Math:** General. **Physical sciences:** Chemistry, physics. **Psychology:** General. **Social sciences:** Economics, political science, sociology. **Visual/performing arts:** Art.

Computing on campus. 4 workstations in dormitories, library, computer center, student center. Dormitories linked to campus network. Commuter students can connect to campus network. Helpline, repair service available.

Student life. **Freshman orientation:** Mandatory. Preregistration for classes offered. **Housing:** Single-sex dorms, wellness housing available. $50 nonrefundable deposit. **Activities:** Choral groups, dance, drama, music ensembles, radio station, student government, student newspaper, Baptist student union, biology club, Afro-American studies group, College Republicans, foreign students club, French club, pre-health club, prelaw club, honor societies, human services clubs.

Athletics. NAIA. **Intercollegiate:** Baseball M, basketball, cross-country, golf, tennis. **Intramural:** Badminton, baseball M, basketball, cheerleading, cross-country M, football (non-tackle) M, golf, soccer M, softball, tennis, volleyball. **Team name:** Bulldogs.

Student services. Adult student services, chaplain/spiritual director, career counseling, student employment services, financial aid counseling, health services, personal counseling, placement for graduates, veterans' counselor.

Contact. E-mail: info@tougaloo.edu
Phone: (601) 977-7765 Toll-free number: (888) 424-2566
Junoesque Jacobs, Director of Admissions, Tougaloo College, 500 West County Line Road, Tougaloo, MS 39174

University of Mississippi

University, Mississippi — **CB member**
www.olemiss.edu — **CB code: 1840**

- Public 4-year university
- Residential campus in large town
- 12,609 degree-seeking undergraduates: 9% part-time, 53% women, 13% African American, 1% Asian American, 1% Hispanic American, 1% international
- 2,422 degree-seeking graduate students
- 83% of applicants admitted

General. Founded in 1844. Regionally accredited. **Degrees:** 2,450 bachelor's awarded; master's, doctoral, first professional offered. **ROTC:** Army, Naval, Air Force. **Location:** 75 miles from Memphis, Tennessee. **Calendar:** Semester, extensive summer session. **Full-time faculty:** 725 total; 19% minority, 61% women. **Part-time faculty:** 142 total; 8% minority, 49% women. **Class size:** 50% < 20, 49% 20-39, less than 1% 40-49, less than 1% 50-99. **Special facilities:** Accredited teaching museum, William Faulkner home and grounds, Southern culture center, National Center for Physical Acoustics, 2 super computers, National Center for the Development of Natural Products, National School Food Service Management Institute, water and wetland resources center.

Freshman class profile. 7,946 applied, 6,630 admitted, 2,473 enrolled.

Mid 50% test scores			
SAT critical reading:	450-580	GPA 3.50-3.74:	14%
SAT math:	460-580	GPA 3.0-3.49:	28%
ACT composite:	20-26	GPA 2.0-2.99:	34%
GPA 3.75 or higher:	23%	International:	1%

Basis for selection. School achievement record and test scores important. SAT or ACT may be required for students with core GPA of under 3.2. Essay required for Croff Institute for International Studies, honors college; audition required for music, theater majors. Portfolio recommended for art majors. **Homeschooled:** Transcript of courses and grades required. **Learning Disabled:** Report and document disabilities to student disabilities office.

High school preparation. College-preparatory program required. 15 units required. Required and recommended units include English 4, mathematics 3-4, social studies 1-2, history 2, science 3-4 (laboratory 2), foreign language 1-2, computer science .5 and academic electives 1. Mathematics units must include algebra and 2 higher courses. Social sciences units must include U.S. history and U.S. government. Academic electives must include 1 year world geography and fourth year math or science.

2008-2009 Annual costs. Tuition/fees: $5,107; $12,468 out-of-state. Room/board: $5,914.

2007-2008 Financial aid. **Need-based:** 1,482 full-time freshmen applied for aid; 955 were judged to have need; 920 of these received aid. Average need met was 76%. Average scholarship/grant was $6,299; average loan $3,809. 44% of total undergraduate aid awarded as scholarships/grants, 56% as loans/jobs. **Non-need-based:** Awarded to 2,934 full-time undergraduates, including 775 freshmen. Scholarships awarded for academics, alumni affiliation, art, athletics, leadership, minority status, music/drama, ROTC, state residency.

Application procedures. **Admission:** Priority date 4/1; deadline 7/20 (postmark date). $25 fee ($50 out-of-state), may be waived for applicants with need. Admission notification on a rolling basis beginning on or about 9/15. Online out-of-state application fee: $50. **Financial aid:** Priority date 3/15; no closing date. FAFSA required. Applicants notified on a rolling basis starting 4/1; must reply within 3 week(s) of notification.

Academics. **Special study options:** Accelerated study, combined bachelor's/graduate degree, cooperative education, distance learning, double major, ESL, exchange student, honors, independent study, internships, study abroad, teacher certification program. **Credit/placement by examination:** AP, CLEP, IB, institutional tests. 63 credit hours maximum toward bachelor's degree. Student must earn 12 hours in residence before any credit-by-examination hours are recorded on transcript. **Support services:** Learning center, reduced course load, remedial instruction, study skills assistance, tutoring, writing center.

Honors college/program. Requires test scores, transcript, essays, and recommendations. 120 students admitted each fall. Unique courses which meet general education requirements taught by senior/master faculty. Senior thesis required.

Majors. **Area/ethnic studies:** African-American. **Biology:** General. **Business:** Accounting, business admin, finance, insurance, management information systems, managerial economics, marketing, real estate. **Communications:** Journalism. **Computer sciences:** General. **Education:** Elementary,

English, foreign languages, mathematics, science, social studies, special. **Engineering:** General, chemical, civil, electrical, geological, mechanical. **Family/consumer sciences:** General. **Foreign languages:** Classics, French, German, linguistics, Spanish. **Health:** Audiology/speech pathology. **History:** General. **Legal studies:** Paralegal. **Liberal arts:** Arts/sciences. **Math:** General. **Parks/recreation:** Exercise sciences, facilities management. **Philosophy/religion:** Philosophy. **Physical sciences:** Chemistry, geology, physics. **Protective services:** Forensics, law enforcement admin. **Psychology:** General. **Public administration:** Policy analysis, social work. **Social sciences:** Anthropology, economics, international relations, political science, sociology. **Visual/performing arts:** General, art history/conservation, dramatic. **Other:** Southern studies.

Most popular majors. Business/marketing 32%, education 9%, health sciences 6%.

Computing on campus. 638 workstations in dormitories, library, computer center. Dormitories wired for high-speed internet access and linked to campus network. Commuter students can connect to campus network. Online course registration, online library, helpline, repair service, student web hosting, wireless network available.

Student life. Freshman orientation: Mandatory. Preregistration for classes offered. 2 days in June, additional session immediately before beginning of term. **Housing:** Guaranteed on-campus for freshmen. Single-sex dorms, apartments, fraternity/sorority housing, wellness housing available. $75 nonrefundable deposit. Intensive study floors available to honors and other students. Special interest, graduate/older students, substance-free, environmental interest housing available. **Activities:** Bands, campus ministries, choral groups, dance, drama, international student organizations, music ensembles, musical theater, opera, radio station, student government, student newspaper, symphony orchestra, TV station, Wesley Foundation, Baptist student union, Black student union, Students for Environmental Awareness, Mortar Board, Habitat for Humanity, Students Envisioning Equality through Diversity.

Athletics. NCAA. **Intercollegiate:** Baseball M, basketball, cheerleading, cross-country, fencing, football (tackle) M, golf, lacrosse M, racquetball M, rifle W, rugby M, skiing M, soccer, softball W, tennis, track and field, volleyball W. **Intramural:** Badminton, basketball, bowling, football (tackle), golf, handball, rifle, soccer, softball, swimming, table tennis, tennis, track and field, volleyball, water polo. **Team name:** Rebels.

Student services. Adult student services, alcohol/substance abuse counseling, chaplain/spiritual director, career counseling, student employment services, financial aid counseling, health services, legal services, minority student services, personal counseling, placement for graduates, veterans' counselor, women's services. **Physically disabled:** Services for visually, speech, hearing impaired.

Contact. E-mail: admissions@olemiss.edu
Phone: (662) 915-7226 Toll-free number: (800) 653-6477
Fax: (662) 915-5869
Charlotte Fant, Director of Admissions and Registrar, University of Mississippi, 145 Martindale, University, MS 38677-1848

University of Mississippi Medical Center

Jackson, Mississippi
www.umc.edu — **CB code: 0358**

- Public two-year upper-division health science college
- Commuter campus in large city

General. Founded in 1955. Regionally accredited. **Degrees:** 201 bachelor's awarded; master's, doctoral, first professional offered. **Location:** 200 miles from Memphis, Tennessee. **Calendar:** Quarter, limited summer session. **Full-time faculty:** 729 total. **Part-time faculty:** 161 total.

Student profile. 575 degree-seeking undergraduates.

Out-of-state:	1%	**25 or older:**	80%
Live on campus:	3%		

Basis for selection. College transcript required. Competitive admission to health science programs based on grades, recommendations, test scores, interviews. Transfer accepted as sophomores, juniors.

2008-2009 Annual costs. Tuition/fees: $5,107; $12,467 out-of-state. Tuition and fees quoted are for semester-based nursing and other health-related undergraduate programs. Books/supplies: $1,596.

Financial aid. All financial aid based on need.

Application procedures. Admission: Deadline 2/11. $10 fee. Admission notification 4/11. Must reply by 5/11. Application closing dates and reply dates vary by program. **Financial aid:** FAFSA, institutional form required.

Academics. Includes schools of medicine, nursing, health-related professions, and dentistry, graduate programs in medical and clinical health sciences, and 623-bed teaching hospital. Certificate programs in emergency medical technology and radiologic technology and clinical nuclear medicine offered. **Special study options:** Liberal arts/career combination. **Credit/placement by examination:** CLEP. **Support services:** Pre-admission summer program, study skills assistance, tutoring.

Majors. Health: Clinical lab science, cytotechnology, dental hygiene, medical records admin.

Computing on campus. 75 workstations in library, computer center. Online library available.

Student life. Housing: Single-sex dorms, apartments available. $75 deposit. **Activities:** Student government, student newspaper, University Christian Fellowship, Catholic Student Organization.

Athletics. Intramural: Baseball, basketball, football (tackle) M, golf, soccer, softball, table tennis.

Student services. Alcohol/substance abuse counseling, chaplain/spiritual director, career counseling, financial aid counseling, health services, minority student services, personal counseling. **Physically disabled:** Services for speech, hearing impaired.

Contact. Phone: (601) 984-1080
Barbara Westerfield, Registrar, University of Mississippi Medical Center, 2500 North State Street, Jackson, MS 39216

University of Southern Mississippi

Hattiesburg, Mississippi — **CB member**
www.usm.edu — **CB code: 1479**

- Public 4-year university
- Residential campus in small city
- 12,062 degree-seeking undergraduates: 14% part-time, 60% women, 29% African American, 1% Asian American, 1% Hispanic American, 1% international
- 2,731 degree-seeking graduate students
- 55% of applicants admitted
- SAT or ACT (ACT writing optional) required
- 44% graduate within 6 years

General. Founded in 1910. Regionally accredited. Dual campus with main campus in Hattiesburg and nonresidential, nontraditional campus in Long Beach, and other sites along Mississippi Gulf Coast. **Degrees:** 2,262 bachelor's awarded; master's, doctoral offered. **ROTC:** Army, Air Force. **Location:** 85 miles from Jackson, 110 miles from New Orleans. **Calendar:** Semester, extensive summer session. **Full-time faculty:** 743 total; 77% have terminal degrees, 14% minority, 45% women. **Part-time faculty:** 186 total; 34% have terminal degrees, 6% minority, 62% women. **Class size:** 48% < 20, 36% 20-39, 5% 40-49, 7% 50-99, 3% >100. **Special facilities:** Marine education center, aquarium.

Freshman class profile. 5,295 applied, 2,910 admitted, 1,527 enrolled.

Mid 50% test scores		**Rank in top quarter:**	47%
SAT critical reading:	460-570	**Rank in top tenth:**	20%
SAT math:	480-570	**End year in good standing:**	74%
ACT composite:	19-24	**Return as sophomores:**	72%
GPA 3.75 or higher:	12%	**Out-of-state:**	22%
GPA 3.50-3.74:	11%	**Live on campus:**	92%
GPA 3.0-3.49:	28%	**Fraternities:**	21%
GPA 2.0-2.99:	48%	**Sororities:**	16%

Basis for selection. Test scores, GPA, class rank important. Applicants who don't meet criteria may be required to participate in screening process that includes testing. Test not required of some students.

High school preparation. College-preparatory program required. 15.5 units required; 17.5 recommended. Required and recommended units include English 4, mathematics 3, social studies 3, science 3, foreign language 2, computer science .5 and academic electives 2. Mathematics must include algebra I and II, geometry or higher mathematics. Social sciences must include US government, US history, world history, and economics or geography. Sciences must be chosen from introductory and advanced biology, physics, and chemistry. 2 units world geography, or additional science or mathematics may be substituted for 1 foreign language. 2 units of electives and .5 units of computer applications required.

2008-2009 Annual costs. Tuition/fees: $5,096; $12,746 out-of-state. Room/board: $5,330. Books/supplies: $1,200. Personal expenses: $2,804.

2007-2008 Financial aid. **Need-based:** 1,227 full-time freshmen applied for aid; 947 were judged to have need; 919 of these received aid. Average need met was 79%. Average scholarship/grant was $3,698; average loan $3,657. 41% of total undergraduate aid awarded as scholarships/grants, 59% as loans/jobs. **Non-need-based:** Awarded to 4,031 full-time undergraduates, including 878 freshmen.

Application procedures. **Admission:** No deadline. $35 fee, may be waived for applicants with need. Admission notification on a rolling basis beginning on or about 9/1. **Financial aid:** Priority date 3/15; no closing date. FAFSA, institutional form required.

Academics. **Special study options:** Accelerated study, combined bachelor's/graduate degree, cooperative education, distance learning, double major, dual enrollment of high school students, ESL, honors, independent study, internships, study abroad, teacher certification program. **Credit/placement by examination:** AP, CLEP, SAT, ACT, institutional tests. 30 credit hours maximum toward bachelor's degree. **Support services:** Learning center, preadmission summer program, reduced course load, remedial instruction, study skills assistance, tutoring, writing center.

Honors college/program. Requires an ACT score of 26 or equivalent GPA requirement, and essay.

Majors. **Architecture:** Interior. **Area/ethnic studies:** American. **Biology:** General, marine. **Business:** Accounting, business admin, finance, hotel/motel admin, human resources, international, management information systems, managerial economics, marketing. **Communications:** General, advertising, journalism, radio/tv. **Computer sciences:** General, data processing. **Education:** Business, Deaf/hearing impaired, elementary, music, physical, special, technology/industrial arts. **Engineering technology:** Architectural, computer, electrical, industrial. **Family/consumer sciences:** Clothing/textiles, family studies, family systems. **Foreign languages:** General. **Health:** Athletic training, audiology/speech pathology, clinical lab science, dietetics, health services, nursing (RN). **History:** General. **Interdisciplinary:** Biological/physical sciences. **Legal studies:** Paralegal. **Liberal arts:** Library science. **Math:** General. **Parks/recreation:** General, sports admin. **Personal/culinary services:** Mortuary science. **Philosophy/religion:** Philosophy, religion. **Physical sciences:** Chemistry, geology, oceanography, physics. **Protective services:** Criminal justice, forensics. **Psychology:** General. **Public administration:** Social work. **Social sciences:** Anthropology, geography, international relations, political science, sociology. **Visual/performing arts:** General, dance, dramatic, music management. **Other:** Tourism.

Most popular majors. Business/marketing 20%, communications/journalism 6%, education 10%, health sciences 13%, parks/recreation 6%, psychology 8%.

Computing on campus. 202 workstations in dormitories, library, computer center. Dormitories wired for high-speed internet access and linked to campus network. Commuter students can connect to campus network. Online course registration, online library, helpline, student web hosting, wireless network available.

Student life. **Freshman orientation:** Available. Preregistration for classes offered. **Policies:** Freshmen who reside in area may live at home. All freshmen who request campus housing required to live in freshman dormitories. **Housing:** Single-sex dorms, special housing for disabled, apartments, fraternity/sorority housing available. $75 nonrefundable deposit, deadline 2/1. **Activities:** Bands, campus ministries, choral groups, dance, drama, film society, international student organizations, literary magazine, music ensembles, musical theater, opera, radio station, student government, student newspaper, symphony orchestra, Honor Societies, Service and Religious Organizations, Young Republicans, Young Democrats.

Athletics. NCAA. **Intercollegiate:** Baseball M, basketball, cross-country, football (tackle) M, golf, rugby M, soccer W, softball W, tennis, track and field, volleyball W. **Intramural:** Badminton, basketball, bowling, golf, racquetball, soccer, softball, squash, swimming, table tennis, tennis, track and field, volleyball. **Team name:** Golden Eagles.

Student services. Adult student services, career counseling, student employment services, health services, minority student services, on-campus daycare, personal counseling, placement for graduates, veterans' counselor, women's services. **Physically disabled:** Services for visually, speech, hearing impaired. **Learning disabled:** Comprehensive services available.

Contact. E-mail: admissions@usm.edu
Phone: (601) 266-5000 Fax: (601) 266-5148
Amanda Belsom, Admissions Operations, University of Southern Mississippi, 118 College Drive #5166, Hattiesburg, MS 39406-0001

Wesley College
Florence, Mississippi
www.wesleycollege.edu **CB code: 1923**

- Private 4-year Bible college affiliated with Congregational Methodist Church
- Residential campus in small town

General. Founded in 1972. Accredited by ABHE. **Location:** 12 miles from Jackson. **Calendar:** Semester.

Annual costs/financial aid. Tuition/fees (2008-2009): $8,748. Room/board: $4,480. Books/supplies: $700. Personal expenses: $650. Need-based financial aid available to full-time and part-time students.

Contact. Phone: (601) 845-5747
Director of Enrollment, PO Box 1070, Florence, MS 39073-0070

William Carey University
Hattiesburg, Mississippi
www.wmcarey.edu **CB code: 1907**

- Private 4-year university and liberal arts college affiliated with Baptist faith
- Commuter campus in small city
- 1,839 degree-seeking undergraduates: 16% part-time, 72% women, 29% African American, 1% Asian American, 1% Hispanic American, 3% international
- 1,132 graduate students
- SAT or ACT (ACT writing optional) required
- 43% graduate within 6 years

General. Founded in 1906. Regionally accredited. **Degrees:** 448 bachelor's awarded; master's offered. **ROTC:** Army, Air Force. **Location:** 110 miles from New Orleans. **Calendar:** Trimester, extensive summer session. **Full-time faculty:** 93 total; 63% have terminal degrees, 3% minority, 53% women. **Part-time faculty:** 95 total; 43% have terminal degrees, 5% minority, 53% women. **Class size:** 57% < 20, 42% 20-39, less than 1% 40-49. **Special facilities:** Center for Study of the Life and Work of William Carey, Lucile Parker art collection and gallery, garden.

Freshman class profile. 498 applied, 470 admitted, 137 enrolled.

Mid 50% test scores		**Out-of-state:**	12%
SAT critical reading:	400-600	**Live on campus:**	82%
SAT math:	420-570	**International:**	7%
ACT composite:	20-28	**Fraternities:**	1%
End year in good standing:	86%	**Sororities:**	1%
Return as sophomores:	77%		

Basis for selection. Open admission, but selective for some programs. ACT of 20 or SAT of 950 (exclusive of Writing) required. **Homeschooled:** Transcript of courses and grades required.

High school preparation. College-preparatory program recommended. 16 units required. Required units include English 4, mathematics 3, social studies 2 and science 3.

2008-2009 Annual costs. Tuition/fees: $9,750. Room/board: $3,810. Books/supplies: $2,850. Personal expenses: $1,350.

2007-2008 Financial aid. **Need-based:** 21% of total undergraduate aid awarded as scholarships/grants, 79% as loans/jobs. **Non-need-based:** Scholarships awarded for academics, alumni affiliation, art, athletics, music/drama, religious affiliation.

Application procedures. **Admission:** Priority date 7/12; no deadline. $30 fee. Admission notification on a rolling basis. Admissions application priority date: 30 days prior to beginning of term. **Financial aid:** Priority date 4/1, closing date 9/1. FAFSA required. Applicants notified on a rolling basis starting 6/1; must reply within 2 week(s) of notification.

Academics. **Special study options:** Accelerated study, cross-registration, distance learning, double major, dual enrollment of high school students, honors, independent study, internships, study abroad, teacher certification program. **Credit/placement by examination:** AP, CLEP, IB, institutional tests. 30 credit hours maximum toward bachelor's degree. **Support services:** Reduced course load, remedial instruction, study skills assistance, tutoring.

Majors. **Biology:** General. **Business:** Business admin. **Communications:** General, journalism. **Education:** Art, biology, drama/dance, elementary, English, mathematics, music, physical, social science, speech. **Health:** Health services, music therapy, nursing (RN). **History:** General. **Math:** General. **Parks/recreation:** Health/fitness. **Physical sciences:** Chemistry. **Psychology:** General. **Social sciences:** General. **Theology:** Bible, sacred music. **Visual/performing arts:** Art, dramatic, music performance, studio arts.

Most popular majors. Business/marketing 9%, education 15%, health sciences 28%, liberal arts 11%, psychology 13%.

Computing on campus. 50 workstations in library, computer center. Dormitories wired for high-speed internet access. Commuter students can connect to campus network. Online library, helpline, wireless network available.

Student life. **Freshman orientation:** Mandatory. Preregistration for classes offered. Orientation for new students is held prior to the start of the fall term. **Policies:** Religious observance required. **Housing:** Guaranteed on-campus for freshmen. Single-sex dorms, apartments, wellness housing available. $150 fully refundable deposit. **Activities:** Bands, campus ministries, choral groups, dance, drama, international student organizations, music ensembles, musical theater, student government, student newspaper, Baptist student union, Afro-American club, psychology club, Fellowship of Christian Athletes, honorary organizations, Church Related Vocations Fellowship, science society, student nurses association, music therapy association.

Athletics. NAIA. **Intercollegiate:** Baseball M, basketball, golf, soccer, softball W. **Intramural:** Basketball, bowling, football (non-tackle) M, football (tackle), soccer, softball, table tennis, tennis, volleyball. **Team name:** Crusaders.

Student services. Adult student services, alcohol/substance abuse counseling, chaplain/spiritual director, career counseling, services for economically disadvantaged, student employment services, financial aid counseling, personal counseling, placement for graduates, veterans' counselor. **Physically disabled:** Services for visually impaired.

Contact. E-mail: admissions@wmcarey.edu
Phone: (601) 318-6103 Toll-free number: (800) 962-5991
Fax: (601) 318-6765
William Curry, Dean of Enrollment Management & Records, William Carey University, 498 Tuscan Avenue, Hattiesburg, MS 39401

Missouri

Avila University

Kansas City, Missouri
www.avila.edu **CB code: 6109**

- Private 4-year university and liberal arts college affiliated with Roman Catholic Church
- Commuter campus in very large city
- 1,163 degree-seeking undergraduates: 18% part-time, 66% women, 13% African American, 1% Asian American, 6% Hispanic American, 1% Native American, 5% international
- 571 degree-seeking graduate students
- 50% of applicants admitted
- SAT or ACT (ACT writing optional) required
- 43% graduate within 6 years

General. Founded in 1916. Regionally accredited. **Degrees:** 229 bachelor's awarded; master's offered. **ROTC:** Army. **Calendar:** Semester, extensive summer session. **Full-time faculty:** 75 total; 75% have terminal degrees, 7% minority, 60% women. **Part-time faculty:** 135 total; 22% have terminal degrees, 6% minority, 60% women. **Class size:** 68% < 20, 30% 20-39, 2% 40-49, less than 1% 50-99. **Special facilities:** Theater, radiological laboratory, 30 off-campus medical-clinical learning sites, campus media production facilities, nursing learning resource center, photography lab.

Freshman class profile. 1,038 applied, 520 admitted, 185 enrolled.

Mid 50% test scores		**GPA 2.0-2.99:**	29%
SAT critical reading:	500-530	**Rank in top quarter:**	13%
SAT math:	480-530	**Rank in top tenth:**	1%
ACT composite:	20-24	**Return as sophomores:**	68%
GPA 3.75 or higher:	17%	**Out-of-state:**	25%
GPA 3.50-3.74:	16%	**Live on campus:**	80%
GPA 3.0-3.49:	38%	**International:**	2%

Basis for selection. Unconditional acceptance for applicants with minimum GPA of 2.5 and ACT composite of 20 or higher. Others may be considered. ACT/SAT not required if student has been out of high school 1 year or more. Use ACT subscores for placement in math and English. Audition recommended for drama, music students. **Homeschooled:** SAT or ACT and home school transcripts required. GED may be requested.

High school preparation. 17 units required. Required units include English 4, mathematics 3, social studies 3, science 3 (laboratory 1) and foreign language 3. One fine arts also recommended.

2008-2009 Annual costs. Tuition/fees: $20,150. Room/board: $5,900. Books/supplies: $800. Personal expenses: $2,200.

2007-2008 Financial aid. **Need-based:** 180 full-time freshmen applied for aid; 178 were judged to have need; 177 of these received aid. Average need met was 32%. Average scholarship/grant was $7,293; average loan $2,519. 41% of total undergraduate aid awarded as scholarships/grants, 59% as loans/jobs. **Non-need-based:** Awarded to 157 full-time undergraduates, including 139 freshmen. Scholarships awarded for academics, alumni affiliation, art, athletics, music/drama, religious affiliation. **Additional information:** Financial aid adjusted for increases in tuition based on need.

Application procedures. **Admission:** No deadline. $25 fee, may be waived for applicants with need, free for online applicants. Admission notification on a rolling basis. **Financial aid:** Priority date 3/1, closing date 4/1. FAFSA, institutional form required. Applicants notified on a rolling basis starting 2/1; must reply within 2 week(s) of notification.

Academics. Outcome-based core curriculum; interdisciplinary course work at junior level required; unique senior experience bridges transition from college to community. **Special study options:** Accelerated study, combined bachelor's/graduate degree, cooperative education, cross-registration, distance learning, double major, dual enrollment of high school students, ESL, exchange student, independent study, internships, liberal arts/career combination, study abroad, teacher certification program, Washington semester, weekend college. **Credit/placement by examination:** AP, CLEP, IB, SAT, ACT, institutional tests. 32 credit hours maximum toward bachelor's degree. **Support services:** Learning center, reduced course load, remedial instruction, study skills assistance, tutoring, writing center.

Majors. **Biology:** General. **Business:** General, accounting, business admin, finance, international, marketing. **Communications:** General. **Computer sciences:** General. **Education:** Elementary, middle, secondary, special. **Health:** Facilities admin, nursing (RN). **History:** General. **Interdisciplinary:** Biological/physical sciences. **Legal studies:** Paralegal. **Philosophy/religion:** Religion. **Physical sciences:** Chemistry. **Psychology:** General. **Public administration:** Social work. **Social sciences:** Political science, sociology. **Visual/performing arts:** Dramatic, music performance, studio arts.

Most popular majors. Business/marketing 23%, education 9%, health sciences 29%, psychology 9%, visual/performing arts 6%.

Computing on campus. 156 workstations in dormitories, library, computer center, student center. Dormitories wired for high-speed internet access and linked to campus network. Commuter students can connect to campus network. Online course registration, online library, helpline, wireless network available.

Student life. **Freshman orientation:** Mandatory. Preregistration for classes offered. Held 3 days prior to first day of classes; programs available for freshmen-adult transfer students and friends/family of new students. **Policies:** First-time, first-year students not living at home with parents/guardians required to live on campus through sophomore year. **Housing:** Guaranteed on-campus for freshmen. Coed dorms, apartments, wellness housing available. Single-sex floors available. **Activities:** Campus ministries, choral groups, dance, drama, international student organizations, literary magazine, musical theater, student government, student newspaper, student nurses association, psychology club, Black Student Union, premedical club, English club, education club, Association of Radiological Science, social work association, National Association of Masters in Psychology, Society of Life Scientists.

Athletics. NAIA. **Intercollegiate:** Baseball M, basketball, cheerleading M, football (tackle) M, golf W, soccer, softball W, volleyball W. **Intramural:** Basketball, table tennis, volleyball. **Team name:** Eagles.

Student services. Adult student services, alcohol/substance abuse counseling, chaplain/spiritual director, career counseling, student employment services, financial aid counseling, health services, on-campus daycare, personal counseling, placement for graduates, veterans' counselor, women's services. **Physically disabled:** Services for visually, speech, hearing impaired.

Contact. E-mail: admission@avila.edu
Phone: (816) 501-2400 Toll-free number: (800) 462-8452
Fax: (816) 501-2453
Patricia Harper, Director of Admission, Avila University, 11901 Wornall Road, Kansas City, MO 64145-1007

Baptist Bible College

Springfield, Missouri
www.gobbc.com **CB code: 0991**

- Private 4-year Bible and seminary college affiliated with Baptist faith
- Residential campus in small city
- 489 degree-seeking undergraduates: 13% part-time, 48% women, 2% African American, 1% Asian American, 4% Hispanic American, 1% Native American, 1% international
- 58 graduate students

General. Founded in 1950. Candidate for regional accreditation; also accredited by ABHE. **Degrees:** 84 bachelor's, 3 associate awarded; master's offered. **Location:** 180 miles from Kansas City, 225 miles from St. Louis. **Calendar:** Semester.

Freshman class profile. 175 applied, 119 admitted, 86 enrolled.

Mid 50% test scores		**ACT composite:**	18-23

Basis for selection. Open admission. Baptist pastor's recommendation required. **Homeschooled:** Ability To Benefit test required.

2008-2009 Annual costs. Tuition/fees: $13,610. Room/board: $5,400. Books/supplies: $840.

2007-2008 Financial aid. **Non-need-based:** Scholarships awarded for academics.

Application procedures. **Admission:** Priority date 8/1; no deadline. $40 fee. Admission notification on a rolling basis. **Financial aid:** Closing date 5/1. FAFSA, institutional form required. Applicants notified on a rolling basis; must reply within 2 week(s) of notification.

Academics. **Special study options:** Distance learning. **Credit/placement by examination:** AP, CLEP. **Support services:** Learning center, reduced course load, study skills assistance, tutoring.

Majors. **Business:** Administrative services. **Education:** Elementary, music. **Philosophy/religion:** Religion. **Theology:** Missionary, pastoral counseling, religious ed, sacred music, theology.

Computing on campus. 70 workstations in library, computer center, student center. Dormitories wired for high-speed internet access and linked to campus network. Online library, helpline, repair service available.

Student life. **Freshman orientation:** Mandatory. Preregistration for classes offered. **Policies:** Religious observance required. **Housing:** Guaranteed on-campus for freshmen. Single-sex dorms, apartments available. **Activities:** Concert band, choral groups, music ensembles, radio station, student government, student newspaper.

Athletics. NCCAA. **Intercollegiate:** Basketball, soccer M, volleyball W. **Intramural:** Basketball. **Team name:** Patriots.

Student services. Chaplain/spiritual director, career counseling, financial aid counseling, health services, on-campus daycare, personal counseling, veterans' counselor.

Contact. E-mail: cmcgee@baptist.edu
Phone: (417) 268-6013 Toll-free number: (800) 228-5754 ext. 6021
Fax: (417) 268-6694
Jon Slayden, Director of Enrollment Services, Baptist Bible College, 628 East Kearney Street, Springfield, MO 65803

Calvary Bible College and Theological Seminary

Kansas City, Missouri
www.calvary.edu **CB code: 6331**

- Private 4-year Bible and seminary college affiliated with nondenominational tradition
- Residential campus in large city
- 230 degree-seeking undergraduates: 23% part-time, 51% women, 7% African American, 1% Hispanic American, 2% Native American
- 58 graduate students

General. Founded in 1932. Regionally accredited; also accredited by ABHE. **Degrees:** 69 bachelor's, 8 associate awarded; master's, first professional offered. **ROTC:** Army. **Location:** 20 miles from Kansas City. **Calendar:** Semester, limited summer session. **Full-time faculty:** 13 total; 38% have terminal degrees, 31% women. **Part-time faculty:** 14 total; 43% have terminal degrees, 7% minority, 29% women.

Freshman class profile. 56 applied, 44 admitted, 42 enrolled.

Mid 50% test scores		**GPA 3.0-3.49:**	19%
ACT composite:	19-24	**GPA 2.0-2.99:**	20%
GPA 3.75 or higher:	36%	**Return as sophomores:**	57%
GPA 3.50-3.74:	22%		

Basis for selection. Open admission, but selective for some programs. Christian character stressed along with academic preparation. Pastor's and personal reference forms required. School achievement record and test scores considered. Applicants are required to submit a written Personal Testimony/ Confirmation and Statement of Faith. Audition required for music students. **Homeschooled:** Transcripts are required in compliance with state's home school policies. **Learning Disabled:** Students should contact the Director of Admissions.

2009-2010 Annual costs. Tuition/fees (projected): $8,872. Room/ board: $4,400. Books/supplies: $500. Personal expenses: $150.

2007-2008 Financial aid. **Need-based:** 33% of total undergraduate aid awarded as scholarships/grants, 67% as loans/jobs. **Non-need-based:** Scholarships awarded for academics, alumni affiliation, job skills, music/drama, religious affiliation, ROTC.

Application procedures. **Admission:** Closing date 7/15 (receipt date). $25 fee. Admission notification on a rolling basis. Must reply by 8/15. **Financial aid:** Priority date 3/1, closing date 4/1. FAFSA, institutional form required. Applicants notified on a rolling basis starting 5/1.

Academics. Each student carries major in Bible and theology and second major in a professional area. These majors prepare students for vocational and/or volunteer involvement in Christian ministry. **Special study options:** Cooperative education, double major, independent study, internships, student-designed major, teacher certification program. **Credit/placement by examination:** AP, CLEP, IB, institutional tests. **Support services:** Learning center, reduced course load, remedial instruction, study skills assistance, tutoring.

Majors. **Business:** Organizational behavior. **Communications:** Broadcast journalism, media studies. **Education:** Elementary, music, secondary. **Social sciences:** Urban studies. **Theology:** Bible, missionary, pastoral counseling, preministerial, religious ed, sacred music, theology, youth ministry. **Visual/ performing arts:** Music performance, piano/organ, voice/opera. **Other:** Christian broadcasting, Christian ministry, Organizational leadership.

Most popular majors. Business/marketing 9%, education 10%, theological studies 78%.

Computing on campus. 21 workstations in library, student center. Dormitories wired for high-speed internet access. Online course registration, repair service, wireless network available.

Student life. **Freshman orientation:** Mandatory, $50 fee. **Policies:** Weekly Christian ministry, chapel and church attendance required. Single students required to live in college housing unless living with parents or at least 23 years of age. Religious observance required. **Housing:** Guaranteed on-campus for all undergraduates. Single-sex dorms, apartments available. $150 nonrefundable deposit, deadline 7/15. Duplexes for married students available. **Activities:** Pep band, campus ministries, choral groups, drama, music ensembles, musical theater, radio station, student government, Missionary Prayer Fellowship, short-term missions.

Athletics. NCCAA. **Intercollegiate:** Basketball, soccer M, volleyball W. **Team name:** Warriors.

Student services. Alcohol/substance abuse counseling, chaplain/ spiritual director, student employment services, financial aid counseling, health services, personal counseling, veterans' counselor, women's services.

Contact. E-mail: admissions@calvary.edu
Phone: (816) 326-3960 Toll-free number: (800) 326-3960
Fax: (816) 331-4474
Robert Crank, Director of Admissions, Calvary Bible College and Theological Seminary, 15800 Calvary Road, Kansas City, MO 64147

Central Bible College

Springfield, Missouri
www.cbcag.edu **CB code: 6085**

- Private 4-year Bible college affiliated with Assemblies of God
- Residential campus in small city
- 697 degree-seeking undergraduates
- 89% of applicants admitted
- Application essay required

General. Founded in 1922. Accredited by ABHE. **Degrees:** 118 bachelor's, 17 associate awarded. **ROTC:** Army, Air Force. **Location:** 210 miles from St. Louis, 174 miles from Kansas City. **Calendar:** Semester, extensive summer session. **Full-time faculty:** 32 total. **Part-time faculty:** 55 total.

Freshman class profile. 255 applied, 228 admitted, 210 enrolled.

Mid 50% test scores		**SAT writing:**	400-620
SAT critical reading:	400-620	**ACT composite:**	18-24
SAT math:	410-600		

Basis for selection. Special consideration given to members of Assemblies of God and all applicants who rank in top half of graduating class who meet entrance requirements. Interview recommended for all students; audition recommended for music students. **Homeschooled:** Transcript of courses and grades required.

High school preparation. Strong background in English, math, and science recommended. Computer literacy course recommended.

2008-2009 Annual costs. Tuition/fees: $10,630. Room/board: $5,032. Books/supplies: $550.

Application procedures. **Admission:** Priority date 8/15; no deadline. $25 fee, may be waived for applicants with need. Admission notification on a rolling basis. **Financial aid:** Priority date 5/1; no closing date. FAFSA required. Applicants notified on a rolling basis starting 5/15; must reply within 3 week(s) of notification.

Academics. **Special study options:** Accelerated study, cooperative education, cross-registration, double major, independent study, internships. **Credit/ placement by examination:** CLEP, SAT, ACT, institutional tests. 24 credit hours maximum toward bachelor's degree. **Support services:** Reduced course load, remedial instruction, tutoring.

Majors. Theology: Bible, missionary, pastoral counseling, religious ed, sacred music, theology, youth ministry. **Other:** Ministry in arts.

Computing on campus. 20 workstations in library, computer center.

Student life. Freshman orientation: Mandatory, $175 fee. Preregistration for classes offered. **Policies:** Practices which are known to be morally wrong by Biblical teaching are not acceptable for members of the college community. Religious observance required. **Housing:** Guaranteed on-campus for freshmen. Single-sex dorms, apartments, wellness housing available. **Activities:** Jazz band, choral groups, drama, music ensembles, radio station, student government, student newspaper, Campus Missions Fellowship, Delta Chi, FOCAL, student government association, student ministries, multicultural club.

Athletics. NCCAA. **Intercollegiate:** Basketball, soccer M, volleyball W. **Intramural:** Basketball, softball. **Team name:** Spartans.

Student services. Student employment services, financial aid counseling, health services, personal counseling, placement for graduates, veterans' counselor. **Physically disabled:** Services for hearing impaired.

Contact. E-mail: info@cbcag.edu
Phone: (417) 833-2551 ext. 1290 Toll-free number: (800) 831-4222
Fax: (417) 833-5141
Bill Davis, Registrar, Central Bible College, 3000 North Grant Avenue, Springfield, MO 65803-1069

Central Christian College of the Bible

Moberly, Missouri
www.cccb.edu **CB code: 6145**

- Private 4-year Bible college affiliated with Christian Church
- Residential campus in large town
- 398 degree-seeking undergraduates
- 97% of applicants admitted
- ACT (writing recommended), application essay required

General. Founded in 1957. Accredited by ABHE. Every full-time student receives a full-tuition scholarship. **Degrees:** 70 bachelor's, 26 associate awarded. **Location:** 35 miles from Columbia. **Calendar:** Semester, limited summer session. **Full-time faculty:** 16 total. **Part-time faculty:** 12 total. **Special facilities:** 71,000 volume library with computer lab and foreign language lab.

Freshman class profile. 203 applied, 197 admitted, 71 enrolled.

Mid 50% test scores			
SAT critical reading:	490-550	SAT writing:	500-590
SAT math:	470-580	ACT composite:	18-23
		Live on campus:	100%

Basis for selection. High school transcript, ACT/SAT scores and references very important. Students with GPA below 2.0 assigned reduced course load.

High school preparation. 15 units recommended. Recommended units include English 2, mathematics 2, social studies 1 and science 2.

2008-2009 Annual costs. Full-time students receive full scholarship for tuition only, $8,800. Room and board $5,650 for two semesters. Required fees $1,950 per semester.Off-campus students pay a $650 facilities usage fee per semester. Books/supplies: $947. Personal expenses: $4,635.

Application procedures. Admission: No deadline. No application fee. Admission notification on a rolling basis beginning on or about 12/1. Admitted applicants must reply within 6 weeks of notification. **Financial aid:** Priority date 3/15, closing date 4/1. FAFSA required. Applicants notified by 5/15; must reply within 2 week(s) of notification.

Academics. Special study options: Cooperative education, distance learning, dual enrollment of high school students, internships. **Credit/placement by examination:** CLEP. 6 credit hours maximum toward bachelor's degree. **Support services:** Reduced course load, study skills assistance, tutoring.

Majors. Philosophy/religion: Religion. **Theology:** Pastoral counseling, religious ed, sacred music, theology.

Computing on campus. 30 workstations in library, student center. Dormitories wired for high-speed internet access and linked to campus network. Commuter students can connect to campus network. Wireless network available.

Student life. Freshman orientation: Mandatory, $250 fee. Preregistration for classes offered. **Policies:** Religious observance required. **Housing:** Guaranteed on-campus for all undergraduates. Single-sex dorms, wellness housing available. **Activities:** Choral groups, international student organizations, music ensembles, student government, Harvesters missions group, Gospel choir.

Athletics. NCCAA. **Intercollegiate:** Basketball, soccer M, volleyball W. **Intramural:** Basketball, bowling, softball, table tennis, tennis, volleyball. **Team name:** Heralds.

Student services. Chaplain/spiritual director, career counseling, financial aid counseling, personal counseling, placement for graduates, veterans' counselor.

Contact. E-mail: admissions2@cccb.edu
Phone: (888) 263-3900 Toll-free number: (888) 263-3900
Fax: (888) 263-3936
Aaron Wright, Director of Admission, Central Christian College of the Bible, 911 East Urbandale Drive, Moberly, MO 65270-1997

Central Methodist University

Fayette, Missouri
www.centralmethodist.edu **CB code: 6089**

- Private 4-year university and liberal arts college affiliated with United Methodist Church
- Residential campus in small town
- 1,031 degree-seeking undergraduates: 3% part-time, 51% women, 9% African American, 2% Hispanic American, 1% Native American, 3% international
- 66% of applicants admitted
- SAT or ACT (ACT writing optional) required
- 40% graduate within 6 years

General. Founded in 1854. Regionally accredited. **Degrees:** 149 bachelor's, 2 associate awarded; master's offered. **ROTC:** Army, Air Force. **Location:** 25 miles from Columbia,150 miles from St. Louis. **Calendar:** Semester, limited summer session. **Full-time faculty:** 55 total; 60% have terminal degrees, 4% minority, 42% women. **Part-time faculty:** 34 total; 18% have terminal degrees, 47% women. **Class size:** 63% < 20, 29% 20-39, 5% 40-49, 3% 50-99. **Special facilities:** Observatory and laboratory, natural history museum, conservatory of music.

Freshman class profile. 1,174 applied, 769 admitted, 300 enrolled.

Mid 50% test scores			
ACT composite:	19-24	Rank in top quarter:	33%
GPA 3.75 or higher:	22%	Rank in top tenth:	12%
GPA 3.50-3.74:	22%	End year in good standing:	90%
GPA 3.0-3.49:	35%	Return as sophomores:	57%
GPA 2.0-2.99:	21%	Out-of-state:	11%
		Live on campus:	96%

Basis for selection. Full acceptance requires 2.5 GPA and 21 ACT or equivalent SAT. Interview required for nursing applicants; audition recommended for drama, music students.

High school preparation. College-preparatory program recommended. 24 units recommended. Recommended units include English 4, mathematics 3, social studies 3, science 3 and foreign language 2. 2 humanities recommended.

2009-2010 Annual costs. Tuition/fees (projected): $18,842. Room/board: $6,000. Books/supplies: $900. Personal expenses: $2,250.

2008-2009 Financial aid. Non-need-based: Scholarships awarded for academics, alumni affiliation, athletics, leadership, music/drama, religious affiliation, ROTC.

Application procedures. Admission: No deadline. $20 fee, may be waived for applicants with need, free for online applicants. Admission notification on a rolling basis beginning on or about 10/1. Must reply by May 1 or within 4 week(s) if notified thereafter. **Financial aid:** Priority date 3/15; no closing date. FAFSA required. Applicants notified on a rolling basis starting 1/30; must reply within 2 week(s) of notification.

Academics. Special study options: Accelerated study, combined bachelor's/graduate degree, distance learning, double major, dual enrollment of high school students, honors, independent study, internships, liberal arts/career combination, student-designed major, study abroad, teacher certification program. 3-year bachelor's degree, 2-week January travel program. **Credit/placement by examination:** AP, CLEP, IB, ACT, institutional tests. 32 credit hours maximum toward associate degree, 32 toward bachelor's. **Support**

services: Learning center, pre-admission summer program, reduced course load, remedial instruction, study skills assistance, tutoring.

Majors. Biology: General, marine. **Business:** General, accounting, banking/financial services, business admin, entrepreneurial studies, international, management science. **Communications:** General. **Computer sciences:** Computer science. **Conservation:** Environmental science. **Education:** Biology, chemistry, early childhood, elementary, foreign languages, middle, music, physical, physics, science, secondary, social science, special. **Family/consumer sciences:** Child development. **Foreign languages:** Spanish. **Health:** Athletic training, nursing (RN). **History:** General. **Math:** General. **Parks/recreation:** Facilities management. **Philosophy/religion:** Philosophy, religion. **Physical sciences:** Chemistry, physics. **Protective services:** Law enforcement admin. **Psychology:** General. **Social sciences:** Political science, sociology. **Visual/performing arts:** Dramatic, music performance. **Other:** Marketing and advertising.

Most popular majors. Business/marketing 28%, education 21%, health sciences 15%.

Computing on campus. 200 workstations in dormitories, library, computer center, student center. Dormitories wired for high-speed internet access and linked to campus network. Commuter students can connect to campus network. Online library, helpline, repair service, wireless network available.

Student life. Freshman orientation: Available. Preregistration for classes offered. **Housing:** Guaranteed on-campus for all undergraduates. Coed dorms, single-sex dorms, apartments, fraternity/sorority housing available. $100 fully refundable deposit. **Activities:** Bands, campus ministries, choral groups, dance, drama, international student organizations, literary magazine, music ensembles, musical theater, radio station, student government, student newspaper, Alpha Phi Omega, prelaw club, religious, service, business, music organizations, Students in Free Enterprise.

Athletics. NAIA. **Intercollegiate:** Baseball M, basketball, cross-country, football (tackle) M, soccer, softball W, track and field, volleyball W. **Intramural:** Basketball, football (tackle) M, golf, racquetball, soccer, softball, tennis, track and field, volleyball. **Team name:** Eagles.

Student services. Alcohol/substance abuse counseling, chaplain/spiritual director, career counseling, student employment services, financial aid counseling, health services, personal counseling, placement for graduates.

Contact. E-mail: admissions@centralmethodist.edu
Phone: (660) 248-6251 Toll-free number: (877) 268-1854
Fax: (660) 248-1872
Lawrence Anderson, Director of Admissions, Central Methodist University, 411 Central Methodist Square, Fayette, MO 65248-1198

Chamberlain College of Nursing

St. Louis, Missouri
www.chamberlain.edu **CB code: 3139**

- For-profit 4-year nursing college affiliated with United Church of Christ
- Commuter campus in very large city
- 2,167 degree-seeking undergraduates
- Application essay required

General. Founded in 1889. Regionally accredited. In addition to the St. Louis campus, there is a second campus in Columbus, OH. Affiliated with Fontbonne College; general education requirements offered on both campuses. **Degrees:** 285 bachelor's, 65 associate awarded. **Calendar:** Semester, limited summer session. **Full-time faculty:** 30 total. **Part-time faculty:** 50 total. **Special facilities:** Hospital, archives.

Basis for selection. High school GPA of 2.5, rank in top third of class, ACT scores, personal statement important. Interview and reference may be considered. SAT or ACT recommended.

High school preparation. Required units include English 4, mathematics 3 and science 3.

2008-2009 Annual costs. Books/supplies: $1,100. Personal expenses: $550.

Financial aid. Non-need-based: Scholarships awarded for academics.

Application procedures. Admission: Closing date 4/15. $50 fee, may be waived for applicants with need. Admission notification on a rolling basis. **Financial aid:** No deadline. FAFSA, institutional form required. Applicants notified on a rolling basis starting 4/1; must reply within 2 week(s) of notification.

Academics. Special study options: Cross-registration, liberal arts/career combination. **Credit/placement by examination:** CLEP, institutional tests. 30 credit hours maximum toward bachelor's degree. **Support services:** Learning center, reduced course load, remedial instruction, tutoring.

Majors. Health: Nursing (RN).

Computing on campus. 20 workstations in computer center.

Student life. Freshman orientation: Mandatory. **Housing:** Single-sex dorms available. $50 deposit. **Activities:** Choral groups, student government, National Student Nurse Association.

Student services. Health services, on-campus daycare, personal counseling.

Contact. Phone: (314) 768-7528 Toll-free number: (800) 942-3410
Fax: (314) 768-5673
Kelly Rowe, Director of Admissions, Chamberlain College of Nursing, 6150 Oakland Avenue, St. Louis, MO 63139

College of the Ozarks

Point Lookout, Missouri
www.cofo.edu **CB code: 6713**

- Private 4-year liberal arts college affiliated with interdenominational tradition
- Residential campus in small town
- 1,320 degree-seeking undergraduates: 1% part-time, 57% women, 1% African American, 1% Asian American, 1% Hispanic American, 1% Native American, 2% international
- 12% of applicants admitted
- SAT or ACT (ACT writing optional), interview required
- 62% graduate within 6 years; 15% enter graduate study

General. Founded in 1906. Regionally accredited. No tuition; students work at a campus job rather than pay tuition. **Degrees:** 291 bachelor's awarded. **ROTC:** Army. **Location:** 2 miles from Branson, 45 miles from Springfield. **Calendar:** Semester. **Full-time faculty:** 91 total; 56% have terminal degrees, 2% minority, 32% women. **Part-time faculty:** 28 total; 14% have terminal degrees, 36% women. **Class size:** 58% < 20, 39% 20-39, less than 1% 40-49, 2% 50-99. **Special facilities:** Greenhouses, college-operated hotel, observatory, nature preserve.

Freshman class profile. 2,698 applied, 316 admitted, 274 enrolled.

Mid 50% test scores		**GPA 2.0-2.99:**	8%
SAT critical reading:	530-590	**Rank in top quarter:**	55%
SAT math:	440-620	**Rank in top tenth:**	20%
SAT writing:	460-620	**End year in good standing:**	75%
ACT composite:	20-25	**Return as sophomores:**	82%
GPA 3.75 or higher:	36%	**Out-of-state:**	27%
GPA 3.50-3.74:	23%	**Live on campus:**	99%
GPA 3.0-3.49:	33%	**International:**	1%

Basis for selection. High school record, financial need, test scores, class rank, recommendations, activities and interview important. Academic interest and growth, development of intellectual skills considered. TOEFL for non-native English speakers. ACT preferred. Audition recommended for music students; portfolio recommended for art students. **Homeschooled:** Pass grades are not acceptable. Candidates must present a transcript with a letter or percentage grade.

High school preparation. College-preparatory program recommended. 24 units recommended. Recommended units include English 4, mathematics 3, social studies 3, science 2 (laboratory 1) and foreign language 2. Public speaking, visual and performing arts recommended.

2009-2010 Annual costs. Cost of full-time tuition met through combination of institutional work program and federal, state, and institutional funding. Required fees: $390. Full-time students participating in work program work 15 hours per week for 16 weeks and one 40-hour work week per semester. Part-time students (commuters only) pay $295 per credit hour for tuition and additional $390 per year as required fees. Room/board: $5,000. Books/supplies: $800. Personal expenses: $390.

2008-2009 Financial aid. Need-based: Average need met was 85%. Average scholarship/grant was $10,937. 78% of total undergraduate aid awarded as scholarships/grants, 22% as loans/jobs. **Non-need-based:** Scholarships awarded for academics, art, athletics, leadership, music/drama, ROTC, state residency.

Application procedures. Admission: Closing date 2/15 (receipt date). No application fee. Admission notification on a rolling basis beginning on or about 3/1. Must reply by May 1 or within 2 week(s) if notified thereafter. Housing deposit due within two weeks of admission offer. **Financial aid:** Priority date 2/15; no closing date. FAFSA required. Applicants notified by 7/1.

Academics. Curriculum offers liberal arts foundation with intensive concentration in special areas. **Special study options:** Accelerated study, combined bachelor's/graduate degree, double major, dual enrollment of high school students, independent study, internships, liberal arts/career combination, student-designed major, teacher certification program. 3-2 engineering program, interdisciplinary programs, paraprofessional counseling certificate, pre-professional programs, dietetics program. **Credit/placement by examination:** AP, CLEP, IB, ACT, institutional tests. Five "credits by exam" classes unless specific approval by academic dean. **Support services:** Learning center, reduced course load, remedial instruction, study skills assistance, tutoring, writing center.

Majors. Agriculture: Agronomy, animal sciences, business, horticultural science, horticulture, mechanization. **Biology:** General. **Business:** Accounting, business admin, hospitality admin, international, managerial economics, marketing, restaurant/food services. **Communications:** General, broadcast journalism, journalism, public relations. **Computer sciences:** General, computer science. **Conservation:** Wildlife. **Education:** Agricultural, art, biology, business, chemistry, early childhood, elementary, English, family/consumer sciences, history, mathematics, music, physical, science, secondary, social studies, technology/industrial arts. **Family/consumer sciences:** General, child development, food/nutrition. **Foreign languages:** Spanish. **Health:** Dietetics, nursing (RN). **History:** General. **Math:** General. **Parks/recreation:** Facilities management, health/fitness. **Philosophy/religion:** Philosophy, religion. **Physical sciences:** Chemistry. **Protective services:** Corrections, police science. **Psychology:** General. **Public administration:** Social work. **Social sciences:** Sociology. **Theology:** Sacred music. **Visual/performing arts:** Art, dramatic, studio arts, theater design.

Most popular majors. Agriculture 9%, business/marketing 22%, education 13%, English 7%, visual/performing arts 8%.

Computing on campus. 160 workstations in dormitories, library. Dormitories wired for high-speed internet access and linked to campus network. Commuter students can connect to campus network. Online course registration, online library, helpline, wireless network available.

Student life. Freshman orientation: Mandatory. Preregistration for classes offered. 10-day program held the week before classes begin. **Policies:** Convocations and chapel attendance required for some students. All full-time students must live in residence halls unless they meet one of the following criteria: 21 years of age or older, married, living with parents, or veteran of armed services. Religious observance required. **Housing:** Guaranteed on-campus for all undergraduates. Single-sex dorms, wellness housing available. $100 fully refundable deposit. **Activities:** Bands, campus ministries, choral groups, drama, film society, literary magazine, music ensembles, musical theater, radio station, student government, student newspaper, Baptist student union, fire department, InterVarsity Christian Fellowship, wilderness activities club, Aggie club, Flying Falcons, business undergraduate society, Bonner Organization, College Republicans, College Democrats.

Athletics. NAIA. **Intercollegiate:** Baseball M, basketball, volleyball W. **Intramural:** Basketball, fencing, football (non-tackle) M, soccer, softball, swimming, tennis, volleyball. **Team name:** Bobcats.

Student services. Chaplain/spiritual director, career counseling, student employment services, financial aid counseling, health services, on-campus daycare, personal counseling, placement for graduates, veterans' counselor.

Contact. E-mail: admiss4@cofo.edu
Phone: (417) 334-6411 ext. 2636 Toll-free number: (800) 222-0525
Fax: (417) 335-2618
Marci Linson, Dean of Admissions, College of the Ozarks, PO Box 17, Point Lookout, MO 65726-0017

Columbia College

Columbia, Missouri
www.ccis.edu **CB code: 6095**

- Private 4-year liberal arts college affiliated with Christian Church (Disciples of Christ)
- Commuter campus in small city
- 1,101 degree-seeking undergraduates: 18% part-time, 59% women, 5% African American, 1% Asian American, 1% Hispanic American, 1% Native American, 7% international
- 182 degree-seeking graduate students
- 53% of applicants admitted
- SAT or ACT (ACT writing optional) required
- 46% graduate within 6 years; 16% enter graduate study

General. Founded in 1851. Regionally accredited. Programs for adult students offered on campus and at 34 teaching locations in United States and Cuba. **Degrees:** 173 bachelor's, 14 associate awarded; master's offered. **ROTC:** Army, Naval, Air Force. **Location:** 120 miles from Kansas City, 120 miles from St. Louis. **Calendar:** Semester, extensive summer session. **Full-time faculty:** 63 total; 78% have terminal degrees, 6% minority, 46% women. **Part-time faculty:** 36 total; 19% have terminal degrees, 3% minority, 42% women. **Class size:** 73% < 20, 27% 20-39.

Freshman class profile. 1,162 applied, 617 admitted, 220 enrolled.

Mid 50% test scores		**Rank in top quarter:**	41%
SAT critical reading:	440-580	**Rank in top tenth:**	23%
SAT math:	520-660	**End year in good standing:**	85%
ACT composite:	19-27	**Return as sophomores:**	58%
GPA 3.75 or higher:	28%	**Out-of-state:**	3%
GPA 3.50-3.74:	15%	**Live on campus:**	71%
GPA 3.0-3.49:	26%	**International:**	12%
GPA 2.0-2.99:	29%		

Basis for selection. School achievement, class rank, test scores most important. Also use IB (International Baccaluareate) for placement. **Homeschooled:** Statement describing homeschool structure and mission, transcript of courses and grades required. ACT/SAT required; no GED requirement.

High school preparation. College-preparatory program recommended. 14 units recommended. Recommended units include English 4, mathematics 3, social studies 2, science 3 and foreign language 2.

2009-2010 Annual costs. Tuition/fees: $14,576. Room/board: $5,898.

2007-2008 Financial aid. Need-based: 100 full-time freshmen applied for aid; 90 were judged to have need; 90 of these received aid. Average need met was 69%. Average scholarship/grant was $9,264; average loan $3,878. 49% of total undergraduate aid awarded as scholarships/grants, 51% as loans/jobs. **Non-need-based:** Awarded to 1,071 full-time undergraduates, including 294 freshmen. Scholarships awarded for academics, alumni affiliation, art, athletics, job skills, leadership, music/drama, religious affiliation, ROTC, state residency.

Application procedures. Admission: Closing date 8/10 (postmark date). $25 fee, may be waived for applicants with need. Admission notification on a rolling basis beginning on or about 9/15. **Financial aid:** No deadline. FAFSA required. Applicants notified on a rolling basis starting 3/1.

Academics. Evening degree program available based on 8-week ongoing terms. **Special study options:** Cross-registration, distance learning, double major, dual enrollment of high school students, ESL, honors, internships, study abroad, teacher certification program. **Credit/placement by examination:** AP, CLEP, IB, SAT, ACT, institutional tests. 45 credit hours maximum toward associate degree, 60 toward bachelor's. **Support services:** Tutoring, writing center.

Honors college/program. High school GPA of 3.5 or greater, ACT in 78th percentile or higher required for admission.

Majors. Area/ethnic studies: American. **Biology:** General. **Business:** Accounting, business admin, finance, international, management science, marketing. **Communications:** General. **Computer sciences:** General, computer science. **Conservation:** Environmental studies. **History:** General. **Liberal arts:** Arts/sciences. **Math:** General. **Physical sciences:** Chemistry. **Protective services:** Forensics, law enforcement admin. **Psychology:** General. **Public administration:** Human services. **Social sciences:** Political science, sociology. **Visual/performing arts:** Art, ceramics, drawing, graphic design, painting, photography, printmaking, studio arts. **Other:** Philosophy and religious atudies.

Most popular majors. Business/marketing 47%, interdisciplinary studies 13%, psychology 15%, security/protective services 12%.

Computing on campus. 83 workstations in dormitories, library, computer center, student center. Dormitories wired for high-speed internet access and linked to campus network. Commuter students can connect to campus network. Online course registration, online library, helpline, repair service, wireless network available.

Student life. Freshman orientation: Available. Preregistration for classes offered. Held weekend before classes start. **Policies:** Alcohol and illegal drugs forbidden on campus. **Housing:** Guaranteed on-campus for freshmen. Coed dorms, single-sex dorms, special housing for disabled, apartments, wellness housing available. $100 fully refundable deposit. **Activities:** Campus ministries, choral groups, drama, international student organizations, literary magazine, music ensembles, Model UN, student government, student newspaper, International Student Association, Mock Trial Association, Student Leaders Advocating Teaching Excellence, Partners in Education,

Criminal Justice Association, Elysium Players, Fellowship of Christian Athletes, Delta Epsilon Chi.

Athletics. NAIA. **Intercollegiate:** Basketball, soccer M, softball W, volleyball W. **Intramural:** Basketball, bowling, football (non-tackle), golf, soccer, softball, volleyball. **Team name:** Cougars.

Student services. Alcohol/substance abuse counseling, career counseling, services for economically disadvantaged, student employment services, financial aid counseling, health services, personal counseling, placement for graduates, veterans' counselor. **Physically disabled:** Services for visually, speech, hearing impaired.

Contact. E-mail: admissions@ccis.edu
Phone: (573) 875-7352 Toll-free number: (800) 231-2391 ext. 7352
Fax: (573) 875-7506
John Wilkerson, Director of Admissions, Columbia College, 1001 Rogers Street, Columbia, MO 65216

Conception Seminary College

Conception, Missouri
www.conception.edu **CB code: 6112**

- Private 4-year seminary college for men affiliated with Roman Catholic Church
- Residential campus in rural community
- 105 degree-seeking undergraduates
- 83% of applicants admitted
- ACT, application essay required

General. Founded in 1883. Regionally accredited. Operated by Benedictine Monks of Conception Abbey, for both independent seminary students and candidates affiliated with sponsoring diocese. Women may enroll on part-time basis. **Degrees:** 14 bachelor's awarded. **Location:** 100 miles from Kansas City, 45 miles from St. Joseph. **Calendar:** Semester. **Full-time faculty:** 10 total. **Part-time faculty:** 18 total. **Special facilities:** Basilica.

Freshman class profile. 12 applied, 10 admitted, 9 enrolled.

Mid 50% test scores		Live on campus:	100%
ACT composite:	20-28		

Basis for selection. ACT composite scores tend to count more heavily than high school grades. Class rank considered. Applicants must be sponsored. Interview recommended.

High school preparation. 16 units required. Required units include English 4, social studies 4 and science 4.

2009-2010 Annual costs. Tuition/fees (projected): $15,786. Room/board: $9,362. Books/supplies: $450. Personal expenses: $800.

Financial aid. Non-need-based: Scholarships awarded for academics.

Application procedures. Admission: Priority date 6/1; deadline 7/31 (receipt date). No application fee. Admission notification on a rolling basis beginning on or about 2/1. Must reply by 8/10. Foreign applications require written certification of financial, ecclesiastical sponsorship. **Financial aid:** No deadline. FAFSA required. Applicants notified on a rolling basis starting 8/1; must reply by 8/20.

Academics. Curriculum combines liberal arts and pre-theology training to accommodate varying degrees of vocational commitment. **Special study options:** ESL, independent study. **Credit/placement by examination:** CLEP, ACT, institutional tests. 12 credit hours maximum toward bachelor's degree. **Support services:** Learning center, reduced course load, remedial instruction, study skills assistance, tutoring.

Majors. Philosophy/religion: Philosophy.

Computing on campus. 15 workstations in dormitories, library, computer center. Dormitories wired for high-speed internet access and linked to campus network. Online library, helpline, repair service available.

Student life. Freshman orientation: Mandatory. Preregistration for classes offered. **Policies:** Religious observance required. **Housing:** Guaranteed on-campus for all undergraduates. Wellness housing available. $50 deposit. **Activities:** Choral groups, drama, music ensembles, musical theater, student government, student newspaper, apostolic work, mission club, social concerns, community council, Inner-Life.

Athletics. Intercollegiate: Basketball M, soccer M, volleyball M. **Intramural:** Basketball M, football (non-tackle) M, racquetball M, soccer M, softball M, swimming M, table tennis M, tennis M, track and field M, volleyball M, weight lifting M. **Team name:** Blue Knights.

Student services. Adult student services, alcohol/substance abuse counseling, chaplain/spiritual director, career counseling, financial aid counseling, health services, personal counseling.

Contact. E-mail: vocations@conception.edu
Phone: (660) 944-2886 Fax: (660) 944-2829
Br. Paul Sheller, Director of Admissions, Conception Seminary College, Box 502, Conception, MO 64433-0502

Cox College

Springfield, Missouri
www.coxcollege.edu **CB code: 3932**

- Private 4-year health science and nursing college
- Commuter campus in small city
- 500 degree-seeking undergraduates

General. Regionally accredited. **Degrees:** 77 bachelor's, 54 associate awarded. **Calendar:** Semester, limited summer session. **Full-time faculty:** 21 total. **Part-time faculty:** 26 total. **Special facilities:** Nursing resource center.

Freshman class profile. 209 applied, 183 admitted, 95 enrolled.

Basis for selection. Open admission, but selective for some programs. Students considered for matriculation based on rankings, which are determined by selection criteria. TOEFL required of non-native English speakers and all international applicants. ACT or SAT scores required for early decision candidates. If ACT or SAT scores are less than 5 years old, student may be exempt from pre-entrance placement testing. **Homeschooled:** Applicants must submit official transcript from a state accredited institution or official GED or high school equivalency score report.

High school preparation. Recommended units include English 4, mathematics 2 and science 2. Early Decision candidates must achieve grade of C or better in biology, chemistry, 4 units English, 2 units math, including algebra.

2008-2009 Annual costs. Tuition/fees: $9,720. Educational fee of $40 per credit hour. Room only: $2,400. Books/supplies: $1,200.

Application procedures. Admission: Closing date 8/1 (receipt date). $45 fee, may be waived for applicants with need. Application must be submitted on paper. Admission notification on a rolling basis. **Financial aid:** Priority date 3/1; no closing date.

Academics. Special study options: Accelerated study. **Credit/placement by examination:** CLEP, SAT, ACT, institutional tests. 6 credit hours maximum toward associate degree, 6 toward bachelor's. **Support services:** Remedial instruction, study skills assistance, tutoring, writing center.

Majors. Health: Nursing (RN).

Computing on campus. 34 workstations in dormitories, library, computer center.

Student life. Freshman orientation: Available. **Housing:** Coed dorms available. $100 deposit. **Activities:** Student government, National Student Nurses Association, student council, residence hall council, Christian Fellowship.

Student services. Financial aid counseling.

Contact. E-mail: admissions@coxcollege.edu
Phone: (417) 269-3068 Toll-free number: (866) 898-5355
Fax: (417) 269-3586
Lindy Biglieni, Director of Admission, Cox College, 1423 North Jefferson Avenue, Springfield, MO 65802

Culver-Stockton College

Canton, Missouri **CB member**
www.culver.edu **CB code: 6123**

- Private 4-year liberal arts college affiliated with Christian Church (Disciples of Christ)
- Residential campus in small town
- 771 degree-seeking undergraduates: 4% part-time, 55% women
- 68% of applicants admitted
- SAT or ACT (ACT writing optional), application essay required
- 53% graduate within 6 years; 13% enter graduate study

General. Founded in 1853. Regionally accredited. **Degrees:** 188 bachelor's awarded. **Location:** 130 miles from St. Louis, 20 miles from Quincy, IL. **Calendar:** Semester, limited summer session. **Full-time faculty:** 46 total; 74% have terminal degrees, 6% minority, 30% women. **Part-time faculty:** 34 total; 12% have terminal degrees, 3% minority, 56% women. **Class size:** 70% < 20, 28% 20-39, less than 1% 40-49, less than 1% 50-99.

Freshman class profile. 1,419 applied, 963 admitted, 232 enrolled.

Mid 50% test scores		**Rank in top tenth:**	11%
SAT critical reading:	380-520	**End year in good standing:**	86%
SAT math:	470-600	**Return as sophomores:**	61%
ACT composite:	19-24	**Out-of-state:**	13%
GPA 3.75 or higher:	20%	**Live on campus:**	92%
GPA 3.50-3.74:	21%	**International:**	5%
GPA 3.0-3.49:	34%	**Fraternities:**	6%
GPA 2.0-2.99:	25%	**Sororities:**	5%
Rank in top quarter:	38%		

Basis for selection. Secondary school record, recommendations, application essay, class rank, test scores most important; extracurricular activities, talent, personal qualities considered. **Learning Disabled:** Must request accommodations and submit appropriate documentation.

High school preparation. College-preparatory program recommended. 15 units required. Required and recommended units include English 4, mathematics 2, social studies 3 and science 4.

2008-2009 Annual costs. Tuition/fees: $21,750. Room/board: $7,200. Books/supplies: $1,000. Personal expenses: $330.

2008-2009 Financial aid. Need-based: 207 full-time freshmen applied for aid; 183 were judged to have need; 183 of these received aid. Average need met was 81%. Average scholarship/grant was $16,514; average loan $4,486. 67% of total undergraduate aid awarded as scholarships/grants, 33% as loans/jobs. **Non-need-based:** Awarded to 292 full-time undergraduates, including 107 freshmen. Scholarships awarded for academics, alumni affiliation, art, athletics, job skills, leadership, music/drama, religious affiliation, state residency.

Application procedures. Admission: Priority date 5/1; no deadline. $25 fee, may be waived for applicants with need, free for online applicants. Admission notification on a rolling basis beginning on or about 10/15. **Financial aid:** Priority date 3/1, closing date 6/1. FAFSA required. Applicants notified on a rolling basis starting 2/15; must reply within 2 week(s) of notification.

Academics. Special study options: Combined bachelor's/graduate degree, distance learning, double major, dual enrollment of high school students, honors, independent study, internships, liberal arts/career combination, semester at sea, student-designed major, study abroad, teacher certification program, Washington semester. **Credit/placement by examination:** AP, CLEP, IB, ACT, institutional tests. 90 credit hours maximum toward bachelor's degree. **Support services:** Learning center, reduced course load, remedial instruction, study skills assistance, tutoring, writing center.

Majors. Biology: General, biochemistry. **Business:** Accounting, business admin, finance. **Communications:** General. **Education:** General, art, elementary, music, physical, speech. **Health:** Athletic training, nursing (RN). **History:** General. **Math:** General. **Parks/recreation:** Sports admin. **Philosophy/religion:** Religion. **Protective services:** Law enforcement admin. **Psychology:** General. **Social sciences:** Political science. **Visual/performing arts:** Art, arts management, dramatic.

Most popular majors. Business/marketing 26%, education 22%, health sciences 15%, psychology 9%, security/protective services 6%, visual/performing arts 8%.

Computing on campus. 110 workstations in dormitories, library, computer center, student center. Dormitories wired for high-speed internet access and linked to campus network. Commuter students can connect to campus network. Online course registration, online library, helpline, repair service, student web hosting, wireless network available.

Student life. Freshman orientation: Mandatory, $150 fee. Preregistration for classes offered. Held for 3 days prior to the beginning of the fall semester. **Policies:** All students under age 21 required to live on campus unless living with parents. Students have voting representation on faculty committees. **Housing:** Guaranteed on-campus for all undergraduates. Coed dorms, single-sex dorms, fraternity/sorority housing, wellness housing available. $200 deposit, deadline 8/15. **Activities:** Bands, campus ministries, choral groups, dance, drama, literary magazine, music ensembles, Model UN, musical theater, radio station, student government, student newspaper, Disciples on Campus, Christian Fellowship Group, Fellowship of Christian Athletes, Student Government Association, Black Student Union, criminal justice club, psychology club, HOPE, student nurses organization.

Athletics. NAIA. **Intercollegiate:** Baseball M, basketball, cheerleading, cross-country, football (tackle) M, golf, soccer, softball W, track and field, volleyball W. **Intramural:** Basketball, football (non-tackle), golf, racquetball, soccer, softball, track and field, volleyball. **Team name:** Wildcats.

Student services. Adult student services, alcohol/substance abuse counseling, chaplain/spiritual director, career counseling, student employment services, financial aid counseling, personal counseling, placement for graduates, veterans' counselor.

Contact. E-mail: enrollment@culver.edu
Phone: (573) 288-6331 Toll-free number: (800) 537-1883
Fax: (573) 288-6618
Jim Lynes, Director of Admissions, Culver-Stockton College, One College Hill, Canton, MO 63435-1299

DevRy University: Kansas City

Kansas City, Missouri
www.devry.edu **CB code: 6092**

- For-profit 4-year university
- Commuter campus in large city
- 945 degree-seeking undergraduates: 47% part-time, 29% women, 17% African American, 3% Asian American, 4% Hispanic American, 1% Native American, 1% international
- 167 degree-seeking graduate students
- Interview required

General. Founded in 1931. Regionally accredited. **Degrees:** 179 bachelor's, 26 associate awarded; master's offered. **Location:** 15 miles from downtown. **Calendar:** Semester, extensive summer session. **Full-time faculty:** 30 total; 7% minority, 27% women. **Part-time faculty:** 58 total; 5% minority, 45% women.

Basis for selection. Applicants must have high school diploma or equivalant degree from accredited postsecondary institution, and be at least 17 years of age on the first day of classes. New students may enter at beginning of any semester. CPT also accepted.

High school preparation. Required units include mathematics 1. Math unit must be algebra or higher.

2008-2009 Annual costs. Tuition/fees: $14,130. Books/supplies: $1,300. Personal expenses: $5,082.

2007-2008 Financial aid. All financial aid based on need.

Application procedures. Admission: No deadline. $50 fee, may be waived for applicants with need. Admission notification on a rolling basis. **Financial aid:** No deadline. FAFSA required. Applicants notified on a rolling basis.

Academics. Special study options: Accelerated study, distance learning, weekend college. **Credit/placement by examination:** CLEP, institutional tests. **Support services:** Learning center, remedial instruction, tutoring.

Majors. Business: Business admin. **Computer sciences:** Networking, systems analysis, web page design. **Engineering technology:** Biomedical, computer, electrical. **Other:** Technical management.

Most popular majors. Business/marketing 47%, computer/information sciences 29%, engineering/engineering technologies 21%.

Computing on campus. 1,300 workstations in library, computer center. Online course registration, online library, helpline available.

Student life. Freshman orientation: Mandatory. **Housing:** Private apartments, student-plan housing, private rooms available. **Activities:** Association of Information Technology Professionals, Campus Crusade for Christ, Institute for Electrical & Electronics Engineers, Phi Beta Lambda, Tau Alpha Pi, professional certification club, drama club, Gamma Beta Phi.

Athletics. Intramural: Volleyball.

Student services. Career counseling, student employment services, financial aid counseling, placement for graduates, veterans' counselor. **Physically disabled:** Services for visually, hearing impaired.

Contact. E-mail: ssmeed@kc.devry.edu
Phone: (816) 941-2810 Toll-free number: (800) 821-3766
Fax: (816) 941-0896
Shane Smeed, Director of Admissions, DeVry University: Kansas City, 11224 Holmes Street, Kansas City, MO 64131-3626

Drury University
Springfield, Missouri
www.drury.edu **CB code: 6169**

- Private 4-year university and liberal arts college affiliated with United Church of Christ and Christian Church (Disciples of Christ)
- Residential campus in large city
- 1,543 degree-seeking undergraduates: 3% part-time, 53% women
- 500 degree-seeking graduate students
- 72% of applicants admitted
- SAT or ACT (ACT writing optional) required
- 64% graduate within 6 years

General. Founded in 1873. Regionally accredited. **Degrees:** 321 bachelor's awarded; master's offered. **ROTC:** Army. **Location:** 220 miles from St. Louis, 170 miles from Kansas City. **Calendar:** Semester, limited summer session. **Full-time faculty:** 127 total; 91% have terminal degrees, 7% minority, 38% women. **Part-time faculty:** 45 total; 7% have terminal degrees, 9% minority, 47% women. **Class size:** 65% < 20, 33% 20-39, 1% 40-49, less than 1% 50-99. **Special facilities:** Science center, greenhouse, astronomical observation station, electronic music lab.

Freshman class profile. 1,108 applied, 801 admitted, 334 enrolled.

Mid 50% test scores		**Rank in top tenth:**	35%
ACT composite:	22-28	**Return as sophomores:**	82%
GPA 3.75 or higher:	60%	**Out-of-state:**	5%
GPA 3.50-3.74:	15%	**Live on campus:**	74%
GPA 3.0-3.49:	15%	**International:**	5%
GPA 2.0-2.99:	10%	**Fraternities:**	29%
Rank in top quarter:	67%	**Sororities:**	44%

Basis for selection. School achievement record, test scores, reference from high school counselor, essay important. Interview recommended for all students. Audition recommended for music, theater students; portfolio recommended for architecture, art students.

High school preparation. College-preparatory program recommended. 12 units required. Required and recommended units include English 4, mathematics 3-4, social studies 3, science 3 and foreign language 2.

2008-2009 Annual costs. Tuition/fees: $18,409. Room/board: $6,384. Books/supplies: $1,500. Personal expenses: $1,500.

2008-2009 Financial aid. Need-based: 317 full-time freshmen applied for aid; 292 were judged to have need; 292 of these received aid. Average need met was 83%. Average scholarship/grant was $6,280; average loan $4,950. 35% of total undergraduate aid awarded as scholarships/grants, 65% as loans/jobs. **Non-need-based:** Awarded to 1,695 full-time undergraduates, including 373 freshmen. Scholarships awarded for academics, alumni affiliation, art, athletics, job skills, leadership, minority status, music/drama, religious affiliation.

Application procedures. Admission: Priority date 1/15; deadline 8/1 (postmark date). $25 fee, may be waived for applicants with need. Admission notification on a rolling basis beginning on or about 10/1. Must reply by May 1 or within 3 week(s) if notified thereafter. Application fee waived if applicant visits campus. **Financial aid:** Closing date 3/15. FAFSA, institutional form required. Applicants notified on a rolling basis starting 3/30; must reply within 2 week(s) of notification.

Academics. General education curriculum leads to minor in global studies for each student. **Special study options:** Accelerated study, combined bachelor's/graduate degree, cooperative education, distance learning, double major, dual enrollment of high school students, ESL, honors, independent study, internships, liberal arts/career combination, student-designed major, study abroad, teacher certification program, Washington semester. Living-learning communities, leadership/community service communities, Drury Center in Volos, Greece. **Credit/placement by examination:** AP, CLEP, IB, institutional tests. **Support services:** Pre-admission summer program, reduced course load, remedial instruction, study skills assistance, tutoring, writing center.

Majors. Architecture: Architecture. **Biology:** General. **Business:** Accounting, business admin, finance. **Communications:** General, advertising, public relations. **Computer sciences:** General, computer science, information systems. **Conservation:** Environmental science, environmental studies. **Education:** General, elementary, music, physical, secondary. **Engineering technology:** General. **Foreign languages:** French, German, Spanish. **Health:** Music therapy, physician assistant, predental, premedicine, prenursing, prepharmacy, preveterinary. **History:** General. **Liberal arts:** Arts/sciences. **Math:** General. **Parks/recreation:** Exercise sciences. **Philosophy/religion:** Philosophy, religion. **Physical sciences:** Applied physics, chemistry. **Psychology:** General. **Social sciences:** Criminology, economics, political science, sociology. **Visual/performing arts:** General, art, art history/conservation, arts management, design, dramatic, music management, music theory/composition, piano/organ, studio arts, voice/opera.

Most popular majors. Architecture 7%, biology 13%, business/marketing 17%, communications/journalism 11%, English 7%, physical sciences 7%, social sciences 6%, visual/performing arts 9%.

Computing on campus. 338 workstations in dormitories, library, computer center, student center. Dormitories wired for high-speed internet access and linked to campus network. Commuter students can connect to campus network. Online course registration, online library, helpline, repair service, student web hosting, wireless network available.

Student life. Freshman orientation: Mandatory, $145 fee. 4-day program; includes parent session. Registration for classes occurs separately in late June. **Housing:** Guaranteed on-campus for freshmen. Coed dorms, single-sex dorms, special housing for disabled, apartments, fraternity/sorority housing available. $200 fully refundable deposit, deadline 6/1. Living-learning, leadership/service communities available. **Activities:** Bands, campus ministries, choral groups, dance, drama, film society, international student organizations, literary magazine, music ensembles, musical theater, opera, radio station, student government, student newspaper, symphony orchestra, TV station, Think Green environmental club, Young Republicans, College Democrats, Student Union Board, Mortar Board, Habitat for Humanity, Students in Free Enterprise, Ad Team, Student Teacher Assocation.

Athletics. NCAA. **Intercollegiate:** Baseball M, basketball, cheerleading, cross-country, diving, golf, soccer, softball W, swimming, tennis, volleyball W. **Intramural:** Basketball, football (non-tackle) M, football (tackle), racquetball, soccer, softball W, volleyball. **Team name:** Panthers.

Student services. Adult student services, alcohol/substance abuse counseling, chaplain/spiritual director, career counseling, services for economically disadvantaged, student employment services, financial aid counseling, health services, minority student services, personal counseling, placement for graduates, veterans' counselor, women's services. **Physically disabled:** Services for visually, speech, hearing impaired.

Contact. E-mail: druryad@drury.edu
Phone: (417) 873-7205 Toll-free number: (800) 922-2274
Fax: (417) 866-3873
Chip Parker, Director of Admission, Drury University, 900 North Benton Avenue, Springfield, MO 65802-3712

Evangel University
Springfield, Missouri
www.evangel.edu **CB code: 6198**

- Private 4-year liberal arts college affiliated with Assemblies of God
- Residential campus in small city
- 1,718 degree-seeking undergraduates: 7% part-time, 58% women
- 153 degree-seeking graduate students
- 67% of applicants admitted
- SAT or ACT with writing required

General. Founded in 1955. Regionally accredited. **Degrees:** 324 bachelor's, 5 associate awarded; master's offered. **ROTC:** Army. **Location:** 170 miles from Kansas City, 212 miles from St. Louis. **Calendar:** Semester, limited summer session. **Full-time faculty:** 105 total. **Part-time faculty:** 54 total. **Class size:** 64% < 20, 29% 20-39, 4% 40-49, 3% 50-99.

Freshman class profile. 1,094 applied, 728 admitted, 338 enrolled.

Mid 50% test scores		**Out-of-state:**	60%
ACT composite:	20-26	**Live on campus:**	90%
End year in good standing:	94%		

Basis for selection. Minimum 2.0 high school GPA, acceptance of college's moral and religious standards, acceptable ACT or SAT scores, rank in top half of graduating class. Statement of Christian faith required. Audition required for music, sport students. Essay and portfolio recommended. **Homeschooled:** Letter of recommendation (nonparent) required. Admissions based upon ACT/SAT scores and letters of recommendation.

High school preparation. Recommended units include English 3, mathematics 2, social studies 2 and science 1.

2008-2009 Annual costs. Tuition/fees: $15,010. Room/board: $5,410.

2007-2008 Financial aid. All financial aid based on need. 321 full-time freshmen applied for aid; 265 were judged to have need; 235 of these received aid. Average need met was 54%. Average scholarship/grant was $6,183;

average loan $3,584. 33% of total undergraduate aid awarded as scholarships/grants, 67% as loans/jobs.

Application procedures. Admission: Closing date 8/1 (receipt date). $25 fee, may be waived for applicants with need. Admission notification on a rolling basis. **Financial aid:** Priority date 4/1, closing date 6/30. FAFSA required. Applicants notified on a rolling basis starting 4/1; must reply within 3 week(s) of notification.

Academics. Special study options: Cross-registration, double major, dual enrollment of high school students, internships, liberal arts/career combination, study abroad, teacher certification program, Washington semester. **Credit/placement by examination:** AP, CLEP, IB, ACT, institutional tests. 30 credit hours maximum toward associate degree, 30 toward bachelor's. **Support services:** Learning center, reduced course load, remedial instruction, study skills assistance, tutoring, writing center.

Majors. Biology: General. **Business:** General, accounting, business admin, marketing. **Communications:** General, broadcast journalism, journalism. **Communications technology:** General. **Computer sciences:** General. **Education:** Art, business, early childhood, elementary, English, foreign languages, mathematics, middle, music, physical, science, secondary, social studies, special. **Foreign languages:** Spanish. **Health:** Clinical lab technology, predental, premedicine, preveterinary. **History:** General. **Interdisciplinary:** Math/computer science. **Legal studies:** Prelaw. **Math:** General. **Parks/recreation:** General. **Physical sciences:** Chemistry. **Protective services:** Criminal justice. **Psychology:** General. **Public administration:** Social work. **Social sciences:** General, criminology, political science, sociology. **Theology:** Bible, missionary, sacred music. **Visual/performing arts:** Dramatic, music performance, studio arts.

Most popular majors. Business/marketing 15%, communications/journalism 9%, education 21%, philosophy/religious studies 12%, psychology 10%, social sciences 7%.

Computing on campus. 407 workstations in dormitories, library, computer center, student center. Dormitories wired for high-speed internet access and linked to campus network. Online library, helpline, wireless network available.

Student life. Freshman orientation: Mandatory. Preregistration for classes offered. **Policies:** Religious observance required. **Housing:** Guaranteed on-campus for freshmen. Coed dorms, single-sex dorms, apartments, wellness housing available. $200 deposit, deadline 8/1. **Activities:** Bands, campus ministries, choral groups, drama, literary magazine, music ensembles, radio station, student government, student newspaper, symphony orchestra, TV station, international students club, honor fraternities, student ministries.

Athletics. NAIA. **Intercollegiate:** Baseball M, basketball, cross-country, football (tackle) M, golf, softball W, tennis, track and field, volleyball W. **Intramural:** Basketball, football (non-tackle), soccer, softball, volleyball W. **Team name:** Crusaders.

Student services. Chaplain/spiritual director, career counseling, student employment services, financial aid counseling, health services, personal counseling, placement for graduates, veterans' counselor. **Physically disabled:** Services for visually, hearing impaired.

Contact. E-mail: admission@evangel.edu
Phone: (417) 865-2811 ext. 7205 Toll-free number: (800) 382-6435
Fax: (417) 865-9599
Jeff Burnett, Director of Admissions, Evangel University, 1111 North Glenstone, Springfield, MO 65802

Everest College: Springfield

Springfield, Missouri
www.springfield-college.com **CB code: 1478**

- For-profit 4-year technical college
- Commuter campus in small city

General. Founded in 1979. Accredited by ACICS. **Location:** 250 miles from St. Louis, 190 miles from Kansas City. **Calendar:** Quarter.

Contact. Phone: (417) 864-7220
Director of Admissions, 1010 West Sunshine, Springfield, MO 65807

Fontbonne University

St. Louis, Missouri **CB member**
www.fontbonne.edu **CB code: 6216**

- Private 4-year university and liberal arts college affiliated with Roman Catholic Church
- Commuter campus in large city
- 2,009 degree-seeking undergraduates: 25% part-time, 71% women, 36% African American, 1% Asian American, 1% Hispanic American, 1% international
- 845 degree-seeking graduate students
- 82% of applicants admitted
- SAT or ACT (ACT writing recommended) required
- 51% graduate within 6 years

General. Founded in 1923. Regionally accredited. **Degrees:** 457 bachelor's awarded; master's offered. **ROTC:** Army, Air Force. **Location:** 6 miles from downtown. **Calendar:** Semester, limited summer session. **Full-time faculty:** 82 total; 76% have terminal degrees, 10% minority, 70% women. **Part-time faculty:** 165 total. **Class size:** 81% < 20, 19% 20-39. **Special facilities:** Theater, speech, language, and hearing clinic, academic resource and ADA accommodations center.

Freshman class profile. 547 applied, 448 admitted, 192 enrolled.

Mid 50% test scores		**Rank in top tenth:**	12%
ACT composite:	19-24	**End year in good standing:**	59%
GPA 3.75 or higher:	13%	**Return as sophomores:**	65%
GPA 3.50-3.74:	13%	**Out-of-state:**	12%
GPA 3.0-3.49:	31%	**Live on campus:**	54%
GPA 2.0-2.99:	43%	**International:**	2%
Rank in top quarter:	32%		

Basis for selection. High school GPA, class rank, test scores considered. Recommendations may be requested. Essay and interview recommended. Audition required for theater students; portfolio required for art students.

High school preparation. College-preparatory program required. 16 units required. Required units include English 4, mathematics 3, social studies 3, science 3 (laboratory 1) and academic electives 3. Core electives 3 units. Must include foreign language and 1 unit visual or performing arts.

2008-2009 Annual costs. Tuition/fees: $19,320. Room/board: $7,210. Books/supplies: $650. Personal expenses: $640.

2007-2008 Financial aid. Need-based: 160 full-time freshmen applied for aid; 139 were judged to have need; 132 of these received aid. Average need met was 18%. Average scholarship/grant was $4,265; average loan $1,234. 45% of total undergraduate aid awarded as scholarships/grants, 55% as loans/jobs. **Non-need-based:** Awarded to 1,267 full-time undergraduates, including 118 freshmen. Scholarships awarded for academics, alumni affiliation, art, leadership, minority status, music/drama, religious affiliation, state residency.

Application procedures. Admission: Priority date 12/15; no deadline. $25 fee, may be waived for applicants with need. Admission notification on a rolling basis. Must reply by May 1 or within 3 week(s) if notified thereafter. **Financial aid:** Closing date 4/1. FAFSA, institutional form required. Applicants notified on a rolling basis starting 2/1; must reply within 2 week(s) of notification.

Academics. Special study options: Accelerated study, cooperative education, cross-registration, distance learning, double major, dual enrollment of high school students, ESL, exchange student, honors, independent study, internships, liberal arts/career combination, semester at sea, student-designed major, study abroad, teacher certification program, weekend college. 3-2 program in social work or engineering with Washington University. **Credit/placement by examination:** AP, CLEP, IB, institutional tests. 30 credit hours maximum toward bachelor's degree. Fontbonne will accept undergraduate credit by exam for non-standardized examinations given by accredited institutions. Course number, title, and credit hours must appear on official transcript. Determination as to fulfillment of certain course requirements will be reviewed and considered by department chairperson. **Support services:** Learning center, reduced course load, remedial instruction, study skills assistance, tutoring, writing center.

Majors. Biology: General. **Business:** Business admin, organizational behavior. **Communications:** General, advertising. **Computer sciences:** General. **Education:** Deaf/hearing impaired, early childhood, elementary, family/consumer sciences, middle, special. **Family/consumer sciences:** Clothing/textiles. **Health:** Dietetics, speech pathology. **History:** General. **Legal studies:** Prelaw. **Liberal arts:** Arts/sciences. **Math:** General. **Parks/recreation:** Sports admin. **Psychology:** General. **Public administration:** Human services. **Social sciences:** Sociology. **Visual/performing arts:** Art, dramatic, studio arts.

Most popular majors. Business/marketing 47%, education 16%.

Computing on campus. 285 workstations in dormitories, library, computer center. Dormitories wired for high-speed internet access and linked to campus network. Commuter students can connect to campus network. Online course registration, online library, helpline, repair service, wireless network available.

Student life. **Freshman orientation:** Mandatory, $75 fee. Preregistration for classes offered. Held during week prior to classes, includes community service. **Housing:** Coed dorms, special housing for disabled, apartments, wellness housing available. $150 fully refundable deposit. Apartment style residence halls available. **Activities:** Campus ministries, choral groups, dance, drama, international student organizations, literary magazine, music ensembles, musical theater, radio station, student government, student newspaper, College Republicans, Fontbonne in Service and Humility, Straights and Gays for Equality, Students for the Enhancement of Black Awareness.

Athletics. NCAA. **Intercollegiate:** Baseball M, basketball, bowling, cross-country, golf, lacrosse, soccer, softball W, tennis, volleyball. **Intramural:** Badminton, basketball, bowling, football (non-tackle), soccer, softball, table tennis, tennis, volleyball. **Team name:** Griffins.

Student services. Adult student services, alcohol/substance abuse counseling, chaplain/spiritual director, career counseling, student employment services, financial aid counseling, health services, minority student services, personal counseling, placement for graduates. **Physically disabled:** Services for speech, hearing impaired.

Contact. Phone: (314) 889-1400 Toll-free number: (800) 205-5862
Fax: (314) 889-1451
Peggy Musen, Vice President for Enrollment Management, Fontbonne University, 6800 Wydown Boulevard, St. Louis, MO 63105

Global University
Springfield, Missouri
www.globaluniversity.edu **CB code: 4916**

- Private 4-year Bible and seminary college affiliated with Assemblies of God
- Commuter campus in small city
- 5,880 degree-seeking undergraduates

General. Founded in 1948. Accredited by DETC. All course work completed via distance education. **Degrees:** 264 bachelor's awarded; master's, first professional offered. **Location:** 200 miles from St. Louis, 170 miles from Kansas City. **Calendar:** Continuous, extensive summer session. **Full-time faculty:** 55 total. **Part-time faculty:** 450 total.

Basis for selection. Open admission.

2009-2010 Annual costs. Tuition/fees (projected): $3,300. Quoted tuition is for U.S. students. Tuition for international students varies by country. Books/supplies: $650.

Application procedures. **Admission:** No deadline. $40 fee. Admission notification on a rolling basis.

Academics. **Special study options:** Distance learning, external degree, independent study. **Credit/placement by examination:** CLEP. 16 credit hours maximum toward associate degree, 32 toward bachelor's. **Support services:** Study skills assistance.

Majors. **Theology:** Bible, missionary, religious ed, theology.

Computing on campus. Online library available.

Student services. Chaplain/spiritual director.

Contact. E-mail: info@globaluniversity.edu
Phone: (417) 862-9533 Toll-free number: (800) 443-1083
Fax: (417) 865-7167
C. Kroh, Registrar and Associate Dean of Student Services, Global University, 1211 South Glenstone Avenue, Springfield, MO 65804

Goldfarb School of Nursing at Barnes-Jewish College
St. Louis, Missouri
www.barnesjewishcollege.edu **CB code: 6329**

- Private two-year upper-division nursing college
- Commuter campus in large city
- 72% of applicants admitted

General. Regionally accredited. Affiliated with Barnes-Jewish Hospital and Washington University Medical Center. **Degrees:** 157 bachelor's, 134 associate awarded; master's offered. **Location:** Downtown. **Calendar:** Trimester, extensive summer session. **Full-time faculty:** 35 total; 9% minority, 89% women. **Class size:** 20% < 20, 50% 20-39, 25% 40-49, 5% 50-99.

Student profile. 511 degree-seeking undergraduates, 114 degree-seeking graduate students. 311 applied as first time-transfer students, 223 admitted, 163 enrolled. 80% transferred from two-year, 20% transferred from four-year institutions.

Women:	89%	**Out-of-state:**	5%
Part-time:	47%	**25 or older:**	85%

Basis for selection. Open admission. College transcript required. Transfer accepted as juniors, seniors.

2008-2009 Annual costs. Tuition/fees: $13,730.

Financial aid. **Need-based:** 13% of total undergraduate aid awarded as scholarships/grants, 87% as loans/jobs. **Non-need-based:** Scholarships awarded for academics, leadership.

Application procedures. **Admission:** Priority date 11/15; deadline 3/1. $50 fee. Application must be submitted on paper. Must reply by 5/1. **Financial aid:** No deadline. Applicants notified on a rolling basis. FAFSA required.

Academics. **Special study options:** Accelerated study, combined bachelor's/graduate degree. **Credit/placement by examination:** AP, CLEP, IB, institutional tests. **Support services:** Tutoring, writing center.

Majors. **Health:** Nursing (RN).

Computing on campus. 60 workstations in library, computer center. Commuter students can connect to campus network. Online library, helpline, wireless network available.

Student life. **Activities:** Student newspaper.

Student services. Financial aid counseling.

Contact. E-mail: bjcon-admissions@bjc.org
Phone: (314) 454-7057 Toll-free number: (800) 832-9009
Fax: (314) 362-9250
Michael Ward, Associate Dean for Student Programs, Goldfarb School of Nursing at Barnes-Jewish College, 4483 Duncan Avenue, St. Louis, MO 63110-1091

Grantham University
Kansas City, Missouri
www.grantham.edu **CB code: 2244**

- For-profit 4-year virtual university
- Large city
- 5,935 degree-seeking undergraduates
- 488 graduate students

General. Founded in 1951. Accredited by DETC. Degree programs are 100 percent online. **Degrees:** 292 bachelor's, 551 associate awarded; master's offered. **Calendar:** Continuous. **Full-time faculty:** 6 total; 67% have terminal degrees, 33% women. **Part-time faculty:** 140 total; 27% have terminal degrees, 48% women.

Basis for selection. Open admission. High school diploma, GED, or equivalent required. Basic computer skills and use of computer with Windows, Internet access, e-mail account, printer also required.

2009-2010 Annual costs. Tuition/fees: $7,980. Grantham's tuition includes required textbooks, software and shipping (within U.S.).

2008-2009 Financial aid. **Additional information:** DANTES and some employer reimbursement programs available.

Application procedures. **Admission:** No deadline. No application fee. Admission notification on a rolling basis. **Financial aid:** No deadline.

Academics. **Special study options:** Accelerated study, combined bachelor's/graduate degree, distance learning, independent study. **Credit/placement by examination:** CLEP, IB. 45 credit hours maximum toward associate degree, 90 toward bachelor's. **Support services:** Learning center, tutoring.

Majors. **Business:** Business admin, human resources, management information systems, office management. **Computer sciences:** General, applications programming, computer science, data processing, information systems, information technology, LAN/WAN management, systems analysis. **Engineering technology:** Computer, electrical. **Protective services:** Law enforcement admin. **Other:** Engineering management, Multidisciplinary studies.

Most popular majors. Business/marketing 52%, computer/information sciences 18%, engineering/engineering technologies 26%.

Computing on campus. PC or laptop required. Online library available.

Student life. **Freshman orientation:** Mandatory.

Student services. Adult student services, financial aid counseling, veterans' counselor.

Contact. E-mail: admissions@grantham.edu
Phone: (800) 955-2527 Toll-free number: (800) 955-2527
Fax: (816) 595-5757
DeAnn Wandler, Vice President of Enrollment Management, Grantham University, 7200 Northwest 86th Street, Kansas City, MO 64153

Hannibal-LaGrange College
Hannibal, Missouri
www.hlg.edu **CB code: 6266**

- Private 4-year liberal arts college affiliated with Southern Baptist Convention
- Commuter campus in large town
- 1,005 degree-seeking undergraduates
- 1,127 graduate students
- SAT or ACT (ACT writing optional), interview required
- 51% graduate within 6 years; 12% enter graduate study

General. Founded in 1858. Regionally accredited. Christian environment. **Degrees:** 228 bachelor's, 31 associate awarded; master's offered. **Location:** 100 miles from St. Louis. **Calendar:** Semester, limited summer session. **Full-time faculty:** 62 total; 27% have terminal degrees, 2% minority, 50% women. **Part-time faculty:** 34 total; 35% have terminal degrees, 9% minority, 65% women. **Class size:** 75% < 20, 24% 20-39, 1% 40-49. **Special facilities:** Nature trail, fine arts theater, mission center.

Freshman class profile. 202 enrolled.

Mid 50% test scores		**Rank in top tenth:**	21%
ACT composite:	18-26	**Return as sophomores:**	77%
Rank in top quarter:	37%	**Live on campus:**	85%

Basis for selection. Most applicants admitted. Test scores important. 20 or above ACT composite required. Applicants with 16-19 ACT composite admitted provisionally. ACT administered on campus on registration day. Applications without English Composition 1 and college algebra must submit ACT scores and take mathematics placement exam. Interviews required for performance and honor students. **Homeschooled:** Transcript of courses and grades required. ACT score required. **Learning Disabled:** Must provide appropriate documentation citing learning disability.

High school preparation. College-preparatory program recommended. Recommended units include English 2, mathematics 1, history 3, science 1 (laboratory 1).

2008-2009 Annual costs. Tuition/fees: $14,506. Room/board: $5,270. Books/supplies: $800. Personal expenses: $2,061.

2008-2009 Financial aid. **Non-need-based:** Scholarships awarded for academics, art, athletics, music/drama, religious affiliation. **Additional information:** Work-study opportunities vary according to on- and off-campus needs.

Application procedures. **Admission:** Closing date 8/26. $25 fee. Admission notification on a rolling basis beginning on or about 9/1. **Financial aid:** Closing date 7/1. FAFSA, institutional form required. Applicants notified on a rolling basis; must reply by 8/31.

Academics. **Special study options:** Accelerated study, distance learning, double major, dual enrollment of high school students, ESL, honors, independent study, internships, student-designed major, study abroad, teacher certification program, weekend college. Student-designed major in Liberal Studies. **Credit/placement by examination:** AP, CLEP, SAT, ACT, institutional tests. 16 credit hours maximum toward associate degree, 30 toward bachelor's. No more than 8 credit hours in one discipline. **Support services:** Reduced course load, remedial instruction, study skills assistance, tutoring.

Honors college/program. Minimum ACT-25, essay. Additional 21 hours plus research project, must maintain requirements for eligibility each semester.

Majors. **Biology:** General. **Business:** General, accounting, business admin, marketing, organizational behavior. **Communications:** General. **Computer sciences:** General. **Education:** General, art, business, early childhood, elementary, English, mathematics, music, physical, science, secondary, social studies. **Health:** Nursing (RN). **History:** General. **Liberal arts:** Arts/sciences. **Math:** General. **Parks/recreation:** Facilities management. **Philosophy/religion:** Christian. **Protective services:** Law enforcement admin. **Psychology:** General. **Public administration:** Human services. **Social sciences:** Sociology. **Theology:** Bible, religious ed, sacred music. **Visual/performing arts:** Art, dramatic, music performance, piano/organ, studio arts, voice/opera. **Other:** Intercultural missions.

Most popular majors. Business/marketing 27%, communications/journalism 6%, education 27%, public administration/social services 7%, security/protective services 9%.

Computing on campus. 91 workstations in library, computer center. Dormitories linked to campus network. Commuter students can connect to campus network. Online library, repair service available.

Student life. **Freshman orientation:** Mandatory, $50 fee. Preregistration for classes offered. Conducted 4 days before classes begin. **Policies:** Students under 21 years of age at beginning of enrollment semester, and not living with parent or guardian, required to live residence housing unless living with approved relative. Religious observance required. **Housing:** Single-sex dorms, special housing for disabled, apartments, wellness housing available. $100 fully refundable deposit, deadline 8/26. **Activities:** Campus ministries, choral groups, drama, music ensembles, student government, student newspaper, Democratic club, Fellowship of Christian Athletes, Phi Beta Delta (men's service), Phi Beta Lambda, Gatekeepers (mentoring), Students for Life, Natures Investigation Circulus, Missouri State Teachers Association, Republican club, art club, science club.

Athletics. NAIA, NCCAA. **Intercollegiate:** Baseball M, basketball, golf, soccer, softball W, swimming, track and field, volleyball, wrestling M. **Intramural:** Baseball M, basketball, racquetball, softball, table tennis, volleyball. **Team name:** Trojans.

Student services. Career counseling, student employment services, personal counseling, placement for graduates. **Physically disabled:** Services for visually, hearing impaired.

Contact. E-mail: admissio@hlg.edu
Phone: (573) 629-3264 Toll-free number: (800) 454-1119
Fax: (573) 221-6594
Ray Carty, Vice President of Enrollment Management, Hannibal-LaGrange College, 2800 Palmyra Road, Hannibal, MO 63401

Harris-Stowe State University
St. Louis, Missouri
www.hssu.edu **CB code: 6269**

- Public 4-year university
- Commuter campus in large city
- 1,799 degree-seeking undergraduates: 27% part-time, 67% women, 91% African American, 1% Hispanic American, 1% international
- 83% of applicants admitted

General. Founded in 1857. Regionally accredited. **Degrees:** 106 bachelor's awarded. **ROTC:** Army, Air Force. **Location:** Midtown. **Calendar:** Semester, limited summer session. **Full-time faculty:** 54 total; 59% have terminal degrees, 43% minority, 50% women. **Part-time faculty:** 108 total; 16% have terminal degrees, 78% minority, 58% women. **Class size:** 70% < 20, 30% 20-39. **Special facilities:** Jazz institute.

Freshman class profile. 1,521 applied, 1,258 admitted, 434 enrolled.

Mid 50% test scores		**Live on campus:**	34%
ACT composite:	14-17	**Fraternities:**	1%
Return as sophomores:	43%	**Sororities:**	1%
Out-of-state:	1%		

Basis for selection. ACT composite score of 21, or combined ACT composite percentile rank and high school class percentile rank greater than or equal to 100. Full-time, first-year freshmen are encouraged to meet the Missouri High School Core Curriculum requirements. SAT or ACT recommended. Applicants with scores below 18 on any section of the ACT or below 440 on any section of the SAT must take Harris-Stowe State University's institutional placement test. **Learning Disabled:** Submit documentation of disability for review by Director of Academic Support Services.

High school preparation. College-preparatory program recommended. Required and recommended units include English 4, mathematics 3, social studies 3, science 3 (laboratory 1), foreign language 2 and academic electives 7. 1 visual/performing arts required. Social studies must include American government. Electives must be from above list.

2008-2009 Annual costs. Tuition/fees: $5,340; $10,092 out-of-state. Books/supplies: $500. Personal expenses: $2,000.

2007-2008 Financial aid. Need-based: Average need met was 85%. Average scholarship/grant was $3,000; average loan $4,000. 92% of total undergraduate aid awarded as scholarships/grants, 8% as loans/jobs. **Non-need-based:** Scholarships awarded for academics, athletics, music/drama, state residency.

Application procedures. Admission: No deadline. $15 fee. Application must be submitted on paper. Admission notification on a rolling basis. **Financial aid:** Priority date 4/1; no closing date. FAFSA, institutional form required. Must reply within 3 week(s) of notification.

Academics. Special study options: Accelerated study, cooperative education, ESL, internships, student-designed major, teacher certification program. **Credit/placement by examination:** CLEP, SAT, ACT, institutional tests. **Support services:** Learning center, pre-admission summer program, reduced course load, remedial instruction, study skills assistance, tutoring, writing center.

Majors. Business: General, accounting, business admin, entrepreneurial studies, hospitality admin, marketing. **Computer sciences:** General, information systems, networking. **Education:** Early childhood, elementary, middle, multi-level teacher, secondary. **Health:** Health services admin. **Protective services:** Juvenile corrections, law enforcement admin. **Public administration:** General. **Social sciences:** Urban studies.

Most popular majors. Business/marketing 38%, computer/information sciences 6%, education 37%, security/protective services 9%.

Computing on campus. 205 workstations in dormitories, library, computer center. Dormitories wired for high-speed internet access. Commuter students can connect to campus network. Wireless network available.

Student life. Freshman orientation: Mandatory. Program directed by counseling staff during semester. **Housing:** Coed dorms available. $500 nonrefundable deposit. **Activities:** Choral groups, drama, international student organizations, literary magazine, music ensembles, student government, student newspaper, African American Studies Society, multicultural council, 100 Strong, Organization for Cultrual Progress, Student Ambassadors.

Athletics. NAIA. **Intercollegiate:** Baseball M, basketball, cheerleading, soccer, softball W, volleyball W. **Intramural:** Basketball, volleyball. **Team name:** Hornets.

Student services. Career counseling, student employment services, financial aid counseling, health services, personal counseling, placement for graduates, veterans' counselor.

Contact. E-mail: admissions@hssu.edu
Phone: (314) 340-3300 Fax: (314) 340-3555
Lashanda Boone, Executive Director of Enrollment Management, Harris-Stowe State University, 3026 Laclede Avenue, St. Louis, MO 63103-2199

Hickey College

St. Louis, Missouri
www.hickeycollege.edu **CB code: 2308**

- For-profit 4-year business and technical college
- Commuter campus in very large city
- 402 degree-seeking undergraduates

General. Founded in 1933. Accredited by ACICS. **Degrees:** 39 bachelor's, 120 associate awarded. **Location:** 15 miles from downtown. **Calendar:** Semester. **Full-time faculty:** 16 total. **Part-time faculty:** 21 total.

Basis for selection. Open admission, but selective for some programs. Selective enrollment for paralegal and veterinary technician programs.

2008-2009 Annual costs. Tuition/fees: $12,520. Room/board: $5,600. Books/supplies: $1,000.

Application procedures. Admission: No deadline. $50 fee. Admission notification on a rolling basis. **Financial aid:** No deadline. FAFSA required. Applicants notified on a rolling basis.

Academics. Credit/placement by examination: CLEP.

Majors. Business: Management science.

Computing on campus. 134 workstations in library, computer center.

Student life. Housing: Apartments available.

Student services. Placement for graduates.

Contact. E-mail: admin@hickeycollege.edu
Phone: (314) 434-2212 Toll-free number: (800) 777-1544
Fax: (314) 434-1974
Michelle Hayes, Admissions Manager, Hickey College, 940 West Port Plaza, St. Louis, MO 63146

ITT Technical Institute: Arnold

Arnold, Missouri
www.itt-tech.edu **CB code: 2691**

- For-profit 4-year technical college
- Commuter campus in large town

General. Accredited by ACICS. **Calendar:** Quarter.

Annual costs/financial aid. Books/supplies: $3,100.

Contact. Phone: (636) 464-6600
Director of Recruitment, 1930 Meyer Drury Drive, Arnold, MO 63010

ITT Technical Institute: Earth City

Earth City, Missouri
www.itt-tech.edu **CB code: 1216**

- For-profit 4-year technical college
- Commuter campus in large city

General. Founded in 1936. Accredited by ACICS. **Location:** 15 miles from St. Louis. **Calendar:** Quarter.

Contact. Phone: (314) 298-7800
Director of Recruitment, 13505 Lakefront Drive, Earth City, MO 63045

Kansas City Art Institute

Kansas City, Missouri
www.kcai.edu **CB code: 6330**

- Private 4-year visual arts college
- Commuter campus in large city
- 656 degree-seeking undergraduates: 1% part-time, 57% women, 3% African American, 4% Asian American, 7% Hispanic American, 1% Native American
- 59% of applicants admitted
- SAT or ACT with writing, application essay required
- 68% graduate within 6 years

General. Founded in 1885. Regionally accredited. **Degrees:** 119 bachelor's awarded. **Location:** 250 miles from St. Louis, 500 miles from Denver. **Calendar:** Semester, limited summer session. **Full-time faculty:** 48 total; 90% have terminal degrees, 4% minority, 42% women. **Part-time faculty:** 50 total; 46% have terminal degrees, 38% women. **Class size:** 82% < 20, 18% 20-39. **Special facilities:** Foundry, arboretum.

Freshman class profile. 688 applied, 409 admitted, 149 enrolled.

Mid 50% test scores		**GPA 2.0-2.99:**	35%
SAT critical reading:	450-590	**Rank in top quarter:**	10%
SAT math:	450-530	**Rank in top tenth:**	1%
SAT writing:	430-550	**End year in good standing:**	90%
ACT composite:	20-25	**Return as sophomores:**	80%
GPA 3.75 or higher:	14%	**Out-of-state:**	75%
GPA 3.50-3.74:	13%	**Live on campus:**	90%
GPA 3.0-3.49:	37%		

Basis for selection. Portfolio, academic record, recommendations, test scores, personal interview important. Acceptable level of studio proficiency required prior to consideration of other credentials. **Homeschooled:** State high school equivalency certificate required.

High school preparation. 20 units recommended. Recommended units include English 4, mathematics 3, social studies 3, science 3 and academic electives 3. 4 fine arts electives recommended.

2008-2009 Annual costs. Tuition/fees: $27,220. Room/board: $8,294. Books/supplies: $1,500. Personal expenses: $2,000.

2008-2009 Financial aid. Need-based: Average need met was 74%. Average scholarship/grant was $15,943; average loan $6,014. 68% of total undergraduate aid awarded as scholarships/grants, 32% as loans/jobs. **Non-need-based:** Scholarships awarded for academics, art. **Additional information:** February 15 and March 15 priority application dates for merit scholarships; deadline July 1.

Application procedures. **Admission:** No deadline. $35 fee, may be waived for applicants with need. Admission notification on a rolling basis beginning on or about 9/1. Must reply by May 1 or within 2 week(s) if notified thereafter. **Financial aid:** Priority date 3/15, closing date 4/1. FAFSA required. Applicants notified on a rolling basis starting 4/1; must reply within 2 week(s) of notification.

Academics. **Special study options:** Double major, exchange student, independent study, internships, study abroad. **Credit/placement by examination:** AP, CLEP, IB. 15 credit hours maximum toward bachelor's degree. **Support services:** Learning center, reduced course load, remedial instruction, study skills assistance, tutoring, writing center.

Majors. **Visual/performing arts:** Art history/conservation, ceramics, cinematography, fiber arts, graphic design, painting, photography, printmaking, sculpture.

Most popular majors. Visual/performing arts 50%.

Computing on campus. 50 workstations in dormitories, library, computer center. Dormitories wired for high-speed internet access and linked to campus network. Commuter students can connect to campus network. Online course registration, online library, helpline, wireless network available.

Student life. **Freshman orientation:** Mandatory. Preregistration for classes offered. 3-day program held prior to start of academic year. **Housing:** Guaranteed on-campus for freshmen. Coed dorms, apartments, wellness housing available. $125 deposit, deadline 5/1. **Activities:** Film society, student government.

Student services. Adult student services, alcohol/substance abuse counseling, career counseling, student employment services, financial aid counseling, minority student services, personal counseling, placement for graduates, veterans' counselor. **Physically disabled:** Services for visually, hearing impaired. **Learning disabled:** Comprehensive services available.

Contact. E-mail: admiss@kcai.edu
Phone: (816) 474-5224 Toll-free number: (800) 522-5224
Fax: (816) 802-3309
Kansas City Art Institute, 4415 Warwick Boulevard, Kansas City, MO 64111-1820

Lincoln University

Jefferson City, Missouri
www.lincolnu.edu **CB code: 6366**

- Public 4-year university and liberal arts college
- Commuter campus in large town
- 2,445 degree-seeking undergraduates: 20% part-time, 60% women, 45% African American, 1% Asian American, 1% Hispanic American, 4% international
- 143 degree-seeking graduate students

General. Founded in 1866. Regionally accredited. 1890 land-grant institution. **Degrees:** 245 bachelor's, 82 associate awarded; master's offered. **ROTC:** Army, Naval, Air Force. **Location:** 132 miles from St. Louis, 157 miles from Kansas City. **Calendar:** Semester, limited summer session. **Full-time faculty:** 120 total; 49% have terminal degrees, 32% minority, 50% women. **Part-time faculty:** 122 total. **Class size:** 55% < 20, 42% 20-39, 2% 40-49, less than 1% 50-99. **Special facilities:** Ethnic studies center and archives, 3 research farms, agriculture and extension information center.

Freshman class profile. 1,566 applied, 1,480 admitted, 575 enrolled.

Mid 50% test scores		**GPA 2.0-2.99:**	56%
SAT critical reading:	340-470	**Rank in top quarter:**	16%
SAT math:	360-480	**Rank in top tenth:**	3%
ACT composite:	15-20	**Return as sophomores:**	53%
GPA 3.75 or higher:	5%	**Out-of-state:**	24%
GPA 3.50-3.74:	8%	**Live on campus:**	59%
GPA 3.0-3.49:	15%	**International:**	2%

Basis for selection. Open admission, but selective for some programs and for out-of-state students. Special requirements for nursing and education programs. ACT or SAT scores required but used for placement purposes only. Audition required for sacred music and music education students. **Homeschooled:** Must submit a transcript with the parent's notarized signature, demonstrating completion of the Missouri Minimum Core Curriculum or its equivalency, as determined by the University. **Learning Disabled:** Comprehensive documentation of disability by qualified professional must be on file to request accommodations.

High school preparation. College-preparatory program recommended. 16 units recommended. Recommended units include English 4, mathematics 3, social studies 3, science 2 (laboratory 1), foreign language 2, visual/performing arts 1 and academic electives 1. Social studies courses should include 1 unit of U.S. history and at least 1 semester of government.

2008-2009 Annual costs. Tuition/fees: $6,175; $10,885 out-of-state. Students enrolled full-time must pay $232.50 per fall/spring semester or $96 per summer semester for health insurance if they do not provide proof of other coverage. Enrollment in the student health insurance program is required for international students. Room/board: $4,660. Books/supplies: $950. Personal expenses: $166.

2008-2009 Financial aid. **Non-need-based:** Scholarships awarded for academics, art, athletics, job skills, leadership, minority status, music/drama, ROTC, state residency.

Application procedures. **Admission:** Closing date 7/15 (postmark date). $20 fee. Admission notification on a rolling basis. **Financial aid:** Priority date 3/1; no closing date. FAFSA, institutional form required. Applicants notified by 3/15; Applicants notified on a rolling basis starting 3/15; must reply within 2 week(s) of notification.

Academics. **Special study options:** Accelerated study, distance learning, double major, dual enrollment of high school students, exchange student, honors, independent study, internships, study abroad, teacher certification program. Senior citizen program. **Credit/placement by examination:** AP, CLEP, institutional tests. 15 credit hours maximum toward associate degree, 20 toward bachelor's. Total number of alternative credit hours cannot exceed 30. Students may receive credit only for courses numbered 100-299. Each examination may be taken only once. Students must be currently enrolled during the semester in which he/she elects to take the exam. **Support services:** Learning center, pre-admission summer program, reduced course load, remedial instruction, study skills assistance, tutoring, writing center.

Majors. **Agriculture:** General, business. **Biology:** General. **Business:** Accounting, business admin, managerial economics, marketing. **Communications:** Journalism. **Computer sciences:** Information systems. **Conservation:** Environmental science. **Education:** Art, biology, business, chemistry, elementary, English, mathematics, music, physical, physics, social science, special. **Engineering technology:** Civil, mechanical. **Foreign languages:** Spanish. **Health:** Clinical lab science, nursing (RN). **History:** General. **Liberal arts:** Arts/sciences. **Math:** General. **Physical sciences:** Chemistry, physics. **Protective services:** Law enforcement admin. **Psychology:** General. **Public administration:** General, social work. **Social sciences:** Political science, sociology. **Theology:** Sacred music. **Visual/performing arts:** Studio arts. **Other:** Wellness.

Most popular majors. Agriculture 7%, business/marketing 28%, computer/information sciences 8%, education 13%, liberal arts 11%, security/protective services 7%.

Computing on campus. 315 workstations in dormitories, library, computer center, student center. Dormitories wired for high-speed internet access and linked to campus network. Online library, helpline, wireless network available.

Student life. **Freshman orientation:** Mandatory, $50 fee. Preregistration for classes offered. Summer orientations are one and a half day programs. Other sessions throughout the year. **Policies:** Unmarried freshmen and sophomores under 21 years of age, whose primary domicile is beyond a 60-mile radius of the University, are required to live in residence halls for four consecutive semesters. Armed Forces veterans and any student who has established a primary domicile one year prior to entering the University are exempted from this policy. **Housing:** Guaranteed on-campus for freshmen. Coed dorms, single-sex dorms, wellness housing available. $125 fully refundable deposit, deadline 7/1. Honors housing available. **Activities:** Bands, campus ministries, choral groups, dance, drama, international student organizations, literary magazine, music ensembles, radio station, student government, student newspaper, TV station, Baptist Student Center, College Republicans, College Democrats, Barrier Breakers, Wesley Foundation, Kathleen McGuire Newman Center.

Athletics. NCAA. **Intercollegiate:** Baseball M, basketball, cheerleading M, cross-country W, football (tackle) M, golf M, softball W, tennis W, track and field. **Intramural:** Basketball, bowling. **Team name:** Blue Tigers.

Student services. Career counseling, services for economically disadvantaged, financial aid counseling, health services, personal counseling, veterans' counselor. **Physically disabled:** Services for visually, speech, hearing impaired.

Contact. E-mail: enroll@lincolnu.edu
Phone: (573) 681-5599 Toll-free number: (800) 521-5052
Fax: (573) 681-5889
Mike Kosher, Director of Admissions, Lincoln University, 820 Chestnut Stree, B7 Young Hall, Jefferson City, MO 65102-0029

Lindenwood University

St. Charles, Missouri
www.lindenwood.edu **CB code: 6367**

- Private 4-year university and liberal arts college affiliated with Presbyterian Church (USA)
- Residential campus in very large city
- 6,330 degree-seeking undergraduates: 6% part-time, 56% women, 11% African American, 1% Asian American, 2% Hispanic American, 10% international
- 3,742 degree-seeking graduate students
- 40% of applicants admitted
- SAT or ACT (ACT writing optional) required
- 43% graduate within 6 years

General. Founded in 1827. Regionally accredited. **Degrees:** 1,177 bachelor's awarded; master's, doctoral offered. **ROTC:** Army. **Location:** 20 miles from St. Louis. **Calendar:** 4-1-4, limited summer session. **Full-time faculty:** 190 total; 65% have terminal degrees, 8% minority, 40% women. **Part-time faculty:** 293 total. **Class size:** 57% < 20, 42% 20-39, less than 1% 40-49, less than 1% >100. **Special facilities:** Greenhouse, wetland program facility, success center.

Freshman class profile. 4,020 applied, 1,598 admitted, 1,106 enrolled.

Mid 50% test scores			
SAT critical reading:	410-490	Rank in top quarter:	30%
SAT math:	480-560	Rank in top tenth:	10%
ACT composite:	20-24	Return as sophomores:	66%
GPA 3.75 or higher:	13%	Out-of-state:	25%
GPA 3.50-3.74:	15%	Live on campus:	86%
GPA 3.0-3.49:	32%	International:	14%
GPA 2.0-2.99:	37%	Fraternities:	1%
		Sororities:	1%

Basis for selection. Class rank, school record, high school GPA very important. **Homeschooled:** Transcript of courses and grades required.

High school preparation. College-preparatory program recommended. 16 units recommended. Recommended units include English 4, mathematics 3, social studies 3, history 3, science 3 (laboratory 1), foreign language 2 and visual/performing arts 1.

2008-2009 Annual costs. Tuition/fees: $13,000. Room/board: $6,860. Books/supplies: $3,000. Personal expenses: $9,000.

2008-2009 Financial aid. Need-based: 974 full-time freshmen applied for aid; 550 were judged to have need; 550 of these received aid. Average need met was 90%. Average scholarship/grant was $2,473; average loan $1,668. 53% of total undergraduate aid awarded as scholarships/grants, 47% as loans/jobs. **Non-need-based:** Awarded to 1,860 full-time undergraduates, including 289 freshmen. Scholarships awarded for academics, alumni affiliation, art, job skills, leadership, music/drama, ROTC.

Application procedures. Admission: No deadline. $30 fee, may be waived for applicants with need. Admission notification on a rolling basis beginning on or about 9/1. Must reply by May 1 or within 4 week(s) if notified thereafter. **Financial aid:** Priority date 4/1; no closing date. FAFSA required. Applicants notified on a rolling basis.

Academics. Special study options: Accelerated study, combined bachelor's/graduate degree, cross-registration, distance learning, double major, dual enrollment of high school students, ESL, honors, independent study, internships, student-designed major, study abroad, teacher certification program. Bachelor of engineering with Washington University, 3-2 Lindenwood University/University of Missouri Columbia dual degree program in engineering and math or computer sciences, 2-2 program in engineering, 2-2 nursing program with Barnes Jewish Medical Center. **Credit/placement by examination:** AP, CLEP, IB, SAT, ACT, institutional tests. **Support services:** Learning center, reduced course load, study skills assistance, tutoring, writing center.

Majors. Area/ethnic studies: American. **Biology:** General, environmental. **Business:** General, accounting, business admin, communications, entrepreneurial studies, finance, hospitality admin, human resources, international, management information systems, marketing, nonprofit/public, retailing. **Communications:** General, advertising, digital media, journalism, media studies, organizational. **Computer sciences:** General, computer science, information technology. **Conservation:** Environmental science. **Education:** Art, biology, business, chemistry, early childhood, early childhood special, elementary, French, history, middle, physical, science, social science, social studies, Spanish, technology/industrial arts, trade/industrial. **Foreign languages:** French, Spanish. **Health:** Athletic training, health care admin. **History:** General. **Interdisciplinary:** Gerontology. **Math:** General. **Parks/recreation:** Exercise sciences, sports admin. **Personal/culinary services:** Funeral direction, mortuary science. **Philosophy/religion:** Christian, philosophy, religion. **Physical sciences:** Chemistry. **Protective services:** Criminal justice, fire services admin. **Psychology:** General. **Public administration:** General, human services, social work. **Social sciences:** Criminology, international relations, political science, sociology. **Theology:** Pastoral counseling, youth ministry. **Visual/performing arts:** General, acting, art, art history/conservation, arts management, dance, directing/producing, dramatic, fashion design, multimedia, music management, music performance, music theory/composition, studio arts, theater arts management, theater design.

Most popular majors. Business/marketing 45%, communications/journalism 9%, education 11%, security/protective services 6%, visual/performing arts 7%.

Computing on campus. 153 workstations in library, computer center, student center. Dormitories wired for high-speed internet access and linked to campus network. Commuter students can connect to campus network. Online course registration, online library, helpline, wireless network available.

Student life. Freshman orientation: Mandatory. Preregistration for classes offered. **Policies:** Zero tolerance of illegal substances. **Housing:** Guaranteed on-campus for all undergraduates. Single-sex dorms, apartments, wellness housing available. $300 nonrefundable deposit. Housing for single parents with children available. **Activities:** Bands, campus ministries, choral groups, dance, drama, international student organizations, literary magazine, music ensembles, musical theater, radio station, student government, student newspaper, symphony orchestra, TV station, Campus Crusade for Christ, intercultural club, American Humanics, Circle K, Reform Campus Fellowship, Lewis & Clark Historical Society, Eastern Debating Society, Christian Life Group, Fellowship of Christian Athletes.

Athletics. NAIA. **Intercollegiate:** Baseball M, basketball, bowling, cheerleading, cross-country, diving, field hockey W, football (tackle) M, golf, ice hockey, rifle, soccer, softball W, swimming, tennis, track and field, volleyball, water polo, wrestling M. **Intramural:** Basketball, bowling, football (non-tackle), soccer, softball, swimming, table tennis, tennis, volleyball, water polo. **Team name:** Lions.

Student services. Adult student services, chaplain/spiritual director, career counseling, student employment services, financial aid counseling, placement for graduates, veterans' counselor. **Physically disabled:** Services for visually, hearing impaired.

Contact. E-mail: admissions@lindenwood.edu
Phone: (636) 949-4949 Fax: (636) 949-4989
Joe Parisi, Dean of Undergraduate Day Admissions, Lindenwood University, 209 South Kingshighway, St. Charles, MO 63301-1695

Maryville University of Saint Louis

St. Louis, Missouri **CB member**
www.maryville.edu **CB code: 6399**

- Private 4-year university
- Commuter campus in very large city
- 2,818 degree-seeking undergraduates: 39% part-time, 76% women, 6% African American, 2% Asian American, 1% Hispanic American, 1% international
- 619 degree-seeking graduate students
- 54% of applicants admitted
- SAT or ACT (ACT writing optional) required
- 56% graduate within 6 years; 9% enter graduate study

General. Founded in 1872. Regionally accredited. **Degrees:** 546 bachelor's awarded; master's, doctoral offered. **ROTC:** Army. **Location:** 20 miles from downtown. **Calendar:** Semester, limited summer session. **Full-time faculty:** 113 total; 86% have terminal degrees, 12% minority, 59% women. **Part-time faculty:** 246 total; 51% have terminal degrees, 9% minority, 63% women. **Class size:** 65% < 20, 34% 20-39, less than 1% 40-49. **Special facilities:** Observatory, auditorium, outdoor walking trails, coffeehouse, teaching laboratory, clinical laboratories, communications laboratory, multimedia classrooms.

Freshman class profile. 1,637 applied, 882 admitted, 355 enrolled.

Mid 50% test scores		**Rank in top tenth:**	25%
ACT composite:	22-26	**End year in good standing:**	94%
GPA 3.75 or higher:	43%	**Return as sophomores:**	80%
GPA 3.50-3.74:	19%	**Out-of-state:**	20%
GPA 3.0-3.49:	25%	**Live on campus:**	66%
GPA 2.0-2.99:	13%	**International:**	1%
Rank in top quarter:	52%		

Basis for selection. School record most important. Recommendations and extracurricular activities considered. ACT or SAT very important. Interview and 20 hours observation in clinical setting required for physical therapy students. Audition required for music therapy students; portfolio required for art education, graphic design, interior design, and studio art majors. **Homeschooled:** Increased weight placed on ACT or SAT scores.

High school preparation. College-preparatory program recommended. 22 units required. Required and recommended units include English 4, mathematics 3, social studies 2, science 2, foreign language 3 and academic electives 8. Applicants for actuarial science, art, education, interior design, clinical laboratory science, nursing, occupational therapy, and physical therapy must meet other specific requirements.

2009-2010 Annual costs. Tuition/fees (projected): $21,145. Room/board: $8,300. Books/supplies: $1,600. Personal expenses: $2,100.

2008-2009 Financial aid. Need-based: 281 full-time freshmen applied for aid; 242 were judged to have need; 242 of these received aid. Average need met was 78%. Average scholarship/grant was $8,590; average loan $2,962. 50% of total undergraduate aid awarded as scholarships/grants, 50% as loans/jobs. **Non-need-based:** Awarded to 472 full-time undergraduates, including 91 freshmen. Scholarships awarded for academics, alumni affiliation, art, leadership, minority status, ROTC.

Application procedures. Admission: Closing date 8/15. $30 fee, may be waived for applicants with need, free for online applicants. Admission notification on a rolling basis. Must reply by May 1 or within 4 week(s) if notified thereafter. **Financial aid:** Priority date 3/1; no closing date. FAFSA required. Applicants notified on a rolling basis starting 3/1; must reply by 5/1 or within 2 week(s) of notification.

Academics. Special study options: Accelerated study, combined bachelor's/graduate degree, cooperative education, cross-registration, distance learning, double major, dual enrollment of high school students, honors, independent study, internships, liberal arts/career combination, semester at sea, student-designed major, study abroad, teacher certification program, Washington semester, weekend college. **Credit/placement by examination:** AP, CLEP, IB, SAT, ACT, institutional tests. 30 credit hours maximum toward bachelor's degree. **Support services:** Learning center, reduced course load, study skills assistance, tutoring, writing center.

Majors. Biology: General, biochemistry, biomedical sciences. **Business:** General, accounting, actuarial science, business admin, e-commerce, management information systems, marketing. **Communications:** Media studies. **Computer sciences:** Computer science. **Conservation:** Environmental science, environmental studies. **Education:** Art, biology, chemistry, early childhood, elementary, English, history, mathematics, middle, secondary. **Health:** Clinical lab science, music therapy, nursing (RN), predental, vocational rehab counseling. **History:** General. **Interdisciplinary:** Biological/physical sciences. **Legal studies:** Paralegal. **Liberal arts:** Arts/sciences. **Math:** General, applied. **Parks/recreation:** Sports admin. **Physical sciences:** Chemistry. **Psychology:** General, industrial, social. **Social sciences:** Criminology, sociology. **Visual/performing arts:** Graphic design, interior design, studio arts.

Most popular majors. Business/marketing 30%, health sciences 31%, psychology 11%, visual/performing arts 7%.

Computing on campus. 489 workstations in dormitories, library, computer center, student center. Dormitories wired for high-speed internet access and linked to campus network. Commuter students can connect to campus network. Online course registration, online library, helpline, student web hosting, wireless network available.

Student life. Freshman orientation: Available. Preregistration for classes offered. 3-day program prior to start of classes. **Housing:** Guaranteed on-campus for all undergraduates. Coed dorms, apartments, wellness housing available. $150 fully refundable deposit, deadline 5/1. **Activities:** Bands, campus ministries, choral groups, dance, drama, literary magazine, music ensembles, student government, student newspaper, symphony orchestra, student academic majors clubs, Baptist student union, Campus Crusade for Christ, Roman Catholic student community, Reformed Campus Fellowship, Association of Black Collegians, multicultural club, community service club.

Athletics. NCAA. **Intercollegiate:** Baseball M, basketball, cross-country, golf, soccer, softball W, tennis, track and field, volleyball W. **Intramural:** Basketball, bowling, cheerleading, football (non-tackle), soccer, softball, table tennis, volleyball. **Team name:** Saints.

Student services. Adult student services, alcohol/substance abuse counseling, chaplain/spiritual director, career counseling, student employment services, financial aid counseling, health services, minority student services, personal counseling, placement for graduates, veterans' counselor. **Physically disabled:** Services for visually, speech, hearing impaired.

Contact. E-mail: admissions@maryville.edu
Phone: (314) 529-9350 Toll-free number: (800) 627-9855 ext. 9350
Fax: (314) 529-9927
Shani Lenore, Assistant Vice President of Enrollment, Maryville University of Saint Louis, 650 Maryville University Drive, St. Louis, MO 63141-7299

Midwest University
Wentzville, Missouri
www.midwest.edu

- Private two-year upper-division university and seminary college
- Large town

General. Regionally accredited. **Degrees:** 9 bachelor's awarded; master's, doctoral, first professional offered. **Calendar:** Semester. **Full-time faculty:** 5 total. **Part-time faculty:** 4 total.

Student profile. 87 degree-seeking undergraduates.

Academics. Credit/placement by examination: CLEP.

Majors. Philosophy/religion: Religion.

Contact. E-mail: usa@midwest.edu
Phone: (636) 327-4645
Jeoung Ham, Registrar and Director of Admissions, Midwest University

Missouri Baptist University
St. Louis, Missouri
www.mobap.edu **CB code: 2258**

- Private 4-year university and liberal arts college affiliated with Baptist faith
- Commuter campus in very large city
- 1,444 degree-seeking undergraduates
- 67% of applicants admitted

General. Founded in 1963. Regionally accredited. **Degrees:** 294 bachelor's, 3 associate awarded; master's offered. **ROTC:** Army. **Location:** 10 miles from downtown. **Calendar:** Semester, limited summer session. **Full-time faculty:** 71 total; 54% have terminal degrees, 44% women. **Part-time faculty:** 165 total; 18% have terminal degrees, 48% women.

Freshman class profile. 543 applied, 365 admitted, 204 enrolled.

Mid 50% test scores		**ACT composite:**	19-24
SAT critical reading:	410-470	**Rank in top quarter:**	51%
SAT math:	380-540	**Rank in top tenth:**	12%

Basis for selection. Minimum 2.0 high school GPA. Minimum score of 20 is required for ACT and/or a minimum score of 950 (exclusive of Writing) on SAT. Final class rank must be in the upper 50 percent of the graduating class. Applicants with high school GPA below 2.0 may be admitted on a probational status. Interview and/or essay required for academically weak students; audition required for music majors. **Learning Disabled:** Students must self-identify to the Special Needs Access Office, provide current written documentation of a disability from a qualified professional or agency, and request accommodations from the university. Documentation must meet institutional documentation criteria, indicate a substantial limitation in the education environment, and be completed at least six weeks prior to the start of the semester or class.

High school preparation. 22 units required. Required and recommended units include English 4, mathematics 3, social studies 2, history 1, science 2 (laboratory 1), foreign language 2 and academic electives 3. One visual and performing arts required.

2008-2009 Annual costs. Tuition/fees: $16,872. Room/board: $7,070.

2007-2008 Financial aid. Non-need-based: Scholarships awarded for academics, alumni affiliation, athletics, leadership, music/drama, religious affiliation.

Application procedures. Admission: No deadline. $30 fee, may be waived for applicants with need. Application must be submitted on paper. Admission notification on a rolling basis. **Financial aid:** Priority date 4/1; no closing date. FAFSA, institutional form required. Applicants notified on a rolling basis starting 4/15; must reply within 2 week(s) of notification.

Academics. Special study options: Accelerated study, combined bachelor's/graduate degree, cooperative education, cross-registration, distance learning, double major, dual enrollment of high school students, independent study, internships, liberal arts/career combination, student-designed major, study abroad, teacher certification program, urban semester, Washington semester. **Credit/placement by examination:** AP, CLEP, institutional tests. 45 credit hours maximum toward bachelor's degree. No single source may account for more than 30 of the 45 credit-hour maximum. **Support services:** Reduced course load, remedial instruction, study skills assistance, tutoring.

Majors. Biology: General, biotechnology. **Business:** Accounting, business admin, marketing, operations. **Communications:** General. **Computer sciences:** General. **Education:** Business, early childhood, elementary, health, middle, music, physical, science. **Family/consumer sciences:** Family studies. **Health:** Athletic training. **History:** General. **Math:** General. **Parks/recreation:** Sports admin. **Philosophy/religion:** Christian. **Physical sciences:** Chemistry. **Protective services:** Criminal justice. **Psychology:** General. **Public administration:** Human services. **Social sciences:** General. **Theology:** Religious ed, sacred music, theology. **Visual/performing arts:** Music performance. **Other:** Worship arts.

Most popular majors. Business/marketing 20%, communications/journalism 6%, education 31%, parks/recreation 7%, psychology 7%, theological studies 7%.

Computing on campus. 55 workstations in dormitories, library, computer center. Dormitories wired for high-speed internet access and linked to campus network. Commuter students can connect to campus network. Online library, helpline, wireless network available.

Student life. Freshman orientation: Mandatory. **Policies:** Religious observance required. **Housing:** Single-sex dorms, apartments, wellness housing available. $250 deposit, deadline 7/1. **Activities:** Bands, choral groups, drama, literary magazine, music ensembles, musical theater, opera, radio station, student government, student newspaper, Baptist Student Union, Fellowship of Christian Athletes, Student Mission, state teachers association, Ministerial Alliance, international club, science club, computer club, College Music Educators National Conference, Students in Free Enterprise.

Athletics. NAIA. **Intercollegiate:** Baseball M, basketball, bowling, cheerleading, cross-country, golf, lacrosse W, soccer, softball W, tennis W, track and field, volleyball, wrestling M. **Intramural:** Basketball, softball, volleyball. **Team name:** Spartans.

Student services. Adult student services, chaplain/spiritual director, career counseling, student employment services, financial aid counseling, personal counseling, placement for graduates, veterans' counselor. **Physically disabled:** Services for visually, hearing impaired.

Contact. E-mail: admissions@mobap.edu
Phone: (314) 392-2290 Toll-free number: (877) 434-1115
Fax: (314) 392-2292
Terry Cruse, Director of Admissions, Missouri Baptist University, One College Park Drive, St. Louis, MO 63141-8698

Missouri Southern State University

Joplin, Missouri
www.mssu.edu **CB code: 6322**

- Public 4-year university and liberal arts college
- Commuter campus in large town
- 5,189 degree-seeking undergraduates: 26% part-time, 60% women
- 45 degree-seeking graduate students
- 96% of applicants admitted
- 33% graduate within 6 years

General. Founded in 1937. Regionally accredited. Extension courses offered in Lamar, Monett, Nevada (evening only), limited weekend courses. Television and online courses offered. **Degrees:** 673 bachelor's, 125 associate awarded; master's offered. **Location:** 138 miles from Kansas City, 126 miles from Tulsa, Oklahoma. **Calendar:** Semester, extensive summer session. **Full-time faculty:** 215 total; 58% have terminal degrees, 10% minority, 40% women. **Part-time faculty:** 89 total; 17% have terminal degrees, 4% minority, 48% women. **Class size:** 55% < 20, 45% 20-39, less than 1% 40-49. **Special facilities:** Biology pond, crime lab, child development center, small business development center, indoor "livefire" firearms range, performing arts center, greenhouse, law library, cyber coffee shop.

Freshman class profile. 1,382 applied, 1,330 admitted, 1,055 enrolled.

Mid 50% test scores		**Rank in top tenth:**	14%
ACT composite:	19-25	**End year in good standing:**	70%
GPA 3.75 or higher:	25%	**Return as sophomores:**	61%
GPA 3.50-3.74:	17%	**Out-of-state:**	14%
GPA 3.0-3.49:	29%	**Live on campus:**	75%
GPA 2.0-2.99:	27%	**Fraternities:**	1%
Rank in top quarter:	39%	**Sororities:**	1%

Basis for selection. Minimum 18 ACT or rank in upper 50% of class. ACT recommended. International students must score in 75th percentile on Michigan Test for English as foreign language.

High school preparation. 16 units required. Required and recommended units include English 4, mathematics 3, social studies 3, science 2 (laboratory 1), foreign language 2 and academic electives 3. 1 unit from visual arts, music, dance or theater required.

2008-2009 Annual costs. Tuition/fees: $4,816; $9,106 out-of-state. Room/board: $5,382. Books/supplies: $800. Personal expenses: $1,500.

2008-2009 Financial aid. Need-based: 572 full-time freshmen applied for aid; 445 were judged to have need; 439 of these received aid. Average need met was 87%. Average scholarship/grant was $2,108; average loan $2,311. 41% of total undergraduate aid awarded as scholarships/grants, 59% as loans/jobs. **Non-need-based:** Awarded to 2,085 full-time undergraduates, including 518 freshmen. Scholarships awarded for academics, art, athletics, leadership, minority status, music/drama.

Application procedures. Admission: Priority date 8/1; no deadline. $15 fee. Admission notification on a rolling basis beginning on or about 9/1. **Financial aid:** Priority date 5/1; no closing date. FAFSA, institutional form required. Applicants notified by 3/1; Applicants notified on a rolling basis starting 2/15; must reply within 3 week(s) of notification.

Academics. Special study options: Accelerated study, combined bachelor's/graduate degree, cooperative education, distance learning, double major, dual enrollment of high school students, ESL, exchange student, honors, independent study, internships, liberal arts/career combination, study abroad, teacher certification program, weekend college. **Credit/placement by examination:** AP, CLEP, IB, SAT, ACT, institutional tests. **Support services:** Learning center, reduced course load, remedial instruction, study skills assistance, tutoring, writing center.

Honors college/program. Entrance by invitation. Approximately 30 students admitted each year. Application closing date March 1. Require 28 ACT or 3.5 GPA.

Majors. Biology: General, bacteriology, biochemistry, biotechnology, conservation, ecology, genetics, marine. **Business:** General, accounting, finance, financial planning, international, management science, marketing, operations. **Communications:** General, media studies. **Computer sciences:** General, computer science, information systems, programming. **Conservation:** General, management/policy. **Education:** General, art, biology, business, chemistry, early childhood, elementary, English, ESL, foreign languages, French, German, health, history, mathematics, middle, multi-level teacher, music, physical, physics, reading, science, secondary, social science, Spanish, special, speech, technology/industrial arts. **Engineering:** Industrial. **Foreign languages:** French, German, Spanish. **Health:** Environmental health, nursing (RN), predental, premedicine, prepharmacy, preveterinary. **History:** General. **Math:** General, computational. **Parks/recreation:** Health/fitness. **Physical sciences:** Chemistry, physics. **Protective services:** Forensics, law enforcement admin. **Psychology:** General. **Social sciences:** General, international relations, political science, sociology. **Visual/performing arts:** Dramatic, studio arts.

Most popular majors. Biology 6%, business/marketing 25%, education 16%, health sciences 10%, liberal arts 6%, security/protective services 11%.

Computing on campus. 522 workstations in library, computer center, student center. Dormitories wired for high-speed internet access and linked to campus network. Commuter students can connect to campus network. Online library, helpline, repair service, student web hosting, wireless network available.

Student life. Freshman orientation: Mandatory, $30 fee. Preregistration for classes offered. One-day introduction to campus and enrollment process during summer, plus 8-week course. **Policies:** Freshmen must live in residence halls if space is available, unless married, residing with relatives, or excused by the Coordinator of Student Housing. **Housing:** Guaranteed on-campus for freshmen. Coed dorms, single-sex dorms, special housing for disabled, apartments, wellness housing available. $150 fully refundable deposit. **Activities:** Bands, campus ministries, choral groups, dance, drama, film society, international student organizations, literary magazine, music ensembles, Model UN, musical theater, radio station, student government, student newspaper, symphony orchestra, TV station, over 90 clubs and organizations available.

Athletics. NCAA. **Intercollegiate:** Baseball M, basketball, cheerleading, cross-country, football (tackle) M, golf M, soccer, softball W, tennis W, track and field, volleyball W. **Intramural:** Basketball, football (non-tackle), golf, racquetball, soccer, softball, table tennis, tennis, volleyball. **Team name:** Lions, Lady Lions.

Student services. Adult student services, alcohol/substance abuse counseling, career counseling, services for economically disadvantaged, student employment services, financial aid counseling, health services, on-campus daycare, personal counseling, placement for graduates, veterans' counselor. **Physically disabled:** Services for visually, hearing impaired. **Learning disabled:** Comprehensive services available.

Contact. E-mail: admissions@mssu.edu
Phone: (417) 625-9378 Toll-free number: (866) 818-6778
Fax: (417) 659-4429
Derek Skaggs, Director of Enrollment Services, Missouri Southern State University, 3950 East Newman Road, Joplin, MO 64801-1595

Missouri State University

Springfield, Missouri
www.missouristate.edu **CB code: 6665**

- Public 4-year university
- Commuter campus in small city
- 14,493 degree-seeking undergraduates: 12% part-time, 55% women, 3% African American, 2% Asian American, 2% Hispanic American, 1% Native American, 2% international
- 2,837 degree-seeking graduate students
- 74% of applicants admitted
- SAT or ACT (ACT writing optional) required
- 53% graduate within 6 years

General. Founded in 1906. Regionally accredited. **Degrees:** 2,795 bachelor's awarded; master's, doctoral offered. **ROTC:** Army. **Location:** 180 miles from Kansas City. **Calendar:** Semester, extensive summer session. **Full-time faculty:** 737 total; 80% have terminal degrees, 8% minority, 43% women. **Part-time faculty:** 356 total; 26% have terminal degrees, 3% minority, 49% women. **Class size:** 39% < 20, 44% 20-39, 8% 40-49, 7% 50-99, 2% >100. **Special facilities:** Observatory, 125-acre agriculture research and demonstration center, summer tent theater, archaeological research center, social research center, agriculture research center.

Freshman class profile. 7,486 applied, 5,552 admitted, 2,568 enrolled.

Mid 50% test scores		**End year in good standing:**	75%
ACT composite:	21-27	**Return as sophomores:**	73%
GPA 3.75 or higher:	39%	**Out-of-state:**	10%
GPA 3.50-3.74:	16%	**Live on campus:**	54%
GPA 3.0-3.49:	29%	**International:**	1%
GPA 2.0-2.99:	16%	**Fraternities:**	24%
Rank in top quarter:	49%	**Sororities:**	30%
Rank in top tenth:	23%		

Basis for selection. Applicant must have 108 or higher on selection index (sum of high school class rank percentile and test score percentile).

High school preparation. College-preparatory program required. 16 units required. Required units include English 4, mathematics 3, social studies 3, science 2 (laboratory 1), visual/performing arts 1 and academic electives 3. Academic electives must include foreign language.

2008-2009 Annual costs. Tuition/fees: $6,256; $11,536 out-of-state. Room/board: $5,576. Books/supplies: $900. Personal expenses: $3,500.

2008-2009 Financial aid. **Need-based:** 2,032 full-time freshmen applied for aid; 1,372 were judged to have need; 1,325 of these received aid. Average need met was 67%. Average scholarship/grant was $5,343; average loan $2,908. 43% of total undergraduate aid awarded as scholarships/grants, 57% as loans/jobs. **Non-need-based:** Scholarships awarded for academics, alumni affiliation, art, athletics, job skills, leadership, minority status, music/drama, ROTC, state residency. **Additional information:** Extensive scholarship program offered to freshmen and transfer students. Out-of-state fee stipends available. Student employment service available to assist students in securing employment on campus and in community.

Application procedures. **Admission:** Priority date 3/1; deadline 7/20 (postmark date). $35 fee, may be waived for applicants with need. Admission notification on a rolling basis beginning on or about 9/1. **Financial aid:** Priority date 5/31; no closing date. FAFSA required. Applicants notified by 6/1.

Academics. **Special study options:** Accelerated study, combined bachelor's/graduate degree, cooperative education, distance learning, double major, dual enrollment of high school students, ESL, exchange student, honors, independent study, internships, student-designed major, study abroad, teacher certification program. London semester. **Credit/placement by examination:** AP, CLEP, IB, SAT, ACT, institutional tests. **Support services:** Learning center, pre-admission summer program, study skills assistance, tutoring, writing center.

Honors college/program. Minimum 27 ACT or 1220 (exclusive of Writing) SAT and rank in top 10th percentile of class required. Approximately 250 to 300 freshmen enroll each year. Program includes freshman honors seminar, honors general education courses, departmental honors courses, senior project, senior honors seminar.

Majors. **Agriculture:** General, agribusiness operations, agronomy, animal sciences, horticultural science. **Architecture:** Urban/community planning. **Biology:** General, cellular/molecular. **Business:** General, accounting, business admin, construction management, finance, hospitality admin, insurance, logistics, management information systems, marketing. **Communications:** General, journalism, media studies. **Computer sciences:** Computer science. **Conservation:** Wildlife. **Education:** Agricultural, art, biology, business, chemistry, early childhood, elementary, English, family/consumer sciences, French, German, history, Latin, mathematics, middle, music, physical, physics, school counseling, science, Spanish, special, technology/industrial arts. **Engineering technology:** Industrial management. **Family/consumer sciences:** Clothing/textiles, family studies, housing. **Foreign languages:** French, German, Latin, Spanish. **Health:** Athletic training, audiology/speech pathology, clinical lab science, dietetics, nursing (RN), preop/surgical nursing, radiologic technology/medical imaging, respiratory therapy technology. **History:** General. **Interdisciplinary:** Gerontology. **Liberal arts:** Humanities. **Math:** General. **Parks/recreation:** General, exercise sciences. **Philosophy/religion:** Philosophy, religion. **Physical sciences:** Chemistry, geology, physics. **Psychology:** General. **Public administration:** General, social work. **Social sciences:** Anthropology, cartography, criminology, economics, geography, political science, sociology. **Visual/performing arts:** General, art history/conservation, dance, design, dramatic, music performance, studio arts. **Other:** Electronic arts, Engineering physics, Entertainment management, Speech and theatre education.

Most popular majors. Business/marketing 34%, communications/journalism 6%, education 14%, psychology 6%, social sciences 7%.

Computing on campus. 1,800 workstations in dormitories, library, computer center, student center. Dormitories wired for high-speed internet access and linked to campus network. Commuter students can connect to campus network. Online library, helpline, student web hosting, wireless network available.

Student life. **Freshman orientation:** Mandatory, $40 fee. Preregistration for classes offered. 2-day program held during summer. **Housing:** Guaranteed on-campus for freshmen. Coed dorms, special housing for disabled, apartments, fraternity/sorority housing available. $100 fully refundable deposit, deadline 7/1. Nontraditional, upper-class, honor, transfer student housing available. **Activities:** Bands, campus ministries, choral groups, dance, drama, film society, international student organizations, literary magazine, music ensembles, Model UN, musical theater, opera, radio station, student government, student newspaper, symphony orchestra, TV station, nearly 300 student organizations available.

Athletics. NCAA. **Intercollegiate:** Baseball M, basketball, cross-country, field hockey W, football (tackle) M, golf, soccer, softball W, swimming, track and field, volleyball W. **Intramural:** Basketball, bowling, football (non-tackle), golf, racquetball, soccer, softball, table tennis, tennis, track and field, volleyball, weight lifting, wrestling. **Team name:** Bears.

Student services. Adult student services, alcohol/substance abuse counseling, chaplain/spiritual director, career counseling, services for economically disadvantaged, student employment services, financial aid counseling, health services, legal services, minority student services, on-campus daycare, personal counseling, placement for graduates, veterans' counselor. **Physically disabled:** Services for visually, speech, hearing impaired. **Learning disabled:** Comprehensive services available.

Contact. E-mail: info@missouristate.edu
Phone: (417) 836-5517 Toll-free number: (800) 492-7900
Fax: (417) 836-6334
Donald Simpson, Director of Admissions, Missouri State University, 901 South National Avenue, Springfield, MO 65897

Missouri Technical School

St. Louis, Missouri
www.motech.edu **CB code: 2383**

- For-profit 4-year engineering and technical college
- Commuter campus in very large city
- 114 degree-seeking undergraduates
- 94% of applicants admitted
- Interview required

General. Founded in 1932. Accredited by ACCSCT. **Degrees:** 14 bachelor's, 25 associate awarded. **Location:** 20 miles from downtown. **Calendar:** Semester, extensive summer session. **Full-time faculty:** 6 total; 83% have terminal degrees. **Part-time faculty:** 9 total.

Freshman class profile. 17 applied, 16 admitted, 11 enrolled.

Basis for selection. Test scores and interview most important. Minimum ACT score of 20 required. TOEFL required for international students. Internal admissions test or ACT score of 20 or higher needed for admission.

High school preparation. Math and science courses recommended.

2008-2009 Annual costs. Tuition is $500 per credit hour. Fees are $95 per 2-month term. Books/supplies: $800.

Financial aid. All financial aid based on need.

Application procedures. Admission: No deadline. $125 fee. Admission notification on a rolling basis. **Financial aid:** No deadline. FAFSA, institutional form required. Applicants notified on a rolling basis.

Academics. Special study options: Accelerated study, double major, independent study, internships. **Credit/placement by examination:** CLEP, IB, institutional tests. **Support services:** Reduced course load, remedial instruction, study skills assistance, tutoring.

Majors. Computer sciences: Computer graphics, computer science, information systems, LAN/WAN management, programming, systems analysis. **Engineering:** Computer, electrical, software. **Engineering technology:** Electrical. **Health:** Substance abuse counseling.

Computing on campus. 120 workstations in library, computer center, student center. Commuter students can connect to campus network. Helpline, repair service available.

Student life. Freshman orientation: Mandatory. Preregistration for classes offered. Held for 2 hours on Saturday before the term starts. **Housing:** Single-sex dorms, wellness housing available. $175 deposit. Apartment housing available, must be applied for. **Activities:** Student government, student newspaper.

Student services. Adult student services, alcohol/substance abuse counseling, career counseling, student employment services, financial aid counseling, placement for graduates. **Physically disabled:** Services for visually, hearing impaired.

Contact. Phone: (314) 569-3600 Toll-free number: (800) 280-3600
Fax: (314) 569-1167
Director of Admissions, Missouri Technical School, 1167 Corporate Lake Drive, St. Louis, MO 63132-1716

Missouri University of Science and Technology

Rolla, Missouri **CB member**
www.mst.edu **CB code: 6876**

- Public 4-year university
- Residential campus in large town
- 4,874 degree-seeking undergraduates: 4% part-time, 22% women, 5% African American, 3% Asian American, 2% Hispanic American, 1% Native American, 3% international
- 1,434 degree-seeking graduate students
- 92% of applicants admitted
- SAT or ACT (ACT writing optional) required
- 61% graduate within 6 years

General. Founded in 1870. Regionally accredited. **Degrees:** 910 bachelor's awarded; master's, doctoral offered. **ROTC:** Army, Naval, Air Force. **Location:** 100 miles from St. Louis, 100 miles from Springfield. **Calendar:** Semester, extensive summer session. **Full-time faculty:** 363 total; 88% have terminal degrees, 26% minority, 19% women. **Part-time faculty:** 83 total; 45% have terminal degrees, 17% minority, 34% women. **Class size:** 36% < 20, 38% 20-39, 13% 40-49, 9% 50-99, 4% >100. **Special facilities:** Computerized manufacturing system, nuclear reactor, observatory, experimental mine, museum of rocks, minerals, and gemstones, centers for environmental research, virtual reality laboratory, student design team center, wind tunnel.

Freshman class profile. 2,379 applied, 2,180 admitted, 1,046 enrolled.

Mid 50% test scores		**Rank in top quarter:**	72%
SAT critical reading:	540-660	**Rank in top tenth:**	39%
SAT math:	610-700	**Return as sophomores:**	87%
ACT composite:	24-30	**Out-of-state:**	22%
GPA 3.75 or higher:	41%	**Live on campus:**	95%
GPA 3.50-3.74:	24%	**International:**	3%
GPA 3.0-3.49:	25%	**Fraternities:**	21%
GPA 2.0-2.99:	10%	**Sororities:**	21%

Basis for selection. Admission based on secondary school record, class rank, and standardized test scores. Recommendations considered. ACT or SAT score percentage, plus high school class rank percentile should equal 120 (minimum). Exceptions may be made on an individual basis. Campus visit and personal statement encouraged. **Homeschooled:** Transcript of courses and grades required. Must submit a standardized test score. **Learning Disabled:** Should submit voluntary declaration of disability to receive accommodation.

High school preparation. College-preparatory program required. 17 units required. Required units include English 4, mathematics 4, social studies 3, science 3 (laboratory 1) and foreign language 2. One fine arts required. Foreign language units must be in same language.

2008-2009 Annual costs. Tuition/fees: $8,488; $19,579 out-of-state. Room/board: $7,035. Books/supplies: $900. Personal expenses: $2,256.

2007-2008 Financial aid. Need-based: 799 full-time freshmen applied for aid; 616 were judged to have need; 616 of these received aid. Average need met was 46%. Average scholarship/grant was $5,227; average loan $3,893. 58% of total undergraduate aid awarded as scholarships/grants, 42% as loans/jobs. **Non-need-based:** Awarded to 1,439 full-time undergraduates, including 550 freshmen. Scholarships awarded for academics, alumni affiliation, athletics, job skills, leadership, minority status, music/drama, religious affiliation, ROTC, state residency.

Application procedures. Admission: Priority date 12/1; deadline 7/1 (postmark date). $35 fee, may be waived for applicants with need. Admission notification on a rolling basis beginning on or about 10/1. Must reply by May 1 or within 3 week(s) if notified thereafter. **Financial aid:** Priority date 3/1; no closing date. FAFSA required. Applicants notified on a rolling basis; must reply within 3 week(s) of notification.

Academics. Special study options: Accelerated study, combined bachelor's/graduate degree, cooperative education, distance learning, double major, dual enrollment of high school students, ESL, honors, independent study, internships, liberal arts/career combination, student-designed major, study abroad, teacher certification program. **Credit/placement by examination:** AP, CLEP, IB, institutional tests. **Support services:** Learning center, pre-admission summer program, reduced course load, study skills assistance, tutoring, writing center.

Majors. Biology: General, biochemistry, biophysics. **Business:** General, business admin, management information systems. **Computer sciences:** General, computer science, information systems, information technology. **Engineering:** Aerospace, architectural, ceramic, chemical, civil, computer, electrical, environmental, geological, mechanical, mechanics, metallurgical, mining, nuclear, petroleum, polymer. **Engineering technology:** Industrial management. **Health:** Predental, premedicine. **History:** General. **Legal studies:** Prelaw. **Math:** Applied. **Philosophy/religion:** Philosophy. **Physical sciences:** Chemistry, geochemistry, geology, geophysics, physics. **Psychology:** General. **Social sciences:** Economics.

Most popular majors. Computer/information sciences 9%, engineering/engineering technologies 72%.

Computing on campus. PC or laptop required. 812 workstations in dormitories, library, computer center. Dormitories wired for high-speed internet access and linked to campus network. Commuter students can connect to campus network. Online course registration, online library, helpline, repair service, student web hosting, wireless network available.

Student life. Freshman orientation: Mandatory, $135 fee. Preregistration for classes offered. Program includes meetings with advisers and placement testing. **Housing:** Guaranteed on-campus for freshmen. Coed dorms, special housing for disabled, apartments, cooperative housing, fraternity/sorority housing, wellness housing available. $160 partly refundable deposit, deadline 6/1. Special accommodations for disabled students in co-ed dormitories. **Activities:** Bands, campus ministries, choral groups, dance, drama, international student organizations, literary magazine, music ensembles, musical theater, radio station, student government, student newspaper, symphony orchestra, over 200 student groups avaliable.

Athletics. NCAA. **Intercollegiate:** Baseball M, basketball, cheerleading, cross-country, football (tackle) M, soccer, softball W, swimming M, track and field, volleyball W. **Intramural:** Badminton, basketball, bowling, cross-country, football (non-tackle), golf, racquetball, soccer, softball, swimming, table tennis, tennis, track and field, volleyball, weight lifting. **Team name:** Miners.

Student services. Adult student services, alcohol/substance abuse counseling, career counseling, student employment services, financial aid counseling, health services, legal services, minority student services, personal counseling, placement for graduates, women's services. **Physically disabled:** Services for visually, speech, hearing impaired. **Learning disabled:** Comprehensive services available.

Contact. E-mail: admissions@mst.edu
Phone: (573) 341-4164 Toll-free number: (800) 522-0938
Fax: (573) 341-4082
Rance Larsen, Director of Admissions, Missouri University of Science and Technology, 106 Parker Hall, Rolla, MO 65409

Missouri Valley College

Marshall, Missouri
www.moval.edu **CB code: 6413**

- Private 4-year liberal arts college affiliated with Presbyterian Church (USA)
- Residential campus in large town
- 1,400 degree-seeking undergraduates
- 30% of applicants admitted
- SAT or ACT (ACT writing optional) required

General. Founded in 1889. Regionally accredited. **Degrees:** 215 bachelor's, 1 associate awarded. **ROTC:** Army. **Location:** 75 miles from Kansas City. **Calendar:** Semester, limited summer session. **Full-time faculty:** 70 total. **Part-time faculty:** 50 total. **Class size:** 45% < 20, 54% 20-39, less than 1% 40-49, less than 1% 50-99.

Freshman class profile. 2,055 applied, 612 admitted, 419 enrolled.

Mid 50% test scores			
SAT critical reading:	410-490	Rank in top tenth:	6%
SAT math:	440-550	Out-of-state:	25%
ACT composite:	17-20	Live on campus:	90%
Rank in top quarter:	19%	Fraternities:	25%
		Sororities:	25%

Basis for selection. Interview, recommendations, high school record, test scores important; extracurricular activities, personal attributes also important; class rank considered. Essay recommended for academically weak students. Audition recommended for drama majors; portfolio recommended for art majors. **Homeschooled:** GED in addition to acceptable ACT/SAT score is sufficient.

High school preparation. Recommended units include English 4, mathematics 3, social studies 1, history 3, science 3 and foreign language 1.

2008-2009 Annual costs. Tuition/fees: $15,950. Room/board: $6,050. Books/supplies: $1,300. Personal expenses: $2,900.

Financial aid. Non-need-based: Scholarships awarded for academics, state residency.

Application procedures. Admission: Priority date 3/1; no deadline. $15 fee, may be waived for applicants with need, free for online applicants. Admission notification on a rolling basis. Must reply by May 1 or within 4 week(s) if notified thereafter. **Financial aid:** Priority date 3/1; no closing date. FAFSA required. Applicants notified on a rolling basis starting 2/1; must reply within 6 week(s) of notification.

Academics. Special study options: Combined bachelor's/graduate degree, double major, dual enrollment of high school students, ESL, external degree, independent study, internships, liberal arts/career combination, student-designed major, teacher certification program. **Credit/placement by examination:** AP, CLEP, SAT, ACT, institutional tests. 30 credit hours maximum toward bachelor's degree. **Support services:** Learning center, reduced course load, remedial instruction, study skills assistance, tutoring, writing center.

Majors. Biology: General. **Business:** Accounting, business admin. **Communications:** Media studies. **Computer sciences:** General. **Education:** Elementary, multiple handicapped, physical, secondary, social studies, special. **Health:** Athletic training, substance abuse counseling. **History:** General. **Interdisciplinary:** Biological/physical sciences. **Liberal arts:** Arts/sciences. **Math:** General. **Parks/recreation:** Exercise sciences, facilities management. **Protective services:** Law enforcement admin. **Psychology:** General. **Public administration:** General. **Social sciences:** Economics, political science, sociology. **Visual/performing arts:** Art, dramatic.

Computing on campus. 172 workstations in library, computer center, student center. Dormitories wired for high-speed internet access and linked to campus network. Commuter students can connect to campus network. Online library, helpline, repair service, wireless network available.

Student life. Freshman orientation: Available. Preregistration for classes offered. **Housing:** Guaranteed on-campus for all undergraduates. Single-sex dorms, apartments, fraternity/sorority housing available. **Activities:** Bands, choral groups, dance, drama, film society, literary magazine, music ensembles, musical theater, radio station, student government, student newspaper, symphony orchestra, TV station, international student organization, American Humanics, minority student union, Fellowship of Christian Athletes, student council for exceptional children.

Athletics. NAIA. **Intercollegiate:** Baseball M, basketball, cheerleading, cross-country, football (tackle) M, golf, rodeo, soccer, softball W, tennis, track and field, volleyball, wrestling. **Intramural:** Badminton, baseball M, basketball, bowling, cross-country, football (non-tackle), soccer, softball, table tennis, track and field, volleyball, weight lifting. **Team name:** Vikings.

Student services. Alcohol/substance abuse counseling, chaplain/spiritual director, career counseling, student employment services, financial aid counseling, health services, placement for graduates, veterans' counselor.

Contact. E-mail: admissions@moval.edu
Phone: (660) 831-4114 Fax: (660) 831-4233
Tennille Langdon, Director of Admissions, Missouri Valley College, 500 East College Street, Marshall, MO 65340

Missouri Western State University

St. Joseph, Missouri
www.missouriwestern.edu **CB code: 6625**

- Public 4-year business and liberal arts college
- Commuter campus in small city
- 5,000 degree-seeking undergraduates

General. Founded in 1915. Regionally accredited. **Degrees:** 587 bachelor's, 52 associate awarded. **ROTC:** Army. **Location:** 48 miles from Kansas City. **Calendar:** Semester, extensive summer session. **Full-time faculty:** 187 total. **Part-time faculty:** 140 total. **Class size:** 40% < 20, 53% 20-39, 3% 40-49, 4% 50-99, less than 1% >100. **Special facilities:** Biology nature study area, planetarium.

Freshman class profile.

Mid 50% test scores			
ACT composite:	16-22	Out-of-state:	6%
		Live on campus:	46%

Basis for selection. Open admission, but selective for some programs. School record, test scores, interview, recommendations important for education, nursing, mathematics, computer science, social work applicants. Special talents important for music, art applicants. High school units mandated by state law may vary by program. Interview required for education, nursing, social work programs. Portfolio recommended for art majors, audition recommended for music majors.

2008-2009 Annual costs. Tuition/fees: $5,460; $9,688 out-of-state. Room/board: $5,868. Books/supplies: $800. Personal expenses: $3,200.

2007-2008 Financial aid. Non-need-based: Scholarships awarded for academics, alumni affiliation, art, athletics, job skills, leadership, minority status, music/drama, state residency.

Application procedures. Admission: Priority date 7/15; deadline 6/1. $15 fee, may be waived for applicants with need. Admission notification on a rolling basis. **Financial aid:** Closing date 3/1. FAFSA, institutional form required. Applicants notified on a rolling basis starting 4/5; must reply within 3 week(s) of notification.

Academics. Special study options: Combined bachelor's/graduate degree, distance learning, double major, dual enrollment of high school students, honors, internships, liberal arts/career combination, teacher certification program, weekend college. **Credit/placement by examination:** AP, CLEP, institutional tests. 30 credit hours maximum toward associate degree, 30 toward bachelor's. **Support services:** Learning center, pre-admission summer program, reduced course load, remedial instruction, study skills assistance, tutoring, writing center.

Majors. **Biology:** General, biochemistry. **Business:** Accounting, business admin, finance, marketing. **Communications:** General. **Computer sciences:** General, information systems. **Education:** Art, elementary, English, French, middle, music, Spanish. **Engineering technology:** Computer, construction, electrical. **Foreign languages:** French, Spanish. **Health:** Clinical lab technology, nursing (RN). **History:** General. **Interdisciplinary:** Natural sciences. **Liberal arts:** Arts/sciences. **Math:** General. **Parks/recreation:** Facilities management, health/fitness. **Physical sciences:** Chemistry. **Protective services:** Criminal justice. **Psychology:** General. **Public administration:** Social work. **Social sciences:** Economics, political science. **Visual/performing arts:** Art, graphic design.

Computing on campus. 300 workstations in dormitories, library, computer center, student center. Dormitories linked to campus network. Commuter students can connect to campus network. Online course registration available.

Student life. **Freshman orientation:** Available, $60 fee. Preregistration for classes offered. **Housing:** Coed dorms, apartments, fraternity/sorority housing available. $100 deposit. **Activities:** Bands, choral groups, dance, drama, music ensembles, musical theater, student government, student newspaper, symphony orchestra, over 70 organizations.

Athletics. NCAA. **Intercollegiate:** Baseball M, basketball, football (tackle) M, golf, soccer W, softball W, tennis W, volleyball W, wrestling M. **Intramural:** Archery, badminton, baseball M, basketball, bowling, golf, handball, racquetball, rugby M, soccer M, softball, table tennis, tennis, volleyball. **Team name:** Griffons.

Student services. Adult student services, alcohol/substance abuse counseling, career counseling, student employment services, financial aid counseling, health services, minority student services, on-campus daycare, personal counseling, placement for graduates, veterans' counselor.

Contact. E-mail: admissions@mwsc.edu
Phone: (816) 271-4200 Toll-free number: (800) 662-7041
Fax: (816) 271-5833
Howard McCauley, Director of Admissions, Missouri Western State University, 4525 Downs Drive, St. Joseph, MO 64507

National American University: Kansas City

Independence, Missouri
www.national.edu **CB code: 5357**

- For-profit 4-year university
- Commuter campus in large city
- 422 degree-seeking undergraduates
- Interview required

General. Founded in 1941. Regionally accredited. **Degrees:** 9 bachelor's, 8 associate awarded. **Location:** 8 miles from downtown. **Calendar:** Quarter, extensive summer session. **Full-time faculty:** 2 total. **Part-time faculty:** 36 total.

Basis for selection. Open admission.

Financial aid. All financial aid based on need.

Application procedures. **Admission:** No deadline. $25 fee. Admission notification on a rolling basis. **Financial aid:** No deadline. FAFSA, institutional form required. Applicants notified on a rolling basis starting 6/4.

Academics. **Special study options:** Accelerated study, distance learning, double major, independent study, internships, liberal arts/career combination. **Credit/placement by examination:** CLEP, institutional tests. **Support services:** Learning center, study skills assistance, tutoring.

Majors. **Business:** Accounting, business admin, management information systems, marketing. **Computer sciences:** Information systems. **Health:** Nursing (RN). **Legal studies:** Paralegal.

Computing on campus. 50 workstations in computer center. Online library available.

Student life. **Freshman orientation:** Mandatory. Preregistration for classes offered. **Activities:** Student government, student newspaper.

Athletics. **Team name:** Mavericks.

Student services. Adult student services, career counseling, student employment services, financial aid counseling, placement for graduates.

Contact. Phone: (866) 628-1288 Fax: (816) 412-7705
Amy King, Director of Admissions, National American University: Kansas City, 3620 Arrowhead Avenue, Independence, MO 64057

Northwest Missouri State University

Maryville, Missouri
www.nwmissouri.edu **CB code: 6488**

- Public 4-year university
- Residential campus in large town
- 5,506 degree-seeking undergraduates: 5% part-time, 55% women
- 1,121 graduate students
- 76% of applicants admitted
- SAT or ACT (ACT writing optional) required
- 52% graduate within 6 years; 99% enter graduate study

General. Founded in 1905. Regionally accredited. **Degrees:** 854 bachelor's, 37 associate awarded; master's offered. **ROTC:** Army. **Location:** 100 miles from Kansas City. **Calendar:** Trimester, extensive summer session. **Full-time faculty:** 253 total; 69% have terminal degrees, 41% women. **Part-time faculty:** 73 total. **Class size:** 42% < 20, 46% 20-39, 4% 40-49, 7% 50-99, less than 1% >100. **Special facilities:** Arboretum, lake-front outdoor education recreation area, laboratory school, dairy operation, swine herd, horticulture complex, experimental farmland.

Freshman class profile. 4,678 applied, 3,542 admitted, 1,429 enrolled.

Mid 50% test scores		**Rank in top quarter:**	40%
SAT critical reading:	420-560	**Rank in top tenth:**	14%
SAT math:	450-610	**Return as sophomores:**	71%
ACT composite:	19-24	**Out-of-state:**	24%
GPA 3.75 or higher:	22%	**Live on campus:**	91%
GPA 3.50-3.74:	19%	**Fraternities:**	24%
GPA 3.0-3.49:	32%	**Sororities:**	18%
GPA 2.0-2.99:	27%		

Basis for selection. School achievement record and test scores most important. Index based on class rank and national test. Audition recommended for dramatic arts and music students; portfolio recommended for art students. **Homeschooled:** Transcript of courses and grades, state high school equivalency certificate required.

High school preparation. College-preparatory program recommended. 16 units required. Required and recommended units include English 4, mathematics 3-4, social studies 3, science 2-3 (laboratory 1), foreign language 2, visual/performing arts 1 and academic electives 3. One fine arts required. Foreign language and additional math and science highly recommended.

2009-2010 Annual costs. Tuition/fees (projected): $6,911; $11,633 out-of-state. Tuition/fees includes free laptop for full-time students and textbook rental for primary textbooks. Room/board: $6,876. Books/supplies: $500. Personal expenses: $1,400.

2007-2008 Financial aid. **Need-based:** 48% of total undergraduate aid awarded as scholarships/grants, 52% as loans/jobs. **Non-need-based:** Scholarships awarded for academics, alumni affiliation, art, athletics, job skills, leadership, minority status, music/drama, state residency.

Application procedures. **Admission:** No deadline. $25 fee, may be waived for applicants with need, free for online applicants. Admission notification on a rolling basis beginning on or about 9/1. **Financial aid:** Priority date 4/1; no closing date. FAFSA required. Applicants notified on a rolling basis starting 3/15; must reply within 2 week(s) of notification.

Academics. **Special study options:** Cross-registration, distance learning, double major, dual enrollment of high school students, ESL, exchange student, honors, independent study, internships, liberal arts/career combination, study abroad, teacher certification program, Washington semester. **Credit/placement by examination:** AP, CLEP, IB, SAT, ACT, institutional tests. **Support services:** Learning center, reduced course load, remedial instruction, study skills assistance, tutoring, writing center.

Majors. **Agriculture:** General, agribusiness operations, agronomy, animal sciences, economics, horticultural science. **Biology:** General, marine. **Business:** Accounting, administrative services, business admin, finance, international, management information systems, managerial economics, marketing. **Communications:** Advertising, journalism, organizational, public relations, radio/tv. **Computer sciences:** General, web page design. **Conservation:** Wildlife. **Education:** Agricultural, art, biology, business, chemistry, curriculum, elementary, English, family/consumer sciences, mathematics, middle, multiple handicapped, music, physical, physics, science, social science, Spanish. **Family/consumer sciences:** Apparel marketing, family studies, institutional food production. **Foreign languages:** Spanish. **Health:** Clinical lab science, dietetics, preveterinary. **History:** General. **Interdisciplinary:** Biological/physical sciences, biopsychology. **Liberal arts:** Humanities. **Math:** General, statistics. **Parks/recreation:** General, facilities management. **Philosophy/religion:** Philosophy. **Physical sciences:** Chemistry, geology, physics. **Psychology:** General, industrial, psychobiology, social. **Public administration:** General. **Social sciences:** Economics, geography, political science, sociology. **Visual/performing arts:** Acting, dramatic, studio arts, theater design. **Other:** Alternative energy, Speech/theatre education.

Most popular majors. Agriculture 8%, business/marketing 25%, communications/journalism 11%, education 19%, psychology 9%.

Computing on campus. 6,450 workstations in dormitories, library, computer center, student center. Dormitories wired for high-speed internet access and linked to campus network. Commuter students can connect to campus network. Online course registration, online library, helpline, repair service, student web hosting, wireless network available.

Student life. Freshman orientation: Mandatory, $100 fee. Preregistration for classes offered. One-day program in June plus 4-day program held before classes begin in August. **Policies:** Alcohol- and smoke-free campus. **Housing:** Guaranteed on-campus for freshmen. Coed dorms, special housing for disabled, apartments, fraternity/sorority housing available. $150 nonrefundable deposit. **Activities:** Bands, choral groups, dance, drama, film society, international student organizations, literary magazine, music ensembles, musical theater, radio station, student government, student newspaper, symphony orchestra, TV station, more than 180 student organizations available.

Athletics. NCAA. **Intercollegiate:** Baseball M, basketball, cheerleading, cross-country, football (tackle) M, golf W, soccer W, softball W, tennis, track and field, volleyball W. **Intramural:** Badminton, basketball, cross-country, football (non-tackle), golf, racquetball, skiing, softball W, swimming, table tennis, tennis, track and field, volleyball. **Team name:** Bearcats.

Student services. Alcohol/substance abuse counseling, chaplain/spiritual director, career counseling, services for economically disadvantaged, student employment services, financial aid counseling, health services, minority student services, personal counseling, placement for graduates. **Physically disabled:** Services for visually, speech, hearing impaired.

Contact. E-mail: admissions@nwmissouri.edu
Phone: (660) 562-1562 Toll-free number: (800) 633-1175
Fax: (660) 562-1121
Beverly Schenkel, Dean of Enrollment Management, Northwest Missouri State University, 800 University Drive, Maryville, MO 64468-6001

Ozark Christian College
Joplin, Missouri
www.occ.edu **CB code: 6542**

- Private 4-year Bible college affiliated with nondenominational tradition
- Residential campus in large town
- 602 degree-seeking undergraduates: 12% part-time, 42% women, 1% African American, 1% Asian American, 1% Hispanic American, 1% Native American, 2% international
- SAT or ACT (ACT writing optional), application essay required
- 38% graduate within 6 years

General. Founded in 1942. Accredited by ABHE. **Degrees:** 121 bachelor's, 8 associate awarded. **Location:** 70 miles from Springfield, 100 miles from Tulsa, Oklahoma. **Calendar:** Semester, limited summer session. **Full-time faculty:** 28 total; 25% have terminal degrees, 7% women. **Part-time faculty:** 39 total; 8% have terminal degrees, 3% minority, 20% women. **Class size:** 67% < 20, 25% 20-39, 5% 40-49, 3% 50-99.

Freshman class profile. 144 enrolled.

Return as sophomores:	80%	**International:**	1%
Live on campus:	90%		

Basis for selection. Secondary school record, test scores, essay important. 2 references required. Audition required for music ministry students. **Homeschooled:** Transcript of courses and grades required. Provide notarized transcript of grades signed by student and parents.

High school preparation. 15 units recommended. Recommended units include English 3, mathematics 2, history 1, science 2 and academic electives 7.

2008-2009 Annual costs. Tuition/fees: $8,188. Room/board: $4,170. Books/supplies: $600. Personal expenses: $1,500.

2007-2008 Financial aid. Need-based: 37% of total undergraduate aid awarded as scholarships/grants, 63% as loans/jobs. **Non-need-based:** Scholarships awarded for academics, leadership.

Application procedures. Admission: Closing date 8/5 (receipt date). $30 fee, may be waived for applicants with need. Admission notification on a rolling basis. Applicant must submit high school transcript through first half of senior year. **Financial aid:** Priority date 4/1; no closing date. FAFSA required. Applicants notified on a rolling basis starting 4/15; must reply within 4 week(s) of notification.

Academics. Special study options: Combined bachelor's/graduate degree, cooperative education, distance learning, double major, independent study, internships. 5-year bachelor's degree program in theology. **Credit/placement by examination:** CLEP, ACT, institutional tests. **Support services:** Learning center, study skills assistance, tutoring.

Majors. Theology: Bible, missionary, religious ed, sacred music, theology.

Computing on campus. 23 workstations in library, computer center, student center. Dormitories wired for high-speed internet access and linked to campus network. Commuter students can connect to campus network. Online library, helpline, repair service, wireless network available.

Student life. Freshman orientation: Mandatory. **Housing:** Guaranteed on-campus for all undergraduates. Single-sex dorms, wellness housing available. $90 deposit, deadline 8/5. **Activities:** Choral groups, drama, music ensembles, musical theater, radio station, student government.

Athletics. NCCAA. **Intercollegiate:** Baseball M, basketball, soccer, volleyball W. **Intramural:** Basketball, racquetball, volleyball. **Team name:** Ambassadors.

Student services. Adult student services, chaplain/spiritual director, career counseling, student employment services, financial aid counseling, health services, personal counseling, placement for graduates, veterans' counselor. **Physically disabled:** Services for hearing impaired.

Contact. E-mail: occadmin@occ.edu
Phone: (417) 624-2518 Fax: (417) 624-0090
Troy Nelson, Director of Admissions, Ozark Christian College, 1111 North Main Street, Joplin, MO 64801

Park University
Parkville, Missouri
www.park.edu **CB code: 6574**

- Private 4-year university
- Commuter campus in small town
- 11,080 degree-seeking undergraduates: 90% part-time, 51% women, 20% African American, 2% Asian American, 16% Hispanic American, 1% Native American, 4% international
- 592 degree-seeking graduate students
- 78% of applicants admitted
- 39% graduate within 6 years

General. Founded in 1875. Regionally accredited. MetroPark School for adult education in Kansas City offers bachelor's degree. School for Extended Learning (SEL) offers degree programs in 21 states. **Degrees:** 2,554 bachelor's, 63 associate awarded; master's offered. **ROTC:** Army. **Location:** 12 miles from downtown Kansas City. **Calendar:** Semester, extensive summer session. **Full-time faculty:** 152 total. **Part-time faculty:** 867 total. **Special facilities:** 700 acres of woodland.

Freshman class profile. 627 applied, 492 admitted, 257 enrolled.

Mid 50% test scores		**Return as sophomores:**	67%
ACT composite:	18-28	**Out-of-state:**	21%
Rank in top quarter:	40%	**Live on campus:**	35%
Rank in top tenth:	8%	**International:**	32%

Basis for selection. GPA (minimum 2.0), followed by test scores and rank in top half of class important. Exceptions considered on individual merit. Students with 3.0 GPA not required to submit SAT/ACT for admission; however, institutional placement test must be substituted. Entering freshmen with GPA of 2.0 to 3.0 must either be in top half of graduating class or submit satisfactory SAT/ACT scores. Interview recommended for academically weak students; audition recommended for music and theater students; portfolio recommended for art students.

High school preparation. 19 units recommended. Recommended units include English 3, mathematics 2, social studies 3, history 1, science 2 (laboratory 1), foreign language 2 and academic electives 6.

2008-2009 Annual costs. Tuition/fees: $8,190. Tuition varies by program and hours taken. Room/board: $5,810. Books/supplies: $1,200. Personal expenses: $2,745.

2007-2008 Financial aid. **Non-need-based:** Scholarships awarded for academics, alumni affiliation, art, athletics, job skills, leadership, minority status, music/drama, religious affiliation, ROTC.

Application procedures. **Admission:** Priority date 4/15; deadline 8/1. $25 fee, may be waived for applicants with need. Admission notification on a rolling basis. **Financial aid:** Priority date 4/1, closing date 8/1. FAFSA, institutional form required. Applicants notified on a rolling basis starting 4/1.

Academics. **Special study options:** Accelerated study, cross-registration, distance learning, double major, dual enrollment of high school students, ESL, honors, independent study, internships, student-designed major, study abroad, teacher certification program, Washington semester, weekend college. **Credit/placement by examination:** AP, CLEP, ACT, institutional tests. **Support services:** Learning center, reduced course load, remedial instruction, study skills assistance, tutoring, writing center.

Majors. **Biology:** General. **Business:** Accounting, accounting/business management, business admin, logistics, management information systems, managerial economics, marketing. **Communications:** General. **Computer sciences:** General, computer science. **Education:** Early childhood, elementary. **Family/consumer sciences:** Child development. **Foreign languages:** Spanish. **Health:** Athletic training. **History:** General. **Interdisciplinary:** Math/computer science, natural sciences. **Legal studies:** General. **Liberal arts:** Arts/sciences. **Math:** General. **Physical sciences:** Chemistry. **Protective services:** Fire services admin, law enforcement admin. **Psychology:** General. **Public administration:** General, social work. **Social sciences:** Economics, geography, political science, sociology. **Transportation:** Aviation management. **Visual/performing arts:** Dramatic, graphic design, interior design, studio arts.

Most popular majors. Business/marketing 66%, psychology 16%, security/protective services 9%.

Computing on campus. 570 workstations in dormitories, library, computer center, student center. Dormitories linked to campus network. Commuter students can connect to campus network. Online course registration available.

Student life. **Freshman orientation:** Mandatory. Preregistration for classes offered. **Housing:** Guaranteed on-campus for freshmen. Coed dorms, apartments available. $100 deposit. **Activities:** Choral groups, drama, literary magazine, radio station, student government, student newspaper, symphony orchestra, service organizations, Christian Fellowship, World Student Union, Brothers and Sisters United, accounting society, Latin American student organization, marketing club, honors club, non-traditional student organization.

Athletics. NAIA. **Intercollegiate:** Baseball M, basketball, cross-country, golf W, soccer, softball W, track and field, volleyball. **Intramural:** Basketball, soccer, softball, volleyball. **Team name:** Pirates.

Student services. Career counseling, student employment services, financial aid counseling, health services, on-campus daycare, personal counseling, placement for graduates, veterans' counselor. **Physically disabled:** Services for visually, speech, hearing impaired.

Contact. E-mail: admissions@park.edu
Phone: (816) 584-6214 Toll-free number: (800) 745-7275
Fax: (816) 741-4462
Cathy Colapietro, Director of Admissions and Student Financial Services, Park University, 8700 NW River Park Drive, Parkville, MO 64152

Research College of Nursing

Kansas City, Missouri
www.researchcollege.edu **CB code: 6612**

- For-profit 4-year nursing college
- Residential campus in very large city
- 302 degree-seeking undergraduates: 1% part-time, 94% women
- 80 degree-seeking graduate students
- 71% of applicants admitted
- SAT or ACT (ACT writing optional) required

General. Founded in 1905. Regionally accredited. Natural science, social science, and liberal arts courses taken at Rockhurst University. Students have access to facilities, organizations, sports and activities on both campuses. Bachelor of Science in Nursing is awarded jointly by Research College of Nursing and Rockhurst University. **Degrees:** 118 bachelor's awarded; master's offered. **ROTC:** Army. **Location:** 5 miles from downtown. **Calendar:** Semester, limited summer session. **Full-time faculty:** 31 total. **Part-time faculty:** 4 total. **Special facilities:** Medical library, 532-bed research medical center.

Freshman class profile. 227 applied, 161 admitted, 50 enrolled.

Mid 50% test scores		Out-of-state:	25%
ACT composite:	22-26	Live on campus:	77%

Basis for selection. Academic record, high school GPA, rank in top half of class, counselor's recommendation, test scores very important. ACT score of 20 required. Interview, high school activities considered. Interview recommended for all; strongly recommended for applicants with ACT scores below 20.

High school preparation. College-preparatory program recommended. 18 units recommended. Recommended units include English 4, mathematics 3, social studies 3, science 4 and foreign language 2. Visual or performing arts also recommended. Mathematics should include algebra II, science should include chemistry.

2008-2009 Annual costs. Tuition/fees: $24,480. Room/board: $6,800. Books/supplies: $720. Personal expenses: $915.

2008-2009 Financial aid. **Non-need-based:** Scholarships awarded for academics, alumni affiliation, leadership. **Additional information:** Financial aid handled by Rockhurst University for freshmen and sophomores.

Application procedures. **Admission:** Priority date 3/1; no deadline. $20 fee, may be waived for applicants with need, free for online applicants. Admission notification on a rolling basis beginning on or about 10/1. Must reply by May 1 or within 4 week(s) if notified thereafter. **Financial aid:** Priority date 3/15; no closing date. FAFSA, institutional form required. Applicants notified on a rolling basis starting 3/15.

Academics. Students admitted into nursing program in freshman year guaranteed place in upper-division nursing courses if academic requirements maintained. **Special study options:** Accelerated study, cross-registration, double major, dual enrollment of high school students, exchange student, honors, independent study, study abroad. **Credit/placement by examination:** AP, CLEP, IB, ACT, institutional tests. 32 credit hours maximum toward bachelor's degree. **Support services:** Learning center, reduced course load, tutoring.

Majors. **Health:** Nursing (RN).

Computing on campus. 300 workstations in dormitories, library, computer center. Dormitories wired for high-speed internet access and linked to campus network. Commuter students can connect to campus network. Online course registration, helpline, wireless network available.

Student life. **Freshman orientation:** Mandatory, $50 fee. Preregistration for classes offered. **Housing:** Guaranteed on-campus for freshmen. Coed dorms, single-sex dorms, apartments, fraternity/sorority housing available. $200 fully refundable deposit. Freshman nursing students not living at home must live on Rockhurst College campus. All other undergraduates may choose to live on Research College campus or at Rockhurst College. **Activities:** Campus ministries, choral groups, drama, music ensembles, musical theater, radio station, student government, student newspaper, Alpha Phi Omega, Black Student Union, Young Republicans, Young Democrats, Missouri Student Nurses Association, National Student Nurses Association, Rockhurst Organization of Collegiate Women.

Athletics. NCAA. **Intercollegiate:** Baseball M, basketball, cross-country, golf, soccer, softball W, tennis, volleyball W. **Intramural:** Basketball, lacrosse, racquetball, rugby, table tennis, volleyball.

Student services. Chaplain/spiritual director, career counseling, student employment services, financial aid counseling, health services, on-campus daycare, personal counseling, placement for graduates, veterans' counselor.

Contact. Phone: (816) 995-2812 Toll-free number: (866) 855-0296
Fax: (816) 995-2813
Lane Ramey, Director of Freshmen Admission, Research College of Nursing, 2525 East Meyer Boulevard, Kansas City, MO 64132-1199

Rockhurst University

Kansas City, Missouri **CB member**
www.rockhurst.edu **CB code: 6611**

- Private 4-year business and liberal arts college affiliated with Roman Catholic Church
- Residential campus in very large city

- 1,578 degree-seeking undergraduates: 9% part-time, 61% women, 5% African American, 3% Asian American, 6% Hispanic American, 1% Native American, 1% international
- 829 degree-seeking graduate students
- 76% of applicants admitted
- SAT or ACT (ACT writing optional) required
- 63% graduate within 6 years; 23% enter graduate study

General. Founded in 1910. Regionally accredited. Students graduate with community service transcript in addition to academic transcript. **Degrees:** 403 bachelor's awarded; master's, doctoral offered. **ROTC:** Army. **Location:** 5 miles from downtown. **Calendar:** Semester, limited summer session. **Full-time faculty:** 129 total; 83% have terminal degrees, 7% minority, 50% women. **Part-time faculty:** 101 total; 35% have terminal degrees, 7% minority, 48% women. **Class size:** 38% < 20, 56% 20-39, 3% 40-49, 3% 50-99, less than 1% >100. **Special facilities:** Science center.

Freshman class profile. 1,943 applied, 1,481 admitted, 358 enrolled.

Mid 50% test scores		**Rank in top quarter:**	57%
SAT critical reading:	500-610	**Rank in top tenth:**	28%
SAT math:	500-660	**End year in good standing:**	97%
ACT composite:	22-28	**Return as sophomores:**	84%
GPA 3.75 or higher:	40%	**Out-of-state:**	59%
GPA 3.50-3.74:	21%	**Live on campus:**	84%
GPA 3.0-3.49:	26%	**International:**	1%
GPA 2.0-2.99:	13%		

Basis for selection. High school GPA, class rank, test scores, recommendations most important; school and community activities considered. Interviews recommended for all students. Essay or personal statement may be required or requested. **Homeschooled:** Transcript of courses and grades, state high school equivalency certificate required. GED requested dependent on quality of grades presented on transcript.

High school preparation. College-preparatory program recommended. 16 units recommended. Recommended units include English 4, mathematics 3, social studies 3, history 2, science 3 (laboratory 3), foreign language 2 and academic electives 4.

2009-2010 Annual costs. Tuition/fees (projected): $25,890. Room/board: $7,080. Books/supplies: $1,400. Personal expenses: $1,029.

2008-2009 Financial aid. Need-based: 356 full-time freshmen applied for aid; 330 were judged to have need; 328 of these received aid. Average need met was 100%. Average scholarship/grant was $6,626; average loan $3,283. 71% of total undergraduate aid awarded as scholarships/grants, 29% as loans/jobs. **Non-need-based:** Awarded to 1,503 full-time undergraduates, including 382 freshmen. Scholarships awarded for academics, alumni affiliation, art, athletics, leadership, music/drama, religious affiliation. **Additional information:** Auditions, portfolios required for some scholarships.

Application procedures. Admission: No deadline. $25 fee, may be waived for applicants with need, free for online applicants. Admission notification on a rolling basis beginning on or about 9/1. Must reply by May 1 or within 2 week(s) if notified thereafter. **Financial aid:** Priority date 3/1, closing date 6/30. FAFSA required. Applicants notified on a rolling basis starting 1/30; must reply within 4 week(s) of notification.

Academics. Core curriculum based on 7 "modes of inquiry," different ways people approach reality to seek truth including artistic, literary, historical, scientific-causal, scientific-relational, philosophical, and theological. **Special study options:** Accelerated study, combined bachelor's/graduate degree, cooperative education, cross-registration, double major, dual enrollment of high school students, exchange student, honors, independent study, internships, liberal arts/career combination, New York semester, study abroad, teacher certification program, Washington semester. **Credit/placement by examination:** AP, CLEP, IB, SAT, ACT, institutional tests. 32 credit hours maximum toward bachelor's degree. **Support services:** Learning center, study skills assistance, tutoring, writing center.

Majors. Biology: General, biochemistry. **Business:** Business admin, communications, nonprofit/public. **Communications:** General. **Education:** Elementary, secondary. **Foreign languages:** French, Spanish. **Health:** Clinical lab science, nursing (RN), speech pathology. **History:** General. **Interdisciplinary:** Global studies. **Math:** General. **Philosophy/religion:** Philosophy, religion. **Physical sciences:** Chemistry, physics. **Psychology:** General. **Public administration:** Community org/advocacy. **Social sciences:** General, economics, political science.

Most popular majors. Biology 8%, business/marketing 22%, health sciences 29%, psychology 11%, social sciences 7%.

Computing on campus. 500 workstations in dormitories, library, computer center, student center. Dormitories wired for high-speed internet access and linked to campus network. Commuter students can connect to campus network. Online course registration, online library, helpline, student web hosting, wireless network available.

Student life. Freshman orientation: Mandatory, $70 fee. Preregistration for classes offered. Programs held 4 days before fall semester begins. Includes participation in community service projects. **Policies:** Full-time unmarried freshmen and sophomores must live on campus if not living with family. **Housing:** Coed dorms, single-sex dorms, special housing for disabled, apartments, fraternity/sorority housing, wellness housing available. $200 nonrefundable deposit. **Activities:** Campus ministries, choral groups, dance, drama, international student organizations, literary magazine, student government, student newspaper, Alpha Phi Omega, Black Student Union, Multicultural Affairs Office, American Humanics, Appalachian Service Project, Peace of the World, Amnesty International, student alumni association.

Athletics. NCAA. **Intercollegiate:** Baseball M, basketball, golf, soccer, softball W, tennis, volleyball W. **Intramural:** Baseball M, basketball, cross-country, football (tackle) M, golf, handball M, racquetball, soccer, softball, table tennis, volleyball, wrestling M. **Team name:** Hawks.

Student services. Alcohol/substance abuse counseling, chaplain/spiritual director, career counseling, student employment services, financial aid counseling, health services, personal counseling, placement for graduates, veterans' counselor.

Contact. E-mail: admission@rockhurst.edu
Phone: (816) 501-4100 Toll-free number: (800) 842-6776
Fax: (816) 501-4241
Lane Ramey, Director of Freshman Admissions, Rockhurst University, 1100 Rockhurst Road, Kansas City, MO 64110-2561

St. Louis Christian College

Florissant, Missouri
www.slcconline.edu **CB code: 0334**

- Private 4-year Bible college affiliated with Christian Churches/Churches of Christ affiliation
- Residential campus in small city
- 303 degree-seeking undergraduates: 15% part-time, 40% women
- ACT (writing optional), application essay required

General. Founded in 1956. Candidate for regional accreditation; also accredited by ABHE. Students highly involved in service and field education. **Degrees:** 36 bachelor's, 18 associate awarded. **Location:** 15 miles from downtown St. Louis. **Calendar:** Semester, limited summer session. **Full-time faculty:** 10 total. **Part-time faculty:** 15 total.

Freshman class profile. 59 enrolled.

Mid 50% test scores		**Out-of-state:**	46%
ACT composite:	20-26	**Live on campus:**	94%

Basis for selection. ACT score, high school class rank, and GPA very important. English and Math placement based on ACT subscores or ACCUPLACER tests. Interview recommended for all. Audition required for religious music students. **Homeschooled:** ACT required, GED recommended.

High school preparation. Recommended units include English 4, mathematics 3, social studies 3, science 3, foreign language 2 and academic electives 4.

2008-2009 Annual costs. Full-time residential students maintaining an acceptable GPA receive full scholarships for tuition; required fees are $1300 annually. Full-time commuter students pay $148 per-credit-hour; required fees, $1300. Room/board: $6,600. Books/supplies: $800. Personal expenses: $600.

2008-2009 Financial aid. Need-based: 33% of total undergraduate aid awarded as scholarships/grants, 67% as loans/jobs. **Non-need-based:** Scholarships awarded for academics, alumni affiliation, leadership, music/drama, religious affiliation.

Application procedures. Admission: Priority date 1/15; deadline 8/1 (receipt date). $15 fee, may be waived for applicants with need. Admission notification on a rolling basis beginning on or about 10/1. **Financial aid:** Closing date 8/1. FAFSA, institutional form required. Applicants notified on a rolling basis starting 7/20; must reply within 2 week(s) of notification.

Academics. Preparation for ministries in preaching, education, youth work, mission fields, music, worship and pre-seminary education. **Special study options:** Cross-registration, internships. **Credit/placement by examination:** CLEP, ACT, institutional tests. 30 credit hours maximum toward associate degree, 30 toward bachelor's. **Support services:** Remedial instruction, tutoring, writing center.

Majors. Education: General. **Theology:** Bible, missionary, religious ed, sacred music, theology.

Computing on campus. 13 workstations in library, computer center. Dormitories linked to campus network.

Student life. **Freshman orientation:** Mandatory, $250 fee. Preregistration for classes offered. Held weekend before first day of class. **Policies:** Students involved in evangelistic activities of area churches. Religious observance required. **Housing:** Guaranteed on-campus for all undergraduates. Single-sex dorms, apartments available. $100 deposit, deadline 8/10. **Activities:** Choral groups, drama, music ensembles, student government, missions interest group, ministry teams.

Athletics. NCCAA. **Intercollegiate:** Baseball M, basketball M, volleyball W. **Intramural:** Baseball M, basketball, softball, tennis, volleyball. **Team name:** Soldiers.

Student services. Adult student services, chaplain/spiritual director, career counseling, student employment services, personal counseling. **Physically disabled:** Services for visually, hearing impaired.

Contact. E-mail: admissions@slcconline.edu
Phone: (314) 837-6777 ext. 8110 Toll-free number: (800) 877-7522
Fax: (314) 837-8291
Carrie Chapman, Director of Admissions, St. Louis Christian College, 1360 Grandview Drive, Florissant, MO 63033

Saint Louis University

St. Louis, Missouri — **CB member**
www.slu.edu — **CB code: 6629**

- Private 4-year university affiliated with Roman Catholic Church
- Residential campus in very large city
- 7,635 degree-seeking undergraduates: 9% part-time, 59% women, 9% African American, 6% Asian American, 3% Hispanic American, 5% international
- 4,823 degree-seeking graduate students
- 72% of applicants admitted
- SAT or ACT (ACT writing optional), application essay required
- 74% graduate within 6 years; 33% enter graduate study

General. Founded in 1818. Regionally accredited. Institution maintains campus with facilities in Madrid, Spain. **Degrees:** 1,538 bachelor's awarded; master's, doctoral, first professional offered. **ROTC:** Army, Air Force. **Location:** Midtown. **Calendar:** Semester, extensive summer session. **Full-time faculty:** 633 total; 90% have terminal degrees, 10% minority, 43% women. **Part-time faculty:** 443 total; 14% have terminal degrees, 8% minority, 55% women. **Class size:** 54% < 20, 37% 20-39, 4% 40-49, 4% 50-99, 2% >100. **Special facilities:** Vatican manuscripts microfilm library, art museums, biological station, entrepreneurial studies center, earthquake research center, supersonic wind tunnel, water tunnel, shock tube, flight simulators, airport, fabrication labs, sculpture/ceramics studio, performing arts center, physiology and gait research labs, practice clinics with actual clients in counseling and family therapy, child development, speech and hearing, psychology, dental, occupational and physical therapy, organic gardening and food service.

Freshman class profile. 10,022 applied, 7,259 admitted, 1,528 enrolled.

Mid 50% test scores		**Rank in top tenth:**	36%
SAT critical reading:	530-640	**End year in good standing:**	92%
SAT math:	540-660	**Return as sophomores:**	84%
ACT composite:	24-29	**Out-of-state:**	63%
GPA 3.75 or higher:	49%	**Live on campus:**	89%
GPA 3.50-3.74:	18%	**International:**	3%
GPA 3.0-3.49:	21%	**Fraternities:**	11%
GPA 2.0-2.99:	12%	**Sororities:**	15%
Rank in top quarter:	65%		

Basis for selection. Secondary school record, standardized test scores important; recommendations, essay, extracurricular activities, character/personal qualities, volunteer work considered. Academic performance is most important for international applicants. Audition recommended for music majors; portfolio recommended for art majors. **Homeschooled:** Appplicants strongly recommended to present 5 academic courses each semester for all four years. Should include 4 years of English, 4 years of mathematics (algebra I & II, and geometry), 3 years each of foreign language, natural science, social science and academic electives. **Learning Disabled:** Students with learning disabilities are responsible for contacting Disabilities Services in order to learn about the accommodation process on campus and to receive academic accommodations within the classroom.

High school preparation. College-preparatory program recommended. 20 units required. Required units include English 4, mathematics 4, social studies 3, science 3, foreign language 3 and academic electives 3.

2008-2009 Annual costs. Tuition/fees: $30,728. Room/board: $8,760. Books/supplies: $1,040. Personal expenses: $3,513.

2007-2008 Financial aid. **Need-based:** 1,241 full-time freshmen applied for aid; 995 were judged to have need; 995 of these received aid. Average need met was 70%. Average scholarship/grant was $16,092; average loan $3,991. 74% of total undergraduate aid awarded as scholarships/grants, 26% as loans/jobs. **Non-need-based:** Awarded to 2,597 full-time undergraduates, including 671 freshmen. Scholarships awarded for academics, art, athletics, leadership, music/drama, religious affiliation, ROTC. **Additional information:** Special assistance for TRIO eligible students applying by the priority date of 3/1; enhanced awards include guarantee of grant aid up to 80% of the cost of attendance for these students.

Application procedures. **Admission:** Closing date 12/1 (receipt date). $25 fee. Admission notification 8/1. Admission notification on a rolling basis beginning on or about 10/1. Must reply by May 1 or within 2 week(s) if notified thereafter. **Financial aid:** Priority date 3/1; no closing date. FAFSA required. Applicants notified on a rolling basis starting 3/1; must reply by 5/1 or within 4 week(s) of notification.

Academics. **Special study options:** Accelerated study, combined bachelor's/graduate degree, cooperative education, cross-registration, distance learning, double major, dual enrollment of high school students, ESL, honors, independent study, internships, liberal arts/career combination, student-designed major, study abroad, teacher certification program. **Credit/placement by examination:** AP, CLEP, IB, SAT, ACT, institutional tests. 30 credit hours maximum toward bachelor's degree. **Support services:** Pre-admission summer program, reduced course load, study skills assistance, tutoring, writing center.

Honors college/program. Admission Requirements: 30 ACT/1320 SAT/3.8 GPA. There are approximately 150 freshman admitted each year. Academic offerings: Honors core classes, honors opportunities in major, senior honors thesis.

Majors. **Area/ethnic studies:** American, women's. **Biology:** General, biochemistry. **Business:** Business admin, human resources, management information systems, management science, marketing, organizational behavior, purchasing. **Communications:** General. **Computer sciences:** General. **Conservation:** Environmental science. **Education:** Multi-level teacher. **Engineering:** Aerospace, biomedical, computer, electrical, mechanical, physics. **Engineering technology:** Aerospace, electrical, industrial management. **Family/consumer sciences:** Food/nutrition. **Foreign languages:** General, classics, French, German, Italian, modern Greek, Russian, Spanish. **Health:** Athletic training, audiology/speech pathology, clinical lab science, cytotechnology, medical radiologic technology/radiation therapy, medical records admin, nuclear medical technology, nursing (RN). **History:** General. **Liberal arts:** Humanities. **Math:** General. **Parks/recreation:** Exercise sciences. **Philosophy/religion:** Philosophy. **Physical sciences:** Atmospheric science, chemistry, geology, geophysics, physics. **Protective services:** Corrections, law enforcement admin. **Psychology:** General. **Public administration:** Social work. **Social sciences:** Economics, international relations, political science, sociology, urban studies. **Theology:** Theology. **Transportation:** Airline/commercial pilot, aviation management. **Visual/performing arts:** Art history/conservation, dramatic, studio arts.

Most popular majors. Biology 6%, business/marketing 23%, communications/journalism 6%, health sciences 17%, social sciences 7%.

Computing on campus. 300 workstations in dormitories, library, computer center, student center. Dormitories wired for high-speed internet access and linked to campus network. Commuter students can connect to campus network. Online course registration, online library, helpline, student web hosting, wireless network available.

Student life. **Freshman orientation:** Mandatory. Preregistration for classes offered. Two day summer program offered seven times prior to fall enrollment. **Housing:** Coed dorms, single-sex dorms, special housing for disabled, apartments, fraternity/sorority housing available. $250 fully refundable deposit, deadline 5/1. Foreign language housing available. **Activities:** Bands, campus ministries, choral groups, dance, drama, film society, international student organizations, literary magazine, music ensembles, Model UN, musical theater, radio station, student government, student newspaper, TV station, Black student alliance, College Democrats, College Republicans, student activities board, Muslim student association, Relay for Life, Amnesty International.

Athletics. NCAA. **Intercollegiate:** Baseball M, basketball, cross-country, diving, field hockey W, soccer, softball W, swimming, tennis, track and field, volleyball W. **Intramural:** Badminton, basketball, bowling, football (non-tackle), golf, handball, racquetball, soccer, softball, squash, swimming, table tennis, tennis, volleyball. **Team name:** Billikens.

Student services. Adult student services, alcohol/substance abuse counseling, chaplain/spiritual director, career counseling, services for economically disadvantaged, student employment services, financial aid counseling, health services, minority student services, personal counseling, veterans' counselor, women's services. **Physically disabled:** Services for visually, speech, hearing impaired.

Contact. E-mail: admitme@slu.edu
Phone: (314) 977-2500 Toll-free number: (800) 758-3678
Fax: (314) 977-7136
Jean Gilman, Dean, Saint Louis University, 221 North Grand Boulevard, St. Louis, MO 63103

St. Luke's College

Kansas City, Missouri
www.saintlukescollege.edu **CB code: 7127**

- Private two-year upper-division nursing college affiliated with Episcopal Church
- Commuter campus in large city
- 18% of applicants admitted
- Application essay, interview required

General. Founded in 1903. Regionally accredited. **Degrees:** 52 bachelor's awarded. **Calendar:** Semester, limited summer session. **Full-time faculty:** 16 total. **Class size:** 100% 20-39. **Special facilities:** Simulated clinical settings for nursing students.

Student profile. 118 degree-seeking undergraduates. 302 applied as first time-transfer students, 55 admitted, 55 enrolled. 100% entered as juniors.

Basis for selection. High school transcript, college transcript, application essay, interview required. Recommendations required. Health care-related work and community service considered. Transfer accepted as juniors.

2009-2010 Annual costs. Tuition/fees (projected): $9,520. Books/supplies: $600.

Financial aid. Need-based: 118 applied for aid; 115 were judged to have need; 115 of these received aid. Average need met was 70%. 84% of total undergraduate aid awarded as scholarships/grants, 16% as loans/jobs.

Application procedures. Admission: Deadline 12/31. $35 fee. Admission notification 3/1. **Financial aid:** FAFSA, institutional form required.

Academics. Special study options: Combined bachelor's/graduate degree. **Credit/placement by examination:** AP, CLEP.

Majors. Health: Nursing (RN).

Computing on campus. 30 workstations in computer center. Helpline available.

Student life. Activities: Student government.

Student services. Career counseling, financial aid counseling, health services, personal counseling.

Contact. E-mail: slc-admissions@saint-lukes.org
Phone: (816) 932-2367 Fax: (816) 932-9064
St. Luke's College, 8320 Ward Parkway, Suite 300, Kansas City, MO 64114

Southeast Missouri State University

Cape Girardeau, Missouri **CB member**
www.semo.edu **CB code: 6655**

- Public 4-year university
- Commuter campus in large town
- 8,632 degree-seeking undergraduates: 19% part-time, 59% women, 9% African American, 1% Asian American, 1% Hispanic American, 1% Native American, 2% international
- 793 degree-seeking graduate students
- 88% of applicants admitted
- SAT or ACT (ACT writing optional) required
- 51% graduate within 6 years

General. Founded in 1873. Regionally accredited. **Degrees:** 1,469 bachelor's, 10 associate awarded; master's offered. **ROTC:** Air Force. **Location:** 120 miles from St. Louis. **Calendar:** Semester, extensive summer session. **Full-time faculty:** 421 total; 76% have terminal degrees, 13% minority, 46% women. **Part-time faculty:** 183 total; 18% have terminal degrees, 5% minority, 54% women. **Class size:** 43% < 20, 53% 20-39, 2% 40-49, 1% 50-99, less than 1% >100. **Special facilities:** Demonstration farm, NASA educator resource center, mobile teaching and learning center, mobile health center, museum of archeology, history, and fine art.

Freshman class profile. 4,244 applied, 3,723 admitted, 1,828 enrolled.

Mid 50% test scores		**Rank in top tenth:**	16%
SAT critical reading:	450-580	**End year in good standing:**	73%
SAT math:	450-620	**Return as sophomores:**	72%
ACT composite:	20-25	**Out-of-state:**	13%
GPA 3.75 or higher:	27%	**Live on campus:**	62%
GPA 3.50-3.74:	16%	**International:**	2%
GPA 3.0-3.49:	29%	**Fraternities:**	18%
GPA 2.0-2.99:	27%	**Sororities:**	9%
Rank in top quarter:	43%		

Basis for selection. Standard test scores, academic GPA, rigor of secondary school records very important. Non-traditional students may take the ASSET exam, but ACT preferred; SAT accepted. Audition required for music and theater majors.

High school preparation. College-preparatory program required. 17 units required. Required units include English 4, mathematics 3, social studies 2, history 1, science 3 (laboratory 1), visual/performing arts 1 and academic electives 3. Of social studies requirements, .5 units must be in U.S. government.

2008-2009 Annual costs. Tuition/fees: $6,255; $10,890 out-of-state. Room/board: $6,065. Books/supplies: $440. Personal expenses: $2,114.

2007-2008 Financial aid. Need-based: 1,317 full-time freshmen applied for aid; 906 were judged to have need; 889 of these received aid. Average need met was 69%. Average scholarship/grant was $5,140; average loan $3,148. 47% of total undergraduate aid awarded as scholarships/grants, 53% as loans/jobs. **Non-need-based:** Awarded to 1,397 full-time undergraduates, including 539 freshmen. Scholarships awarded for academics, alumni affiliation, art, athletics, job skills, leadership, minority status, music/drama, ROTC, state residency.

Application procedures. Admission: Priority date 12/15; deadline 5/1 (postmark date). $25 fee, may be waived for applicants with need. Admission notification on a rolling basis beginning on or about 9/1. Must reply by 5/1. **Financial aid:** Priority date 3/1; no closing date. FAFSA required. Applicants notified on a rolling basis starting 4/1; must reply within 3 week(s) of notification.

Academics. Special study options: Accelerated study, distance learning, double major, dual enrollment of high school students, ESL, honors, independent study, internships, liberal arts/career combination, student-designed major, study abroad, teacher certification program. **Credit/placement by examination:** AP, CLEP, SAT, ACT, institutional tests. 30 credit hours maximum toward associate degree, 30 toward bachelor's. Departmental exams offered. **Support services:** Learning center, pre-admission summer program, reduced course load, remedial instruction, study skills assistance, tutoring, writing center.

Majors. Agriculture: General, agribusiness operations, animal sciences, horticultural science, plant sciences. **Biology:** General. **Business:** Accounting, business admin, finance, marketing, office management. **Communications:** General. **Computer sciences:** General, programming. **Conservation:** Environmental studies. **Education:** Art, business, elementary, English, family/consumer sciences, foreign languages, kindergarten/preschool, mathematics, middle, music, physical, science, social studies, special, speech, technology/industrial arts. **Engineering:** Physics. **Engineering technology:** General, industrial. **Family/consumer sciences:** General. **Foreign languages:** French, German, Spanish. **Health:** Clinical lab science, communication disorders, nursing (RN). **History:** General. **Interdisciplinary:** Global studies. **Liberal arts:** Humanities. **Math:** General. **Parks/recreation:** General, health/fitness, sports admin. **Philosophy/religion:** Philosophy. **Physical sciences:** Chemistry, physics. **Protective services:** Corrections. **Psychology:** General. **Public administration:** Social work. **Social sciences:** Anthropology, economics, political science. **Visual/performing arts:** General, art, dramatic.

Most popular majors. Business/marketing 13%, education 18%, engineering/engineering technologies 6%, family/consumer sciences 6%, health sciences 6%, liberal arts 13%.

Computing on campus. 1,311 workstations in dormitories, library, computer center, student center. Dormitories wired for high-speed internet access and linked to campus network. Online course registration, online library, helpline, student web hosting, wireless network available.

Student life. **Freshman orientation:** Mandatory, $50 fee. Preregistration for classes offered. One-day program offered many times throughout the semester. **Housing:** Coed dorms, fraternity/sorority housing, wellness housing available. $150 partly refundable deposit. Apartments for students with dependents available. **Activities:** Bands, campus ministries, choral groups, dance, drama, international student organizations, literary magazine, music ensembles, Model UN, musical theater, opera, radio station, student government, student newspaper, symphony orchestra, Baptist Student Union, Lutheran Student Fellowship, Association of Black Collegians, College Republicans, College Democrats, Friends Without Borders, Indian Subcontinent Student Association, Catholic Campus Ministries, Chinese Students & Scholars Association.

Athletics. NCAA. **Intercollegiate:** Baseball M, basketball, cheerleading, cross-country, football (tackle) M, gymnastics W, soccer W, softball W, tennis W, track and field, volleyball W. **Intramural:** Badminton, basketball, bowling, football (non-tackle), golf, racquetball, soccer, softball, swimming, table tennis, tennis, volleyball, wrestling. **Team name:** Redhawks.

Student services. Adult student services, alcohol/substance abuse counseling, chaplain/spiritual director, career counseling, services for economically disadvantaged, student employment services, financial aid counseling, health services, minority student services, on-campus daycare, personal counseling, placement for graduates, veterans' counselor. **Physically disabled:** Services for visually, speech, hearing impaired. **Learning disabled:** Comprehensive services available.

Contact. E-mail: admissions@semo.edu
Phone: (573) 651-2590 Fax: (573) 651-5936
Deborah Below, Director, Southeast Missouri State University, One University Plaza, Cape Girardeau, MO 63701

Southwest Baptist University

Bolivar, Missouri
www.sbuniv.edu **CB code: 6664**

- Private 4-year university affiliated with Southern Baptist Convention
- Residential campus in small town
- 2,507 degree-seeking undergraduates: 25% part-time, 66% women, 4% African American, 1% Asian American, 1% Hispanic American, 1% Native American, 1% international
- 505 degree-seeking graduate students
- 74% of applicants admitted
- SAT or ACT (ACT writing optional) required
- 54% graduate within 6 years

General. Founded in 1878. Regionally accredited. **Degrees:** 367 bachelor's, 137 associate awarded; master's, doctoral offered. **ROTC:** Army. **Location:** 25 miles from Springfield, 120 miles from Kansas City. **Calendar:** Semester, extensive summer session. **Full-time faculty:** 116 total; 60% have terminal degrees, 2% minority, 42% women. **Part-time faculty:** 129 total; 22% have terminal degrees, less than 1% minority, 58% women. **Class size:** 64% < 20, 29% 20-39, 5% 40-49, 2% 50-99.

Freshman class profile. 1,380 applied, 1,015 admitted, 453 enrolled.

Mid 50% test scores		**Rank in top quarter:**	50%
SAT critical reading:	440-590	**Rank in top tenth:**	23%
SAT math:	420-600	**End year in good standing:**	86%
ACT composite:	20-26	**Return as sophomores:**	72%
GPA 3.75 or higher:	42%	**Out-of-state:**	30%
GPA 3.50-3.74:	15%	**Live on campus:**	96%
GPA 3.0-3.49:	27%	**International:**	1%
GPA 2.0-2.99:	15%		

Basis for selection. Must meet 2 of 3 qualifiers: 2.50 GPA, 21 ACT or 990 SAT score (exclusive of Writing), top 50% high school class rank. Interview required for conditionally admitted applicants, recommended for all. Audition recommended for music, speech, and theater students.

High school preparation. College-preparatory program recommended. 13 units recommended. Recommended units include English 4, mathematics 3, social studies 2, science 2 and academic electives 2. 2 additional units of foreign language or computer science or 2 units of English, math, social studies or natural sciences recommended.

2009-2010 Annual costs. Tuition/fees: $16,530. Room/board: $5,470. Books/supplies: $1,000. Personal expenses: $1,000.

2008-2009 Financial aid. **Need-based:** 439 full-time freshmen applied for aid; 346 were judged to have need; 343 of these received aid. Average need met was 86%. Average scholarship/grant was $5,852; average loan $3,920. 51% of total undergraduate aid awarded as scholarships/grants, 49% as loans/jobs. **Non-need-based:** Awarded to 1,750 full-time undergraduates, including 481 freshmen. Scholarships awarded for academics, art, athletics, minority status, music/drama, state residency.

Application procedures. **Admission:** No deadline. $30 fee, may be waived for applicants with need. Admission notification on a rolling basis beginning on or about 9/1. **Financial aid:** Priority date 3/15; no closing date. FAFSA, institutional form required. Applicants notified on a rolling basis starting 3/1; must reply within 2 week(s) of notification.

Academics. **Special study options:** Cooperative education, distance learning, double major, dual enrollment of high school students, honors, independent study, internships, student-designed major, study abroad, teacher certification program, Washington semester. **Credit/placement by examination:** AP, CLEP, IB, SAT, ACT, institutional tests. 16 credit hours maximum toward associate degree, 32 toward bachelor's. **Support services:** Learning center, reduced course load, remedial instruction, study skills assistance, tutoring, writing center.

Majors. **Biology:** General. **Business:** Accounting, business admin, customer service, finance, international, marketing, office management. **Communications:** General. **Computer sciences:** General, computer science. **Education:** Art, biology, chemistry, elementary, English, health, middle, music, physical, science, social science. **Foreign languages:** Spanish. **Health:** Athletic training, clinical lab science, nursing (RN). **History:** General. **Math:** General. **Parks/recreation:** General, health/fitness, sports admin. **Philosophy/religion:** Religion. **Physical sciences:** Chemistry. **Protective services:** Law enforcement admin. **Psychology:** General. **Public administration:** Human services. **Social sciences:** Political science, sociology. **Theology:** Bible, missionary, religious ed, sacred music, theology. **Visual/performing arts:** Art, commercial/advertising art, dramatic. **Other:** Science and christian faith.

Most popular majors. Business/marketing 15%, education 20%, health sciences 15%, psychology 13%, theological studies 9%.

Computing on campus. 261 workstations in dormitories, library, computer center, student center. Dormitories linked to campus network. Commuter students can connect to campus network. Online library, helpline, wireless network available.

Student life. **Freshman orientation:** Available. Preregistration for classes offered. 5-days prior to start of the fall semester. **Policies:** Religious observance required. **Housing:** Guaranteed on-campus for freshmen. Single-sex dorms, apartments, wellness housing available. $100 deposit. **Activities:** Bands, campus ministries, choral groups, drama, international student organizations, music ensembles, musical theater, opera, student government, student newspaper, symphony orchestra, University Missions, Habitat for Humanity, Christian Service Organization, Theatrical Evangelism and Mission, Students in Free Enterprise, Discipleship-Now teams.

Athletics. NCAA. **Intercollegiate:** Baseball M, basketball, cheerleading, cross-country, football (tackle) M, golf M, soccer W, softball W, tennis, track and field, volleyball W. **Intramural:** Basketball, football (non-tackle), soccer, softball, table tennis, volleyball. **Team name:** Bearcats.

Student services. Chaplain/spiritual director, career counseling, student employment services, financial aid counseling, health services, personal counseling, placement for graduates.

Contact. E-mail: dcrowder@sbuniv.edu
Phone: (417) 328-1810 Toll-free number: (800) 526-5859
Fax: (417) 328-1514
Darren Crowder, Director of Admissions, Southwest Baptist University, 1600 University Avenue, Bolivar, MO 65613-2597

Stephens College

Columbia, Missouri **CB member**
www.stephens.edu **CB code: 6683**

- Private 4-year liberal arts college for women
- Residential campus in small city
- 923 degree-seeking undergraduates: 17% part-time, 97% women, 10% African American, 1% Asian American, 3% Hispanic American, 1% Native American
- 200 degree-seeking graduate students
- 71% of applicants admitted
- SAT or ACT (ACT writing optional), application essay required
- 58% graduate within 6 years; 23% enter graduate study

General. Founded in 1833. Regionally accredited. **Degrees:** 142 bachelor's, 1 associate awarded; master's offered. **ROTC:** Army, Naval, Air Force. **Location:** 125 miles from St. Louis and Kansas City. **Calendar:** Semester, limited summer session. **Full-time faculty:** 55 total; 47% have terminal degrees, 2% minority, 84% women. **Part-time faculty:** 55 total; 26% have terminal degrees, 2% minority, 69% women. **Class size:** 77% < 20, 21% 20-39, 1% 40-49, 1% 50-99. **Special facilities:** Professional-level theater, private elementary school and child study center, 60-horse stables, historical costume collection.

Freshman class profile. 694 applied, 490 admitted, 223 enrolled.

Mid 50% test scores		**GPA 2.0-2.99:**	26%
SAT critical reading:	490-640	**Rank in top quarter:**	43%
SAT math:	490-600	**Rank in top tenth:**	19%
SAT writing:	530-620	**End year in good standing:**	89%
ACT composite:	20-25	**Return as sophomores:**	77%
GPA 3.75 or higher:	25%	**Out-of-state:**	41%
GPA 3.50-3.74:	15%	**Live on campus:**	92%
GPA 3.0-3.49:	34%	**Sororities:**	7%

Basis for selection. School achievement record most important, followed by test scores. Interview recommended for all students; audition mandatory for dance, recommended for theater, musical theater students. **Homeschooled:** Statement describing homeschool structure and mission, letter of recommendation (nonparent) required. Statement should be short narrative written by person primarily responsible for academic training, and should describe the nature of the secondary-level education.

High school preparation. 12 units recommended. Recommended units include English 4, mathematics 3, social studies 1, science 2 and foreign language 2.

2008-2009 Annual costs. Tuition/fees: $23,000. Room/board: $8,730. Books/supplies: $1,000. Personal expenses: $2,215.

2008-2009 Financial aid. Need-based: 197 full-time freshmen applied for aid; 172 were judged to have need; 172 of these received aid. Average need met was 77%. Average scholarship/grant was $15,911; average loan $2,951. 67% of total undergraduate aid awarded as scholarships/grants, 33% as loans/jobs. **Non-need-based:** Awarded to 254 full-time undergraduates, including 75 freshmen. Scholarships awarded for academics, alumni affiliation, athletics, leadership, music/drama, state residency.

Application procedures. Admission: Priority date 4/1; no deadline. $25 fee, may be waived for applicants with need, free for online applicants. Admission notification on a rolling basis beginning on or about 9/15. **Financial aid:** Priority date 3/15; no closing date. FAFSA required. Applicants notified on a rolling basis starting 3/1.

Academics. Special study options: Combined bachelor's/graduate degree, cross-registration, distance learning, double major, dual enrollment of high school students, external degree, independent study, internships, liberal arts/career combination, semester at sea, student-designed major, study abroad, teacher certification program. **Credit/placement by examination:** AP, CLEP, IB, SAT, ACT. 15 credit hours maximum toward associate degree, 30 toward bachelor's. **Support services:** Learning center, pre-admission summer program, study skills assistance, tutoring, writing center.

Majors. Agriculture: Equine science. **Biology:** General. **Business:** Accounting, business admin, fashion, marketing. **Communications:** General, advertising, broadcast journalism, journalism, public relations. **Education:** General, early childhood, elementary. **Family/consumer sciences:** Clothing/textiles. **Health:** Medical records admin. **Legal studies:** Prelaw. **Liberal arts:** Arts/sciences. **Psychology:** General. **Visual/performing arts:** General, commercial/advertising art, dance, dramatic, fashion design.

Most popular majors. Biology 6%, business/marketing 25%, health sciences 15%, psychology 6%, visual/performing arts 29%.

Computing on campus. 85 workstations in dormitories, library, computer center. Dormitories linked to campus network. Commuter students can connect to campus network. Online library, helpline, repair service, student web hosting, wireless network available.

Student life. Freshman orientation: Mandatory. Preregistration for classes offered. Typically held third week of August, one week prior to start of classes. Registration held mid-June on campus with academic advisor. **Housing:** Guaranteed on-campus for all undergraduates. Apartments available. $100 deposit. Pets allowed in dorm rooms. Freshman academic residence hall available. **Activities:** Choral groups, dance, drama, film society, literary magazine, music ensembles, musical theater, radio station, student government, student newspaper, TV station, more than 45 clubs and organizations.

Athletics. NAIA. **Intercollegiate:** Basketball W, cross-country W, softball W, swimming W, tennis W, volleyball W. **Intramural:** Equestrian W. **Team name:** Stars.

Student services. Adult student services, career counseling, student employment services, financial aid counseling, health services, personal counseling, placement for graduates, women's services.

Contact. E-mail: apply@stephens.edu
Phone: (573) 876-7207 Toll-free number: (800) 876-7207
Fax: (573) 876-7237
David Adams, Dean of Enrollment Management, Stephens College, 1200 East Broadway, Columbia, MO 65215

Truman State University

Kirksville, Missouri — **CB member**
www.truman.edu — **CB code: 6483**

- Public 4-year university and liberal arts college
- Residential campus in large town
- 5,497 degree-seeking undergraduates: 2% part-time, 58% women, 5% African American, 2% Asian American, 2% Hispanic American, 1% Native American, 5% international
- 238 degree-seeking graduate students
- 79% of applicants admitted
- SAT or ACT (ACT writing optional), application essay required
- 69% graduate within 6 years; 50% enter graduate study

General. Founded in 1867. Regionally accredited. State's only public liberal arts and sciences university. **Degrees:** 1,104 bachelor's awarded; master's offered. **ROTC:** Army. **Location:** 195 miles from St. Louis, 170 miles from Kansas City. **Calendar:** Semester, extensive summer session. **Full-time faculty:** 357 total; 84% have terminal degrees, 11% minority, 39% women. **Part-time faculty:** 27 total; 41% have terminal degrees, 7% minority, 59% women. **Class size:** 44% < 20, 48% 20-39, 4% 40-49, 4% 50-99, less than 1% >100. **Special facilities:** Observatory, greenhouse, local history museum, 400-acre farm, human performance laboratory, speech and hearing clinic, biofeedback laboratory, IR and NMR instrumentation, independent learning center for nursing, art gallery, radio station, television studio.

Freshman class profile. 4,280 applied, 3,377 admitted, 1,334 enrolled.

Mid 50% test scores		**Rank in top tenth:**	50%
SAT critical reading:	540-700	**End year in good standing:**	85%
SAT math:	570-690	**Return as sophomores:**	85%
ACT composite:	25-31	**Out-of-state:**	19%
GPA 3.75 or higher:	63%	**Live on campus:**	98%
GPA 3.50-3.74:	18%	**International:**	5%
GPA 3.0-3.49:	17%	**Fraternities:**	15%
GPA 2.0-2.99:	2%	**Sororities:**	13%
Rank in top quarter:	80%		

Basis for selection. High school performance (class rank, GPA, college preparatory curriculum), test scores, essay most important; special ability, talent and achievement considered. Portfolio recommended for fine arts students. Audition required for music students. **Homeschooled:** Transcript of courses and grades required. **Learning Disabled:** Students welcome to provide additional documentation of their learning disability.

High school preparation. College-preparatory program required. 16 units required; 17 recommended. Required and recommended units include English 4, mathematics 3-4, social studies 2, history 1, science 3 (laboratory 1-2), foreign language 2 and visual/performing arts 1.

2008-2009 Annual costs. Tuition/fees: $6,692; $11,542 out-of-state. Room/board: $6,290. Books/supplies: $1,000. Personal expenses: $2,500.

2007-2008 Financial aid. Need-based: 1,124 full-time freshmen applied for aid; 556 were judged to have need; 556 of these received aid. Average need met was 85%. Average scholarship/grant was $3,129; average loan $3,306. 42% of total undergraduate aid awarded as scholarships/grants, 58% as loans/jobs. **Non-need-based:** Awarded to 4,559 full-time undergraduates, including 1,441 freshmen. Scholarships awarded for academics, alumni affiliation, art, athletics, leadership, minority status, music/drama, ROTC, state residency. **Additional information:** Out-of-state students whose parents work in Missouri may deduct $1 for every dollar paid in Missouri income taxes from out-of-state tuition.

Application procedures. Admission: Priority date 12/15; no deadline. No application fee. Admission notification on a rolling basis. Must reply by May 1 or within 3 week(s) if notified thereafter. **Financial aid:** Priority date 4/1; no closing date. FAFSA, institutional form required. Applicants notified on a rolling basis starting 3/1; must reply within 4 week(s) of notification.

Academics. Special study options: Combined bachelor's/graduate degree, double major, dual enrollment of high school students, exchange student, honors, independent study, internships, semester at sea, student-designed major, study abroad, teacher certification program, Washington semester. **Credit/placement by examination:** AP, CLEP, IB, institutional tests. **Support services:** Pre-admission summer program, study skills assistance, tutoring, writing center.

Majors. Agriculture: General, agronomy, animal sciences, business, equestrian studies. **Biology:** General, exercise physiology. **Business:** Accounting, business admin, finance, management information systems, marketing. **Communications:** General, journalism. **Computer sciences:** General. **Education:** Speech impaired. **Foreign languages:** Classics, French, German, linguistics, Romance, Russian, Spanish. **Health:** Athletic training, communication disorders, health services, nursing (RN), predental, premedicine, prepharmacy, preveterinary. **History:** General. **Legal studies:** Prelaw. **Math:** General. **Parks/recreation:** Exercise sciences, health/fitness. **Philosophy/religion:** Philosophy, religion. **Physical sciences:** Chemistry, physics. **Protective services:** Criminal justice. **Psychology:** General. **Social sciences:** Economics, political science, sociology. **Visual/performing arts:** General, art, art history/conservation, commercial/advertising art, dramatic, music performance, studio arts.

Most popular majors. Biology 7%, business/marketing 19%, communications/journalism 7%, English 9%, health sciences 6%, parks/recreation 9%, psychology 9%, visual/performing arts 7%.

Computing on campus. 965 workstations in dormitories, library, computer center, student center. Dormitories wired for high-speed internet access and linked to campus network. Commuter students can connect to campus network. Online course registration, online library, helpline, repair service, student web hosting, wireless network available.

Student life. Freshman orientation: Mandatory, $305 fee. Preregistration for classes offered. Sessions held during June and August, with additional program about a week before fall semester begins. **Housing:** Guaranteed on-campus for freshmen. Coed dorms, special housing for disabled, apartments, fraternity/sorority housing, wellness housing available. $150 partly refundable deposit, deadline 5/1. International roommate options available. **Activities:** Bands, campus ministries, choral groups, dance, drama, film society, international student organizations, literary magazine, music ensembles, Model UN, musical theater, opera, radio station, student government, student newspaper, symphony orchestra, TV station, Alpha Phi Omega, Association of Black Collegians, College Republicans, Campus Christian Fellowship, Amnesty International, Blue Key, Cardinal Key, Circle-K, College Democrats, Baptist Student Union.

Athletics. NCAA. **Intercollegiate:** Baseball M, basketball, cross-country, football (tackle) M, golf, soccer, softball W, swimming, tennis, track and field, volleyball W, wrestling M. **Intramural:** Badminton, basketball, bowling, football (non-tackle), racquetball, soccer, softball, swimming, table tennis, tennis, track and field, volleyball, weight lifting. **Team name:** Bulldogs.

Student services. Career counseling, services for economically disadvantaged, student employment services, financial aid counseling, health services, minority student services, personal counseling, placement for graduates, veterans' counselor, women's services. **Physically disabled:** Services for visually, speech, hearing impaired.

Contact. E-mail: admissions@truman.edu
Phone: (660) 785-4114 Toll-free number: (800) 892-7792
Fax: (660) 785-7456
Melody Chambers, Director of Admission, Truman State University, 100 East Normal Street, Kirksville, MO 63501-9980

University of Central Missouri

Warrensburg, Missouri
www.ucmo.edu **CB code: 6090**

- Public 4-year university
- Commuter campus in large town
- 8,314 degree-seeking undergraduates: 14% part-time, 54% women, 7% African American, 1% Asian American, 2% Hispanic American, 1% Native American, 3% international
- 1,933 degree-seeking graduate students
- 86% of applicants admitted
- SAT or ACT (ACT writing optional) required
- 51% graduate within 6 years

General. Founded in 1871. Regionally accredited. **Degrees:** 1,606 bachelor's, 1 associate awarded; master's offered. **ROTC:** Army, Air Force. **Location:** 50 miles from Kansas City. **Calendar:** Semester, extensive summer session. **Full-time faculty:** 437 total; 68% have terminal degrees, 12% minority, 42% women. **Class size:** 47% < 20, 44% 20-39, 6% 40-49, 3% 50-99, less than 1% >100. **Special facilities:** Airport, 260-acre farm, children's literature collection, musical instruments collection, child development lab, advanced technology library.

Freshman class profile. 3,766 applied, 3,244 admitted, 1,613 enrolled.

Mid 50% test scores		**Rank in top quarter:**	33%
SAT critical reading:	450-580	**Rank in top tenth:**	11%
SAT math:	450-510	**Return as sophomores:**	72%
SAT writing:	420-560	**Out-of-state:**	1%
ACT composite:	20-24	**Live on campus:**	85%
GPA 3.75 or higher:	20%	**International:**	3%
GPA 3.50-3.74:	16%	**Fraternities:**	8%
GPA 3.0-3.49:	30%	**Sororities:**	6%
GPA 2.0-2.99:	32%		

Basis for selection. Applicant must be in top two-thirds of high school class, complete 16-unit core curriculum and have minimum ACT score of 20. TOEFL required for international students. Essay required for some programs; audition recommended for music students. **Homeschooled:** Recommend ACT, GED, or equivalent.

High school preparation. College-preparatory program required. 16 units required. Required and recommended units include English 4, mathematics 3, social studies 3, science 2 (laboratory 1), foreign language 2 and academic electives 3. 1 fine/performing arts required.

2008-2009 Annual costs. Tuition/fees: $6,885; $12,444 out-of-state. Room/board: $6,320. Books/supplies: $700. Personal expenses: $1,450.

2007-2008 Financial aid. Non-need-based: Scholarships awarded for academics, alumni affiliation, art, athletics, leadership, minority status, music/drama, ROTC, state residency.

Application procedures. Admission: Priority date 6/1; no deadline. $30 fee, may be waived for applicants with need. Admission notification on a rolling basis beginning on or about 8/18. **Financial aid:** Priority date 3/1; no closing date. FAFSA required. Applicants notified on a rolling basis starting 3/1; must reply within 2 week(s) of notification.

Academics. Online services and resources include library, technical support, writing center and bookstore. Extensive international exchange program. **Special study options:** Combined bachelor's/graduate degree, cooperative education, cross-registration, distance learning, double major, dual enrollment of high school students, ESL, honors, internships, liberal arts/career combination, student-designed major, study abroad, teacher certification program, weekend college. Engineering program with University of Missouri (Columbia, Rolla) and University of Indiana, MIssouri University of Science & Technology at Rolla. **Credit/placement by examination:** AP, CLEP, IB, SAT, ACT, institutional tests. 15 credit hours maximum toward associate degree, 30 toward bachelor's. **Support services:** Learning center, remedial instruction, study skills assistance, tutoring, writing center.

Honors college/program. Minimum ACT score of 25; 319 freshmen admitted; requires 48 credit hours.

Majors. Agriculture: General, business, economics. **Biology:** General. **Business:** Accounting, actuarial science, business admin, finance, hotel/motel admin, human resources, management information systems, marketing, office management, tourism promotion. **Communications:** General, broadcast journalism, journalism, public relations. **Communications technology:** Graphic/printing. **Computer sciences:** General, data processing. **Education:** Agricultural, art, biology, business, chemistry, elementary, English, family/consumer sciences, foreign languages, French, German, mathematics, middle, music, physical, physics, science, secondary, social studies, Spanish, special, speech, technology/industrial arts. **Engineering technology:** Architectural, construction, drafting, electrical, industrial. **Family/consumer sciences:** General, child development, clothing/textiles, family studies. **Foreign languages:** French, German, Spanish. **Health:** Nursing (RN), speech pathology. **History:** General. **Math:** General. **Parks/recreation:** General, facilities management. **Physical sciences:** Chemistry, geology, physics, planetary. **Protective services:** Law enforcement admin. **Psychology:** General. **Public administration:** Social work. **Social sciences:** Economics, geography, political science, sociology. **Visual/performing arts:** Art, commercial/advertising art, dramatic, interior design, photography, studio arts.

Most popular majors. Business/marketing 18%, education 18%, engineering/engineering technologies 11%, health sciences 7%, security/protective services 7%, visual/performing arts 10%.

Computing on campus. 2,727 workstations in dormitories, library, computer center, student center. Dormitories wired for high-speed internet access and linked to campus network. Commuter students can connect to campus network. Online course registration, online library, helpline, student web hosting, wireless network available.

Student life. Freshman orientation: Mandatory. Preregistration for classes offered. 8 one-day sessions in early summer. **Housing:** Guaranteed on-campus for all undergraduates. Coed dorms, single-sex dorms, special housing for disabled, apartments, fraternity/sorority housing, wellness housing available. $100 nonrefundable deposit, deadline 6/1. Honors hall, economy suites available. **Activities:** Bands, campus ministries, choral groups, dance, drama, film society, international student organizations, literary magazine, music ensembles, musical theater, opera, radio station, student government, student newspaper, symphony orchestra, TV station, Association of Black Collegiates, nontraditional student association, student ambassadors, College Republicans, College Democrats, United Students for Equal Access, Student Government Association.

Athletics. NCAA. **Intercollegiate:** Baseball M, basketball, bowling W, cross-country, football (tackle) M, golf M, soccer W, softball W, track and field, volleyball W, wrestling M. **Intramural:** Archery M, badminton M, basketball, bowling, cross-country, diving, football (tackle), golf, racquetball, rifle, rugby M, soccer, softball, swimming, table tennis, tennis, track and field, volleyball, water polo, weight lifting M, wrestling M. **Team name:** Mules (M), Jennies (W).

Student services. Adult student services, alcohol/substance abuse counseling, chaplain/spiritual director, career counseling, student employment services, financial aid counseling, health services, minority student services, on-campus daycare, personal counseling, placement for graduates, veterans' counselor, women's services. **Physically disabled:** Services for visually, speech, hearing impaired.

Contact. E-mail: admit@ucmovmb.ucmo.edu
Phone: (660) 543-4290 Toll-free number: (877) 729-8266
Fax: (660) 543-8517
Ann Nordyke, Chief Admissions Officer, University of Central Missouri, WDE 1400, Warrensburg, MO 64093

University of Missouri: Columbia

Columbia, Missouri — **CB member**
www.missouri.edu — **CB code: 6875**

- Public 4-year university
- Residential campus in small city
- 22,649 degree-seeking undergraduates: 5% part-time, 52% women, 6% African American, 2% Asian American, 2% Hispanic American, 1% Native American, 2% international
- 6,485 degree-seeking graduate students
- 85% of applicants admitted
- SAT or ACT (ACT writing optional) required

General. Founded in 1839. Regionally accredited. Students with common academic interest housed in same residence hall and enrolled in 3 classes together. **Degrees:** 4,779 bachelor's awarded; master's, doctoral, first professional offered. **ROTC:** Army, Naval, Air Force. **Location:** 125 miles from Kansas City, 125 miles from St. Louis. **Calendar:** Semester, limited summer session. **Full-time faculty:** 1,270 total; 92% have terminal degrees, 18% minority, 35% women. **Part-time faculty:** 67 total; 94% have terminal degrees, 9% minority, 43% women. **Special facilities:** Observatory, research nuclear reactor, freedom of information center, Food for 21st Century program, engineering experiment station, center for research in social behavior, equine center, university research farms, child development laboratory, daily city newspaper production, nightly newscasts, black culture center.

Freshman class profile. 14,491 applied, 12,327 admitted, 5,782 enrolled.

Mid 50% test scores		Out-of-state:	19%
SAT critical reading:	540-660	Live on campus:	85%
SAT math:	540-650	International:	2%
ACT composite:	23-28	Fraternities:	31%
Rank in top quarter:	54%	Sororities:	36%
Rank in top tenth:	25%		

Basis for selection. Admission based on required core courses and combination of high school rank and test scores. Individual programs may have additional requirements. Trial summer admission open to Missouri residents. Students must complete math and English with C or better to continue enrollment on probation in fall. ACT preferred.

High school preparation. College-preparatory program required. 17 units required. Required units include English 4, mathematics 4, social studies 3, science 3 (laboratory 1) and foreign language 2. 1 fine arts required. Math must include algebra I and higher.

2008-2009 Annual costs. Tuition/fees: $8,485; $19,558 out-of-state. Room/board: $8,100. Books/supplies: $1,020. Personal expenses: $1,490.

2007-2008 Financial aid. Need-based: 3,486 full-time freshmen applied for aid; 2,237 were judged to have need; 2,215 of these received aid. Average need met was 91%. Average scholarship/grant was $7,270; average loan $3,723. 52% of total undergraduate aid awarded as scholarships/grants, 48% as loans/jobs. **Non-need-based:** Awarded to 4,976 full-time undergraduates, including 1,550 freshmen. Scholarships awarded for academics, alumni affiliation, art, athletics, leadership, minority status, music/drama, ROTC, state residency. **Additional information:** Scholarship available for international students based on success during 1st semester.

Application procedures. Admission: Priority date 5/1; no deadline. $45 fee, may be waived for applicants with need. Admission notification on a rolling basis. Must reply by May 1 or within 4 week(s) if notified thereafter. **Financial aid:** Priority date 3/1; no closing date. FAFSA required. Applicants notified on a rolling basis starting 4/1; must reply within 4 week(s) of notification.

Academics. Guaranteed admission to School of Law with 30 ACT, and maintenance of 3.3 GPA. Early admission to School of Medicine with 30 ACT, maintenance of 3.4 GPA, and required interview. Early admission to School of Nursing with 29 ACT and rank in top 10% of high school class. Project for Excellence in Teaching offered. **Special study options:** Accelerated study, combined bachelor's/graduate degree, cooperative education, cross-registration, distance learning, double major, dual enrollment of high school students, ESL, exchange student, external degree, honors, independent study, internships, New York semester, student-designed major, study abroad, teacher certification program, Washington semester. **Credit/placement by examination:** AP, CLEP, IB, ACT, institutional tests. Credit by examination policy varies by school/college. **Support services:** Learning center, pre-admission summer program, reduced course load, study skills assistance, tutoring, writing center.

Honors college/program. 29 ACT or 1280 SAT and top 10% of high school graduating class required. If school does not rank, core GPA of 3.71 necessary. Core GPA includes all English courses, all math courses Algebra I and higher, and all science, social studies, and foreign language courses.

Majors. Agriculture: General, animal sciences, business, communications, economics, food science, plant sciences, soil science. **Area/ethnic studies:** African-American, East Asian, European, Latin American, South Asian, women's. **Biology:** General, biochemistry, conservation, microbiology. **Business:** General, accounting, banking/financial services, business admin, hotel/motel admin, international, marketing, real estate, restaurant/food services, travel services. **Communications:** General, advertising, broadcast journalism, journalism, photojournalism, radio/tv. **Computer sciences:** General, computer science, information technology. **Conservation:** Fisheries, forestry, wildlife. **Education:** General, agricultural, art, biology, business, chemistry, early childhood, elementary, English, foreign languages, mathematics, middle, multiple handicapped, music, physics, science, secondary, social studies, Spanish, voc/tech. **Engineering:** Agricultural, biomedical, chemical, civil, computer, electrical, industrial, mechanical. **Family/consumer sciences:** Clothing/textiles, family resources, family studies, food/nutrition, housing, human nutrition. **Foreign languages:** Classics, East Asian, French, German, linguistics, Russian, South Asian, Spanish. **Health:** Audiology/speech pathology, dietetics, health services admin, medical radiologic technology/radiation therapy, nuclear medical technology, nursing (RN), premedicine, prepharmacy, preveterinary, radiologic technology/medical imaging, respiratory therapy technology, sonography. **History:** General. **Interdisciplinary:** Behavioral sciences, nutrition sciences, peace/conflict. **Math:** General, statistics. **Military:** General. **Parks/recreation:** General, exercise sciences. **Philosophy/religion:** Philosophy, religion. **Physical sciences:** Atmospheric science, chemistry, geology, physics. **Psychology:** General. **Public administration:** Social work. **Social sciences:** Anthropology, archaeology, economics, geography, political science, sociology. **Visual/performing arts:** Art, dramatic.

Most popular majors. Biology 6%, business/marketing 19%, communications/journalism 12%, education 6%, engineering/engineering technologies 7%, family/consumer sciences 6%, health sciences 7%, social sciences 7%.

Computing on campus. 1,179 workstations in dormitories, library, computer center, student center. Dormitories wired for high-speed internet access and linked to campus network. Commuter students can connect to campus network. Online course registration, online library, helpline, repair service, student web hosting, wireless network available.

Student life. Freshman orientation: Available. Preregistration for classes offered. Nineteen 2-day sessions during summer; parents invited. **Policies:** Alcohol-free and smoke-free campus buildings, residence halls, and Greek housing. **Housing:** Guaranteed on-campus for freshmen. Coed dorms, single-sex dorms, apartments, fraternity/sorority housing, wellness housing available. $300 fully refundable deposit, deadline 4/1. Specialized living/learning communities and freshman interest groups in residence halls for fine arts, French, Spanish, women in engineering, men in engineering, journalism, service learning, first-time college students, international studies, nursing students. **Activities:** Bands, choral groups, dance, drama, film society, international student organizations, literary magazine, music ensembles, musical theater, opera, radio station, student government, student newspaper, symphony orchestra, TV station, Over 518 clubs available.

Athletics. NCAA. **Intercollegiate:** Baseball M, basketball, cross-country, diving, football (tackle) M, golf, gymnastics W, soccer W, softball W, swimming, tennis W, track and field, volleyball W, wrestling M. **Intramural:** Basketball, football (non-tackle), golf, soccer, softball, volleyball. **Team name:** Tigers.

Student services. Alcohol/substance abuse counseling, chaplain/spiritual director, career counseling, services for economically disadvantaged, student employment services, financial aid counseling, health services, legal services, minority student services, on-campus daycare, personal counseling, placement for graduates, veterans' counselor, women's services. **Physically disabled:** Services for visually, speech, hearing impaired.

Contact. E-mail: mu4u@missouri.edu
Phone: (573) 882-7786 Toll-free number: (800) 225-6075
Fax: (573) 882-7887
Barbara Rupp, Director of Admissions, University of Missouri: Columbia, 230 Jesse Hall, Columbia, MO 65211

University of Missouri: Kansas City

Kansas City, Missouri — **CB member**
www.umkc.edu — **CB code: 6872**

- Public 4-year university
- Commuter campus in large city
- 7,353 degree-seeking undergraduates: 21% part-time, 58% women, 15% African American, 6% Asian American, 4% Hispanic American, 1% Native American, 3% international
- 4,924 degree-seeking graduate students
- 73% of applicants admitted
- SAT or ACT (ACT writing optional) required
- 43% graduate within 6 years

General. Founded in 1929. Regionally accredited. **Degrees:** 1,289 bachelor's awarded; master's, doctoral, first professional offered. **ROTC:** Army. **Location:** 500 miles from Chicago, 250 miles from St. Louis. **Calendar:** Semester, extensive summer session. **Full-time faculty:** 689 total; 79% have terminal degrees, 22% minority, 42% women. **Part-time faculty:** 460 total; 28% have terminal degrees, 11% minority, 50% women. **Class size:** 53% < 20, 34% 20-39, 5% 40-49, 6% 50-99, 2% >100. **Special facilities:** Observatory, science and technology library, music conservatory, miniature toy museum.

Freshman class profile. 3,276 applied, 2,384 admitted, 1,007 enrolled.

Mid 50% test scores		**Rank in top tenth:**	31%
SAT critical reading:	530-650	**End year in good standing:**	63%
SAT math:	520-680	**Return as sophomores:**	76%
ACT composite:	21-27	**Out-of-state:**	23%
GPA 3.75 or higher:	29%	**Live on campus:**	61%
GPA 3.50-3.74:	18%	**International:**	3%
GPA 3.0-3.49:	27%	**Fraternities:**	18%
GPA 2.0-2.99:	25%	**Sororities:**	17%
Rank in top quarter:	58%		

Basis for selection. Admission based on class rank, test scores, and high school course requirements. Admission is very selective to combined arts and sciences/medical; highly selective to pharmacy program; and selective to Conservatory of Music. Interview required for dentistry, medicine, and pharmacy applicants; audition required for dance and conservatory of music applicants. Portfolio recommended. **Homeschooled:** Transcript of courses and grades required. ACT or SAT score required.

High school preparation. College-preparatory program required. 17 units required. Required units include English 4, mathematics 4, social studies 3, science 3 (laboratory 1), foreign language 2 and visual/performing arts 1.

2008-2009 Annual costs. Tuition/fees: $8,272; $19,363 out-of-state. Room/board: $8,096. Books/supplies: $1,180. Personal expenses: $4,900.

2008-2009 Financial aid. Need-based: 787 full-time freshmen applied for aid; 625 were judged to have need; 615 of these received aid. Average need met was 59%. Average scholarship/grant was $7,411; average loan $6,710. 37% of total undergraduate aid awarded as scholarships/grants, 63% as loans/jobs. **Non-need-based:** Awarded to 1,028 full-time undergraduates, including 285 freshmen. Scholarships awarded for academics, alumni affiliation, art, athletics, leadership, minority status, music/drama, state residency.

Application procedures. Admission: Priority date 4/1; no deadline. $45 fee, may be waived for applicants with need. Admission notification on a rolling basis. Architecture, medicine, and pharmacy programs have separate application deadlines and specific admissions requirements. **Financial aid:** Priority date 3/1; no closing date. FAFSA required. Applicants notified on a rolling basis starting 4/15; must reply within 2 week(s) of notification.

Academics. Special study options: Accelerated study, combined bachelor's/graduate degree, distance learning, double major, dual enrollment of high school students, ESL, honors, independent study, internships, liberal arts/career combination, student-designed major, study abroad, teacher certification program. **Credit/placement by examination:** AP, CLEP, IB, institutional tests. 30 credit hours maximum toward bachelor's degree. **Support services:** Learning center, reduced course load, study skills assistance, tutoring, writing center.

Majors. Architecture: Urban/community planning. **Area/ethnic studies:** American. **Biology:** General. **Business:** General, accounting. **Computer sciences:** General, information systems. **Conservation:** Environmental science. **Education:** General, elementary, middle, music, secondary. **Engineering:** Civil, electrical, mechanical. **Foreign languages:** French, German, Spanish. **Health:** Clinical lab science, dental hygiene, nursing (RN). **History:** General. **Liberal arts:** Arts/sciences. **Math:** General. **Philosophy/religion:** Philosophy. **Physical sciences:** Chemistry, geology, physics. **Protective services:** Law enforcement admin. **Psychology:** General. **Social sciences:** Economics, geography, political science, sociology, urban studies. **Visual/performing arts:** Art, art history/conservation, dance, dramatic, music performance, music theory/composition, studio arts. **Other:** Communication studies, Electrical & computer engineering, History and Judaic studies, Mathematics & statistics.

Most popular majors. Business/marketing 14%, communications/journalism 6%, education 8%, health sciences 9%, liberal arts 18%, psychology 6%, social sciences 6%, visual/performing arts 6%.

Computing on campus. 680 workstations in dormitories, library, computer center, student center. Dormitories wired for high-speed internet access and linked to campus network. Commuter students can connect to campus network. Online course registration, online library, helpline, wireless network available.

Student life. Freshman orientation: Mandatory, $40 fee. Preregistration for classes offered. Several 2-day orientations during summer. **Housing:** Coed dorms, apartments, fraternity/sorority housing, wellness housing available. $300 partly refundable deposit. University owned houses available. **Activities:** Bands, choral groups, dance, drama, international student organizations, literary magazine, music ensembles, Model UN, opera, radio station, student government, student newspaper, symphony orchestra, over 200 religious, political, ethnic, and social service organizations.

Athletics. NCAA. **Intercollegiate:** Basketball, cheerleading, cross-country, golf, soccer M, softball W, tennis, track and field, volleyball W. **Intramural:** Basketball, football (tackle), golf, racquetball, softball, table tennis, volleyball. **Team name:** Kangaroos.

Student services. Adult student services, alcohol/substance abuse counseling, chaplain/spiritual director, career counseling, student employment services, financial aid counseling, health services, minority student services, on-campus daycare, personal counseling, placement for graduates, veterans' counselor, women's services. **Physically disabled:** Services for visually, speech, hearing impaired.

Contact. E-mail: admit@umkc.edu
Phone: (816) 235-1111 Toll-free number: (800) 775-8652
Fax: (816) 235-5544
Jennifer DeHaemers, Assistant Vice Chancellor of Student Affairs, University of Missouri: Kansas City, 5100 Rockhill Road, AC120, Kansas City, MO 64110-2499

University of Missouri: St. Louis

St. Louis, Missouri — **CB member**
www.umsl.edu — **CB code: 6889**

- Public 4-year university
- Commuter campus in very large city
- 8,681 degree-seeking undergraduates: 35% part-time, 57% women, 19% African American, 3% Asian American, 2% Hispanic American, 3% international
- 3,152 degree-seeking graduate students
- 58% of applicants admitted
- SAT or ACT (ACT writing optional) required
- 43% graduate within 6 years; 12% enter graduate study

General. Founded in 1963. Regionally accredited. **Degrees:** 2,016 bachelor's awarded; master's, doctoral, first professional offered. **ROTC:** Army, Air Force. **Location:** 7 miles from downtown. **Calendar:** Semester, extensive summer session. **Full-time faculty:** 489 total; 76% have terminal degrees, 19% minority, 48% women. **Part-time faculty:** 411 total; 25% have terminal degrees, 12% minority, 57% women. **Class size:** 44% < 20, 41% 20-39, 7% 40-49, 7% 50-99, 1% >100. **Special facilities:** Mercantile library, observatory, 3 art galleries, performing arts center.

Freshman class profile. 2,107 applied, 1,216 admitted, 469 enrolled.

Mid 50% test scores		**End year in good standing:**	70%
SAT math:	460-560	**Return as sophomores:**	71%
ACT composite:	20-26	**Out-of-state:**	10%
Rank in top quarter:	50%	**International:**	6%
Rank in top tenth:	22%		

Basis for selection. Class rank, test scores and high school course requirements most important. Audition required for music majors; not required for admission but for the purpose of placement with instrument. **Homeschooled:** ACT scores are key factor in determining admission. Students should strive for score of 24 or higher.

High school preparation. College-preparatory program required. 17 units required. Required units include English 4, mathematics 4, social studies 3, science 3 (laboratory 1) and foreign language 2. 1 fine art required.

2008-2009 Annual costs. Tuition/fees: $8,595; $19,686 out-of-state. Room/board: $7,782. Books/supplies: $900. Personal expenses: $5,514.

2008-2009 Financial aid. **Non-need-based:** Scholarships awarded for academics, alumni affiliation, art, athletics, music/drama, ROTC, state residency.

Application procedures. **Admission:** Closing date 8/24. $35 fee, may be waived for applicants with need. Admission notification on a rolling basis beginning on or about 10/1. **Financial aid:** Priority date 4/1; no closing date. FAFSA required. Applicants notified on a rolling basis starting 4/1; must reply within 2 week(s) of notification.

Academics. **Special study options:** Accelerated study, combined bachelor's/graduate degree, cooperative education, cross-registration, distance learning, double major, dual enrollment of high school students, ESL, exchange student, honors, independent study, internships, liberal arts/career combination, semester at sea, student-designed major, study abroad, teacher certification program. **Credit/placement by examination:** AP, CLEP, IB, SAT, ACT, institutional tests. 30 credit hours maximum toward bachelor's degree. **Support services:** Learning center, pre-admission summer program, study skills assistance, tutoring, writing center.

Honors college/program. Selection based on scores, class rank, extracurricular activities, test scores, 2 recommendations, essay, interview with Dean. Approximately 50 freshmen admitted each fall. Academic program includes honors classes.

Majors. **Biology:** General, biochemistry. **Business:** Accounting, business admin, finance, international, logistics, management information systems, marketing, operations, organizational behavior. **Communications:** General, media studies. **Computer sciences:** General. **Education:** General, early childhood, elementary, music, physical, secondary, special. **Engineering:** Civil, electrical, mechanical. **Foreign languages:** French, German, Spanish. **Health:** Health care admin, nursing (RN). **History:** General. **Liberal arts:** Arts/sciences. **Math:** General, applied. **Philosophy/religion:** Philosophy. **Physical sciences:** Chemistry, physics. **Psychology:** General. **Public administration:** General, social work. **Social sciences:** Anthropology, criminology, economics, political science, sociology. **Visual/performing arts:** Art, art history/conservation, dramatic.

Most popular majors. Business/marketing 30%, communications/journalism 6%, education 12%, health sciences 9%, psychology 6%, social sciences 10%.

Computing on campus. 1,200 workstations in dormitories, library, computer center, student center. Dormitories wired for high-speed internet access and linked to campus network. Commuter students can connect to campus network. Online course registration, online library, helpline, student web hosting, wireless network available.

Student life. **Freshman orientation:** Available. Preregistration for classes offered. One day program held several times throughout summer. Spring orientation session offered in January. **Housing:** Guaranteed on-campus for all undergraduates. Coed dorms, special housing for disabled, apartments, fraternity/sorority housing, wellness housing available. $400 partly refundable deposit, deadline 7/1. **Activities:** Bands, choral groups, dance, drama, film society, international student organizations, literary magazine, music ensembles, Model UN, musical theater, opera, radio station, student government, student newspaper, Associated Black Collegians, Spanish club, Alpha Phi Omega, Amnesty International, Pan-Hellenic Council, College Republicans, Catholic Students at Newman Center, Campus Crusade for Christ, UMSL Life Group.

Athletics. NCAA. **Intercollegiate:** Baseball M, basketball, golf, ice hockey M, soccer, softball W, tennis, volleyball W. **Intramural:** Badminton, basketball, bowling, football (non-tackle), football (tackle), golf, racquetball, skiing, soccer, softball, swimming, table tennis, tennis, volleyball, weight lifting. **Team name:** Tritons.

Student services. Adult student services, alcohol/substance abuse counseling, chaplain/spiritual director, career counseling, services for economically disadvantaged, student employment services, financial aid counseling, health services, minority student services, on-campus daycare, personal counseling, placement for graduates, veterans' counselor, women's services. **Physically disabled:** Services for visually, speech, hearing impaired.

Contact. E-mail: admissions@umsl.edu
Phone: (314) 516-5451 Toll-free number: (888) GO2-UMSL
Fax: (314) 516-5310
J. McCalley, Associate Vice Provost, University of Missouri: St. Louis, One University Boulevard, St. Louis, MO 63121-4400

Washington University in St. Louis

St. Louis, Missouri **CB member**
www.wustl.edu **CB code: 6929**

- Private 4-year university
- Residential campus in large city
- 6,339 degree-seeking undergraduates: 5% part-time, 51% women, 10% African American, 13% Asian American, 3% Hispanic American, 4% international
- 6,162 degree-seeking graduate students
- 22% of applicants admitted
- SAT or ACT (ACT writing optional), application essay required
- 94% graduate within 6 years

General. Founded in 1853. Regionally accredited. **Degrees:** 1,760 bachelor's awarded; master's, doctoral, first professional offered. **ROTC:** Army, Air Force. **Location:** 7 miles from downtown. **Calendar:** Semester, extensive summer session. **Full-time faculty:** 907 total; 98% have terminal degrees, 35% women. **Part-time faculty:** 173 total; 43% women. **Class size:** 74% < 20, 14% 20-39, 3% 40-49, 7% 50-99, 2% >100. **Special facilities:** Research center, 59-acre medical campus, observatory, plant growth facility, international writer's center, planetarium, business/economics experimental laboratory, laboratory science building, outdoor research center, theater.

Freshman class profile. 21,979 applied, 4,775 admitted, 1,426 enrolled.

Mid 50% test scores		**Out-of-state:**	90%
SAT critical reading:	680-760	**Live on campus:**	99%
SAT math:	700-780	**International:**	6%
ACT composite:	31-34	**Fraternities:**	25%
Return as sophomores:	96%	**Sororities:**	25%

Basis for selection. Rigor of high school curriculum and academic performance, GPA, test scores, extracurricular activities, essay, recommendations very important. Counselor and teacher recommendations required of all applicants. Portfolio optional for students applying to the College of Art and the College of Architecture. **Homeschooled:** Letter of recommendation (nonparent) required.

High school preparation. College-preparatory program recommended. 20 units recommended. Recommended units include English 4, mathematics 4, social studies 4, history 4, science 4 (laboratory 4) and foreign language 2.

2009-2010 Annual costs. Tuition/fees: $38,864. Room/board: $12,465. Books/supplies: $1,280. Personal expenses: $2,060.

2008-2009 Financial aid. **Need-based:** 935 full-time freshmen applied for aid; 543 were judged to have need; 539 of these received aid. Average need met was 100%. Average scholarship/grant was $28,345; average loan $4,996. 84% of total undergraduate aid awarded as scholarships/grants, 16% as loans/jobs. **Non-need-based:** Awarded to 1,107 full-time undergraduates, including 321 freshmen. Scholarships awarded for academics, ROTC.

Application procedures. **Admission:** Closing date 1/15. $55 fee, may be waived for applicants with need. Admission notification 4/1. Must reply by 5/1. **Financial aid:** Closing date 2/15. FAFSA, CSS PROFILE required. Applicants notified by 4/1; must reply by 5/1.

Academics. Special study options: Accelerated study, combined bachelor's/graduate degree, cooperative education, cross-registration, double major, dual enrollment of high school students, ESL, exchange student, independent study, internships, liberal arts/career combination, student-designed major, study abroad, teacher certification program, Washington semester. University Scholars Program. **Credit/placement by examination:** AP, CLEP, IB, institutional tests. **Support services:** Learning center, pre-admission summer program, reduced course load, study skills assistance, tutoring, writing center.

Majors. Architecture: Architecture, technology. **Area/ethnic studies:** African-American, American, Asian, East Asian, European, German, Latin American, Near/Middle Eastern, women's. **Biology:** General, biochemistry, biophysics. **Business:** General, accounting, business admin, entrepreneurial studies, finance, human resources, international, international finance, managerial economics, marketing, operations. **Communications:** Advertising, journalism. **Computer sciences:** General, computer science, data processing, information systems. **Conservation:** Environmental studies. **Education:** General, art, biology, chemistry, drama/dance, elementary, English, French, German, history, mathematics, middle, physics, science, secondary, social science, social studies, Spanish. **Engineering:** Biomedical, chemical, computer, electrical, mechanical, systems. **Foreign languages:** General, ancient Greek, Arabic, Chinese, classics, comparative lit, French, German, Germanic, Hebrew, Italian, Japanese, Latin, Romance, Spanish. **Health:** Predental, premedicine, prepharmacy, preveterinary. **History:** General. **Interdisciplinary:** Ancient studies, biological/physical sciences, biopsychology, math/computer science, neuroscience, science/society, systems science. **Liberal arts:** Arts/sciences, humanities. **Math:** General, applied, statistics. **Philosophy/religion:** Islamic, Judaic, philosophy, religion. **Physical sciences:** Chemistry, geology, physics, planetary. **Psychology:** General, industrial. **Social sciences:** General, anthropology, archaeology, economics, international relations, political science, urban studies. **Visual/performing arts:** General, art, art history/conservation, ceramics, commercial/advertising art, dance, design, dramatic, drawing, fashion design, film/cinema, graphic design, illustration, music history, music theory/composition, painting, photography, printmaking, sculpture, studio arts, theater history, voice/opera.

Most popular majors. Biology 8%, business/marketing 13%, engineering/engineering technologies 17%, psychology 9%, social sciences 16%, visual/performing arts 7%.

Computing on campus. 2,500 workstations in dormitories, library, computer center, student center. Dormitories wired for high-speed internet access and linked to campus network. Commuter students can connect to campus network. Online course registration, online library, helpline, repair service, student web hosting, wireless network available.

Student life. Freshman orientation: Mandatory. Preregistration for classes offered. **Housing:** Guaranteed on-campus for freshmen. Coed dorms, apartments, cooperative housing, fraternity/sorority housing, wellness housing available. $250 deposit, deadline 5/1. **Activities:** Bands, campus ministries, choral groups, dance, drama, film society, international student organizations, literary magazine, music ensembles, Model UN, musical theater, opera, radio station, student government, student newspaper, symphony orchestra, TV station, over 200 social clubs and organizations.

Athletics. NCAA. **Intercollegiate:** Baseball M, basketball, cross-country, diving, football (tackle) M, golf W, soccer, softball W, swimming, tennis, track and field, volleyball W. **Intramural:** Badminton, basketball, bowling, cross-country, football (non-tackle), golf, racquetball, soccer, softball, swimming, table tennis, tennis, track and field, volleyball, water polo. **Team name:** Bears.

Student services. Adult student services, alcohol/substance abuse counseling, chaplain/spiritual director, career counseling, services for economically disadvantaged, student employment services, financial aid counseling, health services, minority student services, on-campus daycare, personal counseling, placement for graduates, veterans' counselor, women's services. **Physically disabled:** Services for visually, speech, hearing impaired.

Contact. E-mail: admissions@wustl.edu
Phone: (314) 935-6000 Toll-free number: (800) 638-0700
Fax: (314) 935-4290
Nanette Tarbouni, Director of Admissions, Washington University in St. Louis, Campus Box 1089, One Brookings Drive, St. Louis, MO 63130-4899

Webster University

St. Louis, Missouri — **CB member**
www.webster.edu — **CB code: 6933**

- Private 4-year university
- Commuter campus in large city
- 3,463 degree-seeking undergraduates: 25% part-time, 58% women, 13% African American, 2% Asian American, 2% Hispanic American, 2% international
- 4,377 degree-seeking graduate students
- 57% of applicants admitted
- SAT or ACT (ACT writing recommended), application essay required
- 60% graduate within 6 years; 16% enter graduate study

General. Founded in 1915. Regionally accredited. Additional programs offered at five St. Louis area campuses. Undergraduate degrees offered at extended campus locations in California, South Carolina, Florida, as well as international campuses in Vienna, Austria; Leiden, The Netherlands; Geneva, Switzerland; Cha-am, Thailand; and London, United Kingdom. **Degrees:** 919 bachelor's awarded; master's, doctoral offered. **ROTC:** Army, Air Force. **Location:** 12 miles from St. Louis. **Calendar:** Semester, limited summer session. **Full-time faculty:** 184 total; 74% have terminal degrees, 6% minority, 46% women. **Part-time faculty:** 679 total; 6% minority, 45% women. **Class size:** 86% < 20, 14% 20-39, less than 1% 40-49. **Special facilities:** Repertory theater, opera theater, community music school.

Freshman class profile. 1,667 applied, 950 admitted, 420 enrolled.

Mid 50% test scores		**GPA 2.0-2.99:**	22%
SAT critical reading:	570-630	**Rank in top quarter:**	53%
SAT math:	540-620	**Rank in top tenth:**	24%
ACT composite:	21-28	**Return as sophomores:**	77%
GPA 3.75 or higher:	33%	**Out-of-state:**	28%
GPA 3.50-3.74:	19%	**Live on campus:**	65%
GPA 3.0-3.49:	26%		

Basis for selection. School achievement record, test scores important. Rank in top half of class recommended. Recommendation, essay, resume of activities considered. Interview recommended for all students. Audition required for dance, music, music theater, and theater students; portfolio required for art and film students. **Homeschooled:** Transcripts, ACT or SAT scores, recommendations from community leader or employer must be submitted.

High school preparation. College-preparatory program recommended. 21 units recommended. Recommended units include English 4, mathematics 3, social studies 3, science 3 (laboratory 2), foreign language 2 and academic electives 3.

2008-2009 Annual costs. Tuition/fees: $20,440. Tuition $23,940 for theater conservatory students. Room/board: $9,000. Books/supplies: $800. Personal expenses: $1,500.

2007-2008 Financial aid. Need-based: 443 full-time freshmen applied for aid; 361 were judged to have need; 361 of these received aid. Average scholarship/grant was $7,108; average loan $3,602. 60% of total undergraduate aid awarded as scholarships/grants, 40% as loans/jobs. **Non-need-based:** Awarded to 1,719 full-time undergraduates, including 402 freshmen. Scholarships awarded for academics, art, music/drama.

Application procedures. Admission: Priority date 3/1; deadline 6/1. $35 fee, may be waived for applicants with need. Admission notification on a rolling basis beginning on or about 9/1. Must reply by May 1 or within 4 week(s) if notified thereafter. **Financial aid:** Priority date 4/1; no closing date. FAFSA, institutional form required. Applicants notified on a rolling basis starting 2/9; must reply within 2 week(s) of notification.

Academics. Professional Actors Equity theater company in residence for theater program. Internships and practicums available in most areas. **Special study options:** Accelerated study, combined bachelor's/graduate degree, cooperative education, cross-registration, distance learning, double major, dual enrollment of high school students, ESL, exchange student, honors, independent study, internships, liberal arts/career combination, student-designed major, study abroad, teacher certification program. Certificate programs and combination bachelor's/master's degree in many subject areas, student leadership development program, individualized majors. **Credit/placement by examination:** AP, CLEP, IB. 64 credit hours maximum toward bachelor's degree. **Support services:** Learning center, reduced course load, remedial instruction, study skills assistance, tutoring, writing center.

Majors. Area/ethnic studies: American. **Biology:** General. **Business:** General, accounting, accounting/finance, business admin, finance, international, marketing. **Communications:** General, advertising, broadcast journalism, digital media, journalism, public relations. **Communications technology:** Recording arts. **Computer sciences:** Computer science. **Education:** General, music. **Foreign languages:** General, French, German, Spanish. **Health:** Nursing (RN). **History:** General. **Interdisciplinary:** Global studies. **Legal studies:** General, paralegal. **Liberal arts:** Arts/sciences, humanities. **Math:** General. **Philosophy/religion:** Ethics, philosophy, religion. **Psychology:** General. **Social sciences:** General, anthropology, economics, international relations, political science, sociology. **Visual/performing arts:** Acting, art, cinematography, dance, directing/producing, dramatic, film/cinema, photography, studio arts. **Other:** Media literacy.

Most popular majors. Business/marketing 31%, communications/journalism 13%, computer/information sciences 6%, social sciences 9%, visual/performing arts 15%.

Computing on campus. 450 workstations in dormitories, library, computer center, student center. Dormitories wired for high-speed internet access and linked to campus network. Online course registration, online library, helpline, student web hosting, wireless network available.

Student life. Freshman orientation: Available. **Housing:** Guaranteed on-campus for freshmen. Coed dorms, apartments available. $150 fully refundable deposit, deadline 4/1. Pets allowed in dorm rooms. **Activities:** Jazz band, choral groups, dance, drama, film society, international student organizations, literary magazine, music ensembles, musical theater, opera, radio station, student government, student newspaper, symphony orchestra, TV station, African student association, Campus Crusade for Christ, Chinese student association, Colleges Against Cancer, Habitat for Humanity, Latin American student association, Muslim student association, Sustainability Initiative, Webster LGBTQ Alliance.

Athletics. NCAA. **Intercollegiate:** Baseball M, basketball, cross-country W, golf M, soccer, softball W, tennis, volleyball W. **Intramural:** Bowling, soccer, table tennis, volleyball M. **Team name:** Gorloks.

Student services. Alcohol/substance abuse counseling, chaplain/spiritual director, career counseling, student employment services, financial aid counseling, health services, minority student services, personal counseling, placement for graduates, women's services. **Physically disabled:** Services for visually, speech, hearing impaired.

Contact. E-mail: admit@webster.edu
Phone: (314) 968-6991 Toll-free number: (800) 753-6765
Fax: (314) 968-7115
Niel DeVasto, Director of Undergraduate Admissions, Webster University, 470 East Lockwood Avenue, St. Louis, MO 63119-3194

Westminster College

Fulton, Missouri — **CB member**
www.westminster-mo.edu — **CB code: 6937**

- Private 4-year liberal arts college affiliated with Presbyterian Church (USA)
- Residential campus in large town
- 980 degree-seeking undergraduates: 44% women, 5% African American, 1% Asian American, 2% Hispanic American, 2% Native American, 14% international
- 77% of applicants admitted
- SAT or ACT (ACT writing optional) required
- 61% graduate within 6 years; 24% enter graduate study

General. Founded in 1851. Regionally accredited. **Degrees:** 168 bachelor's awarded. **ROTC:** Army, Air Force. **Location:** 100 miles from St. Louis, 24 miles from Jefferson City. **Calendar:** Semester, limited summer session. **Full-time faculty:** 59 total; 78% have terminal degrees, 8% minority, 37% women. **Part-time faculty:** 38 total; 45% have terminal degrees, 58% women. **Class size:** 64% < 20, 36% 20-39. **Special facilities:** Winston Churchill memorial and library, 12th century church re-built on campus.

Freshman class profile. 966 applied, 745 admitted, 244 enrolled.

Mid 50% test scores		**Rank in top quarter:**	51%
SAT critical reading:	480-610	**Rank in top tenth:**	18%
SAT math:	500-620	**Return as sophomores:**	84%
SAT writing:	470-610	**Out-of-state:**	24%
ACT composite:	23-28	**Live on campus:**	97%
GPA 3.75 or higher:	27%	**International:**	12%
GPA 3.50-3.74:	13%	**Fraternities:**	60%
GPA 3.0-3.49:	33%	**Sororities:**	40%
GPA 2.0-2.99:	27%		

Basis for selection. High school achievement (including class rank, involvement, ACT scores, curriculum, GPA) and recommendations most important. Interview recommended for borderline students, required for students with learning disabilities. **Learning Disabled:** Learning Disabilities Program applicants must have completed applications credentials and personal interview prior to April 1, including untimed SAT/ACT results.

High school preparation. College-preparatory program recommended. 16 units required. Required and recommended units include English 4, mathematics 3, social studies 2, science 2 (laboratory 2), foreign language 2 and academic electives 2. Pre-med and pre-dental students should have at least 3 lab science, 1 advanced math.

2009-2010 Annual costs. Tuition/fees: $18,700. Room/board: $7,120. Books/supplies: $800. Personal expenses: $2,480.

2008-2009 Financial aid. Need-based: 198 full-time freshmen applied for aid; 142 were judged to have need; 142 of these received aid. Average need met was 70%. Average scholarship/grant was $13,397; average loan $3,154. 88% of total undergraduate aid awarded as scholarships/grants, 12% as loans/jobs. **Non-need-based:** Awarded to 425 full-time undergraduates, including 97 freshmen. Scholarships awarded for academics, alumni affiliation, leadership, minority status, music/drama, religious affiliation, ROTC, state residency.

Application procedures. Admission: Priority date 2/1; no deadline. No application fee. Admission notification on a rolling basis beginning on or about 10/1. Must reply by May 1 or within 3 week(s) if notified thereafter. **Financial aid:** Priority date 2/15; no closing date. FAFSA required. Applicants notified on a rolling basis starting 3/1; must reply within 3 week(s) of notification.

Academics. First-year seminar fosters communication, critical thinking and study skills. **Special study options:** Combined bachelor's/graduate degree, cooperative education, cross-registration, double major, dual enrollment of high school students, exchange student, honors, independent study, internships, liberal arts/career combination, New York semester, student-designed major, study abroad, teacher certification program, urban semester, Washington semester. **Credit/placement by examination:** AP, CLEP, IB, institutional tests. 30 credit hours maximum toward bachelor's degree. **Support services:** Learning center, reduced course load, remedial instruction, study skills assistance, tutoring, writing center.

Majors. Biology: General, biochemistry. **Business:** Accounting, business admin, management information systems. **Communications:** Advertising, journalism, media studies. **Computer sciences:** General. **Conservation:** General, environmental science, environmental studies. **Education:** Elementary, middle, physical, secondary. **Foreign languages:** French, Spanish. **Health:** Athletic training. **History:** General. **Math:** General. **Philosophy/religion:** Philosophy, religion. **Physical sciences:** Chemistry, physics. **Psychology:** General. **Social sciences:** Anthropology, economics, international relations, political science, sociology.

Most popular majors. Biology 7%, business/marketing 38%, education 9%, English 8%, psychology 8%, social sciences 10%.

Computing on campus. 200 workstations in library, computer center. Dormitories wired for high-speed internet access and linked to campus network. Commuter students can connect to campus network. Online course registration, online library, helpline, student web hosting, wireless network available.

Student life. Freshman orientation: Mandatory. Preregistration for classes offered. Held three days before classes start. **Housing:** Guaranteed on-campus for freshmen. Coed dorms, single-sex dorms, apartments, fraternity/sorority housing available. **Activities:** Pep band, campus ministries, choral groups, international student organizations, literary magazine, music ensembles, Model UN, student government, student newspaper, Young Democrats, Young Republicans, Big Brother-Big Sister program, Environmentally Concerned Students, Chapel Leadership Council, Habitat For Humanity, Fellowship of Christian Athletes.

Athletics. NCAA. **Intercollegiate:** Baseball M, basketball, cheerleading M, cross-country W, football (tackle) M, golf, soccer, softball W, tennis, track and field, volleyball W. **Intramural:** Basketball, football (non-tackle), soccer, softball, volleyball. **Team name:** Blue Jays.

Student services. Alcohol/substance abuse counseling, chaplain/spiritual director, career counseling, student employment services, financial aid counseling, health services, minority student services, personal counseling, placement for graduates, women's services. **Physically disabled:** Services for visually, speech, hearing impaired. **Learning disabled:** Comprehensive services available.

Contact. E-mail: admissions@westminster-mo.edu
Phone: (573) 592-5251 Toll-free number: (800) 475-3361
Fax: (573) 592-5255
George Wolf, Vice President and Dean of Enrollment Services, Westminster College, 501 Westminster Avenue, Fulton, MO 65251-1299

William Jewell College

Liberty, Missouri — **CB member**
www.jewell.edu — **CB code: 6941**

- Private 4-year liberal arts college
- Residential campus in large town
- 1,210 degree-seeking undergraduates: 13% part-time, 60% women

- 63% of applicants admitted
- SAT or ACT (ACT writing recommended), application essay required
- 61% graduate within 6 years; 27% enter graduate study

General. Founded in 1849. Regionally accredited. Campus in Harlaxton, England. **Degrees:** 298 bachelor's awarded. **ROTC:** Army. **Location:** 14 miles from downtown Kansas City. **Calendar:** Semester, limited summer session. **Full-time faculty:** 76 total; 86% have terminal degrees, 5% minority, 50% women. **Part-time faculty:** 76 total; 16% have terminal degrees, 12% minority, 67% women. **Class size:** 75% < 20, 24% 20-39, less than 1% 40-49. **Special facilities:** Observatory, flow cytometer, high and low-ropes course, outdoor environmental learning lab, Quimby pipe organ.

Freshman class profile. 1,585 applied, 994 admitted, 265 enrolled.

Mid 50% test scores			
SAT critical reading:	540-660	Rank in top quarter:	60%
SAT math:	500-610	Rank in top tenth:	33%
ACT composite:	23-28	End year in good standing:	83%
GPA 3.75 or higher:	45%	Return as sophomores:	78%
GPA 3.50-3.74:	21%	Out-of-state:	29%
GPA 3.0-3.49:	26%	Live on campus:	94%
GPA 2.0-2.99:	8%	Fraternities:	28%
		Sororities:	44%

Basis for selection. Admissions based on secondary school record. Class rank, standardized test scores, and essay also important. Audition or portfolio required for scholarship seeking music, theater, or art students.

High school preparation. College-preparatory program required. 15 units required; 19 recommended. Required and recommended units include English 4, mathematics 3-4, social studies 3, science 3 (laboratory 1), foreign language 2-3 and academic electives 2.

2009-2010 Annual costs. Tuition/fees: $24,300. Base tuition covers 12 to 18 credits per semester. Room/board: $6,700. Books/supplies: $1,100. Personal expenses: $2,520.

2008-2009 Financial aid. **Need-based:** 244 full-time freshmen applied for aid; 198 were judged to have need; 198 of these received aid. Average need met was 93%. Average scholarship/grant was $16,925; average loan $4,915. 71% of total undergraduate aid awarded as scholarships/grants, 29% as loans/jobs. **Non-need-based:** Awarded to 998 full-time undergraduates, including 263 freshmen. Scholarships awarded for academics, alumni affiliation, art, athletics, music/drama.

Application procedures. **Admission:** Priority date 12/1; deadline 8/15 (postmark date). $25 fee, may be waived for applicants with need, free for online applicants. Admission notification on a rolling basis beginning on or about 9/15. Must reply by May 1 or within 2 week(s) if notified thereafter. **Financial aid:** Priority date 3/1; no closing date. FAFSA required. Applicants notified on a rolling basis starting 2/15; must reply within 1.5 week(s) of notification.

Academics. Interdisciplinary core curriculum required. **Special study options:** Accelerated study, combined bachelor's/graduate degree, double major, dual enrollment of high school students, honors, independent study, internships, liberal arts/career combination, semester at sea, student-designed major, study abroad, teacher certification program, Washington semester. Pryor Leadership Studies. **Credit/placement by examination:** AP, CLEP, IB, SAT, ACT, institutional tests. No limit to credit by examination, but student must complete 30 hours in residence. **Support services:** Study skills assistance, tutoring, writing center.

Honors college/program. Oxbridge Honors Program allows students to study their major subject using tutorial mode of instruction used at Oxford University and Cambridge University (England). Minimum 3.8 GPA, ACT score of 28 required for admission.

Majors. **Biology:** General, biochemistry, molecular. **Business:** Accounting, business admin, international, managerial economics, nonprofit/public. **Communications:** General, organizational. **Computer sciences:** General, computer science, information systems. **Education:** Art, biology, chemistry, drama/dance, elementary, English, foreign languages, French, mathematics, music, physical, physics, secondary, social studies, Spanish, speech. **Foreign languages:** French, Spanish. **Health:** Clinical lab science, nursing (RN). **History:** General. **Math:** General. **Parks/recreation:** General. **Philosophy/religion:** Philosophy, religion. **Physical sciences:** Chemistry, physics. **Psychology:** General. **Social sciences:** International relations, political science. **Theology:** Sacred music. **Visual/performing arts:** Art, dramatic, music performance, music theory/composition. **Other:** Bioethics, Oxbridge history of ideas, Self-designed.

Most popular majors. Business/marketing 17%, communications/journalism 6%, education 6%, health sciences 21%, psychology 11%, visual/performing arts 6%.

Computing on campus. 232 workstations in library, computer center, student center. Dormitories wired for high-speed internet access and linked to campus network. Commuter students can connect to campus network. Online course registration, online library, helpline, student web hosting, wireless network available.

Student life. **Freshman orientation:** Mandatory. Preregistration for classes offered. 3-day program prior to the first day of classes. **Housing:** Guaranteed on-campus for all undergraduates. Coed dorms, single-sex dorms, special housing for disabled, fraternity/sorority housing, wellness housing available. $300 nonrefundable deposit, deadline 5/1. Off-campus houses utilized as residence halls available. **Activities:** Bands, campus ministries, choral groups, dance, drama, music ensembles, musical theater, opera, radio station, student government, student newspaper, symphony orchestra, Young Democrats, College Republicans, Progressive Students for America, Amnesty International, Student Senate, UNITY, Rotaract, Fellowship of Christian Athletes, TPEXEIN.

Athletics. NAIA. **Intercollegiate:** Baseball M, basketball, cheerleading, cross-country, football (tackle) M, golf, soccer, softball W, tennis, track and field, volleyball W. **Intramural:** Basketball, football (non-tackle), golf, racquetball, soccer, softball, tennis, volleyball. **Team name:** Cardinals.

Student services. Adult student services, alcohol/substance abuse counseling, chaplain/spiritual director, career counseling, student employment services, financial aid counseling, health services, minority student services, personal counseling, placement for graduates. **Physically disabled:** Services for hearing impaired.

Contact. E-mail: admission@william.jewell.edu
Phone: (816) 415-7511 Toll-free number: (888) 253-9355
Fax: (816) 415-5040
Bridget Gramling, Dean of Admission, William Jewell College, 500 College Hill, Liberty, MO 64068

William Woods University

Fulton, Missouri — **CB member**
www.williamwoods.edu — **CB code: 6944**

- Private 4-year university and liberal arts college affiliated with Christian Church (Disciples of Christ)
- Residential campus in large town
- 991 degree-seeking undergraduates: 16% part-time, 75% women, 4% African American, 2% Hispanic American, 1% Native American, 1% international
- 1,298 degree-seeking graduate students
- 83% of applicants admitted
- SAT or ACT (ACT writing recommended) required
- 47% graduate within 6 years

General. Founded in 1870. Regionally accredited. Students may enroll in courses offered at 4 other mid-Missouri colleges and universities. **Degrees:** 249 bachelor's, 24 associate awarded; master's offered. **ROTC:** Army, Naval, Air Force. **Location:** 100 miles from St. Louis, 30 miles from Columbia. **Calendar:** Semester, limited summer session. **Full-time faculty:** 56 total; 54% have terminal degrees, 12% minority, 55% women. **Part-time faculty:** 252 total; 18% have terminal degrees, 4% minority, 34% women. **Class size:** 76% < 20, 23% 20-39, less than 1% 40-49. **Special facilities:** Equestrian studies facilities, observatory, broadcasting laboratory, computer laboratories, model courtroom, ASL interpreting laboratories.

Freshman class profile. 749 applied, 620 admitted, 151 enrolled.

Mid 50% test scores			
SAT critical reading:	460-600	Rank in top quarter:	39%
SAT math:	440-570	Rank in top tenth:	16%
ACT composite:	19-24	Return as sophomores:	79%
GPA 3.75 or higher:	19%	Out-of-state:	44%
GPA 3.50-3.74:	23%	Live on campus:	100%
GPA 3.0-3.49:	33%	Fraternities:	47%
GPA 2.0-2.99:	25%	Sororities:	50%

Basis for selection. Secondary school record, class rank, test scores most important; extracurricular activities, 2 academic references also important; interview considered. Interview recommended for all students. Audition required for performing arts students; portfolio required for visual arts students. **Homeschooled:** Letter of recommendation (nonparent) required. GED required; ACT/SAT should be submitted.

High school preparation. 16 units required; 20 recommended. Required and recommended units include English 4, mathematics 3, social studies 2, history 3, science 3 (laboratory 3) and foreign language 2.

2008-2009 Annual costs. Tuition/fees: $16,690. Commuter students pay additional $50 fee per year. Room/board: $6,750. Books/supplies: $1,200. Personal expenses: $3,000.

2008-2009 Financial aid. Need-based: 145 full-time freshmen applied for aid; 140 were judged to have need; 139 of these received aid. Average need met was 79%. Average scholarship/grant was $12,245; average loan $4,093. 64% of total undergraduate aid awarded as scholarships/grants, 36% as loans/jobs. **Non-need-based:** Awarded to 412 full-time undergraduates, including 48 freshmen. Scholarships awarded for academics, alumni affiliation, art, athletics, leadership, music/drama, religious affiliation.

Application procedures. Admission: Priority date 3/1; no deadline. $25 fee, may be waived for applicants with need, free for online applicants. Admission notification on a rolling basis. Must reply by May 1 or within 3 week(s) if notified thereafter. **Financial aid:** Priority date 3/1; no closing date. FAFSA, institutional form required. Applicants notified on a rolling basis starting 3/15; must reply within 2 week(s) of notification.

Academics. ASL interpreting available. **Special study options:** Accelerated study, combined bachelor's/graduate degree, cross-registration, double major, dual enrollment of high school students, ESL, honors, independent study, internships, liberal arts/career combination, New York semester, student-designed major, study abroad, teacher certification program, Washington semester. Hollywood semester, qualified students may complete bachelor's degree in 3 years through Century Scholars program. **Credit/placement by examination:** AP, CLEP, IB, SAT, ACT, institutional tests. 30 credit hours maximum toward bachelor's degree. **Support services:** Pre-admission summer program, reduced course load, remedial instruction, study skills assistance, tutoring, writing center.

Majors. Agriculture: Equestrian studies. **Biology:** General. **Business:** Accounting, business admin, international, management information systems, managerial economics. **Communications:** General, advertising, broadcast journalism, journalism, public relations. **Computer sciences:** General. **Education:** General, art, elementary, English, mathematics, middle, physical, science, secondary, social science, special. **Foreign languages:** American Sign Language, Spanish. **Health:** Athletic training. **History:** General. **Legal studies:** General, paralegal. **Math:** General. **Parks/recreation:** Sports admin. **Physical sciences:** General. **Psychology:** General. **Public administration:** Social work. **Social sciences:** Political science. **Visual/performing arts:** Art, design, dramatic, graphic design, studio arts.

Most popular majors. Agriculture 15%, business/marketing 37%, communications/journalism 6%, education 7%, health sciences 6%.

Computing on campus. 135 workstations in dormitories, library, computer center, student center. Dormitories wired for high-speed internet access and linked to campus network. Online course registration, online library, helpline, repair service, wireless network available.

Student life. Freshman orientation: Mandatory. Preregistration for classes offered. 7 days prior to start of fall term. **Policies:** All residence halls nonsmoking. Students under 23 must reside on campus unless married or living with parent or guardian; lottery offered to students who wish to move off campus in spring for following fall semester. **Housing:** Guaranteed on-campus for all undergraduates. Coed dorms, single-sex dorms, special housing for disabled, apartments, fraternity/sorority housing, wellness housing available. $250 partly refundable deposit, deadline 8/15. Senior housing, single rooms, independent housing, learning communities, upper-class halls and apartments available. **Activities:** Campus ministries, choral groups, dance, drama, international student organizations, literary magazine, musical theater, radio station, student government, student newspaper, Big Brothers/Big Sisters, campus activities board, Association of Christian Ecumenical Students, community action network, Jesters, Students for Social Work, departmental clubs.

Athletics. NAIA. **Intercollegiate:** Baseball M, basketball, cross-country, golf, soccer, softball W, track and field, volleyball. **Intramural:** Badminton, baseball M, basketball, equestrian, football (non-tackle), softball, table tennis, tennis, volleyball, weight lifting. **Team name:** Owls.

Student services. Adult student services, alcohol/substance abuse counseling, chaplain/spiritual director, career counseling, financial aid counseling, health services, personal counseling. **Physically disabled:** Services for visually, speech, hearing impaired.

Contact. E-mail: admissions@williamwoods.edu
Phone: (573) 592-4221 Toll-free number: (800) 995-3159
Fax: (573) 592-1146
Jimmy Clay, Executive Director and Vice President of Enrollment Services, William Woods University, One University Avenue, Fulton, MO 65251-2388

Montana

Carroll College

Helena, Montana
www.carroll.edu
CB member
CB code: 4041

- Private 4-year liberal arts college affiliated with Roman Catholic Church
- Residential campus in large town
- 1,311 degree-seeking undergraduates: 7% part-time, 56% women, 1% African American, 1% Asian American, 2% Hispanic American, 1% Native American, 1% international
- 76% of applicants admitted
- SAT or ACT (ACT writing recommended) required
- 62% graduate within 6 years

General. Founded in 1909. Regionally accredited. **Degrees:** 315 bachelor's awarded. **ROTC:** Army. **Location:** 90 miles from Great Falls, 240 miles from Billings. **Calendar:** Semester, limited summer session. **Full-time faculty:** 84 total; 67% have terminal degrees, 1% minority, 39% women. **Part-time faculty:** 73 total; 6% have terminal degrees, 51% women. **Special facilities:** Observatory, seismograph station, engineering lab, nursing lab including "SimMan" and "SimBaby".

Freshman class profile. 1,174 applied, 895 admitted, 345 enrolled.

Mid 50% test scores		**GPA 2.0-2.99:**	16%
SAT critical reading:	490-590	**Rank in top quarter:**	59%
SAT math:	500-610	**Rank in top tenth:**	26%
SAT writing:	480-580	**Return as sophomores:**	80%
ACT composite:	21-26	**Out-of-state:**	47%
GPA 3.75 or higher:	33%	**Live on campus:**	95%
GPA 3.50-3.74:	21%	**International:**	1%
GPA 3.0-3.49:	30%		

Basis for selection. School achievement record, test scores, recommendations most important. SAT and SAT Subject Tests required of home schooled and nonaccredited high school graduates. Personal statement required. Interview recommended for academically weak students.

High school preparation. College-preparatory program recommended. 18 units recommended. Recommended units include English 4, mathematics 3, social studies 1, history 2, science 2 (laboratory 1), foreign language 2 and academic electives 2. 1 technology recommended.

2009-2010 Annual costs. Tuition/fees (projected): $22,592. Room/board: $7,118. Books/supplies: $800. Personal expenses: $1,600.

2008-2009 Financial aid. Need-based: 338 full-time freshmen applied for aid; 208 were judged to have need; 208 of these received aid. Average need met was 83%. Average scholarship/grant was $13,109; average loan $4,314. 68% of total undergraduate aid awarded as scholarships/grants, 32% as loans/jobs. **Non-need-based:** Awarded to 313 full-time undergraduates, including 126 freshmen. Scholarships awarded for academics, art, athletics, leadership, minority status, music/drama, religious affiliation, ROTC.

Application procedures. Admission: Priority date 3/1; deadline 6/1 (receipt date). $35 fee, may be waived for applicants with need, free for online applicants. Admission notification on a rolling basis beginning on or about 9/10. Must reply by May 1 or within 2 week(s) if notified thereafter. **Financial aid:** Priority date 3/1; no closing date. FAFSA required. Applicants notified on a rolling basis starting 3/1; must reply by 5/1 or within 2 week(s) of notification.

Academics. Special study options: Accelerated study, cooperative education, double major, dual enrollment of high school students, ESL, exchange student, honors, independent study, internships, liberal arts/career combination, student-designed major, study abroad, teacher certification program. 3-2 engineering program with Notre Dame, Columbia University, USC, Gonzaga University, Montana State University-Bozeman, Montana Tech; complete Civil Engineering program ABATE. **Credit/placement by examination:** AP, CLEP, IB, SAT, ACT, institutional tests. 9 credit hours maximum toward associate degree, 18 toward bachelor's. **Support services:** Learning center, pre-admission summer program, reduced course load, study skills assistance, tutoring, writing center.

Majors. Biology: General. **Business:** Accounting, business admin. **Communications:** General, public relations. **Computer sciences:** Computer science. **Conservation:** Environmental studies. **Education:** Biology, chemistry, elementary, English, ESL, history, mathematics, physical, social science, social studies, Spanish, speech. **Engineering:** Civil. **Foreign languages:** Classics, French, Spanish. **Health:** Community health services, health services, nursing (RN). **History:** General. **Math:** General, applied. **Parks/recreation:** Sports admin. **Philosophy/religion:** Ethics, philosophy. **Physical sciences:** Chemistry. **Psychology:** General. **Public administration:** General. **Social sciences:** International relations, political science, sociology. **Theology:** Theology. **Visual/performing arts:** General.

Computing on campus. 85 workstations in dormitories, library, computer center, student center. Dormitories wired for high-speed internet access and linked to campus network. Commuter students can connect to campus network. Online course registration, helpline, wireless network available.

Student life. Freshman orientation: Mandatory, $100 fee. Preregistration for classes offered. Four-day program. Fee includes cost of meals, entertainment, and various activities. **Policies:** Freshmen and sophomores required to live on campus. **Housing:** Guaranteed on-campus for freshmen. Coed dorms, apartments available. $300 partly refundable deposit, deadline 7/1. **Activities:** Pep band, campus ministries, choral groups, dance, drama, film society, international student organizations, literary magazine, music ensembles, musical theater, radio station, student government, student newspaper, College Democrats, Circle K, cultural exchange club, Into the Streets service organization, peer mentors, social work club, sociology club, student community outreach experience, Young Republicans.

Athletics. NAIA. **Intercollegiate:** Basketball, cross-country, football (tackle) M, golf, soccer W, swimming, volleyball W. **Intramural:** Badminton, basketball, bowling, cross-country, golf, handball, racquetball, skiing, soccer, softball, swimming, table tennis, volleyball, water polo. **Team name:** Saints.

Student services. Adult student services, alcohol/substance abuse counseling, chaplain/spiritual director, career counseling, student employment services, financial aid counseling, health services, personal counseling, placement for graduates, veterans' counselor.

Contact. E-mail: enroll@carroll.edu
Phone: (406) 447-4384 Toll-free number: (800) 992-3648
Fax: (406) 447-4533
Cynthia Thornquist, Director of Admissions and Enrollment, Carroll College, 1601 North Benton Avenue, Helena, MT 59625

Montana State University: Billings

Billings, Montana
www.msubillings.edu
CB member
CB code: 4298

- Public 4-year university and technical college
- Commuter campus in small city
- 4,100 degree-seeking undergraduates: 27% part-time, 64% women, 1% African American, 1% Asian American, 4% Hispanic American, 5% Native American
- 296 degree-seeking graduate students
- 100% of applicants admitted
- SAT or ACT (ACT writing recommended) required
- 33% graduate within 6 years; 8% enter graduate study

General. Founded in 1927. Regionally accredited. College of Professional Studies and Lifelong Learning located in downtown Billings. **Degrees:** 550 bachelor's, 232 associate awarded; master's offered. **ROTC:** Army, Naval, Air Force. **Location:** 224 miles from Helena, 560 miles from Denver. **Calendar:** Semester, limited summer session. **Full-time faculty:** 153 total; 88% have terminal degrees, 3% minority, 39% women. **Part-time faculty:** 157 total; 5% minority, 56% women. **Class size:** 46% < 20, 46% 20-39, 4% 40-49, 4% 50-99, less than 1% >100. **Special facilities:** Biological station, center for business enterprise, Montana Center for Disabilities, special education learning center, center for gerontological studies, small business institute, urban institute, public radio, center for applied economic research.

Freshman class profile. 1,359 applied, 1,356 admitted, 795 enrolled.

Mid 50% test scores		**GPA 2.0-2.99:**	35%
SAT critical reading:	430-570	**Rank in top quarter:**	31%
SAT math:	470-560	**Rank in top tenth:**	10%
ACT composite:	19-24	**End year in good standing:**	65%
GPA 3.75 or higher:	15%	**Return as sophomores:**	54%
GPA 3.50-3.74:	15%	**Out-of-state:**	8%
GPA 3.0-3.49:	33%	**Live on campus:**	36%

Basis for selection. Applicants must meet one of the following: 2.5 GPA, 22 ACT/1030 SAT (exclusive of Writing), or rank in upper half of graduating class. **Homeschooled:** Applicants may be admitted based on GED, ACT, or COMPASS scores.

High school preparation. College-preparatory program required. 14 units required. Required units include English 4, mathematics 3, social studies 3, science 2 (laboratory 2). 2 years foreign language, computer science, visual and performing arts, or vocational education also recommended.

2008-2009 Annual costs. Tuition/fees: $5,172; $13,980 out-of-state. Room/board: $5,270. Books/supplies: $1,000. Personal expenses: $3,300.

2007-2008 Financial aid. Need-based: 568 full-time freshmen applied for aid; 447 were judged to have need; 420 of these received aid. Average need met was 64%. Average scholarship/grant was $3,765; average loan $2,915. 41% of total undergraduate aid awarded as scholarships/grants, 59% as loans/jobs. **Non-need-based:** Awarded to 193 full-time undergraduates, including 46 freshmen. Scholarships awarded for academics, alumni affiliation, art, athletics, job skills, leadership, minority status, music/drama, state residency. **Additional information:** Veterans and honors fee waivers offered.

Application procedures. Admission: Priority date 7/1; no deadline. $30 fee. Application must be submitted on paper. Admission notification on a rolling basis. **Financial aid:** Priority date 3/1; no closing date. FAFSA required. Applicants notified on a rolling basis starting 4/1; must reply within 3 week(s) of notification.

Academics. Full degree programs and many courses designed for working professionals. **Special study options:** Accelerated study, combined bachelor's/graduate degree, cooperative education, cross-registration, distance learning, double major, dual enrollment of high school students, ESL, external degree, honors, independent study, internships, liberal arts/career combination, study abroad, teacher certification program, weekend college. Evening College, with extensive online programs and courses. College of Technology offers training and retraining for employment by combining academics and vocational opportunities. **Credit/placement by examination:** AP, CLEP, SAT, ACT. **Support services:** Learning center, reduced course load, remedial instruction, study skills assistance, tutoring, writing center.

Majors. Biology: General. **Business:** General. **Communications:** General, media studies, public relations. **Conservation:** Environmental studies. **Education:** General, art, biology, chemistry, curriculum, elementary, English, foreign languages, health, history, mathematics, music, physical, physics, science, secondary, social science, social studies, Spanish, special. **Foreign languages:** Spanish. **Health:** Athletic training, health care admin, vocational rehab counseling. **History:** General. **Liberal arts:** Arts/sciences. **Math:** General. **Parks/recreation:** Health/fitness, sports admin. **Physical sciences:** Chemistry. **Protective services:** Criminal justice. **Psychology:** General. **Public administration:** Human services. **Social sciences:** Political science, sociology. **Visual/performing arts:** Art, dramatic, music performance.

Most popular majors. Business/marketing 23%, communications/journalism 6%, education 25%, liberal arts 14%, psychology 7%.

Computing on campus. 1,050 workstations in dormitories, library, computer center, student center. Dormitories wired for high-speed internet access and linked to campus network. Commuter students can connect to campus network. Online course registration, online library, helpline, student web hosting, wireless network available.

Student life. Freshman orientation: Mandatory, $75 fee. Preregistration for classes offered. One-day orientations held throughout summer. **Housing:** Coed dorms, single-sex dorms, special housing for disabled, apartments, wellness housing available. $75 fully refundable deposit. **Activities:** Bands, campus ministries, choral groups, drama, international student organizations, literary magazine, music ensembles, musical theater, radio station, student government, student newspaper, more than 50 student groups available.

Athletics. NCAA. **Intercollegiate:** Baseball M, basketball, cheerleading, cross-country, golf, soccer, softball W, tennis, track and field, volleyball W. **Intramural:** Archery, basketball, cross-country, golf, racquetball, skiing, softball, swimming, table tennis, tennis, volleyball. **Team name:** Yellowjackets.

Student services. Adult student services, alcohol/substance abuse counseling, chaplain/spiritual director, career counseling, services for economically disadvantaged, student employment services, financial aid counseling, health services, legal services, minority student services, on-campus daycare, personal counseling, placement for graduates, veterans' counselor. **Physically disabled:** Services for visually, speech, hearing impaired.

Contact. E-mail: cjohannes@msubillings.edu
Phone: (406) 657-2158 Toll-free number: (800) 656-6782
Fax: (406) 657-2051
Shelly Andersen, Director of Admissions, Montana State University: Billings, 1500 University Drive, Billings, MT 59101-0298

Montana State University: Bozeman

Bozeman, Montana — **CB member**
www.montana.edu — **CB code: 4488**

- Public 4-year university
- Residential campus in large town
- 10,406 degree-seeking undergraduates: 14% part-time, 46% women, 1% Asian American, 1% Hispanic American, 3% Native American, 2% international
- 1,536 degree-seeking graduate students
- 67% of applicants admitted
- SAT or ACT with writing required
- 48% graduate within 6 years

General. Founded in 1893. Regionally accredited. **Degrees:** 1,809 bachelor's awarded; master's, doctoral offered. **ROTC:** Army, Air Force. **Location:** 139 miles from Billings. **Calendar:** Semester, limited summer session. **Full-time faculty:** 552 total; 79% have terminal degrees, 3% minority, 35% women. **Part-time faculty:** 261 total; 36% have terminal degrees, 2% minority, 56% women. **Class size:** 43% < 20, 34% 20-39, 9% 40-49, 8% 50-99, 6% >100. **Special facilities:** Museum of the Rockies, agricultural bioscience center, wind tunnel, electron microscope, center for biofilm engineering, planetarium, telecommunication center, geographic information and analysis center, thermal biology institute, rural dwellers center.

Freshman class profile. 6,245 applied, 4,155 admitted, 2,070 enrolled.

Mid 50% test scores		**Rank in top quarter:**	41%
SAT critical reading:	490-620	**Rank in top tenth:**	18%
SAT math:	510-630	**Return as sophomores:**	72%
ACT composite:	21-27	**Out-of-state:**	37%
GPA 3.75 or higher:	25%	**Live on campus:**	84%
GPA 3.50-3.74:	16%	**International:**	1%
GPA 3.0-3.49:	29%	**Fraternities:**	3%
GPA 2.0-2.99:	29%	**Sororities:**	3%

Basis for selection. Minimum 2.5 GPA or 22 ACT/SAT equivalent, or rank in top half of graduating class. Completion of state college-preparatory requirements important. Students may use SAT/ACT math scores for placement or take departmental exam. Students with 27 ACT English or 640 SAT verbal can waive freshman composition. Varies by program. **Homeschooled:** GED required.

High school preparation. College-preparatory program required. 14 units required. Required units include English 4, mathematics 3, social studies 3, science 2 (laboratory 2). 4 math recommended for science majors. Substitutions for foreign language requirement possible. 2 foreign language, preferably 2 computer science, visual and performing arts, or approved vocational education units.

2008-2009 Annual costs. Tuition/fees: $5,798; $16,997 out-of-state. Room/board: $7,070. Books/supplies: $1,090. Personal expenses: $1,740.

2007-2008 Financial aid. Need-based: 1,237 full-time freshmen applied for aid; 901 were judged to have need; 868 of these received aid. Average need met was 76%. Average scholarship/grant was $4,446; average loan $3,963. 34% of total undergraduate aid awarded as scholarships/grants, 66% as loans/jobs. **Non-need-based:** Awarded to 634 full-time undergraduates, including 156 freshmen. Scholarships awarded for academics, alumni affiliation, art, athletics, job skills, leadership, minority status, music/drama, ROTC, state residency.

Application procedures. Admission: No deadline. $30 fee. Admission notification on a rolling basis. **Financial aid:** Priority date 3/1; no closing date. FAFSA required. Applicants notified on a rolling basis starting 4/1; must reply within 3 week(s) of notification.

Academics. Special study options: Combined bachelor's/graduate degree, cooperative education, cross-registration, distance learning, double major, ESL, exchange student, honors, independent study, internships, student-designed major, study abroad, teacher certification program. Combined bachelor's/master's programs in environmental design/architecture and construction engineering technology/construction engineering management. **Credit/placement by examination:** AP, CLEP, IB, SAT, ACT, institutional tests. No more than 30 semester credits earned by correspondence, extension, or continuing education counted toward bachelor's degree. **Support services:** Learning center, remedial instruction, study skills assistance, tutoring, writing center.

Majors. Agriculture: Business, horticultural science, plant sciences, range science. **Architecture:** Environmental design. **Biology:** General, bacteriology, biotechnology. **Business:** General. **Computer sciences:** Computer science. **Conservation:** General, management/policy. **Education:** Agricultural, elementary, music, secondary, technology/industrial arts. **Engineering:**

Chemical, civil, computer, electrical, mechanical. **Engineering technology:** Construction. **Family/consumer sciences:** General. **Foreign languages:** General. **Health:** Nursing (RN). **History:** General. **Math:** General. **Parks/recreation:** Sports admin. **Philosophy/religion:** Philosophy. **Physical sciences:** Chemistry, physics, planetary. **Psychology:** General. **Social sciences:** Anthropology, economics, political science, sociology. **Visual/performing arts:** Art, cinematography.

Most popular majors. Biology 8%, business/marketing 13%, education 7%, engineering/engineering technologies 16%, family/consumer sciences 6%, health sciences 9%, visual/performing arts 7%.

Computing on campus. 850 workstations in dormitories, library, computer center. Dormitories wired for high-speed internet access and linked to campus network. Commuter students can connect to campus network. Online course registration, helpline, wireless network available.

Student life. Freshman orientation: Mandatory, $65 fee. Preregistration for classes offered. **Housing:** Guaranteed on-campus for freshmen. Coed dorms, single-sex dorms, apartments, fraternity/sorority housing, wellness housing available. $200 nonrefundable deposit. Older student floors available. **Activities:** Bands, campus ministries, choral groups, dance, drama, film society, international student organizations, literary magazine, music ensembles, musical theater, radio station, student newspaper, TV station, campus service organizations, Circle-K, Native American club, international coordinating council, black student union, Campus Crusade for Christ, Intervarsity Christian Fellowship.

Athletics. NCAA. **Intercollegiate:** Basketball, cheerleading, cross-country, football (tackle) M, golf W, rodeo, skiing, tennis, track and field, volleyball W. **Intramural:** Archery, badminton, basketball, bowling, cross-country, golf, gymnastics, handball, racquetball, rodeo, skiing, soccer, softball, swimming, table tennis, tennis, track and field, volleyball, water polo, weight lifting, wrestling M. **Team name:** Bobcats.

Student services. Adult student services, alcohol/substance abuse counseling, chaplain/spiritual director, career counseling, student employment services, financial aid counseling, health services, legal services, minority student services, on-campus daycare, personal counseling, placement for graduates, veterans' counselor, women's services. **Physically disabled:** Services for visually, speech, hearing impaired.

Contact. E-mail: admissions@montana.edu
Phone: (406) 994-2452 Toll-free number: (888) 678-2287
Fax: (406) 994-1923
Ronda Russell, Director, Admissions and Enrollment Services, Montana State University: Bozeman, PO Box 172190, Bozeman, MT 59717-2190

Montana State University: Northern

Havre, Montana
www.msun.edu **CB code: 4538**

- Public 4-year university and liberal arts college
- Commuter campus in large town
- 878 full-time, degree-seeking undergraduates
- 115 graduate students
- SAT or ACT (ACT writing recommended) required

General. Founded in 1929. Regionally accredited. Classes for military personnel available at resident center at Malmstrom Air Force Base, Great Falls. Extended campus in Great Falls. **Degrees:** 170 bachelor's, 97 associate awarded; master's offered. **Location:** 115 miles from Great Falls. **Calendar:** Semester, extensive summer session. **Full-time faculty:** 73 total. **Part-time faculty:** 30 total.

Freshman class profile.

Mid 50% test scores			
SAT critical reading:	420-510	ACT composite:	16-21
SAT math:	400-500	Out-of-state:	10%
		Live on campus:	31%

Basis for selection. Test scores, 2.5 GPA or upper half of class, in conjunction with college preparatory program, important.

High school preparation. 14 units required. Required units include English 4, mathematics 3, social studies 3, science 2 (laboratory 2) and academic electives 2.

2008-2009 Annual costs. Tuition/fees: $4,390; $15,035 out-of-state. Room/board: $5,928. Books/supplies: $800. Personal expenses: $558.

Financial aid. Non-need-based: Scholarships awarded for academics, athletics.

Application procedures. Admission: No deadline. $30 fee, may be waived for applicants with need. Admission notification on a rolling basis. **Financial aid:** Priority date 4/15; no closing date. FAFSA, institutional form required. Applicants notified on a rolling basis; must reply within 2 week(s) of notification.

Academics. Special study options: Accelerated study, combined bachelor's/graduate degree, cooperative education, distance learning, double major, dual enrollment of high school students, honors, independent study, internships, liberal arts/career combination, teacher certification program. **Credit/placement by examination:** AP, CLEP, SAT, ACT, institutional tests. **Support services:** Learning center, pre-admission summer program, reduced course load, remedial instruction, study skills assistance, tutoring.

Majors. Agriculture: Business. **Area/ethnic studies:** Native American. **Biology:** General. **Business:** Business admin. **Communications:** General. **Computer sciences:** General. **Education:** General, elementary, mathematics, physical, science, secondary, social science, technology/industrial arts. **Engineering technology:** Civil, drafting, electrical. **Foreign languages:** French. **Health:** Nursing (RN). **Mechanic/repair:** Electronics/electrical. **Physical sciences:** Chemistry. **Visual/performing arts:** Studio arts.

Computing on campus. 250 workstations in dormitories, library, computer center, student center. Dormitories wired for high-speed internet access and linked to campus network. Commuter students can connect to campus network. Online course registration, online library, helpline, repair service available.

Student life. Freshman orientation: Mandatory. Preregistration for classes offered. **Housing:** Guaranteed on-campus for all undergraduates. Coed dorms, single-sex dorms, apartments available. $75 fully refundable deposit, deadline 9/1. Limited housing available for nontraditional students. **Activities:** Concert band, choral groups, dance, drama, music ensembles, musical theater, radio station, student government, student newspaper, North Star Ambassadors, Inter-Christian fellowship, Delta Alpha Theta, Sweetgrass Society, Northern Vets club.

Athletics. NAIA. **Intercollegiate:** Basketball, cheerleading, football (tackle) M, golf W, rodeo, volleyball W, wrestling M. **Intramural:** Badminton, basketball, bowling, football (non-tackle), racquetball, rodeo, skiing, soccer, softball, swimming, table tennis, tennis, volleyball, weight lifting. **Team name:** Lights, Skylights.

Student services. Adult student services, alcohol/substance abuse counseling, career counseling, services for economically disadvantaged, student employment services, financial aid counseling, health services, minority student services, on-campus daycare, personal counseling, placement for graduates, veterans' counselor. **Physically disabled:** Services for visually, speech, hearing impaired.

Contact. E-mail: admissions@msun.edu
Phone: (406) 265-3704 Toll-free number: (800) 662-6132
Fax: (406) 265-3792
Stacey Gonsalez, Director of Admissions, Montana State University: Northern, Box 7751, Havre, MT 59501

Montana Tech of the University of Montana

Butte, Montana
www.mtech.edu **CB code: 4487**

- Public 4-year engineering and technical college
- Commuter campus in large town
- 2,086 degree-seeking undergraduates: 9% part-time, 38% women, 1% African American, 1% Asian American, 2% Hispanic American, 2% Native American, 7% international
- 103 degree-seeking graduate students
- 90% of applicants admitted
- SAT or ACT (ACT writing recommended) required
- 41% graduate within 6 years; 18% enter graduate study

General. Founded in 1893. Regionally accredited. **Degrees:** 263 bachelor's, 106 associate awarded; master's offered. **Location:** 82 miles from Bozeman, 65 miles from Helena. **Calendar:** Semester, extensive summer session. **Full-time faculty:** 121 total; 54% have terminal degrees, 34% women. **Part-time faculty:** 61 total; 10% have terminal degrees, 48% women. **Class size:** 65% < 20, 26% 20-39, 7% 40-49, 2% 50-99, less than 1% >100. **Special facilities:** Mineral museum, earthquake studies office.

Freshman class profile. 577 applied, 522 admitted, 404 enrolled.

Mid 50% test scores			
SAT math:	490-620	Rank in top quarter:	37%
ACT composite:	20-25	Rank in top tenth:	17%
GPA 3.75 or higher:	24%	Return as sophomores:	69%
GPA 3.50-3.74:	14%	Out-of-state:	11%
GPA 3.0-3.49:	29%	Live on campus:	53%
GPA 2.0-2.99:	31%	International:	4%

Basis for selection. Rank in top half of graduating class, or graduate with minimum cumulative GPA of 2.5, or achieve minimum composite score on ACT of 22, or minimum total score on SAT of 1530; meet math and English standards, and complete preparatory requirements.

High school preparation. College-preparatory program required. Required and recommended units include English 4, mathematics 3-4, social studies 3, history 3, science 2 (laboratory 2). Combined 3 years of foreign language, visual and performing arts, computer science, or vocational education required.

2008-2009 Annual costs. Tuition/fees: $5,713; $15,352 out-of-state. Room/board: $6,140. Books/supplies: $1,000. Personal expenses: $1,600.

2008-2009 Financial aid. **Non-need-based:** Scholarships awarded for academics, alumni affiliation, athletics, minority status, state residency.

Application procedures. **Admission:** No deadline. $30 fee. Admission notification on a rolling basis. **Financial aid:** Priority date 3/1; no closing date. FAFSA, institutional form required. Applicants notified on a rolling basis starting 4/1; must reply within 2 week(s) of notification.

Academics. **Special study options:** Combined bachelor's/graduate degree, cooperative education, cross-registration, distance learning, double major, dual enrollment of high school students, external degree, honors, independent study, internships, teacher certification program. 3-2 liberal arts-engineering program with Carroll College, dual enrollment agreement with Flathead Valley Community College, collaborative programs with UM Helena (BAS Business, BS BIT, BAS General Studies), UM Western (Elementary Education Certification and Secondary Education Certification in Biological Sciences, General Sciences, and Mathematical Sciences), and UM-COT (AAS Surgical Technology). **Credit/placement by examination:** AP, CLEP, IB, SAT, ACT, institutional tests. 10 credit hours maximum toward associate degree, 30 toward bachelor's. **Support services:** Learning center, pre-admission summer program, reduced course load, study skills assistance, tutoring.

Majors. **Biology:** General. **Business:** General. **Computer sciences:** Computer science, networking. **Engineering:** General, electrical, environmental, geological, metallurgical, mining, petroleum, software. **Health:** Medical informatics, nursing (RN), occupational health. **Liberal arts:** Arts/sciences. **Math:** General. **Physical sciences:** General, chemistry. **Other:** Business information technology.

Most popular majors. Business/marketing 13%, computer/information sciences 6%, engineering/engineering technologies 49%, health sciences 15%.

Computing on campus. 491 workstations in dormitories, library, computer center, student center. Dormitories wired for high-speed internet access and linked to campus network. Commuter students can connect to campus network. Online course registration, online library, helpline, repair service, student web hosting, wireless network available.

Student life. **Freshman orientation:** Mandatory. Preregistration for classes offered. Held several days before semester start. **Housing:** Guaranteed on-campus for freshmen. Coed dorms, special housing for disabled, apartments available. $100 fully refundable deposit. **Activities:** Pep band, campus ministries, international student organizations, radio station, student government, student newspaper, Baptist student union, Circle-K, Baha'i club, Prospectors, American Indian Science and Engineering Society, Students in Engineering Programs, Abundant Campus Life Ministry, Newman Club, Catholic Campus Ministries, FRINGE, LDSSA.

Athletics. NAIA. **Intercollegiate:** Basketball, football (tackle) M, golf, volleyball W. **Intramural:** Basketball, football (non-tackle), racquetball, softball, volleyball. **Team name:** Orediggers.

Student services. Adult student services, alcohol/substance abuse counseling, chaplain/spiritual director, career counseling, student employment services, financial aid counseling, health services, minority student services, personal counseling, placement for graduates, veterans' counselor, women's services. **Physically disabled:** Services for visually, hearing impaired.

Contact. E-mail: enrollment@mtech.edu
Phone: (406) 496-4256 Toll-free number: (800) 445-8324
Fax: (406) 496-4710
Tony Campeau, Director of Enrollment Management, Montana Tech of the University of Montana, 1300 West Park Street, Butte, MT 59701-8997

Rocky Mountain College

Billings, Montana
www.rocky.edu **CB code: 4660**

- Private 4-year liberal arts college affiliated with United Church of Christ, United Methodist Church, United Presbyterian Church
- Commuter campus in small city
- 877 degree-seeking undergraduates
- 69% of applicants admitted
- SAT or ACT (ACT writing optional) required

General. Founded in 1878. Regionally accredited. **Degrees:** 168 bachelor's awarded; master's offered. **Calendar:** Semester, limited summer session. **Full-time faculty:** 63 total. **Part-time faculty:** 16 total. **Class size:** 75% < 20, 23% 20-39, less than 1% 40-49, less than 1% 50-99. **Special facilities:** Outdoor recreation center, flight school, equestrian facilities, geology library, rock climbing wall.

Freshman class profile. 720 applied, 498 admitted, 197 enrolled.

Mid 50% test scores			
SAT critical reading:	460-590	GPA 3.0-3.49:	30%
SAT math:	450-570	GPA 2.0-2.99:	25%
ACT composite:	19-24	Rank in top quarter:	43%
GPA 3.75 or higher:	25%	Rank in top tenth:	21%
GPA 3.50-3.74:	20%	Out-of-state:	44%
		Live on campus:	89%

Basis for selection. 2.5 GPA, ACT 21 or combined critical reading/math SAT of 1000 meets requirement for regular admission. Essay recommended for all students. Interview recommended for students not meeting regular admission requirements. Audition recommended for music, theater students. Portfolio recommended for art students. **Homeschooled:** Applicants must either have GED or pass ACT based on college entrance standards.

High school preparation. 13 units required. Required and recommended units include English 4, mathematics 2-3, social studies 2, history 2, science 2 (laboratory 1) and foreign language 1-2.

2008-2009 Annual costs. Tuition/fees: $19,080. Room/board: $6,382. Books/supplies: $1,000. Personal expenses: $1,000.

2007-2008 Financial aid. **Need-based:** 56% of total undergraduate aid awarded as scholarships/grants, 44% as loans/jobs. **Non-need-based:** Scholarships awarded for academics, alumni affiliation, art, athletics, leadership, minority status, music/drama, religious affiliation, state residency.

Application procedures. **Admission:** No deadline. Students who make their decision by Dec. 31 receive priority placement in housing and class selection. **Financial aid:** Priority date 3/1; no closing date. FAFSA, institutional form required. Applicants notified on a rolling basis starting 2/1; must reply within 4 week(s) of notification.

Academics. **Special study options:** Accelerated study, combined bachelor's/graduate degree, distance learning, double major, dual enrollment of high school students, ESL, honors, independent study, internships, student-designed major, study abroad, teacher certification program. 3-2 program in occupational therapy, degree completion program, master's in physician assistant studies. **Credit/placement by examination:** AP, CLEP, IB, SAT, ACT, institutional tests. 15 credit hours maximum toward associate degree, 31 toward bachelor's. **Support services:** Learning center, reduced course load, remedial instruction, study skills assistance, tutoring.

Majors. **Agriculture:** Business, equestrian studies. **Biology:** General. **Business:** Accounting, business admin, management science. **Communications:** General. **Computer sciences:** Computer science, information technology. **Conservation:** Environmental science, environmental studies. **Education:** General, art, biology, drama/dance, elementary, English, history, mathematics, middle, multi-level teacher, music, physical, secondary, social studies. **Health:** Athletic training. **History:** General. **Math:** General. **Parks/recreation:** Exercise sciences, health/fitness. **Physical sciences:** Chemistry, geology. **Psychology:** General. **Social sciences:** Economics, political science, sociology. **Transportation:** Airline/commercial pilot, aviation management. **Visual/performing arts:** Art, dramatic, music performance, theater design. **Other:** Philosophy and religious thought.

Most popular majors. Agriculture 6%, biology 6%, business/marketing 30%, education 11%, psychology 7%, visual/performing arts 8%.

Computing on campus. 104 workstations in dormitories, library, computer center, student center. Dormitories wired for high-speed internet access and linked to campus network. Commuter students can connect to campus network. Online course registration, online library, helpline, student web hosting, wireless network available.

Student life. Freshman orientation: Mandatory. Preregistration for classes offered. Held during the 4 days before classes start; includes mountain getaway trip. **Housing:** Guaranteed on-campus for freshmen. Coed dorms, apartments available. Suites available. **Activities:** Bands, choral groups, drama, literary magazine, music ensembles, student government, student newspaper, Newman Club, intervarsity, American Indian science and engineering society, American Indian cultural association, health occupation groups, business club, precision flying team, ski club, equestrian club, Sojourner's club.

Athletics. NAIA. **Intercollegiate:** Basketball, cheerleading, equestrian, football (tackle) M, golf, skiing, soccer W, volleyball W. **Intramural:** Basketball, football (tackle) M, golf, handball, racquetball, skiing, soccer, softball, swimming, table tennis, tennis, volleyball. **Team name:** Battlin' Bears.

Student services. Adult student services, alcohol/substance abuse counseling, chaplain/spiritual director, career counseling, student employment services, financial aid counseling, health services, on-campus daycare, personal counseling, placement for graduates. **Physically disabled:** Services for visually, speech, hearing impaired.

Contact. E-mail: admissions@rocky.edu
Phone: (406) 657-1021 Toll-free number: (800) 877-6259
Fax: (406) 657-1189
Kelly Edward, Associate Director of Admissions, Rocky Mountain College, 1511 Poly Drive, Billings, MT 59102-1796

Salish Kootenai College

Pablo, Montana
www.skc.edu **CB code: 0898**

- Private 4-year liberal arts college
- Commuter campus in rural community

General. Founded in 1977. Regionally accredited. Native American cultural heritage. **Degrees:** 35 bachelor's, 65 associate awarded. **Location:** 55 miles from Missoula, 65 miles from Kalispell. **Calendar:** Quarter, limited summer session. **Full-time faculty:** 72 total; 61% have terminal degrees, 33% minority, 47% women. **Part-time faculty:** 40 total; 12% have terminal degrees, 52% minority, 58% women.

Basis for selection. Open admission, but selective for some programs. Special requirements for highway construction worker training, social work, dental assisting technology and nursing. Highway construction worker training program has special application which includes drug testing. Third-year applicants to social work program must complete special application which includes background check. Dental assisting technology and nursing also require special applications.

2008-2009 Annual costs. Full-time tuition for Native American students, $2,736 ($76 per credit hour); full-time tuition for students of Native American descent, $3,384 ($94 per credit hour). Academic year required fees, $897. Books/supplies: $750. Personal expenses: $1,800.

Application procedures. Admission: Priority date 7/1; no deadline. No application fee. Application must be submitted on paper. Admission notification on a rolling basis. **Financial aid:** Priority date 3/31; no closing date. FAFSA required. Applicants notified on a rolling basis starting 7/15; must reply within 6 week(s) of notification.

Academics. Special study options: Combined bachelor's/graduate degree, cooperative education, distance learning, double major, dual enrollment of high school students, independent study, internships. **Credit/placement by examination:** CLEP, institutional tests. **Support services:** Learning center, remedial instruction, study skills assistance, tutoring, writing center.

Majors. Business: Administrative services. **Computer sciences:** General. **Conservation:** General. **Health:** Nursing (RN). **Public administration:** Social work.

Most popular majors. Business/marketing 16%, computer/information sciences 8%, health sciences 20%, natural resources/environmental science 12%, public administration/social services 44%.

Computing on campus. 42 workstations in library, computer center, student center. Dormitories wired for high-speed internet access. Online course registration, online library, helpline, wireless network available.

Student life. Freshman orientation: Mandatory. Preregistration for classes offered. Held prior to registration day; one-half to one-day session. **Housing:** Special housing for disabled, apartments available. Housing costs based on income. **Activities:** Student government, student newspaper, TV station.

Athletics. Intercollegiate: Basketball. **Intramural:** Basketball, skiing, softball, volleyball. **Team name:** Bison.

Student services. Career counseling, student employment services, on-campus daycare, personal counseling, placement for graduates, veterans' counselor. **Physically disabled:** Services for visually, speech, hearing impaired.

Contact. E-mail: jackie_moran@skc.edu
Phone: (406) 275-4866 Fax: (406) 275-4810
Elaine Frank, Director of Enrollment Services, Salish Kootenai College, PO Box 70, Pablo, MT 59855

University of Great Falls

Great Falls, Montana
www.ugf.edu **CB code: 4058**

- Private 4-year university and liberal arts college affiliated with Roman Catholic Church
- Residential campus in small city
- 647 degree-seeking undergraduates: 28% part-time, 61% women, 4% African American, 1% Asian American, 7% Hispanic American, 4% Native American, 2% international
- 73 degree-seeking graduate students
- 83% of applicants admitted
- Application essay required

General. Founded in 1932. Regionally accredited. **Degrees:** 116 bachelor's, 11 associate awarded; master's offered. **Location:** 600 miles from Seattle, 370 miles from Spokane, Washington. **Calendar:** Semester, limited summer session. **Full-time faculty:** 41 total; 80% have terminal degrees, 2% minority, 56% women. **Part-time faculty:** 72 total; 15% have terminal degrees, 4% minority, 56% women. **Class size:** 86% < 20, 14% 20-39. **Special facilities:** Herbarium.

Freshman class profile. 338 applied, 282 admitted, 120 enrolled.

Mid 50% test scores		**GPA 3.0-3.49:**	28%
SAT critical reading:	290-410	**GPA 2.0-2.99:**	46%
SAT math:	360-510	**Return as sophomores:**	62%
ACT composite:	18-24	**Out-of-state:**	43%
GPA 3.75 or higher:	9%	**Live on campus:**	90%
GPA 3.50-3.74:	11%	**International:**	3%

Basis for selection. High school record and character most important. ACT/SAT scores may be considered when making scholarship decisions. SAT or ACT, SAT Subject Tests recommended. Interview recommended. **Homeschooled:** Transcript of courses and grades required. Applicants should submit SAT/ACT test scores, bibliography of school literature and essay describing and evaluating preparation for university-level work.

High school preparation. 20 units required; 22 recommended. Required and recommended units include English 4, mathematics 3, social studies 1-2, history 3, science 3 (laboratory 1) and academic electives 5.

2008-2009 Annual costs. Tuition/fees: $17,582. Room/board: $6,490. Books/supplies: $800. Personal expenses: $750.

2008-2009 Financial aid. Need-based: Average need met was 59%. Average scholarship/grant was $4,730; average loan $3,557. 44% of total undergraduate aid awarded as scholarships/grants, 56% as loans/jobs. **Non-need-based:** Scholarships awarded for academics, art, athletics, religious affiliation.

Application procedures. Admission: Priority date 5/1; deadline 9/1 (postmark date). $35 fee, may be waived for applicants with need. Admission notification on a rolling basis beginning on or about 10/1. Must reply by May 1 or within 2 week(s) if notified thereafter. Admission granted with 6th semester transcripts. **Financial aid:** Priority date 5/1; no closing date. FAFSA required. Applicants notified on a rolling basis starting 3/1; must reply within 2 week(s) of notification.

Academics. Trio Title IV Student Support Services program available to eligible students. **Special study options:** Combined bachelor's/graduate degree, cooperative education, distance learning, double major, dual enrollment of high school students, exchange student, honors, independent study, internships, liberal arts/career combination, study abroad, teacher certification program, weekend college. **Credit/placement by examination:** AP, CLEP, IB, SAT, ACT, institutional tests. 30 credit hours maximum toward associate degree, 30 toward bachelor's. **Support services:** Learning center, pre-admission summer program, reduced course load, remedial instruction, study skills assistance, tutoring, writing center.

Majors. **Biology:** General, botany. **Business:** Accounting, accounting/business management, business admin. **Computer sciences:** General, applications programming, computer graphics, computer science, data processing, LAN/WAN management, networking, programming, security, system admin, systems analysis. **Education:** Art, biology, chemistry, early childhood, elementary, English, gifted/talented, health, history, kindergarten/preschool, mathematics, middle, physical, psychology, reading, science, secondary, social science, social studies, special. **Health:** Preveterinary, substance abuse counseling. **History:** General. **Legal studies:** Paralegal. **Math:** General. **Parks/recreation:** Health/fitness. **Philosophy/religion:** Religion. **Physical sciences:** Chemistry. **Protective services:** Corrections, criminal justice, forensics, juvenile corrections, police science. **Psychology:** General. **Social sciences:** General, political science, sociology. **Visual/performing arts:** Art.

Most popular majors. Business/marketing 15%, education 23%, legal studies 7%, psychology 22%, security/protective services 14%.

Computing on campus. 120 workstations in dormitories, library, computer center, student center. Dormitories wired for high-speed internet access and linked to campus network. Commuter students can connect to campus network. Online course registration, online library, helpline, repair service, student web hosting, wireless network available.

Student life. **Freshman orientation:** Mandatory, $75 fee. Preregistration for classes offered. Programs held 3 days prior to fall and spring semesters; includes float trip down Missouri River. **Policies:** No drugs, alcohol, firearms or weapons allowed on campus. **Housing:** Guaranteed on-campus for freshmen. Coed dorms, apartments, wellness housing available. $150 fully refundable deposit, deadline 8/25. **Activities:** Bands, campus ministries, choral groups, dance, drama, film society, music ensembles, musical theater, student government, student newspaper, symphony orchestra, United Tribes Club, Americorps, drama club, art club, Students In Free Enterprise, international law and justice club, medical science club, student Montana education association, paralegal club.

Athletics. NAIA. **Intercollegiate:** Basketball, cross-country, golf, soccer W, softball W, volleyball W, wrestling M. **Intramural:** Baseball, basketball, bowling, cheerleading, football (non-tackle), softball, tennis, volleyball. **Team name:** Argonauts.

Student services. Adult student services, alcohol/substance abuse counseling, chaplain/spiritual director, career counseling, services for economically disadvantaged, student employment services, financial aid counseling, health services, minority student services, on-campus daycare, personal counseling, placement for graduates, veterans' counselor, women's services. **Physically disabled:** Services for visually, hearing impaired.

Contact. E-mail: enroll@ugf.edu
Phone: (406) 791-5200 Toll-free number: (800) 856-9544
Fax: (406) 791-5209
April Clutter, Assistant Director of Admissions, University of Great Falls, 1301 20th Street South, Great Falls, MT 59405

University of Montana

Missoula, Montana — **CB member**
www.umt.edu — **CB code: 4489**

- Public 4-year university and liberal arts college
- Residential campus in small city
- 12,196 degree-seeking undergraduates
- 96% of applicants admitted
- SAT or ACT (ACT writing recommended) required

General. Founded in 1893. Regionally accredited. Two-year technical college provides technical training, education and postsecondary academic preparation through general associate programs. **Degrees:** 1,712 bachelor's, 206 associate awarded; master's, doctoral, first professional offered. **ROTC:** Army. **Location:** 210 miles from Spokane, Washington. **Calendar:** Semester, extensive summer session. **Full-time faculty:** 564 total. **Part-time faculty:** 236 total. **Class size:** 45% < 20, 36% 20-39, 6% 40-49, 8% 50-99, 5% >100. **Special facilities:** Broadcast media center (public radio and TV) and performing arts building; 3 art galleries; wildlife biology museum; 29,000-acre experimental forest; biological research station; geology field camp; biological, biomedical, kinesiology, physiology, and forestry-related research centers and labs; environmental studies laboratory; primate colony; forensics lab; clinical psychology center; practical ethics center; Fort Missoula field research center.

Freshman class profile. 5,342 applied, 5,118 admitted, 2,412 enrolled.

Mid 50% test scores			
SAT critical reading:	480-580	Out-of-state:	27%
SAT math:	480-590	Live on campus:	69%
SAT writing:	450-580	Fraternities:	6%
ACT composite:	20-26	Sororities:	5%

Basis for selection. Must meet one of the following: 2.5 GPA, 22 ACT, 1540 SAT, or rank in top half of graduating class. TOEFL or Michigan Test and statement of intent and personal contribution required for international students. SAT/ACT not required for nontraditional students or international students.

High school preparation. Required and recommended units include English 4, mathematics 3, social studies 3, history 1-2, science 2 (laboratory 2), foreign language 2 and academic electives 2. Computer science, visual and performing arts, and/or vocational education.

2008-2009 Annual costs. Tuition/fees: $5,150; $16,425 out-of-state. Room/board: $6,258. Books/supplies: $850. Personal expenses: $3,700.

2007-2008 Financial aid. **Non-need-based:** Scholarships awarded for academics, art, athletics, leadership, music/drama, ROTC, state residency.

Application procedures. **Admission:** Priority date 3/1; no deadline. $30 fee. Admission notification on a rolling basis beginning on or about 9/15. **Financial aid:** Priority date 2/15; no closing date. FAFSA, institutional form, CSS PROFILE required. Applicants notified on a rolling basis starting 4/1; must reply by 8/1 or within 4 week(s) of notification.

Academics. **Special study options:** Combined bachelor's/graduate degree, cooperative education, cross-registration, distance learning, double major, ESL, exchange student, honors, independent study, internships, study abroad, teacher certification program. English language institute, combined programs with other institutions for bachelor in nursing and master in public administration with Montana State University - Bozeman. **Credit/placement by examination:** AP, CLEP, institutional tests. 10 credit hours maximum toward associate degree. Credit hours awarded determined by academic department. **Support services:** Learning center, pre-admission summer program, reduced course load, remedial instruction, study skills assistance, tutoring, writing center.

Majors. **Architecture:** Urban/community planning. **Area/ethnic studies:** Asian, Native American, women's. **Biology:** General, bacteriology, botany, cellular/molecular, zoology. **Business:** General, business admin, finance, international, management information systems, marketing. **Communications:** General, broadcast journalism, journalism. **Computer sciences:** Computer science. **Conservation:** General, forestry, wildlife. **Education:** General, art, biology, business, elementary, English, mathematics, music, physical, secondary. **Foreign languages:** Classics, French, German, Japanese, Latin, Russian, Spanish. **Health:** Athletic training, clinical lab science. **History:** General. **Interdisciplinary:** Math/computer science. **Liberal arts:** Arts/sciences. **Math:** General. **Parks/recreation:** Exercise sciences, facilities management, health/fitness. **Philosophy/religion:** Philosophy. **Physical sciences:** Chemistry, geology, physics. **Psychology:** General. **Public administration:** Social work. **Social sciences:** Anthropology, cartography, criminology, economics, geography, international relations, political science, sociology. **Visual/performing arts:** General, art, art history/conservation, dance, dramatic, music performance, music theory/composition.

Computing on campus. 1,800 workstations in dormitories, library, computer center, student center. Dormitories wired for high-speed internet access and linked to campus network. Commuter students can connect to campus network. Online course registration, online library, helpline, repair service, wireless network available.

Student life. **Freshman orientation:** Mandatory, $45 fee. Preregistration for classes offered. Three-day summer session which includes parent track. **Housing:** Guaranteed on-campus for freshmen. Coed dorms, single-sex dorms, special housing for disabled, apartments, fraternity/sorority housing available. $120 deposit, deadline 3/1. Honors floors, international floors, quiet floors, activity dorms, personal development housing available. **Activities:** Bands, choral groups, dance, drama, literary magazine, music ensembles, musical theater, opera, radio station, student government, student newspaper, symphony orchestra, TV station, Associated Students of University of Montana, University of Montana Advocates, Mortar Board, Spurs, Circle-K, forestry student association, honors student association, Kyi-Yo (Native American organization), environmental action club, American Indian Business Leaders.

Athletics. NCAA. **Intercollegiate:** Basketball, cheerleading, cross-country, football (tackle) M, golf W, rodeo, soccer W, tennis, track and field, volleyball W. **Intramural:** Badminton, baseball M, basketball, football (tackle), golf, handball, racquetball, soccer, softball, swimming, table tennis, tennis, track and field, triathlon, volleyball. **Team name:** Grizzlies.

Student services. Adult student services, alcohol/substance abuse counseling, chaplain/spiritual director, career counseling, services for economically disadvantaged, student employment services, financial aid counseling, health services, legal services, minority student services, on-campus daycare, personal counseling, placement for graduates, veterans' counselor, women's services. **Physically disabled:** Services for visually, speech, hearing impaired.

Contact. E-mail: admiss@umontana.edu
Phone: (406) 243-6266 Toll-free number: (800) 462-8636
Fax: (406) 243-5711
Jed Liston, Assistant Vice President for Enrollment Services, University of Montana, Lommasson Center 103, Missoula, MT 59812

University of Montana: Western

Dillon, Montana **CB member**
www.umwestern.edu **CB code: 4945**

- Public 4-year liberal arts and teachers college
- Residential campus in small town
- 1,150 degree-seeking undergraduates: 14% part-time, 55% women

General. Founded in 1893. Regionally accredited. **Degrees:** 148 bachelor's, 33 associate awarded. **Location:** 65 miles from Butte, 145 miles from Idaho Falls. **Calendar:** Semester, extensive summer session. **Full-time faculty:** 62 total; 81% have terminal degrees, 47% women. **Part-time faculty:** 26 total; 35% have terminal degrees, 69% women. **Special facilities:** Outdoor education center, wildlife exhibit, office simulation center, public gallery, affiliation with La Cense, Montana Ranch.

Freshman class profile.

Mid 50% test scores			
SAT critical reading:	390-500	Rank in top quarter:	20%
SAT math:	400-520	Rank in top tenth:	4%
ACT composite:	16-21	Out-of-state:	27%
		Live on campus:	99%

Basis for selection. Open admission, but selective for some programs. High school official transcripts, class rank, test scores. Writing and Math scores required. **Homeschooled:** State high school equivalency certificate required.

High school preparation. College-preparatory program required. 16 units recommended. Recommended units include English 4, mathematics 3, social studies 3, science 3 (laboratory 3) and academic electives 2. Vocational education, computer education, foreign language, visual or performing arts recommended.

2008-2009 Annual costs. Tuition/fees: $3,675; $12,491 out-of-state. Room/board: $5,350. Books/supplies: $750. Personal expenses: $2,000.

2007-2008 Financial aid. Non-need-based: Scholarships awarded for academics, alumni affiliation, art, athletics, leadership, minority status, state residency. **Additional information:** Tuition and/or fee waivers for veterans, Native Americans and other minorities.

Application procedures. Admission: Priority date 7/1; no deadline. $30 fee. Admission notification on a rolling basis. **Financial aid:** Priority date 3/1; no closing date. FAFSA required. Applicants notified on a rolling basis starting 3/1; must reply within 2 week(s) of notification.

Academics. Offer classes in block scheduling system. All students take 1 course at a time in 3 week blocks. Blocks end with final exam and are followed by 4 day break prior to next block. 4 blocks per semester; most classes are 4 credits. **Special study options:** Cooperative education, distance learning, double major, dual enrollment of high school students, honors, independent study, internships, liberal arts/career combination, teacher certification program. **Credit/placement by examination:** AP, CLEP, institutional tests. 30 credit hours maximum toward associate degree, 30 toward bachelor's. **Support services:** Learning center, reduced course load, remedial instruction, study skills assistance, tutoring.

Majors. Biology: General. **Business:** General, business admin, communications, tourism/travel. **Conservation:** General, environmental studies, wildlife. **Education:** General, art, biology, business, chemistry, early childhood, elementary, English, health, history, mathematics, multi-level teacher, music, physical, school librarian, science, secondary, social studies, technology/industrial arts. **Liberal arts:** Arts/sciences. **Math:** Applied. **Physical sciences:** Chemistry, geology. **Psychology:** General. **Social sciences:** General. **Visual/performing arts:** General, art, dramatic.

Most popular majors. Business/marketing 24%, education 50%, natural resources/environmental science 6%, social sciences 6%.

Computing on campus. 140 workstations in dormitories, library, computer center. Dormitories linked to campus network. Commuter students can connect to campus network. Online course registration, wireless network available.

Student life. Freshman orientation: Mandatory, $60 fee. Preregistration for classes offered. **Housing:** Guaranteed on-campus for freshmen. Coed dorms, single-sex dorms, special housing for disabled, apartments, wellness housing available. $100 fully refundable deposit. Students with fewer than 30 credits not living with family required to live in dormitory. Transfer students under 21 with fewer than 30 credits not living with parents required to live on campus. **Activities:** Campus ministries, choral groups, drama, literary magazine, music ensembles, radio station, student government, student newspaper, admissions ambassadors, Chi Alpha-Christian fellowship, outdoor club, Polynesian club, rodeo club, IT club, academic clubs, community service.

Athletics. NAIA. **Intercollegiate:** Basketball, equestrian, football (tackle) M, golf, rodeo, volleyball W. **Intramural:** Basketball, golf, racquetball, skiing, soccer, softball, tennis, volleyball. **Team name:** Bulldogs, Lady Bulldogs.

Student services. Alcohol/substance abuse counseling, career counseling, student employment services, financial aid counseling, legal services, on-campus daycare, personal counseling, placement for graduates, veterans' counselor. **Physically disabled:** Services for visually, speech, hearing impaired.

Contact. E-mail: admissions@umwestern.edu
Phone: (406) 683-7331 Toll-free number: (877) 683-7331
Fax: (406) 683-7493
Catherine Redhead, Director of Admissions, University of Montana: Western, 710 South Atlantic Street, Dillon, MT 59725

Nebraska

Bellevue University
Bellevue, Nebraska
www.bellevue.edu **CB code: 6053**

- Private 4-year university and business college
- Commuter campus in large city
- 5,695 degree-seeking undergraduates: 42% part-time, 49% women, 12% African American, 2% Asian American, 8% Hispanic American, 1% Native American, 5% international
- 2,488 degree-seeking graduate students

General. Founded in 1965. Regionally accredited. Satellite operations throughout a five-state area in the Midwest. Focus on adult learners, non-traditional students and customized programs for organizations and corporations. **Degrees:** 1,838 bachelor's awarded; master's, doctoral offered. **ROTC:** Army, Air Force. **Calendar:** Continuous, extensive summer session. **Full-time faculty:** 84 total; 46% have terminal degrees, 11% minority, 45% women. **Part-time faculty:** 248 total; 21% have terminal degrees, 5% minority, 38% women.

Basis for selection. Open admission, but selective for some programs. Students dismissed from another institution for academic or disciplinary reasons will be accepted for admission after 1 year has lapsed since dismissal from that institution. Admission to Professional Studies program requires roughly 60 transfer credit hours from accredited institution. Michigan English Language Assessment Battery used for placement after arrival. IELT also accepted. **Homeschooled:** Students should submit official verification of completion.

High school preparation. Recommended units include English 3, mathematics 3, social studies 3, history 3, science 3 (laboratory 1), foreign language 3 and academic electives 3.

2008-2009 Annual costs. Tuition/fees: $6,165. Prices vary depending on program. Books/supplies: $1,500. Personal expenses: $1,845.

2007-2008 Financial aid. Non-need-based: Scholarships awarded for academics, athletics, leadership.

Application procedures. Admission: No deadline. $50 fee, may be waived for applicants with need. Admission notification on a rolling basis. **Financial aid:** Priority date 4/15; no closing date. FAFSA, institutional form required. Applicants notified on a rolling basis starting 4/15; must reply within 2 week(s) of notification.

Academics. Special study options: Accelerated study, cross-registration, distance learning, double major, dual enrollment of high school students, ESL, independent study, internships, liberal arts/career combination, weekend college. **Credit/placement by examination:** AP, CLEP, IB, institutional tests. Offer 12 computer profiency exams, each worth 1 credit. Maximum of 12 credits allowed. **Support services:** Learning center, remedial instruction, study skills assistance, tutoring, writing center.

Majors. Biology: General. **Business:** General, accounting, business admin, e-commerce, human resources, management information systems, marketing. **Communications:** General. **Computer sciences:** General, information systems, information technology, web page design. **Conservation:** General, environmental science. **Education:** Physical. **Health:** Health care admin, premedicine, substance abuse counseling. **Legal studies:** Prelaw. **Liberal arts:** Arts/sciences. **Parks/recreation:** Sports admin. **Protective services:** Law enforcement admin. **Psychology:** General. **Public administration:** General, human services. **Social sciences:** General, sociology. **Visual/performing arts:** Art, art history/conservation, arts management, commercial/advertising art, studio arts.

Most popular majors. Business/marketing 53%, computer/information sciences 10%, health sciences 7%, security/protective services 10%.

Computing on campus. 600 workstations in library, computer center. Commuter students can connect to campus network. Online course registration, online library, helpline, wireless network available.

Student life. Freshman orientation: Available. Preregistration for classes offered. 2-day programs held the beginning week of fall, winter and spring semesters. **Policies:** No alcohol at any student events. Any event must be coordinated through the Student Activities Office. **Activities:** Student government, Alpha Chi, Campus Crusade for Christ, computer graphic design club, Delta Epsilon Chi, economics club, institute of management accountants, multicultural student organization, student advisory council, toastmasters, chapter of Student Veterans Association.

Athletics. NAIA. **Intercollegiate:** Baseball M, basketball M, soccer, softball W, volleyball W. **Team name:** Bruins.

Student services. Career counseling, student employment services, financial aid counseling, personal counseling, placement for graduates, veterans' counselor. **Physically disabled:** Services for visually, speech, hearing impaired.

Contact. E-mail: info@bellevue.edu
Phone: (402) 293-2000 Toll-free number: (800) 756-7920
Fax: (402) 557-7230
Nick Baker, Director, Undergraduate Admissions, Bellevue University, 1000 Galvin Road South, Bellevue, NE 68005-3098

BryanLGH College of Health Sciences
Lincoln, Nebraska
www.bryanlghcollege.org/

- Private 4-year health science college
- Commuter campus in large city
- 256 degree-seeking undergraduates
- 31 graduate students
- 89% of applicants admitted
- SAT or ACT (ACT writing optional), application essay, interview required

General. Regionally accredited. **Degrees:** 23 bachelor's, 33 associate awarded; master's offered. **Calendar:** Semester, limited summer session. **Full-time faculty:** 32 total; 9% have terminal degrees, 3% minority, 97% women. **Part-time faculty:** 31 total; 16% have terminal degrees, 13% minority, 77% women. **Class size:** 65% < 20, 26% 20-39, 3% 40-49, 6% 50-99. **Special facilities:** William Jennings Bryan home and museum, health system facilities, human patient simulators.

Freshman class profile. 55 applied, 49 admitted, 25 enrolled.

Mid 50% test scores		**GPA 3.50-3.74:**	30%
ACT composite:	21-24	**GPA 3.0-3.49:**	26%
GPA 3.75 or higher:	44%	**Out-of-state:**	3%

Basis for selection. Applicants are reviewed by a faculty admissions committee. Students scoring above a certain rubric level are admitted.

High school preparation. College-preparatory program recommended. 23 units recommended. Recommended units include English 4, mathematics 4, social studies 4, science 4 (laboratory 2), foreign language 4 and computer science 1.

2008-2009 Annual costs. Tuition/fees: $10,580. Books/supplies: $1,000. Personal expenses: $3,120.

2007-2008 Financial aid. Need-based: 22 full-time freshmen applied for aid; 22 were judged to have need; 22 of these received aid. Average scholarship/grant was $2,160. 15% of total undergraduate aid awarded as scholarships/grants, 85% as loans/jobs. **Non-need-based:** Scholarships awarded for academics, leadership.

Application procedures. Admission: No deadline. $25 fee, may be waived for applicants with need. Admission notification on a rolling basis. Must reply by May 1 or within 4 week(s) if notified thereafter. **Financial aid:** Closing date 5/1. FAFSA, institutional form required. Applicants notified on a rolling basis starting 5/1; must reply within 3 week(s) of notification.

Academics. Special study options: Independent study. **Credit/placement by examination:** CLEP, institutional tests. 1 credit hours maximum toward associate degree, 2 toward bachelor's. **Support services:** Learning center, pre-admission summer program, remedial instruction, study skills assistance, tutoring.

Majors. Health: Nursing (RN).

Computing on campus. 30 workstations in library, student center. Commuter students can connect to campus network. Online library, helpline, wireless network available.

Student life. Freshman orientation: Mandatory. Preregistration for classes offered. Held on-campus the Thursday and Friday before classes begin each term. **Activities:** Student government, Red Cross, Caring with Christ, Action for Students, student nurses association, health promotion organization.

Student services. Alcohol/substance abuse counseling, financial aid counseling, health services, personal counseling.

Contact. E-mail: admissions@bryanlghcollege.org
Phone: (402) 481-8697 Toll-free number: (800) 742-7844 ext. 18697
Fax: (402) 481-8697
Kelli Backman, Admissions Counselor, BryanLGH College of Health Sciences, 5035 Everett Street, Lincoln, NE 68506

Chadron State College

Chadron, Nebraska
www.csc.edu **CB code: 6466**

- Public 4-year business, liberal arts and teachers college
- Residential campus in small town
- 2,050 degree-seeking undergraduates

General. Founded in 1911. Regionally accredited. Limited distance education classes and programs offered online and at Scottsbluff, Alliance, Sidney, and throughout western Nebraska and eastern Wyoming. **Degrees:** 358 bachelor's awarded; master's offered. **ROTC:** Army. **Location:** 100 miles from Scottsbluff. **Calendar:** Semester, limited summer session. **Full-time faculty:** 100 total. **Part-time faculty:** 35 total. **Class size:** 65% < 20, 30% 20-39, 4% 40-49, less than 1% 50-99. **Special facilities:** Planetarium, herbarium, geological museum, high plains heritage center.

Freshman class profile.

Mid 50% test scores		**GPA 2.0-2.99:**	28%
ACT composite:	17-24	**Rank in top quarter:**	26%
GPA 3.75 or higher:	20%	**Rank in top tenth:**	11%
GPA 3.50-3.74:	11%	**Out-of-state:**	29%
GPA 3.0-3.49:	22%	**Live on campus:**	90%

Basis for selection. Open admission, but selective for some programs. Test scores must be submitted for placement, but no minimum score required. Audition recommended for music program.

High school preparation. 12 units recommended. Recommended units include English 4, mathematics 3, social studies 3, science 2 (laboratory 2). Units in visual or performing arts, computer literacy, or foreign language recommended.

2008-2009 Annual costs. Tuition/fees: $4,557; $8,052 out-of-state. Room/board: $4,654. Books/supplies: $600. Personal expenses: $972.

Financial aid. Non-need-based: Scholarships awarded for academics, alumni affiliation, art, athletics, leadership, minority status, music/drama, state residency.

Application procedures. Admission: No deadline. $15 fee. Admission notification on a rolling basis. **Financial aid:** Priority date 6/1; no closing date. FAFSA, institutional form required. Applicants notified on a rolling basis starting 4/1; must reply within 2 week(s) of notification.

Academics. Special study options: Accelerated study, combined bachelor's/graduate degree, cooperative education, distance learning, double major, dual enrollment of high school students, honors, independent study, internships, student-designed major, study abroad, teacher certification program. **Credit/placement by examination:** AP, CLEP, SAT, ACT, institutional tests. 65 credit hours maximum toward bachelor's degree. **Support services:** Learning center, pre-admission summer program, reduced course load, remedial instruction, study skills assistance, tutoring, writing center.

Majors. Agriculture: Range science. **Biology:** General. **Business:** Accounting, business admin, finance, management information systems, management science, office management. **Computer sciences:** Information systems. **Education:** Art, biology, business, chemistry, drama/dance, elementary, English, family/consumer sciences, history, mathematics, middle, music, physical, physics, science, secondary, social science, Spanish, technology/industrial arts, trade/industrial. **Family/consumer sciences:** General. **Foreign languages:** Spanish. **History:** General. **Legal studies:** General, prelaw. **Liberal arts:** Arts/sciences, library science. **Math:** General. **Parks/recreation:** General. **Physical sciences:** Chemistry. **Psychology:** General. **Public administration:** Social work. **Social sciences:** General, sociology. **Visual/performing arts:** Art, dramatic.

Most popular majors. Biology 11%, business/marketing 20%, education 27%.

Computing on campus. 120 workstations in dormitories, library, computer center, student center. Dormitories wired for high-speed internet access and linked to campus network. Commuter students can connect to campus network. Online course registration, online library, helpline, wireless network available.

Student life. Freshman orientation: Available, $50 fee. Preregistration for classes offered. Four or five 2-day weekend orientations held prior to start of fall term. **Housing:** Guaranteed on-campus for freshmen. Coed dorms, single-sex dorms, special housing for disabled, apartments, wellness housing available. $100 deposit, deadline 6/1. **Activities:** Bands, choral groups, dance, drama, international student organizations, music ensembles, musical theater, student government, student newspaper, Circle K, student education association, multicultural club, Intervarsity Christian Fellowship, White Buffalo Club.

Athletics. NCAA. **Intercollegiate:** Basketball, football (tackle) M, golf W, track and field, volleyball W, wrestling M. **Intramural:** Archery, badminton, basketball, bowling, golf, racquetball, rugby M, softball, track and field, volleyball, wrestling M. **Team name:** Eagles.

Student services. Adult student services, alcohol/substance abuse counseling, career counseling, services for economically disadvantaged, student employment services, financial aid counseling, health services, on-campus daycare, personal counseling, placement for graduates, veterans' counselor. **Physically disabled:** Services for visually, speech, hearing impaired.

Contact. E-mail: inquire@csc.edu
Phone: (308) 432-6263 Toll-free number: (800) 242-3766
Fax: (308) 432-6229
Tena Cook, Director of Admissions, Chadron State College, 1000 Main Street, Chadron, NE 69337

Clarkson College

Omaha, Nebraska
www.clarksoncollege.edu **CB code: 2250**

- Private 4-year health science college affiliated with Episcopal Church
- Commuter campus in large city
- 738 degree-seeking undergraduates
- 169 graduate students
- Application essay required

General. Founded in 1888. Regionally accredited. **Degrees:** 124 bachelor's, 46 associate awarded; master's offered. **ROTC:** Army, Air Force. **Location:** 50 miles from Lincoln. **Calendar:** Semester, extensive summer session. **Full-time faculty:** 42 total; 52% have terminal degrees, 5% minority, 98% women. **Part-time faculty:** 53 total; 66% have terminal degrees, 4% minority, 72% women. **Class size:** 66% < 20, 30% 20-39, less than 1% 40-49, 3% 50-99. **Special facilities:** Health care clinical facilities for professional education (more than 180 clinical sites), fully energized radiologic technology lab.

Freshman class profile. 87 applied, 48 admitted, 29 enrolled.

Mid 50% test scores		**Out-of-state:**	79%
ACT composite:	21-25		

Basis for selection. Open admission, but selective for some programs. GPA, class rank, test scores, essay important. ACT recommended. **Homeschooled:** Must take GED and submit ACT scores. Essay required. Transcript or portfolio recommended.

High school preparation. 9 units required. Required and recommended units include English 3-4, mathematics 2-4, social studies 2-3, history 2, science 2-4 (laboratory 1-2) and foreign language 2.

2008-2009 Annual costs. Tuition/fees: $13,140. Distance learning fee: $40 per credit hour. Room only: $4,400. Books/supplies: $600. Personal expenses: $1,500.

2007-2008 Financial aid. Non-need-based: Scholarships awarded for academics, alumni affiliation, minority status, religious affiliation.

Application procedures. Admission: No deadline. $35 fee. Application must be submitted on paper. Admission notification on a rolling basis. Must reply by May 1 or within 4 week(s) if notified thereafter. Application deadlines may vary by program. Students should check with admissions office for program deadlines. **Financial aid:** Priority date 4/1; no closing date. FAFSA, institutional form required. Applicants notified on a rolling basis starting 4/13; must reply within 3 week(s) of notification.

Academics. **Special study options:** Accelerated study, combined bachelor's/graduate degree, cooperative education, cross-registration, distance learning, double major, dual enrollment of high school students, external degree, independent study, internships, study abroad. **Credit/placement by examination:** CLEP, institutional tests. 40 credit hours maximum toward associate degree, 88 toward bachelor's. Unlimited number of hours of credit by examination may be counted toward degree if residency requirement of 40 hours is met. **Support services:** Learning center, reduced course load, study skills assistance, tutoring, writing center.

Majors. **Business:** General, business admin. **Health:** Health care admin, medical radiologic technology/radiation therapy, nursing (RN), preop/surgical nursing, radiologic technology/medical imaging.

Computing on campus. 60 workstations in dormitories, library, computer center. Dormitories wired for high-speed internet access. Commuter students can connect to campus network. Online library, helpline, repair service available.

Student life. **Freshman orientation:** Mandatory. Preregistration for classes offered. One-day program held on Friday before classes begin. **Housing:** Guaranteed on-campus for freshmen. Coed dorms, apartments available. $250 deposit, deadline 6/30. Board plan not available, kitchens located in each apartment. **Activities:** Student government, student newspaper, Christian Fellowship, Red Cross, National Student Nurses Association, Fellows club, Ambassador club, student leadership council.

Athletics. **Intercollegiate:** Skiing M.

Student services. Adult student services, alcohol/substance abuse counseling, career counseling, student employment services, financial aid counseling, health services, minority student services, on-campus daycare, personal counseling, placement for graduates. **Physically disabled:** Services for visually, hearing impaired.

Contact. E-mail: admiss@clarksoncollege.edu
Phone: (402) 552-3041 Toll-free number: (800) 647-5500
Fax: (402) 552-6057
Denise Work, Director of Admission, Clarkson College, 101 South 42nd Street, Omaha, NE 68131-2739

College of Saint Mary
Omaha, Nebraska
www.csm.edu **CB code: 6106**

- Private 4-year nursing, liberal arts and teachers college for women affiliated with Roman Catholic Church
- Commuter campus in large city
- 722 degree-seeking undergraduates: 21% part-time, 100% women, 11% African American, 1% Asian American, 8% Hispanic American, 1% Native American
- 205 degree-seeking graduate students
- 45% of applicants admitted
- SAT or ACT (ACT writing optional) required
- 51% graduate within 6 years

General. Founded in 1923. Regionally accredited. Weekend accelerated master's program, integrated service learning. **Degrees:** 109 bachelor's, 78 associate awarded; master's, doctoral offered. **ROTC:** Army, Air Force. **Location:** 10 miles from downtown. **Calendar:** Semester, limited summer session. **Full-time faculty:** 57 total; 58% have terminal degrees, 26% minority, 81% women. **Part-time faculty:** 103 total; 21% have terminal degrees, 9% minority, 77% women. **Class size:** 80% < 20, 20% 20-39, less than 1% 50-99. **Special facilities:** Nursing labs, on-site child development center.

Freshman class profile. 495 applied, 224 admitted, 85 enrolled.

Mid 50% test scores		**Rank in top quarter:**	35%
ACT composite:	18-23	**Rank in top tenth:**	12%
GPA 3.75 or higher:	29%	**End year in good standing:**	74%
GPA 3.50-3.74:	18%	**Return as sophomores:**	60%
GPA 3.0-3.49:	29%	**Out-of-state:**	11%
GPA 2.0-2.99:	23%	**Live on campus:**	82%

Basis for selection. Test scores, secondary school record, class rank important. Recommendations considered. **Homeschooled:** Must take ACT exam and submit scores.

High school preparation. Required and recommended units include English 4, mathematics 2-3, social studies 2 and science 2-3. Chemistry and biology required of nursing, occupational therapy and pre-professional studies students.

2008-2009 Annual costs. Tuition/fees: $21,260. Room/board: $6,400. Books/supplies: $1,100. Personal expenses: $1,656.

2008-2009 Financial aid. **Need-based:** 70 full-time freshmen applied for aid; 67 were judged to have need; 67 of these received aid. Average need met was 75%. Average scholarship/grant was $14,969; average loan $3,781. 46% of total undergraduate aid awarded as scholarships/grants, 54% as loans/jobs. **Non-need-based:** Scholarships awarded for academics, athletics, music/drama.

Application procedures. **Admission:** No deadline. $30 fee, may be waived for applicants with need. Admission notification on a rolling basis. **Financial aid:** Priority date 3/1; no closing date. FAFSA required. Applicants notified on a rolling basis starting 3/1; must reply within 2 week(s) of notification.

Academics. **Special study options:** Accelerated study, combined bachelor's/graduate degree, cooperative education, distance learning, double major, exchange student, honors, independent study, internships, liberal arts/career combination, student-designed major, study abroad, teacher certification program, weekend college. **Credit/placement by examination:** AP, CLEP, IB, ACT, institutional tests. 15 credit hours maximum toward associate degree, 15 toward bachelor's. 10 percent of program may be earned through credit by examination. **Support services:** Learning center, reduced course load, remedial instruction, study skills assistance, tutoring, writing center.

Majors. **Biology:** General. **Business:** Business admin. **Computer sciences:** General. **Education:** Biology, chemistry, early childhood, elementary, English, mathematics, middle, science, secondary, social science, special. **Foreign languages:** Spanish. **Health:** Clinical lab technology, nursing (RN), predental, premedicine, prepharmacy, preveterinary. **Legal studies:** Paralegal. **Liberal arts:** Arts/sciences. **Math:** General. **Physical sciences:** General, chemistry. **Psychology:** General. **Theology:** Theology. **Visual/performing arts:** Studio arts.

Most popular majors. Business/marketing 15%, education 13%, health sciences 43%, legal studies 7%, liberal arts 8%.

Computing on campus. 90 workstations in dormitories, library, computer center, student center. Dormitories wired for high-speed internet access and linked to campus network. Commuter students can connect to campus network. Online course registration, online library, wireless network available.

Student life. **Freshman orientation:** Mandatory. Preregistration for classes offered. One-day program offered several times during late spring and summer. **Policies:** Student Senate and Multicultural Association of Students members must have an overall 2.5 GPA to be eligible. **Housing:** Guaranteed on-campus for freshmen. $125 nonrefundable deposit, deadline 8/1. Residence hall for single mothers with children available. **Activities:** Campus ministries, choral groups, student government, Do Unto Others Board, residence hall council, Golden S, campus activities board, Student Education Association of Nebraska, business student association, College Democrats, Multicultural Association of Students.

Athletics. NAIA. **Intercollegiate:** Basketball W, cheerleading M, cross-country W, soccer W, softball W, volleyball W. **Intramural:** Volleyball W. **Team name:** Flames.

Student services. Adult student services, alcohol/substance abuse counseling, chaplain/spiritual director, career counseling, services for economically disadvantaged, student employment services, financial aid counseling, health services, minority student services, on-campus daycare, personal counseling, placement for graduates, veterans' counselor, women's services. **Physically disabled:** Services for visually, speech, hearing impaired.

Contact. E-mail: enroll@csm.edu
Phone: (402) 399-2355 Toll-free number: (800) 926-5534
Fax: (402) 399-2412
Joe Szejk, Vice President for Enrollment Services and Marketing, College of Saint Mary, 7000 Mercy Road, Omaha, NE 68106

Concordia University
Seward, Nebraska
www.cune.edu **CB code: 6116**

- Private 4-year university affiliated with Lutheran Church - Missouri Synod
- Residential campus in small town
- 1,076 degree-seeking undergraduates: 3% part-time, 52% women, 2% African American, 1% Asian American, 1% Hispanic American
- 226 degree-seeking graduate students
- 68% of applicants admitted

- SAT or ACT (ACT writing optional) required
- 63% graduate within 6 years; 27% enter graduate study

General. Founded in 1894. Regionally accredited. **Degrees:** 225 bachelor's awarded; master's offered. **ROTC:** Army, Air Force. **Location:** 25 miles from Lincoln, 75 miles from Omaha. **Calendar:** Semester, limited summer session. **Full-time faculty:** 58 total; 69% have terminal degrees, 2% minority, 31% women. **Part-time faculty:** 103 total; 39% have terminal degrees, 1% minority, 60% women. **Class size:** 53% < 20, 44% 20-39, 3% 40-49. **Special facilities:** Rock museum, observatory, arboretum.

Freshman class profile. 1,224 applied, 838 admitted, 273 enrolled.

Mid 50% test scores		**GPA 2.0-2.99:**	15%
SAT critical reading:	440-590	**Rank in top quarter:**	45%
SAT math:	460-570	**Rank in top tenth:**	22%
ACT composite:	21-27	**Return as sophomores:**	81%
GPA 3.75 or higher:	42%	**Out-of-state:**	60%
GPA 3.50-3.74:	17%	**Live on campus:**	99%
GPA 3.0-3.49:	25%		

Basis for selection. High school GPA and SAT/ACT scores important in admissions decisions. Audition required for drama, music, and speech programs; portfolio required for art program. **Homeschooled:** Statement describing homeschool structure and mission, transcript of courses and grades, state high school equivalency certificate required.

High school preparation. College-preparatory program recommended. 16 units recommended. Recommended units include English 4, mathematics 3, social studies 3, science 2, foreign language 1 and academic electives 3. One unit each in music, art, and physical education recommended.

2009-2010 Annual costs. Tuition/fees: $21,250. Room/board: $5,520. Books/supplies: $750. Personal expenses: $1,200.

2008-2009 Financial aid. Need-based: 254 full-time freshmen applied for aid; 211 were judged to have need; 211 of these received aid. Average need met was 74%. Average scholarship/grant was $10,006; average loan $3,223. 76% of total undergraduate aid awarded as scholarships/grants, 24% as loans/jobs. **Non-need-based:** Awarded to 441 full-time undergraduates, including 131 freshmen. Scholarships awarded for academics, alumni affiliation, art, athletics, leadership, music/drama, religious affiliation.

Application procedures. Admission: Priority date 7/1; deadline 8/1 (receipt date). No application fee. Admission notification on a rolling basis beginning on or about 9/1. Must reply within 30 days of receipt of acceptance letter or request extension. **Financial aid:** Priority date 3/1; no closing date. FAFSA required. Applicants notified on a rolling basis starting 3/1; must reply within 4 week(s) of notification.

Academics. Curriculum for degree completion program for bachelor of arts in organizational management contains 16 modules taken sequentially one night a week for 18 months. Summer term offering hybrid online and face to face instruction. **Special study options:** Accelerated study, distance learning, double major, dual enrollment of high school students, ESL, exchange student, independent study, internships, study abroad, teacher certification program. Undergraduate students may take graduate level classes. **Credit/placement by examination:** AP, CLEP, IB, SAT, ACT. **Support services:** Learning center, reduced course load, study skills assistance, tutoring, writing center.

Majors. Biology: General. **Business:** General, accounting, business admin, communications, management information systems. **Communications:** General, journalism. **Computer sciences:** Computer science. **Education:** General, art, biology, business, chemistry, computer, elementary, English, ESL, family/consumer sciences, geography, health, history, mathematics, middle, multi-level teacher, music, physical, physics, science, secondary, social studies, Spanish, speech, technology/industrial arts. **Foreign languages:** Spanish. **Health:** Predental, premedicine, prenursing, prepharmacy, preveterinary. **History:** General. **Interdisciplinary:** Behavioral sciences. **Legal studies:** Prelaw. **Math:** General. **Parks/recreation:** Exercise sciences, health/fitness, sports admin. **Physical sciences:** General, chemistry. **Psychology:** General. **Social sciences:** Geography. **Theology:** Preministerial, religious ed, sacred music, theology, youth ministry. **Visual/performing arts:** General, art, dramatic, graphic design, piano/organ, studio arts, voice/opera.

Most popular majors. Business/marketing 20%, education 38%, theological studies 11%, visual/performing arts 7%.

Computing on campus. 186 workstations in dormitories, library, computer center, student center. Dormitories wired for high-speed internet access and linked to campus network. Commuter students can connect to campus network. Online course registration, online library, helpline, student web hosting, wireless network available.

Student life. Freshman orientation: Mandatory. Preregistration for classes offered. 3 days before classes start. Includes community service events and community building. **Policies:** University responsibly maintains Christian standards of conduct among its students, faculty and staff. **Housing:** Guaranteed on-campus for all undergraduates. Single-sex dorms, special housing for disabled, apartments, wellness housing available. $200 fully refundable deposit, deadline 8/24. **Activities:** Bands, campus ministries, choral groups, drama, literary magazine, music ensembles, musical theater, student government, student newspaper, symphony orchestra, Circle K, Ongoing Ambassadors for Christ, multicultural awareness club, Peers and Leaders Serving, Habitat for Humanity, Leaders in Physical Health Education, Mission Minded Students, Students in Free Enterprise, Students with Families Association.

Athletics. NAIA. **Intercollegiate:** Baseball M, basketball, cross-country, football (tackle) M, golf, soccer, softball W, tennis, track and field, volleyball W, wrestling M. **Intramural:** Basketball, bowling, football (non-tackle), racquetball, soccer, softball, table tennis, tennis, track and field, volleyball. **Team name:** Bulldogs.

Student services. Adult student services, alcohol/substance abuse counseling, chaplain/spiritual director, career counseling, student employment services, financial aid counseling, health services, personal counseling, placement for graduates. **Physically disabled:** Services for visually, speech, hearing impaired.

Contact. E-mail: admiss@cune.edu
Phone: (800) 535-5494 Toll-free number: (800) 535-5494
Fax: (402) 643-4073
Aaron Roberts, Director of Undergraduate and Graduate Recruitment, Concordia University, 800 North Columbia Avenue, Seward, NE 68434-1556

Creative Center
Omaha, Nebraska
www.creativecenter.edu

- For-profit 4-year visual arts and career college
- Commuter campus in large city
- 118 degree-seeking undergraduates: 2% part-time, 48% women
- Application essay, interview required

General. Accredited by ACCSCT. **Degrees:** 21 bachelor's, 35 associate awarded. **Calendar:** Semester, limited summer session. **Full-time faculty:** 3 total; 33% women. **Part-time faculty:** 12 total; 42% women. **Class size:** 23% 20-39, 38% 40-49, 38% 50-99.

Basis for selection. Students must provide a letter of recommendation, a letter of intent, a high school transcript and a portfolio to be reviewed and approved. Portfolio required.

2009-2010 Annual costs. Tuition/fees (projected): $20,400. Tuition/fees may vary by program.

Financial aid. Non-need-based: Scholarships awarded for academics, art.

Application procedures. Admission: No deadline. $100 fee. Application must be submitted on paper. Admission notification on a rolling basis. **Financial aid:** No deadline. FAFSA required. Applicants notified on a rolling basis starting 1/1.

Academics. Credit/placement by examination: CLEP. **Support services:** Reduced course load, study skills assistance, tutoring.

Majors. Visual/performing arts: Graphic design.

Computing on campus. PC or laptop required. 8 workstations in library. Online library, helpline, student web hosting, wireless network available.

Student life. Freshman orientation: Mandatory. Orientation held throughout first week of class.

Student services. Career counseling, financial aid counseling, placement for graduates.

Contact. E-mail: admissions@creativecenter.edu
Phone: (402) 898-1000 Toll-free number: (888) 898-1789
Fax: (402) 898-1301
Beth Connor, Admissions and Placement Coordinator, Creative Center, 10850 Emmet Street, Omaha, NE 68164

Creighton University
Omaha, Nebraska **CB member**
www.creighton.edu **CB code: 6121**

- Private 4-year university affiliated with Roman Catholic Church
- Residential campus in very large city

- 4,087 degree-seeking undergraduates: 7% part-time, 59% women, 4% African American, 9% Asian American, 4% Hispanic American, 1% Native American, 1% international
- 2,964 degree-seeking graduate students
- 82% of applicants admitted
- SAT or ACT (ACT writing optional), application essay required
- 76% graduate within 6 years; 40% enter graduate study

General. Founded in 1878. Regionally accredited. **Degrees:** 888 bachelor's, 2 associate awarded; master's, doctoral, first professional offered. **ROTC:** Army, Air Force. **Location:** 167 miles from Kansas City, 290 miles from Minneapolis. **Calendar:** Semester, extensive summer session. **Full-time faculty:** 508 total; 85% have terminal degrees, 11% minority, 41% women. **Part-time faculty:** 213 total; 41% have terminal degrees, 8% minority, 47% women. **Class size:** 48% < 20, 44% 20-39, 3% 40-49, 4% 50-99, less than 1% >100.

Freshman class profile. 4,740 applied, 3,871 admitted, 985 enrolled.

Mid 50% test scores		**Rank in top quarter:**	73%
SAT critical reading:	500-610	**Rank in top tenth:**	42%
SAT math:	540-650	**End year in good standing:**	97%
SAT writing:	510-620	**Return as sophomores:**	87%
ACT composite:	24-29	**Out-of-state:**	68%
GPA 3.75 or higher:	57%	**Live on campus:**	95%
GPA 3.50-3.74:	18%	**International:**	2%
GPA 3.0-3.49:	20%	**Fraternities:**	26%
GPA 2.0-2.99:	5%	**Sororities:**	28%

Basis for selection. School record, high school GPA, test scores, and application essay important. Class rank considered. **Homeschooled:** GED required.

High school preparation. College-preparatory program recommended. 16 units required; 21 recommended. Required and recommended units include English 4, mathematics 3-4, social studies 2-3, history 1, science 2-3, foreign language 2-3 and academic electives 3.

2008-2009 Annual costs. Tuition/fees: $28,542. Room/board: $8,516. Books/supplies: $1,000. Personal expenses: $1,400.

2008-2009 Financial aid. Need-based: 765 full-time freshmen applied for aid; 588 were judged to have need; 588 of these received aid. Average need met was 92%. Average scholarship/grant was $19,524; average loan $6,066. 69% of total undergraduate aid awarded as scholarships/grants, 31% as loans/jobs. **Non-need-based:** Awarded to 3,201 full-time undergraduates, including 896 freshmen. Scholarships awarded for academics, alumni affiliation, art, athletics, leadership, minority status, music/drama, ROTC.

Application procedures. Admission: Priority date 12/1; deadline 2/15. $40 fee, may be waived for applicants with need, free for online applicants. Admission notification on a rolling basis beginning on or about 12/15. Must reply by May 1 or within 2 week(s) if notified thereafter. **Financial aid:** Priority date 3/1; no closing date. FAFSA, institutional form required. Applicants notified on a rolling basis starting 3/15; must reply by 5/1 or within 4 week(s) of notification.

Academics. Sequences of courses offered in preengineering, predentistry, prelaw, premedicine, prepharmacy, prephysical therapy, preveterinary. Institution's students given admissions preference into all of university's professional schools. Core curriculum required (61 semester hours from 5 areas: cultures, ideas and civilizations; theology, philosophy and ethics; natural science; social and behavioral sciences; skills). **Special study options:** Accelerated study, combined bachelor's/graduate degree, cross-registration, distance learning, double major, dual enrollment of high school students, ESL, exchange student, honors, independent study, internships, liberal arts/career combination, study abroad, teacher certification program, Washington semester. 3-3 program in engineering with University of Detroit Mercy, 3-3 Law Program within Creighton University, study abroad opportunities at 110 partner institutions in 40 countries. **Credit/placement by examination:** AP, CLEP, IB, SAT, ACT, institutional tests. CLEP Subject Examinations must be taken with essay where applicable. **Support services:** Learning center, pre-admission summer program, reduced course load, remedial instruction, study skills assistance, tutoring, writing center.

Majors. Area/ethnic studies: American, Native American. **Biology:** General. **Business:** Accounting, business admin, communications, e-commerce, entrepreneurial studies, finance, international, management information systems, marketing. **Communications:** General, journalism, organizational. **Computer sciences:** Computer science. **Education:** Chemistry, elementary, Latin, secondary. **Foreign languages:** Ancient Greek, classics, French, German, Latin, Spanish. **Health:** Athletic training, EMT paramedic, health care admin, nursing (RN). **History:** General. **Math:** General, applied. **Parks/recreation:** Exercise sciences. **Philosophy/religion:** Philosophy, religion. **Physical sciences:** Atmospheric science, chemistry, physics. **Psychology:** General. **Public administration:** Social work. **Social sciences:** Anthropology, economics, international relations, political science, sociology. **Visual/performing arts:** Art, dramatic, graphic design, music performance, studio arts.

Most popular majors. Biology 10%, business/marketing 18%, communications/journalism 7%, health sciences 25%, psychology 6%, social sciences 8%.

Computing on campus. 520 workstations in dormitories, library, computer center, student center. Dormitories wired for high-speed internet access and linked to campus network. Commuter students can connect to campus network. Online course registration, online library, helpline, repair service, student web hosting, wireless network available.

Student life. Freshman orientation: Mandatory, $60 fee. Preregistration for classes offered. Held first week of fall semester. **Housing:** Guaranteed on-campus for freshmen. Coed dorms, single-sex dorms, special housing for disabled, apartments, wellness housing available. $100 fully refundable deposit, deadline 5/1. **Activities:** Bands, campus ministries, choral groups, dance, drama, international student organizations, literary magazine, music ensembles, Model UN, musical theater, student government, student newspaper, symphony orchestra, TV station, world hunger awareness group, Afro-American students association, international relations club, women's resource center, community service center, Christian life community, Young Democrats, Young Republicans.

Athletics. NCAA. **Intercollegiate:** Baseball M, basketball, cross-country, golf, rowing (crew) W, soccer, softball W, tennis, volleyball W. **Intramural:** Badminton, basketball, bowling, football (non-tackle), golf, racquetball, soccer, softball, tennis, volleyball. **Team name:** Bluejays.

Student services. Adult student services, alcohol/substance abuse counseling, chaplain/spiritual director, career counseling, services for economically disadvantaged, student employment services, financial aid counseling, health services, minority student services, on-campus daycare, personal counseling, placement for graduates, veterans' counselor, women's services. **Physically disabled:** Services for visually, speech, hearing impaired. **Learning disabled:** Comprehensive services available.

Contact. E-mail: admissions@creighton.edu
Phone: (402) 280-2703 Toll-free number: (800) 282-5835
Fax: (402) 280-2685
Mary Chase, Director of Admissions, Creighton University, 2500 California Plaza, Omaha, NE 68178-0001

Dana College

Blair, Nebraska — **CB member**
www.dana.edu — **CB code: 6157**

- Private 4-year liberal arts college affiliated with Evangelical Lutheran Church in America
- Residential campus in small town

General. Founded in 1884. Regionally accredited. **Location:** 20 miles from Omaha. **Calendar:** 4-1-4.

Annual costs/financial aid. Tuition/fees (2008-2009): $20,120. Room/board: $6,350. Books/supplies: $750. Personal expenses: $1,150. Need-based financial aid available to full-time and part-time students.

Contact. Phone: (402) 426-7222
Director of Admission, 2848 College Drive, Blair, NE 68008-1099

Doane College

Crete, Nebraska — **CB member**
www.doane.edu — **CB code: 6165**

- Private 4-year liberal arts college affiliated with United Church of Christ
- Residential campus in small town
- 896 degree-seeking undergraduates: 1% part-time, 50% women, 4% African American, 1% Asian American, 3% Hispanic American, 1% international
- 76% of applicants admitted
- SAT or ACT (ACT writing optional) required
- 66% graduate within 6 years

General. Founded in 1872. Regionally accredited. Campuses also in Lincoln and Grand Island. **Degrees:** 188 bachelor's awarded; master's offered. **ROTC:** Army, Air Force. **Location:** 25 miles from Lincoln, 75 miles from Omaha. **Calendar:** 4-1-4, limited summer session. **Full-time faculty:** 73

total; 75% have terminal degrees, 3% minority, 47% women. **Part-time faculty:** 58 total; 16% have terminal degrees, 2% minority, 57% women. **Class size:** 84% < 20, 15% 20-39, less than 1% 40-49, less than 1% 50-99. **Special facilities:** Arboretum, open-air theater, observatory, all-American rose test garden, ropes challenge course, fitness trail.

Freshman class profile. 1,111 applied, 840 admitted, 248 enrolled.

Mid 50% test scores			
SAT critical reading:	440-550	GPA 3.0-3.49:	25%
SAT math:	460-580	GPA 2.0-2.99:	6%
SAT writing:	420-600	Rank in top quarter:	46%
ACT composite:	19-25	Rank in top tenth:	15%
GPA 3.75 or higher:	32%	Return as sophomores:	74%
GPA 3.50-3.74:	37%	Out-of-state:	16%
		Live on campus:	99%

Basis for selection. Academic and personal record, recommendations, test scores important. Class rank considered. Interview required for academically marginal students; audition required for drama, music programs and forensics; portfolio required for art program.

High school preparation. College-preparatory program recommended. 13 units recommended. Recommended units include English 4, mathematics 3, social studies 3 and science 3.

2008-2009 Annual costs. Tuition/fees: $20,150. Room/board: $5,600. Books/supplies: $800. Personal expenses: $1,050.

2008-2009 Financial aid. Need-based: 226 full-time freshmen applied for aid; 198 were judged to have need; 198 of these received aid. Average need met was 97%. Average scholarship/grant was $14,017; average loan $3,891. 62% of total undergraduate aid awarded as scholarships/grants, 38% as loans/jobs. **Non-need-based:** Awarded to 213 full-time undergraduates, including 48 freshmen. Scholarships awarded for academics, art, athletics, music/drama.

Application procedures. Admission: No deadline. No application fee. Admission notification on a rolling basis beginning on or about 9/15. Must reply by May 1 or within 4 week(s) if notified thereafter. **Financial aid:** Priority date 3/1; no closing date. FAFSA required. Applicants notified on a rolling basis starting 3/1; must reply within 2 week(s) of notification.

Academics. Midwest Institute for International Students prepares students to meet English language requirement for admission to Doane and other American colleges. **Special study options:** Combined bachelor's/graduate degree, double major, ESL, honors, independent study, internships, student-designed major, study abroad, teacher certification program. 3-2 programs in engineering with Washington University, Columbia University, 3-2 program in environmental and forestry studies with Duke University. **Credit/placement by examination:** AP, CLEP, IB, SAT, ACT, institutional tests. 36 credit hours maximum toward bachelor's degree. International students who successfully complete Midwest Institute ESL program may be admitted without TOEFL scores. **Support services:** Learning center, reduced course load, remedial instruction, study skills assistance, tutoring, writing center.

Majors. Biology: General, biochemistry. **Business:** Accounting, business admin, human resources. **Communications:** Journalism, organizational. **Computer sciences:** General, computer science, information systems. **Conservation:** Environmental studies. **Education:** Elementary, ESL, physical, special. **Foreign languages:** French, German, Spanish. **History:** General. **Interdisciplinary:** Global studies, natural sciences. **Legal studies:** Paralegal. **Liberal arts:** Arts/sciences. **Math:** General. **Philosophy/religion:** Philosophy, religion. **Physical sciences:** Chemistry, physics. **Psychology:** General. **Public administration:** General. **Social sciences:** General, economics, international relations, political science, sociology. **Visual/performing arts:** Art, dramatic, graphic design.

Most popular majors. Biology 12%, business/marketing 17%, communications/journalism 6%, education 14%, psychology 6%, social sciences 11%, visual/performing arts 9%.

Computing on campus. 400 workstations in dormitories, library, computer center, student center. Dormitories wired for high-speed internet access and linked to campus network. Commuter students can connect to campus network. Online course registration, online library, helpline, student web hosting, wireless network available.

Student life. Freshman orientation: Available. Preregistration for classes offered. **Policies:** Unmarried students under 22 not living with parents expected to live on campus. **Housing:** Guaranteed on-campus for freshmen. Coed dorms, single-sex dorms available. $200 fully refundable deposit. **Activities:** Bands, campus ministries, choral groups, dance, drama, film society, literary magazine, music ensembles, musical theater, radio station, student government, student newspaper, TV station, student education association, Doane speakers, Club Internationale, Fellowship of Christian Athletes, American Minority Student Alliance, College Republicans, Young Democrats.

Athletics. NAIA. **Intercollegiate:** Baseball M, basketball, bowling, cross-country, football (tackle) M, golf, soccer, softball W, tennis, track and field, volleyball W. **Intramural:** Basketball, football (tackle) M, golf, softball, swimming, tennis, volleyball. **Team name:** Tigers.

Student services. Adult student services, chaplain/spiritual director, career counseling, student employment services, financial aid counseling, health services, personal counseling, placement for graduates, veterans' counselor.

Contact. E-mail: admissions@doane.edu
Phone: (402) 826-8222 Toll-free number: (800) 333-6263
Fax: (402) 826-8600
Cezar Mesquita, Dean of Admission, Doane College, 1014 Boswell Avenue, Crete, NE 68333

Grace University
Omaha, Nebraska
www.graceuniversity.edu **CB code: 6248**

- Private 4-year university and Bible college affiliated with interdenominational tradition
- Residential campus in very large city
- 367 degree-seeking undergraduates
- 65 graduate students
- 61% of applicants admitted
- ACT (writing optional), application essay required

General. Founded in 1943. Regionally accredited; also accredited by ABHE. **Degrees:** 69 bachelor's, 3 associate awarded; master's offered. **ROTC:** Air Force. **Calendar:** Semester, limited summer session. **Full-time faculty:** 26 total. **Part-time faculty:** 44 total. **Class size:** 87% < 20, 8% 20-39, 1% 40-49, 3% 50-99, less than 1% >100.

Freshman class profile. 204 applied, 124 admitted, 72 enrolled.

Basis for selection. School achievement record, religious affiliation/commitment, test scores, and student profile important. Conditional admission for students who have not taken SAT/ACT. Audition required for music programs. **Homeschooled:** Transcript of courses and grades required. ACT score of 20 or GED required.

High school preparation. College-preparatory program recommended. Teacher education program requires 4 language arts, 2 mathematics, 2 sciences, 2 social sciences.

2008-2009 Annual costs. Tuition/fees: $14,490. Room/board: $5,590. Books/supplies: $800.

2008-2009 Financial aid. Non-need-based: Scholarships awarded for academics, alumni affiliation, music/drama.

Application procedures. Admission: Priority date 2/1; deadline 8/15 (receipt date). $35 fee, may be waived for applicants with need. Admission notification on a rolling basis. High school students can take up to two courses prior to their high school graduation at a reduced cost. **Financial aid:** Priority date 3/1; no closing date. FAFSA, institutional form required. Applicants notified on a rolling basis starting 3/1; must reply within 2 week(s) of notification.

Academics. Special study options: Distance learning, dual enrollment of high school students, internships, liberal arts/career combination, student-designed major, study abroad. Adult degree completion program. **Credit/placement by examination:** AP, CLEP, ACT. 15 credit hours maximum toward bachelor's degree. **Support services:** Learning center, reduced course load, study skills assistance, tutoring.

Majors. Business: Management science. **Communications:** Broadcast journalism, journalism. **Education:** Business, elementary, English, ESL, history, mathematics, middle, music, secondary, social science. **Health:** Nursing (RN). **Liberal arts:** Arts/sciences. **Psychology:** General. **Theology:** Bible, missionary, religious ed, sacred music, theology.

Computing on campus. 35 workstations in dormitories, library, computer center. Dormitories wired for high-speed internet access and linked to campus network. Commuter students can connect to campus network. Online library, helpline, wireless network available.

Student life. Freshman orientation: Mandatory. Preregistration for classes offered. **Policies:** All on campus housing is alcohol/drug/smoke-free. Religious observance required. **Housing:** Guaranteed on-campus for freshmen. Single-sex dorms, apartments, wellness housing available. $150 partly refundable deposit. **Activities:** Concert band, choral groups, drama, music ensembles, student government, student newspaper.

Athletics. NCCAA. **Intercollegiate:** Basketball, soccer M, volleyball W. **Intramural:** Basketball M, football (tackle), volleyball W. **Team name:** Royals.

Student services. Chaplain/spiritual director, career counseling, student employment services, financial aid counseling, health services, personal counseling, placement for graduates.

Contact. E-mail: admissions@graceuniversity.edu
Phone: (402) 449-2831 Toll-free number: (800) 383-1422
Fax: (402) 449-2999
Angie Wayman, Director of Traditional Undergraduate Admissions, Grace University, 1311 South Ninth Street, Omaha, NE 68108-3629

Hastings College

Hastings, Nebraska — **CB member**
www.hastings.edu — **CB code: 6270**

- Private 4-year liberal arts college affiliated with Presbyterian Church (USA)
- Residential campus in large town

General. Founded in 1882. Regionally accredited. **Location:** 90 miles from Lincoln, 150 miles from Omaha. **Calendar:** 4-1-4.

Annual costs/financial aid. Tuition/fees (2008-2009): $20,782. Room/board: $5,702. Books/supplies: $750. Personal expenses: $1,800. Need-based financial aid available to full-time and part-time students.

Contact. Phone: (402) 461-7403
Director of Admissions, 710 North Turner Avenue, Hastings, NE 68901-7621

ITT Technical Institute: Omaha

Omaha, Nebraska
www.itt-tech.edu — **CB code: 2740**

- For-profit 4-year technical college
- Commuter campus in large city

General. Accredited by ACICS. **Calendar:** Quarter.

Contact. Phone: (402) 331-2900
Director of Recruitment, 9814 M Street, Omaha, NE 68127

Midland Lutheran College

Fremont, Nebraska
www.mlc.edu — **CB code: 6406**

- Private 4-year liberal arts college affiliated with Evangelical Lutheran Church in America
- Residential campus in large town

General. Founded in 1883. Regionally accredited. **Location:** 35 miles from Omaha, 52 miles from Lincoln. **Calendar:** 4-1-4.

Annual costs/financial aid. Tuition/fees (2008-2009): $22,006. Room/board: $5,366. Books/supplies: $800. Personal expenses: $1,430. Need-based financial aid available to full-time and part-time students.

Contact. Phone: (402) 941-6501
Director of Admissions, 900 North Clarkson, Fremont, NE 68025

Nebraska Christian College

Papillion, Nebraska
www.nechristian.edu — **CB code: 1332**

- Private 4-year Bible college affiliated with Christian Church/Churches of Christ
- Residential campus in large town
- 162 degree-seeking undergraduates
- ACT (writing optional) required

General. Founded in 1944. Accredited by ABHE. **Degrees:** 10 bachelor's, 7 associate awarded. **Calendar:** Semester, limited summer session. **Full-time faculty:** 11 total. **Part-time faculty:** 7 total.

Basis for selection. Christian commitment and references very important; high school transcript or GED required. Transcript of any previous college work required.

2008-2009 Annual costs. Tuition/fees: $10,400. Room/board: $4,800. Books/supplies: $600. Personal expenses: $1,900.

2007-2008 Financial aid. Non-need-based: Scholarships awarded for academics, leadership.

Application procedures. Admission: Closing date 9/1. $25 fee, may be waived for applicants with need. Admission notification on a rolling basis. **Financial aid:** Priority date 6/1; no closing date. FAFSA, institutional form required. Applicants notified on a rolling basis starting 5/5.

Academics. Special study options: Combined bachelor's/graduate degree, cooperative education, double major, dual enrollment of high school students, independent study, internships. **Credit/placement by examination:** AP, CLEP. **Support services:** Learning center, reduced course load, study skills assistance, tutoring, writing center.

Majors. Theology: Bible, missionary, religious ed, sacred music, theology.

Computing on campus. 10 workstations in library, computer center. Dormitories wired for high-speed internet access. Wireless network available.

Student life. Freshman orientation: Mandatory. **Policies:** Religious observance required. **Housing:** Single-sex dorms, special housing for disabled, apartments available. $100 deposit. **Activities:** Choral groups, drama, music ensembles, student government.

Athletics. NCCAA. **Intercollegiate:** Basketball, soccer M, volleyball W. **Intramural:** Basketball M, football (non-tackle), soccer, volleyball. **Team name:** Parsons.

Student services. Adult student services, career counseling, student employment services, financial aid counseling, health services, personal counseling, placement for graduates.

Contact. E-mail: admissions@nechristian.edu
Phone: (402) 935-9400 Fax: (402) 935-9500
Tim Snyder, Director of Admissions, Nebraska Christian College, 12550 South 114th Street, Papillion, NE 68046

Nebraska Methodist College of Nursing and Allied Health

Omaha, Nebraska
www.methodistcollege.edu — **CB code: 6510**

- Private 4-year health science and nursing college affiliated with United Methodist Church
- Commuter campus in large city
- 520 degree-seeking undergraduates: 28% part-time, 92% women, 3% African American, 3% Asian American, 1% Hispanic American, 1% Native American
- 83 degree-seeking graduate students
- 50% of applicants admitted
- SAT or ACT (ACT writing optional) required
- 75% graduate within 6 years

General. Founded in 1891. Regionally accredited. Health care classes offered at Josie Harper campus. **Degrees:** 113 bachelor's, 33 associate awarded; master's offered. **ROTC:** Army. **Location:** 120 miles from Des Moines, Iowa, 180 miles from Kansas City, Missouri. **Calendar:** Semester, limited summer session. **Full-time faculty:** 47 total; 28% have terminal degrees, 2% minority, 89% women. **Part-time faculty:** 11 total; 36% have terminal degrees, 100% women. **Class size:** 48% < 20, 46% 20-39, 3% 40-49, 3% 50-99. **Special facilities:** Human cadaver lab.

Freshman class profile. 184 applied, 92 admitted, 65 enrolled.

Mid 50% test scores		**GPA 2.0-2.99:**	13%
ACT composite:	19-23	**Rank in top quarter:**	11%
GPA 3.75 or higher:	18%	**Rank in top tenth:**	11%
GPA 3.50-3.74:	18%	**Out-of-state:**	3%
GPA 3.0-3.49:	51%	**Live on campus:**	20%

Basis for selection. School achievement, test scores most important. Personal statement, interview important. Recommendations, school and community activities considered. Deadlines vary by program. ACT or SAT is required of all current high school graduates and of students making application within two years of high school graduation. Departmental interview for specific programs. **Homeschooled:** Submit GED equivalent. The State of NE does not issue high school diplomas to exempt students.

High school preparation. 10 units required. Required units include English 4, mathematics 2, social studies 2, science 2 (laboratory 2). Chemistry, biology, and algebra required. A background in physics is strongly recommended for applicants for radiologic technology, sonography, and physical therapist assistant.

2009-2010 Annual costs. Tuition/fees (projected): $14,250. Room only: $4,824. Books/supplies: $962. Personal expenses: $1,395.

2007-2008 Financial aid. **Need-based:** 22 full-time freshmen applied for aid; 20 were judged to have need; 20 of these received aid. Average need met was 55%. Average scholarship/grant was $5,956; average loan $3,083. 35% of total undergraduate aid awarded as scholarships/grants, 65% as loans/jobs. **Non-need-based:** Awarded to 18 full-time undergraduates, including 1 freshmen. Scholarships awarded for academics, leadership, religious affiliation, ROTC.

Application procedures. **Admission:** No deadline. $25 fee, may be waived for applicants with need. Admission notification on a rolling basis. Required within two weeks of acceptance. Application deadlines vary by program. **Financial aid:** Priority date 5/1; no closing date. FAFSA, institutional form required. Applicants notified on a rolling basis starting 3/1; must reply within 3 week(s) of notification.

Academics. Peer tutoring available for most courses. **Special study options:** Accelerated study, combined bachelor's/graduate degree, distance learning, independent study, internships. **Credit/placement by examination:** AP, CLEP, institutional tests. 9 credit hours maximum toward associate degree, 9 toward bachelor's. Credit by examination considered on an individual basis. **Support services:** Learning center, reduced course load, remedial instruction, study skills assistance, tutoring, writing center.

Majors. **Health:** Cardiovascular technology, nursing (RN), radiologic technology/medical imaging, respiratory therapy technology, sonography.

Computing on campus. 75 workstations in library, computer center, student center. Dormitories linked to campus network. Online course registration, online library, helpline available.

Student life. **Freshman orientation:** Mandatory. Preregistration for classes offered. 2-days held in August, one-day transfer orientation for allied health students held in May. **Housing:** Guaranteed on-campus for all undergraduates. Coed dorms, apartments, wellness housing available. $150 nonrefundable deposit. **Activities:** Campus ministries, student government, student nurse association (state and national), allied health student association, College Ambassadors, minority student organization, Pathfinders, residence hall council.

Student services. Adult student services, alcohol/substance abuse counseling, chaplain/spiritual director, career counseling, student employment services, financial aid counseling, health services, minority student services, personal counseling, placement for graduates, veterans' counselor.

Contact. E-mail: admissions@methodistcollege.edu
Phone: (402) 354-7200 Toll-free number: (800) 335-5510
Fax: (402) 354-7020
Sarah Bonney, Director of Admissions, Nebraska Methodist College of Nursing and Allied Health, 720 North 87th Street, Omaha, NE 68114

Nebraska Wesleyan University

Lincoln, Nebraska
www.nebrwesleyan.edu **CB code: 6470**

- Private 4-year liberal arts college affiliated with United Methodist Church
- Residential campus in small city
- 1,817 degree-seeking undergraduates: 11% part-time, 58% women, 2% African American, 2% Asian American, 1% Hispanic American
- 216 degree-seeking graduate students
- 80% of applicants admitted
- SAT or ACT (ACT writing optional) required
- 66% graduate within 6 years

General. Founded in 1887. Regionally accredited. Non-traditional programs on accelerated semesters. **Degrees:** 408 bachelor's awarded; master's offered. **ROTC:** Army, Air Force. **Location:** 55 miles from Omaha, 200 miles from Kansas City, Missouri. **Calendar:** Semester, limited summer session. **Full-time faculty:** 105 total; 85% have terminal degrees, 2% minority, 53% women. **Part-time faculty:** 54 total; 22% have terminal degrees, 4% minority, 52% women. **Class size:** 44% < 20, 52% 20-39, 2% 40-49, 2% 50-99. **Special facilities:** Planetarium, laboratory theater, greenhouse, herbarium, nuclear magnetic resonance laboratory, sleep laboratory, art gallery.

Freshman class profile. 1,519 applied, 1,214 admitted, 383 enrolled.

Mid 50% test scores		**Return as sophomores:**	83%
ACT composite:	23-27	**Out-of-state:**	9%
Rank in top quarter:	63%	**Live on campus:**	92%
Rank in top tenth:	26%	**Fraternities:**	23%
End year in good standing:	95%	**Sororities:**	19%

Basis for selection. Students who rank in the top half of their graduating class or achieve an ACT composite score of 20 or an SAT combined score of 950 (exclusive of Writing) are invited to apply for admission. Campus visit recommended for all students; audition required for drama, music scholarships; portfolio required for art scholarships. **Homeschooled:** Transcript of courses and grades required. GED scores.

High school preparation. College-preparatory program recommended. Recommended units include English 4, mathematics 3, social studies 3, science 3 and foreign language 2.

2008-2009 Annual costs. Tuition/fees: $21,274. Room/board: $5,710. Books/supplies: $800. Personal expenses: $1,800.

2008-2009 Financial aid. **Need-based:** 334 full-time freshmen applied for aid; 277 were judged to have need; 277 of these received aid. Average need met was 73%. Average scholarship/grant was $11,847; average loan $4,421. 64% of total undergraduate aid awarded as scholarships/grants, 36% as loans/jobs. **Non-need-based:** Awarded to 515 full-time undergraduates, including 134 freshmen. Scholarships awarded for academics, art, music/drama, religious affiliation.

Application procedures. **Admission:** Closing date 8/15 (postmark date). $20 fee, may be waived for applicants with need, free for online applicants. Admission notification on a rolling basis beginning on or about 1/15. Must reply by May 1 or within 4 week(s) if notified thereafter. **Financial aid:** No deadline. FAFSA required. Applicants notified on a rolling basis starting 3/1; must reply within 4 week(s) of notification.

Academics. **Special study options:** Combined bachelor's/graduate degree, double major, dual enrollment of high school students, exchange student, independent study, internships, liberal arts/career combination, semester at sea, study abroad, teacher certification program, United Nations semester, urban semester, Washington semester. 3-2 engineering with Washington University or Columbia University; Capitol Hill Internship Program; Chicago Center for Urban Life and Culture; summer research fellowships in the natural sciences; faculty led international study tours. **Credit/placement by examination:** AP, CLEP, IB, institutional tests. Unlimited number of hours of credit by examination may be counted toward degree. **Support services:** Reduced course load, study skills assistance, tutoring, writing center.

Majors. **Biology:** General, biochemistry, Biochemistry/biophysics and molecular biology. **Business:** Accounting, business admin, international. **Communications:** General, political. **Computer sciences:** Computer science, information technology. **Education:** Elementary, English, middle, music, physical, science, social science, special. **Foreign languages:** French, German, Spanish. **Health:** Athletic training, nursing (RN). **History:** General. **Interdisciplinary:** Biopsychology, global studies. **Math:** General. **Parks/recreation:** Exercise sciences, health/fitness, sports admin. **Philosophy/religion:** Philosophy, religion. **Physical sciences:** Chemistry, physics. **Psychology:** General, industrial. **Public administration:** Social work. **Social sciences:** Economics, political science, sociology. **Visual/performing arts:** Art, dramatic, music performance, studio arts. **Other:** Business-sociology, Gender studies.

Most popular majors. Biology 9%, business/marketing 27%, education 9%, English 9%, health sciences 10%, parks/recreation 8%, psychology 7%.

Computing on campus. 360 workstations in dormitories, library, computer center, student center. Dormitories wired for high-speed internet access and linked to campus network. Commuter students can connect to campus network. Online course registration, online library, helpline, repair service, student web hosting, wireless network available.

Student life. **Freshman orientation:** Mandatory. Preregistration for classes offered. Summer 1-day registration sessions in June; 4-day orientation program before fall classes begin. **Housing:** Guaranteed on-campus for all undergraduates. Coed dorms, single-sex dorms, special housing for disabled, apartments, fraternity/sorority housing available. $100 nonrefundable deposit, deadline 7/1. Residence hall suites and townhomes. **Activities:** Bands, campus ministries, choral groups, drama, international student organizations, literary magazine, music ensembles, musical theater, opera, student government, student newspaper, Student Fellowship, Fellowship of Christian Athletes, Rainbow Club, College Republicans, Young Democrats, Nebraskans for Peace, international relations organization, Circle K, environmental action, global service learning.

Athletics. NAIA, NCAA. **Intercollegiate:** Baseball M, basketball, cross-country, football (tackle) M, golf, soccer, softball W, tennis, track and field, volleyball W. **Intramural:** Basketball, bowling, football (non-tackle), racquetball, soccer, softball, tennis, volleyball, water polo. **Team name:** Prairie Wolves.

Student services. Adult student services, chaplain/spiritual director, career counseling, student employment services, financial aid counseling, health services, minority student services, personal counseling, placement for graduates, women's services. **Physically disabled:** Services for visually, speech, hearing impaired.

Contact. E-mail: admissions@nebrwesleyan.edu
Phone: (402) 465-2218 Toll-free number: (800) 541-3818
Fax: (402) 465-2177
David Duzik, Director of Admissions, Nebraska Wesleyan University, 5000 St. Paul Avenue, Lincoln, NE 68504

Peru State College

Peru, Nebraska
www.peru.edu **CB code: 6468**

- Public 4-year liberal arts and teachers college
- Residential campus in rural community
- 1,548 degree-seeking undergraduates
- 48% of applicants admitted

General. Founded in 1867. Regionally accredited. Elementary school teacher certification courses offered at Offutt Air Force Base. Online graduate degrees in education and organizational management offered. **Degrees:** 276 bachelor's awarded; master's offered. **Location:** 64 miles from Omaha, 67 miles from Lincoln. **Calendar:** Semester, limited summer session. **Full-time faculty:** 48 total; 92% have terminal degrees, 4% minority, 38% women. **Part-time faculty:** 54 total; 52% women.

Freshman class profile. 839 applied, 402 admitted, 217 enrolled.

Out-of-state:	7%	**Live on campus:**	75%

Basis for selection. SAT/ACT scores required of all, however scores are only used in admissions decisions for out-of-state applicants. Out-of-state applicants must rank in top half of graduating class or have ACT score of 14 or SAT score of 560 (exclusive of Writing), and 2.0 GPA. **Homeschooled:** Transcript of courses and grades required.

High school preparation. 16 units recommended. Recommended units include English 4, mathematics 2, social studies 3, science 2 and foreign language 1.

2008-2009 Annual costs. Tuition/fees: $4,388; $7,883 out-of-state. Room/board: $5,556. Books/supplies: $600. Personal expenses: $1,000.

2007-2008 Financial aid. All financial aid based on need.

Application procedures. Admission: Priority date 12/1; no deadline. No application fee. Admission notification on a rolling basis beginning on or about 9/1. **Financial aid:** Priority date 3/1; no closing date. FAFSA, institutional form required. Applicants notified on a rolling basis starting 3/1; must reply within 2 week(s) of notification.

Academics. Special study options: Cooperative education, cross-registration, distance learning, double major, dual enrollment of high school students, honors, independent study, internships, liberal arts/career combination, study abroad, teacher certification program. **Credit/placement by examination:** CLEP, IB. 16 credit hours maximum toward bachelor's degree. **Support services:** Learning center, reduced course load, remedial instruction, study skills assistance, tutoring.

Majors. Biology: Plant physiology. **Business:** Business admin, office technology. **Computer sciences:** General, computer science, programming. **Education:** General, art, biology, computer, early childhood, elementary, English, history, mathematics, middle, music, physical, physics, science, secondary, social science, special, speech, voc/tech. **Interdisciplinary:** Natural sciences. **Math:** General. **Protective services:** Law enforcement admin. **Psychology:** General. **Social sciences:** General, sociology. **Visual/performing arts:** Art.

Most popular majors. Business/marketing 38%, education 47%, psychology 6%.

Computing on campus. 140 workstations in dormitories, library, computer center, student center. Dormitories linked to campus network.

Student life. Freshman orientation: Mandatory. Preregistration for classes offered. 5 different 1-day sessions in June, July, August. **Housing:** Guaranteed on-campus for freshmen. Coed dorms, single-sex dorms, apartments, wellness housing available. $100 deposit. **Activities:** Bands, choral groups, drama, literary magazine, music ensembles, musical theater, student government, student newspaper, TV station, Fellowship of Christian Athletes, multicultural committee, Phi Beta Lambda, Peru Players, Women's Athletic Association, Ambassadors.

Athletics. NAIA. **Intercollegiate:** Baseball M, basketball, football (tackle) M, golf W, softball W, volleyball W. **Intramural:** Basketball, soccer, softball, swimming, table tennis, tennis, volleyball, water polo M. **Team name:** Bobcats.

Student services. Adult student services, alcohol/substance abuse counseling, chaplain/spiritual director, career counseling, student employment services, financial aid counseling, health services, on-campus daycare, personal counseling, placement for graduates, veterans' counselor. **Physically disabled:** Services for visually, hearing impaired.

Contact. E-mail: admissions@oakmail.peru.edu
Phone: (402) 872-2221 Toll-free number: (800) 742-4412
Fax: (402) 872-2296
Micki Willis, Director of Recruitment and Admissions, Peru State College, Box 10, Peru, NE 68421-0010

Union College

Lincoln, Nebraska
www.ucollege.edu **CB code: 6865**

- Private 4-year liberal arts college affiliated with Seventh-day Adventists
- Residential campus in small city
- 838 degree-seeking undergraduates: 14% part-time, 57% women, 3% African American, 3% Asian American, 6% Hispanic American, 1% Native American, 9% international
- 71 graduate students
- 64% of applicants admitted
- SAT or ACT (ACT writing optional), application essay required
- 52% graduate within 6 years

General. Founded in 1889. Regionally accredited. **Degrees:** 162 bachelor's, 9 associate awarded; master's offered. **Location:** 50 miles from Omaha. **Calendar:** Semester, limited summer session. **Full-time faculty:** 58 total; 41% have terminal degrees, 10% minority, 36% women. **Part-time faculty:** 35 total; 14% have terminal degrees, 11% minority, 60% women. **Class size:** 68% < 20, 28% 20-39, 3% 40-49, less than 1% 50-99. **Special facilities:** Arboretum.

Freshman class profile. 354 applied, 228 admitted, 169 enrolled.

Mid 50% test scores		**Rank in top quarter:**	18%
ACT composite:	20-25	**Rank in top tenth:**	13%
GPA 3.75 or higher:	38%	**Return as sophomores:**	66%
GPA 3.50-3.74:	17%	**Out-of-state:**	86%
GPA 3.0-3.49:	24%	**Live on campus:**	97%
GPA 2.0-2.99:	20%	**International:**	4%

Basis for selection. School achievement record and 3 references (including 1 from pastor) very important. Interview recommended for all students; audition recommended for music program; portfolio recommended for art program.

High school preparation. College-preparatory program recommended. 20 units required. Required and recommended units include English 3-4, mathematics 2-3, social studies 1, history 1, science 2-3 (laboratory 1), foreign language 1 and academic electives 3. 2 algebra, 1 geometry, trigonometry recommended for mathematics and science-related programs. Physics and chemistry recommended for nursing, biology, chemistry, physics, engineering, medical technology, premedicine, and predental programs.

2008-2009 Annual costs. Tuition/fees: $16,920. Room/board: $4,680. Books/supplies: $1,000. Personal expenses: $1,200.

2007-2008 Financial aid. Non-need-based: Scholarships awarded for academics. **Additional information:** Special institutional grants offered to all freshmen and sophomores demonstrating exceptional financial need.

Application procedures. Admission: No deadline. No application fee. Admission notification on a rolling basis. **Financial aid:** Priority date 5/1; no closing date. FAFSA required. Applicants notified on a rolling basis starting 4/15; must reply by 5/1 or within 3 week(s) of notification.

Academics. **Special study options:** Cross-registration, double major, dual enrollment of high school students, ESL, honors, independent study, internships, student-designed major, study abroad, teacher certification program. **Credit/placement by examination:** AP, CLEP, IB, ACT, institutional tests. **Support services:** Learning center, reduced course load, remedial instruction, study skills assistance, tutoring, writing center.

Majors. **Biology:** General, biochemistry. **Business:** Accounting, business admin, finance, international finance, management science. **Communications:** Journalism, public relations. **Computer sciences:** Computer science, information systems, systems analysis. **Education:** General, elementary, secondary. **Foreign languages:** French, German, Spanish. **History:** General. **Math:** General. **Parks/recreation:** Health/fitness, sports admin. **Philosophy/religion:** Religion. **Physical sciences:** Chemistry, physics. **Psychology:** General. **Public administration:** Social work. **Social sciences:** General. **Theology:** Pastoral counseling, religious ed, theology. **Visual/performing arts:** Commercial/advertising art, music performance, studio arts. **Other:** International relief and rescue.

Most popular majors. Business/marketing 16%, communications/journalism 6%, education 12%, health sciences 36%.

Computing on campus. 80 workstations in dormitories, library, computer center, student center. Dormitories wired for high-speed internet access and linked to campus network. Commuter students can connect to campus network. Online library, helpline, student web hosting, wireless network available.

Student life. **Freshman orientation:** Mandatory. Preregistration for classes offered. **Policies:** Religious observance required. **Housing:** Guaranteed on-campus for all undergraduates. Single-sex dorms, apartments available. **Activities:** Concert band, choral groups, drama, literary magazine, music ensembles, student government, student newspaper, Collegiate Adventists for Better Living, Union for Christ, Union for Kids.

Athletics. **Intercollegiate:** Basketball, soccer. **Intramural:** Badminton, basketball, bowling, football (non-tackle), golf, gymnastics, racquetball, soccer, softball, tennis, volleyball. **Team name:** Warriors and Lady Warriors.

Student services. Chaplain/spiritual director, career counseling, student employment services, financial aid counseling, health services, minority student services, personal counseling, placement for graduates. **Physically disabled:** Services for visually, speech, hearing impaired.

Contact. E-mail: ucenroll@ucollege.edu
Phone: (402) 486-2504 Toll-free number: (800) 228-4600
Fax: (402) 486-2895
Huda McClelland, Director of Admission, Union College, 3800 South 48th Street, Lincoln, NE 68506-4300

University of Nebraska - Kearney

Kearney, Nebraska
www.unk.edu **CB code: 6467**

- Public 4-year university
- Residential campus in large town
- 4,911 degree-seeking undergraduates: 8% part-time, 53% women, 1% African American, 1% Asian American, 4% Hispanic American, 8% international
- 1,439 degree-seeking graduate students
- 80% of applicants admitted
- SAT and SAT Subject Tests or ACT (ACT writing optional) required
- 59% graduate within 6 years

General. Founded in 1903. Regionally accredited. **Degrees:** 1,039 bachelor's awarded; master's offered. **Location:** 180 miles from Omaha. **Calendar:** Semester, extensive summer session. **Full-time faculty:** 304 total; 77% have terminal degrees, 7% minority, 46% women. **Part-time faculty:** 96 total; 21% have terminal degrees, 2% minority, 59% women. **Class size:** 39% < 20, 49% 20-39, 7% 40-49, 4% 50-99, less than 1% >100. **Special facilities:** Nebraska state art collection, state arboretum, planetarium.

Freshman class profile. 2,797 applied, 2,244 admitted, 1,045 enrolled.

Mid 50% test scores		**Rank in top quarter:**	38%
SAT critical reading:	400-660	**Rank in top tenth:**	17%
SAT math:	420-680	**Return as sophomores:**	79%
SAT writing:	370-640	**Out-of-state:**	8%
ACT composite:	20-25	**Live on campus:**	86%
GPA 3.75 or higher:	29%	**International:**	5%
GPA 3.50-3.74:	16%	**Fraternities:**	8%
GPA 3.0-3.49:	31%	**Sororities:**	7%
GPA 2.0-2.99:	23%		

Basis for selection. Test scores, school achievement record most important. Applicants who show promise of academic success, but do not meet admission requirements, may be admitted on conditional basis.

High school preparation. 16 units required. Required units include English 4, mathematics 3, social studies 3, science 3 (laboratory 1), foreign language 2 and academic electives 1.

2008-2009 Annual costs. Tuition/fees: $5,426; $10,001 out-of-state. Room/board: $6,330. Books/supplies: $860. Personal expenses: $2,494.

2008-2009 Financial aid. **Non-need-based:** Scholarships awarded for academics, alumni affiliation, art, athletics, leadership, minority status, music/drama, state residency.

Application procedures. **Admission:** Priority date 8/1; no deadline. $45 fee. Admission notification on a rolling basis beginning on or about 10/1. **Financial aid:** Priority date 4/1; no closing date. FAFSA, institutional form required. Applicants notified on a rolling basis starting 3/15; must reply within 2 week(s) of notification.

Academics. **Special study options:** Cooperative education, distance learning, double major, dual enrollment of high school students, ESL, exchange student, honors, independent study, internships, study abroad, teacher certification program. International student exchange program with Sapporo University and Kansai Gaidai, Japan; Nebraska semester abroad. **Credit/placement by examination:** CLEP, SAT, ACT, institutional tests. 45 credit hours maximum toward bachelor's degree. **Support services:** Learning center, study skills assistance, tutoring, writing center.

Majors. **Agriculture:** Business. **Biology:** General. **Business:** Business admin, office management, office/clerical, operations, tourism/travel. **Communications:** General, advertising, broadcast journalism, journalism. **Computer sciences:** General, information systems. **Education:** General, art, biology, business, chemistry, early childhood, elementary, English, ESL, family/consumer sciences, foreign languages, French, German, health, history, learning disabled, mathematics, mentally handicapped, middle, multiple handicapped, music, physical, physically handicapped, physics, science, secondary, social science, Spanish, special, speech, speech impaired, technology/industrial arts, trade/industrial. **Family/consumer sciences:** General, business, clothing/textiles, family studies, housing. **Foreign languages:** French, German, Spanish, translation. **Health:** Medical radiologic technology/radiation therapy, respiratory therapy technology, speech pathology. **History:** General. **Liberal arts:** Arts/sciences. **Math:** General. **Parks/recreation:** Facilities management, sports admin. **Philosophy/religion:** Philosophy. **Physical sciences:** Chemistry, physics. **Protective services:** Criminal justice, police science. **Psychology:** General. **Public administration:** Social work. **Social sciences:** General, economics, geography, international relations, political science, sociology. **Visual/performing arts:** General, art, art history/conservation, commercial/advertising art, dramatic, music performance, studio arts.

Most popular majors. Business/marketing 25%, education 16%, parks/recreation 7%.

Computing on campus. 411 workstations in dormitories, library, computer center, student center. Dormitories wired for high-speed internet access and linked to campus network. Commuter students can connect to campus network. Online course registration, helpline, repair service, wireless network available.

Student life. **Freshman orientation:** Available. Preregistration for classes offered. **Housing:** Guaranteed on-campus for freshmen. Coed dorms, single-sex dorms, apartments, fraternity/sorority housing available. **Activities:** Bands, choral groups, dance, drama, international student organizations, music ensembles, musical theater, radio station, student government, student newspaper, symphony orchestra, TV station, Young Republicans, Young Democrats, Alpha Phi Omega, Fellowship of Christian Athletes, People of Color.

Athletics. NCAA. **Intercollegiate:** Baseball M, basketball, cross-country, diving W, football (tackle) M, golf, softball W, swimming W, tennis, track and field, volleyball W, wrestling M. **Intramural:** Archery, badminton, basketball, bowling, cross-country, diving, football (non-tackle), golf, racquetball, soccer, softball, swimming, table tennis, tennis, track and field, volleyball, water polo, wrestling M. **Team name:** Lopers.

Student services. Alcohol/substance abuse counseling, career counseling, student employment services, financial aid counseling, health services, minority student services, on-campus daycare, personal counseling, placement for graduates, veterans' counselor, women's services. **Physically disabled:** Services for visually, hearing impaired.

Contact. E-mail: admissionsug@unk.edu
Phone: (308) 865-8526 Toll-free number: (800) 532-7639
Fax: (308) 865-8987
Dusty Newton, Director of Admissions, University of Nebraska - Kearney, 905 West 25th, Kearney, NE 68849

University of Nebraska - Lincoln

Lincoln, Nebraska **CB member**
www.unl.edu **CB code: 6877**

- Public 4-year university
- Residential campus in small city
- 18,526 degree-seeking undergraduates: 7% part-time, 46% women, 2% African American, 3% Asian American, 3% Hispanic American, 1% Native American, 3% international
- 4,333 degree-seeking graduate students
- 63% of applicants admitted
- SAT or ACT (ACT writing optional) required
- 64% graduate within 6 years

General. Founded in 1869. Regionally accredited. Nebraska's only land-grant university. Research opportunities impacting state's economic development available to students. **Degrees:** 3,246 bachelor's, 12 associate awarded; master's, doctoral, first professional offered. **ROTC:** Army, Naval, Air Force. **Location:** 50 miles from Omaha. **Calendar:** Semester, extensive summer session. **Full-time faculty:** 1,070 total; 96% have terminal degrees, 17% minority, 29% women. **Part-time faculty:** 11 total; 100% have terminal degrees, 9% minority, 27% women. **Class size:** 39% < 20, 41% 20-39, 6% 40-49, 7% 50-99, 7% >100. **Special facilities:** State museum, planetarium, center for performing arts, arboretum, center for Asian Culture, center for Great Plains studies, center for biomaterials and genetic research.

Freshman class profile. 9,709 applied, 6,122 admitted, 4,200 enrolled.

Mid 50% test scores		Return as sophomores:	84%
SAT critical reading:	510-670	Out-of-state:	20%
SAT math:	530-670	Live on campus:	94%
ACT composite:	22-28	International:	1%
Rank in top quarter:	52%	Fraternities:	18%
Rank in top tenth:	24%	Sororities:	23%

Basis for selection. Students must meet minimum requirements of ACT composite score of 20 or higher, SAT combined score of 950 (exclusive of writing) or rank in top half of class. Audition required for music program. **Homeschooled:** Statement describing homeschool structure and mission, transcript of courses and grades required.

High school preparation. College-preparatory program required. 16 units required. Required and recommended units include English 4, mathematics 4, social studies 3, history 1, science 3 (laboratory 1) and foreign language 2. Mathematics must include algebra I and II, geometry, and 1 higher level math. 2 units of foreign language must be in same language. At least 1 social studies should be U.S. and/or world history and 1 additional unit should be history, American government, and/or geography. College of Engineering & Technology requires 1 pre-calculus/trigonometry, 1 physics and 1 chemistry. Architecture requires 0.5 trigonometry or pre-calculus for pre-architecture.

2008-2009 Annual costs. Tuition/fees: $6,585; $17,205 out-of-state. Room/board: $6,882. Books/supplies: $950. Personal expenses: $2,009.

2007-2008 Financial aid. Need-based: 2,895 full-time freshmen applied for aid; 1,952 were judged to have need; 1,915 of these received aid. Average need met was 75%. Average scholarship/grant was $7,219; average loan $3,266. 51% of total undergraduate aid awarded as scholarships/grants, 49% as loans/jobs. **Non-need-based:** Awarded to 2,500 full-time undergraduates, including 969 freshmen. Scholarships awarded for academics, alumni affiliation, art, athletics, leadership, minority status, music/drama, state residency.

Application procedures. Admission: Priority date 1/15; deadline 5/1 (receipt date). $45 fee, may be waived for applicants with need. Admission notification on a rolling basis beginning on or about 9/1. Must reply by 5/1. **Financial aid:** Priority date 4/15; no closing date. FAFSA required. Applicants notified on a rolling basis starting 4/1.

Academics. Comprehensive Education Program (CEP) is required of all entering students. Master of architecture professional degree available. **Special study options:** Accelerated study, combined bachelor's/graduate degree, cooperative education, cross-registration, distance learning, double major, dual enrollment of high school students, ESL, exchange student, honors, independent study, internships, liberal arts/career combination, student-designed major, study abroad, teacher certification program. **Credit/placement by examination:** AP, CLEP, IB, SAT, ACT, institutional tests. Individual colleges have different policies. **Support services:** Learning center, pre-admission summer program, reduced course load, remedial instruction, study skills assistance, tutoring, writing center.

Honors college/program. Formal application required. Acceptance based on evaluation of the student's potential by the faculty committee.

Majors. Agriculture: General, agronomy, animal sciences, business, communications, economics, food science, horticultural science, landscaping, mechanization, plant protection, products processing, range science, soil science. **Architecture:** Architecture, interior, landscape. **Area/ethnic studies:** Latin American, regional, Western European, women's. **Biology:** General, biochemistry, botany. **Business:** Accounting, actuarial science, business admin, finance, hospitality admin, international, management science, managerial economics, marketing. **Communications:** General, advertising, broadcast journalism, journalism. **Computer sciences:** General. **Conservation:** General, environmental studies, management/policy. **Education:** Agricultural, art, biology, business, chemistry, computer, Deaf/hearing impaired, elementary, English, ESL, foreign languages, French, German, health, history, mathematics, middle, multi-level teacher, music, physical, physics, reading, sales/marketing, science, social science, Spanish, technology/industrial arts, trade/industrial. **Engineering:** Agricultural, architectural, biomedical, chemical, civil, computer, electrical, industrial, mechanical. **Engineering technology:** Construction, electrical, industrial. **Family/consumer sciences:** General, clothing/textiles, food/nutrition, housing. **Foreign languages:** Ancient Greek, classics, French, German, Latin, Russian, Spanish. **Health:** Athletic training, community health services, predental, premedicine, prepharmacy, preveterinary, speech pathology, veterinary technology/assistant. **History:** General. **Interdisciplinary:** Ancient studies, medieval/Renaissance. **Liberal arts:** Arts/sciences, humanities. **Math:** General. **Parks/recreation:** Exercise sciences. **Philosophy/religion:** Philosophy. **Physical sciences:** Atmospheric science, chemistry, geology, hydrology, physics. **Protective services:** Forensics. **Psychology:** General. **Social sciences:** Anthropology, economics, geography, international relations, political science, sociology. **Visual/performing arts:** Art history/conservation, dance, dramatic, film/cinema, studio arts. **Other:** Child, youth and family studies, Ethnic studies, News and editorial, Technical education.

Most popular majors. Agriculture 6%, business/marketing 20%, communications/journalism 7%, education 10%, engineering/engineering technologies 13%, family/consumer sciences 7%, psychology 6%, social sciences 7%.

Computing on campus. 650 workstations in dormitories, library, computer center, student center. Dormitories wired for high-speed internet access and linked to campus network. Commuter students can connect to campus network. Online course registration, online library, helpline, student web hosting, wireless network available.

Student life. Freshman orientation: Available. Preregistration for classes offered. Day-long program conducted from mid-June to mid-July. **Policies:** No smoking allowed in University buildings. No alcohol or firearms on campus. Freshmen required to live on campus if not living with parents or close relatives. **Housing:** Guaranteed on-campus for freshmen. Coed dorms, single-sex dorms, special housing for disabled, apartments, cooperative housing, fraternity/sorority housing available. $250 partly refundable deposit, deadline 5/1. Pets allowed in dorm rooms. Special interest floors available. **Activities:** Bands, campus ministries, choral groups, dance, drama, film society, international student organizations, literary magazine, music ensembles, Model UN, musical theater, opera, radio station, student government, student newspaper, symphony orchestra, TV station, Afrikaan People's Union, University of Nebraska Inter-Tribal Exchange, Mexican-American student association, adult student network, Ecology Now, student foundation, student-alumni association, UNL Entrepreneurial Society.

Athletics. NCAA. **Intercollegiate:** Baseball M, basketball, bowling W, cross-country, diving W, football (tackle) M, golf, gymnastics, rifle W, rodeo, rowing (crew), soccer W, softball W, swimming W, tennis, track and field, volleyball W, wrestling M. **Intramural:** Football (non-tackle), soccer, softball, tennis, track and field, volleyball, water polo, wrestling M. **Team name:** Cornhuskers.

Student services. Adult student services, alcohol/substance abuse counseling, chaplain/spiritual director, career counseling, services for economically disadvantaged, student employment services, financial aid counseling, health services, legal services, minority student services, on-campus daycare, personal counseling, placement for graduates, veterans' counselor, women's services. **Physically disabled:** Services for visually, speech, hearing impaired.

Contact. E-mail: admissions@unl.edu
Phone: (402) 472-2023 Toll-free number: (800) 742-8800
Fax: (402) 472-0670
Alan Cerveny, Dean of Admissions, University of Nebraska - Lincoln, 1410 Q Street, Lincoln, NE 68588-0417

University of Nebraska - Omaha

Omaha, Nebraska **CB member**
www.unomaha.edu **CB code: 6420**

- Public 4-year university
- Commuter campus in large city
- 11,069 degree-seeking undergraduates: 21% part-time, 52% women, 6% African American, 3% Asian American, 4% Hispanic American, 1% Native American, 2% international
- 2,607 degree-seeking graduate students
- 84% of applicants admitted
- SAT or ACT (ACT writing optional) required
- 43% graduate within 6 years; 20% enter graduate study

General. Founded in 1908. Regionally accredited. Cooperative classes at Offutt Air Force Base. Cooperative programs with UNMC medical center. **Degrees:** 1,887 bachelor's awarded; master's, doctoral offered. **ROTC:** Army, Air Force. **Location:** 160 miles from Kansas City, Missouri. **Calendar:** Semester, extensive summer session. **Full-time faculty:** 479 total; 81% have terminal degrees, 18% minority, 43% women. **Part-time faculty:** 401 total; 24% have terminal degrees, 12% minority, 47% women. **Class size:** 35% < 20, 43% 20-39, 9% 40-49, 11% 50-99, 2% >100. **Special facilities:** Outdoor venture center, climbing wall, nature preserve, planetarium, Nebraska Book Arts Center.

Freshman class profile. 4,295 applied, 3,622 admitted, 1,816 enrolled.

Mid 50% test scores		**Rank in top tenth:**	13%
ACT composite:	20-26	**Return as sophomores:**	69%
GPA 3.75 or higher:	26%	**Out-of-state:**	10%
GPA 3.50-3.74:	16%	**Live on campus:**	41%
GPA 3.0-3.49:	28%	**International:**	1%
GPA 2.0-2.99:	29%	**Fraternities:**	5%
Rank in top quarter:	36%	**Sororities:**	4%

Basis for selection. School achievement record, test scores important. Must have ACT score of 20, comparable SAT score or class rank in upper half of graduating class. Admitted for special talent consideration on case by case basis. Open admission for non-degree applicants and non-traditional adult freshman applicants. Audition required for music program. **Homeschooled:** Applicants must submit official GED scores verifying successful completion of the GED. An ACT composite score of 25+ may be substituted in lieu of the GED score.

High school preparation. College-preparatory program required. 16 units required. Required units include English 4, mathematics 3, social studies 1, history 2, science 3 (laboratory 1), foreign language 2 and academic electives 1. Specific course requirements for programs in business administration, human resources and family services for College of Engineering and Technology.

2008-2009 Annual costs. Tuition/fees: $5,880; $15,458 out-of-state. Room/board: $6,980. Books/supplies: $800. Personal expenses: $2,110.

2007-2008 Financial aid. Need-based: 1,093 full-time freshmen applied for aid; 731 were judged to have need; 699 of these received aid. Average scholarship/grant was $1,758; average loan $2,659. 45% of total undergraduate aid awarded as scholarships/grants, 55% as loans/jobs. **Non-need-based:** Awarded to 2,236 full-time undergraduates, including 688 freshmen. Scholarships awarded for academics, alumni affiliation, art, athletics, leadership, minority status, music/drama, ROTC, state residency.

Application procedures. Admission: Closing date 8/1 (postmark date). $45 fee. Admission notification on a rolling basis. **Financial aid:** Priority date 3/1; no closing date. FAFSA required. Applicants notified on a rolling basis starting 4/15; must reply within 2 week(s) of notification.

Academics. Associate degree program available on Omaha campus through University of Nebraska-Lincoln in construction, drafting and design technology, electronic technology, fire control and safety technology, fire protection, manufacturing technology. On-line courses in aviation studies also available. **Special study options:** Combined bachelor's/graduate degree, cooperative education, cross-registration, distance learning, double major, dual enrollment of high school students, ESL, exchange student, honors, independent study, internships, student-designed major, study abroad, teacher certification program. **Credit/placement by examination:** AP, CLEP, ACT, institutional tests. 30 credit hours maximum toward bachelor's degree. CLEP exams in American History and Western Civilization must be accompanied by essay. **Support services:** Reduced course load, study skills assistance, tutoring, writing center.

Majors. Area/ethnic studies: African-American, Latin American, women's. **Biology:** General, bioinformatics, biotechnology. **Business:** General, accounting, banking/financial services, business admin, finance, investments/securities, management information systems, managerial economics, marketing, real estate, small business admin. **Communications:** General, broadcast journalism, journalism. **Computer sciences:** Computer science. **Conservation:** Environmental studies. **Education:** Elementary, music, physical, secondary, special, speech impaired. **Engineering:** Architectural, chemical, civil, computer, electrical, physics. **Engineering technology:** Construction, industrial, manufacturing. **Family/consumer sciences:** General, communication, family resources. **Foreign languages:** French, German, Spanish. **Health:** Community health services, health care admin, premedicine. **History:** General. **Interdisciplinary:** Gerontology, global studies, natural sciences. **Liberal arts:** Library science. **Math:** General. **Parks/recreation:** General, exercise sciences. **Philosophy/religion:** Philosophy, religion. **Physical sciences:** Chemistry, geology, physics. **Protective services:** Criminal justice. **Psychology:** General. **Public administration:** General, social work. **Social sciences:** Geography, political science, sociology, urban studies. **Transportation:** Aviation, aviation management. **Visual/performing arts:** Art, art history/conservation, dramatic, music performance, music theory/composition, piano/organ, stringed instruments, studio arts, voice/opera.

Most popular majors. Biology 6%, business/marketing 25%, education 13%, psychology 6%, security/protective services 9%.

Computing on campus. 2,415 workstations in dormitories, library, computer center, student center. Dormitories wired for high-speed internet access and linked to campus network. Commuter students can connect to campus network. Online course registration, online library, helpline, student web hosting, wireless network available.

Student life. Freshman orientation: Mandatory. Preregistration for classes offered. Held every week April 15 thru August 1st. **Housing:** Coed dorms available. $250 partly refundable deposit. **Activities:** Bands, campus ministries, choral groups, dance, drama, film society, international student organizations, literary magazine, music ensembles, musical theater, opera, radio station, student government, student newspaper, symphony orchestra, TV station, American multi-cultural students, chapter summary Bible study, student government legislative & public relations, Campus Crusade for Christ, honor societies, Greek letter organizations.

Athletics. NCAA. **Intercollegiate:** Baseball M, basketball, cross-country W, football (tackle) M, golf W, ice hockey M, soccer W, softball W, swimming W, tennis W, track and field W, volleyball W, wrestling M. **Intramural:** Badminton, basketball, bowling, golf, gymnastics, handball, racquetball, soccer, softball, squash, swimming, tennis, volleyball, wrestling M. **Team name:** Mavericks.

Student services. Adult student services, alcohol/substance abuse counseling, chaplain/spiritual director, career counseling, services for economically disadvantaged, student employment services, financial aid counseling, health services, minority student services, on-campus daycare, personal counseling, placement for graduates, veterans' counselor, women's services. **Physically disabled:** Services for visually, speech, hearing impaired.

Contact. E-mail: unoadm@mail.unomaha.edu
Phone: (402) 554-2393 Toll-free number: (800) 585-8648
Fax: (402) 554-3472
Jolene Adams, Director of Admissions, University of Nebraska - Omaha, 6001 Dodge Street, Omaha, NE 68182-0005

University of Nebraska Medical Center

Omaha, Nebraska
www.unmc.edu **CB code: 6896**

- Public two-year upper-division health science college
- Commuter campus in very large city
- 48% of applicants admitted

General. Founded in 1869. Regionally accredited. Students must have 30 plus transfer hours to be admitted to UNMC. **Degrees:** 370 bachelor's awarded; master's, doctoral, first professional offered. **ROTC:** Army, Air Force. **Calendar:** Semester, limited summer session. **Full-time faculty:** 848 total; 85% have terminal degrees, 16% minority, 42% women. **Part-time faculty:** 189 total; 83% have terminal degrees, 8% minority, 46% women.

Student profile. 793 degree-seeking undergraduates, 2,388 degree-seeking graduate students. 946 applied as first time-transfer students, 456 admitted, 395 enrolled. 16% entered as juniors, 12% entered as seniors. 5% transferred from two-year, 95% transferred from four-year institutions.

Women:	88%	**International:**	1%
African American:	1%	**Part-time:**	8%
Asian American:	2%	**Out-of-state:**	10%
Hispanic American:	3%	**25 or older:**	31%
Native American:	1%		

Basis for selection. College transcript required. Admissions requirements, application procedures, and closing dates vary by program. Health professions program applicants must have completed prerequisite courses at another institution. Transfer accepted as sophomores, juniors, seniors.

2008-2009 Annual costs. Tuition/fees: $5,773; $16,393 out-of-state. Tuition varies by program. Books/supplies: $900. Personal expenses: $1,500.

Application procedures. Admission: $45 fee, may be waived for applicants with need. **Financial aid:** Priority date 4/1, no deadline. Applicants notified on a rolling basis starting 5/1; must reply within 2 weeks of notification. FAFSA, institutional form required.

Academics. Special study options: Accelerated study, combined bachelor's/graduate degree, distance learning, honors. **Credit/placement by examination:** CLEP, IB, institutional tests. 24 credit hours maximum toward bachelor's degree.

Majors. Health: Clinical lab science, dental hygiene, medical radiologic technology/radiation therapy, nuclear medical technology, nursing (RN), radiologic technology/medical imaging, sonography.

Computing on campus. 108 workstations in library, computer center, student center. Commuter students can connect to campus network. Online library, helpline, repair service, wireless network available.

Student life. Housing: Apartments available. **Activities:** Student government, committee on minority concerns, American Academy of Physician Assistants, Religious Life Council, Christian Fellowship, student association for rural health, student services council, student professional organizations.

Athletics. Intramural: Basketball, softball, volleyball.

Student services. Alcohol/substance abuse counseling, career counseling, services for economically disadvantaged, financial aid counseling, health services, minority student services, on-campus daycare, personal counseling, veterans' counselor. **Physically disabled:** Services for hearing impaired.

Contact. E-mail: ttonjes@unmc.edu
Phone: (402) 559-6468 Toll-free number: (800) 626-8431 ext. 96468
Fax: (402) 559-6796
University of Nebraska Medical Center, 984230 Nebraska Medical Center, Omaha, NE 68198-4230

Wayne State College

Wayne, Nebraska — **CB member**
www.wsc.edu — **CB code: 6469**

- Public 4-year liberal arts and teachers college
- Residential campus in small town
- 2,863 degree-seeking undergraduates: 8% part-time, 54% women, 3% African American, 1% Asian American, 2% Hispanic American, 1% Native American, 1% international
- 581 degree-seeking graduate students
- 46% graduate within 6 years

General. Founded in 1909. Regionally accredited. Campus is state arboretum. **Degrees:** 466 bachelor's awarded; master's offered. **ROTC:** Army. **Location:** 45 miles from Sioux City, Iowa. **Calendar:** Semester, extensive summer session. **Full-time faculty:** 125 total; 78% have terminal degrees, 4% minority, 45% women. **Part-time faculty:** 85 total; 12% have terminal degrees, 5% minority, 62% women. **Class size:** 44% < 20, 48% 20-39, 6% 40-49, 2% 50-99. **Special facilities:** Planetarium, outdoor amphitheater.

Freshman class profile. 1,328 applied, 1,328 admitted, 660 enrolled.

Mid 50% test scores		**Rank in top quarter:**	27%
ACT composite:	18-24	**Rank in top tenth:**	9%
GPA 3.75 or higher:	21%	**Return as sophomores:**	65%
GPA 3.50-3.74:	17%	**Out-of-state:**	18%
GPA 3.0-3.49:	28%	**Live on campus:**	93%
GPA 2.0-2.99:	31%	**International:**	1%

Basis for selection. Open admission.

High school preparation. College-preparatory program required. 18 units recommended. Recommended units include English 4, mathematics 3, social studies 3, science 2, foreign language 2, computer science 2 and visual/performing arts 2.

2008-2009 Annual costs. Tuition/fees: $4,571; $8,066 out-of-state. Room/board: $5,054. Books/supplies: $1,000. Personal expenses: $889.

2008-2009 Financial aid. Need-based: 577 full-time freshmen applied for aid; 421 were judged to have need; 419 of these received aid. Average need met was 38%. Average scholarship/grant was $1,778; average loan $1,624. 45% of total undergraduate aid awarded as scholarships/grants, 55% as loans/jobs. **Non-need-based:** Awarded to 859 full-time undergraduates, including 256 freshmen. Scholarships awarded for academics, art, athletics, leadership, minority status, music/drama, religious affiliation, state residency.

Application procedures. Admission: Priority date 12/1; deadline 8/20. $30 fee. Admission notification on a rolling basis beginning on or about 9/15. Maximum period of postponement: 1 semester. **Financial aid:** Priority date 4/1; no closing date. FAFSA required. Applicants notified on a rolling basis starting 3/1; must reply within 4 week(s) of notification.

Academics. Special study options: Cooperative education, distance learning, double major, dual enrollment of high school students, honors, independent study, internships, student-designed major, study abroad, teacher certification program. Learning Communities, First-Year Experience. **Credit/placement by examination:** AP, CLEP, institutional tests. **Support services:** Learning center, reduced course load, study skills assistance, tutoring, writing center.

Majors. Biology: General. **Business:** Business admin. **Communications:** General, journalism, media studies. **Computer sciences:** General, information systems. **Education:** Art, biology, business, chemistry, drama/dance, early childhood, elementary, English, family/consumer sciences, foreign languages, geography, history, mathematics, middle, music, physical, psychology, social science, special, speech, technology/industrial arts. **Engineering technology:** General. **Family/consumer sciences:** General, food/nutrition. **Foreign languages:** General, Spanish. **Health:** Athletic training. **History:** General. **Math:** General. **Parks/recreation:** Exercise sciences, health/fitness, sports admin. **Physical sciences:** Chemistry. **Protective services:** Criminal justice. **Psychology:** General. **Social sciences:** General, geography, political science, sociology. **Visual/performing arts:** Art, dramatic, graphic design.

Most popular majors. Business/marketing 21%, education 26%, parks/recreation 7%, psychology 7%, security/protective services 8%.

Computing on campus. 365 workstations in library, computer center, student center. Dormitories wired for high-speed internet access and linked to campus network. Commuter students can connect to campus network. Online course registration, helpline, wireless network available.

Student life. Freshman orientation: Available, $75 fee. Preregistration for classes offered. **Housing:** Guaranteed on-campus for freshmen. Coed dorms, wellness housing available. $100 fully refundable deposit. **Activities:** Bands, campus ministries, choral groups, dance, drama, international student organizations, literary magazine, music ensembles, musical theater, radio station, student government, student newspaper, TV station.

Athletics. NCAA. **Intercollegiate:** Baseball M, basketball, cross-country, football (tackle) M, golf, soccer W, softball W, track and field, volleyball W. **Intramural:** Archery, badminton, basketball, bowling, football (non-tackle), golf, handball, racquetball, softball, swimming, table tennis, tennis, track and field, volleyball, weight lifting M, wrestling M. **Team name:** Wildcats.

Student services. Alcohol/substance abuse counseling, chaplain/spiritual director, career counseling, services for economically disadvantaged, student employment services, financial aid counseling, health services, minority student services, personal counseling, placement for graduates, veterans' counselor. **Physically disabled:** Services for visually, speech, hearing impaired.

Contact. E-mail: admit1@wsc.edu
Phone: (402) 375-7234 Toll-free number: (800) 228-9972
Fax: (402) 375-7204
Tammy Young, Director of Admissions, Wayne State College, 1111 Main Street, Wayne, NE 68787

York College
York, Nebraska
www.york.edu **CB code: 6984**

- Private 4-year liberal arts and teachers college affiliated with Church of Christ
- Residential campus in small town
- 382 degree-seeking undergraduates: 3% part-time, 47% women, 5% African American, 1% Asian American, 6% Hispanic American, 1% Native American, 1% international
- 64% of applicants admitted
- SAT or ACT (ACT writing optional) required
- 46% graduate within 6 years

General. Founded in 1956. Regionally accredited. **Degrees:** 62 bachelor's, 11 associate awarded. **ROTC:** Army, Naval, Air Force. **Location:** 50 miles from Lincoln. **Calendar:** Semester, limited summer session. **Full-time faculty:** 24 total; 42% have terminal degrees, 4% minority, 38% women. **Part-time faculty:** 24 total; 21% have terminal degrees, 38% women. **Class size:** 85% < 20, 13% 20-39, 2% 40-49, less than 1% 50-99. **Special facilities:** 35,000 sq. ft. indoor sports practice facility, historic prayer chapel.

Freshman class profile. 404 applied, 257 admitted, 115 enrolled.

Mid 50% test scores		**Rank in top quarter:**	24%
SAT critical reading:	460-560	**Rank in top tenth:**	11%
SAT math:	460-550	**End year in good standing:**	80%
ACT composite:	18-25	**Return as sophomores:**	56%
GPA 3.75 or higher:	21%	**Out-of-state:**	66%
GPA 3.50-3.74:	10%	**Live on campus:**	95%
GPA 3.0-3.49:	30%	**Fraternities:**	66%
GPA 2.0-2.99:	36%	**Sororities:**	76%

Basis for selection. ACT/SAT test scores, high school GPA, class rank very important. Essay recommended but not required. **Homeschooled:** Transcript of courses and grades required. **Learning Disabled:** Submission of high school IEP is recommended for students who self-identify learning disabilities.

High school preparation. College-preparatory program recommended. 15 units required; 21 recommended. Required and recommended units include English 3-4, mathematics 2-4, social studies 1-4, history 1-4, science 2-4 and foreign language 3.

2009-2010 Annual costs. Tuition/fees (projected): $14,000. Room/board: $4,500. Books/supplies: $1,500. Personal expenses: $2,400.

2007-2008 Financial aid. Need-based: Average need met was 24%. Average scholarship/grant was $4,046; average loan $3489.83. 45% of total undergraduate aid awarded as scholarships/grants, 55% as loans/jobs. **Non-need-based:** Scholarships awarded for academics, alumni affiliation, athletics, leadership, music/drama.

Application procedures. Admission: Priority date 3/31; deadline 8/31 (receipt date). $20 fee, may be waived for applicants with need. Admission notification on a rolling basis. Must reply by 9/1. **Financial aid:** Priority date 4/1; no closing date. FAFSA required. Applicants notified on a rolling basis starting 3/1; must reply within 4 week(s) of notification.

Academics. Special study options: Accelerated study, double major, dual enrollment of high school students, independent study, internships, student-designed major, teacher certification program. **Credit/placement by examination:** AP, CLEP, IB, SAT, ACT, institutional tests. 12 credit hours maximum toward associate degree, 32 toward bachelor's. **Support services:** Reduced course load, remedial instruction, study skills assistance, tutoring.

Majors. Biology: General. **Business:** Accounting, business admin, finance, human resources. **Communications:** General. **Education:** General, art, biology, business, drama/dance, elementary, English, history, mathematics, middle, multi-level teacher, music, physical, reading, secondary, social science, special, speech. **History:** General. **Math:** General. **Philosophy/religion:** Religion. **Psychology:** General. **Social sciences:** Criminology. **Theology:** Bible, religious ed. **Visual/performing arts:** Voice/opera. **Other:** Sports management.

Most popular majors. Biology 7%, business/marketing 26%, education 30%, liberal arts 11%, psychology 9%.

Computing on campus. 57 workstations in dormitories, library, computer center. Dormitories wired for high-speed internet access and linked to campus network. Online library, helpline, wireless network available.

Student life. Freshman orientation: Mandatory. Preregistration for classes offered. **Policies:** Students expected to conform to Christian norms. Alcohol and tobacco prohibited. Unmarried, full-time students under 21 required to live on campus or with relatives or staff off campus. **Housing:** Guaranteed on-campus for all undergraduates. Single-sex dorms, apartments, wellness housing available. $100 fully refundable deposit, deadline 8/31. **Activities:** Campus ministries, choral groups, drama, music ensembles, musical theater, student government, student newspaper, service clubs, Chi Rho, spiritual life committee.

Athletics. NAIA. **Intercollegiate:** Baseball M, basketball, soccer, softball W, volleyball W, wrestling M. **Intramural:** Basketball, football (non-tackle), soccer, softball, table tennis, volleyball. **Team name:** Panthers.

Student services. Adult student services, chaplain/spiritual director, career counseling, student employment services, financial aid counseling, personal counseling, placement for graduates, veterans' counselor.

Contact. E-mail: enroll@york.edu
Phone: (402) 363-5627 Toll-free number: (800) 950-9675
Fax: (402) 363-5623
Willie Sanchez, Director of Admissions, York College, 1125 East 8th Street, York, NE 68467

Nevada

Art Institute of Las Vegas

Henderson, Nevada
www.artinstitutes.edu/lasvegas/ **CB code: 3141**

- For-profit 3-year culinary school and visual arts college
- Commuter campus in very large city
- 1,301 degree-seeking undergraduates: 19% part-time, 48% women, 9% African American, 12% Asian American, 14% Hispanic American, 1% Native American
- Application essay, interview required
- 32% graduate within 6 years

General. Accredited by ACCSCT. The Art Institute of Las Vegas occupies approximately 45,000 square feet at 2350 Corporate Circle and 10,500 square feet at 2340 Corporate Circle. **Degrees:** 120 bachelor's, 50 associate awarded. **Location:** 10 miles from Las Vegas. **Calendar:** Quarter, extensive summer session. **Full-time faculty:** 27 total; 7% have terminal degrees, 22% women. **Part-time faculty:** 59 total; 5% have terminal degrees, 46% women. **Class size:** 77% < 20, 19% 20-39, 2% 40-49, 2% 50-99. **Special facilities:** Sound-mixing studio, student-run restaurant, print and service bureaus, photography lab, supply store, learning resource center.

Freshman class profile. 436 applied, 296 admitted, 231 enrolled.

GPA 3.75 or higher:	2%	**Return as sophomores:**	54%
GPA 3.50-3.74:	4%	**Out-of-state:**	7%
GPA 3.0-3.49:	17%	**Live on campus:**	12%
GPA 2.0-2.99:	60%		

Basis for selection. Open admission, but selective for some programs. Proof of high school graduation or GED certificate required before the end of the first quarter. Proof of attaining an associate degree or higher from an accredited institution (or its equivalent, if achieved outside the United States) acceptable. High school diploma and a minimum GPA of 2.5 required of Game Art & Design applicants. High school diploma and a minimum GPA of 2.0 required of Audio Production program applicants. Professional portfolio required of Game Art & Design and Media Arts and Animation program applicants. Face-to-face or phone interview, an original essay of at least 150 words required. Personal portfolio may be required, depending upon the desired academic curriculum. Official transcripts for high school, GED, and/or college, ACCUPLACER test or satisfactory SAT or ACT scores required of all applicants. **Homeschooled:** Institution must be recognized by state or national department of education. **Learning Disabled:** Applicants requiring additional educational or tuition assistance are encouraged to contact the Director of Admissions. Accommodations to qualified students with disabilities available through the Student Affairs office.

2009-2010 Annual costs. Tuition/fees (projected): $22,002.

2008-2009 Financial aid. Non-need-based: Scholarships awarded for academics, state residency.

Application procedures. Admission: No deadline. $150 fee. Application must be submitted on paper. Admission notification on a rolling basis. **Financial aid:** No deadline. Applicants notified on a rolling basis.

Academics. A wide variety of support services available including advising services, study groups, tutoring services, and housing services. **Special study options:** Distance learning, honors, independent study, internships, liberal arts/career combination, study abroad. **Credit/placement by examination:** AP, CLEP, IB, institutional tests. 28 credit hours maximum toward associate degree, 48 toward bachelor's. **Support services:** Learning center, pre-admission summer program, reduced course load, remedial instruction, study skills assistance, tutoring, writing center.

Majors. BACHELOR'S. Communications technology: Animation/special effects, recording arts. **Computer sciences:** Computer graphics. **Personal/culinary services:** Restaurant/catering. **Visual/performing arts:** General, cinematography, design, fashion design, graphic design, interior design, multimedia, photography. **ASSOCIATE. Personal/culinary services:** Baking, chef training.

Most popular majors. Visual/performing arts 30%.

Computing on campus. 221 workstations in library, computer center. Commuter students can connect to campus network. Online course registration, online library, student web hosting, wireless network available.

Student life. Freshman orientation: Mandatory. Preregistration for classes offered. **Policies:** Resident Advisor (RA) available to on-campus students, apartment information and roommate referrals available to off-campus students. **Housing:** Apartments, wellness housing available. $150 partly refundable deposit. **Activities:** Film society.

Student services. Adult student services, alcohol/substance abuse counseling, career counseling, services for economically disadvantaged, student employment services, financial aid counseling, personal counseling, placement for graduates. **Physically disabled:** Services for visually, speech, hearing impaired. **Learning disabled:** Comprehensive services available.

Contact. Phone: (702) 369-9944
Dewey McGuirk, Senior Director of Admissions, Art Institute of Las Vegas, 2350 Corporate Circle, Henderson, NV 89074-7737

DeVry University: Henderson

Henderson, Nevada
www.devry.edu

- For-profit 4-year university
- Commuter campus in large city
- 170 degree-seeking undergraduates: 44% part-time, 45% women, 23% African American, 11% Asian American, 20% Hispanic American, 1% Native American
- 64 degree-seeking graduate students

General. Degrees: 11 bachelor's, 4 associate awarded; master's offered. **Calendar:** Semester. **Full-time faculty:** 1 total. **Part-time faculty:** 36 total; 28% minority, 36% women.

Basis for selection. Academic record and interview most important.

2008-2009 Annual costs. Tuition/fees: $13,930. Books/supplies: $1,300. Personal expenses: $5,082.

2007-2008 Financial aid. Non-need-based: Scholarships awarded for academics.

Application procedures. Admission: No deadline. $50 fee. Admission notification on a rolling basis. **Financial aid:** No deadline. FAFSA required. Applicants notified on a rolling basis.

Academics. Special study options: Accelerated study, distance learning. **Credit/placement by examination:** CLEP.

Majors. Business: Business admin. **Other:** Technology management.

Contact. Phone: (702) 933-9700
DeVry University: Henderson, 2490 Paseo Verde Parkway, Suite 150, Henderson, NV 89074

Great Basin College

Elko, Nevada
www.gbcnv.edu **CB code: 4293**

- Public 4-year community and teachers college
- Commuter campus in large town
- 2,230 degree-seeking undergraduates
- Application essay, interview required

General. Founded in 1967. Regionally accredited. **Degrees:** 47 bachelor's, 196 associate awarded. **Location:** 280 miles from Reno, 220 miles from Salt Lake City. **Calendar:** Semester, limited summer session. **Full-time faculty:** 104 total. **Part-time faculty:** 178 total.

Freshman class profile.

Out-of-state:	5%	**Live on campus:**	3%

Basis for selection. Open admission, but selective for some programs. Placement test required for some English and math courses. Nursing applicants selected on basis of point system. Points given for courses completed, grades, current work experience in health field, certifications, letters of recommendation, and scores obtained on required entrance exam which measures math and reading comprehension skills. Application/selection process for formal admission to last 2 years of bachelor degree programs, including interview and essay.

2008-2009 Annual costs. Tuition/fees: $1,921; $7,629 out-of-state. Discounted tuition (Good Neighbor rates) available for nonresident students residing in certain counties bordering Nevada. Room only: $3,300. Books/supplies: $1,400.

Application procedures. Admission: No deadline. $10 fee. Admission notification on a rolling basis. **Financial aid:** Priority date 6/1; no closing date. FAFSA required. Applicants notified on a rolling basis starting 7/1.

Academics. Special study options: Cooperative education, distance learning, dual enrollment of high school students, ESL, independent study, liberal arts/career combination, teacher certification program. **Credit/placement by examination:** AP, CLEP, institutional tests. 15 credit hours maximum toward associate degree, 30 toward bachelor's. **Support services:** Learning center, reduced course load, remedial instruction, study skills assistance, tutoring, writing center.

Majors. Agriculture: Business. **Business:** Business admin. **Education:** Agricultural, biology, elementary, history, mathematics, science, secondary, social science, trade/industrial. **Engineering:** Surveying. **Health:** Nursing (RN). **Interdisciplinary:** Cultural resource management. **Liberal arts:** Arts/sciences. **Social sciences:** General.

Computing on campus. 200 workstations in dormitories, library, computer center. Dormitories linked to campus network. Commuter students can connect to campus network. Online course registration, online library, helpline, wireless network available.

Student life. Freshman orientation: Mandatory, $26 fee. Preregistration for classes offered. **Housing:** Coed dorms, apartments, wellness housing available. **Activities:** Choral groups, drama, musical theater, student government, vocational clubs, nursing club, rodeo, intramural sports, student ambassadors.

Athletics. Intramural: Rodeo, table tennis, volleyball.

Student services. Adult student services, career counseling, services for economically disadvantaged, student employment services, financial aid counseling, minority student services, on-campus daycare, personal counseling, placement for graduates, veterans' counselor. **Physically disabled:** Services for visually, speech, hearing impaired.

Contact. E-mail: admissions@gbcnv.edu
Phone: (775) 753-2311 Fax: (775) 738-8771
Julie Byrnes, Director of Enrollment Management, Great Basin College, 1500 College Parkway, Elko, NV 89801

International Academy of Design and Technology: Henderson

Henderson, Nevada
www.iadtvegas.com

- For-profit 3-year visual arts and technical college
- Very large city
- 450 degree-seeking undergraduates

General. Accredited by ACICS. **Degrees:** 26 bachelor's, 14 associate awarded. **Location:** 10 miles from Las Vegas. **Calendar:** Quarter. **Full-time faculty:** 6 total. **Part-time faculty:** 36 total. **Class size:** 84% < 20, 16% 20-39.

Freshman class profile. 109 applied, 109 admitted, 108 enrolled.

Basis for selection. Open admission. **Homeschooled:** ACT or SAT scores.

2008-2009 Annual costs. Tuition/fees: $16,560. Costs of books and supplies vary from $4,200 to $9,600 for entire program depending on course of study. Additional fees may apply.

2008-2009 Financial aid. Need-based: 2% of total undergraduate aid awarded as scholarships/grants, 98% as loans/jobs.

Application procedures. Admission: No deadline. $50 fee. **Financial aid:** No deadline.

Academics. Special study options: Distance learning, independent study, internships, study abroad. **Credit/placement by examination:** AP, CLEP. **Support services:** Tutoring.

Majors. BACHELOR'S. Visual/performing arts: Fashion design, graphic design, interior design. **ASSOCIATE. Visual/performing arts:** Fashion design, graphic design, interior design.

Computing on campus. Online course registration, online library, wireless network available.

Student life. Freshman orientation: Mandatory.

Contact. E-mail: vegas_web@iadtvegas.com
Phone: (702) 990-0150 Toll-free number: (866) 400-4238
Maggie Balderas, Director of Admissions, International Academy of Design and Technology: Henderson, 2495 Village View Drive, Henderson, NV 89074

ITT Technical Institute: Henderson

Henderson, Nevada
www.itt-tech.edu **CB code: 2710**

- For-profit 4-year technical college
- Commuter campus in small city

General. Accredited by ACICS. **Calendar:** Quarter.

Contact. Phone: (702) 558-5404
Director of Recruitment, 168 North Gibson Road, Henderson, NV 89014

Morrison University

Reno, Nevada
www.morrison.neumont.edu **CB code: 2114**

- For-profit 4-year university and business college
- Commuter campus in small city
- 105 degree-seeking undergraduates
- Interview required

General. Founded in 1902. Accredited by ACICS. **Degrees:** 21 bachelor's, 8 associate awarded; master's offered. **Location:** Half of mile from downtown. **Calendar:** Quarter, extensive summer session. **Full-time faculty:** 3 total; 33% have terminal degrees, 33% women. **Part-time faculty:** 18 total; 39% have terminal degrees, 11% minority, 44% women. **Class size:** 91% < 20, 9% 20-39.

Freshman class profile.

Out-of-state:	3%	**Live on campus:**	2%

Basis for selection. Open admission.

2008-2009 Annual costs. Books/supplies: $825. Personal expenses: $1,800.

Application procedures. Admission: No deadline. $25 fee, may be waived for applicants with need. Admission notification on a rolling basis. **Financial aid:** No deadline. FAFSA required. Applicants notified on a rolling basis starting 7/1.

Academics. Special study options: Accelerated study, combined bachelor's/graduate degree, double major, dual enrollment of high school students, independent study, internships, liberal arts/career combination, weekend college. **Credit/placement by examination:** CLEP, IB. 9 credit hours maximum toward associate degree, 9 toward bachelor's. Students may take challenge exam for credit within first week of class start. **Support services:** Learning center, reduced course load, remedial instruction, study skills assistance, tutoring, writing center.

Majors. Business: Accounting, business admin, management information systems, office management.

Computing on campus. 62 workstations in library, computer center.

Student life. Freshman orientation: Mandatory. Preregistration for classes offered. **Policies:** Dress code, appropriate conduct policy, zero tolerance for alcohol and drug use while in school. **Activities:** Student government, student newspaper.

Student services. Adult student services, alcohol/substance abuse counseling, career counseling, student employment services, financial aid counseling, personal counseling, placement for graduates, veterans' counselor.

Contact. E-mail: ctiminsky@morrison.neumont.edu
Phone: (775) 850-0700 ext. 101 Fax: (775) 850-0711
Joyce Decker, Director of Enrollment, Morrison University, 10315 Professional Circle, #201, Reno, NV 89521

Nevada State College
Henderson, Nevada
www.nsc.nevada.edu

- Public 4-year nursing, liberal arts and teachers college
- Commuter campus in large city
- 1,667 degree-seeking undergraduates: 51% part-time, 75% women, 8% African American, 12% Asian American, 16% Hispanic American, 1% Native American
- 79% of applicants admitted

General. Regionally accredited. **Degrees:** 188 bachelor's awarded. **Location:** Downtown. **Calendar:** Semester, limited summer session. **Full-time faculty:** 58 total; 64% have terminal degrees, 24% minority, 60% women. **Part-time faculty:** 63 total; 18% minority, 57% women. **Class size:** 40% < 20, 57% 20-39, less than 1% 40-49. **Special facilities:** Liberal arts and sciences building.

Freshman class profile. 902 applied, 716 admitted, 190 enrolled.

Mid 50% test scores			
SAT critical reading:	410-530	GPA 3.0-3.49:	29%
SAT math:	410-520	GPA 2.0-2.99:	59%
SAT writing:	390-520	Rank in top quarter:	23%
ACT composite:	16-23	Rank in top tenth:	4%
GPA 3.75 or higher:	2%	Return as sophomores:	53%
GPA 3.50-3.74:	8%	Out-of-state:	2%

Basis for selection. 2.0 GPA required. **Homeschooled:** Transcript of courses and grades required. SAT/ACT required.

High school preparation. College-preparatory program required. 12 units required. Required units include English 4, mathematics 3, social studies 3 and science 2.

2008-2009 Annual costs. Tuition/fees: $3,045; $11,444 out-of-state. Books/supplies: $1,300. Personal expenses: $2,220.

2008-2009 Financial aid. Need-based: 39% of total undergraduate aid awarded as scholarships/grants, 61% as loans/jobs.

Application procedures. Admission: No deadline. $30 fee. Admission notification on a rolling basis. **Financial aid:** Priority date 3/1, closing date 6/1. FAFSA, institutional form required. Applicants notified on a rolling basis starting 5/1.

Academics. Special study options: Accelerated study, combined bachelor's/graduate degree, distance learning, double major, dual enrollment of high school students, ESL, independent study, internships, teacher certification program. **Credit/placement by examination:** AP, CLEP, SAT, ACT, institutional tests. **Support services:** Learning center, remedial instruction, tutoring, writing center.

Majors. Biology: General. **Business:** Accounting technology, business admin, management science. **Communications:** General. **Computer sciences:** Computer science. **Conservation:** Environmental science. **Education:** General, biology, elementary, English, history, mathematics, secondary, special. **Health:** Nursing (RN), speech pathology. **History:** General. **Interdisciplinary:** Systems science. **Protective services:** Law enforcement admin. **Psychology:** General. **Social sciences:** Economics. **Other:** Area studies, other, Education, other, Occupational therapy/therapist, Psychology, other.

Most popular majors. Business/marketing 9%, education 17%, health sciences 55%, security/protective services 6%.

Computing on campus. 123 workstations in library, computer center, student center. Commuter students can connect to campus network. Online course registration, online library, helpline, student web hosting, wireless network available.

Student life. Freshman orientation: Available. Preregistration for classes offered. A one-day program held the Saturday before Fall classes commence. Concurrently held, there is a separate program for family members. **Activities:** Choral groups, student government, student newspaper, Alpha Phi Omega/Venture Crew, Young Democrats, Asian Pacific Islander Coalition, Black Student Organization, American Sign Language Club.

Athletics. Team name: Scorpions.

Student services. Financial aid counseling, minority student services. **Physically disabled:** Services for visually, speech, hearing impaired.

Contact. E-mail: admissions@nsc.nevada.edu
Phone: (702) 992-2130
Patricia Ring, Admissions/Registrar, Director, Nevada State College, 1125 Nevada State Drive, Henderson, NV 89002

Sierra Nevada College
Incline Village, Nevada
www.sierranevada.edu **CB code: 4757**

- Private 4-year liberal arts college
- Residential campus in small town
- 354 degree-seeking undergraduates
- SAT or ACT with writing, application essay required

General. Founded in 1969. Regionally accredited. **Degrees:** 44 bachelor's awarded; master's offered. **ROTC:** Army. **Location:** 35 miles from Reno. **Calendar:** Semester, limited summer session. **Full-time faculty:** 15 total. **Part-time faculty:** 55 total. **Class size:** 84% < 20, 16% 20-39. **Special facilities:** Entertainment technology lab, center for environmental sciences.

Freshman class profile.

Mid 50% test scores			
SAT critical reading:	440-630	Rank in top quarter:	35%
SAT math:	440-600	Rank in top tenth:	10%
ACT composite:	18-26	Out-of-state:	71%
		Live on campus:	90%

Basis for selection. Motivation as evidenced in personal interview and/or autobiographical statement very important. Applicants with GPA below 2.0 may be admitted provisionally, upon review by faculty admission committee. Interview recommended. **Homeschooled:** Submit any course plans or transcripts along with any home schooling plans that are available.

High school preparation. Recommended units include English 4, mathematics 3, social studies 2, history 2, science 2 and foreign language 2.

2008-2009 Annual costs. Tuition/fees: $22,978. Room/board: $8,824. Books/supplies: $1,454. Personal expenses: $3,147.

2008-2009 Financial aid. Non-need-based: Scholarships awarded for academics, art, athletics.

Application procedures. Admission: Priority date 2/15; no deadline. No application fee. Admission notification on a rolling basis beginning on or about 11/1. Must reply by May 1 or within 3 week(s) if notified thereafter. **Financial aid:** Priority date 4/1; no closing date. FAFSA, institutional form required. Applicants notified on a rolling basis; must reply by 5/1 or within 4 week(s) of notification.

Academics. Interdisciplinary studies in business, environmental science, fine arts, and the humanities. **Special study options:** Combined bachelor's/graduate degree, double major, honors, independent study, internships, liberal arts/career combination, study abroad, teacher certification program. Tuition exchange. **Credit/placement by examination:** AP, CLEP, IB, SAT, ACT, institutional tests. 30 credit hours maximum toward bachelor's degree. **Support services:** Remedial instruction, study skills assistance, tutoring, writing center.

Majors. Biology: General, ecology. **Business:** Business admin, hospitality admin, resort management. **Computer sciences:** General, computer science. **Conservation:** Environmental science, management/policy. **Health:** Premedicine, prenursing, prepharmacy. **Interdisciplinary:** Global studies. **Liberal arts:** Arts/sciences. **Psychology:** General. **Visual/performing arts:** General, ceramics, drawing, painting, printmaking, sculpture, studio arts.

Most popular majors. Business/marketing 31%, English 9%, liberal arts 12%, psychology 7%, visual/performing arts 24%.

Computing on campus. PC or laptop required. 30 workstations in dormitories, library, computer center, student center. Dormitories wired for high-speed internet access and linked to campus network. Commuter students can connect to campus network. Online library, helpline, repair service, wireless network available.

Student life. Freshman orientation: Mandatory. Preregistration for classes offered. Week-long program held the week prior to first day of classes. **Housing:** Guaranteed on-campus for all undergraduates. Coed dorms, wellness housing available. $200 nonrefundable deposit, deadline 5/1. **Activities:** Jazz band, choral groups, drama, literary magazine, music ensembles, musical theater, student government, student newspaper, recycling club, Christian club, Amnesty International.

Athletics. NCAA. **Intercollegiate:** Skiing. **Intramural:** Basketball, bowling, skiing, soccer, softball, volleyball. **Team name:** Eagles.

Student services. Alcohol/substance abuse counseling, career counseling, student employment services, financial aid counseling, health services, personal counseling, placement for graduates, veterans' counselor.

Contact. E-mail: admissions@sierranevada.edu
Phone: (775) 831-1314 Toll-free number: (866) 412-4636
Fax: (775) 831-6223
Bernie McConnell, Director of Admission, Sierra Nevada College, 999 Tahoe Boulevard, Incline Village, NV 89451-4269

University of Nevada: Las Vegas

Las Vegas, Nevada — **CB member**
www.unlv.edu — **CB code: 4861**

- Public 4-year university
- Commuter campus in very large city
- 22,149 degree-seeking undergraduates
- 5,250 graduate students
- 74% of applicants admitted

General. Founded in 1957. Regionally accredited. Credit courses available at Nellis Air Force Base. **Degrees:** 3,696 bachelor's awarded; master's, doctoral, first professional offered. **ROTC:** Army. **Location:** 268 miles from Los Angeles, 290 miles from Phoenix. **Calendar:** Semester, extensive summer session. **Full-time faculty:** 950 total; 88% have terminal degrees, 19% minority, 35% women. **Part-time faculty:** 727 total. **Class size:** 37% < 20, 41% 20-39, 9% 40-49, 10% 50-99, 2% >100. **Special facilities:** National supercomputing center for energy and environment, natural history museum, arboretum, 3 theaters, concert hall, international gaming institute, professional practice school for teachers.

Freshman class profile. 8,217 applied, 6,094 admitted, 3,038 enrolled.

Mid 50% test scores		GPA 2.0-2.99:	21%
SAT critical reading:	450-560	Rank in top quarter:	50%
SAT math:	460-580	Rank in top tenth:	18%
ACT composite:	19-24	Out-of-state:	20%
GPA 3.75 or higher:	13%	Live on campus:	30%
GPA 3.50-3.74:	18%	Fraternities:	8%
GPA 3.0-3.49:	47%	Sororities:	6%

Basis for selection. GED not accepted. High school record must show minimum 3.0 minimum GPA in core courses. ACT/SAT can waive GPA requirements, but all students must have the core. Recommendations, personal essay and test scores considered for students applying through Alternate Criteria program. ACT/SAT required for English and math course placement. SAT or ACT recommended. SAT/ACT required for students appealing admission through alternate criteria and for placement into English/math courses. Audition recommended for music, theater arts programs; portfolio recommended for art program. **Homeschooled:** Transcript of courses and grades, letter of recommendation (nonparent) required. Personal statement, two letters of recommendation, ACT/SAT test scores required.

High school preparation. 13 units required. Required units include English 4, mathematics 3, social studies 3, science 3 (laboratory 2). Algebra or higher level math required.

2008-2009 Annual costs. Tuition/fees: $4,493; $15,588 out-of-state. Discounted tuition (Good Neighbor rates) available for nonresident students residing in certain counties bordering Nevada. Out-of-state per-credit-hour rates: 1-6 hours, $272 per credit plus fees; 7 or more hours, $5,548 per semester plus $130 per credit and fees. Room/board: $9,808. Books/supplies: $850. Personal expenses: $1,800.

2007-2008 Financial aid. Need-based: 1,487 full-time freshmen applied for aid; 1,114 were judged to have need; 1,098 of these received aid. Average need met was 71%. Average scholarship/grant was $4,715. **Non-need-based:** Scholarships awarded for academics, alumni affiliation, art, athletics, job skills, leadership, minority status, music/drama, ROTC, state residency. **Additional information:** Tuition reduction for state residents through consortium programs and for out-of-state students graduating from high schools in designated counties bordering Nevada, for military dependents residing in-state, and for dependents of children of alumni not residing in-state.

Application procedures. Admission: Priority date 2/1; no deadline. $60 fee. Admission notification on a rolling basis beginning on or about 2/28. **Financial aid:** Priority date 2/1; no closing date. FAFSA, institutional form required. Applicants notified on a rolling basis starting 3/20; must reply within 2 week(s) of notification.

Academics. Special study options: Accelerated study, combined bachelor's/graduate degree, cooperative education, cross-registration, distance learning, double major, dual enrollment of high school students, ESL, exchange student, honors, independent study, internships, student-designed major, study abroad, teacher certification program. 2+2 culinary arts program with College of Southern Nevada. **Credit/placement by examination:** AP, CLEP, IB, SAT, ACT, institutional tests. 30 credit hours maximum toward bachelor's degree. **Support services:** Learning center, pre-admission summer program, remedial instruction, study skills assistance, tutoring, writing center.

Honors college/program. Honors College applicants must complete the honors application, letters of recommendation, test scores, personal statements, and essay response.

Majors. Architecture: Architecture, interior, landscape, urban/community planning. **Area/ethnic studies:** Asian, Latin American, women's. **Biology:** General. **Business:** Accounting, finance, hospitality admin, human resources, international marketing, management information systems, managerial economics, marketing, real estate. **Communications:** General. **Computer sciences:** Computer science. **Conservation:** General, environmental studies, management/policy. **Education:** Adult/continuing, computer, early childhood, elementary, health, physical, secondary, special. **Engineering:** Civil, computer, electrical, mechanical, software. **Engineering technology:** Construction. **Foreign languages:** French, German, Spanish. **Health:** Athletic training, clinical lab science, health care admin, medical radiologic technology/radiation therapy, nuclear medical technology, nursing (RN), physics/radiologic health. **History:** General. **Interdisciplinary:** Nutrition sciences. **Liberal arts:** Arts/sciences. **Math:** General, applied. **Parks/recreation:** General, exercise sciences, health/fitness. **Personal/culinary services:** Culinary arts. **Philosophy/religion:** Philosophy. **Physical sciences:** Chemistry, geology, physics. **Psychology:** General. **Public administration:** Social work. **Social sciences:** Anthropology, political science, sociology. **Visual/performing arts:** Art, dance, dramatic, film/cinema, jazz, studio arts.

Most popular majors. Business/marketing 29%, communications/journalism 6%, education 9%, psychology 7%, social sciences 6%, visual/performing arts 6%.

Computing on campus. 1,550 workstations in dormitories, library, computer center, student center. Dormitories wired for high-speed internet access and linked to campus network. Commuter students can connect to campus network. Online course registration, online library, helpline, wireless network available.

Student life. Freshman orientation: Mandatory, $90 fee. Preregistration for classes offered. **Housing:** Guaranteed on-campus for freshmen. Coed dorms, special housing for disabled, fraternity/sorority housing, wellness housing available. $125 partly refundable deposit. All-female, study intensive floors and special interest floors available; handicapped accessible suites in all complexes. **Activities:** Bands, campus ministries, choral groups, dance, drama, film society, international student organizations, literary magazine, music ensembles, musical theater, opera, radio station, student government, student newspaper, symphony orchestra, TV station, Young Democrats/Republicans, Rebel Christian Fellowship, Hillel, ethnic student council, student organization of Latinos, black student association, Latter-day Saints student organization, Hawaii club.

Athletics. NCAA. **Intercollegiate:** Baseball M, basketball, cheerleading, cross-country W, diving, football (tackle) M, golf, soccer, softball W, swimming, tennis, track and field W, volleyball W. **Intramural:** Badminton, basketball, bowling, cross-country, diving W, football (tackle) M, golf, racquetball, soccer, softball, swimming, table tennis, tennis, track and field, volleyball. **Team name:** Rebels.

Student services. Adult student services, alcohol/substance abuse counseling, chaplain/spiritual director, career counseling, services for economically disadvantaged, student employment services, financial aid counseling, health services, minority student services, on-campus daycare, personal counseling, placement for graduates, veterans' counselor, women's services. **Physically disabled:** Services for visually, speech, hearing impaired. **Learning disabled:** Comprehensive services available.

Contact. E-mail: admissions@unlv.edu
Phone: (702) 774-8658 Fax: (702) 774-8008
Luke Schultheis, Executive Director of Admissions & Recruitment, University of Nevada: Las Vegas, 4505 Maryland Parkway Box 451021, Las Vegas, NV 89154-1021

University of Nevada: Reno

Reno, Nevada — **CB member**
www.unr.edu — **CB code: 4844**

- Public 4-year university
- Commuter campus in small city
- 12,789 degree-seeking undergraduates: 18% part-time, 53% women, 3% African American, 7% Asian American, 9% Hispanic American, 1% Native American, 2% international

- 2,734 degree-seeking graduate students
- 91% of applicants admitted
- 48% graduate within 6 years

General. Founded in 1874. Regionally accredited. **Degrees:** 2,118 bachelor's awarded; master's, doctoral, first professional offered. **ROTC:** Army. **Location:** 225 miles from San Francisco, 35 miles from Lake Tahoe. **Calendar:** Semester, extensive summer session. **Full-time faculty:** 668 total; 82% have terminal degrees, 14% minority, 43% women. **Part-time faculty:** 27 total; 63% have terminal degrees, 4% minority, 52% women. **Class size:** 36% < 20, 43% 20-39, 7% 40-49, 8% 50-99, 6% >100. **Special facilities:** Mineral museum, planetarium, arboretum, disability resource center, ethnic student resource center, internship center.

Freshman class profile. 4,874 applied, 4,450 admitted, 2,296 enrolled.

Mid 50% test scores		**GPA 2.0-2.99:**	17%
SAT critical reading:	460-580	**End year in good standing:**	75%
SAT math:	470-590	**Return as sophomores:**	76%
SAT writing:	470-570	**Out-of-state:**	15%
ACT composite:	20-25	**Live on campus:**	54%
GPA 3.75 or higher:	20%	**International:**	2%
GPA 3.50-3.74:	21%	**Fraternities:**	11%
GPA 3.0-3.49:	42%	**Sororities:**	14%

Basis for selection. GED not accepted. Secondary school record most important, with 3.0 GPA in academic core of English, math, social sciences and natural sciences. If student does not meet GPA requirement, 1040 SAT or 22 ACT may be used in place of GPA requirement. All students applying for scholarships must submit test scores. Interview recommended for nursing program; audition recommended for music program; portfolio recommended for fine arts program. **Homeschooled:** Students who do not meet Board of Regents admission requirements to the university may appeal for special admission. This includes students who have been home schooled.

High school preparation. College-preparatory program required. 13 units required. Required units include English 4, mathematics 3, social studies 3, science 3 (laboratory 2).

2008-2009 Annual costs. Tuition/fees: $4,561; $15,656 out-of-state. Discounted tuition (Good Neighbor rates) available for nonresident students residing in certain counties bordering Nevada. Discounted tuition also available for Western Undergraduate Exchange students. Room/board: $9,989. Books/supplies: $1,300. Personal expenses: $2,578.

2007-2008 Financial aid. Need-based: 1,267 full-time freshmen applied for aid; 784 were judged to have need; 765 of these received aid. Average need met was 54%. Average scholarship/grant was $5,324; average loan $3,044. 53% of total undergraduate aid awarded as scholarships/grants, 47% as loans/jobs. **Non-need-based:** Awarded to 7,675 full-time undergraduates, including 1,958 freshmen. Scholarships awarded for academics, alumni affiliation, art, athletics, music/drama. **Additional information:** Reduced out-of-state tuition available for children of alumni and for non-residents from some neighboring counties in California and participants in WUE program.

Application procedures. Admission: Priority date 3/1; no deadline. $60 fee, may be waived for applicants with need. Admission notification on a rolling basis. **Financial aid:** Priority date 2/15; no closing date. FAFSA required. Applicants notified on a rolling basis starting 4/1; must reply within 2 week(s) of notification.

Academics. Special study options: Distance learning, double major, dual enrollment of high school students, ESL, honors, independent study, internships, study abroad, teacher certification program. **Credit/placement by examination:** AP, CLEP, IB, SAT, ACT, institutional tests. 60 credit hours maximum toward bachelor's degree. **Support services:** Learning center, pre-admission summer program, reduced course load, remedial instruction, study skills assistance, tutoring, writing center.

Majors. Agriculture: Animal breeding, animal sciences, economics. **Area/ethnic studies:** Women's. **Biology:** General, biochemistry, biotechnology. **Business:** General, accounting, entrepreneurial studies, finance, hospitality admin, human resources, international, logistics, managerial economics, marketing. **Communications:** General, journalism. **Computer sciences:** General, computer science. **Conservation:** General, environmental science, forestry, management/policy, wildlife. **Education:** Agricultural, art, business, elementary, English, family/consumer sciences, foreign languages, health, mathematics, music, physical, science, secondary, social science, social studies, special, technology/industrial arts, trade/industrial. **Engineering:** Chemical, civil, computer, electrical, environmental, geological, mechanical, metallurgical, mining, physics, water resource. **Engineering technology:** Construction. **Family/consumer sciences:** Child development, family studies, food/nutrition. **Foreign languages:** French, German, Spanish. **Health:** Nursing (RN), preveterinary, speech pathology. **History:** General. **Interdisciplinary:** Neuroscience, nutrition sciences, science/society. **Math:** General. **Philosophy/religion:** Philosophy. **Physical sciences:** Atmospheric science, chemistry, geology, geophysics, physics. **Psychology:** General, social. **Public administration:** Social work. **Social sciences:** Anthropology, criminology, geography, international relations, political science, sociology. **Visual/performing arts:** Art, art history/conservation, dramatic, music performance. **Other:** English language and linguistics, Health ecology, Speech communication teacher education.

Most popular majors. Biology 8%, business/marketing 15%, communications/journalism 6%, education 7%, engineering/engineering technologies 9%, health sciences 9%, liberal arts 6%, psychology 6%, social sciences 10%.

Computing on campus. 500 workstations in dormitories, library, computer center, student center. Dormitories wired for high-speed internet access and linked to campus network. Commuter students can connect to campus network. Online course registration, online library, helpline, repair service, student web hosting, wireless network available.

Student life. Freshman orientation: Mandatory, $99 fee. Preregistration for classes offered. Sessions held before each semester. Family members welcome. **Housing:** Coed dorms, single-sex dorms, special housing for disabled, apartments, wellness housing available. $300 deposit. Special interest floors (fitness, arts and culture, stereo limitation, alcohol prohibition, honors) available. **Activities:** Bands, choral groups, dance, drama, film society, international student organizations, literary magazine, music ensembles, Model UN, musical theater, opera, radio station, student government, student newspaper, symphony orchestra, Intervarsity Christian Fellowship, black student union, American Indian organization, Asian American Alliance, Chinese students association, Young Republicans, Young Democrats, Hillel, MEXA.

Athletics. NCAA. **Intercollegiate:** Baseball M, basketball, cross-country W, diving W, football (tackle) M, golf, rifle, skiing, soccer W, softball W, swimming W, tennis, track and field W, volleyball W. **Intramural:** Badminton, basketball, bowling, football (non-tackle), golf, racquetball, soccer, softball, swimming, table tennis, tennis, track and field, volleyball, water polo, weight lifting. **Team name:** Wolf Pack.

Student services. Adult student services, alcohol/substance abuse counseling, career counseling, services for economically disadvantaged, student employment services, financial aid counseling, health services, legal services, minority student services, on-campus daycare, personal counseling, placement for graduates, veterans' counselor, women's services. **Physically disabled:** Services for visually, speech, hearing impaired.

Contact. E-mail: asknevada@unr.edu
Phone: (775) 784-1110 Toll-free number: (866) 263-8232
Fax: (775) 784-4283
Melisa Choroszy, Associate Vice President, Enrollment Services, University of Nevada: Reno, Mail Stop 120, Reno, NV 89557

University of Southern Nevada
Henderson, Nevada
www.usn.edu

- Private two-year upper-division university
- Commuter campus in very large city
- 73% of applicants admitted
- Application essay, interview required

General. Candidate for regional accreditation. **Degrees:** 55 bachelor's awarded; master's, doctoral, first professional offered. **Location:** 9 miles from Las Vegas. **Calendar:** Differs by program. **Full-time faculty:** 46 total; 100% have terminal degrees, 20% minority, 59% women. **Part-time faculty:** 29 total; 66% have terminal degrees, 45% minority, 69% women. **Class size:** 100% 50-99.

Student profile. 139 degree-seeking undergraduates, 637 degree-seeking graduate students. 129 applied as first time-transfer students, 94 admitted, 72 enrolled. 62% transferred from two-year, 38% transferred from four-year institutions.

Women:	78%	**25 or older:**	59%
Out-of-state:	55%		

Basis for selection. College transcript, application essay, interview required. Must complete specified courses. Transfer accepted as juniors.

2008-2009 Annual costs. Tuition and fees vary by program from $26,200 to $38,000. Books/supplies: $1,000. Personal expenses: $2,000.

Financial aid. Need-based: 136 applied for aid; 119 were judged to have need; 119 of these received aid. Average need met was 59%. 15% of total undergraduate aid awarded as scholarships/grants, 85% as loans/jobs. **Non-need-based:** Awarded to 48 undergraduates. Scholarships awarded for academics.

Application procedures. Admission: Rolling admission. $100 fee. Application must be submitted on paper. **Financial aid:** Priority date 1/1, closing date 4/1. Applicants notified on a rolling basis starting 4/1; must reply within 2 weeks of notification. FAFSA, institutional form required.

Academics. Special study options: Accelerated study, combined bachelor's/graduate degree. **Credit/placement by examination:** CLEP.

Majors. Health: Nursing (RN).

Computing on campus. PC or laptop required. 15 workstations in library. Online library, helpline, repair service, wireless network available.

Student services. Financial aid counseling, placement for graduates.

Contact. E-mail: bsnadmission@usn.edu
Phone: (702) 968-2075 Fax: (702) 990-4435
University of Southern Nevada, 11 Sunset Way, Henderson, NV 89014

Four-Year Colleges

New Hampshire

Chester College of New England

Chester, New Hampshire — **CB member**
www.chestercollege.edu — **CB code: 3977**

- Private 4-year visual arts and liberal arts college
- Residential campus in rural community
- 209 degree-seeking undergraduates: 6% part-time, 66% women, 1% African American, 2% Asian American, 3% Hispanic American, 1% Native American
- 44% of applicants admitted
- Application essay, interview required

General. Founded in 1965. Regionally accredited. **Degrees:** 36 bachelor's awarded. **Location:** 10 miles from Manchester, 50 miles from Boston. **Calendar:** Semester, limited summer session. **Full-time faculty:** 12 total; 100% have terminal degrees, 8% minority, 58% women. **Part-time faculty:** 30 total; 47% have terminal degrees, 60% women. **Class size:** 97% < 20, 3% 20-39.

Freshman class profile. 255 applied, 111 admitted, 63 enrolled.

Mid 50% test scores		**GPA 3.0-3.49:**	34%
SAT critical reading:	440-610	**GPA 2.0-2.99:**	54%
SAT math:	390-550	**End year in good standing:**	88%
ACT composite:	14-21	**Return as sophomores:**	70%
GPA 3.75 or higher:	1%	**Out-of-state:**	43%
GPA 3.50-3.74:	4%	**Live on campus:**	67%

Basis for selection. High school achievement record, recommendations important; SAT/ACT scores considered. Interview and portfolio review required. **Homeschooled:** Statement describing homeschool structure and mission, interview, letter of recommendation (nonparent) required. Students may be required to complete an essay under examination conditions. SAT scores required.

High school preparation. Recommended units include English 4, mathematics 3, social studies 2, history 2, science 3 and foreign language 1.

2008-2009 Annual costs. Tuition/fees: $16,950. Lab fees vary per student; average cost $600. Room/board: $8,086. Books/supplies: $1,100. Personal expenses: $1,000.

2007-2008 Financial aid. Non-need-based: Scholarships awarded for academics, art, state residency.

Application procedures. Admission: No deadline. $35 fee, may be waived for applicants with need. Admission notification on a rolling basis beginning on or about 1/15. Must reply by May 1 or within 2 week(s) if notified thereafter. **Financial aid:** Priority date 3/15; no closing date. FAFSA required. Applicants notified on a rolling basis starting 12/1; must reply within 2 week(s) of notification.

Academics. Special study options: Cross-registration, double major, independent study, internships, liberal arts/career combination, student-designed major, study abroad. **Credit/placement by examination:** AP, CLEP, institutional tests. 60 credit hours maximum toward bachelor's degree. **Support services:** Reduced course load, remedial instruction, study skills assistance, tutoring.

Majors. Communications: Digital media, media studies. **Computer sciences:** Web page design. **Liberal arts:** Arts/sciences. **Visual/performing arts:** Art, graphic design, photography, studio arts.

Most popular majors. English 28%, interdisciplinary studies 22%, visual/performing arts 50%.

Computing on campus. 42 workstations in library, computer center, student center. Dormitories wired for high-speed internet access. Online library available.

Student life. Freshman orientation: Mandatory. Preregistration for classes offered. Three-day orientation. **Housing:** Guaranteed on-campus for all undergraduates. Coed dorms, wellness housing available. $300 nonrefundable deposit, deadline 8/15. **Activities:** Drama, literary magazine, student government.

Student services. Career counseling, financial aid counseling, personal counseling, placement for graduates.

Contact. E-mail: admissions@chestercollege.edu
Phone: (603) 887-7400 Toll-free number: (800) 974-6372
Fax: (603) 887-1777
Sarah Vogell, Director of Admission and Enrollment Management, Chester College of New England, 40 Chester Street, Chester, NH 03036

Colby-Sawyer College

New London, New Hampshire — **CB member**
www.colby-sawyer.edu — **CB code: 3281**

- Private 4-year liberal arts college
- Residential campus in small town
- 989 degree-seeking undergraduates
- 78% of applicants admitted
- Application essay required

General. Founded in 1837. Regionally accredited. **Degrees:** 189 bachelor's, 4 associate awarded. **ROTC:** Army, Air Force. **Location:** 30 miles from Hanover, 35 miles from Concord. **Calendar:** Semester. **Full-time faculty:** 60 total. **Part-time faculty:** 67 total. **Class size:** 65% < 20, 35% 20-39, less than 1% 40-49. **Special facilities:** Fine arts center, laboratory school (preschool, K-3), library learning center, conservatory and greenhouse, science center, weather station.

Freshman class profile. 2,264 applied, 1,776 admitted, 394 enrolled.

GPA 3.75 or higher:	5%	**GPA 2.0-2.99:**	42%
GPA 3.50-3.74:	12%	**Out-of-state:**	67%
GPA 3.0-3.49:	40%	**Live on campus:**	98%

Basis for selection. High school transcript most important. Recommendations, school and community activities, essay also considered. Interviews highly recommended, but not required. Test scores considered if submitted,. Portfolio recommended for art program.

High school preparation. 15 units required. Required units include English 4, mathematics 3, social studies 3, science 3 (laboratory 3) and foreign language 2. Nursing applicants strongly encouraged to have 3 years of college-preparatory lab sciences, including biology and chemistry.

2008-2009 Annual costs. Tuition/fees: $29,620. Room/board: $10,340. Books/supplies: $750. Personal expenses: $1,000.

2008-2009 Financial aid. Non-need-based: Scholarships awarded for academics, alumni affiliation, art, leadership, minority status, music/drama.

Application procedures. Admission: No deadline. $45 fee, may be waived for applicants with need, free for online applicants. Admission notification on a rolling basis beginning on or about 12/15. Must reply by May 1 or within 2 week(s) if notified thereafter. **Financial aid:** Priority date 2/15, closing date 3/1. FAFSA required. Applicants notified on a rolling basis starting 1/1; must reply by 5/1 or within 2 week(s) of notification.

Academics. Liberal arts and experiential education integrated. Internships or senior research projects required in all major programs. **Special study options:** Accelerated study, cross-registration, double major, dual enrollment of high school students, ESL, exchange student, honors, independent study, internships, semester at sea, student-designed major, study abroad, teacher certification program, Washington semester. **Credit/placement by examination:** AP, CLEP, IB, institutional tests. 30 credit hours maximum toward associate degree, 60 toward bachelor's. **Support services:** Learning center, reduced course load, study skills assistance, tutoring.

Majors. Biology: General. **Business:** Business admin. **Communications:** Media studies. **Conservation:** Environmental studies. **Education:** Art, early childhood, English, social studies. **Health:** Athletic training, nursing (RN). **Parks/recreation:** Exercise sciences, sports admin. **Psychology:** General, developmental. **Visual/performing arts:** Art, graphic design, studio arts.

Most popular majors. Business/marketing 12%, communications/journalism 7%, education 12%, health sciences 16%, parks/recreation 11%, psychology 17%, visual/performing arts 12%.

Computing on campus. 150 workstations in library, computer center, student center. Dormitories wired for high-speed internet access and linked to campus network. Commuter students can connect to campus network. Online library, helpline, wireless network available.

Student life. Freshman orientation: Mandatory. Preregistration for classes offered. Two days immediately preceding beginning of fall semester. **Housing:** Guaranteed on-campus for all undergraduates. Coed dorms, single-sex dorms, special housing for disabled, wellness housing available. **Activities:** Choral groups, dance, drama, literary magazine, musical theater, radio station, student government, student newspaper, community service club, Safe Zones, cross cultural club, Christian Fellowship, Coalition for Peace and Justice, Student Democrats.

Athletics. NCAA. **Intercollegiate:** Baseball M, basketball, diving, equestrian, lacrosse W, skiing, soccer, swimming, tennis, track and field, volleyball W. **Intramural:** Basketball, football (non-tackle), golf, soccer, volleyball. **Team name:** Chargers.

Student services. Alcohol/substance abuse counseling, career counseling, student employment services, financial aid counseling, health services, personal counseling. **Physically disabled:** Services for visually, hearing impaired.

Contact. E-mail: admissions@colby-sawyer.edu
Phone: (603) 526-3700 Toll-free number: (800) 272-1015
Fax: (603) 526-3452
Tracey Perkins, Director of Admission Counseling, Colby-Sawyer College, 541 Main Street, New London, NH 03257-7835

Daniel Webster College

Nashua, New Hampshire — **CB member**
www.dwc.edu — **CB code: 3648**

- Private 4-year business and liberal arts college
- Residential campus in small city
- 722 degree-seeking undergraduates: 5% part-time, 21% women
- 286 degree-seeking graduate students
- SAT or ACT (ACT writing optional), application essay required
- 42% graduate within 6 years

General. Founded in 1965. Regionally accredited. STEM institution: Science, Technology, Engineering & Management. **Degrees:** 148 bachelor's, 17 associate awarded; master's offered. **ROTC:** Army, Air Force. **Location:** 17 miles from Manchester, 35 miles from Boston. **Calendar:** Semester, limited summer session. **Full-time faculty:** 36 total; 67% have terminal degrees, 11% minority, 25% women. **Part-time faculty:** 44 total; 73% have terminal degrees, 7% minority, 23% women. **Class size:** 77% < 20, 23% 20-39. **Special facilities:** On-campus flight center, aircraft, 3 flight simulators, air-traffic-control simulation system, windtunnel, ATC tower.

Freshman class profile.

Mid 50% test scores		**GPA 3.50-3.74:**	16%
SAT critical reading:	450-570	**GPA 3.0-3.49:**	40%
SAT math:	470-600	**GPA 2.0-2.99:**	38%
ACT composite:	20-25	**Out-of-state:**	60%
GPA 3.75 or higher:	5%	**Live on campus:**	80%

Basis for selection. High school transcript, recommendations, test scores and essay most important. Extracurricular activities considered. Interviews recommended. **Homeschooled:** Transcript of courses and grades, interview, letter of recommendation (nonparent) required.

High school preparation. 16 units required. Required and recommended units include English 4, mathematics 3-4, social studies 2, history 2, science 3 (laboratory 2), foreign language 2 and computer science 1.

2008-2009 Annual costs. Tuition/fees: $27,032. Room/board: $9,369. Books/supplies: $1,000. Personal expenses: $1,500.

2007-2008 Financial aid. **Need-based:** 8% of total undergraduate aid awarded as scholarships/grants, 92% as loans/jobs. **Non-need-based:** Scholarships awarded for academics, alumni affiliation, leadership.

Application procedures. **Admission:** No deadline. $35 fee, may be waived for applicants with need. Admission notification on a rolling basis beginning on or about 12/1. Must reply by May 1 or within 2 week(s) if notified thereafter. **Financial aid:** Priority date 3/1; no closing date. FAFSA, institutional form required. Applicants notified on a rolling basis starting 3/15; must reply within 2 week(s) of notification.

Academics. Credit granted for pilot licenses. Flight students must have FAA Class II physical examination. Flight operations majors must pass FAA written examinations and flight tests to earn pilot ratings. **Special study options:** Accelerated study, combined bachelor's/graduate degree, cooperative education, cross-registration, distance learning, double major, dual enrollment of high school students, independent study, internships, liberal arts/career combination, study abroad, Washington semester. **Credit/placement by examination:** AP, CLEP, IB, institutional tests. 30 credit hours maximum toward associate degree, 30 toward bachelor's. **Support services:** Learning center, study skills assistance, tutoring, writing center.

Majors. **Business:** General, business admin, management information systems, marketing. **Computer sciences:** General, a.i./robotics, computer science, information systems, LAN/WAN management. **Engineering:** Aerospace, mechanical. **Parks/recreation:** Sports admin. **Protective services:** Emergency management/homeland security. **Psychology:** General. **Social sciences:** General. **Transportation:** Air traffic control, aviation, aviation management.

Most popular majors. Business/marketing 33%, computer/information sciences 10%, engineering/engineering technologies 7%.

Computing on campus. 150 workstations in dormitories, library, computer center, student center. Dormitories wired for high-speed internet access and linked to campus network. Helpline, repair service, wireless network available.

Student life. **Freshman orientation:** Mandatory, $250 fee. 4-day program. **Housing:** Guaranteed on-campus for all undergraduates. Coed dorms, single-sex dorms, apartments, wellness housing available. $400 nonrefundable deposit, deadline 5/1. Townhouses attained by merit. Suites for 4 to 7 students available. **Activities:** Jazz band, choral groups, drama, film society, student government, student newspaper, Campus Crusade for Christ, Gay-Straight Alliance.

Athletics. NCAA. **Intercollegiate:** Baseball M, basketball, cross-country, field hockey W, golf, lacrosse, soccer, softball W, volleyball. **Intramural:** Basketball, football (tackle) M, ice hockey M, skiing, soccer, volleyball. **Team name:** Eagles.

Student services. Adult student services, alcohol/substance abuse counseling, career counseling, student employment services, financial aid counseling, health services, personal counseling, placement for graduates, veterans' counselor.

Contact. E-mail: admissions@dwc.edu
Phone: (603) 577-6600 Toll-free number: (800) 325-6876
Fax: (603) 577-6001
Daniel Monahan, Dean of Admissions and Financial Assistance, Daniel Webster College, 20 University Drive, Nashua, NH 03063

Dartmouth College

Hanover, New Hampshire — **CB member**
www.dartmouth.edu — **CB code: 3351**

- Private 4-year university and liberal arts college
- Residential campus in large town
- 4,067 degree-seeking undergraduates: 50% women, 8% African American, 14% Asian American, 7% Hispanic American, 4% Native American, 7% international
- 1,647 degree-seeking graduate students
- 13% of applicants admitted
- SAT and SAT Subject Tests or ACT with writing, application essay required
- 95% graduate within 6 years

General. Founded in 1769. Regionally accredited. **Degrees:** 1,084 bachelor's awarded; master's, doctoral, first professional offered. **ROTC:** Army. **Location:** 130 miles from Boston. **Calendar:** Quarter, extensive summer session. **Full-time faculty:** 492 total. **Part-time faculty:** 155 total. **Special facilities:** Observatory, centers for humanities, social sciences, physical science, performing arts, ethics, life science, computation.

Freshman class profile. 16,538 applied, 2,228 admitted, 1,095 enrolled.

Mid 50% test scores		**Rank in top tenth:**	90%
SAT critical reading:	660-770	**Return as sophomores:**	98%
SAT math:	670-780	**Out-of-state:**	97%
SAT writing:	680-770	**Live on campus:**	100%
ACT composite:	29-34	**International:**	7%

Basis for selection. Evidence of intellectual capability, motivation, and personal integrity of primary importance. Talent, accomplishment, and involvement in nonacademic areas also evaluated. 2 SAT Subject Tests of student's choice required. Interview optional.

High school preparation. College-preparatory program recommended. Recommended units include English 4, mathematics 4, social studies 3, history 3 and science 3. Strongest academic program available to applicant recommended.

2009-2010 Annual costs. Tuition/fees: $38,789. Room/board: $11,295. Books/supplies: $1,512. Personal expenses: $1,341.

2007-2008 Financial aid. All financial aid based on need. 690 full-time freshmen applied for aid; 557 were judged to have need; 557 of these received aid. Average need met was 100%. Average scholarship/grant was $32,413; average loan $3,341. 85% of total undergraduate aid awarded as scholarships/grants, 15% as loans/jobs.

Application procedures. Admission: Closing date 1/1 (postmark date). $70 fee, may be waived for applicants with need. Admission notification 4/10. Must reply by 5/1. **Financial aid:** Closing date 2/1. FAFSA, CSS PROFILE required. Applicants notified by 4/2; must reply by 5/1.

Academics. Undergraduate research encouraged. **Special study options:** Combined bachelor's/graduate degree, double major, exchange student, honors, independent study, internships, semester at sea, student-designed major, study abroad, teacher certification program, Washington semester. Williams Mystic Seaport Maritime Studies program, study at Eugene O'Neill National Theater Institute, Twelve College Exchange, University of California-San Diego exchange program, McGill University exchange program, exchange programs with over 50 foreign universities, special academic programs in Washington, DC and Tucson, AZ. **Credit/placement by examination:** AP, CLEP, IB, SAT, ACT, institutional tests. **Support services:** Learning center, study skills assistance, tutoring, writing center.

Majors. Area/ethnic studies: African, African-American, Asian, Caribbean, German, Hispanic-American/Latino/Chicano, Latin American, Native American, Near/Middle Eastern, Russian/Slavic, Spanish/Iberian, women's. **Biology:** General, biochemistry, Biochemistry/biophysics and molecular biology, cell/histology, ecology, evolutionary, genetics, molecular. **Computer sciences:** Computer science. **Conservation:** General, environmental studies. **Engineering:** Biomedical, physics, science. **Foreign languages:** Arabic, Chinese, classics, comparative lit, French, German, Hebrew, Italian, Japanese, linguistics, Russian, South Asian, Spanish. **History:** General. **Interdisciplinary:** Ancient studies, classical/archaeology, neuroscience. **Math:** General. **Philosophy/religion:** Philosophy, religion. **Physical sciences:** Astronomy, chemistry, physics, planetary. **Psychology:** General. **Social sciences:** Anthropology, economics, geography, political science, sociology. **Visual/performing arts:** Art history/conservation, dramatic, film/cinema, studio arts.

Most popular majors. Biology 6%, English 6%, foreign language 6%, history 9%, psychology 8%, social sciences 32%.

Computing on campus. PC or laptop required. Dormitories wired for high-speed internet access and linked to campus network. Commuter students can connect to campus network. Online course registration, online library, helpline, repair service, student web hosting, wireless network available.

Student life. Freshman orientation: Mandatory. Held week before fall classes begin; freshmen trips led by Dartmouth outing club. **Housing:** Guaranteed on-campus for freshmen. Coed dorms, apartments, cooperative housing, fraternity/sorority housing, wellness housing available. Academic affinity housing, faculty-in-residence programs, special interest housing available. **Activities:** Bands, campus ministries, choral groups, dance, drama, film society, international student organizations, literary magazine, music ensembles, Model UN, musical theater, opera, radio station, student government, student newspaper, symphony orchestra, TV station, community and service programs, religious groups, and political and ethnic organizations available.

Athletics. NCAA. **Intercollegiate:** Baseball M, basketball, cross-country, diving, equestrian, field hockey W, football (tackle) M, golf, ice hockey, lacrosse, rowing (crew), sailing, skiing, soccer, softball W, squash, swimming, tennis, track and field, volleyball W. **Intramural:** Baseball M, basketball, bowling, cross-country, football (non-tackle), golf, handball, ice hockey, lacrosse, racquetball, skiing, soccer, softball, squash, swimming, table tennis, tennis, track and field, volleyball, water polo, wrestling M. **Team name:** Big Green.

Student services. Alcohol/substance abuse counseling, chaplain/spiritual director, career counseling, student employment services, financial aid counseling, health services, minority student services, on-campus daycare, personal counseling, placement for graduates, women's services. **Physically disabled:** Services for visually, speech, hearing impaired.

Contact. E-mail: admissions.office@dartmouth.edu
Phone: (603) 646-2875 Fax: (603) 646-1216
Maria Laskaris, Dean of Admissions and Financial Aid, Dartmouth College, 6016 McNutt Hall, Hanover, NH 03755

Franklin Pierce University

Rindge, New Hampshire — **CB member**
www.franklinpierce.edu — **CB code: 3395**

- Private 4-year university and liberal arts college
- Residential campus in small town
- 2,061 degree-seeking undergraduates: 15% part-time, 49% women, 2% African American, 1% Asian American, 2% Hispanic American, 3% international
- 450 degree-seeking graduate students
- 77% of applicants admitted
- SAT or ACT with writing, application essay required
- 49% graduate within 6 years; 37% enter graduate study

General. Founded in 1962. Regionally accredited. 4 satellite campuses offer continuing education sequence of 8-week undergraduate and 12-week graduate sessions on-campus and online. Associate, bachelor's, MBA, DPT, MEd, DA and PA offered through graduate and professional studies division campuses in Concord, Lebanon, Manchester and Portsmouth, NH as well as online. **Degrees:** 428 bachelor's, 37 associate awarded; master's, doctoral offered. **ROTC:** Army, Air Force. **Location:** 20 miles from Keene, 60 miles from Boston. **Calendar:** Semester, limited summer session. **Full-time faculty:** 100 total; 68% have terminal degrees, 1% minority, 45% women. **Part-time faculty:** 123 total; 20% have terminal degrees, 3% minority, 43% women. **Class size:** 70% < 20, 30% 20-39. **Special facilities:** Glass blowing studio, ceramic studio and firing kiln, graphic design workshop, archaeological dig site, physical therapy labs, television studio, media production studios.

Freshman class profile. 4,100 applied, 3,171 admitted, 477 enrolled.

Mid 50% test scores			
SAT critical reading:	440-550	GPA 2.0-2.99:	68%
SAT math:	430-540	Rank in top quarter:	20%
SAT writing:	420-520	Rank in top tenth:	7%
GPA 3.75 or higher:	3%	End year in good standing:	92%
GPA 3.50-3.74:	6%	Return as sophomores:	62%
GPA 3.0-3.49:	23%	Out-of-state:	85%
		Live on campus:	98%

Basis for selection. School achievement record, difficulty of course work, recommendations and school involvement primary considerations. Test scores also important. Test of English as a Foreign Language (TOEFL) is required for English speakers of other languages. Interview and campus visit recommended for all. **Homeschooled:** Letter of recommendation (nonparent) required.

High school preparation. College-preparatory program required. 16 units required. Required units include English 4, mathematics 3, social studies 3, science 3 (laboratory 2) and academic electives 4.

2008-2009 Annual costs. Tuition/fees: $28,300. Room/board: $9,200.

2008-2009 Financial aid. Non-need-based: Scholarships awarded for academics, alumni affiliation, athletics, leadership, music/drama.

Application procedures. Admission: No deadline. $40 fee. Admission notification on a rolling basis beginning on or about 10/15. Must reply by May 1 or within 2 week(s) if notified thereafter. **Financial aid:** Closing date 3/1. FAFSA required. Applicants notified on a rolling basis starting 3/1; must reply within 2 week(s) of notification.

Academics. Special study options: Accelerated study, combined bachelor's/graduate degree, distance learning, double major, dual enrollment of high school students, ESL, exchange student, honors, independent study, internships, liberal arts/career combination, student-designed major, study abroad, teacher certification program, Washington semester. Walk Across Europe, Washington Internship, Arcadia Study Abroad, Vienna, Athens. **Credit/placement by examination:** AP, CLEP, IB, SAT, ACT, institutional tests. 12 credit hours maximum toward associate degree, 30 toward bachelor's. **Support services:** Learning center, reduced course load, remedial instruction, study skills assistance, tutoring, writing center.

Majors. Area/ethnic studies: American. **Biology:** General. **Business:** Accounting/finance, management information systems, management science, marketing. **Communications:** Media studies. **Computer sciences:** Information technology. **Conservation:** Environmental science. **Education:** General. **History:** General. **Liberal arts:** Arts/sciences. **Math:** General. **Parks/recreation:** Facilities management. **Protective services:** Criminal justice. **Psychology:** General. **Public administration:** Social work. **Social sciences:** Anthropology, political science. **Visual/performing arts:** Arts management, commercial/advertising art, dance, dramatic, music performance, studio arts.

Most popular majors. Business/marketing 15%, communications/journalism 12%, psychology 6%, security/protective services 12%, social sciences 10%, visual/performing arts 14%.

Computing on campus. 109 workstations in dormitories, library, computer center. Dormitories wired for high-speed internet access and linked to campus network. Commuter students can connect to campus network. Online library, helpline, repair service, wireless network available.

Student life. **Freshman orientation:** Mandatory. Preregistration for classes offered. Held immediately prior to start of semester. **Housing:** Guaranteed on-campus for all undergraduates. Coed dorms, special housing for disabled, apartments, wellness housing available. $250 nonrefundable deposit, deadline 6/20. **Activities:** Jazz band, campus ministries, choral groups, dance, drama, international student organizations, literary magazine, music ensembles, musical theater, radio station, student government, student newspaper, TV station, student senate, law club, business club, black student alliance, Pierce Pals, community service, environmental awareness club, emergency medical services club, education club.

Athletics. NCAA. **Intercollegiate:** Baseball M, basketball, cross-country W, field hockey W, golf M, ice hockey M, lacrosse, rowing (crew), soccer, softball W, tennis, volleyball W. **Intramural:** Baseball M, basketball, cross-country W, field hockey W, sailing, skiing, soccer, softball, table tennis, tennis, volleyball. **Team name:** Ravens.

Student services. Alcohol/substance abuse counseling, chaplain/spiritual director, career counseling, student employment services, financial aid counseling, health services, minority student services, personal counseling, placement for graduates, women's services.

Contact. E-mail: admissions@franklinpierce.edu
Phone: (603) 899-4050 Toll-free number: (800) 437-0048
Fax: (603) 899-4394
Linda Quimby, Director, Admissions, Franklin Pierce University, 40 University Drive, Rindge, NH 03461-0060

Granite State College
Concord, New Hampshire
www.granite.edu **CB code: 0458**

- Public 4-year liberal arts college
- Commuter campus in large town
- 1,174 degree-seeking undergraduates: 54% part-time, 73% women, 1% African American, 1% Asian American, 1% Hispanic American, 1% Native American
- 178 graduate students
- Application essay required
- 51% graduate within 6 years

General. Founded in 1972. Regionally accredited. **Degrees:** 232 bachelor's, 90 associate awarded. **ROTC:** Army. **Calendar:** Trimester, limited summer session. **Part-time faculty:** 147 total; 66% women. **Class size:** 97% < 20, 3% 20-39.

Freshman class profile. 93 applied, 93 admitted, 47 enrolled.

Basis for selection. Open admission. Accuplacer tests used for placement.

2008-2009 Annual costs. Tuition/fees: $7,335; $7,755 out-of-state. Books/supplies: $900. Personal expenses: $2,475.

Application procedures. **Admission:** No deadline. $45 fee. Admission notification on a rolling basis. **Financial aid:** No deadline. FAFSA, institutional form required. Applicants notified on a rolling basis starting 4/15.

Academics. **Special study options:** Accelerated study, cross-registration, distance learning, double major, independent study, internships, liberal arts/career combination, student-designed major, teacher certification program. **Credit/placement by examination:** AP, CLEP, SAT, ACT, institutional tests. 32 credit hours maximum toward associate degree, 64 toward bachelor's. Exams must support degree program. **Support services:** Learning center, remedial instruction, study skills assistance, tutoring.

Majors. **Business:** Management science. **Education:** Early childhood. **Interdisciplinary:** Behavioral sciences. **Liberal arts:** Arts/sciences. **Protective services:** Criminal justice, law enforcement admin. **Other:** Applied Studies.

Most popular majors. Business/marketing 24%, interdisciplinary studies 24%, liberal arts 41%.

Computing on campus. 139 workstations in computer center, student center. Online course registration, online library, helpline, wireless network available.

Student life. **Freshman orientation:** Available. **Activities:** Alumni/learner association.

Student services. Adult student services, career counseling, financial aid counseling, veterans' counselor.

Contact. E-mail: ruth.nawn@granite.edu
Phone: (603) 228-3000 ext. 339 Toll-free number: (888) 228-3000 ext. 339
Fax: (603) 513-1386
Ruth Nawn, Associate Director of Admissions, Granite State College, 8 Old Suncook Road, Concord, NH 03301-7317

Hesser College
Manchester, New Hampshire
www.hesser.edu **CB code: 3452**

- For-profit 4-year business and junior college
- Residential campus in small city
- 3,400 undergraduates
- Application essay, interview required

General. Founded in 1900. Regionally accredited. Courses also available at centers in Nashua, Salem, Portsmouth, and Concord. **Degrees:** 164 bachelor's, 709 associate awarded. **Location:** 50 miles from Boston. **Calendar:** Semester, limited summer session. **Full-time faculty:** 50 total. **Part-time faculty:** 130 total. **Class size:** 68% < 20, 32% 20-39.

Freshman class profile.

Out-of-state:	25%	Live on campus:	18%

Basis for selection. Open admission, but selective for some programs. School achievement record most important. Admission granted to applicants in top 70% of graduating class with 2.0 high school GPA. Physical therapist and graphic design programs are selective. Portfolio recommended for fashion design, interior design and graphic design programs. **Learning Disabled:** Must meet with director of center for teaching, learning and assessment.

2008-2009 Annual costs. Tuition/fees: $14,220. Room/board: $7,160. Books/supplies: $1,200. Personal expenses: $550.

Financial aid. All financial aid based on need. **Additional information:** Two private loans available to assist students in paying their balance; Tree Loan, SLM Loan.

Application procedures. **Admission:** No deadline. $20 fee, may be waived for applicants with need. Admission notification on a rolling basis. **Financial aid:** Priority date 5/1; no closing date. FAFSA, institutional form required. Applicants notified on a rolling basis starting 3/1; must reply within 3 week(s) of notification.

Academics. **Special study options:** Accelerated study, independent study, internships. **Credit/placement by examination:** AP, CLEP, IB, institutional tests. Max of 50% of total program credits awarded via CLEP, DANTES and Advanced Placement exams. Max of 25% of total program credits awarded via institutional exams. **Support services:** Learning center, reduced course load, remedial instruction, tutoring, writing center.

Majors. **Business:** Accounting, business admin. **Protective services:** Law enforcement admin.

Computing on campus. 20 workstations in library, computer center. Dormitories wired for high-speed internet access. Helpline, repair service available.

Student life. **Freshman orientation:** Mandatory. Preregistration for classes offered. **Housing:** Guaranteed on-campus for freshmen. Single-sex dorms, wellness housing available. $125 deposit. **Activities:** Choral groups, radio station, student government, TV station, special interest organizations relating to accounting, business, travel, and retailing, community service club.

Athletics. NJCAA. **Intercollegiate:** Baseball M, basketball, soccer, softball W, volleyball. **Intramural:** Basketball, cheerleading W, football (non-tackle), soccer, volleyball. **Team name:** Blue Devils.

Student services. Alcohol/substance abuse counseling, career counseling, student employment services, financial aid counseling, health services, personal counseling, placement for graduates, veterans' counselor.

Contact. E-mail: admissions@hesser.edu
Phone: (603) 668-6660 ext. 2110 Toll-free number: (800) 526-9231 ext. 2110 Fax: (603) 666-4722
Leann Gray, Director of Admissions, Hesser College, 3 Sundial Avenue, Manchester, NH 03103

Keene State College
Keene, New Hampshire **CB member**
www.keene.edu **CB code: 3472**

- Public 4-year liberal arts and teachers college
- Residential campus in large town
- 4,866 degree-seeking undergraduates: 3% part-time, 57% women, 1% African American, 1% Hispanic American
- 82 degree-seeking graduate students
- 72% of applicants admitted
- SAT or ACT (ACT writing recommended), application essay required
- 58% graduate within 6 years

General. Founded in 1909. Regionally accredited. **Degrees:** 999 bachelor's, 40 associate awarded; master's offered. **ROTC:** Air Force. **Location:** 52 miles from Concord, 85 miles from Boston. **Calendar:** Semester, extensive summer session. **Full-time faculty:** 185 total; 4% minority, 46% women. **Part-time faculty:** 237 total; 53% women. **Class size:** 52% < 20, 42% 20-39, 5% 40-49, 2% 50-99. **Special facilities:** Arboretum and gardens, center for Holocaust studies, child development center, community research center, curriculum materials library, small business institute, college-owned camp, 400-acre preserve, theater complex.

Freshman class profile. 5,057 applied, 3,627 admitted, 2,442 enrolled.

Mid 50% test scores			
SAT critical reading:	440-550	GPA 2.0-2.99:	44%
SAT math:	440-550	Rank in top quarter:	22%
SAT writing:	450-540	Rank in top tenth:	4%
GPA 3.75 or higher:	5%	End year in good standing:	89%
GPA 3.50-3.74:	10%	Return as sophomores:	80%
GPA 3.0-3.49:	40%	Out-of-state:	55%
		Live on campus:	95%

Basis for selection. High school record, including challenging courses, most important. SAT or ACT scores do not hold nearly as much weight as high school performance. Audition required for music education and music performance programs; portfolio required for art program. **Homeschooled:** Statement describing homeschool structure and mission required. **Learning Disabled:** Documented proof of disability required for some services.

High school preparation. College-preparatory program recommended. 14 units required. Required units include English 4, mathematics 3, social studies 2, science 3 and academic electives 2.

2008-2009 Annual costs. Tuition/fees: $8,778; $16,628 out-of-state. New England Regional tuition is 150% of in-state public institution tuition. Room/board: $7,796. Books/supplies: $800. Personal expenses: $750.

2007-2008 Financial aid. **Need-based:** 1,103 full-time freshmen applied for aid; 713 were judged to have need; 699 of these received aid. Average need met was 66%. Average scholarship/grant was $4,960; average loan $3,644. 39% of total undergraduate aid awarded as scholarships/grants, 61% as loans/jobs. **Non-need-based:** Awarded to 871 full-time undergraduates, including 247 freshmen. Scholarships awarded for academics, alumni affiliation, art, music/drama.

Application procedures. **Admission:** Closing date 4/1 (receipt date). $40 fee, may be waived for applicants with need. Admission notification on a rolling basis. Must reply by 5/1. **Financial aid:** Closing date 3/1. FAFSA required. Applicants notified on a rolling basis; must reply within 4 week(s) of notification.

Academics. **Special study options:** Cooperative education, double major, ESL, exchange student, honors, independent study, internships, liberal arts/career combination, student-designed major, study abroad, teacher certification program. **Credit/placement by examination:** AP, CLEP. 30 credit hours maximum toward associate degree, 60 toward bachelor's. **Support services:** Learning center, pre-admission summer program, reduced course load, study skills assistance, tutoring, writing center.

Majors. **Architecture:** Architecture. **Area/ethnic studies:** American. **Biology:** General. **Business:** Business admin. **Communications:** General, journalism. **Computer sciences:** General. **Conservation:** Environmental studies. **Education:** Biology, chemistry, computer, early childhood, elementary, English, French, geography, health, history, mathematics, music, physical, science, secondary, social studies, Spanish, special, technology/industrial arts. **Engineering technology:** Architectural, occupational safety. **Foreign languages:** French, Spanish. **Health:** Athletic training, dietetics, substance abuse counseling. **History:** General, American, European. **Interdisciplinary:** Biological/physical sciences. **Math:** General. **Parks/recreation:** Health/fitness. **Physical sciences:** General, chemistry, geology. **Psychology:** General, clinical, developmental, experimental, social. **Social sciences:** General, economics, geography, sociology. **Visual/performing arts:** Acting, cinematography, commercial/advertising art, dance, directing/producing, film/cinema, graphic design, music history, music performance, music theory/composition, studio arts, theater design, theater history. **Other:** Chemistry physics, Computer mathematics, Individualized, Math physics, Music technology, Technology studies.

Most popular majors. Business/marketing 8%, communications/journalism 8%, education 20%, engineering/engineering technologies 9%, psychology 13%, social sciences 12%, visual/performing arts 7%.

Computing on campus. 500 workstations in dormitories, library, computer center, student center. Dormitories wired for high-speed internet access and linked to campus network. Commuter students can connect to campus network. Online course registration, online library, helpline, repair service, student web hosting, wireless network available.

Student life. **Freshman orientation:** Mandatory. Preregistration for classes offered. **Housing:** Coed dorms, single-sex dorms, apartments, fraternity/sorority housing, wellness housing available. $100 nonrefundable deposit, deadline 5/1. Language/Culture, leadership, quiet study available. **Activities:** Bands, campus ministries, choral groups, dance, drama, film society, international student organizations, literary magazine, music ensembles, musical theater, radio station, student government, student newspaper, TV station, Habitat for Humanity, Amnesty International, student government, campus ecology, civil liberties union, student volunteer organization, environmental outing club, KSC Pride, Circle K.

Athletics. NCAA. **Intercollegiate:** Baseball M, basketball, cheerleading, cross-country, diving, field hockey W, lacrosse, soccer, softball W, swimming, track and field, volleyball W. **Intramural:** Badminton, basketball, cross-country, football (non-tackle), racquetball, soccer, softball, tennis, track and field, volleyball, water polo. **Team name:** Owls.

Student services. Adult student services, alcohol/substance abuse counseling, chaplain/spiritual director, career counseling, student employment services, financial aid counseling, health services, minority student services, on-campus daycare, personal counseling, placement for graduates, veterans' counselor. **Physically disabled:** Services for visually, speech, hearing impaired.

Contact. E-mail: admissions@keene.edu
Phone: (603) 358-2276 Toll-free number: (800) 572-1909
Fax: (603) 358-2767
Margaret Richmond, Director of Admissions, Keene State College, 229 Main Street, Keene, NH 03435-2604

Magdalen College
Warner, New Hampshire
www.magdalen.edu **CB code: 3562**

- Private 4-year liberal arts college affiliated with Roman Catholic Church
- Residential campus in small town
- 59 degree-seeking undergraduates: 56% women, 3% African American, 7% Hispanic American, 2% international
- 81% of applicants admitted
- SAT or ACT (ACT writing recommended), application essay, interview required

General. Regionally accredited. **Degrees:** 14 bachelor's awarded. **Location:** 20 miles from Concord. **Calendar:** Semester. **Full-time faculty:** 7 total. **Part-time faculty:** 2 total. **Special facilities:** Observatory.

Freshman class profile. 42 applied, 34 admitted, 24 enrolled.

Mid 50% test scores			
SAT critical reading:	510-670	End year in good standing:	87%
SAT math:	390-570	Return as sophomores:	93%
ACT composite:	21-24	Out-of-state:	78%
		Live on campus:	100%

Basis for selection. Campus visit required (may be waived due to hardship). Academic GPA and high school transcript important.

High school preparation. 24 units recommended. Recommended units include English 4, mathematics 4, social studies 3, history 2, science 3, foreign language 2 and academic electives 6.

2008-2009 Annual costs. Tuition/fees: $12,250. Room/board: $6,500. Books/supplies: $400. Personal expenses: $200.

Financial aid. All financial aid based on need.

Application procedures. **Admission:** Closing date 5/1 (postmark date). $35 fee. Application must be submitted on paper. Admission notification on a rolling basis. Must reply by May 1 or within 4 week(s) if notified thereafter. **Financial aid:** Closing date 6/30. Institutional form required. Applicants notified by 7/1; must reply by 7/1 or within 4 week(s) of notification.

Academics. Special study options: Study abroad. **Credit/placement by examination:** CLEP. **Support services:** Learning center, pre-admission summer program, remedial instruction, study skills assistance, tutoring.

Majors. Liberal arts: Arts/sciences.

Computing on campus. 20 workstations in dormitories, library. Online library available.

Student life. Freshman orientation: Mandatory. 2-day program in early September. **Policies:** Dress code for class. Required attendance at meals. Curfews in dormitories. No-cut policy for class. Campus service required. Sunday mass required for Catholic students. Religious observance required. **Housing:** Guaranteed on-campus for all undergraduates. Single-sex dorms, wellness housing available. $500 deposit, deadline 6/15. **Activities:** Choral groups, drama, music ensembles, musical theater, campus service organization, college choir.

Athletics. Intramural: Basketball, football (non-tackle) M, soccer, volleyball.

Student services. Chaplain/spiritual director, career counseling, student employment services, financial aid counseling, personal counseling.

Contact. E-mail: admissions@magdalen.edu
Phone: (603) 456-2656 ext. 14 Toll-free number: (877) 498-1723
Fax: (603) 456-2660
Bobbie Anne Abson, Director of Admissions and Financial Aid, Magdalen College, 511 Kearsarge Mountain Road, Warner, NH 03278

New England College

Henniker, New Hampshire
www.nec.edu **CB code: 3657**

- Private 4-year business, liberal arts and teachers college
- Residential campus in small town
- 1,054 degree-seeking undergraduates: 4% part-time, 47% women
- 684 degree-seeking graduate students
- 76% of applicants admitted
- Application essay required
- 42% graduate within 6 years; 22% enter graduate study

General. Founded in 1946. Regionally accredited. Cross-registration with other 4-year institutions available through New Hampshire College and University Council. **Degrees:** 162 bachelor's awarded; master's offered. **ROTC:** Army, Air Force. **Location:** 18 miles from Concord. **Calendar:** Semester, limited summer session. **Full-time faculty:** 62 total; 76% have terminal degrees, 5% minority, 42% women. **Part-time faculty:** 46 total; 35% have terminal degrees, 2% minority, 52% women. **Class size:** 67% < 20, 33% 20-39. **Special facilities:** Center for Educational Innovation.

Freshman class profile. 2,057 applied, 1,557 admitted, 300 enrolled.

Mid 50% test scores		**Rank in top quarter:**	16%
SAT critical reading:	400-510	**Rank in top tenth:**	4%
SAT math:	390-510	**End year in good standing:**	76%
SAT writing:	380-510	**Return as sophomores:**	63%
ACT composite:	16-20	**Out-of-state:**	62%
GPA 3.75 or higher:	2%	**Live on campus:**	90%
GPA 3.50-3.74:	5%	**International:**	3%
GPA 3.0-3.49:	30%	**Fraternities:**	5%
GPA 2.0-2.99:	55%	**Sororities:**	3%

Basis for selection. School achievement record most important, followed by recommendations, essay or personal statement, evidence of leadership and extracurricular activities. Interview recommended for all; portfolio recommended for art program. **Homeschooled:** Transcript of courses and grades, state high school equivalency certificate, letter of recommendation (nonparent) required.

High school preparation. College-preparatory program recommended. 12 units required. Required and recommended units include English 4, mathematics 3, social studies 3, science 3 (laboratory 1-2) and foreign language 2.

2008-2009 Annual costs. Tuition/fees: $26,472. Room/board: $9,288. Books/supplies: $640. Personal expenses: $1,250.

2008-2009 Financial aid. Non-need-based: Scholarships awarded for academics, alumni affiliation, art, job skills, leadership, music/drama.

Application procedures. Admission: No deadline. $30 fee, may be waived for applicants with need. Admission notification on a rolling basis beginning on or about 11/1. **Financial aid:** Priority date 4/1; no closing date. FAFSA, institutional form required. Applicants notified on a rolling basis starting 1/12; must reply within 2 week(s) of notification.

Academics. Special study options: Accelerated study, combined bachelor's/graduate degree, cross-registration, distance learning, double major, dual enrollment of high school students, ESL, exchange student, external degree, honors, independent study, internships, liberal arts/career combination, semester at sea, student-designed major, study abroad, teacher certification program, Washington semester. Exchange programs with Regent's College, London; American University of Paris; 18 colleges in Quebec, Canada; University of the Sunshine Coast, Australia. Students keep all financial aid when abroad. **Credit/placement by examination:** AP, CLEP, IB, institutional tests. 21 credit hours maximum toward associate degree, 21 toward bachelor's. **Support services:** Learning center, reduced course load, remedial instruction, study skills assistance, tutoring, writing center.

Majors. Biology: General. **Business:** Accounting, business admin, entrepreneurial studies, finance, human resources, management information systems, marketing. **Communications:** General, advertising, public relations. **Computer sciences:** General. **Conservation:** Environmental science. **Education:** Art, biology, elementary, English, learning disabled, mathematics, physical, science, secondary, social science, social studies, special. **Engineering:** Civil. **Foreign languages:** Comparative lit. **Health:** Health care admin, premedicine. **History:** General. **Legal studies:** Prelaw. **Liberal arts:** Arts/sciences. **Math:** General. **Parks/recreation:** General, exercise sciences, facilities management, sports admin. **Philosophy/religion:** Philosophy. **Protective services:** Criminal justice. **Psychology:** General. **Social sciences:** Political science, sociology. **Visual/performing arts:** Art, art history/conservation, dramatic, photography.

Most popular majors. Business/marketing 18%, communications/journalism 8%, education 8%, English 7%, parks/recreation 10%, psychology 8%, security/protective services 6%, social sciences 8%, visual/performing arts 13%.

Computing on campus. 200 workstations in library, computer center, student center. Dormitories wired for high-speed internet access and linked to campus network. Commuter students can connect to campus network. Online course registration, online library, helpline, wireless network available.

Student life. Freshman orientation: Available. Preregistration for classes offered. Held 3 days prior to first day of classes and 3 mid-summer options. **Housing:** Guaranteed on-campus for all undergraduates. Coed dorms, apartments, fraternity/sorority housing, wellness housing available. $100 nonrefundable deposit. Quiet study options, special interest housing available. **Activities:** Choral groups, dance, drama, international student organizations, literary magazine, radio station, student government, student newspaper, international student association, Hillel, Servcorps, environmental action committee, Womyn's Network, international diplomacy council, Adventure Bound.

Athletics. NCAA. **Intercollegiate:** Baseball M, basketball, cross-country, field hockey W, ice hockey, lacrosse, soccer, softball W. **Intramural:** Baseball M, basketball, ice hockey, soccer, softball, table tennis, tennis, volleyball. **Team name:** Pilgrims.

Student services. Adult student services, alcohol/substance abuse counseling, career counseling, student employment services, financial aid counseling, health services, personal counseling, placement for graduates, veterans' counselor.

Contact. E-mail: admission@nec.edu
Phone: (603) 428-2223 Toll-free number: (800) 521-7642
Fax: (603) 428-3155
Diane Raymond, Director of Admissions, New England College, 102 Bridge Street, Henniker, NH 03242

Plymouth State University

Plymouth, New Hampshire **CB member**
www.plymouth.edu **CB code: 3690**

- Public 4-year university and teachers college
- Residential campus in small town
- 4,204 degree-seeking undergraduates: 3% part-time, 47% women, 1% Asian American, 1% Hispanic American
- 831 degree-seeking graduate students
- 71% of applicants admitted
- SAT or ACT with writing, application essay required
- 54% graduate within 6 years

General. Founded in 1871. Regionally accredited. **Degrees:** 806 bachelor's, 1 associate awarded; master's offered. **ROTC:** Army, Air Force. **Location:** 60 miles from Manchester, 115 miles from Boston. **Calendar:** Semester, limited summer session. **Full-time faculty:** 182 total. **Part-time faculty:** 207 total. **Class size:** 47% < 20, 48% 20-39, 3% 40-49, 1% 50-99, less than 1% >100. **Special facilities:** Planetarium, cultural arts center, child development and family center, geographic information systems lab, meteorology institute, center for the environment, climbing wall, ropes course.

Freshman class profile. 4,425 applied, 3,136 admitted, 1,085 enrolled.

Mid 50% test scores		**GPA 2.0-2.99:**	65%
SAT critical reading:	430-530	**Rank in top quarter:**	14%
SAT math:	440-530	**Rank in top tenth:**	4%
ACT composite:	14-19	**Return as sophomores:**	81%
GPA 3.75 or higher:	2%	**Out-of-state:**	51%
GPA 3.50-3.74:	6%	**Live on campus:**	94%
GPA 3.0-3.49:	26%		

Basis for selection. Decision made by committee, based on school achievement record (most important) followed by test scores, recommendations, essay and extracurricular activites. SAT/ACT not required for resident or non-resident aliens. Audition required for music and theater programs. Portfolio required for art program. **Homeschooled:** Transcript of any work attempted in secondary school, SAT or ACT, GED or homeschool diploma, outline of homeschool curriculum required.

High school preparation. College-preparatory program required. 13 units required; 18 recommended. Required and recommended units include English 4, mathematics 3, social studies 2-3, history 1-2, science 2-3 (laboratory 1) and foreign language 2.

2008-2009 Annual costs. Tuition/fees: $8,424; $16,274 out-of-state. New England Regional tuition: 150% of in-state public institution tuition. Room/board: $8,150.

2007-2008 Financial aid. **Non-need-based:** Scholarships awarded for academics, minority status, music/drama.

Application procedures. **Admission:** Closing date 4/1 (postmark date). $40 fee, may be waived for applicants with need. Admission notification on a rolling basis beginning on or about 11/1. Must reply by 5/1. **Financial aid:** Priority date 3/1; no closing date. FAFSA required. Applicants notified on a rolling basis starting 2/15; must reply by 5/1.

Academics. **Special study options:** Distance learning, double major, exchange student, honors, independent study, internships, student-designed major, study abroad, teacher certification program. **Credit/placement by examination:** AP, CLEP, institutional tests. 30 credit hours maximum toward bachelor's degree. **Support services:** Study skills assistance, tutoring, writing center.

Majors. **Architecture:** Urban/community planning. **Biology:** General, biotechnology, environmental. **Business:** General, accounting, business admin, marketing. **Communications:** General. **Computer sciences:** Computer science, information technology. **Conservation:** Environmental studies. **Education:** Art, early childhood, elementary, music. **Foreign languages:** French, Spanish. **Health:** Athletic training, public health ed. **History:** General. **Liberal arts:** Humanities. **Math:** General. **Parks/recreation:** Health/fitness. **Philosophy/religion:** Philosophy. **Physical sciences:** Atmospheric science, chemistry. **Protective services:** Criminal justice. **Psychology:** General. **Public administration:** General, social work. **Social sciences:** General, applied economics, geography, political science. **Visual/performing arts:** Art, commercial/advertising art, dramatic, studio arts. **Other:** Adventure education.

Most popular majors. Business/marketing 27%, education 16%, parks/recreation 8%, security/protective services 7%, social sciences 6%, visual/performing arts 8%.

Computing on campus. 500 workstations in dormitories, library, computer center, student center. Dormitories wired for high-speed internet access and linked to campus network. Commuter students can connect to campus network. Online course registration, online library, helpline, repair service, student web hosting, wireless network available.

Student life. **Freshman orientation:** Mandatory, $180 fee. Preregistration for classes offered. 5 sessions in June, one session in September. **Housing:** Guaranteed on-campus for freshmen. Coed dorms, apartments, fraternity/sorority housing, wellness housing available. $90 partly refundable deposit, deadline 5/1. Music/theater/dance housing, honors housing, special interest housing, and community service housing available. Also, non-traditional housing. **Activities:** Bands, choral groups, dance, drama, film society, international student organizations, literary magazine, music ensembles, musical theater, radio station, student government, student newspaper, Chi Alpha Christian Fellowship, multicultural student organization, Nicaragua club, volunteer club, social work club, health and wellness club, peer educators, Alternative Spring Break.

Athletics. NCAA. **Intercollegiate:** Baseball M, basketball, cheerleading M, diving W, field hockey W, football (tackle) M, ice hockey, lacrosse, skiing, soccer, softball W, swimming W, tennis W, volleyball W, wrestling M. **Intramural:** Basketball, bowling, cross-country, football (non-tackle), golf, racquetball, soccer, softball, table tennis, tennis, triathlon, volleyball. **Team name:** Panthers.

Student services. Alcohol/substance abuse counseling, chaplain/spiritual director, career counseling, student employment services, financial aid counseling, health services, on-campus daycare, personal counseling, placement for graduates, veterans' counselor, women's services. **Physically disabled:** Services for visually, hearing impaired.

Contact. E-mail: plymouthadmit@plymouth.edu
Phone: (603) 535-2237 Toll-free number: (800) 842-6900
Fax: (603) 535-2714
Eugene Fahey, Senior Associate Director of Admission, Plymouth State University, 17 High Street MSC 52, Plymouth, NH 03264-1595

Rivier College

Nashua, New Hampshire — **CB member**
www.rivier.edu — **CB code: 3728**

- Private 4-year liberal arts and teachers college affiliated with Roman Catholic Church
- Commuter campus in small city
- 1,402 degree-seeking undergraduates: 28% part-time, 81% women
- 577 degree-seeking graduate students
- SAT or ACT with writing, application essay required
- 62% graduate within 6 years

General. Founded in 1933. Regionally accredited. Founded in 1933 by the Sisters of the Presentation of Mary Convent. **Degrees:** 145 bachelor's, 115 associate awarded; master's, doctoral offered. **ROTC:** Army, Naval, Air Force. **Location:** 19 miles from Manchester, 45 miles from Boston. **Calendar:** Semester, limited summer session. **Full-time faculty:** 75 total. **Part-time faculty:** 110 total. **Class size:** 62% < 20, 35% 20-39, 2% 40-49, less than 1% 50-99. **Special facilities:** Center for finance and economics, early childhood center/laboratory school, biology research lab.

Freshman class profile. 825 applied, 686 admitted, 260 enrolled.

Out-of-state:	45%	**Live on campus:**	68%

Basis for selection. Open admission, but selective for some programs. High school academic record (course selection, course level, grades), test scores, extracurricular activities, application essay, and letters of recommendation considered. Interview recommended for all; portfolio required for art programs. **Homeschooled:** Statement describing homeschool structure and mission required.

High school preparation. College-preparatory program required. 16 units recommended. Recommended units include English 4, mathematics 3, social studies 2, history 1, science 1 (laboratory 1), foreign language 2 and academic electives 3. Nursing program applicants must have completed chemistry and algebra.

2008-2009 Annual costs. Tuition/fees: $23,750. Room/board: $8,673. Books/supplies: $1,200. Personal expenses: $1,500.

2007-2008 Financial aid. **Non-need-based:** Scholarships awarded for academics, alumni affiliation, minority status.

Application procedures. **Admission:** Priority date 3/1; no deadline. $25 fee, may be waived for applicants with need. Admission notification on a rolling basis beginning on or about 12/1. **Financial aid:** Priority date 2/1; no closing date. FAFSA required. Applicants notified on a rolling basis starting 3/1; must reply by 5/1 or within 2 week(s) of notification.

Academics. Formal programs for learning disabled students not offered, but college staffs Office of Special Needs Services with part-time learning disabilities specialist. **Special study options:** Combined bachelor's/graduate degree, cross-registration, double major, ESL, honors, independent study, internships, liberal arts/career combination, study abroad, teacher certification program. **Credit/placement by examination:** AP, CLEP, IB, institutional tests. 12 credit hours maximum toward associate degree, 12 toward bachelor's. **Support services:** Learning center, reduced course load, study skills assistance, tutoring, writing center.

Honors college/program. Honors program limited to 15 students per class. Special application and interview required. Scholarship available to all participants. SAT 1200 plus (exclusive of Writing), top 20% of high school class. Honors classes will fulfill some core requirements.

Majors. **Biology:** General. **Business:** Business admin, management information systems, management science. **Communications:** General, broadcast journalism, journalism, public relations. **Computer sciences:** Computer science. **Education:** General, biology, early childhood, elementary, English, foreign languages, history, mathematics, science, secondary, social science, social studies, Spanish. **Foreign languages:** Spanish. **Health:** Nursing (RN), predental, premedicine, preop/surgical nursing, preveterinary. **History:** General. **Legal studies:** Prelaw. **Liberal arts:** Arts/sciences. **Math:** General. **Psychology:** General. **Social sciences:** General, political science, sociology. **Visual/performing arts:** Design, photography, studio arts.

Most popular majors. Business/marketing 14%, education 24%, health sciences 22%, psychology 12%, social sciences 6%, visual/performing arts 7%.

Computing on campus. 150 workstations in dormitories, library, computer center, student center. Dormitories linked to campus network. Commuter students can connect to campus network. Online course registration, online library, helpline, repair service, wireless network available.

Student life. **Freshman orientation:** Mandatory, $100 fee. Preregistration for classes offered. 2-day on-campus program in June. Parallel program for parents. **Housing:** Guaranteed on-campus for all undergraduates. Coed dorms, special housing for disabled, wellness housing available. $100 deposit, deadline 5/1. **Activities:** Campus ministries, choral groups, dance, drama, international student organizations, literary magazine, Model UN, student government, student newspaper, symphony orchestra, TV station, REACT (Rivier Environmental Activists), Amnesty International, Chinese student association, America Reads, Americorps, Habitat for Humanity.

Athletics. NCAA. **Intercollegiate:** Baseball M, basketball, cross-country, soccer, softball W, track and field, volleyball. **Intramural:** Basketball, soccer, softball, table tennis, volleyball, weight lifting. **Team name:** Raiders.

Student services. Adult student services, alcohol/substance abuse counseling, chaplain/spiritual director, career counseling, student employment services, financial aid counseling, health services, minority student services, on-campus daycare, personal counseling, placement for graduates.

Contact. E-mail: rivadmit@rivier.edu
Phone: (603) 897-8507 Toll-free number: (800) 447-4843
Fax: (603) 891-1799
David Boisvert, Vice President for Enrollment Management, Rivier College, 420 South Main Street, Nashua, NH 03060-5086

St. Anselm College

Manchester, New Hampshire — **CB member**
www.anselm.edu — **CB code: 3748**

- Private 4-year nursing and liberal arts college affiliated with Roman Catholic Church
- Residential campus in small city
- 1,879 degree-seeking undergraduates: 1% part-time, 58% women, 1% African American, 1% Asian American, 2% Hispanic American, 1% Native American, 1% international
- 70% of applicants admitted
- SAT or ACT (ACT writing optional), application essay required

General. Founded in 1889. Regionally accredited. Administered by Order of St. Benedict. **Degrees:** 426 bachelor's awarded. **ROTC:** Army, Air Force. **Location:** 50 miles from Boston. **Calendar:** Semester, limited summer session. **Full-time faculty:** 136 total; 95% have terminal degrees, 7% minority, 50% women. **Part-time faculty:** 65 total; 52% have terminal degrees, 5% minority, 54% women. **Class size:** 59% < 20, 38% 20-39, less than 1% 40-49, 2% 50-99, less than 1% >100. **Special facilities:** Observatory, institute of politics, ice arena, humanities and performing arts center, art center, Abbey Church.

Freshman class profile. 3,835 applied, 2,679 admitted, 501 enrolled.

Mid 50% test scores		**GPA 3.0-3.49:**	45%
SAT critical reading:	490-580	**GPA 2.0-2.99:**	35%
SAT math:	500-590	**Rank in top quarter:**	56%
SAT writing:	500-600	**Rank in top tenth:**	23%
ACT composite:	21-26	**Return as sophomores:**	85%
GPA 3.75 or higher:	7%	**Out-of-state:**	80%
GPA 3.50-3.74:	13%	**Live on campus:**	96%

Basis for selection. School achievement record and character most important, followed by test scores, 2 recommendations, essay. Interview recommended. **Homeschooled:** Statement describing homeschool structure and mission, interview, letter of recommendation (nonparent) required.

High school preparation. College-preparatory program required. 16 units required. Required and recommended units include English 4, mathematics 3-4, social studies 2, science 3-4 (laboratory 2) and foreign language 2-4.

2008-2009 Annual costs. Tuition/fees: $29,170. Room/board: $10,760. Books/supplies: $800.

2008-2009 Financial aid. **Need-based:** 439 full-time freshmen applied for aid; 360 were judged to have need; 360 of these received aid. Average need met was 84%. Average scholarship/grant was $16,099; average loan $5,091. 65% of total undergraduate aid awarded as scholarships/grants, 35% as loans/jobs. **Non-need-based:** Awarded to 460 full-time undergraduates, including 120 freshmen. Scholarships awarded for academics, athletics, state residency.

Application procedures. **Admission:** Priority date 3/1; no deadline. $55 fee, may be waived for applicants with need. Admission notification on a rolling basis beginning on or about 1/1. Must reply by May 1 or within 2 week(s) if notified thereafter. **Financial aid:** Closing date 3/15. FAFSA, CSS PROFILE required. Applicants notified on a rolling basis starting 3/10; must reply by 5/1.

Academics. 4-semester humanities program required of all students. Special studies certificates in addition to major concentrations available in fine arts (visual arts, theater, music), international studies, communications, computational physical science, human relations and work, French, Spanish, German, Latin, Greek, Russian area studies, Latin American studies, Asian studies, Catholic studies, medieval studies, neuroscience, public policy studies, web design. **Special study options:** Cross-registration, honors, independent study, internships, liberal arts/career combination, New York semester, semester at sea, study abroad, teacher certification program, Washington semester. **Credit/placement by examination:** AP, CLEP, IB, institutional tests. 30 credit hours maximum toward bachelor's degree. **Support services:** Learning center, reduced course load, study skills assistance, tutoring, writing center.

Majors. **Biology:** General, biochemistry. **Business:** General, accounting, finance, managerial economics. **Computer sciences:** Computer science. **Conservation:** Environmental science. **Engineering:** General, physics. **Foreign languages:** Classics, French, Spanish. **Health:** Nursing (RN), predental, premedicine. **History:** General. **Interdisciplinary:** Biological/physical sciences, math/computer science. **Legal studies:** Prelaw. **Liberal arts:** Arts/sciences. **Math:** General. **Philosophy/religion:** Philosophy. **Physical sciences:** Chemistry, physics. **Protective services:** Criminal justice. **Psychology:** General. **Social sciences:** Economics, international relations, political science, sociology. **Theology:** Theology. **Visual/performing arts:** Art.

Most popular majors. Biology 6%, business/marketing 25%, health sciences 15%, history 7%, psychology 7%, social sciences 23%.

Computing on campus. 400 workstations in dormitories, library, computer center, student center. Dormitories wired for high-speed internet access and linked to campus network. Commuter students can connect to campus network. Online course registration, online library, helpline, repair service, wireless network available.

Student life. **Freshman orientation:** Available, $25 fee. Preregistration for classes offered. Held 3 days prior to fall semester. **Housing:** Guaranteed on-campus for all undergraduates. Coed dorms, single-sex dorms, special housing for disabled, apartments, wellness housing available. $200 nonrefundable deposit, deadline 5/1. **Activities:** Bands, campus ministries, choral groups, dance, drama, film society, international student organizations, literary magazine, Model UN, musical theater, radio station, student government, student newspaper, TV station, Muslim student associations, black student alliance, Knights of Columbus, College Republicans, College Democrats, rugby club, Oxford Companions, volunteers center, music society, Radio Flyers.

Athletics. NCAA. **Intercollegiate:** Baseball M, basketball, cross-country, field hockey W, football (tackle) M, golf, ice hockey, lacrosse, skiing, soccer, softball W, tennis, volleyball W. **Intramural:** Basketball, football (non-tackle), handball, ice hockey, racquetball, skiing, soccer, softball, table tennis, tennis, volleyball. **Team name:** Hawks.

Student services. Alcohol/substance abuse counseling, chaplain/spiritual director, career counseling, student employment services, financial aid counseling, health services, minority student services, personal counseling, placement for graduates, veterans' counselor.

Contact. E-mail: admission@anselm.edu
Phone: (603) 641-7500 Toll-free number: (888) 426-7356
Fax: (603) 641-7550
Nancy Griffin, Dean of Admission, St. Anselm College, 100 Saint Anselm Drive, Manchester, NH 03102-1310

Southern New Hampshire University

Manchester, New Hampshire **CB member**
www.snhu.edu **CB code: 3649**

- Private 4-year university
- Residential campus in small city
- 2,024 degree-seeking undergraduates: 2% part-time, 54% women, 1% African American, 1% Asian American, 2% Hispanic American, 1% Native American, 4% international
- 1,786 degree-seeking graduate students
- 86% of applicants admitted
- SAT or ACT with writing, application essay required
- 55% graduate within 6 years

General. Founded in 1932. Regionally accredited. Continuing Education Centers in Manchester, Nashua, Salem, Seacoast, Brunswick (ME) and online. Graduate programs in Manchester, Nashua, Seacoast, Salem, Brunswick (ME), and online. **Degrees:** 1,034 bachelor's, 166 associate awarded; master's, doctoral offered. **ROTC:** Army, Air Force. **Location:** 55 miles from Boston. **Calendar:** Differs by program, extensive summer session. **Full-time faculty:** 132 total; 74% have terminal degrees, 11% minority, 39% women. **Part-time faculty:** 256 total; 40% women. **Class size:** 48% < 20, 52% 20-39. **Special facilities:** Culinary institute, financial studies center, advertising agency, audiovisual studio, psychology observation lab, career development center, iMAC graphics lab.

Freshman class profile. 3,124 applied, 2,685 admitted, 599 enrolled.

Mid 50% test scores			
SAT critical reading:	440-520	Rank in top quarter:	25%
SAT math:	440-540	Rank in top tenth:	8%
SAT writing:	430-530	Return as sophomores:	74%
ACT composite:	18-21	Out-of-state:	60%
GPA 3.75 or higher:	4%	Live on campus:	85%
GPA 3.50-3.74:	12%	International:	2%
GPA 3.0-3.49:	33%	Fraternities:	4%
GPA 2.0-2.99:	51%	Sororities:	3%

Basis for selection. High school academic record weighed most heavily, including courses and course levels, grades, and class rank (if applicable). SAT/ACT scores, extracurricular activities, work experience, recommendations, and essay also considered. Interview required for 3-year bachelor's program. Creative writing majors must submit samples of their original writing. Culinary Arts and Baking and Pastry Arts applicants not required to submit SAT or ACT scores. Interview recommended.

High school preparation. College-preparatory program required. 12 units required. Required units include English 4, mathematics 3, social studies 2, history 2, science 3 (laboratory 2) and foreign language 2.

2008-2009 Annual costs. Tuition/fees: $24,954. Room/board: $9,600. Books/supplies: $900. Personal expenses: $1,000.

2008-2009 Financial aid. Non-need-based: Scholarships awarded for academics, alumni affiliation, athletics, leadership, state residency.

Application procedures. Admission: Priority date 3/15; no deadline. $40 fee, may be waived for applicants with need. Admission notification on a rolling basis. Must reply by May 1 or within 4 week(s) if notified thereafter. **Financial aid:** Priority date 3/15; no closing date. FAFSA required. Applicants notified on a rolling basis starting 3/1; must reply within 3 week(s) of notification.

Academics. All undergraduate day students required to have laptop computer. **Special study options:** Accelerated study, combined bachelor's/graduate degree, cooperative education, distance learning, double major, dual enrollment of high school students, ESL, honors, independent study, internships, semester at sea, student-designed major, study abroad, teacher certification program, United Nations semester, Washington semester, weekend college. Three-year honors program in business administration. **Credit/placement by examination:** AP, CLEP, IB, institutional tests. 15 credit hours maximum toward associate degree, 15 toward bachelor's. **Support services:** Learning center, pre-admission summer program, reduced course load, remedial instruction, study skills assistance, tutoring.

Majors. Business: Accounting, business admin, hospitality admin, international, marketing, retailing, tourism/travel. **Communications:** General, advertising, digital media. **Computer sciences:** General. **Conservation:** Environmental studies. **Education:** General, business, early childhood, elementary, English, social studies. **Family/consumer sciences:** Child development. **History:** General. **Interdisciplinary:** Accounting/computer science. **Parks/recreation:** Sports admin. **Psychology:** General. **Public administration:** General. **Social sciences:** General, economics, political science. **Visual/performing arts:** Graphic design. **Other:** Justice Studies, Public Relations, Technical Management.

Most popular majors. Business/marketing 61%, education 6%, psychology 7%.

Computing on campus. PC or laptop required. 674 workstations in library, computer center. Dormitories wired for high-speed internet access and linked to campus network. Commuter students can connect to campus network. Online course registration, online library, helpline, repair service, wireless network available.

Student life. Freshman orientation: Mandatory, $150 fee. Preregistration for classes offered. Five 1-day sessions held in June; 3-day program held at the opening of the fall term. **Housing:** Guaranteed on-campus for all undergraduates. Coed dorms, special housing for disabled, apartments, wellness housing available. $200 fully refundable deposit, deadline 5/1. Women's floor and wellness housing. **Activities:** Campus ministries, choral groups, dance, drama, international student organizations, literary magazine, Model UN, musical theater, radio station, student government, student newspaper, TV station.

Athletics. NCAA. **Intercollegiate:** Baseball M, basketball, cheerleading, cross-country, golf M, ice hockey M, lacrosse, soccer, softball W, tennis, volleyball W. **Intramural:** Badminton, basketball, football (tackle), racquetball, skiing, soccer, softball, table tennis, tennis, volleyball W. **Team name:** Penmen.

Student services. Adult student services, alcohol/substance abuse counseling, chaplain/spiritual director, career counseling, student employment services, financial aid counseling, health services, personal counseling, placement for graduates, veterans' counselor. **Physically disabled:** Services for visually, speech, hearing impaired.

Contact. E-mail: admission@snhu.edu
Phone: (603) 645-9611 Toll-free number: (800) 642-4968
Fax: (603) 645-9693
Steve Soba, Director of Admission, Southern New Hampshire University, 2500 North River Road, Manchester, NH 03106-1045

Thomas More College of Liberal Arts

Merrimack, New Hampshire
www.thomasmorecollege.edu **CB code: 3892**

- Private 4-year liberal arts college affiliated with Roman Catholic Church
- Residential campus in large town
- 95 degree-seeking undergraduates
- 36% of applicants admitted
- SAT or ACT (ACT writing optional), application essay required

General. Founded in 1978. Regionally accredited. **Degrees:** 18 bachelor's awarded. **Location:** 45 miles from Boston. **Calendar:** Semester. **Full-time faculty:** 7 total. **Part-time faculty:** 4 total. **Class size:** 80% < 20, 10% 20-39, 10% 50-99.

Freshman class profile. 100 applied, 36 admitted, 25 enrolled.

Out-of-state:	96%	Live on campus:	90%

Basis for selection. Evidence of student's desire to learn important. Complete application includes essay, 2 academic letters of recommendation, high school transcript, and SAT or ACT scores. Interviews and/or visits are strongly recommended.

High school preparation. 17 units required. Required units include English 4, mathematics 3, social studies 2, history 2, science 2 (laboratory 2) and foreign language 2. Recommended languages: Latin, French, German, Greek. Recommended electives: music, art.

2008-2009 Annual costs. Tuition/fees: $13,200. Room/board: $8,800. Books/supplies: $350. Personal expenses: $150.

2008-2009 Financial aid. Non-need-based: Scholarships awarded for academics.

Application procedures. Admission: No deadline. No application fee. **Financial aid:** Priority date 5/1; no closing date. FAFSA required. Applicants notified on a rolling basis starting 5/15; must reply within 2 week(s) of notification.

Academics. Each student, regardless of major, takes 6-hour humanities course every semester throughout 4 years: philosophy, literature, politics, history, theology taught by faculty from various disciplines. **Special study**

options: Independent study, study abroad. Sophomore semester in Rome. **Credit/placement by examination:** CLEP. **Support services:** Tutoring.

Majors. Biology: General. **Philosophy/religion:** Philosophy. **Social sciences:** Political science.

Most popular majors. English 43%, philosophy/religious studies 21%, social sciences 36%.

Computing on campus. 7 workstations in library.

Student life. Freshman orientation: Mandatory. **Policies:** Students are responsible, in main part, for care of campus. **Housing:** Guaranteed on-campus for all undergraduates. Single-sex dorms available. **Activities:** Choral groups, drama.

Student services. Chaplain/spiritual director, career counseling, financial aid counseling, personal counseling.

Contact. E-mail: admissions@thomasmorecollege.edu
Phone: (603) 880-8308 ext. 14 Toll-free number: (800) 880-8308 ext. 14
Fax: (603) 880-9280
Jessica Rock, Director of Admissions, Thomas More College of Liberal Arts, Six Manchester Street, Merrimack, NH 03054-4818

University of New Hampshire

Durham, New Hampshire — **CB member**
www.unh.edu — **CB code: 3918**

- Public 4-year university
- Residential campus in small town
- 11,845 degree-seeking undergraduates: 2% part-time, 56% women, 1% African American, 2% Asian American, 2% Hispanic American, 1% international
- 2,359 degree-seeking graduate students
- 65% of applicants admitted
- SAT or ACT with writing, application essay required
- 72% graduate within 6 years

General. Founded in 1866. Regionally accredited. **Degrees:** 2,377 bachelor's, 141 associate awarded; master's, doctoral offered. **ROTC:** Army, Air Force. **Location:** 50 miles from Boston, 50 miles from Portland, ME. **Calendar:** Semester, extensive summer session. **Full-time faculty:** 708 total; 83% have terminal degrees, 9% minority, 36% women. **Part-time faculty:** 377 total; 16% have terminal degrees, 1% minority, 60% women. **Class size:** 44% < 20, 35% 20-39, 6% 40-49, 10% 50-99, 6% >100. **Special facilities:** Journalism laboratory, optical observatory, marine research laboratory, experiential learning center, child development center, agricultural and equine facilities, electron microscope, sawmill, nature preserve.

Freshman class profile. 16,246 applied, 10,592 admitted, 2,692 enrolled.

Mid 50% test scores		**Return as sophomores:**	89%
SAT critical reading:	510-610	**Out-of-state:**	54%
SAT math:	520-620	**Live on campus:**	92%
Rank in top quarter:	75%	**Fraternities:**	6%
Rank in top tenth:	24%	**Sororities:**	9%
End year in good standing:	93%		

Basis for selection. School achievement record most important, followed by course selection, class rank, recommendations, test scores. Co-curricular activities, character/leadership considered. SAT Subject Tests can satisfy a foreign language requirement for students in a BA program. Audition required for music programs. **Homeschooled:** Supporting documents include GED scores, transcripts, education plans, syllabi, SAT or ACT scores, homeschool association information.

High school preparation. College-preparatory program required. 17 units required; 22 recommended. Required and recommended units include English 4, mathematics 3-4, social studies 3, science 3-4 (laboratory 2-3), foreign language 2-3 and visual/performing arts 1. Additional requirements determined by intended major.

2008-2009 Annual costs. Tuition/fees: $11,756; $25,236 out-of-state. New England Regional Student Program tuition 175% of in-state public institution tuition. College of Earth and Physical Science charges an extra $748 per year. Whittemore School of Business charges an extra $733 per year. Music majors must pay an additional $800 per year. Room/board: $8,596. Books/supplies: $1,400. Personal expenses: $2,105.

2007-2008 Financial aid. Need-based: 2,030 full-time freshmen applied for aid; 1,516 were judged to have need; 1,485 of these received aid. Average need met was 84%. Average scholarship/grant was $4,122; average loan $2,841. 46% of total undergraduate aid awarded as scholarships/grants, 54% as loans/jobs. **Non-need-based:** Awarded to 2,905 full-time undergraduates, including 579 freshmen. Scholarships awarded for academics, art, athletics, leadership, music/drama, ROTC.

Application procedures. Admission: Closing date 2/1 (postmark date). $50 fee ($65 out-of-state), may be waived for applicants with need. Admission notification 4/15. Admission notification on a rolling basis beginning on or about 11/15. Must reply by 5/1. **Financial aid:** Closing date 3/1. FAFSA required. Applicants notified on a rolling basis starting 3/1.

Academics. General education requirement has 8 components. Students admitted as freshmen or as freshmen transfers must complete 4 writing intensive courses. **Special study options:** Combined bachelor's/graduate degree, cross-registration, double major, ESL, exchange student, honors, independent study, internships, semester at sea, student-designed major, study abroad, teacher certification program, Washington semester. Undergraduate research opportunities, International Undergraduate Opportunities Program. **Credit/placement by examination:** AP, CLEP, IB, institutional tests. 32 credit hours maximum toward associate degree, 64 toward bachelor's. **Support services:** Learning center, reduced course load, study skills assistance, tutoring, writing center.

Majors. Agriculture: Agronomy, animal sciences, business, dairy, dairy husbandry, equestrian studies, food science, horticultural science, plant sciences. **Architecture:** Urban/community planning. **Area/ethnic studies:** European, French, Western European, women's. **Biology:** General, bacteriology, biochemistry, microbiology, plant molecular, plant physiology, zoology. **Business:** General, accounting, business admin, entrepreneurial studies, finance, hospitality admin, hotel/motel admin, tourism/travel. **Communications:** General, digital media, journalism, media studies. **Computer sciences:** General, computer science. **Conservation:** General, economics, environmental science, environmental studies, forestry, wildlife. **Education:** Art, English, mathematics, music, science. **Engineering:** General, chemical, civil, computer, electrical, environmental, materials, materials science, mechanical, ocean. **Family/consumer sciences:** Child development, family studies, family/community services, food/nutrition, human nutrition. **Foreign languages:** Ancient Greek, classics, French, German, Latin, linguistics, modern Greek, Russian, Spanish. **Health:** Athletic training, clinical lab science, clinical lab technology, clinical nutrition, communication disorders, dietetics, health care admin, nursing (RN), recreational therapy, speech pathology. **History:** General. **Interdisciplinary:** Global studies, natural sciences. **Liberal arts:** Humanities. **Math:** General, applied. **Parks/recreation:** General, exercise sciences. **Personal/culinary services:** Restaurant/catering. **Philosophy/religion:** Philosophy. **Physical sciences:** Chemistry, geology, physics. **Psychology:** General. **Public administration:** Social work. **Social sciences:** Anthropology, criminology, economics, international relations, political science, sociology. **Visual/performing arts:** Music performance, music theory/composition, studio arts.

Most popular majors. Biology 6%, business/marketing 16%, communications/journalism 6%, engineering/engineering technologies 6%, English 7%, health sciences 9%, parks/recreation 6%, psychology 9%, social sciences 11%.

Computing on campus. 345 workstations in library, computer center, student center. Dormitories wired for high-speed internet access and linked to campus network. Commuter students can connect to campus network. Online course registration, online library, helpline, repair service, student web hosting, wireless network available.

Student life. Freshman orientation: Mandatory. Preregistration for classes offered. Two-day program held in June with additional session in fall. A minority student orientation is also offered. **Housing:** Guaranteed on-campus for freshmen. Coed dorms, single-sex dorms, apartments, fraternity/sorority housing, wellness housing available. $200 partly refundable deposit, deadline 5/1. **Activities:** Bands, campus ministries, choral groups, dance, drama, film society, international student organizations, literary magazine, music ensembles, Model UN, musical theater, radio station, student government, student newspaper, symphony orchestra, TV station, Diversity Support Coalition, Black student union, Indian student association, United Asian Coalition, Chinese Students and Scholars Association, Intervarsity Christian Fellowship, Young Life, Catholic student organization, College Democrats, College Republicans.

Athletics. NCAA. **Intercollegiate:** Basketball, cross-country, diving W, field hockey W, football (tackle) M, gymnastics W, ice hockey, lacrosse W, skiing, soccer, swimming W, track and field, volleyball W. **Intramural:** Basketball, field hockey W, football (non-tackle), ice hockey, racquetball, soccer, softball, table tennis, tennis, volleyball. **Team name:** Wildcats.

Student services. Adult student services, alcohol/substance abuse counseling, chaplain/spiritual director, career counseling, services for economically disadvantaged, student employment services, financial aid counseling,

health services, legal services, minority student services, on-campus daycare, personal counseling, placement for graduates, veterans' counselor, women's services. **Physically disabled:** Services for visually, speech, hearing impaired.

Contact. E-mail: admissions@unh.edu
Phone: (603) 862-1360 Fax: (603) 862-0077
Robert McGann, Director of Admissions, University of New Hampshire, Grant House, Durham, NH 03824

University of New Hampshire at Manchester

Manchester, New Hampshire — **CB member**
www.unhm.unh.edu — **CB code: 2094**

- Public 4-year university and liberal arts college
- Commuter campus in small city
- 792 degree-seeking undergraduates
- 72% of applicants admitted
- SAT or ACT (ACT writing optional), application essay required

General. Founded in 1985. Regionally accredited. **Degrees:** 141 bachelor's, 24 associate awarded; master's offered. **ROTC:** Army, Air Force. **Location:** 55 miles from Boston, 35 miles from Concord. **Calendar:** Semester, limited summer session. **Full-time faculty:** 36 total. **Part-time faculty:** 104 total.

Freshman class profile. 257 applied, 186 admitted, 109 enrolled.

Mid 50% test scores			
SAT critical reading:	450-550	**SAT writing:**	450-540
SAT math:	450-550	**Out-of-state:**	1%

Basis for selection. Achievement in high school college preparatory program most important. SAT scores should be consistent with achievement. Recommendation, essay, interview very helpful for students of moderate achievement or in nontraditional cases. Non-native speakers of English must submit TOEFL scores. Interview necessary for college transition program. **Homeschooled:** Transcript of courses and grades, state high school equivalency certificate, letter of recommendation (nonparent) required. Encourage GED, SAT, syllabus of curriculum; diploma from homeschool association if available. **Learning Disabled:** To be eligible for services students must provide documentation of their disability as determined by a licensed physician and /or certified psychologist who is skilled in the diagnosis of such disability. This documentation must be current (generally within three years). Detailed guidelines are available at the UNHM Academic Counseling office.

High school preparation. College-preparatory program recommended. Required and recommended units include English 4, mathematics 3-4, social studies 2, science 3-4 (laboratory 3) and foreign language 2-3.

2008-2009 Annual costs. Tuition/fees: $9,291; $23,051 out-of-state. New England Regional Student tuition 150% of in-state public institution tuition. Books/supplies: $700. Personal expenses: $2,020.

2008-2009 Financial aid. **Non-need-based:** Scholarships awarded for academics, state residency.

Application procedures. **Admission:** Priority date 4/1; deadline 6/15 (postmark date). $45 fee ($60 out-of-state), may be waived for applicants with need. Admission notification on a rolling basis. Must reply by May 1 or within 3 week(s) if notified thereafter. **Financial aid:** Closing date 3/1. FAFSA required. Applicants notified on a rolling basis starting 4/1; must reply within 2 week(s) of notification.

Academics. **Special study options:** Combined bachelor's/graduate degree, cross-registration, double major, ESL, exchange student, external degree, independent study, internships, semester at sea, student-designed major, study abroad, teacher certification program, Washington semester. **Credit/placement by examination:** AP, CLEP, IB, institutional tests. 48 credit hours maximum toward associate degree, 64 toward bachelor's. ACT, PEP exams accepted to RN Baccalaureate program. **Support services:** Learning center, pre-admission summer program, reduced course load, remedial instruction, study skills assistance, tutoring, writing center.

Majors. **Biology:** General. **Business:** Business admin. **Communications:** General. **Computer sciences:** General. **Engineering technology:** Electrical. **Foreign languages:** Sign language interpretation. **History:** General. **Liberal arts:** Arts/sciences, humanities. **Psychology:** General. **Social sciences:** Political science.

Computing on campus. 64 workstations in library, computer center. Commuter students can connect to campus network. Online library, helpline, wireless network available.

Student life. **Freshman orientation:** Mandatory, $30 fee. Preregistration for classes offered. 3-day (or evening) program held in June, August, and January. June attendees able to preregister for fall courses. **Housing:** Students may reside in dormitories at New Hampshire Institute of Art. **Activities:** Student government, student newspaper.

Athletics. **Team name:** Wildcats.

Student services. Career counseling, financial aid counseling, veterans' counselor. **Physically disabled:** Services for visually, speech, hearing impaired.

Contact. E-mail: unhm.admissions@unh.edu
Phone: (603) 641-4150 Fax: (603) 641-4342
Miho Bean, Associate Director of Admissions, University of New Hampshire at Manchester, 400 Commercial Street, Manchester, NH 03101-1113

New Jersey

Berkeley College

Woodland Park, New Jersey **CB member**
www.berkeleycollege.edu **CB code: 2061**

- For-profit 4-year business college
- Commuter campus in large town
- 3,435 degree-seeking undergraduates: 14% part-time, 72% women, 25% African American, 5% Asian American, 36% Hispanic American, 1% Native American, 2% international
- 41% graduate within 6 years

General. Founded in 1931. Regionally accredited. Branch campuses in Paramus, Newark, and Woodbridge. **Degrees:** 302 bachelor's, 272 associate awarded. **Location:** 20 miles from New York City. **Calendar:** Quarter, extensive summer session. **Full-time faculty:** 64 total. **Part-time faculty:** 145 total. **Class size:** 36% < 20, 64% 20-39, less than 1% 40-49.

Freshman class profile.

Return as sophomores:	50%	**Out-of-state:**	2%

Basis for selection. Class rank, high school record, interview most important. Passing grade on school entrance/placement exam required. Interviews strongly recommended.

2009-2010 Annual costs. Tuition/fees: $19,950. Room/board: $10,050. Books/supplies: $1,360. Personal expenses: $3,000.

Financial aid. Non-need-based: Scholarships awarded for academics, alumni affiliation. **Additional information:** Alumni scholarship examination given in November and December. Full and partial scholarships awarded.

Application procedures. Admission: No deadline. $50 fee. Admission notification on a rolling basis. Admitted applicants must reply within 2 weeks of notification. **Financial aid:** No deadline. FAFSA required. Applicants notified on a rolling basis starting 3/1; must reply within 6 week(s) of notification.

Academics. Special study options: Accelerated study, distance learning, internships, New York semester, study abroad. **Credit/placement by examination:** AP, CLEP, SAT, ACT, institutional tests. **Support services:** Learning center, remedial instruction, study skills assistance, tutoring, writing center.

Majors. Business: Accounting, business admin, fashion, financial planning, international, marketing. **Health:** Health care admin. **Protective services:** Law enforcement admin. **Other:** Interior design management.

Computing on campus. 358 workstations in library, computer center, student center. Dormitories linked to campus network. Commuter students can connect to campus network. Online library, helpline, wireless network available.

Student life. Freshman orientation: Mandatory. **Housing:** Coed dorms available. $400 deposit. **Activities:** Choral groups, literary magazine, student government, Phi Beta Lambda, paralegal club, interior design club, athletic club, fashion and marketing club, Phi Theta Kappa.

Athletics. Team name: Bulldogs.

Student services. Adult student services, alcohol/substance abuse counseling, career counseling, student employment services, financial aid counseling, on-campus daycare, personal counseling, placement for graduates.

Contact. E-mail: info@berkeleycollege.edu
Phone: (973) 278-5400 ext. 1210 Toll-free number: (800) 446-5400
Fax: (973) 278-9141
Susan Costello, Director for High School Admissions, Berkeley College, 44 Rifle Camp Road, Woodland Park, NJ 07424-0440

Beth Medrash Govoha

Lakewood, New Jersey
CB code: 2166

- Private 4-year rabbinical college for men affiliated with Jewish faith
- Residential campus in small city

General. Founded in 1943. Accredited by AARTS. **Calendar:** Semester.

Annual costs/financial aid. Tuition/fees (2008-2009): $14,228. Room/board: $4,172. Books/supplies: $450.

Contact. Phone: (732) 367-1060
Director of Admissions, 617 Sixth Street, Lakewood, NJ 08701

Bloomfield College

Bloomfield, New Jersey **CB member**
www.bloomfield.edu **CB code: 2044**

- Private 4-year liberal arts and teachers college affiliated with Presbyterian Church (USA)
- Commuter campus in large town
- 2,002 degree-seeking undergraduates: 21% part-time, 66% women, 50% African American, 4% Asian American, 21% Hispanic American, 1% international
- 29% of applicants admitted
- SAT or ACT (ACT writing optional), application essay required

General. Founded in 1868. Regionally accredited. **Degrees:** 277 bachelor's awarded. **ROTC:** Army. **Location:** 7 miles from Newark, 15 miles from New York City. **Calendar:** Semester, limited summer session. **Full-time faculty:** 70 total; 74% have terminal degrees, 21% minority, 60% women. **Part-time faculty:** 172 total; 17% have terminal degrees, 39% minority, 50% women. **Class size:** 78% < 20, 21% 20-39, less than 1% 40-49, less than 1% 50-99, less than 1% >100. **Special facilities:** Technology and multimedia center.

Freshman class profile. 2,690 applied, 767 admitted, 426 enrolled.

Mid 50% test scores		**GPA 2.0-2.99:**	69%
SAT critical reading:	370-450	**Rank in top quarter:**	12%
SAT math:	360-450	**End year in good standing:**	84%
GPA 3.75 or higher:	1%	**Return as sophomores:**	67%
GPA 3.50-3.74:	4%	**Out-of-state:**	4%
GPA 3.0-3.49:	19%	**Live on campus:**	38%

Basis for selection. Acceptance for regular admission requires 900 SAT (exclusive of Writing) and 2.7 GPA. Interviews not required but strongly recommended. Essays must be self-recommendations or reflections on previous educational experiences. Recent graded term paper can be substituted for essay. **Homeschooled:** Transcript of courses and grades, state high school equivalency certificate, interview, letter of recommendation (nonparent) required. Applicants must submit SAT scores and official transcript with information about organization that performed accreditation/conversion. **Learning Disabled:** Students must meet regular admission requirements, and should ask for special accommodations for SAT testing.

High school preparation. College-preparatory program required. 14 units required.

2008-2009 Annual costs. Tuition/fees: $20,080. Room/board: $9,500. Books/supplies: $850. Personal expenses: $1,543.

2008-2009 Financial aid. Need-based: 395 full-time freshmen applied for aid; 367 were judged to have need; 366 of these received aid. Average need met was 68%. Average scholarship/grant was $15,203; average loan $6,888. 69% of total undergraduate aid awarded as scholarships/grants, 31% as loans/jobs. **Non-need-based:** Awarded to 630 full-time undergraduates, including 190 freshmen. Scholarships awarded for academics, alumni affiliation, athletics, leadership, religious affiliation.

Application procedures. Admission: Priority date 3/14; deadline 8/1 (receipt date). $40 fee, may be waived for applicants with need. Admission notification on a rolling basis beginning on or about 10/1. **Financial aid:** Priority date 3/15, closing date 6/1. FAFSA required. Applicants notified on a rolling basis starting 3/1; must reply within 2 week(s) of notification.

Academics. Organized into 7 divisions: Business and Computer Information Systems, Creative Arts and Technology, Humanities, Natural Science and Mathematics, Nursing, and Social and Behavioral Sciences, and Education. **Special study options:** Accelerated study, distance learning, double major, dual enrollment of high school students, ESL, honors, independent study, internships, liberal arts/career combination, student-designed major, study abroad, teacher certification program, weekend college. Four-year clinical laboratory science program and allied health technologies major offered in conjunction with University of Medicine and Dentistry of New Jersey; joint BS/MS in computer information systems program offered with NJIT; special programs offered by the Institute for Technology and Professional Studies. **Credit/placement by examination:** AP, CLEP, institutional tests. 16 credit hours maximum toward bachelor's degree. Maximum of 16 course units may be earned through CLEP examinations, portfolio assessment, and nursing assessment. **Support services:** Learning center, remedial instruction, study skills assistance, tutoring, writing center.

Majors. **Biology:** General. **Business:** Accounting, business admin, e-commerce. **Computer sciences:** General, networking. **Education:** General. **Health:** Nursing (RN). **History:** General. **Math:** General, applied. **Philosophy/religion:** Philosophy, religion. **Physical sciences:** Chemistry. **Psychology:** General. **Social sciences:** Political science, sociology. **Visual/performing arts:** General. **Other:** Allied health technologies.

Most popular majors. Biology 6%, business/marketing 21%, education 7%, English 7%, health sciences 10%, psychology 12%, social sciences 13%, visual/performing arts 15%.

Computing on campus. 100 workstations in dormitories, library, computer center, student center. Dormitories wired for high-speed internet access and linked to campus network. Commuter students can connect to campus network. Online library, helpline, student web hosting, wireless network available.

Student life. **Freshman orientation:** Available. Preregistration for classes offered. Multi-day sessions offered prior to beginning of fall semester. **Policies:** Statement of Shared Values adopted, addressing student conduct and standards for behavior. **Housing:** Coed dorms available. $100 fully refundable deposit, deadline 5/1. **Activities:** Choral groups, dance, drama, international student organizations, literary magazine, radio station, student government, African Student Association, Association of Latin American Students, Team Infinite, Sisters in Support, Christian Fellowship, Caribbean Student Association.

Athletics. NCAA. **Intercollegiate:** Baseball M, basketball, cross-country, soccer, softball W, tennis M, volleyball W. **Intramural:** Basketball, volleyball M. **Team name:** Deacons.

Student services. Adult student services, alcohol/substance abuse counseling, chaplain/spiritual director, career counseling, student employment services, financial aid counseling, health services, personal counseling, placement for graduates. **Physically disabled:** Services for visually, speech, hearing impaired. **Learning disabled:** Comprehensive services available.

Contact. E-mail: admission@bloomfield.edu
Phone: (973) 748-9000 ext. 230 Toll-free number: (800) 848-4555
Fax: (973) 748-0916
Adam Castro, Director of Admissions, Bloomfield College, One Park Place, Bloomfield, NJ 07003

Caldwell College

Caldwell, New Jersey — **CB member**
www.caldwell.edu — **CB code: 2072**

- Private 4-year liberal arts college affiliated with Roman Catholic Church
- Commuter campus in large town
- 1,668 degree-seeking undergraduates
- 606 graduate students
- 60% of applicants admitted
- SAT or ACT with writing, application essay required

General. Founded in 1939. Regionally accredited. **Degrees:** 239 bachelor's awarded; master's offered. **ROTC:** Army. **Location:** 20 miles from New York City. **Calendar:** Semester, limited summer session. **Full-time faculty:** 83 total. **Part-time faculty:** 119 total. **Class size:** 79% < 20, 21% 20-39.

Freshman class profile. 1,850 applied, 1,106 admitted, 290 enrolled.

Mid 50% test scores		**Rank in top tenth:**	10%
SAT critical reading:	440-550	**Out-of-state:**	7%
SAT math:	430-570	**Live on campus:**	56%
Rank in top quarter:	23%		

Basis for selection. Class rank in top half, school achievement record, test scores, interview, extracurricular activities very important. Counselor's recommendation, volunteer work important. Essay, interview recommended for all, audition required for music programs, portfolio required for art programs.

High school preparation. 16 units required. Required units include English 4, mathematics 2, history 1, science 2 (laboratory 1), foreign language 2 and academic electives 5.

2008-2009 Annual costs. Tuition/fees: $23,600. Room/board: $9,650. Books/supplies: $1,200. Personal expenses: $1,000.

2008-2009 Financial aid. **Non-need-based:** Scholarships awarded for academics, alumni affiliation, art, athletics, leadership, music/drama, religious affiliation.

Application procedures. **Admission:** Priority date 12/1; no deadline. $40 fee, may be waived for applicants with need. Admission notification on a rolling basis beginning on or about 12/31. Must reply by May 1 or within 2 week(s) if notified thereafter. **Financial aid:** Priority date 4/1; no closing date. FAFSA, institutional form required. Applicants notified on a rolling basis starting 3/1; must reply within 4 week(s) of notification.

Academics. **Special study options:** Accelerated study, combined bachelor's/graduate degree, cooperative education, distance learning, double major, ESL, external degree, honors, independent study, internships, liberal arts/career combination, student-designed major, study abroad, teacher certification program, Washington semester, weekend college. Offers affiliation programs with institutions such as New York University, Columbia University, Temple University, UMDNJ and others where students earn bachelor's degree, typically in biology, and professional degree from the affiliated school. **Credit/placement by examination:** AP, CLEP, IB, institutional tests. 30 credit hours maximum toward bachelor's degree. Credit by exam only available during first year (30 credits) of matriculation. Credit toward major dependent on departmental approval. Prior Learning Assessment (PLA) for adult students who must attend PLA workshop. **Support services:** Learning center, pre-admission summer program, remedial instruction, study skills assistance, tutoring, writing center.

Majors. **Biology:** General. **Business:** Accounting, business admin, international, management science, marketing. **Communications:** General. **Computer sciences:** General, computer science. **Education:** Elementary. **Foreign languages:** French, Spanish. **Health:** Clinical lab technology. **History:** General. **Math:** General. **Physical sciences:** Chemistry. **Protective services:** Criminal justice. **Psychology:** General. **Social sciences:** General, political science, sociology. **Theology:** Theology. **Visual/performing arts:** Art, studio arts.

Most popular majors. Business/marketing 20%, communications/journalism 8%, education 12%, psychology 13%, security/protective services 9%.

Computing on campus. 210 workstations in dormitories, library, computer center, student center. Dormitories wired for high-speed internet access and linked to campus network. Commuter students can connect to campus network. Online course registration, online library, helpline, student web hosting, wireless network available.

Student life. **Freshman orientation:** Mandatory, $200 fee. Preregistration for classes offered. Held Sunday and Monday prior to beginning of classes in August. **Housing:** Guaranteed on-campus for all undergraduates. Coed dorms, wellness housing available. $200 nonrefundable deposit, deadline 5/1. **Activities:** Jazz band, campus ministries, choral groups, drama, international student organizations, literary magazine, music ensembles, musical theater, student government, student newspaper, Circle K, black students cooperative union, Latin American student association, Portuguese club, Irish club.

Athletics. NCAA. **Intercollegiate:** Baseball M, basketball, cross-country W, golf M, soccer, softball W, tennis. **Intramural:** Basketball, football (non-tackle), soccer, softball, volleyball. **Team name:** Cougars.

Student services. Adult student services, alcohol/substance abuse counseling, chaplain/spiritual director, career counseling, services for economically disadvantaged, student employment services, financial aid counseling, health services, minority student services, personal counseling, placement for graduates, women's services. **Physically disabled:** Services for visually, hearing impaired.

Contact. E-mail: admissions@caldwell.edu
Phone: (973) 618-3500 Toll-free number: (888) 864-9516
Fax: (973) 618-3600
Kathryn Reilly, Executive Director of Admissions and Financial Aid, Caldwell College, 9 Ryerson Avenue, Caldwell, NJ 07006-6195

Centenary College

Hackettstown, New Jersey — **CB member**
www.centenarycollege.edu — **CB code: 2080**

- Private 4-year liberal arts college affiliated with United Methodist Church
- Residential campus in large town
- 2,283 degree-seeking undergraduates: 8% part-time, 65% women, 10% African American, 1% Asian American, 8% Hispanic American, 1% international
- 978 degree-seeking graduate students

- 64% of applicants admitted
- SAT or ACT, application essay required
- 51% graduate within 6 years

General. Founded in 1867. Regionally accredited. **Degrees:** 371 bachelor's, 80 associate awarded; master's offered. **Location:** 55 miles from New York City. **Calendar:** Semester, limited summer session. **Full-time faculty:** 68 total; 56% have terminal degrees, 7% minority, 50% women. **Part-time faculty:** 279 total; 49% women. **Class size:** 60% < 20, 39% 20-39, 1% 40-49. **Special facilities:** Textile laboratory, equestrian center.

Freshman class profile. 1,188 applied, 755 admitted, 310 enrolled.

Mid 50% test scores		**GPA 2.0-2.99:**	70%
SAT critical reading:	410-490	**Rank in top quarter:**	28%
SAT math:	410-490	**Rank in top tenth:**	11%
SAT writing:	400-500	**Return as sophomores:**	80%
ACT composite:	15-23	**Out-of-state:**	21%
GPA 3.75 or higher:	2%	**Live on campus:**	84%
GPA 3.50-3.74:	5%	**Fraternities:**	1%
GPA 3.0-3.49:	20%	**Sororities:**	1%

Basis for selection. School achievement record, standardized test scores most important. Interview, recommendations, community activities also strongly considered. Interviews required for academically marginal students with special needs; recommended for others. Portfolio required for art and design, graphic arts majors. **Homeschooled:** State high school equivalency certificate required. **Learning Disabled:** Interview with Director of Services, documentation of psycho-education evaluation and IEP required for supportive services programs.

High school preparation. College-preparatory program required. 16 units required; 20 recommended. Required and recommended units include English 4, mathematics 3-4, social studies 2, science 2-4 (laboratory 1-2) and foreign language 2. Major-related courses on high school level recommended.

2008-2009 Annual costs. Tuition/fees: $24,930. Additional fees required for equine majors and for comprehensive learning support program. Laptop computers provided to all full-time undergraduate students. Room/board: $8,900. Books/supplies: $1,200. Personal expenses: $850.

2007-2008 Financial aid. **Need-based:** 263 full-time freshmen applied for aid; 224 were judged to have need; 223 of these received aid. Average need met was 75%. Average scholarship/grant was $13,812; average loan $5,558. 45% of total undergraduate aid awarded as scholarships/grants, 55% as loans/jobs. **Non-need-based:** Awarded to 398 full-time undergraduates, including 140 freshmen. Scholarships awarded for academics, alumni affiliation, art, leadership, minority status, music/drama, religious affiliation, state residency.

Application procedures. **Admission:** Priority date 3/1; no deadline. $30 fee ($30 out-of-state), may be waived for applicants with need, free for online applicants. Admission notification on a rolling basis beginning on or about 12/15. Must reply by May 1 or within 4 week(s) if notified thereafter. **Financial aid:** Priority date 4/1, closing date 6/1. FAFSA required. Applicants notified on a rolling basis starting 3/1.

Academics. Core curriculum required. Educational program balances career and liberal arts. **Special study options:** Accelerated study, combined bachelor's/graduate degree, cross-registration, distance learning, double major, dual enrollment of high school students, ESL, exchange student, honors, independent study, internships, liberal arts/career combination, student-designed major, study abroad, teacher certification program, weekend college. **Credit/placement by examination:** AP, CLEP, IB. 15 credit hours maximum toward associate degree, 30 toward bachelor's. **Support services:** Learning center, pre-admission summer program, reduced course load, remedial instruction, study skills assistance, tutoring, writing center.

Majors. **Agriculture:** Equestrian studies. **Biology:** General. **Business:** Accounting, business admin. **Communications:** General. **Computer sciences:** General. **Education:** General. **History:** General. **Math:** General. **Protective services:** Criminal justice. **Psychology:** General. **Social sciences:** Political science, sociology. **Visual/performing arts:** Commercial/advertising art, dramatic, fashion design.

Most popular majors. Business/marketing 39%, English 10%, psychology 9%, social sciences 10%, visual/performing arts 6%.

Computing on campus. PC or laptop required. 750 workstations in dormitories, library, computer center. Dormitories wired for high-speed internet access and linked to campus network. Commuter students can connect to campus network. Online course registration, online library, helpline, repair service, wireless network available.

Student life. **Freshman orientation:** Mandatory. Preregistration for classes offered. Three-day orientation prior to start of classes. **Housing:** Coed dorms, single-sex dorms, special housing for disabled, apartments available. $150 deposit, deadline 5/1. **Activities:** Campus ministries, choral groups, dance, drama, film society, international student organizations, literary magazine, Model UN, musical theater, radio station, student government, student newspaper, TV station, art guild, student activities committee, service groups, fashion group, academic clubs, professional and honor societies, special interest clubs, Students in Free Enterprise.

Athletics. NCAA. **Intercollegiate:** Baseball M, basketball, cross-country, equestrian, golf, lacrosse, soccer, softball W, volleyball W, wrestling M. **Intramural:** Basketball M, equestrian M. **Team name:** Cyclones.

Student services. Adult student services, alcohol/substance abuse counseling, chaplain/spiritual director, career counseling, services for economically disadvantaged, student employment services, financial aid counseling, health services, minority student services, personal counseling, placement for graduates, women's services. **Learning disabled:** Comprehensive services available.

Contact. E-mail: admissions@centenarycollege.edu
Phone: (908) 852-1400 ext. 2217 Toll-free number: (800) 236-8679
Fax: (908) 852-3454
Diane Finnan, Vice President for Enrollment Management and Strategic Branding, Centenary College, 400 Jefferson Street, Hackettstown, NJ 07840-9989

The College of New Jersey

Ewing, New Jersey
www.tcnj.edu **CB code: 2519**

- Public 4-year liberal arts college
- Residential campus in large town
- 6,194 degree-seeking undergraduates: 2% part-time, 59% women, 7% African American, 6% Asian American, 9% Hispanic American
- 462 degree-seeking graduate students
- 42% of applicants admitted
- SAT or ACT (ACT writing optional), application essay required
- 85% graduate within 6 years; 27% enter graduate study

General. Founded in 1855. Regionally accredited. **Degrees:** 1,418 bachelor's awarded; master's offered. **ROTC:** Army, Air Force. **Location:** 35 miles from Philadelphia. **Calendar:** Semester, limited summer session. **Full-time faculty:** 343 total; 87% have terminal degrees, 22% minority, 48% women. **Part-time faculty:** 403 total; 21% have terminal degrees, 8% minority, 54% women. **Class size:** 41% < 20, 55% 20-39, 4% 40-49, less than 1% 50-99. **Special facilities:** Concert hall, electron microscopy lab, nuclear magnetic resonance lab, optical spectroscopy lab, observatory, planetarium, greenhouse.

Freshman class profile. 9,692 applied, 4,112 admitted, 1,295 enrolled.

Mid 50% test scores		**Rank in top tenth:**	66%
SAT critical reading:	560-660	**Return as sophomores:**	95%
SAT math:	590-690	**Out-of-state:**	8%
SAT writing:	570-670	**Live on campus:**	95%
Rank in top quarter:	90%		

Basis for selection. Standardized test scores, high school rank and choice of curriculum very important. Extracurricular service, activities and community involvement considered. Audition required for music; portfolio required for art. **Homeschooled:** Statement describing homeschool structure and mission, transcript of courses and grades, state high school equivalency certificate, letter of recommendation (nonparent) required.

High school preparation. College-preparatory program recommended. 18 units required; 20 recommended. Required and recommended units include English 4, mathematics 3, social studies 2-3, science 3 (laboratory 2-3) and foreign language 2-3.

2008-2009 Annual costs. Tuition/fees: $12,308; $20,415 out-of-state. Room/board: $9,612. Books/supplies: $1,000. Personal expenses: $1,500.

2008-2009 Financial aid. **Need-based:** 1,124 full-time freshmen applied for aid; 633 were judged to have need; 596 of these received aid. Average need met was 47%. Average scholarship/grant was $14,125; average loan $3,285. 43% of total undergraduate aid awarded as scholarships/grants, 57% as loans/jobs. **Non-need-based:** Awarded to 2,068 full-time undergraduates, including 535 freshmen. Scholarships awarded for academics. **Additional information:** Merit scholarships available to New Jersey high school graduates based on academic distinction. Limited number of scholarships available to out-of-state students who demonstrate exceptional academic achievement in high school and on SAT.

Application procedures. **Admission:** Closing date 2/15 (postmark date). $70 fee, may be waived for applicants with need. Admission notification on a rolling basis beginning on or about 1/15. Must reply by May 1 or within 3 week(s) if notified thereafter. **Financial aid:** Priority date 3/1, closing date 10/1. FAFSA required. Applicants notified on a rolling basis starting 6/1.

Academics. **Special study options:** Combined bachelor's/graduate degree, cross-registration, double major, dual enrollment of high school students, exchange student, honors, independent study, internships, liberal arts/career combination, semester at sea, student-designed major, study abroad, teacher certification program, Washington semester. **Credit/placement by examination:** AP, CLEP, IB, SAT, institutional tests. 30 credit hours maximum toward bachelor's degree. **Support services:** Learning center, pre-admission summer program, reduced course load, remedial instruction, study skills assistance, tutoring, writing center.

Majors. **Area/ethnic studies:** Women's. **Biology:** General. **Business:** General, accounting, business admin, finance, international, marketing. **Computer sciences:** General. **Education:** Art, biology, chemistry, Deaf/hearing impaired, early childhood, elementary, English, foreign languages, health, history, mathematics, middle, physical, physics, social science, social studies, Spanish, special, speech, technology/industrial arts. **Engineering:** General, biomedical, civil, computer, electrical, mechanical, science. **Foreign languages:** Spanish. **Health:** Nursing (RN), preop/surgical nursing. **History:** General. **Math:** General, statistics. **Philosophy/religion:** Philosophy. **Physical sciences:** Chemistry, physics. **Protective services:** Law enforcement admin. **Psychology:** General. **Social sciences:** Criminology, economics, international relations, political science, sociology. **Visual/performing arts:** General, art, commercial/advertising art, multimedia, studio arts. **Other:** Self-designed major.

Most popular majors. Biology 7%, business/marketing 14%, education 22%, English 11%, psychology 10%, visual/performing arts 6%.

Computing on campus. 760 workstations in dormitories, library, computer center, student center. Dormitories wired for high-speed internet access and linked to campus network. Commuter students can connect to campus network. Online course registration, online library, helpline, repair service, student web hosting, wireless network available.

Student life. **Freshman orientation:** Mandatory, $165 fee. Preregistration for classes offered. Four-part program including June advisement week, summer readings, welcome week, college seminar. **Housing:** Guaranteed on-campus for freshmen. Coed dorms, single-sex dorms, special housing for disabled, apartments, wellness housing available. $150 nonrefundable deposit, deadline 5/1. Pets allowed in dorm rooms. Housing for transfer students available. **Activities:** Bands, campus ministries, choral groups, dance, drama, international student organizations, literary magazine, music ensembles, Model UN, musical theater, opera, radio station, student government, student newspaper, symphony orchestra, TV station, black student union, Amnesty International, Circle K, EOF Alliance, PRISM, Islamic society, outreach association, students acting for the environment, Jewish student union, ACTION: activist coalition.

Athletics. NCAA. **Intercollegiate:** Baseball M, basketball, cross-country, diving, field hockey W, football (tackle) M, golf M, lacrosse W, soccer, softball W, swimming, tennis, track and field, wrestling M. **Intramural:** Basketball, bowling, fencing, field hockey, football (non-tackle), golf M, ice hockey M, lacrosse M, racquetball, rugby, skiing, soccer, softball, swimming, tennis, volleyball, water polo. **Team name:** Lions.

Student services. Adult student services, alcohol/substance abuse counseling, chaplain/spiritual director, career counseling, services for economically disadvantaged, student employment services, financial aid counseling, health services, minority student services, personal counseling, placement for graduates, veterans' counselor, women's services. **Physically disabled:** Services for visually, speech, hearing impaired.

Contact. E-mail: tcnjinfo@tcnj.edu
Phone: (609) 771-2131 Fax: (609) 637-5174
Lisa Angeloni, Dean of Admissions, The College of New Jersey, Box 7718, Ewing, NJ 08628

College of St. Elizabeth

Morristown, New Jersey **CB member**
www.cse.edu **CB code: 2090**

- Private 4-year liberal arts college for women affiliated with Roman Catholic Church
- Residential campus in large town
- 1,181 degree-seeking undergraduates: 43% part-time, 90% women, 15% African American, 4% Asian American, 15% Hispanic American, 4% international
- 845 degree-seeking graduate students
- 82% of applicants admitted
- SAT or ACT (ACT writing optional), application essay required
- 59% graduate within 6 years

General. Founded in 1899. Regionally accredited. Men admitted to adult undergraduate programs and master's programs. **Degrees:** 251 bachelor's awarded; master's, doctoral offered. **Location:** 40 miles from New York City. **Calendar:** Semester, limited summer session. **Full-time faculty:** 72 total; 83% have terminal degrees, 4% minority, 65% women. **Part-time faculty:** 129 total; 8% minority, 70% women. **Class size:** 86% < 20, 14% 20-39, less than 1% >100. **Special facilities:** Library of rare books and manuscripts, Greek theater, Shakespeare garden, Holocaust education resource center, center for Catholic women's history, center for theological and spiritual development.

Freshman class profile. 458 applied, 377 admitted, 159 enrolled.

Mid 50% test scores		**Rank in top tenth:**	19%
SAT critical reading:	380-490	**Return as sophomores:**	67%
SAT math:	380-480	**Out-of-state:**	4%
SAT writing:	380-490	**Live on campus:**	77%
Rank in top quarter:	34%	**International:**	7%

Basis for selection. School achievement record and recommendations most important, followed by test scores, class rank; interview recommended. **Homeschooled:** Letter of recommendation (nonparent) required. Applicants processed on individual basis. Must provide approved curriculum guide.

High school preparation. College-preparatory program required. 16 units required; 23 recommended. Required and recommended units include English 3-4, mathematics 2-3, history 1-3, science 1-2 (laboratory 1-2), foreign language 2 and academic electives 7.

2008-2009 Annual costs. Tuition/fees: $24,428. Room/board: $10,690. Books/supplies: $1,200. Personal expenses: $1,312.

2007-2008 Financial aid. **Non-need-based:** Scholarships awarded for academics, alumni affiliation, art, leadership, state residency.

Application procedures. **Admission:** Priority date 3/1; deadline 8/15 (receipt date). $35 fee, may be waived for applicants with need. Admission notification on a rolling basis beginning on or about 11/15. Must reply by May 1 or within 2 week(s) if notified thereafter. **Financial aid:** Priority date 3/1; no closing date. FAFSA required. Applicants notified on a rolling basis starting 11/15; must reply by 5/1 or within 2 week(s) of notification.

Academics. Students with 60 undergraduate credits may take accelerated program in business or communication on Saturdays and complete bachelor's degree in 2 years. **Special study options:** Accelerated study, combined bachelor's/graduate degree, cross-registration, distance learning, double major, dual enrollment of high school students, ESL, exchange student, honors, independent study, internships, liberal arts/career combination, student-designed major, study abroad, teacher certification program, United Nations semester, weekend college. Accelerated co-ed baccalaureate program with majors in business, communication, nursing and psychology for adults over age 23 with classes evenings and on Saturdays. **Credit/placement by examination:** AP, CLEP, IB, institutional tests. 30 credit hours maximum toward bachelor's degree. Credit for prior work and/or life experience offered via portfolio. **Support services:** Learning center, pre-admission summer program, reduced course load, remedial instruction, study skills assistance, tutoring.

Majors. **Area/ethnic studies:** American. **Biology:** General, biochemistry. **Business:** Business admin. **Communications:** General. **Computer sciences:** Computer science. **Education:** Elementary, special. **Foreign languages:** Spanish. **Health:** Health care admin. **History:** General. **Interdisciplinary:** Global studies. **Math:** General. **Philosophy/religion:** Philosophy. **Physical sciences:** Chemistry. **Psychology:** General. **Social sciences:** Economics, sociology. **Theology:** Theology. **Visual/performing arts:** Art.

Most popular majors. Business/marketing 9%, communications/journalism 7%, education 12%, English 7%, health sciences 19%, interdisciplinary studies 8%, psychology 13%.

Computing on campus. 127 workstations in dormitories, library, computer center. Dormitories wired for high-speed internet access and linked to campus network. Commuter students can connect to campus network. Helpline, wireless network available.

Student life. **Freshman orientation:** Mandatory, $200 fee. Preregistration for classes offered. Comprehensive program held before start of classes for Women's College students. **Housing:** Guaranteed on-campus for all undergraduates. Wellness housing available. $200 deposit. **Activities:** Campus ministries, choral groups, drama, literary magazine, music ensembles, student government, student newspaper, volunteer services center, international/

intercultural club, Latin Roots, Students Take Action Committee, foreign language club, American Chemical Society Affiliates, psychology club, sociology club.

Athletics. NCAA. **Intercollegiate:** Basketball W, equestrian W, soccer W, softball W, swimming W, tennis W, volleyball W. **Intramural:** Volleyball W. **Team name:** Eagles.

Student services. Adult student services, alcohol/substance abuse counseling, chaplain/spiritual director, career counseling, services for economically disadvantaged, student employment services, financial aid counseling, health services, minority student services, personal counseling, placement for graduates, women's services. **Physically disabled:** Services for visually, speech, hearing impaired.

Contact. E-mail: apply@cse.edu
Phone: (973) 290-4700 Toll-free number: (800) 210-7900
Fax: (973) 290-4710
Donna Tatarka, Dean of Admission, College of St. Elizabeth, 2 Convent Road, Morristown, NJ 07960-6989

DeVry University: North Brunswick

North Brunswick, New Jersey
www.devry.edu **CB code: 2203**

- For-profit 4-year university
- Commuter campus in small city
- 1,281 degree-seeking undergraduates: 35% part-time, 29% women, 25% African American, 10% Asian American, 21% Hispanic American, 1% Native American, 2% international
- Interview required

General. Founded in 1996. Regionally accredited. **Degrees:** 202 bachelor's, 205 associate awarded. **Location:** 30 miles from New York City. **Calendar:** Semester, extensive summer session. **Full-time faculty:** 39 total; 26% minority, 33% women. **Part-time faculty:** 130 total; 28% minority, 46% women.

Basis for selection. Applicants must have high school diploma or equivalent, degree from an accredited postsecondary institution, or submit acceptable test scores and be at least 17 years of age on the first day of classes. New students may enter at beginning of any semester. SAT or ACT recommended. CPT also accepted.

High school preparation. Required units include mathematics 1. Math unit must be algebra or higher.

2008-2009 Annual costs. Tuition/fees: $14,800. Books/supplies: $1,300. Personal expenses: $3,152.

2007-2008 Financial aid. All financial aid based on need.

Application procedures. Admission: No deadline. $50 fee. Admission notification on a rolling basis. **Financial aid:** No deadline. FAFSA required. Applicants notified on a rolling basis.

Academics. Special study options: Accelerated study, cooperative education, distance learning, weekend college. **Credit/placement by examination:** CLEP, institutional tests. **Support services:** Learning center, remedial instruction, tutoring.

Majors. Business: Business admin. **Computer sciences:** Networking, systems analysis. **Engineering technology:** Biomedical, electrical. **Other:** Technical management.

Most popular majors. Business/marketing 21%, computer/information sciences 58%, engineering/engineering technologies 21%.

Computing on campus. 575 workstations in library, computer center. Online course registration, online library, helpline available.

Student life. Freshman orientation: Mandatory. **Activities:** Student government, Phi Theta Kappa, Golden Key, Institution of Electrical and Electronics Engineers, cultural exchange club, chess club, art club, Crusade for Christ.

Student services. Career counseling, student employment services, financial aid counseling, on-campus daycare, placement for graduates, veterans' counselor. **Physically disabled:** Services for visually, hearing impaired.

Contact. E-mail: admissions@devry.edu
Phone: (732) 435-4850 Toll-free number: (800) 333-3879
Fax: (732) 435-4850
Gerald Wargo, Director of Admissions, DeVry University: North Brunswick, 630 US Highway One, North Brunswick, NJ 08902-3362

Drew University

Madison, New Jersey **CB member**
www.drew.edu **CB code: 2193**

- Private 4-year university and liberal arts college affiliated with United Methodist Church
- Residential campus in large town
- 1,575 degree-seeking undergraduates: 2% part-time, 62% women, 7% African American, 5% Asian American, 9% Hispanic American, 2% international
- 911 degree-seeking graduate students
- 68% of applicants admitted
- 73% graduate within 6 years

General. Founded in 1867. Regionally accredited. **Degrees:** 334 bachelor's awarded; master's, doctoral, first professional offered. **Location:** 30 miles from New York City. **Calendar:** Semester, limited summer session. **Full-time faculty:** 159 total; 98% have terminal degrees, 20% minority, 46% women. **Part-time faculty:** 74 total. **Class size:** 74% < 20, 22% 20-39, 3% 40-49, 1% 50-99. **Special facilities:** 80-acre forest preserve, arboretum, photography gallery, observatory, research greenhouse, laser holography laboratory, center for the arts, music hall.

Freshman class profile. 5,219 applied, 3,531 admitted, 390 enrolled.

Mid 50% test scores		**GPA 2.0-2.99:**	19%
SAT critical reading:	520-650	**Rank in top quarter:**	68%
SAT math:	510-620	**Rank in top tenth:**	36%
SAT writing:	510-640	**Return as sophomores:**	83%
ACT composite:	23-28	**Out-of-state:**	47%
GPA 3.75 or higher:	15%	**Live on campus:**	92%
GPA 3.50-3.74:	20%	**International:**	1%
GPA 3.0-3.49:	46%		

Basis for selection. School achievement record most important; test scores also important. Interview recommended. **Homeschooled:** Statement describing homeschool structure and mission, transcript of courses and grades required.

High school preparation. Recommended units include English 4, mathematics 3, social studies 2, history 2, science 2 (laboratory 2), foreign language 2 and academic electives 3.

2008-2009 Annual costs. Tuition/fees: $36,470. Room/board: $9,978. Books/supplies: $3,228. Personal expenses: $2,438.

2007-2008 Financial aid. Need-based: 82% of total undergraduate aid awarded as scholarships/grants, 18% as loans/jobs. **Non-need-based:** Scholarships awarded for academics, art, minority status, music/drama.

Application procedures. Admission: Priority date 12/19; deadline 2/15. $50 fee, may be waived for applicants with need. Applicants notified by third week in March. Must reply by 5/1. **Financial aid:** Closing date 2/15. FAFSA, CSS PROFILE required. Applicants notified by 3/31; must reply by 5/1.

Academics. RISE program enables students to conduct scientific research with retired scientists. **Special study options:** Accelerated study, combined bachelor's/graduate degree, cross-registration, double major, exchange student, independent study, internships, New York semester, student-designed major, study abroad, teacher certification program, United Nations semester, Washington semester. Seven year dual degree (BA/MD) program with UMDNJ - New Jersey Medical School. Five year dual degree (BA/BS or B Eng) programs in engineering and technologies with Columbia University, Stevens Institute of Technology, and Washington University. Five year dual degree (BA/Master of Forestry or Master of Environmental Management) program with Duke University. **Credit/placement by examination:** AP, CLEP, IB, institutional tests. 32 credit hours maximum toward bachelor's degree. **Support services:** Learning center, pre-admission summer program, reduced course load, tutoring, writing center.

Majors. Area/ethnic studies: African, women's. **Biology:** General, Biochemistry/biophysics and molecular biology. **Computer sciences:** Computer science. **Conservation:** Environmental studies. **Foreign languages:** Chinese, classics, French, German, Spanish. **History:** General. **Interdisciplinary:** Behavioral sciences, neuroscience. **Math:** General. **Philosophy/**

religion: Philosophy, religion. **Physical sciences:** Chemistry, physics. **Psychology:** General. **Social sciences:** Anthropology, economics, political science, sociology. **Visual/performing arts:** Art, art history/conservation, dramatic. **Other:** Biological anthropology.

Most popular majors. Biology 7%, English 9%, foreign language 10%, interdisciplinary studies 7%, psychology 10%, social sciences 32%, visual/ performing arts 11%.

Computing on campus. PC or laptop required. 2,500 workstations in library, computer center. Dormitories wired for high-speed internet access and linked to campus network. Commuter students can connect to campus network. Online course registration, online library, helpline, repair service, wireless network available.

Student life. **Freshman orientation:** Mandatory, $250 fee. Preregistration for classes offered. Held the week before start of fall semester. **Housing:** Guaranteed on-campus for all undergraduates. Coed dorms, special housing for disabled, wellness housing available. $250 nonrefundable deposit, deadline 5/1. **Activities:** Campus ministries, choral groups, dance, drama, film society, international student organizations, literary magazine, music ensembles, radio station, student government, student newspaper, symphony orchestra, TV station, Amnesty International, Hispanic student organization, College Democrats, College Republicans, Pan-African student organization, Inter-Varsity Christian Fellowship, Jewish student organization/ Hillel, environmental action league, Students Against Violence Everywhere, The Alliance.

Athletics. NCAA. **Intercollegiate:** Baseball M, basketball, cross-country, equestrian, fencing, field hockey W, lacrosse, soccer, softball W, swimming, tennis. **Intramural:** Basketball, football (non-tackle), racquetball, soccer, softball, squash, table tennis, volleyball. **Team name:** Rangers.

Student services. Adult student services, alcohol/substance abuse counseling, chaplain/spiritual director, career counseling, services for economically disadvantaged, student employment services, financial aid counseling, health services, minority student services, on-campus daycare, personal counseling, placement for graduates, women's services. **Physically disabled:** Services for visually, hearing impaired.

Contact. E-mail: cadm@drew.edu
Phone: (973) 408-3739 Fax: (973) 408-3068
Mary Beth Carey, Dean of College Admissions and Financial Assistance, Drew University, 36 Madison Avenue, Madison, NJ 07940-4063

Fairleigh Dickinson University: College at Florham

Madison, New Jersey
www.fdu.edu **CB code: 2262**

- Private 4-year university
- Residential campus in large town
- 2,410 degree-seeking undergraduates: 6% part-time, 52% women, 8% African American, 3% Asian American, 8% Hispanic American, 1% international
- 987 degree-seeking graduate students
- 62% of applicants admitted
- SAT or ACT (ACT writing optional) required
- 51% graduate within 6 years

General. Regionally accredited. Additional campus locations: Wroxton College, England and Vancouver, Canada. **Degrees:** 504 bachelor's awarded; master's offered. **ROTC:** Army, Air Force. **Location:** 27 miles from New York City. **Calendar:** Semester, extensive summer session. **Full-time faculty:** 120 total. **Part-time faculty:** 200 total. **Special facilities:** ITV multimedia classrooms, web-ilab, regional center for students with learning disabilities, cyber crime lab.

Freshman class profile. 3,496 applied, 2,182 admitted, 606 enrolled.

Mid 50% test scores			
SAT critical reading:	460-550	Rank in top tenth:	15%
SAT math:	460-570	Return as sophomores:	76%
SAT writing:	460-560	Out-of-state:	16%
Rank in top quarter:	35%	Live on campus:	84%
		International:	1%

Basis for selection. GPA, test scores, difficulty of high school curriculum most important. **Learning Disabled:** Separate application along with admissions application.

High school preparation. 16 units required. Required and recommended units include English 4, mathematics 3, social studies 2, history 2, science 2-3 (laboratory 2-3), foreign language 2 and academic electives 3.

2008-2009 Annual costs. Tuition/fees: $30,198. Room/board: $10,548.

2007-2008 Financial aid. **Need-based:** 421 full-time freshmen applied for aid; 366 were judged to have need; 366 of these received aid. Average scholarship/grant was $11,705; average loan $3,000. 64% of total undergraduate aid awarded as scholarships/grants, 36% as loans/jobs. **Non-need-based:** Awarded to 1,181 full-time undergraduates, including 327 freshmen. Scholarships awarded for academics, alumni affiliation, music/drama.

Application procedures. **Admission:** Priority date 3/15; no deadline. $40 fee, may be waived for applicants with need, free for online applicants. Admission notification on a rolling basis beginning on or about 11/1. Must reply by May 1 or within 2 week(s) if notified thereafter. **Financial aid:** Priority date 2/15; no closing date. FAFSA required. Applicants notified on a rolling basis starting 2/1; must reply by 5/1 or within 4 week(s) of notification.

Academics. **Special study options:** Accelerated study, combined bachelor's/ graduate degree, cooperative education, cross-registration, distance learning, double major, external degree, honors, independent study, internships, liberal arts/career combination, study abroad, teacher certification program, Washington semester, weekend college. **Credit/placement by examination:** CLEP, institutional tests. 33 credit hours maximum toward bachelor's degree. **Support services:** Learning center, remedial instruction, study skills assistance, tutoring, writing center.

Majors. **Biology:** General, biochemistry, marine. **Business:** Accounting, business admin, entrepreneurial studies, hospitality admin, managerial economics, marketing. **Communications:** General. **Computer sciences:** General. **Foreign languages:** French, Spanish. **Health:** Clinical lab science, health services, medical radiologic technology/radiation therapy, nursing (RN), respiratory therapy technology. **History:** General. **Liberal arts:** Humanities. **Math:** General. **Philosophy/religion:** Philosophy. **Physical sciences:** Chemistry. **Psychology:** General. **Social sciences:** Economics, political science, sociology. **Visual/performing arts:** General, cinematography, dramatic. **Other:** Allied health technology.

Most popular majors. Business/marketing 34%, communications/ journalism 9%, English 6%, psychology 16%, social sciences 7%, visual/ performing arts 10%.

Computing on campus. 140 workstations in library, computer center. Dormitories wired for high-speed internet access and linked to campus network. Commuter students can connect to campus network. Online course registration, online library, helpline, wireless network available.

Student life. **Freshman orientation:** Mandatory. Preregistration for classes offered. **Housing:** Guaranteed on-campus for freshmen. Coed dorms, special housing for disabled, apartments available. $350 partly refundable deposit, deadline 5/1. **Activities:** Campus ministries, choral groups, dance, drama, international student organizations, literary magazine, Model UN, musical theater, opera, radio station, student government, student newspaper, Latin American student organization, Florham programming committee, green club, Greek organizations, student volunteer association.

Athletics. NCAA. **Intercollegiate:** Baseball M, basketball, cross-country, field hockey W, football (tackle) M, golf M, lacrosse, soccer, softball W, swimming, tennis, volleyball W. **Intramural:** Basketball, bowling, football (non-tackle), ice hockey M, soccer, volleyball. **Team name:** Devils.

Student services. Adult student services, alcohol/substance abuse counseling, chaplain/spiritual director, career counseling, services for economically disadvantaged, student employment services, financial aid counseling, health services, minority student services, personal counseling, placement for graduates, women's services. **Physically disabled:** Services for visually, speech, hearing impaired. **Learning disabled:** Comprehensive services available.

Contact. E-mail: globaleducation@fdu.edu
Phone: (800) 338-8803 Toll-free number: (800) 338-8803
Fax: (973) 443-8088
Jonathan Wexler, Associate Vice President for Admissions and Financial Aid, Fairleigh Dickinson University: College at Florham, 285 Madison Avenue, Madison, NJ 07940

Fairleigh Dickinson University: Metropolitan Campus

Teaneck, New Jersey
www.fdu.edu **CB code: 2263**

- Private 4-year university
- Commuter campus in large town
- 3,415 degree-seeking undergraduates: 37% part-time, 58% women, 15% African American, 6% Asian American, 21% Hispanic American, 7% international

- 2,716 degree-seeking graduate students
- 52% of applicants admitted
- SAT or ACT (ACT writing optional) required

General. Founded in 1942. Regionally accredited. Additional campus at Wroxton College, England and Vancouver, Canada. **Degrees:** 792 bachelor's, 46 associate awarded; master's, doctoral offered. **ROTC:** Army, Air Force. **Location:** 13 miles from New York City. **Calendar:** Semester, extensive summer session. **Full-time faculty:** 185 total. **Part-time faculty:** 440 total. **Special facilities:** Computer labs, ITV multimedia classrooms, photonics lab, learning disabilities center, psychological services center, marine biology lab, cyber crime lab.

Freshman class profile. 3,954 applied, 2,048 admitted, 515 enrolled.

Mid 50% test scores			
SAT critical reading:	440-530	Rank in top tenth:	21%
SAT math:	450-560	Return as sophomores:	71%
SAT writing:	430-540	Out-of-state:	17%
Rank in top quarter:	43%	Live on campus:	47%
		International:	9%

Basis for selection. Rigor of secondary school record and GPA most important. Recommendations, standardized test scores, extracurricular activities important. **Learning Disabled:** Regional Center for College Students with Learning Disabilities requires separate application. Must also apply to university admissions.

High school preparation. College-preparatory program required. 16 units required. Required and recommended units include English 4, mathematics 3, social studies 2, history 2, science 2-3 (laboratory 2-3), foreign language 2 and academic electives 3.

2008-2009 Annual costs. Tuition/fees: $28,084. Room/board: $10,914.

2007-2008 Financial aid. Need-based: 330 full-time freshmen applied for aid; 305 were judged to have need; 305 of these received aid. Average scholarship/grant was $11,250; average loan $2,655. 71% of total undergraduate aid awarded as scholarships/grants, 29% as loans/jobs. **Non-need-based:** Awarded to 1,053 full-time undergraduates, including 274 freshmen. Scholarships awarded for academics, alumni affiliation, athletics, music/drama.

Application procedures. Admission: Priority date 3/15; no deadline. $40 fee, may be waived for applicants with need, free for online applicants. Admission notification on a rolling basis beginning on or about 11/1. Must reply by May 1 or within 2 week(s) if notified thereafter. **Financial aid:** Priority date 2/15; no closing date. FAFSA required. Applicants notified on a rolling basis starting 3/1; must reply by 5/1 or within 2 week(s) of notification.

Academics. Core curriculum consists of 4 interdisciplinary courses. Marine biology majors spend 1 semester at marine station in the Dominican Republic. **Special study options:** Accelerated study, combined bachelor's/graduate degree, cooperative education, distance learning, double major, ESL, honors, independent study, internships, student-designed major, study abroad, teacher certification program, Washington semester, weekend college. **Credit/placement by examination:** AP, CLEP, institutional tests. 33 credit hours maximum toward bachelor's degree. **Support services:** Learning center, pre-admission summer program, reduced course load, remedial instruction, study skills assistance, tutoring, writing center.

Majors. Biology: General, biochemistry, marine. **Business:** Accounting, business admin, entrepreneurial studies, hospitality admin, managerial economics, marketing. **Communications:** General. **Computer sciences:** Computer science, information technology. **Conservation:** Environmental science. **Engineering:** Electrical. **Engineering technology:** Civil, construction, electrical, mechanical. **Foreign languages:** French, Spanish. **Health:** Clinical lab science, nursing (RN), radiologic technology/medical imaging. **History:** General. **Interdisciplinary:** Biological/physical sciences. **Liberal arts:** Humanities. **Math:** General. **Philosophy/religion:** Philosophy. **Physical sciences:** Chemistry, physics. **Protective services:** Criminal justice. **Psychology:** General. **Social sciences:** Economics, international relations, political science, sociology. **Visual/performing arts:** General, dramatic.

Most popular majors. Business/marketing 13%, health sciences 7%, liberal arts 52%, psychology 6%.

Computing on campus. 160 workstations in library, computer center. Dormitories wired for high-speed internet access and linked to campus network. Commuter students can connect to campus network. Online course registration, online library, helpline, wireless network available.

Student life. Freshman orientation: Mandatory. Preregistration for classes offered. **Housing:** Guaranteed on-campus for freshmen. Coed dorms available. $350 partly refundable deposit, deadline 5/1. **Activities:** Pep band, campus ministries, dance, drama, international student organizations, literary magazine, Model UN, radio station, student government, student newspaper, TV station, multicultural council, Indian cultural experience, international student association, Business Leaders of Tomorrow, student programming committee.

Athletics. NCAA. **Intercollegiate:** Baseball M, basketball, bowling W, cross-country, fencing W, golf, soccer, softball W, tennis, track and field, volleyball W. **Intramural:** Badminton, basketball, football (non-tackle), golf M, soccer, volleyball. **Team name:** Knights.

Student services. Adult student services, alcohol/substance abuse counseling, chaplain/spiritual director, career counseling, services for economically disadvantaged, student employment services, financial aid counseling, health services, personal counseling, placement for graduates, women's services. **Physically disabled:** Services for visually, speech, hearing impaired. **Learning disabled:** Comprehensive services available.

Contact. E-mail: globaleducation@fdu.edu
Phone: (201) 692-2553 Toll-free number: (800) 338-8803
Fax: (201) 692-7319
Jonathan Wexler, Associate Vice President for Admissions and Financial Aid, Fairleigh Dickinson University: Metropolitan Campus, 1000 River Road, H-DH3-10, Teaneck, NJ 07666-1996

Felician College
Lodi, New Jersey
www.felician.edu **CB code: 2321**

- Private 4-year liberal arts college affiliated with Roman Catholic Church
- Commuter campus in large city
- 1,766 degree-seeking undergraduates: 24% part-time, 77% women, 12% African American, 10% Asian American, 17% Hispanic American
- 249 degree-seeking graduate students
- 82% of applicants admitted
- SAT or ACT (ACT writing optional) required

General. Founded in 1942. Regionally accredited. Additional campus in Rutherford. All programs spread through both campuses. **Degrees:** 134 bachelor's, 19 associate awarded; master's offered. **Location:** 12 miles from New York City. **Calendar:** Semester, limited summer session. **Full-time faculty:** 95 total; 59% women. **Part-time faculty:** 78 total. **Class size:** 76% < 20, 23% 20-39, less than 1% 40-49, less than 1% 50-99, less than 1% >100. **Special facilities:** Nursing skills laboratory, performance and theater facilities.

Freshman class profile. 1,600 applied, 1,307 admitted, 262 enrolled.

Mid 50% test scores			
SAT critical reading:	400-500	Return as sophomores:	65%
SAT math:	390-490	Out-of-state:	6%

Basis for selection. School achievement record, test scores most important. Interview, school and community activities, recommendations of high school counselor considered. Interview recommended for all; portfolio recommended for art programs.

High school preparation. 19 units recommended. Recommended units include English 4, mathematics 3, social studies 3, science 3 and academic electives 6. Biology, chemistry, algebra required for nursing and medical laboratory technology applicants.

2008-2009 Annual costs. Tuition/fees: $23,500. Room/board: $9,350. Books/supplies: $1,118. Personal expenses: $1,671.

2007-2008 Financial aid. Need-based: 210 full-time freshmen applied for aid; 186 were judged to have need; 186 of these received aid. Average need met was 10%. Average scholarship/grant was $7,700; average loan $3,500. 59% of total undergraduate aid awarded as scholarships/grants, 41% as loans/jobs. **Non-need-based:** Awarded to 573 full-time undergraduates, including 109 freshmen. Scholarships awarded for academics, alumni affiliation, athletics, religious affiliation.

Application procedures. Admission: No deadline. $30 fee, may be waived for applicants with need. Admission notification on a rolling basis beginning on or about 3/15. Must reply by May 1 or within 2 week(s) if notified thereafter. **Financial aid:** Priority date 6/1; no closing date. FAFSA required. Applicants notified on a rolling basis starting 4/1; must reply within 2 week(s) of notification.

Academics. Post-baccalaureate certification available in elementary and secondary education. **Special study options:** Accelerated study, combined bachelor's/graduate degree, cooperative education, cross-registration, distance learning, double major, dual enrollment of high school students, ESL, honors, independent study, internships, liberal arts/career combination, student-designed major, study abroad, teacher certification program, weekend college. **Credit/placement by examination:** AP, CLEP, IB, SAT, institutional tests. 15 credit hours maximum toward associate degree, 30 toward bachelor's. **Support services:** Learning center, writing center.

Majors. **Biology:** General, toxicology. **Business:** Accounting, business admin, marketing. **Communications:** General, broadcast journalism, digital media, journalism. **Computer sciences:** General, computer science. **Education:** Early childhood, early childhood special, elementary, mathematics. **Health:** Cytotechnology, health services, nuclear medical technology, nursing (RN), nursing admin, respiratory therapy technology. **History:** General. **Interdisciplinary:** Natural sciences. **Liberal arts:** Humanities. **Math:** General. **Philosophy/religion:** Philosophy, religion. **Psychology:** General. **Social sciences:** Sociology. **Visual/performing arts:** Art, studio arts.

Computing on campus. 140 workstations in dormitories, library, computer center. Dormitories wired for high-speed internet access and linked to campus network. Commuter students can connect to campus network. Online library, repair service, wireless network available.

Student life. **Freshman orientation:** Mandatory. Three summer programs available. **Policies:** No drugs or alcohol on campus. **Housing:** Guaranteed on-campus for freshmen. Coed dorms, single-sex dorms, special housing for disabled available. $200 deposit. **Activities:** Choral groups, drama, international student organizations, literary magazine, student government, Angelicum club, history club, RCIA, Kappa Sigma Xi, aspiring authors, Students in Free Enterprise, Kappa Gamma Pi.

Athletics. NAIA, NCAA. **Intercollegiate:** Baseball M, basketball, cross-country, golf M, soccer, softball W, track and field, volleyball W. **Intramural:** Basketball M, bowling. **Team name:** Golden Falcons.

Student services. Chaplain/spiritual director, financial aid counseling, health services. **Learning disabled:** Comprehensive services available.

Contact. E-mail: admissions@inet.felician.edu
Phone: (201) 559-6131 Fax: (201) 559-6188
Alexander Scott, Dean of Undergraduate Admissions, Felician College, 262 South Main Street, Lodi, NJ 07644-2198

Georgian Court University

Lakewood, New Jersey — **CB member**
www.georgian.edu — **CB code: 2274**

- Private 4-year university and liberal arts college for women affiliated with Roman Catholic Church
- Residential campus in large town
- 1,756 degree-seeking undergraduates: 16% part-time, 94% women, 10% African American, 2% Asian American, 7% Hispanic American
- 866 degree-seeking graduate students
- 73% of applicants admitted
- 64% graduate within 6 years

General. Founded in 1908. Regionally accredited. Evening and graduate divisions coeducational. **Degrees:** 408 bachelor's awarded; master's offered. **Location:** 60 miles from New York City and Philadelphia. **Calendar:** Semester, limited summer session. **Full-time faculty:** 103 total; 84% have terminal degrees, 13% minority, 64% women. **Part-time faculty:** 206 total; 27% have terminal degrees, 7% minority, 58% women. **Class size:** 76% < 20, 24% 20-39. **Special facilities:** Arboretum, NASA Education Resource Center.

Freshman class profile. 923 applied, 674 admitted, 251 enrolled.

GPA 3.75 or higher:	8%	**Rank in top tenth:**	13%
GPA 3.50-3.74:	13%	**Return as sophomores:**	70%
GPA 3.0-3.49:	26%	**Out-of-state:**	6%
GPA 2.0-2.99:	49%	**Live on campus:**	69%
Rank in top quarter:	37%		

Basis for selection. Completed high school program reviewed for rigor of courses and grades received. Students should be completing program of 16 academic units with grades of 2.5 or higher. Students not meeting criteria referred to faculty committee for review. SAT or ACT recommended. **Homeschooled:** Statement describing homeschool structure and mission required.

High school preparation. College-preparatory program required. 16 units required. Required units include English 4, mathematics 2, history 1, (laboratory 1), foreign language 2 and academic electives 6.

2008-2009 Annual costs. Tuition/fees: $23,360. Room/board: $9,112. Books/supplies: $1,250. Personal expenses: $2,400.

2008-2009 Financial aid. **Need-based:** 234 full-time freshmen applied for aid; 212 were judged to have need; 212 of these received aid. Average need met was 79%. Average scholarship/grant was $18,289; average loan $3,785. 60% of total undergraduate aid awarded as scholarships/grants, 40% as loans/jobs. **Non-need-based:** Awarded to 282 full-time undergraduates, including 67 freshmen. Scholarships awarded for academics, alumni affiliation, art, athletics, leadership, minority status, music/drama, religious affiliation.

Application procedures. **Admission:** Closing date 8/1 (receipt date). $40 fee, may be waived for applicants with need. Admission notification on a rolling basis beginning on or about 10/1. Must reply by May 1 or within 2 week(s) if notified thereafter. **Financial aid:** Priority date 3/1; no closing date. FAFSA, institutional form required. Applicants notified on a rolling basis starting 2/1; must reply within 2 week(s) of notification.

Academics. **Special study options:** Accelerated study, combined bachelor's/graduate degree, distance learning, double major, dual enrollment of high school students, ESL, honors, independent study, internships, liberal arts/career combination, study abroad, teacher certification program. **Credit/placement by examination:** AP, CLEP, institutional tests. 30 credit hours maximum toward bachelor's degree. **Support services:** Learning center, reduced course load, remedial instruction, study skills assistance, tutoring.

Majors. **Biology:** General, biochemistry. **Business:** Accounting, business admin, hospitality admin. **Communications:** General. **Education:** Elementary. **Foreign languages:** Spanish. **Health:** Clinical lab science, nursing (RN). **History:** General. **Interdisciplinary:** Natural sciences. **Liberal arts:** Humanities. **Math:** General. **Parks/recreation:** Exercise sciences. **Philosophy/religion:** Religion. **Physical sciences:** Chemistry, physics. **Protective services:** Criminal justice. **Psychology:** General. **Public administration:** Social work. **Social sciences:** Sociology. **Visual/performing arts:** Art, dance. **Other:** Allied health technologies, Applied arts and sciences.

Most popular majors. Business/marketing 13%, education 28%, English 10%, history 7%, psychology 17%.

Computing on campus. 192 workstations in dormitories, library, computer center. Dormitories wired for high-speed internet access and linked to campus network. Commuter students can connect to campus network. Online course registration, online library, helpline, wireless network available.

Student life. **Freshman orientation:** Mandatory, $155 fee. Held during the week before classes begin. **Housing:** Guaranteed on-campus for all undergraduates. Wellness housing available. $250 deposit, deadline 5/1. **Activities:** Bands, campus ministries, choral groups, dance, international student organizations, literary magazine, music ensembles, Model UN, student government, student newspaper, council for exceptional children, Sisters United, Re-Entry women's club, Alliance Francaise, Amnesty International, black student union, LASO, living/learning communities.

Athletics. NCAA. **Intercollegiate:** Basketball W, cross-country W, lacrosse W, soccer W, softball W, tennis W, track and field W, volleyball W. **Team name:** Lions.

Student services. Chaplain/spiritual director, career counseling, financial aid counseling, health services, personal counseling. **Physically disabled:** Services for visually, speech, hearing impaired.

Contact. E-mail: admissions@georgian.edu
Phone: (732) 987-2200 ext. 2700 Toll-free number: (800) 458-8422 ext. 2760 Fax: (732) 987-2000
Kathie Gallant, Director of Admissions, Georgian Court University, 900 Lakewood Avenue, Lakewood, NJ 08701-2697

Kean University

Union, New Jersey — **CB member**
www.kean.edu — **CB code: 2517**

- Public 4-year university and liberal arts college
- Commuter campus in small city
- 10,907 degree-seeking undergraduates: 22% part-time, 63% women, 20% African American, 6% Asian American, 20% Hispanic American, 2% international
- 1,923 degree-seeking graduate students
- 64% of applicants admitted
- SAT or ACT (ACT writing optional), application essay required
- 44% graduate within 6 years

General. Founded in 1855. Regionally accredited. **Degrees:** 1,908 bachelor's awarded; master's, doctoral offered. **ROTC:** Army, Air Force. **Location:** 12 miles from New York City. **Calendar:** Semester, limited summer session. **Full-time faculty:** 364 total; 90% have terminal degrees, 30% minority, 46% women. **Part-time faculty:** 916 total; 22% minority, 51% women. **Class size:** 39% < 20, 60% 20-39, less than 1% 40-49, less than 1% 50-99. **Special facilities:** Holocaust resource center, ethnic studies center, museum, center for New Jersey science, technology & mathematics education, institute for foreign service and diplomacy.

Freshman class profile. 5,572 applied, 3,570 admitted, 1,469 enrolled.

Mid 50% test scores			
SAT critical reading:	400-500	Rank in top quarter:	24%
SAT math:	410-520	Rank in top tenth:	8%
GPA 3.75 or higher:	5%	Return as sophomores:	78%
GPA 3.50-3.74:	8%	Out-of-state:	4%
GPA 3.0-3.49:	34%	Live on campus:	35%
GPA 2.0-2.99:	52%	International:	1%

Basis for selection. High school GPA at or above 2.50, test scores, counselor recommendations important. Consideration given to class rank, military service, work, personal life experiences. Non-US-educated applicants evaluated based on academic record in home country. If needed, applicants advised of specific additional requirements.

High school preparation. College-preparatory program required. 16 units required. Required and recommended units include English 4, mathematics 3, social studies 2, history 2, science 2 (laboratory 2), foreign language 2 and academic electives 5.

2008-2009 Annual costs. Tuition/fees: $9,179; $13,661 out-of-state. Room/board: $9,677.

2008-2009 Financial aid. **Need-based:** 1,254 full-time freshmen applied for aid; 952 were judged to have need; 887 of these received aid. Average need met was 56%. Average scholarship/grant was $7,210; average loan $3,443. 54% of total undergraduate aid awarded as scholarships/grants, 46% as loans/jobs. **Non-need-based:** Awarded to 746 full-time undergraduates, including 252 freshmen. Scholarships awarded for academics, alumni affiliation, art, leadership, music/drama.

Application procedures. **Admission:** Priority date 5/1; deadline 5/31 (postmark date). $50 fee, may be waived for applicants with need. Admission notification on a rolling basis beginning on or about 11/1. Must reply by May 1 or within 2 week(s) if notified thereafter. **Financial aid:** Priority date 3/15; no closing date. FAFSA required. Applicants notified on a rolling basis starting 3/15; must reply by 5/1.

Academics. **Special study options:** Accelerated study, combined bachelor's/graduate degree, cooperative education, distance learning, double major, dual enrollment of high school students, ESL, honors, independent study, internships, liberal arts/career combination, semester at sea, study abroad, teacher certification program, Washington semester, weekend college. 2-year bachelor's degree program for RNs, Foreign Transfer Programs, TraveLearn. **Credit/placement by examination:** AP, CLEP, IB, SAT, institutional tests. 46 credit hours maximum toward bachelor's degree. **Support services:** Learning center, pre-admission summer program, reduced course load, remedial instruction, study skills assistance, tutoring, writing center.

Majors. **Biology:** General. **Business:** Accounting, business admin, finance, marketing. **Communications:** General. **Communications technology:** Printing management. **Computer sciences:** General, networking. **Education:** Elementary, kindergarten/preschool, music, physical, special, speech. **Engineering technology:** Electrical. **Foreign languages:** Spanish. **Health:** Athletic training, clinical lab science, medical records admin. **History:** General. **Liberal arts:** Arts/sciences. **Math:** General. **Parks/recreation:** Facilities management. **Physical sciences:** Chemistry, geology. **Protective services:** Law enforcement admin. **Psychology:** General. **Public administration:** General, social work. **Social sciences:** Economics, political science, sociology. **Visual/performing arts:** Acting, art, art history/conservation, design, dramatic, film/cinema, industrial design, interior design, studio arts, theater design. **Other:** Philosophy and religion, Psychology rehabilitation, Science and technology, Speech, language & hearing science.

Most popular majors. Business/marketing 21%, education 18%, psychology 11%, visual/performing arts 8%.

Computing on campus. 1,700 workstations in dormitories, library, computer center, student center. Dormitories wired for high-speed internet access and linked to campus network. Commuter students can connect to campus network. Online course registration, student web hosting, wireless network available.

Student life. **Freshman orientation:** Mandatory, $50 fee. Preregistration for classes offered. **Housing:** Coed dorms, single-sex dorms, special housing for disabled, apartments available. $100 nonrefundable deposit, deadline 5/1. **Activities:** Bands, campus ministries, choral groups, dance, drama, film society, international student organizations, literary magazine, music ensembles, Model UN, musical theater, opera, radio station, student government, student newspaper, TV station, Asian culture club, Association of Indian students, Association of Latin American students, Pan African student association, Intervarsity Christian fellowship, international student association, Haitian student association, Hamor's Head Club for Democrats, Jewish culture club, Muslim student association.

Athletics. NCAA. **Intercollegiate:** Baseball M, basketball, field hockey W, football (tackle) M, lacrosse, soccer, softball W, tennis W, track and field, volleyball W. **Intramural:** Basketball, football (non-tackle), soccer, softball, tennis, volleyball, weight lifting. **Team name:** Cougars.

Student services. Adult student services, alcohol/substance abuse counseling, chaplain/spiritual director, career counseling, services for economically disadvantaged, student employment services, financial aid counseling, health services, minority student services, on-campus daycare, personal counseling, placement for graduates, veterans' counselor, women's services. **Physically disabled:** Services for visually, speech, hearing impaired. **Learning disabled:** Comprehensive services available.

Contact. E-mail: admitme@kean.edu
Phone: (908) 737-7100 Fax: (908) 737-7105
Valerie Winslow, Director of Admissions, Kean University, 1000 Morris Avenue, Union, NJ 07083-0411

Monmouth University

West Long Branch, New Jersey — **CB member**
www.monmouth.edu — **CB code: 2416**

- Private 4-year university
- Residential campus in small town
- 4,664 degree-seeking undergraduates: 8% part-time, 57% women, 4% African American, 2% Asian American, 5% Hispanic American
- 1,539 degree-seeking graduate students
- 57% of applicants admitted
- SAT or ACT with writing required
- 59% graduate within 6 years

General. Founded in 1933. Regionally accredited. **Degrees:** 960 bachelor's, 10 associate awarded; master's offered. **ROTC:** Air Force. **Location:** 50 miles from New York City, 75 miles from Philadelphia. **Calendar:** Semester, limited summer session. **Full-time faculty:** 247 total; 84% have terminal degrees, 16% minority, 53% women. **Part-time faculty:** 313 total; 23% have terminal degrees, 6% minority, 50% women. **Class size:** 44% < 20, 56% 20-39, less than 1% 40-49. **Special facilities:** Multimedia communications center with TV and radio station, sculpture garden, ice house-gallery.

Freshman class profile. 7,039 applied, 3,978 admitted, 961 enrolled.

Mid 50% test scores			
SAT critical reading:	490-560	GPA 2.0-2.99:	26%
SAT math:	510-590	Rank in top quarter:	46%
SAT writing:	490-570	Rank in top tenth:	18%
ACT composite:	22-24	End year in good standing:	96%
GPA 3.75 or higher:	15%	Return as sophomores:	75%
GPA 3.50-3.74:	19%	Out-of-state:	18%
GPA 3.0-3.49:	40%	Live on campus:	82%

Basis for selection. School record, GPA, test scores important followed by recommendations and essay. Resume of activities including community involvement and leadership positions encouraged. Audition recommended for music programs; portfolio recommended for art programs. Interview recommended for Music and Theatre Arts Department. **Homeschooled:** State high school equivalency certificate required. All students who submit portfolio of coursework in lieu of transcript must also complete institution's curriculum chart for homeschooled students.

High school preparation. College-preparatory program recommended. 16 units required; 20 recommended. Required and recommended units include English 4, mathematics 3, social studies 2, history 2, science 2 (laboratory 1), foreign language 2 and academic electives 5.

2008-2009 Annual costs. Tuition/fees: $24,098. Room/board: $9,221. Books/supplies: $1,000. Personal expenses: $1,996.

2008-2009 Financial aid. **Need-based:** 801 full-time freshmen applied for aid; 601 were judged to have need; 601 of these received aid. Average need met was 85%. Average scholarship/grant was $12,433; average loan $3,696. 70% of total undergraduate aid awarded as scholarships/grants, 30%

as loans/jobs. **Non-need-based:** Awarded to 1,663 full-time undergraduates, including 393 freshmen. Scholarships awarded for academics, alumni affiliation, art, athletics, leadership.

Application procedures. Admission: Priority date 12/1; deadline 3/1 (receipt date). $50 fee, may be waived for applicants with need. Admission notification 4/1. Must reply by 5/1. All deposits non-refundable after May 1. **Financial aid:** Priority date 2/15; no closing date. FAFSA required. Applicants notified on a rolling basis starting 2/15; must reply within 2 week(s) of notification.

Academics. Special study options: Accelerated study, combined bachelor's/graduate degree, cooperative education, cross-registration, double major, dual enrollment of high school students, honors, independent study, internships, liberal arts/career combination, student-designed major, study abroad, teacher certification program, Washington semester. **Credit/placement by examination:** AP, CLEP, IB, SAT, ACT, institutional tests. 30 credit hours maximum toward bachelor's degree. AP credit awarded only for institutional course equivalents. **Support services:** Learning center, reduced course load, remedial instruction, study skills assistance, tutoring, writing center.

Honors college/program. Students admitted to honors school with 1200 SAT (exclusive of Writing, with Critical Reading score no less than 510) and 3.3 GPA.

Majors. Biology: General, environmental. **Business:** Business admin, international. **Communications:** General. **Computer sciences:** General. **Education:** General, special. **Engineering:** Software. **Foreign languages:** General. **Health:** Clinical lab science, health services, nursing (RN). **History:** General. **Math:** General. **Physical sciences:** Chemistry. **Protective services:** Criminal justice. **Psychology:** General. **Public administration:** Social work. **Social sciences:** General, anthropology, political science. **Visual/performing arts:** Art, dramatic. **Other:** Fine arts, Interdisciplinary studies.

Most popular majors. Business/marketing 29%, communications/journalism 16%, education 15%, psychology 7%, security/protective services 8%, visual/performing arts 7%.

Computing on campus. 698 workstations in dormitories, library, computer center, student center. Dormitories wired for high-speed internet access and linked to campus network. Commuter students can connect to campus network. Online library, helpline, student web hosting, wireless network available.

Student life. Freshman orientation: Mandatory, $200 fee. Preregistration for classes offered. Two-day orientation held in July. **Policies:** No one who has not successfully completed at least 12 credit hours may associate with a fraternity or sorority. Students must have minimum 2.2 cumulative GPA and be registered full-time. Transfer students taking 12 or more credits may also associate. **Housing:** Coed dorms, apartments, wellness housing available. $150 deposit. Honors, 24-hour quiet floors, leadership floors available. **Activities:** Bands, choral groups, dance, drama, international student organizations, literary magazine, music ensembles, musical theater, radio station, student government, student newspaper, TV station, Hillel, Christian Ambassadors, Catholic center, African-American student union, Latin American club, Circle K, Rotaract Club, alternative lifestyles clubs.

Athletics. NCAA. **Intercollegiate:** Baseball M, basketball, cross-country, field hockey W, football (tackle) M, golf, lacrosse W, sailing, soccer, softball W, tennis, track and field. **Intramural:** Badminton, basketball, football (non-tackle), soccer, softball, tennis, volleyball, water polo. **Team name:** Hawks.

Student services. Adult student services, alcohol/substance abuse counseling, chaplain/spiritual director, career counseling, services for economically disadvantaged, student employment services, financial aid counseling, health services, legal services, personal counseling, placement for graduates, veterans' counselor, women's services. **Physically disabled:** Services for visually, speech, hearing impaired.

Contact. E-mail: admission@monmouth.edu
Phone: (732) 571-3456 Toll-free number: (800) 543-9671
Fax: (732) 263-5166
Lauren Cifelli, Director of Undergraduate Admission, Monmouth University, 400 Cedar Avenue, West Long Branch, NJ 07764-1898

Montclair State University

Upper Montclair, New Jersey — **CB member**
www.montclair.edu — **CB code: 2520**

- Public 4-year university
- Residential campus in large town
- 13,101 degree-seeking undergraduates: 15% part-time, 61% women, 9% African American, 6% Asian American, 20% Hispanic American, 2% international
- 2,491 degree-seeking graduate students
- 52% of applicants admitted
- SAT or ACT (ACT writing recommended) required
- 61% graduate within 6 years; 5% enter graduate study

General. Founded in 1908. Regionally accredited. Includes Institute for the Humanities, Institute for the Advancement of Philosophy for Children, Institute for Critical Thinking, New Jersey School of Conservation in Stokes State Forest, Branchville, and Center for Continuing Education. **Degrees:** 2,632 bachelor's awarded; master's, doctoral offered. **ROTC:** Army, Naval, Air Force. **Location:** 14 miles from New York City. **Calendar:** Semester, limited summer session. **Full-time faculty:** 524 total; 92% have terminal degrees, 23% minority, 47% women. **Part-time faculty:** 873 total; 5% have terminal degrees, 9% minority, 55% women.

Freshman class profile. 12,151 applied, 6,357 admitted, 2,271 enrolled.

Mid 50% test scores			
SAT critical reading:	440-530	Rank in top quarter:	33%
SAT math:	450-550	Rank in top tenth:	10%
SAT writing:	450-540	End year in good standing:	95%
GPA 3.75 or higher:	8%	Return as sophomores:	82%
GPA 3.50-3.74:	14%	Out-of-state:	3%
GPA 3.0-3.49:	39%	Live on campus:	47%
GPA 2.0-2.99:	39%	International:	1%

Basis for selection. School achievement record most important. Extracurricular activities, test scores, community activities also important. Consideration given to disadvantaged applicants. Interview required for art, music, music therapy, speech, theater, and dance programs; audition required for dance, music, speech, theater programs; portfolio required for art programs. **Homeschooled:** Statement describing homeschool structure and mission, transcript of courses and grades required.

High school preparation. College-preparatory program required. 16 units required. Required units include English 4, mathematics 3, social studies 2, science 2 (laboratory 2), foreign language 2 and academic electives 3. 4 math (including trigonometry) required of computer science majors. Algebra II required for business administration majors. 3 additional units in English, social studies, science, math, or foreign language required.

2008-2009 Annual costs. Tuition/fees: $9,428; $17,208 out-of-state. Room/board: $9,660. Books/supplies: $1,200. Personal expenses: $3,637.

2008-2009 Financial aid. Need-based: 1,550 full-time freshmen applied for aid; 1,156 were judged to have need; 1,077 of these received aid. Average need met was 66%. Average scholarship/grant was $7,796; average loan $3,528. 49% of total undergraduate aid awarded as scholarships/grants, 51% as loans/jobs. **Non-need-based:** Awarded to 1,134 full-time undergraduates, including 211 freshmen. Scholarships awarded for academics, alumni affiliation, art, leadership, minority status, music/drama, ROTC, state residency.

Application procedures. Admission: Closing date 3/1 (postmark date). $60 fee, may be waived for applicants with need. Admission notification on a rolling basis beginning on or about 10/1. Must reply by 5/1. Immediate decision process available to seniors at some local high schools. **Financial aid:** Priority date 3/1; no closing date. FAFSA required. Applicants notified on a rolling basis starting 4/1; must reply within 2 week(s) of notification.

Academics. Special study options: Combined bachelor's/graduate degree, cooperative education, double major, ESL, honors, independent study, internships, study abroad, teacher certification program, Washington semester. Joint admission with UMDNJ. **Credit/placement by examination:** AP, CLEP, IB, institutional tests. 24 credit hours maximum toward bachelor's degree. **Support services:** Learning center, pre-admission summer program, reduced course load, remedial instruction, tutoring, writing center.

Honors college/program. Two of the following required: rank in top 10% of high school class; 600 SAT verbal or math; 1200 SAT (exclusive of Writing); unusual ability in creative arts or exceptional leadership or other extraordinary accomplishment.

Majors. Area/ethnic studies: Women's. **Biology:** General, biochemistry, molecular. **Business:** Business admin. **Communications:** Broadcast journalism, organizational, radio/tv. **Computer sciences:** General, computer science, information technology. **Education:** Business, drama/dance, health, physical, technology/industrial arts. **Family/consumer sciences:** General, food/nutrition. **Foreign languages:** Classics, French, Italian, Latin, linguistics, Spanish. **Health:** Athletic training, health services, music therapy. **History:** General. **Interdisciplinary:** Peace/conflict. **Liberal arts:** Arts/sciences, humanities. **Math:** General. **Philosophy/religion:** Philosophy, religion.

Physical sciences: Chemistry, geology, physics. **Psychology:** General. **Social sciences:** Anthropology, economics, geography, political science, sociology. **Visual/performing arts:** Art, cinematography, dance, dramatic, fashion design, graphic design, illustration, music performance. **Other:** Animation and illustration, Justice studies.

Most popular majors. Biology 6%, business/marketing 18%, family/consumer sciences 18%, psychology 10%, social sciences 8%, visual/performing arts 9%.

Computing on campus. 700 workstations in dormitories, library, computer center, student center. Dormitories wired for high-speed internet access and linked to campus network. Commuter students can connect to campus network. Online course registration, online library, helpline, repair service, wireless network available.

Student life. **Freshman orientation:** Mandatory, $175 fee. Preregistration for classes offered. **Housing:** Coed dorms, single-sex dorms, special housing for disabled, apartments available. $125 nonrefundable deposit, deadline 5/1. **Activities:** Bands, campus ministries, choral groups, dance, drama, international student organizations, literary magazine, music ensembles, musical theater, opera, radio station, student government, student newspaper, symphony orchestra, TV station, Newman center, college life union board, recreation board, organization for students of African unity, Latin American student organization, LEAD.

Athletics. NCAA. **Intercollegiate:** Baseball M, basketball, diving, field hockey W, football (tackle) M, lacrosse, soccer, softball W, swimming, track and field, volleyball W. **Intramural:** Badminton, basketball, bowling, football (tackle) M, golf, racquetball, softball, tennis, volleyball, water polo. **Team name:** Red Hawks.

Student services. Adult student services, alcohol/substance abuse counseling, chaplain/spiritual director, career counseling, services for economically disadvantaged, student employment services, financial aid counseling, health services, on-campus daycare, personal counseling, placement for graduates, veterans' counselor, women's services. **Physically disabled:** Services for visually, speech, hearing impaired. **Learning disabled:** Comprehensive services available.

Contact. E-mail: undergraduate.admissions@mail.montclair.edu
Phone: (973) 655-4444 Toll-free number: (800) 331-9205
Fax: (973) 655-7700
Jason Langdon, Director of Admissions, Montclair State University, One Normal Avenue, Upper Montclair, NJ 07043-1624

New Jersey City University

Jersey City, New Jersey — **CB member**
www.njcu.edu — **CB code: 2516**

- Public 4-year university
- Commuter campus in small city
- 6,068 degree-seeking undergraduates: 28% part-time, 61% women, 19% African American, 7% Asian American, 35% Hispanic American, 1% international
- 938 degree-seeking graduate students
- 30% of applicants admitted
- SAT or ACT, application essay required

General. Founded in 1927. Regionally accredited. **Degrees:** 1,020 bachelor's awarded; master's offered. **Location:** 5 miles from New York City. **Calendar:** Semester, extensive summer session. **Full-time faculty:** 238 total; 86% have terminal degrees, 34% minority, 50% women. **Part-time faculty:** 433 total; 27% minority, 42% women. **Class size:** 52% < 20, 46% 20-39, less than 1% 40-49, 1% 50-99. **Special facilities:** Laboratory school for multihandicapped children, computer technology center, cooperative education, media studies center.

Freshman class profile. 4,366 applied, 1,309 admitted, 678 enrolled.

Mid 50% test scores		**Out-of-state:**	1%
SAT critical reading:	420-500	**Live on campus:**	4%
SAT math:	430-510	**Fraternities:**	2%
SAT writing:	410-500	**Sororities:**	2%
Return as sophomores:	70%		

Basis for selection. High school courses, grades, class rank, and test scores most important, followed by essay or personal statement. Special program for educationally disadvantaged applicants available with above criteria. Interview recommended for all; audition required for music programs; portfolio recommended for art programs.

High school preparation. Required and recommended units include English 4, mathematics 4, social studies 4, science 4 (laboratory 2-3) and foreign language 2.

2008-2009 Annual costs. Tuition/fees: $8,727; $15,793 out-of-state. Room/board: $8,613. Books/supplies: $1,600. Personal expenses: $1,600.

Application procedures. **Admission:** Closing date 4/1. $35 fee, may be waived for applicants with need, free for online applicants. Admission notification on a rolling basis beginning on or about 1/1. Must reply by May 1 or within 3 week(s) if notified thereafter. **Financial aid:** Priority date 4/15; no closing date. FAFSA required.

Academics. Cooperative education placement offered in all majors. Professional diploma in school psychology offered. **Special study options:** Cooperative education, distance learning, double major, dual enrollment of high school students, ESL, honors, independent study, internships, liberal arts/career combination, study abroad, teacher certification program, Washington semester, weekend college. **Credit/placement by examination:** AP, CLEP, IB, institutional tests. 30 credit hours maximum toward bachelor's degree. **Support services:** Learning center, pre-admission summer program, reduced course load, remedial instruction, tutoring, writing center.

Majors. **Biology:** General. **Business:** Business admin. **Communications:** General. **Computer sciences:** General. **Education:** Early childhood, elementary, reading, special. **Foreign languages:** Spanish. **Health:** Clinical lab science, health services, nursing (RN). **History:** General. **Math:** General. **Philosophy/religion:** Philosophy. **Physical sciences:** Chemistry, geology, physics. **Protective services:** Firefighting, security services. **Psychology:** General. **Social sciences:** Economics, political science, sociology. **Visual/performing arts:** Art, studio arts.

Most popular majors. Business/marketing 27%, psychology 12%, security/protective services 12%, social sciences 8%.

Computing on campus. 1,400 workstations in dormitories, library, computer center, student center. Dormitories wired for high-speed internet access and linked to campus network. Commuter students can connect to campus network. Online course registration, online library, helpline, wireless network available.

Student life. **Freshman orientation:** Mandatory. **Housing:** Coed dorms, apartments available. $150 deposit, deadline 8/13. **Activities:** Bands, campus ministries, choral groups, dance, drama, film society, international student organizations, literary magazine, music ensembles, musical theater, opera, radio station, student government, student newspaper, Campus Christian fellowship, black freedom society, Latin power association, Africana journal.

Athletics. NCAA. **Intercollegiate:** Baseball M, basketball, bowling W, cross-country, soccer, softball W, track and field, volleyball. **Intramural:** Basketball, bowling, racquetball, soccer, softball, swimming, table tennis, volleyball, weight lifting. **Team name:** Gothic Knights.

Student services. Chaplain/spiritual director, career counseling, student employment services, financial aid counseling, health services, on-campus daycare, personal counseling, placement for graduates, veterans' counselor, women's services. **Physically disabled:** Services for visually, speech, hearing impaired.

Contact. E-mail: admissions@njcu.edu
Phone: (201) 200-3234 Toll-free number: (888) 441-6528
Carmen Panlilio, Assistant Vice President for Admissions and Financial Aid, New Jersey City University, 2039 Kennedy Boulevard, Jersey City, NJ 07305-1597

New Jersey Institute of Technology

Newark, New Jersey — **CB member**
www.njit.edu — **CB code: 2513**

- Public 4-year university
- Residential campus in very large city
- 5,213 degree-seeking undergraduates: 17% part-time, 20% women, 10% African American, 21% Asian American, 19% Hispanic American, 1% Native American, 5% international
- 2,698 degree-seeking graduate students
- 69% of applicants admitted
- SAT or ACT with writing required
- 58% graduate within 6 years

General. Founded in 1881. Regionally accredited. **Degrees:** 878 bachelor's awarded; master's, doctoral offered. **ROTC:** Army, Air Force. **Location:** 10 miles from New York City. **Calendar:** Semester, extensive summer session. **Full-time faculty:** 396 total; 100% have terminal degrees, 21% minority, 17% women. **Part-time faculty:** 263 total; 10% minority, 18% women. **Class size:** 69% < 20, 29% 20-39, less than 1% 40-49, less than 1% 50-99, less than 1% >100. **Special facilities:** Computer chip manufacturing laboratory, multi-lifecycle engineering center, numerous government and industry-sponsored research laboratories, hazardous waste management research center, factory floor manufacturing center, observatory.

Freshman class profile. 3,429 applied, 2,379 admitted, 907 enrolled.

Mid 50% test scores		**Return as sophomores:**	83%
SAT critical reading:	480-590	**Out-of-state:**	6%
SAT math:	550-650	**Live on campus:**	51%
SAT writing:	480-580	**International:**	3%
Rank in top quarter:	49%	**Fraternities:**	8%
Rank in top tenth:	25%	**Sororities:**	3%

Basis for selection. Class rank, test scores, secondary school record including grades and curriculum most important. Grades in math and science very important, especially for engineering, engineering science and computer science applicants. Essay and interview required for honors college; interview and portfolio required for architecture programs. Interview required for conditional admission, educational opportunity program.

High school preparation. College-preparatory program required. 16 units required. Required and recommended units include English 4, mathematics 4, social studies 1, history 1, science 2, foreign language 2 and academic electives 2. 3 math required of management majors and science, technology and society majors. One lab science required for management majors.

2008-2009 Annual costs. Tuition/fees: $12,482; $21,942 out-of-state. Room/board: $9,206. Books/supplies: $1,200. Personal expenses: $1,100.

2007-2008 Financial aid. Need-based: 548 full-time freshmen applied for aid; 448 were judged to have need; 448 of these received aid. Average need met was 65%. Average scholarship/grant was $8,591; average loan $3,529. 64% of total undergraduate aid awarded as scholarships/grants, 36% as loans/jobs. **Non-need-based:** Awarded to 2,309 full-time undergraduates, including 544 freshmen. Scholarships awarded for academics, alumni affiliation, art, leadership, minority status, music/drama, ROTC, state residency. **Additional information:** Extensive co-op program for all majors.

Application procedures. Admission: Closing date 4/1. $50 fee, may be waived for applicants with need. Admission notification on a rolling basis beginning on or about 11/15. Must reply by May 1 or within 2 week(s) if notified thereafter. **Financial aid:** Priority date 3/15, closing date 5/15. FAFSA required. Applicants notified on a rolling basis starting 3/1; must reply within 2 week(s) of notification.

Academics. All freshmen given personal computers. Numerous research opportunities available. **Special study options:** Accelerated study, combined bachelor's/graduate degree, cooperative education, cross-registration, distance learning, double major, ESL, honors, independent study, internships, study abroad. Environmental Scholars Program, Career Advancement Plan, University Research Experience. **Credit/placement by examination:** AP, CLEP, SAT, institutional tests. **Support services:** Learning center, preadmission summer program, reduced course load, remedial instruction, study skills assistance, tutoring.

Majors. Architecture: Architecture. **Biology:** General. **Business:** Business admin. **Computer sciences:** General, information systems, information technology. **Conservation:** Environmental science. **Engineering:** Biomedical, chemical, civil, computer, electrical, environmental, geological, industrial, manufacturing, mechanical, science. **Engineering technology:** General. **History:** General. **Interdisciplinary:** Science/society. **Math:** Applied. **Physical sciences:** Chemistry, physics.

Most popular majors. Architecture 10%, business/marketing 8%, computer/information sciences 23%, engineering/engineering technologies 52%.

Computing on campus. PC or laptop required. 1,500 workstations in dormitories, library, computer center, student center. Dormitories wired for high-speed internet access and linked to campus network. Commuter students can connect to campus network. Online course registration, online library, helpline, repair service, student web hosting, wireless network available.

Student life. Freshman orientation: Mandatory. **Housing:** Coed dorms available. $100 nonrefundable deposit, deadline 6/2. **Activities:** Dance, drama, literary magazine, radio station, student government, student newspaper, Arab student association, black student engineers association, Caribbean student association, Chinese student association, Hispanic students in technology association, Intervarsity Christian Federation, Polish student association, Islamic student association, women engineers club.

Athletics. NCAA. **Intercollegiate:** Baseball M, basketball, cross-country, fencing, soccer, swimming, tennis, volleyball. **Intramural:** Badminton, basketball, bowling, cricket, fencing, racquetball, soccer, swimming, table tennis, tennis, track and field, volleyball, weight lifting. **Team name:** Highlanders.

Student services. Alcohol/substance abuse counseling, career counseling, student employment services, health services, on-campus daycare, personal counseling, placement for graduates, veterans' counselor, women's services. **Physically disabled:** Services for visually, speech, hearing impaired.

Contact. E-mail: admissions@njit.edu
Phone: (973) 596-3300 Toll-free number: (800) 925-6548
Fax: (973) 596-3461
Kathy Kelly, Director of Admissions, New Jersey Institute of Technology, University Heights, Newark, NJ 07102

Princeton University

Princeton, New Jersey **CB member**
www.princeton.edu **CB code: 2672**

- Private 4-year university
- Residential campus in large town
- 4,878 degree-seeking undergraduates: 48% women, 8% African American, 15% Asian American, 8% Hispanic American, 1% Native American, 10% international
- 2,452 degree-seeking graduate students
- 10% of applicants admitted
- SAT or ACT with writing, SAT Subject Tests, application essay required
- 96% graduate within 6 years

General. Founded in 1746. Regionally accredited. **Degrees:** 1,137 bachelor's awarded; master's, doctoral offered. **ROTC:** Army, Air Force. **Location:** 50 miles from New York City, 45 miles from Philadelphia. **Calendar:** Semester. **Full-time faculty:** 843 total; 92% have terminal degrees, 18% minority, 29% women. **Part-time faculty:** 201 total; 64% have terminal degrees, 14% minority, 40% women. **Class size:** 74% < 20, 13% 20-39, 4% 40-49, 5% 50-99, 4% >100. **Special facilities:** Institute for integrative genomics, center for theoretical physics, institute in neuroscience, center for creative and performing arts, center for human values, plasma physics laboratory, council of the humanities, institute for international and regional studies, observatory, center for energy and the environment.

Freshman class profile. 21,370 applied, 2,122 admitted, 1,243 enrolled.

Mid 50% test scores		**GPA 3.0-3.49:**	8%
SAT critical reading:	690-790	**Rank in top quarter:**	100%
SAT math:	700-790	**Rank in top tenth:**	97%
SAT writing:	690-780	**Return as sophomores:**	98%
ACT composite:	31-34	**Out-of-state:**	85%
GPA 3.75 or higher:	81%	**Live on campus:**	100%
GPA 3.50-3.74:	11%	**International:**	11%

Basis for selection. GED not accepted. School achievement record and recommendations of guidance counselor and 2 teachers very important. Test scores required, including scores for 3 SAT Subject Tests. Prospective students in engineering should take SAT Subject Tests in physics and either math or chemistry, as well as one other test in subject of their choice. Interview recommended for all; audition or submission of supplementary materials (CD of solo performance) required for music programs; portfolio required for creative writing, dance (video), visual arts programs. Supplementary materials for the visual and performing arts considered. **Homeschooled:** Statement describing homeschool structure and mission required.

High school preparation. College-preparatory program recommended. Recommended units include English 4, mathematics 4, social studies 2, history 2, science 4 (laboratory 2) and foreign language 4. 1 physics or chemistry (preferably both) and 4 math urged for prospective engineering majors.

2008-2009 Annual costs. Tuition/fees: $34,290. Room/board: $11,405. Books/supplies: $1,200. Personal expenses: $2,295.

2007-2008 Financial aid. All financial aid based on need. 793 full-time freshmen applied for aid; 671 were judged to have need; 671 of these received aid. Average need met was 100%. Average scholarship/grant was $31,187. 97% of total undergraduate aid awarded as scholarships/grants, 3% as loans/jobs. **Additional information:** All aid need-based; all aid grant money (no loans); institution meets full demonstrated need.

Application procedures. Admission: Closing date 1/1 (postmark date). $65 fee, may be waived for applicants with need. Admission notification 3/31. Must reply by May 1 or within 1 week(s) if notified thereafter. **Financial aid:** Priority date 2/1; no closing date. FAFSA, institutional form required. Applicants notified by 4/1; must reply by 5/1.

Academics. Independent project in junior year and senior thesis required for graduation. **Special study options:** Cross-registration, exchange student, independent study, student-designed major, study abroad, teacher certification program. **Credit/placement by examination:** AP, CLEP, IB, institutional tests. **Support services:** Learning center, pre-admission summer program, study skills assistance, tutoring, writing center.

Majors. Architecture: Architecture. **Area/ethnic studies:** East Asian, Near/Middle Eastern. **Biology:** Ecology, molecular. **Engineering:** Chemical, civil, computer, electrical, mechanical, operations research. **Foreign languages:** Classics, comparative lit, German, Italian, Slavic, Spanish. **History:** General. **Math:** General. **Philosophy/religion:** Philosophy, religion. **Physical sciences:** Astrophysics, chemistry, geology, physics. **Psychology:** General. **Public administration:** General. **Social sciences:** Anthropology, economics, political science, sociology. **Visual/performing arts:** Art history/conservation.

Most popular majors. Biology 10%, engineering/engineering technologies 17%, English 7%, history 8%, philosophy/religious studies 6%, physical sciences 6%, public administration/social services 8%, social sciences 22%.

Computing on campus. 500 workstations in dormitories, library, computer center, student center. Dormitories wired for high-speed internet access and linked to campus network. Commuter students can connect to campus network. Online course registration, online library, helpline, repair service, student web hosting, wireless network available.

Student life. Freshman orientation: Mandatory. Three-day orientation. Optional 1-week trip with Outdoor Action or Student Volunteer Council. **Housing:** Guaranteed on-campus for all undergraduates. Coed dorms, special housing for disabled, apartments available. Residential colleges for freshmen and sophomores. Kosher dining facilities available. **Activities:** Bands, campus ministries, choral groups, dance, drama, film society, international student organizations, literary magazine, music ensembles, Model UN, musical theater, opera, radio station, student government, student newspaper, symphony orchestra, over 200 student organizations available.

Athletics. NCAA. **Intercollegiate:** Baseball M, basketball, cross-country, diving, fencing, field hockey W, football (tackle), golf, ice hockey, lacrosse, rowing (crew), soccer, softball W, squash, swimming, tennis, track and field, volleyball, water polo, wrestling M. **Intramural:** Badminton, basketball, bowling, football (non-tackle), golf, ice hockey, judo, racquetball, soccer, softball, tennis, water polo. **Team name:** Tigers.

Student services. Alcohol/substance abuse counseling, chaplain/spiritual director, career counseling, student employment services, financial aid counseling, health services, minority student services, personal counseling, placement for graduates, women's services. **Physically disabled:** Services for visually, speech, hearing impaired.

Contact. E-mail: uaoffice@princeton.edu
Phone: (609) 258-3060 Fax: (609) 258-6743
Janet Rapelye, Dean of Admission, Princeton University, Box 430, Princeton, NJ 08544-0430

Rabbi Jacob Joseph School
Edison, New Jersey

- Private 4-year rabbinical college
- Large town

General. Accredited by AARTS. **Calendar:** Semester.

Contact. Phone: (732) 985-6533
One Plainfield Avenue, Edison, NJ 08817

Rabbinical College of America
Morristown, New Jersey

CB code: 1546

- Private 4-year rabbinical college for men affiliated with Jewish faith
- Residential campus in large town

General. Founded in 1956. Accredited by AARTS. **Location:** One mile from downtown, 35 miles from New York City. **Calendar:** Semester.

Annual costs/financial aid. Tuition/fees (2008-2009): $9,700. Room/board: $6,800.

Contact. Phone: (973) 267-9404
Registrar, 226 Sussex Avenue, CN 1996, Morristown, NJ 07962-1996

Ramapo College of New Jersey
Mahwah, New Jersey **CB member**
www.ramapo.edu **CB code: 2884**

- Public 4-year liberal arts college
- Residential campus in large town
- 5,284 degree-seeking undergraduates: 8% part-time, 58% women, 6% African American, 5% Asian American, 9% Hispanic American, 2% international
- 225 degree-seeking graduate students
- 46% of applicants admitted
- SAT, application essay required
- 70% graduate within 6 years

General. Founded in 1969. Regionally accredited. **Degrees:** 1,234 bachelor's awarded; master's offered. **ROTC:** Air Force. **Location:** 35 miles from New York City. **Calendar:** Semester, extensive summer session. **Full-time faculty:** 199 total; 95% have terminal degrees, 20% minority, 46% women. **Part-time faculty:** 195 total; 46% women. **Class size:** 28% < 20, 69% 20-39, 3% 40-49. **Special facilities:** International telecommunications center, electron microscope, Holocaust center, performing arts center, international and intercultural education office, environmental studies/sustainability education center, greenhouse center, astronomical observatory.

Freshman class profile. 5,556 applied, 2,550 admitted, 880 enrolled.

Mid 50% test scores			
SAT critical reading:	520-610	GPA 2.0-2.99:	12%
SAT math:	540-630	Rank in top quarter:	60%
SAT writing:	520-610	Rank in top tenth:	21%
GPA 3.75 or higher:	18%	Return as sophomores:	88%
GPA 3.50-3.74:	22%	Out-of-state:	3%
GPA 3.0-3.49:	48%	Live on campus:	85%
		International:	2%

Basis for selection. School achievement record, test scores most important. Applicants should rank in top 25% of high school class. ESL or TOEFL assessment used to determine English language proficiency. SAT Reading and ACT Reading/English may be used for academic advising. Certain majors have additional entrance requirements.

High school preparation. 18 units required. Required units include English 4, mathematics 3, social studies 3, science 3 (laboratory 3), foreign language 2 and academic electives 3. Math must consist of algebra I, geometry, and algebra II.

2008-2009 Annual costs. Tuition/fees: $10,765; $17,476 out-of-state. Room/board: $10,830. Books/supplies: $1,200. Personal expenses: $2,250.

2007-2008 Financial aid. Need-based: 717 full-time freshmen applied for aid; 476 were judged to have need; 454 of these received aid. Average need met was 73%. Average scholarship/grant was $9,966; average loan $3,326. 48% of total undergraduate aid awarded as scholarships/grants, 52% as loans/jobs. **Non-need-based:** Awarded to 1,069 full-time undergraduates, including 239 freshmen. Scholarships awarded for academics, state residency.

Application procedures. Admission: Closing date 3/1. $60 fee, may be waived for applicants with need. Admission notification on a rolling basis beginning on or about 11/15. Must reply by 5/1. **Financial aid:** Priority date 3/1; no closing date. FAFSA required. Applicants notified on a rolling basis starting 4/1; must reply by 5/1 or within 2 week(s) of notification.

Academics. Thematic learning communities. **Special study options:** Accelerated study, combined bachelor's/graduate degree, cooperative education, cross-registration, distance learning, double major, dual enrollment of high school students, exchange student, external degree, honors, independent study, internships, liberal arts/career combination, student-designed major, study abroad, teacher certification program. **Credit/placement by examination:** AP, CLEP, IB, SAT. 65 credit hours maximum toward bachelor's degree. **Support services:** Learning center, pre-admission summer program, reduced course load, remedial instruction, study skills assistance, tutoring, writing center.

Majors. Area/ethnic studies: American. **Biology:** General, biochemistry, bioinformatics. **Business:** Accounting, business admin, international. **Communications:** General. **Computer sciences:** General, information systems.

Conservation: Environmental science, environmental studies. **Foreign languages:** Comparative lit, Spanish. **Health:** Clinical lab science, health services. **History:** General. **Interdisciplinary:** Biological/physical sciences, global studies. **Legal studies:** General. **Liberal arts:** Arts/sciences, humanities. **Math:** General. **Physical sciences:** Chemistry, physics. **Psychology:** General. **Public administration:** Social work. **Social sciences:** Economics, political science, sociology. **Visual/performing arts:** General, art, dramatic, multimedia.

Most popular majors. Biology 7%, business/marketing 17%, communications/journalism 10%, foreign language 7%, health sciences 8%, legal studies 6%, psychology 13%, visual/performing arts 7%.

Computing on campus. 1,058 workstations in dormitories, library, computer center, student center. Dormitories wired for high-speed internet access and linked to campus network. Commuter students can connect to campus network. Online course registration, online library, helpline, repair service, student web hosting, wireless network available.

Student life. **Freshman orientation:** Mandatory, $130 fee. Preregistration for classes offered. Several sessions held throughout summer. **Policies:** Smoking prohibited in all physical buildings on campus. Smokers must stand 25 feet away from buildings. **Housing:** Guaranteed on-campus for freshmen. Coed dorms, special housing for disabled, apartments, cooperative housing, wellness housing available. $200 partly refundable deposit, deadline 5/1. **Activities:** Campus ministries, choral groups, dance, drama, international student organizations, literary magazine, music ensembles, Model UN, musical theater, radio station, student government, student newspaper, TV station, United Asian Americans, College Democrats, College Republicans, Hillel, Intervarsity Christian Fellowship, Muslim student association, Community Builders Coalition, culture club.

Athletics. NCAA. **Intercollegiate:** Baseball M, basketball, cheerleading M, cross-country, field hockey W, lacrosse W, soccer, softball W, swimming, tennis, track and field, volleyball. **Intramural:** Basketball, bowling, football (non-tackle) M, soccer, softball, volleyball. **Team name:** Roadrunners.

Student services. Adult student services, alcohol/substance abuse counseling, chaplain/spiritual director, career counseling, services for economically disadvantaged, student employment services, financial aid counseling, health services, minority student services, personal counseling, placement for graduates, veterans' counselor, women's services. **Physically disabled:** Services for visually, speech, hearing impaired. **Learning disabled:** Comprehensive services available.

Contact. E-mail: admissions@ramapo.edu
Phone: (201) 684-7300 Toll-free number: (800) 972-6276
Fax: (201) 684-7964
Peter Rice, Director of Admissions, Ramapo College of New Jersey, 505 Ramapo Valley Road, Mahwah, NJ 07430-1680

Freshman class profile. 4,511 applied, 2,411 admitted, 842 enrolled.

Mid 50% test scores		Rank in top tenth:	28%
SAT critical reading:	490-590	End year in good standing:	90%
SAT math:	500-600	Return as sophomores:	83%
ACT composite:	18-22	Out-of-state:	2%
Rank in top quarter:	58%	Live on campus:	86%

Basis for selection. Secondary school record, class rank, test scores most important; essay, recommendations, extracurricular activities also important; interview, work experience considered. **Homeschooled:** Statement describing homeschool structure and mission, transcript of courses and grades required.

High school preparation. College-preparatory program required. 16 units required; 18 recommended. Required and recommended units include English 4, mathematics 3, social studies 2, science 2 (laboratory 2), foreign language 2 and academic electives 5.

2008-2009 Annual costs. Tuition/fees: $9,815; $14,988 out-of-state. Room/board: $10,166. Books/supplies: $1,400. Personal expenses: $1,614.

2008-2009 Financial aid. **Need-based:** 727 full-time freshmen applied for aid; 554 were judged to have need; 538 of these received aid. Average need met was 80%. Average scholarship/grant was $9,341; average loan $3,470. 36% of total undergraduate aid awarded as scholarships/grants, 64% as loans/jobs. **Non-need-based:** Awarded to 1,024 full-time undergraduates, including 314 freshmen. Scholarships awarded for academics, art, leadership, minority status, music/drama, state residency.

Application procedures. **Admission:** Priority date 2/1; deadline 6/1 (postmark date). $50 fee, may be waived for applicants with need. Admission notification on a rolling basis beginning on or about 10/1. Must reply by May 1 or within 2 week(s) if notified thereafter. **Financial aid:** Priority date 3/1; no closing date. FAFSA required. Applicants notified on a rolling basis starting 4/1; must reply within 2 week(s) of notification.

Academics. **Special study options:** Combined bachelor's/graduate degree, cross-registration, distance learning, double major, dual enrollment of high school students, honors, independent study, internships, liberal arts/career combination, semester at sea, study abroad, teacher certification program, Washington semester. Dual degree bachelor's program in engineering with Rutgers University and New Jersey Institute of Technology, preceptorial advising, opportunities for specialized research, extensive Washington internship available. **Credit/placement by examination:** AP, CLEP, IB, SAT, ACT, institutional tests. 32 credit hours maximum toward bachelor's degree. **Support services:** Learning center, pre-admission summer program, reduced course load, remedial instruction, study skills assistance, tutoring, writing center.

Richard Stockton College of New Jersey

Pomona, New Jersey — **CB member**
www.stockton.edu — **CB code: 2889**

- Public 4-year liberal arts college
- Residential campus in large town
- 6,544 degree-seeking undergraduates: 10% part-time, 58% women, 8% African American, 5% Asian American, 6% Hispanic American, 1% Native American
- 533 degree-seeking graduate students
- 53% of applicants admitted
- SAT or ACT (ACT writing optional), application essay required
- 65% graduate within 6 years; 28% enter graduate study

General. Founded in 1969. Regionally accredited. 7-acre marine science field station located off-campus. **Degrees:** 1,723 bachelor's awarded; master's, doctoral offered. **Location:** 12 miles from Atlantic City, 50 miles from Philadelphia. **Calendar:** Semester, extensive summer session. **Full-time faculty:** 281 total; 89% have terminal degrees, 23% minority, 50% women. **Part-time faculty:** 218 total; 30% have terminal degrees. **Class size:** 22% < 20, 73% 20-39, 3% 40-49, less than 1% 50-99, less than 1% >100. **Special facilities:** Arboretum, forestry nursery, ecologic succession plots and study preserve, child care center, interdisciplinary natural sciences laboratory, observatory, Holocaust center, geothermal plant, ITV classroom, performing arts theater, hospital located on college grounds.

Majors. **Biology:** General, biochemistry, marine. **Business:** Business admin, hospitality admin. **Communications:** General. **Computer sciences:** Information systems. **Conservation:** Environmental studies. **Education:** Multi-level teacher. **Foreign languages:** General. **Health:** Audiology/speech pathology, nursing (RN). **History:** General. **Liberal arts:** Arts/sciences. **Math:** General. **Physical sciences:** Chemistry, geology, physics. **Psychology:** General. **Public administration:** Social work. **Social sciences:** Criminology, economics, political science, sociology. **Visual/performing arts:** General. **Other:** Computational science, Philosophy and religion.

Most popular majors. Biology 9%, business/marketing 20%, education 11%, psychology 12%, social sciences 15%.

Computing on campus. 3,375 workstations in dormitories, library, computer center, student center. Dormitories wired for high-speed internet access and linked to campus network. Commuter students can connect to campus network. Online course registration, online library, helpline, student web hosting, wireless network available.

Student life. **Freshman orientation:** Mandatory, $50 fee. Preregistration for classes offered. Program includes parents' sessions. **Housing:** Guaranteed on-campus for freshmen. Coed dorms, special housing for disabled, wellness housing available. $150 partly refundable deposit, deadline 5/1. **Activities:** Concert band, choral groups, dance, drama, international student organizations, literary magazine, music ensembles, radio station, student government, student newspaper, TV station, Books Without Borders, unified black students society, Christian Fellowship, Jewish student union, Circle K International, Amnesty International, action volunteers for the environment, Water Watch, CHANGE, campus religious council.

Athletics. NCAA. **Intercollegiate:** Baseball M, basketball, cheerleading, cross-country, field hockey W, lacrosse M, rowing (crew) W, soccer, softball W, tennis W, track and field, volleyball W. **Intramural:** Basketball, football (non-tackle), soccer, softball, table tennis, volleyball. **Team name:** Ospreys.

Student services. Adult student services, alcohol/substance abuse counseling, chaplain/spiritual director, career counseling, services for economically disadvantaged, student employment services, financial aid counseling, health services, on-campus daycare, personal counseling, placement for graduates, veterans' counselor. **Physically disabled:** Services for visually, speech, hearing impaired. **Learning disabled:** Comprehensive services available.

Contact. E-mail: admissions@stockton.edu
Phone: (609) 652-4261 Toll-free number: (866) 772-2885
Fax: (609) 748-5541
John Iacovelli, Dean of Enrollment Management, Richard Stockton College of New Jersey, Jim Leeds Road, Pomona, NJ 08240-0195

Rider University

Lawrenceville, New Jersey — **CB member**
www.rider.edu — **CB code: 2758**

- Private 4-year university
- Residential campus in large town
- 4,606 degree-seeking undergraduates: 14% part-time, 61% women, 9% African American, 3% Asian American, 5% Hispanic American, 3% international
- 993 degree-seeking graduate students
- 74% of applicants admitted
- SAT or ACT with writing, application essay required
- 58% graduate within 6 years; 16.5% enter graduate study

General. Founded in 1865. Regionally accredited. Westminster College of the Arts, located in Lawrenceville and Princeton campuses. **Degrees:** 895 bachelor's, 5 associate awarded; master's offered. **ROTC:** Army. **Location:** 5 miles from Princeton, 3 miles from Trenton. **Calendar:** Semester, extensive summer session. **Full-time faculty:** 244 total; 96% have terminal degrees, 16% minority, 43% women. **Part-time faculty:** 347 total; 40% have terminal degrees, 8% minority, 51% women. **Class size:** 54% < 20, 41% 20-39, 3% 40-49, less than 1% 50-99, less than 1% >100. **Special facilities:** Holocaust/genocide center, teaching and learning center.

Freshman class profile. 6,829 applied, 5,053 admitted, 880 enrolled.

Mid 50% test scores		**GPA 2.0-2.99:**	29%
SAT critical reading:	470-560	**Rank in top quarter:**	37%
SAT math:	470-570	**Rank in top tenth:**	14%
SAT writing:	460-570	**Return as sophomores:**	80%
ACT composite:	18-24	**Out-of-state:**	25%
GPA 3.75 or higher:	16%	**Live on campus:**	89%
GPA 3.50-3.74:	18%	**International:**	2%
GPA 3.0-3.49:	37%		

Basis for selection. High school curriculum most important, followed by GPA, test scores, essay, and recommendations. Extracurricular activities, interview considered. Interview recommended for all; audition required for music program with Westminster College of the Arts. **Homeschooled:** Information about syllabi, reading lists, and/or course descriptions recommended.

High school preparation. College-preparatory program required. 16 units required. Required and recommended units include English 4, mathematics 3-4, social studies 2, history 2, science 4 (laboratory 4) and foreign language 2. Algebra I and II and geometry required for business administration, science, math majors.

2008-2009 Annual costs. Tuition/fees: $27,730. Room/board: $10,280. Books/supplies: $1,400. Personal expenses: $840.

2008-2009 Financial aid. Need-based: 752 full-time freshmen applied for aid; 634 were judged to have need; 634 of these received aid. Average need met was 73%. Average scholarship/grant was $15,186; average loan $3,923. 54% of total undergraduate aid awarded as scholarships/grants, 46% as loans/jobs. **Non-need-based:** Awarded to 1,476 full-time undergraduates, including 313 freshmen. Scholarships awarded for academics, alumni affiliation, art, athletics, leadership, minority status, music/drama, state residency.

Application procedures. Admission: Priority date 1/15; no deadline. $50 fee, may be waived for applicants with need. Admission notification on a rolling basis beginning on or about 12/15. Must reply by May 1 or within 4 week(s) if notified thereafter. Notification of admission decision sent within 3-4 weeks of receiving application. **Financial aid:** Priority date 3/1; no closing date. FAFSA required. Applicants notified on a rolling basis starting 3/15.

Academics. Special study options: Cooperative education, cross-registration, distance learning, double major, honors, independent study, internships, liberal arts/career combination, study abroad, teacher certification program, weekend college. **Credit/placement by examination:** AP, CLEP, SAT, ACT, institutional tests. Policy varies by major. 30 hours of credit by general examination may be counted toward degree. No limit for subject examinations. Not acceptable for last 30 credits of degree program. 4-8 AP courses (24 credits) required for sophomore standing. **Support services:** Learning center, reduced course load, remedial instruction, study skills assistance, tutoring, writing center.

Majors. Area/ethnic studies: American. **Biology:** General, biochemistry. **Business:** Accounting, actuarial science, administrative services, business admin, entrepreneurial studies, finance, human resources, international, management science, managerial economics, marketing, office management, organizational behavior. **Communications:** Advertising, journalism. **Computer sciences:** General. **Conservation:** Environmental science. **Education:** Business, elementary, music, sales/marketing, science, secondary. **Foreign languages:** French, German, Russian, Spanish. **History:** General. **Interdisciplinary:** Biopsychology. **Liberal arts:** Arts/sciences. **Math:** General. **Philosophy/religion:** Philosophy. **Physical sciences:** Chemistry, geology, oceanography, physics. **Psychology:** General. **Social sciences:** Economics, international relations, political science, sociology. **Theology:** Sacred music. **Visual/performing arts:** Art, arts management, music theory/composition, piano/organ, studio arts, voice/opera. **Other:** Global supply chain management.

Most popular majors. Business/marketing 37%, education 16%, English 11%, liberal arts 8%, psychology 7%.

Computing on campus. 300 workstations in dormitories, library, computer center, student center. Dormitories wired for high-speed internet access and linked to campus network. Commuter students can connect to campus network. Online course registration, online library, helpline, student web hosting, wireless network available.

Student life. Freshman orientation: Mandatory, $250 fee. Preregistration for classes offered. Two-day program for new students and family members. **Housing:** Guaranteed on-campus for freshmen. Coed dorms, single-sex dorms, special housing for disabled, apartments, fraternity/sorority housing, wellness housing available. $300 nonrefundable deposit, deadline 5/1. Faculty-in-residence options, suites available. **Activities:** Bands, campus ministries, choral groups, dance, drama, film society, international student organizations, literary magazine, music ensembles, Model UN, musical theater, opera, radio station, student government, student newspaper, TV station, student entertainment council, residence hall association, finance board, Asian student organization, interfraternity council, hunger and homelessness awareness, College Republicans, Latin American student organization.

Athletics. NCAA. **Intercollegiate:** Baseball M, basketball, cheerleading, cross-country, diving, field hockey W, golf M, soccer, softball W, swimming, tennis, track and field, volleyball W, wrestling M. **Intramural:** Basketball, football (non-tackle), ice hockey M, lacrosse, soccer, softball, track and field, volleyball. **Team name:** Broncs.

Student services. Adult student services, alcohol/substance abuse counseling, chaplain/spiritual director, career counseling, services for economically disadvantaged, student employment services, financial aid counseling, health services, minority student services, personal counseling, placement for graduates, veterans' counselor, women's services. **Physically disabled:** Services for visually, speech, hearing impaired.

Contact. E-mail: admissions@rider.edu
Phone: (609) 896-5042 Toll-free number: (800) 257-9026
Fax: (609) 895-6645
Sue Christian, Director of Undergraduate Admissions, Rider University, 2083 Lawrenceville Road, Lawrenceville, NJ 08648-3099

Rowan University

Glassboro, New Jersey — **CB member**
www.rowan.edu — **CB code: 2515**

- Public 4-year university
- Residential campus in large town
- 8,910 degree-seeking undergraduates: 12% part-time, 52% women
- 1,074 degree-seeking graduate students
- 57% of applicants admitted
- SAT or ACT (ACT writing optional) required
- 66% graduate within 6 years; 4% enter graduate study

General. Founded in 1923. Regionally accredited. **Degrees:** 1,927 bachelor's awarded; master's, doctoral offered. **ROTC:** Army. **Location:** 20 miles from Philadelphia. **Calendar:** Semester, extensive summer session. **Full-time faculty:** 407 total; 84% have terminal degrees, 22% minority, 42%

women. **Part-time faculty:** 530 total; 26% have terminal degrees, 10% minority, 46% women. **Class size:** 39% < 20, 60% 20-39, less than 1% 40-49, less than 1% 50-99, less than 1% >100. **Special facilities:** Observatory, glass-blowing museum, on-campus early childhood demonstration center, animal penthouse, greenhouse for biological studies, concert hall.

Freshman class profile. 7,146 applied, 4,048 admitted, 1,334 enrolled.

Mid 50% test scores		**GPA 2.0-2.99:**	20%
SAT critical reading:	480-580	**Rank in top quarter:**	46%
SAT math:	500-600	**Rank in top tenth:**	15%
SAT writing:	480-580	**Return as sophomores:**	83%
GPA 3.75 or higher:	23%	**Out-of-state:**	5%
GPA 3.50-3.74:	19%	**Live on campus:**	83%
GPA 3.0-3.49:	37%		

Basis for selection. School achievement record and test scores most important, followed by recommendations. Audition required for music, theater programs; portfolio interview required for art program.

High school preparation. College-preparatory program required. 16 units required. Required and recommended units include English 4, mathematics 3, science 2 and foreign language 2. Engineering applicants should have 3 units of laboratory science including physics and chemistry, and 4 units of college preparatory math including precalculus. Calculus strongly recommended.

2008-2009 Annual costs. Tuition/fees: $10,908; $18,016 out-of-state. Room/board: $9,456. Books/supplies: $1,200.

2007-2008 Financial aid. Need-based: 1,054 full-time freshmen applied for aid; 632 were judged to have need; 582 of these received aid. Average need met was 92%. Average scholarship/grant was $7,020; average loan $3,182. 30% of total undergraduate aid awarded as scholarships/grants, 70% as loans/jobs. **Non-need-based:** Awarded to 3,806 full-time undergraduates, including 776 freshmen. Scholarships awarded for academics, art, music/drama.

Application procedures. Admission: Closing date 3/1 (postmark date). $50 fee, may be waived for applicants with need. Admission notification on a rolling basis beginning on or about 11/1. Must reply by 5/1. **Financial aid:** Closing date 3/15. FAFSA, institutional form required. Applicants notified on a rolling basis starting 5/1; must reply within 2 week(s) of notification.

Academics. Camden campus offers general education courses and major programs in elementary education, business administration, law/justice, and sociology. **Special study options:** Accelerated study, distance learning, double major, dual enrollment of high school students, ESL, exchange student, honors, independent study, internships, study abroad, teacher certification program, weekend college. **Credit/placement by examination:** AP, CLEP, IB, SAT, institutional tests. 30 credit hours maximum toward bachelor's degree. **Support services:** Pre-admission summer program, remedial instruction, study skills assistance, tutoring, writing center.

Majors. Biology: General, biochemistry. **Business:** Accounting, business admin, finance, human resources, management information systems, management science, marketing. **Communications:** Advertising, journalism, public relations. **Computer sciences:** Computer science. **Education:** General, art, early childhood, elementary, music, secondary, special. **Engineering:** Chemical, civil, electrical, mechanical. **Foreign languages:** Spanish. **Health:** Athletic training. **History:** General. **Liberal arts:** Arts/sciences. **Math:** General. **Parks/recreation:** Health/fitness, sports admin. **Physical sciences:** Chemistry, physics. **Protective services:** Criminal justice. **Psychology:** General, developmental. **Social sciences:** Economics, geography, political science, sociology. **Visual/performing arts:** Art, dance, dramatic, film/cinema, jazz, music performance, music theory/composition, studio arts.

Most popular majors. Business/marketing 16%, communications/journalism 11%, education 18%, English 6%, security/protective services 6%, social sciences 7%.

Computing on campus. 1,200 workstations in library, computer center. Dormitories linked to campus network. Commuter students can connect to campus network. Online course registration, online library, helpline, repair service, student web hosting, wireless network available.

Student life. Freshman orientation: Available. Preregistration for classes offered. Overnight program for freshmen and their families during summer. **Housing:** Guaranteed on-campus for freshmen. Coed dorms, special housing for disabled, apartments, wellness housing available. $200 fully refundable deposit, deadline 5/1. Townhouses. **Activities:** Bands, choral groups, dance, drama, film society, music ensembles, radio station, student government, student newspaper, symphony orchestra, TV station, Over 100 clubs and student organizations available.

Athletics. NCAA. **Intercollegiate:** Baseball M, basketball, cross-country, diving, field hockey W, football (tackle) M, lacrosse W, soccer, softball W, swimming, track and field, volleyball W. **Intramural:** Basketball, bowling, golf, handball, racquetball, soccer, softball, table tennis, tennis, volleyball. **Team name:** Profs.

Student services. Adult student services, alcohol/substance abuse counseling, chaplain/spiritual director, career counseling, student employment services, financial aid counseling, health services, legal services, minority student services, on-campus daycare, personal counseling, placement for graduates, veterans' counselor, women's services. **Physically disabled:** Services for visually, speech, hearing impaired.

Contact. E-mail: admissions@rowan.edu
Phone: (856) 256-4200 Toll-free number: (877) 787-6926
Fax: (856) 256-4430
Albert Betts, Director of Admissions, Rowan University, Savitz Hall, 201 Mullica Hill Road, Glassboro, NJ 08028

Rutgers, The State University of New Jersey: Camden Regional Campus

Camden, New Jersey — **CB member**
www.rutgers.edu — **CB code: 2742**

- Public 4-year university
- Commuter campus in small city
- 3,840 degree-seeking undergraduates: 19% part-time, 54% women, 16% African American, 8% Asian American, 8% Hispanic American, 1% international
- 1,475 degree-seeking graduate students
- 51% of applicants admitted
- SAT or ACT with writing required
- 63% graduate within 6 years

General. Founded in 1927. Regionally accredited. Undergraduate schools: Camden College of Arts and Sciences, University College-Camden, School of Business-Camden. Graduate degrees available at School of Business. Graduate schools: Graduate School-Camden, School of Law-Camden. **Degrees:** 798 bachelor's awarded; master's, first professional offered. **ROTC:** Army, Air Force. **Location:** One mile from Philadelphia. **Calendar:** Semester, extensive summer session. **Full-time faculty:** 237 total; 99% have terminal degrees, 16% minority, 36% women. **Part-time faculty:** 184 total; 99% have terminal degrees, 13% minority, 37% women. **Class size:** 42% < 20, 42% 20-39, 7% 40-49, 6% 50-99, 3% >100. **Special facilities:** Fine arts center.

Freshman class profile. 5,758 applied, 2,925 admitted, 480 enrolled.

Mid 50% test scores		**Rank in top tenth:**	23%
SAT critical reading:	500-590	**Return as sophomores:**	80%
SAT math:	520-610	**Out-of-state:**	5%
SAT writing:	490-580	**Live on campus:**	65%
Rank in top quarter:	52%	**International:**	2%

Basis for selection. School achievement record (including grades, rank, strength of program, honors) and test scores most important. Extracurricular activities, talent, disadvantaged status considered. SAT Subject Tests required for applicants who will not have diploma from accredited high school by entrance date. May also be required of GED holders. SAT/ACT scores should be submitted by December of senior year. **Homeschooled:** SAT Subject Tests required for applicants who will not have diploma from accredited high school by entrance date.

High school preparation. College-preparatory program required. 16 units required. Required and recommended units include English 4, mathematics 3-4, science 2, foreign language 2 and academic electives 5. Math requirement includes algebra I and II and geometry. 4 math, 1 chemistry, 1 physics required for engineering applicants.

2008-2009 Annual costs. Tuition/fees: $11,358; $21,306 out-of-state. Room/board: $9,378. Books/supplies: $1,431. Personal expenses: $1,631.

2008-2009 Financial aid. Need-based: Average need met was 64%. Average scholarship/grant was $9,323; average loan $3,269. 60% of total undergraduate aid awarded as scholarships/grants, 40% as loans/jobs. **Non-need-based:** Scholarships awarded for academics, alumni affiliation, art, athletics, leadership, minority status, music/drama, state residency.

Application procedures. Admission: Closing date 12/1. $65 fee, may be waived for applicants with need. Application must be submitted online. Admission notification on a rolling basis beginning on or about 2/28. Must reply by May 1 or within 2 week(s) if notified thereafter. May apply to up to 3 Rutgers colleges with 1 application. Students applying by December 1 notified by February 28. **Financial aid:** Priority date 3/15; no closing date. FAFSA required. Applicants notified on a rolling basis starting 2/1; must reply within 2 week(s) of notification.

Academics. Special study options: Accelerated study, combined bachelor's/graduate degree, cooperative education, cross-registration, distance learning, double major, dual enrollment of high school students, ESL, exchange student, honors, independent study, internships, liberal arts/career combination, student-designed major, study abroad, teacher certification program, weekend college. 8-year BA/MD with University of Medicine and Dentistry of New Jersey, 5-year BA or BS/MA in criminal justice with School of Criminal Justice-Newark, 2+2 BS and 2+3 dual bachelor's degree transfer programs with School of Engineering, BA in political science/MPA, BA in economics/MPA, BA/MS in biology, BA/MS in chemistry, BA/MA in English, BA/MA in history, BA/MA in liberal studies, BA/MS in mathematics, articulated bachelor's/dentistry program with University of Medicine and Dentistry of New Jersey. **Credit/placement by examination:** AP, CLEP, IB, institutional tests. No more than 8 credits given for elementary or intermediate levels of any foreign language. Graduating seniors may take no more than one examination in their final term. **Support services:** Learning center, pre-admission summer program, reduced course load, remedial instruction, study skills assistance, tutoring, writing center.

Majors. Area/ethnic studies: African-American. **Biology:** General, biomedical sciences. **Business:** Accounting, business admin, finance, hospitality admin, marketing. **Computer sciences:** Computer science. **Engineering:** Biomedical, ceramic, chemical, civil, electrical, mechanical, science. **Foreign languages:** French, German, Spanish. **Health:** Nursing (RN), predental, premedicine. **History:** General. **Interdisciplinary:** Biological/physical sciences. **Legal studies:** Prelaw. **Liberal arts:** Arts/sciences. **Math:** General. **Philosophy/religion:** Philosophy. **Physical sciences:** Chemistry, physics. **Protective services:** Criminal justice. **Psychology:** General. **Public administration:** Social work. **Social sciences:** Economics, political science, sociology, urban studies. **Visual/performing arts:** Art, dramatic.

Most popular majors. Business/marketing 26%, English 7%, psychology 14%, security/protective services 7%, social sciences 14%.

Computing on campus. 187 workstations in dormitories, library, computer center, student center. Dormitories linked to campus network. Commuter students can connect to campus network. Helpline, repair service available.

Student life. Freshman orientation: Available. **Housing:** Coed dorms, special housing for disabled, apartments available. $200 nonrefundable deposit. **Activities:** Drama, international student organizations, literary magazine, radio station, student government, student newspaper, accounting society, forensics society, political science association, black student union, Latin American students organization, physics society, Jewish student union, marketing association, psychology club.

Athletics. NCAA. **Intercollegiate:** Baseball M, basketball, cross-country, golf M, rowing (crew) W, soccer, softball W, track and field, volleyball W. **Intramural:** Badminton, basketball, football (tackle) M, handball, racquetball, soccer, softball, squash, volleyball. **Team name:** Scarlet Raptors.

Student services. Career counseling, student employment services, health services, on-campus daycare, personal counseling, placement for graduates, veterans' counselor. **Physically disabled:** Services for visually, speech, hearing impaired.

Contact. Phone: (856) 225-6104 Fax: (856) 225-6498
Deborah Bowles, Director of Admissions, Rutgers, The State University of New Jersey: Camden Regional Campus, 406 Penn Street, Camden, NJ 08102

Rutgers, The State University of New Jersey: New Brunswick/Piscataway Campus

Piscataway, New Jersey — **CB member**
www.rutgers.edu — **CB code: 2765**

- Public 4-year university
- Residential campus in large town
- 27,753 degree-seeking undergraduates: 5% part-time, 49% women, 9% African American, 25% Asian American, 9% Hispanic American, 2% international
- 7,089 degree-seeking graduate students
- 56% of applicants admitted
- SAT or ACT with writing required
- 73% graduate within 6 years

General. Founded in 1969. Regionally accredited. Undergraduate schools include Douglass College, Livingston College, Rutgers College, University College-New Brunswick, Cook College, School of Engineering, Mason Gross School of the Arts, Edward J. Bloustein School of Planning and Public Policy, College of Nursing, College of Pharmacy, School of Business-New Brunswick, School of Communication, Information and Library Studies. **Degrees:** 5,652 bachelor's awarded; master's, doctoral, first professional offered. **ROTC:** Army, Air Force. **Location:** 33 miles from New York City. **Calendar:** Semester, extensive summer session. **Full-time faculty:** 1,562 total; 99% have terminal degrees, 18% minority, 34% women. **Part-time faculty:** 833 total; 99% have terminal degrees, 16% minority, 51% women. **Class size:** 41% < 20, 30% 20-39, 7% 40-49, 11% 50-99, 10% >100. **Special facilities:** Geology museum, ecological preserve, 2 theaters, center for urban policy research, institute for health, health care policy and aging research, journalism resources institute, laboratory for computer science research, center for math, science and computer education.

Freshman class profile. 29,547 applied, 16,478 admitted, 5,840 enrolled.

Mid 50% test scores			
SAT critical reading:	530-630	Rank in top tenth:	41%
SAT math:	560-680	Return as sophomores:	91%
SAT writing:	540-640	Out-of-state:	10%
Rank in top quarter:	81%	Live on campus:	88%
		International:	1%

Basis for selection. School achievement record (including grades, rank, strength of program, honors, AP) and test scores most important. Extracurricular activities, leadership talent, minority, disadvantaged status considered. State residents with educationally and economically disadvantaged backgrounds given consideration through state Educational Opportunity Fund program. SAT Subject Tests required of applicants who, by expected date of entrance, will not have diploma from accredited high school. May also be required of GED holders. Recommended that SAT/ACT be submitted by December of senior year. Interview, audition, portfolio review required for Mason Gross School of the Arts. **Homeschooled:** SAT Subject Tests required of graduates from non-accredited high schools.

High school preparation. College-preparatory program required. 16 units required. Required and recommended units include English 4, mathematics 3-4, science 2, foreign language 2 and academic electives 5. Math requirement includes algebra I and II and geometry. 4 math, 1 chemistry, 1 physics required for engineering program. One biology, 1 chemistry required for nursing program. 5-9 academic electives required, depending on college.

2008-2009 Annual costs. Tuition/fees: $11,540; $21,488 out-of-state. Tuition and fees may vary by program. Room/board: $10,232. Books/supplies: $1,431. Personal expenses: $1,631.

2008-2009 Financial aid. Need-based: Average need met was 51%. Average scholarship/grant was $10,191; average loan $3,466. 65% of total undergraduate aid awarded as scholarships/grants, 35% as loans/jobs. **Non-need-based:** Scholarships awarded for academics, alumni affiliation, art, athletics, leadership, minority status, music/drama, state residency.

Application procedures. Admission: Closing date 12/1. $65 fee, may be waived for applicants with need. Application must be submitted online. Admission notification on a rolling basis. Must reply by May 1 or within 2 week(s) if notified thereafter. May apply to up to 3 Rutgers colleges with 1 application. Applications received by December 1 will be answered by February 28. **Financial aid:** Priority date 3/15; no closing date. FAFSA required. Applicants notified on a rolling basis starting 2/1; must reply within 2 week(s) of notification.

Academics. Special study options: Accelerated study, combined bachelor's/graduate degree, cooperative education, cross-registration, distance learning, double major, dual enrollment of high school students, ESL, exchange student, honors, independent study, internships, liberal arts/career combination, student-designed major, study abroad, teacher certification program, Washington semester, weekend college. Washington semester, 8-year BA or BS/MD with University of Medicine and Dentistry of New Jersey, 5-year BA/MBA, 5-year dual degrees in liberal arts and engineering, 5-year BA or BS/MPP with Edward J. Bloustein School of Planning and Public Policy, 5-year BA or BS/MA in criminal justice with School of Criminal Justice in Newark, 6-year BA in biology/MS in physician assistant, 5-year BA or BS/M.Ed. offered in conjunction with the Graduate School of Education, dual admission to Newark School of Law. **Credit/placement by examination:** AP, CLEP, IB, institutional tests. 30 credit hours maximum toward bachelor's degree. **Support services:** Learning center, pre-admission summer program, reduced course load, remedial instruction, study skills assistance, tutoring, writing center.

Majors. Agriculture: Animal sciences, food science, plant sciences. **Architecture:** Environmental design, urban/community planning. **Area/ethnic studies:** African, African-American, American, Caribbean, Central/Eastern European, East Asian, Hispanic-American/Latino/Chicano, Latin American,

Near/Middle Eastern, Russian/Slavic, women's. **Biology:** General, bacteriology, biochemistry, biometrics, biotechnology, cell/histology, genetics, marine, molecular. **Business:** Accounting, business admin, finance, labor relations, management information systems, management science, marketing. **Communications:** General, journalism. **Computer sciences:** Computer science. **Conservation:** General, environmental studies, management/policy. **Engineering:** Biomedical, ceramic, chemical, civil, electrical, environmental, mechanical, science. **Foreign languages:** Chinese, classics, comparative lit, French, German, Italian, linguistics, Portuguese, Russian, Spanish. **Health:** Clinical lab technology, nursing (RN), physician assistant, predental, premedicine. **History:** General. **Interdisciplinary:** Medieval/Renaissance, nutrition sciences. **Legal studies:** Prelaw. **Math:** General, statistics. **Parks/recreation:** Exercise sciences. **Philosophy/religion:** Judaic, philosophy, religion. **Physical sciences:** Atmospheric science, chemistry, geology, physics. **Protective services:** Law enforcement admin. **Psychology:** General. **Public administration:** Social work. **Social sciences:** Anthropology, economics, geography, political science, sociology, urban studies. **Visual/performing arts:** Art, art history/conservation, dance, dramatic.

Most popular majors. Biology 11%, business/marketing 8%, communications/journalism 9%, engineering/engineering technologies 8%, psychology 9%, social sciences 16%.

Computing on campus. 1,450 workstations in dormitories, library, computer center, student center. Dormitories linked to campus network. Commuter students can connect to campus network. Helpline, repair service available.

Student life. **Freshman orientation:** Available. **Housing:** Guaranteed on-campus for freshmen. Coed dorms, single-sex dorms, special housing for disabled, apartments, cooperative housing, fraternity/sorority housing available. $100 deposit, deadline 6/15. Cooperative housing at Cook College only. Residence for single mothers and children available. **Activities:** Bands, campus ministries, choral groups, dance, drama, film society, international student organizations, literary magazine, music ensembles, musical theater, opera, radio station, student government, student newspaper, symphony orchestra, TV station, 400 organizations available.

Athletics. NCAA. **Intercollegiate:** Baseball M, basketball, cross-country, diving, fencing, field hockey W, football (tackle) M, golf, gymnastics W, lacrosse, rowing (crew), soccer, softball W, swimming, tennis, track and field, volleyball W, wrestling M. **Intramural:** Badminton, basketball, bowling, cross-country, golf, racquetball, soccer, softball, squash, swimming, table tennis, tennis, track and field, volleyball, water polo, wrestling M. **Team name:** Scarlet Knights.

Student services. Adult student services, career counseling, student employment services, health services, on-campus daycare, personal counseling, placement for graduates, veterans' counselor. **Physically disabled:** Services for visually, speech, hearing impaired.

Contact. Phone: (732) 932-4636 Fax: (732) 445-0237
Diane Harris, Associate Director of Undergraduate Admissions, Rutgers, The State University of New Jersey: New Brunswick/Piscataway Campus, 65 Davidson Road, Room 202, Piscataway, NJ 08854-8097

Rutgers, The State University of New Jersey: Newark Regional Campus

Newark, New Jersey
www.rutgers.edu **CB code: 2753**

- Public 4-year university
- Commuter campus in large city
- 6,406 degree-seeking undergraduates: 15% part-time, 55% women, 19% African American, 24% Asian American, 21% Hispanic American, 2% international
- 3,739 degree-seeking graduate students
- 50% of applicants admitted
- SAT or ACT with writing required
- 57% graduate within 6 years

General. Founded in 1930. Regionally accredited. **Degrees:** 962 bachelor's awarded; master's, doctoral, first professional offered. **ROTC:** Army, Air Force. **Location:** 10 miles from New York City. **Calendar:** Semester, extensive summer session. **Full-time faculty:** 417 total; 99% have terminal degrees, 19% minority, 37% women. **Part-time faculty:** 260 total; 99% have terminal degrees, 20% minority, 42% women. **Class size:** 26% < 20, 34% 20-39, 18% 40-49, 18% 50-99, 4% >100. **Special facilities:** Biology learning center, jazz institute, animal behavior institute, center for molecular and behavioral neuroscience, center for negotiation and conflict resolution.

Freshman class profile. 11,035 applied, 5,564 admitted, 955 enrolled.

Mid 50% test scores		**Rank in top tenth:**	30%
SAT critical reading:	470-560	**Return as sophomores:**	87%
SAT math:	500-610	**Out-of-state:**	8%
SAT writing:	480-580	**Live on campus:**	47%
Rank in top quarter:	64%	**International:**	2%

Basis for selection. School achievement record and test scores most important. Extracurricular activities, leadership talent, minority, disadvantaged status considered. State residents with educational and economically disadvantaged backgrounds given consideration through state Educational Opportunity Fund program. SAT Subject Tests required of applicants who, by expected date of entrance, will not have diploma from accredited high school. May also be required of GED holders. SAT/ACT scores should be submitted by December of senior year.

High school preparation. College-preparatory program required. 16 units required. Required and recommended units include English 4, mathematics 3-4, science 2, foreign language 2 and academic electives 5. Math requirement includes algebra I, II and geometry. 4 math, 1 chemistry, 1 physics required for engineering program. One biology, 1 chemistry required for nursing program. Foreign language recommended.

2008-2009 Annual costs. Tuition/fees: $11,083; $21,031 out-of-state. Tuition and fees may vary by program. Room/board: $10,639. Books/supplies: $1,431. Personal expenses: $1,631.

2008-2009 Financial aid. **Need-based:** Average need met was 64%. Average scholarship/grant was $9,579; average loan $3,140. 68% of total undergraduate aid awarded as scholarships/grants, 32% as loans/jobs. **Non-need-based:** Scholarships awarded for academics, alumni affiliation, art, athletics, leadership, minority status, music/drama, religious affiliation, state residency.

Application procedures. **Admission:** Priority date 12/1; no deadline. $65 fee, may be waived for applicants with need. Application must be submitted online. Admission notification on a rolling basis beginning on or about 2/28. Must reply by May 1 or within 2 week(s) if notified thereafter. May apply to up to 3 Rutgers colleges with 1 application. Applications completed by December 1 will be answered by February 28. **Financial aid:** Priority date 3/15; no closing date. FAFSA required. Applicants notified on a rolling basis starting 2/1; must reply within 2 week(s) of notification.

Academics. **Special study options:** Accelerated study, combined bachelor's/graduate degree, cooperative education, cross-registration, distance learning, double major, dual enrollment of high school students, ESL, exchange student, honors, independent study, internships, liberal arts/career combination, student-designed major, study abroad, teacher certification program, Washington semester, weekend college. 8-year BA/MD with University of Medicine and Dentistry of New Jersey, 5-year BA or BS/MA in criminal justice, 2-2 and 2-3 in engineering, dual admission to School of Law, 5-year BA/MBA, industrial engineering program with New Jersey Institute of Technology, bachelor's/dentistry program with Universtiy of Medicine and Dentistry of New Jersey. **Credit/placement by examination:** AP, CLEP, IB, institutional tests. 24 credit hours maximum toward bachelor's degree. **Support services:** Learning center, pre-admission summer program, reduced course load, remedial instruction, study skills assistance, tutoring, writing center.

Honors college/program. By invitation.

Majors. **Area/ethnic studies:** African, African-American, American, Caribbean, Hispanic-American/Latino/Chicano, women's. **Biology:** General, botany, zoology. **Business:** Accounting, business admin, finance, marketing. **Communications:** Journalism. **Computer sciences:** Computer science, information systems. **Conservation:** General. **Engineering:** Biomedical, ceramic, chemical, civil, electrical, mechanical. **Foreign languages:** French, Spanish. **Health:** Clinical lab science, clinical lab technology, nursing (RN), predental, premedicine. **History:** General. **Interdisciplinary:** Science/society. **Legal studies:** Prelaw. **Math:** General, applied. **Philosophy/religion:** Philosophy. **Physical sciences:** Chemistry, geology, physics. **Protective services:** Criminal justice. **Psychology:** General. **Public administration:** Social work. **Social sciences:** Anthropology, economics, political science, sociology. **Visual/performing arts:** Art, dramatic.

Most popular majors. Biology 8%, business/marketing 34%, health sciences 13%, psychology 7%, security/protective services 13%, social sciences 7%.

Computing on campus. 450 workstations in dormitories, library, computer center. Dormitories linked to campus network. Commuter students can connect to campus network. Helpline, repair service available.

Student life. **Freshman orientation:** Available. **Housing:** Coed dorms, special housing for disabled, apartments, fraternity/sorority housing available. $100 deposit. **Activities:** Choral groups, drama, international student organizations, radio station, student government, student newspaper, black organization of students, Puerto Rican and Latin American student organizations, political organizations, religious organizations, service organizations.

Athletics. NCAA. **Intercollegiate:** Baseball M, basketball, soccer, softball W, tennis, volleyball. **Intramural:** Basketball, racquetball, soccer, tennis, volleyball. **Team name:** Scarlet Raiders.

Student services. Career counseling, student employment services, health services, personal counseling, placement for graduates, veterans' counselor. **Physically disabled:** Services for visually, speech, hearing impaired.

Contact. Phone: (973) 353-5205 Fax: (973) 353-1440
Bruce Neimeyer, Director of Admissions at Newark, Rutgers, The State University of New Jersey: Newark Regional Campus, 249 University Avenue, Newark, NJ 07102-1896

Saint Peter's College

Jersey City, New Jersey — **CB member**
www.spc.edu — **CB code: 2806**

- Private 4-year liberal arts college affiliated with Roman Catholic Church
- Commuter campus in small city
- 2,326 degree-seeking undergraduates: 11% part-time, 57% women, 22% African American, 10% Asian American, 25% Hispanic American, 4% international
- 581 degree-seeking graduate students
- 61% of applicants admitted
- SAT or ACT (ACT writing optional), application essay required
- 45% graduate within 6 years; 10% enter graduate study

General. Founded in 1872. Regionally accredited. Extensive evening program on main campus, at branch locations at Englewood Cliffs and South Amboy for adult learners, and other locations throughout metropolitan area. **Degrees:** 455 bachelor's, 21 associate awarded; master's offered. **ROTC:** Army, Air Force. **Location:** 3 miles from New York City. **Calendar:** Semester, extensive summer session. **Full-time faculty:** 113 total; 79% have terminal degrees, 12% minority, 44% women. **Part-time faculty:** 171 total; 21% minority, 36% women. **Class size:** 61% < 20, 39% 20-39, less than 1% 40-49.

Freshman class profile. 5,906 applied, 3,606 admitted, 580 enrolled.

Mid 50% test scores		**GPA 3.0-3.49:**	33%
SAT critical reading:	420-520	**GPA 2.0-2.99:**	41%
SAT math:	420-520	**End year in good standing:**	73%
SAT writing:	410-510	**Return as sophomores:**	77%
ACT composite:	16-21	**Out-of-state:**	18%
GPA 3.75 or higher:	12%	**Live on campus:**	55%
GPA 3.50-3.74:	14%	**International:**	4%

Basis for selection. Admissions decision based on (in rank order) school achievement record, test scores, essay, letters of recommendation, class activities. Interview recommended.

High school preparation. 16 units required; 19 recommended. Required and recommended units include English 4, mathematics 3-4, history 2-3, science 2-3 (laboratory 1), foreign language 2 and academic electives 3.

2008-2009 Annual costs. Tuition/fees: $25,666. Room/board: $10,336. Books/supplies: $700. Personal expenses: $600.

2007-2008 Financial aid. **Need-based:** 543 full-time freshmen applied for aid; 482 were judged to have need; 472 of these received aid. Average need met was 71%. Average scholarship/grant was $18,155; average loan $3,266. 73% of total undergraduate aid awarded as scholarships/grants, 27% as loans/jobs. **Non-need-based:** Awarded to 425 full-time undergraduates, including 112 freshmen. Scholarships awarded for academics, athletics. **Additional information:** Cooperative education internships available in all majors, with average salaries exceeding $5,200.

Application procedures. **Admission:** Priority date 4/1; no deadline. No application fee. Admission notification on a rolling basis beginning on or about 11/1. **Financial aid:** Priority date 3/15; no closing date. FAFSA required. Applicants notified on a rolling basis starting 2/15; must reply by 5/1 or within 2 week(s) of notification.

Academics. Joint Pre-Med/MD program with UMDNJ, joint Pre-Law/Law and Occupational Therapy program with Seton Hall University, joint Pharmacy and Physical Therapy program with Rutgers University, joint Engineering Program with New Jersey Institute of Technology. **Special study options:** Accelerated study, combined bachelor's/graduate degree, cooperative education, double major, dual enrollment of high school students, exchange student, honors, independent study, internships, liberal arts/career combination, student-designed major, study abroad, teacher certification program, Washington semester. Joint degree in clinical laboratory sciences with University of Medicine and Dentistry of New Jersey. **Credit/placement by examination:** AP, CLEP, IB, institutional tests. 30 credit hours maximum toward bachelor's degree. **Support services:** Learning center, preadmission summer program, reduced course load, remedial instruction, study skills assistance, tutoring, writing center.

Majors. **Area/ethnic studies:** American. **Biology:** General, biochemistry, toxicology. **Business:** Accounting, actuarial science, banking/financial services, business admin, international, management information systems, managerial economics. **Communications:** General. **Computer sciences:** General, computer science, information systems, programming. **Education:** Elementary. **Foreign languages:** General, classics, Spanish. **Health:** Clinical lab science, cytotechnology, nursing (RN). **History:** General. **Interdisciplinary:** Biological/physical sciences. **Math:** General. **Philosophy/religion:** Philosophy, religion. **Physical sciences:** Chemistry, physics. **Psychology:** General. **Public administration:** Policy analysis. **Social sciences:** General, economics, political science, sociology, urban studies. **Visual/performing arts:** Studio arts.

Most popular majors. Biology 7%, business/marketing 34%, education 8%, health sciences 8%, security/protective services 11%, social sciences 6%.

Computing on campus. 225 workstations in dormitories, library, computer center, student center. Dormitories wired for high-speed internet access and linked to campus network. Commuter students can connect to campus network. Online library, helpline, student web hosting, wireless network available.

Student life. **Freshman orientation:** Mandatory, $200 fee. Preregistration for classes offered. Three-day sessions held throughout July. Program features academic advising, social activities, and introduction to community service. **Housing:** Guaranteed on-campus for all undergraduates. Coed dorms, special housing for disabled, apartments available. $200 partly refundable deposit, deadline 5/1. **Activities:** Choral groups, drama, international student organizations, literary magazine, radio station, student government, student newspaper, Alpha Phi Omega, Emmaus Spiritual Retreats, Circle K, Young Republicans, Hispanic culture club, Irish American club, Asian American student union, Black Action Committee, Indo-Pak culture club.

Athletics. NCAA. **Intercollegiate:** Baseball M, basketball, bowling, cheerleading, cross-country, diving, golf M, soccer, softball W, swimming, tennis, track and field, volleyball W. **Intramural:** Baseball M, basketball, bowling, racquetball, soccer, softball, swimming, table tennis, tennis, volleyball, water polo. **Team name:** Peacocks/Peahens.

Student services. Adult student services, alcohol/substance abuse counseling, chaplain/spiritual director, career counseling, services for economically disadvantaged, student employment services, financial aid counseling, health services, minority student services, personal counseling, placement for graduates, veterans' counselor. **Physically disabled:** Services for visually, speech, hearing impaired.

Contact. E-mail: admissions@spc.edu
Phone: (201) 761-7100 Toll-free number: (888) 772-9933
Fax: (201) 761-7105
Joe Giglio, Director of Admission, Saint Peter's College, 2641 Kennedy Boulevard, Jersey City, NJ 07306

Seton Hall University

South Orange, New Jersey — **CB member**
www.shu.edu — **CB code: 2811**

- Private 4-year university affiliated with Roman Catholic Church
- Residential campus in large town
- 4,963 degree-seeking undergraduates: 6% part-time, 56% women, 12% African American, 7% Asian American, 11% Hispanic American, 2% international
- 4,008 degree-seeking graduate students
- 73% of applicants admitted
- SAT or ACT with writing, application essay required
- 60% graduate within 6 years

General. Founded in 1856. Regionally accredited. Immaculate Conception Seminary and school of theology located on campus. Off-campus sites for nursing and education. **Degrees:** 1,033 bachelor's awarded; master's, doctoral, first professional offered. **ROTC:** Army. **Location:** 14 miles from New York City. **Calendar:** Semester, extensive summer session. **Full-time**

faculty: 452 total; 17% minority, 48% women. **Part-time faculty:** 503 total; 16% minority, 48% women. **Class size:** 50% < 20, 48% 20-39, 1% 40-49, 1% 50-99, less than 1% >100. **Special facilities:** Computer graphics and communications laboratories, educational media center, nursing demonstration room, art center, music laboratories, special collections center.

Freshman class profile. 9,775 applied, 7,146 admitted, 1,219 enrolled.

Mid 50% test scores		**GPA 2.0-2.99:**	27%
SAT critical reading:	490-600	**Rank in top quarter:**	56%
SAT math:	490-600	**Rank in top tenth:**	25%
SAT writing:	500-600	**Return as sophomores:**	85%
ACT composite:	22-27	**Out-of-state:**	32%
GPA 3.75 or higher:	20%	**Live on campus:**	78%
GPA 3.50-3.74:	16%	**International:**	1%
GPA 3.0-3.49:	37%		

Basis for selection. School achievement record, test scores, recommendations, essay most important. Extracurricular activities, volunteer work, work experience important. Class rank, interview, talent/ability, character/personal qualities considered. Interview strongly recommended. Audition required for music majors. **Homeschooled:** Statement describing homeschool structure and mission required. Must submit GED (total score of at least 225 with no individual score below 45) and copy of homeschool curriculum with list of textbooks used for each of the major unit requirements.

High school preparation. College-preparatory program required. 16 units required. Required units include English 4, mathematics 3, social studies 2, science 1 (laboratory 1), foreign language 2 and academic electives 4. Nursing majors must have additional 2 units in science (biology and chemistry).

2008-2009 Annual costs. Tuition/fees: $29,630. Required fees include lease of laptop computer. Room/board: $11,360.

2007-2008 Financial aid. Need-based: 1,056 full-time freshmen applied for aid; 923 were judged to have need; 919 of these received aid. Average need met was 79%. Average scholarship/grant was $2,912; average loan $2,033. 44% of total undergraduate aid awarded as scholarships/grants, 56% as loans/jobs. **Non-need-based:** Awarded to 3,898 full-time undergraduates, including 1,136 freshmen. Scholarships awarded for academics, alumni affiliation, athletics, minority status, ROTC, state residency.

Application procedures. Admission: Priority date 3/1; no deadline. $55 fee, may be waived for applicants with need, free for online applicants. Admission notification on a rolling basis beginning on or about 12/1. Must reply by May 1 or within 4 week(s) if notified thereafter. **Financial aid:** Priority date 2/15; no closing date. FAFSA required. Applicants notified on a rolling basis starting 3/1; must reply by 5/1 or within 4 week(s) of notification.

Academics. Special study options: Accelerated study, combined bachelor's/graduate degree, cooperative education, cross-registration, distance learning, double major, dual enrollment of high school students, ESL, honors, independent study, internships, liberal arts/career combination, study abroad, teacher certification program, Washington semester. **Credit/placement by examination:** AP, CLEP, IB, SAT, institutional tests. 30 credit hours maximum toward bachelor's degree. **Support services:** Pre-admission summer program, reduced course load, remedial instruction, study skills assistance, tutoring, writing center.

Majors. Area/ethnic studies: African-American, Asian, Latin American. **Biology:** General, biochemistry. **Business:** Accounting, business admin, finance, information resources management, labor relations, management information systems, managerial economics, marketing. **Communications:** General, journalism, public relations, radio/tv. **Computer sciences:** General. **Conservation:** Environmental studies. **Education:** Art, early childhood, elementary, secondary, special. **Foreign languages:** General, classics, French, Italian, Spanish. **Health:** Nursing (RN). **History:** General. **Liberal arts:** Arts/sciences, humanities. **Math:** General. **Parks/recreation:** Sports admin. **Philosophy/religion:** Christian, philosophy, religion. **Physical sciences:** Chemistry, physics. **Protective services:** Criminal justice. **Psychology:** General. **Public administration:** Social work. **Social sciences:** Anthropology, economics, international relations, political science, sociology. **Theology:** Religious ed, theology. **Visual/performing arts:** General, art history/conservation, commercial/advertising art, dramatic, music history, music performance, theater arts management.

Most popular majors. Biology 7%, business/marketing 20%, communications/journalism 10%, education 8%, health sciences 11%, security/protective services 6%, social sciences 12%.

Computing on campus. PC or laptop required. 350 workstations in dormitories, library, computer center, student center. Dormitories wired for high-speed internet access and linked to campus network. Online course registration, online library, helpline, repair service, student web hosting, wireless network available.

Student life. Freshman orientation: Mandatory. Preregistration for classes offered. Two-day program held at various times from June through July. **Policies:** 1.8 GPA housing requirement. **Housing:** Coed dorms, special housing for disabled, apartments, wellness housing available. $250 deposit, deadline 5/1. **Activities:** Pep band, campus ministries, choral groups, drama, international student organizations, radio station, student government, student newspaper, TV station, Adelante, black students union, community service organizations, Puerto Rican Institute, Amnesty International, student ambassadors.

Athletics. NCAA. **Intercollegiate:** Baseball M, basketball, cross-country, golf M, soccer, softball W, swimming, tennis W, track and field, volleyball W. **Intramural:** Basketball, football (non-tackle), racquetball, soccer, softball, tennis, volleyball. **Team name:** Pirates.

Student services. Alcohol/substance abuse counseling, chaplain/spiritual director, career counseling, services for economically disadvantaged, student employment services, financial aid counseling, health services, minority student services, personal counseling, placement for graduates. **Physically disabled:** Services for visually, speech, hearing impaired.

Contact. E-mail: thehall@shu.edu
Phone: (973) 761-9332 Toll-free number: (800) 843-4255
Fax: (973) 275-2040
Peter Nacy, Assistant Vice President for Admissions, Seton Hall University, 400 South Orange Avenue, South Orange, NJ 07079-2680

Somerset Christian College

Zarephath, New Jersey
www.somerset.edu **CB code: 3933**

- Private 4-year Bible and liberal arts college affiliated with Pillar of Fire International
- Commuter campus in small town
- 164 degree-seeking undergraduates
- SAT or ACT with writing, application essay required

General. Candidate for regional accreditation; also accredited by ABHE. **Degrees:** 6 bachelor's, 14 associate awarded. **Location:** 45 miles from New York City and Philadelphia. **Calendar:** Semester, limited summer session. **Full-time faculty:** 5 total; 40% have terminal degrees, 20% minority, 20% women. **Part-time faculty:** 2 total; 100% have terminal degrees, 50% minority, 50% women. **Class size:** 48% < 20, 52% 20-39.

Basis for selection. Recommendations most important. High school record, standardized test scores, essay also important. **Homeschooled:** Interview, letter of recommendation (nonparent) required. Transcript of study including subjects, grades and GPA required. Students must send proof of graduation date or GED scores. **Learning Disabled:** Students must have documented diagnosis and portfolio of prior school collaboration in accommodating students' learning disabilities.

High school preparation. 15 units required. Required units include English 4, mathematics 1, social studies 3, science 2, foreign language 2 and academic electives 3.

2008-2009 Annual costs. Tuition/fees: $11,190. Personal expenses: $1,120.

Financial aid. All financial aid based on need.

Application procedures. Admission: Closing date 8/30 (postmark date). $35 fee, may be waived for applicants with need. Application must be submitted online. Admission notification on a rolling basis. **Financial aid:** No deadline. FAFSA required. Applicants notified on a rolling basis starting 1/31.

Academics. Special study options: Distance learning, dual enrollment of high school students, independent study, internships. **Credit/placement by examination:** AP, CLEP, IB, institutional tests. **Support services:** Learning center, reduced course load, remedial instruction, study skills assistance, tutoring, writing center.

Majors. Philosophy/religion: Christian. **Theology:** Bible.

Computing on campus. 30 workstations in library, computer center. Online course registration, online library, wireless network available.

Student life. Freshman orientation: Mandatory. Preregistration for classes offered. **Policies:** Religious observance required. **Activities:** Student government, student newspaper.

Student services. Chaplain/spiritual director, career counseling, financial aid counseling.

Contact. E-mail: info@somerset.edu
Phone: (732) 356-1595 Toll-free number: (800) 234-9305
Fax: (732) 356-4846
James Partin, Director of Admissions, Somerset Christian College, 10 College Way, Zarephath, NJ 08890

Stevens Institute of Technology

Hoboken, New Jersey
www.stevens.edu
CB member
CB code: 2819

- Private 4-year university and engineering college
- Residential campus in small city
- 2,142 degree-seeking undergraduates: 25% women, 4% African American, 13% Asian American, 10% Hispanic American, 4% international
- 3,415 degree-seeking graduate students
- 52% of applicants admitted
- SAT or ACT (ACT writing optional), application essay, interview required
- 75% graduate within 6 years; 10% enter graduate study

General. Founded in 1870. Regionally accredited. **Degrees:** 370 bachelor's awarded; master's, doctoral offered. **ROTC:** Army, Air Force. **Location:** One mile from New York City. **Calendar:** Semester, extensive summer session. **Full-time faculty:** 251 total; 90% have terminal degrees, 13% minority, 18% women. **Part-time faculty:** 187 total. **Class size:** 43% < 20, 47% 20-39, 4% 40-49, 4% 50-99, 2% >100. **Special facilities:** Laboratory for coastal, ocean and naval engineering, environmental laboratory, design and manufacturing institute, advanced telecommunications institute, geoenvironmental laboratory, optical communications lab, quantum cascade laser, center for mass spectrometry, center for microchemical systems, computer visualization laboratory.

Freshman class profile. 2,889 applied, 1,495 admitted, 545 enrolled.

Mid 50% test scores			
SAT critical reading:	540-650	Rank in top quarter:	82%
SAT math:	620-700	Rank in top tenth:	53%
SAT writing:	540-640	Return as sophomores:	89%
ACT composite:	24-29	Out-of-state:	35%
GPA 3.75 or higher:	50%	Live on campus:	92%
GPA 3.50-3.74:	25%	International:	4%
GPA 3.0-3.49:	21%	Fraternities:	27%
GPA 2.0-2.99:	4%	Sororities:	26%

Basis for selection. GED not accepted. Admissions committee meets to review applicant's file once official transcript and standardized test scores received and interview requirement completed. Other information submitted considered as well. SAT Subject Tests required for accelerated premed, predentistry, or prelaw programs and recommended for all others. Students who live outside 250-mile radius and are unable to visit campus may schedule phone interview. Additional interview with departmental committee required of applicants to accelerated premed, predentistry, and prelaw programs. **Homeschooled:** Letter of recommendation (nonparent) required.

High school preparation. College-preparatory program required. 16 units required. Required and recommended units include English 4, mathematics 4, social studies 2, history 2, science 3-4 (laboratory 3-4), foreign language 2 and academic electives 4. Business, engineering, computer science, and applied science programs require 2 algebra, 1 geometry, 1 pre-calculus or calculus, 1 chemistry, 1 physics, 1 biology.

2008-2009 Annual costs. Tuition/fees: $36,800. Room/board: $11,580. Books/supplies: $900. Personal expenses: $750.

2008-2009 Financial aid. Non-need-based: Scholarships awarded for academics, leadership, music/drama, ROTC.

Application procedures. Admission: Priority date 11/15; deadline 2/1 (postmark date). $55 fee, may be waived for applicants with need, free for online applicants. Admission notification 4/1. Must reply by May 1 or within 2 week(s) if notified thereafter. **Financial aid:** Priority date 2/15; no closing date. FAFSA required. Applicants notified on a rolling basis starting 3/30; must reply by 5/1 or within 2 week(s) of notification.

Academics. Special study options: Accelerated study, combined bachelor's/graduate degree, cooperative education, cross-registration, distance learning, double major, dual enrollment of high school students, honors, independent study, internships, study abroad. 4-year bachelor's/master's programs in all engineering and science disciplines; dual enrollment program with New York University. **Credit/placement by examination:** AP, CLEP, IB. **Support services:** Pre-admission summer program, reduced course load, remedial instruction, study skills assistance, tutoring, writing center.

Majors. Biology: Biochemistry, bioinformatics. **Business:** Business admin, management information systems. **Computer sciences:** General, networking, security. **Engineering:** General, biomedical, chemical, civil, computer, electrical, environmental, materials science, mechanical, physics. **Engineering technology:** Industrial management. **History:** General. **Interdisciplinary:** Math/computer science. **Liberal arts:** Arts/sciences. **Math:** Applied. **Philosophy/religion:** Philosophy. **Physical sciences:** Chemistry, physics. **Other:** Music and technology, Quantitative finance.

Most popular majors. Business/marketing 12%, computer/information sciences 9%, engineering/engineering technologies 69%.

Computing on campus. PC or laptop required. 484 workstations in dormitories, library, computer center, student center. Dormitories wired for high-speed internet access and linked to campus network. Commuter students can connect to campus network. Online course registration, online library, helpline, repair service, student web hosting, wireless network available.

Student life. Freshman orientation: Mandatory, $500 fee. Preregistration for classes offered. Three-day program. **Policies:** Honor system observed. Freshmen not living at home must live on campus. **Housing:** Guaranteed on-campus for all undergraduates. Coed dorms, single-sex dorms, apartments, fraternity/sorority housing, wellness housing available. $350 nonrefundable deposit, deadline 6/15. **Activities:** Bands, campus ministries, choral groups, dance, drama, international student organizations, literary magazine, music ensembles, musical theater, radio station, student government, student newspaper, TV station, over 70 organizations.

Athletics. NCAA. **Intercollegiate:** Baseball M, basketball, cross-country, equestrian W, fencing, field hockey W, golf, lacrosse, soccer, softball W, swimming, tennis, track and field, volleyball, wrestling M. **Intramural:** Archery, badminton, basketball, cricket, football (non-tackle), lacrosse M, racquetball, soccer, softball, squash, tennis, volleyball. **Team name:** Ducks.

Student services. Alcohol/substance abuse counseling, chaplain/spiritual director, career counseling, services for economically disadvantaged, student employment services, financial aid counseling, health services, minority student services, personal counseling, placement for graduates, veterans' counselor, women's services. **Physically disabled:** Services for visually, speech, hearing impaired.

Contact. E-mail: admissions@stevens.edu
Phone: (201) 216-5194 Toll-free number: (800) 458-5323
Fax: (201) 216-8348
Daniel Gallagher, Dean of University Admissions, Stevens Institute of Technology, 1 Castle Point on Hudson, Hoboken, NJ 07030

Talmudical Academy of New Jersey

Adelphia, New Jersey
CB code: 0686

- Private 4-year rabbinical college for men affiliated with Jewish faith
- Large town

General. Founded in 1967. Accredited by AARTS. **Calendar:** Semester.

Contact. Phone: (732) 431-1600
Registrar and Admissions Director, Route 524, PO Box 7, Adelphia, NJ 07710

Thomas Edison State College

Trenton, New Jersey
www.tesc.edu
CB member
CB code: 0682

- Public 4-year liberal arts college
- Small city
- 16,797 degree-seeking undergraduates: 100% part-time, 37% women, 16% African American, 3% Asian American, 8% Hispanic American, 1% Native American, 2% international
- 572 degree-seeking graduate students

General. Founded in 1972. Regionally accredited. **Degrees:** 1,911 bachelor's, 492 associate awarded; master's offered. **Location:** 45 miles from Philadelphia, 76 miles from New York City. **Calendar:** Continuous.

Basis for selection. Open admission, but selective for some programs. Applicants should be at least 21 years old. Certain programs in health professions limited to persons holding appropriate certification. Admission to bachelor's degree nursing program limited to registered nurses (RNs) currently licensed in the USA. Admission to Master of Arts in Educational

Leadership degree limited to person with valid Teacher's Certificate. Applicants under the age of 21 may be accepted on case-by-case basis, or if they are member of a special population such as a corporate partner or member of U.S. military.

2008-2009 Annual costs. Tuition/fees: $4,555; $6,520 out-of-state. Two tuition plans available-either the Comprehensive Tuition Plan: $4,555 per year (state residents and military personnel), $6,520 (out-of-state), which covers up to 36 credits per year for all credit-earning options; or the Enrolled Options Plan: $1,350 per year (state residents and military personnel), $2,445 (out-of-state) and $3,340 (international) for annual enrollment tuition and a technology services fee ($100).

2007-2008 Financial aid. **Need-based:** 17% of total undergraduate aid awarded as scholarships/grants, 83% as loans/jobs. **Additional information:** Financial aid applications should be received two months before each new term begins.

Application procedures. **Admission:** No deadline. $75 fee. Admission notification on a rolling basis. **Financial aid:** No deadline. FAFSA, institutional form required. Applicants notified on a rolling basis; must reply within 4 week(s) of notification.

Academics. Provides flexibility to complete degree, including credit by examination, assessment of experiential learning, guided study, online courses, e-pack courses and credit for licenses and certificates, corporate and military training. Contracts with subject matter experts to act as mentors to academic units of college. **Special study options:** Combined bachelor's/graduate degree, distance learning, dual enrollment of high school students, external degree, independent study. Bachelor of Science in Health Sciences program offered in partnership with University of Medicine and Dentistry of New Jersey School of Health-Related Professions. Program designed for those employed in allied health field and requires students to possess professional certifications and licensures. **Credit/placement by examination:** AP, CLEP. 60 credit hours maximum toward associate degree, 120 toward bachelor's.

Majors. **Agriculture:** Horticulture. **Biology:** General. **Business:** Accounting, business admin, entrepreneurial studies, finance, hospitality admin, human resources, international, labor relations, marketing, nonprofit/public, operations, real estate. **Communications:** General, journalism. **Computer sciences:** Computer science, information technology, security. **Conservation:** Environmental science, environmental studies, forestry. **Engineering technology:** Architectural drafting, biomedical, civil, construction, electrical, manufacturing, mechanical, nuclear, surveying. **Family/consumer sciences:** Child care. **Foreign languages:** General. **Health:** Clinical lab science, cytotechnology, dental hygiene, facilities admin, health services, medical radiologic technology/radiation therapy, nuclear medical technology, nursing (RN), perfusion technology, public health ed, radiation protection, respiratory therapy technology, veterinary technology/assistant. **History:** General. **Interdisciplinary:** Gerontology, natural sciences. **Legal studies:** Paralegal. **Liberal arts:** Arts/sciences, humanities. **Math:** General. **Mechanic/repair:** Aircraft. **Parks/recreation:** General. **Philosophy/religion:** Philosophy, religion. **Protective services:** Criminal justice, fire safety technology, law enforcement admin. **Psychology:** General. **Public administration:** General, community org/advocacy, human services. **Social sciences:** General, anthropology, economics, political science, sociology. **Transportation:** Air traffic control. **Visual/performing arts:** Art, dramatic, photography. **Other:** Aviation flight technology, Computer information systems, Emergency disaster services, Engineering graphics, Kitchen and bath design.

Most popular majors. Business/marketing 14%, engineering/engineering technologies 16%, health sciences 7%, liberal arts 27%, psychology 7%, social sciences 8%.

Computing on campus. Commuter students can connect to campus network. Online course registration, online library, wireless network available.

Student life. **Activities:** Student newspaper.

Student services. Adult student services, financial aid counseling, veterans' counselor. **Physically disabled:** Services for visually, hearing impaired.

Contact. E-mail: admissions@tesc.edu
Phone: (888) 442-8372 Toll-free number: (888) 442-8372
Fax: (609) 984-8447
David Hoftiezer, Director, Admissions, Thomas Edison State College, 101 West State Street, Trenton, NJ 08608-1176

University of Medicine and Dentistry of New Jersey: School of Health Related Professions

Newark, New Jersey
www.shrp.umdnj.edu **CB code: 0598**

- Public two-year upper-division health science college
- Commuter campus in large city
- Application essay, interview required

General. Founded in 1976. Regionally accredited. Courses offered through videoconferencing in Newark, Scotch Plains, and Stratford. Possible oppurtunity to cross-enroll in courses offered by other schools within UMDNJ. **Degrees:** 97 bachelor's, 80 associate awarded; master's, doctoral offered. **Location:** 15 miles from New York City. **Calendar:** Semester, limited summer session. **Full-time faculty:** 110 total. **Part-time faculty:** 20 total.

Student profile. 1,450 degree-seeking undergraduates. 1,382 applied as first time-transfer students.

Basis for selection. Open admission. College transcript, application essay, interview required. Admission requirements vary per program; transfer applicants evaluated by faculty and associate dean. Minimum GPA and interview most important; health-related experience and letters of recommendation also important. Qualified minority, disabled and disadvantaged students encouraged to apply. Application procedures and closing dates vary per program. Transfer accepted as sophomores, juniors, seniors.

2008-2009 Annual costs. Tuition/fees: $9,160; $13,420 out-of-state. Books/supplies: $1,000.

Application procedures. **Admission:** Rolling admission. $75 fee. **Financial aid:** FAFSA, institutional form required.

Academics. **Special study options:** Accelerated study, combined bachelor's/graduate degree, cross-registration, distance learning, double major, dual enrollment of high school students, independent study, internships, liberal arts/career combination, student-designed major. **Credit/placement by examination:** CLEP, IB, institutional tests. Maximum of half of graduation requirement credits for professional component may be earned by examination.

Majors. **Health:** Clinical lab science, cytotechnology, dental hygiene, health services, medical radiologic technology/radiation therapy, nuclear medical technology, respiratory therapy technology, sonography.

Computing on campus. Commuter students can connect to campus network. Online course registration, online library, helpline, repair service available.

Student life. **Housing:** Coed dorms available. **Activities:** Student professional organizations.

Student services. Career counseling, services for economically disadvantaged, health services, personal counseling.

Contact. E-mail: shrpadm@umdnj.edu
Phone: (973) 972-5454 Fax: (973) 972-7463
Brian Lewis, Assistant Dean for Enrollment Services, University of Medicine and Dentistry of New Jersey: School of Health Related Professions, 65 Bergen Street, Newark, NJ 07101-1709

University of Medicine and Dentistry of New Jersey: School of Nursing

Newark, New Jersey
www.sn.umdnj.edu **CB code: 0769**

- Public 4-year nursing college
- Commuter campus in large city
- 850 degree-seeking undergraduates

General. Founded in 1992. Regionally accredited. **Degrees:** 1 bachelor's awarded; master's, doctoral offered. **Location:** 10 miles from New York City. **Calendar:** Semester, extensive summer session.

Basis for selection. Each program has established criteria for admissions. Minimum GPA and interview most important. Nursing and health related experiences and letters of recommendation also important. Qualified minority, handicapped, and disadvantaged students encouraged to apply. Essay, interview recommended.

High school preparation. Specific high school course requirements vary by program.

2008-2009 Annual costs. Tuition/fees: $12,221; $16,400 out-of-state. Costs vary by program; costs cited are for BSN program. Additional insurance fee ($1,967) for students not covered by equivalent plan.

Application procedures. **Admission:** No deadline. $50 fee. Admission notification on a rolling basis. Closing date varies for each program. **Financial aid:** Priority date 3/1; no closing date. Applicants notified on a rolling basis.

Academics. **Special study options:** Accelerated study, combined bachelor's/graduate degree, double major, independent study. 3 joint degree programs: AS in nursing with Middlesex County College and BSN with Ramapo College of NJ and New Jersey Institute of Technology, MS in nursing transition option for registered nurses. **Credit/placement by examination:** CLEP. **Support services:** Reduced course load, tutoring.

Computing on campus. Commuter students can connect to campus network. Online library, helpline, repair service, wireless network available.

Student life. **Housing:** Coed dorms available. **Activities:** Student government, student newspaper, Student professional organizations by nursing specialty.

Student services. Health services, personal counseling. **Physically disabled:** Services for visually, hearing impaired.

Contact. E-mail: snadmissions@umdnj.edu
Phone: (973) 972-5336 Fax: (973) 972-7453
Brian Lewis, Assistant Dean of Enrollment Services, University of Medicine and Dentistry of New Jersey: School of Nursing, 65 Bergen Street Room 149, Newark, NJ 07101-1709

William Paterson University of New Jersey

Wayne, New Jersey **CB member**
www.wpunj.edu **CB code: 2518**

- Public 4-year university and liberal arts college
- Commuter campus in large town
- 8,608 degree-seeking undergraduates: 16% part-time, 56% women, 14% African American, 6% Asian American, 18% Hispanic American, 1% international
- 805 degree-seeking graduate students
- 63% of applicants admitted
- SAT or ACT (ACT writing optional) required
- 46% graduate within 6 years

General. Founded in 1855. Regionally accredited. **Degrees:** 1,597 bachelor's awarded; master's offered. **ROTC:** Air Force. **Location:** 20 miles from New York City. **Calendar:** Semester, limited summer session. **Full-time faculty:** 379 total; 90% have terminal degrees, 32% minority, 47% women. **Part-time faculty:** 552 total; 15% minority, 49% women. **Class size:** 47% < 20, 51% 20-39, 2% 40-49, less than 1% 50-99, less than 1% >100. **Special facilities:** 5 Silicon Graphics Iris workstations, satellite uplink and downlink capabilities, 2 theaters.

Freshman class profile. 6,843 applied, 4,344 admitted, 1,345 enrolled.

Mid 50% test scores		**Rank in top tenth:**	6%
SAT critical reading:	440-520	**Return as sophomores:**	77%
SAT math:	450-540	**Out-of-state:**	3%
Rank in top quarter:	24%	**Live on campus:**	49%

Basis for selection. School record and test score most important; recommendations also important; class rank and essay considered. Audition required for music programs; portfolio required for art programs. Essays recommended. **Homeschooled:** Transcript of courses and grades, state high school equivalency certificate required.

High school preparation. College-preparatory program required. 16 units required. Required units include English 4, mathematics 3, social studies 2, science 2 (laboratory 2) and academic electives 5. Five additional college preparatory courses (advanced math, literature, foreign language, social science) also required.

2008-2009 Annual costs. Tuition/fees: $10,492; $17,050 out-of-state. Room/board: $9,990. Books/supplies: $1,300. Personal expenses: $2,300.

2008-2009 Financial aid. **Need-based:** 88% of total undergraduate aid awarded as scholarships/grants, 12% as loans/jobs. **Non-need-based:** Scholarships awarded for academics, alumni affiliation, music/drama.

Application procedures. **Admission:** Priority date 4/1; deadline 5/1 (postmark date). $50 fee, may be waived for applicants with need. Admission notification on a rolling basis beginning on or about 10/1. Must reply by May 1 or within 2 week(s) if notified thereafter. **Financial aid:** Priority date 4/1; no closing date. FAFSA required. Applicants notified on a rolling basis starting 3/15.

Academics. Honors programs available in biopsychology, humanities, cognitive science, life science and environmental ethics, music, nursing, performing and literary arts. **Special study options:** Accelerated study, combined bachelor's/graduate degree, cross-registration, distance learning, double major, dual enrollment of high school students, ESL, exchange student, honors, independent study, internships, study abroad, teacher certification program, Washington semester. Cluster courses (program that provides opportunities for students and faculty to study and learn together in courses grouped in interdisciplinary clusters of three). **Credit/placement by examination:** AP, CLEP, SAT, ACT, institutional tests. 90 credit hours maximum toward bachelor's degree. **Support services:** Learning center, pre-admission summer program, reduced course load, remedial instruction, study skills assistance, tutoring, writing center.

Honors college/program. Generally, accept students with 1200+ SAT scores (math and reading) and a solid B+ or above high school average. About 100 first-year students admitted to Honors College each year.

Majors. **Area/ethnic studies:** African, African-American, Caribbean, French, Latin American, women's. **Biology:** General, biotechnology. **Business:** Accounting, business admin, finance, international finance, managerial economics. **Communications:** General. **Computer sciences:** General, computer science. **Conservation:** General, environmental science. **Education:** General, art, early childhood, elementary, health, kindergarten/preschool, mathematics, music, physical, special. **Foreign languages:** French, Spanish. **Health:** Nursing (RN), public health nursing, speech pathology. **History:** General. **Math:** General. **Parks/recreation:** Exercise sciences. **Philosophy/religion:** Philosophy. **Physical sciences:** Chemistry. **Psychology:** General. **Social sciences:** Anthropology, economics, geography, political science, sociology. **Visual/performing arts:** Art, jazz, music management, music performance.

Most popular majors. Business/marketing 19%, communications/journalism 12%, education 7%, English 9%, health sciences 6%, psychology 12%, social sciences 13%, visual/performing arts 7%.

Computing on campus. 700 workstations in dormitories, library, computer center. Dormitories wired for high-speed internet access and linked to campus network. Commuter students can connect to campus network. Online course registration, online library, helpline, student web hosting, wireless network available.

Student life. **Freshman orientation:** Mandatory, $75 fee. Two-day program held twice in early summer. Freshmen and parents invited to stay overnight for nominal fee. **Housing:** Guaranteed on-campus for all undergraduates. Coed dorms, special housing for disabled, apartments, wellness housing available. $150 nonrefundable deposit, deadline 4/1. Hall reserved for students 21-and-older, apartment-style housing, women's floor, academic interest housing available. **Activities:** Bands, campus ministries, choral groups, dance, drama, film society, international student organizations, literary magazine, music ensembles, Model UN, radio station, student government, student newspaper, TV station, black student association, Christian Fellowship club, Jewish student association, Feminist Collective, organization of Latin American students, United Asian Americans, coalition of lesbians, gays & friends.

Athletics. NCAA. **Intercollegiate:** Baseball M, basketball, field hockey W, football (tackle) M, soccer, softball W, swimming, volleyball W. **Intramural:** Basketball, field hockey W, soccer W, softball, volleyball. **Team name:** Pioneers.

Student services. Adult student services, alcohol/substance abuse counseling, chaplain/spiritual director, career counseling, services for economically disadvantaged, student employment services, financial aid counseling, health services, legal services, minority student services, on-campus daycare, personal counseling, placement for graduates, veterans' counselor, women's services. **Physically disabled:** Services for visually, speech, hearing impaired.

Contact. E-mail: admissions@wpunj.edu
Phone: (973) 720-2125 Toll-free number: (877) 978-3923
Fax: (973) 720-2910
Colleen O'Connor, Director of Admissions, William Paterson University of New Jersey, 300 Pompton Road, Wayne, NJ 07470

Four-Year Colleges

New Mexico

Art Center Design College
Albuquerque, New Mexico
www.theartcenter.edu **CB code: 3039**

- For-profit 4-year visual arts college
- Commuter campus in very large city
- 283 degree-seeking undergraduates
- SAT or ACT (ACT writing optional), application essay, interview required

General. **Degrees:** 23 bachelor's, 10 associate awarded. **Calendar:** Semester, extensive summer session. **Full-time faculty:** 8 total. **Part-time faculty:** 25 total.

Freshman class profile.

Mid 50% test scores		**SAT math:**	370-450
SAT critical reading:	450-520	**ACT composite:**	17-23

Basis for selection. High school transcripts (GED accepted), ACT or SAT scores, essay, interview, personal statement form, and art work for illustration, animation, fine arts and graphic design programs. Applications accepted based on an evaluation of strengths, academic preparedness and communication skills. **Homeschooled:** Transcript of courses and grades required.

High school preparation. College-preparatory program recommended.

2008-2009 Annual costs. Tuition/fees: $16,320. Books/supplies: $1,250. Personal expenses: $3,204.

2008-2009 Financial aid. **Non-need-based:** Scholarships awarded for academics.

Application procedures. **Admission:** No deadline. $25 fee. Admission notification on a rolling basis. **Financial aid:** FAFSA required.

Academics. **Special study options:** Double major, independent study, internships, liberal arts/career combination. **Credit/placement by examination:** AP, CLEP, IB, SAT, ACT, institutional tests. **Support services:** Learning center, reduced course load, remedial instruction, study skills assistance, tutoring, writing center.

Majors. **Business:** Marketing. **Communications:** Advertising. **Communications technology:** Animation/special effects. **Visual/performing arts:** Graphic design, illustration, interior design, photography, studio arts.

Computing on campus. Online course registration, online library, student web hosting, wireless network available.

Student life. **Freshman orientation:** Mandatory. Preregistration for classes offered.

Student services. Adult student services, career counseling, student employment services, financial aid counseling, personal counseling, placement for graduates, veterans' counselor.

Contact. E-mail: inquire@theartcenter.edu
Phone: (505) 254-7575 Toll-free number: (800) 825-8753
Fax: (505) 254-4754
Colleen Gimbel-Froebe, Director of Enrollment Management, Art Center Design College, 5000 Marble Avenue NE, Albuquerque, NM 87119

Eastern New Mexico University
Portales, New Mexico
www.enmu.edu **CB code: 4299**

- Public 4-year university
- Residential campus in large town
- 3,153 degree-seeking undergraduates: 25% part-time, 57% women, 6% African American, 1% Asian American, 30% Hispanic American, 3% Native American, 4% international
- 525 degree-seeking graduate students
- 67% of applicants admitted
- SAT or ACT (ACT writing optional) required

General. Founded in 1927. Regionally accredited. **Degrees:** 496 bachelor's, 13 associate awarded; master's offered. **Location:** 225 miles from Albuquerque, 120 miles from Lubbock, Texas. **Calendar:** Semester, extensive summer session. **Full-time faculty:** 154 total; 79% have terminal degrees, 12% minority, 46% women. **Part-time faculty:** 137 total; 19% have terminal degrees, 17% minority, 44% women. **Class size:** 55% < 20, 38% 20-39, 5% 40-49, 2% 50-99. **Special facilities:** Natural history museum, mineral museum, scanning and transmission electron microscopes.

Freshman class profile. 1,662 applied, 1,110 admitted, 580 enrolled.

Mid 50% test scores		**Rank in top quarter:**	32%
SAT critical reading:	420-530	**Rank in top tenth:**	11%
SAT math:	410-540	**End year in good standing:**	77%
ACT composite:	17-22	**Return as sophomores:**	60%
GPA 3.75 or higher:	16%	**Out-of-state:**	21%
GPA 3.50-3.74:	15%	**Live on campus:**	75%
GPA 3.0-3.49:	36%	**International:**	1%
GPA 2.0-2.99:	32%		

Basis for selection. Test scores, school record, recommendations important. Students not meeting regular admission standards may be admitted on probation. **Homeschooled:** Transcript of courses and grades required.

High school preparation. 14 units recommended. Recommended units include English 4, mathematics 3, social studies 2, science 4 and foreign language 1.

2008-2009 Annual costs. Tuition/fees: $3,342; $8,886 out-of-state. Room/board: $5,222. Books/supplies: $1,200. Personal expenses: $3,000.

2008-2009 Financial aid. **Need-based:** Average need met was 35%. Average scholarship/grant was $3,483; average loan $3,430. 38% of total undergraduate aid awarded as scholarships/grants, 62% as loans/jobs. **Non-need-based:** Scholarships awarded for academics, alumni affiliation, art, athletics, leadership, music/drama, state residency.

Application procedures. **Admission:** Priority date 8/15; no deadline. No application fee. Admission notification on a rolling basis. **Financial aid:** Priority date 3/1; no closing date. FAFSA required. Applicants notified by 4/1; must reply within 3 week(s) of notification.

Academics. **Special study options:** Accelerated study, cooperative education, distance learning, double major, dual enrollment of high school students, exchange student, honors, independent study, internships, student-designed major, study abroad, teacher certification program. **Credit/placement by examination:** AP, CLEP, ACT, institutional tests. 32 credit hours maximum toward associate degree, 50 toward bachelor's. **Support services:** Learning center, pre-admission summer program, remedial instruction, tutoring.

Majors. **Agriculture:** Agribusiness operations, dairy. **Biology:** General. **Business:** Accounting, business admin, finance, human resources, management information systems, managerial economics, marketing. **Communications:** General, broadcast journalism, journalism. **Computer sciences:** General, computer science. **Conservation:** Environmental science, wildlife. **Education:** Agricultural, business, early childhood, elementary, music, physical, sales/marketing, special. **Engineering technology:** General. **Family/consumer sciences:** General. **Foreign languages:** Spanish. **Health:** Audiology/speech pathology, clinical lab science, nursing (RN). **History:** General. **Liberal arts:** Arts/sciences. **Math:** General. **Parks/recreation:** Health/fitness. **Philosophy/religion:** Religion. **Physical sciences:** Chemistry, geology. **Protective services:** Criminal justice, forensics. **Psychology:** General. **Public administration:** Social work. **Social sciences:** General, anthropology, political science, sociology. **Transportation:** Aviation management. **Visual/performing arts:** Art, dramatic.

Most popular majors. Business/marketing 15%, education 19%, health sciences 6%, liberal arts 13%.

Computing on campus. 476 workstations in dormitories, library, computer center. Dormitories linked to campus network. Commuter students can connect to campus network. Repair service available.

Student life. **Freshman orientation:** Mandatory, $60 fee. Preregistration for classes offered. **Housing:** Guaranteed on-campus for freshmen. Coed dorms, single-sex dorms, special housing for disabled, apartments, fraternity/sorority housing, wellness housing available. $150 fully refundable deposit. **Activities:** Bands, choral groups, dance, drama, film society, literary magazine, music ensembles, musical theater, radio station, student government, student newspaper, symphony orchestra, TV station, several religious, political, honorary, and service organization.

Athletics. NCAA. **Intercollegiate:** Baseball M, basketball, cross-country, football (tackle) M, rodeo, soccer, softball W, track and field, volleyball W. **Intramural:** Badminton, basketball, cross-country, football (tackle) M, golf, racquetball, soccer, softball, tennis, volleyball. **Team name:** Greyhounds.

Student services. Adult student services, career counseling, student employment services, financial aid counseling, health services, minority student services, on-campus daycare, personal counseling, placement for graduates, veterans' counselor. **Physically disabled:** Services for visually, speech, hearing impaired.

Contact. Phone: (575) 562-2178 Toll-free number: (800) 367-3668
Fax: (575) 562-2566
Donna Kittrell, Director of Enrollment Services, Eastern New Mexico University, Station Seven, Portales, NM 88130

Institute of American Indian Arts

Santa Fe, New Mexico
www.iaia.edu **CB code: 0180**

- Public 4-year visual arts college
- Residential campus in small city

General. Founded in 1962. Regionally accredited. **Location:** 60 miles from Albuquerque. **Calendar:** Semester.

Annual costs/financial aid. Tuition/fees (2008-2009): $3,150. Room/board: $4,900. Books/supplies: $2,500. Personal expenses: $2,400. Need-based financial aid available to full-time and part-time students.

Contact. Phone: (505) 424-2332
Director of Admissions, Records & Enrollment, 83 Avan Nu Po Road, Santa Fe, NM 87508-1300

ITT Technical Institute: Albuquerque

Albuquerque, New Mexico
www.itt-tech.edu **CB code: 2690**

- For-profit 4-year technical college
- Commuter campus in large city

General. Accredited by ACICS. **Calendar:** Quarter.

Contact. Phone: (505) 828-1114
Director of Recruitment, 5100 Masthead Street NE, Albuquerque, NM 87109

National American University: Rio Rancho

Rio Rancho, New Mexico
www.national.edu **CB code: 5360**

- For-profit 4-year business college
- Large city
- 565 degree-seeking undergraduates

General. Founded in 1941. Regionally accredited. **Degrees:** 37 bachelor's, 13 associate awarded; master's offered. **ROTC:** Naval, Air Force. **Calendar:** Quarter, extensive summer session. **Part-time faculty:** 60 total.

Basis for selection. Open admission.

2009-2010 Annual costs. Tuition/fees (projected): $15,620. Books/supplies: $675.

Application procedures. Admission: No deadline. $25 fee. Admission notification on a rolling basis. **Financial aid:** No deadline. Institutional form required. Applicants notified on a rolling basis.

Academics. Special study options: Combined bachelor's/graduate degree, distance learning, independent study. **Credit/placement by examination:** AP, CLEP. 45 credit hours maximum toward associate degree, 95 toward bachelor's. **Support services:** Tutoring.

Majors. Business: Accounting, business admin, management information systems.

Most popular majors. Business/marketing 82%, computer/information sciences 18%.

Computing on campus. 15 workstations in library, computer center.

Student life. Activities: Choral groups, literary magazine, music ensembles, TV station.

Athletics. Team name: Mavericks.

Student services. Adult student services, career counseling, student employment services, placement for graduates, veterans' counselor.

Contact. Phone: (505) 348-3750 Fax: (505) 348-3755
Nancy Pointer-Meason, Director of Admissions, National American University: Rio Rancho, 4775 Indian School Road NE, Suite 200, Albuquerque, NM 87110

New Mexico Highlands University

Las Vegas, New Mexico **CB member**
www.nmhu.edu **CB code: 4532**

- Public 4-year university
- Commuter campus in large town
- 1,984 degree-seeking undergraduates: 24% part-time, 58% women
- 1,119 degree-seeking graduate students

General. Founded in 1893. Regionally accredited. **Degrees:** 336 bachelor's, 1 associate awarded; master's offered. **Location:** 68 miles from Santa Fe, 120 miles from Albuquerque. **Calendar:** Semester, limited summer session. **Full-time faculty:** 145 total; 32% minority, 48% women.

Freshman class profile. 437 enrolled.

Mid 50% test scores		**GPA 2.0-2.99:**	50%
ACT composite:	16-20	**Rank in top quarter:**	21%
GPA 3.75 or higher:	8%	**Rank in top tenth:**	6%
GPA 3.50-3.74:	10%	**Return as sophomores:**	45%
GPA 3.0-3.49:	26%		

Basis for selection. Minimum 2.0 GPA required. All tests used for placement purposes. COMPASS may be submitted in place of ACT. **Homeschooled:** Transcript of courses and grades, state high school equivalency certificate required.

2008-2009 Annual costs. Tuition/fees: $2,688; $4,052 out-of-state. Room/board: $5,364. Books/supplies: $794. Personal expenses: $1,748.

2007-2008 Financial aid. Need-based: 38% of total undergraduate aid awarded as scholarships/grants, 62% as loans/jobs. **Non-need-based:** Scholarships awarded for academics, athletics, leadership, minority status, music/drama, state residency. **Additional information:** Work study funds available on no-need basis to state residents.

Application procedures. Admission: No deadline. $15 fee, may be waived for applicants with need. Admission notification on a rolling basis. **Financial aid:** Priority date 3/1, closing date 5/1. FAFSA, institutional form required. Applicants notified on a rolling basis starting 5/15; must reply within 2 week(s) of notification.

Academics. Special study options: Combined bachelor's/graduate degree, cooperative education, distance learning, double major, dual enrollment of high school students, ESL, honors, independent study, internships, liberal arts/career combination, teacher certification program. **Credit/placement by examination:** AP, CLEP, institutional tests. As approved by appropriate department. **Support services:** Learning center, study skills assistance, tutoring, writing center.

Majors. Biology: General. **Business:** Accounting, business admin, finance, international, management information systems, marketing. **Communications:** Media studies. **Computer sciences:** Computer science. **Conservation:** Forest management. **Education:** Biology, computer, early childhood, elementary, mathematics, music, physical, science, special. **Foreign languages:** Spanish. **History:** General. **Math:** General. **Parks/recreation:** Health/fitness, sports admin. **Physical sciences:** Chemistry, forensic chemistry, geology. **Protective services:** Criminal justice, forensics. **Psychology:** General. **Public administration:** Social work. **Social sciences:** Anthropology, criminology, political science, sociology. **Visual/performing arts:** Art, music performance, studio arts.

Most popular majors. Business/marketing 21%, education 32%.

Computing on campus. 250 workstations in dormitories, library, computer center, student center. Dormitories wired for high-speed internet access and linked to campus network. Commuter students can connect to campus network. Online library, helpline, repair service, wireless network available.

Student life. Freshman orientation: Mandatory, $50 fee. Preregistration for classes offered. **Housing:** Guaranteed on-campus for freshmen. Coed dorms, single-sex dorms, apartments available. $100 partly refundable deposit. **Activities:** Bands, choral groups, dance, drama, film society, international student organizations, music ensembles, musical theater, radio station, student government, student newspaper, TV station, social work club, international student club, several ethnic and religious groups.

Athletics. NAIA, NCAA. **Intercollegiate:** Baseball M, basketball, cross-country, football (tackle) M, rodeo, soccer W, softball W, track and field W, volleyball W, wrestling M. **Intramural:** Baseball M, basketball, golf, handball, racquetball, rifle, rugby, skiing, softball, swimming, table tennis, tennis, track and field. **Team name:** Cowboys, Cowgirls.

Student services. Adult student services, career counseling, services for economically disadvantaged, student employment services, financial aid counseling, health services, minority student services, on-campus daycare, personal counseling, placement for graduates, veterans' counselor. **Physically disabled:** Services for visually, speech, hearing impaired.

Contact. E-mail: mdbassett@nmhu.edu
Phone: (505) 454-3434 Toll-free number: (877) 850-9064
Fax: (505) 454-3552
John Coca, Director of Admissions, New Mexico Highlands University, Box 9000, Las Vegas, NM 87701

New Mexico Institute of Mining and Technology

Socorro, New Mexico — **CB member**
www.nmt.edu — **CB code: 4533**

- Public 4-year engineering and liberal arts college
- Residential campus in small town
- 1,173 degree-seeking undergraduates: 5% part-time, 26% women, 1% African American, 4% Asian American, 24% Hispanic American, 4% Native American, 3% international
- 423 degree-seeking graduate students
- 35% of applicants admitted
- SAT or ACT (ACT writing optional) required

General. Founded in 1889. Regionally accredited. Student employment opportunities in research facilities and in faculty research. **Degrees:** 194 bachelor's, 4 associate awarded; master's, doctoral offered. **Location:** 75 miles from Albuquerque. **Calendar:** Semester, limited summer session. **Full-time faculty:** 125 total; 98% have terminal degrees, 17% minority, 18% women. **Part-time faculty:** 26 total; 23% have terminal degrees, 15% minority, 27% women. **Class size:** 62% < 20, 29% 20-39, 5% 40-49, 4% 50-99. **Special facilities:** Experimental mine, mineral museum, laboratory for atmospheric physics and chemistry, energetic materials research, seismic research network, scanning electron microscope, scanning transmission electron microscope, transmission electron microscope, New Mexico Bureau of Geology, observatory.

Freshman class profile. 1,045 applied, 370 admitted, 287 enrolled.

Mid 50% test scores		**GPA 3.0-3.49:**	24%
SAT critical reading:	530-660	**GPA 2.0-2.99:**	13%
SAT math:	550-680	**Rank in top quarter:**	65%
ACT composite:	23-29	**Rank in top tenth:**	37%
GPA 3.75 or higher:	41%	**Out-of-state:**	16%
GPA 3.50-3.74:	22%	**International:**	1%

Basis for selection. Test scores and high school GPA most important. Minimum 2.5 GPA required. Minimum 21 ACT or 970 SAT (exclusive of Writing) required. ACT recommended. Writing components accepted but not crucial to admission. Interview and recommendations considered if GPA and test scores are borderline or if other issues need to be addressed. **Home-schooled:** Must supply documentation of courses completed.

High school preparation. College-preparatory program recommended. 15 units required; 18 recommended. Required and recommended units include English 4, mathematics 3-4, social studies 2-3, history 1, science 2-4 (laboratory 2-3), foreign language 2 and academic electives 3.

2008-2009 Annual costs. Tuition/fees: $4,353; $12,545 out-of-state. Room/board: $5,460. Books/supplies: $1,050. Personal expenses: $1,592.

2007-2008 Financial aid. Non-need-based: Scholarships awarded for academics, alumni affiliation, minority status, state residency. **Additional information:** Campus research projects offer student employment based on merit.

Application procedures. Admission: Priority date 3/1; deadline 8/1. $15 fee, may be waived for applicants with need. Admission notification on a rolling basis beginning on or about 3/1. Must reply by May 1 or within 2 week(s) if notified thereafter. **Financial aid:** Priority date 6/1; no closing date. FAFSA, institutional form required. Applicants notified on a rolling basis starting 4/1; must reply within 2 week(s) of notification.

Academics. Special study options: Accelerated study, cooperative education, distance learning, double major, dual enrollment of high school students, exchange student, independent study, internships, student-designed major, teacher certification program. **Credit/placement by examination:** AP, CLEP, institutional tests. No limit to number of credits. Must have permission of instructor. **Support services:** Pre-admission summer program, reduced course load, study skills assistance, tutoring, writing center.

Majors. Biology: General, biochemistry. **Business:** Business admin. **Computer sciences:** General, computer science, information technology. **Conservation:** General, environmental studies. **Engineering:** General, chemical, civil, electrical, environmental, materials, mechanical, metallurgical, mining, petroleum. **Math:** General, applied. **Physical sciences:** Astrophysics, atmospheric physics, chemistry, geology, geophysics, physics. **Psychology:** General.

Most popular majors. Biology 10%, computer/information sciences 14%, engineering/engineering technologies 43%, liberal arts 7%, physical sciences 11%.

Computing on campus. 225 workstations in dormitories, library, computer center, student center. Dormitories wired for high-speed internet access and linked to campus network. Commuter students can connect to campus network. Helpline, student web hosting, wireless network available.

Student life. Freshman orientation: Available, $40 fee. Preregistration for classes offered. 2-day event held weekend before classes start. **Housing:** Coed dorms, single-sex dorms, apartments, wellness housing available. $100 partly refundable deposit, deadline 6/1. Students living on-campus must purchase meal plan. **Activities:** Bands, choral groups, dance, drama, film society, music ensembles, musical theater, radio station, student government, student newspaper, many organizations available.

Athletics. Intramural: Badminton, basketball, fencing, golf, racquetball, rifle, rugby, soccer, softball, table tennis, tennis, volleyball.

Student services. Adult student services, career counseling, student employment services, health services, on-campus daycare, personal counseling, placement for graduates. **Physically disabled:** Services for visually, hearing impaired.

Contact. E-mail: admission@admin.nmt.edu
Phone: (575) 835-5424 Toll-free number: (800) 428-8324
Fax: (575) 835-5989
Mike Kloeppel, Director of Admission, New Mexico Institute of Mining and Technology, 801 Leroy Place, Socorro, NM 87801

New Mexico State University

Las Cruces, New Mexico — **CB member**
www.nmsu.edu — **CB code: 4531**

- Public 4-year university
- Commuter campus in small city
- 13,556 degree-seeking undergraduates: 13% part-time, 55% women, 3% African American, 1% Asian American, 43% Hispanic American, 4% Native American, 5% international
- 3,505 degree-seeking graduate students
- 82% of applicants admitted
- SAT or ACT with writing required
- 42% graduate within 6 years

General. Founded in 1888. Regionally accredited. **Degrees:** 2,250 bachelor's, 21 associate awarded; master's, doctoral offered. **ROTC:** Army, Air Force. **Location:** 42 miles from El Paso, Texas. **Calendar:** Semester, extensive summer session. **Full-time faculty:** 711 total; 76% have terminal degrees, 20% minority, 38% women. **Part-time faculty:** 304 total; 22% have terminal degrees, 17% minority, 61% women. **Class size:** 52% < 20, 32% 20-39, 8% 40-49, 6% 50-99, 3% >100. **Special facilities:** Observatory, horse farm, rodeo grounds, electron microscope, CRAY supercomputer, sports medicine training clinic.

Freshman class profile. 5,960 applied, 4,897 admitted, 2,571 enrolled.

Mid 50% test scores			
SAT critical reading:	430-560	GPA 2.0-2.99:	27%
SAT math:	430-560	Rank in top quarter:	45%
SAT writing:	430-550	Rank in top tenth:	19%
ACT composite:	18-24	End year in good standing:	85%
GPA 3.75 or higher:	25%	Return as sophomores:	79%
GPA 3.50-3.74:	16%	Out-of-state:	21%
GPA 3.0-3.49:	31%	International:	4%

Basis for selection. School achievement record, test scores most important.

High school preparation. 10 units required. Required units include English 4, mathematics 3, science 2 (laboratory 2) and foreign language 1. English must include at least 2 composition, 1 of which must be at junior or senior level. Math must be algebra I, algebra II, geometry, trigonometry or advanced math. Will accept 1 foreign language or 1 fine arts.

2008-2009 Annual costs. Tuition/fees: $4,758; $14,740 out-of-state. Room/board: $5,976. Books/supplies: $998. Personal expenses: $3,660.

2008-2009 Financial aid. **Non-need-based:** Scholarships awarded for academics, alumni affiliation, athletics, leadership, minority status, state residency.

Application procedures. **Admission:** No deadline. $20 fee. Admission notification on a rolling basis. **Financial aid:** No deadline. FAFSA, institutional form required. Applicants notified on a rolling basis starting 3/1.

Academics. **Special study options:** Accelerated study, cooperative education, cross-registration, distance learning, double major, exchange student, honors, independent study, internships, student-designed major, study abroad, teacher certification program, weekend college. **Credit/placement by examination:** AP, CLEP, institutional tests. **Support services:** Learning center, reduced course load, study skills assistance, tutoring, writing center.

Majors. **Agriculture:** General, agribusiness operations, agronomy, animal sciences, horticultural science, range science, soil science, turf management. **Architecture:** Urban/community planning. **Area/ethnic studies:** Women's. **Biology:** General, bacteriology, biochemistry, ecology, plant pathology. **Business:** General, accounting, business admin, finance, hospitality admin, international, marketing, real estate. **Communications:** Journalism. **Computer sciences:** General, information systems, information technology. **Conservation:** Environmental science, wildlife. **Education:** General, agricultural, early childhood, elementary, family/consumer sciences, music, physical, secondary. **Engineering:** Aerospace, agricultural, chemical, civil, electrical, industrial, mechanical, physics. **Engineering technology:** Surveying. **Family/consumer sciences:** Clothing/textiles, family studies, food/nutrition. **Foreign languages:** General. **Health:** Athletic training, clinical lab science, environmental health, nursing (RN), public health ed. **History:** General. **Math:** General. **Parks/recreation:** Facilities management. **Philosophy/religion:** Philosophy. **Physical sciences:** Chemistry, geology, physics. **Protective services:** Criminal justice. **Psychology:** General. **Public administration:** Community org/advocacy, social work. **Social sciences:** Anthropology, economics, geography, political science, sociology. **Visual/performing arts:** General, cinematography, dance, dramatic, music performance, studio arts.

Most popular majors. Business/marketing 17%, education 12%, engineering/engineering technologies 9%, health sciences 11%, security/protective services 7%.

Computing on campus. 743 workstations in dormitories, library, computer center, student center. Dormitories wired for high-speed internet access and linked to campus network. Commuter students can connect to campus network. Online course registration, online library, helpline, repair service, student web hosting, wireless network available.

Student life. **Freshman orientation:** Available. Preregistration for classes offered. **Housing:** Coed dorms, single-sex dorms, special housing for disabled, apartments, fraternity/sorority housing, wellness housing available. $100 deposit, deadline 7/1. Upper division dorms available. **Activities:** Bands, campus ministries, choral groups, dance, drama, literary magazine, music ensembles, musical theater, opera, radio station, student government, student newspaper, symphony orchestra, TV station, Baptist student union, Catholic center, Young Democrats, College Republicans, Black Allied Student Association, Movimiento Estudiantil Chicano de Azatlan, Native American organization.

Athletics. NCAA. **Intercollegiate:** Baseball M, basketball, cross-country, equestrian, football (tackle) M, golf, softball W, swimming W, tennis, track and field W, volleyball W. **Intramural:** Archery, badminton, basketball, cheerleading, football (non-tackle), football (tackle), golf, racquetball, soccer, softball, tennis, volleyball, water polo, weight lifting, wrestling M. **Team name:** Aggies.

Student services. Adult student services, alcohol/substance abuse counseling, career counseling, student employment services, health services, personal counseling, placement for graduates, veterans' counselor. **Physically disabled:** Services for visually, speech, hearing impaired.

Contact. E-mail: admissions@nmsu.edu
Phone: (575) 646-3121 Toll-free number: (800) 662-6678
Fax: (575) 646-6330
Tyler Pruett, Director of Admissions, New Mexico State University, Box 30001, MSC 3A, Las Cruces, NM 88003-8001

St. John's College

Santa Fe, New Mexico — **CB member**
www.sjcsf.edu — **CB code: 4737**

- Private 4-year liberal arts college
- Residential campus in small city
- 431 degree-seeking undergraduates: 1% part-time, 39% women, 3% Asian American, 5% Hispanic American, 1% Native American, 4% international
- 80 degree-seeking graduate students
- 81% of applicants admitted
- Application essay required
- 56% graduate within 6 years; 17% enter graduate study

General. Founded in 1964. Regionally accredited. Second campus in Annapolis, MD, where students may transfer during their 4 years. **Degrees:** 104 bachelor's awarded; master's offered. **Location:** 60 miles from Albuquerque. **Calendar:** Semester, limited summer session. **Full-time faculty:** 68 total; 82% have terminal degrees, 6% minority, 25% women. **Part-time faculty:** 1 total; 100% have terminal degrees, 100% women. **Class size:** 97% < 20, 3% 20-39. **Special facilities:** Search and rescue center, Ptolemy stone, forest with hiking trails.

Freshman class profile. 323 applied, 263 admitted, 119 enrolled.

Mid 50% test scores			
SAT critical reading:	620-730	End year in good standing:	96%
SAT math:	570-680	Return as sophomores:	78%
ACT composite:	25-31	Out-of-state:	87%
Rank in top quarter:	60%	Live on campus:	99%
Rank in top tenth:	27%	International:	6%

Basis for selection. 3 essays describing educational and personal background and goals most important along with 2 letters of reference from teachers; secondary school reference from counselor or other school official also requested. High school achievement record considered. SAT or ACT required of early admission or home schooled applicants. Interview and 24 hour campus visit strongly encouraged. **Homeschooled:** Statement describing homeschool structure and mission, transcript of courses and grades, letter of recommendation (nonparent) required. **Learning Disabled:** Campus visit very strongly encouraged.

High school preparation. College-preparatory program recommended. 5 units required; 22 recommended. Required and recommended units include English 4, mathematics 3, history 2, science 3 (laboratory 3) and foreign language 2-4. Math requirement includes 2 algebra, 1 geometry. Precalculus or trigonometry recommended.

2009-2010 Annual costs. Tuition/fees (projected): $41,096. Room/board: $9,562. Books/supplies: $275. Personal expenses: $750.

2007-2008 Financial aid. All financial aid based on need. 84 full-time freshmen applied for aid; 63 were judged to have need; 63 of these received aid. Average need met was 95%. Average scholarship/grant was $24,425; average loan $3,125. 77% of total undergraduate aid awarded as scholarships/grants, 23% as loans/jobs. **Additional information:** 100% of need met for most of those qualified to receive aid. Families receive individual attention in determining need fairly. Independent students must submit parental data. Financial aid information also required of noncustodial parent in cases of separation or divorce. Aid awarded first-come, first-served until institutional money exhausted. Apply early by February 15; after April 1 aid difficult to obtain.

Application procedures. **Admission:** Priority date 3/1; no deadline. No application fee. Admission notification on a rolling basis. Must reply by May 1 or within 2 week(s) if notified thereafter. Early application encouraged. **Financial aid:** Priority date 2/15; no closing date. FAFSA, CSS PROFILE required. Applicants notified on a rolling basis starting 12/10; must reply by 5/1.

Academics. In addition to formal support structures, students have built in learning community in which all are engaged in the same project. **Special study options:** Accelerated study, internships. Great Books program. **Credit/placement by examination:** CLEP. **Support services:** Tutoring, writing center.

Majors. Liberal arts: Arts/sciences.

Computing on campus. 20 workstations in library, computer center. Dormitories wired for high-speed internet access and linked to campus network. Commuter students can connect to campus network. Helpline, wireless network available.

Student life. Freshman orientation: Mandatory. Four-day program held twice a year. Includes on-campus service day, student activities fair, numerous community meals, and formal welcoming ceremony. **Housing:** Guaranteed on-campus for freshmen. Coed dorms, single-sex dorms, special housing for disabled, apartments, wellness housing available. Single-sex suites available. **Activities:** Bands, choral groups, dance, drama, film society, literary magazine, music ensembles, musical theater, student government, student newspaper, Amnesty International, Hebrew study group, peer counseling, soup kitchen, Beneficial Farm, Habitat for Humanity, primary school tutoring, international affairs study group.

Athletics. Intercollegiate: Fencing. **Intramural:** Badminton, basketball, cross-country, fencing, racquetball, skiing, soccer, softball, squash, table tennis, tennis, volleyball.

Student services. Alcohol/substance abuse counseling, career counseling, student employment services, financial aid counseling, health services, personal counseling, placement for graduates, women's services.

Contact. E-mail: admissions@sjcsf.edu
Phone: (505) 984-6060 Toll-free number: (800) 331-5232
Fax: (505) 984-6162
Lawrence Clendenin, Director of Admissions, St. John's College, 1160 Camino Cruz Blanca, Santa Fe, NM 87505-4599

University of New Mexico

Albuquerque, New Mexico — **CB member**
www.unm.edu — **CB code: 4845**

- Public 4-year university
- Commuter campus in very large city
- 18,394 degree-seeking undergraduates: 19% part-time, 56% women, 3% African American, 4% Asian American, 36% Hispanic American, 7% Native American, 1% international
- 5,711 degree-seeking graduate students
- SAT or ACT (ACT writing recommended) required
- 44% graduate within 6 years

General. Founded in 1889. Regionally accredited. Branch campuses in Valencia County, Los Alamos, Gallup, and Taos. **Degrees:** 3,052 bachelor's, 9 associate awarded; master's, doctoral, first professional offered. **ROTC:** Army, Naval, Air Force. **Location:** 2 miles from downtown. **Calendar:** Semester, limited summer session. **Full-time faculty:** 988 total; 82% have terminal degrees, 23% minority, 46% women. **Part-time faculty:** 455 total; 30% have terminal degrees, 20% minority, 55% women. **Class size:** 43% < 20, 39% 20-39, 5% 40-49, 9% 50-99, 4% >100. **Special facilities:** 5 museums; observatory; meteoritics institute; arboretum; teaching hospital; major research facilities in ceramics, optoelectronics, space nuclear power, high power devices and systems; institute of lithography; Latin American institute.

Freshman class profile.

Mid 50% test scores		**GPA 3.0-3.49:**	34%
SAT critical reading:	470-610	**GPA 2.0-2.99:**	25%
SAT math:	460-600	**Rank in top quarter:**	45%
ACT composite:	19-25	**Rank in top tenth:**	20%
GPA 3.75 or higher:	23%	**Return as sophomores:**	77%
GPA 3.50-3.74:	18%	**International:**	1%

Basis for selection. School achievement record (2.25 GPA required in college-preparatory units) most important. Test scores, class rank second. Essays, recommendations considered. Essay considered if student appeal denied. **Homeschooled:** Applicants must either pass GED, submit SAT Subject Test scores, or have 2.25 GPA and complete 13 college prep academic units. **Learning Disabled:** Student who is not admissable according to numerical admissions and self-discloses disability can be admitted after being approved by Special Admissions Committee.

High school preparation. College-preparatory program required. 13 units required. Required units include English 4, mathematics 3, social studies 1, history 1, science 2 (laboratory 1) and foreign language 2. Foreign language requirements must be in same language. 1 science must be laboratory in biology, chemistry or physics. Math must be algebra I, geometry, algebra II, trigonometry or higher. 1 English must be 11th or 12th grade composition.

2008-2009 Annual costs. Tuition/fees: $4,834; $15,708 out-of-state. Room/board: $7,336. Books/supplies: $920. Personal expenses: $2,966.

Financial aid. Non-need-based: Scholarships awarded for academics, alumni affiliation, art, athletics, job skills, leadership, minority status, music/drama, religious affiliation, ROTC, state residency.

Application procedures. Admission: Closing date 6/15 (postmark date). $20 fee, may be waived for applicants with need. Admission notification on a rolling basis. **Financial aid:** Priority date 3/1; no closing date. FAFSA required. Applicants notified on a rolling basis.

Academics. Special study options: Accelerated study, combined bachelor's/graduate degree, cooperative education, distance learning, double major, dual enrollment of high school students, ESL, exchange student, honors, independent study, internships, semester at sea, student-designed major, study abroad, teacher certification program, Washington semester, weekend college. **Credit/placement by examination:** AP, CLEP, IB, SAT, ACT, institutional tests. **Support services:** Learning center, reduced course load, remedial instruction, tutoring.

Majors. Architecture: Architecture, environmental design. **Area/ethnic studies:** African-American, American, Asian, European, Latin American, Native American, Russian/Slavic, women's. **Biology:** General, biochemistry. **Business:** Business admin. **Communications:** Journalism, media studies. **Computer sciences:** General. **Conservation:** Environmental science. **Education:** Art, early childhood, elementary, health, music, physical, secondary, special, technology/industrial arts. **Engineering:** Chemical, civil, computer, electrical, mechanical, nuclear, science. **Family/consumer sciences:** General, family studies, food/nutrition. **Foreign languages:** General, classics, comparative lit, French, German, linguistics, Portuguese, Russian, sign language interpretation, Spanish. **Health:** Audiology/speech pathology, clinical lab technology, dental hygiene, EMT paramedic, medical radiologic technology/radiation therapy, nursing (RN), physician assistant. **History:** General. **Liberal arts:** Arts/sciences, humanities. **Math:** General, statistics. **Philosophy/religion:** Philosophy, religion. **Physical sciences:** Astrophysics, chemistry, geology, physics. **Protective services:** Corrections. **Psychology:** General. **Public administration:** Community org/advocacy. **Social sciences:** Anthropology, economics, geography, political science, sociology. **Visual/performing arts:** Art, art history/conservation, dance, dramatic, film/cinema, music performance, theater design.

Most popular majors. Biology 6%, business/marketing 15%, education 12%, health sciences 11%, liberal arts 6%, psychology 7%, social sciences 8%, visual/performing arts 6%.

Computing on campus. 470 workstations in dormitories, library, computer center, student center. Dormitories wired for high-speed internet access and linked to campus network. Commuter students can connect to campus network. Online course registration, online library, helpline, student web hosting, wireless network available.

Student life. Freshman orientation: Mandatory, $125 fee. Two-day sessions held June-August. **Housing:** Coed dorms, special housing for disabled, apartments, fraternity/sorority housing, wellness housing available. $300 deposit. Special living options include senior housing, academic floors, scholar's wing, global learning center, freshman living learning community, outdoors/wellness, computer science, engineering units. **Activities:** Bands, campus ministries, choral groups, dance, drama, film society, international student organizations, literary magazine, music ensembles, Model UN, musical theater, opera, radio station, student government, student newspaper, symphony orchestra, TV station, Panhellenic Council, Raza graduate student association, black student union, KIVA club, MEChA, NMPIRG, Hillel, Navigators, New Mexico wilderness alliance, international center.

Athletics. NCAA. **Intercollegiate:** Baseball M, basketball, cross-country, diving W, football (tackle) M, golf, skiing, soccer, softball W, swimming W, tennis, track and field, volleyball W. **Intramural:** Archery, badminton, basketball, bowling, cross-country, fencing, football (non-tackle), football (tackle) M, golf, racquetball, skiing, soccer, softball, swimming, table tennis, tennis, triathlon, volleyball, water polo. **Team name:** Lobos.

Student services. Adult student services, alcohol/substance abuse counseling, chaplain/spiritual director, career counseling, services for economically disadvantaged, student employment services, financial aid counseling, health services, legal services, minority student services, on-campus daycare, personal counseling, placement for graduates, veterans' counselor, women's services. **Physically disabled:** Services for visually, speech, hearing impaired.

Contact. E-mail: apply@unm.edu
Phone: (505) 277-2446 Toll-free number: (800) 225-5866
Fax: (505) 277-6686
Deborah Kieltyka, Director of Admissions and Recruiting Services, University of New Mexico, Office of Admissions, Albuquerque, NM 87196-4895

University of the Southwest
Hobbs, New Mexico
www.usw.edu **CB code: 4116**

- Private 4-year liberal arts and teachers college
- Commuter campus in large town
- 393 degree-seeking undergraduates: 13% part-time, 56% women
- 181 degree-seeking graduate students
- SAT or ACT (ACT writing optional) required

General. Founded in 1956. Regionally accredited. **Degrees:** 93 bachelor's awarded; master's offered. **Location:** 110 miles from Lubbock, Texas. **Calendar:** Semester, extensive summer session. **Full-time faculty:** 18 total; 100% have terminal degrees, 17% minority, 44% women. **Part-time faculty:** 30 total; 100% have terminal degrees, 7% minority, 53% women. **Class size:** 87% < 20, 13% 20-39.

Freshman class profile. 270 applied, 212 admitted, 93 enrolled.

Mid 50% test scores			
SAT critical reading:	290-470	GPA 3.50-3.74:	16%
SAT math:	310-520	GPA 3.0-3.49:	41%
SAT writing:	360-470	GPA 2.0-2.99:	31%
ACT composite:	15-23	Rank in top quarter:	33%
GPA 3.75 or higher:	8%	Rank in top tenth:	11%
		Out-of-state:	9%

Basis for selection. Open admission, but selective for some programs. Applicants must meet 2 of 3 criteria: ACT 19 or SAT 910 (exclusive of Writing), 2.0 GPA; top half of graduating class. **Homeschooled:** Statement describing homeschool structure and mission, transcript of courses and grades, state high school equivalency certificate required. **Learning Disabled:** Students with special needs are required to submit diagnostic test results in which special need was evaluated during last 3 years, Individual Education Plan (IEP), and other supporting documentation.

2008-2009 Annual costs. Tuition/fees: $12,750. Room/board: $5,980. Books/supplies: $1,000. Personal expenses: $750.

2008-2009 Financial aid. **Non-need-based:** Scholarships awarded for academics, alumni affiliation, athletics, leadership, religious affiliation, state residency.

Application procedures. **Admission:** No deadline. $25 fee. Admission notification on a rolling basis beginning on or about 7/1. **Financial aid:** Priority date 4/1, closing date 6/1. FAFSA, institutional form required. Applicants notified on a rolling basis starting 4/1; must reply within 2 week(s) of notification.

Academics. 6 hours religious studies, 3 hours economics required of all students. **Special study options:** Combined bachelor's/graduate degree, cooperative education, distance learning, double major, dual enrollment of high school students, internships, teacher certification program. Internet program for criminal justice degree only. **Credit/placement by examination:** AP, CLEP, IB. 45 credit hours maximum toward bachelor's degree. **Support services:** Reduced course load, remedial instruction, study skills assistance, tutoring.

Majors. **Biology:** General. **Business:** Accounting, business admin, management information systems, marketing. **Conservation:** General, environmental studies. **Education:** Bilingual, elementary, English, mathematics, physical, sales/marketing, science, secondary, social science, special. **History:** General. **Legal studies:** Prelaw. **Liberal arts:** Arts/sciences, humanities. **Math:** General. **Philosophy/religion:** Religion. **Protective services:** Criminal justice. **Psychology:** General. **Social sciences:** General. **Theology:** Pastoral counseling, youth ministry.

Most popular majors. Business/marketing 15%, education 27%, legal studies 11%, liberal arts 6%.

Computing on campus. 35 workstations in library, computer center. Dormitories wired for high-speed internet access. Online library, helpline, wireless network available.

Student life. **Freshman orientation:** Mandatory. Preregistration for classes offered. Held 1 week prior to beginning of classes. **Housing:** Single-sex dorms, apartments, wellness housing available. $150 fully refundable deposit. **Activities:** Drama, literary magazine, music ensembles, student government, student newspaper, debate, teaching, Students in Free Enterprise, Alpha Phi Omega, Southwest Cultural Pride Club, Sigma Tau Delta, USW Alumni Association.

Athletics. NAIA. **Intercollegiate:** Baseball M, basketball M, cross-country, golf, soccer, softball W, track and field, volleyball W. **Intramural:** Badminton M, basketball, football (tackle) M, soccer W, table tennis, volleyball W. **Team name:** Mustangs.

Student services. Chaplain/spiritual director, student employment services, financial aid counseling, personal counseling, placement for graduates, veterans' counselor.

Contact. E-mail: admissions@usw.edu
Phone: (505) 392-6563 Toll-free number: (800) 530-4400 ext. 1007
Fax: (505) 392-6006
Ashley Taylor, Admissions Coordinator, University of the Southwest, 6610 Lovington Highway #506, Hobbs, NM 88240

Western New Mexico University
Silver City, New Mexico **CB member**
www.wnmu.edu **CB code: 4535**

- Public 4-year university
- Commuter campus in large town
- 1,753 degree-seeking undergraduates: 24% part-time, 65% women, 4% African American, 1% Asian American, 47% Hispanic American, 2% Native American, 1% international
- 419 degree-seeking graduate students

General. Founded in 1893. Regionally accredited. **Degrees:** 181 bachelor's, 103 associate awarded; master's offered. **Location:** 155 miles from El Paso, Texas, 193 miles from Tucson, Arizona. **Calendar:** Semester, extensive summer session. **Full-time faculty:** 100 total; 93% have terminal degrees. **Part-time faculty:** 140 total. **Class size:** 79% < 20, 19% 20-39, less than 1% 40-49, 1% 50-99. **Special facilities:** Museum specializing in Native American cultures, fine arts center and gallery, amphitheater.

Freshman class profile.

Mid 50% test scores			
SAT critical reading:	380-460	Return as sophomores:	48.3%
SAT math:	390-500	Out-of-state:	17%
ACT composite:	16-21	Live on campus:	50%
		International:	1%

Basis for selection. Open admission. COMPASS test used for placement. **Homeschooled:** State high school equivalency certificate required. If state high school equivalency certificate not received, student must take GED.

High school preparation. Recommended units include English 4, mathematics 3, social studies 2, history 1 and science 2.

2008-2009 Annual costs. Tuition/fees: $3,430; $12,718 out-of-state. Room/board: $5,145. Books/supplies: $810. Personal expenses: $2,060.

2007-2008 Financial aid. **Non-need-based:** Scholarships awarded for academics, athletics, state residency.

Application procedures. **Admission:** Priority date 8/1; no deadline. No application fee. Admission notification on a rolling basis. **Financial aid:** Closing date 4/1. FAFSA, institutional form required. Applicants notified on a rolling basis starting 4/1; must reply within 2 week(s) of notification.

Academics. **Special study options:** Cooperative education, distance learning, double major, dual enrollment of high school students, honors, independent study, internships, liberal arts/career combination, teacher certification program. **Credit/placement by examination:** AP, CLEP, IB. 12 credit hours maximum toward associate degree, 32 toward bachelor's. **Support services:** Learning center, remedial instruction, study skills assistance, tutoring, writing center.

Majors. **Area/ethnic studies:** Hispanic-American/Latino/Chicano. **Biology:** General, botany, zoology. **Business:** General, accounting, business admin, managerial economics, marketing, operations. **Computer sciences:** General. **Conservation:** Wildlife. **Education:** General, art, biology, business, chemistry, elementary, ESL, health, mathematics, middle, music, physical, science, secondary, social science, social studies, Spanish, special, technology/industrial arts, voc/tech. **Foreign languages:** Spanish. **Health:** Clinical lab technology. **History:** General. **Liberal arts:** Arts/sciences. **Math:** General. **Physical sciences:** Chemistry. **Protective services:** Criminal justice, law enforcement admin. **Psychology:** General. **Public administration:** Social work. **Social sciences:** General, sociology. **Visual/performing arts:** Studio arts.

Most popular majors. Business/marketing 21%, education 20%, health sciences 9%, liberal arts 12%, security/protective services 8%.

Computing on campus. 150 workstations in dormitories, library, computer center. Dormitories linked to campus network. Commuter students can connect to campus network. Online course registration, online library, helpline available.

Student life. Freshman orientation: Available, $10 fee. Preregistration for classes offered. Two-day sessions held once a month from late May through mid-August. **Housing:** Guaranteed on-campus for all undergraduates. Coed dorms, single-sex dorms, special housing for disabled, apartments available. $75 deposit. **Activities:** Bands, campus ministries, choral groups, drama, music ensembles, musical theater, student government, student newspaper, symphony orchestra, Baptist student union, Society for the Advancement of Management, St. Francis Newman club, Chicano student organization, criminal justice, Native American club.

Athletics. NCAA. **Intercollegiate:** Basketball, cross-country, football (tackle) M, golf, softball W, tennis, volleyball W. **Intramural:** Basketball, racquetball, softball, swimming, tennis, volleyball. **Team name:** Mustangs.

Student services. Chaplain/spiritual director, career counseling, student employment services, financial aid counseling, health services, minority student services, on-campus daycare, personal counseling, placement for graduates. **Physically disabled:** Services for visually, speech, hearing impaired.

Contact. E-mail: tresslerd@wnmu.edu
Phone: (505) 538-6106 Toll-free number: (800) 872-9668
Fax: (505) 538-6127
Dan Tressler, Director of Admissions, Western New Mexico University, Castorena 106, Silver City, NM 88062

New York

Adelphi University

Garden City, New York
www.adelphi.edu
CB member
CB code: 2003

- Private 4-year university
- Commuter campus in large town
- 4,933 degree-seeking undergraduates: 14% part-time, 70% women, 12% African American, 6% Asian American, 6% Hispanic American, 3% international
- 2,972 degree-seeking graduate students
- 66% of applicants admitted
- SAT or ACT with writing, application essay required
- 64% graduate within 6 years; 40% enter graduate study

General. Founded in 1896. Regionally accredited. Program for students with learning disabilities. **Degrees:** 1,319 bachelor's, 8 associate awarded; master's, doctoral offered. **ROTC:** Army, Air Force. **Location:** 20 miles from New York City. **Calendar:** Semester, limited summer session. **Full-time faculty:** 295 total; 88% have terminal degrees, 20% minority, 52% women. **Part-time faculty:** 639 total; 17% minority, 70% women. **Class size:** 45% < 20, 50% 20-39, 3% 40-49, 2% 50-99. **Special facilities:** Speech and hearing center, science library, observatory, arboretum.

Freshman class profile. 6,865 applied, 4,551 admitted, 964 enrolled.

Mid 50% test scores		**GPA 2.0-2.99:**	24%
SAT critical reading:	470-580	**Rank in top quarter:**	51%
SAT math:	500-590	**Rank in top tenth:**	23%
SAT writing:	470-580	**End year in good standing:**	85%
ACT composite:	20-26	**Return as sophomores:**	78%
GPA 3.75 or higher:	21%	**Out-of-state:**	10%
GPA 3.50-3.74:	23%	**Live on campus:**	41%
GPA 3.0-3.49:	30%	**International:**	3%

Basis for selection. 3.0 cumulative GPA, and SAT combined critical reading, math and writing SAT score of 1500 or higher very important. Rank in top third of class, school and community activities, references also important. SAT/ACT scores accepted on rolling basis. SAT recommended for General Studies entrants, not required for adult academic programs in University College. Applicants to dance, drama, music, or art require audition and portfolio review, education majors must have 2.75 minimum GPA. Interview required for honors college applicants. **Homeschooled:** State high school equivalency certificate required. GED required if applicant not receiving diploma from accredited high school or academy. **Learning Disabled:** Fee-based learning disability program where students receive academic and counseling support, requires admission: interview required, SAT recommended, WAIS-III, WJ-III required. Accommodations for learning disabled students not in program without cost, including accommodative testing, scribes, academic assistance.

High school preparation. College-preparatory program recommended. 16 units recommended. Recommended units include English 4, mathematics 3, science 3 and foreign language 2. 4 additional units recommended in either social studies, history, English, mathematics, science or foreign language.

2008-2009 Annual costs. Tuition/fees: $25,240. Room/board: $10,000. Books/supplies: $1,000. Personal expenses: $1,200.

2008-2009 Financial aid. Need-based: 818 full-time freshmen applied for aid; 650 were judged to have need; 625 of these received aid. Average need met was 56%. Average scholarship/grant was $5,525; average loan $3,897. 58% of total undergraduate aid awarded as scholarships/grants, 42% as loans/jobs. **Non-need-based:** Awarded to 2,017 full-time undergraduates, including 422 freshmen. Scholarships awarded for academics, alumni affiliation, art, athletics, job skills, leadership, minority status, music/drama, religious affiliation.

Application procedures. Admission: No deadline. $35 fee, may be waived for applicants with need. Admission notification on a rolling basis beginning on or about 10/1. **Financial aid:** Priority date 3/1; no closing date. FAFSA required. Applicants notified on a rolling basis starting 2/15.

Academics. Special study options: Accelerated study, combined bachelor's/graduate degree, cross-registration, distance learning, double major, ESL, honors, independent study, internships, liberal arts/career combination, study abroad, teacher certification program, Washington semester, weekend college. Learning Disabilities program combining matriculation with support services; University College for adults 21 and over; 1-year intensive General Studies program for freshmen with HS records/SAT scores that do not meet school standards. Students who successfully complete this program invited to enroll in other school programs in their sophomore year. **Credit/placement by examination:** AP, CLEP, IB. 30 credit hours maximum toward bachelor's degree. **Support services:** Learning center, pre-admission summer program, reduced course load, study skills assistance, tutoring, writing center.

Honors college/program. SAT, 3.5 GPA, evidence of academic or creative writing and interview required. 60-80 freshmen admitted.

Majors. Area/ethnic studies: Latin American. **Biology:** General, biochemistry. **Business:** Accounting, business admin, finance. **Communications:** Journalism, media studies. **Computer sciences:** General, information systems. **Conservation:** Environmental studies. **Education:** Art, health, physical, secondary. **Foreign languages:** French, Spanish. **Health:** Audiology/speech pathology, nursing (RN). **History:** General. **Interdisciplinary:** Biological/physical sciences, global studies. **Liberal arts:** Humanities. **Math:** General. **Parks/recreation:** Health/fitness, sports admin. **Philosophy/religion:** Philosophy. **Physical sciences:** Chemistry, physics. **Protective services:** Law enforcement admin. **Psychology:** General. **Public administration:** Social work. **Social sciences:** General, anthropology, economics, political science, sociology. **Visual/performing arts:** Art history/conservation, dance, dramatic, studio arts.

Most popular majors. Business/marketing 16%, health sciences 32%, psychology 7%, social sciences 9%, visual/performing arts 6%.

Computing on campus. 664 workstations in dormitories, library, computer center, student center. Dormitories wired for high-speed internet access and linked to campus network. Commuter students can connect to campus network. Online course registration, online library, helpline, repair service, student web hosting, wireless network available.

Student life. Freshman orientation: Mandatory, $255 fee. Preregistration for classes offered. 3-day orientation held on Garden City campus. **Housing:** Coed dorms, special housing for disabled available. $300 nonrefundable deposit, deadline 5/1. Special housing available for students in Honors College, Performing Arts, and Excel Mentoring Program. **Activities:** Concert band, campus ministries, choral groups, dance, drama, film society, international student organizations, literary magazine, music ensembles, Model UN, musical theater, radio station, student government, student newspaper, symphony orchestra, Approximately 80 activities are offered.

Athletics. NCAA. **Intercollegiate:** Baseball M, basketball, bowling W, cross-country, golf M, lacrosse, soccer, softball W, swimming, tennis, track and field, volleyball W. **Intramural:** Badminton, basketball, cheerleading W, football (non-tackle), soccer, volleyball, weight lifting M. **Team name:** Panthers.

Student services. Adult student services, alcohol/substance abuse counseling, chaplain/spiritual director, career counseling, student employment services, financial aid counseling, health services, minority student services, on-campus daycare, personal counseling, placement for graduates, veterans' counselor. **Physically disabled:** Services for visually, speech, hearing impaired. **Learning disabled:** Comprehensive services available.

Contact. E-mail: admissions@adelphi.edu
Phone: (516) 877-3050 Toll-free number: (800) 233-5744
Fax: (516) 877-3039
Christine Murphy, Director of Admissions, Adelphi University, One South Avenue, Levermore 110, Garden City, NY 11530-0701

Albany College of Pharmacy and Health Sciences

Albany, New York
www.acphs.edu
CB code: 2013

- Private 4-year health science and pharmacy college
- Residential campus in small city
- 1,098 degree-seeking undergraduates: 1% part-time, 59% women, 3% African American, 13% Asian American, 1% Hispanic American, 9% international
- 426 graduate students
- 62% of applicants admitted
- SAT or ACT with writing, application essay required
- 54% graduate within 6 years

General. Founded in 1881. Regionally accredited. **Degrees:** 5 bachelor's awarded; first professional offered. **ROTC:** Army, Naval, Air Force. **Location:** 200 miles from New York City. **Calendar:** Semester, limited summer session. **Full-time faculty:** 84 total. **Part-time faculty:** 19 total. **Class size:** 32% < 20, 44% 20-39, 5% 40-49, 3% 50-99, 16% >100. **Special facilities:** Turn-of-the-century antique pharmacy.

Freshman class profile. 1,186 applied, 740 admitted, 292 enrolled.

Mid 50% test scores		**Rank in top quarter:**	76%
SAT critical reading:	490-650	**Rank in top tenth:**	41%
SAT math:	530-680	**End year in good standing:**	82%
ACT composite:	22-29	**Return as sophomores:**	80%
GPA 3.75 or higher:	32%	**Out-of-state:**	11%
GPA 3.50-3.74:	54%	**Live on campus:**	96%
GPA 3.0-3.49:	14%	**International:**	8%

Basis for selection. High school record, test scores, essay, letters of recommendation, New York State Regents Examinations considered. Special emphasis on science and mathematics grades.

High school preparation. College-preparatory program required. 17 units required; 21 recommended. Required and recommended units include English 4, mathematics 3-4, social studies 3, science 4 (laboratory 4) and academic electives 6.

2008-2009 Annual costs. Tuition/fees: $24,450. Fees include mandatory laptop purchase. Room/board: $7,600. Books/supplies: $800. Personal expenses: $700.

2008-2009 Financial aid. Need-based: 262 full-time freshmen applied for aid; 197 were judged to have need; 193 of these received aid. Average need met was 51%. Average scholarship/grant was $8,005; average loan $3,267. 31% of total undergraduate aid awarded as scholarships/grants, 69% as loans/jobs. **Non-need-based:** Awarded to 246 full-time undergraduates, including 87 freshmen. Scholarships awarded for academics, leadership.

Application procedures. Admission: Priority date 3/1; no deadline. $75 fee, may be waived for applicants with need. Admission notification on a rolling basis beginning on or about 3/15. Must reply by May 1 or within 2 week(s) if notified thereafter. **Financial aid:** Priority date 2/1, closing date 5/1. FAFSA required. Applicants notified on a rolling basis starting 3/20; must reply within 2 week(s) of notification.

Academics. Special study options: Combined bachelor's/graduate degree, cross-registration. **Credit/placement by examination:** AP, CLEP, IB. 30 credit hours maximum toward bachelor's degree. **Support services:** Study skills assistance, tutoring, writing center.

Majors. Health: Clinical lab science, cytotechnology, health services, pharmaceutical sciences.

Computing on campus. PC or laptop required. 30 workstations in library. Dormitories wired for high-speed internet access and linked to campus network. Commuter students can connect to campus network. Online library, helpline, repair service, wireless network available.

Student life. Freshman orientation: Mandatory, $250 fee. Usually held over first weekend prior to class start. **Policies:** College observes honor code. Residency required in first 2 years of study except for students living within 30-mile radius of campus. **Housing:** Guaranteed on-campus for freshmen. Coed dorms, apartments available. $250 nonrefundable deposit, deadline 6/1. **Activities:** Choral groups, dance, international student organizations, literary magazine, student government, student newspaper, Academy of Student Pharmacists, student pharmaceutical society of state of NY, Phi Lambda Sigma.

Athletics. Intercollegiate: Basketball, soccer. **Intramural:** Basketball, football (non-tackle), tennis, volleyball. **Team name:** Panthers.

Student services. Alcohol/substance abuse counseling, chaplain/spiritual director, career counseling, student employment services, financial aid counseling, health services, minority student services, personal counseling, placement for graduates.

Contact. E-mail: admissions@acphs.edu
Phone: (518) 694-7221 Toll-free number: (888) 203-8010
Fax: (518) 694-7322
Carly Connors, Director of Admissions, Albany College of Pharmacy and Health Sciences, 106 New Scotland Avenue, Albany, NY 12208-3492

Alfred University

Alfred, New York — **CB member**
www.alfred.edu — **CB code: 2005**

- Private 4-year university
- Residential campus in rural community
- 1,906 degree-seeking undergraduates
- 76% of applicants admitted
- SAT or ACT (ACT writing optional), application essay required

General. Founded in 1836. Regionally accredited. **Degrees:** 416 bachelor's awarded; master's, doctoral offered. **ROTC:** Army. **Location:** 75 miles from Rochester, 65 miles from Elmira. **Calendar:** Semester, limited summer session. **Full-time faculty:** 170 total. **Part-time faculty:** 39 total. **Class size:** 61% < 20, 33% 20-39, 2% 40-49, 4% 50-99, less than 1% >100. **Special facilities:** Observatory, carillon, 3 art galleries, library of ceramics, ceramics museum, equestrian center, Foster Lake.

Freshman class profile. 2,557 applied, 1,945 admitted, 502 enrolled.

Mid 50% test scores		**Rank in top quarter:**	46%
SAT critical reading:	500-610	**Rank in top tenth:**	18%
SAT math:	510-620	**Out-of-state:**	30%
ACT composite:	21-26	**Live on campus:**	95%

Basis for selection. Rigor of high school curriculum, grades, class rank, standardized ACT or SAT test results, extracurricular involvement, letters of recommendation, and character are all factors. International students required to submit TOEFL if they do not take the SAT or ACT. Interview recommended. Portfolio required for students seeking admission to School of Art & Design. **Homeschooled:** Advise students to document courses taken and provide reading list. SAT or ACT mandatory and relied on heavily.

High school preparation. 16 units required. Required units include English 4, mathematics 2, social studies 2, science 2 (laboratory 2). 3-4 math for business college, 2-3 math for liberal arts and science college, 2 math for art and design college, 4 math for engineering school.

2008-2009 Annual costs. Tuition/fees: $24,278. Tuition info provided is for students enrolling in the College of Business or the College of Liberal Arts and Sciences. Costs for students enrolling in the School of Engineering vary by program and/or residency. Costs for students enrolling in the School of Art and Design vary by residency. Room/board: $10,796. Books/supplies: $900. Personal expenses: $500.

2007-2008 Financial aid. Need-based: 73% of total undergraduate aid awarded as scholarships/grants, 27% as loans/jobs. **Non-need-based:** Scholarships awarded for academics, art, leadership, music/drama.

Application procedures. Admission: Priority date 2/1; no deadline. $40 fee, may be waived for applicants with need. Admission notification on a rolling basis beginning on or about 11/15. Must reply by May 1 or within 2 week(s) if notified thereafter. **Financial aid:** Closing date 3/15. FAFSA, institutional form required. Applicants notified on a rolling basis starting 2/15; must reply by 5/1 or within 2 week(s) of notification.

Academics. Credit hours required for graduation vary from 120-138 depending on the major. There is a physical education requirement for all students. Additional graduation requirements vary by college. Preadmission summer program is required for students enrolling at AU through Opportunity Programs (EOP or HEOP). **Special study options:** Combined bachelor's/graduate degree, cooperative education, cross-registration, double major, ESL, exchange student, honors, independent study, internships, liberal arts/career combination, New York semester, semester at sea, student-designed major, study abroad, teacher certification program, United Nations semester, Washington semester. **Credit/placement by examination:** AP, CLEP, IB, SAT, ACT, institutional tests. **Support services:** Reduced course load, study skills assistance, tutoring, writing center.

Majors. Biology: General. **Business:** Accounting, business admin, finance, marketing. **Communications:** General. **Conservation:** Environmental studies. **Education:** Art, biology, business, chemistry, elementary, English, French, mathematics, middle, physics, social studies, Spanish. **Engineering:** Biomedical, ceramic, electrical, materials, materials science, mechanical. **Foreign languages:** French, German, Spanish. **Health:** Athletic training, clinical lab technology, predental, premedicine, preveterinary. **History:** General. **Interdisciplinary:** Biological/physical sciences, gerontology, intercultural. **Liberal arts:** Arts/sciences. **Math:** General. **Philosophy/religion:** Philosophy. **Physical sciences:** Chemistry, geology, physics. **Protective services:** Criminal justice. **Psychology:** General. **Social sciences:** Economics, political science, sociology. **Visual/performing arts:** Ceramics, dramatic, studio arts. **Other:** Glass science engineering.

Most popular majors. Business/marketing 11%, engineering/engineering technologies 15%, psychology 10%, visual/performing arts 32%.

Computing on campus. 450 workstations in dormitories, library, computer center, student center. Dormitories wired for high-speed internet access and linked to campus network. Commuter students can connect to campus network. Online course registration, online library, helpline, student web hosting, wireless network available.

Student life. Freshman orientation: Mandatory. Preregistration for classes offered. Starts the Wednesday before classes begin. Combination of academic and nonacademic activities to acclimate students to life on campus. **Policies:** Students must abide by Code of Honor. Policies against hazing and sexual harassment. All students required to live in residence halls 6 semesters. Students in poor academic standing required to live on campus. Exceptions granted for married students, students 23 and older, students living with parents/legal guardian and commuting from home, students with dependents, and veterans. **Housing:** Guaranteed on-campus for freshmen. Coed dorms, apartments, wellness housing available. $300 nonrefundable deposit, deadline 5/1. Theme housing available (honors, language house, outdoor sports). **Activities:** Bands, choral groups, dance, drama, film society, literary magazine, music ensembles, musical theater, radio station, student government, student newspaper, symphony orchestra, TV station, Hillel, Brothers and Sisters in Christ, Spectrum, Student Volunteers for Community Action, Alpha Phi Omega, Habitat for Humanity, Christian fellowship, women's issues coalition.

Athletics. NCAA. **Intercollegiate:** Basketball, cross-country, diving, equestrian, football (tackle) M, lacrosse, skiing, soccer, softball W, swimming, tennis, track and field, volleyball W. **Intramural:** Basketball, football (non-tackle), lacrosse M, racquetball, skiing, soccer, softball, squash, tennis, volleyball. **Team name:** Saxons.

Student services. Alcohol/substance abuse counseling, chaplain/spiritual director, career counseling, services for economically disadvantaged, student employment services, financial aid counseling, health services, minority student services, personal counseling, placement for graduates, women's services. **Physically disabled:** Services for visually, speech, hearing impaired.

Contact. E-mail: admissions@alfred.edu
Phone: (607) 871-2115 Toll-free number: (800) 541-9229
Fax: (607) 871-2198
Jeremy Spencer, Director of Admissions, Alfred University, Alumni Hall, Alfred, NY 14802-1205

Bard College

Annandale-on-Hudson, New York — **CB member**
www.bard.edu — **CB code: 2037**

- Private 4-year liberal arts college affiliated with Episcopal Church
- Residential campus in small town
- 1,826 degree-seeking undergraduates: 3% part-time, 57% women, 2% African American, 3% Asian American, 3% Hispanic American, 1% Native American, 10% international
- 273 degree-seeking graduate students
- 25% of applicants admitted
- Application essay required
- 76% graduate within 6 years

General. Founded in 1860. Regionally accredited. **Degrees:** 339 bachelor's, 131 associate awarded; master's, doctoral offered. **Location:** 90 miles from New York City, 50 miles from Albany. **Calendar:** Semester. **Full-time faculty:** 141 total; 9% have terminal degrees, 15% minority, 45% women. **Part-time faculty:** 112 total; 12% have terminal degrees, 20% minority, 48% women. **Class size:** 76% < 20, 23% 20-39, less than 1% 40-49, less than 1% 50-99. **Special facilities:** Ecology field station contiguous to Hudson River Estuary Preserves; curatorial studies and art center; museum of late 20th-century art; archaeological field school; economics institute; center for studies in decorative arts, design and culture; Frank Gehry-designed performing arts center; Rafael Vinoly-designed science center.

Freshman class profile. 5,459 applied, 1,378 admitted, 517 enrolled.

Mid 50% test scores		**End year in good standing:**	95%
SAT critical reading:	680-740	**Return as sophomores:**	83%
SAT math:	650-690	**Out-of-state:**	73%
Rank in top quarter:	95%	**Live on campus:**	100%
Rank in top tenth:	63%	**International:**	10%

Basis for selection. School transcripts and achievement record, rigor of high school program, essays, academic recommendations, talents and dedication to activities, love of learning, and personal ambition important. Campus tour and information session recommended. Tape or CD, brief musical autobiography, and audition required of conservatory applicants. **Homeschooled:** Statement describing homeschool structure and mission, transcript of courses and grades required.

High school preparation. College-preparatory program required. 24 units recommended. Recommended units include English 4, mathematics 4, social studies 4, history 4, science 4 (laboratory 3) and foreign language 4.

2008-2009 Annual costs. Tuition/fees: $38,374. Room/board: $10,866. Books/supplies: $850. Personal expenses: $600.

2008-2009 Financial aid. Need-based: 335 full-time freshmen applied for aid; 301 were judged to have need; 301 of these received aid. Average need met was 89%. Average scholarship/grant was $29,351; average loan $3,645. 79% of total undergraduate aid awarded as scholarships/grants, 21% as loans/jobs. **Non-need-based:** Awarded to 46 full-time undergraduates, including 5 freshmen. Scholarships awarded for academics. **Additional information:** Excellence and Equal Cost Program for students who graduate in top 10 of public high school class lowers fees to levels equivalent to those at home state university or college.

Application procedures. Admission: Closing date 1/15 (receipt date). $50 fee, may be waived for applicants with need. Application must be submitted on paper. Admission notification on a rolling basis beginning on or about 4/1. Must reply by May 1 or within 2 week(s) if notified thereafter. Applicants may be admitted through early action, regular procedure, or Immediate Decision Plan, which gives next-day decision after day-long program and individual interview. Sessions scheduled in early fall. **Financial aid:** Priority date 2/1, closing date 2/15. FAFSA, CSS PROFILE required. Applicants notified by 4/1; must reply by 5/1.

Academics. Strong tradition of independent study and tutorial work with faculty member. Writing-intensive, multidisciplinary programs. Extensive programs in languages, human rights and globalization and international affairs. Unique collaboration with The Rockefeller University. **Special study options:** Combined bachelor's/graduate degree, cross-registration, double major, dual enrollment of high school students, ESL, independent study, internships, New York semester, student-designed major, study abroad, Washington semester. Intensive language studies in Italy, Germany, France, Mexico, Russia, China, program in International Education (Central and Eastern Europe and Southern Africa). **Credit/placement by examination:** AP, CLEP, IB. **Support services:** Learning center, reduced course load, remedial instruction, study skills assistance, tutoring, writing center.

Majors. Area/ethnic studies: African, American, Asian, French, German, Italian, Latin American, Near/Middle Eastern, Russian/Slavic, Spanish/Iberian. **Biology:** General. **Computer sciences:** Computer science. **Foreign languages:** General, ancient Greek, Arabic, Chinese, comparative lit, French, German, Hebrew, Italian, Japanese, Làtin, Russian, Sanskrit, Spanish, translation. **Health:** Premedicine. **History:** General, American, Asian, European. **Interdisciplinary:** Global studies, medieval/Renaissance, neuroscience. **Legal studies:** Prelaw. **Liberal arts:** Arts/sciences. **Math:** General. **Philosophy/religion:** Judaic, philosophy, religion. **Physical sciences:** Chemistry, physics. **Psychology:** General. **Social sciences:** General, anthropology, archaeology, economics, political science, sociology. **Visual/performing arts:** General, acting, art history/conservation, cinematography, conducting, dance, directing/producing, dramatic, film/cinema, jazz, multimedia, music history, music performance, music theory/composition, photography, piano/organ, play/screenwriting, stringed instruments, studio arts, theater history, voice/opera. **Other:** Gender and sexuality, Human rights.

Most popular majors. English 12%, foreign language 7%, social sciences 12%, visual/performing arts 37%.

Computing on campus. 425 workstations in library, computer center, student center. Dormitories wired for high-speed internet access and linked to campus network. Commuter students can connect to campus network. Online course registration, online library, helpline, student web hosting, wireless network available.

Student life. Freshman orientation: Mandatory, $550 fee. 3-week writing-intensive Workshop in Language and Thinking held on campus in August immediately prior to fall semester; coincides with Bard Music Festival. **Policies:** All students members of the student government association, a democratic forum that allocates funds, takes action on campus issues, and provides student representation on administrative and faculty committees. **Housing:** Guaranteed on-campus for freshmen. Coed dorms, single-sex dorms, cooperative housing, wellness housing available. Pets allowed in dorm rooms. **Activities:** Bands, campus ministries, choral groups, dance, drama, film society, international student organizations, literary magazine, music ensembles, Model UN, musical theater, opera, radio station, student government, student newspaper, symphony orchestra, over 120 clubs and organizations available.

Athletics. NCAA. **Intercollegiate:** Basketball, cross-country, soccer, squash M, tennis, track and field, volleyball. **Intramural:** Basketball, bowling, soccer, softball, squash. **Team name:** Raptors.

Student services. Adult student services, alcohol/substance abuse counseling, chaplain/spiritual director, career counseling, services for economically disadvantaged, student employment services, financial aid counseling, health services, legal services, minority student services, personal counseling, placement for graduates, women's services. **Physically disabled:** Services for visually, hearing impaired.

Contact. E-mail: admissions@bard.edu
Phone: (845) 758-7472 Fax: (845) 758-5208
Mary Backlund, Director of Admission, Bard College, 30 Campus Road, Annandale-on-Hudson, NY 12504-5000

Barnard College

New York, New York — **CB member**
www.barnard.edu — **CB code: 2038**

- Private 4-year liberal arts college for women
- Residential campus in very large city
- 2,359 degree-seeking undergraduates: 2% part-time, 100% women, 5% African American, 16% Asian American, 9% Hispanic American, 4% international
- 28% of applicants admitted
- SAT and SAT Subject Tests or ACT with writing, application essay required

General. Founded in 1889. Regionally accredited. Cross-registration and shared facilities with Columbia University. Students receive Columbia University degrees. **Degrees:** 572 bachelor's awarded. **Calendar:** Semester. **Full-time faculty:** 204 total; 93% have terminal degrees, 20% minority, 59% women. **Part-time faculty:** 136 total; 85% have terminal degrees, 11% minority, 70% women. **Class size:** 70% < 20, 18% 20-39, 4% 40-49, 6% 50-99, 2% >100. **Special facilities:** Center for toddler development, center for research on women, theater, dance studios, access to 3,600-acre nature preserve in upstate New York, greenhouse, access to geological observatory.

Freshman class profile. 4,274 applied, 1,218 admitted, 576 enrolled.

Mid 50% test scores		**GPA 3.0-3.49:**	9%
SAT critical reading:	640-740	**Rank in top quarter:**	90%
SAT math:	610-700	**Rank in top tenth:**	74%
SAT writing:	650-750	**Out-of-state:**	69%
ACT composite:	28-31	**Live on campus:**	99%
GPA 3.75 or higher:	64%	**International:**	4%
GPA 3.50-3.74:	27%		

Basis for selection. High school record most important. Depth and difficulty of high school program considered. Test scores, recommendations, involvement in school and community activities, special talents, skills considered. Interview recommended.

High school preparation. College-preparatory program required. 16 units recommended. Recommended units include English 4, mathematics 3, science 3 (laboratory 2) and foreign language 3. Additional units in social sciences, art, music also recommended.

2008-2009 Annual costs. Tuition/fees: $37,538. Room/board: $11,926. Books/supplies: $1,146. Personal expenses: $1,366.

2008-2009 Financial aid. All financial aid based on need. 326 full-time freshmen applied for aid; 250 were judged to have need; 250 of these received aid. Average need met was 100%. Average scholarship/grant was $33,907; average loan $2,886. 89% of total undergraduate aid awarded as scholarships/grants, 11% as loans/jobs. **Additional information:** HEOP for NY residents only; no loan. Pell eligible students: no loan for first-year students, loan reduced to $2,000 for sophomores, juniors and seniors.

Application procedures. Admission: Closing date 1/1 (postmark date). $55 fee, may be waived for applicants with need. Application must be submitted on paper. Admission notification 4/1. Must reply by May 1 or within 2 week(s) if notified thereafter. **Financial aid:** Closing date 2/1. FAFSA, CSS PROFILE required. Applicants notified by 3/31; must reply by 5/1.

Academics. Interdisciplinary first year seminar mandatory. Coursework in global cultures, which may also fulfill other degree requirements, is mandatory. **Special study options:** Accelerated study, combined bachelor's/graduate degree, cross-registration, double major, dual enrollment of high school students, exchange student, honors, independent study, internships, liberal arts/career combination, student-designed major, study abroad, teacher certification program. Independent scholars program, BA/BS in engineering and applied science. **Credit/placement by examination:** AP, CLEP, IB, institutional tests. 30 credit hours maximum toward bachelor's degree. **Support services:** Pre-admission summer program, tutoring, writing center.

Majors. Architecture: Architecture, history/criticism. **Area/ethnic studies:** African, American, Asian, European, French, German, Latin American, Near/Middle Eastern, Russian/Slavic, Slavic, Spanish/Iberian, women's. **Biology:** General, biochemistry, biophysics, environmental. **Computer sciences:** General, computer science. **Conservation:** Environmental science, environmental studies. **Engineering:** Physics. **Foreign languages:** Ancient Greek, classics, comparative lit, French, German, Italian, Latin, linguistics, modern Greek, Russian, Spanish. **History:** General. **Interdisciplinary:** Ancient studies, biopsychology, medieval/Renaissance. **Math:** General, applied, statistics. **Philosophy/religion:** Philosophy, religion. **Physical sciences:** Astronomy, astrophysics, chemical physics, chemistry, geology, physics. **Psychology:** General. **Social sciences:** Anthropology, economics, geography, political science, sociology, urban studies. **Visual/performing arts:** General, art history/conservation, dance, dramatic, film/cinema, jazz.

Most popular majors. Area/ethnic studies 9%, English 10%, history 9%, psychology 14%, social sciences 25%, visual/performing arts 12%.

Computing on campus. 208 workstations in dormitories, library, computer center, student center. Dormitories wired for high-speed internet access and linked to campus network. Commuter students can connect to campus network. Online course registration, online library, helpline, repair service, wireless network available.

Student life. Freshman orientation: Mandatory, $275 fee. August 27 for 2 days. **Housing:** Guaranteed on-campus for all undergraduates. Special housing for disabled, apartments available. $400 nonrefundable deposit, deadline 6/15. Coed dorms available through Columbia University. **Activities:** Bands, campus ministries, choral groups, dance, drama, film society, literary magazine, music ensembles, musical theater, opera, radio station, student government, student newspaper, symphony orchestra, TV station, more than 100 organizations.

Athletics. NCAA. **Intercollegiate:** Archery W, basketball W, cross-country W, diving W, fencing W, field hockey W, golf W, lacrosse W, rowing (crew) W, soccer W, softball W, swimming W, tennis W, track and field W, volleyball W. **Intramural:** Archery W, badminton W, basketball W, bowling W, cross-country W, fencing W, racquetball W, sailing W, soccer W, softball W, swimming W, tennis W, volleyball W. **Team name:** Lions.

Student services. Alcohol/substance abuse counseling, career counseling, student employment services, financial aid counseling, health services, personal counseling, placement for graduates, women's services. **Physically disabled:** Services for visually, speech, hearing impaired.

Contact. E-mail: admissions@barnard.edu
Phone: (212) 854-2014 Fax: (212) 854-6220
Jennifer Fondiller, Dean of Admissions, Barnard College, 3009 Broadway, New York, NY 10027-6598

Beis Medrash Heichal Dovid

Far Rockaway, New York

- Private 4-year rabbinical college for men affiliated with Jewish faith
- Large city

General. Accredited by AARTS. **Calendar:** Semester.

Annual costs/financial aid. Tuition/fees (2008-2009): $7,700.

Contact. Phone: (718) 868-2300 ext. 360
Registrar, 257 Beach 17th Street, Far Rockaway, NY 11691

Berkeley College

White Plains, New York
www.berkeleycollege.edu — **CB code: 2064**

- For-profit 4-year business college
- Commuter campus in small city
- 697 degree-seeking undergraduates: 6% part-time, 68% women, 33% African American, 3% Asian American, 27% Hispanic American, 6% international
- 39% graduate within 6 years

General. Founded in 1945. Regionally accredited. **Degrees:** 126 bachelor's, 36 associate awarded. **Location:** 28 miles from New York City. **Calendar:** Quarter, extensive summer session. **Full-time faculty:** 21 total. **Part-time faculty:** 14 total. **Class size:** 39% < 20, 61% 20-39. **Special facilities:** Access to Manhattanville College facilities.

Freshman class profile. 141 enrolled.

Return as sophomores:	50%	**Out-of-state:**	18%

Basis for selection. Class rank, high school record, interview most important. Passing grade on school entrance examination required. SAT/ACT considered if submitted. Interviews strongly recommended.

2009-2010 Annual costs. Tuition/fees: $19,950. Room only: $7,500. Books/supplies: $1,360. Personal expenses: $3,000.

Financial aid. **Non-need-based:** Scholarships awarded for academics, alumni affiliation. **Additional information:** Alumni scholarship examination given in November and December. Full and partial scholarships awarded.

Application procedures. **Admission:** No deadline. $50 fee. Admission notification on a rolling basis. Admitted applicants must reply within 2 weeks of notification. **Financial aid:** No deadline. FAFSA required. Applicants notified on a rolling basis starting 3/1; must reply within 6 week(s) of notification.

Academics. **Special study options:** Accelerated study, distance learning, ESL, internships, New York semester, study abroad. **Credit/placement by examination:** AP, CLEP, SAT, ACT, institutional tests. **Support services:** Learning center, remedial instruction, study skills assistance, tutoring, writing center.

Majors. **Business:** Accounting, business admin, fashion, financial planning, international, management information systems, marketing. **Health:** Health care admin. **Protective services:** Law enforcement admin.

Computing on campus. 150 workstations in library, computer center. Dormitories linked to campus network. Commuter students can connect to campus network. Online library, helpline, wireless network available.

Student life. **Freshman orientation:** Mandatory. **Housing:** Coed dorms available. $400 fully refundable deposit. **Activities:** Student government, accounting club, Berkeley club, Phi Beta Lambda, Phi Theta Kappa, international club, fashion club, paralegal club.

Athletics. **Intramural:** Basketball, cheerleading, soccer. **Team name:** Knights.

Student services. Adult student services, career counseling, student employment services, financial aid counseling, personal counseling, placement for graduates.

Contact. E-mail: info@berkeleycollege.edu
Phone: (914) 694-1122 Toll-free number: (800) 446-5400
Fax: (914) 328-9469
Giselle Rivera, Director, High School Admissions, Berkeley College, 99 Church Street, White Plains, NY 10601

Berkeley College of New York City

New York, New York
www.berkeleycollege.edu **CB code: 0954**

- For-profit 4-year business college
- Commuter campus in very large city
- 3,054 degree-seeking undergraduates: 11% part-time, 70% women, 26% African American, 4% Asian American, 24% Hispanic American, 1% Native American, 18% international
- 39% graduate within 6 years

General. Founded in 1936. Regionally accredited. Extension center located in Lower Manhattan (Financial District) and a branch campus located in Westchester County (White Plains). **Degrees:** 416 bachelor's, 130 associate awarded. **Location:** Midtown Manhattan. **Calendar:** Quarter, extensive summer session. **Full-time faculty:** 76 total. **Part-time faculty:** 126 total. **Class size:** 11% < 20, 89% 20-39.

Freshman class profile. 470 enrolled.

Return as sophomores:	46%	**Out-of-state:**	11%

Basis for selection. High school record and interview most important. Institutional entrance tests required of all applicants. SAT or ACT accepted in lieu of institutional entrance exam.

2009-2010 Annual costs. Tuition/fees: $19,950. Books/supplies: $1,360. Personal expenses: $3,000.

Financial aid. **Non-need-based:** Scholarships awarded for academics, alumni affiliation. **Additional information:** Alumni scholarship examination given in November and December. Full and partial scholarships awarded.

Application procedures. **Admission:** No deadline. $50 fee. Admission notification on a rolling basis. Admitted applicants must reply within 2 weeks of notification. **Financial aid:** No deadline. FAFSA required. Applicants notified on a rolling basis starting 3/1; must reply within 6 week(s) of notification.

Academics. **Special study options:** Accelerated study, distance learning, ESL, internships, study abroad. **Credit/placement by examination:** AP, CLEP, SAT, ACT, institutional tests. **Support services:** Learning center, remedial instruction, study skills assistance, tutoring, writing center.

Majors. **Business:** Accounting, business admin, fashion, financial planning, international, management information systems, marketing. **Health:** Health care admin. **Protective services:** Law enforcement admin.

Computing on campus. 200 workstations in library, computer center. Commuter students can connect to campus network. Online library, helpline, wireless network available.

Student life. **Freshman orientation:** Mandatory. **Housing:** $400 deposit. **Activities:** Student government, international club, multicultural club, fashion club, accounting club, paralegal club, student government.

Athletics. **Intramural:** Basketball, cheerleading, soccer. **Team name:** Knights.

Student services. Adult student services, alcohol/substance abuse counseling, career counseling, student employment services, financial aid counseling, personal counseling, placement for graduates.

Contact. E-mail: info@berkeleycollege.edu
Phone: (212) 986-4343 Toll-free number: (800) 446-5400
Fax: (212) 818-1079
Stephen Weinstein, Enrollment Director, Berkeley College of New York City, 3 East 43rd Street, New York, NY 10017

Beth Hamedrash Shaarei Yosher Institute

Brooklyn, New York
CB code: 0731

- Private 5-year rabbinical college for men affiliated with Jewish faith
- Very large city

General. Founded in 1962. Accredited by AARTS. **Calendar:** Semester.

Annual costs/financial aid. Tuition/fees (2008-2009): $6,010. Room/board: $1,200. Personal expenses: $2,000.

Contact. Phone: (718) 854-2290
Director of Student Financial Aid, 4102-10 16th Avenue, Brooklyn, NY 11204

Beth Hatalmud Rabbinical College

Brooklyn, New York
CB code: 7317

- Private 4-year rabbinical college for men affiliated with Jewish faith
- Very large city

General. Founded in 1950. Accredited by AARTS. **Calendar:** Semester.

Annual costs/financial aid. Tuition/fees (2008-2009): $5,600.

Contact. Phone: (718) 259-2525
Director of Admissions, 2127 82nd Street, Brooklyn, NY 11214

Boricua College

New York, New York
www.boricuacollege.edu **CB code: 2901**

- Private 4-year liberal arts college
- Commuter campus in very large city
- 968 degree-seeking undergraduates
- 84 graduate students
- 38% of applicants admitted
- Application essay, interview required
- 43% graduate within 6 years

General. Founded in 1974. Regionally accredited. Boricua College has four centers: one each in Manhattan and the Bronx, and two in Brooklyn. **Degrees:** 146 bachelor's, 161 associate awarded; master's offered. **Calendar:** Semester, limited summer session. **Full-time faculty:** 58 total; 100% have terminal degrees, 36% women. **Part-time faculty:** 76 total; 100% have terminal degrees. **Class size:** 100% 20-39. **Special facilities:** Art galleries.

Freshman class profile. 827 applied, 316 admitted, 217 enrolled.

Basis for selection. Entrance examination, academic records, interview by the faculty, 2 letters of recommendation. Institutional tests required for admissions and placement. Final interview and approval by the faculty is required. **Learning Disabled:** Evaluation is done based on individual needs of the candidate.

2008-2009 Annual costs. Tuition/fees: $9,000. Books/supplies: $400. Personal expenses: $3,625.

2007-2008 Financial aid. Need-based: 456 full-time freshmen applied for aid; 451 were judged to have need; 441 of these received aid. Average need met was 59%. Average scholarship/grant was $117; average loan $2,093. 87% of total undergraduate aid awarded as scholarships/grants, 13% as loans/jobs. **Non-need-based:** Awarded to 28 full-time undergraduates, including 20 freshmen.

Application procedures. Admission: No deadline. $25 fee, may be waived for applicants with need. Admission notification on a rolling basis. **Financial aid:** Priority date 4/30; no closing date. FAFSA required. Applicants notified on a rolling basis; must reply within 3 week(s) of notification.

Academics. Academic load consists of 5 courses per semester: 3 applied studies courses (individualized instruction, colloquium, experiential), 1 theoretical, and 1 cultural class. Academic support services are available at different hours upon request. **Special study options:** Accelerated study, independent study, internships, liberal arts/career combination, teacher certification program. **Credit/placement by examination:** CLEP, institutional tests. 30 credit hours maximum toward bachelor's degree. **Support services:** Reduced course load, tutoring.

Majors. Area/ethnic studies: Latin American. **Business:** Business admin. **Education:** Elementary. **Liberal arts:** Arts/sciences. **Public administration:** Human services.

Computing on campus. 120 workstations in library, computer center, student center. Online library, helpline, wireless network available.

Student life. Freshman orientation: Mandatory. Preregistration for classes offered. Based on appointments. **Policies:** Student regulations include a sexual harassment policy. **Activities:** Choral groups, dance, drama, opera, student government, student newspaper.

Athletics. Intramural: Basketball, volleyball.

Student services. Adult student services, career counseling, student employment services, personal counseling, placement for graduates.

Contact. E-mail: acruz@boricuacollege.edu
Phone: (212) 694-1000 ext. 650 Fax: (212) 694-1015
Miriam Pfeffer, Director of Admissions, Boricua College, 3755 Broadway, New York, NY 10032

Briarcliffe College

Bethpage, New York
www.briarcliffe.edu **CB code: 3108**

- For-profit 4-year business and technical college
- Commuter campus in large town
- 1,727 degree-seeking undergraduates

General. Founded in 1966. Regionally accredited. **Degrees:** 350 bachelor's, 574 associate awarded. **Location:** 20 miles from New York City. **Calendar:** Semester, extensive summer session. **Full-time faculty:** 65 total. **Part-time faculty:** 128 total. **Class size:** 60% < 20, 39% 20-39, less than 1% 40-49.

Basis for selection. School achievement record important, recommendations suggested. Interviews recommended. **Homeschooled:** Not accepted.

High school preparation. Recommended units include English 4, mathematics 2, social studies 4 and science 1.

2008-2009 Annual costs. Tuition/fees: $17,568.

Financial aid. Non-need-based: Scholarships awarded for academics.

Application procedures. Admission: No deadline. $35 fee. Admission notification on a rolling basis. **Financial aid:** No deadline. FAFSA, institutional form required. Applicants notified on a rolling basis.

Academics. Special study options: Independent study, internships, study abroad. 4-year BFA program with concentration in graphic design available. **Credit/placement by examination:** CLEP, institutional tests. 15 credit hours maximum toward associate degree, 15 toward bachelor's. **Support services:** Learning center, reduced course load, remedial instruction, study skills assistance, tutoring.

Majors. Business: Accounting, business admin, marketing. **Computer sciences:** Information technology, networking, programming. **Visual/performing arts:** General.

Computing on campus. 400 workstations in library, computer center. Commuter students can connect to campus network. Online library available.

Student life. Freshman orientation: Mandatory. Preregistration for classes offered. **Housing:** Single-sex dorms available. **Activities:** Student government, student newspaper.

Athletics. USCAA. **Intercollegiate:** Baseball M, basketball, bowling, lacrosse M, soccer M, softball W, volleyball W. **Team name:** Seahawks.

Student services. Financial aid counseling, placement for graduates.

Contact. E-mail: info@bcl.edu
Phone: (516) 918-3600 Fax: (516) 470-6020
Alan Shikowitz, Director of Admissions, Briarcliffe College, 1055 Stewart Avenue, Bethpage, NY 11714

Canisius College

Buffalo, New York **CB member**
www.canisius.edu **CB code: 2073**

- Private 4-year liberal arts and teachers college affiliated with Roman Catholic Church
- Residential campus in large city
- 3,224 degree-seeking undergraduates: 3% part-time, 54% women, 6% African American, 1% Asian American, 3% Hispanic American, 3% international
- 1,566 degree-seeking graduate students
- 76% of applicants admitted
- SAT or ACT (ACT writing optional) required
- 68% graduate within 6 years

General. Founded in 1870. Regionally accredited. Campus connected by underground tunnel system, rapid transit stations near campus. **Degrees:** 811 bachelor's, 4 associate awarded; master's offered. **ROTC:** Army. **Calendar:** Semester, limited summer session. **Full-time faculty:** 226 total; 92% have terminal degrees, 8% minority, 39% women. **Part-time faculty:** 268 total; 21% have terminal degrees, 5% minority, 48% women. **Class size:** 43% < 20, 53% 20-39, 3% 40-49, less than 1% 50-99. **Special facilities:** Mini-planetarium, seismograph station, rare book room, digital media lab, human performance lab, animal care unit.

Freshman class profile. 3,847 applied, 2,905 admitted, 807 enrolled.

Mid 50% test scores			
SAT critical reading:	500-610	GPA 2.0-2.99:	17%
SAT math:	510-630	Rank in top quarter:	58%
ACT composite:	22-27	Rank in top tenth:	27%
GPA 3.75 or higher:	34%	Return as sophomores:	83%
GPA 3.50-3.74:	18%	Out-of-state:	6%
GPA 3.0-3.49:	31%	Live on campus:	75%
		International:	3%

Basis for selection. Primary emphasis placed on strength of academic record, achievement, class rank and SAT/ACT scores. Essays, recommendations important. Extracurricular activities, alumni affiliation factors. Interview and essay recommended.

High school preparation. College-preparatory program required. 19 units required; 23 recommended. Required and recommended units include English 4, mathematics 3, social studies 4, science 2-3 (laboratory 2), foreign language 2-3 and academic electives 4.

2008-2009 Annual costs. Tuition/fees: $28,157. Room/board: $10,150.

2008-2009 Financial aid. Need-based: 719 full-time freshmen applied for aid; 647 were judged to have need; 647 of these received aid. Average need met was 88%. Average scholarship/grant was $19,506; average loan $3,298. 71% of total undergraduate aid awarded as scholarships/grants, 29% as loans/jobs. **Non-need-based:** Awarded to 1,188 full-time undergraduates, including 327 freshmen. Scholarships awarded for academics, alumni affiliation, art, athletics, job skills, music/drama, religious affiliation, ROTC.

Application procedures. Admission: Priority date 3/1; deadline 5/1. $40 fee, may be waived for applicants with need, free for online applicants. Admission notification on a rolling basis beginning on or about 12/15. Must reply by 5/1. **Financial aid:** Priority date 2/15; no closing date. FAFSA required. Applicants notified on a rolling basis starting 3/1; must reply within 2 week(s) of notification.

Academics. Pre-professional programs include pre-engineering, prelaw, premedical, predentistry, preveterinary medicine, prepharmacy. **Special study options:** Combined bachelor's/graduate degree, cooperative education, cross-registration, distance learning, double major, dual enrollment of high school students, ESL, exchange student, honors, independent study, internships, study abroad, teacher certification program. Early assurance for medical and dental school with SUNY Buffalo Medical and Dental Schools (New York state residents only), and the Upstate Medical School at Syracuse; 7-year joint degree programs with SUNY Buffalo Dental School, the Ohio College of Podiatric Medicine, the New York College of Podiatric Medicine and SUNY State College of Optometry in NYC; AS/BS with Fashion Institute of Technology. **Credit/placement by examination:** AP, CLEP, IB, SAT, ACT, institutional tests. 30 credit hours maximum toward bachelor's degree. **Support services:** Learning center, pre-admission summer program, reduced course load, remedial instruction, study skills assistance, tutoring, writing center.

Majors. **Area/ethnic studies:** European. **Biology:** General, biochemistry, bioinformatics. **Business:** Accounting, accounting technology, entrepreneurial studies, finance, international, management information systems, management science, marketing. **Communications:** General, digital media. **Computer sciences:** Computer science. **Conservation:** Environmental science. **Education:** Early childhood, early childhood special, elementary, physical, secondary. **Foreign languages:** French, Germanic, Spanish. **Health:** Athletic training, clinical lab science. **History:** General. **Liberal arts:** Arts/sciences, humanities. **Math:** General. **Philosophy/religion:** Philosophy, religion. **Physical sciences:** Chemistry, physics. **Protective services:** Criminal justice. **Psychology:** General. **Social sciences:** Anthropology, economics, international relations, political science, sociology, urban studies. **Visual/performing arts:** Art history/conservation.

Most popular majors. Biology 8%, business/marketing 27%, communications/journalism 10%, education 16%, parks/recreation 6%, psychology 10%, social sciences 9%.

Computing on campus. 500 workstations in dormitories, library, computer center, student center. Dormitories wired for high-speed internet access and linked to campus network. Commuter students can connect to campus network. Online course registration, online library, helpline, repair service, student web hosting, wireless network available.

Student life. **Freshman orientation:** Mandatory, $125 fee. Preregistration for classes offered. Program includes testing, advisement, registration, introduction to student services. **Policies:** Religious observance required. **Housing:** Coed dorms, special housing for disabled, apartments, wellness housing available. $200 partly refundable deposit, deadline 5/1. Themed housing, science, honors, townhouses available. **Activities:** Bands, campus ministries, choral groups, dance, drama, film society, international student organizations, literary magazine, music ensembles, musical theater, radio station, student government, student newspaper, TV station, political science association, ethnic and social service organizations, international affairs society, social justice club, Circle K, Global Horizons, German club, Italian club, Little Theater.

Athletics. NCAA. **Intercollegiate:** Baseball M, basketball, cross-country, golf M, ice hockey M, lacrosse, soccer, softball W, swimming, synchronized swimming W, volleyball W. **Intramural:** Cheerleading, golf M, rowing (crew) W, rugby. **Team name:** Golden Griffins.

Student services. Adult student services, alcohol/substance abuse counseling, chaplain/spiritual director, career counseling, services for economically disadvantaged, student employment services, financial aid counseling, health services, minority student services, personal counseling, placement for graduates, veterans' counselor. **Physically disabled:** Services for visually, speech, hearing impaired. **Learning disabled:** Comprehensive services available.

Contact. E-mail: admissions@canisius.edu
Phone: (716) 888-2200 Toll-free number: (800) 843-1517
Fax: (716) 888-3230
Ann Marie Moscovic, Director of Admissions, Canisius College, 2001 Main Street, Buffalo, NY 14208-1098

Cazenovia College

Cazenovia, New York
www.cazenovia.edu **CB code: 2078**

- Private 4-year liberal arts college
- Residential campus in small town
- 1,062 degree-seeking undergraduates: 8% part-time, 75% women, 4% African American, 1% Asian American, 3% Hispanic American, 1% Native American
- 69% of applicants admitted

General. Founded in 1824. Regionally accredited. **Degrees:** 176 bachelor's, 6 associate awarded. **ROTC:** Army, Air Force. **Location:** 20 miles from Syracuse. **Calendar:** Semester, limited summer session. **Full-time faculty:** 59 total; 3% minority, 61% women. **Part-time faculty:** 129 total; 5% minority, 60% women. **Class size:** 84% < 20, 15% 20-39, 1% 40-49. **Special facilities:** 160-acre farm and equine center, art and design facility and gallery.

Freshman class profile. 2,045 applied, 1,404 admitted, 284 enrolled.

Mid 50% test scores			
SAT critical reading:	450-560	GPA 3.0-3.49:	32%
SAT math:	450-570	GPA 2.0-2.99:	31%
ACT composite:	20-25	Rank in top quarter:	40%
GPA 3.75 or higher:	20%	Rank in top tenth:	15%
GPA 3.50-3.74:	17%	Out-of-state:	25%
		Live on campus:	97%

Basis for selection. Rigor of secondary school record very important; interview, recommendations, school activities important. SAT or ACT recommended. Portfolio recommended for art, graphic and interior design, photography programs.

High school preparation. 16 units recommended. Recommended units include English 4, mathematics 2, social studies 4 and science 2. Art courses recommended for art and design majors.

2008-2009 Annual costs. Tuition/fees: $22,894. Room/board: $9,502. Books/supplies: $1,000. Personal expenses: $100.

2008-2009 Financial aid. **Need-based:** 259 full-time freshmen applied for aid; 223 were judged to have need; 223 of these received aid. Average need met was 78%. Average scholarship/grant was $18,105; average loan $3,314. 70% of total undergraduate aid awarded as scholarships/grants, 30% as loans/jobs. **Non-need-based:** Awarded to 196 full-time undergraduates, including 63 freshmen. Scholarships awarded for academics.

Application procedures. **Admission:** Priority date 3/1; no deadline. $30 fee, may be waived for applicants with need, free for online applicants. Admission notification on a rolling basis beginning on or about 11/1. Must reply by May 1 or within 2 week(s) if notified thereafter. **Financial aid:** Priority date 3/15; no closing date. FAFSA required. Applicants notified on a rolling basis starting 11/1; must reply by 5/1 or within 2 week(s) of notification.

Academics. **Special study options:** Combined bachelor's/graduate degree, double major, exchange student, honors, independent study, internships, student-designed major, study abroad, teacher certification program, Washington semester. **Credit/placement by examination:** AP, CLEP, IB, institutional tests. **Support services:** Learning center, pre-admission summer program, reduced course load, remedial instruction, study skills assistance, tutoring, writing center.

Majors. **Agriculture:** Equine science. **Business:** Accounting, business admin, fashion. **Communications:** General. **Conservation:** Environmental studies. **Education:** Early childhood, special. **Liberal arts:** Arts/sciences. **Parks/recreation:** Sports admin. **Protective services:** Criminal justice. **Psychology:** General. **Public administration:** Human services. **Social sciences:** General. **Visual/performing arts:** Design, fashion design, interior design, photography, studio arts.

Most popular majors. Business/marketing 32%, public administration/social services 14%, visual/performing arts 37%.

Computing on campus. Dormitories wired for high-speed internet access and linked to campus network. Commuter students can connect to campus network. Online library, helpline, wireless network available.

Student life. **Freshman orientation:** Mandatory. Preregistration for classes offered. **Housing:** Coed dorms, single-sex dorms available. $200 nonrefundable deposit, deadline 5/1. Single room suites available. **Activities:** Jazz band, campus ministries, choral groups, dance, drama, film society, musical theater, radio station, student government, student newspaper, human services club, overseas travel club, Young Democrats, Young Republicans, Cazventures outdoor club, Certified Peer Educators, You Are Not Alone-LGBT, Student Organization of Ethnic Diversity.

Athletics. NCAA. **Intercollegiate:** Baseball M, basketball, cheerleading, cross-country, equestrian, golf M, lacrosse, rowing (crew), soccer, softball W, volleyball W. **Intramural:** Basketball, bowling, equestrian, football (non-tackle), rowing (crew), skiing, soccer, softball, swimming, volleyball, weight lifting. **Team name:** Wildcats.

Student services. Alcohol/substance abuse counseling, chaplain/spiritual director, career counseling, services for economically disadvantaged, student employment services, financial aid counseling, health services, personal counseling, placement for graduates. **Physically disabled:** Services for visually, speech, hearing impaired.

Contact. E-mail: admission@cazenovia.edu
Phone: (315) 655-7208 Toll-free number: (800) 654-3210
Fax: (315) 655-4860
Robert Croot, Vice President for Enrollment Management and Dean for Admissions and Financial Aid, Cazenovia College, 3 Sullivan Street, Cazenovia, NY 13035

Central Yeshiva Tomchei Tmimim-Lubavitch

Brooklyn, New York

CB code: 0549

- Private 4-year rabbinical college for men affiliated with Jewish faith
- Very large city

General. Accredited by AARTS. **Calendar:** Continuous.

Annual costs/financial aid. Tuition/fees (2008-2009): $5,250. Room/board: $2,300.

Contact. Phone: (718) 859-7600
841-853 Ocean Parkway, Brooklyn, NY 11230

City University of New York: Baruch College

New York, New York **CB member**
www.baruch.cuny.edu **CB code: 2034**

- Public 4-year business and liberal arts college
- Commuter campus in very large city
- 12,473 degree-seeking undergraduates: 23% part-time, 52% women, 10% African American, 31% Asian American, 17% Hispanic American, 12% international
- 3,579 degree-seeking graduate students
- 24% of applicants admitted
- SAT or ACT (ACT writing optional) required
- 57% graduate within 6 years

General. Founded in 1919. Regionally accredited. **Degrees:** 2,611 bachelor's awarded; master's offered. **ROTC:** Army. **Calendar:** Semester, extensive summer session. **Full-time faculty:** 509 total; 84% have terminal degrees, 21% minority, 37% women. **Part-time faculty:** 509 total; 24% have terminal degrees, 23% minority, 39% women. **Class size:** 25% < 20, 57% 20-39, 6% 40-49, 10% 50-99, 2% >100. **Special facilities:** Performing arts center (black box theater, gallery, various theaters and recital halls).

Freshman class profile. 18,834 applied, 4,426 admitted, 1,512 enrolled.

Mid 50% test scores		**Rank in top tenth:**	37%
SAT critical reading:	480-590	**End year in good standing:**	90%
SAT math:	550-660	**Return as sophomores:**	90%
GPA 3.75 or higher:	13%	**Out-of-state:**	5%
GPA 3.50-3.74:	16%	**International:**	6%
GPA 3.0-3.49:	38%	**Fraternities:**	1%
GPA 2.0-2.99:	32%	**Sororities:**	1%
Rank in top quarter:	66%		

Basis for selection. Overall high school performance and 82 average or combined SAT score of 1200 required. **Homeschooled:** 1200 SAT required. **Learning Disabled:** No special requirements; recommended that students call Disability Service Office to discuss available services.

High school preparation. 16 units required. Required and recommended units include English 4, mathematics 3-4, social studies 4, science 2 (laboratory 2), foreign language 2-3 and academic electives 1.

2008-2009 Annual costs. Tuition/fees: $4,370; $11,170 out-of-state. Books/supplies: $1,016. Personal expenses: $2,706.

2008-2009 Financial aid. Need-based: 80% of total undergraduate aid awarded as scholarships/grants, 20% as loans/jobs. **Non-need-based:** Scholarships awarded for academics, state residency.

Application procedures. Admission: Priority date 3/15; no deadline. $65 fee, may be waived for applicants with need. Admission notification on a rolling basis beginning on or about 2/1. Must reply by May 1 or within 2 week(s) if notified thereafter. **Financial aid:** Priority date 3/15, closing date 4/30. FAFSA required. Applicants notified on a rolling basis starting 4/1; must reply by 6/1 or within 6 week(s) of notification.

Academics. 120 credit hours required for BA/BS degrees, 124 for BBA. Optional humanities seminar examining 2 or more disciplines in arts and sciences; joint business/liberal arts and science majors; programs in arts administration, management of musical enterprise, real estate, and metropolitan development. **Special study options:** Accelerated study, combined bachelor's/graduate degree, cross-registration, distance learning, double major, ESL, exchange student, honors, independent study, internships, liberal arts/career combination, student-designed major, study abroad. **Credit/placement by examination:** AP, CLEP, IB, institutional tests. 21 credit hours maximum toward bachelor's degree. No more than 21 credits through AP and/or college courses taken in high school. **Support services:** Learning center, pre-admission summer program, reduced course load, study skills assistance, tutoring, writing center.

Honors college/program. Applicants must have high standardized test scores (1300+ on the SAT, exclusive of Writing) and high school averages (90+). Leadership potential and community involvement sought. Applicants must supply teacher recommendations and essay.

Majors. Architecture: Urban/community planning. **Biology:** General. **Business:** General, accounting, actuarial science, business admin, communications, finance, human resources, labor relations, management information systems, managerial economics, operations, real estate, sales/distribution. **Communications:** General, advertising, journalism. **Computer sciences:** General, computer science, information systems. **Engineering:** Operations research. **Foreign languages:** Comparative lit, Spanish. **History:** General. **Interdisciplinary:** Biological/physical sciences. **Liberal arts:** Arts/sciences. **Math:** General, statistics. **Philosophy/religion:** Philosophy. **Psychology:** General. **Public administration:** General. **Social sciences:** Economics, political science, sociology. **Visual/performing arts:** Arts management, design, music management.

Most popular majors. Business/marketing 76%.

Computing on campus. 1,300 workstations in library, computer center, student center. Online course registration, online library, helpline, wireless network available.

Student life. Freshman orientation: Mandatory. Half day-long, on-campus session offered on multiple days. **Activities:** Campus ministries, choral groups, dance, drama, film society, international student organizations, literary magazine, Model UN, musical theater, radio station, student government, student newspaper, Hillel, National Association of Black Accountants, Golden Key, International Honor Society, Asian Student Association, Muslim Student Association, United International Student Body, Model United Nations, Pre-Law Society, Caribbean Student Association.

Athletics. NCAA. **Intercollegiate:** Baseball M, basketball, cheerleading, cross-country, diving W, soccer M, softball W, swimming, tennis, volleyball. **Intramural:** Badminton, basketball, cross-country, racquetball, swimming, table tennis, volleyball, weight lifting. **Team name:** Bearcats.

Student services. Adult student services, alcohol/substance abuse counseling, chaplain/spiritual director, career counseling, student employment services, financial aid counseling, health services, legal services, personal counseling, placement for graduates, veterans' counselor. **Physically disabled:** Services for visually, speech, hearing impaired.

Contact. Phone: (646) 312-1400 Fax: (646) 312-1363
Marybeth Murphy, Vice President for Enrollment Management Services, City University of New York: Baruch College, One Bernard Baruch Way, Box H-0720, New York, NY 10010-5585

City University of New York: Brooklyn College

Brooklyn, New York **CB member**
www.brooklyn.cuny.edu **CB code: 2046**

- Public 4-year liberal arts college
- Commuter campus in very large city
- 12,160 degree-seeking undergraduates: 25% part-time, 60% women, 26% African American, 14% Asian American, 12% Hispanic American, 6% international
- 3,240 degree-seeking graduate students
- 35% of applicants admitted
- SAT or ACT required
- 44% graduate within 6 years

General. Founded in 1930. Regionally accredited. **Degrees:** 2,154 bachelor's awarded; master's offered. **Location:** 10 miles from Manhattan. **Calendar:** Semester, extensive summer session. **Full-time faculty:** 530 total; 92% have terminal degrees, 28% minority, 43% women. **Part-time faculty:** 650 total; 27% minority, 48% women. **Class size:** 41% < 20, 50% 20-39,

5% 40-49, 3% 50-99, less than 1% >100. **Special facilities:** Astronomical observatory, greenhouse, applied sciences institute, institute for the humanities, infant study center, Brooklyn Center for the Performing Arts, particle accelerator.

Freshman class profile. 16,190 applied, 5,650 admitted, 1,358 enrolled.

Mid 50% test scores		**Rank in top quarter:**	49%
SAT critical reading:	450-560	**Rank in top tenth:**	14%
SAT math:	490-590	**Return as sophomores:**	77%
GPA 3.75 or higher:	5%	**Out-of-state:**	3%
GPA 3.50-3.74:	21%	**International:**	4%
GPA 3.0-3.49:	60%	**Fraternities:**	1%
GPA 2.0-2.99:	14%	**Sororities:**	1%

Basis for selection. Students accepted based on SAT scores and academic average. Essay required for BA/MD, CHC and Scholars, interview recommended for scholars program. Audition required for music conservatory, theater programs; portfolio required for fine arts program.

High school preparation. College-preparatory program recommended. 21 units recommended. Recommended units include English 4, mathematics 3, social studies 4, science 3, foreign language 3 and academic electives 4.

2008-2009 Annual costs. Tuition/fees: $4,431; $11,231 out-of-state. Books/supplies: $1,016. Personal expenses: $1,686.

2008-2009 Financial aid. Need-based: 1,168 full-time freshmen applied for aid; 1,060 were judged to have need; 1,058 of these received aid. Average need met was 99%. Average scholarship/grant was $3,200; average loan $2,650. 62% of total undergraduate aid awarded as scholarships/grants, 38% as loans/jobs. **Non-need-based:** Awarded to 2,737 full-time undergraduates, including 479 freshmen. Scholarships awarded for academics, art, leadership, music/drama, state residency.

Application procedures. Admission: Priority date 3/1; no deadline. $65 fee. Admission notification on a rolling basis beginning on or about 1/30. **Financial aid:** Priority date 4/1; no closing date. FAFSA required. Applicants notified on a rolling basis starting 5/1.

Academics. Special study options: Accelerated study, combined bachelor's/graduate degree, distance learning, double major, dual enrollment of high school students, ESL, honors, independent study, internships, liberal arts/career combination, student-designed major, study abroad, teacher certification program, Washington semester, weekend college. **Credit/placement by examination:** AP, CLEP, IB, institutional tests. 35 credit hours maximum toward bachelor's degree. **Support services:** Learning center, preadmission summer program, reduced course load, study skills assistance, tutoring, writing center.

Majors. Area/ethnic studies: African-American, American, Caribbean, Hispanic-American/Latino/Chicano, Latin American, women's. **Biology:** General. **Business:** Accounting, business admin. **Communications:** General, broadcast journalism, journalism, radio/tv. **Communications technology:** Radio/tv. **Computer sciences:** General. **Conservation:** Environmental studies. **Education:** General, bilingual, biology, chemistry, early childhood, elementary, English, French, kindergarten/preschool, mathematics, music, physical, physics, social studies, Spanish, special, speech, speech impaired. **Family/consumer sciences:** Food/nutrition. **Foreign languages:** Classics, comparative lit, French, Italian, linguistics, Russian, Spanish. **Health:** Audiology/speech pathology, speech pathology. **History:** General. **Interdisciplinary:** Biological/physical sciences, math/computer science. **Math:** General, algebra, computational. **Parks/recreation:** Health/fitness. **Philosophy/religion:** Judaic, philosophy, religion. **Physical sciences:** Chemistry, geology, physics. **Psychology:** General. **Public administration:** Community org/advocacy. **Social sciences:** Anthropology, economics, political science, sociology. **Visual/performing arts:** Acting, art, art history/conservation, cinematography, dramatic, film/cinema, music performance, music theory/composition, play/screenwriting.

Most popular majors. Business/marketing 29%, education 12%, health sciences 6%, psychology 13%, social sciences 7%, visual/performing arts 6%.

Computing on campus. 2,000 workstations in library, computer center, student center. Online library, wireless network available.

Student life. Freshman orientation: Available. **Activities:** Concert band, choral groups, dance, drama, film society, literary magazine, music ensembles, radio station, student government, student newspaper, symphony orchestra, TV station, Hillel, Newman Club, student Christian association, Alpha Phi Omega, Christian fellowship, Islamic society, Caribbean student union, accounting society, lesbian/gay/bisexual/transgender alliance.

Athletics. NCAA. **Intercollegiate:** Basketball, cross-country, soccer M, softball W, tennis, track and field, volleyball. **Intramural:** Badminton W, basketball, racquetball, soccer M, softball W, tennis, track and field, volleyball. **Team name:** Bridges.

Student services. Adult student services, alcohol/substance abuse counseling, chaplain/spiritual director, career counseling, services for economically disadvantaged, student employment services, financial aid counseling, health services, on-campus daycare, personal counseling, placement for graduates, veterans' counselor, women's services. **Physically disabled:** Services for visually, speech, hearing impaired. **Learning disabled:** Comprehensive services available.

Contact. E-mail: adminqry@brooklyn.cuny.edu
Phone: (718) 951-5001 Fax: (718) 951-4506
Penelope Ferry, Director of Undergraduate Admissions, City University of New York: Brooklyn College, 2900 Bedford Avenue, Brooklyn, NY 11210

City University of New York: City College

New York, New York — **CB member**
www.ccny.cuny.edu — **CB code: 2083**

- Public 4-year university
- Commuter campus in very large city
- 11,494 degree-seeking undergraduates: 23% part-time, 50% women, 24% African American, 19% Asian American, 35% Hispanic American, 11% international
- 2,950 degree-seeking graduate students
- 45% of applicants admitted
- SAT or ACT, interview required
- 36% graduate within 6 years

General. Founded in 1847. Regionally accredited. **Degrees:** 1,463 bachelor's awarded; master's, doctoral offered. **Calendar:** Semester, extensive summer session. **Full-time faculty:** 555 total; 90% have terminal degrees, 17% minority, 38% women. **Part-time faculty:** 894 total; 30% have terminal degrees, 23% minority, 47% women. **Class size:** 43% < 20, 52% 20-39, 4% 40-49, less than 1% 50-99, less than 1% >100. **Special facilities:** Planetarium, weather station, ultra-fast laser spectroscopy laboratory, microwave laboratory, computer-aided design facilities, slide library, darkroom facilities, sonic music arts facility, structural biology center.

Freshman class profile. 19,133 applied, 8,598 admitted, 1,805 enrolled.

Mid 50% test scores		**Rank in top quarter:**	34%
SAT critical reading:	430-550	**Rank in top tenth:**	29%
SAT math:	460-590	**End year in good standing:**	81%
GPA 3.75 or higher:	6%	**Return as sophomores:**	1769%
GPA 3.50-3.74:	15%	**Out-of-state:**	2%
GPA 3.0-3.49:	28%	**International:**	8%
GPA 2.0-2.99:	46%		

Basis for selection. Academic average and number of academic units achieved in high school, SAT, or GED score of 325 or better important. Units recommended for admission must be acquired before graduation from any CUNY senior college. SAT section test scores of 450 or 20 ACT on math and verbal exempt student from taking placement exam. Interview required for biomedical education, audition required for music program; portfolio required for electronic design and multimedia. **Homeschooled:** Applicants must obtain GED or diploma through regionally accredited program.

High school preparation. College-preparatory program recommended. 16 units recommended. Recommended units include English 4, mathematics 2, social studies 4, science 2 (laboratory 2) and foreign language 2. One unit of art or music recommended. For science and engineering students, 3 units of mathematics required.

2008-2009 Annual costs. Tuition/fees: $4,329; $11,129 out-of-state. Room only on-campus; there is student housing with rates by apartment size. Books/supplies: $1,016.

2007-2008 Financial aid. Need-based: 1,570 full-time freshmen applied for aid; 1,555 were judged to have need; 1,500 of these received aid. Average need met was 81%. Average scholarship/grant was $5,822; average loan $1,812. 67% of total undergraduate aid awarded as scholarships/grants, 33% as loans/jobs. **Non-need-based:** Awarded to 2,451 full-time undergraduates, including 1,277 freshmen. Scholarships awarded for academics, alumni affiliation, leadership.

Application procedures. Admission: Priority date 3/15; no deadline. $65 fee. Admission notification on a rolling basis beginning on or about 1/15. **Financial aid:** Priority date 4/15; no closing date. FAFSA required. Applicants notified on a rolling basis starting 4/15.

Academics. **Special study options:** Accelerated study, combined bachelor's/graduate degree, cooperative education, cross-registration, double major, dual enrollment of high school students, ESL, exchange student, honors, independent study, internships, liberal arts/career combination, student-designed major, study abroad, teacher certification program. Center for Worker Education, doctoral degrees through CUNY Graduate Center. **Credit/placement by examination:** AP, CLEP, IB, ACT, institutional tests. **Support services:** Learning center, pre-admission summer program, reduced course load, tutoring, writing center.

Honors college/program. Admits only new first-year students, who must apply by special application. The application deadline is November 1 for early admission and December 15 for regular admission. For the class admitted fall 2005 (Class of 2009), the average high school GPA was 93.9 (on a scale of 100) and the average SAT was 1376 (exclusive of Writing). Students are expected to achieve an overall 3.3 GPA by the end of their first year and a 3.5 GPA by the end of their second year, which must be maintained until graduation in four years. Detailed information about additional benefits, including full-tuition scholarships and study grants, and requirements of the CUNY Honors College can be accessed on the college's website.

Majors. **Architecture:** Architecture. **Area/ethnic studies:** African-American, Asian, Caribbean, Latin American. **Biology:** General, biochemistry. **Business:** General. **Communications:** General, advertising, journalism, public relations. **Computer sciences:** Computer science. **Education:** Art, bilingual, biology, chemistry, early childhood, elementary, English, foreign languages, French, history, mathematics, music, physics, science, secondary, social studies, Spanish. **Engineering:** Biomedical, chemical, civil, computer, electrical, mechanical. **Foreign languages:** General, comparative lit, French, Spanish. **Health:** Physician assistant, premedicine, prepharmacy, preveterinary. **History:** General. **Interdisciplinary:** Global studies. **Legal studies:** Prelaw. **Math:** General. **Philosophy/religion:** Judaic, philosophy. **Physical sciences:** Chemistry, geology, physics, planetary. **Psychology:** General. **Social sciences:** Anthropology, economics, international relations, political science, sociology. **Visual/performing arts:** General, art, art history/conservation, cinematography, commercial/advertising art, dramatic, film/cinema, graphic design, jazz, music performance, music theory/composition, studio arts.

Most popular majors. Architecture 6%, communications/journalism 6%, engineering/engineering technologies 16%, health sciences 7%, liberal arts 11%, psychology 10%, social sciences 10%, visual/performing arts 9%.

Computing on campus. 2,000 workstations in library, computer center, student center. Dormitories wired for high-speed internet access and linked to campus network. Commuter students can connect to campus network. Online course registration, online library, helpline, repair service, wireless network available.

Student life. **Freshman orientation:** Mandatory. Full-day program, including registration, held in spring and summer. **Housing:** Guaranteed on-campus for all undergraduates. Apartments, wellness housing available. $400 nonrefundable deposit. **Activities:** Jazz band, choral groups, dance, drama, film society, music ensembles, Model UN, musical theater, radio station, student government, student newspaper, numerous religious, political, ethnic, and social service organizations.

Athletics. NCAA. **Intercollegiate:** Baseball M, basketball, cross-country, fencing, lacrosse M, soccer, tennis, track and field, volleyball. **Intramural:** Badminton M, basketball, fencing, soccer M, softball W, swimming, tennis, track and field, volleyball. **Team name:** Beavers.

Student services. Alcohol/substance abuse counseling, chaplain/spiritual director, career counseling, services for economically disadvantaged, student employment services, financial aid counseling, health services, minority student services, on-campus daycare, personal counseling, placement for graduates, veterans' counselor, women's services. **Physically disabled:** Services for visually, speech, hearing impaired. **Learning disabled:** Comprehensive services available.

Contact. E-mail: admissions@ccny.cuny.edu
Phone: (212) 650-6977 Fax: (212) 650-6417
Joseph Fatozzi, Director of Admissions, City University of New York: City College, 160 Convent Avenue, New York, NY 10031

City University of New York: College of Staten Island

Staten Island, New York — **CB member**
www.csi.cuny.edu — **CB code: 2778**

- Public 4-year liberal arts college
- Commuter campus in very large city
- 11,901 degree-seeking undergraduates: 28% part-time, 59% women, 9% African American, 8% Asian American, 11% Hispanic American, 3% international
- 829 degree-seeking graduate students
- 100% of applicants admitted
- Application essay, interview required
- 46% graduate within 6 years

General. Founded in 1955. Regionally accredited. **Degrees:** 1,060 bachelor's, 766 associate awarded; master's offered. **Location:** 10 miles from downtown Manhattan. **Calendar:** Semester, extensive summer session. **Full-time faculty:** 348 total; 83% have terminal degrees, 22% minority, 42% women. **Part-time faculty:** 596 total; 27% have terminal degrees, 16% minority, 50% women. **Class size:** 30% < 20, 52% 20-39, 15% 40-49, 3% 50-99, less than 1% >100. **Special facilities:** Astrophysical observatory, archives and special collections, artificial intelligence laboratory, center for developmental neuroscience and developmental disabilities, center for engineered polymeric materials, center for environmental science, nuclear magnetic resonance spectrometer, CUNY High Performance Computational Facility.

Freshman class profile. 8,945 applied, 8,945 admitted, 2,514 enrolled.

Mid 50% test scores		**GPA 3.0-3.49:**	27%
SAT critical reading:	440-540	**GPA 2.0-2.99:**	54%
SAT math:	460-560	**End year in good standing:**	76%
SAT writing:	440-540	**Return as sophomores:**	82%
GPA 3.75 or higher:	2%	**Out-of-state:**	1%
GPA 3.50-3.74:	12%	**International:**	2%

Basis for selection. Applicants to the baccalaureate program considered on the basis of high school academic record and SAT scores. Open admission policy for associate degree programs; additional requirements including essays and recommendations for selective programs. SAT or ACT recommended.

High school preparation. College-preparatory program recommended. 15 units required; 16 recommended. Required and recommended units include English 4, mathematics 2-3, social studies 4, science 2-3 and foreign language 2-3.

2008-2009 Annual costs. Tuition/fees: $4,378; $11,178 out-of-state. Books/supplies: $1,016. Personal expenses: $1,686.

2008-2009 Financial aid. **Need-based:** Average need met was 57%. Average scholarship/grant was $5,725; average loan $2,924. 78% of total undergraduate aid awarded as scholarships/grants, 22% as loans/jobs. **Non-need-based:** Scholarships awarded for academics, art, leadership, minority status, music/drama.

Application procedures. **Admission:** Priority date 3/15; no deadline. $65 fee, may be waived for applicants with need. Application must be submitted online. Admission notification on a rolling basis beginning on or about 12/15. **Financial aid:** Priority date 3/31; no closing date. FAFSA required. Applicants notified on a rolling basis starting 6/1.

Academics. Baccalaureate for Unique and Interdisciplinary Studies available, CUNY's individualized, university-wide BA/BS degree, where students formulate proposals for unique areas of concentration, then collaborate with CUNY faculty members to design their degrees. **Special study options:** Cross-registration, distance learning, double major, ESL, honors, independent study, internships, liberal arts/career combination, New York semester, student-designed major, study abroad, teacher certification program, United Nations semester, urban semester, Washington semester, weekend college. Cross-registration at any CUNY. **Credit/placement by examination:** AP, CLEP, IB, SAT, ACT, institutional tests. 30 credit hours maximum toward associate degree, 30 toward bachelor's. **Support services:** Learning center, pre-admission summer program, remedial instruction, study skills assistance, tutoring.

Honors college/program. Minimum 1200 SAT (exclusive of Writing) and 92 high school average required. 20 seats available.

Majors. **Area/ethnic studies:** African-American, American, women's. **Biology:** General, biochemistry. **Business:** General, accounting. **Communications:** General. **Computer sciences:** Computer science, information systems. **Education:** Biology, chemistry, English, history, mathematics, Spanish. **Engineering:** General. **Foreign languages:** Spanish. **Health:** Clinical lab science, nursing (RN). **History:** General. **Liberal arts:** Arts/sciences. **Math:** General. **Philosophy/religion:** Philosophy. **Physical sciences:** Chemistry, physics. **Psychology:** General. **Public administration:** Social work. **Social sciences:** Economics, international relations, political science. **Visual/performing arts:** Dramatic, film/cinema. **Other:** Fine arts and arts studies.

Most popular majors. Business/marketing 22%, English 7%, liberal arts 12%, psychology 12%, social sciences 19%.

Computing on campus. 1,254 workstations in library, computer center, student center. Online course registration, online library, helpline, student web hosting, wireless network available.

Student life. **Freshman orientation:** Mandatory. Scheduled at beginning of each semester, after or during time periods devoted to testing, advisement, and registration. Students with less than 6 credits are required to complete the orientation requirement during the first semester prior to completing 12 credits. **Activities:** Jazz band, campus ministries, dance, drama, film society, international student organizations, literary magazine, music ensembles, radio station, student government, student newspaper, Muslim student association, Israel club, Colleges Against Cancer, Chi Alpha Christian club, Hillel, armed forces club, international cultural dance club, Sri Lankan student association, South Asian student association, Middle Eastern club.

Athletics. NCAA. **Intercollegiate:** Baseball M, basketball, cross-country, diving, soccer, softball W, swimming, tennis, volleyball W. **Intramural:** Cricket, handball, racquetball. **Team name:** Dolphins.

Student services. Adult student services, alcohol/substance abuse counseling, chaplain/spiritual director, career counseling, services for economically disadvantaged, student employment services, financial aid counseling, health services, minority student services, on-campus daycare, personal counseling, placement for graduates, veterans' counselor, women's services. **Physically disabled:** Services for visually, speech, hearing impaired.

Contact. E-mail: admissions@mail.cuny.csi.edu
Phone: (718) 982-2010 Fax: (718) 982-2500
Emmanuel Esperance, Director of Recruitment & Admissions, City University of New York: College of Staten Island, 2800 Victory Boulevard 2A-104, Staten Island, NY 10314

City University of New York: CUNY Online

New York, New York
www.cuny.edu/online

- Public 4-year virtual university
- Very large city
- 669 degree-seeking undergraduates
- Application essay required

General. Regionally accredited. CUNY Online offers a fully asynchronous online bachelor's degree program for students who have at least 30 earned credits, and a new online graduate certificate program in Immigration Law Studies. **Degrees:** 13 bachelor's awarded. **Calendar:** Semester, limited summer session. **Part-time faculty:** 116 total; 72% have terminal degrees, 16% minority, 52% women. **Class size:** 38% < 20, 62% 20-39.

Basis for selection. Open admission, but selective for some programs. Accept only transfer applicants with at least 30 credits earned. SAT or ACT recommended. **Homeschooled:** State high school equivalency certificate required.

2008-2009 Annual costs. Tuition/fees: $4,380; $4,380 out-of-state. Books/supplies: $1,016.

Application procedures. **Admission:** Closing date 8/1 (receipt date). $70 fee, may be waived for applicants with need. Application must be submitted online. Admission notification on a rolling basis. **Financial aid:** Closing date 8/1.

Academics. **Special study options:** Distance learning. **Credit/placement by examination:** AP, CLEP, IB, SAT, ACT. **Support services:** Study skills assistance, tutoring.

Majors. **Business:** General. **Communications:** General.

Computing on campus. PC or laptop required. Helpline available.

Contact. E-mail: onlineba@mail.cuny.edu
Otilia Abraham, Coordinator of Admissions, City University of New York: CUNY Online, 101 West 31st Street, 7th Floor, New York, NY 10001

City University of New York: Hunter College

New York, New York — **CB member**
www.hunter.cuny.edu — **CB code: 2301**

- Public 4-year liberal arts college
- Commuter campus in very large city
- 14,709 degree-seeking undergraduates: 26% part-time, 67% women, 12% African American, 20% Asian American, 20% Hispanic American, 10% international
- 4,311 degree-seeking graduate students
- 28% of applicants admitted
- SAT or ACT required
- 41% graduate within 6 years

General. Founded in 1870. Regionally accredited. **Degrees:** 2,511 bachelor's awarded; master's offered. **Calendar:** Semester, limited summer session. **Full-time faculty:** 684 total; 88% have terminal degrees, 28% minority, 50% women. **Part-time faculty:** 958 total; 38% have terminal degrees, 23% minority, 62% women. **Class size:** 43% < 20, 47% 20-39, 3% 40-49, 5% 50-99, less than 1% >100. **Special facilities:** Mathematics learning center, on-campus elementary and secondary schools.

Freshman class profile. 27,866 applied, 7,861 admitted, 2,043 enrolled.

Mid 50% test scores		**GPA 3.0-3.49:**	31%
SAT critical reading:	490-580	**GPA 2.0-2.99:**	41%
SAT math:	510-610	**Return as sophomores:**	84%
GPA 3.75 or higher:	12%	**Out-of-state:**	5%
GPA 3.50-3.74:	13%	**International:**	8%

Basis for selection. Requirements vary by program. Indexing formula using weighted averages, high school academic units, and SAT scores for admission to some programs. SAT or ACT not required, but recommended, of first-time freshmen who graduated high school more than a year preceding admission.

High school preparation. 16 units recommended. Required and recommended units include English 2-4, mathematics 2-3, social studies 4, science 1-2 (laboratory 1), foreign language 2 and academic electives 1. 1 fine art or performing art recommended.

2008-2009 Annual costs. Tuition/fees: $4,399; $11,199 out-of-state. Dormitory availability very limited. Room only: $3,726. Books/supplies: $1,016. Personal expenses: $4,526.

2007-2008 Financial aid. **Need-based:** 1,489 full-time freshmen applied for aid; 1,005 were judged to have need; 988 of these received aid. Average need met was 77%. Average scholarship/grant was $4,361; average loan $2,367. 78% of total undergraduate aid awarded as scholarships/grants, 22% as loans/jobs. **Non-need-based:** Awarded to 2,542 full-time undergraduates, including 1,064 freshmen. Scholarships awarded for academics.

Application procedures. **Admission:** Closing date 3/15 (postmark date). $65 fee, may be waived for applicants with need. Admission notification on a rolling basis beginning on or about 1/15. **Financial aid:** Priority date 5/1; no closing date. FAFSA required. Applicants notified on a rolling basis starting 5/15.

Academics. **Special study options:** Accelerated study, combined bachelor's/graduate degree, cross-registration, distance learning, double major, dual enrollment of high school students, exchange student, honors, independent study, internships, liberal arts/career combination, student-designed major, study abroad, teacher certification program. BA/MA/MS programs in anthropology, biology/EOPS, economics, English, history, math, music, physics, social research (MS). **Credit/placement by examination:** AP, CLEP, IB, institutional tests. 30 credit hours maximum toward bachelor's degree. **Support services:** Learning center, reduced course load, remedial instruction, study skills assistance, tutoring, writing center.

Majors. **Area/ethnic studies:** African-American, Latin American, Near/Middle Eastern, women's. **Biology:** General, pharmacology. **Business:** Accounting. **Communications:** Media studies. **Computer sciences:** General. **Education:** General, art, biology, chemistry, drama/dance, early childhood, elementary, English, foreign languages, French, geography, German, health, history, Latin, mathematics, music, physical, physics, secondary, social studies, Spanish. **Family/consumer sciences:** Food/nutrition. **Foreign languages:** General, ancient Greek, Chinese, classics, comparative lit, French, German, Hebrew, Italian, Latin, Romance, Russian, Spanish. **Health:** Adult health nursing, clinical lab science, clinical lab technology, maternal/child health nursing, nurse practitioner, nursing (RN), pediatric nursing, psychiatric nursing, public health nursing, speech pathology. **History:** General. **Liberal arts:** Humanities. **Math:** General, statistics. **Philosophy/religion:** Judaic, philosophy, religion. **Physical sciences:** Chemistry, physics. **Psychology:** General. **Social sciences:** Anthropology, archaeology, economics, geography, international relations, political science, sociology, urban studies. **Visual/performing arts:** Art history/conservation, cinematography, dance, dramatic, film/cinema, music performance, music theory/composition, studio arts.

Most popular majors. Business/marketing 6%, communications/journalism 7%, English 13%, health sciences 6%, psychology 14%, social sciences 22%, visual/performing arts 9%.

Computing on campus. 750 workstations in dormitories, library, computer center, student center. Commuter students can connect to campus network. Online course registration, online library, helpline, repair service, student web hosting, wireless network available.

Student life. **Freshman orientation:** Available. Preregistration for classes offered. **Housing:** Coed dorms, wellness housing available. **Activities:** Bands, choral groups, dance, drama, film society, literary magazine, music ensembles, musical theater, radio station, student government, student newspaper, symphony orchestra, TV station, over 100 political, ethnic, social, and religious organizations.

Athletics. NCAA. **Intercollegiate:** Basketball, cross-country, fencing, football (non-tackle) W, soccer M, softball W, swimming W, tennis, track and field, volleyball, wrestling M. **Intramural:** Basketball, bowling, football (non-tackle), racquetball, swimming, table tennis, tennis, volleyball. **Team name:** Hawks.

Student services. Adult student services, alcohol/substance abuse counseling, chaplain/spiritual director, career counseling, services for economically disadvantaged, student employment services, financial aid counseling, health services, legal services, minority student services, on-campus daycare, personal counseling, placement for graduates, veterans' counselor, women's services. **Physically disabled:** Services for visually, speech, hearing impaired.

Contact. E-mail: admissions@hunter.cuny.edu
Phone: (212) 772-4490
William Zlata, Director of Admissions, City University of New York: Hunter College, 695 Park Avenue, New York, NY 10065

City University of New York: John Jay College of Criminal Justice

New York, New York — **CB member**
www.jjay.cuny.edu/ — **CB code: 2115**

- Public 4-year college of criminal justice and public safety
- Commuter campus in very large city
- 12,615 degree-seeking undergraduates: 24% part-time, 58% women, 24% African American, 8% Asian American, 41% Hispanic American, 3% international
- 1,822 degree-seeking graduate students
- 62% of applicants admitted
- SAT or ACT with writing required
- 43% graduate within 6 years; 37% enter graduate study

General. Founded in 1964. Regionally accredited. **Degrees:** 1,717 bachelor's, 186 associate awarded; master's offered. **Calendar:** Semester, limited summer session. **Full-time faculty:** 418 total; 81% have terminal degrees, 34% minority, 44% women. **Part-time faculty:** 596 total; 33% minority, 45% women. **Class size:** 23% < 20, 70% 20-39, 7% 40-49, less than 1% 50-99, less than 1% >100. **Special facilities:** Security laboratory, fire science laboratory, explosion-proof toxicology research laboratory.

Freshman class profile. 9,958 applied, 6,169 admitted, 2,442 enrolled.

Mid 50% test scores		**GPA 2.0-2.99:**	63%
SAT critical reading:	420-520	**End year in good standing:**	84%
SAT math:	420-510	**Return as sophomores:**	72%
SAT writing:	370-420	**Out-of-state:**	7%
GPA 3.0-3.49:	16%	**International:**	2%

Basis for selection. Admission to associate degree programs requires minimum SAT score of 900 (exclusive of Writing), high school average of 72, or GED score of 300. Admission to baccalaureate degree program requires minimum SAT score from 960 to 1020 or minimum high school average of 80 and minimum of 12 academic units with a total of 4 units in English and mathematics with at least 1 unit in each discipline. **Homeschooled:** Applicants must have diploma issued by local registered high school, and minimum SAT of 1100.

High school preparation. College-preparatory program recommended. 14 units required; 19 recommended. Required and recommended units include English 4, mathematics 3-4, social studies 2-4, (laboratory 2-3), foreign language 2-3 and visual/performing arts 1. One unit in fine arts required/recommended.

2008-2009 Annual costs. Tuition/fees: $4,329; $11,129 out-of-state. Books/supplies: $875. Personal expenses: $3,550.

2007-2008 Financial aid. **Need-based:** Average need met was 85%. Average scholarship/grant was $2,926; average loan $2,331. 70% of total undergraduate aid awarded as scholarships/grants, 30% as loans/jobs. **Non-need-based:** Scholarships awarded for academics, state residency.

Application procedures. **Admission:** Priority date 12/1; deadline 5/1 (postmark date). $65 fee. Application must be submitted online. Admission notification on a rolling basis beginning on or about 1/15. Centralized application processing allows students to apply to 6 academic programs within CUNY system at same time. Admission to John Jay on space-available basis. **Financial aid:** No deadline. FAFSA required. Applicants notified on a rolling basis starting 7/15; must reply within 2 week(s) of notification.

Academics. Degree requirements and curriculum combine professional education with the liberal arts. The Baccalaureate for Unique and Interdisciplinary Studies (CUNY BA), is CUNY's individualized, university-wide BA/BS degree, where students formulate proposals for unique areas of concentration, then collaborate with CUNY faculty members to design their degrees. **Special study options:** Combined bachelor's/graduate degree, cooperative education, cross-registration, distance learning, dual enrollment of high school students, ESL, exchange student, honors, independent study, internships, liberal arts/career combination, student-designed major, study abroad, weekend college. **Credit/placement by examination:** AP, CLEP, SAT, ACT, institutional tests. 32 credit hours maximum toward associate degree, 32 toward bachelor's. **Support services:** Learning center, preadmission summer program, reduced course load, remedial instruction, tutoring, writing center.

Majors. **Computer sciences:** General. **Physical sciences:** General. **Protective services:** Law enforcement admin. **Psychology:** General. **Public administration:** General, community org/advocacy. **Social sciences:** Criminology, economics, political science.

Most popular majors. Psychology 26%, security/protective services 55%, social sciences 16%.

Computing on campus. 1,750 workstations in library, computer center. Commuter students can connect to campus network. Online course registration, helpline available.

Student life. **Freshman orientation:** Available. Preregistration for classes offered. **Policies:** Students represented on college committees. **Activities:** Choral groups, dance, drama, musical theater, radio station, student government, student newspaper, Law Society, Irish club, Students against War and Racism, Haitian club, Christian Seekers Fellowship Club, Jewish Students Society, Newman Club, Betances Society, Black Student Society, ethnic organizations.

Athletics. NCAA. **Intercollegiate:** Baseball M, basketball, cross-country, diving W, rifle, soccer, softball W, swimming W, tennis, volleyball W. **Intramural:** Basketball, rifle, soccer M, swimming. **Team name:** Bloodhounds.

Student services. Adult student services, alcohol/substance abuse counseling, career counseling, services for economically disadvantaged, student employment services, financial aid counseling, health services, on-campus daycare, personal counseling, placement for graduates, veterans' counselor, women's services. **Physically disabled:** Services for visually, speech, hearing impaired.

Contact. E-mail: admiss@jjay.cuny.edu
Phone: (212) 237-8865 Fax: (212) 237-8777
Sandra Palleja, Dean of Admissions and Registration, City University of New York: John Jay College of Criminal Justice, 445 West 59th Street, New York, NY 10019

City University of New York: Lehman College

Bronx, New York — **CB member**
www.lehman.cuny.edu — **CB code: 2312**

- Public 4-year liberal arts college
- Commuter campus in very large city
- 8,571 degree-seeking undergraduates: 33% part-time, 70% women, 30% African American, 5% Asian American, 52% Hispanic American, 5% international
- 1,923 degree-seeking graduate students
- 39% of applicants admitted
- SAT or ACT (ACT writing optional) required
- 46% graduate within 6 years

General. Founded in 1931. Regionally accredited. **Degrees:** 1,383 bachelor's awarded; master's offered. **ROTC:** Army. **Location:** 8 miles from Manhattan. **Calendar:** Semester, limited summer session. **Full-time faculty:** 371 total; 75% have terminal degrees, 28% minority, 50% women. **Part-time faculty:** 401 total; 23% have terminal degrees, 37% minority, 53% women. **Class size:** 39% < 20, 59% 20-39, less than 1% 40-49, less than 1% 50-99. **Special facilities:** 2,500-seat performing arts center.

Freshman class profile. 12,971 applied, 5,033 admitted, 1,001 enrolled.

Mid 50% test scores			
SAT critical reading:	410-490	GPA 3.0-3.49:	63%
SAT math:	420-500	GPA 2.0-2.99:	24%
SAT writing:	400-480	End year in good standing:	82%
GPA 3.75 or higher:	3%	Return as sophomores:	72%
GPA 3.50-3.74:	10%	Out-of-state:	1%
		International:	3%

Basis for selection. High school record, GPA, and college preparatory courses most important. Tests are used to exempt students from placement tests. **Homeschooled:** State high school equivalency certificate required.

High school preparation. 16 units required. Required units include English 4, mathematics 3, social studies 4, science 2 (laboratory 1), foreign language 2 and visual/performing arts 1.

2008-2009 Annual costs. Tuition/fees: $4,340; $11,140 out-of-state. Books/supplies: $1,016. Personal expenses: $2,717.

2007-2008 Financial aid. All financial aid based on need. 800 full-time freshmen applied for aid; 800 were judged to have need; 800 of these received aid. Average need met was 11%. Average scholarship/grant was $1,579; average loan $1,529. 71% of total undergraduate aid awarded as scholarships/grants, 29% as loans/jobs.

Application procedures. Admission: $65 fee. Admission notification on a rolling basis. **Financial aid:** No deadline. FAFSA required. Applicants notified on a rolling basis starting 3/1.

Academics. Special study options: Accelerated study, cooperative education, cross-registration, distance learning, double major, dual enrollment of high school students, ESL, honors, independent study, internships, student-designed major, study abroad, teacher certification program. **Credit/placement by examination:** AP, CLEP, IB, institutional tests. 30 credit hours maximum toward bachelor's degree. **Support services:** Learning center, pre-admission summer program, reduced course load, remedial instruction, study skills assistance, tutoring, writing center.

Honors college/program. Criteria for selection include high school academic record, SAT/ACT scores, essay, 2 letters of recommendation and interview.

Majors. Area/ethnic studies: African-American, Latin American. **Biology:** General. **Business:** Accounting, business admin. **Communications:** General. **Computer sciences:** General, information systems. **Education:** Health, mathematics, physical. **Family/consumer sciences:** Food/nutrition. **Foreign languages:** Comparative lit, French, Italian, linguistics, Spanish. **Health:** Audiology/speech pathology, facilities admin, nursing (RN). **History:** General. **Liberal arts:** Arts/sciences. **Math:** General. **Philosophy/religion:** Philosophy. **Physical sciences:** Chemistry, geology, physics. **Psychology:** General. **Public administration:** Social work. **Social sciences:** Anthropology, economics, geography, political science, sociology. **Visual/performing arts:** Art history/conservation, commercial/advertising art, music performance.

Most popular majors. Business/marketing 14%, education 25%, health sciences 22%, public administration/social services 7%, social sciences 11%.

Computing on campus. 88 workstations in library, computer center, student center. Commuter students can connect to campus network. Online library, helpline, repair service, student web hosting, wireless network available.

Student life. Freshman orientation: Mandatory. Preregistration for classes offered. **Activities:** Bands, choral groups, dance, drama, film society, literary magazine, music ensembles, musical theater, opera, radio station, student government, student newspaper, symphony orchestra, TV station, various religious, political, ethnic, and social service organizations.

Athletics. NCAA. **Intercollegiate:** Baseball M, basketball, cross-country, diving, softball W, swimming, tennis, track and field, volleyball. **Intramural:** Badminton, basketball, racquetball, soccer, softball, swimming, table tennis, tennis, volleyball. **Team name:** Lightning.

Student services. Adult student services, chaplain/spiritual director, career counseling, services for economically disadvantaged, student employment services, financial aid counseling, health services, on-campus daycare, personal counseling, placement for graduates, veterans' counselor, women's services. **Physically disabled:** Services for visually, speech, hearing impaired.

Contact. E-mail: enroll@lehman.cuny.edu
Phone: (718) 960-8713 Toll-free number: (877) leh-man-1
Fax: (718) 960-8712
Laurie Austin, Director of Admissions, City University of New York: Lehman College, 250 Bedford Park Boulevard West, Bronx, NY 10468

City University of New York: Medgar Evers College

Brooklyn, New York — **CB member**
www.mec.cuny.edu — **CB code: 2460**

- Public 4-year liberal arts college
- Commuter campus in very large city
- 5,710 degree-seeking undergraduates: 35% part-time, 76% women, 90% African American, 1% Asian American, 4% Hispanic American, 2% international

General. Founded in 1969. Regionally accredited. **Degrees:** 345 bachelor's, 392 associate awarded. **Calendar:** Semester, extensive summer session. **Full-time faculty:** 188 total; 54% have terminal degrees, 85% minority, 46% women. **Part-time faculty:** 226 total; 88% minority, 40% women. **Class size:** 18% < 20, 81% 20-39, less than 1% 40-49.

Freshman class profile. 4,864 applied, 4,649 admitted, 1,049 enrolled.

Mid 50% test scores			
SAT critical reading:	340-440	GPA 2.0-2.99:	77%
SAT math:	330-430	End year in good standing:	45%
GPA 3.75 or higher:	1%	Return as sophomores:	56%
GPA 3.50-3.74:	1%	Out-of-state:	1%
GPA 3.0-3.49:	2%	International:	2%

Basis for selection. Open admission, but selective for some programs. Special requirements for nursing and baccalaureate programs with school record, class rank, and test scores considered. Discretionary policy admits 25 students each semester without high school diplomas. Must be 21 years old, legal residents of New York City.

High school preparation. 15 units recommended. Recommended units include English 4, mathematics 3, history 2, science 2 and academic electives 4.

2008-2009 Annual costs. Tuition/fees: $4,302; $11,102 out-of-state. Books/supplies: $798. Personal expenses: $1,653.

2007-2008 Financial aid. Non-need-based: Scholarships awarded for academics, leadership.

Application procedures. Admission: Priority date 7/8; no deadline. $65 fee, may be waived for applicants with need. Admission notification on a rolling basis. **Financial aid:** Priority date 1/2, closing date 7/31. FAFSA required. Applicants notified on a rolling basis; must reply within 3 week(s) of notification.

Academics. Special study options: Cross-registration, distance learning, ESL, honors, independent study, internships, liberal arts/career combination, student-designed major, study abroad, teacher certification program. 2-year bachelor's program in nursing for RNs. **Credit/placement by examination:** AP, CLEP, IB, institutional tests. 15 credit hours maximum toward associate degree, 30 toward bachelor's. **Support services:** Learning center, pre-admission summer program, reduced course load, remedial instruction, tutoring.

Majors. Biology: General. **Business:** General, accounting, business admin. **Computer sciences:** Information systems. **Conservation:** Environmental studies. **Education:** Elementary, special. **Health:** Nursing (RN). **Liberal arts:** Arts/sciences. **Math:** General. **Psychology:** General. **Public administration:** General.

Most popular majors. Biology 11%, business/marketing 46%, health sciences 10%, psychology 14%.

Computing on campus. 450 workstations in library, computer center, student center. Online course registration, online library, wireless network available.

Student life. Freshman orientation: Available. Preregistration for classes offered. **Activities:** Jazz band, choral groups, dance, drama, literary magazine, radio station, student government, student newspaper, TV station, numerous religious, political, ethnic, and social service clubs.

Athletics. NCAA. **Intercollegiate:** Basketball, cross-country, soccer, softball W, track and field, volleyball. **Intramural:** Basketball, bowling, cheerleading W, soccer M, swimming, track and field W. **Team name:** Cougar.

Student services. Career counseling, student employment services, financial aid counseling, health services, on-campus daycare, personal counseling, placement for graduates, veterans' counselor, women's services. **Physically disabled:** Services for visually, speech, hearing impaired.

Contact. E-mail: enroll@mec.cuny.edu
Phone: (718) 270-6024 Fax: (718) 270-6411
Gloria Leon, Director of Admissions, City University of New York: Medgar Evers College, 1665 Bedford Avenue, Brooklyn, NY 11225-2201

City University of New York: New York City College of Technology

Brooklyn, New York — **CB member**
www.citytech.cuny.edu — **CB code: 2550**

- Public 4-year technical college
- Commuter campus in very large city
- 13,442 degree-seeking undergraduates: 39% part-time, 48% women, 38% African American, 15% Asian American, 27% Hispanic American, 6% international

General. Founded in 1946. Regionally accredited. **Degrees:** 559 bachelor's, 875 associate awarded. **Calendar:** Semester, extensive summer session. **Full-time faculty:** 346 total; 66% have terminal degrees, 33% minority, 44% women. **Part-time faculty:** 645 total; 13% have terminal degrees, 39% minority, 40% women. **Class size:** 34% < 20, 59% 20-39, 7% 40-49. **Special facilities:** Ophthalmic dispensing and dental clinics, laboratory kitchens and dining room.

Freshman class profile. 11,847 applied, 10,507 admitted, 3,158 enrolled.

Mid 50% test scores			
SAT critical reading:	350-440	Return as sophomores:	79%
SAT math:	370-470	Out-of-state:	1%
SAT writing:	350-430	International:	4%

Basis for selection. Open admission, but selective for some programs.

High school preparation. 14 units required; 17 recommended. Required and recommended units include English 4, mathematics 2-3, social studies 2-3, science 2-3 (laboratory 1-2), foreign language 1-2, visual/performing arts 1 and academic electives 1-2.

2008-2009 Annual costs. Tuition/fees: $4,289; $11,089 out-of-state. Books/supplies: $879. Personal expenses: $2,710.

2008-2009 Financial aid. Need-based: 2,274 full-time freshmen applied for aid; 2,029 were judged to have need; 1,970 of these received aid. Average need met was 62%. Average scholarship/grant was $6,250; average loan $2,248. 86% of total undergraduate aid awarded as scholarships/grants, 14% as loans/jobs. **Non-need-based:** Awarded to 481 full-time undergraduates, including 349 freshmen. Scholarships awarded for state residency. **Additional information:** Foreign students applying for aid must have resided in New York for at least 1 year.

Application procedures. Admission: Priority date 3/15; no deadline. $65 fee, may be waived for applicants with need. Admission notification on a rolling basis. **Financial aid:** Priority date 5/15; no closing date. FAFSA required.

Academics. Students in health science programs work under supervision with patients in clinical settings. Industry standard facilities used in hospitality management program. **Special study options:** Distance learning, dual enrollment of high school students, ESL, honors, independent study, internships, student-designed major, study abroad, teacher certification program, weekend college. Bridge programs to higher education or careers in engineering technology, alternate format program for those out of high school 5 years with or without diploma. **Credit/placement by examination:** AP, CLEP, IB, institutional tests. 30 credit hours maximum toward associate degree. **Support services:** Learning center, pre-admission summer program, remedial instruction, study skills assistance, tutoring, writing center.

Majors. Business: Hospitality admin, tourism/travel. **Communications technology:** Graphic/printing. **Computer sciences:** General. **Construction:** Maintenance. **Education:** Technology/industrial arts. **Engineering technology:** Architectural, electromechanical, telecommunications. **Health:** Health services admin. **Legal studies:** Paralegal. **Math:** Applied. **Public administration:** Human services. **Visual/performing arts:** Commercial/advertising art, theater design.

Most popular majors. Architecture 7%, business/marketing 16%, computer/information sciences 30%, engineering/engineering technologies 7%, legal studies 7%, public administration/social services 9%, visual/performing arts 12%.

Computing on campus. Online course registration, online library, helpline, student web hosting, wireless network available.

Student life. Freshman orientation: Available. **Housing:** Some housing available at nearby university. **Activities:** Drama, musical theater, student government, student newspaper, full range of student clubs.

Athletics. NCAA. **Intercollegiate:** Basketball, cross-country, soccer M, softball W, tennis, volleyball. **Intramural:** Basketball, handball, soccer M, table tennis, track and field, volleyball. **Team name:** Yellow Jackets.

Student services. Adult student services, career counseling, services for economically disadvantaged, student employment services, financial aid counseling, health services, minority student services, on-campus daycare, personal counseling, placement for graduates. **Physically disabled:** Services for visually, speech, hearing impaired.

Contact. E-mail: admissions@citytech.cuny.edu
Phone: (718) 260-5500 Fax: (718) 260-5504
Alexis Chaconis, Director of Admissions, City University of New York: New York City College of Technology, 300 Jay Street Namm G17, Brooklyn, NY 11201

City University of New York: Queens College

Flushing, New York
www.qc.cuny.edu — **CB code: 2750**

- Public 4-year liberal arts college
- Commuter campus in very large city
- 14,497 degree-seeking undergraduates: 26% part-time, 60% women, 9% African American, 22% Asian American, 18% Hispanic American, 6% international
- 3,839 degree-seeking graduate students
- 38% of applicants admitted
- SAT or ACT (ACT writing optional) required
- 55% graduate within 6 years

General. Founded in 1937. Regionally accredited. **Degrees:** 2,217 bachelor's awarded; master's offered. **ROTC:** Army, Naval. **Location:** 17 miles from Manhattan. **Calendar:** Semester, extensive summer session. **Full-time faculty:** 630 total; 86% have terminal degrees, 19% minority, 43% women. **Part-time faculty:** 795 total; 31% have terminal degrees, 16% minority, 49% women. **Class size:** 48% < 20, 45% 20-39, 5% 40-49, 1% 50-99, less than 1% >100. **Special facilities:** Louis Armstrong archives, Kupferberg center for the performing arts, center for Byzantine and Modern Greek studies, neuroscience research center.

Freshman class profile. 15,724 applied, 5,915 admitted, 1,675 enrolled.

Mid 50% test scores			
SAT critical reading:	490-550	GPA 2.0-2.99:	3%
SAT math:	490-580	Return as sophomores:	85%
SAT writing:	490-550	Out-of-state:	1%
GPA 3.75 or higher:	5%	International:	6%
GPA 3.50-3.74:	21%	Fraternities:	1%
GPA 3.0-3.49:	71%	Sororities:	1%

Basis for selection. Factors include high school grades, strength of academic program, and test scores. Successful candidates will have chosen well-rounded program of study and attained at least B+ average. SAT scores on Critical Reading and Mathematics are considered. SAT Subject Tests recommended. SAT and SAT Subject Test required of scholarship and honors college applicants. Essay and interview recommended for scholarship, honors program; audition recommended for music, performance; portfolio recommended for bachelor of fine arts. Other criteria considered for appeals. **Homeschooled:** Transcript of courses and grades, state high school equivalency certificate required. Students must submit a letter from the superintendent of their school district confirming that all high school graduation requirements of the district have been met through home schooling. If students cannot obtain the letter from the high school district, they must obtain a General Equivalency Development Diploma (GED). **Learning Disabled:** Untimed SAT/ACT accepted.

High school preparation. College-preparatory program required. 16 units required; 17 recommended. Required and recommended units include English 4, mathematics 3, social studies 4, science 2-3 (laboratory 2-3) and foreign language 3.

2008-2009 Annual costs. Tuition/fees: $4,427; $11,227 out-of-state. Books/supplies: $1,016. Personal expenses: $3,556.

2007-2008 Financial aid. Need-based: 1,333 full-time freshmen applied for aid; 1,213 were judged to have need; 970 of these received aid. Average need met was 77%. Average scholarship/grant was $1,250; average loan $2,625. 68% of total undergraduate aid awarded as scholarships/grants, 32% as loans/jobs. **Non-need-based:** Awarded to 1,398 full-time undergraduates, including 553 freshmen. Scholarships awarded for academics, athletics, music/drama, state residency.

Application procedures. Admission: Priority date 1/1; no deadline. $65 fee, may be waived for applicants with need. Application must be submitted online. Admission notification on a rolling basis beginning on or about 1/15. Admitted applicants must reply by May 1 for some programs, within 4 weeks after notification for others. **Financial aid:** Priority date 2/1; no closing date. FAFSA, institutional form required. Applicants notified on a rolling basis starting 3/1; must reply within 3 week(s) of notification.

Academics. Required core liberal arts curriculum includes courses in the humanities, physical and biological sciences, scientific methodology and quantitative reasoning, social sciences, and pre-industrial/non-western civilization. Core requirements are being revised by the College for Fall 2009. **Special study options:** Accelerated study, cross-registration, double major, dual enrollment of high school students, ESL, honors, independent study, internships, liberal arts/career combination, student-designed major, study abroad, teacher certification program, weekend college. **Credit/placement by examination:** AP, CLEP, SAT, institutional tests. **Support services:** Learning center, pre-admission summer program, study skills assistance, tutoring, writing center.

Honors college/program. 40 students, average SAT of 1300 (exclusive of Writing) or higher, high school average 95 or higher, required to submit SAT Subject Test scores, interview required.

Majors. Area/ethnic studies: African, American, East Asian, Latin American, women's. **Biology:** General. **Business:** Accounting, actuarial science, finance, international, labor studies. **Communications:** Media studies. **Computer sciences:** Computer science. **Conservation:** Environmental science, environmental studies. **Education:** Art, early childhood, elementary, ESL, family/consumer sciences, music, physical, physics. **Family/consumer sciences:** General. **Foreign languages:** Ancient Greek, comparative lit, French, German, Hebrew, Italian, Latin, linguistics, Russian, Spanish. **Health:** Speech pathology. **History:** General. **Liberal arts:** Arts/sciences. **Math:** General. **Parks/recreation:** Exercise sciences. **Philosophy/religion:** Judaic, philosophy, religion. **Physical sciences:** Chemistry, geology, physics. **Psychology:** General. **Social sciences:** General, anthropology, economics, political science, sociology, urban studies. **Visual/performing arts:** Art history/conservation, dramatic, film/cinema, graphic design, music performance, studio arts. **Other:** Byzantine and Modern Greek studies.

Most popular majors. Business/marketing 18%, communications/journalism 6%, education 11%, English 8%, psychology 14%, social sciences 20%.

Computing on campus. 2,300 workstations in library, computer center, student center. Commuter students can connect to campus network. Online course registration, online library, helpline, repair service, student web hosting, wireless network available.

Student life. Freshman orientation: Mandatory. Preregistration for classes offered. Held in June, July, August. **Policies:** Students found guilty of any form of academic dishonesty, such as plagiarism or cheating on an examination, are subject to discipline, including suspension or dismissal from the college. **Housing:** Coed dorms, wellness housing available. Dormitories available on a first-come, first-served basis. Disabled and international students do not have separate accommodations. **Activities:** Bands, choral groups, dance, drama, film society, literary magazine, music ensembles, musical theater, radio station, student government, student newspaper, symphony orchestra, TV station, Catholic, Protestant, Hindu, Jewish, Greek Orthodox, Muslim, African American, Asian, Bangladeshi, Guyanese, Haitian, Hispanic, Italian, Irish, lesbian, and gay student organizations; honor societies; various clubs; political student associations.

Athletics. NCAA. **Intercollegiate:** Baseball M, basketball, cross-country, diving, fencing W, lacrosse W, soccer, softball W, swimming, tennis, track and field, volleyball W, water polo M. **Intramural:** Basketball, cross-country, football (non-tackle), ice hockey M, racquetball, soccer, softball, tennis, track and field, volleyball. **Team name:** Knights.

Student services. Adult student services, alcohol/substance abuse counseling, career counseling, services for economically disadvantaged, student employment services, financial aid counseling, health services, minority student services, on-campus daycare, personal counseling, placement for graduates, veterans' counselor, women's services. **Physically disabled:** Services for visually, speech, hearing impaired.

Contact. E-mail: vincent.angrisani@qc.cuny.edu
Phone: (718) 997-5600 Fax: (718) 997-5617
Vincent Angrisani, Executive Director of Admissions and Enrollment Management, City University of New York: Queens College, 6530 Kissena Boulevard, Jefferson 117, Flushing, NY 11367-1597

City University of New York: York College

Jamaica, New York — **CB member**
www.york.cuny.edu — **CB code: 2992**

- Public 4-year liberal arts college
- Commuter campus in very large city
- 6,208 degree-seeking undergraduates: 30% part-time, 67% women, 43% African American, 12% Asian American, 18% Hispanic American
- 46 graduate students
- SAT or ACT (ACT writing recommended) required

General. Founded in 1966. Regionally accredited. **Degrees:** 746 bachelor's awarded; master's offered. **Location:** 14 miles from midtown Manhattan. **Calendar:** Semester, limited summer session. **Full-time faculty:** 183 total; 42% minority, 55% women. **Part-time faculty:** 287 total; 53% minority, 55% women. **Class size:** 15% < 20, 41% 20-39, 11% 40-49, 14% 50-99, 20% >100. **Special facilities:** Theater, cardio-pneumo-simulator, flight simulator.

Freshman class profile. 1,059 enrolled.

End year in good standing:	72%	**Out-of-state:**	1%
Return as sophomores:	69%		

Basis for selection. 75 average with 12 high school academic units basic admission requirement; allowance made for higher average or test scores. Units recommended for admission must be acquired before graduation from any CUNY senior college. Admission requirements for CUNY senior colleges will be automatically satisfied with completion of our core requirement. Interview required for occupational therapy, nursing, physician assistant, and social work or for appeal.

High school preparation. 12 units required; 20 recommended. Required and recommended units include English 4, mathematics 2, social studies 2, science 2, foreign language 2 and academic electives 8-10.

2008-2009 Annual costs. Tuition/fees: $4,312; $11,112 out-of-state. Books/supplies: $1,016. Personal expenses: $3,186.

2008-2009 Financial aid. Need-based: 838 full-time freshmen applied for aid; 740 were judged to have need; 724 of these received aid. Average need met was 23%. Average scholarship/grant was $1,638; average loan $1,329. 86% of total undergraduate aid awarded as scholarships/grants, 14% as loans/jobs. **Non-need-based:** Awarded to 121 full-time undergraduates, including 78 freshmen. Scholarships awarded for academics.

Application procedures. Admission: Closing date 1/9. $65 fee. Admission notification on a rolling basis beginning on or about 1/1. Centralized application processing allows students to apply to 6 schools within CUNY system at same time. **Financial aid:** Priority date 5/1; no closing date. FAFSA required. Applicants notified on a rolling basis starting 3/1.

Academics. Special study options: Combined bachelor's/graduate degree, cooperative education, distance learning, double major, dual enrollment of high school students, ESL, honors, independent study, internships, liberal arts/career combination, student-designed major, study abroad, teacher certification program. Co-op programs in business, computer science, health professions. **Credit/placement by examination:** AP, CLEP, IB, institutional tests. 16 credit hours maximum toward bachelor's degree. Students with SAT/ACT scores exempt from CUNY skills assessment tests. **Support services:** Learning center, pre-admission summer program, remedial instruction, study skills assistance, tutoring, writing center.

Majors. Area/ethnic studies: African-American. **Biology:** General, biotechnology. **Business:** Accounting, business admin, management information systems, marketing. **Communications technology:** General. **Computer sciences:** General, computer science. **Education:** Health, physical. **Family/consumer sciences:** Aging. **Foreign languages:** French, Spanish. **Health:** Clinical lab technology, environmental health, nursing (RN). **History:** General. **Interdisciplinary:** Gerontology. **Liberal arts:** Arts/sciences. **Math:** General. **Philosophy/religion:** Philosophy. **Physical sciences:** Chemistry, geology, physics. **Psychology:** General. **Public administration:** Social work. **Social sciences:** Anthropology, economics, political science, sociology. **Visual/performing arts:** Art history/conservation, dramatic.

Most popular majors. Business/marketing 33%, education 9%, health sciences 9%, psychology 15%, public administration/social services 9%, social sciences 6%.

Computing on campus. 650 workstations in library, computer center, student center. Online library, wireless network available.

Student life. **Freshman orientation:** Available. Preregistration for classes offered. **Activities:** Jazz band, choral groups, drama, film society, literary magazine, musical theater, student government, student newspaper, TV station, 48 organizations.

Athletics. NCAA. **Intercollegiate:** Basketball, cheerleading, cross-country, soccer, softball W, swimming, tennis, track and field, volleyball, weight lifting. **Intramural:** Badminton, basketball, soccer M, softball W, swimming, table tennis, tennis, track and field, volleyball, weight lifting. **Team name:** Cardinals.

Student services. Adult student services, chaplain/spiritual director, career counseling, student employment services, financial aid counseling, health services, on-campus daycare, personal counseling, placement for graduates, veterans' counselor. **Physically disabled:** Services for visually, speech, hearing impaired.

Contact. E-mail: admissions@york.cuny.edu
Phone: (718) 262-2165 Fax: (718) 262-2601
Diane Warmsley, Director of Admissions/Enrollment, City University of New York: York College, 94-20 Guy R. Brewer Boulevard, Jamaica, NY 11451-9989

Clarkson University

Potsdam, New York — **CB member**
www.clarkson.edu — **CB code: 2084**

- Private 4-year university
- Residential campus in large town
- 2,574 degree-seeking undergraduates: 27% women, 3% African American, 3% Asian American, 3% Hispanic American, 3% international
- 446 degree-seeking graduate students
- 79% of applicants admitted
- SAT or ACT (ACT writing optional), application essay required
- 71% graduate within 6 years; 38% enter graduate study

General. Founded in 1896. Regionally accredited. **Degrees:** 609 bachelor's awarded; master's, doctoral, first professional offered. **ROTC:** Army, Air Force. **Location:** 140 miles from Syracuse, 70 miles from Watertown. **Calendar:** Semester, extensive summer session. **Full-time faculty:** 186 total; 94% have terminal degrees, 11% minority, 26% women. **Part-time faculty:** 31 total; 26% have terminal degrees, 32% women. **Class size:** 47% < 20, 29% 20-39, 7% 40-49, 14% 50-99, 3% >100. **Special facilities:** Design, prototyping and testing facilities for SPEED Team competitions (Student Projects for Engineering Experience & Design), Center for the Environment, Center for Sustainable Energy Systems, Center for Air Resources Engineering and Science, Center for Advanced Materials Processing, Center for Rehabilitation Engineering, Science, and Technology.

Freshman class profile. 3,204 applied, 2,522 admitted, 735 enrolled.

Mid 50% test scores			
SAT critical reading:	500-560	GPA 2.0-2.99:	13%
SAT math:	610-660	Rank in top quarter:	70%
SAT writing:	480-590	Rank in top tenth:	38%
ACT composite:	24-28	End year in good standing:	87%
GPA 3.75 or higher:	20%	Return as sophomores:	83%
GPA 3.50-3.74:	38%	Out-of-state:	28%
GPA 3.0-3.49:	29%	Live on campus:	92%
		International:	4%

Basis for selection. School achievement record, test scores, recommendations, school and community involvement important. SAT Subject Tests recommended. Interview recommended. **Homeschooled:** Transcript of courses and grades required. **Learning Disabled:** Documented information on disabilities necessary.

High school preparation. College-preparatory program recommended. 16 units required. Required and recommended units include English 4, mathematics 3-4 and science 2-3.

2009-2010 Annual costs. Tuition/fees: $32,910. Room/board: $11,118. Books/supplies: $1,100. Personal expenses: $1,000.

2007-2008 Financial aid. **Need-based:** 574 full-time freshmen applied for aid; 499 were judged to have need; 499 of these received aid. Average need met was 86%. Average scholarship/grant was $14,270; average loan $5,100. 66% of total undergraduate aid awarded as scholarships/grants, 34% as loans/jobs. **Non-need-based:** Awarded to 476 full-time undergraduates, including 181 freshmen. Scholarships awarded for academics, alumni affiliation, leadership, minority status, ROTC.

Application procedures. **Admission:** Closing date 1/15 (postmark date). $50 fee, may be waived for applicants with need, free for online applicants. Admission notification on a rolling basis beginning on or about 2/1. Must reply by May 1 or within 2 week(s) if notified thereafter. Candidates encouraged to submit completed application between October 1 and March 1 of their final year in secondary school. **Financial aid:** Priority date 2/15; no closing date. FAFSA required. Applicants notified on a rolling basis starting 3/19; must reply by 5/1 or within 2 week(s) of notification.

Academics. 3-year B.S. degree option. Students must be in top 10 percent of their high school class. Students apply Advanced Placement credits and/or work on special projects during the summer. **Special study options:** Accelerated study, combined bachelor's/graduate degree, cooperative education, cross-registration, double major, dual enrollment of high school students, ESL, honors, independent study, liberal arts/career combination, semester at sea, student-designed major, study abroad. 3-2 agreements with many area colleges; innovation and entrepreneurship development experience under auspices of Shipley Center for innovation and working with: Shipley Center for Innovation, Clarkson Entrepreneurs Organization (CEO) and Center for Global Competitiveness. **Credit/placement by examination:** AP, CLEP, IB, institutional tests. 30 credit hours maximum toward bachelor's degree. **Support services:** Pre-admission summer program, study skills assistance, tutoring, writing center.

Majors. **Area/ethnic studies:** American. **Biology:** General, environmental toxicology, molecular biochemistry. **Business:** Accounting/finance, business admin, e-commerce, entrepreneurial studies. **Communications:** General, digital media. **Computer sciences:** General, computer science. **Conservation:** Environmental studies. **Engineering:** General, aerospace, chemical, civil, computer, electrical, environmental, mechanical, software. **Engineering technology:** Architectural. **Health:** Environmental health, occupational health, predental, premedicine, preveterinary. **History:** General. **Legal studies:** Prelaw. **Liberal arts:** Arts/sciences. **Math:** General, applied, statistics. **Physical sciences:** Chemistry, physics. **Psychology:** General. **Social sciences:** General, political science, sociology.

Most popular majors. Biology 6%, business/marketing 27%, engineering/engineering technologies 49%.

Computing on campus. 400 workstations in library, computer center. Dormitories wired for high-speed internet access and linked to campus network. Commuter students can connect to campus network. Online course registration, online library, helpline, repair service, student web hosting, wireless network available.

Student life. **Freshman orientation:** Available. Students meet housemates, classmates, advisers. Optional pre-orientation outing club trips; $125 charge for students who participate. **Housing:** Guaranteed on-campus for freshmen. Coed dorms, single-sex dorms, special housing for disabled, apartments, fraternity/sorority housing, wellness housing available. **Activities:** Bands, choral groups, drama, international student organizations, literary magazine, musical theater, radio station, student government, student newspaper, symphony orchestra, TV station, InterVarsity Christian Fellowship, American Indian science and engineering society, Black engineers society, Hispanic professional engineers society, women engineers society, special interest clubs.

Athletics. NCAA. **Intercollegiate:** Baseball M, basketball, cross-country, diving, golf M, ice hockey, lacrosse, skiing, soccer, swimming, volleyball W. **Intramural:** Basketball, football (tackle) M, ice hockey, racquetball, rowing (crew) M, soccer, softball, swimming, volleyball. **Team name:** Golden Knights.

Student services. Alcohol/substance abuse counseling, career counseling, services for economically disadvantaged, student employment services, financial aid counseling, health services, minority student services, personal counseling, placement for graduates, veterans' counselor, women's services. **Physically disabled:** Services for visually, speech, hearing impaired. **Learning disabled:** Comprehensive services available.

Contact. E-mail: admission@clarkson.edu
Phone: (315) 268-6480 Toll-free number: (800) 527-6577
Fax: (315) 268-7647
Brian Grant, Director of Admission, Clarkson University, Holcroft House, Potsdam, NY 13699-5605

Colgate University

Hamilton, New York — **CB member**
www.colgate.edu — **CB code: 2086**

- Private 4-year liberal arts college
- Residential campus in small town
- 2,806 degree-seeking undergraduates: 52% women, 6% African American, 6% Asian American, 6% Hispanic American, 1% Native American, 5% international
- 8 degree-seeking graduate students

- 24% of applicants admitted
- SAT or ACT (ACT writing optional), application essay required
- 91% graduate within 6 years; 20% enter graduate study

General. Founded in 1819. Regionally accredited. **Degrees:** 675 bachelor's awarded; master's offered. **ROTC:** Army. **Location:** 38 miles from Syracuse, 25 miles from Utica. **Calendar:** Semester. **Full-time faculty:** 263 total; 98% have terminal degrees, 19% minority, 41% women. **Part-time faculty:** 52 total; 64% have terminal degrees, 19% minority, 65% women. **Class size:** 64% < 20, 33% 20-39, 1% 40-49, 2% 50-99, less than 1% >100. **Special facilities:** Anthropology museum, center for learning, teaching, and research, cable TV station, life sciences complex, geology/fossil collection, observatory, electron microscopes, laser lab, weather lab, geographic information system, center for outreach.

Freshman class profile. 9,416 applied, 2,254 admitted, 738 enrolled.

Mid 50% test scores		**GPA 2.0-2.99:**	6%
SAT critical reading:	630-730	**Rank in top quarter:**	89%
SAT math:	640-730	**Rank in top tenth:**	65%
ACT composite:	29-32	**Return as sophomores:**	94%
GPA 3.75 or higher:	39%	**Out-of-state:**	72%
GPA 3.50-3.74:	28%	**Live on campus:**	100%
GPA 3.0-3.49:	27%	**International:**	4%

Basis for selection. School achievement record of primary importance. Teacher/counselor recommendations, test scores, and major talent or personal accomplishment considered. Disadvantaged, nontraditional, and minority applicants given special consideration. **Homeschooled:** Statement describing homeschool structure and mission, transcript of courses and grades, letter of recommendation (nonparent) required. **Learning Disabled:** Optional self-disclosure of disabilities in admissions process.

High school preparation. College-preparatory program recommended. 16 units required; 20 recommended. Required and recommended units include English 4, mathematics 3-4, social studies 3-4, science 3-4 (laboratory 2-3) and foreign language 3-4. Foreign language units should be in 1 language.

2008-2009 Annual costs. Tuition/fees: $39,545. Room/board: $9,625. Books/supplies: $1,920. Personal expenses: $860.

2007-2008 Financial aid. **Need-based:** 289 full-time freshmen applied for aid; 235 were judged to have need; 235 of these received aid. Average need met was 100%. Average scholarship/grant was $32,574; average loan $1,769. 89% of total undergraduate aid awarded as scholarships/grants, 11% as loans/jobs. **Non-need-based:** Awarded to 158 full-time undergraduates, including 38 freshmen. Scholarships awarded for athletics.

Application procedures. **Admission:** Closing date 1/15 (postmark date). $55 fee, may be waived for applicants with need, free for online applicants. Admission notification 4/1. Must reply by 5/1. **Financial aid:** Closing date 1/15. CSS PROFILE required. Applicants notified by 4/1; must reply by 5/1 or within 2 week(s) of notification.

Academics. **Special study options:** Combined bachelor's/graduate degree, cross-registration, double major, honors, independent study, internships, semester at sea, student-designed major, study abroad, teacher certification program, urban semester, Washington semester. 3-4 architecture program with Washington University (MO), 3-2 program in engineering with Columbia University, Rensselaer Polytechnic Institute, and Washington University; Early Assurance Medical School program with American University; Extended study program during winter or summer breaks offer academic work in 13 locations around world including South Africa, Ireland, and China. **Credit/placement by examination:** AP, CLEP, IB, SAT, institutional tests. **Support services:** Learning center, pre-admission summer program, reduced course load, study skills assistance, tutoring, writing center.

Majors. **Area/ethnic studies:** African, African-American, Asian, Latin American, Native American, Russian/Slavic, women's. **Biology:** General, biochemistry, molecular. **Computer sciences:** General, computer science. **Conservation:** General, environmental studies. **Education:** General. **Foreign languages:** Classics, French, German, Japanese, Latin, modern Greek, Russian, Spanish. **Health:** Predental, premedicine, preveterinary. **History:** General. **Interdisciplinary:** Biological/physical sciences, math/computer science, natural sciences, neuroscience, peace/conflict. **Liberal arts:** Arts/sciences. **Math:** General. **Philosophy/religion:** Philosophy, religion. **Physical sciences:** Astronomy, astrophysics, chemistry, geology, physics. **Psychology:** General. **Social sciences:** General, anthropology, economics, geography, international economic development, international relations, political science, sociology. **Visual/performing arts:** Art, art history/conservation, dramatic, studio arts.

Most popular majors. Biology 8%, English 9%, foreign language 8%, history 9%, social sciences 34%, visual/performing arts 6%.

Computing on campus. 848 workstations in dormitories, library, computer center, student center. Dormitories wired for high-speed internet access and linked to campus network. Commuter students can connect to campus network. Online course registration, helpline, repair service, student web hosting, wireless network available.

Student life. **Freshman orientation:** Mandatory. Preregistration for classes offered. 4-day program held 4 days before first day of classes. **Policies:** All students required to read, sign, and abide by Academic Honor Code. **Housing:** Guaranteed on-campus for all undergraduates. Coed dorms, special housing for disabled, apartments, cooperative housing, fraternity/sorority housing, wellness housing available. $500 nonrefundable deposit, deadline 5/1. Accommodations for students with special needs, townhouses for small groups of students available. **Activities:** Bands, choral groups, dance, drama, film society, literary magazine, music ensembles, musical theater, radio station, student government, student newspaper, symphony orchestra, TV station, over 125 campus organizations.

Athletics. NCAA. **Intercollegiate:** Basketball, cheerleading, cross-country, diving, field hockey W, football (tackle) M, golf M, ice hockey, lacrosse, rowing (crew), soccer, softball W, swimming, tennis, track and field, volleyball W. **Intramural:** Basketball, bowling, football (non-tackle), golf, ice hockey, racquetball, rifle, soccer, softball, squash, table tennis, tennis, volleyball. **Team name:** Raiders.

Student services. Alcohol/substance abuse counseling, chaplain/spiritual director, career counseling, services for economically disadvantaged, student employment services, financial aid counseling, health services, minority student services, personal counseling, placement for graduates, women's services. **Physically disabled:** Services for visually, hearing impaired.

Contact. E-mail: admission@mail.colgate.edu
Phone: (315) 228-7401 Fax: (315) 228-7544
Gary Ross, Dean of Admission, Colgate University, 13 Oak Drive, Hamilton, NY 13346-1383

College of Mount St. Vincent

Riverdale, New York — **CB member**
www.mountsaintvincent.edu — **CB code: 2088**

- Private 4-year liberal arts college affiliated with Roman Catholic Church
- Residential campus in very large city
- 1,448 degree-seeking undergraduates: 9% part-time, 74% women, 13% African American, 11% Asian American, 29% Hispanic American, 1% international
- 111 degree-seeking graduate students
- 67% of applicants admitted
- SAT or ACT, application essay required
- 57% graduate within 6 years; 20% enter graduate study

General. Founded in 1847. Regionally accredited. Dual certification in elementary and special education and secondary and special education. 5-year program for master of science in education. **Degrees:** 281 bachelor's awarded; master's offered. **Location:** 12 miles from midtown Manhattan. **Calendar:** Semester, limited summer session. **Full-time faculty:** 73 total; 92% have terminal degrees, 8% minority, 62% women. **Part-time faculty:** 112 total; 36% minority, 56% women. **Class size:** 49% < 20, 50% 20-39, less than 1% 40-49. **Special facilities:** NMR spectrometer, computer graphics and animation center, computer classrooms, forensic science equipment.

Freshman class profile. 2,224 applied, 1,482 admitted, 375 enrolled.

Mid 50% test scores		**GPA 2.0-2.99:**	55%
SAT critical reading:	440-530	**End year in good standing:**	79%
SAT math:	430-520	**Return as sophomores:**	70%
GPA 3.75 or higher:	4%	**Out-of-state:**	19%
GPA 3.50-3.74:	9%	**Live on campus:**	66%
GPA 3.0-3.49:	28%		

Basis for selection. School achievement record (rank in top half of class, 3.0 high school GPA) most important, test scores and recommendations important, school and community activities considered. Interview recommended. **Learning Disabled:** Must submit IEP or other certification to receive service.

High school preparation. College-preparatory program recommended. 16 units required; 20 recommended. Required and recommended units include English 4, mathematics 2-3, social studies 2-3, science 2-3 and foreign language 2-3. 3 math for nursing, science, and math majors; 3 science with lab for nursing and science majors.

2008-2009 Annual costs. Tuition/fees: $24,600. Room/board: $9,370. Books/supplies: $850. Personal expenses: $900.

2007-2008 Financial aid. Non-need-based: Scholarships awarded for academics, alumni affiliation, leadership.

Application procedures. Admission: No deadline. $35 fee, may be waived for applicants with need, free for online applicants. Admission notification on a rolling basis beginning on or about 2/1. Must reply by May 1 or within 3 week(s) if notified thereafter. **Financial aid:** Priority date 3/1; no closing date. FAFSA required. Applicants notified on a rolling basis starting 3/1; must reply by 5/1 or within 3 week(s) of notification.

Academics. Special study options: Accelerated study, combined bachelor's/graduate degree, double major, honors, independent study, internships, liberal arts/career combination, study abroad, teacher certification program. 3-2 occupational therapy program with Columbia University, 3-2 physical therapy with New York Medical College. **Credit/placement by examination:** AP, CLEP, IB, institutional tests. 18 credit hours maximum toward bachelor's degree. **Support services:** Learning center, pre-admission summer program, reduced course load, remedial instruction, study skills assistance, tutoring, writing center.

Majors. Biology: General, biochemistry. **Business:** General, business admin. **Communications:** General. **Foreign languages:** General, French, Spanish. **Health:** Preop/surgical nursing. **History:** General. **Liberal arts:** Arts/sciences. **Math:** General. **Philosophy/religion:** Philosophy, religion. **Physical sciences:** Chemistry. **Psychology:** General. **Social sciences:** Economics, sociology.

Most popular majors. Biology 7%, business/marketing 19%, communications/journalism 13%, English 6%, health sciences 16%, liberal arts 8%, psychology 18%.

Computing on campus. 323 workstations in library, computer center. Dormitories wired for high-speed internet access and linked to campus network. Commuter students can connect to campus network. Online course registration, online library, helpline, repair service, wireless network available.

Student life. Freshman orientation: Mandatory, $125 fee. Preregistration for classes offered. 3 days with overnight for all freshmen; parent participation overnight optional. **Housing:** Guaranteed on-campus for all undergraduates. Coed dorms, single-sex dorms, special housing for disabled available. $200 fully refundable deposit, deadline 5/1. **Activities:** Campus ministries, choral groups, dance, drama, international student organizations, literary magazine, musical theater, radio station, student government, student newspaper, TV station, Culturally Aware Students of Today, Latino club, student nurses association, Circle-K, Student Action for Viable Earth, black student union, pep club, communications club.

Athletics. NCAA. **Intercollegiate:** Baseball M, basketball, cross-country, lacrosse, soccer, softball W, swimming, tennis, track and field W, volleyball. **Team name:** Dolphins.

Student services. Adult student services, chaplain/spiritual director, career counseling, student employment services, financial aid counseling, health services, personal counseling, placement for graduates. **Physically disabled:** Services for visually, hearing impaired.

Contact. E-mail: admissions.office@mountsaintvincent.edu
Phone: (718) 405-3267 Toll-free number: (800) 665-2678
Fax: (718) 549-7945
Roland Pinzon, Director of Admission, College of Mount St. Vincent, 6301 Riverdale Avenue, Riverdale, NY 10471-1093

College of New Rochelle

New Rochelle, New York **CB member**
www.cnr.edu **CB code: 2089**

- Private 4-year nursing and liberal arts college for women affiliated with Roman Catholic Church
- Residential campus in small city
- 874 degree-seeking undergraduates: 33% part-time, 96% women, 38% African American, 6% Asian American, 16% Hispanic American
- 878 degree-seeking graduate students
- 43% of applicants admitted
- SAT or ACT (ACT writing optional) required
- 52% graduate within 6 years

General. Founded in 1904. Regionally accredited. Independent institution in Roman Catholic tradition. Coeducational school of nursing and graduate school. **Degrees:** 261 bachelor's awarded; master's offered. **ROTC:** Army, Naval. **Location:** 14 miles from New York City. **Calendar:** Semester, limited summer session. **Full-time faculty:** 87 total; 87% have terminal degrees, 10% minority, 71% women. **Part-time faculty:** 145 total; 30% minority, 77% women. **Class size:** 73% < 20, 27% 20-39, less than 1% 50-99. **Special facilities:** 2 learning skills centers (including 1 for nursing), electron microscope, institute for entrepreneurial studies, computer graphics laboratory, model classroom, rare book collections of James Joyce, Thomas More, Ursuline Order.

Freshman class profile. 1,820 applied, 784 admitted, 139 enrolled.

Mid 50% test scores		**GPA 2.0-2.99:**	3%
SAT critical reading:	440-540	**Rank in top quarter:**	62%
SAT math:	450-540	**Rank in top tenth:**	17%
ACT composite:	18-23	**Return as sophomores:**	72%
GPA 3.75 or higher:	4%	**Out-of-state:**	16%
GPA 3.50-3.74:	36%	**Live on campus:**	93%
GPA 3.0-3.49:	57%		

Basis for selection. Admissions based on secondary school record. Class rank and standardized test scores also important. Essay, interview recommended; portfolio required for art program.

High school preparation. 16 units required. Required and recommended units include English 4, mathematics 3, social studies 3, science 3 (laboratory 2) and foreign language 2. Biology, chemistry, 3 math required for nursing and physical therapy.

2008-2009 Annual costs. Tuition/fees: $25,342. All incoming freshmen given laptop at no additional cost. Room/board: $9,200. Books/supplies: $600. Personal expenses: $1,000.

2007-2008 Financial aid. Non-need-based: Scholarships awarded for academics, art, leadership.

Application procedures. Admission: No deadline. $20 fee, may be waived for applicants with need. Admission notification on a rolling basis beginning on or about 11/1. Must reply by May 1 or within 3 week(s) if notified thereafter. **Financial aid:** Priority date 3/1; no closing date. FAFSA, institutional form required. Applicants notified on a rolling basis starting 1/1; must reply within 2 week(s) of notification.

Academics. Laptop computers given to all undergraduate students. **Special study options:** Accelerated study, combined bachelor's/graduate degree, cooperative education, cross-registration, double major, exchange student, honors, independent study, internships, liberal arts/career combination, study abroad, teacher certification program, United Nations semester, Washington semester. Preprofessional programs in law, medicine, health. **Credit/placement by examination:** AP, CLEP, institutional tests. 15 credit hours maximum toward bachelor's degree. **Support services:** Learning center, reduced course load, remedial instruction, study skills assistance, tutoring, writing center.

Majors. Area/ethnic studies: American, women's. **Biology:** General. **Business:** General. **Communications:** Broadcast journalism, media studies. **Conservation:** Environmental studies. **Education:** General, art, elementary, special. **Foreign languages:** Classics, French, Latin, Spanish. **Health:** Art therapy, nursing (RN). **History:** General. **Interdisciplinary:** Biological/physical sciences, global studies. **Legal studies:** Prelaw. **Math:** General. **Philosophy/religion:** Philosophy, religion. **Physical sciences:** Chemistry. **Psychology:** General. **Public administration:** Social work. **Social sciences:** Economics, political science, sociology. **Visual/performing arts:** Art history/conservation, studio arts.

Most popular majors. Health sciences 67%, psychology 9%.

Computing on campus. 223 workstations in dormitories, library, computer center. Dormitories wired for high-speed internet access and linked to campus network. Commuter students can connect to campus network. Online course registration, online library, helpline, wireless network available.

Student life. Freshman orientation: Available. Preregistration for classes offered. **Housing:** Guaranteed on-campus for all undergraduates. Wellness housing available. $100 deposit. **Activities:** Campus ministries, choral groups, dance, drama, film society, literary magazine, musical theater, student government, student newspaper, community services, Latin American Women Society, Black Student Union, CNR Drama, nurses gospel choir.

Athletics. NCAA. **Intercollegiate:** Basketball W, cross-country W, softball W, swimming W, tennis W, volleyball W. **Team name:** Blue Angels.

Student services. Adult student services, alcohol/substance abuse counseling, chaplain/spiritual director, career counseling, services for economically disadvantaged, student employment services, financial aid counseling, health services, personal counseling, placement for graduates, women's services. **Physically disabled:** Services for visually, speech, hearing impaired.

Contact. E-mail: admission@cnr.edu
Phone: (914) 654-5452 Toll-free number: (800) 933-5923
Fax: (914) 654-5464
Stephanie Decker, Director of Admissions, College of New Rochelle, 29 Castle Place, New Rochelle, NY 10805-2339

College of Saint Rose

Albany, New York **CB member**
www.strose.edu **CB code: 2091**

- Private 4-year liberal arts and teachers college affiliated with Roman Catholic Church
- Commuter campus in small city
- 3,051 degree-seeking undergraduates: 7% part-time, 71% women, 3% African American, 1% Asian American, 4% Hispanic American, 1% international
- 2,045 degree-seeking graduate students
- 66% of applicants admitted
- SAT or ACT (ACT writing optional) required
- 73% graduate within 6 years

General. Founded in 1920. Regionally accredited. **Degrees:** 693 bachelor's awarded; master's offered. **ROTC:** Army, Naval, Air Force. **Location:** 140 miles from New York City. **Calendar:** Semester, limited summer session. **Full-time faculty:** 199 total; 80% have terminal degrees, 11% minority, 54% women. **Part-time faculty:** 270 total; 3% minority, 57% women. **Class size:** 59% < 20, 40% 20-39, less than 1% 40-49, less than 1% 50-99. **Special facilities:** Massry Center for the Arts, recital hall, choral rehearsal room, instrument rehearsal room, gallery, Center for Art and Design, one of the largest screen printing facilities in the state, production and recording facility, music library.

Freshman class profile. 4,020 applied, 2,664 admitted, 576 enrolled.

Mid 50% test scores		**Rank in top quarter:**	48%
SAT critical reading:	460-560	**Rank in top tenth:**	16%
SAT math:	470-570	**End year in good standing:**	76%
ACT composite:	20-25	**Return as sophomores:**	81%
GPA 3.75 or higher:	26%	**Out-of-state:**	7%
GPA 3.50-3.74:	15%	**Live on campus:**	84%
GPA 3.0-3.49:	32%	**International:**	2%
GPA 2.0-2.99:	27%		

Basis for selection. School achievement record, test scores, extracurricular activities, recommendations most important; interview also considered. Music applicants must read music, play at least 1 instrument, and pass audition using standard repertoire as guide. Art applicants must submit portfolio.

High school preparation. Required and recommended units include English 4, mathematics 4, social studies 4, history 4, science 4 (laboratory 2), foreign language 3-4 and academic electives 4.

2008-2009 Annual costs. Tuition/fees: $21,972. Room/board: $8,986. Books/supplies: $1,200. Personal expenses: $1,500.

2007-2008 Financial aid. **Need-based:** 582 full-time freshmen applied for aid; 582 were judged to have need; 572 of these received aid. Average need met was 49%. Average scholarship/grant was $3,429; average loan $1,660. 61% of total undergraduate aid awarded as scholarships/grants, 39% as loans/jobs. **Non-need-based:** Awarded to 323 full-time undergraduates, including 43 freshmen. Scholarships awarded for academics, alumni affiliation, art, athletics, minority status, music/drama.

Application procedures. **Admission:** Priority date 12/1; deadline 5/1 (receipt date). $40 fee, may be waived for applicants with need, free for online applicants. Admission notification on a rolling basis beginning on or about 12/1. Must reply by 5/1. **Financial aid:** Priority date 3/1; no closing date. FAFSA required. Applicants notified on a rolling basis starting 3/15; must reply by 5/1 or within 2 week(s) of notification.

Academics. **Special study options:** Accelerated study, combined bachelor's/graduate degree, cross-registration, double major, exchange student, independent study, internships, liberal arts/career combination, student-designed major, study abroad, teacher certification program. **Credit/placement by examination:** AP, CLEP, IB, institutional tests. 15 credit hours maximum toward bachelor's degree. **Support services:** Learning center, preadmission summer program, reduced course load, remedial instruction, study skills assistance, tutoring, writing center.

Majors. **Area/ethnic studies:** American, women's. **Biology:** General, biochemistry, cell/histology. **Business:** Accounting, business admin. **Computer sciences:** General. **Conservation:** Environmental studies. **Education:** Art, biology, chemistry, early childhood, elementary, English, mathematics, music, secondary, social studies, Spanish, special, trade/industrial. **Foreign languages:** Spanish. **Health:** Audiology/speech pathology, clinical lab science. **History:** General. **Liberal arts:** Arts/sciences. **Math:** General. **Philosophy/religion:** Religion. **Physical sciences:** Chemistry. **Protective services:** Law enforcement admin. **Psychology:** General. **Public administration:** Social work. **Social sciences:** Political science, sociology. **Visual/performing arts:** Commercial/advertising art, music performance. **Other:** Public communications.

Most popular majors. Business/marketing 13%, communication technologies 6%, education 45%, psychology 6%, visual/performing arts 7%.

Computing on campus. 575 workstations in dormitories, library, computer center, student center. Dormitories wired for high-speed internet access and linked to campus network. Commuter students can connect to campus network. Online course registration, online library, helpline, student web hosting, wireless network available.

Student life. **Freshman orientation:** Mandatory, $175 fee. Two-part orientation: 2-day overnight summer program and week-long program that begins 2 days prior to start of fall classes. **Housing:** Guaranteed on-campus for freshmen. Coed dorms, single-sex dorms, apartments available. $300 nonrefundable deposit, deadline 5/1. **Activities:** Bands, campus ministries, choral groups, dance, drama, international student organizations, literary magazine, music ensembles, musical theater, radio station, student government, student newspaper, symphony orchestra, TV station, many religious, ethnic, political, and social service organizations available.

Athletics. NCAA. **Intercollegiate:** Baseball M, basketball, cross-country, golf M, soccer, softball W, swimming, tennis W, track and field, volleyball W. **Intramural:** Basketball, football (non-tackle) M, soccer, volleyball. **Team name:** Golden Knights.

Student services. Adult student services, alcohol/substance abuse counseling, chaplain/spiritual director, career counseling, services for economically disadvantaged, student employment services, financial aid counseling, health services, legal services, minority student services, personal counseling, placement for graduates. **Physically disabled:** Services for visually, speech, hearing impaired.

Contact. E-mail: admit@strose.edu
Phone: (518) 454-5111 Toll-free number: (800) 637-8556
Fax: (518) 454-2013
Mary Grondahl, Associate Vice President for Enrollment Planning and Undergraduate Admissions, College of Saint Rose, 432 Western Avenue, Albany, NY 12203

Columbia University

New York, New York **CB member**
www.columbia.edu **CB code: 2116**

- Private 4-year university
- Residential campus in very large city
- 5,667 degree-seeking undergraduates: 47% women, 10% African American, 18% Asian American, 11% Hispanic American, 1% Native American, 10% international
- 11% of applicants admitted
- SAT or ACT with writing, SAT Subject Tests, application essay required
- 95% graduate within 6 years

General. Founded in 1754. Regionally accredited. **Degrees:** 1,396 bachelor's awarded; master's, doctoral offered. **ROTC:** Army, Naval, Air Force. **Calendar:** Semester, extensive summer session. **Special facilities:** Art and architecture galleries, cinemas, theaters, geological observatory, interactive graphics laboratory, telecommunications research center, plasma laboratory, materials laboratory, astronomical observatory.

Freshman class profile. 22,584 applied, 2,417 admitted, 1,356 enrolled.

Mid 50% test scores		**Return as sophomores:**	99%
SAT critical reading:	680-770	**Out-of-state:**	72%
SAT math:	680-780	**Live on campus:**	99%
SAT writing:	690-770	**International:**	10%
ACT composite:	29-34		

Basis for selection. School achievement record most important. Test scores, recommendations, essay, extracurricular activities also important. TOEFL or IELTS exam required of all non-native speakers. Interview recommended for all; audition required for Julliard program. **Homeschooled:** 2 additional SAT Subject Tests.

High school preparation. Recommended units include English 4, mathematics 4, history 4, science 4 (laboratory 4), foreign language 4 and academic electives 4.

2008-2009 Annual costs. Tuition/fees: $39,326. Room/board: $9,980. Books/supplies: $2,100.

2008-2009 Financial aid. All financial aid based on need. 803 full-time freshmen applied for aid; 645 were judged to have need; 645 of these received aid. Average need met was 100%. Average scholarship/grant was $33,901; average loan $3,363. 92% of total undergraduate aid awarded as scholarships/grants, 8% as loans/jobs. **Additional information:** We have eliminated student loans for those receiving Columbia need-based aid and replaced them with additional University grants, and significantly reduced the parent contribution for families making less than $100,000 per year.

Application procedures. Admission: Closing date 1/2 (postmark date). $70 fee, may be waived for applicants with need. Admission notification 4/1. Must reply by 5/1. **Financial aid:** Closing date 3/2. FAFSA, CSS PROFILE required. Applicants notified by 4/1; must reply by 5/1.

Academics. Special study options: Accelerated study, combined bachelor's/graduate degree, cooperative education, cross-registration, double major, dual enrollment of high school students, ESL, exchange student, independent study, internships, liberal arts/career combination, student-designed major, study abroad, teacher certification program. Combined 3-2 program with engineering with over 100 liberal arts colleges around the country. **Credit/placement by examination:** AP, CLEP, IB, institutional tests. 16 credit hours maximum toward bachelor's degree. **Support services:** Pre-admission summer program, study skills assistance, tutoring, writing center.

Majors. Architecture: Architecture. **Area/ethnic studies:** African, African-American, American, Asian, Asian-American, Central/Eastern European, Chinese, East Asian, European, French, German, Hispanic-American/Latino/Chicano, Italian, Japanese, Korean, Latin American, Near/Middle Eastern, Polish, regional, Russian/Slavic, Slavic, Spanish/Iberian, women's. **Biology:** General, biochemistry, biophysics, ecology, environmental, evolutionary. **Computer sciences:** Computer science. **Conservation:** General, environmental science. **Education:** General. **Engineering:** Biomedical, chemical, civil, computer, electrical, environmental, geological, materials, materials science, mechanical, mechanics, metallurgical, mining, operations research. **Engineering technology:** Industrial management. **Foreign languages:** Ancient Greek, Biblical, Chinese, classics, comparative lit, East Asian, French, German, Germanic, Italian, Japanese, Korean, Latin, linguistics, modern Greek, Russian, Slavic, Spanish. **History:** General. **Interdisciplinary:** Ancient studies, classical/archaeology, intercultural, medieval/Renaissance, neuroscience. **Math:** General, applied, statistics. **Philosophy/religion:** Philosophy, religion. **Physical sciences:** Astronomy, astrophysics, chemical physics, chemistry, geochemistry, geology, geophysics, physics, planetary. **Psychology:** General. **Social sciences:** Anthropology, archaeology, economics, political science, sociology, urban studies. **Visual/performing arts:** General, art history/conservation, dance, dramatic, film/cinema, jazz, studio arts, theater history.

Most popular majors. Biology 6%, engineering/engineering technologies 21%, English 6%, history 7%, social sciences 26%.

Computing on campus. 150 workstations in dormitories, library, computer center, student center. Dormitories wired for high-speed internet access and linked to campus network. Commuter students can connect to campus network. Online course registration, online library, helpline, student web hosting, wireless network available.

Student life. Freshman orientation: Mandatory, $480 fee. Preregistration for classes offered. A one-week program offering academic advising sessions, cultural events, parents orientation sessions, and more. Students may also choose to participate in pre-orientation programs like the Columbia Outdoor Orientation Program or the Columbia Urban Experience. **Housing:** Guaranteed on-campus for all undergraduates. Coed dorms, special housing for disabled, fraternity/sorority housing available. Special interest (group) housing available. **Activities:** Bands, campus ministries, choral groups, dance, drama, film society, international student organizations, literary magazine, music ensembles, Model UN, musical theater, opera, radio station, student government, student newspaper, symphony orchestra, TV station, African-American, Hispanic, Native American, Asian-American, Gay/Lesbian student organizations, community service groups, religious groups of all denominations.

Athletics. NCAA. **Intercollegiate:** Archery W, baseball M, basketball, cross-country, diving, fencing, field hockey W, football (tackle) M, golf, lacrosse W, rowing (crew), soccer, softball W, swimming, tennis, track and field, volleyball W, wrestling M. **Intramural:** Basketball, football (non-tackle), racquetball, soccer, softball, squash, tennis, volleyball. **Team name:** Lions.

Student services. Alcohol/substance abuse counseling, chaplain/spiritual director, career counseling, services for economically disadvantaged, student employment services, financial aid counseling, health services, minority student services, personal counseling, placement for graduates, women's services. **Physically disabled:** Services for visually, speech, hearing impaired.

Contact. Phone: (212) 854-2522 Fax: (212) 854-1209
Jessica Marinaccio, Dean of Undergraduate Admissions, Columbia University, 212 Hamilton Hall, MC 2807, New York, NY 10027

Columbia University: School of General Studies

New York, New York
www.gs.columbia.edu **CB code: 2095**

- Private 4-year university and liberal arts college
- Commuter campus in very large city
- 1,245 degree-seeking undergraduates: 39% part-time, 51% women, 5% African American, 7% Asian American, 6% Hispanic American, 13% international
- 40% of applicants admitted
- SAT or ACT (ACT writing optional), application essay required

General. Founded in 1947. Regionally accredited. Liberal arts division of university for nontraditional students whose undergraduate study has been interrupted or postponed for at least 1 year. Postbaccalaureate Premedical Program offered. **Degrees:** 225 bachelor's awarded. **ROTC:** Army, Air Force. **Calendar:** Semester, extensive summer session. **Full-time faculty:** 951 total; 100% have terminal degrees, 24% minority, 32% women. **Part-time faculty:** 219 total; 100% have terminal degrees, 25% minority, 44% women. **Special facilities:** Earth Institute, observatory.

Freshman class profile. 266 applied, 107 admitted, 63 enrolled.

Basis for selection. Maturity and varied backgrounds of students considered. Aptitude and motivation important together with academic performance and test scores. Interview requested when needed.

High school preparation. College-preparatory program recommended.

2008-2009 Annual costs. Tuition/fees: $37,958. Room/board: $11,261. Books/supplies: $2,000.

2008-2009 Financial aid. All financial aid based on need. 61% of total undergraduate aid awarded as scholarships/grants, 39% as loans/jobs.

Application procedures. Admission: Priority date 3/1; deadline 6/1 (postmark date). $65 fee. Admission notification on a rolling basis beginning on or about 2/1. Must reply by May 1 or within 2 week(s) if notified thereafter. **Financial aid:** Priority date 4/15, closing date 6/1. FAFSA, institutional form required. Applicants notified on a rolling basis; must reply within 3 week(s) of notification.

Academics. Special study options: Accelerated study, combined bachelor's/graduate degree, cross-registration, double major, dual enrollment of high school students, ESL, exchange student, honors, independent study, internships, student-designed major, study abroad, teacher certification program. Dual degree program with Jewish Theological Seminary. **Credit/placement by examination:** AP, CLEP, SAT, ACT, institutional tests. 30 credit hours maximum toward bachelor's degree. **Support services:** Learning center, pre-admission summer program, reduced course load, remedial instruction, study skills assistance, tutoring, writing center.

Majors. Architecture: Architecture. **Area/ethnic studies:** African, African-American, American, Asian, East Asian, Hispanic-American/Latino/Chicano, Latin American, Near/Middle Eastern, Russian/Slavic, women's. **Biology:** General, evolutionary. **Computer sciences:** General, computer science. **Conservation:** General, environmental studies. **Education:** Elementary, secondary. **Foreign languages:** Classics, comparative lit, French, German, Italian, Portuguese, Russian, Spanish. **Health:** Premedicine. **History:** General. **Math:** General, applied, statistics. **Philosophy/religion:** Philosophy, religion. **Physical sciences:** Astronomy, astrophysics, chemistry, geochemistry, geology, geophysics, oceanography, physics. **Psychology:** General. **Public administration:** Human services. **Social sciences:** Economics, political science, sociology, urban studies. **Visual/performing arts:** General, art history/conservation, dance, dramatic, film/cinema, music performance, musicology, painting, sculpture, voice/opera.

Most popular majors. English 17%, history 9%, social sciences 28%.

Computing on campus. 347 workstations in dormitories, library, computer center, student center. Dormitories wired for high-speed internet access and linked to campus network. Commuter students can connect to campus network. Online course registration, online library, helpline, repair service, student web hosting, wireless network available.

Student life. Freshman orientation: Mandatory, $125 fee. Preregistration for classes offered. Generally held 1 week before classes start. Academic planning session (held prior to beginning of semester) required of all new students. **Housing:** Coed dorms, single-sex dorms, special housing for disabled, apartments, cooperative housing, fraternity/sorority housing available. $400 nonrefundable deposit. Limited on-campus housing available. Off-campus housing registry provides listings of Columbia-affiliated apartments. **Activities:** Bands, campus ministries, choral groups, dance, drama, film society, international student organizations, literary magazine, music ensembles, Model UN, musical theater, opera, radio station, student government, student newspaper, symphony orchestra, TV station, many religious, political, and ethnic organizations.

Athletics. NCAA. **Intercollegiate:** Archery W, baseball M, basketball, cross-country, diving, fencing, field hockey W, football (tackle) M, golf, lacrosse W, rowing (crew), soccer, softball W, swimming, tennis, track and field, volleyball W, wrestling M. **Intramural:** Baseball M, basketball, boxing, cricket M, diving, fencing, lacrosse, racquetball, skiing, soccer, softball, squash, swimming, tennis, volleyball. **Team name:** Lions.

Student services. Adult student services, alcohol/substance abuse counseling, chaplain/spiritual director, career counseling, services for economically disadvantaged, student employment services, financial aid counseling, health services, minority student services, personal counseling, placement for graduates, veterans' counselor, women's services. **Physically disabled:** Services for visually impaired. **Learning disabled:** Comprehensive services available.

Contact. E-mail: gsdegree@columbia.edu
Phone: (212) 854-2772 Toll-free number: (800) 895-1169
Fax: (212) 854-6316
Curtis Rodgers, Dean of Enrollment Management, Columbia University: School of General Studies, 408 Lewisohn Hall, Mail Code 4101, New York, NY 10027

Concordia College

Bronxville, New York — **CB member**
www.concordia-ny.edu — **CB code: 2096**

- Private 4-year liberal arts college affiliated with Lutheran Church - Missouri Synod
- Residential campus in small town
- 673 degree-seeking undergraduates
- 68% of applicants admitted
- SAT or ACT with writing, application essay required

General. Founded in 1881. Regionally accredited. Christian principles central to program of study. **Degrees:** 123 bachelor's, 5 associate awarded. **Location:** 14 miles from New York City. **Calendar:** Semester, limited summer session. **Full-time faculty:** 33 total; 67% have terminal degrees, 18% minority, 46% women. **Part-time faculty:** 44 total; 18% minority, 41% women. **Class size:** 62% < 20, 37% 20-39, 1% 40-49. **Special facilities:** Electric-piano laboratory, distance learning classroom, new media electronic and digital learning center.

Freshman class profile. 720 applied, 490 admitted, 108 enrolled.

Mid 50% test scores		**GPA 3.50-3.74:**	10%
SAT critical reading:	410-490	**GPA 3.0-3.49:**	23%
SAT math:	390-490	**GPA 2.0-2.99:**	54%
SAT writing:	400-500	**Rank in top quarter:**	27%
ACT composite:	16-19	**Rank in top tenth:**	13%
GPA 3.75 or higher:	6%	**Out-of-state:**	26%

Basis for selection. Test scores, school achievement record, interview important; community and church involvement considered. Interview required for some, recommended for others; audition required for music program. **Homeschooled:** Statement describing homeschool structure and mission, transcript of courses and grades, interview, letter of recommendation (nonparent) required. Show explanation of all course work studied and grades obtained. **Learning Disabled:** Students required to meet with learning specialist and submit most recent psychological assessment.

High school preparation. 15 units recommended. Recommended units include English 4, mathematics 3, social studies 2, science 2 (laboratory 2) and foreign language 2.

2008-2009 Annual costs. Tuition/fees: $22,930. Room/board: $8,745. Books/supplies: $900. Personal expenses: $1,500.

Financial aid. Non-need-based: Scholarships awarded for academics, athletics, leadership, music/drama.

Application procedures. Admission: Closing date 3/15 (postmark date). $50 fee, may be waived for applicants with need. Admission notification on a rolling basis beginning on or about 12/1. Must reply by May 1 or within 4 week(s) if notified thereafter. **Financial aid:** Priority date 4/1; no closing date. FAFSA required. Applicants notified on a rolling basis starting 4/1; must reply by 5/1 or within 3 week(s) of notification.

Academics. Special study options: Combined bachelor's/graduate degree, cooperative education, cross-registration, distance learning, double major, ESL, exchange student, honors, independent study, internships, liberal arts/career combination, student-designed major, study abroad, teacher certification program. **Credit/placement by examination:** AP, CLEP, IB, institutional tests. 30 credit hours maximum toward associate degree, 30 toward bachelor's. **Support services:** Reduced course load, remedial instruction, study skills assistance, tutoring, writing center.

Majors. Biology: General, ecology. **Business:** General, accounting, business admin, finance, international. **Education:** General, elementary. **Health:** Premedicine. **History:** General. **Interdisciplinary:** Behavioral sciences. **Legal studies:** Prelaw. **Liberal arts:** Arts/sciences. **Math:** General. **Philosophy/religion:** Religion. **Physical sciences:** Geology. **Psychology:** General. **Public administration:** Social work. **Social sciences:** General. **Theology:** Religious ed, sacred music.

Computing on campus. 30 workstations in library, computer center. Dormitories wired for high-speed internet access and linked to campus network. Commuter students can connect to campus network. Online course registration, online library, helpline, repair service, wireless network available.

Student life. Freshman orientation: Mandatory. Preregistration for classes offered. Held at beginning of semester with adviser. **Housing:** Guaranteed on-campus for all undergraduates. Single-sex dorms available. $300 deposit, deadline 5/1. **Activities:** Jazz band, campus ministries, choral groups, drama, music ensembles, musical theater, student government, student newspaper, Christian service organizations, Afro-Latino American club, social work club, Prayer Partners, environmental club, In His Name, Lutheran Women League, Rotaract club.

Athletics. NCAA. **Intercollegiate:** Baseball M, basketball, cross-country, soccer, softball W, tennis, volleyball. **Intramural:** Basketball, football (non-tackle), softball W, squash, tennis, volleyball. **Team name:** Clippers.

Student services. Adult student services, alcohol/substance abuse counseling, chaplain/spiritual director, career counseling, student employment services, financial aid counseling, health services, minority student services, personal counseling, placement for graduates. **Learning disabled:** Comprehensive services available.

Contact. E-mail: admission@concordia-ny.edu
Phone: (914) 337-9300 ext. 2155 Toll-free number: (800) 937-2655
Fax: (914) 395-4636
John Bahr, Dean of Enrollment, Concordia College, 171 White Plains Road, Bronxville, NY 10708

Cooper Union for the Advancement of Science and Art

New York, New York — **CB member**
www.cooper.edu — **CB code: 2097**

- Private 4-year visual arts and engineering college
- Commuter campus in very large city
- 898 degree-seeking undergraduates: 38% women, 5% African American, 18% Asian American, 7% Hispanic American, 1% Native American, 15% international
- 52 degree-seeking graduate students
- 9% of applicants admitted
- SAT or ACT (ACT writing optional), application essay required
- 88% graduate within 6 years; 45% enter graduate study

General. Founded in 1859. Regionally accredited. Full-tuition scholarship school of architecture, art, and engineering. **Degrees:** 215 bachelor's awarded; master's offered. **Calendar:** Semester, limited summer session. **Full-time faculty:** 52 total; 86% have terminal degrees, 14% minority, 27% women. **Part-time faculty:** 176 total; 58% have terminal degrees, 14% minority, 32% women. **Class size:** 69% < 20, 31% 20-39, less than 1% 40-49. **Special facilities:** Special labs in: biomechanics, materials, soils, hydraulics, design systems, computers, circuits, signal processing, acoustics and audio engineering, combustion research and demonstration, robotic theater studio, rapid prototyping, energy reclamation and innovation, materials and micro/nano engineering, mechatronics, thermal/fluid/engines, tissue engineering.

Freshman class profile. 3,055 applied, 283 admitted, 206 enrolled.

Mid 50% test scores		**Rank in top quarter:**	98%
SAT critical reading:	620-710	**Rank in top tenth:**	93%
SAT math:	640-780	**End year in good standing:**	91%
ACT composite:	29-33	**Return as sophomores:**	92%
GPA 3.75 or higher:	40%	**Out-of-state:**	40%
GPA 3.50-3.74:	15%	**Live on campus:**	80%
GPA 3.0-3.49:	37%	**International:**	14%
GPA 2.0-2.99:	8%		

Basis for selection. Engineering applicants reviewed on high school record and program, essays, SAT, and required SAT Subject Test scores. Art and architecture applicants selected on basis of home test, high school record and program, SAT. All international students must apply from an address in United States. 2 SAT Subject Tests required for engineering applicants: 1 math and 1 chemistry or 1 math and 1 physics. Portfolios required for art applicants. All art and architecture applicants must complete a home test. **Homeschooled:** Statement describing homeschool structure and mission, transcript of courses and grades, letter of recommendation (nonparent) required. Must present proof of high school graduation certification (national) or equivalent.

High school preparation. College-preparatory program recommended. 16 units required; 18 recommended. Required and recommended units include English 4, mathematics 1-4, social studies 1-4, history 1, science 1-4 (laboratory 3) and academic electives 8. 1 science required for architecture and art. 2 science and 4 math required for engineering including physics, chemistry, and precalculus; calculus preferred. 1 math required for art, 3 math for architecture including trigonometry or precalculus. 18 total units recommended for engineering.

2008-2009 Annual costs. Tuition/fees: $34,650. Every student admitted receives full-tuition scholarship (covering tuition only) for duration of enrollment. International students assessed annual filing fee of $1,750. Room only: $9,900. Books/supplies: $1,400. Personal expenses: $1,575.

2007-2008 Financial aid. Need-based: 123 full-time freshmen applied for aid; 61 were judged to have need; 61 of these received aid. Average need met was 92%. Average scholarship/grant was $3,249; average loan $3,271. 67% of total undergraduate aid awarded as scholarships/grants, 33% as loans/jobs. **Non-need-based:** Awarded to 914 full-time undergraduates, including 206 freshmen. Scholarships awarded for academics. **Additional information:** All students receive full-tuition scholarships valued at approximately $33,000 per year. Students able to document need receive financial aid package that may include combination of grants, loans, work-study, internships.

Application procedures. Admission: Priority date 12/1; deadline 1/1 (postmark date). $65 fee, may be waived for applicants with need. Admission notification 4/1. Must reply by May 1 or within 4 week(s) if notified thereafter. Regular application closing date for architecture January 1, for fine arts January 10, for engineering February 1. **Financial aid:** Priority date 4/15, closing date 6/1. FAFSA, CSS PROFILE required. Applicants notified by 6/1; must reply by 6/30 or within 2 week(s) of notification.

Academics. Engineering tutorials and engineering mentor program available. All freshman engineering majors required to prove or acquire computer literacy. 128 credit hours required for graduation in art program, 135 in engineering, and 160 in architecture. Students may take classes in all 3 schools. Art students encouraged to take courses throughout 7 disciplines. Architecture students take 5 years of design culminating in thesis year. Engineering students encouraged to take coursework in other majors. **Special study options:** Combined bachelor's/graduate degree, cross-registration, exchange student, independent study, internships, student-designed major, study abroad. Research opportunities. Students may take up to 1 year off between studies to pursue related experiences. **Credit/placement by examination:** AP, CLEP, institutional tests. Varies depending upon school and department. **Support services:** Tutoring, writing center.

Majors. Architecture: Architecture. **Engineering:** General, chemical, civil, electrical, mechanical. **Visual/performing arts:** Graphic design, studio arts. **Other:** Interdisciplinary engineering.

Most popular majors. Architecture 14%, engineering/engineering technologies 51%, visual/performing arts 35%.

Computing on campus. 650 workstations in dormitories, library, computer center. Dormitories linked to campus network. Commuter students can connect to campus network. Online library, helpline, repair service, student web hosting, wireless network available.

Student life. Freshman orientation: Available, $100 fee. 2.5 days, of which 1.5 days usually spent away at camp. **Housing:** Coed dorms, wellness housing available. $500 fully refundable deposit, deadline 6/1. **Activities:** Bands, choral groups, dance, drama, film society, literary magazine, music ensembles, musical theater, student government, student newspaper, symphony orchestra, 90 registered clubs available.

Athletics. Intercollegiate: Basketball, cross-country, equestrian W, lacrosse M, soccer M, tennis, volleyball. **Intramural:** Badminton, baseball M, basketball, bowling, cross-country, fencing, golf, judo, soccer, softball, table tennis, tennis, volleyball. **Team name:** Pioneers.

Student services. Alcohol/substance abuse counseling, career counseling, student employment services, financial aid counseling, minority student services, personal counseling, placement for graduates, veterans' counselor. **Physically disabled:** Services for visually, hearing impaired.

Contact. E-mail: admissions@cooper.edu
Phone: (212) 353-4120 Fax: (212) 353-4342
Mitchell Lipton, Dean of Admissions and Records/Registrar, Cooper Union for the Advancement of Science and Art, 30 Cooper Square, Suite 300, New York, NY 10003-7183

Cornell University

Ithaca, New York — **CB member**
www.cornell.edu — **CB code: 2098**

- Private 4-year university
- Residential campus in large town
- 13,772 degree-seeking undergraduates: 49% women, 5% African American, 17% Asian American, 6% Hispanic American, 8% international
- 6,391 degree-seeking graduate students
- 21% of applicants admitted
- SAT or ACT with writing, application essay required
- 93% graduate within 6 years; 30% enter graduate study

General. Founded in 1865. Regionally accredited. 7 undergraduate colleges: agriculture and life sciences; architecture, art, and planning; arts and sciences; engineering; hotel administration; human ecology; industrial and labor relations. 6 graduate/professional colleges. **Degrees:** 3,431 bachelor's awarded; master's, doctoral, first professional offered. **ROTC:** Army, Naval, Air Force. **Location:** 60 miles from Syracuse. **Calendar:** Semester, extensive summer session. **Full-time faculty:** 1,720 total; 92% have terminal degrees, 16% minority, 30% women. **Part-time faculty:** 176 total; 68% have terminal degrees, 4% minority, 35% women. **Class size:** 58% < 20, 20% 20-39, 5% 40-49, 11% 50-99, 6% >100. **Special facilities:** Johnson Museum of Art, Africana studies/research center, particle accelerator, biotechnology institute, supercomputer, national research centers, center for performing arts, observatory, marine laboratory, plantations, ornithology laboratory, life sciences institute.

Freshman class profile. 33,073 applied, 6,834 admitted, 3,139 enrolled.

Mid 50% test scores		**End year in good standing:**	99%
SAT critical reading:	630-730	**Return as sophomores:**	96%
SAT math:	670-770	**Out-of-state:**	67%
ACT composite:	29-33	**Live on campus:**	100%
Rank in top quarter:	98%	**International:**	10%
Rank in top tenth:	88%		

Basis for selection. School achievement record (difficulty of courses, grades earned), test scores, preparation and background for specific programs especially important. Essays, recommendations considered. Subject Test requirements depend upon college/school. Please consult admissions office. Interview required for architecture, hotel administration programs; portfolio required for design programs. **Homeschooled:** Well-documented coursework required.

High school preparation. College-preparatory program recommended. 16 units required. Required and recommended units include English 4, mathematics 3, social studies 3, history 3, science 3 (laboratory 3) and foreign language 3. Requirements vary by college.

2008-2009 Annual costs. Tuition/fees: $36,504. Tuition amounts listed are for Endowed/Private colleges only: Architecture, Art & Planning; Arts & Sciences; Engineering; Hotel Administration. Contract/State college amounts differ and vary by residency and program. Room/board: $11,640. Books/supplies: $740. Personal expenses: $1,500.

2008-2009 Financial aid. All financial aid based on need. 1,414 full-time freshmen applied for aid; 1,246 were judged to have need; 1,246 of these received aid. Average need met was 100%. Average scholarship/grant was $26,649; average loan $2,321. 83% of total undergraduate aid awarded as scholarships/grants, 17% as loans/jobs. **Additional information:** Need-based loans eliminated for undergraduates with family incomes under $60,000, and capped annually at $3,000 for incomes $60,000-$120,000.

Application procedures. **Admission:** Closing date 1/2 (postmark date). $70 fee, may be waived for applicants with need. Early April. Must reply by May 1 or within 2 week(s) if notified thereafter. Notification on rolling basis and dates vary by program/college. **Financial aid:** Closing date 1/5. FAFSA, institutional form, CSS PROFILE required. Applicants notified by 4/1; must reply by 5/1.

Academics. Cornell/Hughes Scholars program for independent research in neurobiology, physiology, genetics and development, and biochemistry (molecular and cell biology), Cornell in Rome program for studies in architecture and fine arts, undergraduate research opportunities in traditional majors as well as in many interdisciplinary fields including American Indian studies, cognitive studies, agriculture, food and society, FALCON language programs. **Special study options:** Accelerated study, cooperative education, cross-registration, distance learning, double major, ESL, exchange student, honors, independent study, internships, liberal arts/career combination, New York semester, semester at sea, student-designed major, study abroad, teacher certification program, urban semester, Washington semester. **Credit/placement by examination:** AP, CLEP, IB, institutional tests. **Support services:** Learning center, pre-admission summer program, reduced course load, study skills assistance, tutoring, writing center.

Majors. **Agriculture:** General, agribusiness operations, agronomy, animal sciences, business, food science, horticultural science, international, ornamental horticulture, plant protection, plant sciences. **Architecture:** Architecture, landscape, urban/community planning. **Area/ethnic studies:** African-American, American, Asian, gay/lesbian, German, Near/Middle Eastern, Russian/Slavic, women's. **Biology:** General, animal genetics, animal physiology, bacteriology, biochemistry, biometrics, ecology, entomology, plant pathology. **Business:** Hotel/motel admin, labor relations, restaurant/food services. **Communications:** General. **Computer sciences:** Computer science, information technology. **Conservation:** General, economics. **Education:** General, agricultural, biology, chemistry, family/consumer sciences, mathematics, physics, science. **Engineering:** General, agricultural, chemical, civil, electrical, environmental, materials, mechanical, operations research, physics. **Family/consumer sciences:** General, consumer economics, family studies, food/nutrition. **Foreign languages:** Classics, comparative lit, French, German, Italian, linguistics, Russian, Spanish. **Health:** Premedicine. **History:** General. **Interdisciplinary:** Neuroscience, science/society. **Liberal arts:** Arts/sciences. **Math:** General. **Philosophy/religion:** Philosophy, religion. **Physical sciences:** Astronomy, atmospheric science, chemistry, geology, physics. **Psychology:** General. **Public administration:** General, community org/advocacy, policy analysis. **Social sciences:** General, anthropology, archaeology, economics, political science, sociology. **Visual/performing arts:** Art history/conservation, dance, dramatic, fiber arts, film/cinema, studio arts, theater design.

Most popular majors. Agriculture 14%, biology 12%, business/marketing 13%, engineering/engineering technologies 19%, social sciences 10%.

Computing on campus. 2,650 workstations in dormitories, library, computer center, student center. Dormitories wired for high-speed internet access and linked to campus network. Commuter students can connect to campus network. Online course registration, online library, helpline, repair service, student web hosting, wireless network available.

Student life. **Freshman orientation:** Mandatory. Preregistration for classes offered. Six days and nights immediately prior to start of classes in August. Over 500 upper-level student Orientation Volunteers participate. All seven undergraduate colleges/schools provide orientations that include academic advising, information sessions, and a number of other programs. **Housing:** Guaranteed on-campus for freshmen. Coed dorms, single-sex dorms, special housing for disabled, apartments, cooperative housing, fraternity/sorority housing available. Ecology House: JAM (Just About Music); Language House; International Living Center; Ujamaa Residential College (Third World house); Risley Residential College (creative & performing arts); Multicultural Living Learning Unit; Akwe:kon (Native American & Nonnative American); Latino Living Center. **Activities:** Bands, campus ministries, choral groups, dance, drama, film society, international student organizations, literary magazine, music ensembles, Model UN, musical theater, radio station, student government, student newspaper, symphony orchestra, TV station, Hillel, Campus Crusade for Christ, La Asociacion Latina, African, Native American, Caribbean, Vietnamese, international, and lesbian/gay/bisexual groups, debate.

Athletics. NCAA. **Intercollegiate:** Baseball M, basketball, cross-country, equestrian W, fencing W, field hockey W, football (tackle) M, golf M, gymnastics W, ice hockey, lacrosse, rowing (crew), soccer, softball W, squash, swimming, tennis, track and field, volleyball W, wrestling M. **Intramural:** Badminton, basketball, bowling, cross-country, football (non-tackle), golf, ice hockey, skiing, soccer, softball, squash, table tennis, tennis, volleyball, water polo, wrestling. **Team name:** Big Red.

Student services. Alcohol/substance abuse counseling, chaplain/spiritual director, career counseling, student employment services, financial aid counseling, health services, minority student services, on-campus daycare, personal counseling, placement for graduates, veterans' counselor, women's services. **Physically disabled:** Services for visually, speech, hearing impaired.

Contact. E-mail: admissions@cornell.edu
Phone: (607) 255-5241 Fax: (607) 255-0659
Jason Locke, Director of Undergraduate Admissions, Cornell University, 410 Thurston Avenue, Ithaca, NY 14850-2488

Culinary Institute of America

Hyde Park, New York — **CB member**
www.ciachef.edu — **CB code: 3301**

- Private 4-year culinary school
- Residential campus in large town
- 2,728 degree-seeking undergraduates: 44% women
- 88% of applicants admitted
- Application essay required
- 51% graduate within 6 years

General. Founded in 1946. Candidate for regional accreditation; also accredited by ACCSCT. **Degrees:** 266 bachelor's, 1,085 associate awarded. **Location:** 80 miles from New York City. **Calendar:** Semester. **Full-time faculty:** 128 total; 6% have terminal degrees, 23% women. **Part-time faculty:** 44 total; 54% women. **Special facilities:** 41 teaching kitchens and bakeshops, 5 restaurants, culinary library with over 70,000 volumes.

Freshman class profile. 919 applied, 805 admitted, 571 enrolled.

GPA 3.75 or higher:	12%	**Rank in top tenth:**	9%
GPA 3.50-3.74:	16%	**End year in good standing:**	92%
GPA 3.0-3.49:	39%	**Return as sophomores:**	78%
GPA 2.0-2.99:	32%	**Out-of-state:**	77%
Rank in top quarter:	29%	**International:**	6%

Basis for selection. School achievement record, 6 months work experience (particularly in hands-on food preparation), and interview important. SAT/ACT not used for admissions, but if tests taken recommended that students submit scores.

High school preparation. Recommended units include English 4, mathematics 3, social studies 2, history 2 and science 2.

2008-2009 Annual costs. Tuition/fees: $23,470. Room and board costs shown for typical undergraduate; costs may vary. Room/board: $7,230. Books/supplies: $975.

2007-2008 Financial aid. **Non-need-based:** Scholarships awarded for academics, alumni affiliation, job skills, leadership, minority status.

Application procedures. **Admission:** No deadline. $50 fee, may be waived for applicants with need. Admission notification on a rolling basis. **Financial aid:** Priority date 12/15; no closing date. FAFSA required. Applicants notified by 4/1; must reply by 5/1 or within 4 week(s) of notification.

Academics. Curriculum devoted exclusively to culinary arts and baking and pastry arts education. Freshmen may enroll in one of 4 enrollment seasons throughout the year. All students complete 18-week paid externship program. Two-thirds of class time involves hands-on cooking, baking, table service, and dining room operations management in kitchens, bakeshops, and 5 student-staffed public restaurants. **Special study options:** Cross-registration, distance learning, internships. **Credit/placement by examination:** CLEP, institutional tests. **Support services:** Learning center, reduced course load, remedial instruction, study skills assistance, tutoring, writing center.

Majors. **Business:** Restaurant/food services. **Personal/culinary services:** Baking.

Computing on campus. 208 workstations in dormitories, library, computer center, student center. Dormitories wired for high-speed internet access and linked to campus network. Commuter students can connect to campus network. Online library, helpline, repair service, wireless network available.

Student life. **Freshman orientation:** Mandatory. **Housing:** Guaranteed on-campus for freshmen. Coed dorms, special housing for disabled, wellness housing available. Hearing impaired student housing available. **Activities:** International student organizations, literary magazine, student government, student newspaper, Alliance, Eta Sigma Delta Honor Society, Baking and Pastry Arts Society, Black Culinarian Society, Chefs Supporting Agriculture, Culinary Christian Fellowship, Ice Carving Society, Global Culinary Society, Garden Society, Oye Me.

Athletics. **Intercollegiate:** Cross-country, soccer. **Intramural:** Basketball, football (non-tackle), ice hockey, racquetball, soccer, softball, tennis, volleyball. **Team name:** Flames.

Student services. Alcohol/substance abuse counseling, chaplain/spiritual director, career counseling, student employment services, financial aid counseling, health services, personal counseling, placement for graduates, veterans' counselor. **Physically disabled:** Services for visually, speech, hearing impaired.

Contact. E-mail: admissions@culinary.edu
Phone: (845) 452-9430 Toll-free number: (800) 285-4627
Fax: (845) 451-1068
Rachel Birchwood, Director of Admissions, Culinary Institute of America, 1946 Campus Drive, Hyde Park, NY 12538-1499

Daemen College

Amherst, New York — **CB member**
www.daemen.edu — **CB code: 2762**

- Private 4-year liberal arts college
- Residential campus in small city
- 1,650 degree-seeking undergraduates: 14% part-time, 75% women, 10% African American, 1% Asian American, 4% Hispanic American, 1% Native American, 1% international
- 907 degree-seeking graduate students
- 66% of applicants admitted
- 49% graduate within 6 years; 40% enter graduate study

General. Founded in 1947. Regionally accredited. **Degrees:** 263 bachelor's awarded; master's, doctoral offered. **ROTC:** Army. **Location:** 9 miles from downtown Buffalo. **Calendar:** Semester, limited summer session. **Full-time faculty:** 99 total; 76% have terminal degrees, 7% minority, 54% women. **Part-time faculty:** 170 total; 14% have terminal degrees, 4% minority, 65% women. **Class size:** 62% < 20, 36% 20-39, 1% 40-49, less than 1% 50-99. **Special facilities:** Natural and health science research center, videoconference center, center for sustainable communities and civic engagement, center for special education and after-school programs.

Freshman class profile. 1,988 applied, 1,313 admitted, 406 enrolled.

Mid 50% test scores		**GPA 3.0-3.49:**	44%
SAT critical reading:	450-540	**End year in good standing:**	78%
SAT math:	460-570	**Return as sophomores:**	71%
SAT writing:	440-550	**Out-of-state:**	5%
ACT composite:	20-25	**Live on campus:**	61%
GPA 3.75 or higher:	17%	**Fraternities:**	1%
GPA 3.50-3.74:	39%		

Basis for selection. Emphasis on academic achievement and test scores with secondary consideration given to school activities and recommendations. Work experience also considered for entry into physician assistant program. 30 credit hour transfer limit on International Baccalaureate coursework. SAT or ACT recommended. Applicants who have been out of high school for more than 2 years not required to submit SAT or ACT scores. Essay, interview required for physician assistant program; portfolio required for art program. **Homeschooled:** State high school equivalency certificate required. Applicants should provide evidence of equivalency of high school education by GED or attestation of equivalency by superintendent of schools in student's public school district of residence. This documentation needed for financial aid eligibility. **Learning Disabled:** Bring to the attention of Admission Office need for special accommodations and submit current medical evidence of disability and limitations that require accommodations. Feasibility determined by nature and cost of accommodation, availability of funding, and whether accommodation will impact fundamental nature of course or program, among other factors.

High school preparation. College-preparatory program recommended. 16 units recommended. Recommended units include English 4, mathematics 4, social studies 4, science 4 (laboratory 1). All science and allied health programs require 3 math and 3 science. Business program requires 3 math. Foreign language programs require 3 foreign language.

2008-2009 Annual costs. Tuition/fees: $19,870. Room/board: $9,050. Books/supplies: $800. Personal expenses: $800.

2007-2008 Financial aid. **Non-need-based:** Scholarships awarded for academics, art, athletics, leadership.

Application procedures. **Admission:** No deadline. $25 fee, may be waived for applicants with need, free for online applicants. Admission notification on a rolling basis beginning on or about 10/15. Must reply by May 1 or within 2 week(s) if notified thereafter. **Financial aid:** Priority date 2/15; no closing date. FAFSA required. Applicants notified on a rolling basis starting 2/1; must reply within 2 week(s) of notification.

Academics. All professional programs require internships or field placements. There is a general service-learning requirement for graduation for all students. **Special study options:** Accelerated study, combined bachelor's/graduate degree, cross-registration, distance learning, double major, dual enrollment of high school students, exchange student, honors, independent study, internships, liberal arts/career combination, student-designed major, study abroad, teacher certification program, Washington semester, weekend college. Post-RN BS program in nursing. Weekend college for candidates of BS in business administration-general business, and MS in childhood education or special education-childhood education, initial and professional certification. **Credit/placement by examination:** AP, CLEP, IB, institutional tests. No limit other than residency of 30 credit hours minimum required in courses completed at school (select programs may require a higher minimum). Veterans may receive credit for military educational experiences. **Support services:** Learning center, pre-admission summer program, remedial instruction, study skills assistance, tutoring, writing center.

Majors. **Biology:** General, biochemistry. **Business:** Accounting, business admin. **Education:** Art, early childhood, elementary, special. **Foreign languages:** French, Spanish. **Health:** Community health, nursing (RN). **History:** General. **Interdisciplinary:** Natural sciences. **Math:** General. **Philosophy/religion:** Religion. **Psychology:** General. **Public administration:** Social work. **Social sciences:** Political science. **Visual/performing arts:** Art, graphic design, printmaking, studio arts.

Most popular majors. Biology 19%, business/marketing 11%, education 19%, health sciences 28%, psychology 6%, visual/performing arts 8%.

Computing on campus. 146 workstations in library, computer center, student center. Dormitories wired for high-speed internet access and linked to campus network. Commuter students can connect to campus network. Online course registration, online library, repair service, wireless network available.

Student life. **Freshman orientation:** Mandatory, $105 fee. Preregistration for classes offered. Two sessions (2 days each) offered in July for incoming freshmen. One day in mid-August for new transfer students. **Housing:** Guaranteed on-campus for freshmen. Coed dorms, wellness housing available. $200 fully refundable deposit, deadline 5/1. Coed apartment-style residence halls; some apartments are handicapped accessible. **Activities:** Choral groups, dance, drama, literary magazine, student government, student newspaper, multicultural association, Students without Borders, environmental club, Voices of Zion.

Athletics. NAIA. **Intercollegiate:** Basketball, cross-country, golf M, soccer, volleyball W. **Intramural:** Basketball, football (non-tackle) M, softball. **Team name:** Wildcats.

Student services. Alcohol/substance abuse counseling, chaplain/spiritual director, career counseling, student employment services, financial aid counseling, personal counseling, placement for graduates. **Physically disabled:** Services for hearing impaired.

Contact. E-mail: admissions@daemen.edu
Phone: (716) 839-8225 Toll-free number: (800) 462-7652
Fax: (716) 839-8229
Donna Shaffner, Dean of Admissions, Daemen College, 4380 Main Street, Amherst, NY 14226-3592

Darkei Noam Rabbinical College

Brooklyn, New York
CB code: 1270

- Private 5-year rabbinical college for men affiliated with Jewish faith
- Very large city

General. Founded in 1977. Accredited by AARTS. **Calendar:** Semester.

Annual costs/financial aid. Books/supplies: $300. Personal expenses: $3,000.

Contact. Phone: (718) 338-6464
Director of Admissions, 2822 Avenue J, Brooklyn, NY 11210

Davis College
Johnson City, New York
www.davisny.edu **CB code: 2233**

- Private 4-year Bible college affiliated with nondenominational tradition
- Large town
- 241 degree-seeking undergraduates
- SAT or ACT (ACT writing optional), application essay required

General. Regionally accredited; also accredited by ABHE. **Degrees:** 42 bachelor's, 9 associate awarded. **Location:** 2 miles from Binghamton. **Calendar:** Semester, limited summer session. **Full-time faculty:** 11 total. **Part-time faculty:** 13 total.

Basis for selection. Pastor recommendation and high school record most important. Must give evidence of personal knowledge of the Lord Jesus Christ as Savior. Applicant lifestyle consistency with biblical principles is important. **Homeschooled:** Must submit evidence of completion of high school requirements such as a high school transcript, home school transcript or GED.

2008-2009 Annual costs. Tuition/fees: $12,250. Room/board: $6,000.

2007-2008 Financial aid. Need-based: 59% of total undergraduate aid awarded as scholarships/grants, 41% as loans/jobs.

Application procedures. Admission: No deadline. $45 fee. Admission notification on a rolling basis. Dual credit opportunities for high school juniors and seniors through on-campus and online courses. Possible for high school students to complete all freshman requirements prior to high school graduation. **Financial aid:** No deadline. FAFSA, institutional form required. Applicants notified on a rolling basis.

Academics. Special study options: Distance learning, dual enrollment of high school students, independent study, internships, student-designed major. **Credit/placement by examination:** CLEP, SAT, ACT. **Support services:** Reduced course load, study skills assistance, tutoring.

Majors. Theology: Religious ed.

Computing on campus. Dormitories linked to campus network. Commuter students can connect to campus network. Wireless network available.

Student life. Freshman orientation: Mandatory. Preregistration for classes offered. **Housing:** Single-sex dorms, apartments available. **Activities:** Campus ministries, choral groups, international student organizations, student government, student newspaper.

Athletics. NCCAA. **Intercollegiate:** Basketball, soccer, volleyball W. **Intramural:** Soccer, volleyball. **Team name:** Falcons.

Student services. Financial aid counseling, health services, personal counseling.

Contact. E-mail: admissions@davisny.edu
Phone: (607) 729-1581 ext. 406 Toll-free number: (800) 331-4137 ext. 406
Fax: (607) 798-7754
Conroy Lewis, Admissions Counselor, Davis College, 400 Riverside Drive, Johnson City, NY 13790

Devry College of New York
Long Island City, New York **CB member**
www.devry.edu **CB code: 4276**

- For-profit 4-year business and technical college
- Commuter campus in very large city
- 936 degree-seeking undergraduates: 22% part-time, 27% women, 37% African American, 9% Asian American, 31% Hispanic American, 1% Native American, 1% international
- 190 degree-seeking graduate students
- Interview required

General. Regionally accredited. **Degrees:** 149 bachelor's, 51 associate awarded; master's offered. **Calendar:** Semester, extensive summer session. **Full-time faculty:** 36 total; 39% minority, 14% women. **Part-time faculty:** 75 total; 40% minority, 27% women.

Basis for selection. Applicants must have high school diploma or equivalent, or degree from an accredited postsecondary institution. Must demonstrate proficiency in basic college-level skills through test scores and/or institutionally administered placement examinations, and be at least 17 years of age on the first day of classes. New students may enter at beginning of any semester. SAT/ACT considered but not required for admission. If applicant chooses not to submit either, must take institution-administered admissions test.

2008-2009 Annual costs. Tuition/fees: $14,800. Books/supplies: $1,300. Personal expenses: $5,082.

2007-2008 Financial aid. All financial aid based on need.

Application procedures. Admission: No deadline. $50 fee. Admission notification on a rolling basis. **Financial aid:** No deadline. FAFSA required. Applicants notified on a rolling basis.

Academics. Special study options: Accelerated study, distance learning. **Credit/placement by examination:** CLEP, institutional tests. **Support services:** Learning center, remedial instruction, tutoring.

Majors. Business: Business admin. **Computer sciences:** Networking, systems analysis. **Engineering technology:** Biomedical, computer, electrical. **Other:** Technical management.

Most popular majors. Business/marketing 49%, computer/information sciences 32%, engineering/engineering technologies 20%.

Computing on campus. 394 workstations in library, computer center. Online course registration, online library, helpline available.

Student life. Freshman orientation: Mandatory. **Housing:** Private apartments, student-plan housing, private rooms available. **Activities:** Muslim student association, martial arts club.

Student services. Career counseling, student employment services, financial aid counseling, placement for graduates, veterans' counselor. **Physically disabled:** Services for visually, hearing impaired.

Contact. Phone: (718) 472-2728
Newton Myvett, Director of Admissions, Devry College of New York, 3020 Thomson Avenue, Long Island City, NY 11101-3051

Dominican College of Blauvelt
Orangeburg, New York **CB member**
www.dc.edu **CB code: 2190**

- Private 4-year The College has six divisions: Allied Health, Arts & Sciences, Business, Nursing, Social Sciences, and Teacher Education.
- Residential campus in small town
- 1,612 degree-seeking undergraduates: 25% part-time, 68% women, 18% African American, 9% Asian American, 18% Hispanic American, 1% international
- 302 degree-seeking graduate students
- 76% of applicants admitted
- SAT or ACT with writing required
- 46% graduate within 6 years

General. Founded in 1952. Regionally accredited. Private non-affiliated institution, Catholic in origin and Dominican in tradition. **Degrees:** 314 bachelor's, 1 associate awarded; master's, doctoral offered. **Location:** 17 miles from midtown Manhattan. **Calendar:** Differs by program, limited summer session. **Full-time faculty:** 70 total; 51% have terminal degrees, 4% minority, 74% women. **Part-time faculty:** 148 total; 7% have terminal degrees, 14% minority, 54% women. **Class size:** 71% < 20, 29% 20-39.

Freshman class profile. 1,347 applied, 1,017 admitted, 304 enrolled.

Mid 50% test scores			
SAT critical reading:	390-490	GPA 3.0-3.49:	31%
SAT math:	390-480	GPA 2.0-2.99:	57%
SAT writing:	400-470	End year in good standing:	63%
ACT composite:	17-24	Return as sophomores:	63%
GPA 3.75 or higher:	4%	Out-of-state:	37%
GPA 3.50-3.74:	5%	Live on campus:	81%
		International:	1%

Basis for selection. Admissions based on secondary school records and standardized test scores. Interviews and written essays required in some cases. Meeting with admissions counselor not always required for admission but always desirable. Some applicants may be asked to meet with member of admissions staff. **Learning Disabled:** Students with current professional documentation of disabilities will be provided with reasonable accommodations to assure access to and full participation in mainstream of educational process.

High school preparation. College-preparatory program recommended. 16 units required; 18 recommended. Required and recommended units include English 4, mathematics 3, social studies 3-4, science 3 (laboratory 1), foreign language 1-2 and academic electives 2.

2008-2009 Annual costs. Tuition/fees: $20,300. Room/board: $9,730. Books/supplies: $1,500.

2008-2009 Financial aid. **Non-need-based:** Scholarships awarded for academics, athletics. **Additional information:** Individual financial aid counseling available.

Application procedures. **Admission:** No deadline. $35 fee, may be waived for applicants with need. Admission notification on a rolling basis. **Financial aid:** Priority date 2/15; no closing date. FAFSA required. Applicants notified on a rolling basis starting 2/1.

Academics. **Special study options:** Accelerated study, combined bachelor's/graduate degree, cooperative education, distance learning, dual enrollment of high school students, honors, independent study, internships, study abroad, teacher certification program, weekend college. Accelerated Bachelor of Science in Nursing for college graduates. **Credit/placement by examination:** AP, CLEP, IB, SAT, ACT, institutional tests. 30 credit hours maximum toward associate degree, 60 toward bachelor's. **Support services:** Learning center, remedial instruction, study skills assistance, tutoring, writing center.

Majors. **Biology:** General. **Business:** Accounting, business admin, finance, human resources, international, management information systems, marketing. **Computer sciences:** General. **Education:** General, biology, elementary, English, mathematics, multiple handicapped, secondary, social science, special. **Foreign languages:** Spanish. **Health:** Athletic training, health services, nursing (RN). **History:** General. **Legal studies:** Prelaw. **Liberal arts:** Humanities. **Math:** General. **Psychology:** General. **Public administration:** Social work. **Social sciences:** General, criminology, economics.

Most popular majors. Business/marketing 21%, education 11%, health sciences 29%, social sciences 12%.

Computing on campus. 140 workstations in dormitories, library, computer center. Dormitories wired for high-speed internet access and linked to campus network. Commuter students can connect to campus network. Online library, repair service, wireless network available.

Student life. **Freshman orientation:** Mandatory. **Policies:** Alcohol-free campus. **Housing:** Guaranteed on-campus for all undergraduates. Coed dorms, wellness housing available. $200 deposit. Suites with multiple bedrooms, a bathroom and kitchen available for upperclass students. **Activities:** Campus ministries, choral groups, dance, drama, literary magazine, Model UN, musical theater, student government, student newspaper, Dominicans Uniting Latinos for Cultural Education (DULCE), Helping Hands (community service).

Athletics. NAIA, NCAA. **Intercollegiate:** Baseball M, basketball, cross-country W, golf M, lacrosse, soccer, softball W, track and field W, volleyball W. **Intramural:** Basketball, handball, softball, volleyball. **Team name:** Chargers.

Student services. Alcohol/substance abuse counseling, chaplain/spiritual director, career counseling, student employment services, financial aid counseling, health services, personal counseling, placement for graduates. **Physically disabled:** Services for visually, hearing impaired.

Contact. E-mail: admissions@dc.edu
Phone: (845) 848-7900 Toll-free number: (866) 432-4636
Fax: (845) 365-3150
Joyce Elbe, Director of Admissions, Dominican College of Blauvelt, 470 Western Highway, Orangeburg, NY 10962-1210

Dowling College

Oakdale, New York — **CB member**
www.dowling.edu — **CB code: 2011**

- Private 4-year liberal arts college
- Commuter campus in large town
- 3,288 degree-seeking undergraduates: 36% part-time, 56% women, 10% African American, 3% Asian American, 10% Hispanic American
- 2,418 degree-seeking graduate students
- 79% of applicants admitted
- 39% graduate within 6 years

General. Founded in 1955. Regionally accredited. School of Aviation situated at Brookhaven Airport. **Degrees:** 640 bachelor's awarded; master's, doctoral offered. **ROTC:** Army, Naval, Air Force. **Location:** 50 miles from New York City. **Calendar:** Semester, extensive summer session. **Full-time faculty:** 119 total; 92% have terminal degrees, 13% minority, 38% women. **Part-time faculty:** 418 total; 26% have terminal degrees, 18% minority, 45% women. **Class size:** 65% < 20, 35% 20-39. **Special facilities:** College-owned fleet of aircraft, FRASCA flight simulators, virtual airport.

Freshman class profile. 2,936 applied, 2,319 admitted, 528 enrolled.

Mid 50% test scores		**GPA 2.0-2.99:**	53%
SAT critical reading:	390-510	**Rank in top quarter:**	22%
SAT math:	400-530	**Rank in top tenth:**	8%
GPA 3.75 or higher:	10%	**Return as sophomores:**	59%
GPA 3.50-3.74:	4%	**Out-of-state:**	7%
GPA 3.0-3.49:	13%	**Live on campus:**	11%

Basis for selection. Program of study, recent achievement, academic rank, school record, standardized test scores, counselor's recommendation considered. SAT or ACT recommended.

High school preparation. College-preparatory program recommended. 16 units required. Required units include English 4, mathematics 3, social studies 4, science 2, foreign language 2 and academic electives 1. 4 additional units recommended.

2008-2009 Annual costs. Tuition/fees: $20,310. Room/board: $9,140. Books/supplies: $1,000. Personal expenses: $1,096.

2008-2009 Financial aid. **Need-based:** 357 full-time freshmen applied for aid; 348 were judged to have need; 348 of these received aid. Average need met was 92%. Average scholarship/grant was $3,545; average loan $3,632. 81% of total undergraduate aid awarded as scholarships/grants, 19% as loans/jobs. **Non-need-based:** Awarded to 951 full-time undergraduates, including 277 freshmen. Scholarships awarded for academics, alumni affiliation, athletics.

Application procedures. **Admission:** No deadline. $35 fee, may be waived for applicants with need. Admission notification on a rolling basis. **Financial aid:** Priority date 4/30; no closing date. FAFSA required. Applicants notified on a rolling basis starting 3/1.

Academics. Optional winter term enables students to take 2 additional courses. **Special study options:** Accelerated study, combined bachelor's/graduate degree, cooperative education, double major, ESL, honors, independent study, internships, liberal arts/career combination, student-designed major, study abroad, teacher certification program, weekend college. Federal Aviation Administration cooperative program. **Credit/placement by examination:** AP, CLEP, IB, SAT, institutional tests. 30 credit hours maximum toward bachelor's degree. **Support services:** Learning center, preadmission summer program, reduced course load, remedial instruction, study skills assistance, tutoring.

Majors. **Biology:** General. **Business:** Accounting, business admin, finance. **Computer sciences:** General, computer science. **Conservation:** Environmental science. **Education:** General, art, biology, business, chemistry, elementary, English, foreign languages, mathematics, middle, multi-level teacher, music, physical, science, secondary, social science, social studies, Spanish, special. **History:** General. **Liberal arts:** Arts/sciences, humanities. **Math:** General. **Philosophy/religion:** Philosophy. **Physical sciences:** Chemistry. **Psychology:** General. **Social sciences:** General, anthropology, economics, political science, sociology. **Transportation:** Aviation, aviation management. **Visual/performing arts:** General, art, dramatic. **Other:** Communications arts, Marine studies.

Most popular majors. Business/marketing 32%, education 21%, liberal arts 8%, psychology 7%, social sciences 11%.

Computing on campus. 180 workstations in library, computer center. Dormitories wired for high-speed internet access and linked to campus network. Online course registration, online library, helpline available.

Student life. **Freshman orientation:** Available. Preregistration for classes offered. **Housing:** Coed dorms available. $200 nonrefundable deposit. **Activities:** Jazz band, choral groups, drama, international student organizations, literary magazine, music ensembles, musical theater, student government, student newspaper, symphony orchestra, 23 clubs and organizations related to academics, honor societies in business, education, economics, and psychology, Circle-K, computer science, scholarship society.

Athletics. NCAA. **Intercollegiate:** Baseball M, basketball, cross-country W, equestrian W, golf M, lacrosse M, rowing (crew), soccer, softball W, tennis, volleyball W. **Intramural:** Basketball, bowling, soccer, softball. **Team name:** Golden Lions.

Student services. Adult student services, alcohol/substance abuse counseling, chaplain/spiritual director, career counseling, services for economically disadvantaged, student employment services, financial aid counseling, health services, personal counseling, placement for graduates. **Physically disabled:** Services for visually, speech, hearing impaired.

Contact. E-mail: admissions@dowling.edu
Phone: (631) 244-3030 Toll-free number: (800) 369-5464
Fax: (631) 244-1059
Glenn Berman, Dean of Admissions, Dowling College, 150 Idle Hour Boulevard, Oakdale, NY 11769-1999

D'Youville College

Buffalo, New York — **CB member**
www.dyc.edu — **CB code: 2197**

- Private 4-year health science and liberal arts college
- Commuter campus in large city
- 1,614 degree-seeking undergraduates: 14% part-time, 75% women, 13% African American, 1% Asian American, 4% Hispanic American, 1% Native American, 11% international
- 1,194 degree-seeking graduate students
- 82% of applicants admitted
- SAT or ACT (ACT writing optional) required
- 59% graduate within 6 years

General. Founded in 1908. Regionally accredited. **Degrees:** 291 bachelor's awarded; master's, doctoral, first professional offered. **ROTC:** Army. **Location:** 1 mile from downtown. **Calendar:** Semester, extensive summer session. **Class size:** 66% < 20, 29% 20-39, 3% 40-49, 1% 50-99, less than 1% >100. **Special facilities:** Equipment for blind and visually impaired including computer system with speech synthesizer, Braille printer, Versabraille, and print enhancer; physical therapy gait analysis lab; professional theater; gross anatomy lab.

Freshman class profile. 1,580 applied, 1,291 admitted, 221 enrolled.

Mid 50% test scores		**Rank in top tenth:**	11%
SAT critical reading:	450-530	**End year in good standing:**	85%
SAT math:	450-560	**Return as sophomores:**	76%
SAT writing:	450-550	**Out-of-state:**	9%
ACT composite:	18-25	**Live on campus:**	39%
Rank in top quarter:	40%	**International:**	7%

Basis for selection. High school GPA, class rank, test scores, type of high school program important. Interview, essay, letters of recommendation optional. 3 recommendations required for physician's assistant program. Interview required for physician's assistant and chiropractic programs. **Homeschooled:** Transcript of courses and grades, state high school equivalency certificate, letter of recommendation (nonparent) required.

High school preparation. College-preparatory program recommended. 16 units recommended. Recommended units include English 4, mathematics 3, social studies 3, science 3 and foreign language 3. Biology and chemistry required for nursing, occupational therapy, physical therapy, dietetics, chiropractic and physician's assistant programs. 3 units of math required for accounting.

2008-2009 Annual costs. Tuition/fees: $19,000. Substantial tuition reduction depending on SAT scores. Room/board: $9,300. Books/supplies: $1,000. Personal expenses: $800.

2007-2008 Financial aid. Need-based: 158 full-time freshmen applied for aid; 141 were judged to have need; 141 of these received aid. Average need met was 82%. Average scholarship/grant was $10,465; average loan $5,365. 46% of total undergraduate aid awarded as scholarships/grants, 54% as loans/jobs. **Non-need-based:** Awarded to 206 full-time undergraduates, including 41 freshmen. Scholarships awarded for academics, leadership, religious affiliation, ROTC.

Application procedures. Admission: No deadline. $25 fee, may be waived for applicants with need, free for online applicants. Admission notification on a rolling basis. Must reply by May 1 or within 2 week(s) if notified thereafter. **Financial aid:** Priority date 3/1; no closing date. FAFSA required. Applicants notified on a rolling basis starting 4/1; must reply within 2 week(s) of notification.

Academics. Special study options: Accelerated study, combined bachelor's/graduate degree, cross-registration, distance learning, double major, dual enrollment of high school students, exchange student, independent study, internships, liberal arts/career combination, study abroad, teacher certification program, weekend college. Career Discovery Program for undecided students; Teacher certification at the graduate level only. **Credit/placement by examination:** AP, CLEP, IB, institutional tests. 15 credit hours maximum toward bachelor's degree. Life experience may be granted credit through local Challenge Examinations. Prior to entering D'Youville, up to 15 credits may be earned via standardized examinations; additional 15 credits may be earned via standardized examinations after enrolling. **Support services:** Learning center, pre-admission summer program, reduced course load, remedial instruction, study skills assistance, tutoring, writing center.

Majors. Biology: General. **Business:** General, accounting, business admin, international. **Computer sciences:** Information technology. **Health:** Health care admin, nursing (RN), physician assistant, predental, premedicine, preop/surgical nursing, prepharmacy, preveterinary. **History:** General. **Interdisciplinary:** Global studies. **Legal studies:** Prelaw. **Math:** General. **Philosophy/religion:** Philosophy. **Physical sciences:** Chemistry. **Psychology:** General. **Social sciences:** Sociology.

Most popular majors. Business/marketing 16%, health sciences 59%, interdisciplinary studies 9%.

Computing on campus. 100 workstations in dormitories, library, computer center, student center. Dormitories wired for high-speed internet access and linked to campus network. Commuter students can connect to campus network. Online library, helpline, repair service, student web hosting, wireless network available.

Student life. Freshman orientation: Mandatory, $60 fee. Preregistration for classes offered. Programs vary for traditional, transfer, and graduate students. **Housing:** Guaranteed on-campus for freshmen. Coed dorms, special housing for disabled, apartments, wellness housing available. $100 fully refundable deposit. Quiet floors for upper level students. **Activities:** Campus ministries, choral groups, drama, international student organizations, literary magazine, Model UN, student government, student newspaper, Black Student Union, Latin American club, Lambda Sigma, writers club, Student Nurses Association, Asian Student Union.

Athletics. NCAA. **Intercollegiate:** Baseball M, basketball, cross-country, golf, rowing (crew) W, soccer, softball W, tennis, volleyball. **Intramural:** Basketball, cheerleading W, table tennis, volleyball. **Team name:** Spartans.

Student services. Adult student services, alcohol/substance abuse counseling, chaplain/spiritual director, career counseling, services for economically disadvantaged, student employment services, financial aid counseling, health services, minority student services, personal counseling, placement for graduates, veterans' counselor. **Physically disabled:** Services for visually, speech, hearing impaired.

Contact. E-mail: admissions@dyc.edu
Phone: (716) 829-7600 Toll-free number: (800) 777-3921
Fax: (716) 829-7900
Steve Smith, Director of Admissions, D'Youville College, 320 Porter Avenue, Buffalo, NY 14201-1084

Eastman School of Music of the University of Rochester

Rochester, New York
www.esm.rochester.edu — **CB code: 2224**

- Private 4-year music and performing arts college
- Residential campus in large city
- 500 degree-seeking undergraduates
- 400 graduate students
- Application essay, interview required

General. Founded in 1921. Regionally accredited. Professional school within University of Rochester. Eastman students may take non-music classes, earn BA or BS degree, and attend social events at University of Rochester's River Campus. **Degrees:** 108 bachelor's awarded; master's, doctoral offered. **ROTC:** Naval. **Location:** 357 miles from New York City, 80 miles from Niagara Falls. **Calendar:** Semester, limited summer session. **Full-time faculty:** 74 total. **Part-time faculty:** 58 total. **Class size:** 89% < 20, 9% 20-39, 1% 40-49, less than 1% 50-99. **Special facilities:** 4 performance halls including 3094-seat theater, computers for synthesis and analysis of music, complete analog and digital recording studios, music library containing over 700,000 items, over 135 practice rooms.

Freshman class profile.

Out-of-state:	75%	**Fraternities:**	7%
Live on campus:	99%	**Sororities:**	11%

Basis for selection. Proficiency in major area most important, in addition to academic record, test scores, interview, recommendations. Composition majors submit portfolio of scores. Some areas (jazz, composition, voice, piano) prescreened in advance of live audition. Candidates encouraged to audition at Eastman in the spring on designated audition dates, but auditions are held across the USA in January, and auditions by recording are also possible in most areas. SAT and SAT Subject Tests or ACT recommended. Candidates who come to Eastman for a live audition are also give a musicianship test, and a music theory test. Audition required for all; research/term paper required for theory majors; portfolio required for composition majors. Interview recommended for all, required for composition, music education, musical arts, theory majors. **Homeschooled:** Statement describing homeschool structure and mission, transcript of courses and grades, state high school equivalency certificate, interview, letter of recommendation (nonparent) required. SAT or ACT, at least 2 SAT Subject Tests required. Taking college credit classes also encouraged. **Learning Disabled:** To facilitate a smooth audition day experience, Admissions Office requests advance notice of any special considerations.

High school preparation. 16 units required. Required units include English 4.

2008-2009 Annual costs. Tuition/fees: $36,100. Room/board: $11,020. Books/supplies: $650. Personal expenses: $1,500.

2007-2008 Financial aid. **Need-based:** 78% of total undergraduate aid awarded as scholarships/grants, 22% as loans/jobs. **Non-need-based:** Scholarships awarded for academics, alumni affiliation, job skills, leadership, minority status, music/drama, state residency.

Application procedures. **Admission:** Closing date 12/1 (postmark date). $100 fee, may be waived for applicants with need. Application must be submitted online. Admission notification on a rolling basis beginning on or about 3/15. Must reply by May 1 or within 2 week(s) if notified thereafter. Admission review occurs following candidate's audition/interview. Regional auditions in Asia occur in fall, regional auditions in United States typically occur in January, auditions at Eastman School of Music occur in February and early March; typically, admission review and decisions following final audition date in Rochester. Separate (additional) application required for dual degree program. **Financial aid:** Closing date 2/28. FAFSA, institutional form required. Applicants notified on a rolling basis starting 3/15; must reply by 5/1 or within 2 week(s) of notification.

Academics. Arts leadership programs; orchestral studies and sacred music diploma programs. **Special study options:** Double major, ESL, independent study, internships, student-designed major, study abroad, teacher certification program. **Credit/placement by examination:** AP, CLEP, institutional tests. **Support services:** Pre-admission summer program, remedial instruction, study skills assistance, tutoring, writing center.

Majors. **Education:** Music. **Visual/performing arts:** Jazz, music performance, music theory/composition, piano/organ, voice/opera.

Most popular majors. Education 16%, visual/performing arts 84%.

Computing on campus. 50 workstations in dormitories, library, computer center, student center. Dormitories wired for high-speed internet access and linked to campus network. Commuter students can connect to campus network. Online course registration, online library, helpline, repair service, student web hosting, wireless network available.

Student life. **Freshman orientation:** Mandatory, $195 fee. Includes mandatory placement testing. **Policies:** Undergraduates required to live in college housing for first 3 years unless released by Assistant Dean of Residential Life. **Housing:** Guaranteed on-campus for freshmen. Coed dorms, single-sex dorms, special housing for disabled, fraternity/sorority housing, wellness housing available. **Activities:** Bands, choral groups, literary magazine, music ensembles, opera, radio station, student government, student newspaper, symphony orchestra, international students association, Amnesty International, Intervarsity Christian Fellowship, Jewish students, Lambda, student association, graduate student association, musical organizations.

Student services. Adult student services, alcohol/substance abuse counseling, chaplain/spiritual director, career counseling, student employment services, financial aid counseling, health services, personal counseling, placement for graduates. **Physically disabled:** Services for visually, speech impaired.

Contact. E-mail: admissions@esm.rochester.edu
Phone: (585) 274-1060 Toll-free number: (800) 388-9695
Fax: (585) 232-8601
Adrian Daly, Director of Admissions, Eastman School of Music of the University of Rochester, 26 Gibbs Street, Rochester, NY 14604-2599

Elmira College

Elmira, New York — **CB member**
www.elmira.edu — **CB code: 2226**

- Private 4-year liberal arts college
- Residential campus in large town
- 1,272 degree-seeking undergraduates: 16% part-time, 72% women, 2% African American, 1% Asian American, 1% Hispanic American, 1% international
- 164 graduate students
- 74% of applicants admitted
- SAT or ACT (ACT writing optional), application essay required
- 60% graduate within 6 years; 52% enter graduate study

General. Founded in 1855. Regionally accredited. **Degrees:** 297 bachelor's, 3 associate awarded; master's offered. **ROTC:** Army, Air Force. **Location:** 106 miles from Rochester, 90 miles from Syracuse, 50 miles from Binghamton. **Calendar:** 4-4-1. Limited summer session. **Full-time faculty:** 82 total; 1% minority. **Part-time faculty:** 119 total; 51% have terminal degrees, 3% minority, 63% women. **Class size:** 81% < 20, 18% 20-39, less than 1% 40-49. **Special facilities:** Center for Mark Twain Studies.

Freshman class profile. 2,090 applied, 1,554 admitted, 350 enrolled.

Mid 50% test scores			
SAT critical reading:	510-620	Rank in top quarter:	65%
SAT math:	500-610	Rank in top tenth:	30%
ACT composite:	24-28	End year in good standing:	96%
GPA 3.75 or higher:	23%	Return as sophomores:	74%
GPA 3.50-3.74:	17%	Out-of-state:	52%
GPA 3.0-3.49:	30%	Live on campus:	98%
GPA 2.0-2.99:	30%	International:	1%

Basis for selection. GED not accepted. School academic record primary. Test scores, recommendations, essay, character and extracurricular activities important. Interview highly recommended. **Homeschooled:** Statement describing homeschool structure and mission, transcript of courses and grades, interview, letter of recommendation (nonparent) required.

High school preparation. College-preparatory program recommended. 16 units required. Required and recommended units include English 4, mathematics 3, social studies 3, history 1, science 3 (laboratory 2), foreign language 2 and academic electives 2. 1 additional unit of foreign language recommended for foreign language, education, and international business programs.

2008-2009 Annual costs. Tuition/fees: $33,250. Room/board: $10,100. Books/supplies: $500. Personal expenses: $550.

2008-2009 Financial aid. **Need-based:** 265 full-time freshmen applied for aid; 246 were judged to have need; 246 of these received aid. Average need met was 80%. Average scholarship/grant was $21,232; average loan $3,818. 71% of total undergraduate aid awarded as scholarships/grants, 29% as loans/jobs. **Non-need-based:** Awarded to 356 full-time undergraduates, including 100 freshmen. Scholarships awarded for academics, leadership, ROTC, state residency. **Additional information:** Sibling Scholarship program provides 50% discounts on second immediate family member's room and board, regardless of need.

Application procedures. **Admission:** Priority date 2/1; deadline 3/1 (postmark date). $50 fee, may be waived for applicants with need. Admission notification on a rolling basis beginning on or about 10/15. Must reply by May 1 or within 2 week(s) if notified thereafter. **Financial aid:** Priority date 2/1, closing date 6/30. FAFSA required. Applicants notified on a rolling basis starting 2/1; must reply by 5/1 or within 3 week(s) of notification.

Academics. Mandatory writing program for all freshmen. 7.5-credit internship/community service, often done during 6-week spring term, required of all students. International study emphasized. **Special study options:** Accelerated study, combined bachelor's/graduate degree, double major, dual enrollment of high school students, ESL, exchange student, independent study, internships, liberal arts/career combination, student-designed major, study abroad, teacher certification program. **Credit/placement by examination:** AP, CLEP, IB. 30 credit hours maximum toward bachelor's degree. **Support services:** Reduced course load, study skills assistance, tutoring, writing center.

Majors. **Area/ethnic studies:** American. **Biology:** General, biochemistry. **Business:** Accounting, business admin, international, managerial economics, marketing. **Conservation:** General, environmental studies. **Education:** Art, biology, chemistry, Deaf/hearing impaired, elementary, English, foreign languages, French, history, mathematics, middle, multi-level teacher, science, secondary, social science, social studies, Spanish, speech, speech impaired. **Foreign languages:** General, ancient Greek, classics, French, Latin, Spanish. **Health:** Audiology/speech pathology, clinical lab science, nursing (RN), predental, premedicine, preveterinary. **History:** General. **Legal studies:** Prelaw. **Math:** General. **Philosophy/religion:** Philosophy, religion. **Physical sciences:** Chemistry. **Protective services:** Criminal justice. **Psychology:** General. **Public administration:** General, human services. **Social sciences:** General, anthropology, economics, international relations, political science, sociology. **Visual/performing arts:** Art, dramatic.

Computing on campus. 145 workstations in library, computer center. Dormitories wired for high-speed internet access and linked to campus network. Commuter students can connect to campus network. Wireless network available.

Student life. **Freshman orientation:** Mandatory, $350 fee. Preregistration for classes offered. 2-day summer registration program for course registration, assessments, and get-acquainted activities. 4-day orientation program in the fall. **Housing:** Guaranteed on-campus for all undergraduates. Coed dorms, single-sex dorms, special housing for disabled, apartments, wellness housing available. Quiet floors. All undergraduates required to live in college housing unless living with family or over the age of 25. **Activities:** Concert band, campus ministries, choral groups, dance, drama, international student organizations, literary magazine, music ensembles, Model UN, musical theater, radio station, student government, student newspaper, More than 100 student interest groups including Christian Fellowship, Hillel, international student club, Habitat for Humanity, ski club, College Democrats, College Republicans, equestrian club, and sports medicine club.

Athletics. NCAA. **Intercollegiate:** Basketball, cheerleading M, equestrian W, field hockey W, golf, ice hockey, lacrosse, soccer, softball W, tennis, volleyball W. **Intramural:** Badminton, basketball, bowling, football (non-tackle), handball, ice hockey, racquetball, skiing, skin diving, soccer, softball, squash, swimming, table tennis, tennis, volleyball. **Team name:** Soaring Eagles.

Student services. Alcohol/substance abuse counseling, chaplain/spiritual director, career counseling, student employment services, financial aid counseling, health services, personal counseling, placement for graduates, veterans' counselor, women's services. **Physically disabled:** Services for visually, speech, hearing impaired.

Contact. E-mail: admissions@elmira.edu
Phone: (607) 735-1724 Toll-free number: (800) 935-6472
Fax: (607) 735-1718
Brett Moore, Director of Admissions, Elmira College, One Park Place, Elmira, NY 14901

Eugene Lang College The New School for Liberal Arts

New York, New York
www.lang.edu **CB code: 2521**

- Private 4-year liberal arts college
- Commuter campus in very large city
- 1,347 degree-seeking undergraduates: 6% part-time, 68% women, 4% African American, 6% Asian American, 7% Hispanic American, 1% Native American, 4% international
- 55% of applicants admitted
- SAT or ACT, application essay, interview required
- 49% graduate within 6 years

General. Founded in 1978. Regionally accredited. Students design own academic programs with advisers. Access to New York University and Cooper Union libraries, ability to select courses within The New School and Cooper Union. **Degrees:** 274 bachelor's awarded. **Location:** Located in Manhattan. **Calendar:** Semester, limited summer session. **Full-time faculty:** 72 total; 72% have terminal degrees, 25% minority, 50% women. **Part-time faculty:** 71 total; 17% minority, 49% women. **Class size:** 80% < 20, 17% 20-39, 2% 40-49, less than 1% 50-99. **Special facilities:** Photography laboratories, screening rooms, art galleries.

Freshman class profile. 1,984 applied, 1,100 admitted, 301 enrolled.

Mid 50% test scores		**GPA 2.0-2.99:**	22%
SAT critical reading:	550-660	**Rank in top quarter:**	73%
SAT math:	500-610	**Rank in top tenth:**	29%
SAT writing:	560-670	**End year in good standing:**	97%
ACT composite:	23-27	**Return as sophomores:**	73%
GPA 3.75 or higher:	11%	**Out-of-state:**	78%
GPA 3.50-3.74:	13%	**Live on campus:**	84%
GPA 3.0-3.49:	54%	**International:**	4%

Basis for selection. Success in college preparatory studies most important supplemented by writing ability, intellectual curiosity, interview. Extracurricular/community activities, evidence of special talents, recommendations important. Telephone interviews available to students who cannot travel to New York. Essay required for BA/BFA; audition required for jazz, BA/BFA; portfolio required for art, BA/BFA.

High school preparation. College-preparatory program recommended. 16 units required; 18 recommended. Required and recommended units include English 4, mathematics 3, social studies 3, history 2, science 3 and foreign language 2. Honors/AP courses recommended.

2008-2009 Annual costs. Tuition/fees: $33,060. Room/board: $12,390. Books/supplies: $2,050. Personal expenses: $1,550.

2008-2009 Financial aid. **Need-based:** 187 full-time freshmen applied for aid; 170 were judged to have need; 170 of these received aid. Average need met was 80%. Average scholarship/grant was $21,287; average loan $8,675. 73% of total undergraduate aid awarded as scholarships/grants, 27% as loans/jobs. **Non-need-based:** Awarded to 235 full-time undergraduates, including 71 freshmen. Scholarships awarded for academics, music/drama.

Application procedures. **Admission:** Closing date 2/1 (postmark date). $50 fee, may be waived for applicants with need. Admission notification on a rolling basis beginning on or about 3/25. Must reply by May 1 or within 3 week(s) if notified thereafter. **Financial aid:** No deadline. FAFSA required. Applicants notified on a rolling basis starting 3/1; must reply within 4 week(s) of notification.

Academics. Students map out individual program of study within 5 broad areas of concentration. Seminars rather than lecture classes. **Special study options:** Accelerated study, combined bachelor's/graduate degree, cross-registration, distance learning, double major, ESL, exchange student, independent study, internships, liberal arts/career combination, student-designed major, study abroad, urban semester. **Credit/placement by examination:** CLEP, IB. **Support services:** Tutoring, writing center.

Majors. **Area/ethnic studies:** African-American, American, Caribbean, European, Latin American, Western European, women's. **Communications:** Journalism. **Education:** Foundations. **Foreign languages:** Comparative lit. **History:** General. **Interdisciplinary:** Science/society. **Liberal arts:** Arts/sciences. **Philosophy/religion:** Philosophy, religion. **Psychology:** General. **Social sciences:** General, anthropology, economics, international relations, political science, sociology, urban studies. **Visual/performing arts:** General, art history/conservation, dance, music history, studio arts, theater history. **Other:** Culture and media.

Computing on campus. 1,200 workstations in library, computer center, student center. Dormitories wired for high-speed internet access and linked to campus network. Commuter students can connect to campus network. Online course registration, online library, helpline, student web hosting, wireless network available.

Student life. **Freshman orientation:** Mandatory. Preregistration for classes offered. One week before classes begin. **Housing:** Guaranteed on-campus for freshmen. Coed dorms, special housing for disabled, apartments, wellness housing available. $250 nonrefundable deposit, deadline 7/1. **Activities:** Jazz band, choral groups, dance, drama, film society, international student organizations, literary magazine, music ensembles, opera, radio station, student government, student newspaper, symphony orchestra, Amnesty International, women's group, student union, Latino and African-American student organizations, gay/lesbian student organizations, volunteer groups, environmental group.

Student services. Career counseling, student employment services, financial aid counseling, health services, minority student services, personal counseling. **Learning disabled:** Comprehensive services available.

Contact. E-mail: lang@newschool.edu
Phone: (212) 229-5665 Toll-free number: (877) 528-3321
Fax: (212) 229-5355
Nicole Curvin, Director of Admissions, Eugene Lang College The New School for Liberal Arts, 65 West 11th Street (3rd floor), New York, NY 10011

Excelsior College

Albany, New York
www.excelsior.edu **CB code: 0759**

- Private 4-year virtual liberal arts college
- Small city
- 32,133 degree-seeking undergraduates
- 996 graduate students

General. Founded in 1970. Regionally accredited. Provides Internet-based courses. No residency required. Professional academic advising provided. **Degrees:** 2,714 bachelor's, 2,481 associate awarded; master's offered. **Calendar:** Continuous, extensive summer session. **Full-time faculty:** 25 total; 60% women. **Part-time faculty:** 667 total; 60% women. **Class size:** 73% < 20, 27% 20-39. **Special facilities:** Comprehensive virtual library.

Basis for selection. Open admission, but selective for some programs. Admission to nursing program open to students with certain health care background.

2008-2009 Annual costs. Students charged $895 enrollment fee and $300 per credit hour. Because of nontraditional pricing, school does not charge set tuition based on 15 credit hours per semester.

2007-2008 Financial aid. All financial aid based on need. 20% of total undergraduate aid awarded as scholarships/grants, 80% as loans/jobs. **Additional information:** Excelsior College is Title IV eligible for certain degree programs. College approved for all veterans educational benefit programs.

Application procedures. Admission: No deadline. $75 fee. Admission notification on a rolling basis. Students may enroll at any time and are not divided into traditional classifications such as freshmen or sophomores. Applicants without high school diploma admitted as special students. **Financial aid:** Priority date 7/1; no closing date. FAFSA, institutional form required. Applicants notified on a rolling basis starting 8/1; must reply within 2 week(s) of notification.

Academics. Portfolio assessment option in subject areas where proficiency or performance examinations unavailable. Failing grades not placed in student records or figured into GPA. **Special study options:** Accelerated study, combined bachelor's/graduate degree, distance learning, external degree, honors, independent study. **Credit/placement by examination:** AP, CLEP. Some degrees can be earned entirely by examination. **Support services:** Reduced course load, study skills assistance, writing center.

Majors. Biology: General. **Business:** Accounting, business admin, finance, hospitality admin, human resources, insurance, international, management information systems, marketing, operations. **Communications:** General. **Computer sciences:** General, information systems, information technology. **Engineering technology:** General, computer systems, instrumentation, manufacturing, mechanical, nuclear. **Foreign languages:** General. **Health:** Health services, nursing (RN), optometric assistant. **History:** General. **Liberal arts:** Arts/sciences. **Math:** General. **Philosophy/religion:** Philosophy. **Physical sciences:** Chemistry, geology, optics, physics. **Protective services:** Criminal justice. **Psychology:** General. **Social sciences:** Economics, geography, political science, sociology. **Other:** Area studies, Electronic instrumentation technology.

Most popular majors. Business/marketing 8%, liberal arts 75%.

Computing on campus. Commuter students can connect to campus network. Online library, helpline available.

Student life. Freshman orientation: Available. Orientation conducted by mail. **Policies:** Students are kept informed of program developments through mailings, web, correspondence, and program newsletters.

Student services. Adult student services, career counseling, financial aid counseling, veterans' counselor.

Contact. E-mail: info@excelsior.edu
Phone: (518) 464-8500 Toll-free number: (888) 647-2388
Fax: (518) 464-8777
Annette Jeffes, Assistant VP for Enrollment Management, Admissions, Excelsior College, 7 Columbia Circle, Albany, NY 12203-5159

Fashion Institute of Technology

New York, New York
www.fitnyc.edu **CB code: 2257**

- Public 4-year visual arts and business college
- Commuter campus in very large city
- 7,706 degree-seeking undergraduates: 12% part-time, 86% women, 6% African American, 9% Asian American, 11% Hispanic American, 11% international
- 207 degree-seeking graduate students
- 39% of applicants admitted
- Application essay required

General. Founded in 1944. Regionally accredited. SUNY institution. Specialized 2-year and 4-year programs provide professional preparation for fashion and design industries. **Degrees:** 1,196 bachelor's, 1,707 associate awarded; master's offered. **Calendar:** Semester, extensive summer session. **Full-time faculty:** 244 total. **Part-time faculty:** 745 total. **Class size:** 35% < 20, 65% 20-39. **Special facilities:** Textile and costume collection, fragrance laboratory, computer-aided design, textile, knitting, communications facility.

Freshman class profile. 4,330 applied, 1,690 admitted, 1,122 enrolled.

Return as sophomores:	85%	**Live on campus:**	67%
Out-of-state:	38%	**International:**	6%

Basis for selection. Rank in class, portfolio, essay, community service, work experience, awards and honors considered. Portfolio required for art and design.

High school preparation. College-preparatory program recommended. College preparatory program recommended.

2008-2009 Annual costs. Tuition/fees: $3,854; $10,682 out-of-state. Room/board: $10,440. Books/supplies: $1,600. Personal expenses: $1,500.

2008-2009 Financial aid. All financial aid based on need.

Application procedures. Admission: Priority date 1/1; deadline 2/1 (receipt date). $40 fee. Admission notification 4/15. Admission notification on a rolling basis. Must reply by 5/1. No transfers can apply under early action. **Financial aid:** Priority date 2/1; no closing date. FAFSA, institutional form required. Applicants notified on a rolling basis starting 4/15; must reply within 2 week(s) of notification.

Academics. Special study options: Distance learning, exchange student, honors, internships, study abroad. One-year programs, evening/weekend programs. **Credit/placement by examination:** AP, CLEP, IB, SAT, ACT, institutional tests. See FIT's website for transfer credit policies. **Support services:** Learning center, pre-admission summer program, remedial instruction, study skills assistance, tutoring, writing center.

Majors. Business: Fashion, international marketing, market research, special products marketing. **Communications:** Advertising. **Communications technology:** Animation/special effects. **Family/consumer sciences:** Clothing/textiles, textile manufacture. **Visual/performing arts:** Arts management, commercial photography, commercial/advertising art, fashion design, graphic design, illustration, industrial design, interior design, studio arts.

Most popular majors. Business/marketing 37%, communications/journalism 14%, visual/performing arts 42%.

Computing on campus. 1,500 workstations in dormitories, library, computer center, student center. Dormitories wired for high-speed internet access and linked to campus network. Commuter students can connect to campus network. Online course registration, helpline, repair service, student web hosting, wireless network available.

Student life. Freshman orientation: Mandatory. Preregistration for classes offered. **Housing:** Coed dorms, single-sex dorms, apartments, wellness housing available. **Activities:** Student newspaper, more than 60 groups and organizations available.

Athletics. NJCAA. **Intercollegiate:** Basketball, cross-country, swimming, tennis, volleyball W. **Intramural:** Bowling. **Team name:** Tigers.

Student services. Adult student services, alcohol/substance abuse counseling, chaplain/spiritual director, career counseling, services for economically disadvantaged, student employment services, financial aid counseling, health services, personal counseling, placement for graduates, veterans' counselor. **Physically disabled:** Services for visually, speech, hearing impaired.

Contact. E-mail: fitinfo@fitnyc.edu
Phone: (212) 217-3760
Dolores Lombardi, Director of Admissions, Fashion Institute of Technology, Seventh Avenue at 27th Street, New York, NY 10001-5992

Five Towns College

Dix Hills, New York
www.ftc.edu **CB code: 3142**

- For-profit 4-year music and liberal arts college
- Commuter campus in large town
- 1,117 degree-seeking undergraduates: 19% African American, 1% Asian American, 12% Hispanic American, 2% international
- 46 graduate students
- SAT or ACT with writing, application essay, interview required

General. Founded in 1972. Regionally accredited. **Degrees:** 178 bachelor's, 7 associate awarded; master's, doctoral offered. **Location:** 40 miles from New York City. **Calendar:** Semester, limited summer session. **Full-time faculty:** 33 total. **Part-time faculty:** 96 total. **Class size:** 51% < 20, 43% 20-39, 6% 40-49, less than 1% 50-99. **Special facilities:** 24-, 48- and 72-track recording studios with ProTools and 5.1 surround sound, Korg MIDI technology studio, professional film/video arts studio and editing labs, theater technology lab.

Freshman class profile.

Mid 50% test scores		ACT composite:	17-19
SAT critical reading:	400-500	Out-of-state:	9%
SAT math:	370-510	Live on campus:	20%
SAT writing:	400-490		

Basis for selection. Minimum 2.5 GPA required. Applicants for music and theater programs must pass audition and demonstrate competency in music, math, and English. SAT/ACT recommended but not required for transfer students. **Learning Disabled:** Provide recent copy of individualized educational program and psychological report.

High school preparation. 18 units recommended. Recommended units include English 4, mathematics 3, social studies 3, science 2 and foreign language 2. Music harmony and other applied music classes recommended for music students.

2008-2009 Annual costs. Tuition/fees: $17,800. Room/board: $11,750. Books/supplies: $1,200. Personal expenses: $3,200.

2008-2009 Financial aid. Need-based: 200 full-time freshmen applied for aid; 172 were judged to have need; 172 of these received aid. Average need met was 48%. Average scholarship/grant was $6,500; average loan $3,500. 62% of total undergraduate aid awarded as scholarships/grants, 38% as loans/jobs. **Non-need-based:** Awarded to 500 full-time undergraduates, including 125 freshmen. Scholarships awarded for academics, music/drama.

Application procedures. Admission: No deadline. $35 fee, may be waived for applicants with need. Admission notification on a rolling basis beginning on or about 11/1. **Financial aid:** Priority date 3/31; no closing date. FAFSA, institutional form required. Applicants notified on a rolling basis; must reply within 4 week(s) of notification.

Academics. Number of credit hours required for students in major field of study varies by program. **Special study options:** Combined bachelor's/graduate degree, distance learning, dual enrollment of high school students, independent study, internships, liberal arts/career combination, teacher certification program. **Credit/placement by examination:** AP, CLEP, institutional tests. **Support services:** Learning center, pre-admission summer program, reduced course load, remedial instruction, tutoring.

Majors. Business: Business admin. **Communications:** General, broadcast journalism, journalism, media studies, radio/tv. **Communications technology:** Recording arts. **Education:** Elementary, music. **Visual/performing arts:** Acting, cinematography, dramatic, film/cinema, jazz, music performance, music theory/composition, piano/organ, stringed instruments, voice/opera.

Most popular majors. Business/marketing 59%, education 8%, visual/performing arts 29%.

Computing on campus. 84 workstations in library, computer center, student center. Dormitories wired for high-speed internet access and linked to campus network. Helpline, repair service available.

Student life. Freshman orientation: Mandatory. **Housing:** Coed dorms, wellness housing available. $250 deposit. **Activities:** Bands, choral groups, dance, drama, film society, music ensembles, musical theater, radio station, student government, student newspaper.

Student services. Alcohol/substance abuse counseling, career counseling, services for economically disadvantaged, student employment services, financial aid counseling, health services, personal counseling, placement for graduates. **Learning disabled:** Comprehensive services available.

Contact. E-mail: admissions@ftc.edu
Phone: (631) 656-2110 Fax: (631) 656-2172
Jerry Cohen, Dean of Enrollment Services, Five Towns College, 305 North Service Road, Dix Hills, NY 11746-6055

Fordham University

Bronx, New York — **CB member**
www.fordham.edu — **CB code: 2259**

- Private 4-year university affiliated with Roman Catholic Church
- Residential campus in very large city
- 7,882 degree-seeking undergraduates: 7% part-time, 55% women, 5% African American, 7% Asian American, 13% Hispanic American, 2% international
- 6,240 degree-seeking graduate students
- 47% of applicants admitted
- SAT or ACT (ACT writing optional), application essay required

General. Founded in 1841. Regionally accredited. Rose Hill campus in Bronx, Lincoln Center campus in Manhattan. **Degrees:** 1,865 bachelor's awarded; master's, doctoral, first professional offered. **ROTC:** Army, Naval, Air Force. **Calendar:** Semester, extensive summer session. **Full-time faculty:** 667 total; 96% have terminal degrees, 16% minority, 40% women. **Part-time faculty:** 736 total; 46% have terminal degrees, 13% minority, 47% women. **Class size:** 49% < 20, 48% 20-39, 1% 40-49, less than 1% 50-99, less than 1% >100. **Special facilities:** Environmental center in Armonk, seismic station, Fordham Hispanic Research, Third Age Center addressing issues of older population.

Freshman class profile. 23,892 applied, 11,172 admitted, 1,904 enrolled.

Mid 50% test scores		GPA 3.0-3.49:	31%
SAT critical reading:	560-660	GPA 2.0-2.99:	7%
SAT math:	570-660	Rank in top quarter:	77%
SAT writing:	570-670	Rank in top tenth:	42%
ACT composite:	25-29	Out-of-state:	50%
GPA 3.75 or higher:	35%	Live on campus:	73%
GPA 3.50-3.74:	26%	International:	3%

Basis for selection. School achievement record most important followed by test scores, class rank, extracurricular activities, recommendations, essay, personal characteristics. Special consideration given to children of alumni. SAT Subject Tests recommended. Audition required for dance and theater programs.

High school preparation. College-preparatory program required. 22 units required; 25 recommended. Required and recommended units include English 4, mathematics 3-4, social studies 2, history 2, science 3-4, foreign language 2-3 and academic electives 6.

2008-2009 Annual costs. Tuition/fees: $35,257. Room/board: $12,980. Books/supplies: $840. Personal expenses: $1,540.

2007-2008 Financial aid. Non-need-based: Scholarships awarded for academics, athletics, ROTC.

Application procedures. Admission: Closing date 2/1 (postmark date). $50 fee, may be waived for applicants with need. Admission notification 4/1. Must reply by May 1 or within 2 week(s) if notified thereafter. **Financial aid:** Closing date 2/1. FAFSA, CSS PROFILE required. Applicants notified by 3/31; must reply by 5/1 or within 2 week(s) of notification.

Academics. Special study options: Combined bachelor's/graduate degree, distance learning, double major, ESL, exchange student, honors, independent study, internships, student-designed major, study abroad, teacher certification program, United Nations semester. Global Program in International Business. **Credit/placement by examination:** AP, CLEP, IB, institutional tests. 32 credit hours maximum toward bachelor's degree. Credit for CLEP examination only offered for liberal studies, adult continuing education school. **Support services:** Pre-admission summer program, tutoring, writing center.

Majors. Area/ethnic studies: African, African-American, American, Latin American, Near/Middle Eastern, Russian/Slavic, women's. **Biology:** General. **Business:** General, accounting, business admin, finance, international, management information systems, managerial economics, market research. **Communications:** General. **Computer sciences:** General. **Foreign languages:** Ancient Greek, classics, comparative lit, French, German, Italian, Latin, modern Greek, Russian, Spanish. **Health:** Predental, premedicine, prepharmacy, preveterinary. **History:** General. **Interdisciplinary:** Intercultural. **Legal studies:** Prelaw. **Math:** General. **Philosophy/religion:** Philosophy, religion. **Physical sciences:** Chemistry, physics. **Protective services:** Criminal justice. **Psychology:** General. **Public administration:** General, social work. **Social sciences:** Anthropology, economics, political science, sociology, urban studies. **Visual/performing arts:** Art, art history/conservation, dance, dramatic, film/cinema, photography, studio arts, theater design.

Most popular majors. Business/marketing 27%, communications/journalism 13%, English 7%, psychology 7%, social sciences 20%, visual/performing arts 6%.

Computing on campus. 900 workstations in dormitories, library, computer center. Dormitories wired for high-speed internet access and linked to campus network. Commuter students can connect to campus network. Online course registration, online library, helpline, repair service, wireless network available.

Student life. Freshman orientation: Mandatory, $110 fee. Comprehensive academic and social orientation 3 days prior to start of classes. **Housing:** Guaranteed on-campus for all undergraduates. Coed dorms, apartments available. $200 partly refundable deposit, deadline 5/1. **Activities:** Bands, campus ministries, choral groups, dance, drama, film society, international student organizations, literary magazine, music ensembles, musical theater, radio station, student government, student newspaper, symphony orchestra, TV station, Rose Hill Ambassadors, international black student union, Progressive Students for Justice, Circle-K, commuter student association, Fordham University Emerging Leaders, Fordham University emergency medical services, weekend activities committee.

Athletics. NCAA. **Intercollegiate:** Baseball M, basketball, cross-country, diving, football (tackle) M, golf M, rowing (crew) W, soccer, softball W, squash M, swimming, tennis, track and field, volleyball W, water polo M. **Intramural:** Basketball, football (tackle), golf W, handball, racquetball, soccer, softball, swimming, tennis, triathlon, volleyball. **Team name:** Rams.

Student services. Adult student services, alcohol/substance abuse counseling, chaplain/spiritual director, career counseling, student employment services, financial aid counseling, health services, personal counseling, placement for graduates. **Physically disabled:** Services for visually, hearing impaired.

Contact. E-mail: enroll@fordham.edu
Phone: (718) 817-4000 Toll-free number: (800) 367-3426
Fax: (718) 367-9404
Peter Farrell, Director of Admissions, Fordham University, East 441 Fordham Road, Bronx, NY 10458

Globe Institute of Technology

New York, New York
www.globe.edu **CB code: 3333**

- For-profit 4-year university and business college
- Commuter campus in very large city

General. Regionally accredited. **Calendar:** Semester.

Annual costs/financial aid. Tuition/fees (2008-2009): $11,040. Room/board: $5,000. Books/supplies: $800. Need-based financial aid available to full-time and part-time students.

Contact. Phone: (212) 349-4330
Admission Director, 291 Broadway, New York, NY 10007

Hamilton College

Clinton, New York **CB member**
www.hamilton.edu **CB code: 2286**

- Private 4-year liberal arts college
- Residential campus in rural community
- 1,834 degree-seeking undergraduates: 52% women, 4% African American, 7% Asian American, 5% Hispanic American, 1% Native American, 5% international
- 28% of applicants admitted
- SAT and SAT Subject Tests or ACT (ACT writing optional), application essay required
- 91% graduate within 6 years

General. Founded in 1812. Regionally accredited. **Degrees:** 442 bachelor's awarded. **ROTC:** Army, Air Force. **Location:** 10 miles from Utica, 50 miles from Syracuse. **Calendar:** Semester. **Full-time faculty:** 174 total; 97% have terminal degrees, 18% minority, 41% women. **Part-time faculty:** 42 total; 45% have terminal degrees, 17% minority, 64% women. **Class size:** 75% < 20, 22% 20-39, 2% 40-49, less than 1% 50-99, less than 1% >100. **Special facilities:** Observatory, nature preserve, electron microscope.

Freshman class profile. 5,073 applied, 1,424 admitted, 462 enrolled.

Mid 50% test scores		**Return as sophomores:**	96%
SAT critical reading:	650-730	**Out-of-state:**	70%
SAT math:	650-720	**Live on campus:**	100%
Rank in top quarter:	95%	**International:**	5%
Rank in top tenth:	76%		

Basis for selection. School achievement record, rank in high school class, school and community activities, application essay, graded example of expository writing, recommendations important. Test scores and interview also considered. Some preference given children of alumni. Special consideration given students from minority groups, disadvantaged backgrounds, and certain geographic regions. Students can fulfill test requirements with SAT or ACT or 3 SAT Subject Tests or 3 AP exams or any combination of these. Interview recommended for all; audition tape recommended for music applicants; audition DVD recommended for theater and dance applicants; portfolio recommended for studio art applicants.

High school preparation. College-preparatory program recommended. 16 units recommended. Recommended units include English 4, mathematics 3, social studies 3, science 3 and foreign language 3.

2008-2009 Annual costs. Tuition/fees: $38,600. Room/board: $9,810. Books/supplies: $1,300. Personal expenses: $1,000.

2008-2009 Financial aid. All financial aid based on need. 241 full-time freshmen applied for aid; 189 were judged to have need; 189 of these received aid. Average need met was 100%. Average scholarship/grant was $28,647; average loan $2,714. 88% of total undergraduate aid awarded as scholarships/grants, 12% as loans/jobs. **Additional information:** Will meet demonstrated need of all aided applicants. Effective with the 2008-2009 academic year, incoming students were no longer awarded merit scholarships. Upperclass students that had been awarded merit scholarships previously will continue to be awarded such until their graduation.

Application procedures. Admission: Closing date 1/1 (postmark date). $75 fee, may be waived for applicants with need, free for online applicants. Admission notification 4/1. Must reply by 5/1. **Financial aid:** Closing date 2/8. FAFSA, institutional form, CSS PROFILE required. Applicants notified by 4/1; must reply by 5/1.

Academics. Sophomores may attain guaranteed early admission to one of 6 participating medical schools. Students must complete senior program or project in their concentration. May participate in Williams College Mystic Seaport Program. **Special study options:** Accelerated study, combined bachelor's/graduate degree, cross-registration, double major, ESL, independent study, internships, New York semester, student-designed major, study abroad, Washington semester. 3-2 program in engineering with Columbia University, Rensselaer Polytechnic Institute, Washington University (St. Louis); 3-3 program in law at Columbia University. **Credit/placement by examination:** AP, CLEP, IB, institutional tests. **Support services:** Learning center, pre-admission summer program, reduced course load, study skills assistance, tutoring, writing center.

Majors. Area/ethnic studies: African-American, American, Asian, Russian/Slavic, women's. **Biology:** General, biochemistry, molecular. **Communications:** General. **Computer sciences:** General. **Conservation:** Environmental studies. **Foreign languages:** General, ancient Greek, Chinese, classics, comparative lit, French, German, Japanese, Latin, Russian, Spanish. **History:** General. **Interdisciplinary:** Neuroscience. **Liberal arts:** Arts/sciences. **Math:** General. **Philosophy/religion:** Philosophy, religion. **Physical sciences:** Chemical physics, chemistry, geology, physics. **Psychology:** General. **Public administration:** Policy analysis. **Social sciences:** Anthropology, archaeology, economics, international relations, political science, sociology. **Visual/performing arts:** Art history/conservation, dance, dramatic, studio arts.

Most popular majors. English 7%, foreign language 12%, mathematics 8%, physical sciences 9%, social sciences 28%, visual/performing arts 8%.

Computing on campus. 625 workstations in library, computer center, student center. Dormitories wired for high-speed internet access and linked to campus network. Commuter students can connect to campus network. Online course registration, online library, helpline, repair service, student web hosting, wireless network available.

Student life. Freshman orientation: Mandatory. One week prior to start of classes. **Policies:** Honor code covers all examinations, papers, research, and use of library. **Housing:** Guaranteed on-campus for all undergraduates. Coed dorms, special housing for disabled, apartments, wellness housing available. Special interest housing available including language houses and international house, quiet areas, substance-free areas. **Activities:** Bands, campus ministries, choral groups, dance, drama, film society, international student organizations, literary magazine, music ensembles, Model UN, musical theater, radio station, student government, student newspaper, symphony orchestra, TV station, Newman Club, Jewish student organization, Black and Latin student union, women's center, La Vanguardia, Amnesty International, Muslim student organization, Asian cultural society, West Indian and African association.

Athletics. NCAA. **Intercollegiate:** Baseball M, basketball, cross-country, diving, field hockey W, football (tackle) M, golf M, ice hockey, lacrosse, rowing (crew), soccer, softball W, squash, swimming, tennis, track and field, volleyball W. **Intramural:** Badminton, basketball, cross-country, diving, fencing W, football (non-tackle), football (tackle) M, golf, handball, ice hockey, lacrosse, racquetball, soccer, softball, squash, swimming, tennis, volleyball. **Team name:** Continentals.

Student services. Adult student services, alcohol/substance abuse counseling, chaplain/spiritual director, career counseling, student employment services, financial aid counseling, health services, minority student services, on-campus daycare, personal counseling, placement for graduates, women's services. **Physically disabled:** Services for visually, speech, hearing impaired.

Contact. E-mail: admission@hamilton.edu
Phone: (315) 859-4421 Toll-free number: (800) 843-2655
Fax: (315) 859-4457
Monica Inzer, Dean of Admissions and Financial Aid, Hamilton College, 198 College Hill Road, Clinton, NY 13323-1293

Hartwick College

Oneonta, New York **CB member**
www.hartwick.edu **CB code: 2288**

- Private 4-year liberal arts college
- Residential campus in large town
- 1,472 degree-seeking undergraduates: 3% part-time, 57% women, 4% African American, 2% Asian American, 4% Hispanic American, 4% international
- 83% of applicants admitted
- Application essay required
- 57% graduate within 6 years; 23% enter graduate study

General. Founded in 1797. Regionally accredited. Additional campus for recreation, research, student residences. **Degrees:** 298 bachelor's awarded. **Location:** 68 miles from Binghamton, 75 miles from Albany. **Calendar:** 4-1-4, limited summer session. **Full-time faculty:** 111 total; 96% have terminal degrees, 8% minority, 40% women. **Part-time faculty:** 55 total; 47% women. **Class size:** 67% < 20, 31% 20-39, 1% 40-49, less than 1% 50-99. **Special facilities:** Environmental field station, museum, Native American artifact and library collections, tissue culture laboratory, electron microscope, 16-inch telescope and observatory, nuclear magnetic resonance spectrometer, fine and performing arts center.

Freshman class profile. 2,532 applied, 2,101 admitted, 446 enrolled.

Mid 50% test scores		**GPA 2.0-2.99:**	39%
SAT critical reading:	490-610	**Rank in top quarter:**	45%
SAT math:	510-610	**Rank in top tenth:**	18%
ACT composite:	21-27	**Return as sophomores:**	70%
GPA 3.75 or higher:	10%	**Out-of-state:**	34%
GPA 3.50-3.74:	21%	**Live on campus:**	97%
GPA 3.0-3.49:	28%	**International:**	3%

Basis for selection. School achievement record, class rank, personal qualities, extracurricular activities, and recommendations considered. Test scores optional except for students applying to nursing program. SAT/ACT score submission not required for admission except for Nursing majors. Interview recommended for all; audition required for music program; portfolio recommended for art program. **Homeschooled:** Transcript of courses and grades, letter of recommendation (nonparent) required. Must meet all stated application requirements and submit SAT or ACT test score. At least 3 SAT Subject Tests strongly recommended. Transcripts should be submitted with course description and/or syllabi.

High school preparation. 19 units recommended. Recommended units include English 4, mathematics 3, social studies 2, history 2, science 3 (laboratory 2) and foreign language 3.

2008-2009 Annual costs. Tuition/fees: $31,900. Room/board: $8,685. Books/supplies: $700. Personal expenses: $400.

2007-2008 Financial aid. Need-based: 412 full-time freshmen applied for aid; 367 were judged to have need; 367 of these received aid. Average need met was 75%. Average scholarship/grant was $18,207; average loan $5,200. 64% of total undergraduate aid awarded as scholarships/grants, 36% as loans/jobs. **Non-need-based:** Awarded to 466 full-time undergraduates, including 162 freshmen. Scholarships awarded for academics, alumni affiliation, athletics, leadership, state residency.

Application procedures. Admission: Closing date 2/15 (postmark date). $35 fee, may be waived for applicants with need, free for online applicants. Admission notification 3/15. Must reply by 5/1. **Financial aid:** Priority date 2/15; no closing date. FAFSA required. Applicants notified by 3/15; must reply within 2 week(s) of notification.

Academics. Curriculum includes first-year seminar, core requirements and contemporary issues seminar. Senior thesis required. First-year students provided with notebook-sized personal computer. **Special study options:** Accelerated study, combined bachelor's/graduate degree, cross-registration, double major, exchange student, honors, independent study, internships, liberal arts/career combination, semester at sea, student-designed major, study abroad, teacher certification program, urban semester, Washington semester. Off-campus January term in Egypt, England, France, Ghana, Greece, South Africa; Philadelphia Urban Semester; Boston Semester; Outward Bound, NOLS programs; cooperative program in law with Albany Law School; 3-2 engineering with Clarkson University, Columbia University. **Credit/placement by examination:** AP, CLEP, IB, institutional tests. **Support services:** Reduced course load, study skills assistance, tutoring, writing center.

Majors. Biology: General, biochemistry. **Business:** Accounting, business admin. **Computer sciences:** General, information systems. **Education:** Music. **Foreign languages:** French, German, Spanish. **Health:** Clinical lab science, nursing (RN). **History:** General. **Liberal arts:** Arts/sciences. **Math:** General. **Philosophy/religion:** Philosophy, religion. **Physical sciences:** Chemistry, geology, physics. **Psychology:** General. **Social sciences:** Anthropology, economics, political science, sociology. **Visual/performing arts:** Art, art history/conservation, dramatic.

Most popular majors. Biology 7%, business/marketing 18%, English 6%, health sciences 9%, history 6%, psychology 6%, social sciences 22%, visual/performing arts 9%.

Computing on campus. PC or laptop required. 56 workstations in library, computer center. Dormitories wired for high-speed internet access and linked to campus network. Commuter students can connect to campus network. Online library, helpline, repair service, student web hosting, wireless network available.

Student life. Freshman orientation: Mandatory, $300 fee. Preregistration for classes offered. Summer registration/parent orientation and 4-day pre-semester in-residence program. **Housing:** Guaranteed on-campus for freshmen. Coed dorms, single-sex dorms, special housing for disabled, apartments, fraternity/sorority housing, wellness housing available. Housing at environmental campus available. **Activities:** Bands, choral groups, dance, drama, literary magazine, music ensembles, musical theater, radio station, student government, student newspaper, over 60 academic and social organizations available.

Athletics. NCAA. **Intercollegiate:** Basketball, cheerleading M, cross-country, diving, equestrian W, field hockey W, football (tackle) M, lacrosse, soccer, swimming, tennis, volleyball W, water polo W. **Intramural:** Basketball, cross-country, equestrian, football (tackle), racquetball, soccer, squash, swimming, table tennis, tennis, volleyball, water polo. **Team name:** Hawks.

Student services. Alcohol/substance abuse counseling, chaplain/spiritual director, career counseling, student employment services, financial aid counseling, health services, personal counseling, placement for graduates. **Physically disabled:** Services for visually, hearing impaired.

Contact. E-mail: admissions@hartwick.edu
Phone: (607) 431-4150 Toll-free number: (888) 427-8942
Fax: (607) 431-4154
Jacqueline Gregory, Director of Admissions, Hartwick College, Box 4022, Oneonta, NY 13820-4022

Hilbert College

Hamburg, New York
www.hilbert.edu **CB code: 2334**

- Private 4-year liberal arts college affiliated with Roman Catholic Church
- Commuter campus in large town
- 957 degree-seeking undergraduates: 26% part-time, 61% women, 8% African American, 3% Hispanic American, 1% Native American
- 75% of applicants admitted
- 49% graduate within 6 years

General. Founded in 1957. Regionally accredited. Affiliated with Franciscan Sisters of St. Joseph. Legal assistant program approved by American Bar Association. **Degrees:** 205 bachelor's, 23 associate awarded. **ROTC:** Army. **Location:** 10 miles from Buffalo. **Calendar:** Semester, limited summer session. **Full-time faculty:** 46 total; 46% have terminal degrees, 4% minority, 50% women. **Part-time faculty:** 80 total; 19% have terminal degrees, 1% minority, 38% women. **Class size:** 64% < 20, 36% 20-39. **Special facilities:** Comprehensive law library.

Freshman class profile. 955 applied, 720 admitted, 223 enrolled.

Mid 50% test scores		**GPA 2.0-2.99:**	54%
SAT critical reading:	380-490	**Rank in top quarter:**	19%
SAT math:	400-500	**Rank in top tenth:**	4%
ACT composite:	17-21	**End year in good standing:**	62%
GPA 3.75 or higher:	1%	**Return as sophomores:**	58%
GPA 3.50-3.74:	14%	**Out-of-state:**	2%
GPA 3.0-3.49:	27%	**Live on campus:**	27%

Basis for selection. School achievement record and course selection important. Candidates must meet minimum academic criteria including high school GPA. SAT or ACT recommended. Essay, interview recommended.

Homeschooled: Transcript of courses and grades, state high school equivalency certificate required. **Learning Disabled:** Separate statement directly to academic services required.

High school preparation. 16 units required; 21 recommended. Required and recommended units include English 4, mathematics 3-4, social studies 3-4, science 2-3 (laboratory 1-2) and foreign language 1-2.

2008-2009 Annual costs. Tuition/fees: $17,350. Room/board: $6,950. Books/supplies: $700. Personal expenses: $800.

2007-2008 Financial aid. Need-based: 222 full-time freshmen applied for aid; 203 were judged to have need; 202 of these received aid. Average need met was 69%. Average scholarship/grant was $7,563; average loan $3,773. 51% of total undergraduate aid awarded as scholarships/grants, 49% as loans/jobs. **Non-need-based:** Awarded to 138 full-time undergraduates, including 32 freshmen. Scholarships awarded for academics, job skills, leadership, minority status, state residency.

Application procedures. Admission: Priority date 6/30; deadline 9/1 (receipt date). $20 fee, may be waived for applicants with need. Admission notification on a rolling basis beginning on or about 6/30. **Financial aid:** Priority date 3/1; no closing date. FAFSA required. Applicants notified on a rolling basis starting 3/15; must reply within 2 week(s) of notification.

Academics. Special study options: Combined bachelor's/graduate degree, cooperative education, cross-registration, distance learning, dual enrollment of high school students, honors, independent study, internships, study abroad, Washington semester. Member of Western New York consortium. **Credit/placement by examination:** AP, CLEP, IB, SAT, institutional tests. 18 credit hours maximum toward associate degree, 32 toward bachelor's. **Support services:** Learning center, reduced course load, study skills assistance, tutoring, writing center.

Majors. Business: Accounting, business admin. **Communications:** Digital media. **Communications technology:** Photo/film/video. **Health:** Health services. **Legal studies:** Paralegal. **Liberal arts:** Arts/sciences. **Protective services:** Criminal justice, forensics, police science. **Psychology:** General. **Public administration:** Human services. **Social sciences:** Political science.

Most popular majors. Business/marketing 28%, legal studies 10%, liberal arts 8%, psychology 6%, security/protective services 38%.

Computing on campus. 146 workstations in dormitories, library, computer center, student center. Dormitories wired for high-speed internet access. Online course registration, online library, helpline, wireless network available.

Student life. Freshman orientation: Mandatory, $25 fee. 1-day programs held in June, July or August. **Housing:** Guaranteed on-campus for all undergraduates. Coed dorms, apartments available. $50 nonrefundable deposit, deadline 8/1. **Activities:** Campus ministries, choral groups, drama, literary magazine, student government, student newspaper, SADD, Human Service Association, Psychology Club, Great Expectations, Criminal Justice Club, Students in Free Enterprise, Common Grounds, Economic Crime Investigation Club.

Athletics. NCAA. **Intercollegiate:** Baseball M, basketball, cross-country, golf, soccer, softball W, volleyball. **Intramural:** Basketball, football (non-tackle), soccer, softball, table tennis, volleyball. **Team name:** Hawks.

Student services. Adult student services, alcohol/substance abuse counseling, chaplain/spiritual director, career counseling, student employment services, financial aid counseling, minority student services, personal counseling, placement for graduates, veterans' counselor. **Physically disabled:** Services for visually, hearing impaired.

Contact. E-mail: admissions@hilbert.edu
Phone: (716) 649-7900 ext. 211 Toll-free number: (800) 649-8003
Fax: (716) 649-1152
Timothy Lee, Director of Admissions, Hilbert College, 5200 South Park Avenue, Hamburg, NY 14075-1597

Hobart and William Smith Colleges

Geneva, New York — **CB member**
www.hws.edu — **CB code: 2294**

- Private 4-year liberal arts college
- Residential campus in large town
- 2,069 degree-seeking undergraduates
- 54% of applicants admitted
- Application essay required

General. Founded in 1822. Regionally accredited. Hobart and William Smith are coordinate colleges. All classes coeducational with one faculty, one President, one Board of Trustees, and one campus, but with separate deans, student governments, and athletic departments. **Degrees:** 399 bachelor's awarded; master's offered. **Location:** 50 miles from Syracuse, 40 miles from Rochester. **Calendar:** Semester. **Full-time faculty:** 202 total. **Part-time faculty:** 19 total. **Class size:** 68% < 20, 29% 20-39, 2% 40-49, 2% 50-99. **Special facilities:** 70-foot research vessel, 100-acre nature preserve, Finger Lakes Institute.

Freshman class profile. 4,306 applied, 2,315 admitted, 546 enrolled.

Mid 50% test scores			
SAT critical reading:	550-660	GPA 3.0-3.49:	39%
SAT math:	560-660	GPA 2.0-2.99:	27%
SAT writing:	550-660	Rank in top quarter:	68%
ACT composite:	25-29	Rank in top tenth:	38%
GPA 3.75 or higher:	17%	Out-of-state:	61%
GPA 3.50-3.74:	17%	Live on campus:	100%

Basis for selection. High school record, school and community activities, recommendations, and test scores important. Interview and talent considered. Economically and educationally disadvantaged NY state residents may apply through Higher Education Opportunity Program. SAT or ACT recommended. Standardized tests only required for those applying for the Trustee or Blackwell scholarships, those who come from a high school without a traditionally graded transcript, or those for whom English is not a first language. Interview recommended for all. Candidates for arts scholars program must submit portfolio or audition on campus. **Homeschooled:** Interview required. Students without a traditional, graded transcript must submit standardized test scores.

High school preparation. 20 units required. Required and recommended units include English 4, mathematics 3, social studies 2-3, history 2, science 3 (laboratory 2), foreign language 2-3 and academic electives 2-4. Mathematics must include algebra, geometry, and trigonometry sequence.

2008-2009 Annual costs. Tuition/fees: $38,860. Room/board: $9,686. Books/supplies: $1,000. Personal expenses: $600.

2007-2008 Financial aid. Need-based: 78% of total undergraduate aid awarded as scholarships/grants, 22% as loans/jobs. **Non-need-based:** Scholarships awarded for academics, art, leadership, music/drama.

Application procedures. Admission: Closing date 2/1 (postmark date). $45 fee, may be waived for applicants with need, free for online applicants. Admission notification 4/1. Must reply by 5/1. **Financial aid:** Closing date 2/15. FAFSA, CSS PROFILE required. Applicants notified by 4/1; must reply by 5/1 or within 2 week(s) of notification.

Academics. All students must complete a major and a minor or a second major, 1 of which must be interdisciplinary. **Special study options:** Combined bachelor's/graduate degree, cross-registration, double major, ESL, exchange student, honors, independent study, internships, semester at sea, student-designed major, study abroad, teacher certification program, Washington semester. **Credit/placement by examination:** AP, CLEP, IB, institutional tests. Credit by examination counted toward degree limited to equivalent of 7 courses. **Support services:** Learning center, pre-admission summer program, reduced course load, study skills assistance, tutoring, writing center.

Majors. Architecture: Architecture. **Area/ethnic studies:** African, African-American, American, Asian, European, gay/lesbian, Hispanic-American/Latino/Chicano, Latin American, Russian/Slavic, women's. **Biology:** General, biochemistry. **Communications:** Media studies. **Computer sciences:** General, computer science. **Conservation:** Environmental studies. **Foreign languages:** Chinese, classics, comparative lit, French, Japanese, Latin, Russian, Spanish. **Health:** Predental, premedicine, preveterinary. **History:** General. **Interdisciplinary:** Math/computer science. **Math:** General. **Philosophy/religion:** Philosophy, religion. **Physical sciences:** Chemistry, geology, physics. **Psychology:** General. **Public administration:** Policy analysis. **Social sciences:** Anthropology, economics, international relations, political science, sociology, urban studies. **Visual/performing arts:** Art history/conservation, dance, dramatic, studio arts.

Computing on campus. 150 workstations in library, computer center. Dormitories wired for high-speed internet access and linked to campus network. Commuter students can connect to campus network. Online course registration, online library, helpline, repair service, student web hosting, wireless network available.

Student life. Freshman orientation: Mandatory. Preregistration for classes offered. 3-day program. **Housing:** Guaranteed on-campus for all undergraduates. Coed dorms, single-sex dorms, apartments, cooperative housing, fraternity/sorority housing, wellness housing available. Upperclassmen townhouses available. Extensive residential education program. **Activities:** Bands, choral groups, dance, drama, film society, literary magazine, music ensembles, musical theater, radio station, student government, student newspaper, symphony orchestra, service network, Literary Corps, international students club, denominational clubs, African-American student coalition, political educational network, Pan-African-Latin Organization, pride network, Big Brothers/Big Sisters, Latin American student organization.

Athletics. NCAA. **Intercollegiate:** Basketball, cross-country, diving W, field hockey W, football (tackle) M, golf, ice hockey M, lacrosse, rowing (crew), sailing, soccer, squash, swimming W, tennis. **Intramural:** Badminton, basketball, bowling, cross-country, diving M, equestrian, fencing, football (non-tackle), golf, ice hockey, lacrosse, racquetball, rugby, skiing, soccer, softball, squash, swimming, table tennis, tennis, track and field, volleyball, water polo. **Team name:** Statesmen (Hobart); Herons (William Smith).

Student services. Adult student services, alcohol/substance abuse counseling, chaplain/spiritual director, career counseling, services for economically disadvantaged, student employment services, financial aid counseling, health services, legal services, minority student services, personal counseling, placement for graduates, women's services. **Physically disabled:** Services for visually, speech, hearing impaired.

Contact. E-mail: admissions@hws.edu
Phone: (315) 781-3622 Toll-free number: (800) 852-2256
Fax: (315) 781-3914
John Young, Director of Admissions, Hobart and William Smith Colleges, 629 South Main Street, Geneva, NY 14456

Hofstra University

Hempstead, New York — **CB member**
www.hofstra.edu — **CB code: 2295**

- Private 4-year university
- Residential campus in large city
- 8,179 degree-seeking undergraduates: 7% part-time, 52% women, 9% African American, 5% Asian American, 8% Hispanic American, 1% international
- 3,834 degree-seeking graduate students
- 53% of applicants admitted
- Application essay required
- 55% graduate within 6 years; 29% enter graduate study

General. Founded in 1935. Regionally accredited. **Degrees:** 1,750 bachelor's awarded; master's, doctoral, first professional offered. **ROTC:** Army. **Location:** 25 miles from New York City. **Calendar:** 4-1-4, extensive summer session. **Full-time faculty:** 551 total; 90% have terminal degrees, 17% minority, 42% women. **Part-time faculty:** 634 total; 38% have terminal degrees, 8% minority, 48% women. **Class size:** 47% < 20, 46% 20-39, 3% 40-49, 4% 50-99, less than 1% >100. **Special facilities:** Financial trading room, comprehensive media production facility, converged newsroom learning center, linux beowolf cluster, digital language lab, technology, science and engineering labs, rooftop observatory, 7 theaters, assessment centers for child observation and counseling, child care institute, cultural center, museum, arboretum, bird sanctuary.

Freshman class profile. 20,071 applied, 10,646 admitted, 1,655 enrolled.

Mid 50% test scores		**Rank in top quarter:**	52%
SAT critical reading:	540-630	**Rank in top tenth:**	26%
SAT math:	550-640	**End year in good standing:**	90%
ACT composite:	23-27	**Return as sophomores:**	80%
GPA 3.75 or higher:	23%	**Out-of-state:**	49%
GPA 3.50-3.74:	15%	**Live on campus:**	79%
GPA 3.0-3.49:	34%	**International:**	1%
GPA 2.0-2.99:	28%		

Basis for selection. Secondary school record, standardized test scores (SAT or ACT, required for some), TOEFL scores for international applicants, personal essay and letters of recommendation most important. For some, interview is required. SAT Subject Tests recommended. No deadline (rolling) for SAT or ACT test scores. Standardized tests not required for admission to New Opportunities at Hofstra (NOAH), School of University Studies, Program for Academic Learning Skills (PALS) or International Applicants (TOEFL is required). Interview required of HEOP, School for University Studies and Program for Academic Learning Skills applicants. Audition recommended for music, theater programs; portfolio recommended for fine arts program. **Homeschooled:** Statement describing homeschool structure and mission, transcript of courses and grades, state high school equivalency certificate required. Must provide at least 2 recommendations, including 1 from primary instructor or person who has primary responsibility for assessing applicant's academic performance. School required to certify completion of secondary school for all enrolled students prior to graduation. **Learning Disabled:** Students may apply to the Program for Academic Learning Skills (PALS). PALS provides auxiliary aids and compensatory services to certified learning disabled students who have been accepted to the University through regular admissions. Application includes copy of psychological testing, WAISR or WISC. In addition an achievement test, full psychoeducational report with diagnostic statement, letter from guidance counselor regarding current special education placement, and WAIS III must also be provided. Testing documentation must be dated within 24 months of application.

High school preparation. College-preparatory program required. 16 units required. Required and recommended units include English 4, mathematics 3-4, social studies 3-4, science 3-4 (laboratory 1-2) and foreign language 2-3. Social studies includes history; 4 math, 1 chemistry, and 1 physics required for engineering.

2008-2009 Annual costs. Tuition/fees: $28,630. Room/board: $10,825. Books/supplies: $1,000. Personal expenses: $1,175.

2007-2008 Financial aid. Need-based: 1,386 full-time freshmen applied for aid; 1,053 were judged to have need; 1,041 of these received aid. Average need met was 61%. Average scholarship/grant was $11,185; average loan $3,575. 44% of total undergraduate aid awarded as scholarships/grants, 56% as loans/jobs. **Non-need-based:** Awarded to 1,834 full-time undergraduates, including 534 freshmen. Scholarships awarded for academics, art, athletics, leadership, music/drama, ROTC, state residency.

Application procedures. Admission: No deadline. $70 fee, may be waived for applicants with need. Admission notification on a rolling basis beginning on or about 2/1. Must reply by May 1 or within 2 week(s) if notified thereafter. **Financial aid:** Priority date 2/15; no closing date. FAFSA required. Applicants notified on a rolling basis starting 3/1; must reply by 5/1 or within 2 week(s) of notification.

Academics. Special study options: Accelerated study, combined bachelor's/graduate degree, cross-registration, distance learning, double major, dual enrollment of high school students, ESL, external degree, honors, independent study, internships, liberal arts/career combination, student-designed major, study abroad, teacher certification program, Washington semester. **Credit/placement by examination:** AP, CLEP, IB, institutional tests. 30 credit hours maximum toward bachelor's degree. **Support services:** Learning center, pre-admission summer program, reduced course load, study skills assistance, tutoring, writing center.

Honors college/program. Students invited to join when applying for admission. Typically only top 10% of admits invited.

Majors. Area/ethnic studies: African, American, Asian, Caribbean, Hispanic-American/Latino/Chicano, Latin American, women's. **Biology:** General, biochemistry. **Business:** General, accounting, actuarial science, business admin, entrepreneurial studies, finance, international, labor studies, management information systems, managerial economics, marketing. **Communications:** General, broadcast journalism, journalism, media studies, public relations, radio/tv. **Computer sciences:** Computer science. **Conservation:** Environmental studies. **Education:** Art, biology, business, chemistry, early childhood, elementary, English, foreign languages, French, German, health, mathematics, multi-level teacher, music, physical, physics, science, secondary, social studies, Spanish. **Engineering:** Biomedical, civil, computer, electrical, environmental, industrial, manufacturing, mechanical, science. **Foreign languages:** Chinese, classics, comparative lit, French, German, Hebrew, Italian, Latin, linguistics, Russian, Spanish. **Health:** Athletic training, audiology/speech pathology, community health, health services, physician assistant, predental, premedicine, preveterinary. **History:** General. **Interdisciplinary:** Math/computer science, natural sciences. **Legal studies:** Prelaw. **Liberal arts:** Arts/sciences, humanities. **Math:** General, applied. **Philosophy/religion:** Judaic, philosophy, religion. **Physical sciences:** Chemistry, geology, physics. **Protective services:** Forensics. **Psychology:** General. **Social sciences:** General, anthropology, econometrics, economics, geography, political science, sociology. **Visual/performing arts:** Acting, art history/conservation, ceramics, dance, directing/producing, dramatic, jazz, metal/jewelry, music history, music management, music performance, music theory/composition, painting, photography, studio arts.

Most popular majors. Business/marketing 33%, communications/journalism 13%, education 8%, English 6%, psychology 8%, social sciences 7%.

Computing on campus. 1,628 workstations in dormitories, library, computer center. Dormitories wired for high-speed internet access and linked to campus network. Commuter students can connect to campus network. Online course registration, online library, helpline, repair service, student web hosting, wireless network available.

Student life. Freshman orientation: Mandatory, $200 fee. Preregistration for classes offered. Several orientation programs. Summer orientation is a 3-day/2-night program in which new students live on campus and begin preparation for the fall semester. The program extends into the entire first year beginning with the full array of programs five days prior to the start of classes and then throughout the year with programs and events designed to acclimate students to student life. **Housing:** Guaranteed on-campus for freshmen. Coed dorms, single-sex dorms, special housing for disabled, apartments available. $300 nonrefundable deposit, deadline 5/1. Honors housing, living-learning community, quiet floors available. **Activities:** Bands, campus ministries, choral groups, dance, drama, film society, international student organizations, literary magazine, music ensembles, musical theater, opera, radio station, student government, student newspaper, symphony orchestra, TV station, Hillel, Muslim student association, African People's Organization, Hofstra Organization of Latin Americans, College Republicans, Hofstra Democrats, Women of Action, Progressive Students Union, Entertainment Unlimited.

Athletics. NCAA. **Intercollegiate:** Baseball M, basketball, cross-country, field hockey W, football (tackle) M, golf, lacrosse, soccer, softball W, tennis, volleyball W, wrestling M. **Intramural:** Badminton, basketball, football (non-tackle) M, soccer, softball, table tennis, tennis, volleyball. **Team name:** Pride.

Student services. Adult student services, alcohol/substance abuse counseling, chaplain/spiritual director, career counseling, student employment services, financial aid counseling, health services, minority student services, on-campus daycare, personal counseling, placement for graduates, veterans' counselor. **Physically disabled:** Services for visually, speech, hearing impaired. **Learning disabled:** Comprehensive services available.

Contact. E-mail: admission@hofstra.edu
Phone: (516) 463-6700 Toll-free number: (800) 463-7872
Fax: (516) 463-5100
Jessica Eads, Vice President for Enrollment & Dean of Admission and Financial Aid, Hofstra University, Admissions Center, 100 Hofstra University, Hempstead, NY 11549

Holy Trinity Orthodox Seminary
Jordanville, New York
www.hts.edu **CB code: 2298**

- Private 5-year seminary college for men affiliated with Russian Orthodox Church
- Residential campus in rural community
- 30 degree-seeking undergraduates
- Application essay required

General. Founded in 1948. Regionally accredited. **Degrees:** 7 bachelor's awarded. **Location:** 20 miles from Utica. **Calendar:** Semester, limited summer session. **Full-time faculty:** 6 total; 17% have terminal degrees, 17% women. **Part-time faculty:** 13 total; 8% have terminal degrees, 8% women. **Class size:** 100% < 20. **Special facilities:** Museum of Russian history, archives, icon painting studio.

Freshman class profile.

Out-of-state:	50%	**Live on campus:**	100%

Basis for selection. Orthodoxy/Orthodox baptism, knowledge of Russian, entrance exam required. Recommendation from spiritual father or parish priest important. **Homeschooled:** Letter of recommendation (nonparent) required.

2009-2010 Annual costs. Tuition/fees (projected): $3,000. Room/board: $2,500. Books/supplies: $200.

Financial aid. Additional information: Work-study program can reasonably pay for room and board over the course of the academic year.

Application procedures. Admission: Closing date 5/1 (postmark date). No application fee.

Academics. Special study options: Distance learning, ESL. **Credit/placement by examination:** CLEP, institutional tests. **Support services:** Remedial instruction, tutoring.

Majors. Theology: Theology.

Computing on campus. 8 workstations in dormitories, library.

Student life. Freshman orientation: Mandatory. **Policies:** Closed campus. Religious observance required. **Housing:** Guaranteed on-campus for all undergraduates. Wellness housing available. **Activities:** Choral groups, student newspaper.

Contact. E-mail: info@hts.edu
Phone: (315) 858-0945
Dc. Vladimir Tsurikov, Dean, Holy Trinity Orthodox Seminary, Box 36, Jordanville, NY 13361

Houghton College
Houghton, New York **CB member**
www.houghton.edu **CB code: 2299**

- Private 4-year liberal arts college affiliated with Wesleyan Church
- Residential campus in rural community
- 1,330 degree-seeking undergraduates: 4% part-time, 64% women, 2% African American, 1% Asian American, 1% Hispanic American, 1% Native American, 4% international
- 32 degree-seeking graduate students
- 89% of applicants admitted
- SAT or ACT (ACT writing optional), application essay required
- 72% graduate within 6 years; 33% enter graduate study

General. Founded in 1883. Regionally accredited. All students receive laptop computer as part of tuition. Extension campuses in suburban Buffalo and in the Adirondack State Park. Study abroad programs in London, Tanzania, and Australia. School of Music accredited by National Association of Schools of Music. **Degrees:** 354 bachelor's, 7 associate awarded; master's offered. **ROTC:** Army. **Location:** 60 miles from Buffalo, 70 miles from Rochester. **Calendar:** Semester, limited summer session. **Full-time faculty:** 88 total; 85% have terminal degrees, 7% minority, 30% women. **Part-time faculty:** 69 total; 14% have terminal degrees, 3% minority, 48% women. **Class size:** 65% < 20, 28% 20-39, 4% 40-49, 3% 50-99. **Special facilities:** Equestrian center with indoor riding ring, ropes/initiatives course, downhill and cross-country skiing facilities, media arts computer lab, hiking and biking trails.

Freshman class profile. 905 applied, 805 admitted, 327 enrolled.

Mid 50% test scores		**GPA 2.0-2.99:**	10%
SAT critical reading:	520-650	**Rank in top quarter:**	66%
SAT math:	510-620	**Rank in top tenth:**	39%
SAT writing:	500-640	**End year in good standing:**	91%
ACT composite:	23-29	**Return as sophomores:**	85%
GPA 3.75 or higher:	39%	**Out-of-state:**	44%
GPA 3.50-3.74:	31%	**Live on campus:**	97%
GPA 3.0-3.49:	20%	**International:**	6%

Basis for selection. Student's high school transcript and standardized test scores of the utmost importance. Application essays, Christian character recommendation, other intangibles also considered. Interview recommended for all applicants. Audition and separate application required for entrance into the School of Music. **Learning Disabled:** Students must provide an IEP to receive services.

High school preparation. College-preparatory program recommended. 16 units recommended. Recommended units include English 4, mathematics 3, social studies 1, history 2, science 2 (laboratory 2) and foreign language 2.

2008-2009 Annual costs. Tuition/fees: $22,990. Tuition includes laptop computer, fees. Room/board: $6,930. Books/supplies: $900. Personal expenses: $750.

2008-2009 Financial aid. Need-based: 291 full-time freshmen applied for aid; 261 were judged to have need; 261 of these received aid. Average need met was 82%. Average scholarship/grant was $15,718; average loan $4,298. 57% of total undergraduate aid awarded as scholarships/grants, 43% as loans/jobs. **Non-need-based:** Awarded to 351 full-time undergraduates, including 96 freshmen. Scholarships awarded for academics, alumni affiliation, art, athletics, music/drama, religious affiliation, ROTC, state residency. **Additional information:** Wesley Full Tuition Grant offered to 25 new students each year. This grant covers the balance of tuition after all state and federal aid is awarded.

Application procedures. Admission: No deadline. $40 fee, may be waived for applicants with need. Admission notification on a rolling basis. Must reply by May 1 or within 4 week(s) if notified thereafter. **Financial aid:** Priority date 3/1; no closing date. FAFSA required. Applicants notified on a rolling basis starting 3/15; must reply by 5/1.

Academics. Special study options: Combined bachelor's/graduate degree, cross-registration, double major, exchange student, honors, independent study, internships, liberal arts/career combination, study abroad, teacher certification program. **Credit/placement by examination:** AP, CLEP, IB, SAT, ACT, institutional tests. 16 credit hours maximum toward associate degree, 32 toward bachelor's. **Support services:** Learning center, reduced course load, study skills assistance, tutoring, writing center.

Honors college/program. Admission to the First-Year Honors Program requires separate application, academic reference, writing sample, and interview.

Majors. **Agriculture:** Equestrian studies. **Biology:** General, biochemistry, environmental. **Business:** General, accounting, business admin. **Communications:** General, digital media, public relations. **Computer sciences:** Computer science, information technology. **Education:** General, biology, chemistry, elementary, English, ESL, foreign languages, French, history, mathematics, music, physical, physics, secondary, social studies, Spanish. **Engineering:** Physics. **Foreign languages:** French, Spanish. **Health:** Predental, premedicine, prepharmacy, preveterinary, recreational therapy. **History:** General. **Interdisciplinary:** Intercultural. **Math:** General. **Parks/recreation:** General, health/fitness. **Philosophy/religion:** Philosophy, religion. **Physical sciences:** Chemistry, physics. **Psychology:** General. **Social sciences:** International relations, political science, sociology. **Theology:** Bible, missionary, preministerial, youth ministry. **Visual/performing arts:** Art, music performance, music theory/composition, piano/organ, stringed instruments, studio arts, voice/opera.

Most popular majors. Area/ethnic studies 6%, biology 10%, business/marketing 28%, education 17%, English 6%, visual/performing arts 6%.

Computing on campus. PC or laptop required. 15 workstations in library, computer center, student center. Dormitories wired for high-speed internet access and linked to campus network. Commuter students can connect to campus network. Online library, helpline, repair service, wireless network available.

Student life. **Freshman orientation:** Mandatory. Preregistration for classes offered. **Policies:** Drinking of alcoholic beverages and smoking on or off campus prohibited. Religious observance required. **Housing:** Guaranteed on-campus for freshmen. Single-sex dorms, special housing for disabled, apartments, wellness housing available. $300 nonrefundable deposit, deadline 5/1. **Activities:** Bands, campus ministries, choral groups, drama, international student organizations, literary magazine, music ensembles, musical theater, opera, student government, student newspaper, symphony orchestra, Allegany County Outreach, Global Christian Fellowship, Habitat for Humanity, Youth for Christ, Fellowship of Christian Athletes, Intercultural Student Organization.

Athletics. NAIA. **Intercollegiate:** Basketball, cross-country, field hockey W, soccer, track and field, volleyball W. **Intramural:** Basketball, equestrian, football (non-tackle) M, racquetball, soccer, table tennis, volleyball, water polo. **Team name:** Highlanders.

Student services. Chaplain/spiritual director, career counseling, student employment services, financial aid counseling, health services, personal counseling, placement for graduates. **Physically disabled:** Services for visually impaired. **Learning disabled:** Comprehensive services available.

Contact. E-mail: admission@houghton.edu
Phone: (585) 567-9353 Toll-free number: (800) 777-2556
Fax: (585) 567-9522
Wayne MacBeth, Vice President for Enrollment Management and Church Relations, Houghton College, 1 Willard Avenue/PO Box 128, Houghton, NY 14744-0128

Iona College

New Rochelle, New York — **CB member**
www.iona.edu — **CB code: 2324**

- Private 4-year business and liberal arts college affiliated with Roman Catholic Church
- Residential campus in small city
- 3,442 degree-seeking undergraduates: 3% part-time, 54% women, 6% African American, 2% Asian American, 11% Hispanic American, 1% international
- 908 degree-seeking graduate students
- 59% of applicants admitted
- SAT or ACT (ACT writing optional), application essay required
- 63% graduate within 6 years; 71% enter graduate study

General. Founded in 1940. Regionally accredited. Independent institution in Roman Catholic, Christian Brothers tradition. **Degrees:** 787 bachelor's awarded; master's offered. **ROTC:** Army, Air Force. **Location:** 20 miles from New York City. **Calendar:** Semester, extensive summer session. **Full-time faculty:** 176 total; 92% have terminal degrees, 11% minority, 34% women. **Part-time faculty:** 220 total; 36% have terminal degrees, 13% minority, 40% women. **Class size:** 42% < 20, 51% 20-39, 7% 40-49. **Special facilities:** Extensive Irish and rare books collection.

Freshman class profile. 6,009 applied, 3,572 admitted, 923 enrolled.

Mid 50% test scores		Rank in top quarter:	54%
SAT critical reading:	540-640	Rank in top tenth:	31%
SAT math:	550-660	Return as sophomores:	87%
GPA 3.75 or higher:	5%	Out-of-state:	29%
GPA 3.50-3.74:	15%	Live on campus:	66%
GPA 3.0-3.49:	53%	International:	1%
GPA 2.0-2.99:	27%		

Basis for selection. High school curriculum and GPA most important, followed by test scores, recommendations, interview, extracurricular activities, essays, grade trends. Interviews recommended. **Homeschooled:** Transcript of courses and grades, interview, letter of recommendation (nonparent) required.

High school preparation. College-preparatory program recommended. 16 units required; 20 recommended. Required and recommended units include English 4, mathematics 3-4, social studies 1-2, history 1-2, science 2-3 (laboratory 2), foreign language 2 and academic electives 1-3.

2009-2010 Annual costs. Tuition/fees: $27,500. Room/board: $11,300. Books/supplies: $1,500. Personal expenses: $1,250.

2008-2009 Financial aid. **Need-based:** 912 full-time freshmen applied for aid; 671 were judged to have need; 669 of these received aid. Average need met was 26%. Average scholarship/grant was $4,391; average loan $2,554. 57% of total undergraduate aid awarded as scholarships/grants, 43% as loans/jobs. **Non-need-based:** Awarded to 3,312 full-time undergraduates, including 967 freshmen. Scholarships awarded for academics, alumni affiliation, athletics, ROTC.

Application procedures. **Admission:** Closing date 2/15 (postmark date). $50 fee, may be waived for applicants with need. Admission notification 3/20. Must reply by 5/1. **Financial aid:** Closing date 4/15. FAFSA, institutional form required. Applicants notified on a rolling basis starting 12/20; must reply by 5/1 or within 2 week(s) of notification.

Academics. **Special study options:** Accelerated study, combined bachelor's/graduate degree, distance learning, double major, honors, independent study, internships, liberal arts/career combination, study abroad, teacher certification program, weekend college. **Credit/placement by examination:** AP, CLEP, SAT, ACT. 60 credit hours maximum toward bachelor's degree. **Support services:** Learning center, pre-admission summer program, reduced course load, tutoring, writing center.

Majors. **Biology:** General, biochemistry, environmental. **Business:** Accounting, business admin, finance, international, management information systems, marketing. **Communications:** General, advertising, journalism, media studies, public relations, radio/tv. **Computer sciences:** Computer science, networking, web page design. **Education:** Biology, early childhood, elementary, English, French, mathematics, secondary, social studies, Spanish. **Foreign languages:** French, Italian, Spanish. **Health:** Audiology/speech pathology, clinical lab science, health care admin. **History:** General. **Interdisciplinary:** Global studies. **Liberal arts:** Arts/sciences. **Math:** General, applied. **Philosophy/religion:** Philosophy, religion. **Physical sciences:** Chemistry, physics. **Protective services:** Law enforcement admin. **Psychology:** General. **Public administration:** Social work. **Social sciences:** Economics, political science, sociology. **Visual/performing arts:** Dramatic. **Other:** Italian teacher education.

Most popular majors. Business/marketing 36%, communications/journalism 14%, education 8%, psychology 10%, security/protective services 7%, social sciences 6%.

Computing on campus. 627 workstations in dormitories, library, computer center, student center. Dormitories wired for high-speed internet access and linked to campus network. Commuter students can connect to campus network. Online course registration, online library, helpline, repair service, wireless network available.

Student life. **Freshman orientation:** Mandatory. Preregistration for classes offered. Overnight summer program in June and July; 1-day welcome program. **Housing:** Coed dorms, special housing for disabled, apartments, wellness housing available. $400 nonrefundable deposit, deadline 5/1. Honors program student housing available. **Activities:** Pep band, campus ministries, choral groups, dance, drama, film society, international student organizations, literary magazine, Model UN, musical theater, radio station, student government, student newspaper, TV station, Gaelic Society, Council of Multicultural Leaders, Italian club, Students of Caribbean Ancestry, Hispanic Organization for Latin Awareness, Amnesty International, Democrats, Republicans, Hellenic Society, Asian Student Association, Students for American Awareness.

Athletics. NCAA. **Intercollegiate:** Baseball M, basketball, cross-country, diving, golf M, lacrosse W, rowing (crew), soccer, softball W, swimming, track and field, volleyball W, water polo. **Intramural:** Basketball, football (non-tackle), soccer, table tennis, volleyball. **Team name:** Gaels.

Student services. Adult student services, alcohol/substance abuse counseling, chaplain/spiritual director, career counseling, student employment services, financial aid counseling, health services, minority student services, personal counseling, placement for graduates, veterans' counselor, women's services. **Physically disabled:** Services for speech impaired. **Learning disabled:** Comprehensive services available.

Contact. E-mail: icad@iona.edu
Phone: (914) 633-2502 Toll-free number: (800) 231-4662
Fax: (914) 633-2182
Kevin Cavanagh, Assistant VP for College Admissions, Iona College, 715 North Avenue, New Rochelle, NY 10801-1890

Ithaca College

Ithaca, New York — **CB member**
www.ithaca.edu — **CB code: 2325**

- Private 4-year health science and liberal arts college
- Residential campus in large town
- 5,968 degree-seeking undergraduates: 1% part-time, 56% women, 3% African American, 4% Asian American, 4% Hispanic American, 2% international
- 404 degree-seeking graduate students
- 66% of applicants admitted
- SAT or ACT with writing, application essay required
- 77% graduate within 6 years

General. Founded in 1892. Regionally accredited. **Degrees:** 1,396 bachelor's awarded; master's, doctoral offered. **ROTC:** Army, Air Force. **Location:** 250 miles from New York City, 60 miles from Syracuse. **Calendar:** Semester, extensive summer session. **Full-time faculty:** 463 total; 92% have terminal degrees, 8% minority, 46% women. **Part-time faculty:** 216 total; 61% have terminal degrees, 7% minority, 55% women. **Class size:** 53% < 20, 41% 20-39, 2% 40-49, 3% 50-99, 1% >100. **Special facilities:** Digital audio/video labs, photography labs, cinematography postproduction studio, film animation lab, lighting studio, physical therapy and occupational therapy clinics, speech and hearing clinic, exercise science labs, greenhouse, tissue culture laboratory, simulated trading room, recording and electroacoustic music studio, observatory.

Freshman class profile. 12,233 applied, 8,014 admitted, 1,441 enrolled.

Mid 50% test scores		**Rank in top tenth:**	35%
SAT critical reading:	540-640	**Return as sophomores:**	84%
SAT math:	550-640	**Out-of-state:**	57%
SAT writing:	540-640	**Live on campus:**	99%
Rank in top quarter:	73%	**International:**	2%

Basis for selection. School achievement record, test scores most important. School and community activities, accomplishments, special talents, interview also important. Audition required for music, theater arts programs; portfolio recommended for BFA program. **Homeschooled:** Transcript of courses and grades, letter of recommendation (nonparent) required. Applicants encouraged to provide in-depth information regarding academic preparation.

High school preparation. College-preparatory program required. 16 units required. Required units include English 4, mathematics 3, social studies 4, science 3, foreign language 2 and academic electives 1.

2008-2009 Annual costs. Tuition/fees: $30,606. Room/board: $11,126. Books/supplies: $1,130. Personal expenses: $1,470.

2008-2009 Financial aid. Need-based: 1,202 full-time freshmen applied for aid; 989 were judged to have need; 989 of these received aid. Average need met was 91%. Average scholarship/grant was $18,510; average loan $5,018. 70% of total undergraduate aid awarded as scholarships/grants, 30% as loans/jobs. **Non-need-based:** Awarded to 1,945 full-time undergraduates, including 622 freshmen. Scholarships awarded for academics, alumni affiliation, leadership, minority status, music/drama, ROTC.

Application procedures. Admission: Closing date 2/1. $60 fee, may be waived for applicants with need. Admission notification 4/15. Admission notification on a rolling basis beginning on or about 11/15. Must reply by May 1 or within 2 week(s) if notified thereafter. **Financial aid:** Priority date 2/1; no closing date. FAFSA required. Applicants notified on a rolling basis starting 2/15.

Academics. Over 50 minors available. **Special study options:** Accelerated study, combined bachelor's/graduate degree, cross-registration, distance learning, double major, dual enrollment of high school students, honors, independent study, internships, liberal arts/career combination, student-designed major, study abroad, teacher certification program, Washington semester. London Center (England), Los Angeles program, study opportunities in over 50 countries. **Credit/placement by examination:** AP, CLEP, IB, institutional tests. 90 credit hours maximum toward bachelor's degree. **Support services:** Study skills assistance, tutoring, writing center.

Majors. Biology: General, biochemistry. **Business:** General, accounting, business admin, finance, international, managerial economics, market research, marketing. **Communications:** General, broadcast journalism, journalism, media studies, organizational, radio/tv. **Communications technology:** Recording arts. **Computer sciences:** General, computer science, information systems, information technology, programming. **Conservation:** General, environmental studies. **Education:** Art, biology, chemistry, Deaf/hearing impaired, English, foreign languages, French, German, health, history, mathematics, multi-level teacher, music, physical, physics, science, secondary, social studies, Spanish, speech impaired. **Foreign languages:** General, French, German, Italian, Spanish. **Health:** Athletic training, facilities admin, occupational therapy assistant, predental, premedicine, preveterinary, public health ed, recreational therapy, speech pathology. **History:** General. **Interdisciplinary:** Gerontology, intercultural, nutrition sciences. **Legal studies:** General, prelaw. **Liberal arts:** Arts/sciences. **Math:** General. **Parks/recreation:** Exercise sciences, health/fitness, sports admin. **Philosophy/religion:** Philosophy. **Physical sciences:** Chemistry, physics. **Psychology:** General, industrial. **Social sciences:** General, anthropology, applied economics, econometrics, economics, political science, sociology. **Visual/performing arts:** General, acting, art, art history/conservation, arts management, cinematography, dance, dramatic, film/cinema, jazz, music performance, music theory/composition, photography, studio arts, theater arts management, theater design. **Other:** Sport studies.

Most popular majors. Business/marketing 11%, communications/journalism 17%, education 6%, English 7%, health sciences 10%, parks/recreation 6%, social sciences 8%, visual/performing arts 17%.

Computing on campus. 640 workstations in library, computer center. Dormitories wired for high-speed internet access and linked to campus network. Commuter students can connect to campus network. Online course registration, online library, helpline, repair service, student web hosting, wireless network available.

Student life. Freshman orientation: Available, $265 fee. Preregistration for classes offered. 2.5 days in summer and 4 days before school highlighted by placement tests and registration. Separate parent orientation program offered in summer. **Housing:** Guaranteed on-campus for all undergraduates. Coed dorms, single-sex dorms, special housing for disabled, apartments, fraternity/sorority housing, wellness housing available. First-year students only, quiet study residence halls, music honor fraternity housing, co-ed by door buildings, honors floor, several freshmen seminar groups housed together, H.O.M.E. Program (Housing Offering a Multicultural Experience) available. **Activities:** Bands, campus ministries, choral groups, dance, drama, film society, international student organizations, literary magazine, music ensembles, musical theater, opera, radio station, student government, student newspaper, symphony orchestra, TV station, Jewish, Christian, Catholic, Muslim, and Christian Science organizations, African-Latino society, Amnesty International, BiGayla, community service network, Habitat for Humanity, Sex and Gender Education, Asia Society, Friends of Israel.

Athletics. NCAA. **Intercollegiate:** Baseball M, basketball, cross-country, diving, field hockey W, football (tackle) M, gymnastics W, lacrosse, rowing (crew), soccer, softball W, swimming, tennis, track and field, volleyball W, wrestling M. **Intramural:** Basketball, bowling, golf, ice hockey M, rowing (crew), rugby W, skiing, soccer, softball, tennis, volleyball. **Team name:** Bombers.

Student services. Adult student services, alcohol/substance abuse counseling, chaplain/spiritual director, career counseling, student employment services, financial aid counseling, health services, minority student services, personal counseling, placement for graduates, veterans' counselor. **Physically disabled:** Services for visually, speech, hearing impaired.

Contact. E-mail: admission@ithaca.edu
Phone: (607) 274-3124 Toll-free number: (800) 429-4274
Fax: (607) 274-1900
Gerard Turbide, Director of Admission, Ithaca College, 953 Danby Road, Ithaca, NY 14850

Jewish Theological Seminary of America

New York, New York
www.jtsa.edu — **CB code: 2339**

- Private 4-year rabbinical and seminary college affiliated with Jewish faith
- Residential campus in very large city

- 190 degree-seeking undergraduates: 4% part-time, 57% women, 1% Hispanic American, 3% international
- 357 degree-seeking graduate students
- 60% of applicants admitted
- SAT or ACT with writing, application essay required
- 91% graduate within 6 years; 15% enter graduate study

General. Founded in 1886. Regionally accredited. **Degrees:** 32 bachelor's awarded; master's, doctoral, first professional offered. **ROTC:** Army, Naval, Air Force. **Calendar:** Semester, extensive summer session. **Full-time faculty:** 63 total; 32% women. **Part-time faculty:** 67 total; 54% women. **Class size:** 86% < 20, 13% 20-39, 1% 40-49. **Special facilities:** Jewish museum containing over 27,000 objects (paintings, sculptures, works on paper, artifacts, etc.), library containing largest collection of Hebraica and Judaica outside of Israel.

Freshman class profile. 124 applied, 74 admitted, 46 enrolled.

Mid 50% test scores			
SAT critical reading:	620-720	GPA 3.75 or higher:	65%
SAT math:	610-700	GPA 3.50-3.74:	10%
SAT writing:	650-750	GPA 3.0-3.49:	25%
ACT composite:	27-32	Return as sophomores:	100%
		Out-of-state:	83%

Basis for selection. GED not accepted. School achievement record, interest in Jewish studies, test scores, recommendations important; leadership potential considered. Interview recommended for residents in the New York area (within 100 mile radius).

High school preparation. Recommended units include English 4, mathematics 4, social studies 1, history 3, science 4, foreign language 4 and academic electives 4. Additional courses in Judaic studies, when available.

2008-2009 Annual costs. Tuition/fees: $15,000. Costs quoted paid to school only; separate costs assessed for dual-degree enrollment at Columbia University/Barnard College. Room only: $9,200. Books/supplies: $500.

2008-2009 Financial aid. Non-need-based: Scholarships awarded for academics, alumni affiliation, leadership.

Application procedures. Admission: Closing date 2/15 (postmark date). $65 fee, may be waived for applicants with need. Application must be submitted on paper. Admission notification 4/1. Must reply by 5/1. Application deadline January 1 for double degree program with Barnard College, February 15 for joint program with Columbia University. **Financial aid:** Priority date 2/1, closing date 3/1. FAFSA, institutional form, CSS PROFILE required. Applicants notified on a rolling basis starting 4/1; must reply within 4 week(s) of notification.

Academics. Special study options: Cross-registration, distance learning, double major, exchange student, honors, independent study, liberal arts/career combination, student-designed major, study abroad. BA/MA program with The Graduate School or William Davidson School of Jewish Education. **Credit/placement by examination:** AP, CLEP, institutional tests. 6 credit hours maximum toward bachelor's degree. **Support services:** Preadmission summer program, remedial instruction, tutoring, writing center.

Majors. Foreign languages: General. **Philosophy/religion:** Judaic. **Theology:** Sacred music. **Visual/performing arts:** Music performance, music theory/composition.

Computing on campus. 50 workstations in dormitories, library, computer center. Dormitories wired for high-speed internet access and linked to campus network. Commuter students can connect to campus network. Online course registration, online library, helpline, wireless network available.

Student life. Freshman orientation: Mandatory. **Policies:** Student life centers around supportive Jewish community. Undergraduates enrolled in joint degree programs with Barnard and Columbia participate in their extracurricular activities. **Housing:** Coed dorms, special housing for disabled available. **Activities:** Concert band, choral groups, dance, musical theater, student government, student newspaper, community service organization.

Athletics. Intramural: Basketball, bowling, field hockey W, lacrosse M, softball, volleyball.

Student services. Career counseling, student employment services, health services, personal counseling, placement for graduates.

Contact. E-mail: lcadmissions@jtsa.edu
Phone: (212) 678-8832 Fax: (212) 280-6022
Reina Cohen, Director of Admissions, Jewish Theological Seminary of America, 3080 Broadway, New York, NY 10027

Juilliard School

New York, New York
www.juilliard.edu **CB code: 2340**

- Private 4-year music and performing arts college
- Commuter campus in very large city
- 500 degree-seeking undergraduates: 47% women, 9% African American, 17% Asian American, 5% Hispanic American, 17% international
- 116 degree-seeking graduate students
- 8% of applicants admitted
- Application essay, interview required
- 85% graduate within 6 years

General. Founded in 1905. Regionally accredited. **Degrees:** 168 bachelor's awarded; master's, doctoral offered. **Calendar:** Semester. **Full-time faculty:** 113 total; 9% minority, 38% women. **Part-time faculty:** 159 total; 18% minority, 28% women. **Class size:** 88% < 20, 12% 20-39. **Special facilities:** Media center, over 100 practice rooms with over 200 pianos, scenery and costume shops, 15 2-story rehearsal studios, 5 theaters, 2 recital halls.

Freshman class profile. 2,138 applied, 162 admitted, 122 enrolled.

Live on campus:	100%	International:	19%

Basis for selection. Quality of performance at audition most important. Foreign students given English proficiency examination at time of audition or may present TOEFL. Audition required. **Homeschooled:** Transcript of courses and grades, letter of recommendation (nonparent) required.

High school preparation. Extensive previous study in major field of dance, drama, or music required.

2008-2009 Annual costs. Tuition/fees: $28,640. Room/board: $11,250. Books/supplies: $700. Personal expenses: $3,400.

2008-2009 Financial aid. Need-based: 113 full-time freshmen applied for aid; 96 were judged to have need; 96 of these received aid. Average need met was 87%. Average scholarship/grant was $23,776; average loan $1,980. 76% of total undergraduate aid awarded as scholarships/grants, 24% as loans/jobs. **Non-need-based:** Awarded to 44 full-time undergraduates, including 9 freshmen. Scholarships awarded for music/drama.

Application procedures. Admission: Closing date 12/1. $100 fee, may be waived for applicants with need. Admission notification 4/1. Must reply by May 1 or within 2 week(s) if notified thereafter. Auditions held in March. Drama auditions in January and Febuary, application closing date December 1; notification by April 1, or 1 month after audition. **Financial aid:** Closing date 3/1. FAFSA, institutional form required. Applicants notified by 4/1; must reply by 5/1.

Academics. 3-year diploma program available in performing arts. **Special study options:** Accelerated study, cross-registration, honors. Eligible students can enroll in courses at Barnard College and Columbia College to fulfill liberal arts elective requirements. **Credit/placement by examination:** AP, CLEP, institutional tests. **Support services:** Tutoring.

Majors. Visual/performing arts: Dance, dramatic, jazz, music performance, music theory/composition, piano/organ, stringed instruments.

Computing on campus. 65 workstations in dormitories, library, computer center. Dormitories wired for high-speed internet access. Online library, wireless network available.

Student life. Freshman orientation: Mandatory, $200 fee. For all new students, begins 10 days before first day of classes. **Housing:** Guaranteed on-campus for freshmen. Coed dorms, wellness housing available. $250 nonrefundable deposit, deadline 5/1. Single-sex floor, quiet floor, graduate student only floor available. **Activities:** Student government, student newspaper, ArtREACH, Korea Campus Crusade for Christ, Christian Fellowship, Amnesty Juilliard.

Student services. Alcohol/substance abuse counseling, career counseling, student employment services, financial aid counseling, health services, minority student services, personal counseling, placement for graduates.

Contact. E-mail: admissions@juilliard.edu
Phone: (212) 799-5000 ext. 223 Fax: (212) 769-6420
Lee Cioppa, Associate Dean for Admissions, Juilliard School, 60 Lincoln Center Plaza, New York, NY 10023-6588

Kehilath Yakov Rabbinical Seminary
Brooklyn, New York

CB code: 0619

- Private 4-year rabbinical college for men affiliated with Jewish faith
- Very large city

General. Accredited by AARTS. **Calendar:** Continuous.

Annual costs/financial aid. Tuition/fees (2008-2009): $5,000.

Contact. Phone: (718) 963-3940
206 Wilson Street, Brooklyn, NY 11211

Keuka College
Keuka Park, New York
www.keuka.edu

CB member
CB code: 2350

- Private 4-year liberal arts college affiliated with American Baptist Churches in the USA
- Residential campus in rural community
- 1,483 degree-seeking undergraduates: 19% part-time, 73% women, 7% African American, 1% Asian American, 2% Hispanic American, 1% Native American
- 131 degree-seeking graduate students
- 81% of applicants admitted
- Application essay required
- 51% graduate within 6 years; 34% enter graduate study

General. Founded in 1890. Regionally accredited. **Degrees:** 322 bachelor's awarded; master's offered. **Location:** 50 miles from Rochester, 60 miles from Syracuse. **Calendar:** 4-1-4, limited summer session. **Full-time faculty:** 65 total; 82% have terminal degrees, 63% women. **Part-time faculty:** 40 total; 28% have terminal degrees, 60% women. **Class size:** 54% < 20, 45% 20-39, 1% 40-49. **Special facilities:** Lakefront for boating, sailing and science projects and research.

Freshman class profile. 805 applied, 655 admitted, 270 enrolled.

Mid 50% test scores			
SAT critical reading:	400-530	GPA 2.0-2.99:	34%
SAT math:	370-580	Rank in top quarter:	28%
SAT writing:	390-530	Rank in top tenth:	8%
GPA 3.75 or higher:	7%	End year in good standing:	89%
GPA 3.50-3.74:	18%	Return as sophomores:	69%
GPA 3.0-3.49:	41%	Out-of-state:	6%
		Live on campus:	97%

Basis for selection. Overall GPA, extracurricular activities, community service, leadership experience, letter of recommendation, quality of essay, SAT/ACT scores considered by committee. Interview recommended for all, required for some.

High school preparation. College-preparatory program recommended. 18 units recommended. Recommended units include English 4, mathematics 3, social studies 3, history 2, science 3 (laboratory 2) and foreign language 3.

2008-2009 Annual costs. Tuition/fees: $21,760. Room/board: $8,850. Books/supplies: $1,200. Personal expenses: $1,000.

2007-2008 Financial aid. Need-based: 278 full-time freshmen applied for aid; 260 were judged to have need; 260 of these received aid. Average need met was 74%. Average scholarship/grant was $12,805; average loan $5,464. 55% of total undergraduate aid awarded as scholarships/grants, 45% as loans/jobs. **Non-need-based:** Awarded to 185 full-time undergraduates, including 45 freshmen. Scholarships awarded for academics, alumni affiliation, leadership, minority status, religious affiliation.

Application procedures. Admission: No deadline. $30 fee, may be waived for applicants with need. Admission notification on a rolling basis beginning on or about 9/1. **Financial aid:** Priority date 3/15; no closing date. FAFSA required. Applicants notified on a rolling basis starting 3/1; must reply by 5/1 or within 2 week(s) of notification.

Academics. All students must complete 1 field period or internship each year, every 30 credit hours (experiential education). Field Period enables students to spend 4 weeks a year participating in an internship or international travel, or undertaking an independent project. **Special study options:** Accelerated study, combined bachelor's/graduate degree, cooperative education, cross-registration, double major, dual enrollment of high school students, independent study, internships, student-designed major, study abroad, teacher certification program. Albany semester; 3-1 in clinical science with New York Chiropractic College. **Credit/placement by examination:** AP, CLEP, institutional tests. 12 credit hours maximum toward bachelor's degree. **Support services:** Learning center, reduced course load, remedial instruction, study skills assistance, tutoring, writing center.

Majors. Biology: General, biochemistry. **Business:** Accounting, business admin, marketing. **Communications:** General. **Conservation:** Environmental science. **Education:** Biology, early childhood, English, mathematics, secondary, social studies, special. **Foreign languages:** American Sign Language, sign language interpretation. **Health:** Clinical lab science, nursing (RN). **Legal studies:** Prelaw. **Liberal arts:** Arts/sciences. **Math:** General. **Protective services:** Law enforcement admin. **Psychology:** General. **Public administration:** Social work. **Social sciences:** General, criminology, sociology.

Most popular majors. Business/marketing 21%, education 19%, health sciences 23%, security/protective services 17%.

Computing on campus. 140 workstations in dormitories, library, computer center. Dormitories wired for high-speed internet access and linked to campus network. Helpline, repair service, wireless network available.

Student life. Freshman orientation: Mandatory, $150 fee. Preregistration for classes offered. 2-session summer program. **Policies:** No smoking allowed in any campus building, including residence halls. **Housing:** Guaranteed on-campus for all undergraduates. Coed dorms, single-sex dorms, special housing for disabled, cooperative housing, wellness housing available. $150 deposit. Leadership and management housing. **Activities:** Bands, campus ministries, choral groups, dance, drama, film society, international student organizations, literary magazine, musical theater, radio station, student government, student newspaper, social work club, Keuka Leaders club, Keuka Circle (community service), Newman Club, minority support group, political action coalition, Student Nurse Association.

Athletics. NCAA. **Intercollegiate:** Baseball M, basketball, cross-country, golf, lacrosse, soccer, softball W, synchronized swimming W, tennis, volleyball W. **Intramural:** Basketball, football (non-tackle), soccer, softball, volleyball. **Team name:** Storm.

Student services. Adult student services, alcohol/substance abuse counseling, chaplain/spiritual director, career counseling, student employment services, financial aid counseling, health services, minority student services, personal counseling, placement for graduates, women's services. **Physically disabled:** Services for visually, speech, hearing impaired.

Contact. E-mail: admissions@mail.keuka.edu
Phone: (315) 279-5254 Toll-free number: (800) 335-3852
Fax: (315) 279-5386
Carolanne Marquis, Executive Vice President, Keuka College, 141 Cental Avenue, Keuka Park, NY 14478-0098

King's College
New York, New York
www.tkc.edu

CB code: 2871

- Private 4-year liberal arts college affiliated with nondenominational tradition
- Residential campus in very large city
- 254 degree-seeking undergraduates: 2% part-time, 61% women, 2% African American, 3% Asian American, 4% Hispanic American, 5% international
- 98% of applicants admitted
- SAT or ACT (ACT writing optional), interview required

General. Regionally accredited. Bibically-based curriculum focused on politics, philosophy, economics and business management. **Degrees:** 38 bachelor's awarded. **Calendar:** Semester, limited summer session. **Full-time faculty:** 16 total; 100% have terminal degrees, 12% women. **Part-time faculty:** 7 total; 71% have terminal degrees, 29% women. **Class size:** 49% < 20, 38% 20-39, 11% 40-49, 2% 50-99.

Freshman class profile. 336 applied, 328 admitted, 68 enrolled.

Mid 50% test scores			
SAT critical reading:	600-690	GPA 2.0-2.99:	9%
SAT math:	570-650	Rank in top quarter:	79%
SAT writing:	570-700	Rank in top tenth:	39%
ACT composite:	25-30	End year in good standing:	100%
GPA 3.75 or higher:	58%	Return as sophomores:	83%
GPA 3.50-3.74:	9%	Out-of-state:	96%
GPA 3.0-3.49:	24%	Live on campus:	96%

Basis for selection. Admissions based on academic preparedness and leadership qualities, primarily assessed through transcript, SAT or ACT scores, and entrance interview. **Learning Disabled:** Documentation required of any learning disabilities that will require special accommodation.

High school preparation. 18 units required; 21 recommended. Required and recommended units include English 4, mathematics 3-4, social studies 2, history 2, science 3-4, foreign language 2-3 and academic electives 2.

2008-2009 Annual costs. Tuition/fees: $22,850. Room only: $8,750.

2008-2009 Financial aid. Need-based: 55 full-time freshmen applied for aid; 44 were judged to have need; 44 of these received aid. Average need met was 59%. Average scholarship/grant was $14,938; average loan $3,500. 71% of total undergraduate aid awarded as scholarships/grants, 29% as loans/jobs. **Non-need-based:** Awarded to 189 full-time undergraduates, including 66 freshmen. Scholarships awarded for academics.

Application procedures. Admission: Priority date 11/15; no deadline. $35 fee, may be waived for applicants with need. Admission notification on a rolling basis beginning on or about 11/1. Must reply by May 1 or within 4 week(s) if notified thereafter. **Financial aid:** Priority date 3/15; no closing date. FAFSA required. Applicants notified on a rolling basis.

Academics. Special study options: Independent study, internships, study abroad. **Credit/placement by examination:** AP, CLEP, IB, institutional tests. **Support services:** Reduced course load, study skills assistance, tutoring.

Majors. Business: Business admin. **Other:** Politics, philosophy, and economics.

Most popular majors. Business/marketing 24%, interdisciplinary studies 76%.

Computing on campus. PC or laptop required. 8 workstations in library. Dormitories wired for high-speed internet access and linked to campus network. Commuter students can connect to campus network. Online course registration, wireless network available.

Student life. Freshman orientation: Mandatory. Preregistration for classes offered. Held two days prior to first day of class. **Policies:** No alcoholic beverages/drug usage permitted on campus or in housing. **Housing:** Guaranteed on-campus for all undergraduates. Coed dorms, single-sex dorms available. $600 fully refundable deposit, deadline 8/1. **Activities:** Campus ministries, dance, drama, literary magazine, student government, student newspaper.

Athletics. Team name: Pride.

Student services. Chaplain/spiritual director, career counseling, student employment services, financial aid counseling.

Contact. E-mail: info@tkc.edu
Phone: (212) 659-3610 Toll-free number: (888) 969-7200 ext. 3610
Fax: (212) 659-3611
Brian Parker, Vice President of Admissions, King's College, 350 Fifth Avenue, Lower Lobby, New York, NY 10118

Laboratory Institute of Merchandising

New York, New York — **CB member**
www.limcollege.edu — **CB code: 2380**

- For-profit 4-year college of fashion business
- Commuter campus in very large city
- 1,308 degree-seeking undergraduates: 4% part-time, 94% women, 11% African American, 6% Asian American, 14% Hispanic American, 1% international
- 56% of applicants admitted
- SAT or ACT (ACT writing optional), application essay, interview required
- 61% graduate within 6 years

General. Founded in 1939. Regionally accredited. **Degrees:** 184 bachelor's, 24 associate awarded; master's offered. **Location:** Located in midtown Manhattan. **Calendar:** Semester, limited summer session. **Full-time faculty:** 26 total; 38% have terminal degrees, 31% minority, 46% women. **Part-time faculty:** 138 total; 8% have terminal degrees, 22% minority, 55% women. **Class size:** 66% < 20, 34% 20-39.

Freshman class profile. 1,069 applied, 597 admitted, 304 enrolled.

Mid 50% test scores		**GPA 2.0-2.99:**	52%
SAT critical reading:	440-520	**Rank in top quarter:**	17%
SAT math:	420-510	**Rank in top tenth:**	3%
SAT writing:	500-520	**Return as sophomores:**	64%
ACT composite:	19-23	**Out-of-state:**	58%
GPA 3.75 or higher:	11%	**Live on campus:**	66%
GPA 3.50-3.74:	5%	**International:**	1%
GPA 3.0-3.49:	29%		

Basis for selection. Interview, high school transcript, SAT/ACT score, letters of recommendation and college transcripts important. **Homeschooled:** Transcript of courses and grades, state high school equivalency certificate, interview, letter of recommendation (nonparent) required.

High school preparation. College-preparatory program recommended.

2008-2009 Annual costs. Tuition/fees: $19,825. Room/board: $18,700. Books/supplies: $1,100. Personal expenses: $2,000.

2007-2008 Financial aid. All financial aid based on need.

Application procedures. Admission: No deadline. $40 fee, may be waived for applicants with need. Admission notification on a rolling basis beginning on or about 12/15. **Financial aid:** Priority date 4/1; no closing date. FAFSA, institutional form required. Applicants notified on a rolling basis starting 2/15; must reply within 2 week(s) of notification.

Academics. Associate degree program distributed among liberal arts, business, and professional courses, including 2 work projects of 3 credits and 5 weeks each. Bachelor's degree programs distributed among liberal arts, business, and professional courses with a semester-long, 13-credit cooperative work project. Freshmen and sophomores participate in 3-credit, 5-week work project. Seniors participate in 16-week full-semester co-op. Curriculum also includes weekly field trips into fashion industry and guest lecturer series featuring fashion professionals. **Special study options:** Combined bachelor's/graduate degree, cooperative education, internships, study abroad. 3-credit trip to Europe in winter/summer. **Credit/placement by examination:** AP, CLEP, SAT, ACT, institutional tests. **Support services:** Learning center, pre-admission summer program, reduced course load, remedial instruction, study skills assistance, tutoring, writing center.

Majors. Business: Business admin, fashion, management science, marketing. **Family/consumer sciences:** Apparel marketing. **Other:** Visual merchandising.

Most popular majors. Business/marketing 40%, family/consumer sciences 51%, visual/performing arts 9%.

Computing on campus. 270 workstations in library, computer center, student center. Dormitories wired for high-speed internet access. Commuter students can connect to campus network. Online library, helpline available.

Student life. Freshman orientation: Mandatory. **Housing:** Coed dorms available. $700 partly refundable deposit. Affiliated with local YW-YMHA and Educational Housing Inc. in which traditional residence life experience available. **Activities:** Student government.

Student services. Alcohol/substance abuse counseling, career counseling, student employment services, financial aid counseling, personal counseling, placement for graduates.

Contact. E-mail: admissions@limcollege.edu
Phone: (212) 752-1530 ext. 289 Toll-free number: (800) 677-1323
Fax: (212) 750-3432
Kristina Gibson, Director of Admissions, Laboratory Institute of Merchandising, 12 East 53rd Street, New York, NY 10022

Le Moyne College

Syracuse, New York — **CB member**
www.lemoyne.edu — **CB code: 2366**

- Private 4-year liberal arts college affiliated with Roman Catholic Church
- Residential campus in small city
- 2,496 degree-seeking undergraduates: 8% part-time, 61% women, 4% African American, 2% Asian American, 5% Hispanic American, 1% international
- 499 degree-seeking graduate students
- 61% of applicants admitted
- SAT or ACT (ACT writing optional), application essay required
- 78% graduate within 6 years; 41% enter graduate study

General. Founded in 1946. Regionally accredited. **Degrees:** 526 bachelor's awarded; master's offered. **ROTC:** Army, Air Force. **Location:** 2 miles from downtown. **Calendar:** Semester, extensive summer session. **Full-time faculty:** 158 total; 94% have terminal degrees, 15% minority, 43% women. **Part-time faculty:** 167 total; 30% have terminal degrees, 4% minority, 50% women. **Class size:** 41% < 20, 57% 20-39, less than 1% 40-49, 1% 50-99. **Special facilities:** Performing arts center.

Freshman class profile. 4,212 applied, 2,579 admitted, 544 enrolled.

Mid 50% test scores		**GPA 2.0-2.99:**	19%
SAT critical reading:	480-580	**Rank in top quarter:**	52%
SAT math:	500-590	**Rank in top tenth:**	22%
ACT composite:	21-25	**End year in good standing:**	93%
GPA 3.75 or higher:	15%	**Return as sophomores:**	84%
GPA 3.50-3.74:	23%	**Out-of-state:**	5%
GPA 3.0-3.49:	43%	**Live on campus:**	90%

Basis for selection. High school courses and performance most important; class rank, test scores, recommendations, essay, interview, extracurricular activities also important. Students from underrepresented populations encouraged. February 1 priority date by which SAT scores must be received for fall term admission. Interview recommended. **Homeschooled:** Statement describing homeschool structure and mission, transcript of courses and grades, interview, letter of recommendation (nonparent) required. **Learning Disabled:** Interview strongly recommended.

High school preparation. College-preparatory program recommended. 17 units required. Required and recommended units include English 4, mathematics 3-4, social studies 4, science 3-4 (laboratory 3) and foreign language 3. 4 math required for science and math majors.

2009-2010 Annual costs. Tuition/fees: $25,830. Room/board: $9,990. Books/supplies: $700. Personal expenses: $1,510.

2007-2008 Financial aid. Need-based: 542 full-time freshmen applied for aid; 480 were judged to have need; 479 of these received aid. Average need met was 82%. Average scholarship/grant was $10,855; average loan $3,807. 61% of total undergraduate aid awarded as scholarships/grants, 39% as loans/jobs. **Non-need-based:** Awarded to 1,402 full-time undergraduates, including 374 freshmen. Scholarships awarded for academics, alumni affiliation, athletics, leadership, minority status, ROTC. **Additional information:** Parent loan program at low interest, monthly payment plans and alternative loans for students.

Application procedures. Admission: Priority date 2/1; no deadline. $35 fee, may be waived for applicants with need, free for online applicants. Admission notification on a rolling basis beginning on or about 1/1. Must reply by May 1 or within 4 week(s) if notified thereafter. **Financial aid:** Priority date 2/1; no closing date. FAFSA, institutional form required. Applicants notified by 3/15; must reply by 5/1 or within 2 week(s) of notification.

Academics. Academic accommodations and services for students with documented disabilities. **Special study options:** Accelerated study, combined bachelor's/graduate degree, double major, dual enrollment of high school students, honors, independent study, internships, liberal arts/career combination, semester at sea, study abroad, teacher certification program, Washington semester. Certificate of Advanced Studies in Educational Leadership and Certificate of Advanced Studies in Nursing. **Credit/placement by examination:** AP, CLEP, IB. **Support services:** Learning center, remedial instruction, study skills assistance, tutoring, writing center.

Majors. Biology: General, biochemistry, ecology. **Business:** Accounting, business admin, finance, labor studies, management information systems, marketing, operations. **Communications:** General. **Computer sciences:** General. **Foreign languages:** French, Spanish. **Health:** Nursing (RN), predental, premedicine, prepharmacy, preveterinary. **History:** General. **Interdisciplinary:** Biological/physical sciences, peace/conflict. **Legal studies:** Prelaw. **Math:** General. **Philosophy/religion:** Philosophy, religion. **Physical sciences:** Chemistry, physics. **Psychology:** General. **Social sciences:** Criminology, economics, political science, sociology. **Visual/performing arts:** Dramatic.

Most popular majors. Biology 11%, business/marketing 28%, English 7%, history 6%, psychology 19%, social sciences 14%.

Computing on campus. 325 workstations in dormitories, library, computer center, student center. Dormitories wired for high-speed internet access and linked to campus network. Commuter students can connect to campus network. Online course registration, online library, helpline, repair service, student web hosting, wireless network available.

Student life. Freshman orientation: Mandatory, $200 fee. Preregistration for classes offered. 4 summer orientation sessions of 2 days each and one fall orientation. **Housing:** Guaranteed on-campus for all undergraduates. Coed dorms, single-sex dorms, special housing for disabled, apartments, wellness housing available. Living/Learning communities available. **Activities:** Bands, campus ministries, choral groups, dance, drama, film society, international student organizations, literary magazine, music ensembles, Model UN, musical theater, radio station, student government, student newspaper, TV station, international club, Amnesty International, Habitat for Humanity, Democrats Club, Republican Club, Gaelic Society, El Progreso, Pride in Our Work Ethnicity and Race, Muslim student association.

Athletics. NCAA. **Intercollegiate:** Baseball M, basketball, cross-country, diving, golf M, lacrosse, soccer, softball W, swimming, tennis, volleyball W. **Intramural:** Basketball, football (non-tackle) M, racquetball, soccer, softball, volleyball. **Team name:** Dolphins.

Student services. Adult student services, alcohol/substance abuse counseling, chaplain/spiritual director, career counseling, student employment services, financial aid counseling, health services, minority student services, personal counseling, placement for graduates. **Physically disabled:** Services for visually, speech, hearing impaired.

Contact. E-mail: admission@lemoyne.edu
Phone: (315) 445-4300 Toll-free number: (800) 333-4733
Fax: (315) 445-4711
Dennis Nicholson, Director of Admission, Le Moyne College, 1419 Salt Springs Road, Syracuse, NY 13214-1301

Long Island University: Brooklyn Campus

Brooklyn, New York — **CB member**
www.liu.edu — **CB code: 2369**

- Private 4-year university and liberal arts college
- Commuter campus in very large city
- 3,830 degree-seeking undergraduates: 18% part-time, 73% women, 36% African American, 12% Asian American, 14% Hispanic American, 1% international
- 4,098 degree-seeking graduate students
- 80% of applicants admitted

General. Founded in 1926. Regionally accredited. **Degrees:** 609 bachelor's, 26 associate awarded; master's, doctoral, first professional offered. **ROTC:** Army. **Calendar:** Semester, extensive summer session. **Full-time faculty:** 306 total; 32% minority, 51% women. **Part-time faculty:** 517 total; 37% minority, 53% women.

Freshman class profile. 4,387 applied, 3,524 admitted, 1,009 enrolled.

Mid 50% test scores		**GPA 2.0-2.99:**	47%
SAT critical reading:	400-510	**End year in good standing:**	65%
SAT math:	400-550	**Return as sophomores:**	48%
GPA 3.75 or higher:	12%	**Out-of-state:**	21%
GPA 3.50-3.74:	11%	**Live on campus:**	25%
GPA 3.0-3.49:	20%	**International:**	1%

Basis for selection. Rigor of secondary school record, class rank, academic GPA, recommendations, test scores, essay considered. ACT or SAT required for admission to computer science, molecular biology, nursing, pharmacy, pre-athletic training, pre-occupational therapy, and pre-physician assistant majors. Interview, audition, and/or personal statement may be required for particular programs.

High school preparation. 16 units recommended. Recommended units include English 4, mathematics 2, social studies 3 and academic electives 4. Academic electives include any electives from fields of foreign languages, social studies, mathematics or natural science. Other electives include 3 credits of any studies except physical education and military science that lead to graduation from accredited high school.

2008-2009 Annual costs. Tuition/fees: $27,365. Room/board: $10,040.

Application procedures. Admission: Priority date 6/1; no deadline. $30 fee, may be waived for applicants with need. Admission notification on a rolling basis. Some programs have February 1 application deadline. **Financial aid:** Priority date 3/15; no closing date. FAFSA required. Applicants notified on a rolling basis.

Academics. Special study options: Accelerated study, combined bachelor's/graduate degree, cooperative education, double major, ESL, honors, independent study, internships, student-designed major, study abroad, teacher certification program, United Nations semester. **Credit/placement by examination:** AP, CLEP, IB, institutional tests. **Support services:** Learning center, pre-admission summer program, reduced course load, remedial instruction, study skills assistance, tutoring, writing center.

Majors. Biology: General, biochemistry. **Business:** Accounting, business admin, finance, sales/distribution. **Communications:** General, journalism.

Computer sciences: General. **Education:** Art, biology, chemistry, elementary, English, mathematics, music, physical, Spanish, speech impaired. **Foreign languages:** General. **Health:** Audiology/speech pathology, clinical lab science, community health, cytotechnology, nursing (RN), physician assistant. **History:** General. **Liberal arts:** Arts/sciences, humanities. **Math:** General. **Parks/recreation:** Exercise sciences. **Philosophy/religion:** Philosophy. **Physical sciences:** Chemistry. **Psychology:** General. **Public administration:** Social work. **Social sciences:** General, economics, political science, sociology. **Visual/performing arts:** General, commercial/advertising art, dance, music performance, studio arts.

Most popular majors. Business/marketing 14%, health sciences 37%, liberal arts 6%, psychology 8%, social sciences 7%.

Computing on campus. 600 workstations in dormitories, library, computer center. Dormitories wired for high-speed internet access and linked to campus network. Online library, wireless network available.

Student life. Freshman orientation: Available, $35 fee. **Housing:** Coed dorms available. $150 deposit. **Activities:** Jazz band, choral groups, dance, drama, literary magazine, music ensembles, musical theater, radio station, student government, student newspaper, TV station.

Athletics. NCAA. **Intercollegiate:** Baseball M, basketball, cross-country, golf, lacrosse W, soccer, softball W, tennis W, track and field, volleyball W. **Team name:** Blackbirds.

Student services. Chaplain/spiritual director, career counseling, student employment services, financial aid counseling, health services, personal counseling, placement for graduates. **Physically disabled:** Services for visually, speech, hearing impaired.

Contact. E-mail: admissions@brooklyn.liu.edu
Phone: (718) 488-1011 Toll-free number: (800) 548-7526
Fax: (718) 797-2399
Richard Sunday, Dean of Admissions, Long Island University: Brooklyn Campus, 1 University Plaza, Brooklyn, NY 11201

Long Island University: C. W. Post Campus

Brookville, New York — **CB member**
www.liu.edu — **CB code: 2070**

- Private 4-year university and liberal arts college
- Commuter campus in small town
- 4,925 degree-seeking undergraduates: 13% part-time, 62% women, 9% African American, 3% Asian American, 8% Hispanic American, 6% international
- 3,080 degree-seeking graduate students
- 84% of applicants admitted
- SAT or ACT (ACT writing optional), application essay required

General. Founded in 1954. Regionally accredited. **Degrees:** 961 bachelor's, 2 associate awarded; master's, doctoral offered. **ROTC:** Army. **Location:** 25 miles from New York City. **Calendar:** Semester, extensive summer session. **Full-time faculty:** 336 total; 15% minority, 45% women. **Part-time faculty:** 524 total; 11% minority, 50% women. **Special facilities:** Tilles center for the performing arts.

Freshman class profile. 5,152 applied, 4,353 admitted, 970 enrolled.

Mid 50% test scores		**GPA 2.0-2.99:**	47%
SAT critical reading:	440-530	**End year in good standing:**	79%
SAT math:	440-550	**Return as sophomores:**	69%
GPA 3.75 or higher:	10%	**Out-of-state:**	13%
GPA 3.50-3.74:	11%	**Live on campus:**	57%
GPA 3.0-3.49:	28%	**International:**	7%

Basis for selection. Rigor of secondary school record, class rank, GPA, recommendations, test scores, essay considered. Audition required for dance, music, and theater programs; interview recommended for communication arts, dance, and theater/film programs; portfolio required for art programs.

High school preparation. 16 units recommended. Recommended units include English 4, mathematics 3, social studies 4, science 3 (laboratory 3) and foreign language 2.

2008-2009 Annual costs. Tuition/fees: $27,400. Room/board: $10,520. Books/supplies: $675.

Application procedures. Admission: Priority date 3/1; no deadline. $30 fee, may be waived for applicants with need. Admission notification on a rolling basis. **Financial aid:** Priority date 3/1; no closing date. FAFSA, CSS PROFILE required. Applicants notified on a rolling basis starting 3/1; must reply by 5/1.

Academics. Special study options: Accelerated study, combined bachelor's/graduate degree, cooperative education, cross-registration, double major, dual enrollment of high school students, ESL, honors, independent study, internships, student-designed major, study abroad, teacher certification program, United Nations semester, Washington semester, weekend college. **Credit/placement by examination:** AP, CLEP, IB, institutional tests. **Support services:** Learning center, pre-admission summer program, reduced course load, remedial instruction, study skills assistance, tutoring, writing center.

Majors. Biology: General, cell/histology. **Business:** Accounting, business admin. **Communications:** Advertising, journalism. **Communications technology:** Radio/tv. **Computer sciences:** Information systems, information technology. **Education:** Art, biology, elementary, English, foreign languages, health, kindergarten/preschool, mathematics, music, physical, social studies, Spanish. **Foreign languages:** General, French, Italian, Spanish. **Health:** Art therapy, audiology/speech pathology, facilities admin, marriage/family therapy, medical radiologic technology/radiation therapy, medical records admin, nursing (RN). **History:** General. **Liberal arts:** Arts/sciences. **Math:** General, applied. **Philosophy/religion:** Philosophy. **Physical sciences:** Chemistry, geology, physics. **Protective services:** Forensics, law enforcement admin. **Psychology:** General. **Public administration:** General, social work. **Social sciences:** Economics, geography, international relations, political science, sociology. **Visual/performing arts:** Art history/conservation, arts management, cinematography, commercial/advertising art, dance, dramatic, music performance, photography, studio arts. **Other:** Earth science education.

Most popular majors. Business/marketing 18%, education 18%, health sciences 8%, psychology 6%, security/protective services 12%, social sciences 7%, visual/performing arts 10%.

Computing on campus. Dormitories wired for high-speed internet access and linked to campus network. Commuter students can connect to campus network. Repair service, wireless network available.

Student life. Freshman orientation: Available, $100 fee. Preregistration for classes offered. 2-day sessions for freshmen held in July and August prior to start of fall classes. **Housing:** Guaranteed on-campus for freshmen. Coed dorms, single-sex dorms available. $300 deposit, deadline 5/1. 24-hour intensified study housing available. **Activities:** Bands, choral groups, dance, drama, film society, literary magazine, music ensembles, musical theater, radio station, student government, student newspaper, TV station.

Athletics. NCAA. **Intercollegiate:** Baseball M, basketball, cross-country, field hockey W, football (tackle) M, lacrosse, soccer, softball W, swimming W, tennis W, volleyball W. **Team name:** Pioneers.

Student services. Adult student services, alcohol/substance abuse counseling, chaplain/spiritual director, career counseling, student employment services, financial aid counseling, health services; personal counseling, placement for graduates, veterans' counselor. **Physically disabled:** Services for visually, speech, hearing impaired. **Learning disabled:** Comprehensive services available.

Contact. E-mail: enroll@cwpost.liu.edu
Phone: (516) 299-2900 Toll-free number: (800) 548-7526
Fax: (516) 299-2137
Joanne Graziano, Admissions Director, Long Island University: C. W. Post Campus, 720 Northern Boulevard, Brookville, NY 11548-1300

Machzikei Hadath Rabbinical College

Brooklyn, New York
CB code: 0726

- Private 5-year rabbinical and seminary college for men affiliated with Jewish faith
- Commuter campus in very large city

General. Founded in 1956. Accredited by AARTS. **Calendar:** Semester.

Annual costs/financial aid. Tuition/fees (2008-2009): $7,000.

Contact. Phone: (718) 854-8777 ext. 23
Director of Admissions, 5407 16th Avenue, Brooklyn, NY 11204

Manhattan College

Riverdale, New York — **CB member**
www.manhattan.edu — **CB code: 2395**

- Private 4-year engineering and liberal arts college affiliated with Roman Catholic Church
- Residential campus in very large city
- 3,025 degree-seeking undergraduates: 3% part-time, 48% women, 3% African American, 3% Asian American, 11% Hispanic American

- 421 degree-seeking graduate students
- 57% of applicants admitted
- SAT or ACT with writing required

General. Founded in 1853. Regionally accredited. Independent institution in the Roman Catholic tradition sponsored by De La Salle Christian Brothers. **Degrees:** 668 bachelor's awarded; master's offered. **ROTC:** Army, Air Force. **Location:** 10 miles from midtown Manhattan. **Calendar:** Semester, extensive summer session. **Full-time faculty:** 180 total. **Part-time faculty:** 140 total. **Class size:** 45% < 20, 54% 20-39, 1% 40-49. **Special facilities:** Plant morphogenesis laboratory.

Freshman class profile. 5,511 applied, 3,123 admitted, 727 enrolled.

Mid 50% test scores		**GPA 2.0-2.99:**	20%
SAT critical reading:	500-590	**Rank in top quarter:**	59%
SAT math:	510-620	**Rank in top tenth:**	21%
ACT composite:	22-26	**Out-of-state:**	31%
GPA 3.75 or higher:	25%	**Live on campus:**	80%
GPA 3.50-3.74:	15%	**Fraternities:**	2%
GPA 3.0-3.49:	40%	**Sororities:**	3%

Basis for selection. School achievement record and test scores most important. Essay, recommendations, and extracurricular activities also reviewed. Interview recommended.

High school preparation. College-preparatory program recommended. 16 units required; 17 recommended. Required and recommended units include English 4, mathematics 3-4, social studies 3, science 2-3, foreign language 2-3 and academic electives 2. 4 mathematics, 4 science (including precalculus, chemistry, and physics) recommended of engineering majors and most science majors.

2009-2010 Annual costs. Tuition/fees (projected): $24,680. Program fees range from $1,000 to $1,900 depending on program. Room/board: $9,770. Books/supplies: $750. Personal expenses: $1,000.

2008-2009 Financial aid. All financial aid based on need. Average need met was 78%. Average scholarship/grant was $9,040; average loan $2,472. 58% of total undergraduate aid awarded as scholarships/grants, 42% as loans/jobs.

Application procedures. Admission: Priority date 3/1; no deadline. $60 fee, may be waived for applicants with need. Admission notification on a rolling basis beginning on or about 12/15. **Financial aid:** Priority date 3/1, closing date 4/1. FAFSA required. Applicants notified on a rolling basis starting 2/15; must reply by 5/1.

Academics. Special study options: Accelerated study, combined bachelor's/graduate degree, cooperative education, cross-registration, distance learning, double major, ESL, exchange student, honors, independent study, internships, liberal arts/career combination, student-designed major, study abroad, teacher certification program, Washington semester. **Credit/placement by examination:** AP, CLEP, institutional tests. 30 credit hours maximum toward bachelor's degree. **Support services:** Learning center, reduced course load, remedial instruction, study skills assistance, tutoring, writing center.

Majors. Biology: General, biochemistry. **Business:** General, accounting, finance, international, management information systems, managerial economics, statistics. **Communications:** General, broadcast journalism, journalism. **Computer sciences:** General, computer science, information systems. **Education:** General, biology, chemistry, computer, early childhood, elementary, English, foreign languages, French, health, history, mathematics, middle, physical, physics, science, secondary, social science, social studies, Spanish, special. **Engineering:** Chemical, civil, electrical, environmental, mechanical. **Foreign languages:** French, Spanish. **Health:** Nuclear medical technology, predental, premedicine, preveterinary. **History:** General. **Interdisciplinary:** Peace/conflict. **Legal studies:** Prelaw. **Math:** General. **Philosophy/religion:** Philosophy, religion. **Physical sciences:** Chemistry, physics. **Psychology:** General. **Social sciences:** Economics, sociology.

Most popular majors. Business/marketing 30%, communications/journalism 9%, education 11%, engineering/engineering technologies 21%.

Computing on campus. 320 workstations in library, computer center, student center. Dormitories wired for high-speed internet access and linked to campus network. Commuter students can connect to campus network. Online course registration, online library, helpline, repair service available.

Student life. Freshman orientation: Mandatory. **Housing:** Guaranteed on-campus for all undergraduates. Coed dorms available. $700 deposit, deadline 5/1. **Activities:** Bands, campus ministries, choral groups, dance, drama, international student organizations, literary magazine, music ensembles, Model UN, musical theater, radio station, student government, student newspaper, symphony orchestra, TV station, African American club, Caribbean society, Chinese student association, Circle-K, Gaelic society, Young Conservatives, Democrats, Republicans, multicultural student union.

Athletics. NCAA. **Intercollegiate:** Baseball M, basketball, cheerleading, cross-country, golf M, lacrosse, soccer, softball W, swimming W, tennis, track and field, volleyball W. **Intramural:** Baseball M, basketball, cross-country, soccer, softball, track and field, volleyball. **Team name:** Jaspers.

Student services. Alcohol/substance abuse counseling, chaplain/spiritual director, career counseling, student employment services, financial aid counseling, health services, personal counseling, placement for graduates, veterans' counselor. **Physically disabled:** Services for visually, hearing impaired.

Contact. E-mail: admit@manhattan.edu
Phone: (718) 862-7200 Toll-free number: (800) 622-9235
Fax: (718) 862-8019
William Bissett, Vice President for Enrollment Management, Manhattan College, 4513 Manhattan College Parkway, Riverdale, NY 10471

Manhattan School of Music
New York, New York
www.msmnyc.edu **CB code: 2396**

- Private 4-year music college
- Residential campus in very large city
- 422 degree-seeking undergraduates: 1% part-time, 49% women, 4% African American, 9% Asian American, 4% Hispanic American, 26% international
- 547 degree-seeking graduate students
- 38% of applicants admitted
- Application essay required
- 60% graduate within 6 years

General. Founded in 1917. Regionally accredited. Extensive performance opportunities on campus and off. **Degrees:** 95 bachelor's awarded; master's, doctoral offered. **Calendar:** Semester. **Full-time faculty:** 64 total; 81% have terminal degrees, 2% minority, 38% women. **Part-time faculty:** 191 total; 17% have terminal degrees, 7% minority, 31% women. **Class size:** 80% < 20, 16% 20-39, less than 1% 50-99, 3% >100. **Special facilities:** 850-seat concert hall, recital halls, state-of-the art-performance spaces, distance learning center, electronic music studios, recording studio, performance library.

Freshman class profile. 963 applied, 362 admitted, 106 enrolled.

GPA 3.75 or higher:	38%	**Return as sophomores:**	91%
GPA 3.50-3.74:	18%	**Out-of-state:**	70%
GPA 3.0-3.49:	36%	**Live on campus:**	98%
GPA 2.0-2.99:	8%	**International:**	29%

Basis for selection. Audition, availability of space in specific performance area, and academic record most important. Audition required. **Homeschooled:** Statement describing homeschool structure and mission, transcript of courses and grades, letter of recommendation (nonparent) required. GED accepted, but if no GED, SAT or ACT required.

High school preparation. College-preparatory program recommended. Recommended units include English 4, mathematics 3, social studies 4, history 4, science 3 and foreign language 4. Extensive music training required.

2008-2009 Annual costs. Tuition/fees: $30,475. Health fee of $2,250 required unless already insured. Room/board: $13,700. Books/supplies: $1,000. Personal expenses: $1,500.

2007-2008 Financial aid. Need-based: 69 full-time freshmen applied for aid; 58 were judged to have need; 55 of these received aid. Average need met was 41%. Average scholarship/grant was $14,869; average loan $3,833. 66% of total undergraduate aid awarded as scholarships/grants, 34% as loans/jobs. **Non-need-based:** Awarded to 37 full-time undergraduates, including 13 freshmen. Scholarships awarded for academics, alumni affiliation, leadership, music/drama.

Application procedures. Admission: Closing date 12/1 (receipt date). $100 fee, may be waived for applicants with need. Application must be submitted online. Admission notification 4/1. Must reply by May 1 or within 2 week(s) if notified thereafter. **Financial aid:** Closing date 3/1. FAFSA, institutional form, CSS PROFILE required. Applicants notified by 4/1; must reply by 5/1 or within 2 week(s) of notification.

Academics. Special study options: Cross-registration, ESL, independent study, study abroad. **Credit/placement by examination:** CLEP, institutional tests. 60 credit hours maximum toward bachelor's degree. **Support services:** Reduced course load, remedial instruction, tutoring.

Majors. **Visual/performing arts:** Music performance, music theory/composition.

Computing on campus. 20 workstations in library, computer center. Dormitories wired for high-speed internet access and linked to campus network. Online library, helpline, wireless network available.

Student life. **Freshman orientation:** Mandatory. Preregistration for classes offered. Held 1-2 weeks before classes start. **Policies:** Undergraduate students required to live in residence hall for first 2 years. Alcohol allowed only for those over 21 and only in designated areas. No smoking in any building. **Housing:** Guaranteed on-campus for freshmen. Coed dorms available. $500 nonrefundable deposit, deadline 6/15. Housing guaranteed only to students who submit documents and pay deposit by set deadline. **Activities:** Bands, choral groups, international student organizations, music ensembles, musical theater, opera, student government, student newspaper, symphony orchestra, Pan-African student union, international student association, chess club, resident community council, student council, gay, lesbian and transgender club, small performance organizations.

Student services. Career counseling, student employment services, financial aid counseling, personal counseling. **Physically disabled:** Services for visually impaired.

Contact. E-mail: admission@msmnyc.edu
Phone: (212) 749-2802 ext. 4436 Fax: (212) 749-3025
Amy Anderson, Associate Dean for Enrollment Management, Manhattan School of Music, 120 Claremont Avenue, New York, NY 10027-4698

Manhattanville College

Purchase, New York — **CB member**
www.manhattanville.edu — **CB code: 2397**

- Private 4-year liberal arts and teachers college
- Residential campus in small town
- 1,842 degree-seeking undergraduates: 7% part-time, 67% women
- 1,177 graduate students
- 52% of applicants admitted
- SAT or ACT, application essay required
- 59% graduate within 6 years; 30% enter graduate study

General. Founded in 1841. Regionally accredited. Strong relationship with United Nations. **Degrees:** 394 bachelor's awarded; master's offered. **Location:** 25 miles from New York City. **Calendar:** Semester, extensive summer session. **Full-time faculty:** 100 total; 96% have terminal degrees, 13% minority, 52% women. **Part-time faculty:** 166 total; 98% have terminal degrees, 12% minority, 51% women. **Class size:** 73% < 20, 25% 20-39, 2% 40-49. **Special facilities:** Photography laboratory, observatory, environmental biology laboratory, TV production studio, blackbox theater.

Freshman class profile. 4,556 applied, 2,350 admitted, 555 enrolled.

Mid 50% test scores		**GPA 2.0-2.99:**	43%
SAT critical reading:	500-610	**Rank in top quarter:**	47%
SAT math:	490-610	**Rank in top tenth:**	22%
SAT writing:	500-610	**End year in good standing:**	75%
ACT composite:	21-24	**Return as sophomores:**	75%
GPA 3.75 or higher:	9%	**Out-of-state:**	45%
GPA 3.50-3.74:	12%	**Live on campus:**	85%
GPA 3.0-3.49:	36%		

Basis for selection. School achievement record, recommendations, test scores or samples of academic work most important. Essay, school and community activities. Interview strongly recommended. Portfolio required for fine arts program; audition recommended for dance, music and theater programs.

High school preparation. 16 units required. Required units include English 4, mathematics 3, social studies 2, science 2 and academic electives 5.

2008-2009 Annual costs. Tuition/fees: $31,620. Room/board: $13,040. Books/supplies: $800. Personal expenses: $1,550.

2007-2008 Financial aid. **Need-based:** 246 full-time freshmen applied for aid; 233 were judged to have need; 231 of these received aid. Average scholarship/grant was $16,338; average loan $4,313. **Non-need-based:** Awarded to 1,317 full-time undergraduates, including 276 freshmen. Scholarships awarded for academics, alumni affiliation, art, leadership, music/drama. **Additional information:** Upper level students may earn additional money and academic credit through internship program.

Application procedures. **Admission:** Closing date 3/1 (postmark date). $65 fee, may be waived for applicants with need. Admission notification on a rolling basis beginning on or about 1/2. Must reply by May 1 or within 2 week(s) if notified thereafter. **Financial aid:** Closing date 3/1. FAFSA required. Applicants notified on a rolling basis starting 2/1; must reply by 5/1 or within 2 week(s) of notification.

Academics. Students must complete portfolio before graduation, which is individualized academic plan and profile. **Special study options:** Accelerated study, combined bachelor's/graduate degree, cooperative education, cross-registration, distance learning, double major, dual enrollment of high school students, ESL, exchange student, external degree, honors, independent study, internships, liberal arts/career combination, New York semester, student-designed major, study abroad, teacher certification program, Washington semester, weekend college. Study abroad programs in Oxford, Paris, Tokyo, Osaka, Madrid, Seville, Florence, Rome, Berlin, Galway and the world capitals program in Jerusalem, Santiago, Brussels, Buenos Aires, Prague, Moscow, and South Africa. **Credit/placement by examination:** AP, CLEP, IB, institutional tests. Up to 60 transfer credits allowed: up to 30 AP credits, up to 18 IB credits, no CLEP limit. **Support services:** Learning center, reduced course load, remedial instruction, study skills assistance, tutoring, writing center.

Majors. **Area/ethnic studies:** American, Asian, French. **Biology:** General, biochemistry. **Business:** Business admin, finance. **Communications:** General. **Computer sciences:** General. **Education:** General. **Foreign languages:** Romance. **History:** General. **Interdisciplinary:** Neuroscience. **Liberal arts:** Arts/sciences. **Math:** General. **Philosophy/religion:** Philosophy, religion. **Physical sciences:** Chemistry, physics. **Psychology:** General. **Social sciences:** Economics, political science, sociology. **Visual/performing arts:** Art history/conservation, dance, dramatic.

Most popular majors. Business/marketing 25%, education 9%, English 6%, history 8%, psychology 13%, social sciences 15%, visual/performing arts 11%.

Computing on campus. 270 workstations in dormitories, library, computer center, student center. Dormitories wired for high-speed internet access and linked to campus network. Commuter students can connect to campus network. Online course registration, online library, helpline, repair service, student web hosting, wireless network available.

Student life. **Freshman orientation:** Mandatory. Preregistration for classes offered. **Housing:** Coed dorms, wellness housing available. $370 deposit, deadline 5/1. **Activities:** Bands, campus ministries, choral groups, dance, drama, film society, international student organizations, literary magazine, music ensembles, Model UN, musical theater, opera, radio station, student government, student newspaper, symphony orchestra, TV station, language and culture clubs, Students Organized Against Racism, women's resource center, gay/straight coalition, political science association, multicultural advisory board, Black student union.

Athletics. NCAA. **Intercollegiate:** Baseball M, basketball, cheerleading M, field hockey W, golf M, ice hockey, lacrosse, soccer, softball W, tennis. **Intramural:** Basketball. **Team name:** Valiants.

Student services. Adult student services, alcohol/substance abuse counseling, chaplain/spiritual director, career counseling, services for economically disadvantaged, student employment services, financial aid counseling, health services, minority student services, personal counseling, placement for graduates, women's services. **Physically disabled:** Services for visually, speech, hearing impaired. **Learning disabled:** Comprehensive services available.

Contact. E-mail: admissions@mville.edu
Phone: (914) 323-5464 Toll-free number: (800) 328-4553
Fax: (914) 694-1732
Erica Padilla, Director of Admissions, Manhattanville College, 2900 Purchase Street, Purchase, NY 10577

Mannes College The New School for Music

New York, New York
www.mannes.edu — **CB code: 2398**

- Private 4-year music college
- Commuter campus in very large city
- 213 degree-seeking undergraduates: 12% part-time, 55% women, 3% African American, 10% Asian American, 4% Hispanic American, 36% international
- 192 degree-seeking graduate students
- 37% of applicants admitted
- 74% graduate within 6 years

General. Founded in 1916. Regionally accredited. Division of The New School. **Degrees:** 29 bachelor's awarded; master's offered. **Location:** Located in Manhattan. **Calendar:** Semester, limited summer session. **Full-time faculty:** 7 total; 14% have terminal degrees, 14% minority, 14% women. **Part-time faculty:** 138 total; 11% minority, 37% women. **Class size:** 96% < 20, 3% 20-39, less than 1% 40-49, less than 1% >100. **Special facilities:** 2 concert halls.

Freshman class profile. 543 applied, 201 admitted, 86 enrolled.

GPA 3.75 or higher:	17%	**Return as sophomores:**	84%
GPA 3.50-3.74:	13%	**Out-of-state:**	71%
GPA 3.0-3.49:	33%	**Live on campus:**	39%
GPA 2.0-2.99:	33%	**International:**	37%
End year in good standing:	100%		

Basis for selection. In order of importance: specific talent for major as evidenced by audition in major instrument or evaluation of previous accomplishment for composers and theory majors, general musicianship skills (ear, theory, etc.), academic record. Institutionally designed entrance examination, including major audition. Written examinations in music theory, dictation, ear training, and English usage. Audition required, essay recommended. Placement exams and interviews required for all Bachelor of Music, Bachelor of Science, Undergraduate Diploma, and Master of Music applicants. If applicant does not complete all sessions, application incomplete and will not be considered for acceptance. Tapes may be submitted for advisory opinion.

High school preparation. Required and recommended units include English 4, mathematics 4, social studies 2, science 4 (laboratory 2) and foreign language 2.

2008-2009 Annual costs. Tuition/fees: $32,150. Room/board: $12,390. Books/supplies: $2,050. Personal expenses: $1,550.

2008-2009 Financial aid. Need-based: 17 full-time freshmen applied for aid; 16 were judged to have need; 16 of these received aid. Average need met was 77%. Average scholarship/grant was $13,798; average loan $17,537. 36% of total undergraduate aid awarded as scholarships/grants, 64% as loans/jobs. **Non-need-based:** Scholarships awarded for academics, music/drama. **Additional information:** Closing date for scholarship applications 2 weeks prior to audition date.

Application procedures. Admission: Closing date 12/1 (postmark date). $100 fee. Admission notification on a rolling basis beginning on or about 4/1. Must reply by May 1 or within 4 week(s) if notified thereafter. **Financial aid:** No deadline. FAFSA required. Applicants notified on a rolling basis starting 3/1; must reply within 4 week(s) of notification.

Academics. Special study options: Accelerated study, double major, ESL, independent study, internships. **Credit/placement by examination:** CLEP. **Support services:** Remedial instruction, tutoring, writing center.

Majors. Visual/performing arts: Conducting, music performance, music theory/composition, piano/organ, stringed instruments, studio arts, voice/opera.

Computing on campus. 15 workstations in library, computer center. Dormitories wired for high-speed internet access and linked to campus network. Commuter students can connect to campus network. Online course registration, helpline, student web hosting, wireless network available.

Student life. Freshman orientation: Mandatory. **Housing:** Coed dorms, special housing for disabled available. $250 nonrefundable deposit, deadline 7/1. **Activities:** Jazz band, choral groups, dance, drama, film society, international student organizations, literary magazine, music ensembles, opera, radio station, student government, student newspaper, symphony orchestra.

Student services. Career counseling, student employment services, financial aid counseling, health services, personal counseling. **Learning disabled:** Comprehensive services available.

Contact. E-mail: mannesadmissions@newschool.edu
Phone: (212) 580-0210 ext. 4862 Toll-free number: (800) 292-3040
Georgia Schmitt, Director of Admissions, Mannes College The New School for Music, 150 West 85th Street, New York, NY 10024

Marist College

Poughkeepsie, New York — **CB member**
www.marist.edu — **CB code: 2400**

- Private 4-year liberal arts college
- Residential campus in small city
- 4,796 degree-seeking undergraduates: 6% part-time, 59% women, 3% African American, 2% Asian American, 6% Hispanic American
- 792 degree-seeking graduate students
- 37% of applicants admitted
- SAT or ACT with writing, application essay required
- 80% graduate within 6 years; 23% enter graduate study

General. Founded in 1929. Regionally accredited. Substantial internship opportunities for all majors. Students participate in community service program. **Degrees:** 1,155 bachelor's awarded; master's offered. **ROTC:** Army. **Location:** 75 miles from New York City, 75 miles from Albany. **Calendar:** Semester, limited summer session. **Full-time faculty:** 222 total; 75% have terminal degrees, 12% minority, 44% women. **Part-time faculty:** 328 total; 10% minority, 43% women. **Class size:** 53% < 20, 46% 20-39, less than 1% 40-49, less than 1% 50-99. **Special facilities:** Bureau of economic research, laboratory for environmental studies, management studies center, institute for public opinion, on-campus arboretum, online journalism laboratory.

Freshman class profile. 9,198 applied, 3,446 admitted, 1,022 enrolled.

Mid 50% test scores		**GPA 3.0-3.49:**	38%
SAT critical reading:	530-620	**GPA 2.0-2.99:**	22%
SAT math:	540-630	**Rank in top quarter:**	73%
SAT writing:	540-630	**Rank in top tenth:**	32%
ACT composite:	23-27	**Return as sophomores:**	88%
GPA 3.75 or higher:	24%	**Out-of-state:**	51%
GPA 3.50-3.74:	16%	**Live on campus:**	95%

Basis for selection. Secondary school achievement record, rank in top third of class primary consideration. Test scores, recommendations, activities, personal and leadership qualities also important. Campus visits and information sessions with admission counselors strongly recommended. **Homeschooled:** Transcript of courses and grades, letter of recommendation (nonparent) required.

High school preparation. 17 units required. Required and recommended units include English 4, mathematics 3-4, social studies 2, history 1, science 3-4 (laboratory 2-3), foreign language 2-3 and academic electives 2. 1 U.S. history required. 4 math recommended for computer science and physical science majors, 2 social studies required, 2 social science recommended.

2008-2009 Annual costs. Tuition/fees: $25,596. Room/board: $10,730. Books/supplies: $1,300. Personal expenses: $90.

2008-2009 Financial aid. Need-based: 854 full-time freshmen applied for aid; 616 were judged to have need; 613 of these received aid. Average need met was 72%. Average scholarship/grant was $12,662; average loan $3,793. 66% of total undergraduate aid awarded as scholarships/grants, 34% as loans/jobs. **Non-need-based:** Awarded to 2,635 full-time undergraduates, including 732 freshmen. Scholarships awarded for academics, athletics, music/drama, ROTC, state residency.

Application procedures. Admission: Closing date 2/15 (postmark date). $50 fee, may be waived for applicants with need. Admission notification 3/30. Must reply by 5/1. **Financial aid:** Priority date 2/15, closing date 5/1. FAFSA, institutional form required. Applicants notified on a rolling basis starting 3/15; must reply by 5/1 or within 2 week(s) of notification.

Academics. Paralegal certificates offered. **Special study options:** Accelerated study, combined bachelor's/graduate degree, cooperative education, cross-registration, distance learning, double major, dual enrollment of high school students, ESL, honors, independent study, internships, liberal arts/career combination, semester at sea, study abroad, teacher certification program, United Nations semester, Washington semester, weekend college. Undergraduates may take graduate classes. Cooperative education in arts, business, computer science, education, humanities, natural science, social/behavioral science, technologies. **Credit/placement by examination:** AP, CLEP, IB, SAT, ACT, institutional tests. ACT-PEP accepted on individual basis. **Support services:** Learning center, reduced course load, study skills assistance, tutoring, writing center.

Majors. Area/ethnic studies: American. **Biology:** General, biochemistry, biomedical sciences. **Business:** Accounting, business admin, fashion. **Communications:** Advertising, digital media, journalism, organizational, public relations, radio/tv. **Computer sciences:** Computer science, information systems, information technology, programming. **Conservation:** Environmental science. **Education:** Biology, chemistry, English, French, mathematics, social studies, Spanish, special. **Foreign languages:** French, Spanish. **Health:** Athletic training, clinical lab science. **History:** General. **Math:** General, applied, computational. **Philosophy/religion:** Philosophy. **Physical sciences:** Chemistry. **Protective services:** Law enforcement admin. **Psychology:** General. **Public administration:** Social work. **Social sciences:** Economics, political science. **Visual/performing arts:** Art, art history/conservation, fashion design, studio arts.

Most popular majors. Business/marketing 26%, communications/journalism 21%, education 12%, liberal arts 7%, psychology 7%.

Computing on campus. 646 workstations in dormitories, library, computer center, student center. Dormitories wired for high-speed internet access and linked to campus network. Commuter students can connect to campus network. Online course registration, online library, helpline, repair service, student web hosting, wireless network available.

Student life. **Freshman orientation:** Mandatory, $90 fee. 1-day orientation in June. **Housing:** Guaranteed on-campus for freshmen. Coed dorms, special housing for disabled, apartments, wellness housing available. Garden apartments, townhouses, suites available. **Activities:** Bands, campus ministries, choral groups, dance, drama, film society, literary magazine, music ensembles, musical theater, radio station, student government, student newspaper, TV station, black student union, Asian Alliance, Circle K, ARCO, community service programs, Habitat for Humanity, political science club, council on theatre arts, social action clubs.

Athletics. NCAA. **Intercollegiate:** Baseball M, basketball, cross-country, diving, football (tackle) M, lacrosse, rowing (crew), soccer, softball W, swimming, tennis, track and field, volleyball W, water polo W. **Intramural:** Basketball, soccer, softball, volleyball. **Team name:** Red Foxes.

Student services. Adult student services, alcohol/substance abuse counseling, chaplain/spiritual director, career counseling, student employment services, financial aid counseling, health services, personal counseling, placement for graduates, veterans' counselor. **Physically disabled:** Services for visually, hearing impaired. **Learning disabled:** Comprehensive services available.

Contact. E-mail: admission@marist.edu
Phone: (845) 575-3226 Toll-free number: (800) 436-5483
Fax: (845) 575-3215
Kent Rinehart, Dean of Undergraduate Admission, Marist College, 3399 North Road, Poughkeepsie, NY 12601-1387

Marymount Manhattan College

New York, New York — **CB member**
www.mmm.edu — **CB code: 2405**

- Private 4-year liberal arts college
- Residential campus in very large city
- 1,897 degree-seeking undergraduates: 12% part-time, 75% women, 11% African American, 3% Asian American, 11% Hispanic American, 3% international
- 69% of applicants admitted
- SAT or ACT (ACT writing optional), application essay required
- 49% graduate within 6 years

General. Founded in 1936. Regionally accredited. **Degrees:** 375 bachelor's, 5 associate awarded. **Calendar:** Semester, limited summer session. **Full-time faculty:** 96 total; 88% have terminal degrees, 14% minority, 55% women. **Part-time faculty:** 170 total; 44% have terminal degrees, 18% minority, 62% women. **Class size:** 73% < 20, 27% 20-39. **Special facilities:** Communications and learning center, communication arts multimedia suite, center for science education.

Freshman class profile. 3,065 applied, 2,130 admitted, 562 enrolled.

Mid 50% test scores			
SAT critical reading:	500-600	GPA 3.0-3.49:	44%
SAT math:	460-560	GPA 2.0-2.99:	32%
ACT composite:	21-25	Return as sophomores:	62%
GPA 3.75 or higher:	10%	Out-of-state:	31%
GPA 3.50-3.74:	14%	Live on campus:	78%
		International:	2%

Basis for selection. High school GPA of 3.0 and SAT verbal and math scores of 450 each recommended. Letters of recommendation from teachers and administrators, extracurricular and community activities important. Rolling deadline for SAT/ACT score receipt. If students submit the Writing part of the SAT or ACT we look at it, but it is not a basis for any decision. Interview recommended for all; audition required for acting, dance, and theater programs; portfolio recommended for art program. **Homeschooled:** Transcript of courses and grades required. Must submit official high school transcripts if high school attended before withdrawing. **Learning Disabled:** Interview and Wechsler Delta Adult Intelligence Scale test required.

High school preparation. College-preparatory program recommended. 17 units required. Required and recommended units include English 4, mathematics 3, social studies 3, science 3 (laboratory 2), foreign language 2 and academic electives 4.

2008-2009 Annual costs. Tuition/fees: $21,792. Room/board: $12,660. Books/supplies: $1,000. Personal expenses: $3,000.

2008-2009 Financial aid. **Need-based:** 436 full-time freshmen applied for aid; 335 were judged to have need; 334 of these received aid. Average need met was 50%. Average scholarship/grant was $10,134; average loan $2,860. 45% of total undergraduate aid awarded as scholarships/grants, 55% as loans/jobs. **Non-need-based:** Awarded to 362 full-time undergraduates, including 355 freshmen. Scholarships awarded for academics, art, leadership, music/drama. **Additional information:** Limited international scholarships for top applicants.

Application procedures. **Admission:** Priority date 3/15; no deadline. $60 fee, may be waived for applicants with need. Admission notification on a rolling basis beginning on or about 9/1. Must reply by May 1 or within 3 week(s) if notified thereafter. **Financial aid:** Priority date 3/15; no closing date. FAFSA required. Applicants notified on a rolling basis starting 3/15; must reply by 5/1 or within 3 week(s) of notification.

Academics. **Special study options:** Accelerated study, distance learning, double major, dual enrollment of high school students, exchange student, independent study, internships, liberal arts/career combination, study abroad, teacher certification program. 5-year bachelor's/master's program in computer science with Polytechnic University, programs with Laboratory Institute of Merchandising, New York School of Interior Design, Deutsches Haus at New York University, China Institute, New York Institute of Finance, American Institute of Banking, Hunter College of CUNY, Martha Graham School of Dance, HEOP. **Credit/placement by examination:** AP, CLEP, IB, SAT, institutional tests. 30 credit hours maximum toward bachelor's degree. Maximum of 12 credits for language proficiency. SAT Subject used for placement if submitted. **Support services:** Learning center, reduced course load, remedial instruction, study skills assistance, tutoring, writing center.

Majors. **Biology:** General. **Business:** Accounting, business admin. **Communications:** General. **Health:** Audiology/speech pathology. **History:** General. **Liberal arts:** Humanities. **Philosophy/religion:** Philosophy, religion. **Psychology:** General. **Social sciences:** International relations, political science, sociology. **Visual/performing arts:** Acting, art, art history/conservation, dance, dramatic, graphic design, studio arts.

Most popular majors. Business/marketing 13%, communications/journalism 20%, English 7%, psychology 9%, visual/performing arts 39%.

Computing on campus. 215 workstations in library, computer center, student center. Dormitories wired for high-speed internet access and linked to campus network. Commuter students can connect to campus network. Wireless network available.

Student life. **Freshman orientation:** Mandatory. Preregistration for classes offered. 3 days of introductions, information, activities, and social engagements. **Housing:** Coed dorms available. $500 nonrefundable deposit, deadline 5/1. **Activities:** Choral groups, dance, drama, international student organizations, literary magazine, musical theater, radio station, student government, student newspaper, ethnic, religious, political, women's, environmental, and cultural groups, student professional organizations, and honor societies.

Student services. Adult student services, alcohol/substance abuse counseling, chaplain/spiritual director, career counseling, student employment services, financial aid counseling, health services, personal counseling, placement for graduates. **Physically disabled:** Services for speech, hearing impaired. **Learning disabled:** Comprehensive services available.

Contact. E-mail: admissions@mmm.edu
Phone: (212) 517-0430 Toll-free number: (800) 627-9668
Fax: (212) 517-0448
Jim Rogers, Dean of Admissions, Marymount Manhattan College, 221 East 71st Street, New York, NY 10021-4597

Medaille College

Buffalo, New York
www.medaille.edu — **CB code: 2422**

- Private 4-year liberal arts college
- Commuter campus in large city
- 1,669 degree-seeking undergraduates: 2% part-time, 62% women, 13% African American, 1% Asian American, 2% Hispanic American, 1% Native American
- 1,195 degree-seeking graduate students
- 73% of applicants admitted
- SAT or ACT with writing, application essay required
- 44% graduate within 6 years; 27% enter graduate study

General. Founded in 1875. Regionally accredited. **Degrees:** 321 bachelor's, 94 associate awarded; master's offered. **ROTC:** Army. **Location:** 3 miles from downtown. **Calendar:** Semester, limited summer session. **Full-time faculty:** 89 total; 58% have terminal degrees, 15% minority, 44% women. **Part-time faculty:** 258 total; 10% have terminal degrees, 6% minority, 51% women. **Class size:** 58% < 20, 41% 20-39, less than 1% 40-49, less than 1% 50-99, less than 1% >100. **Special facilities:** New media institute.

Freshman class profile. 1,319 applied, 963 admitted, 411 enrolled.

Mid 50% test scores		**GPA 3.0-3.49:**	23%
SAT critical reading:	430-520	**GPA 2.0-2.99:**	53%
SAT math:	410-500	**End year in good standing:**	84%
ACT composite:	18-21	**Return as sophomores:**	68%
GPA 3.75 or higher:	7%	**Out-of-state:**	3%
GPA 3.50-3.74:	9%	**Live on campus:**	28%

Basis for selection. Motivation and maturity, as well as academic record and test scores, considered. SAT recommended. Interview strongly recommended.

High school preparation. College-preparatory program recommended. 12 units required; 20 recommended. Required and recommended units include English 4, mathematics 2-3, social studies 4, history 2, science 2-3 (laboratory 2) and foreign language 2. 3 math, 3 science recommended for veterinary technology.

2008-2009 Annual costs. Tuition/fees: $18,230. Continuing students tuition is $17,420. Room/board: $8,846. Books/supplies: $1,100. Personal expenses: $1,100.

2007-2008 Financial aid. Need-based: 381 full-time freshmen applied for aid; 381 were judged to have need; 381 of these received aid. Average need met was 70%. Average scholarship/grant was $8,000; average loan $5,000. 53% of total undergraduate aid awarded as scholarships/grants, 47% as loans/jobs. **Non-need-based:** Awarded to 734 full-time undergraduates, including 397 freshmen. Scholarships awarded for academics, leadership.

Application procedures. Admission: Priority date 8/1; no deadline. $25 fee, may be waived for applicants with need, free for online applicants. Admission notification on a rolling basis beginning on or about 10/1. Must reply by May 1 or within 4 week(s) if notified thereafter. **Financial aid:** Priority date 3/1; no closing date. FAFSA required. Applicants notified on a rolling basis starting 3/1; must reply within 2 week(s) of notification.

Academics. All pre-professional programs require participation in at least 1 internship. Branch campuses in Amherst and Rochester. **Special study options:** Accelerated study, combined bachelor's/graduate degree, cross-registration, double major, honors, independent study, internships, liberal arts/career combination, student-designed major, teacher certification program, weekend college. Module system for full-time evening students and for full-time weekend students. **Credit/placement by examination:** AP, CLEP, IB, SAT. 30 credit hours maximum toward associate degree, 60 toward bachelor's. **Support services:** Learning center, reduced course load, remedial instruction, study skills assistance, tutoring.

Majors. Biology: General. **Business:** General, business admin, management information systems. **Communications:** Media studies. **Computer sciences:** General. **Education:** General, biology, elementary, English, mathematics, middle, secondary, social studies. **Family/consumer sciences:** Child care. **Health:** Veterinary technology/assistant. **Interdisciplinary:** Biopsychology. **Liberal arts:** Arts/sciences. **Math:** General. **Parks/recreation:** Sports admin. **Protective services:** Police science. **Psychology:** General. **Visual/performing arts:** General.

Most popular majors. Business/marketing 47%, education 14%, liberal arts 6%, parks/recreation 7%.

Computing on campus. 120 workstations in dormitories, library, computer center, student center. Dormitories wired for high-speed internet access and linked to campus network. Commuter students can connect to campus network. Online library, wireless network available.

Student life. Freshman orientation: Mandatory. Preregistration for classes offered. **Housing:** Coed dorms, single-sex dorms, apartments, wellness housing available. $100 deposit, deadline 9/1. **Activities:** Drama, film society, literary magazine, musical theater, radio station, student government, student newspaper, TV station, African American student union, child and youth services club, student volunteer center, multicultural association, SADD, international student society, resident student council.

Athletics. NCAA. **Intercollegiate:** Baseball M, basketball, bowling W, cross-country, golf, lacrosse, soccer, softball W, volleyball. **Team name:** Mavericks.

Student services. Adult student services, career counseling, student employment services, financial aid counseling, health services, personal counseling, placement for graduates, veterans' counselor. **Physically disabled:** Services for visually, speech, hearing impaired.

Contact. E-mail: admissionsug@medaille.edu
Phone: (716) 880-2200 Toll-free number: (800) 292-1582
Fax: (716) 880-2007
Greg Florczak, Director of Undergraduate Admissions, Medaille College, 18 Agassiz Circle, Buffalo, NY 14214

Medaille College: Amherst
Williamsville, New York

- Private 4-year liberal arts college
- Small town

General. Calendar: Semester.

Annual costs/financial aid. Tuition/fees (2008-2009): $18,230.

Contact. Phone: (716) 631-1061
30 Wilson Road, Williamsville, NY 14221

Medaille College: Rochester
Rochester, New York

- Private 4-year liberal arts college
- Small city

General. Calendar: Semester.

Annual costs/financial aid. Tuition/fees (2008-2009): $18,230.

Contact. Phone: (585) 272-0030
100 Corporate Woods, Suite 200, Rochester, NY 14623

Mercy College
Dobbs Ferry, New York
www.mercy.edu **CB code: 2409**

- Private 4-year liberal arts college
- Commuter campus in large town
- 5,004 degree-seeking undergraduates: 29% part-time, 69% women, 26% African American, 4% Asian American, 29% Hispanic American, 1% international
- 3,492 degree-seeking graduate students
- 60% of applicants admitted

General. Founded in 1950. Regionally accredited. Campuses in Dobbs Ferry, White Plains, Yorktown Heights, Bronx, Manhattan. **Degrees:** 1,037 bachelor's, 95 associate awarded; master's, doctoral offered. **ROTC:** Army, Air Force. **Calendar:** Semester, extensive summer session. **Full-time faculty:** 169 total; 69% have terminal degrees, 18% minority, 55% women. **Part-time faculty:** 640 total; 18% minority, 52% women. **Class size:** 69% < 20, 31% 20-39, less than 1% 40-49. **Special facilities:** Music and recording studios.

Freshman class profile. 2,584 applied, 1,545 admitted, 774 enrolled.

GPA 3.75 or higher:	3%	**Return as sophomores:**	61%
GPA 3.50-3.74:	5%	**Out-of-state:**	5%
GPA 3.0-3.49:	12%	**Live on campus:**	6%
GPA 2.0-2.99:	52%	**International:**	1%

Basis for selection. SAT/ACT optional. SAT Subject Tests recommended. Additional interview with Program Director required for Nursing, Occupational Therapy, Physical Therapy, Social Work, Veterinary Technology, Computer Arts programs. **Homeschooled:** State high school equivalency certificate required.

High school preparation. College-preparatory program required. 21 units required. Required units include English 4, mathematics 4, social studies 2, history 2, science 3 (laboratory 1), foreign language 3 and academic electives 3.

2008-2009 Annual costs. Tuition/fees: $15,470. Room/board: $9,820. Books/supplies: $1,200. Personal expenses: $1,210.

2008-2009 Financial aid. Need-based: 628 full-time freshmen applied for aid; 605 were judged to have need; 557 of these received aid. Average

need met was 43%. Average scholarship/grant was $9,136; average loan $3,330. 68% of total undergraduate aid awarded as scholarships/grants, 32% as loans/jobs. **Non-need-based:** Awarded to 994 full-time undergraduates, including 337 freshmen. Scholarships awarded for academics, athletics.

Application procedures. **Admission:** No deadline. $40 fee, may be waived for applicants with need. Admission notification on a rolling basis beginning on or about 8/1. Must reply by May 1 or within 3 week(s) if notified thereafter. **Financial aid:** Priority date 2/15; no closing date. FAFSA required. Applicants notified on a rolling basis starting 4/1; must reply within 2 week(s) of notification.

Academics. Some graduate programs on trimester and quarter schedule. Programs leading to provisional state certification offered in education. **Special study options:** Accelerated study, combined bachelor's/graduate degree, cooperative education, distance learning, double major, dual enrollment of high school students, honors, internships, teacher certification program, weekend college. Program for college students with learning disabilities. **Credit/placement by examination:** AP, CLEP, SAT, ACT, institutional tests. 30 credit hours maximum toward associate degree, 30 toward bachelor's. **Support services:** Learning center, reduced course load, remedial instruction, study skills assistance, tutoring.

Honors college/program. Minimum 90 or above high school average required. Approximately 65 freshmen admitted. Students take honors English, speech and math freshmen year and additional four academic honors courses for total of 24 credits.

Majors. **Agriculture:** Animal sciences. **Biology:** General. **Business:** Accounting, accounting/business management, business admin. **Communications:** Media studies. **Computer sciences:** General, information systems, security. **Foreign languages:** Spanish. **Health:** Audiology/speech pathology, clinical lab science, health services, nursing admin. **History:** General. **Liberal arts:** Arts/sciences. **Math:** General. **Protective services:** Law enforcement admin. **Psychology:** General. **Public administration:** Social work. **Social sciences:** General, political science, sociology. **Visual/performing arts:** Commercial/advertising art. **Other:** Music industry and technology.

Most popular majors. Business/marketing 24%, health sciences 16%, psychology 10%, social sciences 29%.

Computing on campus. 680 workstations in dormitories, library, computer center, student center. Dormitories wired for high-speed internet access and linked to campus network. Commuter students can connect to campus network. Online course registration, online library, helpline, repair service, wireless network available.

Student life. **Freshman orientation:** Available. Preregistration for classes offered. **Policies:** Student services geared to commuter population with midday activities and programs. **Housing:** Coed dorms available. $300 nonrefundable deposit, deadline 5/1. **Activities:** Campus ministries, dance, Model UN, student government, student newspaper, Reporter's Impact, Green club, Dance Off Society Showstoppers, chess club, Latin American student association, Mercy College Models, Veterinary Technology club, Italian club, Accounting Society, Creative Minds poetry club.

Athletics. NCAA. **Intercollegiate:** Baseball M, basketball, cross-country, soccer, softball W, tennis M, track and field, volleyball W. **Intramural:** Baseball M, basketball, softball. **Team name:** Mavericks.

Student services. Adult student services, alcohol/substance abuse counseling, career counseling, services for economically disadvantaged, student employment services, financial aid counseling, health services, minority student services, on-campus daycare, personal counseling, placement for graduates. **Physically disabled:** Services for visually, speech, hearing impaired.

Contact. E-mail: admissions@mercy.edu
Phone: (914) 674-7324 Toll-free number: (877) 637-2946
Fax: (914) 674-7608
Deirdre Whitman, Vice President for Enrollment Management, Mercy College, 555 Broadway, Dobbs Ferry, NY 10522

Mesivta Torah Vodaath Seminary

Brooklyn, New York

CB code: 0636

- Private 5-year rabbinical college for men affiliated with Jewish faith
- Very large city

General. Founded in 1918. Accredited by AARTS. **Calendar:** Semester.

Annual costs/financial aid. Tuition/fees (2008-2009): $7,050. Room/board: $4,500.

Contact. Phone: (718) 941-8000
Director of Admissions, 425 East Ninth Street, Brooklyn, NY 11218

Metropolitan College of New York

New York, New York — **CB member**
www.metropolitan.edu — **CB code: 4802**

- Private 4-year business and liberal arts college
- Commuter campus in very large city
- 582 degree-seeking undergraduates
- 42% of applicants admitted
- Application essay, interview required

General. Founded in 1964. Regionally accredited. Students attend 3-semester full year with 1-month break. Off-site extensions for human services program in the Bronx, Staten Island and northeastern Queens. Students receive credit for applying studies to jobs or internship sites. **Degrees:** 222 bachelor's, 54 associate awarded; master's offered. **Location:** In downtown Manhattan. **Calendar:** Semester, extensive summer session. **Full-time faculty:** 27 total. **Part-time faculty:** 156 total; 33% minority, 49% women. **Class size:** 73% < 20, 27% 20-39.

Freshman class profile. 528 applied, 220 admitted, 115 enrolled.

Basis for selection. Academic record, test scores, previous volunteer experience, school and community activities, professional recommendations, motivation and communication skills as demonstrated in interviews considered. Combined SAT score of 1050 (exclusive of Writing) or higher can be substituted for institution-administered Test of Adult Basic Education or ACCUPLACER required for admission.

High school preparation. 16 units required. Required units include English 4, mathematics 2, social studies 2, science 1 and foreign language 4.

2008-2009 Annual costs. Tuition/fees: $16,750. Tuition reported is undergraduate business program; other programs may vary in cost. Books/supplies: $1,500. Personal expenses: $726.

2007-2008 Financial aid. **Non-need-based:** Scholarships awarded for academics. **Additional information:** Limited merit scholarships.

Application procedures. **Admission:** Priority date 8/15; no deadline. $30 fee, may be waived for applicants with need. Admission notification on a rolling basis beginning on or about 3/15. **Financial aid:** Priority date 3/15; no closing date. FAFSA required. Applicants notified on a rolling basis.

Academics. Class work integrated with field work. Class learning applied, documented and assessed in internship or employment setting. **Special study options:** Accelerated study, cooperative education, honors, internships, liberal arts/career combination, study abroad, teacher certification program, weekend college. **Credit/placement by examination:** CLEP, IB. 32 credit hours maximum toward bachelor's degree. **Support services:** Learning center, remedial instruction, tutoring.

Majors. **Area/ethnic studies:** African-American. **Business:** General, business admin, communications, managerial economics. **Communications:** General. **Education:** General. **Legal studies:** Prelaw. **Public administration:** Community org/advocacy, human services, social work. **Social sciences:** General, sociology, urban studies.

Most popular majors. Business/marketing 30%, public administration/social services 70%.

Computing on campus. 130 workstations in library, computer center.

Student life. **Freshman orientation:** Mandatory. **Activities:** Drama, student government, student newspaper, honor societies, networking club, dance committee.

Student services. Adult student services, career counseling, student employment services, financial aid counseling, personal counseling, placement for graduates, veterans' counselor. **Physically disabled:** Services for visually, hearing impaired.

Contact. Phone: (212) 343-1234 ext. 5001 Toll-free number: (800) 338-4465 Fax: (212) 343-8470
Steven Lenhart, Vice President of Enrollment Management, Metropolitan College of New York, 431 Canal Street, New York, NY 10013-1919

Mirrer Yeshiva Central Institute
Brooklyn, New York
CB code: 0661

- Private 4-year rabbinical college for men affiliated with Jewish faith
- Very large city

General. Accredited by AARTS. **Calendar:** Continuous.

Annual costs/financial aid. Tuition/fees (2008-2009): $4,700. Room/board: $4,000.

Contact. Phone: (718) 645-0536
Admissions Director, 1795 Ocean Parkway, Brooklyn, NY 11223

Molloy College
Rockville Centre, New York **CB member**
www.molloy.edu **CB code: 2415**

- Private 4-year liberal arts college affiliated with Roman Catholic Church
- Commuter campus in large town
- 2,817 degree-seeking undergraduates: 25% part-time, 78% women, 18% African American, 7% Asian American, 10% Hispanic American, 1% international
- 920 graduate students
- 56% of applicants admitted
- SAT or ACT with writing, application essay required

General. Founded in 1955. Regionally accredited. Independent institution in Dominican tradition. **Degrees:** 572 bachelor's, 44 associate awarded; master's offered. **ROTC:** Army, Naval, Air Force. **Location:** 20 miles from New York City. **Calendar:** 4-1-4, limited summer session. **Full-time faculty:** 162 total; 67% have terminal degrees, 12% minority, 74% women. **Part-time faculty:** 331 total; 24% have terminal degrees, 10% minority, 67% women. **Class size:** 69% < 20, 31% 20-39, less than 1% 40-49. **Special facilities:** Weather station at Jones Beach, international business center.

Freshman class profile. 1,664 applied, 933 admitted, 404 enrolled.

Mid 50% test scores		**GPA 3.0-3.49:**	56%
SAT critical reading:	440-520	**GPA 2.0-2.99:**	11%
SAT math:	450-550	**Rank in top quarter:**	26%
SAT writing:	440-540	**Rank in top tenth:**	8%
GPA 3.75 or higher:	10%	**International:**	1%
GPA 3.50-3.74:	23%		

Basis for selection. Secondary school achievement with particular attention to grade 11 performance most important. Test scores also important. Recommendations, school and community activities, interview considered. Audition required for music program; portfolio required for art program. **Homeschooled:** State high school equivalency certificate required. **Learning Disabled:** Applicants reviewed by separate committee.

High school preparation. College-preparatory program required. 19 units required. Required units include English 4, mathematics 3, social studies 4, science 3 and foreign language 3. Science, math, and nursing majors must have 1 biology, 1 chemistry, and 3 math.

2008-2009 Annual costs. Tuition/fees: $19,635. Books/supplies: $900. Personal expenses: $2,040.

2008-2009 Financial aid. Need-based: 365 full-time freshmen applied for aid; 297 were judged to have need; 296 of these received aid. Average need met was 65%. Average scholarship/grant was $9,660; average loan $3,952. 41% of total undergraduate aid awarded as scholarships/grants, 59% as loans/jobs. **Non-need-based:** Awarded to 364 full-time undergraduates, including 102 freshmen. Scholarships awarded for academics, art, athletics, leadership, music/drama.

Application procedures. Admission: Priority date 11/15; no deadline. $30 fee, may be waived for applicants with need. Admission notification on a rolling basis beginning on or about 11/1. **Financial aid:** Priority date 4/15, closing date 5/1. FAFSA required. Applicants notified on a rolling basis starting 3/1.

Academics. Special study options: Accelerated study, combined bachelor's/graduate degree, cooperative education, cross-registration, double major, ESL, honors, independent study, internships, liberal arts/career combination, student-designed major, study abroad, teacher certification program, weekend college. **Credit/placement by examination:** AP, CLEP, IB, SAT, ACT, institutional tests. 15 credit hours maximum toward associate degree, 30 toward bachelor's. **Support services:** Learning center, pre-admission summer program, reduced course load, remedial instruction, study skills assistance, tutoring, writing center.

Majors. Biology: General, ecology. **Business:** Accounting, business admin. **Communications:** General. **Computer sciences:** Computer science, information systems. **Education:** General, art, biology, elementary, English, history, mathematics, music, secondary, social studies, Spanish, special. **Foreign languages:** Spanish. **Health:** Audiology/speech pathology, health services admin, music therapy, nursing (RN). **History:** General. **Liberal arts:** Arts/sciences. **Math:** General. **Philosophy/religion:** Philosophy. **Protective services:** Law enforcement admin. **Psychology:** General. **Public administration:** Social work. **Social sciences:** Political science, sociology. **Visual/performing arts:** General, art, music performance.

Most popular majors. Business/marketing 8%, education 12%, health sciences 46%.

Computing on campus. 420 workstations in library, computer center, student center. Commuter students can connect to campus network. Online course registration, online library, helpline, wireless network available.

Student life. Freshman orientation: Mandatory. **Activities:** Jazz band, choral groups, dance, drama, literary magazine, music ensembles, musical theater, student government, student newspaper, African American and Caribbean organization, Gaelic society, Out for Acceptance, social work club, Union Hispana de Molloy, Youth for Christ, HOPE Team.

Athletics. NCAA. **Intercollegiate:** Baseball M, basketball, cross-country, equestrian, lacrosse, soccer, softball W, tennis W, volleyball W. **Team name:** Lions.

Student services. Adult student services, alcohol/substance abuse counseling, chaplain/spiritual director, career counseling, services for economically disadvantaged, student employment services, financial aid counseling, health services, personal counseling, veterans' counselor. **Physically disabled:** Services for visually, hearing impaired.

Contact. E-mail: admissions@molloy.edu
Phone: (516) 678-5000 ext. 6240 Toll-free number: (888) 466-5569
Fax: (516) 256-2247
Marguerite Lane, Director of Admissions, Molloy College, PO Box 5002, Rockville Centre, NY 11570

Monroe College
Bronx, New York
www.monroecollege.edu **CB code: 2463**

- For-profit 4-year business and health science college
- Commuter campus in very large city
- 6,307 degree-seeking undergraduates: 20% part-time, 71% women, 47% African American, 1% Asian American, 41% Hispanic American, 6% international
- 397 degree-seeking graduate students
- 61% of applicants admitted
- Application essay, interview required
- 51% graduate within 6 years; 15% enter graduate study

General. Founded in 1933. Regionally accredited. Branch campus in New Rochelle offers all programs, courses, and services available at main campus. **Degrees:** 685 bachelor's, 1,421 associate awarded; master's offered. **ROTC:** Army. **Calendar:** Semester, extensive summer session. **Full-time faculty:** 79 total; 38% have terminal degrees, 77% minority, 53% women. **Part-time faculty:** 258 total; 10% have terminal degrees, 58% minority, 42% women. **Class size:** 44% < 20, 55% 20-39, less than 1% 50-99.

Freshman class profile. 2,612 applied, 1,592 admitted, 1,295 enrolled.

End year in good standing:	70%	**Live on campus:**	25%
Return as sophomores:	78%	**International:**	4%
Out-of-state:	1%		

Basis for selection. Interview, school achievement record, test scores required. Modified open admissions for students who pass admissions test.

2008-2009 Annual costs. Tuition/fees: $11,212. Room/board: $7,100. Books/supplies: $900. Personal expenses: $5,102.

2007-2008 Financial aid. All financial aid based on need.

Application procedures. Admission: No deadline. $35 fee. Admission notification on a rolling basis. **Financial aid:** Closing date 3/31. FAFSA required. Applicants notified on a rolling basis starting 7/1.

Academics. **Special study options:** Cooperative education, distance learning, dual enrollment of high school students, honors, internships, liberal arts/career combination, study abroad, weekend college. **Credit/placement by examination:** AP, CLEP, IB, institutional tests. 30 credit hours maximum toward associate degree, 30 toward bachelor's. **Support services:** Learning center, pre-admission summer program, remedial instruction, study skills assistance, tutoring, writing center.

Majors. **Business:** Accounting, business admin, hospitality admin. **Computer sciences:** General. **Health:** Health services admin. **Protective services:** Law enforcement admin.

Most popular majors. Business/marketing 60%, computer/information sciences 20%, security/protective services 17%.

Computing on campus. 800 workstations in dormitories, library, computer center. Dormitories wired for high-speed internet access and linked to campus network. Commuter students can connect to campus network. Online course registration, online library, helpline, wireless network available.

Student life. **Freshman orientation:** Mandatory. Preregistration for classes offered. **Housing:** Coed dorms available. $100 deposit. Assistance for foreign students in securing local housing. Student apartments available near New Rochelle campus. On-campus housing at New Rochelle campus. **Activities:** Dance, international student organizations, Students in Free Enterprise, NABA.

Athletics. NJCAA. **Intercollegiate:** Baseball M, basketball, soccer M, volleyball W. **Intramural:** Basketball, softball W. **Team name:** Mustangs.

Student services. Adult student services, career counseling, student employment services, financial aid counseling, personal counseling, placement for graduates, veterans' counselor. **Physically disabled:** Services for visually, speech, hearing impaired.

Contact. E-mail: ejerome@monroecollege.edu
Phone: (718) 933-6700 Toll-free number: (800) 556-6676
Fax: (718) 364-3552
Evan Jerome, Director of Admissions, Monroe College, Monroe College Way, Bronx, NY 10468

Mount St. Mary College

Newburgh, New York — **CB member**
www.msmc.edu — **CB code: 2423**

- Private 4-year liberal arts college affiliated with Roman Catholic Church
- Residential campus in large town
- 2,067 degree-seeking undergraduates: 15% part-time, 74% women, 8% African American, 2% Asian American, 10% Hispanic American
- 493 degree-seeking graduate students
- 77% of applicants admitted
- SAT or ACT with writing required
- 53% graduate within 6 years; 31% enter graduate study

General. Founded in 1954. Regionally accredited. Independent institution in Judeo-Christian tradition, founded by Dominican Sisters of Newburgh. **Degrees:** 437 bachelor's awarded; master's offered. **Location:** 58 miles from New York City. **Calendar:** Semester, limited summer session. **Full-time faculty:** 76 total; 88% have terminal degrees, 10% minority, 59% women. **Part-time faculty:** 141 total; 24% have terminal degrees, 10% minority, 52% women. **Class size:** 39% < 20, 58% 20-39, 2% 40-49, 1% 50-99. **Special facilities:** Elementary school on campus.

Freshman class profile. 1,878 applied, 1,448 admitted, 439 enrolled.

Mid 50% test scores		**GPA 2.0-2.99:**	31%
SAT critical reading:	450-550	**Rank in top quarter:**	37%
SAT math:	450-550	**Rank in top tenth:**	11%
SAT writing:	450-540	**End year in good standing:**	81%
ACT composite:	18-23	**Return as sophomores:**	68%
GPA 3.75 or higher:	9%	**Out-of-state:**	19%
GPA 3.50-3.74:	18%	**Live on campus:**	73%
GPA 3.0-3.49:	40%		

Basis for selection. Admissions decisions based on total admission score which weighs high school average, class rank, and test scores as well as teacher/counselor recommendations. Interview recommended for all; essay required for special consideration, recommended for all others. **Homeschooled:** Transcript of courses and grades required. **Learning Disabled:** Must include IEP with application. Must meet with Director of Counseling and Coordinator of Services for Persons with Disabilities.

High school preparation. College-preparatory program recommended. 20 units recommended. Recommended units include English 4, mathematics 3, social studies 4, science 3, foreign language 3, academic electives 3.5. Recommended math sequence is algebra, geometry, trigonometry. Biology and chemistry required for nursing majors.

2008-2009 Annual costs. Tuition/fees: $20,745. Room/board: $11,030. Books/supplies: $1,000. Personal expenses: $1,000.

2008-2009 Financial aid. **Need-based:** 399 full-time freshmen applied for aid; 327 were judged to have need; 326 of these received aid. Average need met was 68%. Average scholarship/grant was $10,524; average loan $4,197. 46% of total undergraduate aid awarded as scholarships/grants, 54% as loans/jobs. **Non-need-based:** Awarded to 402 full-time undergraduates, including 128 freshmen. Scholarships awarded for academics, ROTC.

Application procedures. **Admission:** Priority date 4/1; no deadline. $40 fee, may be waived for applicants with need, free for online applicants. Admission notification on a rolling basis beginning on or about 9/1. **Financial aid:** Closing date 2/15. FAFSA required. Applicants notified on a rolling basis starting 4/1; must reply within 2 week(s) of notification.

Academics. **Special study options:** Accelerated study, combined bachelor's/graduate degree, cooperative education, cross-registration, distance learning, double major, dual enrollment of high school students, exchange student, honors, independent study, internships, liberal arts/career combination, student-designed major, study abroad, teacher certification program. **Credit/placement by examination:** AP, CLEP, IB, SAT, ACT, institutional tests. 45 credit hours maximum toward bachelor's degree. **Support services:** Learning center, pre-admission summer program, reduced course load, remedial instruction, study skills assistance, tutoring, writing center.

Majors. **Biology:** General. **Business:** Accounting, business admin. **Communications:** Media studies, public relations. **Computer sciences:** Information technology. **Education:** Early childhood, multi-level teacher, secondary. **Foreign languages:** Spanish. **Health:** Clinical lab science, nursing (RN). **History:** General. **Interdisciplinary:** Natural sciences. **Math:** General. **Physical sciences:** Chemistry. **Psychology:** General. **Public administration:** Human services. **Social sciences:** General, sociology. **Other:** Multi-/Interdisciplinary studies.

Most popular majors. Business/marketing 18%, communications/journalism 6%, English 12%, health sciences 15%, history 12%, mathematics 6%, psychology 12%, public administration/social services 7%.

Computing on campus. 570 workstations in dormitories, library, computer center, student center. Dormitories wired for high-speed internet access and linked to campus network. Commuter students can connect to campus network. Online course registration, online library, helpline, student web hosting, wireless network available.

Student life. **Freshman orientation:** Mandatory, $215 fee. Preregistration for classes offered. Held the weekend before classes begin. **Housing:** Coed dorms, single-sex dorms, special housing for disabled available. $450 fully refundable deposit, deadline 5/1. **Activities:** Concert band, campus ministries, choral groups, dance, drama, film society, literary magazine, music ensembles, musical theater, radio station, student government, student newspaper, black student union, Habitat for Humanity, Big Brothers/Big Sisters, Christian fellowship, Latin student union.

Athletics. NCAA. **Intercollegiate:** Baseball M, basketball, cross-country, soccer, softball W, swimming, tennis, volleyball W. **Intramural:** Basketball, bowling, football (non-tackle) M, golf, soccer, softball, swimming, table tennis, volleyball. **Team name:** Blue Knights.

Student services. Adult student services, alcohol/substance abuse counseling, chaplain/spiritual director, career counseling, services for economically disadvantaged, student employment services, financial aid counseling, health services, personal counseling, placement for graduates. **Physically disabled:** Services for visually impaired.

Contact. E-mail: admissions@msmc.edu
Phone: (845) 569-3248 Toll-free number: (888) 937-6762
Fax: (845) 562-6762
J. Randall Ognibene, Director of Admissions, Mount St. Mary College, 330 Powell Avenue, Newburgh, NY 12550

Nazareth College of Rochester

Rochester, New York — **CB member**
www.naz.edu — **CB code: 2511**

- Private 4-year liberal arts college
- Residential campus in large city

- 2,144 degree-seeking undergraduates: 6% part-time, 76% women, 5% African American, 2% Asian American, 3% Hispanic American, 1% international
- 1,036 degree-seeking graduate students
- 74% of applicants admitted
- Application essay required
- 72% graduate within 6 years

General. Founded in 1924. Regionally accredited. **Degrees:** 516 bachelor's awarded; master's, doctoral offered. **ROTC:** Army, Air Force. **Location:** 7 miles from downtown. **Calendar:** Semester, extensive summer session. **Full-time faculty:** 155 total; 88% have terminal degrees, 14% minority, 61% women. **Part-time faculty:** 209 total; 23% have terminal degrees, 9% minority, 63% women. **Class size:** 61% < 20, 38% 20-39, less than 1% 40-49, less than 1% 50-99. **Special facilities:** Arts center, psychology research facility, speech clinic, center for service learning, physical therapy clinic.

Freshman class profile. 2,181 applied, 1,624 admitted, 471 enrolled.

Mid 50% test scores		**GPA 2.0-2.99:**	28%
SAT critical reading:	530-630	**Rank in top quarter:**	67%
SAT math:	530-630	**Rank in top tenth:**	30%
SAT writing:	510-610	**Return as sophomores:**	81%
ACT composite:	23-27	**Out-of-state:**	8%
GPA 3.75 or higher:	19%	**Live on campus:**	90%
GPA 3.50-3.74:	21%	**International:**	1%
GPA 3.0-3.49:	31%		

Basis for selection. School achievement record, strength of high school academic program, class rank, recommendations most heavily considered. Standardized test optional institution. Interview recommended for all; audition required for music and theater arts programs; portfolio required for art programs.

High school preparation. College-preparatory program required. 16 units required; 20 recommended. Required and recommended units include English 4, mathematics 3-4, social studies 3-4, science 3-4 (laboratory 2) and foreign language 3-4.

2008-2009 Annual costs. Tuition/fees: $24,226. Room/board: $9,916.

2007-2008 Financial aid. Need-based: 411 full-time freshmen applied for aid; 357 were judged to have need; 357 of these received aid. Average need met was 79%. Average scholarship/grant was $13,548; average loan $3,694. 57% of total undergraduate aid awarded as scholarships/grants, 43% as loans/jobs. **Non-need-based:** Awarded to 555 full-time undergraduates, including 144 freshmen. Scholarships awarded for academics, alumni affiliation, art, minority status, music/drama, ROTC, state residency.

Application procedures. Admission: Priority date 12/15; deadline 2/15 (postmark date). $40 fee, may be waived for applicants with need, free for online applicants. Admission notification on a rolling basis beginning on or about 3/1. Must reply by May 1 or within 4 week(s) if notified thereafter. **Financial aid:** Priority date 12/15, closing date 5/1. FAFSA required. CSS PROFILE required of early decision applicants only. Applicants notified on a rolling basis starting 2/20; must reply by 5/1 or within 2 week(s) of notification.

Academics. Special study options: Combined bachelor's/graduate degree, cross-registration, distance learning, double major, exchange student, honors, independent study, internships, study abroad, teacher certification program, Washington semester. 2-2 bachelor's degree completion program for registered nurses and Monroe Community College graduates. **Credit/placement by examination:** AP, CLEP, IB, SAT, ACT. 30 credit hours maximum toward bachelor's degree. **Support services:** Reduced course load, remedial instruction, study skills assistance, tutoring, writing center.

Majors. Area/ethnic studies: American. **Biology:** General, biochemistry. **Business:** General, accounting, international. **Communications:** General. **Computer sciences:** Information systems. **Education:** Art, business, elementary, music, secondary, special. **Foreign languages:** French, German, Italian, Spanish. **Health:** Communication disorders, music therapy, speech pathology. **History:** General. **Interdisciplinary:** Peace/conflict. **Math:** General. **Philosophy/religion:** Philosophy, religion. **Physical sciences:** Chemistry. **Psychology:** General. **Public administration:** Social work. **Social sciences:** General, anthropology, economics, political science, sociology. **Visual/performing arts:** Art, art history/conservation, dramatic, music history, music performance, music theory/composition, studio arts. **Other:** Music business.

Most popular majors. Business/marketing 12%, education 6%, English 6%, health sciences 23%, history 6%, psychology 13%, social sciences 8%, visual/performing arts 6%.

Computing on campus. 150 workstations in dormitories, library, computer center. Dormitories wired for high-speed internet access and linked to campus network. Commuter students can connect to campus network. Online library, helpline, wireless network available.

Student life. Freshman orientation: Mandatory, $100 fee. Preregistration for classes offered. Orientation charge included in first-year fees. 3-day weekend program includes community service. **Policies:** First- and second-year students are required to live on campus, unless living with family. **Housing:** Guaranteed on-campus for all undergraduates. Coed dorms, single-sex dorms, special housing for disabled, apartments, wellness housing available. $100 nonrefundable deposit, deadline 5/1. Foreign language houses, special interest and collective housing for students in various majors, quiet floor, honors floor available. **Activities:** Bands, campus ministries, choral groups, dance, drama, international student organizations, music ensembles, musical theater, radio station, student government, student newspaper, symphony orchestra, Amnesty International, Campus Ministry Council, Inter-Ethnic Coalition, Undergraduate Association, French club, Italian club, Rotaract, Women's Resource Network.

Athletics. NCAA. **Intercollegiate:** Basketball, cross-country, diving, equestrian, field hockey W, golf, lacrosse, soccer, softball W, swimming, tennis, track and field, volleyball. **Intramural:** Basketball, racquetball, soccer, softball, swimming, tennis, volleyball. **Team name:** Golden Flyers.

Student services. Adult student services, alcohol/substance abuse counseling, chaplain/spiritual director, career counseling, services for economically disadvantaged, student employment services, financial aid counseling, health services, minority student services, on-campus daycare, personal counseling, placement for graduates, women's services. **Physically disabled:** Services for visually, speech, hearing impaired.

Contact. E-mail: admissions@naz.edu
Phone: (585) 389-2860 Toll-free number: (800) 462-3944
Fax: (585) 389-2826
Thomas DaRin, Vice President for Enrollment Management, Nazareth College of Rochester, 4245 East Avenue, Rochester, NY 14618-3790

New York Institute of Technology

Old Westbury, New York
www.nyit.edu **CB code: 2561**

- Private 4-year university and health science college
- Commuter campus in large town
- 4,767 degree-seeking undergraduates: 15% part-time, 37% women, 10% African American, 12% Asian American, 10% Hispanic American, 9% international
- 3,206 degree-seeking graduate students
- 76% of applicants admitted
- SAT or ACT (ACT writing recommended), application essay required
- 45% graduate within 6 years

General. Founded in 1955. Regionally accredited. Multiple sites, including campuses on Long Island, Manhattan, online, and at sites throughout the world. **Degrees:** 1,389 bachelor's, 40 associate awarded; master's, doctoral, first professional offered. **ROTC:** Army, Air Force. **Location:** 15 miles from New York City. **Calendar:** Semester, extensive summer session. **Full-time faculty:** 335 total; 58% have terminal degrees, 21% minority, 38% women. **Part-time faculty:** 613 total; 15% minority, 41% women. **Class size:** 62% < 20, 33% 20-39, 3% 40-49, 2% 50-99. **Special facilities:** Center for urban/suburban studies, center for neighborhood revitalization, Parkinson's disease treatment center, center for labor and industrial relations, center for energy, environment and economics, center for teaching and learning with technology, culinary arts center, center for entrepreneurial and small business services, center for business information technologies, motion graphics laboratory.

Freshman class profile. 4,025 applied, 3,064 admitted, 998 enrolled.

Mid 50% test scores		**Rank in top quarter:**	55%
SAT critical reading:	470-570	**Rank in top tenth:**	23%
SAT math:	530-630	**Return as sophomores:**	70%
ACT composite:	21-27	**Out-of-state:**	10%
GPA 3.75 or higher:	16%	**Live on campus:**	25%
GPA 3.50-3.74:	30%	**International:**	7%
GPA 3.0-3.49:	44%	**Fraternities:**	2%
GPA 2.0-2.99:	10%	**Sororities:**	1%

Basis for selection. 2 letters of recommendation required for 4-year nursing, occupational therapy, physical therapy, physician assistant and all education programs. Proof of 100 hours of volunteer or work experience required for physical therapy, physician assistant, occupational therapy programs. SAT important, minimum scores vary with program. Interview required for occupational therapy, physician assistant, physical therapy, BS/doctor of osteopathic medicine, and BS/Juris Doctor program applicants.

Portfolio required for fine arts program. **Homeschooled:** State high school equivalency certificate required.

High school preparation. 17 units required. Required and recommended units include English 4, mathematics 3, social studies 3-4, science 3 (laboratory 1) and academic electives 7. Freshmen in selected majors required to prove or acquire computer literacy.

2008-2009 Annual costs. Tuition/fees: $22,750. Room only charges apply to Manhattan campus; board charges vary on other campuses. Tuition/fee costs reported for nontechnology majors, vary for other programs. Room only: $10,310. Books/supplies: $1,400. Personal expenses: $2,550.

2007-2008 Financial aid. **Need-based:** 1,023 full-time freshmen applied for aid; 860 were judged to have need; 851 of these received aid. Average scholarship/grant was $4,141; average loan $3,849. 57% of total undergraduate aid awarded as scholarships/grants, 43% as loans/jobs. **Non-need-based:** Awarded to 2,817 full-time undergraduates, including 1,002 freshmen. Scholarships awarded for academics, athletics.

Application procedures. **Admission:** Closing date 3/1. $50 fee, may be waived for applicants with need. Admission notification on a rolling basis beginning on or about 1/1. Must reply by 5/1. Application closing date for nursing, occupational therapy, physical therapy and physician assistant programs February 1. Notification to applicants to these programs sent March 1. Applicants to these programs must reply by May 1 or within 30 days if notified thereafter. No deferred admission to these programs. **Financial aid:** Priority date 3/1; no closing date. FAFSA required. Applicants notified on a rolling basis starting 3/15; must reply by 5/1 or within 2 week(s) of notification.

Academics. School focuses on career-oriented professional education, applications-oriented research and service in public interest. **Special study options:** Accelerated study, combined bachelor's/graduate degree, cooperative education, cross-registration, distance learning, double major, dual enrollment of high school students, ESL, honors, independent study, internships, liberal arts/career combination, study abroad, teacher certification program, weekend college. Combined bachelor's/professional degree program in life sciences/osteopathic medicine, architectural technology/energy management, architectural technology/MBA, mechanical engineering/energy management, life sciences/physical therapy, life sciences/occupational therapy, behavioral sciences/law at Touro College Law Center. **Credit/placement by examination:** AP, CLEP, IB, institutional tests. 30 credit hours maximum toward associate degree, 60 toward bachelor's. **Support services:** Learning center, pre-admission summer program, reduced course load, remedial instruction, study skills assistance, tutoring, writing center.

Majors. **Architecture:** Architecture, technology. **Biology:** General. **Business:** Accounting, business admin, finance, hotel/motel admin, human resources, management information systems, marketing, tourism/travel. **Communications:** General, advertising, broadcast journalism, radio/tv. **Computer sciences:** General, computer graphics, computer science, networking. **Education:** Art, biology, business, chemistry, elementary, English, health occupations, mathematics, middle, physics, sales/marketing, science, social science, social studies, technology/industrial arts, trade/industrial, voc/tech. **Engineering:** Biomedical, computer, electrical, mechanical. **Engineering technology:** Aerospace, electrical, energy systems, environmental, mechanical. **Health:** Nursing (RN), physician assistant, premedicine. **Interdisciplinary:** Nutrition sciences. **Physical sciences:** Chemistry. **Protective services:** Law enforcement admin. **Psychology:** General. **Social sciences:** Political science, sociology. **Visual/performing arts:** Commercial/advertising art, interior design, studio arts.

Most popular majors. Architecture 14%, biology 7%, business/marketing 17%, communications/journalism 11%, engineering/engineering technologies 12%, health sciences 7%, interdisciplinary studies 9%, visual/performing arts 9%.

Computing on campus. PC or laptop required. 1,210 workstations in dormitories, library, computer center, student center. Dormitories wired for high-speed internet access and linked to campus network. Commuter students can connect to campus network. Online course registration, online library, helpline, student web hosting, wireless network available.

Student life. **Freshman orientation:** Available. Preregistration for classes offered. One day at end of August. **Housing:** Guaranteed on-campus for all undergraduates. Coed dorms, special housing for disabled, apartments available. $275 nonrefundable deposit. Central Islip campus fully residential, special housing for graduate, architecture students. Off-campus housing available for Manhattan campus. **Activities:** Choral groups, dance, drama, film society, literary magazine, musical theater, radio station, student government, student newspaper, TV station, American Institute of Architecture Students, biomedical society, National Society of Black Engineers, Newman Club, Christian fellowship, Jewish student union, African people's organization, Community Connection, South Asian student association, Chinese student association.

Athletics. NCAA. **Intercollegiate:** Baseball M, basketball, cross-country, lacrosse M, soccer, softball W, volleyball W. **Intramural:** Basketball, football (non-tackle), golf, soccer, softball, swimming, table tennis, tennis, volleyball, weight lifting. **Team name:** Bears.

Student services. Adult student services, alcohol/substance abuse counseling, chaplain/spiritual director, career counseling, student employment services, financial aid counseling, health services, personal counseling, placement for graduates, veterans' counselor. **Physically disabled:** Services for hearing impaired.

Contact. E-mail: admissions@nyit.edu
Phone: (516) 686-7520 Toll-free number: (800) 345-6948
Fax: (516) 686-7613
Jacquelyn Nealon, Vice President for Enrollment, New York Institute of Technology, Box 8000, Old Westbury, NY 11568

New York School of Interior Design

New York, New York
www.nysid.edu **CB code: 0333**

- Private 4-year visual arts college
- Commuter campus in very large city
- 705 degree-seeking undergraduates: 74% part-time, 90% women, 3% African American, 10% Asian American, 7% Hispanic American
- 16 degree-seeking graduate students
- 46% of applicants admitted
- Application essay required

General. Founded in 1916. The college is devoted exclusively to interior design education. **Degrees:** 32 bachelor's, 75 associate awarded; master's, first professional offered. **Location:** Located in Manhattan. **Calendar:** Semester, extensive summer session. **Full-time faculty:** 2 total; 50% women. **Part-time faculty:** 77 total; 34% have terminal degrees, 5% minority, 39% women. **Class size:** 91% < 20, 9% 50-99. **Special facilities:** Three galleries for architecture and interior design exhibits, lighting laboratory.

Freshman class profile. 93 applied, 43 admitted, 15 enrolled.

GPA 3.50-3.74:	66%	**End year in good standing:**	65%
GPA 3.0-3.49:	34%	**Return as sophomores:**	25%
Rank in top quarter:	44%	**Out-of-state:**	47%

Basis for selection. High school transcripts, 2 letters of recommendation, essay, and portfolio in art/design. Portfolio required, interview recommended. **Homeschooled:** State high school equivalency certificate required.

High school preparation. 16 units recommended. Recommended units include English 4, mathematics 2, social studies 2, history 2, science 2 and foreign language 2. Studio art or drafting is recommended.

2009-2010 Annual costs. Tuition/fees: $20,840. Books/supplies: $1,000. Personal expenses: $900.

2008-2009 Financial aid. All financial aid based on need. Average scholarship/grant was $2,500; average loan $6,000. 20% of total undergraduate aid awarded as scholarships/grants, 80% as loans/jobs.

Application procedures. **Admission:** Priority date 3/1; no deadline. $50 fee, may be waived for applicants with need. Admission notification on a rolling basis beginning on or about 4/1. Must reply by May 1 or within 4 week(s) if notified thereafter. **Financial aid:** Priority date 5/1; no closing date. FAFSA required. Applicants notified on a rolling basis starting 2/1; must reply within 2 week(s) of notification.

Academics. **Special study options:** Independent study, internships, study abroad, weekend college. **Credit/placement by examination:** AP, CLEP, IB, institutional tests. 17 credit hours maximum toward associate degree, 41 toward bachelor's. **Support services:** Study skills assistance, tutoring, writing center.

Majors. **Visual/performing arts:** Interior design.

Computing on campus. 125 workstations in library, computer center. Dormitories wired for high-speed internet access and linked to campus network. Commuter students can connect to campus network. Online course registration, helpline available.

Student life. **Freshman orientation:** Available. Preregistration for classes offered. General orientation is held the week before classes begin. **Housing:** Coed dorms available. **Activities:** Student chapter of American Society of Interior Designers.

Student services. Adult student services, career counseling, student employment services, financial aid counseling, personal counseling, placement for graduates.

Contact. E-mail: admissions@nysid.edu
Phone: (212) 472-1500 ext. 204 Toll-free number: (800) 336-9743 ext. 204
Fax: (212) 472-1867
David Sprouls, Director of Admissions, New York School of Interior Design, 170 East 70th Street, New York, NY 10021-5110

New York University

New York, New York **CB member**
www.nyu.edu **CB code: 2562**

- Private 4-year university
- Residential campus in very large city
- 20,781 degree-seeking undergraduates: 6% part-time, 61% women, 4% African American, 20% Asian American, 8% Hispanic American, 6% international
- 19,855 degree-seeking graduate students
- 32% of applicants admitted
- SAT or ACT with writing, application essay required
- 84% graduate within 6 years

General. Founded in 1831. Regionally accredited. School of Continuing and Professional Studies also available for adult degree and noncredit programs. **Degrees:** 6,158 bachelor's, 454 associate awarded; master's, doctoral, first professional offered. **ROTC:** Army, Naval. **Calendar:** Semester, extensive summer session. **Full-time faculty:** 2,227 total; 90% have terminal degrees, 18% minority, 40% women. **Part-time faculty:** 2,435 total; 62% have terminal degrees, 47% women. **Class size:** 60% < 20, 25% 20-39, 4% 40-49, 7% 50-99, 5% >100. **Special facilities:** Special academic facilities for arts, business, culture, education, international relations, language, law, media, music, public service, research, and social policy.

Freshman class profile. 37,245 applied, 11,965 admitted, 4,496 enrolled.

Mid 50% test scores			
SAT critical reading:	620-720	Rank in top quarter:	92%
SAT math:	630-720	Rank in top tenth:	68%
SAT writing:	620-720	Return as sophomores:	92%
ACT composite:	28-31	Out-of-state:	71%
GPA 3.75 or higher:	36%	Live on campus:	90%
GPA 3.50-3.74:	37%	International:	8%
GPA 3.0-3.49:	26%	Fraternities:	2%
GPA 2.0-2.99:	1%	Sororities:	2%

Basis for selection. School achievement record most important. Standardized test scores, activities, essay, recommendations also important. Audition and/or submission of creative materials required for applicants to either Tisch School of the Arts or art and music programs within the School of Education. 2 SAT Subject Tests required of all students with exception of fine and performing arts students whose audition/portfolio is used in lieu of Subject Tests. Audition required for dance, drama, and music programs; portfolio required for art, theater design, photography, cinema studies, film, television, radio, and dramatic writing programs. Portfolios may include writing, photography, film or other creative work. **Homeschooled:** Transcript of courses and grades, letter of recommendation (nonparent) required. Home-schooled applicants must submit official score reports from either the SAT Reasoning Test (including the Writing section), or the ACT with the ACT Writing Test. Home-schooled students must also submit at least two SAT Subject Test scores. NYU policy requires certification of completion of secondary school for all enrolled students prior to graduation from the University. As such, homeschooled students must either be able to provide a homeschool diploma or certificate of completion that is considered the equivalent of a high school diploma in the applicant's home state, or they must be willing, if admitted, to apply for a New York State equivalency diploma upon the completion of twenty-four college credits.

High school preparation. College-preparatory program required. 16 units required; 17 recommended. Required and recommended units include English 4, mathematics 3-4, history 4, science 3-4 (laboratory 2) and foreign language 2-3.

2008-2009 Annual costs. Tuition/fees: $37,372. Room/board: $12,810. Books/supplies: $800. Personal expenses: $1,000.

2008-2009 Financial aid. Need-based: 2,975 full-time freshmen applied for aid; 2,371 were judged to have need; 2,361 of these received aid. Average need met was 72%. Average scholarship/grant was $19,391; average loan $4,946. 59% of total undergraduate aid awarded as scholarships/grants, 41% as loans/jobs. **Non-need-based:** Awarded to 1,583 full-time undergraduates, including 232 freshmen. Scholarships awarded for academics. **Additional information:** Both need-based and merit scholarships available to first-time students. Range from $1,000 to $25,000.

Application procedures. Admission: Closing date 1/1 (postmark date). $65 fee, may be waived for applicants with need. Application must be submitted online. Admission notification 4/1. Must reply by May 1 or within 3 week(s) if notified thereafter. **Financial aid:** Closing date 2/15. FAFSA required. Applicants notified on a rolling basis starting 4/1; must reply by 5/1.

Academics. Special study options: Accelerated study, combined bachelor's/graduate degree, cross-registration, distance learning, double major, ESL, exchange student, honors, independent study, internships, liberal arts/career combination, student-designed major, study abroad, teacher certification program, Washington semester, weekend college. NYU offers an exchange program with several historically black colleges including Spelman College, Morehouse College, and Xavier University of Louisiana. **Credit/placement by examination:** AP, CLEP, IB. 32 credit hours maximum toward bachelor's degree. 8 to 32 hours of credit may be awarded for International Baccalaureate. **Support services:** Learning center, pre-admission summer program, reduced course load, study skills assistance, tutoring, writing center.

Majors. Architecture: Urban/community planning. **Area/ethnic studies:** African-American, East Asian, European, Latin American, Near/Middle Eastern. **Biology:** General, biochemistry. **Business:** General, accounting, finance, hotel/motel admin, international, labor relations, managerial economics, real estate, restaurant/food services. **Communications:** General, journalism, radio/tv. **Communications technology:** Radio/tv. **Computer sciences:** General, computer science. **Education:** Art, business, elementary, ESL, kindergarten/preschool, mathematics, music, social studies, special, speech impaired. **Engineering:** Operations research. **Family/consumer sciences:** Food/nutrition. **Foreign languages:** General, classics, comparative lit, French, German, Hebrew, Italian, linguistics, Russian, Spanish. **Health:** Audiology/speech pathology, dental hygiene, nursing (RN). **History:** General. **Interdisciplinary:** Neuroscience. **Liberal arts:** Arts/sciences, humanities. **Math:** General. **Parks/recreation:** Facilities management. **Philosophy/religion:** Philosophy, religion. **Physical sciences:** Chemistry, physics. **Psychology:** General. **Public administration:** General, community org/advocacy, social work. **Social sciences:** General, anthropology, economics, international relations, political science, sociology, urban studies. **Visual/performing arts:** Cinematography, commercial/advertising art, dance, dramatic, music performance, photography, studio arts. **Other:** Fundraising.

Most popular majors. Business/marketing 20%, communications/journalism 9%, liberal arts 7%, social sciences 15%, visual/performing arts 20%.

Computing on campus. 2,600 workstations in dormitories, library, computer center, student center. Dormitories wired for high-speed internet access and linked to campus network. Commuter students can connect to campus network. Online course registration, online library, helpline, repair service, student web hosting, wireless network available.

Student life. Freshman orientation: Available. Preregistration for classes offered. Each undergraduate college handles own orientation. Charge and program determined and vary by school. **Housing:** Guaranteed on-campus for all undergraduates. Coed dorms, special housing for disabled, apartments, fraternity/sorority housing, wellness housing available. $300 nonrefundable deposit, deadline 5/1. First-Year Residential Experience program available for new students. **Activities:** Bands, campus ministries, choral groups, dance, drama, film society, international student organizations, literary magazine, music ensembles, Model UN, musical theater, opera, radio station, student government, student newspaper, symphony orchestra, TV station, over 300 clubs and organizations available.

Athletics. NCAA. **Intercollegiate:** Basketball, cross-country, diving, fencing, golf, soccer, swimming, tennis, track and field, volleyball, wrestling M. **Intramural:** Basketball, bowling, football (non-tackle), soccer, softball, tennis, volleyball. **Team name:** Violets.

Student services. Adult student services, alcohol/substance abuse counseling, chaplain/spiritual director, career counseling, services for economically disadvantaged, student employment services, financial aid counseling, health services, minority student services, personal counseling, placement for graduates, women's services. **Physically disabled:** Services for visually, speech, hearing impaired.

Contact. E-mail: admissions@nyu.edu
Phone: (212) 998-4500 Fax: (212) 995-4902
Barbara Hall, Associate Provost for Admissions and Financial Aid, New York University, 665 Broadway, 11th floor, New York, NY 10012-2339

Niagara University
Niagara University, New York CB member
www.niagara.edu CB code: 2558

- Private 4-year university affiliated with Roman Catholic Church
- Residential campus in small city
- 3,291 degree-seeking undergraduates: 8% part-time, 62% women, 4% African American, 1% Asian American, 2% Hispanic American, 1% Native American, 14% international
- 844 degree-seeking graduate students
- 74% of applicants admitted
- SAT or ACT (ACT writing optional) required
- 64% graduate within 6 years; 24% enter graduate study

General. Founded in 1856. Regionally accredited. Independent institution in the Vincentian tradition. **Degrees:** 700 bachelor's awarded; master's offered. **ROTC:** Army. **Location:** 20 miles from Buffalo; 90 miles from Toronto, Canada. **Calendar:** Semester, extensive summer session. **Full-time faculty:** 150 total; 94% have terminal degrees, 15% minority, 38% women. **Part-time faculty:** 227 total; 9% minority, 49% women. **Class size:** 41% < 20, 54% 20-39, 5% 40-49, less than 1% 50-99. **Special facilities:** Castellani Art Museum, Dwyer Ice Arena.

Freshman class profile. 3,268 applied, 2,403 admitted, 742 enrolled.

Mid 50% test scores		**Rank in top quarter:**	41%
SAT critical reading:	480-590	**Rank in top tenth:**	13%
SAT math:	470-570	**End year in good standing:**	96%
ACT composite:	19-25	**Return as sophomores:**	80%
GPA 3.75 or higher:	13%	**Out-of-state:**	9%
GPA 3.50-3.74:	30%	**Live on campus:**	78%
GPA 3.0-3.49:	51%	**International:**	2%
GPA 2.0-2.99:	6%		

Basis for selection. School achievement record, class rank, test scores most important. School recommendation also important. Character, personality, and extracurricular activities considered. Alumni relationship also considered. Interview, essay recommended for all; audition recommended for theater program. **Homeschooled:** Transcript of courses and grades required. Letter from district superintendent or local district official confirming that the student has received an education "substantially equivalent" to instruction given to students graduating from the public high school in that district.

High school preparation. College-preparatory program recommended. 16 units required. Required units include English 4, mathematics 2, social studies 2, science 2, foreign language 2 and academic electives 4. 3 science (biology, chemistry mandatory, physics recommended) for math, science, nursing applicants. 2 foreign language required of all except business applicants. 3 math required for math, biology, business, biochemistry, chemistry, computer and information sciences, natural sciences, and nursing applicants. 3 social studies required for prospective social studies majors.

2008-2009 Annual costs. Tuition/fees: $23,575. Room/board: $9,750. Books/supplies: $900. Personal expenses: $750.

2008-2009 Financial aid. Need-based: 735 full-time freshmen applied for aid; 704 were judged to have need; 704 of these received aid. Average need met was 79%. Average scholarship/grant was $15,327; average loan $4,619. 57% of total undergraduate aid awarded as scholarships/grants, 43% as loans/jobs. **Non-need-based:** Awarded to 1,490 full-time undergraduates, including 412 freshmen. Scholarships awarded for academics, athletics, music/drama, ROTC. **Additional information:** Opportunity program available for academically and economically disadvantaged students.

Application procedures. Admission: Closing date 8/1 (receipt date). $30 fee, may be waived for applicants with need. Admission notification on a rolling basis. Must reply by May 1 or within 4 week(s) if notified thereafter. **Financial aid:** Priority date 2/15; no closing date. FAFSA required. Applicants notified on a rolling basis starting 3/1; must reply within 3 week(s) of notification.

Academics. Academic exploration program for students undecided about their choice of major. **Special study options:** Accelerated study, combined bachelor's/graduate degree, cooperative education, cross-registration, double major, dual enrollment of high school students, ESL, exchange student, honors, independent study, internships, liberal arts/career combination, New York semester, study abroad, teacher certification program, Washington semester. **Credit/placement by examination:** AP, CLEP, institutional tests. 15 credit hours maximum toward associate degree, 15 toward bachelor's. **Support services:** Learning center, pre-admission summer program, reduced course load, remedial instruction, study skills assistance, tutoring, writing center.

Majors. Biology: General, biochemistry. **Business:** Accounting, finance, hospitality admin, hotel/motel admin, human resources, international, logistics, managerial economics, marketing, restaurant/food services, tourism/travel, training/development. **Communications:** General. **Computer sciences:** General, computer science, information systems. **Education:** General, biology, business, chemistry, early childhood, elementary, English, French, mathematics, secondary, social studies, Spanish, special. **Foreign languages:** French, Spanish. **Health:** Nursing (RN), predental, premedicine, preveterinary. **History:** General. **Legal studies:** Prelaw. **Liberal arts:** Arts/sciences. **Math:** General. **Philosophy/religion:** Philosophy, religion. **Physical sciences:** Chemistry. **Protective services:** Criminal justice. **Psychology:** General. **Public administration:** Social work. **Science technology:** Biological. **Social sciences:** General, criminology, political science, sociology. **Transportation:** General. **Visual/performing arts:** Dramatic.

Most popular majors. Business/marketing 35%, education 20%, security/protective services 8%, social sciences 6%.

Computing on campus. 150 workstations in dormitories, library, computer center, student center. Dormitories wired for high-speed internet access and linked to campus network. Commuter students can connect to campus network. Online course registration, online library, helpline, repair service, wireless network available.

Student life. Freshman orientation: Available. Preregistration for classes offered. **Policies:** Freshmen not within reasonable commuting distance required to live on campus for 2 years. **Housing:** Guaranteed on-campus for all undergraduates. Coed dorms, apartments, wellness housing available. $100 nonrefundable deposit, deadline 5/1. **Activities:** Pep band, campus ministries, choral groups, dance, drama, international student organizations, musical theater, radio station, student government, student newspaper, ethnic awareness society, Knights of Columbus, community action program, Muscular Dystrophy Association, foreign student council, St. Vincent DePaul Society, Black Student Union.

Athletics. NCAA. **Intercollegiate:** Baseball M, basketball, cross-country, diving, golf M, ice hockey, lacrosse, soccer, softball W, swimming, tennis, volleyball W. **Intramural:** Baseball M, basketball, bowling, golf, racquetball, skiing, softball, volleyball W, water polo. **Team name:** Purple Eagles.

Student services. Adult student services, alcohol/substance abuse counseling, chaplain/spiritual director, career counseling, services for economically disadvantaged, student employment services, financial aid counseling, health services, minority student services, personal counseling, placement for graduates, veterans' counselor.

Contact. E-mail: admissions@niagara.edu
Phone: (716) 286-8700 Fax: (716) 286-8733
Harry Gong, Director of Admissions, Niagara University, Niagara University, NY 14109

Nyack College
Nyack, New York
www.nyack.edu CB code: 2560

- Private 4-year liberal arts college affiliated with Christian and Missionary Alliance
- Residential campus in large town
- 1,900 degree-seeking undergraduates
- Application essay required

General. Founded in 1882. Regionally accredited. Extension center in Manhattan. **Degrees:** 519 bachelor's, 12 associate awarded; master's, first professional offered. **Location:** 25 miles from New York City. **Calendar:** Differs by program, limited summer session. **Full-time faculty:** 148 total. **Part-time faculty:** 190 total.

Freshman class profile.

Mid 50% test scores		**GPA 3.0-3.49:**	23%
SAT critical reading:	400-530	**GPA 2.0-2.99:**	42%
SAT math:	380-530	**Rank in top quarter:**	29%
ACT composite:	18-25	**Rank in top tenth:**	12%
GPA 3.75 or higher:	11%	**Live on campus:**	85%
GPA 3.50-3.74:	11%		

Basis for selection. Applicants must have Christian commitment and sign agreement to abide by community life standards. Academic record, class rank, and test scores most important. Pastor's recommendation required for students applying to traditional undergraduate program. Interview recommended for those with unsatisfactory recommendations or academic concerns; audition required for music program. **Homeschooled:** Transcript of courses and grades required. **Learning Disabled:** Students should inform their admissions counselors.

High school preparation. 16 units required. Required and recommended units include English 4, foreign language 2 and academic electives 4. 3 in any combination of math and science and 3 in any combination of history and social science recommended.

2008-2009 Annual costs. Tuition/fees: $18,300. Room/board: $7,800. Books/supplies: $750. Personal expenses: $2,060.

2008-2009 Financial aid. **Non-need-based:** Scholarships awarded for academics, alumni affiliation, art, athletics, leadership, minority status, music/drama, religious affiliation, state residency.

Application procedures. **Admission:** No deadline. $25 fee, may be waived for applicants with need. Admission notification on a rolling basis. **Financial aid:** Priority date 3/1; no closing date. FAFSA required. Applicants notified on a rolling basis starting 3/1; must reply by 4/1 or within 4 week(s) of notification.

Academics. Adult degree completion program offers accelerated study option for adult students, with classes held throughout the New York metropolitan and lower Hudson Valley regions, Washington, DC and Dayton, Ohio. **Special study options:** Accelerated study, distance learning, double major, ESL, honors, independent study, internships, liberal arts/career combination, study abroad, teacher certification program, Washington semester. Adult degree completion program. **Credit/placement by examination:** AP, CLEP, SAT, institutional tests. 30 credit hours maximum toward bachelor's degree. **Support services:** Learning center, pre-admission summer program, reduced course load, remedial instruction, study skills assistance, tutoring, writing center.

Majors. **Business:** Accounting, business admin. **Communications:** General. **Computer sciences:** General. **Education:** Elementary, ESL, music. **History:** General. **Liberal arts:** Arts/sciences. **Math:** General. **Philosophy/religion:** Philosophy, religion. **Psychology:** General. **Public administration:** Social work. **Social sciences:** General. **Theology:** Religious ed, sacred music, theology. **Visual/performing arts:** Music performance, music theory/composition.

Computing on campus. 180 workstations in dormitories, library, computer center, student center. Online library, wireless network available.

Student life. **Freshman orientation:** Mandatory, $100 fee. Preregistration for classes offered. Usually 4 days the week prior to classes starting. **Policies:** Alcohol, tobacco, and narcotic drug use and possession prohibited on and off campus. Religious observance required. **Housing:** Single-sex dorms, apartments, wellness housing available. $150 deposit. **Activities:** Choral groups, drama, literary magazine, music ensembles, musical theater, radio station, student government, student newspaper, symphony orchestra, African American Association of Cultural Exchange, missions committee, drama ensemble, Association of Latin American Students, Asian student organization, mime and interpretive dance group, business club, WNYK Radio, Student Chapter of Music Educators National Conference.

Athletics. NCAA, NCCAA. **Intercollegiate:** Baseball M, basketball, cheerleading, cross-country, golf M, soccer, softball W, volleyball W. **Team name:** Warriors.

Student services. Adult student services, alcohol/substance abuse counseling, chaplain/spiritual director, career counseling, services for economically disadvantaged, student employment services, financial aid counseling, health services, personal counseling, placement for graduates. **Physically disabled:** Services for visually, hearing impaired.

Contact. E-mail: admissions@nyack.edu
Phone: (845) 358-1710 ext. 350 Toll-free number: (800) 336-9225
Fax: (845) 358-3047
Dinesh Mahtani, Director of Admissions, Nyack College, 1 South Boulevard, Nyack, NY 10960-3698

Ohr Somayach Tanenbaum Education Center

Monsey, New York
www.os.edu **CB code: 3357**

- Private 4-year rabbinical college for men affiliated with Jewish faith
- Residential campus in large town
- 91 degree-seeking undergraduates: 11% part-time
- 11 degree-seeking graduate students
- Interview required

General. Founded in 1979. Accredited by AARTS. First and Second Talmudic degrees offered. **Degrees:** 10 bachelor's awarded; first professional offered. **Location:** Half a mile from Spring Valley, 33 miles from New York City. **Calendar:** Semester, extensive summer session. **Full-time faculty:** 3 total. **Part-time faculty:** 2 total; 100% have terminal degrees.

Basis for selection. Potential for scholastic and character achievement evaluated through personal interview, recommendations, departmental examinations, and prior religious and secular studies. Essay recommended.

2008-2009 Annual costs. Books/supplies: $300. Personal expenses: $725.

Application procedures. **Admission:** No deadline. $75 fee, may be waived for applicants with need. Admission notification on a rolling basis. **Financial aid:** No deadline. Applicants notified on a rolling basis starting 7/1; must reply within 4 week(s) of notification.

Academics. **Special study options:** Accelerated study, cross-registration, independent study, study abroad, teacher certification program. **Credit/placement by examination:** CLEP, institutional tests. **Support services:** Pre-admission summer program, reduced course load, tutoring.

Majors. **Philosophy/religion:** Judaic. **Theology:** Talmudic.

Computing on campus. 3 workstations in computer center. Repair service available.

Student life. **Policies:** Religious observance required. **Housing:** Apartments available. $100 deposit. Students above age 30 must arrange own housing off campus. Assistance provided in locating housing. **Activities:** Singing group, community volunteers.

Athletics. **Intramural:** Baseball M, basketball M, skiing M, swimming M.

Student services. Career counseling, student employment services, personal counseling, placement for graduates.

Contact. E-mail: ohr@os.edu
Phone: (845) 425-1370 Fax: (845) 425-8865
Avrohom Braun, Dean of Students, Ohr Somayach Tanenbaum Education Center, 244 Route 306, Monsey, NY 10952

Pace University

New York, New York **CB member**
www.pace.edu **CB code: 2635**

- Private 4-year university
- Residential campus in very large city
- 7,206 degree-seeking undergraduates: 15% part-time, 60% women, 10% African American, 10% Asian American, 12% Hispanic American, 4% international
- 4,828 degree-seeking graduate students
- 75% of applicants admitted
- SAT or ACT (ACT writing optional), application essay required
- 57% graduate within 6 years

General. Founded in 1906. Regionally accredited. Four schools and one college of the university are located on New York City and Pleasantville campuses: Dyson College of Arts and Sciences, Lienhard School of Nursing, School of Education, Lubin School of Business, and Seidenberg School of Computer Science and Information Systems. The School of Law and Lubin Graduate Center are located in White Plains. **Degrees:** 1,635 bachelor's, 99 associate awarded; master's, doctoral, first professional offered. **ROTC:** Army, Air Force. **Calendar:** Semester, limited summer session. **Full-time faculty:** 425 total; 86% have terminal degrees, 16% minority, 43% women. **Part-time faculty:** 706 total; 24% have terminal degrees, 14% minority, 52% women. **Class size:** 49% < 20, 48% 20-39, 2% 40-49, less than 1% 50-99, less than 1% >100. **Special facilities:** Art galleries, multimedia language laboratories, speech and hearing center, studio theater.

Freshman class profile. 9,123 applied, 6,811 admitted, 1,663 enrolled.

Mid 50% test scores		**Rank in top tenth:**	14%
SAT critical reading:	490-580	**End year in good standing:**	94%
SAT math:	490-590	**Return as sophomores:**	74%
ACT composite:	20-26	**Out-of-state:**	42%
GPA 3.75 or higher:	11%	**Live on campus:**	70%
GPA 3.50-3.74:	14%	**International:**	5%
GPA 3.0-3.49:	31%	**Fraternities:**	2%
GPA 2.0-2.99:	43%	**Sororities:**	2%
Rank in top quarter:	41%		

Basis for selection. 85 high school GPA, rank in top half of class, test scores, recommendations, personal statement important. Extracurricular activities also considered. Non-native speakers of English required to take

TOEFL. Official scores must be sent directly to school. Notarized copies not acceptable. Interviews strongly recommended; audition required for dance, dramatic arts, theater; portfolio recommended for art programs. Applicants to Lienhard School of Nursing must be certified in CPR. **Learning Disabled:** Diagnostic tests recommended.

High school preparation. College-preparatory program recommended. 16 units required; 20 recommended. Required and recommended units include English 4, mathematics 3-4, social studies 1-2, history 2-3, science 2 (laboratory 2), foreign language 2-3 and academic electives 2.

2008-2009 Annual costs. Tuition/fees: $31,364. Room/board: $11,180. Books/supplies: $800. Personal expenses: $1,248.

2008-2009 Financial aid. **Need-based:** 1,360 full-time freshmen applied for aid; 1,231 were judged to have need; 1,229 of these received aid. Average need met was 76%. Average scholarship/grant was $21,866; average loan $3,922. 70% of total undergraduate aid awarded as scholarships/grants, 30% as loans/jobs. **Non-need-based:** Awarded to 1,827 full-time undergraduates, including 561 freshmen. Scholarships awarded for academics, athletics, music/drama.

Application procedures. **Admission:** Closing date 3/1 (postmark date). $45 fee, may be waived for applicants with need. Admission notification on a rolling basis beginning on or about 12/15. Must reply by May 1 or within 2 week(s) if notified thereafter. **Financial aid:** Priority date 3/15; no closing date. FAFSA required. Applicants notified on a rolling basis starting 2/25; must reply by 5/1 or within 3 week(s) of notification.

Academics. Adult undergraduate degrees in liberal/general studies, business and computer science. **Special study options:** Accelerated study, combined bachelor's/graduate degree, cooperative education, cross-registration, distance learning, double major, dual enrollment of high school students, ESL, honors, independent study, internships, study abroad, teacher certification program. Evening and freshman studies programs, pre-freshman summer program, learning communities and service learning. **Credit/placement by examination:** AP, CLEP, IB, institutional tests. 30 credit hours maximum toward associate degree, 96 toward bachelor's. **Support services:** Learning center, reduced course load, remedial instruction, study skills assistance, tutoring, writing center.

Honors college/program. Honors Program requires entering freshmen have 90 or higher high school GPA, SAT verbal minimum of 550, SAT math minimum of 550 and a combined SAT score of 1200 (exclusive of Writing). Honors program students may be enrolled in any of undergraduate schools at university.

Majors. **Area/ethnic studies:** American, women's. **Biology:** General, biochemistry. **Business:** General, accounting, business admin, e-commerce, entrepreneurial studies, finance, hotel/motel admin, human resources, international, international marketing, management science, marketing. **Communications:** General, advertising. **Computer sciences:** General, computer science, information systems, systems analysis. **Conservation:** Environmental science, environmental studies. **Education:** Biology, chemistry, early childhood, elementary, English, history, mathematics, science, social studies, Spanish, special, speech impaired. **Foreign languages:** General, Spanish. **Health:** Clinical lab science, communication disorders, nursing (RN). **History:** General. **Liberal arts:** Arts/sciences. **Math:** General. **Philosophy/religion:** Philosophy, religion. **Physical sciences:** Chemistry. **Protective services:** Forensics, law enforcement admin. **Psychology:** General. **Public administration:** Community org/advocacy. **Social sciences:** General, economics, political science. **Visual/performing arts:** Acting, art, art history/conservation, commercial/advertising art, dramatic, film/cinema, studio arts. **Other:** E-business and interactive media, Modern languages and cultures.

Most popular majors. Business/marketing 42%, communications/journalism 9%, computer/information sciences 7%, health sciences 13%, psychology 6%.

Computing on campus. 250 workstations in library, computer center. Dormitories linked to campus network. Commuter students can connect to campus network. Online library, helpline, wireless network available.

Student life. **Freshman orientation:** Mandatory. Preregistration for classes offered. **Housing:** Coed dorms, apartments, wellness housing available. $500 nonrefundable deposit, deadline 5/1. Apartment style housing for upperclassmen available. **Activities:** Choral groups, dance, drama, film society, international student organizations, literary magazine, Model UN, musical theater, radio station, student government, student newspaper, TV station, Collegiate Italian American Organization, Asian Cultural Society, international student organization, Hillel, Pace Christian Fellowship, Caribbean student association, African Students Association at Pace, Sabor Latino, Project Pericles, NATURE (environmental club).

Athletics. NCAA. **Intercollegiate:** Baseball M, basketball, cross-country, equestrian W, football (tackle) M, golf M, lacrosse M, soccer W, softball W, swimming, tennis, track and field, volleyball W. **Intramural:** Football (non-tackle), soccer, softball, volleyball. **Team name:** Setters.

Student services. Adult student services, career counseling, student employment services, health services, personal counseling, placement for graduates, veterans' counselor. **Physically disabled:** Services for visually, speech, hearing impaired.

Contact. E-mail: infoctr@pace.edu
Phone: (212) 346-1323 Toll-free number: (800) 874-7223
Fax: (212) 346-1040
Susan Reantillo, Director, Undergraduate Admissions, Pace University, 1 Pace Plaza, New York, NY 10038

Pace University: Pleasantville/Briarcliff

Pleasantville, New York
www.pace.edu **CB code: 2685**

- Private 4-year university
- Residential campus in small town

General. Regionally accredited. **Location:** 7 miles from White Plains, 30 miles from New York City. **Calendar:** Semester.

Annual costs/financial aid. Tuition/fees (2008-2009): $31,357. Room/board: $11,180. Books/supplies: $800. Personal expenses: $1,248. Need-based financial aid available to full-time and part-time students.

Contact. Phone: (914) 773-3746
Director of Admission, 861 Bedford Road, Pleasantville, NY 10570

Parsons The New School for Design

New York, New York
www.parsons.edu **CB code: 2638**

- Private 4-year visual arts college
- Commuter campus in very large city
- 3,815 degree-seeking undergraduates: 9% part-time, 78% women, 4% African American, 17% Asian American, 7% Hispanic American, 33% international
- 426 degree-seeking graduate students
- 50% of applicants admitted
- SAT or ACT required
- 68% graduate within 6 years

General. Founded in 1896. Regionally accredited. Division of The New School. **Degrees:** 530 bachelor's, 413 associate awarded; master's offered. **Location:** Located in Manhattan. **Calendar:** Semester, extensive summer session. **Full-time faculty:** 129 total; 53% have terminal degrees, 12% minority, 47% women. **Part-time faculty:** 937 total; 1% have terminal degrees, 16% minority, 50% women. **Class size:** 91% < 20, 9% 20-39, less than 1% 40-49, less than 1% 50-99, less than 1% >100. **Special facilities:** Architecture studio, labs, galleries.

Freshman class profile. 2,921 applied, 1,472 admitted, 658 enrolled.

Mid 50% test scores		**GPA 2.0-2.99:**	22%
SAT critical reading:	480-590	**Rank in top quarter:**	38%
SAT math:	490-610	**Rank in top tenth:**	12%
SAT writing:	490-600	**End year in good standing:**	94%
ACT composite:	22-26	**Return as sophomores:**	87%
GPA 3.75 or higher:	18%	**Out-of-state:**	73%
GPA 3.50-3.74:	19%	**Live on campus:**	75%
GPA 3.0-3.49:	40%	**International:**	31%

Basis for selection. Portfolio and home examination most important, followed by school achievement record and test scores. Activities, leadership, motivation considered. Applicants required to complete home examination of 4 specific art and design problems as supplement to portfolio. Portfolio required, essay recommended for all; interview recommended, required for those geographically close.

High school preparation. College-preparatory program recommended.

2008-2009 Annual costs. Tuition/fees: $34,460. Room/board: $12,390. Books/supplies: $2,050. Personal expenses: $1,550.

2008-2009 Financial aid. **Need-based:** 331 full-time freshmen applied for aid; 291 were judged to have need; 291 of these received aid. Average need met was 76%. Average scholarship/grant was $16,073; average loan $11,991. 57% of total undergraduate aid awarded as scholarships/grants,

43% as loans/jobs. **Non-need-based:** Scholarships awarded for academics, music/drama.

Application procedures. Admission: $50 fee, may be waived for applicants with need. Admission notification on a rolling basis. Must reply by May 1 or within 4 week(s) if notified thereafter. **Financial aid:** No deadline. FAFSA required. Applicants notified on a rolling basis starting 3/1; must reply within 4 week(s) of notification.

Academics. Special study options: Accelerated study, cross-registration, distance learning, double major, ESL, exchange student, independent study, internships, liberal arts/career combination, student-designed major, study abroad. Five-year combined BA/BFA, New York Studio Program. **Credit/placement by examination:** CLEP, IB. **Support services:** Pre-admission summer program, remedial instruction, tutoring, writing center.

Majors. Architecture: Architecture, environmental design, interior, landscape. **Business:** Fashion. **Visual/performing arts:** Design, fashion design, illustration, industrial design, interior design, photography, studio arts. **Other:** Design and technology.

Most popular majors. Visual/performing arts 98%.

Computing on campus. 1,200 workstations in library, computer center. Dormitories wired for high-speed internet access and linked to campus network. Commuter students can connect to campus network. Online course registration, helpline, student web hosting, wireless network available.

Student life. Freshman orientation: Mandatory. Orientation to school, programs, services, and New York City. **Housing:** Coed dorms, special housing for disabled, apartments available. $250 nonrefundable deposit, deadline 7/1. **Activities:** Jazz band, choral groups, dance, drama, film society, international student organizations, literary magazine, music ensembles, opera, radio station, student government, student newspaper, symphony orchestra, women's group, student union, Latino and African-American student organizations, gay/lesbian student organizations, volunteer groups, environmental group.

Student services. Alcohol/substance abuse counseling, career counseling, services for economically disadvantaged, student employment services, financial aid counseling, health services, minority student services, personal counseling, placement for graduates.

Contact. E-mail: parsadm@newschool.edu
Phone: (212) 229-8910 Toll-free number: (877) 528-3321
Fax: (212) 229-8975
Anthony Padilla, Director of Admission, Parsons The New School for Design, 65 Fifth Avenue, New York, NY 10011

Paul Smith's College

Paul Smiths, New York
www.paulsmiths.edu **CB code: 2640**

- Private 4-year liberal arts college
- Residential campus in rural community
- 927 degree-seeking undergraduates
- 81% of applicants admitted

General. Founded in 1937. Regionally accredited. Hands-on experience in major, internship programs within college, and externships with leading companies. **Degrees:** 99 bachelor's, 108 associate awarded. **Location:** 150 miles from Albany, 20 miles from Lake Placid. **Calendar:** Semester, limited summer session. **Full-time faculty:** 54 total. **Part-time faculty:** 21 total. **Class size:** 60% < 20, 31% 20-39, 5% 40-49, 4% 50-99. **Special facilities:** Sugar maple plantation, sawmill, on-campus restaurant, 14,200-acre forest, on-campus retail bakery.

Freshman class profile. 943 applied, 766 admitted, 314 enrolled.

Mid 50% test scores		ACT composite:	17-23
SAT critical reading:	410-530	Out-of-state:	35%
SAT math:	410-540	Live on campus:	97%

Basis for selection. Most consideration given to high school or college course work as well as SAT/ACT scores. Personal essays, letters of recommendation, relevant experience and SAT/ACT scores highly encouraged. Interview recommended. **Homeschooled:** Statement describing homeschool structure and mission, transcript of courses and grades, interview, letter of recommendation (nonparent) required.

High school preparation. 4 units required; 8 recommended. Required and recommended units include English 4, mathematics 2, science 2 (laboratory 2) and foreign language 2. High school subject requirements vary according to program.

2009-2010 Annual costs. Tuition/fees: $20,030. Program fees range from $630 to $2,030 depending on program. Room/board: $8,940. Books/supplies: $1,000. Personal expenses: $1,000.

2008-2009 Financial aid. Need-based: 285 full-time freshmen applied for aid; 261 were judged to have need; 261 of these received aid. Average need met was 69%. Average scholarship/grant was $10,337; average loan $2,940. 63% of total undergraduate aid awarded as scholarships/grants, 37% as loans/jobs. **Non-need-based:** Awarded to 178 full-time undergraduates, including 51 freshmen. Scholarships awarded for academics. **Additional information:** Merit aid only for international students; no financial aid application required.

Application procedures. Admission: No deadline. $30 fee, may be waived for applicants with need. Admission notification on a rolling basis beginning on or about 10/1. **Financial aid:** Priority date 3/31; no closing date. FAFSA required. Applicants notified on a rolling basis starting 3/5; must reply within 4 week(s) of notification.

Academics. Special study options: Combined bachelor's/graduate degree, double major, honors, independent study, internships, liberal arts/career combination, study abroad. **Credit/placement by examination:** AP, CLEP, IB, institutional tests. 15 credit hours maximum toward associate degree, 15 toward bachelor's. **Support services:** Learning center, reduced course load, remedial instruction, study skills assistance, tutoring, writing center.

Majors. Biology: General. **Business:** General, business admin, entrepreneurial studies, hospitality admin, hospitality/recreation, hotel/motel admin, resort management, restaurant/food services, tourism promotion, tourism/travel. **Conservation:** General, environmental science, fisheries, forest management, forest resources, forest sciences, forestry, management/policy, wildlife. **Health:** Predental, premedicine, preveterinary. **Interdisciplinary:** Biological/physical sciences. **Liberal arts:** Arts/sciences. **Parks/recreation:** General, facilities management. **Personal/culinary services:** Chef training, culinary arts, restaurant/catering.

Most popular majors. Business/marketing 17%, natural resources/environmental science 41%, parks/recreation 12%, personal/culinary services 27%.

Computing on campus. 140 workstations in library, computer center. Dormitories wired for high-speed internet access and linked to campus network. Commuter students can connect to campus network. Online library, helpline, student web hosting available.

Student life. Freshman orientation: Mandatory, $125 fee. **Housing:** Guaranteed on-campus for all undergraduates. Coed dorms, single-sex dorms, wellness housing available. $100 nonrefundable deposit, deadline 5/1. **Activities:** Choral groups, literary magazine, radio station, student government, student newspaper, outing club, gaming and Anime club, conservation club, Junior American Culinary Federation, Christian Fellowship, fiber arts, fish and game club, ski and snowboard club, campus council.

Athletics. NAIA. **Intercollegiate:** Basketball, cross-country, rugby, soccer, volleyball W. **Intramural:** Basketball, ice hockey M, rugby, skiing, soccer, softball, volleyball, water polo. **Team name:** Bobcats.

Student services. Adult student services, alcohol/substance abuse counseling, chaplain/spiritual director, career counseling, services for economically disadvantaged, student employment services, financial aid counseling, health services, personal counseling, placement for graduates. **Physically disabled:** Services for visually, hearing impaired.

Contact. E-mail: admiss@paulsmiths.edu
Phone: (518) 327-6227 Toll-free number: (800) 421-2605
Fax: (518) 327-6016
Kathy Fitzgerald, Vice President of Enrollment Management, Paul Smith's College, PO Box 265, Routes 30 & 86, Paul Smiths, NY 12970-0265

Polytechnic Institute of New York University

Brooklyn, New York **CB member**
www.poly.edu **CB code: 2668**

- Private 4-year university
- Commuter campus in very large city
- 1,505 degree-seeking undergraduates: 4% part-time, 19% women, 12% African American, 29% Asian American, 12% Hispanic American, 15% international
- 2,287 degree-seeking graduate students
- 55% of applicants admitted
- SAT or ACT, application essay required
- 53% graduate within 6 years; 16% enter graduate study

General. Founded in 1854. Regionally accredited. **Degrees:** 259 bachelor's awarded; master's, doctoral offered. **ROTC:** Army, Air Force. **Location:** 2 miles from New York City. **Calendar:** Semester, extensive summer session. **Full-time faculty:** 138 total; 91% have terminal degrees, 24% minority, 17% women. **Part-time faculty:** 157 total; 50% have terminal degrees, 18% minority, 19% women. **Class size:** 55% < 20, 35% 20-39, 7% 40-49, 3% 50-99. **Special facilities:** Library of science and technology, center for advanced technology in telecommunications, institute of imaging sciences, center for construction management technology, transportation research institute, wireless research institute, urban infrastructure institute.

Freshman class profile. 1,854 applied, 1,013 admitted, 292 enrolled.

Mid 50% test scores		**Rank in top tenth:**	31%
SAT critical reading:	510-610	**Return as sophomores:**	84%
SAT math:	580-680	**Out-of-state:**	8%
GPA 3.75 or higher:	17%	**Live on campus:**	29%
GPA 3.50-3.74:	24%	**International:**	10%
GPA 3.0-3.49:	28%	**Fraternities:**	6%
GPA 2.0-2.99:	27%	**Sororities:**	3%
Rank in top quarter:	61%		

Basis for selection. School achievement record, class rank, test scores, recommendations required. Special emphasis on mathematics and science areas. Interview recommended.

High school preparation. College-preparatory program required. Required and recommended units include English 4, mathematics 4, social studies 3, science 4, foreign language 2 and academic electives 2. Requirements include 1 chemistry, pre-calculus, calculus.

2008-2009 Annual costs. Tuition/fees: $32,644. Room/board: $8,722. Books/supplies: $1,000. Personal expenses: $1,575.

2007-2008 Financial aid. Need-based: 324 full-time freshmen applied for aid; 237 were judged to have need; 237 of these received aid. Average need met was 89%. Average scholarship/grant was $9,964; average loan $3,627. 62% of total undergraduate aid awarded as scholarships/grants, 38% as loans/jobs. **Non-need-based:** Awarded to 1,132 full-time undergraduates, including 287 freshmen. Scholarships awarded for academics.

Application procedures. Admission: Priority date 2/1; no deadline. $50 fee, may be waived for applicants with need, free for online applicants. Admission notification on a rolling basis beginning on or about 2/1. Must reply by May 1 or within 4 week(s) if notified thereafter. **Financial aid:** Priority date 3/1; no closing date. FAFSA, institutional form, CSS PROFILE required. Applicants notified on a rolling basis starting 3/15; must reply within 2 week(s) of notification.

Academics. Special study options: Accelerated study, combined bachelor's/graduate degree, cooperative education, distance learning, double major, honors, internships, study abroad. Joint master's degree program in dental materials science with New York University. **Credit/placement by examination:** AP, CLEP, IB, institutional tests. 16 credit hours maximum toward bachelor's degree. Students with outstanding record or specialized competence may establish 16 credits maximum toward baccalaureate degree by passing comprehensive examinations. Each department determines courses in which examination available and examination format. **Support services:** Learning center, pre-admission summer program, remedial instruction, study skills assistance, tutoring, writing center.

Honors college/program. Students selected for Honors College must have superior high school academic records and interview with member of Honors College Faculty Governing Board.

Majors. Biology: Molecular biochemistry. **Business:** Construction management, management information systems. **Communications:** Digital media, journalism. **Computer sciences:** General, computer science. **Engineering:** Chemical, civil, computer, electrical, mechanical. **Interdisciplinary:** Science/society. **Liberal arts:** Arts/sciences. **Math:** General. **Physical sciences:** Chemistry, physics. **Other:** Sustainable urban environments.

Most popular majors. Business/marketing 6%, computer/information sciences 13%, engineering/engineering technologies 69%.

Computing on campus. PC or laptop required. 104 workstations in dormitories, library, computer center, student center. Dormitories linked to campus network. Commuter students can connect to campus network. Online library, helpline, repair service, student web hosting, wireless network available.

Student life. Freshman orientation: Available. **Housing:** Guaranteed on-campus for freshmen. Coed dorms, fraternity/sorority housing, wellness housing available. $300 nonrefundable deposit. **Activities:** Film society, literary magazine, radio station, student government, student newspaper, Society of Women Engineers, Society of Black Engineers, Ambassador Society, ethnic and service organizations, Society of Hispanic Professional Engineers, Alpha Phi Omega service fraternity.

Athletics. NCAA. **Intercollegiate:** Baseball M, basketball, cross-country, judo, soccer, softball W, tennis, track and field, volleyball. **Intramural:** Basketball, bowling, football (non-tackle), golf, handball M, ice hockey M, racquetball, skiing, soccer, softball W, table tennis, track and field, volleyball, weight lifting. **Team name:** Blue Jays.

Student services. Career counseling, student employment services, placement for graduates.

Contact. E-mail: uadmit@poly.edu
Phone: (718) 260-3100 Toll-free number: (800) 765-9832
Fax: (718) 260-3446
Joy Colelli, Dean of Admissions and New Students, Polytechnic Institute of New York University, 6 Metrotech Center, Brooklyn, NY 11201-2999

Pratt Institute

Brooklyn, New York — **CB member**
www.pratt.edu — **CB code: 2669**

- Private 4-year university and visual arts college
- Residential campus in very large city
- 3,085 degree-seeking undergraduates: 5% part-time, 61% women, 5% African American, 14% Asian American, 8% Hispanic American, 12% international
- 1,639 degree-seeking graduate students
- 42% of applicants admitted
- SAT or ACT with writing, application essay required

General. Founded in 1887. Regionally accredited. Additional campus located in Manhattan with associate degree programs, bachelor's degree in construction management program, and various graduate programs. **Degrees:** 631 bachelor's, 42 associate awarded; master's offered. **Location:** 2 miles from Manhattan. **Calendar:** Semester, extensive summer session. **Full-time faculty:** 127 total; 64% have terminal degrees, 10% minority, 39% women. **Part-time faculty:** 873 total; 16% minority, 41% women. **Class size:** 87% < 20, 12% 20-39, less than 1% 40-49. **Special facilities:** Wood and metal workshops, ceramics kiln studios and casting foundry, digital arts labs, printmaking workshop, fine arts center, center for community development.

Freshman class profile. 5,010 applied, 2,098 admitted, 647 enrolled.

Mid 50% test scores		**GPA 3.0-3.49:**	31%
SAT critical reading:	510-640	**GPA 2.0-2.99:**	15%
SAT math:	540-650	**Return as sophomores:**	88%
ACT composite:	22-28	**Out-of-state:**	72%
GPA 3.75 or higher:	34%	**Live on campus:**	82%
GPA 3.50-3.74:	20%	**International:**	17%

Basis for selection. Admissions committee considers overall academic record which includes academic performance, portfolio, curriculum, test scores, recommendation, and essay. SAT Subject Tests recommended for applicants to architecture program. Interview not required. Letter of recommendation required for all applicants. Portfolio required for architecture, art and design programs.

High school preparation. 16 units recommended. Recommended units include English 4, mathematics 4, social studies 1, science 2 and academic electives 5. 4 math required for architecture and construction management applicants.

2009-2010 Annual costs. Tuition/fees (projected): $34,880. All architecture students required to purchase laptop and software (discounted) during summer. All sophomore interior design majors required to purchase laptop computer. Laptop costs approximately $3,600. Room/board: $9,756. Books/supplies: $3,000. Personal expenses: $1,000.

2008-2009 Financial aid. Need-based: 481 full-time freshmen applied for aid; 407 were judged to have need; 407 of these received aid. Average need met was 69%. Average scholarship/grant was $8,431; average loan $5,663. 52% of total undergraduate aid awarded as scholarships/grants, 48% as loans/jobs. **Non-need-based:** Awarded to 1,978 full-time undergraduates, including 412 freshmen. Scholarships awarded for academics, art.

Application procedures. Admission: Closing date 1/5 (postmark date). $50 fee, may be waived for applicants with need. Admission notification 4/1. Must reply by May 1 or within 2 week(s) if notified thereafter. **Financial aid:** Closing date 2/1. FAFSA, institutional form required. Applicants notified on a rolling basis starting 3/11; must reply within 2 week(s) of notification.

Academics. **Special study options:** ESL, exchange student, independent study, internships, study abroad, teacher certification program. **Credit/placement by examination:** AP, CLEP, institutional tests. **Support services:** Learning center, pre-admission summer program, reduced course load, study skills assistance, tutoring, writing center.

Majors. **Architecture:** Architecture. **Business:** Construction management. **Computer sciences:** Computer graphics. **Construction:** Site management. **Education:** Art. **Visual/performing arts:** Art history/conservation, cinematography, design, fashion design, industrial design, interior design, photography, studio arts. **Other:** Critical and visual studies.

Most popular majors. Architecture 17%, visual/performing arts 74%.

Computing on campus. 300 workstations in dormitories, library, computer center, student center. Dormitories wired for high-speed internet access and linked to campus network. Commuter students can connect to campus network. Online course registration, helpline, repair service, student web hosting, wireless network available.

Student life. **Freshman orientation:** Available. Preregistration for classes offered. **Housing:** Guaranteed on-campus for freshmen. Coed dorms, special housing for disabled, apartments, wellness housing available. $300 fully refundable deposit, deadline 5/1. Quiet floors. **Activities:** Campus ministries, film society, international student organizations, literary magazine, music ensembles, radio station, student government, student newspaper, TV station, Christian Fellowship, Jewish student union, Muslim student association, Asian student organization, The Agenda, Korean student association, environmental resource group, Gay/Lesbian at Pratt, New York Public Interest Research Group, Pratt Projects (socially conscious project design and creation).

Athletics. NCAA. **Intercollegiate:** Basketball M, cross-country, soccer, tennis, track and field, volleyball W. **Intramural:** Badminton, basketball, football (non-tackle) M, weight lifting. **Team name:** Canonneers.

Student services. Alcohol/substance abuse counseling, chaplain/spiritual director, career counseling, student employment services, financial aid counseling, health services, minority student services, personal counseling, placement for graduates, veterans' counselor. **Physically disabled:** Services for visually, speech, hearing impaired.

Contact. E-mail: visit@pratt.edu
Phone: (718) 636-3514 Toll-free number: (800) 331-0834
Fax: (718) 636-3670
William Swan, Director of Admissions, Pratt Institute, 200 Willoughby Avenue, Brooklyn, NY 11205-3817

Rabbinical Academy Mesivta Rabbi Chaim Berlin

Brooklyn, New York

CB code: 0719

- Private 4-year rabbinical college for men affiliated with Jewish faith
- Very large city

General. Accredited by AARTS. **Calendar:** Continuous.

Annual costs/financial aid. Tuition/fees (2008-2009): $9,250. Room/board: $3,000.

Contact. Phone: (718) 377-0777
Admissions Director, 1605 Coney Island Avenue, Brooklyn, NY 11230

Rabbinical College Beth Shraga

Monsey, New York

- Private 4-year rabbinical college for men affiliated with Jewish faith
- Commuter campus in large town

General. **Calendar:** Continuous.

Annual costs/financial aid. Tuition/fees (2008-2009): $8,700. Tuition includes fees. Room/board: $4,200.

Contact. Phone: (845) 356-1980
Admissions Director, PO Box 412, Monsey, NY 10952

Rabbinical College Bobover Yeshiva B'nei Zion

Brooklyn, New York

CB code: 7011

- Private 5-year rabbinical college for men affiliated with Jewish faith
- Very large city

General. Accredited by AARTS. **Calendar:** Continuous.

Annual costs/financial aid. Tuition/fees (2008-2009): $5,500. Room/board: $4,300. Books/supplies: $400. Personal expenses: $500.

Contact. Phone: (718) 438-2018
Director, 1577 48th Street, Brooklyn, NY 11219

Rabbinical College Ch'san Sofer of New York

Brooklyn, New York

CB code: 0714

- Private 4-year rabbinical college for men affiliated with Jewish faith
- Very large city

General. Founded in 1940. Accredited by AARTS. **Calendar:** Semester.

Annual costs/financial aid. Tuition/fees (2008-2009): $6,200.

Contact. Phone: (718) 236-1171
Dean of the College, 1876 50th Street, Brooklyn, NY 11204

Rabbinical College of Long Island

Long Beach, New York

CB code: 0675

- Private 4-year rabbinical and teachers college for men affiliated with Jewish faith
- Large town

General. Founded in 1965. Accredited by AARTS. **Calendar:** Trimester.

Contact. Phone: (516) 431-7414
Director of Admissions, 205 West Beech Street, Long Beach, NY 11561

Rabbinical College of Ohr Shimon Yisroel

Brooklyn, New York

- Private 4-year rabbinical college for men
- Very large city

General. Accredited by AARTS. **Calendar:** Semester.

Annual costs/financial aid. Tuition/fees (2008-2009): $6,600.

Contact. Phone: (718) 855-4092
215-217 Hewes Street, Brooklyn, NY 11211

Rabbinical Seminary Adas Yereim

Brooklyn, New York

CB code: 0666

- Private 4-year rabbinical college for men affiliated with Jewish faith
- Very large city

General. Founded in 1961. Accredited by AARTS. **Calendar:** Semester.

Annual costs/financial aid. Tuition/fees (2008-2009): $5,200.

Contact. Phone: (718) 388-1751
Director of Finances, 185 Wilson Street, Brooklyn, NY 11211

Rabbinical Seminary of America
Flushing, New York
CB code: 2776

- Private 5-year rabbinical and seminary college for men affiliated with Jewish faith
- Very large city

General. Founded in 1933. Accredited by AARTS. **Calendar:** Semester.

Annual costs/financial aid. Tuition/fees (2008-2009): $6,000. Room/board: $5,000.

Contact. Phone: (718) 268-4700
Registrar, 76-01 147th Street, Flushing, NY 11367

Rensselaer Polytechnic Institute
Troy, New York **CB member**
www.rpi.edu **CB code: 2757**

- Private 4-year university
- Residential campus in small city
- 5,367 degree-seeking undergraduates: 28% women, 4% African American, 11% Asian American, 6% Hispanic American, 1% Native American, 2% international
- 2,013 degree-seeking graduate students
- 44% of applicants admitted
- SAT or ACT with writing, application essay required
- 82% graduate within 6 years; 25% enter graduate study

General. Founded in 1824. Regionally accredited. **Degrees:** 1,143 bachelor's awarded; master's, doctoral offered. **ROTC:** Army, Naval, Air Force. **Location:** 10 miles from Albany, 150 miles from New York City. **Calendar:** Semester, extensive summer session. **Full-time faculty:** 401 total; 99% have terminal degrees, 22% minority, 22% women. **Part-time faculty:** 95 total; 61% have terminal degrees, 5% minority, 20% women. **Class size:** 53% < 20, 30% 20-39, 7% 40-49, 9% 50-99, 1% >100. **Special facilities:** Center for terahertz research, nanoscale science and engineering center, linear accelerator laboratory, observatory, incubator center, fresh water institute, lighting research center, social and behavioral research laboratory, center for biotechnology and interdisciplinary studies, computational center for nanotechnology innovations, geotechnical centrifuge research center, artificial intelligence and reasoning lab, human-level intelligence laboratory, experimental media and performing arts center.

Freshman class profile. 11,249 applied, 4,962 admitted, 1,356 enrolled.

Mid 50% test scores			
SAT critical reading:	600-690	Rank in top quarter:	92%
SAT math:	650-730	Rank in top tenth:	64%
SAT writing:	580-680	End year in good standing:	95%
ACT composite:	24-29	Return as sophomores:	95%
GPA 3.75 or higher:	42%	Out-of-state:	65%
GPA 3.50-3.74:	37%	Live on campus:	98%
GPA 3.0-3.49:	20%	International:	3%
GPA 2.0-2.99:	1%	Fraternities:	21%
		Sororities:	13%

Basis for selection. School achievement record important, test scores and essay required, activities considered. SAT Subject Tests in a math and a science required for accelerated program applicants only, or ACT (which must include the optional writing component in lieu of SAT and SAT Subject Tests); students applying from countries (such as China) that do not offer our required standardized tests will be considered without testing on a case-by-case basis. Portfolio required for electronic arts, highly recommended for architecture.

High school preparation. College-preparatory program required. 15 units required. Required and recommended units include English 4, mathematics 4, social studies 2-3 and science 3-4. Best suited applicants will have completed 4 math through pre-calculus, 3 science, and 2 social studies and/or history.

2008-2009 Annual costs. Tuition/fees: $37,990. Room/board: $10,730. Books/supplies: $1,815.

2008-2009 Financial aid. Need-based: 1,116 full-time freshmen applied for aid; 892 were judged to have need; 892 of these received aid. Average need met was 82%. Average scholarship/grant was $23,079; average loan $6,727. 75% of total undergraduate aid awarded as scholarships/grants, 25% as loans/jobs. **Non-need-based:** Awarded to 2,219 full-time undergraduates, including 673 freshmen. Scholarships awarded for academics, alumni affiliation, art, athletics, leadership, minority status, music/drama, ROTC.

Application procedures. Admission: Closing date 1/15 (postmark date). $70 fee, may be waived for applicants with need. Admission notification 3/14. Must reply by 5/1. **Financial aid:** Closing date 2/15. FAFSA, CSS PROFILE required. Applicants notified by 3/25.

Academics. Extensive accelerated program offerings available in virtually all Science departments including Computer Science, Physics, Applied Physics, Biology, Biochemistry and Biophysics, Geology and Hydrology, leading to the BS-PhD. **Special study options:** Accelerated study, combined bachelor's/graduate degree, cooperative education, cross-registration, double major, dual enrollment of high school students, exchange student, honors, independent study, internships, liberal arts/career combination, student-designed major, study abroad. BS/MD with Albany Medical College; BS/JD with Columbia University and Albany Law School. **Credit/placement by examination:** AP, CLEP, IB. **Support services:** Learning center, pre-admission summer program, reduced course load, remedial instruction, study skills assistance, tutoring, writing center.

Majors. Architecture: Architecture. **Biology:** General, biochemistry, biophysics. **Business:** Business admin. **Communications:** General, digital media. **Computer sciences:** General, computer science, information technology. **Conservation:** Environmental science. **Engineering:** General, aerospace, biomedical, chemical, civil, computer, electrical, environmental, industrial, materials, mechanical, mechanics, nuclear, physics, science, systems. **Engineering technology:** Industrial management. **Health:** Predental, premedicine. **Interdisciplinary:** Biological/physical sciences, science/society. **Legal studies:** Prelaw. **Liberal arts:** Arts/sciences. **Math:** General. **Philosophy/religion:** Philosophy. **Physical sciences:** Chemistry, geology, hydrology, physics. **Psychology:** General. **Social sciences:** Economics. **Visual/performing arts:** Studio arts. **Other:** Games and Simulation Arts and Sciences.

Most popular majors. Business/marketing 7%, computer/information sciences 8%, engineering/engineering technologies 63%.

Computing on campus. PC or laptop required. 1,081 workstations in dormitories, library, computer center, student center. Dormitories wired for high-speed internet access and linked to campus network. Commuter students can connect to campus network. Online course registration, online library, helpline, repair service, student web hosting, wireless network available.

Student life. Freshman orientation: Mandatory, $175 fee. Preregistration for classes offered. Held over 2-day period in July or August. **Policies:** College housing required of all freshmen unless student lives within 50-mile radius of campus with parent(s) or legal guardian(s). **Housing:** Guaranteed on-campus for freshmen. Coed dorms, special housing for disabled, apartments, fraternity/sorority housing available. **Activities:** Bands, campus ministries, choral groups, dance, drama, film society, international student organizations, literary magazine, music ensembles, musical theater, radio station, student government, student newspaper, symphony orchestra, TV station, student-run union; more than 160 athletic, service, media, multicultural, performing arts, visual arts, religious clubs and organizations.

Athletics. NCAA. **Intercollegiate:** Baseball M, basketball, cross-country, diving, field hockey W, football (tackle) M, golf M, lacrosse, soccer, softball W, swimming, tennis, track and field. **Intramural:** Badminton, basketball, bowling, football (non-tackle), golf, ice hockey, racquetball, soccer, softball, swimming, tennis, track and field, volleyball. **Team name:** Redhawks, Engineers.

Student services. Alcohol/substance abuse counseling, chaplain/spiritual director, career counseling, services for economically disadvantaged, student employment services, financial aid counseling, health services, legal services, minority student services, personal counseling, placement for graduates, women's services. **Physically disabled:** Services for visually, speech, hearing impaired. **Learning disabled:** Comprehensive services available.

Contact. E-mail: admissions@rpi.edu
Phone: (518) 276-6216 Fax: (518) 276-4072
James Nondorf, Vice President for Enrollment, Rensselaer Polytechnic Institute, 110 Eighth Street, Troy, NY 12180-3590

Roberts Wesleyan College
Rochester, New York **CB member**
www.roberts.edu **CB code: 2759**

- Private 4-year liberal arts college affiliated with Free Methodist Church of North America
- Residential campus in large city
- 1,339 degree-seeking undergraduates: 8% part-time, 69% women

- 521 degree-seeking graduate students
- 66% of applicants admitted
- SAT or ACT (ACT writing recommended), application essay required
- 64% graduate within 6 years

General. Founded in 1866. Regionally accredited. **Degrees:** 389 bachelor's awarded; master's offered. **ROTC:** Army, Air Force. **Location:** 8 miles from downtown. **Calendar:** Semester, limited summer session. **Full-time faculty:** 107 total; 65% have terminal degrees, 10% minority, 46% women. **Part-time faculty:** 128 total; 23% have terminal degrees, 6% minority, 58% women. **Class size:** 62% < 20, 34% 20-39, 2% 40-49, 2% 50-99.

Freshman class profile. 1,499 applied, 982 admitted, 246 enrolled.

Mid 50% test scores			
SAT critical reading:	480-590	GPA 2.0-2.99:	21%
SAT math:	470-600	Rank in top quarter:	53%
SAT writing:	460-580	Rank in top tenth:	25%
ACT composite:	21-27	Return as sophomores:	85%
GPA 3.75 or higher:	27%	Out-of-state:	14%
GPA 3.50-3.74:	22%	Live on campus:	84%
GPA 3.0-3.49:	29%	International:	2%

Basis for selection. Rank in top 30% of high school class, 2.9 GPA, recommendations, test scores, and interview important. Students expected to recognize Christian perspectives and values college upholds. Audition required for music program; portfolio required for art education, studio art. **Homeschooled:** Transcript of courses and grades, state high school equivalency certificate, letter of recommendation (nonparent) required. Strongly recommend applicants visit.

High school preparation. College-preparatory program recommended. 12 units required. Required and recommended units include English 4, mathematics 2-4, social studies 2-3, history 3, science 4 (laboratory 3) and foreign language 3. Biology and chemistry required of nursing applicants.

2008-2009 Annual costs. Tuition/fees: $22,598. Room/board: $8,228. Books/supplies: $1,000. Personal expenses: $1,575.

2007-2008 Financial aid. Need-based: 223 full-time freshmen applied for aid; 203 were judged to have need; 203 of these received aid. Average need met was 81%. Average scholarship/grant was $12,767; average loan $5,379. 56% of total undergraduate aid awarded as scholarships/grants, 44% as loans/jobs. **Non-need-based:** Awarded to 196 full-time undergraduates, including 55 freshmen. Scholarships awarded for academics, alumni affiliation, art, athletics, music/drama, religious affiliation, ROTC, state residency. **Additional information:** Dollars for Scholars offer matching grants of up to $750.

Application procedures. Admission: Priority date 2/1; deadline 8/15 (postmark date). $35 fee, may be waived for applicants with need, free for online applicants. Admission notification on a rolling basis. Must reply by May 1 or within 2 week(s) if notified thereafter. **Financial aid:** Priority date 3/15; no closing date. FAFSA required. Applicants notified on a rolling basis starting 3/15; must reply by 5/1 or within 2 week(s) of notification.

Academics. Special study options: Cross-registration, distance learning, double major, dual enrollment of high school students, ESL, honors, independent study, internships, liberal arts/career combination, study abroad, teacher certification program, Washington semester. **Credit/placement by examination:** AP, CLEP, IB. 30 credit hours maximum toward bachelor's degree. **Support services:** Learning center, reduced course load, remedial instruction, study skills assistance, tutoring, writing center.

Majors. Biology: General, biochemistry. **Business:** General, accounting, business admin, human resources, marketing. **Communications:** General. **Computer sciences:** General, computer science. **Education:** Art, biology, chemistry, early childhood, elementary, English, history, kindergarten/preschool, mathematics, music, physics, science, social science, social studies, Spanish, special. **Foreign languages:** Spanish. **Health:** Nursing (RN), preop/surgical nursing. **History:** General. **Interdisciplinary:** Biological/physical sciences. **Liberal arts:** Arts/sciences, humanities. **Math:** General. **Philosophy/religion:** Religion. **Physical sciences:** Chemistry, physics. **Protective services:** Forensics, law enforcement admin. **Psychology:** General. **Public administration:** Social work. **Social sciences:** General, sociology. **Theology:** Bible, theology. **Visual/performing arts:** Commercial/advertising art, piano/organ, studio arts, voice/opera. **Other:** Economic crime investigation.

Most popular majors. Business/marketing 26%, education 20%, health sciences 19%, visual/performing arts 6%.

Computing on campus. 250 workstations in library, computer center, student center. Dormitories wired for high-speed internet access and linked to campus network. Commuter students can connect to campus network. Online course registration, online library, helpline, wireless network available.

Student life. Freshman orientation: Mandatory. Preregistration for classes offered. **Policies:** Religious observance required. **Housing:** Guaranteed on-campus for freshmen. Single-sex dorms, special housing for disabled, apartments, wellness housing available. $100 nonrefundable deposit, deadline 5/1. **Activities:** Bands, campus ministries, choral groups, dance, drama, international student organizations, music ensembles, musical theater, opera, radio station, student government, student newspaper, symphony orchestra, Chapel, mission trips, At the Foot of the Cross service, Habitat for Humanity, In Jesus' Name, Bible studies, SIFE (Student in Free Enterprise), Acting on Aids, senate, Celebration of Diversity.

Athletics. NAIA, NCCAA. **Intercollegiate:** Basketball, cross-country, golf, soccer, tennis, track and field, volleyball W. **Intramural:** Basketball, cross-country, football (non-tackle), racquetball, skiing, soccer, softball, table tennis, tennis, track and field, volleyball, water polo. **Team name:** Raiders.

Student services. Adult student services, alcohol/substance abuse counseling, chaplain/spiritual director, career counseling, student employment services, financial aid counseling, health services, personal counseling, placement for graduates, veterans' counselor. **Physically disabled:** Services for visually, hearing impaired.

Contact. E-mail: admissions@roberts.edu
Phone: (585) 594-6400 Toll-free number: (800) 777-4792
Fax: (585) 594-6371
Linda Hoffman, Vice President for Admissions and Marketing, Roberts Wesleyan College, 2301 Westside Drive, Rochester, NY 14624-1997

Rochester Institute of Technology

Rochester, New York — **CB member**
www.rit.edu — **CB code: 2760**

- Private 4-year university
- Residential campus in large city
- 13,056 degree-seeking undergraduates: 7% part-time, 33% women
- 2,633 graduate students
- 60% of applicants admitted
- SAT or ACT (ACT writing optional), application essay required
- 65% graduate within 6 years; 11% enter graduate study

General. Founded in 1829. Regionally accredited. University comprises 8 colleges, including National Technical Institute for the Deaf. **Degrees:** 2,452 bachelor's, 348 associate awarded; master's, doctoral offered. **ROTC:** Army, Naval, Air Force. **Location:** 5 miles from downtown, 70 miles from Buffalo. **Calendar:** Quarter, extensive summer session. **Full-time faculty:** 947 total. **Part-time faculty:** 444 total. **Class size:** 42% < 20, 40% 20-39, 11% 40-49, 6% 50-99, 2% >100. **Special facilities:** Laser optics laboratory, observatory, animal care facility, color and black-and-white photography darkrooms, electronic prepress and publishing equipment, ceramic kilns, glass furnaces, blacksmithing area, student-operated restaurant, computer graphics and robotic labs, microelectronic, telecommunications, and computer engineering facilities, access to Internet 2 research network.

Freshman class profile. 12,725 applied, 7,689 admitted, 2,625 enrolled.

Mid 50% test scores			
SAT critical reading:	540-630	Rank in top tenth:	30%
SAT math:	560-670	Return as sophomores:	88%
SAT writing:	520-610	Out-of-state:	47%
ACT composite:	24-29	Live on campus:	95%
Rank in top quarter:	62%	Fraternities:	5%
		Sororities:	5%

Basis for selection. Primary emphasis on high school grades in required courses, which vary by major. SAT or ACT given considerable weight. Class rank important. Candidates allowed to apply for up to 3 majors. ACT preferred for applicants to National Technical Institute for the Deaf. Interview recommended for all; portfolio required for art, crafts, and design programs. **Homeschooled:** Transcript of courses and grades required. Applicants should provide state certification of graduation if available.

High school preparation. College-preparatory program required. 22 units required. Required and recommended units include English 4, mathematics 2-3, social studies 4, science 2-3 (laboratory 1-2), foreign language 2 and academic electives 10. Units required for social studies may be met with history courses. College of Engineering requires 4 math including precalculus.

2008-2009 Annual costs. Tuition/fees: $28,035. Room/board: $9,381. Books/supplies: $900. Personal expenses: $600.

2007-2008 Financial aid. **Need-based:** 2,202 full-time freshmen applied for aid; 1,896 were judged to have need; 1,896 of these received aid. Average need met was 88%. Average scholarship/grant was $13,700; average loan $5,100. 67% of total undergraduate aid awarded as scholarships/grants, 33% as loans/jobs. **Non-need-based:** Awarded to 3,328 full-time undergraduates, including 788 freshmen. Scholarships awarded for academics, art, leadership, ROTC. **Additional information:** Most juniors and seniors participate in cooperative education program, earning an average $4,500-$6,500 per 3-month employment period through paid employment in jobs related to major.

Application procedures. **Admission:** Priority date 2/1; no deadline. $50 fee, may be waived for applicants with need. Admission notification on a rolling basis beginning on or about 3/1. Must reply by May 1 or within 2 week(s) if notified thereafter. Applications received after March 15 will be processed if space available. **Financial aid:** Priority date 3/1; no closing date. FAFSA, institutional form required. Applicants notified on a rolling basis starting 3/15; must reply by 5/1.

Academics. **Special study options:** Accelerated study, combined bachelor's/graduate degree, cooperative education, cross-registration, distance learning, double major, ESL, exchange student, honors, independent study, internships, liberal arts/career combination, student-designed major, study abroad, teacher certification program, weekend college. Accelerated bachelor's/master's degree programs, England semester, Japan semester, summer program in Croatia. **Credit/placement by examination:** AP, CLEP, IB, SAT, ACT, institutional tests. 45 credit hours maximum toward associate degree. **Support services:** Learning center, pre-admission summer program, reduced course load, study skills assistance, tutoring, writing center.

Majors. **Biology:** General, biochemistry, bioinformatics, biomedical sciences, biotechnology. **Business:** General, accounting, accounting/business management, business admin, finance, hospitality admin, hotel/motel admin, international, management information systems, market research, marketing, resort management, restaurant/food services, special products marketing, statistics, tourism promotion, tourism/travel, travel services. **Communications:** General, advertising, digital media, journalism, photojournalism, public relations. **Communications technology:** Animation/special effects, desktop publishing, graphics, photo/film/video, printing management. **Computer sciences:** General, computer graphics, computer science, database management, information technology, LAN/WAN management, networking, security, system admin, systems analysis, web page design, webmaster. **Engineering:** Aerospace, biomedical, chemical, computer, electrical, industrial, manufacturing, mechanical, polymer, software, systems. **Engineering technology:** Civil, computer, electrical, electromechanical, environmental, manufacturing, mechanical, occupational safety, telecommunications. **Family/consumer sciences:** Consumer economics, food/nutrition, human nutrition. **Foreign languages:** American Sign Language, sign language interpretation. **Health:** Medical illustrating, physician assistant, predental, premedicine, prepharmacy, preveterinary, sonography. **Interdisciplinary:** Math/computer science. **Legal studies:** Prelaw. **Math:** Applied, computational, probability, statistics. **Personal/culinary services:** Restaurant/catering. **Philosophy/religion:** Philosophy. **Physical sciences:** Chemistry, physics, polymer chemistry. **Production:** Furniture, woodworking. **Protective services:** Law enforcement admin. **Psychology:** General. **Public administration:** Policy analysis. **Social sciences:** Economics, international relations. **Visual/performing arts:** Ceramics, cinematography, commercial photography, commercial/advertising art, crafts, design, graphic design, illustration, industrial design, interior design, metal/jewelry, multimedia, painting, photography, printmaking, sculpture, studio arts. **Other:** Urban studies.

Most popular majors. Biology 6%, business/marketing 11%, computer/information sciences 16%, engineering/engineering technologies 27%, interdisciplinary studies 8%, visual/performing arts 16%.

Computing on campus. 2,500 workstations in dormitories, library, computer center. Dormitories wired for high-speed internet access and linked to campus network. Commuter students can connect to campus network. Online course registration, online library, helpline, repair service, student web hosting, wireless network available.

Student life. **Freshman orientation:** Mandatory, $165 fee. Preregistration for classes offered. Orientation in September prior to start of classes. **Policies:** Alcohol prohibited in campus residence halls. **Housing:** Guaranteed on-campus for freshmen. Coed dorms, special housing for disabled, apartments, fraternity/sorority housing, wellness housing available. $300 nonrefundable deposit, deadline 5/1. Special interest houses for students in selected majors or groups, single-sex floors within coed dorms, special honors program floor available. **Activities:** Bands, campus ministries, choral groups, dance, drama, film society, international student organizations, literary magazine, music ensembles, musical theater, radio station, student government, student newspaper, Asian Culture Society, Electronic Gaming Society, Gospel Ensemble, Society of Women Engineers, Society of Hispanic Engineers, National Society of Black Engineers, Emerging Black Artists, Feminist Action, Catholic Newman Network, Outing club.

Athletics. NCAA. **Intercollegiate:** Baseball M, basketball, cheerleading, cross-country, diving, ice hockey, lacrosse, rowing (crew), soccer, softball W, swimming, tennis, track and field, volleyball W, wrestling M. **Intramural:** Badminton, basketball, bowling, football (non-tackle) M, golf, ice hockey, racquetball, soccer, softball, table tennis, tennis, volleyball. **Team name:** Tigers.

Student services. Adult student services, alcohol/substance abuse counseling, chaplain/spiritual director, career counseling, services for economically disadvantaged, student employment services, financial aid counseling, health services, legal services, minority student services, on-campus daycare, personal counseling, placement for graduates, veterans' counselor, women's services. **Physically disabled:** Services for visually, speech, hearing impaired. **Learning disabled:** Comprehensive services available.

Contact. E-mail: admissions@rit.edu
Phone: (585) 475-6631 Fax: (585) 475-7424
Daniel Shelley, Assistant Vice President and Director of Undergraduate Admissions, Rochester Institute of Technology, 60 Lomb Memorial Drive, Rochester, NY 14623-5604

Russell Sage College

Troy, New York — **CB member**
www.sage.edu/rsc — **CB code: 2764**

- Private 4-year liberal arts college for women
- Residential campus in small city
- 676 degree-seeking undergraduates: 2% part-time, 99% women, 6% African American, 3% Asian American, 3% Hispanic American
- 74% of applicants admitted
- Application essay required
- 71% graduate within 6 years; 54% enter graduate study

General. Founded in 1916. Regionally accredited. Russell Sage College offers liberal arts and professional degree programs in business, nursing and health sciences, education, performing arts. RSC is a member of The Sage Colleges, including the coeducational Sage College of Albany and Sage Graduate School. **Degrees:** 197 bachelor's awarded. **ROTC:** Army, Naval, Air Force. **Location:** 10 miles from Albany, 150 miles from New York City. **Calendar:** Semester, extensive summer session. **Full-time faculty:** 49 total; 82% have terminal degrees, 6% minority, 65% women. **Part-time faculty:** 36 total; 42% have terminal degrees, 78% women. **Class size:** 54% < 20, 46% 20-39, less than 1% 50-99. **Special facilities:** Center for women's studies, New York State Theater Institute, INVEST nanotechnology business incubator.

Freshman class profile. 378 applied, 281 admitted, 123 enrolled.

Mid 50% test scores		**GPA 2.0-2.99:**	29%
SAT critical reading:	540-610	**Rank in top quarter:**	54%
SAT math:	510-570	**Rank in top tenth:**	19%
ACT composite:	22-25	**End year in good standing:**	92%
GPA 3.75 or higher:	15%	**Return as sophomores:**	82%
GPA 3.50-3.74:	13%	**Out-of-state:**	17%
GPA 3.0-3.49:	43%	**Live on campus:**	85%

Basis for selection. High school record, standardized test scores most important. Recommendations of school officials, intended major, school and community activities considered. Results from SAT or ACT examinations optional for applicants whose secondary school rank is in top 20% of graduating class. Interview recommended. **Homeschooled:** Statement describing homeschool structure and mission, transcript of courses and grades, interview, letter of recommendation (nonparent) required. **Learning Disabled:** The Sage Colleges promote self-advocacy for students with disabilities and facilitates a positive and adaptive learning environment for such students. Students seeking accommodations are required to present a recent evaluation of their disability conducted by a licensed professional. Upon admission, those requesting accommodations must contact the Coordinator of Disability Services in the Campus Life Office.

High school preparation. 16 units required. Required and recommended units include English 4, mathematics 3-4, social studies 4, science 3-4 (laboratory 2-3) and foreign language 2-3. Nursing program applicants must have 6 math/science combination including chemistry. Physical and occupational therapy students must have 4 math/science.

2008-2009 Annual costs. Tuition/fees: $26,740. Room/board: $9,200. Books/supplies: $1,200. Personal expenses: $1,460.

2008-2009 Financial aid. **Need-based:** 123 full-time freshmen applied for aid; 110 were judged to have need; 110 of these received aid. Average scholarship/grant was $6,500; average loan $2,950. 57% of total undergraduate aid awarded as scholarships/grants, 43% as loans/jobs. **Non-need-based:** Awarded to 477 full-time undergraduates, including 191 freshmen. Scholarships awarded for academics, alumni affiliation, leadership, music/drama.

Application procedures. Admission: Priority date 3/1; no deadline. $30 fee, may be waived for applicants with need. Admission notification on a rolling basis beginning on or about 12/15. Must reply by May 1 or within 2 week(s) if notified thereafter. **Financial aid:** Priority date 3/1; no closing date. FAFSA required. Applicants notified on a rolling basis starting 3/1; must reply by 5/1 or within 2 week(s) of notification.

Academics. All students complete internship, field experience, or clinical experience. All students engage in service learning through 2 required courses: Women in the World (first year) and Women Changing the World (senior year). **Special study options:** Accelerated study, combined bachelor's/graduate degree, cross-registration, distance learning, double major, honors, independent study, internships, liberal arts/career combination, student-designed major, study abroad, teacher certification program. Early College for high school juniors, combined bachelor's/master's, bachelor's/doctoral programs with Sage Graduate School, 3+3 BA/JD with Albany Law School, 3+2 BS/BSE with Rensselaer Polytechnic Institute, BA/MS Accelerated Physician Assistant Program with Albany Medical College, BA/MS Early Assurance Program with Albany Medical College, BA/MD Early Assurance Program with Albany Medical College. **Credit/placement by examination:** AP, CLEP, IB, SAT, ACT, institutional tests. 30 credit hours maximum toward bachelor's degree. **Support services:** Learning center, pre-admission summer program, reduced course load, remedial instruction, study skills assistance, tutoring, writing center.

Majors. Biology: General, biochemistry. **Business:** Business admin. **Communications:** Media studies. **Conservation:** Environmental science. **Education:** Elementary. **Family/consumer sciences:** Human nutrition. **Foreign languages:** Spanish. **Health:** Art therapy, nursing (RN). **History:** General. **Interdisciplinary:** Global studies. **Liberal arts:** Arts/sciences. **Math:** General. **Physical sciences:** Chemistry. **Protective services:** Criminal justice, forensics. **Psychology:** General. **Social sciences:** Political science, sociology. **Visual/performing arts:** Dramatic. **Other:** BioPsychology, Interdisciplinary Studies.

Most popular majors. Biology 14%, education 12%, health sciences 35%, liberal arts 7%, psychology 9%, social sciences 8%.

Computing on campus. 157 workstations in library, computer center, student center. Dormitories wired for high-speed internet access and linked to campus network. Commuter students can connect to campus network. Online course registration, online library, helpline, wireless network available.

Student life. Freshman orientation: Available, $200 fee. Preregistration for classes offered. 1-day welcome programs offered in June. 4-day orientation in September. **Policies:** Zero tolerance for drugs, harassment, or violence on campus. **Housing:** Guaranteed on-campus for all undergraduates. Wellness housing available. $100 partly refundable deposit, deadline 5/1. Special houses available for honor students and students interested in language/international awareness activities. Over-21 residence hall available for seniors. 19th-century brownstone residences available. **Activities:** Campus ministries, choral groups, dance, drama, literary magazine, music ensembles, musical theater, student government, student newspaper, Black and Latina student alliance, gay and lesbian alliance, Fellowship of Christian Athletes, Hillel, Newman Community, Rotaract Club, Key Club, Sage Votes.

Athletics. NCAA. **Intercollegiate:** Basketball W, soccer W, softball W, tennis W, volleyball W. **Intramural:** Volleyball W. **Team name:** Gators.

Student services. Adult student services, alcohol/substance abuse counseling, chaplain/spiritual director, career counseling, services for economically disadvantaged, student employment services, financial aid counseling, health services, minority student services, personal counseling, placement for graduates, women's services.

Contact. E-mail: rscadm@sage.edu
Phone: (518) 244-2217 Toll-free number: (888) 837-9724
Fax: (518) 244-6880
Kathy Rusch, Director of Admission, Russell Sage College, 45 Ferry Street, Troy, NY 12180-4115

Sage College of Albany

Albany, New York
www.sage.edu **CB code: 2343**

- Private 4-year business and liberal arts college
- Commuter campus in small city
- 820 degree-seeking undergraduates: 35% part-time, 70% women, 12% African American, 2% Asian American, 3% Hispanic American
- 62% of applicants admitted
- Application essay required
- 31% graduate within 6 years; 31% enter graduate study

General. Founded in 1957. Regionally accredited. **Degrees:** 226 bachelor's, 39 associate awarded. **ROTC:** Army, Air Force. **Location:** 150 miles from New York City. **Calendar:** Semester, extensive summer session. **Full-time faculty:** 39 total; 67% have terminal degrees, 5% minority, 59% women. **Part-time faculty:** 52 total; 19% have terminal degrees, 52% women. **Class size:** 77% < 20, 22% 20-39, less than 1% 50-99. **Special facilities:** Fine arts studio, graphic design and interior design studios, award-winning Opalka Gallery.

Freshman class profile. 296 applied, 183 admitted, 65 enrolled.

Mid 50% test scores		**GPA 2.0-2.99:**	50%
SAT critical reading:	470-520	**Rank in top quarter:**	16%
SAT math:	470-510	**Rank in top tenth:**	4%
ACT composite:	19-21	**End year in good standing:**	93%
GPA 3.75 or higher:	5%	**Return as sophomores:**	76%
GPA 3.50-3.74:	6%	**Out-of-state:**	14%
GPA 3.0-3.49:	28%	**Live on campus:**	77%

Basis for selection. Recommendation of high school guidance counselor or teacher and academic record considered for all applicants. Applications reviewed on individual basis. SAT or ACT optional for applicants with secondary school rank in top 20% of graduating class. Interview recommended for all; portfolio required for art and design programs. **Homeschooled:** Statement describing homeschool structure and mission, transcript of courses and grades, interview, letter of recommendation (nonparent) required.

High school preparation. College-preparatory program required. 16 units required. Required and recommended units include English 4, mathematics 2-3, social studies 4, science 2-3 and foreign language 2.

2008-2009 Annual costs. Tuition/fees: $19,490. Room/board: $9,350. Books/supplies: $1,200. Personal expenses: $1,460.

2008-2009 Financial aid. Need-based: 65 full-time freshmen applied for aid; 61 were judged to have need; 61 of these received aid. Average scholarship/grant was $6,600; average loan $2,950. 67% of total undergraduate aid awarded as scholarships/grants, 33% as loans/jobs. **Non-need-based:** Awarded to 243 full-time undergraduates, including 39 freshmen. Scholarships awarded for academics, art, leadership.

Application procedures. Admission: No deadline. $30 fee, may be waived for applicants with need. Admission notification on a rolling basis beginning on or about 11/1. Must reply by May 1 or within 2 week(s) if notified thereafter. **Financial aid:** Priority date 3/1; no closing date. FAFSA required. Applicants notified on a rolling basis starting 3/1; must reply by 5/1 or within 2 week(s) of notification.

Academics. College of Applied Studies offers specialties in art and design, business and communications, computer technologies, legal studies, creative studies. Four programs in fine arts (photography, graphic design, interior design, and fine arts) accredited by National Association of Schools of Art and Design. Transfer-friendly "two plus two" curriculum with professional study beginning in first 2 years; joint degrees in clinical biology and cytotechnology with Albany College of Pharmacy. Ease of transfer for community college graduates. **Special study options:** Combined bachelor's/graduate degree, cross-registration, distance learning, double major, honors, independent study, internships, liberal arts/career combination, student-designed major, study abroad. **Credit/placement by examination:** AP, CLEP, IB, SAT, ACT, institutional tests. 30 credit hours maximum toward associate degree, 30 toward bachelor's. **Support services:** Learning center, pre-admission summer program, reduced course load, remedial instruction, study skills assistance, tutoring, writing center.

Majors. Biology: General. **Business:** Accounting, business admin. **Communications:** Digital media. **Computer sciences:** General, networking, webmaster. **Education:** Physical. **Health:** Cytotechnology, nursing (RN). **Legal studies:** General. **Liberal arts:** Arts/sciences. **Protective services:** Law enforcement admin. **Psychology:** General. **Public administration:** Policy analysis. **Social sciences:** General. **Visual/performing arts:** Graphic design, interior design, studio arts.

Most popular majors. Business/marketing 19%, education 11%, liberal arts 12%, social sciences 11%, visual/performing arts 24%.

Computing on campus. 183 workstations in library, computer center. Dormitories wired for high-speed internet access and linked to campus network. Commuter students can connect to campus network. Online course registration, online library, helpline, wireless network available.

Student life. Freshman orientation: Available, $125 fee. Preregistration for classes offered. New students may receive academic advising and register for classes (summer, fall, spring) beginning March 1st each year. One-day welcome programs offered in June. 4-day orientation in September.

Policies: Zero tolerance for drugs, harassment or violence on campus. **Housing:** Guaranteed on-campus for freshmen. Coed dorms, apartments, wellness housing available. $100 partly refundable deposit, deadline 5/1. Apartment-style suites available on adjacent campus. **Activities:** Literary magazine, student government, student newspaper, ALDANA (African American, Latino, Desi's, Asian, Native American Alliance), Sage Votes, Association of Campus Events, Gay Straight Alliance.

Athletics. Intercollegiate: Basketball W, lacrosse W, soccer W, softball W, tennis, volleyball W. **Intramural:** Badminton, football (non-tackle). **Team name:** Gators.

Student services. Adult student services, alcohol/substance abuse counseling, chaplain/spiritual director, career counseling, services for economically disadvantaged, student employment services, financial aid counseling, health services, minority student services, personal counseling, placement for graduates, veterans' counselor.

Contact. E-mail: scaadm@sage.adm
Phone: (518) 292-1730 Toll-free number: (888) 837-9724
Fax: (518) 292-1912
Andrew Palumbo, Director of Undergraduate Admission, Sage College of Albany, 140 New Scotland Avenue, Albany, NY 12208

Saint Bonaventure University

St. Bonaventure, New York — **CB member**
www.sbu.edu — **CB code: 2793**

- Private 4-year university affiliated with Roman Catholic Church
- Residential campus in large town
- 1,892 degree-seeking undergraduates: 1% part-time, 51% women, 4% African American, 2% Asian American, 3% Hispanic American, 2% international
- 461 degree-seeking graduate students
- 91% of applicants admitted
- 70% graduate within 6 years

General. Founded in 1858. Regionally accredited. Catholic institution in Franciscan tradition. **Degrees:** 464 bachelor's awarded; master's offered. **ROTC:** Army. **Location:** 75 miles from Buffalo. **Calendar:** Semester, limited summer session. **Full-time faculty:** 145 total; 77% have terminal degrees, 6% minority, 30% women. **Part-time faculty:** 65 total; 3% minority, 52% women. **Class size:** 61% < 20, 39% 20-39. **Special facilities:** Observatory, digital media laboratory, permanent art collection, retreat facility, rare books collection.

Freshman class profile. 1,731 applied, 1,580 admitted, 563 enrolled.

Mid 50% test scores		**GPA 2.0-2.99:**	39%
SAT critical reading:	460-570	**Rank in top quarter:**	42%
SAT math:	450-580	**Rank in top tenth:**	17%
SAT writing:	450-560	**Return as sophomores:**	80%
ACT composite:	19-26	**Out-of-state:**	26%
GPA 3.75 or higher:	22%	**Live on campus:**	95%
GPA 3.50-3.74:	11%	**International:**	1%
GPA 3.0-3.49:	25%		

Basis for selection. Interview, high school GPA and curriculum most important. Recommendation, class rank, test scores, extracurricular activities also considered. Applicants to dual admission premed program with George Washington University must submit Biology SAT Subject Test scores. Essay recommended for all. **Homeschooled:** Statement describing homeschool structure and mission, transcript of courses and grades, letter of recommendation (nonparent) required. Course syllabus, book titles, and all course evaluations required to be considered for admission.

High school preparation. 19 units recommended. Recommended units include English 4, mathematics 3, social studies 4, science 3 and foreign language 2. Science majors must have 4 science, 4 math. Business majors need 4 math. Recommend 3 science lab.

2009-2010 Annual costs. Tuition/fees (projected): $25,785. Room/board: $9,100. Books/supplies: $700. Personal expenses: $650.

Financial aid. Non-need-based: Scholarships awarded for academics, art, athletics, leadership, minority status, music/drama, religious affiliation, ROTC, state residency.

Application procedures. Admission: Priority date 2/1; deadline 4/30 (postmark date). $30 fee, may be waived for applicants with need, free for online applicants. Admission notification on a rolling basis beginning on or about 9/15. Must reply by May 1 or within 1 week(s) if notified thereafter. Applications considered until housing is closed. **Financial aid:** Priority date 2/1; no closing date. FAFSA, institutional form required. Applicants notified on a rolling basis starting 4/1; must reply by 5/1 or within 3 week(s) of notification.

Academics. Special study options: Accelerated study, combined bachelor's/graduate degree, cross-registration, distance learning, double major, dual enrollment of high school students, exchange student, honors, independent study, internships, liberal arts/career combination, student-designed major, study abroad, teacher certification program, Washington semester. **Credit/placement by examination:** AP, CLEP, IB, SAT, ACT, institutional tests. 30 credit hours maximum toward bachelor's degree. **Support services:** Learning center, pre-admission summer program, reduced course load, remedial instruction, study skills assistance, tutoring.

Majors. Area/ethnic studies: Women's. **Biology:** General, biochemistry, bioinformatics. **Business:** Accounting, finance, management information systems, management science. **Communications:** Journalism, media studies. **Computer sciences:** General, computer science. **Conservation:** General. **Education:** Elementary, physical, special. **Foreign languages:** Classics, French, Latin, Spanish. **History:** General. **Interdisciplinary:** Gerontology, global studies. **Math:** General. **Philosophy/religion:** Philosophy. **Physical sciences:** Chemistry, physics. **Psychology:** General. **Social sciences:** General, political science, sociology. **Theology:** Theology. **Visual/performing arts:** General, art history/conservation, dramatic. **Other:** Childhood studies.

Most popular majors. Business/marketing 28%, communications/journalism 15%, education 16%, psychology 6%, social sciences 15%.

Computing on campus. 321 workstations in dormitories, library, computer center, student center. Dormitories wired for high-speed internet access and linked to campus network. Commuter students can connect to campus network. Online course registration, helpline, repair service, student web hosting, wireless network available.

Student life. Freshman orientation: Mandatory, $150 fee. Preregistration for classes offered. 2-day session held in July. **Policies:** Students must live on campus until they are seniors or 21 years old unless they live within commuting distance. **Housing:** Guaranteed on-campus for all undergraduates. Single-sex dorms, special housing for disabled, apartments, wellness housing available. $200 nonrefundable deposit, deadline 5/1. **Activities:** Bands, campus ministries, choral groups, dance, drama, international student organizations, literary magazine, music ensembles, Model UN, radio station, student government, student newspaper, TV station, Knights of Columbus, Irish society, black student union, Students In Free Enterprise, service learning organization.

Athletics. NCAA. **Intercollegiate:** Baseball M, basketball, cross-country, diving, golf M, lacrosse W, soccer, softball W, swimming, tennis. **Intramural:** Basketball, bowling, football (non-tackle) M, golf, racquetball, skiing, soccer, softball, swimming, table tennis, tennis, volleyball, water polo M. **Team name:** Bonnies.

Student services. Alcohol/substance abuse counseling, chaplain/spiritual director, career counseling, services for economically disadvantaged, student employment services, financial aid counseling, health services, personal counseling, placement for graduates, veterans' counselor.

Contact. E-mail: admissions@sbu.edu
Phone: (716) 375-2400 Toll-free number: (800) 462-5050
Fax: (716) 375-4005
James DiRisio, Director of Admissions, Saint Bonaventure University, Route 417, St. Bonaventure, NY 14778-2284

St. Francis College

Brooklyn Heights, New York — **CB member**
www.stfranciscollege.edu — **CB code: 2796**

- Private 4-year liberal arts college affiliated with Roman Catholic Church
- Commuter campus in very large city
- 2,344 degree-seeking undergraduates: 12% part-time, 54% women
- 18 degree-seeking graduate students
- 75% of applicants admitted
- SAT, application essay required
- 53% graduate within 6 years

General. Founded in 1884. Regionally accredited. **Degrees:** 443 bachelor's, 18 associate awarded; master's offered. **ROTC:** Army, Air Force. **Location:** 5 minutes from Manhattan by subway. **Calendar:** Semester, limited summer session. **Full-time faculty:** 78 total; 85% have terminal degrees, 10% minority, 46% women. **Part-time faculty:** 156 total; 23% have terminal degrees, 23% minority, 36% women. **Class size:** 49% < 20, 50%

20-39, less than 1% 40-49, less than 1% 50-99. **Special facilities:** Television production and editing facility with 3 Ikegami cameras and 17 Mac G5 digital editing stations.

Freshman class profile. 1,707 applied, 1,279 admitted, 591 enrolled.

Mid 50% test scores			
SAT critical reading:	410-510	GPA 3.0-3.49:	17%
SAT math:	410-520	GPA 2.0-2.99:	51%
SAT writing:	410-510	Return as sophomores:	76%
GPA 3.75 or higher:	8%	Out-of-state:	2%
GPA 3.50-3.74:	10%	Live on campus:	3%
		International:	8%

Basis for selection. Academic achievement, test scores, counselor's recommendation, school and community activities, and admissions interview important. Degree-seeking students who do not meet criteria may be admitted after review and assessment of their educational background. SAT/ACT scores must be received by first day of class for fall-term admission. Interview required of academically weak applicants. **Homeschooled:** Statement describing homeschool structure and mission, state high school equivalency certificate required.

High school preparation. 18.5 units recommended. Recommended units include English 4, mathematics 2, social studies 4, science 2, visual/performing arts 1, academic electives 5.5. Applicants seeking BS should have completed 11th grade high school math or its equivalent.

2008-2009 Annual costs. Tuition/fees: $15,720. Books/supplies: $1,000. Personal expenses: $4,000.

2008-2009 Financial aid. **Non-need-based:** Scholarships awarded for academics, athletics.

Application procedures. **Admission:** No deadline. $35 fee, may be waived for applicants with need. Admission notification on a rolling basis. Must reply by May 1 or within 2 week(s) if notified thereafter. **Financial aid:** Priority date 2/15; no closing date. FAFSA required. Applicants notified on a rolling basis starting 3/15; must reply within 2 week(s) of notification.

Academics. **Special study options:** Accelerated study, combined bachelor's/graduate degree, cooperative education, cross-registration, double major, dual enrollment of high school students, ESL, exchange student, honors, independent study, internships, student-designed major, study abroad, teacher certification program, Washington semester. Accelerated biomedical science program with New York College of Podiatric Medicine, medical technology program with St. Vincent's Catholic Medical Centers of New York and New York Methodist Hospital, joint affiliation program with St. Vincent's Catholic Medical Centers of New York in radiologic sciences. **Credit/placement by examination:** AP, CLEP, IB, SAT, ACT, institutional tests. 32 credit hours maximum toward associate degree, 98 toward bachelor's. **Support services:** Learning center, pre-admission summer program, remedial instruction, study skills assistance, tutoring, writing center.

Majors. **Biology:** General, biomedical sciences. **Business:** Accounting, business admin. **Communications:** General, digital media, public relations, radio/tv. **Computer sciences:** System admin. **Education:** Biology, chemistry, elementary, English, mathematics, physical, social studies, visually handicapped. **Foreign languages:** Spanish. **Health:** Clinical lab science, medical radiologic technology/radiation therapy, nursing (RN), physician assistant. **History:** General. **Liberal arts:** Arts/sciences. **Math:** General. **Philosophy/religion:** Philosophy, religion. **Physical sciences:** Chemistry. **Protective services:** Criminal justice. **Psychology:** General. **Social sciences:** Economics, political science, sociology. **Other:** Health promotion and science, International cultural studies.

Most popular majors. Biology 6%, business/marketing 22%, communications/journalism 11%, education 9%, liberal arts 16%, psychology 9%.

Computing on campus. 600 workstations in library, computer center, student center. Commuter students can connect to campus network. Helpline, wireless network available.

Student life. **Freshman orientation:** Mandatory. Preregistration for classes offered. During their first semester students are enrolled in a Freshman Seminar course taught by academic advisors. **Housing:** St. Francis has partnered with Educational Housing Services and offers a limited amount of student housing. **Activities:** Campus ministries, choral groups, dance, drama, literary magazine, student government, student newspaper, Latin American Society, Haitian Alliance, Caribbean student association, Christian club, Arab-American Society, French club, College Republicans, History and Political Science Society, Italian Historical Society, Model United Nations.

Athletics. NCAA. **Intercollegiate:** Basketball, cross-country, diving, soccer M, swimming, tennis, track and field, volleyball W, water polo. **Intramural:** Basketball, football (tackle) M, soccer M, volleyball. **Team name:** Terriers.

Student services. Adult student services, chaplain/spiritual director, career counseling, services for economically disadvantaged, student employment services, financial aid counseling, health services, personal counseling, placement for graduates, veterans' counselor. **Physically disabled:** Services for visually, speech, hearing impaired.

Contact. E-mail: admissions@stfranciscollege.edu
Phone: (718) 489-3473 Fax: (718) 802-0453
Bro. George Larkin, Dean of Admissions, St. Francis College, 180 Remsen Street, Brooklyn Heights, NY 11201-9902

St. John Fisher College

Rochester, New York — **CB member**
www.sjfc.edu — **CB code: 2798**

- Private 4-year liberal arts college affiliated with Roman Catholic Church
- Residential campus in large town
- 2,850 degree-seeking undergraduates: 7% part-time, 59% women, 5% African American, 2% Asian American, 3% Hispanic American
- 921 degree-seeking graduate students
- 62% of applicants admitted
- SAT or ACT (ACT writing optional), application essay required
- 73% graduate within 6 years; 35% enter graduate study

General. Founded in 1948. Regionally accredited. **Degrees:** 695 bachelor's awarded; master's, doctoral, first professional offered. **ROTC:** Army, Naval, Air Force. **Location:** 6 miles from downtown. **Calendar:** Semester, extensive summer session. **Full-time faculty:** 201 total; 82% have terminal degrees, 14% minority, 49% women. **Part-time faculty:** 167 total; 7% minority, 62% women. **Class size:** 39% < 20, 58% 20-39, 3% 40-49, less than 1% 50-99. **Special facilities:** 2 electron microscopes, language laboratory, cyber cafe.

Freshman class profile. 3,231 applied, 2,017 admitted, 569 enrolled.

Mid 50% test scores			
SAT critical reading:	480-570	GPA 2.0-2.99:	14%
SAT math:	510-600	Rank in top quarter:	59%
SAT writing:	470-560	Rank in top tenth:	22%
ACT composite:	22-26	End year in good standing:	90%
GPA 3.75 or higher:	25%	Return as sophomores:	84%
GPA 3.50-3.74:	28%	Out-of-state:	2%
GPA 3.0-3.49:	33%	Live on campus:	87%

Basis for selection. GED not accepted. Academic factors considered include high school GPA, strength of curriculum, class rank, and standardized test results. Extracurricular involvements, letters of recommendation, and personal interview also considered. Interview recommended for all. **Homeschooled:** Transcript of courses and grades, letter of recommendation (nonparent) required.

High school preparation. College-preparatory program required. 16 units required. Required and recommended units include English 4, mathematics 4, social studies 4, science 4 and foreign language 3. 4 math required for programs needing college calculus.

2008-2009 Annual costs. Tuition/fees: $23,390. Room/board: $10,040. Books/supplies: $900. Personal expenses: $600.

2007-2008 Financial aid. **Need-based:** 523 full-time freshmen applied for aid; 445 were judged to have need; 445 of these received aid. Average need met was 86%. Average scholarship/grant was $13,456; average loan $5,278. 62% of total undergraduate aid awarded as scholarships/grants, 38% as loans/jobs. **Non-need-based:** Awarded to 1,782 full-time undergraduates, including 343 freshmen. Scholarships awarded for academics, leadership.

Application procedures. **Admission:** Priority date 12/1; no deadline. $30 fee, may be waived for applicants with need. Admission notification on a rolling basis beginning on or about 12/1. Must reply by May 1 or within 3 week(s) if notified thereafter. **Financial aid:** Priority date 2/15; no closing date. FAFSA required. Applicants notified on a rolling basis starting 3/22; must reply by 5/1 or within 3 week(s) of notification.

Academics. All entering freshmen participate in one of the integrative learning communities as part of first-year experience. Experiential learning opportunities integrated into undergraduate programs. **Special study options:** Accelerated study, cross-registration, distance learning, double major, exchange student, honors, independent study, internships, liberal arts/career combination, student-designed major, study abroad, teacher certification program, Washington semester, weekend college. 3-4 optometry program with Pennsylvania College of Optometry, 2-2 environmental science and forestry program with SUNY, 3-2 pre-engineering program with affiliated engineering schools, 2-2 pre-engineering program with University of Detroit and Manhattan College, 4-2 pre-engineering program with Columbia University. **Credit/placement by examination:** AP, CLEP, IB, institutional tests. 66 credit hours maximum toward bachelor's degree. **Support services:** Reduced course load, remedial instruction, study skills assistance, tutoring, writing center.

Majors. **Area/ethnic studies:** American. **Biology:** General. **Business:** Accounting, business admin, finance. **Communications:** General. **Computer sciences:** General, computer science. **Education:** General, biology, chemistry, elementary, English, French, history, mathematics, physics, secondary, social studies, Spanish, special. **Foreign languages:** French, Spanish. **Health:** Nursing (RN). **History:** General. **Liberal arts:** Arts/sciences. **Math:** General, statistics. **Parks/recreation:** Sports admin. **Philosophy/religion:** Philosophy, religion. **Physical sciences:** Chemistry, physics. **Psychology:** General. **Social sciences:** Anthropology, economics, international relations, political science, sociology.

Most popular majors. Business/marketing 23%, communications/journalism 9%, education 19%, health sciences 9%, psychology 8%, social sciences 10%.

Computing on campus. 525 workstations in library, computer center. Dormitories wired for high-speed internet access and linked to campus network. Commuter students can connect to campus network. Online course registration, online library, helpline, student web hosting, wireless network available.

Student life. **Freshman orientation:** Mandatory. Preregistration for classes offered. 3-day program held weekend prior to start of classes. Day-long course registration program held in May, including full day of activities for parents. **Policies:** All housing smoke-free. **Housing:** Guaranteed on-campus for freshmen. Coed dorms, single-sex dorms, special housing for disabled available. $300 nonrefundable deposit, deadline 5/1. All residence halls accessible to students with disabilities. **Activities:** Campus ministries, choral groups, dance, drama, literary magazine, musical theater, student government, student newspaper, TV station, Circle K, Latino student union, Black student union, Asian student union, Fisher Players, gospel choir, resident student association, commuter council, student activities board, Fisher Pride.

Athletics. NCAA. **Intercollegiate:** Baseball M, basketball, football (tackle) M, golf, lacrosse, soccer, softball W, tennis, volleyball W. **Intramural:** Basketball, football (non-tackle) M, soccer, volleyball. **Team name:** Cardinals.

Student services. Adult student services, chaplain/spiritual director, career counseling, services for economically disadvantaged, student employment services, financial aid counseling, health services, on-campus daycare, personal counseling, placement for graduates. **Physically disabled:** Services for visually, hearing impaired.

Contact. E-mail: admissions@sjfc.edu
Phone: (585) 385-8064 Toll-free number: (800) 444-4640
Fax: (585) 385-8386
Stacy Ledermann, Director of Freshman Admissions, St. John Fisher College, 3690 East Avenue, Rochester, NY 14618-3597

St. John's University

Queens, New York — **CB member**
www.stjohns.edu — **CB code: 2799**

- Private 4-year university affiliated with Roman Catholic Church
- Commuter campus in very large city
- 12,326 degree-seeking undergraduates: 3% part-time, 54% women, 16% African American, 17% Asian American, 15% Hispanic American, 4% international
- 4,967 degree-seeking graduate students
- 46% of applicants admitted
- SAT or ACT (ACT writing optional) required
- 61% graduate within 6 years

General. Founded in 1870. Regionally accredited. Branch campuses in Staten Island, Manhattan, and Oakdale; graduate center in Rome, Italy. Study abroad opportunities in Paris, Dublin, Ireland, and Salamanca, Spain. Summer study abroad programs in Korea, Vietnam, China, Dubai, Bermuda, London, Argentina, Spain, the South of France. Winter study abroad programs: Galapagos Islands, Puerto Rico, Italy. **Degrees:** 2,117 bachelor's, 46 associate awarded; master's, doctoral, first professional offered. **ROTC:** Army. **Location:** 10 miles from midtown Manhattan. **Calendar:** Semester, extensive summer session. **Full-time faculty:** 674 total; 86% have terminal degrees, 20% minority, 41% women. **Part-time faculty:** 818 total; 36% have terminal degrees, 18% minority, 40% women. **Class size:** 38% < 20, 50% 20-39, 6% 40-49, 5% 50-99, less than 1% >100. **Special facilities:** Speech and hearing clinic, instructional media center, health education resource center, writing institute, institute of Asian studies.

Freshman class profile. 40,970 applied, 18,670 admitted, 3,268 enrolled.

Mid 50% test scores		**Rank in top quarter:**	42%
SAT critical reading:	480-580	**Rank in top tenth:**	18%
SAT math:	490-610	**Return as sophomores:**	76%
GPA 3.75 or higher:	19%	**Out-of-state:**	27%
GPA 3.50-3.74:	14%	**Live on campus:**	53%
GPA 3.0-3.49:	35%	**International:**	4%
GPA 2.0-2.99:	30%		

Basis for selection. School achievement record, standardized test scores, counselor/teacher recommendations, extracurricular activities, personal essay used. Interview, personal statement, essay recommended for all; portfolio required for creative photography, fine art, graphic design, illustration programs. **Homeschooled:** Statement describing homeschool structure and mission, state high school equivalency certificate required.

High school preparation. College-preparatory program recommended. 4 units required; 12 recommended. Required and recommended units include English 4, mathematics 3, social studies 2, history 2, science 2 (laboratory 2) and foreign language 2. Additional math/science classes highly recommended or required for certain majors.

2008-2009 Annual costs. Tuition/fees: $28,790. Tuition may vary by program and class year. Four-year fixed rate tuition plan available for incoming freshmen. Room/board: $12,570. Books/supplies: $1,000. Personal expenses: $2,700.

2007-2008 Financial aid. **Need-based:** 2,782 full-time freshmen applied for aid; 2,514 were judged to have need; 2,497 of these received aid. Average need met was 72%. Average scholarship/grant was $11,390; average loan $4,290. 61% of total undergraduate aid awarded as scholarships/grants, 39% as loans/jobs. **Non-need-based:** Awarded to 8,599 full-time undergraduates, including 2,436 freshmen. Scholarships awarded for academics, alumni affiliation, art, athletics, leadership, music/drama, religious affiliation, ROTC.

Application procedures. **Admission:** No deadline. $50 fee, may be waived for applicants with need, free for online applicants. Admission notification on a rolling basis beginning on or about 12/1. Must reply by May 1 or within 2 week(s) if notified thereafter. Application closing date for pharmacy students February 1. **Financial aid:** Priority date 2/1; no closing date. FAFSA required. Applicants notified on a rolling basis starting 3/15; must reply within 2 week(s) of notification.

Academics. **Special study options:** Accelerated study, combined bachelor's/graduate degree, cross-registration, distance learning, double major, dual enrollment of high school students, ESL, honors, independent study, internships, liberal arts/career combination, study abroad, teacher certification program, weekend college. **Credit/placement by examination:** AP, CLEP, IB, SAT, ACT, institutional tests. Students must complete at least 50 percent of major courses and at least 30 credits on campus. **Support services:** Learning center, pre-admission summer program, reduced course load, study skills assistance, tutoring, writing center.

Majors. **Area/ethnic studies:** Asian. **Biology:** General, toxicology. **Business:** Accounting, actuarial science, business admin, finance, hospitality admin, insurance, management information systems, marketing. **Communications:** General, advertising, journalism, public relations. **Communications technology:** Photo/film/video. **Computer sciences:** General, security. **Conservation:** Environmental studies. **Education:** Biology, elementary, English, mathematics, physics, secondary, social studies, Spanish, special. **Engineering technology:** Telecommunications. **Foreign languages:** French, Italian, Spanish. **Health:** Audiology/speech pathology, clinical lab science, health care admin, pathology assistant, physician assistant, radiologic technology/medical imaging. **History:** General. **Legal studies:** General. **Liberal arts:** Arts/sciences. **Math:** General. **Parks/recreation:** Sports admin. **Personal/culinary services:** Mortuary science. **Philosophy/religion:** Philosophy. **Physical sciences:** General, chemistry, physics. **Protective services:** Law enforcement admin, security management. **Psychology:** General. **Public administration:** General, human services. **Social sciences:** General, anthropology, economics, political science, sociology. **Theology:** Theology. **Visual/performing arts:** Graphic design, illustration, photography, studio arts.

Most popular majors. Biology 6%, business/marketing 26%, communications/journalism 11%, education 6%, health sciences 7%, legal studies 6%, parks/recreation 6%, psychology 6%, security/protective services 7%.

Computing on campus. PC or laptop required. 1,252 workstations in dormitories, library, computer center, student center. Dormitories wired for high-speed internet access and linked to campus network. Commuter students can connect to campus network. Online course registration, online library, helpline, repair service, student web hosting, wireless network available.

Student life. Freshman orientation: Mandatory, $250 fee. 3-day orientation program includes trip to Manhattan. **Housing:** Coed dorms, apartments available. $500 nonrefundable deposit, deadline 5/1. Limited off-campus apartments available. **Activities:** Bands, campus ministries, choral groups, drama, literary magazine, music ensembles, musical theater, radio station, student government, student newspaper, TV station, over 180 organizations on all campuses.

Athletics. NCAA. **Intercollegiate:** Baseball M, basketball, cross-country W, fencing, golf, lacrosse M, soccer, softball W, tennis, track and field W, volleyball W. **Intramural:** Badminton, basketball, cheerleading, football (non-tackle), soccer, softball, table tennis, tennis, volleyball, weight lifting. **Team name:** Red Storm.

Student services. Adult student services, alcohol/substance abuse counseling, chaplain/spiritual director, career counseling, student employment services, financial aid counseling, health services, minority student services, personal counseling, placement for graduates, veterans' counselor. **Physically disabled:** Services for visually, speech, hearing impaired.

Contact. E-mail: admhelp@stjohns.edu
Phone: (718) 990-2000 Toll-free number: (888) 978-5646
Fax: (718) 990-2096
Karen Vahey, Director of Admission, St. John's University, 8000 Utopia Parkway, Queens, NY 11439

St. Joseph's College

Brooklyn, New York — **CB member**
www.sjcny.edu — **CB code: 2802**

- Private 4-year liberal arts and teachers college
- Commuter campus in very large city
- 1,037 degree-seeking undergraduates: 32% part-time, 76% women, 36% African American, 7% Asian American, 14% Hispanic American
- 219 degree-seeking graduate students
- 74% of applicants admitted
- SAT or ACT with writing required
- 73% graduate within 6 years

General. Founded in 1916. Regionally accredited. **Degrees:** 241 bachelor's awarded; master's offered. **Location:** 8 miles from Manhattan. **Calendar:** Semester, limited summer session. **Full-time faculty:** 50 total; 66% have terminal degrees, 22% minority, 60% women. **Part-time faculty:** 79 total; 30% minority, 48% women. **Class size:** 79% < 20, 20% 20-39, less than 1% 40-49. **Special facilities:** On-campus laboratory preschool for children 3-6 years old, model school for prospective teachers.

Freshman class profile. 849 applied, 626 admitted, 131 enrolled.

Mid 50% test scores			
SAT critical reading:	440-540	GPA 3.50-3.74:	10%
SAT math:	430-550	GPA 3.0-3.49:	34%
GPA 3.75 or higher:	11%	GPA 2.0-2.99:	42%
		Return as sophomores:	81%

Basis for selection. High school achievement record, SAT/ACT scores, class rank, activities, recommendations important. Personal statements encouraged. Essay, interview recommended.

High school preparation. 18 units required. Required and recommended units include English 4, mathematics 3, social studies 4, science 2, foreign language 2-3 and academic electives 3. 3 units science recommended for science majors. No specific course requirements for general studies applicants.

2008-2009 Annual costs. Tuition/fees: $15,963. Books/supplies: $1,000. Personal expenses: $600.

2007-2008 Financial aid. Need-based: 59% of total undergraduate aid awarded as scholarships/grants, 41% as loans/jobs. **Non-need-based:** Scholarships awarded for academics, alumni affiliation, leadership.

Application procedures. Admission: No deadline. $25 fee, may be waived for applicants with need. Admission notification on a rolling basis. **Financial aid:** Priority date 2/25; no closing date. FAFSA, institutional form required. Applicants notified on a rolling basis starting 4/1; must reply by 5/1 or within 2 week(s) of notification.

Academics. Special study options: Accelerated study, honors, independent study, internships, teacher certification program, weekend college. Accelerated biomedical program with New York College of Podiatric Medicine. **Credit/placement by examination:** AP, CLEP, institutional tests. 30 credit hours maximum toward bachelor's degree. **Support services:** Reduced course load, tutoring, writing center.

Majors. Biology: General. **Business:** General, accounting, business admin, human resources. **Education:** General, early childhood, elementary, mathematics, middle, science, secondary, social studies, special. **Foreign languages:** General. **Health:** Health care admin, prenursing. **History:** General. **Liberal arts:** Arts/sciences. **Math:** General. **Physical sciences:** Chemistry. **Psychology:** General. **Social sciences:** General, sociology.

Most popular majors. Business/marketing 22%, education 16%, health sciences 40%.

Computing on campus. 90 workstations in library, computer center. Dormitories wired for high-speed internet access. Commuter students can connect to campus network. Online course registration, online library available.

Student life. Freshman orientation: Mandatory. Preregistration for classes offered. **Activities:** Campus ministries, choral groups, dance, drama, literary magazine, musical theater, student government, student newspaper, Gaelic society, Hispanic awareness club, heritage gallery, Asian awareness, Japanese animation, political affairs, student ambassador club.

Athletics. USCAA. **Intercollegiate:** Basketball, cross-country, softball W, swimming W, tennis M, volleyball. **Intramural:** Basketball, table tennis, volleyball. **Team name:** Bears.

Student services. Adult student services, chaplain/spiritual director, career counseling, student employment services, financial aid counseling, personal counseling, placement for graduates.

Contact. E-mail: asinfob@sjcny.edu
Phone: (718) 636-6868 Fax: (718) 636-8303
Theresa LaRocca-Meyer, Director of Admissions, St. Joseph's College, 245 Clinton Avenue, Brooklyn, NY 11205-3688

St. Joseph's College: Suffolk Campus

Patchogue, New York
www.sjcny.edu — **CB code: 2841**

- Private 4-year branch campus and liberal arts college
- Commuter campus in large town
- 3,727 degree-seeking undergraduates: 22% part-time, 72% women
- 433 graduate students
- 78% of applicants admitted
- SAT or ACT (ACT writing recommended) required
- 68% graduate within 6 years

General. Founded in 1916. Regionally accredited. **Degrees:** 895 bachelor's awarded; master's offered. **ROTC:** Army, Air Force. **Location:** 60 miles from New York City. **Calendar:** 4-1-4, extensive summer session. **Full-time faculty:** 113 total; 66% have terminal degrees, 8% minority, 58% women. **Part-time faculty:** 272 total; 6% minority, 48% women. **Class size:** 55% < 20, 45% 20-39, less than 1% 40-49, less than 1% 50-99. **Special facilities:** Playhouse.

Freshman class profile. 1,391 applied, 1,080 admitted, 493 enrolled.

Mid 50% test scores		GPA 2.0-2.99:	18%
SAT critical reading:	490-550	Rank in top quarter:	55%
SAT math:	490-580	Rank in top tenth:	19%
SAT writing:	450-550	Return as sophomores:	83%
GPA 3.75 or higher:	27%	Fraternities:	1%
GPA 3.50-3.74:	26%	Sororities:	2%
GPA 3.0-3.49:	29%		

Basis for selection. Grades in high school academic classes, GPA and rank in class most important. Performance on standardized tests important. Strongly factored in are letters of recommendation, personal statement and school/community activities. SAT Subject Tests recommended. Interview recommended. Essays required of scholarship candidates, strongly recommended for all others. **Homeschooled:** Transcript of courses and grades required. SAT or ACT required. Interview strongly recommended.

High school preparation. 18 units required. Required and recommended units include English 4, mathematics 3, social studies 4, science 3 (laboratory 3), foreign language 2 and academic electives 2. Social science unit must be American history.

2008-2009 Annual costs. Tuition/fees: $15,963. Books/supplies: $1,000. Personal expenses: $600.

2007-2008 Financial aid. **Need-based:** 53% of total undergraduate aid awarded as scholarships/grants, 47% as loans/jobs. **Non-need-based:** Scholarships awarded for academics.

Application procedures. **Admission:** Priority date 8/15; no deadline. $25 fee, may be waived for applicants with need. Application must be submitted on paper. Admission notification on a rolling basis beginning on or about 11/1. Must reply by May 1 or within 2 week(s) if notified thereafter. **Financial aid:** Priority date 2/25; no closing date. FAFSA, institutional form required. Applicants notified on a rolling basis starting 3/15; must reply within 2 week(s) of notification.

Academics. **Special study options:** Combined bachelor's/graduate degree, distance learning, double major, honors, independent study, internships, liberal arts/career combination, study abroad, teacher certification program, weekend college. 5-year program bachelor's/master's in computer science from Polytechnic University; 5-year BNS/MS in accounting. **Credit/placement by examination:** AP, CLEP, IB, institutional tests. 30 credit hours maximum toward bachelor's degree. **Support services:** Learning center, reduced course load, study skills assistance, tutoring, writing center.

Majors. **Biology:** General. **Business:** Accounting, business admin. **Communications:** General. **Computer sciences:** Computer science, information technology. **Education:** General, biology, early childhood, elementary, English, history, kindergarten/preschool, mathematics, middle, science, secondary, social studies, Spanish, special. **Foreign languages:** Spanish. **Health:** Facilities admin, predental, premedicine, preveterinary, recreational therapy. **History:** General. **Liberal arts:** Arts/sciences. **Math:** General. **Parks/recreation:** General. **Psychology:** General. **Social sciences:** General, criminology, economics, political science, sociology.

Most popular majors. Business/marketing 15%, education 47%, health sciences 8%, psychology 6%.

Computing on campus. 223 workstations in library, computer center. Commuter students can connect to campus network. Online course registration, online library, helpline, wireless network available.

Student life. **Freshman orientation:** Mandatory, $50 fee. Preregistration for classes offered. 1-day orientation in August just prior to start of classes. **Policies:** 2.7 average required to run for student government. **Activities:** Bands, choral groups, dance, drama, literary magazine, music ensembles, musical theater, student government, student newspaper, Amnesty International, student volunteer services, Circle K, Students Taking an Active Role in Society, Spanish club, Diversity Union, Habitat for Humanity, social sciences club, Lion's Club.

Athletics. NCAA. **Intercollegiate:** Baseball M, basketball, cross-country, equestrian, golf M, soccer, softball W, swimming, tennis, track and field, volleyball W. **Intramural:** Football (non-tackle). **Team name:** Golden Eagles.

Student services. Adult student services, alcohol/substance abuse counseling, chaplain/spiritual director, career counseling, student employment services, financial aid counseling, minority student services, personal counseling, veterans' counselor. **Physically disabled:** Services for visually, hearing impaired.

Contact. E-mail: suffolkas@sjcny.edu
Phone: (631) 447-3219 Fax: (631) 447-3601
Gigi Lamens, Director of Admissions and Enrollment Planning, St. Joseph's College: Suffolk Campus, 155 West Roe Boulevard, Patchogue, NY 11772-2603

St. Lawrence University

Canton, New York — **CB member**
www.stlawu.edu — **CB code: 2805**

- Private 4-year liberal arts college
- Residential campus in small town
- 2,187 degree-seeking undergraduates: 55% women, 3% African American, 2% Asian American, 3% Hispanic American, 1% Native American, 5% international
- 96 degree-seeking graduate students
- 34% of applicants admitted
- Application essay required
- 76% graduate within 6 years; 22% enter graduate study

General. Founded in 1856. Regionally accredited. **Degrees:** 499 bachelor's awarded; master's offered. **ROTC:** Army, Air Force. **Location:** 70 miles from Ottawa, Canada. **Calendar:** Semester, limited summer session. **Full-time faculty:** 173 total; 97% have terminal degrees, 17% minority, 48% women. **Part-time faculty:** 21 total; 38% have terminal degrees, 19% minority, 62% women. **Class size:** 70% < 20, 29% 20-39, less than 1% 40-49, less than 1% 50-99, less than 1% >100. **Special facilities:** 1,000 contiguous acres include woods and river habitat for conducting primary research; science facility; center for arts technology; golf course; crew boathouse; Adirondack Semester yurt village.

Freshman class profile. 5,419 applied, 1,829 admitted, 616 enrolled.

Mid 50% test scores			
SAT critical reading:	570-640	GPA 2.0-2.99:	4%
SAT math:	570-640	Rank in top quarter:	74%
SAT writing:	560-650	Rank in top tenth:	44%
ACT composite:	25-29	End year in good standing:	88%
GPA 3.75 or higher:	36%	Return as sophomores:	88%
GPA 3.50-3.74:	23%	Out-of-state:	55%
GPA 3.0-3.49:	37%	Live on campus:	100%
		International:	6%

Basis for selection. Academic record most important; test scores, extracurricular activities, seriousness of purpose and intellectual promise important. Students for whom English is not the native language must submit official TOEFL results and are encouraged to submit SAT or ACT. Interview recommended.

High school preparation. College-preparatory program required. 20 units recommended. Recommended units include English 4, mathematics 4, social studies 2, history 2, science 4 and foreign language 4.

2008-2009 Annual costs. Tuition/fees: $37,915. Room/board: $9,645. Books/supplies: $750.

2008-2009 Financial aid. **Need-based:** 447 full-time freshmen applied for aid; 378 were judged to have need; 377 of these received aid. Average need met was 95%. Average scholarship/grant was $26,792; average loan $3,360. 86% of total undergraduate aid awarded as scholarships/grants, 14% as loans/jobs. **Non-need-based:** Awarded to 631 full-time undergraduates, including 226 freshmen. Scholarships awarded for academics, alumni affiliation, athletics, minority status, ROTC, state residency.

Application procedures. **Admission:** Closing date 2/1 (postmark date). $60 fee, may be waived for applicants with need. Admission notification 3/31. Must reply by May 1 or within 2 week(s) if notified thereafter. **Financial aid:** Closing date 2/1. FAFSA required. Applicants notified by 3/31; must reply by 5/1 or within 2 week(s) of notification.

Academics. Quantitative Resource Center for math assistance. **Special study options:** Combined bachelor's/graduate degree, cross-registration, double major, exchange student, independent study, internships, student-designed major, study abroad, teacher certification program, Washington semester. Community-based learning; 3-2 program in engineering with Clarkson University, Columbia University, Rensselaer Polytechnic Institute, University of Rochester, University of Southern California, Washington University of St. Louis; early assurance programs in medicine with SUNY Health Science Center at Syracuse and in dentistry with SUNY at Buffalo; combined bachelor's/graduate degree program in business administration with Clarkson University, Union College and Rochester Institute of Technology; 14 study abroad programs in Australia, Europe, Kenya, Japan, Costa Rica, India, Canada, Trinidad and Tobago, China. **Credit/placement by examination:** AP, CLEP, IB, institutional tests. 60 credit hours maximum toward bachelor's degree. **Support services:** Pre-admission summer program, reduced course load, study skills assistance, tutoring, writing center.

Majors. **Area/ethnic studies:** African, Asian, Canadian. **Biology:** General, biochemistry, biophysics, conservation, neurobiology/physiology. **Computer sciences:** Computer science. **Conservation:** Environmental studies. **Foreign languages:** General, French, German, Spanish. **History:** General. **Interdisciplinary:** Global studies, neuroscience. **Math:** General. **Philosophy/religion:** Philosophy, religion. **Physical sciences:** Chemistry, geology, geophysics, physics. **Psychology:** General. **Social sciences:** Anthropology, economics, political science, sociology. **Visual/performing arts:** Dramatic, studio arts.

Most popular majors. Biology 8%, English 7%, foreign language 6%, history 8%, psychology 9%, social sciences 33%, visual/performing arts 9%.

Computing on campus. 608 workstations in dormitories, library, computer center, student center. Dormitories wired for high-speed internet access and linked to campus network. Commuter students can connect to campus network. Online course registration, helpline, repair service, student web hosting, wireless network available.

Student life. **Freshman orientation:** Mandatory. Preregistration for classes offered. Orientation is three days preceding the start of fall classes. Programs are focused on academic introductions to the liberal arts, to the living-learning community concept, and St. Lawrence traditions. **Policies:** First-Year Program requires freshmen to reside in college with academic/administrative staff. **Housing:** Guaranteed on-campus for all undergraduates.

Coed dorms, apartments, fraternity/sorority housing, wellness housing available. Townhouse apartments for senior leaders, some suites available. Students can petition to have quiet or single-sex halls within dormitory. **Activities:** Concert band, campus ministries, choral groups, dance, drama, film society, international student organizations, literary magazine, music ensembles, radio station, student government, student newspaper, TV station, Jewish Student organization, Black Student Union, Muslim Students Organization, environmental awareness organization, Habitat for Humanity, outing club, academic honorary societies, Circle K, Amnesty International.

Athletics. NCAA. **Intercollegiate:** Baseball M, basketball, cross-country, diving, equestrian, field hockey W, football (tackle) M, golf, ice hockey, lacrosse, rowing (crew), skiing, soccer, softball W, squash, swimming, tennis, track and field, volleyball W. **Intramural:** Basketball, football (non-tackle) M, football (tackle) M, ice hockey, soccer, softball W, tennis, triathlon, volleyball. **Team name:** Saints.

Student services. Alcohol/substance abuse counseling, chaplain/spiritual director, career counseling, services for economically disadvantaged, student employment services, financial aid counseling, health services, minority student services, personal counseling, placement for graduates. **Physically disabled:** Services for visually, hearing impaired.

Contact. E-mail: admissions@stlawu.edu
Phone: (315) 229-5261 Toll-free number: (800) 285-1856
Fax: (315) 229-5818
Teresa Cowdrey, Vice President and Dean of Admissions and Financial Aid, St. Lawrence University, Payson Hall, Canton, NY 13617

St. Thomas Aquinas College

Sparkill, New York — **CB member**
www.stac.edu — **CB code: 2807**

- Private 4-year liberal arts college
- Commuter campus in large town
- 1,429 degree-seeking undergraduates: 6% part-time, 57% women, 6% African American, 2% Asian American, 15% Hispanic American, 1% international
- 216 degree-seeking graduate students
- 79% of applicants admitted
- SAT or ACT (ACT writing optional) required
- 52% graduate within 6 years

General. Founded in 1952. Regionally accredited. **Degrees:** 294 bachelor's, 8 associate awarded; master's offered. **ROTC:** Air Force. **Location:** 15 miles from New York City. **Calendar:** Semester, extensive summer session. **Full-time faculty:** 63 total; 86% have terminal degrees, 13% minority, 46% women. **Part-time faculty:** 94 total; 23% have terminal degrees, 12% minority, 44% women. **Class size:** 46% < 20, 54% 20-39. **Special facilities:** Arts, sciences and technology center, digital imaging laboratory.

Freshman class profile. 1,443 applied, 1,147 admitted, 352 enrolled.

Mid 50% test scores		**GPA 3.0-3.49:**	12%
SAT critical reading:	420-510	**GPA 2.0-2.99:**	62%
SAT math:	400-530	**Rank in top quarter:**	35%
SAT writing:	410-510	**Rank in top tenth:**	5%
ACT composite:	16-23	**Return as sophomores:**	70%
GPA 3.75 or higher:	6%	**Out-of-state:**	23%
GPA 3.50-3.74:	10%	**Live on campus:**	66%

Basis for selection. School achievement record, test scores, recommendation, and interview considered. Applicants should be in top half of class and have GPA above 3.0. Essay, interview recommended for all; portfolio recommended for art program. **Homeschooled:** Statement describing homeschool structure and mission, transcript of courses and grades, state high school equivalency certificate, letter of recommendation (nonparent) required.

High school preparation. 20 units required. Required units include English 4, mathematics 3, social studies 4, science 3 (laboratory 2) and foreign language 3.

2009-2010 Annual costs. Tuition/fees: $21,170. Room/board: $9,980. Books/supplies: $750. Personal expenses: $1,000.

2007-2008 Financial aid. **Need-based:** 297 full-time freshmen applied for aid; 217 were judged to have need; 214 of these received aid. Average need met was 55%. Average scholarship/grant was $9,524; average loan $3,535. 55% of total undergraduate aid awarded as scholarships/grants, 45% as loans/jobs. **Non-need-based:** Awarded to 300 full-time undergraduates, including 84 freshmen. Scholarships awarded for academics, athletics.

Application procedures. **Admission:** No deadline. $30 fee. Admission notification on a rolling basis beginning on or about 10/1. **Financial aid:** Priority date 2/15; no closing date. FAFSA required. Applicants notified on a rolling basis starting 3/1; must reply by 5/1 or within 4 week(s) of notification.

Academics. **Special study options:** Accelerated study, combined bachelor's/graduate degree, cooperative education, cross-registration, double major, dual enrollment of high school students, ESL, exchange student, honors, independent study, internships, liberal arts/career combination, study abroad, teacher certification program, Washington semester. **Credit/placement by examination:** AP, CLEP, IB, SAT, ACT, institutional tests. 15 credit hours maximum toward associate degree, 30 toward bachelor's. **Support services:** Learning center, pre-admission summer program, reduced course load, remedial instruction, study skills assistance, tutoring, writing center.

Majors. **Biology:** General. **Business:** General, accounting, business admin, finance, international marketing, marketing. **Communications:** General, broadcast journalism, journalism. **Computer sciences:** General. **Education:** General, art, biology, chemistry, elementary, English, foreign languages, history, mathematics, multi-level teacher, physics, science, secondary, social studies, Spanish, special. **Engineering:** General. **Foreign languages:** General, French, Spanish. **Health:** Art therapy, predental, premedicine, prenursing, prepharmacy, preveterinary. **History:** General. **Interdisciplinary:** Biological/physical sciences, math/computer science. **Legal studies:** Prelaw. **Liberal arts:** Arts/sciences. **Math:** General, applied. **Parks/recreation:** Facilities management. **Philosophy/religion:** Philosophy, religion. **Physical sciences:** Chemistry, physics. **Protective services:** Forensics, law enforcement admin. **Psychology:** General. **Social sciences:** General. **Visual/performing arts:** Art, commercial/advertising art, graphic design, studio arts.

Most popular majors. Business/marketing 24%, communications/journalism 8%, education 13%, psychology 12%, security/protective services 11%, social sciences 9%.

Computing on campus. 200 workstations in dormitories, library, computer center, student center. Dormitories wired for high-speed internet access and linked to campus network. Commuter students can connect to campus network. Online library, helpline, wireless network available.

Student life. **Freshman orientation:** Mandatory, $75 fee. Preregistration for classes offered. **Housing:** Guaranteed on-campus for freshmen. Single-sex dorms, apartments, wellness housing available. $250 nonrefundable deposit, deadline 5/1. **Activities:** Choral groups, dance, drama, literary magazine, music ensembles, musical theater, opera, radio station, student government, student newspaper, TV station, political union, business association, community service organization.

Athletics. NAIA, NCAA. **Intercollegiate:** Baseball M, basketball, cross-country, golf, lacrosse W, soccer, softball W, tennis, track and field. **Intramural:** Basketball, skiing, softball, tennis. **Team name:** Spartans.

Student services. Adult student services, alcohol/substance abuse counseling, chaplain/spiritual director, career counseling, student employment services, financial aid counseling, health services, personal counseling, placement for graduates, veterans' counselor, women's services. **Physically disabled:** Services for visually, speech, hearing impaired. **Learning disabled:** Comprehensive services available.

Contact. E-mail: admissions@stac.edu
Phone: (845) 398-4100 Toll-free number: (800) 999-7822
Fax: (845) 398-4114
Danielle Mac Kay, Director of Admissions, St. Thomas Aquinas College, 125 Route 340, Sparkill, NY 10976

Sarah Lawrence College

Bronxville, New York — **CB member**
www.slc.edu — **CB code: 2810**

- Private 4-year liberal arts college
- Residential campus in small city
- 1,309 degree-seeking undergraduates: 3% part-time, 74% women, 4% African American, 6% Asian American, 5% Hispanic American, 3% international
- 326 degree-seeking graduate students
- 46% of applicants admitted
- Application essay required
- 73% graduate within 6 years

General. Founded in 1926. Regionally accredited. **Degrees:** 303 bachelor's awarded; master's offered. **Location:** 15 miles from New York City. **Calendar:** Semester, limited summer session. **Full-time faculty:** 113 total; 20% minority, 50% women. **Part-time faculty:** 221 total; 17% minority,

56% women. **Class size:** 93% < 20, 4% 20-39, 1% 40-49, 2% 50-99. **Special facilities:** Visual arts center, student-run theater, early childhood center, greenhouse.

Freshman class profile. 2,785 applied, 1,293 admitted, 348 enrolled.

GPA 3.75 or higher:	39%	**Rank in top tenth:**	37%
GPA 3.50-3.74:	25%	**Return as sophomores:**	80%
GPA 3.0-3.49:	30%	**Out-of-state:**	80%
GPA 2.0-2.99:	6%	**Live on campus:**	100%
Rank in top quarter:	84%	**International:**	4%

Basis for selection. Student essays (one of which is a graded, analytical writing sample) and transcript most important. Letters of recommendation and extracurricular commitments also important. Interview considered. Students interested in visual art or music encouraged to submit slides, cassette tapes, or compositions. If on-campus interview not possible, applicant may arrange interview with an alumna/us or counselor.

High school preparation. College-preparatory program required. Required and recommended units include English 4, mathematics 2-4, social studies 4, history 2-4, science 2-4 and foreign language 2-4.

2008-2009 Annual costs. Tuition/fees: $40,350. Room/board: $13,716. Books/supplies: $600. Personal expenses: $800.

2008-2009 Financial aid. All financial aid based on need. 229 full-time freshmen applied for aid; 188 were judged to have need; 188 of these received aid. Average need met was 89%. Average scholarship/grant was $25,368; average loan $2,349. 82% of total undergraduate aid awarded as scholarships/grants, 18% as loans/jobs.

Application procedures. **Admission:** Closing date 1/1 (postmark date). $60 fee, may be waived for applicants with need. Admission notification 4/1. Must reply by 5/1. **Financial aid:** Closing date 2/1. FAFSA, CSS PROFILE required. Applicants notified by 4/1; must reply by 5/1.

Academics. 90% of classes are seminars with 11-12 students. Individual biweekly conferences with professors and self-designed independent study available. Students design own course of study with advisor. Based on the Sarah Lawrence College pedagogy providing for one-on-one student-teacher conferences, part-time faculty at SLC often provide student contact hours equal to or greater than full-time faculty at other institutions. Although there are no formal majors, students may de facto create double majors. Course work required in 3 of 4 divisions: humanities, history and the social sciences, natural sciences and mathematics, creative and performing arts. **Special study options:** Combined bachelor's/graduate degree, double major, exchange student, independent study, internships, student-designed major, study abroad, teacher certification program. Academic year in Oxford, Paris, Florence, Catania (Sicily), Cuba, guest year at Reed College (Oregon and its study abroad program) or guest year at Eugene Lang College of the New School (New York City); theater year in London. **Credit/placement by examination:** AP, CLEP, IB. **Support services:** Writing center.

Majors. **Liberal arts:** Arts/sciences. **Philosophy/religion:** Judaic. **Social sciences:** Urban studies.

Computing on campus. 110 workstations in library, computer center. Dormitories wired for high-speed internet access and linked to campus network. Commuter students can connect to campus network. Online library, helpline, student web hosting available.

Student life. **Freshman orientation:** Mandatory. 9-day program held just before fall semester. **Housing:** Guaranteed on-campus for freshmen. Coed dorms, single-sex dorms available. $500 nonrefundable deposit, deadline 5/1. Freshmen required to live on campus unless living at home. **Activities:** Jazz band, campus ministries, choral groups, dance, drama, film society, international student organizations, literary magazine, music ensembles, musical theater, radio station, student government, student newspaper, symphony orchestra, Amnesty International, Harambe (students of African descent), Hillel, Queer Variety Coalition, Beyond Compliance, Asian-Pacific Islander Coalition to Advance Diversity, Unidad (students of Latino descent), Our Time Musical Theater Troupe, The Experimental Music Club, SLC ACTS UP.

Athletics. **Intercollegiate:** Basketball M, equestrian, rowing (crew), softball W, swimming W, tennis, volleyball W. **Team name:** Gryphons.

Student services. Adult student services, alcohol/substance abuse counseling, career counseling, student employment services, financial aid counseling, health services, minority student services, personal counseling, placement for graduates. **Physically disabled:** Services for visually, speech, hearing impaired.

Contact. E-mail: slcadmit@sarahlawrence.edu
Phone: (914) 395-2510 Toll-free number: (800) 888-2858
Fax: (914) 395-2515
Amy Abrams, Dean of Admission, Sarah Lawrence College, One Mead Way, Bronxville, NY 10708-5999

School of Visual Arts

New York, New York — **CB member**
www.sva.edu — **CB code: 2835**

- For-profit 4-year visual arts college
- Commuter campus in very large city
- 3,402 degree-seeking undergraduates
- 449 graduate students
- SAT or ACT (ACT writing optional), application essay required

General. Founded in 1947. Regionally accredited. Faculty composed entirely of working professionals. **Degrees:** 674 bachelor's awarded; master's offered. **Calendar:** Semester, limited summer session. **Full-time faculty:** 161 total. **Part-time faculty:** 810 total. **Class size:** 70% < 20, 28% 20-39, 2% 50-99, less than 1% >100. **Special facilities:** Visual arts museum, Milton Glaser design study center and archives, 8 student galleries including 9,000-square-foot gallery.

Freshman class profile.

Mid 50% test scores		**GPA 3.50-3.74:**	12%
SAT critical reading:	450-580	**GPA 3.0-3.49:**	35%
SAT math:	460-590	**GPA 2.0-2.99:**	44%
SAT writing:	450-580	**Out-of-state:**	56%
ACT composite:	19-24	**Live on campus:**	70%
GPA 3.75 or higher:	8%		

Basis for selection. Portfolio, academic record, interview important. Character and professional recommendations optional. Interview optional. Portfolio required for all programs. **Homeschooled:** Statement describing home-school structure and mission, transcript of courses and grades, state high school equivalency certificate, interview, letter of recommendation (nonparent) required. GED.

High school preparation. Recommended units include English 4, social studies 4, history 4 and visual/performing arts 2.

2008-2009 Annual costs. Tuition/fees: $25,500. Additional fees vary by department. Room only: $11,350. Books/supplies: $2,100. Personal expenses: $1,600.

2008-2009 Financial aid. **Non-need-based:** Scholarships awarded for art.

Application procedures. **Admission:** No deadline. $50 fee, may be waived for applicants with need. Admission notification on a rolling basis beginning on or about 1/15. Admitted applicants are encouraged to reply by May 1. **Financial aid:** Priority date 2/1; no closing date. FAFSA required. Applicants notified on a rolling basis starting 2/15; must reply within 4 week(s) of notification.

Academics. Curriculum designed to prepare students to graduate as working professionals in the arts. **Special study options:** ESL, exchange student, honors, internships, liberal arts/career combination, study abroad, teacher certification program. **Credit/placement by examination:** AP, CLEP, IB. **Support services:** Learning center, pre-admission summer program, reduced course load, remedial instruction, study skills assistance, tutoring, writing center.

Honors college/program. Additional application component.

Majors. **Visual/performing arts:** Art history/conservation, commercial/advertising art, interior design, photography, studio arts. **Other:** Film, video, animation.

Computing on campus. 728 workstations in library, computer center, student center. Dormitories wired for high-speed internet access and linked to campus network. Commuter students can connect to campus network. Online library, helpline, wireless network available.

Student life. **Freshman orientation:** Mandatory. Comprehensive 5-day program. **Housing:** Coed dorms, single-sex dorms, wellness housing available. $800 nonrefundable deposit, deadline 5/1. **Activities:** Campus ministries, film society, international student organizations, literary magazine, radio station, student government, Korean Christian, animal rights, international film club, Campus Crusade for Christ, political, anime film club, fine art club, MFA Speakers, wrestling club.

Athletics. **Intramural:** Baseball, tennis.

Student services. Alcohol/substance abuse counseling, career counseling, student employment services, financial aid counseling, health services, personal counseling, placement for graduates, veterans' counselor, women's services. **Physically disabled:** Services for hearing impaired.

Contact. E-mail: admissions@sva.edu
Phone: (212) 592-2100 Toll-free number: (800) 436-4204
Fax: (212) 592-2116
Adam Rogers, Director of Admissions, School of Visual Arts, 209 East 23rd Street, New York, NY 10010-3994

Shor Yoshuv Rabbinical College

Lawrence, New York
www.shoryoshuv.org **CB code: 7129**

- Private 4-year rabbinical college for men affiliated with Jewish faith
- Very large city

General. Accredited by AARTS. **Calendar:** Continuous.

Annual costs/financial aid. Tuition/fees (2008-2009): $8,360. Room/board: $6,000.

Contact. Phone: (516) 239-9002
Admissions Director, One Cedar Lawn Avenue, Lawrence, NY 11559

Siena College

Loudonville, New York **CB member**
www.siena.edu **CB code: 2814**

- Private 4-year liberal arts college affiliated with Roman Catholic Church
- Residential campus in large town
- 3,242 degree-seeking undergraduates: 4% part-time, 54% women, 2% African American, 3% Asian American, 4% Hispanic American
- 56% of applicants admitted
- SAT or ACT with writing, application essay required
- 80% graduate within 6 years

General. Founded in 1937. Regionally accredited. Affiliated with the Franciscan Friars. **Degrees:** 769 bachelor's awarded. **ROTC:** Army, Naval, Air Force. **Location:** 2 miles from Albany. **Calendar:** Semester, limited summer session. **Full-time faculty:** 187 total; 92% have terminal degrees, 9% minority, 37% women. **Part-time faculty:** 130 total; 46% have terminal degrees, 5% minority, 41% women. **Class size:** 32% < 20, 68% 20-39. **Special facilities:** Financial technology center featuring real-time capital market trading room, accounting lab, stock ticker, plasma data screens, 24 multimedia workstations.

Freshman class profile. 6,490 applied, 3,604 admitted, 832 enrolled.

Mid 50% test scores		**GPA 3.0-3.49:**	37%
SAT critical reading:	500-590	**GPA 2.0-2.99:**	13%
SAT math:	530-630	**Rank in top quarter:**	59%
SAT writing:	500-590	**Rank in top tenth:**	25%
ACT composite:	23-26	**Return as sophomores:**	88%
GPA 3.75 or higher:	25%	**Out-of-state:**	17%
GPA 3.50-3.74:	25%	**Live on campus:**	92%

Basis for selection. School achievement record most important, priority given to students with challenging courses. Test scores, activities, recommendations also important. Interview required for Albany Medical School program finalists; recommended for all others. **Homeschooled:** Transcript of courses and grades required.

High school preparation. College-preparatory program required. 13 units required; 19 recommended. Required and recommended units include English 4, mathematics 3-4, social studies 1, history 2-3, science 3-4 (laboratory 3-4) and foreign language 3.

2008-2009 Annual costs. Tuition/fees: $23,950. Room/board: $9,410. Books/supplies: $930. Personal expenses: $888.

2007-2008 Financial aid. **Need-based:** 690 full-time freshmen applied for aid; 564 were judged to have need; 559 of these received aid. Average need met was 78%. Average scholarship/grant was $13,180; average loan $3,452. 76% of total undergraduate aid awarded as scholarships/grants, 24% as loans/jobs. **Non-need-based:** Awarded to 1,961 full-time undergraduates, including 558 freshmen. Scholarships awarded for academics, athletics, leadership, minority status, ROTC, state residency.

Application procedures. **Admission:** Closing date 3/1 (postmark date). $50 fee, may be waived for applicants with need. Admission notification 3/15. Must reply by 5/1. **Financial aid:** Priority date 2/15, closing date 5/1. FAFSA required. Applicants notified by 4/1; must reply by 5/1.

Academics. Extensive internship program in capital district with state legislature, businesses, social agencies, libraries, and museums. **Special study options:** Accelerated study, combined bachelor's/graduate degree, cross-registration, double major, ESL, honors, independent study, internships, liberal arts/career combination, study abroad, teacher certification program, Washington semester. **Credit/placement by examination:** AP, CLEP, IB, institutional tests. 36 credit hours maximum toward bachelor's degree. 36 total credits permitted by proficiency examination, non-collegiate-sponsored instructional/experiential learning combined. **Support services:** Tutoring, writing center.

Majors. **Area/ethnic studies:** American. **Biology:** General, biochemistry, ecology. **Business:** Accounting, finance, marketing. **Computer sciences:** General. **Foreign languages:** Classics, French, Spanish. **History:** General. **Math:** General, applied, computational. **Philosophy/religion:** Philosophy, religion. **Physical sciences:** Chemistry, physics. **Psychology:** General. **Public administration:** Social work. **Social sciences:** Economics, political science, sociology. **Visual/performing arts:** General.

Most popular majors. Biology 11%, business/marketing 42%, English 7%, history 6%, psychology 11%, social sciences 9%.

Computing on campus. 456 workstations in library, computer center. Dormitories wired for high-speed internet access and linked to campus network. Commuter students can connect to campus network. Online course registration, online library, helpline, wireless network available.

Student life. **Freshman orientation:** Mandatory, $180 fee. Preregistration for classes offered. 3-day summer program. **Housing:** Guaranteed on-campus for freshmen. Coed dorms, special housing for disabled, apartments, wellness housing available. On-campus townhouses (men's and women's), quiet living area. **Activities:** Pep band, dance, drama, literary magazine, musical theater, radio station, student government, student newspaper, TV station, approximately 70 clubs and organizations.

Athletics. NCAA. **Intercollegiate:** Baseball M, basketball, cross-country, diving W, field hockey W, golf, lacrosse, soccer, softball W, swimming W, tennis, volleyball W, water polo W. **Intramural:** Basketball, football (non-tackle), golf, soccer, softball, volleyball. **Team name:** Saints.

Student services. Alcohol/substance abuse counseling, chaplain/spiritual director, career counseling, services for economically disadvantaged, student employment services, financial aid counseling, health services, minority student services, personal counseling, placement for graduates, women's services. **Physically disabled:** Services for visually, speech, hearing impaired.

Contact. E-mail: admit@siena.edu
Phone: (518) 783-2423 Toll-free number: (888) 287-4362
Fax: (518) 783-2436
Heather Renault, Director for Admissions, Siena College, 515 Loudon Road, Loudonville, NY 12211-1462

Skidmore College

Saratoga Springs, New York **CB member**
www.skidmore.edu **CB code: 2815**

- Private 4-year liberal arts college
- Residential campus in large town
- 2,678 degree-seeking undergraduates: 3% part-time, 60% women, 3% African American, 9% Asian American, 5% Hispanic American, 1% Native American, 3% international
- 60 degree-seeking graduate students
- 30% of applicants admitted
- SAT or ACT with writing, application essay required
- 81% graduate within 6 years

General. Founded in 1903. Regionally accredited. **Degrees:** 628 bachelor's awarded; master's offered. **ROTC:** Army, Air Force. **Location:** 30 miles from Albany. **Calendar:** Semester, limited summer session. **Full-time faculty:** 249 total; 80% have terminal degrees, 14% minority, 54% women. **Part-time faculty:** 117 total; 36% have terminal degrees, 13% minority, 53% women. **Class size:** 72% < 20, 27% 20-39, 1% 50-99, less than 1% >100. **Special facilities:** Fine and performing arts facilities, equestrian center, 400 acres of woodlands and trails, teaching museum.

Freshman class profile. 7,316 applied, 2,178 admitted, 652 enrolled.

Mid 50% test scores		GPA 2.0-2.99:	14%
SAT critical reading:	580-680	Rank in top quarter:	79%
SAT math:	590-670	Rank in top tenth:	37%
SAT writing:	590-690	Return as sophomores:	93%
ACT composite:	26-29	Out-of-state:	66%
GPA 3.75 or higher:	20%	Live on campus:	100%
GPA 3.50-3.74:	22%	International:	2%
GPA 3.0-3.49:	44%		

Basis for selection. Rigor of school record very important. Class rank, GPA, recommendations, and test scores also important. SAT Subject Tests recommended. 2 SAT Subject Tests recommended of all applicants. Interview recommended for all.

High school preparation. College-preparatory program required. Recommended units include English 4, mathematics 4, social studies 4, science 4 (laboratory 3) and foreign language 4.

2008-2009 Annual costs. Tuition/fees: $38,888. Room/board: $10,377. Books/supplies: $1,085. Personal expenses: $1,000.

2008-2009 Financial aid. Need-based: 350 full-time freshmen applied for aid; 284 were judged to have need; 284 of these received aid. Average need met was 85%. Average scholarship/grant was $29,699; average loan $2,574. 85% of total undergraduate aid awarded as scholarships/grants, 15% as loans/jobs. **Non-need-based:** Awarded to 209 full-time undergraduates, including 113 freshmen. Scholarships awarded for music/drama.

Application procedures. Admission: Closing date 1/15 (postmark date). $60 fee, may be waived for applicants with need. Admission notification 4/1. Must reply by 5/1. Enrollment deposit of $500 required on or before May 1. **Financial aid:** Closing date 1/15. FAFSA, CSS PROFILE required. Applicants notified by 4/1; must reply by 5/1.

Academics. Special study options: Accelerated study, combined bachelor's/graduate degree, cross-registration, distance learning, double major, dual enrollment of high school students, exchange student, external degree, honors, independent study, internships, liberal arts/career combination, student-designed major, study abroad, teacher certification program, Washington semester. 3+2 programs in engineering with Dartmouth College and Clarkson University, 4+1 MAT with Union College, 4+1 MBA with Clarkson University and the Graduate College at Union University. **Credit/placement by examination:** AP, CLEP, IB, SAT, ACT, institutional tests. Up to 60 hours may be counted toward degree. Maximum of 12 semester hours may be granted in credit through CLEP subject examinations. **Support services:** Pre-admission summer program, study skills assistance, tutoring, writing center.

Majors. Area/ethnic studies: American, Asian, French, women's. **Biology:** General. **Business:** General. **Computer sciences:** General. **Conservation:** Environmental studies. **Education:** Elementary. **Foreign languages:** Classics, French, German, Spanish. **History:** General. **Interdisciplinary:** Biopsychology, neuroscience. **Liberal arts:** Arts/sciences. **Math:** General. **Parks/recreation:** Exercise sciences. **Philosophy/religion:** Philosophy, religion. **Physical sciences:** Chemistry, geology, physics. **Psychology:** General. **Public administration:** Social work. **Social sciences:** Anthropology, economics, international relations, political science, sociology. **Visual/performing arts:** Art history/conservation, dance, dramatic, music history. **Other:** Biology/philosophy.

Most popular majors. Business/marketing 12%, English 8%, liberal arts 6%, psychology 8%, social sciences 17%, visual/performing arts 16%.

Computing on campus. Dormitories wired for high-speed internet access and linked to campus network. Commuter students can connect to campus network. Online course registration, online library, helpline, student web hosting, wireless network available.

Student life. Freshman orientation: Mandatory. Programs on and off campus. Fee for off-campus programs. **Housing:** Guaranteed on-campus for all undergraduates. Coed dorms, single-sex dorms, special housing for disabled, apartments available. $500 nonrefundable deposit, deadline 5/1. There is a gender neutral wing. Townhouse clusters available for upperclassmen. **Activities:** Bands, campus ministries, choral groups, dance, drama, international student organizations, literary magazine, music ensembles, Model UN, musical theater, opera, radio station, student government, student newspaper, symphony orchestra, TV station, 80 clubs and organizations.

Athletics. NCAA. **Intercollegiate:** Baseball M, basketball, diving, equestrian W, field hockey W, golf M, ice hockey M, lacrosse, rowing (crew), soccer, softball W, swimming, tennis, volleyball W. **Intramural:** Basketball, football (tackle) M, racquetball, soccer, softball, tennis, volleyball, water polo. **Team name:** Thoroughbreds.

Student services. Alcohol/substance abuse counseling, chaplain/spiritual director, career counseling, services for economically disadvantaged, student employment services, financial aid counseling, health services, minority student services, on-campus daycare, personal counseling, placement for graduates, veterans' counselor. **Physically disabled:** Services for visually, speech, hearing impaired.

Contact. E-mail: admissions@skidmore.edu
Phone: (518) 580-5570 Toll-free number: (800) 867-6007
Fax: (518) 580-5584
Mary Lou Bates, Dean of Admissions and Financial Aid, Skidmore College, 815 North Broadway, Saratoga Springs, NY 12866

State University of New York at Albany

Albany, New York — **CB member**
www.albany.edu — **CB code: 2532**

- Public 4-year university
- Residential campus in small city
- 12,937 degree-seeking undergraduates: 5% part-time, 48% women, 9% African American, 6% Asian American, 8% Hispanic American, 2% international
- 4,514 degree-seeking graduate students
- 50% of applicants admitted
- SAT or ACT with writing required
- 64% graduate within 6 years; 51% enter graduate study

General. Founded in 1844. Regionally accredited. Extensive internships in New York's Capital Region. International center for research and development in emerging field of nanotechnology. **Degrees:** 2,734 bachelor's awarded; master's, doctoral offered. **ROTC:** Army, Air Force. **Location:** 4 miles from downtown. **Calendar:** Semester, extensive summer session. **Full-time faculty:** 652 total; 92% have terminal degrees, 17% minority, 36% women. **Part-time faculty:** 621 total; 12% minority, 46% women. **Class size:** 24% < 20, 42% 20-39, 11% 40-49, 11% 50-99, 12% >100. **Special facilities:** Northeast Regional Forensic Institute; atmospheric science research center and Whiteface Mountain observation facility, microbeam analysis facility, large fine arts work areas, peptide synthesis facility, recombinant DNA sequencing laboratories, nanoscale science and engineering facilities.

Freshman class profile. 21,892 applied, 11,031 admitted, 2,410 enrolled.

Mid 50% test scores		GPA 2.0-2.99:	19%
SAT critical reading:	490-580	Rank in top quarter:	50%
SAT math:	520-610	Rank in top tenth:	15%
ACT composite:	22-26	Return as sophomores:	84%
GPA 3.75 or higher:	11%	Out-of-state:	8%
GPA 3.50-3.74:	19%	Live on campus:	98%
GPA 3.0-3.49:	51%	International:	3%

Basis for selection. High school record, class rank, GPA, standardized test scores very important; essay, recommendations important. **Homeschooled:** Statement describing homeschool structure and mission, state high school equivalency certificate required.

High school preparation. College-preparatory program required. 18 units required. Required and recommended units include English 4, mathematics 2-4, social studies 3, history 2, science 2-3 (laboratory 2-3), foreign language 1-3 and academic electives 4.

2008-2009 Annual costs. Tuition/fees: $6,078; $12,338 out-of-state. Room/board: $9,778. Books/supplies: $1,000. Personal expenses: $1,792.

2007-2008 Financial aid. Need-based: 2,096 full-time freshmen applied for aid; 1,370 were judged to have need; 1,342 of these received aid. Average need met was 74%. Average scholarship/grant was $5,554; average loan $3,875. 51% of total undergraduate aid awarded as scholarships/grants, 49% as loans/jobs. **Non-need-based:** Awarded to 1,058 full-time undergraduates, including 333 freshmen. Scholarships awarded for academics, athletics, state residency.

Application procedures. Admission: Closing date 3/1 (receipt date). $40 fee, may be waived for applicants with need. Admission notification on a rolling basis beginning on or about 1/1. Must reply by May 1 or within 2 week(s) if notified thereafter. **Financial aid:** Priority date 3/15; no closing date. FAFSA required. Applicants notified on a rolling basis starting 3/15; must reply by 5/1.

Academics. Project Renaissance year-long program for first-year students offers interdisciplinary course of study, close acquaintance with faculty in program, and community living. Participation open to all freshmen on first-come, first-served basis. **Special study options:** Accelerated study, combined bachelor's/graduate degree, cross-registration, distance learning, double major, dual enrollment of high school students, ESL, honors, independent study, internships, liberal arts/career combination, student-designed major, study abroad, Washington semester. Accelerated 5-year bachelor's/master's in 40 fields, internships with New York State Legislature, 3+3 program with Albany Law School, biology/dental program with Boston University Goldman School of Dental Medicine, bachelor's/doctor of optometry with SUNY State College, early assurance program with Albany Medical College and SUNY Upstate Medical University. **Credit/placement by examination:** AP, CLEP, IB. 60 credit hours maximum toward bachelor's degree. **Support services:** Pre-admission summer program, remedial instruction, study skills assistance, tutoring, writing center.

Honors college/program. Applicants admitted as Presidential Scholars & Frederick Douglass Scholars invited to apply to the Honors College. Approximately 125 freshmen will be admitted each fall. An additional 25 current University at Albany students will be admitted at the end of their first year.

Majors. Area/ethnic studies: African-American, Asian, Caribbean, Central/Eastern European, Chinese, East Asian, Japanese, Latin American, Russian/Slavic, women's. **Biology:** General, biochemistry, environmental, molecular. **Business:** Accounting, business admin. **Communications:** General. **Computer sciences:** General, information systems. **Foreign languages:** Classics, French, Italian, linguistics, Russian, Spanish. **Health:** Predental, premedicine, prepharmacy, preveterinary. **History:** General. **Interdisciplinary:** Classical/archaeology, medieval/Renaissance. **Math:** General, applied. **Philosophy/religion:** Judaic, philosophy, religion. **Physical sciences:** Atmospheric science, chemistry, physics. **Protective services:** Criminal justice. **Psychology:** General. **Public administration:** Social work. **Social sciences:** Anthropology, economics, geography, political science, sociology, urban studies. **Visual/performing arts:** Art history/conservation, dramatic, music performance, music theory/composition, studio arts. **Other:** Document studies.

Most popular majors. Biology 6%, business/marketing 16%, communications/journalism 8%, English 8%, history 6%, psychology 12%, social sciences 25%.

Computing on campus. 500 workstations in dormitories, library, computer center. Dormitories wired for high-speed internet access and linked to campus network. Commuter students can connect to campus network. Online course registration, online library, helpline, student web hosting, wireless network available.

Student life. Freshman orientation: Mandatory, $200 fee. Preregistration for classes offered. 2 days in summer with parental participation, 2 days in fall without parental participation. **Housing:** Guaranteed on-campus for freshmen. Coed dorms, apartments, wellness housing available. $125 fully refundable deposit. Individualized services for disabled students available, including accessible housing information. **Activities:** Bands, campus ministries, choral groups, dance, drama, international student organizations, literary magazine, music ensembles, musical theater, radio station, student government, student newspaper, symphony orchestra, over 200 student groups.

Athletics. NCAA. **Intercollegiate:** Baseball M, basketball, cross-country, field hockey W, football (tackle) M, golf W, lacrosse, rugby, soccer, softball W, tennis W, track and field, volleyball W. **Intramural:** Basketball, football (non-tackle), racquetball, soccer, softball, tennis, track and field, volleyball. **Team name:** Great Danes.

Student services. Alcohol/substance abuse counseling, chaplain/spiritual director, career counseling, services for economically disadvantaged, student employment services, financial aid counseling, health services, legal services, minority student services, on-campus daycare, personal counseling, placement for graduates, women's services. **Physically disabled:** Services for visually, speech, hearing impaired. **Learning disabled:** Comprehensive services available.

Contact. E-mail: ugadmissions@albany.edu
Phone: (518) 442-5435 Fax: (518) 442-5383
Robert Andrea, Director of Undergraduate Admissions, State University of New York at Albany, Office of Undergraduate Admissions, University Hall 112, Albany, NY 12222

State University of New York at Binghamton

Binghamton, New York — **CB member**
www.binghamton.edu — **CB code: 2535**

- Public 4-year university
- Residential campus in small city
- 11,760 degree-seeking undergraduates: 3% part-time, 48% women, 5% African American, 13% Asian American, 7% Hispanic American, 9% international
- 2,849 degree-seeking graduate students
- 40% of applicants admitted
- SAT or ACT with writing, application essay required
- 80% graduate within 6 years; 45% enter graduate study

General. Founded in 1946. Regionally accredited. Kosher kitchen, union hall, 4 libraries, residential communities with faculty masters. **Degrees:** 2,819 bachelor's awarded; master's, doctoral offered. **ROTC:** Army, Air Force. **Location:** 50 miles from Ithaca, 70 miles from Syracuse. **Calendar:** Semester, extensive summer session. **Full-time faculty:** 594 total; 91% have terminal degrees, 25% minority, 37% women. **Part-time faculty:** 293 total; 11% minority, 50% women. **Class size:** 46% < 20, 34% 20-39, 7% 40-49, 8% 50-99, 5% >100. **Special facilities:** 190-acre nature preserve, 4-climate greenhouse, performing arts center (5 theaters), art/dance studios, sculpture foundry, research centers, electron microcopy laboratories, geographic information systems core facility, public archeology facility, integrated electronics engineering center, institute for child development, information commons, events center.

Freshman class profile. 26,666 applied, 10,598 admitted, 2,521 enrolled.

Mid 50% test scores			
SAT critical reading:	580-660	Rank in top quarter:	83%
SAT math:	610-690	Rank in top tenth:	48%
ACT composite:	26-29	End year in good standing:	91%
GPA 3.75 or higher:	50%	Return as sophomores:	90%
GPA 3.50-3.74:	20%	Out-of-state:	14%
GPA 3.0-3.49:	22%	Live on campus:	98%
GPA 2.0-2.99:	7%	International:	9%

Basis for selection. Quality of courses, grades and grade trend, and test scores. Evidence of intellectual curiosity, interest in others, and nonacademic pursuits sought through application. Geographic, socioeconomic, and ethnic diversity considered. Audition offered for music; portfolio review offered for art; theater talent also considered. **Homeschooled:** State high school equivalency certificate required. Students required to obtain documentation of equivalency from local school boards.

High school preparation. College-preparatory program required. 16 units required. Required and recommended units include English 4, mathematics 3-4, social studies 2, history 4, science 2-4 and foreign language 3. 3 units of 1 foreign language or 2 each of 2 foreign languages required of liberal arts applicants.

2008-2009 Annual costs. Tuition/fees: $6,072; $12,332 out-of-state. Room/board: $9,774. Books/supplies: $800. Personal expenses: $740.

2008-2009 Financial aid. Need-based: 1,947 full-time freshmen applied for aid; 1,013 were judged to have need; 1,008 of these received aid. Average need met was 75%. Average scholarship/grant was $5,092; average loan $3,547. 34% of total undergraduate aid awarded as scholarships/grants, 66% as loans/jobs. **Non-need-based:** Awarded to 1,913 full-time undergraduates, including 434 freshmen. Scholarships awarded for academics, art, athletics, leadership, minority status, music/drama, state residency.

Application procedures. Admission: Priority date 1/2; no deadline. $40 fee, may be waived for applicants with need. Admission notification on a rolling basis beginning on or about 4/1. Must reply by May 1 or within 4 week(s) if notified thereafter. **Financial aid:** Priority date 2/1; no closing date. FAFSA required. Applicants notified on a rolling basis starting 4/1; must reply within 2 week(s) of notification.

Academics. Learning community program is residentially based and targeted primarily for first-year students. **Special study options:** Accelerated study, combined bachelor's/graduate degree, cross-registration, distance learning, double major, dual enrollment of high school students, ESL, exchange student, honors, independent study, internships, liberal arts/career combination, student-designed major, study abroad, teacher certification program, Washington semester. Individualized major programs; early assurance (premed, special health care, dentistry and optometry); 3-2 and 4-1 combined BA or BS/MA or MS degree programs. **Credit/placement by examination:** AP, CLEP, IB, institutional tests. 32 credit hours maximum toward bachelor's degree. **Support services:** Learning center, pre-admission summer program, study skills assistance, tutoring, writing center.

Majors. Area/ethnic studies: African-American, Asian, East Asian, Latin American, South Asian. **Biology:** General, biochemistry, cellular/molecular. **Business:** Accounting, actuarial science, business admin, entrepreneurial studies, finance, international, management information systems, marketing. **Computer sciences:** General, computer science. **Conservation:** Environmental studies. **Engineering:** General, computer, electrical, industrial, mechanical. **Family/consumer sciences:** Family studies. **Foreign languages:** Arabic, classics, comparative lit, French, German, Hebrew, Italian, Latin, linguistics, Spanish. **Health:** Nursing (RN). **History:** General. **Interdisciplinary:** Medieval/Renaissance. **Math:** General. **Philosophy/religion:**

Judaic, philosophy. **Physical sciences:** Chemistry, geology, physics. **Psychology:** General, psychobiology. **Social sciences:** General, anthropology, applied economics, cartography, economics, geography, international relations, political science, sociology. **Visual/performing arts:** Acting, art, art history/conservation, cinematography, directing/producing, dramatic, music performance, sculpture, studio arts, theater design. **Other:** Multi/Interdisciplinary studies.

Most popular majors. Biology 7%, business/marketing 13%, engineering/engineering technologies 8%, English 10%, health sciences 8%, psychology 11%, social sciences 22%.

Computing on campus. 992 workstations in dormitories, library, computer center. Dormitories wired for high-speed internet access and linked to campus network. Commuter students can connect to campus network. Online course registration, online library, helpline, student web hosting, wireless network available.

Student life. **Freshman orientation:** Available, $190 fee. Preregistration for classes offered. 2-day session held in summer for fall semester. Parents invited to participate. 2-day session held in January for students entering spring semester. **Housing:** Guaranteed on-campus for freshmen. Coed dorms, special housing for disabled, apartments, wellness housing available. $200 nonrefundable deposit, deadline 5/1. Special interest housing and learning communities (residential community faculty masters) available. **Activities:** Bands, campus ministries, choral groups, dance, drama, film society, international student organizations, literary magazine, music ensembles, Model UN, musical theater, opera, radio station, student government, student newspaper, symphony orchestra, TV station, debate team, pre-law, pre-med/pre-health, pre-dental, pre-optometry, pre-vet clubs, student tour guides/ambassadors, honors programs/societies, scholars program, religious, ethnic, minority, women's, public interest, and voluntary service organizations.

Athletics. NCAA. **Intercollegiate:** Baseball M, basketball, cross-country, diving, golf M, lacrosse, soccer, softball W, swimming, tennis, track and field, volleyball W, wrestling M. **Intramural:** Basketball, bowling, football (non-tackle), racquetball, soccer, softball, table tennis, tennis, volleyball. **Team name:** Bearcats.

Student services. Adult student services, alcohol/substance abuse counseling, chaplain/spiritual director, career counseling, services for economically disadvantaged, student employment services, financial aid counseling, health services, legal services, minority student services, on-campus daycare, personal counseling, placement for graduates, veterans' counselor, women's services. **Physically disabled:** Services for visually, speech, hearing impaired. **Learning disabled:** Comprehensive services available.

Contact. E-mail: admit@binghamton.edu
Phone: (607) 777-2171 Fax: (607) 777-4445
Cheryl Brown, Director of Admissions, State University of New York at Binghamton, Box 6001, Binghamton, NY 13902-6001

State University of New York at Buffalo

Buffalo, New York — **CB member**
www.buffalo.edu — **CB code: 2925**

- Public 4-year university
- Commuter campus in large city
- 18,760 degree-seeking undergraduates: 6% part-time, 46% women, 7% African American, 9% Asian American, 4% Hispanic American, 12% international
- 8,831 degree-seeking graduate students
- 52% of applicants admitted
- SAT or ACT with writing required
- 65% graduate within 6 years; 35% enter graduate study

General. Founded in 1846. Regionally accredited. SUNY Buffalo is the largest and most comprehensive in the 64-campus State University of New York system. **Degrees:** 3,966 bachelor's awarded; master's, doctoral, first professional offered. **ROTC:** Army. **Location:** 10 miles from downtown. **Calendar:** Semester, extensive summer session. **Full-time faculty:** 1,237 total; 92% have terminal degrees, 24% minority, 34% women. **Part-time faculty:** 555 total; 75% have terminal degrees, 12% minority, 48% women. **Class size:** 31% < 20, 36% 20-39, 9% 40-49, 15% 50-99, 9% >100. **Special facilities:** Center for the arts, Slee concert hall, anthropology research museum, multidisciplinary center for earthquake engineering research, New York state center of excellence in bioinformatics & life sciences, center for computational research, poetry and rare books collection, center of Excellence for document analysis & recognition, New York State center for engineering design and industrial innovation, pharmacy museum, virtual site museum, electronic poetry center, archaeological survey center, numerous research centers.

Freshman class profile. 19,784 applied, 10,268 admitted, 3,154 enrolled.

Mid 50% test scores		**GPA 2.0-2.99:**	27%
SAT critical reading:	500-600	**Rank in top quarter:**	64%
SAT math:	550-650	**Rank in top tenth:**	25%
ACT composite:	23-27	**Return as sophomores:**	87%
GPA 3.75 or higher:	15%	**Out-of-state:**	7%
GPA 3.50-3.74:	13%	**Live on campus:**	70%
GPA 3.0-3.49:	45%	**International:**	13%

Basis for selection. Freshmen evaluated based on secondary school performance, strength of curriculum, standardized test scores, and, in some cases, supplemental application. SAT Subject Test considered for placement for foreign language. Audition required for music. **Homeschooled:** Transcript of courses and grades, letter of recommendation (nonparent) required. Essay describing educational program, special projects, extracurricular activities, and special accomplishments required as well as 2 letters of recommendation: 1 from parent or other person providing education, 1 from person involved with other activities. If admitted, will need to submit letter from superintendent of local school district attesting to completion of program of home instruction meeting requirements of Section 100.10 of the Regulations of the Commissioner of Education, or passing score on GED. **Learning Disabled:** No separate admissions process: eligibility for services must be established by provision of disability documentation that meets institutional standards.

High school preparation. College-preparatory program recommended. 17 units recommended. Recommended units include English 4, mathematics 3, social studies 4, science 3 and foreign language 3.

2008-2009 Annual costs. Tuition/fees: $6,285; $12,545 out-of-state. Room/board: $9,552. Books/supplies: $947. Personal expenses: $667.

2007-2008 Financial aid. **Need-based:** 2,572 full-time freshmen applied for aid; 1,677 were judged to have need; 1,632 of these received aid. Average need met was 68%. Average scholarship/grant was $3,035; average loan $3,372. 52% of total undergraduate aid awarded as scholarships/grants, 48% as loans/jobs. **Non-need-based:** Awarded to 3,014 full-time undergraduates, including 989 freshmen. Scholarships awarded for academics, athletics, minority status, music/drama, state residency.

Application procedures. **Admission:** Priority date 11/1; no deadline. $40 fee, may be waived for applicants with need. Admission notification on a rolling basis beginning on or about 2/1. Must reply by May 1 or within 2 week(s) if notified thereafter. **Financial aid:** Priority date 3/1; no closing date. FAFSA required. Applicants notified on a rolling basis starting 2/1; must reply by 5/1.

Academics. Over 300 baccalaureate, master's and doctoral degree programs. Comprehensive College of Arts and Sciences plus 11 professional schools including Law, Medicine and Dentistry. **Special study options:** Accelerated study, combined bachelor's/graduate degree, cooperative education, cross-registration, distance learning, double major, dual enrollment of high school students, ESL, exchange student, honors, independent study, internships, liberal arts/career combination, student-designed major, study abroad, teacher certification program, Washington semester. Certificate programs, combined degree programs, early assurance program with School of Medicine and Dentistry, Honors College and Learning Communities. **Credit/placement by examination:** AP, CLEP, IB, SAT, ACT, institutional tests. Maximum of 30 credits from International Baccalaureate. **Support services:** Learning center, pre-admission summer program, reduced course load, remedial instruction, study skills assistance, tutoring, writing center.

Majors. **Architecture:** Architecture, environmental design. **Area/ethnic studies:** African-American, American, Asian, women's. **Biology:** General, biochemistry, bioinformatics, biomedical sciences, biophysics, biostatistics, biotechnology, pharmacology/toxicology. **Business:** Business admin. **Communications:** General, media studies. **Computer sciences:** Computer science, information systems. **Engineering:** General, aerospace, chemical, civil, computer, electrical, environmental, industrial, mechanical, physics, structural. **Foreign languages:** Classics, French, German, Italian, linguistics, Spanish. **Health:** Audiology/speech pathology, clinical lab science, nuclear medical technology, nursing (RN). **History:** General. **Liberal arts:** Humanities. **Math:** General. **Philosophy/religion:** Philosophy. **Physical sciences:** Chemistry, geology, physics, theoretical physics. **Psychology:** General. **Social sciences:** Anthropology, economics, geography, political science, sociology. **Visual/performing arts:** Art, art history/conservation, dance, dramatic, film/cinema, music performance, studio arts. **Other:** Exercise physiology, Multi-interdisciplinary studies.

Most popular majors. Biology 8%, business/marketing 20%, communications/journalism 9%, engineering/engineering technologies 10%, health sciences 7%, liberal arts 7%, psychology 10%, social sciences 8%.

Computing on campus. 2,450 workstations in dormitories, library, computer center, student center. Dormitories wired for high-speed internet access and linked to campus network. Commuter students can connect to campus network. Online course registration, online library, helpline, repair service, student web hosting, wireless network available.

Student life. **Freshman orientation:** Available, $190 fee. Preregistration for classes offered. One-and-a-half-day program. **Policies:** University standards, administrative regulations and student conduct rules apply. **Housing:** Guaranteed on-campus for all undergraduates. Coed dorms, special housing for disabled, apartments, wellness housing available. $200 fully refundable deposit, deadline 5/1. Academic interest, honors. **Activities:** Bands, campus ministries, choral groups, dance, drama, film society, international student organizations, literary magazine, music ensembles, musical theater, radio station, student government, student newspaper, symphony orchestra, TV station, over 300 registered organizations.

Athletics. NCAA. **Intercollegiate:** Baseball M, basketball, cross-country, diving, football (tackle) M, rowing (crew) W, soccer, softball W, swimming, tennis, track and field, volleyball W, wrestling M. **Intramural:** Badminton, basketball, cross-country, football (non-tackle), racquetball, soccer, softball, tennis, volleyball. **Team name:** Bulls.

Student services. Adult student services, alcohol/substance abuse counseling, chaplain/spiritual director, career counseling, services for economically disadvantaged, student employment services, financial aid counseling, health services, legal services, minority student services, on-campus daycare, personal counseling, placement for graduates, veterans' counselor. **Physically disabled:** Services for visually, speech, hearing impaired.

Contact. E-mail: ub-admissions@buffalo.edu
Phone: (716) 645-6900 Toll-free number: (888) 822-3648
Fax: (716) 645-6411
Patricia Armstrong, Director of Admissions, State University of New York at Buffalo, 12 Capen Hall, Buffalo, NY 14260-1660

State University of New York at Farmingdale

Farmingdale, New York — **CB member**
www.farmingdale.edu — **CB code: 2526**

- Public 4-year technical college
- Commuter campus in large town
- 5,951 degree-seeking undergraduates: 23% part-time, 42% women, 10% African American, 5% Asian American, 10% Hispanic American, 1% international
- 40% of applicants admitted
- 40% graduate within 6 years

General. Founded in 1912. Regionally accredited. **Degrees:** 544 bachelor's, 523 associate awarded. **Location:** 30 miles from New York City. **Calendar:** Semester, extensive summer session. **Full-time faculty:** 183 total; 50% have terminal degrees, 18% minority, 45% women. **Part-time faculty:** 356 total; 14% have terminal degrees, 14% minority, 47% women. **Class size:** 25% < 20, 59% 20-39, 14% 40-49, 1% 50-99. **Special facilities:** CAD/CAM laboratory, fleet of single-engine and multi-engine aircraft, dental and health care laboratories, bioscience labs, Cold Spring Harbor Research lab on campus, manufacturing labs with plasmajet and advanced robotic technology, solar cell and hydrogen fuel cell research.

Freshman class profile. 6,365 applied, 2,535 admitted, 1,511 enrolled.

Mid 50% test scores		**GPA 2.0-2.99:**	54%
SAT critical reading:	430-530	**Rank in top quarter:**	21%
SAT math:	450-550	**Rank in top tenth:**	5%
SAT writing:	420-500	**End year in good standing:**	79%
GPA 3.75 or higher:	5%	**Return as sophomores:**	77%
GPA 3.50-3.74:	12%	**Out-of-state:**	1%
GPA 3.0-3.49:	29%		

Basis for selection. School achievement record of primary importance. Applicants apply to and are accepted into a specific curriculum. Requirements vary according to program. SAT required for bachelor's degree students. Interview and portfolio required for advertising art and design, visual communications programs.

High school preparation. 20.5 units required. Required and recommended units include English 4, mathematics 2-4, social studies 4, science 2-4 and foreign language 2. Requirements vary by curriculum.

2008-2009 Annual costs. Tuition/fees: $5,375; $11,635 out-of-state. Room/board: $10,850. Books/supplies: $1,200. Personal expenses: $900.

Financial aid. **Non-need-based:** Scholarships awarded for academics.

Application procedures. **Admission:** No deadline. $40 fee, may be waived for applicants with need. Admission notification on a rolling basis beginning on or about 11/1. Must reply by May 1 or within 4 week(s) if notified thereafter. Priority given to applications received by January 15 for dental hygiene program and nursing program. **Financial aid:** Priority date 4/1; no closing date. FAFSA, institutional form required. Applicants notified on a rolling basis starting 4/1.

Academics. **Special study options:** Distance learning, double major, honors, internships, study abroad. **Credit/placement by examination:** AP, CLEP, institutional tests. **Support services:** Learning center, remedial instruction, study skills assistance, tutoring, writing center.

Majors. **Agriculture:** Horticulture. **Biology:** General. **Business:** Business admin, operations. **Communications:** Media studies. **Computer sciences:** Programming. **Construction:** Maintenance. **Engineering technology:** Architectural, automotive, computer, computer systems, electrical, industrial, manufacturing, mechanical. **Health:** Dental hygiene, nursing (RN). **Interdisciplinary:** Science/society. **Math:** Applied. **Protective services:** Security management, security services. **Psychology:** Industrial. **Social sciences:** Applied economics. **Transportation:** Airline/commercial pilot, aviation management. **Other:** Software technology.

Most popular majors. Biology 7%, business/marketing 39%, communications/journalism 10%, computer/information sciences 9%, engineering/engineering technologies 17%, security/protective services 6%, trade and industry 7%.

Computing on campus. 950 workstations in library, computer center, student center. Dormitories wired for high-speed internet access and linked to campus network. Commuter students can connect to campus network. Online course registration, online library, wireless network available.

Student life. **Freshman orientation:** Mandatory, $125 fee. Preregistration for classes offered. **Housing:** Coed dorms available. $125 deposit. **Activities:** Choral groups, drama, international student organizations, literary magazine, radio station, student government, student newspaper, African student association, Asian student alliance, Caribbean student organization, Christian fellowship.

Athletics. NCAA. **Intercollegiate:** Baseball M, basketball, cross-country, golf M, lacrosse, soccer, softball W, tennis M, track and field, volleyball W. **Intramural:** Basketball, golf, racquetball, soccer, softball, squash, swimming, tennis, volleyball, weight lifting. **Team name:** Rams.

Student services. Alcohol/substance abuse counseling, chaplain/spiritual director, career counseling, services for economically disadvantaged, student employment services, financial aid counseling, health services, on-campus daycare, personal counseling, placement for graduates, veterans' counselor. **Physically disabled:** Services for visually, speech, hearing impaired.

Contact. E-mail: admissions@farmingdale.edu
Phone: (631) 420-2200 Toll-free number: (800) 432-7646
Fax: (631) 420-2633
Jim Hall, Director of Admissions, State University of New York at Farmingdale, 2350 Broadhollow Road, Farmingdale, NY 11735-1021

State University of New York at New Paltz

New Paltz, New York — **CB member**
www.newpaltz.edu — **CB code: 2541**

- Public 4-year liberal arts college
- Residential campus in large town
- 6,195 degree-seeking undergraduates: 9% part-time, 66% women, 6% African American, 3% Asian American, 10% Hispanic American, 3% international
- 1,250 degree-seeking graduate students
- 39% of applicants admitted
- SAT or ACT (ACT writing optional) required
- 69% graduate within 6 years; 48% enter graduate study

General. Founded in 1828. Regionally accredited. More than 16 percent of undergraduates participate in international education each academic year. **Degrees:** 1,461 bachelor's awarded; master's offered. **Location:** 65 miles from Albany, 96 miles from New York City. **Calendar:** Semester, extensive summer session. **Full-time faculty:** 335 total; 82% have terminal degrees, 14% minority, 50% women. **Part-time faculty:** 387 total; 26% have terminal degrees, 11% minority, 59% women. **Class size:** 42% < 20, 50% 20-39, 4% 40-49, 3% 50-99, less than 1% >100. **Special facilities:** 3 theaters, recital hall, speech and hearing clinical center, music therapy training center, observatory, planetarium, theater collection, electronic classrooms.

Freshman class profile. 13,868 applied, 5,452 admitted, 1,335 enrolled.

Mid 50% test scores		**GPA 2.0-2.99:**	14%
SAT critical reading:	500-600	**Return as sophomores:**	84%
SAT math:	500-600	**Out-of-state:**	6%
GPA 3.75 or higher:	10%	**Live on campus:**	93%
GPA 3.50-3.74:	25%	**International:**	4%
GPA 3.0-3.49:	51%		

Basis for selection. Secondary school curriculum and achievement, standardized test scores most important. Applicants, especially academically marginal, encouraged to send personal statements regarding academic work, recommendations from academic teachers, and any other pertinent information. Essay and recommendations encouraged for all; audition required for music, music therapy, theater arts programs; portfolio required for art education, scenography, studio art, and visual arts programs. **Homeschooled:** Must submit all data as required by NYS Commissioner of Education's regulations (Section 100.10).

High school preparation. College-preparatory program required. 17 units required; 21 recommended. Required and recommended units include English 4, mathematics 3-4, social studies 4, history 1, science 3-4 (laboratory 2-4) and foreign language 2-4.

2008-2009 Annual costs. Tuition/fees: $5,419; $11,679 out-of-state. Room/board: $8,690. Books/supplies: $1,250. Personal expenses: $1,100.

2008-2009 Financial aid. All financial aid based on need. 1,084 full-time freshmen applied for aid; 650 were judged to have need; 639 of these received aid. Average need met was 53%. Average scholarship/grant was $4,517; average loan $3,245. 34% of total undergraduate aid awarded as scholarships/grants, 66% as loans/jobs.

Application procedures. Admission: Closing date 4/1 (receipt date). $40 fee, may be waived for applicants with need. Admission notification on a rolling basis beginning on or about 1/1. Must reply by May 1 or within 2 week(s) if notified thereafter. **Financial aid:** Priority date 3/15; no closing date. FAFSA required. Applicants notified on a rolling basis starting 4/1; must reply within 4 week(s) of notification.

Academics. Bachelor's degree completion program for registered nurses. **Special study options:** Combined bachelor's/graduate degree, cooperative education, cross-registration, distance learning, double major, dual enrollment of high school students, ESL, exchange student, honors, independent study, internships, liberal arts/career combination, New York semester, student-designed major, study abroad, teacher certification program, United Nations semester. Student exchange programs in Australia, Brazil, Cuba, Czech Republic, Denmark, Ecuador, England, France, Greece, Ireland, Italy, Japan, The Netherlands, New Zealand, Spain, Uzbekistan, U.S. Virgin Islands and Zimbabwe. **Credit/placement by examination:** AP, CLEP, IB, SAT, institutional tests. 30 credit hours maximum toward bachelor's degree. **Support services:** Learning center, reduced course load, remedial instruction, study skills assistance, tutoring, writing center.

Majors. Area/ethnic studies: African-American, Asian, Latin American, women's. **Biology:** General, biotechnology. **Business:** General, accounting, business admin, finance, international, logistics. **Communications:** General, broadcast journalism, journalism, public relations. **Computer sciences:** General. **Education:** Art, biology, chemistry, early childhood special, elementary, English, foreign languages, French, German, history, learning disabled, mathematics, middle, physics, science, secondary, social science, social studies, Spanish, special, speech, speech impaired. **Engineering:** Computer, electrical. **Foreign languages:** French, German, Spanish. **Health:** Communication disorders, music therapy, nursing (RN). **History:** General. **Interdisciplinary:** Biopsychology. **Legal studies:** Prelaw. **Liberal arts:** Arts/sciences. **Math:** General. **Philosophy/religion:** Philosophy. **Physical sciences:** Chemistry, geochemistry, geology, physics. **Psychology:** General. **Public administration:** Social work. **Social sciences:** General, anthropology, economics, geography, international relations, political science, sociology. **Visual/performing arts:** General, acting, art, art history/conservation, ceramics, commercial/advertising art, dramatic, metal/jewelry, painting, photography, piano/organ, printmaking, sculpture, studio arts, theater design, theater history, voice/opera.

Most popular majors. Business/marketing 13%, communications/journalism 6%, education 33%, English 8%, social sciences 8%, visual/performing arts 10%.

Computing on campus. 950 workstations in dormitories, library, computer center, student center. Dormitories wired for high-speed internet access and linked to campus network. Commuter students can connect to campus network. Online course registration, online library, helpline, student web hosting, wireless network available.

Student life. Freshman orientation: Available, $175 fee. Preregistration for classes offered. 3-day academic and transition program. **Housing:** Guaranteed on-campus for freshmen. Coed dorms, single-sex dorms, special housing for disabled available. $100 partly refundable deposit, deadline 5/1. First-year initiative, honors, art, nursing program housing. **Activities:** Bands, campus ministries, choral groups, dance, drama, international student organizations, literary magazine, music ensembles, musical theater, radio station, student government, student newspaper, symphony orchestra, TV station, Jewish Action Movement, Black Student Union, Habitat for Humanity, Circle K International, equestrian club, NAACP, philosophy club, Korean culture union.

Athletics. NCAA. **Intercollegiate:** Baseball M, basketball, cheerleading M, cross-country, diving, field hockey W, lacrosse W, soccer, softball W, swimming, tennis, volleyball. **Intramural:** Badminton, basketball, football (non-tackle), golf, handball, racquetball, soccer, softball, tennis, volleyball. **Team name:** Hawks.

Student services. Alcohol/substance abuse counseling, chaplain/spiritual director, career counseling, services for economically disadvantaged, student employment services, financial aid counseling, health services, legal services, minority student services, on-campus daycare, personal counseling, placement for graduates, veterans' counselor, women's services. **Physically disabled:** Services for visually, speech, hearing impaired.

Contact. E-mail: admissions@newpaltz.edu
Phone: (845) 257-3200 Toll-free number: (888) 639-7589
Fax: (845) 257-3209
Kimberly Strano, Director of Freshmen and International Admission, State University of New York at New Paltz, 100 Hawk Drive, New Paltz, NY 12561-2443

State University of New York at Oswego

Oswego, New York — **CB member**
www.oswego.edu — **CB code: 2543**

- Public 4-year university
- Residential campus in large town
- 7,095 degree-seeking undergraduates: 6% part-time, 53% women, 4% African American, 2% Asian American, 4% Hispanic American, 1% Native American, 1% international
- 701 degree-seeking graduate students
- 47% of applicants admitted
- SAT or ACT (ACT writing optional), application essay required
- 59% graduate within 6 years; 26% enter graduate study

General. Founded in 1861. Regionally accredited. **Degrees:** 1,440 bachelor's awarded; master's offered. **ROTC:** Army. **Location:** 35 miles from Syracuse, 65 miles from Rochester. **Calendar:** Semester, limited summer session. **Full-time faculty:** 319 total; 79% have terminal degrees, 20% minority, 42% women. **Part-time faculty:** 197 total; 23% have terminal degrees, 8% minority, 48% women. **Class size:** 52% < 20, 33% 20-39, 8% 40-49, 5% 50-99, 2% >100. **Special facilities:** Weather facsimile machine, planetarium, cross-country ski facilities, advanced technology classrooms, biological field station.

Freshman class profile. 9,965 applied, 4,682 admitted, 1,473 enrolled.

Mid 50% test scores		**Rank in top tenth:**	14%
SAT critical reading:	520-590	**End year in good standing:**	89%
SAT math:	520-590	**Return as sophomores:**	78%
ACT composite:	21-25	**Out-of-state:**	2%
GPA 3.75 or higher:	20%	**Live on campus:**	88%
GPA 3.50-3.74:	22%	**International:**	2%
GPA 3.0-3.49:	44%	**Fraternities:**	6%
GPA 2.0-2.99:	14%	**Sororities:**	5%
Rank in top quarter:	52%		

Basis for selection. High school GPA and curriculum most important, followed by test scores, supplemental portion of application and letters of recommendation. Special talents considered. Applicants recommended to send both SAT and ACT; higher score accepted. Interview recommended for all; portfolio required for graphic design and fine arts (BFA). **Home-schooled:** Proof of high school graduation or GED recognized by state of residency required. **Learning Disabled:** Advised to contact Office of Learning Services and/or Disability Services with copy of IEP if applicable.

High school preparation. College-preparatory program required. 18 units required; 20 recommended. Required and recommended units include English 4, mathematics 3-4, social studies 4, science 3-4 (laboratory 2-3) and foreign language 2-4. Combined minimum of 7 units of college prep math and science recommended.

2008-2009 Annual costs. Tuition/fees: $5,531; $11,791 out-of-state. Room/board: $10,170. Books/supplies: $800. Personal expenses: $850.

2008-2009 Financial aid. Need-based: 1,319 full-time freshmen applied for aid; 873 were judged to have need; 843 of these received aid. Average need met was 87%. Average scholarship/grant was $5,313; average loan $5,055. 37% of total undergraduate aid awarded as scholarships/grants, 63% as loans/jobs. **Non-need-based:** Awarded to 2,007 full-time undergraduates, including 640 freshmen. Scholarships awarded for academics, state residency.

Application procedures. Admission: Priority date 1/15; no deadline. $40 fee, may be waived for applicants with need. Admission notification on a rolling basis beginning on or about 1/15. Must reply by May 1 or within 4 week(s) if notified thereafter. **Financial aid:** Priority date 3/1; no closing date. FAFSA required. Applicants notified on a rolling basis starting 3/1; must reply by 5/1 or within 3 week(s) of notification.

Academics. Special study options: Accelerated study, combined bachelor's/graduate degree, cross-registration, distance learning, double major, dual enrollment of high school students, ESL, exchange student, external degree, honors, independent study, internships, liberal arts/career combination, study abroad, teacher certification program, Washington semester. **Credit/placement by examination:** AP, CLEP, IB, SAT. 30 credit hours maximum toward bachelor's degree. **Support services:** Learning center, pre-admission summer program, reduced course load, remedial instruction, study skills assistance, tutoring, writing center.

Honors college/program. Approximately 80 freshmen enroll annually, distinct program of general education classes held in small class settings.

Majors. Area/ethnic studies: American, women's. **Biology:** General, zoology. **Business:** Accounting, business admin, finance, human resources, management science. **Communications:** General, broadcast journalism, journalism, public relations. **Computer sciences:** Computer science, information systems. **Education:** Agricultural, biology, business, chemistry, elementary, English, French, German, health occupations, history, mathematics, physics, science, secondary, social studies, Spanish, technology/industrial arts, trade/industrial, voc/tech. **Family/consumer sciences:** Child development. **Foreign languages:** French, German, linguistics, Spanish. **Health:** Medical radiologic technology/radiation therapy, perfusion technology, public health ed. **History:** General. **Interdisciplinary:** Cognitive science, global studies. **Legal studies:** Prelaw. **Math:** General, applied. **Philosophy/religion:** Philosophy. **Physical sciences:** Chemistry, geochemistry, geology, meteorology, physics. **Psychology:** General. **Social sciences:** Anthropology, econometrics, economics, political science, sociology. **Visual/performing arts:** Art, commercial/advertising art, dramatic.

Most popular majors. Business/marketing 19%, communications/journalism 9%, education 27%, psychology 10%, visual/performing arts 6%.

Computing on campus. 900 workstations in dormitories, library, computer center, student center. Dormitories wired for high-speed internet access and linked to campus network. Commuter students can connect to campus network. Online course registration, online library, helpline, student web hosting, wireless network available.

Student life. Freshman orientation: Mandatory, $159 fee. Preregistration for classes offered. 2-day program for incoming students and families. **Housing:** Guaranteed on-campus for all undergraduates. Coed dorms, wellness housing available. $100 fully refundable deposit, deadline 5/1. Pets allowed in dorm rooms. Global living and learning center, suites for upperclassmen, nontraditional student housing, first-year experience residence hall for incoming freshmen only, housing for 21 and over single suites available. **Activities:** Bands, choral groups, dance, drama, film society, international student organizations, literary magazine, music ensembles, musical theater, radio station, student government, student newspaper, symphony orchestra, TV station, Christian, Jewish, Catholic, and Baptist groups, black student union, Latin student union, Caribbean student association, international student association, Native American Heritage Association, Students Educating Everyone About Disabilities.

Athletics. NCAA. **Intercollegiate:** Baseball M, basketball, cross-country, diving, field hockey W, golf M, ice hockey, lacrosse, soccer, softball W, swimming, tennis, track and field, volleyball W, wrestling M. **Intramural:** Badminton, basketball, football (non-tackle), golf, lacrosse, racquetball, skiing, soccer, softball, swimming, tennis, volleyball, weight lifting M, wrestling M. **Team name:** Lakers.

Student services. Adult student services, alcohol/substance abuse counseling, career counseling, services for economically disadvantaged, student employment services, financial aid counseling, health services, minority student services, on-campus daycare, personal counseling, placement for graduates, veterans' counselor, women's services. **Physically disabled:** Services for visually, speech, hearing impaired.

Contact. E-mail: admiss@oswego.edu
Phone: (315) 312-2250 Fax: (315) 312-3260
Joseph Grant, Vice President for Student Affairs and Enrollment, State University of New York at Oswego, 229 Sheldon Hall, Oswego, NY 13126-3599

State University of New York at Purchase

Purchase, New York
www.purchase.edu **CB code: 2878**

- Public 4-year university
- Residential campus in large town
- 3,790 degree-seeking undergraduates: 6% part-time, 55% women, 8% African American, 3% Asian American, 10% Hispanic American, 2% international
- 145 degree-seeking graduate students
- 24% of applicants admitted
- SAT or ACT (ACT writing optional) required
- 50% graduate within 6 years

General. Founded in 1967. Regionally accredited. **Degrees:** 743 bachelor's awarded; master's offered. **Location:** 25 miles from New York City, 5 miles from White Plains. **Calendar:** Semester, extensive summer session. **Full-time faculty:** 145 total; 84% have terminal degrees, 16% minority, 51% women. **Part-time faculty:** 233 total; 60% have terminal degrees, 9% minority, 43% women. **Class size:** 69% < 20, 23% 20-39, 5% 40-49, 2% 50-99, less than 1% >100. **Special facilities:** Performing arts center, children's center, electron microscope, Neuberger Museum of Art.

Freshman class profile. 8,905 applied, 2,155 admitted, 709 enrolled.

Mid 50% test scores		**GPA 2.0-2.99:**	31%
SAT critical reading:	520-620	**Rank in top quarter:**	39%
SAT math:	490-590	**Rank in top tenth:**	10%
SAT writing:	510-610	**Return as sophomores:**	79%
ACT composite:	22-26	**Out-of-state:**	27%
GPA 3.75 or higher:	13%	**Live on campus:**	90%
GPA 3.50-3.74:	17%	**International:**	1%
GPA 3.0-3.49:	39%		

Basis for selection. For liberal arts and sciences programs, high school achievement record or test scores important. For conservatory, performing arts and visual arts applicants, audition, interview, or portfolio most important. SAT recommended. Interview and essay required for film, theater design/technology programs; audition required for acting, dance, music programs; portfolio required for visual arts program.

High school preparation. College-preparatory program recommended.

2008-2009 Annual costs. Tuition/fees: $5,811; $12,071 out-of-state. Room/board: $9,908. Books/supplies: $1,100. Personal expenses: $700.

2008-2009 Financial aid. Need-based: 597 full-time freshmen applied for aid; 394 were judged to have need; 393 of these received aid. Average need met was 56%. Average scholarship/grant was $5,218; average loan $3,501. 51% of total undergraduate aid awarded as scholarships/grants, 49% as loans/jobs. **Non-need-based:** Awarded to 389 full-time undergraduates, including 58 freshmen. Scholarships awarded for academics, art, music/drama. **Additional information:** All applicants automatically considered for scholarship upon review of applications, essays, auditions, and/or portfolio.

Application procedures. Admission: Priority date 3/1; deadline 7/15 (postmark date). $40 fee, may be waived for applicants with need. Admission notification 5/1. Must reply by May 1 or within 2 week(s) if notified thereafter. Application deadlines vary by program. Priority date of 1/30 for students applying to acting, design/technology, and film programs. **Financial aid:** Priority date 2/1; no closing date. FAFSA required. Applicants notified on a rolling basis starting 3/1; must reply within 2 week(s) of notification.

Academics. Special study options: Cross-registration, distance learning, double major, ESL, independent study, internships, liberal arts/career combination, student-designed major, study abroad. Conservatory master-apprentice training in dance, music, acting, film, theater design technology, visual arts. **Credit/placement by examination:** AP, CLEP, institutional tests. 30 credit hours maximum toward bachelor's degree. **Support services:** Learning center, pre-admission summer program, remedial instruction, tutoring, writing center.

Majors. Area/ethnic studies: Women's. **Biology:** General, ecology. **Communications:** Journalism, media studies. **Conservation:** Environmental science, environmental studies. **Foreign languages:** General. **History:** General. **Interdisciplinary:** Math/computer science. **Liberal arts:** Arts/sciences. **Math:** General. **Philosophy/religion:** Philosophy. **Physical sciences:** Chemistry. **Psychology:** General. **Social sciences:** Anthropology, economics, political science, sociology. **Visual/performing arts:** Art history/conservation, arts management, cinematography, commercial/advertising art, dance, dramatic, drawing, graphic design, music performance, music theory/

composition, painting, photography, play/screenwriting, printmaking, sculpture, theater design, theater history.

Most popular majors. Liberal arts 26%, social sciences 8%, visual/performing arts 46%.

Computing on campus. 600 workstations in dormitories, library, computer center. Dormitories wired for high-speed internet access and linked to campus network. Commuter students can connect to campus network. Online course registration, online library, helpline, repair service, wireless network available.

Student life. **Freshman orientation:** Mandatory, $120 fee. Preregistration for classes offered. **Housing:** Coed dorms, special housing for disabled, apartments, wellness housing available. $100 fully refundable deposit. Freshman residence, non-traditional age hall, presidential scholars, learning community. **Activities:** Jazz band, choral groups, dance, drama, film society, international student organizations, literary magazine, music ensembles, musical theater, radio station, student government, student newspaper, TV station, philosophy club, chemistry society, literature club, dance club, ski club, Purchase Experimental Theatre, Organization of African People in America (OAPIA), Latinos Unidos, Gay/Lesbian/Bisexual and Transgendered Union.

Athletics. NCAA. **Intercollegiate:** Baseball M, basketball, cross-country, soccer, softball W, swimming W, tennis, volleyball. **Intramural:** Badminton, basketball, bowling, cross-country, fencing, golf, racquetball, skiing, soccer, softball, squash, swimming, table tennis, tennis, volleyball, water polo, weight lifting. **Team name:** Panthers.

Student services. Adult student services, alcohol/substance abuse counseling, career counseling, services for economically disadvantaged, student employment services, financial aid counseling, health services, on-campus daycare, personal counseling, placement for graduates, veterans' counselor, women's services. **Physically disabled:** Services for visually, hearing impaired.

Contact. E-mail: admissn@purchase.edu
Phone: (914) 251-6300 Fax: (914) 251-6314
Stephanie McCaine, State University of New York at Purchase, 735 Anderson Hill Road, Purchase, NY 10577-1400

State University of New York at Stony Brook

Stony Brook, New York — **CB member**
www.stonybrook.edu — **CB code: 2548**

- Public 4-year university
- Residential campus in large town
- 15,596 degree-seeking undergraduates: 6% part-time, 49% women, 7% African American, 22% Asian American, 8% Hispanic American, 6% international
- 6,838 degree-seeking graduate students
- 43% of applicants admitted
- SAT or ACT with writing required
- 61% graduate within 6 years

General. Founded in 1957. Regionally accredited. **Degrees:** 3,171 bachelor's awarded; master's, doctoral, first professional offered. **ROTC:** Army, Air Force. **Location:** 60 miles from New York City. **Calendar:** Semester, limited summer session. **Full-time faculty:** 938 total; 97% have terminal degrees, 19% minority, 35% women. **Part-time faculty:** 716 total; 14% minority, 46% women. **Class size:** 37% < 20, 36% 20-39, 7% 40-49, 13% 50-99, 8% >100. **Special facilities:** Nuclear accelerator, natural science museum, 3-theater fine arts center, nature preserve, working arrangements with Cold Spring Harbor Laboratory and Brookhaven National Laboratory.

Freshman class profile. 25,590 applied, 11,090 admitted, 2,894 enrolled.

Mid 50% test scores			
SAT critical reading:	520-610	Rank in top quarter:	72%
SAT math:	570-660	Rank in top tenth:	36%
SAT writing:	510-610	End year in good standing:	88%
GPA 3.75 or higher:	32%	Return as sophomores:	88%
GPA 3.50-3.74:	23%	Out-of-state:	10%
GPA 3.0-3.49:	33%	Live on campus:	80%
GPA 2.0-2.99:	12%	International:	5%

Basis for selection. High school GPA, test scores and level of high school curriculum most important factors. Class rank, interview, letters of recommendation, extracurricular activities, essays considered. SAT Subject Tests recommended. Audition and musicianship examination required for major in music. Supplemental application with essay required for admission to Honors College, WISE (Women in Science & Engineering), Scholars for Medicine, Engineering Scholars for Medicine, Honors Program in Computer Science and for merit scholarship consideration. **Homeschooled:** State high school equivalency certificate required. Applicants required to take 5 Regents exams through their home school district or have their home district verify that they have fulfilled high school graduation requirements through home school curriculum. **Learning Disabled:** Applicants required to submit documentation of learning disability. Psychological and educational evaluation also required.

High school preparation. 16 units required; 19 recommended. Required and recommended units include English 4, mathematics 3-4, social studies 4, science 3-4 and foreign language 2-3. 4 math and 4 science recommended for applicants to science, engineering, and math programs.

2008-2009 Annual costs. Tuition/fees: $5,810; $12,070 out-of-state. Room/board: $9,132. Books/supplies: $900. Personal expenses: $1,292.

2007-2008 Financial aid. **Need-based:** 2,202 full-time freshmen applied for aid; 1,497 were judged to have need; 1,445 of these received aid. Average need met was 68%. Average scholarship/grant was $6,626; average loan $4,212. 54% of total undergraduate aid awarded as scholarships/grants, 46% as loans/jobs. **Non-need-based:** Awarded to 1,288 full-time undergraduates, including 481 freshmen. Scholarships awarded for academics, alumni affiliation, art, athletics, job skills, leadership, music/drama.

Application procedures. **Admission:** Priority date 12/1; no deadline. $40 fee, may be waived for applicants with need. Admission notification on a rolling basis beginning on or about 2/1. Must reply by May 1 or within 2 week(s) if notified thereafter. **Financial aid:** Priority date 3/1; no closing date. FAFSA required. Applicants notified on a rolling basis starting 3/1; must reply by 5/1 or within 2 week(s) of notification.

Academics. **Special study options:** Combined bachelor's/graduate degree, cross-registration, distance learning, double major, dual enrollment of high school students, ESL, exchange student, honors, independent study, internships, New York semester, student-designed major, study abroad, teacher certification program, Washington semester. **Credit/placement by examination:** AP, CLEP, IB, institutional tests. 30 credit hours maximum toward bachelor's degree. **Support services:** Learning center, reduced course load, remedial instruction, tutoring, writing center.

Honors college/program. High grades in major subject areas, minimum cumulative unweighted high school average of 93, minimum combined SAT (exclusive of Writing) of 1300 or ACT score of 30, record of advanced or college-level course work, and evidence of writing ability required.

Majors. **Area/ethnic studies:** African-American, American, European, women's. **Biology:** General, biochemistry, marine, pharmacology. **Business:** Business admin. **Communications:** Journalism. **Computer sciences:** Computer science, information systems. **Conservation:** Environmental studies. **Engineering:** General, biomedical, computer hardware, electrical, mechanical. **Foreign languages:** Comparative lit, French, German, Italian, linguistics, Russian, Spanish. **Health:** Clinical lab science, cytotechnology, nursing (RN), respiratory therapy technology. **History:** General. **Liberal arts:** Humanities. **Math:** General, applied. **Philosophy/religion:** Philosophy, religion. **Physical sciences:** Astronomy, chemistry, geology, physics. **Psychology:** General. **Public administration:** Social work. **Social sciences:** Anthropology, economics, political science, sociology. **Visual/performing arts:** Art history/conservation, dramatic, studio arts.

Most popular majors. Biology 11%, business/marketing 8%, health sciences 20%, psychology 12%, social sciences 14%.

Computing on campus. 2,300 workstations in dormitories, library, computer center, student center. Dormitories wired for high-speed internet access and linked to campus network. Commuter students can connect to campus network. Online course registration, helpline, student web hosting available.

Student life. **Freshman orientation:** Mandatory, $180 fee. Preregistration for classes offered. 1-day session held in June or early August. **Housing:** Coed dorms, special housing for disabled, apartments, wellness housing available. $200 fully refundable deposit, deadline 5/1. Single sex floors in coed dorms available. **Activities:** Bands, choral groups, dance, drama, film society, literary magazine, music ensembles, musical theater, opera, radio station, student government, student newspaper, symphony orchestra, Jewish, Protestant, Catholic, Islamic Society, Baha'i religious organizations, Inter-Varsity Christian Fellowship, international club, Chinese association, Indian student association, Pakistan club, African students association.

Athletics. NCAA. **Intercollegiate:** Baseball M, basketball, cross-country, diving, football (tackle) M, lacrosse, soccer, softball W, swimming, tennis, track and field, volleyball W. **Intramural:** Basketball, softball. **Team name:** Seawolves.

Student services. Adult student services, alcohol/substance abuse counseling, chaplain/spiritual director, career counseling, services for economically disadvantaged, student employment services, financial aid counseling, health services, minority student services, on-campus daycare, personal counseling, placement for graduates, veterans' counselor, women's services. **Physically disabled:** Services for visually, speech, hearing impaired.

Contact. E-mail: enroll@stonybrook.edu
Phone: (631) 632-6868 Toll-free number: (800) 872-7869
Fax: (631) 632-9898
Judith Burke-Berhannan, Dean of Admissions, State University of New York at Stony Brook, 118 Administration Building, Stony Brook, NY 11794-1901

State University of New York College at Brockport

Brockport, New York **CB member**
www.brockport.edu **CB code: 2537**

- Public 4-year liberal arts college
- Residential campus in small town
- 6,892 degree-seeking undergraduates: 9% part-time, 57% women, 6% African American, 1% Asian American, 3% Hispanic American, 1% international
- 1,123 degree-seeking graduate students
- 44% of applicants admitted
- SAT or ACT (ACT writing optional) required
- 63% graduate within 6 years

General. Founded in 1867. Regionally accredited. **Degrees:** 1,610 bachelor's awarded; master's offered. **ROTC:** Army, Naval, Air Force. **Location:** 16 miles from Rochester. **Calendar:** Semester, limited summer session. **Full-time faculty:** 316 total; 84% have terminal degrees, 17% minority, 47% women. **Part-time faculty:** 274 total; 32% have terminal degrees, 8% minority, 52% women. **Class size:** 44% < 20, 49% 20-39, 4% 40-49, 3% 50-99, less than 1% >100. **Special facilities:** Aquaculture ponds, unidata weather information system, weather radio receiver, nuclear laboratory, high resolution germanium detector, research vessel on Lake Ontario, electron microscope, two supercomputers, Doppler radar system, hydrotherapy room, parallel supercomputer, ultramodern dance facilities including green room.

Freshman class profile. 8,545 applied, 3,775 admitted, 994 enrolled.

Mid 50% test scores			
SAT critical reading:	480-570	Rank in top quarter:	55%
SAT math:	500-590	Rank in top tenth:	18%
ACT composite:	21-26	End year in good standing:	100%
GPA 3.75 or higher:	29%	Return as sophomores:	84%
GPA 3.50-3.74:	21%	Out-of-state:	2%
GPA 3.0-3.49:	37%	Live on campus:	89%
GPA 2.0-2.99:	12%	International:	1%

Basis for selection. High school academic record including number of academic units, GPA, class rank, test scores important. Recommendations, essay, extracurricular activities strongly recommended. Recommend student take SAT or ACT for the first time in junior year of high school. Interview required in some cases; auditions required for dance and theater acting. **Homeschooled:** Statement describing homeschool structure and mission, transcript of courses and grades, state high school equivalency certificate, letter of recommendation (nonparent) required. Outline of courses completed at high school level, official test scores (SAT/ACT), personal essay, 2 letters of recommendation, and biography of books read during high school program required.

High school preparation. College-preparatory program recommended. 18 units required. Required and recommended units include English 4, mathematics 3-4, social studies 4, science 3-4 (laboratory 1), foreign language 3, computer science 1, visual/performing arts 1 and academic electives 4.

2008-2009 Annual costs. Tuition/fees: $5,444; $11,704 out-of-state. Room/board: $8,630. Books/supplies: $3,202. Personal expenses: $1,621.

2007-2008 Financial aid. Need-based: 868 full-time freshmen applied for aid; 624 were judged to have need; 620 of these received aid. Average need met was 84%. Average scholarship/grant was $4,198; average loan $4,340. 43% of total undergraduate aid awarded as scholarships/grants, 57% as loans/jobs. **Non-need-based:** Awarded to 796 full-time undergraduates, including 261 freshmen. Scholarships awarded for academics, alumni affiliation, art, leadership, minority status, ROTC, state residency.

Application procedures. Admission: Priority date 2/1; no deadline. $40 fee, may be waived for applicants with need. Admission notification on a rolling basis beginning on or about 11/15. Must reply by May 1 or within 3 week(s) if notified thereafter. **Financial aid:** Priority date 2/15; no closing date. FAFSA required. Applicants notified on a rolling basis starting 3/15; must reply by 5/1 or within 4 week(s) of notification.

Academics. Time/credit-shortened B.S. degree, experiential learning, domestic and international internships through Delta College. 3-1-3 program allows 30 college credits to be earned during student's senior year of high school. **Special study options:** Accelerated study, combined bachelor's/graduate degree, cross-registration, distance learning, double major, dual enrollment of high school students, honors, independent study, internships, New York semester, semester at sea, student-designed major, study abroad, teacher certification program, Washington semester. **Credit/placement by examination:** AP, CLEP, IB, institutional tests. 90 credit hours maximum toward bachelor's degree. **Support services:** Learning center, pre-admission summer program, reduced course load, study skills assistance, tutoring, writing center.

Honors college/program. Freshman applicants should have high school average of at least a 91 and SAT of 1150 (exclusive of Writing) or ACT of 25. The average honors student has a 93 GPA and a 1220 SAT and/or 27 ACT.

Majors. Area/ethnic studies: African, African-American, women's. **Biology:** General, aquatic, biochemistry, biotechnology, cellular/molecular, environmental, exercise physiology. **Business:** Accounting, business admin, finance, international, international marketing. **Communications:** General, broadcast journalism, journalism, media studies. **Computer sciences:** General, computer science. **Conservation:** General, environmental science, environmental studies. **Education:** General, bilingual, biology, chemistry, developmentally delayed, elementary, English, health, history, mathematics, physical, physics, science, secondary, social studies, Spanish, special. **Foreign languages:** General, French, Spanish. **Health:** Athletic training, clinical lab technology, health care admin, nursing (RN), predental, premedicine, preveterinary. **History:** General. **Math:** General. **Parks/recreation:** General, facilities management, sports admin. **Philosophy/religion:** Philosophy. **Physical sciences:** Atmospheric science, chemistry, geology, hydrology, meteorology, physics, planetary. **Protective services:** Police science, security management. **Psychology:** General. **Public administration:** Social work. **Science technology:** Biological. **Social sciences:** Anthropology, international relations, political science, sociology. **Visual/performing arts:** General, art, dance, dramatic, studio arts.

Computing on campus. 750 workstations in dormitories, library, computer center, student center. Dormitories wired for high-speed internet access and linked to campus network. Commuter students can connect to campus network. Online course registration, online library, helpline, wireless network available.

Student life. Freshman orientation: Available. $145 fee. Preregistration for classes offered. 24-hour program held in late June and early July. Students are given their course schedule and take a required Computer Skills Exam. A parent/family program runs parallel to the student orientation. **Housing:** Guaranteed on-campus for freshmen. Coed dorms, special housing for disabled, apartments, wellness housing available. $100 nonrefundable deposit, deadline 5/1. Special living options available include freshman first-year experience program, transfer student program, health club, scholar floors, single-sex areas, adult, 24-hour quiet, academic excellence floors. **Activities:** Campus ministries, choral groups, dance, drama, international student organizations, literary magazine, musical theater, radio station, student government, student newspaper, TV station, Organization for Students of African Descent, Association of Latin American Students, Alpha Chi Honor Society, Caribbean club, women's center, Brockport Adult Student Organization, peer counseling, student alumni association, Native American student organization.

Athletics. NCAA. **Intercollegiate:** Baseball M, basketball, cross-country, diving, field hockey W, football (tackle) M, gymnastics W, ice hockey M, lacrosse, soccer, softball W, swimming, tennis W, track and field, volleyball W, wrestling M. **Intramural:** Badminton, basketball, bowling, football (non-tackle), racquetball, soccer, softball, table tennis, volleyball. **Team name:** Golden Eagles.

Student services. Alcohol/substance abuse counseling, chaplain/spiritual director, career counseling, services for economically disadvantaged, student employment services, financial aid counseling, health services, legal services, minority student services, on-campus daycare, personal counseling, placement for graduates, veterans' counselor, women's services. **Physically disabled:** Services for visually, speech, hearing impaired.

Contact. E-mail: admit@brockport.edu
Phone: (585) 395-2751 Fax: (585) 395-5452
Bernard Valento, Director of Undergraduate Admissions, State University of New York College at Brockport, 350 New Campus Drive, Brockport, NY 14420-2915

State University of New York College at Buffalo

Buffalo, New York **CB member**
www.buffalostate.edu **CB code: 2533**

- Public 4-year liberal arts and teachers college
- Commuter campus in large city
- 9,172 degree-seeking undergraduates: 10% part-time, 59% women, 15% African American, 2% Asian American, 5% Hispanic American, 1% Native American, 1% international
- 1,760 degree-seeking graduate students
- 45% of applicants admitted
- SAT or ACT (ACT writing optional), SAT Subject Tests required
- 43% graduate within 6 years; 6% enter graduate study

General. Founded in 1867. Regionally accredited. **Degrees:** 1,767 bachelor's awarded; master's offered. **ROTC:** Army. **Location:** 450 miles from New York City, 250 miles from Cleveland. **Calendar:** Semester, limited summer session. **Full-time faculty:** 431 total; 74% have terminal degrees, 19% minority, 47% women. **Part-time faculty:** 361 total; 16% have terminal degrees, 8% minority, 53% women. **Special facilities:** Planetarium, performing arts center, center for environmental research and education, child care center, art center, Great Lakes research facility.

Freshman class profile. 10,304 applied, 4,662 admitted, 1,559 enrolled.

Mid 50% test scores		**GPA 2.0-2.99:**	30%
SAT critical reading:	430-530	**Return as sophomores:**	78%
SAT math:	440-540	**Out-of-state:**	2%
GPA 3.75 or higher:	7%	**International:**	1%
GPA 3.50-3.74:	12%	**Fraternities:**	1%
GPA 3.0-3.49:	51%	**Sororities:**	1%

Basis for selection. High school GPA, class rank, test scores important. Recommendations, essay, interview, volunteer work, work experience and extracurricular activities also considered. Portfolio required for fine arts program.

High school preparation. 17 units recommended. Required and recommended units include English 4, mathematics 2-3, science 2-3, foreign language 3 and academic electives 4.

2008-2009 Annual costs. Tuition/fees: $5,375; $11,635 out-of-state. Room/board: $9,064. Books/supplies: $900. Personal expenses: $1,000.

2007-2008 Financial aid. All financial aid based on need. 1,220 full-time freshmen applied for aid; 1,199 were judged to have need; 1,199 of these received aid. Average need met was 71%. Average scholarship/grant was $4,944; average loan $3,128. 52% of total undergraduate aid awarded as scholarships/grants, 48% as loans/jobs.

Application procedures. Admission: No deadline. $40 fee, may be waived for applicants with need. Admission notification on a rolling basis beginning on or about 12/15. Must reply by May 1 or within 4 week(s) if notified thereafter. **Financial aid:** Priority date 3/15, closing date 5/1. FAFSA required. Applicants notified on a rolling basis starting 5/1; must reply within 4 week(s) of notification.

Academics. Special study options: Cooperative education, cross-registration, distance learning, double major, dual enrollment of high school students, ESL, exchange student, honors, independent study, internships, liberal arts/career combination, New York semester, study abroad, teacher certification program, Washington semester. **Credit/placement by examination:** AP, CLEP, IB, institutional tests. 30 credit hours maximum toward bachelor's degree. **Support services:** Learning center, pre-admission summer program, reduced course load, remedial instruction, study skills assistance, tutoring.

Honors college/program. High school students must have GPA of 90 or higher (or rank within the top 10 percent of their graduating class) and SAT scores of 1100 (exclusive of Writing) or higher. Advanced Placement courses with grades of B or better, cocurricular activities, and community involvement also considered.

Majors. Architecture: Urban/community planning. **Biology:** General. **Business:** General, business admin, fashion, hospitality admin, hospitality/recreation, office management. **Communications:** General, broadcast journalism, journalism, media studies. **Computer sciences:** General, information systems, programming. **Education:** General, art, biology, business, chemistry, early childhood, elementary, emotionally handicapped, English, foreign languages, French, health occupations, kindergarten/preschool, mathematics, mentally handicapped, music, physical, physically handicapped, physics, reading, sales/marketing, science, secondary, social studies, Spanish, speech impaired, technology/industrial arts, trade/industrial, voc/tech. **Engineering technology:** Electrical, electromechanical, industrial, mechanical. **Family/consumer sciences:** Clothing/textiles, food/nutrition. **Foreign languages:** French, Spanish. **Health:** Speech pathology. **History:** General. **Liberal arts:** Humanities. **Math:** General. **Parks/recreation:** Health/fitness. **Philosophy/religion:** Philosophy. **Physical sciences:** Chemistry, geology, physics, planetary. **Protective services:** Criminal justice, forensics. **Psychology:** General. **Public administration:** Social work. **Social sciences:** Anthropology, economics, geography, political science, sociology. **Visual/performing arts:** General, art history/conservation, commercial/advertising art, dramatic, fashion design, fiber arts, interior design, metal/jewelry, painting, photography, printmaking, sculpture, studio arts, theater arts management.

Most popular majors. Business/marketing 11%, communications/journalism 6%, education 31%, social sciences 7%, visual/performing arts 6%.

Computing on campus. 900 workstations in dormitories, library, computer center, student center. Dormitories wired for high-speed internet access and linked to campus network. Commuter students can connect to campus network. Online course registration, online library, helpline, repair service, wireless network available.

Student life. Freshman orientation: Mandatory, $175 fee. Preregistration for classes offered. **Housing:** Coed dorms, apartments, wellness housing available. $100 fully refundable deposit, deadline 7/1. Apartments for students with dependent children available. **Activities:** Bands, campus ministries, choral groups, dance, drama, film society, international student organizations, literary magazine, music ensembles, radio station, student government, student newspaper, Newman Club, Amnesty International, public interest groups, African American student organization, Adelante Estudiantes, Native American student organization, Muslim student organization, Caribbean student organization.

Athletics. NCAA. **Intercollegiate:** Basketball, cross-country, diving, football (tackle) M, ice hockey M, lacrosse W, soccer, softball W, swimming, tennis W, track and field, volleyball W. **Intramural:** Basketball, football (tackle) M, racquetball, soccer, softball, volleyball. **Team name:** Bengals.

Student services. Adult student services, career counseling, student employment services, health services, minority student services, on-campus daycare, personal counseling, placement for graduates, veterans' counselor. **Physically disabled:** Services for visually, speech, hearing impaired.

Contact. E-mail: admissions@buffalostate.edu
Phone: (716) 878-4017 Fax: (716) 878-6100
Lesa Loritts, Director of Admissions, State University of New York College at Buffalo, 1300 Elmwood Avenue, Moot Hall, Buffalo, NY 14222-1095

State University of New York College at Cortland

Cortland, New York **CB member**
www.cortland.edu **CB code: 2538**

- Public 4-year liberal arts and teachers college
- Residential campus in large town
- 6,096 degree-seeking undergraduates: 2% part-time, 57% women, 3% African American, 1% Asian American, 6% Hispanic American, 1% Native American, 1% international
- 1,035 degree-seeking graduate students
- 41% of applicants admitted
- SAT or ACT (ACT writing recommended), application essay required
- 63% graduate within 6 years; 50% enter graduate study

General. Founded in 1868. Regionally accredited. **Degrees:** 1,275 bachelor's awarded; master's offered. **ROTC:** Army, Air Force. **Location:** 35 miles from Syracuse, 20 miles from Ithaca. **Calendar:** Semester, limited summer session. **Full-time faculty:** 306 total; 74% have terminal degrees, 12% minority, 49% women. **Part-time faculty:** 269 total; 16% have terminal degrees, 4% minority, 53% women. **Class size:** 40% < 20, 50% 20-39, 4% 40-49, 6% 50-99, 1% >100. **Special facilities:** Raquette Lake outdoor education complex; Brauer education center (geology field station); Hoxie Gorge Nature Preserve; Dowd Art Gallery; Bowers science museum; Brooks ethnographic teaching museum; center for speech & hearing disorders.

Freshman class profile. 11,573 applied, 4,703 admitted, 1,172 enrolled.

Mid 50% test scores		**Rank in top quarter:**	45%
SAT critical reading:	510-590	**Rank in top tenth:**	10%
SAT math:	480-560	**End year in good standing:**	85%
GPA 3.75 or higher:	18%	**Return as sophomores:**	81%
GPA 3.50-3.74:	20%	**Out-of-state:**	3%
GPA 3.0-3.49:	41%	**Live on campus:**	98%
GPA 2.0-2.99:	20%		

Basis for selection. Primary consideration given to course selection and performance. SAT/ACT scores, class rank, extracurricular activities, personal statement/essay, recommendations also enter into decision. Additional consideration for special talents, interview, alumni relation, geographical residence, minority status, volunteer work, work experience. Audition required for musical theater program; portfolio required for art studio program.

High school preparation. College-preparatory program required. Required and recommended units include English 4, mathematics 3-4, social studies 4, science 3-4 and foreign language 3-4. 2 units in math, science, or foreign language can be compensated for by 4+ units or advanced course work in another one of the three areas.

2008-2009 Annual costs. Tuition/fees: $5,499; $11,759 out-of-state. Room/board: $9,170. Books/supplies: $1,000. Personal expenses: $1,665.

2007-2008 Financial aid. Need-based: 1,072 full-time freshmen applied for aid; 673 were judged to have need; 659 of these received aid. Average need met was 73%. Average scholarship/grant was $3,043; average loan $3,747. 44% of total undergraduate aid awarded as scholarships/grants, 56% as loans/jobs. **Non-need-based:** Awarded to 1,386 full-time undergraduates, including 298 freshmen. Scholarships awarded for academics, art, leadership, minority status, music/drama, state residency.

Application procedures. Admission: Priority date 2/28; no deadline. $40 fee, may be waived for applicants with need. Admission notification on a rolling basis beginning on or about 1/2. Must reply by May 1 or within 4 week(s) if notified thereafter. **Financial aid:** Priority date 3/1; no closing date. FAFSA required. Applicants notified on a rolling basis starting 3/15; must reply by 5/1 or within 4 week(s) of notification.

Academics. Special study options: Combined bachelor's/graduate degree, cooperative education, cross-registration, distance learning, double major, dual enrollment of high school students, exchange student, honors, independent study, internships, liberal arts/career combination, student-designed major, study abroad, teacher certification program, Washington semester. **Credit/placement by examination:** AP, CLEP, IB, institutional tests. 30 credit hours maximum toward bachelor's degree. **Support services:** Learning center, pre-admission summer program, reduced course load, study skills assistance, tutoring, writing center.

Honors college/program. Open to entering fall freshmen and rising sophomores. Applicants should have exceptional academic record based on grades, standardized tests, course selection and extracurricular activities. To complete Honors Program, students must take at least 24 credits of honors-level courses, by taking combination of specially designated honors courses, contract courses and a course in which they complete the required honors thesis. Students also may use maximum of 2 Writing Intensive (WRIT) courses beyond the all-college requirements toward completion of the honors program.

Majors. Area/ethnic studies: African-American. **Biology:** General, biomedical sciences. **Communications:** General, organizational. **Education:** Biology, chemistry, elementary, English, ESL, French, health, kindergarten/preschool, mathematics, physical, physics, science, social studies, Spanish, special, speech impaired. **Foreign languages:** French, Spanish. **Health:** Athletic training, audiology/speech pathology, health services, recreational therapy. **History:** General. **Math:** General. **Parks/recreation:** General, exercise sciences, facilities management, sports admin. **Philosophy/religion:** Philosophy. **Physical sciences:** Chemistry, geology, physics. **Psychology:** General. **Public administration:** Community org/advocacy. **Social sciences:** Anthropology, criminology, economics, geography, international relations, political science, sociology. **Visual/performing arts:** Art, commercial/advertising art, studio arts.

Most popular majors. Communications/journalism 6%, education 41%, parks/recreation 16%, social sciences 15%.

Computing on campus. 838 workstations in dormitories, library, computer center, student center. Dormitories wired for high-speed internet access and linked to campus network. Commuter students can connect to campus network. Online course registration, online library, helpline, repair service, wireless network available.

Student life. Freshman orientation: Mandatory, $140 fee. Preregistration for classes offered. 1-1/2 day program during the summer includes overnight with faculty, staff and other students. **Policies:** All students must agree to abide by Code of Student Conduct. Freshmen/sophomores/transfers required to live on campus. **Housing:** Guaranteed on-campus for freshmen. Coed dorms, special housing for disabled, apartments, cooperative housing, wellness housing available. $150 nonrefundable deposit, deadline 5/1. Leadership house, quiet atmosphere, transfer floor. **Activities:** Campus ministries, choral groups, dance, drama, film society, international student organizations, literary magazine, music ensembles, Model UN, musical theater, radio station, student government, student newspaper, symphony orchestra, TV station, Agape, Hillel, Black student union, Caribbean student association, La Familia Latina, Habitat for Humanity, AIDS Prevention & Awareness, Colleges Against Cancer, Cortland Against All Rape, New York public interest research group.

Athletics. NCAA. **Intercollegiate:** Baseball M, basketball, cross-country, diving, field hockey W, football (non-tackle) M, football (tackle) M, golf W, gymnastics W, ice hockey, lacrosse, racquetball, soccer, softball W, swimming, tennis W, track and field, volleyball W, wrestling M. **Intramural:** Archery, badminton, basketball, bowling, football (non-tackle), golf, racquetball, soccer, softball, table tennis, tennis, volleyball, water polo, weight lifting. **Team name:** Red Dragons.

Student services. Adult student services, alcohol/substance abuse counseling, chaplain/spiritual director, career counseling, student employment services, financial aid counseling, health services, on-campus daycare, personal counseling, placement for graduates, veterans' counselor. **Physically disabled:** Services for visually, speech, hearing impaired.

Contact. E-mail: admissions@cortland.edu
Phone: (607) 753-4712 Fax: (607) 753-5998
Mark Yacavone, Director of Admissions, State University of New York College at Cortland, PO Box 2000, Cortland, NY 13045-0900

State University of New York College at Fredonia

Fredonia, New York **CB member**
www.fredonia.edu **CB code: 2539**

- Public 4-year liberal arts college
- Residential campus in large town
- 5,163 degree-seeking undergraduates: 3% part-time, 56% women, 3% African American, 1% Asian American, 3% Hispanic American, 1% international
- 370 degree-seeking graduate students
- 52% of applicants admitted
- SAT or ACT (ACT writing optional), application essay required
- 61% graduate within 6 years

General. Founded in 1826. Regionally accredited. **Degrees:** 1,120 bachelor's awarded; master's offered. **Location:** 45 miles from Buffalo, 50 miles from Erie, Pennsylvania. **Calendar:** Semester, limited summer session. **Full-time faculty:** 242 total; 80% have terminal degrees, 8% minority, 45% women. **Part-time faculty:** 195 total; 14% have terminal degrees, 4% minority, 47% women. **Class size:** 43% < 20, 44% 20-39, 5% 40-49, 6% 50-99, 2% >100. **Special facilities:** Arts center, communication lab, sound recording studios, education and local history museums.

Freshman class profile. 6,489 applied, 3,360 admitted, 1,188 enrolled.

Mid 50% test scores		**Rank in top tenth:**	16%
SAT critical reading:	500-590	**End year in good standing:**	82%
SAT math:	510-600	**Return as sophomores:**	85%
ACT composite:	21-26	**Out-of-state:**	2%
GPA 3.75 or higher:	19%	**Live on campus:**	90%
GPA 3.50-3.74:	26%	**International:**	1%
GPA 3.0-3.49:	41%	**Fraternities:**	3%
GPA 2.0-2.99:	14%	**Sororities:**	3%
Rank in top quarter:	48%		

Basis for selection. Academic achievement, test results and subjects taken given priority. Counselor recommendations, resume with supporting materials important when priority credentials marginal. Audition required for acting, music, musical performance, musical theater, production design. Portfolio required for all Visual Arts and New Media programs. **Home-schooled:** Submit all documentation of subject areas covered.

High school preparation. College-preparatory program recommended. 20 units required; 23 recommended. Required and recommended units include English 4, mathematics 3-4, social studies 4, science 3-4 (laboratory 3), foreign language 3-4, computer science 1, visual/performing arts 1 and academic electives 1.

2008-2009 Annual costs. Tuition/fees: $5,588; $11,848 out-of-state. Room/board: $9,130. Books/supplies: $1,050. Personal expenses: $688.

2008-2009 Financial aid. Need-based: 1,042 full-time freshmen applied for aid; 710 were judged to have need; 705 of these received aid. Average need met was 70%. Average scholarship/grant was $3,628; average loan $3,705. 48% of total undergraduate aid awarded as scholarships/grants, 52% as loans/jobs. **Non-need-based:** Awarded to 776 full-time undergraduates, including 284 freshmen. Scholarships awarded for academics, alumni affiliation, art, athletics, leadership, minority status, music/drama.

Application procedures. Admission: No deadline. $40 fee, may be waived for applicants with need. Admission notification on a rolling basis beginning on or about 12/1. Must reply by May 1 or within 4 week(s) if notified thereafter. **Financial aid:** Priority date 2/1, closing date 5/15. FAFSA required. Applicants notified on a rolling basis starting 3/10; must reply within 4 week(s) of notification.

Academics. Extensive interdisciplinary studies degree programs offered. **Special study options:** Accelerated study, combined bachelor's/graduate degree, cooperative education, distance learning, double major, honors, independent study, internships, student-designed major, study abroad, teacher certification program, Washington semester. Albany semester, over 90 exchange programs within SUNY system, 13 universities in engineering. **Credit/placement by examination:** AP, CLEP, IB. 30 credit hours maximum toward bachelor's degree. **Support services:** Learning center, study skills assistance, tutoring.

Majors. Area/ethnic studies: American. **Biology:** General, biochemistry, biotechnology, human/medical genetics. **Business:** Accounting, business admin, communications, finance, management information systems, management science. **Communications:** General, broadcast journalism, public relations. **Communications technology:** Recording arts. **Computer sciences:** General. **Conservation:** Environmental studies. **Education:** General, biology, chemistry, early childhood, elementary, English, foreign languages, French, mathematics, music, physics, secondary, social studies, Spanish, speech, speech impaired. **Foreign languages:** French, Spanish. **Health:** Audiology/speech pathology, clinical lab technology, communication disorders, music therapy. **History:** General. **Legal studies:** General, prelaw. **Math:** General. **Philosophy/religion:** Philosophy. **Physical sciences:** Chemistry, geochemistry, geology, geophysics, physics, planetary. **Protective services:** Criminal justice. **Psychology:** General. **Public administration:** Social work. **Social sciences:** Economics, political science, sociology. **Visual/performing arts:** Art, art history/conservation, ceramics, commercial/advertising art, dramatic, drawing, music history, music management, music performance, music theory/composition, painting, piano/organ, printmaking, sculpture, studio arts, theater design, voice/opera.

Most popular majors. Business/marketing 14%, communications/journalism 9%, education 30%, interdisciplinary studies 6%, psychology 7%, social sciences 6%, visual/performing arts 9%.

Computing on campus. 500 workstations in dormitories, library, computer center. Dormitories wired for high-speed internet access and linked to campus network. Commuter students can connect to campus network. Online course registration, online library, helpline, repair service, wireless network available.

Student life. Freshman orientation: Available, $105 fee. Preregistration for classes offered. 2-day program with students and parents in late June and early July; attendance strongly recommended. **Housing:** Guaranteed on-campus for all undergraduates. Coed dorms, single-sex dorms, apartments, wellness housing available. $50 fully refundable deposit, deadline 5/1. **Activities:** Bands, campus ministries, choral groups, dance, drama, literary magazine, music ensembles, musical theater, opera, radio station, student government, student newspaper, symphony orchestra, TV station, Newman Club, Black student union, Young Republicans, service fraternities and sororities, Jewish student union, Young Democrats, Native American Student Association, Latinos Unidos, Intervarsity Christian Fellowship.

Athletics. NCAA. **Intercollegiate:** Baseball M, basketball, cross-country, ice hockey M, lacrosse W, soccer, softball W, swimming, tennis W, track and field, volleyball W. **Intramural:** Baseball M, basketball, field hockey W, handball, ice hockey, lacrosse M, racquetball, soccer, softball, volleyball, water polo. **Team name:** Blue Devils.

Student services. Alcohol/substance abuse counseling, chaplain/spiritual director, career counseling, student employment services, financial aid counseling, health services, legal services, minority student services, on-campus daycare, personal counseling, placement for graduates, veterans' counselor. **Physically disabled:** Services for speech impaired.

Contact. E-mail: admissions.office@fredonia.edu
Phone: (716) 673-3251 Toll-free number: (800) 252-1212
Fax: (716) 673-3249
Christopher Dearth, Director of Admissions, State University of New York College at Fredonia, 178 Central Avenue, Fredonia, NY 14063-1136

State University of New York College at Geneseo

Geneseo, New York — **CB member**
www.geneseo.edu — **CB code: 2540**

- Public 4-year liberal arts college
- Residential campus in small town
- 5,441 degree-seeking undergraduates: 1% part-time, 58% women, 2% African American, 6% Asian American, 4% Hispanic American, 3% international
- 121 degree-seeking graduate students
- 37% of applicants admitted
- SAT or ACT (ACT writing optional), application essay required
- 78% graduate within 6 years; 36% enter graduate study

General. Founded in 1871. Regionally accredited. **Degrees:** 1,132 bachelor's awarded; master's offered. **ROTC:** Army, Air Force. **Location:** 30 miles from Rochester. **Calendar:** Semester, limited summer session. **Full-time faculty:** 251 total; 87% have terminal degrees, 15% minority, 42% women. **Part-time faculty:** 101 total; 22% have terminal degrees, 8% minority, 50% women. **Class size:** 28% < 20, 54% 20-39, 9% 40-49, 6% 50-99, 3% >100. **Special facilities:** Nuclear accelerator, planetarium, 3 theaters, ice arena, arboretum.

Freshman class profile. 10,588 applied, 3,915 admitted, 1,081 enrolled.

Mid 50% test scores		**Rank in top quarter:**	83%
SAT critical reading:	620-700	**Rank in top tenth:**	50%
SAT math:	640-690	**End year in good standing:**	87%
ACT composite:	28-30	**Return as sophomores:**	90%
GPA 3.75 or higher:	48%	**Out-of-state:**	2%
GPA 3.50-3.74:	32%	**Live on campus:**	100%
GPA 3.0-3.49:	18%	**International:**	4%
GPA 2.0-2.99:	2%		

Basis for selection. Rigor of high school preparation, high school GPA, class rank, test scores, school and community activities, special talent, leadership, personal essay important. Special consideration given to minority applicants, children and grandchildren of alumni. Audition required for dramatic arts, music programs; portfolio required for art programs. **Homeschooled:** Statement describing homeschool structure and mission, transcript of courses and grades, state high school equivalency certificate, letter of recommendation (nonparent) required. Letter from high school offical or home school agency indicating the student is meeting production requirements.

High school preparation. College-preparatory program recommended. 20 units recommended. Recommended units include English 4, mathematics 4, social studies 4, science 4 and foreign language 4. Music, art also recommended. 4 math required for computer science and business majors.

2008-2009 Annual costs. Tuition/fees: $5,658; $11,918 out-of-state. Room/board: $9,070. Books/supplies: $800. Personal expenses: $800.

2008-2009 Financial aid. Need-based: 884 full-time freshmen applied for aid; 392 were judged to have need; 392 of these received aid. Average need met was 72%. Average scholarship/grant was $2,090; average loan $3,932. 47% of total undergraduate aid awarded as scholarships/grants, 53% as loans/jobs. **Non-need-based:** Awarded to 913 full-time undergraduates, including 253 freshmen. Scholarships awarded for academics, art, leadership, minority status, music/drama, religious affiliation, ROTC, state residency.

Application procedures. Admission: Closing date 1/1 (postmark date). $40 fee, may be waived for applicants with need. Admission notification on a rolling basis beginning on or about 3/1. Must reply by 5/1. **Financial aid:** Closing date 2/15. FAFSA required. Applicants notified on a rolling basis starting 3/15; must reply by 5/1.

Academics. Special study options: Combined bachelor's/graduate degree, cross-registration, double major, ESL, honors, independent study, internships, study abroad, teacher certification program, Washington semester. Albany semester, 3-2 engineering, 3-3 engineering, 4-1 MBA, 3-4 dentistry, 3-4 optometry, 3-4 osteopathic medicine, 3-2 or 3-1 nursing, 3-3 physical therapy, pre-med and pre-law advisory program. **Credit/placement by examination:** AP, CLEP, IB, SAT, ACT, institutional tests. 30 credit hours maximum toward bachelor's degree. **Support services:** Learning center, pre-admission summer program, reduced course load, study skills assistance, tutoring, writing center.

Majors. **Area/ethnic studies:** African-American, American. **Biology:** General, biochemistry, biophysics. **Business:** General, accounting, business admin. **Communications:** General. **Computer sciences:** General. **Education:** Biology, chemistry, early childhood, elementary, English, French, mathematics, physics, science, social studies, Spanish, special. **Foreign languages:** Comparative lit, French, Spanish. **Health:** Communication disorders, speech pathology. **History:** General. **Math:** General. **Philosophy/religion:** Philosophy. **Physical sciences:** Chemistry, geochemistry, geology, geophysics, physics. **Psychology:** General. **Social sciences:** Anthropology, economics, geography, international relations, political science, sociology. **Visual/performing arts:** Art history/conservation, dramatic, music performance, studio arts.

Most popular majors. Biology 10%, business/marketing 15%, communications/journalism 6%, education 27%, psychology 9%, social sciences 13%.

Computing on campus. PC or laptop required. 900 workstations in dormitories, library, computer center, student center. Dormitories wired for high-speed internet access and linked to campus network. Commuter students can connect to campus network. Online course registration, helpline, student web hosting, wireless network available.

Student life. **Freshman orientation:** Available, $140 fee. Preregistration for classes offered. 5 sessions, 2 days each, during June and July. **Housing:** Guaranteed on-campus for freshmen. Coed dorms, wellness housing available. $150 fully refundable deposit, deadline 5/1. Special interest housing available. Some fraternities/sororities have housing independent of college. **Activities:** Bands, campus ministries, choral groups, dance, drama, international student organizations, literary magazine, music ensembles, Model UN, musical theater, radio station, student government, student newspaper, symphony orchestra, TV station, 171 organizations and clubs, interfaith center.

Athletics. NCAA. **Intercollegiate:** Basketball, cross-country, diving, equestrian W, field hockey W, ice hockey M, lacrosse, soccer, softball W, swimming, tennis W, track and field, volleyball W. **Intramural:** Badminton, basketball, football (non-tackle), racquetball, skiing, soccer, softball, squash, table tennis, tennis, volleyball, water polo M. **Team name:** Blue Knights, Lady Knights.

Student services. Alcohol/substance abuse counseling, chaplain/spiritual director, career counseling, services for economically disadvantaged, student employment services, financial aid counseling, health services, legal services, minority student services, on-campus daycare, personal counseling, placement for graduates, veterans' counselor, women's services. **Physically disabled:** Services for visually, speech, hearing impaired.

Contact. E-mail: admissions@geneseo.edu
Phone: (585) 245-5571 Toll-free number: (866) 245-5211
Fax: (585) 245-5550
Kris Shay, Director of Admissions, State University of New York College at Geneseo, 1 College Circle, Geneseo, NY 14454-1471

State University of New York College at Old Westbury

Old Westbury, New York — **CB member**
www.oldwestbury.edu — **CB code: 2866**

- Public 4-year business and liberal arts college
- Commuter campus in small city
- 3,355 degree-seeking undergraduates: 15% part-time, 59% women, 30% African American, 6% Asian American, 18% Hispanic American, 2% international
- 48 degree-seeking graduate students
- 45% of applicants admitted
- SAT or ACT with writing required
- 37% graduate within 6 years; 79% enter graduate study

General. Founded in 1965. Regionally accredited. Curricular focus on interdisciplinary and multicultural academic programs. **Degrees:** 631 bachelor's awarded; master's offered. **ROTC:** Army, Air Force. **Location:** 25 miles from New York City. **Calendar:** Semester, extensive summer session. **Full-time faculty:** 130 total; 86% have terminal degrees, 36% minority, 49% women. **Part-time faculty:** 143 total; 29% have terminal degrees, 22% minority, 55% women. **Class size:** 30% < 20, 69% 20-39, less than 1% 40-49, less than 1% 50-99. **Special facilities:** Language lab, performing arts theatre, recital hall, science laboratories, athletic center.

Freshman class profile. 3,651 applied, 1,630 admitted, 341 enrolled.

Mid 50% test scores			
SAT critical reading:	450-540	Rank in top quarter:	33%
SAT math:	470-550	Rank in top tenth:	7%
SAT writing:	430-510	Return as sophomores:	73%
ACT composite:	21-23	Out-of-state:	3%
GPA 3.75 or higher:	6%	Live on campus:	59%
GPA 3.50-3.74:	11%	International:	2%
GPA 3.0-3.49:	28%	Fraternities:	1%
GPA 2.0-2.99:	52%	Sororities:	1%

Basis for selection. High school GPA, SAT scores, letters of recommendation, interview, personal essay important. SAT Subject Tests recommended. Essay and interview recommended for academically weak students. **Homeschooled:** Statement describing homeschool structure and mission required. Letter from superintendent of local school district verifying home schooling equivalent to high school curriculum required.

High school preparation. 19 units required. Required units include English 4, mathematics 3, social studies 2, history 2, science 3 (laboratory 3), foreign language 2 and academic electives 3. Health and physical education.

2008-2009 Annual costs. Tuition/fees: $5,177; $11,437 out-of-state. Room/board: $9,032. Books/supplies: $800. Personal expenses: $1,210.

2007-2008 Financial aid. **Need-based:** 356 full-time freshmen applied for aid; 353 were judged to have need; 301 of these received aid. Average need met was 45%. Average scholarship/grant was $5,762; average loan $2,088. 51% of total undergraduate aid awarded as scholarships/grants, 49% as loans/jobs. **Non-need-based:** Awarded to 77 full-time undergraduates, including 24 freshmen. Scholarships awarded for academics, alumni affiliation, state residency.

Application procedures. **Admission:** Priority date 12/1; no deadline. $40 fee, may be waived for applicants with need. Admission notification on a rolling basis beginning on or about 1/7. Must reply by May 1 or within 2 week(s) if notified thereafter. **Financial aid:** Priority date 4/1; no closing date. FAFSA, institutional form required. Applicants notified on a rolling basis starting 4/15; must reply within 2 week(s) of notification.

Academics. All freshmen enroll in First-Year Experience program. **Special study options:** Combined bachelor's/graduate degree, cross-registration, distance learning, double major, ESL, exchange student, honors, independent study, internships, liberal arts/career combination, study abroad, teacher certification program, Washington semester. Minority access to research centers, Minority biomedical research. **Credit/placement by examination:** AP, CLEP, IB, SAT, institutional tests. 30 credit hours maximum toward bachelor's degree. Each department has own policy for accepting credit by examination in fulfillment of departmental requirements. 8 credits awarded for minimum of 2 years of active duty in any branch of military service. Veterans may also apply for credit based on specific formal courses of instruction given by military services. **Support services:** Learning center, pre-admission summer program, reduced course load, remedial instruction, study skills assistance, tutoring, writing center.

Honors college/program. High school GPA 90 or above, SAT scores 1100 or higher. The Honors curriculum will be comprised of 24 credits: First-year Seminar; Gen Ed Linked Course; English Composition 2; Internship or Study Abroad or Directed Research (Independent Study) or Civic Engagement Honors Course; Major Course Requirement with Research Component and Capstone Honors Course.

Majors. **Area/ethnic studies:** American. **Biology:** General, biochemistry. **Business:** Accounting, business admin, finance, labor relations, marketing. **Communications:** General. **Computer sciences:** General, information systems. **Education:** Bilingual, biology, chemistry, elementary, mathematics, middle, science, secondary, social studies, Spanish, special. **Foreign languages:** Comparative lit, Spanish. **Liberal arts:** Arts/sciences, humanities. **Math:** General. **Philosophy/religion:** Philosophy. **Physical sciences:** Chemistry. **Psychology:** General. **Social sciences:** General, criminology, sociology. **Visual/performing arts:** General.

Most popular majors. Business/marketing 34%, communications/journalism 8%, education 12%, psychology 12%, social sciences 16%.

Computing on campus. 400 workstations in library, computer center, student center. Dormitories wired for high-speed internet access. Online course registration, online library, helpline, wireless network available.

Student life. **Freshman orientation:** Mandatory, $110 fee. Preregistration for classes offered. Held prior to fall term for 3 days; for new students and parents. A one-day orientation is held prior to the spring term for all new students. **Housing:** Guaranteed on-campus for all undergraduates. Coed dorms, wellness housing available. $50 fully refundable deposit, deadline

5/1. Honors wing. **Activities:** Campus ministries, choral groups, dance, drama, film society, international student organizations, radio station, student government, student newspaper, women's center, Alianza Latina, African People's Organization, Big Brother/Big Sister club, Asian club, Access for All, Council for Unity, Shekinah Chorale.

Athletics. NCAA. **Intercollegiate:** Baseball M, basketball, cross-country, soccer M, softball W, swimming, volleyball W. **Intramural:** Badminton, cheerleading W, equestrian, football (tackle), racquetball, soccer, softball, swimming, tennis, volleyball, weight lifting. **Team name:** Panthers.

Student services. Alcohol/substance abuse counseling, chaplain/spiritual director, career counseling, services for economically disadvantaged, student employment services, financial aid counseling, health services, on-campus daycare, personal counseling, women's services. **Physically disabled:** Services for visually, hearing impaired.

Contact. E-mail: enroll@oldwestbury.edu
Phone: (516) 876-3073 Fax: (516) 876-3307
Mary Marquez Bell, Vice President of Enrollment Services, State University of New York College at Old Westbury, Box 307, Old Westbury, NY 11568-0307

State University of New York College at Oneonta

Oneonta, New York — **CB member**
www.oneonta.edu — **CB code: 2542**

- Public 4-year liberal arts college
- Residential campus in large town
- 5,508 degree-seeking undergraduates: 2% part-time, 58% women, 3% African American, 2% Asian American, 5% Hispanic American, 1% international
- 123 degree-seeking graduate students
- 37% of applicants admitted
- SAT or ACT (ACT writing optional), application essay required
- 60% graduate within 6 years; 42% enter graduate study

General. Founded in 1887. Regionally accredited. **Degrees:** 1,315 bachelor's awarded; master's offered. **Location:** 75 miles from Albany, 175 miles from New York City. **Calendar:** Semester, extensive summer session. **Full-time faculty:** 266 total; 77% have terminal degrees, 18% minority, 47% women. **Part-time faculty:** 223 total; 18% have terminal degrees, 11% minority, 46% women. **Class size:** 42% < 20, 42% 20-39, 12% 40-49, 3% 50-99, less than 1% >100. **Special facilities:** Digital planetarium/theater, observatory, biological field station in Cooperstown, science discovery center, children's center, music recording studio with tunable walls, computer art lab, DNA computing and genomics lab.

Freshman class profile. 12,571 applied, 4,695 admitted, 1,021 enrolled.

Mid 50% test scores			
SAT critical reading:	510-600	GPA 2.0-2.99:	2%
SAT math:	540-610	Rank in top quarter:	65%
ACT composite:	23-26	Rank in top tenth:	23%
GPA 3.75 or higher:	11%	End year in good standing:	94%
GPA 3.50-3.74:	19%	Return as sophomores:	82%
GPA 3.0-3.49:	68%	Out-of-state:	2%
		Live on campus:	98%

Basis for selection. School achievement record, curriculum, test scores most important. Personal experiences, motivations, awards, honors and recommendations considered. Students scoring below 420 on SAT math or below 450 on SAT verbal must take placement tests. High school writing sample can be submitted in place of essay; interview recommended. **Homeschooled:** Statement describing homeschool structure and mission, transcript of courses and grades, state high school equivalency certificate, interview, letter of recommendation (nonparent) required.

High school preparation. College-preparatory program recommended. 16 units required. Required and recommended units include English 4, mathematics 2-3, social studies 3, science 2-3 (laboratory 2) and foreign language 2-3. 15 specific units and 1 additional unit required in math, science, or foreign language.

2008-2009 Annual costs. Tuition/fees: $5,485; $11,745 out-of-state. Room/board: $8,106. Books/supplies: $900. Personal expenses: $1,070.

2008-2009 Financial aid. Need-based: 903 full-time freshmen applied for aid; 565 were judged to have need; 547 of these received aid. Average need met was 58%. Average scholarship/grant was $4,451; average loan $3,494. 52% of total undergraduate aid awarded as scholarships/grants, 48% as loans/jobs. **Non-need-based:** Awarded to 1,247 full-time undergraduates, including 286 freshmen. Scholarships awarded for academics, alumni affiliation, leadership, minority status, music/drama, state residency.

Application procedures. Admission: Priority date 2/1; no deadline. $40 fee, may be waived for applicants with need. Admission notification on a rolling basis beginning on or about 12/1. Must reply by May 1 or within 4 week(s) if notified thereafter. **Financial aid:** Priority date 3/15; no closing date. FAFSA required. Applicants notified on a rolling basis starting 3/1; must reply by 5/1 or within 4 week(s) of notification.

Academics. Special study options: Combined bachelor's/graduate degree, cross-registration, distance learning, double major, ESL, honors, independent study, internships, liberal arts/career combination, New York semester, study abroad, teacher certification program, Washington semester. 3-1 program in fashion with Fashion Institute of Technology; 3-2 program in engineering with Alfred University, Clarkson University, Georgia Institute of Technology, Polytechnic Institute of New York, Rensselaer Polytechnic Institute, SUNY at Binghamton, SUNY Buffalo, Syracuse University; 2-2 program in forestry with SUNY College of Environmental Science and Forestry; 2-2 programs in physical therapy, medical technology, respiratory care, and cytotechnology with SUNY Upstate Medical University, combined bachelor's/graduate degree programs in accounting and management with SUNY Binghamton; 4-1 MBA program with Rochester Institute of Technology; 2-3 option in physical therapy with SUNY Upstate Medical University; 3-1 option in fashion marketing and 2-2 option in fashion design with American Intercontinental University in London. **Credit/placement by examination:** AP, CLEP, IB. 36 credit hours maximum toward bachelor's degree. **Support services:** Learning center, pre-admission summer program, reduced course load, remedial instruction, study skills assistance, tutoring, writing center.

Majors. Area/ethnic studies: African-American, Hispanic-American/Latino/Chicano. **Biology:** General, biochemistry. **Business:** Accounting, fashion, managerial economics. **Communications:** General, media studies. **Communications technology:** Animation/special effects. **Computer sciences:** General, computer graphics, computer science. **Conservation:** Environmental science. **Education:** Biology, chemistry, early childhood, elementary, English, family/consumer sciences, foreign languages, French, history, mathematics, multi-level teacher, physics, science, social science, Spanish. **Family/consumer sciences:** General, child development, clothing/textiles, family studies, food/nutrition. **Foreign languages:** French, Spanish. **History:** General. **Interdisciplinary:** Gerontology. **Math:** General, statistics. **Philosophy/religion:** Philosophy. **Physical sciences:** Atmospheric science, chemistry, geology, hydrology, physics. **Protective services:** Criminal justice. **Psychology:** General. **Social sciences:** Anthropology, economics, geography, political science, sociology. **Visual/performing arts:** Art history/conservation, dramatic, multimedia, music management, studio arts.

Most popular majors. Business/marketing 8%, communications/journalism 10%, education 21%, family/consumer sciences 9%, psychology 6%, social sciences 6%, visual/performing arts 17%.

Computing on campus. 700 workstations in dormitories, library, computer center, student center. Dormitories wired for high-speed internet access and linked to campus network. Commuter students can connect to campus network. Online course registration, online library, helpline, student web hosting, wireless network available.

Student life. Freshman orientation: Available, $100 fee. Preregistration for classes offered. Meet adviser, select courses, register for classes. **Housing:** Guaranteed on-campus for freshmen. Coed dorms, wellness housing available. $100 fully refundable deposit, deadline 5/1. Special interest housing options and apartment-style suites available within residence halls. **Activities:** Bands, campus ministries, choral groups, dance, drama, film society, international student organizations, literary magazine, music ensembles, Model UN, musical theater, opera, radio station, student government, student newspaper, symphony orchestra, TV station, Campus Ambassadors, Newman Club, Hillel, HOLA Hispanic/Latino organization, Indian cultural club, Muslim student association, Students of Color Coalition, international students organization, Democracy Matters, center for social responsibility and community.

Athletics. NCAA. **Intercollegiate:** Baseball M, basketball, cross-country, field hockey W, lacrosse, soccer, softball W, swimming, tennis, track and field, volleyball W, wrestling M. **Intramural:** Basketball, football (non-tackle) W, soccer, softball, volleyball. **Team name:** Red Dragons.

Student services. Adult student services, alcohol/substance abuse counseling, chaplain/spiritual director, career counseling, services for economically disadvantaged, student employment services, financial aid counseling, health services, minority student services, on-campus daycare, personal counseling, placement for graduates, veterans' counselor, women's services. **Physically disabled:** Services for visually, speech, hearing impaired.

Contact. E-mail: admissions@oneonta.edu
Phone: (607) 436-2524 Toll-free number: (800) 786-9123
Fax: (607) 436-3074
Karen Brown, Director of Admissions, State University of New York College at Oneonta, Admissions Office, 116 Alumni Hall, Oneonta, NY 13820-4016

State University of New York College at Plattsburgh

Plattsburgh, New York **CB member**
www.plattsburgh.edu **CB code: 2544**

- Public 4-year liberal arts and teachers college
- Residential campus in large town
- 5,602 degree-seeking undergraduates: 5% part-time, 56% women, 5% African American, 2% Asian American, 4% Hispanic American, 1% Native American, 7% international
- 515 degree-seeking graduate students
- 49% of applicants admitted
- SAT or ACT (ACT writing optional) required
- 54% graduate within 6 years

General. Founded in 1889. Regionally accredited. Residential satellite campus for biotechnology and environmental science majors. **Degrees:** 1,103 bachelor's awarded; master's offered. **ROTC:** Army. **Location:** 60 miles from Montreal, Canada, 30 miles from Burlington, Vermont. **Calendar:** Semester, limited summer session. **Full-time faculty:** 282 total; 83% have terminal degrees, 11% minority, 39% women. **Part-time faculty:** 228 total; 19% have terminal degrees, 7% minority, 60% women. **Class size:** 46% < 20, 40% 20-39, 9% 40-49, 5% 50-99, less than 1% >100. **Special facilities:** Center for art, music, and theater, wilderness tract, planetarium, electron microscope, remote sensing laboratory, NMR spectrophotometer, computer operated infrared spectrophotometer, liquid scintillation counter, auditory research labs, speech and hearing clinic, Alzheimer's disease assistance center, virtual reality simulator lab, traumatic brain injury center.

Freshman class profile. 6,909 applied, 3,410 admitted, 1,028 enrolled.

Mid 50% test scores			
SAT critical reading:	490-570	GPA 2.0-2.99:	37%
SAT math:	500-590	Rank in top quarter:	39%
ACT composite:	21-25	Rank in top tenth:	10%
GPA 3.75 or higher:	4%	Return as sophomores:	79%
GPA 3.50-3.74:	15%	Out-of-state:	6%
GPA 3.0-3.49:	44%	Live on campus:	89%
		International:	4%

Basis for selection. Curriculum, high school GPA, class rank, test scores most important. Trend of grades, school and community activities, personal interview, and recommendations also considered. Equal opportunity program for academically and financially disadvantaged students. Essay and interview recommended for all; audition required for music programs; portfolio required for BFA (bachelor of fine arts) programs. **Homeschooled:** Letter from superintendent of the school district in which the student resides attesting to the completion of program of home institution meeting the requirements of the state of residence.

High school preparation. College-preparatory program required. 14 units required; 21 recommended. Required and recommended units include English 4, mathematics 3-4, social studies 3, history 1, science 3-4, foreign language 3 and academic electives 2.

2008-2009 Annual costs. Tuition/fees: $5,422; $11,682 out-of-state. Room/board: $8,250.

2007-2008 Financial aid. Need-based: 806 full-time freshmen applied for aid; 554 were judged to have need; 546 of these received aid. Average need met was 84%. Average scholarship/grant was $5,434; average loan $4,825. 40% of total undergraduate aid awarded as scholarships/grants, 60% as loans/jobs. **Non-need-based:** Awarded to 2,586 full-time undergraduates, including 600 freshmen. Scholarships awarded for academics, alumni affiliation, art, leadership, minority status, music/drama, ROTC, state residency.

Application procedures. Admission: Priority date 12/1; no deadline. $40 fee, may be waived for applicants with need. Admission notification on a rolling basis beginning on or about 1/15. Must reply by May 1 or within 4 week(s) if notified thereafter. **Financial aid:** Priority date 2/15; no closing date. FAFSA required. Applicants notified on a rolling basis starting 3/15; must reply by 5/1.

Academics. Credit for military experience, pass/fail option. **Special study options:** Combined bachelor's/graduate degree, cooperative education, cross-registration, distance learning, double major, dual enrollment of high school students, ESL, exchange student, honors, independent study, internships, liberal arts/career combination, student-designed major, study abroad, teacher certification program. Semester and academic year programs in Canada, study opportunities abroad in Argentina, Australia, Chile, Uruguay, England, 3-2 program in engineering with Clarkson University, SUNY Stony Brook and Binghamton, Syracuse University, McGill University and University of Vermont, 3-4 BA/OD with SUNY College of Optometry, 4-1 BS/MBA with Clarkson University. **Credit/placement by examination:** AP, CLEP, IB, SAT, ACT, institutional tests. 30 credit hours maximum toward bachelor's degree. **Support services:** Learning center, pre-admission summer program, reduced course load, remedial instruction, study skills assistance, tutoring, writing center.

Majors. Area/ethnic studies: Canadian, Latin American, women's. **Biology:** General, biochemistry, cell/histology, ecology. **Business:** General, accounting, business admin, entrepreneurial studies, finance, hotel/motel admin, international, management information systems, marketing, restaurant/food services, tourism/travel. **Communications:** Journalism, media studies, organizational, radio/tv. **Computer sciences:** General. **Conservation:** General, environmental science. **Education:** Biology, chemistry, computer, early childhood, elementary, English, foreign languages, French, history, mathematics, multi-level teacher, physics, science, social science, social studies, Spanish, special. **Family/consumer sciences:** Family studies, food/nutrition. **Foreign languages:** French, Spanish. **Health:** Audiology/speech pathology, clinical lab science, cytotechnology, nursing (RN). **History:** General. **Liberal arts:** Arts/sciences. **Math:** General. **Parks/recreation:** General. **Philosophy/religion:** Philosophy. **Physical sciences:** Chemistry, geology, physics. **Protective services:** Criminal justice. **Psychology:** General. **Public administration:** Social work. **Social sciences:** Anthropology, economics, geography, political science, sociology. **Visual/performing arts:** General, art, dramatic. **Other:** Fitness and wellness, Global supply chain management.

Most popular majors. Business/marketing 18%, communications/journalism 9%, education 12%, health sciences 7%, psychology 9%, security/protective services 7%, social sciences 7%.

Computing on campus. 566 workstations in dormitories, library, computer center, student center. Dormitories wired for high-speed internet access and linked to campus network. Commuter students can connect to campus network. Online course registration, online library, helpline, repair service, student web hosting, wireless network available.

Student life. Freshman orientation: Available, $75 fee. Preregistration for classes offered. 2-night stay with meals included; simultaneous program for parents; includes course selection and registration. **Housing:** Guaranteed on-campus for all undergraduates. Coed dorms, special housing for disabled, wellness housing available. $50 fully refundable deposit. Living/learning communities available. **Activities:** Bands, choral groups, dance, drama, film society, literary magazine, music ensembles, musical theater, radio station, student government, student newspaper, TV station, Akeba, El Pueblo, environmental action committee, Hillel, Inter-Varsity Christian Fellowship, Newman Association, Points of View, College Democrats, College Republicans.

Athletics. NCAA. **Intercollegiate:** Baseball M, basketball, cross-country, ice hockey, lacrosse M, soccer, softball W, tennis W, track and field, volleyball W. **Intramural:** Basketball, field hockey, football (non-tackle) M, racquetball, softball, tennis, volleyball. **Team name:** Cardinals.

Student services. Adult student services, alcohol/substance abuse counseling, chaplain/spiritual director, career counseling, services for economically disadvantaged, student employment services, financial aid counseling, health services, legal services, minority student services, on-campus daycare, personal counseling, placement for graduates, veterans' counselor, women's services. **Physically disabled:** Services for visually, speech, hearing impaired.

Contact. E-mail: admissions@plattsburgh.edu
Phone: (518) 564-2040 Toll-free number: (888) 673-0012
Fax: (518) 564-2045
Richard Higgins, Associate Vice President for Enrollment Management, State University of New York College at Plattsburgh, Kehoe Administration Building, Plattsburgh, NY 12901

State University of New York College at Potsdam

Potsdam, New York **CB member**
www.potsdam.edu **CB code: 2545**

- Public 4-year liberal arts and teachers college
- Residential campus in large town

- 3,590 degree-seeking undergraduates: 3% part-time, 57% women, 3% African American, 1% Asian American, 3% Hispanic American, 1% Native American, 4% international
- 656 degree-seeking graduate students
- 67% of applicants admitted
- SAT or ACT (ACT writing optional) required
- 51% graduate within 6 years; 42% enter graduate study

General. Founded in 1816. Regionally accredited. **Degrees:** 707 bachelor's awarded; master's offered. **ROTC:** Army, Air Force. **Location:** 150 miles from Syracuse, 80 miles from Montreal, Canada. **Calendar:** Semester, limited summer session. **Full-time faculty:** 271 total; 86% have terminal degrees, 9% minority, 43% women. **Part-time faculty:** 112 total; 30% have terminal degrees, 3% minority, 62% women. **Class size:** 65% < 20, 30% 20-39, 3% 40-49, 2% 50-99, less than 1% >100. **Special facilities:** Electronic music and recording studios, planetarium, seismographic laboratory, 24-hour computer laboratory, concert hall, music theater, anthropology museum, biology museum, teaching resource center.

Freshman class profile. 4,326 applied, 2,910 admitted, 808 enrolled.

Mid 50% test scores		**Rank in top quarter:**	35%
SAT critical reading:	470-570	**Rank in top tenth:**	13%
SAT math:	470-580	**End year in good standing:**	90%
ACT composite:	20-25	**Return as sophomores:**	73%
GPA 3.75 or higher:	19%	**Out-of-state:**	4%
GPA 3.50-3.74:	14%	**Live on campus:**	92%
GPA 3.0-3.49:	34%	**International:**	4%
GPA 2.0-2.99:	33%		

Basis for selection. Admissions decisions based on secondary school record and standardized test scores. Class rank, talent, ability, activities and community service also important. Freshman applicants over the age of 22 are not required to submit SAT or ACT scores. Essays and interviews required for some, but not all applicants. Auditions required for music majors. Auditions encouraged for dance and theatre majors. Portfolios encouraged for art majors. **Homeschooled:** GED required. SAT or ACT required.

High school preparation. College-preparatory program recommended. 13 units required; 21 recommended. Required and recommended units include English 4, mathematics 2-4, social studies 4, science 2-4 (laboratory 1-2), foreign language 4 and visual/performing arts 1.

2008-2009 Annual costs. Tuition/fees: $5,462; $11,722 out-of-state. Room/board: $8,820: Books/supplies: $1,200. Personal expenses: $1,100.

2008-2009 Financial aid. Need-based: 725 full-time freshmen applied for aid; 520 were judged to have need; 515 of these received aid. Average need met was 90%. Average scholarship/grant was $6,153; average loan $3,584. 58% of total undergraduate aid awarded as scholarships/grants, 42% as loans/jobs. **Non-need-based:** Awarded to 1,235 full-time undergraduates, including 441 freshmen. Scholarships awarded for academics, art, leadership, minority status, music/drama, ROTC. **Additional information:** Apply early to access limited, need-based awards.

Application procedures. Admission: No deadline. $40 fee, may be waived for applicants with need. Admission notification on a rolling basis beginning on or about 10/1. Must reply by May 1 for guaranteed enrollment. **Financial aid:** Priority date 3/1; no closing date. FAFSA required. Applicants notified on a rolling basis starting 2/1; must reply by 5/1 or within 4 week(s) of notification.

Academics. Special study options: Combined bachelor's/graduate degree, cross-registration, distance learning, double major, dual enrollment of high school students, exchange student, honors, independent study, internships, liberal arts/career combination, student-designed major, study abroad, teacher certification program. First-year students may enroll in interdisciplinary program to study art, literature, science, and sociology of the Adirondacks. Extension offers undergraduate and graduate courses with emphasis on teacher education. Combined degree options in engineering with Clarkson University and SUNY Binghamton; accounting, engineering or management with SUNY Institute of Technology. **Credit/placement by examination:** AP, CLEP, IB. Credit awarded for International Baccalaureate on course-by-course evaluation. **Support services:** Learning center, pre-admission summer program, reduced course load, study skills assistance, tutoring, writing center.

Majors. Area/ethnic studies: Women's. **Biology:** General, biochemistry. **Business:** Business admin, labor relations, managerial economics. **Computer sciences:** General. **Conservation:** Environmental studies. **Education:** Biology, chemistry, elementary, English, foreign languages, French, mathematics, music, physics, science, social studies, Spanish. **Foreign languages:** French, Spanish. **History:** General. **Math:** General. **Philosophy/religion:** Philosophy. **Physical sciences:** Chemistry, geology, physics. **Protective services:** Criminal justice. **Psychology:** General. **Social sciences:** Anthropology, archaeology, economics, political science, sociology. **Visual/performing arts:** General, art, art history/conservation, dance, dramatic, music management, music performance, music theory/composition.

Most popular majors. Business/marketing 10%, education 27%, English 9%, psychology 9%, social sciences 10%, visual/performing arts 11%.

Computing on campus. 470 workstations in dormitories, library, computer center, student center. Dormitories wired for high-speed internet access and linked to campus network. Commuter students can connect to campus network. Online course registration, online library, helpline, student web hosting, wireless network available.

Student life. Freshman orientation: Available, $165 fee. Preregistration for classes offered. Two-day program. **Policies:** Academic honor code outlines expectations for academic honesty and integrity; code of student rights, responsibilities, and conduct can be found in student handbook. **Housing:** Guaranteed on-campus for all undergraduates. Coed dorms, special housing for disabled, apartments, wellness housing available. $50 fully refundable deposit, deadline 5/1. First-year experience, study intensive. **Activities:** Bands, campus ministries, choral groups, dance, drama, international student organizations, literary magazine, music ensembles, musical theater, opera, radio station, student government, student newspaper, symphony orchestra, Intervarsity Christian Fellowship, Black Student Alliance, Potsdam Association of Native Americans, Caribbean Latin American Student Society, Politics Association, Circle K, Lesbian, Gay, Bisexual and Transgender Association, Students for Peaceful Alternatives, Philosophy Forum, Pagan Studies.

Athletics. NCAA. **Intercollegiate:** Basketball, cheerleading, cross-country, equestrian, golf M, ice hockey, lacrosse, soccer, softball W, swimming, tennis W, volleyball W. **Intramural:** Basketball, football (non-tackle), racquetball, soccer, softball, tennis, volleyball, water polo, weight lifting. **Team name:** Bears.

Student services. Adult student services, alcohol/substance abuse counseling, chaplain/spiritual director, career counseling, services for economically disadvantaged, student employment services, financial aid counseling, health services, legal services, minority student services, on-campus daycare, personal counseling, placement for graduates, veterans' counselor, women's services. **Physically disabled:** Services for visually, speech, hearing impaired.

Contact. E-mail: admissions@potsdam.edu
Phone: (315) 267-2180 Toll-free number: (877) 768-7326
Fax: (315) 267-2163
Thomas Nesbitt, Director of Admissions, State University of New York College at Potsdam, 44 Pierrepont Avenue, Potsdam, NY 13676

State University of New York College of Environmental Science and Forestry

Syracuse, New York — **CB member**
www.esf.edu — **CB code: 2530**

- Public 4-year university and liberal arts college
- Residential campus in small city
- 1,541 degree-seeking undergraduates: 3% part-time, 39% women, 1% African American, 3% Asian American, 3% Hispanic American, 1% Native American, 1% international
- 480 degree-seeking graduate students
- 48% of applicants admitted
- SAT or ACT (ACT writing recommended), application essay required
- 72% graduate within 6 years; 34% enter graduate study

General. Founded in 1911. Regionally accredited. Doctoral granting; focused on the science, engineering, design and management of the environment and natural resources. **Degrees:** 265 bachelor's, 38 associate awarded; master's, doctoral offered. **ROTC:** Army, Air Force. **Location:** 1 mile from downtown. **Calendar:** Semester, limited summer session. **Full-time faculty:** 146 total; 96% have terminal degrees, 11% minority, 24% women. **Part-time faculty:** 27 total; 85% have terminal degrees, 7% minority, 41% women. **Class size:** 77% < 20, 12% 20-39, 4% 40-49, 4% 50-99, 3% >100. **Special facilities:** 6 regional campuses and field stations used for field study and research, 25,000-acre multi-campus forest system, ecological center, wildlife collection, semi-commercial paper mill.

Freshman class profile. 1,568 applied, 756 admitted, 312 enrolled.

Mid 50% test scores		End year in good standing:	96%
SAT critical reading:	520-610	Return as sophomores:	89%
SAT math:	540-630	Out-of-state:	22%
ACT composite:	22-27	Live on campus:	90%
Rank in top quarter:	65%	International:	1%
Rank in top tenth:	25%		

Basis for selection. High school record most important, test scores, essay, and recommendations also important. Applicant should have strong college preparatory program with focus on mathematics and science for most programs and design background preferred for Landscape Architecture. Interview or participation in informational program recommended for all; portfolio required for some landscape architecture applicants. **Homeschooled:** Statement describing homeschool structure and mission required. If no superintendent's statement provided, student must have GED to enroll.

High school preparation. College-preparatory program required. 14 units required; 19 recommended. Required and recommended units include English 4, mathematics 3-4, social studies 3, history 1, science 3-4 (laboratory 3-4) and foreign language 3.

2008-2009 Annual costs. Tuition/fees: $5,136; $11,396 out-of-state. Room and board available through Syracuse University. Books/supplies: $1,200. Personal expenses: $450.

2008-2009 Financial aid. Need-based: 274 full-time freshmen applied for aid; 196 were judged to have need; 196 of these received aid. Average need met was 100%. Average scholarship/grant was $5,000; average loan $5,500. 49% of total undergraduate aid awarded as scholarships/grants, 51% as loans/jobs. **Non-need-based:** Awarded to 337 full-time undergraduates, including 186 freshmen. Scholarships awarded for academics, alumni affiliation, leadership, minority status, ROTC, state residency.

Application procedures. Admission: Priority date 12/1; no deadline. $40 fee, may be waived for applicants with need. Admission notification on a rolling basis beginning on or about 2/1. Must reply by May 1 or within 4 week(s) if notified thereafter. **Financial aid:** Priority date 3/1; no closing date. FAFSA required. Applicants notified on a rolling basis starting 3/15; must reply within 2 week(s) of notification.

Academics. Special study options: Combined bachelor's/graduate degree, cooperative education, cross-registration, dual enrollment of high school students, ESL, honors, independent study, internships, study abroad, teacher certification program. Associate degree programs in forestry technology and land surveying technology offered through The Ranger School in Adirondack Mountains. **Credit/placement by examination:** AP, CLEP, IB, institutional tests. **Support services:** Learning center, pre-admission summer program, reduced course load, study skills assistance, tutoring, writing center.

Majors. Agriculture: Animal sciences, plant protection. **Architecture:** Landscape. **Biology:** Aquatic, biochemistry, biotechnology, conservation, environmental, wildlife. **Business:** Construction management. **Conservation:** General, environmental science, environmental studies, fisheries, forest management, forest resources, forest sciences, forestry, management/policy, wildlife, wood science. **Education:** Biology, chemistry, science. **Engineering:** General, environmental. **Physical sciences:** Chemistry. **Other:** Bioprocess engineering, paper science and engineering, wood products engineering, Natural history and interpretation.

Most popular majors. Architecture 8%, biology 37%, engineering/engineering technologies 22%, natural resources/environmental science 30%.

Computing on campus. 200 workstations in dormitories, library, computer center, student center. Dormitories wired for high-speed internet access and linked to campus network. Commuter students can connect to campus network. Online course registration, online library, helpline, repair service, student web hosting, wireless network available.

Student life. Freshman orientation: Mandatory, $50 fee. Preregistration for classes offered. 4-day program prior to start of fall classes. **Policies:** Freshmen are required to live on campus (in Syracuse University housing) unless they live within commuting distance. **Housing:** Guaranteed on-campus for freshmen. Coed dorms, special housing for disabled, apartments, fraternity/sorority housing, wellness housing available. $400 nonrefundable deposit, deadline 5/1. All on-campus housing available through Syracuse University. SUNY-ESF is located on the campus of Syracuse University. **Activities:** Bands, campus ministries, choral groups, dance, drama, film society, international student organizations, literary magazine, music ensembles, musical theater, radio station, student government, student newspaper, symphony orchestra, undergraduate student association, Alpha Xi Sigma honor society, Wildlife Society, multicultural organization, environmental action coalition, woodsmen's team, creative minds club, green campus initiative, soccer teams, golf team.

Athletics. Intercollegiate: Golf, soccer. **Intramural:** Basketball, football (non-tackle), racquetball, soccer, softball, tennis.

Student services. Alcohol/substance abuse counseling, chaplain/spiritual director, career counseling, services for economically disadvantaged, student employment services, financial aid counseling, health services, legal services, minority student services, personal counseling, placement for graduates, veterans' counselor, women's services. **Physically disabled:** Services for visually, speech, hearing impaired. **Learning disabled:** Comprehensive services available.

Contact. E-mail: esfinfo@esf.edu
Phone: (315) 470-6600 Fax: (315) 470-6933
Susan Sanford, Director of Admissions & Inter-Institutional Relations, State University of New York College of Environmental Science and Forestry, 106 Bray Hall, Syracuse, NY 13210

State University of New York Downstate Medical Center

Brooklyn, New York
www.downstate.edu **CB code: 2534**

- Public two-year upper-division health science and nursing college
- Commuter campus in very large city
- Application essay, interview required

General. Founded in 1858. Regionally accredited. **Degrees:** 189 bachelor's awarded; master's, doctoral, first professional offered. **Articulation:** Agreements with St. Francis College, CUNY Medgar Evers College. **Location:** 4 miles from downtown Brooklyn, 6 miles from downtown Manhattan. **Calendar:** Semester, limited summer session. **Full-time faculty:** 720 total. **Part-time faculty:** 160 total.

Student profile. 324 degree-seeking undergraduates, 1,288 graduate students. 100% entered as juniors. 80% transferred from two-year, 20% transferred from four-year institutions.

Women:	83%	Out-of-state:	4%
Part-time:	43%	25 or older:	72%

Basis for selection. College transcript, application essay, interview required. College of Medicine applicants apply through AMCAS: $65 application fee. Rolling admissions for College of Nursing and College of Health-Related Professions: $30 fee. Each program has different admission requirements. RN/BS program requires New York State Registered Nurse license. Prerequisite courses vary by program. Transfer accepted as juniors.

2008-2009 Annual costs. Tuition/fees: $4,745; $11,005 out-of-state. Reported room-only price is for double standard; other room-only prices vary by accommodation and can range up to $8,504. Room only: $4,663. Books/supplies: $1,358.

Financial aid. Need-based: 55% of total undergraduate aid awarded as scholarships/grants, 45% as loans/jobs.

Application procedures. Admission: Deadline 4/1. $40 fee, may be waived for applicants with need. Application must be submitted on paper. Closing dates for applications differ, depending on program, and begin December 15. **Financial aid:** FAFSA required.

Academics. Special study options: Combined bachelor's/graduate degree, liberal arts/career combination. **Credit/placement by examination:** AP, CLEP. **Support services:** Learning center, reduced course load, tutoring.

Majors. Health: Nursing (RN), physician assistant, sonography.

Student life. Housing: Coed dorms available. **Activities:** Student government, student newspaper.

Athletics. Intramural: Basketball M.

Student services. Health services.

Contact. E-mail: admissions@downstate.edu
Phone: (718) 270-2446 Fax: (718) 270-7592
Shushawna DeOliveira, Director of Admissions & Enrollment, State University of New York Downstate Medical Center, 450 Clarkson Avenue, Box 60, Brooklyn, NY 11203-2098

State University of New York Empire State College

Saratoga Springs, New York — **CB member**
www.esc.edu — **CB code: 2214**

- Public 4-year liberal arts college
- Commuter campus in large town
- 10,993 degree-seeking undergraduates: 63% part-time, 61% women, 13% African American, 2% Asian American, 7% Hispanic American, 5% international
- 815 degree-seeking graduate students
- 81% of applicants admitted
- Application essay required
- 36% graduate within 6 years

General. Founded in 1971. Regionally accredited. No campus or classrooms; students meet with faculty and use facilities at regional centers and units throughout state. Centers in Genesee Valley (Rochester), Long Island (Old Westbury), Metropolitan New York, Hudson Valley (Hartsdale), and Buffalo. Coordinating center at Saratoga Springs. Units in Binghamton, Ithaca, Mid-Hudson (New Paltz), Mohawk Valley (Utica-Rome), North Country (Plattsburgh), Onondaga (Syracuse), Saratoga Springs, Watertown, and International Programs in Athens, Prague, the Dominican Repuplic and several other locations. **Degrees:** 2,167 bachelor's, 611 associate awarded; master's offered. **Calendar:** Continuous, extensive summer session. **Full-time faculty:** 169 total; 98% have terminal degrees, 15% minority, 60% women. **Part-time faculty:** 1,209 total.

Freshman class profile. 1,775 applied, 1,436 admitted, 557 enrolled.

Basis for selection. Requirements for undergraduate admission: completed application, possession of high school diploma or equivalent, ability to pursue college-level work, payment of nonrefundable orientation fee, and completion of the college's orientation process.

2008-2009 Annual costs. Tuition/fees: $4,575; $10,835 out-of-state. Books/supplies: $2,550. Personal expenses: $900.

2007-2008 Financial aid. All financial aid based on need. 36% of total undergraduate aid awarded as scholarships/grants, 64% as loans/jobs.

Application procedures. Admission: Priority date 6/1; no deadline. No application fee. Admission notification on a rolling basis. **Financial aid:** Priority date 4/1; no closing date. FAFSA required. Applicants notified on a rolling basis; must reply within 3 week(s) of notification.

Academics. Special study options: Accelerated study, combined bachelor's/graduate degree, cross-registration, distance learning, double major, external degree, independent study, internships, student-designed major, teacher certification program. Weekend residencies for some specialized programs. **Credit/placement by examination:** AP, CLEP, IB. 40 credit hours maximum toward associate degree, 96 toward bachelor's. **Support services:** Study skills assistance, tutoring, writing center.

Majors. Business: General, labor relations. **Education:** General. **Health:** Nursing (RN). **History:** General. **Interdisciplinary:** Biological/physical sciences. **Liberal arts:** Arts/sciences. **Psychology:** General. **Public administration:** Community org/advocacy. **Social sciences:** General, economics. **Visual/performing arts:** Studio arts.

Most popular majors. Business/marketing 43%, English 7%, physical sciences 7%, psychology 7%, public administration/social services 18%, visual/performing arts 6%.

Computing on campus. 100 workstations in computer center. Commuter students can connect to campus network. Online course registration, online library, helpline available.

Student life. Freshman orientation: Mandatory, $50 fee.

Student services. Adult student services, career counseling, student employment services, veterans' counselor. **Physically disabled:** Services for visually, speech, hearing impaired.

Contact. E-mail: admissions@esc.edu
Phone: (518) 587-2100 Toll-free number: (800) 847-3000
Fax: (518) 587-9759
Jennifer D'Agostino, Director of Admissions, State University of New York Empire State College, 2 Union Avenue, Saratoga Springs, NY 12866

State University of New York Institute of Technology at Utica/Rome

Utica, New York — **CB member**
www.sunyit.edu — **CB code: 0755**

- Public 4-year business and nursing college
- Commuter campus in small city
- 1,993 degree-seeking undergraduates: 25% part-time, 43% women, 8% African American, 3% Asian American, 3% Hispanic American, 1% Native American, 1% international
- 487 degree-seeking graduate students
- 39% of applicants admitted
- SAT or ACT (ACT writing optional) required

General. Founded in 1966. Regionally accredited. **Degrees:** 411 bachelor's awarded; master's offered. **ROTC:** Army. **Location:** 50 miles from Syracuse, 90 miles from Albany. **Calendar:** Semester, limited summer session. **Full-time faculty:** 92 total; 76% have terminal degrees, 17% minority, 39% women. **Part-time faculty:** 105 total; 22% have terminal degrees, 6% minority, 44% women. **Class size:** 59% < 20, 40% 20-39, less than 1% 40-49, less than 1% 50-99.

Freshman class profile. 1,731 applied, 669 admitted, 207 enrolled.

Mid 50% test scores		**End year in good standing:**	88%
SAT critical reading:	480-570	**Return as sophomores:**	70%
SAT math:	510-610	**Out-of-state:**	3%
ACT composite:	20-28	**Live on campus:**	85%
Rank in top quarter:	43%	**International:**	1%
Rank in top tenth:	18%		

Basis for selection. Students must meet minimum SAT/ACT score ranges with competitive high school averages as well as minimum high school unit requirements. **Homeschooled:** Statement describing homeschool structure and mission, transcript of courses and grades, state high school equivalency certificate required. Statement from local public school superintendent that verifies home school curriculum matches NYS Regents Curriculum required.

High school preparation. 17 units required; 25 recommended. Required and recommended units include English 4, mathematics 3-4, social studies 2, history 2, science 3-4 (laboratory 3-4), foreign language 3 and academic electives 2.

2008-2009 Annual costs. Tuition/fees: $5,433; $11,693 out-of-state. Room/board: $8,320. Books/supplies: $900. Personal expenses: $1,315.

2007-2008 Financial aid. Need-based: 186 full-time freshmen applied for aid; 143 were judged to have need; 136 of these received aid. Average scholarship/grant was $2,462; average loan $1,234. 46% of total undergraduate aid awarded as scholarships/grants, 54% as loans/jobs. **Non-need-based:** Awarded to 249 full-time undergraduates, including 11 freshmen. Scholarships awarded for academics.

Application procedures. Admission: No deadline. $40 fee, may be waived for applicants with need. Admission notification on a rolling basis beginning on or about 1/15. Must reply by May 1 or within 4 week(s) if notified thereafter. **Financial aid:** Priority date 3/15; no closing date. FAFSA required. Applicants notified on a rolling basis starting 3/17; must reply within 2 week(s) of notification.

Academics. SUNYIT has four schools that offer professional and technical programs: School of Business, School of Nursing & Health Systems, School of Arts & Sciences and School of Information Systems & Engineering Technologies. **Special study options:** Accelerated study, combined bachelor's/graduate degree, cross-registration, distance learning, double major, dual enrollment of high school students, independent study, internships, liberal arts/career combination. **Credit/placement by examination:** AP, CLEP, IB, SAT, ACT, institutional tests. Credit awarded for International Baccalaureate varies by academic department. **Support services:** Learning center, remedial instruction, study skills assistance, tutoring, writing center.

Majors. Business: General, accounting, business admin, finance. **Computer sciences:** General, information systems. **Engineering:** Electrical. **Engineering technology:** Civil, computer, electrical, industrial, mechanical. **Health:** Health care admin, medical records admin, nursing (RN). **Math:** Applied. **Protective services:** Criminal justice. **Psychology:** General. **Social sciences:** Sociology.

Most popular majors. Business/marketing 28%, communications/journalism 7%, computer/information sciences 10%, engineering/engineering technologies 24%, health sciences 14%, psychology 8%, social sciences 6%.

Computing on campus. 244 workstations in dormitories, library, computer center, student center. Dormitories wired for high-speed internet access and linked to campus network. Commuter students can connect to campus network. Online course registration, online library, student web hosting, wireless network available.

Student life. Freshman orientation: Mandatory. Preregistration for classes offered. **Housing:** Guaranteed on-campus for freshmen. Coed dorms, special housing for disabled available. $150 fully refundable deposit, deadline 5/1. **Activities:** Jazz band, international student organizations, radio station, student government, student newspaper, TV station, black student union, Latino student association.

Athletics. NCAA. **Intercollegiate:** Baseball M, basketball, bowling, cross-country, golf, lacrosse M, soccer, softball W, volleyball W. **Intramural:** Badminton, basketball, bowling, golf, racquetball, soccer, softball, tennis, volleyball. **Team name:** Wildcats.

Student services. Alcohol/substance abuse counseling, chaplain/spiritual director, career counseling, services for economically disadvantaged, student employment services, financial aid counseling, health services, legal services, minority student services, personal counseling, placement for graduates, veterans' counselor, women's services. **Physically disabled:** Services for visually, speech, hearing impaired.

Contact. E-mail: admissions@sunyit.edu
Phone: (315) 792-7500 Toll-free number: (866) 278-6948
Fax: (315) 792-7837
Jennifer Phelan-Ninh, Director of Admissions, State University of New York Institute of Technology at Utica/Rome, Box 3050, Utica, NY 13504-3050

State University of New York Maritime College

Throggs Neck, New York — **CB member**
www.sunymaritime.edu — **CB code: 2536**

- Public 4-year maritime college
- Residential campus in very large city
- 1,432 degree-seeking undergraduates: 6% part-time, 10% women, 6% African American, 4% Asian American, 9% Hispanic American, 7% international
- 184 degree-seeking graduate students
- 80% of applicants admitted
- SAT or ACT (ACT writing optional) required
- 48% graduate within 6 years; 3% enter graduate study

General. Founded in 1874. Regionally accredited. Graduates eligible for commission as officers in Navy, Marine Corps, Coast Guard, Air Force, and commissioned Corps of the National Oceanic and Atmospheric Administration. 3 summer semesters at sea and regiment option required for students interested in obtaining U.S. Merchant Marine Officer's License. **Degrees:** 218 bachelor's, 4 associate awarded; master's offered. **ROTC:** Army, Naval. **Location:** 10 miles from New York City. **Calendar:** Semester, limited summer session. **Full-time faculty:** 66 total; 48% have terminal degrees, 6% minority, 20% women. **Part-time faculty:** 54 total; 28% have terminal degrees, 22% minority, 20% women. **Class size:** 37% < 20, 52% 20-39, 7% 40-49, 2% 50-99, 1% >100. **Special facilities:** 565-foot training ship, training tanker, Center for Simulated Marine Operations, bridge simulator, model basin and towing tank, CAD-CAM facilities, 2 diesel propulsion simulators, maritime museum, sailing center including several 1-ton ocean racers.

Freshman class profile. 1,141 applied, 908 admitted, 398 enrolled.

Mid 50% test scores		**Rank in top quarter:**	24%
SAT critical reading:	460-560	**Rank in top tenth:**	1%
SAT math:	490-590	**End year in good standing:**	81%
ACT composite:	19-24	**Return as sophomores:**	77%
GPA 3.75 or higher:	7%	**Out-of-state:**	27%
GPA 3.50-3.74:	8%	**Live on campus:**	94%
GPA 3.0-3.49:	32%	**International:**	1%
GPA 2.0-2.99:	50%		

Basis for selection. Quality and strength of preparation, school achievement record, including first semester senior grades, class rank, test scores, extracurricular activities considered. Interview and essay recommended. Interviews and essays are not required but highly recommended. **Homeschooled:** Statement describing homeschool structure and mission, transcript of courses and grades, state high school equivalency certificate, letter of recommendation (nonparent) required.

High school preparation. College-preparatory program recommended. 18 units required. Required and recommended units include English 3, mathematics 3-4, social studies 3, history 3, science 3-4 (laboratory 1) and foreign language 3. Math requirement includes algebra, geometry, trigonometry; math beyond trigonometry recommended. Chemistry or physics required; both strongly recommended.

2008-2009 Annual costs. Tuition/fees: $5,426; $11,686 out-of-state. Additional required uniform charges. Room/board: $9,500. Books/supplies: $1,200. Personal expenses: $1,910.

2007-2008 Financial aid. Need-based: 315 full-time freshmen applied for aid; 198 were judged to have need; 196 of these received aid. Average need met was 53%. Average scholarship/grant was $4,958; average loan $3,515. 43% of total undergraduate aid awarded as scholarships/grants, 57% as loans/jobs. **Non-need-based:** Awarded to 230 full-time undergraduates, including 108 freshmen. Scholarships awarded for academics, leadership, ROTC, state residency. **Additional information:** All cadets who are United States citizens, physically qualified for Merchant Marine license, and not yet 25 at time of enrollment eligible to apply for Student Incentive Payment (SIP) of $3,000 per year from Maritime Administration of the Department of Transportation. Out-of-state students who elect to participate in SIP pay in-state tuition fees.

Application procedures. Admission: No deadline. $40 fee, may be waived for applicants with need. Admission notification on a rolling basis beginning on or about 9/15. **Financial aid:** Priority date 3/15, closing date 7/15. FAFSA, institutional form required. Applicants notified on a rolling basis starting 3/15.

Academics. Cadets acquire technical, professional, and leadership experience on training cruises to foreign and domestic ports during annual summer sea terms, while preparing for U.S. Merchant Marine Officer's License. **Special study options:** Cooperative education, distance learning, double major, dual enrollment of high school students, ESL, honors, independent study, internships, semester at sea. United States Coast Guard-issued deck and engine license program. **Credit/placement by examination:** AP, CLEP, IB, institutional tests. 18 credit hours maximum toward associate degree, 18 toward bachelor's. **Support services:** Learning center, pre-admission summer program, reduced course load, study skills assistance, tutoring, writing center.

Majors. Business: General, business admin, marketing, tourism/travel. **Engineering:** General, electrical, industrial, marine, mechanical. **Liberal arts:** Arts/sciences. **Physical sciences:** Atmospheric science.

Most popular majors. Business/marketing 48%, engineering/engineering technologies 45%, physical sciences 6%.

Computing on campus. 130 workstations in dormitories, library, computer center, student center. Dormitories wired for high-speed internet access and linked to campus network. Online course registration, online library, helpline, student web hosting, wireless network available.

Student life. Freshman orientation: Mandatory, $110 fee. Preregistration for classes offered. 2-day, overnight program held in July and August, focusing on small group interaction (each session limited to 85 participants) with the goals of campus knowledge, student networking, and registration. Parents and families can attend an informational brunch. Regimental students required to additionally attend INDOC, a two-week long training period prior to the start of classes. **Policies:** Students can choose from two lifestyle options on campus, either traditional college or Regiment of Cadets. All students governed by the College Code of Conduct and within that all Cadets are governed by the Regimental Rules and Regulations. All students have access to and can participate in student organizations, athletics, student government, and recreation facilities. **Housing:** Coed dorms, special housing for disabled available. $100 fully refundable deposit, deadline 5/1. Most undergraduates required to live in on-campus housing. **Activities:** Bands, campus ministries, choral groups, international student organizations, music ensembles, student government, Newman Club, Eagle Scout Fraternity, culture club, Afro-Caribbean club, Emerald Society, Pershing Rifles, honor guard, Turkish club, Jewish club.

Athletics. NCAA. **Intercollegiate:** Baseball M, basketball, cross-country, football (tackle) M, ice hockey M, lacrosse, rifle, rowing (crew) W, sailing, soccer, softball W, swimming, volleyball W. **Intramural:** Basketball, cross-country, football (tackle) M, soccer, softball, volleyball. **Team name:** Privateers.

Student services. Alcohol/substance abuse counseling, chaplain/spiritual director, career counseling, services for economically disadvantaged, financial aid counseling, health services, legal services, personal counseling, placement for graduates, veterans' counselor. **Physically disabled:** Services for visually, speech, hearing impaired.

Contact. E-mail: admissions@sunymaritime.edu
Phone: (718) 409-7221 Toll-free number: (800) 654-1874
Fax: (718) 409-7465
Jonathan White, Dean of Admissions, State University of New York Maritime College, 6 Pennyfield Avenue, Throggs Neck, NY 10465-4198

State University of New York Upstate Medical University

Syracuse, New York
www.upstate.edu **CB code: 2547**

- Public two-year upper-division health science and nursing college
- Residential campus in small city
- 35% of applicants admitted
- Application essay, interview required

General. Founded in 1834. Regionally accredited. Undergraduate level consists of upper-division programs. Affiliated with Crouse-Irving Memorial Hospital, Veteran's Administration Medical Center, Community General Hospital of Greater Syracuse, St. Joseph's Hospital Health Center, Hutchings Psychiatric Center. **Degrees:** 96 bachelor's awarded; master's, doctoral, first professional offered. **Articulation:** Agreements with SUNY Alfred, SUNY Canton, SUNY Cobleskill, SUNY Cortland, SUNY Delhi, SUNY Geneseo, SUNY Morrisville, SUNY Oswego, SUNY Oneonta, Cayuga CC, Columbia-Greene CC, Finger Lakes CC, Genesee CC, Jefferson CC, Mohawk Valley CC, Monroe CC, Niagara County CC, North Country CC, Onondaga CC, Sullivan CC, Tompkins Cortland CC. **ROTC:** Army. **Location:** 250 miles from New York City, 150 miles from Buffalo. **Calendar:** Semester, limited summer session. **Full-time faculty:** 507 total; 98% have terminal degrees, 18% minority, 31% women. **Part-time faculty:** 245 total; 96% have terminal degrees, 17% minority, 34% women. **Class size:** 86% < 20, 11% 20-39, 2% 40-49, 1% 50-99. **Special facilities:** Institutionally owned and operated 350-bed teaching hospital and Level 1 trauma center.

Student profile. 269 degree-seeking undergraduates, 1,051 degree-seeking graduate students. 481 applied as first time-transfer students, 169 admitted, 121 enrolled. 100% entered as juniors. 60% transferred from two-year, 40% transferred from four-year institutions.

Women:	74%	**Part-time:**	36%
African American:	6%	**Out-of-state:**	4%
Asian American:	5%	**Live on campus:**	56%
Native American:	1%	**25 or older:**	61%
International:	2%		

Basis for selection. High school transcript, college transcript, application essay, interview required. Evaluation of academic performance in courses required for admission. Personal interviews, recommendations, and essay also important. Applicants must complete admissions course requirements prior to admission. Final decision made at discretion of admissions committee, regardless of applicant's prior academic standing. Transfer accepted as juniors, seniors.

2008-2009 Annual costs. Tuition/fees: $4,908; $11,168 out-of-state. Room only: $5,600. Books/supplies: $975. Personal expenses: $1,416.

Financial aid. All financial aid based on need. Average need met was 95%. 27% of total undergraduate aid awarded as scholarships/grants, 73% as loans/jobs.

Application procedures. Admission: Rolling admission. $40 fee, may be waived for applicants with need. Application deadline for physical therapy program March 15. Cardiovascular perfusion program completes admission process March 1. Preference to New York residents. High school seniors may apply for admission 2 years prior to intended date of entry. Transfer students apply in fall 1 year prior to intended date of entry. High school seniors may apply for early admission. **Financial aid:** Applicants notified on a rolling basis; must reply within 2 weeks of notification. FAFSA required.

Academics. Special study options: Combined bachelor's/graduate degree, independent study. **Credit/placement by examination:** AP, CLEP, institutional tests. 36 credit hours maximum toward bachelor's degree. **Support services:** Reduced course load, tutoring.

Majors. Health: Clinical lab science, nursing (RN), perfusion technology, respiratory therapy technology, sonography. **Other:** Medical imaging / X-ray / MRI / CT.

Computing on campus. 50 workstations in dormitories, library, computer center, student center. Dormitories wired for high-speed internet access and linked to campus network. Commuter students can connect to campus network. Helpline, student web hosting, wireless network available.

Student life. Policies: Students under 21 required to live on campus unless living at home. **Housing:** Guaranteed on-campus for all undergraduates. Coed dorms, apartments available. $150 deposit, deadline 8/1. **Activities:** Student government, campus activities governing board, Diversity in Allied Health.

Athletics. Intramural: Basketball, handball, racquetball, softball, table tennis, tennis, volleyball, water polo.

Student services. Alcohol/substance abuse counseling, career counseling, financial aid counseling, health services, minority student services, on-campus daycare, personal counseling, placement for graduates, veterans' counselor.

Contact. E-mail: admiss@upstate.edu
Phone: (315) 464-4570 Toll-free number: (800) 736-2171
Fax: (315) 464-8867
Jennifer Welch, Director of Admissions, State University of New York Upstate Medical University, 766 Irving Avenue, Syracuse, NY 13210

Syracuse University

Syracuse, New York **CB member**
www.syr.edu **CB code: 2823**

- Private 4-year university
- Residential campus in small city
- 13,105 degree-seeking undergraduates: 4% part-time, 56% women, 7% African American, 9% Asian American, 6% Hispanic American, 1% Native American, 5% international
- 5,346 degree-seeking graduate students
- 53% of applicants admitted
- SAT or ACT with writing, application essay required
- 82% graduate within 6 years; 18% enter graduate study

General. Founded in 1870. Regionally accredited. **Degrees:** 2,886 bachelor's, 7 associate awarded; master's, doctoral, first professional offered. **ROTC:** Army, Air Force. **Location:** 150 miles from Albany, 250 miles from New York City. **Calendar:** Semester, extensive summer session. **Full-time faculty:** 943 total; 87% have terminal degrees, 19% minority, 36% women. **Part-time faculty:** 560 total; 8% minority, 49% women. **Class size:** 63% < 20, 24% 20-39, 5% 40-49, 5% 50-99, 3% >100. **Special facilities:** Newhouse Complex media laboratories, digital convergence center, Syracuse Center of Excellence in Environmental and Energy Systems, advanced flight simulator for aerospace engineering, Ballentine Investment Institute, community darkrooms, Syracuse Stage professional theater, Mary Ann Shaw Center for Public Service, Bernice M. Wright Child Development Laboratory School, Belfer Audio Laboratory and Archive, Gebbie Speech, Language, and Hearing Clinic.

Freshman class profile. 22,079 applied, 11,597 admitted, 3,186 enrolled.

Mid 50% test scores		**Rank in top quarter:**	74%
SAT critical reading:	520-620	**Rank in top tenth:**	39%
SAT math:	550-650	**Return as sophomores:**	90%
SAT writing:	530-630	**Out-of-state:**	57%
ACT composite:	23-28	**Live on campus:**	99%
GPA 3.75 or higher:	42%	**International:**	6%
GPA 3.50-3.74:	21%	**Fraternities:**	15%
GPA 3.0-3.49:	30%	**Sororities:**	26%
GPA 2.0-2.99:	7%		

Basis for selection. Most important: strong performance in challenging, rigorous college preparatory curriculum from accredited secondary school, strong qualitative factors, good citizenship. Also important: secondary school counselor evaluation, 2 academic recommendations, standardized test scores. Personal characteristics, talents and interests considered. Applicants not admitted to their first-choice program may be considered for alternate programs on a space-available basis only if they checked this option on the admissions application. Priority given to those applying to first-choice programs. TOEFL exam is required of all applicants whose native language is not English. Portfolio required for art, architecture programs; audition required for drama and music programs. Interviews recommended for all candidates, but not required. **Homeschooled:** Transcript of courses and grades, interview, letter of recommendation (nonparent) required. Submit detailed course descriptions/syllabus used. 2 recommendations from someone outside home required. For financial aid eligibility, letter from local school district must be submitted acknowledging that curriculum taught at home is substantially equivalent to that of the school district; or GED.

High school preparation. College-preparatory program required. 19 units required. Required units include English 4, mathematics 4, social studies 4, science 4 (laboratory 4) and foreign language 3.

2008-2009 Annual costs. Tuition/fees: $33,440. Room/board: $11,656. Books/supplies: $1,268. Personal expenses: $880.

2008-2009 Financial aid. **Need-based:** 2,270 full-time freshmen applied for aid; 1,862 were judged to have need; 1,862 of these received aid. Average need met was 86%. Average scholarship/grant was $20,750; average loan $4,600. 71% of total undergraduate aid awarded as scholarships/grants, 29% as loans/jobs. **Non-need-based:** Awarded to 2,458 full-time undergraduates, including 623 freshmen. Scholarships awarded for academics, art, athletics, music/drama, ROTC.

Application procedures. **Admission:** Closing date 1/1 (postmark date). $70 fee, may be waived for applicants with need. Admission notification on a rolling basis beginning on or about 3/15. Must reply by 5/1. **Financial aid:** Closing date 2/1. FAFSA, CSS PROFILE required. Applicants notified by 3/21; must reply by 5/1.

Academics. **Special study options:** Accelerated study, combined bachelor's/graduate degree, cooperative education, distance learning, double major, dual enrollment of high school students, ESL, honors, independent study, internships, liberal arts/career combination, student-designed major, study abroad, teacher certification program. Syracuse offers many undergraduate research opportunities, pre-professional programs, and minors. **Credit/placement by examination:** AP, CLEP, IB, institutional tests. 30 credit hours maximum toward bachelor's degree. Maximum of 30 semester hours of credit may be accepted from all forms of extra-institutional, experiential learning, and examination programs. **Support services:** Learning center, pre-admission summer program, study skills assistance, tutoring, writing center.

Majors. **Architecture:** Architecture, interior. **Area/ethnic studies:** African, African-American, American, Latin American, Russian/Slavic, women's. **Biology:** General, biochemistry, biophysics. **Business:** Accounting, business admin, entrepreneurial studies, finance, marketing, sales/distribution. **Communications:** General, advertising, journalism, public relations, radio/tv. **Computer sciences:** General, information systems. **Education:** Art, biology, chemistry, Deaf/hearing impaired, elementary, English, family/consumer sciences, mathematics, music, physical, physics, social studies, special. **Engineering:** Aerospace, biomedical, chemical, civil, computer, electrical, environmental, mechanical, operations research, physics. **Family/consumer sciences:** Clothing/textiles, consumer economics, family studies, food/nutrition, institutional food production. **Foreign languages:** General, classics, French, German, Italian, linguistics, Russian, Spanish. **Health:** Audiology/speech pathology, predental, premedicine, preveterinary. **History:** General. **Interdisciplinary:** Nutrition sciences. **Legal studies:** General. **Liberal arts:** Arts/sciences, library science. **Math:** General. **Philosophy/religion:** Philosophy, religion. **Physical sciences:** Chemistry, geology, physics. **Psychology:** General. **Public administration:** General, social work. **Social sciences:** General, anthropology, economics, geography, international relations, political science, sociology. **Visual/performing arts:** Art, art history/conservation, cinematography, commercial/advertising art, dramatic, music history, music performance, music theory/composition, painting, photography, sculpture, studio arts. **Other:** Applied computer technology, Classical civilization, Earth science teacher education, Graphic arts, Health & wellness, Recording & allied entertainment industries, Sports management, Supply chain management.

Most popular majors. Business/marketing 14%, communications/journalism 13%, engineering/engineering technologies 6%, psychology 6%, social sciences 13%, visual/performing arts 12%.

Computing on campus. 2,955 workstations in dormitories, library, computer center, student center. Dormitories wired for high-speed internet access and linked to campus network. Commuter students can connect to campus network. Online course registration, online library, helpline, repair service, student web hosting, wireless network available.

Student life. **Freshman orientation:** Mandatory. Preregistration for classes offered. Held for four days prior to the start of classes each fall. A variety of academic and social activities assist students in the transition from high school to college. **Policies:** Freshmen and sophomores required to live on campus. **Housing:** Guaranteed on-campus for freshmen. Coed dorms, special housing for disabled, apartments, fraternity/sorority housing, wellness housing available. $400 partly refundable deposit, deadline 5/1. International living center, single-sex floors and wings of residence halls, numerous learning communities, and interest housing available. **Activities:** Bands, campus ministries, choral groups, dance, drama, film society, international student organizations, literary magazine, music ensembles, musical theater, radio station, student government, student newspaper, symphony orchestra, TV station, more than 300 student organizations, including arts, cultural, entertainment, environmental, governance, media, political, professional, service, and social interests groups.

Athletics. NCAA. **Intercollegiate:** Basketball, cross-country, diving, field hockey W, football (tackle) M, ice hockey W, lacrosse, rowing (crew), soccer, softball W, swimming, tennis W, track and field, volleyball W. **Intramural:** Basketball, football (non-tackle), racquetball, soccer, softball, tennis, volleyball. **Team name:** Orange.

Student services. Adult student services, alcohol/substance abuse counseling, chaplain/spiritual director, career counseling, services for economically disadvantaged, student employment services, financial aid counseling, health services, legal services, minority student services, on-campus daycare, personal counseling, placement for graduates, veterans' counselor, women's services. **Physically disabled:** Services for visually, speech, hearing impaired.

Contact. E-mail: orange@syr.edu
Phone: (315) 443-3611 Fax: (315) 443-4226
Susan Donovan, Dean of Admissions, Syracuse University, 100 Crouse-Hinds Hall, Syracuse, NY 13244-2130

Talmudical Institute of Upstate New York

Rochester, New York

CB code: 1426

- Private 5-year rabbinical and seminary college for men affiliated with Jewish faith
- Residential campus in large city

General. Founded in 1974. Accredited by AARTS. **Calendar:** Semester.

Annual costs/financial aid. Tuition/fees (2008-2009): $5,000. Room/board: $4,000.

Contact. Phone: (585) 473-2810
769 Park Avenue, Rochester, NY 14607

Talmudical Seminary Oholei Torah

Brooklyn, New York

CB code: 0712

- Private 4-year rabbinical and seminary college for men affiliated with Jewish faith
- Very large city

General. Founded in 1956. Accredited by AARTS. **Calendar:** Semester.

Annual costs/financial aid. Tuition/fees (2008-2009): $6,000. Room/board: $2,800.

Contact. Phone: (718) 774-5215
667 Eastern Parkway, Brooklyn, NY 11213-3397

Torah Temimah Talmudical Seminary

Brooklyn, New York

CB code: 7132

- Private 4-year rabbinical and seminary college for men affiliated with Jewish faith
- Very large city

General. Accredited by AARTS. **Calendar:** Continuous.

Annual costs/financial aid. Tuition/fees (2008-2009): $8,650. Room/board: $3,000.

Contact. Phone: (718) 853-8500
555 Ocean Parkway, Brooklyn, NY 11218

Touro College

New York, New York
www.touro.edu

CB code: 2902

- Private 4-year liberal arts college
- Commuter campus in very large city
- 8,650 degree-seeking undergraduates: 20% part-time, 71% women, 17% African American, 5% Asian American, 11% Hispanic American
- 8,479 degree-seeking graduate students
- 65% of applicants admitted

General. Founded in 1970. Regionally accredited. School of General Studies provides programs for part-time and adult students. **Degrees:** 1,526 bachelor's, 795 associate awarded; master's, doctoral, first professional offered. **Calendar:** Semester, limited summer session. **Full-time faculty:** 551 total. **Part-time faculty:** 988 total.

Freshman class profile. 4,011 applied, 2,602 admitted, 1,337 enrolled.

Basis for selection. For College of Liberal Arts and Sciences, 3.0 high school GPA, SAT verbal and math scores of 500 preferred. Recommendations from high school teachers and counselors and motivation important. High school experience less important for applicants to associate degree programs who take institutional admissions test. SAT or ACT recommended. SAT or ACT required for applicants to school of Health Sciences. Essay and interview recommended for College of Liberal Arts and Sciences.

High school preparation. 17 units recommended. Recommended units include English 4, mathematics 3, social studies 3, science 3 and foreign language 3. Requirements may vary by division.

2008-2009 Annual costs. Tuition/fees: $13,300. Room/board: $6,250. Books/supplies: $750. Personal expenses: $1,764.

Application procedures. **Admission:** No deadline. $50 fee, may be waived for applicants with need. Admission notification on a rolling basis. **Financial aid:** Priority date 5/15, closing date 6/1. FAFSA required. Applicants notified by 8/15.

Academics. **Special study options:** Accelerated study, combined bachelor's/graduate degree, distance learning, dual enrollment of high school students, ESL, honors, independent study, internships, liberal arts/career combination, student-designed major, study abroad, teacher certification program. **Credit/placement by examination:** AP, CLEP, institutional tests. **Support services:** Learning center, reduced course load, remedial instruction, tutoring.

Majors. **Biology:** General. **Business:** General, accounting, business admin, management information systems, managerial economics, marketing. **Communications:** General. **Computer sciences:** General. **Education:** Special. **Foreign languages:** General, Hebrew. **Health:** Communication disorders, medical records technology, nursing (RN), physician assistant, predental, premedicine, prepharmacy, preveterinary. **History:** General. **Interdisciplinary:** Biological/physical sciences. **Liberal arts:** Arts/sciences. **Math:** General. **Philosophy/religion:** Judaic, philosophy. **Physical sciences:** Chemistry. **Psychology:** General. **Social sciences:** General, economics, political science, sociology.

Computing on campus. 400 workstations in library, computer center.

Student life. **Freshman orientation:** Available. **Housing:** Single-sex dorms available. $50 deposit. No board or meal plan available. Kitchen facilities in student housing. **Activities:** Literary magazine, student government, student newspaper, accounting and business society, biology club, debating society, Jewish Affairs Committee, foreign students association, Omicron Delta.

Student services. Adult student services, career counseling, student employment services, personal counseling, placement for graduates, veterans' counselor.

Contact. E-mail: lasadmit@adminm.touro.edu
Phone: (718) 252-7800 ext. 299 Fax: (718) 253-9455
Arthur Wigfall, Director of Admissions, Touro College, 1602 Avenue J, Brooklyn, NY 11230

U.T.A. Mesivta-Kiryas Jocl
Monroe, New York

- Private 4-year rabbinical college for men affiliated with Jewish faith
- Large town

General. Accredited by AARTS. **Calendar:** Semester.

Annual costs/financial aid. Tuition/fees (2008-2009): $5,000. Room/board: $3,000.

Contact. Phone: (845) 783-9901
9 Nickelsburg Road, #312, Monroe, NY 10950-2169

Union College
Schenectady, New York CB member
www.union.edu CB code: 2920

- Private 4-year engineering and liberal arts college
- Residential campus in small city
- 2,199 degree-seeking undergraduates: 49% women, 4% African American, 6% Asian American, 4% Hispanic American, 3% international
- 39% of applicants admitted
- Application essay required
- 85% graduate within 6 years; 35% enter graduate study

General. Founded in 1795. Regionally accredited. **Degrees:** 473 bachelor's awarded. **ROTC:** Army, Naval, Air Force. **Location:** 15 miles from Albany, 175 miles from New York City. **Calendar:** Trimester, limited summer session. **Full-time faculty:** 194 total; 95% have terminal degrees, 11% minority, 41% women. **Part-time faculty:** 42 total; 69% have terminal degrees, 17% minority, 52% women. **Class size:** 70% < 20, 27% 20-39, 3% 40-49, less than 1% 50-99. **Special facilities:** Horticultural garden, superconducting nuclear magnetic resonance spectrometer, electron scanning microscope, tandem pelletron positive ion accelerator, X-ray diffraction equipment, remote-controlled telescope.

Freshman class profile. 5,271 applied, 2,067 admitted, 580 enrolled.

Mid 50% test scores		**GPA 2.0-2.99:**	9%
SAT critical reading:	570-660	**Rank in top quarter:**	82%
SAT math:	600-680	**Rank in top tenth:**	57%
SAT writing:	560-670	**End year in good standing:**	99%
ACT composite:	26-30	**Return as sophomores:**	93%
GPA 3.75 or higher:	33%	**Out-of-state:**	57%
GPA 3.50-3.74:	23%	**Live on campus:**	100%
GPA 3.0-3.49:	35%	**International:**	4%

Basis for selection. GED not accepted. Course selection and grades closely considered along with recommendations from high school and extracurricular record. Ethnic and geographic diversity sought in student body. Testing optional except for combined programs. Applicants for leadership in medicine and law and public policy programs required to submit the SAT and 2 SAT Subject Tests and must complete necessary tests no later than December of senior year. Portfolio recommended for art programs. **Homeschooled:** Interview required.

High school preparation. College-preparatory program required. 16 units required; 24 recommended. Required and recommended units include English 4, mathematics 3-4, social studies 1-2, history 1-2, science 2-4 (laboratory 2-4) and foreign language 2-4.

2008-2009 Annual costs. Comprehensive fee: $48,552. Rebates offered to students living off-campus and/or not using a meal plan. Books/supplies: $450. Personal expenses: $808.

2008-2009 Financial aid. **Need-based:** 296 full-time freshmen applied for aid; 254 were judged to have need; 254 of these received aid. Average need met was 99%. Average scholarship/grant was $28,957; average loan $3,730. 85% of total undergraduate aid awarded as scholarships/grants, 15% as loans/jobs. **Non-need-based:** Awarded to 309 full-time undergraduates, including 109 freshmen. Scholarships awarded for academics, ROTC. **Additional information:** Cancellable loans given to eligible students who engage in public service work after graduation. Loans cancellable at rate of 20% for each year of service.

Application procedures. **Admission:** Closing date 1/15 (postmark date). $50 fee, may be waived for applicants with need, free for online applicants. Admission notification 4/1. Must reply by 5/1. If application filed online, supplemental graded, written essay from 11th or 12th grade required to complete application. **Financial aid:** Priority date 2/1, closing date 2/1. FAFSA, CSS PROFILE required. Applicants notified by 4/1; must reply by 5/1.

Academics. **Special study options:** Accelerated study, combined bachelor's/graduate degree, cross-registration, double major, dual enrollment of high school students, honors, independent study, internships, liberal arts/career combination, student-designed major, study abroad, teacher certification program. **Credit/placement by examination:** AP, CLEP, IB, institutional tests. 4 credit hours maximum toward bachelor's degree. **Support services:** Study skills assistance, tutoring, writing center.

Majors. **Area/ethnic studies:** American. **Biology:** General, biochemistry. **Computer sciences:** General. **Engineering:** Electrical, mechanical. **Foreign languages:** General, classics. **History:** General. **Interdisciplinary:** Biological/physical sciences, neuroscience, science/society. **Liberal arts:** Arts/sciences, humanities. **Math:** General. **Philosophy/religion:** Philosophy. **Physical sciences:** Astronomy, chemistry, geology, physics. **Psychology:** General. **Social sciences:** General, anthropology, economics, political science, sociology. **Visual/performing arts:** General.

Most popular majors. Biology 10%, engineering/engineering technologies 11%, English 6%, history 9%, liberal arts 10%, physical sciences 6%, psychology 10%, social sciences 25%.

Computing on campus. 504 workstations in library, computer center, student center. Dormitories wired for high-speed internet access and linked to campus network. Commuter students can connect to campus network.

Online course registration, online library, helpline, student web hosting, wireless network available.

Student life. Freshman orientation: Mandatory, $250 fee. Preregistration for classes offered. Begins Thursday and ends Sunday before classes begin. Orientation fee included in Admission and Security deposit. **Policies:** All students expected to live on campus during undergraduate years, provided housing is available. **Housing:** Guaranteed on-campus for freshmen. Coed dorms, apartments, fraternity/sorority housing, wellness housing available. $150 nonrefundable deposit, deadline 5/1. Minerva Houses. Up to 45 students live in each. All students and faculty members have house affiliations. Each house contributes intellectual, cultural, and social events to the campus. **Activities:** Bands, campus ministries, choral groups, dance, drama, film society, international student organizations, literary magazine, music ensembles, Model UN, radio station, student government, student newspaper, symphony orchestra, TV station, African and Latino Alliance of Students, Asian Student Union, Big Brothers/Big Sisters, College Republicans, Intervarsity Christian Fellowship, Jewish Student Union, Middle Eastern Civilization and Culture Association, Newman Club, UCARE-a community action club, Union College Democrats.

Athletics. NCAA. **Intercollegiate:** Baseball M, basketball, cross-country, diving, field hockey W, football (tackle) M, ice hockey, lacrosse, rowing (crew), soccer, softball W, swimming, tennis, track and field, volleyball W. **Intramural:** Basketball, football (non-tackle) M, ice hockey, lacrosse W, soccer, softball, tennis, volleyball. **Team name:** Dutchmen, Dutchwomen.

Student services. Alcohol/substance abuse counseling, chaplain/spiritual director, career counseling, services for economically disadvantaged, student employment services, financial aid counseling, health services, minority student services, personal counseling, placement for graduates. **Physically disabled:** Services for visually, hearing impaired.

Contact. E-mail: admissions@union.edu
Phone: (518) 388-6112 Toll-free number: (888) 843-6688
Fax: (518) 388-6986
Ann Brown, Director of Admissions, Union College, Grant Hall, Schenectady, NY 12308-2311

United States Merchant Marine Academy

Kings Point, New York — **CB member**
www.usmma.edu — **CB code: 2923**

- Public 4-year military and maritime college
- Residential campus in large town
- 985 degree-seeking undergraduates: 12% women
- 18 degree-seeking graduate students
- 26% of applicants admitted
- SAT or ACT (ACT writing optional), application essay required

General. Founded in 1943. Regionally accredited. Accepted applicants appointed to academy as midshipmen, USNR. **Degrees:** 213 bachelor's awarded; master's offered. **Location:** 20 miles from midtown Manhattan. **Calendar:** Trimester, limited summer session. **Full-time faculty:** 95 total; 100% have terminal degrees, 10% minority, 15% women. **Class size:** 45% < 20, 54% 20-39, less than 1% 40-49, less than 1% 50-99. **Special facilities:** US Merchant Marine Museum, computer-aided operational research facility, T/V Kings Pointer docked on campus.

Freshman class profile. 1,734 applied, 449 admitted, 307 enrolled.

Mid 50% test scores			
SAT critical reading:	540-640	Rank in top quarter:	23%
SAT math:	600-660	Rank in top tenth:	18%
ACT composite:	25-29	Out-of-state:	86%
		Live on campus:	100%

Basis for selection. Nomination by U.S. representatives or senators. Competitive standing determined by test scores, high school GPA, class rank, motivation, extracurricular activities, interest in academy, industry, citizenship, and recommendations from counselors, teachers, school principal. Must also meet medical requirements and pass physical fitness exercise regimen. Untimed test results not acceptable. Interview recommended. **Homeschooled:** Letter of recommendation (nonparent) required. Must have completed chemistry with lab or physics with lab through state-certified instructor.

High school preparation. 18 units required. Required and recommended units include English 4, mathematics 3-4, social studies 4, science 3-4 (laboratory 1-2), foreign language 2 and academic electives 8.

2008-2009 Annual costs. All midshipmen receive full tuition, room, board, and medical and dental expenses from the federal government. Total required freshmen fees include purchase of laptop computer, color printer, and PDA. International students pay required fees plus additional international student fee. Books/supplies: $692.

2007-2008 Financial aid. Need-based: 64% of total undergraduate aid awarded as scholarships/grants, 36% as loans/jobs. **Additional information:** Students paid by steamship companies while at sea.

Application procedures. Admission: Closing date 3/1 (postmark date). No application fee. Admission notification on a rolling basis beginning on or about 11/1. Must reply by May 1 or within 2 week(s) if notified thereafter. **Financial aid:** Closing date 5/1. FAFSA, institutional form required. Applicants notified on a rolling basis starting 1/31.

Academics. Special study options: Honors, independent study, internships, semester at sea, study abroad. Sea training on merchant vessels. **Credit/placement by examination:** CLEP, institutional tests. **Support services:** Learning center, remedial instruction, study skills assistance, tutoring.

Majors. Engineering: Marine, systems. **Engineering technology:** Industrial management. **Mechanic/repair:** Marine. **Transportation:** General, maritime/Merchant Marine.

Most popular majors. Engineering/engineering technologies 39%, trade and industry 61%.

Computing on campus. PC or laptop required. 1,200 workstations in dormitories, library. Dormitories wired for high-speed internet access and linked to campus network. Helpline, repair service, wireless network available.

Student life. Freshman orientation: Mandatory. 2-week orientation starting in early July. **Housing:** Guaranteed on-campus for all undergraduates. Coed dorms, wellness housing available. Students required to live on campus. **Activities:** Bands, choral groups, drama, musical theater, student government, student newspaper, Christian Fellowship Community, Newman Club.

Athletics. NCAA. **Intercollegiate:** Baseball M, basketball, cross-country, diving, football (tackle) M, golf, lacrosse M, rowing (crew), sailing, soccer M, softball W, swimming, tennis, track and field, volleyball W, wrestling M. **Intramural:** Baseball M, basketball, boxing, cross-country, football (tackle) M, racquetball, rowing (crew), soccer, softball, tennis, track and field, volleyball, water polo, weight lifting. **Team name:** Mariners.

Student services. Alcohol/substance abuse counseling, chaplain/spiritual director, career counseling, student employment services, financial aid counseling, health services, personal counseling, placement for graduates.

Contact. E-mail: admissions@usmma.edu
Phone: (516) 773-5391 Toll-free number: (866) 546-4778
Fax: (516) 773-5390
CAPT. Robert Johnson, Director of Admissions, United States Merchant Marine Academy, 300 Steamboat Road, Admissions Center, Kings Point, NY 11024-1699

United States Military Academy

West Point, New York — **CB member**
www.usma.edu — **CB code: 2924**

- Public 4-year military college
- Residential campus in small town
- 4,553 degree-seeking undergraduates: 15% women, 6% African American, 7% Asian American, 8% Hispanic American, 1% Native American, 1% international
- 16% of applicants admitted
- SAT or ACT with writing, application essay required
- 83% graduate within 6 years; 2% enter graduate study

General. Founded in 1802. Regionally accredited. Cadets receive Bachelor of Science degree designed specifically to meet intellectual requirements of a commissioned officer in the Army. **Degrees:** 992 bachelor's awarded. **Location:** 50 miles from New York City. **Calendar:** Semester, limited summer session. **Full-time faculty:** 637 total; 42% have terminal degrees, 12% minority, 19% women. **Class size:** 96% < 20, 4% 20-39. **Special facilities:** West Point Museum, American Revolutionary-era Fort Putnam, 4,500-seat Eisenhower Hall.

Freshman class profile. 10,140 applied, 1,592 admitted, 1,272 enrolled.

Mid 50% test scores		End year in good standing:	93%
SAT critical reading:	560-670	Return as sophomores:	91%
SAT math:	590-680	Out-of-state:	93%
ACT composite:	25-30	Live on campus:	100%
Rank in top quarter:	75%	International:	1%
Rank in top tenth:	43%		

Basis for selection. ACT/SAT, rigor of high school record, class rank, and faculty recommendations used to determine academic qualification. Demonstrated leadership potential, physical ability, medical exam and Candidate Fitness Assessment also important. Must be U.S. citizen, at least 17 but not yet 23 by July 1 of year admitted, unmarried, not pregnant, and without legal child support obligations. Naturalized citizens must provide documentation. Nomination by member of Congress required. Consideration also given to percentage of students from school who attend 4-year colleges after high school. The number of cadets at the Military Academy and the sources from which they may be nominated and appointed are prescribed in Sections 4341a, 4342-4344, and 4347, Title 10, United States Code (10 USC 4341a, 4342-4344, and 4347). Interview recommended. **Learning Disabled:** No learning disabled at USMA.

High school preparation. 19 units recommended. Recommended units include English 4, mathematics 4, social studies 1, history 1, science 4 (laboratory 2), foreign language 2 and academic electives 3. English units should have strong emphasis on composition, grammar, literature and speech; math should include algebra, geometry, intermediate algebra, and trigonometry; U.S. history should include courses in geography, government and economics. Precalculus, calculus and basic computing course helpful.

2009-2010 Annual costs. All cadets are on active duty as members of the U.S. Army and receive an annual salary of approximately $10,148. Room and board, medical, and dental care are provided by the Army. Deposit of $2,900 required for initial uniforms, books, supplies, equipment and fees. If needed, loans for deposit available from $100 to $2,900.

2007-2008 Financial aid. Additional information: Cadets permitted to receive scholarships, but since there are no tuition, room, or board charges, scholarships stipulated for tuition, room or board only based on need rather than merit cannot be accepted. Scholarships may be used for textbooks, uniforms, and other expenses or used dollar for dollar to offset initial $2,900 deposit.

Application procedures. Admission: Closing date 2/28. No application fee. Application must be submitted online. Admission notification on a rolling basis beginning on or about 11/15. Must reply by 5/1.

Academics. Cadets must complete minimum basic requirement of 40 academic courses. 8 semesters of physical education and 4 military science courses required. Cumulative GPA of at least 2.0 required, while meeting appropriate physical fitness and proper conduct standards. **Special study options:** Double major, exchange student, honors, independent study, internships, study abroad, Washington semester. Opportunities to attend Army Schools (Ariborne, Air Assault, etc.) to learn special skills and to intern with an Army organization during the summer. **Credit/placement by examination:** CLEP. **Support services:** Learning center, reduced course load, remedial instruction, study skills assistance, tutoring.

Majors. Area/ethnic studies: African, East Asian, European, Latin American, Near/Middle Eastern, regional, Russian/Slavic. **Biology:** General. **Business:** Business admin, organizational behavior. **Computer sciences:** Information systems, information technology. **Conservation:** Environmental science, environmental studies. **Engineering:** Chemical, civil, electrical, environmental, mechanical, nuclear, operations research, systems. **Engineering technology:** Civil, environmental, industrial management, mechanical, nuclear. **Foreign languages:** Arabic, Chinese, French, German, Portuguese, Russian, Spanish. **History:** American, European. **Interdisciplinary:** Cognitive science, systems science. **Legal studies:** General. **Liberal arts:** Humanities. **Math:** General. **Military:** General. **Parks/recreation:** Exercise sciences. **Physical sciences:** General, chemistry, physics. **Psychology:** General. **Social sciences:** Economics, geography, international relations, political science, sociology, U.S. government. **Other:** Applied statistics, Chemical engineering studies, Military, Terrorism studies.

Most popular majors. Business/marketing 9%, engineering/engineering technologies 25%, foreign language 11%, history 7%, social sciences 21%.

Computing on campus. PC or laptop required. 1,000 workstations in dormitories, library, computer center. Dormitories wired for high-speed internet access and linked to campus network. Commuter students can connect to campus network. Online library, helpline, repair service, wireless network available.

Student life. Freshman orientation: Mandatory. **Policies:** Honor code. Cadets administer honor system with power to recommend dismissal. Military dress required. All cadets participate in intercollegiate, club or intramural level sport each semester. Seniors and juniors (after spring break) permitted to maintain cars. **Housing:** Guaranteed on-campus for all undergraduates. Coed dorms, wellness housing available. **Activities:** Pep band, campus ministries, choral groups, dance, drama, film society, international student organizations, literary magazine, music ensembles, Model UN, musical theater, radio station, student government, student newspaper, TV station, Arabic language club, Asian-Pacific club, Catholic Cadet Catechists, Big Brothers & Big Sisters, Cadet Alcohol & Drug Intervention Council, Jewish chapel choir, cultural affairs group, domestic affairs forum, Student Conference on US Affairs, Scoutmaster's Council.

Athletics. NCAA. **Intercollegiate:** Baseball M, basketball, cross-country, diving, football (tackle) M, golf, gymnastics M, ice hockey M, lacrosse M, rifle, soccer, softball W, swimming, tennis, track and field, volleyball W, wrestling M. **Intramural:** Basketball, bowling, boxing M, cheerleading, cross-country, football (non-tackle) M, football (tackle) M, handball, lacrosse, racquetball, rugby, skin diving, soccer, softball, squash, swimming, track and field, volleyball, wrestling M. **Team name:** Black Knights.

Student services. Alcohol/substance abuse counseling, chaplain/spiritual director, career counseling, health services, legal services, personal counseling, placement for graduates, women's services.

Contact. E-mail: admissions@usma.edu
Phone: (845) 938-5760
Col. Deborah McDonald, Director of Admissions, United States Military Academy, 646 Swift Road, West Point, NY 10996-1905

United Talmudical Seminary
Brooklyn, New York
CB code: 0696

- Private 5-year rabbinical college for men affiliated with Jewish faith
- Very large city

General. Founded in 1949. Accredited by AARTS. **Calendar:** Semester.

Annual costs/financial aid. Tuition/fees (2008-2009): $6,000. Room/board: $3,000.

Contact. Phone: (718) 963-9260
Director of Admissions, 82 Lee Avenue, Brooklyn, NY 11211

University of Rochester
Rochester, New York **CB member**
www.rochester.edu **CB code: 2928**

- Private 4-year university
- Residential campus in large city
- 5,178 degree-seeking undergraduates: 2% part-time, 51% women, 4% African American, 10% Asian American, 4% Hispanic American, 7% international
- 3,956 degree-seeking graduate students
- 43% of applicants admitted
- SAT or ACT (ACT writing optional), application essay required
- 84% graduate within 6 years; 99% enter graduate study

General. Founded in 1850. Regionally accredited. The Rochester Curriculum commitment means there are no required subjects; instead, students design their education. As they structure their choices, students will eventually choose to major in one of 65 degree programs in science and engineering, humanities, or social sciences, and complete a cluster of at least three related course in each of the other two areas. **Degrees:** 1,232 bachelor's awarded; master's, doctoral, first professional offered. **ROTC:** Army, Naval, Air Force. **Location:** 2 miles from downtown Rochester. **Calendar:** Semester, extensive summer session. **Full-time faculty:** 515 total; 88% have terminal degrees, 12% minority, 27% women. **Part-time faculty:** 248 total; 4% minority, 55% women. **Class size:** 60% < 20, 23% 20-39, 4% 40-49, 9% 50-99, 4% >100. **Special facilities:** Eastman Theatre, Memorial Art Gallery, music library, nuclear structure research laboratory, laser energetics laboratory, African and African-American Studies Institute, Susan B. Anthony Institute for Gender and Women's Studies, observatory, dental center, hospital, visual science center, optics institute, MRI scanner, cancer center, children's hospital, VR lab.

Freshman class profile. 11,633 applied, 4,964 admitted, 1,167 enrolled.

Mid 50% test scores			
SAT critical reading:	600-700	Rank in top quarter:	94%
SAT math:	620-730	Rank in top tenth:	75%
SAT writing:	590-700	End year in good standing:	95%
ACT composite:	27-31	Return as sophomores:	95%
GPA 3.75 or higher:	54%	Out-of-state:	52%
GPA 3.50-3.74:	19%	Live on campus:	100%
GPA 3.0-3.49:	23%	International:	9%
		GPA 2.0-2.99:	4%

Basis for selection. School achievement record, test scores, recommendations most important. Personal qualities, academic GPA, extracurricular activities are important. Alumni relationship, minority status, special talents considered. An audition is required for music programs at Eastman School of Music. **Homeschooled:** Statement describing homeschool structure and mission, transcript of courses and grades, interview, letter of recommendation (nonparent) required. Must submit comprehensive description of the program of study (including syllabi with textbooks, where applicable), complete list of all literary texts completed, method of instruction (specifically for laboratory sciences) and assessment (written essays/multiple choice examinations, homework, etc.), and a personal statement reflecting on the value of the home schooling experience. Most students who successfully gain admission to the University of Rochester have completed four years of English, four years of mathematics, four years of history/social studies, three years of laboratory science, and three years of foreign language study.

High school preparation. College-preparatory program required. 32 units required.

2008-2009 Annual costs. Tuition/fees: $37,250. Room/board: $10,810. Books/supplies: $990. Personal expenses: $1,160.

2008-2009 Financial aid. Need-based: Average need met was 100%. Average scholarship/grant was $27,021; average loan $4,154. 75% of total undergraduate aid awarded as scholarships/grants, 25% as loans/jobs. **Non-need-based:** Scholarships awarded for academics, alumni affiliation, leadership, music/drama, ROTC, state residency. **Additional information:** Alternative loans and financing information available.

Application procedures. Admission: Closing date 1/1 (postmark date). $60 fee, may be waived for applicants with need. Admission notification 4/1. Must reply by 5/1. **Financial aid:** Closing date 2/1. FAFSA, CSS PROFILE required. Applicants notified by 4/1; must reply by 5/1.

Academics. Special study options: Accelerated study, combined bachelor's/graduate degree, cooperative education, cross-registration, double major, dual enrollment of high school students, ESL, honors, independent study, internships, liberal arts/career combination, New York semester, semester at sea, student-designed major, study abroad, teacher certification program, urban semester, Washington semester. Senior scholars research program allows selected undergraduates to devote entire senior year to student-designed research project; Take Five, 5th year tuition-free year to supplement regular requirements; Quest (1st-year course emphasizing how to learn). **Credit/placement by examination:** AP, CLEP, IB, institutional tests. **Support services:** Learning center, pre-admission summer program, reduced course load, study skills assistance, tutoring, writing center.

Majors. Area/ethnic studies: African-American, Russian/Slavic, women's. **Biology:** General, bacteriology, biochemistry, cell/histology, ecology, embryology, molecular, molecular genetics. **Business:** Managerial economics. **Computer sciences:** Computer science. **Conservation:** Environmental science, environmental studies. **Education:** Music. **Engineering:** General, biomedical, chemical, electrical, geological, mechanical, science. **Foreign languages:** General, classics, comparative lit, French, German, Japanese, linguistics, Russian, sign language interpretation, Spanish. **Health:** Nursing (RN). **History:** General. **Interdisciplinary:** Biological/physical sciences, classical/archaeology. **Liberal arts:** Arts/sciences. **Math:** General, applied, statistics. **Philosophy/religion:** Philosophy, religion. **Physical sciences:** Chemistry, geology, optics, physics. **Psychology:** General, experimental. **Social sciences:** Anthropology, economics, international relations, political science. **Visual/performing arts:** Art history/conservation, film/cinema, jazz, music performance, music theory/composition, studio arts. **Other:** Archaeology, engineering and architecture, Health and society, Mathematics and statistics, Physics and astronomy.

Most popular majors. Biology 13%, engineering/engineering technologies 9%, health sciences 11%, physical sciences 6%, psychology 11%, social sciences 16%, visual/performing arts 11%.

Computing on campus. 450 workstations in dormitories, library, computer center, student center. Dormitories wired for high-speed internet access. Commuter students can connect to campus network. Online course registration, online library, helpline, repair service, wireless network available.

Student life. Freshman orientation: Mandatory. Preregistration for classes offered. Held 1 week prior to first day of classes. **Housing:** Guaranteed on-campus for freshmen. Coed dorms, single-sex dorms, special housing for disabled, apartments, fraternity/sorority housing, wellness housing available. Freshman housing, special-interest floors, suite-style living, single-gender floors. **Activities:** Bands, choral groups, dance, drama, film society, international student organizations, literary magazine, music ensembles, Model UN, musical theater, opera, radio station, student government, student newspaper, symphony orchestra, TV station, Hillel, Catholic Newman Society, Muslim students association, debate union, UR Bhangra, Black student union, Charles Drew Pre-Health Society, Grassroots, Colleges Against Cancer, campus activities board.

Athletics. NCAA. **Intercollegiate:** Baseball M, basketball, cross-country, diving, field hockey W, football (tackle) M, golf M, lacrosse W, rowing (crew), soccer, softball W, squash, swimming, tennis, track and field, volleyball W. **Intramural:** Basketball, bowling, boxing, fencing, football (tackle) M, golf M, judo, racquetball, rugby, soccer, softball, squash, table tennis, tennis, volleyball, weight lifting. **Team name:** Yellowjackets.

Student services. Adult student services, alcohol/substance abuse counseling, chaplain/spiritual director, career counseling, services for economically disadvantaged, student employment services, financial aid counseling, health services, minority student services, personal counseling, placement for graduates, veterans' counselor, women's services. **Physically disabled:** Services for visually, hearing impaired.

Contact. E-mail: admit@admissions.rochester.edu
Phone: (585) 275-3221 Toll-free number: (888) 822-2256
Fax: (585) 461-4595
Jonathan Burdick, Dean of Admissions and Financial Aid, University of Rochester, 300 Wilson Boulevard, Rochester, NY 14627-0251

Utica College

Utica, New York — **CB member**
www.utica.edu — **CB code: 2932**

- Private 4-year liberal arts college
- Residential campus in small city
- 2,436 degree-seeking undergraduates: 17% part-time, 58% women, 11% African American, 1% Asian American, 4% Hispanic American, 1% Native American, 2% international
- 580 degree-seeking graduate students
- 74% of applicants admitted
- Application essay required
- 52% graduate within 6 years; 46% enter graduate study

General. Founded in 1946. Regionally accredited. **Degrees:** 487 bachelor's awarded; master's, doctoral, first professional offered. **ROTC:** Army, Air Force. **Location:** 50 miles from Syracuse. **Calendar:** Semester, limited summer session. **Full-time faculty:** 126 total; 89% have terminal degrees, 6% minority, 48% women. **Part-time faculty:** 196 total; 44% women. **Class size:** 75% < 20, 24% 20-39, less than 1% 40-49.

Freshman class profile. 2,911 applied, 2,163 admitted, 574 enrolled.

Mid 50% test scores			
SAT critical reading:	410-520	Rank in top quarter:	29%
SAT math:	420-550	Rank in top tenth:	10%
SAT writing:	400-510	End year in good standing:	89%
ACT composite:	18-23	Return as sophomores:	69%
GPA 3.75 or higher:	19%	Out-of-state:	15%
GPA 3.50-3.74:	2%	Live on campus:	78%
GPA 3.0-3.49:	39%	International:	4%
		GPA 2.0-2.99:	38%

Basis for selection. Academic record, high school course of study, rank in class most important. Extracurricular activities, essay, interview, recommendations also important. SAT or ACT scores required only for freshmen applying to BS Health Studies/DPT Physical Therapy, BS Health Studies/MS Occupational Therapy, Nursing, or joint health professions programs, Higher Education Opportunity Program (HEOP), or for academic merit scholarships. Interview recommended. **Homeschooled:** Applicants must receive GED within first year of attendance. **Learning Disabled:** Written evaluation required, including discrepancy analysis completed by licensed psychologist or certified learning disability specialist indicating specific learning disability or disabilities.

High school preparation. College-preparatory program recommended. 16 units required. Required units include English 4, mathematics 3, social studies 3, science 3, foreign language 2 and academic electives 1.

2008-2009 Annual costs. Tuition/fees: $26,058. Room/board: $10,430.

2008-2009 Financial aid. **Need-based:** 528 full-time freshmen applied for aid; 494 were judged to have need; 492 of these received aid. Average need met was 74%. Average scholarship/grant was $10,042; average loan $3,404. 66% of total undergraduate aid awarded as scholarships/grants, 34% as loans/jobs. **Non-need-based:** Awarded to 246 full-time undergraduates, including 68 freshmen. Scholarships awarded for academics.

Application procedures. **Admission:** No deadline. $40 fee, may be waived for applicants with need. Admission notification on a rolling basis beginning on or about 9/1. January 15 application deadline for all joint medical programs, BS in Health Studies/ MS in Occupational Therapy program, and BS in Health Studies/DPT in Physical Therapy program. February 15 application deadline for nursing program. **Financial aid:** Priority date 2/15; no closing date. FAFSA required. Applicants notified on a rolling basis starting 2/1; must reply by 5/1 or within 4 week(s) of notification.

Academics. **Special study options:** Accelerated study, combined bachelor's/graduate degree, cooperative education, cross-registration, distance learning, double major, dual enrollment of high school students, exchange student, honors, independent study, internships, liberal arts/career combination, study abroad, teacher certification program, United Nations semester, Washington semester, weekend college. BS Health Studies/MS Occupational Therapy weekend program; Economic Crime Investigation online program for transfer students. **Credit/placement by examination:** AP, CLEP, IB, SAT, institutional tests. 30 credit hours maximum toward bachelor's degree. **Support services:** Learning center, pre-admission summer program, reduced course load, remedial instruction, study skills assistance, tutoring, writing center.

Majors. **Biology:** General. **Business:** Accounting, business admin, managerial economics. **Communications:** General, journalism, public relations. **Computer sciences:** General. **Education:** Early childhood, elementary, ESL, secondary, special. **Family/consumer sciences:** Child care. **Foreign languages:** General. **Health:** Facilities admin, health services, nursing (RN), recreational therapy. **History:** General. **Liberal arts:** Arts/sciences. **Math:** General. **Philosophy/religion:** Philosophy. **Physical sciences:** Chemistry, physics. **Protective services:** Criminal justice. **Psychology:** General. **Social sciences:** Economics, international relations, political science, sociology.

Most popular majors. Business/marketing 18%, communications/journalism 7%, English 6%, health sciences 22%, psychology 13%, security/protective services 11%.

Computing on campus. 227 workstations in library, computer center, student center. Dormitories wired for high-speed internet access and linked to campus network. Helpline available.

Student life. **Freshman orientation:** Available, $50 fee. Preregistration for classes offered. Summer program for freshmen and parents held during the third week of July. **Policies:** All freshmen required to live in college residence for first 2 years, unless residing at home. **Housing:** Guaranteed on-campus for freshmen. Coed dorms, special housing for disabled, apartments, wellness housing available. $200 deposit, deadline 5/1. Separate floors for men and women available in select residence halls. **Activities:** Concert band, choral groups, dance, drama, film society, literary magazine, radio station, student government, student newspaper, Latin American student union, Jewish student union, College Republicans, Women's resource center, Asian association, gospel choir, Africa in Motion, Christian Fellowship, West Indian Connection, UC Pride.

Athletics. NCAA. **Intercollegiate:** Baseball M, basketball, cross-country, diving, field hockey W, football (tackle) M, golf M, ice hockey, lacrosse, soccer, softball W, swimming, tennis, volleyball W, water polo W. **Intramural:** Basketball, bowling, football (non-tackle), racquetball, soccer, softball, tennis, volleyball, water polo. **Team name:** Pioneers.

Student services. Adult student services, alcohol/substance abuse counseling, chaplain/spiritual director, career counseling, services for economically disadvantaged, student employment services, financial aid counseling, health services, minority student services, personal counseling, placement for graduates, veterans' counselor, women's services. **Physically disabled:** Services for visually, speech, hearing impaired.

Contact. E-mail: admiss@utica.edu
Phone: (315) 792-3006 Toll-free number: (800) 782-8884
Fax: (315) 792-3003
Patrick Quinn, Vice President for Enrollment Management, Utica College, 1600 Burrstone Road, Utica, NY 13502-4892

Vassar College

Poughkeepsie, New York — **CB member**
www.vassar.edu — **CB code: 2956**

- Private 4-year liberal arts college
- Residential campus in small city
- 2,343 degree-seeking undergraduates: 1% part-time, 58% women, 5% African American, 10% Asian American, 7% Hispanic American, 6% international
- 25% of applicants admitted
- SAT and SAT Subject Tests or ACT with writing, application essay required
- 92% graduate within 6 years; 17% enter graduate study

General. Founded in 1861. Regionally accredited. **Degrees:** 638 bachelor's awarded; master's offered. **Location:** 75 miles from New York City. **Calendar:** Semester, limited summer session. **Full-time faculty:** 299 total; 89% have terminal degrees, 26% minority, 46% women. **Part-time faculty:** 37 total; 54% have terminal degrees, 16% minority, 60% women. **Class size:** 70% < 20, 28% 20-39, less than 1% 40-49, less than 1% 50-99, less than 1% >100. **Special facilities:** Environmental nature center, observatory, electron microscope, nursery school, experimental theater, art center and geology museum, intercultural center and outdoor amphitheater.

Freshman class profile. 7,361 applied, 1,839 admitted, 640 enrolled.

Mid 50% test scores		**Rank in top quarter:**	96%
SAT critical reading:	670-750	**Rank in top tenth:**	70%
SAT math:	650-720	**End year in good standing:**	98%
SAT writing:	660-750	**Return as sophomores:**	96%
ACT composite:	29-33	**Out-of-state:**	74%
GPA 3.75 or higher:	55%	**Live on campus:**	99%
GPA 3.50-3.74:	30%	**International:**	7%
GPA 3.0-3.49:	15%		

Basis for selection. Academic credentials most important. Personal achievements, essay, and recommendations also considered carefully. Evidence that students have elected most demanding program available crucial. Disadvantaged status considered. 2 SAT Subject Tests of student's choice required. Optional interviews available with alumni.

High school preparation. College-preparatory program recommended. 20 units recommended. Recommended units include English 4, mathematics 4, social studies 2, history 2, science 4 (laboratory 3) and foreign language 4. Advanced and accelerated courses recommended whenever possible. Minimum of 20 units recommended with additional unit in science, foreign language, and studies.

2008-2009 Annual costs. Tuition/fees: $40,210. Room/board: $9,040. Books/supplies: $860. Personal expenses: $1,200.

2008-2009 Financial aid. All financial aid based on need. 438 full-time freshmen applied for aid; 366 were judged to have need; 366 of these received aid. Average need met was 100%. Average scholarship/grant was $33,145; average loan $1,698. 88% of total undergraduate aid awarded as scholarships/grants, 12% as loans/jobs. **Additional information:** No loans in the initial financial aid packages for students from families with total income used in need analysis of $60,000 or less.

Application procedures. **Admission:** Closing date 1/1 (receipt date). $60 fee, may be waived for applicants with need. Admission notification 4/1. Must reply by 5/1. **Financial aid:** Closing date 2/1. FAFSA, CSS PROFILE required. Applicants notified by 3/30; must reply by 5/1.

Academics. Introductory-level college course emphasizing written and oral communication required for freshmen. Majors declared through department, interdepartmental programs, multidisciplinary programs, and independent programs. Summer research with faculty. **Special study options:** Combined bachelor's/graduate degree, cooperative education, cross-registration, double major, exchange student, independent study, internships, liberal arts/career combination, student-designed major, study abroad, teacher certification program, urban semester, Washington semester. Independently designed junior year abroad programs; exchange programs with institutions in 12-college exchange as well as Fisk University, Hampton Institute, Howard University, Morehouse College, and Spelman College; 3-2 engineering program with Dartmouth College. **Credit/placement by examination:** AP, CLEP, IB, institutional tests. 4 credit hours maximum toward bachelor's degree. **Support services:** Learning center, reduced course load, study skills assistance, tutoring, writing center.

Majors. **Area/ethnic studies:** African, American, Asian, Latin American, women's. **Biology:** General, biochemistry. **Communications:** Media studies. **Computer sciences:** General. **Conservation:** Environmental studies. **Foreign languages:** Ancient Greek, Chinese, French, German, Italian, Japanese, Latin, Russian, Spanish. **History:** General. **Interdisciplinary:** Ancient studies, cognitive science, medieval/Renaissance, neuroscience, science/society. **Liberal arts:** Arts/sciences. **Math:** General. **Philosophy/religion:** Judaic, philosophy, religion. **Physical sciences:** Astronomy, chemistry, geology, physics. **Psychology:** General. **Social sciences:** Anthropology, economics, geography, international relations, political science, sociology, urban studies. **Visual/performing arts:** Art, dramatic, film/cinema.

Most popular majors. English 7%, foreign language 11%, interdisciplinary studies 6%, psychology 8%, social sciences 26%, visual/performing arts 13%.

Computing on campus. 432 workstations in dormitories, library, computer center, student center. Dormitories wired for high-speed internet access and linked to campus network. Commuter students can connect to campus network. Online course registration, helpline, repair service, student web hosting, wireless network available.

Student life. Freshman orientation: Mandatory. Preregistration for classes offered. Held one week prior to start of classes. **Housing:** Guaranteed on-campus for all undergraduates. Coed dorms, single-sex dorms, special housing for disabled, apartments, cooperative housing, wellness housing available. Quiet housing. **Activities:** Bands, choral groups, dance, drama, film society, international student organizations, literary magazine, music ensembles, Model UN, musical theater, opera, radio station, student government, student newspaper, symphony orchestra, TV station, Catholic community, Jewish union, Promoting Equality and Community Everywhere, Amnesty International, Young Socialists, Republican/Libertarian Coalition, AIDS education committee, Habitat for Humanity, Step Beyond (community service), African students union.

Athletics. NCAA. **Intercollegiate:** Baseball M, basketball, cross-country, diving, fencing, field hockey W, golf W, lacrosse, rowing (crew), soccer, squash, swimming, tennis, track and field, volleyball. **Intramural:** Badminton, basketball, bowling, football (non-tackle), golf, handball, soccer, softball, squash, tennis, volleyball, water polo. **Team name:** Brewers.

Student services. Alcohol/substance abuse counseling, chaplain/spiritual director, career counseling, student employment services, financial aid counseling, health services, minority student services, on-campus daycare, personal counseling, placement for graduates, veterans' counselor, women's services. **Physically disabled:** Services for visually, hearing impaired.

Contact. E-mail: admissons@vassar.edu
Phone: (845) 437-7300 Toll-free number: (800) 827-7270
Fax: (845) 437-7063
David Borus, Dean of Admission and Financial Aid, Vassar College, Box 10, 124 Raymond Avenue, Poughkeepsie, NY 12604-0077

Vaughn College of Aeronautics and Technology

Flushing, New York — **CB member**
www.vaughn.edu — **CB code: 2001**

- Private 4-year engineering and technical college
- Commuter campus in very large city
- 1,071 degree-seeking undergraduates: 24% part-time, 13% women, 20% African American, 12% Asian American, 37% Hispanic American, 1% Native American, 3% international
- 6 degree-seeking graduate students
- 95% of applicants admitted
- SAT or ACT (ACT writing recommended), application essay required
- 34% graduate within 6 years; 6% enter graduate study

General. Founded in 1932. Regionally accredited. Engineering technology programs accredited by the Accreditation Board for Engineering and Technology. Management programs accredited by the International Assembly of Collegiate Business Education. **Degrees:** 114 bachelor's, 117 associate awarded; master's offered. **ROTC:** Army, Air Force. **Location:** 5 miles from Manhattan. **Calendar:** Semester, extensive summer session. **Full-time faculty:** 38 total; 32% have terminal degrees, 53% minority, 10% women. **Part-time faculty:** 83 total; 6% have terminal degrees, 53% minority, 13% women. **Class size:** 69% < 20, 31% 20-39. **Special facilities:** Fiber optic Unix-Novell computer system, 65-foot tower overlooking LaGuardia Airport, Frasca 142 flight simulator, nondestructive testing laboratory, composite materials laboratory and computerized engine test-cell.

Freshman class profile. 443 applied, 423 admitted, 223 enrolled.

Mid 50% test scores			
SAT critical reading:	470-630	GPA 2.0-2.99:	13%
SAT math:	510-610	End year in good standing:	47%
GPA 3.75 or higher:	13%	Return as sophomores:	63%
GPA 3.50-3.74:	15%	Live on campus:	12%
GPA 3.0-3.49:	59%	International:	4%

Basis for selection. High school transcripts or GED scores most important followed by SAT, ACT, or TOEFL. B.S. programs require strong performance in high school math and sciences courses. Open admissions to associate degree programs. SAT or ACT with Writing exam required for all first-time, first-year applicants to BS program. Interview recommended. **Homeschooled:** Statement describing homeschool structure and mission, transcript of courses and grades, state high school equivalency certificate required. **Learning Disabled:** IEP documentation required.

High school preparation. College-preparatory program recommended. 14 units required; 18 recommended. Required and recommended units include English 4, mathematics 3-4, social studies 1-4 and science 2-4. Precalculus and physics required.

2008-2009 Annual costs. Tuition/fees: $15,900. Room/board: $10,130. Books/supplies: $1,050. Personal expenses: $1,200.

2008-2009 Financial aid. Need-based: 173 full-time freshmen applied for aid; 173 were judged to have need; 173 of these received aid. Average need met was 82%. Average scholarship/grant was $1,100; average loan $1,776. 49% of total undergraduate aid awarded as scholarships/grants, 51% as loans/jobs. **Non-need-based:** Awarded to 395 full-time undergraduates, including 108 freshmen. Scholarships awarded for academics, alumni affiliation, job skills, leadership, ROTC, state residency.

Application procedures. Admission: Priority date 3/1; no deadline. $40 fee, may be waived for applicants with need. Admission notification on a rolling basis beginning on or about 2/1. **Financial aid:** Priority date 3/1; no closing date. FAFSA required. Applicants notified by 4/15; must reply within 2 week(s) of notification.

Academics. Special study options: Accelerated study, distance learning, double major, independent study, internships, liberal arts/career combination. **Credit/placement by examination:** AP, CLEP, IB, SAT, ACT, institutional tests. 30 credit hours maximum toward associate degree, 60 toward bachelor's. **Support services:** Learning center, pre-admission summer program, reduced course load, remedial instruction, study skills assistance, tutoring, writing center.

Majors. Business: General. **Engineering technology:** CAD/CADD, electrical. **Mechanic/repair:** Aircraft, aircraft powerplant, avionics, communications systems. **Transportation:** Airline/commercial pilot, aviation, aviation management. **Other:** Mechatronic engineering.

Most popular majors. Business/marketing 6%, engineering/engineering technologies 24%, trade and industry 70%.

Computing on campus. 70 workstations in dormitories, library, computer center, student center. Dormitories wired for high-speed internet access and linked to campus network. Commuter students can connect to campus network. Online library, helpline, repair service, wireless network available.

Student life. Freshman orientation: Mandatory. Preregistration for classes offered. One-day session held before classes begin. **Housing:** Guaranteed on-campus for all undergraduates. Coed dorms, wellness housing available. $250 partly refundable deposit, deadline 6/15. **Activities:** Student government, American Institute of Aeronautics and Astronautics, Society of Automotive Engineers, Institute of Electrical and Electronics Engineers, flying club, Women in Aviation-International.

Athletics. Intercollegiate: Basketball M. **Intramural:** Basketball, soccer. **Team name:** Warriors.

Student services. Chaplain/spiritual director, career counseling, services for economically disadvantaged, student employment services, financial aid counseling, health services, legal services, minority student services, personal counseling, placement for graduates, veterans' counselor.

Contact. E-mail: admitme@vaughn.edu
Phone: (718) 429-6600 ext. 118 Toll-free number: (800) 866-6828
Fax: (718) 779-2231
Vincent Papandrea, Assistant Vice President of Enrollment, Vaughn College of Aeronautics and Technology, 86-01 23rd Avenue, Flushing, NY 11369

Wagner College

Staten Island, New York — **CB member**
www.wagner.edu — **CB code: 2966**

- Private 4-year liberal arts college affiliated with Lutheran Church in America
- Residential campus in very large city
- 1,911 degree-seeking undergraduates: 2% part-time, 62% women, 5% African American, 2% Asian American, 6% Hispanic American, 1% international
- 349 degree-seeking graduate students
- 61% of applicants admitted
- SAT or ACT (ACT writing optional), application essay required
- 66% graduate within 6 years; 39% enter graduate study

General. Founded in 1883. Regionally accredited. **Degrees:** 384 bachelor's awarded; master's offered. **ROTC:** Army. **Location:** 10 miles from New York City. **Calendar:** Semester, limited summer session. **Full-time faculty:** 101 total; 92% have terminal degrees, 10% minority, 48% women. **Part-time faculty:** 155 total; 13% have terminal degrees, 46% women. **Class size:** 57% < 20, 43% 20-39, less than 1% 50-99. **Special facilities:** Planetarium, electron microscopes.

Freshman class profile. 3,012 applied, 1,831 admitted, 481 enrolled.

Mid 50% test scores		**GPA 2.0-2.99:**	10%
SAT critical reading:	530-640	**Rank in top quarter:**	70%
SAT math:	530-650	**Rank in top tenth:**	17%
SAT writing:	520-650	**Return as sophomores:**	77%
ACT composite:	23-28	**Out-of-state:**	61%
GPA 3.75 or higher:	19%	**Live on campus:**	85%
GPA 3.50-3.74:	23%	**International:**	1%
GPA 3.0-3.49:	48%		

Basis for selection. School achievement, test scores, recommendations, interview, special talents, essay all considered. Interview recommended for all; audition required for music, theater programs; portfolio recommended for art programs. Interview required for Physician Assistant program. **Homeschooled:** Transcript of courses and grades required.

High school preparation. College-preparatory program required. 21 units required. Required units include English 4, mathematics 3, social studies 1, history 3, science 2 (laboratory 1), foreign language 2 and academic electives 6. 4 economics, arts, computers, or other elective areas of study required.

2008-2009 Annual costs. Tuition/fees: $31,050. Room/board: $9,250. Books/supplies: $725. Personal expenses: $1,260.

2008-2009 Financial aid. Need-based: 384 full-time freshmen applied for aid; 303 were judged to have need; 303 of these received aid. Average need met was 74%. Average scholarship/grant was $11,797; average loan $4,028. 52% of total undergraduate aid awarded as scholarships/grants, 48% as loans/jobs. **Non-need-based:** Awarded to 670 full-time undergraduates, including 187 freshmen. Scholarships awarded for academics, athletics, music/drama.

Application procedures. Admission: Priority date 2/1; deadline 2/15 (postmark date). $50 fee, may be waived for applicants with need. Admission notification on a rolling basis beginning on or about 3/1. Must reply by May 1 or within 2 week(s) if notified thereafter. **Financial aid:** Priority date 2/15; no closing date. FAFSA, institutional form required. Applicants notified on a rolling basis starting 3/1; must reply within 3 week(s) of notification.

Academics. Special study options: Combined bachelor's/graduate degree, double major, exchange student, honors, independent study, internships, study abroad, teacher certification program, United Nations semester, Washington semester. Learning community. **Credit/placement by examination:** AP, CLEP, IB, institutional tests. 9 credit hours maximum toward bachelor's degree. Up to 9 units may be awarded for credit by exam and prior experience. Each unit is equivalent to 3.3 credit hours. **Support services:** Reduced course load, tutoring, writing center.

Majors. Biology: General, bacteriology. **Business:** Accounting, business admin, finance, international, managerial economics, marketing. **Computer sciences:** Computer science. **Education:** General, early childhood, middle, secondary. **Foreign languages:** French, Spanish. **Health:** Nursing (RN), physician assistant, predental, premedicine. **History:** General. **Liberal arts:** Arts/sciences. **Math:** General. **Philosophy/religion:** Philosophy. **Physical sciences:** Chemistry, physics. **Psychology:** General. **Public administration:** Policy analysis. **Social sciences:** Anthropology, political science, sociology. **Visual/performing arts:** Arts management, dramatic, music performance, studio arts, theater design.

Most popular majors. Business/marketing 18%, education 6%, English 6%, health sciences 16%, psychology 7%, social sciences 12%, visual/performing arts 20%.

Computing on campus. 230 workstations in dormitories, library, computer center. Dormitories wired for high-speed internet access and linked to campus network. Commuter students can connect to campus network. Online library, helpline, wireless network available.

Student life. Freshman orientation: Mandatory. Freshmen move on-campus 3 days prior to start of fall semester. Orientation involves academic advisement and registration, social activities, and trip to Manhattan. **Housing:** Guaranteed on-campus for all undergraduates. Coed dorms, apartments, fraternity/sorority housing, wellness housing available. $300 nonrefundable deposit, deadline 5/1. **Activities:** Bands, campus ministries, choral groups, dance, drama, literary magazine, music ensembles, musical theater, radio station, student government, student newspaper, Lutheran student club, Newman Society, Hillel, national honor societies, Amnesty International, Young Democrats, Young Republicans, Nubian Society, Muslim student association.

Athletics. NCAA. **Intercollegiate:** Baseball M, basketball, cross-country, football (tackle) M, golf, lacrosse, soccer W, softball W, swimming W, tennis, track and field, volleyball W, water polo W, wrestling M. **Intramural:** Basketball, bowling, cheerleading W, football (tackle) M, soccer, softball, table tennis, tennis, volleyball. **Team name:** Seahawks.

Student services. Alcohol/substance abuse counseling, chaplain/spiritual director, career counseling, student employment services, financial aid counseling, health services, personal counseling, placement for graduates, women's services. **Physically disabled:** Services for visually, hearing impaired.

Contact. E-mail: adm@wagner.edu
Phone: (718) 390-3411 Toll-free number: (800) 221-1010
Fax: (718) 390-3105
Leigh-Ann Nowicki, Dean of Admissions, Wagner College, One Campus Road, Staten Island, NY 10301-4495

Webb Institute

Glen Cove, New York — **CB member**
www.webb-institute.edu — **CB code: 2970**

- Private 4-year engineering and maritime college
- Residential campus in large town
- 90 degree-seeking undergraduates: 18% women, 4% Asian American, 2% Hispanic American
- 41% of applicants admitted
- SAT, SAT Subject Tests, interview required
- 61% graduate within 6 years; 25% enter graduate study

General. Founded in 1889. Regionally accredited. All students participate in 2-month paid winter work program in marine industry each year. **Degrees:** 24 bachelor's awarded. **Location:** 22 miles from New York City. **Calendar:** Semester. **Full-time faculty:** 11 total; 54% have terminal degrees, 9% women. **Part-time faculty:** 4 total; 50% women. **Class size:** 24% < 20, 76% 20-39. **Special facilities:** Adjoining nature preserve, model testing tank.

Freshman class profile. 73 applied, 30 admitted, 22 enrolled.

Mid 50% test scores		**Rank in top tenth:**	71%
SAT critical reading:	610-670	**End year in good standing:**	96%
SAT math:	670-740	**Return as sophomores:**	88%
SAT writing:	610-680	**Out-of-state:**	68%
GPA 3.75 or higher:	100%	**Live on campus:**	100%
Rank in top quarter:	93%		

Basis for selection. GED not accepted. High school record, class rank, test scores, and interview with President of college most important. Character, motivation, and outside activities considered. **Homeschooled:** Statement describing homeschool structure and mission, transcript of courses and grades, letter of recommendation (nonparent) required.

High school preparation. College-preparatory program recommended. 16 units required. Required units include English 4, mathematics 4, social studies 2, science 2 (laboratory 2) and academic electives 4.

2009-2010 Annual costs. All students receive 4-year, full-tuition scholarships. Room/board: $10,200. Books/supplies: $750. Personal expenses: $3,700.

2007-2008 Financial aid. All financial aid based on need.

Application procedures. Admission: Closing date 2/15 (postmark date). $25 fee, may be waived for applicants with need. Application must be submitted on paper. Admission notification on a rolling basis beginning on or about 3/15. Must reply by May 1 or within 2 week(s) if notified thereafter. **Financial aid:** Closing date 7/1. FAFSA required. Applicants notified by 8/1; must reply within 2 week(s) of notification.

Academics. Intensive single curriculum program demands high career motivation. **Special study options:** Double major, independent study, internships. **Credit/placement by examination:** CLEP. **Support services:** Study skills assistance.

Majors. Engineering: Marine.

Computing on campus. PC or laptop required. 100 workstations in dormitories, library, computer center, student center. Dormitories wired for

high-speed internet access and linked to campus network. Repair service, wireless network available.

Student life. Freshman orientation: Mandatory. Held 1 week before classes start. **Housing:** Guaranteed on-campus for all undergraduates. Coed dorms, single-sex dorms, wellness housing available. $150 deposit. **Activities:** Choral groups, drama, music ensembles, student government, free membership available to local YMCA, women engineers, society of American naval engineers, WebbWomen, society of naval architects and marine engineers.

Athletics. Intercollegiate: Basketball, cross-country, sailing, soccer, tennis, track and field, volleyball. **Intramural:** Basketball, cross-country, soccer, softball, triathlon, volleyball.

Student services. Alcohol/substance abuse counseling, career counseling, student employment services, financial aid counseling, health services, personal counseling, placement for graduates.

Contact. E-mail: admissions@webb-institute.edu
Phone: (516) 671-2213 Toll-free number: (866) 708-9322
Fax: (516) 674-9838
William Murray, Director of Enrollment Management, Webb Institute, 298 Crescent Beach Road, Glen Cove, NY 11542-1398

Wells College

Aurora, New York — **CB member**
www.wells.edu — **CB code: 2971**

- Private 4-year liberal arts college
- Residential campus in rural community
- 563 degree-seeking undergraduates: 1% part-time, 69% women, 7% African American, 2% Asian American, 5% Hispanic American, 1% Native American, 1% international
- 64% of applicants admitted
- SAT or ACT (ACT writing recommended), application essay required
- 52% graduate within 6 years; 27% enter graduate study

General. Founded in 1868. Regionally accredited. **Degrees:** 82 bachelor's awarded. **ROTC:** Army, Air Force. **Location:** 30 miles from Ithaca, 50 miles from Syracuse. **Calendar:** Semester. **Full-time faculty:** 44 total; 84% have terminal degrees, 20% minority, 48% women. **Part-time faculty:** 44 total; 30% have terminal degrees, 7% minority, 59% women. **Class size:** 89% < 20, 11% 20-39, less than 1% 40-49. **Special facilities:** Book arts center, lithography presses, digital imaging laboratory, boathouse with access to Cayuga Lake, indoor tennis courts, 9-hole golf course, science facility with growth chamber, cold room.

Freshman class profile. 1,117 applied, 713 admitted, 155 enrolled.

Mid 50% test scores		**GPA 2.0-2.99:**	19%
SAT critical reading:	500-620	**Rank in top quarter:**	67%
SAT math:	490-600	**Rank in top tenth:**	35%
SAT writing:	470-600	**End year in good standing:**	80%
ACT composite:	21-27	**Return as sophomores:**	72%
GPA 3.75 or higher:	15%	**Out-of-state:**	36%
GPA 3.50-3.74:	41%	**Live on campus:**	99%
GPA 3.0-3.49:	25%	**International:**	2%

Basis for selection. Academic achievement record most important. Test scores, class rank, recommendations, essay, school and community extracurricular activities also important. Evidence of leadership ability through academic and cocurricular activities also considered. Interviews highly recommended. **Homeschooled:** Statement describing homeschool structure and mission, transcript of courses and grades, state high school equivalency certificate required. Please contact Admissions Office for additional information.

High school preparation. College-preparatory program recommended. 17 units required; 23 recommended. Required and recommended units include English 4, mathematics 3-4, social studies 1, history 3, science 2-3 (laboratory 2-3), foreign language 1-2 and academic electives 2-3. Students encouraged to take 2 computer science, art, and/or music. AP and honors courses recommended.

2009-2010 Annual costs. Tuition/fees: $29,680. Room/board: $9,000. Books/supplies: $800. Personal expenses: $800.

2008-2009 Financial aid. Need-based: 135 full-time freshmen applied for aid; 113 were judged to have need; 113 of these received aid. Average need met was 87%. Average scholarship/grant was $14,486; average loan $2,865. 71% of total undergraduate aid awarded as scholarships/grants, 29% as loans/jobs. **Non-need-based:** Awarded to 301 full-time undergraduates, including 99 freshmen. Scholarships awarded for academics, alumni affiliation, leadership.

Application procedures. Admission: Priority date 12/15; deadline 3/1 (postmark date). $40 fee, may be waived for applicants with need. Admission notification 4/1. Must reply by 5/1. **Financial aid:** Priority date 2/15; no closing date. FAFSA required. CSS PROFILE required of early decision candidates only. Applicants notified on a rolling basis starting 3/1; must reply by 5/1.

Academics. Experiential learning integrated through internship and off-campus study programs, study abroad, research with professors, and community service. **Special study options:** Accelerated study, combined bachelor's/graduate degree, cross-registration, double major, independent study, internships, student-designed major, study abroad, teacher certification program, Washington semester. **Credit/placement by examination:** AP, CLEP, IB, SAT, ACT, institutional tests. 6 credit hours maximum toward bachelor's degree. **Support services:** Learning center, reduced course load, study skills assistance, tutoring, writing center.

Majors. Area/ethnic studies: African-American, American, women's. **Biology:** General, biochemistry, molecular. **Business:** General, managerial economics. **Computer sciences:** Computer science. **Conservation:** General, environmental science, environmental studies. **Foreign languages:** General, comparative lit, French, German, Spanish. **Health:** Predental, premedicine, preveterinary. **History:** General. **Interdisciplinary:** Global studies. **Legal studies:** Prelaw. **Liberal arts:** Humanities. **Math:** General. **Philosophy/religion:** Ethics, philosophy, religion. **Physical sciences:** Chemistry, physics. **Psychology:** General. **Public administration:** Policy analysis. **Social sciences:** Anthropology, economics, international relations, sociology, U.S. government. **Visual/performing arts:** General, art, art history/conservation, dance, dramatic, studio arts.

Most popular majors. Biology 10%, English 12%, history 6%, psychology 22%, social sciences 17%.

Computing on campus. 85 workstations in dormitories, library, computer center. Dormitories wired for high-speed internet access and linked to campus network. Commuter students can connect to campus network. Online course registration, online library, repair service, wireless network available.

Student life. Freshman orientation: Mandatory. Preregistration for classes offered. General introduction held during 5-day orientation before classes begin. **Policies:** Honor code governs academic and co-curricular life. **Housing:** Guaranteed on-campus for all undergraduates. Coed dorms, single-sex dorms, wellness housing available. $300 nonrefundable deposit, deadline 5/1. **Activities:** Choral groups, dance, drama, literary magazine, music ensembles, Model UN, student government, student newspaper, Amnesty International, American Red Cross Club, College Democrats, College Republicans, Praising Our Work, social and cultural organization, Women in Life-Long Learning.

Athletics. NCAA. **Intercollegiate:** Basketball, cross-country, field hockey W, golf, lacrosse, soccer, softball W, swimming, tennis W. **Intramural:** Basketball, field hockey, golf, sailing, skiing, soccer, tennis, volleyball. **Team name:** Express.

Student services. Adult student services, chaplain/spiritual director, career counseling, financial aid counseling, health services, minority student services, personal counseling, women's services.

Contact. E-mail: admissions@wells.edu
Phone: (315) 364-3264 Toll-free number: (800) 952-9355
Fax: (315) 364-3227
Susan Sloan, Director of Admissions, Wells College, 170 Main Street, Aurora, NY 13026

Yeshiva and Kolel Bais Medrash Elyon

Monsey, New York

- Private 4-year rabbinical college for men affiliated with Jewish faith
- Small city

General. Accredited by AARTS. **Calendar:** Semester.

Annual costs/financial aid. Tuition/fees (2008-2009): $7,800.

Contact. Phone: (845) 356-7064
Admissions Director, 73 Main Street, Monsey, NY 10952

Yeshiva and Kollel Harbotzas Torah

Brooklyn, New York

- Private 4-year rabbinical college for men affiliated with Jewish faith
- Very large city

General. Accredited by AARTS. **Calendar:** Semester.

Annual costs/financial aid. Tuition/fees (2008-2009): $5,400.

Contact. Phone: (718) 692-0208
1049 East 15th Street, Brooklyn, NY 11230

Yeshiva Derech Chaim
Brooklyn, New York
CB code: 0552

- Private 5-year rabbinical college for men affiliated with Jewish faith
- Very large city

General. Founded in 1975. Accredited by AARTS. **Calendar:** Semester.

Annual costs/financial aid. Tuition/fees (2008-2009): $9,500. Tuition includes board expenses. Room: $3,000. Books/supplies: $400.

Contact. Phone: (718) 438-3070
Admissions Director, 1573 39th Street, Brooklyn, NY 11218

Yeshiva D'Monsey Rabbinical College
Monsey, New York

- Private 4-year rabbinical college for men affiliated with Jewish faith
- Large town

General. Accredited by AARTS. **Calendar:** Semester.

Annual costs/financial aid. Tuition/fees (2008-2009): $3,000. Room/board: $3,000.

Contact. Phone: (845) 352-5852
2 Roman Boulevard, Monsey, NY 10952

Yeshiva Gedolah Imrei Yosef D'Spinka
Brooklyn, New York

- Private 4-year rabbinical college for men affiliated with Jewish faith
- Very large city

General. Accredited by AARTS. **Calendar:** Semester.

Annual costs/financial aid. Tuition/fees (2008-2009): $5,500.

Contact. Phone: (718) 851-1600
Admissions Director, 1466 56th Street, Brooklyn, NY 11219

Yeshiva Gedolah Zichron Moshe
South Fallsburg, New York
CB code: 0750

- Private 4-year rabbinical college for men affiliated with Jewish faith
- Small town

General. Founded in 1969. Accredited by AARTS. **Calendar:** Semester.

Annual costs/financial aid. Tuition/fees (2008-2009): $8,300. Room/board: $2,800. Books/supplies: $200. Personal expenses: $3,003.

Contact. Phone: (845) 434-5240
Dean of Admissions, Laurel Park Road, South Fallsburg, NY 12779

Yeshiva Karlin Stolin
Brooklyn, New York
CB code: 1582

- Private 4-year rabbinical college for men affiliated with Jewish faith
- Very large city

General. Accredited by AARTS. **Calendar:** Semester.

Annual costs/financial aid. Tuition/fees (2008-2009): $6,000. Room/board: $3,200.

Contact. Phone: (718) 232-7800
1818 54th Street, Brooklyn, NY 11204-1545

Yeshiva Mikdash Melech
Brooklyn, New York
www.mikdashmelech.net **CB code: 1432**

- Private 5-year rabbinical college for men affiliated with Jewish faith
- Residential campus in very large city
- 79 degree-seeking undergraduates: 15% international
- 10 degree-seeking graduate students
- Interview required

General. Accredited by AARTS. **Degrees:** 2 bachelor's awarded; master's, first professional offered. **Calendar:** Semester, extensive summer session. **Full-time faculty:** 6 total; 67% have terminal degrees. **Class size:** 100% < 20.

Freshman class profile.

End year in good standing:	98%	**International:**	20%
Live on campus:	70%		

Basis for selection. Open admission, but selective for some programs. Recommendations, school record, test scores, and class rank considered. **Homeschooled:** Statement describing homeschool structure and mission required.

High school preparation. Required units include English 3, mathematics 3, social studies 1, history 1, science 2 (laboratory 1), foreign language 1 and academic electives 1.

2009-2010 Annual costs. Tuition/fees: $6,500. Room/board: $3,800.

2007-2008 Financial aid. Non-need-based: Scholarships awarded for academics, leadership, religious affiliation.

Application procedures. Admission: No deadline. Application must be submitted on paper. Admission notification on a rolling basis. **Financial aid:** No deadline. FAFSA required. Applicants notified on a rolling basis starting 5/1.

Academics. Special study options: Independent study, study abroad. **Credit/placement by examination:** CLEP. **Support services:** Remedial instruction, tutoring.

Majors. Philosophy/religion: Judaic. **Theology:** Talmudic.

Computing on campus. Wireless network available.

Student life. Freshman orientation: Available. Preregistration for classes offered. **Policies:** Religious observance required. **Housing:** Guaranteed on-campus for freshmen. Wellness housing available.

Student services. Adult student services, chaplain/spiritual director, financial aid counseling.

Contact. E-mail: mikdashmelech@verizon.net
Phone: (718) 339-1090 Fax: (718) 998-9321
Rabbi. Shmuel Beyda, Admissions Director, Yeshiva Mikdash Melech, 1326 Ocean Parkway, Brooklyn, NY 11230

Yeshiva of Nitra
Mount Kisco, New York
CB code: 7131

- Private 4-year rabbinical college for men affiliated with Jewish faith
- Small city

General. Accredited by AARTS. **Calendar:** Continuous.

Annual costs/financial aid. Tuition/fees (2008-2009): $6,000. Room/board: $3,000.

Contact. Phone: (718) 387-0422
Pine Bridge Road, Mount Kisco, NY 10549

Yeshiva of the Telshe Alumni
Riverdale, New York

- Private 4-year rabbinical college for men affiliated with Jewish faith
- Very large city

General. Accredited by AARTS. **Calendar:** Semester.

Annual costs/financial aid. Tuition/fees (2008-2009): $7,900. Room/board: $4,600.

Contact. Phone: (718) 601-3523
4904 Independence Avenue, Riverdale, NY 10471

Yeshiva Shaar Hatorah
Kew Gardens, New York
CB code: 0743

- Private 4-year rabbinical college for men affiliated with Jewish faith
- Very large city

General. Founded in 1976. Accredited by AARTS. **Calendar:** Semester.

Annual costs/financial aid. Comprehensive fee (2008-2009): $13,500.

Contact. Phone: (718) 846-1940
Admissions Director, 117-06 84th Avenue, Kew Gardens, NY 11418

Yeshiva Shaarei Torah of Rockland
Suffern, New York

- Private 4-year rabbinical college for men affiliated with Jewish faith
- Commuter campus in large town

General. Accredited by AARTS. **Calendar:** Semester.

Annual costs/financial aid. Tuition/fees (2008-2009): $7,000. Room/board: $3,000.

Contact. Phone: (845) 352-3431
Admissions Director, 91 West Carlton Road, Suffern, NY 10901

Yeshiva University
New York, New York
www.yu.edu
CB member
CB code: 2990

- Private 4-year university
- Residential campus in very large city
- 3,017 degree-seeking undergraduates
- 67% of applicants admitted
- SAT or ACT with writing, application essay, interview required

General. Founded in 1886. Regionally accredited. Campus locations in Manhattan and the Bronx. **Degrees:** 646 bachelor's, 292 associate awarded; master's, doctoral, first professional offered. **Calendar:** Semester, limited summer session. **Full-time faculty:** 863 total. **Part-time faculty:** 389 total.

Freshman class profile. 2,108 applied, 1,402 admitted, 981 enrolled.

Mid 50% test scores		**SAT math:**	540-670
SAT critical reading:	540-670	**ACT composite:**	23-28

Basis for selection. Equal weight given to high school GPA, test scores, ability and motivation as indicated in interview, school and community activities, recommendations of principal, guidance counselor, and/or employer. **Homeschooled:** Statement describing homeschool structure and mission, transcript of courses and grades, state high school equivalency certificate, interview required.

2008-2009 Annual costs. Tuition/fees: $32,094. Room/board: $9,880. Books/supplies: $1,166. Personal expenses: $3,101.

2008-2009 Financial aid. Additional information: Essays required of Distinguished Scholarship applicants.

Application procedures. Admission: Priority date 2/1; no deadline. $65 fee, may be waived for applicants with need. Admission notification on a rolling basis beginning on or about 12/15. Must reply by May 1 or within 2 week(s) if notified thereafter. **Financial aid:** Priority date 4/15, closing date 5/1. FAFSA, institutional form required. Applicants notified on a rolling basis starting 4/1.

Academics. Special study options: Combined bachelor's/graduate degree, cross-registration, double major, dual enrollment of high school students, exchange student, honors, independent study, internships, student-designed major, study abroad, teacher certification program. **Credit/placement by examination:** CLEP, institutional tests. 44 credit hours maximum toward bachelor's degree. **Support services:** Reduced course load, tutoring, writing center.

Honors college/program. 1400 SAT (exclusive of Writing) or ACT equivalent, 2 nominations, interview required.

Majors. Biology: General. **Business:** Accounting, business admin. **Computer sciences:** General, computer science. **Education:** Elementary, foreign languages. **Engineering:** General. **Foreign languages:** Classics, French, Hebrew. **Health:** Audiology/speech pathology, premedicine. **History:** General. **Math:** General. **Philosophy/religion:** Judaic, philosophy. **Physical sciences:** Chemistry, physics. **Psychology:** General. **Social sciences:** Economics, political science, sociology.

Computing on campus. 350 workstations in library, computer center, student center. Dormitories wired for high-speed internet access and linked to campus network. Online library, helpline, repair service, wireless network available.

Student life. Freshman orientation: Mandatory. Held the week before classes. **Policies:** Students participate in university governance through college senates. **Housing:** Guaranteed on-campus for all undergraduates. Single-sex dorms, apartments available. $250 nonrefundable deposit, deadline 6/1. **Activities:** Jazz band, choral groups, drama, literary magazine, music ensembles, musical theater, radio station, student government, student newspaper, neighborhood social service, preprofessional, special interest, and political clubs.

Athletics. NCAA. **Intercollegiate:** Baseball M, basketball, cross-country M, fencing M, golf M, soccer M, tennis M, volleyball M, wrestling M. **Intramural:** Basketball, tennis M, volleyball W. **Team name:** Macs.

Student services. Career counseling, student employment services, health services, personal counseling, placement for graduates.

Contact. E-mail: yuadmit@yu.edu
Phone: (212) 960-5277 Fax: (212) 960-0086
Michael Kranzler, Director of Undergraduate Admissions, Yeshiva University, 500 West 185th Street, New York, NY 10033

Yeshivas Novominsk
Brooklyn, New York

- Private 4-year rabbinical college for men affiliated with Jewish faith
- Very large city

General. Accredited by AARTS. **Calendar:** Semester.

Annual costs/financial aid. Tuition/fees (2008-2009): $8,400. Room/board: $3,500.

Contact. Phone: (718) 438-2727
1569 47th Street, Brooklyn, NY 11219

Yeshivath Viznitz
Monsey, New York

- Private 4-year rabbinical college for men
- Large town

General. Accredited by AARTS. **Calendar:** Semester.

Annual costs/financial aid. Tuition/fees (2008-2009): $4,900. Room/board: $1,650.

Contact. Phone: (914) 356-1010
25 Phyllis Terrace, Monsey, NY 10952

North Carolina

Apex School of Theology
Durham, North Carolina
www.apexsot.edu

- Public 4-year Bible college
- Small city
- 67 degree-seeking undergraduates

General. Regionally accredited. **Calendar:** Semester. **Full-time faculty:** 4 total.

Freshman class profile. 7 enrolled.

Basis for selection. Open admission.

Academics. Credit/placement by examination: CLEP.

Majors. Theology: Theology.

Contact. Apex School of Theology, 2945 South Miami Boulevard, Suite 114, Durham, NC 27703

Appalachian State University
Boone, North Carolina — **CB member**
www.appstate.edu — **CB code: 5010**

- Public 4-year university
- Residential campus in large town
- 14,373 degree-seeking undergraduates: 5% part-time, 51% women, 3% African American, 1% Asian American, 2% Hispanic American
- 1,926 degree-seeking graduate students
- 58% of applicants admitted
- SAT or ACT with writing required
- 61% graduate within 6 years

General. Founded in 1899. Regionally accredited. **Degrees:** 2,634 bachelor's awarded; master's, doctoral offered. **ROTC:** Army. **Location:** 87 miles from Winston-Salem. **Calendar:** Semester, extensive summer session. **Full-time faculty:** 779 total; 100% have terminal degrees, 8% minority, 43% women. **Part-time faculty:** 353 total; 79% have terminal degrees, 5% minority, 51% women. **Class size:** 41% < 20, 43% 20-39, 7% 40-49, 7% 50-99, 2% >100. **Special facilities:** Observatory, cultural museum, visual arts center, year round outdoor adventure camp.

Freshman class profile. 13,182 applied, 7,655 admitted, 2,781 enrolled.

Mid 50% test scores			
SAT critical reading:	530-620	Rank in top quarter:	58%
SAT math:	550-630	Rank in top tenth:	23%
SAT writing:	510-600	Return as sophomores:	87%
ACT composite:	22-26	Out-of-state:	14%
GPA 3.75 or higher:	61%	Live on campus:	98%
GPA 3.50-3.74:	18%	International:	1%
GPA 3.0-3.49:	18%	Fraternities:	4%
GPA 2.0-2.99:	3%	Sororities:	3%

Basis for selection. GED not accepted. Satisfactory combination of grades and/or class rank and required test scores. SAT Math used for placement; CE clarification: no date, but on space basis. Audition required for music majors; portfolio required for art majors.

High school preparation. 13 units required. Required units include English 4, mathematics 4, social studies 1, history 1, science 3 (laboratory 1) and foreign language 2. Specific math units required.

2008-2009 Annual costs. Tuition/fees: $4,275; $14,334 out-of-state. Room/board: $6,160. Books/supplies: $700. Personal expenses: $1,400.

2008-2009 Financial aid. Non-need-based: Scholarships awarded for academics, alumni affiliation, art, athletics, job skills, leadership, minority status, music/drama, religious affiliation, ROTC, state residency.

Application procedures. Admission: No deadline. $50 fee, may be waived for applicants with need. Must reply by 5/1. Postponement allowed on individual basis for one term during academic year. **Financial aid:** Priority date 3/15; no closing date. FAFSA required. Applicants notified by 4/1; Applicants notified on a rolling basis starting 4/1; must reply within 3 week(s) of notification.

Academics. Special study options: Distance learning, double major, dual enrollment of high school students, ESL, exchange student, honors, independent study, internships, liberal arts/career combination, student-designed major, study abroad, teacher certification program. **Credit/placement by examination:** AP, CLEP, IB, SAT, ACT, institutional tests. **Support services:** Learning center, pre-admission summer program, remedial instruction, study skills assistance, tutoring, writing center.

Majors. Architecture: Urban/community planning. **Area/ethnic studies:** Women's. **Biology:** General, ecology. **Business:** Accounting, actuarial science, business admin, construction management, finance, hospitality admin, insurance, international, management information systems, marketing. **Communications:** General, advertising, journalism, public relations, radio/tv. **Computer sciences:** Computer science. **Conservation:** Environmental science, environmental studies. **Education:** Art, biology, business, chemistry, drama/dance, elementary, English, family/consumer sciences, French, health, history, kindergarten/preschool, learning disabled, mathematics, middle, music, physical, physics, social studies, Spanish, technology/industrial arts. **Engineering technology:** Solar energy. **Family/consumer sciences:** Child development, clothing/textiles, food/nutrition. **Foreign languages:** French, Spanish. **Health:** Athletic training, clinical lab science, communication disorders, health care admin, music therapy, nursing (RN), public health ed. **History:** General. **Interdisciplinary:** Global studies. **Liberal arts:** Arts/sciences. **Math:** General, statistics. **Parks/recreation:** Exercise sciences, facilities management. **Philosophy/religion:** Philosophy, religion. **Physical sciences:** Chemistry, geology, physics. **Protective services:** Criminal justice. **Psychology:** General. **Public administration:** Social work. **Social sciences:** Anthropology, economics, geography, political science, sociology. **Visual/performing arts:** Art, arts management, commercial photography, dance, dramatic, graphic design, industrial design, interior design, music management, music performance, studio arts. **Other:** Appalachian studies, Geology, secondary education.

Most popular majors. Business/marketing 19%, communications/journalism 8%, education 16%, psychology 7%, social sciences 8%, visual/performing arts 8%.

Computing on campus. 2,500 workstations in dormitories, library, computer center, student center. Dormitories wired for high-speed internet access and linked to campus network. Commuter students can connect to campus network. Online course registration, online library, helpline, repair service, wireless network available.

Student life. Freshman orientation: Mandatory. Preregistration for classes offered. 2-day program throughout summer and at beginning of each semester and summer school session. **Policies:** Student must be full-time and live on campus to join a fraternity or sorority. **Housing:** Guaranteed on-campus for freshmen. Coed dorms, single-sex dorms, special housing for disabled, apartments, wellness housing available. $100 nonrefundable deposit, deadline 5/1. Sorority housing available. **Activities:** Bands, campus ministries, choral groups, dance, drama, film society, international student organizations, literary magazine, music ensembles, Model UN, musical theater, opera, radio station, student government, student newspaper, symphony orchestra, TV station, Campus Crusade for Christ, Habitat for Humanity, Order of the Black and Gold, ACLU, College Democrats/Republicans, Wesley Foundation, Westminster Canterbury Fellowship, Circle K.

Athletics. NCAA. **Intercollegiate:** Baseball M, basketball, cross-country, field hockey W, football (tackle) M, golf, soccer, softball W, tennis, track and field, volleyball W, wrestling M. **Intramural:** Archery, badminton, basketball, cheerleading, cross-country, fencing, field hockey W, football (non-tackle), football (tackle), golf, gymnastics, handball, racquetball, rugby M, soccer, softball, squash, swimming, table tennis, tennis, track and field, triathlon, volleyball, water polo, wrestling M. **Team name:** Mountaineers.

Student services. Adult student services, alcohol/substance abuse counseling, chaplain/spiritual director, career counseling, student employment services, financial aid counseling, health services, minority student services, on-campus daycare, personal counseling, placement for graduates, veterans' counselor, women's services. **Physically disabled:** Services for visually, speech, hearing impaired. **Learning disabled:** Comprehensive services available.

Contact. E-mail: admissions@appstate.edu
Phone: (828) 262-2000 Fax: (828) 262-3296
Paul Hiatt, Director of Admissions, Appalachian State University, ASU Box 32004, Boone, NC 28608

Art Institute of Charlotte

Charlotte, North Carolina
www.artinstitutes.edu/charlotte **CB code: 3834**

- For-profit 4-year visual arts and career college
- Commuter campus in very large city
- 974 degree-seeking undergraduates: 29% part-time, 66% women, 36% African American, 2% Asian American, 5% Hispanic American
- Application essay, interview required

General. Accredited by ACICS. **Degrees:** 81 bachelor's, 79 associate awarded. **Location:** 8 miles from Center City. **Calendar:** Quarter, extensive summer session. **Full-time faculty:** 47 total; 19% have terminal degrees, 30% minority, 49% women. **Part-time faculty:** 35 total; 23% have terminal degrees, 9% minority, 43% women. **Class size:** 77% < 20, 23% 20-39. **Special facilities:** Computer labs, interior design lighting laboratory, photography studio, audio/video production studios, teaching restaurant open to the public.

Basis for selection. Open admission, but selective for some programs. Interviews required. Applicant must provide a written essay and high school transcripts with minimum 2.0 GPA. Students with a 2.0 average or lower required to take Accuplacer placement test. SAT or ACT recommended. **Homeschooled:** Statement describing homeschool structure and mission, transcript of courses and grades, interview required.

2009-2010 Annual costs. Tuition/fees (projected): $21,996. Annual tuition and fees vary by program. First-time students pay kit fee $810-$2150. Room only: $4,866.

Application procedures. Admission: No deadline. $150 fee. Admission notification on a rolling basis.

Academics. Students begin studies in the majors alongside general education classes from the first quarter. **Special study options:** Distance learning, internships, study abroad. **Credit/placement by examination:** AP, CLEP, SAT, ACT, institutional tests. **Support services:** Learning center, remedial instruction, study skills assistance, tutoring, writing center.

Majors. Business: Apparel. **Computer sciences:** Web page design. **Personal/culinary services:** Culinary arts. **Visual/performing arts:** Graphic design, interior design.

Computing on campus. 224 workstations in library, computer center, student center. Commuter students can connect to campus network. Online library, helpline, student web hosting, wireless network available.

Student life. Freshman orientation: Mandatory. Preregistration for classes offered. Orientation is held the Saturday prior to the first day of classes which is typically on Monday. **Policies:** No weapons, drugs, or alcohol permitted on campus or in on-campus housing apts. **Housing:** Apartments available. $450 fully refundable deposit. **Activities:** Campus ministries, choral groups, student newspaper, Campus Crusade for Christ.

Student services. Alcohol/substance abuse counseling, career counseling, student employment services, financial aid counseling, personal counseling, placement for graduates, veterans' counselor.

Contact. E-mail: aichadm@aii.edu
Phone: (704) 357-8020 Toll-free number: (800) 872-4417
Fax: (704) 357-1133
Pamela Rogers, Senior Director of Admissions, Art Institute of Charlotte, Three LakePointe Plaza, Charlotte, NC 28217-4536

Barton College

Wilson, North Carolina **CB member**
www.barton.edu **CB code: 5016**

- Private 4-year liberal arts college affiliated with Christian Church (Disciples of Christ)
- Residential campus in large town
- 1,125 degree-seeking undergraduates: 21% part-time, 70% women, 24% African American, 1% Asian American, 3% Hispanic American, 1% Native American, 2% international
- 48% of applicants admitted
- SAT or ACT (ACT writing optional) required
- 42% graduate within 6 years

General. Founded in 1902. Regionally accredited. **Degrees:** 210 bachelor's awarded. **Location:** 45 miles from Raleigh. **Calendar:** 4-1-4, limited summer session. **Full-time faculty:** 70 total; 63% have terminal degrees, 10% minority, 50% women. **Part-time faculty:** 34 total; 12% have terminal degrees, 9% minority, 65% women. **Class size:** 63% < 20, 36% 20-39, less than 1% 40-49, less than 1% 50-99. **Special facilities:** Lula E. Rackley Gallery and the Virginia Thompson Graves Gallery of the Barton Museum, greenhouse, TV and music recording studios, photo developing labs and darkroom.

Freshman class profile. 2,468 applied, 1,176 admitted, 249 enrolled.

Mid 50% test scores		**GPA 2.0-2.99:**	46%
SAT critical reading:	390-570	**Rank in top quarter:**	31%
SAT math:	400-590	**Rank in top tenth:**	5%
SAT writing:	380-540	**Return as sophomores:**	71%
ACT composite:	16-24	**Out-of-state:**	27%
GPA 3.75 or higher:	9%	**Live on campus:**	81%
GPA 3.50-3.74:	11%	**International:**	1%
GPA 3.0-3.49:	34%		

Basis for selection. High school GPA, test scores, strong academic course study important. Interview recommended for marginal students; portfolio recommended for art students. **Homeschooled:** State high school equivalency certificate required.

High school preparation. 13 units required. Required and recommended units include English 4, mathematics 3, social studies 2, science 2 (laboratory 1), foreign language 2 and academic electives 1.

2008-2009 Annual costs. Tuition/fees: $19,938. Room/board: $6,782.

2008-2009 Financial aid. Need-based: 229 full-time freshmen applied for aid; 207 were judged to have need; 207 of these received aid. Average need met was 82%. Average scholarship/grant was $5,477; average loan $4,361. 28% of total undergraduate aid awarded as scholarships/grants, 72% as loans/jobs. **Non-need-based:** Awarded to 896 full-time undergraduates, including 251 freshmen. Scholarships awarded for academics, alumni affiliation, art, athletics, leadership, minority status, music/drama, religious affiliation, state residency.

Application procedures. Admission: No deadline. $25 fee, may be waived for applicants with need, free for online applicants. Admission notification on a rolling basis. Must reply by May 1 or within 2 week(s) if notified thereafter. **Financial aid:** Priority date 4/1; no closing date. FAFSA required. Applicants notified on a rolling basis starting 5/1; must reply within 2 week(s) of notification.

Academics. Special study options: Cooperative education, double major, ESL, honors, independent study, internships, liberal arts/career combination, study abroad, teacher certification program, Washington semester, weekend college. **Credit/placement by examination:** AP, CLEP, IB, SAT, ACT, institutional tests. 30 credit hours maximum toward bachelor's degree. **Support services:** Remedial instruction, study skills assistance, tutoring, writing center.

Majors. Biology: General. **Business:** Accounting, business admin, human resources. **Communications:** Media studies. **Computer sciences:** General. **Conservation:** Environmental science. **Education:** Art, Deaf/hearing impaired, elementary, learning disabled, middle, physical, social studies. **Foreign languages:** Spanish. **Health:** Athletic training, nursing (RN). **History:** General. **Interdisciplinary:** Gerontology. **Liberal arts:** Arts/sciences. **Math:** General. **Parks/recreation:** Health/fitness, sports admin. **Philosophy/religion:** Religion. **Physical sciences:** Chemistry. **Protective services:** Criminal justice. **Psychology:** General. **Public administration:** Social work. **Social sciences:** Political science. **Visual/performing arts:** Dramatic, studio arts.

Most popular majors. Business/marketing 26%, education 13%, health sciences 15%, parks/recreation 6%, public administration/social services 6%, social sciences 8%.

Computing on campus. 176 workstations in dormitories, library, computer center, student center. Dormitories wired for high-speed internet access and linked to campus network. Commuter students can connect to campus network. Online library, helpline, wireless network available.

Student life. Freshman orientation: Mandatory, $75 fee. Preregistration for classes offered. Two-day sessions held during June. **Housing:** Guaranteed on-campus for freshmen. Coed dorms, single-sex dorms, special housing for disabled, fraternity/sorority housing, wellness housing available. $150 nonrefundable deposit, deadline 5/1. Full-time freshmen and sophomores not living with parents required to live on campus. Special permission required for students under 23 to live off-campus. **Activities:** Pep band, campus ministries, choral groups, dance, drama, literary magazine, musical theater, student government, student newspaper, symphony orchestra, TV station, Disciples on Campus, Fellowship of Christian Athletes, Habitat for Humanity, Alpha Phi Omega, Campus Conservatives, College Democrats, diversity education team, political science club, Campus Crusade for Christ.

Athletics. NCAA. **Intercollegiate:** Baseball M, basketball, cross-country, golf M, soccer, softball W, tennis, volleyball W. **Intramural:** Badminton, basketball, football (non-tackle), soccer, softball, tennis, volleyball. **Team name:** Bulldogs.

Student services. Adult student services, chaplain/spiritual director, career counseling, student employment services, financial aid counseling, health services, personal counseling, placement for graduates. **Physically disabled:** Services for visually, hearing impaired.

Contact. E-mail: enroll@barton.edu
Phone: (252) 399-6317 Toll-free number: (800) 345-4973
Fax: (252) 399-6572
Amanda Metts, Director of Admissions, Barton College, Box 5000, Wilson, NC 27893-7000

Belmont Abbey College

Belmont, North Carolina — **CB member**
www.belmontabbeycollege.edu — **CB code: 5055**

- Private 4-year liberal arts college affiliated with Roman Catholic Church
- Residential campus in small town
- 1,459 degree-seeking undergraduates: 6% part-time, 62% women, 23% African American, 2% Asian American, 4% Hispanic American, 3% international
- 65% of applicants admitted
- SAT or ACT with writing required
- 32% graduate within 6 years; 15% enter graduate study

General. Founded in 1876. Regionally accredited. **Degrees:** 161 bachelor's awarded. **ROTC:** Army, Naval, Air Force. **Location:** 10 miles from Charlotte. **Calendar:** Semester, limited summer session. **Full-time faculty:** 62 total; 74% have terminal degrees, 3% minority, 42% women. **Part-time faculty:** 69 total; 17% have terminal degrees, 4% minority, 49% women. **Class size:** 66% < 20, 33% 20-39, less than 1% 40-49, less than 1% 50-99.

Freshman class profile. 1,466 applied, 950 admitted, 286 enrolled.

Mid 50% test scores		**Rank in top tenth:**	10%
SAT critical reading:	450-570	**End year in good standing:**	65%
SAT math:	460-550	**Return as sophomores:**	58%
ACT composite:	17-23	**Out-of-state:**	52%
GPA 3.75 or higher:	12%	**Live on campus:**	90%
GPA 3.50-3.74:	13%	**International:**	4%
GPA 3.0-3.49:	22%	**Fraternities:**	20%
GPA 2.0-2.99:	52%	**Sororities:**	20%
Rank in top quarter:	29%		

Basis for selection. GPA, class rank, high school curriculum, and test scores most important. Personal accomplishments, extracurricular activities, and letters of recommendation strongly considered.

High school preparation. College-preparatory program recommended. 16 units required. Required and recommended units include English 4, mathematics 3-4, social studies 1, history 1, science 2, foreign language 2-3 and academic electives 3. For science majors 4 math, 1 chemistry, 1 physics, 1 additional science recommended.

2008-2009 Annual costs. Tuition/fees: $21,039. Room/board: $9,866. Books/supplies: $900. Personal expenses: $1,800.

2008-2009 Financial aid. Need-based: 50% of total undergraduate aid awarded as scholarships/grants, 50% as loans/jobs. **Non-need-based:** Scholarships awarded for academics, athletics, leadership, religious affiliation, state residency.

Application procedures. Admission: Closing date 8/1 (postmark date). $35 fee, may be waived for applicants with need, free for online applicants. Admission notification on a rolling basis beginning on or about 9/15. Must reply by May 1 or within 3 week(s) if notified thereafter. **Financial aid:** Priority date 4/1; no closing date. FAFSA required. Applicants notified on a rolling basis starting 3/1; must reply within 2 week(s) of notification.

Academics. Special study options: Accelerated study, double major, dual enrollment of high school students, honors, independent study, internships, liberal arts/career combination, study abroad, teacher certification program, weekend college. **Credit/placement by examination:** AP, CLEP, IB, institutional tests. 30 credit hours maximum toward bachelor's degree. **Support services:** Learning center, study skills assistance, tutoring, writing center.

Majors. Biology: General. **Business:** Accounting, business admin, international. **Computer sciences:** Programming. **Education:** General, elementary. **Health:** Predental, premedicine, prepharmacy, preveterinary. **History:** General. **Legal studies:** Prelaw. **Liberal arts:** Arts/sciences. **Math:** General. **Philosophy/religion:** Philosophy, religion. **Protective services:** Criminal justice. **Psychology:** General. **Social sciences:** General, criminology, economics, political science, sociology. **Other:** Applied psychology.

Most popular majors. Business/marketing 42%, education 26%, psychology 7%.

Computing on campus. 56 workstations in library, computer center, student center. Dormitories wired for high-speed internet access and linked to campus network. Commuter students can connect to campus network. Online course registration, online library, helpline, wireless network available.

Student life. Freshman orientation: Mandatory. Preregistration for classes offered. 4 days prior to class start. **Housing:** Guaranteed on-campus for all undergraduates. Coed dorms, single-sex dorms, special housing for disabled, apartments available. $400 deposit, deadline 8/24. 24-hour quiet (honors) dorm available. **Activities:** Campus ministries, choral groups, drama, international student organizations, literary magazine, musical theater, student government, student newspaper, BAC College Republicans, Belmont Abbey College Democrats, Delta Psi Theta Sorority, International Club, Association of Latino Professionals in Finance & Accounting.

Athletics. NCAA. **Intercollegiate:** Baseball M, basketball, cheerleading, cross-country, golf, lacrosse, soccer, softball W, volleyball W, wrestling M. **Intramural:** Basketball, bowling, cross-country, football (non-tackle) M, golf, softball, table tennis, volleyball. **Team name:** Crusaders.

Student services. Adult student services, alcohol/substance abuse counseling, chaplain/spiritual director, career counseling, student employment services, financial aid counseling, health services, personal counseling, placement for graduates, veterans' counselor. **Physically disabled:** Services for visually, speech, hearing impaired.

Contact. E-mail: admissions@bac.edu
Phone: (704) 461-6665 Toll-free number: (888) 222-0110
Fax: (704) 461-6220
Roger Jones, Director of Admissions, Belmont Abbey College, 100 Belmont - Mt. Holly Road, Belmont, NC 28012-2795

Bennett College

Greensboro, North Carolina — **CB member**
www.bennett.edu — **CB code: 5058**

- Private 4-year liberal arts college for women affiliated with United Methodist Church
- Residential campus in small city
- 673 degree-seeking undergraduates: 1% part-time, 100% women, 98% African American, 1% Hispanic American
- 45% of applicants admitted
- Application essay required
- 37% graduate within 6 years

General. Founded in 1873. Regionally accredited. **Degrees:** 108 bachelor's awarded. **ROTC:** Army, Air Force. **Location:** 26 miles from Winston-Salem, 96 miles from Charlotte. **Calendar:** Semester, limited summer session. **Full-time faculty:** 55 total; 54% have terminal degrees, 69% minority, 71% women. **Part-time faculty:** 27 total; 15% have terminal degrees, 78% minority, 59% women. **Class size:** 73% < 20, 26% 20-39, less than 1% 50-99. **Special facilities:** Women's Leadership Institute, Carnegie Negro Library.

Freshman class profile. 1,337 applied, 601 admitted, 195 enrolled.

Mid 50% test scores		**GPA 2.0-2.99:**	69%
SAT critical reading:	360-470	**Rank in top quarter:**	16%
SAT math:	340-420	**Rank in top tenth:**	2%
ACT composite:	15-18	**End year in good standing:**	78%
GPA 3.75 or higher:	2%	**Return as sophomores:**	77%
GPA 3.50-3.74:	4%	**Out-of-state:**	76%
GPA 3.0-3.49:	18%	**Live on campus:**	98%

Basis for selection. School achievement record, test scores, recommendations of counselors, and applicant's personal statement important. SAT or ACT recommended. Interview recommended for borderline students. **Homeschooled:** Transcript of courses and grades, letter of recommendation (nonparent) required.

High school preparation. 18 units required. Required units include English 4, mathematics 3, social studies 2, science 2, foreign language 2 and academic electives 5.

2008-2009 Annual costs. Tuition/fees: $14,648. Room/board: $6,478. Books/supplies: $1,200. Personal expenses: $3,000.

2008-2009 Financial aid. **Need-based:** 192 full-time freshmen applied for aid; 181 were judged to have need; 173 of these received aid. Average need met was 45%. Average scholarship/grant was $8,418; average loan $3,170. 43% of total undergraduate aid awarded as scholarships/grants, 57% as loans/jobs. **Non-need-based:** Awarded to 45 full-time undergraduates, including 17 freshmen. Scholarships awarded for state residency.

Application procedures. **Admission:** No deadline. $30 fee, may be waived for applicants with need. Admission notification on a rolling basis. **Financial aid:** Closing date 4/15. FAFSA, institutional form required. Applicants notified by 7/15.

Academics. Accepted students who do not meet required SAT or ACT score admitted to Academic Enrichment Program which provides tutoring, counseling and other support services. **Special study options:** Accelerated study, cooperative education, cross-registration, double major, exchange student, honors, independent study, internships, liberal arts/career combination, student-designed major, study abroad, teacher certification program, Washington semester. Dual degree programs in nursing and engineering with North Carolina Agricultural and Technical State University. **Credit/placement by examination:** AP, CLEP, SAT, ACT, institutional tests. **Support services:** Learning center, pre-admission summer program, reduced course load, remedial instruction, tutoring, writing center.

Majors. **Biology:** General. **Business:** Accounting, business admin. **Communications:** Media studies. **Computer sciences:** General. **Education:** Elementary, English, mathematics, mentally handicapped, middle, music. **Math:** General. **Physical sciences:** Chemistry. **Psychology:** General. **Public administration:** Social work. **Social sciences:** Political science, sociology. **Visual/performing arts:** General, arts management.

Most popular majors. Biology 11%, business/marketing 17%, communications/journalism 7%, education 9%, interdisciplinary studies 10%, psychology 14%, public administration/social services 13%, social sciences 6%, visual/performing arts 6%.

Computing on campus. 130 workstations in dormitories, library, computer center. Dormitories wired for high-speed internet access. Commuter students can connect to campus network. Online library, wireless network available.

Student life. **Freshman orientation:** Mandatory, $100 fee. Preregistration for classes offered. **Housing:** Guaranteed on-campus for all undergraduates. Wellness housing available. $100 deposit. Students with GPA of 3.0 may reside in honor residence hall. **Activities:** Choral groups, dance, drama, film society, literary magazine, music ensembles, radio station, student government, student newspaper, TV station, Student Christian Fellowship, NAACP, social work club, Women in Communications, student teachers association, psychology club, political science club.

Athletics. NCAA. **Intercollegiate:** Basketball W, cross-country W, softball W, tennis W, track and field W, volleyball W. **Intramural:** Basketball W, softball W, swimming W, tennis W, volleyball W. **Team name:** Belles.

Student services. Chaplain/spiritual director, career counseling, student employment services, financial aid counseling, health services, on-campus daycare, personal counseling, placement for graduates.

Contact. E-mail: admiss@bennett.edu
Phone: (336) 370-8624 Toll-free number: (800) 413-5323
Fax: (336) 517-2166
Tisa Frederick, Assistant Director of Admissions, Bennett College, 900 East Washington Street, Greensboro, NC 27401-3239

Brevard College

Brevard, North Carolina — **CB member**
www.brevard.edu — **CB code: 5067**

- Private 4-year liberal arts college affiliated with United Methodist Church
- Residential campus in small town
- 632 degree-seeking undergraduates: 2% part-time, 44% women, 10% African American, 1% Asian American, 2% Hispanic American, 3% international
- 47% of applicants admitted
- SAT or ACT (ACT writing recommended), application essay required
- 33% graduate within 6 years

General. Founded in 1853. Regionally accredited. **Degrees:** 128 bachelor's awarded. **Location:** 33 miles from Asheville. **Calendar:** Semester. **Full-time faculty:** 56 total; 71% have terminal degrees, 45% women. **Part-time faculty:** 30 total; 37% have terminal degrees, 43% women. **Class size:** 80% < 20, 20% 20-39. **Special facilities:** Mountain climbing wall, ropes challenge course, Appalachian center for environmental solutions, fitness appraisal lab, transformational leadership, forest institute, performing arts center, policy center, academic enrichment center.

Freshman class profile. 1,127 applied, 526 admitted, 183 enrolled.

Mid 50% test scores		**Rank in top quarter:**	15%
SAT critical reading:	430-550	**Rank in top tenth:**	2%
SAT math:	430-540	**End year in good standing:**	80%
ACT composite:	15-22	**Return as sophomores:**	57%
GPA 3.75 or higher:	19%	**Out-of-state:**	47%
GPA 3.50-3.74:	12%	**Live on campus:**	93%
GPA 3.0-3.49:	24%	**International:**	3%
GPA 2.0-2.99:	43%		

Basis for selection. High school record, class rank, SAT/ACT scores, references, extracurricular activities, recommendations, essay, interview, talent/ability, character/personal qualities, volunteer work important. Essay, interview recommended for all students; portfolio required for art students; audition required for music students. **Homeschooled:** Statement describing homeschool structure and mission, transcript of courses and grades required. Legal documentation from homeschool agency, local school district, or State Department of Education and admissions interview required. **Learning Disabled:** Evaluation by licensed professional within past 3 years.

High school preparation. 22 units recommended. Recommended units include English 4, mathematics 3, social studies 4, history 1, science 3 (laboratory 1), foreign language 2 and academic electives 4. Math units should include 2 algebra and 1 geometry.

2008-2009 Annual costs. Tuition/fees: $20,050. Room/board: $7,540. Books/supplies: $1,000. Personal expenses: $1,000.

2008-2009 Financial aid. **Non-need-based:** Scholarships awarded for academics, art, athletics, job skills, leadership, minority status, music/drama, religious affiliation, state residency.

Application procedures. **Admission:** No deadline. $30 fee, may be waived for applicants with need. Admission notification on a rolling basis beginning on or about 7/1. **Financial aid:** Priority date 4/15; no closing date. FAFSA required. Applicants notified on a rolling basis starting 2/1; must reply within 4 week(s) of notification.

Academics. **Special study options:** Double major, dual enrollment of high school students, honors, independent study, internships, student-designed major, study abroad, teacher certification program. **Credit/placement by examination:** AP, CLEP, IB, SAT, ACT, institutional tests. 92 credit hours maximum toward bachelor's degree. **Support services:** Learning center, reduced course load, remedial instruction, study skills assistance, tutoring, writing center.

Majors. **Biology:** Ecology. **Business:** Business admin. **Conservation:** Environmental science, environmental studies. **Education:** General, art, drama/dance, elementary, English, mathematics, multi-level teacher, music, physical, science, secondary, social studies. **Health:** Health services, predental, premedicine, prenursing, preveterinary. **History:** General. **Interdisciplinary:** Biological/physical sciences. **Liberal arts:** Arts/sciences. **Math:** General. **Parks/recreation:** Exercise sciences, facilities management. **Philosophy/religion:** Religion. **Protective services:** Law enforcement admin. **Psychology:** General. **Visual/performing arts:** Art, dramatic, music performance.

Most popular majors. Business/marketing 16%, interdisciplinary studies 14%, parks/recreation 24%, psychology 7%, visual/performing arts 11%.

Computing on campus. 100 workstations in dormitories, library, computer center, student center. Dormitories wired for high-speed internet access and linked to campus network. Online library, helpline, wireless network available.

Student life. **Freshman orientation:** Mandatory, $95 fee. Preregistration for classes offered. Orientations held in August prior to start of classes. **Housing:** Guaranteed on-campus for all undergraduates. Coed dorms, single-sex dorms, special housing for disabled, wellness housing available. All non-county or non-adjacent-county residents required to live on campus until age 21. **Activities:** Bands, campus ministries, choral groups, dance, drama, literary magazine, music ensembles, musical theater, opera, student government, student newspaper, Recycling Club, Fellowship of Christian Athletes, Omicron Delta Kappa, Outing Club, Environmental Educators, History Club, Young Politicians of America, Business Club, Debate Society.

Athletics. NCAA. **Intercollegiate:** Baseball M, basketball, cheerleading M, cross-country, football (tackle) M, golf, soccer, softball W, tennis, track and field, volleyball W. **Intramural:** Archery, badminton, basketball, bowling, cross-country, equestrian, football (tackle) M, golf, skiing, soccer, softball, swimming, tennis, track and field, volleyball. **Team name:** Tornados.

Student services. Alcohol/substance abuse counseling, chaplain/spiritual director, career counseling, student employment services, financial aid counseling, health services, personal counseling, placement for graduates, veterans' counselor. **Physically disabled:** Services for visually, speech, hearing impaired.

Contact. E-mail: admissions@brevard.edu
Phone: (828) 883-8292 Toll-free number: (800) 527-9090
Fax: (828) 884-3790
Ken Sigler, Director of Admissions, Brevard College, One Brevard College Drive, Brevard, NC 28712

Cabarrus College of Health Sciences

Concord, North Carolina
www.cabarruscollege.edu **CB code: 5136**

- Private 4-year health science and nursing college
- Commuter campus in small city
- 372 degree-seeking undergraduates
- 44% of applicants admitted
- Application essay required

General. Regionally accredited. **Degrees:** 15 bachelor's, 92 associate awarded. **Location:** 25 miles from Charlotte. **Calendar:** Semester, limited summer session. **Full-time faculty:** 25 total. **Part-time faculty:** 28 total. **Class size:** 67% < 20, 24% 20-39, 7% 40-49, 2% 50-99.

Freshman class profile. 131 applied, 58 admitted, 25 enrolled.

Mid 50% test scores		**GPA 3.50-3.74:**	14%
SAT critical reading:	450-520	**GPA 3.0-3.49:**	23%
SAT math:	440-560	**GPA 2.0-2.99:**	14%
ACT composite:	19-23	**Rank in top quarter:**	55%
GPA 3.75 or higher:	49%	**Rank in top tenth:**	6%

Basis for selection. School record, class rank, essay, test scores, and recommendations most important.

High school preparation. Required and recommended units include English 4, mathematics 2, science 2 (laboratory 2) and foreign language 2.

2008-2009 Annual costs. Tuition/fees: $9,450. Books/supplies: $1,300.

2008-2009 Financial aid. Need-based: 60% of total undergraduate aid awarded as scholarships/grants, 40% as loans/jobs.

Application procedures. Admission: Priority date 3/1; no deadline. $35 fee.

Academics. Special study options: Cross-registration, distance learning, liberal arts/career combination. **Credit/placement by examination:** AP, CLEP, institutional tests. 15 credit hours maximum toward associate degree, 15 toward bachelor's. **Support services:** Learning center, pre-admission summer program, study skills assistance.

Majors. Health: Health care admin, health services admin, nursing (RN).

Computing on campus. 24 workstations in library, computer center, student center. Commuter students can connect to campus network. Online library, wireless network available.

Student life. Freshman orientation: Mandatory. Preregistration for classes offered. 2-day orientation before start of first semester. **Activities:** Student government, student newspaper, Christian student union, association of nursing students, Rotaract.

Student services. Career counseling, financial aid counseling, on-campus daycare, personal counseling. **Physically disabled:** Services for hearing impaired.

Contact. E-mail: admissions@cabarruscollege.edu
Phone: (704) 403-1556 Fax: (704) 403-2077
Mark Ellison, Director of Admissions, Cabarrus College of Health Sciences, 401 Medical Park Drive, Concord, NC 28025-2405

Campbell University

Buies Creek, North Carolina **CB member**
www.campbell.edu **CB code: 5100**

- Private 4-year university and liberal arts college
- Residential campus in small town
- 2,906 degree-seeking undergraduates: 5% part-time, 52% women, 12% African American, 3% Hispanic American, 1% Native American, 4% international
- 1,737 degree-seeking graduate students
- 60% of applicants admitted
- SAT or ACT (ACT writing recommended) required
- 52% graduate within 6 years

General. Founded in 1887. Regionally accredited. **Degrees:** 838 bachelor's, 122 associate awarded; master's, doctoral, first professional offered. **ROTC:** Army. **Location:** 30 miles from Raleigh, 30 miles from Fayetteville. **Calendar:** Semester, extensive summer session. **Full-time faculty:** 196 total; 90% have terminal degrees, 36% women. **Part-time faculty:** 109 total; 50% have terminal degrees, 50% women. **Class size:** 55% < 20, 27% 20-39, 7% 40-49, 10% 50-99, less than 1% >100. **Special facilities:** Golf course, animal museum, drug information center, nature trail.

Freshman class profile. 3,440 applied, 2,065 admitted, 813 enrolled.

Mid 50% test scores		**GPA 2.0-2.99:**	6%
SAT critical reading:	520-640	**Rank in top quarter:**	81%
SAT math:	510-650	**Rank in top tenth:**	41%
SAT writing:	520-640	**Return as sophomores:**	70%
ACT composite:	22-	**Out-of-state:**	20%
GPA 3.75 or higher:	63%	**Live on campus:**	80%
GPA 3.50-3.74:	11%	**International:**	2%
GPA 3.0-3.49:	20%		

Basis for selection. 1425 SAT, GPA, course selection, class rank, and standardized test scores considered. Students with less than the acceptable threshold may be considered for probational admission. Candidates reviewed on an individual basis. Interview recommended on a case by case basis. Essay recommended for all students; audition recommended for music programs.

High school preparation. College-preparatory program recommended. 13 units recommended. Recommended units include English 4, mathematics 3, social studies 2, science 2 (laboratory 1) and foreign language 2. One social science should be U.S. History. Math units must include algebra I and II as well as geometry.

2008-2009 Annual costs. Tuition/fees: $20,350. Room/board: $6,830. Books/supplies: $1,200. Personal expenses: $3,080.

2008-2009 Financial aid. Non-need-based: Scholarships awarded for academics, athletics, music/drama, religious affiliation, ROTC, state residency.

Application procedures. Admission: No deadline. $35 fee, may be waived for applicants with need. Admission notification on a rolling basis. **Financial aid:** Priority date 3/15; no closing date. FAFSA required. Applicants notified on a rolling basis starting 4/15; must reply within 2 week(s) of notification.

Academics. Special study options: Accelerated study, combined bachelor's/graduate degree, cooperative education, distance learning, double major, dual enrollment of high school students, exchange student, honors, independent study, internships, liberal arts/career combination, study abroad, teacher certification program, Washington semester. **Credit/placement by examination:** AP, CLEP, IB, SAT, ACT, institutional tests. **Support services:** Reduced course load, remedial instruction, study skills assistance, tutoring, writing center.

Majors. Biology: General, biochemistry. **Business:** General, accounting, business admin, communications, financial planning, international, management information systems. **Communications:** Advertising, broadcast journalism, journalism, public relations, radio/tv. **Computer sciences:** Computer graphics, computer science, information systems. **Education:** General, biology, elementary, English, family/consumer sciences, French, history, mathematics, middle, music, physical, social studies, Spanish. **Family/consumer sciences:** General, child development, family studies. **Foreign languages:** French, Spanish. **Health:** Athletic training, predental, premedicine, prepharmacy, preveterinary. **History:** General. **Legal studies:** Prelaw. **Math:** General. **Parks/recreation:** Exercise sciences, facilities management, health/fitness, sports admin. **Philosophy/religion:** Religion. **Physical sciences:** Chemistry. **Protective services:** Criminal justice. **Psychology:** General. **Public administration:** General, social work. **Social sciences:** Economics, international relations, political science. **Theology:** Sacred music. **Visual/performing arts:** Commercial/advertising art, dramatic, piano/organ, studio arts, voice/opera.

Most popular majors. Business/marketing 28%, health sciences 6%, liberal arts 12%, psychology 10%, social sciences 6%.

Computing on campus. Dormitories wired for high-speed internet access and linked to campus network. Commuter students can connect to campus network. Helpline, wireless network available.

Student life. Freshman orientation: Mandatory. Preregistration for classes offered. Two weekend sessions in summer available to incoming freshmen and their families for students entering in Fall. Short program before classes start for students entering in Spring. **Policies:** Religious observance required. **Housing:** Guaranteed on-campus for all undergraduates. Single-sex dorms, special housing for disabled, apartments, wellness housing available. $100 fully refundable deposit. **Activities:** Bands, campus ministries, choral groups, drama, international student organizations, literary magazine, music ensembles, musical theater, radio station, student government, student newspaper, Baptist Student Union, College Democrats/Republicans, Fellowship of Christian Athletes, North Carolina Student Legislators, Campus Crusade, Christians in Action, Campbell Catholic Community, Circle K.

Athletics. NCAA. **Intercollegiate:** Baseball M, basketball, cheerleading, cross-country, football (tackle) M, golf, soccer, softball W, swimming W, tennis, track and field, volleyball W, wrestling M. **Intramural:** Basketball, football (non-tackle), soccer, softball, swimming, table tennis, tennis, volleyball, water polo. **Team name:** Fighting Camels.

Student services. Adult student services, alcohol/substance abuse counseling, chaplain/spiritual director, career counseling, student employment services, financial aid counseling, health services, personal counseling, placement for graduates, veterans' counselor. **Physically disabled:** Services for visually, speech, hearing impaired.

Contact. E-mail: buildyourfuture@campbell.edu
Phone: (910) 893-1200 ext. 1290 Toll-free
number: (800) 334-4111 ext. 1290 Fax: (910) 893-1288
Jason Hall, Assistant Vice President for Admissions, Campbell University, PO Box 546, Buies Creek, NC 27506

Carolina Christian College

Winston-Salem, North Carolina
www.carolina.edu

- Private 4-year Bible college affiliated with Church of Christ
- Commuter campus in large city
- 24 degree-seeking undergraduates: 8% part-time, 42% women, 79% African American
- Application essay required

General. Accredited by ABHE. **Degrees:** 5 bachelor's, 2 associate awarded. **Calendar:** Differs by program, limited summer session. **Full-time faculty:** 1 total. **Part-time faculty:** 7 total; 29% have terminal degrees, 71% minority, 71% women.

Freshman class profile. 9 applied, 9 admitted, 6 enrolled.

Basis for selection. Open admission. COMPASS test required.

2008-2009 Annual costs. Tuition/fees: $4,700. Books/supplies: $400.

Application procedures. Admission: No deadline. $50 fee, may be waived for applicants with need. Application must be submitted on paper. Admission notification on a rolling basis. **Financial aid:** No deadline. FAFSA required. Applicants notified on a rolling basis.

Academics. Special study options: Accelerated study, independent study. **Credit/placement by examination:** CLEP, institutional tests. 12 credit hours maximum toward associate degree, 24 toward bachelor's. **Support services:** Remedial instruction.

Majors. Theology: Bible.

Computing on campus. 8 workstations in library. Wireless network available.

Student life. Freshman orientation: Available. **Activities:** Campus ministries, student government.

Contact. Phone: (336) 744-0900 ext. 103 Fax: (336) 744-0901
LaTanya Lucas, Academic Dean, Carolina Christian College, Box 777, Winston-Salem, NC 27105

Catawba College

Salisbury, North Carolina — **CB member**
www.catawba.edu — **CB code: 5103**

- Private 4-year liberal arts college affiliated with United Church of Christ
- Residential campus in large town
- 1,225 degree-seeking undergraduates: 5% part-time, 53% women, 15% African American, 1% Hispanic American, 2% international
- 36 degree-seeking graduate students
- 61% of applicants admitted
- SAT or ACT (ACT writing recommended), application essay required
- 34% graduate within 6 years; 13% enter graduate study

General. Founded in 1851. Regionally accredited. **Degrees:** 281 bachelor's awarded; master's offered. **ROTC:** Army. **Location:** 30 miles from Charlotte, 50 miles from Greensboro. **Calendar:** Semester, limited summer session. **Full-time faculty:** 72 total; 88% have terminal degrees, 6% minority, 42% women. **Part-time faculty:** 25 total; 52% have terminal degrees, 48% women. **Class size:** 60% < 20, 39% 20-39, less than 1% 40-49, less than 1% 50-99. **Special facilities:** Comprehensive three-manual Casavant pipe-organ, observatory, 45-acre outdoor biological laboratory, nature preserve.

Freshman class profile. 992 applied, 601 admitted, 497 enrolled.

Mid 50% test scores		**GPA 2.0-2.99:**	17%
SAT critical reading:	450-580	**Rank in top quarter:**	50%
SAT math:	480-590	**Rank in top tenth:**	21%
ACT composite:	19-25	**Return as sophomores:**	68%
GPA 3.75 or higher:	39%	**Out-of-state:**	32%
GPA 3.50-3.74:	16%	**Live on campus:**	87%
GPA 3.0-3.49:	27%	**International:**	4%

Basis for selection. School achievement record, class rank, standardized test scores, school recommendations important. SAT preferred, but ACT also accepted. Interview recommended for all students; audition recommended for drama, music programs.

High school preparation. College-preparatory program recommended. 16 units required. Required and recommended units include English 4, mathematics 2-3, social studies 3, science 2-3 (laboratory 3), foreign language 2 and academic electives 1. Required credits must be academic subjects at college preparatory level.

2008-2009 Annual costs. Tuition/fees: $22,290. Room/board: $7,700. Books/supplies: $800. Personal expenses: $1,200.

2007-2008 Financial aid. Need-based: 234 full-time freshmen applied for aid; 199 were judged to have need; 199 of these received aid. Average need met was 89%. Average scholarship/grant was $5,105; average loan $4,436. 44% of total undergraduate aid awarded as scholarships/grants, 56% as loans/jobs. **Non-need-based:** Awarded to 1,323 full-time undergraduates, including 315 freshmen. Scholarships awarded for academics, athletics, music/drama, state residency.

Application procedures. Admission: Priority date 8/1; no deadline. $25 fee, may be waived for applicants with need. Admission notification on a rolling basis beginning on or about 10/1. **Financial aid:** Priority date 3/15; no closing date. FAFSA required. Applicants notified on a rolling basis starting 11/1; must reply within 2 week(s) of notification.

Academics. Special study options: Cross-registration, double major, dual enrollment of high school students, honors, independent study, internships, liberal arts/career combination, student-designed major, study abroad, teacher certification program. **Credit/placement by examination:** AP, CLEP, IB, institutional tests. 30 credit hours maximum toward bachelor's degree. **Support services:** Learning center, study skills assistance, tutoring, writing center.

Majors. Biology: General. **Business:** Accounting, business admin, management information systems. **Communications:** General. **Conservation:** Environmental science, environmental studies. **Education:** Elementary, gifted/talented, middle, music, physical. **Foreign languages:** French, Spanish. **Health:** Athletic training, recreational therapy. **History:** General. **Legal studies:** Prelaw. **Math:** General. **Parks/recreation:** General, health/fitness, sports admin. **Philosophy/religion:** Religion. **Physical sciences:** Chemistry. **Protective services:** Law enforcement admin. **Psychology:** General. **Public administration:** General. **Social sciences:** Political science, sociology. **Visual/performing arts:** Arts management, dramatic, music performance.

Most popular majors. Business/marketing 38%, education 8%, parks/recreation 6%, security/protective services 6%, visual/performing arts 13%.

Computing on campus. 100 workstations in dormitories, library, computer center. Dormitories wired for high-speed internet access and linked to campus network. Commuter students can connect to campus network. Helpline, repair service, wireless network available.

Student life. Freshman orientation: Mandatory. Orientation program week prior to start of fall classes includes advising and registration for classes. Optional summer orientation programs for students and parents at additional cost. **Housing:** Guaranteed on-campus for all undergraduates. Coed dorms, single-sex dorms, wellness housing available. $200 nonrefundable deposit. **Activities:** Bands, campus ministries, choral groups, dance, drama, international student organizations, literary magazine, music ensembles, musical theater, student government, student newspaper, symphony orchestra, Alpha program, Athenian society, Helen Foil Beard Society, political science association, environmental service clubs, Fellowship of Christian Athletes, multi-cultural club, Philomathean club, volunteer club.

Athletics. NCAA. **Intercollegiate:** Baseball M, basketball, cross-country, field hockey W, football (tackle) M, golf, lacrosse M, soccer, softball W, swimming, tennis, volleyball W. **Intramural:** Basketball, cross-country, football (tackle) M, golf, handball, racquetball, soccer, softball, table tennis, tennis, volleyball. **Team name:** Catawba Indians.

Student services. Adult student services, alcohol/substance abuse counseling, chaplain/spiritual director, career counseling, student employment services, financial aid counseling, health services, personal counseling, placement for graduates. **Physically disabled:** Services for hearing impaired.

Contact. E-mail: admission@catawba.edu
Phone: (704) 637-4402 Toll-free number: (800) 228-2922
Fax: (704) 637-4422
Lois Williams, Dean of Admissions, Catawba College, 2300 West Innes Street, Salisbury, NC 28144-2488

Chowan University

Murfreesboro, North Carolina — **CB member**
www.chowan.edu — **CB code: 5107**

- Private 4-year university and liberal arts college affiliated with Southern Baptist Convention
- Residential campus in rural community
- 897 degree-seeking undergraduates
- SAT or ACT (ACT writing optional) required

General. Founded in 1848. Regionally accredited. **Degrees:** 93 bachelor's, 9 associate awarded. **Location:** 80 miles from Norfolk Virginia, 130 miles from Raleigh. **Calendar:** Semester, limited summer session. **Full-time faculty:** 50 total. **Part-time faculty:** 20 total. **Class size:** 64% < 20, 33% 20-39, 2% 40-49, less than 1% 50-99. **Special facilities:** Graphic communications center.

Freshman class profile.

Mid 50% test scores			
SAT critical reading:	380-470	Out-of-state:	55%
SAT math:	380-480	Live on campus:	84%
SAT writing:	380-470	Fraternities:	11%
ACT composite:	15-21	Sororities:	20%

Basis for selection. School achievement record most important. Essay, interview recommended for all students; audition required for music majors; portfolio required for graphic design and studio art majors. **Homeschooled:** State high school equivalency certificate required.

High school preparation. College-preparatory program recommended. Recommended units include English 4, mathematics 3, social studies 2, science 2 (laboratory 2) and academic electives 7.

2008-2009 Annual costs. Tuition/fees: $18,120. $120 Communications fee for residents only. Room/board: $7,210. Books/supplies: $864. Personal expenses: $1,000.

2007-2008 Financial aid. Non-need-based: Scholarships awarded for academics, athletics, leadership, music/drama, religious affiliation, state residency.

Application procedures. Admission: No deadline. $20 fee, may be waived for applicants with need. Admission notification on a rolling basis. Must reply by May 1 or within 2 week(s) if notified thereafter. **Financial aid:** Priority date 3/1; no closing date. FAFSA required. Applicants notified on a rolling basis starting 3/1; must reply within 2 week(s) of notification.

Academics. Special study options: Distance learning, double major, dual enrollment of high school students, honors, independent study, internships, liberal arts/career combination, teacher certification program. **Credit/placement by examination:** AP, CLEP, IB, SAT. 15 credit hours maximum toward associate degree, 15 toward bachelor's. **Support services:** Learning center, reduced course load, remedial instruction, study skills assistance, tutoring.

Majors. Biology: General. **Business:** Accounting/business management, business admin, information resources management, marketing, small business admin. **Communications technology:** Graphics. **Education:** General, elementary, English, history, music, physical, secondary. **Health:** Athletic training, predental, premedicine, prenursing, prepharmacy, preveterinary. **History:** General. **Liberal arts:** Arts/sciences. **Parks/recreation:** Exercise sciences, health/fitness, sports admin. **Philosophy/religion:** Religion. **Physical sciences:** General. **Protective services:** Law enforcement admin. **Psychology:** General. **Visual/performing arts:** Graphic design, music performance, studio arts.

Most popular majors. Biology 12%, business/marketing 11%, communications/journalism 12%, education 17%, history 8%, parks/recreation 7%, psychology 7%, security/protective services 10%, visual/performing arts 10%.

Computing on campus. 219 workstations in dormitories, library, computer center. Dormitories wired for high-speed internet access and linked to campus network. Commuter students can connect to campus network. Online course registration, online library, helpline, repair service available.

Student life. Freshman orientation: Mandatory, $50 fee. Preregistration for classes offered. **Policies:** No alcohol on campus; restricted dorm visitation; academic honor code. **Housing:** Guaranteed on-campus for all undergraduates. Single-sex dorms, wellness housing available. $200 partly refundable deposit, deadline 5/1. **Activities:** Bands, choral groups, drama, literary magazine, music ensembles, student government, Christian student union, Student National Education Association, Fellowship of Christian Athletes, Rotaract, international student association, Voices of Inspiration, College Democrats, College Republicans, history club, women's club.

Athletics. NCAA, NCCAA. **Intercollegiate:** Baseball M, basketball, cheerleading, cross-country W, football (tackle) M, golf, soccer, softball W, tennis, volleyball W. **Intramural:** Badminton, basketball, football (non-tackle) M, golf, handball, racquetball, softball, swimming, table tennis, tennis, volleyball W. **Team name:** Hawks.

Student services. Chaplain/spiritual director, career counseling, student employment services, financial aid counseling, health services, personal counseling, placement for graduates, veterans' counselor.

Contact. E-mail: admissions@chowan.edu
Phone: (252) 398-1235 Toll-free number: (800) 488-4101
Fax: (252) 398-1190
Jonathan Wirt, Vice President for Enrollment Management, Chowan University, One University Place, Murfreesboro, NC 27855-9901

Davidson College

Davidson, North Carolina — **CB member**
www.davidson.edu — **CB code: 5150**

- Private 4-year liberal arts college affiliated with Presbyterian Church (USA)
- Residential campus in small town
- 1,661 degree-seeking undergraduates: 51% women, 6% African American, 4% Asian American, 4% Hispanic American, 1% Native American, 4% international
- 26% of applicants admitted
- SAT or ACT (ACT writing optional), application essay required
- 94% graduate within 6 years

General. Founded in 1837. Regionally accredited. **Degrees:** 432 bachelor's awarded. **ROTC:** Army, Air Force. **Location:** 19 miles from Charlotte. **Calendar:** Semester. **Full-time faculty:** 168 total; 97% have terminal degrees, 16% minority, 37% women. **Part-time faculty:** 9 total; 78% have terminal degrees, 11% minority, 44% women. **Class size:** 71% < 20, 28% 20-39, less than 1% 40-49. **Special facilities:** Laser facility, electron microscope, campus arboretum.

Freshman class profile. 4,412 applied, 1,133 admitted, 482 enrolled.

Mid 50% test scores			
SAT critical reading:	630-730	Rank in top quarter:	97%
SAT math:	640-730	Rank in top tenth:	81%
SAT writing:	630-730	Return as sophomores:	96%
ACT composite:	28-32	Out-of-state:	81%
GPA 3.75 or higher:	86%	Live on campus:	100%
GPA 3.50-3.74:	8%	International:	4%
GPA 3.0-3.49:	6%	Fraternities:	40%

Basis for selection. GED not accepted. Course selection, rigor of program, grades, recommendations, essays, test scores, class rank considered. SAT and SAT Subject Tests or ACT recommended. Campus visit strongly recommended.

High school preparation. College-preparatory program required. 16 units required. Required and recommended units include English 4, mathematics

3-4, science 2-4 and foreign language 2-4. Foreign language units should be in same language. 2 required, 4 recommended for social studies or history units.

2008-2009 Annual costs. Tuition/fees: $33,479. Room/board: $9,471. Books/supplies: $1,000. Personal expenses: $1,325.

2007-2008 Financial aid. Need-based: 243 full-time freshmen applied for aid; 159 were judged to have need; 155 of these received aid. Average need met was 100%. Average scholarship/grant was $20,793; average loan $2,208. 93% of total undergraduate aid awarded as scholarships/grants, 7% as loans/jobs. **Non-need-based:** Awarded to 614 full-time undergraduates, including 151 freshmen. Scholarships awarded for academics, art, athletics, leadership, minority status, music/drama, ROTC. **Additional information:** The college has increased the money it provides for grants in financial aid packages and eliminated mandatory loans.

Application procedures. Admission: Closing date 1/2 (postmark date). $50 fee, may be waived for applicants with need. Admission notification 4/1. Must reply by 5/1. **Financial aid:** Closing date 2/15. FAFSA, CSS PROFILE required. Applicants notified by 4/1; must reply by 5/1.

Academics. 2-year interdisciplinary course in humanities available for freshmen and sophomores. Center for Special Studies supervises student-designed majors. **Special study options:** Cross-registration, double major, exchange student, honors, independent study, student-designed major, study abroad, teacher certification program, Washington semester. Visiting student program with Howard University and Morehouse College; Dean Rusk program in International Studies; Philadelphia Center Pro-School for Field Studies. **Credit/placement by examination:** AP, CLEP, IB, institutional tests. **Support services:** Tutoring, writing center.

Majors. Biology: General. **Foreign languages:** Classics, French, German, Spanish. **History:** General. **Math:** General. **Philosophy/religion:** Philosophy, religion. **Physical sciences:** Chemistry, physics. **Psychology:** General. **Social sciences:** Anthropology, economics, political science, sociology. **Visual/performing arts:** Art, dramatic.

Most popular majors. Biology 10%, English 14%, foreign language 11%, history 10%, psychology 8%, social sciences 27%, visual/performing arts 8%.

Computing on campus. 142 workstations in dormitories, library, computer center, student center. Dormitories wired for high-speed internet access and linked to campus network. Commuter students can connect to campus network. Online course registration, helpline, repair service, wireless network available.

Student life. Freshman orientation: Mandatory, $100 fee. Preregistration for classes offered. **Housing:** Guaranteed on-campus for freshmen. Coed dorms, apartments, wellness housing available. Substance-free, suite/apartment-style housing available. **Activities:** Bands, campus ministries, choral groups, dance, drama, international student organizations, literary magazine, music ensembles, musical theater, radio station, student government, student newspaper, symphony orchestra, black student coalition, Amnesty International, Young Democrats, College Republicans, Habitat for Humanity, Asia 3D, gender resource center.

Athletics. NCAA. **Intercollegiate:** Baseball M, basketball, cross-country, diving, field hockey W, football (tackle) M, golf M, lacrosse W, soccer, swimming, tennis, track and field, volleyball W, wrestling M. **Intramural:** Basketball, football (non-tackle), soccer, softball, volleyball. **Team name:** Wildcats.

Student services. Alcohol/substance abuse counseling, chaplain/spiritual director, career counseling, financial aid counseling, health services, minority student services, personal counseling, placement for graduates. **Physically disabled:** Services for visually, hearing impaired.

Contact. E-mail: admission@davidson.edu
Phone: (704) 894-2230 Toll-free number: (800) 768-0380
Fax: (704) 894-2016
Christopher Gruber, Vice President and Dean of Admission and Financial Aid, Davidson College, Box 7156, Davidson, NC 28035-7156

DeVry University: Charlotte

Charlotte, North Carolina
www.devry.edu

- For-profit 4-year university
- Commuter campus in very large city
- 163 degree-seeking undergraduates: 54% part-time, 55% women, 66% African American, 1% Asian American, 6% Hispanic American
- 153 degree-seeking graduate students
- Interview required

General. Degrees: 23 bachelor's awarded; master's offered. **Calendar:** Semester. **Full-time faculty:** 3 total; 33% minority.

Basis for selection. Academic record considered.

2008-2009 Annual costs. Tuition/fees: $13,930. Books/supplies: $1,300. Personal expenses: $5,082.

2007-2008 Financial aid. Non-need-based: Scholarships awarded for academics.

Application procedures. Admission: No deadline. $50 fee. Admission notification on a rolling basis. **Financial aid:** No deadline. FAFSA required. Applicants notified on a rolling basis.

Academics. Special study options: Accelerated study, distance learning. **Credit/placement by examination:** CLEP.

Majors. Business: Business admin. **Computer sciences:** General. **Other:** Technology management.

Contact. Phone: (704) 362-2345
DeVry University: Charlotte, 4521 Sharon Road, Charlotte, NC 28211

Duke University

Durham, North Carolina — **CB member**
www.duke.edu — **CB code: 5156**

- Private 4-year university affiliated with United Methodist Church
- Residential campus in small city
- 6,352 degree-seeking undergraduates: 49% women, 10% African American, 22% Asian American, 6% Hispanic American, 6% international
- 7,375 degree-seeking graduate students
- 22% of applicants admitted
- SAT and SAT Subject Tests or ACT with writing, application essay required
- 94% graduate within 6 years

General. Founded in 1838. Regionally accredited. **Degrees:** 1,620 bachelor's awarded; master's, doctoral, first professional offered. **ROTC:** Army, Naval, Air Force. **Location:** 30 miles from Raleigh, 170 miles from Richmond, Virginia. **Calendar:** Semester, extensive summer session. **Full-time faculty:** 1,027 total; 96% have terminal degrees, 19% minority, 28% women. **Class size:** 69% < 20, 22% 20-39, 3% 40-49, 3% 50-99, 2% >100. **Special facilities:** 4,500-square-foot residence/laboratory, marine laboratory, museum of art, Duke forest, teaching and research center, herbarium, science research center, French science center, global health institute, institute for genome sciences and policy, humanities institute, institute for ethics, Duke phytotron, institute for public policy, institute for environmental policy solutions, social science research institute, center for black culture.

Freshman class profile. 18,774 applied, 4,202 admitted, 1,703 enrolled.

Mid 50% test scores		**Rank in top tenth:**	90%
SAT critical reading:	660-760	**Return as sophomores:**	97%
SAT math:	680-780	**Out-of-state:**	85%
SAT writing:	660-760	**Live on campus:**	100%
ACT composite:	29-34	**International:**	7%
Rank in top quarter:	97%		

Basis for selection. GED not accepted. Courses, school achievement record, school and community activities, essays, recommendations, test scores considered. Special consideration to alumni children and minority applicants. Applicants requesting alumni interview must submit Part I of application by 10/1 for Early Decision or by 12/1 for regular decision. Students using ACT for admission need to submit SAT Subject Tests or AP scores for foreign language and mathematics placement. Applicants to Arts and Sciences submitting SAT must submit 2 SAT Subject Tests. Applicants to School of Engineering submitting SAT must take SAT Subject Test in mathematics and 1 other subject. Interview with alumnus/a in student's home area recommended, but not required; audition recommended for drama, music majors; portfolio recommended for art majors. **Homeschooled:** Transcript of courses and grades, letter of recommendation (nonparent) required.

High school preparation. Recommended units include English 4, mathematics 4, social studies 4, science 4 and foreign language 4. 4 math and 1 physics or chemistry required for engineering applicants, with calculus required before enrolling.

2009-2010 Annual costs. Tuition/fees: $38,741. Room/board: $11,154. Books/supplies: $1,105. Personal expenses: $1,840.

Financial aid. Non-need-based: Scholarships awarded for academics, alumni affiliation, art, athletics, leadership, minority status, religious affiliation, ROTC, state residency.

Application procedures. Admission: Closing date 1/2 (postmark date). $75 fee, may be waived for applicants with need. Admission notification 4/1. Must reply by 5/1. **Financial aid:** Closing date 3/1. FAFSA, CSS PROFILE required. Applicants notified by 4/1; must reply by 5/1 or within 4 week(s) of notification.

Academics. International comparative studies with an emphasis in one or more areas. Special Focus Program for freshmen: engineering frontiers, evolution and humankind, forging social ideals, genome revolution, global health, memory and invention, visions of freedom. **Special study options:** Combined bachelor's/graduate degree, cross-registration, distance learning, double major, ESL, exchange student, honors, independent study, internships, New York semester, semester at sea, student-designed major, study abroad, teacher certification program, Washington semester. Art program/internship in New York City, marine biology semester in Beaufort. **Credit/placement by examination:** AP, CLEP, IB. **Support services:** Learning center, preadmission summer program, tutoring, writing center.

Majors. Area/ethnic studies: African-American, Asian, women's. **Biology:** General, anatomy. **Computer sciences:** General. **Conservation:** General. **Engineering:** Biomedical, civil, electrical, mechanical. **Foreign languages:** Ancient Greek, classics, East Asian, French, German, Italian, Latin, Russian, Slavic, Spanish. **History:** General. **Interdisciplinary:** Medieval/Renaissance, neuroscience. **Math:** General. **Philosophy/religion:** Philosophy, religion. **Physical sciences:** Chemistry, geology, physics. **Psychology:** General. **Public administration:** Policy analysis. **Social sciences:** Anthropology, economics, political science, sociology. **Visual/performing arts:** Art history/conservation, design, dramatic.

Most popular majors. Biology 9%, engineering/engineering technologies 14%, English 9%, history 6%, psychology 10%, public administration/social services 7%, social sciences 28%.

Computing on campus. 450 workstations in dormitories, library, computer center, student center. Dormitories wired for high-speed internet access and linked to campus network. Commuter students can connect to campus network. Online course registration, online library, helpline, repair service, student web hosting, wireless network available.

Student life. Freshman orientation: Mandatory. Preregistration for classes offered. Held week prior to start of classes. **Housing:** Guaranteed on-campus for freshmen. Coed dorms, single-sex dorms, special housing for disabled, apartments, wellness housing available. Special interest housing available for students in women's studies, the arts, languages, service (Alpha Phi Omega). All first-year students live together on East Campus. Most first-year residence halls have a faculty member in residence. All sophomores must live on West Campus. **Activities:** Bands, campus ministries, choral groups, dance, drama, film society, international student organizations, literary magazine, music ensembles, musical theater, opera, radio station, student government, student newspaper, symphony orchestra, TV station, Black Student Alliance, Hillel, Newman Club, Spanish American-Latin Student Association, Volunteers for Youth, Big Brother/Big Sister, Campus Crusade for Christ, Duke Democrats, College Republicans, Habitat for Humanity.

Athletics. NCAA. **Intercollegiate:** Baseball M, basketball, cross-country, diving, fencing, field hockey W, football (tackle) M, golf, lacrosse, rowing (crew) W, soccer, swimming, tennis, track and field, volleyball W, wrestling M. **Intramural:** Badminton, baseball, basketball, football (tackle) M, golf, racquetball, soccer M, softball, squash, swimming, table tennis, tennis, volleyball. **Team name:** Blue Devils.

Student services. Adult student services, alcohol/substance abuse counseling, chaplain/spiritual director, career counseling, student employment services, financial aid counseling, health services, minority student services, on-campus daycare, personal counseling, placement for graduates, veterans' counselor, women's services. **Physically disabled:** Services for visually, speech, hearing impaired.

Contact. Phone: (919) 684-3214 Fax: (919) 681-8941
Christoph Guttentag, Dean of Undergraduate Admissions, Duke University, 2138 Campus Drive, Durham, NC 27708

East Carolina University

Greenville, North Carolina — **CB member**
www.ecu.edu — **CB code: 5180**

- Public 4-year university
- Residential campus in small city
- 20,717 degree-seeking undergraduates: 12% part-time, 58% women, 15% African American, 2% Asian American, 2% Hispanic American, 1% Native American, 1% international
- 5,335 degree-seeking graduate students
- 74% of applicants admitted
- SAT or ACT with writing required
- 54% graduate within 6 years

General. Founded in 1907. Regionally accredited. **Degrees:** 3,549 bachelor's awarded; master's, doctoral, first professional offered. **ROTC:** Army, Air Force. **Location:** 80 miles from Raleigh. **Calendar:** Semester, extensive summer session. **Full-time faculty:** 1,280 total; 79% have terminal degrees, 14% minority, 46% women. **Part-time faculty:** 49 total; 55% have terminal degrees, 6% minority, 45% women. **Class size:** 40% < 20, 40% 20-39, 8% 40-49, 9% 50-99, 3% >100. **Special facilities:** 2 accelerators, climbing wall, ropes course, global classroom, field station.

Freshman class profile. 14,459 applied, 10,680 admitted, 4,538 enrolled.

Mid 50% test scores			
SAT critical reading:	450-540	GPA 2.0-2.99:	23%
SAT math:	470-570	Rank in top quarter:	37%
SAT writing:	440-530	Rank in top tenth:	12%
ACT composite:	19-23	Return as sophomores:	76%
GPA 3.75 or higher:	21%	Out-of-state:	16%
GPA 3.50-3.74:	17%	Live on campus:	81%
GPA 3.0-3.49:	39%	International:	1%

Basis for selection. Freshman admission decisions based on a formula that weighs class rank, high school GPA (unweighted), and standardized test scores. GED accepted for non-traditional freshmen. SAT preferred, ACT also accepted. Audition, statement of purpose and letter of recommendation required for music programs. **Homeschooled:** Transcript of courses and grades required.

High school preparation. College-preparatory program recommended. 20 units required. Required units include English 4, mathematics 4, social studies 1, history 1, science 3 (laboratory 1), foreign language 2 and visual/performing arts 1. Recommended that during senior year student take the 4th math requirement, 1 foreign language, 1 natural science, 1 English. Social studies units must include 1 U.S. history. 1 fine art recommended.

2008-2009 Annual costs. Tuition/fees: $4,406; $14,920 out-of-state. Room/board: $7,630. Books/supplies: $900. Personal expenses: $3,000.

2008-2009 Financial aid. Non-need-based: Scholarships awarded for academics, alumni affiliation, art, athletics, minority status, ROTC.

Application procedures. Admission: Closing date 3/15 (postmark date). $60 fee, may be waived for applicants with need. Admission notification on a rolling basis beginning on or about 10/1. Must reply by May 1 or within 2 week(s) if notified thereafter. Out-of-state freshman enrollment limited to 18% of incoming freshman class, and processed on space-available basis. Applications received prior to December 31 receive priority. **Financial aid:** Priority date 4/15; no closing date. FAFSA required. Applicants notified on a rolling basis starting 3/15; must reply within 3 week(s) of notification.

Academics. Special study options: Accelerated study, combined bachelor's/graduate degree, cooperative education, distance learning, double major, dual enrollment of high school students, exchange student, honors, independent study, internships, student-designed major, study abroad, teacher certification program, Washington semester. **Credit/placement by examination:** AP, CLEP, IB, SAT, institutional tests. **Support services:** Learning center, reduced course load, remedial instruction, study skills assistance, tutoring, writing center.

Majors. Architecture: Urban/community planning. **Area/ethnic studies:** African-American, women's. **Biology:** General, biochemistry, exercise physiology. **Business:** Accounting, accounting/business management, business admin, finance, hotel/motel admin, management information systems, marketing, office technology. **Communications:** General, broadcast journalism. **Computer sciences:** Computer science, information technology. **Education:** Art, business, drama/dance, elementary, English, family/consumer sciences, French, German, health, kindergarten/preschool, learning disabled, mathematics, middle, music, physical, sales/marketing, science, social studies, Spanish, special. **Engineering:** General. **Engineering technology:** Construction, drafting, industrial, manufacturing. **Family/consumer sciences:** Child development, clothing/textiles, family/community services. **Foreign languages:** French, German, Spanish. **Health:** Athletic training, audiology/speech pathology, clinical lab science, clinical nutrition, dietetics, environmental health, health services, marriage/family therapy, medical records admin, music therapy, nursing (RN), public health ed, recreational therapy, vocational rehab counseling. **History:** General, public archives. **Liberal arts:**

Arts/sciences. **Math:** General. **Parks/recreation:** Exercise sciences, facilities management, sports admin. **Philosophy/religion:** Philosophy. **Physical sciences:** Chemistry, geology, physics. **Protective services:** Criminal justice. **Psychology:** General. **Public administration:** Social work. **Social sciences:** Anthropology, economics, geography, political science, sociology. **Visual/performing arts:** Acting, art, art history/conservation, ceramics, cinematography, dance, directing/producing, dramatic, drawing, fiber arts, graphic design, illustration, interior design, jazz, metal/jewelry, music performance, music theory/composition, painting, photography, piano/organ, printmaking, sculpture, stringed instruments, studio arts, voice/opera.

Computing on campus. 2,188 workstations in dormitories, library, computer center, student center. Dormitories wired for high-speed internet access and linked to campus network. Commuter students can connect to campus network. Online course registration, online library, helpline, repair service, student web hosting, wireless network available.

Student life. Freshman orientation: Mandatory, $100 fee. Preregistration for classes offered. 2-phase program: 1 summer session (overnight stay) and 1 session the day prior to start of classes. **Housing:** Guaranteed on-campus for freshmen. Coed dorms, single-sex dorms, fraternity/sorority housing available. $200 partly refundable deposit, deadline 5/1. First-year student floor, leadership hall, extended quiet-hours floor, academic year residence halls available. **Activities:** Bands, campus ministries, choral groups, dance, drama, film society, international student organizations, literary magazine, music ensembles, Model UN, musical theater, radio station, student government, student newspaper, symphony orchestra, 280 registered organizations.

Athletics. NCAA. **Intercollegiate:** Baseball M, basketball, cheerleading, cross-country, diving, football (tackle) M, golf, soccer W, softball W, swimming, tennis, track and field, volleyball. **Intramural:** Basketball, bowling, cross-country, football (non-tackle), golf, racquetball, softball, table tennis, tennis, volleyball. **Team name:** Pirates.

Student services. Adult student services, alcohol/substance abuse counseling, chaplain/spiritual director, career counseling, student employment services, financial aid counseling, health services, minority student services, personal counseling, placement for graduates, veterans' counselor. **Physically disabled:** Services for visually, speech, hearing impaired.

Contact. E-mail: admis@ecu.edu
Phone: (252) 328-6640 Fax: (252) 328-6945
Donald Joyner, Director of Admissions, East Carolina University, Office of Undergraduate Admissions, Greenville, NC 27858-4353

Elizabeth City State University

Elizabeth City, North Carolina — **CB member**
www.ecsu.edu — **CB code: 5629**

- Public 4-year liberal arts college
- Commuter campus in large town
- 3,097 degree-seeking undergraduates
- 39% of applicants admitted
- SAT or ACT (ACT writing optional) required

General. Founded in 1891. Regionally accredited. **Degrees:** 389 bachelor's awarded; master's offered. **ROTC:** Army. **Location:** 50 miles from Norfolk, Virginia. **Calendar:** Semester, extensive summer session. **Full-time faculty:** 168 total; 51% have terminal degrees, 42% minority. **Part-time faculty:** 77 total; 6% have terminal degrees, 62% minority. **Class size:** 61% < 20, 31% 20-39, 7% 40-49, less than 1% 50-99. **Special facilities:** Recording studio, boardwalk in nature preserves/wetlands, golf driving range.

Freshman class profile. 4,000 applied, 1,567 admitted, 638 enrolled.

Mid 50% test scores			
SAT critical reading:	380-460	Rank in top quarter:	13%
SAT math:	380-460	Rank in top tenth:	8%
GPA 3.75 or higher:	6%	Out-of-state:	15%
GPA 3.50-3.74:	6%	Live on campus:	79%
GPA 3.0-3.49:	23%	Fraternities:	3%
GPA 2.0-2.99:	60%	Sororities:	6%

Basis for selection. GPA and test scores considered. Special consideration given to residents from 21 neighboring counties. All applicants to any campus in the UNC system, except those exempted by current campus policies, must submit standardized test scores. SAT preferred, ACT accepted. **Homeschooled:** Statement describing homeschool structure and mission, transcript of courses and grades, letter of recommendation (nonparent) required. **Learning Disabled:** Important to ascertain in advance the extent of the learning disability in order to provide the available service(s).

High school preparation. 20 units required. Required units include English 4, mathematics 3, social studies 2, science 2 (laboratory 1) and foreign language 2. One additional laboratory science also required. Mathematics must include 1 algebra and 1 geometry. Social science must include 1 history.

2008-2009 Annual costs. Tuition/fees: $2,914; $11,928 out-of-state. Room/board: $5,159. Books/supplies: $670. Personal expenses: $1,200.

Financial aid. Non-need-based: Scholarships awarded for academics, athletics, minority status, ROTC, state residency.

Application procedures. Admission: Priority date 5/1; deadline 6/30. $30 fee, may be waived for applicants with need. Admission notification on a rolling basis. **Financial aid:** Priority date 3/1, closing date 3/15. FAFSA required. Applicants notified on a rolling basis starting 6/1; must reply within 3 week(s) of notification.

Academics. Special study options: Combined bachelor's/graduate degree, cooperative education, distance learning, double major, honors, independent study, internships, liberal arts/career combination, teacher certification program, weekend college. **Credit/placement by examination:** AP, CLEP, IB, SAT. 48 credit hours maximum toward bachelor's degree. **Support services:** Learning center, pre-admission summer program, reduced course load, remedial instruction, study skills assistance, tutoring, writing center.

Majors. Biology: General. **Business:** Accounting, business admin. **Computer sciences:** Computer science. **Education:** Art, business, chemistry, elementary, English, history, learning disabled, mathematics, middle, physical, special, technology/industrial arts. **Engineering technology:** Industrial. **History:** General. **Math:** General. **Physical sciences:** Chemistry, geology, oceanography, physics. **Protective services:** Criminal justice. **Psychology:** General. **Public administration:** Social work. **Social sciences:** General, political science, sociology. **Transportation:** Aviation. **Visual/performing arts:** Music management, studio arts.

Computing on campus. 350 workstations in dormitories, library, computer center, student center. Dormitories wired for high-speed internet access and linked to campus network. Commuter students can connect to campus network. Online course registration, online library, helpline, repair service, wireless network available.

Student life. Freshman orientation: Mandatory, $100 fee. Preregistration for classes offered. Three sessions held during summer months covering 2 1/2 days each. **Housing:** Guaranteed on-campus for freshmen. Coed dorms, single-sex dorms, apartments, wellness housing available. $100 deposit, deadline 8/1. College-leased housing available. **Activities:** Bands, choral groups, dance, drama, literary magazine, music ensembles, radio station, student government, student newspaper, symphony orchestra, TV station, United Campus Religious Fellowship, honor and recognition societies in education, science, dramatics, journalism, student union program.

Athletics. NCAA. **Intercollegiate:** Baseball M, basketball, bowling W, boxing W, cheerleading, cross-country, football (tackle) M, golf, softball W, tennis, track and field, volleyball W, wrestling M. **Intramural:** Baseball M, basketball, boxing, football (non-tackle) M, softball, volleyball. **Team name:** Vikings.

Student services. Alcohol/substance abuse counseling, chaplain/spiritual director, career counseling, student employment services, financial aid counseling, health services, personal counseling, placement for graduates, veterans' counselor. **Physically disabled:** Services for visually, speech, hearing impaired.

Contact. E-mail: gdeese@mail.ecsu.edu
Phone: (252) 335-3305 Toll-free number: (800) 347-3278
Fax: (252) 335-3537
Grady Deese, Director of Admissions, Elizabeth City State University, 1704 Weeksville Road, Campus Box 901, Elizabeth City, NC 27909

Elon University

Elon, North Carolina — **CB member**
www.elon.edu — **CB code: 5183**

- Private 4-year university and liberal arts college affiliated with United Church of Christ
- Residential campus in large town
- 4,992 degree-seeking undergraduates: 2% part-time, 59% women, 6% African American, 1% Asian American, 2% Hispanic American, 2% international
- 636 degree-seeking graduate students
- 42% of applicants admitted

- SAT or ACT with writing, application essay required
- 78% graduate within 6 years; 16% enter graduate study

General. Founded in 1889. Regionally accredited. **Degrees:** 1,203 bachelor's awarded; master's, doctoral, first professional offered. **ROTC:** Army, Air Force. **Location:** 15 miles from Greensboro. **Calendar:** 4-1-4, extensive summer session. **Full-time faculty:** 333 total; 86% have terminal degrees, 9% minority, 46% women. **Part-time faculty:** 124 total; 54% have terminal degrees, 5% minority, 44% women. **Class size:** 51% < 20, 49% 20-39, less than 1% 40-49, less than 1% 50-99. **Special facilities:** Fine arts center, science center, academic pavilions.

Freshman class profile. 9,434 applied, 3,990 admitted, 1,291 enrolled.

Mid 50% test scores		**GPA 2.0-2.99:**	6%
SAT critical reading:	560-650	**Rank in top quarter:**	68%
SAT math:	570-660	**Rank in top tenth:**	33%
SAT writing:	570-660	**End year in good standing:**	97%
ACT composite:	25-29	**Return as sophomores:**	90%
GPA 3.75 or higher:	64%	**Out-of-state:**	74%
GPA 3.50-3.74:	12%	**Live on campus:**	100%
GPA 3.0-3.49:	18%	**International:**	3%

Basis for selection. School achievement record most important, followed by test scores. Class rank, school and community activities, personal statement, recommendations also considered. Audition required for all performing arts programs. **Homeschooled:** Statement describing homeschool structure and mission, transcript of courses and grades, state high school equivalency certificate, letter of recommendation (nonparent) required.

High school preparation. College-preparatory program required. Required and recommended units include English 4, mathematics 3-4, social studies 1, history 2-3, science 3 (laboratory 1) and foreign language 2-3. Algebra I, II and geometry required.

2008-2009 Annual costs. Tuition/fees: $24,076. Room/board: $7,770. Books/supplies: $900. Personal expenses: $1,500.

2008-2009 Financial aid. Need-based: 704 full-time freshmen applied for aid; 405 were judged to have need; 405 of these received aid. Average need met was 77%. Average scholarship/grant was $10,090; average loan $3,382. 64% of total undergraduate aid awarded as scholarships/grants, 36% as loans/jobs. **Non-need-based:** Awarded to 2,600 full-time undergraduates, including 505 freshmen. Scholarships awarded for academics, art, athletics, leadership, music/drama, ROTC, state residency.

Application procedures. Admission: Priority date 11/1; deadline 1/10 (postmark date). $50 fee, may be waived for applicants with need. Admission notification 3/15. Must reply by May 1 or within 1 week(s) if notified thereafter. **Financial aid:** Priority date 2/15; no closing date. FAFSA, institutional form, CSS PROFILE required. Applicants notified on a rolling basis starting 3/30.

Academics. Special study options: Accelerated study, combined bachelor's/graduate degree, cross-registration, distance learning, double major, dual enrollment of high school students, ESL, exchange student, honors, independent study, internships, liberal arts/career combination, student-designed major, study abroad, teacher certification program, Washington semester. **Credit/placement by examination:** AP, CLEP, IB, SAT, ACT, institutional tests. **Support services:** Learning center, reduced course load, remedial instruction, study skills assistance, tutoring, writing center.

Majors. Biology: General. **Business:** Accounting, business admin, entrepreneurial studies, finance, international, management information systems, marketing. **Communications:** General, broadcast journalism, journalism. **Computer sciences:** General, computer science, information systems. **Conservation:** Environmental studies. **Education:** General, curriculum, elementary, middle, secondary, special. **Engineering:** General, chemical, computer, environmental, physics. **Engineering technology:** Environmental. **Foreign languages:** General, French, Spanish. **Health:** Predental, premedicine, staff services technology. **History:** General. **Legal studies:** Prelaw. **Math:** General, applied. **Parks/recreation:** Exercise sciences, facilities management, sports admin. **Philosophy/religion:** Philosophy, religion. **Physical sciences:** Chemistry, physics. **Protective services:** Criminal justice. **Psychology:** General. **Public administration:** General, human services. **Social sciences:** Anthropology, economics, international relations, political science, sociology. **Visual/performing arts:** Art, art history/conservation, ceramics, dance, dramatic, music performance, painting, photography, theater design. **Other:** Cinema, Music technology, Professional writing and rhetoric.

Most popular majors. Business/marketing 22%, communications/journalism 17%, parks/recreation 8%, psychology 7%, social sciences 14%, visual/performing arts 6%.

Computing on campus. 850 workstations in dormitories, library, computer center, student center. Dormitories wired for high-speed internet access and linked to campus network. Commuter students can connect to campus network. Online course registration, online library, helpline, repair service, student web hosting, wireless network available.

Student life. Freshman orientation: Mandatory. Preregistration for classes offered. Optional orientation during spring of high school senior year. Required orientation in August. **Policies:** Freshmen and sophomores are required to live on campus; housing is guaranteed. **Housing:** Guaranteed on-campus for freshmen. Coed dorms, single-sex dorms, apartments, fraternity/sorority housing, wellness housing available. $500 fully refundable deposit, deadline 5/1. **Activities:** Bands, campus ministries, choral groups, dance, drama, film society, literary magazine, music ensembles, Model UN, musical theater, radio station, student government, student newspaper, symphony orchestra, TV station, Intervarsity Christian Fellowship, Young Republicans, Black cultural society, Epsilon Sigma Alpha, liberal arts forum, Hillel, student media, Habitat for Humanity.

Athletics. NCAA. **Intercollegiate:** Baseball M, basketball, cheerleading, cross-country, football (tackle) M, golf, soccer, softball W, tennis, track and field W, volleyball W. **Intramural:** Basketball, bowling, football (non-tackle), golf, racquetball, soccer, table tennis, tennis, volleyball. **Team name:** Phoenix.

Student services. Adult student services, alcohol/substance abuse counseling, chaplain/spiritual director, career counseling, student employment services, financial aid counseling, health services, minority student services, personal counseling, placement for graduates, veterans' counselor, women's services. **Physically disabled:** Services for visually, speech, hearing impaired.

Contact. E-mail: admissions@elon.edu
Phone: (336) 278-3566 Toll-free number: (800) 334-8448
Fax: (336) 278-7699
Greg Zaiser, Dean of Admissions, Elon University, 2700 Campus Box, Elon, NC 27244-2010

Fayetteville State University

Fayetteville, North Carolina — **CB member**
www.uncfsu.edu — **CB code: 5212**

- Public 4-year university
- Commuter campus in small city
- 5,608 degree-seeking undergraduates
- SAT or ACT with writing required

General. Founded in 1867. Regionally accredited. Courses leading to bachelor's degree also available at the Fort Bragg/Pope AFB Center, Seymour Johnson AFB, and online. **Degrees:** 775 bachelor's awarded; master's, doctoral offered. **ROTC:** Army, Air Force. **Location:** 60 miles from Raleigh. **Calendar:** Semester, limited summer session. **Full-time faculty:** 200 total. **Part-time faculty:** 40 total. **Special facilities:** Greenhouse, observatory, planetarium.

Freshman class profile.

Mid 50% test scores		**Rank in top tenth:**	5%
SAT critical reading:	380-460	**Out-of-state:**	16%
SAT math:	370-470	**Live on campus:**	74%
Rank in top quarter:	21%		

Basis for selection. 2.0 GPA, SAT scores, completion of 18 prescribed high school units required. All applicants, except those exempted by current campus policies, must submit a standardized test score. SAT preferred, ACT also accepted.

High school preparation. 19 units required. Required and recommended units include English 4, mathematics 3, social studies 2, history 1, science 3, foreign language 2 and academic electives 6. Foreign language units can be used as academic elective units.

2008-2009 Annual costs. Tuition/fees: $3,301; $13,483 out-of-state. Application fees-$25, Orientation fees-$45, Car registration-$45, Ins.-$378, Room breakage Deposit-$125, Bronco card-$24, Late registration fee-$20. Room/board: $5,010. Books/supplies: $350. Personal expenses: $750.

Financial aid. Non-need-based: Scholarships awarded for academics, alumni affiliation, athletics, music/drama, ROTC, state residency.

Application procedures. Admission: Closing date 7/1 (postmark date). $25 fee, may be waived for applicants with need. Admission notification on a rolling basis beginning on or about 1/15. Must reply by 7/1. **Financial aid:** Priority date 3/1, closing date 4/1. FAFSA required. Applicants notified on a rolling basis starting 4/15; must reply within 2 week(s) of notification.

Academics. Special study options: Accelerated study, combined bachelor's/graduate degree, cooperative education, distance learning, double major, dual enrollment of high school students, honors, independent study, internships, study abroad, teacher certification program, weekend college. **Credit/**

placement by examination: AP, CLEP, institutional tests. 30 credit hours maximum toward bachelor's degree. **Support services:** Learning center, pre-admission summer program, remedial instruction, tutoring.

Majors. **Biology:** General. **Business:** Accounting, business admin, office management. **Computer sciences:** General. **Education:** Business, English, health, mathematics, middle, music, physical, secondary, social science. **History:** General. **Math:** General. **Physical sciences:** Chemistry. **Protective services:** Criminal justice. **Psychology:** General. **Public administration:** General. **Social sciences:** General, geography, political science, sociology. **Visual/performing arts:** General, dramatic.

Most popular majors. Business/marketing 22%, education 14%, psychology 11%, security/protective services 13%, social sciences 19%.

Computing on campus. 600 workstations in dormitories, library, computer center, student center. Dormitories wired for high-speed internet access and linked to campus network. Commuter students can connect to campus network. Online course registration, online library, helpline, wireless network available.

Student life. **Freshman orientation:** Mandatory, $45 fee. 3 Saturdays in July and August. **Housing:** Single-sex dorms available. $125 deposit, deadline 7/1. **Activities:** Bands, choral groups, drama, music ensembles, radio station, student government, student newspaper, TV station, Baptist student union, Federation of Young Democrats, NAACP, NCNW, Honda Campus All-Stars, art guild, Illusions modeling club.

Athletics. NCAA. **Intercollegiate:** Basketball, bowling W, cross-country, football (tackle) M, golf, softball W, tennis, track and field, volleyball W. **Intramural:** Baseball M, basketball, bowling, football (tackle) M, golf, gymnastics, swimming, tennis M, volleyball. **Team name:** Broncos.

Student services. Alcohol/substance abuse counseling, career counseling, student employment services, financial aid counseling, health services, on-campus daycare, personal counseling, placement for graduates, veterans' counselor. **Physically disabled:** Services for visually impaired.

Contact. E-mail: admissions@uncfsu.edu
Phone: (910) 672-1371 Toll-free number: (800) 222-2594
Fax: (910) 672-1414
Charles Darlington, Director of Admissions, Fayetteville State University, 1200 Murchison Road, Fayetteville, NC 28301-4298

Gardner-Webb University

Boiling Springs, North Carolina — **CB member**
www.gardner-webb.edu — **CB code: 5242**

- Private 4-year university and liberal arts college affiliated with Southern Baptist Convention
- Residential campus in small town
- 2,600 degree-seeking undergraduates: 17% part-time, 66% women
- 1,246 degree-seeking graduate students
- 63% of applicants admitted
- SAT or ACT (ACT writing optional) required
- 49% graduate within 6 years

General. Founded in 1905. Regionally accredited. **Degrees:** 601 bachelor's, 68 associate awarded; master's, doctoral, first professional offered. **ROTC:** Army, Air Force. **Location:** 45 miles from Charlotte, 60 miles from Greenville, SC. **Calendar:** Semester, extensive summer session. **Full-time faculty:** 142 total; 79% have terminal degrees, 49% women. **Part-time faculty:** 186 total. **Class size:** 69% < 20, 30% 20-39, less than 1% 40-49. **Special facilities:** Observatory, adventure and ropes course, Lake Hollifield and Carillon.

Freshman class profile. 3,227 applied, 2,042 admitted, 441 enrolled.

Mid 50% test scores		**GPA 2.0-2.99:**	24%
SAT critical reading:	440-580	**Rank in top quarter:**	41%
SAT math:	450-560	**Rank in top tenth:**	16%
GPA 3.75 or higher:	36%	**Return as sophomores:**	76%
GPA 3.50-3.74:	14%	**Out-of-state:**	35%
GPA 3.0-3.49:	26%	**Live on campus:**	98%

Basis for selection. School achievement record most important, followed by test scores, recommendations, and school and community activities. Expected 2.5 GPA. The Accuplacer placement test is required of students whose SAT or ACT scores fall below a certain minimum. This test will be used to determine whether the student is to be placed in remedial courses or college level English and Math courses. Interview, portfolio, essay recommended for all students; audition required for music scholarships. Interview may be required for conditionally admitted students.

High school preparation. College-preparatory program recommended. Recommended units include English 4, mathematics 3, social studies 2, science 2 and foreign language 2.

2008-2009 Annual costs. Tuition/fees: $20,465. Room/board: $6,500. Books/supplies: $1,000.

2007-2008 Financial aid. **Need-based:** 359 full-time freshmen applied for aid; 285 were judged to have need; 285 of these received aid. Average need met was 60%. Average scholarship/grant was $7,375; average loan $4,109. 57% of total undergraduate aid awarded as scholarships/grants, 43% as loans/jobs. **Non-need-based:** Awarded to 1,099 full-time undergraduates, including 371 freshmen. Scholarships awarded for academics, athletics, leadership, music/drama, religious affiliation, ROTC, state residency.

Application procedures. **Admission:** No deadline. $40 fee, may be waived for applicants with need, free for online applicants. Admission notification on a rolling basis. **Financial aid:** Priority date 3/15; no closing date. FAFSA required. Applicants notified on a rolling basis starting 3/1; must reply within 2 week(s) of notification.

Academics. Special program offerings possible (including interpreters, notetakers) for students who have tested learning or physically disabled. **Special study options:** Accelerated study, combined bachelor's/graduate degree, double major, dual enrollment of high school students, honors, independent study, internships, liberal arts/career combination, study abroad, teacher certification program. Spring break in New York, fall break in Washington, summer Costa Rica and Quebec language trips. **Credit/placement by examination:** AP, CLEP, IB, SAT, ACT, institutional tests. 64 credit hours maximum toward bachelor's degree. **Support services:** Learning center, pre-admission summer program, reduced course load, remedial instruction, study skills assistance, tutoring, writing center.

Honors college/program. Students with 1170 SAT (exclusive of Writing) and 3.8 GPA average admitted.

Majors. **Biology:** General, ecology. **Business:** General, accounting, business admin, finance, international, management information systems. **Communications:** General, broadcast journalism, journalism, public relations. **Computer sciences:** General, computer science. **Education:** General, biology, chemistry, elementary, English, foreign languages, French, health, history, mathematics, middle, multi-level teacher, music, physical, science, secondary, social science, Spanish. **Foreign languages:** General, American Sign Language, French, sign language interpretation, Spanish. **Health:** Athletic training, health care admin, nursing (RN), predental, premedicine, prepharmacy, preveterinary. **History:** General. **Interdisciplinary:** Math/computer science. **Legal studies:** Prelaw. **Math:** General. **Philosophy/religion:** Philosophy, religion. **Physical sciences:** Chemistry. **Psychology:** General. **Social sciences:** General, political science, sociology. **Theology:** Missionary, religious ed, sacred music, youth ministry. **Visual/performing arts:** Art, ceramics, dramatic, drawing, music management, music performance, music theory/composition, painting, photography, piano/organ, printmaking, sculpture, stringed instruments, studio arts, voice/opera. **Other:** Biblical languages and literature, Electronic publishing, English as a second language with teacher licensure.

Most popular majors. Business/marketing 33%, health sciences 11%, social sciences 30%.

Computing on campus. 150 workstations in library, computer center. Dormitories wired for high-speed internet access and linked to campus network. Commuter students can connect to campus network. Online course registration, online library, helpline, wireless network available.

Student life. **Freshman orientation:** Mandatory, $75 fee. Preregistration for classes offered. 3-day program typically held near the end of August, just before fall semester commences. **Policies:** Limited visitation hours: 12:00 noon to 12:00 midnight in dorm rooms. Lobbies open for visitation until 2:00 am., no alcohol or tobacco allowed on campus, and "quiet hours" observed from 10 pm through 10 am. **Housing:** Guaranteed on-campus for all undergraduates. Single-sex dorms, special housing for disabled, apartments, wellness housing available. $150 fully refundable deposit. Honors student residence hall available. **Activities:** Bands, campus ministries, choral groups, dance, drama, literary magazine, music ensembles, musical theater, opera, radio station, student government, student newspaper, symphony orchestra, The Verge, Fellowship of Christian Athletes, student volunteer groups, prison ministry, student YMCA, gospel choir, Bible studies, College Republicans and College Democrats.

Athletics. NCAA. **Intercollegiate:** Baseball M, basketball, cheerleading, cross-country, football (tackle) M, golf, soccer, softball W, swimming, tennis, track and field, volleyball W, wrestling M. **Intramural:** Badminton, baseball, basketball, football (non-tackle), racquetball, skiing, soccer, softball, swimming, table tennis, tennis, volleyball. **Team name:** Runnin' Bulldogs.

Student services. Alcohol/substance abuse counseling, chaplain/spiritual director, career counseling, student employment services, financial aid counseling, personal counseling, placement for graduates, veterans' counselor. **Physically disabled:** Services for visually, speech, hearing impaired. **Learning disabled:** Comprehensive services available.

Contact. E-mail: admissions@gardner-webb.edu
Phone: (704) 406-4498 Toll-free number: (800) 253-6472
Fax: (704) 406-4488
Nathan Alexander, Assistant Vice President of Enrollment Management and Admissions, Gardner-Webb University, Box 817, Boiling Springs, NC 28017

Greensboro College

Greensboro, North Carolina — **CB member**
www.greensborocollege.edu — **CB code: 5260**

- Private 4-year liberal arts college affiliated with United Methodist Church
- Residential campus in large city
- 1,043 degree-seeking undergraduates: 15% part-time, 52% women
- 83 degree-seeking graduate students
- 63% of applicants admitted
- SAT or ACT with writing, application essay required
- 40% graduate within 6 years; 10% enter graduate study

General. Founded in 1838. Regionally accredited. **Degrees:** 191 bachelor's awarded; master's offered. **ROTC:** Army, Air Force. **Location:** 90 miles from Charlotte, 75 miles from Raleigh. **Calendar:** Semester, limited summer session. **Full-time faculty:** 68 total; 7% minority, 48% women. **Part-time faculty:** 79 total. **Class size:** 83% < 20, 17% 20-39. **Special facilities:** Historical museum, computer writing center, computerized music laboratories.

Freshman class profile. 1,048 applied, 660 admitted, 212 enrolled.

Mid 50% test scores			
SAT critical reading:	410-520	GPA 3.0-3.49:	25%
SAT math:	410-520	GPA 2.0-2.99:	45%
SAT writing:	410-520	Rank in top quarter:	24%
ACT composite:	15-21	Rank in top tenth:	7%
GPA 3.75 or higher:	19%	Return as sophomores:	57%
GPA 3.50-3.74:	10%	Out-of-state:	27%
		Live on campus:	93%

Basis for selection. High school curriculum most important, followed by grades, class rank, test scores, personal statement, school and community activities, high school caliber. Recommendations, interview considered. Interview recommended for all students. Audition required for music, theater majors; portfolio required for art majors. **Homeschooled:** Interview highly recommended and SAT/ACT required. **Learning Disabled:** Students wishing to receive accommodations facilitated by the Office of Disability Services are responsible for disclosure of physical, psychological, and learning disabilities. Accommodation of learning and psychological disabilities must be accompanied by appropriate documentation that includes professional evaluation, diagnosis, and recommendations.

High school preparation. College-preparatory program recommended. Recommended units include English 4, mathematics 3, history 2, science 2 (laboratory 1) and foreign language 2. Remaining units must be selected from art, music, social science and physical education.

2008-2009 Annual costs. Tuition/fees: $22,248. Room/board: $8,420. Books/supplies: $900. Personal expenses: $900.

2008-2009 Financial aid. Non-need-based: Scholarships awarded for academics, alumni affiliation, art, leadership, music/drama, religious affiliation, state residency.

Application procedures. Admission: Priority date 12/15; no deadline. $35 fee, may be waived for applicants with need. Admission notification on a rolling basis. Must reply by May 1 or within 4 week(s) if notified thereafter. **Financial aid:** Priority date 4/15; no closing date. FAFSA, institutional form required. Applicants notified on a rolling basis starting 2/1; must reply within 2 week(s) of notification.

Academics. Special study options: Accelerated study, cross-registration, double major, dual enrollment of high school students, ESL, honors, independent study, internships, liberal arts/career combination, student-designed major, study abroad, teacher certification program, weekend college. Academic success program, minor in ethics across the curriculum, minor in women's and gender studies, minor in computer science. **Credit/placement by examination:** AP, CLEP, IB, institutional tests. 45 credit hours maximum toward bachelor's degree. **Support services:** Learning center, reduced course load, study skills assistance, tutoring, writing center.

Majors. Biology: General. **Business:** Accounting, managerial economics. **Communications:** General. **Education:** General, art, biology, drama/dance, early childhood, elementary, emotionally handicapped, English, history, learning disabled, mathematics, mentally handicapped, middle, multiple handicapped, music, physical, social studies, Spanish, special. **Foreign languages:** French, Spanish. **Health:** Athletic training. **History:** General. **Liberal arts:** Arts/sciences. **Math:** General. **Parks/recreation:** Exercise sciences, health/fitness, sports admin. **Philosophy/religion:** Religion. **Physical sciences:** Chemistry. **Psychology:** General. **Social sciences:** Political science, sociology. **Visual/performing arts:** Dramatic, music performance, studio arts, theater design.

Most popular majors. Biology 7%, business/marketing 25%, education 15%, social sciences 12%, visual/performing arts 16%.

Computing on campus. 152 workstations in dormitories, library, computer center, student center. Dormitories wired for high-speed internet access and linked to campus network. Commuter students can connect to campus network. Online library, helpline, repair service, wireless network available.

Student life. Freshman orientation: Mandatory. Preregistration for classes offered. Orientations held in May, June, July and August. **Housing:** Guaranteed on-campus for all undergraduates. Coed dorms, single-sex dorms, apartments, wellness housing available. $200 partly refundable deposit. All students who have earned less than 58 credit hours required to live in college housing unless married, veterans, or residing with parents. All students encouraged to do so. **Activities:** Bands, choral groups, dance, drama, international student organizations, literary magazine, music ensembles, Model UN, musical theater, opera, student government, student newspaper, Student Christian Fellowship, United African American Society, Student National Education Association, campus activity board, Fellowship of Christian Athletes, Los Amigos.

Athletics. NCAA. **Intercollegiate:** Baseball M, basketball, cheerleading, cross-country, football (tackle) M, golf M, lacrosse, soccer, softball W, swimming W, tennis, volleyball W. **Intramural:** Baseball M, basketball, football (non-tackle), skiing. **Team name:** The Pride.

Student services. Adult student services, alcohol/substance abuse counseling, chaplain/spiritual director, career counseling, student employment services, financial aid counseling, health services, personal counseling, placement for graduates. **Physically disabled:** Services for visually, speech, hearing impaired.

Contact. E-mail: admissions@greensborocollege.edu
Phone: (336) 272-7102 ext. 211 Toll-free number: (800) 346-8226
Fax: (336) 378-0154
Tim Jackson, Director of Admissions, Greensboro College, 815 West Market Street, Greensboro, NC 27401-1875

Guilford College

Greensboro, North Carolina — **CB member**
www.guilford.edu — **CB code: 5261**

- Private 4-year liberal arts college affiliated with Society of Friends (Quaker)
- Residential campus in small city
- 2,641 degree-seeking undergraduates: 16% part-time, 60% women, 23% African American, 2% Asian American, 3% Hispanic American, 1% Native American, 1% international
- 60% of applicants admitted
- Application essay required
- 58% graduate within 6 years

General. Founded in 1837. Regionally accredited. **Degrees:** 521 bachelor's awarded. **ROTC:** Army, Naval, Air Force. **Location:** 90 miles from Raleigh, 100 miles from Charlotte. **Calendar:** Semester, limited summer session. **Full-time faculty:** 128 total; 83% have terminal degrees, 17% minority, 48% women. **Part-time faculty:** 91 total; 41% have terminal degrees, 13% minority, 50% women. **Class size:** 69% < 20, 30% 20-39, less than 1% 40-49. **Special facilities:** Observatory, multimedia learning center for cultures and languages, telecommunications center, photography studio, outdoor sculpture studio, computer visualization laboratory.

Freshman class profile. 3,610 applied, 2,163 admitted, 436 enrolled.

Mid 50% test scores		**GPA 3.0-3.49:**	30%
SAT critical reading:	500-620	**GPA 2.0-2.99:**	40%
SAT math:	500-600	**Rank in top quarter:**	45%
SAT writing:	480-610	**Return as sophomores:**	67%
ACT composite:	21-26	**Out-of-state:**	63%
GPA 3.75 or higher:	12%	**Live on campus:**	98%
GPA 3.50-3.74:	18%		

Basis for selection. School achievement record and essay most important. Test scores, interview, recommendations, interests, leadership ability also important. Minimum SAT composite score of 1000 (exclusive of Writing) or ACT score of 22 recommended. SAT or ACT recommended. Applicant may choose to submit portfolio instead of standardized test scores. Portfolio should reflect student's academic, creative, and personal interests and accomplishments. It must include, but is not limited to, 3-5 writing samples (at least one should be a graded expository written work) and, if available, a junior/senior reading list. Auditions and portfolios recommended in music, theatre and art. **Homeschooled:** Interview required. Provide reason for homeschool.

High school preparation. 12 units recommended. Recommended units include English 4, mathematics 3, science 3 and foreign language 2.

2008-2009 Annual costs. Tuition/fees: $26,030. Parking fee $70, required athletic insurance $183. Room/board: $7,140. Books/supplies: $900. Personal expenses: $1,200.

2007-2008 Financial aid. Need-based: 341 full-time freshmen applied for aid; 271 were judged to have need; 271 of these received aid. Average scholarship/grant was $12,419; average loan $4,903. 45% of total undergraduate aid awarded as scholarships/grants, 55% as loans/jobs. **Non-need-based:** Awarded to 718 full-time undergraduates, including 153 freshmen. Scholarships awarded for academics.

Application procedures. Admission: Priority date 1/15; deadline 2/15 (postmark date). $25 fee, may be waived for applicants with need, free for online applicants. Admission notification on a rolling basis beginning on or about 11/1. Must reply by May 1 or within 3 week(s) if notified thereafter. **Financial aid:** Priority date 3/1; no closing date. FAFSA required. Applicants notified on a rolling basis starting 2/15; must reply within 2 week(s) of notification.

Academics. Faculty tutoring for skills development and student tutoring for course-specific help available. Assistance available for non-remedial writing, organizational/time-management skills, and students with learning disabilities. Remedial assistance and reader service for the blind available. **Special study options:** Accelerated study, combined bachelor's/graduate degree, cooperative education, cross-registration, double major, ESL, exchange student, honors, independent study, internships, liberal arts/career combination, student-designed major, study abroad, teacher certification program, Washington semester, weekend college. 3-2 degree programs available in forestry and environmental studies with Duke University, and in physician assistant training with Bowman Gray School of Medicine at Wake Forest University. Many internships, work-study programs, accelerated degree programs in business management, computer information systems, psychology, and biology, dual majors, student-designed majors, study abroad in 9 countries, and cross-registration with members of the Greater Greensboro Consortium (8 colleges/universities). **Credit/placement by examination:** AP, CLEP, IB, SAT, ACT, institutional tests. 32 credit hours maximum toward bachelor's degree. **Support services:** Learning center, pre-admission summer program, reduced course load, remedial instruction, study skills assistance, tutoring, writing center.

Majors. Area/ethnic studies: African-American, women's. **Biology:** General, biomedical sciences. **Business:** Accounting, business admin. **Computer sciences:** General, information systems. **Conservation:** Environmental studies. **Education:** Elementary, physical, secondary. **Foreign languages:** French, German, Germanic, Spanish. **Health:** Athletic training. **History:** General. **Interdisciplinary:** Peace/conflict. **Math:** General. **Parks/recreation:** Exercise sciences, health/fitness, sports admin. **Philosophy/religion:** Philosophy, religion. **Physical sciences:** Chemistry, geology, physics. **Protective services:** Criminal justice, forensics. **Psychology:** General. **Social sciences:** Economics, international relations, political science, sociology. **Visual/performing arts:** Art, dramatic.

Most popular majors. Biology 9%, business/marketing 18%, English 7%, psychology 12%, security/protective services 11%, social sciences 10%, visual/performing arts 6%.

Computing on campus. 348 workstations in dormitories, library, computer center, student center. Dormitories wired for high-speed internet access and linked to campus network. Commuter students can connect to campus network. Helpline, repair service, wireless network available.

Student life. Freshman orientation: Mandatory, $75 fee. Preregistration for classes offered. One-day event in Spring; parents invited. **Policies:** Consistent with its Quaker heritage, college promotes and encourages student involvement in community service projects. **Housing:** Guaranteed on-campus for freshmen. Coed dorms, single-sex dorms, special housing for disabled, apartments, cooperative housing, wellness housing available. $400 fully refundable deposit, deadline 5/1. Special interest housing available. **Activities:** Bands, campus ministries, choral groups, dance, drama, film society, international student organizations, literary magazine, music ensembles, musical theater, radio station, student government, student newspaper, African American cultural society, Amnesty International, Project Community, community senate, Christian fellowship, Native American club, Hillel, Quaker Concerns, Guilford Action Network.

Athletics. NCAA. **Intercollegiate:** Baseball, basketball, cross-country, football (tackle) M, golf M, lacrosse, rugby, soccer, softball W, swimming W, tennis, volleyball W. **Intramural:** Baseball, basketball, cheerleading W, football (non-tackle), soccer, softball, table tennis, tennis, volleyball, water polo. **Team name:** Quakers.

Student services. Adult student services, alcohol/substance abuse counseling, chaplain/spiritual director, career counseling, student employment services, financial aid counseling, health services, minority student services, personal counseling, placement for graduates, veterans' counselor, women's services. **Physically disabled:** Services for visually, speech, hearing impaired. **Learning disabled:** Comprehensive services available.

Contact. E-mail: admission@guilford.edu
Phone: (336) 316-2100 Toll-free number: (800) 992-7759
Fax: (336) 316-2954
Randy Doss, Vice President, Enrollment and Campus Life, Guilford College, Admissions, New Garden Hall, Greensboro, NC 27410-4108

High Point University

High Point, North Carolina — **CB member**
www.highpoint.edu — **CB code: 5293**

- Private 4-year university and liberal arts college affiliated with United Methodist Church
- Residential campus in small city
- 3,046 degree-seeking undergraduates: 8% part-time, 64% women
- 328 degree-seeking graduate students
- 74% of applicants admitted
- SAT or ACT (ACT writing optional) required
- 56% graduate within 6 years; 40% enter graduate study

General. Founded in 1924. Regionally accredited. **Degrees:** 479 bachelor's awarded; master's offered. **ROTC:** Army, Air Force. **Location:** 15 miles from Greensboro. **Calendar:** Semester, limited summer session. **Full-time faculty:** 153 total; 76% have terminal degrees, 11% minority, 42% women. **Part-time faculty:** 124 total. **Class size:** 74% < 20, 26% 20-39. **Special facilities:** Athletic/convocation center, fine arts center.

Freshman class profile. 3,428 applied, 2,549 admitted, 881 enrolled.

Mid 50% test scores		**GPA 2.0-2.99:**	45%
SAT critical reading:	480-570	**Rank in top quarter:**	41%
SAT math:	480-580	**Rank in top tenth:**	17%
SAT writing:	480-570	**Return as sophomores:**	81%
ACT composite:	20-24	**Out-of-state:**	72%
GPA 3.75 or higher:	10%	**Live on campus:**	97%
GPA 3.50-3.74:	10%	**Fraternities:**	10%
GPA 3.0-3.49:	35%	**Sororities:**	18%

Basis for selection. The most important factors are the academic transcript, including grades received and course selection, followed by standardized test scores (SAT or ACT). Other important factors are demonstrated leadership, extracurricular and community involvement, and special talent. Students who speak English as a second language must demonstrate proficiency in English. TOEFL preferred, other instruments considered. International students may submit TOEFL in lieu of SAT or ACT, unless they wish to play on intercollegiate athletic teams in which case either SAT or ACT required. Interview strongly encouraged. Applicants asked to provide short essay answers to specific questions, but personal essays invited and considered. **Learning Disabled:** Regardless of disability status, a person must meet the academic and technical standards required for admission.

High school preparation. 14 units required. Required and recommended units include English 4, mathematics 3, social studies 3, science 2 (laboratory 1), foreign language 2 and academic electives 2.

2009-2010 Annual costs. Comprehensive fee: (projected) $34,000. Books/supplies: $1,500. Personal expenses: $2,000.

2007-2008 Financial aid. Non-need-based: Scholarships awarded for academics, alumni affiliation, art, athletics, leadership, music/drama, religious affiliation, state residency.

Application procedures. Admission: Priority date 11/3; deadline 3/14 (postmark date). $40 fee, may be waived for applicants with need. Admission notification on a rolling basis beginning on or about 1/1. Must reply by May 1 or within 4 week(s) if notified thereafter. **Financial aid:** Priority date 3/1; no closing date. FAFSA required. Applicants notified on a rolling basis starting 4/1; must reply within 3 week(s) of notification.

Academics. Special study options: Accelerated study, combined bachelor's/graduate degree, cooperative education, cross-registration, double major, dual enrollment of high school students, ESL, honors, independent study, internships, liberal arts/career combination, student-designed major, study abroad, teacher certification program. Dual degree programs with Duke University (forestry and environmental science) and Wake Forest University School of Medicine (medical technology). **Credit/placement by examination:** AP, CLEP, IB, SAT, ACT, institutional tests. 31 credit hours maximum toward bachelor's degree. **Support services:** Learning center, pre-admission summer program, reduced course load, study skills assistance, tutoring, writing center.

Majors. Area/ethnic studies: American. **Biology:** General. **Business:** Accounting, business admin, entrepreneurial studies, human resources, international, management information systems, marketing, organizational behavior. **Communications:** General, digital media, journalism. **Computer sciences:** General, computer science, security. **Conservation:** Forestry. **Education:** Art, early childhood, elementary, middle, physical, secondary, special. **Foreign languages:** General, French, Spanish. **Health:** Athletic training, clinical lab science. **History:** General. **Interdisciplinary:** Global studies. **Math:** General. **Parks/recreation:** Exercise sciences, facilities management, sports admin. **Philosophy/religion:** Philosophy, religion. **Physical sciences:** Chemistry. **Protective services:** Criminal justice. **Psychology:** General. **Social sciences:** Political science, sociology. **Visual/performing arts:** Art, dramatic, interior design, theater design. **Other:** Games design and interactive communication, Home furnishings marketing.

Most popular majors. Business/marketing 42%, education 10%, psychology 6%, social sciences 7%.

Computing on campus. 950 workstations in library, computer center, student center. Dormitories wired for high-speed internet access and linked to campus network. Commuter students can connect to campus network. Online course registration, online library, helpline, repair service, student web hosting, wireless network available.

Student life. Freshman orientation: Mandatory. Preregistration for classes offered. **Housing:** Guaranteed on-campus for freshmen. Coed dorms, single-sex dorms, special housing for disabled, apartments, cooperative housing, fraternity/sorority housing, wellness housing available. $200 fully refundable deposit, deadline 5/1. **Activities:** Bands, choral groups, dance, drama, literary magazine, music ensembles, musical theater, radio station, student government, student newspaper, TV station, Alpha Phi Omega, black cultural awareness, Board of Stewards, College Republicans, College Democrats, Fellowship of Christian Athletes, Model United Nations, Phi Theta Kappa Alumni Association, volunteer center.

Athletics. NCAA. **Intercollegiate:** Baseball M, basketball, cheerleading, cross-country, golf, soccer, tennis, track and field, volleyball W. **Intramural:** Badminton, basketball, bowling, golf, racquetball, soccer, softball, swimming, table tennis, tennis, track and field M, volleyball, water polo. **Team name:** Panthers.

Student services. Adult student services, alcohol/substance abuse counseling, chaplain/spiritual director, career counseling, student employment services, financial aid counseling, health services, personal counseling, placement for graduates, veterans' counselor.

Contact. E-mail: admiss@highpoint.edu
Phone: (336) 841-9216 Toll-free number: (800) 345-6993
Fax: (336) 888-6382
Andy Bills, Vice President for Enrollment, High Point University, 833 Montlieu Avenue, High Point, NC 27262-3598

John Wesley College

High Point, North Carolina
www.johnwesley.edu **CB code: 5348**

- Private 4-year Bible college affiliated with interdenominational tradition
- Commuter campus in small city
- 78 degree-seeking undergraduates
- Application essay, interview required

General. Founded in 1932. Accredited by ABHE. **Degrees:** 39 bachelor's, 1 associate awarded. **Location:** 15 miles from Greensboro, 60 miles from Charlotte. **Calendar:** Semester, limited summer session. **Full-time faculty:** 3 total. **Part-time faculty:** 25 total. **Class size:** 98% < 20, 2% 20-39.

Basis for selection. Future career in church-related vocations and motivation; religious commitment and personal statement very important. Positive personal testimony required. Finding and following God's will foremost. **Homeschooled:** Transcript of courses and grades required. Junior or higher standing, GPA 3.2 or higher, 16 or older, and recommendation from high school administrator or guidance counselor required.

High school preparation. 20 units recommended. Recommended units include English 4, mathematics 3, social studies 2, science 2 (laboratory 2).

2008-2009 Annual costs. Tuition/fees: $10,730. Room only: $2,344. Books/supplies: $1,000. Personal expenses: $2,600.

2007-2008 Financial aid. Additional information: Early Acceptance Scholarships, Academic Honor Scholarships, Married Student Credit and Minister/Missionary Dependent Scholarship available.

Application procedures. Admission: Closing date 8/8 (postmark date). $35 fee, may be waived for applicants with need. Admission notification on a rolling basis. **Financial aid:** Priority date 3/15; no closing date. FAFSA required. Applicants notified on a rolling basis starting 6/1; must reply within 3 week(s) of notification.

Academics. All students major in Bible; second major optional. **Special study options:** Accelerated study, cooperative education, distance learning, double major, dual enrollment of high school students, independent study, internships, student-designed major. **Credit/placement by examination:** AP, CLEP, IB, institutional tests. 15 credit hours maximum toward associate degree, 30 toward bachelor's. **Support services:** Reduced course load.

Majors. Business: Business admin. **Education:** Elementary. **Theology:** Pastoral counseling, religious ed, theology.

Most popular majors. Business/marketing 45%, philosophy/religious studies 45%.

Computing on campus. 6 workstations in library, computer center. Dormitories wired for high-speed internet access. Online library available.

Student life. Freshman orientation: Mandatory. Preregistration for classes offered. Orientation activities held 2 business days before classes begin. **Policies:** Religious observance required. **Housing:** Apartments, wellness housing available. $50 deposit, deadline 7/15. **Activities:** Campus ministries, drama, literary magazine, student government, evangelistic ministries, prison ministry, gospel music team, foreign missions involvement team.

Athletics. Intramural: Basketball, bowling, golf, table tennis, volleyball.

Student services. Chaplain/spiritual director, student employment services, financial aid counseling, personal counseling, veterans' counselor.

Contact. E-mail: aziemba@johnwesley.edu
Phone: (336) 889-2262 ext. 127 Fax: (336) 889-2261
Amanda Ziemba, Admissions Officer, John Wesley College, 2314 North Centennial, High Point, NC 27265-3197

Johnson & Wales University: Charlotte

Charlotte, North Carolina
www.jwu.edu **CB code: 4360**

- Private 4-year university
- Commuter campus in very large city
- 2,436 degree-seeking undergraduates: 2% part-time, 58% women, 24% African American, 2% Asian American, 3% Hispanic American, 2% international
- 62% of applicants admitted

General. Degrees: 365 bachelor's, 547 associate awarded. **Location:** Downtown. **Calendar:** Quarter. **Full-time faculty:** 83 total; 20% minority, 42% women. **Part-time faculty:** 17 total; 6% minority, 53% women. **Class size:** 34% < 20, 59% 20-39, 7% 40-49, less than 1% 50-99.

Freshman class profile. 5,598 applied, 3,452 admitted, 636 enrolled.

Mid 50% test scores		**GPA 3.0-3.49:**	32%
SAT critical reading:	410-530	**GPA 2.0-2.99:**	48%
SAT math:	420-520	**Out-of-state:**	64%
GPA 3.75 or higher:	11%	**Live on campus:**	81%
GPA 3.50-3.74:	8%	**International:**	1%

Basis for selection. Secondary school record, class rank, and interview important. SAT or ACT recommended of all; required for applicants to the honors programs.

High school preparation. 12 units recommended. Required and recommended units include English 4, mathematics 3, social studies 2 and science 3.

2009-2010 Annual costs. Tuition/fees: $23,490. Room/board: $9,249. Books/supplies: $1,500. Personal expenses: $594.

2008-2009 Financial aid. Need-based: 626 full-time freshmen applied for aid; 521 were judged to have need; 521 of these received aid. Average need met was 66%. Average scholarship/grant was $8,733; average loan $3,314. 41% of total undergraduate aid awarded as scholarships/grants, 59% as loans/jobs. **Non-need-based:** Awarded to 1,894 full-time undergraduates, including 559 freshmen. Scholarships awarded for academics, alumni affiliation, job skills, leadership, state residency.

Application procedures. Admission: No deadline. No application fee. Admission notification on a rolling basis beginning on or about 11/1. Must reply by May 1 or within 2 week(s) if notified thereafter. **Financial aid:** No deadline. FAFSA required. Applicants notified on a rolling basis starting 3/1.

Academics. Math center. **Special study options:** Accelerated study, cooperative education, dual enrollment of high school students, ESL, exchange student, honors, independent study, internships, study abroad. **Credit/placement by examination:** CLEP, institutional tests. **Support services:** Learning center, pre-admission summer program, reduced course load, remedial instruction, study skills assistance, tutoring, writing center.

Majors. Business: Accounting, hotel/motel admin, management science, marketing, restaurant/food services, tourism/travel. **Other:** Sports/entertainment/event management.

Most popular majors. Business/marketing 41%, family/consumer sciences 46%, parks/recreation 13%.

Computing on campus. 160 workstations in library. Dormitories wired for high-speed internet access and linked to campus network. Commuter students can connect to campus network. Online library, helpline, wireless network available.

Student life. Freshman orientation: Available. **Housing:** Coed dorms available. $300 nonrefundable deposit. **Activities:** Campus ministries, international student organizations, student government, student newspaper.

Athletics. Intramural: Basketball, soccer, softball, volleyball. **Team name:** Wildcats.

Student services. Career counseling, student employment services, financial aid counseling, health services, personal counseling, veterans' counselor. **Physically disabled:** Services for visually, speech, hearing impaired.

Contact. E-mail: admissions.clt@jwu.edu
Phone: (866) 598-2427 Toll-free number: (800) DIA-LJWU
Fax: (980) 598-1111
Joseph Campos, Director of Admissions, Johnson & Wales University: Charlotte, 801 West Trade Street, Charlotte, NC 28202

Johnson C. Smith University

Charlotte, North Carolina — **CB member**
www.jcsu.edu — **CB code: 5333**

- Private 4-year university and liberal arts college
- Residential campus in very large city
- 1,571 degree-seeking undergraduates: 2% part-time, 60% women, 99% African American
- 49% of applicants admitted
- SAT or ACT (ACT writing optional) required
- 38% graduate within 6 years; 23% enter graduate study

General. Founded in 1867. Regionally accredited. **Degrees:** 213 bachelor's awarded. **ROTC:** Army, Air Force. **Location:** 244 miles from Atlanta. **Calendar:** Semester, limited summer session. **Full-time faculty:** 103 total; 77% have terminal degrees, 71% minority, 52% women. **Part-time faculty:** 22 total; 18% have terminal degrees, 82% minority, 59% women. **Class size:** 44% < 20, 54% 20-39, 2% 40-49.

Freshman class profile. 5,049 applied, 2,491 admitted, 557 enrolled.

Mid 50% test scores		**GPA 2.0-2.99:**	70%
SAT critical reading:	380-460	**Rank in top quarter:**	13%
SAT math:	370-490	**Rank in top tenth:**	3%
ACT composite:	15-18	**End year in good standing:**	80%
GPA 3.75 or higher:	2%	**Return as sophomores:**	63%
GPA 3.50-3.74:	4%	**Out-of-state:**	74%
GPA 3.0-3.49:	15%	**Live on campus:**	97%

Basis for selection. High school GPA, SAT or ACT scores very important. Interviews are accepted but not required.

High school preparation. College-preparatory program required. 16 units required. Required units include English 4, mathematics 3, social studies 2, science 2 (laboratory 1), foreign language 2 and academic electives 3.

2008-2009 Annual costs. Tuition/fees: $15,754. Room/board: $6,132. Books/supplies: $1,500. Personal expenses: $2,400.

2007-2008 Financial aid. Need-based: 431 full-time freshmen applied for aid; 405 were judged to have need; 405 of these received aid. Average need met was 59%. Average scholarship/grant was $4,493; average loan $3,500. 33% of total undergraduate aid awarded as scholarships/grants, 67% as loans/jobs. **Non-need-based:** Awarded to 412 full-time undergraduates, including 250 freshmen. Scholarships awarded for academics, athletics, ROTC, state residency.

Application procedures. Admission: Closing date 7/1 (postmark date). $25 fee, may be waived for applicants with need. Admission notification on a rolling basis beginning on or about 10/1. **Financial aid:** Priority date 3/1; no closing date. FAFSA required. Applicants notified on a rolling basis starting 3/1; must reply within 2 week(s) of notification.

Academics. Requirements include 10 hours per year of community service, assessments in basic competencies, and exit exams in major field for seniors. Freshmen who have completed liberal studies program with honors may apply to enter Honors College as sophomores. **Special study options:** Accelerated study, cooperative education, cross-registration, double major, exchange student, honors, independent study, internships, liberal arts/career combination, study abroad, teacher certification program. **Credit/placement by examination:** AP, CLEP, institutional tests. **Support services:** Learning center, pre-admission summer program, reduced course load, study skills assistance, tutoring, writing center.

Honors college/program. Currently, students receiving academic scholarships are expected to enroll in the Advanced Freshman Studies Program, which is preparatory for admission into the Honors College during the sophomore year. Students who complete the freshman year of the Liberal Studies Program with honors may be admitted into the Honors College in the sophomore year. Other students are invited to join the program based on their grades, high school preparation, and SAT scores as well as on references from both University and high school instructors.

Majors. Biology: General. **Business:** Business admin. **Communications:** Media studies. **Computer sciences:** General, information technology. **Education:** Elementary, health, mathematics, physical. **Engineering:** Computer. **Foreign languages:** French, Spanish. **Health:** Community health services. **History:** General. **Interdisciplinary:** Natural sciences. **Liberal arts:** Arts/sciences. **Math:** General. **Parks/recreation:** Sports admin. **Physical sciences:** Chemistry. **Psychology:** General. **Public administration:** Social work. **Social sciences:** General, criminology, economics, political science. **Visual/performing arts:** Music management.

Most popular majors. Biology 10%, business/marketing 15%, communications/journalism 12%, computer/information sciences 9%, English 7%, parks/recreation 7%, security/protective services 12%.

Computing on campus. PC or laptop required. 335 workstations in dormitories, library, computer center. Dormitories wired for high-speed internet access and linked to campus network. Commuter students can connect to campus network. Online course registration, online library, helpline, repair service, wireless network available.

Student life. Freshman orientation: Available, $100 fee. Three-day program in July for students and parents. **Housing:** Guaranteed on-campus for freshmen. Coed dorms, single-sex dorms available. $150 nonrefundable deposit, deadline 7/15. Limited honors housing available. **Activities:** Bands, choral groups, drama, music ensembles, student government, student newspaper, Student Christian Association, NAACP, National Association of Black Accountants, National Association of Black Engineers, Habitat for Humanity, College Democrats, Young Republicans.

Athletics. NCAA. **Intercollegiate:** Basketball, bowling W, cross-country, football (tackle) M, golf, softball W, tennis, track and field, volleyball W. **Intramural:** Basketball, football (non-tackle), table tennis. **Team name:** Golden Bulls.

Student services. Adult student services, alcohol/substance abuse counseling, career counseling, services for economically disadvantaged, student employment services, financial aid counseling, health services, minority student services, personal counseling, veterans' counselor. **Physically disabled:** Services for visually, speech, hearing impaired.

Contact. E-mail: admissions@jcsu.edu
Phone: (704) 378-1010 Toll-free number: (800) 782-7303
Fax: (704) 378-1242
Ronice Johnson, Assistant Director of Admissions, Johnson C. Smith University, 100 Beatties Ford Road, Charlotte, NC 28216-5398

Lees-McRae College

Banner Elk, North Carolina — **CB member**
www.lmc.edu — **CB code: 5364**

- Private 4-year liberal arts college affiliated with Presbyterian Church (USA)
- Residential campus in rural community
- 948 degree-seeking undergraduates
- 74% of applicants admitted
- SAT or ACT (ACT writing optional) required

General. Founded in 1900. Regionally accredited. **Degrees:** 225 bachelor's awarded. **Location:** 17 miles from Boone, 40 miles from Johnson City, Tennessee. **Calendar:** Semester, limited summer session. **Full-time faculty:** 52 total. **Part-time faculty:** 13 total. **Class size:** 71% < 20, 29% 20-39. **Special facilities:** Wireless campus, biology field station, Blue Ridge Wildlife Rehabilitation Institute.

Freshman class profile. 1,120 applied, 827 admitted, 277 enrolled.

Mid 50% test scores		**ACT composite:**	19-24
SAT critical reading:	420-540	**Out-of-state:**	50%
SAT math:	430-530	**Live on campus:**	96%

Basis for selection. High school record and rank in top half of class preferred. Test scores optional. Recommendations considered. Interview recommended for all students; portfolio recommended for performing arts programs. Audition required for athletic, performing arts programs.

High school preparation. 18 units required. Required and recommended units include English 4, mathematics 3, social studies 2, history 1, science 2 (laboratory 1), foreign language 2 and academic electives 6.

2008-2009 Annual costs. Tuition/fees: $20,500. Room/board: $7,000. Books/supplies: $900. Personal expenses: $1,945.

2008-2009 Financial aid. **Non-need-based:** Scholarships awarded for academics, alumni affiliation, athletics, leadership, minority status, music/drama, religious affiliation, state residency.

Application procedures. **Admission:** Priority date 5/1; no deadline. No application fee. Admission notification on a rolling basis beginning on or about 12/1. Accepting and notifying applicants of acceptance status begins after completion of 6 semesters in high school. **Financial aid:** Priority date 3/15; no closing date. FAFSA required. Applicants notified on a rolling basis starting 3/1; must reply within 2 week(s) of notification.

Academics. **Special study options:** Double major, ESL, honors, independent study, internships, liberal arts/career combination, student-designed major, study abroad, teacher certification program. 3-2 program Environmental Science/Forestry with Duke University. **Credit/placement by examination:** AP, CLEP, IB, ACT, institutional tests. 16 credit hours maximum toward bachelor's degree. **Support services:** Learning center, remedial instruction, study skills assistance, tutoring, writing center.

Majors. **Biology:** General. **Business:** Business admin. **Communications:** General. **Computer sciences:** Computer science, information systems. **Education:** Drama/dance, elementary, physical. **Health:** Predental, premedicine, preveterinary. **History:** General. **Liberal arts:** Arts/sciences. **Math:** General. **Philosophy/religion:** Religion. **Protective services:** Criminal justice. **Psychology:** General. **Social sciences:** International relations, sociology. **Visual/performing arts:** Dramatic.

Most popular majors. Biology 13%, business/marketing 17%, education 29%, psychology 10%, security/protective services 13%.

Computing on campus. 125 workstations in dormitories, library, computer center, student center. Dormitories wired for high-speed internet access and linked to campus network. Commuter students can connect to campus network. Online course registration, online library, helpline, wireless network available.

Student life. **Freshman orientation:** Mandatory. Preregistration for classes offered. 6 summer Freshmen Experience sessions (1 required) followed by August orientation. **Housing:** Guaranteed on-campus for freshmen. Coed dorms, single-sex dorms, wellness housing available. **Activities:** Choral groups, dance, drama, international student organizations, music ensembles, musical theater, student government, Order of the Tower, student ambassadors, residence hall association, sports medicine club, Phi Beta Lambda, Circle K, campus after the class hours, EMS club.

Athletics. NCAA. **Intercollegiate:** Basketball, cheerleading, cross-country, golf M, lacrosse, soccer, softball W, tennis, track and field, volleyball. **Intramural:** Basketball, cross-country, football (non-tackle), golf, skiing, soccer, softball, table tennis, tennis, volleyball. **Team name:** Bobcats.

Student services. Alcohol/substance abuse counseling, chaplain/spiritual director, career counseling, student employment services, financial aid counseling, health services, personal counseling, veterans' counselor.

Contact. E-mail: admissions@lmc.edu
Phone: (828) 898-8723 Toll-free number: (800) 280-4562
Fax: (828) 898-8707
Frank OHagan, Director of Admissions, Lees-McRae College, Box 128, Banner Elk, NC 28604

Lenoir-Rhyne University

Hickory, North Carolina — **CB member**
www.lr.edu — **CB code: 5365**

- Private 4-year liberal arts college affiliated with Evangelical Lutheran Church in America
- Residential campus in large town
- 1,347 degree-seeking undergraduates: 5% part-time, 64% women, 9% African American, 3% Asian American, 2% Hispanic American, 1% international
- 159 degree-seeking graduate students
- 81% of applicants admitted
- SAT or ACT with writing required
- 55% graduate within 6 years

General. Founded in 1891. Regionally accredited. **Degrees:** 284 bachelor's awarded; master's offered. **ROTC:** Army, Naval. **Location:** 50 miles from Charlotte. **Calendar:** Semester, limited summer session. **Full-time faculty:** 93 total; 81% have terminal degrees, 4% minority, 46% women. **Part-time faculty:** 82 total; 38% have terminal degrees, 5% minority, 43% women. **Class size:** 68% < 20, 30% 20-39, 1% 40-49, less than 1% 50-99. **Special facilities:** Observatory, multimedia classrooms, outdoor classroom.

Freshman class profile. 2,248 applied, 1,829 admitted, 346 enrolled.

Mid 50% test scores		**GPA 3.0-3.49:**	22%
SAT critical reading:	440-550	**GPA 2.0-2.99:**	19%
SAT math:	460-580	**Rank in top quarter:**	48%
SAT writing:	460-550	**Rank in top tenth:**	19%
ACT composite:	19-24	**Return as sophomores:**	70%
GPA 3.75 or higher:	43%	**Out-of-state:**	22%
GPA 3.50-3.74:	16%	**Live on campus:**	78%

Basis for selection. School achievement record most important. Interview recommended for all students; audition required for music majors. **Homeschooled:** Transcript of courses and grades required.

High school preparation. 12 units required. Required units include English 4, mathematics 3, history 1, science 1 (laboratory 1) and foreign language 2. Chemistry required for nursing program. "History" refers to U.S. History; mathematics needs to include algebra I, algebra II, geometry.

2009-2010 Annual costs. Tuition/fees: $24,200. Room/board: $8,540. Books/supplies: $1,100. Personal expenses: $1,500.

2007-2008 Financial aid. **Non-need-based:** Scholarships awarded for academics, athletics, job skills, leadership, minority status, music/drama, ROTC, state residency.

Application procedures. **Admission:** Priority date 12/1; deadline 8/15 (receipt date). $35 fee, may be waived for applicants with need. Admission notification on a rolling basis beginning on or about 6/1. Must reply by May 1 or within 2 week(s) if notified thereafter. Students will not be put on the housing roster until the deposit is received. **Financial aid:** Priority date

3/1, closing date 8/1. FAFSA required. Applicants notified on a rolling basis starting 3/1; must reply within 2 week(s) of notification.

Academics. Special program for deaf, hearing-impaired and disabled students. **Special study options:** Accelerated study, combined bachelor's/graduate degree, cross-registration, distance learning, double major, dual enrollment of high school students, ESL, exchange student, external degree, honors, independent study, internships, liberal arts/career combination, student-designed major, study abroad, teacher certification program, Washington semester. **Credit/placement by examination:** AP, CLEP, IB, SAT, ACT, institutional tests. 16 credit hours maximum toward bachelor's degree. **Support services:** Learning center, pre-admission summer program, remedial instruction, study skills assistance, tutoring, writing center.

Majors. Area/ethnic studies: American. **Biology:** General. **Business:** Accounting, finance, international, management information systems, management science, marketing. **Communications:** General. **Computer sciences:** General, information systems. **Conservation:** Environmental studies, forestry. **Education:** Art, biology, chemistry, Deaf/hearing impaired, early childhood, elementary, English, ESL, history, mathematics, middle, music, physical, psychology, science, social science, social studies. **Engineering technology:** General. **Family/consumer sciences:** Child development. **Foreign languages:** French, German, Latin, Spanish. **Health:** Athletic training, clinical lab science, nursing (RN), premedicine. **History:** General. **Legal studies:** Prelaw. **Liberal arts:** Arts/sciences. **Math:** General. **Parks/recreation:** Sports admin. **Philosophy/religion:** Philosophy, religion. **Physical sciences:** Chemistry, physics. **Psychology:** General. **Public administration:** Human services. **Science technology:** Chemical. **Social sciences:** Economics, international relations, political science, sociology. **Theology:** Sacred music. **Visual/performing arts:** Arts management, dramatic, graphic design, music performance.

Most popular majors. Business/marketing 14%, education 18%, health sciences 24%, psychology 8%.

Computing on campus. 112 workstations in library, computer center, student center. Dormitories wired for high-speed internet access and linked to campus network. Commuter students can connect to campus network. Online library, helpline, wireless network available.

Student life. Freshman orientation: Mandatory. Preregistration for classes offered. Held 2 days before start of classes. **Housing:** Guaranteed on-campus for all undergraduates. Coed dorms, special housing for disabled, fraternity/sorority housing available. $200 deposit. **Activities:** Bands, campus ministries, choral groups, dance, drama, literary magazine, music ensembles, Model UN, musical theater, radio station, student government, student newspaper, symphony orchestra, Black Student Alliance, Campus Crusade for Christ, Fellowship of Christian Athletes, North Carolina Student Legislature, Intervarsity Christian Fellowship, College Democrats, Lutheran Student Movement, Student Occupational Therapy Association, Gay Straight Alliance, College Republicans, College Democrats.

Athletics. NCAA. **Intercollegiate:** Baseball M, basketball, cheerleading, cross-country, football (tackle) M, golf, soccer, softball W, swimming W, tennis, track and field, volleyball W. **Intramural:** Basketball, football (non-tackle), lacrosse M, soccer, softball, volleyball. **Team name:** Bears.

Student services. Adult student services, chaplain/spiritual director, career counseling, student employment services, financial aid counseling, health services, minority student services, personal counseling, veterans' counselor. **Physically disabled:** Services for hearing impaired.

Contact. E-mail: admission@lr.edu
Phone: (828) 328-7300 Toll-free number: (800) 277-5721
Fax: (828) 328-7378
Karen Feezor, Director of Admissions, Lenoir-Rhyne University, PO Box 7227, Hickory, NC 28603

Livingstone College

Salisbury, North Carolina — **CB member**
www.livingstone.edu — **CB code: 5367**

- Private 4-year liberal arts college affiliated with African Methodist Episcopal Zion Church
- Residential campus in large town
- 994 degree-seeking undergraduates
- 63% of applicants admitted
- SAT or ACT (ACT writing optional) required

General. Founded in 1879. Regionally accredited. **Degrees:** 118 bachelor's awarded. **ROTC:** Army. **Location:** 44 miles from Charlotte. **Calendar:** Semester. **Full-time faculty:** 54 total. **Part-time faculty:** 11 total. **Class size:** 64% < 20, 28% 20-39, 4% 40-49, 1% 50-99, 2% >100. **Special facilities:** Center for Negro and African life, literature and international studies.

Freshman class profile. 1,979 applied, 1,237 admitted, 336 enrolled.

Mid 50% test scores			
SAT critical reading:	330-420	Rank in top quarter:	6%
SAT math:	330-430	Rank in top tenth:	4%
SAT writing:	320-420	Out-of-state:	59%
ACT composite:	13-16	Live on campus:	85%

Basis for selection. School achievement record, test scores, recommendations important. College's placement test, instead of ELPT, used for advising and placement. Audition required for music majors; interview recommended for academically weak students.

High school preparation. 10 units required. Required and recommended units include English 4, mathematics 3, social studies 2, history 1, science 2 and foreign language 2.

2008-2009 Annual costs. Tuition/fees: $12,915. Room/board: $6,040. Books/supplies: $800. Personal expenses: $3,000.

2007-2008 Financial aid. Non-need-based: Scholarships awarded for academics, alumni affiliation, athletics, leadership, music/drama, religious affiliation, ROTC, state residency.

Application procedures. Admission: Priority date 5/15; no deadline. $25 fee, may be waived for applicants with need. Admission notification on a rolling basis. Must reply by May 1 or within 4 week(s) if notified thereafter. **Financial aid:** Priority date 3/15, closing date 6/30. FAFSA required. Applicants notified by 5/1; must reply within 4 week(s) of notification.

Academics. Special study options: Accelerated study, cross-registration, double major, independent study, internships, teacher certification program. **Credit/placement by examination:** CLEP, institutional tests. **Support services:** Learning center, reduced course load, study skills assistance, tutoring.

Majors. Biology: General. **Business:** Accounting, business admin. **Computer sciences:** General. **Education:** Elementary. **Engineering:** General. **Health:** Predental, prepharmacy. **History:** General. **Legal studies:** General. **Math:** General. **Parks/recreation:** Sports admin. **Physical sciences:** Chemistry. **Protective services:** Criminal justice. **Psychology:** General. **Public administration:** Social work. **Social sciences:** General, political science, sociology. **Theology:** Theology. **Visual/performing arts:** Dramatic.

Most popular majors. Business/marketing 25%, parks/recreation 9%, psychology 17%, security/protective services 15%, social sciences 13%.

Computing on campus. 200 workstations in dormitories, library, computer center. Dormitories wired for high-speed internet access and linked to campus network.

Student life. Freshman orientation: Mandatory, $100 fee. Preregistration for classes offered. **Housing:** Single-sex dorms, special housing for disabled, apartments available. $100 deposit. **Activities:** Bands, choral groups, dance, drama, film society, music ensembles, musical theater, radio station, student government, pre-theological union, AME Zion Council.

Athletics. NCAA. **Intercollegiate:** Basketball, bowling, cross-country, football (tackle) M, softball W, tennis, track and field, volleyball W. **Intramural:** Basketball. **Team name:** Blue Bears.

Student services. Career counseling, student employment services, health services, personal counseling, placement for graduates, veterans' counselor.

Contact. Phone: (704) 216-6001 Toll-free number: (800) 835-3435
Fax: (704) 216-6215
Nicole Daniels, Director of Enrollment Management and Admission, Livingstone College, 701 West Monroe Street, Salisbury, NC 28144-5213

Mars Hill College

Mars Hill, North Carolina — **CB member**
www.mhc.edu — **CB code: 5395**

- Private 4-year liberal arts college affiliated with Baptist faith
- Residential campus in small town
- 1,203 degree-seeking undergraduates: 6% part-time, 52% women
- 60% of applicants admitted
- SAT or ACT (ACT writing optional) required
- 38% graduate within 6 years

General. Founded in 1856. Regionally accredited. **Degrees:** 214 bachelor's awarded. **Location:** 17 miles from Asheville. **Calendar:** Semester, extensive summer session. **Full-time faculty:** 71 total; 69% have terminal degrees, 1% minority, 44% women. **Part-time faculty:** 84 total. **Class size:** 88% < 20, 12% 20-39. **Special facilities:** Satellite receiver for foreign language study, Appalachian archives and artifacts museum.

Freshman class profile. 1,667 applied, 993 admitted, 300 enrolled.

Mid 50% test scores		**GPA 3.0-3.49:**	21%
SAT critical reading:	410-520	**GPA 2.0-2.99:**	43%
SAT math:	430-550	**Return as sophomores:**	69%
ACT composite:	16-21	**Out-of-state:**	40%
GPA 3.75 or higher:	24%	**International:**	2%
GPA 3.50-3.74:	11%		

Basis for selection. School achievement record, test scores, school and community activities, recommendations from school officials all important. Students interested in early admission must apply as full-time students, achieve A average in courses, minimum SAT 1000 (exclusive of Writing) or ACT 22, and submit 2 recommendations from high school personnel. Audition required for music, theater programs. Essay, portfolio recommended; interview recommended for students who do not meet other admissions criteria. **Homeschooled:** Transcript of courses and grades required. **Learning Disabled:** Letter of documentation required.

High school preparation. 11 units required. Required and recommended units include English 4, mathematics 3, social studies 2, history 2, science 2, foreign language 2 and computer science 1.

2008-2009 Annual costs. Tuition/fees: $19,894. Room/board: $6,891. Books/supplies: $1,000. Personal expenses: $1,000.

2008-2009 Financial aid. **Non-need-based:** Scholarships awarded for academics, art, athletics, religious affiliation, state residency.

Application procedures. **Admission:** No deadline. $25 fee, may be waived for applicants with need. Admission notification on a rolling basis. **Financial aid:** No deadline. FAFSA, institutional form required. Applicants notified on a rolling basis; must reply within 2 week(s) of notification.

Academics. **Special study options:** Accelerated study, cross-registration, distance learning, double major, dual enrollment of high school students, ESL, exchange student, independent study, internships, liberal arts/career combination, student-designed major, study abroad, teacher certification program. 3-2 physician assistant, 3-1 medical technology, 2-2 allied health programs. **Credit/placement by examination:** AP, CLEP, IB, SAT, ACT, institutional tests. 32 credit hours maximum toward bachelor's degree. **Support services:** Learning center, reduced course load, remedial instruction, study skills assistance, tutoring, writing center.

Majors. **Biology:** General, botany, zoology. **Business:** General, accounting, business admin, finance, international. **Communications:** General. **Computer sciences:** Computer science. **Education:** General, art, elementary, English, middle, music, physical, secondary. **Foreign languages:** Spanish. **Health:** Athletic training, clinical lab assistant, physician assistant, predental, premedicine, prepharmacy, preveterinary. **History:** General. **Interdisciplinary:** Biological/physical sciences. **Legal studies:** Prelaw. **Liberal arts:** Arts/sciences. **Math:** General. **Parks/recreation:** Facilities management, health/fitness. **Philosophy/religion:** Religion. **Physical sciences:** Chemistry. **Psychology:** General. **Public administration:** Social work. **Social sciences:** International relations, political science, sociology. **Visual/performing arts:** Art, dramatic, fashion design, music performance.

Most popular majors. Business/marketing 21%, education 30%, social sciences 6%, visual/performing arts 10%.

Computing on campus. 180 workstations in library, computer center, student center. Dormitories wired for high-speed internet access and linked to campus network. Commuter students can connect to campus network. Online library, helpline, repair service, wireless network available.

Student life. **Freshman orientation:** Mandatory. Preregistration for classes offered. **Housing:** Guaranteed on-campus for all undergraduates. Single-sex dorms, special housing for disabled, apartments available. $250 deposit. College townhouses and apartments available to upperclassmen. **Activities:** Bands, campus ministries, choral groups, dance, drama, literary magazine, music ensembles, musical theater, student government, student newspaper, Christian Student Movement, Fellowship of Christian Athletes, The Refuge, Ladies of Distinction, Black Student Alliance, health care society, Green Students United, Bailey Mountain Cloggers.

Athletics. NCAA. **Intercollegiate:** Baseball M, basketball, cross-country, football (tackle) M, golf, lacrosse M, soccer, softball W, swimming, tennis, track and field, volleyball W. **Intramural:** Badminton, basketball, football (non-tackle), soccer, softball, tennis, volleyball, water polo M. **Team name:** Lions.

Student services. Adult student services, chaplain/spiritual director, career counseling, services for economically disadvantaged, student employment services, financial aid counseling, health services, personal counseling, veterans' counselor.

Contact. E-mail: admissions@mhc.edu
Phone: (828) 689-1201 Toll-free number: (866) 642-4968
Fax: (828) 689-1473
Ed Hoffmeyer, Dean of Admissions, Mars Hill College, Blackwell Hall, Box 370, Mars Hill, NC 28754

Meredith College

Raleigh, North Carolina — **CB member**
www.meredith.edu — **CB code: 5410**

- Private 4-year liberal arts college for women
- Residential campus in large city
- 1,901 degree-seeking undergraduates: 9% part-time, 100% women, 11% African American, 2% Asian American, 2% Hispanic American, 2% international
- 205 degree-seeking graduate students
- 69% of applicants admitted
- SAT or ACT (ACT writing optional) required

General. Founded in 1891. Regionally accredited. **Degrees:** 363 bachelor's awarded; master's offered. **ROTC:** Army, Air Force. **Location:** 250 miles from Washington, DC, 375 miles from Atlanta. **Calendar:** Semester, limited summer session. **Full-time faculty:** 147 total; 88% have terminal degrees, 10% minority, 67% women. **Part-time faculty:** 109 total; 30% have terminal degrees, 6% minority, 69% women. **Class size:** 72% < 20, 26% 20-39, 1% 40-49, less than 1% 50-99, less than 1% >100. **Special facilities:** Amphitheatre, child care laboratory, experimental and clinical psychology laboratories, autism laboratory, astronomy observation deck, electron microscope suite, 15 student/faculty research laboratories, greenhouse.

Freshman class profile. 1,557 applied, 1,080 admitted, 397 enrolled.

Mid 50% test scores		**GPA 2.0-2.99:**	26%
SAT critical reading:	470-560	**Rank in top quarter:**	48%
SAT math:	470-570	**Rank in top tenth:**	18%
ACT composite:	19-24	**Out-of-state:**	10%
GPA 3.75 or higher:	15%	**Live on campus:**	93%
GPA 3.50-3.74:	17%	**International:**	5%
GPA 3.0-3.49:	42%		

Basis for selection. GED not accepted. School record (courses taken, grades on academic subjects, and class rank), test scores, and recommendations important. Meredith seeks to enroll qualified students of varying backgrounds, interests and talents and has a need-blind admission policy. Essay and/or interview may be required of some; audition recommended for music majors; portfolio recommended for art majors. **Homeschooled:** SAT Reasoning and SAT Subject Tests (English, math, and foreign language or one of applicant's choice) required.

High school preparation. 16 units required. Required units include English 4, mathematics 3, science 3 and foreign language 2. 3 units required in social studies or history. At least 1 elective required, preferably from core academic subjects.

2008-2009 Annual costs. Tuition/fees: $23,550. Tuition includes a new laptop computer for each full-time freshman, which will be replaced with a new laptop during her junior year. Upon graduation from Meredith, the laptop remains the property of the student. Room/board: $6,740. Books/supplies: $750. Personal expenses: $1,250.

2008-2009 Financial aid. **Non-need-based:** Scholarships awarded for academics, art, leadership, minority status, music/drama, religious affiliation, state residency.

Application procedures. **Admission:** Priority date 2/15; no deadline. $40 fee, may be waived for applicants with need. Admission notification on a rolling basis beginning on or about 11/1. Must reply by May 1 or within 2 week(s) if notified thereafter. **Financial aid:** Priority date 2/15; no closing date. FAFSA required. Applicants notified on a rolling basis starting 3/15; must reply by 5/1 or within 2 week(s) of notification.

Academics. Undergraduate research program available to students in all disciplines. Post-baccalaureate dietetic internship program and post-baccalaureate certificate in paralegal studies available. **Special study options:** Accelerated study, combined bachelor's/graduate degree, cooperative education, cross-registration, double major, dual enrollment of high school students, honors, independent study, internships, liberal arts/career combination, New York semester, student-designed major, study abroad, teacher certification program, United Nations semester, Washington semester. Study

Abroad includes summer programs, semester/year abroad opportunities, and individually-tailored semesters. 3-2 in engineering with N.C. State University. **Credit/placement by examination:** AP, CLEP, IB, institutional tests. **Support services:** Learning center, reduced course load, remedial instruction, study skills assistance, tutoring, writing center.

Majors. **Area/ethnic studies:** Women's. **Biology:** General, molecular. **Business:** Accounting, business admin, fashion. **Communications:** General, media studies. **Computer sciences:** General, computer science. **Conservation:** Environmental science, environmental studies. **Education:** Art, drama/dance, music, physical. **Family/consumer sciences:** General, child development. **Foreign languages:** French, Spanish. **Health:** Dietetics, health services. **History:** General, public archives. **Interdisciplinary:** Global studies. **Math:** General. **Parks/recreation:** Health/fitness. **Philosophy/religion:** Religion. **Physical sciences:** Chemistry. **Psychology:** General. **Public administration:** Social work. **Social sciences:** Economics, political science, sociology, U.S. government. **Visual/performing arts:** Dance, dramatic, fashion design, graphic design, interior design, music pedagogy, music performance, studio arts.

Most popular majors. Business/marketing 12%, communications/journalism 8%, family/consumer sciences 10%, health sciences 6%, psychology 12%, visual/performing arts 18%.

Computing on campus. PC or laptop required. 145 workstations in dormitories, library, computer center, student center. Dormitories wired for high-speed internet access and linked to campus network. Commuter students can connect to campus network. Online course registration, online library, helpline, repair service, wireless network available.

Student life. **Freshman orientation:** Mandatory. Preregistration for classes offered. 4-day program before start of classes with extra day for athletes, international students, and students with disabilities. **Policies:** Honor Code is a long-standing tradition that requires individual integrity and community responsibility of all students. Traditional-aged freshmen and sophomores must live on campus except if married or living with parents or other relatives by special permission. **Housing:** Guaranteed on-campus for freshmen. Wellness housing available. $100 nonrefundable deposit, deadline 5/1. Pets allowed in dorm rooms. Campus housing available for all 4 years. All on-campus housing is "wellness housing.". **Activities:** Concert band, choral groups, dance, drama, international student organizations, literary magazine, music ensembles, Model UN, musical theater, student government, student newspaper, symphony orchestra, association for cultural awareness, unity council, service council, Habitat for Humanity, Angels for the Environment, College Democrats, College Republicans, Christian Association, Catholic Angels.

Athletics. NCAA. **Intercollegiate:** Basketball W, cross-country W, soccer W, softball W, tennis W, volleyball W. **Team name:** Avenging Angels.

Student services. Adult student services, alcohol/substance abuse counseling, chaplain/spiritual director, career counseling, student employment services, financial aid counseling, health services, minority student services, personal counseling, placement for graduates. **Physically disabled:** Services for visually, speech, hearing impaired.

Contact. E-mail: admissions@meredith.edu
Phone: (919) 760-8581 Toll-free number: (800) 637-3348
Fax: (919) 760-2348
Cristan Trahey, Director of Admissions, Meredith College, 3800 Hillsborough Street, Raleigh, NC 27607-5298

Methodist University
Fayetteville, North Carolina
www.methodist.edu **CB code: 5426**

- Private 4-year liberal arts college affiliated with United Methodist Church
- Residential campus in small city
- 1,929 degree-seeking undergraduates: 15% part-time, 44% women, 19% African American, 1% Asian American, 6% Hispanic American, 1% Native American, 4% international
- 145 degree-seeking graduate students
- 66% of applicants admitted
- SAT or ACT (ACT writing optional) required
- 39% graduate within 6 years

General. Founded in 1956. Regionally accredited. **Degrees:** 336 bachelor's, 15 associate awarded; master's offered. **ROTC:** Army, Air Force. **Location:** 50 miles from Raleigh-Durham. **Calendar:** Semester, extensive summer session. **Full-time faculty:** 127 total; 77% have terminal degrees, 12% minority, 49% women. **Part-time faculty:** 86 total; 91% have terminal degrees, 17% minority, 43% women. **Class size:** 74% < 20, 25% 20-39, less than 1% 40-49, less than 1% 50-99. **Special facilities:** Computer-assisted English composition laboratory, psychology computer-experimental laboratory, nature trail, professional golf and tennis management center, 18-hole golf course and driving range, environmental simulation center (virtual reality laboratory).

Freshman class profile. 2,937 applied, 1,946 admitted, 468 enrolled.

Mid 50% test scores			
SAT critical reading:	440-540	Rank in top quarter:	33%
SAT math:	440-560	Rank in top tenth:	12%
SAT writing:	410-510	Return as sophomores:	67%
ACT composite:	18-23	Out-of-state:	47%
GPA 3.75 or higher:	21%	Live on campus:	91%
GPA 3.50-3.74:	10%	International:	4%
GPA 3.0-3.49:	28%	Fraternities:	3%
GPA 2.0-2.99:	41%	Sororities:	3%

Basis for selection. High school record (GPA), curriculum, test scores carefully considered. All prospective student files reviewed on individual basis. Extracurricular achievements and teacher/counselor recommendations also considered. Students who transfer English 101 credits must take institutional English Placement Exam. SAT/ACT scores not required of transfer students with more than 31 semester hours of transferable credit. Essay and interview recommended for all students; audition recommended for drama and music majors; portfolio recommended for art majors. **Homeschooled:** Transcript of courses and grades required.

High school preparation. College-preparatory program required. 16 units required; 20 recommended. Required and recommended units include English 4, mathematics 3-4, social studies 2, history 1-2, science 2-3 (laboratory 1-2), foreign language 2 and academic electives 4.

2009-2010 Annual costs. Tuition/fees: $23,038. Professional golf management, professional tennis management, and music students have additional fees. Room/board: $8,400. Books/supplies: $1,000. Personal expenses: $1,500.

2007-2008 Financial aid. **Non-need-based:** Scholarships awarded for academics, alumni affiliation, leadership, music/drama, religious affiliation, ROTC, state residency.

Application procedures. **Admission:** No deadline. $25 fee, may be waived for applicants with need, free for online applicants. Admission notification on a rolling basis beginning on or about 9/1. Must reply by May 1 or within 2 week(s) if notified thereafter. **Financial aid:** Priority date 5/1, closing date 7/1. FAFSA required. Applicants notified on a rolling basis starting 3/1; must reply within 2 week(s) of notification.

Academics. **Special study options:** Accelerated study, distance learning, double major, dual enrollment of high school students, ESL, exchange student, honors, independent study, internships, liberal arts/career combination, student-designed major, study abroad, teacher certification program, Washington semester, weekend college. **Credit/placement by examination:** AP, CLEP, IB, SAT, ACT, institutional tests. 45 credit hours maximum toward associate degree, 45 toward bachelor's. **Support services:** Learning center, reduced course load, remedial instruction, study skills assistance, tutoring, writing center.

Majors. **Biology:** General, botany, cellular/molecular, conservation, ecology, exercise physiology, microbiology, zoology. **Business:** Accounting, business admin, finance, hospitality admin, hospitality/recreation, management information systems, marketing, resort management, tourism/travel. **Communications:** General, journalism, media studies, organizational. **Computer sciences:** General, computer graphics, computer science, web page design. **Education:** General, art, biology, chemistry, elementary, English, foreign languages, mathematics, middle, music, physical, secondary, social studies, special. **Engineering technology:** Occupational safety. **Foreign languages:** French, Spanish. **Health:** Athletic training, facilities admin, health care admin, physician assistant, predental, premedicine, prenursing, prepharmacy, preveterinary. **History:** General. **Legal studies:** Prelaw. **Liberal arts:** Arts/sciences. **Math:** General. **Parks/recreation:** Exercise sciences, facilities management, health/fitness, sports admin. **Philosophy/religion:** Philosophy, religion. **Physical sciences:** Chemistry, forensic chemistry. **Protective services:** Criminal justice, emergency management/homeland security, forensics, law enforcement admin. **Psychology:** General. **Public administration:** Social work. **Social sciences:** Political science, sociology. **Theology:** Religious ed. **Visual/performing arts:** General, art, ceramics, graphic design, music performance, painting, printmaking, sculpture, studio arts. **Other:** Professional tennis management.

Most popular majors. Biology 6%, business/marketing 44%, education 7%, parks/recreation 8%, social sciences 8%.

Computing on campus. 220 workstations in library, computer center, student center. Dormitories wired for high-speed internet access and linked to campus network. Commuter students can connect to campus network. Online course registration, online library, helpline, wireless network available.

Student life. **Freshman orientation:** Available. Preregistration for classes offered. Typically held the weekend (Friday and Saturday) after July 4th. **Housing:** Guaranteed on-campus for all undergraduates. Coed dorms, single-sex dorms, apartments, wellness housing available. $100 nonrefundable deposit, deadline 5/1. Health/wellness hall, first-year experience hall available. Students must live on-campus through sophomore year unless living with parents/guardians. All residence halls are non-smoking facilities. **Activities:** Bands, campus ministries, choral groups, dance, drama, international student organizations, literary magazine, music ensembles, Model UN, musical theater, radio station, student government, student newspaper, symphony orchestra, Fellowship of Christian Athletes, Young Democrats/ Republicans, African American culture society, student activities committee, commuting student organization.

Athletics. NCAA. **Intercollegiate:** Baseball M, basketball, cheerleading, cross-country, football (tackle) M, golf, lacrosse W, soccer, softball W, tennis, track and field, volleyball W. **Intramural:** Basketball, cheerleading W, football (non-tackle), golf, racquetball, soccer, softball, table tennis, tennis, volleyball. **Team name:** Monarchs.

Student services. Alcohol/substance abuse counseling, chaplain/ spiritual director, career counseling, student employment services, financial aid counseling, health services, personal counseling, placement for graduates, veterans' counselor, women's services. **Physically disabled:** Services for visually impaired.

Contact. E-mail: admissions@methodist.edu
Phone: (910) 630-7027 Toll-free number: (800) 488-7110
Fax: (910) 630-7285
Jamie Legg, Director of Admissions, Methodist University, 5400 Ramsey Street, Fayetteville, NC 28311-1498

Miller-Motte Technical College

Wilmington, North Carolina
www.miller-motte.edu **CB code: 3342**

- For-profit 4-year business and technical college
- Commuter campus in small city
- 747 degree-seeking undergraduates
- Interview required

General. Accredited by ACICS. **Degrees:** 45 bachelor's, 175 associate awarded. **Location:** 145 miles from Raleigh. **Calendar:** Quarter, extensive summer session. **Full-time faculty:** 35 total. **Part-time faculty:** 30 total.

Basis for selection. Open admission, but selective for some programs. Minimum test score of 15 on Wonderlic test for admission, 18 for Medical Assisting, 21 for Surgical Technology, 20 for Computer Systems Network Administrator, 18 for Criminal Justice, 18 for Paralegal, and 18 for Dental Assisting. **Homeschooled:** Transcript of courses and grades required.

High school preparation. 17 units recommended. Recommended units include English 4, mathematics 4, social studies 4, science 4 (laboratory 1).

2008-2009 Annual costs. Tuition/fees: $10,890. Books/supplies: $1,000. Personal expenses: $2,250.

2007-2008 Financial aid. All financial aid based on need.

Application procedures. **Admission:** No deadline. $35 fee. Application must be submitted on paper. Admission notification on a rolling basis. **Financial aid:** No deadline. FAFSA, institutional form required.

Academics. **Special study options:** Distance learning, double major, internships. **Credit/placement by examination:** CLEP, institutional tests. 46 credit hours maximum toward associate degree. **Support services:** Learning center, reduced course load, remedial instruction, study skills assistance, tutoring.

Majors. **Business:** Business admin. **Health:** Health services. **Protective services:** Law enforcement admin.

Most popular majors. Business/marketing 50%, health sciences 50%.

Computing on campus. 120 workstations in library, computer center. Commuter students can connect to campus network. Online library, repair service, student web hosting available.

Student life. **Freshman orientation:** Mandatory. Preregistration for classes offered. **Activities:** Student newspaper.

Athletics. **Team name:** Marlin.

Student services. Career counseling, financial aid counseling, placement for graduates.

Contact. Phone: (910) 392-4660 Toll-free number: (800) 784-2110
Fax: (910) 799-6224
Tom Bogush, Director of Admissions, Miller-Motte Technical College, 5000 Market Street, Wilmington, NC 28405

Montreat College

Montreat, North Carolina **CB member**
www.montreat.edu **CB code: 5423**

- Private 4-year liberal arts college affiliated with Presbyterian Church Reformed and Independent
- Residential campus in small town
- 932 degree-seeking undergraduates: 1% part-time, 62% women
- 170 degree-seeking graduate students
- SAT or ACT (ACT writing recommended), application essay required

General. Founded in 1916. Regionally accredited. North Carolina's only member institute of the Council for Christian Colleges and Universities. **Degrees:** 152 bachelor's, 43 associate awarded; master's offered. **Location:** 16 miles from Asheville. **Calendar:** Semester, limited summer session. **Full-time faculty:** 46 total; 67% have terminal degrees, 13% minority, 35% women. **Class size:** 72% < 20, 26% 20-39, 2% 40-49. **Special facilities:** Ropes course, climbing wall, chapel of the prodigal, Black Mountain Campus.

Freshman class profile. 401 applied, 253 admitted, 120 enrolled.

Mid 50% test scores		**Out-of-state:**	31%
SAT critical reading:	430-540	**Live on campus:**	100%
SAT math:	440-550		

Basis for selection. Open admission, but selective for some programs. Decisions are criteria-based, using GPA and SAT/ACT scores as initial qualifiers. Essay, recommendation, and extracurricular activities also considered. Interview required for students who do not meet standard admission requirements. **Homeschooled:** Transcript of courses and grades, letter of recommendation (nonparent) required. **Learning Disabled:** Students with documented learning disabilities are referred to the Director of Student Success before an admissions decision is made.

High school preparation. College-preparatory program required. 16 units required. Required units include English 4, mathematics 3, social studies 3, science 3, foreign language 1 and academic electives 2.

2008-2009 Annual costs. Tuition/fees: $18,700. Room/board: $6,000. Books/supplies: $975. Personal expenses: $1,910.

2007-2008 Financial aid. **Need-based:** 148 full-time freshmen applied for aid; 129 were judged to have need; 129 of these received aid. Average need met was 62%. Average scholarship/grant was $9,660; average loan $3,167. 57% of total undergraduate aid awarded as scholarships/grants, 43% as loans/jobs. **Non-need-based:** Awarded to 163 full-time undergraduates, including 34 freshmen. Scholarships awarded for academics, alumni affiliation, athletics, leadership, music/drama, religious affiliation, state residency.

Application procedures. **Admission:** Priority date 5/15; deadline 8/1 (postmark date). $30 fee, may be waived for applicants with need. Admission notification on a rolling basis beginning on or about 9/15. **Financial aid:** Priority date 3/15; no closing date. FAFSA, institutional form required. Applicants notified on a rolling basis starting 1/15; must reply within 2 week(s) of notification.

Academics. **Special study options:** Accelerated study, double major, dual enrollment of high school students, independent study, internships, student-designed major, study abroad, teacher certification program, Washington semester. **Credit/placement by examination:** AP, CLEP, IB, institutional tests. 15 credit hours maximum toward associate degree, 30 toward bachelor's. **Support services:** Reduced course load, study skills assistance, tutoring, writing center.

Majors. **Area/ethnic studies:** American. **Biology:** General. **Business:** Accounting, business admin, international, marketing. **Communications:** Media studies. **Computer sciences:** General. **Conservation:** Environmental studies. **Education:** Elementary. **History:** General, American. **Parks/ recreation:** General. **Philosophy/religion:** Christian. **Psychology:** General. **Public administration:** Human services. **Theology:** Bible, missionary, religious ed, youth ministry. **Visual/performing arts:** Music management, music performance.

Most popular majors. Business/marketing 72%.

Computing on campus. 60 workstations in library, computer center, student center. Dormitories wired for high-speed internet access and linked to campus network. Helpline, repair service, wireless network available.

Student life. Freshman orientation: Mandatory. Preregistration for classes offered. 5 days before classes start. There is also a pre-orientation program, Wilderness Journey, available at extra cost. **Policies:** No alcohol on campus. Religious observance required. **Housing:** Guaranteed on-campus for all undergraduates. Single-sex dorms, wellness housing available. $100 nonrefundable deposit, deadline 4/1. 351 spaces available for undergraduate students. **Activities:** Choral groups, dance, drama, music ensembles, musical theater, student government, student newspaper, missions club, Fellowship of Christian Athletes, Young Life.

Athletics. NAIA. **Intercollegiate:** Baseball M, basketball, cross-country, golf, soccer, softball W, track and field, volleyball W. **Intramural:** Basketball, football (non-tackle), soccer, softball, table tennis, tennis, volleyball. **Team name:** Cavaliers.

Student services. Adult student services, alcohol/substance abuse counseling, chaplain/spiritual director, career counseling, student employment services, financial aid counseling, health services, personal counseling, placement for graduates, veterans' counselor. **Physically disabled:** Services for visually, speech, hearing impaired.

Contact. E-mail: admissions@montreat.edu
Phone: (828) 669-8012 ext. 3781 Toll-free number: (800) 622-6968
Fax: (828) 669-0120
Tony Robinson, Director of Enrollment Development & Outreach, Montreat College, Box 1267, Montreat, NC 28757-1267

Mount Olive College

Mount Olive, North Carolina — **CB member**
www.moc.edu — **CB code: 5435**

- Private 4-year liberal arts college affiliated with Free Will Baptists
- Residential campus in small town
- 3,390 degree-seeking undergraduates: 23% part-time, 65% women, 34% African American, 1% Asian American, 3% Hispanic American

General. Founded in 1951. Regionally accredited. **Degrees:** 637 bachelor's, 210 associate awarded. **Location:** 13 miles from Goldsboro. **Calendar:** Semester, extensive summer session. **Full-time faculty:** 89 total; 86% have terminal degrees, 16% minority, 33% women. **Part-time faculty:** 233 total; 24% have terminal degrees, 13% minority, 46% women. **Class size:** 71% < 20, 29% 20-39, less than 1% >100.

Freshman class profile. 1,949 applied, 1,082 admitted, 383 enrolled.

Mid 50% test scores			
SAT critical reading:	420-510	**GPA 3.0-3.49:**	28%
SAT math:	430-530	**GPA 2.0-2.99:**	40%
ACT composite:	15-21	**Rank in top quarter:**	36%
GPA 3.75 or higher:	21%	**Rank in top tenth:**	9%
GPA 3.50-3.74:	8%	**Out-of-state:**	11%

Basis for selection. Open admission, but selective for some programs. School record, test scores, class rank important. Personal recommendations considered. Interview recommended for all students; portfolio recommended for art majors. Audition required for music majors.

High school preparation. College-preparatory program recommended. 17 units required. Required units include English 4, mathematics 3, social studies 3, science 3 (laboratory 1) and academic electives 3.

2009-2010 Annual costs. Tuition/fees: $13,776. Room/board: $5,540. Books/supplies: $1,400.

2007-2008 Financial aid. Need-based: Average need met was 69%. Average scholarship/grant was $7,196; average loan $2,492. 46% of total undergraduate aid awarded as scholarships/grants, 54% as loans/jobs. **Non-need-based:** Awarded to 134 full-time undergraduates, including 9 freshmen. Scholarships awarded for academics, art, athletics, leadership, music/drama, religious affiliation.

Application procedures. Admission: No deadline. $20 fee, may be waived for applicants with need, free for online applicants. Admission notification on a rolling basis beginning on or about 10/1. **Financial aid:** No deadline. FAFSA required. Applicants notified on a rolling basis starting 2/14; must reply within 2 week(s) of notification.

Academics. Special study options: Accelerated study, cooperative education, distance learning, double major, dual enrollment of high school students, external degree, honors, independent study, internships, liberal arts/career combination, teacher certification program. Accelerated extension program at Seymour Johnson Air Force Base in Goldsboro; 55-week degree completion program in business offered in New Bern, Wilmington, and Raleigh-Research Triangle Park. **Credit/placement by examination:** AP, CLEP, institutional tests. 15 credit hours maximum toward associate degree, 30 toward bachelor's. **Support services:** Learning center, reduced course load, remedial instruction, study skills assistance, tutoring, writing center.

Majors. Biology: General. **Business:** Accounting, business admin, human resources, management information systems, organizational behavior. **Communications:** General. **Computer sciences:** General. **History:** General. **Liberal arts:** Arts/sciences. **Math:** General. **Parks/recreation:** General. **Philosophy/religion:** Religion. **Protective services:** Criminal justice. **Psychology:** General. **Visual/performing arts:** Design, studio arts.

Most popular majors. Business/marketing 49%, education 16%, security/protective services 16%.

Computing on campus. 50 workstations in library, computer center. Dormitories wired for high-speed internet access and linked to campus network. Commuter students can connect to campus network. Online library, repair service, wireless network available.

Student life. Freshman orientation: Available. **Policies:** Religious observance required. **Housing:** Guaranteed on-campus for freshmen. Single-sex dorms, apartments available. $50 nonrefundable deposit, deadline 2/26. **Activities:** Concert band, campus ministries, choral groups, international student organizations, music ensembles, musical theater, student government, English society, political forum, recreation majors club, Fellowship of Christian Athletes, Phi Beta Lambda, minority students' organization, Fellowship of Christian Students, Free Spirit.

Athletics. NCAA. **Intercollegiate:** Baseball M, basketball, cross-country, golf, soccer, softball W, tennis, volleyball. **Intramural:** Badminton, baseball M, basketball, football (tackle) M, handball, racquetball, softball, table tennis, tennis, volleyball.

Student services. Adult student services, career counseling, student employment services, health services, personal counseling, placement for graduates, veterans' counselor.

Contact. E-mail: admissions@moc.edu
Phone: (919) 658-2502 Toll-free number: (800) 653-0854
Fax: (919) 658-9816
Tim Woodard, Director of Admissions, Mount Olive College, 634 Henderson Street, Mount Olive, NC 28365

North Carolina Agricultural and Technical State University

Greensboro, North Carolina — **CB member**
www.ncat.edu — **CB code: 5003**

- Public 4-year university
- Residential campus in small city
- 8,632 degree-seeking undergraduates: 9% part-time, 52% women, 91% African American, 1% Asian American, 1% Hispanic American, 1% international
- 1,433 degree-seeking graduate students
- 53% of applicants admitted
- SAT or ACT with writing, SAT Subject Tests required

General. Founded in 1891. Regionally accredited. **Degrees:** 1,172 bachelor's awarded; master's, doctoral offered. **ROTC:** Army, Air Force. **Location:** 91 miles from Charlotte. **Calendar:** Semester. **Full-time faculty:** 520 total. **Part-time faculty:** 138 total. **Special facilities:** African heritage center, planetarium, herbarium, Olympic track.

Freshman class profile. 5,538 applied, 2,915 admitted, 1,607 enrolled.

Mid 50% test scores			
SAT critical reading:	400-500	**GPA 3.0-3.49:**	30%
SAT math:	410-510	**GPA 2.0-2.99:**	46%
ACT composite:	17-22	**Rank in top quarter:**	5%
GPA 3.75 or higher:	6%	**Return as sophomores:**	74%
GPA 3.50-3.74:	18%	**Out-of-state:**	21%
		International:	1%

Basis for selection. High school GPA, class rank, test scores, recommendations, course selection reviewed. SAT preferred, but ACT accepted. Audition recommended for music programs; portfolio recommended for art programs.

High school preparation. 19 units required. Required units include English 4, mathematics 4, social studies 1, history 1, science 3 (laboratory 1), foreign language 2 and academic electives 4.

2008-2009 Annual costs. Tuition/fees: $3,593; $13,035 out-of-state. Room/board: $5,336. Books/supplies: $1,400. Personal expenses: $1,500.

2008-2009 Financial aid. Non-need-based: Scholarships awarded for academics, athletics, music/drama, ROTC.

Application procedures. Admission: Priority date 6/1; no deadline. $45 fee. Admission notification on a rolling basis beginning on or about 9/15. Must reply by May 1 or within 2 week(s) if notified thereafter. **Financial aid:** Priority date 3/15; no closing date. FAFSA required. Applicants notified on a rolling basis starting 4/1; must reply within 2 week(s) of notification.

Academics. Special study options: Cooperative education, cross-registration, distance learning, double major, dual enrollment of high school students, honors, internships, study abroad, teacher certification program, weekend college. **Credit/placement by examination:** AP, CLEP, SAT, ACT, institutional tests. **Support services:** Learning center, reduced course load, remedial instruction, study skills assistance, tutoring, writing center.

Majors. Agriculture: Animal sciences, business, economics, plant sciences. **Architecture:** Landscape. **Biology:** General. **Business:** General, accounting, business admin, finance, managerial economics, marketing, transportation. **Communications:** General, broadcast journalism, journalism, public relations. **Computer sciences:** General. **Education:** General, agricultural, biology, business, chemistry, driver/safety, early childhood, elementary, English, family/consumer sciences, foreign languages, French, history, mathematics, music, physical, physics, social science, special, speech, technology/industrial arts, trade/industrial. **Engineering:** Agricultural, architectural, chemical, civil, electrical, materials, mechanical. **Engineering technology:** Industrial management, occupational safety. **Family/consumer sciences:** General, clothing/textiles, family studies, family/community services, food/nutrition. **Foreign languages:** French. **Health:** Occupational health. **History:** General. **Math:** General. **Parks/recreation:** Facilities management, health/fitness. **Physical sciences:** Chemistry, physics. **Psychology:** General. **Public administration:** Social work. **Social sciences:** General, political science, sociology. **Visual/performing arts:** General, art, dramatic.

Most popular majors. Business/marketing 17%, communications/journalism 7%, engineering/engineering technologies 15%, health sciences 6%, psychology 9%, visual/performing arts 7%.

Computing on campus. 675 workstations in library, computer center. Dormitories wired for high-speed internet access and linked to campus network. Commuter students can connect to campus network. Online course registration, helpline available.

Student life. Freshman orientation: Mandatory, $10 fee. Preregistration for classes offered. **Housing:** Guaranteed on-campus for freshmen. Coed dorms, single-sex dorms, wellness housing available. $150 deposit. **Activities:** Bands, choral groups, dance, drama, international student organizations, music ensembles, radio station, student government, student newspaper, symphony orchestra, TV station.

Athletics. NCAA. **Intercollegiate:** Baseball M, basketball, bowling W, cross-country, football (tackle) M, softball W, swimming W, tennis W, track and field, volleyball W, wrestling M. **Intramural:** Badminton, baseball M, basketball, bowling W, cross-country, football (tackle) M, golf, handball, racquetball, soccer, softball, swimming, table tennis, tennis, track and field, volleyball. **Team name:** Aggies.

Student services. Adult student services, alcohol/substance abuse counseling, career counseling, student employment services, financial aid counseling, health services, minority student services, personal counseling, placement for graduates, veterans' counselor. **Physically disabled:** Services for visually, speech, hearing impaired.

Contact. E-mail: uadmit@ncat.edu
Phone: (336) 334-7946 Toll-free number: (800) 443-8964
Fax: (336) 334-7478
Yvette Murph, Associate Vice Chancellor for Enrollment Management, North Carolina Agricultural and Technical State University, Webb Hall, Greensboro, NC 27411-0001

North Carolina Central University

Durham, North Carolina — **CB member**
www.nccu.edu — **CB code: 5495**

- Public 4-year university
- Commuter campus in small city
- 5,497 degree-seeking undergraduates
- 70% of applicants admitted
- SAT or ACT with writing required

General. Founded in 1910. Regionally accredited. Historically, the majority of students have been African American. **Degrees:** 882 bachelor's awarded; master's, first professional offered. **ROTC:** Army, Air Force. **Location:** 23 miles from Raleigh. **Calendar:** Semester, extensive summer session. **Full-time faculty:** 388 total. **Part-time faculty:** 222 total. **Class size:** 36% < 20, 47% 20-39, 11% 40-49, 6% 50-99, less than 1% >100. **Special facilities:** Collection of primary resources on black life and culture, art museum with works of Afro-American culture.

Freshman class profile. 3,233 applied, 2,260 admitted, 1,035 enrolled.

Mid 50% test scores			
SAT critical reading:	380-460	GPA 3.0-3.49:	20%
SAT math:	380-470	GPA 2.0-2.99:	60%
SAT writing:	370-450	Rank in top quarter:	16%
ACT composite:	15-19	Rank in top tenth:	5%
GPA 3.75 or higher:	7%	Out-of-state:	16%
GPA 3.50-3.74:	5%	Live on campus:	80%

Basis for selection. Academic achievement, class rank, test scores important. SAT preferred, ACT also accepted. Audition required for music programs. **Homeschooled:** Transcript of courses and grades, state high school equivalency certificate required.

High school preparation. 14 units required. Required units include English 4, mathematics 4, social studies 2, history 1, science 3 (laboratory 2) and foreign language 2. Social studies units must include 1 U.S. history. One foreign language, and 1 math recommended during 12th grade. Students who graduate high school in and after 2006 must have one additional math course from the following: pre-calculus, AP statistics, AP calculus, IB math level II, integrated math IV, discrete math, advanced models and functions.

2008-2009 Annual costs. Tuition/fees: $3,751; $13,495 out-of-state. Room/board: $5,743. Books/supplies: $1,500. Personal expenses: $1,575.

Financial aid. Non-need-based: Scholarships awarded for academics, alumni affiliation, athletics, minority status, music/drama, state residency. **Additional information:** Departmental grants based on need plus other available criteria.

Application procedures. Admission: Priority date 5/1; deadline 7/1. $40 fee. Admission notification on a rolling basis. Early admission available with permission from high school principal and academic dean. **Financial aid:** Priority date 4/1; no closing date. FAFSA required. Applicants notified by 5/1; must reply within 2 week(s) of notification.

Academics. Special study options: Cooperative education, distance learning, double major, ESL, honors, independent study, internships, study abroad, teacher certification program. **Credit/placement by examination:** AP, CLEP, SAT, ACT, institutional tests. 30 credit hours maximum toward bachelor's degree. **Support services:** Learning center, remedial instruction, study skills assistance, tutoring, writing center.

Majors. Biology: General. **Business:** Accounting, business admin, hospitality admin. **Communications:** Media studies. **Computer sciences:** Computer science, information systems. **Conservation:** Environmental science. **Education:** Art, biology, chemistry, drama/dance, elementary, English, family/consumer sciences, French, health, history, kindergarten/preschool, mathematics, middle, music, physical, physics, Spanish. **Family/consumer sciences:** General. **Foreign languages:** French, Spanish. **Health:** Athletic training, nursing (RN), public health ed. **History:** General. **Math:** General. **Parks/recreation:** Facilities management, health/fitness. **Physical sciences:** Chemistry, physics. **Protective services:** Law enforcement admin. **Psychology:** General. **Public administration:** Social work. **Social sciences:** Geography, political science, sociology. **Visual/performing arts:** Art, dramatic, jazz.

Most popular majors. Business/marketing 18%, education 9%, family/consumer sciences 6%, health sciences 6%, psychology 7%, security/protective services 10%, social sciences 11%.

Computing on campus. 400 workstations in dormitories, library, computer center. Dormitories wired for high-speed internet access and linked to campus network. Commuter students can connect to campus network. Online course registration, online library, helpline, repair service, wireless network available.

Student life. Freshman orientation: Mandatory. Preregistration for classes offered. **Housing:** Coed dorms, single-sex dorms available. $100 deposit, deadline 6/1. Coed honors dormitory available. **Activities:** Bands, choral groups, dance, drama, literary magazine, radio station, student government, student newspaper.

Athletics. NAIA, NCAA. **Intercollegiate:** Basketball, bowling, cheerleading W, cross-country, football (tackle) M, golf, softball W, tennis, track and field, volleyball W. **Team name:** Eagles.

Student services. Career counseling, student employment services, health services, on-campus daycare, personal counseling, placement for graduates, veterans' counselor.

Contact. E-mail: admissions@nccu.edu
Phone: (919) 560-6298 Toll-free number: (877) 667-7533
Fax: (919) 530-7625
Jocelyn Foy, Director of Admissions, North Carolina Central University, PO Box 19717, Durham, NC 27707

North Carolina State University

Raleigh, North Carolina — **CB member**
www.ncsu.edu — **CB code: 5496**

- Public 4-year university
- Residential campus in large city
- 22,839 degree-seeking undergraduates: 7% part-time, 43% women, 9% African American, 5% Asian American, 3% Hispanic American, 1% Native American, 1% international
- 7,241 degree-seeking graduate students
- 59% of applicants admitted
- SAT or ACT with writing required
- 69% graduate within 6 years

General. Founded in 1887. Regionally accredited. **Degrees:** 4,535 bachelor's, 132 associate awarded; master's, doctoral, first professional offered. **ROTC:** Army, Naval, Air Force. **Location:** One mile from downtown. **Calendar:** Semester, extensive summer session. **Full-time faculty:** 1,760 total; 89% have terminal degrees, 20% minority, 31% women. **Part-time faculty:** 195 total; 63% have terminal degrees, 12% minority, 44% women. **Class size:** 32% < 20, 45% 20-39, 7% 40-49, 11% 50-99, 5% >100. **Special facilities:** 3 electron microscopes, phytotron, research farms, 2 campus theaters, craft center, stable isotope laboratory, teaching forest, wood products laboratory, coastal marine science laboratory, 80,000 acres of research forests and research farm lands, fiber, fabric, and garment manufacturing equipment.

Freshman class profile. 17,652 applied, 10,362 admitted, 4,669 enrolled.

Mid 50% test scores			
SAT critical reading:	520-610	Rank in top quarter:	78%
SAT math:	550-660	Rank in top tenth:	34%
SAT writing:	510-610	Return as sophomores:	90%
ACT composite:	22-27	Out-of-state:	9%
GPA 3.75 or higher:	85%	Live on campus:	77%
GPA 3.50-3.74:	10%	International:	1%
GPA 3.0-3.49:	4%	Fraternities:	7%
GPA 2.0-2.99:	1%	Sororities:	12%

Basis for selection. GED not accepted. School academic record, standardized test scores important. Counselor evaluations, extracurricular activities also considered. Preference given to students with exceptionally strong high school record. Level and difficulty of courses considered. Weighted grades for advanced, honors, AP courses considered. All applicants to the UNC system, except those exempted by current campus policies, must submit standardized test scores. SAT preferred, ACT also accepted. Essay recommended for all students. Interview and portfolio required for College of Design applicants. Verification of golf playing ability required for Professional Golf Management Program.

High school preparation. 16 units required; 20 recommended. Required and recommended units include English 4, mathematics 4, social studies 1, history 1, science 3-4 (laboratory 1-2), foreign language 2 and academic electives 1-4. Science units should include 1 life or biological science, 1 physical science, and 1 laboratory science. Honors, advanced, AP and IB courses given extra weight.

2008-2009 Annual costs. Tuition/fees: $5,274; $17,572 out-of-state. Room/board: $7,982. Books/supplies: $930. Personal expenses: $1,250.

2008-2009 Financial aid. **Need-based:** 3,364 full-time freshmen applied for aid; 2,038 were judged to have need; 2,019 of these received aid. Average need met was 90%. Average scholarship/grant was $9,282; average loan $2,427. 75% of total undergraduate aid awarded as scholarships/grants, 25% as loans/jobs. **Non-need-based:** Awarded to 2,212 full-time undergraduates, including 614 freshmen. Scholarships awarded for academics, alumni affiliation, athletics, leadership, ROTC, state residency. **Additional information:** Freshman Merit Scholarships; students submitting complete admissions application by the November 1 Early Action deadline automatically considered, additional information may be required after initial review.

Application procedures. **Admission:** Priority date 11/1; deadline 2/1 (postmark date). $70 fee, may be waived for applicants with need. Must reply by 5/1. Students applying under regular admission to College of Design must submit application by 12/1. Selected candidates will be invited to interview. **Financial aid:** Priority date 3/1; no closing date. FAFSA, institutional form required. CSS PROFILE recommended for early scholarship consideration. Applicants notified on a rolling basis starting 4/1.

Academics. **Special study options:** Accelerated study, combined bachelor's/graduate degree, cooperative education, cross-registration, distance learning, double major, dual enrollment of high school students, ESL, exchange student, external degree, honors, independent study, internships, liberal arts/career combination, student-designed major, study abroad, teacher certification program. 2+2 Engineering with University of North Carolina-Asheville and selected community colleges. **Credit/placement by examination:** AP, CLEP, IB, SAT, ACT, institutional tests. **Support services:** Learning center, pre-admission summer program, reduced course load, remedial instruction, study skills assistance, tutoring, writing center.

Majors. **Agriculture:** Agribusiness operations, agronomy, animal sciences, education services, food science, horticultural science, mechanization, poultry. **Architecture:** Architecture, environmental design, landscape. **Area/ethnic studies:** African-American, women's. **Biology:** General, biochemistry, botany, microbiology, zoology. **Business:** Accounting, business admin, managerial economics. **Communications:** General. **Computer sciences:** Computer science. **Conservation:** General, environmental science, forest management, management/policy, wood science. **Education:** General, agricultural, elementary, English, French, health occupations, mathematics, middle, sales/marketing, science, social studies, Spanish, technology/industrial arts. **Engineering:** General, aerospace, agricultural, biomedical, chemical, civil, computer, construction, electrical, environmental, industrial, materials, mechanical, nuclear, textile. **Engineering technology:** Environmental. **Family/consumer sciences:** Apparel marketing, clothing/textiles. **Foreign languages:** French, Spanish. **History:** General. **Interdisciplinary:** Global studies, science/society. **Liberal arts:** Arts/sciences. **Math:** General, applied, statistics. **Parks/recreation:** Facilities management, sports admin. **Philosophy/religion:** Philosophy, religion. **Physical sciences:** Atmospheric science, chemistry, geology, oceanography, physics, polymer chemistry. **Psychology:** General. **Public administration:** Social work. **Social sciences:** Anthropology, criminology, geography, political science, sociology. **Visual/performing arts:** Arts management, design, graphic design, industrial design.

Most popular majors. Agriculture 6%, biology 11%, business/marketing 15%, communications/journalism 6%, engineering/engineering technologies 22%, social sciences 8%.

Computing on campus. 3,000 workstations in dormitories, library, computer center, student center. Dormitories wired for high-speed internet access and linked to campus network. Commuter students can connect to campus network. Online course registration, helpline, repair service, student web hosting, wireless network available.

Student life. **Freshman orientation:** Mandatory, $100 fee. Preregistration for classes offered. 2-day program. **Housing:** Coed dorms, single-sex dorms, special housing for disabled, apartments, fraternity/sorority housing, wellness housing available. International student dormitory, Residential Scholars Program, residence hall for students interested in computers and visual and performing arts, first year college living and learning experience. **Activities:** Bands, campus ministries, choral groups, dance, drama, international student organizations, literary magazine, music ensembles, musical theater, radio station, student government, student newspaper, symphony orchestra, Alpha Phi Omega, Baptist Student Union, Campus Crusade for Christ, Circle-K, international student board, Young Democrats, Young Republicans, Society of Afro-American Culture, YMCA.

Athletics. NCAA. **Intercollegiate:** Baseball M, basketball, cheerleading, cross-country, diving, football (tackle) M, golf, gymnastics W, rifle, soccer, softball W, swimming, tennis, track and field, volleyball W, wrestling M. **Intramural:** Archery, badminton, baseball M, basketball, bowling, cross-country, fencing, field hockey W, football (non-tackle), golf, gymnastics, handball, ice hockey M, lacrosse M, racquetball, rugby M, sailing, skiing, skin diving, soccer, softball, squash, swimming, table tennis, tennis, track and field, volleyball, wrestling M. **Team name:** Wolfpack.

Student services. Adult student services, alcohol/substance abuse counseling, chaplain/spiritual director, career counseling, student employment services, financial aid counseling, health services, legal services, minority student services, on-campus daycare, personal counseling, placement for graduates, veterans' counselor, women's services. **Physically disabled:** Services for visually, speech, hearing impaired.

Contact. E-mail: undergrad_admissions@ncsu.edu
Phone: (919) 515-2434 Fax: (919) 515-5039
Thomas Griffin, Director of Undergraduate Admissions, North Carolina State University, 203 Peele Hall, Box 7103, Raleigh, NC 27695-7103

North Carolina Wesleyan College

Rocky Mount, North Carolina
www.ncwc.edu **CB code: 5501**

- Private 4-year liberal arts college affiliated with United Methodist Church
- Residential campus in small city
- 1,318 degree-seeking undergraduates: 21% part-time, 58% women
- 63% of applicants admitted
- SAT or ACT (ACT writing optional) required

General. Founded in 1956. Regionally accredited. Adult students, 22 and older, can attend classes at sites in Raleigh, Goldsboro, and Rocky Mount. There is a free Silver Scholars Program for age 60 and above. **Degrees:** 386 bachelor's awarded. **ROTC:** Army. **Location:** 57 miles from Raleigh. **Calendar:** Semester, extensive summer session. **Full-time faculty:** 49 total; 76% have terminal degrees, 4% minority, 45% women. **Part-time faculty:** 107 total; 48% have terminal degrees, 20% minority. **Class size:** 82% < 20, 18% 20-39. **Special facilities:** Black Mountain archival collection, center for the performing arts.

Freshman class profile. 1,245 applied, 781 admitted, 245 enrolled.

Mid 50% test scores			
SAT critical reading:	410-520	Rank in top quarter:	18%
SAT math:	420-550	Rank in top tenth:	8%
SAT writing:	400-510	Out-of-state:	42%
ACT composite:	16-22	Live on campus:	85%

Basis for selection. High school GPA most important, followed by SAT or ACT score, rigor of high school curriculum, and recommendations. Essay, school and community activities considered. SAT preferred. Essay, interview recommended for all students. **Homeschooled:** Statement describing homeschool structure and mission, interview required.

High school preparation. College-preparatory program recommended. Recommended units include English 4, mathematics 3, social studies 2, science 2 (laboratory 2) and foreign language 2.

2008-2009 Annual costs. Tuition/fees: $20,790. Room/board: $7,380. Books/supplies: $1,000. Personal expenses: $1,200.

2007-2008 Financial aid. All financial aid based on need. **Additional information:** Scholarships based on GPA. Various scholarship and leadership awards available.

Application procedures. Admission: No deadline. $25 fee, may be waived for applicants with need. Admission notification on a rolling basis. **Financial aid:** Priority date 3/1; no closing date. FAFSA required. Applicants notified on a rolling basis starting 1/1; must reply within 2 week(s) of notification.

Academics. Special study options: Accelerated study, cooperative education, cross-registration, distance learning, double major, dual enrollment of high school students, honors, independent study, internships, liberal arts/career combination, teacher certification program, weekend college. **Credit/placement by examination:** AP, CLEP, institutional tests. **Support services:** Learning center, pre-admission summer program, reduced course load, remedial instruction, study skills assistance, tutoring, writing center.

Majors. Biology: General. **Business:** Accounting, business admin. **Computer sciences:** Information systems. **Conservation:** General. **Education:** Elementary, middle, physical. **Health:** Premedicine. **History:** General. **Math:** General. **Philosophy/religion:** Religion. **Physical sciences:** Chemistry. **Protective services:** Criminal justice. **Psychology:** General. **Social sciences:** Political science, sociology. **Visual/performing arts:** Dramatic.

Computing on campus. 223 workstations in dormitories, library, computer center, student center. Dormitories wired for high-speed internet access and linked to campus network. Commuter students can connect to campus network. Online course registration, helpline, repair service available.

Student life. Freshman orientation: Mandatory. Preregistration for classes offered. Takes place prior to start of fall classes. **Housing:** Guaranteed on-campus for freshmen. Coed dorms, single-sex dorms, special housing for disabled, wellness housing available. $100 deposit, deadline 7/15. **Activities:** Bands, choral groups, drama, literary magazine, music ensembles, student government, student newspaper, Black Student Association, Fellowship of Christian Athletes, College Republicans, Wesleyan Christian Fellowship.

Athletics. NCAA. **Intercollegiate:** Baseball M, basketball, cheerleading M, cross-country W, football (tackle) M, golf M, lacrosse W, soccer, softball W, tennis, volleyball W. **Intramural:** Basketball, football (tackle) M, lacrosse W, soccer, softball, table tennis, tennis, volleyball. **Team name:** Bishops.

Student services. Adult student services, alcohol/substance abuse counseling, chaplain/spiritual director, career counseling, student employment services, financial aid counseling, health services, personal counseling, placement for graduates, veterans' counselor. **Physically disabled:** Services for visually, hearing impaired.

Contact. E-mail: adm@ncwc.edu
Phone: (252) 985-5200 Toll-free number: (800) 488-6292
Fax: (252) 985-5295
Cecilia Summers, Director of Admissions, North Carolina Wesleyan College, 3400 North Wesleyan Boulevard, Rocky Mount, NC 27804

Peace College

Raleigh, North Carolina **CB member**
www.peace.edu **CB code: 5533**

- Private 4-year liberal arts college for women affiliated with Presbyterian Church (USA)
- Residential campus in large city
- 665 degree-seeking undergraduates: 4% part-time, 100% women
- 65% of applicants admitted
- SAT or ACT (ACT writing optional) required
- 35% graduate within 6 years; 16% enter graduate study

General. Founded in 1857. Regionally accredited. **Degrees:** 126 bachelor's awarded. **ROTC:** Army, Naval, Air Force. **Location:** Downtown. **Calendar:** Semester, limited summer session. **Full-time faculty:** 44 total; 86% have terminal degrees, 11% minority, 64% women. **Part-time faculty:** 47 total; 49% have terminal degrees, 13% minority, 55% women. **Class size:** 74% < 20, 25% 20-39, less than 1% 50-99.

Freshman class profile. 1,005 applied, 651 admitted, 185 enrolled.

Mid 50% test scores		GPA 2.0-2.99:	44%
SAT critical reading:	420-510	Rank in top quarter:	22%
SAT math:	400-510	Rank in top tenth:	7%
ACT composite:	14-22	End year in good standing:	82%
GPA 3.75 or higher:	15%	Return as sophomores:	65%
GPA 3.50-3.74:	11%	Out-of-state:	12%
GPA 3.0-3.49:	28%	Live on campus:	89%

Basis for selection. School achievement record, test scores, 2.0 GPA on college preparatory courses recommended. SAT combined score of 800 (exclusive of Writing) and above preferred or ACT of 17 minimum. Interview recommended for all students. Audition required for theatre, drama, and music majors; portfolio required for art programs. **Learning Disabled:** Students with learning disabilities are encouraged to contact disabilities resource center regarding their needs.

High school preparation. 15 units required; 17 recommended. Required and recommended units include English 4, mathematics 3-4, social studies 2, history 2, science 2-3 and foreign language 2.

2009-2010 Annual costs. Tuition/fees: $22,993. Room/board: $7,820. Books/supplies: $1,300. Personal expenses: $2,200.

2008-2009 Financial aid. Need-based: 158 full-time freshmen applied for aid; 143 were judged to have need; 143 of these received aid. Average need met was 78%. Average scholarship/grant was $17,208; average loan $3,103. 66% of total undergraduate aid awarded as scholarships/grants, 34% as loans/jobs. **Non-need-based:** Awarded to 202 full-time undergraduates, including 67 freshmen. Scholarships awarded for academics, art, music/drama, state residency.

Application procedures. Admission: Priority date 4/1; no deadline. $25 fee, may be waived for applicants with need. Admission notification on a rolling basis beginning on or about 8/1. Must reply by May 1 or within 2 week(s) if notified thereafter. Prefer early admission candidates with SAT 1100 or above, 3.5 GPA in college preparatory courses, and rank in top 25% of class. On-campus interview required. **Financial aid:** Priority date 3/15; no closing date. FAFSA required. Applicants notified on a rolling basis starting 3/1; must reply within 4 week(s) of notification.

Academics. Special study options: Cross-registration, double major, dual enrollment of high school students, honors, independent study, internships, liberal arts/career combination, study abroad, teacher certification program. **Credit/placement by examination:** AP, CLEP, IB, SAT, ACT, institutional tests. 6 credit hours maximum toward bachelor's degree. CLEP credit is granted to students who have achieved the minimum score in designated subject tests. Students may petition program coordinators for additional or alternative credit, if warranted. **Support services:** Learning center, reduced course load, remedial instruction, study skills assistance, tutoring, writing center.

Majors. Biology: General. **Business:** Business admin, human resources. **Communications:** General. **Education:** Early childhood, multi-level teacher. **Family/consumer sciences:** Child development. **Foreign languages:** Spanish. **History:** General. **Liberal arts:** Arts/sciences. **Psychology:** General. **Social sciences:** Anthropology, political science. **Visual/performing arts:** Design, music performance. **Other:** Leadership studies.

Most popular majors. Biology 6%, business/marketing 21%, communications/journalism 14%, liberal arts 6%, psychology 10%, social sciences 10%.

Computing on campus. 180 workstations in dormitories, library, computer center, student center. Dormitories wired for high-speed internet access and linked to campus network. Commuter students can connect to campus network. Online course registration, online library, helpline, repair service, student web hosting, wireless network available.

Student life. Freshman orientation: Mandatory, $150 fee. Preregistration for classes offered. 2-day program offered prior to start of classes. **Policies:** Honor code and Student Code of Conduct. Religious observance required. **Housing:** Guaranteed on-campus for freshmen. Special housing for disabled, wellness housing available. $150 nonrefundable deposit, deadline 7/1. Freshmen and sophomores required to live on campus unless living with relatives in area. **Activities:** Campus ministries, choral groups, dance, drama, literary magazine, music ensembles, musical theater, opera, student government, student newspaper, Christian Association, honor societies, recreation association, Young Democrats/Republicans, Phi Theta Kappa, Student Environmental Action Coalition.

Athletics. NCAA. **Intercollegiate:** Basketball W, cross-country W, soccer W, softball W, tennis W, volleyball W. **Intramural:** Badminton W, basketball W, equestrian W, soccer W, softball W, swimming W, table tennis W, tennis W, volleyball W. **Team name:** Peace Pacers.

Student services. Adult student services, chaplain/spiritual director, career counseling, student employment services, financial aid counseling, health services, personal counseling, placement for graduates.

Contact. E-mail: admissions@peace.edu
Phone: (919) 508-2000 Toll-free number: (800) 732-2347
Fax: (919) 508-2306
Matt Green, Dean of Enrollment, Peace College, 15 East Peace Street, Raleigh, NC 27604-1194

Pfeiffer University

Misenheimer, North Carolina — **CB member**
www.pfeiffer.edu — **CB code: 5536**

- Private 4-year university and liberal arts college affiliated with United Methodist Church
- Residential campus in rural community
- 1,089 degree-seeking undergraduates: 13% part-time, 57% women
- 930 degree-seeking graduate students
- 71% of applicants admitted
- SAT or ACT (ACT writing optional) required
- 59% graduate within 6 years

General. Founded in 1885. Regionally accredited. **Degrees:** 234 bachelor's awarded; master's offered. **ROTC:** Army. **Location:** 35 miles from Charlotte, 60 miles from Winston-Salem. **Calendar:** Semester, limited summer session. **Full-time faculty:** 74 total; 69% have terminal degrees, 10% minority, 32% women. **Part-time faculty:** 68 total; 35% women. **Class size:** 78% < 20, 21% 20-39, less than 1% 40-49, less than 1% 50-99. **Special facilities:** Retreat center.

Freshman class profile. 912 applied, 648 admitted, 218 enrolled.

Mid 50% test scores		**Rank in top quarter:**	30%
SAT critical reading:	420-520	**Rank in top tenth:**	17%
SAT math:	430-540	**Return as sophomores:**	66%
GPA 3.75 or higher:	21%	**Out-of-state:**	36%
GPA 3.50-3.74:	11%	**Live on campus:**	75%
GPA 3.0-3.49:	24%	**International:**	2%
GPA 2.0-2.99:	43%		

Basis for selection. School achievement record, class rank, recommendations, and test scores reviewed. Interview recommended for all students; audition required for music programs.

High school preparation. 12 units required; 16 recommended. Required and recommended units include English 4, mathematics 3, social studies 2-4, history 2, science 2-3 (laboratory 1) and foreign language 2. Math should include algebra I and geometry.

2008-2009 Annual costs. Tuition/fees: $18,570. Room/board: $7,360. Books/supplies: $750. Personal expenses: $600.

2007-2008 Financial aid. Need-based: 190 full-time freshmen applied for aid; 155 were judged to have need; 155 of these received aid. Average need met was 80%. Average scholarship/grant was $11,529; average loan $2,959. 65% of total undergraduate aid awarded as scholarships/grants, 35% as loans/jobs. **Non-need-based:** Awarded to 372 full-time undergraduates, including 112 freshmen. Scholarships awarded for academics, alumni affiliation, athletics, leadership, music/drama, religious affiliation, state residency.

Application procedures. Admission: No deadline. $25 fee, may be waived for applicants with need. Admission notification on a rolling basis beginning on or about 9/1. **Financial aid:** Priority date 5/1; no closing date. FAFSA required. Applicants notified on a rolling basis starting 3/1; must reply within 2 week(s) of notification.

Academics. Special study options: Accelerated study, combined bachelor's/graduate degree, cooperative education, distance learning, double major, dual enrollment of high school students, honors, independent study, internships, liberal arts/career combination, study abroad, teacher certification program, Washington semester, weekend college. **Credit/placement by examination:** AP, CLEP, IB, SAT, ACT, institutional tests. **Support services:** Learning center, reduced course load, remedial instruction, study skills assistance, tutoring.

Majors. Biology: General. **Business:** General, accounting, business admin. **Communications:** General. **Computer sciences:** General. **Conservation:** Environmental studies. **Education:** Elementary, music, physical, secondary, social science, special. **Engineering:** General. **Health:** Athletic training, health care admin, predental, premedicine, preveterinary. **History:** General. **Legal studies:** Prelaw. **Liberal arts:** Arts/sciences. **Math:** General. **Parks/recreation:** Facilities management, sports admin. **Philosophy/religion:** Religion. **Physical sciences:** Chemistry. **Protective services:** Criminal justice, police science. **Psychology:** General. **Social sciences:** Economics, sociology. **Theology:** Missionary, religious ed, sacred music, youth ministry. **Visual/performing arts:** Arts management, dramatic.

Most popular majors. Business/marketing 31%, communications/journalism 6%, education 11%, parks/recreation 7%, security/protective services 11%.

Computing on campus. 114 workstations in library, computer center. Dormitories linked to campus network. Commuter students can connect to campus network. Online library, repair service, wireless network available.

Student life. Freshman orientation: Available, $35 fee. **Housing:** Guaranteed on-campus for all undergraduates. Coed dorms, single-sex dorms, special housing for disabled, apartments, wellness housing available. $150 deposit. Apartment-style housing with shared kitchen and bath available for older students not married. **Activities:** Bands, choral groups, dance, drama, literary magazine, music ensembles, musical theater, student government, student newspaper, religious organizations, political groups, service clubs, professional clubs.

Athletics. NCAA. **Intercollegiate:** Baseball M, basketball, cross-country, golf, lacrosse, soccer, softball W, swimming, tennis, volleyball W. **Intramural:** Basketball, lacrosse, soccer, softball, table tennis, tennis, volleyball. **Team name:** Falcons.

Student services. Alcohol/substance abuse counseling, chaplain/spiritual director, career counseling, student employment services, financial aid counseling, health services, personal counseling, placement for graduates, veterans' counselor.

Contact. E-mail: admiss@pfeiffer.edu
Phone: (704) 463-1360 ext. 2060 Toll-free number: (800) 338-2060
Fax: (704) 463-1363
Steven Cumming, Director of Admissions, Pfeiffer University, Box 960, Misenheimer, NC 28109

Piedmont Baptist College

Winston-Salem, North Carolina
www.pbc.edu — **CB code: 5555**

- Private 4-year Bible and seminary college affiliated with Baptist faith
- Small city

- 273 degree-seeking undergraduates: 27% part-time, 38% women
- 129 degree-seeking graduate students
- ACT (writing optional), application essay required

General. Founded in 1945. Regionally accredited. **Degrees:** 44 bachelor's, 8 associate awarded; master's, doctoral offered. **Location:** 75 miles from Charlotte, 100 miles from Raleigh. **Calendar:** Semester, limited summer session. **Full-time faculty:** 20 total. **Part-time faculty:** 15 total. **Class size:** 77% < 20, 17% 20-39, 4% 40-49, 1% 50-99. **Special facilities:** Restored 18th Century Moravian community, Old Salem.

Freshman class profile. 61 enrolled.

Out-of-state:	55%	**Live on campus:**	44%

Basis for selection. Student's life objectives and previous academic record important. Interview recommended for all students; audition required for music program.

High school preparation. Recommended units include English 4, mathematics 3, social studies 3, science 3 and foreign language 2.

2008-2009 Annual costs. Tuition/fees: $10,800. Room/board: $5,560. Books/supplies: $600. Personal expenses: $600.

Application procedures. Admission: Priority date 7/31; no deadline. $60 fee. Admission notification on a rolling basis beginning on or about 12/1. Must reply by May 1 or within 2 week(s) if notified thereafter. **Financial aid:** No deadline. Institutional form required. Applicants notified on a rolling basis starting 3/1.

Academics. Special study options: Cooperative education, distance learning, double major, dual enrollment of high school students, independent study, internships, teacher certification program. **Credit/placement by examination:** AP, CLEP, institutional tests. **Support services:** Learning center, reduced course load, remedial instruction, study skills assistance, tutoring.

Majors. Education: Elementary, English, music, physical. **Theology:** Bible, missionary, youth ministry.

Most popular majors. Education 33%, philosophy/religious studies 60%.

Computing on campus. 26 workstations in library, computer center, student center. Dormitories linked to campus network. Commuter students can connect to campus network. Online course registration, online library, helpline, wireless network available.

Student life. Freshman orientation: Mandatory. Preregistration for classes offered. Held 2 days prior to registration, overviews basic rules and guidelines. **Policies:** Religious observance required. **Housing:** Guaranteed on-campus for freshmen. Single-sex dorms, apartments available. **Activities:** Choral groups, drama, music ensembles, student government, student newspaper, missions fellowship, preachers' fellowship, youth leaders' fellowship, educators' fellowship, music fellowship.

Athletics. NCCAA. **Intercollegiate:** Basketball, soccer M, volleyball W. **Team name:** Conquerors.

Student services. Chaplain/spiritual director, career counseling, financial aid counseling, health services, personal counseling, placement for graduates, veterans' counselor.

Contact. E-mail: admissions@pbc.edu
Phone: (336) 725-8344 ext. 7900 Toll-free number: (800) 937-5097
Fax: (336) 725-5522
Kathy Holritz, Director of Admissions, Piedmont Baptist College, 420 South Boad Street, Winston-Salem, NC 27101-5133

Queens University of Charlotte

Charlotte, North Carolina — **CB member**
www.queens.edu — **CB code: 5560**

- Private 4-year university affiliated with Presbyterian Church (USA)
- Residential campus in very large city
- 1,718 degree-seeking undergraduates: 31% part-time, 77% women, 17% African American, 2% Asian American, 5% Hispanic American, 5% international
- 494 degree-seeking graduate students
- 77% of applicants admitted
- SAT or ACT with writing required
- 61% graduate within 6 years

General. Founded in 1857. Regionally accredited. **Degrees:** 255 bachelor's, 124 associate awarded; master's offered. **ROTC:** Army, Air Force. **Calendar:** Semester, limited summer session. **Full-time faculty:** 103 total; 70% have terminal degrees, 12% minority, 67% women. **Part-time faculty:** 96 total; 38% have terminal degrees, 7% minority, 60% women. **Class size:** 70% < 20, 26% 20-39, 3% 40-49, 2% 50-99. **Special facilities:** Rare books museum, recital hall.

Freshman class profile. 1,538 applied, 1,179 admitted, 309 enrolled.

Mid 50% test scores		**Rank in top quarter:**	47%
SAT critical reading:	470-570	**Rank in top tenth:**	20%
SAT math:	480-580	**Return as sophomores:**	69%
SAT writing:	470-570	**Out-of-state:**	43%
ACT composite:	20-24	**Live on campus:**	90%
GPA 3.75 or higher:	36%	**International:**	2%
GPA 3.50-3.74:	17%	**Fraternities:**	17%
GPA 3.0-3.49:	29%	**Sororities:**	23%
GPA 2.0-2.99:	18%		

Basis for selection. High school courses taken, school achievement record, class rank, test scores important. Extracurricular activities, recommendations also considered. Official test scores must be received prior to admission. Interview recommended for all students. Audition required for drama, music, music therapy programs; portfolio recommended for art program. **Homeschooled:** Transcript of courses and grades required. Evidence of Home School registration in the home state (copy of Home School License) required.

High school preparation. College-preparatory program required. Required units include English 4, mathematics 3, social studies 2, science 2 (laboratory 1) and foreign language 2. Chemistry recommended for nursing majors.

2008-2009 Annual costs. Tuition/fees: $22,068. Room/board: $7,882. Books/supplies: $1,200. Personal expenses: $1,500.

2008-2009 Financial aid. Need-based: 238 full-time freshmen applied for aid; 195 were judged to have need; 195 of these received aid. Average need met was 81%. Average scholarship/grant was $14,560; average loan $3,084. 56% of total undergraduate aid awarded as scholarships/grants, 44% as loans/jobs. **Non-need-based:** Awarded to 522 full-time undergraduates, including 154 freshmen.

Application procedures. Admission: Priority date 12/1; no deadline. $40 fee, may be waived for applicants with need, free for online applicants. Admission notification on a rolling basis beginning on or about 10/1. Must reply by May 1 or within 3 week(s) if notified thereafter. Admission can be deferred up to one year. **Financial aid:** Priority date 3/1; no closing date. FAFSA required. Applicants notified on a rolling basis starting 3/15; must reply by 5/1 or within 3 week(s) of notification.

Academics. 6 credit hours of internships required to enhance job placement and career opportunities. **Special study options:** Cross-registration, double major, dual enrollment of high school students, honors, independent study, internships, student-designed major, study abroad, teacher certification program, Washington semester, weekend college. John Belk International Program (3-week study tours in Europe and Asia), interdisciplinary core curriculum, professional golf management, Harvard Model UN, European internship program offered. **Credit/placement by examination:** AP, CLEP, IB, institutional tests. 43 credit hours maximum toward bachelor's degree. **Support services:** Learning center, reduced course load, study skills assistance, tutoring, writing center.

Majors. Area/ethnic studies: American, European. **Biology:** General, biochemistry, environmental. **Business:** Business admin, international, marketing. **Communications:** General, journalism, media studies, organizational. **Computer sciences:** Information systems. **Education:** General, elementary. **Foreign languages:** General. **Health:** Music therapy, nursing (RN), predental, premedicine, preop/surgical nursing, prepharmacy, preveterinary. **History:** General. **Interdisciplinary:** Global studies. **Legal studies:** Prelaw. **Math:** General, statistics. **Philosophy/religion:** Religion. **Physical sciences:** Chemistry. **Psychology:** General. **Social sciences:** Political science, sociology. **Visual/performing arts:** Dramatic, music performance, studio arts.

Computing on campus. Dormitories wired for high-speed internet access and linked to campus network. Commuter students can connect to campus network. Online library, helpline, wireless network available.

Student life. Freshman orientation: Mandatory. Preregistration for classes offered. 2-day program held at beginning of academic year. Pre-orientation held in spring for all deposited freshmen. **Housing:** Guaranteed on-campus for freshmen. Coed dorms, special housing for disabled, wellness housing available. $250 fully refundable deposit, deadline 5/1. Apartment style residence hall available for traditional undergraduates only. **Activities:** Pep band, campus ministries, choral groups, dance, drama, international student organizations, literary magazine, music ensembles, Model UN, musical theater, student government, student newspaper, Students for Black Awareness, College Republicans, College Democrats, North Carolina Student Legislature, Justinian Society.

Athletics. NCAA. **Intercollegiate:** Basketball, cheerleading, cross-country, golf, lacrosse, soccer, softball W, tennis, track and field, volleyball W. **Intramural:** Basketball, football (non-tackle) M, soccer, softball, volleyball. **Team name:** Royals.

Student services. Alcohol/substance abuse counseling, chaplain/spiritual director, career counseling, student employment services, financial aid counseling, health services, minority student services, personal counseling, placement for graduates. **Physically disabled:** Services for visually impaired.

Contact. E-mail: admissions@queens.edu
Phone: (704) 337-2212 Toll-free number: (800) 849-0202
Fax: (704) 337-2403
William Lee, Director of Admissions, Queens University of Charlotte, 1900 Selwyn Ave, Charlotte, NC 28274

Roanoke Bible College

Elizabeth City, North Carolina
www.roanokebible.edu **CB code: 5597**

- Private 4-year Bible college affiliated with Church of Christ
- Residential campus in large town
- 166 degree-seeking undergraduates
- 56% of applicants admitted
- SAT or ACT (ACT writing optional), application essay required
- 58% graduate within 6 years

General. Founded in 1948. Regionally accredited; also accredited by ABHE. **Degrees:** 19 bachelor's, 6 associate awarded. **Location:** 50 miles from Norfolk, Virginia. **Calendar:** Semester, limited summer session. **Full-time faculty:** 9 total; 56% have terminal degrees, 33% women. **Part-time faculty:** 19 total; 32% have terminal degrees, 5% minority, 26% women. **Class size:** 85% < 20, 15% 20-39.

Freshman class profile. 127 applied, 71 admitted, 41 enrolled.

Mid 50% test scores		**GPA 3.0-3.49:**	17%
SAT critical reading:	410-570	**GPA 2.0-2.99:**	43%
SAT math:	420-590	**Rank in top quarter:**	41%
ACT composite:	19-24	**Rank in top tenth:**	14%
GPA 3.75 or higher:	17%	**Return as sophomores:**	52%
GPA 3.50-3.74:	13%		

Basis for selection. Evidence of Christian character, school achievement record, test scores, school and community activities, recommendations important. Interview recommended if questions arise from references or academic record. **Homeschooled:** Transcript of courses and grades, state high school equivalency certificate required.

High school preparation. 20 units required. Required and recommended units include English 4, mathematics 3, social studies 2, history 2, science 3 (laboratory 2), foreign language 2, computer science 1 and academic electives 4.

2008-2009 Annual costs. Tuition/fees: $9,150. Room/board: $5,890. Books/supplies: $900. Personal expenses: $2,500.

2007-2008 Financial aid. Need-based: 33 full-time freshmen applied for aid; 31 were judged to have need; 31 of these received aid. Average need met was 78%. Average scholarship/grant was $3,390; average loan $2,625. 43% of total undergraduate aid awarded as scholarships/grants, 57% as loans/jobs. **Non-need-based:** Awarded to 34 full-time undergraduates, including 11 freshmen. Scholarships awarded for academics, alumni affiliation, leadership, music/drama, religious affiliation.

Application procedures. Admission: No deadline. $50 fee, may be waived for applicants with need. Admission notification on a rolling basis beginning on or about 9/1. Must reply by May 1 or within 2 week(s) if notified thereafter. **Financial aid:** Priority date 3/15; no closing date. FAFSA, institutional form required. Applicants notified on a rolling basis starting 4/1; must reply within 2 week(s) of notification.

Academics. Special study options: Distance learning, double major, dual enrollment of high school students, internships. Semester-long mission intern class overseas. **Credit/placement by examination:** AP, CLEP, institutional tests. 8 credit hours maximum toward associate degree, 16 toward bachelor's. **Support services:** Learning center, reduced course load, remedial instruction, study skills assistance, writing center.

Majors. Business: Nonprofit/public. **Foreign languages:** Linguistics. **Philosophy/religion:** Religion. **Theology:** Bible, missionary, pastoral counseling, religious ed, theology, youth ministry.

Computing on campus. 24 workstations in dormitories, library, computer center. Dormitories wired for high-speed internet access and linked to campus network. Commuter students can connect to campus network.

Student life. Freshman orientation: Mandatory, $130 fee. Preregistration for classes offered. **Policies:** All students have opportunity to travel in choral group throughout country. Religious observance required. **Housing:** Guaranteed on-campus for all undergraduates. Single-sex dorms, special housing for disabled, apartments, wellness housing available. $75 nonrefundable deposit, deadline 4/1. **Activities:** Campus ministries, choral groups, drama, music ensembles, musical theater, student government.

Athletics. Intercollegiate: Basketball, volleyball. **Intramural:** Basketball, football (non-tackle), golf, soccer, softball, table tennis, tennis, volleyball. **Team name:** Flames.

Student services. Career counseling, student employment services, financial aid counseling, personal counseling, placement for graduates. **Physically disabled:** Services for hearing impaired.

Contact. E-mail: admissions@roanokebible.edu
Phone: (252) 334-2028 Toll-free number: (800) 722-8980
Fax: (252) 334-2064
Garrett Lewis, Director of Enrollment Management, Roanoke Bible College, 715 North Poindexter Street, Elizabeth City, NC 27909

St. Andrews Presbyterian College

Laurinburg, North Carolina **CB member**
www.sapc.edu **CB code: 5214**

- Private 4-year liberal arts college affiliated with Presbyterian Church (USA)
- Residential campus in large town
- 603 degree-seeking undergraduates: 4% part-time, 60% women, 10% African American, 1% Asian American, 3% Hispanic American, 1% international
- 78% of applicants admitted
- SAT or ACT (ACT writing optional) required
- 54% graduate within 6 years

General. Founded in 1958. Regionally accredited. **Degrees:** 171 bachelor's awarded. **Location:** 40 miles from Fayetteville, 20 miles from Pinehurst. **Calendar:** Semester, limited summer session. **Full-time faculty:** 40 total; 75% have terminal degrees, 2% minority, 40% women. **Part-time faculty:** 43 total; 30% have terminal degrees, 2% minority, 56% women. **Class size:** 74% < 20, 26% 20-39, less than 1% 40-49. **Special facilities:** Psychology laboratory complex, equestrian facilities, nature preserve, electronic fine arts center.

Freshman class profile. 845 applied, 662 admitted, 138 enrolled.

Mid 50% test scores		**GPA 3.0-3.49:**	39%
SAT critical reading:	440-560	**GPA 2.0-2.99:**	35%
SAT math:	430-530	**Rank in top quarter:**	19%
SAT writing:	430-530	**Rank in top tenth:**	12%
ACT composite:	18-23	**Return as sophomores:**	62%
GPA 3.75 or higher:	8%	**Out-of-state:**	65%
GPA 3.50-3.74:	16%	**Live on campus:**	99%

Basis for selection. High school GPA, test scores, curriculum, type of high school very important. Recommendations important. Interview required for academically weak students, recommended for all other applicants. **Homeschooled:** Standardized test scores and interview required.

High school preparation. College-preparatory program recommended. Required units include English 4, mathematics 3, social studies 2, science 3, foreign language 2 and academic electives 2.

2008-2009 Annual costs. Tuition/fees: $20,375. Private living, lab fees, and equestrian fees additional. Room/board: $8,425. Books/supplies: $1,200. Personal expenses: $1,900.

2007-2008 Financial aid. Need-based: 187 full-time freshmen applied for aid; 149 were judged to have need; 149 of these received aid. Average need met was 77%. Average scholarship/grant was $10,974; average loan $3,473. 67% of total undergraduate aid awarded as scholarships/grants, 33% as loans/jobs. **Non-need-based:** Awarded to 414 full-time undergraduates,

including 151 freshmen. Scholarships awarded for academics, alumni affiliation, art, athletics, leadership, music/drama.

Application procedures. Admission: Priority date 5/1; no deadline. $30 fee, may be waived for applicants with need. Admission notification on a rolling basis beginning on or about 9/1. Housing deposit fully refundable until May 1st. **Financial aid:** Priority date 5/1; no closing date. FAFSA required. Applicants notified on a rolling basis starting 10/1; must reply within 2 week(s) of notification.

Academics. Academic programs include St. Andrew's General Education. **Special study options:** Double major, honors, independent study, internships, student-designed major, study abroad, teacher certification program, Washington semester, weekend college. Courses offered abroad during winter or summer in Britain, Greece, India, Switzerland, Venezuela, China, Hawaii, former Soviet Union; exchange programs with Stirling University, Scotland and Kansai Gaidai University, Japan; study at Brunnenburg Castle, Italy, and Beijing Normal College of Foreign Languages. **Credit/placement by examination:** AP, CLEP, IB, institutional tests. 30 credit hours maximum toward bachelor's degree. **Support services:** Reduced course load, tutoring, writing center.

Majors. Agriculture: Equestrian studies. **Area/ethnic studies:** Asian. **Biology:** General. **Business:** General, business admin, international. **Communications:** Media studies. **Education:** Elementary, physical. **Health:** Athletic training, premedicine, prepharmacy, preveterinary. **History:** General, public archives. **Legal studies:** Prelaw. **Liberal arts:** Arts/sciences. **Math:** General. **Philosophy/religion:** Philosophy, religion. **Physical sciences:** Chemistry. **Psychology:** General. **Social sciences:** Political science. **Visual/performing arts:** General, art.

Most popular majors. Biology 7%, business/marketing 35%, communications/journalism 6%, education 15%, English 6%, liberal arts 6%, parks/recreation 10%.

Computing on campus. 100 workstations in library, computer center, student center. Dormitories wired for high-speed internet access and linked to campus network. Online library, repair service available.

Student life. Freshman orientation: Mandatory, $100 fee. 3 days prior to start of fall term. **Policies:** Honor code enforced. **Housing:** Guaranteed on-campus for all undergraduates. Coed dorms, single-sex dorms available. $250 deposit, deadline 8/25. **Activities:** Campus ministries, choral groups, drama, literary magazine, student government, student newspaper, Christian Student Fellowship, black student union, women's issues group, writer's forum, world culture club, Eco-Action, student activities union.

Athletics. NCAA. **Intercollegiate:** Baseball M, basketball, cross-country, equestrian, golf, lacrosse, soccer, softball W, tennis, track and field, volleyball W. **Intramural:** Basketball, bowling, racquetball, soccer, softball W, table tennis, volleyball. **Team name:** Knights.

Student services. Adult student services, alcohol/substance abuse counseling, career counseling, student employment services, financial aid counseling, health services, personal counseling, placement for graduates, women's services. **Physically disabled:** Services for visually, speech, hearing impaired.

Contact. E-mail: admissions@sapc.edu
Phone: (910) 277-5555 Toll-free number: (800) 763-0198
Fax: (910) 277-5087
Kirsten Simmons, Director of Admission, St. Andrews Presbyterian College, 1700 Dogwood Mile, Laurinburg, NC 28352

St. Augustine's College

Raleigh, North Carolina — **CB member**
www.st-aug.edu — **CB code: 5596**

- Private 4-year liberal arts college affiliated with Episcopal Church
- Residential campus in large city
- 1,417 degree-seeking undergraduates
- 53% of applicants admitted
- Interview required

General. Founded in 1867. Regionally accredited. Home to historic St. Augustine's College Chapel and St. Agnes Hospital. **Degrees:** 168 bachelor's awarded. **ROTC:** Army, Air Force. **Location:** One mile from downtown. **Calendar:** Semester, limited summer session. **Full-time faculty:** 78 total. **Part-time faculty:** 42 total. **Class size:** 65% < 20, 33% 20-39, 2% 40-49, less than 1% 50-99. **Special facilities:** Archival collection tracing history of African-Americans in North Carolina and Delaney family.

Freshman class profile. 2,914 applied, 1,544 admitted, 485 enrolled.

SAT critical reading:	-430	**Out-of-state:**	65%
SAT math:	-430	**Live on campus:**	92%
ACT composite:	-17	**Fraternities:**	6%
Rank in top quarter:	44%	**Sororities:**	12%
Rank in top tenth:	15%		

Basis for selection. High school record (GPA and rank), standardized test scores and letters of recommendation reviewed. Alumni affiliation also considered. SAT or ACT recommended. Institutionally administered Accuplacer test is used for pre- and post-testing evaluation and placement purposes. Essay recommended. Auditions and interviews required of music majors. **Learning Disabled:** Students must self-identify. ADA Coordinator will assess level of disability and arrange for student to access the needed equipment or tutorials.

High school preparation. 20 units required. Required units include English 4, mathematics 3, social studies 2, science 2 and academic electives 9. One unit of algebra required, 2 units of laboratory recommended.

2008-2009 Annual costs. Tuition/fees: $14,124. Room/board: $6,652. Books/supplies: $900. Personal expenses: $1,530.

2008-2009 Financial aid. Need-based: 65% of total undergraduate aid awarded as scholarships/grants, 35% as loans/jobs. **Non-need-based:** Scholarships awarded for academics, art, athletics, leadership, minority status, music/drama, religious affiliation, ROTC, state residency.

Application procedures. Admission: Closing date 8/1 (postmark date). $25 fee, may be waived for applicants with need. Admission notification on a rolling basis beginning on or about 1/1. **Financial aid:** Closing date 3/15. FAFSA, institutional form required. Applicants notified on a rolling basis starting 5/1; must reply within 2 week(s) of notification.

Academics. Required "Learning Community" program for all new freshmen and transfers. First year program includes skills enhancement and college survival tips. Community service requirement is part of course. **Special study options:** Accelerated study, cooperative education, cross-registration, double major, dual enrollment of high school students, honors, independent study, internships, liberal arts/career combination, study abroad, teacher certification program, weekend college. **Credit/placement by examination:** CLEP, IB, institutional tests. 15 credit hours maximum toward bachelor's degree. **Support services:** Learning center, pre-admission summer program, reduced course load, remedial instruction, study skills assistance, tutoring, writing center.

Majors. Area/ethnic studies: African-American. **Biology:** General, biomedical sciences. **Business:** Accounting, business admin, management science, real estate. **Communications:** General. **Computer sciences:** General, computer science. **Education:** Elementary. **Engineering:** General. **Health:** Occupational health, premedicine. **History:** General. **Legal studies:** Prelaw. **Math:** General. **Parks/recreation:** Health/fitness, sports admin. **Philosophy/religion:** Religion. **Physical sciences:** Chemistry. **Protective services:** Criminal justice, forensics. **Psychology:** General. **Social sciences:** Political science, sociology. **Visual/performing arts:** General, art, cinematography, music performance.

Most popular majors. Business/marketing 35%, communications/journalism 7%, computer/information sciences 12%, security/protective services 10%, social sciences 14%.

Computing on campus. 250 workstations in dormitories, library, computer center. Dormitories wired for high-speed internet access and linked to campus network. Commuter students can connect to campus network. Online course registration, online library, helpline, repair service available.

Student life. Freshman orientation: Mandatory, $60 fee. Preregistration for classes offered. 2-day orientations held in June, July, and August with students and parents. **Policies:** Alcohol and drug-free campus. No tolerance policy. No firearm policy. No smoking policy for all campus administrative buildings. Religious observance required. **Housing:** Guaranteed on-campus for freshmen. Single-sex dorms, wellness housing available. $150 deposit. **Activities:** Bands, choral groups, dance, drama, film society, music ensembles, musical theater, radio station, student government, student newspaper, symphony orchestra, TV station, Christian Fellowship Organization, Young Democrats of America, Falcons for the Cause, NAACP, foreign language club, Falcon Battalion/Army ROTC, Student Service Corps, SAC Association for Black Journalists, International student association, Latin American students organization.

Athletics. NCAA. **Intercollegiate:** Baseball M, basketball, bowling W, cheerleading W, cross-country, football (tackle) M, golf, softball W, tennis, track and field, volleyball W. **Intramural:** Baseball M, basketball, softball W, volleyball. **Team name:** Falcons.

Student services. Adult student services, alcohol/substance abuse counseling, chaplain/spiritual director, career counseling, services for economically disadvantaged, student employment services, financial aid counseling, health services, minority student services, personal counseling, placement for graduates, veterans' counselor. **Physically disabled:** Services for visually impaired.

Contact. E-mail: admissions@st-aug.edu
Phone: (919) 516-4012 Toll-free number: (800) 948-1126
Fax: (919) 516-5805
Jorge Sousa, Director of Admissions, St. Augustine's College, 1315 Oakwood Avenue, Raleigh, NC 27610-2298

Salem College

Winston-Salem, North Carolina — **CB member**
www.salem.edu — **CB code: 5607**

- Private 4-year liberal arts college for women affiliated with Moravian Church in America
- Residential campus in small city
- 699 degree-seeking undergraduates: 18% part-time, 97% women, 18% African American, 1% Asian American, 4% Hispanic American, 10% international
- 199 degree-seeking graduate students
- 59% of applicants admitted
- SAT or ACT (ACT writing optional), application essay required
- 53% graduate within 6 years; 28% enter graduate study

General. Founded in 1772. Regionally accredited. Male students age 23 and over may enroll in adult program only; male students may not reside at the college. **Degrees:** 157 bachelor's awarded; master's offered. **ROTC:** Army. **Location:** 80 miles from Charlotte, 25 miles from Greensboro. **Calendar:** 4-1-4, limited summer session. **Full-time faculty:** 56 total; 89% have terminal degrees, 9% minority, 61% women. **Part-time faculty:** 49 total; 37% have terminal degrees, 12% minority, 63% women. **Class size:** 84% < 20, 16% 20-39.

Freshman class profile. 429 applied, 253 admitted, 119 enrolled.

Mid 50% test scores		**GPA 2.0-2.99:**	6%
SAT critical reading:	480-610	**Rank in top quarter:**	67%
SAT math:	470-580	**Rank in top tenth:**	39%
SAT writing:	480-590	**End year in good standing:**	96%
ACT composite:	22-28	**Return as sophomores:**	88%
GPA 3.75 or higher:	48%	**Out-of-state:**	35%
GPA 3.50-3.74:	22%	**Live on campus:**	98%
GPA 3.0-3.49:	24%	**International:**	1%

Basis for selection. School achievement record, essay or personal statement, test scores important. Recommendations, interview, extracurricular and community activities, talent, minority status considered. Interview recommended for all students. Audition required for music program; portfolio recommended for art program.

High school preparation. College-preparatory program required. 16 units required. Required units include English 4, mathematics 3, social studies 2, science 3, foreign language 2 and academic electives 3. Math requirement includes 2 algebra and 1 geometry. On a case by case basis, a portion of this requirement may be waived for adult students.

2008-2009 Annual costs. Tuition/fees: $20,415. Room/board: $10,705. Books/supplies: $950. Personal expenses: $845.

2007-2008 Financial aid. Need-based: 73% of total undergraduate aid awarded as scholarships/grants, 27% as loans/jobs. **Non-need-based:** Scholarships awarded for academics, alumni affiliation, leadership, minority status, music/drama, state residency.

Application procedures. Admission: Priority date 3/1; no deadline. $30 fee, may be waived for applicants with need, free for online applicants. Admission notification on a rolling basis beginning on or about 10/1. Must reply by May 1 or within 2 week(s) if notified thereafter. **Financial aid:** Priority date 3/1; no closing date. FAFSA required. Applicants notified on a rolling basis starting 3/1; must reply by 5/1 or within 2 week(s) of notification.

Academics. Special study options: Cross-registration, double major, dual enrollment of high school students, exchange student, honors, independent study, internships, liberal arts/career combination, student-designed major, study abroad, teacher certification program, Washington semester. 3-1 clinical laboratory sciences/medical technology program with Wake Forest University's Baptist Medical Center; various study abroad options available through Brethren Colleges of America (BCA); St. Peters, Oxford; and St. Clare's, Oxford. **Credit/placement by examination:** AP, CLEP, IB, institutional tests. A maximum of 16 courses credit awarded through CLEP exam. **Support services:** Learning center, reduced course load, study skills assistance, tutoring, writing center.

Majors. Area/ethnic studies: American. **Biology:** General. **Business:** Accounting, business admin, international, nonprofit/public. **Communications:** General. **Education:** Early childhood, elementary, music, secondary. **Foreign languages:** French, German, Spanish. **Health:** Clinical lab technology. **History:** General. **Math:** General. **Philosophy/religion:** Philosophy, religion. **Physical sciences:** Chemistry. **Psychology:** General. **Social sciences:** Economics, international relations, sociology. **Visual/performing arts:** Art history/conservation, arts management, interior design, music performance, studio arts.

Most popular majors. Biology 9%, business/marketing 12%, communications/journalism 9%, English 12%, foreign language 7%, psychology 9%, social sciences 18%, visual/performing arts 9%.

Computing on campus. 54 workstations in library, computer center. Dormitories wired for high-speed internet access and linked to campus network. Commuter students can connect to campus network. Online library, helpline, wireless network available.

Student life. Freshman orientation: Mandatory. Preregistration for classes offered. 3 days before fall term begins. Separate orientation program for adult students. **Housing:** Guaranteed on-campus for freshmen. Apartments, wellness housing available. $250 nonrefundable deposit, deadline 5/1. All full-time students under 23 years required to reside on-campus unless they reside with family within a 30 mile radius of the college. **Activities:** Marching band, choral groups, dance, drama, international student organizations, literary magazine, music ensembles, Model UN, musical theater, student government, student newspaper, College Democrats, College Republicans, Green Party, Catholic Student Association, Campus Activities Council, Intervarsity Fellowship, Habitat for Humanity.

Athletics. NCAA. **Intercollegiate:** Basketball W, cross-country W, soccer W, swimming W, tennis W, volleyball W. **Team name:** Spirits.

Student services. Adult student services, chaplain/spiritual director, career counseling, financial aid counseling, health services, personal counseling, placement for graduates, women's services.

Contact. E-mail: admissions@salem.edu
Phone: (336) 721-2621 Toll-free number: (800) 327-2536
Fax: (336) 917-5572
Katherine Watts, Dean of Admissions and Financial Aid, Salem College, 601 South Church Street, Winston-Salem, NC 27108

Shaw University

Raleigh, North Carolina — **CB member**
www.shawuniversity.edu — **CB code: 5612**

- Private 4-year university and liberal arts college affiliated with Baptist faith
- Residential campus in large city
- 2,453 degree-seeking undergraduates
- SAT or ACT (ACT writing optional), application essay required

General. Founded in 1865. Regionally accredited. **Degrees:** 421 bachelor's, 10 associate awarded; master's, first professional offered. **ROTC:** Army, Air Force. **Location:** 139 miles from Charlotte. **Calendar:** Semester, limited summer session. **Full-time faculty:** 116 total; 66% have terminal degrees, 82% minority, 33% women. **Part-time faculty:** 156 total; 38% have terminal degrees, 88% minority, 40% women. **Class size:** 70% < 20, 26% 20-39, 2% 40-49, 2% 50-99.

Freshman class profile.

Mid 50% test scores		**GPA 3.0-3.49:**	11%
SAT critical reading:	330-430	**GPA 2.0-2.99:**	74%
SAT math:	320-420	**Rank in top quarter:**	12%
SAT writing:	320-420	**Rank in top tenth:**	3%
ACT composite:	11-16	**Out-of-state:**	52%
GPA 3.75 or higher:	2%	**Live on campus:**	72%
GPA 3.50-3.74:	2%		

Basis for selection. 2.0 high school GPA desired. Interview, portfolio recommended for some. **Homeschooled:** Transcript of courses and grades, state high school equivalency certificate required.

High school preparation. 18 units required. Required units include English 3, mathematics 2, social studies 2, science 2 and academic electives 9. 9 electives in English, foreign language, mathematics, science.

2008-2009 Annual costs. Tuition/fees: $11,696. Room/board: $7,200. Books/supplies: $700. Personal expenses: $1,000.

2007-2008 Financial aid. **Non-need-based:** Scholarships awarded for academics, alumni affiliation, art, athletics, music/drama, religious affiliation.

Application procedures. **Admission:** Closing date 7/30. $25 fee, may be waived for applicants with need. Admission notification on a rolling basis beginning on or about 8/1. **Financial aid:** Priority date 3/1; no closing date. FAFSA required. Applicants notified on a rolling basis starting 3/15; must reply within 2 week(s) of notification.

Academics. **Special study options:** Accelerated study, cross-registration, distance learning, double major, dual enrollment of high school students, external degree, honors, independent study, liberal arts/career combination, student-designed major, study abroad, teacher certification program, weekend college. **Credit/placement by examination:** CLEP, SAT, ACT, institutional tests. 30 credit hours maximum toward associate degree, 60 toward bachelor's. **Support services:** Learning center, reduced course load, study skills assistance, tutoring, writing center.

Majors. **Biology:** General. **Business:** Business admin, international. **Communications:** Media studies. **Computer sciences:** General, computer science. **Conservation:** General. **Education:** Elementary, English, mathematics. **Foreign languages:** Spanish. **Health:** Athletic training, audiology/speech pathology, recreational therapy. **Liberal arts:** Arts/sciences. **Math:** General. **Parks/recreation:** General, exercise sciences. **Philosophy/religion:** Religion. **Physical sciences:** Chemistry, physics. **Protective services:** Criminal justice. **Psychology:** General. **Public administration:** General, social work. **Social sciences:** International relations, political science, sociology. **Visual/performing arts:** Dramatic.

Most popular majors. Business/marketing 29%, philosophy/religious studies 6%, psychology 9%, public administration/social services 6%, security/protective services 16%, social sciences 12%.

Computing on campus. 150 workstations in dormitories, library, computer center, student center. Dormitories wired for high-speed internet access and linked to campus network. Commuter students can connect to campus network. Online course registration, online library, helpline, repair service, student web hosting, wireless network available.

Student life. **Freshman orientation:** Available. **Housing:** Single-sex dorms, wellness housing available. $100 deposit. **Activities:** Bands, campus ministries, choral groups, dance, drama, international student organizations, music ensembles, musical theater, radio station, student government, student newspaper, NAACP, business, sociology, criminal justice, accounting clubs, Christian Fellowship, northern exposure, Order of the Eastern Star.

Athletics. NCAA. **Intercollegiate:** Baseball M, basketball, bowling W, cross-country, football (tackle) M, softball W, tennis, track and field, volleyball W. **Intramural:** Basketball, tennis, volleyball. **Team name:** Bears.

Student services. Adult student services, alcohol/substance abuse counseling, chaplain/spiritual director, career counseling, student employment services, financial aid counseling, health services, personal counseling, placement for graduates, veterans' counselor. **Physically disabled:** Services for visually, speech, hearing impaired.

Contact. E-mail: admissions@shawu.edu
Phone: (919) 546-8275 Toll-free number: (800) 214-6683
Fax: (919) 546-8271
Cassandra Clifton, Interim Director of Admissions and International Counselor, Shaw University, 118 East South Street, Raleigh, NC 27601

Southeastern Baptist Theological Seminary

Wake Forest, North Carolina
www.sebts.edu **CB code: 7050**

- Private 4-year Bible and seminary college affiliated with Southern Baptist Convention
- Small town

General. Founded in 1950. Regionally accredited. **Location:** 20 miles from Raleigh, 30 miles from Durham. **Calendar:** Semester.

Annual costs/financial aid. Tuition/fees (2008-2009): $6,860. Non-Southern Baptist students per credit hour charge is $416. Books/supplies: $400.

Contact. Phone: (919) 761-2280
Dean of Students, PO Box 1889, Wake Forest, NC 27588

University of North Carolina at Asheville

Asheville, North Carolina **CB member**
www.unca.edu **CB code: 5013**

- Public 4-year university and liberal arts college
- Residential campus in small city
- 3,150 degree-seeking undergraduates: 11% part-time, 58% women, 3% African American, 1% Asian American, 3% Hispanic American, 1% international
- 24 degree-seeking graduate students
- 73% of applicants admitted
- SAT or ACT with writing, application essay required
- 60% graduate within 6 years; 21% enter graduate study

General. Founded in 1927. Regionally accredited. **Degrees:** 704 bachelor's awarded; master's offered. **Location:** 130 miles from Charlotte, 200 miles from Atlanta. **Calendar:** Semester, limited summer session. **Full-time faculty:** 207 total; 86% have terminal degrees, 14% minority, 41% women. **Part-time faculty:** 124 total; 40% have terminal degrees, 6% minority, 48% women. **Class size:** 54% < 20, 44% 20-39, less than 1% 40-49, 1% 50-99, less than 1% >100. **Special facilities:** Botanical gardens, Jewish studies center, arboretum, environmental quality institute, distance learning facility, music recording studio, National Environmental Modeling and Analysis Center (NEMAC), astronomical research institute, National Climatic Data Center.

Freshman class profile. 2,464 applied, 1,807 admitted, 586 enrolled.

Mid 50% test scores		**GPA 2.0-2.99:**	2%
SAT critical reading:	530-640	**Rank in top quarter:**	59%
SAT math:	520-630	**Rank in top tenth:**	22%
SAT writing:	510-620	**End year in good standing:**	88%
ACT composite:	21-27	**Return as sophomores:**	79%
GPA 3.75 or higher:	63%	**Out-of-state:**	17%
GPA 3.50-3.74:	20%	**Live on campus:**	95%
GPA 3.0-3.49:	15%	**International:**	1%

Basis for selection. GED not accepted. High school curriculum, GPA, and class rank (top third), most important. Test scores important. Counselor recommendation and essay question required. Interview, extracurricular activities that support academic achievement considered. Students expected to have completed advanced coursework. Personal statements helpful. Interviews recommended. **Homeschooled:** Must provide a transcript documenting all courses taken, particularly UNC system minimum admissions requirements, units of credit received. Transcript must be signed by homeschool administrator. For North Carolina residents, a copy of the school's registration with the North Carolina Department of Non-Public Instruction is required. **Learning Disabled:** Untimed SAT accepted.

High school preparation. College-preparatory program required. 15 units required. Required and recommended units include English 4, mathematics 4, social studies 1, history 1, science 3 (laboratory 1), foreign language 2 and academic electives 4. Science units should include biology and physical science such as chemistry or physics. One unit US history, 1 unit other social studies required. Math must include algebra I, II and geometry and 1 math course with algebra II as pre-requisite.

2008-2009 Annual costs. Tuition/fees: $4,255; $15,585 out-of-state. Room/board: $6,620. Books/supplies: $850. Personal expenses: $1,400.

2007-2008 Financial aid. **Need-based:** 405 full-time freshmen applied for aid; 215 were judged to have need; 215 of these received aid. Average need met was 79%. Average scholarship/grant was $4,554; average loan $3,004. 54% of total undergraduate aid awarded as scholarships/grants, 46% as loans/jobs. **Non-need-based:** Awarded to 417 full-time undergraduates, including 95 freshmen. Scholarships awarded for academics, alumni affiliation, art, athletics, job skills, leadership, minority status, music/drama, state residency.

Application procedures. **Admission:** Priority date 11/10; deadline 2/15 (postmark date). $50 fee, may be waived for applicants with need. Admission notification on a rolling basis beginning on or about 4/1. Must reply by 5/1. **Financial aid:** Priority date 3/1; no closing date. FAFSA required. Applicants notified on a rolling basis starting 3/15.

Academics. **Special study options:** Cross-registration, distance learning, double major, dual enrollment of high school students, exchange student, honors, independent study, internships, liberal arts/career combination, semester at sea, student-designed major, study abroad, teacher certification program, Washington semester. **Credit/placement by examination:** AP, CLEP, IB, institutional tests. 30 credit hours maximum toward bachelor's degree. AP and CLEP exam grades required for credit are subject to change. **Support services:** Learning center, reduced course load, remedial instruction, study skills assistance, tutoring, writing center.

Majors. **Area/ethnic studies:** Women's. **Biology:** General. **Business:** Accounting, business admin, operations. **Communications:** Media studies. **Computer sciences:** Computer science, web page design. **Conservation:** Environmental studies. **Engineering:** General. **Foreign languages:** Classics, French, German, Spanish. **Health:** Public health ed. **History:** General. **Liberal arts:** Arts/sciences. **Math:** General. **Philosophy/religion:** Philosophy, religion. **Physical sciences:** Atmospheric science, chemistry, physics. **Psychology:** General. **Social sciences:** Economics, political science, sociology. **Visual/performing arts:** Art, dramatic, studio arts.

Most popular majors. Business/marketing 9%, communications/journalism 6%, English 8%, natural resources/environmental science 8%, physical sciences 6%, psychology 14%, social sciences 11%, visual/performing arts 9%.

Computing on campus. 216 workstations in dormitories, library, computer center, student center. Dormitories wired for high-speed internet access and linked to campus network. Commuter students can connect to campus network. Online course registration, online library, helpline, repair service, student web hosting, wireless network available.

Student life. **Freshman orientation:** Mandatory, $55 fee. Preregistration for classes offered. 2-day program for incoming freshmen held in June; 1-day program for transfer students held in June and August. Additional 3-day orientation conducted immediately prior to the start of classes. **Housing:** Guaranteed on-campus for freshmen. Coed dorms, single-sex dorms, special housing for disabled, wellness housing available. $150 deposit, deadline 5/1. 24-hour quiet floors available. **Activities:** Bands, campus ministries, choral groups, dance, drama, international student organizations, literary magazine, music ensembles, musical theater, radio station, student government, student newspaper, Baptist student union, international student association, InterVarsity Christian Fellowship, African American student association, Active Students for a Healthy Environment, University Ambassadors, Jewish student association, Asian Students in Asheville.

Athletics. NCAA. **Intercollegiate:** Baseball M, basketball, cheerleading, cross-country, soccer, tennis, track and field, volleyball W. **Intramural:** Basketball, football (non-tackle), golf, racquetball, soccer, softball, tennis, volleyball, water polo. **Team name:** Bulldogs.

Student services. Adult student services, alcohol/substance abuse counseling, chaplain/spiritual director, career counseling, student employment services, financial aid counseling, health services, minority student services, personal counseling, placement for graduates, veterans' counselor, women's services. **Physically disabled:** Services for visually, hearing impaired.

Contact. E-mail: admissions@unca.edu
Phone: (828) 251-6481 Toll-free number: (800) 531-9842
Fax: (828) 251-6482
Patrice Mitchell, Dean of Admissions, University of North Carolina at Asheville, CPO#1320, UNCA, Asheville, NC 28804-8510

University of North Carolina at Chapel Hill

Chapel Hill, North Carolina — **CB member**
www.unc.edu — **CB code: 5816**

- Public 4-year university
- Residential campus in large town
- 17,422 degree-seeking undergraduates: 2% part-time, 59% women, 11% African American, 7% Asian American, 5% Hispanic American, 1% Native American, 1% international
- 9,434 degree-seeking graduate students
- 34% of applicants admitted
- SAT or ACT with writing, application essay required

General. Founded in 1789. Regionally accredited. Entering freshmen required to own laptop meeting university specifications, as a part of the Carolina Computing Initiative; qualified students will receive special loans or grants. **Degrees:** 4,131 bachelor's awarded; master's, doctoral, first professional offered. **ROTC:** Army, Naval, Air Force. **Location:** 8 miles from Durham, 26 miles from Raleigh. **Calendar:** Semester, extensive summer session. **Full-time faculty:** 1,600 total; 87% have terminal degrees, 20% minority, 42% women. **Part-time faculty:** 146 total; 68% have terminal degrees, 10% minority, 45% women. **Class size:** 44% < 20, 40% 20-39, 6% 40-49, 5% 50-99, 5% >100. **Special facilities:** Planetarium, observatory, arboretum, botanical garden.

Freshman class profile. 21,543 applied, 7,315 admitted, 3,865 enrolled.

Mid 50% test scores		**GPA 2.0-2.99:**	1%
SAT critical reading:	590-690	**Rank in top quarter:**	96%
SAT math:	620-700	**Rank in top tenth:**	79%
SAT writing:	590-690	**End year in good standing:**	99%
ACT composite:	26-31	**Return as sophomores:**	97%
GPA 3.75 or higher:	95%	**Out-of-state:**	16%
GPA 3.50-3.74:	2%	**Live on campus:**	82%
GPA 3.0-3.49:	2%	**International:**	1%

Basis for selection. GED not accepted. High school record, including course selection and performance, very important. Test scores, essays, activities, and recommendations also receive strong consideration. Separate consideration given to out-of-state children of alumni. SAT preferred, ACT also accepted. Test score submission deadlines may vary. Audition required for drama and music programs; portfolio recommended for art program. **Homeschooled:** SAT Subject Tests recommended. Students should follow curriculum equivalent to that of high school students taking Advanced Placement and honors courses. **Learning Disabled:** Students may voluntarily supply documentation regarding disability and impact on educational experiences with application.

High school preparation. College-preparatory program required. 17 units required; 19 recommended. Required and recommended units include English 4, mathematics 4, social studies 2-3, science 3-4 (laboratory 1), foreign language 2-4 and academic electives 2. One social studies must be U.S. history.

2008-2009 Annual costs. Tuition/fees: $5,397; $22,295 out-of-state. Fees may be higher for dental programs. Room/board: $7,334. Books/supplies: $1,000. Personal expenses: $1,250.

2007-2008 Financial aid. **Non-need-based:** Scholarships awarded for academics, alumni affiliation, art, athletics, leadership, music/drama, religious affiliation, state residency. **Additional information:** Carolina meets 100% of all need documented for both resident and non-resident undergraduates who quality for need based aid, with a favorable mix of approximately 2/3 grants and scholarships and 1/3 loans and work study.

Application procedures. **Admission:** Closing date 1/15 (postmark date). $70 fee, may be waived for applicants with need. On or around 01/15 for early notification; on or around 03/20 for regular notification. Must reply by 5/1. **Financial aid:** Priority date 3/1; no closing date. FAFSA, CSS PROFILE required. Applicants notified on a rolling basis starting 3/15; must reply by 5/1.

Academics. **Special study options:** Combined bachelor's/graduate degree, cross-registration, distance learning, double major, dual enrollment of high school students, honors, independent study, internships, student-designed major, study abroad, teacher certification program. **Credit/placement by examination:** AP, CLEP, IB, SAT, ACT, institutional tests. Credit by examination is non-transferable. **Support services:** Learning center, pre-admission summer program, reduced course load, study skills assistance, tutoring, writing center.

Majors. **Area/ethnic studies:** African-American, American, Asian, European, Latin American, Russian/Slavic, women's. **Biology:** General, biostatistics, pathology. **Business:** Business admin, human resources. **Communications:** General, media studies. **Computer sciences:** Computer science, information systems. **Conservation:** Environmental science, environmental studies. **Education:** Early childhood, elementary, middle. **Family/consumer sciences:** Food/nutrition. **Foreign languages:** Classics, comparative lit, German, linguistics. **Health:** Clinical lab science, dental hygiene, environmental health, health care admin, medical radiologic technology/radiation therapy, nursing (RN). **History:** General. **Interdisciplinary:** Peace/conflict. **Liberal arts:** Arts/sciences. **Math:** General, applied. **Parks/recreation:** Facilities management, health/fitness. **Philosophy/religion:** Philosophy, religion. **Physical sciences:** Chemistry, geology, physics. **Psychology:** General. **Public administration:** Policy analysis. **Social sciences:** Anthropology, archaeology, economics, geography, political science, sociology. **Visual/performing arts:** Art history/conservation, dramatic, music performance, studio arts. **Other:** Applied science, International studies, Romance languages French, Italian, Portuguese, Spanish.

Most popular majors. Area/ethnic studies 6%, biology 9%, business/marketing 9%, communications/journalism 12%, health sciences 8%, psychology 9%, social sciences 16%.

Computing on campus. PC or laptop required. 600 workstations in dormitories, library, computer center, student center. Dormitories wired for high-speed internet access and linked to campus network. Commuter students can connect to campus network. Online course registration, online library, helpline, repair service, student web hosting, wireless network available.

Student life. **Freshman orientation:** Mandatory, $160 fee. Preregistration for classes offered. 2-day summer orientation. **Policies:** Policies exist regarding: illegal drugs, honor code, student organizations, nondiscrimination policy, no smoking policy, student possession and consumption of alcoholic beverages in facilities, harassment. **Housing:** Coed dorms, single-sex dorms, special housing for disabled, apartments, wellness housing available. $200 nonrefundable deposit, deadline 5/15. Special options in housing - Learning communities such as RELIC (Religion as Explorative Learning Integrated in our Community), language houses, The Carolina Experience, Men@Carolina, W.E.L.L. (Women's Experiences: Learning and Leadership), Connected Learning Program, service and leadership, substance free environments, sustainability, UNITAS. **Activities:** Bands, campus ministries, choral groups, dance, drama, film society, international student organizations, literary magazine, music ensembles, Model UN, musical theater, opera, radio station, student government, student newspaper, symphony orchestra, TV station, Alpha Phi Omega co-ed service fraternity, Asian students association, Black Student Movement, Campus Crusade for Christ, Carolina Cancer Focus, Carolina Hispanic Association, College Republicans, Habitat for Humanity, Young Democrats.

Athletics. NCAA. **Intercollegiate:** Baseball M, basketball, cross-country, diving, fencing, field hockey W, football (tackle) M, golf, gymnastics W, lacrosse, rowing (crew) W, soccer, softball W, swimming, tennis, track and field, volleyball W, wrestling M. **Intramural:** Badminton, basketball, football (non-tackle), golf, handball, racquetball, soccer, softball, swimming, table tennis, tennis, triathlon, volleyball, water polo. **Team name:** Tarheels.

Student services. Alcohol/substance abuse counseling, chaplain/spiritual director, career counseling, student employment services, financial aid counseling, health services, legal services, minority student services, on-campus daycare, personal counseling, placement for graduates, veterans' counselor, women's services. **Physically disabled:** Services for visually, speech, hearing impaired. **Learning disabled:** Comprehensive services available.

Contact. E-mail: unchelp@admissions.unc.edu
Phone: (919) 966-3621 Fax: (919) 962-3045
Stephen Farmer, Assistant Provost and Director of Undergraduate Admissions, University of North Carolina at Chapel Hill, Jackson Hall CB #2200, Chapel Hill, NC 27599-2200

University of North Carolina at Charlotte

Charlotte, North Carolina — **CB member**
www.uncc.edu — **CB code: 5105**

- Public 4-year university
- Residential campus in very large city
- 18,216 degree-seeking undergraduates: 15% part-time, 52% women, 15% African American, 5% Asian American, 4% Hispanic American, 2% international
- 3,722 degree-seeking graduate students
- 76% of applicants admitted
- SAT or ACT with writing required
- 51% graduate within 6 years

General. Founded in 1946. Regionally accredited. **Degrees:** 3,375 bachelor's awarded; master's, doctoral offered. **ROTC:** Army, Air Force. **Location:** 10 miles from downtown. **Calendar:** Semester, limited summer session. **Full-time faculty:** 989 total; 85% have terminal degrees, 20% minority, 42% women. **Part-time faculty:** 420 total; 26% have terminal degrees, 15% minority, 60% women. **Class size:** 31% < 20, 45% 20-39, 8% 40-49, 9% 50-99, 6% >100. **Special facilities:** Botanical and horticultural complex with controlled environment, 100-acre experimental ecological reserve, tropical rain forest conservatory, 46-acre wildlife refuge, 9,600-seat multipurpose student activity center.

Freshman class profile. 10,336 applied, 7,906 admitted, 3,090 enrolled.

Mid 50% test scores			
SAT critical reading:	470-560	**Rank in top quarter:**	43%
SAT math:	490-590	**Rank in top tenth:**	15%
SAT writing:	460-550	**End year in good standing:**	77%
ACT composite:	20-24	**Return as sophomores:**	77%
GPA 3.75 or higher:	35%	**Out-of-state:**	11%
GPA 3.50-3.74:	20%	**Live on campus:**	76%
GPA 3.0-3.49:	38%	**International:**	2%
GPA 2.0-2.99:	7%	**Fraternities:**	6%
		Sororities:	6%

Basis for selection. Overall performance in high school academic courses, senior year academic courses in progress, and SAT scores considered. SAT preferred, but ACT also accepted. Audition required for music; interview required for art, architecture, and music programs; portfolio required for art, architecture programs. **Learning Disabled:** Students can submit documentation of their learning disability in the admissions process if they choose to disclose.

High school preparation. College-preparatory program required. 16 units required. Required and recommended units include English 4, mathematics 4, social studies 2, history 1, science 3 (laboratory 1), foreign language 2 and academic electives 1. English should emphasize grammar, composition & literature; science should include at least 1 unit in a life or biological science and at least 1 unit in a physical science and 1 lab; foreign language units should be in same language. 1 social studies unit must be in U.S. history.

2008-2009 Annual costs. Tuition/fees: $4,279; $14,691 out-of-state. Room/board: $6,800. Books/supplies: $1,200. Personal expenses: $1,520.

2007-2008 Financial aid. **Need-based:** 2,092 full-time freshmen applied for aid; 1,390 were judged to have need; 1,354 of these received aid. Average need met was 73%. Average scholarship/grant was $5,065; average loan $3,108. 49% of total undergraduate aid awarded as scholarships/grants, 51% as loans/jobs. **Non-need-based:** Awarded to 1,084 full-time undergraduates, including 225 freshmen. Scholarships awarded for academics, athletics, leadership, music/drama.

Application procedures. **Admission:** Closing date 7/1 (postmark date). $50 fee, may be waived for applicants with need. Admission notification on a rolling basis beginning on or about 11/1. Must reply by 11/1. Must reply by May 1 or within 2 week(s) if notified thereafter. **Financial aid:** Priority date 4/1; no closing date. FAFSA required. Applicants notified on a rolling basis starting 4/1; must reply within 3 week(s) of notification.

Academics. **Special study options:** Accelerated study, cooperative education, cross-registration, distance learning, double major, dual enrollment of high school students, ESL, honors, independent study, internships, study abroad, teacher certification program, Washington semester, weekend college. Wilderness exploration program. **Credit/placement by examination:** AP, CLEP, IB, institutional tests. 30 credit hours maximum toward bachelor's degree. **Support services:** Learning center, pre-admission summer program, reduced course load, study skills assistance, tutoring, writing center.

Honors college/program. Minimum GPA 3.0 or high school rank and SAT scores predictive of 3.0 GPA. Must submit 2-3 page essay describing educational goals and objectives, as well as one letter of recommendation from a person who can address potential for success in Honors Program. Brief interview may be scheduled.

Majors. **Architecture:** Architecture. **Area/ethnic studies:** African-American, Latin American. **Biology:** General. **Business:** Accounting, business admin, finance, international, management information systems, managerial economics, marketing, operations. **Communications:** General. **Computer sciences:** Computer science. **Education:** Art, chemistry, drama/dance, elementary, English, French, German, history, kindergarten/preschool, mathematics, mentally handicapped, middle, music, Spanish. **Engineering:** Civil, computer, electrical, mechanical, systems. **Engineering technology:** Civil, electrical, mechanical. **Family/consumer sciences:** Family studies. **Foreign languages:** French, German, Spanish. **Health:** Athletic training, clinical lab science, nursing (RN), public health ed. **History:** General. **Math:** General. **Parks/recreation:** Health/fitness. **Philosophy/religion:** Philosophy, religion. **Physical sciences:** Chemistry, geology, meteorology, physics. **Protective services:** Criminal justice, fire services admin. **Psychology:** General. **Public administration:** Social work. **Social sciences:** Anthropology, economics, geography, political science, sociology. **Visual/performing arts:** Art, art history/conservation, dance, dramatic, music performance, studio arts. **Other:** Construction management, International studies, Mathematics for business.

Most popular majors. Business/marketing 23%, communications/journalism 7%, education 9%, engineering/engineering technologies 10%, psychology 8%, social sciences 7%.

Computing on campus. 1,500 workstations in dormitories, library, computer center, student center. Dormitories wired for high-speed internet access and linked to campus network. Commuter students can connect to campus network. Online course registration, online library, helpline, student web hosting, wireless network available.

Student life. **Freshman orientation:** Available, $85 fee. Preregistration for classes offered. 2-day program for freshmen and parents. Parents fee $32. **Policies:** Students must follow code of student responsibility, code of student academic integrity, and university policy statements. **Housing:** Coed dorms, single-sex dorms, special housing for disabled, apartments, fraternity/sorority housing, wellness housing available. $100 deposit. Housing for disabled students limited. Suite housing, honors housing, Greek village housing available. **Activities:** Bands, choral groups, dance, drama, literary magazine, music ensembles, musical theater, opera, student government, student newspaper, TV station, Campus Crusade for Christ, Hillel, College Democrats,

College Republicans, feminist union, black student union, Latin American student organization, Muslim student association, Native American student organization, Asian student union.

Athletics. NCAA. **Intercollegiate:** Baseball M, basketball, cross-country, golf M, soccer, softball W, tennis, track and field, volleyball W. **Intramural:** Badminton, basketball, bowling, field hockey, football (non-tackle), golf, handball, lacrosse, racquetball, rugby, soccer, softball, swimming, table tennis, tennis, track and field, volleyball, water polo. **Team name:** Fortyniners.

Student services. Adult student services, alcohol/substance abuse counseling, chaplain/spiritual director, career counseling, student employment services, financial aid counseling, health services, minority student services, personal counseling, placement for graduates, veterans' counselor, women's services. **Physically disabled:** Services for visually, speech, hearing impaired.

Contact. E-mail: unccadm@uncc.edu
Phone: (704) 687-2213 Fax: (704) 687-6483
Tina McEntire, Director of Admissions, University of North Carolina at Charlotte, 9201 University City Boulevard, Charlotte, NC 28223-0001

University of North Carolina at Greensboro

Greensboro, North Carolina — **CB member**
www.uncg.edu — **CB code: 5913**

- Public 4-year university
- Commuter campus in small city
- 13,545 degree-seeking undergraduates: 12% part-time, 67% women, 22% African American, 4% Asian American, 3% Hispanic American, 1% international
- 3,071 degree-seeking graduate students
- 72% of applicants admitted
- SAT or ACT with writing required
- 53% graduate within 6 years

General. Founded in 1891. Regionally accredited. **Degrees:** 2,389 bachelor's awarded; master's, doctoral offered. **ROTC:** Army, Air Force. **Location:** 90 miles from Raleigh. **Calendar:** Semester, extensive summer session. **Full-time faculty:** 816 total; 80% have terminal degrees, 15% minority, 50% women. **Part-time faculty:** 389 total; 46% have terminal degrees, 13% minority, 63% women. **Class size:** 43% < 20, 40% 20-39, 5% 40-49, 10% 50-99, 3% >100. **Special facilities:** Observatory, Silva cello music collection, Randall Jarrell collection, women's studies collection.

Freshman class profile. 9,187 applied, 6,634 admitted, 2,492 enrolled.

Mid 50% test scores		**GPA 2.0-2.99:**	7%
SAT critical reading:	460-560	**Rank in top quarter:**	45%
SAT math:	470-570	**Rank in top tenth:**	13%
SAT writing:	450-550	**Return as sophomores:**	76%
GPA 3.75 or higher:	42%	**Out-of-state:**	8%
GPA 3.50-3.74:	19%	**Live on campus:**	79%
GPA 3.0-3.49:	32%	**International:**	1%

Basis for selection. GED not accepted. Combined test scores and high school GPA based on academic courses most important. High school recommendations and activities considered. SAT preferred, but ACT accepted. Audition required for music program.

High school preparation. 15 units required. Required units include English 4, mathematics 4, social studies 2, science 3 (laboratory 1) and foreign language 2.

2008-2009 Annual costs. Tuition/fees: $4,135; $15,629 out-of-state. Room/board: $6,188. Books/supplies: $1,662. Personal expenses: $2,196.

2008-2009 Financial aid. Need-based: 1,997 full-time freshmen applied for aid; 1,835 were judged to have need; 1,832 of these received aid. Average need met was 64%. Average scholarship/grant was $8,512; average loan $2,586. 55% of total undergraduate aid awarded as scholarships/grants, 45% as loans/jobs. **Non-need-based:** Awarded to 6,582 full-time undergraduates, including 1,490 freshmen. Scholarships awarded for academics, alumni affiliation, art, athletics, leadership, music/drama, state residency.

Application procedures. Admission: Priority date 11/1; deadline 3/1 (postmark date). $45 fee, may be waived for applicants with need. Application must be submitted on paper. Admission notification on a rolling basis beginning on or about 3/1. Must reply by May 1 or within 4 week(s) if notified thereafter. **Financial aid:** Priority date 3/1; no closing date. FAFSA required. Applicants notified on a rolling basis starting 3/15; must reply within 3 week(s) of notification.

Academics. Special study options: Accelerated study, combined bachelor's/graduate degree, cross-registration, distance learning, double major, dual enrollment of high school students, honors, independent study, internships, study abroad, teacher certification program, Washington semester. Evening university. **Credit/placement by examination:** AP, CLEP, institutional tests. Up to 64 semester hours of any combination of transfer, correspondence, examination or other will be accepted. SAT Subject Test scores in some subjects may qualify for credit. **Support services:** Learning center, reduced course load, remedial instruction, study skills assistance, tutoring, writing center.

Majors. Area/ethnic studies: African-American, women's. **Biology:** General, biochemistry. **Business:** Accounting, business admin, finance, hospitality admin, international, managerial economics. **Communications:** Media studies. **Computer sciences:** Computer science, networking. **Education:** Art, biology, Deaf/hearing impaired, drama/dance, elementary, English, French, mathematics, middle, music, physical, social science, social studies, Spanish, special. **Family/consumer sciences:** Child development, clothing/textiles, family studies. **Foreign languages:** Classics, French, German, Spanish. **Health:** Audiology/speech pathology, clinical lab science, nursing (RN), public health ed. **History:** General. **Interdisciplinary:** Nutrition sciences. **Liberal arts:** Arts/sciences. **Math:** General. **Parks/recreation:** General, exercise sciences. **Philosophy/religion:** Philosophy, religion. **Physical sciences:** Chemistry, physics. **Psychology:** General. **Public administration:** Social work. **Social sciences:** Anthropology, economics, geography, political science, sociology. **Visual/performing arts:** Art, dance, dramatic, interior design, music performance, music theory/composition, studio arts.

Most popular majors. Business/marketing 16%, education 12%, English 8%, health sciences 10%, social sciences 8%, visual/performing arts 10%.

Computing on campus. 600 workstations in dormitories, library, computer center, student center. Dormitories linked to campus network. Commuter students can connect to campus network. Online course registration, online library, helpline, wireless network available.

Student life. Freshman orientation: Mandatory. Preregistration for classes offered. **Housing:** Coed dorms, single-sex dorms, apartments available. $150 nonrefundable deposit, deadline 5/1. Residential college (academic/residential program), International House available. **Activities:** Bands, choral groups, dance, drama, film society, international student organizations, literary magazine, music ensembles, Model UN, musical theater, opera, radio station, student government, student newspaper, symphony orchestra, neo-black society, environmental awareness foundation, political awareness club, Habitat for Humanity, Rotaract Club, gay, lesbian and bisexual student association.

Athletics. NCAA. **Intercollegiate:** Baseball M, basketball, cross-country, golf, soccer, softball W, tennis, volleyball W, wrestling M. **Intramural:** Badminton, basketball, bowling, golf, racquetball, soccer, softball, swimming, table tennis, tennis, track and field, volleyball. **Team name:** Spartans.

Student services. Adult student services, chaplain/spiritual director, career counseling, student employment services, financial aid counseling, health services, personal counseling, placement for graduates, veterans' counselor. **Physically disabled:** Services for visually, speech, hearing impaired.

Contact. E-mail: admissions@uncg.edu
Phone: (336) 334-5243 Fax: (336) 334-4180
Lise Keller, Director of Admissions, University of North Carolina at Greensboro, 1400 Spring Garden Street, Greensboro, NC 27402-6170

University of North Carolina at Pembroke

Pembroke, North Carolina — **CB member**
www.uncp.edu — **CB code: 5534**

- Public 4-year university and liberal arts college
- Commuter campus in small town
- 5,280 degree-seeking undergraduates: 19% part-time, 62% women, 29% African American, 2% Asian American, 3% Hispanic American, 18% Native American, 1% international
- 643 degree-seeking graduate students
- 87% of applicants admitted
- SAT or ACT with writing required
- 34% graduate within 6 years; 32% enter graduate study

General. Founded in 1887. Regionally accredited. **Degrees:** 687 bachelor's awarded; master's offered. **ROTC:** Army, Air Force. **Location:** 31 miles from Fayetteville. **Calendar:** Semester, limited summer session. **Full-time faculty:** 311 total; 70% have terminal degrees, 21% minority, 46% women. **Part-time faculty:** 139 total; 20% have terminal degrees, 28% minority, 55% women. **Class size:** 43% < 20, 40% 20-39, 16% 40-49, 2%

50-99, less than 1% >100. **Special facilities:** Native American Resource Center, performing arts center.

Freshman class profile. 2,533 applied, 2,204 admitted, 1,073 enrolled.

Mid 50% test scores			
SAT critical reading:	410-490	Rank in top quarter:	31%
SAT math:	420-510	Rank in top tenth:	9%
SAT writing:	390-480	End year in good standing:	68%
ACT composite:	16-19	Return as sophomores:	67%
GPA 3.75 or higher:	16%	Out-of-state:	5%
GPA 3.50-3.74:	12%	Live on campus:	72%
GPA 3.0-3.49:	27%	Fraternities:	7%
GPA 2.0-2.99:	45%	Sororities:	6%

Basis for selection. High school record, class standing, GPA, test scores, and college preparatory courses important. Tests not required for students over 21. Auditions and interviews may be required for acceptance to obtain programs.

High school preparation. College-preparatory program required. 15 units required. Required units include English 4, mathematics 4, social studies 1, history 1, science 3 (laboratory 1) and foreign language 2.

2008-2009 Annual costs. Tuition/fees: $3,608; $12,868 out-of-state. Room/board: $6,190. Books/supplies: $1,000. Personal expenses: $1,505.

2008-2009 Financial aid. Need-based: 969 full-time freshmen applied for aid; 755 were judged to have need; 742 of these received aid. Average need met was 76%. Average scholarship/grant was $5,928; average loan $3,195. 48% of total undergraduate aid awarded as scholarships/grants, 52% as loans/jobs. **Non-need-based:** Awarded to 365 full-time undergraduates, including 132 freshmen. Scholarships awarded for academics, alumni affiliation, art, athletics, music/drama, state residency.

Application procedures. Admission: Priority date 7/15; deadline 7/31. $40 fee, may be waived for applicants with need. Admission notification on a rolling basis beginning on or about 9/15. **Financial aid:** Priority date 3/15; no closing date. FAFSA required. Applicants notified by 4/15; Applicants notified on a rolling basis starting 4/15; must reply within 2 week(s) of notification.

Academics. Certification on secondary teaching level in English, biology, mathematics, social studies, and science education. **Special study options:** Accelerated study, cooperative education, cross-registration, distance learning, double major, dual enrollment of high school students, ESL, exchange student, external degree, honors, independent study, internships, study abroad, teacher certification program, Washington semester. **Credit/placement by examination:** AP, CLEP, SAT, ACT, institutional tests. 30 credit hours maximum toward bachelor's degree. **Support services:** Learning center, pre-admission summer program, reduced course load, remedial instruction, tutoring, writing center.

Honors college/program. Approximately 35 students are chosen yearly to participate in the Esther G. Maynor Honors College. Selected students have distinguished themselves through academic achievement, leadership, and community involvement. These students do have additional acceptance requirements, which includes average SAT score of 1150 and GPA above 3.5. Academic program offers interdisciplinary educational opportunities that enhance the general curriculum as well as social and cultural opportunities.

Majors. Area/ethnic studies: American, Native American. **Biology:** General. **Business:** Accounting, business admin. **Communications:** Media studies. **Computer sciences:** Computer science, information technology. **Conservation:** Environmental science. **Education:** Art, biology, elementary, English, kindergarten/preschool, mathematics, middle, music, physical, science, social studies, special. **Foreign languages:** Spanish. **Health:** Athletic training, nursing (RN), public health ed. **History:** General. **Math:** General. **Parks/recreation:** Facilities management, health/fitness. **Physical sciences:** Chemistry, physics. **Protective services:** Criminal justice. **Psychology:** General. **Public administration:** Social work. **Social sciences:** Political science, sociology. **Visual/performing arts:** Dramatic, music performance, studio arts. **Other:** BIS multi-interdisciplinary studies, Philosophy and religion.

Most popular majors. Biology 7%, business/marketing 10%, communications/journalism 7%, education 16%, health sciences 8%, parks/recreation 6%, security/protective services 8%, social sciences 11%.

Computing on campus. 875 workstations in dormitories, library, computer center, student center. Dormitories wired for high-speed internet access and linked to campus network. Commuter students can connect to campus network. Online course registration, online library, helpline, wireless network available.

Student life. Freshman orientation: Mandatory, $50 fee. **Housing:** Coed dorms, single-sex dorms, apartments available. $125 fully refundable deposit, deadline 7/15. Freshmen given preference for on-campus housing. Apartments available. **Activities:** Bands, campus ministries, choral groups, dance, drama, film society, international student organizations, literary magazine, music ensembles, Model UN, musical theater, radio station, student government, student newspaper, TV station, Native American Organization, African American Student Organization, Baptist Student Union, International Student Organization, Methodist Campus Ministry, Fellowship of Christian Athletes, Campus Association of Social Workers, American Medical Student Association, criminal justice club, Student Government Association.

Athletics. NCAA. **Intercollegiate:** Baseball M, basketball, cheerleading, cross-country, football (tackle) M, golf, soccer, softball W, tennis W, track and field, volleyball W, wrestling M. **Intramural:** Basketball, bowling, football (tackle) M, golf M, racquetball, soccer M, softball, volleyball, wrestling M. **Team name:** Braves.

Student services. Chaplain/spiritual director, career counseling, student employment services, financial aid counseling, health services, personal counseling, veterans' counselor. **Physically disabled:** Services for visually, hearing impaired.

Contact. E-mail: admissons@uncp.edu
Phone: (910) 521-6262 Toll-free number: (800) 949-8627
Fax: (910) 521-6497
Jackie Clark, Vice Chancellor for Enrollment Management, University of North Carolina at Pembroke, Box 1510, Pembroke, NC 28372

University of North Carolina at Wilmington

Wilmington, North Carolina — **CB member**
www.uncw.edu — **CB code: 5907**

- Public 4-year university
- Commuter campus in small city
- 10,625 degree-seeking undergraduates: 7% part-time, 58% women, 5% African American, 2% Asian American, 3% Hispanic American, 1% Native American
- 1,080 degree-seeking graduate students
- 59% of applicants admitted
- SAT or ACT with writing, application essay required

General. Founded in 1947. Regionally accredited. **Degrees:** 2,741 bachelor's awarded; master's, doctoral offered. **Location:** 125 miles from Raleigh. **Calendar:** Semester, extensive summer session. **Full-time faculty:** 580 total; 84% have terminal degrees, 13% minority, 43% women. **Part-time faculty:** 353 total; 31% have terminal degrees, 7% minority, 52% women. **Class size:** 31% < 20, 53% 20-39, 8% 40-49, 7% 50-99, 2% >100. **Special facilities:** Wildlife preserve, research vessel for marine biology laboratory.

Freshman class profile. 9,311 applied, 5,449 admitted, 2,073 enrolled.

Mid 50% test scores			
SAT critical reading:	530-610	GPA 3.0-3.49:	16%
SAT math:	550-630	GPA 2.0-2.99:	3%
SAT writing:	510-600	Rank in top quarter:	62%
ACT composite:	22-26	Rank in top tenth:	23%
GPA 3.75 or higher:	62%	Out-of-state:	15%
GPA 3.50-3.74:	19%	Live on campus:	38%

Basis for selection. High school record; rank in class, if provided; standardized test scores; and rigor of courses completed in high school are very important. SAT or ACT with writing required. Auditions for Music majors required. **Homeschooled:** Statement describing homeschool structure and mission, transcript of courses and grades, letter of recommendation (nonparent) required.

High school preparation. Required units include English 4, mathematics 4, social studies 2, history 1, science 3 (laboratory 1) and foreign language 2. Of the 2 social studies units, 1 unit must be U.S. history.

2008-2009 Annual costs. Tuition/fees: $4,527; $14,694 out-of-state. Room/board: $7,280. Books/supplies: $934. Personal expenses: $1,100.

2008-2009 Financial aid. Need-based: 1,012 full-time freshmen applied for aid; 554 were judged to have need; 545 of these received aid. Average need met was 88%. Average scholarship/grant was $3,763; average loan $2,792. 57% of total undergraduate aid awarded as scholarships/grants, 43% as loans/jobs. **Non-need-based:** Awarded to 386 full-time undergraduates, including 89 freshmen. Scholarships awarded for academics, athletics, leadership, minority status, music/drama, state residency.

Application procedures. Admission: Priority date 11/1; deadline 2/1 (postmark date). $60 fee, may be waived for applicants with need. Admission notification 4/1. Must reply by May 1 or within 4 week(s) if notified thereafter. **Financial aid:** Priority date 3/15; no closing date. FAFSA, institutional form required. Applicants notified on a rolling basis starting 4/1; must reply within 3 week(s) of notification.

Academics. **Special study options:** Accelerated study, cooperative education, cross-registration, distance learning, double major, dual enrollment of high school students, ESL, exchange student, honors, independent study, internships, study abroad, teacher certification program. 2+2 engineering programs. **Credit/placement by examination:** AP, CLEP, IB, institutional tests. **Support services:** Learning center, reduced course load, remedial instruction, tutoring, writing center.

Majors. **Biology:** General, marine. **Business:** Accounting, business admin, finance, management information systems, managerial economics, marketing. **Communications:** General. **Computer sciences:** Computer science. **Conservation:** Environmental science, environmental studies. **Education:** Biology, chemistry, elementary, emotionally handicapped, English, French, history, kindergarten/preschool, learning disabled, mathematics, mentally handicapped, middle, multiple handicapped, music, physical, Spanish, special. **Foreign languages:** French, German, Spanish. **Health:** Athletic training, nursing (RN), public health ed, recreational therapy. **History:** General. **Math:** General, statistics. **Parks/recreation:** Facilities management, health/fitness. **Philosophy/religion:** Philosophy, religion. **Physical sciences:** Chemistry, geology, physics. **Protective services:** Criminal justice. **Psychology:** General. **Public administration:** Social work. **Social sciences:** Anthropology, economics, geography, political science, sociology. **Visual/performing arts:** Art history/conservation, cinematography, dramatic, music performance, studio arts. **Other:** Health professions and Related Clinical Sciences, other, Teacher education and professional development, specific subject areas, other.

Most popular majors. Biology 8%, business/marketing 24%, communications/journalism 8%, education 8%, English 6%, parks/recreation 6%, psychology 7%, social sciences 6%, visual/performing arts 6%.

Computing on campus. 1,020 workstations in dormitories, library, computer center, student center. Dormitories wired for high-speed internet access and linked to campus network. Commuter students can connect to campus network. Online course registration, online library, helpline, repair service, student web hosting, wireless network available.

Student life. **Freshman orientation:** Mandatory, $80 fee. Preregistration for classes offered. **Housing:** Coed dorms, single-sex dorms, apartments, wellness housing available. $105 nonrefundable deposit, deadline 5/1. Honors housing. **Activities:** Bands, campus ministries, choral groups, dance, drama, film society, international student organizations, literary magazine, music ensembles, musical theater, opera, radio station, student government, student newspaper, symphony orchestra, TV station, Baptist student union, black student alliance, College Republicans, Fellowship of Christian University Students, Global Serve, Alpha Phi Omega, Young Democrats, Newman Catholic Student Center, African American-Hispanic-Asian-Native American organizations.

Athletics. NCAA. **Intercollegiate:** Baseball M, basketball, cheerleading, cross-country, diving, golf, soccer, softball W, swimming, tennis, track and field, volleyball W. **Intramural:** Basketball, football (non-tackle), golf, soccer, softball, tennis, volleyball. **Team name:** Seahawks.

Student services. Adult student services, alcohol/substance abuse counseling, chaplain/spiritual director, career counseling, student employment services, financial aid counseling, health services, minority student services, personal counseling, placement for graduates, veterans' counselor. **Physically disabled:** Services for visually, speech, hearing impaired.

Contact. E-mail: admissions@uncw.edu
Phone: (910) 962-3243 Toll-free number: (800) 228-5571
Fax: (910) 962-3038
Janice Rockwell, Director, University of North Carolina at Wilmington, 601 South College Road, Wilmington, NC 28403-5904

University of North Carolina School of the Arts

Winston-Salem, North Carolina — **CB member**
www.ncarts.edu — **CB code: 5512**

- Public 4-year visual arts and performing arts college
- Residential campus in small city
- 765 degree-seeking undergraduates
- 114 graduate students
- 44% of applicants admitted
- Interview required

General. Founded in 1963. Regionally accredited. State Conservatory with high school, undergraduate and graduate facilities. **Degrees:** 120 bachelor's awarded; master's offered. **Location:** 90 miles from Charlotte, 75 miles from Raleigh. **Calendar:** Trimester, limited summer session. **Full-time faculty:** 144 total; 38% have terminal degrees, 1% minority, 33% women. **Part-time faculty:** 39 total; 15% have terminal degrees, 46% women. **Class size:** 84% < 20, 14% 20-39, less than 1% 40-49, 1% 50-99. **Special facilities:** Stage production shop, film village with sound and recording stages.

Freshman class profile. 695 applied, 303 admitted, 166 enrolled.

Mid 50% test scores			
SAT critical reading:	510-630	SAT writing:	490-610
SAT math:	460-630	Out-of-state:	62%
		Live on campus:	95%

Basis for selection. Talent, achievement, career potential most important. Admission heavily dependent on audition. SAT combined score of 800 (exclusive of Writing) or ACT composite score of 19, school record, recommendations important. SAT or ACT recommended. Interview recommended for all students. Audition required for dance, drama, music programs; portfolio required for design, filmmaking, production programs.

High school preparation. College-preparatory program recommended. 20 units required. Required and recommended units include English 4, mathematics 3, social studies 2, history 1, science 3 (laboratory 1), foreign language 2 and academic electives 4.

2008-2009 Annual costs. Tuition/fees: $5,216; $17,096 out-of-state. Required fees may vary by program. Room/board: $6,831. Books/supplies: $865. Personal expenses: $1,889.

2007-2008 Financial aid. **Need-based:** 50% of total undergraduate aid awarded as scholarships/grants, 50% as loans/jobs. **Non-need-based:** Scholarships awarded for academics, art, leadership, music/drama, state residency.

Application procedures. **Admission:** Priority date 3/1; no deadline. $60 fee, may be waived for applicants with need. Admission notification on a rolling basis beginning on or about 4/1. Must reply by May 1 or within 3 week(s) if notified thereafter. Application closing date dependent upon audition. Applications must be submitted at least 2 weeks before audition date. Dance, drama and filmmaking interviews begin in January and end in early March. Music and technical theater auditions begin in November and end in early March. Decisions generally are made by April 1, or about 2 weeks after audition if later than April 1. **Financial aid:** Priority date 3/1; no closing date. FAFSA required. Applicants notified on a rolling basis starting 4/1; must reply within 2 week(s) of notification.

Academics. Professional training supplemented by strong general studies curriculum, small classes 7:1 student-teacher ratio. **Special study options:** Independent study, internships. **Credit/placement by examination:** AP, CLEP. **Support services:** Remedial instruction, study skills assistance, tutoring, writing center.

Majors. **Liberal arts:** Arts/sciences. **Visual/performing arts:** Cinematography, dance, dramatic, music performance, theater design.

Computing on campus. 28 workstations in dormitories, library, student center. Dormitories wired for high-speed internet access and linked to campus network. Online course registration available.

Student life. **Freshman orientation:** Mandatory, $75 fee. Orientation is the first three days in the academic year. All art schools have separate orientations which include academic assessment. **Housing:** Guaranteed on-campus for freshmen. Coed dorms, single-sex dorms, apartments available. $200 deposit, deadline 5/1. **Activities:** Jazz band, dance, drama, music ensembles, musical theater, opera, student government, student newspaper, symphony orchestra, spirituality committee, ADAPT-drug prevention team, C.A.R.E.-AIDS awareness and prevention team, Awareness for Gay and Lesbian Equality, Artists for Christ, Awareness of Black Arts, Minorities on the Move.

Athletics. **Team name:** Fighting Pickles.

Student services. Alcohol/substance abuse counseling, career counseling, student employment services, financial aid counseling, health services, personal counseling.

Contact. E-mail: admissions@ncarts.edu
Phone: (336) 770-3291 Fax: (336) 770-3370
Sheeler Lawson, Director of Admissions, University of North Carolina School of the Arts, 1533 South Main Street, Winston-Salem, NC 27127-2188

Wake Forest University

Winston-Salem, North Carolina — **CB member**
www.wfu.edu — **CB code: 5885**

- Private 4-year university
- Residential campus in small city

- 4,466 degree-seeking undergraduates: 2% part-time, 51% women, 7% African American, 5% Asian American, 3% Hispanic American, 1% Native American, 1% international
- 2,349 degree-seeking graduate students
- 38% of applicants admitted
- Application essay required
- 88% graduate within 6 years

General. Founded in 1834. Regionally accredited. All freshmen receive a personal computer and a color printer/scanner/copier. **Degrees:** 1,028 bachelor's awarded; master's, doctoral, first professional offered. **ROTC:** Army. **Location:** 4 miles from downtown. **Calendar:** Semester, limited summer session. **Full-time faculty:** 471 total; 88% have terminal degrees, 14% minority, 38% women. **Part-time faculty:** 113 total; 6% minority, 44% women. **Class size:** 56% < 20, 37% 20-39, 5% 40-49, 2% 50-99, less than 1% >100. **Special facilities:** Museum of anthropology, center for nanotechnology and molecular materials, Reynolda house museum of American art, art gallery, archaeology laboratory, biomechanics laboratory, laser physics laboratory.

Freshman class profile. 9,050 applied, 3,473 admitted, 1,202 enrolled.

Mid 50% test scores			
SAT critical reading:	610-690	Return as sophomores:	93%
SAT math:	630-710	Out-of-state:	74%
ACT composite:	27-31	Live on campus:	99%
Rank in top quarter:	91%	International:	1%
Rank in top tenth:	64%	Fraternities:	33%
		Sororities:	46%

Basis for selection. High school curriculum and achievement, test scores, school and community activities, essay, personal recommendations, special talents all important. Audition recommended for those competing for a Presidential Scholarship (for students with special talents in music, theater, art, dance, and debate).

High school preparation. College-preparatory program required. 16 units required; 20 recommended. Required and recommended units include English 4, mathematics 3-4, social studies 2-4, science 1-4 and foreign language 2-4.

2008-2009 Annual costs. Tuition/fees: $36,975. Tuition covers cost of an IBM Thinkpad computer and inkjet printer for freshmen. Room/board: $9,945. Books/supplies: $850. Personal expenses: $1,350.

2008-2009 Financial aid. **Need-based:** 430 full-time freshmen applied for aid; 344 were judged to have need; 338 of these received aid. Average need met was 99%. Average scholarship/grant was $23,682; average loan $6,536. 66% of total undergraduate aid awarded as scholarships/grants, 34% as loans/jobs. **Non-need-based:** Awarded to 1,540 full-time undergraduates, including 372 freshmen. Scholarships awarded for academics, alumni affiliation, art, athletics, leadership, music/drama, religious affiliation, ROTC, state residency. **Additional information:** In fall 2008, freshmen with an annual family income of less than $40,000 will have their student loans capped at $4,000 per year during their college years. Other financial aid to the students will come from grant and scholarship increases and work-study opportunities.

Application procedures. **Admission:** Closing date 1/15. $50 fee, may be waived for applicants with need. Admission notification 4/1. Must reply by 5/1. **Financial aid:** Priority date 2/1, closing date 3/1. FAFSA, CSS PROFILE required. Applicants notified on a rolling basis starting 4/1; must reply by 5/1 or within 4 week(s) of notification.

Academics. Language courses at all levels in Russian, Greek, Italian, Hebrew; elementary and intermediate courses in Chinese, Japanese and Arabic; elementary courses in Hindi, Portuguese. **Special study options:** Combined bachelor's/graduate degree, cross-registration, double major, dual enrollment of high school students, honors, independent study, internships, study abroad, teacher certification program, Washington semester. Semester in London, Venice, or Vienna and semester at universities in Dijon, Salamanca, Berlin, Moscow, Beijing, and Japan. **Credit/placement by examination:** AP, CLEP, IB, institutional tests. **Support services:** Learning center, reduced course load, study skills assistance, tutoring, writing center.

Majors. **Biology:** General, bacteriology. **Business:** General, accounting, finance, management science. **Communications:** General. **Computer sciences:** Computer science. **Education:** Elementary, social studies. **Foreign languages:** Ancient Greek, Chinese, classics, French, German, Japanese, Latin, Russian, Spanish. **Health:** Clinical lab science. **History:** General. **Math:** General. **Parks/recreation:** Exercise sciences. **Philosophy/religion:** Philosophy, religion. **Physical sciences:** Chemistry, physics. **Psychology:** General. **Social sciences:** Anthropology, econometrics, economics, political science, sociology. **Visual/performing arts:** Art history/conservation, dramatic, music history, music performance, studio arts.

Most popular majors. Business/marketing 18%, communications/journalism 7%, foreign language 8%, history 8%, psychology 9%, social sciences 22%.

Computing on campus. PC or laptop required. 4,412 workstations in dormitories, library, computer center, student center. Dormitories wired for high-speed internet access and linked to campus network. Commuter students can connect to campus network. Online course registration, online library, helpline, repair service, student web hosting, wireless network available.

Student life. **Freshman orientation:** Mandatory. Preregistration for classes offered. Six days before Fall classes start. **Policies:** First- and second-year students with residential status required to live on campus. **Housing:** Guaranteed on-campus for all undergraduates. Coed dorms, apartments, fraternity/sorority housing, wellness housing available. **Activities:** Bands, campus ministries, choral groups, dance, drama, film society, international student organizations, literary magazine, music ensembles, Model UN, radio station, student government, student newspaper, symphony orchestra, TV station, Black Student Alliance, College Democrats, College Republicans, Alpha Phi Omega, InterVarsity Christian Fellowship, Amnesty International, Habitat for Humanity, volunteer service corps.

Athletics. NCAA. **Intercollegiate:** Baseball M, basketball, cheerleading, cross-country, field hockey W, football (tackle) M, golf, soccer, tennis, track and field, volleyball W. **Intramural:** Basketball, bowling, cross-country, diving, equestrian W, football (non-tackle), golf, racquetball, soccer, softball, table tennis, tennis, volleyball, water polo, wrestling M. **Team name:** Demon Deacons.

Student services. Alcohol/substance abuse counseling, chaplain/spiritual director, career counseling, student employment services, financial aid counseling, health services, minority student services, personal counseling, placement for graduates. **Physically disabled:** Services for visually, speech, hearing impaired.

Contact. E-mail: admissions@wfu.edu
Phone: (336) 758-5201 Fax: (336) 758-4324
Martha Allman, Director of Admissions, Wake Forest University, PO Box 7305, Winston-Salem, NC 27109-7305

Warren Wilson College

Asheville, North Carolina — **CB member**
www.warren-wilson.edu — **CB code: 5886**

- Private 4-year liberal arts college affiliated with Presbyterian Church (USA)
- Residential campus in small city
- 955 degree-seeking undergraduates
- SAT or ACT (ACT writing optional), application essay required

General. Founded in 1894. Regionally accredited. **Degrees:** 177 bachelor's awarded; master's offered. **Location:** One mile from Asheville. **Calendar:** 4 consecutive 8-week terms. **Full-time faculty:** 62 total; 94% have terminal degrees, 11% minority, 48% women. **Part-time faculty:** 14 total; 71% have terminal degrees, 14% minority, 50% women. **Class size:** 81% < 20, 19% 20-39, less than 1% 40-49. **Special facilities:** 300-acre college farm, archaeological site, climbing wall, adventure challenge course, hiking trails.

Freshman class profile.

Mid 50% test scores			
SAT critical reading:	540-670	Rank in top quarter:	42%
SAT math:	500-610	Rank in top tenth:	21%
SAT writing:	530-610	Out-of-state:	80%
ACT composite:	22-27	Live on campus:	98%

Basis for selection. In order of importance: high school achievement, class rank, personal statement, recommendations, test scores, school and community activities. All records of examinations taken overseas plus TOEFL required of foreign applicants. Interview, portfolio recommended. **Homeschooled:** Submit transcript listing course titles and content, partial portfolio of sample work completed (graded papers), document that serves as diploma, copy of state rules under which school was formed or is recognized.

High school preparation. Required and recommended units include English 4, mathematics 3, history 3, science 2 (laboratory 2) and foreign language 2. Math requirement includes algebra I, II and geometry. Sciences must include 2 laboratories.

2008-2009 Annual costs. Tuition/fees: $22,666. All resident students required to work 15 hours per week in college's work program. $3,144 earnings credited toward tuition costs. Room/board: $7,116. Books/supplies: $900. Personal expenses: $1,509.

2008-2009 Financial aid. **Non-need-based:** Scholarships awarded for academics, art, job skills, leadership, religious affiliation, state residency.

Application procedures. **Admission:** Priority date 1/15; deadline 3/15 (receipt date). No application fee. Admission notification on a rolling basis beginning on or about 2/1. Must reply by 5/1. **Financial aid:** Priority date 4/1; no closing date. FAFSA, institutional form required. Applicants notified on a rolling basis starting 3/1; must reply within 3 week(s) of notification.

Academics. **Special study options:** Cross-registration, double major, dual enrollment of high school students, ESL, exchange student, honors, independent study, internships, liberal arts/career combination, student-designed major, study abroad, teacher certification program, Washington semester. **Credit/placement by examination:** AP, CLEP, institutional tests. **Support services:** Reduced course load, study skills assistance, tutoring, writing center.

Majors. **Biology:** General. **Business:** Business admin. **Conservation:** General. **Education:** General, early childhood, elementary, middle, secondary. **Foreign languages:** General. **Health:** Premedicine, preveterinary. **History:** General. **Liberal arts:** Arts/sciences. **Math:** General. **Parks/recreation:** General. **Philosophy/religion:** Philosophy, religion. **Physical sciences:** Chemistry. **Psychology:** General. **Public administration:** Social work. **Social sciences:** Anthropology, economics, political science, sociology. **Visual/performing arts:** Art.

Most popular majors. Biology 7%, education 8%, history 8%, interdisciplinary studies 14%, natural resources/environmental science 16%, psychology 8%, social sciences 14%.

Computing on campus. 91 workstations in library, computer center, student center. Dormitories wired for high-speed internet access and linked to campus network. Commuter students can connect to campus network. Online course registration, online library, helpline, wireless network available.

Student life. **Freshman orientation:** Mandatory, $200 fee. 7-day orientation (late August) includes full day community service, dinner/discussion with faculty. **Policies:** Triad program requires students to work 15 hours/week at an on-campus job and do 100 hours community service by graduation, in addition to academics. **Housing:** Guaranteed on-campus for all undergraduates. Coed dorms, single-sex dorms, apartments, cooperative housing, wellness housing available. **Activities:** Jazz band, choral groups, dance, drama, international student organizations, literary magazine, music ensembles, musical theater, student government, student newspaper, Amnesty International, Emmaus, Interfaith, Jewish student group, Buddhist experience, earth first, sustainable living.

Athletics. USCAA. **Intercollegiate:** Basketball, cross-country, soccer, swimming. **Intramural:** Basketball, football (non-tackle), soccer, table tennis, tennis, triathlon, volleyball. **Team name:** Owls.

Student services. Alcohol/substance abuse counseling, chaplain/spiritual director, career counseling, student employment services, financial aid counseling, health services, minority student services, personal counseling, placement for graduates.

Contact. E-mail: admit@warren-wilson.edu
Phone: (828) 771-2073 Toll-free number: (800) 934-3536
Fax: (828) 298-1440
Richard Blomgren, Dean of Admission, Warren Wilson College, Office of Admission, Asheville, NC 28815-9000

Western Carolina University

Cullowhee, North Carolina **CB member**
www.wcu.edu **CB code: 5897**

- Public 4-year university
- Residential campus in small town
- 6,896 degree-seeking undergraduates: 16% part-time, 52% women, 6% African American, 1% Asian American, 2% Hispanic American, 1% Native American, 1% international
- 1,638 degree-seeking graduate students
- 51% of applicants admitted
- SAT or ACT with writing required
- 50% graduate within 6 years

General. Founded in 1889. Regionally accredited. **Degrees:** 1,525 bachelor's awarded; master's, doctoral offered. **Location:** 53 miles from Asheville, 157 miles from Atlanta, GA. **Calendar:** Semester, extensive summer session. **Full-time faculty:** 488 total; 76% have terminal degrees, 6% minority, 45% women. **Part-time faculty:** 217 total; 27% have terminal degrees, 3% minority, 57% women. **Class size:** 39% < 20, 53% 20-39, 6% 40-49, less than 1% 50-99, less than 1% >100. **Special facilities:** Center for applied technology, fine and performing arts center, collection of historical Native American artifacts and documents, center for the advancement of teaching, public policy institute, mountain heritage center.

Freshman class profile. 7,331 applied, 3,743 admitted, 1,224 enrolled.

Mid 50% test scores		**GPA 3.0-3.49:**	29%
SAT critical reading:	460-550	**GPA 2.0-2.99:**	20%
SAT math:	480-570	**Rank in top quarter:**	39%
SAT writing:	440-530	**Rank in top tenth:**	14%
ACT composite:	19-23	**Return as sophomores:**	71%
GPA 3.75 or higher:	35%	**Out-of-state:**	8%
GPA 3.50-3.74:	16%	**Live on campus:**	96%

Basis for selection. The most important admission factors are secondary school record, class rank, GPA, standardized test scores, talent/ability, and applicant's interest. SAT recommended. All applicants, except those exempted by current campus policies, must submit standardized test scores. SAT preferred, ACT also accepted. Essays not required but will be considered if submitted. Auditions and/or portfolios are required for some art/music/theater programs. **Homeschooled:** Must submit official transcript of all work completed and meet standards equivalent to those used for applicants from approved secondary schools.

High school preparation. College-preparatory program required. 20 units required; 24 recommended. Required and recommended units include English 4, mathematics 4, social studies 2, history 1, science 3 (laboratory 3), foreign language 2 and academic electives 4-8.

2008-2009 Annual costs. Tuition/fees: $4,413; $13,996 out-of-state. Room/board: $5,626.

2008-2009 Financial aid. **Need-based:** 972 full-time freshmen applied for aid; 670 were judged to have need; 662 of these received aid. Average need met was 87%. Average scholarship/grant was $7,868; average loan $3,644. 60% of total undergraduate aid awarded as scholarships/grants, 40% as loans/jobs. **Non-need-based:** Awarded to 1,021 full-time undergraduates, including 280 freshmen. Scholarships awarded for academics, art, athletics, leadership, music/drama, state residency.

Application procedures. **Admission:** Priority date 3/1; deadline 4/1 (postmark date). $40 fee, may be waived for applicants with need. Admission notification on a rolling basis beginning on or about 1/30. Must reply by 5/1. Housing deposit due upon receipt of student's acceptance. **Financial aid:** Priority date 3/31; no closing date. FAFSA, institutional form required. Applicants notified on a rolling basis starting 4/1.

Academics. **Special study options:** Combined bachelor's/graduate degree, cooperative education, distance learning, double major, dual enrollment of high school students, exchange student, honors, independent study, internships, student-designed major, study abroad, teacher certification program. Service learning. **Credit/placement by examination:** AP, CLEP, IB, institutional tests. 45 credit hours maximum toward bachelor's degree. **Support services:** Learning center, pre-admission summer program, reduced course load, study skills assistance, tutoring, writing center.

Honors college/program. For first-year students to be considered, they need to meet at least one of the following criteria: 1875 SAT or 30 ACT, 4.0 weighted cumulative HS GPA, rank in the top 10% of HS class. Other requirements apply to transfer students and students currently enrolled.

Majors. **Biology:** General. **Business:** Accounting, business admin, entrepreneurial studies, finance, hospitality admin, international, management information systems, marketing. **Communications:** General. **Computer sciences:** Computer science. **Conservation:** Environmental science, management/policy. **Education:** Art, elementary, English, German, kindergarten/preschool, mathematics, middle, music, physical, science, social studies, Spanish, special. **Engineering:** Electrical. **Engineering technology:** General, construction, electrical, industrial, manufacturing. **Foreign languages:** French, German, Spanish. **Health:** Athletic training, clinical lab science, communication disorders, dietetics, EMT paramedic, environmental health, health care admin, medical records admin, nursing (RN), recreational therapy. **History:** General. **Liberal arts:** Arts/sciences. **Math:** General. **Parks/recreation:** Facilities management, sports admin. **Philosophy/religion:** Philosophy. **Physical sciences:** Chemistry, geology. **Protective services:** Criminal justice, forensics. **Psychology:** General. **Public administration:** General, social work. **Social sciences:** General, anthropology, geography, political science, sociology. **Visual/performing arts:** Art, dramatic, interior design, music performance, studio arts. **Other:** Entrepreneurship, Motion picture and television production.

Most popular majors. Business/marketing 16%, education 23%, engineering/engineering technologies 8%, health sciences 13%, security/protective services 7%.

Computing on campus. PC or laptop required. 181 workstations in library, computer center, student center. Dormitories wired for high-speed internet access and linked to campus network. Commuter students can connect to campus network. Online course registration, online library, helpline, repair service, student web hosting, wireless network available.

Student life. **Freshman orientation:** Mandatory, $115 fee. Preregistration for classes offered. 2-day orientation sessions are held in June and July. Sessions are for both students and parents. **Housing:** Guaranteed on-campus for freshmen. Coed dorms, single-sex dorms, special housing for disabled, apartments, fraternity/sorority housing, wellness housing available. $150 nonrefundable deposit, deadline 6/1. **Activities:** Bands, campus ministries, choral groups, dance, drama, film society, international student organizations, literary magazine, music ensembles, Model UN, musical theater, radio station, student government, student newspaper, TV station, financial planning club, Fellowship of Christian Athletes, Black theater ensemble, Catholic Campus Ministries, Japanese Animation Society, Organization of Ebony Students, WCU College Republicans, WCU College Democrats, La Voz Latina, Pagan student association.

Athletics. NCAA. **Intercollegiate:** Baseball M, basketball, cheerleading, cross-country, football (tackle) M, golf, soccer W, softball W, tennis W, track and field, volleyball W. **Intramural:** Badminton, basketball, bowling, cross-country, football (non-tackle), football (tackle), racquetball, soccer, softball, swimming, table tennis, tennis, track and field, volleyball, water polo, weight lifting, wrestling. **Team name:** Catamounts.

Student services. Alcohol/substance abuse counseling, chaplain/spiritual director, career counseling, student employment services, financial aid counseling, health services, minority student services, on-campus daycare, personal counseling, placement for graduates, women's services. **Physically disabled:** Services for visually, speech, hearing impaired.

Contact. E-mail: admiss@wcu.edu
Phone: (828) 227-7317 Toll-free number: (877) 928-4968
Fax: (828) 227-7319
Alan Kines, Director of Admissions, Western Carolina University, 102 Camp Building, Cullowhee, NC 28723

Wingate University

Wingate, North Carolina — **CB member**
www.wingate.edu — **CB code: 5908**

- Private 4-year university and liberal arts college affiliated with Baptist faith
- Residential campus in small town
- 1,440 degree-seeking undergraduates: 3% part-time, 47% women, 12% African American, 2% Asian American, 2% Hispanic American, 1% Native American, 3% international
- 573 degree-seeking graduate students
- 54% graduate within 6 years

General. Founded in 1896. Regionally accredited. **Degrees:** 260 bachelor's awarded; master's, doctoral, first professional offered. **ROTC:** Army, Air Force. **Location:** 25 miles from Charlotte. **Calendar:** Semester, limited summer session. **Full-time faculty:** 109 total; 94% have terminal degrees, 8% minority, 47% women. **Part-time faculty:** 62 total. **Class size:** 52% < 20, 47% 20-39, less than 1% 40-49, less than 1% 50-99. **Special facilities:** Outdoor recreation laboratory, 11-acre lake, performing arts center.

Freshman class profile. 3,897 applied, 2,151 admitted, 432 enrolled.

Mid 50% test scores		**GPA 2.0-2.99:**	21%
SAT critical reading:	440-550	**Rank in top quarter:**	50%
SAT math:	470-580	**Rank in top tenth:**	22%
SAT writing:	440-540	**End year in good standing:**	94%
ACT composite:	19-24	**Return as sophomores:**	72%
GPA 3.75 or higher:	40%	**Out-of-state:**	20%
GPA 3.50-3.74:	15%	**Live on campus:**	91%
GPA 3.0-3.49:	24%	**International:**	5%

Basis for selection. Open admission, but selective for some programs. Decisions based on secondary school record (GPA, class rank) and the rigor of secondary school record. Test scores are considered. SAT/ACT not required, but strongly recommended. SAT or ACT recommended. Interview recommended for all students; portfolio recommended for art majors; audition required for music majors.

High school preparation. 13 units recommended. Recommended units include English 4, mathematics 3, social studies 2, science 2 (laboratory 1) and foreign language 2.

2008-2009 Annual costs. Tuition/fees: $19,350. Some music and art courses carry a fee. Room/board: $7,700. Books/supplies: $1,000. Personal expenses: $900.

2008-2009 Financial aid. **Non-need-based:** Scholarships awarded for academics, alumni affiliation, art, athletics, music/drama, state residency. **Additional information:** Institutional aid may not be available after June 1.

Application procedures. **Admission:** Priority date 4/1; no deadline. $30 fee, may be waived for applicants with need. Admission notification on a rolling basis beginning on or about 9/15. Must reply by May 1 or within 4 week(s) if notified thereafter. **Financial aid:** Priority date 5/1; no closing date. FAFSA required. Applicants notified on a rolling basis starting 3/1; must reply within 2 week(s) of notification.

Academics. Attendance to cultural events required as part of Lyceum program. Travel abroad available. Internships and undergraduate research under faculty supervision available. **Special study options:** Combined bachelor's/graduate degree, cross-registration, double major, dual enrollment of high school students, honors, independent study, internships, study abroad, teacher certification program. Adult Completion Program at the Wingate University School of Graduate Programs and Adult Education in downtown Matthews, NC. The program offers undergraduate courses in the evening for working adults. **Credit/placement by examination:** AP, CLEP, IB, SAT, ACT, institutional tests. 30 credit hours maximum toward bachelor's degree. **Support services:** Learning center, reduced course load, study skills assistance, tutoring, writing center.

Majors. **Area/ethnic studies:** American. **Biology:** General, environmental. **Business:** Accounting, business admin, finance, marketing. **Communications:** General, broadcast journalism, journalism, public relations. **Computer sciences:** Computer science. **Education:** Art, biology, elementary, English, mathematics, middle, music, physical, reading, social studies. **Foreign languages:** Spanish. **Health:** Athletic training, predental, premedicine, prepharmacy, preveterinary. **History:** General. **Interdisciplinary:** Math/computer science. **Legal studies:** Prelaw. **Liberal arts:** Arts/sciences. **Math:** General. **Parks/recreation:** Facilities management, sports admin. **Philosophy/religion:** Philosophy, religion. **Physical sciences:** Chemistry. **Psychology:** General. **Public administration:** Human services. **Social sciences:** Sociology. **Visual/performing arts:** Art, music management, music performance, piano/organ, studio arts, voice/opera. **Other:** Pre-engineering studies.

Most popular majors. Biology 6%, business/marketing 16%, communications/journalism 8%, education 12%, liberal arts 6%, psychology 6%, visual/performing arts 9%.

Computing on campus. 75 workstations in library, computer center, student center. Dormitories wired for high-speed internet access. Commuter students can connect to campus network. Wireless network available.

Student life. **Freshman orientation:** Mandatory. Preregistration for classes offered. Begins 4 days before classes. **Policies:** Honor Code. **Housing:** Guaranteed on-campus for all undergraduates. Single-sex dorms, special housing for disabled, apartments, wellness housing available. $300 deposit. **Activities:** Bands, campus ministries, choral groups, drama, international student organizations, literary magazine, music ensembles, student government, student newspaper, TV station, academic honors societies, Greek life, Christian Student Union, minority student association, university and community assistance network, gospel choir, College Republicans, outdoor recreation and adventure club, running club.

Athletics. NCAA. **Intercollegiate:** Baseball M, basketball, cross-country, football (tackle) M, golf, lacrosse M, soccer, softball W, swimming, tennis, volleyball W. **Intramural:** Basketball, bowling, diving, football (tackle) M, golf, lacrosse W, racquetball, soccer, softball, swimming, table tennis, tennis, volleyball, water polo. **Team name:** Bulldogs.

Student services. Chaplain/spiritual director, career counseling, student employment services, financial aid counseling, health services, minority student services, personal counseling, placement for graduates.

Contact. E-mail: admit@wingate.edu
Phone: (704) 233-8200 Toll-free number: (800) 755-5550
Fax: (704) 233-8110
Thomas Brown, Dean of Enrollment Management, Wingate University, Campus Box 3059, Wingate, NC 28174-0157

Winston-Salem State University

Winston-Salem, North Carolina — **CB member**
www.wssu.edu — **CB code: 5909**

- Public 4-year university and health science college
- Commuter campus in small city
- 5,948 degree-seeking undergraduates
- 54% of applicants admitted
- SAT or ACT with writing required

General. Founded in 1892. Regionally accredited. **Degrees:** 867 bachelor's awarded; master's offered. **ROTC:** Army. **Location:** 28 miles from Greensboro, 75 miles from Charlotte. **Calendar:** Semester, limited summer session. **Full-time faculty:** 420 total; 48% minority. **Part-time faculty:** 69 total; 44% minority. **Class size:** 42% < 20, 50% 20-39, 6% 40-49, 2% 50-99.

Freshman class profile. 4,069 applied, 2,194 admitted, 1,357 enrolled.

Mid 50% test scores		**GPA 3.0-3.49:**	33%
SAT critical reading:	390-470	**GPA 2.0-2.99:**	52%
SAT math:	400-480	**Rank in top quarter:**	3%
ACT composite:	16-19	**Rank in top tenth:**	1%
GPA 3.75 or higher:	5%	**Out-of-state:**	12%
GPA 3.50-3.74:	8%	**Live on campus:**	82%

Basis for selection. Admissions based on secondary school record, class rank, and standardized tests scores. Campus interview very important. Extracurricular activities also important. SAT preferred. Interview recommended for all students; audition required for music program.

High school preparation. 15 units required. Required units include English 4, mathematics 4, social studies 1, history 1, science 3 and foreign language 2. Mathematics units must include or exceed algebra I, geometry and algebra II.

2008-2009 Annual costs. Tuition/fees: $3,389; $12,029 out-of-state. Room/board: $5,942. Personal expenses: $2,100.

2007-2008 Financial aid. Need-based: 57% of total undergraduate aid awarded as scholarships/grants, 43% as loans/jobs. **Non-need-based:** Scholarships awarded for academics, athletics, ROTC, state residency.

Application procedures. Admission: Closing date 2/16. $40 fee, may be waived for applicants with need. Admission notification on a rolling basis. **Financial aid:** Priority date 5/1; no closing date. FAFSA required. Applicants notified by 5/15; must reply within 2 week(s) of notification.

Academics. Special study options: Accelerated study, cross-registration, distance learning, double major, ESL, honors, independent study, internships, liberal arts/career combination, study abroad, teacher certification program, Washington semester, weekend college. **Credit/placement by examination:** AP, CLEP, IB, institutional tests. 36 credit hours maximum toward bachelor's degree. **Support services:** Learning center, reduced course load, remedial instruction, study skills assistance, tutoring.

Majors. Area/ethnic studies: African-American. **Biology:** General, biotechnology, molecular. **Business:** Accounting, business admin, managerial economics. **Communications:** Media studies. **Computer sciences:** Computer science, information technology. **Education:** Art, early childhood, elementary, English, mathematics, middle, music, physical, social studies, Spanish, special. **Foreign languages:** Spanish. **Health:** Clinical lab science, nursing (RN), recreational therapy, vocational rehab counseling. **History:** General. **Interdisciplinary:** Gerontology. **Liberal arts:** Arts/sciences. **Math:** General. **Parks/recreation:** Exercise sciences, sports admin. **Physical sciences:** Chemistry. **Protective services:** Criminal justice. **Psychology:** General. **Public administration:** Social work. **Social sciences:** Political science, sociology. **Visual/performing arts:** Art, music management.

Most popular majors. Business/marketing 13%, health sciences 42%, parks/recreation 7%, social sciences 7%.

Computing on campus. PC or laptop required. 500 workstations in dormitories, library, computer center, student center. Dormitories wired for high-speed internet access and linked to campus network. Commuter students can connect to campus network. Online course registration, online library, wireless network available.

Student life. Freshman orientation: Available, $300 fee. Preregistration for classes offered. Held on a summer weekend. **Housing:** Coed dorms, single-sex dorms available. $75 nonrefundable deposit, deadline 5/14. **Activities:** Bands, dance, drama, radio station, student government, student newspaper, TV station, student religious council.

Athletics. NCAA. **Intercollegiate:** Basketball, bowling W, cheerleading M, cross-country, football (tackle) M, golf M, softball W, tennis, track and field, volleyball W. **Intramural:** Basketball M. **Team name:** Rams.

Student services. Adult student services, career counseling, student employment services, financial aid counseling, health services, personal counseling, veterans' counselor. **Physically disabled:** Services for visually impaired.

Contact. E-mail: admissions@wssu.edu
Phone: (336) 750-2070 Toll-free number: (800) 257-4052
Fax: (336) 750-2079
Douglas Kilgore, Director of Admissions, Winston-Salem State University, 601 Martin Luther King Jr Drive, Winston-Salem, NC 27110

North Dakota

Dickinson State University
Dickinson, North Dakota
www.dsu.nodak.edu **CB code: 6477**

- Public 4-year university
- Residential campus in large town
- 2,730 degree-seeking undergraduates: 31% part-time, 61% women, 2% African American, 1% Asian American, 2% Hispanic American, 2% Native American, 16% international
- 31% graduate within 6 years

General. Founded in 1918. Regionally accredited. **Degrees:** 424 bachelor's, 57 associate awarded. **Location:** 100 miles from Bismarck, 300 miles from Billings, Montana. **Calendar:** Semester, limited summer session. **Full-time faculty:** 89 total; 53% have terminal degrees, 4% minority, 49% women. **Part-time faculty:** 154 total; 8% have terminal degrees, 1% minority, 62% women. **Class size:** 64% < 20, 29% 20-39, 4% 40-49, 3% 50-99. **Special facilities:** Nature preserve.

Freshman class profile. 620 applied, 583 admitted, 335 enrolled.

Mid 50% test scores			
SAT critical reading:	430-530	Rank in top tenth:	5%
SAT math:	470-590	Return as sophomores:	64%
ACT composite:	18-23	Out-of-state:	45%
Rank in top quarter:	15%	International:	10%

Basis for selection. Open admission, but selective for some programs. Minimum 20 ACT composite or minimum 2.0 GPA required for nursing program. To be accepted into our Honors Leadership Program students must have a 3.5 high school GPA and/or a 26 on ACT. **Homeschooled:** Transcript of courses and grades, letter of recommendation (nonparent) required.

High school preparation. College-preparatory program required. 13 units recommended. Recommended units include English 4, mathematics 3, social studies 3 and science 3. One algebra, 1 chemistry required for nursing program.

2008-2009 Annual costs. Tuition/fees: $5,084; $11,796 out-of-state. Tuition for Minnesota residents: $4,197. Tuition for South Dakota, Montana, Manitoba, Saskatchewan residents: $5,024. Room/board: $4,280. Books/supplies: $900. Personal expenses: $1,325.

2007-2008 Financial aid. Need-based: 23% of total undergraduate aid awarded as scholarships/grants, 77% as loans/jobs. **Non-need-based:** Scholarships awarded for academics, alumni affiliation, art, athletics, job skills, leadership, minority status, music/drama, religious affiliation, state residency. **Additional information:** Scholarships available to new students, priority deadline December 1.

Application procedures. Admission: No deadline. $35 fee. Admission notification on a rolling basis. **Financial aid:** Priority date 3/15; no closing date. FAFSA required. Must reply within 2 week(s) of notification.

Academics. Limited evening classes available. **Special study options:** Accelerated study, combined bachelor's/graduate degree, cooperative education, distance learning, double major, dual enrollment of high school students, ESL, honors, independent study, internships, liberal arts/career combination, student-designed major, study abroad, teacher certification program. **Credit/placement by examination:** AP, CLEP, institutional tests. 8 credit hours maximum toward associate degree, 15 toward bachelor's. **Support services:** Learning center, remedial instruction, study skills assistance, tutoring, writing center.

Honors college/program. 25 freshmen admitted each fall and there is a special academic track that concludes with a leadership minor. Must submit a resume, essay and two letters of recommendation.

Majors. Agriculture: Business. **Biology:** General. **Business:** General, accounting, administrative services, business admin, finance, management information systems, office management. **Communications:** General. **Computer sciences:** Computer science. **Education:** Art, biology, business, chemistry, computer, drama/dance, early childhood, elementary, English, foreign languages, health, history, mathematics, middle, music, physical, reading, science, secondary, social science, Spanish, speech. **Foreign languages:** Spanish. **Health:** Nursing (RN), predental, premedicine, preveterinary. **History:** General. **Interdisciplinary:** Behavioral sciences, natural sciences. **Legal studies:** Prelaw. **Liberal arts:** Arts/sciences. **Math:** General. **Parks/recreation:** Health/fitness. **Physical sciences:** Chemistry. **Psychology:** General. **Social sciences:** General, political science. **Visual/performing arts:** Art, dramatic, studio arts, theater design.

Most popular majors. Biology 6%, business/marketing 36%, education 16%, health sciences 7%, liberal arts 13%.

Computing on campus. 235 workstations in dormitories, library, computer center, student center. Dormitories wired for high-speed internet access and linked to campus network. Commuter students can connect to campus network. Online course registration, online library, helpline, repair service, wireless network available.

Student life. Freshman orientation: Mandatory, $35 fee. Preregistration for classes offered. **Housing:** Guaranteed on-campus for all undergraduates. Coed dorms, single-sex dorms, special housing for disabled, apartments, wellness housing available. $50 fully refundable deposit. **Activities:** Bands, choral groups, dance, drama, film society, literary magazine, music ensembles, musical theater, student government, student newspaper.

Athletics. NAIA. **Intercollegiate:** Baseball M, basketball, cross-country, football (tackle) M, golf, rodeo, softball W, track and field, volleyball W, wrestling M. **Intramural:** Basketball, football (non-tackle), soccer, softball, volleyball. **Team name:** Blue Hawks.

Student services. Adult student services, career counseling, services for economically disadvantaged, student employment services, financial aid counseling, health services, minority student services, personal counseling, placement for graduates. **Physically disabled:** Services for visually, speech, hearing impaired. **Learning disabled:** Comprehensive services available.

Contact. E-mail: dsu.hawks@dickinsonstate.edu
Phone: (701) 483-2175 Toll-free number: (800) 279-4295
Fax: (701) 483-2409
Steve Glasser, Director of Enrollment Services, Dickinson State University, 291 Campus Drive, Dickinson, ND 58601-4896

Jamestown College
Jamestown, North Dakota
www.jc.edu **CB code: 6318**

- Private 4-year liberal arts college affiliated with Presbyterian Church (USA)
- Residential campus in large town
- 990 degree-seeking undergraduates: 5% part-time, 52% women, 2% African American, 2% Asian American, 2% Hispanic American, 1% Native American, 5% international
- 67% of applicants admitted
- 43% graduate within 6 years; 7% enter graduate study

General. Founded in 1883. Regionally accredited. **Degrees:** 172 bachelor's awarded. **Location:** 100 miles from Fargo and Bismarck. **Calendar:** Semester, limited summer session. **Full-time faculty:** 55 total; 51% have terminal degrees, 7% minority, 46% women. **Part-time faculty:** 32 total; 9% have terminal degrees, 3% minority, 47% women. **Class size:** 48% < 20, 43% 20-39, 7% 40-49, 2% 50-99, less than 1% >100.

Freshman class profile. 883 applied, 592 admitted, 270 enrolled.

Mid 50% test scores			
SAT critical reading:	420-530	GPA 2.0-2.99:	24%
SAT math:	440-540	Rank in top quarter:	45%
ACT composite:	20-25	Rank in top tenth:	18%
GPA 3.75 or higher:	29%	Return as sophomores:	74%
GPA 3.50-3.74:	18%	Out-of-state:	56%
GPA 3.0-3.49:	29%	Live on campus:	95%
		International:	8%

Basis for selection. Applicants with minimum 2.5 high school GPA or 18 ACT or 850 SAT (exclusive of writing) generally accepted. Applicants may be admitted on standard, conditional, or probationary basis. Interview recommended for all students. Audition required for music program; portfolio recommended for art program. **Homeschooled:** Letter of recommendation (nonparent) required.

High school preparation. College-preparatory program recommended. Recommended units include English 4, mathematics 3, social studies 3, science 4 and foreign language 2.

2009-2010 Annual costs. Tuition/fees (projected): $15,886. Room/board: $5,156. Books/supplies: $1,000. Personal expenses: $1,300.

2008-2009 Financial aid. **Need-based:** 243 full-time freshmen applied for aid; 188 were judged to have need; 187 of these received aid. Average need met was 85%. Average scholarship/grant was $9,840; average loan $3,794. 56% of total undergraduate aid awarded as scholarships/grants, 44% as loans/jobs. **Non-need-based:** Awarded to 616 full-time undergraduates, including 198 freshmen. Scholarships awarded for academics, alumni affiliation, art, athletics, leadership, music/drama, religious affiliation. **Additional information:** FAFSA must be received by March 15th for North Dakota residents to be considered for North Dakota state grants.

Application procedures. **Admission:** Priority date 7/1; no deadline. $20 fee, may be waived for applicants with need, free for online applicants. Admission notification on a rolling basis. **Financial aid:** Priority date 3/15; no closing date. FAFSA required. Applicants notified on a rolling basis starting 2/1.

Academics. **Special study options:** Combined bachelor's/graduate degree, cooperative education, double major, dual enrollment of high school students, honors, independent study, internships, liberal arts/career combination, student-designed major, study abroad, teacher certification program. **Credit/placement by examination:** AP, CLEP, IB, SAT, ACT, institutional tests. Unlimited number of hours of credit by examination may be counted toward degree. **Support services:** Learning center, reduced course load, remedial instruction, study skills assistance, tutoring, writing center.

Majors. **Biology:** General, biochemistry. **Business:** Accounting, business admin, finance, financial planning, hospitality admin, international, management information systems, managerial economics, marketing, tourism/travel. **Communications:** General. **Computer sciences:** Computer science, information technology. **Education:** Biology, chemistry, early childhood, elementary, English, history, mathematics, music, physical, secondary, special. **Foreign languages:** French, German, Spanish. **Health:** Clinical lab science, nursing (RN), radiologic technology/medical imaging. **History:** General. **Math:** General, applied. **Parks/recreation:** Sports admin. **Philosophy/religion:** Religion. **Physical sciences:** Chemistry. **Protective services:** Criminal justice. **Psychology:** General. **Social sciences:** Political science. **Visual/performing arts:** Dramatic, music performance, studio arts.

Most popular majors. Biology 10%, business/marketing 22%, education 15%, health sciences 20%, security/protective services 7%, social sciences 8%.

Computing on campus. 359 workstations in dormitories, library, computer center, student center. Dormitories wired for high-speed internet access and linked to campus network. Commuter students can connect to campus network. Online course registration, online library, helpline, repair service, student web hosting, wireless network available.

Student life. **Freshman orientation:** Mandatory. 3 days prior to classes. **Policies:** Weekly chapel service available on campus. Non-alcoholic nightclub available. **Housing:** Guaranteed on-campus for all undergraduates. Coed dorms, special housing for disabled, wellness housing available. $100 fully refundable deposit. **Activities:** Bands, campus ministries, choral groups, dance, drama, music ensembles, musical theater, student government, student newspaper, honor societies, Students of Service, Fellowship of Christian Athletes, Jimmie Janes, Jimmie Ambassadors, Ignition.

Athletics. NAIA. **Intercollegiate:** Baseball M, basketball, cheerleading M, cross-country, football (tackle) M, golf, soccer, softball W, track and field, volleyball W, wrestling. **Intramural:** Basketball, bowling, football (non-tackle), racquetball, soccer, softball, volleyball. **Team name:** Jimmies.

Student services. Alcohol/substance abuse counseling, chaplain/spiritual director, career counseling, student employment services, financial aid counseling, on-campus daycare, personal counseling, placement for graduates.

Contact. E-mail: admissions@jc.edu
Phone: (701) 252-3467 ext. 5562 Toll-free number: (800) 336-2554
Fax: (701) 253-4318
Judy Erickson, Director of Admissions, Jamestown College, 6081 College Lane, Jamestown, ND 58405

Mayville State University

Mayville, North Dakota
www.mayvillestate.edu **CB code: 6478**

- Public 4-year business and teachers college
- Residential campus in small town
- 789 degree-seeking undergraduates: 43% part-time, 62% women, 5% African American, 1% Asian American, 2% Hispanic American, 3% Native American, 3% international
- 31% graduate within 6 years; 10% enter graduate study

General. Founded in 1889. Regionally accredited. Every student issued laptop computer. All students complete an Information Technology Certificate as part of their bachelor's degree. **Degrees:** 108 bachelor's, 2 associate awarded. **ROTC:** Army, Air Force. **Location:** 60 miles from Fargo, 40 miles from Grand Forks. **Calendar:** Semester, limited summer session. **Full-time faculty:** 36 total; 47% have terminal degrees, 3% minority, 36% women. **Part-time faculty:** 31 total; 10% have terminal degrees, 3% minority, 68% women. **Class size:** 78% < 20, 22% 20-39, less than 1% 40-49. **Special facilities:** Nature area, business incubation technology center, head start and child development center, undergraduate research labs.

Freshman class profile. 204 applied, 178 admitted, 90 enrolled.

Mid 50% test scores		**Out-of-state:**	42%
ACT composite:	17-22	**Live on campus:**	95%
End year in good standing:	80%	**International:**	1%
Return as sophomores:	60%		

Basis for selection. Open admission, but selective for some programs. Admission to teacher education programs based on meeting GPA criteria, completion of PPST, and completion of specific prerequisites. ACT math scores used for placement. Interview recommended. **Homeschooled:** Transcript of courses and grades required. Must provide documentation equivalent to high school diploma.

High school preparation. College-preparatory program required. 17 units required; 18 recommended. Required and recommended units include English 4, mathematics 3, social studies 3, science 3 (laboratory 3) and foreign language 2. One unit of computer studies recommended.

2008-2009 Annual costs. Tuition/fees: $5,654; $7,646 out-of-state. Full-time tuition for South Dakota, Montana, Kansas, Michigan, Missouri, Nebraska, Manitoba, and Saskatchewan residents: $4,981. Full-time tuition for Minnesota residents: $4,162. All other states and Canadian provinces: $5,977. Room/board: $4,272. Books/supplies: $800. Personal expenses: $2,800.

2008-2009 Financial aid. **Need-based:** 86 full-time freshmen applied for aid; 79 were judged to have need; 79 of these received aid. Average need met was 100%. Average scholarship/grant was $2,815; average loan $2,591. 36% of total undergraduate aid awarded as scholarships/grants, 64% as loans/jobs. **Non-need-based:** Awarded to 278 full-time undergraduates, including 82 freshmen. Scholarships awarded for academics, athletics, leadership, minority status, music/drama, state residency.

Application procedures. **Admission:** No deadline. $35 fee. Admission notification on a rolling basis beginning on or about 1/1. **Financial aid:** Priority date 2/15; no closing date. FAFSA required. Applicants notified on a rolling basis starting 5/1; must reply within 2 week(s) of notification.

Academics. **Special study options:** Accelerated study, cooperative education, distance learning, double major, dual enrollment of high school students, internships, student-designed major, teacher certification program. 3-year business administration degree with cooperative education internship. **Credit/placement by examination:** AP, CLEP, institutional tests. 30 credit hours maximum toward bachelor's degree. **Support services:** Learning center, pre-admission summer program, remedial instruction, study skills assistance, tutoring.

Majors. **Biology:** General. **Business:** Business admin, office management. **Computer sciences:** General. **Education:** Biology, business, chemistry, elementary, English, geography, health, history, mathematics, physical, social science. **Family/consumer sciences:** Child care. **Health:** Athletic training, clinical lab science, predental, premedicine, prenursing, prepharmacy, preveterinary. **Legal studies:** Prelaw. **Math:** General. **Parks/recreation:** Health/fitness. **Physical sciences:** Chemistry. **Psychology:** General. **Social sciences:** General. **Other:** Health Education.

Most popular majors. Business/marketing 22%, education 50%, family/consumer sciences 7%, parks/recreation 8%, psychology 6%.

Computing on campus. PC or laptop required. Dormitories wired for high-speed internet access and linked to campus network. Commuter students can connect to campus network. Online course registration, online library, helpline, repair service, wireless network available.

Student life. **Freshman orientation:** Mandatory, $35 fee. Preregistration for classes offered. Half-day events held in June and July. **Housing:** Guaranteed on-campus for all undergraduates. Single-sex dorms, apartments, wellness housing available. $50 nonrefundable deposit. **Activities:** Bands, choral groups, drama, international student organizations, music ensembles, musical theater, radio station, student government, student newspaper, campus crusade, student education association, residence hall association, health and physical education club, student activities council, alumni ambassadors, minority/international student association.

Athletics. NAIA. **Intercollegiate:** Baseball M, basketball, football (tackle) M, softball W, volleyball W. **Intramural:** Badminton, basketball, bowling, football (non-tackle), golf, ice hockey M, racquetball, soccer, softball, table tennis, tennis, track and field, volleyball, weight lifting. **Team name:** Comets.

Student services. Adult student services, career counseling, student employment services, financial aid counseling, health services, on-campus daycare, personal counseling, placement for graduates, veterans' counselor. **Physically disabled:** Services for visually, hearing impaired.

Contact. E-mail: admit@mayvillestate.edu
Phone: (701) 788-4842 Toll-free number: (800) 437-4104
Fax: (701) 788-4748
Ray Gerszewski, Vice President for Student Affairs and Enrollment Management, Mayville State University, 330 Third Street, NE, Mayville, ND 58257-1299

Medcenter One College of Nursing

Bismarck, North Dakota
www.medcenterone.com/collegeofnursing CB code: 7051

- Private two-year upper-division nursing college
- Commuter campus in small city
- 61% of applicants admitted
- Application essay, interview required

General. Founded in 1988. Regionally accredited. Small college affiliated with a health system which provides a variety of clinical experiences. **Degrees:** 43 bachelor's awarded. **Articulation:** Agreement with Bismarck State College. **Location:** 190 miles from Fargo, 105 miles from Minot. **Calendar:** Semester, limited summer session. **Full-time faculty:** 10 total; 10% have terminal degrees, 10% minority, 100% women. **Part-time faculty:** 3 total; 100% women. **Class size:** 15% < 20, 23% 20-39, 62% 40-49.

Student profile. 91 degree-seeking undergraduates. 88 applied as first time-transfer students, 54 admitted, 48 enrolled. 100% entered as juniors. 80% transferred from two-year, 20% transferred from four-year institutions.

Women:	86%	**Part-time:**	2%
African American:	1%	**Out-of-state:**	7%
Hispanic American:	1%	**25 or older:**	35%
Native American:	1%		

Basis for selection. High school transcript, college transcript, application essay, interview required. All students must transfer with minimum 64 credits of general education prerequisites, including 5 prerequisite science courses. Students not required to complete all prerequisites prior to applying but must have a minimum of 2 required sciences completed. Credits not completed at time of application must be completed prior to starting 300 level nursing courses fall semester. Overall college GPA, science GPA important. Transfer accepted as sophomores, juniors, seniors.

2008-2009 Annual costs. Tuition/fees: $10,017. Books/supplies: $1,069. Personal expenses: $1,000.

Financial aid. Need-based: 89 applied for aid; 72 were judged to have need; 72 of these received aid. Average need met was 96%. 46% of total undergraduate aid awarded as scholarships/grants, 54% as loans/jobs. **Non-need-based:** Awarded to 25 undergraduates.

Application procedures. Admission: Priority date 11/7. $40 fee. Application must be submitted on paper. **Financial aid:** Priority date 3/1, no deadline. Applicants notified on a rolling basis starting 6/1; must reply within 2 weeks of notification.

Academics. Special study options: Internships. **Credit/placement by examination:** CLEP, institutional tests. 30 credit hours maximum toward bachelor's degree.

Majors. Health: Nursing (RN).

Computing on campus. 17 workstations in library, computer center. Online library, wireless network available.

Student life. Activities: Student government, Student Nurse Association, Student Organization.

Student services. Financial aid counseling, health services, personal counseling, placement for graduates.

Contact. E-mail: msmith@mohs.org
Phone: (701) 323-6833 Fax: (701) 323-6289
Mary Smith, Director of Student Services, Medcenter One College of Nursing, 512 North 7th Street, Bismarck, ND 58501-4425

Minot State University

Minot, North Dakota
www.minotstateu.edu CB code: 6479

- Public 4-year university and liberal arts college
- Commuter campus in large town
- 3,172 degree-seeking undergraduates: 29% part-time, 61% women
- 260 graduate students
- 72% of applicants admitted
- SAT or ACT (ACT writing optional) required
- 31% graduate within 6 years

General. Founded in 1913. Regionally accredited. **Degrees:** 498 bachelor's, 1 associate awarded; master's offered. **Location:** 105 miles from Bismarck, 225 miles from Grand Forks. **Calendar:** Semester, limited summer session. **Full-time faculty:** 176 total; 53% have terminal degrees, 8% minority, 53% women. **Part-time faculty:** 86 total; 2% minority, 63% women. **Class size:** 65% < 20, 31% 20-39, 3% 40-49, 2% 50-99. **Special facilities:** Natural history museum, center for persons with disabilities, Native American collection, observatory, rural crime and justice center.

Freshman class profile. 643 applied, 460 admitted, 437 enrolled.

Mid 50% test scores		**GPA 3.0-3.49:**	37%
SAT critical reading:	440-530	**GPA 2.0-2.99:**	24%
SAT math:	430-510	**Return as sophomores:**	68%
SAT writing:	390-520	**Out-of-state:**	10%
ACT composite:	19-24	**Live on campus:**	21%
GPA 3.75 or higher:	20%	**International:**	11%
GPA 3.50-3.74:	18%		

Basis for selection. Secondary school record very important; ACT/SAT test scores, ACT composite score must be no less than 17; those below the recommended composite score are reviewed on an individual basis.

High school preparation. 13 units required. Required units include English 4, mathematics 3, social studies 3, science 3 (laboratory 3). Science should include at least 3 units of biology, chemistry, physics, or physical science. Social science should not include consumer education, cooperative marketing, orientation to social science, or marriage/family. Math must be algebra I or above.

2008-2009 Annual costs. Tuition/fees: $5,043; $12,022 out-of-state. Room/board: $4,450. Books/supplies: $900.

2007-2008 Financial aid. Need-based: 401 full-time freshmen applied for aid; 259 were judged to have need; 258 of these received aid. Average need met was 85%. Average scholarship/grant was $3,216; average loan $3,170. 38% of total undergraduate aid awarded as scholarships/grants, 62% as loans/jobs. **Non-need-based:** Awarded to 545 full-time undergraduates, including 137 freshmen. Scholarships awarded for academics, alumni affiliation, art, athletics, minority status, music/drama, state residency. **Additional information:** Scholarship application deadline is 2/15.

Application procedures. Admission: Priority date 4/1; no deadline. $35 fee. Admission notification on a rolling basis. **Financial aid:** Priority date 3/15; no closing date. FAFSA, institutional form required. Applicants notified on a rolling basis starting 5/1; must reply within 2 week(s) of notification.

Academics. Wide variety of distance courses offered. **Special study options:** Cooperative education, distance learning, double major, dual enrollment of high school students, ESL, external degree, honors, independent study, internships, liberal arts/career combination, student-designed major, study abroad, teacher certification program. **Credit/placement by examination:** AP, CLEP, institutional tests. **Support services:** Learning center, reduced course load, remedial instruction, study skills assistance, tutoring, writing center.

Majors. Biology: General. **Business:** Accounting, business admin, finance, international, management information systems, marketing. **Communications:** Broadcast journalism, radio/tv. **Communications technology:** General. **Computer sciences:** General. **Education:** Art, biology, business, chemistry, Deaf/hearing impaired, elementary, English, foreign languages, French,

German, history, mathematics, mentally handicapped, music, physical, physics, science, social science, Spanish, speech impaired. **Foreign languages:** General, French, German, Spanish. **Health:** Clinical lab science, communication disorders, health care admin, medical radiologic technology/radiation therapy, nursing (RN), substance abuse counseling. **History:** General. **Liberal arts:** Arts/sciences. **Math:** General. **Parks/recreation:** Sports admin. **Physical sciences:** General, chemistry, geology, physics. **Protective services:** Criminal justice. **Psychology:** General. **Public administration:** Social work. **Social sciences:** General, economics, geography, sociology. **Visual/performing arts:** Art, arts management, dramatic, music performance.

Most popular majors. Business/marketing 24%, education 22%, health sciences 15%, liberal arts 6%, security/protective services 10%.

Computing on campus. 300 workstations in dormitories, library, computer center, student center. Dormitories wired for high-speed internet access and linked to campus network. Commuter students can connect to campus network. Online course registration, online library, helpline, repair service, wireless network available.

Student life. Freshman orientation: Mandatory, $35 fee. Preregistration for classes offered. **Policies:** First-year students required to live in university housing (exceptions exist). **Housing:** Guaranteed on-campus for freshmen. Coed dorms, single-sex dorms, apartments, wellness housing available. $100 deposit. **Activities:** Marching band, campus ministries, choral groups, drama, international student organizations, music ensembles, musical theater, radio station, student government, student newspaper, TV station, disability awareness organization, Democratic Party, Republican Party, Intervarsity Christian Fellowship, Native American cultural awareness club, United Campus Ministries, Catholic student association, international awareness club, Student Education of Hard of Hearing/Deaf, National Student Speech/Hearing Association.

Athletics. NAIA. **Intercollegiate:** Baseball M, basketball, cheerleading M, cross-country, football (tackle) M, golf, softball W, track and field, volleyball W. **Intramural:** Basketball, bowling, ice hockey M, racquetball, softball, track and field, volleyball. **Team name:** Beavers.

Student services. Adult student services, alcohol/substance abuse counseling, chaplain/spiritual director, career counseling, services for economically disadvantaged, student employment services, financial aid counseling, health services, minority student services, personal counseling, placement for graduates, veterans' counselor, women's services. **Physically disabled:** Services for visually, speech, hearing impaired.

Contact. E-mail: askmsu@minotstateu.edu
Phone: (701) 858-3350 Toll-free number: (800) 777-0750
Fax: (701) 839-6933
Kevin Harmon, Dean of Admissions, Minot State University, 500 University Avenue West, Minot, ND 58707-5002

North Dakota State University

Fargo, North Dakota — **CB member**
www.ndsu.edu — **CB code: 6474**

- Public 4-year university
- Residential campus in small city
- 10,799 degree-seeking undergraduates: 7% part-time, 43% women, 2% African American, 1% Asian American, 1% Hispanic American, 1% Native American, 4% international
- 1,962 degree-seeking graduate students
- 80% of applicants admitted
- SAT or ACT (ACT writing optional) required
- 51% graduate within 6 years

General. Founded in 1890. Regionally accredited. **Degrees:** 1,763 bachelor's awarded; master's, doctoral, first professional offered. **ROTC:** Army, Air Force. **Location:** 250 miles from Minneapolis-St. Paul. **Calendar:** Semester, limited summer session. **Full-time faculty:** 612 total; 80% have terminal degrees, 18% minority, 33% women. **Part-time faculty:** 128 total; 28% have terminal degrees, 7% minority, 46% women. **Class size:** 36% < 20, 43% 20-39, 7% 40-49, 9% 50-99, 5% >100. **Special facilities:** Fine arts center, regional studies institute, biotechnology institute, engineering computer center, center for writers, wellness center, technology park, downtown campus for art and architecture, equine center.

Freshman class profile. 5,678 applied, 4,542 admitted, 2,661 enrolled.

Mid 50% test scores			
SAT critical reading:	480-660	Rank in top quarter:	40%
SAT math:	510-670	Rank in top tenth:	16%
ACT composite:	20-25	End year in good standing:	75%
GPA 3.75 or higher:	26%	Return as sophomores:	81%
GPA 3.50-3.74:	21%	Out-of-state:	65%
GPA 3.0-3.49:	32%	Live on campus:	91%
GPA 2.0-2.99:	20%	International:	2%

Basis for selection. All applicants must have completed college preparatory program in high school. Admission based on overall performance in high school, performance in college preparatory courses and standardized test scores. Admission to nursing, veterinary technology, architecture, pharmacy, electrical engineering, mechanical engineering programs based on academic record and test scores. Campus visit recommended for all students. Audition required for music programs. Secondary admission requirements for many programs. **Homeschooled:** Applicants advised to work with local school district for issuance of a Certificate of Graduation.

High school preparation. College-preparatory program required. 13 units required. Required units include English 4, mathematics 3, social studies 3, science 3 (laboratory 3).

2008-2009 Annual costs. Tuition/fees: $6,226; $15,015 out-of-state. Tuition for for MSEP and WUE state residents: $7,895. Room/board: $6,220. Books/supplies: $650. Personal expenses: $2,230.

2007-2008 Financial aid. Need-based: 2,037 full-time freshmen applied for aid; 1,365 were judged to have need; 1,336 of these received aid. Average need met was 38%. Average scholarship/grant was $3,729; average loan $3,853. 30% of total undergraduate aid awarded as scholarships/grants, 70% as loans/jobs. **Non-need-based:** Awarded to 2,519 full-time undergraduates, including 808 freshmen. Scholarships awarded for academics, alumni affiliation, art, athletics, leadership, minority status, music/drama, ROTC, state residency.

Application procedures. Admission: Closing date 8/15 (receipt date). $35 fee. Admission notification on a rolling basis. **Financial aid:** Closing date 3/15. FAFSA required. Applicants notified on a rolling basis starting 3/15.

Academics. Special study options: Combined bachelor's/graduate degree, cooperative education, cross-registration, distance learning, double major, dual enrollment of high school students, ESL, honors, independent study, internships, student-designed major, study abroad, teacher certification program. Tri-college, collaborative enrollment (ND University System) Pathway program with ND sister institution with remedial coursework for students not meeting admission requirements. **Credit/placement by examination:** AP, CLEP, IB, ACT, institutional tests. **Support services:** Reduced course load, remedial instruction, study skills assistance, tutoring, writing center.

Majors. Agriculture: General, agribusiness operations, animal sciences, communications, crop production, economics, equestrian studies, food science, horticultural science, mechanization, plant protection, soil science, turf management. **Architecture:** Environmental design, landscape. **Area/ethnic studies:** Women's. **Biology:** General, Biochemistry/biophysics and molecular biology, biotechnology, botany, microbiology, zoology. **Business:** Accounting, business admin, communications, construction management, finance, financial planning, hospitality admin, management information systems, marketing. **Communications:** Health, journalism, public relations. **Computer sciences:** Computer science. **Conservation:** Management/policy. **Education:** Agricultural, biology, chemistry, elementary, English, family/consumer sciences, French, German, health, history, mathematics, music, physical, physics, science, social science, social studies, Spanish, speech. **Engineering:** Agricultural, civil, computer, construction, electrical, industrial, manufacturing, mechanical. **Family/consumer sciences:** Clothing/textiles, family studies. **Foreign languages:** Classics, French, Spanish. **Health:** Clinical lab science, dietetics, nursing (RN), preveterinary, radiologic technology/medical imaging, respiratory therapy technology, veterinary technology/assistant. **History:** General, public archives. **Interdisciplinary:** Global studies. **Legal studies:** Prelaw. **Liberal arts:** Humanities. **Math:** General, statistics. **Parks/recreation:** General, sports admin. **Philosophy/religion:** Philosophy. **Physical sciences:** Chemistry, geology, physics. **Protective services:** Criminal justice, emergency management/homeland security. **Psychology:** General, psychometrics. **Social sciences:** General, anthropology, economics, political science, sociology. **Visual/performing arts:** Art, dramatic, interior design.

Most popular majors. Agriculture 7%, biology 6%, business/marketing 16%, engineering/engineering technologies 13%, family/consumer sciences 6%, health sciences 12%.

Computing on campus. 500 workstations in dormitories, library, computer center, student center. Dormitories wired for high-speed internet access. Online course registration, online library, helpline, repair service, student web hosting, wireless network available.

Student life. Freshman orientation: Available, $10 fee. Offered in June, July or August and day before classes. **Policies:** No alcoholic beverages allowed on campus, code of student conduct. **Housing:** Guaranteed on-campus for freshmen. Coed dorms, single-sex dorms, apartments, fraternity/sorority housing, wellness housing available. $50 partly refundable deposit. Housing is handicap accessible. **Activities:** Bands, choral groups, dance, drama, international student organizations, music ensembles, radio station, student government, student newspaper, Newman Center, Lutheran Student Fellowship, United Campus Ministry, College Republicans, College Democrats, Circle-K, Mortar Board, Black Student Alliance, Native American student association.

Athletics. NCAA. **Intercollegiate:** Baseball M, basketball, cross-country, football (tackle) M, golf, soccer W, softball W, track and field, volleyball W, wrestling M. **Intramural:** Basketball, football (non-tackle), softball, volleyball. **Team name:** Bison.

Student services. Adult student services, alcohol/substance abuse counseling, career counseling, student employment services, financial aid counseling, health services, minority student services, on-campus daycare, personal counseling, veterans' counselor. **Physically disabled:** Services for visually, speech, hearing impaired. **Learning disabled:** Comprehensive services available.

Contact. E-mail: ndsu.admission@ndsu.edu
Phone: (701) 231-8643 Toll-free number: (800) 488-6378
Fax: (701) 231-8802
Jobey Lichtblau, Director of Admission, North Dakota State University, Ceres Hall 124, Fargo, ND 58105-5454

Rasmussen College: Fargo

Fargo, North Dakota
www.rasmussen.edu **CB code: 3343**

- For-profit 4-year career college
- Commuter campus in small city
- 505 full-time, degree-seeking undergraduates

General. Degrees: 1 bachelor's, 164 associate awarded. **Calendar:** Quarter, extensive summer session. **Full-time faculty:** 9 total. **Part-time faculty:** 15 total.

Basis for selection. Open admission, but selective for some programs. Some programs require placement examinations.

2008-2009 Annual costs. Tuition/fees: $16,800.

Application procedures. Admission: No deadline. $60 fee. Admission notification on a rolling basis. **Financial aid:** No deadline. FAFSA, institutional form required. Applicants notified on a rolling basis.

Academics. Special study options: Distance learning, double major, independent study, internships, liberal arts/career combination. **Credit/placement by examination:** AP, CLEP, IB, institutional tests. 45 credit hours maximum toward associate degree, 90 toward bachelor's. 50% of a student's program must be completed through coursework at Rasmussen College. **Support services:** Learning center, remedial instruction, study skills assistance, tutoring, writing center.

Majors. Business: Accounting, business admin. **Other:** Criminal justice (general / other).

Computing on campus. 100 workstations in library, computer center, student center. Online course registration, online library, helpline, wireless network available.

Student life. Freshman orientation: Mandatory. **Activities:** Student government.

Student services. Adult student services, career counseling, services for economically disadvantaged, student employment services, financial aid counseling, placement for graduates.

Contact. E-mail: peter.limvere@rasmussen.edu
Phone: (701) 277-3889 Toll-free number: (800) 817-0009
Fax: (701) 277-5604
Peter Limvere, Director of Admissions, Rasmussen College: Fargo, 4012 19th Avenue SW, Fargo, ND 58103

Trinity Bible College

Ellendale, North Dakota
www.trinitybiblecollege.edu **CB code: 0356**

- Private 4-year Bible college affiliated with Assemblies of God
- Residential campus in rural community

General. Founded in 1948. Regionally accredited. **Location:** 60 miles from Jamestown, 38 miles from Aberdeen. **Calendar:** Semester.

Annual costs/financial aid. Tuition/fees (2008-2009): $12,940. Room/board: $4,590. Books/supplies: $800. Personal expenses: $1,636. Need-based financial aid available to full-time and part-time students.

Contact. Phone: (701) 349-3621
Director of Enrollment Services, 50 6th Avenue South, Ellendale, ND 58436-7150

University of Mary

Bismarck, North Dakota
www.umary.edu **CB code: 6428**

- Private 4-year university affiliated with Roman Catholic Church
- Residential campus in small city
- 2,052 degree-seeking undergraduates: 20% part-time, 61% women
- 765 degree-seeking graduate students
- 81% of applicants admitted
- SAT or ACT (ACT writing optional) required
- 57% graduate within 6 years; 23% enter graduate study

General. Founded in 1959. Regionally accredited. Additional centers in Bismarck and Fargo. **Degrees:** 500 bachelor's, 1 associate awarded; master's, doctoral offered. **Location:** 6 miles from downtown. **Calendar:** Semester, limited summer session. **Full-time faculty:** 100 total; 47% have terminal degrees, 1% minority, 55% women. **Part-time faculty:** 180 total; 20% have terminal degrees, 11% minority, 49% women. **Class size:** 57% < 20, 32% 20-39, 2% 40-49, 7% 50-99, 1% >100. **Special facilities:** Climbing wall.

Freshman class profile. 1,020 applied, 830 admitted, 374 enrolled.

Mid 50% test scores		**Rank in top tenth:**	14%
ACT composite:	20-26	**End year in good standing:**	95%
GPA 3.75 or higher:	28%	**Return as sophomores:**	69%
GPA 3.50-3.74:	18%	**Out-of-state:**	36%
GPA 3.0-3.49:	35%	**Live on campus:**	93%
GPA 2.0-2.99:	19%	**International:**	1%
Rank in top quarter:	40%		

Basis for selection. Automatic acceptance for applicants in top half of class with 2.5 GPA and 19 ACT. Applicants not meeting these standards may be admitted with specific conditions for enrollment. Audition required for music program; interview recommended for academically weak students. **Homeschooled:** State high school equivalency certificate required.

High school preparation. College-preparatory program recommended. Recommended units include English 4, mathematics 3, social studies 4 and science 3.

2009-2010 Annual costs. Tuition/fees (projected): $12,584. Room/board: $4,940. Books/supplies: $900. Personal expenses: $920.

2007-2008 Financial aid. Need-based: 336 full-time freshmen applied for aid; 270 were judged to have need; 270 of these received aid. 33% of total undergraduate aid awarded as scholarships/grants, 67% as loans/jobs. **Non-need-based:** Awarded to 2,470 full-time undergraduates, including 571 freshmen. Scholarships awarded for academics, athletics, leadership, music/drama, state residency.

Application procedures. Admission: No deadline. $25 fee, may be waived for applicants with need. Admission notification on a rolling basis. Must reply by May 1 or within 4 week(s) if notified thereafter. **Financial aid:** Priority date 3/15; no closing date. FAFSA required. Must reply within 2 week(s) of notification.

Academics. Special study options: Accelerated study, combined bachelor's/graduate degree, cooperative education, distance learning, double major, dual enrollment of high school students, external degree, independent study, internships, liberal arts/career combination, semester at sea, study abroad, teacher certification program, weekend college. **Credit/placement by examination:** AP, CLEP, IB, ACT, institutional tests. 32 credit hours maximum toward associate degree, 96 toward bachelor's. **Support services:** Learning center, reduced course load, remedial instruction, study skills assistance, tutoring, writing center.

Majors. Biology: General. **Business:** Accounting, business admin, communications, finance, management science. **Communications:** General, public relations. **Computer sciences:** General, information systems. **Education:** Biology, business, early childhood, elementary, English, history, mathematics, mentally handicapped, music, physical, social science. **Engineering:**

General. **Health:** Athletic training, clinical lab science, medical radiologic technology/radiation therapy, nursing (RN), respiratory therapy technology, substance abuse counseling. **Math:** General. **Parks/recreation:** Exercise sciences, health/fitness, sports admin. **Philosophy/religion:** Religion. **Protective services:** Criminal justice, law enforcement admin. **Psychology:** General. **Public administration:** Social work. **Social sciences:** General. **Theology:** Theology. **Visual/performing arts:** Music performance.

Most popular majors. Business/marketing 39%, education 12%, health sciences 22%, liberal arts 8%.

Computing on campus. 235 workstations in dormitories, library, computer center. Dormitories wired for high-speed internet access and linked to campus network. Commuter students can connect to campus network. Online course registration, online library, student web hosting, wireless network available.

Student life. **Freshman orientation:** Mandatory. Preregistration for classes offered. Two-day orientation for freshmen at beginning of fall term. **Housing:** Guaranteed on-campus for freshmen. Single-sex dorms, special housing for disabled, apartments, wellness housing available. $100 fully refundable deposit. **Activities:** Bands, campus ministries, choral groups, dance, drama, international student organizations, literary magazine, music ensembles, musical theater, radio station, student government, student newspaper, campus ministry, Spurs, Circle-K, student nurses association, Young Democrats, College Republicans, student education association, social work club, music educators national conference.

Athletics. NCAA. **Intercollegiate:** Baseball M, basketball, cross-country, football (tackle) M, golf, soccer, softball W, tennis, track and field, volleyball W, wrestling M. **Intramural:** Badminton, basketball, bowling, football (non-tackle), golf, racquetball, soccer, softball, swimming, table tennis, tennis, volleyball, weight lifting. **Team name:** Marauders.

Student services. Adult student services, alcohol/substance abuse counseling, chaplain/spiritual director, career counseling, services for economically disadvantaged, student employment services, financial aid counseling, health services, minority student services, personal counseling, placement for graduates, veterans' counselor. **Physically disabled:** Services for hearing impaired.

Contact. E-mail: marauder@umary.edu
Phone: (701) 355-8030 Toll-free number: (800) 288-6279
Fax: (701) 255-7687
Cheryl Kalberer, Director of Admissions, University of Mary, 7500 University Drive, Bismarck, ND 58504-9652

University of North Dakota

Grand Forks, North Dakota
www.und.edu **CB code: 6878**

- Public 4-year university
- Residential campus in small city
- 10,129 degree-seeking undergraduates: 14% part-time, 45% women; 1% African American, 1% Asian American, 1% Hispanic American, 3% Native American, 4% international
- 2,619 degree-seeking graduate students
- 75% of applicants admitted
- SAT or ACT (ACT writing optional) required
- 54% graduate within 6 years; 18% enter graduate study

General. Founded in 1883. Regionally accredited. **Degrees:** 1,836 bachelor's awarded; master's, doctoral, first professional offered. **ROTC:** Army, Air Force. **Location:** 320 miles from Minneapolis-St. Paul, 150 miles from Winnipeg, Canada. **Calendar:** Semester, extensive summer session. **Full-time faculty:** 565 total; 79% have terminal degrees, 11% minority, 39% women. **Part-time faculty:** 64 total; 34% have terminal degrees, 53% women. **Class size:** 40% < 20, 45% 20-39, 6% 40-49, 6% 50-99, 3% >100. **Special facilities:** Art museum, atmospherium, supercomputing center, native media center, American Indian center, biomedical research center, climate change and CO2 center, instructional and learning technologies center, peace studies center, renewable energy center, rural health center, children and family services training center, clinical education center, environmental training institute, ecological studies institute, hydrogen technology center, Native American aging resource center, behavioral research center, Indian law center, wellness center.

Freshman class profile. 4,069 applied, 3,067 admitted, 1,942 enrolled.

Mid 50% test scores		**End year in good standing:**	82%
ACT composite:	20-25	**Return as sophomores:**	78%
GPA 3.75 or higher:	29%	**Out-of-state:**	61%
GPA 3.50-3.74:	18%	**Live on campus:**	89%
GPA 3.0-3.49:	32%	**International:**	1%
GPA 2.0-2.99:	21%	**Fraternities:**	10%
Rank in top quarter:	40%	**Sororities:**	9%
Rank in top tenth:	16%		

Basis for selection. High school record and test scores most important. **Homeschooled:** Transcript of courses and grades required.

High school preparation. College-preparatory program required. 13 units required. Required and recommended units include English 4, mathematics 3, social studies 3, science 3 (laboratory 3) and foreign language 1. Math must be algebra I and above.

2008-2009 Annual costs. Tuition/fees: $6,513; $15,325 out-of-state. Tuition for South Dakota, Montana, Saskatchewan, Manitoba residents: $7,914. Room/board: $5,735. Books/supplies: $800. Personal expenses: $2,070.

2007-2008 Financial aid. **Need-based:** 1,577 full-time freshmen applied for aid; 1,105 were judged to have need; 1,085 of these received aid. Average need met was 37%. Average scholarship/grant was $3,267; average loan $4,512. 22% of total undergraduate aid awarded as scholarships/grants, 78% as loans/jobs. **Non-need-based:** Awarded to 2,607 full-time undergraduates, including 738 freshmen. Scholarships awarded for academics, alumni affiliation, art, athletics, job skills, leadership, music/drama, religious affiliation, ROTC.

Application procedures. **Admission:** No deadline. $35 fee. Admission notification on a rolling basis beginning on or about 9/1. **Financial aid:** Priority date 3/15; no closing date. FAFSA required. Applicants notified on a rolling basis starting 5/15; must reply within 4 week(s) of notification.

Academics. **Special study options:** Accelerated study, combined bachelor's/graduate degree, cooperative education, cross-registration, distance learning, double major, dual enrollment of high school students, ESL, exchange student, external degree, honors, independent study, internships, liberal arts/career combination, semester at sea, student-designed major, study abroad, teacher certification program, weekend college. **Credit/placement by examination:** AP, CLEP, IB, ACT, institutional tests. **Support services:** Learning center, pre-admission summer program, reduced course load, remedial instruction, study skills assistance, tutoring, writing center.

Majors. **Area/ethnic studies:** Chinese, Native American. **Biology:** General, animal behavior, wildlife. **Business:** Accounting, accounting/finance, entrepreneurial studies, finance, human resources, management information systems, managerial economics, marketing, operations. **Communications:** General. **Communications technology:** Graphics. **Computer sciences:** General, systems analysis. **Education:** Art, business, early childhood, elementary, mathematics, middle, music, physical, sales/marketing, science, social science. **Engineering:** Chemical, civil, electrical, environmental, geological, mechanical. **Engineering technology:** Industrial, occupational safety. **Family/consumer sciences:** Food/nutrition. **Foreign languages:** General, classics, French, German, Scandinavian, Spanish. **Health:** Athletic training, audiology/speech pathology, clinical lab science, clinical nutrition, communication disorders, cytotechnology, dietetics, music therapy, nursing (RN), vocational rehab counseling. **History:** General. **Interdisciplinary:** Global studies. **Math:** General. **Parks/recreation:** Facilities management. **Philosophy/religion:** Philosophy, religion. **Physical sciences:** General, atmospheric science, chemistry, geology, physics. **Protective services:** Criminal justice, forensics. **Psychology:** General. **Public administration:** General, social work. **Social sciences:** General, anthropology, economics, geography, political science, sociology. **Transportation:** Air traffic control, airline/commercial pilot, aviation, aviation management, flight instructor. **Visual/performing arts:** General, art, dramatic, graphic design, music performance. **Other:** Fisheries and wildlife biology.

Most popular majors. Business/marketing 14%, education 9%, health sciences 11%, trade and industry 16%.

Computing on campus. 1,100 workstations in dormitories, library, computer center, student center. Dormitories wired for high-speed internet access and linked to campus network. Commuter students can connect to campus network. Online course registration, online library, helpline, student web hosting, wireless network available.

Student life. **Freshman orientation:** Available, $15 fee. Preregistration for classes offered. Held weekend before school opens in August. **Housing:** Guaranteed on-campus for freshmen. Coed dorms, single-sex dorms, special housing for disabled, apartments, fraternity/sorority housing, wellness housing available. $250 partly refundable deposit, deadline 5/1. **Activities:** Bands, campus ministries, choral groups, dance, drama, film society, international student organizations, literary magazine, music ensembles, musical theater, opera, radio station, student government, student newspaper, symphony orchestra, TV station, over 230 organizations available.

Athletics. NCAA. **Intercollegiate:** Baseball M, basketball, cross-country, diving, football (tackle) M, golf, ice hockey, soccer W, softball W, swimming, tennis W, track and field, volleyball W. **Intramural:** Badminton, basketball, cross-country, golf, ice hockey, racquetball, soccer W, softball W, swimming, tennis W, track and field, volleyball W. **Team name:** Fighting Sioux.

Student services. Adult student services, alcohol/substance abuse counseling, chaplain/spiritual director, career counseling, services for economically disadvantaged, student employment services, financial aid counseling, health services, legal services, minority student services, on-campus daycare, personal counseling, placement for graduates, veterans' counselor, women's services. **Physically disabled:** Services for visually, speech, hearing impaired.

Contact. E-mail: enrollmentservices@mail.und.nodak.edu
Phone: (701) 777-3821 Toll-free number: (800) 225-5863
Fax: (701) 777-2721
Deborah Melby, Director, University of North Dakota, Twamley Hall Room 205 264 Centennial Drive Stop 8357, Grand Forks, ND 58202-8357

Valley City State University

Valley City, North Dakota
www.vcsu.edu **CB code: 6480**

- Public 4-year liberal arts and teachers college
- Residential campus in small town
- 900 degree-seeking undergraduates: 25% part-time, 54% women, 3% African American, 1% Asian American, 2% Hispanic American, 2% Native American, 5% international
- 119 degree-seeking graduate students
- 97% of applicants admitted
- SAT or ACT (ACT writing optional) required
- 50% graduate within 6 years

General. Founded in 1889. Regionally accredited. All full-time undergraduate students are provided a laptop computer. **Degrees:** 170 bachelor's awarded; master's offered. **Location:** 60 miles from Fargo. **Calendar:** Semester, limited summer session. **Full-time faculty:** 57 total; 54% have terminal degrees, 5% minority, 47% women. **Part-time faculty:** 32 total; 34% have terminal degrees, 59% women. **Special facilities:** Planetarium, medicine wheel, undergraduate research labs.

Freshman class profile. 262 applied, 255 admitted, 156 enrolled.

Mid 50% test scores		Rank in top quarter:	24%
SAT math:	370-510	Rank in top tenth:	9%
ACT composite:	18-23	Out-of-state:	25%
GPA 3.75 or higher:	20%	Live on campus:	90%
GPA 3.50-3.74:	16%	International:	8%
GPA 3.0-3.49:	29%	Fraternities:	1%
GPA 2.0-2.99:	35%	Sororities:	1%

Basis for selection. School achievement record and test scores important. **Homeschooled:** Transcript of courses and grades required.

High school preparation. 13 units required. Required and recommended units include English 4, mathematics 3, social studies 3, science 3 (laboratory 3) and foreign language 1.

2008-2009 Annual costs. Tuition/fees: $5,781; $12,691 out-of-state. Full-time tuition for South Dakota, Montana, Manitoba, Saskatchewan residents: $5,172. Full-time tuition for WUE students: $6,209. Room/board: $4,248. Books/supplies: $800. Personal expenses: $1,827.

2008-2009 Financial aid. Need-based: 160 full-time freshmen applied for aid; 134 were judged to have need; 134 of these received aid. Average need met was 86%. Average scholarship/grant was $3,364; average loan $2,614. 40% of total undergraduate aid awarded as scholarships/grants, 60% as loans/jobs. **Non-need-based:** Awarded to 303 full-time undergraduates, including 134 freshmen. Scholarships awarded for academics, alumni affiliation, athletics, leadership, minority status, music/drama.

Application procedures. Admission: No deadline. $35 fee. Admission notification on a rolling basis beginning on or about 9/15. **Financial aid:** Priority date 3/15; no closing date. FAFSA required. Applicants notified on a rolling basis starting 2/1; must reply within 4 week(s) of notification.

Academics. Special study options: Combined bachelor's/graduate degree, cooperative education, distance learning, double major, dual enrollment of high school students, internships, liberal arts/career combination, student-designed major, study abroad, teacher certification program. **Credit/placement by examination:** AP, CLEP, SAT, ACT, institutional tests. **Support services:** Reduced course load, study skills assistance, tutoring.

Majors. Biology: General. **Business:** Business admin, human resources, office management. **Computer sciences:** General. **Education:** Art, biology, business, chemistry, elementary, English, health, history, instructional media, mathematics, music, physical, science, secondary, social science, Spanish, technology/industrial arts, trade/industrial, voc/tech. **Foreign languages:** Spanish. **Health:** Predental, premedicine, prenursing, prepharmacy, preveterinary. **History:** General. **Legal studies:** Prelaw. **Liberal arts:** Arts/sciences. **Math:** General. **Parks/recreation:** Health/fitness. **Physical sciences:** Chemistry. **Psychology:** General. **Social sciences:** General. **Visual/performing arts:** Art.

Most popular majors. Business/marketing 21%, education 47%.

Computing on campus. 925 workstations in dormitories, library, computer center, student center. Dormitories wired for high-speed internet access and linked to campus network. Commuter students can connect to campus network. Online course registration, online library, helpline, repair service, student web hosting, wireless network available.

Student life. Freshman orientation: Available, $10 fee. Half-day sessions for students with concurrent sessions for parents; held on 2 separate days in June. **Policies:** Tobacco-free campus. **Housing:** Guaranteed on-campus for all undergraduates. Coed dorms, single-sex dorms, special housing for disabled, apartments, fraternity/sorority housing, wellness housing available. $50 fully refundable deposit. Apartments for students with children. **Activities:** Bands, choral groups, drama, international student organizations, literary magazine, music ensembles, student government, student newspaper, symphony orchestra, inter-residence hall council, inter-fraternity/sorority council, inter-varsity Christian fellowship, Music Educators National Conference, Student National Education Association, Newman Club, Association of Information Technology Professionals, Faith Lutheran student club.

Athletics. NAIA. **Intercollegiate:** Baseball M, basketball, football (tackle) M, golf, softball W, volleyball W. **Intramural:** Basketball, bowling, cross-country, football (non-tackle), golf, ice hockey, racquetball, softball, track and field, volleyball. **Team name:** Vikings.

Student services. Career counseling, student employment services, financial aid counseling, health services, on-campus daycare, personal counseling, placement for graduates, veterans' counselor.

Contact. E-mail: enrollment.services@vcsu.edu
Phone: (701) 845-7101 Toll-free number: (800) 532-8641 ext. 7101
Fax: (701) 845-7299
Charlene Stenson, Director of Enrollment Services, Valley City State University, 101 College Street SW, Valley City, ND 58072-4098

Ohio

Allegheny Wesleyan College
Salem, Ohio
www.awc.edu **CB code: 4120**

- Private 4-year Bible college affiliated with Allegheny Wesleyan Methodist Connection
- Residential campus in small town

General. Accredited by ABHE. **Calendar:** Semester.

Annual costs/financial aid. Tuition/fees (2008-2009): $5,550. Room/board: $3,300. Books/supplies: $550. Personal expenses: $800.

Contact. Phone: (330) 337-6403
Director of Admissions, 2161 Woodside Road, Salem, OH 44460-9598

Antioch University McGregor
Yellow Springs, Ohio
www.mcgregor.edu **CB code: 4527**

- Private 4-year university, branch campus and liberal arts college
- Commuter campus in small town
- 160 degree-seeking undergraduates: 58% part-time, 76% women
- 470 degree-seeking graduate students
- Application essay, interview required

General. Founded in 1988. Regionally accredited. **Degrees:** 30 bachelor's awarded; master's offered. **Location:** 18 miles from Dayton. **Calendar:** Quarter, limited summer session. **Full-time faculty:** 18 total. **Part-time faculty:** 43 total. **Special facilities:** Nature reserve.

Basis for selection. Applicants must be over 21. Recommendations and motivation most important.

2008-2009 Annual costs. Tuition/fees: $14,760. Books/supplies: $1,800.

Application procedures. Admission: Priority date 6/1; deadline 11/1. $45 fee. Admission notification on a rolling basis. **Financial aid:** No deadline. Applicants notified on a rolling basis.

Academics. Special study options: Combined bachelor's/graduate degree, double major, independent study, student-designed major, weekend college. **Credit/placement by examination:** CLEP. 45 credit hours maximum toward bachelor's degree. **Support services:** Reduced course load, writing center.

Majors. Business: Business admin, human resources. **Health:** Health services. **Liberal arts:** Arts/sciences, humanities. **Math:** General. **Public administration:** Human services.

Most popular majors. Business/marketing 43%, liberal arts 24%, psychology 26%.

Computing on campus. 35 workstations in computer center. Commuter students can connect to campus network. Online course registration, online library, helpline, wireless network available.

Student life. Freshman orientation: Mandatory, $25 fee. **Activities:** Radio station, student newspaper.

Student services. Adult student services, financial aid counseling.

Contact. E-mail: sas@mcgregor.edu
Phone: (937) 769-1818 Fax: (937) 769-1804
Oscar Robinson, Director of Admissions, Antioch University McGregor, 900 Dayton Street, Yellow Springs, OH 45387

Art Academy of Cincinnati
Cincinnati, Ohio
www.artacademy.edu **CB code: 1002**

- Private 4-year visual arts college
- Commuter campus in large city
- 159 degree-seeking undergraduates: 4% part-time, 64% women, 4% African American, 1% Asian American, 1% Hispanic American, 1% international
- 1 degree-seeking graduate students
- 21% of applicants admitted
- SAT or ACT (ACT writing optional), application essay required

General. Founded in 1869. Regionally accredited. **Degrees:** 33 bachelor's awarded; master's offered. **Location:** One mile from downtown. **Calendar:** Semester, limited summer session. **Full-time faculty:** 14 total; 57% women. **Part-time faculty:** 30 total. **Special facilities:** Glass-blowing facility, three art galleries.

Freshman class profile. 541 applied, 116 admitted, 49 enrolled.

Mid 50% test scores			
SAT critical reading:	480-600	Out-of-state:	36%
SAT math:	420-570	Live on campus:	51%
ACT composite:	18-24	International:	2%

Basis for selection. Academic background based upon GPA and ACT/SAT scores; portfolio review and interview very important; 1-page artist statement and 1 letter of recommendation required. Portfolio required for all; interview required for those within 150 miles of campus. **Home-schooled:** Transcript of courses and grades, state high school equivalency certificate required.

High school preparation. 12 units recommended. Recommended units include English 4, mathematics 3, social studies 1 and science 2. 3-4 units art recommended.

2008-2009 Annual costs. Tuition/fees: $21,300. Room/board: $6,800. Books/supplies: $1,200.

Financial aid. Non-need-based: Scholarships awarded for academics, art.

Application procedures. Admission: Priority date 3/1; deadline 6/30 (postmark date). No application fee. Admission notification on a rolling basis. **Financial aid:** Priority date 4/1; no closing date. FAFSA required. Applicants notified on a rolling basis starting 3/1.

Academics. Special study options: Cross-registration, double major, exchange student, independent study, internships, New York semester, student-designed major, study abroad. **Credit/placement by examination:** AP, CLEP, institutional tests. **Support services:** Learning center, study skills assistance, tutoring, writing center.

Majors. Visual/performing arts: Art history/conservation, design, drawing, illustration, painting, photography, printmaking, sculpture, studio arts.

Computing on campus. 40 workstations in computer center. Dormitories wired for high-speed internet access.

Student life. Freshman orientation: Mandatory. Preregistration for classes offered. Held 5 days before school begins. **Housing:** Coed dorms available. $250 nonrefundable deposit, deadline 6/1. **Activities:** Film society, literary magazine, student government.

Student services. Career counseling, student employment services, financial aid counseling, personal counseling, placement for graduates, veterans' counselor. **Physically disabled:** Services for hearing impaired.

Contact. E-mail: admissions@artacademy.edu
Phone: (513) 562-8740 Toll-free number: (800) 323-5692
Fax: (513) 562-8778
John Wadell, Director of Admissions, Art Academy of Cincinnati, 1212 Jackson Street, Cincinnati, OH 45202

Ashland University
Ashland, Ohio
www.ashland.edu **CB code: 1021**

- Private 4-year university and liberal arts college affiliated with Brethren Church
- Residential campus in large town

- 2,594 degree-seeking undergraduates: 9% part-time, 51% women, 10% African American, 1% Asian American, 3% Hispanic American, 2% international
- 2,645 degree-seeking graduate students
- 82% of applicants admitted
- SAT or ACT (ACT writing optional) required
- 61% graduate within 6 years

General. Founded in 1878. Regionally accredited. **Degrees:** 564 bachelor's, 9 associate awarded; master's, doctoral, first professional offered. **Location:** 60 miles from Cleveland, 80 miles from Columbus. **Calendar:** Semester, limited summer session. **Full-time faculty:** 234 total; 84% have terminal degrees, 6% minority, 42% women. **Part-time faculty:** 347 total; 33% have terminal degrees, 4% minority, 53% women. **Class size:** 58% < 20, 42% 20-39, less than 1% 40-49, less than 1% 50-99. **Special facilities:** Centers for public affairs, business and economic research, convocation, numismatic, nonviolence, educational improvement, entrepreneurial studies; institute for middle level education.

Freshman class profile. 2,766 applied, 2,266 admitted, 585 enrolled.

Mid 50% test scores		**Rank in top quarter:**	42%
SAT critical reading:	440-560	**Rank in top tenth:**	16%
SAT math:	460-570	**End year in good standing:**	78%
SAT writing:	440-550	**Return as sophomores:**	71%
ACT composite:	19-24	**Out-of-state:**	6%
GPA 3.75 or higher:	20%	**Live on campus:**	87%
GPA 3.50-3.74:	16%	**International:**	1%
GPA 3.0-3.49:	32%	**Fraternities:**	2%
GPA 2.0-2.99:	32%	**Sororities:**	4%

Basis for selection. School achievement record most important; test scores also important. Counselor's recommendation considered. Interview recommended for all; audition recommended for music, theater programs; portfolio recommended for art. **Homeschooled:** Transcript of courses and grades required.

High school preparation. College-preparatory program recommended. Required and recommended units include English 3-4, mathematics 2-3, social studies 2-3, history 1, science 2-3, foreign language 2 and academic electives 1.

2008-2009 Annual costs. Tuition/fees: $24,342. Room/board: $8,876. Books/supplies: $800. Personal expenses: $1,461.

2008-2009 Financial aid. Need-based: 553 full-time freshmen applied for aid; 499 were judged to have need; 499 of these received aid. Average need met was 90%. Average scholarship/grant was $17,268; average loan $4,244. 61% of total undergraduate aid awarded as scholarships/grants, 39% as loans/jobs. **Non-need-based:** Scholarships awarded for academics, alumni affiliation, art, athletics, job skills, leadership, minority status, music/drama, religious affiliation.

Application procedures. Admission: No deadline. No application fee. Admission notification on a rolling basis beginning on or about 9/15. Must reply by May 1 or within 4 week(s) if notified thereafter. **Financial aid:** Priority date 3/15; no closing date. FAFSA, institutional form required. Applicants notified on a rolling basis starting 3/15; must reply within 5 week(s) of notification.

Academics. Special study options: Double major, ESL, honors, independent study, internships, student-designed major, study abroad, teacher certification program, weekend college. Pre-MBA courses for graduated nonbusiness majors, bachelor's degree completion program for RNs, teacher licensure for those with non-teaching degrees, pre-seminary. **Credit/placement by examination:** AP, CLEP, IB, SAT, ACT, institutional tests. 32 credit hours maximum toward associate degree, 32 toward bachelor's. **Support services:** Learning center, study skills assistance, tutoring, writing center.

Majors. Area/ethnic studies: American. **Biology:** General. **Business:** General, accounting, business admin, finance, franchise operations, management information systems, marketing, purchasing. **Communications:** General, journalism, radio/tv. **Computer sciences:** Computer science. **Conservation:** Environmental science. **Education:** Art, biology, business, chemistry, drama/dance, early childhood, English, family/consumer sciences, French, kindergarten/preschool, mathematics, middle, music, physical, science, social studies, Spanish, special. **Family/consumer sciences:** Family systems, food/nutrition. **Foreign languages:** French, Spanish. **Health:** Athletic training, nursing admin, recreational therapy. **History:** General. **Legal studies:** Prelaw. **Liberal arts:** Arts/sciences. **Math:** General. **Parks/recreation:** General, facilities management, sports admin. **Philosophy/religion:** Philosophy, religion. **Physical sciences:** Chemistry, geology, physics, planetary. **Protective services:** Law enforcement admin. **Psychology:** General. **Public administration:** Social work. **Social sciences:** Economics, political science, sociology. **Theology:** Bible, missionary, religious ed. **Visual/performing arts:** Commercial/advertising art, dramatic, music performance, music theory/composition, studio arts.

Most popular majors. Business/marketing 23%, education 33%.

Computing on campus. 1,500 workstations in dormitories, library, computer center, student center. Dormitories wired for high-speed internet access and linked to campus network. Commuter students can connect to campus network. Online course registration, online library, helpline, repair service, wireless network available.

Student life. Freshman orientation: Available, $100 fee. Preregistration for classes offered. One-day program usually held in June and July. **Housing:** Guaranteed on-campus for all undergraduates. Coed dorms, single-sex dorms, apartments, fraternity/sorority housing, wellness housing available. $200 fully refundable deposit, deadline 5/1. Scholar hall available. Apartments available to seniors. **Activities:** Bands, campus ministries, choral groups, dance, drama, international student organizations, literary magazine, music ensembles, musical theater, radio station, student government, student newspaper, symphony orchestra, TV station, Christian Fellowship, Newman Club, Fellowship of Christian Athletes, international club, black student union, campus activities board, community care, adventure club, Republican/Democratic club.

Athletics. NCAA. **Intercollegiate:** Baseball M, basketball, cheerleading, cross-country, diving, football (tackle) M, golf, soccer, softball W, swimming, tennis W, track and field, volleyball W, wrestling M. **Intramural:** Badminton, basketball, bowling, football (non-tackle), golf, racquetball, soccer, softball, swimming, table tennis, tennis, volleyball, wrestling M. **Team name:** Eagles.

Student services. Adult student services, alcohol/substance abuse counseling, chaplain/spiritual director, career counseling, student employment services, financial aid counseling, health services, minority student services, personal counseling, placement for graduates, veterans' counselor. **Physically disabled:** Services for visually, speech, hearing impaired.

Contact. E-mail: enrollme@ashland.edu
Phone: (419) 289-5052 Toll-free number: (800) 882-1548 ext. 5052
Fax: (419) 289-5999
Thomas Mansperger, Director of Admissions, Ashland University, 401 College Avenue, Ashland, OH 44805-9981

Baldwin-Wallace College

Berea, Ohio — **CB member**
www.bw.edu — **CB code: 1050**

- Private 4-year liberal arts college affiliated with United Methodist Church
- Residential campus in large town
- 3,535 degree-seeking undergraduates: 12% part-time, 57% women, 7% African American, 1% Asian American, 3% Hispanic American, 1% international
- 674 degree-seeking graduate students
- 67% of applicants admitted
- SAT or ACT (ACT writing optional), application essay required
- 73% graduate within 6 years

General. Founded in 1845. Regionally accredited. Campus in Beachwood, offering evening and Saturday classes for bachelor's and master's degrees in business, professional development and executive education. **Degrees:** 753 bachelor's awarded; master's offered. **ROTC:** Army, Air Force. **Location:** 15 miles from Cleveland. **Calendar:** Semester, limited summer session. **Full-time faculty:** 164 total; 80% have terminal degrees, 9% minority, 40% women. **Part-time faculty:** 238 total; 17% have terminal degrees, 10% minority, 47% women. **Class size:** 53% < 20, 46% 20-39, less than 1% 40-49, less than 1% 50-99. **Special facilities:** Observatory, 2 art galleries, 2 theaters, conservatory of music, 2 dance studios, cybercafe, arboretum, Lyceum Square (historical site).

Freshman class profile. 3,321 applied, 2,213 admitted, 738 enrolled.

Mid 50% test scores		**Rank in top quarter:**	47%
SAT critical reading:	500-610	**Rank in top tenth:**	27%
SAT math:	490-600	**End year in good standing:**	93%
SAT writing:	490-600	**Return as sophomores:**	83%
ACT composite:	21-26	**Out-of-state:**	16%
GPA 3.75 or higher:	32%	**Live on campus:**	84%
GPA 3.50-3.74:	22%	**Fraternities:**	14%
GPA 3.0-3.49:	28%	**Sororities:**	25%
GPA 2.0-2.99:	16%		

Basis for selection. Academic achievement (preferably 3.2 GPA) and class rank (preferably top 30%) most important. Test scores used to support data from high school record. 23 ACT, 550 SAT verbal, 550 SAT math recommended. Applicants must be graduates of accredited secondary school. Test optional for full-time, first-time freshmen (not home schooled or international) for admissions. In lieu of test scores, recent graded writing sample required. Test scores required for all enrolling students for use in placement and research. Interview recommended for all; audition required for music, music education, music theater, and music therapy programs; portfolio recommended for art program. **Homeschooled:** Statement describing homeschool structure and mission, transcript of courses and grades, letter of recommendation (nonparent) required.

High school preparation. College-preparatory program required. 17 units required; 24 recommended. Required and recommended units include English 4, mathematics 3-4, social studies 3-4, history 1, science 3-4 (laboratory 2), foreign language 2 and computer science 3. Some flexibility in choice of subjects permitted.

2008-2009 Annual costs. Tuition/fees: $23,524. Conservatory tuition is higher. Room/board: $7,728. Books/supplies: $1,000. Personal expenses: $1,500.

2008-2009 Financial aid. **Need-based:** 668 full-time freshmen applied for aid; 586 were judged to have need; 586 of these received aid. Average need met was 93%. Average scholarship/grant was $14,522; average loan $4,389. 69% of total undergraduate aid awarded as scholarships/grants, 31% as loans/jobs. **Non-need-based:** Awarded to 962 full-time undergraduates, including 160 freshmen. Scholarships awarded for academics, alumni affiliation, leadership, minority status, music/drama, religious affiliation.

Application procedures. **Admission:** Priority date 3/1; no deadline. $25 fee, may be waived for applicants with need, free for online applicants. Admission notification on a rolling basis beginning on or about 10/1. Must reply by May 1 or within 3 week(s) if notified thereafter. New Student Fee of $200 refundable until May 1. **Financial aid:** Priority date 5/1, closing date 9/1. FAFSA required. Applicants notified on a rolling basis starting 2/14.

Academics. Weekend classes limited to nontraditional students. **Special study options:** Accelerated study, combined bachelor's/graduate degree, cross-registration, distance learning, double major, dual enrollment of high school students, ESL, exchange student, honors, independent study, internships, liberal arts/career combination, semester at sea, student-designed major, study abroad, teacher certification program, Washington semester, weekend college. 3-2 in engineering with Case Western Reserve University, Columbia University (NY) and Washington University (MO); 3-2 in Social Work with Case Western Reserve University; 3/2 Accounting MBA, 3/2 Human Resources MBA and 3/2 Computer Science/Info. Systems MBA Programs. **Credit/placement by examination:** AP, CLEP, IB, SAT, ACT, institutional tests. **Support services:** Learning center, reduced course load, remedial instruction, study skills assistance, tutoring, writing center.

Majors. **Biology:** General, exercise physiology. **Business:** Accounting, business admin, finance, human resources, international, marketing, small business admin. **Communications:** General, media studies, public relations. **Computer sciences:** Computer science, networking, systems analysis. **Conservation:** Economics. **Education:** General, early childhood, learning disabled, middle, music. **Foreign languages:** French, German, Spanish. **Health:** Athletic training, communication disorders, health care admin, music therapy, predental, premedicine, prepharmacy, preveterinary. **History:** General. **Interdisciplinary:** Biological/physical sciences, global studies, neuroscience. **Math:** General. **Parks/recreation:** Health/fitness, sports admin. **Philosophy/religion:** Philosophy, religion. **Physical sciences:** Chemistry, physics. **Protective services:** Criminal justice. **Psychology:** General. **Social sciences:** Econometrics, economics, political science, sociology. **Visual/performing arts:** Acting, art, art history/conservation, film/cinema, music history, music performance, music theory/composition, piano/organ, studio arts, theater arts management, voice/opera. **Other:** Organizational leadership, Pre-Engineering.

Most popular majors. Biology 6%, business/marketing 25%, communications/journalism 6%, education 12%, visual/performing arts 9%.

Computing on campus. 543 workstations in dormitories, library, computer center, student center. Dormitories wired for high-speed internet access and linked to campus network. Commuter students can connect to campus network. Online course registration, online library, helpline, student web hosting, wireless network available.

Student life. **Freshman orientation:** Mandatory, $75 fee. Preregistration for classes offered. Two-day program held in June, July, August. **Policies:** All full-time students required to live on campus first and second year. Residency exemptions made for commuting students living with families. **Housing:** Guaranteed on-campus for freshmen. Coed dorms, single-sex dorms, special housing for disabled, apartments, fraternity/sorority housing available. Sprout Houses (for single mothers and children), Carmel Living and Learning Center. **Activities:** Bands, campus ministries, choral groups, dance, drama, film society, international student organizations, literary magazine, music ensembles, Model UN, musical theater, opera, radio station, student government, student newspaper, symphony orchestra, TV station, Campus Crusade for Christ, Hillel, Newman Student Organization, College Democrats, College Republicans, Black Student Alliance, Hispanic American Student Association, Middle Eastern Student Alliance, Certified Peer Educators, Habitat for Humanity.

Athletics. NCAA. **Intercollegiate:** Baseball M, basketball, cross-country, diving, football (tackle) M, golf, soccer, softball W, swimming, tennis, track and field, volleyball W, wrestling M. **Intramural:** Badminton, basketball, football (non-tackle), football (tackle) M, golf, racquetball, soccer, softball, tennis, volleyball, wrestling M. **Team name:** Yellow Jackets.

Student services. Adult student services, alcohol/substance abuse counseling, chaplain/spiritual director, career counseling, student employment services, financial aid counseling, health services, minority student services, personal counseling. **Physically disabled:** Services for visually, speech, hearing impaired.

Contact. E-mail: admission@bw.edu
Phone: (440) 826-2222 Toll-free number: (877) 292-7759
Fax: (440) 826-3830
Susan Dileno, VP of Enrollment Management, Baldwin-Wallace College, 275 Eastland Road, Berea, OH 44017-2088

Bluffton University

Bluffton, Ohio
www.bluffton.edu **CB code: 1067**

- Private 4-year liberal arts college affiliated with Mennonite Church
- Residential campus in small town
- 957 degree-seeking undergraduates: 3% part-time, 54% women, 4% African American, 1% Asian American, 2% Hispanic American, 2% international
- 115 degree-seeking graduate students
- 58% of applicants admitted
- SAT or ACT (ACT writing optional) required
- 63% graduate within 6 years

General. Founded in 1899. Regionally accredited. Christian faith, values, and service to others in the Anabaptist, peace church tradition. **Degrees:** 253 bachelor's awarded; master's offered. **Location:** 15 miles from Lima, 75 miles from Toledo. **Calendar:** Semester, limited summer session. **Full-time faculty:** 64 total; 73% have terminal degrees, 9% minority, 33% women. **Part-time faculty:** 49 total; 8% have terminal degrees, 6% minority, 43% women. **Class size:** 57% < 20, 35% 20-39, 6% 40-49, less than 1% 50-99, less than 1% >100. **Special facilities:** Nature preserve.

Freshman class profile. 1,492 applied, 858 admitted, 272 enrolled.

Mid 50% test scores		**GPA 2.0-2.99:**	28%
SAT critical reading:	450-580	**Rank in top quarter:**	40%
SAT math:	450-570	**Rank in top tenth:**	16%
ACT composite:	19-25	**Return as sophomores:**	76%
GPA 3.75 or higher:	26%	**Out-of-state:**	9%
GPA 3.50-3.74:	13%	**Live on campus:**	97%
GPA 3.0-3.49:	33%	**International:**	1%

Basis for selection. Class rank, school achievement record, and test scores very important. Campus visit and interview strongly recommended. Essay required for academically weak students; audition and portfolio required for scholarships in music and art. **Homeschooled:** Interview required.

High school preparation. College-preparatory program recommended. 16 units recommended. Recommended units include English 4, mathematics 3, social studies 3, science 3 and foreign language 3.

2008-2009 Annual costs. Tuition/fees: $22,920. Room/board: $7,596. Books/supplies: $1,150. Personal expenses: $1,430.

2008-2009 Financial aid. **Need-based:** 261 full-time freshmen applied for aid; 242 were judged to have need; 242 of these received aid. Average need met was 97%. Average scholarship/grant was $16,137; average loan $4,682. 54% of total undergraduate aid awarded as scholarships/grants, 46% as loans/jobs. **Non-need-based:** Awarded to 144 full-time undergraduates, including 36 freshmen. Scholarships awarded for academics, art, job skills, leadership, minority status, music/drama, state residency.

Application procedures. **Admission:** Priority date 5/1; deadline 8/20 (receipt date). $20 fee, may be waived for applicants with need, free for online applicants. Admission notification on a rolling basis beginning on or about 6/1. **Financial aid:** Priority date 5/1, closing date 10/1. FAFSA required. Applicants notified on a rolling basis starting 3/1; must reply within 3 week(s) of notification.

Academics. **Special study options:** Accelerated study, combined bachelor's/graduate degree, double major, dual enrollment of high school students, honors, independent study, internships, liberal arts/career combination, student-designed major, study abroad, teacher certification program, Washington semester. Degree-completion program for working adults 25 years and older. **Credit/placement by examination:** AP, CLEP, SAT, ACT, institutional tests. 20 credit hours maximum toward bachelor's degree. **Support services:** Learning center, remedial instruction, tutoring, writing center.

Majors. **Biology:** General. **Business:** Accounting, business admin, management information systems, organizational behavior. **Communications:** General. **Computer sciences:** Computer science, information systems, information technology. **Education:** Art, biology, business, chemistry, early childhood, elementary, English, family/consumer sciences, health, history, kindergarten/preschool, mathematics, mentally handicapped, middle, music, physical, physics, science, secondary, social studies, special. **Family/consumer sciences:** General, clothing/textiles, food/nutrition. **Foreign languages:** Spanish. **Health:** Premedicine. **History:** General. **Interdisciplinary:** Peace/conflict. **Math:** General. **Parks/recreation:** Facilities management, health/fitness, sports admin. **Philosophy/religion:** Religion. **Physical sciences:** Chemistry, physics. **Protective services:** Criminal justice. **Psychology:** General. **Public administration:** Social work. **Social sciences:** General, economics, sociology. **Theology:** Youth ministry. **Visual/performing arts:** Art.

Most popular majors. Business/marketing 32%, education 20%, public administration/social services 6%, visual/performing arts 6%.

Computing on campus. 125 workstations in dormitories, library, computer center, student center. Dormitories wired for high-speed internet access and linked to campus network. Commuter students can connect to campus network. Online course registration, online library, helpline, repair service, student web hosting, wireless network available.

Student life. **Freshman orientation:** Mandatory. Preregistration for classes offered. Fall orientation begins Friday before classes and continues through first week of classes. Additional 1-day event held over summer; students can choose 1 of 4 dates. **Policies:** No alcoholic beverages or tobacco allowed on campus. Honor system applies to all student activities. Students should feel comfortable with emphasis on faith and values. Voluntary chapel service once each week. All traditional undergraduate students required to live on campus or commute from home. **Housing:** Guaranteed on-campus for all undergraduates. Coed dorms, single-sex dorms available. **Activities:** Bands, campus ministries, choral groups, dance, drama, international student organizations, literary magazine, music ensembles, musical theater, radio station, student government, student newspaper, departmental clubs, Brothers and Sisters in Christ, peace club, Habitat for Humanity, Fellowship of Christian Athletes, African American student organization, peer awareness leaders, College Republicans, Young Democrats.

Athletics. NCAA. **Intercollegiate:** Baseball M, basketball, cheerleading M, cross-country, football (tackle) M, soccer, softball W, tennis, track and field, volleyball W. **Intramural:** Basketball, bowling, football (non-tackle), softball, volleyball. **Team name:** Beavers.

Student services. Alcohol/substance abuse counseling, chaplain/spiritual director, career counseling, student employment services, financial aid counseling, health services, minority student services, personal counseling, placement for graduates. **Physically disabled:** Services for visually, hearing impaired. **Learning disabled:** Comprehensive services available.

Contact. E-mail: admissions@bluffton.edu
Phone: (419) 358-3257 Toll-free number: (800) 488-3257
Fax: (419) 358-3081
Chris Jebsen, Director of Admissions, Bluffton University, 1 University Drive, Bluffton, OH 45817-2104

Bowling Green State University

Bowling Green, Ohio — **CB member**
www.bgsu.edu — **CB code: 1069**

- Public 4-year university
- Residential campus in large town
- 14,596 degree-seeking undergraduates: 6% part-time, 53% women, 10% African American, 1% Asian American, 3% Hispanic American, 1% Native American, 2% international
- 2,488 degree-seeking graduate students
- 87% of applicants admitted
- SAT and SAT Subject Tests or ACT (ACT writing optional) required
- 58% graduate within 6 years

General. Founded in 1910. Regionally accredited. **Degrees:** 3,310 bachelor's awarded; master's, doctoral offered. **ROTC:** Army, Air Force. **Location:** 23 miles from Toledo. **Calendar:** Semester, limited summer session. **Full-time faculty:** 851 total; 75% have terminal degrees, 16% minority, 44% women. **Part-time faculty:** 171 total; 5% minority, 52% women. **Class size:** 40% < 20, 48% 20-39, 6% 40-49, 5% 50-99, less than 1% >100. **Special facilities:** Planetarium, film theater, sound recording archives, popular culture library, marine biology laboratory, educational memorabilia center.

Freshman class profile. 11,111 applied, 9,712 admitted, 3,098 enrolled.

Mid 50% test scores		**GPA 2.0-2.99:**	36%
SAT critical reading:	440-560	**Rank in top quarter:**	33%
SAT math:	450-550	**Rank in top tenth:**	12%
SAT writing:	440-540	**End year in good standing:**	74%
ACT composite:	19-24	**Return as sophomores:**	73%
GPA 3.75 or higher:	16%	**Out-of-state:**	12%
GPA 3.50-3.74:	14%	**Live on campus:**	90%
GPA 3.0-3.49:	34%	**International:**	1%

Basis for selection. Admissions decision based on high school sixth semester GPA and ACT or SAT test scores. Interview recommended for all; audition required for music; portfolio required for art programs. Essays required for honors program. **Homeschooled:** Transcript of courses and grades required.

High school preparation. College-preparatory program recommended. Recommended units include English 4, mathematics 3, social studies 3, science 3 (laboratory 2), foreign language 2 and visual/performing arts 1.

2008-2009 Annual costs. Tuition/fees: $9,060; $16,368 out-of-state. Room/board: $7,220. Books/supplies: $1,174. Personal expenses: $2,344.

2007-2008 Financial aid. **Need-based:** 3,000 full-time freshmen applied for aid; 2,231 were judged to have need; 2,163 of these received aid. Average need met was 73%. Average scholarship/grant was $6,213; average loan $6,365. 36% of total undergraduate aid awarded as scholarships/grants, 64% as loans/jobs. **Non-need-based:** Awarded to 2,504 full-time undergraduates, including 572 freshmen. Scholarships awarded for academics, alumni affiliation, art, athletics, leadership, minority status, music/drama, ROTC, state residency.

Application procedures. **Admission:** Priority date 2/1; deadline 7/15 (postmark date). $40 fee, may be waived for applicants with need. Admission notification on a rolling basis beginning on or about 10/1. Must reply by 5/1. **Financial aid:** No deadline. FAFSA required. Applicants notified on a rolling basis starting 4/15; must reply within 3 week(s) of notification.

Academics. Evening degree programs and career counseling offered for adults in the greater community. **Special study options:** Accelerated study, combined bachelor's/graduate degree, cooperative education, cross-registration, distance learning, double major, dual enrollment of high school students, exchange student, honors, independent study, internships, liberal arts/career combination, student-designed major, study abroad, teacher certification program, Washington semester. **Credit/placement by examination:** AP, CLEP, SAT, ACT, institutional tests. 30 hours toward bachelor's degree through portfolio program. **Support services:** Learning center, preadmission summer program, reduced course load, remedial instruction, study skills assistance, tutoring, writing center.

Majors. **Architecture:** Environmental design, interior. **Area/ethnic studies:** African, American, Asian, women's. **Biology:** General, bacteriology, ecology, marine. **Business:** General, accounting, fashion, finance, hospitality admin, international, logistics, management information systems, managerial economics, tourism promotion, tourism/travel. **Communications:** General, broadcast journalism, journalism, public relations. **Computer sciences:** General. **Conservation:** Management/policy, water/wetlands/marine. **Education:** General, art, biology, business, Deaf/hearing impaired, drama/dance, English, foreign languages, French, kindergarten/preschool, mathematics, middle, music, physical, sales/marketing, science, social studies, special, voc/tech. **Engineering technology:** Aerospace, construction, electrical, electromechanical, industrial, mechanical, quality control. **Family/consumer sciences:** Aging, child development, family studies, food/nutrition. **Foreign languages:** Classics, French, German, Latin, Russian, Spanish. **Health:** Athletic training, clinical lab science, communication disorders, community health, dietetics, environmental health, health care admin, nursing (RN). **History:** General. **Interdisciplinary:** Gerontology, neuroscience. **Legal studies:** Prelaw. **Liberal arts:** Arts/sciences. **Math:** General, applied, statistics. **Parks/recreation:** General, sports admin. **Philosophy/religion:** Philosophy. **Physical sciences:** Chemistry, geology, physics. **Protective services:** Criminal justice. **Psychology:** General. **Public administration:** General, social work. **Social sciences:** Applied economics, economics, geography, international relations, political science, sociology. **Transportation:** Aviation management. **Visual/performing arts:** Acting, art, art history/conservation, cinematography, design, dramatic, film/cinema, jazz, music history, music performance, music theory/composition, piano/organ, studio arts, theater design, voice/opera. **Other:** Digital/computer art, Ethnic Studies, Exercise, movement, Information systems auditing, Popular Culture, Technology, Telecommunications.

Most popular majors. Business/marketing 15%, education 21%, English 6%, health sciences 8%, visual/performing arts 9%.

Computing on campus. 1,563 workstations in dormitories, library, computer center, student center. Dormitories wired for high-speed internet access and linked to campus network. Commuter students can connect to campus network. Online course registration, helpline, repair service, wireless network available.

Student life. Freshman orientation: Available. Preregistration for classes offered. Normally held in summer. **Housing:** Guaranteed on-campus for freshmen. Coed dorms, fraternity/sorority housing, wellness housing available. $200 deposit, deadline 5/1. No-alcohol wings, nonsmoking areas, residential housing communities available. **Activities:** Bands, choral groups, dance, drama, film society, international student organizations, literary magazine, music ensembles, musical theater, radio station, student government, student newspaper, symphony orchestra, TV station, Active Christians Today, African Peoples Association, Asian Communities, United Latino Student Union, World Student Association, Women's Group, College Democrats, College Republicans, Habitat for Humanity, Environmental Action Group.

Athletics. NCAA. **Intercollegiate:** Baseball M, basketball, cross-country, diving, football (tackle) M, golf, gymnastics W, ice hockey M, soccer, softball W, swimming, tennis, track and field, volleyball W. **Intramural:** Basketball, cross-country, football (non-tackle), golf, handball, ice hockey, racquetball, soccer, softball, swimming, tennis, track and field, volleyball. **Team name:** Falcons.

Student services. Adult student services, alcohol/substance abuse counseling, career counseling, services for economically disadvantaged, student employment services, financial aid counseling, health services, legal services, minority student services, personal counseling, placement for graduates, veterans' counselor, women's services. **Physically disabled:** Services for visually, speech, hearing impaired.

Contact. E-mail: admissions@bgsu.edu
Phone: (419) 372-2478 Toll-free number: (866) Cho-osebgsu
Fax: (419) 372-6955
Gary Swegan, Assistant Vice Provost/Director of Admissions, Bowling Green State University, 110 McFall Center, Bowling Green, OH 43403-0085

Bryant & Stratton College: Eastlake

Eastlake, Ohio
www.bryantstratton.edu **CB code: 3251**

- For-profit 4-year business college
- Commuter campus in small town
- 709 degree-seeking undergraduates
- Interview required

General. Degrees: 1 bachelor's, 9 associate awarded. **Location:** 15 miles from downtown Cleveland. **Calendar:** Continuous, limited summer session. **Full-time faculty:** 20 total. **Part-time faculty:** 35 total.

Basis for selection. Open admission. Student's evaluation and diagnostic tests must show qualification for at least pre-college, preparatory math and English courses. **Learning Disabled:** Students with learning disability must provide instructional effectiveness plan from high school counselor.

2008-2009 Annual costs. Tuition/fees: $15,230. Books/supplies: $1,800. Personal expenses: $300.

2007-2008 Financial aid. Non-need-based: Scholarships awarded for academics.

Application procedures. Admission: Closing date 9/12 (receipt date). $35 fee. Admission notification on a rolling basis. **Financial aid:** No deadline. FAFSA required. Applicants notified on a rolling basis.

Academics. ACTIVUM learning system facilitates students in developing technical and career-based skills through field trips, portfolio presentations, computer simulations and internship opportunities. **Special study options:** Accelerated study, distance learning, double major, dual enrollment of high school students, independent study, internships. Professional skills center offers medical coding courses and computer certification. **Credit/placement by examination:** AP, CLEP, institutional tests. 12 credit hours maximum toward associate degree, 12 toward bachelor's. **Support services:** Remedial instruction, study skills assistance, tutoring.

Majors. Business: Business admin.

Computing on campus. 400 workstations in library, computer center. Commuter students can connect to campus network. Online library, helpline, repair service, wireless network available.

Student life. Freshman orientation: Mandatory. Preregistration for classes offered. Various 4-hour sessions over 1-2 days prior to start of each term. **Activities:** Student government, student newspaper, student council, Institute of Management Accountants, PC users group, campus ambassador society.

Athletics. NJCAA. **Intercollegiate:** Soccer M. **Team name:** Bobcats.

Student services. Adult student services, student employment services, financial aid counseling, placement for graduates. **Physically disabled:** Services for visually, speech, hearing impaired.

Contact. E-mail: mejohnson@bryantstratton.edu
Phone: (440) 510-1112 Fax: (440) 306-2015
Melanie Johnson, Director of Admissions, Bryant & Stratton College: Eastlake, 35350 Curtis Boulevard, Eastlake, OH 44095

Bryant & Stratton College: Parma

Parma, Ohio
www.bryantstratton.edu **CB code: 0577**

- For-profit 4-year nursing and junior college
- Commuter campus in small city

General. Founded in 1854. Regionally accredited. **Location:** 10 miles from Cleveland. **Calendar:** Semester.

Annual costs/financial aid. Tuition/fees (2008-2009): $13,740. Books/supplies: $1,600. Personal expenses: $3,111. Need-based financial aid available to full-time and part-time students.

Contact. Phone: (216) 265-3151 ext. 229
Director of Admissions, 12955 Snow Road, Parma, OH 44130-1013

Capital University

Columbus, Ohio **CB member**
www.capital.edu **CB code: 1099**

- Private 4-year university affiliated with Evangelical Lutheran Church in America
- Residential campus in very large city
- 2,552 degree-seeking undergraduates: 9% part-time, 61% women, 10% African American, 1% Asian American, 2% Hispanic American, 1% international
- 950 degree-seeking graduate students
- 77% of applicants admitted
- SAT or ACT (ACT writing optional) required
- 63% graduate within 6 years; 29% enter graduate study

General. Founded in 1830. Regionally accredited. **Degrees:** 594 bachelor's awarded; master's, first professional offered. **ROTC:** Army, Air Force. **Location:** 5 miles from downtown. **Calendar:** Semester, limited summer session. **Full-time faculty:** 199 total; 68% have terminal degrees, 11% minority, 46% women. **Part-time faculty:** 208 total; 24% have terminal degrees, 14% minority, 48% women. **Class size:** 62% < 20, 37% 20-39, less than 1% 40-49, less than 1% 50-99.

Freshman class profile. 3,441 applied, 2,658 admitted, 644 enrolled.

Mid 50% test scores		**GPA 2.0-2.99:**	22%
SAT critical reading:	490-580	**Rank in top quarter:**	51%
SAT math:	480-600	**Rank in top tenth:**	21%
SAT writing:	460-590	**Return as sophomores:**	71%
ACT composite:	21-26	**Out-of-state:**	8%
GPA 3.75 or higher:	29%	**Live on campus:**	83%
GPA 3.50-3.74:	16%	**International:**	1%
GPA 3.0-3.49:	33%		

Basis for selection. Academic achievement in college-preparatory curriculum most important. Recommendations, test scores, and extracurricular activities considered. Interview recommended for all; audition required for music program; portfolio recommended for art, art therapy programs. **Homeschooled:** Statement describing homeschool structure and mission, transcript of courses and grades, letter of recommendation (nonparent) required.

High school preparation. College-preparatory program recommended. 18 units recommended. Recommended units include English 4, mathematics 3, social studies 3, science 3 (laboratory 2), foreign language 2 and visual/performing arts 1. Chemistry and algebra II for nursing applicants. One fine arts recommended.

2008-2009 Annual costs. Tuition/fees: $27,680. Room/board: $7,150. Books/supplies: $1,000. Personal expenses: $1,730.

2007-2008 Financial aid. **Need-based:** 579 full-time freshmen applied for aid; 518 were judged to have need; 518 of these received aid. Average need met was 23%. Average scholarship/grant was $6,317; average loan $2,820. 41% of total undergraduate aid awarded as scholarships/grants, 59% as loans/jobs. **Non-need-based:** Awarded to 2,133 full-time undergraduates, including 629 freshmen. Scholarships awarded for academics, alumni affiliation, art, minority status, music/drama, religious affiliation, ROTC, state residency.

Application procedures. **Admission:** Priority date 4/1; no deadline. $25 fee, may be waived for applicants with need, free for online applicants. Admission notification on a rolling basis beginning on or about 9/30. Must reply by May 1 or within 2 week(s) if notified thereafter. **Financial aid:** Priority date 2/28; no closing date. FAFSA required. Applicants notified on a rolling basis starting 3/1; must reply by 5/1.

Academics. Teacher certification for learning disabilities and reading. Paralegal certification available from law school. **Special study options:** Accelerated study, combined bachelor's/graduate degree, cooperative education, cross-registration, double major, dual enrollment of high school students, ESL, exchange student, external degree, honors, independent study, internships, liberal arts/career combination, student-designed major, study abroad, teacher certification program, Washington semester. Dual degree engineering program with Washington University, St. Louis, and Case Western Reserve; 3-2 occupational therapy program with Washington University, St. Louis. **Credit/placement by examination:** AP, CLEP, IB, SAT, ACT, institutional tests. 27 credit hours maximum toward bachelor's degree. **Support services:** Learning center, reduced course load, remedial instruction, study skills assistance, tutoring, writing center.

Majors. **Biology:** General, biochemistry. **Business:** Accounting, business admin, managerial economics, marketing. **Communications:** General, organizational, public relations, radio/tv. **Computer sciences:** Computer science. **Conservation:** Environmental science. **Education:** Early childhood, middle, music, physical, special. **Engineering:** Computer. **Foreign languages:** French, Spanish. **Health:** Art therapy, athletic training, nursing (RN), nursing admin. **History:** General. **Math:** General. **Parks/recreation:** Exercise sciences, health/fitness. **Philosophy/religion:** Philosophy, religion. **Physical sciences:** Chemistry. **Psychology:** General. **Public administration:** General, social work. **Social sciences:** Criminology, economics, international relations, political science, sociology. **Visual/performing arts:** Art, dramatic, jazz, music management, music performance, music theory/composition, piano/organ, voice/opera.

Most popular majors. Business/marketing 12%, education 12%, health sciences 23%, public administration/social services 9%, social sciences 7%, visual/performing arts 7%.

Computing on campus. 454 workstations in dormitories, library, computer center, student center. Dormitories wired for high-speed internet access and linked to campus network. Commuter students can connect to campus network. Online course registration, online library, helpline, wireless network available.

Student life. **Freshman orientation:** Mandatory, $200 fee. One-day program in summer, 5-day program before start of classes. **Housing:** Guaranteed on-campus for freshmen. Coed dorms, special housing for disabled, apartments, fraternity/sorority housing available. $100 nonrefundable deposit, deadline 5/1. Honors housing, self-governing areas, and group cluster housing available. **Activities:** Bands, campus ministries, choral groups, dance, drama, international student organizations, literary magazine, music ensembles, musical theater, radio station, student government, student newspaper, symphony orchestra, TV station, black student union, Young Republicans, Campus Democrats, Circle K, Ebony Brotherhood Association, international student association, Capateers (volunteers), Habitat for Humanity, university programming.

Athletics. NCAA. **Intercollegiate:** Baseball M, basketball, cross-country, football (tackle) M, golf, soccer, softball W, tennis, track and field, volleyball W. **Intramural:** Basketball, bowling, football (non-tackle), softball, volleyball. **Team name:** Crusaders.

Student services. Chaplain/spiritual director, career counseling, student employment services, financial aid counseling, health services, minority student services, personal counseling, placement for graduates, veterans' counselor.

Contact. E-mail: admissions@capital.edu
Phone: (614) 236-6101 Toll-free number: (866) 544-6175
Fax: (614) 236-6926
Amanda Steiner, Director of Admission, Capital University, 1 College and Main, Columbus, OH 43209-2394

Case Western Reserve University

Cleveland, Ohio — **CB member**
www.case.edu — **CB code: 1105**

- Private 4-year university
- Residential campus in very large city
- 4,267 degree-seeking undergraduates: 2% part-time, 43% women, 6% African American, 17% Asian American, 2% Hispanic American, 3% international
- 5,263 degree-seeking graduate students
- 73% of applicants admitted
- SAT or ACT with writing, application essay required
- 80% graduate within 6 years; 44% enter graduate study

General. Founded in 1826. Regionally accredited. **Degrees:** 793 bachelor's awarded; master's, doctoral, first professional offered. **ROTC:** Army, Air Force. **Location:** 4 miles from downtown. **Calendar:** Semester, extensive summer session. **Full-time faculty:** 737 total; 90% have terminal degrees, 15% minority, 42% women. **Part-time faculty:** 163 total; 64% have terminal degrees, 6% minority, 42% women. **Class size:** 59% < 20, 23% 20-39, 7% 40-49, 7% 50-99, 4% >100. **Special facilities:** Biology field station, observatory, interdisciplinary research centers, natural history museum, historical society, botanical garden.

Freshman class profile. 7,351 applied, 5,390 admitted, 1,026 enrolled.

Mid 50% test scores		**Return as sophomores:**	92%
SAT critical reading:	590-690	**Out-of-state:**	50%
SAT math:	620-720	**Live on campus:**	97%
SAT writing:	580-680	**International:**	3%
ACT composite:	26-32	**Fraternities:**	34%
Rank in top quarter:	87%	**Sororities:**	29%
Rank in top tenth:	63%		

Basis for selection. School achievement record and test scores most important. School and community activities, essays, recommendations, and interview also considered. Special consideration to applicants from culturally, educationally, or economically disadvantaged backgrounds. IELTS, AP International English test, or TOEFL required for all international students. Interview recommended for all; audition required for music, music education programs; portfolio required for art education program. Writing sample required. **Homeschooled:** Transcript of courses and grades, interview required. At least 3 SAT Subject Tests highly recommended. Students encouraged to submit at least 2 letters from outside instructors or employers.

High school preparation. College-preparatory program required. 16 units required. Required and recommended units include English 4, mathematics 3-4, social studies 3-4, science 3 (laboratory 2-3) and foreign language 2-3. 3 laboratory science recommended. 4 math, 1 chemistry and physics recommended for engineering. 3 laboratory science (1 chemistry) recommended for science, math, and premedical.

2008-2009 Annual costs. Tuition/fees: $35,572. Room/board: $10,450.

2008-2009 Financial aid. **Need-based:** 912 full-time freshmen applied for aid; 761 were judged to have need; 730 of these received aid. Average need met was 88%. Average scholarship/grant was $23,465; average loan $6,898. 67% of total undergraduate aid awarded as scholarships/grants, 33% as loans/jobs. **Non-need-based:** Awarded to 3,049 full-time undergraduates, including 791 freshmen. Scholarships awarded for academics, art, leadership, music/drama.

Application procedures. **Admission:** Closing date 1/15 (postmark date). No application fee. Application must be submitted online. Admission notification 4/1. Must reply by 5/1. **Financial aid:** Priority date 2/1; no closing date. FAFSA, institutional form required. Applicants notified on a rolling basis starting 2/15; must reply by 5/1 or within 2 week(s) of notification.

Academics. Preprofessional Scholars Program gives talented undergraduates conditional acceptances to graduate schools of medicine, dentistry, law, and social work. Most programs allow students to pursue combined bachelor's/master's. **Special study options:** Accelerated study, combined bachelor's/graduate degree, cooperative education, cross-registration, double major, dual enrollment of high school students, ESL, exchange student, honors, independent study, internships, liberal arts/career combination, student-designed major, study abroad, teacher certification program, Washington semester. Exchange program with Fisk University, 3-2 binary program in engineering, biochemistry, and astronomy. **Credit/placement by examination:** AP, CLEP, IB, institutional tests. **Support services:** Learning center, pre-admission summer program, reduced course load, study skills assistance, tutoring, writing center.

Majors. **Area/ethnic studies:** American, Asian, French, German, Japanese, women's. **Biology:** General, biochemistry, evolutionary. **Business:** Accounting, business admin. **Computer sciences:** General, computer science. **Conservation:** Environmental studies. **Education:** Art, music. **Engineering:** General, aerospace, biomedical, chemical, civil, computer, electrical, materials, materials science, mechanical, physics, polymer, systems. **Family/consumer sciences:** Human nutrition. **Foreign languages:** Classics, comparative lit, French, German, Spanish. **Health:** Communication disorders, dietetics, nursing (RN). **History:** General, science/technology. **Interdisciplinary:** Cognitive science, gerontology, natural sciences, nutrition sciences. **Math:** General, applied, statistics. **Philosophy/religion:** Philosophy, religion. **Physical sciences:** Astronomy, chemistry, geology, physics. **Psychology:** General. **Social sciences:** Anthropology, economics, international relations, political science, sociology. **Visual/performing arts:** Art history/conservation, dramatic. **Other:** Systems biology.

Most popular majors. Biology 11%, business/marketing 8%, engineering/engineering technologies 24%, health sciences 10%, physical sciences 6%, psychology 8%, social sciences 12%.

Computing on campus. 415 workstations in dormitories, library, computer center, student center. Dormitories wired for high-speed internet access and linked to campus network. Commuter students can connect to campus network. Online course registration, online library, helpline, repair service, student web hosting, wireless network available.

Student life. **Freshman orientation:** Mandatory, $370 fee. Preregistration for classes offered. Four 3-day sessions beginning in July. **Housing:** Guaranteed on-campus for freshmen. Coed dorms, apartments, fraternity/sorority housing, wellness housing available. Residential colleges for first-year students. Secured female-only floor available. Special-interest housing available. **Activities:** Bands, campus ministries, choral groups, dance, drama, film society, international student organizations, literary magazine, music ensembles, Model UN, musical theater, radio station, student government, student newspaper, symphony orchestra, University Christian Movement, Hillel Foundation, African-American Society, College Democrats, College Republicans, Habitat for Humanity.

Athletics. NCAA. **Intercollegiate:** Baseball M, basketball, cross-country, football (tackle) M, soccer, softball W, swimming, tennis, track and field, volleyball W, wrestling M. **Intramural:** Badminton, basketball, bowling, cross-country, football (non-tackle), football (tackle) M, golf, racquetball, soccer, softball, squash, swimming, table tennis, tennis, track and field, volleyball, water polo, weight lifting, wrestling M. **Team name:** Spartans.

Student services. Adult student services, alcohol/substance abuse counseling, chaplain/spiritual director, career counseling, student employment services, financial aid counseling, health services, legal services, minority student services, personal counseling, placement for graduates, veterans' counselor, women's services. **Physically disabled:** Services for visually, speech, hearing impaired.

Contact. E-mail: admission@case.edu
Phone: (216) 368-4450 Fax: (216) 368-5111
Rae DiBaggio, Co-Director of Undergraduate Admission, Case Western Reserve University, Wolstein Hall, Cleveland, OH 44106-7055

Cedarville University
Cedarville, Ohio
www.cedarville.edu **CB code: 1151**

- Private 4-year university and liberal arts college affiliated with Baptist faith
- Residential campus in small town
- 2,940 degree-seeking undergraduates: 2% part-time, 54% women, 1% African American, 1% Asian American, 2% Hispanic American, 1% international
- 55 degree-seeking graduate students
- SAT or ACT (ACT writing recommended), application essay required
- 66% graduate within 6 years

General. Founded in 1887. Regionally accredited. **Degrees:** 317 bachelor's awarded; master's offered. **ROTC:** Army, Air Force. **Location:** 12 miles from Springfield, 20 miles from Dayton. **Calendar:** Semester, limited summer session. **Full-time faculty:** 212 total; 61% have terminal degrees, 6% minority, 27% women. **Part-time faculty:** 20 total; 5% minority, 60% women. **Class size:** 64% < 20, 28% 20-39, 1% 40-49, 6% 50-99, 1% >100.

Freshman class profile.

Mid 50% test scores			
SAT critical reading:	540-650	GPA 2.0-2.99:	7%
SAT math:	530-640	Rank in top quarter:	59%
SAT writing:	520-630	Rank in top tenth:	32%
ACT composite:	22-27	End year in good standing:	96%
GPA 3.75 or higher:	44%	Return as sophomores:	83%
GPA 3.50-3.74:	23%	Out-of-state:	65%
GPA 3.0-3.49:	26%	Live on campus:	98%
		International:	1%

Basis for selection. Clear testimony of personal faith in Jesus Christ, evidence of consistent Christian lifestyle, above-average academic performance (academic records, class rank, test scores), personal references considered. Applications reviewed on a rolling basis. SAT and SAT Subject Tests or ACT recommended. Audition required for music majors; interview recommended for academically marginal students. Interview required for pre-pharmacy students. **Learning Disabled:** Students encouraged to contact Coordinator of Disabilities Services.

High school preparation. Recommended units include English 4, mathematics 4, social studies 3, science 3 (laboratory 3) and foreign language 3. Additional math and science recommended for nursing, science, engineering, and math applicants.

2008-2009 Annual costs. Tuition/fees: $20,992. Room/board: $5,010. Books/supplies: $900. Personal expenses: $1,450.

2007-2008 Financial aid. **Need-based:** 701 full-time freshmen applied for aid; 558 were judged to have need; 554 of these received aid. Average need met was 31%. Average scholarship/grant was $2,801; average loan $3,178. 49% of total undergraduate aid awarded as scholarships/grants, 51% as loans/jobs. **Non-need-based:** Awarded to 2,124 full-time undergraduates, including 755 freshmen. Scholarships awarded for academics, alumni affiliation, athletics, leadership, minority status, music/drama, ROTC, state residency.

Application procedures. **Admission:** Priority date 3/1; no deadline. $30 fee, may be waived for applicants with need. Admission notification on a rolling basis beginning on or about 8/1. Must reply by May 1 or within 2 week(s) if notified thereafter. **Financial aid:** Priority date 3/1; no closing date. FAFSA required. Applicants notified on a rolling basis starting 3/1; must reply within 4 week(s) of notification.

Academics. **Special study options:** Accelerated study, cooperative education, distance learning, double major, dual enrollment of high school students, honors, independent study, internships, liberal arts/career combination, student-designed major, study abroad, teacher certification program, Washington semester. **Credit/placement by examination:** AP, CLEP, IB, SAT, ACT, institutional tests. 40 credit hours maximum toward bachelor's degree. **Support services:** Reduced course load, remedial instruction, study skills assistance, tutoring, writing center.

Majors. **Area/ethnic studies:** American. **Biology:** General, cellular/molecular. **Business:** Accounting, business admin, finance, international, management information systems, marketing. **Communications:** General, journalism, media studies, organizational, political, radio/tv. **Communications technology:** General. **Computer sciences:** General, computer science. **Education:** Biology, early childhood, elementary, English, mathematics, middle, music, physical, physics, science, social studies, Spanish, special. **Engineering:** Computer, electrical, mechanical. **Foreign languages:** Spanish. **Health:** Athletic training, clinical lab science, nursing (RN), predental, premedicine, preveterinary. **History:** General. **Interdisciplinary:** Global studies. **Legal studies:** Prelaw. **Math:** General. **Parks/recreation:** Exercise sciences, health/fitness, sports admin. **Philosophy/religion:** Philosophy. **Physical sciences:** Chemistry, physics. **Protective services:** Forensics, law enforcement admin. **Psychology:** General. **Public administration:** General, social work. **Social sciences:** General, political science, sociology. **Theology:** Missionary, pastoral counseling, religious ed, sacred music, theology, youth ministry. **Visual/performing arts:** Dramatic, graphic design, music pedagogy, music performance, music theory/composition, studio arts.

Most popular majors. Business/marketing 15%, education 14%, engineering/engineering technologies 6%, health sciences 12%, theological studies 11%.

Computing on campus. 1,800 workstations in dormitories, library, student center. Dormitories linked to campus network. Commuter students can connect to campus network. Online course registration, helpline, repair service, wireless network available.

Student life. **Freshman orientation:** Mandatory, $105 fee. **Policies:** Alcohol, tobacco, and drugs prohibited. Religious observance required. **Housing:** Guaranteed on-campus for all undergraduates. Single-sex dorms, apartments available. $250 nonrefundable deposit, deadline 5/1. **Activities:** Bands, campus ministries, choral groups, drama, music ensembles, musical theater, radio station, student government, student newspaper, symphony orchestra,

College Republicans, Emergency Medical Squad, Earth Stewardship Organization, Fellowship for World Missions, Students for Social Justice, Society for Technical Communicators, Society of Automotive Engineers International.

Athletics. NAIA, NCCAA. **Intercollegiate:** Baseball M, basketball, cheerleading, cross-country, golf M, soccer, softball W, tennis, track and field, volleyball W. **Intramural:** Badminton, basketball, bowling, cross-country, football (tackle) M, golf, racquetball, soccer, softball, table tennis, tennis, volleyball. **Team name:** Yellow Jackets.

Student services. Chaplain/spiritual director, career counseling, student employment services, financial aid counseling, health services, personal counseling, placement for graduates, veterans' counselor. **Physically disabled:** Services for visually impaired.

Contact. E-mail: admissions@cedarville.edu
Phone: (937) 766-7700 Toll-free number: (800) 233-2784
Fax: (937) 766-7575
Scott VanLoo, Director of Admissions, Cedarville University, 251 North Main Street, Cedarville, OH 45314

Central State University

Wilberforce, Ohio
www.centralstate.edu
CB member
CB code: 1107

- Public 4-year university and liberal arts college
- Residential campus in rural community
- 2,107 degree-seeking undergraduates: 7% part-time, 50% women, 94% African American, 1% Hispanic American
- 29 degree-seeking graduate students
- 40% of applicants admitted
- SAT or ACT (ACT writing optional) required

General. Founded in 1887. Regionally accredited. Ohio's only public historically black university. **Degrees:** 170 bachelor's awarded; master's offered. **ROTC:** Army, Air Force. **Location:** 18 miles from Dayton. **Calendar:** Semester, limited summer session. **Full-time faculty:** 107 total; 67% have terminal degrees, 71% minority, 34% women. **Part-time faculty:** 87 total; 75% minority, 51% women. **Class size:** 57% < 20, 40% 20-39, 2% 40-49, 1% 50-99. **Special facilities:** Afro-American museum, hydraulics laboratory, computer numerically controlled equipment for machining and robotic welding, business incubator.

Freshman class profile. 6,175 applied, 2,483 admitted, 662 enrolled.

Mid 50% test scores		**GPA 3.0-3.49:**	12%
SAT critical reading:	340-440	**GPA 2.0-2.99:**	64%
SAT math:	340-440	**Return as sophomores:**	51%
ACT composite:	15-18	**Out-of-state:**	51%
GPA 3.75 or higher:	1%	**Live on campus:**	78%
GPA 3.50-3.74:	3%		

Basis for selection. Out-of-state residents must have 2.5 GPA and 19 ACT or 910 SAT. Ohio residents must have 2.0 GPA and 15 ACT or 720 SAT. Interview recommended. Personal essay required for admissions appeal process. **Homeschooled:** Transcript of courses and grades, state high school equivalency certificate, interview, letter of recommendation (nonparent) required. Ohio students need ONGP test results or OGT.

High school preparation. 16 units recommended. Recommended units include English 4, mathematics 3, social studies 3, science 3 and foreign language 2. 1 art recommended.

2008-2009 Annual costs. Tuition/fees: $5,294; $11,462 out-of-state. Room/board: $7,402. Books/supplies: $1,000. Personal expenses: $1,400.

2008-2009 Financial aid. Non-need-based: Scholarships awarded for academics, alumni affiliation, art, athletics, leadership, music/drama, religious affiliation, ROTC.

Application procedures. Admission: No deadline. $20 fee, may be waived for applicants with need. Admission notification on a rolling basis. **Financial aid:** Priority date 2/15; no closing date. FAFSA, institutional form required. Applicants notified on a rolling basis starting 5/1.

Academics. Special study options: Combined bachelor's/graduate degree, cooperative education, cross-registration, double major, honors, independent study, internships, study abroad, teacher certification program. **Credit/placement by examination:** AP, CLEP, SAT, ACT, institutional tests. 30 credit hours maximum toward bachelor's degree. **Support services:** Learning center, pre-admission summer program, reduced course load, tutoring, writing center.

Majors. Biology: General. **Business:** General, accounting. **Communications:** Broadcast journalism, journalism. **Computer sciences:** Computer science. **Education:** Early childhood, middle, multi-level teacher, secondary, special. **Engineering:** Environmental, manufacturing, water resource. **Engineering technology:** Industrial. **History:** General. **Math:** General. **Parks/recreation:** General. **Physical sciences:** Chemistry, geology. **Protective services:** Criminal justice. **Psychology:** General. **Public administration:** Social work. **Social sciences:** Economics, political science, sociology. **Visual/performing arts:** Art, jazz, music performance.

Most popular majors. Business/marketing 25%, communications/journalism 8%, education 19%, psychology 8%, social sciences 14%, visual/performing arts 6%.

Computing on campus. 400 workstations in library, computer center, student center. Dormitories wired for high-speed internet access and linked to campus network. Online course registration, online library, helpline, wireless network available.

Student life. Freshman orientation: Mandatory, $125 fee. Preregistration for classes offered. **Housing:** Guaranteed on-campus for freshmen. Coed dorms, single-sex dorms available. $195 fully refundable deposit, deadline 8/1. **Activities:** Bands, campus ministries, choral groups, dance, drama, music ensembles, radio station, student government, student newspaper, TV station.

Athletics. NCAA. **Intercollegiate:** Basketball, cross-country, football (tackle) M, golf, tennis, track and field, volleyball. **Intramural:** Basketball, cross-country, football (non-tackle) M, racquetball, tennis. **Team name:** Marauders.

Student services. Alcohol/substance abuse counseling, chaplain/spiritual director, career counseling, services for economically disadvantaged, student employment services, financial aid counseling, health services, on-campus daycare, personal counseling, placement for graduates.

Contact. E-mail: admissions@centralstate.edu
Phone: (937) 376-6348 Toll-free number: (800) 388-2781
Fax: (937) 376-6648
Robin Rucker, Associate Director of Admissions, Central State University, PO Box 1004, Wilberforce, OH 45384-1004

Chancellor University

Cleveland, Ohio
www.myers.edu
CB code: 1178

- Private 4-year university
- Commuter campus in very large city

General. Founded in 1848. Regionally accredited. **Location:** Downtown. **Calendar:** Semester.

Annual costs/financial aid. Tuition/fees (2008-2009): $13,500. Room/board: $5,933. Books/supplies: $1,250.

Contact. Phone: (216) 432-8992
Vice President for Enrollment Management, 3921 Chester Avenue, Cleveland, OH 44114

Cincinnati Christian University

Cincinnati, Ohio
www.ccuniversity.edu
CB code: 1091

- Private 4-year university affiliated with Church of Christ/Christian Church
- Residential campus in very large city
- 800 degree-seeking undergraduates: 18% part-time, 46% women, 13% African American, 1% Hispanic American
- 291 degree-seeking graduate students
- 75% of applicants admitted
- SAT or ACT (ACT writing optional), application essay required

General. Founded in 1924. Regionally accredited; also accredited by ABHE. Member of Greater Cincinnati Consortium of Colleges and Universities. **Degrees:** 120 bachelor's, 6 associate awarded; master's, first professional offered. **Location:** 10 miles from downtown. **Calendar:** Semester, limited summer session. **Full-time faculty:** 36 total; 69% have terminal degrees, 6% minority, 22% women. **Part-time faculty:** 74 total; 20% have terminal degrees, 4% minority, 24% women. **Class size:** 68% < 20, 23% 20-39, 4% 40-49, 5% 50-99.

Freshman class profile. 352 applied, 264 admitted, 114 enrolled.

Mid 50% test scores			
SAT critical reading:	440-560	GPA 3.50-3.74:	14%
SAT math:	420-570	GPA 3.0-3.49:	18%
SAT writing:	410-560	GPA 2.0-2.99:	49%
ACT composite:	18-24	Return as sophomores:	62%
GPA 3.75 or higher:	14%	Out-of-state:	31%
		Live on campus:	77%

Basis for selection. High school academic record and standardized test scores important. 2.5 GPA, 17 ACT/1215 SAT required for unconditional admission. Applicants age 25 or older can substitute English proficiency test and essay for SAT/ACT requirement. Audition required for music programs.

2008-2009 Annual costs. Tuition/fees: $12,143. Room/board: $6,350. Books/supplies: $800. Personal expenses: $1,950.

2007-2008 Financial aid. **Need-based:** 152 full-time freshmen applied for aid; 126 were judged to have need; 123 of these received aid. Average need met was 52%. Average scholarship/grant was $4,838; average loan $3,830. 40% of total undergraduate aid awarded as scholarships/grants, 60% as loans/jobs. **Non-need-based:** Awarded to 223 full-time undergraduates, including 73 freshmen. Scholarships awarded for academics, athletics, leadership, music/drama, religious affiliation, state residency.

Application procedures. **Admission:** Priority date 3/1; deadline 7/1 (postmark date). $40 fee, may be waived for applicants with need. Admission notification on a rolling basis. **Financial aid:** Priority date 3/1; no closing date. FAFSA required. Applicants notified on a rolling basis starting 4/1; must reply within 2 week(s) of notification.

Academics. **Special study options:** Cooperative education, cross-registration, distance learning, double major, honors, independent study, internships, teacher certification program. Adult degree completion program. **Credit/placement by examination:** AP, CLEP, IB, institutional tests. 15 credit hours maximum toward associate degree, 30 toward bachelor's. **Support services:** Learning center, reduced course load, remedial instruction, study skills assistance, tutoring, writing center.

Majors. **Computer sciences:** Data processing, information technology, LAN/WAN management, programming. **Education:** Early childhood, elementary, middle, secondary, special. **Philosophy/religion:** Christian. **Psychology:** General. **Theology:** Bible, missionary, religious ed, sacred music.

Most popular majors. Business/marketing 6%, education 6%, psychology 9%, theological studies 79%.

Computing on campus. 57 workstations in dormitories, library, computer center, student center. Dormitories wired for high-speed internet access and linked to campus network. Online library, helpline, repair service, wireless network available.

Student life. **Freshman orientation:** Mandatory. Preregistration for classes offered. **Housing:** Guaranteed on-campus for all undergraduates. Single-sex dorms, apartments, wellness housing available. $35 nonrefundable deposit, deadline 7/1. **Activities:** Concert band, campus ministries, choral groups, drama, international student organizations, music ensembles, musical theater, student government.

Athletics. NCCAA. **Intercollegiate:** Baseball M, basketball, soccer, volleyball W. **Intramural:** Basketball, cheerleading, football (tackle) M, soccer, track and field, volleyball. **Team name:** Eagles.

Student services. Career counseling, student employment services, financial aid counseling, health services, personal counseling. **Physically disabled:** Services for hearing impaired.

Contact. E-mail: cbcadmission@ccuniversity.edu
Phone: (513) 244-8141 Toll-free number: (800) 949-4228
Fax: (513) 244-8140
Jenny Baker, Admissions Director, Cincinnati Christian University, 2700 Glenway Avenue, Cincinnati, OH 45204-3200

Cincinnati College of Mortuary Science

Cincinnati, Ohio
www.ccms.edu **CB code: 0945**

- Private 4-year school of mortuary science
- Commuter campus in large city
- 100 degree-seeking undergraduates

General. Founded in 1882. Regionally accredited. **Degrees:** 40 bachelor's, 53 associate awarded. **Location:** 3 miles from downtown. **Calendar:** Quarter. **Full-time faculty:** 6 total. **Part-time faculty:** 6 total. **Class size:** 100% 50-99.

Basis for selection. Open admission.

High school preparation. 15 units recommended. Recommended units include English 3, mathematics 1, social studies 2 and science 2.

2008-2009 Annual costs. Tuition/fees: $8,775. Tuition for 4-quarter A.A.S. $16,875; 5-quarter B.M.S. $120,250; 6-quarter A.A.S. $22,725. Books and supplies for 4-quarter students $1,400; 6-quarter students $1,800; 5th quarter only $100.

2008-2009 Financial aid. All financial aid based on need. 24% of total undergraduate aid awarded as scholarships/grants, 76% as loans/jobs.

Application procedures. **Admission:** No deadline. $25 fee. Admission notification on a rolling basis. **Financial aid:** Priority date 7/1; no closing date. FAFSA required. Applicants notified on a rolling basis starting 3/1; must reply within 2 week(s) of notification.

Academics. Program of study contingent on licensing requirements of state in which student will practice. **Special study options:** Internships. **Credit/placement by examination:** AP, CLEP, institutional tests. 41 credit hours maximum toward associate degree, 56 toward bachelor's. **Support services:** Reduced course load, tutoring.

Majors. **Personal/culinary services:** Mortuary science.

Student life. **Freshman orientation:** Mandatory. Preregistration for classes offered. **Housing:** Some housing available in local funeral homes.

Student services. Career counseling, student employment services, personal counseling, veterans' counselor. **Physically disabled:** Services for hearing impaired.

Contact. Phone: (513) 761-2020 Fax: (513) 761-3333
Pat Sullivan, Executive Director Enrollment Management, Cincinnati College of Mortuary Science, 645 West North Bend Road, Cincinnati, OH 45224-1428

Cleveland Institute of Art

Cleveland, Ohio **CB member**
www.cia.edu **CB code: 1152**

- Private 4-year visual arts college
- Commuter campus in very large city
- 492 degree-seeking undergraduates: 1% part-time, 52% women, 5% African American, 5% Asian American, 5% Hispanic American, 2% international
- 87% of applicants admitted
- SAT or ACT (ACT writing optional), application essay required
- 66% graduate within 6 years

General. Founded in 1882. Regionally accredited. **Degrees:** 74 bachelor's awarded; master's offered. **ROTC:** Army, Naval, Air Force. **Location:** 5 miles from downtown. **Calendar:** Semester, limited summer session. **Full-time faculty:** 45 total; 87% have terminal degrees, 9% minority, 49% women. **Part-time faculty:** 51 total; 61% have terminal degrees, 8% minority, 47% women. **Class size:** 83% < 20, 17% 20-39. **Special facilities:** Individual studio spaces, wood shop, metal shop, art galleries.

Freshman class profile. 422 applied, 366 admitted, 101 enrolled.

Mid 50% test scores			
SAT critical reading:	470-580	Rank in top quarter:	40%
SAT math:	470-540	Rank in top tenth:	13%
ACT composite:	20-25	End year in good standing:	91%
GPA 3.75 or higher:	15%	Return as sophomores:	86%
GPA 3.50-3.74:	19%	Out-of-state:	41%
GPA 3.0-3.49:	37%	Live on campus:	76%
GPA 2.0-2.99:	29%	International:	3%

Basis for selection. Portfolio of 12 to 20 pieces, high school transcripts, statement of purpose, test scores, and 1 letter of recommendation required. Interview strongly recommended. **Homeschooled:** Transcript of courses and grades, state high school equivalency certificate, letter of recommendation (nonparent) required. GED required.

High school preparation. 20 units recommended. Recommended units include English 4, mathematics 3, social studies 3, science 3 and academic electives 6. 2 years of art recommended.

2008-2009 Annual costs. Tuition/fees: $31,010. Room/board: $9,148. Books/supplies: $1,910. Personal expenses: $1,940.

2008-2009 Financial aid. **Need-based:** 93 full-time freshmen applied for aid; 86 were judged to have need; 86 of these received aid. Average need met was 71%. Average scholarship/grant was $17,599; average loan $4,707. 20% of total undergraduate aid awarded as scholarships/grants, 80% as loans/jobs. **Non-need-based:** Awarded to 110 full-time undergraduates, including 24 freshmen. Scholarships awarded for academics, art.

Application procedures. **Admission:** Priority date 7/1; no deadline. $30 fee, may be waived for applicants with need. Admission notification on a rolling basis beginning on or about 10/1. Must reply by May 1 or within 2 week(s) if notified thereafter. **Financial aid:** Priority date 3/15; no closing date. FAFSA, institutional form required. Applicants notified on a rolling basis starting 3/16; must reply within 4 week(s) of notification.

Academics. **Special study options:** Cooperative education, cross-registration, exchange student, honors, independent study, internships, New York semester, study abroad. Study for up to 2 semesters at any Alliance of Independent Colleges of Art and Design. **Credit/placement by examination:** AP, CLEP, IB. 63 credit hours maximum toward bachelor's degree. **Support services:** Reduced course load, remedial instruction, study skills assistance, tutoring, writing center.

Majors. **Health:** Medical illustrating. **Visual/performing arts:** Ceramics, commercial/advertising art, drawing, fiber arts, illustration, industrial design, interior design, metal/jewelry, painting, photography, printmaking, sculpture.

Computing on campus. 303 workstations in dormitories, library, computer center. Dormitories wired for high-speed internet access and linked to campus network. Online course registration, online library, student web hosting, wireless network available.

Student life. **Freshman orientation:** Mandatory, $130 fee. Preregistration for classes offered. Summer overnight program for students/parents and fall orientation for students only. **Housing:** Coed dorms, apartments, fraternity/sorority housing available. $150 nonrefundable deposit, deadline 6/15. **Activities:** Campus ministries, film society, student government, student newspaper, student artist association, student leadership council, nature and hiking club, student activities program board, student independent exhibition committee, gay/lesbian association, Artists for Christ, cinema club, community service club.

Student services. Alcohol/substance abuse counseling, chaplain/spiritual director, career counseling, student employment services, financial aid counseling, health services, personal counseling. **Learning disabled:** Comprehensive services available.

Contact. E-mail: admiss@cia.edu
Phone: (216) 421-7418 Toll-free number: (800) 223-4700
Fax: (216) 754-3634
Sheila Cowman, Director of Admissions, Cleveland Institute of Art, 11141 East Boulevard, Cleveland, OH 44106-1710

Cleveland Institute of Music

Cleveland, Ohio
www.cim.edu **CB code: 1124**

- Private 4-year music college
- Residential campus in very large city
- 230 degree-seeking undergraduates
- SAT or ACT (ACT writing optional), application essay required

General. Founded in 1920. Regionally accredited. **Degrees:** 50 bachelor's awarded; master's, doctoral offered. **Location:** 2 miles from downtown. **Calendar:** Semester, limited summer session. **Full-time faculty:** 42 total. **Part-time faculty:** 69 total. **Special facilities:** Electronic music studios, audio recording facilities, large record, tape, CD library, technology learning center.

Freshman class profile.

Out-of-state:	77%	**Live on campus:**	100%

Basis for selection. Audition most important. High school record, test scores, and letters of recommendation also reviewed. Incoming students must have scholastic and musical skills prerequisite to entering highly intensive, professionally oriented program. Institutional examinations including sight singing, ear training, and keyboard harmony required. Audition required. **Homeschooled:** Transcript of courses and grades required.

High school preparation. 16 units recommended. Recommended units include English 4, mathematics 3, social studies 3, science 3 and foreign language 3.

2009-2010 Annual costs. Tuition/fees (projected): $36,674. Room/board: $10,567. Books/supplies: $1,240. Personal expenses: $1,000.

2007-2008 Financial aid. **Non-need-based:** Scholarships awarded for academics, music/drama.

Application procedures. **Admission:** Closing date 12/1 (receipt date). $100 fee. Application must be submitted online. Admission notification on a rolling basis beginning on or about 3/1. Must reply by 5/1. Deferred admission from fall to spring semesters is dependent upon space availability. **Financial aid:** Priority date 2/15; no closing date. FAFSA, institutional form required. Applicants notified on a rolling basis starting 4/1; must reply by 5/1 or within 2 week(s) of notification.

Academics. **Special study options:** Cross-registration, double major, ESL, independent study, study abroad. **Credit/placement by examination:** AP, CLEP, IB, SAT, ACT, institutional tests. **Support services:** Learning center, reduced course load, remedial instruction, study skills assistance, tutoring, writing center.

Majors. **Communications technology:** Recording arts. **Visual/performing arts:** Music performance, music theory/composition, voice/opera.

Computing on campus. 36 workstations in dormitories, library, computer center, student center. Dormitories wired for high-speed internet access and linked to campus network. Helpline, repair service, wireless network available.

Student life. **Freshman orientation:** Mandatory. Held before the start of classes. **Policies:** Library privileges available through Case Western Reserve University. **Housing:** Coed dorms, wellness housing available. **Activities:** Jazz band, choral groups, dance, drama, music ensembles, opera, student government, student newspaper, symphony orchestra, most student activities, athletics and student services available through Case Western Reserve University.

Student services. Alcohol/substance abuse counseling, career counseling, student employment services, financial aid counseling, health services, personal counseling, placement for graduates, veterans' counselor.

Contact. E-mail: cimadmission@po.cwru.edu
Phone: (216) 795-3107 Fax: (216) 795-3161
William Fay, Director of Admission, Cleveland Institute of Music, 11021 East Boulevard, Cleveland, OH 44106

Cleveland State University

Cleveland, Ohio **CB member**
www.csuohio.edu **CB code: 1221**

- Public 4-year university
- Commuter campus in very large city
- 9,375 degree-seeking undergraduates: 25% part-time, 56% women, 22% African American, 3% Asian American, 3% Hispanic American, 2% international
- 4,951 degree-seeking graduate students
- 65% of applicants admitted

General. Founded in 1964. Regionally accredited. **Degrees:** 1,695 bachelor's awarded; master's, doctoral, first professional offered. **ROTC:** Army, Naval. **Location:** Downtown. **Calendar:** Semester, extensive summer session. **Full-time faculty:** 549 total; 93% have terminal degrees, 21% minority, 39% women. **Part-time faculty:** 519 total; 18% have terminal degrees, 18% minority, 48% women. **Class size:** 45% < 20, 42% 20-39, 5% 40-49, 7% 50-99, less than 1% >100.

Freshman class profile. 3,991 applied, 2,600 admitted, 1,044 enrolled.

Mid 50% test scores		**Rank in top quarter:**	33%
SAT critical reading:	420-560	**Rank in top tenth:**	12%
SAT math:	420-570	**Return as sophomores:**	59%
ACT composite:	18-23	**Out-of-state:**	6%
GPA 3.75 or higher:	15%	**Live on campus:**	31%
GPA 3.50-3.74:	9%	**International:**	2%
GPA 3.0-3.49:	27%	**Fraternities:**	3%
GPA 2.0-2.99:	48%	**Sororities:**	3%

Basis for selection. 2.3 GPA, 16 ACT/750 SAT, and successful completion of 13 core academic units required. 2.5 GPA and 20 ACT/950 SAT required for education applicants; 2.7 GPA and 23 ACT/1070 SAT required for engineering applicants. SAT/ACT must be submitted for counseling purposes, but scores not considered in admission decisions. Audition required for music majors.

High school preparation. College-preparatory program required. 13 units required; 17 recommended. Required and recommended units include English 4, mathematics 3, social studies 3, science 3 (laboratory 1), foreign language 2 and visual/performing arts 1.

2009-2010 Annual costs. Tuition/fees (projected): $7,970; $10,774 out-of-state. Room/board: $8,700. Books/supplies: $800. Personal expenses: $4,300.

2008-2009 Financial aid. **Need-based:** 723 full-time freshmen applied for aid; 642 were judged to have need; 626 of these received aid. Average need met was 48%. Average scholarship/grant was $5,994; average loan $3,270. 34% of total undergraduate aid awarded as scholarships/grants, 66% as loans/jobs. **Non-need-based:** Awarded to 1,059 full-time undergraduates, including 151 freshmen. Scholarships awarded for academics, alumni affiliation, art, athletics, leadership, minority status, music/drama, religious affiliation, ROTC.

Application procedures. **Admission:** Priority date 7/15; deadline 8/15. $30 fee, may be waived for applicants with need. Admission notification on a rolling basis beginning on or about 9/1. **Financial aid:** Priority date 2/15; no closing date. FAFSA required. Applicants notified on a rolling basis starting 3/15; must reply within 4 week(s) of notification.

Academics. **Special study options:** Accelerated study, cooperative education, cross-registration, distance learning, double major, dual enrollment of high school students, ESL, exchange student, honors, independent study, internships, liberal arts/career combination, student-designed major, study abroad, teacher certification program. **Credit/placement by examination:** AP, CLEP, IB, institutional tests. 90 credit hours maximum toward bachelor's degree. Unlimited AP exam credits accepted. **Support services:** Learning center, reduced course load, remedial instruction, study skills assistance, tutoring, writing center.

Majors. **Area/ethnic studies:** French, German, Italian, Spanish/Iberian, women's. **Business:** Accounting, finance, international, labor relations, management information systems, managerial economics, marketing, statistics. **Communications:** General. **Computer sciences:** General. **Conservation:** General, environmental studies. **Education:** Early childhood, elementary, physical, special. **Engineering:** Chemical, civil, electrical, mechanical. **Engineering technology:** Electrical. **Foreign languages:** French, German, linguistics, Spanish. **Health:** Audiology/hearing, nursing (RN). **History:** General. **Liberal arts:** Arts/sciences. **Math:** General. **Philosophy/religion:** Philosophy, religion. **Physical sciences:** Chemistry, geology, physics. **Psychology:** General. **Public administration:** Social work. **Social sciences:** General, anthropology, economics, political science, sociology, urban studies. **Visual/performing arts:** Art, dramatic.

Most popular majors. Business/marketing 22%, communications/journalism 8%, education 9%, engineering/engineering technologies 6%, health sciences 11%, psychology 7%, public administration/social services 6%, social sciences 12%.

Computing on campus. 711 workstations in dormitories, library, computer center, student center. Dormitories wired for high-speed internet access and linked to campus network. Online library, helpline, wireless network available.

Student life. **Freshman orientation:** Available, $25 fee. Preregistration for classes offered. All-day program during summer. **Housing:** Coed dorms, fraternity/sorority housing available. $150 nonrefundable deposit, deadline 1/19. **Activities:** Bands, choral groups, dance, drama, film society, international student organizations, literary magazine, musical theater, opera, radio station, student government, student newspaper, symphony orchestra, Newman Center, Los Latinos Unidos, Hillel, University Christian Movement, Organization for Afro-American Unity, NAACP, environmental action group, College Democrats and Republicans.

Athletics. NCAA. **Intercollegiate:** Baseball M, basketball, cross-country W, diving, fencing, golf, soccer, softball W, swimming, tennis, track and field W, volleyball W, wrestling M. **Intramural:** Badminton, basketball, bowling, cross-country, fencing, field hockey W, golf, handball, racquetball, rowing (crew), sailing, soccer, squash, swimming, table tennis, tennis, track and field, volleyball, water polo, wrestling M. **Team name:** Vikings.

Student services. Adult student services, career counseling, student employment services, health services, personal counseling, placement for graduates, veterans' counselor. **Physically disabled:** Services for visually, speech, hearing impaired. **Learning disabled:** Comprehensive services available.

Contact. E-mail: admissions@csuohio.edu
Phone: (216) 687-2100 Toll-free number: (800) 278-6446
Fax: (216) 687-5501
Mark Nazario, Director, Undergraduate Admissions, Cleveland State University, 2121 Euclid Avenue, Cleveland, OH 44115-2214

College of Mount St. Joseph

Cincinnati, Ohio — **CB member**
www.msj.edu — **CB code: 1129**

- Private 4-year liberal arts college affiliated with Roman Catholic Church
- Commuter campus in very large city
- 1,817 degree-seeking undergraduates: 27% part-time, 65% women, 9% African American, 1% Hispanic American
- 289 degree-seeking graduate students
- 70% of applicants admitted
- SAT or ACT (ACT writing recommended) required
- 52% graduate within 6 years

General. Founded in 1920. Regionally accredited. **Degrees:** 392 bachelor's, 9 associate awarded; master's, doctoral offered. **ROTC:** Army, Air Force. **Location:** 7 miles from downtown. **Calendar:** Semester, extensive summer session. **Full-time faculty:** 121 total; 69% have terminal degrees, 3% minority, 60% women. **Part-time faculty:** 119 total; 24% have terminal degrees, 2% minority, 66% women. **Class size:** 58% < 20, 41% 20-39, less than 1% 40-49.

Freshman class profile. 1,264 applied, 887 admitted, 308 enrolled.

Mid 50% test scores		**GPA 2.0-2.99:**	35%
SAT critical reading:	440-550	**Rank in top quarter:**	38%
SAT math:	440-560	**Rank in top tenth:**	12%
ACT composite:	19-24	**Return as sophomores:**	73%
GPA 3.75 or higher:	15%	**Out-of-state:**	18%
GPA 3.50-3.74:	14%	**Live on campus:**	54%
GPA 3.0-3.49:	35%		

Basis for selection. Criteria for admission include college prep high school curriculum, strong GPA, standardized test scores, evidence of leadership and extracurricular involvement, and personal background. Essays, recommendations and interviews may be required for some students. Audition required for music programs. Portfolio recommended for art programs. **Homeschooled:** Transcripts required along with any documentation from state or national home schooling accreditation agency. Description of completed courses required. **Learning Disabled:** May apply for Project EXCEL, which helps students with learning disabilities.

High school preparation. College-preparatory program recommended. 14 units required; 22 recommended. Required and recommended units include English 4, mathematics 2-4, social studies 1-2, history 1-2, science 2-4 (laboratory 1-2), foreign language 2, visual/performing arts 2 and academic electives 1-2. Math must include a minimum of 1 year each of algebra and geometry. 1 fine arts required. May substitute 2 additional credits from other subjects in place of foreign language.

2008-2009 Annual costs. Tuition/fees: $22,000. Room/board: $6,900. Books/supplies: $800. Personal expenses: $600.

2008-2009 Financial aid. **Need-based:** 282 full-time freshmen applied for aid; 247 were judged to have need; 247 of these received aid. Average need met was 84%. Average scholarship/grant was $13,901; average loan $3,908. 52% of total undergraduate aid awarded as scholarships/grants, 48% as loans/jobs. **Non-need-based:** Awarded to 391 full-time undergraduates, including 78 freshmen. Scholarships awarded for academics, art, leadership, music/drama, ROTC, state residency.

Application procedures. **Admission:** Priority date 4/1; deadline 8/15 (postmark date). $25 fee, may be waived for applicants with need. Admission notification on a rolling basis beginning on or about 10/1. Must reply by May 1 or within 4 week(s) if notified thereafter. **Financial aid:** Priority date 3/1; no closing date. FAFSA required. Applicants notified on a rolling basis starting 2/15; must reply by 5/1 or within 4 week(s) of notification.

Academics. **Special study options:** Accelerated study, cooperative education, cross-registration, distance learning, double major, honors, independent study, internships, liberal arts/career combination, study abroad, teacher certification program. **Credit/placement by examination:** AP, CLEP, IB, SAT, ACT, institutional tests. 32 credit hours maximum toward associate degree, 64 toward bachelor's. **Support services:** Learning center, reduced course load, remedial instruction, study skills assistance, tutoring, writing center.

Majors. **Biology:** General, biochemistry. **Business:** Accounting, business admin. **Communications:** General. **Computer sciences:** General. **Education:** Art, early childhood, middle, special. **Health:** Athletic training, nursing (RN). **History:** General. **Interdisciplinary:** Natural sciences. **Legal studies:** Paralegal. **Liberal arts:** Arts/sciences. **Math:** General. **Parks/recreation:** Sports admin. **Philosophy/religion:** Religion. **Physical sciences:** Chemistry. **Psychology:** General. **Public administration:** Social work. **Social sciences:** Criminology, sociology. **Theology:** Pastoral counseling, religious ed. **Visual/performing arts:** Art, graphic design, interior design, studio arts.

Most popular majors. Business/marketing 15%, education 9%, health sciences 34%, liberal arts 7%, visual/performing arts 13%.

Computing on campus. 278 workstations in library, computer center, student center. Commuter students can connect to campus network. Online course registration, online library, helpline, repair service, student web hosting, wireless network available.

Student life. **Freshman orientation:** Mandatory, $150 fee. Preregistration for classes offered. Two-part orientation: summer session, which includes a 2-day, 1-night stay in dorms, and welcome weekend consisting of service learning event and river cruise over the weekend before start of classes. **Policies:** Smoke-free campus. All unmarried freshmen and sophomores under age 21 who live outside 35-mile radius of college required to live on campus and participate in meal program. **Housing:** Guaranteed on-campus for freshmen. Coed dorms, special housing for disabled available. $100 fully refundable deposit, deadline 8/15. **Activities:** Bands, campus ministries, choral groups, dance, drama, literary magazine, music ensembles, musical theater, student government, student newspaper, Nippon Enthusiasts and Knowledgeable Otaku (Japanese cultural appreciation), black student union, Alpha Phi Omega service organization, Lions for Life, Habitat for Humanity.

Athletics. NCAA. **Intercollegiate:** Baseball M, basketball, cheerleading M, cross-country, football (tackle) M, golf, lacrosse, soccer, softball W, tennis, track and field, volleyball W, wrestling M. **Intramural:** Basketball, football (non-tackle), racquetball, soccer, softball, tennis, volleyball. **Team name:** Lions.

Student services. Adult student services, alcohol/substance abuse counseling, chaplain/spiritual director, career counseling, services for economically disadvantaged, student employment services, financial aid counseling, health services, minority student services, on-campus daycare, personal counseling, placement for graduates, veterans' counselor, women's services. **Physically disabled:** Services for visually, speech, hearing impaired. **Learning disabled:** Comprehensive services available.

Contact. E-mail: admission@mail.msj.edu
Phone: (513) 244-4531 Toll-free number: (800) 654-9314
Fax: (513) 244-4629
Peggy Minnich, Director of Admission, College of Mount St. Joseph, 5701 Delhi Road, Cincinnati, OH 45233-1670

College of Wooster

Wooster, Ohio — **CB member**
www.wooster.edu — **CB code: 1134**

- Private 4-year liberal arts college
- Residential campus in large town
- 1,868 degree-seeking undergraduates: 53% women, 5% African American, 2% Asian American, 2% Hispanic American, 5% international
- 81% of applicants admitted
- SAT or ACT with writing, application essay required
- 77% graduate within 6 years; 40% enter graduate study

General. Founded in 1866. Regionally accredited. **Degrees:** 398 bachelor's awarded. **Location:** 55 miles from Cleveland, 30 miles from Akron. **Calendar:** Semester, limited summer session. **Full-time faculty:** 162 total; 92% have terminal degrees, 51% women. **Part-time faculty:** 38 total; 55% women. **Class size:** 63% < 20, 34% 20-39, 3% 40-49, less than 1% 50-99.

Freshman class profile. 3,445 applied, 2,783 admitted, 516 enrolled.

Mid 50% test scores		Return as sophomores:	88%
SAT critical reading:	540-670	Out-of-state:	38%
SAT math:	540-660	Live on campus:	100%
ACT composite:	23-29	International:	5%
Rank in top quarter:	63%	Fraternities:	10%
Rank in top tenth:	25%	Sororities:	13%

Basis for selection. Course pattern and academic performance most important. Recommendations, extracurricular activities, class rank, test scores, interview considered. Interview recommended for all; audition recommended for music; portfolio recommended for art programs. **Homeschooled:** Statement describing homeschool structure and mission, interview, letter of recommendation (nonparent) required.

High school preparation. College-preparatory program required. Required and recommended units include English 4, mathematics 3-4, social studies 3-4, science 3-4, foreign language 2-3 and academic electives 2. Math recommendation includes 2 algebra.

2008-2009 Annual costs. Tuition/fees: $33,770. Room/board: $8,650. Books/supplies: $900. Personal expenses: $600.

2008-2009 Financial aid. **Need-based:** 388 full-time freshmen applied for aid; 318 were judged to have need; 318 of these received aid. Average need met was 92%. Average scholarship/grant was $22,343; average loan $4,495. 81% of total undergraduate aid awarded as scholarships/grants, 19% as loans/jobs. **Non-need-based:** Awarded to 882 full-time undergraduates, including 228 freshmen. Scholarships awarded for academics, minority status, music/drama, religious affiliation, state residency.

Application procedures. **Admission:** Closing date 2/15 (postmark date). $40 fee, may be waived for applicants with need, free for online applicants. Admission notification 4/1. Admission notification on a rolling basis. Must reply by May 1 or within 2 week(s) if notified thereafter. **Financial aid:** Priority date 2/15; no closing date. FAFSA, institutional form required. Either CSS PROFILE or institution application from prospectives. Applicants notified by 4/1; must reply by 5/1.

Academics. **Special study options:** Combined bachelor's/graduate degree, cooperative education, double major, exchange student, independent study, internships, New York semester, student-designed major, study abroad, teacher certification program, United Nations semester, urban semester, Washington semester. **Credit/placement by examination:** AP, CLEP, IB, institutional tests. 32 credit hours maximum toward bachelor's degree. **Support services:** Learning center, study skills assistance, tutoring, writing center.

Majors. **Area/ethnic studies:** African, African-American, East Asian, Latin American, Near/Middle Eastern, Russian/Slavic, South Asian, Western European, women's. **Biology:** General, biochemistry, Biochemistry/biophysics and molecular biology, molecular. **Business:** Managerial economics. **Communications:** General. **Computer sciences:** General. **Education:** Music. **Foreign languages:** General, classics, comparative lit, French, German, Russian, Spanish. **Health:** Audiology/speech pathology, music therapy. **History:** General. **Interdisciplinary:** Neuroscience. **Math:** General. **Philosophy/religion:** Philosophy, religion. **Physical sciences:** Chemical physics, chemistry, geology, molecular physics, physics. **Psychology:** General. **Public administration:** Social work. **Social sciences:** Anthropology, archaeology, economics, international relations, political science, sociology, urban studies. **Visual/performing arts:** Art history/conservation, dance, dramatic, music history, music performance, music theory/composition, studio arts. **Other:** Classical studies.

Most popular majors. Biology 6%, communications/journalism 6%, English 8%, philosophy/religious studies 9%, physical sciences 7%, psychology 12%, social sciences 23%, visual/performing arts 7%.

Computing on campus. 275 workstations in dormitories, library, computer center, student center. Dormitories wired for high-speed internet access and linked to campus network. Commuter students can connect to campus network. Online course registration, online library, helpline, repair service, student web hosting, wireless network available.

Student life. **Freshman orientation:** Mandatory. Held during 3 days prior to start of semester. **Housing:** Guaranteed on-campus for all undergraduates. Coed dorms, single-sex dorms, fraternity/sorority housing, wellness housing available. Special housing for students participating in volunteer activities. **Activities:** Bands, campus ministries, choral groups, dance, drama, film society, international student organizations, literary magazine, music ensembles, Model UN, musical theater, radio station, student government, student newspaper, symphony orchestra, variety of religious, ethnic, and social service organizations available.

Athletics. NCAA. **Intercollegiate:** Baseball M, basketball, cross-country, diving, field hockey W, football (tackle) M, golf M, lacrosse, soccer, softball W, swimming, tennis, track and field, volleyball W. **Intramural:** Badminton, basketball, bowling, football (non-tackle), golf, racquetball, soccer, softball, swimming, tennis, volleyball, water polo M. **Team name:** Fighting Scots.

Student services. Alcohol/substance abuse counseling, chaplain/spiritual director, career counseling, student employment services, financial aid counseling, health services, minority student services, personal counseling, placement for graduates. **Physically disabled:** Services for visually impaired.

Contact. E-mail: admissions@wooster.edu
Phone: (330) 263-2322 Toll-free number: (800) 877-9905
Fax: (330) 263-2621
Mary Karen Vellines, Vice President for Enrollment Management, College of Wooster, 847 College Avenue, Wooster, OH 44691-2363

Columbus College of Art and Design

Columbus, Ohio
www.ccad.edu **CB code: 1085**

- Private 4-year visual arts college
- Residential campus in very large city
- 1,391 degree-seeking undergraduates: 5% part-time, 58% women, 7% African American, 3% Asian American, 4% Hispanic American, 4% international
- 72% of applicants admitted
- SAT or ACT (ACT writing optional), application essay required
- 64% graduate within 6 years

General. Founded in 1879. Regionally accredited. **Degrees:** 265 bachelor's awarded. **Location:** Downtown. **Calendar:** Semester, limited summer session. **Full-time faculty:** 78 total; 68% have terminal degrees, 9% minority, 33% women. **Part-time faculty:** 105 total; 25% have terminal degrees, 9% minority, 49% women. **Class size:** 61% < 20, 39% 20-39. **Special facilities:** Student exhibition hall.

Freshman class profile. 560 applied, 402 admitted, 323 enrolled.

Mid 50% test scores		**GPA 2.0-2.99:**	54%
SAT critical reading:	460-580	**Rank in top quarter:**	15%
SAT math:	450-550	**Rank in top tenth:**	2%
SAT writing:	440-550	**End year in good standing:**	95%
ACT composite:	19-24	**Return as sophomores:**	78%
GPA 3.75 or higher:	9%	**Out-of-state:**	13%
GPA 3.50-3.74:	15%	**Live on campus:**	69%
GPA 3.0-3.49:	22%	**International:**	9%

Basis for selection. Portfolio and 2.0 GPA important. Portfolio required; interview recommended.

High school preparation. Recommended units include English 4, mathematics 2, science 2 and foreign language 2. 4 units art recommended.

2008-2009 Annual costs. Tuition/fees: $23,564. Room/board: $6,750. Books/supplies: $2,000. Personal expenses: $1,300.

2008-2009 Financial aid. Need-based: Average need met was 65%. Average scholarship/grant was $13,620; average loan $5,085. 60% of total undergraduate aid awarded as scholarships/grants, 40% as loans/jobs. **Non-need-based:** Scholarships awarded for academics, art, ROTC, state residency.

Application procedures. Admission: No deadline. $25 fee, may be waived for applicants with need. Admission notification on a rolling basis. **Financial aid:** Priority date 3/2, closing date 6/4. FAFSA required. Applicants notified on a rolling basis starting 3/15; must reply within 2 week(s) of notification.

Academics. Special study options: Accelerated study, cooperative education, cross-registration, double major, ESL, independent study, internships, New York semester, study abroad. **Credit/placement by examination:** AP, CLEP, SAT, ACT, institutional tests. **Support services:** Learning center, reduced course load, remedial instruction, study skills assistance, tutoring.

Majors. Visual/performing arts: Commercial/advertising art, fashion design, illustration, industrial design, interior design, photography, studio arts.

Computing on campus. 485 workstations in library, computer center, student center. Dormitories wired for high-speed internet access. Online library available.

Student life. Freshman orientation: Mandatory. Held 3 days before first day of classes. **Housing:** Guaranteed on-campus for freshmen. Coed dorms, apartments, wellness housing available. $225 fully refundable deposit, deadline 5/11. **Activities:** Literary magazine, student government, student newspaper, student Bible study, student spirituality group, gay/lesbian/bisexual group.

Athletics. Intramural: Basketball M, soccer M, volleyball.

Student services. Adult student services, career counseling, student employment services, financial aid counseling, personal counseling, placement for graduates.

Contact. E-mail: admissions@ccad.edu
Phone: (614) 224-9101 ext. 3261 Toll-free number: (877) 997-2223
Fax: (614) 232-8344
Thomas Green, Director of Admissions, Columbus College of Art and Design, 107 North Ninth Street, Columbus, OH 43215-3875

Defiance College

Defiance, Ohio **CB member**
www.defiance.edu **CB code: 1162**

- Private 4-year liberal arts college affiliated with United Church of Christ
- Residential campus in large town
- 891 degree-seeking undergraduates: 19% part-time, 53% women
- 107 degree-seeking graduate students
- 73% of applicants admitted
- SAT or ACT (ACT writing optional) required
- 51% graduate within 6 years; 18% enter graduate study

General. Founded in 1850. Regionally accredited. **Degrees:** 179 bachelor's, 7 associate awarded; master's offered. **Location:** 55 miles from Toledo; 45 miles from Fort Wayne, Indiana. **Calendar:** Semester, extensive summer session. **Full-time faculty:** 44 total; 54% have terminal degrees, 7% minority, 41% women. **Part-time faculty:** 57 total; 16% have terminal degrees, 4% minority, 42% women. **Class size:** 69% < 20, 29% 20-39, 1% 40-49, less than 1% 50-99. **Special facilities:** Wildlife sanctuary.

Freshman class profile. 1,085 applied, 792 admitted, 221 enrolled.

Mid 50% test scores		**GPA 2.0-2.99:**	38%
SAT critical reading:	440-560	**Rank in top quarter:**	36%
SAT math:	430-560	**Rank in top tenth:**	15%
SAT writing:	420-560	**End year in good standing:**	76%
ACT composite:	19-24	**Return as sophomores:**	62%
GPA 3.75 or higher:	18%	**Out-of-state:**	19%
GPA 3.50-3.74:	15%	**Live on campus:**	90%
GPA 3.0-3.49:	28%		

Basis for selection. School achievement record, test scores, college preparatory curriculum important. 2.25 GPA, 18 ACT or 870 SAT (exclusive of Writing) required.

High school preparation. College-preparatory program recommended. 16 units recommended. Recommended units include English 4, mathematics 3, social studies 2, science 3, foreign language 2 and visual/performing arts 2. One unit fine arts and 1 unit of computer proficiency recommended.

2008-2009 Annual costs. Tuition/fees: $21,830. Room/board: $7,150. Books/supplies: $1,350. Personal expenses: $1,200.

2007-2008 Financial aid. Non-need-based: Scholarships awarded for academics, leadership.

Application procedures. Admission: No deadline. $25 fee, may be waived for applicants with need, free for online applicants. Admission notification on a rolling basis beginning on or about 9/1. Must reply by May 1 or within 4 week(s) if notified thereafter. **Financial aid:** Priority date 3/1; no closing date. FAFSA required. Applicants notified on a rolling basis starting 3/15; must reply within 3 week(s) of notification.

Academics. Evening sessions available in many areas. Weekend college program for nontraditional students to pursue bachelor's or master's degree in several business majors. **Special study options:** Accelerated study, cooperative education, distance learning, double major, dual enrollment of high school students, honors, independent study, internships, student-designed major, study abroad, teacher certification program, weekend college. **Credit/placement by examination:** AP, CLEP, IB, institutional tests. 15 credit hours maximum toward associate degree, 30 toward bachelor's. **Support services:** Learning center, reduced course load, study skills assistance, tutoring, writing center.

Majors. Biology: General. **Business:** General, accounting, business admin, management information systems. **Communications:** General, journalism, public relations. **Computer sciences:** Computer forensics. **Conservation:** General, environmental studies. **Education:** General, art, biology, business, chemistry, early childhood, elementary, English, health, history, mathematics, middle, multi-level teacher, physical, science, secondary, social science, social studies, speech. **Health:** Athletic training, clinical lab technology, health services, predental, premedicine, preveterinary. **History:** General. **Interdisciplinary:** Biological/physical sciences, math/computer science, natural sciences. **Legal studies:** Prelaw. **Liberal arts:** Arts/sciences. **Math:** General. **Parks/recreation:** Health/fitness, sports admin. **Philosophy/religion:**

Religion. **Protective services:** Forensics. **Psychology:** General. **Public administration:** Social work. **Social sciences:** General, criminology. **Theology:** Religious ed. **Visual/performing arts:** Art, commercial/advertising art, graphic design.

Most popular majors. Business/marketing 30%, education 19%, parks/recreation 9%, science technologies 6%, security/protective services 12%, social sciences 8%.

Computing on campus. 200 workstations in dormitories, library, computer center, student center. Dormitories wired for high-speed internet access and linked to campus network. Commuter students can connect to campus network. Online library, helpline, wireless network available.

Student life. Freshman orientation: Mandatory. Preregistration for classes offered. One-day sessions held in April, May, June, and August. **Policies:** Students must live and take meals on campus unless they are seniors, married, veterans, or living with parents or close relatives within approved commuting distance. **Housing:** Guaranteed on-campus for freshmen. Coed dorms, single-sex dorms, apartments, wellness housing available. ADA-compliant rooms available in each hall. Service floors available. **Activities:** Bands, campus ministries, choral groups, dance, drama, literary magazine, musical theater, student government, student newspaper, American Marketing Association, Black Action Student Association, campus activities board, criminal justice society, Fellowship of Christian Athletes, student ecology club, Habitat for Humanity.

Athletics. NCAA. **Intercollegiate:** Baseball M, basketball, cross-country, football (tackle) M, golf, soccer, softball W, tennis, track and field, volleyball W. **Intramural:** Basketball, football (non-tackle), football (tackle) M, racquetball, volleyball. **Team name:** Yellow Jackets.

Student services. Adult student services, alcohol/substance abuse counseling, chaplain/spiritual director, career counseling, student employment services, financial aid counseling, health services, minority student services, personal counseling, placement for graduates. **Physically disabled:** Services for hearing impaired.

Contact. E-mail: admissions@defiance.edu
Phone: (419) 783-2359 Toll-free number: (800) 520-4632
Fax: (419) 783-2468
Brad Harsha, Director of Admissions, Defiance College, 701 North Clinton Street, Defiance, OH 43512-1695

Denison University

Granville, Ohio — **CB member**
www.denison.edu — **CB code: 1164**

- Private 4-year liberal arts college
- Residential campus in small town
- 2,180 degree-seeking undergraduates: 56% women, 5% African American, 2% Asian American, 3% Hispanic American, 5% international
- 38% of applicants admitted
- Application essay required
- 82% graduate within 6 years

General. Founded in 1831. Regionally accredited. **Degrees:** 541 bachelor's awarded. **ROTC:** Army. **Location:** 27 miles from Columbus. **Calendar:** Semester. **Full-time faculty:** 195 total; 97% have terminal degrees, 15% minority, 44% women. **Part-time faculty:** 23 total; 35% have terminal degrees, 13% minority, 52% women. **Class size:** 70% < 20, 29% 20-39, less than 1% 40-49, less than 1% 50-99. **Special facilities:** Field research station in 350-acre biological reserve, high resolution spectrometer lab, nuclear magnetic resonance spectrometer, planetarium, economics computer lab, harmonic systems lab, digital media lab, fine and performing arts MIX lab (intermedia experimental lab), geographic information systems lab.

Freshman class profile. 5,305 applied, 2,027 admitted, 605 enrolled.

Mid 50% test scores		**GPA 2.0-2.99:**	6%
SAT critical reading:	580-690	**Return as sophomores:**	88%
SAT math:	570-680	**Out-of-state:**	68%
ACT composite:	25-30	**Live on campus:**	100%
GPA 3.75 or higher:	35%	**International:**	6%
GPA 3.50-3.74:	25%	**Fraternities:**	22%
GPA 3.0-3.49:	34%	**Sororities:**	35%

Basis for selection. Academic record, recommendations, talent and ability, character and personal qualities most important. School and community activities, essay and personal potential also important. Test scores considered. Interview recommended for all; audition required for visual and performing arts program; portfolio recommended for studio art programs.

High school preparation. College-preparatory program required. 19 units required. Required units include English 4, mathematics 4, social studies 2, history 1, science 4, foreign language 3 and academic electives 1. 1 unit fine arts recommended.

2008-2009 Annual costs. Tuition/fees: $35,300. Room/board: $8,830. Books/supplies: $650. Personal expenses: $1,200.

2008-2009 Financial aid. Need-based: 373 full-time freshmen applied for aid; 290 were judged to have need; 290 of these received aid. Average need met was 97%. Average scholarship/grant was $26,212; average loan $3,734. 83% of total undergraduate aid awarded as scholarships/grants, 17% as loans/jobs. **Non-need-based:** Awarded to 1,927 full-time undergraduates, including 545 freshmen. Scholarships awarded for academics, art, leadership, music/drama, state residency.

Application procedures. Admission: Priority date 12/1; deadline 1/15 (postmark date). $40 fee, may be waived for applicants with need, free for online applicants. Admission notification 4/1. Must reply by May 1 or within 2 week(s) if notified thereafter. **Financial aid:** Priority date 2/15; no closing date. FAFSA required. Applicants notified by 3/30; must reply by 5/1 or within 2 week(s) of notification.

Academics. Special study options: Double major, honors, independent study, internships, New York semester, semester at sea, student-designed major, study abroad, teacher certification program, Washington semester. **Credit/placement by examination:** AP, CLEP, IB, institutional tests. **Support services:** Learning center, reduced course load, study skills assistance, tutoring, writing center.

Majors. Area/ethnic studies: African-American, East Asian, gay/lesbian, Latin American, Western European, women's. **Biology:** General, biochemistry. **Business:** Organizational behavior. **Communications:** General, digital media. **Computer sciences:** General. **Conservation:** General. **Education:** General, physical. **Foreign languages:** Classics, French, German, Spanish. **History:** General. **Math:** General. **Philosophy/religion:** Philosophy, religion. **Physical sciences:** Chemistry, geology, physics. **Psychology:** General. **Social sciences:** Anthropology, economics, political science, sociology. **Visual/performing arts:** Art history/conservation, dance, dramatic, film/cinema, studio arts.

Most popular majors. Biology 10%, communications/journalism 11%, education 6%, English 8%, psychology 8%, social sciences 24%, visual/performing arts 9%.

Computing on campus. Dormitories wired for high-speed internet access and linked to campus network. Commuter students can connect to campus network. Online library, helpline, student web hosting, wireless network available.

Student life. Freshman orientation: Mandatory. Preregistration for classes offered. Mandatory no-fee August orientation program and optional but highly recommended June program costing $175. **Housing:** Guaranteed on-campus for all undergraduates. Coed dorms, single-sex dorms, apartments, cooperative housing, wellness housing available. 3 student-constructed buildings using alternative energy resources accommodate 12 students. Apartment-style housing for high-GPA upper division students. **Activities:** Jazz band, campus ministries, choral groups, dance, drama, film society, international student organizations, literary magazine, music ensembles, musical theater, radio station, student government, student newspaper, TV station, over 130 organizations available.

Athletics. NCAA. **Intercollegiate:** Baseball M, basketball, cross-country, diving, field hockey W, football (tackle) M, golf M, lacrosse, soccer, softball W, swimming, tennis, track and field, volleyball W. **Intramural:** Basketball, equestrian, football (non-tackle), golf, ice hockey M, lacrosse M, racquetball, rifle, rugby, skiing, soccer, softball, squash, tennis, volleyball, water polo, wrestling M. **Team name:** Big Red.

Student services. Alcohol/substance abuse counseling, chaplain/spiritual director, career counseling, student employment services, financial aid counseling, health services, minority student services, personal counseling, placement for graduates.

Contact. E-mail: admissions@denison.edu
Phone: (740) 587-6276 Toll-free number: (800) 336-4766
Fax: (740) 587-6306
Perry Robinson, VP and Director of Admissions, Denison University, Box H, Granville, OH 43023

DeVry University: Columbus

Columbus, Ohio — **CB member**
www.devry.edu — **CB code: 1605**

- For-profit 4-year university
- Commuter campus in very large city

- 2,520 degree-seeking undergraduates: 41% part-time, 41% women, 25% African American, 2% Asian American, 2% Hispanic American
- 249 degree-seeking graduate students
- Interview required

General. Founded in 1952. Regionally accredited. **Degrees:** 371 bachelor's, 108 associate awarded; master's offered. **ROTC:** Army. **Location:** 5 miles from downtown. **Calendar:** Semester, extensive summer session. **Full-time faculty:** 45 total; 13% minority, 22% women. **Part-time faculty:** 191 total; 12% minority, 44% women.

Basis for selection. Applicants must have high school diploma or equivalent, demonstrate proficiency in basic college-level skills through SAT or ACT scores or institution-administered placement examinations, and be 17 years of age. New students may enter at beginning of any semester. SAT or ACT recommended. CPT also accepted.

High school preparation. Required units include mathematics 1. Math unit must be algebra or higher.

2008-2009 Annual costs. Tuition/fees: $14,130. Books/supplies: $1,300. Personal expenses: $5,082.

2007-2008 Financial aid. All financial aid based on need.

Application procedures. **Admission:** No deadline. $50 fee. Admission notification on a rolling basis. **Financial aid:** No deadline. FAFSA required. Applicants notified on a rolling basis.

Academics. **Special study options:** Accelerated study, distance learning. **Credit/placement by examination:** CLEP, institutional tests. **Support services:** Learning center, tutoring.

Majors. **Business:** Business admin. **Computer sciences:** Networking, systems analysis. **Engineering technology:** Biomedical, computer, electrical. **Other:** Technical management.

Most popular majors. Business/marketing 49%, computer/information sciences 31%, engineering/engineering technologies 19%.

Computing on campus. 408 workstations in library, computer center, student center. Online course registration, online library, helpline available.

Student life. **Freshman orientation:** Mandatory. **Housing:** Private apartments, student-plan housing, private rooms available. **Activities:** Student association, Tau Alpha Pi, Christian Alliance, Asian American student association, Future Accounting Society, Institute of Electrical and Electronics Engineers, Association of IT Professionals, minority student union.

Athletics. **Intramural:** Basketball, soccer, volleyball.

Student services. Career counseling, student employment services, financial aid counseling, placement for graduates, veterans' counselor. **Physically disabled:** Services for visually, hearing impaired.

Contact. E-mail: admissions@devry.edu
Phone: (614) 253-1525 Toll-free number: (800) 426-2206
Fax: (614) 253-0843
Bill Holtry, Dean of Admissions, DeVry University: Columbus, 1350 Alum Creek Drive, Columbus, OH 43209-2705

Franciscan University of Steubenville

Steubenville, Ohio — **CB member**
www.franciscan.edu — **CB code: 1133**

- Private 4-year university affiliated with Roman Catholic Church
- Residential campus in large town
- 2,002 degree-seeking undergraduates
- 72% of applicants admitted
- SAT or ACT (ACT writing optional), application essay required

General. Founded in 1946. Regionally accredited. **Degrees:** 425 bachelor's, 43 associate awarded; master's offered. **ROTC:** Army. **Location:** 40 miles from Pittsburgh. **Calendar:** Semester, limited summer session. **Full-time faculty:** 113 total. **Part-time faculty:** 101 total. **Class size:** 48% < 20, 37% 20-39, 11% 40-49, 3% 50-99, less than 1% >100. **Special facilities:** Replica of Portiuncula (St. Mary of the Angels) Chapel as rebuilt by St. Francis of Assisi in 1207, Tomb of the Unborn Child.

Freshman class profile. 1,328 applied, 957 admitted, 389 enrolled.

Mid 50% test scores		**GPA 3.0-3.49:**	25%
SAT critical reading:	540-650	**GPA 2.0-2.99:**	12%
SAT math:	520-600	**Rank in top quarter:**	56%
SAT writing:	520-630	**Rank in top tenth:**	33%
ACT composite:	22-28	**Out-of-state:**	80%
GPA 3.75 or higher:	44%	**Live on campus:**	88%
GPA 3.50-3.74:	19%	**Sororities:**	1%

Basis for selection. Admission requirements include 2.4 GPA, recommendations, interview when available, 1000 SAT (exclusive of Writing) or 21 ACT. Interview recommended. **Homeschooled:** Applicants should contact Admissions Office for requirements.

High school preparation. 15 units required. Required and recommended units include English 4, mathematics 3, social studies 2, history 2, science 3, foreign language 3 and academic electives 1. 10 units in 4 of the following fields: English, foreign language, social science, math, natural sciences. Remaining 5 units may be in other subjects counted toward graduation. Majors in chemistry, engineering science, or math should have 2 units algebra and 2 units geometry/trigonometry.

2008-2009 Annual costs. Tuition/fees: $19,100. Room/board: $6,600. Books/supplies: $800. Personal expenses: $1,200.

2007-2008 Financial aid. **Need-based:** 44% of total undergraduate aid awarded as scholarships/grants, 56% as loans/jobs. **Non-need-based:** Scholarships awarded for academics, leadership, religious affiliation.

Application procedures. **Admission:** Priority date 1/31; no deadline. $20 fee, may be waived for applicants with need, free for online applicants. Admission notification on a rolling basis beginning on or about 9/1. **Financial aid:** No deadline. FAFSA required. Applicants notified on a rolling basis starting 3/15; must reply within 3 week(s) of notification.

Academics. Students encouraged to spend 1 semester of sophomore year in study abroad program in Gaming, Austria. **Special study options:** Accelerated study, combined bachelor's/graduate degree, distance learning, double major, honors, independent study, internships, liberal arts/career combination, study abroad, teacher certification program. **Credit/placement by examination:** AP, CLEP, IB, institutional tests. 30 credit hours maximum toward associate degree, 30 toward bachelor's. **Support services:** Learning center, reduced course load, study skills assistance, tutoring, writing center.

Honors college/program. 1180 SAT (exclusive of Writing) or 26 ACT, 3.4 GPA, and series of essays required. 40 freshmen admitted. Academic program consists of a great books seminar sequence.

Majors. **Biology:** General. **Business:** Accounting, business admin. **Communications:** General. **Computer sciences:** General, computer science. **Education:** Elementary. **Foreign languages:** Classics, French, German, Spanish. **Health:** Mental health services, nursing (RN). **History:** General. **Legal studies:** General. **Liberal arts:** Humanities. **Math:** General. **Philosophy/religion:** Philosophy. **Physical sciences:** Chemistry. **Psychology:** General. **Public administration:** Social work. **Social sciences:** Anthropology, economics, political science, sociology. **Theology:** Religious ed, sacred music, theology. **Visual/performing arts:** Dramatic.

Most popular majors. Business/marketing 11%, education 9%, health sciences 15%, theological studies 27%.

Computing on campus. 126 workstations in library, computer center. Commuter students can connect to campus network. Online library, helpline available.

Student life. **Freshman orientation:** Mandatory, $150 fee. Preregistration for classes offered. Held weekend before fall classes begin, from Friday morning to Sunday afternoon. **Housing:** Guaranteed on-campus for freshmen. Single-sex dorms available. $300 nonrefundable deposit. Household groups of 10-20 students in residence halls may develop distinctive environment for their group within the context of Christian and Franciscan perspective. **Activities:** Campus ministries, choral groups, drama, international student organizations, literary magazine, music ensembles, radio station, student government, student newspaper, international student organization, Human Life Concerns (pro-life), Works of Mercy Program, leadership development.

Athletics. **Intercollegiate:** Baseball M, basketball, cross-country, rugby M, soccer, tennis M, volleyball W. **Intramural:** Basketball, bowling, football (non-tackle), racquetball, soccer, softball, tennis, volleyball, weight lifting, wrestling M. **Team name:** Barons.

Student services. Adult student services, chaplain/spiritual director, career counseling, student employment services, financial aid counseling, health services, personal counseling, veterans' counselor. **Physically disabled:** Services for visually, speech, hearing impaired.

Contact. E-mail: admissions@franciscan.edu
Phone: (740) 283-6226 Toll-free number: (800) 783-6220
Fax: (740) 284-5456
Margaret Weber, Director of Admissions, Franciscan University of Steubenville, 1235 University Boulevard, Steubenville, OH 43952-1763

Franklin University

Columbus, Ohio
www.franklin.edu **CB code: 1229**

- Private 4-year university and business college
- Commuter campus in very large city
- 7,688 degree-seeking undergraduates

General. Founded in 1902. Regionally accredited. Credit courses offered at suburban campuses and online. **Degrees:** 1,159 bachelor's, 92 associate awarded; master's offered. **ROTC:** Army. **Location:** Downtown. **Calendar:** Trimester, extensive summer session. **Full-time faculty:** 38 total. **Part-time faculty:** 552 total; 19% have terminal degrees, 29% minority, 42% women. **Class size:** 75% < 20, 24% 20-39, less than 1% 40-49. **Special facilities:** Student learning center.

Basis for selection. Open admission, but selective for some programs. Admission tests not required but considered for placement if submitted. Selective admission for international (nonresident alien) students.

High school preparation. Recommended units include mathematics 3.

2008-2009 Annual costs. Tuition/fees: $8,400. Books/supplies: $900. Personal expenses: $2,150.

2007-2008 Financial aid. **Non-need-based:** Scholarships awarded for academics, leadership, minority status.

Application procedures. **Admission:** No deadline. No application fee. Admission notification on a rolling basis. **Financial aid:** Priority date 6/15; no closing date. FAFSA required. Applicants notified on a rolling basis; must reply within 2 week(s) of notification.

Academics. Accelerated 6-week course offerings in addition to 12- and 15-week formats. **Special study options:** Accelerated study, combined bachelor's/graduate degree, cooperative education, cross-registration, distance learning, double major, dual enrollment of high school students, ESL, independent study, internships, study abroad, weekend college. **Credit/placement by examination:** AP, CLEP, institutional tests. 32 credit hours maximum toward associate degree, 84 toward bachelor's. **Support services:** Learning center, reduced course load, remedial instruction, study skills assistance, tutoring, writing center.

Majors. **Business:** General, accounting, finance, human resources, management information systems, management science, marketing, operations. **Communications:** Digital media. **Computer sciences:** General, computer science, information technology, web page design. **Health:** Health care admin, medical records technology.

Most popular majors. Business/marketing 78%, computer/information sciences 15%.

Computing on campus. 370 workstations in library, computer center, student center. Commuter students can connect to campus network. Online course registration, online library, helpline, wireless network available.

Student life. **Freshman orientation:** Available. **Activities:** International student association.

Student services. Adult student services, career counseling, financial aid counseling, veterans' counselor. **Physically disabled:** Services for visually, speech, hearing impaired.

Contact. E-mail: info@franklin.edu
Phone: (614) 797-4700 Toll-free number: (877) 341-6300
Fax: (614) 224-8027
Wendi Robison, Director of Undergraduate Student Services, Franklin University, 201 South Grant Avenue, Columbus, OH 43215-5399

God's Bible School and College

Cincinnati, Ohio
www.gbs.edu **CB code: 1238**

- Private 4-year Bible college affiliated with interdenominational tradition
- Residential campus in large city
- 278 degree-seeking undergraduates

General. Founded in 1900. Accredited by ABHE. **Degrees:** 30 bachelor's, 17 associate awarded. **Location:** One mile from downtown. **Calendar:** Semester. **Full-time faculty:** 13 total. **Part-time faculty:** 14 total.

Freshman class profile. 74 applied, 74 admitted, 67 enrolled.

Basis for selection. Open admission. Three references recommended (two required); SAT required for placement.

High school preparation. 17 units recommended. Recommended units include English 3, mathematics 2, social studies 2 and science 2.

2008-2009 Annual costs. Tuition/fees: $5,580. Room/board: $3,450. Books/supplies: $650. Personal expenses: $2,600.

2008-2009 Financial aid. **Need-based:** 71% of total undergraduate aid awarded as scholarships/grants, 29% as loans/jobs. **Non-need-based:** Scholarships awarded for academics, leadership, music/drama, religious affiliation. **Additional information:** Institutional work scholarships available.

Application procedures. **Admission:** Priority date 6/1; no deadline. $50 fee. Application must be submitted on paper. Admission notification on a rolling basis. **Financial aid:** Priority date 4/30; no closing date. FAFSA required. Applicants notified on a rolling basis.

Academics. **Special study options:** Distance learning, double major, independent study, internships, liberal arts/career combination. **Credit/placement by examination:** CLEP, SAT, institutional tests. **Support services:** Learning center.

Majors. **Education:** Elementary, English, music. **Theology:** Missionary, pastoral counseling, religious ed, sacred music, theology, youth ministry. **Other:** Church/Family Ministry.

Computing on campus. Dormitories wired for high-speed internet access. Wireless network available.

Student life. **Freshman orientation:** Mandatory. Preregistration for classes offered. Takes place week before classes begin, lasting for several days. **Policies:** Students agree to follow all rules, policies and regulations by matriculating. Please contact Office of Student Affairs for specific information. Religious observance required. **Housing:** Guaranteed on-campus for freshmen. Single-sex dorms, wellness housing available. **Activities:** Choral groups, drama, music ensembles, student government, student newspaper, symphony orchestra.

Athletics. **Intramural:** Basketball, volleyball.

Student services. Chaplain/spiritual director, student employment services, financial aid counseling, health services, personal counseling, placement for graduates, veterans' counselor.

Contact. E-mail: jhood@gbs.edu
Phone: (513) 721-7944 ext. 205 Toll-free number: (800) 486-4637 ext. 205
Fax: (513) 721-1357
Steve Buckland, Director of Admissions, God's Bible School and College, 1810 Young Street, Cincinnati, OH 45202-6838

Heidelberg University

Tiffin, Ohio **CB member**
www.heidelberg.edu **CB code: 1292**

- Private 4-year liberal arts college affiliated with United Church of Christ
- Residential campus in large town
- 1,255 degree-seeking undergraduates: 5% part-time, 46% women, 8% African American, 2% Hispanic American, 3% international
- 138 degree-seeking graduate students
- 73% of applicants admitted
- SAT or ACT (ACT writing optional) required
- 53% graduate within 6 years

General. Founded in 1850. Regionally accredited. **Degrees:** 240 bachelor's awarded; master's offered. **ROTC:** Army, Air Force. **Location:** 52 miles from Toledo, 80 miles from Cleveland. **Calendar:** Semester, limited summer session. **Full-time faculty:** 62 total; 86% have terminal degrees, 10% minority, 45% women. **Part-time faculty:** 92 total; 24% have terminal degrees, 10% minority, 47% women. **Class size:** 33% < 20, 16% 20-39, 1% 40-49, less than 1% 50-99, 50% >100. **Special facilities:** National center for water quality research, cadaver laboratory, four wooded lots for science research, archaeology laboratory, historic and military archaeology center.

Freshman class profile. 2,059 applied, 1,502 admitted, 396 enrolled.

Mid 50% test scores			
SAT critical reading:	440-580	Rank in top quarter:	37%
SAT math:	440-590	Rank in top tenth:	12%
SAT writing:	420-550	Return as sophomores:	66%
ACT composite:	18-24	Out-of-state:	15%
GPA 3.75 or higher:	16%	Live on campus:	91%
GPA 3.50-3.74:	15%	International:	2%
GPA 3.0-3.49:	27%	Fraternities:	11%
GPA 2.0-2.99:	41%	Sororities:	18%

Basis for selection. School achievement record most important, followed by test scores. Special talents, community activities, and leadership qualities also considered. Audition required for music; interview recommended for academically weak students. **Learning Disabled:** Students with learning disabilites are strongly encouraged to self-report to the Academic Success Center after deciding to attend the College. Appointments to discuss possible services/accommodations are welcome.

High school preparation. 21 units recommended. Recommended units include English 4, mathematics 3, social studies 3, history 2, science 3 (laboratory 1), foreign language 2 and academic electives 3.

2008-2009 Annual costs. Tuition/fees: $19,922. Room/board: $8,138. Books/supplies: $1,000. Personal expenses: $500.

2008-2009 Financial aid. Need-based: 368 full-time freshmen applied for aid; 328 were judged to have need; 328 of these received aid. Average need met was 84%. Average scholarship/grant was $13,019; average loan $4,079. 52% of total undergraduate aid awarded as scholarships/grants, 48% as loans/jobs. **Non-need-based:** Awarded to 180 full-time undergraduates, including 69 freshmen. Scholarships awarded for academics, music/drama, religious affiliation, state residency.

Application procedures. Admission: Priority date 1/1; deadline 8/1 (receipt date). $25 fee, may be waived for applicants with need, free for online applicants. Admission notification on a rolling basis beginning on or about 10/15. Must reply by May 1 or within 2 week(s) if notified thereafter. **Financial aid:** Priority date 3/1; no closing date. FAFSA required. Applicants notified on a rolling basis starting 3/15; must reply by 5/1 or within 2 week(s) of notification.

Academics. Freshman-level credit courses and graduate education course work offered at Sapporo, Japan campus. Program in Sport Management and Business Administration offered at Royal Racing Football Club, Montagnee in Belgium. **Special study options:** Accelerated study, combined bachelor's/graduate degree, cooperative education, cross-registration, double major, dual enrollment of high school students, ESL, exchange student, honors, independent study, internships, liberal arts/career combination, study abroad, teacher certification program, Washington semester. **Credit/placement by examination:** AP, CLEP, IB, SAT, ACT, institutional tests. 30 credit hours maximum toward bachelor's degree. **Support services:** Learning center, reduced course load, study skills assistance, tutoring, writing center.

Majors. Biology: General, environmental. **Business:** Accounting, business admin, management science. **Communications:** General, public relations. **Computer sciences:** General, computer science. **Conservation:** Management/policy. **Education:** Music, physical. **Foreign languages:** German, Spanish. **Health:** Athletic training, health care admin, predental, premedicine, prenursing, preveterinary. **History:** General. **Interdisciplinary:** Biological/physical sciences. **Legal studies:** Prelaw. **Math:** General. **Parks/recreation:** Sports admin. **Philosophy/religion:** Religion. **Physical sciences:** Chemistry, physics. **Protective services:** Law enforcement admin. **Psychology:** General. **Public administration:** General. **Social sciences:** General, anthropology, economics, political science. **Visual/performing arts:** Music management, music performance, music theory/composition.

Most popular majors. Biology 7%, business/marketing 25%, communications/journalism 6%, education 15%, history 6%, parks/recreation 13%, psychology 9%.

Computing on campus. 125 workstations in dormitories, library, computer center, student center. Dormitories wired for high-speed internet access and linked to campus network. Online course registration, helpline, repair service, wireless network available.

Student life. Freshman orientation: Mandatory. Preregistration for classes offered. Five 2-day summer sessions offered. **Housing:** Guaranteed on-campus for all undergraduates. Coed dorms, single-sex dorms, special housing for disabled, apartments, cooperative housing, wellness housing available. $250 fully refundable deposit, deadline 8/1. Undergraduate specialty houses by major, interest, service groups available. **Activities:** Bands, campus ministries, choral groups, dance, drama, film society, international student organizations, literary magazine, music ensembles, Model UN, musical theater, opera, radio station, student government, student newspaper, symphony orchestra, TV station, black student union, Young Democrats, Young Republicans, Circle-K, religious organizations, World Student Union, Beta Beta Beta, political science organization.

Athletics. NCAA. **Intercollegiate:** Baseball M, basketball, cheerleading, cross-country, football (tackle) M, golf, soccer, softball W, tennis, track and field, volleyball W, wrestling M. **Intramural:** Archery, baseball M, basketball, bowling, golf, soccer, softball, table tennis, volleyball. **Team name:** Student Princes.

Student services. Adult student services, chaplain/spiritual director, career counseling, student employment services, financial aid counseling, health services, minority student services, personal counseling, placement for graduates, women's services. **Physically disabled:** Services for visually, hearing impaired.

Contact. E-mail: adminfo@heidelberg.edu
Phone: (419) 448-2330 Toll-free number: (800) 434-3352
Fax: (419) 448-2334
Lindsay Sooy, Director of Admission, Heidelberg University, 310 East Market Street, Tiffin, OH 44883-2462

Hiram College

Hiram, Ohio — **CB member**
www.hiram.edu — **CB code: 1297**

- Private 4-year liberal arts college affiliated with Christian Church (Disciples of Christ)
- Residential campus in rural community
- 1,313 degree-seeking undergraduates: 14% part-time, 54% women, 11% African American, 1% Asian American, 2% Hispanic American, 1% Native American, 5% international
- 25 degree-seeking graduate students
- 75% of applicants admitted
- SAT or ACT (ACT writing optional), application essay required
- 62% graduate within 6 years

General. Founded in 1850. Regionally accredited. Affiliated with John Cabot University in Rome (Italy), Shoals Marine Laboratory (Appledore Island near Maine/New Hampshire coast), Institute of European Studies (Chicago). Exchange programs with Kansai University of Foreign Studies in Osaka (Japan) and Bosphorus University in Istanbul (Turkey). **Degrees:** 232 bachelor's awarded; master's offered. **Location:** 35 miles from Cleveland. **Calendar:** Semester, limited summer session. **Full-time faculty:** 74 total; 93% have terminal degrees, 3% minority, 49% women. **Part-time faculty:** 110 total; 42% women. **Class size:** 71% < 20, 28% 20-39, less than 1% 40-49, less than 1% 50-99. **Special facilities:** 2 nature/science field research stations, observatory, center for literature and medicine.

Freshman class profile. 1,513 applied, 1,138 admitted, 334 enrolled.

Mid 50% test scores		GPA 2.0-2.99:	32%
SAT critical reading:	480-610	Rank in top quarter:	42%
SAT math:	470-590	Rank in top tenth:	18%
ACT composite:	20-26	Return as sophomores:	80%
GPA 3.75 or higher:	22%	Out-of-state:	26%
GPA 3.50-3.74:	13%	Live on campus:	94%
GPA 3.0-3.49:	33%	International:	7%

Basis for selection. School record, test scores, counselor and teacher recommendations emphasized. Extracurricular participation, alumni relationship considered. Interview required for scholarship candidates or academically marginal applicants; recommended for all others.

High school preparation. 20 units required; 21 recommended. Required and recommended units include English 4, mathematics 3, social studies 3, history 1, science 3 (laboratory 2), foreign language 2-3 and academic electives 2. One course in fine arts recommended.

2009-2010 Annual costs. Tuition/fees (projected): $27,135. Room/board: $9,010. Books/supplies: $700. Personal expenses: $1,408.

2008-2009 Financial aid. Need-based: 52% of total undergraduate aid awarded as scholarships/grants, 48% as loans/jobs. **Non-need-based:** Scholarships awarded for academics, alumni affiliation, music/drama, religious affiliation, state residency.

Application procedures. Admission: Priority date 2/15; no deadline. $35 fee, may be waived for applicants with need, free for online applicants. Admission notification on a rolling basis beginning on or about 10/1. Must reply by May 1 or within 2 week(s) if notified thereafter. **Financial aid:** Priority date 2/15; no closing date. FAFSA required. Applicants notified on a rolling basis starting 2/15; must reply by 5/1 or within 2 week(s) of notification.

Academics. Prelaw, premed and preveterinary programs offered. **Special study options:** Accelerated study, combined bachelor's/graduate degree, cross-registration, double major, dual enrollment of high school students, ESL, exchange student, independent study, internships, student-designed major, study abroad, teacher certification program, Washington semester, weekend college. **Credit/placement by examination:** AP, CLEP, IB, institutional tests. 60 credit hours maximum toward bachelor's degree. **Support services:** Reduced course load, study skills assistance, tutoring, writing center.

Majors. **Biology:** General, biochemistry, biomedical sciences. **Business:** Accounting/finance, business admin. **Communications:** General. **Computer sciences:** General, computer science. **Conservation:** Environmental studies. **Education:** General, elementary. **Foreign languages:** Classics, French, German, Spanish. **History:** General. **Interdisciplinary:** Math/computer science. **Legal studies:** Prelaw. **Math:** General. **Philosophy/religion:** Philosophy, religion. **Physical sciences:** Chemistry, physics. **Psychology:** General. **Social sciences:** General, economics, political science, sociology. **Visual/performing arts:** Art history/conservation, dramatic, studio arts.

Most popular majors. Biology 13%, business/marketing 25%, communications/journalism 7%, education 7%, English 7%, social sciences 14%.

Computing on campus. 100 workstations in dormitories, library, computer center, student center. Dormitories wired for high-speed internet access and linked to campus network. Commuter students can connect to campus network. Online course registration, online library, helpline, student web hosting, wireless network available.

Student life. **Freshman orientation:** Mandatory, $240 fee. Preregistration for classes offered. Several orientation sessions held throughout late spring and summer. **Housing:** Guaranteed on-campus for all undergraduates. Coed dorms, single-sex dorms, special housing for disabled, wellness housing available. $200 nonrefundable deposit, deadline 5/1. Dormitories include 24-hour and 12-hour quiet floors. **Activities:** Bands, campus ministries, choral groups, dance, drama, international student organizations, literary magazine, music ensembles, Model UN, opera, radio station, student government, student newspaper, symphony orchestra, African-American Students United, environmental awareness club, Christian Fellowship, Network for Progressive Action, conservative student forum, volunteer association, international organization, Intercultural Forum, Newman Club, Islamic Society.

Athletics. NCAA. **Intercollegiate:** Baseball M, basketball, cross-country, diving, football (tackle) M, golf, soccer, softball W, swimming, tennis, track and field, volleyball W. **Intramural:** Archery, basketball, football (non-tackle), soccer, softball, tennis, volleyball, water polo. **Team name:** Terriers.

Student services. Chaplain/spiritual director, career counseling, student employment services, health services, minority student services, personal counseling, placement for graduates, veterans' counselor.

Contact. E-mail: admission@hiram.edu
Phone: (330) 569-5169 Toll-free number: (800) 362-5280
Fax: (330) 569-5944
Sherman Dean, Director of Admission, Hiram College, Teachout Price Hall, Hiram, OH 44234

John Carroll University

University Heights, Ohio — **CB member**
www.jcu.edu — **CB code: 1342**

- Private 4-year university and liberal arts college affiliated with Roman Catholic Church
- Residential campus in large town
- 3,081 degree-seeking undergraduates: 2% part-time, 51% women, 6% African American, 2% Asian American, 3% Hispanic American
- 661 degree-seeking graduate students
- 80% of applicants admitted
- SAT or ACT (ACT writing recommended), application essay required
- 82% graduate within 6 years; 74% enter graduate study

General. Founded in 1886. Regionally accredited. **Degrees:** 678 bachelor's awarded; master's offered. **ROTC:** Army. **Location:** 10 miles from Cleveland. **Calendar:** Semester, extensive summer session. **Full-time faculty:** 220 total; 85% have terminal degrees, 10% minority, 41% women. **Part-time faculty:** 175 total; 39% have terminal degrees, 6% minority, 50% women. **Class size:** 42% < 20, 58% 20-39, less than 1% 40-49. **Special facilities:** Science and technology center containing research facilities.

Freshman class profile. 3,481 applied, 2,771 admitted, 792 enrolled.

Mid 50% test scores		**Rank in top quarter:**	49%
SAT critical reading:	490-590	**Rank in top tenth:**	20%
SAT math:	490-600	**End year in good standing:**	87%
SAT writing:	480-590	**Return as sophomores:**	90%
ACT composite:	21-26	**Out-of-state:**	34%
GPA 3.75 or higher:	24%	**Live on campus:**	92%
GPA 3.50-3.74:	18%	**Fraternities:**	9%
GPA 3.0-3.49:	36%	**Sororities:**	10%
GPA 2.0-2.99:	22%		

Basis for selection. High school academic record, rigor of curricula most important. Other criteria include test scores, extracurricular activities, essay. **Homeschooled:** State high school equivalency certificate, interview, letter of recommendation (nonparent) required. Extra emphasis placed on standardized testing.

High school preparation. College-preparatory program required. 16 units required; 21 recommended. Required and recommended units include English 4, mathematics 3-4, social studies 2-4, science 2-3 (laboratory 2-3), foreign language 2-3 and academic electives 3. 2-4 units among social studies, history, social science.

2008-2009 Annual costs. Tuition/fees: $28,090. Room/board: $7,934.

2008-2009 Financial aid. **Need-based:** 695 full-time freshmen applied for aid; 584 were judged to have need; 584 of these received aid. Average need met was 90%. Average scholarship/grant was $19,700; average loan $3,171. 60% of total undergraduate aid awarded as scholarships/grants, 40% as loans/jobs. **Non-need-based:** Awarded to 1,100 full-time undergraduates, including 275 freshmen. Scholarships awarded for academics, alumni affiliation, leadership, minority status, ROTC, state residency. **Additional information:** Institutional form for need analysis required from upperclassmen and transfer students only.

Application procedures. **Admission:** Priority date 12/1; deadline 2/1. No application fee. Admission notification on a rolling basis beginning on or about 12/15. Must reply by May 1 or within 4 week(s) if notified thereafter. **Financial aid:** Priority date 2/15, closing date 3/15. FAFSA required. Applicants notified on a rolling basis starting 2/15; must reply by 5/1 or within 4 week(s) of notification.

Academics. Online course registration available for second semester freshmen. **Special study options:** Accelerated study, combined bachelor's/graduate degree, cooperative education, cross-registration, double major, dual enrollment of high school students, exchange student, honors, independent study, internships, liberal arts/career combination, student-designed major, study abroad, teacher certification program, Washington semester. **Credit/placement by examination:** AP, CLEP, IB, institutional tests. 30 credit hours maximum toward bachelor's degree. **Support services:** Learning center, reduced course load, study skills assistance, tutoring, writing center.

Majors. **Biology:** General. **Business:** Accounting, business admin, finance, logistics, managerial economics. **Communications:** General. **Computer sciences:** General, computer science. **Conservation:** Environmental studies. **Education:** Elementary, physical. **Engineering:** Physics. **Foreign languages:** Ancient Greek, comparative lit, French, German, Latin, Spanish. **Health:** Predental, premedicine, preveterinary. **History:** General. **Interdisciplinary:** Gerontology. **Legal studies:** Prelaw. **Liberal arts:** Arts/sciences. **Math:** General. **Philosophy/religion:** Philosophy, religion. **Physical sciences:** Chemistry, physics. **Psychology:** General. **Social sciences:** Economics, political science, sociology. **Visual/performing arts:** Art history/conservation.

Most popular majors. Biology 8%, business/marketing 27%, communications/journalism 10%, education 8%, psychology 12%, social sciences 11%.

Computing on campus. 200 workstations in dormitories, library, computer center, student center. Dormitories wired for high-speed internet access and linked to campus network. Commuter students can connect to campus network. Online course registration, online library, helpline, repair service, student web hosting, wireless network available.

Student life. **Freshman orientation:** Mandatory, $325 fee. Two-day, one overnight for parents and students. Students take placement tests. **Policies:** Students must adhere to the Student Code of Conduct. All incoming freshman students required to live on campus freshman and sophomore years. **Housing:** Guaranteed on-campus for all undergraduates. Coed dorms, single-sex dorms, special housing for disabled, apartments, fraternity/sorority housing available. $300 fully refundable deposit, deadline 5/1. Suite-style housing available. **Activities:** Pep band, campus ministries, choral groups, dance, drama, literary magazine, music ensembles, radio station, student government, student newspaper, TV station, Christian Life Community, African American Alliance, EMS Association, Habitat for Humanity, Labre Project, Students in Free Enterprise, Public Relations Student Society of America.

Athletics. NCAA. **Intercollegiate:** Baseball M, basketball, cheerleading M, cross-country, diving, football (tackle) M, golf, soccer, softball W, swimming, tennis, track and field, volleyball W, wrestling M. **Intramural:** Basketball, football (non-tackle), golf, racquetball, soccer, softball, table tennis, tennis, volleyball, water polo. **Team name:** Blue Streaks.

Student services. Adult student services, alcohol/substance abuse counseling, chaplain/spiritual director, career counseling, student employment services, financial aid counseling, health services, minority student services, personal counseling, placement for graduates, veterans' counselor. **Physically disabled:** Services for visually, speech, hearing impaired.

Contact. E-mail: admission@jcu.edu
Phone: (216) 397-4294 Toll-free number: (888) 335-6800
Fax: (216) 397-4981
Thomas Fanning, Director of Admission and Retention, John Carroll University, 20700 North Park Boulevard, University Heights, OH 44118-4581

Kent State University

Kent, Ohio — **CB member**
www.kent.edu — **CB code: 1367**

- Public 4-year university
- Residential campus in large town
- 17,660 degree-seeking undergraduates: 11% part-time, 59% women, 9% African American, 2% Asian American, 2% Hispanic American, 1% international
- 4,352 degree-seeking graduate students
- 74% of applicants admitted
- SAT or ACT (ACT writing recommended) required

General. Founded in 1910. Regionally accredited. **Degrees:** 3,795 bachelor's awarded; master's, doctoral offered. **ROTC:** Army, Air Force. **Location:** 50 miles from Cleveland, 11 miles from Akron. **Calendar:** Semester, extensive summer session. **Full-time faculty:** 881 total; 15% minority, 48% women. **Part-time faculty:** 595 total; 7% minority, 55% women. **Class size:** 51% < 20, 38% 20-39, 4% 40-49, 4% 50-99, 3% >100. **Special facilities:** 287-acre airport, liquid crystal institute, fashion museum, planetarium, ice arena, 18-hole golf course.

Freshman class profile. 13,277 applied, 9,808 admitted, 3,777 enrolled.

Mid 50% test scores			
SAT critical reading:	450-580	Rank in top quarter:	33%
SAT math:	450-570	Rank in top tenth:	12%
ACT composite:	19-24	Return as sophomores:	73%
GPA 3.75 or higher:	14%	Out-of-state:	13%
GPA 3.50-3.74:	14%	Live on campus:	82%
GPA 3.0-3.49:	36%	International:	1%
GPA 2.0-2.99:	36%	Fraternities:	4%
		Sororities:	4%

Basis for selection. Academic record, course work, test scores important. Varying criteria for nursing, education, flight, fashion design and merchandising, architecture, interior design, journalism and mass communication, 6-year medical program, music, dance, and honors college applicants. Interview required for 6-year medical program, recommended for all others. Audition required for dance, music, and musical theater students.

High school preparation. College-preparatory program recommended. 16 units recommended. Recommended units include English 4, mathematics 3, social studies 3, science 3 (laboratory 2) and foreign language 3. One fine arts or third unit of foreign language recommended.

2008-2009 Annual costs. Tuition/fees: $8,430; $15,862 out-of-state. Room/board: $7,200. Books/supplies: $990. Personal expenses: $1,590.

2008-2009 Financial aid. Need-based: 3,102 full-time freshmen applied for aid; 2,478 were judged to have need; 2,478 of these received aid. Average need met was 65%. Average scholarship/grant was $5,676; average loan $3,553. 30% of total undergraduate aid awarded as scholarships/grants, 70% as loans/jobs. **Non-need-based:** Awarded to 2,957 full-time undergraduates, including 1,131 freshmen. Scholarships awarded for academics, alumni affiliation, art, athletics, leadership, minority status, music/drama, ROTC, state residency. **Additional information:** Participant in US Department of Education's Quality Assurance Program and Experimental Sites Program.

Application procedures. Admission: Priority date 3/15; deadline 5/1 (postmark date). $30 fee, may be waived for applicants with need. Admission notification on a rolling basis beginning on or about 10/1. **Financial aid:** Priority date 3/1; no closing date. FAFSA required. Applicants notified on a rolling basis starting 3/15; must reply within 2 week(s) of notification.

Academics. Special study options: Accelerated study, combined bachelor's/graduate degree, cooperative education, cross-registration, distance learning, double major, dual enrollment of high school students, ESL, exchange student, external degree, honors, independent study, internships, liberal arts/career combination, New York semester, student-designed major, study abroad, teacher certification program, Washington semester, weekend college. BS/MD. **Credit/placement by examination:** AP, CLEP, IB, SAT, ACT, institutional tests. 30 credit hours maximum toward bachelor's degree. **Support services:** Learning center, pre-admission summer program, reduced course load, remedial instruction, study skills assistance, tutoring, writing center.

Honors college/program. Approximately 250 incoming freshman admitted; based on class rank within top 10%; 3.5 GPA; 25 ACT/1140 SAT (exclusive of Writing); small interactive classes (20 maximum); eight courses culminating with thesis project, portfolio, or course; two study abroad programs.

Majors. Architecture: Architecture. **Area/ethnic studies:** African-American, American, Latin American, Russian/Slavic. **Biology:** General, biotechnology, botany, zoology. **Business:** Accounting, business admin, fashion, finance, management information systems, management science, managerial economics, marketing. **Communications:** General, advertising, broadcast journalism, digital media, journalism, photojournalism, public relations, radio/tv. **Computer sciences:** Systems analysis. **Conservation:** General. **Education:** General, art, business, chemistry, early childhood, health, mathematics, middle, music, physical, science, social studies, special, technology/industrial arts, trade/industrial. **Engineering:** General, industrial. **Family/consumer sciences:** Family studies, food/nutrition. **Foreign languages:** French, German, Latin, Russian, sign language interpretation, Spanish. **Health:** Athletic training, audiology/speech pathology, clinical lab science, nursing (RN), predental, premedicine, preveterinary. **History:** General. **Interdisciplinary:** Peace/conflict. **Legal studies:** Paralegal. **Liberal arts:** Arts/sciences, humanities. **Math:** General, applied. **Parks/recreation:** Facilities management. **Philosophy/religion:** Philosophy. **Physical sciences:** Chemistry, geology, physics. **Protective services:** Criminal justice. **Psychology:** General. **Social sciences:** Anthropology, geography, international relations, political science, sociology. **Transportation:** Aviation. **Visual/performing arts:** Art history/conservation, commercial/advertising art, crafts, dance, dramatic, fashion design, interior design, painting. **Other:** Ethnic Heritage.

Most popular majors. Business/marketing 23%, communications/journalism 7%, education 12%, health sciences 8%, psychology 6%, visual/performing arts 7%.

Computing on campus. 2,100 workstations in dormitories, library, computer center, student center. Dormitories wired for high-speed internet access and linked to campus network. Commuter students can connect to campus network. Online course registration, online library, helpline, repair service, student web hosting, wireless network available.

Student life. Freshman orientation: Mandatory, $100 fee. Preregistration for classes offered. **Housing:** Guaranteed on-campus for freshmen. Coed dorms, single-sex dorms, special housing for disabled, apartments, fraternity/sorority housing available. $200 nonrefundable deposit, deadline 6/4. Single undergraduate students must live in college housing first 4 semesters with some exemptions granted. Learning communities available. **Activities:** Bands, choral groups, dance, drama, film society, literary magazine, music ensembles, musical theater, opera, radio station, student government, student newspaper, TV station, social service, political and religious organizations available.

Athletics. NCAA. **Intercollegiate:** Baseball M, basketball, cross-country, field hockey W, football (tackle) M, golf, gymnastics W, soccer W, softball W, track and field, volleyball W, wrestling M. **Intramural:** Badminton, basketball, bowling, football (non-tackle), golf, racquetball, soccer, softball, table tennis, tennis, water polo, wrestling M. **Team name:** Golden Flashes.

Student services. Adult student services, alcohol/substance abuse counseling, chaplain/spiritual director, career counseling, services for economically disadvantaged, student employment services, financial aid counseling, health services, legal services, minority student services, personal counseling, placement for graduates, veterans' counselor, women's services. **Physically disabled:** Services for visually, speech, hearing impaired.

Contact. E-mail: admissions@kent.edu
Phone: (330) 672-2444 Toll-free number: (800) 988-5368
Fax: (330) 672-2499
Nancy DellaVecchia, Director of Admissions, Kent State University, PO Box 5190, Kent, OH 44242-0001

Kenyon College

Gambier, Ohio — **CB member**
www.kenyon.edu — **CB code: 1370**

- Private 4-year liberal arts college
- Residential campus in rural community

- 1,635 degree-seeking undergraduates: 53% women, 4% African American, 5% Asian American, 3% Hispanic American, 1% Native American, 4% international
- 31% of applicants admitted
- SAT or ACT (ACT writing optional), application essay required
- 88% graduate within 6 years; 21% enter graduate study

General. Founded in 1824. Regionally accredited. **Degrees:** 429 bachelor's awarded. **Location:** 50 miles from Columbus. **Calendar:** Semester. **Full-time faculty:** 152 total; 98% have terminal degrees, 13% minority, 41% women. **Part-time faculty:** 36 total; 64% have terminal degrees, 11% minority, 53% women. **Class size:** 67% < 20, 30% 20-39, 2% 40-49, 2% 50-99. **Special facilities:** Observatory, environmental center and nature preserve, science center.

Freshman class profile. 4,509 applied, 1,413 admitted, 456 enrolled.

Mid 50% test scores		**GPA 2.0-2.99:**	2%
SAT critical reading:	630-730	**Rank in top quarter:**	87%
SAT math:	610-700	**Rank in top tenth:**	61%
SAT writing:	630-720	**End year in good standing:**	98%
ACT composite:	28-32	**Return as sophomores:**	94%
GPA 3.75 or higher:	59%	**Out-of-state:**	82%
GPA 3.50-3.74:	19%	**Live on campus:**	100%
GPA 3.0-3.49:	20%	**International:**	4%

Basis for selection. Secondary school record and personal character most important followed by test scores, class rank, recommendations, essay, talent, activities and interview. Alumni relationship, ethnicity, geographical residence and work experience considered. Non-native speakers of English required to submit TOEFL results. **Homeschooled:** Provide complete curriculum with texts and books used.

High school preparation. College-preparatory program required. 21 units required; 24 recommended. Required and recommended units include English 4, mathematics 3-4, social studies 1, history 2-3, science 3-4 (laboratory 3), foreign language 3-4 and academic electives 3. 1 fine arts recommended.

2009-2010 Annual costs. Tuition/fees: $40,980. Room/board: $7,260. Books/supplies: $1,300.

2008-2009 Financial aid. Need-based: 270 full-time freshmen applied for aid; 189 were judged to have need; 189 of these received aid. Average need met was 98%. Average scholarship/grant was $28,512; average loan $3,067. 85% of total undergraduate aid awarded as scholarships/grants, 15% as loans/jobs. **Non-need-based:** Awarded to 520 full-time undergraduates, including 170 freshmen. Scholarships awarded for academics, leadership, minority status.

Application procedures. Admission: Closing date 1/15 (postmark date). $50 fee, may be waived for applicants with need, free for online applicants. Admission notification 4/1. Must reply by 5/1. **Financial aid:** Closing date 2/15. FAFSA, CSS PROFILE required. Applicants notified by 4/1; must reply by 5/1.

Academics. Special study options: Accelerated study, combined bachelor's/graduate degree, double major, exchange student, honors, independent study, internships, liberal arts/career combination, semester at sea, student-designed major, study abroad, Washington semester. Cooperative 3-2 or 4-1 masters and teacher certification program with Bank Street College of Education; 3-2 engineering program with Case Western Reserve, Rensselaer Polytechnic Institute and Washington University; 3-2 environmental studies program with Duke University. Special off-campus semester programs: Historically Black Colleges; Boston University Marine Program (BUMP); The International Partnership for Service Learning: Appalachia, South Dakota; Marine Laboratory; National Theater Institute; Newberry Library Program in the Humanities; New York Arts Program; Oak Ridge Science Semester, Tennessee; The Philadelphia Center; SEA Semester; Semester in Environmental Science; Washington Semester Programs. **Credit/placement by examination:** AP, CLEP, IB, institutional tests. Credit determined for AP, IB or School Articulation Program (SCAP) counts toward 16 units required for graduation. No diversification requirements may be satisfied with AP credit. **Support services:** Study skills assistance, tutoring, writing center.

Majors. Area/ethnic studies: American, women's. **Biology:** General, biochemistry, molecular. **Foreign languages:** General, ancient Greek, classics, French, German, Latin, Spanish. **History:** General. **Interdisciplinary:** Neuroscience. **Math:** General. **Philosophy/religion:** Philosophy, religion. **Physical sciences:** Chemistry, physics. **Psychology:** General. **Social sciences:** Anthropology, economics, international relations, political science, sociology. **Visual/performing arts:** Art history/conservation, dance, dramatic, studio arts.

Most popular majors. English 16%, history 7%, interdisciplinary studies 11%, philosophy/religious studies 6%, psychology 8%, social sciences 23%, visual/performing arts 14%.

Computing on campus. 530 workstations in dormitories, library, computer center. Dormitories wired for high-speed internet access and linked to campus network. Commuter students can connect to campus network. Online library, helpline, student web hosting, wireless network available.

Student life. Freshman orientation: Mandatory. Held 4 days prior to start of classes. **Housing:** Guaranteed on-campus for all undergraduates. Coed dorms, single-sex dorms, special housing for disabled, apartments, fraternity/sorority housing, wellness housing available. $350 nonrefundable deposit, deadline 5/1. Special accommodations can be made for married, international and disabled students. Fraternity and sorority housing available in room blocks only. Wellness and community service and social group halls on campus. **Activities:** Bands, campus ministries, choral groups, dance, drama, film society, international student organizations, literary magazine, music ensembles, Model UN, musical theater, opera, radio station, student government, student newspaper, symphony orchestra, black student union, Christian Fellowship, Hillel, Asian student alliance, Associacion de Estudiantes Latino Americanos y de Naciones Tropicales Exoticas, Archon Society (community service organization), allied sexual orientations, Amnesty International, Zen meditation group, political affairs club.

Athletics. NCAA. **Intercollegiate:** Baseball M, basketball, cross-country, diving, field hockey W, football (tackle) M, golf M, lacrosse, soccer, softball W, swimming, tennis, track and field, volleyball W. **Intramural:** Basketball, football (non-tackle), racquetball, soccer, softball, squash, tennis, volleyball. **Team name:** Lords/Ladies.

Student services. Alcohol/substance abuse counseling, chaplain/spiritual director, career counseling, student employment services, financial aid counseling, health services, minority student services, personal counseling, placement for graduates, women's services. **Physically disabled:** Services for visually, hearing impaired.

Contact. E-mail: admissions@kenyon.edu
Phone: (740) 427-5776 Toll-free number: (800) 848-2468
Fax: (740) 427-5770
Jennifer Delahunty, Dean of Admissions, Kenyon College, Ransom Hall, Gambier, OH 43022

Kettering College of Medical Arts

Kettering, Ohio
www.kcma.edu **CB code: 0602**

- Private 4-year health science and nursing college affiliated with Seventh-day Adventists
- Commuter campus in large city
- 761 degree-seeking undergraduates
- 53% of applicants admitted
- Application essay required

General. Founded in 1967. Regionally accredited. Institution is educational division of Kettering Health Network. **Degrees:** 26 bachelor's awarded; master's offered. **Location:** 5 miles from Dayton. **Calendar:** Semester, limited summer session. **Full-time faculty:** 53 total; 19% have terminal degrees, 9% minority, 66% women. **Part-time faculty:** 22 total; 9% have terminal degrees, 18% minority, 73% women. **Class size:** 65% < 20, 27% 20-39, 5% 40-49, 2% 50-99.

Freshman class profile. 175 applied, 92 admitted, 68 enrolled.

Mid 50% test scores		**GPA 3.0-3.49:**	31%
SAT critical reading:	450-560	**GPA 2.0-2.99:**	17%
SAT math:	410-570	**Rank in top quarter:**	53%
SAT writing:	430-510	**Rank in top tenth:**	22%
ACT composite:	19-22	**Out-of-state:**	3%
GPA 3.75 or higher:	31%	**Live on campus:**	3%
GPA 3.50-3.74:	21%		

Basis for selection. High school GPA, test scores, personal statements important. Essay required for all applicants; interview required for physician assistant applicants.

High school preparation. 14 units recommended. Recommended units include English 4, mathematics 2 and science 3. Strong mathematics and science background recommended.

2008-2009 Annual costs. Tuition/fees: $9,690. Tuition and fees may vary by program. Room only: $2,900. Books/supplies: $1,100. Personal expenses: $2,792.

Financial aid. Non-need-based: Scholarships awarded for academics.

Application procedures. Admission: No deadline. $25 fee, may be waived for applicants with need, free for online applicants. Admission notification on a rolling basis. **Financial aid:** Priority date 3/31; no closing date. FAFSA, institutional form required. Applicants notified on a rolling basis starting 5/15; must reply within 3 week(s) of notification.

Academics. Special study options: Accelerated study, cross-registration, distance learning, double major, dual enrollment of high school students, external degree, honors. **Credit/placement by examination:** AP, CLEP, SAT, ACT, institutional tests. **Support services:** Learning center, reduced course load, study skills assistance, tutoring, writing center.

Majors. Health: Nursing (RN), predental, premedicine, respiratory therapy technology, sonography.

Computing on campus. 32 workstations in library, computer center. Dormitories wired for high-speed internet access and linked to campus network. Online library, wireless network available.

Student life. Freshman orientation: Mandatory. Preregistration for classes offered. **Policies:** Religious observance required. **Housing:** Single-sex dorms, wellness housing available. $75 nonrefundable deposit. **Activities:** Campus ministries, religious life organizations.

Student services. Chaplain/spiritual director, career counseling, student employment services, financial aid counseling, health services, personal counseling, placement for graduates, veterans' counselor.

Contact. E-mail: studentadmissions@kcma.edu
Phone: (937) 395-8628 Toll-free number: (800) 433-5262
Fax: (937) 395-8338
Becky McDonald, Director of Enrollment Services, Kettering College of Medical Arts, 3737 Southern Boulevard, Kettering, OH 45429-1299

Lake Erie College

Painesville, Ohio — **CB member**
www.lec.edu — **CB code: 1391**

- Private 4-year liberal arts college
- Residential campus in large town
- 728 degree-seeking undergraduates
- 62% of applicants admitted
- SAT or ACT (ACT writing optional), application essay required

General. Founded in 1856. Regionally accredited. **Degrees:** 152 bachelor's awarded; master's offered. **Location:** 30 miles from Cleveland. **Calendar:** Semester, limited summer session. **Full-time faculty:** 51 total. **Part-time faculty:** 60 total. **Class size:** 82% < 20, 18% 20-39. **Special facilities:** Equestrian center.

Freshman class profile. 987 applied, 615 admitted, 252 enrolled.

Mid 50% test scores		**GPA 3.0-3.49:**	28%
SAT critical reading:	410-550	**GPA 2.0-2.99:**	49%
SAT math:	420-550	**Rank in top quarter:**	25%
SAT writing:	410-530	**Rank in top tenth:**	11%
ACT composite:	18-23	**Out-of-state:**	32%
GPA 3.75 or higher:	15%	**Live on campus:**	70%
GPA 3.50-3.74:	7%	**Sororities:**	8%

Basis for selection. School achievement record, test scores, essay, reference letters and interview strongly considered. Special consideration of test scores for some applicants. Interview strongly recommended. **Homeschooled:** Statement describing homeschool structure and mission, transcript of courses and grades, interview, letter of recommendation (nonparent) required. **Learning Disabled:** Documentation of learning disability required.

High school preparation. Recommended units include English 4, mathematics 3, social studies 3, science 3 (laboratory 2) and foreign language 2. 1 fine arts and 1 physical education or health recommended.

2008-2009 Annual costs. Tuition/fees: $25,220. Equestrian fee $880 per course. Room/board: $7,650. Books/supplies: $900. Personal expenses: $1,304.

2007-2008 Financial aid. Non-need-based: Scholarships awarded for academics, art, leadership, music/drama, state residency. **Additional information:** Twins' scholarship, sibling discount.

Application procedures. Admission: Priority date 3/1; deadline 8/1. $30 fee, may be waived for applicants with need, free for online applicants. Admission notification on a rolling basis beginning on or about 9/15. **Financial aid:** No deadline. FAFSA required. Applicants notified on a rolling basis; must reply within 2 week(s) of notification.

Academics. Special study options: Accelerated study, cross-registration, double major, dual enrollment of high school students, honors, independent study, internships, liberal arts/career combination, student-designed major, study abroad, teacher certification program, weekend college. **Credit/placement by examination:** AP, CLEP, IB, SAT, ACT, institutional tests. 32 credit hours maximum toward bachelor's degree. **Support services:** Learning center, reduced course load, study skills assistance, tutoring, writing center.

Majors. Agriculture: Animal breeding, equestrian studies, equine science, farm/ranch. **Biology:** General. **Business:** Accounting, business admin, entrepreneurial studies, international, marketing, training/development. **Communications:** General. **Conservation:** General, environmental studies. **Education:** General, curriculum, elementary, reading, secondary. **Foreign languages:** General, French, German, Italian, Spanish. **History:** General. **Legal studies:** Paralegal, prelaw. **Math:** General. **Physical sciences:** Chemistry. **Protective services:** Law enforcement admin. **Psychology:** General. **Social sciences:** General, sociology. **Visual/performing arts:** General, dance, studio arts, theater arts management.

Most popular majors. Agriculture 12%, biology 6%, business/marketing 24%, education 13%, interdisciplinary studies 8%, physical sciences 6%.

Computing on campus. 112 workstations in dormitories, library, computer center, student center. Dormitories wired for high-speed internet access and linked to campus network. Commuter students can connect to campus network. Online course registration, online library, helpline, repair service, wireless network available.

Student life. Freshman orientation: Mandatory, $200 fee. Preregistration for classes offered. One-day program during summer; extended 3-day orientation for freshman a week prior to start of classes. **Housing:** Guaranteed on-campus for freshmen. Coed dorms, single-sex dorms, wellness housing available. $150 nonrefundable deposit. Residence halls equipped with laundry and kitchen areas available. **Activities:** Choral groups, dance, drama, literary magazine, music ensembles, radio station, student government, student newspaper, honor association, academic association, athletic association, foreign language clubs, professional organizations, equestrian clubs, student activities council.

Athletics. NCAA. **Intercollegiate:** Baseball M, basketball, cross-country, equestrian, football (non-tackle) M, golf, lacrosse M, soccer, softball W, volleyball W. **Team name:** Storm.

Student services. Career counseling, student employment services, financial aid counseling, placement for graduates. **Physically disabled:** Services for visually impaired.

Contact. E-mail: admissions@lec.edu
Phone: (440) 375-7050 Toll-free number: (800) 916-0904
Fax: (440) 375-7005
Eric Felver, Director of Admissions, Lake Erie College, 391 West Washington Street, Painesville, OH 44077-3389

Laura and Alvin Siegal College of Judaic Studies

Cleveland, Ohio
www.siegalcollege.edu — **CB code: 1190**

- Private 4-year liberal arts and teachers college affiliated with Jewish faith
- Commuter campus in large town
- 11 degree-seeking undergraduates
- 50% of applicants admitted
- Application essay, interview required

General. Founded in 1963. Regionally accredited. **Degrees:** 4 bachelor's awarded; master's offered. **Location:** 10 miles from Cleveland. **Calendar:** Semester, extensive summer session. **Full-time faculty:** 8 total. **Part-time faculty:** 23 total.

Freshman class profile. 2 applied, 1 admitted, 1 enrolled.

Basis for selection. Interview and 2 recommendations most important. Essay important; high school record and community activities considered.

High school preparation. Graduation from Hebrew high school or good background in Hebrew language and Judaic subjects.

2008-2009 Annual costs. Tuition/fees: $15,775. Books/supplies: $500.

Application procedures. **Admission:** No deadline. $50 fee. Admission notification on a rolling basis. **Financial aid:** No deadline. Institutional form required. Applicants notified on a rolling basis.

Academics. College specializes in Judaic and Hebrew studies and teacher education. **Special study options:** Cross-registration, distance learning, independent study, internships. **Credit/placement by examination:** AP, CLEP, IB. 45 credit hours maximum toward bachelor's degree. **Support services:** Reduced course load, study skills assistance.

Majors. **Foreign languages:** General, Hebrew. **Philosophy/religion:** Judaic. **Theology:** Bible, religious ed.

Computing on campus. 8 workstations in library. Online library, wireless network available.

Student life. **Freshman orientation:** Available. Preregistration for classes offered.

Student services. Adult student services, career counseling, financial aid counseling. **Physically disabled:** Services for hearing impaired.

Contact. E-mail: admissions@siegalcollege.edu
Phone: (216) 464-4050 Toll-free number: (888) 336-2257
Fax: (216) 464-5827
Ruth Kronick, Director of Student Services, Laura and Alvin Siegal College of Judaic Studies, 26500 Shaker Boulevard, Cleveland, OH 44122

Lourdes College

Sylvania, Ohio — **CB member**
www.lourdes.edu — **CB code: 1427**

- Private 4-year liberal arts college affiliated with Roman Catholic Church
- Commuter campus in large town
- 1,744 degree-seeking undergraduates: 45% part-time, 82% women, 15% African American, 1% Asian American, 4% Hispanic American
- 221 degree-seeking graduate students
- 84% of applicants admitted
- 49% graduate within 6 years

General. Founded in 1958. Regionally accredited. **Degrees:** 260 bachelor's, 33 associate awarded; master's offered. **ROTC:** Army, Air Force. **Location:** 10 miles from Toledo. **Calendar:** Semester, limited summer session. **Full-time faculty:** 80 total; 45% have terminal degrees, 4% minority, 70% women. **Part-time faculty:** 144 total; 20% have terminal degrees, 10% minority, 69% women. **Class size:** 66% < 20, 34% 20-39. **Special facilities:** Planetarium, life lab.

Freshman class profile. 395 applied, 330 admitted, 155 enrolled.

Mid 50% test scores		**Rank in top quarter:**	26%
ACT composite:	17-22	**Rank in top tenth:**	11%
GPA 3.75 or higher:	10%	**End year in good standing:**	89%
GPA 3.50-3.74:	10%	**Return as sophomores:**	60%
GPA 3.0-3.49:	24%	**Out-of-state:**	7%
GPA 2.0-2.99:	47%		

Basis for selection. Academic GPA very important, recommendations and interview considered. Conditional admission may be granted at discretion of the Director of Admission to high school graduates with no prior college experience who have below a 2.0 GPA. **Homeschooled:** Transcript of courses and grades required.

High school preparation. College-preparatory program recommended. 17 units recommended. Recommended units include English 4, mathematics 3, social studies 3, science 3 (laboratory 2), foreign language 2 and visual/performing arts 1.

2008-2009 Annual costs. Tuition/fees: $14,730. Books/supplies: $1,008. Personal expenses: $3,578.

2008-2009 Financial aid. **Need-based:** 96 full-time freshmen applied for aid; 73 were judged to have need; 73 of these received aid. Average scholarship/grant was $6,796; average loan $3,303. 33% of total undergraduate aid awarded as scholarships/grants, 67% as loans/jobs. **Non-need-based:** Awarded to 761 full-time undergraduates, including 73 freshmen. Scholarships awarded for academics, art, minority status, state residency.

Application procedures. **Admission:** No deadline. $25 fee, may be waived for applicants with need, free for online applicants. Admission notification on a rolling basis. **Financial aid:** Priority date 3/1; no closing date. FAFSA required. Applicants notified on a rolling basis starting 3/1; must reply within 4 week(s) of notification.

Academics. **Special study options:** Distance learning, double major, dual enrollment of high school students, independent study, internships, liberal arts/career combination, student-designed major, study abroad, teacher certification program. **Credit/placement by examination:** AP, CLEP, institutional tests. 15 credit hours maximum toward associate degree, 30 toward bachelor's. **Support services:** Learning center, reduced course load, remedial instruction, study skills assistance, tutoring, writing center.

Majors. **Biology:** General. **Business:** Accounting/finance, business admin, human resources, management science, marketing. **Conservation:** Environmental science. **Education:** Early childhood, middle, secondary. **Health:** Health care admin, nursing (RN). **History:** General. **Philosophy/religion:** Religion. **Protective services:** Criminal justice. **Psychology:** General. **Public administration:** Social work. **Social sciences:** Sociology. **Visual/performing arts:** Art, art history/conservation. **Other:** Interdisciplinary Studies.

Most popular majors. Business/marketing 23%, education 10%, health sciences 32%, interdisciplinary studies 9%.

Computing on campus. 177 workstations in library, computer center, student center. Commuter students can connect to campus network. Helpline, wireless network available.

Student life. **Freshman orientation:** Available. Preregistration for classes offered. **Activities:** Campus ministries, choral groups, drama, literary magazine, student government, black student union, Lationo student union, LINK, Young Democrats, Zelta Delta Chi.

Athletics. **Team name:** Gray Wolves.

Student services. Adult student services, alcohol/substance abuse counseling, chaplain/spiritual director, career counseling, services for economically disadvantaged, financial aid counseling, personal counseling. **Physically disabled:** Services for visually, speech, hearing impaired.

Contact. E-mail: lcadmits@lourdes.edu
Phone: (419) 885-5291 ext. 3680 Toll-free number: (800) 878-3210 ext. 3680 Fax: (419) 882-3987
Amy Mergen, Director of Admissions, Lourdes College, 6832 Convent Boulevard, Sylvania, OH 43560-2898

Malone University

Canton, Ohio
www.malone.edu — **CB code: 1439**

- Private 4-year university affiliated with Evangelical Friends Church-Eastern Region
- Residential campus in small city
- 1,929 degree-seeking undergraduates: 10% part-time, 60% women, 7% African American, 1% Asian American, 1% Hispanic American, 1% international
- 403 degree-seeking graduate students
- 71% of applicants admitted
- SAT or ACT (ACT writing optional), application essay required
- 56% graduate within 6 years; 24% enter graduate study

General. Founded in 1892. Regionally accredited. Interdenominational Christian environment. **Degrees:** 541 bachelor's awarded; master's offered. **ROTC:** Army, Air Force. **Location:** 55 miles from Cleveland. **Calendar:** Semester, limited summer session. **Full-time faculty:** 110 total; 70% have terminal degrees, 4% minority, 48% women. **Part-time faculty:** 98 total; 18% have terminal degrees, 3% minority, 56% women. **Special facilities:** Child development center.

Freshman class profile. 1,339 applied, 952 admitted, 391 enrolled.

Mid 50% test scores		**GPA 2.0-2.99:**	27%
SAT critical reading:	470-590	**Rank in top quarter:**	46%
SAT math:	470-590	**Rank in top tenth:**	17%
SAT writing:	460-580	**End year in good standing:**	88%
ACT composite:	20-25	**Return as sophomores:**	75%
GPA 3.75 or higher:	26%	**Out-of-state:**	15%
GPA 3.50-3.74:	20%	**Live on campus:**	85%
GPA 3.0-3.49:	27%	**International:**	1%

Basis for selection. High school record, test scores and recommendations most important. Interview considered and encouraged. Audition required for entrance into music programs; portfolio required during first semester for art programs. **Homeschooled:** Transcript of courses and grades required. **Learning Disabled:** Students disclosing learning disabilities must interview with Director of the Student Access Center.

High school preparation. College-preparatory program required. 18 units required. Required units include English 4, mathematics 3, social studies 2, history 1, science 3 (laboratory 1), foreign language 2, visual/performing arts 1 and academic electives 2.

2008-2009 Annual costs. Tuition/fees: $20,020. Room/board: $6,830. Books/supplies: $930. Personal expenses: $1,250.

2008-2009 Financial aid. Need-based: 362 full-time freshmen applied for aid; 329 were judged to have need; 329 of these received aid. Average need met was 77%. Average scholarship/grant was $12,614; average loan $4,111. 51% of total undergraduate aid awarded as scholarships/grants, 49% as loans/jobs. **Non-need-based:** Awarded to 1,494 full-time undergraduates, including 374 freshmen. Scholarships awarded for academics, alumni affiliation, athletics, leadership, music/drama, religious affiliation. **Additional information:** Prepayment discounts and employer deferred payments available for students in adult degree-completion programs. Employer deferred payment plan is available for traditional undergraduate students.

Application procedures. Admission: Closing date 7/1 (postmark date). $20 fee, may be waived for applicants with need. Admission notification on a rolling basis beginning on or about 9/1. **Financial aid:** Priority date 3/1, closing date 7/31. FAFSA required. Applicants notified on a rolling basis starting 3/1; must reply within 2 week(s) of notification.

Academics. 50-56 hours of general education courses organized under the 3 areas of Foundations of Faith and Learning, Foundational Skills, and Engaging God's World. **Special study options:** Accelerated study, cross-registration, distance learning, double major, dual enrollment of high school students, exchange student, honors, independent study, internships, student-designed major, study abroad, teacher certification program, Washington semester, weekend college. 2 degree-completion programs for adult students in management, nursing; American Studies Program (Washington, D.C.), Australia Studies Centre (Sydney), China Studies Program (Shanghai), Latin American Studies Program (San Jose, Costa Rica), Middle East Studies Program (Cairo, Egypt), Russian Studies Program, Ugandan Studies Program, Los Angeles Film Studies Center, Contemporary Music Center (Martha's Vineyard), Washington Journalism Center, Daystar University in Kenya, Malone University Teacher Education semester in Guatemala. **Credit/placement by examination:** AP, CLEP, SAT, ACT, institutional tests. 62 credit hours maximum toward bachelor's degree. External credit by exam limit is 20, excluding AP credit for which an additional 30 credits are available. Other credits available by in house exams. **Support services:** Reduced course load, remedial instruction, study skills assistance, tutoring, writing center.

Majors. Biology: General, zoology. **Business:** Accounting, business admin. **Communications:** General, journalism, public relations, radio/tv. **Communications technology:** Recording arts. **Computer sciences:** Computer science. **Education:** Art, early childhood, English, health, learning disabled, middle, music, physical, science, social studies, Spanish. **Foreign languages:** Spanish. **Health:** Clinical lab science, nursing (RN), public health ed. **History:** General. **Liberal arts:** Arts/sciences. **Math:** General. **Parks/recreation:** Exercise sciences, health/fitness, sports admin. **Philosophy/religion:** Philosophy. **Physical sciences:** Chemistry. **Psychology:** General. **Public administration:** Social work. **Social sciences:** Political science. **Theology:** Bible, pastoral counseling, sacred music, theology, youth ministry. **Visual/performing arts:** Dramatic, studio arts.

Most popular majors. Business/marketing 38%, education 15%, health sciences 18%.

Computing on campus. 225 workstations in dormitories, library, computer center. Dormitories wired for high-speed internet access and linked to campus network. Commuter students can connect to campus network. Online course registration, online library, helpline, student web hosting, wireless network available.

Student life. Freshman orientation: Mandatory. Preregistration for classes offered. Held 5 days prior to start of semester; some on-campus events, community service, relationship-building activities. **Policies:** Christian institution with conservative campus lifestyle. Full-time students required to live on campus unless 22 or older, holding senior status, married or commuting from home; exceptions considered. Religious observance required. **Housing:** Single-sex dorms, wellness housing available. $50 nonrefundable deposit. **Activities:** Bands, campus ministries, choral groups, dance, drama, film society, international student organizations, literary magazine, music ensembles, musical theater, radio station, student government, student newspaper, TV station, Campus Crusade for Christ, Habitat for Humanity, Helping Hands, multicultural student union, Nurses Christian Fellowship, Rotoract, spiritual life committee, Students in Action, Unity Under Christ, Fellowship of Christian Athletes.

Athletics. NAIA, NCCAA. **Intercollegiate:** Baseball M, basketball, cheerleading, cross-country, football (tackle) M, golf, soccer, softball W, tennis, track and field, volleyball W. **Intramural:** Basketball, bowling, football (non-tackle), skiing, soccer, softball, table tennis, volleyball, weight lifting. **Team name:** Pioneers.

Student services. Adult student services, chaplain/spiritual director, career counseling, student employment services, financial aid counseling, health services, minority student services, personal counseling, placement for graduates. **Physically disabled:** Services for visually, speech, hearing impaired.

Contact. E-mail: admissions@malone.edu
Phone: (330) 471-8100 ext. 8145 Toll-free number: (800) 521-1146
Fax: (330) 471-8149
John Russell, Director of Admissions, Malone University, 2600 Cleveland Avenue NW, Canton, OH 44709-3897

Marietta College

Marietta, Ohio — **CB member**
www.marietta.edu — **CB code: 1444**

- Private 4-year liberal arts college
- Residential campus in large town
- 1,438 degree-seeking undergraduates: 3% part-time, 50% women, 4% African American, 1% Asian American, 2% Hispanic American, 9% international
- 117 degree-seeking graduate students
- 77% of applicants admitted
- SAT or ACT (ACT writing optional) required
- 65% graduate within 6 years; 32% enter graduate study

General. Founded in 1835. Regionally accredited. **Degrees:** 345 bachelor's awarded; master's offered. **Location:** 120 miles from Columbus, 110 miles from Pittsburgh. **Calendar:** Semester, limited summer session. **Full-time faculty:** 103 total; 80% have terminal degrees, 5% minority, 43% women. **Part-time faculty:** 42 total; 33% have terminal degrees, 5% minority, 50% women. **Class size:** 77% < 20, 22% 20-39, less than 1% 40-49, less than 1% 50-99. **Special facilities:** Observatory, center for leadership development, greenhouse, cadaver lab, extensive fossil collection, many historically important documents from the beginning of the old Northwest Territory, planetarium.

Freshman class profile. 2,440 applied, 1,883 admitted, 385 enrolled.

Mid 50% test scores		**Rank in top tenth:**	27%
SAT critical reading:	500-600	**End year in good standing:**	97%
SAT math:	490-630	**Return as sophomores:**	73%
ACT composite:	20-26	**Out-of-state:**	32%
GPA 3.75 or higher:	32%	**Live on campus:**	96%
GPA 3.50-3.74:	14%	**International:**	6%
GPA 3.0-3.49:	31%	**Fraternities:**	14%
GPA 2.0-2.99:	23%	**Sororities:**	21%
Rank in top quarter:	50%		

Basis for selection. High school curriculum, GPA, test scores most important. Recommendations and essay important. Interview recommended for all. Portfolio recommended for arts programs. Auditions required for some music programs. **Homeschooled:** Statement describing homeschool structure and mission, transcript of courses and grades, interview required. Chronicle of study required.

High school preparation. College-preparatory program recommended. 16 units required. Required units include English 4, mathematics 3, social studies 2, history 2, science 3 (laboratory 2), foreign language 2 and academic electives 1.

2008-2009 Annual costs. Tuition/fees: $26,080. Room/board: $7,764. Books/supplies: $712. Personal expenses: $640.

2008-2009 Financial aid. Need-based: 371 full-time freshmen applied for aid; 324 were judged to have need; 324 of these received aid. Average need met was 91%. Average scholarship/grant was $14,366; average loan $3,954. 74% of total undergraduate aid awarded as scholarships/grants, 26% as loans/jobs. **Non-need-based:** Awarded to 968 full-time undergraduates, including 279 freshmen. Scholarships awarded for academics, alumni affiliation, art, leadership, minority status, music/drama, state residency. **Additional information:** Auditions/portfolios for art, creative writing, music and theater required for competitive fine art scholarships.

Application procedures. Admission: Priority date 3/1; deadline 5/1 (postmark date). $25 fee, may be waived for applicants with need, free for online applicants. Admission notification on a rolling basis beginning on or about

9/1. Must reply by May 1 or within 2 week(s) if notified thereafter. **Financial aid:** Priority date 3/1, closing date 4/15. FAFSA, institutional form required. Applicants notified on a rolling basis starting 3/15; must reply by 5/1 or within 2 week(s) of notification.

Academics. Early Alert Program whereby professors can contact the Academic Resource Center to assist those students demonstrating need for additional academic support. **Special study options:** Combined bachelor's/graduate degree, double major, dual enrollment of high school students, ESL, exchange student, honors, independent study, internships, liberal arts/career combination, student-designed major, study abroad, teacher certification program, Washington semester. Leadership program, investigative studies. **Credit/placement by examination:** AP, CLEP, IB, SAT, ACT, institutional tests. 36 credit hours maximum toward bachelor's degree. **Support services:** Reduced course load, remedial instruction, study skills assistance, tutoring, writing center.

Majors. Biology: General, biochemistry. **Business:** Accounting, communications, finance, human resources, international, management information systems, marketing. **Communications:** General, advertising, broadcast journalism, journalism, organizational, public relations, radio/tv. **Computer sciences:** General, computer science, information systems. **Conservation:** Environmental science, environmental studies. **Education:** General, early childhood, elementary, middle, multi-level teacher, secondary. **Engineering:** Petroleum. **Foreign languages:** Spanish. **Health:** Athletic training. **History:** General. **Math:** General. **Physical sciences:** Chemistry, geology, physics. **Psychology:** General. **Social sciences:** Economics, political science. **Visual/performing arts:** Commercial/advertising art, dramatic, studio arts.

Most popular majors. Business/marketing 27%, communications/journalism 14%, education 6%, health sciences 7%, psychology 6%, visual/performing arts 8%.

Computing on campus. 350 workstations in library, computer center, student center. Dormitories wired for high-speed internet access and linked to campus network. Commuter students can connect to campus network. Online library, helpline, student web hosting, wireless network available.

Student life. Freshman orientation: Mandatory, $250 fee. Preregistration for classes offered. Four-and-one-half day program. Culminating event either white-water rafting trip or dinner theater production. **Policies:** Student code of conduct, judicial system, no alcohol policy for students under age of 21. **Housing:** Guaranteed on-campus for freshmen. Coed dorms, single-sex dorms, special housing for disabled, apartments, fraternity/sorority housing, wellness housing available. $200 deposit, deadline 5/1. Special interest theme housing (honors, arts and humanities house) available. **Activities:** Bands, campus ministries, choral groups, dance, drama, international student organizations, literary magazine, music ensembles, Model UN, musical theater, radio station, student government, student newspaper, TV station, InterVarsity Christian Fellowship, Circle K, MC Democrats, MC Republicans, Habitat for Humanity, Feminist Majority Leadership, coalition for social change, American International Association, Charles Sumner Harrison organization, student global AIDS campaign.

Athletics. NCAA. **Intercollegiate:** Baseball M, basketball, cross-country, football (tackle) M, rowing (crew), soccer, softball W, tennis, track and field, volleyball W. **Intramural:** Badminton, basketball, bowling, football (non-tackle), golf, handball, racquetball, soccer, softball, table tennis, tennis, volleyball. **Team name:** Pioneers.

Student services. Adult student services, alcohol/substance abuse counseling, career counseling, student employment services, financial aid counseling, health services, minority student services, personal counseling, placement for graduates. **Physically disabled:** Services for visually, speech, hearing impaired. **Learning disabled:** Comprehensive services available.

Contact. E-mail: admit@marietta.edu
Phone: (740) 376-4600 Toll-free number: (800) 331-7896
Fax: (740) 376-8888
Jason Turley, Director of Admission, Marietta College, 215 Fifth Street, Marietta, OH 45750-4005

MedCentral College of Nursing

Mansfield, Ohio
www.medcentral.edu **CB code: 3935**

- Private 4-year nursing college
- Commuter campus in small city
- 391 degree-seeking undergraduates: 4% African American, 1% Asian American, 1% Hispanic American
- 73% of applicants admitted
- SAT or ACT (ACT writing recommended) required

General. Regionally accredited. General electives taken at the Ohio State University-Mansfield. **Degrees:** 121 bachelor's awarded. **Location:** 60 miles from Cleveland, 60 miles from Columbus. **Calendar:** Quarter, extensive summer session. **Full-time faculty:** 24 total; 17% have terminal degrees, 75% women.

Freshman class profile. 181 applied, 132 admitted, 100 enrolled.

Mid 50% test scores		**GPA 2.0-2.99:**	10%
ACT composite:	18-28	**Rank in top quarter:**	80%
GPA 3.75 or higher:	8%	**Rank in top tenth:**	5%
GPA 3.50-3.74:	21%	**Return as sophomores:**	86%
GPA 3.0-3.49:	61%	**Live on campus:**	20%

Basis for selection. Previous high school and college academic credentials very important. Co-curricular activities, work experience, students character also considered. **Homeschooled:** Transcript of courses and grades required. ACT/SAT required.

High school preparation. 17 units required; 20 recommended. Required and recommended units include English 4, mathematics 3-4, social studies 2, history 1, science 3-4 (laboratory 2-3), foreign language 2, computer science 1 and academic electives 2.

2008-2009 Annual costs. Tuition/fees: $11,420. Room only: $5,130. Books/supplies: $2,000. Personal expenses: $3,000.

2007-2008 Financial aid. Need-based: 41% of total undergraduate aid awarded as scholarships/grants, 59% as loans/jobs. **Non-need-based:** Scholarships awarded for academics, leadership.

Application procedures. Admission: Priority date 5/1; deadline 7/1 (postmark date). $50 fee, may be waived for applicants with need. Application must be submitted on paper. Admission notification on a rolling basis beginning on or about 10/1. Must reply by 8/5. **Financial aid:** Priority date 4/2, closing date 9/15. FAFSA, institutional form required. Applicants notified on a rolling basis starting 4/1; must reply by 5/1 or within 2 week(s) of notification.

Academics. Special study options: Accelerated study, combined bachelor's/graduate degree, dual enrollment of high school students, independent study. **Credit/placement by examination:** AP, CLEP, SAT, ACT, institutional tests. 48 credit hours maximum toward bachelor's degree. **Support services:** Learning center, remedial instruction, study skills assistance, tutoring, writing center.

Majors. Health: Nursing (RN).

Computing on campus. 150 workstations in dormitories, library, computer center. Dormitories wired for high-speed internet access and linked to campus network. Commuter students can connect to campus network. Online course registration, online library, helpline, wireless network available.

Student life. Freshman orientation: Mandatory. Held the beginning of academic quarter. **Housing:** Guaranteed on-campus for freshmen. Coed dorms, apartments, wellness housing available. $100 nonrefundable deposit, deadline 6/15. **Activities:** Choral groups, drama, musical theater, student government, National Student Nurses Association, student government association, SCRUBS Society, Sigma Theta, Tau International.

Student services. Adult student services, alcohol/substance abuse counseling, chaplain/spiritual director, career counseling, student employment services, financial aid counseling, health services, on-campus daycare, personal counseling.

Contact. E-mail: admissions@medcentral.edu
Phone: (419) 520-2600 Toll-free number: (877) 645-4360
Fax: (419) 520-2662
Christopher Harris, Dean of Student Affairs, MedCentral College of Nursing, 335 Glessner Avenue, Mansfield, OH 44903-2265

Mercy College of Northwest Ohio

Toledo, Ohio
www.mercycollege.edu **CB code: 4685**

- Private 4-year health science and nursing college affiliated with Roman Catholic Church
- Commuter campus in large city
- 921 degree-seeking undergraduates: 51% part-time, 86% women, 6% African American, 1% Asian American, 3% Hispanic American
- 73% of applicants admitted
- SAT or ACT (ACT writing optional) required
- 47% graduate within 6 years

General. Degrees: 46 bachelor's, 161 associate awarded. **Calendar:** Semester, limited summer session. **Full-time faculty:** 60 total; 27% have terminal degrees, 5% minority, 87% women. **Part-time faculty:** 53 total; 8% have terminal degrees, 6% minority, 76% women. **Class size:** 49% < 20, 41% 20-39, 5% 40-49, 5% 50-99.

Freshman class profile. 211 applied, 154 admitted, 68 enrolled.

End year in good standing:	94%	**Out-of-state:**	10%
Return as sophomores:	88%	**Live on campus:**	41%

Basis for selection. Students reviewed by admission, progression and graduation committee. 2.3 GPA required. Admission to programs of study may have higher GPA and specific course grade requirements.

High school preparation. College-preparatory program recommended. 11 units required; 23 recommended. Required and recommended units include English 3-4, mathematics 2-4, social studies 2-3, history 1, science 2-4 (laboratory 2-3), foreign language 2, computer science 1 and visual/performing arts 1.

2008-2009 Annual costs. Tuition/fees: $9,546. Books/supplies: $1,344. Personal expenses: $3,184.

2007-2008 Financial aid. Need-based: Average need met was 37%. Average scholarship/grant was $3,604; average loan $2,969. 38% of total undergraduate aid awarded as scholarships/grants, 62% as loans/jobs. **Non-need-based:** Scholarships awarded for academics, alumni affiliation, leadership, religious affiliation, state residency.

Application procedures. Admission: Priority date 1/31; no deadline. $25 fee, may be waived for applicants with need. Admission notification on a rolling basis. Must reply by May 1 or within 2 week(s) if notified thereafter. **Financial aid:** Priority date 3/1; no closing date. FAFSA required. Applicants notified on a rolling basis starting 3/1; must reply within 2 week(s) of notification.

Academics. Special study options: Combined bachelor's/graduate degree, distance learning, double major, independent study, internships. **Credit/placement by examination:** AP, CLEP, institutional tests. **Support services:** Learning center, reduced course load, remedial instruction, study skills assistance, tutoring, writing center.

Majors. Health: Health care admin, nursing (RN).

Computing on campus. 24 workstations in library, computer center, student center. Online course registration, online library, wireless network available.

Student life. Freshman orientation: Mandatory. Preregistration for classes offered. **Housing:** Apartments available. $100 fully refundable deposit. **Activities:** Campus ministries, student government, student newspaper, student senate, Phi Theta Kappa, national student nurses association, Sigma Theta Tau, Go Green, College Ambassadors, American Society of Radiologic Technologists.

Student services. Adult student services, alcohol/substance abuse counseling, chaplain/spiritual director, career counseling, services for economically disadvantaged, student employment services, financial aid counseling, personal counseling. **Physically disabled:** Services for visually, hearing impaired.

Contact. E-mail: admissions@mercycollege.edu
Phone: (419) 251-1313 Toll-free number: (888) 806-3729
Fax: (419) 251-1462
Shelly McCoy Grissom, Chief Admissions Officer, Mercy College of Northwest Ohio, 2221 Madison Avenue, Toledo, OH 43604

Miami University: Oxford Campus

Oxford, Ohio — **CB member**
www.muohio.edu — **CB code: 1463**

- Public 4-year university
- Residential campus in large town
- 14,699 degree-seeking undergraduates: 2% part-time, 54% women, 4% African American, 3% Asian American, 2% Hispanic American, 1% Native American, 2% international
- 1,378 degree-seeking graduate students
- 80% of applicants admitted
- SAT or ACT with writing, application essay required
- 81% graduate within 6 years

General. Founded in 1809. Regionally accredited. Associate degree programs and certificates offered at regional campuses in Hamilton and Middletown, with degrees conferred by main (Oxford) campus. **Degrees:** 3,956 bachelor's, 283 associate awarded; master's, doctoral offered. **ROTC:** Army, Naval, Air Force. **Location:** 35 miles from Cincinnati, 46 miles from Dayton. **Calendar:** Semester, extensive summer session. **Full-time faculty:** 867 total; 87% have terminal degrees, 16% minority, 41% women. **Part-time faculty:** 394 total; 29% have terminal degrees, 11% minority, 50% women. **Class size:** 34% < 20, 50% 20-39, 6% 40-49, 7% 50-99, 3% >100. **Special facilities:** Zoology museum.

Freshman class profile. 15,009 applied, 12,067 admitted, 3,609 enrolled.

Mid 50% test scores		**GPA 2.0-2.99:**	6%
SAT critical reading:	540-640	**Rank in top quarter:**	71%
SAT math:	560-650	**Rank in top tenth:**	37%
ACT composite:	24-29	**Return as sophomores:**	90%
GPA 3.75 or higher:	42%	**Out-of-state:**	32%
GPA 3.50-3.74:	21%	**Live on campus:**	98%
GPA 3.0-3.49:	31%	**International:**	3%

Basis for selection. Admission based upon academic performance, test scores, secondary school experience, community activities, and recommendations from the high school. Diversity of student body, applicant's special abilities, talents and achievements also considered. Audition required for music, theater programs; portfolio required for art, architecture programs. **Homeschooled:** Students who have not earned GED may present credentials that demonstrate levels of academic achievement, ability, and performance equivalent to that of high school graduates. Applicants may be requested to submit samples of work in various areas.

High school preparation. College-preparatory program recommended. 16 units recommended. Recommended units include English 4, mathematics 3, social studies 3, science 3, foreign language 2 and visual/performing arts 1.

2008-2009 Annual costs. Tuition/fees: $11,887; $25,771 out-of-state. Reported in-state tuition represents maximum range that freshmen will be charged. Room/board: $8,998.

2008-2009 Financial aid. Need-based: 2,538 full-time freshmen applied for aid; 1,505 were judged to have need; 1,492 of these received aid. Average need met was 77%. Average scholarship/grant was $6,716; average loan $5,571. 49% of total undergraduate aid awarded as scholarships/grants, 51% as loans/jobs. **Non-need-based:** Awarded to 5,456 full-time undergraduates, including 1,645 freshmen. Scholarships awarded for academics, art, athletics, leadership, minority status, music/drama, ROTC, state residency.

Application procedures. Admission: Priority date 12/1; deadline 2/1 (postmark date). $45 fee, may be waived for applicants with need. Admission notification 3/15. Must reply by 5/1. **Financial aid:** Priority date 2/15; no closing date. FAFSA required. Applicants notified on a rolling basis starting 3/20; must reply by 5/1 or within 3 week(s) of notification.

Academics. Special study options: Combined bachelor's/graduate degree, cooperative education, cross-registration, double major, exchange student, honors, independent study, internships, liberal arts/career combination, semester at sea, student-designed major, study abroad, teacher certification program, Washington semester. Undergraduate associates, undergraduate research program, science and engineering research semester, 3-2 engineering with Case Western Reserve University and Columbia University, 3-2 forestry/environmental studies with Duke University, 3-1 and 4-1 in Clinical Laboratory Science, 3-1 Arts/Professional A.B./Professional degree. **Credit/placement by examination:** AP, CLEP, IB, institutional tests. 32 credit hours maximum toward associate degree, 32 toward bachelor's. **Support services:** Learning center, study skills assistance, tutoring, writing center.

Majors. Architecture: History/criticism, interior, urban/community planning. **Area/ethnic studies:** African-American, American, Italian, Latin American, women's. **Biology:** Bacteriology, biochemistry, botany, zoology. **Business:** Accounting, business admin, finance, management information systems, managerial economics, marketing, operations. **Communications:** General, digital media, journalism, media studies, public relations. **Computer sciences:** Computer science, systems analysis. **Conservation:** Environmental science, environmental studies, wood science. **Education:** Art, biology, chemistry, early childhood, English, foreign languages, French, German, health, Latin, mathematics, middle, music, physical, physics, science, secondary, social studies, Spanish, special, speech. **Engineering:** General, chemical, computer, electrical, manufacturing, mechanical, physics. **Engineering technology:** General, industrial management. **Family/consumer sciences:** Family studies, food/nutrition. **Foreign languages:** Classics, East Asian, French, German, linguistics, Russian, Spanish. **Health:** Athletic training, clinical lab science, nursing (RN), speech pathology. **History:** General. **Interdisciplinary:** Gerontology. **Math:** General, statistics. **Parks/recreation:** Exercise sciences, health/fitness, sports admin. **Philosophy/religion:** Philosophy, religion. **Physical sciences:** Chemistry, geology, physics. **Psychology:**

General. **Public administration:** General, social work. **Social sciences:** Anthropology, economics, geography, international relations, political science, sociology. **Visual/performing arts:** Art history/conservation, commercial/advertising art, dramatic, music performance, studio arts.

Most popular majors. Biology 7%, business/marketing 26%, communications/journalism 6%, education 11%, social sciences 14%.

Computing on campus. 1,200 workstations in dormitories, library, computer center, student center. Dormitories wired for high-speed internet access and linked to campus network. Commuter students can connect to campus network. Online course registration, online library, helpline, repair service, student web hosting, wireless network available.

Student life. **Freshman orientation:** Mandatory, $80 fee. Preregistration for classes offered. Held for 2 days during June and July. **Housing:** Guaranteed on-campus for freshmen. Coed dorms, single-sex dorms, special housing for disabled, apartments, cooperative housing, fraternity/sorority housing, wellness housing available. $425 nonrefundable deposit, deadline 5/1. Special arrangements include sorority suites in residence halls. **Activities:** Bands, campus ministries, choral groups, dance, drama, film society, international student organizations, literary magazine, music ensembles, Model UN, musical theater, opera, radio station, student government, student newspaper, symphony orchestra, TV station, service network, black student action association, Campus Crusade for Christ, Jewish students association, College Democrats/College Republicans, Asian-American association, Alpha Phi Omega.

Athletics. NCAA. **Intercollegiate:** Baseball M, basketball, cross-country, diving, field hockey W, football (tackle) M, golf M, ice hockey M, soccer W, softball W, swimming, tennis W, track and field, volleyball W. **Intramural:** Baseball, basketball, football (non-tackle), ice hockey, racquetball, soccer, softball, tennis, volleyball. **Team name:** Red Hawks.

Student services. Alcohol/substance abuse counseling, chaplain/spiritual director, career counseling, services for economically disadvantaged, student employment services, financial aid counseling, health services, legal services, minority student services, on-campus daycare, personal counseling, placement for graduates, veterans' counselor, women's services. **Physically disabled:** Services for visually, speech, hearing impaired. **Learning disabled:** Comprehensive services available.

Contact. E-mail: admission@muohio.edu
Phone: (513) 529-2531 Fax: (513) 529-1550
Laurie Koehler, Director of Admissions, Miami University: Oxford Campus, 301 South Campus Avenue, Oxford, OH 45056

Mount Carmel College of Nursing

Columbus, Ohio — **CB member**
www.mccn.edu — **CB code: 1502**

- Private 4-year nursing college affiliated with Roman Catholic Church
- Very large city
- 690 degree-seeking undergraduates
- 60% of applicants admitted

General. Regionally accredited. **Degrees:** 198 bachelor's awarded; master's offered. **Location:** Downtown. **Calendar:** Semester, limited summer session. **Full-time faculty:** 40 total. **Part-time faculty:** 30 total.

Freshman class profile. 219 applied, 132 admitted, 77 enrolled.

Mid 50% test scores		**ACT composite:**	19-23

Basis for selection. High school record and standardized test score most important.

2008-2009 Annual costs. Tuition/fees: $8,681. Books/supplies: $600. Personal expenses: $1,614.

2008-2009 Financial aid. **Need-based:** 26% of total undergraduate aid awarded as scholarships/grants, 74% as loans/jobs.

Application procedures. **Admission:** Priority date 2/1; no deadline. $30 fee. **Financial aid:** Priority date 3/1; no closing date. FAFSA, institutional form required. Applicants notified on a rolling basis.

Academics. **Credit/placement by examination:** CLEP.

Majors. **Health:** Nursing (RN).

Contact. E-mail: mccnadmissions@mchs.com
Phone: (614) 234-1085 Toll-free number: (800) 556-6942
Fax: (614) 234-2875
Kim Campbell, Director of Admissions, Mount Carmel College of Nursing, 127 South Davis Avenue, Columbus, OH 43222-1589

Mount Union College

Alliance, Ohio — **CB member**
www.muc.edu — **CB code: 1492**

- Private 4-year liberal arts college affiliated with United Methodist Church
- Residential campus in large town
- 2,203 degree-seeking undergraduates: 3% part-time, 50% women
- 77% of applicants admitted
- SAT or ACT (ACT writing optional), application essay required
- 65% graduate within 6 years; 23% enter graduate study

General. Founded in 1846. Regionally accredited. **Degrees:** 434 bachelor's awarded. **ROTC:** Army, Air Force. **Location:** 55 miles from Cleveland, 75 miles from Pittsburgh. **Calendar:** Semester, limited summer session. **Full-time faculty:** 125 total; 85% have terminal degrees, 10% minority, 36% women. **Part-time faculty:** 107 total; 4% minority, 49% women. **Class size:** 57% < 20, 42% 20-39, less than 1% 40-49, less than 1% 50-99. **Special facilities:** 2 astronomical observatories, 141-acre nature center for ecological studies, bird observatory, scanning electron microscope facility.

Freshman class profile. 2,326 applied, 1,782 admitted, 663 enrolled.

Mid 50% test scores		**GPA 2.0-2.99:**	36%
SAT critical reading:	420-550	**Rank in top quarter:**	41%
SAT math:	450-570	**Rank in top tenth:**	19%
ACT composite:	19-25	**Return as sophomores:**	78%
GPA 3.75 or higher:	18%	**Out-of-state:**	14%
GPA 3.50-3.74:	11%	**Live on campus:**	96%
GPA 3.0-3.49:	34%	**International:**	3%

Basis for selection. Class rank, rigor of secondary school record, standardized test scores, academic GPA very important. Rolling deadline for SAT, ACT scores. Interview recommended for all. Audition recommended for communications, music, and theater programs. Portfolio recommended for art and communications programs. **Homeschooled:** Statement describing homeschool structure and mission required.

High school preparation. 18 units recommended. Recommended units include English 4, mathematics 3, social studies 3, science 3 (laboratory 2), foreign language 2 and academic electives 1.

2008-2009 Annual costs. Tuition/fees: $23,120. Room/board: $7,050. Books/supplies: $750. Personal expenses: $590.

2007-2008 Financial aid. **Need-based:** 547 full-time freshmen applied for aid; 480 were judged to have need; 479 of these received aid. Average need met was 83%. Average scholarship/grant was $13,776; average loan $5,071. 67% of total undergraduate aid awarded as scholarships/grants, 33% as loans/jobs. **Non-need-based:** Awarded to 460 full-time undergraduates, including 140 freshmen. Scholarships awarded for academics, alumni affiliation, art, job skills, leadership, music/drama, religious affiliation, ROTC, state residency.

Application procedures. **Admission:** Priority date 3/1; no deadline. No application fee. Admission notification on a rolling basis beginning on or about 10/1. Admission determined by space availability after May 1. **Financial aid:** Priority date 4/1; no closing date. FAFSA required. Applicants notified on a rolling basis starting 3/15; must reply within 4 week(s) of notification.

Academics. All freshmen must take Liberal Arts Experience course. **Special study options:** Accelerated study, cooperative education, double major, ESL, honors, independent study, internships, student-designed major, study abroad, teacher certification program. **Credit/placement by examination:** AP, CLEP, IB, institutional tests. 15 credit hours maximum toward bachelor's degree. **Support services:** Learning center, study skills assistance, tutoring, writing center.

Majors. **Area/ethnic studies:** American, Asian. **Biology:** General, biochemistry. **Business:** Accounting, business admin, international. **Communications:** General. **Computer sciences:** Programming, web page design. **Conservation:** Environmental science. **Education:** Early childhood, health, middle, music, physical, special. **Foreign languages:** French, German, Japanese, Spanish. **Health:** Athletic training, clinical lab science. **History:** General. **Interdisciplinary:** Neuroscience. **Math:** General. **Parks/recreation:** Exercise sciences, sports admin. **Philosophy/religion:** Philosophy, religion. **Physical sciences:** Chemistry, geology, physics. **Protective services:** Criminalistics. **Psychology:** General. **Social sciences:** Criminology, economics, international relations, political science, sociology. **Visual/performing arts:** Dramatic, music performance, studio arts.

Most popular majors. Business/marketing 18%, education 21%, parks/recreation 13%, social sciences 9%.

Computing on campus. 220 workstations in dormitories, library, computer center, student center. Dormitories wired for high-speed internet access and linked to campus network. Commuter students can connect to campus network. Online course registration, online library, helpline, repair service, student web hosting, wireless network available.

Student life. **Freshman orientation:** Available. Preregistration for classes offered. Two-day summer orientation includes program for parents. Fall orientation held week before registration for students only. **Housing:** Guaranteed on-campus for all undergraduates. Coed dorms, single-sex dorms, special housing for disabled, fraternity/sorority housing, wellness housing available. **Activities:** Bands, choral groups, dance, drama, literary magazine, music ensembles, musical theater, radio station, student government, student newspaper, academic clubs, academic honoraries, religious clubs, service organizations, Alpha Phi Omega, black student union, international students association, women students association, religious life council, student activities council.

Athletics. NCAA. **Intercollegiate:** Baseball M, basketball, cheerleading, cross-country, diving, football (tackle) M, golf, soccer, softball W, swimming, tennis, track and field, volleyball W, wrestling M. **Intramural:** Badminton, basketball, bowling, diving, football (non-tackle), golf, gymnastics, racquetball, soccer, softball, swimming, tennis, volleyball, water polo, weight lifting. **Team name:** Purple Raiders.

Student services. Adult student services, alcohol/substance abuse counseling, chaplain/spiritual director, career counseling, student employment services, financial aid counseling, health services, minority student services, personal counseling, placement for graduates. **Physically disabled:** Services for visually impaired.

Contact. E-mail: admission@muc.edu
Phone: (330) 823-2590 Toll-free number: (800) 334-6682
Fax: (330) 823-5097
Vince Heslop, Director of Enrollment Technology, Mount Union College, 1972 Clark Avenue, Alliance, OH 44601-3993

Mount Vernon Nazarene University

Mount Vernon, Ohio
www.mvnu.edu **CB code: 1531**

- Private 4-year university affiliated with Church of the Nazarene
- Residential campus in large town
- 1,984 degree-seeking undergraduates: 9% part-time, 61% women, 5% African American, 1% Asian American, 1% Hispanic American, 1% international
- 468 degree-seeking graduate students
- 79% of applicants admitted
- SAT or ACT (ACT writing optional), application essay required
- 56% graduate within 6 years; 15% enter graduate study

General. Founded in 1964. Regionally accredited. **Degrees:** 545 bachelor's, 10 associate awarded; master's offered. **Location:** 45 miles from Columbus. **Calendar:** 4-1-4, limited summer session. **Full-time faculty:** 119 total; 64% have terminal degrees, 5% minority, 34% women. **Part-time faculty:** 152 total; 19% have terminal degrees, 3% minority, 36% women. **Class size:** 76% < 20, 19% 20-39, 2% 40-49, 3% 50-99. **Special facilities:** 70-acre biological research area and nature center, weather station.

Freshman class profile. 813 applied, 640 admitted, 368 enrolled.

Mid 50% test scores		**GPA 2.0-2.99:**	22%
SAT critical reading:	500-610	**Rank in top quarter:**	48%
SAT math:	450-580	**Rank in top tenth:**	22%
ACT composite:	23-27	**End year in good standing:**	86%
GPA 3.75 or higher:	30%	**Return as sophomores:**	75%
GPA 3.50-3.74:	19%	**Out-of-state:**	14%
GPA 3.0-3.49:	28%	**Live on campus:**	95%

Basis for selection. High school record, ACT or SAT scores, recommendations important. Interview recommended. **Homeschooled:** Transcript of courses and grades, letter of recommendation (nonparent) required. Family members cannot complete either academic or character references. Employer can complete academic reference. Students who participate in accredited program must provide transcript from accrediting agency; otherwise, must provide a list of classes completed.

High school preparation. College-preparatory program recommended. 21 units recommended. Required and recommended units include English 4, mathematics 3, social studies 3, science 3 (laboratory 3), foreign language 2-3, visual/performing arts 1 and academic electives 4. 1 health and physical education.

2009-2010 Annual costs. Tuition/fees (projected): $20,580. Room/board: $5,890. Books/supplies: $1,000. Personal expenses: $1,885.

2008-2009 Financial aid. **Need-based:** 368 full-time freshmen applied for aid; 335 were judged to have need; 335 of these received aid. Average need met was 68%. Average scholarship/grant was $9,983; average loan $3,882. 46% of total undergraduate aid awarded as scholarships/grants, 54% as loans/jobs. **Non-need-based:** Awarded to 444 full-time undergraduates, including 107 freshmen. Scholarships awarded for academics, athletics, minority status, music/drama, religious affiliation, state residency.

Application procedures. **Admission:** Priority date 3/15; deadline 7/15 (receipt date). $25 fee, may be waived for applicants with need. Admission notification on a rolling basis beginning on or about 9/1. **Financial aid:** Priority date 3/15; no closing date. FAFSA, institutional form required. Applicants notified on a rolling basis starting 2/28; must reply within 2 week(s) of notification.

Academics. Off-campus January term offers unique educational opportunities, including urban and international studies. **Special study options:** Combined bachelor's/graduate degree, cooperative education, cross-registration, distance learning, double major, dual enrollment of high school students, honors, independent study, internships, liberal arts/career combination, study abroad, teacher certification program, Washington semester. Cooperative pre-engineering program with Olivet Nazarene University, cooperative pre-occupational therapy/physical therapy/physician's assistant programs with Chatham College, and articulation agreements with Zane State College, Central Ohio Technical College, and North Central State College. Several opportunities for students to participate in service learning or mission trips. During the academic year, students may participate in one of the following trips: Germany, Hungary, Venezuela, Costa Rica, Nicaragua, Belize, Benin, Romania, or several out-of-state USA trips. **Credit/placement by examination:** AP, CLEP, IB, SAT, ACT, institutional tests. 30 credit hours maximum toward bachelor's degree. **Support services:** Reduced course load, study skills assistance.

Majors. **Biology:** General. **Business:** Accounting, business admin, finance, international, management information systems, marketing, office management. **Communications:** General, journalism, public relations. **Computer sciences:** General, computer science. **Education:** General, art, biology, business, chemistry, early childhood, elementary, English, family/consumer sciences, health, history, mathematics, middle, music, physical, physics, science, secondary, social studies, Spanish, special. **Family/consumer sciences:** General. **Foreign languages:** Spanish. **Health:** Clinical lab science, nursing (RN), staff services technology. **History:** General. **Math:** General. **Parks/recreation:** Exercise sciences, health/fitness, sports admin. **Philosophy/religion:** Philosophy, religion. **Physical sciences:** Chemistry, physics. **Protective services:** Criminal justice, law enforcement admin. **Psychology:** General. **Public administration:** Social work. **Social sciences:** Sociology. **Theology:** Bible, pastoral counseling, religious ed, sacred music, youth ministry. **Visual/performing arts:** Art, design, dramatic, graphic design, music performance. **Other:** Applied business technology, Intercultural studies, Video and radio broadcasting.

Most popular majors. Business/marketing 59%, education 9%.

Computing on campus. 232 workstations in dormitories, library, computer center, student center. Dormitories wired for high-speed internet access and linked to campus network. Commuter students can connect to campus network. Online course registration, online library, helpline, wireless network available.

Student life. **Freshman orientation:** Mandatory, $25 fee. Preregistration for classes offered. Sessions held in June, July, and August. **Policies:** Students expected to comply with university's published lifestyle guidelines. Religious observance required. **Housing:** Guaranteed on-campus for freshmen. Single-sex dorms, special housing for disabled, apartments, wellness housing available. $100 fully refundable deposit, deadline 5/1. **Activities:** Bands, campus ministries, choral groups, drama, international student organizations, music ensembles, musical theater, opera, radio station, student government, student newspaper, Students in Free Enterprise, Fellowship of Christian Athletes, Young Republicans club, Young Democratic club, men's association, women's association, computing machinery association, American Sign Language club, Students with Concern, Mandate.

Athletics. NAIA, NCCAA. **Intercollegiate:** Baseball M, basketball, cross-country, golf M, soccer, softball W, volleyball W. **Intramural:** Basketball, bowling, football (non-tackle), soccer, softball, volleyball. **Team name:** Cougars.

Student services. Adult student services, alcohol/substance abuse counseling, chaplain/spiritual director, career counseling, student employment services, financial aid counseling, health services, minority student services, personal counseling, placement for graduates. **Physically disabled:** Services for visually, speech, hearing impaired.

Contact. E-mail: admissions@mvnu.edu
Phone: (740) 392-6868 ext. 4510 Toll-free number: (866) 462-6868
Fax: (740) 393-0511
James Smith, Director of Admissions, Mount Vernon Nazarene University, 800 Martinsburg Road, Mount Vernon, OH 43050

Muskingum College

New Concord, Ohio — **CB member**
www.muskingum.edu — **CB code: 1496**

- Private 4-year liberal arts college affiliated with Presbyterian Church (USA)
- Residential campus in small town
- 1,664 degree-seeking undergraduates: 7% part-time, 52% women, 5% African American, 1% Asian American, 1% Hispanic American, 1% international
- 367 degree-seeking graduate students
- 78% of applicants admitted
- SAT or ACT (ACT writing optional) required
- 60% graduate within 6 years; 16% enter graduate study

General. Founded in 1837. Regionally accredited. **Degrees:** 299 bachelor's awarded; master's offered. **Location:** 70 miles from Columbus, 125 miles from Pittsburgh. **Calendar:** Semester, limited summer session. **Full-time faculty:** 101 total; 85% have terminal degrees, 10% minority, 44% women. **Part-time faculty:** 36 total; 11% have terminal degrees, 6% minority, 58% women. **Class size:** 63% < 20, 35% 20-39, 2% 40-49. **Special facilities:** Biology field station, conservation facility.

Freshman class profile. 2,051 applied, 1,607 admitted, 482 enrolled.

Mid 50% test scores			
SAT critical reading:	460-580	Rank in top quarter:	49%
SAT math:	480-590	Rank in top tenth:	24%
SAT writing:	450-590	End year in good standing:	80%
ACT composite:	19-25	Return as sophomores:	69%
GPA 3.75 or higher:	22%	Out-of-state:	7%
GPA 3.50-3.74:	15%	Live on campus:	92%
GPA 3.0-3.49:	30%	International:	1%
GPA 2.0-2.99:	33%	Fraternities:	20%
		Sororities:	25%

Basis for selection. School achievement record most important. Test scores, recommendations, extracurricular activities, interview considered. Special consideration to children of alumni. Essay and interview recommended for all; audition recommended for music programs; portfolio recommended for art programs. **Homeschooled:** Transcript of courses and grades, state high school equivalency certificate required. Portfolio of curriculum; statement of compliance with state truancy laws in cases where state certificate is not issued. **Learning Disabled:** PLUS Program available for students with handicapping learning conditions, including learning disabilities. Students must indicate interest in program when applying for admission, and must submit psychological evaluations to complete application process. Application preferred filing date of March 1.

High school preparation. College-preparatory program required. 12 units required; 15 recommended. Required and recommended units include English 4, mathematics 2-3, social studies 2-3, science 2-3 (laboratory 2) and foreign language 2-3.

2008-2009 Annual costs. Tuition/fees: $19,125. Room/board: $7,350. Books/supplies: $1,000. Personal expenses: $900.

2008-2009 Financial aid. Non-need-based: Scholarships awarded for academics, alumni affiliation, art, leadership, minority status, music/drama, religious affiliation, state residency. **Additional information:** Scholarship priority date February 1.

Application procedures. Admission: Closing date 8/1. No application fee. Admission notification on a rolling basis beginning on or about 10/1. Must reply by May 1 or within 2 week(s) if notified thereafter. **Financial aid:** Priority date 3/15, closing date 8/1. FAFSA required. Applicants notified on a rolling basis starting 3/1; must reply by 5/1 or within 2 week(s) of notification.

Academics. Special study options: Accelerated study, distance learning, double major, dual enrollment of high school students, ESL, exchange student, honors, independent study, internships, liberal arts/career combination, student-designed major, study abroad, teacher certification program, United Nations semester, Washington semester. **Credit/placement by examination:** AP, CLEP, IB, SAT, ACT, institutional tests. **Support services:** Learning center, pre-admission summer program, reduced course load, study skills assistance, tutoring, writing center.

Majors. Biology: General, conservation, molecular. **Business:** General, accounting, international marketing, managerial economics. **Communications:** General, digital media, journalism. **Computer sciences:** General, computer science. **Conservation:** Environmental science. **Education:** Early childhood, elementary, middle, secondary, special. **Engineering:** General, science. **Foreign languages:** French, German, Spanish. **Health:** Clinical lab technology, nursing (RN), predental, premedicine, prepharmacy, preveterinary, speech pathology. **History:** General. **Interdisciplinary:** Neuroscience. **Legal studies:** Prelaw. **Liberal arts:** Humanities. **Math:** General. **Philosophy/religion:** Philosophy, religion. **Physical sciences:** Chemistry, geology, physics, planetary. **Protective services:** Police science. **Psychology:** General. **Social sciences:** Anthropology, economics, international relations, political science, sociology. **Theology:** Religious ed, theology. **Visual/performing arts:** Art, dramatic.

Most popular majors. Business/marketing 22%, communications/journalism 6%, education 26%, history 7%, security/protective services 6%, social sciences 7%.

Computing on campus. 217 workstations in dormitories, library, computer center, student center. Dormitories wired for high-speed internet access and linked to campus network. Commuter students can connect to campus network. Online course registration, online library, helpline, repair service, student web hosting, wireless network available.

Student life. Freshman orientation: Available. Preregistration for classes offered. Six 1-day sessions held on weekdays in May and June. **Housing:** Coed dorms, single-sex dorms, apartments, fraternity/sorority housing, wellness housing available. $150 deposit, deadline 5/1. **Activities:** Bands, campus ministries, choral groups, dance, drama, international student organizations, literary magazine, music ensembles, Model UN, musical theater, radio station, student government, student newspaper, symphony orchestra, TV station, Christian Fellowship, Fellowship of Christian Athletes, political awareness program, SADD, Habitat for Humanity, Young Democrats, Young Republicans.

Athletics. NCAA. **Intercollegiate:** Baseball M, basketball, cheerleading, cross-country, football (tackle) M, golf, soccer, softball W, tennis, track and field, volleyball W, wrestling M. **Intramural:** Basketball, bowling, cross-country, football (non-tackle), golf, lacrosse, racquetball, rugby, soccer, softball, table tennis M, tennis, track and field, volleyball, wrestling M. **Team name:** Muskies.

Student services. Alcohol/substance abuse counseling, chaplain/spiritual director, career counseling, student employment services, financial aid counseling, health services, on-campus daycare, personal counseling, placement for graduates. **Physically disabled:** Services for hearing impaired. **Learning disabled:** Comprehensive services available.

Contact. E-mail: adminfo@muskingum.edu
Phone: (740) 826-8137 Toll-free number: (800) 752-6082
Fax: (740) 826-8100
Beth DaLonzo, Senior Director of Admissions and Student Financial Services, Muskingum College, 163 Stormont Street, New Concord, OH 43762-1199

Notre Dame College

Cleveland, Ohio — **CB member**
www.notredamecollege.edu — **CB code: 1566**

- Private 4-year liberal arts college affiliated with Roman Catholic Church
- Commuter campus in very large city
- 1,803 degree-seeking undergraduates
- 39% of applicants admitted
- SAT or ACT, application essay required

General. Founded in 1922. Regionally accredited. Weekend college for adults who have graduated from high school 5 or more years prior to their first term of enrollment. **Degrees:** 97 bachelor's, 8 associate awarded; master's offered. **ROTC:** Army. **Location:** 10 miles from downtown Cleveland. **Calendar:** Semester, limited summer session. **Full-time faculty:** 38 total. **Part-time faculty:** 80 total. **Special facilities:** Science research center.

Freshman class profile. 1,950 applied, 770 admitted, 229 enrolled.

Mid 50% test scores			
SAT critical reading:	410-520	Rank in top quarter:	20%
SAT math:	420-550	Rank in top tenth:	6%
ACT composite:	17-22	Out-of-state:	17%
		Live on campus:	70%

Basis for selection. School achievement record and test scores most important. Applicants should be in top half of class and have 2.5 high school

GPA for unconditional admission. Extracurricular activities also considered. Interview recommended.

High school preparation. Recommended units include English 4, mathematics 3, social studies 2, history 1, science 3 (laboratory 3) and foreign language 3.

2008-2009 Annual costs. Tuition/fees: $22,096. Room/board: $7,372. Books/supplies: $1,428. Personal expenses: $1,470.

Financial aid. **Non-need-based:** Scholarships awarded for academics, state residency.

Application procedures. **Admission:** No deadline. $30 fee, may be waived for applicants with need, free for online applicants. Admission notification on a rolling basis. **Financial aid:** Closing date 5/1. FAFSA required. Applicants notified on a rolling basis starting 1/1; must reply within 2 week(s) of notification.

Academics. **Special study options:** Cooperative education, cross-registration, distance learning, double major, dual enrollment of high school students, exchange student, independent study, internships, student-designed major, study abroad, teacher certification program, weekend college. **Credit/placement by examination:** AP, CLEP, SAT, ACT, institutional tests. **Support services:** Learning center, reduced course load, remedial instruction, tutoring, writing center.

Majors. **Biology:** General, biochemistry, environmental. **Business:** Accounting, business admin, human resources, international, management information systems, marketing. **Communications:** General, digital media, public relations. **Communications technology:** Graphics. **Education:** Early childhood, elementary, secondary. **Health:** Nursing (RN), prenursing. **History:** General. **Math:** General. **Physical sciences:** Chemistry. **Psychology:** General. **Social sciences:** Criminology, political science. **Theology:** Theology. **Visual/performing arts:** General, graphic design, studio arts. **Other:** Public administration.

Most popular majors. Business/marketing 41%, education 25%, psychology 14%.

Computing on campus. 67 workstations in dormitories, library, computer center.

Student life. **Freshman orientation:** Mandatory, $100 fee. Preregistration for classes offered. Three 2-day sessions held in June, July, and August. Evening orientation sessions held in August and January for adult students. **Housing:** Coed dorms, wellness housing available. $150 deposit. **Activities:** Pep band, choral groups, drama, literary magazine, music ensembles, student government, student newspaper, campus ministry board, Black Scholars, multicultural student advisory board, St. Julie Scholars, psychology council, science and business clubs, Achievement in Research and Scholarship.

Athletics. NAIA. **Intercollegiate:** Baseball M, basketball, cross-country, diving W, field hockey W, golf, lacrosse W, soccer, softball W, swimming W, tennis M, track and field, volleyball W, wrestling M. **Intramural:** Soccer W, softball W, tennis, volleyball W. **Team name:** Falcons.

Student services. Adult student services, alcohol/substance abuse counseling, chaplain/spiritual director, career counseling, student employment services, financial aid counseling, health services, personal counseling, placement for graduates. **Learning disabled:** Comprehensive services available.

Contact. E-mail: admissions@ndc.edu
Phone: (216) 373-5355 Toll-free number: (877) 632-6446 ext. 5355
Fax: (216) 381-3802
David Armstrong, Vice President for Enrollment, Notre Dame College, 4545 College Road, Cleveland, OH 44121-4293

Oberlin College

Oberlin, Ohio — **CB member**
www.oberlin.edu — **CB code: 1587**

- Private 4-year music and liberal arts college
- Residential campus in small town
- 2,839 degree-seeking undergraduates: 2% part-time, 55% women, 6% African American, 7% Asian American, 5% Hispanic American, 1% Native American, 6% international
- 26 degree-seeking graduate students
- 33% of applicants admitted
- SAT or ACT with writing required
- 83% graduate within 6 years

General. Founded in 1833. Regionally accredited. **Degrees:** 701 bachelor's awarded; master's offered. **Location:** 34 miles from Cleveland. **Calendar:** 4-1-4. **Full-time faculty:** 285 total; 96% have terminal degrees, 11% minority, 39% women. **Class size:** 68% < 20, 27% 20-39, 2% 40-49, 2% 50-99, less than 1% >100. **Special facilities:** Observatory, bog, environmental studies building, arboretum.

Freshman class profile. 7,006 applied, 2,288 admitted, 768 enrolled.

Mid 50% test scores		**GPA 2.0-2.99:**	4%
SAT critical reading:	640-740	**Rank in top quarter:**	91%
SAT math:	620-710	**Rank in top tenth:**	69%
SAT writing:	640-730	**Return as sophomores:**	94%
ACT composite:	27-32	**Out-of-state:**	91%
GPA 3.75 or higher:	38%	**Live on campus:**	100%
GPA 3.50-3.74:	28%	**International:**	5%
GPA 3.0-3.49:	30%		

Basis for selection. For college of arts and sciences: school achievement record, test scores, school and community leadership activities, recommendations, and interview important. Special consideration to applicants from minority and first generation college families and to foreign applicants. For conservatory: audition most important factor; admission selective. SAT Subject Tests recommended. Interview required for early admission candidates; recommended for all others. Audition required of applicants to conservatory; essay required of applicants to college of arts and sciences. **Homeschooled:** Interview, SAT Subject Tests, detailed portfolio required.

High school preparation. Required units include English 4, mathematics 4, social studies 3, science 3 and foreign language 3.

2008-2009 Annual costs. Tuition/fees: $36,282. Room/board: $9,280. Books/supplies: $830. Personal expenses: $978.

2008-2009 Financial aid. **Need-based:** 452 full-time freshmen applied for aid; 399 were judged to have need; 399 of these received aid. Average need met was 100%. Average scholarship/grant was $27,323; average loan $2,754. 81% of total undergraduate aid awarded as scholarships/grants, 19% as loans/jobs. **Non-need-based:** Scholarships awarded for academics, music/drama.

Application procedures. **Admission:** Closing date 1/15 (postmark date). $35 fee, may be waived for applicants with need. Admission notification 4/1. Must reply by May 1 or within 2 week(s) if notified thereafter. 12/1 application closing date for Conservatory of Music; $100 application fee. **Financial aid:** Priority date 1/15, closing date 2/1. FAFSA, institutional form, CSS PROFILE required. Applicants notified by 4/1; must reply by 5/1 or within 2 week(s) of notification.

Academics. No core curriculum. Students required to take 9 credit hours in each academic division (Humanities, Social Sciences, and Math and Natural Science) and 9 hours related to cultural diversity. **Special study options:** Cross-registration, double major, dual enrollment of high school students, exchange student, honors, independent study, internships, liberal arts/career combination, New York semester, student-designed major, study abroad, teacher certification program, urban semester, Washington semester. 5-year dual degree program with music conservatory and liberal arts college, 3-2 engineering. **Credit/placement by examination:** AP, CLEP, IB, institutional tests. 30 credit hours maximum toward bachelor's degree. **Support services:** Learning center, remedial instruction, study skills assistance, tutoring, writing center.

Majors. **Area/ethnic studies:** African, African-American, American, East Asian, Latin American, Russian/Slavic, women's. **Biology:** General, biochemistry. **Computer sciences:** General. **Conservation:** Environmental studies. **Education:** Music. **Foreign languages:** Ancient Greek, classics, comparative lit, French, German, Latin, Russian, Spanish. **Health:** Predental, premedicine, preveterinary. **History:** General. **Interdisciplinary:** Neuroscience. **Legal studies:** Prelaw. **Math:** General. **Philosophy/religion:** Judaic, philosophy, religion. **Physical sciences:** Chemistry, geology, physics. **Psychology:** General. **Social sciences:** Anthropology, economics, political science, sociology. **Visual/performing arts:** Art history/conservation, conducting, dance, dramatic, film/cinema, jazz, music history, music theory/composition, piano/organ, stringed instruments, studio arts, voice/opera.

Most popular majors. Area/ethnic studies 8%, biology 10%, English 9%, history 7%, philosophy/religious studies 6%, social sciences 12%, visual/performing arts 26%.

Computing on campus. 340 workstations in dormitories, library, computer center. Dormitories wired for high-speed internet access and linked to campus network. Commuter students can connect to campus network. Online course registration, helpline, repair service, wireless network available.

Student life. **Freshman orientation:** Mandatory. Preregistration for classes offered. Held week prior to fall classes. Includes day of service. **Policies:**

Students agree to follow honor code. **Housing:** Guaranteed on-campus for all undergraduates. Coed dorms, single-sex dorms, cooperative housing, wellness housing available. **Activities:** Bands, campus ministries, choral groups, dance, drama, film society, international student organizations, literary magazine, music ensembles, musical theater, opera, radio station, student government, student newspaper, symphony orchestra, religious, political, intercultural, ethnic, social service, and gay/lesbian/bisexual organizations.

Athletics. NCAA. **Intercollegiate:** Baseball M, basketball, cross-country, diving, field hockey W, football (tackle) M, golf, lacrosse, soccer, softball W, swimming, tennis, track and field, volleyball W. **Intramural:** Baseball M, basketball, bowling, football (non-tackle), handball, racquetball, rugby M, skin diving, soccer, softball, squash, table tennis, tennis, track and field, volleyball, weight lifting. **Team name:** Yeomen.

Student services. Alcohol/substance abuse counseling, chaplain/spiritual director, career counseling, services for economically disadvantaged, student employment services, financial aid counseling, health services, minority student services, personal counseling, placement for graduates, women's services. **Physically disabled:** Services for visually, speech, hearing impaired.

Contact. E-mail: college.admissions@oberlin.edu
Phone: (440) 775-8411 Toll-free number: (800) 622-6243
Fax: (440) 775-6905
Debra Chermonte, Dean of Admissions and Financial Aid, Oberlin College, Carnegie Building, 101 North Professor Street, Oberlin, OH 44074

Ohio Christian University

Circleville, Ohio
www.ohiochristian.edu **CB code: 1088**

- Private 4-year Bible college affiliated with Churches of Christ in Christian Union
- Residential campus in large town
- 769 degree-seeking undergraduates: 13% part-time, 51% women
- 90% of applicants admitted
- SAT or ACT (ACT writing optional), application essay required
- 66% graduate within 6 years

General. Founded in 1948. Candidate for regional accreditation; also accredited by ABHE. **Degrees:** 104 bachelor's, 5 associate awarded. **Location:** 25 miles from Columbus. **Calendar:** Semester, limited summer session. **Full-time faculty:** 14 total; 57% have terminal degrees, 7% minority, 21% women. **Part-time faculty:** 37 total. **Class size:** 74% < 20, 22% 20-39, 2% 40-49, 3% 50-99.

Freshman class profile. 311 applied, 279 admitted, 81 enrolled.

Mid 50% test scores		Return as sophomores:	59%
SAT critical reading:	480-560	Out-of-state:	15%
SAT math:	440-540	Live on campus:	37%
ACT composite:	19-24	International:	3%

Basis for selection. Positive Christian testimony, potential for Christian service, sound academic performance, and personal character references important. Students without SAT or ACT may be admitted conditionally but must meet test requirement at earliest opportunity. Interview recommended for all; audition required for music majors.

High school preparation. 15 units recommended. Recommended units include English 4, mathematics 3, social studies 3, science 3 and foreign language 2.

2009-2010 Annual costs. Tuition/fees (projected): $15,050. Room/board: $5,990. Books/supplies: $500. Personal expenses: $2,606.

2007-2008 Financial aid. All financial aid based on need. 238 full-time freshmen applied for aid; 190 were judged to have need; 188 of these received aid. Average need met was 75%. Average scholarship/grant was $3,000; average loan $2,660. 54% of total undergraduate aid awarded as scholarships/grants, 46% as loans/jobs. **Additional information:** Religious affiliation tuition discount.

Application procedures. Admission: Priority date 4/1; no deadline. $50 fee, may be waived for applicants with need. Admission notification on a rolling basis. Must reply by May 1 or within 2 week(s) if notified thereafter. **Financial aid:** Priority date 5/7; no closing date. FAFSA, institutional form required. Applicants notified on a rolling basis starting 5/1; must reply within 2 week(s) of notification.

Academics. Every student required to complete minimum of 30 hours in Bible and theology courses. **Special study options:** Accelerated study, combined bachelor's/graduate degree, distance learning, double major, dual enrollment of high school students, honors, independent study, internships, liberal arts/career combination, student-designed major, study abroad. **Credit/placement by examination:** AP, CLEP, ACT, institutional tests. **Support services:** Reduced course load, remedial instruction, study skills assistance, tutoring, writing center.

Majors. Business: General, accounting, accounting/business management, business admin. **Education:** General, early childhood, elementary, music, secondary. **Philosophy/religion:** Religion. **Psychology:** General. **Theology:** Missionary, pastoral counseling, religious ed, sacred music, theology, youth ministry.

Most popular majors. Education 8%, psychology 11%.

Computing on campus. 58 workstations in dormitories, library, computer center. Dormitories wired for high-speed internet access and linked to campus network. Online library, helpline, repair service, wireless network available.

Student life. Freshman orientation: Mandatory. Preregistration for classes offered. Held 2-days prior to start of classes. **Policies:** Curfew of 11:30 pm (Monday-Thursday), 1:00 am (Friday), 12:00 am (Saturday-Sunday); dress code. Religious observance required. **Housing:** Guaranteed on-campus for freshmen. Single-sex dorms, apartments available. $50 deposit, deadline 8/1. **Activities:** Choral groups, music ensembles, student government, ministerial association, prison ministries, S.H.I.N.E., world gospel mission student involvement, summer camp ministries.

Athletics. NCCAA. **Intercollegiate:** Archery, baseball M, basketball, soccer M, softball W, volleyball W. **Intramural:** Basketball, golf, skiing, soccer, table tennis, volleyball. **Team name:** Trailblazers.

Student services. Adult student services, chaplain/spiritual director, career counseling, student employment services, financial aid counseling, health services, minority student services, personal counseling, veterans' counselor. **Physically disabled:** Services for visually impaired.

Contact. E-mail: enroll@ohiochristian.edu
Phone: (740) 477-7701 Toll-free number: (877) 762-8669
Fax: (740) 477-7755
Mike Egenreider, Director of Admissions, Ohio Christian University, 1476 Lancaster Pike, Circleville, OH 43113

Ohio Dominican University

Columbus, Ohio **CB member**
www.ohiodominican.edu **CB code: 1131**

- Private 4-year university and liberal arts college affiliated with Roman Catholic Church
- Commuter campus in very large city
- 2,106 degree-seeking undergraduates: 25% part-time, 61% women, 24% African American, 1% Asian American, 2% Hispanic American, 1% international
- 687 degree-seeking graduate students
- 68% of applicants admitted
- SAT or ACT (ACT writing optional), application essay required
- 45% graduate within 6 years

General. Founded in 1911. Regionally accredited. **Degrees:** 451 bachelor's, 77 associate awarded; master's offered. **ROTC:** Army. **Location:** 4 miles from downtown. **Calendar:** Semester, limited summer session. **Full-time faculty:** 72 total; 90% have terminal degrees, 8% minority, 56% women. **Part-time faculty:** 151 total; 32% have terminal degrees, 12% minority, 60% women. **Class size:** 55% < 20, 45% 20-39, less than 1% 40-49.

Freshman class profile. 2,555 applied, 1,749 admitted, 366 enrolled.

Mid 50% test scores		Rank in top quarter:	28%
ACT composite:	19-23	Rank in top tenth:	9%
GPA 3.75 or higher:	10%	Return as sophomores:	61%
GPA 3.50-3.74:	10%	Out-of-state:	7%
GPA 3.0-3.49:	35%	Live on campus:	80%
GPA 2.0-2.99:	42%	International:	1%

Basis for selection. High school GPA, curriculum most important, followed by class rank, test scores, interview, recommendations, and activities. Interview required for in-state applicants; recommended for out-of-state. **Homeschooled:** Transcript of courses and grades, state high school equivalency certificate required.

High school preparation. College-preparatory program recommended. 16 units recommended. Recommended units include English 4, mathematics 3, social studies 3, science 3 and foreign language 3.

2008-2009 Annual costs. Tuition/fees: $23,215. Room/board: $7,590. Books/supplies: $1,000. Personal expenses: $2,500.

Financial aid. Non-need-based: Scholarships awarded for academics, athletics, state residency.

Application procedures. Admission: Priority date 4/1; no deadline. $25 fee. Admission notification on a rolling basis beginning on or about 9/1. **Financial aid:** Priority date 4/1; no closing date. FAFSA required. Applicants notified on a rolling basis starting 3/1; must reply within 2 week(s) of notification.

Academics. Special study options: Cross-registration, distance learning, double major, dual enrollment of high school students, honors, independent study, internships, study abroad, teacher certification program, Washington semester. **Credit/placement by examination:** AP, CLEP, IB, ACT. No limit on credit hours by examination, but residency requirement must be met. **Support services:** Learning center, reduced course load, remedial instruction, study skills assistance, tutoring.

Majors. Biology: General. **Business:** Accounting, business admin, communications, finance, international. **Communications:** General, public relations. **Computer sciences:** Information systems. **Education:** Art, biology, chemistry, elementary, English, mathematics, middle, multiple handicapped, physics, science, secondary, social studies, special. **History:** General. **Liberal arts:** Arts/sciences. **Math:** General. **Philosophy/religion:** Philosophy. **Physical sciences:** Chemistry. **Protective services:** Criminal justice. **Psychology:** General. **Public administration:** Social work. **Social sciences:** Economics, political science, sociology. **Theology:** Theology. **Visual/performing arts:** Art, graphic design.

Most popular majors. Business/marketing 46%, education 20%, social sciences 8%.

Computing on campus. 330 workstations in dormitories, library, computer center. Dormitories wired for high-speed internet access and linked to campus network. Commuter students can connect to campus network. Online course registration, online library, helpline, student web hosting available.

Student life. Freshman orientation: Mandatory, $125 fee. Preregistration for classes offered. Held 2 days in August. **Housing:** Coed dorms available. $150 partly refundable deposit, deadline 8/15. **Activities:** Bands, choral groups, drama, literary magazine, music ensembles, radio station, student government, student newspaper, campus ministry, black student union, American international membership club, resident student association, commuter student association, social work club, pallete club, psychology club.

Athletics. NAIA. **Intercollegiate:** Baseball M, basketball, cheerleading, cross-country, football (tackle) M, golf, soccer, softball W, tennis, volleyball W. **Intramural:** Badminton, basketball, golf, soccer, table tennis, tennis, volleyball. **Team name:** Panthers.

Student services. Adult student services, chaplain/spiritual director, career counseling, student employment services, financial aid counseling, health services, minority student services, personal counseling, placement for graduates, veterans' counselor.

Contact. E-mail: admissions@ohiodominican.edu
Phone: (614) 251-4500 Toll-free number: (800) 955-6446
Fax: (614) 251-4772
Nicole Evans, Director of Admissions, Ohio Dominican University, 1216 Sunbury Road, Columbus, OH 43219

Ohio Northern University

Ada, Ohio — **CB member**
www.onu.edu — **CB code: 1591**

- Private 4-year university affiliated with United Methodist Church
- Residential campus in small town
- 2,591 degree-seeking undergraduates: 2% part-time, 47% women, 4% African American, 2% Asian American, 2% Hispanic American, 2% international
- 976 degree-seeking graduate students
- 88% of applicants admitted
- SAT or ACT (ACT writing optional) required
- 69% graduate within 6 years

General. Founded in 1871. Regionally accredited. **Degrees:** 448 bachelor's awarded; master's, doctoral, first professional offered. **ROTC:** Army, Air Force. **Location:** 15 miles from Lima, 80 miles from Columbus. **Calendar:** Quarter, limited summer session. **Full-time faculty:** 235 total; 77% have terminal degrees, 10% minority, 37% women. **Part-time faculty:** 87 total; 29% have terminal degrees, 5% minority, 47% women. **Class size:** 49% < 20, 48% 20-39, 3% 40-49, less than 1% 50-99, less than 1% >100. **Special facilities:** Nature center, drug information center (College of Pharmacy), pharmacy museum.

Freshman class profile. 3,032 applied, 2,662 admitted, 749 enrolled.

Mid 50% test scores			
SAT critical reading:	500-620	Rank in top quarter:	69%
SAT math:	530-650	Rank in top tenth:	41%
SAT writing:	490-620	Return as sophomores:	86%
ACT composite:	23-28	Out-of-state:	17%
GPA 3.75 or higher:	51%	Live on campus:	97%
GPA 3.50-3.74:	15%	International:	2%
GPA 3.0-3.49:	21%	Fraternities:	15%
GPA 2.0-2.99:	13%	Sororities:	24%

Basis for selection. 20 ACT preferred; secondary school record very important. Colleges of Pharmacy and Engineering have higher test score credentials for consideration. GPA, class rank, test scores, college prep curriculum, extracurricular activities considered in admission decisions. Essay and interview recommended for all; audition required for music, performing arts programs; portfolio recommended for art program. **Homeschooled:** Statement describing homeschool structure and mission required.

High school preparation. College-preparatory program required. 16 units required; 24 recommended. Required and recommended units include English 4, mathematics 2-4, social studies 2-3, history 2, science 2-3 (laboratory 2), foreign language 2, computer science 1, visual/performing arts 1 and academic electives 4. 4 units math and science required for engineering and pharmacy applicants.

2008-2009 Annual costs. Tuition/fees: $30,765. Room/board: $7,890. Books/supplies: $1,500. Personal expenses: $1,229.

2008-2009 Financial aid. Non-need-based: Scholarships awarded for academics, alumni affiliation, art, leadership, music/drama, ROTC, state residency.

Application procedures. Admission: Priority date 12/1; deadline 8/15 (receipt date). $30 fee, may be waived for applicants with need. Admission notification on a rolling basis. Must reply by 5/1. Priority date for scholarship eligibility December 1. Pharmacy deadline is November 1 of senior year. **Financial aid:** Priority date 4/15, closing date 6/1. FAFSA, institutional form required. Applicants notified on a rolling basis starting 2/15; must reply within 2 week(s) of notification.

Academics. Pharmacy students admitted directly to 6-year PharmD. program. **Special study options:** Combined bachelor's/graduate degree, cooperative education, distance learning, double major, dual enrollment of high school students, ESL, exchange student, honors, independent study, internships, liberal arts/career combination, study abroad, teacher certification program, Washington semester. **Credit/placement by examination:** AP, CLEP, IB, SAT, ACT, institutional tests. 45 credit hours maximum toward bachelor's degree. **Support services:** Pre-admission summer program, reduced course load, remedial instruction, study skills assistance, tutoring, writing center.

Majors. Biology: General, biochemistry, exercise physiology, molecular. **Business:** Accounting, business admin, finance, international, management science, marketing. **Communications:** General, broadcast journalism, journalism, organizational, public relations. **Computer sciences:** Computer graphics. **Conservation:** General, environmental studies. **Education:** General, art, biology, chemistry, early childhood, elementary, English, foreign languages, French, health, history, mathematics, middle, music, physical, physics, science, secondary, social studies, Spanish, technology/industrial arts. **Engineering:** General, civil, computer, electrical, mechanical. **Engineering technology:** Industrial. **Foreign languages:** French, German, Germanic, Spanish. **Health:** Athletic training, nursing (RN), physician assistant, predental, premedicine, preveterinary. **History:** General. **Liberal arts:** Arts/sciences. **Math:** General, statistics. **Parks/recreation:** Exercise sciences, health/fitness, sports admin. **Philosophy/religion:** Philosophy, religion. **Physical sciences:** Astronomy, chemistry, physics. **Protective services:** Criminal justice, forensics, law enforcement admin, police science. **Psychology:** General. **Social sciences:** General, international relations, political science, sociology. **Visual/performing arts:** Art, commercial/advertising art, dramatic, music management, music performance, music theory/composition, studio arts. **Other:** Pharmacy business.

Most popular majors. Biology 9%, business/marketing 19%, education 9%, engineering/engineering technologies 21%.

Computing on campus. 550 workstations in dormitories, library, computer center, student center. Dormitories wired for high-speed internet access and linked to campus network. Commuter students can connect to campus network. Online course registration, online library, helpline, repair service, wireless network available.

Student life. Freshman orientation: Mandatory. Preregistration for classes offered. Five 1-day orientations in June on Mondays and Fridays. **Policies:** All students must reside on campus until 135 credit hours completed. No smoking in residence halls. **Housing:** Guaranteed on-campus for freshmen. Coed dorms, single-sex dorms, special housing for disabled, apartments, cooperative housing, fraternity/sorority housing, wellness housing available. $200 fully refundable deposit, deadline 5/1. Honors residence halls available. **Activities:** Bands, campus ministries, choral groups, dance, drama, international student organizations, literary magazine, music ensembles, Model UN, musical theater, opera, radio station, student government, student newspaper, symphony orchestra, TV station, Christian legal society, Fellowship of Christian Athletes, university religious association council, black student union, Amnesty International, College Republicans, black law student association, Habitat for Humanity, world student organization.

Athletics. NCAA. **Intercollegiate:** Baseball M, basketball, cross-country, diving, football (tackle) M, golf, soccer, softball W, swimming, tennis, track and field, volleyball W, wrestling M. **Intramural:** Badminton, basketball, bowling, football (non-tackle) M, racquetball, soccer, softball, swimming, table tennis M, tennis, track and field, volleyball, wrestling M. **Team name:** Polar Bears.

Student services. Alcohol/substance abuse counseling, chaplain/spiritual director, career counseling, student employment services, financial aid counseling, health services, legal services, minority student services, personal counseling, placement for graduates. **Physically disabled:** Services for visually, speech, hearing impaired.

Contact. E-mail: admissions-ug@onu.edu
Phone: (419) 772-2260 Toll-free number: (888) 408-4668
Fax: (419) 772-2821
Deborah Miller, Director of Admissions, Ohio Northern University, 525 South Main Street, Ada, OH 45810

Ohio State University: Columbus Campus

Columbus, Ohio — **CB member**
www.osu.edu — **CB code: 1592**

- Public 4-year university
- Residential campus in very large city
- 38,719 degree-seeking undergraduates: 6% part-time, 46% women, 7% African American, 5% Asian American, 3% Hispanic American, 3% international
- 13,503 degree-seeking graduate students
- 62% of applicants admitted
- SAT or ACT with writing, application essay required
- 73% graduate within 6 years

General. Founded in 1870. Regionally accredited. Additional campuses in Wooster, Marion, Lima, Newark, Mansfield. **Degrees:** 9,131 bachelor's, 435 associate awarded; master's, doctoral, first professional offered. **ROTC:** Army, Naval, Air Force. **Location:** 2 miles from downtown. **Calendar:** Quarter, extensive summer session. **Full-time faculty:** 3,224 total; 99% have terminal degrees, 20% minority, 31% women. **Part-time faculty:** 1,127 total; 14% minority, 49% women. **Class size:** 35% < 20, 38% 20-39, 8% 40-49, 11% 50-99, 7% >100. **Special facilities:** Radio telescope, dance notation bureau, extension center for educational research, biological science laboratory on Lake Erie, campus airport, environmental studies center, research vessel on Lake Erie, nuclear research reactor, supercomputer facility, arts center, cultural center, public service and public policy institute, polar research center, health policy studies center, mapping center, materials research center.

Freshman class profile. 20,932 applied, 13,041 admitted, 6,173 enrolled.

Mid 50% test scores			
SAT critical reading:	540-650	End year in good standing:	95%
SAT math:	590-680	Return as sophomores:	93%
SAT writing:	540-640	Out-of-state:	15%
ACT composite:	25-30	Live on campus:	92%
Rank in top quarter:	89%	International:	4%
Rank in top tenth:	53%	Fraternities:	9%
		Sororities:	12%

Basis for selection. Secondary school record, class rank, test scores most important. Audition required for dance, music programs; portfolio required for art programs. **Homeschooled:** May be required to provide GED.

High school preparation. Required and recommended units include English 4, mathematics 3-4, social studies 2-3, science 2-3 (laboratory 2-3), foreign language 2-3, visual/performing arts 1 and academic electives 1.

2008-2009 Annual costs. Tuition/fees: $8,679; $21,918 out-of-state. Room/board: $7,755. Books/supplies: $1,383. Personal expenses: $3,996.

2008-2009 Financial aid. Need-based: 4,880 full-time freshmen applied for aid; 3,117 were judged to have need; 3,115 of these received aid. Average need met was 69%. Average scholarship/grant was $7,667; average loan $3,248. 39% of total undergraduate aid awarded as scholarships/grants, 61% as loans/jobs. **Non-need-based:** Awarded to 9,056 full-time undergraduates, including 2,263 freshmen. Scholarships awarded for academics, alumni affiliation, art, athletics, job skills, leadership, minority status, music/drama, ROTC, state residency.

Application procedures. Admission: Closing date 2/1 (postmark date). $40 fee, may be waived for applicants with need. Admission notification on a rolling basis beginning on or about 12/1. Must reply by May 1 or within 4 week(s) if notified thereafter. **Financial aid:** Priority date 2/15; no closing date. FAFSA required. Must reply by 5/1 or within 4 week(s) of notification.

Academics. Special study options: Accelerated study, combined bachelor's/graduate degree, cooperative education, cross-registration, distance learning, double major, dual enrollment of high school students, ESL, exchange student, honors, independent study, internships, liberal arts/career combination, semester at sea, student-designed major, study abroad, teacher certification program, Washington semester. **Credit/placement by examination:** AP, CLEP, IB, SAT, ACT, institutional tests. 45 credit hours maximum toward bachelor's degree. **Support services:** Learning center, pre-admission summer program, reduced course load, remedial instruction, study skills assistance, tutoring, writing center.

Majors. Agriculture: Agronomy, animal sciences, business, communications, economics, food processing, food science, landscaping, plant protection, plant sciences, turf management. **Architecture:** Architecture, environmental design, interior, landscape. **Area/ethnic studies:** African, African-American, Central/Eastern European, East Asian, Latin American, Near/Middle Eastern, Russian/Slavic, Western European, women's. **Biology:** General, biochemistry, botany, ecology, entomology, genetics, microbiology, molecular genetics, zoology. **Business:** General, accounting, actuarial science, fashion, finance, hospitality admin, hospitality/recreation, human resources, insurance, international, logistics, management information systems, managerial economics, marketing, operations, real estate, transportation. **Communications:** General, journalism, public relations. **Computer sciences:** General, computer science, information systems. **Conservation:** General, fisheries, forestry, management/policy, wildlife. **Education:** Agricultural, art, music, physical, special, technology/industrial arts, trade/industrial. **Engineering:** Aerospace, agricultural, ceramic, chemical, civil, computer, electrical, industrial, materials, materials science, mechanical, metallurgical, physics, systems. **Engineering technology:** Construction, surveying. **Family/consumer sciences:** General, clothing/textiles, family resources, family studies, family/community services, food/nutrition. **Foreign languages:** Arabic, Chinese, classics, comparative lit, French, German, Hebrew, Italian, Japanese, Latin, linguistics, modern Greek, Portuguese, Russian, Spanish. **Health:** Audiology/hearing, audiology/speech pathology, clinical lab science, dental hygiene, dietetics, medical radiologic technology/radiation therapy, medical records admin, perfusion technology, respiratory therapy technology. **History:** General. **Interdisciplinary:** Ancient studies, medieval/Renaissance, nutrition sciences, peace/conflict. **Liberal arts:** Arts/sciences. **Math:** General. **Parks/recreation:** Exercise sciences, facilities management, health/fitness, sports admin. **Philosophy/religion:** Islamic, Judaic, philosophy, religion. **Physical sciences:** Astronomy, chemistry, geology, geophysics, physics. **Production:** Welding. **Psychology:** General. **Public administration:** Social work. **Social sciences:** General, anthropology, criminology, economics, geography, international relations, political science, sociology, urban studies. **Transportation:** Aviation. **Visual/performing arts:** Art, art history/conservation, ceramics, dance, design, dramatic, drawing, industrial design, interior design, jazz, music history, music performance, music theory/composition, painting, photography, piano/organ, printmaking, sculpture, studio arts, voice/opera.

Most popular majors. Biology 6%, business/marketing 16%, communications/journalism 6%, engineering/engineering technologies 7%, family/consumer sciences 8%, health sciences 7%, psychology 6%, social sciences 15%.

Computing on campus. 800 workstations in dormitories, library, computer center, student center. Dormitories wired for high-speed internet access and linked to campus network. Commuter students can connect to campus network. Online course registration, online library, helpline, wireless network available.

Student life. Freshman orientation: Mandatory, $50 fee. Preregistration for classes offered. Numerous 2-day programs held June-August prior to enrollment. **Housing:** Guaranteed on-campus for freshmen. Coed dorms, special housing for disabled, apartments, cooperative housing, fraternity/sorority housing, wellness housing available. $200 nonrefundable deposit. **Activities:** Bands, campus ministries, choral groups, dance, drama, film society, international student organizations, literary magazine, music ensembles, musical theater, opera, radio station, student government, student newspaper, symphony orchestra, TV station, over 800 organizations available.

Four-Year Colleges

Athletics. NCAA. **Intercollegiate:** Baseball M, basketball, cheerleading, cross-country, diving, fencing, field hockey W, football (tackle) M, golf, gymnastics, ice hockey, lacrosse, rifle, soccer, softball W, swimming, synchronized swimming W, tennis, track and field, volleyball, wrestling M. **Intramural:** Badminton, baseball M, basketball, cricket, cross-country, football (non-tackle), golf, ice hockey, racquetball, soccer, softball, swimming, table tennis, tennis, volleyball, wrestling. **Team name:** Buckeyes.

Student services. Adult student services, alcohol/substance abuse counseling, chaplain/spiritual director, career counseling, services for economically disadvantaged, student employment services, financial aid counseling, health services, legal services, minority student services, on-campus daycare, personal counseling, veterans' counselor, women's services. **Physically disabled:** Services for visually, speech, hearing impaired.

Contact. E-mail: askabuckeye@osu.edu
Phone: (614) 292-3980 Fax: (614) 292-4818
Mabel Freeman, Assistant Vice President for Undergraduate Admissions and First Year Experience, Ohio State University: Columbus Campus, 110 Enarson Hall, Columbus, OH 43210

Ohio State University: Lima Campus

Lima, Ohio
www.lima.ohio-state.edu **CB code: 1541**

- Public 4-year branch campus college
- Commuter campus in large town
- 1,268 degree-seeking undergraduates: 10% part-time, 51% women, 4% African American, 1% Asian American, 2% Hispanic American
- 58 degree-seeking graduate students
- Application essay required

General. Founded in 1960. Regionally accredited. Branch campus of Ohio State University; all degrees awarded through main campus. **Degrees:** 110 bachelor's, 33 associate awarded; master's offered. **ROTC:** Army, Naval, Air Force. **Location:** 90 miles from Columbus. **Calendar:** Quarter, limited summer session. **Full-time faculty:** 37 total; 97% have terminal degrees, 14% minority, 35% women. **Part-time faculty:** 45 total; 11% minority, 53% women. **Class size:** 45% < 20, 39% 20-39, 8% 40-49, 6% 50-99, less than 1% >100. **Special facilities:** Greenhouse, nature trails, dinosaur museum.

Freshman class profile. 1,162 applied, 1,157 admitted, 502 enrolled.

Mid 50% test scores			
SAT critical reading:	440-570	Rank in top quarter:	28%
SAT math:	470-610	Rank in top tenth:	9%
SAT writing:	410-540	Return as sophomores:	67%
ACT composite:	19-24	Out-of-state:	1%

Basis for selection. Open admission, but selective for out-of-state students. Out-of-state students evaluated on basis of GPA, class rank, principal/counselor recommendation, and SAT/ACT scores.

High school preparation. Required and recommended units include English 4, mathematics 3-4, social studies 2-3, science 2-3 (laboratory 2), foreign language 2-3, visual/performing arts 1 and academic electives 1.

2008-2009 Annual costs. Tuition/fees: $5,664; $18,903 out-of-state. Books/supplies: $1,383. Personal expenses: $3,420.

2008-2009 Financial aid. Need-based: 442 full-time freshmen applied for aid; 339 were judged to have need; 335 of these received aid. Average need met was 58%. Average scholarship/grant was $3,787; average loan $3,344. 30% of total undergraduate aid awarded as scholarships/grants, 70% as loans/jobs. **Non-need-based:** Awarded to 159 full-time undergraduates, including 107 freshmen. Scholarships awarded for academics, alumni affiliation, art, athletics, job skills, leadership, minority status, music/drama, religious affiliation, ROTC, state residency.

Application procedures. Admission: Closing date 7/1 (postmark date). $40 fee, may be waived for applicants with need. Admission notification on a rolling basis beginning on or about 12/1. Must reply by May 1 or within 4 week(s) if notified thereafter. **Financial aid:** Priority date 3/1; no closing date. FAFSA required. Applicants notified on a rolling basis starting 4/1; must reply within 4 week(s) of notification.

Academics. Students often leave campus after 1-3 years and complete bachelor's degree on Columbus campus. **Special study options:** Accelerated study, cooperative education, cross-registration, distance learning, double major, dual enrollment of high school students, ESL, exchange student, honors, independent study, internships, liberal arts/career combination, student-designed major, study abroad, teacher certification program, weekend college. **Credit/placement by examination:** AP, CLEP, SAT, ACT, institutional tests. 45 credit hours maximum toward bachelor's degree. **Support services:** Learning center, remedial instruction, tutoring, writing center.

Majors. Biology: General. **Business:** General, financial planning, hospitality admin. **Education:** General. **Health:** Health services. **History:** General. **Math:** General. **Psychology:** General.

Computing on campus. 104 workstations in library, computer center. Commuter students can connect to campus network. Online course registration, online library, helpline available.

Student life. Freshman orientation: Mandatory. Preregistration for classes offered. Orientation services available throughout year, days and evenings. **Activities:** Campus ministries, choral groups, drama, international student organizations, music ensembles, musical theater, student government, Bible club, biology club, Buckeye Ag, Buckeye Scholars, Challengers club, English club, psychology club, gaming club.

Athletics. Intramural: Basketball, bowling, golf M, soccer, softball, volleyball. **Team name:** Barons.

Student services. Adult student services, chaplain/spiritual director, career counseling, student employment services, financial aid counseling, on-campus daycare, personal counseling, placement for graduates. **Physically disabled:** Services for visually, speech, hearing impaired.

Contact. E-mail: admissions@lima.ohio-state.edu
Phone: (419) 995-8396 Fax: (419) 995-8483
Beth Keehn, Director of Admissions, Ohio State University: Lima Campus, 4240 Campus Drive, Lima, OH 45804-3596

Ohio State University: Mansfield Campus

Mansfield, Ohio
www.mansfield.ohio-state.edu **CB code: 0744**

- Public 4-year branch campus college
- Commuter campus in small city
- 1,143 degree-seeking undergraduates: 13% part-time, 53% women, 8% African American, 2% Asian American, 2% Hispanic American, 1% Native American
- 69 degree-seeking graduate students
- Application essay required
- 33% graduate within 6 years

General. Founded in 1958. Regionally accredited. Branch campus of Ohio State University; all degrees awarded through main campus. **Degrees:** 87 bachelor's, 115 associate awarded; master's offered. **ROTC:** Army, Naval, Air Force. **Location:** 67 miles from Columbus. **Calendar:** Quarter, limited summer session. **Full-time faculty:** 44 total; 98% have terminal degrees, 9% minority, 41% women. **Part-time faculty:** 59 total; 5% minority, 63% women. **Class size:** 53% < 20, 36% 20-39, 7% 40-49, 4% 50-99. **Special facilities:** Archives and reading room, educational enrichment laboratory, language laboratory, elementary education suite.

Freshman class profile. 1,469 applied, 1,460 admitted, 506 enrolled.

Mid 50% test scores			
SAT critical reading:	430-550	Rank in top tenth:	4%
SAT math:	430-580	End year in good standing:	77%
SAT writing:	410-520	Return as sophomores:	68%
ACT composite:	19-24	Out-of-state:	1%
Rank in top quarter:	25%	Live on campus:	35%

Basis for selection. Open admission, but selective for out-of-state students. Out-of-state applicants evaluated on basis of GPA, class rank, principal/counselor recommendations and SAT/ACT scores.

High school preparation. Recommended units include English 4, mathematics 4, social studies 3, science 3 (laboratory 3), foreign language 3, visual/performing arts 1 and academic electives 1.

2008-2009 Annual costs. Tuition/fees: $5,664; $18,903 out-of-state. Room/board: $4,440. Books/supplies: $1,383. Personal expenses: $3,996.

2008-2009 Financial aid. Need-based: 395 full-time freshmen applied for aid; 328 were judged to have need; 327 of these received aid. Average need met was 61%. Average scholarship/grant was $4,866; average loan $3,331. 36% of total undergraduate aid awarded as scholarships/grants, 64% as loans/jobs. **Non-need-based:** Awarded to 101 full-time undergraduates, including 54 freshmen. Scholarships awarded for academics, alumni affiliation, art, athletics, job skills, leadership, minority status, music/drama, ROTC, state residency.

Application procedures. **Admission:** Closing date 7/1 (postmark date). $40 fee, may be waived for applicants with need. Admission notification on a rolling basis beginning on or about 12/1. **Financial aid:** Priority date 3/1; no closing date. FAFSA required. Applicants notified on a rolling basis starting 4/5; must reply within 4 week(s) of notification.

Academics. Students often leave campus after 1-3 years and complete bachelor's degree on Columbus campus. **Special study options:** Accelerated study, cooperative education, cross-registration, distance learning, double major, dual enrollment of high school students, ESL, exchange student, honors, independent study, internships, liberal arts/career combination, student-designed major, study abroad, teacher certification program. **Credit/placement by examination:** AP, CLEP, SAT, ACT, institutional tests. 45 credit hours maximum toward bachelor's degree. **Support services:** Learning center, remedial instruction, tutoring, writing center.

Majors. **Business:** Business admin. **Education:** Elementary. **History:** General. **Psychology:** General.

Computing on campus. 103 workstations in library, computer center, student center. Commuter students can connect to campus network. Online course registration, online library, helpline, repair service available.

Student life. **Freshman orientation:** Mandatory. Preregistration for classes offered. **Housing:** Coed dorms, wellness housing available. $100 nonrefundable deposit. **Activities:** Campus ministries, dance, drama, film society, student government, African American student union, campus acitivities board, College Crusade for Christ, College Democrats/Republicans, Diversity Alliance, economics and business club, Habitat for Humanity, single parent network, Spanish club, Theta Alpha Pi.

Athletics. **Intercollegiate:** Soccer. **Intramural:** Basketball, bowling, golf, softball, table tennis, volleyball.

Student services. Adult student services, career counseling, student employment services, financial aid counseling, minority student services, personal counseling, placement for graduates. **Physically disabled:** Services for visually, speech, hearing impaired.

Contact. E-mail: admissions@mansfield.ohio-state.edu
Phone: (419) 755-4226 Fax: (419) 755-4241
Henry Thomas, Coordinator of Admissions and Financial Aid, Ohio State University: Mansfield Campus, 1680 University Drive, Mansfield, OH 44906

Ohio State University: Marion Campus

Marion, Ohio
www.marion.ohio-state.edu **CB code: 0752**

- Public 4-year branch campus college
- Commuter campus in large town
- 1,507 degree-seeking undergraduates: 12% part-time, 53% women, 8% African American, 4% Asian American, 2% Hispanic American
- 79 degree-seeking graduate students
- Application essay required
- 36% graduate within 6 years

General. Founded in 1958. Regionally accredited. Branch campus of Ohio State University; all degrees awarded through main campus. **Degrees:** 96 bachelor's, 150 associate awarded; master's offered. **ROTC:** Army, Naval, Air Force. **Location:** 44 miles from Columbus. **Calendar:** Quarter, limited summer session. **Full-time faculty:** 37 total; 97% have terminal degrees, 8% minority, 35% women. **Part-time faculty:** 72 total; 12% minority, 49% women. **Class size:** 41% < 20, 46% 20-39, 10% 40-49, 2% 50-99, less than 1% >100.

Freshman class profile. 1,001 applied, 998 admitted, 553 enrolled.

Mid 50% test scores			
SAT critical reading:	440-540	**Rank in top quarter:**	32%
SAT math:	460-570	**Rank in top tenth:**	10%
SAT writing:	430-530	**End year in good standing:**	77%
ACT composite:	19-23	**Return as sophomores:**	73%
		Out-of-state:	1%

Basis for selection. Open admission, but selective for out-of-state students. Out-of-state students evaluated on basis of GPA class rank, principal/counselor recommendation, and SAT/ACT scores.

High school preparation. Recommended units include English 4, mathematics 4, social studies 3, science 3 (laboratory 3), foreign language 3, visual/performing arts 1 and academic electives 1.

2008-2009 Annual costs. Tuition/fees: $5,664; $18,903 out-of-state. Books/supplies: $1,383. Personal expenses: $3,420.

2008-2009 Financial aid. **Need-based:** 425 full-time freshmen applied for aid; 333 were judged to have need; 333 of these received aid. Average need met was 63%. Average scholarship/grant was $4,425; average loan $3,247. 35% of total undergraduate aid awarded as scholarships/grants, 65% as loans/jobs. **Non-need-based:** Awarded to 167 full-time undergraduates, including 74 freshmen. Scholarships awarded for academics, alumni affiliation, art, athletics, job skills, leadership, minority status, music/drama, ROTC, state residency.

Application procedures. **Admission:** Closing date 7/1 (postmark date). $40 fee, may be waived for applicants with need. Admission notification on a rolling basis beginning on or about 12/1. Must reply by May 1 or within 4 week(s) if notified thereafter. **Financial aid:** Priority date 3/1; no closing date. FAFSA required. Applicants notified on a rolling basis starting 5/1; must reply within 4 week(s) of notification.

Academics. Students often leave campus after 1-3 years and complete bachelor's degree on Columbus campus. **Special study options:** Accelerated study, cooperative education, cross-registration, distance learning, double major, dual enrollment of high school students, ESL, exchange student, honors, independent study, internships, liberal arts/career combination, student-designed major, study abroad, teacher certification program. **Credit/placement by examination:** AP, CLEP, SAT, ACT, institutional tests. 45 credit hours maximum toward bachelor's degree. **Support services:** Learning center, reduced course load, remedial instruction, tutoring, writing center.

Majors. **Business:** Business admin. **Education:** Elementary. **History:** General. **Psychology:** General.

Computing on campus. 174 workstations in library, computer center. Commuter students can connect to campus network. Online course registration, online library, helpline, repair service available.

Student life. **Freshman orientation:** Mandatory. Preregistration for classes offered. **Activities:** Campus ministries, choral groups, literary magazine, music ensembles, student government, Buckeye Ambassador, Christian and Pagan religious organizations, Democratic/Republican political organizations, education society, honors organizations, language organizations, theater and improv troupe, diversity student organization.

Athletics. **Intercollegiate:** Basketball, cheerleading, golf, soccer, volleyball W. **Intramural:** Basketball, softball, volleyball. **Team name:** Scarlet Wave.

Student services. Career counseling, student employment services, financial aid counseling, legal services, on-campus daycare, personal counseling, placement for graduates. **Physically disabled:** Services for visually, speech, hearing impaired.

Contact. E-mail: moreau.1@osu.edu
Phone: (740) 389-6786 ext. 6242 Fax: (740) 386-2439
Matt Moreau, Coordinator of Admissions, Ohio State University: Marion Campus, 1465 Mount Vernon Avenue, Marion, OH 43302

Ohio State University: Newark Campus

Newark, Ohio
www.newark.osu.edu **CB code: 0824**

- Public 4-year branch campus college
- Commuter campus in large town
- 2,259 degree-seeking undergraduates: 10% part-time, 52% women, 9% African American, 2% Asian American, 2% Hispanic American, 1% Native American
- 108 degree-seeking graduate students
- Application essay required

General. Founded in 1957. Regionally accredited. Branch campus of Ohio State University; all degrees awarded through main campus. **Degrees:** 117 bachelor's, 137 associate awarded; master's offered. **ROTC:** Army, Naval, Air Force. **Location:** 28 miles from Columbus. **Calendar:** Quarter, limited summer session. **Full-time faculty:** 52 total; 98% have terminal degrees, 12% minority, 40% women. **Part-time faculty:** 79 total; 5% minority, 53% women. **Class size:** 39% < 20, 55% 20-39, 5% 40-49, less than 1% 50-99. **Special facilities:** Math laboratory, writing laboratory.

Freshman class profile. 2,535 applied, 2,521 admitted, 1,091 enrolled.

Mid 50% test scores			
SAT critical reading:	450-540	Rank in top tenth:	5%
SAT math:	450-570	End year in good standing:	71%
SAT writing:	430-520	Return as sophomores:	66%
ACT composite:	18-24	Out-of-state:	1%
Rank in top quarter:	25%	Live on campus:	15%

Basis for selection. Open admission, but selective for out-of-state students. Out-of-state applicants evaluated based on GPA, class rank, recommendation by principal/counselor, and SAT/ACT score.

High school preparation. Recommended units include English 4, mathematics 4, social studies 3, science 3 (laboratory 3), foreign language 3, visual/performing arts 1 and academic electives 1.

2008-2009 Annual costs. Tuition/fees: $5,664; $18,903 out-of-state. Room only: $5,475. Books/supplies: $1,383. Personal expenses: $3,996.

2008-2009 Financial aid. Need-based: 880 full-time freshmen applied for aid; 669 were judged to have need; 668 of these received aid. Average need met was 59%. Average scholarship/grant was $5,149; average loan $3,272. 31% of total undergraduate aid awarded as scholarships/grants, 69% as loans/jobs. **Non-need-based:** Awarded to 63 full-time undergraduates, including 27 freshmen. Scholarships awarded for academics, alumni affiliation, art, athletics, job skills, leadership, minority status, music/drama, ROTC, state residency.

Application procedures. Admission: Closing date 7/1 (postmark date). $40 fee, may be waived for applicants with need. Admission notification on a rolling basis beginning on or about 12/1. **Financial aid:** Priority date 3/1; no closing date. FAFSA required. Applicants notified on a rolling basis starting 5/1; must reply within 4 week(s) of notification.

Academics. Students often leave campus after 1-3 years and complete bachelor's degree on Columbus campus. **Special study options:** Accelerated study, cooperative education, cross-registration, distance learning, double major, dual enrollment of high school students, ESL, exchange student, honors, independent study, internships, liberal arts/career combination, student-designed major, study abroad, teacher certification program. **Credit/placement by examination:** AP, CLEP, SAT, ACT, institutional tests. 45 credit hours maximum toward bachelor's degree. **Support services:** Learning center, remedial instruction, tutoring, writing center.

Majors. Business: Business admin. **Education:** General. **Psychology:** General.

Computing on campus. 36 workstations in library, computer center, student center. Commuter students can connect to campus network. Online course registration, online library, helpline, repair service available.

Student life. Freshman orientation: Mandatory. Preregistration for classes offered. **Housing:** Coed dorms, wellness housing available. $100 nonrefundable deposit. University-owned student apartments within 2-minute walk from campus. **Activities:** Campus ministries, choral groups, drama, international student organizations, literary magazine, Model UN, musical theater, student government, support groups, minority organization, international multicultural association, ski club, gay/straight alliance, academic and honors organizations.

Athletics. Intercollegiate: Baseball M, basketball, cross-country, golf M, softball W, volleyball. **Intramural:** Badminton, baseball M, basketball, football (non-tackle), soccer, softball, table tennis, tennis, volleyball. **Team name:** Titans.

Student services. Career counseling, student employment services, financial aid counseling, minority student services, on-campus daycare, personal counseling, placement for graduates. **Physically disabled:** Services for visually, speech, hearing impaired.

Contact. E-mail: barclay.3@osu.edu
Phone: (740) 366-3333 Fax: (740) 364-9645
Ann Donahue, Coordinator of Admissions, Ohio State University: Newark Campus, 1179 University Drive, Newark, OH 43055

Ohio University

Athens, Ohio — **CB member**
www.ohio.edu — **CB code: 1593**

- Public 4-year university
- Residential campus in large town
- 17,085 degree-seeking undergraduates: 5% part-time, 51% women, 5% African American, 1% Asian American, 2% Hispanic American, 2% international
- 3,732 degree-seeking graduate students
- 78% of applicants admitted
- SAT or ACT (ACT writing optional) required
- 71% graduate within 6 years; 29% enter graduate study

General. Founded in 1804. Regionally accredited. **Degrees:** 4,025 bachelor's, 606 associate awarded; master's, doctoral, first professional offered. **ROTC:** Army, Air Force. **Location:** 75 miles from Columbus. **Calendar:** Quarter, extensive summer session. **Full-time faculty:** 854 total; 89% have terminal degrees, 18% minority, 36% women. **Part-time faculty:** 319 total; 56% have terminal degrees, 6% minority, 47% women. **Class size:** 44% < 20, 40% 20-39, 5% 40-49, 6% 50-99, 4% >100. **Special facilities:** University airport, nuclear accelerator, biotechnology research center, greenhouse, cartography center, meteorology center, contemporary history institute.

Freshman class profile. 14,046 applied, 10,931 admitted, 3,985 enrolled.

Mid 50% test scores			
SAT critical reading:	480-600	Rank in top quarter:	44%
SAT math:	490-600	Rank in top tenth:	15%
SAT writing:	470-580	End year in good standing:	90%
ACT composite:	21-26	Return as sophomores:	80%
GPA 3.75 or higher:	20%	Out-of-state:	10%
GPA 3.50-3.74:	19%	Live on campus:	97%
GPA 3.0-3.49:	45%	International:	3%
GPA 2.0-2.99:	16%	Fraternities:	13%
		Sororities:	16%

Basis for selection. High school record as represented by rank in class, GPA, and curriculum completed most important. Secondary criteria test scores and recommendation. Rank in top third of class preferred. Audition required for dance and music programs.

High school preparation. 16 units required. Required units include English 4, mathematics 3, social studies 3, science 3 and foreign language 2. One unit visual or performing art recommended.

2008-2009 Annual costs. Tuition/fees: $8,907; $17,871 out-of-state. Room/board: $8,906. Books/supplies: $873. Personal expenses: $1,071.

2008-2009 Financial aid. Need-based: 3,513 full-time freshmen applied for aid; 2,194 were judged to have need; 2,147 of these received aid. Average need met was 58%. Average scholarship/grant was $6,141; average loan $3,423. 38% of total undergraduate aid awarded as scholarships/grants, 62% as loans/jobs. **Non-need-based:** Awarded to 5,286 full-time undergraduates, including 1,917 freshmen. Scholarships awarded for academics, art, athletics, minority status, music/drama, religious affiliation, ROTC.

Application procedures. Admission: Closing date 2/1 (receipt date). $45 fee, may be waived for applicants with need. Admission notification on a rolling basis beginning on or about 10/1. Must reply by 5/1. **Financial aid:** Priority date 3/15, closing date 4/1. FAFSA required. Applicants notified on a rolling basis starting 4/1; must reply within 3 week(s) of notification.

Academics. Extensive learning community opportunities. **Special study options:** Accelerated study, combined bachelor's/graduate degree, cooperative education, cross-registration, distance learning, double major, dual enrollment of high school students, ESL, external degree, honors, independent study, internships, liberal arts/career combination, student-designed major, study abroad, teacher certification program. **Credit/placement by examination:** AP, CLEP, IB, institutional tests. Sophomore standing available by earning 45 quarter hours of credit based on AP scores. **Support services:** Learning center, pre-admission summer program, remedial instruction, study skills assistance, tutoring, writing center.

Honors college/program. Honors Tutorial College application deadline December 15, interview required.

Majors. Area/ethnic studies: African, African-American, Asian, European, Latin American, women's. **Biology:** General, botany, cellular/molecular, microbiology, wildlife, zoology. **Business:** Accounting, actuarial science, business admin, finance, human resources, international, management information systems, managerial economics, marketing. **Communications:** General, broadcast journalism, digital media, journalism, photojournalism, radio/tv. **Computer sciences:** Computer science, information technology. **Education:** Art, early childhood, family/consumer sciences, French, German, physical, secondary, Spanish, special. **Engineering:** Chemical, civil, electrical, industrial, mechanical. **Engineering technology:** Industrial. **Family/consumer sciences:** Child development, clothing/textiles, family resources, family studies, food/nutrition, housing, institutional food production. **Foreign languages:** Ancient Greek, classics, French, German, Latin, linguistics, Russian, Spanish. **Health:** Athletic training, audiology/speech pathology, community health services, dietetics, environmental health, health care admin, nursing (RN), occupational health. **History:** General. **Interdisciplinary:** Neuroscience. **Math:** General, applied. **Parks/recreation:** General, exercise sciences, health/fitness. **Philosophy/religion:** Philosophy, religion. **Physical sciences:** Astrophysics, atmospheric science, chemistry, geology, physics. **Psychology:** General. **Public administration:** Social work. **Social sciences:** Anthropology, criminology, economics, geography, political science, sociology, urban studies. **Transportation:** Aviation, aviation management. **Visual/performing arts:** Acting, art, art history/conservation, ceramics, cinematography, dance, dramatic, graphic design, music history, music performance, music theory/composition, painting, photography, piano/organ, play/screenwriting, printmaking, sculpture, theater arts management, voice/opera.

Most popular majors. Business/marketing 13%, communications/journalism 15%, education 11%, family/consumer sciences 7%, health sciences 7%, liberal arts 6%, parks/recreation 6%, social sciences 8%.

Computing on campus. 1,000 workstations in library, computer center, student center. Dormitories wired for high-speed internet access and linked to campus network. Commuter students can connect to campus network. Online course registration, online library, helpline, repair service, student web hosting, wireless network available.

Student life. Freshman orientation: Mandatory. Preregistration for classes offered. Weekends in summer. **Housing:** Guaranteed on-campus for freshmen. Coed dorms, single-sex dorms, special housing for disabled, apartments, cooperative housing, fraternity/sorority housing, wellness housing available. $200 nonrefundable deposit, deadline 5/1. International, intensive-study residence halls available. **Activities:** Bands, choral groups, dance, drama, film society, literary magazine, music ensembles, musical theater, opera, radio station, student government, student newspaper, symphony orchestra, TV station, over 300 professional, religious, ethnic, political, and social service organizations.

Athletics. NCAA. **Intercollegiate:** Baseball M, basketball, cross-country, diving, field hockey W, football (tackle) M, golf, soccer W, softball W, swimming W, track and field W, volleyball W, wrestling M. **Intramural:** Baseball M, basketball, bowling, cross-country, football (non-tackle), golf, racquetball, soccer, softball, swimming W, table tennis, tennis. **Team name:** Bobcats.

Student services. Adult student services, alcohol/substance abuse counseling, career counseling, services for economically disadvantaged, student employment services, financial aid counseling, health services, legal services, minority student services, personal counseling, placement for graduates, veterans' counselor, women's services. **Physically disabled:** Services for visually, hearing impaired.

Contact. E-mail: admissions@ohio.edu
Phone: (740) 593-4100 Fax: (740) 593-0560
T Garcia, Director of Undergraduate Admissions, Ohio University, 120 Chubb Hall, Athens, OH 45701-2979

Ohio University: Chillicothe Campus

Chillicothe, Ohio
www.chillicothe.ohiou.edu **CB code: 0775**

- Public 4-year branch campus college
- Commuter campus in large town
- 1,855 undergraduates

General. Founded in 1946. Regionally accredited. **Degrees:** 183 associate awarded; master's offered. **Location:** 45 miles from Columbus. **Calendar:** Quarter, limited summer session. **Full-time faculty:** 45 total. **Part-time faculty:** 100 total.

Basis for selection. Open admission, but selective for some programs. Business, communications, education, and engineering colleges require high school GPA and ACT/SAT test scores. **Homeschooled:** State high school equivalency certificate required. Passing scores on Ohio graduation test or GED required.

High school preparation. Recommended units include English 4, mathematics 3, social studies 3, science 3 and foreign language 2. College-preparatory program strongly recommended including 1 visual or performing art.

2008-2009 Annual costs. Tuition/fees: $4,581; $8,904 out-of-state. Books/supplies: $848.

Application procedures. Admission: No deadline. $20 fee, may be waived for applicants with need. Admission notification on a rolling basis. **Financial aid:** No deadline. FAFSA required. Applicants notified on a rolling basis.

Academics. Bachelor's programs in management, elementary education, criminal justice, nursing, technical and applied studies and self-designed major. Degree granted by Ohio University main campus. **Special study options:** Distance learning, double major, dual enrollment of high school students, external degree, independent study, internships, student-designed major, study abroad, teacher certification program. **Credit/placement by examination:** AP, CLEP, institutional tests. **Support services:** Learning center, pre-admission summer program, remedial instruction, study skills assistance, tutoring, writing center.

Majors. Business: Business admin. **Communications:** Organizational. **Education:** Early childhood, middle. **Engineering technology:** Environmental. **Health:** Nursing (RN). **Protective services:** Criminal justice. **Psychology:** General.

Computing on campus. 275 workstations in library, computer center, student center. Commuter students can connect to campus network. Online course registration, online library, helpline, student web hosting, wireless network available.

Student life. Freshman orientation: Available. Preregistration for classes offered. One-day session conducted prior to fall, winter and spring quarters. **Activities:** Drama, student government, student newspaper, National Communication Association, Ross County Association of Future Teachers, anime club, nursing student club, student programming club, human services association, law enforcement association, psychology club.

Athletics. Team name: Hilltoppers.

Student services. Adult student services, career counseling, services for economically disadvantaged, student employment services, financial aid counseling, personal counseling. **Physically disabled:** Services for visually, hearing impaired.

Contact. E-mail: lowej@ohio.edu
Phone: (740) 774-7240 Toll-free number: (877) 462-6824 ext. 240
Fax: (740) 774-7295
Jaime Lowe, Coordinator of Enrollment Services, Ohio University: Chillicothe Campus, 101 University Drive, Chillicothe, OH 45601

Ohio University: Eastern Campus

St. Clairsville, Ohio
www.eastern.ohiou.edu **CB code: 0828**

- Public 4-year branch campus college
- Commuter campus in small town
- 774 degree-seeking undergraduates

General. Founded in 1957. Regionally accredited. **Degrees:** 9 associate awarded; master's offered. **Location:** 7 miles from downtown; 14 miles from Wheeling, West Virginia. **Calendar:** Quarter, limited summer session. **Full-time faculty:** 30 total; 77% have terminal degrees, 23% women. **Part-time faculty:** 40 total. **Special facilities:** Primeval oak forest laboratory, Great Western School (Little Red Schoolhouse).

Basis for selection. Open admission, but selective for some programs. Special requirements for education, business, communication programs. SAT/ACT scores required for admission to education program.

High school preparation. Recommended units include English 4, mathematics 4, social studies 3, science 3 and foreign language 2.

2008-2009 Annual costs. Tuition/fees: $4,395; $5,715 out-of-state.

2007-2008 Financial aid. Non-need-based: Scholarships awarded for academics, alumni affiliation, minority status.

Application procedures. Admission: No deadline. $20 fee, may be waived for applicants with need. Admission notification on a rolling basis. **Financial aid:** Priority date 3/15; no closing date. FAFSA required. Applicants notified by 5/15.

Academics. Several degree programs offered through cross-registration with main campus. **Special study options:** Accelerated study, cooperative education, cross-registration, distance learning, double major, dual enrollment of high school students, external degree, independent study, internships, student-designed major, teacher certification program. **Credit/placement by examination:** CLEP, institutional tests. **Support services:** Learning center, reduced course load, remedial instruction, study skills assistance, tutoring, writing center.

Majors. Education: Elementary. **Liberal arts:** Arts/sciences.

Computing on campus. 11 workstations in library, computer center. Online course registration available.

Student life. **Freshman orientation:** Available. Preregistration for classes offered. **Activities:** Drama.

Athletics. **Intercollegiate:** Basketball, golf M, volleyball W. **Intramural:** Basketball. **Team name:** Panthers.

Student services. Adult student services, career counseling, on-campus daycare, personal counseling.

Contact. Phone: (740) 695-1720 Fax: (740) 695-7077
Kevin Chenoweth, Student Services Manager, Ohio University: Eastern Campus, 45425 National Road West, St. Clairsville, OH 43950-9724

Ohio University: Lancaster Campus

Lancaster, Ohio
www.lancaster.ohiou.edu **CB code: 0826**

- Public 4-year branch campus college
- Large town
- 1,632 degree-seeking undergraduates

General. Founded in 1968. Regionally accredited. Some bachelor's and master's degrees available, awarded through Athens campus. **Degrees:** 74 associate awarded; master's offered. **ROTC:** Army, Naval, Air Force. **Location:** 30 miles from Columbus. **Calendar:** Quarter, extensive summer session. **Full-time faculty:** 30 total. **Part-time faculty:** 70 total.

Basis for selection. Open admission, but selective for some programs. Special requirements for business, education, engineering and communication programs. ACT or SAT scores used in admission decisions to colleges of education, engineering. International students must take English fluency test through Ohio Program of Intensive English.

2008-2009 Annual costs. Tuition/fees: $4,581; $8,904 out-of-state. Books/supplies: $500.

Financial aid. **Additional information:** Scholarship application deadline April 1.

Application procedures. **Admission:** No deadline. $20 fee, may be waived for applicants with need. Admission notification on a rolling basis. **Financial aid:** Priority date 2/15; no closing date. FAFSA required. Applicants notified on a rolling basis; must reply within 2 week(s) of notification.

Academics. **Special study options:** Combined bachelor's/graduate degree, cross-registration, double major, independent study, internships, student-designed major. **Credit/placement by examination:** CLEP, institutional tests. **Support services:** Learning center, remedial instruction, tutoring.

Computing on campus. 98 workstations in library, computer center, student center. Online course registration, online library, helpline, student web hosting available.

Student life. **Freshman orientation:** Available. **Activities:** Choral groups, drama, student government, outdoor club, Young Democrats, Young Republicans, Christian Fellowship, adult support group.

Athletics. **Intercollegiate:** Baseball M, basketball, golf, softball W, tennis. **Intramural:** Skiing, table tennis, volleyball. **Team name:** Cougars.

Student services. Career counseling, student employment services, financial aid counseling, on-campus daycare, placement for graduates, veterans' counselor. **Physically disabled:** Services for visually, speech, hearing impaired.

Contact. Phone: (740) 654-6711 ext. 215 Toll-free number: (888) 446-4468 Fax: (740) 687-9497
Pat Fox, Enrollment Manager, Ohio University: Lancaster Campus, 1570 Granville Pike, Lancaster, OH 43130

Ohio University: Southern Campus at Ironton

Ironton, Ohio
www.southern.ohiou.edu **CB code: 1912**

- Public 4-year branch campus college
- Commuter campus in large town
- 1,166 full-time, degree-seeking undergraduates

General. Founded in 1956. Regionally accredited. Student body reflects both traditional (65%) and non-traditional (45%) students who commute to classes from 3-state area (OH, KY, WV). **Degrees:** 130 associate awarded; master's offered. **Location:** 20 miles from Huntington, West Virginia. **Calendar:** Quarter. **Full-time faculty:** 32 total. **Part-time faculty:** 122 total. **Special facilities:** Microwave link with main campus and other regional campuses, Ohio horse park, nature center, Proctorville center.

Basis for selection. Open admission. **Homeschooled:** Transcript of courses and grades, state high school equivalency certificate required. Written verification from appropriate school district excusing attendance, personal statement discussing academic preparation for college, ACT, SAT required.

High school preparation. College-preparatory program recommended.

2008-2009 Annual costs. Tuition/fees: $4,395; $5,715 out-of-state. Books/supplies: $600. Personal expenses: $1,200.

Financial aid. **Non-need-based:** Scholarships awarded for academics, state residency.

Application procedures. **Admission:** No deadline. $20 fee, may be waived for applicants with need. Admission notification on a rolling basis. **Financial aid:** Priority date 3/15; no closing date. FAFSA required. Applicants notified on a rolling basis starting 4/1.

Academics. **Special study options:** Double major, dual enrollment of high school students, student-designed major, teacher certification program. **Credit/placement by examination:** CLEP, institutional tests. **Support services:** Learning center, remedial instruction, study skills assistance, tutoring, writing center.

Majors. **Business:** Business admin. **Communications:** General, health, organizational, political. **Health:** Health services, nursing (RN). **History:** General. **Protective services:** Criminal justice. **Other:** Long term health care administration, Specialized studies.

Computing on campus. Online course registration, online library, helpline, wireless network available.

Student life. **Freshman orientation:** Mandatory. Preregistration for classes offered. Summer and online orientations available. **Activities:** Concert band, international student organizations, literary magazine, music ensembles, radio station, student government, TV station, Phi Alpha Xi service honor society, Los Amigos Internacionales club, diversity student council, student nurses association, psychology club, art club.

Athletics. **Intercollegiate:** Equestrian.

Student services. Career counseling, financial aid counseling, personal counseling.

Contact. E-mail: askousc@ohiou.edu
Phone: (740) 533-4600 Toll-free number: (800) 626-0513
Fax: (740) 533-4632
Robert Pleasant, Director of Enrollment and Student Services, Ohio University: Southern Campus at Ironton, 1804 Liberty Avenue, Ironton, OH 45638

Ohio University: Zanesville Campus

Zanesville, Ohio
www.zanesville.ohiou.edu **CB code: 0846**

- Public 4-year branch campus college
- Commuter campus in large town
- 1,789 degree-seeking undergraduates: 43% part-time, 75% women, 4% African American, 1% Hispanic American, 1% international

General. Founded in 1946. Regionally accredited. **Degrees:** 116 bachelor's, 152 associate awarded; master's offered. **Location:** 55 miles from Columbus. **Calendar:** Quarter, limited summer session. **Full-time faculty:** 35 total. **Part-time faculty:** 75 total.

Basis for selection. Open admission, but selective for some programs. Nursing admissions based on National League for Nursing test scores, high school GPA, and class rank. Admission to Colleges of Business, Engineering, and Communication based on high school rank and ACT scores. Essay, audition, and portfolio recommended for all; interview recommended for nursing program.

High school preparation. Recommended units include English 4, mathematics 3, social studies 3, science 3 and foreign language 2. One year of visual or performing arts recommended.

2008-2009 Annual costs. Tuition/fees: $4,581; $8,904 out-of-state. Books/supplies: $1,000. Personal expenses: $879.

Application procedures. **Admission:** No deadline. $20 fee, may be waived for applicants with need. Admission notification on a rolling basis beginning on or about 1/1. **Financial aid:** Priority date 3/15; no closing date. FAFSA required. Applicants notified on a rolling basis starting 4/15; must reply within 2 week(s) of notification.

Academics. **Special study options:** Cross-registration, double major, dual enrollment of high school students, independent study, student-designed major, study abroad, teacher certification program. **Credit/placement by examination:** AP, CLEP, institutional tests. **Support services:** Learning center, reduced course load, remedial instruction, tutoring.

Majors. **Business:** General. **Communications:** Health, organizational. **Education:** Early childhood, middle. **Public administration:** Human services.

Computing on campus. 50 workstations in library, computer center. Commuter students can connect to campus network. Online course registration, online library, wireless network available.

Student life. **Freshman orientation:** Mandatory. Preregistration for classes offered. **Activities:** Literary magazine, radio station, student government, cultural events committee, student nursing association.

Athletics. **Intercollegiate:** Baseball M, basketball, golf, tennis, volleyball W. **Intramural:** Badminton, basketball, bowling, golf, skiing, table tennis, tennis, volleyball. **Team name:** Tracers.

Student services. Chaplain/spiritual director, career counseling, student employment services, personal counseling, placement for graduates, veterans' counselor.

Contact. E-mail: ouzservices@ohio.edu
Phone: (740) 588-1439 Fax: (740) 588-1444
Monica Jones, Director of Student Services, Ohio University: Zanesville Campus, 1425 Newark Road, Zanesville, OH 43701

Ohio Wesleyan University

Delaware, Ohio — **CB member**
www.owu.edu — **CB code: 1594**

- Private 4-year liberal arts college affiliated with United Methodist Church
- Residential campus in large town
- 1,947 degree-seeking undergraduates: 53% women, 5% African American, 2% Asian American, 1% Hispanic American, 1% Native American, 9% international
- 64% of applicants admitted
- SAT or ACT (ACT writing optional), application essay required
- 63% graduate within 6 years

General. Founded in 1842. Regionally accredited. **Degrees:** 380 bachelor's awarded. **ROTC:** Army, Air Force. **Location:** 25 miles from Columbus. **Calendar:** Semester, limited summer session. **Full-time faculty:** 135 total; 96% have terminal degrees, 7% minority, 36% women. **Part-time faculty:** 69 total; 42% have terminal degrees, 6% minority, 52% women. **Class size:** 59% < 20, 38% 20-39, 2% 40-49, less than 1% 50-99. **Special facilities:** 2 observatories, US Department of Agriculture laboratories, 2 nature field study preserves, science center, art museum.

Freshman class profile. 4,238 applied, 2,723 admitted, 577 enrolled.

Mid 50% test scores		**Rank in top quarter:**	59%
SAT critical reading:	520-640	**Rank in top tenth:**	30%
SAT math:	520-650	**Return as sophomores:**	79%
ACT composite:	24-29	**Out-of-state:**	47%
GPA 3.75 or higher:	32%	**Live on campus:**	96%
GPA 3.50-3.74:	15%	**International:**	9%
GPA 3.0-3.49:	32%	**Fraternities:**	22%
GPA 2.0-2.99:	20%	**Sororities:**	17%

Basis for selection. High school record (level of challenge and success) most important, followed by class rank, recommendations, test scores, essay, extracurricular activities, general aptitude, character, volunteerism, alumni affiliation. Special consideration given to music, fine art and theater talent. Interview recommended for all. Audition required for music programs. Portfolio recommended for art programs. Essay required of all applicants. **Homeschooled:** Statement describing homeschool structure and mission, state high school equivalency certificate, letter of recommendation (nonparent) required.

High school preparation. College-preparatory program required. 15 units required. Required and recommended units include English 4, mathematics 3-4, social studies 3-4, science 3-4 and foreign language 2-3.

2008-2009 Annual costs. Tuition/fees: $33,660. Room/board: $8,270. Books/supplies: $2,050. Personal expenses: $1,250.

2008-2009 Financial aid. **Need-based:** 461 full-time freshmen applied for aid; 363 were judged to have need; 363 of these received aid. Average need met was 88%. Average scholarship/grant was $21,924; average loan $5,380. 79% of total undergraduate aid awarded as scholarships/grants, 21% as loans/jobs. **Non-need-based:** Awarded to 866 full-time undergraduates, including 277 freshmen. Scholarships awarded for academics, alumni affiliation, art, leadership, minority status, music/drama, religious affiliation, state residency.

Application procedures. **Admission:** Priority date 3/1; deadline 5/1 (postmark date). $35 fee, may be waived for applicants with need, free for online applicants. Admission notification on a rolling basis beginning on or about 10/1. Must reply by May 1 or within 2 week(s) if notified thereafter. **Financial aid:** Priority date 3/1, closing date 5/1. FAFSA, institutional form required. Applicants notified on a rolling basis starting 2/15; must reply by 5/1 or within 2 week(s) of notification.

Academics. Quantitative Skills Center provides individualized and alternative modes of instruction and tutoring to students who need assistance with math skills in any area of study. **Special study options:** Double major, dual enrollment of high school students, exchange student, honors, independent study, internships, New York semester, student-designed major, study abroad, teacher certification program, United Nations semester, urban semester, Washington semester. 3-2 engineering programs with Washington University (MO), Case Western Reserve University, California Institute of Technology (CA), Rensselaer Polytechnic Institute (NY), Alfred College of Ceramics (NY), and Polytechnic Institute of New York. **Credit/placement by examination:** AP, CLEP, IB, SAT, ACT, institutional tests. International Baccalaureate credit given for specific performance levels on higher exams. Students may receive exemption from certain requirements for test scores on SAT, SAT Subject Tests or ACT. **Support services:** Learning center, reduced course load, study skills assistance, tutoring, writing center.

Majors. **Area/ethnic studies:** African-American, East Asian, women's. **Biology:** General, bacteriology, biochemistry, botany, genetics, microbiology, zoology. **Business:** Accounting, international, managerial economics. **Communications:** Broadcast journalism, journalism. **Computer sciences:** General, computer science. **Conservation:** Environmental studies. **Education:** General, art, biology, chemistry, drama/dance, early childhood, elementary, foreign languages, French, German, health, kindergarten/preschool, Latin, mathematics, middle, multi-level teacher, music, physical, physics, science, secondary, social science, social studies, Spanish. **Foreign languages:** Biblical, classics, comparative lit, French, German, Latin, Spanish. **Health:** Predental, premedicine, preveterinary. **History:** General. **Interdisciplinary:** Ancient studies, medieval/Renaissance, neuroscience. **Legal studies:** Prelaw. **Liberal arts:** Arts/sciences. **Math:** General, statistics. **Philosophy/religion:** Philosophy, religion. **Physical sciences:** Astronomy, chemistry, geology, physics. **Psychology:** General. **Social sciences:** Anthropology, economics, geography, international relations, political science, sociology, U.S. government, urban studies. **Theology:** Preministerial. **Visual/performing arts:** Art history/conservation, dance, dramatic, music performance, studio arts.

Most popular majors. Biology 12%, business/marketing 12%, English 6%, psychology 10%, social sciences 17%, visual/performing arts 7%.

Computing on campus. 300 workstations in dormitories, library, computer center, student center. Dormitories wired for high-speed internet access and linked to campus network. Commuter students can connect to campus network. Online library, helpline, repair service, student web hosting, wireless network available.

Student life. **Freshman orientation:** Mandatory. Preregistration for classes offered. Two-day session held in June and during the week before classes begin in August. **Housing:** Guaranteed on-campus for all undergraduates. Coed dorms, single-sex dorms, apartments, fraternity/sorority housing, wellness housing available. $400 nonrefundable deposit, deadline 5/1. Pets allowed in dorm rooms. Small living units for groups of 10-15 students. **Activities:** Bands, campus ministries, choral groups, dance, drama, international student organizations, literary magazine, music ensembles, Model UN, musical theater, opera, radio station, student government, student newspaper, symphony orchestra, B'nai B'rith Hillel Chapter, Christian Fellowship, Young Democrats, College Republicans, student union on black awareness, Sisters United, Tauheed, gay/lesbian/bisexual/transgender center, women's resource center, Habitat for Humanity.

Athletics. NCAA. **Intercollegiate:** Baseball M, basketball, cross-country, diving, field hockey W, football (tackle) M, golf M, lacrosse, soccer, softball W, swimming, tennis, track and field, volleyball W. **Intramural:** Badminton, basketball, equestrian, football (non-tackle) M, golf, handball, lacrosse, racquetball, soccer, softball, squash, swimming, tennis, track and field, volleyball, water polo. **Team name:** Battling Bishops.

Student services. Alcohol/substance abuse counseling, chaplain/spiritual director, career counseling, student employment services, financial aid counseling, health services, minority student services, on-campus day-care, personal counseling.

Contact. E-mail: owuadmit@owu.edu
Phone: (740) 368-3020 Toll-free number: (800) 922-8953
Fax: (740) 368-3314
Carol DelPropost, Assistant Vice President of Admission and Financial Aid, Ohio Wesleyan University, 75 South Sandusky Street, Delaware, OH 43015-2398

Otterbein College

Westerville, Ohio — **CB member**
www.otterbein.edu — **CB code: 1597**

- Private 4-year liberal arts college affiliated with United Methodist Church
- Residential campus in large town
- 2,748 degree-seeking undergraduates
- 82% of applicants admitted
- SAT or ACT (ACT writing optional) required

General. Founded in 1847. Regionally accredited. **Degrees:** 544 bachelor's awarded; master's offered. **ROTC:** Army, Air Force. **Location:** 12 miles from Columbus. **Calendar:** Quarter, limited summer session. **Full-time faculty:** 161 total; 92% have terminal degrees, 11% minority, 55% women. **Part-time faculty:** 140 total. **Special facilities:** Observatory, 3 performance stages, stables, 3 art galleries.

Freshman class profile. 3,381 applied, 2,774 admitted, 673 enrolled.

Mid 50% test scores			
SAT critical reading:	470-600	GPA 3.50-3.74:	21%
SAT math:	480-590	GPA 3.0-3.49:	28%
SAT writing:	460-600	GPA 2.0-2.99:	21%
ACT composite:	19-25	Rank in top quarter:	55%
GPA 3.75 or higher:	30%	Rank in top tenth:	24%
		Live on campus:	80%

Basis for selection. School achievement record most important; test scores also important. Recommendations, essay, interview, and extracurricular activities considered. Students applying between May 1 and June 1 accepted on space-available basis. Visit recommended for all; audition required for music and theater programs; portfolio recommended for visual art program. Essays required for scholarships. **Homeschooled:** Statement describing homeschool structure and mission, transcript of courses and grades required. Submit written documentation of successful completion of college preparatory high school equivalency. Transcripts from cooperating school district preferred. **Learning Disabled:** Students with diagnosed learning disabilities recommended to send documentation with admission application.

High school preparation. College-preparatory program recommended. Recommended units include English 4, mathematics 3, social studies 3, science 3 and foreign language 2. One unit in fine arts recommended.

2008-2009 Annual costs. Tuition/fees: $26,319. Room/board: $7,461. Books/supplies: $1,017. Personal expenses: $1,293.

Financial aid. Non-need-based: Scholarships awarded for academics, alumni affiliation, art, leadership, minority status, music/drama, state residency.

Application procedures. Admission: Priority date 2/1; no deadline. $25 fee, may be waived for applicants with need, free for online applicants. Admission notification on a rolling basis beginning on or about 10/1. Must reply by May 1 or within 4 week(s) if notified thereafter. **Financial aid:** Priority date 4/1; no closing date. FAFSA required. Applicants notified on a rolling basis starting 2/15.

Academics. Special study options: Accelerated study, combined bachelor's/graduate degree, cross-registration, double major, dual enrollment of high school students, exchange student, honors, independent study, internships, liberal arts/career combination, student-designed major, study abroad, teacher certification program, Washington semester, weekend college. BA/BS in engineering with Washington University (MO) or Case Western Reserve University. **Credit/placement by examination:** AP, CLEP, IB, SAT, ACT, institutional tests. 60 credit hours maximum toward bachelor's degree. **Support services:** Learning center, reduced course load, remedial instruction, study skills assistance, tutoring, writing center.

Honors college/program. Presidential Scholars or must be in top 10% of high school class and have 25 ACT.

Majors. Agriculture: Equestrian studies. **Biology:** General, biochemistry, molecular. **Business:** General, accounting, actuarial science, business admin, finance, managerial economics. **Communications:** General, broadcast journalism, journalism, organizational, public relations. **Computer sciences:** Computer science. **Conservation:** General, environmental studies, management/policy. **Education:** General, art, biology, chemistry, early childhood, elementary, English, foreign languages, French, health, history, mathematics, middle, multi-level teacher, music, physical, physics, science, secondary, social studies, Spanish, special. **Foreign languages:** French, Spanish. **Health:** Athletic training, nursing (RN), predental, premedicine, prepharmacy, preveterinary. **History:** General. **Legal studies:** Prelaw. **Math:** General. **Parks/recreation:** Health/fitness, sports admin. **Philosophy/religion:** Philosophy, religion. **Physical sciences:** Chemistry, physics. **Psychology:** General. **Social sciences:** Economics, international relations, political science, sociology. **Visual/performing arts:** General, acting, art, dramatic, music history, music performance, music theory/composition, theater design.

Most popular majors. Business/marketing 17%, communications/journalism 14%, education 15%, health sciences 10%, visual/performing arts 13%.

Computing on campus. 124 workstations in dormitories, library, computer center. Dormitories wired for high-speed internet access and linked to campus network. Commuter students can connect to campus network. Online course registration, helpline, wireless network available.

Student life. Freshman orientation: Mandatory. Preregistration for classes offered. One-day orientation held in July or August. **Housing:** Guaranteed on-campus for freshmen. Coed dorms, single-sex dorms, apartments, fraternity/sorority housing available. **Activities:** Bands, choral groups, dance, drama, international student organizations, literary magazine, music ensembles, musical theater, opera, radio station, student government, student newspaper, symphony orchestra, TV station, Fellowship of Christian Athletes, Christian support group, Afro-American student union, Asian American student union, international students association, religious life council.

Athletics. NCAA. **Intercollegiate:** Baseball M, basketball, cross-country, equestrian, football (tackle) M, golf, lacrosse M, soccer, softball W, tennis, track and field, volleyball W. **Intramural:** Basketball, bowling, football (non-tackle) M, handball, racquetball, soccer, softball, volleyball. **Team name:** Cardinals.

Student services. Adult student services, chaplain/spiritual director, career counseling, student employment services, financial aid counseling, health services, minority student services, personal counseling, placement for graduates, veterans' counselor. **Physically disabled:** Services for visually, hearing impaired.

Contact. E-mail: uotterb@otterbein.edu
Phone: (614) 823-1500 Toll-free number: (800) 488-8144
Fax: (614) 823-1200
Cass Johnson, Director of Admission, Otterbein College, One Otterbein College, Westerville, OH 43081

Pontifical College Josephinum

Columbus, Ohio
www.pcj.edu — **CB code: 1348**

- Private 4-year liberal arts and seminary college for men affiliated with Roman Catholic Church
- Residential campus in very large city
- 164 degree-seeking undergraduates
- 100% of applicants admitted
- SAT or ACT (ACT writing optional), application essay, interview required

General. Founded in 1892. Regionally accredited; also accredited by ATS. **Degrees:** 29 bachelor's awarded; master's, first professional offered. **Calendar:** Semester. **Full-time faculty:** 11 total; 54% have terminal degrees, 36% women. **Part-time faculty:** 20 total; 35% have terminal degrees, 40% women. **Class size:** 82% < 20, 18% 20-39.

Freshman class profile. 11 applied, 11 admitted, 11 enrolled.

Mid 50% test scores			
SAT critical reading:	510-670	ACT composite:	17-31
SAT math:	340-700	Out-of-state:	56%
SAT writing:	450-560	Live on campus:	100%

Basis for selection. School achievement record, recommendations from pastor and director of vocations required. **Homeschooled:** Transcript of courses and grades required.

High school preparation. College-preparatory program recommended. 10 units required; 18 recommended. Required and recommended units include English 4, mathematics 2-4, social studies 2-4, science 1-4 and foreign language 1-2.

2008-2009 Annual costs. Tuition/fees: $16,304. Room/board: $7,798. Books/supplies: $500.

2007-2008 Financial aid. All financial aid based on need.

Application procedures. Admission: Priority date 8/1; no deadline. $25 fee, may be waived for applicants with need. Application must be submitted on paper. Admission notification on a rolling basis beginning on or about 5/1. **Financial aid:** Priority date 9/2; no closing date. FAFSA, institutional form required. Applicants notified on a rolling basis starting 8/15; must reply within 2 week(s) of notification.

Academics. Students participate in supervised field experience and clinical pastoral education. **Special study options:** Double major, ESL, honors, independent study. **Credit/placement by examination:** AP, CLEP, IB, institutional tests. 30 credit hours maximum toward bachelor's degree. **Support services:** Learning center, reduced course load, remedial instruction, tutoring, writing center.

Majors. Area/ethnic studies: Hispanic-American/Latino/Chicano, Latin American. **History:** General. **Liberal arts:** Humanities. **Philosophy/religion:** Philosophy, religion.

Most popular majors. Philosophy/religious studies 82%.

Computing on campus. 16 workstations in library, computer center. Dormitories wired for high-speed internet access and linked to campus network. Online library, wireless network available.

Student life. Freshman orientation: Mandatory. **Policies:** Daily chapel, morning and evening prayer. Religious observance required. **Activities:** Choral groups, music ensembles, student government, Latin American studies organization.

Athletics. Intramural: Basketball M, soccer M, softball M.

Student services. Chaplain/spiritual director, career counseling, financial aid counseling, health services, personal counseling.

Contact. Phone: (614) 985-2241 Toll-free number: (888) 252-5812
Fax: (614) 885-2307
Perry Cahall, Director of Admissions, Pontifical College Josephinum, 7625 North High Street, Columbus, OH 43235-1499

Rabbinical College of Telshe

Wickliffe, Ohio
CB code: 1660

- Private 4-year rabbinical and teachers college for men affiliated with Jewish faith
- Small city
- 23 degree-seeking undergraduates
- 16 degree-seeking graduate students
- 100% of applicants admitted
- 45% graduate within 6 years

General. Founded in 1941. Accredited by AARTS. **Degrees:** 4 bachelor's awarded; master's, doctoral offered. **Calendar:** Semester. **Full-time faculty:** 10 total. **Part-time faculty:** 15 total.

Freshman class profile. 12 applied, 12 admitted, 12 enrolled.

End year in good standing:	100%	**Return as sophomores:**	47%

Basis for selection. GED not accepted. Personal interview and religious commitment most important. **Homeschooled:** Interview required.

2008-2009 Annual costs. Tuition/fees: $7,500. Room/board: $3,600. Books/supplies: $300. Personal expenses: $1,000.

Application procedures. Admission: Closing date 8/15. $100 fee.

Academics. Credit/placement by examination: CLEP.

Majors. Theology: Talmudic.

Student life. Freshman orientation: Mandatory. Preregistration for classes offered.

Contact. Phone: (440) 943-5300 ext. 17 Fax: (440) 943-5303
Rabbi Abraham Matitia, Registrar, Rabbinical College of Telshe, 28400 Euclid Avenue, Wickliffe, OH 44092-2584

Shawnee State University

Portsmouth, Ohio **CB member**
www.shawnee.edu **CB code: 1790**

- Public 4-year university
- Commuter campus in large town
- 2,919 degree-seeking undergraduates: 17% part-time, 57% women
- 41 degree-seeking graduate students

General. Founded in 1986. Regionally accredited. **Degrees:** 286 bachelor's, 234 associate awarded; master's offered. **Location:** 90 miles from Columbus, 90 miles from Cincinnati. **Calendar:** Semester, extensive summer session. **Full-time faculty:** 152 total; 55% have terminal degrees, 8% minority, 41% women. **Part-time faculty:** 152 total; 51% women. **Class size:** 61% < 20, 33% 20-39, 3% 40-49, 2% 50-99, less than 1% >100. **Special facilities:** Planetarium.

Freshman class profile. 3,692 applied, 3,692 admitted, 643 enrolled.

Mid 50% test scores		**Out-of-state:**	7%
ACT composite:	18-22	**Live on campus:**	42%
Rank in top quarter:	33%	**Fraternities:**	6%
Rank in top tenth:	13%	**Sororities:**	7%

Basis for selection. Open admission, but selective for some programs. ACT required, interview recommended for admission to allied health programs. **Homeschooled:** GED required.

High school preparation. 16 units recommended. Recommended units include English 4, mathematics 3, social studies 3, science 3 and foreign language 2. Algebra, biology, chemistry required for allied health programs.

2008-2009 Annual costs. Tuition/fees: $5,832; $10,176 out-of-state. Room/board: $7,670. Books/supplies: $1,440. Personal expenses: $2,090.

Financial aid. Non-need-based: Scholarships awarded for academics. **Additional information:** ACT recommended for scholarship applicants.

Application procedures. Admission: No deadline. No application fee. Admission notification on a rolling basis. Applicants to allied health programs advised to apply by February 1. **Financial aid:** Priority date 6/15; no closing date. FAFSA, institutional form required. Applicants notified on a rolling basis starting 5/1; must reply within 4 week(s) of notification.

Academics. Special study options: Cross-registration, distance learning, double major, dual enrollment of high school students, ESL, honors, independent study, internships, student-designed major, study abroad, teacher certification program, Washington semester. **Credit/placement by examination:** AP, CLEP, institutional tests. SAT or ACT may be used in lieu of university-developed placement test. **Support services:** Learning center, preadmission summer program, reduced course load, remedial instruction, study skills assistance, tutoring, writing center.

Majors. Biology: General. **Business:** Business admin, management information systems. **Education:** General, biology, chemistry, early childhood, history, kindergarten/preschool, mathematics, multi-level teacher, science, social science. **Engineering technology:** Computer, electrical, environmental, plastics. **Health:** Athletic training, nursing (RN), premedicine, prepharmacy, preveterinary. **History:** General. **Math:** General. **Parks/recreation:** Health/fitness, sports admin. **Physical sciences:** Atmospheric science, chemistry. **Psychology:** General. **Social sciences:** General, international relations, sociology. **Visual/performing arts:** General, ceramics, drawing, painting, photography, studio arts.

Most popular majors. Biology 8%, business/marketing 21%, education 9%, English 6%, health sciences 7%, liberal arts 6%, parks/recreation 8%, social sciences 13%, visual/performing arts 9%.

Computing on campus. 620 workstations in library, computer center, student center. Dormitories wired for high-speed internet access. Commuter students can connect to campus network. Online course registration, helpline, wireless network available.

Student life. Freshman orientation: Mandatory. Preregistration for classes offered. One-day programs held throughout the summer. **Housing:** Coed dorms available. $35 nonrefundable deposit, deadline 6/30. **Activities:** Campus ministries, choral groups, drama, literary magazine, music ensembles, musical theater, student government, student newspaper, health executives and administrators learning society, student programming board.

Athletics. NAIA. **Intercollegiate:** Baseball M, basketball, cross-country, golf M, soccer, softball W, tennis W, volleyball W. **Intramural:** Basketball, bowling, golf, racquetball, softball M, swimming, table tennis, tennis, volleyball. **Team name:** Bears.

Student services. Alcohol/substance abuse counseling, career counseling, services for economically disadvantaged, student employment services, financial aid counseling, health services, on-campus daycare, personal counseling, placement for graduates, veterans' counselor. **Physically disabled:** Services for visually, speech, hearing impaired.

Contact. E-mail: to_ssu@shawnee.edu
Phone: (740) 351-4778 Toll-free number: (800) 959-2778
Fax: (740) 351-3111
Bob Trusz, Director of Admissions, Shawnee State University, 940 Second Street, Portsmouth, OH 45662

Temple Baptist College

Cincinnati, Ohio
www.templebaptist.edu

- Private 4-year liberal arts college
- Very large city
- 60 degree-seeking undergraduates

General. Regionally accredited. **Degrees:** 11 bachelor's awarded. **Calendar:** Quarter. **Full-time faculty:** 12 total. **Part-time faculty:** 19 total.

Basis for selection. Letter of recommendation from pastor required.

2008-2009 Annual costs. Tuition/fees: $10,650.

Application procedures. Admission: No deadline. $50 fee. **Financial aid:** Closing date 10/1.

Academics. Credit/placement by examination: CLEP.

Majors. Business: Business admin. **Education:** General, elementary. **Theology:** Religious ed. **Other:** Christian ministries.

Student life. Freshman orientation: Mandatory.

Contact. E-mail: infotbc@templebaptist.edu
Phone: (513) 851-3800
Tanmay Pramanik, Vice President of Student Affairs, Temple Baptist College, 11965 Kenn Road, Cincinnati, OH 45240

Tiffin University

Tiffin, Ohio — **CB member**
www.tiffin.edu — **CB code: 1817**

- Private 4-year university and business college
- Residential campus in large town
- 1,716 degree-seeking undergraduates: 9% part-time, 55% women, 17% African American, 1% Asian American, 3% Hispanic American, 5% international
- 864 degree-seeking graduate students
- 66% of applicants admitted
- SAT or ACT (ACT writing optional) required
- 43% graduate within 6 years

General. Founded in 1888. Regionally accredited. Off-campus courses offered in Lima, Lorain, Columbus, Elyria and online. **Degrees:** 271 bachelor's, 3 associate awarded; master's offered. **ROTC:** Army. **Location:** 50 miles from Toledo, 90 miles from Columbus. **Calendar:** Semester, limited summer session. **Full-time faculty:** 51 total; 65% have terminal degrees, 14% minority, 49% women. **Part-time faculty:** 141 total; 20% have terminal degrees, 38% minority, 47% women. **Class size:** 62% < 20, 32% 20-39, 6% 40-49.

Freshman class profile. 2,212 applied, 1,452 admitted, 358 enrolled.

Mid 50% test scores		**End year in good standing:**	85%
SAT critical reading:	420-490	**Return as sophomores:**	64%
SAT math:	400-500	**Out-of-state:**	24%
ACT composite:	17-22	**Live on campus:**	98%
GPA 3.75 or higher:	10%	**International:**	3%
GPA 3.50-3.74:	12%	**Fraternities:**	2%
GPA 3.0-3.49:	31%	**Sororities:**	2%
GPA 2.0-2.99:	47%		

Basis for selection. Test scores, GPA very important. Students with below 2.0 GPA may be admitted conditionally into Learning Assistance Program. Interview required for academically weak applicants.

High school preparation. College-preparatory program recommended. Required and recommended units include English 4, mathematics 3, social studies 3, science 3 and foreign language 2.

2009-2010 Annual costs. Tuition/fees (projected): $17,730. Room/board: $7,985. Books/supplies: $1,200. Personal expenses: $2,300.

2008-2009 Financial aid. Need-based: 405 full-time freshmen applied for aid; 363 were judged to have need; 363 of these received aid. Average need met was 11%. Average scholarship/grant was $5,720; average loan $3,375. 47% of total undergraduate aid awarded as scholarships/grants, 53% as loans/jobs. **Non-need-based:** Awarded to 1,514 full-time undergraduates, including 342 freshmen. Scholarships awarded for academics, alumni affiliation, athletics, leadership, music/drama, state residency.

Application procedures. Admission: No deadline. $20 fee, may be waived for applicants with need, free for online applicants. Admission notification on a rolling basis beginning on or about 9/15. **Financial aid:** No deadline. FAFSA required. Applicants notified on a rolling basis starting 1/15; must reply within 2 week(s) of notification.

Academics. Special study options: Accelerated study, combined bachelor's/graduate degree, cross-registration, distance learning, double major, dual enrollment of high school students, honors, independent study, internships, study abroad, teacher certification program, Washington semester. **Credit/placement by examination:** AP, CLEP, IB, SAT, ACT, institutional tests. 15 credit hours maximum toward associate degree, 30 toward bachelor's. **Support services:** Learning center, pre-admission summer program, reduced course load, remedial instruction, study skills assistance, tutoring.

Majors. Agriculture: Equine science. **Business:** Accounting, business admin, e-commerce, finance, hospitality admin, human resources, international, logistics, marketing, nonprofit/public, operations. **Communications:** General, digital media, journalism, media studies, public relations. **Computer sciences:** General, information systems, information technology. **Education:** General. **Health:** Substance abuse counseling. **History:** General. **Liberal arts:** Arts/sciences. **Parks/recreation:** Sports admin. **Protective services:** Corrections, emergency management/homeland security, forensics, law enforcement admin. **Psychology:** General, experimental, industrial. **Public administration:** Human services. **Social sciences:** International relations. **Visual/performing arts:** Art, arts management. **Other:** Interdisciplinary studies.

Most popular majors. Business/marketing 48%, psychology 10%, security/protective services 30%.

Computing on campus. 80 workstations in library, computer center, student center. Dormitories wired for high-speed internet access and linked to campus network. Commuter students can connect to campus network. Online course registration, online library, helpline, repair service, wireless network available.

Student life. Freshman orientation: Available, $25 fee. Preregistration for classes offered. Three-part program; first part occurs on a Saturday in April or May, or on a Friday in June; second part is a weekend in late July; third part occurs during first weekend of classes. **Policies:** Lower-division residential students required to be on meal plan. All undergraduates complete 26 hours of co-curricular credit. **Housing:** Guaranteed on-campus for freshmen. Coed dorms, single-sex dorms, special housing for disabled, apartments, fraternity/sorority housing available. $49 partly refundable deposit, deadline 4/9. Theme housing, performing arts, leadership society, house units, junior/senior house units. **Activities:** Bands, campus ministries, choral groups, dance, drama, international student organizations, literary magazine, music ensembles, musical theater, student government, student newspaper, black united students, Chamber of Fools, world student organization, Greek council, Campus Crusade for Christ, Delta Sigma Kappa, gospel choir, Habitat for Humanity.

Athletics. NAIA, NCAA. **Intercollegiate:** Baseball M, basketball, cross-country, football (tackle) M, golf, soccer, softball, squash W, tennis, track and field, volleyball W. **Team name:** Dragons.

Student services. Adult student services, career counseling, student employment services, financial aid counseling, personal counseling, placement for graduates, veterans' counselor.

Contact. E-mail: admissions@tiffin.edu
Phone: (419) 447-6443 Toll-free number: (800) 968-6446 ext. 3423
Fax: (419) 443-5006
Cam Cruickshank, Vice President for Admissions & Student Affairs, Tiffin University, 155 Miami Street, Tiffin, OH 44883

Tri-State Bible College

South Point, Ohio
www.tsbc.edu

- Private 4-year Bible college
- Commuter campus in rural community
- 49 degree-seeking undergraduates

General. Accredited by ABHE. **Degrees:** 3 bachelor's, 2 associate awarded. **Location:** 5 miles from Huntington, WV. **Calendar:** Semester, limited summer session. **Full-time faculty:** 4 total. **Part-time faculty:** 9 total.

Basis for selection. Open admission.

2008-2009 Annual costs. Tuition/fees: $5,690. Books/supplies: $530. Personal expenses: $2,016.

Application procedures. Admission: No deadline. $25 fee.

Academics. Credit/placement by examination: CLEP.

Majors. Other: Theology and religious vocations.

Student life. Activities: Student newspaper.

Contact. E-mail: cmark@zoominternet.net
Phone: (740) 377-2520 Toll-free number: (800) 261-2947
Fax: (740) 377-0001
Michael Burdick, Director of Admission, Tri-State Bible College, 506 Margaret Street, South Point, OH 45680-0445

Union Institute & University

Cincinnati, Ohio — **CB member**
www.tui.edu — **CB code: 0732**

- Private 4-year university
- Commuter campus in very large city
- 916 degree-seeking undergraduates: 33% part-time, 58% women, 24% African American, 2% Asian American, 11% Hispanic American, 1% Native American
- 782 degree-seeking graduate students
- Application essay, interview required

General. Founded in 1964. Regionally accredited. Additional academic centers in Montpelier, Brattleboro, North Miami Beach, Los Angeles and Sacramento. **Degrees:** 471 bachelor's awarded; master's, doctoral offered. **Location:** 2 miles from downtown. **Calendar:** Differs by program, extensive summer session. **Full-time faculty:** 32 total; 100% have terminal degrees, 12% minority, 53% women. **Part-time faculty:** 284 total; 40% have terminal degrees, 20% minority, 55% women.

Basis for selection. Maturity and evidence of ability to engage in self-directed learning is important. Programs designed for adult learners; majority are over age 25.

2008-2009 Annual costs. Tuition/fees: $10,528.

2007-2008 Financial aid. Non-need-based: Scholarships awarded for academics, state residency.

Application procedures. Admission: No deadline. $35 fee, may be waived for applicants with need. Admission notification on a rolling basis. **Financial aid:** No deadline. FAFSA, institutional form required. Must reply within 4 week(s) of notification.

Academics. Many courses available through distance (internet-based) learning. Serves adult learners through individualized programs, carried out through faculty-mentored independent study and research. **Special study options:** Distance learning, independent study, student-designed major, teacher certification program, weekend college. **Credit/placement by examination:** CLEP, institutional tests. 30 credit hours maximum toward bachelor's degree. **Support services:** Reduced course load.

Majors. Business: Business admin, human resources, management information systems, marketing. **Education:** General, early childhood, elementary, ESL, mathematics, multi-level teacher, physical, reading, secondary, social studies, special. **Health:** Maternal/child health, substance abuse counseling. **Liberal arts:** Arts/sciences. **Protective services:** Criminal justice, law enforcement admin. **Psychology:** General. **Public administration:** General, social work.

Most popular majors. Business/marketing 7%, education 13%, liberal arts 26%, public administration/social services 6%, security/protective services 38%.

Computing on campus. 49 workstations in library, computer center. Commuter students can connect to campus network. Online course registration, online library, helpline available.

Student life. Freshman orientation: Available. Preregistration for classes offered. **Policies:** Programs for working adults. **Housing:** Short term on-campus residencies for some programs may require housing.

Student services. Adult student services, career counseling, financial aid counseling. **Physically disabled:** Services for visually, speech, hearing impaired.

Contact. E-mail: admissions@myunion.edu
Phone: (800) 486-3116 Toll-free number: (800) 486-3116
Fax: (802) 828-8565
Gregory Stewart, Vice President, Enrollment Management, Union Institute & University, 440 East McMillan Street, Cincinnati, OH 45206

University of Akron

Akron, Ohio — **CB member**
www.uakron.edu — **CB code: 1829**

- Public 4-year university
- Commuter campus in small city
- 18,521 degree-seeking undergraduates: 19% part-time, 49% women, 13% African American, 2% Asian American, 1% Hispanic American, 1% international
- 4,008 degree-seeking graduate students
- 75% of applicants admitted
- SAT or ACT (ACT writing optional) required

General. Founded in 1870. Regionally accredited. **Degrees:** 2,183 bachelor's, 361 associate awarded; master's, doctoral, first professional offered. **ROTC:** Army, Air Force. **Location:** 40 miles from Cleveland. **Calendar:** Semester, limited summer session. **Full-time faculty:** 757 total; 82% have terminal degrees, 16% minority, 42% women. **Part-time faculty:** 859 total; 28% have terminal degrees, 8% minority, 52% women. **Class size:** 41% < 20, 47% 20-39, 6% 40-49, 4% 50-99, 2% >100. **Special facilities:** Polymer training center, bath nature preserve field station, gas turbine testing facility, training center for fire and hazardous materials.

Freshman class profile. 13,519 applied, 10,107 admitted, 4,006 enrolled.

Mid 50% test scores			
SAT critical reading:	440-570	GPA 2.0-2.99:	38%
SAT math:	440-590	Rank in top quarter:	31%
ACT composite:	18-24	Rank in top tenth:	12%
GPA 3.75 or higher:	15%	Return as sophomores:	69%
GPA 3.50-3.74:	12%	Out-of-state:	3%
GPA 3.0-3.49:	28%	Live on campus:	43%
		International:	1%

Basis for selection. School record, class rank, GPA, and test scores most important. Open access to Summit College Student Success Program and Wayne College. Essay, interview required for honors program; audition required for dance, music programs. **Homeschooled:** Students required to obtain letter of exemption from school district.

High school preparation. College-preparatory program recommended. 15 units recommended. Recommended units include English 4, mathematics 3, social studies 3, science 3 and foreign language 2.

2008-2009 Annual costs. Tuition/fees: $8,612; $17,861 out-of-state. Room/board: $8,311. Books/supplies: $900. Personal expenses: $1,520.

2007-2008 Financial aid. Need-based: 3,263 full-time freshmen applied for aid; 2,650 were judged to have need; 2,650 of these received aid. Average need met was 50%. Average scholarship/grant was $4,956; average loan $3,371. 37% of total undergraduate aid awarded as scholarships/grants, 63% as loans/jobs. **Non-need-based:** Awarded to 5,126 full-time undergraduates, including 1,732 freshmen. Scholarships awarded for academics, art, athletics, leadership, music/drama, ROTC, state residency.

Application procedures. Admission: Closing date 8/11 (receipt date). $30 fee, may be waived for applicants with need. Admission notification on a rolling basis beginning on or about 9/15. **Financial aid:** Priority date 2/1; no closing date. FAFSA, institutional form required. Applicants notified on a rolling basis starting 4/1; must reply within 2 week(s) of notification.

Academics. Special study options: Accelerated study, combined bachelor's/graduate degree, cooperative education, distance learning, double major, ESL, external degree, honors, independent study, internships, student-designed major, study abroad, teacher certification program, weekend college. Undergraduates may take graduate level classes. Co-op programs in arts, business, computer science, engineering, family & consumer sciences, humanities, natural science, technologies. Dual enrollment offered for select graduate level programs. **Credit/placement by examination:** AP, CLEP, IB, SAT, ACT, institutional tests. 38 credit hours maximum toward associate degree, 38 toward bachelor's. **Support services:** Learning center, reduced course load, remedial instruction, study skills assistance, tutoring, writing center.

Honors college/program. Must have 2 out of 3 of following criteria: 3.5 GPA; high school class rank in highest 10%; 27 ACT or 1200 SAT (exclusive of Writing). Some students with other unique qualifications may be admitted.

Majors. Architecture: Urban/community planning. **Biology:** General, animal physiology, biochemistry, botany, ecology, microbiology, zoology. **Business:** Accounting, business admin, e-commerce, financial planning, hotel/motel admin, human resources, international, management information systems, marketing, operations, sales/distribution. **Communications:** General, organizational, public relations, radio/tv. **Computer sciences:** Computer science, networking. **Education:** Art, drama/dance, early childhood, early childhood special, English, family/consumer sciences, French, mathematics, middle, music, physical, science, social studies, Spanish, special, voc/tech. **Engineering:** General, biomedical, chemical, civil, computer, electrical, mechanical, polymer. **Engineering technology:** Construction, electrical, manufacturing, mechanical, surveying. **Family/consumer sciences:** Child development, clothing/textiles, family systems, housing. **Foreign languages:** Classics, French, Spanish. **Health:** Athletic training, audiology/speech pathology, communication disorders, dietetics, licensed practical nurse, nursing (RN), recreational therapy, respiratory therapy technology. **History:** General. **Liberal arts:** Arts/sciences, humanities. **Math:** General, applied, statistics. **Parks/recreation:** Exercise sciences, sports admin. **Philosophy/religion:** Philosophy. **Physical sciences:** Chemistry, geology, geophysics, physics, polymer chemistry. **Protective services:** Criminal justice, fire safety technology. **Psychology:** General. **Public administration:** Social work. **Social sciences:** General, cartography, criminology, economics, geography, international relations, sociology, U.S. government. **Visual/performing arts:** Art history/conservation, ceramics, dance, dramatic, graphic design, jazz, metal/jewelry, music history, music performance, music theory/composition, photography, piano/organ, printmaking, sculpture, stringed instruments, studio arts, voice/opera.

Most popular majors. Business/marketing 20%, communications/journalism 8%, education 14%, engineering/engineering technologies 11%, health sciences 14%.

Computing on campus. 3,100 workstations in dormitories, library, student center. Dormitories wired for high-speed internet access and linked to campus network. Commuter students can connect to campus network. Online course registration, online library, helpline, repair service, student web hosting, wireless network available.

Student life. Freshman orientation: Mandatory, $50 fee. Preregistration for classes offered. One-day program. **Policies:** All student organizations make own criteria for members, but some criteria stipulated through university, such as 2.0 GPA requirement and good standing within university. **Housing:** Coed dorms, single-sex dorms, special housing for disabled, fraternity/sorority housing available. $150 nonrefundable deposit, deadline 2/1. Honors student dormitory. **Activities:** Bands, campus ministries, choral groups, dance, drama, international student organizations, music ensembles, musical theater, radio station, student government, student newspaper, symphony orchestra, TV station, Chinese students and scholars association, Indian students association, Muslim students association, black united students, H.O.L.A., Hillel, College Republicans, College Democrats, Campus Focus, gospel choir.

Athletics. NCAA. **Intercollegiate:** Baseball M, basketball, cheerleading, cross-country, diving W, football (tackle) M, golf M, rifle, soccer, softball W, swimming W, tennis W, track and field, volleyball W. **Intramural:** Badminton, basketball, bowling, cross-country, golf, racquetball, skiing, soccer, softball, swimming, table tennis, track and field, volleyball W, wrestling M. **Team name:** Zips.

Student services. Adult student services, alcohol/substance abuse counseling, career counseling, student employment services, financial aid counseling, health services, minority student services, on-campus daycare, personal counseling, placement for graduates, veterans' counselor, women's services. **Physically disabled:** Services for visually, speech, hearing impaired.

Contact. E-mail: admissions@uakron.edu
Phone: (330) 972-7100 Toll-free number: (800) 655-4884
Fax: (330) 972-7022
Diane Raybuck, Director of Admissions, University of Akron, The University of Akron, Akron, OH 44325-2001

University of Cincinnati

Cincinnati, Ohio — **CB member**
www.uc.edu — **CB code: 1833**

- Public 4-year university
- Commuter campus in large city
- 20,183 degree-seeking undergraduates: 15% part-time, 51% women, 11% African American, 3% Asian American, 2% Hispanic American, 1% international
- 7,997 degree-seeking graduate students
- 61% of applicants admitted
- SAT or ACT with writing, application essay required
- 55% graduate within 6 years

General. Founded in 1819. Regionally accredited. **Degrees:** 3,607 bachelor's, 174 associate awarded; master's, doctoral, first professional offered. **ROTC:** Army, Air Force. **Location:** 2 miles from downtown. **Calendar:** Quarter, extensive summer session. **Full-time faculty:** 1,208 total; 58% have terminal degrees, 18% minority, 41% women. **Part-time faculty:** 41 total; 12% have terminal degrees, 10% minority, 56% women. **Class size:** 45% < 20, 42% 20-39, 5% 40-49, 5% 50-99, 3% >100.

Freshman class profile. 14,333 applied, 8,798 admitted, 3,166 enrolled.

Mid 50% test scores		**GPA 2.0-2.99:**	18%
SAT critical reading:	500-610	**Rank in top quarter:**	49%
SAT math:	520-640	**Rank in top tenth:**	22%
SAT writing:	490-600	**Return as sophomores:**	83%
ACT composite:	22-27	**Out-of-state:**	8%
GPA 3.75 or higher:	26%	**Live on campus:**	72%
GPA 3.50-3.74:	20%	**International:**	1%
GPA 3.0-3.49:	35%		

Basis for selection. Secondary school record, test scores most important. Interview required for music programs; audition required for dance, music programs. **Homeschooled:** Transcript of courses and grades required. Release for home schooling from local Board of Education required.

High school preparation. College-preparatory program recommended. 16 units required. Required and recommended units include English 4, mathematics 3-4, social studies 2, history 1, science 2-3, foreign language 2 and academic electives 2. Specific requirements may vary for each college.

2008-2009 Annual costs. Tuition/fees: $9,399; $23,922 out-of-state. Room/board: $9,240. Books/supplies: $1,275. Personal expenses: $3,725.

2008-2009 Financial aid. Non-need-based: Scholarships awarded for academics, alumni affiliation, art, athletics, leadership, minority status, music/drama, ROTC, state residency.

Application procedures. Admission: Priority date 1/15; deadline 9/1 (postmark date). $40 fee, may be waived for applicants with need. Admission notification on a rolling basis beginning on or about 10/1. **Financial aid:** No deadline. FAFSA required. Applicants notified on a rolling basis starting 3/10; must reply within 2 week(s) of notification.

Academics. Some engineering programs require students to acquire personal computers. **Special study options:** Accelerated study, combined bachelor's/graduate degree, cooperative education, distance learning, double major, ESL, honors, independent study, internships, liberal arts/career combination, study abroad, teacher certification program, Washington semester, weekend college. Learning at Large (students earn college credit without attending regularly scheduled classes). **Credit/placement by examination:** AP, CLEP, institutional tests. **Support services:** Pre-admission summer program, remedial instruction, study skills assistance, tutoring, writing center.

Majors. Architecture: Architecture, urban/community planning. **Area/ethnic studies:** African-American, Asian, French, German, Latin American, Spanish/Iberian. **Biology:** General. **Business:** Accounting, business admin, finance, management information systems, management science, operations, real estate. **Communications:** General, radio/tv. **Computer sciences:** General. **Education:** Art, early childhood, elementary, health, music, secondary. **Engineering:** General, aerospace, chemical, civil, computer, electrical, mechanical, mechanics, metallurgical, nuclear. **Family/consumer sciences:** Food/nutrition. **Foreign languages:** Classics, comparative lit, French, German, Latin, linguistics, Spanish. **Health:** Audiology/speech pathology, clinical lab science, health care admin, nuclear medical technology, nursing (RN), predental, premedicine, prepharmacy, preveterinary. **History:** General. **Interdisciplinary:** Neuroscience. **Liberal arts:** Arts/sciences. **Math:** General. **Philosophy/religion:** Judaic, philosophy. **Physical sciences:** Chemistry, geology, physics. **Protective services:** Criminal justice. **Psychology:** General. **Public administration:** Social work. **Social sciences:** Anthropology, economics, geography, international relations, political science, sociology, urban studies. **Visual/performing arts:** Art history/conservation, commercial/advertising art, conducting, dance, dramatic, fashion design, industrial design, interior design, jazz, music history, music performance, music theory/composition, piano/organ, studio arts, theater design, voice/opera. **Other:** Electronic media.

Most popular majors. Business/marketing 16%, education 6%, engineering/engineering technologies 12%, English 7%, health sciences 15%, security/protective services 6%, visual/performing arts 11%.

Computing on campus. 560 workstations in library, computer center. Dormitories linked to campus network. Commuter students can connect to campus network. Online course registration, helpline, repair service, wireless network available.

Student life. Freshman orientation: Available. Preregistration for classes offered. **Housing:** Guaranteed on-campus for freshmen. Coed dorms, single-sex dorms, apartments, fraternity/sorority housing available. **Activities:** Bands, choral groups, dance, drama, film society, music ensembles, musical theater, opera, radio station, student government, student newspaper, symphony orchestra, Women's Initiative Network, College Democrats, College Republicans.

Athletics. NCAA. **Intercollegiate:** Baseball M, basketball, cross-country, diving, football (tackle) M, golf, lacrosse W, soccer, swimming, tennis, track and field, volleyball W. **Intramural:** Archery W, badminton, baseball M, basketball, bowling, diving, golf, gymnastics W, handball, lacrosse, racquetball, soccer, softball, squash, swimming, table tennis, tennis, track and field, volleyball, wrestling M. **Team name:** Bearcats.

Student services. Adult student services, alcohol/substance abuse counseling, chaplain/spiritual director, career counseling, services for economically disadvantaged, student employment services, financial aid counseling, health services, legal services, minority student services, on-campus daycare, personal counseling, placement for graduates, veterans' counselor, women's services. **Physically disabled:** Services for visually, speech, hearing impaired.

Contact. E-mail: admissions@uc.edu
Phone: (513) 556-1100 Toll-free number: (800) 827-8728
Fax: (513) 556-1105
Thomas Canepa, Assistant Vice President, Admissions, University of Cincinnati, PO Box 210091, Cincinnati, OH 45221-0091

University of Dayton

Dayton, Ohio — **CB member**
www.udayton.edu — **CB code: 1834**

- Private 4-year university affiliated with Roman Catholic Church
- Residential campus in small city
- 7,420 degree-seeking undergraduates: 4% part-time, 49% women, 3% African American, 1% Asian American, 2% Hispanic American, 2% international
- 2,624 degree-seeking graduate students
- 74% of applicants admitted
- SAT or ACT (ACT writing optional), application essay required
- 75% graduate within 6 years

General. Founded in 1850. Regionally accredited. **Degrees:** 1,584 bachelor's awarded; master's, doctoral, first professional offered. **ROTC:** Army, Air Force. **Location:** 2 miles from downtown, 50 miles from Cincinnati. **Calendar:** Semester, extensive summer session. **Full-time faculty:** 462 total; 90% have terminal degrees, 13% minority, 35% women. **Part-time faculty:** 354 total; 7% minority, 47% women. **Class size:** 37% < 20, 52% 20-39, 6% 40-49, 4% 50-99, less than 1% >100. **Special facilities:** Research institute, portfolio management center, learning-teaching center, information sciences center, student-operated stores and coffee bars.

Freshman class profile. 11,610 applied, 8,552 admitted, 1,995 enrolled.

Mid 50% test scores			
SAT critical reading:	520-620	GPA 2.0-2.99:	13%
SAT math:	530-640	Rank in top quarter:	51%
ACT composite:	23-28	Rank in top tenth:	21%
GPA 3.75 or higher:	34%	Return as sophomores:	86%
GPA 3.50-3.74:	18%	Out-of-state:	42%
GPA 3.0-3.49:	35%	Live on campus:	95%
		International:	1%

Basis for selection. Selection of courses in preparation for college, grade record and pattern in high school, class rank, SAT or ACT, character, and record of leadership and service. Will review PAA if presented. Interview recommended for all; audition required for all music programs. **Homeschooled:** Transcript of courses and grades required. Description of courses taken required, including bibliography of texts used for instruction. Examples of projects, homework or writing samples helpful. **Learning Disabled:** Prefer applicant provide documentation explaining disability for assessment.

High school preparation. College-preparatory program recommended. 16 units recommended. Recommended units include English 4, mathematics 3, social studies 3, science 2 (laboratory 1) and academic electives 4. 2 units of foreign language required for admission to the College of Arts and Sciences.

2008-2009 Annual costs. Tuition/fees: $27,330. $1,299 additional cost to all new incoming students for purchase of computer from university. International students pay additional $75 per month for health and accident insurance. Engineering majors required to pay additional $750 per semester in fees. Room/board: $7,980. Books/supplies: $800. Personal expenses: $1,600.

2007-2008 Financial aid. Need-based: 1,380 full-time freshmen applied for aid; 1,040 were judged to have need; 1,036 of these received aid. Average need met was 95%. Average scholarship/grant was $12,448; average loan $6,877. 55% of total undergraduate aid awarded as scholarships/grants, 45% as loans/jobs. **Non-need-based:** Awarded to 6,238 full-time undergraduates, including 875 freshmen. Scholarships awarded for academics, alumni affiliation, art, athletics, leadership, music/drama, ROTC, state residency.

Application procedures. Admission: Priority date 12/15; no deadline. $50 fee, may be waived for applicants with need. Application must be submitted online. Admission notification on a rolling basis beginning on or about 10/31. Must reply by May 1 or within 2 week(s) if notified thereafter. **Financial aid:** Priority date 3/31; no closing date. FAFSA required. Applicants notified on a rolling basis starting 3/1; must reply by 5/1 or within 3 week(s) of notification.

Academics. Special study options: Accelerated study, combined bachelor's/graduate degree, cooperative education, cross-registration, distance learning, double major, dual enrollment of high school students, ESL, exchange student, honors, independent study, internships, liberal arts/career combination, semester at sea, student-designed major, study abroad, teacher certification program, Washington semester. Domestic exchange program with other Marianist institutions; student-designed major in general studies only. **Credit/placement by examination:** AP, CLEP, IB, SAT, ACT, institutional tests. 24 credit hours maximum toward bachelor's degree. **Support services:** Learning center, pre-admission summer program, reduced course load, remedial instruction, study skills assistance, tutoring, writing center.

Majors. Area/ethnic studies: American. **Biology:** General, biochemistry, environmental. **Business:** General, accounting, business admin, entrepreneurial studies, finance, international, management information systems, managerial economics, marketing, operations. **Communications:** General, digital media, journalism, media studies, public relations. **Computer sciences:** General, computer science. **Conservation:** Environmental science. **Education:** Art, early childhood, foreign languages, French, German, middle, multi-level teacher, music, physical, secondary, Spanish, special. **Engineering:** Chemical, civil, computer, electrical, mechanical. **Engineering technology:** General, computer, electrical, industrial, manufacturing, mechanical. **Family/consumer sciences:** Food/nutrition. **Foreign languages:** French, German, Spanish. **Health:** Dietetics, music therapy, predental, premedicine. **History:** General. **Interdisciplinary:** Global studies. **Legal studies:** Prelaw. **Math:** General. **Parks/recreation:** Exercise sciences, facilities management, sports admin. **Philosophy/religion:** Philosophy, religion. **Physical sciences:** General, chemistry, geology, physics. **Protective services:** Criminal justice. **Psychology:** General. **Social sciences:** Econometrics, economics, political science, sociology. **Visual/performing arts:** Art history/conservation, design, dramatic, music performance, music theory/composition, photography, studio arts. **Other:** Human rights.

Most popular majors. Business/marketing 24%, communications/journalism 11%, education 10%, engineering/engineering technologies 16%, psychology 6%.

Computing on campus. PC or laptop required. Dormitories wired for high-speed internet access and linked to campus network. Commuter students can connect to campus network. Online course registration, online library, helpline, repair service, student web hosting, wireless network available.

Student life. Freshman orientation: Mandatory, $115 fee. Preregistration for classes offered. Held 2-3 days preceding the first day of classes. Virtual orientation also available online. **Housing:** Guaranteed on-campus for freshmen. Coed dorms, single-sex dorms, special housing for disabled, apartments, fraternity/sorority housing; wellness housing available. $400 nonrefundable deposit, deadline 5/1. University-owned houses available. **Activities:** Bands, campus ministries, choral groups, dance, drama, international student organizations, literary magazine, music ensembles, Model UN, musical theater, opera, radio station, student government, student newspaper, symphony orchestra, TV station, Catholic Life, Campus Crusade for Christ, College Democrats, College Republicans, diversity discussion group, Indian student association, NAACP, Irish club, Italian club.

Athletics. NCAA. **Intercollegiate:** Baseball M, basketball, cheerleading, cross-country, football (tackle) M, golf, rowing (crew) W, soccer, softball W, tennis, track and field W, volleyball W. **Intramural:** Badminton, basketball, bowling, football (non-tackle), golf, racquetball, soccer, softball, tennis, volleyball, water polo, wrestling. **Team name:** Flyers.

Student services. Adult student services, alcohol/substance abuse counseling, chaplain/spiritual director, career counseling, services for economically disadvantaged, student employment services, financial aid counseling,

health services, minority student services, on-campus daycare, personal counseling, placement for graduates, women's services. **Physically disabled:** Services for visually, speech, hearing impaired. **Learning disabled:** Comprehensive services available.

Contact. E-mail: admission@udayton.edu
Phone: (937) 229-4411 Toll-free number: (800) 837-7433
Fax: (937) 229-4729
Robert Durkle, Dean of Admission, University of Dayton, 300 College Park, Dayton, OH 45469-1300

University of Findlay

Findlay, Ohio
www.findlay.edu **CB code: 1223**

- Private 4-year university and health science college affiliated with Church of God
- Residential campus in large town
- 3,011 degree-seeking undergraduates: 11% part-time, 63% women, 3% African American, 1% Asian American, 1% Hispanic American, 7% international
- 1,256 degree-seeking graduate students
- 68% of applicants admitted
- SAT or ACT (ACT writing optional) required
- 53% graduate within 6 years

General. Founded in 1882. Regionally accredited. **Degrees:** 540 bachelor's, 68 associate awarded; master's, first professional offered. **ROTC:** Army, Air Force. **Location:** 45 miles from Toledo, 90 miles from Columbus. **Calendar:** Semester, limited summer session. **Full-time faculty:** 190 total; 55% have terminal degrees, 11% minority, 46% women. **Part-time faculty:** 173 total; 12% have terminal degrees, 6% minority, 53% women. **Class size:** 58% < 20, 33% 20-39, 6% 40-49, 3% 50-99. **Special facilities:** Two equestrian farms, cadaver lab, environmental resource training center, planetarium, center for habitat studies, museum.

Freshman class profile. 2,914 applied, 1,974 admitted, 640 enrolled.

Mid 50% test scores			
SAT critical reading:	460-570	Rank in top quarter:	55%
SAT math:	480-590	Rank in top tenth:	30%
SAT writing:	480-580	End year in good standing:	88%
ACT composite:	20-26	Return as sophomores:	76%
GPA 3.75 or higher:	35%	Out-of-state:	22%
GPA 3.50-3.74:	18%	Live on campus:	86%
GPA 3.0-3.49:	30%	Fraternities:	2%
GPA 2.0-2.99:	17%	Sororities:	2%

Basis for selection. School achievement record, curriculum, class rank, and recommendations. Essay required for special admissions program and interview is recommended. **Homeschooled:** Statement describing homeschool structure and mission, state high school equivalency certificate, letter of recommendation (nonparent) required. Greater weight placed on standardized entrance exam scores for admission, evaluation of GED if taken. **Learning Disabled:** Strongly encourage interview or campus visit.

High school preparation. College-preparatory program recommended. 16 units recommended. Recommended units include English 4, mathematics 3, social studies 3, history 1, science 4, foreign language 3 and academic electives 1. One fine arts unit recommended. Additional 1 math and 1 science for preveterinary and environmental programs.

2008-2009 Annual costs. Tuition/fees: $24,670. Pre-veterinary and equestrian students pay higher tuition in years one and two; pharmacy students pay higher tuition throughout the program. Room/board: $8,306. Books/supplies: $1,700.

2007-2008 Financial aid. Need-based: Average need met was 71%. Average scholarship/grant was $11,972; average loan $3,029. 62% of total undergraduate aid awarded as scholarships/grants, 38% as loans/jobs. **Non-need-based:** Scholarships awarded for academics, alumni affiliation, athletics, music/drama, state residency.

Application procedures. Admission: Closing date 6/1 (receipt date). No application fee. Admission notification on a rolling basis beginning on or about 9/1. Must reply by May 1 or within 4 week(s) if notified thereafter. Part-time applicants may be admitted year round to any of the six different program start dates. **Financial aid:** Priority date 8/1, closing date 9/1. FAFSA required. Applicants notified on a rolling basis starting 3/1; must reply within 2 week(s) of notification.

Academics. Special study options: Accelerated study, combined bachelor's/graduate degree, cooperative education, distance learning, double major, dual enrollment of high school students, ESL, external degree, honors, independent study, internships, liberal arts/career combination, semester at sea, student-designed major, study abroad, teacher certification program, Washington semester, weekend college. BS in nursing with Mount Carmel College of Nursing and Lourdes College, 3-1 BA prgram with Art Institute Consortium. **Credit/placement by examination:** AP, CLEP, institutional tests. 15 credit hours maximum toward associate degree, 30 toward bachelor's. **Support services:** Learning center, reduced course load, remedial instruction, study skills assistance, tutoring, writing center.

Majors. Agriculture: Equestrian studies, farm/ranch. **Biology:** General. **Business:** General, accounting, business admin, entrepreneurial studies, finance, hospitality admin, hospitality/recreation, human resources, international, marketing. **Communications:** General, journalism, public relations. **Computer sciences:** General, computer science, systems analysis. **Education:** General, art, bilingual, biology, curriculum, developmentally delayed, drama/dance, driver/safety, early childhood, early childhood special, emotionally handicapped, English, ESL, evaluation, foreign languages, foundations, geography, health, history, kindergarten/preschool, learning disabled, mathematics, mentally handicapped, middle, multi-level teacher, multicultural, multiple handicapped, physical, psychology, reading, science, secondary, social science, social studies, Spanish, special, speech, testing/assessment. **Engineering technology:** Hazardous materials. **Foreign languages:** Japanese, Spanish. **Health:** Athletic training, environmental health, health care admin, nuclear medical technology, occupational health, physician assistant, premedicine, prenursing, preveterinary. **History:** General. **Legal studies:** Prelaw. **Math:** General. **Parks/recreation:** Exercise sciences, health/fitness, sports admin. **Philosophy/religion:** Philosophy, religion. **Protective services:** Law enforcement admin. **Psychology:** General. **Public administration:** Social work. **Social sciences:** General, economics, political science, sociology. **Theology:** Theology. **Visual/performing arts:** Art, commercial/advertising art, dramatic, theater design.

Most popular majors. Agriculture 8%, business/marketing 23%, education 14%, health sciences 25%.

Computing on campus. 400 workstations in dormitories, library, computer center, student center. Dormitories wired for high-speed internet access and linked to campus network. Commuter students can connect to campus network. Online course registration, online library, helpline, repair service, student web hosting, wireless network available.

Student life. Freshman orientation: Mandatory, $100 fee. Preregistration for classes offered. One-day registrations for students and orientation for parents during summer. 2-day orientation for students 2 days before classes begin. **Policies:** All freshmen, sophomores, and juniors under the age of 22 required to live on-campus. **Housing:** Guaranteed on-campus for freshmen. Coed dorms, single-sex dorms, special housing for disabled, apartments, fraternity/sorority housing, wellness housing available. $150 nonrefundable deposit, deadline 7/1. Honors house and special interest houses. **Activities:** Bands, campus ministries, choral groups, dance, drama, international student organizations, literary magazine, music ensembles, musical theater, opera, radio station, student government, student newspaper, symphony orchestra, TV station, Circle-K, black student union, wilderness club, Campus Compact, College Democrats, College Republicans, Fellowship of Christian Athletes, Habitat for Humanity, international club, student government association.

Athletics. NCAA. **Intercollegiate:** Baseball M, basketball, cheerleading, cross-country, diving, equestrian, football (tackle) M, golf, soccer, softball W, swimming, tennis, track and field, volleyball W, wrestling M. **Intramural:** Basketball, bowling, football (non-tackle), golf, skiing, soccer, softball, table tennis, tennis, volleyball, water polo. **Team name:** Oilers.

Student services. Adult student services, alcohol/substance abuse counseling, chaplain/spiritual director, career counseling, services for economically disadvantaged, student employment services, financial aid counseling, health services, minority student services, personal counseling, placement for graduates, veterans' counselor, women's services. **Physically disabled:** Services for visually, speech, hearing impaired.

Contact. E-mail: admissions@findlay.edu
Phone: (419) 434-4540 Toll-free number: (800) 548-0932
Fax: (419) 434-4898
Donna Gruber, Director of Undergraduate Admissions, University of Findlay, 1000 North Main Street, Findlay, OH 45840-3653

University of Rio Grande

Rio Grande, Ohio
www.rio.edu **CB code: 1663**

- Private 4-year community and liberal arts college
- Commuter campus in rural community
- 1,484 degree-seeking undergraduates: 17% part-time, 59% women, 3% African American, 1% Asian American, 1% Hispanic American

- 177 graduate students
- 38% graduate within 6 years

General. Founded in 1876. Regionally accredited. Institution is both public and private. First 2 years are state subsidized, second 2 years are private, with higher tuition. Affiliated with Rio Grande Community College. **Degrees:** 222 bachelor's, 192 associate awarded; master's offered. **ROTC:** Army. **Location:** 12 miles from Gallipolis. **Calendar:** Semester, limited summer session. **Full-time faculty:** 92 total; 45% have terminal degrees, 8% minority, 40% women. **Part-time faculty:** 92 total; 3% have terminal degrees, 1% minority, 61% women. **Class size:** 76% < 20, 21% 20-39, 1% 40-49, 2% 50-99. **Special facilities:** Early childhood care center.

Freshman class profile. 2,569 applied, 1,943 admitted, 566 enrolled.

GPA 3.75 or higher:	11%	**Rank in top tenth:**	10%
GPA 3.50-3.74:	13%	**End year in good standing:**	87%
GPA 3.0-3.49:	26%	**Return as sophomores:**	59%
GPA 2.0-2.99:	45%	**Out-of-state:**	3%
Rank in top quarter:	20%	**Live on campus:**	32%

Basis for selection. Open admission, but selective for some programs. ACT required for nursing, medical laboratory technician, radiologic technology, diagnostic medical sonography, respiratory therapy, and education programs. Deferred admission for students demonstrating need for remedial work. Acceptance to Education department occurs at end of sophomore year. **Learning Disabled:** Students with any kind of special needs asked to meet with Director of Accessibility to determine education plan and for academic advising purposes.

High school preparation. College-preparatory program recommended. 21 units recommended. Recommended units include English 4, mathematics 3, social studies 3, history 2, science 3 (laboratory 2), foreign language 2 and academic electives 9. Chemistry, algebra, biology required for nursing applicants.

2008-2009 Annual costs. Tuition/fees: $18,260. Tuition reported is for private university sector of institution. Public community college in-state in-district tuition: $2,880 ($96 per credit hour); in-state out-of-district, $3,450 ($115 per credit hour). All public community college undergraduates pay $632 in required fees. Out-of-state community college students charged private tuition rate. Room/board: $7,000. Books/supplies: $1,000. Personal expenses: $1,571.

2007-2008 Financial aid. Need-based: 313 full-time freshmen applied for aid; 251 were judged to have need; 241 of these received aid. Average need met was 55%. Average scholarship/grant was $2,655; average loan $1,595. 62% of total undergraduate aid awarded as scholarships/grants, 38% as loans/jobs. **Non-need-based:** Awarded to 849 full-time undergraduates, including 236 freshmen. Scholarships awarded for academics, alumni affiliation, athletics, leadership, music/drama, state residency.

Application procedures. Admission: No deadline. $25 fee, may be waived for applicants with need, free for online applicants. Admission notification on a rolling basis. **Financial aid:** Priority date 3/15; no closing date. FAFSA, institutional form required. Applicants notified on a rolling basis starting 1/15; must reply within 3 week(s) of notification.

Academics. Special study options: Accelerated study, combined bachelor's/graduate degree, cooperative education, distance learning, double major, dual enrollment of high school students, ESL, honors, independent study, internships, liberal arts/career combination, student-designed major, study abroad, teacher certification program. **Credit/placement by examination:** AP, CLEP, institutional tests. **Support services:** Learning center, pre-admission summer program, reduced course load, remedial instruction, tutoring.

Majors. Agriculture: Business. **Area/ethnic studies:** American. **Biology:** General. **Business:** General, accounting, accounting technology, business admin, entrepreneurial studies, finance, human resources, international, managerial economics, marketing, office management, office technology, operations, real estate, restaurant/food services, retailing. **Communications:** General, journalism, media studies, public relations. **Computer sciences:** General, applications programming, computer science. **Conservation:** General, environmental studies, wildlife. **Education:** General, art, biology, business, chemistry, early childhood, elementary, English, health, history, mathematics, middle, multi-level teacher, music, physical, physics, reading, science, secondary, social science, special, speech. **Engineering technology:** Manufacturing. **Health:** Clinical lab science, health care admin, nursing (RN), premedicine. **History:** General. **Legal studies:** Prelaw. **Liberal arts:** Humanities. **Math:** General. **Parks/recreation:** Sports admin. **Physical sciences:** General, chemistry, physics. **Psychology:** General. **Public administration:** General, social work. **Social sciences:** General, archaeology, economics. **Theology:** Preministerial. **Visual/performing arts:** General, art, commercial/advertising art, dramatic, music management, studio arts.

Most popular majors. Business/marketing 10%, education 21%, health sciences 18%, natural resources/environmental science 14%, public administration/social services 7%.

Computing on campus. 300 workstations in library, computer center, student center. Dormitories wired for high-speed internet access and linked to campus network. Online course registration, online library, student web hosting, wireless network available.

Student life. Freshman orientation: Available, $50 fee. Preregistration for classes offered. Offered 4 times during the summer. **Policies:** Smoke free dorms and buildings. **Housing:** Guaranteed on-campus for all undergraduates. Coed dorms, single-sex dorms, special housing for disabled, wellness housing available. $200 fully refundable deposit, deadline 7/15. **Activities:** Bands, choral groups, dance, drama, literary magazine, music ensembles, musical theater, radio station, student government, student newspaper, TV station, international student organization, Valley Artist Services, Handicapped Coalition, Young Republicans, Rio Christian Fellowship, Student Ambassadors, Students in Free Enterprise.

Athletics. NAIA. **Intercollegiate:** Baseball M, basketball, cheerleading, cross-country, soccer, softball W, track and field, volleyball W. **Intramural:** Archery, badminton, basketball, equestrian, handball, racquetball, softball, swimming, tennis, water polo, wrestling M. **Team name:** Redstorm.

Student services. Career counseling, student employment services, financial aid counseling, health services, on-campus daycare, personal counseling, placement for graduates, veterans' counselor. **Physically disabled:** Services for visually, speech, hearing impaired.

Contact. E-mail: admissions@rio.edu
Phone: (740) 245-7206 Toll-free number: (800) 282-7201
Fax: (740) 245-7260
Rebecca Long, Director of Admissions, University of Rio Grande, 218 North College Avenue, Rio Grande, OH 45674

University of Toledo

Toledo, Ohio — **CB member**
www.utoledo.edu — **CB code: 1845**

- Public 4-year university
- Commuter campus in large city
- 16,737 degree-seeking undergraduates: 16% part-time, 49% women, 14% African American, 2% Asian American, 3% Hispanic American, 3% international
- 4,488 degree-seeking graduate students
- 46% graduate within 6 years

General. Founded in 1872. Regionally accredited. **Degrees:** 2,651 bachelor's, 118 associate awarded; master's, doctoral, first professional offered. **ROTC:** Army, Air Force. **Location:** 6 miles from downtown. **Calendar:** Semester, extensive summer session. **Full-time faculty:** 1,118 total; 19% minority, 38% women. **Part-time faculty:** 474 total; 10% minority, 51% women. **Class size:** 33% < 20, 48% 20-39, 8% 40-49, 6% 50-99, 4% >100. **Special facilities:** 2 observatories, ion accelerator, arboretum, planetarium, linear laser and nuclear physics laboratory, Lake Erie Research Center.

Freshman class profile. 12,042 applied, 11,045 admitted, 4,195 enrolled.

Mid 50% test scores		**Rank in top quarter:**	36%
SAT critical reading:	440-560	**Rank in top tenth:**	14%
SAT math:	460-590	**Return as sophomores:**	70%
SAT writing:	430-550	**Out-of-state:**	10%
ACT composite:	19-24	**Live on campus:**	63%
GPA 3.75 or higher:	19%	**International:**	2%
GPA 3.50-3.74:	12%	**Fraternities:**	5%
GPA 3.0-3.49:	27%	**Sororities:**	3%
GPA 2.0-2.99:	34%		

Basis for selection. Open admission, but selective for some programs and for out-of-state students. Out-of-state students need 2.0 GPA and 21 ACT or 980 SAT. Applicants to BS program in engineering need 3.0 GPA and 22 ACT or 1020 SAT. For admission to premedicine, predentistry, or preveterinary programs, 3.0 GPA and 25 ACT or 1130 SAT required. Applicants to computer science-engineering program need 3.0 GPA and 25 ACT or 1130 SAT, engineering technology 2.0 GPA and 21 ACT or 980 SAT, business college 2.25 GPA or 25 ACT or 1130 SAT. All SAT scores exclusive of Writing. Audition required for music program. **Homeschooled:** Official recognized transcript required. **Learning Disabled:** Registering with the Office of Accessibility recommended.

High school preparation. College-preparatory program required. Recommended units include English 4, mathematics 3, social studies 3 and science 3.

2008-2009 Annual costs. Tuition/fees: $7,926; $16,738 out-of-state. Room/board: $8,814. Books/supplies: $750. Personal expenses: $2,204.

2008-2009 Financial aid. Need-based: 3,368 full-time freshmen applied for aid; 2,482 were judged to have need; 2,481 of these received aid. Average need met was 66%. Average scholarship/grant was $6,536; average loan $3,604. 40% of total undergraduate aid awarded as scholarships/grants, 60% as loans/jobs. **Non-need-based:** Awarded to 5,328 full-time undergraduates, including 1,942 freshmen. Scholarships awarded for academics, alumni affiliation, art, athletics, leadership, minority status, music/drama, ROTC, state residency. **Additional information:** March priority date for federal aid. Students encouraged to apply as early as December for priority consideration for institutional aid.

Application procedures. Admission: No deadline. $40 fee, may be waived for applicants with need. Admission notification on a rolling basis beginning on or about 10/1. Freshman applicants desiring on-campus housing encouraged to apply early. **Financial aid:** Priority date 3/1; no closing date. FAFSA required. Applicants notified on a rolling basis starting 3/1; must reply within 8 week(s) of notification.

Academics. Special study options: Accelerated study, combined bachelor's/graduate degree, cooperative education, cross-registration, distance learning, double major, dual enrollment of high school students, exchange student, honors, independent study, internships, liberal arts/career combination, student-designed major, study abroad, teacher certification program, weekend college. **Credit/placement by examination:** AP, CLEP, institutional tests. 30 credit hours maximum toward associate degree, 30 toward bachelor's. **Support services:** Learning center, pre-admission summer program, reduced course load, remedial instruction, study skills assistance, tutoring, writing center.

Majors. Area/ethnic studies: African-American, American, Asian, European, Latin American, Near/Middle Eastern, women's. **Biology:** General. **Business:** General, accounting, business admin, entrepreneurial studies, finance, human resources, international, logistics, management information systems, management science, market research, marketing, operations, organizational behavior. **Communications:** General, media studies. **Computer sciences:** Information systems, information technology. **Conservation:** Environmental studies. **Education:** General, art, business, English, French, German, health, kindergarten/preschool, mathematics, music, physical, science, secondary, social studies, Spanish, speech impaired, trade/industrial. **Engineering:** General, biomedical, chemical, civil, computer, electrical, industrial, mechanical. **Engineering technology:** Civil, electromechanical, mechanical. **Foreign languages:** French, German, linguistics, Spanish. **Health:** Facilities admin, medical records admin, nursing (RN), pharmaceutical sciences, predental, premedicine, preveterinary, public health ed, recreational therapy, respiratory therapy technology. **History:** General. **Interdisciplinary:** Medieval/Renaissance. **Legal studies:** Paralegal, prelaw. **Liberal arts:** Arts/sciences, humanities. **Math:** General. **Parks/recreation:** General, exercise sciences, health/fitness. **Philosophy/religion:** Philosophy, religion. **Physical sciences:** Astronomy, chemistry, geology, physics. **Protective services:** Criminal justice. **Psychology:** General. **Public administration:** Social work. **Social sciences:** Anthropology, economics, geography, international relations, political science, sociology, urban studies. **Visual/performing arts:** Art, art history/conservation, dramatic, film/cinema, studio arts.

Most popular majors. Business/marketing 22%, education 11%, engineering/engineering technologies 14%, health sciences 14%, interdisciplinary studies 7%.

Computing on campus. 2,800 workstations in dormitories, library, computer center, student center. Dormitories linked to campus network. Commuter students can connect to campus network. Online course registration, online library, helpline, repair service, wireless network available.

Student life. Freshman orientation: Available, $60 fee. **Housing:** Coed dorms, special housing for disabled, fraternity/sorority housing available. $200 partly refundable deposit, deadline 6/1. **Activities:** Bands, campus ministries, choral groups, dance, drama, international student organizations, literary magazine, music ensembles, opera, radio station, student government, student newspaper, TV station, black student union, Campus Crusade for Christ, Hillel, Latino student union, University YMCA, gay and lesbian student union, international student association, Habitat for Humanity, Toledo Campus Ministry Fellowship.

Athletics. NCAA. **Intercollegiate:** Baseball M, basketball, cross-country, diving W, football (tackle) M, golf, soccer W, softball W, swimming W, tennis, track and field W, volleyball W. **Intramural:** Badminton, basketball, bowling, cheerleading W, diving W, fencing, football (tackle), golf, lacrosse, racquetball, soccer, softball, swimming W, table tennis, tennis, track and field W, volleyball, weight lifting. **Team name:** Rockets.

Student services. Adult student services, alcohol/substance abuse counseling, chaplain/spiritual director, career counseling, services for economically disadvantaged, student employment services, financial aid counseling, health services, legal services, minority student services, on-campus daycare, personal counseling, placement for graduates, veterans' counselor, women's services. **Physically disabled:** Services for visually, speech, hearing impaired.

Contact. E-mail: enroll@utnet.utoledo.edu
Phone: (419) 530-8700 Toll-free number: (800) 586-5336
Fax: (419) 530-4504
William Pierce, Director of Admission, University of Toledo, 2801 West Bancroft Street, Toledo, OH 43606-3398

Urbana University

Urbana, Ohio
www.urbana.edu **CB code: 1847**

- Private 4-year liberal arts college
- Commuter campus in large town
- 829 full-time, degree-seeking undergraduates
- SAT or ACT (ACT writing optional) required

General. Founded in 1850. Regionally accredited. **Degrees:** 208 bachelor's, 59 associate awarded; master's offered. **ROTC:** Army, Air Force. **Location:** 42 miles from Columbus, 49 miles from Dayton. **Calendar:** Semester, limited summer session. **Full-time faculty:** 50 total. **Part-time faculty:** 70 total. **Special facilities:** Johnny Appleseed museum, rare books collection.

Freshman class profile.

Mid 50% test scores		Out-of-state:	1%
ACT composite:	18-21	Live on campus:	50%

Basis for selection. School achievement record, class rank, GPA, test scores, extra-curricular activities and honors important. Special consideration given to children of alumni. Recommendations and interviews encouraged. **Homeschooled:** Transcript of courses and grades, state high school equivalency certificate required.

High school preparation. College-preparatory program required. 15 units recommended. Required and recommended units include English 4, mathematics 2, social studies 2, science 2, foreign language 1 and academic electives 2.

2008-2009 Annual costs. Tuition/fees: $19,864. Room/board: $7,570. Books/supplies: $1,000. Personal expenses: $666.

2008-2009 Financial aid. Non-need-based: Scholarships awarded for academics, alumni affiliation, athletics, music/drama.

Application procedures. Admission: No deadline. $25 fee, may be waived for applicants with need. Admission notification on a rolling basis. **Financial aid:** Closing date 4/1. FAFSA required. Applicants notified on a rolling basis starting 3/1; must reply within 4 week(s) of notification.

Academics. Special study options: Accelerated study, combined bachelor's/graduate degree, cooperative education, cross-registration, double major, honors, independent study, internships, liberal arts/career combination, student-designed major, study abroad, teacher certification program. **Credit/placement by examination:** AP, CLEP, SAT, ACT, institutional tests. 15 credit hours maximum toward associate degree, 15 toward bachelor's. **Support services:** Learning center, pre-admission summer program, reduced course load, remedial instruction, study skills assistance, tutoring, writing center.

Majors. Business: Accounting, accounting/business management, business admin, communications, e-commerce, human resources, managerial economics, marketing, organizational behavior. **Communications:** General, journalism. **Computer sciences:** Information systems. **Education:** General, biology, elementary, English, mathematics, middle, science, secondary, social studies, special. **Health:** Athletic training, health services, predental, premedicine. **History:** General. **Interdisciplinary:** Biological/physical sciences. **Legal studies:** Prelaw. **Liberal arts:** Arts/sciences. **Math:** General. **Parks/recreation:** General, exercise sciences, sports admin. **Philosophy/religion:** Philosophy, religion. **Protective services:** Criminal justice, law enforcement admin. **Psychology:** General. **Public administration:** Community org/advocacy. **Social sciences:** General, political science, sociology.

Computing on campus. 69 workstations in dormitories, library, computer center, student center. Dormitories wired for high-speed internet access and linked to campus network. Commuter students can connect to campus network. Online course registration, online library, helpline, repair service, wireless network available.

Student life. Freshman orientation: Mandatory. Held during the summer. **Housing:** Guaranteed on-campus for freshmen. Single-sex dorms available. $125 deposit, deadline 5/1. **Activities:** Bands, choral groups, drama, literary magazine, music ensembles, musical theater, student government, student newspaper, black student union, College Against Cancer, commuter club, gay/straight alliacnce, Knights for Christ, sports medicine association, student activities committee, student business association, Univeristy Players theatre group, University Singers.

Athletics. NAIA, NCAA. **Intercollegiate:** Baseball M, basketball, football (tackle) M, golf M, soccer, softball W, swimming, volleyball W. **Intramural:** Basketball, racquetball, swimming, synchronized swimming W, table tennis, volleyball, weight lifting. **Team name:** Blue Knights.

Student services. Adult student services, alcohol/substance abuse counseling, career counseling, student employment services, financial aid counseling, health services, personal counseling, placement for graduates, veterans' counselor.

Contact. E-mail: admissions@urbana.edu
Phone: (937) 484-1356 Toll-free number: (800) 787-2262 ext. 1356
Fax: (937) 652-6871
James Weisgerber, Executive Director of Enrollment, Urbana University, 579 College Way, Urbana, OH 43078

Ursuline College

Pepper Pike, Ohio — **CB member**
www.ursuline.edu — **CB code: 1848**

- Private 4-year liberal arts college for women affiliated with Roman Catholic Church
- Residential campus in small town
- 1,093 degree-seeking undergraduates: 32% part-time, 93% women, 27% African American, 2% Asian American, 1% Hispanic American
- 323 degree-seeking graduate students
- 43% of applicants admitted
- SAT or ACT (ACT writing optional), application essay required
- 48% graduate within 6 years

General. Founded in 1871. Regionally accredited. Primarily women's college, but some men admitted. **Degrees:** 165 bachelor's awarded; master's offered. **ROTC:** Army. **Location:** 10 miles from Cleveland. **Calendar:** Semester, limited summer session. **Full-time faculty:** 74 total; 62% have terminal degrees, 4% minority, 85% women. **Part-time faculty:** 142 total; 28% have terminal degrees, 11% minority, 69% women. **Class size:** 80% < 20, 20% 20-39.

Freshman class profile. 339 applied, 145 admitted, 113 enrolled.

Mid 50% test scores		**GPA 2.0-2.99:**	33%
SAT critical reading:	370-510	**Rank in top quarter:**	48%
SAT math:	390-520	**Rank in top tenth:**	19%
ACT composite:	18-23	**End year in good standing:**	84%
GPA 3.75 or higher:	14%	**Return as sophomores:**	73%
GPA 3.50-3.74:	19%	**Out-of-state:**	4%
GPA 3.0-3.49:	33%	**Live on campus:**	67%

Basis for selection. Secondary school record, recommendations, standardized test scores and essay very important. Community activities considered. Interview recommended for all. **Homeschooled:** Transcript of courses and grades, state high school equivalency certificate, interview, letter of recommendation (nonparent) required. Official transcript from accrediting agency needed.

High school preparation. College-preparatory program recommended. 18 units recommended. Recommended units include English 4, mathematics 3, social studies 3, science 3 (laboratory 2), foreign language 2 and visual/performing arts 1. One physical education unit recommended. Nursing students should have chemistry.

2008-2009 Annual costs. Tuition/fees: $22,060. Room/board: $7,352. Books/supplies: $1,000. Personal expenses: $700.

2007-2008 Financial aid. **Need-based:** 96 full-time freshmen applied for aid; 86 were judged to have need; 86 of these received aid. Average need met was 87%. Average scholarship/grant was $13,674; average loan $4,615. 46% of total undergraduate aid awarded as scholarships/grants, 54% as loans/jobs. **Non-need-based:** Awarded to 131 full-time undergraduates, including 31 freshmen. Scholarships awarded for academics, art, athletics, leadership, religious affiliation, ROTC.

Application procedures. **Admission:** No deadline. $25 fee, may be waived for applicants with need, free for online applicants. Applicants notified within 3 weeks of application. Must reply by May 1 or within 4 week(s) if notified thereafter. **Financial aid:** Priority date 3/15; no closing date. FAFSA required. Applicants notified on a rolling basis starting 3/1; must reply within 2 week(s) of notification.

Academics. **Special study options:** Accelerated study, combined bachelor's/graduate degree, cooperative education, cross-registration, distance learning, double major, independent study, internships, liberal arts/career combination, New York semester, teacher certification program, weekend college. Optional junior year program in fashion merchandising or design at Fashion Institute of Technology in New York City for enrichment electives only. **Credit/placement by examination:** AP, CLEP, SAT, ACT, institutional tests. 43 credit hours maximum toward bachelor's degree. **Support services:** Learning center, reduced course load, remedial instruction, study skills assistance, tutoring, writing center.

Majors. **Area/ethnic studies:** American. **Biology:** General, biomedical sciences, biotechnology, environmental. **Business:** Accounting, business admin, fashion, human resources, management information systems, marketing. **Communications:** Public relations. **Education:** Art, early childhood, English, mathematics, middle, science, social studies, special. **Family/consumer sciences:** Work/family studies. **Health:** Facilities admin, health care admin, health services, nursing (RN), prenursing, preop/surgical nursing. **History:** General. **Interdisciplinary:** Historic preservation. **Legal studies:** Paralegal. **Liberal arts:** Humanities. **Math:** General. **Philosophy/religion:** Christian, philosophy. **Psychology:** General. **Public administration:** Social work. **Social sciences:** Sociology. **Visual/performing arts:** Art history/conservation, fashion design, graphic design, interior design, studio arts.

Most popular majors. Business/marketing 18%, education 6%, health sciences 44%, legal studies 6%, visual/performing arts 8%.

Computing on campus. 72 workstations in dormitories, library, computer center, student center. Dormitories wired for high-speed internet access and linked to campus network. Online library, wireless network available.

Student life. **Freshman orientation:** Available. Preregistration for classes offered. Three-day program offered prior to start of fall semester. **Housing:** Coed dorms available. $100 fully refundable deposit. **Activities:** Choral groups, drama, literary magazine, student government, student nurses, education association, campus service and spiritual life committees, ethnic groups, public relations society, peer mentors.

Athletics. NAIA. **Intercollegiate:** Basketball W, cross-country W, golf W, soccer W, softball W, tennis W, track and field W, volleyball W. **Team name:** Arrows.

Student services. Adult student services, chaplain/spiritual director, career counseling, student employment services, financial aid counseling, minority student services, personal counseling. **Physically disabled:** Services for visually, speech, hearing impaired.

Contact. E-mail: admission@ursuline.edu
Phone: (440) 449-4203 Toll-free number: (888) 877-8546
Fax: (440) 684-6138
Kimberly Shepherd, Director of Admissions, Ursuline College, 2550 Lander Road, Pepper Pike, OH 44124-4398

Walsh University

North Canton, Ohio — **CB member**
www.walsh.edu — **CB code: 1926**

- Private 4-year university and liberal arts college affiliated with Roman Catholic Church
- Residential campus in small city
- 2,291 degree-seeking undergraduates: 19% part-time, 65% women
- 450 degree-seeking graduate students
- 81% of applicants admitted
- SAT or ACT (ACT writing optional) required
- 54% graduate within 6 years; 26% enter graduate study

General. Founded in 1958. Regionally accredited. **Degrees:** 366 bachelor's awarded; master's, doctoral offered. **Location:** 20 miles from Akron, 60 miles from Cleveland. **Calendar:** Semester, limited summer session. **Full-time faculty:** 108 total; 73% have terminal degrees, 11% minority, 51% women. **Part-time faculty:** 152 total; 13% have terminal degrees, 3% minority, 49% women. **Class size:** 73% < 20, 27% 20-39, less than 1% 40-49. **Special facilities:** Bioinformatics laboratory, prayer garden, museum.

Freshman class profile. 1,493 applied, 1,211 admitted, 516 enrolled.

Mid 50% test scores		**GPA 2.0-2.99:**	30%
SAT critical reading:	440-540	**Rank in top quarter:**	37%
SAT math:	460-560	**Rank in top tenth:**	14%
ACT composite:	19-24	**End year in good standing:**	97%
GPA 3.75 or higher:	22%	**Return as sophomores:**	74%
GPA 3.50-3.74:	17%	**Out-of-state:**	4%
GPA 3.0-3.49:	31%	**Live on campus:**	41%

Basis for selection. Secondary school record and standardized test scores very important; class rank, recommendations, essay, and character important. Essay, interview recommended for all. **Homeschooled:** Transcript of courses and grades required.

High school preparation. College-preparatory program recommended. 16 units recommended. Recommended units include English 4, mathematics 3, social studies 3, science 3, foreign language 2 and academic electives 1. Algebra, biology, and chemistry required for nursing applicants.

2008-2009 Annual costs. Tuition/fees: $20,050. Room/board: $7,760. Books/supplies: $1,000. Personal expenses: $1,158.

2008-2009 Financial aid. Need-based: 513 full-time freshmen applied for aid; 451 were judged to have need; 451 of these received aid. Average need met was 73%. Average scholarship/grant was $4,008; average loan $2,816. 59% of total undergraduate aid awarded as scholarships/grants, 41% as loans/jobs. **Non-need-based:** Awarded to 1,828 full-time undergraduates, including 701 freshmen. Scholarships awarded for academics, alumni affiliation, athletics, music/drama, religious affiliation, state residency.

Application procedures. Admission: Closing date 8/15 (postmark date). $25 fee, may be waived for applicants with need. Admission notification on a rolling basis beginning on or about 10/1. Must reply by 8/15. **Financial aid:** Priority date 3/15; no closing date. FAFSA, institutional form required. Applicants notified on a rolling basis starting 2/15.

Academics. Accelerated degree completion program for adults with evening and weekend classes, multiple locations. Structured first semester available for selected students. **Special study options:** Accelerated study, combined bachelor's/graduate degree, cross-registration, double major, dual enrollment of high school students, ESL, exchange student, external degree, honors, independent study, internships, liberal arts/career combination, study abroad, teacher certification program, Washington semester. CCSA Consortium for Study Abroad, Rome Experience. **Credit/placement by examination:** AP, CLEP, institutional tests. 45 credit hours maximum toward bachelor's degree. **Support services:** Learning center, reduced course load, remedial instruction, study skills assistance, tutoring, writing center.

Honors college/program. 3.75 high school GPA, 27 ACT or 1200 SAT (exclusive of Writing), writing sample and interview required. Special English and history courses, upper-level seminar and thesis courses.

Majors. Biology: General. **Business:** General, accounting, business admin, finance, management information systems, marketing. **Communications:** General. **Computer sciences:** General. **Education:** Early childhood, elementary, emotionally handicapped, English, mathematics, mentally handicapped, middle, multiple handicapped, physical, reading, science, secondary, social science, social studies. **Foreign languages:** French, Spanish. **Health:** Clinical lab science, nursing (RN), predental, premedicine, preveterinary. **History:** General. **Interdisciplinary:** Biological/physical sciences, natural sciences. **Math:** General. **Philosophy/religion:** Philosophy, religion. **Physical sciences:** Chemistry. **Psychology:** General. **Social sciences:** Political science, sociology. **Theology:** Theology.

Most popular majors. Biology 7%, business/marketing 36%, communications/journalism 8%, education 17%, health sciences 11%, psychology 8%.

Computing on campus. 357 workstations in dormitories, library, student center. Dormitories wired for high-speed internet access and linked to campus network. Online course registration, online library, helpline, repair service, wireless network available.

Student life. Freshman orientation: Mandatory, $200 fee. Preregistration for classes offered. Offered 5 weekends before classes begin in August. **Policies:** All full-time undergraduate students 23 and younger must live on campus (some exceptions permitted). **Housing:** Guaranteed on-campus for all undergraduates. Coed dorms, special housing for disabled, apartments, wellness housing available. $200 deposit, deadline 8/15. Apartment-style residence hall with kitchens; quiet, themed floors for first-year students. **Activities:** Pep band, campus ministries, choral groups, dance, drama, international student organizations, literary magazine, music ensembles, radio station, student government, student newspaper, Circle-K, Black student union, Habitat for Humanity, Institute for Justice and Peace, College Democrats, College Republicans, international club, Students for Life.

Athletics. NAIA. **Intercollegiate:** Baseball M, basketball, cheerleading, cross-country, football (tackle) M, golf, soccer, softball W, tennis, track and field, volleyball W. **Intramural:** Basketball, bowling, football (non-tackle), golf, soccer, softball, swimming, table tennis, tennis, volleyball. **Team name:** Cavaliers.

Student services. Adult student services, alcohol/substance abuse counseling, chaplain/spiritual director, career counseling, student employment services, financial aid counseling, health services, minority student services, personal counseling, placement for graduates, veterans' counselor. **Physically disabled:** Services for visually, speech impaired.

Contact. E-mail: admissions@walsh.edu
Phone: (330) 490-7172 Toll-free number: (800) 362-9846
Fax: (330) 490-7165
Brett Freshour, Vice President for Enrollment Management, Walsh University, 2020 East Maple Street NW, North Canton, OH 44720-3396

Wilberforce University

Wilberforce, Ohio — **CB member**
www.wilberforce.edu — **CB code: 1906**

- Private 4-year liberal arts college affiliated with African Methodist Episcopal Church
- Residential campus in rural community
- 807 degree-seeking undergraduates
- 50% of applicants admitted

General. Founded in 1856. Regionally accredited. Cooperative education program required of all students. **Degrees:** 172 bachelor's awarded; master's offered. **ROTC:** Army, Air Force. **Location:** 18 miles from Dayton. **Calendar:** Semester, extensive summer session. **Full-time faculty:** 340 total. **Part-time faculty:** 39 total. **Special facilities:** African Methodist Episcopal Church archives.

Freshman class profile. 2,717 applied, 1,367 admitted, 182 enrolled.

Out-of-state:	67%	**Live on campus:**	94%

Basis for selection. Class rank (top two-thirds), high school GPA, test scores most important. SAT or ACT recommended. Essay, interview recommended.

High school preparation. 15 units required. Required and recommended units include English 4, mathematics 2-3, social studies 2, science 2-3 and foreign language 2.

2008-2009 Annual costs. Tuition/fees: $11,560. Room/board: $5,320. Books/supplies: $1,000. Personal expenses: $1,500.

Application procedures. Admission: Priority date 1/1; deadline 4/1. $25 fee, may be waived for applicants with need. Admission notification on a rolling basis. **Financial aid:** Priority date 3/15, closing date 6/1. FAFSA, institutional form required. Applicants notified on a rolling basis starting 3/15; must reply within 2 week(s) of notification.

Academics. Special study options: Cooperative education, cross-registration, honors, internships, study abroad. **Credit/placement by examination:** AP, CLEP, institutional tests. 30 credit hours maximum toward bachelor's degree. **Support services:** Remedial instruction, tutoring.

Majors. Biology: General. **Business:** Accounting, business admin, finance, managerial economics. **Communications:** Journalism. **Computer sciences:** General, information systems. **Engineering:** Chemical, civil, electrical, mechanical. **Foreign languages:** Comparative lit. **Health:** Health care admin. **Interdisciplinary:** Biological/physical sciences. **Liberal arts:** Arts/sciences. **Math:** General. **Physical sciences:** Chemistry. **Psychology:** General. **Social sciences:** Economics, political science, sociology. **Visual/performing arts:** Studio arts.

Computing on campus. 49 workstations in library, computer center.

Student life. Housing: Guaranteed on-campus for freshmen. Single-sex dorms, apartments available. **Activities:** Choral groups, dance, drama, music ensembles, radio station, student government, student newspaper, Inter-Faith Fellowship, Interdenominational Ministerial Alliance, Alpha-Omega.

Athletics. NAIA. **Intercollegiate:** Basketball, cross-country, golf, track and field. **Intramural:** Baseball M, basketball, softball, table tennis, tennis, volleyball.

Student services. Career counseling, student employment services, health services, personal counseling, placement for graduates, veterans' counselor.

Contact. E-mail: admissions@wilberforce.edu
Phone: (937) 708-5721 Toll-free number: (800) 367-8568
Fax: (937) 376-4751
Kenya Messer, Vice President for Stidemt Development, Wilberforce University, 1055 North Bickett Road, Wilberforce, OH 45384-1001

Wilmington College

Wilmington, Ohio — **CB member**
www.wilmington.edu — **CB code: 1909**

- Private 4-year liberal arts college affiliated with Society of Friends (Quaker)
- Residential campus in large town
- 1,440 degree-seeking undergraduates: 17% part-time, 55% women, 10% African American, 1% Hispanic American, 1% international
- 46 graduate students
- 90% of applicants admitted
- SAT or ACT (ACT writing optional) required
- 55% graduate within 6 years

General. Founded in 1870. Regionally accredited. Affiliated with Wilmington Yearly Meeting of the Religious Society of Friends. Branch campuses in Cincinnati and other locations. BA in business offered at Cincinnati branch and Wilmington evening program. **Degrees:** 307 bachelor's awarded; master's offered. **Location:** 50 miles from Cincinnati, 60 miles from Columbus. **Calendar:** Semester, limited summer session. **Full-time faculty:** 72 total; 69% have terminal degrees, 1% minority, 43% women. **Part-time faculty:** 50 total; 52% women. **Class size:** 65% < 20, 33% 20-39, 2% 40-49. **Special facilities:** Greenhouse, herbarium, observatory, electron microscope, live animal area, sports medicine center, Peace Resource Center containing Hiroshima/Nagasaki Memorial collection.

Freshman class profile. 1,709 applied, 1,538 admitted, 354 enrolled.

Mid 50% test scores		**GPA 2.0-2.99:**	40%
SAT critical reading:	410-540	**Rank in top quarter:**	39%
SAT math:	410-540	**Rank in top tenth:**	16%
ACT composite:	17-22	**Return as sophomores:**	63%
GPA 3.75 or higher:	21%	**Out-of-state:**	2%
GPA 3.50-3.74:	12%	**Live on campus:**	80%
GPA 3.0-3.49:	26%	**International:**	1%

Basis for selection. Previous academic record, test scores, counselor recommendation, and interview important. Essay, interview recommended for all.

High school preparation. College-preparatory program recommended. 16 units required. Required and recommended units include English 4, mathematics 2, social studies 2, science 2 (laboratory 2), foreign language 2 and academic electives 4. 6 art units recommended.

2008-2009 Annual costs. Tuition/fees: $23,372. Room/board: $8,010. Books/supplies: $500. Personal expenses: $450.

Financial aid. Non-need-based: Scholarships awarded for academics, alumni affiliation, religious affiliation, state residency.

Application procedures. Admission: No deadline. $25 fee, may be waived for applicants with need, free for online applicants. Admission notification on a rolling basis. Online application does not require application fee. **Financial aid:** Priority date 3/31, closing date 6/1. FAFSA required. Applicants notified on a rolling basis starting 3/1; must reply by 5/1 or within 2 week(s) of notification.

Academics. Special study options: Cross-registration, double major, dual enrollment of high school students, honors, independent study, internships, liberal arts/career combination, student-designed major, study abroad, teacher certification program, Washington semester, weekend college. **Credit/placement by examination:** AP, CLEP, IB, SAT, ACT, institutional tests. 30 credit hours maximum toward bachelor's degree. **Support services:** Learning center, reduced course load, remedial instruction, study skills assistance, tutoring, writing center.

Majors. Agriculture: Agribusiness operations, agronomy, animal sciences, business, equine science, farm/ranch, production. **Biology:** General, bacteriology, biochemistry, environmental. **Business:** Accounting, business admin, management science, marketing, sales/distribution. **Communications:** General, journalism, media studies, public relations. **Computer sciences:** General, computer science. **Education:** General, agricultural, biology, chemistry, early childhood, elementary, English, health, history, mathematics, middle, multi-level teacher, physical, science, secondary, social science, social studies. **Foreign languages:** Spanish. **History:** General. **Legal studies:** Prelaw. **Liberal arts:** Arts/sciences. **Math:** General. **Parks/recreation:** Sports admin. **Physical sciences:** Astronomy, chemistry, geology, planetary. **Protective services:** Criminal justice. **Psychology:** General. **Public administration:** Social work. **Social sciences:** General, economics, political science, sociology. **Visual/performing arts:** Art, commercial/advertising art, dramatic.

Most popular majors. Business/marketing 25%, education 23%, psychology 7%.

Computing on campus. 156 workstations in library, computer center. Dormitories wired for high-speed internet access and linked to campus network. Commuter students can connect to campus network. Online course registration, helpline, student web hosting available.

Student life. Freshman orientation: Mandatory. Held 3 days prior to start of fall semester. **Housing:** Guaranteed on-campus for all undergraduates. Coed dorms, single-sex dorms, apartments, fraternity/sorority housing available. $100 nonrefundable deposit, deadline 8/15. Living/learning units available. **Activities:** Campus ministries, choral groups, drama, international student organizations, literary magazine, music ensembles, musical theater, student government, student newspaper, social service, international club, education club, agriculture club, Christian Students, Young Friends (Quaker-Christian group), sports medicine association.

Athletics. NCAA. **Intercollegiate:** Baseball M, basketball, cheerleading, cross-country, football (tackle), golf, soccer, softball W, swimming, tennis, track and field, volleyball W, wrestling M. **Intramural:** Basketball, football (non-tackle), racquetball, soccer, softball, squash, table tennis, tennis, volleyball, weight lifting. **Team name:** Quakers.

Student services. Adult student services, alcohol/substance abuse counseling, chaplain/spiritual director, career counseling, student employment services, financial aid counseling, health services, minority student services, personal counseling, placement for graduates, veterans' counselor.

Contact. E-mail: admissions@wilmington.edu
Phone: (800) 341-9318 ext. 260 Fax: (937) 382-7077
Tina Garland, Director of Admission, Wilmington College, Box 1325 Pyle Center, Wilmington, OH 45177

Wittenberg University

Springfield, Ohio — **CB member**
www.wittenberg.edu — **CB code: 1922**

- Private 4-year liberal arts college affiliated with Evangelical Lutheran Church in America
- Residential campus in small city
- 1,811 degree-seeking undergraduates: 1% part-time, 56% women
- 4 degree-seeking graduate students
- 69% of applicants admitted
- Application essay required
- 61% graduate within 6 years

General. Founded in 1845. Regionally accredited. **Degrees:** 452 bachelor's awarded; master's offered. **ROTC:** Army, Air Force. **Location:** 25 miles from Dayton, 45 miles from Columbus. **Calendar:** Semester, limited summer session. **Full-time faculty:** 142 total; 92% have terminal degrees, 7% minority, 42% women. **Part-time faculty:** 54 total; 28% have terminal degrees, 7% minority, 50% women. **Class size:** 61% < 20, 38% 20-39, less than 1% 40-49, less than 1% 50-99, less than 1% >100. **Special facilities:** Observatory, East Asian art collection, Martin Luther library collection, humanities and technology center.

Freshman class profile. 3,344 applied, 2,299 admitted, 510 enrolled.

Mid 50% test scores		**GPA 2.0-2.99:**	20%
SAT critical reading:	520-640	**Rank in top quarter:**	61%
SAT math:	540-590	**Rank in top tenth:**	33%
ACT composite:	23-29	**Return as sophomores:**	73%
GPA 3.75 or higher:	36%	**Out-of-state:**	34%
GPA 3.50-3.74:	16%	**Live on campus:**	95%
GPA 3.0-3.49:	27%	**International:**	3%

Basis for selection. In order of importance: school achievement record, courses taken, school attended, trend in work, test scores, counselor recommendation, extracurricular activities, and interview. Special consideration for children of alumni, minorities, Lutherans, residents of Clark County, and international students. Math and foreign language placement tests required. Interview recommended for all; portfolio required for art program; audition recommended for dance, music, theater programs. **Homeschooled:** On-campus interview.

High school preparation. Required and recommended units include English 4, mathematics 3-4, history 2-3, science 3-5 (laboratory 2) and foreign language 2-3.

2008-2009 Annual costs. Tuition/fees: $33,236. Room/board: $8,314. Books/supplies: $1,000. Personal expenses: $1,200.

2007-2008 Financial aid. All financial aid based on need. **Additional information:** Auditions required from applicants for music, theater, and dance scholarships. Portfolio required of applicants for art scholarships.

Application procedures. Admission: Closing date 3/15 (postmark date). $40 fee, may be waived for applicants with need. Admission notification on a rolling basis. Must reply by May 1 or within 2 week(s) if notified thereafter. **Financial aid:** Priority date 3/15; no closing date. FAFSA required. Applicants notified on a rolling basis starting 3/1; must reply by 5/1 or within 2 week(s) of notification.

Academics. Special study options: Combined bachelor's/graduate degree, cross-registration, double major, dual enrollment of high school students, honors, independent study, internships, liberal arts/career combination, student-designed major, study abroad, teacher certification program, urban semester, Washington semester, weekend college. Semester programs with Duke University (marine biology), School of Visual Arts in New York, Camarillo Hospital in California, National Institutes of Health in Washington, D.C., Washington University (MO) (occupational therapy), Johns Hopkins Nursing Program; 3-2 engineering with Washington University (MO), Case Western Reserve University. **Credit/placement by examination:** AP, CLEP, IB, institutional tests. **Support services:** Learning center, pre-admission summer program, reduced course load, study skills assistance, tutoring, writing center.

Majors. Area/ethnic studies: American, East Asian, European, Russian/Slavic. **Biology:** General, biochemistry, molecular. **Business:** General, business admin, managerial economics, marketing. **Communications:** General. **Computer sciences:** Computer science. **Conservation:** Environmental studies. **Education:** General, elementary. **Foreign languages:** French, German, Spanish. **History:** General. **Interdisciplinary:** Biological/physical sciences, biopsychology, global studies, math/computer science. **Liberal arts:** Arts/sciences. **Math:** General. **Philosophy/religion:** Philosophy, religion. **Physical sciences:** General, chemistry, geology, physics. **Psychology:** General. **Social sciences:** General, economics, geography, political science, sociology, urban studies. **Visual/performing arts:** General, art.

Most popular majors. Biology 13%, business/marketing 12%, communications/journalism 7%, education 9%, English 8%, psychology 9%, social sciences 16%.

Computing on campus. 900 workstations in dormitories, library, computer center, student center. Dormitories wired for high-speed internet access and linked to campus network. Commuter students can connect to campus network. Online course registration, online library, helpline, student web hosting, wireless network available.

Student life. Freshman orientation: Mandatory. Preregistration for classes offered. Pre-orientation days offered 3 times during the summer. Full orientation held 3 days before the beginning of fall classes. **Housing:** Guaranteed on-campus for all undergraduates. Coed dorms, single-sex dorms, apartments, fraternity/sorority housing, wellness housing available. $400 deposit, deadline 7/1. Substance-free residence hall, honors residence hall, special theme halls available. **Activities:** Bands, campus ministries, choral groups, dance, drama, international student organizations, literary magazine, music ensembles, Model UN, musical theater, opera, radio station, student government, student newspaper, symphony orchestra, Newman club, Concerned Black Students, community volunteer service, Weaver Chapel Association, Project Woman, East Asian studies club, Hillel, Amnesty International, Habitat for Humanity.

Athletics. NCAA. **Intercollegiate:** Baseball M, basketball, cheerleading, cross-country, diving, field hockey W, football (tackle) M, golf, lacrosse, soccer, softball W, swimming, tennis, track and field, volleyball W. **Intramural:** Badminton, basketball, bowling, cricket M, diving, fencing, football (non-tackle), golf, gymnastics, handball M, ice hockey M, judo, racquetball, rugby, sailing, skiing, skin diving, soccer, softball, squash, swimming, table tennis, tennis, track and field, volleyball, water polo M, weight lifting. **Team name:** Tigers.

Student services. Adult student services, alcohol/substance abuse counseling, chaplain/spiritual director, career counseling, student employment services, financial aid counseling, health services, minority student services, personal counseling, placement for graduates, veterans' counselor, women's services.

Contact. E-mail: admission@wittenberg.edu
Phone: (937) 327-6314 Toll-free number: (877) 206-0332 ext. 6314
Fax: (937) 327-6379
Karen Hunt, Director of Admission, Wittenberg University, Ward Street and North Wittenberg, Springfield, OH 45501-0720

Wright State University

Dayton, Ohio — **CB member**
www.wright.edu — **CB code: 1179**

- Public 4-year university
- Commuter campus in small city
- 12,326 degree-seeking undergraduates: 12% part-time, 55% women, 15% African American, 3% Asian American, 2% Hispanic American, 1% international
- 3,574 degree-seeking graduate students
- 85% of applicants admitted
- 42% graduate within 6 years

General. Founded in 1964. Regionally accredited. **Degrees:** 2,382 bachelor's, 59 associate awarded; master's, doctoral, first professional offered. **ROTC:** Army, Air Force. **Location:** 10 miles from downtown. **Calendar:** Quarter, extensive summer session. **Full-time faculty:** 840 total; 42% women. **Part-time faculty:** 23 total; 30% women. **Class size:** 39% < 20, 45% 20-39, 6% 40-49, 6% 50-99, 2% >100. **Special facilities:** Biological preserve, disabled-accessible garden of the senses.

Freshman class profile. 6,143 applied, 5,252 admitted, 2,502 enrolled.

Mid 50% test scores		**Rank in top quarter:**	35%
SAT critical reading:	440-550	**Rank in top tenth:**	14%
SAT math:	430-570	**Return as sophomores:**	70%
ACT composite:	18-24	**Out-of-state:**	3%
GPA 3.75 or higher:	17%	**Live on campus:**	58%
GPA 3.50-3.74:	12%	**International:**	1%
GPA 3.0-3.49:	28%	**Fraternities:**	5%
GPA 2.0-2.99:	40%	**Sororities:**	3%

Basis for selection. Liberal admission policy. College-preparatory curriculum, 2.0 GPA required. Test scores important for selected programs. Audition required for acting, dance, directing/stage management, music programs; portfolio required for art, art education programs.

High school preparation. 15 units required. Required units include English 4, mathematics 3, social studies 3, science 3 (laboratory 3) and foreign language 2. Math requirement includes 2 algebra. Art, music or theater recommended. Students not meeting course recommendations must make up deficiency prior to admission to program.

2008-2009 Annual costs. Tuition/fees: $7,278; $14,004 out-of-state. Room/board: $7,180.

2007-2008 Financial aid. Need-based: 1,926 full-time freshmen applied for aid; 1,569 were judged to have need; 1,562 of these received aid. Average need met was 62%. Average scholarship/grant was $4,362; average loan $3,602. 30% of total undergraduate aid awarded as scholarships/grants, 70% as loans/jobs. **Non-need-based:** Awarded to 1,388 full-time undergraduates, including 432 freshmen. Scholarships awarded for academics, alumni affiliation, art, athletics, leadership, minority status, music/drama, ROTC.

Application procedures. Admission: No deadline. $30 fee. Admission notification on a rolling basis beginning on or about 10/1. Application by January recommended for students desiring on-campus housing. **Financial aid:** Priority date 2/15; no closing date. FAFSA required. Applicants notified on a rolling basis starting 3/15.

Academics. Special study options: Cooperative education, cross-registration, distance learning, double major, ESL, honors, independent study, internships, student-designed major, study abroad, teacher certification program. **Credit/placement by examination:** AP, CLEP, institutional tests. **Support services:** Learning center, pre-admission summer program, reduced course load, remedial instruction, tutoring, writing center.

Majors. Area/ethnic studies: African-American, women's. **Biology:** General, anatomy, biochemistry, pharmacology/toxicology. **Business:** Accounting, business admin, human resources, management information systems, management science, managerial economics, marketing, statistics. **Communications:** General, media studies, organizational. **Computer sciences:** General, computer science, information systems. **Education:** Art, business, early childhood, elementary, English, foreign languages, learning disabled, mathematics, mentally handicapped, multiple handicapped, music, physical, science, social studies. **Engineering:** General, biomedical, computer, electrical, materials, mechanical, physics, science, systems. **Engineering technology:** Biomedical, environmental. **Foreign languages:** General, classics, French, German, Latin, linguistics, modern Greek, Spanish. **Health:** Adult health nursing, clinical lab science, environmental health, nursing (RN), predental, premedicine, prepharmacy, preveterinary, vocational rehab counseling. **History:** General. **Interdisciplinary:** Systems science. **Legal studies:** Prelaw. **Liberal arts:** Arts/sciences. **Math:** General, applied, statistics. **Military:** General. **Philosophy/religion:** Philosophy, religion. **Physical sciences:** Chemistry, geology, physics. **Protective services:** Police science. **Psychology:**

General. **Public administration:** General, social work. **Social sciences:** Anthropology, criminology, economics, geography, international relations, political science, sociology, urban studies. **Visual/performing arts:** Art, art history/conservation, arts management, dance, dramatic, drawing, film/cinema, music history, music performance, music theory/composition, photography, theater design.

Most popular majors. Business/marketing 18%, education 23%, engineering/engineering technologies 7%, health sciences 11%, psychology 7%.

Computing on campus. 600 workstations in dormitories, library, computer center, student center. Dormitories wired for high-speed internet access. Commuter students can connect to campus network. Online course registration, online library, helpline, repair service, student web hosting, wireless network available.

Student life. Freshman orientation: Available. Preregistration for classes offered. **Housing:** Coed dorms, special housing for disabled, apartments available. Honors dorm available. **Activities:** Bands, choral groups, dance, drama, literary magazine, music ensembles, musical theater, opera, radio station, student government, student newspaper, symphony orchestra, TV station, Black Student Union, Baptist Student Union, Student Association for Escorts (SAFE), College Students for Special Wish, Fellowship of Christian Students, Circle-K, Model United Nations, Campus Crusade for Christ, Ohio College Democrats, Jewish Student Union.

Athletics. NCAA. **Intercollegiate:** Baseball M, basketball, cheerleading, cross-country, diving, golf M, soccer, softball W, swimming, tennis, track and field W, volleyball W. **Intramural:** Archery, baseball M, basketball, cricket M, cross-country, football (tackle), golf, handball, lacrosse M, soccer, softball, squash, tennis, volleyball W. **Team name:** Raiders.

Student services. Adult student services, chaplain/spiritual director, career counseling, student employment services, financial aid counseling, health services, legal services, minority student services, personal counseling, placement for graduates, veterans' counselor, women's services. **Physically disabled:** Services for visually, speech, hearing impaired.

Contact. E-mail: admissions@wright.edu
Phone: (937) 775-5700 Toll-free number: (800) 247-1770
Fax: (937) 775-5795
Cathy Davis, Director of Admissions, Wright State University, 3640 Colonel Glenn Highway, Dayton, OH 45435

Xavier University

Cincinnati, Ohio — **CB member**
www.xavier.edu — **CB code: 1965**

- Private 4-year university affiliated with Roman Catholic Church
- Residential campus in large city
- 3,780 degree-seeking undergraduates: 10% part-time, 56% women, 12% African American, 2% Asian American, 3% Hispanic American, 2% international
- 2,428 degree-seeking graduate students
- 76% of applicants admitted
- SAT or ACT (ACT writing optional), application essay required
- 79% graduate within 6 years; 19% enter graduate study

General. Founded in 1831. Regionally accredited. **Degrees:** 930 bachelor's, 18 associate awarded; master's, doctoral offered. **ROTC:** Army, Air Force. **Location:** 5 miles from downtown. **Calendar:** Semester, limited summer session. **Full-time faculty:** 311 total; 80% have terminal degrees, 17% minority, 47% women. **Part-time faculty:** 319 total; 24% have terminal degrees, 9% minority, 52% women. **Class size:** 50% < 20, 48% 20-39, 1% 40-49, less than 1% 50-99, less than 1% >100.

Freshman class profile. 6,151 applied, 4,699 admitted, 860 enrolled.

Mid 50% test scores		**GPA 2.0-2.99:**	17%
SAT critical reading:	500-610	**Rank in top quarter:**	60%
SAT math:	500-610	**Rank in top tenth:**	27%
SAT writing:	500-600	**End year in good standing:**	90%
ACT composite:	22-28	**Return as sophomores:**	87%
GPA 3.75 or higher:	36%	**Out-of-state:**	44%
GPA 3.50-3.74:	18%	**Live on campus:**	89%
GPA 3.0-3.49:	29%	**International:**	1%

Basis for selection. Curriculum, grades, ACT or SAT scores, counselor recommendations, essay, and activities. Campus visit recommended for all students. **Homeschooled:** Statement describing homeschool structure and mission, transcript of courses and grades, interview, letter of recommendation (nonparent) required.

High school preparation. College-preparatory program recommended. 21 units recommended. Recommended units include English 4, mathematics 3, social studies 3, science 3, foreign language 2 and academic electives 5. 1 health/physical education recommended.

2008-2009 Annual costs. Tuition/fees: $26,860. Room/board: $9,270.

2008-2009 Financial aid. Need-based: 676 full-time freshmen applied for aid; 531 were judged to have need; 530 of these received aid. Average need met was 78%. Average scholarship/grant was $11,289; average loan $4,470. 60% of total undergraduate aid awarded as scholarships/grants, 40% as loans/jobs. **Non-need-based:** Awarded to 1,522 full-time undergraduates, including 374 freshmen. Scholarships awarded for academics, alumni affiliation, art, athletics, leadership, music/drama, religious affiliation.

Application procedures. Admission: Closing date 2/1. $35 fee, may be waived for applicants with need, free for online applicants. Admission notification on a rolling basis beginning on or about 10/15. Must reply by May 1 or within 2 week(s) if notified thereafter. **Financial aid:** Priority date 2/15; no closing date. FAFSA required. Applicants notified on a rolling basis starting 2/15; must reply by 5/1.

Academics. Strong emphasis on ethics and values in core curriculum. **Special study options:** Combined bachelor's/graduate degree, cooperative education, cross-registration, double major, dual enrollment of high school students, ESL, honors, independent study, internships, study abroad, teacher certification program, urban semester, Washington semester, weekend college. Cooperative science-engineering program (physics and chemistry) with University of Cincinnati, forestry program and environmental management programs with Duke University, Service Learning Semester. **Credit/placement by examination:** AP, CLEP, IB, institutional tests. 30 credit hours maximum toward associate degree, 60 toward bachelor's. **Support services:** Learning center, pre-admission summer program, reduced course load, remedial instruction, study skills assistance, tutoring, writing center.

Majors. Biology: General. **Business:** General, accounting, business admin, entrepreneurial studies, finance, human resources, international, management information systems, managerial economics, marketing. **Communications:** Advertising, organizational, public relations, radio/tv. **Computer sciences:** Computer science. **Conservation:** Management/policy. **Education:** General, biology, chemistry, early childhood, middle, Montessori teacher, music, physics, secondary, special. **Foreign languages:** Classics, French, German, Spanish. **Health:** Athletic training, clinical lab science, nursing (RN). **History:** General. **Interdisciplinary:** Natural sciences. **Liberal arts:** Arts/sciences. **Math:** General. **Parks/recreation:** Sports admin. **Philosophy/religion:** Philosophy. **Physical sciences:** Chemistry, physics. **Protective services:** Criminal justice. **Psychology:** General. **Public administration:** Social work. **Social sciences:** Economics, international relations, political science, sociology. **Theology:** Theology. **Visual/performing arts:** Studio arts.

Most popular majors. Business/marketing 26%, communications/journalism 7%, education 6%, health sciences 7%, liberal arts 16%, social sciences 7%.

Computing on campus. 250 workstations in dormitories, library, student center. Dormitories wired for high-speed internet access and linked to campus network. Commuter students can connect to campus network. Online course registration, online library, helpline, repair service, student web hosting, wireless network available.

Student life. Freshman orientation: Mandatory, $175 fee. Preregistration for classes offered. Held the weekend before the start of classes. **Policies:** Student handbook, responsible computer use, university alcohol policy, harassment code accountability procedures. **Housing:** Guaranteed on-campus for freshmen. Coed dorms, special housing for disabled, apartments available. $200 fully refundable deposit, deadline 5/1. **Activities:** Bands, campus ministries, choral groups, dance, drama, film society, international student organizations, literary magazine, music ensembles, musical theater, opera, radio station, student government, student newspaper, symphony orchestra, TV station, Life after Sunday, Xavier Interfaith, South Asian Society, St. Vincent DePaul Society, Natural Ties, Black student association, College Republicans, College Democrats, Voices of Solidarity, Student Organization of Latinos.

Athletics. NCAA. **Intercollegiate:** Baseball M, basketball, cheerleading, cross-country, golf, soccer, swimming, tennis, track and field, volleyball W. **Intramural:** Basketball, bowling, football (non-tackle), racquetball, soccer, softball, tennis, volleyball. **Team name:** Musketeers.

Student services. Adult student services, alcohol/substance abuse counseling, chaplain/spiritual director, career counseling, services for economically disadvantaged, student employment services, financial aid counseling, health services, minority student services, personal counseling, placement for graduates, veterans' counselor. **Physically disabled:** Services for visually, speech, hearing impaired. **Learning disabled:** Comprehensive services available.

Contact. E-mail: xuadmit@xavier.edu
Phone: (513) 745-3301 Toll-free number: (877) 982-3648
Fax: (513) 745-4319
Aaron Meis, Dean of Admissions, Xavier University, 3800 Victory Parkway, Cincinnati, OH 45207-5311

Youngstown State University
Youngstown, Ohio
www.ysu.edu **CB code: 1975**

- Public 4-year university
- Commuter campus in small city
- 12,090 degree-seeking undergraduates: 19% part-time, 54% women, 15% African American, 1% Asian American, 2% Hispanic American, 1% international
- 1,181 degree-seeking graduate students
- 35% graduate within 6 years

General. Founded in 1908. Regionally accredited. **Degrees:** 1,478 bachelor's, 226 associate awarded; master's, doctoral offered. **ROTC:** Army, Air Force. **Location:** 60 miles from Cleveland, 60 miles from Pittsburgh. **Calendar:** Semester, limited summer session. **Full-time faculty:** 430 total. **Part-time faculty:** 570 total. **Special facilities:** Planetarium, historic preservation center.

Freshman class profile. 4,489 applied, 3,652 admitted, 2,175 enrolled.

Mid 50% test scores			
SAT critical reading:	400-520	GPA 2.0-2.99:	42%
SAT math:	410-540	Rank in top quarter:	23%
SAT writing:	390-510	Rank in top tenth:	8%
ACT composite:	17-23	Out-of-state:	14%
GPA 3.75 or higher:	10%	Live on campus:	19%
GPA 3.50-3.74:	11%	Fraternities:	2%
GPA 3.0-3.49:	26%	Sororities:	3%

Basis for selection. Open admission, but selective for some programs and for out-of-state students. Out-of-state applicants must be in top two-thirds of class, or have 17 ACT or 820 SAT. Open admission policy for Ohio residents and Mercer and Lawrence County, Pennsylvania residents. Special requirements for nursing, engineering and some other programs. Interview required for BS/MD program; audition required for music, BFA theater programs. **Homeschooled:** Transcript of courses and grades required. ACT or SAT required unless out of high school 2 or more years. Copy of academic assessment reports submitted to appropriate superintendent of school and copy of Superintendent's Exemption Notice showing the student is excused to receive home schooling required. Curriculum outline, detailing course content, textbooks used and any other relevant information regarding coursework must be submitted.

High school preparation. College-preparatory program recommended. 16 units recommended. Recommended units include English 4, mathematics 3, social studies 3, science 2 (laboratory 1) and foreign language 2. 1 fine and performing arts recommended. Recommended coursework should include English composition; algebra I and II, geometry; laboratory science; and US history and government.

2008-2009 Annual costs. Tuition/fees: $6,721; $12,394 out-of-state. Residents of any out-of-state area within 100 miles of campus are charged $9,414 yearly tuition. Per credit hour charge is $392. Room/board: $7,090. Books/supplies: $1,140. Personal expenses: $500.

2007-2008 Financial aid. Need-based: 33% of total undergraduate aid awarded as scholarships/grants, 67% as loans/jobs. **Non-need-based:** Scholarships awarded for academics, alumni affiliation, athletics, ROTC, state residency.

Application procedures. Admission: Priority date 2/15; deadline 8/15. $30 fee, may be waived for applicants with need. Admission notification on a rolling basis. Students who apply by February 15 eligible for early registration and orientation. **Financial aid:** Priority date 2/15; no closing date. FAFSA, institutional form required. Applicants notified on a rolling basis starting 5/30; must reply within 2 week(s) of notification.

Academics. Special study options: Accelerated study, combined bachelor's/graduate degree, cooperative education, cross-registration, distance learning, double major, ESL, exchange student, honors, internships, student-designed major, study abroad, teacher certification program, urban semester, Washington semester, weekend college. Off-campus study with Lorain County Community College. **Credit/placement by examination:** AP, CLEP, IB, institutional tests. In select CLEP and AP tests, higher grade may make student eligible for more credits. **Support services:** Learning center, pre-admission summer program, reduced course load, remedial instruction, study skills assistance, tutoring, writing center.

Majors. Area/ethnic studies: African-American, American. **Biology:** General. **Business:** General, accounting, apparel, banking/financial services, business admin, fashion, finance, financial planning, hospitality admin, hospitality/recreation, human resources, management information systems, managerial economics, marketing, merchandising, office management, operations, public finance, purchasing, retailing, sales/distribution, selling, tourism promotion, tourism/travel. **Communications:** General, advertising, journalism, public relations, radio/tv. **Computer sciences:** General, computer science, information systems, information technology, programming. **Conservation:** Environmental science. **Education:** General, art, autistic, biology, business, chemistry, computer, drama/dance, early childhood, elementary, emotionally handicapped, English, family/consumer sciences, foreign languages, French, health, health occupations, history, kindergarten/preschool, learning disabled, mathematics, mentally handicapped, middle, multi-level teacher, multiple handicapped, music, physical, physics, science, secondary, social science, social studies, Spanish, special, speech. **Engineering:** General, chemical, civil, computer, electrical, industrial, materials, mechanical, structural. **Engineering technology:** General, civil, electrical, mechanical. **Family/consumer sciences:** General, clothing/textiles, family studies, family/community services, food/nutrition, work/family studies. **Foreign languages:** General, French, German, Italian, Spanish. **Health:** Athletic training, clinical lab science, community health, community health services, dietetics, facilities admin, nursing (RN), predental, premedicine, prepharmacy, preveterinary, public health ed, respiratory therapy technology. **History:** General. **Legal studies:** Prelaw. **Math:** General. **Parks/recreation:** Exercise sciences, health/fitness, sports admin. **Philosophy/religion:** Philosophy, religion. **Physical sciences:** General, astronomy, chemistry, geology, physics, planetary. **Protective services:** Corrections, criminal justice, forensics, law enforcement admin, security services. **Psychology:** General. **Public administration:** General, social work. **Social sciences:** General, anthropology, econometrics, economics, geography, international economics, political science, sociology. **Visual/performing arts:** General, acting, art, art history/conservation, commercial/advertising art, dramatic, jazz, music history, music performance, music theory/composition, painting, photography, piano/organ, printmaking, stringed instruments, studio arts, theater design, voice/opera.

Most popular majors. Business/marketing 15%, engineering/engineering technologies 7%, health sciences 11%, liberal arts 6%, security/protective services 6%.

Computing on campus. 170 workstations in dormitories, library, student center. Dormitories wired for high-speed internet access and linked to campus network. Commuter students can connect to campus network. Online course registration, online library, helpline, repair service, student web hosting, wireless network available.

Student life. Freshman orientation: Available, $50 fee. Orientation held in June, July, and August. **Housing:** Guaranteed on-campus for all undergraduates. Coed dorms, single-sex dorms, apartments, fraternity/sorority housing, wellness housing available. $200 deposit. University scholars program honors facility available. **Activities:** Bands, choral groups, dance, drama, literary magazine, music ensembles, musical theater, opera, radio station, student government, student newspaper, symphony orchestra, College Republicans, Student Democrats, Pan-African student union, National Panhellenic Council, Hispanic-American organization, student athlete advisory council, interfraternity council, Golden Key, Omicron Delta Kappa, gospel choir, Panhellenic Council.

Athletics. NCAA. **Intercollegiate:** Baseball M, basketball, cross-country, football (tackle) M, golf, soccer W, softball W, swimming W, tennis, track and field, volleyball W. **Intramural:** Badminton, basketball, bowling, football (non-tackle), golf, handball, ice hockey, lacrosse, racquetball, soccer, softball, swimming, table tennis, tennis, volleyball, water polo. **Team name:** Penguins.

Student services. Adult student services, alcohol/substance abuse counseling, chaplain/spiritual director, career counseling, student employment services, financial aid counseling, health services, minority student services, on-campus daycare, personal counseling, placement for graduates, veterans' counselor, women's services. **Physically disabled:** Services for visually, speech, hearing impaired.

Contact. E-mail: enroll@ysu.edu
Phone: (330) 941-2000 Toll-free number: (877) 468-6978
Fax: (330) 941-3674
Sue Davis, Director of Undergraduate Admissions, Youngstown State University, One University Plaza, Youngstown, OH 44555-0001

Oklahoma

Bacone College
Muskogee, Oklahoma
www.bacone.edu **CB code: 6030**

- Private 4-year liberal arts college affiliated with American Baptist Churches in the USA
- Residential campus in large town
- 928 degree-seeking undergraduates: 12% part-time, 52% women, 24% African American, 1% Asian American, 6% Hispanic American, 30% Native American
- 55% of applicants admitted
- SAT or ACT required

General. Founded in 1880. Regionally accredited. American Indian heritage and commitment to serving Native Americans. Guided by Christian principles. **Degrees:** 80 bachelor's, 84 associate awarded. **Location:** 50 miles from Tulsa. **Calendar:** Semester, limited summer session. **Full-time faculty:** 26 total; 54% have terminal degrees, 35% minority, 73% women. **Part-time faculty:** 42 total; 17% have terminal degrees, 36% minority, 62% women. **Class size:** 70% < 20, 25% 20-39, 5% 40-49. **Special facilities:** Native American museum and collection.

Freshman class profile. 1,261 applied, 697 admitted, 245 enrolled.

Mid 50% test scores		**GPA 2.0-2.99:**	56%
SAT critical reading:	380-460	**Rank in top quarter:**	17%
SAT math:	360-460	**Rank in top tenth:**	5%
ACT composite:	16-20	**End year in good standing:**	54%
GPA 3.75 or higher:	6%	**Return as sophomores:**	29%
GPA 3.50-3.74:	10%	**Out-of-state:**	39%
GPA 3.0-3.49:	26%	**Live on campus:**	78%

Basis for selection. 2.0 GPA and 18 ACT required. Additional standards for admission to nursing and radiography programs. ACT results used as basis for counseling. Interview recommended for nursing, radiologic technology programs. **Homeschooled:** Official transcript from accredited homeschool organization or GED required.

High school preparation. College-preparatory program recommended. Recommended units include English 4, mathematics 3, history 2, science 2 (laboratory 2).

2009-2010 Annual costs. Tuition/fees (projected): $11,700. Room/board: $8,000. Books/supplies: $1,000. Personal expenses: $500.

2008-2009 Financial aid. All financial aid based on need.

Application procedures. Admission: No deadline. $25 fee, may be waived for applicants with need, free for online applicants. Admission notification on a rolling basis. **Financial aid:** Priority date 3/31; no closing date. FAFSA required. Applicants notified on a rolling basis starting 4/1; must reply within 2 week(s) of notification.

Academics. Special study options: Accelerated study, cross-registration, double major, dual enrollment of high school students, independent study, internships, liberal arts/career combination, student-designed major, teacher certification program. **Credit/placement by examination:** AP, CLEP, SAT, ACT, institutional tests. 15 credit hours maximum toward associate degree. **Support services:** Learning center, pre-admission summer program, remedial instruction, study skills assistance, tutoring.

Majors. Area/ethnic studies: Native American. **Business:** Business admin. **Education:** Early childhood, elementary, health, physical. **Health:** Medical radiologic technology/radiation therapy, nursing (RN). **Parks/recreation:** Exercise sciences, facilities management, sports admin. **Protective services:** Criminal justice. **Other:** Christian ministry.

Most popular majors. Business/marketing 12%, education 61%, parks/recreation 13%, social sciences 11%.

Computing on campus. 84 workstations in library, computer center. Dormitories wired for high-speed internet access and linked to campus network. Commuter students can connect to campus network. Online library, wireless network available.

Student life. Freshman orientation: Mandatory. Preregistration for classes offered. **Policies:** No alcohol or tobacco products allowed on campus. **Housing:** Single-sex dorms available. $100 deposit. **Activities:** Campus ministries, choral groups, dance, drama, student government, student newspaper, Native learning work community, Native American students of promise, journalism club, praise team club, praise band, American Indian stickball club, criminal justice studies club, Native American student association, black student association, American Indian dance and song.

Athletics. NAIA. **Intercollegiate:** Baseball M, basketball, cheerleading, cross-country, football (tackle) M, golf, rodeo, soccer, softball W, tennis, track and field, volleyball W, wrestling M. **Intramural:** Basketball, football (tackle) M, soccer, softball, table tennis. **Team name:** Warriors.

Student services. Chaplain/spiritual director, career counseling, student employment services, financial aid counseling, health services, personal counseling, placement for graduates. **Physically disabled:** Services for visually, speech, hearing impaired.

Contact. E-mail: admissionsoffice@bacone.edu
Phone: (918) 683-4581 ext. 7342 Toll-free number: (888) 682-5514 ext. 7342 Fax: (918) 781-7416
Leroy Thompson, Director of Admissions, Bacone College, 2299 Old Bacone Road, Muskogee, OK 74403

Cameron University
Lawton, Oklahoma **CB member**
www.cameron.edu **CB code: 6080**

- Public 4-year university and liberal arts college
- Commuter campus in small city
- 4,700 degree-seeking undergraduates: 32% part-time, 60% women, 16% African American, 3% Asian American, 8% Hispanic American, 8% Native American, 5% international
- 366 degree-seeking graduate students
- 100% of applicants admitted
- SAT or ACT required

General. Founded in 1909. Regionally accredited. **Degrees:** 553 bachelor's, 198 associate awarded; master's offered. **ROTC:** Army. **Location:** 90 miles from Oklahoma City. **Calendar:** Semester, limited summer session. **Full-time faculty:** 161 total; 75% have terminal degrees, 16% minority, 40% women. **Part-time faculty:** 172 total; 17% have terminal degrees, 12% minority, 54% women. **Class size:** 49% < 20, 44% 20-39, 5% 40-49, 2% 50-99.

Freshman class profile. 1,134 applied, 1,133 admitted, 799 enrolled.

Mid 50% test scores		**Rank in top quarter:**	26%
ACT composite:	16-21	**Rank in top tenth:**	9%
GPA 3.75 or higher:	16%	**Out-of-state:**	3%
GPA 3.50-3.74:	14%	**Live on campus:**	7%
GPA 3.0-3.49:	29%	**Fraternities:**	2%
GPA 2.0-2.99:	38%	**Sororities:**	2%

Basis for selection. 2.7 GPA and rank in top half of class, or 20 ACT required for bachelor's degree, associate of science or associate of arts programs. Open admissions for associate of applied science degree candidates only. Those who do not meet bachelor's criteria admitted as associate degree candidates.

High school preparation. College-preparatory program required. 15 units required. Required and recommended units include English 4, mathematics 3, history 3, science 2-3 (laboratory 2), foreign language 1 and academic electives 3. One unit in government, geography, economics or non-Western culture.

2008-2009 Annual costs. Tuition/fees: $4,110; $9,975 out-of-state. Room/board: $3,560. Books/supplies: $1,050.

2007-2008 Financial aid. Need-based: 498 full-time freshmen applied for aid; 443 were judged to have need; 385 of these received aid. Average need met was 85%. Average scholarship/grant was $3,500; average loan $1,000. 58% of total undergraduate aid awarded as scholarships/grants, 42% as loans/jobs. **Non-need-based:** Awarded to 1,009 full-time undergraduates, including 453 freshmen. Scholarships awarded for academics, alumni affiliation, art, athletics, leadership, music/drama, ROTC.

Application procedures. Admission: Priority date 8/1; no deadline. $15 fee, may be waived for applicants with need. Admission notification on a rolling basis beginning on or about 6/10. **Financial aid:** Priority date 5/1; no closing date. FAFSA required. Applicants notified on a rolling basis starting 4/1; must reply by 8/7 or within 2 week(s) of notification.

Academics. **Special study options:** Accelerated study, combined bachelor's/graduate degree, cooperative education, distance learning, double major, dual enrollment of high school students, honors, independent study, internships, liberal arts/career combination, teacher certification program, weekend college. **Credit/placement by examination:** AP, CLEP, IB, institutional tests. **Support services:** Learning center, pre-admission summer program, reduced course load, remedial instruction, study skills assistance, tutoring, writing center.

Majors. **Agriculture:** General, agronomy, animal sciences, horticultural science. **Biology:** General. **Business:** Accounting, business admin. **Communications:** General, broadcast journalism, journalism, public relations. **Computer sciences:** General, computer science, web page design. **Education:** General, art, biology, chemistry, early childhood, elementary, English, history, mathematics, music, physical, science, secondary, social studies. **Engineering technology:** Electrical, mechanical drafting. **Family/consumer sciences:** General. **Foreign languages:** General, linguistics. **Health:** Clinical lab technology. **History:** General. **Interdisciplinary:** Biological/physical sciences, natural sciences. **Math:** General. **Parks/recreation:** Health/fitness. **Physical sciences:** Chemistry, physics. **Protective services:** Criminal justice. **Psychology:** General. **Science technology:** Biological. **Social sciences:** Political science, sociology. **Visual/performing arts:** Art, dramatic, studio arts.

Most popular majors. Business/marketing 20%, education 9%, interdisciplinary studies 7%, parks/recreation 8%, psychology 7%, security/protective services 12%.

Computing on campus. 450 workstations in dormitories, library, computer center. Dormitories wired for high-speed internet access and linked to campus network. Commuter students can connect to campus network. Online library, helpline, student web hosting, wireless network available.

Student life. **Freshman orientation:** Mandatory. 7 sessions annually, held June through August. **Policies:** Student code of conduct; no alcohol on campus. **Housing:** Guaranteed on-campus for all undergraduates. Single-sex dorms, special housing for disabled, apartments, wellness housing available. $200 fully refundable deposit, deadline 7/1. Quiet areas available. **Activities:** Bands, campus ministries, choral groups, drama, film society, international student organizations, literary magazine, music ensembles, musical theater, opera, radio station, student government, student newspaper, symphony orchestra, TV station, Ebony Society, Students of the Caribbean Alliance, American Indian student association, Latin alliance, Asian/Pacific Islander student association, Chi Alpha, Young Republicans.

Athletics. NCAA. **Intercollegiate:** Baseball M, basketball, cross-country M, golf, softball W, tennis, volleyball W. **Intramural:** Badminton, basketball, bowling, football (non-tackle), golf, racquetball, softball, tennis, volleyball. **Team name:** Aggies.

Student services. Chaplain/spiritual director, career counseling, services for economically disadvantaged, student employment services, financial aid counseling, minority student services, veterans' counselor. **Physically disabled:** Services for visually, speech, hearing impaired.

Contact. E-mail: zoed@cameron.edu
Phone: (580) 581-2200 Toll-free number: (888) 454-7600
Fax: (580) 581-5514
Zoe DuRant, Director of Admissions, Cameron University, 2800 West Gore Boulevard, Lawton, OK 73505-6377

DeVry University: Oklahoma City Center
Oklahoma City, Oklahoma
www.devry.edu

- For-profit 4-year university and business college
- Very large city
- 59 degree-seeking undergraduates: 41% part-time, 32% women, 27% African American, 2% Asian American, 3% Hispanic American, 8% Native American
- 22 degree-seeking graduate students

General. Regionally accredited. **Degrees:** 3 bachelor's, 1 associate awarded; master's offered. **Calendar:** Semester. **Part-time faculty:** 8 total; 25% women.

Basis for selection. Applicants must have high school diploma or equivalent, or degree from accredited post-secondary institution, demonstrate proficiency in basic college-level skills through SAT or ACT scores or institution-administered placement examinations, and be at least 17 years of age. DeVry-administered admissions test required if SAT or ACT test scores are not submitted.

2008-2009 Annual costs. Tuition/fees: $13,930. Books/supplies: $1,300. Personal expenses: $5,082.

2007-2008 Financial aid. **Non-need-based:** Scholarships awarded for academics.

Application procedures. **Admission:** No deadline. $50 fee. Admission notification on a rolling basis. **Financial aid:** No deadline. FAFSA required. Applicants notified on a rolling basis.

Academics. **Special study options:** Accelerated study, distance learning. **Credit/placement by examination:** CLEP.

Majors. **Business:** Business admin. **Computer sciences:** Networking.

Contact. DeVry University: Oklahoma City Center, Lakepointe Towers, 4013 NW Expressway Street, Oklahoma City, OK 73116

East Central University
Ada, Oklahoma
www.ecok.edu **CB code: 6186**

- Public 4-year university
- Commuter campus in large town
- 2,850 full-time, degree-seeking undergraduates
- 816 graduate students
- 96% of applicants admitted
- SAT or ACT (ACT writing optional) required

General. Founded in 1909. Regionally accredited. **Degrees:** 654 bachelor's awarded; master's offered. **Location:** 86 miles from Oklahoma City. **Calendar:** Semester, extensive summer session. **Full-time faculty:** 161 total; 70% have terminal degrees, 9% minority, 43% women. **Part-time faculty:** 92 total; 18% have terminal degrees, 11% minority, 56% women.

Freshman class profile. 792 applied, 761 admitted, 555 enrolled.

Mid 50% test scores		**Rank in top quarter:**	42%
ACT composite:	18-22	**Rank in top tenth:**	17%
GPA 3.75 or higher:	24%	**Out-of-state:**	2%
GPA 3.50-3.74:	18%	**Live on campus:**	40%
GPA 3.0-3.49:	32%	**Fraternities:**	55%
GPA 2.0-2.99:	25%	**Sororities:**	45%

Basis for selection. Rank in top 50% of graduating class, 20 ACT or SAT equivalent, 2.7 GPA and required course work important.

High school preparation. 15 units required. Required and recommended units include English 4, mathematics 3, social studies 2, history 1, science 2 (laboratory 2) and academic electives 3. Additional courses from English, math, science, history, social sciences, foreign language, or computer science.

2008-2009 Annual costs. Tuition/fees: $4,221; $10,236 out-of-state. Room/board: $4,080. Books/supplies: $900.

2008-2009 Financial aid. **Non-need-based:** Scholarships awarded for academics, athletics.

Application procedures. **Admission:** No deadline. $20 fee. Admission notification on a rolling basis. **Financial aid:** Closing date 3/1. FAFSA required. Applicants notified on a rolling basis starting 4/15; must reply within 2 week(s) of notification.

Academics. **Special study options:** Distance learning, double major, dual enrollment of high school students, exchange student, honors, independent study, internships, teacher certification program. **Credit/placement by examination:** AP, CLEP, ACT, institutional tests. 94 credit hours maximum toward bachelor's degree. Students do not receive CLEP or AP credit until 12 hours completed in residence with 2.0 GPA. **Support services:** Learning center, pre-admission summer program, reduced course load, remedial instruction, study skills assistance, tutoring, writing center.

Majors. **Biology:** General. **Business:** General, accounting, administrative services, business admin, finance, managerial economics, marketing, office management, operations, sales/distribution. **Communications:** General, broadcast journalism, journalism. **Computer sciences:** General. **Education:** Agricultural, business, drama/dance, early childhood, elementary, English, family/consumer sciences, history, mathematics, mentally handicapped, music, physical, physically handicapped, science, social studies, special, speech, technology/industrial arts, trade/industrial. **Family/consumer sciences:** General, clothing/textiles. **Foreign languages:** Comparative lit. **Health:** Athletic training, environmental health, medical records technology, predental, premedicine, prepharmacy, preveterinary, vocational rehab counseling. **History:** General. **Legal studies:** Paralegal, prelaw. **Math:** General, applied. **Parks/recreation:** General, exercise sciences, health/fitness. **Physical sciences:** Chemistry, physics. **Protective services:** Criminal justice, police science.

Psychology: General. **Public administration:** Community org/advocacy, human services, social work. **Social sciences:** General, cartography, criminology, political science, sociology. **Visual/performing arts:** Art, dramatic, piano/organ, studio arts, voice/opera.

Most popular majors. Business/marketing 11%, education 20%, health sciences 14%, public administration/social services 16%.

Computing on campus. 650 workstations in library, computer center. Online library, helpline, repair service, wireless network available.

Student life. Freshman orientation: Mandatory. Preregistration for classes offered. **Housing:** Coed dorms, single-sex dorms, special housing for disabled, apartments, fraternity/sorority housing available. **Activities:** Bands, choral groups, dance, drama, film society, literary magazine, music ensembles, musical theater, student government, student newspaper, association of black students, Native American student association, Baptist student union, united campus ministry, students with disabilities, Church of Christ Bible Chair, Life House, Sigma Society, Panhellenic, silent friends club.

Athletics. NCAA. **Intercollegiate:** Baseball M, basketball, cross-country, football (tackle) M, golf, soccer W, softball W, tennis, volleyball W. **Intramural:** Basketball, soccer, softball, volleyball. **Team name:** Tigers.

Student services. Adult student services, career counseling, student employment services, financial aid counseling, health services, minority student services, on-campus daycare, personal counseling, placement for graduates, veterans' counselor. **Physically disabled:** Services for visually, speech, hearing impaired.

Contact. E-mail: parmstro@ecok.edu
Phone: (580) 332-8000 Fax: (580) 559-5432
Pamla Armstrong, Registrar and Director of Admissions, East Central University, PMBJ8, 1100 East 14th Street, Ada, OK 74820

Family of Faith College
Shawnee, Oklahoma
www.familyoffaithcollege.edu

- Private 4-year Bible college
- Residential campus in rural community
- 52 degree-seeking undergraduates
- 100% of applicants admitted
- SAT or ACT (ACT writing optional), application essay required

General. Regionally accredited; also accredited by ABHE. **Degrees:** 5 bachelor's awarded. **Location:** 6 miles from Shawnee, 30 miles from Oklahoma City. **Calendar:** Semester, limited summer session. **Full-time faculty:** 8 total. **Part-time faculty:** 4 total.

Freshman class profile. 4 applied, 4 admitted, 4 enrolled.

Mid 50% test scores		**SAT math:**	400-450
SAT critical reading:	500-550	**ACT composite:**	20-24

Basis for selection. SAT/ACT not required for certificate programs. Academic and personal references required. **Homeschooled:** Transcript of courses and grades, state high school equivalency certificate, letter of recommendation (nonparent) required.

2008-2009 Annual costs. Tuition/fees: $5,110. Room only: $1,600.

Application procedures. Admission: Closing date 6/1 (receipt date). $25 fee.

Academics. Credit/placement by examination: CLEP.

Majors. Theology: Bible, theology.

Student life. Housing: $50 fully refundable deposit.

Contact. E-mail: ffc@allegiance.tv
Phone: (405) 273-5331 Fax: (405) 273-8535
Rhonda Gaines, Vice President of Student Affairs, Family of Faith College, PO Box 1805, Shawnee, OK 74802-1805

Hillsdale Free Will Baptist College
Moore, Oklahoma
www.hc.edu

- Private 4-year liberal arts college
- Small city
- 236 degree-seeking undergraduates

General. Regionally accredited. **Calendar:** Semester. **Full-time faculty:** 14 total. **Part-time faculty:** 29 total.

Freshman class profile. 85 enrolled.

Application procedures. Financial aid: Closing date 9/15.

Academics. Credit/placement by examination: CLEP.

Majors. Biology: Exercise physiology. **Business:** General. **Education:** Multi-level teacher. **Psychology:** General. **Theology:** Theology. **Other:** Christian education.

Contact. E-mail: rgiles@hc.edu
Phone: (415) 912-9011
Sue Chaffin, Director of Records and Registration, Hillsdale Free Will Baptist College, P.O. Box 7208, Moore, OK 73153

ITT Technical Institute: Tulsa
Tulsa, Oklahoma

- For-profit 4-year business and technical college
- Large city

General. Accredited by ACICS. **Calendar:** Quarter.

Contact. 4943 South 78th East Avenue, Tulsa, OK 74145

Langston University
Langston, Oklahoma **CB member**
www.lunet.edu **CB code: 6361**

- Public 4-year university and liberal arts college
- Residential campus in rural community
- 2,441 degree-seeking undergraduates: 16% part-time, 59% women, 84% African American, 1% Asian American, 1% Hispanic American, 2% Native American, 1% international
- 275 degree-seeking graduate students
- 43% of applicants admitted
- SAT or ACT (ACT writing optional), application essay required
- 40% graduate within 6 years

General. Founded in 1897. Regionally accredited. Branch campuses in Oklahoma City, Tulsa. **Degrees:** 320 bachelor's, 14 associate awarded; master's, doctoral offered. **ROTC:** Army, Air Force. **Location:** 40 miles from Oklahoma City, 90 miles from Tulsa. **Calendar:** Semester, limited summer session. **Full-time faculty:** 145 total; 74% minority, 46% women. **Part-time faculty:** 72 total; 72% minority, 61% women. **Class size:** 64% < 20, 29% 20-39, 3% 40-49, 3% 50-99. **Special facilities:** International dairy goat research facility.

Freshman class profile. 2,683 applied, 1,146 admitted, 786 enrolled.

GPA 3.50-3.74:	3%	**Return as sophomores:**	58%
GPA 3.0-3.49:	14%	**Out-of-state:**	40%
GPA 2.0-2.99:	59%	**International:**	1%

Basis for selection. 2.7 GPA, 20 ACT or SAT equivalent required. March 1 priority date for SAT or ACT scores. Audition recommended for music program.

High school preparation. 15 units required. Required and recommended units include English 4, mathematics 3, social studies 2, history 1, science 2-8 (laboratory 2), foreign language 1-4 and academic electives 4. Remaining units must be additional work in these areas or in computer science, speech, economics, geography, government, psychology, or sociology. Required units must begin with algebra I. Required social sciences units must include 1 US history.

2008-2009 Annual costs. Tuition/fees: $3,827; $9,407 out-of-state. Housing is apartment-style. Room/board: $6,890. Books/supplies: $800. Personal expenses: $2,037.

2007-2008 Financial aid. All financial aid based on need.

Application procedures. Admission: Priority date 3/1; no deadline. $25 fee. Admission notification on a rolling basis. **Financial aid:** Priority date 3/1, closing date 5/1. CSS PROFILE required. Applicants notified on a rolling basis starting 7/15; must reply within 2 week(s) of notification.

Academics. Special study options: Cooperative education, distance learning, double major, dual enrollment of high school students, honors, internships, liberal arts/career combination, study abroad, teacher certification program. **Credit/placement by examination:** AP, CLEP, SAT, ACT, institutional tests. 16 credit hours maximum toward associate degree, 30 toward bachelor's. **Support services:** Learning center, reduced course load, remedial instruction, tutoring.

Majors. Agriculture: Animal sciences, business, economics, farm/ranch. **Biology:** General, zoology. **Business:** Accounting, administrative services, business admin, human resources. **Communications:** General, broadcast journalism, journalism. **Communications technology:** General. **Computer sciences:** General. **Education:** General, business, elementary, family/consumer sciences, mathematics, music, physical, secondary, social studies, special, technology/industrial arts. **Family/consumer sciences:** General, clothing/textiles, family studies, food/nutrition. **Health:** Health care admin, preveterinary. **History:** General. **Legal studies:** Prelaw. **Math:** General. **Physical sciences:** Chemistry. **Protective services:** Corrections, police science. **Psychology:** General. **Social sciences:** General, economics, geography, sociology, urban studies. **Visual/performing arts:** Art, music performance.

Most popular majors. Business/marketing 23%, education 7%, health sciences 21%, liberal arts 9%, psychology 9%, security/protective services 8%, social sciences 6%.

Computing on campus. 300 workstations in library, computer center. Dormitories wired for high-speed internet access and linked to campus network.

Student life. Freshman orientation: Mandatory. Preregistration for classes offered. Begins 7 days prior to fall enrollment; includes social, cultural, and institutional activities along with registration and enrollment processes. **Policies:** All freshman and sophomore students required to live on campus. Students must have 2.0 GPA to join student organizations. Students must have 2.5 GPA to be in student government, campus royalty, or fraternities and sororities. **Housing:** Guaranteed on-campus for all undergraduates. Apartments available. $200 fully refundable deposit. **Activities:** Bands, choral groups, dance, drama, music ensembles, radio station, student government, student newspaper, TV station, Pan hellenic fraternities and sororities, NAACP, NCNW.

Athletics. NAIA. **Intercollegiate:** Basketball, cheerleading, cross-country, football (tackle) M, softball W, track and field, volleyball W. **Intramural:** Basketball, football (non-tackle), track and field, volleyball. **Team name:** Lions.

Student services. Alcohol/substance abuse counseling, chaplain/spiritual director, career counseling, services for economically disadvantaged, student employment services, financial aid counseling, health services, on-campus daycare, personal counseling, placement for graduates, veterans' counselor. **Physically disabled:** Services for visually, speech, hearing impaired.

Contact. E-mail: gtrobertson@lunet.edu
Phone: (405) 466-3428 Fax: (405) 466-3391
Gayle Robertson, Director of Enrollment Management, Langston University, Box 728, Langston, OK 73050

Mid-America Christian University

Oklahoma City, Oklahoma
www.macu.edu **CB code: 0918**

- Private 4-year university and liberal arts college affiliated with Church of God
- Residential campus in very large city
- 758 degree-seeking undergraduates
- 149 graduate students
- SAT or ACT (ACT writing optional) required

General. Founded in 1953. Regionally accredited. **Degrees:** 178 bachelor's, 4 associate awarded; master's offered. **Location:** 10 miles from downtown. **Calendar:** Semester, limited summer session. **Full-time faculty:** 20 total; 35% have terminal degrees, 10% minority. **Part-time faculty:** 30 total; 20% minority. **Class size:** 67% < 20, 26% 20-39, 2% 40-49, 4% 50-99.

Freshman class profile.

Out-of-state:	64%	**Live on campus:**	82%

Basis for selection. Open admission. Applicants admitted who feel calling to full-time Christian vocations or seek God's will for their lives in a spiritual environment. 2 references required. Interview, audition recommended. **Homeschooled:** Applicants without GED must have 15 ACT English and 14 ACT math.

High school preparation. 16 units recommended. Recommended units include English 4, mathematics 2, social studies 2, science 2 and foreign language 2.

2008-2009 Annual costs. Tuition/fees: $12,800. Room/board: $5,176. Books/supplies: $800. Personal expenses: $660.

2008-2009 Financial aid. Non-need-based: Scholarships awarded for academics, leadership, minority status, music/drama.

Application procedures. Admission: Priority date 8/15; no deadline. $25 fee, may be waived for applicants with need, free for online applicants. Admission notification on a rolling basis beginning on or about 2/1. Students may provisionally enroll without graduation posted in senior year. **Financial aid:** Priority date 5/1; no closing date. FAFSA required. Applicants notified on a rolling basis starting 5/1.

Academics. Degree-completion program available for enrollees 25 years of age and above with approximately 2 years of college experience. Link program available for student lacking general education courses. **Special study options:** Combined bachelor's/graduate degree, distance learning, double major, dual enrollment of high school students, external degree, independent study, internships, liberal arts/career combination, teacher certification program, weekend college. **Credit/placement by examination:** AP, CLEP, SAT, ACT, institutional tests. 30 credit hours maximum toward associate degree, 30 toward bachelor's. Must be completed before accruing 30 credit hours. **Support services:** Remedial instruction, tutoring, writing center.

Majors. Business: Business admin, management information systems, management science, marketing. **Education:** Elementary, English, mathematics, music, secondary, social science, social studies. **Interdisciplinary:** Behavioral sciences. **Math:** General. **Philosophy/religion:** Religion. **Protective services:** Law enforcement admin. **Psychology:** Social. **Social sciences:** General. **Theology:** Bible, pastoral counseling, sacred music, theology. **Visual/performing arts:** Music performance.

Most popular majors. Computer/information sciences 7%, history 27%, philosophy/religious studies 15%, psychology 16%, theological studies 28%.

Computing on campus. 40 workstations in library, computer center, student center. Dormitories wired for high-speed internet access and linked to campus network. Online library, wireless network available.

Student life. Freshman orientation: Mandatory. Preregistration for classes offered. Held 1 day prior to start of classes. **Policies:** No smoking or drinking allowed on campus. Religious observance required. **Housing:** Guaranteed on-campus for freshmen. Single-sex dorms, wellness housing available. $50 deposit. **Activities:** Concert band, choral groups, drama, music ensembles, musical theater, student government, Missions Club, Student Ministerial Fellowship, Ministry Refresher Institute.

Athletics. NCCAA. **Intercollegiate:** Baseball M, basketball, golf, soccer M, softball W, volleyball W. **Intramural:** Basketball, bowling, softball W, table tennis, volleyball. **Team name:** Evangels.

Student services. Chaplain/spiritual director, career counseling, student employment services, financial aid counseling, health services, personal counseling, placement for graduates, veterans' counselor. **Physically disabled:** Services for speech impaired.

Contact. E-mail: info@macu.edu
Phone: (405) 692-3188 Toll-free number: (888) 436-3035
Fax: (405) 692-3165
Jason Duda, Director of Admissions, Mid-America Christian University, 3500 SW 119th Street, Oklahoma City, OK 73170

Northeastern State University

Tahlequah, Oklahoma
www.nsuok.edu **CB code: 6485**

- Public 4-year university
- Commuter campus in large town
- 7,727 degree-seeking undergraduates: 27% part-time, 61% women, 5% African American, 1% Asian American, 2% Hispanic American, 30% Native American, 3% international
- 1,093 degree-seeking graduate students
- 70% of applicants admitted
- ACT (writing optional) required

General. Founded in 1851. Regionally accredited. **Degrees:** 1,525 bachelor's awarded; master's, first professional offered. **ROTC:** Army. **Location:** 60 miles from Tulsa, 30 miles from Muskogee. **Calendar:** Semester, extensive summer session. **Full-time faculty:** 312 total; 72% have terminal degrees, 17% minority, 47% women. **Part-time faculty:** 141 total; 24%

have terminal degrees, 18% minority, 52% women. **Class size:** 52% < 20, 41% 20-39, 4% 40-49, 3% 50-99. **Special facilities:** Literacy study center, tribal studies center, Oklahoma Institute for Learning Styles.

Freshman class profile. 2,344 applied, 1,645 admitted, 999 enrolled.

Mid 50% test scores		End year in good standing:	70%
ACT composite:	18-23	Return as sophomores:	64%
GPA 3.75 or higher:	23%	Out-of-state:	8%
GPA 3.50-3.74:	17%	Live on campus:	69%
GPA 3.0-3.49:	30%	International:	1%
GPA 2.0-2.99:	29%	Fraternities:	15%
Rank in top quarter:	44%	Sororities:	8%
Rank in top tenth:	19%		

Basis for selection. Admissions based on secondary school record, class rank, and standardized test scores. Audition required, interview recommended for music program. Interview recommended for drama program; portfolio recommended for graphic art program. Interview required for alternative admission. **Homeschooled:** Transcript of courses and grades required.

High school preparation. College-preparatory program required. 15 units required. Required and recommended units include English 4, mathematics 3, social studies 2, history 1, science 2 (laboratory 2) and foreign language 2. 3 from English, lab science, math, history, social studies, computer science, or foreign language.

2008-2009 Annual costs. Tuition/fees: $4,155; $10,245 out-of-state. Room/board: $4,784. Books/supplies: $1,000. Personal expenses: $1,080.

2008-2009 Financial aid. Need-based: 824 full-time freshmen applied for aid; 615 were judged to have need; 587 of these received aid. Average need met was 69%. Average scholarship/grant was $4,710; average loan $2,032. 56% of total undergraduate aid awarded as scholarships/grants, 44% as loans/jobs. **Non-need-based:** Awarded to 4,717 full-time undergraduates, including 908 freshmen. Scholarships awarded for academics, alumni affiliation, art, athletics, job skills, leadership, minority status, music/drama, religious affiliation, ROTC, state residency. **Additional information:** Participates in off-campus job location & development program to assist students with off-campus employers to earn money for college expenses.

Application procedures. Admission: Priority date 8/1; no deadline. No application fee. Admission notification on a rolling basis. **Financial aid:** Priority date 3/15; no closing date. FAFSA, institutional form required. Applicants notified on a rolling basis starting 3/15.

Academics. NSU College of Optometry on campus. **Special study options:** Combined bachelor's/graduate degree, distance learning, double major, dual enrollment of high school students, honors, independent study, internships, student-designed major, teacher certification program, weekend college. **Credit/placement by examination:** AP, CLEP, IB, ACT, institutional tests. 30 credit hours maximum toward bachelor's degree. **Support services:** Learning center, pre-admission summer program, reduced course load, remedial instruction, study skills assistance, tutoring, writing center.

Majors. Area/ethnic studies: Native American. **Biology:** General, cell/histology, wildlife. **Business:** Accounting, business admin, entrepreneurial studies, finance, human resources, international, logistics, management information systems, marketing, operations, tourism/travel. **Communications:** Advertising, journalism, public relations. **Computer sciences:** Computer science. **Conservation:** Environmental science. **Education:** Art, biology, chemistry, early childhood, elementary, English, learning disabled, mathematics, music, Native American, physical, physics, science, social studies, Spanish, speech. **Engineering:** Environmental. **Engineering technology:** General, industrial safety. **Family/consumer sciences:** General, food/nutrition. **Foreign languages:** Spanish. **Health:** Audiology/speech pathology, clinical lab science, facilities admin, nursing (RN). **History:** General. **Math:** General. **Parks/recreation:** Exercise sciences. **Physical sciences:** Chemistry. **Protective services:** Law enforcement admin. **Psychology:** General, developmental. **Public administration:** Social work. **Social sciences:** Geography, political science, sociology. **Visual/performing arts:** Art, commercial/advertising art, design, dramatic, photography, studio arts. **Other:** Organizational leadership, Vision science.

Most popular majors. Business/marketing 24%, education 27%, psychology 7%, security/protective services 6%.

Computing on campus. 897 workstations in dormitories, library, computer center. Dormitories wired for high-speed internet access and linked to campus network. Commuter students can connect to campus network. Online library, helpline, student web hosting, wireless network available.

Student life. Freshman orientation: Mandatory. Preregistration for classes offered. **Housing:** Guaranteed on-campus for freshmen. Coed dorms, special housing for disabled, apartments, fraternity/sorority housing, wellness housing available. $75 fully refundable deposit, deadline 7/1. **Activities:** Bands, campus ministries, choral groups, dance, drama, international student organizations, literary magazine, music ensembles, Model UN, musical theater, student government, student newspaper, symphony orchestra, TV station, Native American student association, American Indian science and engineering society, Association of Black Collegians, government and international studies society, Campus Christian Fellowship, Baptist Campus Ministries, Chi Alpha Campus Ministries, Habitat for Humanity, Sigma Theta Epsilon, RiverHawks for Christ.

Athletics. NCAA. **Intercollegiate:** Baseball M, basketball, football (tackle) M, golf, soccer, softball W, tennis W. **Intramural:** Basketball, football (non-tackle), golf, racquetball, soccer, softball, tennis, volleyball. **Team name:** RiverHawks.

Student services. Adult student services, alcohol/substance abuse counseling, career counseling, services for economically disadvantaged, student employment services, financial aid counseling, health services, personal counseling, placement for graduates, veterans' counselor. **Physically disabled:** Services for visually, speech, hearing impaired.

Contact. E-mail: nsuinfo@nsuok.edu
Phone: (918) 444-2200 Toll-free number: (800) 722-9614
Fax: (918) 458-2342
Dawn Cain, Director of Admissions, Northeastern State University, 600 North Grand Avenue, Tahlequah, OK 74464-2399

Northwestern Oklahoma State University

Alva, Oklahoma
www.nwosu.edu **CB code: 6493**

- Public 4-year university and teachers college
- Commuter campus in small town
- 1,747 degree-seeking undergraduates: 28% part-time, 58% women, 5% African American, 1% Asian American, 4% Hispanic American, 5% Native American, 2% international
- 179 degree-seeking graduate students
- 100% of applicants admitted
- SAT or ACT (ACT writing optional) required

General. Founded in 1897. Regionally accredited. **Degrees:** 317 bachelor's awarded; master's offered. **Location:** 160 miles from Oklahoma City, 70 miles from Enid. **Calendar:** Semester, limited summer session. **Full-time faculty:** 88 total; 48% have terminal degrees, 7% minority, 53% women. **Part-time faculty:** 63 total; 8% have terminal degrees, 6% minority, 67% women. **Class size:** 75% < 20, 23% 20-39, 1% 40-49, less than 1% 50-99. **Special facilities:** Farm.

Freshman class profile. 701 applied, 701 admitted, 330 enrolled.

Mid 50% test scores		GPA 3.0-3.49:	33%
SAT critical reading:	380-460	GPA 2.0-2.99:	31%
SAT math:	360-480	Rank in top quarter:	25%
ACT composite:	17-22	Rank in top tenth:	7%
GPA 3.75 or higher:	19%	Out-of-state:	21%
GPA 3.50-3.74:	16%	Live on campus:	70%

Basis for selection. Applicants with 2.7 GPA and in top 50% of class or with 19 ACT admitted unconditionally. Others admitted provisionally. Audition recommended for music program. **Homeschooled:** Transcript of courses and grades required.

High school preparation. 15 units required. Required and recommended units include English 4, mathematics 3, history 2, science 2 (laboratory 2), foreign language 2 and academic electives 3. 1 unit required from either government, economics, geography or non-Western culture.

2008-2009 Annual costs. Tuition/fees: $4,110; $10,140 out-of-state. Room/board: $3,560. Books/supplies: $1,200. Personal expenses: $1,200.

2007-2008 Financial aid. Non-need-based: Scholarships awarded for academics, alumni affiliation, art, athletics, leadership, music/drama.

Application procedures. Admission: No deadline. $15 fee. Admission notification on a rolling basis. **Financial aid:** No deadline. FAFSA required. Applicants notified on a rolling basis starting 5/1.

Academics. Special study options: Distance learning, double major, dual enrollment of high school students, honors, independent study, internships, study abroad, teacher certification program. 2-2 programs in many professional fields. **Credit/placement by examination:** AP, CLEP, SAT, ACT, institutional tests. **Support services:** Learning center, reduced course load, remedial instruction, tutoring, writing center.

Majors. **Agriculture:** General, business. **Biology:** General. **Business:** Accounting, business admin, e-commerce. **Communications:** Broadcast journalism, journalism, public relations. **Computer sciences:** General, information systems, programming. **Conservation:** Management/policy. **Education:** General, business, early childhood, elementary, English, health, learning disabled, mathematics, mentally handicapped, music, physical, science, social science, Spanish, special, technology/industrial arts. **Health:** Nursing (RN). **History:** General. **Legal studies:** Prelaw. **Math:** General. **Parks/recreation:** Health/fitness. **Physical sciences:** Chemistry. **Protective services:** Police science. **Psychology:** General. **Public administration:** Social work. **Social sciences:** General, political science, sociology. **Visual/performing arts:** Dramatic, music performance, piano/organ, voice/opera.

Most popular majors. Agriculture 7%, business/marketing 21%, education 24%, health sciences 6%, parks/recreation 6%, psychology 10%.

Computing on campus. 116 workstations in library, computer center, student center. Dormitories wired for high-speed internet access. Commuter students can connect to campus network. Online library, wireless network available.

Student life. **Freshman orientation:** Mandatory. Preregistration for classes offered. **Housing:** Single-sex dorms, special housing for disabled available. $75 fully refundable deposit. **Activities:** Bands, campus ministries, choral groups, drama, international student organizations, music ensembles, radio station, student government, student newspaper, TV station.

Athletics. NAIA. **Intercollegiate:** Baseball M, basketball, cross-country, football (tackle) M, golf, rodeo, soccer W, softball W. **Intramural:** Basketball, bowling, football (non-tackle), racquetball, softball, volleyball. **Team name:** Rangers.

Student services. Adult student services, career counseling, student employment services, financial aid counseling, health services, personal counseling, placement for graduates, veterans' counselor, women's services. **Physically disabled:** Services for visually, speech, hearing impaired.

Contact. E-mail: recruit@nwosu.edu
Phone: (580) 327-8546 Fax: (580) 327-8413
Matt Adair, Director of Recruitment, Northwestern Oklahoma State University, 709 Oklahoma Boulevard, Alva, OK 73717-2799

Oklahoma Baptist University

Shawnee, Oklahoma — **CB member**
www.okbu.edu — **CB code: 6541**

- Private 4-year university and liberal arts college affiliated with Southern Baptist Convention
- Residential campus in large town
- 1,425 degree-seeking undergraduates
- 25 graduate students
- 63% of applicants admitted
- SAT or ACT (ACT writing optional) required

General. Founded in 1910. Regionally accredited. Each summer approximately 250 students, faculty and staff serve in projects around the world. About 300 students participate in local service projects during the year. **Degrees:** 257 bachelor's awarded; master's offered. **ROTC:** Air Force. **Location:** 35 miles from Oklahoma City, 90 miles from Tulsa. **Calendar:** Semester, limited summer session. **Full-time faculty:** 105 total. **Part-time faculty:** 55 total. **Class size:** 62% < 20, 31% 20-39, 3% 40-49, 3% 50-99. **Special facilities:** Planetarium (operated by students), greenhouse, music technology laboratory, biblical research library.

Freshman class profile. 3,207 applied, 2,013 admitted, 389 enrolled.

Mid 50% test scores		**GPA 3.0-3.49:**	24%
SAT critical reading:	460-600	**GPA 2.0-2.99:**	10%
SAT math:	450-590	**Rank in top quarter:**	59%
ACT composite:	20-26	**Rank in top tenth:**	28%
GPA 3.75 or higher:	46%	**Out-of-state:**	38%
GPA 3.50-3.74:	20%	**Live on campus:**	94%

Basis for selection. 20 ACT or 950 SAT (exclusive of Writing), 3.0 GPA or class rank in top half required. Interview recommended for borderline applicants; audition recommended for drama, music programs; portfolio recommended for art program.

High school preparation. College-preparatory program recommended. 17 units recommended. Recommended units include English 4, mathematics 3, social studies 2, history 1, science 3 (laboratory 2), foreign language 2 and academic electives 2. Math recommendation includes 2 algebra and 1 plane geometry.

2008-2009 Annual costs. Tuition/fees: $16,790. Room/board: $5,200. Books/supplies: $1,000. Personal expenses: $1,575.

2007-2008 Financial aid. **Non-need-based:** Scholarships awarded for academics, alumni affiliation, art, athletics, job skills, leadership, music/drama, religious affiliation, ROTC, state residency.

Application procedures. **Admission:** Priority date 4/1; deadline 8/1 (postmark date). No application fee. Admission notification on a rolling basis beginning on or about 6/1. **Financial aid:** Priority date 3/1; no closing date. FAFSA, institutional form required. Applicants notified on a rolling basis starting 3/1; must reply by 5/1 or within 2 week(s) of notification.

Academics. Opportunities for January-term travel to Europe, Russia, South America; also opportunity to teach English in China and Hungary. **Special study options:** Accelerated study, combined bachelor's/graduate degree, cooperative education, double major, ESL, exchange student, honors, independent study, internships, liberal arts/career combination, student-designed major, study abroad, teacher certification program. Exchange program with Seinan Gakuin University, Japan, and Hong Kong Baptist College; opportunities for January-term travel to Europe, Russia, South America. **Credit/placement by examination:** AP, CLEP, IB, SAT, ACT, institutional tests. 32 credit hours maximum toward bachelor's degree. Essay required for English, government, history exams; oral exam required for French, German and Spanish; lab exam required for information systems. **Support services:** Learning center, pre-admission summer program, reduced course load, remedial instruction, study skills assistance, tutoring.

Majors. **Biology:** General, biochemistry. **Business:** General, accounting, business admin, finance, international, international finance, management information systems, management science, marketing. **Communications:** General, broadcast journalism, journalism, public relations. **Computer sciences:** General, applications programming, computer science, information systems, systems analysis. **Education:** Art, biology, chemistry, early childhood, elementary, English, foreign languages, French, German, health, history, learning disabled, mathematics, mentally handicapped, music, physical, physics, science, secondary, social science, social studies, Spanish, special, speech. **Foreign languages:** General, French, German, Spanish. **Health:** Athletic training, nursing (RN). **History:** General. **Interdisciplinary:** Math/computer science. **Liberal arts:** Arts/sciences. **Math:** General. **Parks/recreation:** Exercise sciences, facilities management, health/fitness, sports admin. **Philosophy/religion:** Philosophy, religion. **Physical sciences:** Chemistry, physics. **Psychology:** General. **Public administration:** Social work. **Social sciences:** General, anthropology, political science, sociology. **Theology:** Bible, missionary, religious ed, sacred music, theology. **Visual/performing arts:** Art, dramatic, music performance, music theory/composition, piano/organ, studio arts, voice/opera.

Computing on campus. 200 workstations in dormitories, library, computer center. Dormitories wired for high-speed internet access and linked to campus network. Online course registration, online library available.

Student life. **Freshman orientation:** Mandatory. Preregistration for classes offered. Held during the 3 days immediately prior to start of fall semester. **Policies:** Campus is alcohol/drug/smoke free. **Housing:** Guaranteed on-campus for all undergraduates. Single-sex dorms, apartments, wellness housing available. **Activities:** Bands, choral groups, drama, literary magazine, music ensembles, musical theater, opera, student government, student newspaper, symphony orchestra, TV station, Campus Crusade, FCA, Baptist Collegiate Ministries, Collegiate Republicans, Young Democrats, black student fellowship, international student union, Native American heritage association, residence hall association.

Athletics. NAIA. **Intercollegiate:** Baseball M, basketball, cross-country, golf, soccer, softball W, tennis, track and field. **Intramural:** Badminton, basketball, bowling, racquetball, soccer, softball, swimming, table tennis, tennis, volleyball. **Team name:** Bison.

Student services. Chaplain/spiritual director, career counseling, student employment services, financial aid counseling, health services, personal counseling, placement for graduates, veterans' counselor. **Physically disabled:** Services for visually, hearing impaired.

Contact. E-mail: admissions@mail.okbu.edu
Phone: (405) 878-2033 Toll-free number: (800) 654-3285
Fax: (405) 878-2046
Bruce Perkins, Director of Admissions, Oklahoma Baptist University, 500 West University, Shawnee, OK 74804

Oklahoma Christian University

Oklahoma City, Oklahoma
www.oc.edu — **CB code: 6086**

- Private 4-year liberal arts college affiliated with Church of Christ
- Residential campus in very large city

- 1,904 degree-seeking undergraduates: 50% women, 4% African American, 3% Asian American, 4% Hispanic American, 4% Native American
- 257 degree-seeking graduate students
- 49% of applicants admitted
- SAT or ACT (ACT writing optional) required
- 46% graduate within 6 years

General. Founded in 1950. Regionally accredited. Every student receives MacBook and choice of iPhone or iPod touch upon enrollment. **Degrees:** 267 bachelor's awarded; master's offered. **ROTC:** Army, Air Force. **Calendar:** Semester, extensive summer session. **Full-time faculty:** 103 total; 68% have terminal degrees, 7% minority, 29% women. **Part-time faculty:** 91 total; 25% have terminal degrees, 6% minority, 38% women. **Class size:** 53% < 20, 38% 20-39, 3% 40-49, 4% 50-99, less than 1% >100.

Freshman class profile. 1,472 applied, 714 admitted, 455 enrolled.

Mid 50% test scores		**GPA 3.0-3.49:**	32%
SAT critical reading:	450-520	**GPA 2.0-2.99:**	16%
SAT math:	460-540	**Rank in top quarter:**	47%
SAT writing:	450-500	**Rank in top tenth:**	22%
ACT composite:	19-26	**Return as sophomores:**	68%
GPA 3.75 or higher:	25%	**Live on campus:**	96%
GPA 3.50-3.74:	19%		

Basis for selection. Students evaluated on both merit and character. Interview/campus visit strongly recommended.

High school preparation. College-preparatory program recommended. 15 units recommended. Required and recommended units include English 4, mathematics 4, social studies 3, science 4 (laboratory 2) and foreign language 2.

2008-2009 Annual costs. Tuition/fees: $16,566. Room/board: $6,390. Books/supplies: $800. Personal expenses: $1,360.

2007-2008 Financial aid. **Non-need-based:** Scholarships awarded for academics, art, athletics, leadership, music/drama, religious affiliation, ROTC.

Application procedures. **Admission:** Priority date 5/1; no deadline. $25 fee, may be waived for applicants with need. Admission notification on a rolling basis beginning on or about 9/1. Must reply by May 1 or within 2 week(s) if notified thereafter. **Financial aid:** Priority date 3/15, closing date 8/31. FAFSA required. Applicants notified on a rolling basis starting 1/15; must reply within 4 week(s) of notification.

Academics. **Special study options:** Accelerated study, combined bachelor's/graduate degree, cross-registration, distance learning, double major, dual enrollment of high school students, ESL, exchange student, honors, independent study, internships, liberal arts/career combination, study abroad, teacher certification program. **Credit/placement by examination:** AP, CLEP, IB, SAT, ACT, institutional tests. 60 credit hours maximum toward bachelor's degree. **Support services:** Learning center, reduced course load, remedial instruction, study skills assistance, tutoring, writing center.

Majors. **Biology:** General, biochemistry. **Business:** General, accounting, business admin, management science, market research. **Communications:** General, advertising, broadcast journalism, journalism, public relations. **Computer sciences:** General, computer science, information systems. **Education:** Art, early childhood, elementary, English, ESL, mathematics, middle, music, physical, science, secondary, social studies, speech. **Engineering:** Computer, electrical, mechanical, physics. **Engineering technology:** Mechanical. **Family/consumer sciences:** Family studies, family/community services. **Foreign languages:** Spanish. **Health:** Clinical lab science, predental, premedicine, prenursing, prepharmacy, preveterinary. **History:** General. **Interdisciplinary:** Biological/physical sciences, math/computer science. **Legal studies:** Prelaw. **Liberal arts:** Arts/sciences. **Math:** General. **Parks/recreation:** Health/fitness. **Philosophy/religion:** Christian, religion. **Physical sciences:** Chemistry. **Psychology:** General. **Social sciences:** Political science. **Theology:** Bible, missionary, religious ed, theology, youth ministry. **Visual/performing arts:** Art, commercial/advertising art, design, dramatic, graphic design, interior design, music performance, piano/organ, studio arts, voice/opera.

Computing on campus. PC or laptop required. 1,850 workstations in dormitories, library, computer center, student center. Dormitories wired for high-speed internet access and linked to campus network. Commuter students can connect to campus network. Online course registration, online library, helpline, repair service, student web hosting, wireless network available.

Student life. **Freshman orientation:** Mandatory, $200 fee. Preregistration for classes offered. Two-part program includes 1-day summer event and week-long event the week before school starts. **Policies:** Single students must live on campus or with parents. Special arrangements considered. Religious observance required. **Housing:** Guaranteed on-campus for all undergraduates. Single-sex dorms, special housing for disabled, apartments, wellness housing available. $100 partly refundable deposit, deadline 5/1. **Activities:** Bands, campus ministries, choral groups, drama, international student organizations, literary magazine, music ensembles, musical theater, opera, radio station, student government, student newspaper, symphony orchestra, TV station.

Athletics. NAIA. **Intercollegiate:** Baseball M, basketball, cheerleading W, cross-country, golf M, soccer, softball W, tennis, track and field. **Intramural:** Basketball, bowling, cross-country, football (non-tackle), golf M, soccer, softball, swimming, table tennis, tennis, track and field, volleyball. **Team name:** Eagles.

Student services. Alcohol/substance abuse counseling, chaplain/spiritual director, career counseling, student employment services, financial aid counseling, health services, minority student services, personal counseling, placement for graduates, veterans' counselor. **Physically disabled:** Services for visually, speech, hearing impaired.

Contact. E-mail: info@oc.edu
Phone: (405) 425-5050 Toll-free number: (800) 877-5050
Fax: (405) 425-5069
Darci Thompson, Director of Admissions, Oklahoma Christian University, Box 11000, Oklahoma City, OK 73136-1100

Oklahoma City University

Oklahoma City, Oklahoma **CB member**
www.okcu.edu **CB code: 6543**

- Private 4-year university and liberal arts college affiliated with United Methodist Church
- Residential campus in very large city
- 2,190 degree-seeking undergraduates: 17% part-time, 62% women, 9% African American, 4% Asian American, 5% Hispanic American, 5% Native American, 16% international
- 1,707 degree-seeking graduate students
- 79% of applicants admitted
- SAT or ACT (ACT writing optional), application essay required
- 51% graduate within 6 years

General. Founded in 1904. Regionally accredited. Institution embraces the United Methodist tradition of scholarship and service and welcomes all faiths. Service learning incorporated throughout the curriculum. **Degrees:** 467 bachelor's awarded; master's, first professional offered. **ROTC:** Army, Air Force. **Location:** 180 miles from Dallas, 350 miles from Kansas City. **Calendar:** Semester, limited summer session. **Full-time faculty:** 198 total; 78% have terminal degrees, 16% minority, 45% women. **Part-time faculty:** 131 total; 63% have terminal degrees, 12% minority, 50% women. **Class size:** 71% < 20, 26% 20-39, 1% 40-49, 1% 50-99. **Special facilities:** Art center, entrepreneurship center, urban wilderness laboratory.

Freshman class profile. 1,065 applied, 842 admitted, 355 enrolled.

Mid 50% test scores		**Rank in top quarter:**	67%
SAT critical reading:	490-600	**Rank in top tenth:**	39%
SAT math:	480-590	**Return as sophomores:**	78%
ACT composite:	22-27	**Out-of-state:**	50%
GPA 3.75 or higher:	34%	**Live on campus:**	94%
GPA 3.50-3.74:	30%	**International:**	5%
GPA 3.0-3.49:	27%	**Fraternities:**	18%
GPA 2.0-2.99:	9%	**Sororities:**	30%

Basis for selection. School achievement record, which includes class rank, and test scores most important. Counselor recommendations, essays, and activities also considered. Interview recommended for all; audition required for dance, music programs; portfolio required for art, graphic design programs. **Homeschooled:** Must demonstrate that individual is graduating no earlier than their class in the public school system.

High school preparation. College-preparatory program recommended. 15 units required. Required units include English 4, mathematics 3, social studies 3, science 3 (laboratory 1) and foreign language 2. Math requirement includes 2 algebra and 1 geometry, trigonometry, math analysis, or calculus. Social studies requirement includes 1 world history, 1 state history or civics, and 1 U.S. history.

2008-2009 Annual costs. Tuition/fees: $23,400. Room/board: $7,056. Books/supplies: $1,500. Personal expenses: $1,000.

2007-2008 Financial aid. **Need-based:** 303 full-time freshmen applied for aid; 238 were judged to have need; 237 of these received aid. Average need met was 72%. Average scholarship/grant was $15,669; average loan $3,651. 81% of total undergraduate aid awarded as scholarships/grants, 19% as loans/jobs. **Non-need-based:** Awarded to 456 full-time undergraduates, including 108 freshmen. Scholarships awarded for academics, art, athletics, job skills, leadership, music/drama, religious affiliation, ROTC.

Application procedures. Admission: Priority date 3/30; deadline 8/21 (postmark date). $30 fee, may be waived for applicants with need. Admission notification on a rolling basis beginning on or about 10/15. Must reply by May 1 or within 2 week(s) if notified thereafter. **Financial aid:** Priority date 3/1, closing date 6/30. FAFSA, institutional form required. Applicants notified on a rolling basis starting 2/24; must reply within 2 week(s) of notification.

Academics. Special study options: Accelerated study, cooperative education, distance learning, double major, dual enrollment of high school students, ESL, exchange student, external degree, honors, independent study, internships, New York semester, student-designed major, study abroad, teacher certification program, Washington semester. **Credit/placement by examination:** AP, CLEP, IB, SAT, ACT, institutional tests. 30 credit hours maximum toward bachelor's degree. **Support services:** Learning center, reduced course load, study skills assistance, tutoring, writing center.

Majors. Area/ethnic studies: American. **Biology:** General, biochemistry, biomedical sciences, cell/histology. **Business:** General, accounting, business admin, finance, international, management information systems, management science, managerial economics, marketing. **Communications:** Advertising, broadcast journalism, journalism, media studies, public relations, radio/tv. **Computer sciences:** General, computer science. **Education:** General, art, business, early childhood, elementary, English, foreign languages, French, German, health, history, mathematics, Montessori teacher, music, physical, science, secondary, social studies, Spanish, speech. **Foreign languages:** French, German, Spanish. **Health:** Athletic training, nursing (RN), predental, premedicine, prepharmacy, preveterinary. **History:** General. **Interdisciplinary:** Biological/physical sciences. **Legal studies:** Prelaw. **Liberal arts:** Arts/sciences, humanities. **Math:** General. **Parks/recreation:** Health/fitness. **Philosophy/religion:** Philosophy, religion. **Physical sciences:** Chemistry, physics. **Protective services:** Corrections, law enforcement admin, police science. **Psychology:** General. **Public administration:** Social work. **Social sciences:** Economics, political science, sociology. **Theology:** Bible, religious ed, sacred music, youth ministry. **Visual/performing arts:** General, acting, art, art history/conservation, arts management, cinematography, dance, dramatic, film/cinema, graphic design, music management, music performance, music theory/composition, photography, piano/organ, stringed instruments, studio arts, theater arts management, theater design, voice/opera. **Other:** Entertainment business, Environmental sciences, Kinesiology & exercise studies, World religions.

Most popular majors. Business/marketing 7%, health sciences 13%, liberal arts 37%, visual/performing arts 20%.

Computing on campus. 489 workstations in dormitories, library, computer center, student center. Dormitories wired for high-speed internet access and linked to campus network. Commuter students can connect to campus network. Online course registration, online library, helpline, repair service, student web hosting, wireless network available.

Student life. Freshman orientation: Mandatory, $50 fee. Preregistration for classes offered. **Housing:** Guaranteed on-campus for all undergraduates. Coed dorms, single-sex dorms, apartments, fraternity/sorority housing, wellness housing available. $100 deposit. Learning communities available. **Activities:** Bands, campus ministries, choral groups, dance, drama, international student organizations, literary magazine, music ensembles, musical theater, opera, student government, student newspaper, symphony orchestra, TV station, Kappa Phi, Sigma Theta Epsilon, Association for People of Color, United Methodist Student Fellowship, Students of Arts Management, Alpha Phi Sorority, Gamma Phi Beta Sorority, Lambda Chi Alpha Fraternity, Kappa Sigma Fraternity.

Athletics. NAIA. **Intercollegiate:** Baseball M, basketball, cheerleading, golf, rowing (crew), soccer, softball W, track and field, volleyball W, wrestling. **Intramural:** Basketball, fencing, football (non-tackle) M, golf, softball, table tennis, volleyball. **Team name:** Stars.

Student services. Adult student services, chaplain/spiritual director, career counseling, student employment services, financial aid counseling, health services, minority student services, personal counseling, placement for graduates, veterans' counselor. **Physically disabled:** Services for visually, hearing impaired.

Contact. E-mail: uadmissions@okcu.edu
Phone: (405) 208-5050 Toll-free number: (800) 633-7242
Fax: (405) 208-5916
Eduardo Prieto, Dean of Enrollment Services, Oklahoma City University, 2501 North Blackwelder Avenue, Oklahoma City, OK 73106-1493

Oklahoma Panhandle State University

Goodwell, Oklahoma
www.opsu.edu **CB code: 6571**

- Public 4-year agricultural and liberal arts college
- Residential campus in rural community
- 1,124 degree-seeking undergraduates: 13% part-time, 49% women, 9% African American, 14% Hispanic American, 3% Native American, 4% international
- 100% of applicants admitted
- 52% graduate within 6 years

General. Founded in 1909. Regionally accredited. **Degrees:** 183 bachelor's, 22 associate awarded. **Location:** 110 miles from Amarillo, Texas; 10 miles from Guymon. **Calendar:** Semester, limited summer session. **Full-time faculty:** 67 total; 31% have terminal degrees, 4% minority, 39% women. **Part-time faculty:** 26 total; 50% women. **Class size:** 77% < 20, 20% 20-39, less than 1% 40-49, 2% 50-99, less than 1% >100. **Special facilities:** Agronomy experiment station, historical museum, livestock facilities, farming area, rodeo arena, meat lab.

Freshman class profile. 317 applied, 317 admitted, 288 enrolled.

Mid 50% test scores			
SAT critical reading:	380-490	GPA 3.0-3.49:	36%
SAT math:	410-570	GPA 2.0-2.99:	35%
ACT composite:	16-21	Out-of-state:	32%
GPA 3.75 or higher:	18%	Live on campus:	90%
GPA 3.50-3.74:	11%	International:	3%

Basis for selection. Secondary school record, test scores and class rank most important. SAT or ACT recommended. Incoming students without ACT, or with score of 19 or below, must take ACCUPLACER test. **Home-schooled:** Transcript of courses and grades required.

High school preparation. 15 units required. Required units include English 4, mathematics 3, social studies 2, history 1, science 2 (laboratory 2) and academic electives 3.

2008-2009 Annual costs. Tuition/fees: $4,202; $9,542 out-of-state. Room/board: $3,270. Books/supplies: $240.

2007-2008 Financial aid. All financial aid based on need.

Application procedures. Admission: No deadline. No application fee. Admission notification on a rolling basis. **Financial aid:** Priority date 3/15; no closing date. FAFSA, institutional form required. Applicants notified by 5/1.

Academics. Special study options: Cooperative education, distance learning, double major, dual enrollment of high school students, ESL, independent study, internships, liberal arts/career combination, teacher certification program. **Credit/placement by examination:** AP, CLEP, SAT, ACT, institutional tests. 34 credit hours maximum toward associate degree, 60 toward bachelor's. **Support services:** Learning center, reduced course load, remedial instruction, study skills assistance, tutoring, writing center.

Majors. Agriculture: Agribusiness operations, agronomy, animal sciences, equine science. **Biology:** General. **Business:** Accounting, business admin. **Computer sciences:** General. **Education:** Agricultural, business, elementary. **Engineering technology:** Industrial. **Foreign languages:** Spanish. **Health:** Nursing (RN). **History:** General. **Interdisciplinary:** Biological/physical sciences. **Math:** General. **Parks/recreation:** Health/fitness. **Physical sciences:** Chemistry. **Psychology:** General. **Social sciences:** General. **Visual/performing arts:** Art.

Most popular majors. Agriculture 22%, biology 12%, business/marketing 11%, computer/information sciences 6%, health sciences 6%, parks/recreation 7%, psychology 8%, visual/performing arts 6%.

Computing on campus. 150 workstations in library, computer center, student center. Dormitories wired for high-speed internet access. Online library, wireless network available.

Student life. Freshman orientation: Mandatory. Preregistration for classes offered. **Housing:** Guaranteed on-campus for all undergraduates. Single-sex dorms, apartments, wellness housing available. **Activities:** Bands, choral groups, drama, music ensembles, musical theater, radio station, student government, student newspaper, Wesley Foundation, Baptist student union, Church of Christ student center, Circle-K, Newman club, Methodist student center.

Athletics. NCAA. **Intercollegiate:** Baseball M, basketball, cheerleading, cross-country, football (tackle) M, golf, softball W, volleyball W. **Intramural:** Basketball, football (non-tackle), golf, soccer, softball, table tennis, volleyball. **Team name:** Aggies.

Student services. Adult student services, alcohol/substance abuse counseling, chaplain/spiritual director, career counseling, student employment services, financial aid counseling, health services, minority student services, personal counseling, placement for graduates. **Physically disabled:** Services for visually, speech, hearing impaired.

Contact. E-mail: jolie@opsu.edu
Phone: (580) 349-1312 Toll-free number: (800) 664-6778
Fax: (580) 349-1371
Bobby Jenkins, Registrar and Director of Admissions, Oklahoma Panhandle State University, OPSU Admissions, Goodwell, OK 73939-0430

Oklahoma State University

Stillwater, Oklahoma — **CB member**
www.osu.okstate.edu — **CB code: 6546**

- Public 4-year university
- Residential campus in small city
- 17,701 degree-seeking undergraduates: 13% part-time, 48% women, 4% African American, 2% Asian American, 3% Hispanic American, 10% Native American, 2% international
- 4,371 degree-seeking graduate students
- 89% of applicants admitted
- SAT or ACT (ACT writing optional) required
- 60% graduate within 6 years

General. Founded in 1890. Regionally accredited. Campuses in Oklahoma City, Okmulgee, Tulsa and Center for Health Sciences (includes College of Osteopathic Medicine) at Tulsa. Stillwater campus includes the Center for Veterinary Health Sciences. **Degrees:** 3,819 bachelor's awarded; master's, doctoral, first professional offered. **ROTC:** Army, Air Force. **Location:** 65 miles from Tulsa, 65 miles from Oklahoma City. **Calendar:** Semester, extensive summer session. **Full-time faculty:** 991 total; 91% have terminal degrees, 10% minority, 32% women. **Part-time faculty:** 272 total; 31% have terminal degrees, 11% minority, 51% women. **Class size:** 37% < 20, 38% 20-39, 11% 40-49, 10% 50-99, 4% >100. **Special facilities:** Laser research center with 8 laboratories and 30 laser systems, biotechnology and genetic engineering research center, telecommunication center.

Freshman class profile. 6,406 applied, 5,702 admitted, 3,073 enrolled.

Mid 50% test scores		**Rank in top quarter:**	56%
SAT critical reading:	480-600	**Rank in top tenth:**	27%
SAT math:	500-620	**Return as sophomores:**	77%
ACT composite:	22-27	**Out-of-state:**	22%
GPA 3.75 or higher:	35%	**Live on campus:**	88%
GPA 3.50-3.74:	23%	**International:**	1%
GPA 3.0-3.49:	32%	**Fraternities:**	21%
GPA 2.0-2.99:	10%	**Sororities:**	28%

Basis for selection. Applicants must have 3.0 GPA and rank in top 33% of class, or 24 ACT/1090 SAT (exclusive of Writing), or have 3.0 GPA in 15 required curricular units and have 21 ACT/980 SAT(exclusive of Writing), or have 3.0 GPA in 15 required curricular units or 22 ACT/1020 SAT and answer 7 undergraduate application questions. Early application encouraged. Test scores must be received no later than Friday before classes begin for fall-term admission. Interview recommended for academically borderline students.

High school preparation. College-preparatory program required. 15 units required; 18 recommended. Required and recommended units include English 4, mathematics 3, social studies 2, history 1, science 2 (laboratory 2), foreign language 2, computer science 1 and academic electives 3.

2008-2009 Annual costs. Tuition/fees: $6,887; $17,241 out-of-state. Room/board: $6,358. Books/supplies: $980. Personal expenses: $2,440.

2007-2008 Financial aid. Need-based: 2,050 full-time freshmen applied for aid; 1,489 were judged to have need; 1,454 of these received aid. Average need met was 72%. Average scholarship/grant was $5,687; average loan $3,158. 57% of total undergraduate aid awarded as scholarships/grants, 43% as loans/jobs. **Non-need-based:** Awarded to 7,469 full-time undergraduates, including 1,820 freshmen. Scholarships awarded for academics, alumni affiliation, art, athletics, leadership, minority status, music/drama, ROTC, state residency.

Application procedures. Admission: No deadline. $40 fee, may be waived for applicants with need. Admission notification on a rolling basis. Deferred admission allowed based on military deployments. **Financial aid:** No deadline. FAFSA required. Applicants notified on a rolling basis starting 10/1; must reply within 4 week(s) of notification.

Academics. Special study options: Accelerated study, combined bachelor's/graduate degree, cross-registration, distance learning, double major, dual enrollment of high school students, ESL, exchange student, honors, independent study, internships, semester at sea, student-designed major, study abroad, teacher certification program, Washington semester. **Credit/placement by examination:** AP, CLEP, IB, SAT, ACT. Maximum number of credit hours towards degree is subject to university "residence credit" policy. **Support services:** Learning center, pre-admission summer program, reduced course load, remedial instruction, study skills assistance, tutoring, writing center.

Honors college/program. 27 ACT/1220 SAT (exclusive of Writing) and 3.74 GPA required.

Majors. Agriculture: Animal sciences, business, communications, economics, food science, horticultural science, landscaping, soil science. **Architecture:** Architecture, landscape. **Area/ethnic studies:** American. **Biology:** General, biochemistry, botany, entomology, microbiology, physiology, zoology. **Business:** Accounting, business admin, finance, hospitality admin, international, management information systems, managerial economics, marketing. **Communications:** Journalism. **Computer sciences:** General. **Conservation:** Environmental science, forestry. **Education:** General, agricultural, elementary, music, physical, secondary, voc/tech. **Engineering:** Aerospace, agricultural, architectural, chemical, civil, computer, electrical, industrial, mechanical. **Engineering technology:** Construction, electrical, mechanical. **Family/consumer sciences:** Family studies, food/nutrition, housing. **Foreign languages:** French, German, Russian, Spanish. **Health:** Athletic training, public health ed, speech pathology. **History:** General. **Liberal arts:** Arts/sciences. **Math:** General, statistics. **Parks/recreation:** General. **Philosophy/religion:** Philosophy. **Physical sciences:** Chemistry, geology, physics. **Protective services:** Fire safety technology. **Psychology:** General. **Social sciences:** Economics, geography, political science, sociology. **Transportation:** Aviation. **Visual/performing arts:** Art, dramatic.

Most popular majors. Agriculture 8%, business/marketing 29%, education 8%, engineering/engineering technologies 10%, family/consumer sciences 8%.

Computing on campus. Dormitories wired for high-speed internet access and linked to campus network. Commuter students can connect to campus network. Online course registration, online library, helpline, repair service, wireless network available.

Student life. Freshman orientation: Mandatory. Preregistration for classes offered. One-day programs in June. Additional program held week before classes begin each fall semester for a fee. **Housing:** Guaranteed on-campus for freshmen. Coed dorms, single-sex dorms, special housing for disabled, apartments, fraternity/sorority housing, wellness housing available. $150 fully refundable deposit. Learning communities, special interest housing available. **Activities:** Bands, campus ministries, choral groups, dance, drama, international student organizations, literary magazine, music ensembles, musical theater, opera, radio station, student government, student newspaper, symphony orchestra, TV station, Campus Crusade for Christ, Flying Aggies, rodeo club, Young Democrats, Young Republicans, fire protection society, Alpha Pi Omega, National Organization for Women, African American student association, Hispanic student association.

Athletics. NCAA. **Intercollegiate:** Baseball M, basketball, cross-country, equestrian W, football (tackle) M, golf, soccer W, softball W, tennis, track and field, wrestling M. **Intramural:** Archery, badminton, basketball, bowling, cross-country, football (tackle), golf, racquetball, soccer, softball, squash, swimming, table tennis, tennis, track and field, volleyball, water polo, weight lifting, wrestling M. **Team name:** Cowboys, Cowgirls.

Student services. Adult student services, alcohol/substance abuse counseling, chaplain/spiritual director, career counseling, student employment services, financial aid counseling, health services, legal services, minority student services, personal counseling, placement for graduates, veterans' counselor, women's services. **Physically disabled:** Services for visually, speech, hearing impaired.

Contact. E-mail: admissions@okstate.edu
Phone: (405) 744-5358 Toll-free number: (800) 233-5019 ext. 1
Fax: (405) 744-7092
Karen Lucas, Director of Undergraduate Admissions, Oklahoma State University, 219 Student Union, Stillwater, OK 74078

Oklahoma Wesleyan University

Bartlesville, Oklahoma — **CB member**
www.okwu.edu — **CB code: 6135**

- Private 4-year university and liberal arts college affiliated with Wesleyan Church
- Residential campus in large town

- 1,015 degree-seeking undergraduates
- 60 graduate students
- 50% of applicants admitted
- SAT or ACT required

General. Founded in 1909. Regionally accredited. **Degrees:** 276 bachelor's, 36 associate awarded; master's offered. **Location:** 40 miles from Tulsa. **Calendar:** Differs by program, limited summer session. **Full-time faculty:** 27 total; 44% have terminal degrees, 4% minority, 30% women. **Part-time faculty:** 3 total; 33% have terminal degrees, 67% women. **Class size:** 89% < 20, 10% 20-39, 1% 40-49, less than 1% 50-99. **Special facilities:** Historic mansion, fine arts center, city bike path.

Freshman class profile. 452 applied, 225 admitted, 93 enrolled.

Mid 50% test scores			
SAT critical reading:	430-520	GPA 3.50-3.74:	13%
SAT math:	420-550	GPA 3.0-3.49:	26%
ACT composite:	19-25	GPA 2.0-2.99:	12%
GPA 3.75 or higher:	49%	Out-of-state:	60%
		Live on campus:	90%

Basis for selection. In addition to required high school study, students must fulfill 2 of the following: rank in top half of class, have 2.0 GPA, or have 18 ACT. **Homeschooled:** Statement describing homeschool structure and mission, transcript of courses and grades required.

High school preparation. 15 units required. Required units include English 4, mathematics 2, social studies 2, science 1 (laboratory 1).

2008-2009 Annual costs. Tuition/fees: $16,585. Room/board: $6,050.

2008-2009 Financial aid. Need-based: 21% of total undergraduate aid awarded as scholarships/grants, 79% as loans/jobs. **Non-need-based:** Scholarships awarded for academics, alumni affiliation, athletics, leadership, music/drama, religious affiliation, state residency.

Application procedures. Admission: No deadline. $25 fee, may be waived for applicants with need, free for online applicants. Admission notification on a rolling basis. Students must be accepted prior to beginning of classes. **Financial aid:** Priority date 4/1; no closing date. FAFSA, institutional form required. Applicants notified on a rolling basis starting 4/1; must reply by 5/1 or within 2 week(s) of notification.

Academics. Special study options: Distance learning, double major, dual enrollment of high school students, independent study, internships, student-designed major, study abroad, teacher certification program, Washington semester. **Credit/placement by examination:** AP, CLEP, institutional tests. 30 credit hours maximum toward associate degree, 36 toward bachelor's. **Support services:** Learning center, reduced course load, remedial instruction, study skills assistance, tutoring, writing center.

Majors. Biology: General. **Business:** General, business admin. **Communications:** General. **Computer sciences:** General, computer science. **Education:** Business, elementary, English, mathematics, music, physical, science, social studies. **History:** General. **Interdisciplinary:** Behavioral sciences. **Math:** General. **Parks/recreation:** Exercise sciences. **Philosophy/religion:** Christian. **Physical sciences:** Chemistry. **Psychology:** General. **Social sciences:** General, political science. **Theology:** Bible, missionary, sacred music, theology.

Computing on campus. 40 workstations in library, computer center, student center. Dormitories wired for high-speed internet access and linked to campus network. Online course registration, online library, helpline, repair service, wireless network available.

Student life. Freshman orientation: Mandatory, $100 fee. Preregistration for classes offered. **Policies:** Religious observance required. **Housing:** Guaranteed on-campus for all undergraduates. Single-sex dorms, apartments available. $200 fully refundable deposit. **Activities:** Bands, campus ministries, choral groups, music ensembles, student government, student newspaper, campus missionary fellowship, theology fellowship, Fellowship of Christian Athletes, Operation Saturation, Sudan fellowship, College Republicans.

Athletics. NAIA, NCCAA. **Intercollegiate:** Baseball M, basketball, cross-country, golf M, soccer, tennis, track and field, volleyball W. **Intramural:** Basketball, football (non-tackle), racquetball, softball, table tennis, volleyball. **Team name:** Eagles.

Student services. Adult student services, chaplain/spiritual director, career counseling, student employment services, financial aid counseling, health services, placement for graduates, veterans' counselor.

Contact. E-mail: admissions@okwu.edu
Phone: (918) 335-6219 Toll-free number: (800) 468-6292
Fax: (918) 335-6229
Robert Myers, Executive Vice President, Oklahoma Wesleyan University, 2201 Silver Lake Road, Bartlesville, OK 74006

Oral Roberts University

Tulsa, Oklahoma — **CB member**
www.oru.edu — **CB code: 6552**

- Private 4-year university and liberal arts college affiliated with nondenominational tradition
- Residential campus in large city
- 2,558 degree-seeking undergraduates: 9% part-time, 58% women
- 509 graduate students
- 73% of applicants admitted
- SAT or ACT (ACT writing optional), application essay required
- 52% graduate within 6 years

General. Founded in 1965. Regionally accredited. Integrated math and science academy sponsored by Oklahoma State Regents for Higher Education. **Degrees:** 556 bachelor's awarded; master's, doctoral, first professional offered. **ROTC:** Air Force. **Location:** 7 miles from downtown. **Calendar:** Semester, limited summer session. **Full-time faculty:** 186 total; 64% have terminal degrees, 12% minority, 41% women. **Part-time faculty:** 105 total; 17% have terminal degrees, 17% minority, 49% women. **Class size:** 66% < 20, 27% 20-39, 3% 40-49, 5% 50-99, less than 1% >100. **Special facilities:** Prayer tower, mineralogical museum.

Freshman class profile. 1,127 applied, 819 admitted, 481 enrolled.

Mid 50% test scores			
SAT critical reading:	470-590	GPA 3.0-3.49:	29%
SAT math:	460-570	GPA 2.0-2.99:	24%
ACT composite:	20-26	Rank in top quarter:	45%
GPA 3.75 or higher:	31%	Rank in top tenth:	23%
GPA 3.50-3.74:	16%	Out-of-state:	68%
		Live on campus:	75%

Basis for selection. Academic record, test scores, personal essay, minister's recommendation, other recommendations, extracurricular activities considered. Students must provide immunization records. Interview recommended for all; audition required for music program; portfolio recommended for art program. **Homeschooled:** Under special circumstances, applicants may be required to submit additional curricular information and/or proof of high school equivalency.

High school preparation. College-preparatory program recommended. 16 units recommended. Recommended units include English 4, mathematics 2, social studies 2, science 1 (laboratory 1), foreign language 2 and academic electives 4. Students matriculating in bachelor of science program may substitute additional math units for foreign language.

2008-2009 Annual costs. Tuition/fees: $18,386. Room/board: $7,610. Books/supplies: $1,500. Personal expenses: $1,500.

2007-2008 Financial aid. Need-based: Average need met was 86%. Average scholarship/grant was $9,759; average loan $6,534. 18% of total undergraduate aid awarded as scholarships/grants, 82% as loans/jobs. **Non-need-based:** Awarded to 1,237 full-time undergraduates, including 168 freshmen. Scholarships awarded for academics, alumni affiliation, art, athletics, leadership, music/drama.

Application procedures. Admission: Priority date 11/15; no deadline. $35 fee, may be waived for applicants with need. Admission notification on a rolling basis. **Financial aid:** Priority date 3/15; no closing date. FAFSA required. Must reply by 7/15.

Academics. Special study options: Accelerated study, combined bachelor's/graduate degree, distance learning, double major, dual enrollment of high school students, ESL, external degree, honors, independent study, internships, liberal arts/career combination, student-designed major, study abroad, teacher certification program, Washington semester, weekend college. **Credit/placement by examination:** AP, CLEP, institutional tests. 30 credit hours maximum toward associate degree, 30 toward bachelor's. **Support services:** Learning center, reduced course load, remedial instruction, study skills assistance, tutoring.

Majors. Biology: General, biochemistry. **Business:** Accounting, business admin, finance, international, international marketing, management information systems, management science, marketing, organizational behavior. **Communications:** General. **Computer sciences:** General, computer science. **Education:** Art, business, early childhood, elementary, English, foreign languages, health, mathematics, music, physical, science, social studies, Spanish, special. **Engineering:** General, biomedical, computer, electrical, mechanical, physics. **Foreign languages:** French, German, Spanish. **Health:** Clinical lab science, nursing (RN). **History:** General. **Liberal arts:** Arts/sciences. **Math:** General. **Parks/recreation:** Exercise sciences, facilities management, health/fitness. **Physical sciences:** Chemistry, physics. **Psychology:** General. **Public administration:** Social work. **Social sciences:** International relations, political science. **Theology:** Bible, missionary, pastoral counseling, religious ed, sacred music, theology. **Visual/performing arts:** Acting, art, commercial/advertising art, dance, design, dramatic, music performance, music theory/composition, piano/organ, studio arts, theater design, voice/opera.

Most popular majors. Business/marketing 25%, communications/journalism 12%, education 9%, health sciences 6%, psychology 6%, theological studies 12%, visual/performing arts 6%.

Computing on campus. 382 workstations in library, computer center. Dormitories linked to campus network. Commuter students can connect to campus network. Online course registration, online library, wireless network available.

Student life. Freshman orientation: Mandatory. Preregistration for classes offered. **Policies:** Single undergraduate students under 25 years of age must live in university housing or with parents. Religious observance required. **Housing:** Guaranteed on-campus for all undergraduates. Single-sex dorms available. $125 nonrefundable deposit, deadline 8/8. **Activities:** Bands, campus ministries, choral groups, dance, drama, international student organizations, music ensembles, Model UN, musical theater, radio station, student government, student newspaper, TV station, community outreach, missions club, Young Republicans, Young Democrats, student activist society, Model United Nations.

Athletics. NCAA. **Intercollegiate:** Baseball M, basketball, cross-country, golf, soccer, tennis, track and field, volleyball W. **Intramural:** Badminton, basketball, bowling, cross-country, football (non-tackle), golf, racquetball, softball, swimming, table tennis, tennis, volleyball, wrestling M. **Team name:** Golden Eagles.

Student services. Chaplain/spiritual director, career counseling, student employment services, financial aid counseling, health services, personal counseling, placement for graduates, veterans' counselor. **Physically disabled:** Services for visually, speech, hearing impaired.

Contact. E-mail: admissions@oru.edu
Phone: (918) 496-6518 Toll-free number: (800) 678-8876
Fax: (918) 495-6222
Chris Belcher, Director of Admissions, Oral Roberts University, 7777 South Lewis Avenue, Tulsa, OK 74171

Rogers State University
Claremore, Oklahoma
www.rsu.edu **CB code: 6545**

- Public 4-year university
- Commuter campus in large town
- 3,788 degree-seeking undergraduates: 40% part-time, 63% women, 3% African American, 1% Asian American, 2% Hispanic American, 30% Native American, 1% international
- 56% of applicants admitted

General. Founded in 1909. Regionally accredited. **Degrees:** 159 bachelor's, 197 associate awarded. **ROTC:** Air Force. **Location:** 25 miles from Tulsa. **Calendar:** Semester, extensive summer session. **Full-time faculty:** 98 total; 62% have terminal degrees, 10% minority, 45% women. **Part-time faculty:** 124 total; 13% have terminal degrees, 12% minority, 66% women. **Class size:** 38% < 20, 59% 20-39, 2% 40-49, less than 1% 50-99. **Special facilities:** Conservation education reserve.

Freshman class profile. 1,686 applied, 941 admitted, 750 enrolled.

Mid 50% test scores		**Rank in top tenth:**	7%
ACT composite:	17-22	**End year in good standing:**	64%
GPA 3.75 or higher:	13%	**Return as sophomores:**	47%
GPA 3.50-3.74:	13%	**Out-of-state:**	3%
GPA 3.0-3.49:	34%	**Live on campus:**	14%
GPA 2.0-2.99:	35%	**International:**	1%
Rank in top quarter:	27%		

Basis for selection. Bachelor degree programs require 20 ACT and no curricular deficiencies. Open admission for associate degree programs. Test scores not required for associate degree applicants. Essay required for returning suspension students only.

High school preparation. College-preparatory program recommended. 15 units required; 19 recommended. Required and recommended units include English 4, mathematics 3-4, social studies 1, history 2, science 2-3 (laboratory 2-3), foreign language 2, computer science 1, visual/performing arts 2 and academic electives 3. Math should include algebra I and II; 1 computer science also recommended; history should include 1 unit of U.S. history and 1 of citizenship (government, geography, etc.).

2008-2009 Annual costs. Tuition/fees: $4,277; $9,734 out-of-state. Room/board: $7,095. Books/supplies: $700.

2008-2009 Financial aid. Need-based: 538 full-time freshmen applied for aid; 396 were judged to have need; 388 of these received aid. Average need met was 61%. Average scholarship/grant was $1,852; average loan $1,051. 37% of total undergraduate aid awarded as scholarships/grants, 63% as loans/jobs. **Non-need-based:** Awarded to 471 full-time undergraduates, including 229 freshmen. Scholarships awarded for academics, athletics, leadership, music/drama.

Application procedures. Admission: No deadline. No application fee. Admission notification on a rolling basis. **Financial aid:** Priority date 6/1; no closing date. FAFSA, institutional form required. Applicants notified on a rolling basis starting 4/1; must reply within 3 week(s) of notification.

Academics. Special study options: Combined bachelor's/graduate degree, cooperative education, distance learning, double major, dual enrollment of high school students, honors, independent study, internships, liberal arts/career combination, study abroad, Washington semester. **Credit/placement by examination:** AP, CLEP, IB, institutional tests. 30 credit hours maximum toward associate degree, 45 toward bachelor's. **Support services:** Learning center, reduced course load, remedial instruction, study skills assistance, tutoring, writing center.

Majors. Biology: General. **Business:** Business admin. **Communications:** General. **Computer sciences:** General, computer graphics. **Health:** Nursing (RN). **Liberal arts:** Arts/sciences. **Parks/recreation:** Sports admin. **Protective services:** Law enforcement admin. **Psychology:** Community. **Public administration:** General. **Social sciences:** General. **Visual/performing arts:** General. **Other:** Applied technology, Business information technology.

Most popular majors. Biology 14%, business/marketing 38%, engineering/engineering technologies 14%, liberal arts 10%, social sciences 14%.

Computing on campus. 320 workstations in dormitories, library, student center. Dormitories wired for high-speed internet access and linked to campus network. Online library, wireless network available.

Student life. Freshman orientation: Available. Preregistration for classes offered. **Housing:** Coed dorms, special housing for disabled, apartments, wellness housing available. $200 fully refundable deposit. **Activities:** Jazz band, campus ministries, choral groups, drama, international student organizations, literary magazine, radio station, student government, TV station, Native American association, Baptist campus ministries, Defenders of Mother Earth, student art association, criminal justice association, student nursing association, Society for Computing and Business Machines, horse and agriculture club.

Athletics. NAIA. **Intercollegiate:** Baseball M, basketball, cheerleading, rodeo, soccer, softball W. **Intramural:** Basketball, bowling, football (non-tackle), soccer, softball, volleyball. **Team name:** Hillcats.

Student services. Adult student services, career counseling, services for economically disadvantaged, student employment services, financial aid counseling, health services, on-campus daycare, personal counseling, placement for graduates, veterans' counselor. **Physically disabled:** Services for visually, hearing impaired.

Contact. E-mail: admissions@rsu.edu
Phone: (918) 343-7546 Toll-free number: (800) 256-7511
Fax: (918) 343-7595
Julie Rampey, Director of Admissions, Rogers State University, 1701 West Will Rogers Boulevard, Claremore, OK 74017

St. Gregory's University
Shawnee, Oklahoma
www.stgregorys.edu **CB code: 6621**

- Private 4-year university and liberal arts college affiliated with Roman Catholic Church
- Residential campus in large town
- 700 degree-seeking undergraduates: 58% part-time, 62% women, 6% African American, 7% Hispanic American, 8% Native American, 5% international
- 44 degree-seeking graduate students

- 97% of applicants admitted
- SAT or ACT (ACT writing optional), application essay required

General. Founded in 1875. Regionally accredited. Roman Catholic and Benedictine tradition. **Degrees:** 160 bachelor's, 42 associate awarded; master's offered. **ROTC:** Air Force. **Location:** 30 miles from Oklahoma City. **Calendar:** Semester, limited summer session. **Full-time faculty:** 39 total; 62% have terminal degrees, 5% minority, 46% women. **Part-time faculty:** 88 total; 23% have terminal degrees, 6% minority, 52% women. **Class size:** 93% < 20, 7% 20-39. **Special facilities:** Benedictine abbey, art museum.

Freshman class profile.

Mid 50% test scores		**GPA 3.0-3.49:**	36%
SAT critical reading:	430-560	**GPA 2.0-2.99:**	28%
SAT math:	440-500	**Rank in top quarter:**	23%
ACT composite:	18-23	**Rank in top tenth:**	13%
GPA 3.75 or higher:	22%	**Out-of-state:**	21%
GPA 3.50-3.74:	14%		

Basis for selection. Core classes, GPA most important; test scores, class rank important. Interview required for students admitted on probation; audition required for dance, drama, and choral scholarships; portfolio required for art scholarships. **Homeschooled:** Interview required. **Learning Disabled:** Students with need beyond ADA standards may apply to Partners in Learning Program. Additional fee of approximately $7,000 required if admitted.

High school preparation. 17 units recommended. Recommended units include English 4, mathematics 3, social studies 2, history 2, science 2 (laboratory 2) and foreign language 2.

2008-2009 Annual costs. Tuition/fees: $15,560. Room/board: $6,288. Books/supplies: $900. Personal expenses: $2,000.

2007-2008 Financial aid. Non-need-based: Scholarships awarded for academics, alumni affiliation, art, athletics, job skills, leadership, music/drama, religious affiliation.

Application procedures. Admission: Priority date 8/1; no deadline. $25 fee, may be waived for applicants with need. Admission notification on a rolling basis. **Financial aid:** Priority date 4/1; no closing date. FAFSA, institutional form required. Applicants notified on a rolling basis starting 2/15; must reply within 3 week(s) of notification.

Academics. Discussion-based seminars on Western and Catholic intellectual traditions required of all freshmen and sophomore students. Special accelerated programs for non-traditional students in Shawnee and Tulsa, Oklahoma. **Special study options:** Accelerated study, cooperative education, double major, ESL, honors, independent study, internships, student-designed major, study abroad, teacher certification program. **Credit/placement by examination:** AP, CLEP, IB, SAT, ACT. 12 credit hours maximum toward associate degree, 30 toward bachelor's. Course proficiency exams available in areas where no CLEP exams offered. **Support services:** Remedial instruction, study skills assistance, tutoring.

Majors. Business: Business admin. **Education:** General, elementary, secondary. **Interdisciplinary:** Natural sciences. **Liberal arts:** Arts/sciences, humanities. **Social sciences:** General. **Theology:** Theology.

Most popular majors. Biology 7%, business/marketing 45%, liberal arts 10%, social sciences 23%, theological studies 8%.

Computing on campus. 60 workstations in dormitories, library, computer center, student center. Dormitories wired for high-speed internet access and linked to campus network. Commuter students can connect to campus network. Online library, helpline, repair service, student web hosting, wireless network available.

Student life. Freshman orientation: Mandatory. Preregistration for classes offered. Three-day program held prior to start of fall term, plus evenings in first week of fall semester. **Policies:** Smoke-free; alcohol/drug-free; on-campus residency required under age 22. **Housing:** Guaranteed on-campus for freshmen. Single-sex dorms, wellness housing available. $100 fully refundable deposit. **Activities:** Jazz band, choral groups, dance, drama, student government, student newspaper, Knights of Columbus, academic honor society, Fellowship of Christian Athletes, Buckley Retreat Team, history club, student alumni council, Students in Free Enterprise, Hispanic awareness student association.

Athletics. NAIA. **Intercollegiate:** Baseball M, basketball, soccer, softball W, volleyball W. **Intramural:** Basketball, football (non-tackle), racquetball, soccer, softball, table tennis, tennis, volleyball. **Team name:** Cavaliers.

Student services. Adult student services, alcohol/substance abuse counseling, chaplain/spiritual director, career counseling, services for economically disadvantaged, student employment services, financial aid counseling, minority student services, personal counseling, placement for graduates, veterans' counselor. **Learning disabled:** Comprehensive services available.

Contact. E-mail: admissions@stgregorys.edu
Phone: (405) 878-5444 Toll-free number: (888) 784-7347
Fax: (405) 878-5198
Director of Admissions, St. Gregory's University, 1900 West MacArthur Drive, Shawnee, OK 74804

Southeastern Oklahoma State University

Durant, Oklahoma
www.sosu.edu **CB code: 6657**

- Public 4-year liberal arts and teachers college
- Commuter campus in large town
- 3,465 degree-seeking undergraduates: 21% part-time, 55% women, 5% African American, 1% Asian American, 3% Hispanic American, 31% Native American, 1% international
- 321 degree-seeking graduate students
- 82% of applicants admitted
- SAT or ACT (ACT writing optional) required

General. Founded in 1909. Regionally accredited. Degree programs offered through satellite campus at Idabel and Higher Education Centers at Ardmore, McAlester, Tinker Air Force Base, Oklahoma City Community College, and Grayson County College. **Degrees:** 662 bachelor's awarded; master's offered. **Location:** 90 miles from Dallas. **Calendar:** Semester, extensive summer session. **Full-time faculty:** 143 total; 74% have terminal degrees, 17% minority, 41% women. **Part-time faculty:** 109 total; 25% have terminal degrees, 20% minority, 47% women. **Class size:** 47% < 20, 43% 20-39, 6% 40-49, 4% 50-99, less than 1% >100. **Special facilities:** Herbarium, equestrian facilities.

Freshman class profile. 916 applied, 748 admitted, 612 enrolled.

Mid 50% test scores		**GPA 2.0-2.99:**	24%
ACT composite:	18-23	**Rank in top quarter:**	43%
GPA 3.75 or higher:	18%	**Rank in top tenth:**	15%
GPA 3.50-3.74:	22%	**Out-of-state:**	22%
GPA 3.0-3.49:	36%		

Basis for selection. High school transcript and test scores important. Must have 2.7 GPA and rank in top half of class, 20 ACT or 940 SAT (exclusive of Writing), score in top half of applicants on ACT scores, or attain 2.7 GPA in 15 core units. Audition required for drama, music programs. Interview required for alternative admissions. **Homeschooled:** 20 ACT required.

High school preparation. College-preparatory program recommended. 15 units required. Required and recommended units include English 4, mathematics 3, social studies 1, history 3, science 2 (laboratory 2), foreign language 1, computer science 1 and academic electives 3. 1 citizenship required.

2008-2009 Annual costs. Tuition/fees: $4,316; $10,687 out-of-state. Room/board: $4,650. Books/supplies: $800. Personal expenses: $1,447.

2007-2008 Financial aid. Need-based: 434 full-time freshmen applied for aid; 407 were judged to have need; 398 of these received aid. Average need met was 64%. Average scholarship/grant was $1,055; average loan $1,199. 58% of total undergraduate aid awarded as scholarships/grants, 42% as loans/jobs. **Non-need-based:** Awarded to 632 full-time undergraduates, including 232 freshmen. Scholarships awarded for academics, alumni affiliation, art, athletics, job skills, leadership, minority status, music/drama, state residency.

Application procedures. Admission: No deadline. $20 fee. Admission notification on a rolling basis. Open admission for adults over 21. **Financial aid:** Priority date 3/1; no closing date. FAFSA, institutional form required. Applicants notified on a rolling basis starting 4/15; must reply within 2 week(s) of notification.

Academics. Programs in aviation, ecology, energy, health-related sciences, and criminology. **Special study options:** Combined bachelor's/graduate degree, distance learning, double major, honors, independent study, internships, teacher certification program. **Credit/placement by examination:** AP, CLEP, IB, SAT, ACT, institutional tests. 60 credit hours maximum toward bachelor's degree. **Support services:** Learning center, preadmission summer program, reduced course load, remedial instruction, study skills assistance, tutoring, writing center.

Majors. **Biology:** General, biotechnology. **Business:** Accounting, business admin, finance, management science, marketing. **Communications:** General. **Computer sciences:** General, information systems. **Conservation:** General. **Education:** Art, elementary, English, mathematics, music, physical, science, secondary, social studies, Spanish, special. **Engineering:** Aerospace. **Engineering technology:** Occupational safety. **Foreign languages:** Spanish. **History:** General. **Math:** General. **Mechanic/repair:** Aircraft. **Parks/recreation:** General. **Physical sciences:** Chemistry. **Protective services:** Criminal justice. **Psychology:** General. **Social sciences:** Political science, sociology. **Transportation:** Airline/commercial pilot. **Visual/performing arts:** Art, dramatic, graphic design, music performance.

Most popular majors. Biology 7%, business/marketing 11%, education 21%, engineering/engineering technologies 12%, liberal arts 13%, parks/recreation 6%.

Computing on campus. 2,138 workstations in dormitories, library, computer center, student center. Dormitories wired for high-speed internet access and linked to campus network. Commuter students can connect to campus network. Online course registration, online library, helpline, student web hosting, wireless network available.

Student life. **Freshman orientation:** Available, $20 fee. Preregistration for classes offered. **Policies:** No alcohol at university events on/off campus. **Housing:** Coed dorms, single-sex dorms, special housing for disabled available. $100 nonrefundable deposit. **Activities:** Bands, campus ministries, choral groups, dance, drama, international student organizations, literary magazine, music ensembles, musical theater, opera, radio station, student government, student newspaper, black American society, Wesley center, student Bible center, Chi Alpha, Young Democrats, College Republicans, Muslim student association.

Athletics. NCAA. **Intercollegiate:** Baseball M, basketball, cross-country W, football (tackle) M, golf M, rodeo, softball W, tennis, volleyball W. **Intramural:** Basketball, bowling, football (non-tackle), football (tackle) M, rodeo, soccer, softball, volleyball W. **Team name:** Savage Storm.

Student services. Adult student services, alcohol/substance abuse counseling, chaplain/spiritual director, career counseling, student employment services, financial aid counseling, health services, minority student services, personal counseling, placement for graduates, veterans' counselor. **Physically disabled:** Services for visually, speech, hearing impaired.

Contact. E-mail: admissions@se.edu
Phone: (580) 745-2060 Toll-free number: (800) 435-1327
Fax: (580) 745-7502
Kristie Luke, Associate Dean of Admissions and Records/Registrar, Southeastern Oklahoma State University, 1405 North Fourth Avenue, PMB 4225, Durant, OK 74701-0607

Southern Nazarene University

Bethany, Oklahoma — **CB member**
www.snu.edu — **CB code: 6036**

- Private 4-year university and liberal arts college affiliated with Church of the Nazarene
- Residential campus in large town
- 1,611 degree-seeking undergraduates: 3% part-time, 52% women
- 441 degree-seeking graduate students

General. Founded in 1899. Regionally accredited. **Degrees:** 538 bachelor's, 1 associate awarded; master's offered. **ROTC:** Army, Air Force. **Location:** 10 miles from Oklahoma City. **Calendar:** Semester, limited summer session. **Full-time faculty:** 85 total. **Part-time faculty:** 60 total. **Special facilities:** Human cadaver laboratory, physics laser laboratory, laboratory school for children.

Freshman class profile.

Mid 50% test scores		**GPA 2.0-2.99:**	24%
ACT composite:	18-26	**Rank in top quarter:**	45%
GPA 3.75 or higher:	32%	**Rank in top tenth:**	22%
GPA 3.50-3.74:	16%	**Live on campus:**	85%
GPA 3.0-3.49:	27%		

Basis for selection. Open admission. Interview recommended for all; audition recommended for music program. **Homeschooled:** Transcript of courses and grades required.

High school preparation. 13 units recommended. Recommended units include English 4, mathematics 3, social studies 2, science 2 and foreign language 2. One computer course recommended.

2008-2009 Annual costs. Tuition/fees: $17,224. Room/board: $5,772. Books/supplies: $600. Personal expenses: $1,200.

2007-2008 Financial aid. **Need-based:** 45% of total undergraduate aid awarded as scholarships/grants, 55% as loans/jobs. **Non-need-based:** Scholarships awarded for academics, athletics, ROTC, state residency.

Application procedures. **Admission:** Priority date 5/1; deadline 8/1. $25 fee, may be waived for applicants with need. Admission notification on a rolling basis. **Financial aid:** Priority date 3/1; no closing date. FAFSA, institutional form required. Applicants notified on a rolling basis starting 5/1; must reply within 2 week(s) of notification.

Academics. **Special study options:** Combined bachelor's/graduate degree, distance learning, double major, dual enrollment of high school students, external degree, honors, independent study, internships, liberal arts/career combination, student-designed major, study abroad, teacher certification program, urban semester, Washington semester. **Credit/placement by examination:** AP, CLEP, IB, institutional tests. 30 credit hours maximum toward bachelor's degree. **Support services:** Remedial instruction, study skills assistance, tutoring, writing center.

Majors. **Area/ethnic studies:** American. **Biology:** General, biochemistry. **Business:** General, accounting, business admin, finance, marketing. **Communications:** General, journalism. **Communications technology:** General. **Computer sciences:** General, networking. **Conservation:** General. **Education:** General, early childhood, elementary, English, history, mathematics, music, physical, reading, science, secondary, Spanish, speech. **Foreign languages:** Spanish. **Health:** Athletic training, clinical lab technology. **History:** General. **Interdisciplinary:** Behavioral sciences. **Legal studies:** Prelaw. **Liberal arts:** Arts/sciences. **Math:** General. **Parks/recreation:** Exercise sciences. **Philosophy/religion:** Philosophy, religion. **Physical sciences:** Chemistry, physics. **Protective services:** Criminal justice. **Psychology:** General. **Social sciences:** General, political science, sociology. **Theology:** Missionary, religious ed, sacred music, theology. **Transportation:** Aviation management. **Visual/performing arts:** General, graphic design.

Most popular majors. Business/marketing 54%, computer/information sciences 6%, education 6%, family/consumer sciences 9%, health sciences 7%.

Computing on campus. 120 workstations in library, computer center. Dormitories wired for high-speed internet access and linked to campus network. Helpline, repair service, wireless network available.

Student life. **Freshman orientation:** Mandatory. Preregistration for classes offered. **Policies:** Single students under 23 required to live on campus or with relatives. Religious observance required. **Housing:** Guaranteed on-campus for freshmen. Single-sex dorms, apartments available. $50 deposit, deadline 8/1. **Activities:** Bands, choral groups, drama, film society, music ensembles, student government, student newspaper, symphony orchestra, TV station, Gospel team, Mission Crusaders, Circle-K, Spanish club, Mortar Board.

Athletics. NAIA. **Intercollegiate:** Baseball M, basketball, cheerleading, cross-country, equestrian, football (tackle) M, golf, soccer, softball W, tennis, track and field, volleyball W. **Intramural:** Basketball, football (non-tackle), football (tackle) M, softball, tennis, track and field, volleyball. **Team name:** Crimson Storm.

Student services. Alcohol/substance abuse counseling, chaplain/spiritual director, career counseling, services for economically disadvantaged, student employment services, financial aid counseling, health services, personal counseling, placement for graduates. **Physically disabled:** Services for visually, speech, hearing impaired.

Contact. E-mail: wrogers@snu.edu
Phone: (405) 491-6324 Toll-free number: (800) 648-9899
Fax: (405) 491-6320
Warren Rogers, Director of Admissions, Southern Nazarene University, 6729 NW 39th Expressway, Bethany, OK 73008

Southwestern Christian University

Bethany, Oklahoma
www.swcu.edu — **CB code: 1433**

- Private 4-year liberal arts college affiliated with Pentecostal Holiness Church
- Residential campus in large town
- 190 degree-seeking undergraduates
- SAT or ACT with writing, application essay, interview required

General. Founded in 1946. Regionally accredited. **Degrees:** 28 bachelor's, 3 associate awarded; master's offered. **Location:** 10 miles from Oklahoma

City. **Calendar:** Semester, limited summer session. **Full-time faculty:** 8 total; 25% have terminal degrees, 12% minority, 62% women. **Part-time faculty:** 26 total; 38% have terminal degrees, 15% minority, 42% women.

Freshman class profile.

Out-of-state:	13%	**Live on campus:**	62%

Basis for selection. 2.5 GPA or 19 ACT required. Additonal materials and interview may be requested.

High school preparation. Required units include English 4, mathematics 2, social studies 2, history 2, science 2 (laboratory 2).

2008-2009 Annual costs. Tuition/fees: $9,800. Adult education program $350 per credit hour. Room/board: $4,600. Books/supplies: $750. Personal expenses: $1,100.

2008-2009 Financial aid. Non-need-based: Scholarships awarded for academics, alumni affiliation, leadership, music/drama, religious affiliation.

Application procedures. Admission: No deadline. No application fee. Application must be submitted on paper. Admission notification on a rolling basis. **Financial aid:** Priority date 8/1; no closing date. FAFSA required. Applicants notified on a rolling basis starting 5/1; must reply within 2 week(s) of notification.

Academics. Applied Biblical Leadership Education (ABLE), an adult studies completion program. **Special study options:** Accelerated study, cross-registration, double major, dual enrollment of high school students, honors, independent study, internships, liberal arts/career combination. **Credit/placement by examination:** AP, CLEP, institutional tests. 30 credit hours maximum toward bachelor's degree. **Support services:** Learning center, reduced course load, remedial instruction, tutoring.

Majors. Business: Business admin. **Philosophy/religion:** Religion. **Theology:** Bible, missionary, pastoral counseling, religious ed, sacred music, theology, youth ministry. **Visual/performing arts:** Music performance.

Computing on campus. 9 workstations in library. Dormitories wired for high-speed internet access and linked to campus network. Online library, wireless network available.

Student life. Freshman orientation: Mandatory. Preregistration for classes offered. Held the week prior to classes; includes academic, financial aid and spiritual life orientation. **Policies:** Extracurricular Christian programs and activities emphasized. Mandatory dress code. Students sign lifestyle covenant agreeing to certain behaviors. Religious observance required. **Housing:** Single-sex dorms available. $100 nonrefundable deposit, deadline 8/15. **Activities:** Choral groups, drama, music ensembles, musical theater, student government, student newspaper, Southwestern Ministerial Association, missionary society, Christian education association.

Athletics. NCCAA. **Intercollegiate:** Basketball M, cross-country, golf M, soccer M, softball, volleyball W. **Intramural:** Baseball M, basketball, cheerleading, football (non-tackle) M, softball, table tennis, volleyball. **Team name:** Eagles.

Student services. Adult student services, chaplain/spiritual director, career counseling, student employment services, financial aid counseling, personal counseling, placement for graduates, veterans' counselor.

Contact. E-mail: megan.miles@swcu.edu
Phone: (405) 789-7661 ext. 3442 Toll-free number: (888) 418-9272
Fax: (405) 495-0078
Rebecca Thompson, Director of Admissions, Southwestern Christian University, Box 340, Bethany, OK 73008

Southwestern Oklahoma State University

Weatherford, Oklahoma — **CB member**
www.swosu.edu — **CB code: 6673**

- Public 4-year university
- Residential campus in large town
- 4,059 degree-seeking undergraduates: 12% part-time, 58% women
- 673 graduate students
- 90% of applicants admitted
- SAT or ACT (ACT writing optional) required

General. Founded in 1901. Regionally accredited. Campus at Sayre offers lower division and remedial courses, as well as associate degrees. **Degrees:** 593 bachelor's, 101 associate awarded; master's, first professional offered. **Location:** 75 miles from Oklahoma City. **Calendar:** Semester, extensive summer session. **Full-time faculty:** 215 total; 59% have terminal degrees, 10% minority, 43% women. **Part-time faculty:** 15 total. **Class size:** 48% < 20, 40% 20-39, 7% 40-49, 6% 50-99.

Freshman class profile. 1,359 applied, 1,227 admitted, 950 enrolled.

Mid 50% test scores		**Rank in top quarter:**	39%
ACT composite:	18-23	**Rank in top tenth:**	18%
GPA 3.75 or higher:	29%	**Return as sophomores:**	63%
GPA 3.50-3.74:	19%	**Out-of-state:**	11%
GPA 3.0-3.49:	31%	**Live on campus:**	57%
GPA 2.0-2.99:	20%	**International:**	1%

Basis for selection. Bachelor degree programs require 19 ACT and no curricular deficiencies. Open admission for certificate and associate degree programs. Last date to submit test scores is first day of classes. Essay required for returning suspension students only.

High school preparation. 15 units required; 17 recommended. Required and recommended units include English 4, mathematics 3, social studies 1, history 2, science 2 (laboratory 2), computer science 1 and academic electives 2-4. Social studies unit must be citizenship. Academic electives should be in fine arts. 3 units computer science or foreign language required.

2008-2009 Annual costs. Tuition/fees: $4,110; $9,450 out-of-state. Room/board: $3,900. Books/supplies: $1,230. Personal expenses: $996.

2008-2009 Financial aid. Need-based: 679 full-time freshmen applied for aid; 513 were judged to have need; 505 of these received aid. Average need met was 90%. Average scholarship/grant was $1,155; average loan $1,351. 45% of total undergraduate aid awarded as scholarships/grants, 55% as loans/jobs. **Non-need-based:** Awarded to 2,311 full-time undergraduates, including 598 freshmen. Scholarships awarded for academics, alumni affiliation, art, athletics, job skills, leadership, music/drama, state residency.

Application procedures. Admission: No deadline. $15 fee. Admission notification on a rolling basis. **Financial aid:** Priority date 3/1; no closing date. FAFSA, institutional form required. Applicants notified on a rolling basis starting 1/1.

Academics. Special study options: Accelerated study, combined bachelor's/graduate degree, distance learning, double major, independent study, internships, student-designed major, teacher certification program, weekend college. Weekend college for nursing only. **Credit/placement by examination:** AP, CLEP, IB, ACT, institutional tests. 62 credit hours maximum toward bachelor's degree. **Support services:** Pre-admission summer program, reduced course load, remedial instruction, study skills assistance, tutoring, writing center.

Majors. Biology: General, biophysics. **Business:** General, accounting, business admin, human resources, management information systems. **Communications:** General. **Computer sciences:** General, computer science, information systems. **Education:** Art, early childhood, elementary, English, health, history, learning disabled, mathematics, mentally handicapped, music, physical, science, social science, special, technology/industrial arts. **Engineering:** General, physics. **Engineering technology:** Manufacturing. **Health:** Athletic training, clinical lab technology, health care admin, medical records admin, music therapy, nursing (RN). **History:** General. **Math:** General. **Parks/recreation:** General, facilities management. **Physical sciences:** Chemistry, physics. **Protective services:** Criminal justice. **Psychology:** General. **Public administration:** Social work. **Social sciences:** Political science, sociology. **Theology:** Sacred music. **Visual/performing arts:** Commercial/advertising art, music management, music performance, music theory/composition, piano/organ, voice/opera.

Most popular majors. Business/marketing 21%, education 19%, health sciences 18%, parks/recreation 9%, visual/performing arts 8%.

Computing on campus. 200 workstations in library, computer center. Dormitories wired for high-speed internet access. Commuter students can connect to campus network. Online library, wireless network available.

Student life. Freshman orientation: Mandatory, $60 fee. Preregistration for classes offered. **Housing:** Guaranteed on-campus for all undergraduates. Single-sex dorms, apartments available. $100 fully refundable deposit, deadline 8/1. **Activities:** Bands, campus ministries, choral groups, drama, international student organizations, literary magazine, music ensembles, Model UN, musical theater, student government, student newspaper, symphony orchestra, 7 religious organizations, 4 political organizations, and approximately 75 social and professional clubs.

Athletics. NCAA. **Intercollegiate:** Baseball M, basketball, cheerleading, cross-country W, football (tackle) M, golf, rodeo, soccer, softball W. **Intramural:** Basketball, bowling, football (non-tackle), golf, racquetball, soccer, softball, swimming, tennis, volleyball. **Team name:** Bulldogs.

Student services. Adult student services, alcohol/substance abuse counseling, career counseling, student employment services, financial aid counseling, health services, personal counseling, placement for graduates, veterans' counselor. **Physically disabled:** Services for visually, hearing impaired.

Contact. E-mail: admissions@swosu.edu
Phone: (580) 774-3009 Fax: (580) 774-3795
Todd Boyd, Director of Admissions, Southwestern Oklahoma State University, 100 Campus Drive, Weatherford, OK 73096

Spartan College of Aeronautics and Technology

Tulsa, Oklahoma
www.spartan.edu **CB code: 0336**

- For-profit 4-year technical college
- Commuter campus in large city
- 1,239 degree-seeking undergraduates
- 50% of applicants admitted
- Interview required

General. Founded in 1928. Accredited by ACCSCT. Multi-campus institution with 2 technical campuses at Tulsa International Airport and one on Jones Airport in South Tulsa. **Degrees:** 20 bachelor's, 136 associate awarded. **Location:** 100 miles from Oklahoma City. **Calendar:** Differs by program, extensive summer session. **Full-time faculty:** 63 total; 3% have terminal degrees, 13% women. **Part-time faculty:** 34 total; 3% have terminal degrees, 9% women. **Class size:** 62% < 20, 38% 20-39.

Freshman class profile. 844 applied, 419 admitted, 98 enrolled.

Out-of-state:	81%	**Live on campus:**	25%

Basis for selection. Applicants must demonstrate proficiency in college-level skills by submission of examination scores deemed appropriate by Spartan for the chosen program of study. Students wishing to attend flight training must obtain FAA Class II flight certificate. SAT or ACT recommended. **Homeschooled:** Statement describing homeschool structure and mission, transcript of courses and grades, state high school equivalency certificate, interview required.

2009-2010 Annual costs. Tuition/fees (projected): $15,345.

Application procedures. Admission: No deadline. $100 fee. Admission notification on a rolling basis. **Financial aid:** No deadline. FAFSA, institutional form required. Applicants notified on a rolling basis starting 2/1; must reply within 2 week(s) of notification.

Academics. Special study options: Independent study. **Credit/placement by examination:** CLEP, institutional tests. No more than half of credits required for degree may be earned through examination. **Support services:** Remedial instruction, tutoring.

Majors. Mechanic/repair: Avionics. **Transportation:** Aviation management. **Other:** Aviation maintenance technician.

Computing on campus. 100 workstations in library, student center. Dormitories wired for high-speed internet access. Online library, wireless network available.

Student life. Freshman orientation: Mandatory. Usually held on Friday immediately preceding start of classes. **Policies:** All student subject to random drug testing. **Housing:** Apartments, wellness housing available. **Activities:** Student government.

Athletics. Intramural: Basketball M, bowling, soccer M, softball M, table tennis M, volleyball M.

Student services. Career counseling, student employment services, financial aid counseling, personal counseling, placement for graduates, veterans' counselor.

Contact. E-mail: spartan@mail.spartan.edu
Phone: (918) 836-6886 Toll-free number: (800) 331-1204
Fax: (918) 831-5287
Damon Bowling, Vice President, Marketing, Spartan College of Aeronautics and Technology, Box 582833, Tulsa, OK 74158-2833

University of Central Oklahoma

Edmond, Oklahoma **CB member**
www.uco.edu **CB code: 6091**

- Public 4-year university
- Commuter campus in small city
- 14,019 degree-seeking undergraduates: 31% part-time, 58% women, 9% African American, 3% Asian American, 4% Hispanic American, 5% Native American, 6% international
- 1,524 degree-seeking graduate students
- 69% of applicants admitted
- SAT or ACT (ACT writing optional) required

General. Founded in 1890. Regionally accredited. **Degrees:** 2,194 bachelor's awarded; master's offered. **ROTC:** Army. **Location:** 12 miles from Oklahoma City. **Calendar:** Semester, extensive summer session. **Full-time faculty:** 434 total; 68% have terminal degrees, 15% minority, 48% women. **Part-time faculty:** 400 total; 14% have terminal degrees, 10% minority, 57% women. **Class size:** 30% < 20, 53% 20-39, 12% 40-49, 4% 50-99, less than 1% >100. **Special facilities:** Jazz lab.

Freshman class profile. 4,614 applied, 3,204 admitted, 2,131 enrolled.

Mid 50% test scores		**Rank in top tenth:**	12%
ACT composite:	19-23	**Out-of-state:**	2%
GPA 3.75 or higher:	18%	**Live on campus:**	40%
GPA 3.50-3.74:	17%	**International:**	6%
GPA 3.0-3.49:	39%	**Fraternities:**	12%
GPA 2.0-2.99:	25%	**Sororities:**	9%
Rank in top quarter:	35%		

Basis for selection. Must have 2.7 GPA and rank in top 50% of class, or 2.7 GPA in 15 unit high school core, or 20 ACT.

High school preparation. College-preparatory program recommended. 17 units required; 18 recommended. Required and recommended units include English 4, mathematics 3-4, social studies 1, history 2, science 2-3 (laboratory 2-3), foreign language 2 and academic electives 3.

2008-2009 Annual costs. Tuition/fees: $4,223; $10,652 out-of-state. Room/board: $5,623. Books/supplies: $1,000. Personal expenses: $2,000.

2007-2008 Financial aid. Need-based: 1,079 full-time freshmen applied for aid; 771 were judged to have need; 691 of these received aid. Average need met was 67%. Average scholarship/grant was $7,524; average loan $2,942. 34% of total undergraduate aid awarded as scholarships/grants, 66% as loans/jobs. **Non-need-based:** Awarded to 6,378 full-time undergraduates, including 273 freshmen. Scholarships awarded for academics, alumni affiliation, art, athletics, leadership, minority status, music/drama, ROTC, state residency.

Application procedures. Admission: No deadline. $25 fee. Admission notification on a rolling basis beginning on or about 4/1. **Financial aid:** Priority date 5/31; no closing date. FAFSA, institutional form required. Applicants notified on a rolling basis starting 5/1; must reply by 6/30 or within 4 week(s) of notification.

Academics. Special study options: Accelerated study, distance learning, double major, dual enrollment of high school students, ESL, honors, independent study, internships, teacher certification program. **Credit/placement by examination:** AP, CLEP, ACT, institutional tests. 94 credit hours maximum toward bachelor's degree. **Support services:** Learning center, reduced course load, remedial instruction, tutoring, writing center.

Majors. Biology: General. **Business:** Accounting, actuarial science, apparel, business admin, finance, human resources, insurance, management information systems, managerial economics, marketing, nonprofit/public, operations. **Communications:** General, advertising, broadcast journalism, journalism, photojournalism, public relations. **Computer sciences:** General, information technology. **Education:** General, art, biology, business, chemistry, curriculum, drama/dance, early childhood, elementary, ESL, family/consumer sciences, French, German, health occupations, history, instructional media, mathematics, music, physical, physics, reading, science, social studies, Spanish, special, technology/industrial arts. **Engineering:** Biomedical, physics. **Engineering technology:** General, industrial safety. **Family/consumer sciences:** General, aging, child development, family systems, food/nutrition. **Foreign languages:** French, German, Spanish. **Health:** Audiology/speech pathology, clinical lab science, nursing (RN), public health ed, speech pathology. **History:** General. **Liberal arts:** Arts/sciences. **Math:** General, applied, statistics. **Parks/recreation:** General, exercise sciences. **Personal/culinary services:** Mortuary science. **Philosophy/religion:** Philosophy. **Physical sciences:** Chemistry, physics. **Protective services:** Corrections, criminal justice, forensics, juvenile corrections, police science. **Psychology:** General. **Social sciences:** Applied economics, economics, geography, political science, sociology, urban studies. **Visual/performing arts:** Art, art history/conservation, dance, dramatic, graphic design, interior design, music performance, piano/organ, stringed instruments, voice/opera.

Most popular majors. Business/marketing 29%, communications/journalism 8%, education 10%, health sciences 6%, liberal arts 13%.

Computing on campus. 450 workstations in dormitories, library, computer center, student center. Dormitories wired for high-speed internet access. Commuter students can connect to campus network. Helpline, wireless network available.

Student life. Freshman orientation: Mandatory, $35 fee. Preregistration for classes offered. 3-day orientation held the week before classes start in August. **Housing:** Coed dorms, single-sex dorms, apartments, fraternity/sorority housing, wellness housing available. $150 fully refundable deposit. **Activities:** Bands, choral groups, dance, drama, international student organizations, music ensembles, musical theater, radio station, student government, student newspaper, symphony orchestra, TV station, Baptist Student Union, Fellowship of Christian Athletes, Young Democrats, Collegiate Republicans, Black student association, Malaysian student association, Association of Women Students, Webmasters.

Athletics. NCAA. **Intercollegiate:** Baseball M, basketball, cross-country, football (tackle) M, golf, soccer W, softball W, tennis, track and field, volleyball W, wrestling M. **Intramural:** Badminton, baseball M, basketball, bowling, football (non-tackle), golf, handball, soccer, softball, swimming, table tennis, tennis, track and field, volleyball, wrestling M. **Team name:** Bronchos.

Student services. Career counseling, student employment services, health services, personal counseling, placement for graduates, veterans' counselor. **Physically disabled:** Services for visually, speech, hearing impaired.

Contact. E-mail: admituco@uco.edu
Phone: (405) 974-2338 Toll-free number: (800) 254-4215
Fax: (405) 341-4964
Linda Lofton, Director, Admissions & Records, University of Central Oklahoma, 100 North University Drive, Edmond, OK 73034-0151

University of Oklahoma

Norman, Oklahoma — **CB member**
www.ou.edu — **CB code: 6879**

- Public 4-year university
- Residential campus in small city
- 20,350 degree-seeking undergraduates: 13% part-time, 52% women, 6% African American, 6% Asian American, 4% Hispanic American, 7% Native American, 2% international
- 9,335 graduate students
- 82% of applicants admitted
- SAT or ACT (ACT writing optional) required
- 62% graduate within 6 years

General. Founded in 1890. Regionally accredited. Faculty-in-residence program has faculty live in student dorms and mix with students. **Degrees:** 4,513 bachelor's awarded; master's, doctoral, first professional offered. **ROTC:** Army, Naval, Air Force. **Location:** 20 miles from Oklahoma City, 200 miles from Dallas. **Calendar:** Semester, extensive summer session. **Full-time faculty:** 1,434 total; 83% have terminal degrees, 18% minority, 41% women. **Part-time faculty:** 416 total; 48% have terminal degrees, 13% minority, 46% women. **Class size:** 48% < 20, 37% 20-39, 5% 40-49, 7% 50-99, 3% >100. **Special facilities:** Museum of science and history, biological station, history of science collection, western history collection, national severe storms laboratory, energy center, national weather center, art museum, museum of natural history.

Freshman class profile. 9,764 applied, 7,961 admitted, 3,803 enrolled.

Mid 50% test scores		**GPA 3.0-3.49:**	27%
SAT critical reading:	520-640	**GPA 2.0-2.99:**	4%
SAT math:	540-650	**Rank in top quarter:**	72%
ACT composite:	23-28	**Rank in top tenth:**	36%
GPA 3.75 or higher:	41%	**Return as sophomores:**	83%
GPA 3.50-3.74:	28%	**International:**	2%

Basis for selection. Standardized test scores, class rank, and secondary school record very important. Prescribed set of requirements for residents and nonresidents that guarantee admission. Applicants who do not meet requirements for guaranteed admission, but do meet certain performance minimums, will be placed on wait list and admitted on space-available basis, with preference given to most academically qualified. Audition required for dance, drama, music programs. **Homeschooled:** Transcript of courses and grades required. **Learning Disabled:** Students must self-identify after admission and provide documentation to receive special services.

High school preparation. College-preparatory program required. 15 units required. Required and recommended units include English 4, mathematics 3, social studies 2, history 1, science 2 (laboratory 2), foreign language 2, computer science 1 and academic electives 3. Must have 1 U.S. history and 2 additional units from history, economics, geography, government, or non-western culture.

2008-2009 Annual costs. Tuition/fees: $7,423; $17,404 out-of-state. Computer course fees and other college level fees vary by college. Room/board: $7,376. Books/supplies: $958. Personal expenses: $2,372.

2007-2008 Financial aid. Need-based: 2,405 full-time freshmen applied for aid; 2,303 were judged to have need; 2,303 of these received aid. Average need met was 93%. Average scholarship/grant was $5,004; average loan $3,732. 40% of total undergraduate aid awarded as scholarships/grants, 60% as loans/jobs. **Non-need-based:** Awarded to 7,927 full-time undergraduates, including 2,338 freshmen. Scholarships awarded for academics, alumni affiliation, art, athletics, leadership, music/drama, religious affiliation, ROTC. **Additional information:** Institutional loans are available for early applicants who do not qualify for federal or state need-based aid.

Application procedures. Admission: Closing date 4/1 (receipt date). $40 fee, may be waived for applicants with need. Admission notification on a rolling basis. Freshman applicants encouraged to apply as soon as junior year in high school is completed or by scholarship deadline of February 1. Online application fee may be waived, with appropriate documentation, for applicants with financial need. **Financial aid:** Priority date 3/1; no closing date. FAFSA required. Applicants notified on a rolling basis starting 3/15; must reply within 6 week(s) of notification.

Academics. College of Liberal Studies through distance learning provides non-traditional students with coherent interdisciplinary liberal arts programs. **Special study options:** Accelerated study, combined bachelor's/graduate degree, cooperative education, distance learning, double major, dual enrollment of high school students, ESL, external degree, honors, independent study, internships, liberal arts/career combination, semester at sea, student-designed major, study abroad, teacher certification program, Washington semester, weekend college. **Credit/placement by examination:** AP, CLEP, IB, SAT, ACT, institutional tests. Credit for prior work/life experience awarded according to recommendations of American Council on Education. Applicability of credits toward a degree vary depending on the college. Credit by examination may be counted toward bachelor's degree, but total number of hours that may be applied vary depending on college. **Support services:** Learning center, pre-admission summer program, remedial instruction, study skills assistance, tutoring, writing center.

Honors college/program. 733 incoming freshmen were accepted for Fall 2008.

Majors. Architecture: Architecture, environmental design. **Area/ethnic studies:** African-American, Native American, women's. **Biology:** Biochemistry, botany, microbiology, zoology. **Business:** Accounting, business admin, construction management, finance, management information systems, management science, managerial economics, marketing. **Communications:** General, advertising, broadcast journalism, journalism. **Computer sciences:** Computer science, information systems. **Conservation:** Environmental science. **Education:** Early childhood, elementary, English, foreign languages, mathematics, music, science, social studies, special. **Engineering:** General, aerospace, architectural, chemical, civil, computer, electrical, environmental, industrial, mechanical, petroleum, physics. **Foreign languages:** Chinese, classics, French, Germanic, linguistics, Russian, Spanish. **Health:** Clinical lab science, communication disorders, dental hygiene, medical radiologic technology/radiation therapy, nuclear medical technology, nursing (RN), sonography. **History:** General. **Interdisciplinary:** Global studies. **Liberal arts:** Arts/sciences, humanities. **Math:** General. **Parks/recreation:** Exercise sciences. **Philosophy/religion:** Philosophy, religion. **Physical sciences:** Astronomy, astrophysics, chemistry, geology, geophysics, meteorology, physics. **Psychology:** General. **Public administration:** General, social work. **Social sciences:** Anthropology, economics, geography, political science, sociology. **Transportation:** Aviation. **Visual/performing arts:** General, art history/conservation, dance, dramatic, film/cinema, interior design, music pedagogy, studio arts. **Other:** Geosciences, Human relations, Multidisciplinary studies.

Most popular majors. Biology 6%, business/marketing 16%, communications/journalism 9%, engineering/engineering technologies 8%, health sciences 13%, social sciences 9%.

Computing on campus. 3,600 workstations in dormitories, library, computer center, student center. Dormitories wired for high-speed internet access and linked to campus network. Commuter students can connect to campus network. Online course registration, online library, helpline, repair service, student web hosting, wireless network available.

Student life. Freshman orientation: Available. Preregistration for classes offered. **Housing:** Guaranteed on-campus for freshmen. Coed dorms, single-sex dorms, special housing for disabled, apartments, fraternity/sorority housing, wellness housing available. $175 fully refundable deposit. Honors, cultural, scholastic, National Merit housing available. **Activities:** Bands, campus ministries, choral groups, dance, drama, film society, international student organizations, literary magazine, music ensembles, Model UN, musical theater, opera, radio station, student government, student newspaper, symphony orchestra, TV station, American Indian, black, Hispanic-American, Asian-American student associations; College Republicans; Young Democrats; Hillel Jewish student organization; Chi Alpha Christian Fellowship; Muslim student association; Alpha Phi Omega.

Athletics. NCAA. **Intercollegiate:** Baseball M, basketball, cheerleading, cross-country, football (tackle) M, golf, gymnastics, rowing (crew) W, soccer W, softball W, tennis, track and field, volleyball W, wrestling M. **Intramural:** Badminton, basketball, football (non-tackle), golf, racquetball, soccer, softball, table tennis, tennis, volleyball, water polo. **Team name:** Sooners.

Student services. Adult student services, alcohol/substance abuse counseling, chaplain/spiritual director, career counseling, services for economically disadvantaged, student employment services, financial aid counseling, health services, legal services, minority student services, on-campus daycare, personal counseling, placement for graduates, veterans' counselor, women's services. **Physically disabled:** Services for visually, speech, hearing impaired.

Contact. E-mail: admrec@ou.edu
Phone: (405) 325-2252 Toll-free number: (800) 234-6868
Fax: (405) 325-7124
Patricia Lynch, Director of Admissions and Records, University of Oklahoma, 1000 Asp Avenue, Norman, OK 73019-4076

University of Science and Arts of Oklahoma

Chickasha, Oklahoma
www.usao.edu **CB code: 6544**

- Public 4-year university and liberal arts college
- Residential campus in large town
- 1,041 degree-seeking undergraduates: 10% part-time, 64% women, 4% African American, 1% Asian American, 5% Hispanic American, 14% Native American, 5% international
- 93% of applicants admitted
- SAT or ACT (ACT writing optional) required

General. Founded in 1908. Regionally accredited. Offers trimester system classes, allowing for 3-year graduation. **Degrees:** 220 bachelor's awarded. **Location:** 45 miles from Oklahoma City. **Calendar:** Trimester, extensive summer session. **Full-time faculty:** 52 total; 88% have terminal degrees, 10% minority, 50% women. **Part-time faculty:** 37 total; 19% have terminal degrees, 8% minority, 49% women. **Class size:** 62% < 20, 30% 20-39, 4% 40-49, 3% 50-99, less than 1% >100. **Special facilities:** Speech and hearing clinic, herbarium, child development center, school for the deaf.

Freshman class profile. 392 applied, 366 admitted, 225 enrolled.

Mid 50% test scores		**Rank in top quarter:**	45%
SAT math:	450-580	**Rank in top tenth:**	19%
ACT composite:	19-25	**End year in good standing:**	75%
GPA 3.75 or higher:	26%	**Return as sophomores:**	61%
GPA 3.50-3.74:	20%	**Out-of-state:**	5%
GPA 3.0-3.49:	39%	**Live on campus:**	74%
GPA 2.0-2.99:	14%	**International:**	7%

Basis for selection. One of the following required for admission: 24 ACT/1090 SAT (exclusive of Writing), 3.0 GPA and ranking in top 33% of high school graduating class, or 3.0 GPA in the 15-unit high school core curriculum and 21 ACT/940 SAT. **Homeschooled:** Transcript of courses and grades required.

High school preparation. College-preparatory program required. 15 units required; 21 recommended. Required and recommended units include English 4, mathematics 3-4, social studies 1, history 2, science 2-3 (laboratory 2-3), foreign language 2 and academic electives 3. 2 units of fine arts, drama and/or speech recommended.

2008-2009 Annual costs. Tuition/fees: $4,440; $10,560 out-of-state. Room/board: $4,860.

2008-2009 Financial aid. Need-based: 165 full-time freshmen applied for aid; 127 were judged to have need; 127 of these received aid. Average need met was 74%. Average scholarship/grant was $6,861; average loan $2,671. 61% of total undergraduate aid awarded as scholarships/grants, 39% as loans/jobs. **Non-need-based:** Awarded to 340 full-time undergraduates, including 97 freshmen. Scholarships awarded for academics, art, athletics, leadership, music/drama, state residency.

Application procedures. Admission: Closing date 8/31 (postmark date). $15 fee, may be waived for applicants with need. Admission notification on a rolling basis beginning on or about 2/10. **Financial aid:** Priority date 3/15; no closing date. FAFSA, institutional form required. Applicants notified on a rolling basis starting 3/15; must reply within 4 week(s) of notification.

Academics. Special study options: Accelerated study, double major, dual enrollment of high school students, independent study, internships, liberal arts/career combination, student-designed major, teacher certification program. **Credit/placement by examination:** AP, CLEP, ACT, institutional tests. 62 credit hours maximum toward bachelor's degree. **Support services:** Learning center, pre-admission summer program, reduced course load, remedial instruction, study skills assistance, tutoring, writing center.

Majors. Area/ethnic studies: Native American. **Biology:** General. **Business:** Business admin. **Communications:** General. **Computer sciences:** Computer science. **Education:** Deaf/hearing impaired, early childhood, elementary. **Health:** Speech pathology. **History:** General. **Interdisciplinary:** Natural sciences. **Math:** General. **Parks/recreation:** Health/fitness. **Physical sciences:** Chemistry, physics. **Psychology:** General. **Social sciences:** Economics, political science, sociology. **Visual/performing arts:** Art, dramatic, studio arts.

Most popular majors. Business/marketing 24%, communications/journalism 6%, education 18%, history 6%, psychology 11%, visual/performing arts 10%.

Computing on campus. 175 workstations in library, computer center, student center. Dormitories wired for high-speed internet access and linked to campus network. Online library, helpline, repair service, student web hosting, wireless network available.

Student life. Freshman orientation: Mandatory. Preregistration for classes offered. **Housing:** Guaranteed on-campus for freshmen. Coed dorms, apartments available. $100 fully refundable deposit, deadline 4/1. **Activities:** Bands, campus ministries, choral groups, dance, drama, international student organizations, literary magazine, music ensembles, musical theater, student government, student newspaper, TV station, Ameslan culture club, Chi Alpha Christian Fellowship, College Democrats, College Republicans, African American student association, international student association, intertribal heritage club, student ambassadors, students with children club, feminist collective.

Athletics. NAIA. **Intercollegiate:** Baseball M, basketball, cheerleading, soccer, softball W. **Intramural:** Basketball, golf, softball M, volleyball. **Team name:** Drovers.

Student services. Alcohol/substance abuse counseling, career counseling, services for economically disadvantaged, student employment services, financial aid counseling, health services, minority student services, personal counseling, placement for graduates, veterans' counselor. **Physically disabled:** Services for visually, hearing impaired.

Contact. E-mail: usao-admissions@usao.edu
Phone: (405) 574-1357 Toll-free number: (800) 933-8726
Fax: (405) 574-1220
Joe Evans, Director of Admissions and Records, University of Science and Arts of Oklahoma, 1727 West Alabama, Chickasha, OK 73018-5322

University of Tulsa

Tulsa, Oklahoma **CB member**
www.utulsa.edu **CB code: 6883**

- Private 4-year university affiliated with Presbyterian Church (USA)
- Residential campus in large city
- 2,981 degree-seeking undergraduates: 4% part-time, 48% women, 6% African American, 3% Asian American, 4% Hispanic American, 4% Native American, 12% international
- 1,113 degree-seeking graduate students
- 46% of applicants admitted
- SAT or ACT (ACT writing optional) required
- 63% graduate within 6 years; 42% enter graduate study

General. Founded in 1894. Regionally accredited. **Degrees:** 610 bachelor's awarded; master's, doctoral, first professional offered. **ROTC:** Air Force. **Location:** 100 miles from Oklahoma City. **Calendar:** Semester, limited summer session. **Full-time faculty:** 317 total; 96% have terminal degrees, 15% minority, 33% women. **Part-time faculty:** 80 total; 96% have terminal degrees, 12% minority, 51% women. **Class size:** 58% < 20, 35% 20-39, 6% 40-49, 2% 50-99. **Special facilities:** Biotechnology institute, center for communicative disorders, communication lab, tall grass prairie preserve.

Freshman class profile. 4,713 applied, 2,180 admitted, 695 enrolled.

Mid 50% test scores			
SAT critical reading:	540-700	Rank in top tenth:	64%
SAT math:	550-700	End year in good standing:	89%
ACT composite:	25-31	Return as sophomores:	88%
GPA 3.75 or higher:	55%	Out-of-state:	48%
GPA 3.50-3.74:	15%	Live on campus:	87%
GPA 3.0-3.49:	22%	International:	8%
GPA 2.0-2.99:	8%	Fraternities:	21%
Rank in top quarter:	82%	Sororities:	23%

Basis for selection. Primary requirements are school achievement records and test scores. High school guidance counselor recommendation required. Extracurricular activities, community involvement, and talents are considered. Essays and interviews are recommended for all; audition required for music, theater programs; portfolio required for art program. **Homeschooled:** Statement describing homeschool structure and mission, transcript of courses and grades, letter of recommendation (nonparent) required.

High school preparation. College-preparatory program recommended. 16 units recommended. Recommended units include English 4, mathematics 3, social studies 1, history 2, science 3 (laboratory 2), foreign language 2 and academic electives 1. 4 math and 4 physical science recommended for engineering and natural science students.

2008-2009 Annual costs. Tuition/fees: $23,940. A one-time $425 fee is charged first-time students for orientation, lifetime transcripts, course drop/add transactions, and graduation/commencement. Room/board: $7,776. Books/supplies: $1,200. Personal expenses: $2,726.

2007-2008 Financial aid. **Need-based:** 591 full-time freshmen applied for aid; 287 were judged to have need; 287 of these received aid. Average need met was 88%. Average scholarship/grant was $5,332; average loan $5,486. 31% of total undergraduate aid awarded as scholarships/grants, 69% as loans/jobs. **Non-need-based:** Awarded to 2,462 full-time undergraduates, including 604 freshmen. Scholarships awarded for academics, alumni affiliation, art, athletics, leadership, minority status, music/drama, religious affiliation.

Application procedures. **Admission:** Priority date 2/1; no deadline. $35 fee, may be waived for applicants with need. Admission notification on a rolling basis beginning on or about 10/1. Must reply by May 1 or within 2 week(s) if notified thereafter. **Financial aid:** Priority date 4/1; no closing date. FAFSA, institutional form required. Applicants notified on a rolling basis starting 3/1; must reply by 5/1 or within 2 week(s) of notification.

Academics. **Special study options:** Accelerated study, combined bachelor's/graduate degree, double major, ESL, honors, independent study, internships, liberal arts/career combination, student-designed major, study abroad, teacher certification program, Washington semester. **Credit/placement by examination:** AP, CLEP, IB, SAT, ACT, institutional tests. 36 credit hours maximum toward bachelor's degree. **Support services:** Learning center, reduced course load, study skills assistance, tutoring, writing center.

Majors. **Area/ethnic studies:** Russian/Slavic. **Biology:** General, biochemistry. **Business:** Accounting, business admin, finance, international, management information systems, marketing, organizational behavior. **Communications:** General. **Computer sciences:** General, computer science, information technology. **Conservation:** Environmental studies. **Education:** Chemistry, Deaf/hearing impaired, early childhood, elementary, mathematics, music. **Engineering:** Chemical, electrical, mechanical, petroleum, physics. **Engineering technology:** Energy systems. **Foreign languages:** French, German, Spanish. **Health:** Athletic training, audiology/speech pathology, communication disorders, nursing (RN). **History:** General. **Interdisciplinary:** Global studies. **Legal studies:** General, prelaw. **Liberal arts:** Arts/sciences. **Math:** Applied. **Parks/recreation:** Exercise sciences. **Philosophy/religion:** Philosophy, religion. **Physical sciences:** Chemistry, geology, geophysics, physics. **Psychology:** General. **Social sciences:** Anthropology, economics, political science, sociology. **Visual/performing arts:** Art, art history/conservation, arts management, dramatic, film/cinema, music performance, music theory/composition, piano/organ, voice/opera.

Most popular majors. Business/marketing 24%, engineering/engineering technologies 13%, visual/performing arts 10%.

Computing on campus. 900 workstations in dormitories, library, computer center, student center. Dormitories wired for high-speed internet access and linked to campus network. Commuter students can connect to campus network. Online course registration, online library, helpline, student web hosting, wireless network available.

Student life. **Freshman orientation:** Available. Preregistration for classes offered. Held the week prior to fall term, designed to help students form relationships with faculty, staff, and fellow students. **Housing:** Guaranteed on-campus for freshmen. Coed dorms, single-sex dorms, special housing for disabled, apartments, fraternity/sorority housing, wellness housing available. $250 partly refundable deposit. Honors and language houses available. **Activities:** Bands, campus ministries, choral groups, dance, drama, international student organizations, literary magazine, music ensembles, Model UN, musical theater, opera, radio station, student government, student newspaper, symphony orchestra, TV station, Baptist Student Union, Fellowship of Christian Athletes, Jewish student association, Young Democrats, Women's Law Caucus, Hispanic student association, College Republicans, International Fellowship House, Association of Black Collegians, volunteer income tax assistance project.

Athletics. NCAA. **Intercollegiate:** Basketball, cheerleading, cross-country, football (tackle) M, golf, rowing (crew) W, soccer, softball W, tennis, track and field, volleyball W. **Intramural:** Badminton, basketball, bowling, cross-country, diving, football (non-tackle), golf, racquetball, soccer, softball, squash, swimming, table tennis, tennis, track and field, volleyball, water polo, wrestling M. **Team name:** Golden Hurricane.

Student services. Adult student services, alcohol/substance abuse counseling, chaplain/spiritual director, career counseling, student employment services, financial aid counseling, health services, legal services, minority student services, on-campus daycare, personal counseling, placement for graduates, veterans' counselor, women's services. **Physically disabled:** Services for visually, speech, hearing impaired.

Contact. E-mail: admission@utulsa.edu
Phone: (918) 631-2307 Toll-free number: (800) 331-3050
Fax: (918) 631-5003
John Corso, Associate Vice President of Enrollment and Student Services, University of Tulsa, 800 South Tucker Drive, Tulsa, OK 74104-3189

Oregon

Art Institute of Portland

Portland, Oregon
www.aipd.artinstitutes.edu
CB member
CB code: 4231

- For-profit 4-year visual arts and liberal arts college
- Commuter campus in large city
- 1,776 degree-seeking undergraduates
- 54% of applicants admitted
- Application essay, interview required

General. Founded in 1963. Regionally accredited. **Degrees:** 238 bachelor's, 22 associate awarded. **Calendar:** Quarter, extensive summer session. **Full-time faculty:** 39 total. **Part-time faculty:** 94 total. **Special facilities:** Specialized library, design laboratories, audio/visual laboratory.

Freshman class profile. 476 applied, 258 admitted, 255 enrolled.

Basis for selection. Proof of graduation from secondary school/GED required. Interview, essay, college transcripts, and/or English/math placement exam considered.

2008-2009 Annual costs. Tuition/fees: $19,395. Room only: $8,274. Books/supplies: $2,457. Personal expenses: $2,700.

2008-2009 Financial aid. **Need-based:** 31% of total undergraduate aid awarded as scholarships/grants, 69% as loans/jobs. **Non-need-based:** Scholarships awarded for art. **Additional information:** Applicants encouraged to apply early for financial aid. Scholarship deadlines range from January 1 to March 1.

Application procedures. **Admission:** No deadline. $50 fee. Admission notification on a rolling basis. **Financial aid:** Priority date 3/1; no closing date. FAFSA required. Applicants notified on a rolling basis starting 1/1; must reply within 5 week(s) of notification.

Academics. **Special study options:** Accelerated study, distance learning, honors, independent study, internships, liberal arts/career combination, study abroad. **Credit/placement by examination:** AP, CLEP, IB, SAT, ACT, institutional tests. Credit by examination only offered for courses in writing, computing, graphics, drawing, and math. **Support services:** Learning center, reduced course load, remedial instruction, study skills assistance, tutoring.

Majors. **Business:** Fashion. **Computer sciences:** Applications programming, computer graphics, web page design. **Visual/performing arts:** Art history/conservation, arts management, cinematography, commercial/ advertising art, design, fashion design, graphic design, industrial design, interior design, multimedia.

Most popular majors. Computer/information sciences 24%, visual/ performing arts 76%.

Computing on campus. 240 workstations in library, computer center. Dormitories wired for high-speed internet access. Commuter students can connect to campus network. Student web hosting, wireless network available.

Student life. **Freshman orientation:** Mandatory. Preregistration for classes offered. Held before each quarter-registration, advising and community services available. **Policies:** Student code of conduct published in catalog. No alcohol or drugs on campus or in housing. **Housing:** Special housing for disabled, apartments, wellness housing available. $250 partly refundable deposit. Apartments for 2 or 4 students. **Activities:** Film society, student government, student newspaper.

Student services. Alcohol/substance abuse counseling, career counseling, student employment services, financial aid counseling, personal counseling, placement for graduates, veterans' counselor. **Physically disabled:** Services for visually, speech, hearing impaired.

Contact. E-mail: aipdadm@aii.edu
Phone: (503) 228-6528 Toll-free number: (888) 228-6528
Fax: (503) 227-1945
Alan Yanda, Director of Admissions, Art Institute of Portland, 1122 Northwest Davis Street, Portland, OR 97209-2911

Concordia University

Portland, Oregon
www.cu-portland.edu
CB code: 4079

- Private 4-year liberal arts and teachers college affiliated with Lutheran Church - Missouri Synod
- Commuter campus in very large city
- 995 degree-seeking undergraduates: 12% part-time, 65% women, 7% African American, 5% Asian American, 6% Hispanic American, 1% Native American, 1% international
- 545 degree-seeking graduate students
- 60% of applicants admitted
- SAT or ACT (ACT writing optional) required
- 54% graduate within 6 years

General. Founded in 1905. Regionally accredited. **Degrees:** 251 bachelor's awarded; master's offered. **ROTC:** Air Force. **Location:** 5 miles from downtown. **Calendar:** Semester, limited summer session. **Full-time faculty:** 49 total; 67% have terminal degrees, 2% minority, 49% women. **Part-time faculty:** 123 total; 20% have terminal degrees, 3% minority, 54% women. **Class size:** 67% < 20, 32% 20-39, less than 1% 40-49, 1% 50-99. **Special facilities:** Environmental research center, children's literature center, Shakespeare authorship research center.

Freshman class profile. 898 applied, 536 admitted, 164 enrolled.

Mid 50% test scores		**GPA 2.0-2.99:**	20%
SAT critical reading:	450-590	**Rank in top quarter:**	38%
SAT math:	450-580	**Rank in top tenth:**	16%
ACT composite:	18-25	**Return as sophomores:**	74%
GPA 3.75 or higher:	27%	**Out-of-state:**	54%
GPA 3.50-3.74:	17%	**Live on campus:**	93%
GPA 3.0-3.49:	35%		

Basis for selection. 2.5 GPA, 480 SAT verbal, or 18 ACT required. **Homeschooled:** Statement describing homeschool structure and mission, state high school equivalency certificate, letter of recommendation (nonparent) required. Interview may be required.

High school preparation. College-preparatory program recommended. 19 units recommended. Recommended units include English 4, mathematics 3, social studies 3, science 3, foreign language 2 and academic electives 3. One computer/keyboarding recommended.

2008-2009 Annual costs. Tuition/fees: $22,100. Room/board: $6,400. Books/supplies: $800. Personal expenses: $1,600.

2008-2009 Financial aid. **Non-need-based:** Scholarships awarded for academics, athletics, leadership, music/drama, religious affiliation.

Application procedures. **Admission:** Priority date 3/1; deadline 7/1 (postmark date). $20 fee, may be waived for applicants with need, free for online applicants. Admission notification on a rolling basis beginning on or about 1/1. Must reply by May 1 or within 2 week(s) if notified thereafter. **Financial aid:** No deadline. FAFSA required. Applicants notified on a rolling basis starting 3/15; must reply by 5/1 or within 3 week(s) of notification.

Academics. **Special study options:** Accelerated study, cross-registration, distance learning, double major, dual enrollment of high school students, ESL, honors, independent study, internships, semester at sea, study abroad, teacher certification program. **Credit/placement by examination:** AP, CLEP, institutional tests. **Support services:** Learning center, remedial instruction, tutoring, writing center.

Majors. **Biology:** General. **Business:** General, business admin, international. **Education:** General, biology, business, chemistry, early childhood, elementary, English, health, history, mathematics, middle, multi-level teacher, physical, science, secondary, social studies. **Health:** Athletic training, health care admin, nursing (RN), premedicine. **History:** General. **Liberal arts:** Arts/sciences. **Parks/recreation:** Health/fitness, sports admin. **Philosophy/ religion:** Religion. **Physical sciences:** Chemistry. **Psychology:** General. **Public administration:** Social work. **Social sciences:** General. **Theology:** Religious ed, theology.

Most popular majors. Business/marketing 25%, education 23%, health sciences 26%, liberal arts 6%, public administration/social services 8%.

Computing on campus. PC or laptop required. 75 workstations in dormitories, library, computer center, student center. Dormitories wired for high-speed internet access and linked to campus network. Commuter students can connect to campus network. Online course registration, online library, helpline, repair service, wireless network available.

Student life. Freshman orientation: Mandatory. Preregistration for classes offered. Usually held the day before classes begin. **Policies:** Optional attendance for chapel services. Lutheran format, mixture of traditional and contemporary services offered. **Housing:** Guaranteed on-campus for freshmen. Coed dorms, apartments, wellness housing available. $50 deposit, deadline 5/1. Homestay option for international students. **Activities:** Campus ministries, choral groups, drama, international student organizations, literary magazine, music ensembles, student government, student newspaper, social service organization, Circle K, Spiritual Life, El Club Latino.

Athletics. NAIA. **Intercollegiate:** Baseball M, basketball, cross-country, golf, soccer, softball W, track and field, volleyball W. **Intramural:** Badminton, basketball, softball, tennis, volleyball. **Team name:** Cavaliers.

Student services. Adult student services, chaplain/spiritual director, career counseling, financial aid counseling, health services, personal counseling, placement for graduates, veterans' counselor.

Contact. E-mail: admissions@cu-portland.edu
Phone: (503) 280-8501 Toll-free number: (800) 321-9371
Fax: (503) 280-8531
Bobi Swan, Dean of Admission, Concordia University, 2811 Northeast Holman Street, Portland, OR 97211-6099

Corban College
Salem, Oregon
www.corban.edu **CB code: 4956**

- Private 4-year liberal arts college affiliated with Baptist faith
- Residential campus in small city
- 812 degree-seeking undergraduates: 9% part-time, 60% women
- 68 degree-seeking graduate students
- 82% of applicants admitted
- SAT or ACT (ACT writing recommended), application essay required
- 50% graduate within 6 years

General. Founded in 1935. Regionally accredited. **Degrees:** 191 bachelor's, 4 associate awarded; master's offered. **ROTC:** Army, Air Force. **Location:** 45 miles from Portland. **Calendar:** Semester, limited summer session. **Full-time faculty:** 40 total; 52% have terminal degrees, 5% minority, 25% women. **Part-time faculty:** 61 total; 16% have terminal degrees, 43% women. **Class size:** 63% < 20, 31% 20-39, 5% 40-49, less than 1% 50-99. **Special facilities:** Archaeological museum.

Freshman class profile. 498 applied, 408 admitted, 187 enrolled.

Mid 50% test scores		**GPA 3.0-3.49:**	26%
SAT critical reading:	480-580	**GPA 2.0-2.99:**	10%
SAT math:	450-580	**Rank in top quarter:**	52%
SAT writing:	440-570	**Rank in top tenth:**	23%
ACT composite:	19-25	**Return as sophomores:**	69%
GPA 3.75 or higher:	41%	**Out-of-state:**	46%
GPA 3.50-3.74:	22%	**Live on campus:**	93%

Basis for selection. Commitment to Christianity, high school GPA, test scores, recommendations, essays, school and community activities considered. Audition required for music program.

High school preparation. College-preparatory program recommended. 14 units recommended. Recommended units include English 4, mathematics 3, social studies 3, science 2 and foreign language 2.

2009-2010 Annual costs. Tuition/fees (projected): $23,202. Room/board: $8,068. Books/supplies: $900. Personal expenses: $1,602.

2007-2008 Financial aid. Need-based: 159 full-time freshmen applied for aid; 141 were judged to have need; 141 of these received aid. Average need met was 65%. Average scholarship/grant was $12,878; average loan $3,588. 59% of total undergraduate aid awarded as scholarships/grants, 41% as loans/jobs. **Non-need-based:** Awarded to 196 full-time undergraduates, including 63 freshmen. Scholarships awarded for academics, alumni affiliation, athletics, leadership, music/drama, ROTC.

Application procedures. Admission: Priority date 3/1; deadline 8/1 (receipt date). No application fee. Admission notification on a rolling basis beginning on or about 10/1. **Financial aid:** Priority date 2/15; no closing date. FAFSA required. Applicants notified on a rolling basis starting 3/1.

Academics. Special study options: Accelerated study, combined bachelor's/graduate degree, cooperative education, cross-registration, distance learning, double major, external degree, honors, independent study, internships, liberal arts/career combination, student-designed major, study abroad, teacher certification program, Washington semester, weekend college. **Credit/placement by examination:** AP, CLEP, institutional tests. 20 credit hours maximum toward associate degree, 32 toward bachelor's. **Support services:** Learning center, reduced course load, tutoring.

Majors. Business: General, accounting, accounting/business management, accounting/finance, business admin, communications, finance, management information systems. **Communications:** General, journalism. **Computer sciences:** Computer science. **Education:** General, biology, business, elementary, English, history, mathematics, middle, multi-level teacher, music, physical, science, secondary, social science, social studies. **Health:** Predental, premedicine, prenursing, prepharmacy, preveterinary. **History:** General. **Legal studies:** Prelaw. **Liberal arts:** Arts/sciences, humanities. **Math:** General. **Parks/recreation:** Health/fitness, sports admin. **Philosophy/religion:** Religion. **Psychology:** General. **Public administration:** Community org/advocacy. **Social sciences:** General. **Theology:** Bible, missionary, pastoral counseling, preministerial, religious ed, sacred music, theology, youth ministry. **Visual/performing arts:** Music performance, piano/organ, voice/opera.

Most popular majors. Business/marketing 18%, education 19%, English 9%, liberal arts 7%, psychology 28%.

Computing on campus. 34 workstations in dormitories, library, computer center, student center. Dormitories wired for high-speed internet access and linked to campus network. Commuter students can connect to campus network. Online library, helpline, repair service, wireless network available.

Student life. Freshman orientation: Mandatory. Preregistration for classes offered. Students assigned to core group of 12-18 students, with adviser to answer questions and schedule classes for fall semester. Core group advisers often visit students in their homes. **Policies:** Religious observance required. **Housing:** Guaranteed on-campus for freshmen. Single-sex dorms, special housing for disabled, apartments, cooperative housing available. $100 nonrefundable deposit, deadline 8/1. **Activities:** Bands, campus ministries, choral groups, drama, literary magazine, music ensembles, musical theater, radio station, student government, student newspaper, symphony orchestra, Christian fellowships.

Athletics. NAIA, NCCAA. **Intercollegiate:** Baseball M, basketball, cross-country, golf M, soccer, softball W, volleyball W. **Intramural:** Basketball, football (non-tackle), soccer, softball, volleyball, weight lifting. **Team name:** Warriors.

Student services. Adult student services, chaplain/spiritual director, career counseling, student employment services, financial aid counseling, health services, personal counseling, placement for graduates. **Physically disabled:** Services for visually, hearing impaired.

Contact. E-mail: admissions@corban.edu
Phone: (503) 375-7005 Toll-free number: (800) 845-3005
Fax: (503) 585-4316
Marty Ziesemer, Director of Admissions, Corban College, 5000 Deer Park Drive SE, Salem, OR 97317-9392

DeVry University: Portland
Portland, Oregon
www.devry.edu

- For-profit 4-year university
- Commuter campus in very large city
- 101 degree-seeking undergraduates: 46% part-time, 38% women, 10% African American, 4% Asian American, 7% Hispanic American, 1% international
- 54 degree-seeking graduate students

General. Degrees: 7 bachelor's awarded; master's offered. **Calendar:** Semester. **Part-time faculty:** 23 total; 9% minority, 9% women.

Basis for selection. Applicants must have high school diploma or equivalent, or a degree from accredited postsecondary institution, demonstrate proficiency in basic college-level skills through SAT or ACT scores or institution-administered placement exams, and be at least 17 years of age on the first day of classes. SAT/ACT tests considered but not required for admission. If applicant chooses not to submit either, must take DeVry-administered admissions test.

2008-2009 Annual costs. Tuition/fees: $13,930. Books/supplies: $1,300. Personal expenses: $5,082.

2007-2008 Financial aid. Non-need-based: Scholarships awarded for academics.

Application procedures. Admission: No deadline. $50 fee. Admission notification on a rolling basis. **Financial aid:** No deadline. FAFSA required. Applicants notified on a rolling basis.

Academics. **Special study options:** Accelerated study, distance learning. **Credit/placement by examination:** CLEP.

Majors. **Computer sciences:** Systems analysis. **Engineering technology:** Biomedical. **Other:** Technical management.

Student life. **Housing:** Private apartments, student-plan housing, private rooms available.

Contact. Phone: (866) 543-3879
DeVry University: Portland, Peterkort Center II, Portland, OR 97225

Eastern Oregon University

La Grande, Oregon
www.eou.edu **CB code: 4300**

- Public 4-year university and liberal arts college
- Residential campus in large town
- 2,823 degree-seeking undergraduates: 37% part-time, 62% women, 2% African American, 2% Asian American, 4% Hispanic American, 3% Native American, 1% international
- 283 degree-seeking graduate students
- 39% of applicants admitted
- SAT or ACT (ACT writing optional) required

General. Founded in 1929. Regionally accredited. **Degrees:** 626 bachelor's awarded; master's offered. **ROTC:** Army. **Location:** 260 miles from Portland; 180 miles from Boise, Idaho. **Calendar:** Quarter, limited summer session. **Full-time faculty:** 99 total; 86% have terminal degrees, 12% minority, 39% women. **Part-time faculty:** 25 total; 36% have terminal degrees, 20% minority, 64% women. **Class size:** 65% < 20, 29% 20-39, 2% 40-49, 4% 50-99. **Special facilities:** Wildlife habitat laboratory, agriculture experiment station.

Freshman class profile. 932 applied, 367 admitted, 350 enrolled.

Mid 50% test scores		**GPA 2.0-2.99:**	32%
SAT critical reading:	410-530	**Rank in top quarter:**	34%
SAT math:	410-510	**Rank in top tenth:**	12%
SAT writing:	390-510	**Return as sophomores:**	58%
ACT composite:	19-22	**Out-of-state:**	27%
GPA 3.75 or higher:	12%	**Live on campus:**	57%
GPA 3.50-3.74:	17%	**International:**	1%
GPA 3.0-3.49:	37%		

Basis for selection. Secondary school record most important; 3.0 GPA in 14 subject areas required. Students not meeting requirements must submit portfolio including essay and 2 letters of recommendation. Limited number of students not meeting requirements may be admitted. **Homeschooled:** State high school equivalency certificate, letter of recommendation (nonparent) required. Applicants must present certificate of completion and portfolio including essay, letters of recommendation, standardized test scores.

High school preparation. College-preparatory program required. Required and recommended units include English 4, mathematics 3, science 2 (laboratory 1) and foreign language 2.

2008-2009 Annual costs. Tuition/fees: $6,240; $6,240 out-of-state. Room/board: $9,100. Books/supplies: $1,152. Personal expenses: $1,353.

2008-2009 Financial aid. **Need-based:** 278 full-time freshmen applied for aid; 228 were judged to have need; 227 of these received aid. Average need met was 48%. Average scholarship/grant was $5,520; average loan $2,166. 46% of total undergraduate aid awarded as scholarships/grants, 54% as loans/jobs. **Non-need-based:** Awarded to 780 full-time undergraduates, including 222 freshmen. Scholarships awarded for academics, art, leadership, minority status, music/drama, state residency.

Application procedures. **Admission:** Priority date 12/1; deadline 9/15 (postmark date). $50 fee, may be waived for applicants with need. Admission notification on a rolling basis beginning on or about 10/1. **Financial aid:** Priority date 3/1; no closing date. FAFSA required. Applicants notified on a rolling basis starting 4/1; must reply within 4 week(s) of notification.

Academics. Regional advisers for distance education students. **Special study options:** Combined bachelor's/graduate degree, cooperative education, cross-registration, distance learning, double major, dual enrollment of high school students, exchange student, external degree, honors, independent study, internships, liberal arts/career combination, semester at sea, student-designed major, study abroad, teacher certification program, weekend college. **Credit/placement by examination:** AP, CLEP, IB, institutional tests. 45 credit hours maximum toward bachelor's degree. **Support services:** Learning center, study skills assistance, tutoring, writing center.

Majors. **Agriculture:** Agronomy, business, economics, range science, soil science. **Biology:** General. **Business:** General, accounting, business admin, managerial economics. **Computer sciences:** General, computer science, web page design. **Conservation:** General. **Education:** General, early childhood, elementary, ESL, German, middle, science, secondary, social science, social studies, Spanish. **Health:** Nursing (RN), ophthalmic lab technology, predental, premedicine, preop/surgical nursing, prepharmacy, preveterinary. **History:** General. **Legal studies:** Prelaw. **Liberal arts:** Arts/sciences. **Math:** General. **Parks/recreation:** Health/fitness. **Physical sciences:** Chemistry, physics. **Protective services:** Fire services admin. **Psychology:** General. **Social sciences:** Anthropology, political science, sociology. **Visual/performing arts:** Dramatic, studio arts.

Most popular majors. Business/marketing 29%, education 15%, liberal arts 24%.

Computing on campus. 150 workstations in dormitories, library, computer center, student center. Dormitories wired for high-speed internet access and linked to campus network. Commuter students can connect to campus network. Online course registration, online library, helpline, repair service, wireless network available.

Student life. **Freshman orientation:** Available. Preregistration for classes offered. **Housing:** Guaranteed on-campus for freshmen. Coed dorms, apartments available. **Activities:** Bands, choral groups, dance, drama, international student organizations, literary magazine, music ensembles, Model UN, musical theater, radio station, student government, student newspaper, symphony orchestra, international relations club, outdoor club, biology club, Fellowship of Christian Athletes, Latter-day Saints student association.

Athletics. NAIA. **Intercollegiate:** Basketball, cheerleading, cross-country, football (tackle) M, rodeo, soccer W, softball W, track and field, volleyball W. **Intramural:** Badminton, basketball, football (non-tackle), racquetball, softball, swimming, tennis, volleyball. **Team name:** Mountaineers.

Student services. Alcohol/substance abuse counseling, career counseling, student employment services, financial aid counseling, health services, minority student services, personal counseling, placement for graduates, veterans' counselor, women's services. **Physically disabled:** Services for visually, hearing impaired.

Contact. E-mail: admissions@eou.edu
Phone: (541) 962-3393 Toll-free number: (800) 452-8639
Fax: (541) 962-3418
Michael Dannells, Director of Admissions, Eastern Oregon University, One University Boulevard, La Grande, OR 97850

Eugene Bible College

Eugene, Oregon
www.ebc.edu **CB code: 4274**

- Private 4-year Bible college affiliated with Open Bible Standard Churches
- Residential campus in small city
- 103 degree-seeking undergraduates: 20% part-time, 49% women
- 50% of applicants admitted
- Application essay required
- 56% graduate within 6 years

General. Founded in 1925. Accredited by ABHE. **Degrees:** 53 bachelor's awarded. **Location:** 100 miles from Portland. **Calendar:** Quarter, extensive summer session. **Full-time faculty:** 6 total; 33% have terminal degrees, 50% minority, 33% women. **Part-time faculty:** 15 total; 20% have terminal degrees, 7% minority, 53% women. **Class size:** 54% < 20, 38% 20-39, 6% 40-49, 2% 50-99.

Freshman class profile. 90 applied, 45 admitted, 31 enrolled.

Mid 50% test scores		**GPA 2.0-2.99:**	32%
SAT critical reading:	450-580	**Rank in top quarter:**	40%
SAT math:	430-610	**Rank in top tenth:**	9%
ACT composite:	19-24	**Return as sophomores:**	57%
GPA 3.75 or higher:	11%	**Out-of-state:**	26%
GPA 3.50-3.74:	16%	**Live on campus:**	81%
GPA 3.0-3.49:	34%		

Basis for selection. School achievement and activities, test scores, recommendations, personal essay most important. Religious affiliation or commitment important factor. **Homeschooled:** CAT test, SAT Subject Test, or ITBS recommended.

High school preparation. College-preparatory program recommended.

2009-2010 Annual costs. Tuition/fees (projected): $10,958. Room/board: $5,670. Books/supplies: $900. Personal expenses: $1,500.

2007-2008 Financial aid. Need-based: 92% of total undergraduate aid awarded as scholarships/grants, 8% as loans/jobs. **Non-need-based:** Scholarships awarded for academics, athletics, leadership, religious affiliation. **Additional information:** Some early acceptance awards possible for those admitted by May 15. Distance awards to those coming from over 1,000 miles away. Some awards for husbands and wives enrolled at same time.

Application procedures. Admission: Priority date 12/31; deadline 9/1 (receipt date). $30 fee, may be waived for applicants with need. Admission notification on a rolling basis beginning on or about 12/31. **Financial aid:** Priority date 5/1, closing date 9/1. FAFSA required. Applicants notified on a rolling basis starting 7/15; must reply within 4 week(s) of notification.

Academics. Transfer-track programs available in elementary education: first 2 years at college, final 2-3 years at other institutions. **Special study options:** Distance learning, double major, independent study, internships. **Credit/placement by examination:** AP, CLEP, institutional tests. **Support services:** Reduced course load, remedial instruction, study skills assistance, tutoring.

Majors. Philosophy/religion: Christian, religion. **Theology:** Bible, missionary, pastoral counseling, religious ed, sacred music, theology, youth ministry.

Computing on campus. 18 workstations in dormitories, library, computer center, student center. Dormitories wired for high-speed internet access. Repair service available.

Student life. Freshman orientation: Mandatory. Preregistration for classes offered. Week-long program ends with camping retreat to mountains with fellow students and faculty. **Policies:** Students required to sign Code of Conduct agreement. Student ministry/community service required. Religious observance required. **Housing:** Guaranteed on-campus for freshmen. Single-sex dorms, apartments available. $75 partly refundable deposit, deadline 9/1. **Activities:** Concert band, campus ministries, choral groups, drama, music ensembles, musical theater, student government.

Athletics. Intramural: Basketball, soccer, volleyball. **Team name:** Deacons.

Student services. Chaplain/spiritual director, student employment services, financial aid counseling, personal counseling, placement for graduates, veterans' counselor.

Contact. E-mail: admissions@ebc.edu
Phone: (541) 485-1780 Toll-free number: (800) 322-2638
Fax: (541) 343-5801
Scott Thomas, Student Recruitment Coordinator, Eugene Bible College, 2155 Bailey Hill Road, Eugene, OR 97405

George Fox University

Newberg, Oregon — **CB member**
www.georgefox.edu — **CB code: 4325**

- Private 4-year university and seminary college affiliated with Society of Friends (Quaker)
- Residential campus in large town
- 1,962 degree-seeking undergraduates: 14% part-time, 61% women, 2% African American, 5% Asian American, 4% Hispanic American, 2% Native American, 4% international
- 1,201 degree-seeking graduate students
- 83% of applicants admitted
- SAT or ACT (ACT writing optional), application essay required
- 61% graduate within 6 years; 26% enter graduate study

General. Founded in 1891. Regionally accredited. Volunteer service encouraged through all-campus Serve Day and serve trips during school breaks. Freshmen receive laptop computer to keep upon graduating. **Degrees:** 546 bachelor's awarded; master's, doctoral, first professional offered. **ROTC:** Air Force. **Location:** 23 miles from Portland. **Calendar:** Semester, limited summer session. **Full-time faculty:** 162 total; 67% have terminal degrees, 7% minority, 37% women. **Part-time faculty:** 196 total; 16% have terminal degrees, 5% minority, 54% women. **Class size:** 61% < 20, 33% 20-39, 5% 40-49, 1% 50-99. **Special facilities:** Center for retreats and outdoor ministries, electron microscope, art galleries.

Freshman class profile. 1,212 applied, 1,003 admitted, 401 enrolled.

Mid 50% test scores		**GPA 2.0-2.99:**	11%
SAT critical reading:	480-620	**Rank in top quarter:**	53%
SAT math:	480-600	**Rank in top tenth:**	32%
SAT writing:	470-590	**End year in good standing:**	88%
ACT composite:	20-26	**Return as sophomores:**	76%
GPA 3.75 or higher:	39%	**Out-of-state:**	32%
GPA 3.50-3.74:	25%	**Live on campus:**	94%
GPA 3.0-3.49:	25%		

Basis for selection. Decision based on grade transcript, test scores, recommendations from teacher and counselor, church, school, and community activities. Interview recommended for all; audition recommended for drama, music programs. **Homeschooled:** Statement describing homeschool structure and mission, transcript of courses and grades, letter of recommendation (nonparent) required.

High school preparation. College-preparatory program recommended. 16 units recommended. Recommended units include English 4, mathematics 3, social studies 2, history 2, science 2 (laboratory 2) and foreign language 2. 1 unit in health and physical education.

2008-2009 Annual costs. Tuition/fees: $25,190. Room/board: $8,000. Books/supplies: $700. Personal expenses: $1,380.

2008-2009 Financial aid. Need-based: 351 full-time freshmen applied for aid; 314 were judged to have need; 314 of these received aid. Average need met was 89%. Average scholarship/grant was $9,095; average loan $3,402. 64% of total undergraduate aid awarded as scholarships/grants, 36% as loans/jobs. **Non-need-based:** Awarded to 1,322 full-time undergraduates, including 330 freshmen. Scholarships awarded for academics, alumni affiliation, art, job skills, leadership, minority status, music/drama, religious affiliation. **Additional information:** Audition required for music and drama scholarships.

Application procedures. Admission: Priority date 2/1; no deadline. $40 fee, may be waived for applicants with need. Admission notification on a rolling basis beginning on or about 10/1. Must reply by May 1 or within 2 week(s) if notified thereafter. **Financial aid:** Priority date 2/1; no closing date. FAFSA required. Applicants notified on a rolling basis starting 3/1; must reply within 6 week(s) of notification.

Academics. Special study options: Accelerated study, cross-registration, double major, dual enrollment of high school students, ESL, exchange student, honors, independent study, internships, student-designed major, study abroad, teacher certification program, Washington semester. **Credit/placement by examination:** AP, CLEP, IB, SAT, ACT, institutional tests. 32 credit hours maximum toward bachelor's degree. **Support services:** Learning center, reduced course load, remedial instruction, study skills assistance, tutoring, writing center.

Majors. Biology: General. **Business:** Accounting, business admin, management information systems. **Communications:** General, organizational. **Computer sciences:** General. **Education:** Elementary, health, music, physical. **Engineering:** General, electrical, mechanical. **Family/consumer sciences:** General. **Foreign languages:** Spanish. **Health:** Athletic training, nursing (RN). **History:** General. **Interdisciplinary:** Behavioral sciences, cognitive science, global studies. **Math:** General. **Parks/recreation:** Health/fitness. **Philosophy/religion:** Philosophy, religion. **Physical sciences:** Chemistry. **Psychology:** General. **Public administration:** Social work. **Social sciences:** Economics, political science, sociology. **Theology:** Bible. **Visual/performing arts:** Art, cinematography, dramatic. **Other:** Christian ministries.

Most popular majors. Business/marketing 34%, health sciences 6%, interdisciplinary studies 11%, visual/performing arts 7%.

Computing on campus. 140 workstations in dormitories, library, computer center, student center. Dormitories wired for high-speed internet access and linked to campus network. Commuter students can connect to campus network. Online course registration, online library, helpline, repair service, wireless network available.

Student life. Freshman orientation: Mandatory. Preregistration for classes offered. One-day programs available during summer. New students attend 3-day program at start of semester. **Policies:** 3-year residency requirement for undergraduates. Required spiritual formation program and chapel program. Religious observance required. **Housing:** Guaranteed on-campus for all undergraduates. Single-sex dorms, special housing for disabled, apartments, wellness housing available. Pets allowed in dorm rooms. Houses, living-learning communities. **Activities:** Bands, campus ministries, choral groups, drama, international student organizations, literary magazine, music ensembles, musical theater, radio station, student government, student newspaper, symphony orchestra, Christian services committee, associated student community, multicultural club, Fellowship of Christian Athletes, Young Life, residence life, leadership development program, Little Bruin.

Athletics. NCAA. **Intercollegiate:** Baseball M, basketball, cross-country, golf, soccer, softball W, tennis, track and field, volleyball W. **Intramural:** Badminton, basketball, football (non-tackle), golf, racquetball, soccer, table tennis, tennis, volleyball. **Team name:** Bruins.

Student services. Adult student services, alcohol/substance abuse counseling, chaplain/spiritual director, career counseling, student employment services, financial aid counseling, health services, minority student services, personal counseling, veterans' counselor. **Physically disabled:** Services for visually, speech, hearing impaired.

Contact. E-mail: admissions@georgefox.edu
Phone: (503) 554-2240 Toll-free number: (800) 765-4369 ext. 2240
Fax: (503) 554-3110
Ryan Dougherty, Director of Undergraduate Admissions, George Fox University, 414 North Meridian Street, Newberg, OR 97132-2697

Gutenberg College
Eugene, Oregon
www.gutenberg.edu **CB code: 2605**

- Private 4-year liberal arts college
- Small city
- 42 degree-seeking undergraduates
- SAT, application essay required

General. Candidate for regional accreditation. "Great Books" education from a biblical worldview. **Degrees:** 2 bachelor's awarded. **Calendar:** Quarter. **Full-time faculty:** 8 total. **Part-time faculty:** 2 total.

Freshman class profile. 11 enrolled.

Basis for selection. Admissions decision based on application, essays, 2 references (academic and character), SAT, transcripts, and course of study. 2 written essays required.

2008-2009 Annual costs. Tuition/fees: $11,853.

Application procedures. Admission: Closing date 3/1. $40 fee. Late applications after 3/1 may be considered; application fee is $60 for late applicants. **Financial aid:** Closing date 6/1. CSS PROFILE required.

Academics. Credit/placement by examination: CLEP.

Majors. Liberal arts: Arts/sciences.

Contact. E-mail: admissions@gutenberg.edu
Phone: (541) 683-5141
Kasey Pilcher, Director of Admissions, Gutenberg College, 1883 University Street, Eugene, OR 97403

ITT Technical Institute: Portland
Portland, Oregon
www.itt-tech.edu **CB code: 0947**

- For-profit 4-year technical college
- Commuter campus in large city

General. Founded in 1979. Accredited by ACICS. **Location:** 10 miles from downtown. **Calendar:** Quarter.

Contact. Phone: (503) 255-6500
Director of Recruitment, 6035 Northeast 78th Court, Portland, OR 97218

Lewis & Clark College
Portland, Oregon **CB member**
www.lclark.edu **CB code: 4384**

- Private 4-year liberal arts college
- Residential campus in very large city
- 1,921 degree-seeking undergraduates: 1% part-time, 61% women, 2% African American, 6% Asian American, 5% Hispanic American, 1% Native American, 5% international
- 1,566 degree-seeking graduate students
- 58% of applicants admitted
- Application essay required
- 71% graduate within 6 years; 24% enter graduate study

General. Founded in 1867. Regionally accredited. **Degrees:** 464 bachelor's awarded; master's, doctoral, first professional offered. **Calendar:** Semester, limited summer session. **Full-time faculty:** 222 total; 97% have terminal degrees, 10% minority, 46% women. **Part-time faculty:** 154 total; 46% have terminal degrees, 4% minority, 56% women. **Class size:** 61% < 20, 34% 20-39, 3% 40-49, 1% 50-99. **Special facilities:** Scanning electron microscope, 3 diode array UV/visible spectrometers, gas chromatography/mass spectrometer, X-ray fluorescence spectrometer, atomic absorption spectrometer, solar telescope with spectrograph, imaging laboratory with high resolution optical microscope, research astronomical observatory, holographic laboratory, electro-acoustic music studio, 85-rank Casavant organ, multi-media foreign language lab, greenhouse.

Freshman class profile. 5,551 applied, 3,227 admitted, 533 enrolled.

Mid 50% test scores		**GPA 2.0-2.99:**	3%
SAT critical reading:	630-720	**Rank in top quarter:**	83%
SAT math:	590-680	**Rank in top tenth:**	43%
SAT writing:	610-700	**End year in good standing:**	99%
ACT composite:	27-31	**Return as sophomores:**	86%
GPA 3.75 or higher:	56%	**Out-of-state:**	87%
GPA 3.50-3.74:	23%	**Live on campus:**	99%
GPA 3.0-3.49:	18%	**International:**	5%

Basis for selection. School curriculum and achievement most important. Standardized tests, recommendations, extracurricular involvement, essay, and interview also considered. Portfolio Path option offered for admission, requiring academic portfolio (including 5 graded writing samples) and 2 additional teacher recommendations; standardized test scores optional. Interviews optional. Audition recommended for music scholarships; portfolio required for Portfolio Path applicants. **Homeschooled:** School's Portfolio Path for admissions recommended. GED required, interview recommended.

High school preparation. College-preparatory program recommended. Recommended units include English 4, mathematics 4, social studies 4, science 3 (laboratory 2) and foreign language 3. One unit fine arts recommended.

2008-2009 Annual costs. Tuition/fees: $33,726. Room/board: $8,820. Books/supplies: $1,050. Personal expenses: $990.

2008-2009 Financial aid. Need-based: 378 full-time freshmen applied for aid; 275 were judged to have need; 275 of these received aid. Average need met was 88%. Average scholarship/grant was $17,363; average loan $4,342. 79% of total undergraduate aid awarded as scholarships/grants, 21% as loans/jobs. **Non-need-based:** Awarded to 404 full-time undergraduates, including 121 freshmen. Scholarships awarded for academics, leadership, music/drama.

Application procedures. Admission: Closing date 2/1 (receipt date). $50 fee, may be waived for applicants with need, free for online applicants. Admission notification 4/1. Must reply by 5/1. **Financial aid:** Priority date 2/15; no closing date. FAFSA, CSS PROFILE required. Applicants notified on a rolling basis starting 3/1.

Academics. Special study options: Accelerated study, combined bachelor's/graduate degree, cross-registration, double major, dual enrollment of high school students, ESL, honors, independent study, internships, New York semester, student-designed major, study abroad, Washington semester. 3-2 engineering program with Columbia University, University of Southern California, Oregon Graduate Institute of Science and Engineering at OHSU, Washington University (St. Louis). **Credit/placement by examination:** AP, CLEP, IB, institutional tests. Up to 24 semester hours awarded for International Baccalaureate full diploma with score of 36 (16 hours for diploma with 32-35). Scores of 5 on higher level AP exams get 4 credits. **Support services:** Learning center, reduced course load, study skills assistance, tutoring, writing center.

Majors. Area/ethnic studies: East Asian. **Biology:** General, biochemistry. **Communications:** General. **Computer sciences:** Computer science. **Conservation:** Environmental studies. **Foreign languages:** General, French, German, Spanish. **History:** General. **Interdisciplinary:** Math/computer science. **Liberal arts:** Arts/sciences. **Math:** General. **Philosophy/religion:** Philosophy, religion. **Physical sciences:** Chemistry, physics. **Psychology:** General. **Social sciences:** Anthropology, economics, international relations, political science, sociology. **Visual/performing arts:** Art, dramatic, music performance, studio arts.

Most popular majors. Biology 9%, English 8%, foreign language 10%, history 7%, psychology 14%, social sciences 26%, visual/performing arts 7%.

Computing on campus. 158 workstations in library, computer center, student center. Dormitories wired for high-speed internet access and linked to campus network. Commuter students can connect to campus network. Online library, helpline, repair service, student web hosting, wireless network available.

Student life. Freshman orientation: Mandatory. Preregistration for classes offered. Held 4 days preceding class in late August. **Housing:** Guaranteed on-campus for freshmen. Coed dorms, single-sex dorms available. Apartment-style residence halls available for upperclassmen. **Activities:** Bands, campus ministries, choral groups, dance, drama, international student organizations, literary magazine, music ensembles, Model UN, musical theater, radio station, student government, student newspaper, symphony orchestra, TV station, Jewish student union, InterVarsity Christian Fellowship, Fellowship of Christian Athletes, Hawaii club, Amnesty International, black student union, Circle K, Forensics, Gringos y Latinos.

Athletics. NCAA. **Intercollegiate:** Baseball M, basketball, cross-country, football (tackle) M, golf, rowing (crew), soccer W, softball W, swimming, tennis, track and field, volleyball W. **Intramural:** Badminton, basketball, cross-country, softball, swimming, table tennis, tennis, volleyball, water polo. **Team name:** Pioneers, Pios.

Student services. Adult student services, alcohol/substance abuse counseling, chaplain/spiritual director, career counseling, services for economically disadvantaged, student employment services, financial aid counseling, health services, legal services, minority student services, personal counseling, placement for graduates, veterans' counselor, women's services. **Physically disabled:** Services for visually, speech, hearing impaired.

Contact. E-mail: admissions@lclark.edu
Phone: (503) 768-7040 Toll-free number: (800) 444-4111
Fax: (503) 768-7055
Michael Sexton, Dean of Admissions, Lewis & Clark College, 0615 SW Palatine Hill Road, Portland, OR 97219-7899

Linfield College

McMinnville, Oregon — **CB member**
www.linfield.edu — **CB code: 4387**

- Private 4-year liberal arts college affiliated with American Baptist Churches in the USA
- Residential campus in large town
- 1,678 degree-seeking undergraduates: 1% part-time, 56% women, 1% African American, 9% Asian American, 5% Hispanic American, 2% Native American, 3% international
- 79% of applicants admitted
- SAT or ACT (ACT writing optional), application essay required
- 72% graduate within 6 years; 15% enter graduate study

General. Founded in 1849. Regionally accredited. Students interested in nursing or health sciences degree may transfer to the Portland Campus as juniors or seniors. Part-time students who wish to complete a bachelor's degree online served through Division of Continuing Education. **Degrees:** 338 bachelor's awarded. **ROTC:** Air Force. **Location:** 38 miles from Portland. **Calendar:** 4-1-4, limited summer session. **Full-time faculty:** 108 total; 94% have terminal degrees, 7% minority, 44% women. **Part-time faculty:** 83 total; 18% have terminal degrees, 49% women. **Class size:** 65% < 20, 33% 20-39, 2% 40-49, less than 1% 50-99, less than 1% >100. **Special facilities:** Cadaver lab, field station, anthropology museum, music technology lab, interactive writing laboratory, speaking center.

Freshman class profile. 2,066 applied, 1,623 admitted, 478 enrolled.

Mid 50% test scores		**Rank in top quarter:**	67%
SAT critical reading:	490-610	**Rank in top tenth:**	33%
SAT math:	500-610	**End year in good standing:**	92%
SAT writing:	490-590	**Return as sophomores:**	81%
ACT composite:	21-27	**Out-of-state:**	48%
GPA 3.75 or higher:	36%	**Live on campus:**	99%
GPA 3.50-3.74:	27%	**International:**	4%
GPA 3.0-3.49:	28%	**Fraternities:**	5%
GPA 2.0-2.99:	9%	**Sororities:**	14%

Basis for selection. High school grades, official transcripts, counselor's recommendation and/or teacher recommendation, test scores, and essay important. Interview recommended.

High school preparation. College-preparatory program recommended. 17 units recommended. Recommended units include English 4, mathematics 4, social studies 3, science 3 and foreign language 2.

2008-2009 Annual costs. Tuition/fees: $27,414. Room/board: $7,860. Books/supplies: $650. Personal expenses: $1,100.

2008-2009 Financial aid. Need-based: 327 full-time freshmen applied for aid; 327 were judged to have need; 327 of these received aid. Average need met was 87%. Average scholarship/grant was $6,269; average loan $3,870. 62% of total undergraduate aid awarded as scholarships/grants, 38% as loans/jobs. **Non-need-based:** Awarded to 1,072 full-time undergraduates, including 307 freshmen. Scholarships awarded for academics, music/drama.

Application procedures. Admission: $40 fee, may be waived for applicants with need. Admission notification 4/1. Must reply by May 1 or within 2 week(s) if notified thereafter. **Financial aid:** Priority date 2/1; no closing date. FAFSA required. Applicants notified by 4/1; must reply by 5/1.

Academics. Special study options: Cross-registration, distance learning, double major, ESL, external degree, independent study, internships, liberal arts/career combination, semester at sea, student-designed major, study abroad, teacher certification program, Washington semester. Semester abroad programs at Linfield centers in Australia, Austria, China (Beijing and Hong Kong), Costa Rica, Ecuador, England, France, Ireland, Japan, Korea, Mexico, New Zealand, and Norway; shorter term study abroad opportunities through one-month January term. **Credit/placement by examination:** AP, CLEP, IB, institutional tests. 30 credit hours maximum toward bachelor's degree. **Support services:** Learning center, reduced course load, study skills assistance, tutoring, writing center.

Majors. Area/ethnic studies: German. **Biology:** General. **Business:** General, accounting, finance, international. **Communications:** General, media studies. **Computer sciences:** Computer science. **Conservation:** Environmental studies. **Education:** Elementary, music. **Foreign languages:** French, German, Japanese, Spanish. **Health:** Athletic training, health services, nursing (RN). **History:** General. **Math:** General. **Parks/recreation:** Exercise sciences, health/fitness. **Philosophy/religion:** Philosophy, religion. **Physical sciences:** General, applied physics, chemistry, physics. **Psychology:** General. **Social sciences:** Anthropology, economics, political science, sociology. **Visual/performing arts:** Art, design, dramatic, music performance, music theory/composition, studio arts.

Most popular majors. Business/marketing 27%, education 9%, English 7%, parks/recreation 8%, social sciences 8%.

Computing on campus. 250 workstations in dormitories, library, computer center, student center. Dormitories wired for high-speed internet access and linked to campus network. Commuter students can connect to campus network. Online course registration, online library, helpline, repair service, student web hosting, wireless network available.

Student life. Freshman orientation: Mandatory. Preregistration for classes offered. Four-day program held at beginning of fall semester; includes advising, peer mentoring. **Policies:** All students required to live on-campus unless they are of senior standing, married, or living with parents locally. **Housing:** Guaranteed on-campus for all undergraduates. Coed dorms, single-sex dorms, special housing for disabled, apartments, fraternity/sorority housing, wellness housing available. **Activities:** Bands, choral groups, dance, drama, international student organizations, literary magazine, music ensembles, musical theater, opera, radio station, student government, student newspaper, symphony orchestra, multicultural student club, Greenfield, Hawaiian club, Fellowship of Christian Athletes, progressive student union, Circle-K, Habitat for Humanity, gay straight alliance, Republican club.

Athletics. NCAA. **Intercollegiate:** Baseball M, basketball, cross-country, football (tackle) M, golf, lacrosse W, soccer, softball, swimming, tennis, track and field, volleyball W. **Intramural:** Basketball, bowling, football (non-tackle), racquetball, soccer, softball, volleyball. **Team name:** Wildcats.

Student services. Adult student services, alcohol/substance abuse counseling, chaplain/spiritual director, career counseling, student employment services, financial aid counseling, health services, minority student services, personal counseling, placement for graduates, veterans' counselor, women's services. **Physically disabled:** Services for visually, speech, hearing impaired.

Contact. E-mail: admission@linfield.edu
Phone: (503) 883-2213 Toll-free number: (800) 640-2287
Fax: (503) 883-2472
Lisa Knodle-Bragiel, Director of Admission, Linfield College, 900 Southeast Baker Street, McMinnville, OR 97218-6894

Marylhurst University

Marylhurst, Oregon
www.marylhurst.edu — **CB code: 0440**

- Private 4-year university and liberal arts college affiliated with Roman Catholic Church
- Commuter campus in large town
- 870 degree-seeking undergraduates: 74% part-time, 70% women, 3% African American, 2% Asian American, 2% Hispanic American, 1% international
- 856 degree-seeking graduate students

General. Founded in 1893. Regionally accredited. **Degrees:** 141 bachelor's awarded; master's, first professional offered. **Location:** 10 miles from Portland. **Calendar:** Quarter, extensive summer session. **Full-time faculty:** 35 total. **Part-time faculty:** 340 total. **Class size:** 98% < 20, 2% 20-39.

Freshman class profile. 40 applied, 27 admitted, 25 enrolled.

Basis for selection. Open admission, but selective for some programs. High school GPA, record and recommendations considered for selective programs.

2008-2009 Annual costs. Tuition/fees: $16,200. Books/supplies: $600. Personal expenses: $1,800.

2007-2008 Financial aid. Need-based: 6 full-time freshmen applied for aid; 4 were judged to have need; 4 of these received aid. Average need met was 43%. Average scholarship/grant was $7,010; average loan $4,791. 29% of total undergraduate aid awarded as scholarships/grants, 71% as loans/jobs. **Non-need-based:** Awarded to 12 full-time undergraduates, including 6 freshmen. Scholarships awarded for academics.

Application procedures. Admission: No deadline. $20 fee. Admission notification on a rolling basis. **Financial aid:** Priority date 6/1; no closing date. FAFSA, institutional form required. Applicants notified on a rolling basis starting 5/1.

Academics. Special study options: Accelerated study, distance learning, double major, ESL, honors, independent study, internships, student-designed major, weekend college. **Credit/placement by examination:** AP, CLEP, IB, institutional tests. 45 credit hours maximum toward bachelor's degree. **Support services:** Learning center, reduced course load, study skills assistance, tutoring, writing center.

Majors. Business: General, business admin, communications, real estate. **Communications:** General. **Conservation:** Environmental studies. **Liberal arts:** Arts/sciences. **Philosophy/religion:** Philosophy, religion. **Psychology:** General. **Social sciences:** General. **Visual/performing arts:** Art, interior design, studio arts.

Most popular majors. Business/marketing 21%, communications/journalism 12%, English 9%, interdisciplinary studies 11%, psychology 9%, visual/performing arts 11%.

Computing on campus. 41 workstations in library. Commuter students can connect to campus network. Online course registration, wireless network available.

Student life. Activities: Jazz band, choral groups, music ensembles, musical theater, symphony orchestra.

Student services. Adult student services, career counseling, financial aid counseling, personal counseling, veterans' counselor. **Physically disabled:** Services for visually, hearing impaired.

Contact. E-mail: admissions@marylhurst.edu
Phone: (503) 699-6268 Toll-free number: (800) 634-9982 ext. 6268
Fax: (503) 635-6585
Gretchen Potter, Director of Admissions, Marylhurst University, PO Box 261, Marylhurst, OR 97036-0261

Mount Angel Seminary
St. Benedict, Oregon
www.mtangel.edu **CB code: 4491**

- Private 4-year seminary college for men affiliated with Roman Catholic Church
- Residential campus in small town
- 79 degree-seeking undergraduates

General. Founded in 1887. Regionally accredited; also accredited by ATS. All undergraduates candidates for Roman Catholic priesthood. **Degrees:** 17 bachelor's awarded; master's, first professional offered. **Location:** 40 miles from Portland. **Calendar:** Semester. **Full-time faculty:** 25 total. **Part-time faculty:** 15 total.

Freshman class profile.

Out-of-state:	75%	**Live on campus:**	100%

Basis for selection. Primarily recommendations from sponsoring dioceses or clergymen, personal interview important. Test scores considered. SAT or ACT recommended. Interview recommended.

2008-2009 Annual costs. Tuition/fees: $14,462. Formation fee of $3,111 per year. Room/board: $9,381. Books/supplies: $800. Personal expenses: $1,000.

Application procedures. Admission: Closing date 6/15. $27 fee, may be waived for applicants with need. Admission notification on a rolling basis beginning on or about 9/1. **Financial aid:** No deadline. Institutional form required. Applicants notified on a rolling basis; must reply within 2 week(s) of notification.

Academics. Special study options: Cross-registration, double major, ESL. Interdivisional program, 3-week full-time pursuit of single approved course of study. **Credit/placement by examination:** CLEP, institutional tests.

Majors. Liberal arts: Arts/sciences. **Philosophy/religion:** Philosophy. **Theology:** Theology.

Computing on campus. 10 workstations in dormitories, library, computer center.

Student life. Policies: All full-time students working toward priesthood required to live on campus. Religious observance required. **Housing:** Guaranteed on-campus for all undergraduates. **Activities:** Student government.

Athletics. Intramural: Basketball M, racquetball M, soccer M, swimming M, volleyball M.

Student services. Health services, personal counseling.

Contact. Phone: (503) 845-3951 Fax: (503) 845-3126
Sr. Virginia Schroeder, Admissions Director, Mount Angel Seminary, One Abbey Drive, St. Benedict, OR 97373

Multnomah University
Portland, Oregon
www.multnomah.edu **CB code: 4496**

- Private 4-year Bible and seminary college affiliated with interdenominational tradition
- Residential campus in very large city
- 582 degree-seeking undergraduates: 12% part-time, 45% women, 1% African American, 3% Asian American, 2% Hispanic American, 1% Native American, 1% international
- 255 degree-seeking graduate students
- 71% of applicants admitted
- SAT or ACT (ACT writing recommended), application essay required
- 43% graduate within 6 years

General. Founded in 1936. Regionally accredited; also accredited by ABHE. Emphasis on preparation for Christian ministries. **Degrees:** 113 bachelor's awarded; master's, first professional offered. **Location:** 5 miles from downtown. **Calendar:** Semester, limited summer session. **Full-time faculty:** 36 total; 75% have terminal degrees, 8% minority, 14% women. **Part-time faculty:** 50 total; 44% have terminal degrees, 4% minority, 18% women. **Class size:** 69% < 20, 24% 20-39, 3% 40-49, 3% 50-99, less than 1% >100.

Freshman class profile. 159 applied, 113 admitted, 72 enrolled.

Mid 50% test scores		**GPA 3.50-3.74:**	22%
SAT critical reading:	470-620	**GPA 3.0-3.49:**	31%
SAT math:	460-580	**GPA 2.0-2.99:**	19%
SAT writing:	470-580	**Rank in top quarter:**	56%
ACT composite:	19-27	**Rank in top tenth:**	28%
GPA 3.75 or higher:	28%	**Return as sophomores:**	62%

Basis for selection. School achievement record, test scores, recommendations most important. **Homeschooled:** If official transcript cannot be supplied, parental statement verifying student has met high school graduation requirements for home schoolers for their home state or GED test scores required.

High school preparation. College-preparatory program recommended. Recommended units include English 4, mathematics 2, social studies 3, history 2, science 3 (laboratory 1) and foreign language 2.

2008-2009 Annual costs. Tuition/fees: $14,100. Cost of health insurance if student is not covered is $1,200. Room/board: $5,840. Books/supplies: $1,000. Personal expenses: $1,600.

2007-2008 Financial aid. Need-based: 60 full-time freshmen applied for aid; 49 were judged to have need; 48 of these received aid. Average need met was 51%. Average scholarship/grant was $4,979; average loan $2,709. 44% of total undergraduate aid awarded as scholarships/grants, 56%

as loans/jobs. **Non-need-based:** Awarded to 36 full-time undergraduates, including 6 freshmen. Scholarships awarded for academics.

Application procedures. Admission: Priority date 3/1; deadline 7/15 (postmark date). $40 fee. Admission notification on a rolling basis. Must reply by 8/15. **Financial aid:** Priority date 3/1, closing date 8/1. FAFSA, institutional form required. Applicants notified on a rolling basis starting 4/1; must reply within 3 week(s) of notification.

Academics. Special study options: Cooperative education, double major, internships, liberal arts/career combination, teacher certification program. **Credit/placement by examination:** AP, CLEP, IB, institutional tests. 20 credit hours maximum toward bachelor's degree. **Support services:** Reduced course load, study skills assistance, tutoring, writing center.

Majors. Communications: General, journalism. **Education:** Elementary. **Foreign languages:** Ancient Greek, Hebrew. **History:** General. **Theology:** Bible, missionary, pastoral counseling, religious ed, sacred music, theology, youth ministry.

Computing on campus. 42 workstations in dormitories, library, computer center, student center. Dormitories wired for high-speed internet access and linked to campus network. Commuter students can connect to campus network. Online library, helpline, wireless network available.

Student life. Freshman orientation: Mandatory. Preregistration for classes offered. Held 3 days before start of classes. **Policies:** No alcohol, smoking, gambling. Religious observance required. **Housing:** Guaranteed on-campus for freshmen. Single-sex dorms, apartments available. $125 fully refundable deposit, deadline 7/15. Houses for married students. **Activities:** Choral groups, drama, music ensembles, student government, student newspaper.

Athletics. NCCAA. **Intercollegiate:** Basketball, volleyball W. **Intramural:** Basketball, football (non-tackle), soccer, volleyball. **Team name:** Lions.

Student services. Chaplain/spiritual director, career counseling, student employment services, financial aid counseling, health services, personal counseling, placement for graduates, veterans' counselor.

Contact. E-mail: admiss@multnomah.edu
Phone: (503) 255-0332 ext. 485 Toll-free number: (800) 275-4672
Fax: (503) 254-1268
John Mayner, Director of Admissions, Multnomah University, 8435 Northeast Glisan Street, Portland, OR 97220-5898

Northwest Christian University
Eugene, Oregon
www.northwestchristian.edu **CB code: 4543**

- Private 4-year university affiliated with Christian Church (Disciples of Christ)
- Commuter campus in small city
- 429 degree-seeking undergraduates: 28% part-time, 59% women, 3% African American, 2% Asian American, 4% Hispanic American, 2% Native American
- 97 degree-seeking graduate students
- 98% of applicants admitted
- SAT or ACT (ACT writing recommended), application essay required
- 42% graduate within 6 years

General. Founded in 1895. Regionally accredited. **Degrees:** 86 bachelor's, 9 associate awarded; master's offered. **ROTC:** Army. **Location:** 110 miles from Portland. **Calendar:** Semester, limited summer session.

Freshman class profile. 512 applied, 502 admitted, 80 enrolled.

Mid 50% test scores			
SAT critical reading:	460-560	GPA 3.0-3.49:	21%
SAT math:	460-570	GPA 2.0-2.99:	25%
SAT writing:	430-560	Rank in top quarter:	44%
ACT composite:	20-28	Rank in top tenth:	24%
GPA 3.75 or higher:	36%	Return as sophomores:	57%
GPA 3.50-3.74:	18%	Out-of-state:	28%
		Live on campus:	81%

Basis for selection. Admission based on evidence of ability to succeed academically and whether applicant is an appropriate fit. Students who fail to meet minimum admissions standards referred to admissions committee for final decision if there is other evidence of potential. Interview recommended, personal statement required.

High school preparation. College-preparatory program recommended.

2009-2010 Annual costs. Tuition/fees (projected): $22,900. Room/board: $6,800. Books/supplies: $900. Personal expenses: $2,340.

2008-2009 Financial aid. Need-based: 75 full-time freshmen applied for aid; 70 were judged to have need; 70 of these received aid. Average need met was 79%. Average scholarship/grant was $13,962; average loan $2,385. 70% of total undergraduate aid awarded as scholarships/grants, 30% as loans/jobs. **Non-need-based:** Scholarships awarded for academics, athletics, leadership, music/drama, religious affiliation.

Application procedures. Admission: Priority date 7/1; no deadline. No application fee. Admission notification on a rolling basis beginning on or about 10/15. **Financial aid:** Priority date 3/1; no closing date. FAFSA required. Applicants notified on a rolling basis starting 3/1; must reply within 2 week(s) of notification.

Academics. Special study options: Accelerated study, distance learning, double major, ESL, independent study, internships, liberal arts/career combination, student-designed major, study abroad, teacher certification program. **Credit/placement by examination:** AP, CLEP, IB, institutional tests. 15 credit hours maximum toward associate degree, 30 toward bachelor's. **Support services:** Reduced course load, remedial instruction, tutoring, writing center.

Majors. Biology: Exercise physiology. **Business:** Accounting, business admin. **Communications:** General. **Education:** Multi-level teacher. **Health:** Health services admin. **History:** General. **Interdisciplinary:** Intercultural. **Math:** General. **Psychology:** General. **Theology:** Bible, missionary, pastoral counseling, sacred music, theology, youth ministry. **Visual/performing arts:** Music management. **Other:** Global studies.

Most popular majors. Business/marketing 39%, education 17%, health sciences 9%, theological studies 9%.

Computing on campus. Dormitories wired for high-speed internet access and linked to campus network. Commuter students can connect to campus network. Online library, helpline, wireless network available.

Student life. Freshman orientation: Mandatory. Preregistration for classes offered. 4-day program; opportunity to meet administrators, staff, faculty members and fellow classmates. **Policies:** Attendance at chapel is required of all students. Religious observance required. **Housing:** Guaranteed on-campus for freshmen. Coed dorms, apartments available. $100 fully refundable deposit, deadline 6/1. **Activities:** Concert band, campus ministries, choral groups, drama, literary magazine, music ensembles, student government, student newspaper.

Athletics. NAIA, USCAA. **Intercollegiate:** Basketball, cross-country, golf, soccer, softball W, track and field, volleyball W. **Intramural:** Basketball, volleyball W. **Team name:** Beacons.

Student services. Adult student services, alcohol/substance abuse counseling, chaplain/spiritual director, career counseling, student employment services, financial aid counseling, health services, personal counseling, placement for graduates, veterans' counselor.

Contact. E-mail: admissions@northwestchristian.edu
Phone: (541) 684-7201 Toll-free number: (877) 463-6622
Fax: (541) 684-7317
Jennifer Samples, Director of Admissions, Northwest Christian University, 828 East 11th Avenue, Eugene, OR 97401-3745

Oregon College of Art & Craft
Portland, Oregon
www.ocac.edu

- Private 4-year visual arts college
- Very large city
- 115 degree-seeking undergraduates: 19% part-time, 71% women, 4% Asian American, 2% Hispanic American, 3% Native American
- 93% of applicants admitted
- Application essay, interview required

General. Candidate for regional accreditation. **Degrees:** 23 bachelor's awarded. **Calendar:** Semester. **Full-time faculty:** 9 total; 89% have terminal degrees, 11% minority, 44% women. **Part-time faculty:** 14 total; 71% have terminal degrees, 7% minority, 57% women. **Class size:** 94% < 20, 6% 20-39.

Freshman class profile. 27 applied, 25 admitted, 8 enrolled.

Mid 50% test scores			
SAT critical reading:	-560	GPA 3.50-3.74:	13%
SAT math:	-640	GPA 3.0-3.49:	25%
SAT writing:	-560	GPA 2.0-2.99:	37%
ACT composite:	17-24	Return as sophomores:	76%
GPA 3.75 or higher:	25%	Out-of-state:	25%
		Live on campus:	37%

Basis for selection. Talent and ability, GPA, essay and interview very important. Portfolio required. **Homeschooled:** Statement describing home-school structure and mission required.

High school preparation. Recommended units include English 4, mathematics 3, social studies 1, history 3, science 3, foreign language 2 and visual/performing arts 2.

2008-2009 Annual costs. Tuition/fees: $20,416. Fees vary by area of concentration. Room/board: $1,800. Books/supplies: $1,800.

2008-2009 Financial aid. Need-based: Average need met was 56%. Average scholarship/grant was $2,281; average loan $3,500. 41% of total undergraduate aid awarded as scholarships/grants, 59% as loans/jobs. **Non-need-based:** Scholarships awarded for academics, art.

Application procedures. Admission: Priority date 3/1; no deadline. $35 fee, may be waived for applicants with need. Admission notification on a rolling basis beginning on or about 1/1. Must reply by May 1 or within 4 week(s) if notified thereafter. **Financial aid:** Priority date 3/1; no closing date. FAFSA required. Applicants notified on a rolling basis starting 3/15.

Academics. Special study options: Cross-registration, exchange student, independent study, internships, study abroad. **Credit/placement by examination:** AP, CLEP, IB, institutional tests. **Support services:** Tutoring.

Majors. Production: Furniture, woodworking. **Visual/performing arts:** Ceramics, drawing, fiber arts, metal/jewelry, painting, photography. **Other:** Book arts.

Computing on campus. Dormitories wired for high-speed internet access. Helpline, wireless network available.

Student life. Freshman orientation: Mandatory. Preregistration for classes offered. Two-day orientation includes field trip to Portland Art Museum. **Housing:** Cooperative housing available. $150 nonrefundable deposit, deadline 5/1. Small number of on-campus housing available for new students straight from high school. **Activities:** Student government, student newspaper.

Student services. Career counseling, financial aid counseling, personal counseling.

Contact. E-mail: admissions@ocac.edu
Phone: (503) 297-5544 ext. 129 Toll-free number: (800) 390-0632
Oregon College of Art & Craft, 8245 SW Barnes Road, Portland, OR 97225-6349

Oregon Health & Science University

Portland, Oregon — **CB member**
www.ohsu.edu — **CB code: 4900**

- Public 3-year university and health science college
- Commuter campus in very large city
- 604 degree-seeking undergraduates: 1% African American, 3% Asian American, 5% Hispanic American, 2% Native American, 1% international
- 1,820 graduate students

General. Founded in 1887. Regionally accredited. **Degrees:** 209 bachelor's awarded; master's, doctoral, first professional offered. **Calendar:** Quarter, limited summer session. **Full-time faculty:** 2,215 total; 47% have terminal degrees, 15% minority, 51% women. **Part-time faculty:** 516 total; 58% have terminal degrees, 11% minority, 44% women.

Basis for selection. Admission requirements vary by program.

2008-2009 Annual costs. Tuition/fees: $18,341; $29,321 out-of-state. Tuition shown is for undergraduate nursing program; costs for other programs vary. Books/supplies: $1,368.

2008-2009 Financial aid. Need-based: 20% of total undergraduate aid awarded as scholarships/grants, 80% as loans/jobs. **Non-need-based:** Scholarships awarded for academics, minority status, state residency.

Application procedures. Admission: Closing date 1/15 (postmark date). $120 fee, may be waived for applicants with need. Application must be submitted online. Admission notification on a rolling basis. Must reply by 5/1. **Financial aid:** Priority date 3/1; no closing date.

Academics. Services offered in OHSU's Center for Diversity and Multicultural Affairs. **Special study options:** Accelerated study, combined bachelor's/graduate degree, distance learning. **Credit/placement by examination:** CLEP, IB. **Support services:** Pre-admission summer program, study skills assistance, tutoring.

Majors. Health: Clinical lab science, EMT paramedic, medical radiologic technology/radiation therapy, nursing (RN).

Computing on campus. 60 workstations in library, computer center, student center. Commuter students can connect to campus network. Online library, helpline, wireless network available.

Student life. Freshman orientation: Available. Orientation varies by program. **Activities:** Student government, student newspaper.

Athletics. Intramural: Basketball, soccer, swimming, table tennis, tennis, volleyball.

Student services. Career counseling, financial aid counseling, health services, personal counseling.

Contact. E-mail: proginfo@ohsu.edu
Phone: (503) 494-2998 Fax: (503) 494-3400
Jennifer Anderson, Director of Admissions, Oregon Health & Science University, 3181 SW Sam Jackson Park Road, Portland, OR 97239

Oregon Institute of Technology

Klamath Falls, Oregon — **CB member**
www.oit.edu — **CB code: 4587**

- Public 4-year career college
- Commuter campus in small city
- 2,603 degree-seeking undergraduates: 1% African American, 6% Asian American, 4% Hispanic American, 2% Native American, 1% international
- 13 graduate students
- 92% of applicants admitted
- SAT or ACT with writing required

General. Founded in 1947. Regionally accredited. Upper-division courses offered in electronics engineering technology, manufacturing engineering technology. Software engineering technology offered at OIT Portland West in Beaverton area. **Degrees:** 489 bachelor's, 96 associate awarded; master's offered. **ROTC:** Army. **Location:** 280 miles from Portland; 270 miles from Reno, Nevada. **Calendar:** Quarter, limited summer session. **Full-time faculty:** 124 total; 44% have terminal degrees, 6% minority, 40% women. **Part-time faculty:** 90 total; 18% have terminal degrees, 7% minority, 36% women. **Class size:** 54% < 20, 40% 20-39, 3% 40-49, 4% 50-99. **Special facilities:** Center for research on geothermal energy, renewable energy center, center for health professions.

Freshman class profile. 630 applied, 581 admitted, 287 enrolled.

Mid 50% test scores			
SAT critical reading:	450-580	GPA 3.0-3.49:	38%
SAT math:	480-610	GPA 2.0-2.99:	17%
ACT composite:	18-24	Rank in top quarter:	52%
GPA 3.75 or higher:	22%	Rank in top tenth:	18%
GPA 3.50-3.74:	23%	Out-of-state:	11%
		Live on campus:	51%

Basis for selection. Secondary school record and standardized test scores very important. Class rank, recommendations, essay, interview, character/personal qualities and work experience all considered. Applicants from non-standard or unaccredited high schools must take 3 SAT Subject Tests: 1 English, 1 math, 1 other of student's choice. **Learning Disabled:** Tech opportunities available.

High school preparation. 14 units required. Required units include English 4, mathematics 3, social studies 3, science 2 (laboratory 1) and foreign language 2.

2008-2009 Annual costs. Tuition/fees: $6,297; $16,692 out-of-state. Room/board: $7,132. Books/supplies: $1,000. Personal expenses: $2,438.

2007-2008 Financial aid. Need-based: 210 full-time freshmen applied for aid; 182 were judged to have need; 178 of these received aid. Average need met was 22%. Average scholarship/grant was $3,034; average loan $2,456. 36% of total undergraduate aid awarded as scholarships/grants, 64%

as loans/jobs. **Non-need-based:** Awarded to 79 full-time undergraduates, including 17 freshmen. Scholarships awarded for academics, athletics, leadership, minority status.

Application procedures. Admission: Priority date 2/1; deadline 10/1. $50 fee. Admission notification on a rolling basis beginning on or about 10/15. Must reply by May 1 or within 4 week(s) if notified thereafter. **Financial aid:** Priority date 3/1; no closing date. FAFSA required. Applicants notified on a rolling basis starting 4/1; must reply within 3 week(s) of notification.

Academics. Special study options: Combined bachelor's/graduate degree, cooperative education, cross-registration, distance learning, double major, dual enrollment of high school students, external degree, internships, liberal arts/career combination, study abroad. **Credit/placement by examination:** AP, CLEP, SAT, ACT, institutional tests. No more than 25% of credits submitted for graduation may be credit by examination. **Support services:** Learning center, reduced course load, remedial instruction, study skills assistance, tutoring.

Majors. Business: Accounting, business admin, entrepreneurial studies, management information systems, marketing, operations, small business admin. **Communications:** General. **Computer sciences:** Information systems. **Conservation:** General. **Engineering technology:** Computer hardware, electrical, energy systems, manufacturing, mechanical, software, surveying. **Health:** Clinical lab science, dental hygiene, health services, medical radiologic technology/radiation therapy, radiologic technology/medical imaging, sonography. **Psychology:** General.

Most popular majors. Business/marketing 17%, engineering/engineering technologies 33%, health sciences 31%, psychology 11%.

Computing on campus. 656 workstations in dormitories, library, computer center. Dormitories wired for high-speed internet access. Commuter students can connect to campus network. Online course registration, online library, helpline, repair service, student web hosting, wireless network available.

Student life. Freshman orientation: Mandatory. Preregistration for classes offered. **Housing:** Coed dorms available. $150 partly refundable deposit, deadline 5/1. **Activities:** Choral groups, radio station, student government, student newspaper, symphony orchestra, TV station, Newman club, Latter-day Saints, Christian Fellowship, Native American club, international student club, Circle K, Latin American club, residence hall association, Phi Delta Theta, College Republicans.

Athletics. NAIA. **Intercollegiate:** Baseball M, basketball, cross-country, soccer W, softball W, track and field, volleyball W. **Intramural:** Basketball, cheerleading, cross-country, football (tackle) M, lacrosse M, soccer, softball, track and field, volleyball. **Team name:** Owls.

Student services. Adult student services, alcohol/substance abuse counseling, career counseling, student employment services, financial aid counseling, health services, personal counseling, placement for graduates, veterans' counselor. **Physically disabled:** Services for visually, hearing impaired.

Contact. E-mail: oit@oit.edu
Phone: (541) 885-1150 Toll-free number: (800) 422-2017
Fax: (541) 885-1115
John Duarte, Director of Admissions, Oregon Institute of Technology, 3201 Campus Drive, Klamath Falls, OR 97601

Oregon State University

Corvallis, Oregon — **CB member**
www.oregonstate.edu — **CB code: 4586**

- Public 4-year university
- Residential campus in small city
- 15,907 degree-seeking undergraduates: 12% part-time, 46% women, 2% African American, 9% Asian American, 5% Hispanic American, 1% Native American, 1% international
- 3,150 degree-seeking graduate students
- 85% of applicants admitted
- SAT or ACT with writing, application essay required
- 62% graduate within 6 years

General. Founded in 1868. Regionally accredited. **Degrees:** 3,269 bachelor's awarded; master's, doctoral, first professional offered. **ROTC:** Army, Naval, Air Force. **Location:** 80 miles from Portland, 45 miles from Eugene. **Calendar:** Quarter, extensive summer session. **Full-time faculty:** 880 total; 75% have terminal degrees, 14% minority, 43% women. **Part-time faculty:** 232 total; 41% have terminal degrees, 7% minority, 55% women. **Class size:** 41% < 20, 33% 20-39, 7% 40-49, 13% 50-99, 6% >100. **Special facilities:** Arboretum, 13,429-acre forest, radiation center (with TRIGA Mark II Nuclear Reactor), wave research facility, marine science center museum and aquarium.

Freshman class profile. 4,654 applied, 3,951 admitted, 3,106 enrolled.

Mid 50% test scores			
SAT critical reading:	460-600	Rank in top quarter:	51%
SAT math:	480-610	Rank in top tenth:	21%
SAT writing:	440-560	Return as sophomores:	81%
ACT composite:	20-26	Out-of-state:	15%
GPA 3.75 or higher:	30%	Live on campus:	79%
GPA 3.50-3.74:	23%	International:	1%
GPA 3.0-3.49:	37%	Fraternities:	16%
GPA 2.0-2.99:	10%	Sororities:	11%

Basis for selection. GPA and essay most important. Students not meeting admission requirements may petition for exception. Students who do not meet subject requirements, who graduated from nonstandard or unaccredited high schools, or who graduated prior to 1987 must submit SAT Subject Test scores in addition to SAT or ACT. Applicants with GED not required to submit test scores. **Homeschooled:** Must submit SAT or ACT, and SAT Subject Tests.

High school preparation. College-preparatory program required. 14 units required. Required and recommended units include English 4, mathematics 3, social studies 3, science 2 (laboratory 1-2) and foreign language 2.

2008-2009 Annual costs. Tuition/fees: $6,187; $18,823 out-of-state. Room/board: $8,208. Books/supplies: $1,527. Personal expenses: $2,403.

2008-2009 Financial aid. Need-based: 2,288 full-time freshmen applied for aid; 1,449 were judged to have need; 1,411 of these received aid. Average need met was 63%. Average scholarship/grant was $2,738; average loan $3,278. 39% of total undergraduate aid awarded as scholarships/grants, 61% as loans/jobs. **Non-need-based:** Awarded to 593 full-time undergraduates, including 107 freshmen. Scholarships awarded for academics, athletics, job skills, leadership, minority status, ROTC, state residency.

Application procedures. Admission: Priority date 2/1; deadline 9/1. $50 fee. Admission notification on a rolling basis beginning on or about 10/1. Must reply by May 1 or within 3 week(s) if notified thereafter. **Financial aid:** Priority date 2/1, closing date 5/1. FAFSA required. Applicants notified on a rolling basis starting 4/1; must reply within 4 week(s) of notification.

Academics. Special study options: Accelerated study, cooperative education, cross-registration, distance learning, double major, dual enrollment of high school students, ESL, exchange student, external degree, honors, independent study, internships, liberal arts/career combination, student-designed major, study abroad, teacher certification program. **Credit/placement by examination:** AP, CLEP, IB, SAT, ACT, institutional tests. **Support services:** Learning center, remedial instruction, study skills assistance, tutoring.

Majors. Agriculture: General, agronomy, animal sciences, business, economics, food science, horticultural science, plant sciences, range science. **Area/ethnic studies:** American. **Biology:** General, bacteriology, biochemistry, biophysics, biotechnology, botany, entomology, zoology. **Business:** Business admin. **Computer sciences:** General. **Conservation:** General, environmental science, fisheries, forest management, forest resources, management/policy, wildlife. **Education:** Technology/industrial arts. **Engineering:** Biomedical, chemical, civil, computer, construction, electrical, environmental, forest, industrial, manufacturing, mechanical, mining, nuclear, physics. **Family/consumer sciences:** Clothing/textiles, family studies, food/nutrition, housing, merchandising. **Foreign languages:** French, German, Spanish. **Health:** Clinical lab technology, environmental health, health care admin, physics/radiologic health, public health ed. **History:** General. **Interdisciplinary:** Biological/physical sciences, global studies. **Liberal arts:** Arts/sciences. **Math:** General. **Parks/recreation:** General, health/fitness. **Philosophy/religion:** Philosophy. **Physical sciences:** Chemistry, geology, physics. **Psychology:** General. **Social sciences:** Anthropology, economics, geography, political science, sociology. **Visual/performing arts:** General, art, fashion design, interior design.

Most popular majors. Agriculture 6%, biology 7%, business/marketing 16%, engineering/engineering technologies 13%, family/consumer sciences 11%.

Computing on campus. 3,000 workstations in dormitories, library, computer center. Dormitories wired for high-speed internet access and linked to campus network. Commuter students can connect to campus network. Online course registration, helpline, repair service, student web hosting, wireless network available.

Student life. **Freshman orientation:** Available. Preregistration for classes offered. **Housing:** Coed dorms, special housing for disabled, apartments, cooperative housing, fraternity/sorority housing available. $45 nonrefundable deposit. **Activities:** Bands, campus ministries, choral groups, dance, drama, film society, international student organizations, literary magazine, music ensembles, Model UN, musical theater, opera, radio station, student government, student newspaper, symphony orchestra, TV station, 253 student organizations, 47 student honor and recognition societies.

Athletics. NCAA. **Intercollegiate:** Baseball M, basketball, cheerleading, cross-country W, football (tackle) M, golf, gymnastics W, rowing (crew), soccer, softball W, swimming W, volleyball W, wrestling M. **Intramural:** Badminton, basketball, bowling, cross-country, football (tackle) M, golf, racquetball, soccer, softball, swimming, tennis, track and field, volleyball, water polo, wrestling M. **Team name:** Beavers.

Student services. Adult student services, career counseling, student employment services, financial aid counseling, health services, legal services, minority student services, on-campus daycare, personal counseling, placement for graduates, veterans' counselor, women's services. **Physically disabled:** Services for visually, speech, hearing impaired.

Contact. E-mail: osuadmit@orst.edu
Phone: (541) 737-4411 Toll-free number: (800) 291-4192
Fax: (541) 737-2482
Michele Sandlin, Director of Admissions, Oregon State University, 104 Kerr Administration Building, Corvallis, OR 97331-2130

Pacific Northwest College of Art
Portland, Oregon
www.pnca.edu **CB code: 4504**

- Private 4-year visual arts college
- Commuter campus in large city
- 477 degree-seeking undergraduates: 8% part-time, 65% women, 2% African American, 3% Asian American, 6% Hispanic American, 1% Native American, 1% international
- 30 degree-seeking graduate students
- 51% of applicants admitted
- Application essay required
- 44% graduate within 6 years

General. Founded in 1909. Regionally accredited. **Degrees:** 56 bachelor's awarded; master's offered. **Calendar:** Semester, limited summer session. **Full-time faculty:** 22 total. **Part-time faculty:** 62 total. **Class size:** 96% < 20, 4% 20-39. **Special facilities:** Student art galleries, printmaking center, individual studio spaces for seniors.

Freshman class profile. 355 applied, 181 admitted, 93 enrolled.

GPA 3.75 or higher:	15%	**Return as sophomores:**	63%
GPA 3.50-3.74:	15%	**Out-of-state:**	52%
GPA 3.0-3.49:	24%	**Live on campus:**	58%
GPA 2.0-2.99:	38%	**International:**	1%

Basis for selection. Portfolio, essays important. 2.0 GPA recommended for academic courses. Greater emphasis on portfolio. Interview recommended. **Homeschooled:** Statement describing homeschool structure and mission, transcript of courses and grades, state high school equivalency certificate, letter of recommendation (nonparent) required. SAT/ACT exam recommended.

High school preparation. Recommended units include English 4, mathematics 3, social studies 3 and science 3. Visual arts classes recommended.

2009-2010 Annual costs. Tuition/fees (projected): $23,304. Books/supplies: $985. Personal expenses: $615.

2008-2009 Financial aid. **Non-need-based:** Scholarships awarded for academics, art.

Application procedures. **Admission:** Priority date 3/1; no deadline. $35 fee, may be waived for applicants with need, free for online applicants. Admission notification on a rolling basis. Must reply by May 1 or within 4 week(s) if notified thereafter. **Financial aid:** Priority date 3/1; no closing date. FAFSA required. Applicants notified on a rolling basis starting 4/1; must reply by 5/1 or within 4 week(s) of notification.

Academics. Thesis required during fourth year. **Special study options:** Cooperative education, cross-registration, dual enrollment of high school students, exchange student, independent study, internships, New York semester, student-designed major, study abroad. 5-year BA/BFA program with Reed College. **Credit/placement by examination:** AP, CLEP. **Support services:** Study skills assistance, tutoring, writing center.

Majors. **Visual/performing arts:** Design, illustration, multimedia, painting, photography, printmaking, sculpture, studio arts.

Computing on campus. 130 workstations in library, computer center, student center. Commuter students can connect to campus network. Online library, wireless network available.

Student life. **Freshman orientation:** Available. Preregistration for classes offered. Three-day program held immediately prior to start of semester. **Housing:** Coed dorms available. $450 partly refundable deposit, deadline 6/15. Pets allowed in dorm rooms. Student housing available through partnership with College Housing Northwest. **Activities:** Film society, radio station, student government.

Student services. Career counseling, financial aid counseling, personal counseling.

Contact. E-mail: admissions@pnca.edu
Phone: (503) 821-8972 Fax: (503) 821-8978
Chris Sweet, Director of Admissions, Pacific Northwest College of Art, 1241 NW Johnson Street, Portland, OR 97209

Pacific University
Forest Grove, Oregon
www.pacificu.edu **CB code: 4601**

- Private 4-year university affiliated with United Church of Christ
- Residential campus in large town
- 1,451 degree-seeking undergraduates: 3% part-time, 64% women, 1% African American, 23% Asian American, 5% Hispanic American, 1% Native American
- 1,643 degree-seeking graduate students
- 78% of applicants admitted
- SAT or ACT (ACT writing optional), application essay required
- 67% graduate within 6 years

General. Founded in 1849. Regionally accredited. Branch campuses in Hillsboro, Portland, and Eugene for selected professional programs. **Degrees:** 236 bachelor's awarded; master's, doctoral, first professional offered. **ROTC:** Army, Air Force. **Location:** 25 miles from Portland. **Calendar:** Semester, limited summer session. **Full-time faculty:** 205 total; 83% have terminal degrees, 14% minority, 48% women. **Part-time faculty:** 148 total; 32% have terminal degrees, 12% minority, 59% women. **Class size:** 67% < 20, 27% 20-39, 2% 40-49, 3% 50-99, less than 1% >100. **Special facilities:** Permaculture project, wildlife refuge, performing arts center, arboretum, center for Internet studies, English language institute, humanitarian center, institute for ethics and social policy, center for gender equity.

Freshman class profile. 1,516 applied, 1,179 admitted, 345 enrolled.

GPA 3.75 or higher:	44%	**Return as sophomores:**	76%
GPA 3.50-3.74:	24%	**Out-of-state:**	51%
GPA 3.0-3.49:	26%	**Live on campus:**	92%
GPA 2.0-2.99:	6%	**Fraternities:**	11%
Rank in top quarter:	69%	**Sororities:**	9%
Rank in top tenth:	39%		

Basis for selection. Strength of high school program, GPA, test scores, course selection, interview most important. 1000 SAT (exclusive of Writing) plus 3.0 GPA recommended. Recommendation, essay, extracurricular activities, leadership involvement also important. Audition required for music program; portfolio recommended for art program. **Homeschooled:** Statement describing homeschool structure and mission, transcript of courses and grades, state high school equivalency certificate, interview, letter of recommendation (nonparent) required.

High school preparation. College-preparatory program recommended. 21 units recommended. Recommended units include English 4, mathematics 3, social studies 3, history 1, science 3 (laboratory 1), foreign language 2 and academic electives 4.

2008-2009 Annual costs. Tuition/fees: $28,270. Room/board: $7,482.

2008-2009 Financial aid. **Need-based:** 310 full-time freshmen applied for aid; 255 were judged to have need; 255 of these received aid. Average need met was 88%. Average scholarship/grant was $14,223; average loan $7,789. 59% of total undergraduate aid awarded as scholarships/grants, 41% as loans/jobs. **Non-need-based:** Awarded to 377 full-time undergraduates, including 116 freshmen. Scholarships awarded for academics, alumni affiliation, art, music/drama.

Application procedures. **Admission:** Priority date 2/15; deadline 8/15. $40 fee, may be waived for applicants with need. Admission notification on a rolling basis beginning on or about 11/1. Must reply by May 1 or within 2 week(s) if notified thereafter. **Financial aid:** Priority date 3/1; no closing date. FAFSA required. Applicants notified on a rolling basis starting 3/1.

Academics. **Special study options:** Combined bachelor's/graduate degree, cross-registration, double major, ESL, independent study, internships, liberal arts/career combination, study abroad, teacher certification program, Washington semester. 3-2 engineering programs with Oregon Graduate Institute and Washington University, 3-2 applied physics program, 4-1 computer science, 4-1 environmental science programs with Oregon Graduate Institute, exchange programs with University of Vienna, Beijing Normal University, University of Edinburgh, other institutions in Europe and Asia; cooperative arrangement with Northwest Film Center. **Credit/placement by examination:** AP, CLEP, IB, SAT, ACT, institutional tests. **Support services:** Learning center, reduced course load, tutoring, writing center.

Majors. **Area/ethnic studies:** American, Asian, Latin American, Western European, women's. **Biology:** General, biochemistry, bioinformatics. **Business:** Business admin. **Communications:** General, journalism. **Computer sciences:** General. **Conservation:** Environmental science, environmental studies. **Education:** General. **Foreign languages:** General, Chinese, French, German, Japanese, Spanish. **History:** General. **Liberal arts:** Arts/sciences. **Math:** General. **Parks/recreation:** Exercise sciences. **Philosophy/religion:** Philosophy. **Physical sciences:** Chemistry, physics. **Psychology:** General. **Public administration:** Social work. **Social sciences:** Economics, international relations, political science, sociology. **Visual/performing arts:** General, art, dramatic, multimedia, music performance.

Most popular majors. Biology 10%, business/marketing 15%, education 6%, parks/recreation 14%, psychology 8%, social sciences 12%, visual/performing arts 6%.

Computing on campus. 200 workstations in dormitories, library, computer center, student center. Dormitories wired for high-speed internet access and linked to campus network. Commuter students can connect to campus network. Online library, helpline, repair service, student web hosting, wireless network available.

Student life. **Freshman orientation:** Mandatory. Preregistration for classes offered. **Policies:** Unmarried freshmen and sophomores under age 21 must live on campus unless living near campus with family. **Housing:** Guaranteed on-campus for freshmen. Coed dorms, special housing for disabled, apartments available. $100 fully refundable deposit, deadline 5/1. 1 wing designated for females. **Activities:** Bands, campus ministries, choral groups, dance, drama, film society, international student organizations, literary magazine, music ensembles, musical theater, radio station, student government, student newspaper, symphony orchestra, Hawaii club, Christian Fellowship, politics and law forum, Circle K, humanitarian center, gay and lesbian support group, ethnic diversity appreciation club, United Church of Christ student organization.

Athletics. NCAA. **Intercollegiate:** Baseball M, basketball, cheerleading, cross-country, golf, lacrosse W, soccer, softball W, swimming, tennis, track and field, volleyball W, wrestling. **Intramural:** Basketball, football (tackle), golf, handball, racquetball, soccer, softball, tennis, volleyball. **Team name:** Boxers.

Student services. Alcohol/substance abuse counseling, career counseling, student employment services, financial aid counseling, health services, minority student services, personal counseling, placement for graduates, veterans' counselor.

Contact. E-mail: admissions@pacificu.edu
Phone: (503) 352-2218 Toll-free number: (800) 677-6712
Fax: (503) 352-2975
Karen Dunston, Director of Undergraduate Admission, Pacific University, 2043 College Way, Forest Grove, OR 97116-1797

Portland State University

Portland, Oregon — **CB member**
www.pdx.edu — **CB code: 4610**

- Public 4-year university
- Commuter campus in very large city
- 17,930 degree-seeking undergraduates: 30% part-time, 53% women, 3% African American, 10% Asian American, 6% Hispanic American, 1% Native American, 5% international
- 6,052 graduate students
- 90% of applicants admitted
- SAT or ACT with writing required

General. Founded in 1946. Regionally accredited. Courses offered at off-campus locations. **Degrees:** 3,289 bachelor's awarded; master's, doctoral offered. **ROTC:** Army, Air Force. **Location:** Downtown. **Calendar:** Quarter, extensive summer session. **Full-time faculty:** 800 total; 73% have terminal degrees, 44% women. **Part-time faculty:** 524 total; 23% have terminal degrees, 51% women. **Class size:** 30% < 20, 43% 20-39, 11% 40-49, 14% 50-99, 2% >100. **Special facilities:** Native American center.

Freshman class profile. 3,757 applied, 3,373 admitted, 1,766 enrolled.

Mid 50% test scores			
SAT critical reading:	460-600	GPA 3.75 or higher:	14%
SAT math:	460-570	GPA 3.50-3.74:	19%
SAT writing:	440-560	GPA 3.0-3.49:	42%
ACT composite:	18-24	GPA 2.0-2.99:	25%
		Out-of-state:	20%

Basis for selection. 3.0 GPA or 1000 SAT (exclusive of Writing)/21 ACT required for automatic admission. Various combinations of test scores and GPA also qualify for automatic admissions. Others may qualify under special action by admissions committee. Interview recommended for those who do not meet regular admission requirement.

High school preparation. 14 units required. Required and recommended units include English 4, mathematics 3, social studies 2, history 1, science 2 (laboratory 1) and foreign language 2. One unit laboratory science recommended.

2008-2009 Annual costs. Tuition/fees: $6,147; $18,837 out-of-state. Room/board: $9,486. Books/supplies: $1,854. Personal expenses: $1,932.

2008-2009 Financial aid. **Non-need-based:** Scholarships awarded for academics, art, athletics, music/drama, state residency.

Application procedures. **Admission:** Priority date 6/1; no deadline. $50 fee. Application must be submitted on paper. Admission notification on a rolling basis. **Financial aid:** Priority date 2/28; no closing date. FAFSA required. Applicants notified on a rolling basis; must reply within 4 week(s) of notification.

Academics. Community based service and research projects offered in Portland area. All students required to complete 45 credit hour multidisciplinary core curriculum, including community service learning experience. Teaching certification only offered at graduate level. **Special study options:** Accelerated study, combined bachelor's/graduate degree, cooperative education, distance learning, double major, ESL, exchange student, honors, independent study, internships, liberal arts/career combination, study abroad, teacher certification program, Washington semester. Haystack Summer Program in the arts and sciences. **Credit/placement by examination:** AP, CLEP, institutional tests. 45 credit hours maximum toward bachelor's degree. **Support services:** Pre-admission summer program, reduced course load, tutoring, writing center.

Honors college/program. Students with 1200 SAT (exclusive of Writing) and 3.5 GPA eligible to apply. Limited to 200 participants.

Majors. **Architecture:** Architecture, urban/community planning. **Area/ethnic studies:** African, Central/Eastern European, East Asian, European, Latin American, Near/Middle Eastern, women's. **Biology:** General, biochemistry. **Business:** General, accounting, business admin, finance, human resources, logistics, management information systems, marketing. **Computer sciences:** Computer science. **Conservation:** General. **Education:** Health. **Engineering:** Civil, computer, electrical, mechanical. **Family/consumer sciences:** Family studies. **Foreign languages:** Chinese, French, German, Japanese, linguistics, Russian, Spanish. **Health:** Audiology/hearing, public health ed. **History:** General. **Interdisciplinary:** Biological/physical sciences. **Liberal arts:** Arts/sciences. **Math:** General. **Philosophy/religion:** Philosophy. **Physical sciences:** Chemistry, geology, physics. **Protective services:** Criminal justice, law enforcement admin. **Psychology:** General. **Public administration:** Social work. **Social sciences:** General, anthropology, economics, geography, international relations, political science, sociology, urban studies. **Visual/performing arts:** Art, art history/conservation, commercial/advertising art, design, dramatic, drawing, music performance, painting, printmaking, sculpture, studio arts.

Most popular majors. Business/marketing 20%, liberal arts 9%, psychology 8%, social sciences 16%.

Computing on campus. 725 workstations in dormitories, library, computer center, student center. Dormitories wired for high-speed internet access and linked to campus network. Commuter students can connect to campus network. Online course registration, online library, helpline, repair service, student web hosting, wireless network available.

Student life. **Freshman orientation:** Available. Preregistration for classes offered. **Policies:** Dormitory and meal service not managed by University available on campus. **Housing:** Coed dorms, special housing for disabled, apartments, fraternity/sorority housing available. Pets allowed in dorm rooms. **Activities:** Bands, campus ministries, choral groups, dance, drama, film society, international student organizations, literary magazine, music ensembles, musical theater, opera, radio station, student government, student newspaper, symphony orchestra, student public interest research group, black cultural affairs board, United Indian Students in Higher Education, women's union, outdoor program, disabled student union, Hispanic student union.

Athletics. NCAA. **Intercollegiate:** Baseball M, basketball, cross-country, football (tackle) M, golf, soccer W, softball W, tennis, track and field, volleyball W, wrestling M. **Intramural:** Archery, basketball, football (tackle) M, golf, racquetball, soccer W, softball, volleyball. **Team name:** Vikings.

Student services. Adult student services, alcohol/substance abuse counseling, chaplain/spiritual director, career counseling, student employment services, financial aid counseling, health services, minority student services, on-campus daycare, personal counseling, placement for graduates, veterans' counselor, women's services. **Physically disabled:** Services for visually, speech, hearing impaired.

Contact. E-mail: admissions@pdx.edu
Phone: (503) 725-3511 Toll-free number: (800) 547-8887 ext. 3511
Fax: (503) 725-5525
Agnes Hoffman, Vice Provost for Enrollment Management, Portland State University, PO Box 751-ADM, Portland, OR 97207-0751

Reed College

Portland, Oregon — **CB member**
www.reed.edu — **CB code: 4654**

- Private 4-year liberal arts college
- Residential campus in very large city
- 1,408 degree-seeking undergraduates: 56% women, 3% African American, 9% Asian American, 7% Hispanic American, 1% Native American, 6% international
- 29 degree-seeking graduate students
- 32% of applicants admitted
- SAT or ACT (ACT writing optional), application essay required
- 77% graduate within 6 years; 65% enter graduate study

General. Founded in 1909. Regionally accredited. **Degrees:** 301 bachelor's awarded; master's offered. **Location:** 5 miles from downtown. **Calendar:** Semester. **Full-time faculty:** 128 total; 89% have terminal degrees, 12% minority, 38% women. **Part-time faculty:** 9 total; 89% have terminal degrees, 33% minority, 44% women. **Class size:** 73% < 20, 23% 20-39, less than 1% 40-49, 2% 50-99, 1% >100. **Special facilities:** Nuclear research reactor, wildlife refuge, fish ladder.

Freshman class profile. 3,485 applied, 1,132 admitted, 330 enrolled.

Mid 50% test scores		**GPA 2.0-2.99:**	1%
SAT critical reading:	660-760	**Rank in top quarter:**	89%
SAT math:	630-710	**Rank in top tenth:**	65%
SAT writing:	650-740	**Return as sophomores:**	89%
ACT composite:	29-32	**Out-of-state:**	91%
GPA 3.75 or higher:	70%	**Live on campus:**	98%
GPA 3.50-3.74:	18%	**International:**	4%
GPA 3.0-3.49:	11%		

Basis for selection. Academic achievement, essay, recommendations, test scores most important. Qualities of character, such as motivation, intellectual curiosity, individual responsibility, social consciousness are important. SAT Subject Tests recommended. Interview recommended. **Homeschooled:** Transcript of courses and grades, letter of recommendation (nonparent) required. High school diploma waived in some cases. Must be above age of compulsory education in home state, submit writing sample, essay.

High school preparation. College-preparatory program recommended. Recommended units include English 4, mathematics 3, social studies 1, history 3, science 3 and foreign language 3.

2008-2009 Annual costs. Tuition/fees: $38,190. Room/board: $9,920. Books/supplies: $950. Personal expenses: $900.

2008-2009 Financial aid. All financial aid based on need. 213 full-time freshmen applied for aid; 169 were judged to have need; 169 of these received aid. Average need met was 100%. Average scholarship/grant was $31,668; average loan $3,043. 85% of total undergraduate aid awarded as scholarships/grants, 15% as loans/jobs. **Additional information:** College meets demonstrated need of continuing students who have attended Reed minimum of 2 semesters, who file financial aid applications on time, and who maintain satisfactory academic progress. Institutional aid consideration is for total of 8 semesters.

Application procedures. Admission: Closing date 1/15 (postmark date). $50 fee, may be waived for applicants with need. Admission notification 4/1. Must reply by May 1 or within 2 week(s) if notified thereafter. **Financial aid:** Closing date 1/15. FAFSA, institutional form, CSS PROFILE required. Applicants notified by 4/1; must reply by 5/1 or within 2 week(s) of notification.

Academics. All students take 1-year course in humanities. After declaring major, students must pass qualifying exam prior to senior year. Seniors engage in 1-year research project in major field and prepare and defend thesis. **Special study options:** Combined bachelor's/graduate degree, cooperative education, cross-registration, double major, dual enrollment of high school students, exchange student, independent study, internships, liberal arts/career combination, study abroad. Computer science program with University of Washington; engineering arrangement with California Institute of Technology, Columbia University School of Engineering and Applied Sciences, Rensselaer Polytechnic Institute; forestry-environmental sciences degree arrangement with Nicholas School of the Environment of Duke University; joint 5-year art program with Pacific Northwest College of Art. **Credit/placement by examination:** AP, CLEP, IB, institutional tests. 30 credit hours maximum toward bachelor's degree. **Support services:** Learning center, study skills assistance, tutoring, writing center.

Majors. Area/ethnic studies: American. **Biology:** General, biochemistry, molecular. **Foreign languages:** Chinese, classics, comparative lit, French, German, linguistics, Russian, Spanish. **History:** General. **Math:** General. **Philosophy/religion:** Philosophy, religion. **Physical sciences:** Chemistry, physics. **Psychology:** General. **Social sciences:** Anthropology, economics, international relations, political science, sociology. **Visual/performing arts:** Art, dramatic. **Other:** Multi/Interdisciplinary Studies.

Most popular majors. Biology 10%, English 15%, history 6%, interdisciplinary studies 9%, physical sciences 9%, psychology 10%, social sciences 21%, visual/performing arts 6%.

Computing on campus. 424 workstations in dormitories, library, computer center, student center. Dormitories wired for high-speed internet access and linked to campus network. Commuter students can connect to campus network. Online course registration, online library, helpline, repair service, student web hosting, wireless network available.

Student life. Freshman orientation: Mandatory. Preregistration for classes offered. Held 5 days before start of classes. **Policies:** Honor code in effect. First-year students required to live on campus. **Housing:** Guaranteed on-campus for freshmen. Coed dorms, single-sex dorms, special housing for disabled, apartments, cooperative housing, wellness housing available. $100 partly refundable deposit, deadline 6/15. Chinese, French, German, Russian, and Spanish language houses available for upper division students. **Activities:** Campus ministries, choral groups, dance, drama, film society, international student organizations, literary magazine, music ensembles, Model UN, radio station, student government, student newspaper, symphony orchestra, Christian Fellowship, Jewish Student Union, women's center, environmental coalition, politically active student groups, volunteer tutoring, language and outing clubs, poetry forum.

Athletics. Intramural: Archery, badminton, basketball M, equestrian, fencing, golf, judo, rowing (crew), rugby, sailing, skiing, soccer, softball, squash, swimming, tennis, volleyball. **Team name:** Griffins.

Student services. Adult student services, alcohol/substance abuse counseling, career counseling, student employment services, financial aid counseling, health services, minority student services, personal counseling, placement for graduates. **Physically disabled:** Services for visually, speech, hearing impaired.

Contact. E-mail: admission@reed.edu
Phone: (503) 777-7511 Toll-free number: (800) 547-4750
Fax: (503) 777-7553
Paul Marthers, Dean of Admission, Reed College, 3203 SE Woodstock Boulevard, Portland, OR 97202-8199

Southern Oregon University

Ashland, Oregon — **CB member**
www.sou.edu — **CB code: 4702**

- Public 4-year university and liberal arts college
- Residential campus in large town
- 4,084 degree-seeking undergraduates: 20% part-time, 58% women, 2% African American, 5% Asian American, 5% Hispanic American, 2% Native American, 2% international
- 457 degree-seeking graduate students
- 89% of applicants admitted
- SAT or ACT (ACT writing recommended) required

General. Founded in 1926. Regionally accredited. Designated by National Aeronautical and Space Administration to cooperate in NASA-directed joint space research by undergraduates. **Degrees:** 676 bachelor's awarded; master's offered. **Location:** 180 miles from Eugene, 285 miles from Portland. **Calendar:** Quarter, extensive summer session. **Full-time faculty:** 207 total; 81% have terminal degrees. **Part-time faculty:** 104 total. **Class size:** 46% < 20, 42% 20-39, 6% 40-49, 5% 50-99, 1% >100. **Special facilities:** Herbarium, U.S. Fish and Wildlife forensics laboratory, public radio network studios, preschool and kindergarten, community television studio, center for visual arts, biotechnology center, institute for environmental economic and civic studies.

Freshman class profile. 1,610 applied, 1,429 admitted, 706 enrolled.

Mid 50% test scores		**GPA 3.0-3.49:**	38%
SAT critical reading:	450-580	**GPA 2.0-2.99:**	30%
SAT math:	460-570	**Out-of-state:**	24%
ACT composite:	20-25	**Live on campus:**	70%
GPA 3.75 or higher:	14%	**International:**	1%
GPA 3.50-3.74:	18%		

Basis for selection. Admissions based on 2.75 GPA from regionally accredited high school, 21 ACT, 1010 SAT (exclusive of Writing), and 14 required high school academic units. For students from non-regionally accredited high schools and home schooled students: 1010 combined scores on SAT Critical Reading & Math, 470 on SAT Writing, and two SAT Subject tests (Math Level I or Math Level IIc and one other subject area of students choice). Requests for special admission for undergraduates reviewed individually. SAT Subject Tests required of students graduating from nonstandard or unaccredited high schools.

High school preparation. College-preparatory program recommended. 14 units required. Required units include English 4, mathematics 3, social studies 3, science 2 (laboratory 1) and foreign language 2.

2008-2009 Annual costs. Tuition/fees: $5,718; $18,264 out-of-state. Room/board: $7,875. Books/supplies: $1,155. Personal expenses: $2,475.

2008-2009 Financial aid. Non-need-based: Scholarships awarded for academics, alumni affiliation, art, athletics, leadership, minority status, music/drama, religious affiliation, state residency.

Application procedures. Admission: No deadline. $50 fee, may be waived for applicants with need. Admission notification on a rolling basis. **Financial aid:** No deadline. FAFSA required. Applicants notified on a rolling basis starting 3/1; must reply within 2 week(s) of notification.

Academics. Special study options: Accelerated study, combined bachelor's/graduate degree, cooperative education, cross-registration, distance learning, double major, dual enrollment of high school students, ESL, exchange student, honors, independent study, internships, liberal arts/career combination, student-designed major, study abroad, teacher certification program. **Credit/placement by examination:** AP, CLEP, IB, institutional tests. 24 credit hours maximum toward bachelor's degree. **Support services:** Learning center, reduced course load, remedial instruction, study skills assistance, tutoring, writing center.

Majors. Biology: General. **Business:** General, accounting, business admin, hospitality admin, marketing. **Communications:** General, journalism, public relations. **Computer sciences:** General, computer science, programming, security. **Conservation:** Environmental studies. **Education:** General. **Foreign languages:** General, Spanish. **Health:** Athletic training, nursing (RN), predental, premedicine, preop/surgical nursing, prepharmacy, preveterinary. **History:** General. **Interdisciplinary:** Biological/physical sciences, math/computer science. **Legal studies:** Prelaw. **Math:** General. **Parks/recreation:** Health/fitness, sports admin. **Physical sciences:** Chemistry, geology, physics. **Protective services:** Criminal justice, law enforcement admin, police science. **Psychology:** General. **Social sciences:** General, anthropology, criminology, economics, geography, political science, sociology. **Visual/performing arts:** Art, dramatic, music management.

Most popular majors. Business/marketing 17%, communications/journalism 10%, psychology 12%, security/protective services 10%, social sciences 9%, visual/performing arts 10%.

Computing on campus. 750 workstations in dormitories, library, computer center, student center. Dormitories wired for high-speed internet access and linked to campus network. Commuter students can connect to campus network. Online course registration, online library, helpline, student web hosting, wireless network available.

Student life. Freshman orientation: Mandatory. Preregistration for classes offered. Early registration in July; orientation few days before start of classes. **Housing:** Guaranteed on-campus for freshmen. Coed dorms, special housing for disabled, apartments, wellness housing available. $50 deposit. Special quiet, nonsmoking, older student or freshmen residence halls available. **Activities:** Bands, campus ministries, choral groups, dance, drama, international student organizations, literary magazine, music ensembles, musical theater, opera, radio station, student government, student newspaper, symphony orchestra, TV station, 100 clubs available.

Athletics. NAIA. **Intercollegiate:** Basketball, cross-country, football (tackle) M, soccer W, softball W, tennis W, track and field, volleyball W, wrestling M. **Intramural:** Badminton, baseball M, basketball, bowling, golf, racquetball, rugby, sailing, skiing, soccer, softball, swimming, table tennis, tennis, track and field, volleyball, water polo. **Team name:** Raiders.

Student services. Adult student services, alcohol/substance abuse counseling, career counseling, services for economically disadvantaged, student employment services, financial aid counseling, health services, legal services, minority student services, on-campus daycare, personal counseling, placement for graduates, veterans' counselor, women's services. **Physically disabled:** Services for visually, speech, hearing impaired. **Learning disabled:** Comprehensive services available.

Contact. E-mail: admissions@sou.edu
Phone: (541) 552-6411 Toll-free number: (800) 482-7672 ext. 6411
Fax: (541) 552-8403
Mark Bottorff, Director of Admissions, Southern Oregon University, 1250 Siskiyou Boulevard, Ashland, OR 97520-5032

University of Oregon

Eugene, Oregon — **CB member**
www.uoregon.edu — **CB code: 4846**

- Public 4-year university
- Residential campus in small city
- 17,356 degree-seeking undergraduates: 7% part-time, 51% women, 2% African American, 7% Asian American, 4% Hispanic American, 1% Native American, 5% international
- 3,352 degree-seeking graduate students
- 85% of applicants admitted
- SAT or ACT with writing required
- 67% graduate within 6 years; 28% enter graduate study

General. Founded in 1876. Regionally accredited. **Degrees:** 3,988 bachelor's awarded; master's, doctoral, first professional offered. **ROTC:** Army, Air Force. **Location:** 110 miles from Portland. **Calendar:** Quarter, extensive summer session. **Full-time faculty:** 844 total; 96% have terminal degrees, 21% minority, 43% women. **Part-time faculty:** 365 total; 86% have terminal degrees, 17% minority, 48% women. **Class size:** 38% < 20, 42% 20-39, 4% 40-49, 9% 50-99, 7% >100. **Special facilities:** Art museum, natural and cultural history museum, sports marketing center, entrepreneurship center, Native American community center, instrumentation center, computer music center, observatory, marine biology institute.

Freshman class profile. 15,013 applied, 12,801 admitted, 4,260 enrolled.

Mid 50% test scores		**Rank in top tenth:**	26%
SAT critical reading:	490-610	**End year in good standing:**	87%
SAT math:	500-610	**Return as sophomores:**	84%
GPA 3.75 or higher:	26%	**Out-of-state:**	40%
GPA 3.50-3.74:	23%	**Live on campus:**	72%
GPA 3.0-3.49:	41%	**International:**	2%
GPA 2.0-2.99:	10%	**Fraternities:**	14%
Rank in top quarter:	58%	**Sororities:**	18%

Basis for selection. Students with 3.25 GPA and 16 college preparatory units guaranteed admission. For all others, secondary school record and test scores most important. Audition required for dance and music programs. Portfolio required for arts, architecture, and interior architecture programs. Essay required for all students with fewer than 16 college preparatory units or GPA below 3.25. **Homeschooled:** 1540 SAT or 22 ACT with writing required. 470 SAT Subject Tests in Math I or II and 470 on second SAT Subject Test required. Foreign language subject test strongly recommended. **Learning Disabled:** If student does not meet admission requirements and has self-identified a documented disability, then a secondary review will take place by the disability review committee.

High school preparation. College-preparatory program required. 14 units required; 16 recommended. Required and recommended units include English 4, mathematics 3, social studies 3, science 2 (laboratory 1) and foreign language 2.

2008-2009 Annual costs. Tuition/fees: $6,435; $19,992 out-of-state. Additional program-specific fees may apply. Room/board: $8,478. Books/supplies: $1,050. Personal expenses: $2,412.

2008-2009 Financial aid. Need-based: 2,687 full-time freshmen applied for aid; 1,559 were judged to have need; 1,429 of these received aid. Average need met was 55%. Average scholarship/grant was $6,114; average loan $3,755. 45% of total undergraduate aid awarded as scholarships/grants, 55% as loans/jobs. **Non-need-based:** Awarded to 3,126 full-time undergraduates, including 1,252 freshmen. Scholarships awarded for academics, athletics, leadership, minority status, music/drama, ROTC, state residency.

Application procedures. Admission: Priority date 11/1; deadline 1/15 (postmark date). $50 fee, may be waived for applicants with need. Admission notification on a rolling basis. Must reply by May 1 or within 4 week(s) if notified thereafter. Additional application deadlines: Clark Honors College, 11/1 early notification, 1/15 standard notification; Architecture, 1/15; Interior Architecture, 1/15; Digital Arts, 2/1; Landscape Architecture, 2/15; Art, 3/1; School of Music and Dance, 1/15. **Financial aid:** Closing date 2/1. FAFSA required. Applicants notified on a rolling basis starting 4/15; must reply within 4 week(s) of notification.

Academics. Special study options: Cross-registration, distance learning, double major, ESL, exchange student, honors, independent study, internships, liberal arts/career combination, semester at sea, student-designed major, study abroad, teacher certification program. Dual enrollment with Lane Community College and Southwestern Oregon Community College. Professional distinctions program (certificate program) in which students gain direct professional preparation through internships, special courses, professional mentor, and development of electronic resume and portfolio. **Credit/placement by examination:** AP, CLEP, IB, SAT, ACT, institutional tests. **Support services:** Learning center, remedial instruction, study skills assistance, tutoring.

Honors college/program. SAT/ACT scores, unweighted GPA, rigor and breadth of coursework, diversity, 2 teacher recommendations and personal essay considered. Approximately 150 spaces available per year.

Majors. Architecture: Architecture, interior, landscape. **Area/ethnic studies:** Asian, Russian/Slavic, women's. **Biology:** General, biochemistry, marine, physiology. **Business:** General, accounting. **Communications:** Advertising, digital media, journalism, media studies, public relations. **Computer sciences:** General. **Conservation:** Environmental science, environmental studies. **Education:** General, music. **Foreign languages:** Ancient Greek, Chinese, classics, comparative lit, French, German, Italian, Japanese, Latin, linguistics, Romance, Russian, Spanish. **Health:** Communication disorders. **History:** General. **Interdisciplinary:** Ancient studies, biological/physical sciences, global studies, math/computer science, medieval/Renaissance. **Liberal arts:** Humanities. **Math:** General. **Philosophy/religion:** Judaic, philosophy, religion. **Physical sciences:** Chemistry, geology, physics. **Psychology:** General. **Public administration:** General, human services. **Social sciences:** General, anthropology, economics, geography, political science, sociology. **Visual/performing arts:** Art, art history/conservation, ceramics, dance, design, dramatic, fiber arts, jazz, metal/jewelry, multimedia, music performance, music theory/composition, painting, photography, printmaking, sculpture, studio arts. **Other:** Product design.

Most popular majors. Business/marketing 13%, communications/journalism 9%, foreign language 7%, interdisciplinary studies 6%, psychology 7%, social sciences 22%, visual/performing arts 7%.

Computing on campus. 1,700 workstations in dormitories, library, computer center, student center. Dormitories wired for high-speed internet access and linked to campus network. Commuter students can connect to campus network. Online course registration, online library, helpline, repair service, student web hosting, wireless network available.

Student life. Freshman orientation: Mandatory. Preregistration for classes offered. Two-day session for students and family held during the summer. **Housing:** Coed dorms, apartments, fraternity/sorority housing, wellness housing available. $250 partly refundable deposit, deadline 3/31. Single-sex halls, residential academic programs, family housing available. **Activities:** Bands, campus ministries, choral groups, dance, drama, film society, international student organizations, literary magazine, music ensembles, musical theater, opera, radio station, student government, student newspaper, symphony orchestra.

Athletics. NCAA. **Intercollegiate:** Baseball M, basketball, cheerleading M, cross-country, football (tackle) M, golf, lacrosse W, soccer W, softball W, tennis, track and field, volleyball W. **Intramural:** Badminton, basketball, cross-country, football (non-tackle), golf, racquetball, soccer, softball, swimming, tennis, track and field, volleyball. **Team name:** Ducks.

Student services. Adult student services, alcohol/substance abuse counseling, career counseling, services for economically disadvantaged, student employment services, financial aid counseling, health services, legal services, minority student services, on-campus daycare, personal counseling, placement for graduates, veterans' counselor, women's services. **Physically disabled:** Services for visually, speech, hearing impaired. **Learning disabled:** Comprehensive services available.

Contact. E-mail: uoadmit@uoregon.edu
Phone: (541) 346-3201 Toll-free number: (800) 232-3825
Fax: (541) 346-5815
Brian Henley, Director of Admissions, University of Oregon, 1217 University of Oregon, Eugene, OR 97403-1217

University of Portland

Portland, Oregon — **CB member**
www.up.edu — **CB code: 4847**

- Private 4-year university affiliated with Roman Catholic Church
- Residential campus in large city
- 2,997 degree-seeking undergraduates: 2% part-time, 63% women, 1% African American, 10% Asian American, 5% Hispanic American, 1% Native American, 2% international
- 540 degree-seeking graduate students
- 79% of applicants admitted
- SAT or ACT (ACT writing optional), application essay required
- 72% graduate within 6 years; 25% enter graduate study

General. Founded in 1901. Regionally accredited. **Degrees:** 719 bachelor's awarded; master's, doctoral offered. **ROTC:** Army, Air Force. **Calendar:** Semester, limited summer session. **Full-time faculty:** 205 total; 90% have terminal degrees, 4% minority, 46% women. **Part-time faculty:** 102 total; 6% have terminal degrees, 4% minority, 43% women. **Class size:** 35% < 20, 55% 20-39, 6% 40-49, 3% 50-99, less than 1% >100.

Freshman class profile. 6,156 applied, 4,867 admitted, 794 enrolled.

Mid 50% test scores		**Rank in top quarter:**	74%
SAT critical reading:	540-660	**Rank in top tenth:**	44%
SAT math:	540-650	**Return as sophomores:**	86%
GPA 3.75 or higher:	48%	**Out-of-state:**	60%
GPA 3.50-3.74:	25%	**Live on campus:**	92%
GPA 3.0-3.49:	24%	**International:**	1%
GPA 2.0-2.99:	3%		

Basis for selection. School achievement record, test scores, counselor recommendation, essay important. **Homeschooled:** Transcript of courses and grades required. Interview strongly encouraged.

High school preparation. College-preparatory program recommended. Required and recommended units include English 3-4, mathematics 2-3, social studies 2, history 2, science 2 and academic electives 7. Engineering, math, and some science majors require additional math and science courses.

2008-2009 Annual costs. Tuition/fees: $30,450. Room/board: $8,756. Books/supplies: $1,000. Personal expenses: $800.

2008-2009 Financial aid. Need-based: 672 full-time freshmen applied for aid; 479 were judged to have need; 479 of these received aid. Average need met was 93%. Average scholarship/grant was $17,548; average loan $3,896. 87% of total undergraduate aid awarded as scholarships/grants, 13% as loans/jobs. **Non-need-based:** Awarded to 2,087 full-time undergraduates, including 552 freshmen. Scholarships awarded for academics, alumni affiliation, athletics, music/drama, religious affiliation, ROTC.

Application procedures. Admission: Priority date 2/1; deadline 6/1 (postmark date). $50 fee, may be waived for applicants with need. Admission notification on a rolling basis beginning on or about 10/1. Must reply by May 1 or within 2 week(s) if notified thereafter. **Financial aid:** Priority date 3/1; no closing date. FAFSA required. Applicants notified on a rolling basis starting 3/15; must reply within 3 week(s) of notification.

Academics. Special study options: Cross-registration, double major, honors, independent study, internships, liberal arts/career combination, study abroad, teacher certification program, Washington semester. **Credit/placement by examination:** AP, CLEP, IB, institutional tests. 45 credit hours maximum toward bachelor's degree. **Support services:** Learning center, study skills assistance, tutoring, writing center.

Majors. Biology: General. **Business:** Accounting, business admin, finance, international, marketing. **Communications:** Media studies, organizational. **Computer sciences:** Computer science. **Conservation:** Environmental science, environmental studies. **Education:** Elementary, music, secondary. **Engineering:** Civil, computer, electrical, environmental, mechanical. **Foreign languages:** French, German, Spanish. **Health:** Nursing (RN). **History:** General. **Math:** General. **Philosophy/religion:** Philosophy. **Physical sciences:** Chemistry, physics. **Psychology:** General. **Public administration:** Social work. **Social sciences:** Political science, sociology. **Theology:** Theology. **Visual/performing arts:** Dramatic, theater arts management.

Most popular majors. Biology 8%, business/marketing 16%, education 6%, engineering/engineering technologies 11%, foreign language 6%, health sciences 21%, social sciences 8%.

Computing on campus. 400 workstations in dormitories, library, computer center, student center. Dormitories wired for high-speed internet access and linked to campus network. Commuter students can connect to campus network. Online course registration, online library, helpline, student web hosting, wireless network available.

Student life. Freshman orientation: Available. Preregistration for classes offered. Held 3 days before classes begin. **Housing:** Guaranteed on-campus for freshmen. Coed dorms, single-sex dorms available. $100 nonrefundable deposit, deadline 5/1. Rental houses available. **Activities:** Bands, campus ministries, choral groups, dance, drama, film society, international student organizations, literary magazine, music ensembles, musical theater, radio station, student government, student newspaper, symphony orchestra, volunteer services, black student union, international club, Hawaiian club, Society of Women Engineeers, feminist discussion group, Bible study group.

Athletics. NCAA. **Intercollegiate:** Baseball M, basketball, cross-country, golf, soccer, tennis, track and field, volleyball W. **Intramural:** Basketball, bowling, football (non-tackle), golf, skiing, soccer, softball, swimming, table tennis, tennis, volleyball, water polo, weight lifting. **Team name:** Pilots.

Student services. Adult student services, alcohol/substance abuse counseling, chaplain/spiritual director, career counseling, student employment services, financial aid counseling, health services, personal counseling, placement for graduates, veterans' counselor. **Physically disabled:** Services for visually, speech, hearing impaired.

Contact. E-mail: admissions@up.edu
Phone: (503) 943-7147 Toll-free number: (888) 627-5601
Fax: (503) 943-7315
Jason McDonald, Dean of Admissions, University of Portland, 5000 North Willamette Boulevard, Portland, OR 97203-5798

Warner Pacific College
Portland, Oregon
www.warnerpacific.edu **CB code: 4595**

- Private 4-year liberal arts college affiliated with Church of God
- Residential campus in very large city
- 874 degree-seeking undergraduates: 2% part-time, 62% women, 7% African American, 3% Asian American, 5% Hispanic American, 1% Native American
- 96 degree-seeking graduate students
- 46% of applicants admitted
- SAT or ACT, application essay required

General. Founded in 1937. Regionally accredited. **Degrees:** 192 bachelor's, 17 associate awarded; master's offered. **ROTC:** Army, Naval, Air Force. **Location:** 44 miles from Salem; 10 miles from Vancouver, Washington. **Calendar:** Semester, limited summer session. **Full-time faculty:** 26 total; 77% have terminal degrees, 4% minority, 23% women. **Part-time faculty:** 73 total; 15% have terminal degrees, 63% women. **Class size:** 72% < 20, 27% 20-39, less than 1% 40-49. **Special facilities:** Field station for wildlife observation and study.

Freshman class profile. 731 applied, 337 admitted, 81 enrolled.

Mid 50% test scores			
SAT critical reading:	450-580	GPA 3.50-3.74:	14%
SAT math:	490-580	GPA 3.0-3.49:	37%
SAT writing:	430-550	GPA 2.0-2.99:	35%
ACT composite:	17-25	End year in good standing:	59%
GPA 3.75 or higher:	14%	Out-of-state:	32%
		Live on campus:	69%

Basis for selection. High school GPA important; test scores, essay, and signed lifestyle agreement required. **Homeschooled:** Statement describing homeschool structure and mission, transcript of courses and grades, state high school equivalency certificate, interview, letter of recommendation (nonparent) required.

High school preparation. 11 units recommended. Recommended units include English 4, mathematics 2, social studies 3 and science 2.

2008-2009 Annual costs. Tuition/fees: $16,630. Room/board: $6,328. Books/supplies: $1,100. Personal expenses: $1,556.

2007-2008 Financial aid. Need-based: 78 full-time freshmen applied for aid; 72 were judged to have need; 72 of these received aid. Average need met was 75%. Average scholarship/grant was $6,472; average loan $3,998. 58% of total undergraduate aid awarded as scholarships/grants, 42% as loans/jobs. **Non-need-based:** Awarded to 391 full-time undergraduates, including 102 freshmen. Scholarships awarded for academics, alumni affiliation, athletics, leadership, minority status, music/drama, religious affiliation.

Application procedures. Admission: No deadline. $50 fee, may be waived for applicants with need. Admission notification on a rolling basis. **Financial aid:** Priority date 3/1, closing date 8/30. FAFSA required. Applicants notified on a rolling basis starting 3/1; must reply within 4 week(s) of notification.

Academics. Special study options: Accelerated study, cooperative education, cross-registration, double major, independent study, internships, liberal arts/career combination, student-designed major, study abroad, teacher certification program, Washington semester. 2-2 nursing program with Walla Walla School of Nursing. **Credit/placement by examination:** AP, CLEP, institutional tests. 30 credit hours maximum toward associate degree, 30 toward bachelor's. No more than 45 total alternative credits (maximum 30 of any one type). **Support services:** Learning center, reduced course load, remedial instruction, study skills assistance, tutoring.

Majors. Area/ethnic studies: American. **Biology:** General. **Business:** Business admin, international. **Communications:** General. **Education:** Elementary, music, physical, secondary. **Family/consumer sciences:** Family studies. **History:** General. **Interdisciplinary:** Accounting/computer science, biopsychology. **Liberal arts:** Arts/sciences. **Parks/recreation:** Exercise sciences, health/fitness, sports admin. **Philosophy/religion:** Religion. **Physical sciences:** General. **Psychology:** General, developmental. **Public administration:** Social work. **Social sciences:** General, urban studies. **Theology:** Preministerial.

Most popular majors. Business/marketing 29%, education 7%, family/consumer sciences 43%, visual/performing arts 6%.

Computing on campus. 25 workstations in dormitories, library, computer center. Dormitories wired for high-speed internet access and linked to campus network. Online library, helpline, wireless network available.

Student life. Freshman orientation: Available. Preregistration for classes offered. **Policies:** Religious observance required. **Housing:** Guaranteed on-campus for freshmen. Single-sex dorms, special housing for disabled, apartments available. $100 deposit. **Activities:** Bands, campus ministries, choral groups, drama, music ensembles, student government.

Athletics. NAIA, NCCAA. **Intercollegiate:** Basketball, cross-country, golf, soccer, track and field, volleyball W. **Intramural:** Badminton, basketball, football (non-tackle), volleyball. **Team name:** Knights.

Student services. Adult student services, chaplain/spiritual director, career counseling, student employment services, financial aid counseling, health services, minority student services, personal counseling, placement for graduates.

Contact. E-mail: admissions@warnerpacific.edu
Phone: (503) 517-1020 Toll-free number: (800) 804-1510
Fax: (503) 517-1352
Shannon Mackey, Executive Director of Enrollment Management, Warner Pacific College, 2219 SE 68th Avenue, Portland, OR 97215-4026

Western Oregon University
Monmouth, Oregon **CB member**
www.wou.edu **CB code: 4585**

- Public 4-year liberal arts and teachers college
- Residential campus in small town
- 4,703 degree-seeking undergraduates: 15% part-time, 57% women
- 668 degree-seeking graduate students
- 45% of applicants admitted
- SAT or ACT with writing required
- 40% graduate within 6 years

General. Founded in 1856. Regionally accredited. **Degrees:** 739 bachelor's, 3 associate awarded; master's offered. **ROTC:** Army, Naval, Air Force. **Location:** 15 miles from Salem, 60 miles from Portland. **Calendar:** Quarter, limited summer session. **Full-time faculty:** 177 total; 82% have terminal degrees, 10% minority, 45% women. **Part-time faculty:** 157 total; 10% have terminal degrees, 16% minority, 55% women. **Class size:** 52% < 20, 38% 20-39, 5% 40-49, 4% 50-99, less than 1% >100. **Special facilities:** Arctic museum, teaching research institute, early childhood and training development center.

Freshman class profile. 2,098 applied, 938 admitted, 906 enrolled.

Mid 50% test scores			
SAT critical reading:	420-530	GPA 2.0-2.99:	30%
SAT math:	430-530	Rank in top quarter:	37%
SAT writing:	470-560	Rank in top tenth:	12%
ACT composite:	17-22	Return as sophomores:	72%
GPA 3.75 or higher:	15%	Out-of-state:	13%
GPA 3.50-3.74:	19%	Live on campus:	90%
GPA 3.0-3.49:	36%	International:	3%

Basis for selection. 2.75 GPA required. 1000 SAT (exclusive of Writing) strongly recommended, but only used in admissions decision if applicant does not meet GPA or college preparation requirements. If applicant does not meet academic requirements, other evidence of potential in the form of interviews, portfolios, auditions, and essays considered. **Homeschooled:** 1000 SAT (exclusive of Writing) or 21 ACT or 1410 SAT Subject Tests combined score in 3 subjects required; must take 1 SAT Reasoning Test, 1 SAT Subject Test in math, and second exam in foreign language.

High school preparation. College-preparatory program required. 14 units required. Required and recommended units include English 4, mathematics 3, social studies 2, history 1, science 2 (laboratory 1) and foreign language 2.

2008-2009 Annual costs. Tuition/fees: $6,318; $16,893 out-of-state. Resident tuition reflects a four-year tuition commitment. Room/board: $7,710. Books/supplies: $1,125. Personal expenses: $2,475.

2008-2009 Financial aid. Need-based: Average need met was 70%. Average scholarship/grant was $6,539; average loan $3,390. 42% of total undergraduate aid awarded as scholarships/grants, 58% as loans/jobs. **Non-need-based:** Scholarships awarded for academics, alumni affiliation, art, athletics, leadership, music/drama.

Application procedures. Admission: No deadline. $50 fee. Admission notification on a rolling basis. **Financial aid:** Priority date 3/1; no closing date. FAFSA required. Applicants notified on a rolling basis starting 2/28; must reply within 3 week(s) of notification.

Academics. Special study options: Distance learning, double major, dual enrollment of high school students, ESL, honors, independent study, internships, student-designed major, study abroad, teacher certification program. Preprofessional studies, interdisciplinary studies, nondegree licensure programs, service learning and career development. **Credit/placement by examination:** AP, CLEP, IB, SAT, ACT, institutional tests. 48 credit hours maximum toward bachelor's degree. **Support services:** Learning center, remedial instruction, study skills assistance, tutoring, writing center.

Majors. Biology: General. **Business:** General. **Communications:** General. **Computer sciences:** General. **Education:** General, biology, chemistry, elementary, health, instructional media, middle, multi-level teacher, physical, reading, science, secondary, social studies, Spanish. **Foreign languages:** Sign language interpretation, Spanish. **History:** General. **Interdisciplinary:** Biological/physical sciences, math/computer science, natural sciences. **Liberal arts:** Arts/sciences. **Math:** General. **Philosophy/religion:** Philosophy. **Physical sciences:** Chemistry, geology, planetary. **Protective services:** Corrections, fire services admin, law enforcement admin. **Psychology:** General. **Public administration:** General. **Social sciences:** General, anthropology, economics, geography, political science, sociology. **Visual/performing arts:** General, art, dance, dramatic, studio arts, theater arts management.

Most popular majors. Business/marketing 18%, education 22%, English 7%, interdisciplinary studies 8%, psychology 8%, security/protective services 7%, social sciences 9%.

Computing on campus. 411 workstations in dormitories, library, computer center, student center. Dormitories wired for high-speed internet access and linked to campus network. Commuter students can connect to campus network. Online course registration, online library, helpline, repair service, wireless network available.

Student life. Freshman orientation: Available. Held last weekend in June and 2nd and 3rd weekends in July on Friday and/or Saturday. **Policies:** No alcohol permitted in residence halls. **Housing:** Guaranteed on-campus for freshmen. Coed dorms, special housing for disabled, apartments, wellness housing available. Family housing, housing by learning communities, community living options available. **Activities:** Bands, campus ministries, choral groups, dance, drama, international student organizations, literary magazine, music ensembles, musical theater, student government, student newspaper, symphony orchestra, TV station, Baptist student union, Big Brother/Big Sister, multicultural student union, Campus Crusade for Christ, Circle K, environmental action committee.

Athletics. NCAA. **Intercollegiate:** Baseball M, basketball, cheerleading, cross-country, football (tackle) M, soccer W, softball W, track and field, volleyball W. **Intramural:** Basketball, bowling, cross-country, football (non-tackle), football (tackle) M, golf, racquetball, rifle, skiing, soccer, softball, swimming, table tennis, tennis, track and field, triathlon, volleyball, water polo, weight lifting, wrestling. **Team name:** Wolves.

Student services. Adult student services, alcohol/substance abuse counseling, chaplain/spiritual director, career counseling, services for economically disadvantaged, student employment services, financial aid counseling, health services, minority student services, on-campus daycare, personal counseling, placement for graduates, veterans' counselor, women's services. **Physically disabled:** Services for visually, speech, hearing impaired.

Contact. E-mail: wolfgram@wou.edu
Phone: (503) 838-8211 Toll-free number: (877) 877-1593
Fax: (503) 838-8067
David McDonald, Dean of Admissions, Enrollment Management, and Retention, Western Oregon University, 345 North Monmouth Avenue, Monmouth, OR 97361

Willamette University

Salem, Oregon — **CB member**
www.willamette.edu — **CB code: 4954**

- Private 4-year university and liberal arts college affiliated with United Methodist Church
- Residential campus in small city
- 1,758 degree-seeking undergraduates: 1% part-time, 56% women, 2% African American, 8% Asian American, 5% Hispanic American, 1% Native American, 1% international
- 786 degree-seeking graduate students
- 76% of applicants admitted
- SAT or ACT with writing, application essay required
- 71% graduate within 6 years; 24% enter graduate study

General. Founded in 1842. Regionally accredited. Sister school to Tokyo International University of America. **Degrees:** 457 bachelor's awarded; master's, first professional offered. **ROTC:** Air Force. **Location:** 45 miles from Portland. **Calendar:** Semester. **Full-time faculty:** 207 total; 96% have terminal degrees, 14% minority, 41% women. **Part-time faculty:** 76 total; 71% have terminal degrees, 8% minority, 42% women. **Class size:** 67% < 20, 33% 20-39, less than 1% 40-49. **Special facilities:** Art museum, American headquarters for International Debate Education Association, papers and memorabilia of Senator Mark O. Hatfield, botanical gardens, Japanese gardens, rose gardens, rural retreat center, wildlife refuge field station, digital art and music studios, 2 electron microscopes (scanning and transmission), 500 MHz Nuclear Magnetic Resonance spectrometer, 305 acre Zena research forest.

Freshman class profile. 3,501 applied, 2,676 admitted, 482 enrolled.

Mid 50% test scores			
SAT critical reading:	570-680	GPA 3.0-3.49:	22%
SAT math:	550-660	GPA 2.0-2.99:	2%
SAT writing:	550-660	Rank in top quarter:	77%
ACT composite:	25-29	Rank in top tenth:	43%
GPA 3.75 or higher:	53%	Return as sophomores:	86%
GPA 3.50-3.74:	23%	Out-of-state:	64%
		Live on campus:	98%

Basis for selection. School record most important, followed by test scores, essay, recommendations, school and community activities, and interview. Audition recommended for music, theater programs; portfolio recommended for art program. **Homeschooled:** Recommend submission of accredited transcript from governing agency, if available.

High school preparation. College-preparatory program required. 20 units required. Required and recommended units include English 4, mathematics 4, social studies 1, history 2, science 3 (laboratory 3), foreign language 3 and visual/performing arts 1.

2008-2009 Annual costs. Tuition/fees: $33,960. Optional health insurance: $405. Room/board: $7,950. Books/supplies: $900.

2008-2009 Financial aid. Need-based: 371 full-time freshmen applied for aid; 278 were judged to have need; 278 of these received aid. Average need met was 93%. Average scholarship/grant was $21,412; average loan $4,430. 73% of total undergraduate aid awarded as scholarships/grants, 27% as loans/jobs. **Non-need-based:** Awarded to 841 full-time undergraduates, including 294 freshmen. Scholarships awarded for academics, alumni affiliation, leadership, minority status, music/drama, religious affiliation.

Application procedures. Admission: Closing date 2/1 (postmark date). $50 fee, may be waived for applicants with need, free for online applicants. Admission notification 4/1. Must reply by May 1 or within 2 week(s) if notified thereafter. **Financial aid:** Closing date 2/1. FAFSA required. CSS

PROFILE recommended of early action applicants. Applicants notified by 4/1; must reply by 5/1 or within 2 week(s) of notification.

Academics. Special study options: Accelerated study, combined bachelor's/graduate degree, double major, exchange student, independent study, internships, student-designed major, study abroad, teacher certification program, urban semester, Washington semester. Interdisciplinary freshman study program, undergraduate research grants, field studies program in ecology in Hawaii, Ecuador, American Southwest, Oregon; 3-2 program, master's degree in management; 3-2 program, bachelor's degree in computer science with Oregon Graduate Institute, University of Oregon; 3-2 program, master's degree in forestry with Duke University. **Credit/placement by examination:** AP, CLEP, IB, institutional tests. 28 credit hours maximum toward bachelor's degree. **Support services:** Reduced course load, study skills assistance, tutoring, writing center.

Majors. Area/ethnic studies: American, Asian, Japanese, Latin American, women's. **Biology:** General. **Computer sciences:** General. **Conservation:** Environmental science. **Education:** Music. **Foreign languages:** Classics, comparative lit, French, German, Spanish. **History:** General. **Interdisciplinary:** Global studies. **Liberal arts:** Humanities. **Math:** General. **Parks/recreation:** Exercise sciences. **Philosophy/religion:** Philosophy, religion. **Physical sciences:** Chemistry, physics. **Psychology:** General. **Social sciences:** Anthropology, economics, political science, sociology. **Visual/performing arts:** Art history/conservation, dramatic, film/cinema, music performance, music theory/composition, piano/organ, stringed instruments, studio arts, voice/opera. **Other:** Science studies.

Most popular majors. Biology 8%, English 10%, foreign language 11%, history 7%, psychology 7%, social sciences 25%, visual/performing arts 7%.

Computing on campus. 400 workstations in dormitories, library, computer center, student center. Dormitories wired for high-speed internet access and linked to campus network. Commuter students can connect to campus network. Online course registration, online library, helpline, repair service, student web hosting, wireless network available.

Student life. Freshman orientation: Mandatory. Preregistration for classes offered. Five-day program before start of semester. **Housing:** Guaranteed on-campus for freshmen. Coed dorms, apartments, fraternity/sorority housing, wellness housing available. International studies house, nonsmoking residence hall, quiet study residence hall, substance-free hall available. **Activities:** Bands, campus ministries, choral groups, dance, drama, film society, international student organizations, literary magazine, music ensembles, Model UN, musical theater, opera, student government, student newspaper, symphony orchestra, More than 100 student organizations available.

Athletics. NCAA. **Intercollegiate:** Baseball M, basketball, cross-country, football (tackle) M, golf, rowing (crew), soccer, softball W, swimming, tennis, track and field, volleyball W. **Intramural:** Badminton, basketball, bowling, football (non-tackle), racquetball, soccer, softball, table tennis, tennis, volleyball, water polo, weight lifting. **Team name:** Bearcats.

Student services. Alcohol/substance abuse counseling, chaplain/spiritual director, career counseling, student employment services, financial aid counseling, health services, minority student services, personal counseling, veterans' counselor, women's services. **Physically disabled:** Services for visually, speech, hearing impaired.

Contact. E-mail: libarts@willamette.edu
Phone: (503) 370-6303 Toll-free number: (877) 542-2787
Fax: (503) 375-5363
Madeleine Rhyneer, Vice President for Admissions and Financial Aid,
Willamette University, 900 State Street, Salem, OR 97301-3922

Pennsylvania

Albright College

Reading, Pennsylvania — **CB member**
www.albright.edu — **CB code: 2004**

- Private 4-year liberal arts college affiliated with United Methodist Church
- Residential campus in small city
- 2,209 degree-seeking undergraduates: 57% women, 10% African American, 2% Asian American, 5% Hispanic American, 6% international
- 9 degree-seeking graduate students
- 62% of applicants admitted
- Application essay required
- 64% graduate within 6 years

General. Founded in 1856. Regionally accredited. **Degrees:** 491 bachelor's awarded; master's offered. **Location:** 50 miles from Philadelphia. **Calendar:** 4-1-4, limited summer session. **Full-time faculty:** 118 total; 81% have terminal degrees, 15% minority, 51% women. **Part-time faculty:** 49 total; 26% have terminal degrees, 6% minority, 63% women. **Class size:** 64% < 20, 35% 20-39, less than 1% 40-49, less than 1% 50-99, less than 1% >100. **Special facilities:** Satellite dish for foreign language program, transmission and scanning electron microscopes, Holocaust resource center, center for local government, center for cultural ecology, center for Latin American studies.

Freshman class profile. 4,561 applied, 2,814 admitted, 509 enrolled.

Mid 50% test scores		**Rank in top tenth:**	16%
SAT critical reading:	440-550	**End year in good standing:**	90%
SAT math:	450-560	**Return as sophomores:**	73%
ACT composite:	18-21	**Out-of-state:**	42%
GPA 3.75 or higher:	21%	**Live on campus:**	91%
GPA 3.50-3.74:	19%	**International:**	8%
GPA 3.0-3.49:	29%	**Fraternities:**	3%
GPA 2.0-2.99:	31%	**Sororities:**	4%
Rank in top quarter:	45%		

Basis for selection. High school performance (with emphasis on difficulty of curriculum pursued), personal statement, and recommendations most important. Community service, extracurricular activity and test scores considered. Interview recommended.

High school preparation. College-preparatory program required. 16 units required; 20 recommended. Required and recommended units include English 4, mathematics 2-3, social studies 2, history 1-2, science 3-4 (laboratory 1-2), foreign language 2-3 and academic electives 2. Bachelor of science applicants should have 1 additional unit in science and 1 in math. 2 units of laboratory science recommended.

2008-2009 Annual costs. Tuition/fees: $30,570. Room/board: $8,670. Books/supplies: $800. Personal expenses: $1,000.

2008-2009 Financial aid. Need-based: Average need met was 78%. Average scholarship/grant was $17,832; average loan $4,990. 32% of total undergraduate aid awarded as scholarships/grants, 68% as loans/jobs. **Non-need-based:** Scholarships awarded for academics, alumni affiliation, art, leadership, minority status, music/drama, religious affiliation.

Application procedures. Admission: Priority date 3/1; no deadline. $25 fee, may be waived for applicants with need. Admission notification on a rolling basis beginning on or about 10/1. Must reply by May 1 or within 2 week(s) if notified thereafter. **Financial aid:** Priority date 3/1; no closing date. FAFSA required. Applicants notified on a rolling basis starting 2/15; must reply by 5/1 or within 2 week(s) of notification.

Academics. Flexible curriculum combines liberal arts education with hands-on experiences. Institution emphasizes faculty-student collaboration and has an active undergraduate research program, which also funds summer projects with faculty. **Special study options:** Accelerated study, combined bachelor's/graduate degree, cross-registration, double major, dual enrollment of high school students, ESL, exchange student, honors, independent study, internships, liberal arts/career combination, semester at sea, student-designed major, study abroad, teacher certification program, urban semester, Washington semester. Interdisciplinary studies, student research. **Credit/placement by examination:** AP, CLEP, IB, SAT, ACT. 28 credit hours maximum toward bachelor's degree. **Support services:** Learning center, pre-admission summer program, reduced course load, study skills assistance, tutoring, writing center.

Majors. Area/ethnic studies: American, Latin American, women's. **Biology:** General, biochemistry. **Business:** Accounting, business admin, finance, international, marketing. **Communications:** General. **Computer sciences:** General, information systems. **Conservation:** General, environmental science, environmental studies. **Education:** Art, early childhood, elementary, secondary, special. **Family/consumer sciences:** Clothing/textiles. **Foreign languages:** French, Spanish. **Health:** Predental, premedicine, preveterinary. **History:** General. **Math:** General. **Philosophy/religion:** Philosophy, religion. **Physical sciences:** Chemistry, optics, physics. **Psychology:** General. **Social sciences:** Anthropology, criminology, economics, political science, sociology. **Visual/performing arts:** Dramatic, studio arts.

Most popular majors. Business/marketing 24%, psychology 14%, social sciences 16%, visual/performing arts 11%.

Computing on campus. 250 workstations in dormitories, library, computer center, student center. Dormitories wired for high-speed internet access and linked to campus network. Online library, helpline, wireless network available.

Student life. Freshman orientation: Mandatory. Preregistration for classes offered. Held the 4 days prior to start of fall classes. **Housing:** Guaranteed on-campus for freshmen. Coed dorms, wellness housing available. $100 nonrefundable deposit, deadline 6/1. Honors housing, break housing suite, all freshmen housing, all-female floors, all-male floors, single rooms, single-sex suites/apartments/wings. **Activities:** Bands, campus ministries, choral groups, dance, drama, international student organizations, literary magazine, music ensembles, musical theater, radio station, student government, student newspaper, TV station, Newman Association, Hillel, Christian Fellowship, African American society, Asian American society, environmental action group, American Association of University Women, human services organization.

Athletics. NCAA. **Intercollegiate:** Baseball M, basketball, cheerleading, cross-country, field hockey W, football (tackle) M, golf M, soccer, softball W, swimming, tennis, track and field, volleyball W. **Intramural:** Basketball, bowling, football (non-tackle), soccer, softball, volleyball. **Team name:** Lions.

Student services. Adult student services, chaplain/spiritual director, career counseling, student employment services, financial aid counseling, health services, minority student services, personal counseling, women's services. **Physically disabled:** Services for visually, hearing impaired.

Contact. E-mail: admission@albright.edu
Phone: (610) 921-7700 Toll-free number: (800) 252-1856
Fax: (610) 921-7729
Gregory Eichhorn, Vice-President for Enrollment Management and Dean of Admissions, Albright College, 13th & Bern Streets, Reading, PA 19612-5234

Allegheny College

Meadville, Pennsylvania — **CB member**
www.allegheny.edu — **CB code: 2006**

- Private 4-year liberal arts college affiliated with United Methodist Church
- Residential campus in large town
- 2,099 degree-seeking undergraduates: 1% part-time, 56% women, 3% African American, 3% Asian American, 2% Hispanic American, 1% international
- 61% of applicants admitted
- SAT or ACT (ACT writing recommended), application essay required
- 74% graduate within 6 years; 54% enter graduate study

General. Founded in 1815. Regionally accredited. **Degrees:** 534 bachelor's awarded. **Location:** 90 miles from Pittsburgh and Cleveland. **Calendar:** Semester, limited summer session. **Full-time faculty:** 150 total; 94% have terminal degrees, 13% minority, 45% women. **Part-time faculty:** 33 total; 30% have terminal degrees, 48% women. **Class size:** 57% < 20, 39% 20-39, 2% 40-49, 2% 50-99, less than 1% >100. **Special facilities:** Science complex, planetarium, observatory, Geographic Information Systems (GIS) learning lab, smart classrooms, solid-volume glass sculpture grouping, environmental research preserve, 80-acre protected forest, Lamont-Doherty Cooperative Seismographic Network Station, art studios, dance studio and performance area, art galleries.

Freshman class profile. 4,243 applied, 2,572 admitted, 565 enrolled.

Mid 50% test scores		**Rank in top tenth:**	46%
SAT critical reading:	550-660	**End year in good standing:**	98%
SAT math:	560-650	**Return as sophomores:**	88%
ACT composite:	23-28	**Out-of-state:**	49%
GPA 3.75 or higher:	50%	**Live on campus:**	99%
GPA 3.50-3.74:	26%	**International:**	1%
GPA 3.0-3.49:	18%	**Fraternities:**	16%
GPA 2.0-2.99:	6%	**Sororities:**	35%
Rank in top quarter:	78%		

Basis for selection. Rigor of high school program most important, followed by high school achievement. Test scores important. Essay, minority status, alumni ties, geography considered. One recommendation from guidance counselor and 1 from teacher required. Interview recommended. **Homeschooled:** Campus visit and individual interview with admissions counselor to discuss portfolios recommended. Recommendation from a non-family member, description of the level of instruction. **Learning Disabled:** Recommended interview with Director of Student Support Services.

High school preparation. College-preparatory program required. 16 units required. Required units include English 4, mathematics 3, social studies 3, science 3, foreign language 2 and academic electives 1.

2008-2009 Annual costs. Tuition/fees: $32,000. Room/board: $8,000.

2008-2009 Financial aid. Need-based: 468 full-time freshmen applied for aid; 389 were judged to have need; 389 of these received aid. Average need met was 95%. Average scholarship/grant was $20,833; average loan $4,662. 76% of total undergraduate aid awarded as scholarships/grants, 24% as loans/jobs. **Non-need-based:** Awarded to 809 full-time undergraduates, including 228 freshmen. Scholarships awarded for academics, leadership, minority status, state residency.

Application procedures. Admission: Closing date 2/15 (postmark date). $35 fee, may be waived for applicants with need, free for online applicants. Admission notification 4/1. Must reply by 5/1. **Financial aid:** Priority date 2/15; no closing date. FAFSA required. Applicants notified on a rolling basis starting 3/1; must reply by 5/1 or within 4 week(s) of notification.

Academics. Experiential learning term; teaeher partnerships with Columbia University Teachers College, Xavier School of Education and University of Pittsburgh; business school partnership with Simon Graduate School of Business Administration at University of Rochester; medical school partnerships with Jefferson Medical College and Drexel College of Medicine; accelerated master's degree program with Carnegie Mellon University for public policy and management, arts management, health policy and management, information systems management, and information technology; accelerated master's degree program with Chatham College for physician assistant; marine biology study programs. **Special study options:** Combined bachelor's/graduate degree, double major, dual enrollment of high school students, ESL, exchange student, independent study, internships, student-designed major, study abroad, Washington semester. Graduate school partnerships, marine biology study program, combined degree programs (3-2, 3-4), summer study program, double minor, pre-professional programs, domestic off-campus semester away study programs. **Credit/placement by examination:** AP, CLEP, IB, institutional tests. 20 credit hours maximum toward bachelor's degree. **Support services:** Learning center, reduced course load, study skills assistance, tutoring, writing center.

Majors. Area/ethnic studies: Women's. **Biology:** General, biochemistry. **Business:** Managerial economics. **Communications:** General, journalism, media studies. **Computer sciences:** Computer science. **Conservation:** Environmental science, environmental studies. **Education:** General. **Engineering:** Software. **Foreign languages:** French, German, Spanish. **Health:** Predental, premedicine, prenursing, prepharmacy, preveterinary. **History:** General. **Interdisciplinary:** Neuroscience. **Legal studies:** Prelaw. **Math:** General. **Philosophy/religion:** Philosophy, religion. **Physical sciences:** Chemistry, geology, physics. **Psychology:** General. **Social sciences:** Applied economics, economics, international relations, political science. **Visual/performing arts:** Art, art history/conservation, dramatic, music performance, studio arts. **Other:** Art and technology, Environmental geology, Health/medical preparatory.

Most popular majors. Biology 15%, English 7%, interdisciplinary studies 7%, natural resources/environmental science 6%, psychology 12%, social sciences 22%.

Computing on campus. 390 workstations in library, computer center, student center. Dormitories wired for high-speed internet access and linked to campus network. Commuter students can connect to campus network. Online library, helpline, repair service, student web hosting, wireless network available.

Student life. Freshman orientation: Mandatory. 4-day session held 4 days before fall classes begin. **Policies:** Honor code. **Housing:** Guaranteed on-campus for all undergraduates. Coed dorms, single-sex dorms, special housing for disabled, apartments, fraternity/sorority housing available. Environmentally-sensitive townhouses, LEED certified, low fume material; quiet study floors. **Activities:** Bands, campus ministries, choral groups, dance, drama, international student organizations, literary magazine, music ensembles, Model UN, musical theater, radio station, student government, student newspaper, symphony orchestra, TV station, Association for Asian and Asian-American Awareness, Advancement of Black Culture, Union Latina, Habitat for Humanity, Newman Association, Hillel, Christian Outreach, Alpha Phi Omega, Americorps Bonner Leaders, College Democrats.

Athletics. NCAA. **Intercollegiate:** Baseball M, basketball, cross-country, diving, football (tackle) M, golf, lacrosse W, soccer, softball W, swimming, tennis, track and field, volleyball W. **Intramural:** Basketball, bowling, football (non-tackle), golf, racquetball, soccer, softball, tennis, volleyball. **Team name:** Gators.

Student services. Adult student services, chaplain/spiritual director, career counseling, student employment services, financial aid counseling, health services, minority student services, personal counseling, placement for graduates. **Physically disabled:** Services for visually, hearing impaired.

Contact. E-mail: admissions@allegheny.edu
Phone: (814) 332-4351 Toll-free number: (800) 521-5293
Fax: (814) 337-0431
Jennifer Winge, Director of Admissions, Allegheny College, Box 5, 520 North Main Street, Meadville, PA 16335

Alvernia University

Reading, Pennsylvania — **CB member**
www.alvernia.edu — **CB code: 2431**

- Private 4-year university and liberal arts college affiliated with Roman Catholic Church
- Residential campus in small city
- 1,918 degree-seeking undergraduates: 18% part-time, 69% women, 11% African American, 1% Asian American, 6% Hispanic American, 1% international
- 585 degree-seeking graduate students
- 77% of applicants admitted
- SAT or ACT (ACT writing optional) required
- 54% graduate within 6 years

General. Founded in 1958. Regionally accredited. Affiliated with Bernardine Sisters, Third Order of St. Francis. **Degrees:** 457 bachelor's, 17 associate awarded; master's, doctoral offered. **ROTC:** Army. **Location:** 60 miles from Philadelphia. **Calendar:** Semester, limited summer session. **Full-time faculty:** 86 total; 59% have terminal degrees, 7% minority, 56% women. **Part-time faculty:** 222 total; 19% have terminal degrees, 13% minority, 51% women. **Class size:** 62% < 20, 37% 20-39, less than 1% 40-49, less than 1% 50-99.

Freshman class profile. 1,575 applied, 1,209 admitted, 389 enrolled.

Mid 50% test scores		**GPA 2.0-2.99:**	43%
SAT critical reading:	430-520	**Rank in top quarter:**	22%
SAT math:	420-530	**Rank in top tenth:**	5%
SAT writing:	430-520	**End year in good standing:**	90%
ACT composite:	17-22	**Return as sophomores:**	69%
GPA 3.75 or higher:	10%	**Out-of-state:**	25%
GPA 3.50-3.74:	14%	**Live on campus:**	77%
GPA 3.0-3.49:	32%	**International:**	1%

Basis for selection. Important factors include academic performance, standardized test scores, class rank, extracurricular activities, and community involvement. Essay, interview recommended for all. Interview required of nursing, occupational therapy and physical therapist assistant applicants.

High school preparation. College-preparatory program recommended. 16 units recommended. Recommended units include English 4, mathematics 4, social studies 3, science 2 and foreign language 2.

2009-2010 Annual costs. Tuition/fees (projected): $24,350. Room/board: $9,212. Books/supplies: $1,400. Personal expenses: $1,196.

2007-2008 Financial aid. Need-based: 288 full-time freshmen applied for aid; 268 were judged to have need; 233 of these received aid. Average need met was 57%. Average scholarship/grant was $10,437; average loan $5,173. 58% of total undergraduate aid awarded as scholarships/grants, 42% as loans/jobs. **Non-need-based:** Awarded to 189 full-time undergraduates, including 47 freshmen. Scholarships awarded for academics, state residency.

Application procedures. Admission: No deadline. $25 fee, may be waived for applicants with need. Admission notification on a rolling basis beginning on or about 10/1. Must reply by May 1 or within 2 week(s) if notified thereafter. **Financial aid:** Priority date 5/1; no closing date. FAFSA required. Applicants notified on a rolling basis starting 2/20; must reply within 2 week(s) of notification.

Academics. Special study options: Accelerated study, combined bachelor's/graduate degree, cross-registration, distance learning, double major, dual enrollment of high school students, ESL, honors, independent study, internships, student-designed major, study abroad, teacher certification program, Washington semester. **Credit/placement by examination:** AP, CLEP, IB, institutional tests. 30 credit hours maximum toward associate degree, 30 toward bachelor's. Total of 30 credits allowed for all experiential credit, CLEP, life experience, challenge exam. **Support services:** Learning center, pre-admission summer program, reduced course load, remedial instruction, study skills assistance, tutoring, writing center.

Majors. Biology: General, biochemistry. **Business:** General, accounting, human resources, marketing. **Communications:** General. **Computer sciences:** General. **Education:** General, biology, chemistry, computer, early childhood, elementary, English, mathematics, science, social studies, special. **Health:** Athletic training, nursing (RN), substance abuse counseling. **History:** General. **Interdisciplinary:** Biological/physical sciences. **Liberal arts:** Arts/sciences. **Math:** General. **Parks/recreation:** Sports admin. **Philosophy/religion:** Religion. **Physical sciences:** Chemistry. **Protective services:** Forensics, law enforcement admin. **Psychology:** General. **Public administration:** Social work. **Social sciences:** General, political science. **Theology:** Theology.

Most popular majors. Business/marketing 19%, education 16%, health sciences 26%, security/protective services 20%.

Computing on campus. 273 workstations in dormitories, library, computer center, student center. Dormitories wired for high-speed internet access and linked to campus network. Commuter students can connect to campus network. Online course registration, online library, helpline, wireless network available.

Student life. Freshman orientation: Mandatory. Preregistration for classes offered. Held weekend before classes start. **Housing:** Guaranteed on-campus for freshmen. Coed dorms, single-sex dorms, special housing for disabled available. $250 nonrefundable deposit, deadline 6/1. Single-sex townhouses available. Single-sex floors in dorms. **Activities:** Choral groups, dance, drama, literary magazine, music ensembles, student government, student newspaper.

Athletics. NCAA. **Intercollegiate:** Baseball M, basketball, cross-country, field hockey W, golf M, ice hockey M, lacrosse, soccer, softball W, tennis, volleyball W. **Intramural:** Basketball, cheerleading W, lacrosse M, volleyball M. **Team name:** Crusaders.

Student services. Adult student services, chaplain/spiritual director, career counseling, services for economically disadvantaged, student employment services, financial aid counseling, health services, minority student services, personal counseling, placement for graduates, veterans' counselor. **Physically disabled:** Services for visually impaired.

Contact. E-mail: admissions@alvernia.edu
Phone: (610) 796-8269 Toll-free number: (888) 258-3764
Fax: (610) 796-2873
Jeff Dittman, Dean of Undergraduate Admission, Alvernia University, 400 St. Bernardine Street, Reading, PA 19607-1799

Arcadia University

Glenside, Pennsylvania — **CB member**
www.arcadia.edu — **CB code: 2039**

- Private 4-year university affiliated with Presbyterian Church (USA)
- Residential campus in large town
- 2,143 degree-seeking undergraduates: 7% part-time, 73% women, 7% African American, 3% Asian American, 4% Hispanic American, 2% international
- 1,372 degree-seeking graduate students
- 70% of applicants admitted
- SAT or ACT with writing, application essay required
- 68% graduate within 6 years

General. Founded in 1853. Regionally accredited. **Degrees:** 461 bachelor's awarded; master's, doctoral offered. **ROTC:** Army. **Location:** 10 miles from Philadelphia. **Calendar:** Semester, limited summer session. **Full-time faculty:** 107 total; 17% minority, 49% women. **Part-time faculty:** 308 total; 10% minority, 57% women. **Class size:** 66% < 20, 32% 20-39, 1% 40-49, less than 1% 50-99, less than 1% >100. **Special facilities:** Observatory housing 14-inch Schmidt-Cassegrain telescope with extensive astrophotography capabilities, Grey Towers Castle (national historic landmark) used as residence hall.

Freshman class profile. 4,651 applied, 3,237 admitted, 597 enrolled.

Mid 50% test scores		**GPA 3.0-3.49:**	30%
SAT critical reading:	500-610	**GPA 2.0-2.99:**	14%
SAT math:	480-590	**Rank in top quarter:**	58%
SAT writing:	500-600	**Rank in top tenth:**	29%
ACT composite:	20-26	**Return as sophomores:**	75%
GPA 3.75 or higher:	39%	**Out-of-state:**	48%
GPA 3.50-3.74:	17%	**Live on campus:**	86%

Basis for selection. Emphasis placed on academic records, including type of program followed, courses taken, grades earned, class rank. Standardized test scores, counselor/ teacher recommendations, participation in school and community activities important. Character references also considered. Supplementary materials demonstrating student's talents and potential recommended. Portfolio review required for fine arts department. Auditions required for BFA in acting. **Homeschooled:** Statement describing homeschool structure and mission, letter of recommendation (nonparent) required. Portfolio representing academic record/work and level of achievement for grades 9-12 required.

High school preparation. College-preparatory program required. 19 units recommended. Recommended units include English 4, mathematics 3, social studies 2, history 2, science 3 (laboratory 3) and foreign language 2. Additional units in foreign language, math, and/or laboratory science recommended. Math includes algebra II and geometry.

2008-2009 Annual costs. Tuition/fees: $29,700. Room/board: $10,280. Books/supplies: $1,000. Personal expenses: $650.

2008-2009 Financial aid. Non-need-based: Scholarships awarded for academics, alumni affiliation, art, leadership, music/drama.

Application procedures. Admission: Priority date 1/15; deadline 3/1. $30 fee, may be waived for applicants with need, free for online applicants. Admission notification on a rolling basis beginning on or about 9/1. Must reply by May 1 or within 2 week(s) if notified thereafter. **Financial aid:** Priority date 3/1; no closing date. FAFSA, institutional form required. Applicants notified on a rolling basis starting 2/15; must reply by 5/1.

Academics. Special study options: Accelerated study, combined bachelor's/graduate degree, cooperative education, cross-registration, distance learning, double major, dual enrollment of high school students, exchange student, honors, independent study, internships, liberal arts/career combination, student-designed major, study abroad, teacher certification program, Washington semester. Combined programs leading to graduate degrees in physical therapy, physician assistant studies (option to combine with public health), forensic science, international peace and conflict resolution. Combined with other universities for degrees in engineering, nursing, optometry. **Credit/placement by examination:** AP, CLEP, IB, institutional tests. 64 credit hours maximum toward bachelor's degree. **Support services:** Learning center, pre-admission summer program, reduced course load, remedial instruction, study skills assistance, tutoring, writing center.

Majors. Biology: General. **Business:** General, accounting, business admin, finance, human resources, international, management information systems, marketing. **Communications:** General, media studies, radio/tv. **Computer sciences:** General, computer science, programming. **Conservation:** Environmental studies. **Education:** General, art, biology, chemistry, early childhood, elementary, English, mathematics, multi-level teacher, science, secondary, social science, social studies, special. **Engineering:** General. **Foreign languages:** Spanish. **Health:** Art therapy, health care admin, health services admin, medical illustrating. **History:** General. **Interdisciplinary:** Biological/physical sciences. **Legal studies:** General. **Liberal arts:** Arts/sciences. **Math:** General. **Philosophy/religion:** Philosophy. **Physical sciences:** Chemistry. **Psychology:** General. **Social sciences:** International relations, political science, sociology. **Visual/performing arts:** General, acting, art history/conservation, ceramics, commercial/advertising art, dramatic, graphic design, interior design, metal/jewelry, painting, photography, printmaking, studio arts, theater history. **Other:** Global legal studies, Sound and music, Sport psychology.

Most popular majors. Biology 8%, business/marketing 15%, communications/journalism 8%, education 11%, psychology 11%, social sciences 8%, visual/performing arts 14%.

Computing on campus. 200 workstations in library, computer center. Dormitories wired for high-speed internet access and linked to campus network. Commuter students can connect to campus network. Online course registration, helpline, repair service, wireless network available.

Student life. Freshman orientation: Mandatory. Preregistration for classes offered. **Housing:** Guaranteed on-campus for all undergraduates. Coed dorms, single-sex dorms, special housing for disabled, apartments, wellness housing available. $300 nonrefundable deposit, deadline 5/1. Living and learning community available. **Activities:** Choral groups, dance, drama, literary magazine, music ensembles, musical theater, radio station, student government, student newspaper, TV station, approximately 45 clubs and organizations.

Athletics. NCAA. **Intercollegiate:** Baseball M, basketball, equestrian, field hockey W, golf, lacrosse W, soccer, softball W, swimming, tennis, volleyball W. **Intramural:** Basketball, field hockey W, football (non-tackle), skiing, soccer, softball, swimming M, tennis, volleyball, weight lifting. **Team name:** Scarlet Knights.

Student services. Adult student services, alcohol/substance abuse counseling, career counseling, services for economically disadvantaged, student employment services, financial aid counseling, health services, minority student services, personal counseling, placement for graduates.

Contact. E-mail: admiss@arcadia.edu
Phone: (215) 572-2910 Toll-free number: (887) 272-2342
Fax: (215) 881-8767
Mark Lapreziosa, Associate Vice President of Enrollment Management, Arcadia University, 450 South Easton Road, Glenside, PA 19038-3295

Art Institute of Philadelphia
Philadelphia, Pennsylvania
www.artinstitutes.edu/Philadelphia **CB code: 2033**

- For-profit 4-year visual arts college
- Commuter campus in very large city
- 3,602 degree-seeking undergraduates
- Application essay, interview required

General. Founded in 1966. Accredited by ACICS. **Degrees:** 405 bachelor's, 298 associate awarded. **Calendar:** Quarter, extensive summer session. **Full-time faculty:** 99 total. **Part-time faculty:** 120 total. **Special facilities:** Recording studio utilizing Pro-tools software, digital photography laboratory, nonlinear digital editing suites, and full-service chef instructor/student-run restaurant.

Freshman class profile. 760 enrolled.

Basis for selection. High school transcript most important. Essay and interview required. Portfolio recommended.

High school preparation. Background or strong interest in chosen major preferred.

Financial aid. Additional information: Institute-sponsored scholarships available.

Application procedures. Admission: No deadline. $50 fee. Admission notification on a rolling basis. **Financial aid:** No deadline. FAFSA, institutional form required. Applicants notified on a rolling basis starting 3/1; must reply within 2 week(s) of notification.

Academics. Academic program designed to simulate working environment, focusing course work on job-related skills. **Special study options:** Independent study, internships. **Credit/placement by examination:** CLEP, IB, SAT, ACT, institutional tests. **Support services:** Learning center, reduced course load, remedial instruction, study skills assistance, tutoring.

Majors. Communications technology: Animation/special effects. **Computer sciences:** Web page design. **Visual/performing arts:** Cinematography, commercial/advertising art, design, industrial design, interior design.

Computing on campus. 507 workstations in dormitories, library, computer center. Dormitories wired for high-speed internet access. Online library, student web hosting available.

Student life. Freshman orientation: Available. **Housing:** Coed dorms, apartments available. **Activities:** Student government.

Student services. Career counseling, student employment services, financial aid counseling, personal counseling, placement for graduates.

Contact. E-mail: aiphadm@aii.edu
Phone: (215) 567-7080 Toll-free number: (800) 275-2474
Fax: (215) 405-6399
Larry McHugh, Director of Admissions, Art Institute of Philadelphia, 1622 Chestnut Street, Philadelphia, PA 19103-5198

Art Institute of Pittsburgh
Pittsburgh, Pennsylvania
www.artinstitutes.edu/pittsburgh **CB code: 2029**

- For-profit 4-year visual arts and technical college
- Commuter campus in large city
- 11,120 degree-seeking undergraduates
- Application essay, interview required

General. Founded in 1921. Regionally accredited; also accredited by ACICS. **Degrees:** 537 bachelor's, 191 associate awarded. **Calendar:** Continuous, extensive summer session. **Full-time faculty:** 386 total. **Part-time faculty:** 798 total. **Special facilities:** Photography laboratory, art gallery for students and faculty, traveling exhibits, 24-track recording studio, restaurant.

Freshman class profile.

Out-of-state:	50%	Live on campus:	50%

Basis for selection. High school transcript most important. Essay required. Interview required. Limited portfolio required for some programs. **Homeschooled:** Statement describing homeschool structure and mission, transcript of courses and grades, state high school equivalency certificate, letter of recommendation (nonparent) required.

High school preparation. Prefer students with demonstrated interest in chosen major.

2009-2010 Annual costs. Tuition/fees (projected): $20,580. Tuition and fees may vary. Culinary lab fee for food courses, $250; $100 lab fee per online course. Books/supplies: $1,445. Personal expenses: $2,160.

Application procedures. Admission: No deadline. $50 fee. Admission notification on a rolling basis. **Financial aid:** No deadline. FAFSA, institutional form required. Applicants notified on a rolling basis starting 4/15.

Academics. Special study options: Distance learning, internships, study abroad. **Credit/placement by examination:** AP, CLEP. **Support services:** Learning center, remedial instruction, tutoring, writing center.

Majors. Business: Fashion. **Communications technology:** Animation/special effects. **Computer sciences:** Web page design. **Personal/culinary services:** Chef training, restaurant/catering. **Visual/performing arts:** Cinematography, commercial/advertising art, design, industrial design, interior design, photography.

Computing on campus. 225 workstations in dormitories, library, computer center. Dormitories wired for high-speed internet access and linked to campus network. Commuter students can connect to campus network. Online course registration, online library, helpline, student web hosting, wireless network available.

Student life. Freshman orientation: Mandatory. Preregistration for classes offered. One-day program held before start of classes. **Housing:** Coed dorms, apartments, wellness housing available. $100 deposit. **Activities:** Drama, film society, international student organizations, student government, student newspaper, community relations activities, student success task force, student council.

Athletics. Intramural: Basketball M.

Student services. Career counseling, student employment services, financial aid counseling, personal counseling, placement for graduates, veterans' counselor. **Physically disabled:** Services for visually, speech, hearing impaired.

Contact. E-mail: aipadm@aii.edu
Phone: (412) 263-6600 Toll-free number: (800) 275-2470
Fax: (412) 263-6667
Melanie Gibson, Senior Director of Admissions, Art Institute of Pittsburgh, 420 Boulevard of the Allies, Pittsburgh, PA 15219-1328

Art Institute Online
Pittsburgh, Pennsylvania
www.aionline.edu **CB code: 3835**

- For-profit 4-year virtual college
- Large city
- 9,050 undergraduates

General. Accredited by ACICS. A division of The Art Institute of Pittsburgh. **Degrees:** 181 bachelor's, 89 associate awarded. **Calendar:** Quarter. **Full-time faculty:** 285 total. **Part-time faculty:** 285 total.

Basis for selection. 2.0 high school GPA required. Applicants must submit completed enrollment agreement and $100 enrollment fee within 10 days of application. Applicants not accepted for admission will receive full refund of all fees paid.

Application procedures. Admission: No deadline. $50 fee. Admission notification on a rolling basis.

Academics. Credit/placement by examination: CLEP.

Majors. Business: Hotel/motel admin. **Communications:** Advertising. **Computer sciences:** Web page design. **Family/consumer sciences:** Merchandising. **Personal/culinary services:** Restaurant/catering. **Visual/performing arts:** Graphic design, interior design. **Other:** Game art and design.

Student life. Freshman orientation: Mandatory. Online student orientation teaches use of online software program and acquaints students with overall classroom environment. Conducted prior to beginning of classes.

Contact. E-mail: aioadm@aii.edu
Phone: (877) 872-8869 Toll-free number: (877) 872-8869
Fax: (412) 995-4320
Ken Boutelle, Admissions Director, Art Institute Online, 1400 Penn Avenue, Pittsburgh, PA 15222

Baptist Bible College of Pennsylvania

Clarks Summit, Pennsylvania
www.bbc.edu **CB code: 2036**

- Private 4-year Bible and seminary college affiliated with Baptist faith
- Residential campus in small city
- 549 degree-seeking undergraduates
- 70% of applicants admitted
- SAT or ACT (ACT writing optional), application essay required

General. Founded in 1932. Regionally accredited; also accredited by ABHE. Part of each student's curriculum includes ministry/service experiences in churches or social agencies. **Degrees:** 143 bachelor's, 8 associate awarded; master's, doctoral, first professional offered. **Location:** 7 miles from Scranton, 20 miles from Wilkes-Barre. **Calendar:** Semester, limited summer session. **Full-time faculty:** 40 total. **Part-time faculty:** 26 total. **Class size:** 70% < 20, 20% 20-39, 4% 40-49, 6% 50-99, 1% >100.

Freshman class profile. 350 applied, 245 admitted, 106 enrolled.

Mid 50% test scores		**GPA 3.50-3.74:**	24%
SAT critical reading:	450-600	**GPA 3.0-3.49:**	25%
SAT math:	420-570	**GPA 2.0-2.99:**	22%
ACT composite:	17-23	**Out-of-state:**	70%
GPA 3.75 or higher:	24%	**Live on campus:**	96%

Basis for selection. Academic record, test scores, references/recommendations most important. Audition required, interview recommended for all; portfolio required for music programs.

2008-2009 Annual costs. Tuition/fees: $15,840. Room/board: $5,900. Books/supplies: $600. Personal expenses: $1,770.

2007-2008 Financial aid. Non-need-based: Scholarships awarded for academics, leadership, music/drama, religious affiliation.

Application procedures. Admission: Priority date 5/1; deadline 8/15 (postmark date). $30 fee. Admission notification on a rolling basis. Must reply by May 1 or within 4 week(s) if notified thereafter. **Financial aid:** Closing date 5/1. FAFSA, institutional form required. Applicants notified on a rolling basis starting 4/1.

Academics. Special study options: Combined bachelor's/graduate degree, distance learning, double major, dual enrollment of high school students, independent study, internships, study abroad, teacher certification program. **Credit/placement by examination:** AP, CLEP, IB, SAT, ACT, institutional tests. **Support services:** Reduced course load, remedial instruction, study skills assistance, tutoring, writing center.

Majors. Business: Administrative services. **Communications:** General. **Education:** Early childhood, elementary, health, mathematics, multi-level teacher, music, physical, science, secondary, social studies. **Parks/recreation:** Health/fitness. **Theology:** Missionary, preministerial, sacred music, youth ministry.

Most popular majors. Communications/journalism 9%, education 27%, psychology 11%, theological studies 52%.

Computing on campus. 30 workstations in library, computer center. Dormitories wired for high-speed internet access and linked to campus network. Online course registration, online library, wireless network available.

Student life. Freshman orientation: Mandatory. Preregistration for classes offered. Parent and student orientation weekend includes sessions on academics, student life, finances, and interaction with faculty. **Policies:** Religious observance required. **Housing:** Guaranteed on-campus for all undergraduates. Single-sex dorms, special housing for disabled, wellness housing available. $250 deposit, deadline 5/1. **Activities:** Choral groups, drama, music ensembles, student government, student newspaper, several religious and service groups.

Athletics. NCAA, NCCAA. **Intercollegiate:** Baseball M, basketball, cheerleading W, cross-country, golf M, soccer, softball W, tennis W, track and field, volleyball, wrestling M. **Intramural:** Basketball, soccer, softball M, volleyball. **Team name:** Defenders.

Student services. Adult student services, alcohol/substance abuse counseling, career counseling, student employment services, financial aid counseling, health services, personal counseling, placement for graduates.

Contact. E-mail: admissions@bbc.edu
Phone: (570) 586-2400 ext. 9271 Toll-free number: (800) 585-9271
Fax: (570) 585-9299
Ken Shepard, Vice President for Enrollment and Marketing Services, Baptist Bible College of Pennsylvania, 538 Venard Road, Clarks Summit, PA 18411-1297

Bloomsburg University of Pennsylvania

Bloomsburg, Pennsylvania **CB member**
www.bloomu.edu **CB code: 2646**

- Public 4-year university and liberal arts college
- Residential campus in large town
- 7,840 degree-seeking undergraduates: 4% part-time, 58% women, 7% African American, 1% Asian American, 3% Hispanic American, 1% international
- 747 degree-seeking graduate students
- 59% of applicants admitted
- SAT or ACT (ACT writing optional) required
- 65% graduate within 6 years; 20% enter graduate study

General. Founded in 1839. Regionally accredited. **Degrees:** 1,545 bachelor's awarded; master's, doctoral offered. **ROTC:** Army, Air Force. **Location:** 40 miles from Wilkes-Barre, 80 miles from Harrisburg. **Calendar:** Semester, extensive summer session. **Full-time faculty:** 378 total; 88% have terminal degrees, 14% minority, 43% women. **Part-time faculty:** 79 total; 22% have terminal degrees, 2% minority, 57% women. **Class size:** 24% < 20, 63% 20-39, 6% 40-49, 4% 50-99, 3% >100.

Freshman class profile. 10,840 applied, 6,350 admitted, 1,811 enrolled.

Mid 50% test scores		**GPA 2.0-2.99:**	22%
SAT critical reading:	460-540	**Rank in top quarter:**	38%
SAT math:	470-570	**Rank in top tenth:**	9%
SAT writing:	440-540	**Return as sophomores:**	80%
GPA 3.75 or higher:	29%	**Out-of-state:**	13%
GPA 3.50-3.74:	14%	**Live on campus:**	91%
GPA 3.0-3.49:	35%		

Basis for selection. School achievement record and class rank most important. School's recommendation considered in borderline cases.

High school preparation. College-preparatory program required. 16 units required; 19 recommended. Required and recommended units include English 4, mathematics 3-4, social studies 2, history 2, science 3-4, foreign language 2, computer science 1 and academic electives 2.

2008-2009 Annual costs. Tuition/fees: $6,848; $14,886 out-of-state. Room/board: $6,292. Books/supplies: $1,200. Personal expenses: $2,800.

2008-2009 Financial aid. Need-based: 1,619 full-time freshmen applied for aid; 1,538 were judged to have need; 1,375 of these received aid. Average need met was 69%. Average scholarship/grant was $5,852; average loan $3,296. 45% of total undergraduate aid awarded as scholarships/grants, 55% as loans/jobs. **Non-need-based:** Awarded to 1,527 full-time undergraduates, including 478 freshmen. Scholarships awarded for academics, art, athletics, job skills, leadership, minority status, music/drama, ROTC, state residency.

Application procedures. Admission: Priority date 12/1; no deadline. $30 fee, may be waived for applicants with need. Admission notification on a rolling basis beginning on or about 9/18. Must reply by May 1 or within 2 week(s) if notified thereafter. **Financial aid:** Priority date 3/15; no closing date. FAFSA required. Applicants notified on a rolling basis starting 4/1.

Academics. Special study options: Combined bachelor's/graduate degree, cooperative education, distance learning, double major, dual enrollment of high school students, ESL, honors, independent study, internships, study abroad, teacher certification program. **Credit/placement by examination:** AP, CLEP, SAT, institutional tests. 64 credit hours maximum toward bachelor's degree. **Support services:** Learning center, pre-admission summer program, reduced course load, remedial instruction, study skills assistance, tutoring, writing center.

Majors. Biology: General. **Business:** Accounting, business admin, managerial economics. **Communications:** General, media studies. **Computer sciences:** General, computer forensics, computer science. **Education:** Business, early childhood, elementary, science, social studies, special. **Engineering:** Electrical. **Foreign languages:** French, German, sign language interpretation, Spanish. **Health:** Audiology/speech pathology, clinical lab science, medical radiologic technology/radiation therapy, nursing (RN), physics/radiologic health. **History:** General. **Math:** General. **Parks/recreation:** Exercise sciences. **Philosophy/religion:** Philosophy. **Physical sciences:** Chemistry, geology, physics. **Protective services:** Criminal justice. **Psychology:** General. **Public administration:** Social work. **Social sciences:** Anthropology, economics, geography, political science, sociology. **Visual/performing arts:** Art history/conservation, dramatic, studio arts.

Most popular majors. Business/marketing 22%, education 17%, English 7%, health sciences 11%, social sciences 8%.

Computing on campus. 1,440 workstations in dormitories, library, computer center, student center. Dormitories wired for high-speed internet access and linked to campus network. Commuter students can connect to campus network. Online course registration, online library, helpline, wireless network available.

Student life. Freshman orientation: Mandatory, $77 fee. Preregistration for classes offered. One-day program in July and 3-day program prior to start of classes. **Housing:** Guaranteed on-campus for freshmen. Coed dorms, apartments, cooperative housing, wellness housing available. $100 nonrefundable deposit, deadline 5/1. **Activities:** Bands, campus ministries, choral groups, dance, drama, international student organizations, literary magazine, music ensembles, Model UN, radio station, student government, student newspaper, symphony orchestra, TV station, Bloomsburg Christian Fellowship, Hillel, University Democrats, College Republicans, community government association, Black Cultural Society, Student Organization of Latinos, Habitat for Humanity.

Athletics. NCAA. **Intercollegiate:** Baseball M, basketball, cross-country, field hockey W, football (tackle) M, lacrosse W, soccer, softball W, swimming, tennis, track and field, wrestling M. **Intramural:** Basketball, field hockey W, football (non-tackle) M, racquetball, soccer, softball, tennis, volleyball, wrestling M. **Team name:** Huskies.

Student services. Adult student services, alcohol/substance abuse counseling, chaplain/spiritual director, career counseling, services for economically disadvantaged, student employment services, financial aid counseling, health services, legal services, minority student services, on-campus daycare, personal counseling, placement for graduates, veterans' counselor, women's services. **Physically disabled:** Services for visually, speech, hearing impaired.

Contact. E-mail: buadmiss@bloomu.edu
Phone: (570) 389-4316 Fax: (570) 389-4741
Christopher Keller, Director of Admissions and Records, Bloomsburg University of Pennsylvania, 104 Student Service Center, Bloomsburg, PA 17815

Bryn Athyn College of the New Church

Bryn Athyn, Pennsylvania
www.brynathyn.edu **CB code: 2002**

- Private 4-year liberal arts college affiliated with General Church of the New Jerusalem (Swedenborgian)
- Residential campus in small town
- 141 degree-seeking undergraduates: 4% part-time, 45% women, 1% African American, 1% Asian American, 20% international
- 19 degree-seeking graduate students
- 88% of applicants admitted
- SAT or ACT with writing, application essay required

General. Founded in 1876. Regionally accredited. **Degrees:** 11 bachelor's, 14 associate awarded; master's, first professional offered. **Location:** 15 miles from Philadelphia. **Calendar:** Trimester. **Full-time faculty:** 21 total; 76% have terminal degrees, 38% women. **Part-time faculty:** 45 total; 36% have terminal degrees, 2% minority, 40% women. **Class size:** 95% < 20, 5% 20-39. **Special facilities:** Performing arts center, archives, ecological restoration trust.

Freshman class profile. 58 applied, 51 admitted, 43 enrolled.

Mid 50% test scores		**GPA 2.0-2.99:**	32%
SAT critical reading:	430-570	**End year in good standing:**	89%
SAT math:	500-580	**Return as sophomores:**	81%
SAT writing:	410-550	**Out-of-state:**	26%
GPA 3.75 or higher:	12%	**Live on campus:**	65%
GPA 3.50-3.74:	21%	**International:**	21%
GPA 3.0-3.49:	35%		

Basis for selection. Applicants expected to have interest in the New Church. School achievement record important; test scores considered. TOEFL required of non-native English speakers. SAT may be required of some Canadian applicants. Interview recommended; may be required. **Home-schooled:** SAT Subject Tests in literature and math recommended.

High school preparation. 15 units recommended. Recommended units include English 4, mathematics 3, history 3, science 3 and foreign language 2. 3 units social studies and/or history required.

2008-2009 Annual costs. Tuition/fees: $10,620. Room/board: $5,853. Books/supplies: $950. Personal expenses: $650.

2008-2009 Financial aid. Need-based: 83% of total undergraduate aid awarded as scholarships/grants, 17% as loans/jobs. **Non-need-based:** Scholarships awarded for academics, leadership, religious affiliation.

Application procedures. Admission: Priority date 2/1; deadline 7/1 (receipt date). $30 fee, may be waived for applicants with need, free for online applicants. Admission notification on a rolling basis beginning on or about 2/1. Must reply by 8/1. **Financial aid:** Closing date 6/1. FAFSA, institutional form required. Applicants notified on a rolling basis starting 4/30; must reply by 9/30.

Academics. Special study options: Accelerated study, cooperative education, cross-registration, distance learning, ESL, independent study, internships, student-designed major, study abroad, teacher certification program. Students can combine multiple curricular areas to design an educational program tailored to meet their particular interests, abilities, and needs. The areas which can be combined are the following: biological sciences, business, classical languages, computer science, education, English, history, mathematics, philosophy, physical sciences, psychology, religion, and social sciences. **Credit/placement by examination:** AP, CLEP, IB, SAT, ACT, institutional tests. **Support services:** Remedial instruction, study skills assistance, tutoring, writing center.

Majors. Biology: General. **Business:** General. **Computer sciences:** General. **Education:** General, biology, English, history. **History:** General. **Math:** General. **Philosophy/religion:** Religion.

Most popular majors. Biology 18%, English 36%, history 9%, interdisciplinary studies 27%, philosophy/religious studies 9%.

Computing on campus. 55 workstations in dormitories, library, computer center, student center. Dormitories wired for high-speed internet access and linked to campus network. Online library, helpline, repair service, wireless network available.

Student life. Freshman orientation: Mandatory. **Policies:** No alcohol on campus, restricted dorm visiting, required chapel attendance. Religious observance required. **Housing:** Guaranteed on-campus for all undergraduates. Single-sex dorms available. $150 fully refundable deposit, deadline 7/15. Satellite housing available. **Activities:** Choral groups, drama, international student organizations, student government, student newspaper, CARE.

Athletics. Intercollegiate: Badminton, ice hockey M, lacrosse, soccer, volleyball W. **Team name:** Blaze.

Student services. Chaplain/spiritual director, career counseling, student employment services, financial aid counseling, health services, personal counseling.

Contact. E-mail: admissions@brynathyn.edu
Phone: (267) 502-2511 Fax: (267) 502-2593
Sean Lawing, Director of Admissions, Bryn Athyn College of the New Church, PO Box 717, Bryn Athyn, PA 19009-0717

Bryn Mawr College

Bryn Mawr, Pennsylvania
www.brynmawr.edu
CB member
CB code: 2049

- Private 4-year liberal arts college for women
- Residential campus in very large city
- 1,274 degree-seeking undergraduates: 1% part-time, 100% women, 6% African American, 12% Asian American, 4% Hispanic American, 7% international
- 436 degree-seeking graduate students
- 49% of applicants admitted
- SAT and SAT Subject Tests or ACT (ACT writing optional), application essay required
- 86% graduate within 6 years; 26% enter graduate study

General. Founded in 1885. Regionally accredited. Academic exchange with Haverford College, Swarthmore College, and University of Pennsylvania. Extracurricular and social coordination with Haverford. **Degrees:** 311 bachelor's awarded; master's, doctoral offered. **ROTC:** Air Force. **Location:** 11 miles from Philadelphia. **Calendar:** Semester, limited summer session. **Full-time faculty:** 158 total; 94% have terminal degrees, 15% minority, 49% women. **Part-time faculty:** 52 total; 29% have terminal degrees, 10% minority, 85% women. **Class size:** 69% < 20, 25% 20-39, 3% 40-49, 3% 50-99. **Special facilities:** Collections of minerals, archaeological and anthropological artifacts.

Freshman class profile. 2,150 applied, 1,049 admitted, 366 enrolled.

Mid 50% test scores		**Rank in top tenth:**	65%
SAT critical reading:	620-730	**Return as sophomores:**	90%
SAT math:	580-680	**Out-of-state:**	88%
SAT writing:	620-710	**Live on campus:**	100%
ACT composite:	27-31	**International:**	10%
Rank in top quarter:	96%		

Basis for selection. School achievement record, recommendations, essay most important. Test scores, school and community activities, extracurricular achievements important. For those submitting SAT, 2 SAT Subject Tests required. Interview recommended. **Homeschooled:** Statement describing homeschool structure and mission, transcript of courses and grades, state high school equivalency certificate, interview, letter of recommendation (nonparent) required. Interview required, but may be completed with admissions officer or alumna.

High school preparation. 16 units recommended. Required and recommended units include English 4, mathematics 3, social studies 2, history 2, science 2 (laboratory 1), foreign language 3 and academic electives 2.

2009-2010 Annual costs. Tuition/fees: $38,034. Room/board: $12,000. Books/supplies: $1,000. Personal expenses: $1,000.

2008-2009 Financial aid. All financial aid based on need. 231 full-time freshmen applied for aid; 175 were judged to have need; 175 of these received aid. Average need met was 100%. Average scholarship/grant was $28,170; average loan $4,496. 79% of total undergraduate aid awarded as scholarships/grants, 21% as loans/jobs.

Application procedures. Admission: Closing date 1/15 (postmark date). $50 fee, may be waived for applicants with need. Admission notification 4/1. Must reply by 5/1. **Financial aid:** Priority date 2/5, closing date 3/1. FAFSA, CSS PROFILE required. Applicants notified by 3/23; must reply by 5/1.

Academics. Most examinations self-scheduled. **Special study options:** Accelerated study, combined bachelor's/graduate degree, cross-registration, double major, dual enrollment of high school students, exchange student, independent study, internships, liberal arts/career combination, student-designed major, study abroad, teacher certification program. 3-2 Program in City and Regional Planning with the University of Pennsylvania. A.B./B.S. 3-2 engineering programs with University of Pennsylvania. **Credit/placement by examination:** AP, CLEP, IB, institutional tests. 32 credit hours maximum toward bachelor's degree. **Support services:** Preadmission summer program, reduced course load, study skills assistance, tutoring, writing center.

Majors. Architecture: Urban/community planning. **Area/ethnic studies:** East Asian. **Biology:** General. **Computer sciences:** Computer science. **Foreign languages:** Ancient Greek, classics, comparative lit, French, German, Italian, Latin, Russian, Spanish. **History:** General. **Interdisciplinary:** Classical/archaeology. **Math:** General. **Philosophy/religion:** Philosophy, religion. **Physical sciences:** Astronomy, chemistry, geology, physics. **Psychology:** General. **Social sciences:** Anthropology, archaeology, economics, political science, sociology, urban studies. **Visual/performing arts:** Art history/conservation, studio arts.

Most popular majors. Biology 9%, English 7%, foreign language 11%, mathematics 7%, physical sciences 10%, psychology 9%, social sciences 30%, visual/performing arts 6%.

Computing on campus. 200 workstations in dormitories, library, computer center, student center. Dormitories linked to campus network. Commuter students can connect to campus network. Online course registration, online library, helpline, repair service, student web hosting, wireless network available.

Student life. Freshman orientation: Mandatory. Week-long program; students divided into groups of 10-20 students based on residence hall assignments. **Policies:** Self-governing student body, academic and social honor code, Customs and Traditions programs. **Housing:** Guaranteed on-campus for all undergraduates. Coed dorms, apartments, cooperative housing, wellness housing available. $200 fully refundable deposit, deadline 6/1. Students may live at Haverford. Foreign language houses available (Chinese, French, German, Hebrew, Italian, Russian, Spanish). Special housing available for non-traditional-aged students. **Activities:** Jazz band, campus ministries, choral groups, dance, drama, film society, international student organizations, literary magazine, music ensembles, Model UN, musical theater, radio station, student government, student newspaper, Mujeres, Rainbow Alliance, investment group, Jewish student union.

Athletics. NCAA. **Intercollegiate:** Badminton W, basketball W, cross-country W, field hockey W, lacrosse W, rowing (crew) W, soccer W, swimming W, tennis W, track and field W, volleyball W. **Intramural:** Tennis W, volleyball W. **Team name:** Owls.

Student services. Adult student services, alcohol/substance abuse counseling, chaplain/spiritual director, career counseling, services for economically disadvantaged, student employment services, financial aid counseling, health services, minority student services, personal counseling, placement for graduates, women's services. **Physically disabled:** Services for visually, speech, hearing impaired.

Contact. E-mail: admissions@brynmawr.edu
Phone: (610) 526-5152 Toll-free number: (800) 262-1885
Fax: (610) 526-7471
Jennifer Rickard, Dean of Admissions and Financial Aid, Bryn Mawr College, 101 North Merion Avenue, Bryn Mawr, PA 19010-2899

Bucknell University

Lewisburg, Pennsylvania
www.bucknell.edu
CB member
CB code: 2050

- Private 4-year university
- Residential campus in small town
- 3,560 degree-seeking undergraduates: 53% women, 3% African American, 6% Asian American, 4% Hispanic American, 3% international
- 98 degree-seeking graduate students
- 30% of applicants admitted
- SAT or ACT with writing, application essay required
- 89% graduate within 6 years; 26% enter graduate study

General. Founded in 1846. Regionally accredited. **Degrees:** 898 bachelor's awarded; master's offered. **ROTC:** Army. **Location:** 75 miles from Harrisburg, 195 miles from Philadelphia. **Calendar:** Semester, limited summer session. **Full-time faculty:** 334 total; 95% have terminal degrees, 13% minority, 39% women. **Part-time faculty:** 24 total; 54% have terminal degrees, 42% women. **Class size:** 55% < 20, 41% 20-39, 2% 40-49, 2% 50-99, less than 1% >100. **Special facilities:** Observatory, 63-acre nature preserve, center for performing arts, poetry center, greenhouse, outdoor naturalistic primate facility, engineering structural test lab, gas chromatograph/mass spectrometer, nuclear magnetic resonance spectrometer, herbarium, 18-hole golf course, small business development center.

Freshman class profile. 8,024 applied, 2,395 admitted, 957 enrolled.

Mid 50% test scores		**Rank in top tenth:**	69%
SAT critical reading:	600-680	**End year in good standing:**	99%
SAT math:	630-710	**Return as sophomores:**	95%
SAT writing:	610-700	**Out-of-state:**	75%
ACT composite:	27-31	**Live on campus:**	99%
Rank in top quarter:	90%	**International:**	4%

Basis for selection. Emphasis on school achievement. Test scores, recommendations, special talents and abilities, evidence of volunteer work, personal qualities important. If English is not student's first language and student submits SAT scores with Critical Reading score below 550, TOEFL required. Audition required for music program; portfolio recommended for art program. **Homeschooled:** Statement describing homeschool structure and mission, interview required. Interview, SAT, graded English paper, writing sample (not from English class), program description or certification from homeschooler's accrediting agency or school district, name/address/ phone number of homeschool supervisor required.

High school preparation. College-preparatory program required. 16 units required; 20 recommended. Required and recommended units include English 4, mathematics 3-4, social studies 2, history 2, science 2-3, foreign language 2-4 and academic electives 1.

2009-2010 Annual costs. Tuition/fees: $40,816. Room/board: $9,504. Books/supplies: $880. Personal expenses: $1,000.

2008-2009 Financial aid. Need-based: 473 full-time freshmen applied for aid; 399 were judged to have need; 399 of these received aid. Average need met was 95%. Average scholarship/grant was $22,400; average loan $4,500. 74% of total undergraduate aid awarded as scholarships/grants, 26% as loans/jobs. **Non-need-based:** Awarded to 324 full-time undergraduates, including 107 freshmen. Scholarships awarded for academics, art, athletics, leadership, music/drama, ROTC.

Application procedures. Admission: Closing date 1/15 (postmark date). $60 fee, may be waived for applicants with need. Admission notification 4/1. Must reply by 5/1. **Financial aid:** Closing date 1/1. FAFSA, CSS PROFILE required. Applicants notified by 4/1; must reply by 5/1.

Academics. Special study options: Combined bachelor's/graduate degree, double major, dual enrollment of high school students, honors, independent study, internships, liberal arts/career combination, student-designed major, study abroad, teacher certification program, Washington semester. **Credit/placement by examination:** AP, CLEP, IB, institutional tests. No policy limit on number of credits; only a few courses offer this option. **Support services:** Learning center, study skills assistance, tutoring, writing center.

Majors. Area/ethnic studies: East Asian, Latin American, women's. **Biology:** General, animal behavior, biochemistry, cellular/molecular. **Business:** Accounting, business admin. **Computer sciences:** General. **Conservation:** Environmental studies. **Education:** General, early childhood, elementary, music, secondary. **Engineering:** Biomedical, chemical, civil, computer, electrical, mechanical. **Foreign languages:** Classics, French, German, Russian, Spanish. **History:** General. **Interdisciplinary:** Neuroscience. **Liberal arts:** Humanities. **Math:** General. **Philosophy/religion:** Philosophy, religion. **Physical sciences:** Chemistry, geology, physics. **Psychology:** General. **Social sciences:** Anthropology, econometrics, economics, geography, international relations, political science, sociology. **Visual/performing arts:** General, art history/conservation, dramatic, music history, music performance, music theory/ composition, studio arts. **Other:** Economics and mathematics studies.

Most popular majors. Biology 11%, business/marketing 15%, engineering/ engineering technologies 16%, English 7%, psychology 6%, social sciences 20%.

Computing on campus. 970 workstations in dormitories, library, computer center, student center. Dormitories wired for high-speed internet access and linked to campus network. Commuter students can connect to campus network. Online course registration, online library, helpline, repair service, wireless network available.

Student life. Freshman orientation: Mandatory, $50 fee. Preregistration for classes offered. Held 5 days prior to start of classes. **Policies:** All first-year students must sign statement of student responsibility. **Housing:** Guaranteed on-campus for all undergraduates. Coed dorms, single-sex dorms, special housing for disabled, apartments, fraternity/sorority housing, wellness housing available. Seven residential colleges with themes: arts, humanities, global, environment, social justice, technology and society; language and culture; quiet floors available. **Activities:** Bands, campus ministries, choral groups, dance, drama, film society, international student organizations, literary magazine, music ensembles, Model UN, musical theater, opera, radio station, student government, student newspaper, symphony orchestra, Hillel, Fellowship of Christians, Chinese culture association, Brothers and Sisters Empowered, Japan Society, Muslim student association, O.H.L.A.S. (formerly Le Cumbre Hispanic), College Democrats, College Republicans.

Athletics. NCAA. **Intercollegiate:** Baseball M, basketball, cross-country, diving, field hockey W, football (tackle) M, golf, lacrosse, rowing (crew) W, soccer, softball W, swimming, tennis, track and field, volleyball W, water polo, wrestling M. **Intramural:** Badminton, basketball, bowling, cross-country, football (non-tackle), golf, racquetball, soccer, softball, squash, table tennis, tennis, volleyball, weight lifting M. **Team name:** Bison.

Student services. Alcohol/substance abuse counseling, chaplain/ spiritual director, career counseling, financial aid counseling, health services, minority student services, personal counseling, placement for graduates, women's services. **Physically disabled:** Services for visually, hearing impaired.

Contact. E-mail: admissions@bucknell.edu
Phone: (570) 577-1101 Fax: (570) 577-3538
Kurt Thiede, Vice President for Enrollment Management and Dean of Admissions, Bucknell University, Freas Hall, Lewisburg, PA 17837-9988

Cabrini College

Radnor, Pennsylvania — **CB member**
www.cabrini.edu — **CB code: 2071**

- Private 4-year liberal arts college affiliated with Roman Catholic Church
- Residential campus in large town
- 1,807 degree-seeking undergraduates: 7% part-time, 66% women, 7% African American, 2% Asian American, 2% Hispanic American
- 1,723 degree-seeking graduate students
- 70% of applicants admitted
- SAT or ACT (ACT writing optional) required
- 56% graduate within 6 years

General. Founded in 1957. Regionally accredited. College sponsored by Missionary Sisters of the Sacred Heart (international religious order serving six continents). **Degrees:** 316 bachelor's awarded; master's offered. **ROTC:** Army, Air Force. **Location:** 18 miles from Philadelphia, 5 miles from King of Prussia. **Calendar:** Semester, limited summer session. **Full-time faculty:** 68 total; 82% have terminal degrees, 7% minority, 57% women. **Part-time faculty:** 237 total; 18% have terminal degrees, 8% minority, 54% women. **Class size:** 57% < 20, 42% 20-39, less than 1% 40-49, less than 1% 50-99. **Special facilities:** College-operated preschool (off-campus), human performance lab, video studio, graphic design lab.

Freshman class profile. 4,630 applied, 3,234 admitted, 527 enrolled.

Mid 50% test scores		Rank in top quarter:	14%
SAT critical reading:	440-520	Rank in top tenth:	3%
SAT math:	420-520	End year in good standing:	87%
GPA 3.75 or higher:	10%	Return as sophomores:	66%
GPA 3.50-3.74:	12%	Out-of-state:	43%
GPA 3.0-3.49:	31%	Live on campus:	88%
GPA 2.0-2.99:	47%		

Basis for selection. School achievement record, test scores, academic potential, and personal qualities most important. Special consideration for children of alumni and students with special backgrounds, skills or abilities. Community action required. Non-English-speaking international students may take TOEFL instead of SAT/ACT. Interview recommended for all; portfolio recommended for studio art program. **Homeschooled:** Transcript of courses and grades, state high school equivalency certificate required. Provide as much external testing data as possible. Standardized test scores given more weight for homeschooled students.

High school preparation. College-preparatory program required. 18 units required; 21 recommended. Required and recommended units include English 4, mathematics 3-4, social studies 3, science 3, foreign language 2 and academic electives 2. Two arts and humanities also recommended. Additional math and science units recommended for science students.

2008-2009 Annual costs. Tuition/fees: $30,010. Room/board: $10,890. Books/supplies: $960. Personal expenses: $360.

2008-2009 Financial aid. Non-need-based: Scholarships awarded for academics, alumni affiliation.

Application procedures. Admission: Priority date 5/1; no deadline. $35 fee, may be waived for applicants with need, free for online applicants. Admission notification on a rolling basis. **Financial aid:** Closing date 4/1. FAFSA required. Applicants notified on a rolling basis starting 3/1.

Academics. Education fieldwork opportunities provided to education majors from sophomore to senior years. Students participate in community service. Internship or co-op programs offered in all majors. **Special study options:** Accelerated study, combined bachelor's/graduate degree, cooperative education, cross-registration, double major, honors, independent study, internships, liberal arts/career combination, student-designed major, study abroad, teacher certification program, Washington semester. Exchange programs with Eastern University, Rosemont College, Valley Forge Military College; cross-registration with Southeastern Pennsylvania Consortium for Higher Education (8-member consortium of private colleges/universities). **Credit/placement by examination:** AP, CLEP, IB, SAT, institutional tests. 30 credit hours maximum toward bachelor's degree. DANTES. **Support services:** Learning center, reduced course load, remedial instruction, study skills assistance, tutoring, writing center.

Majors. **Area/ethnic studies:** American. **Biology:** General. **Business:** Accounting, business admin, finance, human resources, management information systems, marketing. **Communications:** General. **Computer sciences:** General, information technology. **Education:** General, elementary, kindergarten/preschool, special. **Foreign languages:** French, Spanish. **Health:** Clinical lab science, premedicine. **History:** General. **Liberal arts:** Arts/sciences. **Math:** General. **Parks/recreation:** Exercise sciences. **Philosophy/religion:** Philosophy, religion. **Physical sciences:** Chemistry. **Psychology:** General. **Public administration:** Social work. **Social sciences:** Criminology, political science, sociology. **Visual/performing arts:** Graphic design.

Most popular majors. Business/marketing 31%, communications/journalism 10%, education 23%, psychology 8%.

Computing on campus. 426 workstations in dormitories, library, computer center. Dormitories wired for high-speed internet access and linked to campus network. Commuter students can connect to campus network. Online course registration, online library, helpline, student web hosting, wireless network available.

Student life. **Freshman orientation:** Mandatory, $210 fee. Preregistration for classes offered. 3-day program prior to the beginning of the fall semester. **Housing:** Coed dorms, single-sex dorms, special housing for disabled, apartments available. $350 fully refundable deposit, deadline 5/1. Special interest housing options designated for intensified study, honors, Hispanic culture and community service. **Activities:** Campus ministries, choral groups, dance, drama, film society, international student organizations, literary magazine, music ensembles, musical theater, radio station, student government, student newspaper, TV station, Black Student Union, Habitat for Humanity, Cavaliers for Life, La Raza, Up 'til Dawn, Search Club, Student Democratic Association.

Athletics. NCAA. **Intercollegiate:** Basketball, cross-country, field hockey W, golf M, lacrosse, soccer, softball W, swimming, tennis, track and field, volleyball W. **Intramural:** Badminton, basketball, cricket, football (non-tackle), lacrosse, racquetball, rugby, soccer, softball, squash, swimming, tennis, volleyball, water polo. **Team name:** Cavaliers.

Student services. Adult student services, alcohol/substance abuse counseling, chaplain/spiritual director, career counseling, student employment services, financial aid counseling, health services, minority student services, personal counseling, placement for graduates. **Physically disabled:** Services for visually, hearing impaired.

Contact. E-mail: admit@cabrini.edu
Phone: (610) 902-8552 Toll-free number: (800) 848-1003
Fax: (610) 902-8508
Charles Spencer, Director of Admissions, Cabrini College, 610 King of Prussia Road, Radnor, PA 19087-3698

California University of Pennsylvania

California, Pennsylvania **CB member**
www.cup.edu **CB code: 2647**

- Public 4-year university
- Commuter campus in small town
- 6,872 degree-seeking undergraduates
- 1,594 graduate students
- 61% of applicants admitted
- SAT required

General. Founded in 1852. Regionally accredited. Green-oriented; utilizes geothermal technologies to reduce energy consumption. **Degrees:** 1,242 bachelor's, 47 associate awarded; master's offered. **ROTC:** Army, Air Force. **Location:** 38 miles from Pittsburgh. **Calendar:** Semester, limited summer session. **Full-time faculty:** 308 total. **Part-time faculty:** 99 total. **Class size:** 28% < 20, 50% 20-39, 11% 40-49, 10% 50-99, less than 1% >100. **Special facilities:** International corporate art collection, 98-acre farm with recreational facilities.

Freshman class profile. 4,599 applied, 2,807 admitted, 1,370 enrolled.

Mid 50% test scores		**GPA 3.0-3.49:**	36%
SAT critical reading:	460-530	**GPA 2.0-2.99:**	39%
SAT math:	470-540	**Rank in top quarter:**	28%
SAT writing:	450-540	**Rank in top tenth:**	7%
ACT composite:	19-21	**Out-of-state:**	7%
GPA 3.75 or higher:	11%	**Live on campus:**	75%
GPA 3.50-3.74:	13%		

Basis for selection. School achievement record, test scores, activities, recommendations, interview considered. Essay recommended. **Homeschooled:** Transcript of courses and grades required.

High school preparation. 19 units required; 21 recommended. Required and recommended units include English 4, mathematics 3, social studies 2, history 2, science 1 (laboratory 1), foreign language 2 and academic electives 6.

2008-2009 Annual costs. Tuition/fees: $7,315; $10,531 out-of-state. Room/board: $8,886. Books/supplies: $900. Personal expenses: $1,628.

2007-2008 Financial aid. **Non-need-based:** Scholarships awarded for academics, alumni affiliation, art, athletics, leadership, minority status, music/drama, religious affiliation, ROTC, state residency.

Application procedures. **Admission:** Priority date 5/1; no deadline. $25 fee, may be waived for applicants with need. Admission notification on a rolling basis. **Financial aid:** Priority date 5/1; no closing date. FAFSA required. Applicants notified on a rolling basis starting 4/1; must reply within 3 week(s) of notification.

Academics. **Special study options:** Accelerated study, combined bachelor's/graduate degree, cooperative education, cross-registration, distance learning, double major, dual enrollment of high school students, exchange student, external degree, honors, independent study, internships, liberal arts/career combination, student-designed major, study abroad, teacher certification program, urban semester, Washington semester, weekend college. **Credit/placement by examination:** AP, CLEP, IB, SAT, institutional tests. **Support services:** Learning center, pre-admission summer program, reduced course load, remedial instruction, study skills assistance, tutoring, writing center.

Honors college/program. Minimum 1100 SAT (exclusive of Writing), 3.0 GPA, letter of recommendation required. Admitted students work with adviser and dean to design course of study.

Majors. **Biology:** General. **Business:** Accounting, business admin. **Communications:** General. **Computer sciences:** General. **Conservation:** Environmental science. **Education:** General, elementary, kindergarten/preschool, special. **Engineering technology:** General, computer, electrical. **Foreign languages:** General, French, German, Russian, Spanish. **Health:** Athletic training, clinical lab technology, communication disorders, nursing (RN). **History:** General. **Interdisciplinary:** Gerontology. **Liberal arts:** Arts/sciences. **Math:** General. **Parks/recreation:** Facilities management, sports admin. **Philosophy/religion:** Philosophy. **Physical sciences:** General, chemistry, geology, physics. **Protective services:** Criminal justice. **Psychology:** General. **Public administration:** Social work. **Social sciences:** General, geography, political science. **Visual/performing arts:** Art, commercial/advertising art, dramatic, graphic design.

Most popular majors. Business/marketing 12%, education 21%, engineering/engineering technologies 8%, health sciences 8%, parks/recreation 6%, psychology 6%, security/protective services 8%.

Computing on campus. 1,220 workstations in dormitories, library, computer center, student center. Dormitories wired for high-speed internet access and linked to campus network. Commuter students can connect to campus network. Online course registration, online library, helpline available.

Student life. **Freshman orientation:** Mandatory. Preregistration for classes offered. One-day session held in July or August. **Policies:** Freshman students under 21 and not commuting from parental home required to live in dormitory. **Housing:** Coed dorms, special housing for disabled, fraternity/sorority housing, wellness housing available. $235 deposit. **Activities:** Bands, campus ministries, choral groups, dance, drama, film society, international student organizations, literary magazine, music ensembles, musical theater, opera, radio station, student government, student newspaper, symphony orchestra, TV station.

Athletics. NCAA. **Intercollegiate:** Baseball M, basketball, cheerleading, cross-country, football (tackle) M, golf, rugby, soccer, softball, swimming W, tennis W, track and field, volleyball. **Intramural:** Archery, badminton, baseball M, basketball, bowling, cheerleading, cross-country, fencing, football (non-tackle), football (tackle), golf, gymnastics, handball, ice hockey, judo, lacrosse, racquetball, rugby, skiing, skin diving M, soccer, softball W, swimming W, table tennis, tennis W, track and field, triathlon, volleyball, weight lifting, wrestling M. **Team name:** Vulcans.

Student services. Adult student services, alcohol/substance abuse counseling, chaplain/spiritual director, career counseling, services for economically disadvantaged, student employment services, financial aid counseling, health services, legal services, minority student services, personal counseling, placement for graduates, veterans' counselor, women's services. **Physically disabled:** Services for visually, speech, hearing impaired. **Learning disabled:** Comprehensive services available.

Contact. E-mail: inquiry@cup.edu
Phone: (724) 938-4404 Fax: (724) 938-4564
William Edmonds, Dean of Admissions, California University of Pennsylvania, 250 University Avenue, California, PA 15419-1394

Carlow University
Pittsburgh, Pennsylvania
www.carlow.edu **CB code: 2421**

- Private 4-year university and liberal arts college for women affiliated with Roman Catholic Church
- Commuter campus in large city
- 1,502 degree-seeking undergraduates: 24% part-time, 94% women, 17% African American, 1% Asian American, 1% Hispanic American, 1% Native American
- 605 degree-seeking graduate students
- 60% of applicants admitted
- SAT or ACT (ACT writing optional) required
- 47% graduate within 6 years; 18% enter graduate study

General. Founded in 1929. Regionally accredited. Founded by the Sisters of Mercy in 1929 and member of the Conference for Mercy Higher Education. **Degrees:** 341 bachelor's awarded; master's, doctoral offered. **ROTC:** Army, Naval, Air Force. **Location:** 3 miles from downtown. **Calendar:** Semester, limited summer session. **Full-time faculty:** 93 total; 71% have terminal degrees, 8% minority, 74% women. **Part-time faculty:** 143 total; 75% have terminal degrees, 7% minority, 70% women. **Class size:** 86% < 20, 13% 20-39, less than 1% 40-49. **Special facilities:** Early learning center and school, science and technology research labs, communications lab, greenhouse, darkroom, biochamber, children's science lab, International Poetry Forum archives, Women of Spirit Institute.

Freshman class profile. 1,063 applied, 637 admitted, 245 enrolled.

Mid 50% test scores		**GPA 2.0-2.99:**	26%
SAT critical reading:	440-530	**Rank in top quarter:**	39%
SAT math:	440-540	**Rank in top tenth:**	12%
SAT writing:	420-540	**End year in good standing:**	70%
ACT composite:	18-23	**Return as sophomores:**	73%
GPA 3.75 or higher:	15%	**Out-of-state:**	1%
GPA 3.50-3.74:	20%	**Live on campus:**	62%
GPA 3.0-3.49:	39%		

Basis for selection. Secondary school GPA, rank, record, and course work most important. SAT or ACT also considered. 2.5 GPA and class ranking in upper two-fifths of graduating class strengthen the application. International students must take TOEFL and ACT or SAT exams. Essay, interview recommended for all and in some cases required. Portfolio recommended for all art programs. **Homeschooled:** Personal interview and portfolio from most recent year highly recommended.

High school preparation. College-preparatory program recommended. 18 units required. Required and recommended units include English 4, mathematics 3-4, social studies 2, history 2, science 3-4 (laboratory 2) and academic electives 4. Applicants to professional nursing programs must have 4 units English, 3 units social sciences, 2 units math (1 must be algebra), and 2 units laboratory science, including chemistry.

2009-2010 Annual costs. Tuition/fees (projected): $21,718. Nursing supplemental tuition is $170 per credit; student teaching fee is $295 for 3 to 6 credits. Room/board: $8,554. Books/supplies: $1,000. Personal expenses: $1,300.

2007-2008 Financial aid. Need-based: 57% of total undergraduate aid awarded as scholarships/grants, 43% as loans/jobs. **Non-need-based:** Scholarships awarded for academics, alumni affiliation, athletics, leadership.

Application procedures. Admission: Priority date 2/15; no deadline. $20 fee, may be waived for applicants with need, free for online applicants. Admission notification on a rolling basis. Must reply by May 1 or within 2 week(s) if notified thereafter. **Financial aid:** Priority date 4/1; no closing date. FAFSA required. Applicants notified on a rolling basis starting 2/15; must reply within 4 week(s) of notification.

Academics. Special study options: Accelerated study, combined bachelor's/graduate degree, cross-registration, distance learning, double major, dual enrollment of high school students, honors, independent study, internships, liberal arts/career combination, semester at sea, student-designed major, study abroad, teacher certification program, weekend college. 3+2 programs: biology/environmental engineering, chemistry/chemical engineering, math/engineering with Carnegie Mellon University, biology/environmental science and management with Duquesne University. 3+3 JD Law Program. First Year Experience for freshmen, graduate certificates and minors in nursing, social sciences, education, and accounting. **Credit/placement by examination:** AP, CLEP, IB, institutional tests. 30 credit hours maximum toward bachelor's degree. **Support services:** Learning center, reduced course load, remedial instruction, study skills assistance, tutoring.

Majors. Biology: General, environmental. **Business:** General, accounting, auditing, communications, human resources. **Communications:** General, media studies. **Conservation:** Environmental science. **Education:** Art, early childhood, elementary, middle, social studies, special. **Engineering:** Environmental. **Foreign languages:** Spanish. **Health:** Art therapy, health services admin, nursing (RN). **History:** General. **Liberal arts:** Arts/sciences. **Math:** General. **Philosophy/religion:** Philosophy. **Physical sciences:** Chemistry. **Psychology:** General. **Public administration:** Policy analysis, social work. **Social sciences:** Political science, sociology. **Theology:** Theology. **Visual/performing arts:** Art, art history/conservation, commercial/advertising art, graphic design, multimedia, photography. **Other:** Chemistry/chemical engineering, Management in health services, Mathematics/engineering, Scientific/medical marketing.

Most popular majors. Biology 10%, business/marketing 15%, education 15%, health sciences 28%, psychology 7%.

Computing on campus. 134 workstations in dormitories, library, computer center, student center. Dormitories wired for high-speed internet access and linked to campus network. Commuter students can connect to campus network. Online course registration, online library, helpline, repair service, student web hosting, wireless network available.

Student life. Freshman orientation: Mandatory. Preregistration for classes offered. Held 2 days prior to semester, includes seminars, team-building activities, social events. **Housing:** $100 deposit. **Activities:** Marching band, campus ministries, choral groups, drama, international student organizations, literary magazine, student government, student newspaper, community outreach, Alpha Phi Omega, eco club, social work association, united Black students, Alternative Spring Break, FEMME, PRIDE, Chi Eta Phi.

Athletics. NAIA. **Intercollegiate:** Basketball W, soccer W, softball W, tennis W, volleyball W. **Team name:** The Celtics.

Student services. Adult student services, alcohol/substance abuse counseling, chaplain/spiritual director, career counseling, student employment services, financial aid counseling, health services, minority student services, on-campus daycare, personal counseling, placement for graduates, women's services. **Physically disabled:** Services for visually, speech, hearing impaired.

Contact. E-mail: admissions@carlow.edu
Phone: (412) 578-6059 Toll-free number: (800) 333-2275
Fax: (412) 578-6668
Susan Winstel, Associate Director of Admissions, Carlow University, 3333 Fifth Avenue, Pittsburgh, PA 15213-3165

Carnegie Mellon University
Pittsburgh, Pennsylvania **CB member**
www.cmu.edu **CB code: 2074**

- Private 4-year university
- Residential campus in large city
- 5,892 degree-seeking undergraduates: 2% part-time, 40% women, 5% African American, 24% Asian American, 5% Hispanic American, 15% international
- 5,066 degree-seeking graduate students
- 38% of applicants admitted
- SAT or ACT with writing, application essay required
- 87% graduate within 6 years

General. Founded in 1900. Regionally accredited. **Degrees:** 1,295 bachelor's awarded; master's, doctoral offered. **ROTC:** Army, Naval, Air Force. **Location:** 5 miles from downtown. **Calendar:** Semester, limited summer session. **Full-time faculty:** 872 total; 98% have terminal degrees, 16% minority, 26% women. **Part-time faculty:** 164 total; 98% have terminal degrees, 10% minority, 39% women. **Class size:** 64% < 20, 22% 20-39, 3% 40-49, 8% 50-99, 3% >100. **Special facilities:** Botanical institute, rare books collection, recording studios, design studios, photo shoot studio, music halls.

Freshman class profile. 13,527 applied, 5,129 admitted, 1,465 enrolled.

Mid 50% test scores		**GPA 2.0-2.99:**	2%
SAT critical reading:	620-720	**Rank in top quarter:**	93%
SAT math:	670-780	**Rank in top tenth:**	73%
SAT writing:	620-710	**Return as sophomores:**	95%
ACT composite:	29-33	**Out-of-state:**	80%
GPA 3.75 or higher:	45%	**Live on campus:**	99%
GPA 3.50-3.74:	28%	**International:**	12%
GPA 3.0-3.49:	25%		

Basis for selection. Academic and artistic potential, standardized tests, activities, jobs, interests, and other personalized information important. Deadline for fine arts applicants is 12/1. SAT Subject Test required for drama, design, art, or music school applicants. All other applicants must take appropriate tests, preferably by December, but no later than January. College of Fine Arts deadline for application December 1. Interview recommended for all; audition required for drama, music programs; portfolio required for art, design programs. **Homeschooled:** Transcript of courses and grades, letter of recommendation (nonparent) required. Submit syllabus/course descriptions of work done; transcript of grades/evaluations; recommendation from counselor, representative of state board of education, homeschool association, or other person of authority.

High school preparation. 4 units required. Required and recommended units include English 4, mathematics 3, science 3 (laboratory 3), foreign language 2 and academic electives 3-4. Requirements vary by program.

2009-2010 Annual costs. Tuition/fees: $40,920. Room/board: $10,340. Books/supplies: $990. Personal expenses: $1,356.

2008-2009 Financial aid. Need-based: 1,008 full-time freshmen applied for aid; 757 were judged to have need; 753 of these received aid. Average need met was 84%. Average scholarship/grant was $23,539; average loan $3,775. 74% of total undergraduate aid awarded as scholarships/grants, 26% as loans/jobs. **Non-need-based:** Awarded to 1,306 full-time undergraduates, including 387 freshmen. Scholarships awarded for academics, art, leadership, minority status, music/drama, state residency. **Additional information:** Early need analysis offered; merit awards available. Students notified within week to 10 days of receipt of financial aid application.

Application procedures. Admission: Closing date 1/1 (postmark date). $70 fee, may be waived for applicants with need. Admission notification 4/15. Must reply by 5/1. **Financial aid:** Priority date 2/15; no closing date. FAFSA, institutional form required. Applicants notified by 3/15.

Academics. Special study options: Combined bachelor's/graduate degree, cooperative education, cross-registration, distance learning, double major, dual enrollment of high school students, exchange student, independent study, internships, liberal arts/career combination, student-designed major, study abroad, teacher certification program, Washington semester. **Credit/placement by examination:** AP, CLEP, IB, institutional tests. **Support services:** Learning center, pre-admission summer program, study skills assistance, tutoring, writing center.

Majors. Architecture: Architecture, history/criticism, technology. **Area/ethnic studies:** European, Latin American, Russian/Slavic. **Biology:** General, biophysics. **Business:** Business admin, managerial economics. **Communications:** General. **Computer sciences:** Computer science, information systems. **Conservation:** Management/policy. **Engineering:** General, biomedical, chemical, civil, computer, electrical, environmental, materials, materials science, mechanical, metallurgical, operations research. **Foreign languages:** General, Chinese, French, German, Japanese, Spanish. **History:** General, European. **Interdisciplinary:** Behavioral sciences, biopsychology, cognitive science, systems science. **Liberal arts:** Arts/sciences. **Math:** General, applied, computational, probability, statistics. **Philosophy/religion:** Ethics, logic, philosophy. **Physical sciences:** Astrophysics, chemical physics, chemistry, physics. **Psychology:** General, cognitive, psychobiology. **Public administration:** Policy analysis. **Social sciences:** General, economics, international relations, political science. **Visual/performing arts:** Art, design, dramatic, industrial design, jazz, music performance, music theory/composition, piano/organ, stringed instruments, voice/opera.

Most popular majors. Biology 6%, business/marketing 12%, computer/information sciences 11%, engineering/engineering technologies 28%, interdisciplinary studies 6%, physical sciences 6%, visual/performing arts 10%.

Computing on campus. 388 workstations in dormitories, library. Dormitories wired for high-speed internet access and linked to campus network. Commuter students can connect to campus network. Online course registration, online library, helpline, repair service, student web hosting, wireless network available.

Student life. Freshman orientation: Mandatory, $192 fee. Week-long program held one week before start of classes. **Policies:** Freshmen required to live on campus. **Housing:** Guaranteed on-campus for freshmen. Coed dorms, single-sex dorms, special housing for disabled, apartments, fraternity/sorority housing, wellness housing available. $600 nonrefundable deposit, deadline 5/1. Special interest group housing available. **Activities:** Bands, campus ministries, choral groups, dance, drama, film society, international student organizations, literary magazine, music ensembles, Model UN, musical theater, radio station, student government, student newspaper, symphony orchestra, TV station, Alpha Phi Omega, Hillel, minority women's club, service clubs, National Society of Black Engineers, Society of Women Engineers, Phi Beta Kappa, fraternities and sororities.

Athletics. NCAA. **Intercollegiate:** Basketball, cheerleading, cross-country, diving, football (tackle) M, golf M, soccer, swimming, tennis, track and field, volleyball W. **Intramural:** Badminton, basketball, bowling, cross-country, fencing, football (non-tackle), golf, racquetball, soccer, softball, squash, swimming, table tennis, tennis, track and field, volleyball, water polo. **Team name:** Tartans.

Student services. Alcohol/substance abuse counseling, chaplain/spiritual director, career counseling, student employment services, financial aid counseling, health services, on-campus daycare, personal counseling, placement for graduates, women's services. **Physically disabled:** Services for visually, speech, hearing impaired. **Learning disabled:** Comprehensive services available.

Contact. E-mail: undergraduate-admissions@andrew.cmu.edu
Phone: (412) 268-2082 Fax: (412) 268-7838
Michael Steidel, Director of Admissions, Carnegie Mellon University, 5000 Forbes Avenue, Pittsburgh, PA 15213-3890

Cedar Crest College

Allentown, Pennsylvania — **CB member**
www.cedarcrest.edu — **CB code: 2079**

- Private 4-year liberal arts college for women
- Residential campus in small city
- 1,653 degree-seeking undergraduates: 42% part-time, 95% women, 6% African American, 3% Asian American, 7% Hispanic American, 1% Native American, 1% international
- 158 degree-seeking graduate students
- 58% of applicants admitted
- SAT or ACT (ACT writing optional) required
- 59% graduate within 6 years

General. Founded in 1867. Regionally accredited. Men admitted to evening and weekend classes and daytime programs in nursing and nuclear medicine. **Degrees:** 329 bachelor's awarded; master's offered. **ROTC:** Army. **Location:** 55 miles from Philadelphia, 100 miles from New York City. **Calendar:** Semester, extensive summer session. **Full-time faculty:** 92 total; 72% have terminal degrees, 3% minority, 60% women. **Part-time faculty:** 81 total; 22% have terminal degrees, 4% minority, 78% women. **Class size:** 68% < 20, 27% 20-39, 2% 40-49, 3% 50-99. **Special facilities:** Wildlife sanctuary, outdoor Greek theater, arboretum, sculpture garden, aquatic center, college-operated museums.

Freshman class profile. 1,725 applied, 1,007 admitted, 196 enrolled.

Mid 50% test scores		**GPA 2.0-2.99:**	31%
SAT critical reading:	480-590	**Rank in top quarter:**	61%
SAT math:	480-580	**Rank in top tenth:**	24%
SAT writing:	470-570	**End year in good standing:**	88%
ACT composite:	21-27	**Return as sophomores:**	74%
GPA 3.75 or higher:	17%	**Out-of-state:**	38%
GPA 3.50-3.74:	14%	**Live on campus:**	82%
GPA 3.0-3.49:	38%	**International:**	1%

Basis for selection. Secondary school curriculum and grades most important. Test scores important. Special talents, potential for academic and personal growth considered. Interview and essay recommended for all.

High school preparation. College-preparatory program recommended. 16 units required. Required and recommended units include English 4, mathematics 3, social studies 3, science 2 (laboratory 2), foreign language 2 and academic electives 3. Special natural science requirements for nuclear medicine and nursing.

2008-2009 Annual costs. Tuition/fees: $26,668. On-campus students pay $300 resident communication fee; continuing education program's average per-credit-hour cost, $570. Room/board: $9,009.

2008-2009 Financial aid. Need-based: 189 full-time freshmen applied for aid; 169 were judged to have need; 169 of these received aid. Average need met was 79%. Average scholarship/grant was $17,395; average loan $3,879. 63% of total undergraduate aid awarded as scholarships/grants, 37% as loans/jobs. **Non-need-based:** Scholarships awarded for academics, alumni affiliation, art, leadership, music/drama.

Application procedures. Admission: No deadline. $30 fee, may be waived for applicants with need, free for online applicants. Admission notification on a rolling basis beginning on or about 9/15. Must reply by May 1 or within 2 week(s) if notified thereafter. **Financial aid:** Priority date 5/1; no closing date. FAFSA required. Applicants notified on a rolling basis starting 1/1; must reply within 2 week(s) of notification.

Academics. Special study options: Accelerated study, combined bachelor's/graduate degree, cross-registration, distance learning, double major, dual enrollment of high school students, ESL, honors, independent study, internships, liberal arts/career combination, student-designed major, study abroad, teacher certification program, Washington semester, weekend college. **Credit/placement by examination:** AP, CLEP, IB, institutional tests. 18 credit hours maximum toward bachelor's degree. **Support services:** Reduced course load, remedial instruction, study skills assistance, tutoring, writing center.

Majors. Biology: General, biochemistry, environmental, genetics. **Business:** Accounting, business admin, marketing. **Communications:** General. **Computer sciences:** General. **Education:** Elementary, secondary. **Family/consumer sciences:** Food/nutrition. **Foreign languages:** Spanish. **Health:** Nuclear medical technology. **History:** General. **Interdisciplinary:** Neuroscience. **Math:** General. **Physical sciences:** Chemistry. **Psychology:** General. **Public administration:** Social work. **Social sciences:** Criminology, political science. **Visual/performing arts:** General, art, dance, dramatic, studio arts.

Most popular majors. Biology 12%, business/marketing 12%, health sciences 29%, psychology 12%.

Computing on campus. 195 workstations in dormitories, library, computer center, student center. Dormitories wired for high-speed internet access and linked to campus network. Commuter students can connect to campus network. Online course registration, online library, helpline, repair service, student web hosting, wireless network available.

Student life. Freshman orientation: Available. Preregistration for classes offered. 5-day academic and social program in August mandatory. 2-day academic testing and advising program in June suggested. **Policies:** Drinking under age 21 prohibited; honor philosophy exists. **Housing:** Guaranteed on-campus for all undergraduates. Special housing for disabled available. $100 fully refundable deposit. **Activities:** Concert band, campus ministries, choral groups, dance, drama, international student organizations, literary magazine, music ensembles, musical theater, radio station, student government, student newspaper, Amnesty International, Black Awareness Student Union, Best Buddies, Cedar Crest Christian Fellowship, Hillel Society, international student organization, Muslim student association, Peace Coalition, The Political Society, Sisters Inc.

Athletics. NCAA. **Intercollegiate:** Basketball W, cross-country W, field hockey W, lacrosse W, soccer W, softball W, tennis W, volleyball W. **Intramural:** Basketball W, soccer W, softball W, triathlon W, volleyball W. **Team name:** Falcons.

Student services. Adult student services, alcohol/substance abuse counseling, chaplain/spiritual director, career counseling, student employment services, financial aid counseling, health services, personal counseling, placement for graduates, women's services. **Physically disabled:** Services for visually, speech, hearing impaired.

Contact. E-mail: cccadmis@cedarcrest.edu
Phone: (610) 740-3780 Toll-free number: (800) 360-1222
Fax: (610) 606-4647
Judith Neyhart, Executive Vice President for Enrollment, Cedar Crest College, 100 College Drive, Allentown, PA 18104-6196

Central Pennsylvania College
Summerdale, Pennsylvania
www.centralpenn.edu **CB code: 1061**

- For-profit 4-year business and technical college
- Commuter campus in rural community
- 1,086 degree-seeking undergraduates: 43% part-time, 67% women, 20% African American, 2% Asian American, 5% Hispanic American, 1% Native American
- Application essay, interview required
- 61% graduate within 6 years

General. Founded in 1881. Regionally accredited. **Degrees:** 168 bachelor's, 116 associate awarded. **Location:** 5 miles from Harrisburg. **Calendar:** Trimester, extensive summer session. **Full-time faculty:** 24 total. **Part-time faculty:** 88 total. **Special facilities:** Student-staffed restaurant, travel agency, online campus store, mock courtroom, optometric room, multimedia lab, child-care facility, advanced technology education center, conference facility, crime lab.

Freshman class profile.

Out-of-state:	11%	**Live on campus:**	56%

Basis for selection. Open admission, but selective for some programs. High school achievement record very important for admission to physical therapist assistant and paralegal programs. Minimum SAT score of 900 (exclusive of Writing) required for admission into physical therapy assistant program. **Homeschooled:** Provide transcript of courses completed with grades and include parent/teacher/academy signatures. **Learning Disabled:** Students meet with academic dean to discuss provisions needed for individual learning experience.

2008-2009 Annual costs. Tuition/fees: $16,425. Room/board: $6,015. Books/supplies: $1,200. Personal expenses: $1,000.

Financial aid. Non-need-based: Scholarships awarded for academics, alumni affiliation, job skills, leadership, minority status, state residency.

Application procedures. Admission: Priority date 5/1; no deadline. No application fee. Admission notification on a rolling basis. **Financial aid:** Priority date 3/15; no closing date. FAFSA, institutional form required. Applicants notified on a rolling basis starting 2/1; must reply within 2 week(s) of notification.

Academics. Special study options: Distance learning, double major, dual enrollment of high school students, honors, independent study, internships, study abroad. **Credit/placement by examination:** AP, CLEP, IB, institutional tests. 15 credit hours maximum toward associate degree, 15 toward bachelor's. **Support services:** Learning center, reduced course load, remedial instruction, study skills assistance, tutoring, writing center.

Majors. Business: Accounting, business admin. **Communications:** General. **Computer sciences:** Computer science, web page design. **Legal studies:** General. **Protective services:** Criminal justice, emergency management/homeland security.

Most popular majors. Business/marketing 42%, communications/journalism 9%, computer/information sciences 16%, security/protective services 33%.

Computing on campus. 150 workstations in library, computer center. Dormitories wired for high-speed internet access and linked to campus network. Commuter students can connect to campus network. Online course registration, online library, helpline, wireless network available.

Student life. Freshman orientation: Mandatory. Preregistration for classes offered. **Policies:** Dress code, mandatory attendance, ethics policies, no alcohol or drugs. **Housing:** Guaranteed on-campus for freshmen. Apartments, wellness housing available. $250 deposit. All resident housing is either single-gender townhouses or apartments. **Activities:** Choral groups, literary magazine, student government, student newspaper, Debit Debit Credit, Gamma Beta Phi, Delta Epsilon Chi, technology club, Club MED, Toastmasters, Young Republicans.

Athletics. NJCAA. **Intercollegiate:** Basketball, bowling, golf. **Intramural:** Basketball, football (non-tackle), softball, tennis, volleyball. **Team name:** Silver Knights.

Student services. Adult student services, alcohol/substance abuse counseling, career counseling, student employment services, financial aid counseling, on-campus daycare, personal counseling, placement for graduates.

Contact. E-mail: admissions@centralpenn.edu
Phone: (717) 728-2201 Toll-free number: (800) 759-2727
Fax: (717) 732-5254
Heather Armstrong, Assistant Director of Admissions, Central Pennsylvania College, College Hill & Valley Roads, Summerdale, PA 17093-0309

Chatham University
Pittsburgh, Pennsylvania **CB member**
www.chatham.edu **CB code: 2081**

- Private 4-year university and liberal arts college for women
- Residential campus in large city
- 763 degree-seeking undergraduates: 11% part-time, 99% women, 11% African American, 1% Asian American, 2% Hispanic American, 7% international
- 1,080 degree-seeking graduate students
- 71% of applicants admitted
- Application essay required
- 52% graduate within 6 years

General. Founded in 1869. Regionally accredited. **Degrees:** 134 bachelor's awarded; master's, doctoral offered. **ROTC:** Army, Naval, Air Force. **Location:** 5 miles from downtown. **Calendar:** Semester, limited summer session. **Full-time faculty:** 88 total; 93% have terminal degrees, 4% minority, 68% women. **Part-time faculty:** 150 total; 11% minority, 70% women.

Class size: 70% < 20, 29% 20-39, 1% 50-99. **Special facilities:** Broadcast studio, science complex and greenhouse, proscenium theater, arboretum.

Freshman class profile. 638 applied, 450 admitted, 176 enrolled.

Mid 50% test scores		**GPA 2.0-2.99:**	19%
SAT critical reading:	480-590	**Rank in top quarter:**	50%
SAT math:	450-560	**Rank in top tenth:**	28%
ACT composite:	20-24	**Return as sophomores:**	70%
GPA 3.75 or higher:	30%	**Out-of-state:**	27%
GPA 3.50-3.74:	20%	**Live on campus:**	80%
GPA 3.0-3.49:	30%	**International:**	15%

Basis for selection. School achievement record, essays, and test scores most important, though test scores are not required. Students who do not submit SAT/ACT scores required to submit a graded writing sample and resume/list of activities. Portfolios may also be submitted. Activities, talents, volunteer work, paid work, alumnae relationship, class rank, recommendations considered. TOEFL or IELTS required for international students. Campus visit or interviews recommended for all.

High school preparation. College-preparatory program recommended. 11 units required; 15 recommended. Required and recommended units include English 4, mathematics 2-3, science 2-3 and foreign language 2. Require 3 units of social science.

2008-2009 Annual costs. Tuition/fees: $27,496. Required fees ($1,020) cover technology fee, which includes cost of HP tablet computer (required for all first-time first-year students) and the campus fee. Room/board: $8,286. Books/supplies: $860. Personal expenses: $2,862.

2008-2009 Financial aid. Need-based: 141 full-time freshmen applied for aid; 130 were judged to have need; 130 of these received aid. Average need met was 81%. Average scholarship/grant was $4,391; average loan $5,205. 52% of total undergraduate aid awarded as scholarships/grants, 48% as loans/jobs. **Non-need-based:** Awarded to 619 full-time undergraduates, including 163 freshmen. Scholarships awarded for academics, alumni affiliation, leadership, music/drama, state residency.

Application procedures. Admission: Priority date 3/15; deadline 8/1. $35 fee, may be waived for applicants with need, free for online applicants. Admission notification on a rolling basis beginning on or about 10/15. Must reply by May 1 or within 2 week(s) if notified thereafter. **Financial aid:** Priority date 5/1; no closing date. FAFSA required. Applicants notified on a rolling basis starting 2/15; must reply by 5/1 or within 2 week(s) of notification.

Academics. All students eligible through PACE Center to receive free tutoring in every course offered. Specialized courses offered for students having academic difficulties, as well as career preparation courses to help students choose a career path. **Special study options:** Accelerated study, combined bachelor's/graduate degree, cooperative education, cross-registration, distance learning, double major, dual enrollment of high school students, ESL, exchange student, honors, independent study, internships, liberal arts/career combination, semester at sea, student-designed major, study abroad, teacher certification program, Washington semester. Five-year bachelor's/master's programs on campus and with other institutions. **Credit/placement by examination:** AP, CLEP, IB. 12 credit hours maximum toward bachelor's degree. **Support services:** Learning center, reduced course load, remedial instruction, study skills assistance, tutoring, writing center.

Majors. Architecture: Interior. **Area/ethnic studies:** Women's. **Biology:** General, biochemistry. **Business:** Accounting, business admin, international, managerial economics, marketing. **Communications:** General, broadcast journalism, journalism, public relations. **Conservation:** Environmental science, environmental studies. **Education:** Early childhood, elementary. **Engineering:** General. **Foreign languages:** French, Spanish. **Health:** Nursing (RN). **History:** General. **Legal studies:** Prelaw. **Liberal arts:** Arts/sciences. **Math:** General. **Parks/recreation:** Exercise sciences. **Physical sciences:** Chemistry, physics. **Protective services:** Forensics. **Psychology:** General. **Public administration:** Policy analysis, social work. **Social sciences:** Economics, international relations, political science. **Visual/performing arts:** Art history/conservation, arts management, photography, studio arts. **Other:** Film and digitial technology.

Most popular majors. Biology 12%, English 8%, psychology 20%, visual/performing arts 14%.

Computing on campus. PC or laptop required. 300 workstations in dormitories, library, computer center. Dormitories wired for high-speed internet access and linked to campus network. Commuter students can connect to campus network. Online course registration, online library, helpline, repair service, student web hosting, wireless network available.

Student life. Freshman orientation: Mandatory. Preregistration for classes offered. Held immediately before classes begin in late August. Mini-orientations held during late spring and summer when students can register for courses. **Policies:** Honor code. **Housing:** Guaranteed on-campus for all undergraduates. Apartments, wellness housing available. $150 nonrefundable deposit, deadline 5/1. Intercultural residence hall, community service floor and environmental floor within larger residence hall available. **Activities:** Choral groups, dance, drama, international student organizations, literary magazine, music ensembles, musical theater, student government, student newspaper, Black student union, Christian Fellowship, Jewish organization, Feminist collective, Gateway student association, Green Horizons, Mortar Board, Students Against Sexual Oppression.

Athletics. NCAA. **Intercollegiate:** Basketball W, cross-country W, ice hockey W, soccer W, softball W, swimming W, tennis W, volleyball W, water polo W. **Team name:** Cougars.

Student services. Adult student services, chaplain/spiritual director, career counseling, services for economically disadvantaged, student employment services, financial aid counseling, health services, personal counseling, placement for graduates, women's services. **Physically disabled:** Services for visually, speech, hearing impaired.

Contact. E-mail: admissions@chatham.edu
Phone: (412) 365-1825 Toll-free number: (800) 837-1290
Fax: (412) 365-1609
Michael Poll, Vice President of Admissions, Chatham University, Woodland Road, Pittsburgh, PA 15232

Chestnut Hill College

Philadelphia, Pennsylvania — **CB member**
www.chc.edu — **CB code: 2082**

- Private 4-year liberal arts college affiliated with Roman Catholic Church
- Residential campus in very large city
- 1,277 degree-seeking undergraduates: 20% part-time, 70% women, 39% African American, 2% Asian American, 5% Hispanic American, 1% international
- 700 degree-seeking graduate students
- 72% of applicants admitted
- SAT or ACT (ACT writing optional), application essay required
- 55% graduate within 6 years; 30% enter graduate study

General. Founded in 1924. Regionally accredited. Extended campus at adjacent Sugar Loaf Hill. **Degrees:** 233 bachelor's awarded; master's, doctoral offered. **Location:** 17 miles from center city. **Calendar:** Semester, limited summer session. **Full-time faculty:** 76 total; 82% have terminal degrees, 8% minority, 68% women. **Part-time faculty:** 223 total; 28% have terminal degrees, 11% minority, 52% women. **Class size:** 84% < 20, 16% 20-39. **Special facilities:** Observatory, planetarium, Irish literature collection, multimedia center, smart classrooms.

Freshman class profile. 1,589 applied, 1,151 admitted, 196 enrolled.

Mid 50% test scores		**GPA 2.0-2.99:**	42%
SAT critical reading:	460-540	**Rank in top quarter:**	29%
SAT math:	470-540	**Rank in top tenth:**	9%
SAT writing:	440-530	**End year in good standing:**	85%
ACT composite:	19-20	**Return as sophomores:**	70%
GPA 3.75 or higher:	10%	**Out-of-state:**	33%
GPA 3.50-3.74:	9%	**Live on campus:**	70%
GPA 3.0-3.49:	38%	**International:**	1%

Basis for selection. Secondary school record, essay very important. Standardized test scores, recommendations, character, interview, extracurricular activities important. Alumni connection, talent, volunteer activity, work experience considered. Open admissions to accelerated program in the School of Continuing and Professional Studies. Students are placed in writing, math, and language courses on basis of placement tests administered by the college. **Homeschooled:** Must subscribe to a homeschool agency.

High school preparation. 16 units recommended. Recommended units include English 4, mathematics 3, social studies 4, science 3 and foreign language 2.

2009-2010 Annual costs. Tuition/fees: $27,100. Room/board: $8,800. Books/supplies: $1,000. Personal expenses: $1,400.

2008-2009 Financial aid. Need-based: 180 full-time freshmen applied for aid; 163 were judged to have need; 161 of these received aid. Average need met was 72%. Average scholarship/grant was $15,170; average loan $3,736. 38% of total undergraduate aid awarded as scholarships/grants, 62% as loans/jobs. **Non-need-based:** Awarded to 186 full-time undergraduates, including 61 freshmen. Scholarships awarded for academics, alumni affiliation, athletics, leadership, religious affiliation. **Additional information:** Application priority date 1/15 for merit-based scholarships.

Application procedures. Admission: Priority date 1/20; no deadline. $35 fee, may be waived for applicants with need. Admission notification on a rolling basis. Must reply by May 1 or within 3 week(s) if notified thereafter. **Financial aid:** Closing date 4/15. FAFSA required. Applicants notified on a rolling basis starting 1/31; must reply by 5/1 or within 3 week(s) of notification.

Academics. Montessori certification available with elementary and preelementary education. Secondary education certification available in major field of study. Interdisciplinary bachelor's degree in international business, language, and culture. **Special study options:** Combined bachelor's/graduate degree, cooperative education, cross-registration, double major, dual enrollment of high school students, ESL, exchange student, honors, independent study, internships, student-designed major, study abroad, teacher certification program. 2-2 double bachelor's program in biology or chemistry and medical technology with Thomas Jefferson University School of Allied Health Sciences, 3-2 BA/MS psychology, 3-2 BS/MS applied technology, 5-year BS/MEd elementary education with emphasis in special education, dual degree bachelor's in biology or chemistry, master's in physician assistant at Arcadia University, dual degree bachelor's in biology or chemistry, Doctor of Podiatric Medicine at Temple University. **Credit/placement by examination:** AP, CLEP, IB, institutional tests. 12 credit hours maximum toward bachelor's degree. **Support services:** Learning center, preadmission summer program, reduced course load, remedial instruction, study skills assistance, tutoring, writing center.

Majors. Biology: General, biochemistry, molecular. **Business:** Accounting, accounting/business management, business admin, communications, human resources, international, marketing. **Communications:** General. **Communications technology:** General. **Computer sciences:** General, information technology. **Conservation:** Environmental science. **Education:** Early childhood, elementary, multi-level teacher, music. **Family/consumer sciences:** Child care. **Foreign languages:** French, Spanish. **Health:** Health care admin. **History:** General. **Interdisciplinary:** Math/computer science. **Liberal arts:** Arts/sciences. **Math:** General. **Physical sciences:** Chemistry. **Protective services:** Forensics, law enforcement admin. **Psychology:** General. **Public administration:** Human services. **Social sciences:** Political science, sociology.

Most popular majors. Business/marketing 20%, education 12%, psychology 9%, public administration/social services 17%, security/protective services 12%.

Computing on campus. PC or laptop required. 40 workstations in library, computer center. Commuter students can connect to campus network. Helpline, wireless network available.

Student life. Freshman orientation: Available. Preregistration for classes offered. Held 2 or 3 times during the summer. Additional program held the few days before classes begin. **Housing:** Coed dorms, wellness housing available. $200 nonrefundable deposit, deadline 5/1. **Activities:** Jazz band, campus ministries, choral groups, drama, international student organizations, literary magazine, music ensembles, musical theater, radio station, student government, student newspaper, symphony orchestra, TV station, African-American awareness society, Caribbean Culture Club, ecology club, gay/straight alliance, hospitality club, Hispanics in Action, Mosaic of Cultures club, Students for Peace and Justice, College Democrats, College Republicans.

Athletics. NCAA. **Intercollegiate:** Baseball M, basketball, cross-country, golf, lacrosse W, soccer, softball W, tennis, volleyball W. **Team name:** Griffins.

Student services. Adult student services, alcohol/substance abuse counseling, chaplain/spiritual director, career counseling, financial aid counseling, health services, personal counseling.

Contact. E-mail: chcapply@chc.edu
Phone: (215) 248-7001 Toll-free number: (800) 248-0052
Fax: (215) 248-7082
Director of Admissions, School of Undergraduate Studies, Chestnut Hill College, 9601 Germantown Avenue, Philadelphia, PA 19118-2693

Cheyney University of Pennsylvania

Cheyney, Pennsylvania — **CB member**
www.cheyney.edu — **CB code: 2648**

- Public 4-year university
- Residential campus in small town
- 1,315 degree-seeking undergraduates: 7% part-time, 54% women
- 111 degree-seeking graduate students
- 34% of applicants admitted
- SAT or ACT, application essay required
- 31% graduate within 6 years

General. Founded in 1837. Regionally accredited. Courses offered at Philadelphia Urban Center. **Degrees:** 205 bachelor's awarded; master's offered. **ROTC:** Army. **Location:** 25 miles from Philadelphia. **Calendar:** Semester, limited summer session. **Full-time faculty:** 73 total; 66% have terminal degrees, 75% minority, 47% women. **Part-time faculty:** 27 total; 41% have terminal degrees, 82% minority, 59% women. **Special facilities:** Planetarium, weather station, theater arts center.

Freshman class profile. 2,644 applied, 912 admitted, 301 enrolled.

GPA 3.75 or higher:	1%	**Return as sophomores:**	62%
GPA 3.50-3.74:	4%	**Out-of-state:**	35%
GPA 3.0-3.49:	10%	**Live on campus:**	91%
GPA 2.0-2.99:	48%		

Basis for selection. Test scores, class rank, GPA, counselor recommendation, extracurricular activities important. 830 SAT (exclusive of Writing) or 17 ACT required. SAT Subject Tests recommended. Interview recommended.

High school preparation. 13 units required. Required units include English 4, mathematics 3, history 2, science 2 and foreign language 2.

2008-2009 Annual costs. Tuition/fees: $7,089; $15,127 out-of-state. Tuition for residents of MD, NY, NJ and DE is $10,716. Room/board: $7,156. Books/supplies: $1,300.

Financial aid. Non-need-based: Scholarships awarded for academics, athletics.

Application procedures. Admission: Priority date 6/15; deadline 3/31. $20 fee, may be waived for applicants with need. Admission notification on a rolling basis. **Financial aid:** Priority date 3/15; no closing date. FAFSA required. Applicants notified on a rolling basis starting 4/1; must reply within 2 week(s) of notification.

Academics. Health and physical education courses required of most students. **Special study options:** Cooperative education, cross-registration, distance learning, double major, independent study, internships, teacher certification program. **Credit/placement by examination:** AP, CLEP, institutional tests. 23 credit hours maximum toward bachelor's degree. **Support services:** Learning center, pre-admission summer program, reduced course load, remedial instruction, tutoring.

Majors. Biology: General. **Business:** Business admin, hospitality admin. **Communications:** General. **Computer sciences:** General. **Education:** Early childhood, elementary, special. **Family/consumer sciences:** Clothing/textiles. **Foreign languages:** French, Spanish. **Health:** Clinical lab science. **Interdisciplinary:** Biological/physical sciences. **Math:** General. **Parks/recreation:** Facilities management. **Physical sciences:** Chemistry. **Psychology:** General. **Social sciences:** General, economics, political science, sociology. **Visual/performing arts:** Art, dramatic. **Other:** Geographic information science.

Most popular majors. Business/marketing 29%, communications/journalism 13%, psychology 11%, social sciences 34%.

Computing on campus. 296 workstations in dormitories, library, computer center, student center. Dormitories wired for high-speed internet access and linked to campus network. Online course registration, helpline, repair service available.

Student life. Freshman orientation: Mandatory. **Policies:** Ecumenical services held on campus. **Housing:** Guaranteed on-campus for freshmen. Coed dorms, single-sex dorms available. $100 fully refundable deposit, deadline 5/11. Freshmen-only dormitory available. **Activities:** Bands, choral groups, dance, drama, film society, music ensembles, radio station, student government, student newspaper, TV station, Shades of Unity, Toastmasters, business club, education club, NAACP, Latino Students in Action, LaOriginale, Commuter Students Association.

Athletics. NCAA. **Intercollegiate:** Basketball, bowling W, cross-country, football (tackle) M, tennis W, track and field, volleyball W. **Intramural:** Basketball, football (tackle) M. **Team name:** Wolves.

Student services. Career counseling, student employment services, health services, personal counseling, placement for graduates, veterans' counselor.

Contact. E-mail: abrown@cheyney.edu
Phone: (610) 399-2275 Toll-free number: (800) 243-9639
Fax: (610) 399-2099
Angela Brown, Director of Admissions, Cheyney University of Pennsylvania, 1837 University Circle, Cheyney, PA 19319-0019

Clarion University of Pennsylvania

Clarion, Pennsylvania — **CB member**
www.clarion.edu — **CB code: 2649**

- Public 4-year business and teachers college
- Residential campus in small town
- 5,724 degree-seeking undergraduates: 11% part-time, 60% women, 6% African American, 1% Asian American, 1% Hispanic American, 1% international
- 927 degree-seeking graduate students
- 69% of applicants admitted
- SAT or ACT (ACT writing optional) required
- 51% graduate within 6 years

General. Founded in 1867. Regionally accredited. **Degrees:** 822 bachelor's, 130 associate awarded; master's offered. **ROTC:** Army. **Location:** 85 miles from Pittsburgh, 75 miles from Erie. **Calendar:** Semester, limited summer session. **Full-time faculty:** 245 total; 13% minority, 46% women. **Part-time faculty:** 91 total; 2% minority, 54% women. **Class size:** 22% < 20, 58% 20-39, 9% 40-49, 7% 50-99, 3% >100. **Special facilities:** Planetarium.

Freshman class profile. 4,365 applied, 2,999 admitted, 1,370 enrolled.

Mid 50% test scores		**Return as sophomores:**	75%
SAT critical reading:	420-520	**Out-of-state:**	5%
SAT math:	420-530	**Live on campus:**	89%
SAT writing:	410-510	**International:**	1%
Rank in top quarter:	28%	**Fraternities:**	1%
Rank in top tenth:	10%	**Sororities:**	6%

Basis for selection. School achievement record, class rank, GPA, test scores considered. Audition required of music program applicants; Nursing students must complete NLN entrance exam. **Homeschooled:** Transcript of courses and grades required.

High school preparation. 13 units required; 19 recommended. Required and recommended units include English 4, mathematics 3-4, social studies 3-4, science 3-4 (laboratory 1) and foreign language 2.

2008-2009 Annual costs. Tuition/fees: $7,104; $12,462 out-of-state. Tuition for incoming out-of-state residents with SAT of 1100 or higher and at least a 3.5 GPA or the top 20% of their graduating class is $7,766. Room/board: $6,068. Books/supplies: $850. Personal expenses: $2,200.

2007-2008 Financial aid. Need-based: 1,274 full-time freshmen applied for aid; 1,025 were judged to have need; 993 of these received aid. Average need met was 68%. Average scholarship/grant was $5,676; average loan $3,253. 52% of total undergraduate aid awarded as scholarships/grants, 48% as loans/jobs. **Non-need-based:** Awarded to 1,392 full-time undergraduates, including 413 freshmen. Scholarships awarded for academics, art, athletics, leadership, minority status, music/drama, state residency.

Application procedures. Admission: No deadline. $30 fee, may be waived for applicants with need. Admission notification on a rolling basis beginning on or about 9/1. **Financial aid:** Closing date 4/15. FAFSA required. Applicants notified on a rolling basis starting 3/1.

Academics. Special study options: Accelerated study, combined bachelor's/graduate degree, cooperative education, distance learning, double major, dual enrollment of high school students, honors, independent study, internships, liberal arts/career combination, study abroad, teacher certification program. Co-op program in engineering with two participating schools; co-op in speech pathology and audiology with Gallaudet University. Joint and collaborative programs in MSLS/JD, pharmacy, osteopathic medicine, nanotechnology, master of nursing, language, radiologic science, respiratory care and industrial technology. **Credit/placement by examination:** AP, CLEP, IB, institutional tests. 38 credit hours maximum toward bachelor's degree. **Support services:** Learning center, pre-admission summer program, remedial instruction, study skills assistance, tutoring, writing center.

Majors. Biology: General, molecular. **Business:** Accounting, business admin, finance, international, labor relations, managerial economics, marketing, real estate. **Communications:** General. **Computer sciences:** General, information systems. **Conservation:** Environmental science. **Education:** Early childhood, elementary, special. **Foreign languages:** French, Spanish. **Health:** Audiology/speech pathology, clinical lab technology, medical radiologic technology/radiation therapy, nursing (RN). **History:** General. **Interdisciplinary:** Biological/physical sciences. **Liberal arts:** Arts/sciences, library science. **Math:** General, applied. **Philosophy/religion:** Philosophy. **Physical sciences:** Chemistry, geology, physics. **Psychology:** General, social. **Social sciences:** Anthropology, economics, political science, sociology. **Visual/performing arts:** Art, dramatic, music management.

Most popular majors. Business/marketing 10%, communications/journalism 10%, education 19%, health sciences 12%, liberal arts 7%, social sciences 6%.

Computing on campus. 1,143 workstations in dormitories, library, computer center, student center. Dormitories wired for high-speed internet access and linked to campus network. Commuter students can connect to campus network. Online course registration, online library, helpline, student web hosting, wireless network available.

Student life. Freshman orientation: Mandatory, $150 fee. Preregistration for classes offered. One-day session held in January, spring and summer. **Policies:** Students who live on campus are guaranteed a room on campus the following year. **Housing:** Coed dorms, single-sex dorms, apartments, fraternity/sorority housing, wellness housing available. $100 nonrefundable deposit. **Activities:** Bands, choral groups, dance, drama, literary magazine, music ensembles, musical theater, radio station, student government, student newspaper, TV station, Koinonia Christian Fellowship, African American Caucus, Newman Association, Hip Hop Dance Team, NAACP, Young Democrats, Eagle Ambassadors, People Reaching Out and Understanding Disabilities, Students Together Against Rape, University Activities Board.

Athletics. NCAA. **Intercollegiate:** Baseball M, basketball, cross-country W, diving, football (tackle) M, golf M, soccer W, softball W, swimming, tennis W, track and field W, volleyball W, wrestling M. **Intramural:** Badminton, basketball, bowling, golf, racquetball, soccer, softball, swimming, table tennis, tennis, track and field, volleyball, water polo, wrestling. **Team name:** Golden Eagles.

Student services. Adult student services, alcohol/substance abuse counseling, chaplain/spiritual director, career counseling, services for economically disadvantaged, student employment services, financial aid counseling, health services, minority student services, on-campus daycare, personal counseling, placement for graduates, veterans' counselor, women's services. **Physically disabled:** Services for visually, speech, hearing impaired.

Contact. E-mail: admissions@clarion.edu
Phone: (814) 393-2306 Toll-free number: (800) 672-7171
Fax: (814) 393-2030
William Bailey, Dean of Enrollment Management, Clarion University of Pennsylvania, 840 Wood Street, Clarion, PA 16214

Curtis Institute of Music

Philadelphia, Pennsylvania
www.curtis.edu — **CB code: 2100**

- Private 4-year music college
- Commuter campus in very large city
- 132 degree-seeking undergraduates: 46% women, 5% African American, 11% Asian American, 2% Hispanic American, 39% international
- 29 degree-seeking graduate students
- 11% of applicants admitted
- SAT required
- 75% graduate within 6 years

General. Founded in 1924. Regionally accredited. **Degrees:** 21 bachelor's awarded; master's offered. **Calendar:** Semester. **Full-time faculty:** 1 total; 100% women. **Part-time faculty:** 93 total; 9% have terminal degrees, 12% minority, 33% women. **Special facilities:** More than 82,000 titles in audio-visual materials, sheet music, and books.

Freshman class profile. 243 applied, 26 admitted, 22 enrolled.

End year in good standing:	100%	**Out-of-state:**	81%
Return as sophomores:	100%	**International:**	20%

Basis for selection. Admission based on audition. Preference given to applicants demonstrating potential rather than proficiency. Test scores considered for applicants to bachelor's degree program. **Homeschooled:** Transcript of courses and grades, state high school equivalency certificate required.

High school preparation. Major emphasis on applied music activities.

2008-2009 Annual costs. All students awarded a full-tuition scholarship. For 2008-09, Bachelor of Music, required fees $2,185 and additional expenses $16,560,which covers supplies, off-campus room/board, and miscellaneous expenses for the academic year. All other students pay $2,085 (required fees) for academic year. Students required to have adequate health insurance coverage. Curtis can provide comprehensive health insurance policy for about $2,300 for 12 months of coverage.

2008-2009 Financial aid. All financial aid based on need. Average need met was 80%. Average scholarship/grant was $7,016; average loan $3,832. 53% of total undergraduate aid awarded as scholarships/grants, 47% as loans/jobs. **Additional information:** All admitted students receive a full tuition scholarship. The estimated value of this scholarship is $33,500.

Application procedures. Admission: Closing date 12/11 (postmark date). $150 fee, may be waived for applicants with need. Application must be submitted on paper. Admission notification 4/1. Must reply by 5/1. **Financial aid:** Priority date 3/1; no closing date. FAFSA, institutional form required. Applicants notified by 4/1; must reply by 5/1 or within 2 week(s) of notification.

Academics. Special study options: Double major, ESL. **Credit/placement by examination:** AP, CLEP, institutional tests. 47 credit hours maximum toward bachelor's degree. **Support services:** Remedial instruction, study skills assistance, tutoring.

Majors. Visual/performing arts: Music performance, music theory/composition.

Computing on campus. 16 workstations in library, computer center, student center. Online library, repair service, wireless network available.

Student life. Freshman orientation: Mandatory. Preregistration for classes offered. Orientation for international students begins 2 weeks before classes start. The general orientation for all students (including international students) begins 1 week before classes begin. **Housing:** Apartments available. **Activities:** Music ensembles, opera, student government, symphony orchestra.

Student services. Alcohol/substance abuse counseling, career counseling, financial aid counseling, health services, personal counseling, veterans' counselor.

Contact. E-mail: admissions@curtis.edu
Phone: (215) 893-5262 Fax: (215) 893-7900
Christopher Hodges, Admissions Officer, Curtis Institute of Music, 1726 Locust Street, Philadelphia, PA 19103-6187

Delaware Valley College

Doylestown, Pennsylvania — **CB member**
www.delval.edu — **CB code: 2510**

- Private 4-year agricultural and liberal arts college
- Residential campus in large town
- 1,798 degree-seeking undergraduates: 9% part-time, 60% women, 3% African American, 1% Asian American, 2% Hispanic American
- 130 degree-seeking graduate students
- 71% of applicants admitted
- Application essay required
- 50% graduate within 6 years; 15% enter graduate study

General. Founded in 1896. Regionally accredited. **Degrees:** 332 bachelor's, 4 associate awarded; master's offered. **Location:** 20 miles from Philadelphia, 70 miles from New York City. **Calendar:** Semester, extensive summer session. **Full-time faculty:** 84 total; 61% have terminal degrees, 8% minority, 40% women. **Part-time faculty:** 112 total; 13% have terminal degrees, 4% minority, 33% women. **Class size:** 57% < 20, 35% 20-39, 5% 40-49, 3% 50-99, less than 1% >100. **Special facilities:** Equine facility with indoor and outdoor arenas, animal farms, dairy, farm market, arboretum greenhouses, tissue culture laboratories.

Freshman class profile. 1,847 applied, 1,303 admitted, 430 enrolled.

Mid 50% test scores			
SAT critical reading:	460-550	Rank in top quarter:	37%
SAT math:	470-560	Rank in top tenth:	13%
SAT writing:	440-540	End year in good standing:	92%
ACT composite:	20-23	Return as sophomores:	74%
GPA 3.75 or higher:	34%	Out-of-state:	45%
GPA 3.50-3.74:	17%	Live on campus:	89%
GPA 3.0-3.49:	35%	Fraternities:	4%
GPA 2.0-2.99:	14%	Sororities:	5%

Basis for selection. Academic achievement, class rank, test scores, letters of recommendation from math or science teacher and guidance counselor, grades in math and science considered. Interview, essay recommended. **Homeschooled:** State high school equivalency certificate required.

High school preparation. College-preparatory program required. 15 units required. Required units include English 3, mathematics 2, social studies 2, science 2 (laboratory 1) and academic electives 6. For business administration 1 unit science only. Agriculture, biology, and chemistry majors need 6 additional units, business majors 7.

2008-2009 Annual costs. Tuition/fees: $27,078. Room/board: $9,502. Books/supplies: $1,000. Personal expenses: $900.

2007-2008 Financial aid. Need-based: 385 full-time freshmen applied for aid; 333 were judged to have need; 333 of these received aid. Average need met was 69%. Average scholarship/grant was $14,578; average loan $3,240. 78% of total undergraduate aid awarded as scholarships/grants, 22% as loans/jobs. **Non-need-based:** Awarded to 534 full-time undergraduates, including 168 freshmen. Scholarships awarded for academics, alumni affiliation, music/drama.

Application procedures. Admission: Priority date 5/1; no deadline. $35 fee, may be waived for applicants with need, free for online applicants. Admission notification on a rolling basis beginning on or about 10/31. Must reply by May 1 or within 4 week(s) if notified thereafter. **Financial aid:** Priority date 4/1; no closing date. FAFSA required. Applicants notified on a rolling basis starting 2/1; must reply by 5/1.

Academics. Students complete 500-hour employment program related to major. **Special study options:** Accelerated study, combined bachelor's/graduate degree, cooperative education, cross-registration, distance learning, double major, honors, independent study, internships, study abroad, teacher certification program, weekend college. **Credit/placement by examination:** AP, CLEP, institutional tests. Credit for 5 courses may be granted through examination. **Support services:** Learning center, pre-admission summer program, reduced course load, remedial instruction, study skills assistance, tutoring, writing center.

Majors. Agriculture: Agribusiness operations, agronomy, animal sciences, crop production, dairy, food science, horticultural science, ornamental horticulture, turf management. **Biology:** General, zoology. **Business:** Accounting, business admin, management information systems, marketing. **Computer sciences:** General. **Conservation:** Wildlife. **Education:** Secondary. **Math:** General. **Physical sciences:** Chemistry. **Protective services:** Law enforcement admin. **Psychology:** Counseling.

Most popular majors. Agriculture 43%, biology 11%, business/marketing 21%, natural resources/environmental science 6%, security/protective services 10%.

Computing on campus. 150 workstations in dormitories, library, computer center, student center. Dormitories wired for high-speed internet access and linked to campus network. Online library, helpline, repair service, wireless network available.

Student life. Freshman orientation: Mandatory. **Housing:** Guaranteed on-campus for freshmen. Coed dorms, single-sex dorms available. $200 deposit, deadline 5/1. **Activities:** Concert band, choral groups, drama, literary magazine, music ensembles, radio station, student government, student newspaper, Christian Fellowship, Hillel, Future Farmers of America, Minority Leadership Coalition, environmental awareness club, Alpha Phi Omega, DVC Volunteer Corps, Newman Club, equine club, business club.

Athletics. NCAA. **Intercollegiate:** Baseball M, basketball, cheerleading M, cross-country, field hockey W, football (tackle) M, golf M, soccer, softball W, track and field, volleyball W, wrestling M. **Intramural:** Basketball, equestrian, football (tackle) M, softball, volleyball. **Team name:** Aggies.

Student services. Adult student services, career counseling, student employment services, health services, personal counseling, placement for graduates. **Physically disabled:** Services for visually, speech, hearing impaired.

Contact. E-mail: admitme@delval.edu
Phone: (215) 489-2211 Toll-free number: (800) 2DE-LVAL
Fax: (215) 230-2968
Stephen Zenko, Director of Admissions, Delaware Valley College, 700 East Butler Avenue, Doylestown, PA 18901-2697

DeSales University

Center Valley, Pennsylvania — **CB member**
www.desales.edu — **CB code: 2021**

- Private 4-year university affiliated with Roman Catholic Church
- Residential campus in small town
- 2,389 degree-seeking undergraduates: 24% part-time, 60% women, 2% African American, 2% Asian American, 3% Hispanic American
- 773 degree-seeking graduate students
- 75% of applicants admitted
- SAT or ACT required
- 68% graduate within 6 years; 26% enter graduate study

General. Founded in 1964. Regionally accredited. **Degrees:** 420 bachelor's awarded; master's offered. **ROTC:** Army. **Location:** 7 miles from Allentown, 50 miles from Philadelphia. **Calendar:** Semester, limited summer session. **Full-time faculty:** 100 total; 73% have terminal degrees, 10% minority, 47% women. **Part-time faculty:** 125 total; 22% have terminal degrees, 37% women.

Freshman class profile. 1,975 applied, 1,473 admitted, 402 enrolled.

Mid 50% test scores			
SAT critical reading:	490-600	Rank in top quarter:	52%
SAT math:	490-600	Rank in top tenth:	22%
SAT writing:	480-590	Return as sophomores:	84%
ACT composite:	19-25	Out-of-state:	36%
		Live on campus:	90%

Basis for selection. High school achievement most important. Test scores and recommendations also considered. Essay, interview recommended for all; audition required for dance, theater programs. Interview required for physician assistant program.

High school preparation. 16 units required; 18 recommended. Required and recommended units include English 4, mathematics 3-4, social studies 3-4, science 2 (laboratory 2) and foreign language 2. Biology, chemistry, 3 math recommended for biology major. 3 math, including 2 algebra, recommended for business major. Chemistry, physics, 3 math recommended for chemistry major. Biology, chemistry, physics, 2 math recommended for nursing major. 2 biology, chemistry, or physics, and 3 math recommended for pre-med major. 4 math recommended for math major.

2008-2009 Annual costs. Tuition/fees: $25,800. Room/board: $9,330. Books/supplies: $1,200. Personal expenses: $3,000.

2008-2009 Financial aid. **Need-based:** Average need met was 65%. Average scholarship/grant was $9,146; average loan $3,322. 53% of total undergraduate aid awarded as scholarships/grants, 47% as loans/jobs. **Non-need-based:** Scholarships awarded for academics, leadership, music/drama.

Application procedures. **Admission:** Priority date 3/1; deadline 8/1. $30 fee, may be waived for applicants with need. Admission notification on a rolling basis. Must reply by May 1 or within 2 week(s) if notified thereafter. **Financial aid:** Priority date 2/1, closing date 5/1. FAFSA required. Applicants notified on a rolling basis starting 2/15; must reply by 5/1 or within 2 week(s) of notification.

Academics. **Special study options:** Accelerated study, cross-registration, distance learning, double major, dual enrollment of high school students, ESL, honors, independent study, internships, liberal arts/career combination, semester at sea, study abroad, teacher certification program, weekend college. BS in medical studies, MS in physician assistant studies; cross-registration at consortium schools: Cedar Crest, Moravian, Muhlenberg, Lafayette, Lehigh. **Credit/placement by examination:** AP, CLEP, institutional tests. 24 credit hours maximum toward bachelor's degree. For AP credit for Physics B must complete lab component. Must submit research paper for CLEP English Composition with Essay to obtain 6 credits. **Support services:** Learning center, pre-admission summer program, reduced course load, study skills assistance, tutoring.

Majors. **Biology:** General, biochemistry. **Business:** General, accounting, business admin, e-commerce, finance, human resources, management information systems, management science, marketing. **Communications:** General. **Computer sciences:** General, computer science. **Conservation:** Environmental science. **Education:** Elementary, special. **Foreign languages:** Spanish. **Health:** Clinical lab science, nursing (RN), physician assistant. **History:** General. **Legal studies:** General. **Liberal arts:** Arts/sciences. **Math:** General. **Parks/recreation:** Exercise sciences, sports admin. **Philosophy/religion:** Philosophy. **Physical sciences:** Chemistry. **Protective services:** Criminal justice. **Psychology:** General. **Social sciences:** Political science. **Theology:** Theology. **Visual/performing arts:** Dance, dramatic, film/cinema.

Most popular majors. Business/marketing 23%, education 8%, health sciences 19%, parks/recreation 6%, security/protective services 8%, visual/performing arts 9%.

Computing on campus. 150 workstations in library, computer center, student center. Dormitories wired for high-speed internet access and linked to campus network. Commuter students can connect to campus network. Online course registration, online library, helpline, student web hosting, wireless network available.

Student life. **Freshman orientation:** Mandatory, $200 fee. Preregistration for classes offered. One-day academic orientation in June; 4-day social and academic orientation in August. **Policies:** Students under 21 cannot possess or be in presence of alcohol. Access to dorm rooms of opposite sex restricted during certain hours. **Housing:** Guaranteed on-campus for all undergraduates. Single-sex dorms, wellness housing available. Town houses for upperclassmen, common-interest housing available. **Activities:** Pep band, campus ministries, choral groups, dance, drama, film society, international student organizations, literary magazine, music ensembles, Model UN, musical theater, radio station, student government, student newspaper, TV station, pro-life club, accounting and finance club, Habitat For Humanity, Spanish Alliance, Best Buddies, Esto Vir, Lion's Club, natural science club.

Athletics. NCAA. **Intercollegiate:** Baseball M, basketball, cross-country, field hockey W, golf M, lacrosse M, soccer, softball W, tennis, track and field, volleyball W. **Intramural:** Basketball, football (non-tackle), soccer, softball, volleyball. **Team name:** Bulldogs.

Student services. Adult student services, alcohol/substance abuse counseling, chaplain/spiritual director, career counseling, services for economically disadvantaged, student employment services, financial aid counseling, health services, minority student services, personal counseling, placement for graduates, veterans' counselor.

Contact. E-mail: admiss@desales.edu
Phone: (610) 282-4443 Toll-free number: (877) 433-7253
Fax: (610) 282-0131
Mary Birkhead, Dean of Enrollment Management, DeSales University, 2755 Station Avenue, Center Valley, PA 18034-9568

DeVry University: Fort Washington

Fort Washington, Pennsylvania
www.devry.edu **CB code: 3866**

- For-profit 4-year university
- Commuter campus in large town
- 889 degree-seeking undergraduates: 49% part-time, 34% women, 39% African American, 4% Asian American, 6% Hispanic American, 1% international
- 156 degree-seeking graduate students
- Interview required

General. **Degrees:** 122 bachelor's, 20 associate awarded; master's offered. **Location:** 35 miles from Philadelphia. **Calendar:** Semester, extensive summer session. **Full-time faculty:** 26 total; 31% minority, 31% women. **Part-time faculty:** 145 total; 12% minority, 46% women.

Basis for selection. Applicants must have high school diploma or equivalent, or a degree from accredited postsecondary institution, demonstrate proficiency in basic college-level skills through SAT or ACT scores or institution-administered placement exams, and be at least 17 years of age on the first day of classes. New students may enter at beginning of any semester. CPT also accepted.

High school preparation. Math unit must be algebra or higher.

2008-2009 Annual costs. Tuition/fees: $14,800. Books/supplies: $1,300. Personal expenses: $5,082.

2007-2008 Financial aid. All financial aid based on need.

Application procedures. **Admission:** No deadline. $50 fee. Admission notification on a rolling basis. **Financial aid:** No deadline. FAFSA required. Applicants notified on a rolling basis.

Academics. **Special study options:** Accelerated study, distance learning. **Credit/placement by examination:** CLEP. **Support services:** Learning center, remedial instruction, tutoring.

Majors. **Business:** Business admin. **Computer sciences:** Networking, systems analysis. **Engineering:** Software. **Engineering technology:** Biomedical, computer, electrical. **Other:** Technical management.

Most popular majors. Business/marketing 51%, computer/information sciences 30%, engineering/engineering technologies 18%.

Computing on campus. 407 workstations in library, computer center. Online course registration, online library, helpline available.

Student life. **Freshman orientation:** Mandatory. **Activities:** Campus Crusade for Christ, electronic gamers club, creative arts club.

Athletics. **Intramural:** Volleyball.

Student services. Career counseling, student employment services, financial aid counseling, placement for graduates, veterans' counselor. **Physically disabled:** Services for visually, hearing impaired.

Four-Year Colleges

Contact. E-mail: admissions@phi.devry.edu
Phone: (215) 591-5701 Toll-free number: (866) 303-3879
Fax: (215) 591-5745
Steve Cohen, Director of Admission, DeVry University: Fort Washington, 1140 Virginia Drive, Fort Washington, PA 19034-3204

Dickinson College

Carlisle, Pennsylvania **CB member**
www.dickinson.edu **CB code: 2186**

- Private 4-year liberal arts college
- Residential campus in large town
- 2,364 degree-seeking undergraduates: 55% women, 4% African American, 5% Asian American, 5% Hispanic American, 6% international
- 44% of applicants admitted
- Application essay required
- 84% graduate within 6 years; 35% enter graduate study

General. Founded in 1783. Regionally accredited. **Degrees:** 528 bachelor's awarded. **ROTC:** Army. **Location:** 100 miles from Philadelphia, 90 miles from Washington, DC. **Calendar:** Semester, limited summer session. **Full-time faculty:** 194 total; 92% have terminal degrees, 9% minority, 43% women. **Part-time faculty:** 46 total; 52% have terminal degrees, 6% minority, 44% women. **Class size:** 68% < 20, 31% 20-39, 2% 40-49. **Special facilities:** Arts center, planetarium and multiple telescope observatory, intercontinental satellite communications for study-abroad programs, study of contemporary issues center.

Freshman class profile. 5,282 applied, 2,334 admitted, 613 enrolled.

Mid 50% test scores		End year in good standing:	98%
SAT critical reading:	600-700	Return as sophomores:	92%
SAT math:	590-690	Out-of-state:	78%
ACT composite:	26-31	Live on campus:	100%
Rank in top quarter:	87%	International:	5%
Rank in top tenth:	50%		

Basis for selection. Academic potential as shown by school achievement record most important. Extracurricular activities very important. Counselor recommendation required. Motivation, personal character considered. Special consideration given to applicants of color. Preference given to academically qualified children of alumni if they satisfy above criteria. Standardized tests optional. SAT or ACT recommended. Interview recommended.

High school preparation. College-preparatory program recommended. 16 units required. Required and recommended units include English 4, mathematics 3, social studies 2, science 3 (laboratory 2), foreign language 2-3 and academic electives 2.

2009-2010 Annual costs. Tuition/fees: $40,139. Room/board: $10,080. Books/supplies: $1,000. Personal expenses: $1,200.

2008-2009 Financial aid. Need-based: 392 full-time freshmen applied for aid; 307 were judged to have need; 305 of these received aid. Average need met was 98%. Average scholarship/grant was $26,387; average loan $3,887. 79% of total undergraduate aid awarded as scholarships/grants, 21% as loans/jobs. **Non-need-based:** Awarded to 306 full-time undergraduates, including 100 freshmen. Scholarships awarded for academics, leadership, ROTC.

Application procedures. Admission: Closing date 2/1 (postmark date). $65 fee, may be waived for applicants with need. Admission notification 3/31. Must reply by May 1 or within 2 week(s) if notified thereafter. **Financial aid:** Closing date 2/1. FAFSA, CSS PROFILE required. Applicants notified by 3/31; must reply by 5/1 or within 2 week(s) of notification.

Academics. Certificates in interdepartmental programs offered in Latin American studies in conjunction with bachelor's degree. Prebusiness, prelaw and premedical preparation available in conjunction with majors listed. **Special study options:** Accelerated study, combined bachelor's/graduate degree, cross-registration, double major, ESL, exchange student, independent study, internships, liberal arts/career combination, student-designed major, study abroad, teacher certification program, Washington semester. 3-2 engineering programs with University of Pennsylvania, Case Western Reserve University, Rensselaer Polytechnic Institute; 3-3 law degree with Dickinson School of Law of Penn State University. **Credit/placement by examination:** AP, CLEP, IB, institutional tests. **Support services:** Tutoring, writing center.

Majors. Area/ethnic studies: African, American, East Asian, Italian, Near/Middle Eastern, women's. **Biology:** General, biochemistry. **Business:** International. **Computer sciences:** General. **Conservation:** Environmental science, environmental studies. **Foreign languages:** Classics, French, German, Italian, Russian, Spanish. **History:** General. **Interdisciplinary:** Medieval/Renaissance, neuroscience. **Legal studies:** General, prelaw. **Math:** General. **Philosophy/religion:** Judaic, philosophy, religion. **Physical sciences:** Chemistry, geology, physics. **Psychology:** General. **Public administration:** Policy analysis. **Social sciences:** Anthropology, archaeology, economics, international relations, political science, sociology. **Visual/performing arts:** Dramatic, studio arts. **Other:** Dance and music.

Most popular majors. Area/ethnic studies 8%, biology 7%, business/marketing 9%, English 7%, foreign language 7%, psychology 7%, social sciences 26%.

Computing on campus. 621 workstations in dormitories, library, computer center, student center. Dormitories wired for high-speed internet access and linked to campus network. Commuter students can connect to campus network. Online course registration, online library, helpline, repair service, wireless network available.

Student life. Freshman orientation: Mandatory. Preregistration for classes offered. **Housing:** Guaranteed on-campus for all undergraduates. Coed dorms, special housing for disabled, apartments, fraternity/sorority housing available. Foreign language, arts, environmental, multicultural housing available. **Activities:** Bands, choral groups, dance, drama, film society, international student organizations, literary magazine, music ensembles, Model UN, musical theater, radio station, student government, student newspaper, symphony orchestra, public affairs, social service, religious, multicultural, foreign student organizations, College Democrats, Young Republicans, debate club.

Athletics. NCAA. **Intercollegiate:** Baseball M, basketball, cross-country, field hockey W, football (tackle) M, golf, lacrosse, soccer, softball W, swimming, tennis, track and field, volleyball W. **Intramural:** Badminton, basketball M, bowling M, field hockey W, football (non-tackle) M, football (tackle) M, golf, racquetball, soccer, softball, squash, table tennis, tennis, volleyball M. **Team name:** Red Devils.

Student services. Adult student services, alcohol/substance abuse counseling, career counseling, student employment services, financial aid counseling, health services, minority student services, on-campus daycare, personal counseling, placement for graduates. **Physically disabled:** Services for visually, speech, hearing impaired.

Contact. E-mail: admit@dickinson.edu
Phone: (717) 245-1231 Toll-free number: (800) 644-1773
Fax: (717) 245-1442
Stephanie Balmer, Dean of Admissions and Financial Aid, Dickinson College, PO Box 1773, Carlisle, PA 17013-2896

Drexel University

Philadelphia, Pennsylvania **CB member**
www.drexel.edu **CB code: 2194**

- Private 5-year university
- Commuter campus in very large city
- 13,139 degree-seeking undergraduates: 17% part-time, 45% women, 8% African American, 12% Asian American, 3% Hispanic American, 6% international
- 7,843 degree-seeking graduate students
- 68% of applicants admitted
- SAT or ACT (ACT writing optional) required

General. Founded in 1891. Regionally accredited. Most undergraduate programs require up to 18 months work experience within 5-year program of study. **Degrees:** 2,488 bachelor's, 30 associate awarded; master's, doctoral, first professional offered. **ROTC:** Army, Naval, Air Force. **Calendar:** Quarter, extensive summer session. **Class size:** 51% < 20, 40% 20-39, 3% 40-49, 5% 50-99, 2% >100. **Special facilities:** Art collection, observatory, rifle range.

Freshman class profile. 21,454 applied, 14,621 admitted, 2,577 enrolled.

Mid 50% test scores			
SAT critical reading:	540-630	GPA 2.0-2.99:	11%
SAT math:	570-660	Rank in top quarter:	62%
ACT composite:	23-28	Rank in top tenth:	31%
GPA 3.75 or higher:	33%	Out-of-state:	54%
GPA 3.50-3.74:	24%	Live on campus:	87%
GPA 3.0-3.49:	32%	International:	9%

Basis for selection. Academic average, counselor's recommendation and test scores most important, followed by class rank, school, community and church activities. Employment also considered. Essay required for most majors for media arts and design programs. Portfolio required for graphic design, music industry, photography and fashion design. Audition required for dance.

High school preparation. Required and recommended units include mathematics 3, science 1 (laboratory 1) and foreign language 1. Engineering applicants required to have 4 units math (including algebra I and II, geometry, trigonometry, and pre-calculus) and 2 units lab science (including chemistry and physics). Science applicants required to have 4 units math (including algebra I and II, geometry, and trigonometry) and 2 units lab science (including biology, chemistry, or physics). Most other applicants must have algebra I and II and geometry as required math units and one lab science.

2009-2010 Annual costs. Tuition/fees: $31,835. Tuition listed is for 5-year program with co-op quarter terms. Room/board: $12,680. Books/supplies: $1,875. Personal expenses: $3,050.

2008-2009 Financial aid. Non-need-based: Scholarships awarded for academics, alumni affiliation, art, athletics, leadership, music/drama, ROTC.

Application procedures. Admission: Closing date 3/1 (postmark date). $75 fee, may be waived for applicants with need, free for online applicants. Admission notification on a rolling basis. Must reply by May 1 or within 2 week(s) if notified thereafter. **Financial aid:** Closing date 3/1. FAFSA required. Applicants notified on a rolling basis starting 3/15.

Academics. Special study options: Accelerated study, combined bachelor's/graduate degree, cooperative education, distance learning, double major, ESL, honors, independent study, internships, semester at sea, study abroad, teacher certification program, weekend college. 3-3 programs in engineering with Lincoln University, Indiana University of Pennsylvania and Eastern Mennonite College. **Credit/placement by examination:** AP, CLEP, IB, institutional tests. 30 credit hours maximum toward bachelor's degree. **Support services:** Learning center, pre-admission summer program, reduced course load, remedial instruction, study skills assistance, tutoring, writing center.

Majors. Architecture: Architecture. **Biology:** General. **Business:** General, hotel/motel admin, managerial economics. **Computer sciences:** Computer science, information systems, security, web page design. **Conservation:** Environmental science, environmental studies. **Engineering:** Architectural, biomedical, chemical, civil, computer, construction, electrical, environmental, industrial, materials, mechanical, software. **Engineering technology:** General. **Health:** Clinical lab assistant, health care admin, nursing (RN), physician assistant, substance abuse counseling. **History:** General. **Interdisciplinary:** Biological/physical sciences, nutrition sciences. **Liberal arts:** Humanities. **Math:** General. **Parks/recreation:** Sports admin. **Personal/culinary services:** Chef training, restaurant/catering. **Physical sciences:** Chemistry, physics. **Protective services:** Law enforcement admin. **Psychology:** General. **Social sciences:** Anthropology, international relations, political science, sociology. **Visual/performing arts:** Cinematography, dance, design, fashion design, graphic design, interior design, photography, play/screenwriting, theater arts management. **Other:** Communications and applied technology, Design and merchandising.

Most popular majors. Business/marketing 22%, computer/information sciences 10%, engineering/engineering technologies 22%, health sciences 19%, visual/performing arts 8%.

Computing on campus. PC or laptop required. 610 workstations in dormitories, library, computer center, student center. Dormitories wired for high-speed internet access and linked to campus network. Commuter students can connect to campus network. Online course registration, online library, helpline, repair service, student web hosting, wireless network available.

Student life. Freshman orientation: Available. Preregistration for classes offered. 2-day overnight sessions held in July; 3-day program prior to start of classes. **Policies:** Freshmen required to live on campus unless living with parents. **Housing:** Guaranteed on-campus for freshmen. Coed dorms, special housing for disabled, apartments, fraternity/sorority housing available. $200 nonrefundable deposit, deadline 7/1. **Activities:** Bands, campus ministries, choral groups, dance, drama, film society, literary magazine, music ensembles, musical theater, radio station, student government, student newspaper, TV station, Newman Center, Hillel, Alpha Phi Omega, NAACP, Eye Openers, Disciples in Deed, Drexel Christian Fellowship, Jewish Heritage Program.

Athletics. NCAA. **Intercollegiate:** Basketball, diving, field hockey W, golf M, lacrosse, rowing (crew), soccer, softball W, swimming, tennis, wrestling M. **Intramural:** Badminton, basketball, football (non-tackle), soccer, softball, squash, table tennis, tennis, volleyball. **Team name:** Dragons.

Student services. Adult student services, career counseling, student employment services, financial aid counseling, health services, minority student services, personal counseling, placement for graduates. **Physically disabled:** Services for visually, speech, hearing impaired.

Contact. E-mail: enroll@drexel.edu
Phone: (215) 895-2400 Toll-free number: (800) 237-3935
Fax: (215) 895-5939
Joan McDonald, Vice President of Enrollment Management, Drexel University, 3141 Chestnut Street, Philadelphia, PA 19104-2875

Duquesne University

Pittsburgh, Pennsylvania — **CB member**
www.duq.edu — **CB code: 2196**

- Private 4-year university affiliated with Roman Catholic Church
- Residential campus in large city
- 5,616 degree-seeking undergraduates: 4% part-time, 58% women, 4% African American, 2% Asian American, 1% Hispanic American, 2% international
- 4,450 graduate students
- 76% of applicants admitted
- SAT or ACT with writing, application essay required
- 72% graduate within 6 years; 33% enter graduate study

General. Founded in 1878. Regionally accredited. **Degrees:** 1,184 bachelor's awarded; master's, doctoral, first professional offered. **ROTC:** Army, Naval, Air Force. **Calendar:** Semester, extensive summer session. **Full-time faculty:** 447 total; 86% have terminal degrees, 5% minority, 40% women. **Part-time faculty:** 465 total; 4% minority, 49% women. **Class size:** 49% < 20, 38% 20-39, 6% 40-49, 4% 50-99, 3% >100. **Special facilities:** Recording complex, recital hall, electronic studio, keyboard lab, music technology center, academic research center for pharmaceutical information, pharmaceutical technology center, pharmacy manufacturing lab, phenomenology center, health sciences cadaver lab, computational sciences liberal arts center, international nursing center, nurse managed wellness center, business school investment center, health sciences simulation technology laboratory, center for computational sciences, liberal arts living-learning communities, center for nursing research, center for international nursing, confocal microscopes, mass spectrometry facilities, 400- and 500- MHZ NMR spectrometers, electron microscopes, x-ray diffraction spectrometers.

Freshman class profile. 5,715 applied, 4,320 admitted, 1,438 enrolled.

Mid 50% test scores		Rank in top quarter:	55%
SAT critical reading:	510-600	Rank in top tenth:	23%
SAT math:	520-610	End year in good standing:	98%
SAT writing:	510-600	Return as sophomores:	88%
ACT composite:	22-26	Out-of-state:	26%
GPA 3.75 or higher:	40%	Live on campus:	91%
GPA 3.50-3.74:	18%	International:	2%
GPA 3.0-3.49:	32%	Fraternities:	11%
GPA 2.0-2.99:	10%	Sororities:	8%

Basis for selection. School achievement record, standardized test scores, recommendations, essay very important. Decisions based on overall GPA, standardized test scores, curriculum, volunteer activities. Interview recommended for all; audition required for music program. **Homeschooled:** Transcript of courses and grades required. **Learning Disabled:** Documentation of learning disabilities may be required.

High school preparation. College-preparatory program required. 16 units recommended. Recommended units include English 4, mathematics 2, social studies 2, science 2, foreign language 2 and academic electives 4.

2008-2009 Annual costs. Tuition/fees: $25,475. Room/board: $8,888. Books/supplies: $600. Personal expenses: $600.

2007-2008 Financial aid. Need-based: 1,200 full-time freshmen applied for aid; 961 were judged to have need; 961 of these received aid. Average need met was 89%. Average scholarship/grant was $12,428; average loan $4,331. 52% of total undergraduate aid awarded as scholarships/grants, 48% as loans/jobs. **Non-need-based:** Awarded to 4,692 full-time undergraduates, including 1,377 freshmen. Scholarships awarded for academics, athletics, music/drama, ROTC.

Application procedures. **Admission:** Priority date 11/1; deadline 7/1 (receipt date). $50 fee, may be waived for applicants with need. Admission notification on a rolling basis beginning on or about 9/15. Must reply by May 1 or within 2 week(s) if notified thereafter. **Financial aid:** Closing date 5/1. FAFSA, institutional form required. Applicants notified on a rolling basis starting 3/1; must reply by 5/1 or within 3 week(s) of notification.

Academics. **Special study options:** Accelerated study, combined bachelor's/graduate degree, cross-registration, distance learning, double major, dual enrollment of high school students, ESL, exchange student, external degree, honors, independent study, internships, liberal arts/career combination, semester at sea, student-designed major, study abroad, teacher certification program, Washington semester, weekend college. **Credit/placement by examination:** AP, CLEP, IB, institutional tests. 90 credit hours maximum toward bachelor's degree. **Support services:** Learning center, pre-admission summer program, reduced course load, remedial instruction, study skills assistance, tutoring, writing center.

Honors college/program. 1300 SAT or ACT equivalent, 3.5 GPA and ranking in the top 10% of graduating class (if high school ranks seniors). Other well qualified students may apply. Approximately 100 incoming freshmen admitted each year.

Majors. **Biology:** General, biochemistry. **Business:** General, accounting, business admin, communications, entrepreneurial studies, finance, international, investments/securities, logistics, management information systems, management science, managerial economics, marketing, nonprofit/public. **Communications:** General, journalism, public relations. **Computer sciences:** Computer science, programming, web page design, webmaster. **Conservation:** Environmental science. **Education:** General, early childhood, elementary, English, Latin, mathematics, multi-level teacher, music, secondary, social studies, Spanish, special. **Foreign languages:** General, ancient Greek, classics, Latin, Spanish. **Health:** Athletic training, health care admin, music therapy, nursing (RN), pharmacy assistant, premedicine. **History:** General. **Liberal arts:** Arts/sciences. **Math:** General. **Philosophy/religion:** Philosophy. **Physical sciences:** Chemistry, physics. **Protective services:** Security management. **Psychology:** General. **Social sciences:** Economics, international relations, political science, sociology. **Theology:** Theology. **Visual/performing arts:** Art history/conservation, dramatic, music performance, studio arts. **Other:** Public relations, advertising, and applied communications.

Most popular majors. Biology 6%, business/marketing 24%, communications/journalism 6%, education 9%, health sciences 22%, liberal arts 6%.

Computing on campus. 917 workstations in dormitories, library, computer center, student center. Dormitories wired for high-speed internet access and linked to campus network. Commuter students can connect to campus network. Online course registration, online library, helpline, repair service, student web hosting, wireless network available.

Student life. **Freshman orientation:** Mandatory, $150 fee. Preregistration for classes offered. 5-day program in August; includes volunteer opportunities. **Policies:** All recognized student organizations must have faculty or staff adviser, have purpose consistent with university mission, and abide by Code of Rights, Responsibilities and Conduct. **Housing:** Guaranteed on-campus for freshmen. Coed dorms, special housing for disabled, apartments, fraternity/sorority housing, wellness housing available. $300 nonrefundable deposit, deadline 5/1. Club wings available. **Activities:** Bands, choral groups, dance, drama, film society, international student organizations, literary magazine, music ensembles, Model UN, musical theater, opera, radio station, student government, student newspaper, symphony orchestra, TV station, black student union, university volunteers, Latin American student association, Evergreen, Indian student association, St. Vincent de Paul Society, College Republicans, Asian student association, Young Democrats.

Athletics. NCAA. **Intercollegiate:** Baseball M, basketball, cross-country, football (tackle) M, golf M, lacrosse W, rowing (crew) W, soccer, swimming, tennis, track and field, volleyball W, wrestling M. **Intramural:** Badminton, basketball, football (non-tackle), racquetball, skiing, soccer, softball, swimming, table tennis, tennis, track and field, volleyball. **Team name:** Dukes.

Student services. Adult student services, alcohol/substance abuse counseling, chaplain/spiritual director, career counseling, services for economically disadvantaged, student employment services, financial aid counseling, health services, minority student services, on-campus daycare, personal counseling, placement for graduates, women's services. **Physically disabled:** Services for visually, speech, hearing impaired.

Contact. E-mail: admissions@duq.edu
Phone: (412) 396-6222 Toll-free number: (800) 456-0590
Fax: (412) 396-6223
Paul-James Cukanna, Associate Vice President, Enrollment Management, Duquesne University, 600 Forbes Avenue, Administration Building, Pittsburgh, PA 15282-0201

East Stroudsburg University of Pennsylvania

East Stroudsburg, Pennsylvania — **CB member**
www4.esu.edu — **CB code: 2650**

- Public 4-year university
- Residential campus in large town
- 5,995 degree-seeking undergraduates: 7% part-time, 55% women, 5% African American, 1% Asian American, 5% Hispanic American
- 928 degree-seeking graduate students
- 71% of applicants admitted
- SAT or ACT (ACT writing optional) required
- 53% graduate within 6 years

General. Founded in 1893. Regionally accredited. **Degrees:** 1,236 bachelor's awarded; master's offered. **ROTC:** Army, Air Force. **Location:** 40 miles from Allentown and Scranton. **Calendar:** Semester, extensive summer session. **Full-time faculty:** 272 total; 79% have terminal degrees, 13% minority, 43% women. **Part-time faculty:** 74 total; 24% have terminal degrees, 7% minority, 64% women. **Class size:** 28% < 20, 50% 20-39, 19% 40-49, 3% 50-99, less than 1% >100. **Special facilities:** 30-acre ecological studies area, business accelerator program.

Freshman class profile. 6,137 applied, 4,338 admitted, 1,270 enrolled.

Mid 50% test scores			
SAT critical reading:	440-520	Rank in top tenth:	6%
SAT math:	450-540	Return as sophomores:	76%
SAT writing:	430-510	Out-of-state:	28%
Rank in top quarter:	24%	Live on campus:	85%

Basis for selection. Academic achievement primary factor in selection process. Whole-person assessment also used, taking into account school and community activities, achievements and aspirations. SAT recommended.

High school preparation. College-preparatory program recommended. 17 units recommended. Recommended units include English 4, mathematics 4, social studies 3, science 3 (laboratory 1) and foreign language 2.

2008-2009 Annual costs. Tuition/fees: $7,089; $15,127 out-of-state. Tuition for incoming out of state residents who are high achieving science and technology majors (biology, chemistry, computer science, mathematics, and physics) is $8,038. Room/board: $6,148. Books/supplies: $1,000. Personal expenses: $1,951.

2007-2008 Financial aid. **Need-based:** 933 full-time freshmen applied for aid; 666 were judged to have need; 592 of these received aid. Average need met was 81%. Average scholarship/grant was $4,372; average loan $3,279. 45% of total undergraduate aid awarded as scholarships/grants, 55% as loans/jobs. **Non-need-based:** Awarded to 1,300 full-time undergraduates, including 339 freshmen. Scholarships awarded for academics, alumni affiliation, art, athletics, leadership, minority status, music/drama, religious affiliation, state residency.

Application procedures. **Admission:** Closing date 4/1 (postmark date). $35 fee, may be waived for applicants with need. Admission notification on a rolling basis beginning on or about 11/15. Must reply by May 1 or within 3 week(s) if notified thereafter. **Financial aid:** Closing date 3/1. FAFSA required. Applicants notified by 4/1; must reply by 5/1.

Academics. **Special study options:** Accelerated study, combined bachelor's/graduate degree, cross-registration, distance learning, double major, dual enrollment of high school students, exchange student, honors, independent study, internships, student-designed major, study abroad, teacher certification program, urban semester. **Credit/placement by examination:** AP, CLEP, SAT, ACT, institutional tests. 24 credit hours maximum toward bachelor's degree. **Support services:** Learning center, pre-admission summer program, reduced course load, remedial instruction, study skills assistance, tutoring, writing center.

Majors. **Biology:** General, biochemistry, biotechnology, ecology, marine. **Business:** Business admin, hospitality admin. **Communications:** General. **Communications technology:** General. **Computer sciences:** General, security. **Education:** Early childhood, elementary, health, physical, special. **Foreign languages:** French, Spanish. **Health:** Athletic training, audiology/

speech pathology, clinical lab science, health services admin, nursing (RN). **History:** General. **Interdisciplinary:** Biological/physical sciences. **Liberal arts:** Arts/sciences, humanities. **Math:** General. **Parks/recreation:** Exercise sciences, facilities management. **Philosophy/religion:** Philosophy. **Physical sciences:** General, chemistry, geology, physics. **Psychology:** General. **Social sciences:** General, economics, geography, political science, sociology. **Visual/performing arts:** General, dramatic, graphic design.

Most popular majors. Biology 6%, business/marketing 14%, education 23%, health sciences 10%, parks/recreation 10%, psychology 6%, social sciences 11%.

Computing on campus. 397 workstations in dormitories, library, computer center, student center. Dormitories linked to campus network. Online course registration, helpline, wireless network available.

Student life. **Freshman orientation:** Available, $65 fee. Preregistration for classes offered. 2-day event during summer with joint and separate sessions for parents. **Housing:** Guaranteed on-campus for freshmen. Coed dorms, single-sex dorms, special housing for disabled, apartments, wellness housing available. $150 nonrefundable deposit, deadline 5/1. **Activities:** Bands, campus ministries, choral groups, dance, drama, literary magazine, music ensembles, musical theater, radio station, student government, student newspaper, symphony orchestra, Latin American Students Association, Campus Democrats, Young Republicans, African American Student Alliance, Fellowship of Christian Athletes, Newman Club, Women for Awareness.

Athletics. NCAA. **Intercollegiate:** Baseball M, basketball, cross-country, field hockey W, football (tackle) M, lacrosse W, soccer, softball W, swimming W, tennis, track and field, wrestling M. **Intramural:** Badminton, basketball, football (non-tackle), racquetball, soccer, softball, tennis, water polo. **Team name:** Warriors.

Student services. Adult student services, chaplain/spiritual director, career counseling, student employment services, financial aid counseling, health services, minority student services, on-campus daycare, personal counseling, placement for graduates, veterans' counselor, women's services. **Physically disabled:** Services for visually, speech, hearing impaired.

Contact. E-mail: undergrads@po-box.esu.edu
Phone: (570) 422-3542 Toll-free number: (877) 230-5547
Fax: (570) 422-3933
Jeff Jones, Director of Admissions, East Stroudsburg University of Pennsylvania, 200 Prospect Street, East Stroudsburg, PA 18301-2999

Eastern University

St. Davids, Pennsylvania
www.eastern.edu **CB code: 2220**

- Private 4-year university affiliated with American Baptist Churches in the USA
- Residential campus in small town
- 2,537 degree-seeking undergraduates: 5% part-time, 68% women, 20% African American, 2% Asian American, 10% Hispanic American, 2% international
- 1,696 graduate students
- 77% of applicants admitted
- SAT or ACT (ACT writing recommended), application essay required
- 60% graduate within 6 years

General. Founded in 1952. Regionally accredited. **Degrees:** 538 bachelor's, 83 associate awarded; master's, doctoral, first professional offered. **ROTC:** Army, Air Force. **Location:** 10 miles from Philadelphia. **Calendar:** Semester, limited summer session. **Full-time faculty:** 115 total; 86% have terminal degrees, 22% minority, 42% women. **Part-time faculty:** 275 total; 28% have terminal degrees, 21% minority, 48% women. **Class size:** 70% < 20, 29% 20-39, less than 1% 40-49, less than 1% 50-99, less than 1% >100. **Special facilities:** Planetarium, observatory.

Freshman class profile. 1,229 applied, 951 admitted, 443 enrolled.

Mid 50% test scores			
SAT critical reading:	470-600	Return as sophomores:	73%
SAT math:	450-580	Out-of-state:	47%
SAT writing:	470-580	Live on campus:	93%
ACT composite:	17-22	International:	1%

Basis for selection. SAT, GPA, and class rank most important. Interest in school mission, slope of grades, attendance, interviews also evaluated. Interview recommended.

High school preparation. College-preparatory program required. Recommended units include English 4, mathematics 3, social studies 2, science 3 and foreign language 3.

2008-2009 Annual costs. Tuition/fees: $22,715. Room/board: $8,610. Books/supplies: $1,000. Personal expenses: $1,800.

Application procedures. **Admission:** No deadline. $25 fee, may be waived for applicants with need. Admission notification on a rolling basis. **Financial aid:** No deadline. FAFSA, institutional form required. Applicants notified on a rolling basis starting 4/1.

Academics. **Special study options:** Accelerated study, cross-registration, double major, honors, independent study, student-designed major, study abroad, teacher certification program, Washington semester. **Credit/placement by examination:** AP, CLEP, IB, SAT, ACT. 30 credit hours maximum toward associate degree, 60 toward bachelor's. **Support services:** Pre-admission summer program, remedial instruction, study skills assistance, tutoring, writing center.

Honors college/program. Students must be in top 9% of class and have 1300 SAT (exclusive of Writing) or 30 ACT, or have extraordinary leadership abilities with significant academic achievements.

Majors. **Biology:** General, biochemistry. **Business:** Accounting/finance, business admin, entrepreneurial studies, international. **Communications:** General. **Conservation:** General. **Education:** Elementary. **Foreign languages:** Spanish. **Health:** Athletic training, nursing (RN). **History:** General. **Math:** General. **Parks/recreation:** Exercise sciences. **Physical sciences:** Chemistry. **Psychology:** General. **Public administration:** Social work. **Social sciences:** Political science, sociology. **Theology:** Bible, missionary, theology, youth ministry. **Visual/performing arts:** Dance. **Other:** Organizational leadership.

Most popular majors. Business/marketing 26%, education 12%, health sciences 15%, theological studies 12%.

Computing on campus. 131 workstations in dormitories, library, computer center, student center. Dormitories wired for high-speed internet access and linked to campus network. Commuter students can connect to campus network. Repair service available.

Student life. **Freshman orientation:** Mandatory. Preregistration for classes offered. Held 3 days before fall semester. **Policies:** Smoke-free campus. **Housing:** Coed dorms, apartments, wellness housing available. $150 nonrefundable deposit, deadline 8/1. Students required to live on campus unless they receive permission from Dean of Students Office. **Activities:** Bands, choral groups, dance, drama, literary magazine, music ensembles, musical theater, student government, student newspaper, black student league, Penn State Education Association, yacht club, gospel outreach, Fellowship of Christian Athletes, Habitat for Humanity, Evangelicals for Social Action, students organized against racism, prison ministry, Latinos Unidos.

Athletics. NCAA. **Intercollegiate:** Baseball M, basketball, cross-country W, field hockey W, golf, lacrosse, soccer, softball W, tennis, volleyball W. **Intramural:** Basketball, cheerleading, golf, soccer, tennis, volleyball. **Team name:** Eagles.

Student services. Adult student services, alcohol/substance abuse counseling, chaplain/spiritual director, career counseling, financial aid counseling, health services, legal services, minority student services, personal counseling, veterans' counselor, women's services. **Physically disabled:** Services for visually, speech, hearing impaired.

Contact. E-mail: ugadm@eastern.edu
Phone: (610) 341-5967 Toll-free number: (800) 452-0996
Fax: (610) 341-1723
David Urban, Executive Director for Enrollment, Eastern University, 1300 Eagle Road, St. Davids, PA 19087-3696

Edinboro University of Pennsylvania

Edinboro, Pennsylvania **CB member**
www.edinboro.edu **CB code: 2651**

- Public 4-year university and teachers college
- Commuter campus in small town
- 5,928 degree-seeking undergraduates: 10% part-time, 56% women, 9% African American, 1% Asian American, 2% Hispanic American, 1% international
- 1,230 degree-seeking graduate students
- 74% of applicants admitted
- 64% graduate within 6 years

General. Founded in 1857. Regionally accredited. Extensive programs and services for physically and learning disabled students available. Credit courses, continuing education, workshops, and seminars offered at Porreco Extension Center in Erie. **Degrees:** 1,062 bachelor's, 83 associate awarded; master's offered. **ROTC:** Army. **Location:** 18 miles from Erie. **Calendar:** Semester, extensive summer session. **Special facilities:** Observatory, planetarium, natural wildlife museum, robotics laboratory, center for performing arts, speech and hearing clinic, Ft. LeBoeuf Museum.

Freshman class profile. 3,833 applied, 2,839 admitted, 1,257 enrolled.

Mid 50% test scores		**GPA 2.0-2.99:**	38%
SAT critical reading:	420-520	**Rank in top quarter:**	78%
SAT math:	420-530	**Rank in top tenth:**	41%
ACT composite:	16-21	**Return as sophomores:**	70%
GPA 3.75 or higher:	18%	**Out-of-state:**	14%
GPA 3.50-3.74:	14%	**Live on campus:**	77%
GPA 3.0-3.49:	28%	**International:**	1%

Basis for selection. High school curriculum, test scores, GPA, and class rank most important. Recommendations and activities record also reviewed. Interview and essay recommended for all; audition required for music program; portfolio recommended for art program. **Homeschooled:** Transcript of courses and grades, interview, letter of recommendation (nonparent) required.

High school preparation. College-preparatory program recommended. 15 units recommended. Recommended units include English 4, mathematics 3, social studies 4, science 3, foreign language 2 and computer science 1.

2008-2009 Annual costs. Tuition/fees: $7,042; $9,722 out-of-state. Room/board: $6,734. Books/supplies: $900. Personal expenses: $1,300.

2007-2008 Financial aid. Need-based: 1,214 full-time freshmen applied for aid; 1,034 were judged to have need; 1,004 of these received aid. Average need met was 49%. Average scholarship/grant was $4,076; average loan $2,909. 51% of total undergraduate aid awarded as scholarships/grants, 49% as loans/jobs. **Non-need-based:** Awarded to 4,374 full-time undergraduates, including 996 freshmen. Scholarships awarded for academics, alumni affiliation, art, athletics, job skills, leadership, minority status, music/drama, religious affiliation, ROTC, state residency.

Application procedures. Admission: No deadline. $30 fee, may be waived for applicants with need. Admission notification on a rolling basis beginning on or about 9/15. Must reply by May 1 or within 4 week(s) if notified thereafter. **Financial aid:** Priority date 3/15, closing date 5/1. FAFSA required. Applicants notified on a rolling basis starting 3/20; must reply within 2 week(s) of notification.

Academics. 60 credits of general education electives required for bachelor's degree. Associate degree counseling, peer tutoring, peer mentors, academic advising center, and trial admissions program offered. **Special study options:** Combined bachelor's/graduate degree, cooperative education, cross-registration, distance learning, double major, dual enrollment of high school students, honors, independent study, internships, liberal arts/career combination, student-designed major, study abroad, teacher certification program. **Credit/placement by examination:** AP, CLEP, SAT, ACT, institutional tests. 30 credit hours maximum toward associate degree, 30 toward bachelor's. **Support services:** Learning center, pre-admission summer program, reduced course load, remedial instruction, study skills assistance, tutoring, writing center.

Majors. Area/ethnic studies: Latin American, women's. **Biology:** General. **Business:** Accounting, business admin, marketing, operations. **Communications:** General, broadcast journalism, journalism, media studies. **Computer sciences:** General. **Conservation:** Environmental science. **Education:** Elementary, special. **Foreign languages:** German, Spanish. **Health:** Clinical lab technology, communication disorders, nursing (RN), predental, premedicine, preveterinary. **History:** General. **Interdisciplinary:** Biological/physical sciences. **Liberal arts:** Arts/sciences, humanities. **Math:** General. **Parks/recreation:** Health/fitness, sports admin. **Philosophy/religion:** Philosophy. **Physical sciences:** Chemistry, geology, physics, planetary. **Protective services:** Criminal justice. **Psychology:** General. **Public administration:** Social work. **Social sciences:** General, anthropology, economics, geography, political science, sociology. **Visual/performing arts:** Art, art history/conservation, ceramics, dramatic, drawing, fiber arts, graphic design, painting, photography, printmaking, sculpture.

Most popular majors. Business/marketing 10%, communications/journalism 9%, education 10%, health sciences 7%, parks/recreation 6%, psychology 6%, security/protective services 8%, social sciences 6%, visual/performing arts 16%.

Computing on campus. 997 workstations in dormitories, library, computer center, student center. Dormitories wired for high-speed internet access and linked to campus network. Commuter students can connect to campus network. Online course registration, online library, helpline, repair service, student web hosting, wireless network available.

Student life. Freshman orientation: Mandatory. Preregistration for classes offered. Summer and spring programs. **Policies:** Zero tolerance policy for alcohol and drugs on campus. **Housing:** Guaranteed on-campus for freshmen. Coed dorms, single-sex dorms, special housing for disabled, wellness housing available. $75 partly refundable deposit, deadline 5/1. Living/learning communities and suite-style apartments available. **Activities:** Bands, campus ministries, choral groups, dance, drama, film society, international student organizations, literary magazine, music ensembles, opera, radio station, student government, student newspaper, TV station, 169 organizations on campus.

Athletics. NCAA. **Intercollegiate:** Basketball, cross-country, football (tackle) M, lacrosse W, soccer W, softball W, swimming, track and field, volleyball W, wrestling M. **Intramural:** Basketball, football (non-tackle), racquetball, soccer, softball, volleyball, wrestling M. **Team name:** The Fighting Scots.

Student services. Adult student services, alcohol/substance abuse counseling, chaplain/spiritual director, career counseling, student employment services, financial aid counseling, health services, minority student services, personal counseling, placement for graduates, veterans' counselor. **Physically disabled:** Services for visually, speech, hearing impaired. **Learning disabled:** Comprehensive services available.

Contact. E-mail: eup_admissions@edinboro.edu
Phone: (814) 732-2761 Toll-free number: (888) 846-2676
Fax: (814) 732-2420
James Cooney, Director of Undergraduate Admissions, Edinboro University of Pennsylvania, 200 East Normal Street, Edinboro, PA 16444

Elizabethtown College

Elizabethtown, Pennsylvania — **CB member**
www.etown.edu — **CB code: 2225**

- Private 4-year liberal arts college affiliated with Church of the Brethren
- Residential campus in large town
- 2,178 degree-seeking undergraduates: 16% part-time, 65% women
- 46 degree-seeking graduate students
- 65% of applicants admitted
- SAT or ACT (ACT writing optional), application essay required
- 69% graduate within 6 years

General. Founded in 1899. Regionally accredited. **Degrees:** 517 bachelor's, 20 associate awarded; master's offered. **Location:** 20 miles from Harrisburg, 90 miles from Philadelphia. **Calendar:** Semester, limited summer session. **Full-time faculty:** 129 total; 88% have terminal degrees, 10% minority, 48% women. **Part-time faculty:** 173 total; 24% have terminal degrees, 5% minority, 45% women. **Class size:** 73% < 20, 26% 20-39, less than 1% 40-49, less than 1% 50-99, less than 1% >100. **Special facilities:** Anabaptist and Pietist groups center, global citizenship center, Brethren Colleges Abroad headquarters.

Freshman class profile. 3,315 applied, 2,148 admitted, 517 enrolled.

Mid 50% test scores		**Rank in top tenth:**	36%
SAT critical reading:	520-620	**Return as sophomores:**	85%
SAT math:	520-630	**Out-of-state:**	37%
ACT composite:	21-26	**Live on campus:**	97%
Rank in top quarter:	65%		

Basis for selection. School achievement record most important. College preparatory program strongly recommended. Co-curricular activities also considered, particularly service-oriented activities. Applicants should be in top quarter of class. Students may waive SAT/ACT score from admissions and merit-based scholarship decisions if they are ranked in top 10% of class or have 3.5 GPA if school does not rank. Interview required for occupational therapy and honors program. For international business applicants, essay must demonstrate interest in that subject area. Audition required for music, music education, music therapy programs; portfolio required for art program. **Homeschooled:** Letter of recommendation (nonparent) required.

High school preparation. 15 units required; 20 recommended. Required and recommended units include English 4, mathematics 3-4, social studies 2, history 2, science 2-4 (laboratory 2-3), foreign language 2 and academic electives 2.

2008-2009 Annual costs. Tuition/fees: $30,650. Room/board: $7,950. Books/supplies: $800. Personal expenses: $700.

2008-2009 Financial aid. Need-based: 456 full-time freshmen applied for aid; 387 were judged to have need; 387 of these received aid. Average need met was 83%. Average scholarship/grant was $17,932; average loan $3,557. 71% of total undergraduate aid awarded as scholarships/grants, 29% as loans/jobs. **Non-need-based:** Awarded to 570 full-time undergraduates,

including 163 freshmen. Scholarships awarded for academics, art, music/drama, religious affiliation.

Application procedures. **Admission:** Priority date 3/1; no deadline. $30 fee, may be waived for applicants with need, free for online applicants. Admission notification on a rolling basis beginning on or about 12/1. Must reply by May 1 or within 2 week(s) if notified thereafter. December 15 closing date for occupational therapy program. March 1 closing date for international business. January 15 closing date for honors program. **Financial aid:** Priority date 3/15; no closing date. FAFSA, institutional form required. Applicants notified on a rolling basis starting 3/1; must reply by 5/1 or within 2 week(s) of notification.

Academics. **Special study options:** Combined bachelor's/graduate degree, double major, dual enrollment of high school students, ESL, exchange student, external degree, honors, independent study, internships, liberal arts/career combination, study abroad, teacher certification program, Washington semester. 2-2 program with Thomas Jefferson University in nursing, laboratory sciences, diagnostic imaging; 3-3 program in physical therapy (DPT) with Thomas Jefferson University: 3-2 in engineering with Penn State; 3-2 with Duke University in forestry and environmental management; 3-3 in physical therapy with Widener University and University of Maryland, Baltimore; 3+4 in dentistry with Temple University; agreements for MBA programs at Lehigh University, Rutgers University, Loyola College (MD), Penn State University, Harrisburg. **Credit/placement by examination:** AP, CLEP, IB, institutional tests. Credit by examination unlimited provided student is able to fulfill residency requirement. Credit for International Baccalaureate awarded only for subject exams and only for earned scores from 4-7. **Support services:** Learning center, reduced course load, study skills assistance, tutoring, writing center.

Majors. **Biology:** General, biochemistry, biotechnology, environmental. **Business:** Accounting, actuarial science, business admin, international, management information systems, managerial economics, marketing. **Communications:** Media studies. **Computer sciences:** General, information systems. **Conservation:** Forest management. **Education:** Elementary, multi-level teacher, science. **Engineering:** General, computer, industrial. **Foreign languages:** French, German, Japanese, Spanish. **Health:** Music therapy, occupational health. **History:** General. **Math:** General, applied. **Philosophy/religion:** Christian, philosophy, religion. **Physical sciences:** Chemistry, physics. **Psychology:** General. **Public administration:** Social work. **Social sciences:** General, anthropology, criminology, economics, political science, sociology. **Visual/performing arts:** Dramatic, studio arts. **Other:** Corporate communications.

Most popular majors. Biology 7%, business/marketing 27%, communications/journalism 6%, education 11%, health sciences 9%, social sciences 9%.

Computing on campus. 200 workstations in dormitories, library, computer center, student center. Dormitories wired for high-speed internet access and linked to campus network. Commuter students can connect to campus network. Online course registration, online library, helpline, student web hosting, wireless network available.

Student life. **Freshman orientation:** Mandatory. One-day summer program in June and multi-day program at beginning of fall semester. **Policies:** All residence halls are smoke-free. **Housing:** Guaranteed on-campus for all undergraduates. Coed dorms, single-sex dorms, special housing for disabled, apartments, wellness housing available. Special housing available for students involved in service learning and community service. **Activities:** Bands, choral groups, dance, drama, international student organizations, literary magazine, music ensembles, musical theater, radio station, student government, student newspaper, symphony orchestra, TV station, Newman club, Intervarsity Christian Fellowship, Hillel, Circle-K, Habitat for Humanity, Amnesty International, Colors United, College Democrats, Republican club.

Athletics. NCAA. **Intercollegiate:** Baseball M, basketball, cross-country, field hockey W, golf M, lacrosse, soccer, softball W, swimming, tennis, track and field, volleyball W, wrestling M. **Intramural:** Basketball, football (non-tackle) M, racquetball, soccer, softball, tennis, volleyball. **Team name:** Blue Jays.

Student services. Adult student services, alcohol/substance abuse counseling, chaplain/spiritual director, career counseling, student employment services, financial aid counseling, health services, minority student services, personal counseling, placement for graduates, veterans' counselor, women's services. **Physically disabled:** Services for visually, hearing impaired. **Learning disabled:** Comprehensive services available.

Contact. E-mail: admissions@etown.edu
Phone: (717) 361-1400 Fax: (717) 361-1365
Debra Murray, Director of Admissions, Elizabethtown College, One Alpha Drive, Elizabethtown, PA 17022-2298

Franklin & Marshall College

Lancaster, Pennsylvania — **CB member**
www.fandm.edu — **CB code: 2261**

- Private 4-year liberal arts college
- Residential campus in small city
- 2,118 degree-seeking undergraduates: 52% women, 4% African American, 4% Asian American, 4% Hispanic American, 8% international
- 36% of applicants admitted
- Application essay required
- 79% graduate within 6 years; 25% enter graduate study

General. Founded in 1787. Regionally accredited. **Degrees:** 480 bachelor's awarded. **Location:** 60 miles from Philadelphia, 120 miles from Washington, DC. **Calendar:** Semester, limited summer session. **Full-time faculty:** 192 total; 95% have terminal degrees, 10% minority, 37% women. **Part-time faculty:** 41 total; 46% have terminal degrees, 15% minority, 56% women. **Class size:** 52% < 20, 46% 20-39, 1% 40-49, less than 1% 50-99. **Special facilities:** Observatory, science library, retail sales complex, bronze casting foundry, field house, planetarium, natural history museum, concert hall, performing arts center, Writers House.

Freshman class profile. 5,632 applied, 2,021 admitted, 588 enrolled.

Mid 50% test scores		**Rank in top quarter:**	87%
SAT critical reading:	600-690	**Rank in top tenth:**	57%
SAT math:	610-690	**Return as sophomores:**	94%
GPA 3.75 or higher:	33%	**Out-of-state:**	68%
GPA 3.50-3.74:	30%	**Live on campus:**	99%
GPA 3.0-3.49:	30%	**International:**	9%
GPA 2.0-2.99:	7%		

Basis for selection. School achievement record, test scores or graded writing samples, extracurricular activities, recommendations, essay considered. SAT or ACT recommended. Submission of standardized test scores optional for all students. If students choose to omit scores, two recent graded writing samples must then be submitted. Interview required for early decision applicants, strongly recommended for others. Auditions and portfolios recommended for all students who wish to demonstrate particular talent. **Homeschooled:** Interview required. Interview, accrediting and evaluative documentation from home state, and SAT or ACT required. 3 SAT Subject Tests highly recommended.

High school preparation. College-preparatory program required. Required and recommended units include English 4, mathematics 3-4, social studies 1-3, history 2-3, science 2-3 (laboratory 2-3), foreign language 2-4 and visual/performing arts 1.

2008-2009 Annual costs. Tuition/fees: $38,630. Room/board: $9,870. Books/supplies: $650. Personal expenses: $950.

2008-2009 Financial aid. **Non-need-based:** Scholarships awarded for academics, art, leadership, music/drama.

Application procedures. **Admission:** Closing date 2/1 (postmark date). $50 fee, may be waived for applicants with need. Admission notification 4/1. Must reply by May 1 or within 2 week(s) if notified thereafter. **Financial aid:** Priority date 2/1, closing date 3/1. FAFSA, institutional form, CSS PROFILE required. Applicants notified by 3/15; must reply by 5/1.

Academics. Interdisciplinary minors offered. **Special study options:** Accelerated study, combined bachelor's/graduate degree, cross-registration, double major, dual enrollment of high school students, exchange student, honors, independent study, internships, liberal arts/career combination, New York semester, semester at sea, student-designed major, study abroad, teacher certification program, Washington semester. 3-2 programs in forestry, engineering, environmental studies; Columbia University's New York/Paris program. **Credit/placement by examination:** AP, CLEP, IB, institutional tests. 64 credit hours maximum toward bachelor's degree. **Support services:** Preadmission summer program, reduced course load, tutoring, writing center.

Majors. **Area/ethnic studies:** African, African-American, American. **Biology:** General, biochemistry. **Business:** Business admin. **Conservation:** Environmental science, environmental studies. **Foreign languages:** Ancient Greek, classics, French, German, Latin, Spanish. **History:** General. **Interdisciplinary:** Behavioral sciences, biopsychology, neuroscience. **Math:** General. **Philosophy/religion:** Philosophy, religion. **Physical sciences:** Astronomy, astrophysics, chemistry, geology, physics. **Psychology:** General. **Social sciences:** Anthropology, economics, political science, sociology. **Visual/performing arts:** Art history/conservation, dance, dramatic, studio arts.

Most popular majors. Biology 10%, business/marketing 14%, English 9%, foreign language 6%, interdisciplinary studies 9%, social sciences 25%, visual/performing arts 6%.

Computing on campus. 125 workstations in library, computer center. Dormitories wired for high-speed internet access and linked to campus network. Commuter students can connect to campus network. Online course registration, online library, helpline, repair service, student web hosting, wireless network available.

Student life. **Freshman orientation:** Mandatory, $200 fee. Preregistration for classes offered. 5 days prior to start of classes, includes noncredit pre-semester academic experience. **Policies:** Freshmen and sophomores required to live in college housing. **Housing:** Guaranteed on-campus for freshmen. Coed dorms, special housing for disabled, apartments, wellness housing available. French house, arts house, international house available to upperclassmen, community outreach house, men's and women's floors. **Activities:** Bands, choral groups, dance, drama, literary magazine, music ensembles, musical theater, opera, radio station, student government, student newspaper, symphony orchestra, TV station, East Asian society, Catholic Campus Community, Hillel, Christian Fellowship, Habitat for Humanity, Voices for Women, Coalition for Choice, Environmental Action Alliance, Black student union, Mi Gente Latina.

Athletics. NCAA. **Intercollegiate:** Baseball M, basketball, cross-country, field hockey W, football (tackle) M, golf, lacrosse, rowing (crew) W, soccer, softball W, squash, swimming, tennis, track and field, volleyball W, wrestling M. **Intramural:** Archery, badminton, basketball, bowling, cross-country, football (non-tackle) M, soccer, softball, squash, table tennis, tennis, volleyball. **Team name:** Diplomats.

Student services. Alcohol/substance abuse counseling, chaplain/spiritual director, career counseling, student employment services, financial aid counseling, health services, minority student services, on-campus daycare, personal counseling, placement for graduates, women's services.

Contact. E-mail: admission@fandm.edu
Phone: (717) 291-3953 Fax: (717) 291-4389
Sara Harberson, Dean of Admission, Franklin & Marshall College, PO Box 3003, Lancaster, PA 17604-3003

Gannon University

Erie, Pennsylvania — **CB member**
www.gannon.edu — **CB code: 2270**

- Private 4-year university affiliated with Roman Catholic Church
- Residential campus in small city
- 2,495 degree-seeking undergraduates: 6% part-time, 60% women, 5% African American, 1% Asian American, 2% Hispanic American, 1% international
- 1,359 degree-seeking graduate students
- 82% of applicants admitted
- SAT or ACT (ACT writing optional) required
- 65% graduate within 6 years

General. Founded in 1925. Regionally accredited. **Degrees:** 442 bachelor's, 44 associate awarded; master's, doctoral offered. **ROTC:** Army. **Location:** 120 miles from Pittsburgh, 90 miles from Cleveland. **Calendar:** Semester, extensive summer session. **Full-time faculty:** 197 total; 71% have terminal degrees, 12% minority, 43% women. **Part-time faculty:** 139 total; 24% have terminal degrees, 5% minority, 43% women. **Class size:** 55% < 20, 43% 20-39, 2% 40-49, less than 1% 50-99. **Special facilities:** Environmental studies center, computer integrated enterprise manufacturing center, floating laboratory providing hands-on environmental study on Lake Erie.

Freshman class profile. 3,021 applied, 2,487 admitted, 634 enrolled.

Mid 50% test scores		Rank in top quarter:	43%
SAT critical reading:	460-560	Rank in top tenth:	20%
SAT math:	450-580	End year in good standing:	82%
ACT composite:	19-25	Return as sophomores:	79%
GPA 3.75 or higher:	33%	Out-of-state:	28%
GPA 3.50-3.74:	16%	Live on campus:	75%
GPA 3.0-3.49:	28%	International:	1%
GPA 2.0-2.99:	23%		

Basis for selection. High school record important, including course selection, GPA, class rank, standardized test scores, recommendations, personal statement. Admission requirements vary by program. Limited number of students who do not meet all admissions requirements may be accepted into General Studies program. **Homeschooled:** Interview required. **Learning Disabled:** Applicants screened through director must be interviewed.

High school preparation. College-preparatory program required. 16 units required. Required units include English 4. Remaining 12 required academic units based on planned major.

2008-2009 Annual costs. Tuition/fees: $22,662. Room/board: $8,710. Books/supplies: $1,200. Personal expenses: $1,518.

2008-2009 Financial aid. **Need-based:** 601 full-time freshmen applied for aid; 526 were judged to have need; 525 of these received aid. Average need met was 77%. Average scholarship/grant was $13,599; average loan $3,347. 64% of total undergraduate aid awarded as scholarships/grants, 36% as loans/jobs. **Non-need-based:** Awarded to 779 full-time undergraduates, including 212 freshmen. Scholarships awarded for academics, athletics, leadership, music/drama, religious affiliation, ROTC.

Application procedures. **Admission:** No deadline. $25 fee, may be waived for applicants with need. Admission notification on a rolling basis beginning on or about 9/1. Early application especially recommended for health science programs since space is limited. Closing date for occupational therapy, physician's assistant, radiological science programs January 15. Closing date for medical program December 15. **Financial aid:** Priority date 3/15; no closing date. FAFSA, institutional form required. Applicants notified on a rolling basis starting 11/1; must reply by 5/1 or within 4 week(s) of notification.

Academics. Preferred admission to doctorate physical therapy program granted to students with bachelor's degree from Gannon in physical therapy. Occupational therapy and physician assistant programs are 5-year master's degree programs. **Special study options:** Accelerated study, combined bachelor's/graduate degree, distance learning, double major, dual enrollment of high school students, honors, independent study, internships, liberal arts/career combination, study abroad, teacher certification program, Washington semester. **Credit/placement by examination:** AP, CLEP, IB, institutional tests. 36 credit hours maximum toward bachelor's degree. **Support services:** Learning center, reduced course load, remedial instruction, study skills assistance, tutoring, writing center.

Honors college/program. Minimum 1150 SAT score (exclusive of Writing), 3.0 GPA, rank in top tenth of high school class, college preparatory curriculum, extracurricular activities, community service. Recommendation, interview and essay required. Approximately 50 freshmen admitted per year.

Majors. **Biology:** General, bioinformatics. **Business:** Accounting, business admin, finance, insurance, international, management information systems, marketing. **Communications:** Advertising, journalism. **Communications technology:** Radio/tv. **Computer sciences:** General, programming. **Conservation:** Environmental science, environmental studies. **Education:** Business, early childhood, elementary, foreign languages, multi-level teacher, secondary, social studies, special. **Engineering:** Chemical, electrical, environmental, industrial, mechanical. **Foreign languages:** General. **Health:** Clinical lab science, dietetics, nursing (RN), physician assistant, premedicine, respiratory therapy technology. **History:** General. **Legal studies:** Paralegal, prelaw. **Liberal arts:** Arts/sciences. **Math:** General. **Parks/recreation:** Sports admin. **Personal/culinary services:** Mortuary science. **Philosophy/religion:** Philosophy. **Physical sciences:** Chemistry. **Protective services:** Criminal justice. **Psychology:** General. **Public administration:** Social work. **Science technology:** Biological. **Social sciences:** General, political science. **Theology:** Theology. **Visual/performing arts:** General, dramatic. **Other:** International studies.

Most popular majors. Biology 9%, business/marketing 13%, education 7%, health sciences 25%, security/protective services 7%.

Computing on campus. 350 workstations in dormitories, library, computer center, student center. Dormitories wired for high-speed internet access and linked to campus network. Commuter students can connect to campus network. Online library, helpline, wireless network available.

Student life. **Freshman orientation:** Mandatory, $60 fee. Preregistration for classes offered. 4 separate sessions during summer. Open to parents and students. **Housing:** Guaranteed on-campus for freshmen. Coed dorms, special housing for disabled, apartments available. $100 fully refundable deposit. **Activities:** Bands, campus ministries, choral groups, dance, drama, international student organizations, literary magazine, music ensembles, Model UN, musical theater, radio station, student government, student newspaper, Social Concerns, minority student union, College Democrats, College Republicans, activities programming board, debate, Vitality Through Exercise, residence union.

Athletics. NCAA. **Intercollegiate:** Baseball M, basketball, cross-country, diving, football (tackle) M, golf, lacrosse W, soccer, softball W, swimming, volleyball W, water polo, wrestling M. **Intramural:** Basketball, football (non-tackle), handball, racquetball, soccer, volleyball, wrestling M. **Team name:** Golden Knights.

Student services. Adult student services, alcohol/substance abuse counseling, chaplain/spiritual director, career counseling, services for economically disadvantaged, student employment services, financial aid counseling, health services, minority student services, personal counseling, placement for graduates, veterans' counselor. **Learning disabled:** Comprehensive services available.

Contact. E-mail: admissions@gannon.edu
Phone: (814) 871-7240 Toll-free number: (800) 426-6668
Fax: (814) 871-5803
Terrance Kizina, Director of Admission, Gannon University, 109 University Square, Erie, PA 16541-0001

Geneva College

Beaver Falls, Pennsylvania — **CB member**
www.geneva.edu — **CB code: 2273**

- Private 4-year liberal arts college affiliated with Reformed Presbyterian Church of North America
- Residential campus in large town
- 1,381 degree-seeking undergraduates: 2% part-time, 51% women, 4% African American, 1% Asian American, 1% Hispanic American, 1% international
- 232 graduate students
- 81% of applicants admitted
- SAT or ACT (ACT writing optional), application essay required
- 55% graduate within 6 years

General. Founded in 1848. Regionally accredited. **Degrees:** 332 bachelor's, 7 associate awarded; master's offered. **ROTC:** Army. **Location:** 35 miles from Pittsburgh. **Calendar:** Semester, limited summer session. **Full-time faculty:** 79 total; 77% have terminal degrees, 8% minority, 35% women. **Class size:** 62% < 20, 33% 20-39, 1% 40-49, 2% 50-99, 2% >100. **Special facilities:** Collection of artifacts and records of Pittsburgh steel industry, technology development center, observatory, high adventure ropes course.

Freshman class profile. 1,262 applied, 1,019 admitted, 386 enrolled.

Mid 50% test scores		**GPA 2.0-2.99:**	21%
SAT critical reading:	470-600	**Rank in top quarter:**	43%
SAT math:	470-590	**Rank in top tenth:**	15%
ACT composite:	20-25	**Return as sophomores:**	78%
GPA 3.75 or higher:	30%	**Out-of-state:**	29%
GPA 3.50-3.74:	17%	**Live on campus:**	88%
GPA 3.0-3.49:	32%	**International:**	1%

Basis for selection. Academic performance and test scores most important. Recommendations and extracurricular activities considered. Interview recommended for all; audition required for music program. **Homeschooled:** Transcript of courses and grades required. Help in preparing homeschooler's transcript available if necessary.

High school preparation. 16 units required. Required units include English 4, mathematics 2, social studies 3, science 1, foreign language 2 and academic electives 4. Engineering students should have 1 unit of chemistry and physics, 4 units of college-preparatory mathematics including trigonometry or precalculus.

2008-2009 Annual costs. Tuition/fees: $20,400. Room/board: $7,450. Books/supplies: $900. Personal expenses: $1,150.

2008-2009 Financial aid. Need-based: 354 full-time freshmen applied for aid; 318 were judged to have need; 318 of these received aid. Average need met was 81%. Average scholarship/grant was $13,070; average loan $3,791. 63% of total undergraduate aid awarded as scholarships/grants, 37% as loans/jobs. **Non-need-based:** Awarded to 309 full-time undergraduates, including 80 freshmen. Scholarships awarded for academics, music/drama, religious affiliation.

Application procedures. Admission: No deadline. $40 fee, may be waived for applicants with need, free for online applicants. Admission notification on a rolling basis beginning on or about 9/1. Must reply by May 1 or within 3 week(s) if notified thereafter. **Financial aid:** Priority date 3/15; no closing date. FAFSA required. Applicants notified on a rolling basis starting 3/1; must reply by 5/1 or within 4 week(s) of notification.

Academics. Special study options: Accelerated study, cooperative education, cross-registration, double major, dual enrollment of high school students, honors, independent study, internships, liberal arts/career combination, student-designed major, study abroad, teacher certification program, Washington semester. **Credit/placement by examination:** AP, CLEP, IB, SAT, ACT, institutional tests. 30 credit hours maximum toward bachelor's degree. **Support services:** Pre-admission summer program, reduced course load, remedial instruction, study skills assistance, tutoring, writing center.

Majors. Biology: General. **Business:** Accounting, business admin, human resources. **Communications:** General. **Computer sciences:** General. **Education:** General, biology, chemistry, elementary, English, history, mathematics, music, physics, social studies, special. **Engineering:** General, chemical. **Health:** Speech pathology. **History:** General. **Liberal arts:** Arts/sciences. **Math:** Applied. **Philosophy/religion:** Philosophy. **Physical sciences:** Chemistry, physics. **Psychology:** General. **Public administration:** Social work. **Social sciences:** Political science, sociology. **Theology:** Bible, youth ministry. **Visual/performing arts:** Music management, music performance.

Most popular majors. Biology 6%, business/marketing 17%, communications/journalism 7%, education 15%, engineering/engineering technologies 7%, psychology 16%, theological studies 9%.

Computing on campus. 50 workstations in dormitories, library, computer center, student center. Dormitories wired for high-speed internet access and linked to campus network. Commuter students can connect to campus network. Online library, helpline, repair service, wireless network available.

Student life. Freshman orientation: Mandatory. Held 5 days prior to start of classes. **Policies:** Smoking, drinking, social or ballroom dancing not permitted on campus. Students must live on campus unless married, commuting, or over age 24. Religious observance required. **Housing:** Guaranteed on-campus for all undergraduates. Single-sex dorms, apartments, wellness housing available. $150 fully refundable deposit. **Activities:** Bands, campus ministries, choral groups, dance, drama, international student organizations, literary magazine, music ensembles, radio station, student government, student newspaper, Acting on Aids, American Society of Civil Engineering, American Society of Mechanical Engineers, Black student organization, Business and Professional Women, Creation Stewardship Club, International Justice Mission, Young Republicans, Young Democrats.

Athletics. NCAA, NCCAA. **Intercollegiate:** Baseball M, basketball, cross-country, football (tackle) M, soccer, softball W, tennis W, track and field, volleyball W. **Intramural:** Basketball, football (non-tackle), racquetball, soccer, softball, volleyball. **Team name:** Golden Tornadoes.

Student services. Alcohol/substance abuse counseling, chaplain/spiritual director, career counseling, student employment services, financial aid counseling, health services, minority student services, personal counseling, placement for graduates. **Physically disabled:** Services for visually, hearing impaired.

Contact. E-mail: admissions@geneva.edu
Phone: (724) 847-6500 Toll-free number: (800) 847-8255
Fax: (724) 847-6776
David Layton, Dean of Enrollment, Geneva College, 3200 College Avenue, Beaver Falls, PA 15010

Gettysburg College

Gettysburg, Pennsylvania — **CB member**
www.gettysburg.edu — **CB code: 2275**

- Private 4-year liberal arts college
- Residential campus in large town
- 2,457 degree-seeking undergraduates: 53% women, 5% African American, 2% Asian American, 3% Hispanic American, 2% international
- 38% of applicants admitted
- SAT or ACT (ACT writing optional), application essay required
- 82% graduate within 6 years

General. Founded in 1832. Regionally accredited. **Degrees:** 645 bachelor's awarded. **ROTC:** Army. **Location:** 36 miles from Harrisburg, 80 miles from Washington, DC. **Calendar:** Semester. **Full-time faculty:** 204 total; 91% have terminal degrees, 14% minority, 44% women. **Part-time faculty:** 74 total; 8% have terminal degrees, 8% minority, 47% women. **Class size:** 69% < 20, 29% 20-39, 2% 40-49, less than 1% 50-99. **Special facilities:** Observatory, planetarium, intercultural resource center, women's resource center, child study center, public service center, optics and plasma physics laboratories, infrared and NMR spectrometers, proton accelerator, science center, outdoor climbing wall, Sunderman Conservatory of Music.

Freshman class profile. 5,790 applied, 2,190 admitted, 714 enrolled.

Mid 50% test scores		**Out-of-state:**	74%
SAT critical reading:	610-690	**Live on campus:**	94%
SAT math:	610-670	**International:**	3%
Rank in top quarter:	89%	**Fraternities:**	40%
Rank in top tenth:	66%	**Sororities:**	26%
Return as sophomores:	90%		

Basis for selection. Academic record, recommendations, and activities most important. Audition required for the Sunderman Conservatory of Music; portfolio recommended for art program. Interview strongly recommended. **Homeschooled:** Statement describing homeschool structure and mission, transcript of courses and grades, interview, letter of recommendation (nonparent) required.

High school preparation. College-preparatory program required. Required and recommended units include English 4, mathematics 3-4, history 3-4, science 3-4 (laboratory 3-4) and foreign language 3-4. History requirement can be fulfilled with social studies units, depending on available high school courses.

2008-2009 Annual costs. Tuition/fees: $37,950. Room/board: $9,100. Books/supplies: $1,000. Personal expenses: $1,209.

2008-2009 Financial aid. Need-based: 483 full-time freshmen applied for aid; 388 were judged to have need; 388 of these received aid. Average need met was 100%. Average scholarship/grant was $25,221; average loan $3,758. 85% of total undergraduate aid awarded as scholarships/grants, 15% as loans/jobs. **Non-need-based:** Scholarships awarded for academics, music/drama.

Application procedures. Admission: Closing date 2/1 (postmark date). $55 fee, may be waived for applicants with need. Admission notification 4/1. Must reply by May 1 or within 2 week(s) if notified thereafter. **Financial aid:** Closing date 2/15. FAFSA, CSS PROFILE required. Applicants notified by 3/26; must reply by 5/1.

Academics. Special study options: Combined bachelor's/graduate degree, double major, independent study, internships, semester at sea, student-designed major, study abroad, teacher certification program, United Nations semester, Washington semester. 3-2 programs in engineering with Columbia University, Rensselaer Polytechnic Institute, and Washington University in St. Louis; 3-2 program in nursing with Johns Hopkins University; pre-law and health professions advising available. **Credit/placement by examination:** AP, CLEP, IB, SAT, institutional tests. **Support services:** Study skills assistance, tutoring, writing center.

Majors. Area/ethnic studies: African-American, American, Asian, Asian-American, East Asian, Japanese, Latin American, women's. **Biology:** General, biochemistry, conservation, molecular. **Business:** Business admin, finance, international, management science, marketing, nonprofit/public. **Communications:** General, journalism. **Computer sciences:** General, computer science. **Conservation:** General, environmental science, environmental studies, forestry, management/policy, water/wetlands/marine. **Education:** Music. **Engineering:** General, biomedical, chemical, civil, computer, electrical, environmental, mechanical, mechanics, physics, science. **Foreign languages:** Classics, comparative lit, French, German, Japanese, Latin, Spanish. **Health:** Health services, nursing (RN), predental, premedicine, prepharmacy, preveterinary. **History:** General, American, Asian, European. **Interdisciplinary:** Behavioral sciences, biological/physical sciences, global studies, math/computer science, medieval/Renaissance, natural sciences, neuroscience, peace/conflict. **Legal studies:** Prelaw. **Liberal arts:** Arts/sciences. **Math:** General. **Parks/recreation:** Exercise sciences, health/fitness, sports admin. **Philosophy/religion:** Philosophy, religion. **Physical sciences:** Astronomy, chemistry, physics. **Psychology:** General. **Social sciences:** Anthropology, economics, international relations, political science, sociology, U.S. government. **Theology:** Preministerial. **Visual/performing arts:** General, art, art history/conservation, dramatic, film/cinema, music performance, music theory/composition, piano/organ, studio arts, theater arts management, voice/opera.

Most popular majors. Biology 14%, business/marketing 14%, English 9%, history 6%, psychology 9%, social sciences 20%.

Computing on campus. 620 workstations in library, computer center, student center. Dormitories wired for high-speed internet access and linked to campus network. Commuter students can connect to campus network. Online course registration, online library, helpline, repair service, student web hosting, wireless network available.

Student life. Freshman orientation: Mandatory. Preregistration for classes offered. Begins 5 days prior to the start of fall semester classes. **Housing:** Guaranteed on-campus for all undergraduates. Coed dorms, single-sex dorms, apartments, fraternity/sorority housing, wellness housing available. $500 nonrefundable deposit, deadline 5/1. **Activities:** Bands, choral groups, dance, drama, film society, international student organizations, literary magazine, music ensembles, musical theater, opera, radio station, student government, student newspaper, symphony orchestra, TV station, over 120 clubs available.

Athletics. NCAA. **Intercollegiate:** Baseball M, basketball, cheerleading, cross-country, field hockey W, football (tackle) M, golf, lacrosse, soccer, softball W, swimming, tennis, track and field, volleyball W, wrestling M. **Intramural:** Badminton, basketball, field hockey, football (non-tackle), golf, lacrosse W, skiing, soccer, softball, volleyball, weight lifting. **Team name:** Bullets.

Student services. Chaplain/spiritual director, career counseling, student employment services, financial aid counseling, health services, minority student services, personal counseling, placement for graduates, women's services.

Contact. E-mail: admiss@gettysburg.edu
Phone: (717) 337-6100 Toll-free number: (800) 431-0803
Fax: (717) 337-6145
Gail Sweezey, Director of Admissions, Gettysburg College, 300 North Washington Street, Gettysburg, PA 17325-1484

Gratz College

Melrose Park, Pennsylvania
www.gratz.edu **CB code: 2280**

- Private 4-year college of Jewish studies affiliated with Jewish faith
- Commuter campus in very large city
- 10 degree-seeking undergraduates
- 225 graduate students
- Application essay required

General. Founded in 1895. Regionally accredited. **Location:** 6 miles from Philadelphia. **Calendar:** Semester, limited summer session. **Full-time faculty:** 10 total. **Part-time faculty:** 125 total. **Special facilities:** Jewish music library and rare book collection, oral history Holocaust archives, Holocaust Awareness Museum.

Basis for selection. Application, personal statement, transcripts, and two recommendations important. Interview recommended. **Learning Disabled:** Students asked to submit written documentation concerning learning disability to Dean of Students.

2008-2009 Annual costs. Tuition/fees: $12,300. Undergraduate students may take as many as 18 hours per semester for the full-time (academic year) tuition rate of $12,200. Books/supplies: $550. Personal expenses: $500.

Application procedures. Admission: No deadline. $50 fee, may be waived for applicants with need. Admission notification on a rolling basis. **Financial aid:** Priority date 6/1; no closing date. FAFSA, institutional form required. Applicants notified on a rolling basis starting 11/1.

Academics. All education programs relate specifically to Jewish Studies. For bachelor's in Jewish Studies, 42 liberal arts credits from another accredited college or university required. **Special study options:** Cross-registration, distance learning, double major, independent study, internships, study abroad, teacher certification program. **Credit/placement by examination:** CLEP, institutional tests. **Support services:** Reduced course load, remedial instruction, tutoring.

Majors. Philosophy/religion: Judaic, religion.

Computing on campus. 4 workstations in library, student center. Wireless network available.

Student life. Freshman orientation: Available. Preregistration for classes offered. **Activities:** Choral groups, student government.

Student services. Adult student services, career counseling, financial aid counseling, personal counseling, placement for graduates.

Contact. E-mail: admissions@gratz.edu
Phone: (215) 635-7300 ext. 140 Toll-free number: (800) 475-4635 ext. 140
Fax: (215) 635-7399
Ruthann Crosby, Director of Student Life, Gratz College, 7605 Old York Road, Melrose Park, PA 19027

Grove City College

Grove City, Pennsylvania **CB member**
www.gcc.edu **CB code: 2277**

- Private 4-year liberal arts college affiliated with Presbyterian Church (USA)
- Residential campus in small town
- 2,480 degree-seeking undergraduates: 49% women, 1% African American, 2% Asian American, 1% Hispanic American, 1% international
- 56% of applicants admitted

- SAT or ACT (ACT writing optional), application essay, interview required
- 85% graduate within 6 years; 22% enter graduate study

General. Founded in 1876. Regionally accredited. **Degrees:** 568 bachelor's awarded. **Location:** 60 miles from Pittsburgh. **Calendar:** Semester, extensive summer session. **Full-time faculty:** 140 total; 83% have terminal degrees, 2% minority, 26% women. **Part-time faculty:** 69 total; 17% have terminal degrees, 3% minority, 45% women. **Class size:** 40% < 20, 47% 20-39, 7% 40-49, 5% 50-99, 1% >100. **Special facilities:** Observatory.

Freshman class profile. 1,847 applied, 1,040 admitted, 621 enrolled.

Mid 50% test scores		**GPA 2.0-2.99:**	1%
SAT critical reading:	570-700	**Rank in top quarter:**	81%
SAT math:	580-690	**Rank in top tenth:**	52%
ACT composite:	26-30	**Return as sophomores:**	92%
GPA 3.75 or higher:	64%	**Out-of-state:**	53%
GPA 3.50-3.74:	18%	**Live on campus:**	93%
GPA 3.0-3.49:	17%		

Basis for selection. High school record, GPA or class rank, test scores, recommendations, interview, character, and extracurricular activities very important. Audition required for music program. **Homeschooled:** Transcript of courses and grades, interview, letter of recommendation (nonparent) required. Outside activities important.

High school preparation. College-preparatory program recommended. 17 units recommended. Recommended units include English 4, mathematics 3, social studies 2, history 2, science 3 (laboratory 2) and foreign language 3. Engineering, science, and math applicants must have 4 math and 4 science.

2008-2009 Annual costs. Tuition/fees: $12,074. Tuition includes cost of tablet PC and printer. Room/board: $6,440. Books/supplies: $900. Personal expenses: $350.

2008-2009 Financial aid. Need-based: 356 full-time freshmen applied for aid; 250 were judged to have need; 246 of these received aid. Average need met was 60%. Average scholarship/grant was $6,371. 65% of total undergraduate aid awarded as scholarships/grants, 35% as loans/jobs. **Non-need-based:** Awarded to 446 full-time undergraduates, including 83 freshmen. Scholarships awarded for academics, leadership, minority status. **Additional information:** Institutional aid applications required for institutional scholarships, loans, and student employment.

Application procedures. Admission: Closing date 2/1 (postmark date). $50 fee, may be waived for applicants with need. Decision letters mailed 3/15. Must reply by 5/1. **Financial aid:** Closing date 4/15. Institutional form required. Applicants notified on a rolling basis starting 3/15; must reply by 5/1.

Academics. All students required to complete 3-year humanities sequence, which includes religion, philosophy, history, philosophy of science, science/faith/technology, literature, art, and music. **Special study options:** Accelerated study, double major, independent study, internships, study abroad, teacher certification program, Washington semester. **Credit/placement by examination:** AP, CLEP, IB. **Support services:** Reduced course load, study skills assistance, tutoring.

Majors. Biology: General, biochemistry, molecular. **Business:** Accounting, business admin, communications, entrepreneurial studies, international, managerial economics, marketing. **Communications:** General. **Computer sciences:** General, applications programming, systems analysis. **Education:** Biology, chemistry, early childhood, elementary, English, French, history, mathematics, music, physics, science, secondary, social studies, Spanish. **Engineering:** Electrical, mechanical. **Engineering technology:** Industrial management. **Foreign languages:** French, Spanish. **Health:** Predental, premedicine, preveterinary. **History:** General. **Interdisciplinary:** Math/computer science. **Legal studies:** Prelaw. **Math:** General. **Philosophy/religion:** Philosophy, religion. **Physical sciences:** Chemistry, physics. **Psychology:** General. **Social sciences:** Economics, political science, sociology. **Visual/performing arts:** Music management, music performance.

Most popular majors. Biology 10%, business/marketing 18%, communications/journalism 7%, education 12%, engineering/engineering technologies 10%, English 6%, history 6%, philosophy/religious studies 6%, social sciences 9%.

Computing on campus. PC or laptop required. 50 workstations in library, computer center. Dormitories wired for high-speed internet access and linked to campus network. Commuter students can connect to campus network. Online course registration, online library, helpline, repair service, student web hosting, wireless network available.

Student life. Freshman orientation: Available. Preregistration for classes offered. One-day programs in June. **Policies:** Alcohol not permitted on campus. Chapel program consists of lectures, vespers, and seminars. Students must attend 16 chapels per semester. Religious observance required. **Housing:** Guaranteed on-campus for all undergraduates. Single-sex dorms, apartments, wellness housing available. **Activities:** Bands, campus ministries, choral groups, dance, drama, international student organizations, literary magazine, music ensembles, musical theater, opera, radio station, student government, student newspaper, symphony orchestra, TV station, Fellowship of Christian Athletes, Salt Company, Warriors for Christ, Young Life, Neuman club, College Republicans, College Democrats, outing club, orientation board, Life Advocates.

Athletics. NCAA. **Intercollegiate:** Baseball M, basketball, cheerleading M, cross-country, diving, football (tackle) M, golf, soccer, softball W, swimming, tennis, track and field, volleyball W, water polo W. **Intramural:** Badminton, basketball, bowling, football (non-tackle), golf M, handball M, racquetball, soccer W, softball, swimming W, tennis, volleyball. **Team name:** Wolverines.

Student services. Chaplain/spiritual director, career counseling, student employment services, financial aid counseling, health services, minority student services, personal counseling, placement for graduates.

Contact. E-mail: admissions@gcc.edu
Phone: (724) 458-2100 Fax: (724) 458-3395
Jeffrey Mincey, Director of Admissions, Grove City College, 100 Campus Drive, Grove City, PA 16127-2104

Gwynedd-Mercy College

Gwynedd Valley, Pennsylvania — **CB member**
www.gmc.edu — **CB code: 2278**

- Private 4-year health science and liberal arts college affiliated with Roman Catholic Church
- Residential campus in large town
- 1,963 degree-seeking undergraduates: 26% part-time, 73% women, 18% African American, 3% Asian American, 2% Hispanic American, 1% Native American, 1% international
- 503 degree-seeking graduate students
- 60% of applicants admitted
- SAT or ACT (ACT writing optional) required
- 64% graduate within 6 years

General. Founded in 1948. Regionally accredited. Affiliated with the Religious Sisters of Mercy. 8-week evening sessions running 12 months for business and accounting majors. Accelerated degree program begins every 6 weeks. **Degrees:** 391 bachelor's, 228 associate awarded; master's offered. **Location:** 20 miles from Philadelphia. **Calendar:** Semester, limited summer session. **Full-time faculty:** 82 total; 61% have terminal degrees, 2% minority, 68% women. **Part-time faculty:** 215 total; 21% have terminal degrees, 8% minority, 56% women. **Class size:** 65% < 20, 32% 20-39, less than 1% 40-49, 3% 50-99, less than 1% >100. **Special facilities:** Lincolnera collection, nursery laboratory school for early childhood education.

Freshman class profile. 2,043 applied, 1,219 admitted, 346 enrolled.

Mid 50% test scores		**Return as sophomores:**	84%
SAT critical reading:	440-540	**Out-of-state:**	17%
SAT math:	440-540	**Live on campus:**	79%
Rank in top quarter:	26%	**International:**	1%
Rank in top tenth:	4%		

Basis for selection. School achievement record most important, followed by test scores and recommendations. Extracurricular activities considered. Nursing program very competitive.

High school preparation. 16 units required. Required units include English 4, mathematics 3, history 1, science 3 and academic electives 3. Chemistry required for applicants to nursing, cardiovascular, biology, medical technology programs. Biology required for cardiovascular, health information technology programs. Physics required for radiation therapy, medical technology, biology programs. Chemistry or physics required for respiratory therapy.

2008-2009 Annual costs. Tuition/fees: $22,790. Tuition and fees for nursing and allied health programs $23,840 for full-time, and $570 per credit hour for part-time. Room/board: $8,990. Books/supplies: $650. Personal expenses: $1,000.

2007-2008 Financial aid. Need-based: 264 full-time freshmen applied for aid; 211 were judged to have need; 211 of these received aid. Average need met was 75%. Average scholarship/grant was $12,370; average loan

$3,225. 65% of total undergraduate aid awarded as scholarships/grants, 35% as loans/jobs. **Non-need-based:** Awarded to 937 full-time undergraduates, including 234 freshmen. Scholarships awarded for academics, leadership.

Application procedures. Admission: Closing date 8/20 (receipt date). $25 fee, may be waived for applicants with need, free for online applicants. Admission notification on a rolling basis beginning on or about 9/20. Must reply by May 1 or within 3 week(s) if notified thereafter. Nursing program usually filled by May 1. **Financial aid:** Priority date 3/1, closing date 7/15. FAFSA, institutional form required. Applicants notified on a rolling basis starting 2/15; must reply by 5/1 or within 2 week(s) of notification.

Academics. Special study options: Accelerated study, cooperative education, cross-registration, double major, dual enrollment of high school students, ESL, honors, independent study, internships, liberal arts/career combination, teacher certification program, weekend college. **Credit/placement by examination:** AP, CLEP, institutional tests. Credit by examination cannot be applied to open electives. **Support services:** Learning center, reduced course load, remedial instruction, study skills assistance, tutoring, writing center.

Majors. Biology: General. **Business:** Accounting, business admin. **Computer sciences:** General. **Education:** Biology, business, elementary, mathematics, special. **Family/consumer sciences:** Aging. **Health:** Cardiovascular technology, clinical lab science, medical radiologic technology/radiation therapy, medical records admin, nursing (RN), premedicine, preveterinary, respiratory therapy technology. **History:** General. **Math:** General. **Protective services:** Law enforcement admin. **Psychology:** General. **Social sciences:** Sociology.

Computing on campus. 217 workstations in library, computer center, student center. Dormitories wired for high-speed internet access and linked to campus network. Commuter students can connect to campus network. Online course registration, online library, helpline, wireless network available.

Student life. Freshman orientation: Available. Preregistration for classes offered. Multiple full-day sessions offered during the summer. **Housing:** Coed dorms, special housing for disabled available. $250 deposit, deadline 5/1. **Activities:** Campus ministries, choral groups, drama, literary magazine, musical theater, student government, student newspaper, business society, honor societies, Mercy Corps, resident council, commuter club, education club, peer counseling, psychology/sociology club.

Athletics. NCAA. **Intercollegiate:** Baseball M, basketball, cross-country, field hockey W, golf M, lacrosse W, soccer, softball W, tennis, track and field, volleyball W. **Intramural:** Volleyball. **Team name:** Griffins.

Student services. Adult student services, chaplain/spiritual director, career counseling, student employment services, financial aid counseling, health services, minority student services, on-campus daycare, personal counseling, placement for graduates.

Contact. E-mail: admissions@gmc.edu
Phone: (215) 646-7300 ext. 530 Toll-free number: (800) 342-5462
Fax: (215) 641-5556
James Abbuhl, Vice President for Enrollment Management,
Gwynedd-Mercy College, 1325 Sumneytown Pike, Gwynedd Valley, PA 19437-0901

Harrisburg University of Science and Technology
Harrisburg, Pennsylvania
www.HarrisburgU.net

- Private 4-year university
- Commuter campus in small city
- 157 degree-seeking undergraduates: 16% part-time, 48% women
- 24 degree-seeking graduate students

General. Regionally accredited. **Degrees:** 8 bachelor's awarded; master's offered. **Calendar:** Trimester, limited summer session. **Full-time faculty:** 10 total; 90% have terminal degrees, 20% minority, 50% women. **Part-time faculty:** 25 total; 20% have terminal degrees, 28% women. **Class size:** 95% < 20, 5% 20-39.

Freshman class profile.

End year in good standing:	75%	**Out-of-state:**	10%
Return as sophomores:	70%		

Basis for selection. Admissions based on high school record. SAT or ACT recommended. Interview and essay or personal statement recommended. **Homeschooled:** Statement describing homeschool structure and mission required.

2009-2010 Annual costs. Tuition/fees (projected): $18,000. Laptop required. Estimated Cost: $1,800. Books/supplies: $1,000. Personal expenses: $1,700.

2007-2008 Financial aid. Need-based: 33 full-time freshmen applied for aid; 28 were judged to have need; 28 of these received aid. Average need met was 85%. Average scholarship/grant was $3,000; average loan $3,500. 34% of total undergraduate aid awarded as scholarships/grants, 66% as loans/jobs. **Non-need-based:** Scholarships awarded for academics, leadership, state residency.

Application procedures. Admission: No deadline. No application fee. Admission notification on a rolling basis. **Financial aid:** No deadline. FAFSA required. Applicants notified on a rolling basis; must reply within 2 week(s) of notification.

Academics. Special study options: Dual enrollment of high school students, internships. **Credit/placement by examination:** AP, CLEP, institutional tests. **Support services:** Reduced course load, remedial instruction, study skills assistance, tutoring.

Majors. Biology: Biotechnology. **Business:** E-commerce. **Computer sciences:** General, information technology. **Conservation:** Environmental science. **Science technology:** Biological. **Social sciences:** Geography. **Other:** Geospatial imaging.

Most popular majors. Computer/information sciences 37%, science technologies 62%.

Computing on campus. PC or laptop required. 12 workstations in computer center. Commuter students can connect to campus network. Online library, wireless network available.

Student life. Freshman orientation: Mandatory. Preregistration for classes offered.

Student services. Financial aid counseling.

Contact. E-mail: admissions@HarrisburgU.net
Phone: (717) 901-5160 Fax: (717) 901-3160
Timothy Dawson, Director of Admissions and Enrollment Systems,
Harrisburg University of Science and Technology, 326 Market Street,
Harrisburg, PA 17101-2208

Haverford College
Haverford, Pennsylvania — **CB member**
www.haverford.edu — **CB code: 2289**

- Private 4-year liberal arts college
- Residential campus in large town
- 1,169 degree-seeking undergraduates: 53% women, 8% African American, 10% Asian American, 9% Hispanic American, 1% Native American, 3% international
- 27% of applicants admitted
- SAT or ACT with writing, SAT Subject Tests, application essay required
- 94% graduate within 6 years; 19% enter graduate study

General. Founded in 1833. Regionally accredited. Founded by the Society of Friends (Quakers), but now independent. **Degrees:** 301 bachelor's awarded. **Location:** 10 miles from Philadelphia. **Calendar:** Semester. **Full-time faculty:** 115 total; 96% have terminal degrees, 27% minority, 47% women. **Part-time faculty:** 17 total; 71% have terminal degrees, 24% minority, 47% women. **Class size:** 80% < 20, 17% 20-39, 1% 40-49, 2% 50-99. **Special facilities:** Observatory, arboretum, fine arts foundry.

Freshman class profile. 3,311 applied, 895 admitted, 327 enrolled.

Mid 50% test scores		**Rank in top tenth:**	91%
SAT critical reading:	650-740	**Return as sophomores:**	96%
SAT math:	650-740	**Out-of-state:**	83%
SAT writing:	660-750	**Live on campus:**	100%
Rank in top quarter:	97%	**International:**	3%

Basis for selection. School record, test scores, extracurricular achievements, and recommendations important. College seeks diversity of social, economic, and geographic backgrounds. Some preference given to children of alumni. First-year applicants must take SAT or ACT plus 2 SAT Subject

Tests before deadline for decision plan chosen. Interview required of applicants living within 150 miles of college, recommended for others. **Homeschooled:** Statement describing homeschool structure and mission, transcript of courses and grades, interview, letter of recommendation (nonparent) required.

High school preparation. College-preparatory program recommended. No specific high school curriculum required, but recommend inclusion of four years of English and at least three years of mathematics, the sciences, history and social studies, and one or two foreign languages.

2008-2009 Annual costs. Tuition/fees: $37,525. Room/board: $11,450. Books/supplies: $1,194. Personal expenses: $1,468.

2008-2009 Financial aid. All financial aid based on need. 208 full-time freshmen applied for aid; 169 were judged to have need; 169 of these received aid. Average need met was 100%. Average scholarship/grant was $31,983; average loan $539. 91% of total undergraduate aid awarded as scholarships/grants, 9% as loans/jobs.

Application procedures. **Admission:** Closing date 1/15. $60 fee, may be waived for applicants with need. Admission notification 4/15. Must reply by May 1 or within 2 week(s) if notified thereafter. **Financial aid:** Closing date 1/31. FAFSA, CSS PROFILE required. Applicants notified by 4/8; must reply by 5/1.

Academics. Academic Flexibility Program allows for advanced independent work and interdepartmental majors. Ample opportunity for student-faculty research. Senior seminars, comprehensive examination and/or senior thesis required for completion of all major programs. **Special study options:** Combined bachelor's/graduate degree, cross-registration, double major, exchange student, independent study, internships, liberal arts/career combination, student-designed major, study abroad, teacher certification program. Exchange programs with Spelman College (GA), Claremont McKenna College and Pitzer College (CA), Fisk University (TN); cross-registration with Bryn Mawr College, Swarthmore College, noncredit internships also available; 3-2 engineering program with California Institute of Technology. **Credit/placement by examination:** AP, CLEP, IB, institutional tests. **Support services:** Learning center, study skills assistance, tutoring, writing center.

Majors. **Architecture:** Urban/community planning. **Area/ethnic studies:** East Asian. **Biology:** General. **Computer sciences:** General. **Foreign languages:** Ancient Greek, classics, comparative lit, French, German, Italian, Latin, Russian, Spanish. **History:** General. **Liberal arts:** Arts/sciences. **Math:** General. **Philosophy/religion:** Philosophy, religion. **Physical sciences:** Astronomy, chemistry, geology, physics. **Psychology:** General. **Social sciences:** Anthropology, archaeology, economics, political science, sociology, urban studies. **Visual/performing arts:** Art history/conservation, studio arts.

Most popular majors. Biology 12%, English 9%, foreign language 7%, history 7%, philosophy/religious studies 7%, physical sciences 12%, psychology 8%, social sciences 25%.

Computing on campus. 300 workstations in dormitories, library, computer center, student center. Dormitories wired for high-speed internet access and linked to campus network. Commuter students can connect to campus network. Online course registration, online library, helpline, student web hosting, wireless network available.

Student life. **Freshman orientation:** Mandatory, $180 fee. Preregistration for classes offered. Directly precedes the start of the fall semester. **Policies:** Student conduct regulated by academic and social honor code, which allows for unsupervised examinations. Students serve on campus governance and policy-making committees. **Housing:** Guaranteed on-campus for all undergraduates. Coed dorms, single-sex dorms, apartments, wellness housing available. Students may live at Bryn Mawr College through dormitory exchange program. Students at both colleges may eat meals on either campus. **Activities:** Campus ministries, choral groups, dance, drama, international student organizations, literary magazine, music ensembles, musical theater, radio station, student government, student newspaper, Quaker activities committee, Hillel, Christian Fellowship, environmental action committee, black students league, Puerto Rican students association, Asian students association, Bisexual/Gay/Lesbian alliance, Eighth Dimension Volunteer Service Program.

Athletics. NCAA. **Intercollegiate:** Baseball M, basketball, cricket M, cross-country, fencing, field hockey W, lacrosse, soccer, softball W, squash, tennis, track and field, volleyball W. **Intramural:** Basketball, soccer, tennis.

Student services. Alcohol/substance abuse counseling, career counseling, student employment services, financial aid counseling, health services, minority student services, personal counseling, placement for graduates, women's services. **Physically disabled:** Services for visually, speech, hearing impaired.

Contact. E-mail: admission@haverford.edu
Phone: (610) 896-1350 Fax: (610) 896-1338
Jess Lord, Dean of Admission and Financial Aid, Haverford College, 370 Lancaster Avenue, Haverford, PA 19041-1392

Holy Family University

Philadelphia, Pennsylvania — **CB member**
www.holyfamily.edu — **CB code: 2297**

- Private 4-year university and liberal arts college affiliated with Roman Catholic Church
- Commuter campus in very large city
- 2,184 degree-seeking undergraduates: 28% part-time, 75% women, 7% African American, 5% Asian American, 4% Hispanic American, 1% international
- 1,084 degree-seeking graduate students
- 72% of applicants admitted
- 69% graduate within 6 years; 5% enter graduate study

General. Founded in 1954. Regionally accredited. Additional campuses in Newtown, Bensalem, and South Philadelphia. **Degrees:** 401 bachelor's, 22 associate awarded; master's offered. **Location:** 12 miles from downtown. **Calendar:** Semester, extensive summer session. **Full-time faculty:** 98 total; 71% have terminal degrees, 12% minority, 66% women. **Part-time faculty:** 286 total; 14% have terminal degrees, 15% minority, 54% women. **Class size:** 79% < 20, 21% 20-39. **Special facilities:** Early childhood center with nursery school and kindergarten.

Freshman class profile. 1,301 applied, 932 admitted, 404 enrolled.

Mid 50% test scores		**GPA 3.0-3.49:**	64%
SAT critical reading:	420-510	**GPA 2.0-2.99:**	23%
SAT math:	420-510	**End year in good standing:**	77%
SAT writing:	410-490	**Return as sophomores:**	77%
ACT composite:	19-20	**Out-of-state:**	20%
GPA 3.75 or higher:	3%	**Live on campus:**	29%
GPA 3.50-3.74:	10%		

Basis for selection. High school record most important, followed by recommendations, interview and test scores. Motivation, schoolwork and community activities considered. Essay, interview recommended. **Homeschooled:** State-issued equivalency diploma required. **Learning Disabled:** Students must meet with Counseling Center to be evaluated. Results and formal report shared with Admission department and acceptance decision is made. Results discussed with student.

High school preparation. 14 units required; 16 recommended. Required and recommended units include English 4, mathematics 3, history 2, science 2, foreign language 2 and academic electives 3. All students must have algebra I, algebra II, and geometry. Math majors need trigonometry. Nursing requires biology, chemistry, and science electives. Science requires biology, chemistry, and trigonometry.

2009-2010 Annual costs. Tuition/fees (projected): $22,990. Room/board: $9,900. Books/supplies: $972. Personal expenses: $600.

2007-2008 Financial aid. **Need-based:** Average need met was 90%. 44% of total undergraduate aid awarded as scholarships/grants, 56% as loans/jobs. **Non-need-based:** Scholarships awarded for academics, alumni affiliation, athletics.

Application procedures. **Admission:** No deadline. $25 fee, may be waived for applicants with need. Admission notification on a rolling basis. Must reply by May 1 or within 2 week(s) if notified thereafter. **Financial aid:** Priority date 3/1; no closing date. FAFSA, institutional form required. Applicants notified on a rolling basis starting 3/15; must reply within 2 week(s) of notification.

Academics. **Special study options:** Accelerated study, combined bachelor's/graduate degree, cooperative education, double major, dual enrollment of high school students, independent study, internships, study abroad, teacher certification program. **Credit/placement by examination:** AP, CLEP, IB, institutional tests. 30 credit hours maximum toward bachelor's degree. **Support services:** Pre-admission summer program, remedial instruction, study skills assistance, tutoring, writing center.

Majors. **Biology:** General, biochemistry. **Business:** Accounting, business admin, finance, human resources, international, management information systems. **Communications:** Media studies. **Education:** Art, biology, chemistry, early childhood, elementary, English, French, history, mathematics, social science, social studies, Spanish, special. **Foreign languages:** French, Spanish. **Health:** Clinical lab science, nursing (RN), radiologic technology/

medical imaging. **History:** General. **Liberal arts:** Humanities. **Math:** General. **Parks/recreation:** Sports admin. **Philosophy/religion:** Religion. **Physical sciences:** Chemistry. **Protective services:** Criminal justice, fire services admin. **Psychology:** General, industrial. **Public administration:** Social work. **Social sciences:** Economics, sociology. **Visual/performing arts:** Studio arts.

Most popular majors. Business/marketing 14%, education 24%, health sciences 36%, psychology 8%.

Computing on campus. 450 workstations in dormitories, library, computer center. Dormitories wired for high-speed internet access and linked to campus network. Commuter students can connect to campus network. Online course registration, online library, helpline, repair service, wireless network available.

Student life. **Freshman orientation:** Mandatory. **Policies:** Mature and intelligent student conduct expected in accordance with college's interests, standards, and ideals. **Housing:** Guaranteed on-campus for freshmen. Coed dorms, special housing for disabled, apartments, wellness housing available. $300 nonrefundable deposit, deadline 3/15. On-campus housing available for some athletes. **Activities:** Campus ministries, choral groups, drama, literary magazine, music ensembles, musical theater, radio station, student government, student newspaper, TV station, community health and welfare organizations, social and departmental clubs, honor societies, ministry team, Habitat for Humanity.

Athletics. NCAA. **Intercollegiate:** Basketball, cross-country, golf M, lacrosse W, soccer, softball W, tennis W, track and field, volleyball W. **Intramural:** Basketball, bowling, cheerleading W, football (non-tackle), racquetball, table tennis, volleyball. **Team name:** Tigers.

Student services. Adult student services, alcohol/substance abuse counseling, chaplain/spiritual director, career counseling, student employment services, financial aid counseling, health services, minority student services, personal counseling, placement for graduates. **Physically disabled:** Services for visually, speech, hearing impaired. **Learning disabled:** Comprehensive services available.

Contact. E-mail: admissions@holyfamily.edu
Phone: (215) 637-3050 Toll-free number: (800) 637-1191
Fax: (215) 281-1022
Lauren Campbell, Director of Admissions, Holy Family University, 9801 Frankford Avenue, Philadelphia, PA 19114-2009

Immaculata University

Immaculata, Pennsylvania — **CB member**
www.immaculata.edu — **CB code: 2320**

- Private 4-year university and liberal arts college affiliated with Roman Catholic Church
- Residential campus in large town
- 2,776 degree-seeking undergraduates: 61% part-time, 77% women, 12% African American, 2% Asian American, 2% Hispanic American, 1% international
- 952 degree-seeking graduate students
- 80% of applicants admitted
- SAT or ACT (ACT writing recommended) required
- 47% graduate within 6 years

General. Founded in 1920. Regionally accredited. **Degrees:** 500 bachelor's, 25 associate awarded; master's, doctoral offered. **Location:** 20 miles from Philadelphia. **Calendar:** Semester, limited summer session. **Full-time faculty:** 100 total; 73% have terminal degrees, 8% minority, 73% women. **Part-time faculty:** 326 total; 24% have terminal degrees, 62% women. **Class size:** 74% < 20, 26% 20-39.

Freshman class profile. 1,459 applied, 1,165 admitted, 239 enrolled.

Mid 50% test scores			
SAT critical reading:	420-520	GPA 3.50-3.74:	13%
SAT math:	410-530	GPA 3.0-3.49:	26%
SAT writing:	430-530	GPA 2.0-2.99:	43%
ACT composite:	17-24	Return as sophomores:	66%
GPA 3.75 or higher:	17%	Out-of-state:	31%
		Live on campus:	82%

Basis for selection. Class rank, academic program, test scores, counselor recommendation important. Minimum 2.3 GPA preferred. Interviews, essay recommended. Audition required for music program. **Homeschooled:** Transcript of courses and grades required. **Learning Disabled:** Proof of psychological or educational testing date must be supplied.

High school preparation. College-preparatory program required. 16 units required; 20 recommended. Required and recommended units include English 4, mathematics 2-3, social studies 2-3, science 2-4 (laboratory 1), foreign language 2-3 and visual/performing arts 4. Music required for music majors.

2008-2009 Annual costs. Tuition/fees: $24,575. Tuition and fees for entering freshmen guaranteed to not increase for the 4 years of enrollment. Room/board: $10,400. Books/supplies: $1,306.

2008-2009 Financial aid. **Non-need-based:** Scholarships awarded for academics, alumni affiliation, art, job skills, leadership, minority status, music/drama, religious affiliation, state residency.

Application procedures. **Admission:** Priority date 3/1; no deadline. $35 fee, may be waived for applicants with need. Admission notification on a rolling basis beginning on or about 9/15. Must reply by May 1 or within 2 week(s) if notified thereafter. **Financial aid:** Priority date 2/15, closing date 4/15. FAFSA required. Applicants notified on a rolling basis starting 2/1; must reply within 2 week(s) of notification.

Academics. **Special study options:** Accelerated study, combined bachelor's/graduate degree, cross-registration, distance learning, double major, dual enrollment of high school students, honors, independent study, internships, liberal arts/career combination, semester at sea, study abroad, teacher certification program, Washington semester. **Credit/placement by examination:** AP, CLEP, IB, SAT, ACT, institutional tests. 30 credit hours maximum toward associate degree, 63 toward bachelor's. **Support services:** Learning center, reduced course load, remedial instruction, study skills assistance, tutoring, writing center.

Majors. **Biology:** General. **Business:** Accounting, business admin, fashion, finance, human resources. **Computer sciences:** Information systems. **Conservation:** Environmental studies. **Education:** Business, elementary, family/consumer sciences, music. **Foreign languages:** French, German, Spanish. **Health:** Dietetics, health care admin, music therapy, nursing (RN), premedicine. **History:** General. **Interdisciplinary:** Biological/physical sciences, biopsychology, math/computer science. **Math:** General. **Parks/recreation:** Exercise sciences. **Physical sciences:** Chemistry. **Protective services:** Criminal justice. **Psychology:** General. **Public administration:** Policy analysis. **Social sciences:** Economics, international relations, political science, sociology. **Theology:** Theology. **Visual/performing arts:** Music performance.

Most popular majors. Business/marketing 38%, health sciences 42%.

Computing on campus. 326 workstations in dormitories, library, computer center, student center. Dormitories wired for high-speed internet access and linked to campus network. Commuter students can connect to campus network. Online course registration, online library, helpline, wireless network available.

Student life. **Freshman orientation:** Mandatory. Preregistration for classes offered. 2-day session held in summer. **Housing:** Coed dorms, single-sex dorms, special housing for disabled, apartments available. $250 partly refundable deposit. **Activities:** Bands, campus ministries, choral groups, dance, drama, international student organizations, literary magazine, music ensembles, musical theater, student government, student newspaper, symphony orchestra, African American cultural society, American Music Therapy Association, Modern Foreign Language Association.

Athletics. NCAA. **Intercollegiate:** Basketball, cross-country W, field hockey W, golf, lacrosse, soccer, softball W, tennis, volleyball W. **Intramural:** Basketball, cross-country W, field hockey W, lacrosse W, soccer W, softball W, swimming W, tennis W, volleyball W. **Team name:** Mighty Macs.

Student services. Adult student services, alcohol/substance abuse counseling, chaplain/spiritual director, career counseling, student employment services, financial aid counseling, health services, minority student services, personal counseling, placement for graduates. **Physically disabled:** Services for visually, hearing impaired.

Contact. E-mail: admiss@immaculata.edu
Phone: (610) 647-4400 ext. 3060 Toll-free number: (877) 428-6329
Fax: (610) 640-0836
Rebecca Bowlby, Director of Admission, Immaculata University, PO Box 642, Immaculata, PA 19345-0642

Indiana University of Pennsylvania

Indiana, Pennsylvania — **CB member**
www.iup.edu — **CB code: 2652**

- Public 4-year university
- Residential campus in large town

- 11,565 degree-seeking undergraduates: 5% part-time, 55% women, 11% African American, 1% Asian American, 2% Hispanic American, 1% international
- 2,254 degree-seeking graduate students
- 64% of applicants admitted
- SAT or ACT (ACT writing optional) required
- 51% graduate within 6 years

General. Founded in 1875. Regionally accredited. Branch campuses located in Punxsutawney and Armstrong County. **Degrees:** 2,101 bachelor's, 13 associate awarded; master's, doctoral offered. **ROTC:** Army. **Location:** 50 miles from Pittsburgh. **Calendar:** Semester, extensive summer session. **Full-time faculty:** 648 total; 15% minority, 48% women. **Part-time faculty:** 64 total; 6% minority, 55% women. **Special facilities:** Museums, ski slopes, nature preserve, lodge, and sailing base.

Freshman class profile. 11,030 applied, 7,065 admitted, 3,090 enrolled.

Mid 50% test scores		**Rank in top tenth:**	8%
SAT critical reading:	440-540	**Return as sophomores:**	73%
SAT math:	440-540	**Out-of-state:**	7%
SAT writing:	430-520	**Live on campus:**	84%
Rank in top quarter:	26%	**International:**	1%

Basis for selection. School achievement record, recommendations and extracurricular activities considered, test scores, and high school rank important. Audition required for music program; portfolio required for art program. **Homeschooled:** Transcript of courses and grades required.

High school preparation. 4 units recommended. Recommended units include English 3, mathematics 3, social studies 3, science 3 and foreign language 2. Additional .5 unit computer science recommended.

2008-2009 Annual costs. Tuition/fees: $6,958; $14,996 out-of-state. Additional fees of $92 for out-of-state students. Tuition is $8,038 for students in any of these categories: OH, VA, WV, IN and MI residents; branch campus students from any state; out-of-state students with high school GPA of at least 3.0; any transfer student with GPA of at least 3.0. Room/board: $5,578. Books/supplies: $1,000. Personal expenses: $3,059.

2007-2008 Financial aid. Need-based: Average need met was 83%. Average scholarship/grant was $5,285; average loan $3,779. 44% of total undergraduate aid awarded as scholarships/grants, 56% as loans/jobs. **Non-need-based:** Awarded to 2,188 full-time undergraduates, including 172 freshmen. Scholarships awarded for academics, alumni affiliation, art, athletics, job skills, leadership, music/drama, ROTC, state residency.

Application procedures. Admission: Priority date 12/31; no deadline. $35 fee, may be waived for applicants with need. Admission notification on a rolling basis beginning on or about 9/1. Must reply by May 1 or within 2 week(s) if notified thereafter. **Financial aid:** Priority date 4/15; no closing date. FAFSA required. Applicants notified on a rolling basis starting 3/15.

Academics. Special study options: Accelerated study, combined bachelor's/graduate degree, cooperative education, cross-registration, distance learning, double major, dual enrollment of high school students, ESL, exchange student, external degree, honors, independent study, internships, liberal arts/career combination, student-designed major, study abroad, teacher certification program, urban semester, Washington semester, weekend college. **Credit/placement by examination:** AP, CLEP, IB, SAT, ACT, institutional tests. Unlimited number of hours of credit by examination may be counted toward degree. **Support services:** Learning center, pre-admission summer program, remedial instruction, study skills assistance, tutoring, writing center.

Majors. Architecture: Urban/community planning. **Biology:** General, biochemistry. **Business:** General, accounting, business admin, fashion, finance, hospitality admin, human resources, international, management information systems, marketing, office management. **Communications:** General, journalism. **Computer sciences:** General. **Education:** Deaf/hearing impaired, early childhood, elementary, physically handicapped, social science, special, speech impaired, trade/industrial. **Engineering technology:** Occupational safety. **Family/consumer sciences:** General, consumer economics, family studies, food/nutrition. **Foreign languages:** French, German, Spanish. **Health:** Clinical lab science, environmental health, nuclear medical technology, nursing (RN), respiratory therapy technology. **History:** General. **Interdisciplinary:** Biological/physical sciences. **Math:** General, applied. **Parks/recreation:** Health/fitness. **Philosophy/religion:** Philosophy, religion. **Physical sciences:** General, applied physics, chemistry, geology, physics. **Psychology:** General. **Social sciences:** Anthropology, criminology, economics, geography, international relations, political science, sociology. **Visual/performing arts:** Art, dramatic, multimedia, music performance, studio arts. **Other:** Disability services, Economics and mathematics, French for international trade.

Most popular majors. Business/marketing 20%, communications/journalism 8%, education 10%, health sciences 8%, parks/recreation 6%, social sciences 17%, visual/performing arts 8%.

Computing on campus. 3,500 workstations in dormitories, library, computer center. Dormitories wired for high-speed internet access and linked to campus network. Commuter students can connect to campus network. Online course registration, helpline, repair service, student web hosting, wireless network available.

Student life. Freshman orientation: Mandatory, $140 fee. Preregistration for classes offered. **Housing:** Guaranteed on-campus for freshmen. Coed dorms, special housing for disabled, apartments, wellness housing available. $80 nonrefundable deposit, deadline 5/15. Honors college dormitory, substance-free housing, academic specialty floors available. **Activities:** Bands, campus ministries, choral groups, dance, drama, international student organizations, music ensembles, musical theater, radio station, student government, student newspaper, symphony orchestra, TV station, Alpha Phi Omega National Service Fraternity (coeducational), Gamma Sigma Sigma Service Sorority, African American Cultural Center, Campus Crusade for Christ, Coalition for Christian Outreach, Newman Center, Panhellenic Association, NAACP.

Athletics. NCAA. **Intercollegiate:** Baseball M, basketball, cross-country, diving, field hockey W, football (tackle) M, golf M, lacrosse W, soccer W, softball W, swimming, tennis W, track and field, volleyball W. **Intramural:** Archery, badminton, basketball, bowling, cross-country, fencing, football (non-tackle), golf, racquetball, soccer, softball, table tennis, tennis, track and field, volleyball, water polo, weight lifting, wrestling M. **Team name:** Crimson Hawks.

Student services. Adult student services, alcohol/substance abuse counseling, chaplain/spiritual director, career counseling, services for economically disadvantaged, student employment services, financial aid counseling, health services, legal services, minority student services, on-campus daycare, personal counseling, placement for graduates, veterans' counselor, women's services. **Physically disabled:** Services for visually, speech, hearing impaired.

Contact. E-mail: admissions_inquiry@iup.edu
Phone: (724) 357-2230 Toll-free number: (800) 442-6830
Fax: (724) 357-6281
Rhonda Luckey, Vice President for Student Affairs, Indiana University of Pennsylvania, 117 John Sutton Hall, 1011 South Drive, Indiana, PA 15705-1088

Juniata College

Huntingdon, Pennsylvania — **CB member**
www.juniata.edu — **CB code: 2341**

- Private 4-year liberal arts college
- Residential campus in small town
- 1,402 degree-seeking undergraduates: 56% women, 1% African American, 2% Asian American, 2% Hispanic American, 4% international
- 69% of applicants admitted
- Application essay required
- 80% graduate within 6 years; 19% enter graduate study

General. Founded in 1876. Regionally accredited. **Degrees:** 328 bachelor's awarded. **Location:** 30 miles from Altoona and State College. **Calendar:** Semester, limited summer session. **Full-time faculty:** 103 total; 85% have terminal degrees, 5% minority, 38% women. **Part-time faculty:** 49 total; 33% have terminal degrees, 57% women. **Class size:** 70% < 20, 26% 20-39, 3% 40-49, less than 1% 50-99, less than 1% >100. **Special facilities:** Nature preserve, environmental studies field station, observatory, early childhood education center.

Freshman class profile. 2,349 applied, 1,626 admitted, 461 enrolled.

Mid 50% test scores		**Rank in top quarter:**	79%
SAT critical reading:	550-650	**Rank in top tenth:**	44%
SAT math:	550-640	**End year in good standing:**	95%
GPA 3.75 or higher:	55%	**Return as sophomores:**	84%
GPA 3.50-3.74:	18%	**Out-of-state:**	32%
GPA 3.0-3.49:	22%	**Live on campus:**	96%
GPA 2.0-2.99:	5%	**International:**	3%

Basis for selection. School achievement record most important. Standardized test scores, school and community activities, recommendations and essay also important. SAT or ACT recommended. Students may submit SAT or ACT scores either directly from the testing agency or from the guidance counselor. If a student chooses not to submit standardized test scores, then must submit two graded papers. Interview recommended. **Homeschooled:** Interview required.

High school preparation. College-preparatory program required. 16 units required; 18 recommended. Required and recommended units include English 4, mathematics 3-4, social studies 1, history 3, science 3-4 (laboratory 2) and foreign language 2.

2008-2009 Annual costs. Tuition/fees: $30,280. Room/board: $8,420. Books/supplies: $600. Personal expenses: $1,000.

2008-2009 Financial aid. Need-based: 386 full-time freshmen applied for aid; 328 were judged to have need; 328 of these received aid. Average need met was 87%. Average scholarship/grant was $18,469; average loan $3,822. 75% of total undergraduate aid awarded as scholarships/grants, 25% as loans/jobs. **Non-need-based:** Awarded to 587 full-time undergraduates, including 197 freshmen. Scholarships awarded for academics, art.

Application procedures. Admission: Priority date 12/1; deadline 3/15 (postmark date). $30 fee, may be waived for applicants with need, free for online applicants. Admission notification on a rolling basis beginning on or about 2/28. Must reply by May 1 or within 2 week(s) if notified thereafter. **Financial aid:** Closing date 3/1. FAFSA required. Applicants notified on a rolling basis starting 2/21; must reply by 5/1.

Academics. Majors replaced by Programs of Emphasis. Over 50% of students design individualized POE. **Special study options:** Combined bachelor's/graduate degree, double major, dual enrollment of high school students, ESL, exchange student, honors, independent study, internships, student-designed major, study abroad, teacher certification program, urban semester, Washington semester. Marine biology with Oregon Marine Program; 3-3 law with Duquesne University; 3-2 engineering with Columbia University, Pennsylvania State University, Clarkson University, Washington University; 3-4 dentistry with Temple University; 3-4 medicine with Tulane University School of Medicine, Lake Erie College of Osteopathic Medicine; 3-4 optometry with Pennsylvania College of Optometry; 3-4 podiatry with Temple University School of Podiatric Medicine and Ohio College of Podiatric Medicine; nursing with Johns Hopkins University, Case Western Reserve University; biotechnology, cytogenetics/cytotechnology with Jefferson College of Health Professions; physical therapy with Widener University, Drexel University; medical technology with Jefferson College of Health Professions, Altoona Regional Health Systems, Lancaster General College of Nursing & Health Sciences. **Credit/placement by examination:** AP, CLEP, IB, institutional tests. Unlimited number of hours of credit by examination may be counted toward degree. **Support services:** Reduced course load, study skills assistance, tutoring, writing center.

Majors. Biology: General, biochemistry, botany, cell/histology, ecology, marine, microbiology, molecular, zoology. **Business:** General, accounting, business admin, entrepreneurial studies, finance, human resources, information resources management, international, marketing. **Communications:** General, digital media, health. **Computer sciences:** General, information technology. **Conservation:** Environmental science, environmental studies, wildlife. **Education:** General, biology, chemistry, early childhood, early childhood special, elementary, English, French, German, mathematics, multi-level teacher, physics, science, secondary, social studies, Spanish, special. **Engineering:** General, physics. **Foreign languages:** General, French, German, Russian, Spanish. **Health:** Predental, premedicine, prenursing, prepharmacy, preveterinary. **History:** General. **Interdisciplinary:** Global studies, museum, natural sciences, peace/conflict. **Legal studies:** Prelaw. **Liberal arts:** Arts/sciences, humanities. **Math:** General. **Philosophy/religion:** Philosophy, religion. **Physical sciences:** General, chemistry, geology, physics. **Psychology:** General. **Public administration:** General, social work. **Social sciences:** General, anthropology, criminology, international relations, political science, sociology. **Visual/performing arts:** Art history/conservation, dramatic, studio arts, theater arts management.

Most popular majors. Biology 16%, business/marketing 15%, education 6%, natural resources/environmental science 6%, physical sciences 9%, social sciences 10%.

Computing on campus. 360 workstations in library, computer center, student center. Dormitories wired for high-speed internet access and linked to campus network. Commuter students can connect to campus network. Online course registration, online library, helpline, repair service, wireless network available.

Student life. Freshman orientation: Available. Preregistration for classes offered. 2 days in summer, parallel programs for new students and their parents. **Housing:** Guaranteed on-campus for all undergraduates. Coed dorms, single-sex dorms, apartments, wellness housing available. $400 nonrefundable deposit, deadline 5/1. Special interest housing available. **Activities:** Bands, campus ministries, choral groups, dance, drama, film society, international student organizations, literary magazine, music ensembles, Model UN, musical theater, radio station, student government, student newspaper, symphony orchestra, Christian Ministry Board, Catholic Council, Hillel, Muslim Student, Religious Studies Association, United Spiritual Council.

Athletics. NCAA. **Intercollegiate:** Baseball M, basketball, cross-country, field hockey W, football (tackle) M, soccer, softball W, swimming W, tennis, track and field, volleyball. **Intramural:** Basketball, bowling, soccer, volleyball. **Team name:** Eagles.

Student services. Adult student services, alcohol/substance abuse counseling, chaplain/spiritual director, career counseling, student employment services, financial aid counseling, health services, personal counseling, placement for graduates. **Physically disabled:** Services for visually, hearing impaired.

Contact. E-mail: admissions@juniata.edu
Phone: (814) 641-3420 Toll-free number: (877) 586-4282
Fax: (814) 641-3100
Michelle Bartol, Dean of Enrollment, Juniata College, 1700 Moore Street, Huntingdon, PA 16652-2196

Keystone College

La Plume, Pennsylvania — **CB member**
www.keystone.edu — **CB code: 2351**

- Private 4-year junior and liberal arts college
- Residential campus in small town
- 1,687 degree-seeking undergraduates: 23% part-time, 61% women, 1% African American, 1% Hispanic American
- 93% of applicants admitted
- SAT or ACT (ACT writing optional), application essay required

General. Founded in 1868. Regionally accredited. Students may enroll in up to 12 credits as nonmatriculating prior to making formal application to college. Trimester system for Adult Weekender Program. **Degrees:** 261 bachelor's, 85 associate awarded. **ROTC:** Army, Air Force. **Location:** 15 miles from Scranton. **Calendar:** Differs by program, limited summer session. **Full-time faculty:** 65 total; 38% have terminal degrees, 3% minority, 62% women. **Part-time faculty:** 196 total; 11% have terminal degrees, 3% minority, 56% women. **Class size:** 80% < 20, 20% 20-39, less than 1% 40-49, less than 1% 50-99. **Special facilities:** Observatory, children's center, Microsoft-certified systems engineer training site, Willary Water Resource center, U.S. Mid-Atlantic Urban Forestry Center, restaurant (operated by culinary students), delayed harvest trout stream, Countryside Conservancy, PRAXIS testing location, Nightshade Press, WKCV radio station.

Freshman class profile. 904 applied, 838 admitted, 344 enrolled.

Mid 50% test scores		**GPA 2.0-2.99:**	48%
SAT critical reading:	400-490	**Rank in top quarter:**	12%
SAT math:	390-500	**Rank in top tenth:**	5%
SAT writing:	380-480	**Return as sophomores:**	61%
ACT composite:	15-20	**Out-of-state:**	16%
GPA 3.75 or higher:	4%	**Live on campus:**	50%
GPA 3.50-3.74:	8%	**International:**	1%
GPA 3.0-3.49:	27%		

Basis for selection. School achievement record, extracurricular activities, test scores, recommendations, class rank, preparation in proposed major area of study considered. Portfolio and interview required for all art and art education applications. Admissions interview required for some on a case-by-case basis. **Homeschooled:** Statement describing homeschool structure and mission, interview required. Portfolio of high school level work also required. **Learning Disabled:** Current psychological report and Individualized Educational Program or 504 plan should be submitted at time of application. On-campus interview generally required to ensure that the college provides a level of support needed for the student to be academically successful.

High school preparation. College-preparatory program required. 16 units required; 20 recommended. Required and recommended units include English 4, mathematics 3-4, social studies 2, history 1, science 3-4 (laboratory 1), foreign language 2 and academic electives 2. Foreign language recommended for art, communications, and liberal arts curricula. 4 math and 3 science (including 2 lab) recommended for allied health, environmental science, pre-medical tracks, and forensic biology.

2009-2010 Annual costs. Tuition/fees (projected): $18,125. Room/board: $8,580. Books/supplies: $1,500.

2007-2008 Financial aid. Need-based: Average need met was 71%. Average scholarship/grant was $15,158; average loan $2,625. 57% of total undergraduate aid awarded as scholarships/grants, 43% as loans/jobs. **Non-need-based:** Awarded to 54 full-time undergraduates, including 48 freshmen. Scholarships awarded for academics, leadership, ROTC.

Application procedures. Admission: Priority date 5/1; deadline 7/1 (receipt date). $30 fee, may be waived for applicants with need. Admission notification on a rolling basis beginning on or about 11/1. Must reply by May 1 or within 2 week(s) if notified thereafter. **Financial aid:** Priority date 5/1; no closing date. FAFSA required. Applicants notified on a rolling basis starting 2/2; must reply within 2 week(s) of notification.

Academics. Students in good academic and financial standing who have not received at least 1 job offer or acceptance into a transfer or graduate program within 6 months after graduating and fulfilling requirements of Career Development Center will be provided with additional courses and career counseling at no extra charge. **Special study options:** Combined bachelor's/graduate degree, cooperative education, cross-registration, distance learning, double major, dual enrollment of high school students, ESL, honors, independent study, internships, study abroad, teacher certification program, weekend college. 2+2, 2+3, 3+3, 4+3 programs with various 4-year institutions for students studying allied health, health sciences, and environmental sciences. **Credit/placement by examination:** AP, CLEP, IB, SAT, ACT, institutional tests. 12 credit hours maximum toward associate degree, 18 toward bachelor's. Maximum of 32 credits for associate degree-seekers and 64 credits for bachelor's degree-seekers awarded for prior work and/or life experience. **Support services:** Learning center, pre-admission summer program, reduced course load, remedial instruction, study skills assistance, tutoring, writing center.

Honors college/program. Admissions requirements: 1100 SAT (exclusive of Writing) or 24 composite ACT, and top 10% of class or 3.0 GPA. Students who do not meet criteria considered on case-by-case basis.

Majors. Biology: General, biochemistry, biomedical sciences, environmental. **Business:** General, accounting, accounting/business management, business admin, management information systems. **Communications:** General, journalism. **Computer sciences:** General, information systems, information technology, LAN/WAN management, networking, systems analysis. **Conservation:** General, management/policy, water/wetlands/marine. **Education:** General, art, early childhood, elementary, mathematics, multi-level teacher, social studies. **Family/consumer sciences:** General, child care, child development, family systems. **Health:** Predental, premedicine, prepharmacy, preveterinary. **Interdisciplinary:** Biological/physical sciences, natural sciences. **Legal studies:** Prelaw. **Parks/recreation:** General, facilities management, sports admin. **Protective services:** Criminal justice, criminalistics, law enforcement admin. **Psychology:** General. **Social sciences:** General. **Visual/performing arts:** Art, ceramics, drawing, illustration, painting, printmaking, sculpture, studio arts.

Most popular majors. Business/marketing 26%, communications/journalism 8%, education 18%, interdisciplinary studies 7%, parks/recreation 8%, security/protective services 17%, visual/performing arts 10%.

Computing on campus. 120 workstations in dormitories, library, computer center, student center. Dormitories wired for high-speed internet access and linked to campus network. Commuter students can connect to campus network. Online course registration, helpline, wireless network available.

Student life. Freshman orientation: Mandatory, $125 fee. Preregistration for classes offered. One-day program during summer for scheduling classes. Multi-day overnight program prior to start of classes; options include canoeing, rafting, hiking, camping, volunteer service, theater/improv, creative writing, film review, and fine arts. **Policies:** Alcohol and drug-free campus. **Housing:** Guaranteed on-campus for freshmen. Coed dorms, single-sex dorms, special housing for disabled, wellness housing available. $100 nonrefundable deposit, deadline 5/1. **Activities:** Campus ministries, choral groups, drama, international student organizations, literary magazine, musical theater, radio station, student government, student newspaper, Multicultural Affairs Student Organization, Opposing Prejudice Ending Negativity, Prevention Activities Committee, Students in Free Enterprise, Keystone Service Club, campus prayer and Bible study club.

Athletics. NCAA. **Intercollegiate:** Baseball M, basketball, cross-country, field hockey W, golf M, soccer, softball W, tennis, track and field, volleyball W. **Intramural:** Basketball, football (non-tackle), lacrosse, soccer, softball, table tennis, tennis, volleyball, weight lifting. **Team name:** Giants.

Student services. Adult student services, alcohol/substance abuse counseling, chaplain/spiritual director, career counseling, services for economically disadvantaged, student employment services, financial aid counseling, health services, minority student services, on-campus daycare, personal counseling, placement for graduates, veterans' counselor, women's services.

Contact. E-mail: admissions@keystone.edu
Phone: (570) 945-8111 Toll-free number: (800) 824-2764
Fax: (570) 945-7916
Sarah Keating, Vice President for Enrollment and Director of Admissions, Keystone College, One College Green, La Plume, PA 18440-1099

King's College

Wilkes-Barre, Pennsylvania — **CB member**
www.kings.edu — **CB code: 2353**

- Private 4-year business and liberal arts college affiliated with Roman Catholic Church
- Residential campus in small city
- 2,070 degree-seeking undergraduates: 4% part-time, 50% women, 3% African American, 1% Asian American, 4% Hispanic American
- 207 degree-seeking graduate students
- 75% of applicants admitted
- 73% graduate within 6 years; 28% enter graduate study

General. Founded in 1946. Regionally accredited. **Degrees:** 436 bachelor's, 2 associate awarded; master's offered. **ROTC:** Army, Air Force. **Location:** 110 miles from Philadelphia, 140 miles from New York City. **Calendar:** Semester, extensive summer session. **Full-time faculty:** 129 total; 83% have terminal degrees, 5% minority, 40% women. **Part-time faculty:** 80 total; 20% have terminal degrees, 46% women. **Class size:** 59% < 20, 40% 20-39, less than 1% 40-49. **Special facilities:** Rooftop greenhouse, molecular biology laboratory.

Freshman class profile. 2,233 applied, 1,685 admitted, 560 enrolled.

Mid 50% test scores		**GPA 3.0-3.49:**	35%
SAT critical reading:	450-550	**GPA 2.0-2.99:**	29%
SAT math:	450-560	**Rank in top quarter:**	36%
SAT writing:	450-550	**Rank in top tenth:**	17%
ACT composite:	19-24	**Return as sophomores:**	79%
GPA 3.75 or higher:	25%	**Out-of-state:**	32%
GPA 3.50-3.74:	11%	**Live on campus:**	76%

Basis for selection. Class rank and academic GPA very important. Standardized test scores important. SAT or ACT recommended. Students may choose a standardized test option/essay choice in which an official graded writing sample from either junior or senior year is submitted and notarized by the high school guidance office. Students choosing this option are required to notify the Office of Admission on the application. A student's decision is non-reversible and must be made prior to application review. Interview recommended. **Homeschooled:** Transcript of courses and grades, state high school equivalency certificate required. **Learning Disabled:** Learning-disabled students applying for the first-year academic studies program must submit supplemental application with appropriate documentation. Contact Director of Academic Skills Center during admission process.

High school preparation. College-preparatory program required. 16 units required; 22 recommended. Required and recommended units include English 4, mathematics 3-4, social studies 3-4, science 3-4 (laboratory 2) and foreign language 2-3.

2008-2009 Annual costs. Tuition/fees: $24,680. Room/board: $9,370. Books/supplies: $1,160. Personal expenses: $1,206.

2008-2009 Financial aid. Need-based: 528 full-time freshmen applied for aid; 452 were judged to have need; 452 of these received aid. Average need met was 79%. Average scholarship/grant was $13,487; average loan $4,046. 58% of total undergraduate aid awarded as scholarships/grants, 42% as loans/jobs. **Non-need-based:** Awarded to 527 full-time undergraduates, including 152 freshmen. Scholarships awarded for academics, leadership, ROTC. **Additional information:** Any minority student with financial need may receive some aid in the form of a diversity scholarship.

Application procedures. Admission: No deadline. $30 fee, may be waived for applicants with need, free for online applicants. Admission notification on a rolling basis beginning on or about 10/1. Must reply by May 1 or within 2 week(s) if notified thereafter. **Financial aid:** Priority date 2/15; no closing date. FAFSA, institutional form required. Applicants notified on a rolling basis starting 3/1; must reply within 2 week(s) of notification.

Academics. Special study options: Accelerated study, cross-registration, distance learning, double major, dual enrollment of high school students, ESL, honors, independent study, internships, student-designed major, study abroad, teacher certification program, Washington semester, weekend college. Preprofessional programs in dentistry, medicine, pharmacy, veterinary science. **Credit/placement by examination:** AP, CLEP, IB, SAT, ACT, institutional tests. 15 credit hours maximum toward associate degree, 30 toward bachelor's. **Support services:** Learning center, pre-admission summer program, reduced course load, study skills assistance, tutoring, writing center.

Majors. Biology: General. **Business:** Accounting, business admin, finance, human resources, international, marketing. **Communications:** Media studies. **Computer sciences:** General, computer science. **Conservation:** Environmental science, environmental studies. **Education:** Early childhood, elementary, special. **Foreign languages:** French, Spanish. **Health:** Athletic training, clinical lab science, health services. **History:** General. **Interdisciplinary:** Biological/physical sciences, neuroscience. **Math:** General. **Philosophy/religion:** Philosophy. **Physical sciences:** Chemistry. **Protective services:** Criminal justice. **Psychology:** General. **Social sciences:** Economics, political science, sociology. **Theology:** Theology. **Visual/performing arts:** Dramatic.

Most popular majors. Biology 6%, business/marketing 30%, communications/journalism 8%, education 10%, health sciences 6%, psychology 6%, security/protective services 10%.

Computing on campus. 470 workstations in dormitories, library, computer center, student center. Dormitories wired for high-speed internet access and linked to campus network. Commuter students can connect to campus network. Online course registration, helpline, repair service, student web hosting, wireless network available.

Student life. **Freshman orientation:** Mandatory, $160 fee. Preregistration for classes offered. Held the 4 days prior to start of fall classes. **Housing:** Guaranteed on-campus for all undergraduates. Coed dorms, single-sex dorms, apartments available. $200 nonrefundable deposit. **Activities:** Campus ministries, choral groups, dance, drama, literary magazine, music ensembles, radio station, student government, student newspaper, association of campus events, organizations of various majors, Campion Society, Blood Council, Circle K, politics society, environmental awareness and outdoors club, residence hall council, service fraternity and sorority.

Athletics. NCAA. **Intercollegiate:** Baseball M, basketball, cheerleading, cross-country, field hockey W, football (tackle) M, golf M, lacrosse, soccer, softball W, swimming, tennis, volleyball W, wrestling M. **Intramural:** Basketball, soccer. **Team name:** Monarchs.

Student services. Adult student services, chaplain/spiritual director, career counseling, student employment services, financial aid counseling, health services, personal counseling, placement for graduates.

Contact. E-mail: admissions@kings.edu
Phone: (570) 208-5858 Toll-free number: (888) 546-4772
Fax: (570) 208-5971
Michelle Lawrence-Schmude, Director of Admissions, King's College, 133 North River Street, Wilkes-Barre, PA 18711

Kutztown University of Pennsylvania

Kutztown, Pennsylvania — **CB member**
www.kutztown.edu — **CB code: 2653**

- Public 4-year university
- Residential campus in small town
- 8,813 degree-seeking undergraduates: 5% part-time, 57% women, 6% African American, 1% Asian American, 4% Hispanic American, 1% international
- 722 degree-seeking graduate students
- 61% of applicants admitted
- SAT or ACT (ACT writing optional) required
- 53% graduate within 6 years; 26% enter graduate study

General. Founded in 1866. Regionally accredited. **Degrees:** 1,652 bachelor's awarded; master's offered. **ROTC:** Army. **Location:** 20 miles from Allentown and Reading. **Calendar:** Semester, extensive summer session. **Full-time faculty:** 479 total; 58% have terminal degrees, 14% minority, 47% women. **Part-time faculty:** 61 total; 7% minority, 49% women. **Class size:** 30% < 20, 56% 20-39, 4% 40-49, 6% 50-99, 5% >100. **Special facilities:** Observatory, on-campus preschool, Pennsylvania German heritage cultural center, planetarium.

Freshman class profile. 9,501 applied, 5,815 admitted, 1,823 enrolled.

Mid 50% test scores			
SAT critical reading:	450-540	Rank in top quarter:	24%
SAT math:	450-550	Rank in top tenth:	6%
SAT writing:	430-520	End year in good standing:	80%
ACT composite:	18-22	Return as sophomores:	78%
GPA 3.75 or higher:	8%	Out-of-state:	13%
GPA 3.50-3.74:	10%	Live on campus:	89%
GPA 3.0-3.49:	37%	International:	1%
GPA 2.0-2.99:	44%	Fraternities:	4%
		Sororities:	5%

Basis for selection. School records and academic aptitude tests most important. Recommendations, essays, extracurricular activities considered. SAT Subject Tests (biology and chemistry) required for medical technology program. Audition required for music program; portfolio and/or art test required for art education, communication design, crafts, and fine arts programs. **Homeschooled:** Applicants must submit supporting data from Pennsylvania Home Schooling Association.

High school preparation. College-preparatory program recommended. 18 units recommended. Recommended units include English 4, mathematics 4, social studies 4, science 4 and foreign language 2. Course recommendations vary for specific programs.

2008-2009 Annual costs. Tuition/fees: $7,126; $15,164 out-of-state. Room/board: $7,330. Books/supplies: $1,100. Personal expenses: $2,600.

2007-2008 Financial aid. **Need-based:** 1,713 full-time freshmen applied for aid; 1,212 were judged to have need; 1,170 of these received aid. Average need met was 58%. Average scholarship/grant was $5,390; average loan $3,265. 40% of total undergraduate aid awarded as scholarships/grants, 60% as loans/jobs. **Non-need-based:** Awarded to 734 full-time undergraduates, including 151 freshmen. Scholarships awarded for academics, art, athletics, leadership, minority status, music/drama.

Application procedures. **Admission:** Priority date 12/1; no deadline. $35 fee, may be waived for applicants with need. Admission notification on a rolling basis beginning on or about 10/1. Must reply by May 1 or by date stated on notification letter. **Financial aid:** Priority date 2/15; no closing date. FAFSA required. Applicants notified on a rolling basis starting 3/30; must reply by 5/1 or within 4 week(s) of notification.

Academics. **Special study options:** Combined bachelor's/graduate degree, cross-registration, distance learning, double major, dual enrollment of high school students, honors, independent study, internships, liberal arts/career combination, student-designed major, study abroad, teacher certification program. **Credit/placement by examination:** AP, CLEP, IB, SAT, ACT, institutional tests. **Support services:** Learning center, pre-admission summer program, remedial instruction, study skills assistance, tutoring, writing center.

Majors. **Biology:** General. **Business:** Accounting, business admin, finance, human resources, international, management science, marketing. **Communications:** General, digital media. **Computer sciences:** Information technology. **Conservation:** Environmental science. **Education:** General, early childhood, elementary, kindergarten/preschool, reading, secondary, special, speech impaired, visually handicapped. **Foreign languages:** French, German, Russian, Spanish. **Health:** Clinical lab science, nursing (RN). **History:** General. **Interdisciplinary:** Biological/physical sciences. **Liberal arts:** Arts/sciences, library science. **Math:** General. **Philosophy/religion:** Philosophy. **Physical sciences:** Chemistry, geology, oceanography, physics. **Protective services:** Criminal justice. **Psychology:** General. **Public administration:** General, social work. **Social sciences:** General, anthropology, geography, political science, sociology. **Visual/performing arts:** General, art, commercial/advertising art, crafts, dramatic, studio arts.

Most popular majors. Business/marketing 14%, education 16%, English 9%, psychology 8%, security/protective services 6%, social sciences 7%, visual/performing arts 13%.

Computing on campus. 800 workstations in dormitories, library, computer center, student center. Dormitories wired for high-speed internet access and linked to campus network. Commuter students can connect to campus network. Online course registration, online library, helpline, student web hosting, wireless network available.

Student life. **Freshman orientation:** Mandatory, $115 fee. Preregistration for classes offered. 2-day, one overnight session in June, plus 1-day informational program preceding fall semester. **Policies:** No alcohol or drugs. **Housing:** Guaranteed on-campus for freshmen. Coed dorms, single-sex dorms, apartments, cooperative housing available. $125 fully refundable deposit, deadline 5/1. **Activities:** Bands, campus ministries, choral groups, dance, drama, film society, international student organizations, literary magazine, music ensembles, Model UN, musical theater, radio station, student government, student newspaper, symphony orchestra, TV station, Student Alliance for Learning, Success and Achievement, black student union, Minority Achievement Coalition, Brothers and Sisters Seeking Excellence, Feminist Majority Leadership Alliance, Circle K, volunteer center, social work club.

Athletics. NCAA. **Intercollegiate:** Baseball M, basketball, bowling W, cheerleading M, cross-country, field hockey W, football (tackle) M, golf W, lacrosse W, soccer, softball W, swimming, tennis, track and field, volleyball W, wrestling M. **Intramural:** Badminton, basketball, cross-country, football (non-tackle), golf, racquetball, soccer, softball, swimming, table tennis, tennis, volleyball, weight lifting. **Team name:** Golden Bears.

Student services. Adult student services, alcohol/substance abuse counseling, career counseling, services for economically disadvantaged, student employment services, financial aid counseling, health services, minority student services, on-campus daycare, personal counseling, veterans' counselor, women's services. **Physically disabled:** Services for visually, speech, hearing impaired.

Contact. E-mail: admission@kutztown.edu
Phone: (610) 683-4060 Toll-free number: (877) 628-1915
Fax: (610) 683-1375
William Stahler, Director of Admissions, Kutztown University of Pennsylvania, Admissions Office, Kutztown, PA 19530-0730

La Roche College

Pittsburgh, Pennsylvania — **CB member**
www.laroche.edu — **CB code: 2379**

- Private 4-year liberal arts college affiliated with Roman Catholic Church
- Commuter campus in large city
- 1,228 degree-seeking undergraduates: 13% part-time, 65% women, 5% African American, 1% Asian American, 1% Hispanic American, 12% international
- 100 degree-seeking graduate students
- 57% of applicants admitted
- SAT or ACT (ACT writing optional) required
- 63% graduate within 6 years

General. Founded in 1963. Regionally accredited. Founded and sponsored by Sisters of Divine Providence. **Degrees:** 236 bachelor's, 22 associate awarded; master's offered. **ROTC:** Army, Air Force. **Calendar:** Semester, limited summer session. **Full-time faculty:** 63 total; 86% have terminal degrees, 8% minority, 51% women. **Part-time faculty:** 119 total; 52% women. **Class size:** 73% < 20, 27% 20-39.

Freshman class profile. 1,114 applied, 638 admitted, 228 enrolled.

Mid 50% test scores		**GPA 2.0-2.99:**	45%
SAT critical reading:	440-520	**Rank in top quarter:**	25%
SAT math:	400-510	**Rank in top tenth:**	8%
SAT writing:	430-540	**Return as sophomores:**	66%
ACT composite:	16-21	**Out-of-state:**	10%
GPA 3.75 or higher:	7%	**Live on campus:**	71%
GPA 3.50-3.74:	14%	**International:**	16%
GPA 3.0-3.49:	31%		

Basis for selection. Depth and rigor of curriculum considered. Standardized test scores considered in relation to other factors. Recommendation from guidance counselor important. Extracurricular involvement considered. Essay, interview recommended.

High school preparation. 16 units required; 18 recommended. Required and recommended units include English 4, mathematics 3, social studies 3, history 3, science 3 (laboratory 2) and foreign language 2.

2008-2009 Annual costs. Tuition/fees: $20,330. Room/board: $8,338. Books/supplies: $1,000. Personal expenses: $1,350.

2008-2009 Financial aid. Need-based: 217 full-time freshmen applied for aid; 213 were judged to have need; 213 of these received aid. Average need met was 92%. Average scholarship/grant was $2,581; average loan $3,222. 48% of total undergraduate aid awarded as scholarships/grants, 52% as loans/jobs. **Non-need-based:** Awarded to 1,123 full-time undergraduates, including 256 freshmen. Scholarships awarded for academics.

Application procedures. Admission: No deadline. $50 fee, may be waived for applicants with need. Admission notification on a rolling basis beginning on or about 10/1. **Financial aid:** Priority date 2/15, closing date 5/1. FAFSA required. Applicants notified on a rolling basis starting 2/15; must reply within 2 week(s) of notification.

Academics. Special study options: Accelerated study, combined bachelor's/graduate degree, cross-registration, distance learning, double major, ESL, honors, independent study, internships, student-designed major, study abroad, teacher certification program, Washington semester. **Credit/placement by examination:** AP, CLEP, institutional tests. 60 credit hours maximum toward bachelor's degree. **Support services:** Learning center, reduced course load, remedial instruction, study skills assistance, tutoring, writing center.

Majors. Architecture: Interior. **Biology:** General. **Business:** Accounting, finance, international, management science, marketing, real estate. **Communications:** General, media studies. **Computer sciences:** General, computer science, information technology. **Education:** Elementary, English. **Foreign languages:** Spanish. **Health:** Medical radiologic technology/radiation therapy, nursing (RN), respiratory therapy technology. **History:** General. **Liberal arts:** Arts/sciences. **Math:** General. **Philosophy/religion:** Religion. **Physical sciences:** Chemistry. **Protective services:** Criminal justice, emergency management/homeland security. **Psychology:** General. **Public administration:** Human services. **Social sciences:** International relations, sociology. **Theology:** Religious ed. **Visual/performing arts:** Dance, design.

Most popular majors. Architecture 12%, business/marketing 22%, education 9%, health sciences 9%, psychology 7%, security/protective services 8%, visual/performing arts 11%.

Computing on campus. 200 workstations in dormitories, library, computer center. Dormitories wired for high-speed internet access and linked to campus network. Commuter students can connect to campus network. Online course registration, online library, helpline, wireless network available.

Student life. Freshman orientation: Mandatory. Preregistration for classes offered. **Housing:** Coed dorms available. $100 nonrefundable deposit, deadline 5/1. **Activities:** Campus ministries, choral groups, dance, drama, international student organizations, literary magazine, radio station, student government, student newspaper, professional organizations, multicultural student organization, Project Achievement, environment club, Black student coalition, African Student Forum, GLOBE (international students), Rotaract club, community service.

Athletics. NCAA. **Intercollegiate:** Baseball M, basketball, cross-country, golf M, soccer, softball W, volleyball W. **Intramural:** Basketball, racquetball, soccer, softball, table tennis, tennis, volleyball. **Team name:** Redhawks.

Student services. Adult student services, alcohol/substance abuse counseling, chaplain/spiritual director, career counseling, services for economically disadvantaged, student employment services, financial aid counseling, health services, minority student services, personal counseling, placement for graduates, veterans' counselor. **Physically disabled:** Services for visually impaired. **Learning disabled:** Comprehensive services available.

Contact. E-mail: admissions@laroche.edu
Phone: (412) 536-1271 Toll-free number: (800) 838-4572
Fax: (412) 536-1048
David McFarland, Director of Admissions, La Roche College, 9000 Babcock Boulevard, Pittsburgh, PA 15237

La Salle University

Philadelphia, Pennsylvania — **CB member**
www.lasalle.edu — **CB code: 2363**

- Private 4-year university and liberal arts college affiliated with Roman Catholic Church
- Residential campus in very large city
- 4,151 degree-seeking undergraduates: 25% part-time, 64% women, 17% African American, 4% Asian American, 8% Hispanic American, 1% international
- 1,900 degree-seeking graduate students
- 64% of applicants admitted
- SAT or ACT (ACT writing optional), application essay required
- 68% graduate within 6 years

General. Founded in 1863. Regionally accredited. **Degrees:** 893 bachelor's, 40 associate awarded; master's, doctoral offered. **ROTC:** Army, Air Force. **Location:** 6 miles from downtown. **Calendar:** Semester, extensive summer session. **Full-time faculty:** 230 total; 81% have terminal degrees, 10% minority, 48% women. **Part-time faculty:** 172 total; 10% minority, 59% women. **Class size:** 52% < 20, 46% 20-39, 2% 40-49. **Special facilities:** Art museum, cable-access television station, restored home and gardens of 18th-century American portrait painter Charles Wilson Peale.

Freshman class profile. 5,822 applied, 3,718 admitted, 922 enrolled.

Mid 50% test scores		**Rank in top tenth:**	13%
SAT critical reading:	460-560	**Return as sophomores:**	80%
SAT math:	450-560	**Out-of-state:**	45%
GPA 3.75 or higher:	26%	**Live on campus:**	85%
GPA 3.50-3.74:	15%	**International:**	1%
GPA 3.0-3.49:	33%	**Fraternities:**	7%
GPA 2.0-2.99:	26%	**Sororities:**	18%
Rank in top quarter:	37%		

Basis for selection. High school GPA and standardized test scores most important. Activities, recommendations considered. Admission through Academic Discovery Program, provides counseling and tutorial support for students who need academic assistance and meet certain criteria of financial need. Interview recommended. **Homeschooled:** Statement describing homeschool structure and mission required.

High school preparation. College-preparatory program required. 16 units required. Required units include English 4, mathematics 3, history 1, science 1 (laboratory 1), foreign language 2 and academic electives 5.

2008-2009 Annual costs. Tuition/fees: $31,320. Room/board: $10,690. Books/supplies: $500. Personal expenses: $1,119.

2008-2009 Financial aid. Need-based: 772 full-time freshmen applied for aid; 679 were judged to have need; 679 of these received aid. Average need met was 76%. Average scholarship/grant was $17,476; average loan $3,853. 64% of total undergraduate aid awarded as scholarships/grants, 36% as loans/jobs. **Non-need-based:** Awarded to 962 full-time undergraduates, including 279 freshmen. Scholarships awarded for academics, athletics, ROTC.

Application procedures. Admission: No deadline. $35 fee, may be waived for applicants with need, free for online applicants. Admission notification on a rolling basis beginning on or about 12/15. Must reply by May 1 or within 2 week(s) if notified thereafter. **Financial aid:** Priority date 2/15; no closing date. FAFSA required. Applicants notified on a rolling basis starting 3/15; must reply by 5/1 or within 2 week(s) of notification.

Academics. Special study options: Accelerated study, combined bachelor's/graduate degree, cooperative education, double major, dual enrollment of high school students, ESL, honors, independent study, internships, study abroad, teacher certification program. 3-2 with Thomas Jefferson University. **Credit/placement by examination:** AP, CLEP, SAT, ACT, institutional tests. 70 credit hours maximum toward bachelor's degree. **Support services:** Learning center, pre-admission summer program, reduced course load, remedial instruction, tutoring, writing center.

Majors. Area/ethnic studies: Central/Eastern European, regional, Russian/Slavic. **Biology:** General, biochemistry. **Business:** General, accounting, banking/financial services, business admin, communications, finance, human resources, insurance, international, international marketing, labor relations, management science, managerial economics, market research, marketing, nonprofit/public, operations, organizational behavior, statistics. **Communications:** General, broadcast journalism, digital media, journalism, media studies, public relations, radio/tv. **Communications technology:** Desktop publishing, radio/tv. **Computer sciences:** General, applications programming, computer graphics, computer science, database management, information systems, information technology, programming, web page design. **Conservation:** General, environmental science. **Education:** General, bilingual, biology, chemistry, developmentally delayed, early childhood, early childhood special, elementary, emotionally handicapped, English, foreign languages, French, German, history, mathematics, mentally handicapped, middle, multi-level teacher, physically handicapped, science, secondary, social science, social studies, Spanish, special. **Foreign languages:** General, Biblical, classics, comparative lit, French, German, Italian, Latin, Spanish. **Health:** Audiology/hearing, audiology/speech pathology, nursing (RN), predental, premedicine, preveterinary, speech pathology. **History:** General, American. **Interdisciplinary:** Biological/physical sciences, math/computer science, nutrition sciences, peace/conflict, systems science. **Legal studies:** Prelaw. **Liberal arts:** Arts/sciences. **Math:** General, applied, statistics. **Philosophy/religion:** Philosophy, religion. **Physical sciences:** Chemistry, geology, planetary. **Protective services:** Criminal justice. **Psychology:** General. **Public administration:** General, social work. **Social sciences:** General, criminology, economics, international economics, international relations, political science, sociology, U.S. government. **Theology:** Religious ed. **Visual/performing arts:** Art history/conservation, cinematography, film/cinema, music history, studio arts.

Most popular majors. Business/marketing 23%, communications/journalism 12%, education 7%, health sciences 27%, psychology 6%, public administration/social services 8%.

Computing on campus. 181 workstations in library, computer center. Dormitories wired for high-speed internet access and linked to campus network. Commuter students can connect to campus network. Online course registration, online library, helpline, repair service, student web hosting, wireless network available.

Student life. Freshman orientation: Mandatory, $100 fee. Preregistration for classes offered. **Policies:** Nonalcoholic nightclub and eatery available 7 days a week. **Housing:** Guaranteed on-campus for all undergraduates. Coed dorms, special housing for disabled, apartments, wellness housing available. $200 nonrefundable deposit, deadline 5/1. Campus owned and operated townhouses available. **Activities:** Jazz band, campus ministries, choral groups, dance, drama, film society, international student organizations, literary magazine, musical theater, radio station, student government, student newspaper, TV station, black student union, Hillel, women's center, social work association, veterans club, Young Socialist Alliance, student council for exceptional children, urban center.

Athletics. NCAA. **Intercollegiate:** Baseball M, basketball, cheerleading, cross-country, diving, field hockey W, golf, lacrosse W, rowing (crew), soccer, softball W, swimming, tennis, track and field, volleyball W. **Intramural:** Basketball, football (non-tackle), football (tackle), rugby M, softball, volleyball. **Team name:** Explorers.

Student services. Adult student services, alcohol/substance abuse counseling, chaplain/spiritual director, career counseling, services for economically disadvantaged, student employment services, health services, minority student services, on-campus daycare, personal counseling, placement for graduates, veterans' counselor.

Contact. E-mail: admiss@lasalle.edu
Phone: (215) 951-1500 Toll-free number: (800) 328-1910
Fax: (215) 951-1656
James Plunkett, Director of Admission, La Salle University, 1900 West Olney Avenue, Philadelphia, PA 19141-1199

Lafayette College

Easton, Pennsylvania **CB member**
www.lafayette.edu **CB code: 2361**

- Private 4-year engineering and liberal arts college affiliated with Presbyterian Church (USA)
- Residential campus in large town
- 2,352 degree-seeking undergraduates: 1% part-time, 46% women, 5% African American, 4% Asian American, 5% Hispanic American, 7% international
- 37% of applicants admitted
- SAT or ACT with writing, application essay required
- 89% graduate within 6 years

General. Founded in 1826. Regionally accredited. **Degrees:** 599 bachelor's awarded. **ROTC:** Army. **Location:** 80 miles from New York City, 60 miles from Philadelphia. **Calendar:** Semester, limited summer session. **Full-time faculty:** 194 total; 100% have terminal degrees, 10% minority, 31% women. **Part-time faculty:** 68 total; 47% have terminal degrees, 7% minority, 41% women. **Class size:** 58% < 20, 38% 20-39, 2% 40-49, 2% 50-99. **Special facilities:** Advanced computer-aided design laboratory, satellite downlink capability.

Freshman class profile. 6,357 applied, 2,366 admitted, 601 enrolled.

Mid 50% test scores		**GPA 2.0-2.99:**	7%
SAT critical reading:	580-670	**Rank in top quarter:**	93%
SAT math:	610-700	**Rank in top tenth:**	65%
SAT writing:	590-680	**Return as sophomores:**	94%
ACT composite:	26-30	**Out-of-state:**	74%
GPA 3.75 or higher:	30%	**Live on campus:**	100%
GPA 3.50-3.74:	27%	**International:**	6%
GPA 3.0-3.49:	36%		

Basis for selection. Academic performance, class rank, quality of courses taken, personal qualities, extracurricular record, recommendations, and standardized test results important. Special consideration to applicants who will contribute diversity to student body. SAT Subject Tests recommended. SAT Subject Tests, if submitted, may be considered for placement in math and foreign languages. Interview recommended for all; portfolio recommended for art program.

High school preparation. College-preparatory program recommended. 18 units recommended. Recommended units include English 4, mathematics 3, science 2 (laboratory 2), foreign language 2 and academic electives 5. 4 math, chemistry, physics required of bachelor of science degree candidates.

2008-2009 Annual costs. Tuition/fees: $36,090. Room/board: $11,248.

2007-2008 Financial aid. Need-based: 403 full-time freshmen applied for aid; 331 were judged to have need; 306 of these received aid. Average need met was 100%. Average scholarship/grant was $26,383; average loan $3,984. 84% of total undergraduate aid awarded as scholarships/grants, 16% as loans/jobs. **Non-need-based:** Awarded to 281 full-time undergraduates, including 95 freshmen. Scholarships awarded for academics, athletics, leadership, ROTC. **Additional information:** Parent loans, up to $7,500 annually, available with college absorbing interest while student is enrolled. Family has 8 years after graduation to repay. Not limited to those demonstrating need.

Application procedures. Admission: Closing date 1/1. $60 fee, may be waived for applicants with need. Admission notification 4/1. Must reply by May 1 or within 2 week(s) if notified thereafter. **Financial aid** riority date 2/15, closing date 3/15. FAFSA, CSS PROFILE required. Applicants notified by 4/1; must reply by 5/1.

Academics. Self-designed majors include psychobiology, pre-architecture, area studies. Interdisciplinary minors also offered. **Special study options:** Cross-registration, double major, dual enrollment of high school students, exchange student, honors, independent study, internships, New York semester, semester at sea, student-designed major, study abroad, urban semester, Washington semester. Interim sessions here and abroad. **Credit/placement by examination:** AP, CLEP, institutional tests. **Support services:** Reduced course load, tutoring, writing center.

Majors. **Area/ethnic studies:** African, American, Russian/Slavic. **Biology:** General, biochemistry. **Computer sciences:** General. **Engineering:** General, chemical, civil, electrical, mechanical. **Foreign languages:** French, German, Russian, Spanish. **History:** General. **Interdisciplinary:** Neuroscience. **Math:** General. **Philosophy/religion:** Philosophy, religion. **Physical sciences:** Chemistry, geology, physics. **Psychology:** General. **Social sciences:** Anthropology, econometrics, economics, international economics, international relations, political science, sociology. **Visual/performing arts:** Art, music history, studio arts.

Most popular majors. Biology 9%, engineering/engineering technologies 14%, English 7%, psychology 7%, social sciences 36%.

Computing on campus. 600 workstations in library, computer center, student center. Dormitories wired for high-speed internet access and linked to campus network. Commuter students can connect to campus network. Online course registration, online library, helpline, repair service, student web hosting, wireless network available.

Student life. **Freshman orientation:** Mandatory. Preregistration for classes offered. **Housing:** Guaranteed on-campus for all undergraduates. Coed dorms, single-sex dorms, special housing for disabled, apartments, fraternity/sorority housing, wellness housing available. Scholars houses, Hillel House, arts houses. **Activities:** Bands, campus ministries, choral groups, dance, drama, film society, international student organizations, literary magazine, music ensembles, musical theater, radio station, student government, student newspaper, symphony orchestra, Hillel Society, Muslim student association, Newman Association, Association of Black Collegians, Association for Lafayette Feminists, international students association, Lafayette Environmental Awareness and Protection, College Democrats, College Republicans, Students for Social Justice.

Athletics. NCAA. **Intercollegiate:** Baseball M, basketball, cheerleading, cross-country, diving, fencing, field hockey W, football (tackle) M, golf, lacrosse, soccer, softball W, swimming, tennis, track and field, volleyball W. **Intramural:** Badminton, basketball, bowling, football (non-tackle), golf, racquetball, soccer, softball, squash, table tennis, tennis, volleyball, water polo. **Team name:** Leopards.

Student services. Adult student services, alcohol/substance abuse counseling, chaplain/spiritual director, career counseling, services for economically disadvantaged, student employment services, financial aid counseling, health services, minority student services, personal counseling, placement for graduates, women's services. **Physically disabled:** Services for visually impaired. **Learning disabled:** Comprehensive services available.

Contact. E-mail: admissions@lafayette.edu
Phone: (610) 330-5100 Fax: (610) 330-5355
Carol Rowlands, Director of Admissions, Lafayette College, 118 Markle Hall, Easton, PA 18042

Lancaster Bible College

Lancaster, Pennsylvania
www.lbc.edu **CB code: 2388**

- Private 4-year Bible college affiliated with nondenominational tradition
- Residential campus in small city
- 659 degree-seeking undergraduates: 20% part-time, 49% women
- 142 degree-seeking graduate students
- 67% of applicants admitted
- SAT or ACT (ACT writing recommended), application essay required

General. Founded in 1933. Regionally accredited; also accredited by ABHE. **Degrees:** 128 bachelor's, 26 associate awarded; master's offered. **Location:** 64 miles from Philadelphia. **Calendar:** Semester, limited summer session. **Full-time faculty:** 48 total; 52% have terminal degrees, 4% minority, 25% women. **Part-time faculty:** 43 total; 37% have terminal degrees, 42% women. **Class size:** 57% < 20, 33% 20-39, 4% 40-49, 6% 50-99.

Freshman class profile. 285 applied, 192 admitted, 124 enrolled.

Mid 50% test scores			
SAT critical reading:	480-580	Rank in top quarter:	34%
SAT math:	460-570	Rank in top tenth:	16%
ACT composite:	17-23	Out-of-state:	34%
		Live on campus:	92%

Basis for selection. Application must include personal spiritual testimony, academic transcripts, SAT or ACT scores, and 3 references. Interview recommended for all; audition required for religious music program. **Homeschooled:** Yearly evaluations should be included with application.

2008-2009 Annual costs. Tuition/fees: $15,290. Room/board: $6,540. Books/supplies: $700. Personal expenses: $1,750.

2007-2008 Financial aid. **Non-need-based:** Scholarships awarded for academics, alumni affiliation, leadership, music/drama, state residency.

Application procedures. **Admission:** Priority date 8/1; no deadline. $25 fee, may be waived for applicants with need. Admission notification on a rolling basis. **Financial aid:** Priority date 5/1; no closing date. FAFSA required. Applicants notified on a rolling basis starting 3/15; must reply within 3 week(s) of notification.

Academics. **Special study options:** Accelerated study, distance learning, double major, independent study, internships, study abroad, teacher certification program. **Credit/placement by examination:** AP, CLEP, SAT, ACT, institutional tests. 15 credit hours maximum toward associate degree, 30 toward bachelor's. **Support services:** Learning center, reduced course load, remedial instruction, study skills assistance, tutoring.

Majors. **Education:** Elementary, physical. **Theology:** Bible.

Most popular majors. Education 13%, theological studies 88%.

Computing on campus. 35 workstations in library, student center. Dormitories wired for high-speed internet access and linked to campus network. Commuter students can connect to campus network. Online library, helpline available.

Student life. **Freshman orientation:** Mandatory, $40 fee. Preregistration for classes offered. 2 days prior to start of classes. **Policies:** Religious observance required. **Housing:** Guaranteed on-campus for freshmen. Single-sex dorms available. **Activities:** Concert band, choral groups, drama, international student organizations, music ensembles, student government, student newspaper, Christian Counseling Fellowship, married couples fellowship, Helpers in Service teams, student missionary fellowship, resident affairs council, commuter affairs council.

Athletics. NCCAA. **Intercollegiate:** Baseball M, basketball, cheerleading, cross-country, lacrosse W, soccer, volleyball. **Intramural:** Basketball, football (non-tackle) M, soccer, softball, table tennis, tennis, volleyball. **Team name:** Chargers.

Student services. Chaplain/spiritual director, career counseling, student employment services, financial aid counseling, health services, personal counseling, placement for graduates. **Learning disabled:** Comprehensive services available.

Contact. E-mail: admissions@lbc.edu
Phone: (717) 560-8271 Toll-free number: (866) 522-4968
Fax: (717) 560-8213
Jeffrey Hoover, Associate Vice President for Enrollment Services/Registrar, Lancaster Bible College, 901 Eden Road, Lancaster, PA 17601-5036

Lebanon Valley College

Annville, Pennsylvania **CB member**
www.lvc.edu **CB code: 2364**

- Private 4-year liberal arts college affiliated with United Methodist Church
- Residential campus in small town
- 1,655 degree-seeking undergraduates: 4% part-time, 55% women, 1% African American, 2% Asian American, 2% Hispanic American
- 159 degree-seeking graduate students
- 73% of applicants admitted
- 68% graduate within 6 years; 34% enter graduate study

General. Founded in 1866. Regionally accredited. **Degrees:** 398 bachelor's, 1 associate awarded; master's, doctoral offered. **ROTC:** Army. **Location:** 7 miles from Hershey, 25 miles from Harrisburg. **Calendar:** Semester, limited summer session. **Full-time faculty:** 99 total; 86% have terminal degrees, 6% minority, 35% women. **Part-time faculty:** 91 total; 15% have terminal degrees, 1% minority, 36% women. **Class size:** 56% < 20, 42% 20-39, 2% 40-49, less than 1% 50-99. **Special facilities:** Electronic pianos, sound recording studio, transmission electron microscope, scanning electron microscope, Fourier transform infrared spectrometer, atomic absorption spectrometer, nuclear magnetic resonance spectrometer, molecular modeling lab, arboretum, physical therapy wellness pool.

Freshman class profile. 1,885 applied, 1,367 admitted, 396 enrolled.

Mid 50% test scores			
SAT critical reading:	490-600	Rank in top tenth:	38%
SAT math:	510-610	End year in good standing:	89%
SAT writing:	490-600	Return as sophomores:	81%
ACT composite:	20-27	Out-of-state:	21%
Rank in top quarter:	75%	Live on campus:	89%

Basis for selection. Record of high school achievement in challenging college prep courses is most important. Recommendations, test scores (optional), school and community activities evaluated. Submission of standardized test scores is optional for all applicants. Essay and interview recommended for all; audition required for music program.

High school preparation. College-preparatory program required. 16 units required. Required and recommended units include English 4, mathematics 3, social studies 1, history 2, science 2-3 (laboratory 2) and foreign language 2-3.

2008-2009 Annual costs. Tuition/fees: $29,350. Room/board: $7,760. Books/supplies: $1,000. Personal expenses: $1,000.

2008-2009 Financial aid. Need-based: 371 full-time freshmen applied for aid; 316 were judged to have need; 316 of these received aid. Average need met was 86%. Average scholarship/grant was $17,604; average loan $4,566. 75% of total undergraduate aid awarded as scholarships/grants, 25% as loans/jobs. **Non-need-based:** Awarded to 427 full-time undergraduates, including 109 freshmen. Scholarships awarded for academics, alumni affiliation, music/drama.

Application procedures. Admission: No deadline. $30 fee, may be waived for applicants with need. Admission notification on a rolling basis beginning on or about 10/15. Must reply by May 1 or within 2 week(s) if notified thereafter. For early admission of high school students, regular application procedures apply. Permission from school district necessary. **Financial aid:** Priority date 3/1; no closing date. FAFSA, institutional form required. Applicants notified on a rolling basis starting 3/1; must reply by 5/1 or within 2 week(s) of notification.

Academics. Special study options: Combined bachelor's/graduate degree, double major, dual enrollment of high school students, independent study, internships, liberal arts/career combination, student-designed major, study abroad, teacher certification program, urban semester, Washington semester. **Credit/placement by examination:** AP, CLEP, IB, institutional tests. 15 credit hours maximum toward associate degree, 30 toward bachelor's. **Support services:** Reduced course load, study skills assistance, tutoring, writing center.

Majors. Area/ethnic studies: American. **Biology:** General, Biochemistry/biophysics and molecular biology. **Business:** Accounting, actuarial science, business admin. **Communications:** Digital media. **Communications technology:** Recording arts. **Computer sciences:** Computer science. **Education:** Elementary, music. **Foreign languages:** French, German, Spanish. **Health:** Clinical lab science, health care admin, health services. **History:** General. **Math:** General. **Philosophy/religion:** Philosophy, religion. **Physical sciences:** Chemistry, physics. **Psychology:** General, psychobiology. **Social sciences:** Criminology, economics, political science, sociology. **Visual/performing arts:** Music management, music performance, studio arts.

Most popular majors. Biology 6%, business/marketing 16%, education 17%, health sciences 8%, psychology 8%, social sciences 10%, visual/performing arts 10%.

Computing on campus. 187 workstations in library, computer center, student center. Dormitories wired for high-speed internet access and linked to campus network. Commuter students can connect to campus network. Online course registration, online library, helpline, student web hosting, wireless network available.

Student life. Freshman orientation: Mandatory. Preregistration for classes offered. One-day programs in May and July; 3-day program in August. **Housing:** Guaranteed on-campus for all undergraduates. Coed dorms, single-sex dorms, special housing for disabled, apartments available. Suites. **Activities:** Bands, campus ministries, choral groups, drama, international student organizations, literary magazine, music ensembles, musical theater, radio station, student government, student newspaper, symphony orchestra, College Republicans, College Democrats, Cornerstone, Best Buddies, L.E.A.D., Student Action for Earth, The F Word, Servants of Christ, Council of Christian Organizations.

Athletics. NCAA. **Intercollegiate:** Baseball M, basketball, cross-country, field hockey W, football (tackle) M, golf M, ice hockey M, soccer, softball W, swimming, tennis, track and field, volleyball W. **Intramural:** Basketball, football (non-tackle), racquetball, softball, volleyball. **Team name:** Flying Dutchmen.

Student services. Alcohol/substance abuse counseling, chaplain/spiritual director, career counseling, student employment services, financial aid counseling, health services, minority student services, personal counseling, placement for graduates. **Physically disabled:** Services for visually, speech impaired. **Learning disabled:** Comprehensive services available.

Contact. E-mail: admission@lvc.edu
Phone: (717) 867-6181 Toll-free number: (866) 582-4236
Fax: (717) 867-6026
Susan Sarisky, Director of Admission, Lebanon Valley College, 101 North College Avenue, Annville, PA 17003-1400

Lehigh University

Bethlehem, Pennsylvania — **CB member**
www.lehigh.edu — **CB code: 2365**

- Private 4-year university
- Residential campus in small city
- 4,856 degree-seeking undergraduates: 1% part-time, 42% women, 3% African American, 6% Asian American, 5% Hispanic American, 3% international
- 1,908 degree-seeking graduate students
- 28% of applicants admitted
- SAT or ACT with writing, application essay required
- 85% graduate within 6 years; 31% enter graduate study

General. Founded in 1865. Regionally accredited. **Degrees:** 1,092 bachelor's awarded; master's, doctoral offered. **ROTC:** Army. **Location:** 50 miles from Philadelphia, 75 miles from New York City. **Calendar:** Semester, limited summer session. **Full-time faculty:** 443 total; 99% have terminal degrees, 14% minority, 27% women. **Part-time faculty:** 205 total; 8% minority, 46% women. **Class size:** 48% < 20, 36% 20-39, 6% 40-49, 7% 50-99, 3% >100. **Special facilities:** Two aberration-corrected electron microscopes, financial service laboratory, broadband seismic station, multi-directional experimental laboratory, electron optical labs, particle accelerator, rock climbing wall.

Freshman class profile. 12,941 applied, 3,612 admitted, 1,205 enrolled.

Mid 50% test scores			
SAT critical reading:	590-680	Return as sophomores:	94%
SAT math:	640-720	Out-of-state:	79%
Rank in top quarter:	99%	Live on campus:	99%
Rank in top tenth:	93%	International:	6%

Basis for selection. All submitted material considered. TOEFL recommended for international students. Campus visit recommended.

High school preparation. 16 units required. Required units include English 4, mathematics 3, social studies 2, (laboratory 2), foreign language 2 and academic electives 3. Chemistry required, physics recommended for engineering and science candidates. Waivers in math granted by some departments to well-qualified candidates.

2008-2009 Annual costs. Tuition/fees: $37,550. Room/board: $9,770. Books/supplies: $1,000. Personal expenses: $1,220.

2008-2009 Financial aid. Need-based: 758 full-time freshmen applied for aid; 522 were judged to have need; 522 of these received aid. Average need met was 96%. Average scholarship/grant was $27,552; average loan $3,420. 83% of total undergraduate aid awarded as scholarships/grants, 17% as loans/jobs. **Non-need-based:** Awarded to 644 full-time undergraduates, including 130 freshmen. Scholarships awarded for academics, art, athletics, leadership, music/drama, ROTC. **Additional information:** Loans eliminated for students eligible for financial aid and whose family income is less than $50,000.

Application procedures. Admission: Closing date 1/1 (postmark date). $70 fee, may be waived for applicants with need. Admission notification 4/1. Must reply by 5/1. **Financial aid:** Closing date 2/15. FAFSA, CSS PROFILE required. Applicants notified by 3/30; must reply by 5/1 or within 3 week(s) of notification.

Academics. Special study options: Accelerated study, combined bachelor's/graduate degree, cooperative education, cross-registration, distance learning, double major, ESL, exchange student, external degree, honors, independent study, internships, liberal arts/career combination, study abroad, urban semester, Washington semester. **Credit/placement by examination:** AP, CLEP, IB, institutional tests. **Support services:** Learning center, study skills assistance, tutoring, writing center.

Majors. Architecture: Architecture. **Area/ethnic studies:** African-American, American, Asian, Russian/Slavic, women's. **Biology:** General, biochemistry, ecology, molecular. **Business:** General, accounting, finance, logistics, management science, managerial economics, marketing. **Communications:** Journalism. **Computer sciences:** Computer science, information systems. **Conservation:** Environmental science. **Engineering:** Aerospace, biomedical, chemical, civil, computer, electrical, environmental, industrial, materials, mechanical, mechanics, physics, structural. **Foreign languages:** Classics, French, German, Spanish. **Health:** Predental, premedicine. **History:** General. **Interdisciplinary:** Biological/physical sciences, biopsychology, cognitive science, global studies, science/society. **Math:** General, statistics. **Philosophy/religion:** Philosophy, religion. **Physical sciences:** Astronomy, astrophysics, chemistry, geology, physics. **Psychology:** General. **Social sciences:** General, anthropology, international relations, political science, sociology, urban studies. **Visual/performing arts:** Art, art history/conservation, design, dramatic, music history. **Other:** Applied science, Classical civilization.

Most popular majors. Business/marketing 28%, engineering/engineering technologies 23%, psychology 6%, social sciences 8%.

Computing on campus. 634 workstations in dormitories, library, computer center. Dormitories wired for high-speed internet access and linked to campus network. Commuter students can connect to campus network. Online course registration, online library, helpline, repair service, student web hosting, wireless network available.

Student life. **Freshman orientation:** Mandatory, $225 fee. Preregistration for classes offered. Four-day program held prior to the first day of classes. **Policies:** Project Impact program strives to alter drinking culture and bring about enduring changes in pattern of student life. **Housing:** Guaranteed on-campus for freshmen. Coed dorms, special housing for disabled, apartments, fraternity/sorority housing, wellness housing available. $500 nonrefundable deposit, deadline 5/1. Residential college (Taylor College) available. **Activities:** Bands, campus ministries, choral groups, dance, drama, film society, international student organizations, literary magazine, music ensembles, Model UN, musical theater, radio station, student government, student newspaper, symphony orchestra, Global Union, Asian cultural society, Fellowship of Christian Athletes, Omicron Delta Kappa, Chinese culture club, Black student union, Muslim students association, Alpha Phi Omega Service Fraternity, Best Buddies.

Athletics. NCAA. **Intercollegiate:** Baseball M, basketball, cross-country, diving, field hockey W, football (tackle) M, golf, lacrosse, rowing (crew) W, soccer, softball W, swimming, tennis, track and field, volleyball W, wrestling M. **Intramural:** Basketball, football (non-tackle), soccer, softball, volleyball. **Team name:** Mountain Hawks.

Student services. Alcohol/substance abuse counseling, chaplain/spiritual director, career counseling, student employment services, financial aid counseling, health services, minority student services, on-campus daycare, personal counseling, placement for graduates, veterans' counselor, women's services.

Contact. E-mail: admissions@lehigh.edu
Phone: (610) 758-3100 Fax: (610) 758-4361
Bruce Gardiner, Director of Admissions, Lehigh University, 27 Memorial Drive West, Bethlehem, PA 18015-3094

Lincoln University

Lincoln University, Pennsylvania
www.lincoln.edu **CB code: 2367**

- Public 4-year university and liberal arts college
- Residential campus in small town
- 1,966 degree-seeking undergraduates: 2% part-time, 60% women, 94% African American, 1% Hispanic American, 2% international
- 551 degree-seeking graduate students
- 35% of applicants admitted
- SAT or ACT (ACT writing optional), application essay required
- 37% graduate within 6 years

General. Founded in 1854. Regionally accredited. **Degrees:** 224 bachelor's awarded; master's offered. **ROTC:** Army. **Location:** 45 miles from Philadelphia. **Calendar:** Semester, limited summer session. **Full-time faculty:** 103 total; 72% have terminal degrees, 65% minority, 36% women. **Part-time faculty:** 91 total; 31% have terminal degrees, 71% minority. **Class size:** 41% < 20, 57% 20-39, 2% 40-49.

Freshman class profile. 5,892 applied, 2,081 admitted, 533 enrolled.

Mid 50% test scores		**GPA 2.0-2.99:**	52%
SAT critical reading:	380-450	**Rank in top quarter:**	17%
SAT math:	370-450	**Rank in top tenth:**	5%
ACT composite:	15-20	**Return as sophomores:**	68%
GPA 3.75 or higher:	3%	**Out-of-state:**	62%
GPA 3.50-3.74:	4%	**Live on campus:**	99%
GPA 3.0-3.49:	33%	**International:**	1%

Basis for selection. Admissions based on secondary school record and class rank; recommendations, standardized test scores, talent, and ability also important.

High school preparation. 21 units required. Required units include English 4, mathematics 3, social studies 3, science 3 and academic electives 5. 2 arts or humanities required.

2008-2009 Annual costs. Tuition/fees: $8,240; $12,846 out-of-state. Out-of-state students pay additional $612 in fees, which are included in out-of-state tuition figure. Room/board: $7,850. Books/supplies: $1,380. Personal expenses: $1,544.

2008-2009 Financial aid. **Non-need-based:** Scholarships awarded for academics, alumni affiliation, leadership, music/drama.

Application procedures. **Admission:** Priority date 4/1; no deadline. $20 fee, may be waived for applicants with need. Admission notification on a rolling basis beginning on or about 2/15. **Financial aid:** Closing date 5/1. FAFSA required. Applicants notified on a rolling basis starting 4/1; must reply within 3 week(s) of notification.

Academics. **Special study options:** Exchange student, honors, independent study, internships, study abroad, teacher certification program. 3-2 in advanced science/engineering with Drexel University; Penn State University; Howard University; University of Delaware, Temple University, Widener University, and New Jersey Institute of Technology. **Credit/placement by examination:** AP, CLEP, IB, SAT, institutional tests. **Support services:** Learning center, reduced course load, remedial instruction, study skills assistance, tutoring, writing center.

Majors. **Biology:** General. **Business:** Accounting, actuarial science, business admin, finance, human resources. **Communications:** General, journalism. **Computer sciences:** General, information technology. **Conservation:** Environmental science. **Education:** Early childhood, elementary, English, mathematics, music, secondary, special. **Engineering:** General. **Foreign languages:** French, Spanish. **Health:** Recreational therapy. **History:** General. **Math:** General. **Parks/recreation:** Health/fitness. **Philosophy/religion:** Philosophy, religion. **Physical sciences:** General, chemistry, physics. **Protective services:** Criminal justice. **Psychology:** General, industrial, psychobiology. **Public administration:** General, human services. **Social sciences:** Anthropology, economics, international relations, political science, sociology. **Visual/performing arts:** Studio arts.

Most popular majors. Business/marketing 19%, communications/journalism 9%, education 8%, English 6%, parks/recreation 11%, public administration/social services 8%, security/protective services 12%, social sciences 14%.

Computing on campus. 181 workstations in dormitories, library, computer center. Dormitories wired for high-speed internet access and linked to campus network. Commuter students can connect to campus network. Online library, repair service, wireless network available.

Student life. **Freshman orientation:** Mandatory, $164 fee. Preregistration for classes offered. **Housing:** Guaranteed on-campus for freshmen. Coed dorms, single-sex dorms, apartments available. $275 deposit. **Activities:** Jazz band, choral groups, dance, drama, international student organizations, music ensembles, radio station, student government, student newspaper, TV station, Music Educator National Conference, Mu Phi Alpha, Tolson Society, law society, Phi Kappa Epsilon honor society, fashion club, religious organizations, and social clubs.

Athletics. NCAA. **Intercollegiate:** Baseball M, basketball, cross-country, football (tackle) M, soccer, softball, tennis, track and field, volleyball W. **Intramural:** Baseball M, basketball, bowling, boxing W, cheerleading W, cross-country, diving, softball, swimming, tennis, track and field, volleyball. **Team name:** Lions.

Student services. Alcohol/substance abuse counseling, chaplain/spiritual director, career counseling, student employment services, financial aid counseling, health services, personal counseling, women's services.

Contact. E-mail: admiss@lincoln.edu
Phone: (484) 365-7206 Toll-free number: (800) 790-0191
Fax: (484) 365-8109
Germel Eaton-Clarke, Director of Admissions, Lincoln University, 1570 Baltimore Pike, Lincoln University, PA 19352-0999

Lock Haven University of Pennsylvania

Lock Haven, Pennsylvania **CB member**
www.lhup.edu **CB code: 2654**

- Public 4-year university and liberal arts college
- Residential campus in small town
- 4,817 degree-seeking undergraduates: 6% part-time, 57% women, 7% African American, 1% Asian American, 3% Hispanic American, 1% international
- 250 degree-seeking graduate students
- 74% of applicants admitted
- SAT or ACT (ACT writing optional) required
- 55% graduate within 6 years

General. Founded in 1870. Regionally accredited. Branch campus in Clearfield. **Degrees:** 824 bachelor's, 74 associate awarded; master's offered. **ROTC:** Army. **Location:** 26 miles from Williamsport, 35 miles from State College. **Calendar:** Semester, limited summer session. **Full-time faculty:** 235 total; 75% have terminal degrees, 13% minority, 46% women. **Part-time faculty:** 22 total; 9% minority, 50% women. **Class size:** 32% < 20, 50% 20-39, 14% 40-49, 4% 50-99, less than 1% >100. **Special facilities:** Rural retreat conference center, cadaver dissection laboratory, electron microscope, primate laboratory.

Freshman class profile. 4,448 applied, 3,307 admitted, 1,193 enrolled.

Mid 50% test scores		**GPA 3.0-3.49:**	35%
SAT critical reading:	420-510	**GPA 2.0-2.99:**	35%
SAT math:	420-520	**Rank in top quarter:**	24%
SAT writing:	410-510	**Rank in top tenth:**	9%
ACT composite:	17-22	**Out-of-state:**	9%
GPA 3.75 or higher:	10%	**Live on campus:**	80%
GPA 3.50-3.74:	19%		

Basis for selection. Course selection, grades received, and test scores most important. Preferred test score report date February 1. Interview required for nursing program; audition required for music programs. **Homeschooled:** Provide as much documentation as possible. Interview required.

High school preparation. College-preparatory program required. 16 units required; 21 recommended. Required and recommended units include English 4, mathematics 3-4, social studies 2, history 2, science 3-4 (laboratory 2-3) and foreign language 2. 4 units math required for math, computer science, biology, physics, and chemistry majors. 1 unit each biology, chemistry, physics required for health science majors. 1 unit each biology, anatomy and physiology, chemistry recommended for health and physical education majors.

2008-2009 Annual costs. Tuition/fees: $6,917; $12,955 out-of-state. All freshman students are required to have a laptop computer for use in the classroom. Computers can be purchased through the university; cost of computer is not included in mandatory fees. The university has a small number of laptops available to students who cannot afford to make such a purchase. Room/board: $6,448. Books/supplies: $1,100. Personal expenses: $1,922.

2008-2009 Financial aid. Need-based: 1,246 full-time freshmen applied for aid; 971 were judged to have need; 971 of these received aid. Average need met was 73%. Average scholarship/grant was $4,634; average loan $3,500. 46% of total undergraduate aid awarded as scholarships/grants, 54% as loans/jobs. **Non-need-based:** Awarded to 780 full-time undergraduates, including 195 freshmen. Scholarships awarded for academics, art, athletics, leadership, minority status, music/drama, ROTC, state residency.

Application procedures. Admission: Priority date 3/1; no deadline. $25 fee, may be waived for applicants with need. Admission notification on a rolling basis beginning on or about 10/1. Must reply by May 1 or within 2 week(s) if notified thereafter. **Financial aid:** Closing date 3/15. FAFSA required. Applicants notified on a rolling basis starting 4/1; must reply within 2 week(s) of notification.

Academics. Special study options: Combined bachelor's/graduate degree, cross-registration, distance learning, double major, dual enrollment of high school students, honors, independent study, internships, student-designed major, study abroad, teacher certification program. Exchange program with institutions in Taiwan, Russia, Australia, France, England, Poland, Germany, Scotland, Costa Rica, China, Japan, Croatia, Italy, Kenya, Mexico. 2-2 program in music education with Clarion University of Pennsylvania and Millersville University of Pennsylvania. **Credit/placement by examination:** AP, CLEP, IB, SAT, institutional tests. 30 credit hours maximum toward bachelor's degree. **Support services:** Learning center, preadmission summer program, reduced course load, remedial instruction, study skills assistance, tutoring, writing center.

Majors. Biology: General. **Business:** Accounting, business admin. **Communications:** Journalism. **Computer sciences:** General, computer science. **Education:** Elementary, kindergarten/preschool, special. **Foreign languages:** French, German, Spanish. **History:** General. **Interdisciplinary:** Biological/physical sciences. **Legal studies:** Paralegal. **Liberal arts:** Arts/sciences. **Math:** General. **Parks/recreation:** Facilities management, sports admin. **Philosophy/religion:** Philosophy. **Physical sciences:** Chemistry, geology, physics. **Protective services:** Law enforcement admin. **Psychology:** General. **Public administration:** Social work. **Social sciences:** General, economics, geography, international relations, political science, sociology. **Visual/performing arts:** Art, dramatic, studio arts. **Other:** Health and physical education.

Most popular majors. Business/marketing 9%, education 14%, health sciences 9%, parks/recreation 21%, security/protective services 11%.

Computing on campus. PC or laptop required. 290 workstations in dormitories, library, computer center, student center. Dormitories wired for high-speed internet access and linked to campus network. Commuter students can connect to campus network. Online course registration, online library, helpline, repair service, student web hosting, wireless network available.

Student life. Freshman orientation: Available, $75 fee. Overnight new student and parent programs, run concurrently, held during June. **Housing:** Guaranteed on-campus for freshmen. Coed dorms, apartments available. $200 nonrefundable deposit, deadline 5/1. **Activities:** Bands, campus ministries, choral groups, dance, drama, international student organizations, literary magazine, music ensembles, musical theater, radio station, student government, student newspaper, symphony orchestra, TV station, Newman Club, Black Cultural Society, Campus Crusade, Commonwealth Association of Students, Fellowship of Christian Athletes, social service society, Full Gospel Fellowship, New Life Student Fellowship.

Athletics. NCAA. **Intercollegiate:** Baseball M, basketball, boxing, cheerleading, cross-country, field hockey W, football (tackle) M, lacrosse W, soccer, softball W, swimming W, track and field, volleyball W, wrestling M. **Intramural:** Badminton, basketball, cross-country, field hockey W, golf, racquetball, skiing, soccer, softball, tennis, volleyball, water polo, wrestling M. **Team name:** Bald Eagles, Lady Eagles.

Student services. Adult student services, alcohol/substance abuse counseling, chaplain/spiritual director, career counseling, student employment services, financial aid counseling, health services, minority student services, personal counseling, placement for graduates, veterans' counselor, women's services. **Physically disabled:** Services for visually, speech impaired.

Contact. E-mail: admissions@lhup.edu
Phone: (570) 484-2027 Toll-free number: (800) 332-8900
Fax: (570) 484-2201
Stephen Lee, Director of Admissions, Lock Haven University of Pennsylvania, Akeley Hall, Lock Haven, PA 17745

Lycoming College

Williamsport, Pennsylvania **CB member**
www.lycoming.edu **CB code: 2372**

- Private 4-year liberal arts college affiliated with United Methodist Church
- Residential campus in small city
- 1,325 degree-seeking undergraduates: 55% women, 3% African American, 1% Asian American, 2% Hispanic American, 1% international
- 69% of applicants admitted
- SAT or ACT (ACT writing optional), application essay required
- 70% graduate within 6 years; 20% enter graduate study

General. Founded in 1812. Regionally accredited. **Degrees:** 331 bachelor's awarded. **ROTC:** Army. **Location:** 90 miles from Harrisburg, 170 miles from Philadelphia. **Calendar:** Semester, limited summer session. **Full-time faculty:** 89 total; 86% have terminal degrees, 7% minority, 37% women. **Part-time faculty:** 37 total; 16% have terminal degrees, 43% women. **Class size:** 65% < 20, 32% 20-39, 2% 40-49, less than 1% 50-99, less than 1% >100. **Special facilities:** Planetarium, Clean Water Institute, graphics computer lab, Polling Institute.

Freshman class profile. 1,601 applied, 1,111 admitted, 340 enrolled.

Mid 50% test scores			
SAT critical reading:	470-580	Rank in top tenth:	19%
SAT math:	470-580	End year in good standing:	90%
SAT writing:	460-570	Return as sophomores:	79%
ACT composite:	20-27	Out-of-state:	37%
Rank in top quarter:	43%	Live on campus:	95%

Basis for selection. Academic achievement as reflected in school record, class rank, and test scores most important. Curriculum, counselor and teacher recommendations also considered. Interview recommended for all; portfolio recommended for art program and creative writing program; audition recommended for music and theater programs.

High school preparation. College-preparatory program required. 16 units required; 21 recommended. Required and recommended units include English 4, mathematics 3-4, social studies 3-4, science 2-3 (laboratory 2-3), foreign language 2-3 and academic electives 2.

2008-2009 Annual costs. Tuition/fees: $28,764. Room/board: $7,672. Books/supplies: $800. Personal expenses: $800.

2008-2009 Financial aid. Need-based: 325 full-time freshmen applied for aid; 289 were judged to have need; 289 of these received aid. Average need met was 82%. Average scholarship/grant was $18,116; average loan $4,274. 68% of total undergraduate aid awarded as scholarships/grants, 32% as loans/jobs. **Non-need-based:** Awarded to 302 full-time undergraduates, including 81 freshmen. Scholarships awarded for academics, art, leadership, minority status, music/drama.

Application procedures. Admission: Priority date 4/1; deadline 7/1 (receipt date). $35 fee, may be waived for applicants with need, free for online applicants. Admission notification on a rolling basis beginning on or about 12/15. Must reply by May 1 or within 4 week(s) if notified thereafter. **Financial aid:** Priority date 3/1; no closing date. FAFSA, institutional form required. Applicants notified on a rolling basis starting 3/1; must reply by 5/1.

Academics. Teacher certification offered on elementary and secondary levels; special education certification as part of bachelor of arts program. **Special study options:** Accelerated study, combined bachelor's/graduate degree, cross-registration, double major, honors, independent study, internships, student-designed major, study abroad, teacher certification program, United Nations semester, urban semester, Washington semester. **Credit/placement by examination:** AP, CLEP, IB, institutional tests. 64 credit hours maximum toward bachelor's degree. **Support services:** Learning center, study skills assistance, tutoring, writing center.

Majors. Area/ethnic studies: American. **Biology:** General, anatomy, ecology, molecular. **Business:** Accounting, actuarial science, business admin, communications, finance, international finance, managerial economics, marketing. **Communications:** General, digital media. **Computer sciences:** General. **Foreign languages:** French, German, Spanish. **History:** General, American, European. **Interdisciplinary:** Classical/archaeology. **Math:** General. **Philosophy/religion:** Philosophy, religion. **Physical sciences:** Astronomy, chemistry, physics. **Protective services:** Criminal justice. **Psychology:** General. **Social sciences:** Anthropology, archaeology, criminology, economics, political science, sociology, U.S. government. **Visual/performing arts:** General, acting, art, art history/conservation, commercial/advertising art, directing/producing, dramatic, painting, photography, printmaking, sculpture, studio arts. **Other:** Actuarial mathematics.

Most popular majors. Biology 9%, business/marketing 16%, physical sciences 6%, psychology 14%, social sciences 17%, visual/performing arts 11%.

Computing on campus. 137 workstations in library, computer center, student center. Dormitories wired for high-speed internet access and linked to campus network. Commuter students can connect to campus network. Online course registration, online library, helpline, repair service, student web hosting, wireless network available.

Student life. Freshman orientation: Mandatory, $200 fee. Preregistration for classes offered. 2-day, 1-night event for students and parents. Choose 1 of 3 dates. **Policies:** Students must live in college-owned residence halls or apartments. **Housing:** Guaranteed on-campus for all undergraduates. Coed dorms, single-sex dorms, special housing for disabled, apartments, fraternity/sorority housing, wellness housing available. $100 nonrefundable deposit, deadline 5/1. Study-intensive housing, Creative Arts Society housing available. **Activities:** Bands, campus ministries, choral groups, dance, drama, film society, international student organizations, literary magazine, music ensembles, musical theater, radio station, student government, student newspaper, symphony orchestra, TV station, Circle K, Habitat for Humanity, College Democrats, College Republicans, environmental awareness foundation, Black Student Union, Big Brothers/Big Sisters, Colleges Against Cancer, Religious Experiences at Lycoming.

Athletics. NCAA. **Intercollegiate:** Basketball, cross-country, football (tackle) M, golf, lacrosse, soccer, softball W, swimming, tennis, volleyball W, wrestling M. **Intramural:** Basketball, football (non-tackle), soccer, softball, table tennis, volleyball. **Team name:** Warriors.

Student services. Alcohol/substance abuse counseling, chaplain/spiritual director, career counseling, student employment services, financial aid counseling, health services, personal counseling, placement for graduates, women's services. **Physically disabled:** Services for visually, hearing impaired.

Contact. E-mail: admissions@lycoming.edu
Phone: (570) 321-4026 Toll-free number: (800) 345-3920 ext. 4026
Fax: (570) 321-4317
James Spencer, Dean of Admissions and Financial Aid, Lycoming College, 700 College Place, Williamsport, PA 17701

Mansfield University of Pennsylvania

Mansfield, Pennsylvania
www.mansfield.edu **CB code: 2655**

- Public 4-year university and liberal arts college
- Residential campus in small town
- 2,877 degree-seeking undergraduates: 7% part-time, 62% women, 6% African American, 1% Asian American, 2% Hispanic American, 1% Native American, 1% international
- 418 degree-seeking graduate students
- 73% of applicants admitted
- SAT or ACT (ACT writing optional) required
- 48% graduate within 6 years; 16% enter graduate study

General. Founded in 1857. Regionally accredited. **Degrees:** 501 bachelor's, 29 associate awarded; master's offered. **Location:** 50 miles from Williamsport, 30 miles from Corning, New York. **Calendar:** Semester, limited summer session. **Full-time faculty:** 167 total; 65% have terminal degrees, 14% minority, 46% women. **Part-time faculty:** 63 total; 11% have terminal degrees, 8% minority, 59% women. **Class size:** 44% < 20, 46% 20-39, 5% 40-49, 4% 50-99, less than 1% >100. **Special facilities:** Planetarium, solar collector, science museum, animal collection, fisheries research boat, leadership institute.

Freshman class profile. 4,076 applied, 2,992 admitted, 1,015 enrolled.

Mid 50% test scores			
SAT critical reading:	430-530	Rank in top quarter:	31%
SAT math:	430-540	Rank in top tenth:	11%
SAT writing:	420-510	Return as sophomores:	71%
GPA 3.75 or higher:	29%	Out-of-state:	20%
GPA 3.50-3.74:	16%	Live on campus:	80%
GPA 3.0-3.49:	26%	Fraternities:	3%
GPA 2.0-2.99:	28%	Sororities:	1%

Basis for selection. Class rank, high school curriculum, test scores important; counselor's recommendation, extracurricular activities considered. Special consideration given to applicants eligible for Equal Education Opportunity Program. Entry competitive in X-ray technology, respiratory therapy, fisheries, music, art programs, premed, nursing, biology, chemistry. Essay recommended for all; interview required for radiology program; audition required for music program; portfolio required for art program. **Homeschooled:** Statement describing homeschool structure and mission, transcript of courses and grades required.

High school preparation. 21 units required; 25 recommended. Required and recommended units include English 4, mathematics 3-4, history 4, science 2-3 (laboratory 2-3), foreign language 2-4 and academic electives 6.

2008-2009 Annual costs. Tuition/fees: $7,359; $15,397 out-of-state. Tuition for NY residents is $8,842; per-credit-hour charge for NY residents is $368. Room/board: $6,672. Books/supplies: $1,200. Personal expenses: $800.

2007-2008 Financial aid. Non-need-based: Scholarships awarded for academics, art, athletics, leadership, music/drama, state residency.

Application procedures. Admission: No deadline. $25 fee, may be waived for applicants with need. Admission notification on a rolling basis beginning on or about 7/1. Must reply by May 1 or within 2 week(s) if notified thereafter. Applicants to competitive programs should apply by January 15. **Financial aid:** Priority date 3/15; no closing date. FAFSA, institutional form required. Applicants notified on a rolling basis starting 3/15; must reply within 2 week(s) of notification.

Academics. **Special study options:** Cooperative education, cross-registration, distance learning, double major, dual enrollment of high school students, ESL, exchange student, external degree, honors, independent study, internships, liberal arts/career combination, student-designed major, study abroad, teacher certification program, Washington semester. Online programs. **Credit/placement by examination:** AP, CLEP, IB, SAT, institutional tests. **Support services:** Learning center, pre-admission summer program, reduced course load, remedial instruction, study skills assistance, tutoring, writing center.

Majors. **Architecture:** Urban/community planning. **Biology:** General, biochemistry, cell/histology, marine, molecular. **Business:** Accounting, actuarial science, business admin, human resources, international, marketing, tourism promotion, tourism/travel. **Communications:** General, broadcast journalism, journalism, public relations. **Computer sciences:** General, computer science, information systems. **Conservation:** General, environmental studies, fisheries. **Education:** Art, biology, chemistry, early childhood, elementary, English, foreign languages, French, German, history, mathematics, middle, multi-level teacher, music, physics, secondary, social studies, Spanish, special. **Foreign languages:** French, German, Spanish. **Health:** Clinical lab science, clinical lab technology, music therapy, predental, premedicine, preop/surgical nursing, prepharmacy, preveterinary. **History:** General. **Legal studies:** Prelaw. **Liberal arts:** Arts/sciences. **Math:** General. **Philosophy/religion:** Philosophy. **Physical sciences:** Chemistry, geology, physics. **Protective services:** Law enforcement admin. **Psychology:** General. **Public administration:** Social work. **Social sciences:** General, anthropology, economics, geography, political science, sociology. **Visual/performing arts:** Art, art history/conservation, dramatic, music management, music performance, piano/organ, studio arts, voice/opera.

Computing on campus. 840 workstations in dormitories, library, computer center, student center. Dormitories wired for high-speed internet access and linked to campus network. Commuter students can connect to campus network. Online course registration, online library, helpline, wireless network available.

Student life. **Freshman orientation:** Mandatory, $65 fee. Preregistration for classes offered. 2-day program for students and parents. **Housing:** Guaranteed on-campus for all undergraduates. Coed dorms, fraternity/sorority housing available. **Activities:** Bands, choral groups, dance, drama, literary magazine, music ensembles, musical theater, radio station, student government, student newspaper, symphony orchestra, TV station, Black Awarenesss Association, Inter-Varsity Christian Fellowship, Commonwealth Association of Students.

Athletics. NCAA. **Intercollegiate:** Baseball M, basketball, cross-country, diving W, field hockey W, soccer W, softball W, swimming W, track and field. **Intramural:** Basketball, football (non-tackle) M, soccer, softball, tennis, volleyball, water polo. **Team name:** Mounties.

Student services. Adult student services, alcohol/substance abuse counseling, chaplain/spiritual director, career counseling, services for economically disadvantaged, student employment services, financial aid counseling, health services, minority student services, on-campus daycare, personal counseling, placement for graduates, veterans' counselor, women's services. **Physically disabled:** Services for visually, speech, hearing impaired.

Contact. E-mail: admissions@mansfield.edu
Phone: (570) 662-4243 Toll-free number: (800) 577-6826
Fax: (570) 662-4121
Brian Barden, Executive Director of Enrollment Services, Mansfield University of Pennsylvania, South Hall, Mansfield, PA 16933

Marywood University

Scranton, Pennsylvania — **CB member**
www.marywood.edu — **CB code: 2407**

- Private 4-year university affiliated with Roman Catholic Church
- Residential campus in small city
- 2,039 degree-seeking undergraduates: 5% part-time, 70% women, 1% African American, 2% Asian American, 3% Hispanic American, 2% international
- 1,156 degree-seeking graduate students
- 78% of applicants admitted
- SAT or ACT (ACT writing optional) required
- 310% graduate within 6 years; 35% enter graduate study

General. Founded in 1915. Regionally accredited. **Degrees:** 355 bachelor's awarded; master's, doctoral offered. **ROTC:** Army, Air Force. **Location:** 110 miles from Philadelphia, 120 miles from New York City. **Calendar:** Semester, extensive summer session. **Full-time faculty:** 133 total; 84% have terminal degrees, 6% minority, 53% women. **Part-time faculty:** 190 total; 5% minority, 53% women. **Class size:** 54% < 20, 44% 20-39, less than 1% 40-49, 1% 50-99. **Special facilities:** Arboretum, technology lab, science multimedia laboratory, interactive voice laboratory, music computer laboratory, nursing laboratory, video conferencing facility, speech and hearing clinic, healthy family center, early childhood center, center for athletics and wellness.

Freshman class profile. 1,774 applied, 1,377 admitted, 426 enrolled.

Mid 50% test scores		**GPA 2.0-2.99:**	43%
SAT critical reading:	480-560	**Rank in top quarter:**	49%
SAT math:	470-570	**Rank in top tenth:**	15%
SAT writing:	460-550	**Return as sophomores:**	81%
GPA 3.75 or higher:	9%	**Out-of-state:**	35%
GPA 3.50-3.74:	12%	**Live on campus:**	70%
GPA 3.0-3.49:	35%		

Basis for selection. Class rank and high school achievement weighed alongside performance on SAT/ACT. Course selection, achievement outside classroom, involvement in activities in and out of school, and letters or recommendations also considered. TOEFL used for admission of non-native English speakers. Essay recommended for all. Interview required for physician's assistant program; recommended for all others. Audition required for music program; portfolio recommended for art program. **Learning Disabled:** Students may request accommodation by submitting documentation to admissions office or coordinator of services for students with disabilities.

High school preparation. College-preparatory program recommended. 16 units required. Required units include English 4, mathematics 2, social studies 3, science 1 (laboratory 1) and academic electives 6. Biological science must be laboratory science.

2009-2010 Annual costs. Tuition/fees: $26,270. Room/board: $11,498. Books/supplies: $900. Personal expenses: $800.

2008-2009 Financial aid. **Need-based:** 394 full-time freshmen applied for aid; 345 were judged to have need; 344 of these received aid. Average need met was 80%. Average scholarship/grant was $15,206; average loan $3,661. 77% of total undergraduate aid awarded as scholarships/grants, 23% as loans/jobs. **Non-need-based:** Awarded to 492 full-time undergraduates, including 128 freshmen. Scholarships awarded for academics, alumni affiliation, art, leadership, music/drama, ROTC.

Application procedures. **Admission:** No deadline. $35 fee, may be waived for applicants with need, free for online applicants. Admission notification on a rolling basis beginning on or about 10/1. Must reply by May 1 or within 3 week(s) if notified thereafter. Students applying for early admission must submit letter from their high school principal recommending them for early admission. **Financial aid:** Priority date 2/15; no closing date. FAFSA required. Applicants notified on a rolling basis starting 2/15; must reply by 5/1 or within 3 week(s) of notification.

Academics. Healthy Family Center provides opportunities for study and research in nutrition, dietetics, and athletic performance; Robert J. Mellow Center for Athletics and Wellness provides full support for athletic training program. **Special study options:** Combined bachelor's/graduate degree, cross-registration, distance learning, double major, dual enrollment of high school students, ESL, honors, independent study, internships, semester at sea, student-designed major, study abroad, teacher certification program. Students may study in any accredited school in any country that is approved by Marywood, or Marywood also has faculty-led, short-term study abroad programs. **Credit/placement by examination:** AP, CLEP, IB, institutional tests. 30 credit hours maximum toward associate degree, 66 toward bachelor's. **Support services:** Learning center, pre-admission summer program, reduced course load, remedial instruction, study skills assistance, tutoring, writing center.

Majors. **Biology:** General, biotechnology. **Business:** Accounting, business admin, financial planning, hospitality admin, international, marketing. **Communications:** Digital media. **Conservation:** Environmental science. **Education:** Art, biology, elementary, emotionally handicapped, ESL, family/consumer sciences, French, mathematics, music, science, social science, Spanish, special. **Foreign languages:** French, Spanish. **Health:** Art therapy, athletic training, audiology/speech pathology, clinical lab science, dietetics, health care admin, music therapy, nursing (RN). **History:** General. **Math:** General. **Parks/recreation:** Health/fitness. **Philosophy/religion:** Religion. **Psychology:** General, industrial. **Public administration:** Social work. **Social sciences:** General. **Transportation:** Aviation management. **Visual/performing arts:** Arts management, ceramics, dramatic, graphic design, illustration, interior design, music performance, painting, photography, sculpture.

Most popular majors. Business/marketing 9%, education 20%, health sciences 25%, psychology 7%, visual/performing arts 12%.

Computing on campus. 382 workstations in dormitories, library, computer center, student center. Dormitories wired for high-speed internet access and linked to campus network. Commuter students can connect to campus network. Online course registration, online library, helpline, repair service, student web hosting available.

Student life. **Freshman orientation:** Mandatory, $200 fee. Preregistration for classes offered. Includes program for families, held in July for 3 days. Additional 3-day program prior to start of classes. **Policies:** First- and second-year students under 21 not living at home with families in area required to live on campus. **Housing:** Guaranteed on-campus for freshmen. Coed dorms, single-sex dorms, special housing for disabled, apartments, wellness housing available. Volunteer services residential community and international students residential community available. **Activities:** Jazz band, campus ministries, dance, drama, international student organizations, music ensembles, musical theater, radio station, student government, student newspaper, TV station, Amnesty International, Collegiate Volunteers, environmental club, Volunteers in Action, Psi Chi, Peer Mediators, Gay-Straight Alliance, Americorps.

Athletics. NCAA. **Intercollegiate:** Baseball M, basketball, cross-country, field hockey W, lacrosse, soccer, softball W, tennis, volleyball W. **Intramural:** Badminton, basketball, football (non-tackle), racquetball, soccer, softball, table tennis, tennis, volleyball, water polo. **Team name:** Pacers.

Student services. Adult student services, alcohol/substance abuse counseling, chaplain/spiritual director, career counseling, services for economically disadvantaged, student employment services, financial aid counseling, health services, minority student services, on-campus daycare, personal counseling, placement for graduates, women's services. **Physically disabled:** Services for visually, speech, hearing impaired. **Learning disabled:** Comprehensive services available.

Contact. E-mail: yourfuture@marywood.edu
Phone: (570) 348-6234 Toll-free number: (866) 279-9663
Fax: (570) 961-4763
Robert Reese, Director of University Admissions, Marywood University, 2300 Adams Avenue, Scranton, PA 18509-1598

Mercyhurst College

Erie, Pennsylvania — **CB member**
www.mercyhurst.edu — **CB code: 2410**

- Private 4-year liberal arts college affiliated with Roman Catholic Church
- Residential campus in small city
- 3,842 degree-seeking undergraduates: 12% part-time, 59% women, 5% African American, 1% Asian American, 2% Hispanic American, 5% international
- 307 degree-seeking graduate students
- 70% of applicants admitted
- SAT or ACT (ACT writing recommended) required
- 64% graduate within 6 years; 28% enter graduate study

General. Founded in 1926. Regionally accredited. **Degrees:** 658 bachelor's, 213 associate awarded; master's offered. **ROTC:** Air Force. **Location:** 100 miles from Pittsburgh; 90 miles from Buffalo, New York. **Calendar:** Trimester, limited summer session. **Full-time faculty:** 166 total; 51% have terminal degrees, 3% minority, 51% women. **Part-time faculty:** 116 total; 6% have terminal degrees, 3% minority, 47% women. **Class size:** 55% < 20, 44% 20-39, 1% 40-49, less than 1% 50-99. **Special facilities:** Observatory, archaeological materials preservation laboratory.

Freshman class profile. 3,174 applied, 2,236 admitted, 643 enrolled.

Mid 50% test scores		**GPA 2.0-2.99:**	19%
SAT critical reading:	470-570	**Rank in top quarter:**	18%
SAT math:	460-580	**Rank in top tenth:**	15%
SAT writing:	450-570	**End year in good standing:**	92%
ACT composite:	20-25	**Return as sophomores:**	74%
GPA 3.75 or higher:	34%	**Out-of-state:**	52%
GPA 3.50-3.74:	17%	**Live on campus:**	91%
GPA 3.0-3.49:	30%	**International:**	5%

Basis for selection. Admissions based on secondary school record. Class rank, standardized test scores, talent, ability, character, and personal qualities also important. Essay, interview recommended for all; audition required for dance, music programs; portfolio required for art program. **Homeschooled:** SAT/ACT and transcript preferred.

High school preparation. College-preparatory program recommended. 16 units required. Required and recommended units include English 4, mathematics 3, social studies 5, science 2 (laboratory 2) and foreign language 2.

2008-2009 Annual costs. Tuition/fees: $23,286. Room/board: $8,196. Books/supplies: $1,000. Personal expenses: $600.

2008-2009 Financial aid. **Non-need-based:** Scholarships awarded for academics, alumni affiliation, art, athletics, leadership, minority status, music/drama, religious affiliation, ROTC.

Application procedures. **Admission:** Priority date 3/15; no deadline. $30 fee, may be waived for applicants with need, free for online applicants. Admission notification on a rolling basis beginning on or about 11/15. Must reply by May 1 or within 2 week(s) if notified thereafter. **Financial aid:** Priority date 3/1; no closing date. FAFSA required. Applicants notified on a rolling basis starting 2/15; must reply by 5/1 or within 2 week(s) of notification.

Academics. Education department offers graduate student-taught special education programs for learning disabled students. **Special study options:** Combined bachelor's/graduate degree, cooperative education, cross-registration, distance learning, double major, honors, independent study, internships, liberal arts/career combination, New York semester, semester at sea, student-designed major, study abroad, teacher certification program, Washington semester, weekend college. **Credit/placement by examination:** AP, CLEP, IB, SAT, ACT, institutional tests. 30 credit hours maximum toward bachelor's degree. **Support services:** Learning center, preadmission summer program, reduced course load, remedial instruction, study skills assistance, tutoring, writing center.

Majors. **Biology:** General, biochemistry. **Business:** Accounting, business admin, fashion, finance, hospitality admin, international. **Communications:** General. **Computer sciences:** General. **Education:** Art, biology, business, chemistry, early childhood, elementary, English, family/consumer sciences, foreign languages, mathematics, music, science, secondary, social science, special. **Foreign languages:** General. **Health:** Art therapy, health services, medical records technology. **History:** General. **Interdisciplinary:** Global studies. **Math:** General. **Philosophy/religion:** Philosophy, religion. **Physical sciences:** Chemistry, geology. **Protective services:** Criminal justice, forensics. **Psychology:** General. **Public administration:** Social work. **Social sciences:** Anthropology, political science, sociology. **Theology:** Religious ed. **Visual/performing arts:** Dance, interior design, music performance, studio arts.

Most popular majors. Biology 6%, business/marketing 21%, communications/journalism 6%, education 13%, family/consumer sciences 6%, health sciences 6%, interdisciplinary studies 11%, security/protective services 8%.

Computing on campus. 375 workstations in dormitories, library, computer center, student center. Dormitories wired for high-speed internet access and linked to campus network. Commuter students can connect to campus network. Online course registration, online library, helpline, repair service, student web hosting, wireless network available.

Student life. **Freshman orientation:** Mandatory, $150 fee. Preregistration for classes offered. 3 days prior to start of classes. **Housing:** Guaranteed on-campus for all undergraduates. Single-sex dorms, apartments, wellness housing available. $350 fully refundable deposit, deadline 8/1. **Activities:** Bands, campus ministries, choral groups, dance, drama, international student organizations, literary magazine, music ensembles, musical theater, opera, radio station, student government, student newspaper, symphony orchestra, campus ministry, Association of Black Collegians, Habitat for Humanity, Amnesty International, ambassadors club.

Athletics. NCAA. **Intercollegiate:** Baseball M, basketball, cheerleading, cross-country, field hockey W, football (tackle) M, golf, ice hockey, lacrosse, rowing (crew), soccer, softball W, swimming M, tennis, volleyball W, water polo, wrestling M. **Intramural:** Basketball, bowling, football (non-tackle) M, ice hockey, skiing, soccer, softball, table tennis. **Team name:** Lakers.

Student services. Adult student services, alcohol/substance abuse counseling, chaplain/spiritual director, career counseling, services for economically disadvantaged, student employment services, financial aid counseling, health services, personal counseling, placement for graduates, veterans' counselor. **Physically disabled:** Services for hearing impaired. **Learning disabled:** Comprehensive services available.

Contact. E-mail: admissions@mercyhurst.edu
Phone: (814) 824-2202 Toll-free number: (800) 825-1926
Fax: (814) 824-2071
Christopher Coons, Director of Undergraduate Admissions, Mercyhurst College, 501 East 38th Street, Erie, PA 16546-0001

Messiah College

Grantham, Pennsylvania — **CB member**
www.messiah.edu — **CB code: 2411**

- Private 4-year liberal arts college affiliated with interdenominational tradition
- Residential campus in small town
- 2,763 degree-seeking undergraduates: 1% part-time, 63% women, 2% African American, 2% Asian American, 1% Hispanic American, 2% international

- 70% of applicants admitted
- Application essay required
- 76% graduate within 6 years; 13% enter graduate study

General. Founded in 1909. Regionally accredited. Students able to take coursework at Temple University. **Degrees:** 627 bachelor's awarded. **Location:** 10 miles from Harrisburg, 20 miles from Gettysburg. **Calendar:** Semester, limited summer session. **Full-time faculty:** 173 total; 83% have terminal degrees, 5% minority, 38% women. **Part-time faculty:** 114 total; 5% minority, 53% women. **Class size:** 49% < 20, 48% 20-39, 2% 40-49, 1% 50-99, less than 1% >100. **Special facilities:** Historical library and archives, natural history museum, service and learning center, Anabaptist, Pietist, Wesleyan studies institute, community-supported agriculture, solar panel array and pavilion.

Freshman class profile. 2,844 applied, 1,997 admitted, 709 enrolled.

Mid 50% test scores		**GPA 2.0-2.99:**	3%
SAT critical reading:	520-630	**Rank in top quarter:**	70%
SAT math:	520-640	**Rank in top tenth:**	33%
SAT writing:	520-640	**End year in good standing:**	97%
ACT composite:	22-27	**Return as sophomores:**	83%
GPA 3.75 or higher:	56%	**Out-of-state:**	45%
GPA 3.50-3.74:	22%	**Live on campus:**	97%
GPA 3.0-3.49:	19%	**International:**	3%

Basis for selection. Admitted students normally in top third of class and have B average or better. Statement of Christian commitment required. SAT or ACT recommended. Tests required of standard choice applicants. Students in the top 20% of high school class may apply without test scores, but must submit graded writing sample and have on-campus interview. Interview required for students who apply by the "Write Choice" application method, strongly recommended for all others. **Homeschooled:** Comprehensive transcript of senior year academic program as well as courses and course evaluations of 9th through 11th grades required. Include independent evaluation by qualified educator if available. **Learning Disabled:** Autobiographical statement required. Psychoeducational report (done within last 4 years) and interview required only after admissions decision. High school IEP recommended.

High school preparation. College-preparatory program required. 16 units required; 20 recommended. Required and recommended units include English 4, mathematics 2-3, social studies 2, history 2, science 2-3 (laboratory 2-3), foreign language 2 and academic electives 4.

2008-2009 Annual costs. Tuition/fees: $25,670. Room/board: $7,610. Books/supplies: $960. Personal expenses: $1,200.

2008-2009 Financial aid. Need-based: 612 full-time freshmen applied for aid; 510 were judged to have need; 510 of these received aid. Average need met was 75%. Average scholarship/grant was $13,204; average loan $3,640. 59% of total undergraduate aid awarded as scholarships/grants, 41% as loans/jobs. **Non-need-based:** Awarded to 959 full-time undergraduates, including 259 freshmen. Scholarships awarded for academics, art, leadership, music/drama, religious affiliation.

Application procedures. Admission: Priority date 5/1; no deadline. $30 fee, may be waived for applicants with need. Admission notification on a rolling basis beginning on or about 7/1. Must reply by May 1 or within 4 week(s) if notified thereafter. **Financial aid:** Priority date 4/1; no closing date. FAFSA required. Applicants notified on a rolling basis starting 3/15; must reply by 5/1 or within 4 week(s) of notification.

Academics. Supplemental instructional support available. **Special study options:** Accelerated study, double major, dual enrollment of high school students, ESL, exchange student, honors, independent study, internships, student-designed major, study abroad, teacher certification program, urban semester, Washington semester. Pass/Fail option. **Credit/placement by examination:** AP, CLEP, IB, institutional tests. 32 credit hours maximum toward bachelor's degree. **Support services:** Learning center, pre-admission summer program, reduced course load, remedial instruction, study skills assistance, tutoring, writing center.

Majors. Biology: General, biochemistry. **Business:** Accounting, business admin, e-commerce, entrepreneurial studies, human resources, international, managerial economics, marketing. **Communications:** General, journalism, radio/tv. **Computer sciences:** Computer science, information systems. **Conservation:** Environmental science, environmental studies. **Education:** Art, biology, chemistry, early childhood, elementary, English, family/consumer sciences, French, German, mathematics, music, physical, social studies, Spanish. **Engineering:** General. **Family/consumer sciences:** Family/community services. **Foreign languages:** French, German, Spanish. **Health:** Athletic training, clinical nutrition, nursing (RN), recreational therapy. **History:** General. **Interdisciplinary:** Biopsychology. **Liberal arts:** Humanities. **Math:** General. **Parks/recreation:** General, exercise sciences, sports admin. **Philosophy/religion:** Philosophy, religion. **Physical sciences:** Chemistry, physics. **Protective services:** Criminal justice. **Psychology:** General. **Public administration:** Social work. **Social sciences:** Economics, political science, sociology. **Theology:** Bible, religious ed. **Visual/performing arts:** Art history/conservation, arts management, dramatic, studio arts.

Most popular majors. Business/marketing 10%, communications/journalism 7%, education 16%, health sciences 8%, parks/recreation 6%, visual/performing arts 6%.

Computing on campus. 571 workstations in dormitories, library, computer center, student center. Dormitories wired for high-speed internet access and linked to campus network. Commuter students can connect to campus network. Online course registration, online library, helpline, student web hosting, wireless network available.

Student life. Freshman orientation: Mandatory. Preregistration for classes offered. 4-day orientation for students and parents during fall welcome weekend; includes placement exams and service day. **Policies:** Students generally required to live on campus unless married or living with relatives. Religious observance required. **Housing:** Guaranteed on-campus for all undergraduates. Coed dorms, single-sex dorms, special housing for disabled, apartments, wellness housing available. $200 partly refundable deposit, deadline 5/1. **Activities:** Bands, campus ministries, choral groups, dance, drama, film society, international student organizations, literary magazine, music ensembles, musical theater, radio station, student government, student newspaper, symphony orchestra, outreach teams, World Christian Fellowship, Nurses Christian Fellowship, Newman Club, Powerhouse band, Acclamation dance, Alliance of Confessing Theologies, service trips.

Athletics. NCAA. **Intercollegiate:** Baseball M, basketball, cross-country, field hockey W, golf M, lacrosse, soccer, softball W, swimming, tennis, track and field, volleyball W, wrestling M. **Intramural:** Basketball, football (non-tackle), racquetball, soccer, softball, volleyball. **Team name:** Falcons.

Student services. Chaplain/spiritual director, career counseling, student employment services, financial aid counseling, health services, minority student services, on-campus daycare, personal counseling, placement for graduates. **Physically disabled:** Services for visually, speech, hearing impaired.

Contact. E-mail: admiss@messiah.edu
Phone: (717) 691-6000 Toll-free number: (800) 233-4220
Fax: (717) 796-5374
Chopka John, Dean for Enrollment Management, Messiah College, PO Box 3005, Grantham, PA 17027-0800

Millersville University of Pennsylvania

Millersville, Pennsylvania — **CB member**
www.millersville.edu — **CB code: 2656**

- Public 4-year university and liberal arts college
- Residential campus in small town
- 7,098 degree-seeking undergraduates: 8% part-time, 56% women, 7% African American, 1% Asian American, 4% Hispanic American
- 674 degree-seeking graduate students
- 55% of applicants admitted
- SAT or ACT (ACT writing recommended) required
- 62% graduate within 6 years

General. Founded in 1855. Regionally accredited. **Degrees:** 1,477 bachelor's, 5 associate awarded; master's offered. **ROTC:** Army. **Location:** 3 miles from Lancaster, 35 miles from Harrisburg. **Calendar:** 4-1-4, limited summer session. **Full-time faculty:** 314 total; 93% have terminal degrees, 17% minority, 46% women. **Part-time faculty:** 131 total; 34% have terminal degrees, 5% minority, 56% women. **Class size:** 23% < 20, 68% 20-39, 5% 40-49, 3% 50-99, 1% >100. **Special facilities:** Early childhood center, teleconferencing center, weather station, foreign language lab, art galleries.

Freshman class profile. 6,689 applied, 3,678 admitted, 1,323 enrolled.

Mid 50% test scores		**Rank in top tenth:**	14%
SAT critical reading:	470-570	**Return as sophomores:**	81%
SAT math:	490-580	**Out-of-state:**	4%
SAT writing:	460-560	**Live on campus:**	84%
Rank in top quarter:	45%		

Basis for selection. High school record most important, followed by class rank, test scores, and recommendations. Special consideration to students with special talents. Educationally and economically disadvantaged students may be admitted to Aim for Success enrichment program if they demonstrate potential for college success. Applicants without SAT scores may enroll as non-degree students and be admitted to degree-seeking status after completing 12 credits with 2.0 GPA. Interview required for applicants to disadvantaged program; recommended for all others. Audition required for music applicants; portfolio required for art applicants. RN required for nursing program.

High school preparation. College-preparatory program required. 15 units required; 21 recommended. Required and recommended units include English 4, mathematics 3, social studies 3, history 2, science 3 (laboratory 1), foreign language 2 and academic electives 4.

2008-2009 Annual costs. Tuition/fees: $6,866; $14,904 out-of-state. Room/board: $7,308. Books/supplies: $1,000. Personal expenses: $1,687.

2007-2008 Financial aid. **Need-based:** 1,152 full-time freshmen applied for aid; 784 were judged to have need; 758 of these received aid. Average need met was 76%. Average scholarship/grant was $5,320; average loan $3,271. 47% of total undergraduate aid awarded as scholarships/grants, 53% as loans/jobs. **Non-need-based:** Awarded to 771 full-time undergraduates, including 214 freshmen. Scholarships awarded for academics, athletics, minority status.

Application procedures. **Admission:** Priority date 1/1; no deadline. $50 fee, may be waived for applicants with need. Admission notification on a rolling basis beginning on or about 9/15. Extensions of reply date for accepted applicants granted upon request until May 1. **Financial aid:** Closing date 3/15. FAFSA required. Applicants notified on a rolling basis starting 3/19; must reply within 2 week(s) of notification.

Academics. **Special study options:** Accelerated study, combined bachelor's/graduate degree, cooperative education, cross-registration, distance learning, double major, dual enrollment of high school students, honors, independent study, internships, study abroad, teacher certification program. Off-campus study, learning disabilities services, adult continuing education program. **Credit/placement by examination:** AP, CLEP, IB, institutional tests. **Support services:** Learning center, reduced course load, remedial instruction, study skills assistance, tutoring, writing center.

Majors. **Biology:** General. **Business:** Business admin. **Communications:** General. **Computer sciences:** General. **Education:** Elementary, secondary, special. **Engineering technology:** Industrial, occupational safety. **Foreign languages:** French, German, Spanish. **Health:** Nursing (RN). **History:** General. **Math:** General. **Philosophy/religion:** Philosophy. **Physical sciences:** Atmospheric science, chemistry, geology, oceanography, physics. **Psychology:** General. **Public administration:** Social work. **Social sciences:** Anthropology, economics, geography, international relations, political science, sociology. **Visual/performing arts:** Art. **Other:** International studies, Social studies, Technology education.

Most popular majors. Biology 6%, business/marketing 12%, communications/journalism 7%, education 16%, engineering/engineering technologies 6%, physical sciences 6%, psychology 9%, social sciences 11%, visual/performing arts 7%.

Computing on campus. 705 workstations in dormitories, library, computer center, student center. Dormitories wired for high-speed internet access and linked to campus network. Commuter students can connect to campus network. Online course registration, online library, helpline, repair service, wireless network available.

Student life. **Freshman orientation:** Mandatory, $290 fee. Six-day program in August includes parents. **Housing:** Guaranteed on-campus for freshmen. Coed dorms, apartments, wellness housing available. $125 partly refundable deposit, deadline 4/1. Academic interest housing available for several subject areas. University-affiliated apartments and dormitory for single students adjacent to campus. **Activities:** Bands, campus ministries, choral groups, dance, drama, literary magazine, music ensembles, musical theater, radio station, student government, student newspaper, symphony orchestra, TV station, Black Student Union, commuting student association, Circle-K, College Republicans, Marauder Graphics, Asian & Friends Affiliation, College Democrats, NAACP, Society on Latino Affairs.

Athletics. NCAA. **Intercollegiate:** Baseball M, basketball, cheerleading M, cross-country, field hockey W, football (tackle) M, golf M, lacrosse W, soccer, softball W, swimming W, tennis, track and field, volleyball W, wrestling M. **Intramural:** Badminton, basketball, golf, racquetball, soccer, softball, tennis, volleyball. **Team name:** Marauders.

Student services. Adult student services, alcohol/substance abuse counseling, chaplain/spiritual director, career counseling, services for economically disadvantaged, student employment services, financial aid counseling, health services, minority student services, personal counseling, placement for graduates, veterans' counselor, women's services. **Physically disabled:** Services for visually, speech, hearing impaired.

Contact. E-mail: admissions@millersville.edu
Phone: (717) 872-3371 Toll-free number: (800) 682-3648
Fax: (717) 871-2147
Douglas Zander, Director of Admissions, Millersville University of Pennsylvania, PO Box 1002, Millersville, PA 17551-0302

Misericordia University

Dallas, Pennsylvania — **CB member**
www.misericordia.edu — **CB code: 2087**

- Private 4-year health science and liberal arts college affiliated with Roman Catholic Church
- Residential campus in large town
- 2,120 degree-seeking undergraduates: 26% part-time, 71% women, 1% African American, 1% Asian American, 1% Hispanic American
- 318 degree-seeking graduate students
- 71% of applicants admitted
- SAT or ACT (ACT writing optional) required
- 71% graduate within 6 years; 4% enter graduate study

General. Founded in 1924. Regionally accredited. Guaranteed Placement Program (within six months of graduation); Women with Children program for single women. **Degrees:** 434 bachelor's awarded; master's, doctoral offered. **ROTC:** Army, Air Force. **Location:** 9 miles from Wilkes-Barre, 20 miles from Scranton. **Calendar:** Semester, limited summer session. **Full-time faculty:** 95 total; 81% have terminal degrees, 7% minority, 52% women. **Part-time faculty:** 173 total; 14% have terminal degrees, 1% minority, 55% women. **Class size:** 60% < 20, 38% 20-39, 2% 40-49, less than 1% 50-99.

Freshman class profile. 1,430 applied, 1,014 admitted, 384 enrolled.

Mid 50% test scores		**GPA 2.0-2.99:**	22%
SAT critical reading:	460-560	**Rank in top quarter:**	51%
SAT math:	470-570	**Rank in top tenth:**	18%
ACT composite:	21-26	**End year in good standing:**	87%
GPA 3.75 or higher:	13%	**Return as sophomores:**	83%
GPA 3.50-3.74:	19%	**Out-of-state:**	23%
GPA 3.0-3.49:	45%	**Live on campus:**	79%

Basis for selection. In order of importance: high school achievement, test scores, character, recommendations from school teachers or counselors. Test scores weighed more heavily for health science programs. Essay, interview recommended. Essay required for occupational therapy applicants. **Homeschooled:** Transcript of courses and grades required. If applicant not affiliated with specific organization, college will accept transcript from home schooling parent that shows course work completed and grades achieved. GED not required. **Learning Disabled:** Essay, 3 letters of recommendation, documentation of disability, test results (i.e., WAIS) required. SAT/ACT not required.

High school preparation. College-preparatory program recommended. 16 units required. Required units include English 4, mathematics 4, social studies 4 and science 4. 2 units science and algebra required for allied health applicants. Strong math background required for computer science, physical therapy, chemistry and biology applicants.

2008-2009 Annual costs. Tuition/fees: $23,150. Room/board: $9,650. Books/supplies: $850. Personal expenses: $500.

2008-2009 Financial aid. **Need-based:** 359 full-time freshmen applied for aid; 319 were judged to have need; 319 of these received aid. Average need met was 73%. Average scholarship/grant was $12,295; average loan $5,385. 59% of total undergraduate aid awarded as scholarships/grants, 41% as loans/jobs. **Non-need-based:** Awarded to 275 full-time undergraduates, including 76 freshmen. Scholarships awarded for academics, alumni affiliation, leadership, minority status, state residency.

Application procedures. **Admission:** No deadline. $25 fee, may be waived for applicants with need. Admission notification on a rolling basis beginning on or about 9/1. Must reply by May 1 or within 4 week(s) if notified thereafter. Essay required for applicants to 5-year occupational therapy bachelor's/master's program. Closing date for applications to 5-year physical therapy bachelor's/master's program is February 1. **Financial aid:** Priority date 3/1, closing date 5/1. FAFSA, institutional form required. Applicants notified on a rolling basis starting 3/15; must reply by 5/1.

Academics. **Special study options:** Accelerated study, combined bachelor's/graduate degree, cross-registration, distance learning, double major, dual enrollment of high school students, honors, independent study, internships, student-designed major, study abroad, teacher certification program, weekend college. **Credit/placement by examination:** AP, CLEP, IB, SAT, ACT, institutional tests. 40 credit hours maximum toward bachelor's degree. **Support services:** Learning center, pre-admission summer program, study skills assistance, tutoring, writing center.

Majors. **Biology:** General, biochemistry. **Business:** Accounting, business admin, management science, marketing. **Communications:** General. **Computer sciences:** General, information technology. **Education:** Elementary, special. **Health:** Clinical lab science, medical radiologic technology/radiation therapy, nursing (RN). **History:** General. **Liberal arts:** Arts/

sciences. **Math:** General. **Parks/recreation:** Sports admin. **Philosophy/ religion:** Philosophy. **Physical sciences:** Chemistry. **Psychology:** General. **Public administration:** Social work.

Most popular majors. Business/marketing 16%, education 16%, health sciences 40%, psychology 7%.

Computing on campus. 100 workstations in dormitories, library, computer center, student center. Dormitories wired for high-speed internet access and linked to campus network. Commuter students can connect to campus network. Online course registration, online library, helpline, repair service, wireless network available.

Student life. **Freshman orientation:** Mandatory, $200 fee. Preregistration for classes offered. One-day testing for math and English placement. **Housing:** Coed dorms, wellness housing available. $100 nonrefundable deposit, deadline 5/1. Leadership house, apartment building for women with children located adjacent to campus. **Activities:** Jazz band, campus ministries, choral groups, dance, drama, literary magazine, music ensembles, radio station, student government, student newspaper, TV station, student nurses association, Council for Exceptional Children, Circle-K, Peer Associates, Diversity Institute.

Athletics. NCAA. **Intercollegiate:** Baseball M, basketball, cheerleading M, cross-country, field hockey W, golf M, lacrosse, soccer, softball W, swimming, tennis W, track and field, volleyball W. **Intramural:** Basketball, cross-country, football (non-tackle), racquetball, soccer, softball, tennis, volleyball. **Team name:** Cougars.

Student services. Adult student services, alcohol/substance abuse counseling, chaplain/spiritual director, career counseling, services for economically disadvantaged, student employment services, financial aid counseling, health services, minority student services, personal counseling, placement for graduates, women's services. **Physically disabled:** Services for visually, speech, hearing impaired. **Learning disabled:** Comprehensive services available.

Contact. E-mail: admiss@misericordia.edu
Phone: (570) 674-6264 Toll-free number: (866) 262-6363
Fax: (570) 675-2441
Glenn Bozinski, Director of Admissions, Misericordia University, 301 Lake Street, Dallas, PA 18612-1098

Moore College of Art and Design

Philadelphia, Pennsylvania
www.moore.edu **CB code: 2417**

- Private 4-year visual arts college for women
- Commuter campus in very large city
- 525 degree-seeking undergraduates: 6% part-time, 100% women, 12% African American, 2% Asian American, 6% Hispanic American, 1% Native American, 2% international
- 31 degree-seeking graduate students
- 59% of applicants admitted
- Interview required

General. Founded in 1848. Regionally accredited. **Degrees:** 86 bachelor's awarded. **Location:** 90 miles from New York City. **Calendar:** Semester, limited summer session. **Full-time faculty:** 30 total; 70% have terminal degrees, 7% minority, 53% women. **Part-time faculty:** 108 total; 30% have terminal degrees, 11% minority, 68% women. **Class size:** 85% < 20, 15% 20-39. **Special facilities:** Professional and student galleries.

Freshman class profile. 549 applied, 326 admitted, 108 enrolled.

Mid 50% test scores		**GPA 3.0-3.49:**	42%
SAT critical reading:	450-570	**GPA 2.0-2.99:**	45%
SAT math:	430-550	**Return as sophomores:**	76%
ACT composite:	18-25	**Out-of-state:**	41%
GPA 3.75 or higher:	6%	**Live on campus:**	65%
GPA 3.50-3.74:	7%	**International:**	2%

Basis for selection. High school record, interview, portfolio, and test scores important. 850 SAT (exclusive of writing) or 18 ACT and 2.5 GPA required. Students must complete writing placement essay. Portfolio required; essay recommended for all. **Homeschooled:** State high school equivalency certificate required. **Learning Disabled:** Students who request accommodations must provide qualifying documentation on professional letterhead and contain dates of assessment, signatures, titles, and license/certification numbers of diagnosing professionals. Documentation should be no more than 3 years old.

High school preparation. 14 units recommended. Recommended units include English 4, mathematics 2, social studies 4, science 2, foreign language 2 and visual/performing arts 3. Portfolio review required.

2008-2009 Annual costs. Tuition/fees: $27,718. Room/board: $10,501. Books/supplies: $2,060. Personal expenses: $2,000.

2008-2009 Financial aid. **Non-need-based:** Scholarships awarded for academics, art, leadership.

Application procedures. **Admission:** $40 fee, may be waived for applicants with need. Admission notification on a rolling basis beginning on or about 11/15. Must reply by May 1 or within 3 week(s) if notified thereafter. **Financial aid:** Priority date 3/1, closing date 5/1. FAFSA required. Applicants notified on a rolling basis starting 2/15; must reply within 2 week(s) of notification.

Academics. **Special study options:** Double major, exchange student, independent study, internships, teacher certification program. **Credit/ placement by examination:** AP, CLEP, IB, institutional tests. 6 credit hours maximum toward bachelor's degree. **Support services:** Pre-admission summer program, reduced course load, study skills assistance, tutoring.

Majors. **Education:** Art. **Interdisciplinary:** Museum. **Visual/performing arts:** Art history/conservation, fashion design, fiber arts, graphic design, illustration, interior design, photography, studio arts.

Most popular majors. Visual/performing arts 97%.

Computing on campus. PC or laptop required. 125 workstations in dormitories, library, computer center. Dormitories wired for high-speed internet access. Commuter students can connect to campus network. Online course registration, wireless network available.

Student life. **Freshman orientation:** Mandatory, $55 fee. Held 4 days prior to beginning of semester. **Housing:** Guaranteed on-campus for freshmen. Wellness housing available. $200 partly refundable deposit, deadline 7/15. **Activities:** Student government, student newspaper, environmental committee, Emerging Leaders in the Arts, judicial board, residence life mentors, student orientation staff.

Student services. Adult student services, career counseling, student employment services, financial aid counseling, health services, personal counseling.

Contact. E-mail: admiss@moore.edu
Phone: (215) 965-4014 Toll-free number: (800) 523-2025
Fax: (215) 568-3547
Heeseung Lee, Director of Admissions, Moore College of Art and Design, The Parkway at 20th Street, Philadelphia, PA 19103-1179

Moravian College

Bethlehem, Pennsylvania **CB member**
www.moravian.edu **CB code: 2418**

- Private 4-year liberal arts college affiliated with Moravian Church in America
- Residential campus in small city
- 1,668 degree-seeking undergraduates: 6% part-time, 59% women, 2% African American, 2% Asian American, 4% Hispanic American, 1% international
- 224 graduate students
- 70% of applicants admitted
- SAT or ACT with writing, application essay required
- 76% graduate within 6 years

General. Founded in 1742. Regionally accredited. Member of Lehigh Valley Association of Independent Colleges Consortium. Sixth oldest college in country. **Degrees:** 383 bachelor's awarded; master's, first professional offered. **ROTC:** Army. **Location:** 60 miles from Philadelphia, 90 miles from New York City. **Calendar:** Semester, extensive summer session. **Full-time faculty:** 124 total; 88% have terminal degrees, 8% minority, 51% women. **Part-time faculty:** 103 total; 65% have terminal degrees, 2% minority, 52% women. **Class size:** 55% < 20, 44% 20-39, 1% 40-49.

Freshman class profile. 2,098 applied, 1,462 admitted, 387 enrolled.

Mid 50% test scores		**Return as sophomores:**	83%
SAT critical reading:	500-600	**Out-of-state:**	44%
SAT math:	510-610	**Live on campus:**	91%
SAT writing:	500-600	**International:**	1%
ACT composite:	19-23	**Fraternities:**	6%
Rank in top quarter:	57%	**Sororities:**	7%
Rank in top tenth:	27%		

Basis for selection. High school record and standardized test scores important. Academic credentials, character, extracurricular involvement, volunteer work and potential for contribution considered. Interviews strongly recommended; audition required for music applicants; portfolio required for art applicants. **Homeschooled:** Letter of recommendation (nonparent) required. Interview strongly encouraged in order to share educational background in detail.

High school preparation. College-preparatory program required. 16 units required; 18 recommended. Required and recommended units include English 4, mathematics 3-4, social studies 4, science 3 (laboratory 2) and foreign language 2-3. 4 math units recommended for business, science, or math students.

2008-2009 Annual costs. Tuition/fees: $30,062. Room/board: $8,312. Books/supplies: $900. Personal expenses: $1,370.

2008-2009 Financial aid. Need-based: 341 full-time freshmen applied for aid; 292 were judged to have need; 291 of these received aid. Average need met was 81%. Average scholarship/grant was $17,213; average loan $4,025. 62% of total undergraduate aid awarded as scholarships/grants, 38% as loans/jobs. **Non-need-based:** Awarded to 370 full-time undergraduates, including 105 freshmen. Scholarships awarded for academics, alumni affiliation, leadership, minority status, music/drama, religious affiliation, ROTC.

Application procedures. Admission: Closing date 3/1 (postmark date). $40 fee, may be waived for applicants with need, free for online applicants. Admission notification 3/15. Must reply by 5/1. **Financial aid:** Priority date 2/14, closing date 3/15. FAFSA, CSS PROFILE required. Applicants notified on a rolling basis starting 4/1; must reply by 5/1 or within 2 week(s) of notification.

Academics. Learning Center offers partial but responsive program for learning disabled students. **Special study options:** Combined bachelor's/graduate degree, cross-registration, double major, honors, independent study, internships, student-designed major, study abroad, Washington semester. Allied health program with Thomas Jefferson University, forestry program cooperative with Duke University, engineering programs cooperative with Lehigh University and Washington University (MO), dental program cooperative with Temple University. **Credit/placement by examination:** AP, CLEP, IB, SAT, ACT, institutional tests. Some courses not included in credit-by-examination option. **Support services:** Learning center, study skills assistance, tutoring, writing center.

Majors. Area/ethnic studies: German. **Biology:** General, biochemistry. **Business:** Accounting, business admin, international. **Computer sciences:** Computer science. **Conservation:** Environmental science, environmental studies. **Education:** Music, science, social science. **Foreign languages:** Classics, French, German, Spanish. **Health:** Clinical lab science, nursing (RN). **History:** General. **Interdisciplinary:** Neuroscience. **Math:** General. **Philosophy/religion:** Philosophy, religion. **Physical sciences:** Chemistry, geology, physics. **Protective services:** Criminal justice. **Psychology:** General. **Social sciences:** Economics, political science, sociology. **Theology:** Sacred music. **Visual/performing arts:** Art, art history/conservation, dramatic, graphic design, music performance, music theory/composition, studio arts. **Other:** Neuroscience.

Most popular majors. Biology 8%, business/marketing 21%, English 6%, history 7%, psychology 10%, social sciences 16%, visual/performing arts 11%.

Computing on campus. 263 workstations in library, computer center. Dormitories wired for high-speed internet access and linked to campus network. Commuter students can connect to campus network. Online library, helpline, repair service, wireless network available.

Student life. Freshman orientation: Mandatory, $100 fee. Preregistration for classes offered. Three-day program held immediately prior to fall semester. **Housing:** Guaranteed on-campus for all undergraduates. Coed dorms, single-sex dorms, apartments, fraternity/sorority housing, wellness housing available. $400 nonrefundable deposit, deadline 5/1. Townhouses and suites available. **Activities:** Bands, campus ministries, choral groups, dance, drama, international student organizations, literary magazine, music ensembles, musical theater, radio station, student government, student newspaper, symphony orchestra, Hillel Society, Newman Association, international club, Moravian College Christian Fellowship, Spectrum, Catacombs, Campus Community Connection, The Forum, multicultural club, The Learning Connection.

Athletics. NCAA. **Intercollegiate:** Baseball M, basketball, cross-country, field hockey W, football (tackle) M, golf M, lacrosse, soccer, softball W, tennis, track and field, volleyball W. **Intramural:** Basketball, football (non-tackle), soccer, softball, table tennis, tennis, volleyball. **Team name:** Greyhounds.

Student services. Adult student services, alcohol/substance abuse counseling, chaplain/spiritual director, career counseling, student employment services, financial aid counseling, health services, minority student services, personal counseling, placement for graduates. **Physically disabled:** Services for visually, speech, hearing impaired.

Contact. E-mail: admissions@moravian.edu
Phone: (610) 861-1320 Toll-free number: (800) 441-3191
Fax: (610) 625-7930
James Mackin, Director of Admission, Moravian College, 1200 Main Street, Bethlehem, PA 18018

Mount Aloysius College

Cresson, Pennsylvania — **CB member**
www.mtaloy.edu — **CB code: 2420**

- Private 4-year liberal arts college affiliated with Roman Catholic Church
- Commuter campus in small town
- 1,523 degree-seeking undergraduates: 25% part-time, 72% women, 3% African American, 1% Hispanic American, 1% international
- 50 degree-seeking graduate students
- 74% of applicants admitted
- SAT or ACT (ACT writing optional), application essay required
- 34% graduate within 6 years

General. Founded in 1939. Regionally accredited. **Degrees:** 158 bachelor's, 189 associate awarded; master's offered. **Location:** 12 miles from Altoona, 90 miles from Pittsburgh. **Calendar:** Semester, limited summer session. **Full-time faculty:** 58 total; 38% have terminal degrees, 71% women. **Part-time faculty:** 112 total; less than 1% minority, 49% women. **Class size:** 65% < 20, 34% 20-39, less than 1% 40-49. **Special facilities:** Health and science center with mock operating room, telehealth/telenursing, ecumenical library.

Freshman class profile. 1,158 applied, 858 admitted, 336 enrolled.

Mid 50% test scores		**GPA 3.0-3.49:**	40%
SAT critical reading:	410-500	**GPA 2.0-2.99:**	31%
SAT math:	410-510	**Return as sophomores:**	59%
SAT writing:	400-490	**Out-of-state:**	8%
ACT composite:	16-19	**Live on campus:**	50%
GPA 3.75 or higher:	11%	**International:**	1%
GPA 3.50-3.74:	15%		

Basis for selection. School record, test scores, activities, talent, and character most important. Nursing entrance test not required for students with SAT of 900 (exclusive of Writing) or higher. Placement test waived if student scores 500 or higher in either section. Interview required for students with lower SAT scores and GPA. Interviews and essays required for physical therapist assistant majors. **Learning Disabled:** Admission interview required.

High school preparation. 16 units required; 21 recommended. Required and recommended units include English 4, mathematics 3, social studies 3, history 3, science 3, foreign language 2 and academic electives 3. Algebra and 2 lab sciences required for nursing. Algebra, chemistry required for physical therapist assistant, radiography and medical imaging applicants. Biology required for occupational therapy assistant applicants.

2008-2009 Annual costs. Tuition/fees: $16,580. Room/board: $6,950. Books/supplies: $2,000. Personal expenses: $3,000.

2007-2008 Financial aid. Need-based: 326 full-time freshmen applied for aid; 301 were judged to have need; 301 of these received aid. Average need met was 25%. Average scholarship/grant was $2,242; average loan $3,210. 53% of total undergraduate aid awarded as scholarships/grants, 47% as loans/jobs. **Non-need-based:** Awarded to 60 full-time undergraduates, including 50 freshmen. Scholarships awarded for academics, art, leadership, music/drama, religious affiliation.

Application procedures. Admission: No deadline. $30 fee, may be waived for applicants with need. Admission notification on a rolling basis beginning on or about 8/1. **Financial aid:** Priority date 4/1; no closing date. FAFSA required. Applicants notified on a rolling basis starting 3/15; must reply within 4 week(s) of notification.

Academics. **Special study options:** Accelerated study, combined bachelor's/graduate degree, distance learning, honors, independent study, internships, student-designed major, teacher certification program. **Credit/placement by examination:** AP, CLEP, institutional tests. 15 credit hours maximum toward associate degree, 30 toward bachelor's. **Support services:** Learning center, pre-admission summer program, reduced course load, remedial instruction, study skills assistance, tutoring, writing center.

Majors. **Business:** Accounting, accounting/business management, business admin. **Computer sciences:** General, information technology. **Education:** Early childhood, elementary. **Foreign languages:** Sign language interpretation. **Health:** Health services, nursing (RN), physician assistant, radiologic technology/medical imaging. **History:** General. **Interdisciplinary:** Behavioral sciences, math/computer science. **Legal studies:** Prelaw. **Liberal arts:** Arts/sciences, humanities. **Protective services:** Criminal justice. **Psychology:** General. **Social sciences:** General, criminology, political science.

Most popular majors. Business/marketing 20%, education 7%, health sciences 29%, liberal arts 20%, security/protective services 8%.

Computing on campus. 175 workstations in dormitories, library, computer center, student center. Dormitories linked to campus network. Helpline, repair service available.

Student life. **Freshman orientation:** Mandatory. **Housing:** Guaranteed on-campus for all undergraduates. Coed dorms available. **Activities:** Campus ministries, choral groups, drama, student government, student newspaper, nursing, occupational therapy assistant, business, Phi Theta Kappa, student programming council.

Athletics. NCAA. **Intercollegiate:** Baseball M, basketball, cross-country, golf, soccer, softball W, volleyball W. **Intramural:** Baseball M, basketball, football (tackle), golf, skiing, soccer, softball W, table tennis, tennis, volleyball. **Team name:** Mounties.

Student services. Alcohol/substance abuse counseling, chaplain/spiritual director, career counseling, student employment services, financial aid counseling, health services, on-campus daycare, personal counseling, placement for graduates, veterans' counselor. **Physically disabled:** Services for hearing impaired.

Contact. E-mail: admissions@mtaloy.edu
Phone: (814) 886-6383 Toll-free number: (888) 823-2220
Fax: (814) 886-6441
Frank Crouse, Vice President for Enrollment Management/Dean of Admissions, Mount Aloysius College, 7373 Admiral Peary Highway, Cresson, PA 16630

Muhlenberg College

Allentown, Pennsylvania
www.muhlenberg.edu
CB member
CB code: 2424

- Private 4-year liberal arts college affiliated with Evangelical Lutheran Church in America
- Residential campus in small city
- 2,372 degree-seeking undergraduates: 4% part-time, 58% women, 2% African American, 2% Asian American, 4% Hispanic American
- 40% of applicants admitted
- Application essay required
- 85% graduate within 6 years

General. Founded in 1848. Regionally accredited. **Degrees:** 562 bachelor's, 4 associate awarded. **ROTC:** Army. **Location:** 55 miles from Philadelphia, 90 miles from New York City. **Calendar:** Semester, limited summer session. **Full-time faculty:** 175 total; 89% have terminal degrees, 6% minority, 50% women. **Part-time faculty:** 91 total; 22% have terminal degrees, 8% minority, 38% women. **Class size:** 59% < 20, 40% 20-39, less than 1% 40-49, less than 1% 50-99, less than 1% >100. **Special facilities:** 3-theater complex, electronic music studio, natural history museum, 38-acre environmental field station, greenhouse, two electron microscopes, isolation laboratories, DNA sequencer, 20-foot boat for marine studies, 60-acre arboretum.

Freshman class profile. 4,846 applied, 1,927 admitted, 597 enrolled.

Mid 50% test scores		**GPA 2.0-2.99:**	18%
SAT critical reading:	560-660	**Rank in top quarter:**	81%
SAT math:	560-660	**Rank in top tenth:**	50%
SAT writing:	560-660	**End year in good standing:**	97%
ACT composite:	24-29	**Return as sophomores:**	93%
GPA 3.75 or higher:	19%	**Out-of-state:**	77%
GPA 3.50-3.74:	20%	**Live on campus:**	99%
GPA 3.0-3.49:	43%		

Basis for selection. High school courses, grades, class rank, test scores, personal qualities, essay, recommendations, special talents and activities important. Interview strongly recommended. Test scores optional; SAT/ACT required for consideration for Assured Admission Medical and Dental Programs, merit scholarships, honors programs. Audition recommended for dance, drama, music programs; portfolio recommended for art program. **Homeschooled:** Statement describing homeschool structure and mission, transcript of courses and grades, state high school equivalency certificate, letter of recommendation (nonparent) required. Interview strongly recommended.

High school preparation. 16 units required; 20 recommended. Required and recommended units include English 4, mathematics 3-4, social studies 1, history 2-3, science 2-4 (laboratory 2), foreign language 2-3 and academic electives 2. Advanced placement and accelerated courses encouraged.

2008-2009 Annual costs. Tuition/fees: $35,375. Room/board: $8,060. Books/supplies: $1,000. Personal expenses: $1,125.

2008-2009 Financial aid. **Need-based:** 390 full-time freshmen applied for aid; 278 were judged to have need; 273 of these received aid. Average need met was 92%. Average scholarship/grant was $20,683; average loan $3,326. 81% of total undergraduate aid awarded as scholarships/grants, 19% as loans/jobs. **Non-need-based:** Awarded to 855 full-time undergraduates, including 278 freshmen. Scholarships awarded for academics, art, leadership, music/drama.

Application procedures. **Admission:** Closing date 2/15 (postmark date). $50 fee, may be waived for applicants with need. Admission notification 3/15. Must reply by 5/1. **Financial aid:** Closing date 2/15. FAFSA, institutional form, CSS PROFILE required. Applicants notified by 4/1; must reply by 5/1.

Academics. **Special study options:** Accelerated study, combined bachelor's/graduate degree, cross-registration, double major, exchange student, honors, independent study, internships, student-designed major, study abroad, teacher certification program, Washington semester. Study abroad with Lehigh Valley Association of Independent Colleges; over 60 agreements with foreign universities for study abroad; 3-2 or 4-2 combined Degree Program in Engineering with Columbia University or Washington University. MC/Penn Dental Program-University of Pennsylvania. Combined program with Drexel University College of Medicine. 7-year Optometry Program-State University of New York 3-2 or 4-2. Combined Degree Program in Environmental Science or Forestry. **Credit/placement by examination:** AP, CLEP, IB, SAT, ACT, institutional tests. 68 credit hours maximum toward bachelor's degree. 68 credit hours equivalent to 17 course units. **Support services:** Learning center, reduced course load, study skills assistance, tutoring, writing center.

Majors. **Area/ethnic studies:** American, German, Russian/Slavic. **Biology:** General, biochemistry. **Business:** Accounting, business admin, finance, human resources, management information systems. **Communications:** General. **Computer sciences:** General. **Conservation:** Environmental science. **Foreign languages:** General, French, German, Spanish. **History:** General. **Interdisciplinary:** Natural sciences, neuroscience. **Math:** General. **Philosophy/religion:** Philosophy, religion. **Physical sciences:** General, chemistry, physics. **Psychology:** General. **Social sciences:** Anthropology, economics, international relations, political science, sociology. **Visual/performing arts:** Art, dance, dramatic, film/cinema.

Most popular majors. Biology 6%, business/marketing 22%, communications/journalism 10%, English 6%, health sciences 15%, psychology 10%, social sciences 13%.

Computing on campus. 490 workstations in dormitories, library, computer center. Dormitories wired for high-speed internet access and linked to campus network. Commuter students can connect to campus network. Helpline, repair service, wireless network available.

Student life. **Freshman orientation:** Mandatory, $120 fee. Preregistration for classes offered. 3-day program prior to start of classes in August. **Policies:** Students share responsibility for maintaining high standards and must pledge to abide by Academic Behavior Code. **Housing:** Guaranteed on-campus for all undergraduates. Coed dorms, single-sex dorms, special housing for disabled, apartments, fraternity/sorority housing, wellness housing available. $400 deposit, deadline 5/1. College-owned houses in neighborhood surrounding campus. **Activities:** Bands, campus ministries, choral groups, dance, drama, international student organizations, literary magazine, music ensembles, musical theater, radio station, student government, student newspaper, TV station, over 100 clubs and organizations.

Athletics. NCAA. **Intercollegiate:** Baseball M, basketball, cheerleading, cross-country, field hockey W, football (tackle) M, golf, lacrosse, soccer, softball W, tennis, track and field, volleyball W, wrestling M. **Intramural:** Basketball, cross-country, football (non-tackle) M, racquetball, soccer, softball, swimming, tennis, volleyball. **Team name:** Mules.

Student services. Adult student services, alcohol/substance abuse counseling, chaplain/spiritual director, career counseling, student employment services, financial aid counseling, health services, minority student services, personal counseling, placement for graduates, women's services. **Physically disabled:** Services for visually, speech, hearing impaired.

Contact. E-mail: admissions@muhlenberg.edu
Phone: (484) 664-3200 Fax: (484) 664-3234
Christopher Hooker-Haring, Dean of Admission and Financial Aid, Muhlenberg College, 2400 Chew Street, Allentown, PA 18104

Neumann College

Aston, Pennsylvania — **CB member**
www.neumann.edu — **CB code: 2628**

- Private 4-year liberal arts college affiliated with Roman Catholic Church
- Residential campus in large town
- 2,484 degree-seeking undergraduates: 18% part-time, 66% women
- 553 degree-seeking graduate students
- 95% of applicants admitted
- SAT or ACT required
- 55% graduate within 6 years; 20% enter graduate study

General. Founded in 1965. Regionally accredited. Provides Catholic education in Franciscan tradition. **Degrees:** 407 bachelor's, 27 associate awarded; master's, doctoral offered. **ROTC:** Army. **Location:** 19 miles from Philadelphia. **Calendar:** Semester, limited summer session. **Full-time faculty:** 88 total; 68% have terminal degrees, 4% minority, 66% women. **Part-time faculty:** 207 total; 14% have terminal degrees, 5% minority, 66% women. **Class size:** 43% < 20, 55% 20-39, less than 1% 40-49, 1% 50-99, less than 1% >100. **Special facilities:** Franciscan studies institute, Betty Neumann archives.

Freshman class profile. 2,333 applied, 2,206 admitted, 539 enrolled.

Mid 50% test scores		**Rank in top quarter:**	50%
SAT critical reading:	400-490	**Rank in top tenth:**	30%
SAT math:	400-490	**End year in good standing:**	80%
GPA 3.75 or higher:	2%	**Return as sophomores:**	70%
GPA 3.50-3.74:	3%	**Out-of-state:**	32%
GPA 3.0-3.49:	45%	**Live on campus:**	72%
GPA 2.0-2.99:	50%	**International:**	2%

Basis for selection. Acceptance depends on major applied for, SAT scores and high school GPA. Interview recommended. **Homeschooled:** State high school equivalency certificate required.

High school preparation. College-preparatory program recommended. 16 units required; 17 recommended. Required and recommended units include English 4, mathematics 2, social studies 2, science 2-3, foreign language 2 and academic electives 4.

2008-2009 Annual costs. Tuition/fees: $20,402. Room/board: $9,258. Books/supplies: $1,200. Personal expenses: $2,000.

2007-2008 Financial aid. All financial aid based on need. 487 full-time freshmen applied for aid; 487 were judged to have need; 487 of these received aid. Average scholarship/grant was $18,000; average loan $3,000. 53% of total undergraduate aid awarded as scholarships/grants, 47% as loans/jobs.

Application procedures. Admission: No deadline. $35 fee, may be waived for applicants with need, free for online applicants. Admission notification on a rolling basis. Must reply by May 1 or within 2 week(s) if notified thereafter. **Financial aid:** No deadline. FAFSA required. Applicants notified on a rolling basis; must reply within 2 week(s) of notification.

Academics. Special study options: Accelerated study, combined bachelor's/graduate degree, cooperative education, distance learning, double major, exchange student, honors, independent study, internships, liberal arts/career combination, student-designed major, study abroad, teacher certification program, weekend college. **Credit/placement by examination:** AP, CLEP, SAT, institutional tests. 15 credit hours maximum toward associate degree, 30 toward bachelor's. **Support services:** Learning center, pre-admission summer program, reduced course load, remedial instruction, study skills assistance, tutoring, writing center.

Majors. Biology: General. **Business:** Accounting, business admin, international, marketing. **Communications:** General. **Computer sciences:** General. **Conservation:** Environmental studies. **Education:** Early childhood, elementary. **Health:** Clinical lab technology, nursing (RN). **Liberal arts:** Arts/sciences. **Parks/recreation:** Health/fitness, sports admin. **Philosophy/religion:** Religion. **Protective services:** Criminal justice. **Psychology:** General. **Social sciences:** Political science.

Most popular majors. Business/marketing 10%, communications/journalism 6%, education 16%, health sciences 13%, liberal arts 28%, parks/recreation 6%, psychology 6%.

Computing on campus. 400 workstations in dormitories, library, computer center. Dormitories wired for high-speed internet access and linked to campus network. Commuter students can connect to campus network. Online library, helpline, wireless network available.

Student life. Freshman orientation: Mandatory. Preregistration for classes offered. Held the last weekend before classes begin. **Policies:** Alcohol-free campus. **Housing:** Guaranteed on-campus for all undergraduates. Coed dorms, apartments available. $200 deposit, deadline 8/1. **Activities:** Jazz band, campus ministries, choral groups, dance, drama, international student organizations, literary magazine, music ensembles, musical theater, radio station, student government, student newspaper, TV station, Black student union, environmental club, bio/sci club, business association, professional education society, student nurses association, psychology club.

Athletics. NCAA. **Intercollegiate:** Baseball M, basketball, field hockey W, golf M, ice hockey, lacrosse, soccer, softball W, tennis, volleyball W. **Intramural:** Basketball, lacrosse M, softball W, table tennis, tennis, volleyball. **Team name:** Knights.

Student services. Adult student services, alcohol/substance abuse counseling, chaplain/spiritual director, career counseling, services for economically disadvantaged, student employment services, financial aid counseling, health services, on-campus daycare, personal counseling, placement for graduates.

Contact. E-mail: neumann@neumann.edu
Phone: (610) 558-5616 Toll-free number: (800) 963-8626
Fax: (610) 558-5652
Dennis Murphy, Vice President for Enrollment Management, Neumann College, One Neumann Drive, Aston, PA 19014-1298

Peirce College

Philadelphia, Pennsylvania — **CB member**
www.peirce.edu — **CB code: 2674**

- Private 4-year business and technical college
- Commuter campus in very large city
- 2,033 degree-seeking undergraduates: 61% part-time, 74% women, 58% African American, 1% Asian American, 6% Hispanic American, 2% international
- 100% graduate within 6 years

General. Founded in 1865. Regionally accredited. **Degrees:** 268 bachelor's, 215 associate awarded. **Calendar:** Semester, limited summer session. **Full-time faculty:** 31 total; 61% have terminal degrees, 32% minority, 52% women. **Part-time faculty:** 118 total; 27% have terminal degrees, 26% minority, 35% women. **Class size:** 93% < 20, 7% 20-39.

Freshman class profile.

End year in good standing:	78%	**International:**	1%
Out-of-state:	11%		

Basis for selection. Open admission.

2008-2009 Annual costs. Tuition/fees: $14,350. Books/supplies: $1,000. Personal expenses: $2,000.

2007-2008 Financial aid. Need-based: 6 full-time freshmen applied for aid; 6 were judged to have need; 6 of these received aid. Average need met was 46%. Average scholarship/grant was $4,761; average loan $3,908. 48% of total undergraduate aid awarded as scholarships/grants, 52% as loans/

jobs. **Non-need-based:** Scholarships awarded for alumni affiliation, leadership. **Additional information:** Tuition discounts available for US students serving in US military and in protect-and-serve fields.

Application procedures. **Admission:** No deadline. $50 fee, may be waived for applicants with need. Admission notification on a rolling basis. **Financial aid:** Priority date 5/1; no closing date. FAFSA required. Applicants notified on a rolling basis; must reply within 3 week(s) of notification.

Academics. **Special study options:** Accelerated study, cooperative education, distance learning, independent study. **Credit/placement by examination:** AP, CLEP, IB, institutional tests. 30 credit hours maximum toward associate degree, 90 toward bachelor's. **Support services:** Learning center, reduced course load, study skills assistance, tutoring.

Majors. **Business:** Business admin. **Computer sciences:** Information systems. **Legal studies:** Paralegal.

Most popular majors. Business/marketing 57%, computer/information sciences 24%, legal studies 19%.

Computing on campus. PC or laptop required. 36 workstations in library, student center. Online course registration, online library, helpline, wireless network available.

Student life. **Freshman orientation:** Mandatory, $503 fee. Preregistration for classes offered. **Activities:** International student organizations, Chi Alpha Epsilon Honor Society, Delta Mu Delta Honor Society, paralegal student association, information technology student association.

Student services. Adult student services, career counseling, services for economically disadvantaged, student employment services, financial aid counseling, health services. **Physically disabled:** Services for visually, hearing impaired.

Contact. E-mail: info@peirce.edu
Phone: (215) 670-9214 Toll-free number: (888) 467-3472 ext. 9214
Fax: (215) 670-9366
Nadine Maher, Dean of Enrollment Management, Peirce College, 1420 Pine Street, Philadelphia, PA 19102-4699

Penn State Abington

Abington, Pennsylvania
www.abington.psu.edu **CB code: 2660**

- Public 4-year branch campus college
- Commuter campus in small city
- 2,857 degree-seeking undergraduates: 11% part-time, 47% women, 13% African American, 15% Asian American, 6% Hispanic American
- 18 graduate students
- 78% of applicants admitted
- SAT or ACT with writing required
- 47% graduate within 6 years

General. Founded in 1950. Regionally accredited. **Degrees:** 352 bachelor's, 32 associate awarded. **ROTC:** Army, Air Force. **Location:** 15 miles from Philadelphia. **Calendar:** Semester, limited summer session. **Full-time faculty:** 104 total; 58% have terminal degrees, 11% minority, 45% women. **Part-time faculty:** 121 total; 30% have terminal degrees, 9% minority, 41% women. **Class size:** 35% < 20, 56% 20-39, 3% 40-49, 4% 50-99, 2% >100.

Freshman class profile. 3,505 applied, 2,742 admitted, 813 enrolled.

Mid 50% test scores			
SAT critical reading:	400-520	**GPA 2.0-2.99:**	48%
SAT math:	430-550	**Rank in top quarter:**	26%
GPA 3.75 or higher:	8%	**Rank in top tenth:**	7%
GPA 3.50-3.74:	10%	**Return as sophomores:**	75%
GPA 3.0-3.49:	34%	**Out-of-state:**	7%
		International:	1%

Basis for selection. Admission decisions based upon high school GPA, standardized test scores, class rank, personal statements, activities. Essay considered if submitted; portfolios required for select majors. **Home-schooled:** Provide complete documentation showing courses studied and all evaluations presented from home school evaluator or supervisor assigned to student in cooperation with local school district or evaluator approved through program.

High school preparation. College-preparatory program recommended. Required units include English 4, mathematics 3, social studies 3, science 3 and foreign language 2.

2008-2009 Annual costs. Tuition/fees: $11,800; $17,590 out-of-state. Books/supplies: $1,264. Personal expenses: $1,854.

2007-2008 Financial aid. **Need-based:** 746 full-time freshmen applied for aid; 560 were judged to have need; 544 of these received aid. Average need met was 67%. Average scholarship/grant was $6,519; average loan $3,183. 51% of total undergraduate aid awarded as scholarships/grants, 49% as loans/jobs. **Non-need-based:** Awarded to 527 full-time undergraduates, including 342 freshmen. Scholarships awarded for academics, alumni affiliation, athletics, ROTC.

Application procedures. **Admission:** Priority date 11/30; no deadline. $50 fee, may be waived for applicants with need. Admission notification on a rolling basis beginning on or about 11/1. Must reply by May 1 or within 2 week(s) if notified thereafter. All freshmen applications processed at University Park Campus. **Financial aid:** Priority date 2/15; no closing date. FAFSA required. Applicants notified on a rolling basis starting 3/1.

Academics. **Special study options:** Accelerated study, combined bachelor's/graduate degree, cooperative education, distance learning, double major, dual enrollment of high school students, ESL, exchange student, external degree, honors, independent study, internships, liberal arts/career combination, student-designed major, study abroad, teacher certification program. **Credit/placement by examination:** AP, CLEP, IB, SAT. 60 credit hours maximum toward bachelor's degree. **Support services:** Learning center, pre-admission summer program, remedial instruction, study skills assistance, tutoring, writing center.

Majors. **Agriculture:** General, agribusiness operations, agronomy, animal sciences, education services, food science, horticultural science, landscaping, mechanization, soil science, turf management. **Area/ethnic studies:** African-American, East Asian, Latin American, women's. **Biology:** General, bacteriology, biochemistry, biomedical sciences, pathology, toxicology. **Business:** General, accounting, actuarial science, finance, hospitality admin, labor relations, management information systems, managerial economics, marketing, organizational behavior. **Communications:** General, advertising, journalism. **Computer sciences:** General, information systems. **Conservation:** General, forest sciences, forest technology. **Education:** Adult/continuing, art, elementary, foreign languages, secondary, special, testing/assessment. **Engineering:** General, aerospace, architectural, biomedical, chemical, civil, computer, electrical, environmental, industrial, materials science, mechanical, mining, nuclear, petroleum, science. **Engineering technology:** Electrical. **Family/consumer sciences:** Family studies, human nutrition. **Foreign languages:** Classics, comparative lit, French, German, Italian, Japanese, Russian, Spanish. **Health:** Communication disorders, health care admin, nursing (RN), premedicine. **History:** General. **Interdisciplinary:** Biological/physical sciences, medieval/Renaissance. **Liberal arts:** Arts/sciences. **Math:** General, statistics. **Parks/recreation:** General, exercise sciences. **Philosophy/religion:** Judaic, philosophy, religion. **Physical sciences:** Astronomy, atmospheric science, chemistry, geology, physics. **Protective services:** Criminal justice, forensics, law enforcement admin. **Psychology:** General. **Science technology:** Biological. **Social sciences:** Anthropology, archaeology, economics, geography, international economic development, international relations, political science, sociology. **Visual/performing arts:** General, acting, art, art history/conservation, film/cinema, graphic design, theater design. **Other:** Design and applied arts, Rehabilitation and therapeutic studies, Security and protective services.

Most popular majors. Business/marketing 40%, English 6%, liberal arts 6%, psychology 15%, security/protective services 16%.

Computing on campus. 150 workstations in library, computer center. Commuter students can connect to campus network. Online course registration, online library, helpline, repair service, student web hosting, wireless network available.

Student life. **Freshman orientation:** Mandatory, $30 fee. Preregistration for classes offered. Three-part process before classes start: 1-day orientation, advising appointment, and new student day. **Policies:** Acts of intolerance and high-risk drinking discouraged at all locations. All facilities designated smoke-free. Students expected to abide by The Penn State Principles. **Activities:** Campus ministries, dance, drama, film society, literary magazine, music ensembles, student government, student newspaper, Christian Fellowship, Asian club, black student union, Hillel, lesbian and gay alliance, Latino student association, Italian American organization, Muslim student association, Praise and Worship gospel association.

Athletics. **Intercollegiate:** Baseball M, basketball, golf, lacrosse, soccer, softball, tennis, volleyball W. **Intramural:** Basketball, cross-country, football (non-tackle) M, handball, soccer, softball, tennis, volleyball. **Team name:** Nittany Lions.

Student services. Adult student services, alcohol/substance abuse counseling, career counseling, services for economically disadvantaged, student employment services, financial aid counseling, health services, minority student services, personal counseling, placement for graduates, veterans' counselor. **Physically disabled:** Services for visually, speech, hearing impaired.

Contact. E-mail: abingtonadmissions@psu.edu
Phone: (215) 881-7600 Fax: (215) 881-7655
Anne Rohrbach, Executive Director for Undergraduate Admissions, Penn State Abington, 201 Shields Building, University Park, PA 16802-1294

Penn State Altoona

Altoona, Pennsylvania
www.aa.psu.edu **CB code: 2660**

- Public 4-year branch campus college
- Residential campus in small city
- 3,870 degree-seeking undergraduates: 5% part-time, 50% women, 7% African American, 2% Asian American, 3% Hispanic American, 1% international
- 75% of applicants admitted
- SAT or ACT with writing required
- 66% graduate within 6 years

General. Founded in 1929. Regionally accredited. **Degrees:** 299 bachelor's, 94 associate awarded. **ROTC:** Army, Air Force. **Location:** 2 miles from downtown. **Calendar:** Semester, limited summer session. **Full-time faculty:** 161 total; 73% have terminal degrees, 8% minority, 41% women. **Part-time faculty:** 154 total; 19% have terminal degrees, 3% minority, 47% women. **Class size:** 39% < 20, 45% 20-39, 5% 40-49, 10% 50-99, less than 1% >100. **Special facilities:** MAC lab, CAD lab, robotics lab, manufacturing lab, automation lab, environmental studies lab, comprehensive art studio space.

Freshman class profile. 6,180 applied, 4,615 admitted, 1,476 enrolled.

Mid 50% test scores		**Rank in top quarter:**	30%
SAT critical reading:	440-540	**Rank in top tenth:**	8%
SAT math:	470-570	**Return as sophomores:**	87%
GPA 3.75 or higher:	2%	**Out-of-state:**	21%
GPA 3.50-3.74:	9%	**International:**	1%
GPA 3.0-3.49:	47%	**Fraternities:**	4%
GPA 2.0-2.99:	42%	**Sororities:**	2%

Basis for selection. Admission decisions based upon high school GPA, test scores, class rank, personal statements, and activities. Essay considered if submitted; portfolios required for select majors. **Homeschooled:** Provide complete documentation showing courses studied and all evaluations presented from home school evaluator or supervisor assigned to student in cooperation with local school district or evaluator approved through program.

High school preparation. College-preparatory program recommended. Required units include English 4, mathematics 3, social studies 3, science 3 and foreign language 2.

2008-2009 Annual costs. Tuition/fees: $12,182; $18,270 out-of-state. Room/board: $8,270. Books/supplies: $1,264. Personal expenses: $2,916.

2007-2008 Financial aid. **Need-based:** 1,221 full-time freshmen applied for aid; 936 were judged to have need; 902 of these received aid. Average need met was 59%. Average scholarship/grant was $5,676; average loan $3,553. 39% of total undergraduate aid awarded as scholarships/grants, 61% as loans/jobs. **Non-need-based:** Awarded to 764 full-time undergraduates, including 306 freshmen. Scholarships awarded for academics, alumni affiliation, athletics, ROTC.

Application procedures. **Admission:** Priority date 11/30; no deadline. $50 fee, may be waived for applicants with need. Admission notification on a rolling basis beginning on or about 11/1. Must reply by May 1 or within 2 week(s) if notified thereafter. All freshmen applications processed at University Park Campus. **Financial aid:** Priority date 2/15; no closing date. FAFSA required. Applicants notified on a rolling basis starting 3/1.

Academics. **Special study options:** Cooperative education, cross-registration, distance learning, double major, dual enrollment of high school students, ESL, exchange student, honors, independent study, internships, liberal arts/career combination, student-designed major, study abroad, teacher certification program. **Credit/placement by examination:** AP, CLEP, IB, SAT. 60 credit hours maximum toward bachelor's degree. **Support services:** Learning center, remedial instruction, study skills assistance, tutoring, writing center.

Majors. **Agriculture:** General, agribusiness operations, agronomy, animal sciences, education services, food science, horticultural science, landscaping, mechanization, soil science, turf management. **Area/ethnic studies:** African-American, East Asian, Latin American, women's. **Biology:** General, bacteriology, biochemistry, biomedical sciences, pathology, toxicology. **Business:** General, accounting, actuarial science, finance, hospitality admin, labor relations, management information systems, managerial economics, marketing, organizational behavior. **Communications:** General, advertising, journalism. **Computer sciences:** General, information systems. **Conservation:** General, environmental studies, forest sciences, forest technology. **Education:** Adult/continuing, art, elementary, evaluation, foreign languages, secondary, special. **Engineering:** General, aerospace, architectural, biomedical, chemical, civil, computer, electrical, environmental, industrial, materials science, mechanical, mining, nuclear, petroleum, science. **Engineering technology:** Electrical. **Family/consumer sciences:** Family studies, human nutrition. **Foreign languages:** Classics, comparative lit, French, German, Italian, Japanese, Russian, Spanish. **Health:** Communication disorders, health care admin, nursing (RN), premedicine. **History:** General. **Interdisciplinary:** Biological/physical sciences, medieval/Renaissance. **Liberal arts:** Arts/sciences. **Math:** General, statistics. **Parks/recreation:** Exercise sciences, facilities management. **Philosophy/religion:** Judaic, philosophy, religion. **Physical sciences:** Astronomy, atmospheric science, chemistry, geology, physics. **Protective services:** Criminal justice, forensics, law enforcement admin. **Psychology:** General. **Science technology:** Biological. **Social sciences:** Anthropology, archaeology, economics, geography, international economic development, international relations, political science, sociology. **Visual/performing arts:** General, acting, art, art history/conservation, film/cinema, graphic design, theater design. **Other:** Design and applied arts, Rehabilitation and therapeutic studies, Security and protective services.

Most popular majors. Business/marketing 19%, communications/journalism 8%, education 17%, engineering/engineering technologies 8%, family/consumer sciences 6%, psychology 12%, security/protective services 13%.

Computing on campus. 450 workstations in dormitories, library, computer center. Dormitories wired for high-speed internet access and linked to campus network. Commuter students can connect to campus network. Online course registration, online library, helpline, student web hosting, wireless network available.

Student life. **Freshman orientation:** Mandatory. Preregistration for classes offered. Begins Saturday prior to start of classes and runs 2 weeks. **Policies:** Acts of intolerance and high-risk drinking discouraged at all locations. All facilities designated as smoke-free. **Housing:** Coed dorms, special housing for disabled available. $100 partly refundable deposit, deadline 5/1. Suites, special interest housing available. **Activities:** Bands, campus ministries, choral groups, dance, drama, film society, international student organizations, literary magazine, music ensembles, student government, student newspaper, black student union, Circle K, Latin American student association, Catholic campus community, Students About Living Truth, Jewish student association, Asian student association, German club, Eco-Action, Being United for Social Transformation.

Athletics. NAIA. **Intercollegiate:** Baseball M, basketball, cross-country, diving, golf, soccer, softball W, swimming, tennis, volleyball W. **Intramural:** Badminton, basketball, football (non-tackle), football (tackle), racquetball, soccer, softball, table tennis, track and field, triathlon, volleyball, weight lifting. **Team name:** Nittany Lions.

Student services. Adult student services, alcohol/substance abuse counseling, chaplain/spiritual director, career counseling, services for economically disadvantaged, student employment services, financial aid counseling, health services, minority student services, personal counseling, placement for graduates, veterans' counselor, women's services. **Physically disabled:** Services for visually, speech, hearing impaired.

Contact. E-mail: aaadmit@psu.edu
Phone: (814) 949-5466 Toll-free number: (800) 848-9843
Fax: (814) 949-5564
Anne Rohrbach, Executive Director for Undergraduate Admissions, Penn State Altoona, 201 Shields Building, University Park, PA 16802-1294

Penn State Beaver

Monaca, Pennsylvania
www.br.psu.edu **CB code: 2660**

- Public 4-year branch campus college
- Residential campus in small town
- 711 degree-seeking undergraduates: 5% part-time, 37% women, 8% African American, 3% Asian American, 2% Hispanic American
- 8 degree-seeking graduate students
- 90% of applicants admitted
- SAT or ACT with writing required
- 44% graduate within 6 years

General. Founded in 1964. Regionally accredited. **Degrees:** 62 bachelor's, 5 associate awarded; master's offered. **Location:** 30 miles from Pittsburgh.

Calendar: Semester, limited summer session. **Full-time faculty:** 32 total; 69% have terminal degrees, 22% minority, 53% women. **Part-time faculty:** 27 total; 15% have terminal degrees, 44% women. **Class size:** 39% < 20, 53% 20-39, 5% 40-49, 3% 50-99.

Freshman class profile. 739 applied, 662 admitted, 296 enrolled.

Mid 50% test scores		**GPA 2.0-2.99:**	57%
SAT critical reading:	410-520	**Rank in top quarter:**	25%
SAT math:	430-560	**Rank in top tenth:**	6%
GPA 3.75 or higher:	1%	**Return as sophomores:**	70%
GPA 3.50-3.74:	10%	**Out-of-state:**	10%
GPA 3.0-3.49:	31%		

Basis for selection. Admission decisions based upon high school GPA as well as other factors, including standardized verbal and math test scores, class rank, personal statements, activities lists. Essay considered if submitted; portfolios required for select majors. **Homeschooled:** Helpful if applicants provide complete documentation showing courses studied and all evaluations from home school evaluator or supervisor assigned to student in cooperation with local school district or evaluator approved through program.

High school preparation. College-preparatory program recommended. Required units include English 4, mathematics 3, social studies 3, science 3 and foreign language 2.

2008-2009 Annual costs. Tuition/fees: $11,800; $17,590 out-of-state. Room/board: $8,270. Books/supplies: $1,264. Personal expenses: $2,916.

2007-2008 Financial aid. **Need-based:** 257 full-time freshmen applied for aid; 204 were judged to have need; 199 of these received aid. Average need met was 64%. Average scholarship/grant was $6,024; average loan $3,310. 46% of total undergraduate aid awarded as scholarships/grants, 54% as loans/jobs. **Non-need-based:** Awarded to 196 full-time undergraduates, including 112 freshmen. Scholarships awarded for academics, alumni affiliation, athletics, ROTC.

Application procedures. **Admission:** Priority date 11/30; no deadline. $50 fee, may be waived for applicants with need. Admission notification on a rolling basis beginning on or about 11/1. Must reply by May 1 or within 2 week(s) if notified thereafter. All freshmen applications processed at University Park Campus. **Financial aid:** Priority date 2/15; no closing date. FAFSA required. Applicants notified on a rolling basis starting 3/1.

Academics. **Special study options:** Accelerated study, cross-registration, distance learning, double major, dual enrollment of high school students, ESL, honors, independent study, internships, semester at sea, study abroad. **Credit/placement by examination:** AP, CLEP, IB, SAT. 60 credit hours maximum toward bachelor's degree. **Support services:** Learning center, pre-admission summer program, reduced course load, remedial instruction, study skills assistance, tutoring, writing center.

Majors. **Agriculture:** General, agribusiness operations, agronomy, animal sciences, education services, food science, horticultural science, landscaping, mechanization, soil science, turf management. **Area/ethnic studies:** African-American, East Asian, Latin American, women's. **Biology:** General, bacteriology, biochemistry, biomedical sciences, pathology, toxicology. **Business:** Accounting, actuarial science, business admin, finance, hospitality admin, labor relations, management information systems, managerial economics, marketing, organizational behavior. **Communications:** General, advertising, journalism. **Computer sciences:** General, information systems. **Conservation:** General, forest sciences, forest technology. **Education:** Adult/continuing, art, elementary, evaluation, foreign languages, secondary, special. **Engineering:** General, aerospace, architectural, biomedical, chemical, civil, computer, electrical, environmental, industrial, materials science, mechanical, mining, nuclear, petroleum, science. **Engineering technology:** Electrical. **Family/consumer sciences:** Family studies, human nutrition. **Foreign languages:** Classics, comparative lit, French, German, Italian, Japanese, Russian, Spanish. **Health:** Communication disorders, health care admin, nursing (RN), premedicine. **History:** General. **Interdisciplinary:** Biological/physical sciences, medieval/Renaissance. **Liberal arts:** Arts/sciences. **Math:** General, statistics. **Parks/recreation:** Exercise sciences, facilities management. **Philosophy/religion:** Judaic, philosophy, religion. **Physical sciences:** Astronomy, atmospheric science, chemistry, geology, physics. **Protective services:** Forensics, law enforcement admin. **Psychology:** General. **Science technology:** Biological. **Social sciences:** Anthropology, archaeology, economics, geography, international economic development, international relations, political science, sociology. **Visual/performing arts:** General, acting, art, art history/conservation, film/cinema, graphic design, theater design. **Other:** Design and applied arts, Rehabilitation and therapeutic studies, Security and protective services.

Most popular majors. Business/marketing 47%, communications/journalism 10%, computer/information sciences 13%, psychology 30%.

Computing on campus. 127 workstations in library, computer center, student center. Dormitories wired for high-speed internet access and linked to campus network. Commuter students can connect to campus network. Online course registration, online library, helpline, repair service, student web hosting, wireless network available.

Student life. **Freshman orientation:** Mandatory, $30 fee. Preregistration for classes offered. One-day orientation session just before classes begin. **Policies:** Acts of intolerance and high-risk drinking discouraged at all locations. All facilities designated as smoke-free. **Housing:** Coed dorms available. $100 partly refundable deposit, deadline 5/1. Townhouses available. **Activities:** Campus ministries, drama, film society, literary magazine, radio station, student government, student newspaper, Common Ground Christian club, Big Brothers/Big Sisters mentoring program.

Athletics. NJCAA. **Intercollegiate:** Baseball M, basketball, soccer M, softball W, volleyball W. **Intramural:** Basketball, bowling, football (non-tackle), table tennis, volleyball. **Team name:** Nittany Lions.

Student services. Adult student services, alcohol/substance abuse counseling, chaplain/spiritual director, career counseling, services for economically disadvantaged, student employment services, financial aid counseling, health services, personal counseling, placement for graduates, veterans' counselor. **Physically disabled:** Services for visually, speech, hearing impaired.

Contact. E-mail: br-admissions@psu.edu
Phone: (724) 773-3800 Fax: (724) 773-3658
Anne Rohrbach, Executive Director for Undergraduate Admissions, Penn State Beaver, 201 Shields Building, University Park, PA 16802-1294

Penn State Berks

Reading, Pennsylvania
www.bk.psu.edu **CB code: 2660**

- Public 4-year branch campus college
- Residential campus in small city
- 2,576 degree-seeking undergraduates: 7% part-time, 40% women, 7% African American, 4% Asian American, 5% Hispanic American, 1% international
- 57 graduate students
- 81% of applicants admitted
- SAT or ACT with writing required
- 60% graduate within 6 years

General. Founded in 1924. Regionally accredited. **Degrees:** 193 bachelor's, 74 associate awarded. **ROTC:** Army. **Location:** 5 miles from downtown. **Calendar:** Semester, limited summer session. **Full-time faculty:** 112 total; 66% have terminal degrees, 11% minority, 46% women. **Part-time faculty:** 88 total; 16% have terminal degrees, 3% minority, 51% women. **Class size:** 37% < 20, 42% 20-39, 12% 40-49, 10% 50-99.

Freshman class profile. 3,260 applied, 2,648 admitted, 1,000 enrolled.

Mid 50% test scores		**GPA 2.0-2.99:**	59%
SAT critical reading:	430-530	**Rank in top quarter:**	22%
SAT math:	440-550	**Rank in top tenth:**	5%
GPA 3.75 or higher:	2%	**Return as sophomores:**	78%
GPA 3.50-3.74:	4%	**Out-of-state:**	11%
GPA 3.0-3.49:	34%	**International:**	2%

Basis for selection. Admission decisions based upon high school GPA, test scores, class rank, personal statements, and activities. Essay considered if submitted; portfolios required for select majors. **Homeschooled:** Complete documentation showing courses studied and all evaluations presented from home school evaluator or supervisor assigned to student in cooperation with local school district or evaluator approved through program required.

High school preparation. College-preparatory program recommended. Required units include English 4, mathematics 3, social studies 3, science 3 and foreign language 2.

2008-2009 Annual costs. Tuition/fees: $12,282; $18,370 out-of-state. Room/board: $8,990. Books/supplies: $1,264. Personal expenses: $2,916.

2007-2008 Financial aid. **Need-based:** 754 full-time freshmen applied for aid; 552 were judged to have need; 530 of these received aid. Average need met was 58%. Average scholarship/grant was $5,493; average loan $3,392. 40% of total undergraduate aid awarded as scholarships/grants, 60% as loans/jobs. **Non-need-based:** Awarded to 343 full-time undergraduates, including 150 freshmen. Scholarships awarded for academics, alumni affiliation, athletics, ROTC.

Application procedures. Admission: Priority date 11/30; no deadline. $50 fee, may be waived for applicants with need. Admission notification on a rolling basis beginning on or about 11/1. Must reply by May 1 or within 2 week(s) if notified thereafter. All freshmen applications processed at University Park Campus. **Financial aid:** Priority date 2/15; no closing date. FAFSA required. Applicants notified on a rolling basis starting 3/1.

Academics. Special study options: Accelerated study, cooperative education, cross-registration, distance learning, dual enrollment of high school students, ESL, honors, independent study, internships, study abroad, teacher certification program. **Credit/placement by examination:** AP, CLEP, IB, SAT. 60 credit hours maximum toward bachelor's degree. **Support services:** Learning center, pre-admission summer program, remedial instruction, study skills assistance, tutoring, writing center.

Majors. Agriculture: General, agribusiness operations, agronomy, animal sciences, education services, food science, horticultural science, landscaping, mechanization, soil science, turf management. **Area/ethnic studies:** African-American, American, East Asian, Latin American, women's. **Biology:** General, bacteriology, biochemistry, biomedical sciences, pathology, toxicology. **Business:** General, accounting, actuarial science, finance, hospitality admin, labor relations, management information systems, managerial economics, marketing, organizational behavior. **Communications:** General, advertising, journalism. **Computer sciences:** General, information systems. **Conservation:** General, forest sciences, forest technology. **Education:** Adult/continuing, art, elementary, evaluation, foreign languages, secondary, special. **Engineering:** General, aerospace, architectural, biomedical, chemical, civil, computer, electrical, environmental, industrial, materials science, mechanical, mining, nuclear, petroleum, science. **Engineering technology:** Electrical. **Family/consumer sciences:** Family studies, human nutrition. **Foreign languages:** General, classics, comparative lit, French, German, Italian, Japanese, Russian, Spanish. **Health:** Communication disorders, health care admin, nursing (RN), premedicine. **History:** General. **Interdisciplinary:** Biological/physical sciences, medieval/Renaissance. **Liberal arts:** Arts/sciences. **Math:** General, statistics. **Parks/recreation:** Exercise sciences, facilities management. **Philosophy/religion:** Judaic, philosophy, religion. **Physical sciences:** Astronomy, atmospheric science, chemistry, geology, physics. **Protective services:** Forensics, law enforcement admin. **Psychology:** General. **Science technology:** Biological. **Social sciences:** Anthropology, archaeology, economics, geography, international economic development, international relations, political science, sociology. **Visual/performing arts:** General, acting, art, art history/conservation, film/cinema, graphic design, theater design. **Other:** Design and applied arts, Rehabilitation and therapeutic studies, Security and protective services.

Most popular majors. Business/marketing 30%, computer/information sciences 7%, education 9%, engineering/engineering technologies 10%, English 12%, foreign language 6%, interdisciplinary studies 7%, parks/recreation 7%, psychology 9%.

Computing on campus. 311 workstations in dormitories, library, computer center, student center. Dormitories wired for high-speed internet access and linked to campus network. Commuter students can connect to campus network. Online course registration, online library, helpline, repair service, student web hosting, wireless network available.

Student life. Freshman orientation: Mandatory. Preregistration for classes offered. Week prior to the start of classes. **Policies:** All facilities smoke-free. **Housing:** Coed dorms, special housing for disabled available. $100 partly refundable deposit, deadline 5/1. Honor students, suites, special interest houses available. **Activities:** Pep band, campus ministries, choral groups, dance, drama, film society, international student organizations, literary magazine, radio station, student government, student newspaper, TV station, Christian Fellowship, Dimensions-the Ethnic Society, multicultural dance group, substance free, Rainbow Alliance, political science club, spiritual praise choir, yoga and meditation society.

Athletics. NCAA. **Intercollegiate:** Baseball M, basketball, cross-country, golf M, soccer, softball W, tennis, volleyball W. **Intramural:** Badminton, basketball, football (non-tackle), golf, table tennis, volleyball. **Team name:** NIttany Lions.

Student services. Adult student services, alcohol/substance abuse counseling, career counseling, services for economically disadvantaged, student employment services, financial aid counseling, health services, minority student services, personal counseling, placement for graduates, veterans' counselor. **Physically disabled:** Services for visually, speech, hearing impaired. **Learning disabled:** Comprehensive services available.

Contact. E-mail: admissionsbk@psu.edu
Phone: (610) 396-6060 Fax: (610) 396-6077
Anne Rohrbach, Executive Director for Undergraduate Admissions, Penn State Berks, 201 Shields Building, University Park, PA 16802-1294

Penn State Brandywine

Media, Pennsylvania
www.de.psu.edu **CB code: 2660**

- Public 4-year branch campus college
- Commuter campus in small town
- 1,439 degree-seeking undergraduates: 9% part-time, 42% women, 13% African American, 8% Asian American, 2% Hispanic American
- 78% of applicants admitted
- SAT or ACT with writing required
- 36% graduate within 6 years

General. Founded in 1966. Regionally accredited. **Degrees:** 160 bachelor's, 15 associate awarded. **ROTC:** Army, Air Force. **Location:** 20 miles from Philadelphia. **Calendar:** Semester, limited summer session. **Full-time faculty:** 63 total; 59% have terminal degrees, 14% minority, 48% women. **Part-time faculty:** 64 total; 19% have terminal degrees, 5% minority, 56% women. **Class size:** 37% < 20, 53% 20-39, 6% 40-49, 3% 50-99, less than 1% >100.

Freshman class profile. 1,398 applied, 1,089 admitted, 400 enrolled.

Mid 50% test scores		**GPA 2.0-2.99:**	60%
SAT critical reading:	420-520	**Rank in top quarter:**	17%
SAT math:	430-550	**Rank in top tenth:**	5%
GPA 3.75 or higher:	4%	**Return as sophomores:**	72%
GPA 3.50-3.74:	8%	**Out-of-state:**	4%
GPA 3.0-3.49:	28%		

Basis for selection. Admission decisions based on high school GPA, as well as other factors, which may include standardized verbal and math test scores, class rank, personal statements, and list of activities. Essay considered if submitted; portfolios required for select majors. **Homeschooled:** Applicants should provide complete documentation showing courses studied and all evaluations presented from evaluator or supervisor assigned to student in cooperation with local school district or evaluator approved through program.

High school preparation. College-preparatory program recommended. Required units include English 4, mathematics 3, social studies 3, science 3 and foreign language 2.

2008-2009 Annual costs. Tuition/fees: $11,700; $17,490 out-of-state. Books/supplies: $1,264. Personal expenses: $1,854.

2007-2008 Financial aid. Need-based: 346 full-time freshmen applied for aid; 246 were judged to have need; 240 of these received aid. Average need met was 66%. Average scholarship/grant was $5,542; average loan $3,131. 50% of total undergraduate aid awarded as scholarships/grants, 50% as loans/jobs. **Non-need-based:** Awarded to 322 full-time undergraduates, including 182 freshmen. Scholarships awarded for academics, alumni affiliation, athletics, ROTC.

Application procedures. Admission: Priority date 11/30; no deadline. $50 fee, may be waived for applicants with need. Admission notification on a rolling basis beginning on or about 11/1. Must reply by May 1 or within 2 week(s) if notified thereafter. All freshmen applications processed at University Park Campus. **Financial aid:** Priority date 2/15; no closing date. FAFSA required. Applicants notified on a rolling basis starting 3/1.

Academics. Special study options: Combined bachelor's/graduate degree, distance learning, double major, dual enrollment of high school students, ESL, honors, independent study, internships, study abroad, teacher certification program. **Credit/placement by examination:** AP, CLEP, IB, SAT. 60 credit hours maximum toward bachelor's degree. **Support services:** Learning center, pre-admission summer program, reduced course load, remedial instruction, study skills assistance, tutoring, writing center.

Majors. Agriculture: General, agribusiness operations, agronomy, animal sciences, education services, food science, horticultural science, landscaping, mechanization, soil science, turf management. **Area/ethnic studies:** African-American, American, East Asian, Latin American, women's. **Biology:** General, bacteriology, biochemistry, biomedical sciences, pathology, toxicology. **Business:** Accounting, actuarial science, business admin, finance, hospitality admin, labor relations, management information systems, managerial economics, marketing, organizational behavior. **Communications:** General, advertising, journalism. **Computer sciences:** General, information systems. **Conservation:** General, forest sciences, forest technology. **Education:** Adult/continuing, art, elementary, evaluation, foreign languages, secondary, special. **Engineering:** General, aerospace, architectural, biomedical, chemical, civil, computer, electrical, environmental, industrial, materials science, mechanical, mining, nuclear, petroleum, science. **Engineering technology:** Electrical. **Family/consumer sciences:** Family studies, human nutrition. **Foreign languages:** Classics, comparative lit, French,

German, Italian, Japanese, Russian, Spanish. **Health:** Communication disorders, health care admin, nursing (RN), premedicine. **History:** General. **Interdisciplinary:** Biological/physical sciences, medieval/Renaissance. **Liberal arts:** Arts/sciences. **Math:** General, statistics. **Parks/recreation:** Exercise sciences, facilities management. **Philosophy/religion:** Judaic, philosophy, religion. **Physical sciences:** Astronomy, atmospheric science, chemistry, geology, physics. **Protective services:** Forensics, law enforcement admin. **Psychology:** General. **Science technology:** Biological. **Social sciences:** Anthropology, archaeology, economics, geography, international economic development, international relations, political science, sociology. **Visual/performing arts:** General, acting, art, art history/conservation, film/cinema, graphic design, theater design. **Other:** Design and applied arts, Rehabilitation and therapeutic studies, Security and protective services.

Most popular majors. Business/marketing 36%, communications/journalism 14%, computer/information sciences 12%, education 8%, family/consumer sciences 19%, liberal arts 8%.

Computing on campus. 142 workstations in library, computer center, student center. Commuter students can connect to campus network. Online course registration, online library, helpline, repair service, student web hosting, wireless network available.

Student life. Freshman orientation: Available. Preregistration for classes offered. Held in summer, prior to fall semester. **Policies:** Acts of intolerance and high-risk drinking discouraged at all locations. All facilities designated smoke-free. **Activities:** Choral groups, dance, film society, literary magazine, student government, student newspaper, black student league, Nittany Christian Fellowship, gay-straight alliance, gospel ensemble, Jewish student league.

Athletics. Intercollegiate: Baseball M, basketball, soccer, tennis, volleyball W. **Intramural:** Basketball, soccer. **Team name:** Nittany Lions.

Student services. Adult student services, alcohol/substance abuse counseling, career counseling, services for economically disadvantaged, student employment services, financial aid counseling, health services, minority student services, personal counseling, placement for graduates, veterans' counselor, women's services. **Physically disabled:** Services for visually, speech, hearing impaired.

Contact. E-mail: admissions-delco@psu.edu
Phone: (610) 892-1200 Fax: (610) 892-1320
Anne Rohrbach, Executive Director for Undergraduate Admissions, Penn State Brandywine, 201 Shields Building, University Park, PA 16802-1294

Penn State Dubois

DuBois, Pennsylvania
www.ds.psu.edu **CB code: 2660**

- Public 4-year branch campus college
- Commuter campus in small town
- 769 degree-seeking undergraduates: 15% part-time, 52% women, 1% African American, 1% Asian American, 1% Hispanic American
- 1 graduate students
- 87% of applicants admitted
- SAT or ACT with writing required
- 61% graduate within 6 years

General. Founded in 1935. Regionally accredited. **Degrees:** 51 bachelor's, 77 associate awarded; master's offered. **Location:** 120 miles from Pittsburgh. **Calendar:** Semester, limited summer session. **Full-time faculty:** 44 total; 61% have terminal degrees, 14% minority, 46% women. **Part-time faculty:** 40 total; 12% have terminal degrees, 48% women. **Class size:** 68% < 20, 28% 20-39, less than 1% 40-49, 2% 50-99, less than 1% >100.

Freshman class profile. 518 applied, 449 admitted, 244 enrolled.

Mid 50% test scores			
SAT critical reading:	410-510	GPA 2.0-2.99:	49%
SAT math:	440-550	Rank in top quarter:	29%
GPA 3.75 or higher:	2%	Rank in top tenth:	6%
GPA 3.50-3.74:	13%	Return as sophomores:	82%
GPA 3.0-3.49:	36%	Out-of-state:	3%

Basis for selection. Admission decisions based upon high school GPA, as well as other factors, which may include standardized verbal and math test scores, class rank, personal statements, and list of activities. Essay considered if submitted; portfolios required for select majors. **Homeschooled:** Applicants should provide complete documentation showing the courses studied and all evaluations presented from evaluator or supervisor assigned to student in cooperation with local school district or evaluator who is approved through the program.

High school preparation. College-preparatory program recommended. Required units include English 4, mathematics 3, social studies 3, science 3 and foreign language 2.

2008-2009 Annual costs. Tuition/fees: $11,680; $17,470 out-of-state. Books/supplies: $1,264. Personal expenses: $1,854.

2007-2008 Financial aid. Need-based: 204 full-time freshmen applied for aid; 189 were judged to have need; 187 of these received aid. Average need met was 66%. Average scholarship/grant was $5,908; average loan $3,252. 51% of total undergraduate aid awarded as scholarships/grants, 49% as loans/jobs. **Non-need-based:** Awarded to 193 full-time undergraduates, including 90 freshmen. Scholarships awarded for academics, alumni affiliation, athletics, ROTC.

Application procedures. Admission: Priority date 11/30; no deadline. $50 fee, may be waived for applicants with need. Admission notification on a rolling basis beginning on or about 11/1. Must reply by May 1 or within 2 week(s) if notified thereafter. All freshmen applications processed at University Park Campus. **Financial aid:** Priority date 2/15; no closing date. FAFSA required. Applicants notified on a rolling basis starting 3/1.

Academics. Special study options: Accelerated study, cross-registration, distance learning, double major, dual enrollment of high school students, honors, independent study, internships, student-designed major, study abroad. **Credit/placement by examination:** AP, CLEP, IB, SAT. 60 credit hours maximum toward bachelor's degree. **Support services:** Learning center, reduced course load, remedial instruction, study skills assistance, tutoring, writing center.

Majors. Agriculture: General, agribusiness operations, agronomy, animal sciences, education services, food science, horticultural science, landscaping, mechanization, soil science, turf management. **Area/ethnic studies:** African-American, East Asian, Latin American, women's. **Biology:** General, bacteriology, biochemistry, biomedical sciences, pathology, toxicology. **Business:** Accounting, actuarial science, business admin, finance, hospitality admin, labor relations, management information systems, managerial economics, marketing, organizational behavior. **Communications:** General, advertising, journalism. **Computer sciences:** General, information systems. **Conservation:** General, forest sciences, forest technology. **Education:** Art, elementary, foreign languages, secondary, special. **Engineering:** General, aerospace, architectural, biomedical, chemical, civil, computer, electrical, environmental, industrial, materials science, mechanical, mining, nuclear, petroleum, science. **Engineering technology:** Electrical. **Family/consumer sciences:** Family studies, human nutrition. **Foreign languages:** Classics, comparative lit, French, German, Italian, Japanese, Russian, Spanish. **Health:** Communication disorders, health care admin, nursing (RN), premedicine. **History:** General. **Interdisciplinary:** Biological/physical sciences, medieval/Renaissance. **Liberal arts:** Arts/sciences. **Math:** General, statistics. **Parks/recreation:** Exercise sciences, facilities management. **Philosophy/religion:** Judaic, philosophy, religion. **Physical sciences:** Astronomy, atmospheric science, chemistry, geology, physics. **Protective services:** Forensics, law enforcement admin. **Psychology:** General. **Science technology:** Biological. **Social sciences:** Anthropology, archaeology, economics, geography, international economic development, international relations, political science, sociology. **Visual/performing arts:** General, acting, art, art history/conservation, film/cinema, graphic design, theater design. **Other:** Adult and continuing education, Design and applied arts, Rehabilitation and therapeutic studies, Security and protective services.

Most popular majors. Business/marketing 39%, family/consumer sciences 43%, liberal arts 18%.

Computing on campus. 212 workstations in computer center, student center. Commuter students can connect to campus network. Online course registration, online library, helpline, repair service, student web hosting available.

Student life. Freshman orientation: Available. Preregistration for classes offered. Both fall and spring orientations available. **Policies:** Acts of intolerance and high risk drinking discouraged at all locations. All facilities designated smoke free. Students expected to abide by The Penn State Principles. **Housing:** Independently owned housing available nearby. **Activities:** Choral groups, drama, film society, literary magazine, student government, student newspaper, diversity club, women's liaison committee, veterans club, adult learner student organization, environmental conservation and outing club, Campus Crusade for Christ, world cultures club.

Athletics. Intercollegiate: Basketball M, cross-country, volleyball W. **Intramural:** Basketball, table tennis, volleyball. **Team name:** Nittany Lions.

Student services. Adult student services, alcohol/substance abuse counseling, career counseling, services for economically disadvantaged, student employment services, financial aid counseling, health services, personal counseling, placement for graduates, veterans' counselor, women's services. **Physically disabled:** Services for visually, speech, hearing impaired.

Contact. E-mail: duboisinfo@psu.edu
Phone: (814) 375-4720 Toll-free number: (800) 346-7627
Fax: (814) 375-4784
Anne Rohrbach, Executive Director for Undergraduate Admissions, Penn State Dubois, 201 Shields Building, University Park, PA 16802-1294

Penn State Erie, The Behrend College

Erie, Pennsylvania
www.pserie.psu.edu **CB code: 2660**

- Public 4-year branch campus college
- Residential campus in small city
- 4,029 degree-seeking undergraduates: 4% part-time, 37% women, 4% African American, 2% Asian American, 2% Hispanic American, 1% international
- 115 degree-seeking graduate students
- 78% of applicants admitted
- SAT or ACT with writing required
- 64% graduate within 6 years

General. Founded in 1926. Regionally accredited. **Degrees:** 624 bachelor's, 18 associate awarded; master's offered. **ROTC:** Army. **Calendar:** Semester, limited summer session. **Full-time faculty:** 214 total; 56% have terminal degrees, 12% minority, 33% women. **Part-time faculty:** 69 total; 13% have terminal degrees, 1% minority, 41% women. **Class size:** 32% < 20, 44% 20-39, 18% 40-49, 4% 50-99, 2% >100. **Special facilities:** Observatory, natural area for science field trips and experimentation, hiking trails, cross-country skiing.

Freshman class profile. 3,423 applied, 2,681 admitted, 1,085 enrolled.

Mid 50% test scores		**GPA 2.0-2.99:**	30%
SAT critical reading:	460-560	**Rank in top quarter:**	42%
SAT math:	490-600	**Rank in top tenth:**	14%
GPA 3.75 or higher:	8%	**Return as sophomores:**	87%
GPA 3.50-3.74:	15%	**Out-of-state:**	9%
GPA 3.0-3.49:	47%	**International:**	2%

Basis for selection. Admission decisions based on high school GPA, standardized test scores, class rank, personal statements, and activities. Essay considered if submitted; portfolios required for select majors. **Homeschooled:** Complete documentation helpful, showing courses studied and all evaluations presented from home school evaluator, supervisor assigned to student in cooperation with local school district, or evaluator approved through program.

High school preparation. College-preparatory program recommended. Required units include English 4, mathematics 3, social studies 3, science 3 and foreign language 2.

2008-2009 Annual costs. Tuition/fees: $12,282; $18,370 out-of-state. Room/board: $8,270. Books/supplies: $1,264. Personal expenses: $2,916.

2007-2008 Financial aid. Need-based: 1,026 full-time freshmen applied for aid; 843 were judged to have need; 819 of these received aid. Average need met was 62%. Average scholarship/grant was $5,822; average loan $3,712. 41% of total undergraduate aid awarded as scholarships/grants, 59% as loans/jobs. **Non-need-based:** Awarded to 848 full-time undergraduates, including 282 freshmen. Scholarships awarded for academics, alumni affiliation, athletics, ROTC.

Application procedures. Admission: Priority date 11/30; no deadline. $50 fee, may be waived for applicants with need. Admission notification on a rolling basis beginning on or about 11/1. Must reply by May 1 or within 2 week(s) if notified thereafter. All freshmen applications processed at University Park Campus. **Financial aid:** Priority date 2/15; no closing date. FAFSA required. Applicants notified on a rolling basis starting 3/1.

Academics. Special study options: Accelerated study, combined bachelor's/graduate degree, cooperative education, distance learning, double major, dual enrollment of high school students, honors, independent study, internships, liberal arts/career combination, semester at sea, study abroad, teacher certification program. **Credit/placement by examination:** AP, CLEP, IB, SAT, institutional tests. 60 credit hours maximum toward bachelor's degree. **Support services:** Learning center, pre-admission summer program, remedial instruction, study skills assistance, tutoring, writing center.

Majors. Agriculture: General, agribusiness operations, agronomy, animal sciences, education services, food science, horticultural science, landscaping, mechanization, soil science, turf management. **Area/ethnic studies:** African-American, East Asian, Latin American, women's. **Biology:** General, bacteriology, biochemistry, biomedical sciences, pathology, toxicology. **Business:** Accounting, actuarial science, business admin, finance, hospitality admin, international, labor relations, management information systems, managerial economics, marketing, organizational behavior. **Communications:** General, advertising, journalism. **Computer sciences:** General, computer science, information systems. **Conservation:** General, forest sciences, forest technology. **Education:** Adult/continuing, art, elementary, evaluation, foreign languages, secondary, special. **Engineering:** General, aerospace, architectural, biomedical, chemical, civil, computer, electrical, environmental, industrial, materials science, mechanical, mining, nuclear, petroleum, polymer, science, software. **Engineering technology:** Electrical, mechanical. **Family/consumer sciences:** Family studies, human nutrition. **Foreign languages:** Classics, comparative lit, French, German, Italian, Japanese, Russian, Spanish. **Health:** Communication disorders, health care admin, nursing (RN), premedicine. **History:** General. **Interdisciplinary:** Biological/physical sciences, medieval/Renaissance. **Liberal arts:** Arts/sciences. **Math:** General, statistics. **Parks/recreation:** Exercise sciences, facilities management. **Philosophy/religion:** Judaic, philosophy, religion. **Physical sciences:** General, astronomy, atmospheric science, chemistry, geology, physics. **Protective services:** Forensics, law enforcement admin. **Psychology:** General. **Science technology:** Biological. **Social sciences:** Anthropology, archaeology, economics, geography, international economic development, international relations, political science, sociology. **Visual/performing arts:** General, acting, art, art history/conservation, film/cinema, graphic design, theater design. **Other:** Design and applied arts, Multi-/Interdisciplinary studies, Rehabilitation and therapeutic studies, Security and protective services.

Most popular majors. Biology 6%, business/marketing 34%, engineering/engineering technologies 30%, psychology 7%.

Computing on campus. 778 workstations in dormitories, library, computer center, student center. Dormitories wired for high-speed internet access and linked to campus network. Commuter students can connect to campus network. Online course registration, online library, helpline, repair service, student web hosting, wireless network available.

Student life. Freshman orientation: Mandatory. Preregistration for classes offered. Held during the 3 days before start of classes. **Policies:** Acts of intolerance and high-risk drinking discouraged at all locations. All facilities designated as smoke-free. **Housing:** Coed dorms, single-sex dorms, special housing for disabled, apartments available. $100 partly refundable deposit, deadline 5/1. Suites, special interest housing available. **Activities:** Bands, campus ministries, choral groups, dance, drama, film society, international student organizations, literary magazine, music ensembles, radio station, student government, student newspaper, Asian student organization, Association of Black Collegians, National Society of Black Engineers, human relations programming council, multicultural council, Irish American society, Women Today, College Republicans, InterVarsity Christian Fellowship, gospel choir.

Athletics. NCAA. **Intercollegiate:** Baseball M, basketball, cross-country, golf, soccer, softball W, swimming, tennis, track and field, volleyball W, water polo. **Intramural:** Badminton, basketball, bowling, football (non-tackle), golf, soccer, softball, swimming, table tennis, track and field, triathlon, volleyball. **Team name:** Behrend Lions.

Student services. Adult student services, alcohol/substance abuse counseling, chaplain/spiritual director, career counseling, services for economically disadvantaged, student employment services, financial aid counseling, health services, minority student services, on-campus daycare, personal counseling, placement for graduates, veterans' counselor, women's services. **Physically disabled:** Services for visually, speech, hearing impaired.

Contact. E-mail: behrend.admissions@psu.edu
Phone: (814) 898-6100 Toll-free number: (866) 374-3378
Fax: (814) 898-6044
Anne Rohrbach, Executive Director for Undergraduate Admissions, Penn State Erie, The Behrend College, 201 Shields Building, University Park, PA 16801-1294

Penn State Fayette, The Eberly Campus

Uniontown, Pennsylvania
www.fe.psu.edu **CB code: 2660**

- Public 4-year branch campus college
- Commuter campus in large town
- 899 degree-seeking undergraduates: 19% part-time, 60% women, 7% African American, 1% Hispanic American
- 88% of applicants admitted
- SAT or ACT with writing required
- 41% graduate within 6 years

General. Founded in 1934. Regionally accredited. **Degrees:** 86 bachelor's, 110 associate awarded. **Location:** 40 miles from Pittsburgh. **Calendar:** Semester, limited summer session. **Full-time faculty:** 56 total; 48% have terminal degrees, 4% minority, 39% women. **Part-time faculty:** 39 total; 28%

have terminal degrees, 8% minority, 56% women. **Class size:** 53% < 20, 41% 20-39, 5% 40-49, 2% 50-99.

Freshman class profile. 530 applied, 469 admitted, 209 enrolled.

Mid 50% test scores		**GPA 2.0-2.99:**	46%
SAT critical reading:	400-520	**Rank in top quarter:**	33%
SAT math:	400-530	**Rank in top tenth:**	12%
GPA 3.75 or higher:	6%	**Return as sophomores:**	72%
GPA 3.50-3.74:	10%	**Out-of-state:**	3%
GPA 3.0-3.49:	35%		

Basis for selection. Admission decisions based on high school GPA, as well as other factors, which may include standardized verbal and math test scores, class rank, personal statements, and activities lists. Essay considered if submitted; portfolios required for select majors. **Homeschooled:** Complete documentation helpful, showing courses studied and all evaluations presented from home school evaluator, supervisor assigned to student in cooperation with local school district, or evaluator approved through program. **Learning Disabled:** Prospective students with disabilities are encouraged to contact or visit the Office for Disability Services in their junior or senior years in high school in order to find out more about disability services at the college level.

High school preparation. College-preparatory program recommended. Required units include English 4, mathematics 3, social studies 3, science 3 and foreign language 2.

2008-2009 Annual costs. Tuition/fees: $11,700; $17,490 out-of-state. Books/supplies: $1,264. Personal expenses: $1,854.

2007-2008 Financial aid. Need-based: 224 full-time freshmen applied for aid; 195 were judged to have need; 194 of these received aid. Average need met was 68%. Average scholarship/grant was $5,724; average loan $3,362. 46% of total undergraduate aid awarded as scholarships/grants, 54% as loans/jobs. **Non-need-based:** Awarded to 256 full-time undergraduates, including 94 freshmen. Scholarships awarded for academics, alumni affiliation, athletics, ROTC.

Application procedures. Admission: Priority date 11/30; no deadline. $50 fee, may be waived for applicants with need. Admission notification on a rolling basis beginning on or about 11/1. Must reply by May 1 or within 2 week(s) if notified thereafter. All freshmen applications processed at University Park Campus. **Financial aid:** Priority date 2/15; no closing date. FAFSA required. Applicants notified on a rolling basis starting 3/1.

Academics. Special study options: Accelerated study, cross-registration, distance learning, double major, dual enrollment of high school students, honors, independent study, internships, student-designed major, study abroad, weekend college. **Credit/placement by examination:** AP, CLEP, IB, SAT. 60 credit hours maximum toward bachelor's degree. **Support services:** Learning center, remedial instruction, study skills assistance, tutoring, writing center.

Majors. Agriculture: General, agribusiness operations, agronomy, animal sciences, education services, food science, horticultural science, landscaping, mechanization, soil science, turf management. **Area/ethnic studies:** African-American, East Asian, Latin American, women's. **Biology:** General, bacteriology, biochemistry, biomedical sciences, pathology, toxicology. **Business:** Accounting, actuarial science, business admin, finance, labor relations, management information systems, managerial economics, marketing, organizational behavior. **Communications:** General, advertising, journalism. **Computer sciences:** General, information systems. **Conservation:** General, forest sciences, forest technology. **Education:** Adult/continuing, art, elementary, evaluation, foreign languages, secondary, special. **Engineering:** General, aerospace, architectural, biomedical, chemical, civil, computer, electrical, environmental, industrial, materials science, mechanical, mining, nuclear, petroleum, science. **Engineering technology:** Electrical. **Family/consumer sciences:** Family studies, human nutrition. **Foreign languages:** Classics, comparative lit, French, German, Italian, Japanese, Russian, Spanish. **Health:** Communication disorders, health care admin, nursing (RN), premedicine. **History:** General. **Interdisciplinary:** Biological/physical sciences, medieval/Renaissance. **Liberal arts:** Arts/sciences. **Math:** General, statistics. **Parks/recreation:** Exercise sciences, facilities management. **Philosophy/religion:** Judaic, philosophy, religion. **Physical sciences:** Astronomy, atmospheric science, chemistry, geology, physics. **Protective services:** Criminal justice, forensics, law enforcement admin. **Psychology:** General. **Science technology:** Biological. **Social sciences:** Anthropology, archaeology, economics, geography, international economic development, international relations, political science, sociology. **Visual/performing arts:** General, acting, art, art history/conservation, film/cinema, graphic design, theater design. **Other:** Design and applied arts, Rehabilitation and therapeutic studies.

Most popular majors. Business/marketing 22%, English 6%, family/consumer sciences 24%, liberal arts 8%, security/protective services 40%.

Computing on campus. 196 workstations in library, computer center, student center. Commuter students can connect to campus network. Online course registration, online library, helpline, repair service, student web hosting available.

Student life. Freshman orientation: Available. Preregistration for classes offered. **Policies:** Acts of intolerance and high-risk drinking discouraged at all locations. All facilities designated smoke-free. **Housing:** Privately owned, off-campus housing available. **Activities:** Drama, literary magazine, musical theater, student government, student newspaper, adult student organization, humanities society, Christian club, minority students association, Women in Science Engineering & Technology, Students Against Destructive Decisions.

Athletics. Intercollegiate: Baseball M, basketball, golf M, softball W, volleyball W. **Intramural:** Basketball, football (non-tackle), racquetball, softball, tennis. **Team name:** Nittany Lions.

Student services. Adult student services, alcohol/substance abuse counseling, career counseling, services for economically disadvantaged, student employment services, financial aid counseling, health services, on-campus daycare, personal counseling, placement for graduates, veterans' counselor. **Physically disabled:** Services for visually, speech, hearing impaired.

Contact. E-mail: feadm@psu.edu
Phone: (724) 430-4130 Toll-free number: (877) 568-4130
Fax: (724) 430-4175
Anne Rohrbach, Executive Director for Undergraduate Admissions, Penn State Fayette, The Eberly Campus, 201 Shields Building, University Park, PA 16802-1294

Penn State Greater Allegheny
McKeesport, Pennsylvania
www.mk.psu.edu

- Public 4-year branch campus college
- Residential campus in large town
- 643 degree-seeking undergraduates: 6% part-time, 41% women, 23% African American, 4% Asian American, 4% Hispanic American, 2% international
- 78% of applicants admitted
- SAT or ACT with writing required
- 48% graduate within 6 years

General. Founded in 1947. Regionally accredited. **Degrees:** 71 bachelor's, 3 associate awarded. **Location:** 15 miles from Pittsburgh. **Calendar:** Semester, limited summer session. **Full-time faculty:** 38 total; 74% have terminal degrees, 21% minority, 47% women. **Part-time faculty:** 30 total; 17% have terminal degrees, 3% minority, 47% women. **Class size:** 57% < 20, 39% 20-39, 2% 40-49, 2% 50-99. **Special facilities:** Computer-based lab science equipment, special computer labs for systems integration and networking.

Freshman class profile. 689 applied, 539 admitted, 234 enrolled.

Mid 50% test scores		**Rank in top quarter:**	33%
SAT critical reading:	390-530	**Rank in top tenth:**	11%
SAT math:	390-540	**Return as sophomores:**	75%
GPA 3.75 or higher:	3%	**Out-of-state:**	22%
GPA 3.50-3.74:	8%	**Live on campus:**	43%
GPA 3.0-3.49:	28%	**International:**	3%
GPA 2.0-2.99:	58%		

Basis for selection. Admission decisions based upon high school GPA, as well as other factors, which may include standardized verbal and math test scores, class rank, personal statements, and list of activities. Essay considered if submitted; portfolios required for select majors. **Homeschooled:** Complete documentation showing the courses studied and all evaluations presented from evaluator or supervisor assigned to student in cooperation with local school district or evaluator who is approved through the program.

High school preparation. College-preparatory program recommended. Required units include English 4, mathematics 3, social studies 3, science 3 and foreign language 2.

2008-2009 Annual costs. Tuition/fees: $11,800; $17,590 out-of-state. Room/board: $8,270. Books/supplies: $1,264. Personal expenses: $2,916.

2007-2008 Financial aid. Need-based: 247 full-time freshmen applied for aid; 214 were judged to have need; 211 of these received aid. Average need met was 65%. Average scholarship/grant was $6,037; average loan $3,357. 52% of total undergraduate aid awarded as scholarships/grants, 48% as loans/jobs. **Non-need-based:** Awarded to 235 full-time undergraduates,

including 134 freshmen. Scholarships awarded for academics, alumni affiliation, athletics, ROTC.

Application procedures. **Admission:** Priority date 11/30; no deadline. $50 fee, may be waived for applicants with need. Admission notification on a rolling basis beginning on or about 11/1. Must reply by May 1 or within 2 week(s) if notified thereafter. **Financial aid:** Priority date 2/15; no closing date. FAFSA required. Applicants notified on a rolling basis starting 3/1.

Academics. **Special study options:** Cross-registration, distance learning, double major, dual enrollment of high school students, ESL, honors, independent study, internships, liberal arts/career combination, student-designed major, study abroad. **Credit/placement by examination:** AP, CLEP, IB, SAT. 60 credit hours maximum toward bachelor's degree. **Support services:** Learning center, pre-admission summer program, remedial instruction, study skills assistance, tutoring, writing center.

Majors. **Agriculture:** General, agribusiness operations, agronomy, animal sciences, education services, food science, horticultural science, landscaping, mechanization, soil science, turf management. **Area/ethnic studies:** African-American, East Asian, Latin American, women's. **Biology:** General, bacteriology, biochemistry, biomedical sciences, pathology, toxicology. **Business:** Accounting, actuarial science, business admin, finance, hospitality admin, labor relations, management information systems, managerial economics, marketing, organizational behavior. **Communications:** General, advertising, journalism. **Computer sciences:** General, information systems. **Conservation:** General, forest sciences, forest technology. **Education:** Adult/continuing, art, elementary, evaluation, foreign languages, secondary, special. **Engineering:** General, aerospace, architectural, biomedical, chemical, civil, computer, electrical, environmental, industrial, materials science, mechanical, mining, nuclear, petroleum, science. **Engineering technology:** Electrical. **Family/consumer sciences:** Family studies, human nutrition. **Foreign languages:** Classics, comparative lit, French, German, Italian, Japanese, Russian, Spanish. **Health:** Communication disorders, health care admin, nursing (RN), premedicine. **History:** General. **Interdisciplinary:** Biological/physical sciences, medieval/Renaissance. **Liberal arts:** Arts/sciences. **Math:** General, statistics. **Parks/recreation:** Exercise sciences, facilities management. **Philosophy/religion:** Judaic, philosophy, religion. **Physical sciences:** Astronomy, atmospheric science, chemistry, geology, physics. **Protective services:** Forensics, law enforcement admin. **Psychology:** General. **Science technology:** Biological. **Social sciences:** Anthropology, archaeology, economics, geography, international economic development, international relations, political science, sociology. **Visual/performing arts:** General, acting, art, art history/conservation, film/cinema, graphic design, theater design. **Other:** Adult and continuing education, Design and applied arts, Rehabilitation and therapeutic studies, Security and protective services.

Most popular majors. Business/marketing 42%, communications/journalism 9%, computer/information sciences 24%, psychology 23%.

Computing on campus. 203 workstations in dormitories, library, computer center, student center. Dormitories wired for high-speed internet access and linked to campus network. Commuter students can connect to campus network. Online course registration, online library, helpline, student web hosting, wireless network available.

Student life. **Freshman orientation:** Mandatory. Preregistration for classes offered. Orientation held prior to start of semester. **Policies:** Acts of intolerance and high-risk drinking discouraged at all locations. All facilities designated as smoke-free. Students expected to abide by The Penn State Principles. **Housing:** Coed dorms available. $100 partly refundable deposit, deadline 5/1. **Activities:** Dance, drama, literary magazine, radio station, student government, student newspaper, black student union, Christian Fellowship, gospel choir, Spanish club, multicultural organization.

Athletics. **Intercollegiate:** Baseball M, basketball, golf, soccer M, softball W, volleyball W. **Intramural:** Basketball, football (non-tackle), soccer, softball, volleyball.

Student services. Adult student services, alcohol/substance abuse counseling, chaplain/spiritual director, career counseling, services for economically disadvantaged, student employment services, financial aid counseling, health services, minority student services, personal counseling, placement for graduates, veterans' counselor, women's services. **Physically disabled:** Services for visually, speech, hearing impaired.

Contact. E-mail: psumk@psu.edu
Phone: (412) 675-9010 Fax: (412) 675-9046
Anne Rohrbach, Executive Director for Undergraduate Admissions, Penn State Greater Allegheny, 201 Shields Building, University Park, PA 16802-1294

Penn State Harrisburg
Middletown, Pennsylvania
www.hbg.psu.edu **CB code: 2660**

- Public 4-year branch campus college
- Residential campus in small town
- 2,420 degree-seeking undergraduates: 16% part-time, 45% women, 9% African American, 7% Asian American, 4% Hispanic American, 2% international
- 1,254 degree-seeking graduate students
- 73% of applicants admitted
- SAT or ACT with writing required
- 83% graduate within 6 years

General. Founded in 1966. Regionally accredited. **Degrees:** 539 bachelor's, 11 associate awarded; master's, doctoral offered. **ROTC:** Army. **Location:** 8 miles from Harrisburg. **Calendar:** Semester, limited summer session. **Full-time faculty:** 195 total; 85% have terminal degrees, 29% minority, 38% women. **Part-time faculty:** 97 total; 35% have terminal degrees, 8% minority, 41% women. **Class size:** 44% < 20, 51% 20-39, 4% 40-49, less than 1% 50-99. **Special facilities:** Black cultural arts center, humanities gallery, American studies archives.

Freshman class profile. 2,736 applied, 1,985 admitted, 449 enrolled.

Mid 50% test scores		**GPA 2.0-2.99:**	40%
SAT critical reading:	450-560	**Rank in top quarter:**	36%
SAT math:	470-590	**Rank in top tenth:**	9%
GPA 3.75 or higher:	4%	**Return as sophomores:**	80%
GPA 3.50-3.74:	9%	**Out-of-state:**	29%
GPA 3.0-3.49:	47%	**International:**	4%

Basis for selection. Admissions based on secondary school record and standardized test scores.

High school preparation. College-preparatory program recommended. Required units include English 4, mathematics 3, social studies 3, science 3 and foreign language 2.

2008-2009 Annual costs. Tuition/fees: $12,282; $18,370 out-of-state. Room/board: $9,380. Books/supplies: $1,264. Personal expenses: $2,916.

2007-2008 Financial aid. **Need-based:** 348 full-time freshmen applied for aid; 247 were judged to have need; 237 of these received aid. Average need met was 55%. Average scholarship/grant was $6,129; average loan $3,578. 38% of total undergraduate aid awarded as scholarships/grants, 62% as loans/jobs. **Non-need-based:** Awarded to 315 full-time undergraduates, including 69 freshmen. Scholarships awarded for academics, alumni affiliation, athletics, ROTC.

Application procedures. **Admission:** Priority date 11/30; no deadline. $50 fee, may be waived for applicants with need. Admission notification on a rolling basis beginning on or about 11/1. Must reply by May 1 or within 2 week(s) if notified thereafter. All freshmen applications processed at University Park Campus. **Financial aid:** Priority date 2/15; no closing date. FAFSA required. Applicants notified on a rolling basis starting 3/1.

Academics. **Special study options:** Cooperative education, cross-registration, distance learning, double major, dual enrollment of high school students, honors, independent study, internships, student-designed major, study abroad, teacher certification program. **Credit/placement by examination:** AP, CLEP, IB, SAT. 60 credit hours maximum toward bachelor's degree. **Support services:** Learning center, study skills assistance, tutoring, writing center.

Majors. **Area/ethnic studies:** American. **Business:** Business admin, finance, international, management information systems, marketing, organizational behavior. **Communications:** General. **Computer sciences:** General, information systems. **Education:** Elementary, social studies. **Engineering:** Civil, electrical, environmental, mechanical, structural. **Family/consumer sciences:** Family studies. **Health:** Nursing (RN). **Liberal arts:** Humanities. **Math:** Applied. **Protective services:** Criminal justice. **Psychology:** General. **Public administration:** Policy analysis. **Social sciences:** Sociology. **Other:** Multi-/Interdisciplinary studies, Security and protective services.

Most popular majors. Business/marketing 32%, communications/journalism 8%, computer/information sciences 6%, education 11%, engineering/engineering technologies 16%, psychology 7%, security/protective services 8%.

Computing on campus. 520 workstations in library, computer center. Dormitories wired for high-speed internet access and linked to campus network. Commuter students can connect to campus network. Online course registration, online library, helpline, repair service, student web hosting, wireless network available.

Student life. **Freshman orientation:** Available. Preregistration for classes offered. Held 2 days prior to the start of classes. **Policies:** Acts of intolerance and high-risk drinking discouraged at all locations. All facilities designated smoke-free. **Housing:** Special housing for disabled, apartments available. $100 partly refundable deposit, deadline 5/1. Special interest housing available. **Activities:** Choral groups, dance, drama, literary magazine, music ensembles, radio station, student government, student newspaper, black student union, Christian Fellowship, resident community council.

Athletics. Intercollegiate: Baseball M, basketball, cross-country, golf, soccer, softball W, tennis, volleyball W. **Intramural:** Badminton, basketball, racquetball, tennis. **Team name:** Nittany Lions.

Student services. Adult student services, alcohol/substance abuse counseling, career counseling, services for economically disadvantaged, student employment services, financial aid counseling, health services, minority student services, on-campus daycare, personal counseling, placement for graduates, veterans' counselor, women's services. **Physically disabled:** Services for visually, speech, hearing impaired.

Contact. E-mail: hbgadmit@psu.edu
Phone: (717) 948-6250 Toll-free number: (800) 222-2056
Fax: (717) 948-6325
Anne Rohrbach, Executive Director for Undergraduate Admissions, Penn State Harrisburg, 201 Shields Building, University Park, PA 16802-1294

Penn State Hazleton

Hazleton, Pennsylvania
www.hn.psu.edu **CB code: 2660**

- Public 4-year branch campus college
- Residential campus in large town
- 1,186 degree-seeking undergraduates: 3% part-time, 42% women, 9% African American, 4% Asian American, 8% Hispanic American
- 86% of applicants admitted
- SAT or ACT (ACT writing optional) required
- 60% graduate within 6 years

General. Founded in 1934. Regionally accredited. **Degrees:** 29 bachelor's, 50 associate awarded; master's offered. **ROTC:** Army, Air Force. **Location:** 4 miles from Hazleton. **Calendar:** Semester, limited summer session. **Full-time faculty:** 55 total; 64% have terminal degrees, 18% minority, 40% women. **Part-time faculty:** 28 total; 25% have terminal degrees, 11% minority, 46% women. **Class size:** 43% < 20, 45% 20-39, 5% 40-49, 6% 50-99. **Special facilities:** Weather station.

Freshman class profile. 1,454 applied, 1,255 admitted, 542 enrolled.

Mid 50% test scores		**GPA 2.0-2.99:**	59%
SAT critical reading:	420-520	**Rank in top quarter:**	29%
SAT math:	430-550	**Rank in top tenth:**	9%
GPA 3.75 or higher:	2%	**Return as sophomores:**	81%
GPA 3.50-3.74:	5%	**Out-of-state:**	29%
GPA 3.0-3.49:	32%		

Basis for selection. Admission decisions based on high school GPA, as well as other factors, which may include standardized verbal and math test scores, class rank, personal statements, and activities lists. Essay considered if submitted; portfolios required for select majors. **Homeschooled:** Complete documentation helpful, showing courses studied and all evaluations presented from home school evaluator, supervisor assigned to student in cooperation with local school district, or evaluator approved through program.

High school preparation. College-preparatory program recommended. Required units include English 4, mathematics 3, social studies 3, science 3 and foreign language 2.

2008-2009 Annual costs. Tuition/fees: $11,600; $17,390 out-of-state. Room/board: $8,270. Books/supplies: $1,264. Personal expenses: $2,916.

2007-2008 Financial aid. Need-based: 507 full-time freshmen applied for aid; 408 were judged to have need; 394 of these received aid. Average need met was 61%. Average scholarship/grant was $5,607; average loan $3,340. 43% of total undergraduate aid awarded as scholarships/grants, 57% as loans/jobs. **Non-need-based:** Awarded to 350 full-time undergraduates, including 207 freshmen. Scholarships awarded for academics, alumni affiliation, athletics, ROTC.

Application procedures. Admission: Priority date 11/30; no deadline. $50 fee, may be waived for applicants with need. Admission notification on a rolling basis beginning on or about 11/1. Must reply by May 1 or within 2 week(s) if notified thereafter. All freshman applications processed at University Park Campus. **Financial aid:** Priority date 2/15; no closing date. FAFSA required. Applicants notified on a rolling basis starting 3/1.

Academics. Special study options: Accelerated study, cross-registration, distance learning, double major, dual enrollment of high school students, ESL, honors, independent study, internships, student-designed major, study abroad. **Credit/placement by examination:** AP, CLEP, IB, SAT. 60 credit hours maximum toward bachelor's degree. **Support services:** Learning center, remedial instruction, study skills assistance, tutoring, writing center.

Honors college/program. 300 admitted university-wide each year.

Majors. Agriculture: General, agribusiness operations, agronomy, animal sciences, education services, food science, horticultural science, landscaping, mechanization, soil science, turf management. **Area/ethnic studies:** African-American, East Asian, Latin American, women's. **Biology:** General, bacteriology, biochemistry, biomedical sciences, pathology, toxicology. **Business:** Accounting, actuarial science, business admin, finance, hospitality admin, labor relations, management information systems, managerial economics, marketing, organizational behavior. **Communications:** General, advertising, journalism. **Computer sciences:** General, information systems. **Conservation:** General, forest sciences, forest technology. **Education:** Art, elementary, foreign languages, secondary, special. **Engineering:** General, aerospace, architectural, biomedical, chemical, civil, computer, electrical, environmental, industrial, materials science, mechanical, mining, nuclear, petroleum, science. **Engineering technology:** Electrical. **Family/consumer sciences:** Family studies, human nutrition. **Foreign languages:** Classics, comparative lit, French, German, Italian, Japanese, Russian, Spanish. **Health:** Communication disorders, health care admin, nursing (RN), premedicine. **History:** General. **Interdisciplinary:** Biological/physical sciences, medieval/Renaissance. **Liberal arts:** Arts/sciences. **Math:** General, statistics. **Parks/recreation:** Exercise sciences, facilities management. **Philosophy/religion:** Judaic, philosophy, religion. **Physical sciences:** Astronomy, atmospheric science, chemistry, geology, physics. **Protective services:** Forensics, law enforcement admin. **Psychology:** General. **Science technology:** Biological. **Social sciences:** Anthropology, archaeology, economics, geography, international economic development, international relations, political science, sociology. **Visual/performing arts:** General, acting, art, art history/conservation, film/cinema, graphic design, theater design. **Other:** Design and applied arts, Rehabilitation and therapeutic studies, Security and protective services.

Most popular majors. Business/marketing 41%, computer/information sciences 28%, liberal arts 31%.

Computing on campus. 166 workstations in library, student center. Dormitories wired for high-speed internet access and linked to campus network. Commuter students can connect to campus network. Online course registration, online library, helpline, repair service, student web hosting, wireless network available.

Student life. Freshman orientation: Available. Preregistration for classes offered. Testing and academic advising in June; formal orientation in August and September. **Policies:** Acts of intolerance and high-risk drinking discouraged at all locations. All facilities designated as smoke-free. Students expected to abide by The Penn State Principles. **Housing:** Coed dorms available. $100 partly refundable deposit, deadline 5/1. Townhouses, suites available. **Activities:** Campus ministries, choral groups, dance, drama, literary magazine, radio station, student government, student newspaper, multicultural club, Circle K, Allies, Fellowship of Christian Athletes, Helping Hands.

Athletics. Intercollegiate: Baseball M, basketball, cheerleading, golf, soccer M, softball W, tennis, volleyball W. **Intramural:** Rifle, softball, table tennis, tennis, volleyball. **Team name:** Nittany Lions.

Student services. Adult student services, alcohol/substance abuse counseling, chaplain/spiritual director, career counseling, services for economically disadvantaged, student employment services, financial aid counseling, health services, legal services, minority student services, personal counseling, placement for graduates, veterans' counselor, women's services. **Physically disabled:** Services for visually, speech, hearing impaired.

Contact. E-mail: admissions-hn@psu.edu
Phone: (570) 450-3142 Toll-free number: (800) 279-8495
Fax: (570) 450-3182
Anne Rohrbach, Executive Director for Undergraduate Admissions, Penn State Hazleton, 201 Shields Building, University Park, PA 16802-1294

Penn State Lehigh Valley

Fogelsville, Pennsylvania
www.lv.psu.edu **CB code: 2660**

- Public 4-year branch campus college
- Commuter campus in rural community
- 676 degree-seeking undergraduates: 13% part-time, 39% women, 4% African American, 8% Asian American, 9% Hispanic American, 1% international
- 37 graduate students

- 81% of applicants admitted
- SAT or ACT with writing required
- 55% graduate within 6 years

General. Regionally accredited. **Degrees:** 74 bachelor's, 10 associate awarded. **ROTC:** Army. **Location:** 15 miles from Allentown, 30 miles from Easton. **Calendar:** Semester, limited summer session. **Full-time faculty:** 32 total; 69% have terminal degrees, 12% minority, 50% women. **Part-time faculty:** 50 total; 20% have terminal degrees, 2% minority, 42% women. **Class size:** 68% < 20, 26% 20-39, 4% 40-49, 2% 50-99.

Freshman class profile. 932 applied, 752 admitted, 213 enrolled.

Mid 50% test scores		**GPA 2.0-2.99:**	58%
SAT critical reading:	440-550	**Rank in top quarter:**	30%
SAT math:	430-580	**Rank in top tenth:**	9%
GPA 3.75 or higher:	4%	**Return as sophomores:**	76%
GPA 3.50-3.74:	6%	**Out-of-state:**	5%
GPA 3.0-3.49:	30%		

Basis for selection. Admission decisions based on high school GPA, standardized test scores, class rank, personal statements, and activities. Essay considered if submitted; portfolios required for select majors. **Homeschooled:** Applicants should provide complete documentation showing courses studied and all evaluations presented from evaluator or supervisor assigned to student in cooperation with local school district or evaluator approved through program.

High school preparation. College-preparatory program recommended. Required units include English 4, mathematics 3, social studies 3, science 3 and foreign language 2.

2008-2009 Annual costs. Tuition/fees: $11,750; $17,540 out-of-state. Books/supplies: $1,264. Personal expenses: $1,854.

2007-2008 Financial aid. Need-based: 201 full-time freshmen applied for aid; 149 were judged to have need; 141 of these received aid. Average need met was 63%. Average scholarship/grant was $5,936; average loan $3,537. 47% of total undergraduate aid awarded as scholarships/grants, 53% as loans/jobs. **Non-need-based:** Awarded to 119 full-time undergraduates, including 63 freshmen. Scholarships awarded for academics, alumni affiliation, athletics, ROTC.

Application procedures. Admission: Priority date 11/30; no deadline. $50 fee, may be waived for applicants with need. Admission notification on a rolling basis beginning on or about 11/1. Must reply by May 1 or within 2 week(s) if notified thereafter. All freshmen applications processed at University Park Campus. **Financial aid:** Priority date 2/15; no closing date. FAFSA required. Applicants notified on a rolling basis starting 3/1.

Academics. Special study options: Accelerated study, cooperative education, cross-registration, distance learning, dual enrollment of high school students, honors, independent study, internships, study abroad. **Credit/placement by examination:** AP, CLEP, IB, SAT. 60 credit hours maximum toward bachelor's degree. **Support services:** Learning center, reduced course load, study skills assistance, tutoring, writing center.

Majors. Agriculture: General, agribusiness operations, agronomy, animal sciences, education services, food science, horticultural science, landscaping, mechanization, soil science, turf management. **Area/ethnic studies:** African-American, East Asian, Latin American, women's. **Biology:** General, bacteriology, biochemistry, biomedical sciences, pathology, toxicology. **Business:** General, accounting, actuarial science, business admin, finance, hospitality admin, labor relations, management information systems, managerial economics, marketing, organizational behavior. **Communications:** General, advertising, journalism. **Computer sciences:** General, information systems. **Conservation:** General, forest sciences, forest technology. **Education:** Adult/continuing, art, elementary, evaluation, foreign languages, secondary, special. **Engineering:** General, aerospace, architectural, biomedical, chemical, civil, computer, electrical, environmental, industrial, materials science, mechanical, mining, nuclear, petroleum, science. **Engineering technology:** Electrical. **Family/consumer sciences:** Family studies, human nutrition. **Foreign languages:** General, classics, comparative lit, French, German, Italian, Japanese, Russian, Spanish. **Health:** Communication disorders, health care admin, nursing (RN), premedicine. **History:** General. **Interdisciplinary:** Biological/physical sciences, medieval/Renaissance. **Liberal arts:** Arts/sciences. **Math:** General, statistics. **Parks/recreation:** Exercise sciences, facilities management. **Philosophy/religion:** Judaic, philosophy, religion. **Physical sciences:** Astronomy, atmospheric science, chemistry, geology, physics. **Protective services:** Forensics, law enforcement admin. **Psychology:** General. **Science technology:** Biological. **Social sciences:** Anthropology, archaeology, economics, geography, international economic development, international relations, political science, sociology. **Visual/performing arts:** General, acting, art, art history/conservation, film/cinema, graphic design, theater design. **Other:** Design and applied arts, Rehabilitation and therapeutic studies, Security and protective services.

Most popular majors. Business/marketing 59%, computer/information sciences 14%, psychology 19%.

Computing on campus. 155 workstations in dormitories, library, computer center, student center. Commuter students can connect to campus network. Online course registration, online library, helpline, repair service, student web hosting, wireless network available.

Student life. Freshman orientation: Mandatory. Preregistration for classes offered. One-day program held prior to start of classes. **Policies:** Acts of intolerance and high-risk drinking discouraged at all locations. All facilities designated as smoke-free. Students expected to abide by The Penn State Principles. **Activities:** Dance, drama, student government, student newspaper, Asian club, Christian Fellowship, Habitat for Humanity.

Athletics. Intercollegiate: Golf, tennis. **Intramural:** Basketball, football (non-tackle), soccer. **Team name:** Nittany Lions.

Student services. Adult student services, alcohol/substance abuse counseling, career counseling, services for economically disadvantaged, student employment services, financial aid counseling, health services, minority student services, personal counseling, placement for graduates, veterans' counselor. **Physically disabled:** Services for visually, speech, hearing impaired. **Learning disabled:** Comprehensive services available.

Contact. E-mail: admissions-lv@psu.edu
Phone: (610) 285-5035 Fax: (610) 285-5220
Anne Rohrbach, Executive Director for Undergraduate Admissions, Penn State Lehigh Valley, 201 Shields Building, University Park, PA 16802-1294

Penn State Mont Alto

Mont Alto, Pennsylvania
www.ma.psu.edu **CB code: 2660**

- Public 4-year branch campus college
- Residential campus in rural community
- 1,025 degree-seeking undergraduates: 22% part-time, 58% women, 12% African American, 3% Asian American, 3% Hispanic American
- 86% of applicants admitted
- SAT or ACT with writing required
- 47% graduate within 6 years

General. Founded in 1929. Regionally accredited. **Degrees:** 37 bachelor's, 102 associate awarded. **ROTC:** Army. **Location:** 12 miles from Chambersburg. **Calendar:** Semester, limited summer session. **Full-time faculty:** 57 total; 49% have terminal degrees, 7% minority, 53% women. **Part-time faculty:** 51 total; 12% have terminal degrees, 67% women. **Class size:** 52% < 20, 39% 20-39, 6% 40-49, 3% 50-99.

Freshman class profile. 880 applied, 754 admitted, 385 enrolled.

Mid 50% test scores		**GPA 2.0-2.99:**	56%
SAT critical reading:	420-530	**Rank in top quarter:**	30%
SAT math:	410-550	**Rank in top tenth:**	11%
GPA 3.75 or higher:	3%	**Return as sophomores:**	82%
GPA 3.50-3.74:	7%	**Out-of-state:**	26%
GPA 3.0-3.49:	33%	**International:**	1%

Basis for selection. Admission decisions based upon high school GPA, as well as other factors, which may include standardized verbal and math test scores, class rank, personal statements, and list of activities. Essay considered if submitted; portfolios required for select majors. **Homeschooled:** Applicants should provide complete documentation showing courses studied and all evaluations presented from evaluator or supervisor assigned to student in cooperation with local school district or evaluator who is approved through the program.

High school preparation. College-preparatory program recommended. Required units include English 4, mathematics 3, social studies 3, science 3 and foreign language 2.

2008-2009 Annual costs. Tuition/fees: $11,800; $17,590 out-of-state. Room/board: $8,270. Books/supplies: $1,264. Personal expenses: $2,916.

2007-2008 Financial aid. Need-based: 309 full-time freshmen applied for aid; 241 were judged to have need; 238 of these received aid. Average need met was 61%. Average scholarship/grant was $4,650; average loan $3,387. 43% of total undergraduate aid awarded as scholarships/grants, 57% as loans/jobs. **Non-need-based:** Awarded to 255 full-time undergraduates, including 143 freshmen. Scholarships awarded for academics, alumni affiliation, athletics, ROTC.

Application procedures. Admission: Priority date 11/30; no deadline. $50 fee, may be waived for applicants with need. Admission notification on a rolling basis beginning on or about 11/1. Must reply by May 1 or within 2 week(s) if notified thereafter. All freshmen applications processed at University Park Campus. **Financial aid:** Priority date 2/15; no closing date. FAFSA required. Applicants notified on a rolling basis starting 3/1.

Academics. Special study options: Accelerated study, cross-registration, distance learning, double major, dual enrollment of high school students, honors, independent study, internships, study abroad. **Credit/placement by examination:** AP, CLEP, IB, SAT. 60 credit hours maximum toward bachelor's degree. **Support services:** Learning center, remedial instruction, study skills assistance, tutoring, writing center.

Majors. Agriculture: General, agribusiness operations, agronomy, animal sciences, business, education services, food science, horticultural science, landscaping, mechanization, soil science, turf management. **Area/ethnic studies:** African-American, East Asian, Latin American, women's. **Biology:** General, bacteriology, biochemistry, biomedical sciences, pathology, toxicology. **Business:** Accounting, actuarial science, business admin, finance, hospitality admin, labor relations, management information systems, managerial economics, marketing, organizational behavior. **Communications:** General, advertising, journalism. **Computer sciences:** General, information systems. **Conservation:** General, forest sciences, forest technology. **Education:** Adult/continuing, art, elementary, evaluation, foreign languages, secondary, special. **Engineering:** General, aerospace, architectural, biomedical, chemical, civil, computer, electrical, environmental, industrial, materials science, mechanical, mining, nuclear, petroleum, science. **Engineering technology:** Electrical. **Family/consumer sciences:** Family studies, human nutrition. **Foreign languages:** Classics, comparative lit, French, German, Italian, Japanese, Russian, Spanish. **Health:** Communication disorders, health care admin, nursing (RN), premedicine. **History:** General. **Interdisciplinary:** Biological/physical sciences, medieval/Renaissance. **Liberal arts:** Arts/sciences. **Math:** General, statistics. **Parks/recreation:** Exercise sciences, facilities management. **Philosophy/religion:** Judaic, philosophy, religion. **Physical sciences:** Astronomy, atmospheric science, chemistry, geology, physics. **Protective services:** Forensics, law enforcement admin. **Psychology:** General. **Science technology:** Biological. **Social sciences:** Anthropology, archaeology, economics, geography, international economic development, international relations, political science, sociology. **Visual/performing arts:** General, acting, art, art history/conservation, film/cinema, graphic design, theater design. **Other:** Design and applied arts, Rehabilitation and therapeutic studies, Security and protective services.

Most popular majors. Business/marketing 30%, English 16%, family/consumer sciences 54%.

Computing on campus. 164 workstations in computer center, student center. Dormitories wired for high-speed internet access and linked to campus network. Commuter students can connect to campus network. Online course registration, online library, helpline, repair service, student web hosting, wireless network available.

Student life. Freshman orientation: Available. Preregistration for classes offered. **Policies:** Acts of intolerance and high-risk drinking discouraged at all locations. All facilities designated as smoke-free. **Housing:** Coed dorms, special housing for disabled available. $100 partly refundable deposit, deadline 5/1. Suites, special interest housing, townhouses available. **Activities:** Jazz band, campus ministries, dance, drama, student government, student newspaper, Christian Fellowship, language club, multicultural club, volunteer club, black student union, Asian student association.

Athletics. Intercollegiate: Basketball, cheerleading, cross-country, golf, soccer, softball W, tennis, volleyball W. **Intramural:** Badminton, basketball, racquetball, soccer, softball, volleyball. **Team name:** Nittany Lions.

Student services. Adult student services, alcohol/substance abuse counseling, chaplain/spiritual director, career counseling, services for economically disadvantaged, student employment services, financial aid counseling, health services, minority student services, placement for graduates, veterans' counselor, women's services. **Physically disabled:** Services for visually, speech, hearing impaired.

Contact. E-mail: psuma@psu.edu
Phone: (717) 749-6130 Toll-free number: (800) 392-6173
Fax: (717) 749-6132
Anne Rohrbach, Executive Director for Undergraduate Admissions, Penn State Mont Alto, 201 Shields Building, University Park, PA 16802-1294

Penn State New Kensington

New Kensington, Pennsylvania
www.nk.psu.edu **CB code: 2660**

- Public 4-year branch campus college
- Commuter campus in large town
- 707 degree-seeking undergraduates: 18% part-time, 42% women, 3% African American, 1% Asian American, 1% Hispanic American
- 2 degree-seeking graduate students
- 84% of applicants admitted
- SAT or ACT with writing required
- 39% graduate within 6 years

General. Founded in 1958. Regionally accredited. **Degrees:** 64 bachelor's, 49 associate awarded; master's offered. **Location:** 22 miles from Pittsburgh. **Calendar:** Semester, limited summer session. **Full-time faculty:** 40 total; 62% have terminal degrees, 15% minority, 42% women. **Part-time faculty:** 47 total; 23% have terminal degrees, 11% minority, 38% women. **Class size:** 63% < 20, 32% 20-39, 3% 40-49, 3% 50-99.

Freshman class profile. 520 applied, 439 admitted, 192 enrolled.

Mid 50% test scores			
SAT critical reading:	420-540	GPA 2.0-2.99:	54%
SAT math:	430-550	Rank in top quarter:	21%
GPA 3.75 or higher:	6%	Rank in top tenth:	6%
GPA 3.50-3.74:	7%	Return as sophomores:	75%
GPA 3.0-3.49:	32%	Out-of-state:	3%

Basis for selection. Admission decisions based upon high school GPA, as well as other factors, which may include standardized verbal and math test scores, class rank, personal statements, and list of activities. Essay considered if submitted; portfolios required for select majors. **Homeschooled:** Applicants should provide complete documentation showing the courses studied and all evaluations presented from evaluator or supervisor assigned to student in cooperation with local school district or evaluator who is approved through the program.

High school preparation. College-preparatory program recommended. Required units include English 4, mathematics 3, social studies 3, science 3 and foreign language 2.

2008-2009 Annual costs. Tuition/fees: $11,700; $17,490 out-of-state. Books/supplies: $1,264. Personal expenses: $1,854.

2007-2008 Financial aid. Need-based: 190 full-time freshmen applied for aid; 152 were judged to have need; 149 of these received aid. Average need met was 65%. Average scholarship/grant was $4,987; average loan $3,067. 47% of total undergraduate aid awarded as scholarships/grants, 53% as loans/jobs. **Non-need-based:** Awarded to 184 full-time undergraduates, including 88 freshmen. Scholarships awarded for academics, alumni affiliation, athletics, ROTC.

Application procedures. Admission: Priority date 11/30; no deadline. $50 fee, may be waived for applicants with need. Admission notification on a rolling basis beginning on or about 11/1. Must reply by May 1 or within 2 week(s) if notified thereafter. All freshmen applications processed at University Park Campus. **Financial aid:** Priority date 2/15; no closing date. FAFSA required. Applicants notified on a rolling basis starting 3/1.

Academics. Special study options: Cross-registration, distance learning, double major, dual enrollment of high school students, external degree, honors, independent study, internships, study abroad. **Credit/placement by examination:** AP, CLEP, IB, SAT. 60 credit hours maximum toward bachelor's degree. **Support services:** Learning center, remedial instruction, study skills assistance, tutoring, writing center.

Majors. Agriculture: General, agribusiness operations, agronomy, animal sciences, education services, food science, horticultural science, landscaping, mechanization, soil science, turf management. **Area/ethnic studies:** African-American, East Asian, Latin American, women's. **Biology:** General, bacteriology, biochemistry, biomedical sciences, pathology, toxicology. **Business:** Accounting, actuarial science, business admin, finance, hospitality admin, labor relations, management information systems, managerial economics, marketing, organizational behavior. **Communications:** General, advertising, journalism. **Computer sciences:** General, information systems. **Conservation:** General, forest sciences, forest technology. **Education:** Adult/continuing, art, elementary, evaluation, foreign languages, secondary, special. **Engineering:** General, aerospace, architectural, biomedical, chemical, civil, computer, electrical, environmental, industrial, materials science, mechanical, mining, nuclear, petroleum, science. **Engineering technology:** Electrical. **Family/consumer sciences:** Family studies, human nutrition. **Foreign languages:** Classics, comparative lit, French, German, Italian, Japanese, Russian, Spanish. **Health:** Communication disorders, health care admin, nursing (RN), premedicine. **History:** General. **Interdisciplinary:** Biological/physical sciences, medieval/Renaissance. **Liberal arts:** Arts/sciences. **Math:** General, statistics. **Parks/recreation:** Exercise sciences, facilities management. **Philosophy/religion:** Judaic, philosophy, religion. **Physical sciences:** Astronomy, atmospheric science, chemistry, geology, physics. **Protective services:** Forensics, law enforcement admin. **Psychology:** General. **Science technology:** Biological. **Social sciences:** Anthropology, archaeology, economics, geography, international economic development, international relations, political science, sociology. **Visual/performing arts:** General, acting, art, art history/conservation, film/cinema, graphic design, theater design. **Other:** Design and applied arts, Rehabilitation and therapeutic studies, Security and protective services.

Most popular majors. Business/marketing 39%, communications/journalism 14%, computer/information sciences 19%, engineering/engineering technologies 11%, psychology 17%.

Computing on campus. 265 workstations in computer center. Commuter students can connect to campus network. Online course registration, online library, helpline, repair service, student web hosting, wireless network available.

Student life. Freshman orientation: Mandatory, $25 fee. Preregistration for classes offered. 2-day program held prior to beginning of classes. **Policies:** Acts of intolerance and high-risk drinking discouraged at all locations. All facilities designated as smoke-free. Students expected to abide by The Penn State Principles. **Activities:** Jazz band, choral groups, dance, drama, literary magazine, musical theater, student government, student newspaper, multicultural club, Society of Women Engineers, Spanish culture club.

Athletics. Intercollegiate: Basketball, cheerleading, golf, volleyball W. **Intramural:** Basketball, football (non-tackle), racquetball, soccer, softball, table tennis, volleyball. **Team name:** Nittany Lions.

Student services. Adult student services, alcohol/substance abuse counseling, chaplain/spiritual director, career counseling, services for economically disadvantaged, student employment services, financial aid counseling, health services, minority student services, placement for graduates, veterans' counselor, women's services. **Physically disabled:** Services for visually, speech, hearing impaired.

Contact. E-mail: nkadmissions@psu.edu
Phone: (724) 334-5466 Toll-free number: (888) 968-7297
Fax: (724) 334-6111
Anne Rohrbach, Executive Director for Undergraduate Admissions, Penn State New Kensington, 201 Shields Building, University Park, PA 16802-1294

Penn State Schuylkill

Schuylkill Haven, Pennsylvania
www.sl.psu.edu **CB code: 2660**

- Public 4-year branch campus college
- Residential campus in small town
- 905 degree-seeking undergraduates: 9% part-time, 55% women, 33% African American, 3% Asian American, 3% Hispanic American
- 14 degree-seeking graduate students
- 78% of applicants admitted
- SAT or ACT with writing required
- 50% graduate within 6 years

General. Founded in 1934. Regionally accredited. **Degrees:** 52 bachelor's, 26 associate awarded; master's offered. **Location:** 4 miles from Pottsville. **Calendar:** Semester, limited summer session. **Full-time faculty:** 42 total; 71% have terminal degrees, 5% minority, 40% women. **Part-time faculty:** 26 total; 15% have terminal degrees, 8% minority, 46% women. **Class size:** 41% < 20, 52% 20-39, 6% 40-49, 1% 50-99, less than 1% >100.

Freshman class profile. 972 applied, 756 admitted, 371 enrolled.

Mid 50% test scores		**GPA 2.0-2.99:**	65%
SAT critical reading:	380-490	**Rank in top quarter:**	24%
SAT math:	380-500	**Rank in top tenth:**	5%
GPA 3.75 or higher:	2%	**Return as sophomores:**	79%
GPA 3.50-3.74:	4%	**Out-of-state:**	26%
GPA 3.0-3.49:	28%		

Basis for selection. Admission decisions based upon high school GPA, standardized test scores, class rank, personal statements, and activities. Essay considered if submitted; portfolios required for select majors. **Homeschooled:** Complete documentation showing courses studied and all evaluations presented from evaluator or supervisor assigned to student in cooperation with local school district or evaluator approved through program.

High school preparation. College-preparatory program recommended. Required units include English 4, mathematics 3, social studies 3, science 3 and foreign language 2.

2008-2009 Annual costs. Tuition/fees: $11,700; $17,490 out-of-state. Books/supplies: $1,264. Personal expenses: $1,854.

2007-2008 Financial aid. Need-based: 315 full-time freshmen applied for aid; 270 were judged to have need; 267 of these received aid. Average need met was 59%. Average scholarship/grant was $6,478; average loan $3,448. 52% of total undergraduate aid awarded as scholarships/grants, 48% as loans/jobs. **Non-need-based:** Awarded to 264 full-time undergraduates, including 162 freshmen. Scholarships awarded for academics, alumni affiliation, athletics, ROTC.

Application procedures. Admission: Priority date 11/30; no deadline. $50 fee, may be waived for applicants with need. Admission notification on a rolling basis beginning on or about 11/1. Must reply by May 1 or within 2 week(s) if notified thereafter. All freshmen applications processed at University Park Campus. **Financial aid:** Priority date 2/15; no closing date. FAFSA required. Applicants notified on a rolling basis starting 3/1.

Academics. Special study options: Accelerated study, cooperative education, distance learning, double major, dual enrollment of high school students, honors, independent study, internships, student-designed major, study abroad. **Credit/placement by examination:** AP, CLEP, IB, SAT. 60 credit hours maximum toward bachelor's degree. **Support services:** Learning center, study skills assistance, tutoring, writing center.

Majors. Agriculture: General, agribusiness operations, agronomy, animal sciences, business, education services, food science, horticultural science, landscaping, mechanization, soil science, turf management. **Area/ethnic studies:** African-American, East Asian, Latin American, women's. **Biology:** General, bacteriology, biochemistry, biomedical sciences, pathology, toxicology. **Business:** Accounting, actuarial science, business admin, finance, hospitality admin, labor relations, management information systems, managerial economics, marketing, organizational behavior. **Communications:** General, advertising, journalism. **Computer sciences:** General, information systems. **Conservation:** General, forest sciences, forest technology. **Education:** Adult/continuing, art, elementary, evaluation, foreign languages, secondary, special. **Engineering:** Aerospace, architectural, biomedical, chemical, civil, computer, electrical, environmental, industrial, materials science, mechanical, mining, nuclear, petroleum, science. **Engineering technology:** Electrical. **Family/consumer sciences:** Family studies, human nutrition. **Foreign languages:** Classics, comparative lit, French, German, Italian, Japanese, Russian, Spanish. **Health:** Communication disorders, health care admin, nursing (RN), premedicine. **History:** General. **Interdisciplinary:** Biological/physical sciences, medieval/Renaissance. **Liberal arts:** Arts/sciences, humanities. **Math:** General, statistics. **Parks/recreation:** Exercise sciences, facilities management. **Philosophy/religion:** Judaic, philosophy, religion. **Physical sciences:** Astronomy, atmospheric science, chemistry, geology, physics. **Protective services:** Criminal justice, forensics, law enforcement admin. **Psychology:** General. **Science technology:** Biological. **Social sciences:** Anthropology, archaeology, economics, geography, international economic development, international relations, political science, sociology. **Visual/performing arts:** General, acting, art, art history/conservation, film/cinema, graphic design, theater design. **Other:** Design and applied arts, Rehabilitation and therapeutic studies, Security and protective services.

Most popular majors. Business/marketing 33%, psychology 34%, security/protective services 29%.

Computing on campus. 165 workstations in computer center, student center. Dormitories wired for high-speed internet access and linked to campus network. Commuter students can connect to campus network. Online course registration, online library, helpline, repair service, student web hosting, wireless network available.

Student life. Freshman orientation: Available. Preregistration for classes offered. 3-day program held prior to start of classes. **Policies:** Acts of intolerance and high-risk drinking discouraged at all locations. All facilities designated as smoke-free. Students expected to abide by The Penn State Principles. **Housing:** $100 partly refundable deposit. **Activities:** Campus ministries, choral groups, dance, drama, musical theater, student government, student newspaper, Campus Crusade for Christ, criminal justice club, religious and philosophical forum, united minority leaders, Keystone honor society.

Athletics. Intercollegiate: Basketball, cross-country, golf M, soccer M, softball W, volleyball W. **Intramural:** Basketball, football (non-tackle) M, soccer, softball, table tennis, volleyball. **Team name:** Nittany Lions.

Student services. Adult student services, career counseling, services for economically disadvantaged, student employment services, financial aid counseling, health services, minority student services, personal counseling, placement for graduates, veterans' counselor. **Physically disabled:** Services for visually impaired.

Contact. E-mail: sl-admissions@psu.edu
Phone: (570) 385-6252 Fax: (570) 385-6272
Anne Rohrbach, Executive Director for Undergraduate Admissions, Penn State Schuylkill, 201 Shields Building, University Park, PA 16802-1294

Penn State Shenango

Sharon, Pennsylvania
www.shenango.psu.edu **CB code: 2660**

- Public 4-year branch campus college
- Commuter campus in large town
- 641 degree-seeking undergraduates: 28% part-time, 68% women, 7% African American, 1% Hispanic American
- 85% of applicants admitted
- SAT or ACT with writing required
- 34% graduate within 6 years

General. Founded in 1965. Regionally accredited. **Degrees:** 50 bachelor's, 50 associate awarded; master's offered. **Location:** 17 miles from Youngstown, Ohio. **Calendar:** Semester, limited summer session. **Full-time faculty:** 27 total; 48% have terminal degrees, 11% minority, 41% women. **Part-time faculty:** 44 total; 16% have terminal degrees, 4% minority, 48% women. **Class size:** 64% < 20, 31% 20-39, 4% 40-49, 1% 50-99. **Special facilities:** Scanning electron microscope.

Freshman class profile. 247 applied, 209 admitted, 139 enrolled.

Mid 50% test scores		**GPA 2.0-2.99:**	54%
SAT critical reading:	420-500	**Rank in top quarter:**	19%
SAT math:	390-490	**Rank in top tenth:**	4%
GPA 3.75 or higher:	5%	**Return as sophomores:**	66%
GPA 3.50-3.74:	9%	**Out-of-state:**	12%
GPA 3.0-3.49:	30%		

Basis for selection. Admission decisions based upon GPA, as well as other factors which may include standardized verbal and math test scores, class rank, personal statements, and activities lists. Essay considered if submitted; portfolios required for select majors. **Homeschooled:** Complete documentation showing courses studied and all evaluations presented from home school evaluator or supervisor assigned to the student in cooperation with the local school district or evaluator who is approved through the program.

High school preparation. College-preparatory program recommended. Required units include English 4, mathematics 3, social studies 3, science 3 and foreign language 2.

2008-2009 Annual costs. Tuition/fees: $11,600; $17,390 out-of-state. Books/supplies: $1,264. Personal expenses: $1,854.

2007-2008 Financial aid. Need-based: 125 full-time freshmen applied for aid; 111 were judged to have need; 111 of these received aid. Average need met was 64%. Average scholarship/grant was $5,651; average loan $3,405. 47% of total undergraduate aid awarded as scholarships/grants, 53% as loans/jobs. **Non-need-based:** Awarded to 184 full-time undergraduates, including 72 freshmen. Scholarships awarded for academics, alumni affiliation, athletics, ROTC.

Application procedures. Admission: Priority date 11/30; no deadline. $50 fee, may be waived for applicants with need. Admission notification on a rolling basis beginning on or about 11/1. Must reply by May 1 or within 2 week(s) if notified thereafter. All freshmen applications processed at University Park Campus. **Financial aid:** Priority date 2/15; no closing date. FAFSA required. Applicants notified on a rolling basis starting 3/1.

Academics. Special study options: Accelerated study, cross-registration, distance learning, double major, dual enrollment of high school students, honors, independent study, internships, student-designed major, study abroad. **Credit/placement by examination:** AP, CLEP, IB, SAT. 60 credit hours maximum toward bachelor's degree. **Support services:** Learning center, remedial instruction, study skills assistance, tutoring, writing center.

Majors. Agriculture: General, agribusiness operations, agronomy, animal sciences, business, education services, food science, horticultural science, landscaping, mechanization, soil science, turf management. **Area/ethnic studies:** African-American, East Asian, Latin American, women's. **Biology:** General, bacteriology, biochemistry, biomedical sciences, pathology, toxicology. **Business:** Accounting, actuarial science, business admin, finance, hospitality admin, labor relations, management information systems, managerial economics, marketing, organizational behavior. **Communications:** General, advertising, journalism. **Computer sciences:** General, information systems. **Conservation:** General, forest sciences, forest technology. **Education:** Adult/continuing, art, elementary, evaluation, foreign languages, secondary, special. **Engineering:** General, aerospace, architectural, biomedical, chemical, civil, computer, electrical, environmental, industrial, materials science, mechanical, mining, nuclear, petroleum, science. **Engineering technology:** Electrical. **Family/consumer sciences:** Family studies, human nutrition. **Foreign languages:** Classics, comparative lit, French, German, Italian, Japanese, Russian, Spanish. **Health:** Communication disorders, health care admin, nursing (RN), premedicine. **History:** General. **Interdisciplinary:** Biological/physical sciences, medieval/Renaissance. **Liberal arts:** Arts/sciences. **Math:** General, statistics. **Parks/recreation:** Exercise sciences, facilities management. **Philosophy/religion:** Judaic, philosophy, religion. **Physical sciences:** Astronomy, atmospheric science, chemistry, geology, physics. **Protective services:** Forensics, law enforcement admin. **Psychology:** General. **Science technology:** Biological. **Social sciences:** Anthropology, archaeology, economics, geography, international economic development, international relations, political science, sociology. **Visual/performing arts:** General, acting, art, art history/conservation, film/cinema, graphic design, theater design. **Other:** Design and applied arts, Rehabilitation and therapeutic studies, Security and protective services.

Most popular majors. Business/marketing 38%, family/consumer sciences 48%, liberal arts 14%.

Computing on campus. 132 workstations in library, computer center, student center. Commuter students can connect to campus network. Online course registration, online library, helpline, repair service, student web hosting, wireless network available.

Student life. Freshman orientation: Mandatory. Preregistration for classes offered. One-day program held prior to start of semester. **Policies:** Acts of intolerance and high-risk drinking discouraged at all locations. All facilities designated as smoke-free. Students expected to abide by The Penn State Principles. **Activities:** Literary magazine, student government, environmental club, Students for Cultural Diversity, Women in Transition, Word of God Bible study club, Adults Seeking Knowledge.

Athletics. Intramural: Basketball, golf, softball, volleyball. **Team name:** Nittany Lions.

Student services. Adult student services, alcohol/substance abuse counseling, career counseling, student employment services, financial aid counseling, health services, minority student services, placement for graduates, veterans' counselor, women's services. **Physically disabled:** Services for visually, speech, hearing impaired.

Contact. E-mail: psushenango@psu.edu
Phone: (724) 983-2800 Fax: (724) 983-2820
Anne Rohrbach, Executive Director for Undergraduate Admissions, Penn State Shenango, 201 Shields Building, University Park, PA 16802-1294

Penn State University Park

University Park, Pennsylvania **CB member**
www.psu.edu **CB code: 2660**

- Public 4-year university
- Residential campus in large town
- 37,171 degree-seeking undergraduates: 2% part-time, 45% women, 4% African American, 6% Asian American, 4% Hispanic American, 3% international
- 6,164 degree-seeking graduate students
- 51% of applicants admitted
- SAT or ACT with writing required
- 85% graduate within 6 years

General. Founded in 1855. Regionally accredited. **Degrees:** 9,442 bachelor's, 102 associate awarded; master's, doctoral, first professional offered. **ROTC:** Army, Naval, Air Force. **Location:** 90 miles from Harrisburg. **Calendar:** Semester, extensive summer session. **Full-time faculty:** 2,392 total; 77% have terminal degrees, 19% minority, 37% women. **Part-time faculty:** 353 total; 31% have terminal degrees, 7% minority, 49% women. **Class size:** 33% < 20, 42% 20-39, 8% 40-49, 10% 50-99, 8% >100. **Special facilities:** Art museum, earth and mineral science museum and art gallery, anthropology museum, entomological museum, sports museum, land-grant frescoes, agricultural museum, Pennsylvania space grant consortium.

Freshman class profile. 39,089 applied, 20,011 admitted, 7,241 enrolled.

Mid 50% test scores		**GPA 2.0-2.99:**	4%
SAT critical reading:	530-630	**Rank in top quarter:**	81%
SAT math:	570-670	**Rank in top tenth:**	43%
GPA 3.75 or higher:	30%	**Return as sophomores:**	92%
GPA 3.50-3.74:	33%	**Out-of-state:**	34%
GPA 3.0-3.49:	33%	**International:**	6%

Basis for selection. Admission decisions based upon high school GPA, standardized test scores, class rank, personal statements, and activities. Essay considered if submitted; portfolios required for select majors. **Homeschooled:** Complete documentation showing courses studied and all evaluations presented from evaluator or supervisor assigned to student in cooperation with local school district or evaluator approved through program.

High school preparation. College-preparatory program recommended. Required units include English 4, mathematics 3, social studies 3, science 3 and foreign language 2. 3 units required in arts and humanities. Additional requirements for some programs.

2008-2009 Annual costs. Tuition/fees: $13,706; $24,940 out-of-state. Room/board: $8,270. Books/supplies: $1,264. Personal expenses: $2,916.

2007-2008 Financial aid. Need-based: 4,805 full-time freshmen applied for aid; 3,110 were judged to have need; 2,929 of these received aid. Average need met was 61%. Average scholarship/grant was $6,266; average loan $3,492. 39% of total undergraduate aid awarded as scholarships/grants, 61% as loans/jobs. **Non-need-based:** Awarded to 9,017 full-time undergraduates, including 1,926 freshmen. Scholarships awarded for academics, alumni affiliation, athletics, ROTC.

Application procedures. Admission: Priority date 11/30; no deadline. $50 fee, may be waived for applicants with need. Admission notification on a rolling basis beginning on or about 11/1. Must reply by May 1 or within 2 week(s) if notified thereafter. **Financial aid:** Priority date 2/15; no closing date. FAFSA required. Applicants notified on a rolling basis starting 3/1.

Academics. Special study options: Accelerated study, combined bachelor's/graduate degree, cooperative education, cross-registration, distance learning, double major, dual enrollment of high school students, ESL, exchange student, external degree, honors, independent study, internships, liberal arts/career combination, student-designed major, study abroad, teacher certification program, Washington semester, weekend college. **Credit/placement by examination:** AP, CLEP, IB, SAT, institutional tests. 60 credit hours maximum toward bachelor's degree. **Support services:** Learning center, pre-admission summer program, study skills assistance, tutoring, writing center.

Honors college/program. Schreyer Scholars represent the top 5% of students at Penn State, and therefore should also be at the top of their respective high school class. The Schreyer Honors College does not set a minimum standardized test score or grade point average for its applicants. Candidates will be assessed based on the academic and extracurricular documents submitted with the application, as well as responses to essay questions and letters of recommendation.

Majors. Agriculture: General, agribusiness operations, agronomy, animal sciences, education services, food science, horticultural science, landscaping, mechanization, soil science, turf management. **Architecture:** Architecture, landscape. **Area/ethnic studies:** African-American, East Asian, Latin American, women's. **Biology:** General, bacteriology, biochemistry, biomedical sciences, pathology, toxicology. **Business:** Accounting, actuarial science, finance, hospitality admin, labor relations, management information systems, managerial economics, marketing, organizational behavior. **Communications:** General, advertising, journalism. **Computer sciences:** General, information systems. **Conservation:** General, forest sciences, forest technology. **Education:** Adult/continuing, art, elementary, evaluation, foreign languages, music, secondary, special. **Engineering:** General, aerospace, architectural, biomedical, chemical, civil, computer, electrical, environmental, industrial, materials science, mechanical, mining, nuclear, petroleum, science. **Engineering technology:** Electrical. **Family/consumer sciences:** Family studies, human nutrition. **Foreign languages:** Classics, comparative lit, French, German, Italian, Japanese, Russian, Spanish. **Health:** Communication disorders, health care admin, nursing (RN), premedicine. **History:** General. **Interdisciplinary:** Biological/physical sciences, medieval/Renaissance. **Liberal arts:** Arts/sciences. **Math:** General, statistics. **Parks/recreation:** Exercise sciences, facilities management. **Philosophy/religion:** Judaic, philosophy, religion. **Physical sciences:** Astronomy, atmospheric science, chemistry, geology, physics. **Protective services:** Criminal justice, forensics, law enforcement admin. **Psychology:** General. **Science technology:** Biological. **Social sciences:** Anthropology, archaeology, economics, geography, international economic development, international relations, political science, sociology. **Visual/performing arts:** General, acting, art, art history/conservation, film/cinema, graphic design, music performance, theater design. **Other:** Design and applied arts, Rehabilitation and therapeutic, Security and protective services, Women's studies.

Most popular majors. Business/marketing 17%, communications/journalism 9%, education 6%, engineering/engineering technologies 14%, health sciences 6%, social sciences 7%.

Computing on campus. 6,150 workstations in dormitories, library, computer center, student center. Dormitories wired for high-speed internet access and linked to campus network. Commuter students can connect to campus network. Online course registration, online library, helpline, repair service, student web hosting, wireless network available.

Student life. Freshman orientation: Mandatory. Preregistration for classes offered. Held the 2 days prior to start of classes. **Policies:** Acts of intolerance and high-risk drinking discouraged at all locations. All facilites designated as smoke-free. **Housing:** Coed dorms, single-sex dorms, special housing for disabled, apartments, fraternity/sorority housing, wellness housing available. $100 partly refundable deposit, deadline 5/1. Suites, special interest housing available. **Activities:** Bands, campus ministries, choral groups, dance, drama, film society, international student organizations, literary magazine, music ensembles, Model UN, musical theater, opera, radio station, student government, student newspaper, symphony orchestra, TV station, adult learners, eco-action, Habitat for Humanity, minorities in agriculture and natural resources, National Society of Black Engineers, College Democrats, College Libertarians, Womyn's Concerns, Black Caucus, Alliance Christian Fellowship.

Athletics. NCAA. **Intercollegiate:** Baseball M, basketball, cheerleading, cross-country, diving, fencing, field hockey W, football (tackle) M, golf, gymnastics, lacrosse, soccer, softball W, swimming, tennis, track and field, volleyball, wrestling M. **Intramural:** Badminton, basketball, bowling, cross-country, diving, football (non-tackle), football (tackle), golf, gymnastics, racquetball, soccer, softball, squash, swimming, tennis, track and field, volleyball, wrestling. **Team name:** Nittany Lions.

Student services. Adult student services, alcohol/substance abuse counseling, chaplain/spiritual director, career counseling, services for economically disadvantaged, student employment services, financial aid counseling, health services, legal services, minority student services, on-campus daycare, personal counseling, placement for graduates, veterans' counselor, women's services. **Physically disabled:** Services for visually, speech, hearing impaired.

Contact. E-mail: admissions@psu.edu
Phone: (814) 865-5471 Fax: (814) 863-7590
Anne Rohrbach, Executive Director for Undergraduate Admissions, Penn State University Park, 201 Shields Building, University Park, PA 16802-1294

Penn State Wilkes-Barre

Lehman, Pennsylvania
www.wb.psu.edu **CB code: 2660**

- Public 4-year branch campus college
- Commuter campus in small city
- 534 degree-seeking undergraduates: 9% part-time, 31% women, 3% African American, 3% Asian American, 1% Hispanic American
- 65 graduate students
- 85% of applicants admitted
- SAT or ACT with writing required
- 48% graduate within 6 years

General. Founded in 1916. Regionally accredited. **Degrees:** 73 bachelor's, 25 associate awarded; master's offered. **ROTC:** Army, Air Force. **Location:** 10 miles from Wilkes-Barre. **Calendar:** Semester, limited summer session. **Full-time faculty:** 36 total; 58% have terminal degrees, 17% minority, 17% women. **Part-time faculty:** 27 total; 15% have terminal degrees, 52% women. **Class size:** 62% < 20, 36% 20-39, 2% 40-49, less than 1% 50-99.

Freshman class profile. 640 applied, 546 admitted, 179 enrolled.

Mid 50% test scores		**GPA 2.0-2.99:**	49%
SAT critical reading:	420-550	**Rank in top quarter:**	31%
SAT math:	430-570	**Rank in top tenth:**	12%
GPA 3.75 or higher:	2%	**Return as sophomores:**	76%
GPA 3.50-3.74:	11%	**Out-of-state:**	7%
GPA 3.0-3.49:	37%		

Basis for selection. Admission decisions based upon high school GPA, standardized test scores, class rank, personal statements, and activities. Essay considered if submitted; portfolios required for select majors. **Homeschooled:** Complete documentation showing courses studied and all evaluations presented from evaluator or supervisor assigned to student in cooperation with local school district or evaluator approved through program. **Learning Disabled:** Prospective students with disabilities encouraged to contact or visit the Office for Disability Services in their junior or senior years in high school in order to find out more about disability services at the college level.

High school preparation. College-preparatory program recommended. Required units include English 4, mathematics 3, social studies 3, science 3 and foreign language 2.

2008-2009 Annual costs. Tuition/fees: $11,700; $17,490 out-of-state. Books/supplies: $1,264. Personal expenses: $1,854.

2007-2008 Financial aid. Need-based: 165 full-time freshmen applied for aid; 125 were judged to have need; 124 of these received aid. Average need met was 64%. Average scholarship/grant was $5,458; average loan

$3,042. 50% of total undergraduate aid awarded as scholarships/grants, 50% as loans/jobs. **Non-need-based:** Awarded to 205 full-time undergraduates, including 98 freshmen. Scholarships awarded for academics, alumni affiliation, athletics, ROTC.

Application procedures. Admission: Priority date 11/30; no deadline. $50 fee, may be waived for applicants with need. Admission notification on a rolling basis beginning on or about 11/30. Must reply by May 1 or within 2 week(s) if notified thereafter. All freshmen applications processed at University Park Campus. **Financial aid:** Priority date 2/15; no closing date. FAFSA required. Applicants notified on a rolling basis starting 3/1.

Academics. Special study options: Accelerated study, cross-registration, distance learning, double major, dual enrollment of high school students, honors, independent study, internships, student-designed major, study abroad. **Credit/placement by examination:** AP, CLEP, IB, SAT. 60 credit hours maximum toward bachelor's degree. **Support services:** Learning center, study skills assistance, tutoring, writing center.

Majors. Agriculture: General, agribusiness operations, agronomy, animal sciences, education services, food science, horticultural science, landscaping, mechanization, soil science, turf management. **Area/ethnic studies:** African-American, East Asian, Latin American, women's. **Biology:** General, bacteriology, biochemistry, biomedical sciences, pathology, toxicology. **Business:** Accounting, actuarial science, business admin, finance, hospitality admin, labor relations, management information systems, managerial economics, marketing, organizational behavior. **Communications:** General, advertising, journalism. **Computer sciences:** General, information systems. **Conservation:** General, forest sciences, forest technology. **Education:** Adult/continuing, art, elementary, evaluation, foreign languages, secondary, special. **Engineering:** General, aerospace, architectural, biomedical, chemical, civil, computer, electrical, environmental, industrial, materials science, mechanical, mining, nuclear, petroleum, science, surveying. **Engineering technology:** Electrical. **Family/consumer sciences:** Family studies, human nutrition. **Foreign languages:** Classics, comparative lit, French, German, Italian, Japanese, Russian, Spanish. **Health:** Communication disorders, health care admin, nursing (RN), premedicine. **History:** General. **Interdisciplinary:** Biological/physical sciences, medieval/Renaissance. **Liberal arts:** Arts/sciences. **Math:** General, statistics. **Parks/recreation:** General, exercise sciences. **Philosophy/religion:** Judaic, philosophy, religion. **Physical sciences:** Astronomy, atmospheric science, chemistry, geology, physics. **Protective services:** Criminal justice, forensics, law enforcement admin. **Psychology:** General. **Science technology:** Biological. **Social sciences:** Anthropology, archaeology, economics, geography, international economic development, international relations, political science, sociology. **Visual/performing arts:** General, acting, art, art history/conservation, film/cinema, graphic design, theater design. **Other:** Design and applied arts, Rehabilitation and therapeutic studies, Security and protective services.

Most popular majors. Business/marketing 32%, computer/information sciences 12%, liberal arts 14%, security/protective services 38%.

Computing on campus. 196 workstations in library, computer center, student center. Commuter students can connect to campus network. Online course registration, online library, helpline, repair service, student web hosting, wireless network available.

Student life. Freshman orientation: Mandatory. Preregistration for classes offered. One-day session held prior to start of classes. **Policies:** Acts of intolerance and high-risk drinking discouraged at all locations. All facilities designated smoke-free. Students expected to abide by The Penn State Principles. **Activities:** Dance, Model UN, radio station, student government, student newspaper, students for justice club.

Athletics. Intercollegiate: Baseball M, basketball M, cross-country, golf, soccer, volleyball W. **Intramural:** Basketball, football (tackle), racquetball, softball, volleyball. **Team name:** Nittany Lions.

Student services. Adult student services, alcohol/substance abuse counseling, chaplain/spiritual director, career counseling, services for economically disadvantaged, student employment services, financial aid counseling, health services, minority student services, personal counseling, placement for graduates. **Physically disabled:** Services for visually, hearing impaired.

Contact. E-mail: wbadmissions@psu.edu
Phone: (570) 675-9238 Toll-free number: (800) 966-6613
Fax: (570) 675-9113
Anne Rohrbach, Executive Director for Undergraduate Admissions, Penn State Wilkes-Barre, 201 Shields Building, University Park, PA 16802-1294

Penn State Worthington Scranton

Dunmore, Pennsylvania
www.sn.psu.edu **CB code: 2660**

- Public 4-year branch campus college
- Commuter campus in large town
- 1,222 degree-seeking undergraduates: 16% part-time, 53% women, 1% African American, 1% Asian American, 3% Hispanic American
- 83% of applicants admitted
- SAT or ACT with writing required
- 40% graduate within 6 years

General. Founded in 1923. Regionally accredited. **Degrees:** 98 bachelor's, 55 associate awarded; master's offered. **ROTC:** Army, Air Force. **Location:** One mile from Scranton. **Calendar:** Semester, limited summer session. **Full-time faculty:** 57 total; 61% have terminal degrees, 16% minority, 53% women. **Part-time faculty:** 48 total; 17% have terminal degrees, 4% minority, 60% women. **Class size:** 40% < 20, 54% 20-39, 3% 40-49, 2% 50-99.

Freshman class profile. 837 applied, 695 admitted, 330 enrolled.

Mid 50% test scores		**GPA 2.0-2.99:**	56%
SAT critical reading:	420-520	**Rank in top quarter:**	23%
SAT math:	410-530	**Rank in top tenth:**	7%
GPA 3.75 or higher:	3%	**Return as sophomores:**	74%
GPA 3.50-3.74:	9%	**Out-of-state:**	2%
GPA 3.0-3.49:	31%		

Basis for selection. Admission decisions based upon high school GPA, as well as other factors, which may include standardized verbal and math test scores, class rank, personal statements, and list of activities. Essay considered if submitted; portfolios required for select majors. **Homeschooled:** Provide complete documentation showing courses studied and all evaluations presented from evaluator or supervisor assigned to student in cooperation with local school district or evaluator who is approved through the program.

High school preparation. College-preparatory program recommended. Required units include English 4, mathematics 3, social studies 3, science 3 and foreign language 2.

2008-2009 Annual costs. Tuition/fees: $11,660; $17,450 out-of-state. Books/supplies: $1,168. Personal expenses: $1,854.

2007-2008 Financial aid. Need-based: 275 full-time freshmen applied for aid; 226 were judged to have need; 221 of these received aid. Average need met was 65%. Average scholarship/grant was $5,185; average loan $3,220. 45% of total undergraduate aid awarded as scholarships/grants, 55% as loans/jobs. **Non-need-based:** Awarded to 212 full-time undergraduates, including 106 freshmen. Scholarships awarded for academics, alumni affiliation, athletics, ROTC.

Application procedures. Admission: Priority date 11/30; no deadline. $50 fee, may be waived for applicants with need. Admission notification on a rolling basis beginning on or about 11/1. Must reply by May 1 or within 2 week(s) if notified thereafter. All freshmen applications processed at University Park Campus. **Financial aid:** Priority date 2/15; no closing date. FAFSA required. Applicants notified on a rolling basis starting 3/1.

Academics. Special study options: Accelerated study, cooperative education, cross-registration, distance learning, double major, dual enrollment of high school students, honors, independent study, internships, study abroad. **Credit/placement by examination:** AP, CLEP, IB, SAT. 60 credit hours maximum toward bachelor's degree. **Support services:** Learning center, remedial instruction, study skills assistance, tutoring, writing center.

Majors. Agriculture: General, agribusiness operations, agronomy, animal sciences, education services, food science, horticultural science, landscaping, mechanization, soil science, turf management. **Area/ethnic studies:** African-American, American, East Asian, Latin American, women's. **Biology:** General, bacteriology, biochemistry, biomedical sciences. **Business:** Accounting, actuarial science, business admin, finance, hospitality admin, labor relations, management information systems, managerial economics, marketing, organizational behavior. **Communications:** General, advertising, journalism. **Computer sciences:** General, information systems. **Conservation:** General, forest sciences, forest technology. **Education:** Art, elementary, evaluation, foreign languages, secondary, special. **Engineering:** General, aerospace, architectural, biomedical, chemical, civil, computer, electrical, environmental, industrial, materials science, mechanical, mining, nuclear, petroleum, science. **Engineering technology:** Electrical. **Family/consumer sciences:** Family studies, human nutrition. **Foreign languages:** Classics, comparative lit, French, German, Italian, Japanese, Russian, Spanish. **Health:** Communication disorders, health care admin, nursing (RN), premedicine. **History:** General. **Interdisciplinary:** Biological/physical sciences, medieval/Renaissance. **Liberal arts:** Arts/sciences. **Math:** General, statistics. **Parks/recreation:** Exercise sciences, facilities management. **Philosophy/religion:** Judaic, philosophy, religion. **Physical sciences:** Astronomy, atmospheric science, chemistry, geology, physics. **Protective services:** Forensics, law enforcement admin. **Psychology:** General. **Science technology:** Biological. **Social sciences:** Anthropology, archaeology, economics, geography, international economic development, international relations, political science, sociology. **Visual/performing arts:** General, acting, art, art history/conservation, film/cinema, graphic design, theater design. **Other:** Adult and continuing education, Design and applied arts, Rehabilitation and therapeutic studies, Security and protective services.

Most popular majors. Business/marketing 64%, computer/information sciences 15%, family/consumer sciences 11%.

Computing on campus. 180 workstations in library, computer center, student center. Commuter students can connect to campus network. Online course registration, online library, helpline, repair service, student web hosting, wireless network available.

Student life. Freshman orientation: Available. Preregistration for classes offered. **Policies:** Acts of intolerance and high-risk drinking discouraged at all locations. All facilities designated as smoke-free. Students expected to abide by The Penn State Principles. **Activities:** Jazz band, choral groups, drama, literary magazine, music ensembles, student government, student newspaper, community human service organization, Faith and Values, German club, Lighthouse club, multicultural club, veterans club, public affairs club.

Athletics. Intercollegiate: Baseball M, basketball, cross-country, soccer M, softball W. **Intramural:** Basketball, soccer, softball, volleyball, weight lifting. **Team name:** Nittany Lions.

Student services. Adult student services, alcohol/substance abuse counseling, career counseling, services for economically disadvantaged, student employment services, financial aid counseling, health services, personal counseling, placement for graduates, veterans' counselor, women's services. **Physically disabled:** Services for visually, speech, hearing impaired.

Contact. E-mail: wsadmissions@psu.edu
Phone: (570) 963-2500 Fax: (570) 963-2524
Anne Rohrbach, Executive Director for Undergraduate Admissions, Penn State Worthington Scranton, 201 Shields Building, University Park, PA 16802-1294

Penn State York

York, Pennsylvania
www.yk.psu.edu **CB code: 2660**

- Public 4-year branch campus college
- Commuter campus in large town
- 1,149 degree-seeking undergraduates: 24% part-time, 44% women, 6% African American, 5% Asian American, 5% Hispanic American, 1% international
- 116 degree-seeking graduate students
- 82% of applicants admitted
- SAT or ACT with writing required
- 39% graduate within 6 years

General. Founded in 1926. Regionally accredited. **Degrees:** 89 bachelor's, 62 associate awarded; master's offered. **Calendar:** Semester, extensive summer session. **Full-time faculty:** 58 total; 59% have terminal degrees, 17% minority, 33% women. **Part-time faculty:** 57 total; 18% have terminal degrees, 2% minority, 49% women. **Class size:** 59% < 20, 37% 20-39, 2% 40-49, 2% 50-99.

Freshman class profile. 1,338 applied, 1,096 admitted, 339 enrolled.

Mid 50% test scores		**GPA 2.0-2.99:**	55%
SAT critical reading:	430-540	**Rank in top quarter:**	29%
SAT math:	430-570	**Rank in top tenth:**	8%
GPA 3.75 or higher:	4%	**Return as sophomores:**	76%
GPA 3.50-3.74:	6%	**Out-of-state:**	13%
GPA 3.0-3.49:	34%	**International:**	1%

Basis for selection. Admission decisions based upon high school GPA and other factors, which may include standardized verbal and math test scores, class rank, personal statements, activities lists. Essay considered if submitted; portfolios required for select majors. **Homeschooled:** Complete documentation showing courses studied and all evaluations from home school evaluator or supervisor assigned to student in cooperation with local school district or evaluator approved through program.

High school preparation. College-preparatory program recommended. Required units include English 4, mathematics 3, social studies 3, science 3 and foreign language 2.

2008-2009 Annual costs. Tuition/fees: $11,660; $17,450 out-of-state. Books/supplies: $1,264. Personal expenses: $1,854.

2007-2008 Financial aid. Need-based: 274 full-time freshmen applied for aid; 205 were judged to have need; 200 of these received aid. Average need met was 58%. Average scholarship/grant was $4,878; average loan $3,200. 46% of total undergraduate aid awarded as scholarships/grants, 54% as loans/jobs. **Non-need-based:** Awarded to 217 full-time undergraduates, including 104 freshmen. Scholarships awarded for academics, alumni affiliation, athletics, ROTC.

Application procedures. Admission: Priority date 11/30; no deadline. $50 fee, may be waived for applicants with need. Admission notification on a rolling basis beginning on or about 11/1. Must reply by May 1 or within 2 week(s) if notified thereafter. All freshmen applications processed at University Park Campus. **Financial aid:** Priority date 2/15; no closing date. FAFSA required. Applicants notified on a rolling basis starting 3/1.

Academics. Special study options: Accelerated study, cross-registration, distance learning, double major, dual enrollment of high school students, ESL, honors, independent study, internships, student-designed major, study abroad. **Credit/placement by examination:** AP, CLEP, IB, SAT. 60 credit hours maximum toward bachelor's degree. **Support services:** Learning center, pre-admission summer program, reduced course load, remedial instruction, study skills assistance, tutoring, writing center.

Majors. Agriculture: General, agribusiness operations, agronomy, animal sciences, education services, food science, horticultural science, landscaping, mechanization, soil science, turf management. **Area/ethnic studies:** African-American, American, East Asian, Latin American, women's. **Biology:** General, bacteriology, biochemistry, biomedical sciences, pathology, toxicology. **Business:** Accounting, actuarial science, business admin, finance, hospitality admin, labor relations, management information systems, managerial economics, marketing, organizational behavior. **Communications:** General, advertising, journalism. **Computer sciences:** General, information systems. **Conservation:** General, forest sciences, forest technology. **Education:** Adult/continuing, art, elementary, evaluation, foreign languages, secondary, special. **Engineering:** General, aerospace, architectural, biomedical, chemical, civil, computer, electrical, environmental, industrial, materials science, mechanical, mining, nuclear, petroleum, science. **Engineering technology:** Electrical. **Family/consumer sciences:** Family studies, human nutrition. **Foreign languages:** Classics, comparative lit, French, German, Italian, Japanese, Russian, Spanish. **Health:** Communication disorders, health care admin, nursing (RN), premedicine. **History:** General. **Interdisciplinary:** Biological/physical sciences, medieval/Renaissance. **Liberal arts:** Arts/sciences. **Math:** General, statistics. **Parks/recreation:** Exercise sciences, facilities management. **Philosophy/religion:** Judaic, philosophy, religion. **Physical sciences:** Astronomy, atmospheric science, chemistry, geology, physics. **Protective services:** Forensics, law enforcement admin. **Psychology:** General. **Science technology:** Biological. **Social sciences:** Anthropology, archaeology, economics, geography, international economic development, international relations, political science, sociology. **Visual/performing arts:** General, acting, art, art history/conservation, film/cinema, graphic design, theater design. **Other:** Design and applied arts, Rehabilitation and therapeutic studies, Security and protective services.

Most popular majors. Business/marketing 41%, communications/journalism 8%, computer/information sciences 9%, engineering/engineering technologies 10%, English 8%, family/consumer sciences 9%, interdisciplinary studies 12%.

Computing on campus. 169 workstations in computer center. Commuter students can connect to campus network. Online course registration, online library, helpline, repair service, student web hosting, wireless network available.

Student life. Freshman orientation: Mandatory. Preregistration for classes offered. Full-day event in August. **Policies:** Acts of intolerance and high-risk drinking discouraged at all locations. All facilities designated as smoke-free. Students expected to abide by The Penn State Principles. **Housing:** Room, apartment, house rentals in the local community available. **Activities:** Campus ministries, dance, drama, international student organizations, literary magazine, Model UN, student government, student newspaper, black student union, Christian Fellowship, Hispanic students association, Rainbow Alliance, veterans club, Asian culture club, foreign policy club, debate club.

Athletics. Intercollegiate: Baseball M, basketball, soccer, tennis, volleyball. **Intramural:** Badminton, basketball, football (non-tackle) M, handball, soccer, softball, table tennis, tennis, volleyball. **Team name:** Nittany Lions.

Student services. Adult student services, alcohol/substance abuse counseling, chaplain/spiritual director, career counseling, services for economically disadvantaged, student employment services, financial aid counseling, health services, minority student services, personal counseling, placement for graduates, veterans' counselor, women's services. **Physically disabled:** Services for visually, speech, hearing impaired. **Learning disabled:** Comprehensive services available.

Contact. E-mail: ykadmissions@psu.edu
Phone: (717) 771-4040 Toll-free number: (800) 778-6227
Fax: (717) 771-4005
Anne Rohrbach, Executive Director for Undergraduate Admissions, Penn State York, 201 Shields Building, University Park, PA 16802-1294

Pennsylvania College of Art and Design

Lancaster, Pennsylvania
www.pcad.edu **CB code: 2681**

- Private 4-year visual arts college
- Commuter campus in small city
- 297 degree-seeking undergraduates: 8% part-time, 62% women, 2% African American, 3% Asian American, 4% Hispanic American, 1% Native American
- 51% of applicants admitted
- Application essay, interview required
- 30% graduate within 6 years; 5% enter graduate study

General. Regionally accredited. **Degrees:** 38 bachelor's awarded. **Location:** 75 miles from Philadelphia, 75 miles from Baltimore. **Calendar:** Semester, limited summer session. **Full-time faculty:** 14 total; 7% minority, 29% women. **Part-time faculty:** 33 total; 33% women. **Class size:** 86% < 20, 13% 20-39, less than 1% 40-49. **Special facilities:** Visual arts gallery.

Freshman class profile. 293 applied, 150 admitted, 97 enrolled.

GPA 3.75 or higher:	13%	**End year in good standing:**	83%
GPA 3.50-3.74:	20%	**Return as sophomores:**	70%
GPA 3.0-3.49:	15%	**Out-of-state:**	25%
GPA 2.0-2.99:	50%		

Basis for selection. Portfolio review, interview, personal statement, and high school transcripts required. Students with a GPA below 2.5 are required to submit two letters of recommendation. Portfolio required. **Homeschooled:** Transcript of courses and grades, state high school equivalency certificate, interview required.

High school preparation. College-preparatory program recommended.

2008-2009 Annual costs. Tuition/fees: $16,655. Books/supplies: $1,265. Personal expenses: $1,111.

Application procedures. Admission: No deadline. $40 fee, may be waived for applicants with need. Application must be submitted on paper. Admission notification on a rolling basis. Must reply by May 1 or within 2 week(s) if notified thereafter.

Academics. Special study options: Dual enrollment of high school students, internships. **Credit/placement by examination:** AP, CLEP, institutional tests.

Majors. Visual/performing arts: Graphic design, illustration, photography, studio arts.

Computing on campus. Online library, wireless network available.

Student life. Freshman orientation: Mandatory. **Housing:** Housing referral service available. **Activities:** Student government.

Student services. Career counseling, student employment services.

Contact. E-mail: admissions@pcad.edu
Phone: (717) 396-7833 Fax: (717) 396-1339
Natalie Lascek-Speakman, Director of Admission Marketing & Recruitment, Pennsylvania College of Art and Design, PO Box 59, Lancaster, PA 17608-0059

Pennsylvania College of Technology

Williamsport, Pennsylvania **CB member**
www.pct.edu **CB code: 2989**

- Public 4-year technical college
- Commuter campus in small city
- 6,427 degree-seeking undergraduates: 13% part-time, 36% women, 3% African American, 1% Asian American, 1% Hispanic American, 1% Native American
- 50% graduate within 6 years

General. Founded in 1965. Regionally accredited. **Degrees:** 546 bachelor's, 1,109 associate awarded. **ROTC:** Army. **Location:** 85 miles from Harrisburg, 70 miles from Wilkes-Barre. **Calendar:** Semester, limited summer session. **Full-time faculty:** 297 total; 3% minority, 29% women. **Part-time faculty:** 198 total; 2% minority, 53% women. **Special facilities:** Automotive technology center, aviation center, plastics manufacturing center, community arts center, earth science center.

Freshman class profile. 3,002 applied, 2,837 admitted, 1,449 enrolled.

Basis for selection. Open admission, but selective for some programs. Competitive admissions to health science programs, using GPA, SAT scores, high school rank, selected course grades, completed developmental course work. Some programs have more specific requirements. SAT recommended for all bachelor's programs, dental hygiene, radiography, occupational therapy assistant, nursing applicants; college placement exams required for all applicants. **Homeschooled:** Transcript of courses and grades, state high school equivalency certificate required. Must provide proof of graduation from an organization governed by the State Board of Education, such as Pennsylvania Home Schoolers Accreditation Agency. Otherwise must present GED.

2008-2009 Annual costs. Tuition/fees: $11,790; $14,820 out-of-state. Room and board plans vary. Room/board: $8,250. Books/supplies: $1,000. Personal expenses: $2,450.

2007-2008 Financial aid. Non-need-based: Scholarships awarded for academics, alumni affiliation.

Application procedures. Admission: Closing date 7/1 (postmark date). $50 fee, may be waived for applicants with need. Admission notification on a rolling basis. **Financial aid:** Priority date 4/1; no closing date. FAFSA, institutional form required. Applicants notified on a rolling basis starting 6/1; must reply by 7/1 or within 4 week(s) of notification.

Academics. Special study options: Accelerated study, cooperative education, cross-registration, distance learning, dual enrollment of high school students, exchange student, honors, independent study, internships, student-designed major, study abroad, weekend college. **Credit/placement by examination:** AP, CLEP, institutional tests. 30 credit hours maximum toward associate degree, 30 toward bachelor's. **Support services:** Learning center, pre-admission summer program, remedial instruction, study skills assistance, tutoring.

Majors. Business: Accounting, business admin, management information systems. **Communications technology:** Graphic/printing. **Computer sciences:** Networking, security, web page design. **Construction:** Masonry. **Engineering technology:** General, architectural, automotive, civil, construction, electrical, heat/ac/refrig, industrial, manufacturing, mechanical, plastics. **Health:** Adult health nursing, cardiovascular technology, dental hygiene, EMT paramedic, health services, medical records admin, mental health services, surgical technology. **Legal studies:** General. **Mechanic/repair:** Avionics, electronics/electrical, heating/ac/refrig, industrial electronics. **Parks/recreation:** Exercise sciences. **Personal/culinary services:** Chef training. **Visual/performing arts:** Commercial/advertising art.

Most popular majors. Business/marketing 18%, computer/information sciences 19%, engineering/engineering technologies 36%, health sciences 14%.

Computing on campus. 2,200 workstations in dormitories, library, computer center, student center. Dormitories wired for high-speed internet access and linked to campus network. Commuter students can connect to campus network. Online course registration, online library, helpline, student web hosting, wireless network available.

Student life. Freshman orientation: Available. Preregistration for classes offered. 2-day sessions offered throughout summer. **Policies:** No alcohol or illegal drugs on campus. Smoke-free buildings and housing environments. **Housing:** Coed dorms, wellness housing available. $300 partly refundable deposit. **Activities:** Campus ministries, dance, international student organizations, radio station, student government, Alpha Omega Fellowship, Campus Crusade for Christ, Earth Smart, human services club, multicultural society, occupational therapy assistant club, physicians assistant club, Skills USA, student nurses association.

Athletics. USCAA. **Intercollegiate:** Archery, baseball M, basketball, bowling, cross-country, golf, soccer, softball W, tennis, volleyball. **Intramural:** Archery, badminton, basketball, bowling, football (non-tackle), golf, lacrosse, racquetball, soccer, softball, table tennis, tennis, volleyball, weight lifting, wrestling M. **Team name:** Wildcats.

Student services. Adult student services, alcohol/substance abuse counseling, career counseling, student employment services, financial aid counseling, health services, on-campus daycare, personal counseling, placement for graduates, veterans' counselor, women's services. **Physically disabled:** Services for visually, speech, hearing impaired.

Contact. E-mail: admissions@pct.edu
Phone: (570) 327-4761 Toll-free number: (800) 367-9222
Fax: (570) 321-5551
Dennis Correll, Associate Dean for Admissions and Financial Aid, Pennsylvania College of Technology, One College Avenue, Williamsport, PA 17701

Philadelphia Biblical University

Langhorne, Pennsylvania
www.pbu.edu **CB code: 2661**

- Private 4-year university and Bible college affiliated with Protestant Evangelical tradition
- Residential campus in small town
- 1,049 degree-seeking undergraduates: 6% part-time, 55% women, 12% African American, 4% Asian American, 3% Hispanic American, 2% international
- 293 degree-seeking graduate students
- 94% of applicants admitted
- SAT or ACT (ACT writing optional), application essay required
- 52% graduate within 6 years; 31% enter graduate study

General. Founded in 1913. Regionally accredited; also accredited by ABHE. **Degrees:** 264 bachelor's awarded; master's, first professional offered. **ROTC:** Air Force. **Location:** 17 miles from Philadelphia; 5 miles from Trenton, New Jersey. **Calendar:** Semester, limited summer session. **Full-time faculty:** 55 total; 66% have terminal degrees, 13% minority, 33% women. **Part-time faculty:** 74 total; 18% have terminal degrees, 8% minority, 34% women. **Class size:** 59% < 20, 36% 20-39, 2% 40-49, 2% 50-99. **Special facilities:** Wooded walking trail.

Freshman class profile. 387 applied, 363 admitted, 197 enrolled.

Mid 50% test scores			
SAT critical reading:	480-580	Rank in top quarter:	38%
SAT math:	460-560	Rank in top tenth:	11%
ACT composite:	21-26	End year in good standing:	99%
GPA 3.75 or higher:	27%	Return as sophomores:	83%
GPA 3.50-3.74:	20%	Out-of-state:	48%
GPA 3.0-3.49:	27%	Live on campus:	90%
GPA 2.0-2.99:	24%	International:	1%

Basis for selection. High school GPA, pastor's references, autobiography, SAT or ACT scores required for some. Some applicants not meeting academic admissions requirements may be admitted and placed in remedial program. Interview recommended for all; audition required for music program. **Homeschooled:** Letter of recommendation (nonparent) required.

High school preparation. College-preparatory program recommended. 15 units recommended. Recommended units include English 4, mathematics 1, social studies 3, science 2 and foreign language 2.

2008-2009 Annual costs. Tuition/fees: $17,785. Room/board: $7,150. Books/supplies: $1,000. Personal expenses: $1,500.

2008-2009 Financial aid. Need-based: 151 full-time freshmen applied for aid; 137 were judged to have need; 136 of these received aid. Average need met was 71%. Average scholarship/grant was $10,474; average loan $4,000. 61% of total undergraduate aid awarded as scholarships/grants, 39% as loans/jobs. **Non-need-based:** Awarded to 112 full-time undergraduates, including 26 freshmen. Scholarships awarded for academics, leadership, minority status.

Application procedures. Admission: No deadline. $25 fee, may be waived for applicants with need. Admission notification on a rolling basis beginning on or about 7/1. **Financial aid:** Priority date 3/1; no closing date. FAFSA required. Applicants notified on a rolling basis starting 2/15.

Academics. Students may participate in semester studies in Israel. **Special study options:** Accelerated study, combined bachelor's/graduate degree, double major, honors, internships, study abroad, teacher certification program. **Credit/placement by examination:** AP, CLEP, IB, SAT, ACT, institutional tests. 12 credit hours maximum toward bachelor's degree. **Support services:** Learning center, reduced course load, remedial instruction, study skills assistance, tutoring, writing center.

Majors. Business: Business admin. **Education:** Early childhood, elementary, English, mathematics, music, physical, social studies. **Parks/recreation:** Health/fitness. **Public administration:** Social work. **Theology:** Bible, missionary, pastoral counseling, religious ed, sacred music, theology. **Visual/performing arts:** Music performance, music theory/composition.

Most popular majors. Education 11%, philosophy/religious studies 76%, public administration/social services 7%.

Computing on campus. 79 workstations in dormitories, library, student center. Dormitories wired for high-speed internet access and linked to campus network. Commuter students can connect to campus network. Online course registration, online library, helpline, wireless network available.

Student life. Freshman orientation: Mandatory. Preregistration for classes offered. **Policies:** Religious observance required. **Housing:** Guaranteed on-campus for freshmen. Single-sex dorms, special housing for disabled, apartments available. $250 deposit. **Activities:** Concert band, campus ministries, choral groups, drama, international student organizations, music ensembles, musical theater, opera, student government, student newspaper, symphony orchestra, student missionary fellowship, commuter council, resident council, student theological society, cultural awareness association, student business club, social committee.

Athletics. NCAA, NCCAA. **Intercollegiate:** Baseball M, basketball, field hockey W, golf M, soccer, softball W, tennis, volleyball. **Intramural:** Basketball, football (non-tackle), soccer, table tennis, tennis, volleyball. **Team name:** Eagles.

Student services. Alcohol/substance abuse counseling, chaplain/spiritual director, career counseling, student employment services, financial aid counseling, health services, personal counseling, placement for graduates. **Physically disabled:** Services for visually, hearing impaired.

Contact. E-mail: admissions@pbu.edu
Phone: (215) 702-4235 Toll-free number: (800) 366-0049
Fax: (215) 702-4248
Lisa Yoder, Director of Admissions, Philadelphia Biblical University, 200 Manor Avenue, Langhorne, PA 19047-2990

Philadelphia University

Philadelphia, Pennsylvania **CB member**
www.philau.edu **CB code: 2666**

- Private 4-year university
- Residential campus in very large city
- 2,768 degree-seeking undergraduates: 6% part-time, 69% women, 10% African American, 4% Asian American, 3% Hispanic American, 2% international
- 563 degree-seeking graduate students
- 69% of applicants admitted
- SAT or ACT (ACT writing optional) required
- 58% graduate within 6 years; 14% enter graduate study

General. Founded in 1884. Regionally accredited. **Degrees:** 561 bachelor's, 11 associate awarded; master's, doctoral offered. **Location:** 7 miles from Center City. **Calendar:** Semester, limited summer session. **Full-time faculty:** 111 total; 72% have terminal degrees, 12% minority, 43% women. **Part-time faculty:** 322 total; 10% minority, 41% women. **Class size:** 64% < 20, 35% 20-39, less than 1% 40-49, less than 1% 50-99. **Special facilities:** Computer-aided design laboratories in architecture, graphic design and fashion design; CAD facilities, university design center, rapid prototyping.

Freshman class profile. 3,949 applied, 2,731 admitted, 731 enrolled.

Mid 50% test scores			
SAT critical reading:	480-560	Rank in top quarter:	45%
SAT math:	490-590	Rank in top tenth:	13%
SAT writing:	470-560	End year in good standing:	95%
ACT composite:	22-26	Return as sophomores:	74%
GPA 3.75 or higher:	23%	Out-of-state:	60%
GPA 3.50-3.74:	22%	Live on campus:	92%
GPA 3.0-3.49:	37%	International:	2%
GPA 2.0-2.99:	18%	Fraternities:	1%
		Sororities:	1%

Basis for selection. Academic record, GPA, and test scores most important. Extracurricular activities, counselor's recommendation and interview considered. Interview, essay recommended.

High school preparation. College-preparatory program recommended. 15 units required; 19 recommended. Required and recommended units include English 4, mathematics 3-4, social studies 2-3, history 1-2, science 3-4 (laboratory 2), foreign language 2 and academic electives 2.

2008-2009 Annual costs. Tuition/fees: $26,700. Room/board: $8,692. Books/supplies: $1,600. Personal expenses: $1,789.

2008-2009 Financial aid. Need-based: 635 full-time freshmen applied for aid; 546 were judged to have need; 546 of these received aid. Average need met was 73%. Average scholarship/grant was $14,673; average loan

$3,853. 53% of total undergraduate aid awarded as scholarships/grants, 47% as loans/jobs. **Non-need-based:** Awarded to 851 full-time undergraduates, including 235 freshmen. Scholarships awarded for academics, athletics.

Application procedures. **Admission:** No deadline. $35 fee, may be waived for applicants with need. Admission notification on a rolling basis beginning on or about 11/1. Must reply by May 1 or within 1 week(s) if notified thereafter. **Financial aid:** Closing date 4/15. FAFSA required. Applicants notified on a rolling basis starting 2/10; must reply by 5/1.

Academics. **Special study options:** Combined bachelor's/graduate degree, distance learning, double major, honors, independent study, internships, liberal arts/career combination, semester at sea, study abroad. **Credit/placement by examination:** AP, CLEP, SAT, institutional tests. 60 credit hours maximum toward bachelor's degree. **Support services:** Learning center, reduced course load, remedial instruction, study skills assistance, tutoring, writing center.

Majors. **Architecture:** Architecture, interior, landscape. **Biology:** General, biochemistry, environmental. **Business:** Accounting, apparel, business admin, fashion, finance, international, management information systems, marketing. **Communications:** Digital media. **Communications technology:** Animation/special effects, graphics. **Conservation:** Environmental studies. **Engineering:** General, architectural, industrial, mechanical, textile. **Family/consumer sciences:** Apparel marketing, clothing/textiles, textile science. **Health:** Health care admin, premedicine. **Interdisciplinary:** Biopsychology. **Legal studies:** Prelaw. **Physical sciences:** Chemistry. **Psychology:** General. **Visual/performing arts:** Fashion design, fiber arts, graphic design, industrial design, interior design. **Other:** Professional communications.

Most popular majors. Architecture 22%, business/marketing 40%, visual/performing arts 20%.

Computing on campus. 400 workstations in library, computer center, student center. Dormitories wired for high-speed internet access and linked to campus network. Commuter students can connect to campus network. Online course registration, online library, helpline, student web hosting, wireless network available.

Student life. **Freshman orientation:** Mandatory, $100 fee. Preregistration for classes offered. Three-day residential program in summer. **Housing:** Guaranteed on-campus for freshmen. Coed dorms, single-sex dorms, special housing for disabled, apartments, wellness housing available. $250 deposit, deadline 5/1. Townhouses available. **Activities:** Campus ministries, choral groups, dance, drama, international student organizations, student government, student newspaper, professional (major-related) organizations, Black awareness society, Hillel, Christian fellowship, community service corps, Minaret, Gemini Theatre, Phila Capella, Gay Lesbian Bisexual Allies Coalition.

Athletics. NCAA. **Intercollegiate:** Baseball M, basketball, cross-country, field hockey W, golf M, lacrosse W, rowing (crew), soccer, softball W, tennis, volleyball W. **Intramural:** Basketball, cross-country, football (tackle) M, skiing, soccer, softball, swimming, tennis, volleyball W. **Team name:** Rams.

Student services. Adult student services, alcohol/substance abuse counseling, career counseling, student employment services, financial aid counseling, health services, personal counseling, placement for graduates. **Physically disabled:** Services for visually, hearing impaired. **Learning disabled:** Comprehensive services available.

Contact. E-mail: admissions@philau.edu
Phone: (215) 951-2800 Toll-free number: (800) 951-7287
Fax: (215) 951-2907
Christine Greb, Director of Admissions, Philadelphia University, School House Lane and Henry Avenue, Philadelphia, PA 19144-5497

Point Park University

Pittsburgh, Pennsylvania — **CB member**
www.pointpark.edu — **CB code: 2676**

- Private 4-year university
- Commuter campus in large city
- 3,241 degree-seeking undergraduates: 21% part-time, 60% women, 19% African American, 1% Asian American, 2% Hispanic American, 1% international
- 518 degree-seeking graduate students
- 74% of applicants admitted
- SAT or ACT (ACT writing optional), application essay, interview required
- 47% graduate within 6 years

General. Founded in 1960. Regionally accredited. **Degrees:** 626 bachelor's, 6 associate awarded; master's offered. **ROTC:** Army, Air Force. **Location:** Downtown. **Calendar:** Semester, extensive summer session. **Full-time faculty:** 117 total; 62% have terminal degrees, 5% minority, 38% women. **Part-time faculty:** 319 total. **Class size:** 78% < 20, 22% 20-39, less than 1% 40-49, less than 1% 50-99. **Special facilities:** Children's school, Pittsburgh Playhouse, 3-theater performing arts center.

Freshman class profile. 3,130 applied, 2,329 admitted, 538 enrolled.

Mid 50% test scores		**GPA 2.0-2.99:**	29%
SAT critical reading:	460-570	**Rank in top quarter:**	38%
SAT math:	450-560	**Rank in top tenth:**	14%
SAT writing:	450-570	**Return as sophomores:**	71%
ACT composite:	19-24	**Out-of-state:**	34%
GPA 3.75 or higher:	14%	**Live on campus:**	75%
GPA 3.50-3.74:	19%	**International:**	1%
GPA 3.0-3.49:	37%		

Basis for selection. High school record, class rank, test scores most important. Recommendations, extracurricular activities, talent, character also important. Audition required for some majors, portfolio recommended for multimedia, technical theater, stage management programs.

High school preparation. College-preparatory program recommended. 15 units recommended. Recommended units include English 4, mathematics 4, social studies 4, history 4, science 4 and foreign language 2.

2008-2009 Annual costs. Tuition/fees: $20,570. Room/board: $8,940. Books/supplies: $1,000. Personal expenses: $1,100.

2007-2008 Financial aid. **Need-based:** 429 full-time freshmen applied for aid; 355 were judged to have need; 355 of these received aid. Average need met was 68%. Average scholarship/grant was $8,684; average loan $5,229. 51% of total undergraduate aid awarded as scholarships/grants, 49% as loans/jobs. **Non-need-based:** Awarded to 665 full-time undergraduates, including 234 freshmen. Scholarships awarded for academics, alumni affiliation, art, athletics, leadership, music/drama.

Application procedures. **Admission:** No deadline. $40 fee, may be waived for applicants with need, free for online applicants. Admission notification on a rolling basis beginning on or about 10/1. Must reply by May 1 or within 2 week(s) if notified thereafter. **Financial aid:** Priority date 4/15; no closing date. FAFSA required. Applicants notified on a rolling basis starting 2/16; must reply by 8/30 or within 2 week(s) of notification.

Academics. **Special study options:** Accelerated study, cooperative education, cross-registration, distance learning, double major, ESL, exchange student, honors, independent study, internships, liberal arts/career combination, student-designed major, study abroad, teacher certification program, weekend college. Numerous off-campus programs for college credits. Several accelerated programs available. Offers professionally oriented programs in arts, business, communications, and technology. **Credit/placement by examination:** AP, CLEP, IB, SAT, ACT, institutional tests. 30 credit hours maximum toward associate degree, 60 toward bachelor's. **Support services:** Learning center, pre-admission summer program, reduced course load, remedial instruction, study skills assistance, tutoring.

Majors. **Biology:** General, biotechnology. **Business:** Accounting, business admin, human resources. **Communications:** Advertising, broadcast journalism, journalism, media studies, photojournalism. **Computer sciences:** Information technology. **Conservation:** Environmental science. **Education:** Biology, drama/dance, early childhood, elementary, English, mathematics. **Engineering technology:** Civil, mechanical. **History:** General. **Interdisciplinary:** Behavioral sciences. **Legal studies:** General. **Personal/culinary services:** Mortuary science. **Protective services:** Criminal justice, law enforcement admin. **Psychology:** General. **Public administration:** General. **Social sciences:** General, international relations, political science. **Visual/performing arts:** Cinematography, dance, dramatic, photography.

Most popular majors. Business/marketing 22%, communications/journalism 9%, education 7%, engineering/engineering technologies 6%, security/protective services 14%, visual/performing arts 25%.

Computing on campus. 183 workstations in library, computer center, student center. Dormitories wired for high-speed internet access and linked to campus network. Commuter students can connect to campus network. Online course registration, online library, helpline, student web hosting, wireless network available.

Student life. **Freshman orientation:** Mandatory. Preregistration for classes offered. Held in summer months, includes placement testing if needed for major. **Policies:** Policies regarding student conduct, plagiarism and resident life. **Housing:** Guaranteed on-campus for all undergraduates. Coed dorms, special housing for disabled, apartments available. $400 deposit. Living & learning communities; suite style housing. **Activities:** Choral groups, dance, drama, film society, international student organizations, literary magazine, musical theater, radio station, student government, student newspaper, TV station, black student union, Amnesty International.

Athletics. NAIA. **Intercollegiate:** Baseball M, basketball, cross-country, soccer, softball W, volleyball W. **Intramural:** Basketball M, tennis, volleyball, weight lifting M. **Team name:** Pioneers.

Student services. Adult student services, alcohol/substance abuse counseling, career counseling, student employment services, financial aid counseling, health services, on-campus daycare, personal counseling, placement for graduates, veterans' counselor. **Physically disabled:** Services for visually, speech, hearing impaired.

Contact. E-mail: enroll@pointpark.edu
Phone: (412) 392-3430 Toll-free number: (800) 321-0129
Fax: (412) 392-3902
Joell Minford, Director of Admissions, Point Park University, 201 Wood Street, Pittsburgh, PA 15222-1984

Restaurant School at Walnut Hill College

Philadelphia, Pennsylvania
www.walnuthillcollege.edu **CB code: 4883**

- For-profit 4-year culinary school and business college
- Commuter campus in very large city
- 543 degree-seeking undergraduates
- 70% of applicants admitted
- Application essay, interview required

General. Accredited by ACCSCT. Emphasis on fine dining and upscale hotels. **Degrees:** 40 bachelor's, 175 associate awarded. **Calendar:** Quarter. **Full-time faculty:** 21 total. **Part-time faculty:** 3 total. **Special facilities:** Students interact with numerous food and beverage outlets open to public. 4 uniquely themed restaurants and pastry shop/cafe.

Freshman class profile. 213 applied, 149 admitted, 149 enrolled.

Out-of-state:	51%	**Live on campus:**	30%

Basis for selection. Students must submit two letters of reference and a 250-word essay and take a basic skills evaluation. SAT or ACT recommended. Students who score below 900 combined on SAT/ACT math and critical reading, or who did not take either test, must take in-house assessment test. **Homeschooled:** Interview required.

2008-2009 Financial aid. Need-based: 27% of total undergraduate aid awarded as scholarships/grants, 73% as loans/jobs.

Application procedures. Admission: No deadline. $50 fee. Admission notification on a rolling basis. **Financial aid:** No deadline.

Academics. Special study options: Independent study, internships. **Credit/placement by examination:** CLEP. **Support services:** Study skills assistance, tutoring.

Majors. Business: Hotel/motel admin, restaurant/food services.

Computing on campus. 24 workstations in dormitories, library, computer center. Dormitories linked to campus network. Online library available.

Student life. Freshman orientation: Mandatory. 3-day orientation held week prior to start of classes. **Housing:** Coed dorms available. $850 deposit. **Activities:** Literary magazine, student newspaper.

Student services. Career counseling, student employment services, financial aid counseling.

Contact. E-mail: info@walnuthillcollege.edu
Phone: (215) 222-4200 ext. 3011 Toll-free number: (877) 925-6884 ext. 3011 Fax: (215) 222-2811
Becky Smith, Director of Admissions, Restaurant School at Walnut Hill College, 4207 Walnut Street, Philadelphia, PA 19104

Robert Morris University

Moon Township, Pennsylvania **CB member**
www.rmu.edu **CB code: 2769**

- Private 4-year university
- Commuter campus in large town
- 3,681 degree-seeking undergraduates: 15% part-time, 44% women, 8% African American, 1% Asian American, 1% Hispanic American, 2% international
- 968 degree-seeking graduate students
- 75% of applicants admitted
- SAT or ACT (ACT writing optional) required
- 56% graduate within 6 years; 8% enter graduate study

General. Founded in 1921. Regionally accredited. **Degrees:** 835 bachelor's awarded; master's, doctoral offered. **ROTC:** Army, Air Force. **Location:** 17 miles from Pittsburgh. **Calendar:** Semester, limited summer session. **Full-time faculty:** 177 total; 81% have terminal degrees, 13% minority, 37% women. **Part-time faculty:** 200 total; 31% have terminal degrees, 6% minority, 48% women. **Class size:** 40% < 20, 50% 20-39, 9% 40-49, 1% 50-99.

Freshman class profile. 3,611 applied, 2,704 admitted, 649 enrolled.

Mid 50% test scores		**Rank in top quarter:**	30%
SAT critical reading:	450-540	**Rank in top tenth:**	10%
SAT math:	460-580	**Return as sophomores:**	74%
SAT writing:	430-530	**Out-of-state:**	15%
ACT composite:	19-23	**Live on campus:**	77%
GPA 3.75 or higher:	18%	**International:**	3%
GPA 3.50-3.74:	21%	**Fraternities:**	4%
GPA 3.0-3.49:	34%	**Sororities:**	6%
GPA 2.0-2.99:	27%		

Basis for selection. Academic potential, high school GPA, class rank, test scores, and evidence of motivation important. Interview required of restricted-status applicants, recommended for all others.

High school preparation. College-preparatory program required. 16 units required; 18 recommended. Required and recommended units include English 4, mathematics 3, social studies 4, science 2, foreign language 2 and academic electives 3.

2008-2009 Annual costs. Tuition/fees: $19,740. Room/board: $9,880. Books/supplies: $1,200. Personal expenses: $1,500.

2008-2009 Financial aid. Need-based: 594 full-time freshmen applied for aid; 517 were judged to have need; 517 of these received aid. Average need met was 77%. Average scholarship/grant was $11,744; average loan $4,444. 39% of total undergraduate aid awarded as scholarships/grants, 61% as loans/jobs. **Non-need-based:** Awarded to 854 full-time undergraduates, including 205 freshmen. Scholarships awarded for academics, athletics.

Application procedures. Admission: Priority date 12/1; deadline 7/1 (postmark date). $30 fee, may be waived for applicants with need, free for online applicants. Admission notification on a rolling basis beginning on or about 8/1. Must reply by May 1 or within 3 week(s) if notified thereafter. **Financial aid:** No deadline. FAFSA required. Applicants notified on a rolling basis starting 3/15.

Academics. Special study options: Combined bachelor's/graduate degree, cooperative education, cross-registration, distance learning, double major, honors, independent study, internships, study abroad, teacher certification program, weekend college. **Credit/placement by examination:** AP, CLEP, SAT, ACT, institutional tests. 30 credit hours maximum toward bachelor's degree. **Support services:** Pre-admission summer program, reduced course load, remedial instruction, study skills assistance, tutoring.

Majors. Biology: General. **Business:** Accounting, actuarial science, business admin, finance, hospitality admin, management information systems, marketing, organizational behavior. **Communications:** General. **Computer sciences:** Information systems. **Conservation:** Environmental science. **Education:** Business, elementary. **Engineering:** Manufacturing, software. **Health:** Health services admin, medical radiologic technology/radiation therapy, nursing (RN). **Math:** Applied. **Parks/recreation:** Sports admin. **Psychology:** General. **Social sciences:** General, economics. **Visual/performing arts:** Design. **Other:** Competitive intelligence systems, information technology project management, Professional communications.

Most popular majors. Business/marketing 53%, communications/journalism 6%, education 6%, health sciences 7%.

Computing on campus. 300 workstations in library, computer center, student center. Dormitories wired for high-speed internet access and linked to campus network. Commuter students can connect to campus network. Online course registration, online library, helpline, wireless network available.

Student life. Freshman orientation: Mandatory, $100 fee. Preregistration for classes offered. 3-day program. **Housing:** Coed dorms, single-sex dorms, special housing for disabled, apartments, wellness housing available. $150 nonrefundable deposit, deadline 5/1. **Activities:** Bands, campus ministries, choral groups, drama, international student organizations, literary magazine, musical theater, radio station, student government, student newspaper, TV station, minority student organization, campus activities board, inter-residence hall council, inter-fraternity council/Panhellenic council, honor societies, major-related organizations, campus Republicans and Democrats, community service and volunteer organizations.

Athletics. NCAA. **Intercollegiate:** Basketball, cross-country, field hockey W, football (tackle) M, golf, ice hockey, lacrosse, rowing (crew) W, soccer, softball W, tennis, track and field, volleyball W. **Intramural:** Basketball, football (non-tackle) M, softball, volleyball W. **Team name:** Colonials.

Student services. Adult student services, alcohol/substance abuse counseling, chaplain/spiritual director, career counseling, services for economically disadvantaged, student employment services, financial aid counseling, health services, minority student services, personal counseling, placement for graduates, veterans' counselor. **Physically disabled:** Services for visually, speech, hearing impaired. **Learning disabled:** Comprehensive services available.

Contact. E-mail: admissionsoffice@rmu.edu
Phone: (412) 397-5200 Toll-free number: (800) 762-0097
Fax: (412) 397-2425
Robert Morris University, 6001 University Boulevard, Moon Township, PA 15108-1189

Rosemont College

Rosemont, Pennsylvania — **CB member**
www.rosemont.edu — **CB code: 2763**

- Private 4-year liberal arts college affiliated with Roman Catholic Church
- Residential campus in small town
- 506 degree-seeking undergraduates: 23% part-time, 95% women, 44% African American, 6% Asian American, 8% Hispanic American, 1% international
- 385 degree-seeking graduate students
- 62% of applicants admitted
- SAT or ACT, application essay required
- 75% graduate within 6 years; 19% enter graduate study

General. Founded in 1921. Regionally accredited. Starting with the Fall 2009 semester, Rosemont College welcomes women and men into the undergraduate college. **Degrees:** 146 bachelor's awarded; master's offered. **ROTC:** Army, Air Force. **Location:** 11 miles from Philadelphia. **Calendar:** Semester, limited summer session. **Full-time faculty:** 26 total; 92% have terminal degrees, 65% women. **Part-time faculty:** 127 total; 80% have terminal degrees, 11% minority, 58% women. **Class size:** 81% < 20, 19% 20-39.

Freshman class profile. 614 applied, 383 admitted, 126 enrolled.

Mid 50% test scores			
SAT critical reading:	430-570	GPA 2.0-2.99:	40%
SAT math:	420-520	Rank in top quarter:	45%
SAT writing:	440-560	Rank in top tenth:	25%
GPA 3.75 or higher:	17%	End year in good standing:	95%
GPA 3.50-3.74:	13%	Return as sophomores:	68%
GPA 3.0-3.49:	30%	Out-of-state:	30%
		Live on campus:	90%

Basis for selection. School achievement record and curriculum, recommendations, test scores, extracurricular activities strongly considered. Interview recommended. **Homeschooled:** Statement describing homeschool structure and mission, transcript of courses and grades, letter of recommendation (nonparent) required.

High school preparation. College-preparatory program recommended. 18 units required. Required units include English 4, mathematics 2, social studies 2, history 2, science 2 (laboratory 2), foreign language 2 and academic electives 2.

2008-2009 Annual costs. Tuition/fees: $24,810. Room/board: $9,980. Books/supplies: $1,500. Personal expenses: $1,000.

2008-2009 Financial aid. Need-based: 125 full-time freshmen applied for aid; 111 were judged to have need; 111 of these received aid. Average need met was 75%. Average scholarship/grant was $20,209; average loan $3,555. 72% of total undergraduate aid awarded as scholarships/grants, 28% as loans/jobs. **Non-need-based:** Scholarships awarded for academics, art, leadership, religious affiliation.

Application procedures. Admission: No deadline. $35 fee, may be waived for applicants with need, free for online applicants. Admission notification on a rolling basis. Must reply by May 1 or within 2 week(s) if notified thereafter. $300 deposit required of all students intending to enroll. Refundable only if college notified by May 1 of decision not to attend. **Financial aid:** Priority date 2/15; no closing date. FAFSA required. Applicants notified on a rolling basis starting 2/15; must reply within 4 week(s) of notification.

Academics. Special study options: Accelerated study, combined bachelor's/graduate degree, cross-registration, distance learning, double major, ESL, exchange student, honors, independent study, internships, liberal arts/career combination, student-designed major, study abroad, teacher certification program, Washington semester. **Credit/placement by examination:** AP, CLEP, IB, SAT, institutional tests. 30 credit hours maximum toward bachelor's degree. Students may be exempted if they demonstrate mastery of subject as determined by particular department. **Support services:** Learning center, pre-admission summer program, reduced course load, remedial instruction, study skills assistance, tutoring, writing center.

Majors. Area/ethnic studies: Asian, women's. **Biology:** General, biochemistry. **Business:** General, accounting, business admin, communications, hospitality admin, human resources, management science, managerial economics, organizational behavior. **Communications:** General. **Conservation:** Environmental science. **Education:** Elementary, secondary. **Foreign languages:** General, French, German, Italian, Spanish. **History:** General. **Liberal arts:** Arts/sciences, humanities. **Math:** General. **Philosophy/religion:** Philosophy, religion. **Physical sciences:** Chemistry. **Protective services:** Criminal justice. **Psychology:** General. **Social sciences:** General, economics, political science, sociology. **Visual/performing arts:** Art history/conservation.

Most popular majors. Biology 12%, business/marketing 14%, communications/journalism 9%, English 9%, foreign language 8%, history 6%, psychology 14%, social sciences 6%, visual/performing arts 13%.

Computing on campus. 100 workstations in dormitories, library, computer center, student center. Dormitories wired for high-speed internet access and linked to campus network. Commuter students can connect to campus network. Online course registration, online library, helpline, student web hosting, wireless network available.

Student life. Freshman orientation: Mandatory, $280 fee. Preregistration for classes offered. Orientation approximately 3 days; includes academics component. **Housing:** Guaranteed on-campus for all undergraduates. Single-sex dorms, wellness housing available. **Activities:** Bands, campus ministries, choral groups, dance, drama, international student organizations, literary magazine, music ensembles, Model UN, musical theater, opera, radio station, student government, student newspaper, premed club, politics club, Rosemont Alcohol and Drug Awareness Resource, multicultural society, Best Buddies, Triad, art society.

Athletics. NCAA. **Intercollegiate:** Basketball W, field hockey W, lacrosse W, softball W, tennis W, volleyball W. **Team name:** Ramblers.

Student services. Adult student services, alcohol/substance abuse counseling, chaplain/spiritual director, career counseling, student employment services, financial aid counseling, health services, legal services, minority student services, on-campus daycare, personal counseling, placement for graduates, veterans' counselor, women's services. **Physically disabled:** Services for visually, speech, hearing impaired.

Contact. E-mail: admissions@rosemont.edu
Phone: (610) 526-2966 Toll-free number: (800) 331-0708
Fax: (610) 520-4399
Rennie Andrews, Dean of Undergraduate College Admissions, Rosemont College, 1400 Montgomery Avenue, Rosemont, PA 19010-1699

St. Charles Borromeo Seminary - Overbrook

Wynnewood, Pennsylvania
www.scs.edu — **CB code: 2794**

- Private 4-year seminary college for men affiliated with Roman Catholic Church
- Residential campus in large town
- 52 degree-seeking undergraduates: 2% African American, 6% Hispanic American, 8% international
- 112 degree-seeking graduate students
- 100% of applicants admitted
- Application essay, interview required
- 63% graduate within 6 years

General. Founded in 1832. Regionally accredited; also accredited by ATS. College and theology divisions enroll full-time seminary students. Religious studies division enrolls part-time undergraduate and graduate students who wish to pursue theological studies. Part-time programs open to men and women. **Degrees:** 10 bachelor's awarded; master's, first professional offered. **Location:** 4 miles from central Philadelphia. **Calendar:** Semester, limited summer session. **Full-time faculty:** 14 total; 64% have terminal degrees, 21% women. **Part-time faculty:** 11 total; 27% have terminal degrees, 36% women. **Class size:** 93% < 20, 7% 20-39. **Special facilities:** Rare book and special collections.

Freshman class profile. 6 applied, 6 admitted, 6 enrolled.

End year in good standing:	84%	**Out-of-state:**	50%
Return as sophomores:	84%	**Live on campus:**	100%

Basis for selection. Sponsorship by diocese or religious community required for admission to college and theology divisions. Seminary applicants holding bachelor's degree from accredited institution may enter special pre-theology program. SAT or ACT recommended. **Homeschooled:** Transcript of courses and grades, letter of recommendation (nonparent) required.

High school preparation. College-preparatory program recommended. 20 units recommended. Recommended units include English 4, mathematics 3, social studies 3, science 3 and foreign language 3. 3 to 4 units of religious education recommended. GED accepted on individual basis.

2008-2009 Annual costs. Tuition/fees: $13,306. Room/board: $8,931. Books/supplies: $800. Personal expenses: $600.

2008-2009 Financial aid. **Need-based:** 5 full-time freshmen applied for aid; 3 were judged to have need; 3 of these received aid. Average need met was 30%. Average scholarship/grant was $2,521; average loan $3,500. 42% of total undergraduate aid awarded as scholarships/grants, 58% as loans/jobs. **Non-need-based:** Scholarships awarded for religious affiliation.

Application procedures. **Admission:** Priority date 3/1; deadline 7/15. No application fee. Admission notification on a rolling basis beginning on or about 4/1. Level of admission dependent on academic background in philosophy, theology, and classical languages. **Financial aid:** No deadline. FAFSA, institutional form required. Applicants notified on a rolling basis starting 6/1; must reply within 4 week(s) of notification.

Academics. Strong emphasis on philosophy, theology, classical languages, and liberal arts. **Special study options:** Accelerated study, ESL, independent study. **Credit/placement by examination:** AP, CLEP, institutional tests. 30 credit hours maximum toward bachelor's degree. **Support services:** Reduced course load, tutoring.

Majors. **Philosophy/religion:** Philosophy.

Computing on campus. 60 workstations in library, computer center. Online library, wireless network available.

Student life. **Freshman orientation:** Mandatory. **Policies:** Religious observance required. **Housing:** Guaranteed on-campus for all undergraduates. Wellness housing available. On-campus housing available for seminarians in college and theology divisions. On-campus housing available to students in religious studies division during summer session. **Activities:** Choral groups, drama, music ensembles, student government, student newspaper, Seminarians for Life.

Athletics. **Intramural:** Basketball M, football (tackle) M, soccer M, volleyball M.

Student services. Chaplain/spiritual director, financial aid counseling, health services, personal counseling.

Contact. E-mail: frdd@adphila.org
Phone: (610) 785-6271 Fax: (610) 617-9267
Rev. David Diamond, Vice Rector, St. Charles Borromeo Seminary - Overbrook, 100 East Wynnewood Road, Wynnewood, PA 19096

St. Francis University

Loretto, Pennsylvania — **CB member**
www.francis.edu — **CB code: 2797**

- Private 4-year university and liberal arts college affiliated with Roman Catholic Church
- Residential campus in rural community
- 1,571 degree-seeking undergraduates: 6% part-time, 60% women, 5% African American, 1% Asian American, 1% Hispanic American
- 582 degree-seeking graduate students
- 75% of applicants admitted
- SAT or ACT (ACT writing optional), application essay required
- 56% graduate within 6 years

General. Founded in 1847. Regionally accredited. **Degrees:** 328 bachelor's, 4 associate awarded; master's, doctoral offered. **ROTC:** Army. **Location:** 90 miles from Pittsburgh, 20 miles from Altoona. **Calendar:** Semester, limited summer session. **Full-time faculty:** 105 total. **Part-time faculty:** 104 total. **Class size:** 53% < 20, 41% 20-39, 4% 40-49, 2% 50-99. **Special facilities:** Rural health and wellness institute, small business development center, global competitiveness center, Southern Alleghenies art museum, center for remote and medically underserved areas, nature trail.

Freshman class profile. 1,533 applied, 1,156 admitted, 414 enrolled.

Mid 50% test scores		**GPA 2.0-2.99:**	15%
SAT critical reading:	460-550	**Return as sophomores:**	84%
SAT math:	460-580	**Out-of-state:**	29%
ACT composite:	19-26	**Live on campus:**	85%
GPA 3.75 or higher:	35%	**Fraternities:**	13%
GPA 3.50-3.74:	22%	**Sororities:**	10%
GPA 3.0-3.49:	27%		

Basis for selection. High school record most important, followed by test scores, counselor's recommendations, major area of interest, activities, honors. Relationship to alumni also considered. Campus visit highly recommended. Admission to professional track programs places more weight on test scores. Interview highly recommended. **Learning Disabled:** Send documentation to the Academic Center for Enrichment.

High school preparation. College-preparatory program recommended. Required and recommended units include English 4, mathematics 2-4, social studies 2, science 1, foreign language 2 and academic electives 7. One natural science for nonscience majors, 2 for science majors also required. One science unit must include laboratory. Remaining units in academic electives. 4 math and 2 science required for physician assistant and occupational therapy. 4 math and 4 science required for physical therapy.

2008-2009 Annual costs. Tuition/fees: $24,840. Room/board: $8,422. Books/supplies: $800. Personal expenses: $1,250.

2007-2008 Financial aid. **Need-based:** 372 full-time freshmen applied for aid; 326 were judged to have need; 319 of these received aid. Average need met was 66%. Average scholarship/grant was $13,069; average loan $2,775. 65% of total undergraduate aid awarded as scholarships/grants, 35% as loans/jobs. **Non-need-based:** Awarded to 457 full-time undergraduates, including 146 freshmen. Scholarships awarded for academics, alumni affiliation, athletics, music/drama, religious affiliation.

Application procedures. **Admission:** Priority date 3/1; deadline 7/30 (postmark date). $30 fee, may be waived for applicants with need. Admission notification on a rolling basis beginning on or about 10/1. Must reply by May 1 or within 2 week(s) if notified thereafter. Application closing date for physical therapy, occupational therapy and physican assistant January 15. Notification by February 1. **Financial aid:** Priority date 5/1; no closing date. FAFSA required. Applicants notified on a rolling basis starting 3/1.

Academics. **Special study options:** Combined bachelor's/graduate degree, cooperative education, distance learning, double major, honors, independent study, internships, liberal arts/career combination, semester at sea, student-designed major, study abroad, teacher certification program, Washington semester. **Credit/placement by examination:** AP, CLEP, IB, SAT, ACT, institutional tests. 15 credit hours maximum toward associate degree, 30 toward bachelor's. **Support services:** Learning center, pre-admission summer program, reduced course load, remedial instruction, study skills assistance, tutoring, writing center.

Honors college/program. 3.25 GPA, 1150 SAT (580 Critical Reading, exclusive of Writing), and position in top 20% of high school class required. About 40 applicants admitted.

Majors. **Area/ethnic studies:** American, French. **Biology:** General, marine. **Business:** Accounting, business admin, finance, management information systems, marketing. **Communications:** General, public relations. **Computer sciences:** General, computer science, information systems, programming. **Conservation:** Environmental science, environmental studies, forest management, forestry. **Education:** General, biology, chemistry, elementary, English, foreign languages, French, history, mathematics, multi-level teacher, psychology, secondary, social science, social studies, Spanish, special, speech. **Engineering:** General, environmental. **Foreign languages:** General, French, Spanish. **Health:** Clinical lab technology, nursing (RN), physician assistant. **History:** General. **Interdisciplinary:** Biological/physical sciences, math/computer science. **Math:** General. **Philosophy/religion:** Philosophy, religion. **Physical sciences:** Chemistry. **Psychology:** General. **Public administration:** General, social work. **Social sciences:** Economics, political science, sociology. **Other:** Exercise physiology.

Most popular majors. Business/marketing 31%, education 12%, health sciences 24%, psychology 6%.

Computing on campus. PC or laptop required. 40 workstations in dormitories, library, computer center, student center. Dormitories wired for high-speed internet access and linked to campus network. Commuter students can connect to campus network. Online library, helpline, repair service, wireless network available.

Student life. Freshman orientation: Mandatory. Preregistration for classes offered. Held at various times during spring and summer. **Policies:** All students required to live on campus until 21st birthday unless commuter status or a senior by September 1 of academic year. **Housing:** Guaranteed on-campus for freshmen. Coed dorms, single-sex dorms, special housing for disabled, apartments, fraternity/sorority housing, wellness housing available. $100 deposit, deadline 5/1. **Activities:** Bands, choral groups, drama, music ensembles, musical theater, radio station, student government, student newspaper, TV station, Secular Franciscan Order, student activities organization, multicultural awareness club, Historians' Round Table, Knights of Columbus, Peace and Justice Center, current affairs club, pro-life club, prelaw club.

Athletics. NCAA. **Intercollegiate:** Basketball, cross-country, diving W, field hockey W, football (tackle) M, golf, lacrosse W, soccer, softball W, swimming W, tennis, track and field, volleyball. **Intramural:** Basketball, cross-country, football (non-tackle), golf, skiing, soccer, softball, swimming, table tennis, tennis, track and field, volleyball. **Team name:** Red Flash.

Student services. Adult student services, alcohol/substance abuse counseling, chaplain/spiritual director, career counseling, student employment services, financial aid counseling, health services, minority student services, personal counseling, placement for graduates, veterans' counselor.

Contact. E-mail: admissions@francis.edu
Phone: (814) 472-3100 Toll-free number: (800) 342-5732
Fax: (814) 472-3335
Erin McCloskey, Vice President for Enrollment Management, St. Francis University, Box 600, Loretto, PA 15940

Saint Joseph's University

Philadelphia, Pennsylvania — **CB member**
www.sju.edu — **CB code: 2801**

- Private 4-year university affiliated with Roman Catholic Church
- Residential campus in very large city
- 5,161 degree-seeking undergraduates: 13% part-time, 53% women, 7% African American, 2% Asian American, 4% Hispanic American, 2% international
- 2,126 degree-seeking graduate students
- 86% of applicants admitted
- SAT or ACT (ACT writing optional), application essay required
- 79% graduate within 6 years

General. Founded in 1851. Regionally accredited. Founded by the Society of Jesus. **Degrees:** 1,119 bachelor's, 11 associate awarded; master's, doctoral offered. **ROTC:** Army, Naval, Air Force. **Location:** 8 miles from downtown. **Calendar:** Semester, extensive summer session. **Full-time faculty:** 290 total; 90% have terminal degrees, 13% minority, 39% women. **Part-time faculty:** 334 total; 10% minority, 41% women. **Class size:** 38% < 20, 55% 20-39, 5% 40-49, 2% 50-99.

Freshman class profile. 7,012 applied, 6,029 admitted, 1,478 enrolled.

Mid 50% test scores		**GPA 2.0-2.99:**	17%
SAT critical reading:	500-600	**Rank in top quarter:**	48%
SAT math:	510-610	**Rank in top tenth:**	19%
SAT writing:	510-600	**End year in good standing:**	94%
ACT composite:	22-26	**Return as sophomores:**	88%
GPA 3.75 or higher:	19%	**Out-of-state:**	60%
GPA 3.50-3.74:	22%	**Live on campus:**	97%
GPA 3.0-3.49:	42%	**International:**	1%

Basis for selection. GED not accepted. Careful consideration given to applicant's high school curriculum, extracurricular activities, recalculated academic GPA, and standardized test scores. Preference is given to those applicants who have taken more demanding curriculum.

High school preparation. College-preparatory program recommended. 12 units required. Required units include English 4, mathematics 3, history 1, science 2 (laboratory 1) and foreign language 2.

2008-2009 Annual costs. Tuition/fees: $32,860. Room/board: $11,180.

2008-2009 Financial aid. Need-based: Average need met was 83%. Average scholarship/grant was $14,746; average loan $3,685. 52% of total undergraduate aid awarded as scholarships/grants, 48% as loans/jobs. **Non-need-based:** Scholarships awarded for academics, art, athletics, minority status, music/drama, ROTC.

Application procedures. Admission: Closing date 2/1 (postmark date). $60 fee, may be waived for applicants with need. Admission notification 3/1. Must reply by May 1 or within 2 week(s) if notified thereafter. **Financial aid:** Priority date 2/15; no closing date. FAFSA required. Applicants notified on a rolling basis starting 3/1; must reply by 5/1.

Academics. Special study options: Accelerated study, combined bachelor's/graduate degree, cooperative education, distance learning, double major, dual enrollment of high school students, ESL, honors, independent study, internships, student-designed major, study abroad, teacher certification program, Washington semester, weekend college. Jesuit student exchange. **Credit/placement by examination:** AP, CLEP, IB, institutional tests. **Support services:** Learning center, pre-admission summer program, reduced course load, study skills assistance, tutoring, writing center.

Majors. Area/ethnic studies: European, French. **Biology:** General, biochemistry. **Business:** Accounting, actuarial science, business admin, finance, international, international marketing, management information systems, marketing, purchasing, special products marketing. **Communications:** General. **Computer sciences:** General, information systems. **Conservation:** Environmental studies. **Education:** Elementary, English, foreign languages, mathematics, science, secondary, social studies, special. **Foreign languages:** French, German, Italian, Latin, Spanish. **Health:** Facilities admin, health services. **History:** General. **Legal studies:** General. **Liberal arts:** Humanities. **Math:** General. **Philosophy/religion:** Philosophy, religion. **Physical sciences:** Chemistry, physics. **Psychology:** General. **Public administration:** General. **Social sciences:** General, criminology, economics, international relations, political science, sociology. **Visual/performing arts:** General.

Most popular majors. Business/marketing 49%, education 8%, English 7%, psychology 6%, social sciences 14%.

Computing on campus. 675 workstations in dormitories, library, computer center, student center. Dormitories wired for high-speed internet access and linked to campus network. Commuter students can connect to campus network. Online course registration, online library, helpline, repair service, student web hosting, wireless network available.

Student life. Freshman orientation: Available, $225 fee. **Housing:** Guaranteed on-campus for freshmen. Coed dorms, single-sex dorms, special housing for disabled, apartments, wellness housing available. $250 nonrefundable deposit, deadline 5/1. **Activities:** Bands, campus ministries, choral groups, dance, drama, film society, international student organizations, literary magazine, music ensembles, musical theater, radio station, student government, student newspaper, Black Student Union, Hand-in-Hand, College Democrats, College Republicans, Up-Til-Dawn, campus ministry immersion programs, Habitat for Humanity, Students for Life, community service weekly programs.

Athletics. NCAA. **Intercollegiate:** Baseball M, basketball, cheerleading, cross-country, field hockey W, golf M, lacrosse, rowing (crew), soccer, softball W, tennis, track and field. **Intramural:** Basketball, football (non-tackle), golf M, rugby, soccer, softball, tennis, volleyball. **Team name:** Hawks.

Student services. Adult student services, alcohol/substance abuse counseling, chaplain/spiritual director, career counseling, services for economically disadvantaged, student employment services, financial aid counseling, health services, minority student services, personal counseling, women's services. **Physically disabled:** Services for visually, speech, hearing impaired. **Learning disabled:** Comprehensive services available.

Contact. E-mail: admit@sju.edu
Phone: (610) 660-1300 Toll-free number: (888) 232-4295
Fax: (610) 660-1314
Maureen Mathis, Executive Director of Undergraduate Admissions, Saint Joseph's University, 5600 City Avenue, Philadelphia, PA 19131

St. Vincent College

Latrobe, Pennsylvania — **CB member**
www.stvincent.edu — **CB code: 2808**

- Private 4-year liberal arts college affiliated with Roman Catholic Church
- Residential campus in large town
- 1,676 degree-seeking undergraduates: 2% part-time, 47% women, 4% African American, 1% Asian American, 2% Hispanic American, 1% international

- 238 degree-seeking graduate students
- 65% of applicants admitted
- SAT or ACT (ACT writing optional), application essay required
- 72% graduate within 6 years

General. Founded in 1846. Regionally accredited. Affiliated with Order of Saint Benedict. **Degrees:** 302 bachelor's awarded; master's offered. **ROTC:** Army, Air Force. **Location:** 35 miles from Pittsburgh. **Calendar:** Semester, extensive summer session. **Full-time faculty:** 98 total; 84% have terminal degrees, 3% minority, 26% women. **Part-time faculty:** 97 total; 28% have terminal degrees, 1% minority, 41% women. **Class size:** 39% < 20, 59% 20-39, 1% 40-49. **Special facilities:** Planetarium, observatory, radio telescope, wetlands program, rare book collection, spectrophotometer, spectrometer, physiograph workstations, nature reserve, digital imaging lab, Fred Rogers archives.

Freshman class profile. 1,843 applied, 1,204 admitted, 447 enrolled.

Mid 50% test scores		**GPA 2.0-2.99:**	13%
SAT critical reading:	470-570	**Rank in top quarter:**	48%
SAT math:	480-590	**Rank in top tenth:**	22%
SAT writing:	460-570	**Return as sophomores:**	82%
ACT composite:	19-24	**Out-of-state:**	15%
GPA 3.75 or higher:	48%	**Live on campus:**	89%
GPA 3.50-3.74:	15%	**International:**	1%
GPA 3.0-3.49:	24%		

Basis for selection. High school curriculum and grades most important; class rank, test scores, and essay important. Recommendations from school counselor considered. Interview recommended for all; audition required for music programs; portfolio required for art programs. **Learning Disabled:** All prior test results related to learning disability should be submitted.

High school preparation. College-preparatory program recommended. 16 units required; 20 recommended. Required and recommended units include English 4, mathematics 3, social studies 3, science 1-3 (laboratory 1), foreign language 2 and academic electives 5. One plane geometry, 1 intermediate algebra, .5 trigonometry, and 1 physics required for 3-2 engineering program applicants.

2008-2009 Annual costs. Tuition/fees: $25,290. Room/board: $8,280. Books/supplies: $1,050. Personal expenses: $1,600.

2008-2009 Financial aid. **Need-based:** 440 full-time freshmen applied for aid; 359 were judged to have need; 359 of these received aid. Average need met was 87%. Average scholarship/grant was $15,630; average loan $4,208. 85% of total undergraduate aid awarded as scholarships/grants, 15% as loans/jobs. **Non-need-based:** Scholarships awarded for academics, alumni affiliation, leadership, minority status, music/drama, religious affiliation.

Application procedures. **Admission:** Priority date 2/1; deadline 4/1 (postmark date). $25 fee, may be waived for applicants with need, free for online applicants. Admission notification on a rolling basis beginning on or about 10/1. Must reply by May 1 or within 3 week(s) if notified thereafter. **Financial aid:** Priority date 3/1, closing date 5/1. FAFSA required. Applicants notified on a rolling basis starting 3/1; must reply within 2 week(s) of notification.

Academics. College attempts to place career orientation in context of broader human and religious values with emphasis on liberal arts core curriculum. **Special study options:** Accelerated study, combined bachelor's/graduate degree, cooperative education, cross-registration, double major, dual enrollment of high school students, external degree, honors, independent study, internships, liberal arts/career combination, study abroad, teacher certification program. 3-2 engineering BA/BS program with University of Pittsburgh, Catholic University of America, Pennsylvania State; 4-1 BS/MBA, 3-3 BA/JD, 3-2 occupational therapy, physical therapy, and physician's assistant, 2-4 pharmacy programs with Duquesne University; 3-4 podiatry with Ohio College of Pediatric Medicine and Pennsylvania College of Pediatric Medicine. **Credit/placement by examination:** AP, CLEP, IB, institutional tests. 62 credit hours maximum toward bachelor's degree. **Support services:** Learning center, pre-admission summer program, remedial instruction, study skills assistance, tutoring, writing center.

Majors. **Biology:** General, biochemistry, bioinformatics. **Business:** Accounting, business admin, finance, international, marketing. **Communications:** General. **Communications technology:** General. **Computer sciences:** General. **Conservation:** General, environmental science, environmental studies, management/policy. **Education:** Business, elementary, physics, psychology. **Engineering:** General. **Foreign languages:** French, Spanish. **Health:** Predental, premedicine, prepharmacy, preveterinary. **History:** General. **Liberal arts:** Arts/sciences. **Math:** General. **Philosophy/religion:** Philosophy. **Physical sciences:** Chemistry, physics. **Psychology:** General. **Public administration:** Policy analysis. **Social sciences:** Anthropology, economics, political science, sociology. **Theology:** Religious ed, theology. **Visual/performing arts:** Art history/conservation, arts management, graphic design, music performance, studio arts.

Most popular majors. Biology 12%, business/marketing 20%, communications/journalism 9%, history 7%, mathematics 6%, psychology 15%, social sciences 9%.

Computing on campus. 286 workstations in dormitories, library, computer center, student center. Dormitories wired for high-speed internet access and linked to campus network. Online course registration, helpline, repair service, wireless network available.

Student life. **Freshman orientation:** Mandatory, $125 fee. Four weeks of activities are planned to acclimate students to college on academic and social levels. Upperclassmen volunteer to serve as mentors to first-year students through the program. **Housing:** Guaranteed on-campus for freshmen. Coed dorms, apartments available. $200 nonrefundable deposit, deadline 5/1. **Activities:** Pep band, campus ministries, choral groups, dance, drama, international student organizations, literary magazine, music ensembles, radio station, student government, student newspaper, TV station, Respect for Life club, Democrats club, College Republicans, Students for Social Justice, pre-law society, Student Council for Exceptional Children, Italian club, Habitat for Humanity.

Athletics. NCAA. **Intercollegiate:** Baseball M, basketball, cross-country, field hockey W, football (tackle) M, golf, lacrosse, soccer, softball W, swimming, tennis, track and field M, volleyball W. **Intramural:** Basketball, football (non-tackle), soccer, softball, table tennis, volleyball. **Team name:** Bearcats.

Student services. Adult student services, alcohol/substance abuse counseling, chaplain/spiritual director, career counseling, student employment services, financial aid counseling, health services, minority student services, personal counseling, placement for graduates. **Physically disabled:** Services for visually, speech, hearing impaired. **Learning disabled:** Comprehensive services available.

Contact. E-mail: admission@stvincent.edu
Phone: (724) 805-2500 Toll-free number: (800) 782-5549
Fax: (724) 532-5069
David Collins, Assistant Vice President of Admission and Financial Aid, St. Vincent College, 300 Fraser Purchase Road, Latrobe, PA 15650-2690

Seton Hill University

Greensburg, Pennsylvania — **CB member**
www.setonhill.edu — **CB code: 2812**

- Private 4-year university and liberal arts college affiliated with Roman Catholic Church
- Residential campus in large town
- 1,480 degree-seeking undergraduates: 10% part-time, 63% women, 8% African American, 1% Asian American, 1% Hispanic American, 2% international
- 427 degree-seeking graduate students
- 64% of applicants admitted
- Application essay required
- 60% graduate within 6 years; 23% enter graduate study

General. Founded in 1918. Regionally accredited. **Degrees:** 264 bachelor's awarded; master's offered. **ROTC:** Army, Air Force. **Location:** 35 miles from Pittsburgh. **Calendar:** Semester, limited summer session. **Full-time faculty:** 75 total; 79% have terminal degrees, 8% minority, 53% women. **Part-time faculty:** 122 total; 30% have terminal degrees, less than 1% minority, 54% women. **Class size:** 62% < 20, 35% 20-39, 2% 40-49, 1% 50-99. **Special facilities:** Child development center, kindergarten, women in business center, Catholic Holocaust education center.

Freshman class profile. 1,754 applied, 1,130 admitted, 361 enrolled.

Mid 50% test scores		**Rank in top quarter:**	49%
SAT critical reading:	440-560	**Rank in top tenth:**	21%
SAT math:	440-570	**End year in good standing:**	94%
ACT composite:	18-25	**Return as sophomores:**	81%
GPA 3.75 or higher:	31%	**Out-of-state:**	23%
GPA 3.50-3.74:	19%	**Live on campus:**	89%
GPA 3.0-3.49:	24%	**International:**	3%
GPA 2.0-2.99:	26%		

Basis for selection. School achievement record most important, followed by test scores and recommendations. Applicants from minorities or low-income families encouraged, accepted on basis of motivation and potential. SAT or ACT recommended. Students who have not taken SAT or ACT may submit 2 graded writing samples for consideration. Interview recommended for all; audition required for music, theater programs; portfolio required for art program. Additional application required for physician assistant program. **Homeschooled:** Must provide SAT/ACT scores and official transcript issued by a school district or agency approving the curriculum, or GED.

High school preparation. 15 units required. Required and recommended units include English 4, mathematics 2, social studies 2, science 1 (laboratory 1), foreign language 2 and academic electives 4. 4 math units recommended for science majors.

2008-2009 Annual costs. Tuition/fees: $26,006. Room/board: $8,420. Books/supplies: $1,000. Personal expenses: $2,500.

2008-2009 Financial aid. Need-based: 337 full-time freshmen applied for aid; 300 were judged to have need; 299 of these received aid. Average need met was 80%. Average scholarship/grant was $17,828; average loan $5,133. 66% of total undergraduate aid awarded as scholarships/grants, 34% as loans/jobs. **Non-need-based:** Awarded to 393 full-time undergraduates, including 114 freshmen. Scholarships awarded for academics, alumni affiliation, art, athletics, leadership, minority status, music/drama, state residency.

Application procedures. Admission: Priority date 5/1; deadline 8/15 (receipt date). $35 fee, may be waived for applicants with need, free for online applicants. Admission notification on a rolling basis beginning on or about 9/1. **Financial aid:** Priority date 5/1; no closing date. FAFSA, institutional form required. Applicants notified on a rolling basis starting 11/15; must reply by 5/1 or within 2 week(s) of notification.

Academics. Special study options: Accelerated study, combined bachelor's/graduate degree, cross-registration, distance learning, double major, ESL, exchange student, honors, independent study, internships, liberal arts/career combination, New York semester, semester at sea, student-designed major, study abroad, teacher certification program, United Nations semester, Washington semester, weekend college. **Credit/placement by examination:** AP, CLEP, IB, SAT, ACT. 30 credit hours maximum toward bachelor's degree. **Support services:** Learning center, pre-admission summer program, reduced course load, remedial instruction, study skills assistance, tutoring, writing center.

Majors. Biology: General, biochemistry. **Business:** Accounting, actuarial science, business admin, entrepreneurial studies, finance, hospitality admin, human resources, international, management information systems, marketing, sales/distribution. **Communications:** General, journalism. **Computer sciences:** Computer science. **Education:** Art, biology, chemistry, English, family/consumer sciences, foreign languages, mathematics, music, Spanish. **Engineering:** General. **Family/consumer sciences:** General, child care, child development. **Foreign languages:** Spanish. **Health:** Art therapy, clinical lab science, dietetics, music therapy, nursing (RN), physician assistant. **History:** General. **Legal studies:** Prelaw. **Math:** General. **Philosophy/religion:** Religion. **Physical sciences:** Chemistry. **Protective services:** Criminal justice, forensics. **Psychology:** General. **Public administration:** Human services, social work. **Social sciences:** Economics, international relations, political science, sociology. **Theology:** Sacred music. **Visual/performing arts:** Acting, art history/conservation, arts management, ceramics, commercial/advertising art, dramatic, drawing, metal/jewelry, music performance, painting, printmaking, sculpture, studio arts, theater arts management, theater design. **Other:** Actuary science.

Most popular majors. Business/marketing 29%, health sciences 7%, psychology 12%, public administration/social services 6%, social sciences 6%, visual/performing arts 10%.

Computing on campus. 350 workstations in dormitories, library, computer center, student center. Dormitories wired for high-speed internet access and linked to campus network. Commuter students can connect to campus network. Online course registration, helpline, repair service, student web hosting, wireless network available.

Student life. Freshman orientation: Mandatory, $25 fee. Preregistration for classes offered. One-day, on-campus family orientation in summer. Four-day orientation during weekend and weekdays prior to start of classes. **Policies:** Residence hall students involved in setting community standards. **Housing:** Guaranteed on-campus for all undergraduates. Coed dorms, single-sex dorms, wellness housing available. **Activities:** Bands, campus ministries, choral groups, dance, drama, international student organizations, literary magazine, music ensembles, musical theater, student government, student newspaper, symphony orchestra, social work club, liturgical groups, Respect Life, Operation Christmas Basket, Association of Black Collegians, National Coalition Building Institute, Helping Hands, Habitat for Humanity.

Athletics. NCAA. **Intercollegiate:** Baseball M, basketball, cross-country, equestrian W, field hockey W, football (tackle) M, golf, lacrosse, soccer, softball W, tennis, track and field, volleyball W, wrestling M. **Intramural:** Basketball W, equestrian W, soccer W, softball W, volleyball W. **Team name:** Griffins.

Student services. Adult student services, alcohol/substance abuse counseling, chaplain/spiritual director, career counseling, services for economically disadvantaged, student employment services, financial aid counseling, health services, minority student services, on-campus daycare, personal counseling, placement for graduates, veterans' counselor. **Physically disabled:** Services for visually, speech, hearing impaired.

Contact. E-mail: admit@setonhill.edu
Phone: (724) 838-4255 Toll-free number: (800) 826-6234
Fax: (724) 830-1294
Sherri Bett, Director of Admissions, Seton Hill University, 1 Seton Hill Drive, Greensburg, PA 15601

Shippensburg University of Pennsylvania

Shippensburg, Pennsylvania — **CB member**
www.ship.edu — **CB code: 2657**

- Public 4-year university
- Residential campus in small town
- 6,634 degree-seeking undergraduates: 4% part-time, 53% women, 7% African American, 2% Asian American, 2% Hispanic American
- 1,043 degree-seeking graduate students
- 71% of applicants admitted
- SAT or ACT (ACT writing optional) required
- 64% graduate within 6 years

General. Founded in 1871. Regionally accredited. **Degrees:** 1,273 bachelor's awarded; master's offered. **ROTC:** Army. **Location:** 40 miles from Harrisburg. **Calendar:** Semester, extensive summer session. **Full-time faculty:** 324 total; 90% have terminal degrees, 14% minority, 41% women. **Part-time faculty:** 73 total; 29% have terminal degrees, 1% minority, 48% women. **Class size:** 29% < 20, 56% 20-39, 14% 40-49, less than 1% 50-99. **Special facilities:** On-campus elementary school for student teachers, planetarium, vertebrate museum, greenhouse, herbarium, electron microscope, NMR spectrometer, fashion archives, interfaith spiritual center, women's center, performing arts center.

Freshman class profile. 6,765 applied, 4,791 admitted, 1,724 enrolled.

Mid 50% test scores			
SAT critical reading:	450-550	Rank in top quarter:	26%
SAT math:	440-540	Rank in top tenth:	7%
GPA 3.75 or higher:	14%	End year in good standing:	70%
GPA 3.50-3.74:	12%	Return as sophomores:	72%
GPA 3.0-3.49:	36%	Out-of-state:	8%
GPA 2.0-2.99:	37%	Live on campus:	88%

Basis for selection. Secondary school record and test scores important. Summer Bridge Program provides access and academic support to students who do not meet regular admission criteria but have demonstrated potential, desire, and motivation to succeed in college. Rolling date for test scores, but application cannot be considered for admission until test scores are received. Interviews advisable in some situations. **Homeschooled:** Transcript of courses and grades, state high school equivalency certificate required. Those working with accredited agency must submit copy of both annual evaluation and homeschool diploma. All others encouraged to schedule interview and present portfolio, and must provide GED results. Grade transcripts required (if available). **Learning Disabled:** Students must register with Office of Disability Services and provide documentation from qualified professional that verifies disability. Documentation must be less than 3 years old. Reasonable accommodations provided.

High school preparation. College-preparatory program required. 16 units recommended. Recommended units include English 4, mathematics 3, social studies 3, science 3 (laboratory 3) and foreign language 3.

2008-2009 Annual costs. Tuition/fees: $7,099; $15,137 out-of-state. Room/board: $6,604. Books/supplies: $1,090. Personal expenses: $659.

2008-2009 Financial aid. Need-based: 1,476 full-time freshmen applied for aid; 961 were judged to have need; 901 of these received aid. Average need met was 68%. Average scholarship/grant was $5,264; average loan $3,244. 39% of total undergraduate aid awarded as scholarships/grants, 61% as loans/jobs. **Non-need-based:** Awarded to 901 full-time undergraduates, including 293 freshmen. Scholarships awarded for academics, athletics.

Application procedures. Admission: No deadline. $30 fee, may be waived for applicants with need. Admission notification on a rolling basis. Must reply by April 1 or request a May 1 extension in writing. **Financial aid:** Priority date 3/15; no closing date. FAFSA required. Applicants notified on a rolling basis; must reply within 2 week(s) of notification.

Academics. Web-based online courses and programs also available. **Special study options:** Accelerated study, combined bachelor's/graduate degree, cooperative education, distance learning, double major, dual enrollment of high school students, honors, independent study, internships, semester at sea, study abroad, teacher certification program, Washington semester. **Credit/placement by examination:** AP, CLEP, IB, SAT, ACT, institutional tests. 30 credit hours maximum toward bachelor's degree. **Support services:** Learning center, pre-admission summer program, reduced course load, remedial instruction, study skills assistance, tutoring, writing center.

Majors. Biology: General. **Business:** Accounting, business admin, finance, logistics, management science, marketing. **Communications:** Journalism. **Computer sciences:** General, systems analysis. **Conservation:** Environmental studies. **Education:** Elementary. **Foreign languages:** French, Spanish. **Health:** Health care admin. **History:** General. **Math:** General. **Parks/recreation:** Exercise sciences. **Physical sciences:** Chemistry, geology, physics. **Protective services:** Criminal justice. **Psychology:** General. **Public administration:** General, social work. **Social sciences:** Economics, geography, political science, sociology. **Visual/performing arts:** Art. **Other:** Multi-interdisciplinary studies, interdisciplinary arts.

Most popular majors. Business/marketing 24%, communications/journalism 6%, education 13%, English 7%, history 6%, psychology 7%, public administration/social services 6%, security/protective services 7%, social sciences 6%.

Computing on campus. 800 workstations in dormitories, library, computer center, student center. Dormitories wired for high-speed internet access and linked to campus network. Commuter students can connect to campus network. Online course registration, online library, helpline, student web hosting, wireless network available.

Student life. Freshman orientation: Mandatory, $50 fee. Orientation held in summer and prior to fall and spring semesters. **Policies:** University student code of conduct in effect. **Housing:** Guaranteed on-campus for freshmen. Coed dorms, apartments, wellness housing available. $100 partly refundable deposit, deadline 4/1. **Activities:** Bands, campus ministries, choral groups, dance, drama, international student organizations, literary magazine, music ensembles, musical theater, radio station, student government, student newspaper, symphony orchestra, TV station, African American organization, Fellowship of Christian Athletes, Christian Fellowship, College Republicans, Jewish student organization, Big Brother-Big Sister, nontraditional student organization, Latino student organization, Asian-American association, Young Democrats.

Athletics. NCAA. **Intercollegiate:** Baseball M, basketball, cross-country, field hockey W, football (tackle) M, lacrosse W, soccer, softball W, swimming, tennis W, track and field, volleyball W, wrestling M. **Intramural:** Basketball, racquetball, soccer, softball, tennis, volleyball. **Team name:** Raiders.

Student services. Adult student services, chaplain/spiritual director, career counseling, student employment services, financial aid counseling, health services, minority student services, on-campus daycare, personal counseling, placement for graduates, veterans' counselor, women's services. **Physically disabled:** Services for visually, hearing impaired.

Contact. E-mail: admiss@ship.edu
Phone: (717) 477-1231 Toll-free number: (800) 822-8028
Fax: (717) 477-4016
Thomas Speakman, Dean of Enrollment Services, Shippensburg University of Pennsylvania, 1871 Old Main Drive, Shippensburg, PA 17257-2299

Slippery Rock University of Pennsylvania

Slippery Rock, Pennsylvania — **CB member**
www.sru.edu — **CB code: 2658**

- Public 4-year university
- Residential campus in rural community
- 7,620 degree-seeking undergraduates: 6% part-time, 56% women, 5% African American, 1% Asian American, 1% Hispanic American, 1% international
- 767 degree-seeking graduate students
- 59% of applicants admitted
- SAT or ACT (ACT writing optional) required
- 59% graduate within 6 years

General. Founded in 1889. Regionally accredited. Campus located near a state park. **Degrees:** 1,506 bachelor's awarded; master's, doctoral offered. **ROTC:** Army. **Location:** 50 miles from Pittsburgh. **Calendar:** Semester, extensive summer session. **Full-time faculty:** 338 total; 87% have terminal degrees, 18% minority, 47% women. **Part-time faculty:** 49 total; 24% have terminal degrees, 16% minority, 65% women. **Class size:** 18% <20, 58% 20-39, 16% 40-49, 5% 50-99, 3% >100. **Special facilities:** Environmental education centers, crime scene investigation house.

Freshman class profile. 5,779 applied, 3,433 admitted, 1,547 enrolled.

Mid 50% test scores		**Rank in top quarter:**	40%
SAT critical reading:	460-550	**Rank in top tenth:**	12%
SAT math:	470-570	**Return as sophomores:**	79%
SAT writing:	440-550	**Out-of-state:**	13%
ACT composite:	19-24	**Live on campus:**	95%
GPA 3.75 or higher:	21%	**International:**	1%
GPA 3.50-3.74:	22%	**Fraternities:**	5%
GPA 3.0-3.49:	38%	**Sororities:**	5%
GPA 2.0-2.99:	19%		

Basis for selection. Recommended minimum 2.5 GPA, or 76 percent or higher average. Minimum score of 900 SAT (exclusive of Writing) or 20 ACT recommended. Audition required for music and dance majors. **Homeschooled:** Documentation of homeschool diploma or certification information regarding how homeschool material was covered.

High school preparation. College-preparatory program recommended. 16 units recommended. Recommended units include English 4, mathematics 3, social studies 3, history 3, science 3 (laboratory 1) and foreign language 2.

2008-2009 Annual costs. Tuition/fees: $6,934; $9,614 out-of-state. Tuition for out-of-state students with at least 3.0 GPA is $8,038; all out-of-state undergraduates pay an additional $92 in required fees. Room/board: $8,066. Books/supplies: $1,322. Personal expenses: $1,742.

2008-2009 Financial aid. Need-based: 1,437 full-time freshmen applied for aid; 1,022 were judged to have need; 1,004 of these received aid. Average need met was 64%. Average scholarship/grant was $3,106; average loan $3,172. 42% of total undergraduate aid awarded as scholarships/grants, 58% as loans/jobs. **Non-need-based:** Awarded to 2,767 full-time undergraduates, including 805 freshmen. Scholarships awarded for academics, alumni affiliation, art, athletics, job skills, leadership, minority status, music/drama, ROTC, state residency. **Additional information:** May 1 closing date for Pennsylvania state grants.

Application procedures. Admission: No deadline. $30 fee, may be waived for applicants with need. Admission notification on a rolling basis beginning on or about 6/15. Must reply by May 1 or within 2 week(s) if notified thereafter. **Financial aid:** Priority date 5/1; no closing date. FAFSA required. Applicants notified on a rolling basis starting 3/15.

Academics. Exploratory Program for undecided majors, First Year Student Seminar, Living-Learning Environments in the Residence Halls, Learning Communities based on academic majors. **Special study options:** Combined bachelor's/graduate degree, distance learning, double major, exchange student, honors, independent study, internships, liberal arts/career combination, study abroad, teacher certification program. **Credit/placement by examination:** AP, CLEP, IB, SAT, ACT, institutional tests. 45 credit hours maximum toward bachelor's degree. **Support services:** Learning center, pre-admission summer program, reduced course load, remedial instruction, study skills assistance, tutoring, writing center.

Majors. Biology: General, biochemistry, biomedical sciences. **Business:** Accounting, business admin, finance, international, marketing. **Communications:** General, digital media, journalism, public relations. **Computer sciences:** Computer science, information technology. **Education:** Elementary, special. **Engineering technology:** Occupational safety. **Foreign languages:** French, Spanish. **Health:** Athletic training, clinical/medical social work, cytotechnology, health services admin, music therapy, nursing (RN). **History:** General. **Interdisciplinary:** Science/society. **Math:** General, statistics. **Parks/recreation:** Exercise sciences, facilities management, health/fitness, sports admin. **Philosophy/religion:** Philosophy. **Physical sciences:** Chemistry, forensic chemistry, geology, physics. **Psychology:** General. **Public administration:** Social work. **Social sciences:** Criminology, economics, geography, political science. **Visual/performing arts:** Acting, art, dance, music performance, play/screenwriting, studio arts, theater arts management, theater design. **Other:** Chemistry, environmental, Information systems, International business, Spanish, Mathematics, actuarial science, Professional studies.

Most popular majors. Business/marketing 16%, education 22%, health sciences 13%, parks/recreation 11%, social sciences 6%.

Computing on campus. 1,323 workstations in dormitories, library, computer center, student center. Dormitories wired for high-speed internet access and linked to campus network. Commuter students can connect to campus network. Online course registration, online library, helpline, repair service, wireless network available.

Student life. Freshman orientation: Mandatory, $90 fee. Preregistration for classes offered. Several sessions held during summer months. **Housing:**

Guaranteed on-campus for freshmen. Coed dorms, single-sex dorms, special housing for disabled, apartments available. $175 partly refundable deposit. Living-learning communities available. **Activities:** Bands, campus ministries, choral groups, dance, drama, film society, international student organizations, literary magazine, music ensembles, Model UN, musical theater, radio station, student government, student newspaper, symphony orchestra, TV station, Campus Crusade for Christ, SRU College Democrats, SRU College Republicans, Black Action Society, student union for minority affairs, Council for Exceptional Children, Best Buddies, American Sign Language club, bodybuilding/fitness club, outdoor adventure club.

Athletics. NCAA. **Intercollegiate:** Baseball M, basketball, cheerleading, cross-country, field hockey W, football (tackle) M, lacrosse W, soccer, softball W, tennis W, track and field, volleyball W. **Intramural:** Badminton, basketball, bowling, football (non-tackle), racquetball, soccer, softball, tennis, volleyball, water polo. **Team name:** Pride.

Student services. Adult student services, alcohol/substance abuse counseling, chaplain/spiritual director, career counseling, services for economically disadvantaged, student employment services, financial aid counseling, health services, legal services, minority student services, on-campus daycare, personal counseling, placement for graduates, veterans' counselor, women's services. **Physically disabled:** Services for visually, speech, hearing impaired.

Contact. E-mail: asktherock@sru.edu
Phone: (724) 738-2015 Toll-free number: (800) 929-4778
Fax: (724) 738-2913
W.C. Vance, Director of Admissions, Slippery Rock University of Pennsylvania, 1 Morrow Way, Slippery Rock, PA 16057-1383

Susquehanna University

Selinsgrove, Pennsylvania — **CB member**
www.susqu.edu — **CB code: 2820**

- Private 4-year university and liberal arts college affiliated with Evangelical Lutheran Church in America
- Residential campus in small town
- 2,066 degree-seeking undergraduates: 1% part-time, 53% women, 3% African American, 2% Asian American, 2% Hispanic American, 1% international
- 73% of applicants admitted
- Application essay required
- 82% graduate within 6 years; 23% enter graduate study

General. Founded in 1858. Regionally accredited. **Degrees:** 455 bachelor's, 7 associate awarded. **ROTC:** Army. **Location:** 50 miles from Harrisburg. **Calendar:** Semester, limited summer session. **Full-time faculty:** 128 total; 92% have terminal degrees, 16% minority, 43% women. **Part-time faculty:** 121 total; 23% have terminal degrees, 4% minority, 50% women. **Class size:** 52% < 20, 48% 20-39, less than 1% 40-49. **Special facilities:** Ecology field station, film library, music library, rare book room, 24-hour study center, arboretum, observatory, 450-seat teaching theater, child development center, satellite dishes, distribution system for foreign language broadcasts, video conferencing facility, high technology center for business and communications.

Freshman class profile. 2,777 applied, 2,015 admitted, 616 enrolled.

Mid 50% test scores		**GPA 2.0-2.99:**	32%
SAT critical reading:	500-610	**Rank in top quarter:**	60%
SAT math:	520-600	**Rank in top tenth:**	25%
SAT writing:	500-610	**End year in good standing:**	89%
ACT composite:	21-26	**Return as sophomores:**	85%
GPA 3.75 or higher:	18%	**Out-of-state:**	51%
GPA 3.50-3.74:	17%	**Live on campus:**	97%
GPA 3.0-3.49:	32%		

Basis for selection. School record and class rank most important, test scores secondary. Application essay, interview, teacher and counselor evaluations, activities, and interest in the university considered. Students have option of submitting 2 graded writing samples in place of SAT or ACT scores. Interview highly recommended for all. Audition required for music majors. Portfolio required for writing and graphic design majors. **Homeschooled:** Student should have detailed description of course work taken.

High school preparation. College-preparatory program required. 18 units required; 25 recommended. Required and recommended units include English 4, mathematics 3-4, social studies 2-4, history 2, science 3-4 (laboratory 2-3), foreign language 2-4 and academic electives 2-3.

2008-2009 Annual costs. Tuition/fees: $31,080. Room/board: $8,800. Books/supplies: $850. Personal expenses: $750.

2008-2009 Financial aid. Need-based: 508 full-time freshmen applied for aid; 417 were judged to have need; 417 of these received aid. Average need met was 82%. Average scholarship/grant was $19,812; average loan $3,711. 77% of total undergraduate aid awarded as scholarships/grants, 23% as loans/jobs. **Non-need-based:** Awarded to 692 full-time undergraduates, including 233 freshmen. Scholarships awarded for academics, alumni affiliation, leadership, minority status, music/drama, ROTC. **Additional information:** Graduated pay scale for federal work-study program.

Application procedures. Admission: Closing date 3/1 (postmark date). $35 fee, may be waived for applicants with need, free for online applicants. Admission notification 5/1. Admission notification on a rolling basis beginning on or about 1/15. Must reply by 5/1. **Financial aid:** Priority date 3/1, closing date 5/1. FAFSA, CSS PROFILE required. Applicants notified by 3/1; must reply by 5/1.

Academics. Special study options: Accelerated study, combined bachelor's/graduate degree, cross-registration, distance learning, double major, dual enrollment of high school students, exchange student, honors, independent study, internships, liberal arts/career combination, semester at sea, student-designed major, study abroad, teacher certification program, United Nations semester, urban semester, Washington semester. Internships abroad, 3-2 forestry or environmental management with Duke University, semester in London for junior business majors, 150-hour option in accounting to meet American Institute of CPA requirements, dentistry with Temple University, 2-2 allied health with Thomas Jefferson University. **Credit/placement by examination:** AP, CLEP, IB, SAT, ACT, institutional tests. 65 credit hours maximum toward bachelor's degree. **Support services:** Reduced course load, study skills assistance, tutoring, writing center.

Majors. Biology: General, biochemistry, ecology. **Business:** Accounting, business admin. **Communications:** General. **Computer sciences:** Computer science, information systems. **Conservation:** Environmental science. **Education:** Early childhood, elementary, music. **Foreign languages:** French, German, Spanish. **History:** General. **Interdisciplinary:** Global studies. **Liberal arts:** Arts/sciences. **Math:** General. **Philosophy/religion:** Philosophy, religion. **Physical sciences:** Chemistry, physics. **Psychology:** General. **Social sciences:** Economics, political science, sociology. **Visual/performing arts:** Art, art history/conservation, dramatic, graphic design, music performance.

Most popular majors. Biology 6%, business/marketing 26%, communications/journalism 14%, English 7%, liberal arts 6%, psychology 7%, social sciences 9%, visual/performing arts 6%.

Computing on campus. 450 workstations in dormitories, library, computer center, student center. Dormitories wired for high-speed internet access and linked to campus network. Commuter students can connect to campus network. Online course registration, online library, helpline, student web hosting, wireless network available.

Student life. Freshman orientation: Mandatory. Preregistration for classes offered. Four-day program; includes community service projects. **Housing:** Guaranteed on-campus for all undergraduates. Coed dorms, special housing for disabled, apartments, fraternity/sorority housing available. $400 nonrefundable deposit, deadline 5/1. Volunteer services living groups, scholars' house, townhouses available. **Activities:** Bands, campus ministries, choral groups, dance, drama, film society, international student organizations, literary magazine, music ensembles, musical theater, opera, radio station, student government, student newspaper, symphony orchestra, TV station, volunteer services program, investment club, Habitat for Humanity, Student Environmental Action Coalition, Hispanic and Latino student organization, black student organization, Asian student organization, Big Brothers/Big Sisters, Hillel.

Athletics. NCAA. **Intercollegiate:** Baseball M, basketball, cheerleading, cross-country, field hockey W, football (tackle) M, golf, lacrosse, rowing (crew), soccer, softball W, swimming, tennis, track and field, volleyball W. **Intramural:** Baseball M, basketball, football (non-tackle), ice hockey M, racquetball, soccer, softball, tennis, volleyball. **Team name:** Crusaders.

Student services. Adult student services, alcohol/substance abuse counseling, chaplain/spiritual director, career counseling, student employment services, financial aid counseling, health services, minority student services, on-campus daycare, personal counseling, placement for graduates, veterans' counselor, women's services. **Physically disabled:** Services for visually, speech, hearing impaired.

Contact. E-mail: suadmiss@susqu.edu
Phone: (570) 372-4260 Toll-free number: (800) 326-9672
Fax: (570) 372-2722
Chris Markle, Director of Admissions, Susquehanna University, 514 University Avenue, Selinsgrove, PA 17870-1164

Swarthmore College
Swarthmore, Pennsylvania **CB member**
www.swarthmore.edu **CB code: 2821**

- Private 4-year liberal arts college
- Residential campus in small town
- 1,477 degree-seeking undergraduates: 52% women, 9% African American, 17% Asian American, 11% Hispanic American, 1% Native American, 7% international
- 16% of applicants admitted
- SAT and SAT Subject Tests or ACT with writing, application essay required
- 92% graduate within 6 years; 21% enter graduate study

General. Founded in 1864. Regionally accredited. Quaker tradition. **Degrees:** 374 bachelor's awarded. **ROTC:** Army, Naval, Air Force. **Location:** 11 miles from Philadelphia. **Calendar:** Semester. **Full-time faculty:** 169 total; 100% have terminal degrees, 13% minority, 41% women. **Part-time faculty:** 39 total; 54% have terminal degrees, 23% minority, 54% women. **Class size:** 75% < 20, 22% 20-39, 1% 40-49, 2% 50-99, less than 1% >100. **Special facilities:** 399-acre arboretum, observatory, performing arts center, solar energy laboratory, Friends historical library, peace collection, LEED certified science center, 400-meter dual durometer track, civic and social responsibility center.

Freshman class profile. 6,121 applied, 963 admitted, 372 enrolled.

Mid 50% test scores		**Rank in top tenth:**	87%
SAT critical reading:	680-760	**End year in good standing:**	99%
SAT math:	670-760	**Return as sophomores:**	96%
SAT writing:	660-760	**Out-of-state:**	88%
ACT composite:	28-33	**Live on campus:**	100%
Rank in top quarter:	98%	**International:**	8%

Basis for selection. High school record, recommendations, class rank, test scores, essay, reading and experience in school and out, intellectual capacity and character important. Social responsibility considered. Interview strongly recommended. Both on and off-campus interviews are available to prospective students. Students may submit supplemental materials for review by the creative writing, dance, music, theater, and/or visual arts faculty. **Homeschooled:** Include supplementary materials giving evidence of intellectual passion, personal commitments, special talents and interests. Information about the curricula used, including transcripts from any formal classes is requested. Additional essay on reasons for decision to homeschool and its consequences would be helpful. **Learning Disabled:** Proper documentation required.

High school preparation. Recommended units include English 4, mathematics 3 and science 3. 3 history/social studies, study of 1 or 2 foreign languages, and coursework in art and music recommended.

2008-2009 Annual costs. Tuition/fees: $36,490. Room/board: $11,314. Books/supplies: $1,110. Personal expenses: $1,081.

2008-2009 Financial aid. Need-based: 242 full-time freshmen applied for aid; 181 were judged to have need; 181 of these received aid. Average need met was 100%. Average scholarship/grant was $33,328. 95% of total undergraduate aid awarded as scholarships/grants, 5% as loans/jobs. **Non-need-based:** Awarded to 12 full-time undergraduates, including 1 freshmen. Scholarships awarded for academics, leadership, state residency. **Additional information:** 100% of demonstrated financial need met for all admitted students.

Application procedures. Admission: Closing date 1/2 (postmark date). $60 fee, may be waived for applicants with need. Admission notification 4/1. Must reply by 5/1. **Financial aid:** Closing date 2/15. FAFSA, institutional form, CSS PROFILE required. Applicants notified by 4/1; must reply by 5/1.

Academics. Special study options: Accelerated study, cross-registration, double major, exchange student, honors, independent study, internships, student-designed major, study abroad, teacher certification program. Cooperative exchange programs with Rice and Tufts universities and Harvey Mudd, Pomona, Mills, and Middlebury colleges. **Credit/placement by examination:** AP, CLEP, IB, institutional tests. **Support services:** Study skills assistance, tutoring, writing center.

Majors. Area/ethnic studies: Asian, German, women's. **Biology:** General, biochemistry. **Computer sciences:** General. **Education:** General. **Engineering:** General. **Foreign languages:** Ancient Greek, Chinese, classics, comparative lit, French, German, Japanese, Latin, linguistics, Russian, Spanish. **History:** General. **Interdisciplinary:** Medieval/Renaissance. **Math:** General. **Philosophy/religion:** Philosophy, religion. **Physical sciences:** Astronomy, astrophysics, chemical physics, chemistry, physics. **Psychology:** General, psychobiology. **Social sciences:** Anthropology, economics, political science, sociology. **Visual/performing arts:** Art history/conservation, dance, dramatic, film/cinema, studio arts.

Most popular majors. Biology 13%, English 6%, foreign language 7%, history 7%, philosophy/religious studies 9%, psychology 6%, social sciences 26%, visual/performing arts 8%.

Computing on campus. 189 workstations in dormitories, library, computer center, student center. Dormitories wired for high-speed internet access and linked to campus network. Commuter students can connect to campus network. Online course registration, online library, helpline, repair service, student web hosting, wireless network available.

Student life. Freshman orientation: Mandatory. Four-day program held in August. Optional pre-orientation programs available. **Policies:** New students are required to live on campus. **Housing:** Guaranteed on-campus for all undergraduates. Coed dorms, single-sex dorms available. Gender-neutral housing (sharing rooms and/or bathrooms). **Activities:** Jazz band, campus ministries, choral groups, dance, drama, film society, international student organizations, literary magazine, music ensembles, opera, radio station, student government, student newspaper, symphony orchestra, Earthlust, Hillel, Muslim students organization, Saturdays of Service, Swarthmore Christian Fellowship, Swarthmore Sudan, War News Radio.

Athletics. NCAA. **Intercollegiate:** Badminton W, baseball M, basketball, cross-country, field hockey W, golf M, lacrosse, soccer, softball W, swimming, tennis, track and field, volleyball W. **Intramural:** Basketball, football (non-tackle), soccer, softball, table tennis, tennis, volleyball. **Team name:** Garnet Tide, Garnet.

Student services. Alcohol/substance abuse counseling, chaplain/spiritual director, career counseling, services for economically disadvantaged, student employment services, financial aid counseling, health services, minority student services, personal counseling, placement for graduates, women's services. **Physically disabled:** Services for visually, hearing impaired.

Contact. E-mail: admissions@swarthmore.edu
Phone: (610) 328-8300 Toll-free number: (800) 667-3110
Fax: (610) 328-8580
James Bock, Dean of Admissions and Financial Aid, Swarthmore College, 500 College Avenue, Swarthmore, PA 19081

Talmudical Yeshiva of Philadelphia
Philadelphia, Pennsylvania
CB code: 1037

- Private 4-year rabbinical college for men affiliated with Jewish faith
- Residential campus in very large city
- 112 degree-seeking undergraduates: 4% international
- 82% of applicants admitted
- Interview required

General. Founded in 1953. Accredited by AARTS. First Talmudic degree and ordination available. **Degrees:** 22 bachelor's awarded; first professional offered. **Calendar:** Trimester, extensive summer session. **Full-time faculty:** 5 total. **Part-time faculty:** 1 total.

Freshman class profile. 51 applied, 42 admitted, 34 enrolled.

End year in good standing:	97%	**Out-of-state:**	92%
Return as sophomores:	85%	**Live on campus:**	100%

Basis for selection. Institutional examinations required.

High school preparation. 20 units required. Required and recommended units include English 4, social studies 3, science 3 and foreign language 2.

2008-2009 Annual costs. Tuition/fees: $7,300. Room/board: $6,000. Books/supplies: $900.

2007-2008 Financial aid. All financial aid based on need. 22 full-time freshmen applied for aid; 22 were judged to have need; 22 of these received aid. 97% of total undergraduate aid awarded as scholarships/grants, 3% as loans/jobs.

Application procedures. Admission: Priority date 1/15; no deadline. No application fee. Admission notification on a rolling basis beginning on or about 7/15. **Financial aid:** Priority date 8/1, closing date 5/1. FAFSA, institutional form required. Applicants notified on a rolling basis starting 3/15; must reply within 2 week(s) of notification.

Academics. **Credit/placement by examination:** CLEP, IB, institutional tests. **Support services:** Tutoring.

Majors. **Theology:** Talmudic.

Student life. **Policies:** Religious observance required. **Housing:** Guaranteed on-campus for all undergraduates.

Student services. Career counseling, health services, personal counseling, placement for graduates.

Contact. Phone: (215) 473-1212 Fax: (215) 477-5065
Rabbi. Uri Mandelbaum, Admissions Director, Talmudical Yeshiva of Philadelphia, 6063 Drexel Road, Philadelphia, PA 19131

Temple University

Philadelphia, Pennsylvania **CB member**
www.temple.edu **CB code: 2906**

- Public 4-year university
- Commuter campus in very large city
- 25,598 degree-seeking undergraduates: 11% part-time, 54% women, 17% African American, 10% Asian American, 4% Hispanic American, 3% international
- 8,029 degree-seeking graduate students
- 61% of applicants admitted
- SAT or ACT with writing, application essay required
- 64% graduate within 6 years

General. Founded in 1884. Regionally accredited. Campuses in Ambler, Fort Washington, downtown Philadelphia, Harrisburg, Rome, Japan and other international locations. **Degrees:** 4,978 bachelor's, 9 associate awarded; master's, doctoral, first professional offered. **ROTC:** Army, Naval, Air Force. **Location:** 2 miles from downtown. **Calendar:** Semester, extensive summer session. **Full-time faculty:** 1,306 total; 70% have terminal degrees, 16% minority, 37% women. **Part-time faculty:** 1,447 total; 14% minority, 43% women. **Class size:** 36% < 20, 48% 20-39, 9% 40-49, 4% 50-99, 3% >100. **Special facilities:** Observatory, planetarium, arboretum, technology center.

Freshman class profile. 18,670 applied, 11,349 admitted, 3,769 enrolled.

Mid 50% test scores		**GPA 2.0-2.99:**	18%
SAT critical reading:	500-600	**Rank in top quarter:**	53%
SAT math:	510-610	**Rank in top tenth:**	20%
SAT writing:	490-590	**Return as sophomores:**	87%
ACT composite:	21-26	**Out-of-state:**	26%
GPA 3.75 or higher:	20%	**Live on campus:**	79%
GPA 3.50-3.74:	21%	**International:**	1%
GPA 3.0-3.49:	41%		

Basis for selection. Admissions process holistic; every aspect of student's academic history considered. Interview and essay required for health professions applicants. Audition required for dance, music programs; portfolio required for art. **Homeschooled:** Statement describing homeschool structure and mission, transcript of courses and grades, letter of recommendation (nonparent) required.

High school preparation. College-preparatory program required. 16 units required; 22 recommended. Required and recommended units include English 4, mathematics 3-4, social studies 2, history 1-2, science 2-3 (laboratory 1-2), foreign language 2 and academic electives 1-3.

2008-2009 Annual costs. Tuition/fees: $11,448; $20,468 out-of-state. Room/board: $8,884. Books/supplies: $1,000. Personal expenses: $3,947.

2007-2008 Financial aid. **Need-based:** 4,058 full-time freshmen applied for aid; 2,962 were judged to have need; 2,910 of these received aid. Average need met was 87%. Average scholarship/grant was $5,617; average loan $3,328. 55% of total undergraduate aid awarded as scholarships/grants, 45% as loans/jobs. **Non-need-based:** Awarded to 10,494 full-time undergraduates, including 2,547 freshmen. Scholarships awarded for academics, art, athletics, music/drama, ROTC.

Application procedures. **Admission:** Closing date 3/1 (postmark date). $50 fee, may be waived for applicants with need. Admission notification on a rolling basis beginning on or about 10/15. Must reply by May 1 or within 2 week(s) if notified thereafter. **Financial aid:** Closing date 3/1. FAFSA required. Applicants notified on a rolling basis starting 2/15; must reply by 5/1 or within 3 week(s) of notification.

Academics. **Special study options:** Combined bachelor's/graduate degree, cooperative education, cross-registration, distance learning, double major, dual enrollment of high school students, ESL, exchange student, honors, independent study, internships, liberal arts/career combination, student-designed major, study abroad, teacher certification program. Programs in Japan, Italy, Costa Rica, France, Germany, Ghana, India, Spain, Turkey, United Kingdom and Brazil. **Credit/placement by examination:** AP, CLEP, IB, institutional tests. **Support services:** Learning center, pre-admission summer program, reduced course load, remedial instruction, study skills assistance, tutoring, writing center.

Majors. **Agriculture:** Horticultural science. **Architecture:** Architecture, landscape, urban/community planning. **Area/ethnic studies:** African-American, American, Asian, Latin American, women's. **Biology:** General, biochemistry, biophysics. **Business:** General, accounting, actuarial science, business admin, entrepreneurial studies, finance, hospitality admin, insurance, international, labor relations, management information systems, marketing, real estate. **Communications:** Advertising, broadcast journalism, journalism, organizational, public relations, radio/tv. **Computer sciences:** General, information technology. **Conservation:** Environmental science, environmental studies. **Education:** Art, business, elementary, English, foreign languages, mathematics, music, science, social studies, trade/industrial. **Engineering:** Civil, computer, electrical, mechanical. **Engineering technology:** General, civil, computer hardware, construction, electromechanical, energy systems, environmental, manufacturing. **Foreign languages:** Classics, French, German, Hebrew, Italian, linguistics, Russian, Spanish. **Health:** Athletic training, audiology/speech pathology, medical records admin, music therapy, nursing (RN), public health ed, recreational therapy. **History:** General. **Interdisciplinary:** Math/computer science. **Liberal arts:** Arts/sciences. **Math:** General, statistics. **Parks/recreation:** Exercise sciences, facilities management. **Philosophy/religion:** Judaic, philosophy, religion. **Physical sciences:** General, chemistry, geology, physics. **Protective services:** Criminal justice. **Psychology:** General. **Public administration:** Social work. **Social sciences:** Anthropology, economics, international relations, political science, sociology. **Visual/performing arts:** Acting, art, art history/conservation, ceramics, dance, dramatic, fiber arts, film/cinema, graphic design, jazz, metal/jewelry, music history, music pedagogy, music performance, music theory/composition, painting, photography, printmaking, sculpture, voice/opera. **Other:** Public communications.

Most popular majors. Business/marketing 22%, communications/journalism 11%, education 10%, psychology 6%, social sciences 6%, visual/performing arts 11%.

Computing on campus. 3,587 workstations in dormitories, library, computer center, student center. Dormitories wired for high-speed internet access and linked to campus network. Commuter students can connect to campus network. Online course registration, online library, helpline, repair service, student web hosting, wireless network available.

Student life. **Freshman orientation:** Mandatory. Preregistration for classes offered. Includes placement testing. **Housing:** Guaranteed on-campus for freshmen. Coed dorms, special housing for disabled, apartments available. $250 fully refundable deposit, deadline 5/1. Living/learning centers available. **Activities:** Bands, campus ministries, choral groups, dance, drama, film society, international student organizations, literary magazine, music ensembles, musical theater, opera, radio station, student government, student newspaper, symphony orchestra, Newman Club, Hillel, Young Democrats, Young Republicans, professional organizations, public service organization, cultural organization.

Athletics. NCAA. **Intercollegiate:** Baseball M, basketball, cheerleading, cross-country, fencing W, field hockey W, football (tackle) M, golf M, gymnastics, lacrosse W, rowing (crew), soccer, softball W, tennis, track and field, volleyball W. **Intramural:** Basketball, football (non-tackle) M, soccer M, softball, volleyball. **Team name:** Owls.

Student services. Adult student services, alcohol/substance abuse counseling, chaplain/spiritual director, career counseling, services for economically disadvantaged, student employment services, financial aid counseling, health services, legal services, personal counseling, placement for graduates, veterans' counselor. **Physically disabled:** Services for visually, speech, hearing impaired. **Learning disabled:** Comprehensive services available.

Contact. E-mail: tuadm@temple.edu
Phone: (215) 204-7200 Toll-free number: (888) 340-2222
Fax: (215) 204-5694
Karin Mormando, Director, Undergraduate Admissions, Temple University, 103 Conwell Hall, Philadelphia, PA 19122-6096

Thiel College

Greenville, Pennsylvania **CB member**
www.thiel.edu **CB code: 2910**

- Private 4-year liberal arts college affiliated with Evangelical Lutheran Church in America
- Residential campus in small town

- 1,091 degree-seeking undergraduates: 2% part-time, 47% women, 7% African American, 1% Asian American, 1% Hispanic American, 5% international
- 71% of applicants admitted
- SAT or ACT with writing, interview required
- 36% graduate within 6 years

General. Founded in 1866. Regionally accredited. **Degrees:** 182 bachelor's awarded. **Location:** 75 miles from Pittsburgh, 75 miles from Cleveland. **Calendar:** Semester, limited summer session. **Full-time faculty:** 65 total; 68% have terminal degrees, 9% minority, 40% women. **Part-time faculty:** 54 total; 15% have terminal degrees, 2% minority, 63% women. **Class size:** 66% < 20, 31% 20-39, 2% 40-49, less than 1% >100. **Special facilities:** Wildlife sanctuary, black box theater.

Freshman class profile. 1,439 applied, 1,025 admitted, 317 enrolled.

Mid 50% test scores			
SAT critical reading:	400-510	Rank in top quarter:	40%
SAT math:	420-550	Rank in top tenth:	19%
ACT composite:	17-24	End year in good standing:	60%
GPA 3.75 or higher:	18%	Return as sophomores:	59%
GPA 3.50-3.74:	10%	Out-of-state:	45%
GPA 3.0-3.49:	30%	Live on campus:	91%
GPA 2.0-2.99:	38%	International:	5%

Basis for selection. High school GPA, class rank, curriculum, and recommendation important. Essay required. **Learning Disabled:** Students with disabilities must submit evidence of disability to Office of Special Needs.

High school preparation. College-preparatory program recommended. 16 units recommended. Recommended units include English 4, mathematics 2, social studies 3, science 2 (laboratory 2), foreign language 2 and academic electives 1. Engineering, math, and science majors should complete 3 years of college preparatory math and science.

2008-2009 Annual costs. Tuition/fees: $21,406. Room/board: $8,192. Books/supplies: $1,000. Personal expenses: $3,000.

2008-2009 Financial aid. **Need-based:** 281 full-time freshmen applied for aid; 267 were judged to have need; 267 of these received aid. Average need met was 75%. Average scholarship/grant was $14,779; average loan $5,719. 64% of total undergraduate aid awarded as scholarships/grants, 36% as loans/jobs. **Non-need-based:** Awarded to 197 full-time undergraduates, including 49 freshmen. Scholarships awarded for academics, alumni affiliation, leadership, music/drama, religious affiliation, state residency.

Application procedures. **Admission:** Priority date 4/1; deadline 6/30 (receipt date). $35 fee, may be waived for applicants with need, free for online applicants. Admission notification on a rolling basis beginning on or about 9/15. Must reply by May 1 or within 2 week(s) if notified thereafter. **Financial aid:** Priority date 3/15; no closing date. FAFSA required. Applicants notified on a rolling basis starting 2/15; must reply within 2 week(s) of notification.

Academics. **Special study options:** Combined bachelor's/graduate degree, cooperative education, distance learning, double major, dual enrollment of high school students, honors, independent study, internships, liberal arts/career combination, semester at sea, study abroad, teacher certification program, United Nations semester, Washington semester. 3-2 engineering with Case Western Reserve University and University of Pittsburgh, 3-2 engineering technologies with Point Park College, Pittsburgh, cooperative program with Art Institute of Pittsburgh, cooperative engineering with Youngstown State University, exchange with Duke University in forestry. **Credit/placement by examination:** AP, CLEP, IB, SAT, ACT, institutional tests. 30 credit hours maximum toward bachelor's degree. **Support services:** Learning center, reduced course load, remedial instruction, study skills assistance, tutoring, writing center.

Majors. **Biology:** General. **Business:** Accounting, actuarial science, business admin, communications, international, management information systems. **Communications:** General. **Communications technology:** Radio/tv. **Computer sciences:** General, information systems. **Conservation:** General, environmental studies. **Education:** Biology, chemistry, elementary, English, history, mathematics, physics, science, social studies. **Health:** Audiology/speech pathology, clinical lab technology, cytotechnology. **History:** General. **Interdisciplinary:** Neuroscience. **Math:** General. **Personal/culinary services:** General, mortuary science. **Philosophy/religion:** Philosophy, religion. **Physical sciences:** Chemistry, physics. **Protective services:** Criminal justice. **Psychology:** General. **Social sciences:** Political science, sociology. **Theology:** Religious ed. **Visual/performing arts:** General, art, commercial/advertising art. **Other:** Binary engineering, Neuroscience.

Most popular majors. Biology 8%, business/marketing 25%, education 13%, English 8%, history 6%, psychology 9%, security/protective services 7%.

Computing on campus. PC or laptop required. 300 workstations in dormitories, library, computer center, student center. Dormitories wired for high-speed internet access and linked to campus network. Commuter students can connect to campus network. Online course registration, helpline, wireless network available.

Student life. **Freshman orientation:** Mandatory, $275 fee. Preregistration for classes offered. Weekend before classes start. **Housing:** Guaranteed on-campus for all undergraduates. Coed dorms, apartments, fraternity/sorority housing, wellness housing available. $150 partly refundable deposit, deadline 6/30. Special interest housing, learning/living environment available. **Activities:** Bands, campus ministries, choral groups, dance, drama, international student organizations, literary magazine, music ensembles, musical theater, radio station, student government, student newspaper, symphony orchestra, TV station, Organization of Black Collegiates, Lutheran student movement, Circle K.

Athletics. NCAA. **Intercollegiate:** Baseball M, basketball, cheerleading, cross-country, football (tackle) M, golf M, soccer, softball W, track and field, volleyball W, wrestling M. **Intramural:** Badminton, basketball, softball, table tennis, volleyball. **Team name:** Tomcats.

Student services. Alcohol/substance abuse counseling, chaplain/spiritual director, career counseling, student employment services, financial aid counseling, health services, minority student services, personal counseling, placement for graduates. **Physically disabled:** Services for visually, hearing impaired.

Contact. E-mail: admission@thiel.edu
Phone: (724) 589-2345 Toll-free number: (800) 248-4435
Fax: (724) 589-2013
Sonya Lapikas, Director of Admissions, Thiel College, 75 College Avenue, Greenville, PA 16125-2181

Thomas Jefferson University: College of Health Professions

Philadelphia, Pennsylvania
www.jefferson.edu/jchp **CB code: 2903**

- Private two-year upper-division health science and nursing college
- Residential campus in very large city
- Application essay required

General. Founded in 1824. Regionally accredited. Associate degree programs available in evening division. **Degrees:** 330 bachelor's, 89 associate awarded; master's, doctoral, first professional offered. **Articulation:** Agreements with Bloomsburg U of Pennsylvania, Bucks County CC, Cabrini College, CC of Philadelphia, Delaware County CC, Elizabethtown College, Juniata College, Keystone JC, La Salle U, Lebanon Valley College of Pennsylvania, Manor JC, Moravian College, Penn State: Delaware County Campus, St. Joseph's U, Shippensburg U of Pennsylvania, Susquehanna U, Villanova U, Gordon College, Burlington County College, Camden County College, Gloucester County College, Penn State: Abington Campus, Rider U, Muhlenberg College, Middlesex County College, Cumberland County College, Arcadia U. **ROTC:** Naval, Air Force. **Calendar:** Semester, limited summer session. **Full-time faculty:** 150 total. **Part-time faculty:** 55 total. **Special facilities:** Rare book collection, simulation labs, human performance lab (gait research), simulation building.

Student profile. 893 degree-seeking undergraduates, 1,991 degree-seeking graduate students. 80% entered as juniors, 20% entered as seniors. 55% transferred from two-year, 45% transferred from four-year institutions.

Women:	84%	International:	1%
African American:	9%	Part-time:	16%
Asian American:	7%	Out-of-state:	27%
Hispanic American:	2%	Live on campus:	30%

Basis for selection. College transcript, application essay required. Decisions based on review of college transcripts, recommendations, written personal statement, and interview. Specific prerequisite credit requirements for each program. Volunteer experiences strongly recommended; 2 site visits required for OT applicants. Transfer accepted as sophomores, juniors, seniors.

2008-2009 Annual costs. Tuition/fees: $24,514. Books/supplies: $1,495. Personal expenses: $855.

Financial aid. **Non-need-based:** Scholarships awarded for academics, leadership, state residency.

Application procedures. **Admission:** Priority date 3/1. $50 fee, may be waived for applicants with need. **Financial aid:** Applicants notified on a rolling basis starting 11/15; must reply within 2 weeks of notification. FAFSA, institutional form required.

Academics. Plan College Education Program allows qualified high school seniors to reserve a place for future enrollment after completion of required college program. **Special study options:** Accelerated study, combined bachelor's/graduate degree, distance learning, independent study, internships, study abroad. **Credit/placement by examination:** AP, CLEP, institutional tests. 30 credit hours maximum toward bachelor's degree. **Support services:** Preadmission summer program, study skills assistance, tutoring, writing center.

Majors. Biology: Biotechnology. **Health:** Cardiovascular technology, clinical lab science, cytotechnology, nursing (RN), preop/surgical nursing, sonography. **Science technology:** Biological.

Computing on campus. 100 workstations in library, computer center, student center. Dormitories wired for high-speed internet access. Commuter students can connect to campus network. Online course registration, online library, helpline, wireless network available.

Student life. Housing: Guaranteed on-campus for all undergraduates. Coed dorms, special housing for disabled, apartments available. **Activities:** Choral groups, international student organizations, student government, African American student society, Chinese students and scholars society, Hands of Hope, Jewish student association, Medical Professionals for Choice, Asian professional society, Latino health organization, occupational therapy association, physical therapy association, Student Nurses Association of Pennsylvania.

Athletics. Intramural: Basketball, football (non-tackle) M, golf, racquetball, rugby, softball, squash, swimming, table tennis, tennis, volleyball, water polo.

Student services. Adult student services, alcohol/substance abuse counseling, career counseling, student employment services, financial aid counseling, health services, minority student services, on-campus daycare, personal counseling, placement for graduates, veterans' counselor.

Contact. E-mail: jchp@jefferson.edu
Phone: (215) 503-8890 Toll-free number: (877) 533-3247
Fax: (215) 503-7241
Karen Astle, Assistant Dean for Admission, Thomas Jefferson University: College of Health Professions, 130 South Ninth Street, Edison Building, Suite 100, Philadelphia, PA 19107

University of Pennsylvania

Philadelphia, Pennsylvania **CB member**
www.upenn.edu **CB code: 2926**

- Private 4-year university
- Residential campus in very large city
- 9,756 degree-seeking undergraduates: 2% part-time, 50% women, 8% African American, 18% Asian American, 6% Hispanic American, 10% international
- 9,262 degree-seeking graduate students
- 17% of applicants admitted
- SAT and SAT Subject Tests or ACT with writing, application essay required
- 95% graduate within 6 years; 20% enter graduate study

General. Founded in 1740. Regionally accredited. **Degrees:** 2,766 bachelor's awarded; master's, doctoral, first professional offered. **ROTC:** Army, Naval, Air Force. **Location:** One mile from downtown. **Calendar:** Semester, limited summer session. **Full-time faculty:** 1,406 total; 100% have terminal degrees, 18% minority, 35% women. **Part-time faculty:** 1,383 total; 100% have terminal degrees, 14% minority, 44% women. **Class size:** 73% < 20, 17% 20-39, 3% 40-49, 6% 50-99, 1% >100. **Special facilities:** Arthropology museum, contemporary art institute, arboretum, astronomical observatory, large animal research center, women's center, undergraduate research center, wind tunnel, Kelly Writer's House, Hillel Foundation.

Freshman class profile. 22,935 applied, 3,883 admitted, 2,430 enrolled.

Mid 50% test scores		**Rank in top quarter:**	100%
SAT critical reading:	650-740	**Rank in top tenth:**	99%
SAT math:	680-780	**End year in good standing:**	97%
SAT writing:	670-760	**Return as sophomores:**	98%
ACT composite:	30-33	**Out-of-state:**	83%
GPA 3.75 or higher:	72%	**Live on campus:**	100%
GPA 3.50-3.74:	17%	**International:**	10%
GPA 3.0-3.49:	10%	**Fraternities:**	29%
GPA 2.0-2.99:	1%	**Sororities:**	26%

Basis for selection. Transcript indicating rigor of course work and achievement/evaluation most important criteria. Co-curricular involvements and testing strongly considered, as are counselor and faculty recommendations. Personal commentary (essays) and interview considered as well. Interested in diverse geographic, economic, racial, ethnic student body. Students must submit their entire ACT and/or SAT test score history. Portfolio suggested for Architecture and Fine Arts programs. **Homeschooled:** Statement describing homeschool structure and mission, transcript of courses and grades, letter of recommendation (nonparent) required. Commentary from primary instructor most important, and at least 1 other academic reference highly recommended. SAT subject tests in major academic areas highly recommended.

High school preparation. College-preparatory program recommended. 21 units recommended. Recommended units include English 4, mathematics 4, history 3, science 3 (laboratory 3) and foreign language 4.

2008-2009 Annual costs. Tuition/fees: $37,526. Room/board: $10,622. Books/supplies: $1,042. Personal expenses: $2,067.

2007-2008 Financial aid. All financial aid based on need. 1,243 full-time freshmen applied for aid; 923 were judged to have need; 923 of these received aid. Average need met was 100%. Average scholarship/grant was $29,284; average loan $1,912. 85% of total undergraduate aid awarded as scholarships/grants, 15% as loans/jobs.

Application procedures. Admission: Closing date 1/1 (postmark date). $75 fee, may be waived for applicants with need. Admission notification 4/1. Must reply by 5/1. **Financial aid:** Priority date 2/15; no closing date. FAFSA, institutional form, CSS PROFILE required. Applicants notified by 4/1; must reply by 5/1.

Academics. Special study options: Accelerated study, combined bachelor's/graduate degree, cross-registration, double major, dual enrollment of high school students, ESL, exchange student, honors, independent study, internships, liberal arts/career combination, student-designed major, study abroad, teacher certification program, Washington semester. **Credit/placement by examination:** AP, CLEP, IB, institutional tests. No maximum number of semester hours of credit by examination counted toward degree. **Support services:** Learning center, pre-admission summer program, remedial instruction, study skills assistance, tutoring, writing center.

Majors. Architecture: Architecture, environmental design. **Area/ethnic studies:** African, African-American, American, East Asian, South Asian, women's. **Biology:** General, biochemistry, bioinformatics, biomedical sciences, biophysics. **Business:** Accounting, actuarial science, business admin, e-commerce, finance, human resources, insurance, international, management information systems, marketing, operations, real estate, sales/distribution, transportation. **Communications:** General. **Computer sciences:** General, computer graphics, networking. **Conservation:** Environmental studies. **Education:** General, elementary. **Engineering:** Biomedical, chemical, computer, electrical, environmental, materials, materials science, mechanical, systems. **Foreign languages:** Classics, comparative lit, East Asian, French, German, Italian, linguistics, Russian, Semitic, Spanish. **Health:** Community health services, health care admin, nursing (RN). **History:** General, science/technology. **Interdisciplinary:** Cognitive science, global studies, natural sciences, neuroscience. **Legal studies:** General. **Liberal arts:** Arts/sciences, humanities. **Math:** General, statistics. **Philosophy/religion:** Judaic, logic, philosophy, religion. **Physical sciences:** Chemistry, geology, physics. **Psychology:** General. **Public administration:** Policy analysis. **Social sciences:** General, anthropology, economics, international relations, political science, sociology, urban studies. **Visual/performing arts:** General, art history/conservation, dramatic, film/cinema, studio arts.

Most popular majors. Business/marketing 23%, engineering/engineering technologies 9%, health sciences 7%, interdisciplinary studies 6%, social sciences 16%.

Computing on campus. 1,295 workstations in dormitories, library, computer center, student center. Dormitories wired for high-speed internet access and linked to campus network. Commuter students can connect to campus network. Online course registration, online library, helpline, repair service, student web hosting, wireless network available.

Student life. Freshman orientation: Mandatory. Preregistration for classes offered. **Housing:** Guaranteed on-campus for freshmen. Coed dorms, special housing for disabled, apartments, fraternity/sorority housing, wellness housing available. $200 nonrefundable deposit, deadline 5/1. Private off-campus housing available. **Activities:** Bands, choral groups, dance, drama, film society, literary magazine, music ensembles, musical theater, opera, radio station, student government, student newspaper, symphony orchestra, TV station, various religious, political, ethnic, social service, performing arts, cultural, and sports organizations.

Athletics. NCAA. **Intercollegiate:** Baseball M, basketball, cross-country, diving, fencing, field hockey W, football (tackle) M, golf, gymnastics W, lacrosse, rowing (crew), soccer, softball W, squash, swimming, tennis, track and field, volleyball W, wrestling M. **Intramural:** Basketball, football (non-tackle), soccer, softball, tennis, volleyball. **Team name:** Quakers.

Student services. Adult student services, alcohol/substance abuse counseling, chaplain/spiritual director, career counseling, services for economically disadvantaged, student employment services, financial aid counseling, health services, legal services, minority student services, on-campus daycare, personal counseling, placement for graduates, veterans' counselor, women's services. **Physically disabled:** Services for visually, speech, hearing impaired. **Learning disabled:** Comprehensive services available.

Contact. E-mail: info@admissions.ugao.upenn.edu
Phone: (215) 898-7507 Fax: (215) 898-9670
Eric Furda, Dean of Admissions, University of Pennsylvania, 1 College Hall, Philadelphia, PA 19104

University of Pittsburgh

Pittsburgh, Pennsylvania — **CB member**
www.pitt.edu — **CB code: 2927**

- Public 4-year university
- Residential campus in large city
- 17,054 degree-seeking undergraduates: 6% part-time, 51% women, 8% African American, 5% Asian American, 1% Hispanic American, 1% international
- 9,800 degree-seeking graduate students
- 55% of applicants admitted
- SAT or ACT (ACT writing optional) required
- 76% graduate within 6 years; 38% enter graduate study

General. Founded in 1787. Regionally accredited. Regional campuses in Johnstown, Bradford, Titusville, and Greensburg. **Degrees:** 3,914 bachelor's awarded; master's, doctoral, first professional offered. **ROTC:** Army, Naval, Air Force. **Location:** 3 miles from downtown. **Calendar:** Semester, extensive summer session. **Full-time faculty:** 1,550 total. **Part-time faculty:** 535 total. **Class size:** 44% < 20, 34% 20-39, 6% 40-49, 10% 50-99, 6% >100. **Special facilities:** Observatory, nationality rooms, performance hall, American music center, ecology laboratory.

Freshman class profile. 20,685 applied, 11,467 admitted, 3,488 enrolled.

Mid 50% test scores		**Rank in top quarter:**	85%
SAT critical reading:	570-680	**Rank in top tenth:**	48%
SAT math:	590-680	**Return as sophomores:**	91%
ACT composite:	25-30	**Out-of-state:**	25%
GPA 3.75 or higher:	64%	**Live on campus:**	95%
GPA 3.50-3.74:	16%	**International:**	2%
GPA 3.0-3.49:	17%	**Fraternities:**	7%
GPA 2.0-2.99:	3%	**Sororities:**	8%

Basis for selection. GED not accepted. High school record, class rank, test scores, and activities considered. College of General Studies applicants must apply directly to that college, not through Admissions and Financial Aid. Students admitted as freshmen into School of Arts and Sciences, School of Engineering, School of Nursing, and College of Business Administration. Students may be conditionally accepted into the School of Pharmacy, PharmD program with the provision that they successfully complete 4 terms (2 years) of preprofessional study in School of Arts and Sciences. Interview and essay recommended for all; audition required for music program; portfolio recommended for studio art program; essay required for pharmacy applicants. **Homeschooled:** Statement describing homeschool structure and mission, transcript of courses and grades required.

High school preparation. College-preparatory program required. 17 units required; 23 recommended. Required and recommended units include English 4, mathematics 3, social studies 2-3, science 3-4, foreign language 2-3 and academic electives 3-5.

2008-2009 Annual costs. Tuition/fees: $13,642; $23,290 out-of-state. Room/board: $8,600.

2008-2009 Financial aid. **Need-based:** 2,792 full-time freshmen applied for aid; 1,900 were judged to have need; 1,861 of these received aid. Average need met was 82%. Average scholarship/grant was $9,170; average loan $5,356. 54% of total undergraduate aid awarded as scholarships/grants, 46% as loans/jobs. **Non-need-based:** Awarded to 3,982 full-time undergraduates, including 1,221 freshmen. Scholarships awarded for academics, athletics.

Application procedures. **Admission:** No deadline. $45 fee, may be waived for applicants with need. Admission notification on a rolling basis beginning on or about 10/1. Must reply by May 1 or within 3 week(s) if notified thereafter. **Financial aid:** Priority date 3/1; no closing date. FAFSA required. Applicants notified on a rolling basis starting 3/15.

Academics. Accelerated high school program enables students to take courses in School of Arts and Sciences while in high school. **Special study options:** Accelerated study, combined bachelor's/graduate degree, cooperative education, cross-registration, distance learning, double major, dual enrollment of high school students, ESL, exchange student, external degree, honors, independent study, internships, liberal arts/career combination, student-designed major, study abroad, teacher certification program, Washington semester. Freshman seminars, early admission to some graduate programs for exceptional students. **Credit/placement by examination:** AP, CLEP, IB, SAT, ACT, institutional tests. 60 credit hours maximum toward bachelor's degree. College of Arts and Sciences does not accept CLEP. **Support services:** Learning center, pre-admission summer program, reduced course load, remedial instruction, study skills assistance, tutoring, writing center.

Majors. **Area/ethnic studies:** African-American. **Biology:** General, ecology, microbiology, molecular. **Business:** Accounting, business admin, finance, marketing. **Communications:** Media studies. **Computer sciences:** Computer science, information systems. **Education:** Physical. **Engineering:** Biomedical, chemical, civil, computer, electrical, industrial, materials, mechanical, physics. **Foreign languages:** Chinese, classics, French, German, Italian, Japanese, linguistics, Polish, Russian, Slavic, Spanish. **Health:** Audiology/speech pathology, dental hygiene, dietetics, medical records admin, nursing (RN), orthotics/prosthetics. **History:** General, science/technology. **Interdisciplinary:** Biological/physical sciences. **Liberal arts:** Arts/sciences, humanities. **Math:** General, applied, statistics. **Philosophy/religion:** Philosophy, religion. **Physical sciences:** General, chemistry, geology, physics. **Protective services:** Corrections. **Psychology:** General, educational. **Public administration:** General, social work. **Social sciences:** General, anthropology, economics, political science, sociology, urban studies. **Visual/performing arts:** Art history/conservation, dramatic, film/cinema, studio arts.

Most popular majors. Business/marketing 13%, engineering/engineering technologies 10%, English 11%, health sciences 9%, psychology 9%, social sciences 13%.

Computing on campus. 600 workstations in dormitories, library, computer center, student center. Dormitories wired for high-speed internet access and linked to campus network. Commuter students can connect to campus network. Online library, helpline, repair service, wireless network available.

Student life. **Freshman orientation:** Available. Preregistration for classes offered. **Housing:** Guaranteed on-campus for freshmen. Coed dorms, single-sex dorms, fraternity/sorority housing available. $325 fully refundable deposit. Rooms can be adapted to meet disabled students' particular needs. **Activities:** Bands, campus ministries, choral groups, dance, drama, film society, international student organizations, literary magazine, music ensembles, Model UN, radio station, student government, student newspaper, TV station, approximately 450 student organizations.

Athletics. NCAA. **Intercollegiate:** Baseball M, basketball, cross-country, diving, football (tackle) M, gymnastics W, soccer, softball W, swimming, tennis W, track and field, volleyball W, wrestling M. **Intramural:** Badminton, basketball, football (tackle) M, racquetball, soccer, squash, swimming, volleyball, wrestling M. **Team name:** Panthers.

Student services. Adult student services, alcohol/substance abuse counseling, chaplain/spiritual director, career counseling, student employment services, financial aid counseling, health services, personal counseling, placement for graduates, veterans' counselor. **Physically disabled:** Services for visually, speech, hearing impaired.

Contact. E-mail: oafa@pitt.edu
Phone: (412) 624-7488 Fax: (412) 648-8815
Betsy Porter, Director, Office of Admissions and Financial Aid, University of Pittsburgh, 4227 Fifth Avenue, 1st Floor, Alumni Hall, Pittsburgh, PA 15260

University of Pittsburgh at Bradford

Bradford, Pennsylvania — **CB member**
www.upb.pitt.edu — **CB code: 2935**

- Public 4-year university
- Residential campus in large town
- 1,456 degree-seeking undergraduates: 9% part-time, 56% women, 5% African American, 3% Asian American, 1% Hispanic American, 1% international
- 62% of applicants admitted
- SAT or ACT (ACT writing optional) required
- 46% graduate within 6 years; 22% enter graduate study

General. Founded in 1963. Regionally accredited. **Degrees:** 202 bachelor's, 34 associate awarded. **ROTC:** Army. **Location:** 160 miles from Pittsburgh, 79 miles from Buffalo, New York. **Calendar:** Semester, extensive summer session. **Full-time faculty:** 71 total; 65% have terminal degrees, 16% minority, 31% women. **Part-time faculty:** 79 total; 13% have terminal degrees, 5% minority, 58% women. **Class size:** 52% < 20, 42% 20-39, 3% 40-49, 4% 50-99. **Special facilities:** Located in the Allegheny National Forest.

Freshman class profile. 1,032 applied, 639 admitted, 379 enrolled.

Mid 50% test scores		**GPA 2.0-2.99:**	36%
SAT critical reading:	440-540	**Rank in top quarter:**	31%
SAT math:	440-550	**Rank in top tenth:**	8%
SAT writing:	430-540	**End year in good standing:**	72%
ACT composite:	19-24	**Return as sophomores:**	72%
GPA 3.75 or higher:	18%	**Out-of-state:**	19%
GPA 3.50-3.74:	11%	**Live on campus:**	85%
GPA 3.0-3.49:	31%	**International:**	1%

Basis for selection. School achievement record, test scores, interview most important. Essay and recommendations considered. **Homeschooled:** Required: Complete listing of courses taken/completed/in progress, syllabus for each course, textbook used, 1 recommendation from educator, 1 outside recommendation, personal essay, personal interview, state requirement satisfaction.

High school preparation. College-preparatory program recommended. 15 units required. Required and recommended units include English 4, mathematics 2-2.5, history 1, science 1-2 (laboratory 1-2), foreign language 2 and academic electives 5. Engineering and math students must have trigonometry and physics with a lab. Nursing majors must have 3 social science and 1 each of chemistry and biology with labs in both.

2008-2009 Annual costs. Tuition/fees: $11,722; $21,282 out-of-state. Room/board: $7,050. Books/supplies: $1,030. Personal expenses: $1,540.

2008-2009 Financial aid. Need-based: 355 full-time freshmen applied for aid; 304 were judged to have need; 304 of these received aid. Average need met was 89%. Average scholarship/grant was $8,782; average loan $3,245. 63% of total undergraduate aid awarded as scholarships/grants, 37% as loans/jobs. **Non-need-based:** Awarded to 33 full-time undergraduates, including 11 freshmen. Scholarships awarded for academics, alumni affiliation, ROTC, state residency.

Application procedures. Admission: Priority date 5/1; no deadline. $45 fee, may be waived for applicants with need. Admission notification on a rolling basis beginning on or about 10/8. Must reply by May 1 or within 2 week(s) if notified thereafter. **Financial aid:** Priority date 3/1; no closing date. FAFSA required. Applicants notified on a rolling basis starting 4/1; must reply within 2 week(s) of notification.

Academics. Student services include: on-going individual academic, personal and career counseling; strategies for maintaining and improving GPA; assistance with study skills and life management issues; cultural enrichment activities; computer learning lab services; graduate school assistance. **Special study options:** Combined bachelor's/graduate degree, cross-registration, distance learning, double major, dual enrollment of high school students, external degree, independent study, internships, semester at sea, study abroad, teacher certification program. 3-4 pre-optometry program with Pennsylvania College of Optometry, 1-4 pharmacy program with Oakland campus, 3+4 program with LECOM in Osteopathic Medicine. **Credit/placement by examination:** AP, CLEP, IB, SAT, ACT, institutional tests. 30 credit hours maximum toward associate degree, 90 toward bachelor's. **Support services:** Learning center, reduced course load, remedial instruction, study skills assistance, tutoring.

Majors. Biology: General. **Business:** General, accounting, business admin, entrepreneurial studies, hospitality admin. **Communications:** Public relations, radio/tv. **Computer sciences:** Applications programming, computer science. **Conservation:** Environmental studies. **Education:** General, elementary, physical, secondary, social science. **Engineering:** General, chemical, civil, electrical, industrial, mechanical, science. **Engineering technology:** Petroleum. **Health:** Athletic training, nursing (RN), radiologic technology/medical imaging. **Interdisciplinary:** Biological/physical sciences. **Liberal arts:** Humanities. **Math:** Applied. **Parks/recreation:** Sports admin. **Physical sciences:** General, chemistry. **Protective services:** Corrections, law enforcement admin. **Psychology:** General. **Social sciences:** General, demography, economics, political science, sociology. **Visual/performing arts:** General.

Most popular majors. Business/marketing 21%, communications/journalism 7%, education 7%, health sciences 20%, security/protective services 9%, social sciences 13%.

Computing on campus. 118 workstations in library, computer center, student center. Dormitories wired for high-speed internet access and linked to campus network. Commuter students can connect to campus network. Online library, helpline, repair service, student web hosting, wireless network available.

Student life. Freshman orientation: Mandatory, $90 fee. Preregistration for classes offered. 2-day program for students and parents in July; additional 3-day program immediately prior to start of classes. **Housing:** Guaranteed on-campus for freshmen. Coed dorms, special housing for disabled, apartments available. $125 nonrefundable deposit, deadline 5/1. Townhouse/apartment style housing available. **Activities:** Campus ministries, choral groups, dance, drama, literary magazine, radio station, student government, student newspaper, black action committee, Christ in Action, Collegiate Liberals of America, Conservative Union, Habitat for Humanity, ideology expression club.

Athletics. NCAA. **Intercollegiate:** Baseball M, basketball, cross-country, golf, soccer, softball W, swimming, volleyball W. **Intramural:** Basketball, football (non-tackle), golf, ice hockey, soccer, softball, swimming, table tennis, tennis, volleyball, water polo. **Team name:** Panthers.

Student services. Adult student services, alcohol/substance abuse counseling, chaplain/spiritual director, career counseling, student employment services, financial aid counseling, health services, personal counseling, placement for graduates, veterans' counselor.

Contact. E-mail: admissions@upb.pitt.edu
Phone: (814) 362-7555 Toll-free number: (800) 872-1787
Fax: (814) 362-5150
Alexander Nazemetz, Director of Admissions, University of Pittsburgh at Bradford, 300 Campus Drive, Bradford, PA 16701

University of Pittsburgh at Greensburg

Greensburg, Pennsylvania
www.upg.pitt.edu **CB code: 2936**

- Public 4-year branch campus and liberal arts college
- Commuter campus in large town
- 1,807 degree-seeking undergraduates: 7% part-time, 50% women, 5% African American, 3% Asian American, 1% Hispanic American
- 73% of applicants admitted
- SAT or ACT with writing required
- 53% graduate within 6 years

General. Founded in 1963. Regionally accredited. **Degrees:** 225 bachelor's awarded. **ROTC:** Army, Air Force. **Location:** 35 miles from Pittsburgh. **Calendar:** Semester, limited summer session. **Full-time faculty:** 74 total. **Part-time faculty:** 60 total. **Class size:** 37% < 20, 51% 20-39, 4% 40-49, 8% 50-99. **Special facilities:** Wildlife sanctuary and nature trail, humanities village, behavioral science village, natural sciences and new technologies village, international village.

Freshman class profile. 1,436 applied, 1,055 admitted, 462 enrolled.

Mid 50% test scores		**GPA 2.0-2.99:**	25%
SAT critical reading:	460-550	**Rank in top quarter:**	35%
SAT math:	470-560	**Rank in top tenth:**	9%
SAT writing:	440-540	**Return as sophomores:**	75%
ACT composite:	19-23	**Out-of-state:**	5%
GPA 3.75 or higher:	17%	**Live on campus:**	64%
GPA 3.50-3.74:	18%	**International:**	1%
GPA 3.0-3.49:	40%		

Basis for selection. High school curriculum and grades most important, followed by class rank and SAT/ACT scores. Interviews, essays and letters of recommendation all optional. **Homeschooled:** Transcript of courses and grades required.

High school preparation. 15 units required; 20 recommended. Required and recommended units include English 4, mathematics 2-4, social studies 2, history 2, science 1-2 (laboratory 1), foreign language 3, computer science 1 and academic electives 1-3. If student is missing foreign language unit, must have enough academic elective units to meet the minimum total units required (15).

2008-2009 Annual costs. Tuition/fees: $11,782; $21,342 out-of-state. Room/board: $7,530. Books/supplies: $1,000. Personal expenses: $1,500.

2008-2009 Financial aid. Need-based: 406 full-time freshmen applied for aid; 342 were judged to have need; 340 of these received aid. Average need met was 53%. Average scholarship/grant was $6,177; average loan $3,592. 39% of total undergraduate aid awarded as scholarships/grants, 61% as loans/jobs. **Non-need-based:** Awarded to 301 full-time undergraduates, including 111 freshmen. Scholarships awarded for academics, leadership, minority status.

Application procedures. Admission: No deadline. $45 fee, may be waived for applicants with need. Admission notification on a rolling basis beginning on or about 9/1. Must reply by May 1 or within 3 week(s) if notified thereafter. **Financial aid:** Priority date 2/15; no closing date. FAFSA required. Applicants notified on a rolling basis starting 3/15; must reply within 3 week(s) of notification.

Academics. Special study options: Combined bachelor's/graduate degree, cross-registration, double major, dual enrollment of high school students, exchange student, independent study, internships, liberal arts/career combination, student-designed major, study abroad. **Credit/placement by examination:** AP, CLEP, SAT, ACT, institutional tests. 30 credit hours maximum toward bachelor's degree. **Support services:** Learning center, reduced course load, remedial instruction, study skills assistance, tutoring, writing center.

Majors. Area/ethnic studies: American. **Biology:** General. **Business:** Accounting, business admin, management information systems. **Communications:** General, journalism, public relations. **Computer sciences:** Information systems. **Health:** Predental, premedicine, prepharmacy, preveterinary. **History:** General. **Liberal arts:** Arts/sciences. **Math:** Applied. **Physical sciences:** Chemistry. **Protective services:** Law enforcement admin. **Psychology:** General. **Social sciences:** General, anthropology, criminology, political science.

Most popular majors. Biology 10%, business/marketing 26%, English 19%, psychology 18%, security/protective services 11%, social sciences 6%.

Computing on campus. 400 workstations in dormitories, library, computer center. Dormitories wired for high-speed internet access and linked to campus network. Commuter students can connect to campus network. Online course registration, online library, helpline, repair service, student web hosting, wireless network available.

Student life. Freshman orientation: Mandatory, $55 fee. **Housing:** Coed dorms, wellness housing available. $150 fully refundable deposit, deadline 5/1. **Activities:** Choral groups, dance, drama, international student organizations, literary magazine, musical theater, radio station, student government, student newspaper, student activities board, honor societies, academic societies, Alpha Phi Omega, Circle K, Amnesty International, Christian fellowship club, College Republicans, College Democrats.

Athletics. NCAA. **Intercollegiate:** Baseball M, basketball, cross-country, golf, soccer, softball W, tennis, volleyball W. **Intramural:** Baseball M, basketball, golf, racquetball, skiing, soccer, softball, table tennis, tennis, volleyball. **Team name:** Bobcats.

Student services. Adult student services, alcohol/substance abuse counseling, career counseling, student employment services, financial aid counseling, health services, personal counseling, placement for graduates. **Physically disabled:** Services for visually, hearing impaired.

Contact. E-mail: upgadmit@pitt.edu
Phone: (724) 836-9880 Fax: (724) 836-7471
Heather Kabala, Director of Admissions, University of Pittsburgh at Greensburg, 150 Finoli Drive, Greensburg, PA 15601

University of Pittsburgh at Johnstown

Johnstown, Pennsylvania — **CB member**
www.upj.pitt.edu — **CB code: 2934**

- Public 4-year engineering and liberal arts college
- Residential campus in small city
- 3,024 degree-seeking undergraduates: 5% part-time, 47% women, 2% African American, 1% Asian American, 1% Hispanic American
- 89% of applicants admitted
- SAT or ACT (ACT writing recommended) required
- 59% graduate within 6 years

General. Founded in 1927. Regionally accredited. **Degrees:** 533 bachelor's, 21 associate awarded. **Location:** 70 miles from Pittsburgh. **Calendar:** Semester, limited summer session. **Full-time faculty:** 143 total; 68% have terminal degrees, 8% minority, 37% women. **Part-time faculty:** 51 total; 37% have terminal degrees, 2% minority, 37% women. **Class size:** 32% < 20, 58% 20-39, 5% 40-49, 3% 50-99, less than 1% >100. **Special facilities:** 40-acre nature preserve maintained by biology department, performing arts center.

Freshman class profile. 1,704 applied, 1,513 admitted, 835 enrolled.

Mid 50% test scores		**Rank in top quarter:**	32%
SAT critical reading:	440-540	**Rank in top tenth:**	9%
SAT math:	460-560	**Return as sophomores:**	72%
SAT writing:	440-540	**Out-of-state:**	2%
ACT composite:	19-24	**Live on campus:**	80%
GPA 3.75 or higher:	22%	**International:**	1%
GPA 3.50-3.74:	19%	**Fraternities:**	4%
GPA 3.0-3.49:	35%	**Sororities:**	4%
GPA 2.0-2.99:	24%		

Basis for selection. College preparatory curriculum, high school achievement, test scores, and class rank very important. Recommendations and essay considered. Interview recommended.

High school preparation. 15 units required. Required and recommended units include English 4, mathematics 2-3, social studies 4, science 2 (laboratory 1-2) and foreign language 2. One each of trigonometry, physics, and chemistry required for engineering technology program.

2008-2009 Annual costs. Tuition/fees: $11,754; $21,314 out-of-state. Room/board: $6,860. Books/supplies: $1,030. Personal expenses: $1,550.

2008-2009 Financial aid. Need-based: 716 full-time freshmen applied for aid; 712 were judged to have need; 589 of these received aid. Average need met was 56%. Average scholarship/grant was $5,321; average loan $3,602. 47% of total undergraduate aid awarded as scholarships/grants, 53% as loans/jobs. **Non-need-based:** Awarded to 839 full-time undergraduates, including 248 freshmen. Scholarships awarded for academics, athletics, leadership, minority status, state residency.

Application procedures. Admission: No deadline. $45 fee, may be waived for applicants with need. Admission notification on a rolling basis beginning on or about 9/1. Must reply by May 1 or within 2 week(s) if notified thereafter. **Financial aid:** Priority date 4/1; no closing date. FAFSA required. Applicants notified on a rolling basis starting 3/15; must reply within 2 week(s) of notification.

Academics. Special study options: Accelerated study, combined bachelor's/graduate degree, cooperative education, cross-registration, distance learning, double major, dual enrollment of high school students, independent study, internships, liberal arts/career combination, student-designed major, study abroad, teacher certification program. **Credit/placement by examination:** AP, CLEP, IB, SAT, ACT, institutional tests. 90 credit hours maximum toward bachelor's degree. **Support services:** Learning center, reduced course load, study skills assistance, tutoring, writing center.

Majors. Area/ethnic studies: American. **Biology:** General. **Business:** General, accounting, finance, managerial economics, marketing. **Communications:** General, journalism. **Computer sciences:** General. **Conservation:** Environmental studies. **Education:** Biology, chemistry, elementary, English, mathematics, science, secondary, social science, social studies. **Engineering technology:** Civil, electrical, mechanical. **Health:** Predental, premedicine, preveterinary. **History:** General. **Legal studies:** Prelaw. **Liberal arts:** Arts/sciences. **Math:** General. **Physical sciences:** Chemistry, geology. **Psychology:** General. **Social sciences:** General, economics, geography, political science, sociology. **Visual/performing arts:** Dramatic.

Most popular majors. Biology 7%, business/marketing 23%, communications/journalism 10%, education 16%, engineering/engineering technologies 12%, psychology 6%, social sciences 7%.

Computing on campus. 150 workstations in library, computer center. Dormitories wired for high-speed internet access and linked to campus network. Commuter students can connect to campus network. Online course registration, online library, helpline, student web hosting, wireless network available.

Student life. Freshman orientation: Mandatory, $55 fee. Preregistration for classes offered. One-day program. **Policies:** To be eligible to hold office within group or organization, student must be full-time and have minimum 2.0 GPA. **Housing:** Guaranteed on-campus for all undergraduates. Coed dorms, special housing for disabled, apartments, wellness housing available. $350 fully refundable deposit, deadline 7/1. Townhouses, lodges, and single-sex residences available. **Activities:** Concert band, campus ministries, choral groups, dance, drama, literary magazine, music ensembles, Model UN, musical theater, radio station, student government, student newspaper, TV station, Newman Students Association, Black Action Society, Student Outreach Through Service, Time Out Christian Fellowship, Student Council on World Affairs, political science club, honor societies, academic clubs, Habitat for Humanity.

Athletics. NCAA. **Intercollegiate:** Baseball M, basketball, cross-country W, golf, soccer, track and field W, volleyball W, wrestling M. **Intramural:** Basketball, football (non-tackle), softball, volleyball. **Team name:** Mountain Cats.

Student services. Adult student services, alcohol/substance abuse counseling, chaplain/spiritual director, career counseling, student employment services, financial aid counseling, health services, personal counseling, placement for graduates, veterans' counselor. **Physically disabled:** Services for visually, speech, hearing impaired.

Contact. E-mail: upjadmit@pitt.edu
Phone: (814) 269-7050 Toll-free number: (800) 765-4875
Fax: (814) 269-7044
BJ Sarneso, Director of Admissions, University of Pittsburgh at Johnstown, 450 Schoolhouse Road, 157 Blackington Hall, Johnstown, PA 15904-1200

University of Scranton

Scranton, Pennsylvania — **CB member**
www.scranton.edu — **CB code: 2929**

- Private 4-year university and liberal arts college affiliated with Roman Catholic Church
- Residential campus in small city
- 4,010 degree-seeking undergraduates: 4% part-time, 57% women, 1% African American, 2% Asian American, 4% Hispanic American, 1% international
- 1,461 degree-seeking graduate students
- 66% of applicants admitted
- SAT or ACT (ACT writing optional), application essay required
- 81% graduate within 6 years

General. Founded in 1888. Regionally accredited. **Degrees:** 871 bachelor's, 6 associate awarded; master's, doctoral offered. **ROTC:** Army, Air Force. **Location:** 125 miles from Philadelphia, 125 miles from New York City. **Calendar:** Semester, limited summer session. **Full-time faculty:** 260 total; 84% have terminal degrees, 10% minority, 40% women. **Part-time faculty:** 273 total; 19% have terminal degrees, 2% minority, 50% women. **Class size:** 46% < 20, 52% 20-39, 2% 40-49, less than 1% 50-99. **Special facilities:** 2 cyber-cafes, conference and retreat center at Chapman Lake, performing arts center with seating for 700.

Freshman class profile. 7,890 applied, 5,205 admitted, 968 enrolled.

Mid 50% test scores			
SAT critical reading:	510-600	GPA 2.0-2.99:	17%
SAT math:	520-610	Rank in top quarter:	40%
GPA 3.75 or higher:	19%	Rank in top tenth:	30%
GPA 3.50-3.74:	22%	Return as sophomores:	91%
GPA 3.0-3.49:	42%	Out-of-state:	55%
		Live on campus:	85%

Basis for selection. Program taken, GPA, SAT scores, class rank most important. Essay, extracurricular/leadership activities, recommendations important. **Homeschooled:** State high school equivalency certificate required.

High school preparation. College-preparatory program recommended. 16 units required. Required and recommended units include English 4, mathematics 3-4, social studies 2-3, history 2-3, science 3 (laboratory 1), foreign language 2 and academic electives 4. Science and business students should have 4 math; science students should have 4 science.

2008-2009 Annual costs. Tuition/fees: $31,576. Room/board: $10,990. Books/supplies: $1,100. Personal expenses: $1,100.

2008-2009 Financial aid. Non-need-based: Scholarships awarded for academics, minority status, ROTC.

Application procedures. Admission: Closing date 3/1 (postmark date). Admission notification on a rolling basis beginning on or about 1/15. Must reply by May 1 or within 2 week(s) if notified thereafter. **Financial aid:** Priority date 2/15; no closing date. FAFSA required. Applicants notified on a rolling basis starting 3/1; must reply by 5/1 or within 2 week(s) of notification.

Academics. Special study options: Accelerated study, combined bachelor's/graduate degree, cross-registration, distance learning, double major, dual enrollment of high school students, ESL, exchange student, honors, independent study, internships, semester at sea, study abroad, teacher certification program, United Nations semester, Washington semester. Baccalaureate/master's degree programs available. **Credit/placement by examination:** AP, CLEP, IB, SAT, ACT, institutional tests. 30 credit hours maximum toward bachelor's degree. **Support services:** Learning center, pre-admission summer program, remedial instruction, study skills assistance, tutoring, writing center.

Majors. Biology: General, biochemistry, biophysics, molecular. **Business:** Accounting, business admin, finance, human resources, international, management science, marketing, operations. **Communications:** General. **Computer sciences:** General, information systems. **Conservation:** General. **Education:** Early childhood, elementary, secondary, special. **Engineering:** Electrical. **Foreign languages:** Ancient Greek, classics, French, German, Latin, Spanish. **Health:** Clinical lab science, health care admin, nursing (RN). **History:** General. **Interdisciplinary:** Neuroscience. **Math:** General. **Philosophy/religion:** Philosophy, religion. **Physical sciences:** Chemistry, physics. **Protective services:** Criminal justice, forensics. **Psychology:** General. **Public administration:** Human services. **Social sciences:** Economics, international relations, political science, sociology. **Visual/performing arts:** Dramatic.

Most popular majors. Biology 9%, business/marketing 23%, communications/journalism 7%, education 11%, health sciences 11%, social sciences 8%.

Computing on campus. Dormitories wired for high-speed internet access and linked to campus network. Commuter students can connect to campus network. Online course registration, online library, helpline, repair service, student web hosting, wireless network available.

Student life. Freshman orientation: Mandatory, $275 fee. Preregistration for classes offered. Overnight program (1.5 days) for students and parents, held between end of June and mid-July. **Housing:** Guaranteed on-campus for all undergraduates. Coed dorms, single-sex dorms, apartments, wellness housing available. $150 nonrefundable deposit, deadline 5/1. **Activities:** Bands, campus ministries, choral groups, dance, drama, international student organizations, literary magazine, music ensembles, radio station, student government, student newspaper, TV station, religious and social service organizations, veterans club, Young Democrats, Young Republicans, professional clubs, collegiate volunteers, multicultural club, debating club.

Athletics. NCAA. **Intercollegiate:** Baseball M, basketball, cross-country, field hockey W, golf M, ice hockey M, lacrosse, soccer, softball W, swimming, tennis, volleyball W, wrestling M. **Intramural:** Baseball M, basketball, bowling, cross-country, football (tackle) M, golf, handball, lacrosse, racquetball, rugby, skiing, soccer, softball, swimming, table tennis, tennis, track and field, volleyball, water polo M, wrestling M. **Team name:** Royals.

Student services. Adult student services, alcohol/substance abuse counseling, chaplain/spiritual director, career counseling, student employment services, health services, personal counseling, placement for graduates, veterans' counselor. **Physically disabled:** Services for visually, hearing impaired.

Contact. E-mail: admissions@scranton.edu
Phone: (570) 941-7540 Toll-free number: (888) 727-2686
Fax: (570) 941-5928
Joseph Roback, Assistant Vice President for Admissions and Enrollment, University of Scranton, 800 Linden Street, Scranton, PA 18510-4699

University of the Arts

Philadelphia, Pennsylvania — **CB member**
www.uarts.edu — **CB code: 2664**

- Private 4-year visual arts and performing arts college
- Residential campus in very large city
- 2,167 degree-seeking undergraduates: 1% part-time, 57% women, 10% African American, 3% Asian American, 5% Hispanic American, 1% Native American, 4% international
- 218 degree-seeking graduate students
- SAT or ACT (ACT writing optional), application essay required
- 61% graduate within 6 years

General. Founded in 1870. Regionally accredited. **Degrees:** 452 bachelor's awarded; master's offered. **Calendar:** Semester, limited summer session. **Full-time faculty:** 118 total; 58% have terminal degrees, 8% minority, 36% women. **Part-time faculty:** 376 total; 7% minority, 45% women. **Class size:** 79% < 20, 21% 20-39, less than 1% 50-99, less than 1% >100. **Special facilities:** Digital multimedia laboratories, Oxberry animation stand, MIDI and recording studios, analog and digital electronic music studios, music calligraphy laboratory, center for publication arts, industrial design computer-aided product design center, genre-specific art galleries.

Freshman class profile. 549 enrolled.

Mid 50% test scores			
SAT critical reading:	480-590	GPA 3.0-3.49:	28%
SAT math:	450-560	GPA 2.0-2.99:	53%
SAT writing:	460-580	Return as sophomores:	79%
ACT composite:	20-25	Out-of-state:	69%
GPA 3.75 or higher:	8%	Live on campus:	87%
GPA 3.50-3.74:	9%	International:	4%

Basis for selection. Academic records, art work portfolio, audition very important. SAT or ACT scores considered in relation to the former. Statement of purpose and letters of recommendation also important. Class placement in English composition through SAT/ACT scores. August 15 score deadline for placement, counseling and/or credit. Interview recommended for all; audition required for performing arts programs; portfolio required for multimedia, visual arts, writing programs; essay required for media arts, performing arts, and visual arts programs. **Homeschooled:** Statement describing homeschool structure and mission, transcript of courses and grades, state high school equivalency certificate, letter of recommendation (nonparent) required. Interview not required but recommended; GED accepted in lieu of state high school equivalency certificate.

High school preparation. Required and recommended units include English 4, mathematics 3, social studies 2, history 2, science 2 and foreign language 2. Coursework in art, dance, music, creative writing, or theater as appropriate for specific programs recommended.

2008-2009 Annual costs. Tuition/fees: $30,600. Room only: $8,712. Books/supplies: $2,100. Personal expenses: $1,665.

Financial aid. Non-need-based: Scholarships awarded for academics, art, music/drama.

Application procedures. Admission: Priority date 3/1; no deadline. $60 fee, may be waived for applicants with need. Admission notification on a rolling basis beginning on or about 11/1. Must reply by May 1 or within 3 week(s) if notified thereafter. **Financial aid:** Priority date 3/1; no closing date. FAFSA required. Applicants notified on a rolling basis starting 3/15; must reply within 2 week(s) of notification.

Academics. Credit for course work may be given to entering freshmen by portfolio review (awarded after first year) or audition and placement testing. Art and design students declare major at end of first year, dance students at end of second year. **Special study options:** Accelerated study, cross-registration, double major, dual enrollment of high school students, ESL, exchange student, independent study, internships, study abroad, teacher certification program. **Credit/placement by examination:** AP, CLEP, IB, SAT, ACT, institutional tests. Credit by examination counted toward bachelor's degree varies by program. **Support services:** Learning center, pre-admission summer program, reduced course load, remedial instruction, study skills assistance, tutoring, writing center.

Majors. Communications: Digital media. **Communications technology:** Animation/special effects. **Education:** Drama/dance. **Visual/performing arts:** Acting, cinematography, crafts, dance, directing/producing, graphic design, illustration, industrial design, multimedia, music performance, music theory/composition, painting, photography, play/screenwriting, printmaking, sculpture, studio arts, theater design.

Most popular majors. Visual/performing arts 96%.

Computing on campus. PC or laptop required. 400 workstations in library, computer center, student center. Dormitories wired for high-speed internet access and linked to campus network. Commuter students can connect to campus network. Online course registration, online library, helpline, wireless network available.

Student life. Freshman orientation: Available. Preregistration for classes offered. Includes educational sessions on various social issues of university life. **Policies:** Campus code of conduct. **Housing:** Coed dorms, apartments, wellness housing available. $300 deposit, deadline 6/1. All housing in apartment-style units. **Activities:** Jazz band, choral groups, dance, drama, film society, international student organizations, literary magazine, music ensembles, musical theater, radio station, student government, African American Student Union; Alpha Psi Omega (honor organization that promotes community service); GBLT Student Union; Global Exchange; JewArts; Latino Student Union; Remedy (student-driven green initiative); UArts Christian Fellowship.

Athletics. Intramural: Volleyball.

Student services. Adult student services, alcohol/substance abuse counseling, career counseling, services for economically disadvantaged, student employment services, financial aid counseling, health services, personal counseling, placement for graduates, veterans' counselor. **Physically disabled:** Services for visually, speech, hearing impaired.

Contact. E-mail: admissions@uarts.edu
Phone: (215) 717-6049 Toll-free number: (800) 616-2787
Fax: (215) 717-6045
Susan Gandy, Director of Admission, University of the Arts, 320 South Broad Street, Philadelphia, PA 19102

University of the Sciences in Philadelphia

Philadelphia, Pennsylvania — **CB member**
www.usp.edu — **CB code: 2663**

- Private 4-year health science and pharmacy college
- Residential campus in very large city
- 2,063 degree-seeking undergraduates: 1% part-time, 60% women, 5% African American, 36% Asian American, 2% Hispanic American, 1% international
- 851 degree-seeking graduate students
- 58% of applicants admitted
- SAT or ACT with writing required
- 65% graduate within 6 years

General. Founded in 1821. Regionally accredited. **Degrees:** 178 bachelor's awarded; master's, doctoral, first professional offered. **ROTC:** Army, Air Force. **Calendar:** Semester, limited summer session. **Full-time faculty:** 157 total; 78% have terminal degrees, 15% minority, 46% women. **Part-time faculty:** 101 total; 14% minority, 60% women. **Class size:** 43% < 20, 41% 20-39, 4% 40-49, 4% 50-99, 8% >100. **Special facilities:** History of pharmacy museum, advanced pharmacy studies lab, research labs, science and technology center, wet labs.

Freshman class profile. 3,836 applied, 2,227 admitted, 534 enrolled.

Mid 50% test scores		**Rank in top quarter:**	76%
SAT critical reading:	520-600	**Rank in top tenth:**	39%
SAT math:	560-650	**End year in good standing:**	90%
ACT composite:	22-27	**Return as sophomores:**	86%
GPA 3.75 or higher:	44%	**Out-of-state:**	55%
GPA 3.50-3.74:	22%	**Live on campus:**	88%
GPA 3.0-3.49:	27%	**International:**	1%
GPA 2.0-2.99:	7%		

Basis for selection. High school curriculum, GPA, class rank if provided by high school, and SAT or ACT test scores most important criteria. Essay and/or letters of recommendation not required, but reviewed if provided. **Homeschooled:** Transcript of courses and grades, state high school equivalency certificate required. **Learning Disabled:** If admitted under current admission process, students will be provided with necessary additional services to assist in academic success.

High school preparation. 19 units required. Required and recommended units include English 4, mathematics 3-4, social studies 1, history 1, science 3-4 (laboratory 3) and academic electives 4.

2008-2009 Annual costs. Tuition/fees: $28,506. Room/board: $11,146. Books/supplies: $1,050. Personal expenses: $2,660.

2007-2008 Financial aid. Need-based: 490 full-time freshmen applied for aid; 490 were judged to have need; 490 of these received aid. Average need met was 78%. Average scholarship/grant was $9,954; average loan $3,600. 51% of total undergraduate aid awarded as scholarships/grants, 49% as loans/jobs. **Non-need-based:** Awarded to 2,326 full-time undergraduates, including 525 freshmen. Scholarships awarded for academics, athletics.

Application procedures. Admission: No deadline. $45 fee, may be waived for applicants with need. Admission notification on a rolling basis beginning on or about 10/1. Must reply by May 1 or within 2 week(s) if notified thereafter. **Financial aid:** Closing date 3/15. FAFSA required. Applicants notified on a rolling basis starting 1/15; must reply by 5/1 or within 2 week(s) of notification.

Academics. Direct-entry admission for freshman pharmacy, DPT and MPT physical therapy program, occupational therapy and physician assistant programs. Students not required to reapply to professional phase of their majors. **Special study options:** Combined bachelor's/graduate degree, double major, ESL, honors, internships, liberal arts/career combination, teacher certification program. **Credit/placement by examination:** AP, CLEP, IB, SAT, ACT, institutional tests. **Support services:** Learning center, pre-admission summer program, reduced course load, remedial instruction, study skills assistance, tutoring, writing center.

Majors. Biology: General, biochemistry, bioinformatics, microbiology, pharmacology/toxicology. **Business:** Marketing. **Computer sciences:** Computer science. **Conservation:** Environmental science. **Health:** Clinical lab science, health services, physician assistant. **Parks/recreation:** Sports admin. **Physical sciences:** Chemistry. **Psychology:** General, medical. **Other:** Humanities and science.

Most popular majors. Biology 13%, business/marketing 7%, health sciences 77%.

Computing on campus. 190 workstations in dormitories, library, computer center, student center. Dormitories wired for high-speed internet access and linked to campus network. Commuter students can connect to campus network. Online course registration, online library, helpline, repair service, wireless network available.

Student life. **Freshman orientation:** Mandatory. Programs for parents and students; placement testing. **Policies:** Campus alcohol free. **Housing:** Guaranteed on-campus for freshmen. Coed dorms, apartments, fraternity/sorority housing, wellness housing available. $175 nonrefundable deposit, deadline 5/1. Honor halls. **Activities:** Concert band, choral groups, dance, drama, literary magazine, musical theater, student government, student newspaper, professional organizations, Greek letter organizations, religious groups, honor societies, student community involvement program, ethnic/diversity groups, student chapters of scientific organizations, student publications.

Athletics. NAIA, NCAA. **Intercollegiate:** Baseball M, basketball, cross-country, golf, rifle, softball W, tennis, volleyball W. **Intramural:** Archery, badminton, basketball, bowling, rifle, table tennis, volleyball. **Team name:** Devils.

Student services. Adult student services, alcohol/substance abuse counseling, career counseling, student employment services, financial aid counseling, health services, personal counseling, placement for graduates, veterans' counselor. **Physically disabled:** Services for visually, speech, hearing impaired.

Contact. E-mail: admit@usp.edu
Phone: (215) 596-8810 Toll-free number: (888) 996-8747
Fax: (215) 596-8821
Louis Hegyes, Director of Admission, University of the Sciences in Philadelphia, 600 South 43rd Street, Philadelphia, PA 19104-4495

Ursinus College

Collegeville, Pennsylvania — **CB member**
www.ursinus.edu — **CB code: 2931**

- Private 4-year liberal arts college
- Residential campus in small town
- 1,655 degree-seeking undergraduates: 55% women, 6% African American, 4% Asian American, 3% Hispanic American, 1% international
- 55% of applicants admitted
- Application essay required
- 76% graduate within 6 years; 34% enter graduate study

General. Founded in 1869. Regionally accredited. All freshmen receive laptop computers (updated at beginning of junior year). **Degrees:** 343 bachelor's awarded. **Location:** 28 miles from Philadelphia. **Calendar:** Semester. **Full-time faculty:** 123 total; 91% have terminal degrees, 14% minority, 46% women. **Part-time faculty:** 45 total; 36% have terminal degrees, 13% minority, 73% women. **Class size:** 79% < 20, 20% 20-39, less than 1% 40-49, less than 1% 50-99, less than 1% >100. **Special facilities:** Performing arts center, art museum, observatory, outdoor sculpture collection, public walking trails.

Freshman class profile. 6,192 applied, 3,387 admitted, 545 enrolled.

Mid 50% test scores		**Rank in top quarter:**	78%
SAT critical reading:	570-680	**Rank in top tenth:**	48%
SAT math:	570-670	**End year in good standing:**	99%
SAT writing:	560-660	**Return as sophomores:**	88%
ACT composite:	25-29	**Out-of-state:**	47%
GPA 3.75 or higher:	54%	**Live on campus:**	98%
GPA 3.50-3.74:	20%	**Fraternities:**	20%
GPA 3.0-3.49:	21%	**Sororities:**	30%
GPA 2.0-2.99:	5%		

Basis for selection. Academic achievement most important, including courses taken, grades received. Test scores also important. Motivation and activities considered. Rank in top fifth of class preferred. Alumni children and minorities receive special consideration. SAT/ACT optional for students ranking in top 10% of class, or with minimum 3.5 GPA from non-ranking school. Interview recommended.

High school preparation. College-preparatory program required. 17 units required; 22 recommended. Required and recommended units include English 4, mathematics 3-4, social studies 1-4, science 1-4 (laboratory 1-2), foreign language 2-4, academic electives 2.5. An additional 2.5 credits spread among academic or arts electives.

2008-2009 Annual costs. Tuition/fees: $36,910. Room/board: $8,800. Books/supplies: $1,000. Personal expenses: $1,200.

2008-2009 Financial aid. **Need-based:** Average need met was 84%. Average scholarship/grant was $22,007; average loan $3,832. 60% of total undergraduate aid awarded as scholarships/grants, 40% as loans/jobs. **Non-need-based:** Scholarships awarded for academics, alumni affiliation, art, leadership, music/drama.

Application procedures. **Admission:** Closing date 2/15 (receipt date). $50 fee, may be waived for applicants with need, free for online applicants. Admission notification 4/1. Must reply by 4/1. Rolling notification for Early Action within 7 weeks of receipt of application. **Financial aid:** Closing date 2/15. FAFSA, institutional form, CSS PROFILE required. Applicants notified by 4/1; must reply by 5/1 or within 2 week(s) of notification.

Academics. Summer undergraduate research fellowships available. Independent Learning Experience required of all. Study abroad encouraged. All first-year students complete overview of human thought, creativity, culture, history in a 2-semester seminar called the Common Intellectual Experience (CIE). **Special study options:** Combined bachelor's/graduate degree, double major, dual enrollment of high school students, ESL, exchange student, independent study, internships, semester at sea, student-designed major, study abroad, teacher certification program, United Nations semester, Washington semester. Howard University semester. **Credit/placement by examination:** AP, CLEP, IB, institutional tests. **Support services:** Pre-admission summer program, reduced course load, tutoring, writing center.

Majors. **Area/ethnic studies:** American, East Asian. **Biology:** General. **Communications:** General. **Computer sciences:** Computer science. **Conservation:** Environmental studies. **Foreign languages:** Classics, French, German, Spanish. **History:** General. **Interdisciplinary:** Biological/physical sciences, neuroscience. **Math:** General. **Parks/recreation:** Health/fitness. **Philosophy/religion:** Philosophy. **Physical sciences:** Chemistry, physics. **Psychology:** General. **Social sciences:** Anthropology, economics, international relations, political science, sociology. **Visual/performing arts:** Art, art history/conservation, dance, dramatic.

Most popular majors. Biology 14%, communications/journalism 7%, English 7%, parks/recreation 7%, psychology 11%, social sciences 27%.

Computing on campus. PC or laptop required. 1,655 workstations in dormitories, library, computer center, student center. Dormitories wired for high-speed internet access and linked to campus network. Commuter students can connect to campus network. Online course registration, online library, helpline, repair service, student web hosting, wireless network available.

Student life. **Freshman orientation:** Mandatory. Preregistration for classes offered. Two-day session in June and 4-day session in August before start of classes. **Housing:** Guaranteed on-campus for all undergraduates. Coed dorms, single-sex dorms, wellness housing available. $500 nonrefundable deposit, deadline 5/1. Multicultural, community service, art, physical science, literature houses and quiet halls available. **Activities:** Bands, campus ministries, choral groups, dance, drama, film society, literary magazine, music ensembles, Model UN, musical theater, radio station, student government, student newspaper, TV station, Relay for Life, Association of Latinos Motivated to Achieve, Best Buddies, College Democrats, College Republicans, Hillel, Inter-Faith Outreach, Buddhist meditation group.

Athletics. NCAA. **Intercollegiate:** Baseball M, basketball, cross-country, field hockey W, football (tackle) M, golf, gymnastics W, lacrosse, soccer, softball W, swimming, tennis, track and field, volleyball W, wrestling M. **Intramural:** Basketball, football (non-tackle) M, soccer, softball, squash, swimming, tennis, volleyball. **Team name:** Bears.

Student services. Adult student services, alcohol/substance abuse counseling, chaplain/spiritual director, career counseling, student employment services, financial aid counseling, health services, minority student services, personal counseling, placement for graduates. **Physically disabled:** Services for visually, speech, hearing impaired.

Contact. E-mail: admissions@ursinus.edu
Phone: (610) 409-3200 Fax: (610) 409-3662
Robert McCullough, Dean of Admission, Ursinus College, PO Box 1000, Collegeville, PA 19426-1000

Valley Forge Christian College

Phoenixville, Pennsylvania
www.vfcc.edu — **CB code: 2579**

- Private 4-year liberal arts college affiliated with Assemblies of God
- Residential campus in large town
- 969 degree-seeking undergraduates: 16% part-time, 55% women, 8% African American, 3% Asian American, 10% Hispanic American, 1% international
- 13 degree-seeking graduate students

- 81% of applicants admitted
- SAT or ACT with writing, application essay required
- 52% graduate within 6 years

General. Founded in 1938. Regionally accredited. **Degrees:** 106 bachelor's, 11 associate awarded; master's offered. **Location:** 25 miles from Philadelphia. **Calendar:** Semester, limited summer session. **Full-time faculty:** 29 total; 48% have terminal degrees, 10% minority, 34% women. **Part-time faculty:** 49 total; 20% have terminal degrees, 10% minority, 33% women. **Class size:** 53% < 20, 31% 20-39, 5% 40-49, 10% 50-99.

Freshman class profile. 343 applied, 279 admitted, 188 enrolled.

End year in good standing:	80%	**Live on campus:**	80%
Return as sophomores:	70%	**International:**	2%
Out-of-state:	10%		

Basis for selection. School achievement record, pastor recommendation, written essay, test scores important. Bible test required for all; music, computer, English, and math tests required for some. Interview recommended. **Homeschooled:** Statement describing homeschool structure and mission required. Student must sign and date a VFCC home schooled self-certification form. **Learning Disabled:** Academic recommendation from counselor IEP or other.

High school preparation. 16 units recommended. Recommended units include English 4, mathematics 2, social studies 4, science 4 and foreign language 2.

2009-2010 Annual costs. Tuition/fees: $14,232. Room/board: $6,896. Books/supplies: $828. Personal expenses: $1,838.

2007-2008 Financial aid. Need-based: 170 full-time freshmen applied for aid; 149 were judged to have need; 147 of these received aid. Average need met was 52%. Average scholarship/grant was $6,059; average loan $3,187. 41% of total undergraduate aid awarded as scholarships/grants, 59% as loans/jobs. **Non-need-based:** Awarded to 262 full-time undergraduates, including 112 freshmen. Scholarships awarded for academics, leadership, music/drama, religious affiliation, state residency.

Application procedures. Admission: Priority date 5/1; deadline 8/1 (receipt date). $25 fee, may be waived for applicants with need, free for online applicants. Admission notification 8/15. Admission notification on a rolling basis. **Financial aid:** Priority date 5/1; no closing date. FAFSA required. Applicants notified on a rolling basis starting 3/15; must reply within 3 week(s) of notification.

Academics. Special study options: Accelerated study, distance learning, dual enrollment of high school students, ESL, independent study, internships, liberal arts/career combination, study abroad, teacher certification program, weekend college. **Credit/placement by examination:** AP, CLEP, IB, SAT, ACT, institutional tests. 30 credit hours maximum toward bachelor's degree. **Support services:** Learning center, pre-admission summer program, reduced course load, remedial instruction, study skills assistance, tutoring.

Majors. Business: Business admin. **Communications:** Digital media. **Education:** Early childhood, elementary, music. **Foreign languages:** Translation. **Public administration:** Social work. **Theology:** Bible, missionary, pastoral counseling, religious ed, sacred music, theology. **Visual/performing arts:** Music performance.

Most popular majors. Business/marketing 9%, education 17%, psychology 15%, theological studies 56%.

Computing on campus. PC or laptop required. 54 workstations in library, computer center. Dormitories wired for high-speed internet access and linked to campus network. Commuter students can connect to campus network. Online course registration, online library, helpline, repair service, wireless network available.

Student life. Freshman orientation: Mandatory, $55 fee. Preregistration for classes offered. Held weekend prior to beginning of classes. **Policies:** Religious observance required. **Housing:** Guaranteed on-campus for all undergraduates. Single-sex dorms, apartments, wellness housing available. $100 nonrefundable deposit. **Activities:** Bands, campus ministries, choral groups, dance, drama, music ensembles, student government, student newspaper.

Athletics. NCCAA. **Intercollegiate:** Baseball M, basketball, soccer, volleyball W. **Intramural:** Basketball, bowling, football (non-tackle), soccer, softball. **Team name:** Patriots.

Student services. Chaplain/spiritual director, career counseling, student employment services, financial aid counseling, health services, personal counseling, placement for graduates.

Contact. E-mail: admission@vfcc.edu
Phone: (610) 935-0450 Toll-free number: (800) 432-8322
Fax: (610) 917-2069
William Chenco, Director of Admissions, Valley Forge Christian College, 1401 Charlestown Road, Phoenixville, PA 19460

Villanova University

Villanova, Pennsylvania — **CB member**
www.villanova.edu — **CB code: 2959**

- Private 4-year university affiliated with Roman Catholic Church
- Residential campus in large town
- 6,884 degree-seeking undergraduates: 4% part-time, 51% women, 5% African American, 7% Asian American, 6% Hispanic American, 3% international
- 2,970 degree-seeking graduate students
- 39% of applicants admitted
- SAT or ACT with writing, application essay required
- 89% graduate within 6 years

General. Founded in 1842. Regionally accredited. **Degrees:** 1,838 bachelor's, 7 associate awarded; master's, doctoral, first professional offered. **ROTC:** Army, Naval, Air Force. **Location:** 12 miles from Philadelphia. **Calendar:** Semester, extensive summer session. **Full-time faculty:** 579 total; 89% have terminal degrees, 14% minority, 36% women. **Part-time faculty:** 361 total; 37% have terminal degrees, 6% minority, 44% women. **Class size:** 42% < 20, 55% 20-39, 1% 40-49, 2% 50-99, less than 1% >100. **Special facilities:** Astronomy and astrophysics observatories, electron microscope, research with NASA, arboretum, structural engineering teaching and research laboratory.

Freshman class profile. 15,102 applied, 5,963 admitted, 1,604 enrolled.

Mid 50% test scores		**Rank in top quarter:**	81%
SAT critical reading:	580-680	**Rank in top tenth:**	60%
SAT math:	620-710	**Return as sophomores:**	95%
GPA 3.75 or higher:	57%	**Out-of-state:**	77%
GPA 3.50-3.74:	25%	**Live on campus:**	97%
GPA 3.0-3.49:	15%	**International:**	3%
GPA 2.0-2.99:	3%		

Basis for selection. High school record, class rank, standardized test scores, counselor recommendation, essay, extracurricular activities considered. Interview required for finalists of health affiliation programs and Presidential Scholarship consideration. **Homeschooled:** Objective third-party evaluation (state high school association, for example), including syllabi, required.

High school preparation. 22 units required; 25 recommended. Required and recommended units include English 4, mathematics 4, science 4 (laboratory 2-3), foreign language 2-4 and academic electives 2. 4 social studies and/or history required. Total units required varies by academic college.

2009-2010 Annual costs. Tuition/fees (projected): $37,655. Full-time tuition includes laptop for all students. Room/board: $10,070. Books/supplies: $950. Personal expenses: $950.

2008-2009 Financial aid. Need-based: 1,045 full-time freshmen applied for aid; 755 were judged to have need; 748 of these received aid. Average need met was 84%. Average scholarship/grant was $23,198; average loan $3,692. 62% of total undergraduate aid awarded as scholarships/grants, 38% as loans/jobs. **Non-need-based:** Awarded to 1,312 full-time undergraduates, including 315 freshmen. Scholarships awarded for academics, alumni affiliation, athletics, leadership, minority status, religious affiliation, ROTC.

Application procedures. Admission: Priority date 12/15; deadline 1/7 (receipt date). $75 fee, may be waived for applicants with need. Admission notification 4/1. Must reply by 5/1. November 1 priority application date for scholarship consideration. **Financial aid:** Closing date 2/7. FAFSA, institutional form required. Applicants notified by 4/1; must reply by 5/1 or within 2 week(s) of notification.

Academics. Special study options: Accelerated study, combined bachelor's/graduate degree, cooperative education, cross-registration, distance learning, double major, dual enrollment of high school students, ESL, exchange student, honors, independent study, internships, liberal arts/career combination, study abroad, teacher certification program, Washington semester. Cooperative certification programs in elementary education with Rosemont College. **Credit/placement by examination:** AP, CLEP, IB, institutional tests. 30 credit hours maximum toward bachelor's degree. Deans make decisions regarding prior work and life experiences on individual basis. **Support services:** Reduced course load, study skills assistance, tutoring, writing center.

Majors. Biology: General. **Business:** Accounting, business admin, finance, management information systems, managerial economics, marketing. **Communications:** General. **Computer sciences:** General, information systems. **Education:** Elementary, secondary. **Engineering:** Chemical, civil, computer, electrical, mechanical. **Foreign languages:** Classics, French, German, Italian, Spanish. **Health:** Nursing (RN), predental, premedicine. **History:** General. **Interdisciplinary:** Biological/physical sciences. **Liberal arts:** Arts/sciences. **Math:** General. **Philosophy/religion:** Philosophy, religion. **Physical sciences:** Astronomy, astrophysics, chemistry, physics. **Protective services:** Law enforcement admin. **Psychology:** General. **Public administration:** Human services. **Social sciences:** Economics, geography, political science, sociology. **Visual/performing arts:** Art history/conservation.

Most popular majors. Biology 6%, business/marketing 33%, communications/journalism 9%, engineering/engineering technologies 11%, health sciences 9%, social sciences 9%.

Computing on campus. PC or laptop required. 2,530 workstations in dormitories, library, computer center, student center. Dormitories wired for high-speed internet access and linked to campus network. Commuter students can connect to campus network. Online course registration, online library, helpline, repair service, student web hosting, wireless network available.

Student life. Freshman orientation: Mandatory, $125 fee. 4-day on-campus program prior to start of fall term. **Housing:** Guaranteed on-campus for freshmen. Coed dorms, single-sex dorms, apartments, wellness housing available. $700 nonrefundable deposit, deadline 5/1. On-campus housing available for transfer students on space-available basis. **Activities:** Bands, campus ministries, choral groups, dance, drama, film society, international student organizations, literary magazine, music ensembles, musical theater, radio station, student government, student newspaper, symphony orchestra, TV station, Special Olympics, Amnesty International, Villanovans for Life, Black Cultural Society, Big Brother/Sister, Committee for the Homeless, Project Sunshine, Habitat for Humanity, Blue Key Society.

Athletics. NCAA. **Intercollegiate:** Baseball M, basketball, bowling W, cheerleading, cross-country, diving, field hockey W, football (tackle) M, golf M, lacrosse, rowing (crew) W, soccer, softball W, swimming, tennis, track and field, volleyball W, water polo W. **Intramural:** Basketball, cross-country, field hockey W, football (non-tackle), skiing, soccer, softball, tennis, volleyball. **Team name:** Wildcats.

Student services. Adult student services, alcohol/substance abuse counseling, chaplain/spiritual director, career counseling, services for economically disadvantaged, student employment services, financial aid counseling, health services, minority student services, personal counseling, placement for graduates. **Physically disabled:** Services for visually, hearing impaired.

Contact. E-mail: gotovu@villanova.edu
Phone: (610) 519-4000 Fax: (610) 519-6450
Michael Gaynor, Director of University Admission, Villanova University, 800 Lancaster Avenue, Villanova, PA 19085-1672

Washington & Jefferson College

Washington, Pennsylvania — **CB member**
www.washjeff.edu — **CB code: 2967**

- Private 4-year liberal arts college
- Residential campus in large town
- 1,488 degree-seeking undergraduates: 1% part-time, 46% women, 3% African American, 1% Asian American, 1% Hispanic American
- 38% of applicants admitted
- SAT or ACT (ACT writing optional), application essay required
- 73% graduate within 6 years; 34% enter graduate study

General. Founded in 1781. Regionally accredited. **Degrees:** 356 bachelor's awarded. **ROTC:** Army, Air Force. **Location:** 27 miles from Pittsburgh. **Calendar:** 4-1-4, limited summer session. **Full-time faculty:** 112 total; 92% have terminal degrees, 12% minority, 39% women. **Part-time faculty:** 37 total; 38% have terminal degrees, 11% minority, 49% women. **Class size:** 71% < 20, 29% 20-39, less than 1% 40-49. **Special facilities:** Microplate reader, cell culture labs, isolator lab, X-ray diffraction unit, neuropsychology lab, atomic absorption unit, nuclear magnetic resonance lab, refrigerated centrifuge, global learning unit, language lab, spectrometers, laser scanning confocal microscope facility, Abernathy Field Station.

Freshman class profile. 6,826 applied, 2,611 admitted, 399 enrolled.

Mid 50% test scores		**GPA 2.0-2.99:**	15%
SAT critical reading:	510-610	**Rank in top quarter:**	74%
SAT math:	530-630	**Rank in top tenth:**	39%
ACT composite:	22-26	**End year in good standing:**	92%
GPA 3.75 or higher:	24%	**Return as sophomores:**	87%
GPA 3.50-3.74:	18%	**Out-of-state:**	28%
GPA 3.0-3.49:	41%	**Live on campus:**	96%

Basis for selection. Entire high school record including difficulty of schedule, GPA, class rank, extracurricular activities, essay, letters of recommendation important. **Homeschooled:** Letter of recommendation (nonparent) required.

High school preparation. College-preparatory program required. 15 units required. Required units include English 3, mathematics 3, history 1, foreign language 2 and academic electives 6. Six or more academic elective courses from English, math, foreign language, history, and social or natural history required.

2008-2009 Annual costs. Tuition/fees: $31,496. Room/board: $8,488. Books/supplies: $800. Personal expenses: $700.

2008-2009 Financial aid. Need-based: 348 full-time freshmen applied for aid; 299 were judged to have need; 299 of these received aid. Average need met was 80%. Average scholarship/grant was $16,433; average loan $3,934. 66% of total undergraduate aid awarded as scholarships/grants, 34% as loans/jobs. **Non-need-based:** Awarded to 1,260 full-time undergraduates, including 372 freshmen. Scholarships awarded for academics, alumni affiliation.

Application procedures. Admission: Priority date 1/15; deadline 3/1 (postmark date). $25 fee, may be waived for applicants with need, free for online applicants. Admission notification on a rolling basis beginning on or about 10/1. Must reply by 5/1. **Financial aid:** Priority date 2/15; no closing date. FAFSA required. Applicants notified on a rolling basis starting 3/1; must reply by 5/1.

Academics. Special study options: Accelerated study, combined bachelor's/graduate degree, double major, dual enrollment of high school students, honors, independent study, internships, student-designed major, study abroad, teacher certification program, Washington semester. Advanced placement credit. **Credit/placement by examination:** AP, CLEP, IB, institutional tests. 68 credit hours maximum toward bachelor's degree. **Support services:** Learning center, reduced course load, study skills assistance, tutoring.

Majors. Biology: General, biochemistry, biophysics, cellular/anatomical. **Business:** General, accounting, international. **Computer sciences:** Information technology. **Conservation:** Environmental studies. **Education:** General, art. **Foreign languages:** French, German, Spanish. **History:** General. **Interdisciplinary:** Global studies. **Math:** General. **Philosophy/religion:** Philosophy, religion. **Physical sciences:** Chemistry, physics. **Psychology:** General. **Social sciences:** Economics, political science, sociology. **Visual/performing arts:** Art, theater history. **Other:** Multi-/interdisciplinary studies.

Most popular majors. Biology 7%, business/marketing 26%, English 11%, foreign language 6%, history 6%, psychology 15%, social sciences 9%.

Computing on campus. 450 workstations in library, computer center, student center. Dormitories wired for high-speed internet access and linked to campus network. Commuter students can connect to campus network. Online course registration, online library, helpline, repair service, student web hosting, wireless network available.

Student life. Freshman orientation: Mandatory. Preregistration for classes offered. Includes placement tests. **Policies:** All students required to live in campus housing unless granted written approval or living with parents 15 miles or less from the college. Students not permitted to smoke in rooms, hallways, or lounges. **Housing:** Guaranteed on-campus for all undergraduates. Coed dorms, single-sex dorms, special housing for disabled, apartments, fraternity/sorority housing, wellness housing available. Pets allowed in dorm rooms. On-campus suites available. **Activities:** Bands, campus ministries, choral groups, dance, drama, film society, international student organizations, literary magazine, music ensembles, Model UN, musical theater, radio station, student government, student newspaper, symphony orchestra, Newman Club, Hillel Society, Young Republicans, College Democrats, Liberal Student Union, Black Student Union, Alpha Phi Omega, Get Involved in Volunteer Experiences, Asian Student Association, Gay Straight Alliance.

Athletics. NCAA. **Intercollegiate:** Baseball M, basketball, cheerleading, cross-country, diving, field hockey W, football (tackle) M, golf, lacrosse, soccer, softball W, swimming, tennis, track and field, volleyball W, water polo, wrestling M. **Intramural:** Basketball, bowling, cross-country, football (non-tackle), racquetball, soccer, softball, table tennis, tennis, triathlon, volleyball. **Team name:** Presidents.

Student services. Adult student services, alcohol/substance abuse counseling, chaplain/spiritual director, career counseling, student employment services, financial aid counseling, health services, minority student services, personal counseling, placement for graduates, women's services.

Contact. E-mail: admission@washjeff.edu
Phone: (724) 223-6025 Toll-free number: (888) 926-3529
Fax: (724) 223-6534
Alton Newell, Vice President for Enrollment, Washington & Jefferson College, 60 South Lincoln Street, Washington, PA 15301

Waynesburg University

Waynesburg, Pennsylvania — **CB member**
www.waynesburg.edu — **CB code: 2969**

- Private 4-year liberal arts college affiliated with Presbyterian Church (USA)
- Residential campus in small town
- 1,640 degree-seeking undergraduates: 4% part-time, 62% women, 2% African American, 1% Hispanic American
- 721 degree-seeking graduate students
- 89% of applicants admitted
- SAT or ACT with writing required
- 51% graduate within 6 years

General. Founded in 1849. Regionally accredited. Member of the Council for Christian Colleges and Universities. **Degrees:** 408 bachelor's, 5 associate awarded; master's, doctoral offered. **ROTC:** Army. **Location:** 50 miles from Pittsburgh. **Calendar:** Semester, limited summer session. **Full-time faculty:** 67 total; 61% have terminal degrees, 4% minority, 48% women. **Part-time faculty:** 99 total; 18% have terminal degrees, 48% women. **Class size:** 60% < 20, 36% 20-39, 3% 40-49, less than 1% 50-99. **Special facilities:** Geological museum, historical museum, constitutional studies and moral leadership center, research and economic development center, service leadership center.

Freshman class profile. 1,477 applied, 1,320 admitted, 380 enrolled.

Mid 50% test scores		**GPA 2.0-2.99:**	14%
SAT critical reading:	450-560	**Rank in top quarter:**	43%
SAT math:	460-580	**Rank in top tenth:**	36%
GPA 3.75 or higher:	30%	**Return as sophomores:**	74%
GPA 3.50-3.74:	18%	**Out-of-state:**	16%
GPA 3.0-3.49:	38%	**Live on campus:**	83%

Basis for selection. High school classes taken, grades, test scores, activities, community activities, interview, and recommendations considered. Essay, interview recommended. **Homeschooled:** Statement describing homeschool structure and mission, transcript of courses and grades, state high school equivalency certificate required. College should be apprised if homeschooled applicant enrolled in program approved by state's department of education.

High school preparation. 16 units required. Required and recommended units include English 4, mathematics 3, social studies 2, science 2-3, foreign language 2 and academic electives 5.

2008-2009 Annual costs. Tuition/fees: $17,080. Room/board: $7,050. Books/supplies: $1,100. Personal expenses: $230.

2008-2009 Financial aid. Need-based: Average need met was 82%. Average scholarship/grant was $10,892; average loan $3,747. 61% of total undergraduate aid awarded as scholarships/grants, 39% as loans/jobs. **Non-need-based:** Scholarships awarded for academics, alumni affiliation, job skills, leadership, religious affiliation, state residency.

Application procedures. Admission: No deadline. $20 fee, may be waived for applicants with need, free for online applicants. Admission notification on a rolling basis. Rolling date as specified in deposit letter. **Financial aid:** Priority date 3/15; no closing date. FAFSA required. Applicants notified on a rolling basis starting 2/15; must reply within 2 week(s) of notification.

Academics. Nursing majors must complete 126 credit hours for bachelor of science degree. **Special study options:** Accelerated study, combined bachelor's/graduate degree, distance learning, double major, dual enrollment of high school students, ESL, honors, independent study, internships, liberal arts/career combination, study abroad, teacher certification program, Washington semester. 3-2 program in engineering with Penn State University in state College, PA and Washington University in St Louis; 3-1 program in marine biology with Florida Institute of Technology; 3-3 law program with Duquesne University. **Credit/placement by examination:** AP, CLEP, IB, SAT, ACT, institutional tests. 15 credit hours maximum toward bachelor's degree. **Support services:** Learning center, reduced course load, study skills assistance, tutoring, writing center.

Majors. Biology: General, environmental, marine. **Business:** General, accounting, business admin, finance, international, international marketing. **Communications:** General, advertising, broadcast journalism, digital media, journalism, public relations. **Computer sciences:** General, computer science, information technology, networking. **Education:** Art, biology, chemistry, elementary, English, history, mathematics, science, secondary, social studies, special. **Family/consumer sciences:** Family studies. **Health:** Athletic training, nursing (RN), predental, premedicine, preveterinary. **History:** General. **Legal studies:** Prelaw. **Math:** General. **Parks/recreation:** Exercise sciences, sports admin. **Philosophy/religion:** Religion. **Physical sciences:** Chemistry. **Protective services:** Forensics, law enforcement admin. **Psychology:** General. **Public administration:** Human services. **Social sciences:** General, political science, sociology. **Theology:** Theology. **Visual/performing arts:** Art, arts management, commercial/advertising art, music management, theater arts management. **Other:** Forensic accounting.

Most popular majors. Biology 6%, business/marketing 19%, communications/journalism 6%, health sciences 38%, public administration/social services 9%.

Computing on campus. 160 workstations in dormitories, library, computer center, student center. Dormitories wired for high-speed internet access and linked to campus network. Commuter students can connect to campus network. Online course registration, online library, helpline, wireless network available.

Student life. Freshman orientation: Mandatory. Preregistration for classes offered. One-day summer program for parents and students; 2-day program prior to start of classes. **Policies:** No alcohol or drugs permitted on campus. **Housing:** Guaranteed on-campus for all undergraduates. Coed dorms, single-sex dorms, wellness housing available. $150 partly refundable deposit. **Activities:** Bands, choral groups, dance, drama, international student organizations, literary magazine, music ensembles, musical theater, radio station, student government, student newspaper, TV station, Fellowship of Christian Athletes, Newman Club, Black Student Union, Waynesburg Christian Fellowship, Bonner Scholars (service group), Alpha Phi Omega, Habitat for Humanity, Leadership program.

Athletics. NCAA. **Intercollegiate:** Baseball M, basketball, cross-country, football (tackle) M, golf, lacrosse W, soccer, softball W, tennis, track and field, volleyball W, wrestling M. **Intramural:** Basketball, bowling, football (non-tackle), racquetball, softball, table tennis, volleyball W. **Team name:** Yellow Jackets.

Student services. Adult student services, chaplain/spiritual director, career counseling, student employment services, financial aid counseling, health services, minority student services, personal counseling, placement for graduates.

Contact. E-mail: admissions@waynesburg.edu
Phone: (724) 852-3248 Toll-free number: (800) 225-7393
Fax: (724) 627-8124
Sarah Zwinger, Director of Admissions, Waynesburg University, 51 West College Street, Waynesburg, PA 15370-1222

West Chester University of Pennsylvania

West Chester, Pennsylvania — **CB member**
www.wcupa.edu — **CB code: 2659**

- Public 4-year university
- Commuter campus in large town
- 11,127 degree-seeking undergraduates: 8% part-time, 61% women, 9% African American, 2% Asian American, 3% Hispanic American
- 1,579 degree-seeking graduate students
- 47% of applicants admitted
- SAT or ACT with writing, application essay required
- 63% graduate within 6 years

General. Founded in 1871. Regionally accredited. **Degrees:** 2,114 bachelor's awarded; master's offered. **ROTC:** Army. **Location:** 23 miles from Philadelphia. **Calendar:** Semester, extensive summer session. **Special facilities:** Herbarium, 151-acre natural area for environmental studies, planetarium, speech and hearing clinic, autism clinic, center for government and community affairs, mineral museum.

Freshman class profile. 13,353 applied, 6,317 admitted, 2,002 enrolled.

Mid 50% test scores			
SAT critical reading:	480-560	Rank in top quarter:	35%
SAT math:	490-580	Rank in top tenth:	10%
SAT writing:	470-570	Return as sophomores:	84%
GPA 3.75 or higher:	18%	Out-of-state:	14%
GPA 3.50-3.74:	19%	Live on campus:	91%
GPA 3.0-3.49:	41%	Fraternities:	6%
GPA 2.0-2.99:	22%	Sororities:	7%

Basis for selection. College preparatory curriculum in high school, standardized test scores, and personal statement required. Specific course prerequisites depend on major selection. Additional documentation is required of candidates for the summer academic development program. Interview required for athletic training, premedical, and pharmaceutical product development programs. Audition required for music. **Homeschooled:** Students must have work certified by PA Homeschoolers' Association or their high school.

High school preparation. College-preparatory program required. 16 units required; 25 recommended. Required and recommended units include English 4, mathematics 3-4, social studies 2, history 2, science 2-3 (laboratory 1-2), foreign language 2, computer science 1, visual/performing arts 1 and academic electives 1-2.

2008-2009 Annual costs. Tuition/fees: $6,737; $14,775 out-of-state. Room/board: $6,874. Books/supplies: $1,296. Personal expenses: $2,113.

2007-2008 Financial aid. Need-based: 1,650 full-time freshmen applied for aid; 1,039 were judged to have need; 976 of these received aid. Average need met was 61%. Average scholarship/grant was $5,251; average loan $3,523. 33% of total undergraduate aid awarded as scholarships/grants, 67% as loans/jobs. **Non-need-based:** Awarded to 372 full-time undergraduates, including 139 freshmen.

Application procedures. Admission: Priority date 1/1; no deadline. $35 fee, may be waived for applicants with need. Admission notification on a rolling basis beginning on or about 10/1. Must reply by May 1 or within 4 week(s) if notified thereafter. **Financial aid:** Priority date 3/1; no closing date. FAFSA required. Must reply within 4 week(s) of notification.

Academics. Special study options: Cooperative education, cross-registration, distance learning, double major, dual enrollment of high school students, ESL, exchange student, honors, independent study, internships, liberal arts/career combination, student-designed major, study abroad, teacher certification program, Washington semester. **Credit/placement by examination:** AP, CLEP, IB, SAT, institutional tests. 32 credit hours maximum toward bachelor's degree. **Support services:** Learning center, pre-admission summer program, reduced course load, remedial instruction, study skills assistance, tutoring, writing center.

Majors. Area/ethnic studies: American, women's. **Biology:** General, biochemistry. **Business:** General, accounting, business admin, finance, managerial economics, sales/distribution. **Communications:** General. **Computer sciences:** General. **Education:** Early childhood, elementary, special. **Foreign languages:** French, German, Latin, Russian, Spanish. **Health:** Athletic training, audiology/speech pathology, dietetics, health care admin, nursing (RN), premedicine. **History:** General. **Liberal arts:** Arts/sciences. **Math:** General. **Parks/recreation:** Health/fitness. **Philosophy/religion:** Philosophy. **Physical sciences:** Analytical chemistry, chemistry, geology, physics. **Protective services:** Criminal justice. **Psychology:** General. **Public administration:** Social work. **Social sciences:** Anthropology, geography, political science, sociology. **Visual/performing arts:** Art, dramatic, music performance, studio arts.

Most popular majors. Business/marketing 14%, education 17%, English 8%, health sciences 12%, liberal arts 10%, psychology 6%, visual/performing arts 6%.

Computing on campus. 1,200 workstations in dormitories, library, computer center, student center. Dormitories wired for high-speed internet access and linked to campus network. Commuter students can connect to campus network. Online course registration, helpline, repair service, wireless network available.

Student life. Freshman orientation: Mandatory, $155 fee. One-day program in late June/early July followed by 3-day program prior to start of classes in August. **Policies:** Code of conduct applicable on and off campus. **Housing:** Coed dorms, single-sex dorms, special housing for disabled, apartments, fraternity/sorority housing, wellness housing available. $100 nonrefundable deposit, deadline 5/1. **Activities:** Bands, campus ministries, choral groups, dance, drama, international student organizations, literary magazine, music ensembles, musical theater, opera, radio station, student government, student newspaper, symphony orchestra, TV station, lesbian, gay, bisexual, and transgender association, Hillel, Newman Club, Crusade for Christ, Black Student Union, Latino American student organization, College Democrats, College Republicans.

Athletics. NCAA. **Intercollegiate:** Baseball M, basketball, cheerleading M, cross-country, diving, field hockey W, football (tackle) M, golf, gymnastics W, lacrosse W, rugby W, soccer, softball W, swimming, tennis, track and field, volleyball W. **Intramural:** Basketball, field hockey, football (non-tackle), soccer, softball, tennis, volleyball. **Team name:** Golden Rams.

Student services. Adult student services, alcohol/substance abuse counseling, chaplain/spiritual director, career counseling, services for economically disadvantaged, student employment services, financial aid counseling, health services, legal services, minority student services, on-campus daycare, personal counseling, placement for graduates, veterans' counselor, women's services. **Physically disabled:** Services for visually, speech, hearing impaired. **Learning disabled:** Comprehensive services available.

Contact. E-mail: ugadmiss@wcupa.edu
Phone: (610) 436-3411 Toll-free number: (877) 315-2165
Fax: (610) 436-2907
Marsha Haug, Assistant Vice President for Admissions and Enrollment Services, West Chester University of Pennsylvania, Messikomer Hall, West Chester, PA 19383

Westminster College

New Wilmington, Pennsylvania **CB member**
www.westminster.edu **CB code: 2975**

- Private 4-year liberal arts college affiliated with Presbyterian Church (USA)
- Residential campus in small town
- 1,408 degree-seeking undergraduates
- 59% of applicants admitted
- Application essay required

General. Founded in 1852. Regionally accredited. General studies curriculum with a freshman common experience. Semester at Oxford. **Degrees:** 380 bachelor's awarded; master's offered. **ROTC:** Army. **Location:** 60 miles from Pittsburgh; 17 miles from Youngstown, Ohio. **Calendar:** Semester, limited summer session. **Full-time faculty:** 103 total. **Part-time faculty:** 51 total. **Class size:** 63% < 20, 36% 20-39, less than 1% 40-49, less than 1% 50-99. **Special facilities:** Observatory, environmental outdoor laboratory, planetarium, electron microscopes, radar defractor.

Freshman class profile. 2,945 applied, 1,728 admitted, 448 enrolled.

Mid 50% test scores			
SAT critical reading:	470-580	GPA 2.0-2.99:	19%
SAT math:	480-530	Rank in top quarter:	59%
SAT writing:	470-570	Rank in top tenth:	26%
ACT composite:	20-25	Out-of-state:	19%
GPA 3.75 or higher:	29%	Live on campus:	97%
GPA 3.50-3.74:	20%	Fraternities:	33%
GPA 3.0-3.49:	32%	Sororities:	35%

Basis for selection. Class rank most important. Test scores also important. SAT or ACT recommended. Interview recommended for all; audition recommended for music; portfolio recommended for art.

High school preparation. 16 units required. Required units include English 4, mathematics 3, social studies 2, history 1, science 2 (laboratory 2), foreign language 2 and academic electives 3.

2008-2009 Annual costs. Tuition/fees: $28,100. Room/board: $8,100. Books/supplies: $900. Personal expenses: $685.

2008-2009 Financial aid. Non-need-based: Scholarships awarded for academics, athletics.

Application procedures. Admission: Closing date 5/1. $35 fee, may be waived for applicants with need. Admission notification on a rolling basis beginning on or about 11/1. Must reply by May 1 or within 2 week(s) if notified thereafter. **Financial aid:** Closing date 5/1. FAFSA, institutional form required. Applicants notified on a rolling basis starting 11/1; must reply by 5/1 or within 3 week(s) of notification.

Academics. Special study options: Double major, exchange student, honors, independent study, internships, liberal arts/career combination, semester at sea, student-designed major, study abroad, teacher certification program, Washington semester. 3-2 engineering programs with Case Western Reserve University (OH), Penn State, Washington University (MO), 3-2 law program with Duquesne University. **Credit/placement by examination:** AP, CLEP, institutional tests. **Support services:** Learning center, reduced course load, tutoring.

Majors. **Biology:** General, biochemistry, biophysics, ecology, molecular. **Business:** Accounting, business admin, finance, international, international finance, management science, managerial economics, organizational behavior. **Communications:** Broadcast journalism, public relations. **Computer sciences:** General, computer science, programming. **Education:** General, elementary, English, foreign languages, middle, multi-level teacher, secondary, social studies. **Engineering:** General. **Foreign languages:** General, classics, French, German, Latin, Spanish. **Health:** Predental, premedicine, prepharmacy, preveterinary. **History:** General. **Interdisciplinary:** Biopsychology, math/computer science. **Legal studies:** Prelaw. **Math:** General. **Philosophy/religion:** Philosophy, religion. **Physical sciences:** Chemistry, physics. **Protective services:** Criminal justice. **Psychology:** General. **Public administration:** Social work. **Social sciences:** Economics, international relations, political science, sociology. **Theology:** Religious ed. **Visual/performing arts:** Art, dramatic, music performance, music theory/composition, piano/organ, studio arts, voice/opera.

Computing on campus. 160 workstations in library, computer center. Dormitories linked to campus network. Commuter students can connect to campus network. Helpline available.

Student life. **Freshman orientation:** Mandatory, $105 fee. 4-day general social and academic orientation. **Housing:** Guaranteed on-campus for freshmen. Coed dorms, single-sex dorms, special housing for disabled, fraternity/sorority housing available. **Activities:** Bands, campus ministries, choral groups, dance, drama, film society, literary magazine, music ensembles, musical theater, radio station, student government, student newspaper, symphony orchestra, TV station, Fellowship of Christian Athletes, mock convention, service organizations, social awareness and action groups, Students in Action Who Value the Environment, Habitat for Humanity, Alpha Phi Omega.

Athletics. NCAA. **Intercollegiate:** Baseball M, basketball, cross-country, football (tackle) M, golf, soccer, softball W, swimming, tennis, track and field, volleyball W. **Intramural:** Archery, badminton, basketball, equestrian, racquetball, rugby M, softball, track and field W, volleyball. **Team name:** Titans.

Student services. Adult student services, career counseling, student employment services, health services, personal counseling, placement for graduates.

Contact. E-mail: admis@westminster.edu
Phone: (724) 946-7100 Fax: (724) 946-7171
Bradley Tokar, Dean of Admissions, Westminster College, Admissions, Westminster College, New Wilmington, PA 16172-0001

Widener University

Chester, Pennsylvania — **CB member**
www.widener.edu — **CB code: 2642**

- Private 4-year university
- Residential campus in large town
- 3,206 degree-seeking undergraduates: 17% part-time, 54% women, 13% African American, 2% Asian American, 3% Hispanic American, 2% international
- 2,976 degree-seeking graduate students
- 67% of applicants admitted
- SAT or ACT (ACT writing optional) required
- 56% graduate within 6 years

General. Founded in 1821. Regionally accredited. **Degrees:** 602 bachelor's, 17 associate awarded; master's, doctoral, first professional offered. **ROTC:** Army, Naval, Air Force. **Location:** 10 miles from Philadelphia, 10 miles from Wilmington, Delaware. **Calendar:** Semester, limited summer session. **Full-time faculty:** 310 total; 89% have terminal degrees, 11% minority, 51% women. **Part-time faculty:** 358 total; 49% have terminal degrees, 11% minority, 44% women. **Class size:** 61% < 20, 37% 20-39, less than 1% 40-49, less than 1% 50-99. **Special facilities:** Astronomical observatory, rock climbing wall, restaurant lab, executive seminar facility, child development center, recording studio, education lab, commercial graphics lab, physical therapy lab.

Freshman class profile. 4,690 applied, 3,152 admitted, 730 enrolled.

Mid 50% test scores			
SAT critical reading:	450-540	Rank in top tenth:	14%
SAT math:	450-570	Return as sophomores:	72%
GPA 3.75 or higher:	21%	Out-of-state:	38%
GPA 3.50-3.74:	17%	Live on campus:	83%
GPA 3.0-3.49:	35%	International:	1%
GPA 2.0-2.99:	27%	Fraternities:	9%
Rank in top quarter:	32%	Sororities:	8%

Basis for selection. Strength of curriculum, GPA, standardized test scores, class rank most important; recommendations, strength of character important. Interview recommended. **Homeschooled:** Transcript of courses and grades required. Curriculum validation and interview with director of admissions required.

High school preparation. 18 units required; 23 recommended. Required and recommended units include English 4, mathematics 3-4, social studies 3-4, science 3-4 (laboratory 2), foreign language 2 and academic electives 3.

2008-2009 Annual costs. Tuition/fees: $30,450. $950 additional fee for engineering students; $200 additional fee for junior/senior nursing students. Room/board: $10,840. Books/supplies: $1,080. Personal expenses: $1,170.

2008-2009 Financial aid. **Need-based:** 648 full-time freshmen applied for aid; 587 were judged to have need; 587 of these received aid. Average need met was 80%. Average scholarship/grant was $10,523; average loan $4,370. 53% of total undergraduate aid awarded as scholarships/grants, 47% as loans/jobs. **Non-need-based:** Awarded to 1,956 full-time undergraduates, including 583 freshmen. Scholarships awarded for academics, leadership, music/drama, ROTC.

Application procedures. **Admission:** Priority date 2/15; no deadline. $35 fee, may be waived for applicants with need, free for online applicants. Admission notification on a rolling basis beginning on or about 10/1. Must reply by May 1 or within 2 week(s) if notified thereafter. **Financial aid:** Priority date 2/15; no closing date. FAFSA required. Applicants notified on a rolling basis starting 3/15; must reply within 4 week(s) of notification.

Academics. **Special study options:** Accelerated study, combined bachelor's/graduate degree, cooperative education, distance learning, double major, ESL, honors, independent study, internships, liberal arts/career combination, student-designed major, study abroad, teacher certification program, weekend college. **Credit/placement by examination:** AP, CLEP, IB, institutional tests. Students can earn up to 2 years of credit in some fields via CLEP, challenge exams, and Advanced Placement exams. **Support services:** Learning center, pre-admission summer program, reduced course load, remedial instruction, study skills assistance, tutoring, writing center.

Majors. **Area/ethnic studies:** Women's. **Biology:** General, biochemistry. **Business:** Accounting, business admin, finance, financial planning, hospitality admin, human resources, international, management information systems, managerial economics, operations. **Communications:** General. **Computer sciences:** General, computer science, information systems. **Education:** Early childhood, elementary, science, special. **Engineering:** General, chemical, civil, electrical, mechanical. **Foreign languages:** French, Spanish. **Health:** Health services, nursing (RN), predental, premedicine, prenursing, preveterinary. **History:** General. **Legal studies:** Prelaw. **Liberal arts:** Arts/sciences. **Math:** General. **Physical sciences:** Chemistry, physics. **Protective services:** Law enforcement admin. **Psychology:** General. **Public administration:** Social work. **Social sciences:** Anthropology, economics, international relations, political science, sociology. **Visual/performing arts:** Studio arts.

Most popular majors. Business/marketing 24%, education 6%, engineering/engineering technologies 8%, health sciences 23%, psychology 11%, social sciences 6%.

Computing on campus. 720 workstations in library, student center. Dormitories wired for high-speed internet access and linked to campus network. Commuter students can connect to campus network. Online course registration, online library, helpline, repair service, student web hosting, wireless network available.

Student life. **Freshman orientation:** Mandatory. Preregistration for classes offered. **Housing:** Guaranteed on-campus for freshmen. Coed dorms, single-sex dorms, apartments, cooperative housing, fraternity/sorority housing, wellness housing available. $100 nonrefundable deposit. Special interest housing. **Activities:** Bands, campus ministries, choral groups, dance, drama, film society, international student organizations, literary magazine, music ensembles, radio station, student government, student newspaper, TV station, Hillel, black student union, political affairs club, Young Republicans, Young Democrats, environmental society, Widener Big Friends, Crusade for Christ, Alpha Phi Omega, Asian student association, presidential service corps.

Athletics. NCAA. **Intercollegiate:** Baseball M, basketball, cheerleading M, cross-country, field hockey W, football (tackle) M, golf M, lacrosse, soccer, softball W, swimming, track and field, volleyball W. **Intramural:** Basketball, cricket M, football (non-tackle), skiing, soccer, softball, volleyball, water polo M. **Team name:** Pride.

Student services. Adult student services, alcohol/substance abuse counseling, chaplain/spiritual director, career counseling, services for economically disadvantaged, student employment services, financial aid counseling, health services, on-campus daycare, personal counseling, placement for graduates, veterans' counselor, women's services. **Physically disabled:** Services for visually, speech, hearing impaired. **Learning disabled:** Comprehensive services available.

Contact. E-mail: admissions.office@widener.edu
Phone: (610) 499-4126 Toll-free number: (888) 943-3637
Fax: (610) 499-4676
Edwin Wright, Director of Admissions, Widener University, One University Place, Chester, PA 19013

Wilkes University

Wilkes-Barre, Pennsylvania **CB member**
www.wilkes.edu **CB code: 2977**

- Private 4-year university
- Residential campus in small city
- 2,211 degree-seeking undergraduates: 6% part-time, 50% women, 4% African American, 2% Asian American, 2% Hispanic American, 3% international
- 3,592 degree-seeking graduate students
- 75% of applicants admitted
- SAT or ACT required
- 58% graduate within 6 years

General. Founded in 1933. Regionally accredited. **Degrees:** 485 bachelor's awarded; master's, doctoral, first professional offered. **ROTC:** Army, Air Force. **Location:** 100 miles from Philadelphia, 140 miles from New York City. **Calendar:** Semester, extensive summer session. **Full-time faculty:** 146 total; 89% have terminal degrees, 7% minority, 45% women. **Part-time faculty:** 283 total; 4% minority, 45% women. **Class size:** 47% < 20, 47% 20-39, 2% 40-49, 4% 50-99, less than 1% >100. **Special facilities:** Performing arts center, field station, telecommunications center, indoor recreation and athletic center.

Freshman class profile. 2,778 applied, 2,091 admitted, 565 enrolled.

Mid 50% test scores		**Rank in top tenth:**	22%
SAT critical reading:	460-570	**Return as sophomores:**	78%
SAT math:	460-600	**Out-of-state:**	25%
SAT writing:	450-560	**Live on campus:**	75%
Rank in top quarter:	52%	**International:**	2%

Basis for selection. 920 SAT (exclusive of Writing) and/or rank in top 50% of high school class required for unconditional admission. Conditional admission may be offered to some applicants who do not meet these standards; must attend summer program prior to first semester. Interview recommended for all; audition required for theater arts programs.

High school preparation. Recommended units include English 4, mathematics 3, social studies 3, science 2 (laboratory 2) and computer science 1.

2008-2009 Annual costs. Tuition/fees: $25,170. Room/board: $10,780. Books/supplies: $1,100. Personal expenses: $1,000.

2008-2009 Financial aid. Non-need-based: Scholarships awarded for academics, leadership, minority status, music/drama.

Application procedures. Admission: No deadline. $45 fee, may be waived for applicants with need. Admission notification on a rolling basis. Must reply by May 1 or within 2 week(s) if notified thereafter. **Financial aid:** Priority date 3/1; no closing date. FAFSA required. Applicants notified on a rolling basis starting 3/1.

Academics. Special study options: Combined bachelor's/graduate degree, cooperative education, cross-registration, distance learning, double major, dual enrollment of high school students, ESL, external degree, honors, independent study, internships, student-designed major, study abroad, teacher certification program, weekend college. **Credit/placement by examination:** AP, CLEP, institutional tests. Credit by examination may be given to within 30 credits of graduation. **Support services:** Learning center, preadmission summer program, reduced course load, remedial instruction, study skills assistance, tutoring, writing center.

Majors. Biology: General, biochemistry. **Business:** Accounting, business admin, entrepreneurial studies. **Communications:** General, digital media. **Computer sciences:** General, information systems. **Education:** Elementary, special. **Engineering:** Electrical, environmental, mechanical. **Engineering technology:** Industrial management. **Foreign languages:** Spanish. **Health:** Clinical lab science, nursing (RN), pharmaceutical sciences. **History:** General. **Liberal arts:** Arts/sciences. **Math:** General. **Philosophy/religion:** Philosophy. **Physical sciences:** Chemistry, geology. **Protective services:** Criminal justice. **Psychology:** General. **Social sciences:** International relations, political science, sociology. **Visual/performing arts:** Dramatic, music performance.

Most popular majors. Biology 9%, business/marketing 16%, communications/journalism 6%, education 10%, English 6%, health sciences 11%, liberal arts 12%, psychology 8%.

Computing on campus. 530 workstations in library, computer center, student center. Dormitories wired for high-speed internet access and linked to campus network. Commuter students can connect to campus network. Online course registration, online library, helpline, wireless network available.

Student life. Freshman orientation: Mandatory, $125 fee. Preregistration for classes offered. **Housing:** Guaranteed on-campus for all undergraduates. Coed dorms, single-sex dorms, apartments available. $100 nonrefundable deposit. **Activities:** Bands, choral groups, dance, drama, literary magazine, music ensembles, musical theater, radio station, student government, student newspaper, TV station.

Athletics. NCAA. **Intercollegiate:** Baseball M, basketball, cross-country, field hockey W, football (tackle) M, golf M, lacrosse W, soccer, softball W, tennis, volleyball W, wrestling M. **Intramural:** Basketball M, bowling, football (tackle) M, ice hockey M, racquetball, rowing (crew), rugby M, skiing, softball, table tennis, volleyball. **Team name:** Colonels.

Student services. Adult student services, career counseling, student employment services, financial aid counseling, health services, personal counseling, placement for graduates, veterans' counselor. **Physically disabled:** Services for visually, hearing impaired.

Contact. E-mail: admissions@wilkes.edu
Phone: (570) 408-4400 Toll-free number: (800) 945-5378
Fax: (570) 408-4904
Michael Frantz, Vice President of Enrollment Services, Wilkes University, 84 West South Street, Wilkes-Barre, PA 18766

Wilson College

Chambersburg, Pennsylvania **CB member**
www.wilson.edu **CB code: 2979**

- Private 4-year liberal arts college for women affiliated with Presbyterian Church (USA)
- Residential campus in large town
- 497 degree-seeking undergraduates: 36% part-time, 95% women, 4% African American, 1% Asian American, 2% Hispanic American, 5% international
- 18 degree-seeking graduate students
- 55% of applicants admitted
- Application essay required
- 57% graduate within 6 years; 30% enter graduate study

General. Founded in 1869. Regionally accredited. Men admitted to adult degree program, post-baccalaureate teacher intern program. Residential program for single mothers with children. **Degrees:** 89 bachelor's, 10 associate awarded; master's offered. **ROTC:** Army. **Location:** 90 miles from Washington, DC; 145 miles from Philadelphia. **Calendar:** 4-1-4, limited summer session. **Full-time faculty:** 42 total; 88% have terminal degrees, 5% minority, 50% women. **Part-time faculty:** 41 total; 17% have terminal degrees, 2% minority, 73% women. **Class size:** 84% < 20, 16% 20-39. **Special facilities:** Equestrian center, sustainable living center, veterinary medical center, archival center.

Freshman class profile. 477 applied, 262 admitted, 87 enrolled.

Mid 50% test scores		**GPA 2.0-2.99:**	18%
SAT critical reading:	460-550	**Rank in top quarter:**	37%
SAT math:	420-540	**Rank in top tenth:**	10%
SAT writing:	430-540	**End year in good standing:**	87%
ACT composite:	18-22	**Return as sophomores:**	82%
GPA 3.75 or higher:	22%	**Out-of-state:**	40%
GPA 3.50-3.74:	16%	**Live on campus:**	86%
GPA 3.0-3.49:	44%		

Basis for selection. Admissions based on secondary school record. Class rank, recommendations, character, and personal qualities also important. SAT/ACT optional for students with 3.0 GPA in specified college prep curriculum from a regionally accredited secondary school. Interview recommended. **Homeschooled:** Transcript of courses and grades, letter of recommendation (nonparent) required.

High school preparation. College-preparatory program recommended. 15 units required. Required units include English 4, mathematics 3, social studies 4, science 2 (laboratory 2) and foreign language 2.

2008-2009 Annual costs. Tuition/fees: $25,900. Room/board: $8,630. Books/supplies: $1,000. Personal expenses: $800.

2008-2009 Financial aid. **Non-need-based:** Scholarships awarded for academics, alumni affiliation, religious affiliation, state residency.

Application procedures. **Admission:** Priority date 4/30; no deadline. $35 fee, may be waived for applicants with need, free for online applicants. Admission notification on a rolling basis beginning on or about 9/15. Must reply by May 1 or within 3 week(s) if notified thereafter. **Financial aid:** Priority date 4/30; no closing date. FAFSA, institutional form required. Applicants notified on a rolling basis starting 2/15.

Academics. **Special study options:** Cooperative education, cross-registration, double major, ESL, honors, independent study, internships, liberal arts/career combination, student-designed major, study abroad, teacher certification program, Washington semester. **Credit/placement by examination:** AP, CLEP, IB, SAT, ACT, institutional tests. 4 credit hours maximum toward associate degree, 4 toward bachelor's. **Support services:** Learning center, reduced course load, remedial instruction, study skills assistance, tutoring, writing center.

Majors. **Agriculture:** Equestrian studies. **Biology:** General. **Business:** Accounting, business admin, management information systems. **Communications:** Media studies. **Conservation:** Environmental science. **Education:** Elementary. **Foreign languages:** French, Spanish. **Health:** Veterinary technology/assistant. **Math:** General. **Parks/recreation:** Exercise sciences. **Philosophy/religion:** Philosophy, religion. **Physical sciences:** Chemistry. **Psychology:** General, psychobiology. **Social sciences:** General, economics, international relations, sociology. **Visual/performing arts:** Art.

Most popular majors. Agriculture 10%, business/marketing 15%, education 7%, English 8%, health sciences 29%.

Computing on campus. 96 workstations in dormitories, library, computer center, student center. Dormitories wired for high-speed internet access and linked to campus network. Commuter students can connect to campus network. Online course registration, online library, helpline, repair service, wireless network available.

Student life. **Freshman orientation:** Mandatory, $250 fee. Preregistration for classes offered. Held in August. **Policies:** Honor principle, shared governance. **Housing:** Guaranteed on-campus for all undergraduates. Wellness housing available. $300 nonrefundable deposit. Pets allowed in dorm rooms. Students of junior standing or above guaranteed single residence hall room. Housing for single mothers with children available. **Activities:** Choral groups, dance, drama, international student organizations, literary magazine, music ensembles, radio station, student government, student newspaper, religious activities committee, language clubs, interfaith support group, black student union, Curran Scholars, Alternative Spring Break, Bible study, Habitat for Humanity.

Athletics. NCAA. **Intercollegiate:** Basketball W, field hockey W, gymnastics W, lacrosse W, soccer W, softball W, tennis W. **Team name:** Phoenix.

Student services. Adult student services, alcohol/substance abuse counseling, chaplain/spiritual director, career counseling, student employment services, financial aid counseling, health services, on-campus daycare, personal counseling, placement for graduates, women's services.

Contact. E-mail: admissions@wilson.edu
Phone: (717) 262-2002 Toll-free number: (800) 421-8402
Fax: (717) 262-2546
Mary Ann Naso, Vice President for Enrollment and Admissions, Wilson College, 1015 Philadelphia Avenue, Chambersburg, PA 17201-1285

Yeshivath Beth Moshe
Scranton, Pennsylvania
CB code: 1657

- Private 4-year rabbinical college for men affiliated with Jewish faith
- Small city

General. Founded in 1965. Accredited by AARTS. **Calendar:** Continuous.

Contact. Phone: (717) 346-1747
Admissions Director, 930 Hickory Street, Scranton, PA 18505

York College of Pennsylvania
York, Pennsylvania — **CB member**
www.ycp.edu — **CB code: 2991**

- Private 4-year liberal arts college
- Residential campus in small city
- 5,126 degree-seeking undergraduates: 10% part-time, 55% women, 3% African American, 1% Asian American, 2% Hispanic American, 1% international
- 296 degree-seeking graduate students
- 60% of applicants admitted
- SAT or ACT with writing required
- 65% graduate within 6 years

General. Founded in 1787. Regionally accredited. **Degrees:** 983 bachelor's, 38 associate awarded; master's offered. **ROTC:** Army. **Location:** 46 miles from Baltimore, 95 miles from Philadelphia. **Calendar:** Semester, extensive summer session. **Full-time faculty:** 154 total; 86% have terminal degrees, 42% women. **Part-time faculty:** 372 total; 14% have terminal degrees, 53% women. **Class size:** 41% < 20, 56% 20-39, 3% 40-49, less than 1% 50-99, less than 1% >100. **Special facilities:** Engineering innovation center, telecommunications center, rare books collection, oral history room, video production studios, nursing education center.

Freshman class profile. 7,395 applied, 4,431 admitted, 1,104 enrolled.

Mid 50% test scores		**GPA 2.0-2.99:**	13%
SAT critical reading:	490-570	**Rank in top quarter:**	67%
SAT math:	500-590	**Rank in top tenth:**	11%
SAT writing:	480-570	**End year in good standing:**	86%
ACT composite:	21-25	**Return as sophomores:**	77%
GPA 3.75 or higher:	42%	**Out-of-state:**	44%
GPA 3.50-3.74:	16%	**Live on campus:**	71%
GPA 3.0-3.49:	29%		

Basis for selection. High school record, standardized test results, personal qualities most important. Interviews, essays recommended for academically borderline students; audition required for music programs; portfolio recommended for art programs. **Homeschooled:** Statement describing homeschool structure and mission, transcript of courses and grades, state high school equivalency certificate, letter of recommendation (nonparent) required. Diploma required from home school association or local school district; portfolio evaluation conducted by certified teacher; syllabus for each course.

High school preparation. College-preparatory program recommended. 15 units required. Required and recommended units include English 4, mathematics 3-4, social studies 3, science 3 and foreign language 2. One biology, 2 chemistry, and 2 algebra required of nursing applicants.

2009-2010 Annual costs. Tuition/fees: $14,460. Room/board: $8,080. Books/supplies: $1,200. Personal expenses: $1,000.

2008-2009 Financial aid. **Need-based:** 950 full-time freshmen applied for aid; 625 were judged to have need; 615 of these received aid. Average need met was 73%. Average scholarship/grant was $5,103; average loan $5,248. 51% of total undergraduate aid awarded as scholarships/grants, 49% as loans/jobs. **Non-need-based:** Awarded to 1,358 full-time undergraduates, including 536 freshmen. Scholarships awarded for academics, alumni affiliation, music/drama.

Application procedures. **Admission:** No deadline. $30 fee, may be waived for applicants with need, free for online applicants. Admission notification on a rolling basis beginning on or about 10/1. **Financial aid:** No deadline. FAFSA required. Applicants notified on a rolling basis starting 3/1; must reply within 4 week(s) of notification.

Academics. **Special study options:** Combined bachelor's/graduate degree, cooperative education, double major, dual enrollment of high school students, honors, independent study, internships, liberal arts/career combination, student-designed major, study abroad, teacher certification program. **Credit/placement by examination:** AP, CLEP, IB, SAT, ACT, institutional tests. 30 credit hours maximum toward associate degree, 30 toward bachelor's. **Support services:** Learning center, reduced course load, remedial instruction, study skills assistance, tutoring, writing center.

Majors. **Biology:** General. **Business:** Accounting, business admin, entrepreneurial studies, finance, knowledge management, marketing. **Communications:** General, media studies, public relations. **Communications technology:** Recording arts. **Computer sciences:** General, computer science. **Education:** Biology, elementary, English, mathematics, music, science, social studies. **Engineering:** Computer, electrical, mechanical. **Engineering technology:** Industrial management. **Foreign languages:** Spanish. **Health:** Clinical lab science, licensed practical nurse, nuclear medical technology, nursing (RN), respiratory therapy technology. **History:** General. **Interdisciplinary:** Behavioral sciences. **Math:** General. **Parks/recreation:** General, sports admin. **Philosophy/religion:** Philosophy. **Physical sciences:** Chemistry. **Protective services:** Forensics, law enforcement admin. **Psychology:** General. **Social sciences:** Political science, sociology. **Visual/performing arts:** Commercial/advertising art, dramatic, studio arts.

Most popular majors. Business/marketing 18%, communications/journalism 10%, education 11%, health sciences 13%, parks/recreation 6%, security/protective services 7%.

Computing on campus. 650 workstations in library, computer center. Dormitories wired for high-speed internet access and linked to campus network. Commuter students can connect to campus network. Online course registration, online library, helpline, wireless network available.

Student life. Freshman orientation: Mandatory. Preregistration for classes offered. 4-day program prior to fall semester. **Housing:** Guaranteed on-campus for freshmen. Coed dorms, single-sex dorms, special housing for disabled, apartments, wellness housing available. $200 fully refundable deposit. Minidorms featuring units of 10 students, suites, sponsored houses, and apartments available. **Activities:** Bands, choral groups, drama, film society, literary magazine, music ensembles, musical theater, radio station, student government, student newspaper, symphony orchestra, TV station, over 80 student organizations.

Athletics. NCAA. **Intercollegiate:** Baseball M, basketball, cheerleading, cross-country, field hockey W, golf M, lacrosse, soccer, softball W, swimming, tennis, track and field, volleyball W, wrestling M. **Intramural:** Badminton, basketball, football (non-tackle), lacrosse M, rugby M, skiing, soccer M, softball, swimming, tennis, track and field, volleyball, water polo M, wrestling M. **Team name:** Spartans.

Student services. Adult student services, alcohol/substance abuse counseling, chaplain/spiritual director, career counseling, services for economically disadvantaged, student employment services, financial aid counseling, health services, minority student services, personal counseling, placement for graduates, veterans' counselor. **Physically disabled:** Services for visually, hearing impaired.

Contact. E-mail: admissions@ycp.edu
Phone: (717) 849-1600 Toll-free number: (800) 455-8018
Fax: (717) 849-1607
Nancy Spataro, Director of Admissions, York College of Pennsylvania, 441 Country Club Road, York, PA 17403-3651

Puerto Rico

American University of Puerto Rico

Bayamon, Puerto Rico — **CB member**
www.aupr.edu — **CB code: 0961**

- Private 4-year university and business college
- Commuter campus in large city
- 2,934 degree-seeking undergraduates
- 166 graduate students

General. Founded in 1963. Regionally accredited. Branch campus at Manati. **Degrees:** 382 bachelor's, 39 associate awarded; master's offered. **ROTC:** Army. **Location:** 12 miles from San Juan. **Calendar:** Semester, limited summer session. **Full-time faculty:** 53 total. **Part-time faculty:** 123 total. **Special facilities:** Fully computerized classrooms.

Basis for selection. Open admission. SAT required for English-speaking applicants and NCAA student athletes. Interview recommended. **Homeschooled:** Transcript of courses and grades, state high school equivalency certificate required.

High school preparation. 18 units recommended. Recommended units include English 3, mathematics 2, social studies 2, history 1, science 2, foreign language 3 and academic electives 5.

2008-2009 Annual costs. Tuition/fees: $5,010. Books/supplies: $800.

2008-2009 Financial aid. All financial aid based on need.

Application procedures. Admission: No deadline. $25 fee, may be waived for applicants with need. Admission notification on a rolling basis. **Financial aid:** Priority date 4/30, closing date 5/31. FAFSA, institutional form required. Applicants notified by 6/1; must reply within 2 week(s) of notification.

Academics. Special study options: Honors, independent study, internships, liberal arts/career combination. **Credit/placement by examination:** AP, CLEP, institutional tests. **Support services:** Learning center, reduced course load, tutoring.

Majors. Business: General, accounting, administrative services, business admin, office technology, office/clerical, purchasing. **Communications:** General. **Communications technology:** General. **Education:** General, business, elementary, ESL, mathematics, physical, secondary, Spanish, special. **Social sciences:** General.

Computing on campus. 75 workstations in computer center.

Student life. Freshman orientation: Mandatory. Preregistration for classes offered. **Activities:** Student government.

Athletics. NCAA. **Intercollegiate:** Basketball, cross-country, swimming, tennis, track and field, volleyball. **Intramural:** Basketball, cross-country, softball M, table tennis, track and field, volleyball. **Team name:** Pirates.

Student services. Career counseling, student employment services, health services, personal counseling, veterans' counselor. **Physically disabled:** Services for speech impaired.

Contact. E-mail: oficinaadmisiones@aupr.edu
Phone: (787) 620-2040 ext. 2020 Fax: (787) 785-7377
Margarita Cruz, Director of Admissions, American University of Puerto Rico, PO Box 2037, Bayamon, PR 00960-2037

Atlantic College

Guaynabo, Puerto Rico
www.atlanticcollege.edu — **CB code: 7137**

- Private 4-year liberal arts college
- Commuter campus in small city

General. Founded in 1983. Accredited by ACICS. **Degrees:** 126 bachelor's, 20 associate awarded; master's offered. **Location:** 20 miles from San Juan. **Calendar:** Quarter, extensive summer session. **Full-time faculty:** 22 total. **Part-time faculty:** 24 total. **Special facilities:** Motion caption laboratories, audio laboratories (for study of digital graphic design, computerized animation technology).

Basis for selection. Open admission.

High school preparation. 16 units recommended. Recommended units include English 3, mathematics 2, social studies 1, history 2, science 2, foreign language 3 and academic electives 3.

2008-2009 Annual costs. Tuition/fees: $6,175. Books/supplies: $500.

Financial aid. All financial aid based on need.

Application procedures. Admission: No deadline. $30 fee. Admission notification on a rolling basis. **Financial aid:** Closing date 6/30. FAFSA, institutional form required. Applicants notified on a rolling basis starting 4/1; must reply within 2 week(s) of notification.

Academics. Special study options: Combined bachelor's/graduate degree, honors, internships, liberal arts/career combination, student-designed major. **Credit/placement by examination:** CLEP. **Support services:** Learning center, pre-admission summer program, remedial instruction, tutoring.

Majors. Business: Accounting, administrative services, business admin. **Computer sciences:** Security. **Education:** Early childhood special. **Visual/performing arts:** Commercial/advertising art.

Most popular majors. Business/marketing 6%, computer/information sciences 12%, visual/performing arts 74%.

Computing on campus. 16 workstations in library, computer center. Online library, repair service, wireless network available.

Student life. Freshman orientation: Available. **Activities:** Dance, drama, student government, student newspaper.

Athletics. Intercollegiate: Basketball. **Intramural:** Basketball, volleyball.

Student services. Alcohol/substance abuse counseling, career counseling, financial aid counseling, health services, personal counseling, placement for graduates. **Physically disabled:** Services for hearing impaired.

Contact. E-mail: admisiones@atlanticcollege.edu
Phone: (787) 720-1022 ext. 1027 Fax: (787) 720-1092
Zaida Perez, Admissions Officer, Atlantic College, PO Box 3918, Guaynabo, PR 00970

Bayamon Central University

Bayamon, Puerto Rico — **CB member**
www.ucb.edu.pr — **CB code: 0840**

- Private 4-year university affiliated with Roman Catholic Church
- Commuter campus in large city
- 20% of applicants admitted

General. Founded in 1970. Regionally accredited. Member of consortium of U.S. and South American universities. Virtually all students come from Spanish-speaking backgrounds. **Degrees:** 280 bachelor's, 8 associate awarded; master's offered. **ROTC:** Army, Air Force. **Location:** 9 miles from San Juan. **Calendar:** Semester, limited summer session. **Full-time faculty:** 49 total. **Part-time faculty:** 114 total. **Special facilities:** Library of Dominican Order.

Freshman class profile. 2,586 applied, 509 admitted, 378 enrolled.

Basis for selection. School achievement record and test scores most important. Minimum 2.0 high school GPA. Fluency in Spanish, basic knowledge of English necessary. Conditional admission to those identified as having underdeveloped academic potential. SAT or ACT accepted from English-speaking students. Score report must be received by 04/15. Essay recommended for all; interview recommended for academically weak. **Homeschooled:** Transcript of courses and grades required.

High school preparation. Required units include English 3, mathematics 3, social studies 3 and science 1. 3 units of Spanish required.

2008-2009 Annual costs. Tuition/fees: $7,250. Books/supplies: $800. Personal expenses: $1,200.

2008-2009 Financial aid. All financial aid based on need.

Application procedures. Admission: Priority date 12/6; deadline 4/6 (postmark date). $15 fee, may be waived for applicants with need. Admission notification on a rolling basis beginning on or about 3/4. **Financial aid:** Priority date 5/31, closing date 7/2. FAFSA, institutional form required.

Academics. All classroom instruction conducted in Spanish. Core curriculum includes courses in Spanish. Course in methodology of learning must be satisfactorily completed. **Special study options:** Double major, independent study, teacher certification program. **Credit/placement by examination:** AP, CLEP. **Support services:** Learning center, reduced course load, tutoring.

Majors. Biology: General. **Business:** General, accounting, administrative services, business admin, finance, human resources, management information systems, management science, marketing. **Communications:** Journalism. **Conservation:** General. **Education:** Early childhood, elementary, English, instructional media, mathematics, physical, science, secondary, Spanish, special. **Foreign languages:** Spanish. **Health:** Occupational health. **Interdisciplinary:** Biological/physical sciences, natural sciences. **Philosophy/religion:** Philosophy, religion. **Physical sciences:** Chemistry. **Psychology:** General. **Public administration:** General, social work.

Computing on campus. 130 workstations in computer center. Online library available.

Student life. Freshman orientation: Mandatory. Preregistration for classes offered. **Activities:** Choral groups, drama, student government, student newspaper, various cultural, religious, and social activities.

Athletics. Intercollegiate: Basketball, cross-country, softball, swimming, table tennis, tennis, track and field, volleyball. **Intramural:** Basketball, track and field, volleyball. **Team name:** Halcones.

Student services. Career counseling, student employment services, financial aid counseling, health services, on-campus daycare, personal counseling, placement for graduates. **Physically disabled:** Services for visually, hearing impaired.

Contact. E-mail: chernandez@ucb.edu.pr
Phone: (787) 786-3030 ext. 2100 Fax: (787) 740-2200
Cristina Hernandez, Director of Admissions, Bayamon Central University, PO Box 1725, Bayamon, PR 00960-1725

Caribbean University

Bayamon, Puerto Rico — **CB member**
www.caribbean.edu — **CB code: 0779**

- Private 4-year health science and liberal arts college
- Commuter campus in large city
- 4,600 degree-seeking undergraduates
- 1,550 graduate students

General. Founded in 1969. Regionally accredited. Extension centers in Carolina, Vega Baja, and Ponce. **Degrees:** 246 bachelor's, 54 associate awarded; master's, first professional offered. **ROTC:** Army, Naval, Air Force. **Location:** 12 miles from San Juan. **Calendar:** Differs by program, limited summer session. **Full-time faculty:** 60 total. **Part-time faculty:** 80 total. **Special facilities:** College-operated museum program at Bayamon campus.

Freshman class profile.

End year in good standing:	62%	**Out-of-state:**	5%
Return as sophomores:	72%		

Basis for selection. School achievement record, test scores important, and interview considered. SAT required of English-speaking applicants. PAA score reports by August 15. Interview recommended for academically weak. **Homeschooled:** State high school equivalency certificate required.

High school preparation. College-preparatory program recommended.

2009-2010 Annual costs. Tuition/fees (projected): $4,520. Annual full-time tuition for engineering program: $3,960; per-credit-hour charge: $165. Books/supplies: $640. Personal expenses: $1,950.

2007-2008 Financial aid. All financial aid based on need. 65% of total undergraduate aid awarded as scholarships/grants, 35% as loans/jobs.

Application procedures. Admission: No deadline. $25 fee, may be waived for applicants with need. Admission notification on a rolling basis beginning on or about 3/1. **Financial aid:** Priority date 5/30; no closing date. FAFSA required. Applicants notified on a rolling basis starting 7/30; must reply within 2 week(s) of notification.

Academics. Special study options: Combined bachelor's/graduate degree, distance learning, honors, liberal arts/career combination, teacher certification program, weekend college. **Credit/placement by examination:** CLEP, institutional tests. **Support services:** Learning center, remedial instruction, tutoring.

Majors. Biology: General. **Business:** Accounting, administrative services, business admin. **Computer sciences:** General. **Education:** Business, elementary, English, mathematics, science, secondary, special. **Engineering:** Civil, petroleum. **Foreign languages:** Spanish. **Health:** Nursing (RN), premedicine, speech pathology. **Legal studies:** Prelaw. **Parks/recreation:** General. **Public administration:** Social work. **Social sciences:** General, criminology.

Computing on campus. 100 workstations in library, computer center, student center. Online course registration, online library, student web hosting, wireless network available.

Student life. Freshman orientation: Mandatory. Preregistration for classes offered. **Activities:** Choral groups, drama, music ensembles, student government, student newspaper.

Athletics. Intercollegiate: Cheerleading. **Intramural:** Basketball, cross-country, football (tackle), gymnastics, judo, table tennis, tennis, track and field, volleyball. **Team name:** Gryphoms.

Student services. Alcohol/substance abuse counseling, career counseling, services for economically disadvantaged, student employment services, financial aid counseling, health services, personal counseling, placement for graduates, veterans' counselor. **Physically disabled:** Services for visually, speech, hearing impaired.

Contact. E-mail: admissiones@caribbean.edu
Phone: (787) 780-0070 ext. 1111 Toll-free number: (787) 780-0070
Fax: (787) 785-0101
Ida Alvarado, Admissions Coordinator, Caribbean University, PO Box 493, Bayamon, PR 00960-0493

Carlos Albizu University: San Juan

San Juan, Puerto Rico
www.albizu.edu — **CB code: 2104**

- Private two-year upper-division university
- Large town
- Test scores, application essay, interview required

General. Regionally accredited. **Degrees:** 82 bachelor's awarded; master's, doctoral offered. **Calendar:** Semester, limited summer session. **Full-time faculty:** 22 total. **Part-time faculty:** 5 total.

Student profile. 181 degree-seeking undergraduates.

Basis for selection. College transcript, application essay, interview, standardized test scores required. Transfer accepted as sophomores.

2008-2009 Annual costs. Books/supplies: $2,606. Personal expenses: $3,681.

Financial aid. Need-based: 71% of total undergraduate aid awarded as scholarships/grants, 29% as loans/jobs.

Application procedures. Admission: $75 fee. Application must be submitted on paper.

Academics. Special study options: Combined bachelor's/graduate degree, distance learning. **Credit/placement by examination:** CLEP.

Majors. Education: Speech impaired. **Interdisciplinary:** Behavioral sciences.

Computing on campus. 30 workstations in computer center.

Contact. Phone: (787) 725-6500 ext. 21 Fax: (787) 721-7187
Carlos Rodriguez-Irizarry, Director of Admissions, Carlos Albizu University: San Juan, 151 Tanca Street, San Juan, PR 00902-3711

Colegio Biblico Pentecostal

Saint Just, Puerto Rico
www.cbp.edu

- Private 4-year Bible and seminary college
- Small city

General. Accredited by ABHE. **Calendar:** Semester.

Contact. Phone: (787) 761-0808
Registrar, PO Box 901, Saint Just, PR 00978-0901

Colegio Pentecostal Mizpa
San Juan, Puerto Rico
www.colmizpa.edu

- Private 4-year Bible college affiliated with Pentecostal Holiness Church
- Commuter campus in very large city
- 237 degree-seeking undergraduates: 62% part-time, 47% women
- 100% of applicants admitted
- Interview required

General. Accredited by ABHE. **Degrees:** 10 bachelor's, 16 associate awarded. **Calendar:** Semester, limited summer session. **Full-time faculty:** 1 total; 100% women. **Part-time faculty:** 25 total; 20% have terminal degrees, 48% women. **Class size:** 88% < 20, 12% 20-39.

Freshman class profile. 23 applied, 23 admitted, 22 enrolled.

GPA 3.75 or higher:	4%	**GPA 2.0-2.99:**	30%
GPA 3.50-3.74:	9%	**End year in good standing:**	41%
GPA 3.0-3.49:	55%	**Return as sophomores:**	1%

Basis for selection. Academic GPA, religious affiliation very important, rigor of secondary school record considered. **Homeschooled:** State high school equivalency certificate, interview required. **Learning Disabled:** Certified information concerning disability must be provided by student.

2008-2009 Annual costs. Books/supplies: $500. Personal expenses: $1,200.

2007-2008 Financial aid. All financial aid based on need.

Application procedures. Admission: No deadline. $40 fee ($40 out-of-state). Application must be submitted on paper. **Financial aid:** No deadline. FAFSA required.

Academics. Special study options: External degree. **Credit/placement by examination:** CLEP, institutional tests. **Support services:** Learning center, writing center.

Majors. Theology: Bible, pastoral counseling, religious ed.

Computing on campus. Online library, wireless network available.

Student life. Freshman orientation: Mandatory. Preregistration for classes offered. **Policies:** Religious observance required. **Housing:** Single-sex dorms, wellness housing available. $125 fully refundable deposit. **Activities:** Radio station, student government, TV station.

Student services. Adult student services, chaplain/spiritual director, career counseling, services for economically disadvantaged, student employment services, financial aid counseling, personal counseling.

Contact. E-mail: decanatoestudiante@colmizpa.edu
Phone: (787) 720-4476 Fax: (787) 720-2012
Jorge Burgos, Admissions Director and Dean of Students, Colegio Pentecostal Mizpa, PO Box 20966, San Juan, PR 00928-0966

Columbia Centro Universitario: Caguas
Caguas, Puerto Rico
www.columbiaco.edu **CB code: 2315**

- For-profit 4-year business and technical college
- Commuter campus in small city
- 999 degree-seeking undergraduates: 53% part-time, 70% women
- 77 degree-seeking graduate students
- Interview required

General. Founded in 1966. Regionally accredited. **Degrees:** 80 bachelor's, 135 associate awarded; master's offered. **Location:** 15 miles from San Juan. **Calendar:** Differs by program, extensive summer session. **Full-time faculty:** 12 total; 33% have terminal degrees, 42% women. **Part-time faculty:** 73 total; 7% have terminal degrees, 62% women. **Class size:** 60% < 20, 40% 20-39.

Freshman class profile. 404 applied, 351 admitted, 181 enrolled.

Basis for selection. Open admission, but selective for some programs. Parent signature and vaccination certificate required for students under age 21. Portfolio required for adult education students.

High school preparation. 15 units required. Required units include English 3, mathematics 2, social studies 2, history 2, science 3 and academic electives 3.

2008-2009 Annual costs. Tuition/fees: $4,360. Books/supplies: $467. Personal expenses: $1,809.

2007-2008 Financial aid. All financial aid based on need.

Application procedures. Admission: No deadline. $50 fee. Application must be submitted on paper. Admission notification on a rolling basis.

Academics. Credit/placement by examination: AP, CLEP. **Support services:** Tutoring.

Majors. Business: Business admin. **Health:** Nursing (RN).

Most popular majors. Business/marketing 45%, health sciences 55%.

Computing on campus. 27 workstations in library, computer center.

Student life. Freshman orientation: Mandatory.

Student services. Career counseling, student employment services, financial aid counseling, personal counseling, placement for graduates, veterans' counselor.

Contact. E-mail: info@columbiaco.edu
Phone: (787) 743-4041 ext. 240 Toll-free number: (800) 981-4877 ext. 240
Fax: (787) 744-7031
Xiomara Sanchez, Admissions Coordinator, Columbia Centro Universitario: Caguas, PO Box 8517, Caguas, PR 00726

Conservatory of Music of Puerto Rico
San Juan, Puerto Rico
www.cmpr.edu **CB code: 1115**

- Public 4-year music college
- Commuter campus in large city
- 402 degree-seeking undergraduates: 25% part-time, 28% women
- 32 degree-seeking graduate students
- 70% of applicants admitted
- 52% graduate within 6 years; 19% enter graduate study

General. Founded in 1959. Regionally accredited. **Degrees:** 45 bachelor's awarded; master's offered. **Calendar:** Semester, limited summer session. **Full-time faculty:** 46 total; 6% have terminal degrees, 94% minority. **Part-time faculty:** 28 total; 18% have terminal degrees, 93% minority. **Class size:** 96% < 20, 3% 20-39, less than 1% 40-49, less than 1% 50-99. **Special facilities:** Library with more than 26,000 musical scores, technology lab (computers applied to music), piano lab, theater.

Freshman class profile. 104 applied, 73 admitted, 63 enrolled.

GPA 3.75 or higher:	30%	**End year in good standing:**	95%
GPA 3.50-3.74:	26%	**Return as sophomores:**	100%
GPA 3.0-3.49:	30%	**International:**	3%
GPA 2.0-2.99:	13%		

Basis for selection. Musical ability very important. School achievement record, test scores important. Recommendations considered. Must take entrance examination in both theory and instrument. SAT is accepted from applicants from US mainland. Audition required for music performance. Essays and interview also required for music education. **Homeschooled:** State high school equivalency certificate required.

High school preparation. College-preparatory program recommended. Required and recommended units include English 3, mathematics 3, history 3, science 3, foreign language 3 and academic electives 3.

2008-2009 Annual costs. Tuition/fees: $2,750. Books/supplies: $1,650. Personal expenses: $950.

2007-2008 Financial aid. All financial aid based on need. 55 full-time freshmen applied for aid; 55 were judged to have need; 55 of these received aid. Average need met was 52%. Average scholarship/grant was $3,096; average loan $2,625. 43% of total undergraduate aid awarded as scholarships/grants, 57% as loans/jobs.

Application procedures. Admission: Closing date 12/15 (receipt date). $35 fee. Application must be submitted on paper. Admission notification 4/30. **Financial aid:** Priority date 12/15; no closing date. FAFSA, institutional form required. Applicants notified on a rolling basis starting 4/30.

Academics. Special study options: Cross-registration, dual enrollment of high school students, liberal arts/career combination, teacher certification program. **Credit/placement by examination:** AP, CLEP, institutional tests. 12 credit hours maximum toward bachelor's degree. **Support services:** Learning center, pre-admission summer program, reduced course load, remedial instruction, tutoring.

Majors. Education: Music. **Visual/performing arts:** Jazz, music performance, piano/organ, stringed instruments, voice/opera.

Most popular majors. Education 22%, visual/performing arts 78%.

Computing on campus. 17 workstations in library, computer center. Online library, wireless network available.

Student life. Freshman orientation: Mandatory. Preregistration for classes offered. **Activities:** Bands, choral groups, music ensembles, opera, student government, symphony orchestra.

Student services. Career counseling, student employment services, financial aid counseling, personal counseling, placement for graduates.

Contact. E-mail: esantiag@cmpr.gobierno.pr
Phone: (787) 751-0160 ext. 275 Fax: (787) 758-8268
Eutimia Santiago, Director, Admissions Office and Institutional Research, Conservatory of Music of Puerto Rico, Rafael Lamar #350 Esq. Roosevelt, San Juan, PR 00918-2199

Electronic Data Processing College of Puerto Rico

Hato Rey, Puerto Rico
www.edpcollege.edu **CB code: 2243**

- For-profit 4-year business and technical college
- Commuter campus in very large city

General. Founded in 1968. Candidate for regional accreditation. **Calendar:** Semester.

Annual costs/financial aid. Books/supplies: $465. Personal expenses: $1,455.

Contact. Phone: (787) 765-3560
Admissions Director, PO Box 1923, Hato Rey, PR 00919-2303

Electronic Data Processing College: San Sebastian

San Sebastian, Puerto Rico
www.edpcollege.edu **CB code: 3219**

- For-profit 4-year business and health science college
- Commuter campus in small city

General. Location: 28 miles from Mayaguez. **Calendar:** Semester.

Contact. Phone: (787) 896-2252 ext. 225
Admissions Officer, PO Box 1674, San Sebastian, PR 00685

Escuela de Artes Plasticas de Puerto Rico

San Juan, Puerto Rico
www.eap.edu **CB code: 7036**

- Public 4-year visual arts college
- Commuter campus in large city
- 512 degree-seeking undergraduates: 33% part-time, 57% women
- 57% of applicants admitted
- Interview required
- 35% graduate within 6 years; 5% enter graduate study

General. Founded in 1965. Regionally accredited. **Degrees:** 63 bachelor's awarded. **Location:** 12 miles from Carolina and Bayamon. **Calendar:** Semester, limited summer session. **Full-time faculty:** 16 total. **Part-time faculty:** 60 total. **Class size:** 86% <20, 14% 20-39. **Special facilities:** Art gallery and student design center.

Freshman class profile. 147 applied, 84 admitted, 74 enrolled.

Basis for selection. Applicants must complete pre-admissions studio course during the summer. Admissions committee interviews each candidate and reviews portfolio. Test scores and high school GPA very important. SAT for mainland U.S. applicants. Portfolio required. **Homeschooled:** State high school equivalency certificate required.

2008-2009 Annual costs. Tuition/fees: $2,611. Books/supplies: $2,250. Personal expenses: $1,750.

2007-2008 Financial aid. All financial aid based on need. 99% of total undergraduate aid awarded as scholarships/grants, 1% as loans/jobs.

Application procedures. Admission: Closing date 3/3 (receipt date). $25 fee. Application must be submitted on paper. Admission notification on a rolling basis. **Financial aid:** Priority date 4/25, closing date 5/23. FAFSA, institutional form required. Applicants notified by 7/11.

Academics. Special study options: Internships, liberal arts/career combination, teacher certification program. **Credit/placement by examination:** CLEP. **Support services:** Learning center, pre-admission summer program, reduced course load, study skills assistance, tutoring.

Majors. Education: Art. **Visual/performing arts:** General, design, fashion design, industrial design, painting, printmaking, sculpture.

Most popular majors. Education 17%, visual/performing arts 83%.

Computing on campus. 22 workstations in library, computer center.

Student life. Freshman orientation: Available. Preregistration for classes offered. **Policies:** Policies in effect regarding drugs and alcohol, academic progress, sexual harassment; security workshops; handicap policies. **Activities:** Literary magazine, music ensembles, student government.

Student services. Adult student services, alcohol/substance abuse counseling, career counseling, financial aid counseling, personal counseling. **Physically disabled:** Services for speech impaired.

Contact. Phone: (787) 725-8120 ext. 333 Fax: (787) 725-3798
Janet Centeno, Director of Admissions, Escuela de Artes Plasticas de Puerto Rico, PO Box 9021112, San Juan, PR 00902-1112

Inter American University of Puerto Rico: Aguadilla Campus

Aguadilla, Puerto Rico
www.aguadilla.inter.edu **CB code: 2042**

- Private 4-year university and liberal arts college
- Commuter campus in small city
- 4,224 degree-seeking undergraduates: 17% part-time, 55% women
- 243 degree-seeking graduate students

General. Founded in 1957. Regionally accredited. Adult higher education program, continuing education program. **Degrees:** 255 bachelor's, 31 associate awarded; master's offered. **ROTC:** Army, Air Force. **Location:** 10 miles from Aguadilla City, 17 miles from Mayaguez. **Calendar:** Semester, extensive summer session. **Full-time faculty:** 77 total; 100% have terminal degrees, 57% women. **Part-time faculty:** 147 total; 100% have terminal degrees, 48% women. **Special facilities:** Manuel Mendez Bellester special collection.

Freshman class profile. 1,494 applied, 992 admitted, 953 enrolled.

Basis for selection. Open admission, but selective for some programs. Regular program requires minimum 2.0 GPA from accredited secondary school and combined score of 800 on SAT (exclusive of Writing) or PAA. SAT accepted for English-speaking applicants. School achievement record, test scores very important. Pilot Program requires minimum 1.75 GPA from accredited secondary school and College Board examination test. Interview required for AVANCE, adult higher education, and Educational Services programs.

High school preparation. 18 units required. Required units include English 3, mathematics 2, history 2, science 2, foreign language 3 and academic electives 6.

2009-2010 Annual costs. Tuition/fees (projected): $5,308.

Financial aid. Non-need-based: Scholarships awarded for academics.

Application procedures. Admission: Priority date 5/1; deadline 5/15 (receipt date). No application fee. Admission notification on a rolling basis.

Financial aid: Closing date 4/30. FAFSA required. Applicants notified by 6/15; must reply by 8/8.

Academics. Special study options: Cross-registration, distance learning, dual enrollment of high school students, exchange student, honors, independent study, internships, teacher certification program. **Credit/placement by examination:** AP, CLEP. **Support services:** Learning center, remedial instruction, study skills assistance, tutoring.

Majors. Biology: General, biotechnology, microbiology. **Business:** Accounting, administrative services, business admin, hotel/motel admin, management information systems, marketing. **Computer sciences:** Computer science, networking. **Education:** Early childhood, elementary, secondary. **Engineering technology:** Electrical. **Health:** Nursing (RN). **Parks/recreation:** Facilities management. **Protective services:** Criminal justice. **Other:** Psychosocial human services.

Most popular majors. Business/marketing 23%, education 43%, health sciences 7%, legal studies 7%, psychology 6%.

Computing on campus. 493 workstations in library, computer center. Commuter students can connect to campus network. Online course registration, online library, wireless network available.

Student life. Freshman orientation: Mandatory. One-day program in August. **Activities:** Choral groups, drama, radio station, student government, Juventud Universitaria Catolica, Asociacion Evangelica Universitaria, Future Teachers Association, Criminal Justice Association, Secretarial Sciences Association, Psychosocial Human Services Association, Hotel Management Association, Marketing Association, Honors Society.

Athletics. Intercollegiate: Baseball M, basketball, cheerleading, cross-country, judo, soccer M, softball, table tennis, tennis, track and field, volleyball, weight lifting. **Intramural:** Basketball, cross-country, softball, table tennis, tennis, track and field, volleyball, weight lifting. **Team name:** Tigers.

Student services. Adult student services, chaplain/spiritual director, career counseling, student employment services, financial aid counseling, health services, personal counseling, placement for graduates, veterans' counselor.

Contact. Phone: (787) 891-0925 ext. 2101 Fax: (787) 882-3020
Doris Perez, Director of Admissions, Inter American University of Puerto Rico: Aguadilla Campus, Box 20000, Aguadilla, PR 00605

Inter American University of Puerto Rico: Arecibo Campus

Arecibo, Puerto Rico
www.arecibo.inter.edu **CB code: 1411**

- Private 4-year liberal arts college
- Commuter campus in small city
- 4,454 degree-seeking undergraduates
- 88% of applicants admitted

General. Founded in 1957. Regionally accredited. **Degrees:** 380 bachelor's, 40 associate awarded; master's offered. **ROTC:** Army. **Location:** 45 miles from San Juan. **Calendar:** Semester, limited summer session. **Full-time faculty:** 88 total. **Part-time faculty:** 205 total.

Freshman class profile. 1,260 applied, 1,108 admitted, 1,055 enrolled.

Basis for selection. Minimum 2.0 high school GPA. Test scores important; minimum admission index of 800 required. Special admissions policies apply to adults 21 years or older. SAT required of English-speaking applicants. Score reports by August 3. Interview recommended for academically weak.

High school preparation. 15 units required. Required units include English 3, mathematics 3, social studies 3, science 3 and foreign language 3.

2008-2009 Annual costs. Tuition/fees: $5,382. Books/supplies: $890. Personal expenses: $880.

2007-2008 Financial aid. Need-based: 66% of total undergraduate aid awarded as scholarships/grants, 34% as loans/jobs. **Non-need-based:** Scholarships awarded for academics, athletics.

Application procedures. Admission: No application fee. Admission notification on a rolling basis. **Financial aid:** Priority date 5/1; no closing date. FAFSA, institutional form required. Applicants notified on a rolling basis.

Academics. Special study options: Cooperative education, distance learning, honors, independent study, internships, study abroad, teacher certification program. **Credit/placement by examination:** AP, CLEP, institutional tests. 15 credit hours maximum toward associate degree, 15 toward bachelor's. **Support services:** Pre-admission summer program, remedial instruction, study skills assistance, tutoring.

Majors. Biology: General, bacteriology. **Business:** Accounting, administrative services, business admin, management science. **Computer sciences:** General, computer science. **Education:** Biology, chemistry, early childhood, elementary, secondary, Spanish, special. **Health:** Nursing (RN). **Physical sciences:** Chemistry. **Protective services:** Criminal justice. **Public administration:** Social work.

Computing on campus. 350 workstations in library, computer center. Commuter students can connect to campus network. Helpline, wireless network available.

Student life. Freshman orientation: Mandatory. **Activities:** Drama, student government, Baptist Unity, Young Catholics Association, Criminal Justice Association, Haziel Evangelical Association, Future Social Workers Association, Bahai Association, Student Counseling Association, Society for Human Resources.

Athletics. Intercollegiate: Basketball, soccer, softball, table tennis, tennis, track and field, volleyball. **Intramural:** Basketball, cheerleading, soccer, softball, table tennis, tennis, track and field, volleyball. **Team name:** Tigers.

Student services. Adult student services, alcohol/substance abuse counseling, chaplain/spiritual director, career counseling, student employment services, health services, personal counseling, veterans' counselor. **Physically disabled:** Services for visually, hearing impaired.

Contact. E-mail: pmontalvo@arecibo.inter.edu
Phone: (787) 878-5195 Fax: (787) 880-1624
Provi Montalvo, Director of Admissions, Inter American University of Puerto Rico: Arecibo Campus, PO Box 4050, Arecibo, PR 00614-4050

Inter American University of Puerto Rico: Barranquitas Campus

Barranquitas, Puerto Rico
www.br.inter.edu **CB code: 2067**

- Private 4-year university and branch campus college
- Commuter campus in large town

General. Founded in 1957. Regionally accredited. **Location:** 35 miles from San Juan. **Calendar:** Semester.

Annual costs/financial aid. Tuition/fees (2008-2009): $5,332. Books/supplies: $900. Personal expenses: $2,731. Need-based financial aid available to full-time and part-time students.

Contact. Phone: (787) 857-3600 ext. 2011
Director of Admissions, PO Box 517, Barranquitas, PR 00794

Inter American University of Puerto Rico: Bayamon Campus

Bayamon, Puerto Rico
bc.inter.edu **CB code: 2043**

- Private 4-year university and engineering college
- Commuter campus in small city
- 5,114 degree-seeking undergraduates: 16% part-time, 44% women, 100% Hispanic American
- 77 degree-seeking graduate students
- 38% of applicants admitted

General. Founded in 1912. Regionally accredited. **Degrees:** 446 bachelor's, 29 associate awarded; master's offered. **ROTC:** Army, Naval, Air Force. **Location:** 15 miles from San Juan. **Calendar:** Semester, limited summer session. **Full-time faculty:** 101 total; 36% have terminal degrees, 46% women. **Part-time faculty:** 246 total; 8% have terminal degrees, 48% women. **Special facilities:** Wetland used as a natural laboratory, mata de platano field station.

Freshman class profile. 3,857 applied, 1,476 admitted, 1,242 enrolled.

GPA 3.75 or higher:	8%	GPA 2.0-2.99:	50%
GPA 3.50-3.74:	10%	Return as sophomores:	73%
GPA 3.0-3.49:	28%		

Basis for selection. High school GPA and test scores most important. Minimum GPA of 2.0, minimum admission index (based on college formula) of 800. Achievement tests required for placement in math, English, and Spanish. Interview recommended.

High school preparation. Required units include English 3, mathematics 3, social studies 1, history 2, science 3 and foreign language 3.

2008-2009 Annual costs. Tuition/fees: $5,382. Books/supplies: $890.

2008-2009 Financial aid. All financial aid based on need. 1,213 full-time freshmen applied for aid; 1,192 were judged to have need; 974 of these received aid. Average need met was 2%. Average scholarship/grant was $233; average loan $242. 36% of total undergraduate aid awarded as scholarships/grants, 64% as loans/jobs.

Application procedures. Admission: Closing date 5/1 (receipt date). No application fee. Admission notification on a rolling basis. Must reply by 8/1. **Financial aid:** Priority date 6/30; no closing date. FAFSA required. Applicants notified on a rolling basis starting 5/10.

Academics. Special study options: Accelerated study, cooperative education, distance learning, honors, independent study, internships, study abroad. **Credit/placement by examination:** AP, CLEP. 225 credit hours maximum toward associate degree, 225 toward bachelor's. **Support services:** Learning center, pre-admission summer program, study skills assistance, tutoring.

Majors. Biology: General, bioinformatics, biomedical sciences, biotechnology, environmental, microbiology. **Business:** Accounting, administrative services, business admin, entrepreneurial studies, executive assistant, finance, human resources, management information systems, management science, managerial economics, marketing, office technology. **Communications technology:** General. **Computer sciences:** Computer science, information systems. **Conservation:** General, environmental science. **Engineering:** General, electrical, industrial, mechanical. **Engineering technology:** Electrical, industrial management. **Interdisciplinary:** Math/computer science. **Math:** General, applied. **Mechanic/repair:** Computer. **Physical sciences:** Chemistry. **Protective services:** Forensics. **Public administration:** General. **Science technology:** Chemical. **Transportation:** Air traffic control, airline/commercial pilot, aviation, aviation management, flight instructor.

Most popular majors. Biology 9%, business/marketing 41%, communication technologies 13%, engineering/engineering technologies 15%, trade and industry 11%.

Computing on campus. 510 workstations in library, computer center. Commuter students can connect to campus network. Online course registration, online library, repair service, wireless network available.

Student life. Freshman orientation: Mandatory. Preregistration for classes offered. **Housing:** Wellness housing available. **Activities:** Concert band, choral groups, drama, student council, business administration students association, Catholic students association, Christian university brotherhood association, society of joined students for science, photography club, ANCLA group, senior class association, engineering students association.

Athletics. Intercollegiate: Baseball M, basketball, cross-country, soccer M, softball, swimming, table tennis, tennis, track and field, volleyball, wrestling M. **Intramural:** Basketball, cross-country, softball, swimming, table tennis, tennis, track and field, volleyball, wrestling M. **Team name:** Tigers.

Student services. Adult student services, alcohol/substance abuse counseling, chaplain/spiritual director, career counseling, student employment services, financial aid counseling, health services, on-campus daycare, personal counseling, placement for graduates, veterans' counselor. **Physically disabled:** Services for visually, speech, hearing impaired.

Contact. E-mail: calicea@bc.inter.edu
Phone: (787) 279-1912 ext. 2017 Fax: (787) 279-2205
Carlos Alicea, Director of Admissions, Inter American University of Puerto Rico: Bayamon Campus, 500 Dr. John Will Harris Road, Bayamon, PR 00957

Inter American University of Puerto Rico: Fajardo Campus

Fajardo, Puerto Rico
fajardo.inter.edu **CB code: 2065**

- Private 4-year university and branch campus college
- Commuter campus in large town
- 2,130 degree-seeking undergraduates
- 21 graduate students
- 25% of applicants admitted

General. Regionally accredited. **Degrees:** 190 bachelor's, 13 associate awarded; master's offered. **ROTC:** Air Force. **Location:** 34 miles from San Juan. **Calendar:** Semester, limited summer session. **Full-time faculty:** 40 total; 32% have terminal degrees, 58% women. **Part-time faculty:** 124 total; 9% have terminal degrees, 57% women.

Freshman class profile. 1,697 applied, 416 admitted, 416 enrolled.

GPA 3.50-3.74:	14%	GPA 2.0-2.99:	46%
GPA 3.0-3.49:	29%		

Basis for selection. High school students must have 2.0 GPA and average of 400 on first three parts of PAA. Special admissions policies apply to adults age 21 or older. PAA test required for Spanish-speaking applicants; SAT or ACT required for English-speaking applicants. Interview required for adult education program.

High school preparation. 15 units required. Required units include English 3, mathematics 2, social studies 2 and science 3. 3 units Spanish required for Puerto Rican students.

2008-2009 Annual costs. Tuition/fees: $5,382. Books/supplies: $686.

2007-2008 Financial aid. Need-based: 81% of total undergraduate aid awarded as scholarships/grants, 19% as loans/jobs.

Application procedures. Admission: Closing date 5/15. No application fee. Admission notification on a rolling basis. **Financial aid:** Closing date 4/30. FAFSA, institutional form required. Applicants notified on a rolling basis.

Academics. Special study options: Cross-registration, distance learning, double major, dual enrollment of high school students, ESL, honors, independent study, internships, Washington semester. Adult education program. **Credit/placement by examination:** CLEP, institutional tests. 15 credit hours maximum toward bachelor's degree. Maximum 24 credit hours counted for adult education students. **Support services:** Tutoring.

Majors. Business: General, accounting, administrative services, business admin. **Education:** General, biology, early childhood, elementary, ESL, secondary, social studies, Spanish. **Protective services:** Criminal justice.

Most popular majors. Business/marketing 41%, education 34%, science technologies 6%, social sciences 15%.

Computing on campus. 188 workstations in library, computer center. Commuter students can connect to campus network. Online library, wireless network available.

Student life. Freshman orientation: Mandatory. **Activities:** Dance, student government, student council, young Christian students fraternity, tourism student association, history club, human resources students association, future teachers association, criminal justice student association, multilingual student association, special education students association, computer science student association.

Athletics. Intramural: Basketball, boxing M, cheerleading W, softball, table tennis, tennis, track and field, volleyball.

Student services. Adult student services, chaplain/spiritual director, career counseling, student employment services, financial aid counseling, health services, personal counseling, placement for graduates, veterans' counselor.

Contact. E-mail: adcaraba@fajardo.inter.edu
Phone: (787) 860-3100 Fax: (787) 860-3470
Ada Caraballo, Admissions Director, Inter American University of Puerto Rico: Fajardo Campus, Call Box 70003, Fajardo, PR 00738-7003

Inter American University of Puerto Rico: Guayama Campus

Guayama, Puerto Rico
www.guayama.inter.edu **CB code: 2077**

- Private 4-year university
- Commuter campus in large town
- 2,157 degree-seeking undergraduates: 33% part-time, 69% women, 100% Hispanic American
- 24 degree-seeking graduate students

- 56% of applicants admitted
- Interview required

General. Founded in 1957. Regionally accredited. **Degrees:** 211 bachelor's, 63 associate awarded; master's offered. **ROTC:** Army. **Location:** 18 miles from Ponce. **Calendar:** Semester, limited summer session. **Full-time faculty:** 46 total; 24% have terminal degrees, 54% women. **Part-time faculty:** 134 total; 8% have terminal degrees, 48% women. **Class size:** 41% < 20, 38% 20-39, 18% 40-49, 3% 50-99.

Freshman class profile. 572 applied, 323 admitted, 244 enrolled.

Basis for selection. High school graduates must have 2.0 GPA and 800 admission index.

2008-2009 Annual costs. Tuition/fees: $5,332. Books/supplies: $894. Personal expenses: $3,878.

2008-2009 Financial aid. All financial aid based on need. Average need met was 1%. Average scholarship/grant was $70; average loan $168. 18% of total undergraduate aid awarded as scholarships/grants, 82% as loans/jobs.

Application procedures. Admission: Priority date 5/15; no deadline. No application fee. Admission notification on a rolling basis beginning on or about 4/1. **Financial aid:** Closing date 4/29. FAFSA, institutional form required. Applicants notified by 6/15; must reply by 7/30.

Academics. Special study options: Accelerated study, distance learning, dual enrollment of high school students, exchange student, external degree, honors, internships, study abroad, teacher certification program, weekend college. **Credit/placement by examination:** CLEP. **Support services:** Learning center, remedial instruction, tutoring.

Majors. Biology: General, biotechnology. **Business:** Accounting, business admin, human resources, office management. **Education:** Early childhood special, elementary, ESL, kindergarten/preschool, physical. **Health:** Nursing (RN), respiratory therapy technology. **Mechanic/repair:** Computer. **Philosophy/religion:** Religion. **Protective services:** Law enforcement admin.

Most popular majors. Biology 6%, business/marketing 17%, computer/information sciences 6%, education 42%, science technologies 7%, security/protective services 15%.

Computing on campus. 232 workstations in library, computer center, student center. Online course registration, online library, wireless network available.

Student life. Freshman orientation: Mandatory. **Activities:** Choral groups, dance, student government, religious circle.

Athletics. Intercollegiate: Baseball M, basketball, cross-country, soccer M. **Intramural:** Baseball M, basketball, cross-country M, softball, table tennis W, tennis W, track and field. **Team name:** Tigers.

Student services. Adult student services, chaplain/spiritual director, career counseling, student employment services, health services, personal counseling, placement for graduates, veterans' counselor. **Physically disabled:** Services for visually impaired.

Contact. E-mail: lferrer@inter.edu
Phone: (787) 864-7059 Fax: (787) 864-8232
Laura Ferrer-Sanchez, Director of Admissions, Inter American University of Puerto Rico: Guayama Campus, PO Box 10004, Guayama, PR 00785

Inter American University of Puerto Rico: Metropolitan Campus

San Juan, Puerto Rico — **CB member**
www.metro.inter.edu — **CB code: 0873**

- Private 4-year branch campus college
- Commuter campus in large city
- 6,821 degree-seeking undergraduates: 40% part-time, 54% women, 100% Hispanic American
- 3,486 degree-seeking graduate students
- 24% of applicants admitted

General. Founded in 1962. Regionally accredited. **Degrees:** 1,016 bachelor's, 47 associate awarded; master's, doctoral offered. **ROTC:** Army, Air Force. **Location:** 9 miles from San Juan. **Calendar:** Semester, limited summer session. **Full-time faculty:** 213 total; 55% have terminal degrees, 54% women. **Part-time faculty:** 413 total; 38% have terminal degrees, 55% women. **Class size:** 38% < 20, 46% 20-39, 11% 40-49, 6% 50-99.

Freshman class profile. 4,104 applied, 1,001 admitted, 411 enrolled.

Basis for selection. School grade average and test scores important. Minimum GPA of 2.0 plus score average of 400 in SAT. Special admissions policies apply to adults 21 years of age or older. SAT required of English-speaking applicants.

High school preparation. Required units include English 3, mathematics 3 and science 3.

2008-2009 Annual costs. Tuition/fees: $5,382. Books/supplies: $894. Personal expenses: $3,878.

2008-2009 Financial aid. Need-based: Average need met was 1%. Average scholarship/grant was $39; average loan $123. 41% of total undergraduate aid awarded as scholarships/grants, 59% as loans/jobs.

Application procedures. Admission: Closing date 5/15 (receipt date). No application fee. Admission notification on a rolling basis. Must reply by 8/15. **Financial aid:** Closing date 4/30. FAFSA required. Applicants notified on a rolling basis.

Academics. Adult education programs available. **Special study options:** Accelerated study, distance learning, ESL, honors, independent study, internships. **Credit/placement by examination:** AP, CLEP. 12 credit hours maximum toward associate degree, 12 toward bachelor's. Departmental convalidation test. **Support services:** Learning center, pre-admission summer program, remedial instruction, study skills assistance, tutoring, writing center.

Majors. Biology: General, biomedical sciences. **Business:** Accounting, administrative services, business admin, finance, human resources, management information systems, marketing, office/clerical. **Computer sciences:** General. **Education:** Bilingual, biology, chemistry, early childhood, elementary, English, ESL, history, learning disabled, mathematics, mentally handicapped, multi-level teacher, multiple handicapped, physical, science, secondary, social science, social studies, Spanish, special, speech impaired. **Foreign languages:** Spanish. **Health:** Clinical lab science, nursing (RN). **History:** General. **Math:** General. **Physical sciences:** Chemistry. **Protective services:** Criminal justice. **Psychology:** General. **Public administration:** Social work. **Social sciences:** General, anthropology, political science, sociology.

Computing on campus. 720 workstations in library, computer center. Commuter students can connect to campus network. Online course registration, online library available.

Student life. Freshman orientation: Mandatory. Preregistration for classes offered. Held 2 weeks before regular classes begin. **Activities:** Choral groups, drama, international student organizations, student government, student newspaper, Asociacion Justicia Criminal, Futuros Trabajadores Sociales, Asociacion Cristiana Universitaria, Asociacion Circulo de Psicologia, Asociacion de Estudiantes de Microbiologia, Asociacion Futuros Maestros en Accion, English Trimester Psychology Students Association, English Trimester Association, Asociacion de Estudiantes de Contabilidad, Asociacion Estudiantes de Quimica, Asociacion de Estudiantes de Tecnologia Medica.

Athletics. Intercollegiate: Baseball M, basketball, judo M, softball, swimming, tennis, track and field, volleyball. **Intramural:** Basketball, softball, table tennis, tennis, volleyball. **Team name:** Tigres.

Student services. Adult student services, alcohol/substance abuse counseling, chaplain/spiritual director, career counseling, student employment services, financial aid counseling, health services, on-campus daycare, personal counseling, placement for graduates, veterans' counselor. **Physically disabled:** Services for visually, speech, hearing impaired.

Contact. E-mail: jolivieri@metro.inter.edu
Phone: (787) 250-1912 ext. 2188 Fax: (787) 250-1025
Janies Olivieri, Admissions, Inter American University of Puerto Rico: Metropolitan Campus, Box 191293, San Juan, PR 00919-1293

Inter American University of Puerto Rico: Ponce Campus

Mercedita, Puerto Rico
ponce.inter.edu — **CB code: 3531**

- Private 4-year university
- Large town
- 5,673 degree-seeking undergraduates: 39% part-time, 62% women
- 282 degree-seeking graduate students
- 70% of applicants admitted

General. Regionally accredited. **Degrees:** 691 bachelor's, 133 associate awarded; master's offered. **ROTC:** Naval. **Calendar:** Semester. **Full-time**

faculty: 90 total; 33% have terminal degrees, 52% women. **Part-time faculty:** 207 total; 13% have terminal degrees, 55% women. **Class size:** 22% < 20, 55% 20-39, 17% 40-49, 6% 50-99.

Freshman class profile. 1,672 applied, 1,163 admitted, 1,011 enrolled.

Basis for selection. 2.0 high school GPA and average of 400 on first three parts of PAA. Interview required for AVANCE program.

High school preparation. 18 units required. Required units include English 3, mathematics 3, social studies 1, history 3, science 3 (laboratory 1), foreign language 3 and academic electives 1.

2008-2009 Annual costs. Tuition/fees: $5,382. Books/supplies: $925. Personal expenses: $3,878.

2008-2009 Financial aid. All financial aid based on need. Average need met was 3%. Average scholarship/grant was $303; average loan $415. 28% of total undergraduate aid awarded as scholarships/grants, 72% as loans/jobs.

Application procedures. Admission: Closing date 5/15 (receipt date). No application fee. Admission notification on a rolling basis. **Financial aid:** No deadline. FAFSA required.

Academics. Special study options: Cooperative education, distance learning, honors, independent study, internships, study abroad, teacher certification program, weekend college. Adult programs (AVANCE), development programs, PREAD program. **Credit/placement by examination:** CLEP. **Support services:** Learning center, study skills assistance, tutoring.

Majors. Biology: General. **Business:** Accounting, administrative services, business admin, finance, hotel/motel admin, human resources, international, management information systems, management science, marketing, office technology, operations, training/development. **Communications:** Journalism, public relations. **Computer sciences:** Computer science, information systems. **Conservation:** General. **Education:** Biology, early childhood, elementary, ESL, secondary, special. **Health:** Nursing (RN). **Protective services:** Law enforcement admin.

Most popular majors. Business/marketing 31%, computer/information sciences 11%, education 28%, health sciences 12%, legal studies 12%.

Computing on campus. PC or laptop required. 490 workstations in library, computer center, student center. Commuter students can connect to campus network. Online course registration, online library, helpline available.

Student life. Freshman orientation: Available. Includes workshops, seminars, and social activities. **Activities:** Concert band, choral groups, dance, student government, student newspaper.

Athletics. Intercollegiate: Baseball M, basketball, judo, softball, swimming, table tennis, track and field, triathlon, volleyball, weight lifting, wrestling. **Intramural:** Baseball M, basketball M, softball, table tennis, track and field, volleyball, weight lifting. **Team name:** Tigers.

Student services. Adult student services, alcohol/substance abuse counseling, chaplain/spiritual director, career counseling, student employment services, financial aid counseling, health services, on-campus daycare, personal counseling, placement for graduates, women's services. **Physically disabled:** Services for visually, speech, hearing impaired.

Contact. E-mail: fldiaz@poce.inter.edu
Phone: (787) 841-0110 Fax: (787) 841-0103
Franco Diaz Vega, Director of Admissions, Inter American University of Puerto Rico: Ponce Campus, 104 Turpo Industrial Park Road #1, Mercedita, PR 00715-1602

Inter American University of Puerto Rico: San German Campus

San German, Puerto Rico
www.sg.inter.edu CB code: 0946

- Private 4-year university
- Commuter campus in large town
- 4,798 degree-seeking undergraduates: 27% part-time, 52% women
- 908 degree-seeking graduate students
- 98% of applicants admitted
- SAT or ACT (ACT writing optional) required
- 31% graduate within 6 years

General. Founded in 1912. Regionally accredited. San German Inter American School (pre-school to grade 12). **Degrees:** 460 bachelor's, 40 associate awarded; master's, doctoral offered. **ROTC:** Army, Air Force. **Location:** 14 miles from Mayaguez, 104 miles from San Juan. **Calendar:** Semester, extensive summer session. **Full-time faculty:** 126 total; 47% have terminal degrees, 58% women. **Part-time faculty:** 182 total; 13% have terminal degrees, 56% women. **Class size:** 42% < 20, 53% 20-39, 4% 40-49, less than 1% 50-99. **Special facilities:** Nature preserve, botanical garden.

Freshman class profile. 1,460 applied, 1,426 admitted, 1,005 enrolled.

GPA 3.75 or higher:	9%	**End year in good standing:**	95%
GPA 3.50-3.74:	9%	**Return as sophomores:**	77%
GPA 3.0-3.49:	22%	**Out-of-state:**	2%
GPA 2.0-2.99:	51%		

Basis for selection. High school GPA and test scores important. SAT required of English-speaking applicants. Essay, interview recommended for all; audition recommended for music; portfolio recommended for art programs. **Homeschooled:** Statement describing homeschool structure and mission, transcript of courses and grades, state high school equivalency certificate required.

High school preparation. 11 units required; 18 recommended. Required and recommended units include English 3, mathematics 2-3, social studies 2-3, history 2-3, science 2-3, foreign language 3 and academic electives 3. 3 units of Spanish required of Spanish-speaking students.

2008-2009 Annual costs. Tuition/fees: $5,382. Room/board: $2,500. Books/supplies: $894. Personal expenses: $880.

2007-2008 Financial aid. Need-based: 1,044 full-time freshmen applied for aid; 1,024 were judged to have need; 758 of these received aid. Average need met was 3%. Average scholarship/grant was $310; average loan $398. 61% of total undergraduate aid awarded as scholarships/grants, 39% as loans/jobs. **Non-need-based:** Awarded to 117 full-time undergraduates, including 35 freshmen. Scholarships awarded for academics, athletics.

Application procedures. Admission: Closing date 5/15 (receipt date). No application fee. Admission notification on a rolling basis beginning on or about 2/15. **Financial aid:** Closing date 5/14. FAFSA, institutional form required. Applicants notified on a rolling basis; must reply by 8/1.

Academics. Bilingual program enables students to learn English or Spanish while taking courses in their native language. **Special study options:** Accelerated study, cooperative education, cross-registration, distance learning, double major, dual enrollment of high school students, ESL, honors, independent study, internships, liberal arts/career combination, study abroad, teacher certification program, weekend college. Weekend college in some graduate programs. **Credit/placement by examination:** AP, CLEP, institutional tests. 12 credit hours maximum toward associate degree, 18 toward bachelor's. **Support services:** Learning center, reduced course load, remedial instruction, tutoring.

Majors. Architecture: Architecture. **Biology:** General. **Business:** Accounting, administrative services, business admin, finance, human resources, management information systems, management science, marketing, office management. **Computer sciences:** General, computer science. **Education:** General, art, biology, chemistry, early childhood, elementary, English, ESL, history, kindergarten/preschool, mathematics, music, physical, secondary, social studies, Spanish, special, voc/tech. **Engineering technology:** Electrical. **Health:** Clinical lab science, licensed practical nurse, nursing (RN). **Math:** General. **Parks/recreation:** Health/fitness. **Physical sciences:** Chemistry. **Psychology:** General. **Public administration:** General. **Social sciences:** Political science, sociology. **Visual/performing arts:** General, ceramics, drawing, music performance, painting, photography, sculpture.

Most popular majors. Biology 12%, business/marketing 25%, education 33%, psychology 6%.

Computing on campus. 800 workstations in dormitories, library, computer center, student center. Dormitories wired for high-speed internet access and linked to campus network. Commuter students can connect to campus network. Online course registration, online library, wireless network available.

Student life. Freshman orientation: Mandatory. Preregistration for classes offered. General orientation program offered in spring, summer and fall. **Housing:** Single-sex dorms, apartments, wellness housing available. $25 fully refundable deposit, deadline 6/30. **Activities:** Bands, choral groups, dance, drama, international student organizations, music ensembles, student government, student newspaper, Bahai association, student bible union, counselors student association, Catholic student organization, bilingual English-Spanish organization.

Athletics. Intercollegiate: Baseball M, basketball, cross-country, soccer M, softball, swimming, table tennis, tennis, track and field, volleyball, weight lifting. **Intramural:** Basketball, cross-country, softball, table tennis, tennis, track and field, volleyball. **Team name:** Tigers.

Student services. Adult student services, alcohol/substance abuse counseling, chaplain/spiritual director, career counseling, student employment services, financial aid counseling, health services, on-campus daycare, personal counseling, placement for graduates, veterans' counselor.

Contact. E-mail: milcama@sg.inter.edu
Phone: (787) 892-3090 Fax: (787) 892-6350
Mildred Camacho, Director of Admissions, Inter American University of Puerto Rico: San German Campus, Box 5100, San German, PR 00683-9801

National College of Business and Technology: Arecibo

Arecibo, Puerto Rico
www.nationalcollegepr.edu **CB code: 3222**

- For-profit 3-year business and technical college
- Commuter campus in small city
- 2,014 degree-seeking undergraduates

General. Accredited by ACICS. **Degrees:** 84 bachelor's, 172 associate awarded. **Calendar:** Trimester. **Full-time faculty:** 35 total; 74% women. **Part-time faculty:** 51 total; 67% women. **Class size:** 53% < 20, 47% 20-39.

Freshman class profile. 1,296 applied, 715 admitted, 565 enrolled.

Basis for selection. Admissions based on high school record and test scores. College Entrance Examination Board test or institutional tests required for admissions. **Homeschooled:** Transcript of courses and grades, state high school equivalency certificate required.

High school preparation. 18 units required. Required units include English 3, mathematics 3, history 3, science 3, foreign language 3 and academic electives 3.

2008-2009 Annual costs. Tuition/fees: $6,655.

2007-2008 Financial aid. All financial aid based on need. 646 full-time freshmen applied for aid; 646 were judged to have need; 636 of these received aid. Average need met was 3%. Average scholarship/grant was $2,946; average loan $583. 92% of total undergraduate aid awarded as scholarships/grants, 8% as loans/jobs.

Application procedures. Admission: Priority date 8/8; deadline 1/8. $25 fee. Application must be submitted on paper. Admission notification on a rolling basis. **Financial aid:** Priority date 12/31, closing date 4/29. FAFSA required. Applicants notified on a rolling basis starting 5/2; must reply by 5/15 or within 2 week(s) of notification.

Academics. Special study options: Distance learning, independent study, internships. **Credit/placement by examination:** AP, CLEP. **Support services:** Tutoring.

Majors. BACHELOR'S. Business: Administrative services. **Computer sciences:** General, information technology. **Education:** Kindergarten/preschool. **Health:** Nursing (RN). **ASSOCIATE. Business:** Administrative services, business admin, tourism/travel. **Computer sciences:** General. **Engineering technology:** Electrical. **Health:** Dental assistant, medical secretary, nursing (RN), pharmacy assistant. **Legal studies:** Legal secretary.

Most popular majors. Business/marketing 16%, computer/information sciences 6%, education 46%, health sciences 31%.

Computing on campus. 175 workstations in library, computer center, student center. Online library, helpline, student web hosting, wireless network available.

Student life. Freshman orientation: Mandatory. Preregistration for classes offered. **Housing:** Wellness housing available. **Activities:** Drama, student newspaper.

Athletics. Intramural: Basketball, softball, table tennis, volleyball.

Student services. Alcohol/substance abuse counseling, career counseling, financial aid counseling, personal counseling, placement for graduates, veterans' counselor.

Contact. E-mail: aaviles@nationalcollegepr.edu
Phone: (787) 879-5044 ext. 5203 Toll-free number: (800) 780-5134
Fax: (787) 879-5047
Mercedes Pagan, Admissions Director, National College of Business and Technology: Arecibo, PO Box 4035, MSC 452, Arecibo, PR 00614

National College of Business and Technology: Bayamon

Bayamon, Puerto Rico **CB member**
www.nationalcollegepr.edu **CB code: 7135**

- For-profit 3-year business and technical college
- Commuter campus in small city
- 2,443 degree-seeking undergraduates

General. Accredited by ACICS. **Degrees:** 71 bachelor's, 333 associate awarded. **Location:** 25 miles from San Juan. **Calendar:** Trimester. **Full-time faculty:** 44 total; 61% women. **Part-time faculty:** 72 total; 71% women. **Class size:** 38% < 20, 58% 20-39, 4% 40-49.

Freshman class profile. 2,978 applied, 1,095 admitted, 824 enrolled.

Basis for selection. Open admission, but selective for some programs. **Homeschooled:** Transcript of courses and grades, state high school equivalency certificate required.

High school preparation. 18 units required. Required units include English 3, mathematics 3, history 3, science 3, foreign language 3 and academic electives 3.

2008-2009 Annual costs. Tuition/fees: $6,655.

2007-2008 Financial aid. All financial aid based on need. 1,101 full-time freshmen applied for aid; 1,101 were judged to have need; 1,071 of these received aid. Average need met was 2%. Average scholarship/grant was $2,946; average loan $583. 95% of total undergraduate aid awarded as scholarships/grants, 5% as loans/jobs.

Application procedures. Admission: $25 fee. Application must be submitted on paper. Admission notification on a rolling basis. **Financial aid:** Priority date 12/31, closing date 4/29. FAFSA required. Applicants notified on a rolling basis starting 5/2; must reply by 5/15 or within 2 week(s) of notification.

Academics. Special study options: Distance learning, independent study, internships. **Credit/placement by examination:** AP, CLEP. 15 credit hours maximum toward associate degree, 30 toward bachelor's. **Support services:** Tutoring.

Majors. BACHELOR'S. Business: Administrative services. **Computer sciences:** Information systems, programming. **Education:** Kindergarten/preschool, technology/industrial arts. **Health:** Nursing (RN). **ASSOCIATE. Business:** Accounting, administrative services, entrepreneurial studies, office technology, tourism/travel. **Computer sciences:** Information systems, programming. **Engineering technology:** Electrical. **Health:** Dental assistant, nursing (RN), pharmacy assistant. **Legal studies:** Legal secretary.

Most popular majors. Business/marketing 6%, computer/information sciences 19%, education 37%, health sciences 37%.

Computing on campus. 216 workstations in library, computer center, student center. Online library, student web hosting, wireless network available.

Student life. Freshman orientation: Mandatory. Preregistration for classes offered. **Housing:** Wellness housing available. **Activities:** Drama, student newspaper.

Athletics. Intramural: Basketball M, softball M, table tennis, volleyball W.

Student services. Alcohol/substance abuse counseling, career counseling, financial aid counseling, personal counseling, placement for graduates, veterans' counselor.

Contact. E-mail: mepagan@nationalcollegepr.edu
Phone: (787) 780-5134 ext. 4000 Toll-free number: (800) 780-5134
Fax: (787) 779-4909
Mercedes Pagan, Admissions and Marketing Director, National College of Business and Technology: Bayamon, PO Box 2036, Bayamon, PR 00960

National College of Business and Technology: Rio Grande

Rio Grande, Puerto Rico
www.nationalcollegepr.edu

- For-profit 3-year business and technical college
- Commuter campus in small town

- 1,505 degree-seeking undergraduates
- 57% of applicants admitted

General. Accredited by ACICS. **Degrees:** 27 bachelor's, 177 associate awarded. **Calendar:** Trimester. **Full-time faculty:** 15 total; 67% women. **Part-time faculty:** 72 total; 72% women. **Class size:** 59% < 20, 37% 20-39, 4% 40-49.

Freshman class profile. 1,245 applied, 705 admitted, 552 enrolled.

Basis for selection. College Entrance Examination Board test or institutional tests required for admissions. **Homeschooled:** Transcript of courses and grades, state high school equivalency certificate required.

High school preparation. 18 units required. Required units include English 3, mathematics 3, history 3, science 3, foreign language 3 and academic electives 3.

2008-2009 Annual costs. Tuition/fees: $6,655.

2007-2008 Financial aid. All financial aid based on need. 738 full-time freshmen applied for aid; 738 were judged to have need; 702 of these received aid. Average need met was 3%. Average scholarship/grant was $2,946; average loan $583. 88% of total undergraduate aid awarded as scholarships/grants, 12% as loans/jobs.

Application procedures. Admission: $25 fee. Application must be submitted on paper. Admission notification 8/8. Admission notification on a rolling basis beginning on or about 1/8. **Financial aid:** FAFSA required. Must reply by 5/15 or within 2 week(s) of notification.

Academics. Special study options: ESL, independent study, internships, weekend college. **Credit/placement by examination:** AP, CLEP. **Support services:** Tutoring.

Majors. BACHELOR'S. Computer sciences: Information technology. **Health:** Nursing (RN). **ASSOCIATE. Business:** Accounting, entrepreneurial studies, tourism/travel. **Computer sciences:** Information technology. **Health:** Dental assistant, medical secretary, nursing (RN), pharmacy assistant. **Legal studies:** Legal secretary.

Most popular majors. Business/marketing 44%, health sciences 56%.

Computing on campus. 85 workstations in library, computer center, student center. Online library, helpline, student web hosting, wireless network available.

Student life. Freshman orientation: Mandatory. Preregistration for classes offered. **Housing:** Wellness housing available. **Activities:** Choral groups, drama.

Athletics. Intramural: Basketball, softball, table tennis, volleyball.

Student services. Alcohol/substance abuse counseling, career counseling, financial aid counseling, personal counseling.

Contact. E-mail: mepagan@nationalcollegepr.edu
Phone: (800) 981-0812 Fax: (787) 888-8280
Mercedes Pagan, Admissions Director, National College of Business and Technology: Rio Grande, PO Box 3064, Rio Grande, PR 00745

Pontifical Catholic University of Puerto Rico

Ponce, Puerto Rico — **CB member**
www.pucpr.edu — **CB code: 0910**

- Private 4-year university affiliated with Roman Catholic Church
- Commuter campus in small city
- 5,246 undergraduates
- 2,189 graduate students
- 81% of applicants admitted
- SAT or ACT (ACT writing optional) required
- 34% graduate within 6 years

General. Founded in 1948. Regionally accredited. Branch campuses in Arecibo and Mayaguez. **Degrees:** 707 bachelor's, 10 associate awarded; master's, doctoral, first professional offered. **ROTC:** Army, Air Force. **Location:** 60 miles from San Juan. **Calendar:** Semester, limited summer session. **Full-time faculty:** 192 total. **Part-time faculty:** 188 total.

Freshman class profile. 1,540 applied, 1,248 admitted, 896 enrolled.

Mid 50% test scores			
SAT critical reading:	400-530	Live on campus:	4%
SAT math:	390-530	Fraternities:	1%
		Sororities:	1%

Basis for selection. School achievement record, test scores important. SAT required of English-speaking applicants. Interview required for special program. **Homeschooled:** Transcript of courses and grades required.

High school preparation. 15 units required. Required units include English 4, mathematics 3, history 2, science 2 and foreign language 4. 3 units English, 3 units foreign language, 2 units mathematics, 1 unit science, 1 unit history required for 3-year high schools.

2008-2009 Annual costs. Tuition/fees: $5,478. Room only: $1,275. Books/supplies: $600. Personal expenses: $316.

2008-2009 Financial aid. Non-need-based: Scholarships awarded for academics, athletics.

Application procedures. Admission: Priority date 3/15; deadline 7/15 (receipt date). $15 fee, may be waived for applicants with need. Admission notification on a rolling basis beginning on or about 2/15. **Financial aid:** Priority date 5/1; no closing date. FAFSA, institutional form required. Applicants notified by 6/15; must reply within 4 week(s) of notification.

Academics. Special study options: Accelerated study, combined bachelor's/graduate degree, double major, dual enrollment of high school students, ESL, exchange student, honors, independent study, internships, liberal arts/career combination, study abroad. **Credit/placement by examination:** AP, CLEP, institutional tests. 30 credit hours maximum toward bachelor's degree. **Support services:** Learning center, pre-admission summer program, reduced course load, remedial instruction, tutoring.

Majors. Area/ethnic studies: Hispanic-American/Latino/Chicano. **Biology:** General. **Business:** General, accounting, administrative services, business admin, communications, entrepreneurial studies, finance, human resources, international, management information systems, managerial economics, marketing, tourism/travel, transportation. **Communications:** General. **Conservation:** General, environmental studies. **Education:** Art, biology, business, chemistry, early childhood, elementary, English, ESL, family/consumer sciences, history, mathematics, music, physical, science, secondary, social studies, Spanish, special. **Family/consumer sciences:** General. **Foreign languages:** Spanish. **Health:** Cardiovascular technology, clinical lab science, health services, nursing (RN), premedicine. **History:** General. **Interdisciplinary:** Gerontology. **Legal studies:** General, prelaw. **Liberal arts:** Arts/sciences. **Math:** General. **Philosophy/religion:** Philosophy. **Physical sciences:** Chemistry, physics. **Psychology:** General. **Public administration:** General, social work. **Social sciences:** Criminology, political science, sociology. **Transportation:** Maritime/Merchant Marine. **Visual/performing arts:** Studio arts.

Most popular majors. Business/marketing 17%, education 32%, health sciences 13%, liberal arts 7%, public administration/social services 8%.

Computing on campus. 448 workstations in library, computer center, student center. Commuter students can connect to campus network. Online course registration, online library, wireless network available.

Student life. Freshman orientation: Mandatory. **Housing:** Single-sex dorms available. $25 nonrefundable deposit. **Activities:** Choral groups, dance, drama, musical theater, radio station, student government, student newspaper, TV station, Pi Gamma Mu, Phi Alpha Theta, Beta Beta Beta, Alpha Beta Chi, Phi Delta Kappa, honor society for business students, Pioneer Students in Christ and Mary, Miles Jesu, Knights of Columbus, Phi Sigma Kappa.

Athletics. Intercollegiate: Basketball, cross-country, diving, judo, soccer, softball M, swimming, table tennis, tennis, track and field, volleyball, water polo M, wrestling M. **Intramural:** Archery, basketball, cross-country, diving, softball, swimming, table tennis, tennis, track and field, volleyball, wrestling M. **Team name:** Pioneers.

Student services. Chaplain/spiritual director, career counseling, student employment services, health services, on-campus daycare, personal counseling, placement for graduates, veterans' counselor. **Learning disabled:** Comprehensive services available.

Contact. E-mail: admisiones@pucpr.edu
Phone: (787) 841-2000 ext. 1000 Fax: (787) 840-4295
Ana Bonilla, Director of Admissions, Pontifical Catholic University of Puerto Rico, 2250 Las Americas Avenue, Suite 284, Ponce, PR 00717-9777

Turabo University
Gurabo, Puerto Rico
www.suagm.edu/ut **CB code: 0780**

- Private 4-year university and liberal arts college
- Commuter campus in small city
- 13,056 degree-seeking undergraduates: 21% part-time, 60% women, 100% Hispanic American
- 4,073 degree-seeking graduate students

General. Founded in 1972. Regionally accredited. 5 off-campus sites. **Degrees:** 926 bachelor's, 85 associate awarded; master's, doctoral offered. **ROTC:** Army. **Location:** 17 miles from San Juan. **Calendar:** Semester, limited summer session. **Full-time faculty:** 157 total. **Part-time faculty:** 817 total. **Class size:** 49% < 20, 50% 20-39, 1% 40-49, less than 1% 50-99. **Special facilities:** Museum.

Freshman class profile. 6,247 applied, 3,131 admitted, 2,319 enrolled.

GPA 3.75 or higher:	5%	**GPA 2.0-2.99:**	56%
GPA 3.50-3.74:	8%	**Return as sophomores:**	72%
GPA 3.0-3.49:	23%		

Basis for selection. Open admission, but selective for some programs. SAT required for admission to honors and science programs.

High school preparation. 15 units required. Required units include English 3, mathematics 3, social studies 2, science 2 and foreign language 3.

2008-2009 Annual costs. Tuition/fees: $4,584. Room/board: $6,735. Books/supplies: $896.

2008-2009 Financial aid. All financial aid based on need.

Application procedures. Admission: No deadline. $15 fee, may be waived for applicants with need. Admission notification on a rolling basis beginning on or about 3/1. **Financial aid:** Priority date 5/30; no closing date. FAFSA required. Applicants notified by 8/30.

Academics. Special study options: Accelerated study, combined bachelor's/graduate degree, distance learning, honors, independent study, internships, liberal arts/career combination, weekend college. **Credit/placement by examination:** CLEP, institutional tests. **Support services:** Remedial instruction, study skills assistance, tutoring.

Majors. Biology: General, biotechnology. **Business:** Accounting, business admin, management information systems, marketing, office management. **Communications:** General. **Conservation:** Environmental science. **Education:** Biology, chemistry, early childhood, elementary, English, history, mathematics, physical, science, social science, Spanish, special, trade/industrial. **Engineering:** Computer, electrical, mechanical. **Engineering technology:** Industrial management. **Foreign languages:** Sign language interpretation. **Health:** Dietetics, nursing (RN), speech pathology. **Interdisciplinary:** Natural sciences. **Liberal arts:** Humanities. **Physical sciences:** Chemistry. **Psychology:** General. **Public administration:** General, social work. **Social sciences:** General, criminology, political science. **Visual/performing arts:** Graphic design, industrial design, interior design.

Most popular majors. Business/marketing 39%, education 25%, engineering/engineering technologies 7%, social sciences 13%.

Computing on campus. Commuter students can connect to campus network. Helpline available.

Student life. Freshman orientation: Available. Preregistration for classes offered. **Activities:** Choral groups, dance, drama, music ensembles, radio station, student government, student newspaper, TV station.

Athletics. NAIA. **Intercollegiate:** Baseball M, basketball, cross-country, judo, soccer M, softball, swimming, tennis, track and field, volleyball, weight lifting. **Intramural:** Basketball, softball, table tennis, tennis W, volleyball, weight lifting. **Team name:** Tainos.

Student services. Adult student services, alcohol/substance abuse counseling, career counseling, services for economically disadvantaged, student employment services, financial aid counseling, health services, personal counseling, placement for graduates, veterans' counselor. **Physically disabled:** Services for visually, speech, hearing impaired.

Contact. Phone: (787) 746-3009 Toll-free number: (800) 747-8362
Fax: (787) 743-7940
Virginia Gonzalez, Associate Director of Admissions and Financial Aid, Turabo University, PO Box 3030, Gurabo, PR 00778

Universidad Adventista de las Antillas
Mayaguez, Puerto Rico **CB member**
www.uaa.edu **CB code: 1020**

- Private 4-year university and liberal arts college affiliated with Seventh-day Adventists
- Commuter campus in small city
- 883 degree-seeking undergraduates: 10% part-time, 56% women
- 49 graduate students

General. Founded in 1957. Regionally accredited. **Degrees:** 101 bachelor's, 23 associate awarded; master's, first professional offered. **Location:** 100 miles from San Juan. **Calendar:** Semester, limited summer session. **Full-time faculty:** 41 total; 20% have terminal degrees, 46% women. **Part-time faculty:** 33 total; 12% have terminal degrees, 42% women. **Class size:** 30% < 20, 52% 20-39, 9% 40-49, 10% 50-99.

Freshman class profile. 464 applied, 250 admitted, 175 enrolled.

Basis for selection. Open admission, but selective for some programs. SAT or ACT recommended for English-speaking applicants. Interview required for nursing program. **Homeschooled:** Unless homeschool is accredited, applicant must take GED.

High school preparation. 18 units recommended. Recommended units include English 3, mathematics 3, social studies 3, science 3 and academic electives 3. 3 Spanish units recommended.

2008-2009 Annual costs. Tuition/fees: $9,922. Tuition for nonresident aliens is the sum of private tuition ($4,408 per semester) and the Form I-20 deposit ($4,000 only in the first year); after the first year, these students receive credit refund at registration ($500 per semester). An average of $150 per semester is included in tuition for lab expenses. Room/board: $3,300. Books/supplies: $1,000. Personal expenses: $750.

Application procedures. Admission: No deadline. $20 fee, may be waived for applicants with need. Admission notification on a rolling basis. **Financial aid:** No deadline. FAFSA, institutional form required. Applicants notified on a rolling basis starting 8/15; must reply within 3 week(s) of notification.

Academics. Special study options: Cooperative education, double major, ESL, internships, liberal arts/career combination, teacher certification program. **Credit/placement by examination:** AP, CLEP, institutional tests. 12 credit hours maximum toward associate degree, 12 toward bachelor's. **Support services:** Learning center, reduced course load, remedial instruction, tutoring.

Majors. Biology: General. **Business:** General, administrative services. **Computer sciences:** General, computer science, information systems. **Education:** Elementary, music, secondary. **Foreign languages:** Spanish. **Health:** Respiratory therapy technology. **History:** General. **Physical sciences:** Chemistry. **Psychology:** General. **Theology:** Theology.

Most popular majors. Biology 6%, business/marketing 11%, computer/information sciences 7%, education 14%, health sciences 42%, theological studies 12%.

Computing on campus. 62 workstations in dormitories, library, computer center. Commuter students can connect to campus network. Online course registration, online library, repair service available.

Student life. Freshman orientation: Mandatory. Preregistration for classes offered. 2-day program at beginning of each semester. **Policies:** Religious environment designed for Seventh-day Adventist students. **Housing:** Guaranteed on-campus for freshmen. Single-sex dorms, apartments available. **Activities:** Concert band, choral groups, drama, music ensembles, student government, student newspaper, L.I.F.E., S.C.O.R., international club, ministerial club.

Athletics. Intramural: Basketball, bowling, gymnastics, soccer, softball M, swimming, table tennis, tennis, track and field, volleyball. **Team name:** Eagles Gym Team.

Student services. Alcohol/substance abuse counseling, chaplain/spiritual director, career counseling, student employment services, financial aid counseling, health services, personal counseling, veterans' counselor.

Contact. E-mail: admissions@uaa.edu
Phone: (787) 834-9595 ext. 2208 Fax: (787) 834-9597
Evelyn del Valle, Director of Admissions, Universidad Adventista de las Antillas, PO Box 118, Mayaguez, PR 00681-0118

Universidad Central del Caribe
Bayamon, Puerto Rico
www.uccaribe.edu/
CB code: 1549

- Private 4-year university
- Small city

General. Regionally accredited. **Degrees:** 8 bachelor's, 20 associate awarded; master's, first professional offered. **Calendar:** Differs by program. **Full-time faculty:** 15 total. **Part-time faculty:** 1 total.

2008-2009 Annual costs. Tuition/fees: $7,620.

Academics. Credit/placement by examination: CLEP.

Majors. Health: Radiologic technology/medical imaging.

Contact. E-mail: icordero@uccaribe.edu
Phone: (787) 740-1611 Fax: (787) 269-7550
Aristides Cruz, Dean for Academic Affairs, Universidad Central del Caribe, Decanato de Admisiones y Asuntos Estudiantiles, Bayamon, PR 00960-6032

Universidad del Este
Carolina, Puerto Rico
www.suagm.edu/une
CB member
CB code: 0883

- Private 4-year university and liberal arts college
- Commuter campus in small city
- 11,920 degree-seeking undergraduates: 31% part-time, 67% women, 100% Hispanic American
- 1,264 degree-seeking graduate students

General. Founded in 1949. Regionally accredited. **Degrees:** 889 bachelor's, 140 associate awarded; master's offered. **ROTC:** Army. **Location:** 5 miles from San Juan. **Calendar:** Semester, limited summer session. **Full-time faculty:** 82 total; 34% have terminal degrees, 100% minority, 62% women. **Part-time faculty:** 1,088 total; 9% have terminal degrees, 100% minority. **Class size:** 45% < 20, 52% 20-39, 3% 40-49.

Freshman class profile. 8,091 applied, 3,632 admitted, 2,273 enrolled.

GPA 3.75 or higher:	3%	**GPA 2.0-2.99:**	57%
GPA 3.50-3.74:	5%	**Return as sophomores:**	70%
GPA 3.0-3.49:	20%		

Basis for selection. Open admission, but selective for some programs. Special requirements for health and science programs; interview recommended. SAT required of English-speaking freshman applicants.

2008-2009 Annual costs. Tuition/fees: $4,584. Room/board: $6,735. Books/supplies: $1,500.

2008-2009 Financial aid. Non-need-based: Scholarships awarded for academics, athletics.

Application procedures. Admission: Priority date 3/30; no deadline. $15 fee, may be waived for applicants with need. Admission notification on a rolling basis. **Financial aid:** Priority date 5/30; no closing date. FAFSA, institutional form required. Applicants notified by 7/30.

Academics. Special study options: Accelerated study, combined bachelor's/graduate degree, distance learning, honors, independent study, internships, liberal arts/career combination, teacher certification program, weekend college. **Credit/placement by examination:** CLEP. **Support services:** Reduced course load, remedial instruction, study skills assistance, tutoring.

Majors. Biology: General, biotechnology, microbiology. **Business:** Accounting, administrative services, business admin, hospitality/recreation, hotel/motel admin, insurance, management information systems, marketing. **Education:** Early childhood, health, physical, science. **Family/consumer sciences:** Facilities/event planning. **Health:** Critical care nursing, health care admin, medical radiologic technology/radiation therapy, nursing (RN), sonography. **Legal studies:** Paralegal. **Personal/culinary services:** Restaurant/catering. **Protective services:** Law enforcement admin. **Psychology:** General. **Public administration:** Social work. **Social sciences:** General, political science.

Most popular majors. Business/marketing 45%, education 17%, health sciences 6%, public administration/social services 17%, security/protective services 12%.

Computing on campus. Commuter students can connect to campus network. Online library, helpline, repair service, wireless network available.

Student life. Freshman orientation: Available. **Activities:** Choral groups, dance, drama, student government, student newspaper, Phi Theta Kappa, Future Secretaries of America, nursing club.

Athletics. Intercollegiate: Baseball M, basketball, cross-country, softball W, track and field, volleyball, weight lifting. **Intramural:** Basketball, volleyball. **Team name:** Pitirre.

Student services. Adult student services, alcohol/substance abuse counseling, career counseling, services for economically disadvantaged, student employment services, financial aid counseling, health services, personal counseling, placement for graduates, veterans' counselor. **Physically disabled:** Services for visually, speech, hearing impaired.

Contact. E-mail: admisiones_une@suagm.edu
Phone: (787) 257-8080 Toll-free number: (800) 981-6570
Fax: (787) 257-8601 ext. 3307
Magda Ostolaza, Director of Marketing and Recruitment, Universidad del Este, PO Box 2010, Carolina, PR 00984-2010

Universidad Metropolitana
Rio Piedras, Puerto Rico
www.suagm.edu/umet
CB member
CB code: 1519

- Private 4-year university and liberal arts college
- Commuter campus in large city
- 9,797 degree-seeking undergraduates: 20% part-time, 67% women, 100% Hispanic American
- 2,595 degree-seeking graduate students
- 53% of applicants admitted
- 21% graduate within 6 years

General. Founded in 1985. Regionally accredited. **Degrees:** 734 bachelor's, 70 associate awarded; master's, doctoral offered. **ROTC:** Army, Naval, Air Force. **Location:** 3 miles from San Juan. **Calendar:** Semester, limited summer session. **Full-time faculty:** 105 total; 40% have terminal degrees, 100% minority, 66% women. **Part-time faculty:** 799 total; 18% have terminal degrees, 113% minority, 54% women. **Class size:** 51% < 20, 48% 20-39, 1% 40-49.

Freshman class profile. 7,582 applied, 4,018 admitted, 1,872 enrolled.

GPA 3.75 or higher:	3%	**GPA 2.0-2.99:**	55%
GPA 3.50-3.74:	6%	**Return as sophomores:**	73%
GPA 3.0-3.49:	21%		

Basis for selection. School achievement record and test scores considered. SAT required of English-speaking applicants. Interview required for academically weak. **Homeschooled:** State high school equivalency certificate required.

2008-2009 Annual costs. Tuition/fees: $4,584. Room/board: $6,735. Books/supplies: $1,500.

Financial aid. All financial aid based on need.

Application procedures. Admission: Closing date 8/15 (receipt date). $15 fee, may be waived for applicants with need. Admission notification on a rolling basis. **Financial aid:** Priority date 5/30; no closing date. FAFSA required. Applicants notified by 7/30.

Academics. Flexible admissions policy allows Universidad Metropolitana to accept challenge of providing all students with increased opportunities for success. **Special study options:** Accelerated study, combined bachelor's/graduate degree, distance learning, honors, independent study, internships, liberal arts/career combination, teacher certification program, Washington semester, weekend college. Off-campus full-degree sites. **Credit/placement by examination:** CLEP. **Support services:** Remedial instruction, tutoring.

Majors. Biology: General, cellular/anatomical. **Business:** Accounting, banking/financial services, business admin, entrepreneurial studies, management information systems, managerial economics, marketing, sales/distribution, special products marketing. **Communications:** General, public relations. **Computer sciences:** Computer science. **Conservation:** Environmental science, environmental studies, management/policy. **Education:** Biology, early childhood, elementary, English, history, mathematics, multi-level teacher, physical, Spanish, special. **Health:** Environmental health, nursing (RN), respiratory therapy technology. **Physical sciences:** General, chemistry. **Protective services:** Criminal justice, law enforcement admin. **Psychology:** General. **Public administration:** Social work. **Social sciences:** General.

Most popular majors. Business/marketing 39%, education 23%, health sciences 6%, public administration/social services 12%, security/protective services 9%.

Computing on campus. Commuter students can connect to campus network. Helpline, repair service available.

Student life. **Freshman orientation:** Mandatory. Preregistration for classes offered. Held 4 weeks before the beginning of the academic year. **Activities:** Choral groups, drama, student government, student newspaper, TV station, Business Students Association, Hermandad, Social Work, Students Association, Communication Students Association.

Athletics. **Intercollegiate:** Baseball, basketball, cross-country, softball, table tennis, tennis, track and field, volleyball, weight lifting M. **Intramural:** Baseball, basketball, cross-country, softball, table tennis, track and field, volleyball. **Team name:** Cocodrilo.

Student services. Adult student services, alcohol/substance abuse counseling, career counseling, services for economically disadvantaged, student employment services, financial aid counseling, health services, on-campus daycare, personal counseling, placement for graduates, veterans' counselor, women's services. **Physically disabled:** Services for visually, hearing impaired.

Contact. E-mail: admisiones-umet@suagm.edu
Phone: (787) 766-1717 ext. 6587 Toll-free number: (787) 747-8362
Fax: (787) 751-0992
Julio Rodriguez, Director of Admission and Financial Aid, Universidad Metropolitana, Apartado 21150, San Juan, PR 00928

Universidad Politecnica de Puerto Rico

Hato Rey, Puerto Rico — **CB member**
www.pupr.edu — **CB code: 0614**

- Private 5-year university and engineering college
- Commuter campus in large city
- 5,133 degree-seeking undergraduates: 100% Hispanic American
- 715 graduate students
- 96% of applicants admitted

General. Founded in 1966. Regionally accredited. **Degrees:** 422 bachelor's awarded; master's offered. **ROTC:** Army, Air Force. **Location:** 3 miles from San Juan. **Calendar:** Trimester, extensive summer session. **Full-time faculty:** 167 total. **Part-time faculty:** 135 total.

Freshman class profile. 941 applied, 900 admitted, 866 enrolled.

Basis for selection. Minimum 2.5 high school GPA and PAA combined score of 1300 required. SAT in English or Spanish required. **Homeschooled:** Statement describing homeschool structure and mission, transcript of courses and grades, state high school equivalency certificate required.

High school preparation. 15 units required. Required units include English 3, mathematics 3, social studies 3, science 3, foreign language 3 and academic electives 3.

2008-2009 Annual costs. Tuition/fees: $6,393. Room/board: $5,886. Books/supplies: $2,310.

2007-2008 Financial aid. **Non-need-based:** Scholarships awarded for academics, music/drama.

Application procedures. **Admission:** Closing date 8/1. $30 fee. Admission notification on a rolling basis. **Financial aid:** Priority date 5/15, closing date 6/30. FAFSA required. Applicants notified by 7/15.

Academics. **Special study options:** Cooperative education, distance learning, honors. **Credit/placement by examination:** AP, CLEP. **Support services:** Pre-admission summer program, remedial instruction, study skills assistance, tutoring.

Majors. **Architecture:** Architecture. **Business:** General, business admin. **Computer sciences:** Computer science. **Engineering:** Chemical, civil, computer, electrical, industrial, mechanical. **Engineering technology:** Surveying.

Most popular majors. Engineering/engineering technologies 90%.

Computing on campus. 550 workstations in library, computer center. Online library, wireless network available.

Student life. **Freshman orientation:** Available. Preregistration for classes offered. Week-long orientation offered every trimester. **Activities:** Choral groups, drama, student government, TV station, University Bible Association, drugs and alcohol committee.

Athletics. **Intercollegiate:** Baseball M, basketball, cross-country, soccer M, table tennis, tennis, track and field, volleyball. **Intramural:** Basketball, cross-country W, table tennis, tennis, track and field, volleyball. **Team name:** Beavers.

Student services. Alcohol/substance abuse counseling, career counseling, services for economically disadvantaged, student employment services, financial aid counseling, health services, personal counseling, placement for graduates, veterans' counselor. **Physically disabled:** Services for hearing impaired.

Contact. Phone: (787) 754-8000 ext. 309 Fax: (787) 764-8712
Teresa Cardona, Director of Admissions, Universidad Politecnica de Puerto Rico, PO Box 192017, San Juan, PR 00919-2017

University College of San Juan

San Juan, Puerto Rico — **CB member**
www.cunisanjuan.edu — **CB code: 0391**

- Public 4-year community and technical college
- Commuter campus in very large city
- 1,355 degree-seeking undergraduates: 100% Hispanic American
- 83% of applicants admitted

General. Founded in 1972. Regionally accredited. **Degrees:** 69 bachelor's, 121 associate awarded. **Calendar:** Semester, limited summer session. **Full-time faculty:** 27 total. **Part-time faculty:** 73 total. **Class size:** 48% < 20, 50% 20-39, 2% 40-49. **Special facilities:** Language laboratory, learning resource center, amphitheater.

Freshman class profile. 879 applied, 730 admitted, 496 enrolled.

Basis for selection. Combined College Board PAA test scores of 2000 and 2.0 high school GPA required for regular students. Special consideration and priority to applicants from low-income families. SAT/ACT accepted from US applicants. Interview required for nursing program.

High school preparation. 16 units required. Required units include English 3, mathematics 2, social studies 2, history 2, science 1 and academic electives 2. 3 Spanish courses required.

2008-2009 Annual costs. Tuition/fees: $3,150. Books/supplies: $1,200. Personal expenses: $920.

2007-2008 Financial aid. All financial aid based on need.

Application procedures. **Admission:** Closing date 5/1. $15 fee. Admission notification 6/1. Admission after July 31 on space-available basis. **Financial aid:** Closing date 9/30. FAFSA, institutional form required. Applicants notified by 10/30.

Academics. **Special study options:** Cooperative education, double major, exchange student, honors, study abroad. **Credit/placement by examination:** AP, CLEP. **Support services:** Remedial instruction, tutoring.

Majors. **Business:** Accounting. **Computer sciences:** General. **Health:** Nursing (RN). **Protective services:** Police science.

Most popular majors. Business/marketing 13%, computer/information sciences 19%, health sciences 39%, security/protective services 29%.

Computing on campus. 240 workstations in library, computer center. Commuter students can connect to campus network. Online library, wireless network available.

Student life. **Freshman orientation:** Mandatory. One-day program in summer that offers opportunity to meet faculty and staff. **Activities:** Choral groups, dance, drama, student government.

Athletics. **Intercollegiate:** Basketball M, cross-country, softball, table tennis, tennis, track and field, volleyball, weight lifting. **Intramural:** Basketball, bowling, cross-country, handball, racquetball, softball M, table tennis, tennis, track and field, volleyball. **Team name:** Falcons.

Student services. Career counseling, student employment services, health services, personal counseling, placement for graduates, veterans' counselor. **Physically disabled:** Services for visually, speech, hearing impaired.

Contact. E-mail: admisiones@cts.sanjuancapital.com
Phone: (787) 250-7375 Fax: (787) 250-7395
Sandra Rivera, Admissions Officer, University College of San Juan, 180 Jose R. Oliver Avenue, San Juan, PR 00918

University of Puerto Rico: Aguadilla

Aguadilla, Puerto Rico
www.uprag.edu **CB code: 0983**

- Public 4-year liberal arts and technical college
- Commuter campus in small city
- 2,934 degree-seeking undergraduates: 9% part-time, 62% women, 100% Hispanic American
- 86% of applicants admitted
- 637% graduate within 6 years

General. Founded in 1972. Regionally accredited. **Degrees:** 327 bachelor's, 32 associate awarded. **ROTC:** Army. **Location:** 81 miles from San Juan. **Calendar:** Semester, limited summer session. **Full-time faculty:** 124 total; 21% have terminal degrees, 98% minority, 56% women. **Part-time faculty:** 34 total; 9% have terminal degrees, 100% minority, 56% women. **Class size:** 18% < 20, 82% 20-39.

Freshman class profile. 934 applied, 800 admitted, 726 enrolled.

GPA 3.75 or higher:	31%	**GPA 2.0-2.99:**	16%
GPA 3.50-3.74:	21%	**End year in good standing:**	76%
GPA 3.0-3.49:	32%	**Return as sophomores:**	76%

Basis for selection. Admissions based on secondary school record and standardized test scores. Talent and ability considered. SAT and SAT Subject Tests in Spanish and math level I required of English-speaking applicants. **Homeschooled:** Copy of curriculum required.

High school preparation. Recommended units include English 3, mathematics 2 and social studies 2. 3 Spanish recommended.

2008-2009 Annual costs. Tuition/fees: $1,752; $4,077 out-of-state. Books/supplies: $1,825. Personal expenses: $1,200.

2007-2008 Financial aid. All financial aid based on need. 83% of total undergraduate aid awarded as scholarships/grants, 17% as loans/jobs.

Application procedures. Admission: Priority date 11/17; deadline 1/30 (receipt date). $20 fee, may be waived for applicants with need. Application must be submitted on paper. Admission notification 4/2. Admission notification on a rolling basis. Must reply by 4/30. **Financial aid:** Closing date 5/6. FAFSA, institutional form required. Applicants notified on a rolling basis starting 4/1; must reply within 1 week(s) of notification.

Academics. Special study options: Honors, liberal arts/career combination, teacher certification program. **Credit/placement by examination:** CLEP, institutional tests. **Support services:** Learning center, remedial instruction, tutoring.

Majors. Biology: General. **Business:** General, accounting, executive assistant, finance, human resources, management information systems, marketing. **Education:** Elementary, English. **Engineering technology:** Electrical, environmental.

Computing on campus. 427 workstations in library, computer center, student center. Online library, student web hosting, wireless network available.

Student life. Freshman orientation: Available. **Housing:** Family community housing and private guest house available. **Activities:** Concert band, choral groups, drama, student government, Organizacion Juventud en Cristo, Estudiantes Orientadores, Teatro Experimental 80, Bio-Study, Kayukembo Association, Companeros Alertas Ante Un Mundo Buscando Alternativas, alcohol and drug prevention organization, Centro de Reciclaje y Orientacion Ambiental.

Athletics. Intercollegiate: Baseball M, basketball, cross-country, softball W, table tennis, tennis, track and field, volleyball, weight lifting. **Intramural:** Baseball M, basketball, cross-country, softball W, table tennis, tennis, track and field, volleyball, weight lifting. **Team name:** Tiburones.

Student services. Alcohol/substance abuse counseling, career counseling, student employment services, financial aid counseling, health services, personal counseling, placement for graduates. **Physically disabled:** Services for visually impaired.

Contact. E-mail: meserrano@uprag.edu
Phone: (787) 890-2681 ext. 280
Melba Serrano, Admissions Officer, University of Puerto Rico: Aguadilla, Box 6150, Aguadilla, PR 00604-6150

University of Puerto Rico: Arecibo

Arecibo, Puerto Rico
www.upra.edu **CB code: 0911**

- Public 4-year university
- Commuter campus in small city

General. Founded in 1967. Regionally accredited. **Degrees:** 441 bachelor's, 60 associate awarded. **ROTC:** Army. **Location:** 48 miles from San Juan. **Calendar:** Semester, limited summer session. **Full-time faculty:** 217 total. **Part-time faculty:** 60 total. **Class size:** 25% < 20, 75% 20-39.

Basis for selection. Admissions considered according to admission index (defined and published for each academic program) based equally on high school GPA and SAT scores. Those who apply for UPR admission must take the Academic Aptitude Test and Achievement Test offered by the College Entrance Examination Board (CEEB). Interviews sometimes required. **Homeschooled:** State high school equivalency certificate required.

2008-2009 Annual costs. Tuition/fees: $1,752; $4,077 out-of-state. Books/supplies: $1,320. Personal expenses: $1,000.

2007-2008 Financial aid. All financial aid based on need.

Application procedures. Admission: Closing date 11/30. $20 fee. Admission notification 3/18. **Financial aid:** Closing date 4/27. FAFSA, institutional form required.

Academics. Special study options: ESL, exchange student, honors, internships, liberal arts/career combination, study abroad, Washington semester. Evening college, continuing education program, and professional improvement program. **Credit/placement by examination:** AP, CLEP, IB. **Support services:** Learning center, pre-admission summer program, remedial instruction, study skills assistance, tutoring, writing center.

Majors. Biology: Bacteriology. **Business:** Accounting, administrative services, business admin, finance, marketing. **Communications:** Radio/tv. **Communications technology:** Radio/tv. **Computer sciences:** Computer science. **Education:** Elementary, physical. **Engineering technology:** Industrial. **Health:** Nursing (RN). **Psychology:** Industrial.

Most popular majors. Biology 9%, business/marketing 26%, communications/journalism 15%, education 25%, health sciences 9%, psychology 7%.

Computing on campus. 269 workstations in library, computer center. Commuter students can connect to campus network. Online library, student web hosting, wireless network available.

Student life. Freshman orientation: Mandatory. Preregistration for classes offered. 4-day program held (mornings) in summer. **Activities:** Concert band, choral groups, dance, drama, film society, music ensembles, student government, student newspaper, Cheerleaders UPRA, Rhythm Busters, Federacion de Estudiantes de Iberoamericana, Asociacion de Estudiantes Coro de Concierto, Asociacion Nacional de Estudiantes de Educacion, writers club, Capitulo de Estudiantes de Microbiologia, Asociacion Intercesores Cristiana, ACTRE.

Athletics. Intercollegiate: Baseball M, basketball, cross-country, judo, softball W, track and field, volleyball, weight lifting, wrestling M. **Intramural:** Basketball, softball W, volleyball. **Team name:** Los Lobos (Wolves).

Student services. Alcohol/substance abuse counseling, career counseling, services for economically disadvantaged, student employment services, financial aid counseling, health services, personal counseling, placement for graduates, women's services. **Physically disabled:** Services for visually, hearing impaired.

Contact. E-mail: mmendez@upra.edu
Phone: (787) 815-0000 ext. 4110 Fax: (787) 817-3461
Magaly Mendez, Admissions Officer, University of Puerto Rico: Arecibo, PO Box 4010, Arecibo, PR 00614-4010

University of Puerto Rico: Bayamon University College

Bayamon, Puerto Rico
www.uprb.edu **CB code: 0852**

- Public 4-year university and technical college
- Commuter campus in small city

- 5,014 degree-seeking undergraduates: 16% part-time, 54% women, 100% Hispanic American
- 24% of applicants admitted
- 36% graduate within 6 years

General. Founded in 1971. Regionally accredited. **Degrees:** 451 bachelor's, 53 associate awarded. **ROTC:** Army. **Location:** 9 miles from San Juan. **Calendar:** Semester, limited summer session. **Full-time faculty:** 193 total; 34% have terminal degrees, 100% minority, 55% women. **Part-time faculty:** 115 total; 21% have terminal degrees, 100% minority, 59% women. **Special facilities:** Multimedia laboratory.

Freshman class profile. 5,698 applied, 1,376 admitted, 1,252 enrolled.

End year in good standing:	79%	**Out-of-state:**	1%
Return as sophomores:	83%		

Basis for selection. High school GPA and test scores most important. Higher scores required of applicants to bachelor's programs. Special consideration given to applicants with special talents or handicaps. SAT and 2 SAT Subject Tests (Spanish, mathematics) accepted for English-speaking applicants from U.S. mainland. PAA required of Spanish-speaking applicants.

High school preparation. 12 units required. Required and recommended units include English 2, mathematics 2, social studies 1-2 and science 1. 3 units Spanish also required.

2008-2009 Annual costs. Tuition/fees: $1,752; $4,077 out-of-state. Books/supplies: $800. Personal expenses: $600.

Financial aid. All financial aid based on need.

Application procedures. Admission: Priority date 12/10; deadline 1/31 (receipt date). $15 fee. Application must be submitted on paper. Admission notification on a rolling basis beginning on or about 4/25. Must reply by 5/30. **Financial aid:** Closing date 6/15. Institutional form required. Applicants notified by 7/12; must reply within 4 week(s) of notification.

Academics. Special study options: Cooperative education, cross-registration, double major, ESL, exchange student, honors, internships. **Credit/placement by examination:** AP, CLEP. **Support services:** Pre-admission summer program, reduced course load, study skills assistance, tutoring.

Majors. Biology: General. **Business:** Accounting, business admin, executive assistant, finance, logistics, marketing. **Computer sciences:** General. **Education:** Multi-level teacher, physically handicapped. **Engineering technology:** Electrical.

Most popular majors. Biology 11%, business/marketing 41%, computer/information sciences 9%, education 29%, engineering/engineering technologies 10%.

Computing on campus. 370 workstations in computer center. Commuter students can connect to campus network. Wireless network available.

Student life. Freshman orientation: Available. **Activities:** Bands, choral groups, drama, student government, student newspaper, Confraternidad de Cristianos Unidos, Asociacion Juventud Catolica, Society for Human Resource Management, Asociacion de Estudiantes Orientadores, American Marketing Association, Asociacion de Estudiantes de Computadoras, Asociacion de Gerencia de Materiales.

Athletics. NCAA. **Intercollegiate:** Baseball M, basketball, cheerleading, cross-country, swimming, table tennis, tennis, track and field, volleyball, weight lifting, wrestling M. **Intramural:** Table tennis, tennis, volleyball. **Team name:** Vaqueros.

Student services. Adult student services, career counseling, student employment services, health services, personal counseling, placement for graduates.

Contact. E-mail: cmontes@uprb.edu
Phone: (787) 993-8952 Fax: (787) 993-8929
Carmen Montes, Director of Admissions, University of Puerto Rico: Bayamon University College, 174 street #170 Minillas Industrial Park, Bayamon, PR 00959

University of Puerto Rico: Carolina Regional College

Carolina, Puerto Rico
www.uprc.edu **CB code: 3891**

- Public 4-year university
- Commuter campus in small city
- 4,154 degree-seeking undergraduates: 24% part-time, 64% women
- 34% of applicants admitted
- 36% graduate within 6 years

General. Founded in 1974. Regionally accredited. **Degrees:** 410 bachelor's, 124 associate awarded. **Location:** 10 miles from San Juan. **Calendar:** Quarter, limited summer session. **Full-time faculty:** 112 total; 29% have terminal degrees, 45% women. **Part-time faculty:** 113 total; 14% have terminal degrees, 41% women.

Freshman class profile. 3,692 applied, 1,251 admitted, 1,050 enrolled.

GPA 3.75 or higher:	20%	**GPA 2.0-2.99:**	20%
GPA 3.50-3.74:	23%	**End year in good standing:**	77%
GPA 3.0-3.49:	37%	**Return as sophomores:**	78%

Basis for selection. High school GPA and test scores important. SAT and SAT Subject Tests in Spanish, Math Level 1 required of English-speaking applicants. Interview recommended for those with exceptional ability; portfolio recommended for art. **Homeschooled:** Transcript of courses and grades, state high school equivalency certificate required.

High school preparation. 15 units required; 17 recommended. Required and recommended units include English 3, mathematics 3, social studies 3, history 2, science 2, foreign language 3 and academic electives 1.

2008-2009 Annual costs. Tuition/fees: $2,910; $4,248 out-of-state. Books/supplies: $2,735. Personal expenses: $1,200.

2007-2008 Financial aid. All financial aid based on need. 741 full-time freshmen applied for aid; 741 were judged to have need; 741 of these received aid. Average need met was 42%. Average scholarship/grant was $393. 88% of total undergraduate aid awarded as scholarships/grants, 12% as loans/jobs.

Application procedures. Admission: Closing date 1/31 (receipt date). $20 fee ($20 out-of-state). Must reply by 6/12. **Financial aid:** Closing date 6/30. FAFSA, institutional form required. Applicants notified by 6/30; Applicants notified on a rolling basis starting 6/10.

Academics. Special study options: Honors, internships, liberal arts/career combination, study abroad. **Credit/placement by examination:** AP, CLEP, SAT. **Support services:** Learning center, pre-admission summer program, remedial instruction, study skills assistance, tutoring, writing center.

Majors. Business: Administrative services, business admin, finance, hotel/motel admin, tourism promotion. **Communications:** Advertising. **Communications technology:** Graphic/printing. **Protective services:** Forensics, law enforcement admin.

Most popular majors. Business/marketing 20%, communications/journalism 37%, communication technologies 9%, security/protective services 29%.

Computing on campus. 160 workstations in library, computer center. Online course registration, online library, wireless network available.

Student life. Freshman orientation: Mandatory. Preregistration for classes offered. **Activities:** Concert band, choral groups, dance, drama, international student organizations, student government, Asociacion estudiantil de coro y banda y circulo teatral, asociacion juvenil pro-ayuda social, coalicion de universitarios pro-ambiente, consejo de estudiantes, estudiantes de adm. de hoteles y restaurantes, estudiantes de justicia criminal, estudiantes de medios graficos y de publicidad comercial, estudiantes turisticos universitarios (ESTU), innovative interior design association (IDEA), universitarios cristianos en accion (UCA).

Athletics. Intercollegiate: Baseball M, basketball, cheerleading, cross-country, soccer M, softball W, table tennis, tennis, track and field, volleyball, weight lifting. **Intramural:** Basketball M.

Student services. Alcohol/substance abuse counseling, career counseling, services for economically disadvantaged, student employment services, financial aid counseling, health services, personal counseling, veterans' counselor.

Contact. Phone: (787) 757-1485 Fax: (787) 750-7940
Celia Mendez, Director of Admissions, University of Puerto Rico: Carolina Regional College, PO Box 4800, Carolina, PR 00984-4800

University of Puerto Rico: Cayey University College

Cayey, Puerto Rico **CB member**
www.cayey.upr.edu **CB code: 0981**

- Public 4-year liberal arts and teachers college
- Commuter campus in large town

- 3,691 degree-seeking undergraduates: 10% part-time, 72% women, 100% Hispanic American
- 46% of applicants admitted
- 41% graduate within 6 years

General. Founded in 1967. Regionally accredited. **Degrees:** 528 bachelor's awarded. **ROTC:** Army. **Location:** 30 miles from San Juan. **Calendar:** Semester, limited summer session. **Full-time faculty:** 139 total. **Part-time faculty:** 35 total. **Class size:** 31% < 20, 68% 20-39, less than 1% 40-49. **Special facilities:** Museum, eco-park, ecological learning center, interdisciplinary research center, violence prevention center.

Freshman class profile. 2,471 applied, 1,130 admitted, 818 enrolled.

Mid 50% test scores		**GPA 3.50-3.74:**	24%
SAT critical reading:	470-600	**GPA 3.0-3.49:**	25%
SAT math:	470-620	**GPA 2.0-2.99:**	14%
GPA 3.75 or higher:	37%	**Return as sophomores:**	90%

Basis for selection. School achievement record, test scores most important. SAT required for English-speaking applicants. Students from Puerto Rico must submit their CEEB test scores for math and verbal aptitude. SAT critical reading will be used to evaluate verbal aptitude. Audition, portfolio required for admission of candidates based on special talents such as sports; interview recommended for music, theater programs.

High school preparation. 18 units required. Required units include English 3, mathematics 3, social studies 3, history 3, science 2 and academic electives 3. 3 units of Spanish required.

2008-2009 Annual costs. Tuition/fees: $1,752; $4,077 out-of-state. Books/supplies: $1,520. Personal expenses: $1,000.

2008-2009 Financial aid. All financial aid based on need.

Application procedures. Admission: Closing date 11/30 (postmark date). $20 fee. Admission notification 4/4. Must reply by 5/4. **Financial aid:** Closing date 6/30. FAFSA required. Applicants notified by 7/30.

Academics. Special study options: Accelerated study, combined bachelor's/graduate degree, ESL, exchange student, honors, liberal arts/career combination, study abroad, teacher certification program. **Credit/placement by examination:** AP, CLEP, institutional tests. 72 credit hours maximum toward associate degree, 135 toward bachelor's. **Support services:** Pre-admission summer program, remedial instruction, tutoring, writing center.

Majors. Biology: General. **Business:** General, accounting, administrative services, business admin, office management. **Education:** English, history, mathematics, physical, science, social science, social studies, Spanish, special. **Foreign languages:** Spanish. **History:** General. **Interdisciplinary:** Natural sciences. **Liberal arts:** Humanities. **Math:** General. **Physical sciences:** Chemistry. **Psychology:** General. **Social sciences:** General, economics, sociology. **Other:** Psychology and mental health.

Most popular majors. Biology 12%, business/marketing 23%, education 37%, interdisciplinary studies 6%, psychology 11%.

Computing on campus. 1,000 workstations in library, computer center. Online course registration, online library, wireless network available.

Student life. Freshman orientation: Mandatory. Preregistration for classes offered. **Housing:** Housing available for some athletes and exchange students. **Activities:** Bands, choral groups, dance, drama, student government, symphony orchestra, Asociacion de Estudiantes del Programa de Estudios de Honor, Asociacion de Estudiantes de Psicologia Psy-Chi, Circulo de Historia, The English Club, Circulo de Quimica, American Medical Student Association, GAIA, Circulo de Matematica, Asociacion de Estudiantes de Contabilidad, Club de Leones UPR de Cayey.

Athletics. NCAA. **Intercollegiate:** Baseball M, basketball, cross-country, soccer M, softball, swimming, table tennis, tennis, track and field, volleyball, weight lifting. **Intramural:** Baseball M, basketball, cross-country, soccer M, softball, swimming, table tennis, tennis, track and field, volleyball, weight lifting. **Team name:** Toritos.

Student services. Alcohol/substance abuse counseling, career counseling, services for economically disadvantaged, student employment services, financial aid counseling, health services, on-campus daycare, personal counseling, placement for graduates, veterans' counselor. **Physically disabled:** Services for visually impaired.

Contact. E-mail: admisiones@cayey.upr.edu
Phone: (787) 738-5633 Fax: (787) 738-5633
Wilfredo Lopez, Director of Admissions, University of Puerto Rico: Cayey University College, Oficina de Admisiones UPR- Cayey, Cayey, PR 00736

University of Puerto Rico: Humacao

Humacao, Puerto Rico
www.uprh.edu **CB code: 0874**

- Public 4-year university and liberal arts college
- Commuter campus in small city
- 4,500 degree-seeking undergraduates: 8% part-time, 68% women, 99% Hispanic American
- 43% of applicants admitted
- 46% graduate within 6 years

General. Founded in 1962. Regionally accredited. **Degrees:** 485 bachelor's, 123 associate awarded. **Location:** 30 miles from San Juan. **Calendar:** Semester, limited summer session. **Full-time faculty:** 278 total; 48% have terminal degrees, 56% women. **Part-time faculty:** 29 total; 14% have terminal degrees, 52% women. **Special facilities:** Observatory, census data center, communication competencies center.

Freshman class profile. 2,929 applied, 1,253 admitted, 1,135 enrolled.

GPA 3.75 or higher:	39%	**GPA 2.0-2.99:**	8%
GPA 3.50-3.74:	26%	**Out-of-state:**	1%
GPA 3.0-3.49:	27%		

Basis for selection. High school achievement record, test scores important. Non-native speakers of Spanish required to prove fluency through institutional examinations, interviews. Applicants for admission must take the Spanish version of Puerto Rico CEEB of the College Board: aptitude test (verbal and mathematics) and achievement test battery (Spanish, English and mathematics). In lieu of the above, applicants make take SAT and SAT Subject Tests (Spanish Composition and Spanish Reading). SAT and SAT Subject Tests (Spanish and Mathematics Level I) required of English-speaking applicants. **Homeschooled:** Sworn statement indicating that student received formal education at home. **Learning Disabled:** Director of Disabled Students Services Office (SERPI) evaluates learning disabled students to determine if they qualify for special admission.

High school preparation. 18 units recommended. Recommended units include English 3, mathematics 3, social studies 1, history 2, science 3, foreign language 3 and academic electives 3. Foreign language must be Spanish.

2008-2009 Annual costs. Tuition/fees: $1,752; $4,077 out-of-state. Books/supplies: $1,825. Personal expenses: $1,200.

2008-2009 Financial aid. Non-need-based: Scholarships awarded for academics, athletics, music/drama.

Application procedures. Admission: Priority date 11/15; deadline 11/30 (receipt date). $20 fee. Admission notification 4/15. Admission notification on a rolling basis. Must reply by 5/1. **Financial aid:** Closing date 7/31. FAFSA, institutional form required. Applicants notified by 9/30.

Academics. Course work conducted in Spanish. **Special study options:** Exchange student, honors, internships, teacher certification program. Students can travel to Europe during summer and earn 6 credits in elective courses. **Credit/placement by examination:** AP, CLEP. 40 credit hours maximum toward associate degree, 40 toward bachelor's. **Support services:** Learning center, pre-admission summer program, reduced course load, remedial instruction, study skills assistance, tutoring, writing center.

Majors. Biology: General, marine, microbiology. **Business:** General, accounting, administrative services, business admin, human resources, international. **Conservation:** Wildlife. **Education:** Elementary, ESL. **Health:** Nursing (RN). **Math:** Computational. **Physical sciences:** Chemistry, physics. **Public administration:** Social work. **Social sciences:** General.

Most popular majors. Biology 13%, business/marketing 41%, education 26%, physical sciences 9%, public administration/social services 7%.

Computing on campus. 438 workstations in library, computer center. Commuter students can connect to campus network. Online course registration, online library, wireless network available.

Student life. Freshman orientation: Available. Preregistration for classes offered. One-day program. **Activities:** Bands, choral groups, dance, drama, literary magazine, student government, various religious and social service organizations.

Athletics. Intercollegiate: Baseball M, basketball, cheerleading, cross-country, judo, softball W, swimming, tennis W, track and field, volleyball, weight lifting, wrestling M. **Intramural:** Basketball, softball W, volleyball, weight lifting. **Team name:** Buhos.

Student services. Alcohol/substance abuse counseling, career counseling, student employment services, health services, legal services, personal counseling, placement for graduates. **Physically disabled:** Services for visually, speech, hearing impaired.

Contact. E-mail: milagros.alvarez@upr.edu
Phone: (787) 850-9301 Fax: (787) 850-9428
Milagros Alvarez, Director of Admissions, University of Puerto Rico: Humacao, 100 Road 908 CUH Station, Humacao, PR 00791

University of Puerto Rico: Mayaguez

Mayaguez, Puerto Rico — **CB member**
www.uprm.edu — **CB code: 0912**

- Public 5-year university
- Commuter campus in small city
- 12,011 degree-seeking undergraduates: 6% part-time, 49% women, 100% Hispanic American
- 1,066 degree-seeking graduate students
- 77% of applicants admitted

General. Founded in 1911. Regionally accredited. Most courses conducted in Spanish. Students must have working knowledge of Spanish and English. **Degrees:** 1,481 bachelor's awarded; master's, doctoral offered. **ROTC:** Army, Air Force. **Location:** 100 miles from San Juan. **Calendar:** Semester, limited summer session. **Full-time faculty:** 672 total. **Part-time faculty:** 42 total. **Special facilities:** Planetarium, botanical garden, agricultural extension service, agricultural experimental station, natural history collection, resource center for science and engineering.

Freshman class profile. 3,364 applied, 2,580 admitted, 2,448 enrolled.

Mid 50% test scores		**GPA 3.0-3.49:**	21%
SAT critical reading:	530-630	**GPA 2.0-2.99:**	6%
SAT math:	560-690	**Return as sophomores:**	90%
GPA 3.75 or higher:	51%	**Out-of-state:**	1%
GPA 3.50-3.74:	22%		

Basis for selection. Applicants must have high school diploma or its equivalent from educational institution duly accredited by Department of Education of Puerto Rico. Prospective applicants must take University Evaluation and Admissions Tests (PEAU in Spanish) administered by the College Board. First-year applicants only considered for admission in August of first semester. Applications should be submitted before November 30 of year prior to admission. SAT and SAT Subject Tests required for English-speaking applicants. Students from Puerto Rico are required to submit scores from the College Board Entrance Examination aptitude tests. **Home-schooled:** Must supply notarized document (sworn statement) that functions as certification of student educated in home.

High school preparation. 18 units recommended. Recommended units include English 3, mathematics 2, social studies 2, history 2, science 2, foreign language 3 and academic electives 4.

2008-2009 Annual costs. Tuition/fees: $1,752; $4,077 out-of-state. Books/supplies: $1,520. Personal expenses: $1,000.

2007-2008 Financial aid. All financial aid based on need. 1,764 full-time freshmen applied for aid; 1,634 were judged to have need; 1,634 of these received aid. Average need met was 65%. Average scholarship/grant was $4,553; average loan $3,500. 71% of total undergraduate aid awarded as scholarships/grants, 29% as loans/jobs.

Application procedures. Admission: Closing date 12/15 (postmark date). $20 fee. Admission notification on a rolling basis beginning on or about 4/1. Must reply by 4/15. **Financial aid:** Priority date 1/30, closing date 6/30. FAFSA, institutional form required. Applicants notified by 5/30; Applicants notified on a rolling basis starting 5/30.

Academics. Online support available. Spanish language skills (reading, writing) required to read most online course materials. **Special study options:** Cooperative education, distance learning, double major, ESL, exchange student, honors, internships, study abroad, teacher certification program. **Credit/placement by examination:** AP, CLEP, institutional tests. 22 credit hours maximum toward bachelor's degree. **Support services:** Reduced course load, remedial instruction, tutoring, writing center.

Majors. Agriculture: Agribusiness operations, agronomy, animal sciences, business, economics, education services, horticultural science, plant protection, soil science. **Biology:** General, biotechnology, marine, microbiology. **Business:** Accounting, administrative services, business admin, finance, human resources, marketing, office management, organizational behavior, sales/distribution. **Computer sciences:** General, computer science, systems analysis. **Education:** Agricultural, mathematics, physical. **Engineering:** General, chemical, civil, computer, electrical, industrial, mechanical. **Engineering technology:** Surveying. **Foreign languages:** Comparative lit, French, Spanish. **Health:** Athletic training, nursing (RN), premedicine. **History:** General. **Interdisciplinary:** Math/computer science. **Math:** General. **Parks/recreation:** Facilities management, health/fitness. **Philosophy/religion:** Philosophy. **Physical sciences:** General, chemistry, geology, physics. **Psychology:** General. **Social sciences:** General, economics, political science, sociology. **Visual/performing arts:** Art history/conservation, studio arts.

Most popular majors. Agriculture 7%, biology 14%, business/marketing 12%, engineering/engineering technologies 40%, social sciences 6%.

Computing on campus. 1,000 workstations in library, computer center. Commuter students can connect to campus network. Online library, wireless network available.

Student life. Freshman orientation: Mandatory. Orientation session (4 days) held during week preceding classes in the fall semester. **Housing:** Housing available near campus. **Activities:** Bands, choral groups, dance, drama, literary magazine, radio station, student government, student newspaper, Asoc. de Colegiales Evangelicos, Federacion Adventista de Universitarios, Grupo de Apostolado Catolico, Hermandad Colegial de Avivamiento, Jovenes Cristianos del Parque, Asociacion de Colombianos del RUM, Asociacion de Estudiantes Dominicanos del RUM, Juventud Popular Universitaria, Universitarios Estadistas en Accion.

Athletics. NCAA. **Intercollegiate:** Baseball M, basketball, cross-country, gymnastics, soccer M, softball W, swimming, table tennis, tennis, track and field, volleyball, water polo M, wrestling M. **Intramural:** Archery, baseball M, basketball, cross-country, racquetball, soccer M, softball, swimming, table tennis, tennis, volleyball, water polo M, wrestling M. **Team name:** Tarzanes "Bulldogs".

Student services. Alcohol/substance abuse counseling, career counseling, student employment services, health services, personal counseling, placement for graduates, veterans' counselor, women's services. **Physically disabled:** Services for visually, speech, hearing impaired.

Contact. E-mail: admisiones@upr.edu
Phone: (787) 265-3811 Fax: (787) 834-5265
Norma Torres, Director of Admissions, University of Puerto Rico: Mayaguez, Admissions Office, Mayaguez, PR 00681-9021

University of Puerto Rico: Medical Sciences

San Juan, Puerto Rico
www.rcm.upr.edu — **CB code: 0631**

- Public 4-year university
- Commuter campus in large city
- 462 degree-seeking undergraduates: 13% part-time, 82% women, 100% Hispanic American
- 1,849 degree-seeking graduate students

General. Founded in 1950. Regionally accredited. First-time freshmen not admitted. **Degrees:** 95 bachelor's, 24 associate awarded; master's, doctoral, first professional offered. **Calendar:** Differs by program, limited summer session. **Full-time faculty:** 639 total. **Part-time faculty:** 180 total. **Class size:** 72% < 20, 26% 20-39, 2% 40-49, less than 1% 50-99.

Basis for selection. Candidates are admitted on a competitive basis. Applicants must present evidence of successful completion of all admission requirements for the program in which they are interested. In most programs, an admissions committee will also consider nonacademic factors as additional criteria in screening applicants.

2008-2009 Annual costs. Tuition/fees: $1,752; $4,077 out-of-state. Books/supplies: $1,200. Personal expenses: $800.

2008-2009 Financial aid. All financial aid based on need.

Application procedures. Admission: $20 fee. **Financial aid:** Priority date 4/30, closing date 6/15. FAFSA, institutional form required. Applicants notified on a rolling basis starting 8/1; must reply within 2 week(s) of notification.

Academics. Special study options: Combined bachelor's/graduate degree, exchange student, honors, internships. **Credit/placement by examination:** CLEP. **Support services:** Tutoring.

Majors. Health: Clinical lab science, clinical lab technology, nuclear medical technology, nursing (RN), public health ed, speech pathology, veterinary technology/assistant.

Computing on campus. 216 workstations in library, computer center. Commuter students can connect to campus network. Helpline, repair service available.

Student life. **Activities:** Choral groups, dance, drama, student government.

Athletics. **Intramural:** Basketball M, soccer M, softball M, volleyball.

Student services. Career counseling, student employment services, financial aid counseling, health services, legal services, personal counseling, women's services. **Physically disabled:** Services for visually impaired.

Contact. E-mail: marrivera@rcm.upr.edu
Phone: (787) 758-2525 ext. 5211 Fax: (787) 282-7117
Margarita Rivera, Director, Central Office of Admissions, University of Puerto Rico: Medical Sciences, PO Box 365067, San Juan, PR 00936-5067

University of Puerto Rico: Ponce

Ponce, Puerto Rico
www.uprp.edu **CB code: 0836**

- Public 4-year university and branch campus college
- Commuter campus in small city
- 3,232 degree-seeking undergraduates: 12% part-time, 61% women, 100% Hispanic American
- 37% of applicants admitted
- 40% graduate within 6 years

General. Founded in 1970. Regionally accredited. **Degrees:** 355 bachelor's, 87 associate awarded. **ROTC:** Army. **Location:** 68 miles from San Juan, 46 miles from Mayaguez. **Calendar:** Semester, limited summer session. **Full-time faculty:** 158 total; 30% have terminal degrees, 100% minority, 61% women. **Part-time faculty:** 39 total; 3% have terminal degrees, 100% minority, 46% women. **Class size:** 26% < 20, 74% 20-39.

Freshman class profile. 2,468 applied, 916 admitted, 883 enrolled.

Mid 50% test scores		**GPA 3.50-3.74:**	27%
SAT critical reading:	490-590	**GPA 3.0-3.49:**	29%
SAT math:	490-610	**GPA 2.0-2.99:**	5%
SAT writing:	420-590	**End year in good standing:**	83%
GPA 3.75 or higher:	39%	**Return as sophomores:**	651%

Basis for selection. Admission based on general application index (GAI), combination of high school GPA and College Board test scores (50% each). Programs have their own GAI requirements. Interview required for academically weak and special ability. **Homeschooled:** State high school equivalency certificate required.

High school preparation. 18 units required. Required units include English 3, mathematics 3, social studies 3, science 3 and academic electives 2. 3 units Spanish, 1 unit fine arts.

2008-2009 Annual costs. Tuition/fees: $1,752; $4,077 out-of-state. Books/supplies: $1,825. Personal expenses: $800.

2007-2008 Financial aid. All financial aid based on need. 86% of total undergraduate aid awarded as scholarships/grants, 14% as loans/jobs.

Application procedures. **Admission:** Closing date 11/30. $20 fee. Admission notification on a rolling basis beginning on or about 4/15. Must reply by May 1 or within 3 week(s) if notified thereafter. **Financial aid:** Closing date 5/30. FAFSA, institutional form required.

Academics. **Special study options:** Dual enrollment of high school students, honors, internships. **Credit/placement by examination:** CLEP. **Support services:** Remedial instruction, tutoring.

Majors. **Biology:** General. **Business:** Accounting, administrative services, business admin, finance, marketing. **Computer sciences:** General. **Education:** Elementary. **Health:** Athletic training. **Math:** General. **Protective services:** Forensics. **Psychology:** General.

Most popular majors. Biology 8%, business/marketing 31%, education 36%, health sciences 12%, psychology 10%.

Computing on campus. 344 workstations in library, computer center, student center. Wireless network available.

Student life. **Freshman orientation:** Mandatory. **Activities:** Bands, choral groups, dance, drama, student government, Christian youth organizations, including those devoted to Catholic and Baptist students.

Athletics. **Intercollegiate:** Basketball, cross-country, softball, table tennis, tennis, track and field, volleyball. **Intramural:** Basketball, cross-country, gymnastics, softball, table tennis, tennis, track and field, volleyball.

Student services. Career counseling, student employment services, health services, on-campus daycare, personal counseling, placement for graduates, veterans' counselor. **Physically disabled:** Services for visually impaired.

Contact. E-mail: avelazquez@uprp.edu
Phone: (787) 844-8181 ext. 2531 Fax: (787) 840-8108
Acmin Velazquez, Admissions Director, University of Puerto Rico: Ponce, Box 7186, Ponce, PR 00732

University of Puerto Rico: Rio Piedras

San Juan, Puerto Rico **CB member**
www.uprrp.edu **CB code: 0979**

- Public 4-year university
- Commuter campus in large city
- 15,177 degree-seeking undergraduates: 15% part-time, 66% women
- 3,467 graduate students
- 37% of applicants admitted
- 47% graduate within 6 years

General. Founded in 1903. Regionally accredited. Most courses conducted in Spanish. Students must have working knowledge of Spanish and English. **Degrees:** 2,405 bachelor's awarded; master's, doctoral, first professional offered. **ROTC:** Army, Air Force. **Calendar:** Semester, limited summer session. **Full-time faculty:** 1,006 total; 75% have terminal degrees, 49% women. **Part-time faculty:** 350 total; 14% have terminal degrees, 49% women. **Class size:** 44% < 20, 54% 20-39, less than 1% 40-49, less than 1% 50-99, less than 1% >100. **Special facilities:** Museum of history, anthropology and art; theater; warm-blooded animal house; herbarium; biology museum; high-technology microscopy; nanotechnology lasers; virtual astronomy lab.

Freshman class profile. 8,196 applied, 3,050 admitted, 2,817 enrolled.

Mid 50% test scores		**GPA 3.0-3.49:**	22%
SAT critical reading:	540-650	**GPA 2.0-2.99:**	8%
SAT math:	550-680	**Return as sophomores:**	90%
GPA 3.75 or higher:	46%	**Live on campus:**	10%
GPA 3.50-3.74:	24%		

Basis for selection. Admissions based on secondary school record and standardized test scores. Talent and ability considered. Applicants must take Academic Aptitude Test and Achievement Test offered by the College Board. Otherwise, SAT scores must be submitted. Environmental Design requires separate application form and school test; Fine Arts requires departmental test. **Homeschooled:** Notarized homeschooling certificate.

High school preparation. Required and recommended units include English 3, mathematics 2, social studies 1, history 1, science 2 and academic electives 6. 3 units Spanish required.

2008-2009 Annual costs. Tuition/fees: $1,752; $4,077 out-of-state. Room/board: $8,180. Books/supplies: $1,825. Personal expenses: $1,200.

2008-2009 Financial aid. All financial aid based on need. **Additional information:** Tuition waived for honor students, athletes, members of chorus, and others with special talents.

Application procedures. **Admission:** Closing date 12/15 (postmark date). $20 fee. Admission notification 4/15. Must reply by 5/10. **Financial aid:** FAFSA required.

Academics. **Special study options:** Combined bachelor's/graduate degree, cooperative education, double major, exchange student, external degree, honors, internships, liberal arts/career combination, semester at sea, student-designed major, study abroad, teacher certification program, Washington semester. **Credit/placement by examination:** AP, CLEP, institutional tests. 30 credit hours maximum toward bachelor's degree. **Support services:** Remedial instruction, study skills assistance, tutoring, writing center.

Majors. **Architecture:** Environmental design. **Biology:** General. **Business:** General, accounting, administrative services, business admin, finance, human resources, labor relations, management information systems, managerial economics, marketing, operations, statistics. **Communications:** Digital media, journalism, media studies, public relations. **Computer sciences:** Computer science. **Conservation:** General. **Education:** Elementary, family/consumer sciences, secondary. **Family/consumer sciences:** General, food/nutrition. **Foreign languages:** General, comparative lit, French, Spanish.

History: General. **Interdisciplinary:** Intercultural, natural sciences. **Legal studies:** Prelaw. **Liberal arts:** Arts/sciences. **Math:** General. **Philosophy/religion:** Philosophy. **Physical sciences:** Chemistry, physics. **Psychology:** General. **Public administration:** Social work. **Social sciences:** General, anthropology, economics, geography, political science, sociology. **Visual/performing arts:** General, art, art history/conservation, dramatic, drawing, multimedia, painting, sculpture, studio arts.

Most popular majors. Business/marketing 21%, communications/journalism 6%, education 21%, interdisciplinary studies 12%, social sciences 10%.

Computing on campus. 154 workstations in dormitories, library, computer center, student center. Dormitories wired for high-speed internet access and linked to campus network. Commuter students can connect to campus network. Online library, wireless network available.

Student life. **Freshman orientation:** Available. Preregistration for classes offered. Session held for 1 day in summer. **Policies:** Students represented in university administration. **Housing:** Coed dorms, wellness housing available. $35 deposit, deadline 10/29. **Activities:** Jazz band, choral groups, dance, drama, literary magazine, musical theater, radio station, student government, Club Avanza, Confraternidad Universitaria de Avivamiento, Jovenes Cristianos Universitarios, Juventud Universitaria Popular, Club de la Cruz Roja Americana del Recinto de Rio Piedras.

Athletics. NAIA, NCAA. **Intercollegiate:** Basketball, cross-country, gymnastics, soccer M, softball, swimming, table tennis, tennis, track and field, volleyball, water polo M, wrestling M. **Intramural:** Basketball, cross-country, gymnastics, soccer M, softball, swimming, table tennis, tennis, track and field, volleyball, water polo, wrestling M. **Team name:** Gallitos/Jerezanas.

Student services. Adult student services, alcohol/substance abuse counseling, career counseling, student employment services, health services, on-campus daycare, personal counseling, placement for graduates, veterans' counselor. **Physically disabled:** Services for visually, speech, hearing impaired.

Contact. E-mail: admisiones@uprrp.edu
Phone: (787) 764-7290 Toll-free number: (888) 966-2877
Fax: (787) 763-4265
Cruz Valentin, Director of Admissions, University of Puerto Rico: Rio Piedras, Box 23344, San Juan, PR 00931-3344

University of Puerto Rico: Utuado

Utuado, Puerto Rico — CB member
www.uprutuado.edu — CB code: 3893

- Public 4-year agricultural college
- Commuter campus in large town
- 1,596 degree-seeking undergraduates
- Interview required

General. Founded in 1979. Regionally accredited. **Degrees:** 86 bachelor's, 56 associate awarded. **ROTC:** Army. **Location:** 20 miles from Arecibo. **Calendar:** Semester, limited summer session. **Full-time faculty:** 75 total; 51% have terminal degrees, 100% minority, 43% women. **Part-time faculty:** 43 total; 12% have terminal degrees, 100% minority, 67% women. **Special facilities:** 118-acre farm.

Basis for selection. GED not accepted. High school GPA, test scores important. SAT required of English-speaking students.

High school preparation. Required units include English 3, mathematics 2, history 3, science 2 and foreign language 3. 3 fine arts required.

2008-2009 Annual costs. Tuition/fees: $1,752; $4,077 out-of-state. Books/supplies: $1,825. Personal expenses: $1,200.

Financial aid. All financial aid based on need.

Application procedures. **Admission:** Priority date 11/15; no deadline. $20 fee, may be waived for applicants with need. Must reply by May 1 or within 2 week(s) if notified thereafter. **Financial aid:** Priority date 5/31; no closing date. FAFSA required. Applicants notified on a rolling basis starting 9/30; must reply within 4 week(s) of notification.

Academics. **Special study options:** Cooperative education, honors, internships, teacher certification program. **Credit/placement by examination:** AP, CLEP. **Support services:** Reduced course load, remedial instruction, tutoring.

Majors. **Business:** Accounting, office/clerical. **Education:** Elementary.

Most popular majors. Business/marketing 23%, education 77%.

Computing on campus. 90 workstations in library, computer center. Online library available.

Student life. **Freshman orientation:** Mandatory. **Housing:** Wellness housing available. **Activities:** Concert band, choral groups, dance, drama, student government.

Athletics. **Intercollegiate:** Baseball M, basketball, cross-country, softball, tennis, track and field, volleyball, weight lifting. **Intramural:** Baseball M, basketball, cross-country, softball, table tennis, tennis, track and field, volleyball, weight lifting. **Team name:** Guaraguao.

Student services. Alcohol/substance abuse counseling, career counseling, financial aid counseling, health services, personal counseling, placement for graduates, veterans' counselor.

Contact. Phone: (787) 894-2316 Fax: (787) 894-2891
Maria Robles, Admissions Officer, University of Puerto Rico: Utuado, PO Box 2500, Utuado, PR 00641

University of the Sacred Heart

Santurce, Puerto Rico — CB member
www.sagrado.edu — CB code: 0913

- Private 4-year university and liberal arts college affiliated with Roman Catholic Church
- Commuter campus in large city
- 4,552 degree-seeking undergraduates: 18% part-time, 61% women, 100% Hispanic American
- 1,031 degree-seeking graduate students
- 40% graduate within 6 years

General. Founded in 1935. Regionally accredited. **Degrees:** 457 bachelor's, 110 associate awarded; master's offered. **Location:** Located in the San Juan metropolitan area, near the Luis Munos Marin International Airport. **Calendar:** Semester, extensive summer session. **Full-time faculty:** 121 total. **Part-time faculty:** 243 total. **Class size:** 47% < 20, 53% 20-39. **Special facilities:** Jardin Escultorico, Museo de la Radio, Pabellon de las Artes, Patio de las Artes, Galeria Jose (Pepin) Mendez y Teatro Emilio S. Belaval.

Freshman class profile.

GPA 3.75 or higher:	9%	**GPA 2.0-2.99:**	49%
GPA 3.50-3.74:	12%	**Return as sophomores:**	75%
GPA 3.0-3.49:	29%	**Out-of-state:**	2%

Basis for selection. High school GPA and highest score CEEB important. SAT scores accepted in place of CEEB. Interview required for nursing program.

High school preparation. 15 units required. Required and recommended units include English 3, mathematics 3, social studies 2, science 3, foreign language 3 and academic electives 3.

2008-2009 Annual costs. Tuition/fees: $5,820. Room only: $2,400. Books/supplies: $1,706. Personal expenses: $3,960.

Financial aid. **Non-need-based:** Scholarships awarded for academics, athletics.

Application procedures. **Admission:** Priority date 12/15; deadline 6/30. $15 fee, may be waived for applicants with need. Admission notification on a rolling basis. **Financial aid:** Priority date 4/30, closing date 5/30. FAFSA, institutional form required. Applicants notified on a rolling basis starting 6/15; must reply by 8/30.

Academics. **Special study options:** Combined bachelor's/graduate degree, cooperative education, cross-registration, double major, dual enrollment of high school students, exchange student, external degree, honors, independent study, internships, liberal arts/career combination, semester at sea, teacher certification program. International programs with universities in Mexico and Spain. **Credit/placement by examination:** AP, CLEP, institutional tests. **Support services:** Pre-admission summer program, reduced course load, remedial instruction, tutoring.

Majors. **Biology:** General. **Business:** Accounting, business admin, tourism promotion. **Communications:** General, advertising, journalism. **Computer sciences:** Computer science, information systems. **Education:** General, bilingual, elementary, secondary. **Health:** Nursing (RN). **Interdisciplinary:**

Natural sciences. **Math:** General. **Parks/recreation:** Health/fitness. **Physical sciences:** Chemistry. **Psychology:** General. **Public administration:** Social work. **Social sciences:** General. **Visual/performing arts:** General, dramatic, photography.

Most popular majors. Business/marketing 17%, communications/journalism 46%, education 9%, psychology 7%, social sciences 7%.

Computing on campus. 500 workstations in dormitories, library, computer center, student center. Commuter students can connect to campus network. Repair service available.

Student life. Freshman orientation: Available. **Housing:** Single-sex dorms available. $150 deposit, deadline 6/15. **Activities:** Choral groups, drama, film society, literary magazine, radio station, student government, student newspaper, TV station, pastoral services organization, health and allied sciences organization, student council, senior class organization, judo club, soccer club, nursing club, Christian club, microbioloby club, psychology club, chemistry club, justice system, telecommunication club.

Athletics. Intercollegiate: Basketball M, cross-country, swimming, tennis M, track and field, volleyball, wrestling M. **Intramural:** Basketball M, softball M, swimming, table tennis, volleyball. **Team name:** Dolphins.

Student services. Alcohol/substance abuse counseling, career counseling, student employment services, financial aid counseling, health services, personal counseling, placement for graduates, veterans' counselor. **Physically disabled:** Services for visually, hearing impaired.

Contact. E-mail: admision@sagrado.edu
Phone: (787) 728-1515 ext. 3236 Fax: (787) 728-2066
Luis Henriquez, Director of Admissions and Promotion, University of the Sacred Heart, Universidad del Sagrado Corazon Oficina de Nuevo Ingreso, San Juan, PR 00914-0383

Rhode Island

Brown University

Providence, Rhode Island **CB member**
www.brown.edu **CB code: 3094**

- Private 4-year university and liberal arts college
- Residential campus in small city
- 5,874 degree-seeking undergraduates: 52% women, 7% African American, 16% Asian American, 9% Hispanic American, 1% Native American, 8% international
- 2,146 degree-seeking graduate students
- 14% of applicants admitted
- SAT and SAT Subject Tests or ACT with writing, application essay required
- 94% graduate within 6 years; 36% enter graduate study

General. Founded in 1764. Regionally accredited. **Degrees:** 1,542 bachelor's awarded; master's, doctoral, first professional offered. **ROTC:** Army. **Location:** 45 miles from Boston. **Calendar:** Semester, limited summer session. **Full-time faculty:** 689 total. **Part-time faculty:** 191 total. **Special facilities:** Museum of anthropology, observatory, center for the performing arts, center for information technology, institute for education, institute for international studies.

Freshman class profile. 20,633 applied, 2,828 admitted, 1,550 enrolled.

Mid 50% test scores		**Rank in top tenth:**	93%
SAT critical reading:	650-760	**Return as sophomores:**	98%
SAT math:	670-780	**Out-of-state:**	86%
SAT writing:	660-770	**Live on campus:**	100%
ACT composite:	28-33	**International:**	10%
Rank in top quarter:	99%		

Basis for selection. GED not accepted. Strength of academic course load and student's achievement in courses most important. Extracurricular activities, recommendations, personal essay important; test scores strongly considered. Students submitting SAT should submit 2 SAT Subject Tests of their choice. ACT with Writing may take place of both SAT and SAT Subject Tests. Portfolio recommended for art, music programs. Alumni interviews are available, but not required, for all applicants. **Learning Disabled:** Untimed standardized tests accepted.

High school preparation. 19 units recommended. Recommended units include English 4, mathematics 4, history 2, science 4 (laboratory 3), foreign language 4 and academic electives 1. At least 1 art unit (music or art) recommended. Familiarity with computers recommended. Physics, chemistry, and advanced mathematics recommended for prospective science or engineering majors.

2008-2009 Annual costs. Tuition/fees: $37,718. Room/board: $10,022. Books/supplies: $1,230. Personal expenses: $1,590.

2008-2009 Financial aid. All financial aid based on need. 918 full-time freshmen applied for aid; 685 were judged to have need; 685 of these received aid. Average need met was 100%. Average scholarship/grant was $30,375; average loan $2,234. 88% of total undergraduate aid awarded as scholarships/grants, 12% as loans/jobs.

Application procedures. Admission: Closing date 1/1 (postmark date). $70 fee, may be waived for applicants with need. Admission notification 4/1. Must reply by 5/1. **Financial aid:** Closing date 2/1. FAFSA, CSS PROFILE required. Applicants notified by 4/1; Applicants notified on a rolling basis; must reply by 5/1.

Academics. Students must complete course requirements in major(s) of choice, but are free to choose courses without a core curriculum prior to designating a major. **Special study options:** Accelerated study, combined bachelor's/graduate degree, cross-registration, double major, exchange student, honors, independent study, internships, student-designed major, study abroad, teacher certification program. 8-year medical program, cross-registration with Rhode Island School of Design, early childhood certification (in teaching) program via Wheaton College courses. **Credit/placement by examination:** AP, CLEP, institutional tests. **Support services:** Reduced course load, study skills assistance, tutoring, writing center.

Majors. Architecture: History/criticism. **Area/ethnic studies:** African, African-American, American, Asian, East Asian, European, French, German, Hispanic-American/Latino/Chicano, Italian, Latin American, Near/Middle Eastern, Slavic, South Asian, women's. **Biology:** General, aquatic, biochemistry, biophysics, cell/histology, molecular. **Computer sciences:** Computer science. **Conservation:** Environmental science, environmental studies. **Education:** General. **Engineering:** Biomedical, chemical, civil, computer, electrical, materials, mechanical, physics. **Foreign languages:** Ancient Greek, classics, comparative lit, French, German, Italian, Latin, linguistics, Portuguese, Slavic, Spanish. **Health:** Community health services. **History:** General. **Interdisciplinary:** Ancient studies, biological/physical sciences, cognitive science, math/computer science, medieval/Renaissance, neuroscience. **Math:** General, applied, statistics. **Philosophy/religion:** Judaic, philosophy, religion. **Physical sciences:** Chemical physics, chemistry, geochemistry, geology, geophysics, physics. **Psychology:** General. **Public administration:** Policy analysis. **Social sciences:** Anthropology, archaeology, economics, international economic development, international relations, political science, sociology, urban studies. **Visual/performing arts:** General, art history/conservation, dramatic, musicology, studio arts.

Most popular majors. Biology 19%, physical sciences 11%, social sciences 45%.

Computing on campus. 500 workstations in dormitories, library, computer center, student center. Dormitories wired for high-speed internet access and linked to campus network. Commuter students can connect to campus network. Online course registration, online library, helpline, repair service, wireless network available.

Student life. Freshman orientation: Mandatory. Preregistration for classes offered. 5-day program, beginning Wednesday prior to Labor Day. **Policies:** Students must live in on-campus housing for first 3 years; those entering 7th semester may request off-campus residence. **Housing:** Guaranteed on-campus for all undergraduates. Coed dorms, single-sex dorms, cooperative housing, fraternity/sorority housing, wellness housing available. Language houses, social dormitories, cultural houses, special program housing (international students, technology students, environmental studies) available. **Activities:** Bands, choral groups, dance, drama, film society, literary magazine, music ensembles, musical theater, radio station, student government, student newspaper, symphony orchestra, TV station, African students association, ACLU, Amnesty International, Asian American students association, Big Brothers, Community Outreach, Catholic Pastoral Council, Latino American students association, International Organization, Canadian club.

Athletics. NCAA. **Intercollegiate:** Baseball M, basketball, cross-country, diving, equestrian W, fencing, field hockey W, football (tackle) M, golf, gymnastics W, ice hockey, lacrosse, rowing (crew), skiing W, soccer, softball W, squash, swimming, tennis, track and field, volleyball W, water polo, wrestling M. **Intramural:** Badminton, basketball, fencing, field hockey W, ice hockey, lacrosse, racquetball, rugby, soccer, softball, squash, swimming, tennis, volleyball, water polo. **Team name:** Bears.

Student services. Adult student services, alcohol/substance abuse counseling, chaplain/spiritual director, career counseling, student employment services, financial aid counseling, health services, minority student services, personal counseling, placement for graduates, women's services. **Physically disabled:** Services for visually, hearing impaired.

Contact. E-mail: admission_undergraduate@brown.edu
Phone: (401) 863-2378 Fax: (401) 863-9300
James Miller, Director of Admission, Brown University, 45 Prospect Street, Providence, RI 02912

Bryant University

Smithfield, Rhode Island **CB member**
www.bryant.edu **CB code: 3095**

- Private 4-year business and liberal arts college
- Residential campus in large town
- 3,474 degree-seeking undergraduates: 4% part-time, 43% women
- 282 degree-seeking graduate students
- 45% of applicants admitted
- SAT or ACT (ACT writing optional), application essay required
- 68% graduate within 6 years

General. Founded in 1863. Regionally accredited. **Degrees:** 724 bachelor's awarded; master's offered. **ROTC:** Army. **Location:** 12 miles from Providence, 40 miles from Boston. **Calendar:** Semester, extensive summer session. **Full-time faculty:** 161 total; 84% have terminal degrees, 18% minority, 35% women. **Part-time faculty:** 99 total; 14% minority, 46% women. **Class size:** 19% < 20, 80% 20-39, 2% 40-49. **Special facilities:** Technology center, simulated financial trading floor, digital library, digital TV studio, high speed Unix lab with 20 Sun workstations.

Freshman class profile. 6,253 applied, 2,822 admitted, 911 enrolled.

Mid 50% test scores		**GPA 2.0-2.99:**	14%
SAT critical reading:	510-600	**Rank in top quarter:**	63%
SAT math:	560-630	**Rank in top tenth:**	25%
SAT writing:	520-600	**Return as sophomores:**	91%
ACT composite:	23-26	**Out-of-state:**	86%
GPA 3.75 or higher:	23%	**Live on campus:**	95%
GPA 3.50-3.74:	19%	**International:**	4%
GPA 3.0-3.49:	43%		

Basis for selection. Secondary school curriculum, GPA, guidance counselor's recommendation, personal essay very important, class rank and test scores important. Evidence of math ability important for consideration to business programs. **Homeschooled:** Must be completing a state-accredited program. Course descriptions and progress reports required as part of application process. **Learning Disabled:** Foreign language requirement may be waived.

High school preparation. College-preparatory program required. 16 units required; 18 recommended. Required and recommended units include English 4, mathematics 4, history 2-3, science 2-3 (laboratory 2) and foreign language 2. Mathematics must include a year beyond algebra II, with a preference for pre-calculus or calculus in senior year. History includes social sciences.

2008-2009 Annual costs. Tuition/fees: $30,871. Tuition includes cost of laptop computer. $800 non-refundable enrollment commitment deposit is required of both residents and commuters. Room/board: $11,251. Books/supplies: $1,200. Personal expenses: $1,000.

2007-2008 Financial aid. Need-based: 668 full-time freshmen applied for aid; 567 were judged to have need; 567 of these received aid. Average need met was 70%. Average scholarship/grant was $11,010; average loan $4,459. 65% of total undergraduate aid awarded as scholarships/grants, 35% as loans/jobs. **Non-need-based:** Awarded to 1,671 full-time undergraduates, including 595 freshmen. Scholarships awarded for academics, athletics, minority status, ROTC.

Application procedures. Admission: Closing date 2/1 (postmark date). $50 fee, may be waived for applicants with need: Admission notification 3/21. Must reply by 5/1. **Financial aid:** Closing date 2/15. FAFSA required. Applicants notified by 3/24; must reply by 5/1.

Academics. Business majors must minor in Arts & Sciences. Arts & Sciences majors must minor in Business. All students may select further minors. New students complete a one-credit Foundations for Learning course. International Business majors share residence and must complete 12 credit hours in study abroad. **Special study options:** Double major, ESL, honors, independent study, internships, study abroad. **Credit/placement by examination:** AP, CLEP, IB, institutional tests. 30 credit hours maximum toward bachelor's degree. **Support services:** Learning center, study skills assistance, tutoring, writing center.

Majors. Business: Accounting, accounting technology, actuarial science, business admin, finance, financial planning, international, international finance, marketing. **Communications:** General. **Computer sciences:** General, information technology. **Conservation:** Environmental science. **History:** General. **Math:** Applied, statistics. **Psychology:** General. **Social sciences:** Applied economics, economics, international relations, sociology.

Most popular majors. Business/marketing 83%.

Computing on campus. PC or laptop required. 478 workstations in library, computer center. Dormitories wired for high-speed internet access and linked to campus network. Commuter students can connect to campus network. Online course registration, online library, helpline, repair service, student web hosting, wireless network available.

Student life. Freshman orientation: Mandatory, $75 fee. Preregistration for classes offered. 2-day program in June during which students and parents/guardians are housed in campus residence halls overnight. Students also take mathematics placement exam and register for elective courses. **Policies:** All residence halls are smoke free; students 21 and over may drink in privacy of room, quiet study hour policy in effect through academic year. **Housing:** Guaranteed on-campus for freshmen. Coed dorms, single-sex dorms, special housing for disabled, apartments available. Honors. **Activities:** Jazz band, campus ministries, choral groups, dance, drama, international student organizations, musical theater, radio station, student government, student newspaper, TV station, Christian fellowship, Hillel, College Democrats and Republicans, multicultural student union, Alliance for Women's Awareness, Amnesty International, Big Brothers/Big Sisters.

Athletics. NCAA. **Intercollegiate:** Baseball M, basketball, cross-country, field hockey W, football (tackle) M, golf M, lacrosse, soccer, softball W, swimming, tennis, track and field, volleyball W, wrestling M. **Intramural:** Basketball, football (non-tackle) M, soccer, softball, volleyball. **Team name:** Bulldogs.

Student services. Adult student services, alcohol/substance abuse counseling, chaplain/spiritual director, career counseling, services for economically disadvantaged, student employment services, financial aid counseling, health services, minority student services, personal counseling, placement for graduates, veterans' counselor, women's services. **Physically disabled:** Services for visually, hearing impaired.

Contact. E-mail: admission@bryant.edu
Phone: (401) 232-6100 Toll-free number: (800) 622-7001
Fax: (401) 232-6741
Michelle Beauregard, Director of Admission, Bryant University, 1150 Douglas Pike, Smithfield, RI 02917

Johnson & Wales University: Providence

Providence, Rhode Island — **CB member**
www.jwu.edu — **CB code: 3465**

- Private 4-year university
- Residential campus in small city
- 9,395 degree-seeking undergraduates: 9% part-time, 53% women, 7% African American, 3% Asian American, 7% Hispanic American, 6% international
- 386 degree-seeking graduate students
- 71% of applicants admitted
- 54% graduate within 6 years

General. Founded in 1914. Regionally accredited. **Degrees:** 1,523 bachelor's, 1,455 associate awarded; master's, doctoral offered. **ROTC:** Army. **Location:** 200 miles from New York City, 50 miles from Boston. **Calendar:** Quarter, limited summer session. **Full-time faculty:** 287 total; 5% minority, 43% women. **Part-time faculty:** 163 total; 6% minority, 44% women. **Class size:** 38% < 20, 47% 20-39, 15% 40-49, less than 1% 50-99. **Special facilities:** 3 University-operated hotels and restaurants, banquet facilities, information kiosk, culinary archives and museum, equine center.

Freshman class profile. 14,804 applied, 10,450 admitted, 2,555 enrolled.

Mid 50% test scores		**GPA 2.0-2.99:**	50%
SAT critical reading:	410-520	**Return as sophomores:**	74%
SAT math:	400-500	**Out-of-state:**	87%
GPA 3.75 or higher:	10%	**Live on campus:**	86%
GPA 3.50-3.74:	11%	**International:**	4%
GPA 3.0-3.49:	29%		

Basis for selection. Academic record, secondary school curriculum, GPA, class rank, test scores important; student motivation and interest given strong consideration. SAT or ACT required for honors, paralegal, and electronics engineering programs. Interview and letter of recommendation generally required of students in bottom quarter of class; essay and interview recommended for others.

High school preparation. College-preparatory program recommended. Required units include English 4, mathematics 3, social studies 2 and science 3.

2009-2010 Annual costs. Tuition/fees (projected): $23,490. Freshman required fees include $265 orientation fee. Weekend meal plan available for $1,026. Books/supplies: $1,500. Personal expenses: $1,623.

2008-2009 Financial aid. Need-based: 2,364 full-time freshmen applied for aid; 1,786 were judged to have need; 1,778 of these received aid. Average need met was 66%. Average scholarship/grant was $7,848; average loan $3,272. 38% of total undergraduate aid awarded as scholarships/grants, 62% as loans/jobs. **Non-need-based:** Awarded to 5,184 full-time undergraduates, including 1,881 freshmen. Scholarships awarded for academics, alumni affiliation, job skills, leadership, state residency.

Application procedures. Admission: No deadline. No application fee. Admission notification on a rolling basis beginning on or about 11/1. Must reply by May 1 or within 2 week(s) if notified thereafter. **Financial aid:** No deadline. FAFSA required. Applicants notified on a rolling basis starting 3/1; must reply within 2 week(s) of notification.

Academics. Special study options: Accelerated study, cooperative education, dual enrollment of high school students, ESL, exchange student, honors, independent study, internships, study abroad. Externships, practicums (hands-on learning). **Credit/placement by examination:** CLEP, institutional tests. **Support services:** Learning center, pre-admission summer

program, reduced course load, remedial instruction, study skills assistance, tutoring, writing center.

Majors. Agriculture: Equestrian studies, equine science, farm/ranch. **Business:** Accounting, business admin, entrepreneurial studies, fashion, finance, hospitality admin, hotel/motel admin, international, investments/securities, marketing, public finance, tourism promotion, tourism/travel. **Communications:** General. **Computer sciences:** Information systems, systems analysis, web page design, webmaster. **Engineering:** Computer, systems. **Engineering technology:** Drafting. **Interdisciplinary:** Nutrition sciences. **Legal studies:** Paralegal. **Parks/recreation:** Facilities management, sports admin. **Personal/culinary services:** Baking, chef training, culinary arts, food service, restaurant/catering. **Protective services:** Law enforcement admin.

Most popular majors. Business/marketing 44%, family/consumer sciences 13%, parks/recreation 10%, personal/culinary services 14%.

Computing on campus. 400 workstations in library, computer center. Dormitories wired for high-speed internet access and linked to campus network. Commuter students can connect to campus network. Online library, helpline, wireless network available.

Student life. Freshman orientation: Mandatory, $265 fee. Preregistration for classes offered. **Housing:** Guaranteed on-campus for freshmen. Coed dorms, wellness housing available. $300 deposit. Dormitory for National Student Organization scholarship winners, single rooms, women's floors available. **Activities:** Campus ministries, international student organizations, student government, student newspaper, Hillel, Christian student union, ACLU, Latin-American club, Asian club, T.R.U.E. (Together Realizing Unity Can Exist), College Republicans.

Athletics. NCAA. **Intercollegiate:** Baseball M, basketball, cross-country, equestrian, golf, ice hockey, soccer, softball W, tennis, volleyball, wrestling M. **Intramural:** Basketball, golf, soccer, softball, tennis. **Team name:** Wildcats.

Student services. Career counseling, student employment services, financial aid counseling, health services, personal counseling, placement for graduates, veterans' counselor, women's services. **Physically disabled:** Services for visually, speech, hearing impaired.

Contact. E-mail: admissions.pvd@jwu.edu
Phone: (401) 598-2310 Toll-free number: (800) 342-5598
Fax: (401) 598-2948
Maureen Dumas, Dean of Admissions, Johnson & Wales University: Providence, 8 Abbott Park Place, Providence, RI 02903-3703

New England Institute of Technology
Warwick, Rhode Island
www.neit.edu **CB code: 0339**

- Private 4-year technical college
- Commuter campus in small city
- 3,134 degree-seeking undergraduates
- Interview required

General. Founded in 1940. Regionally accredited. **Degrees:** 209 bachelor's, 824 associate awarded. **Location:** 10 miles from Providence, 50 miles from Boston. **Calendar:** Quarter, extensive summer session. **Full-time faculty:** 105 total; 10% have terminal degrees. **Part-time faculty:** 193 total; 4% have terminal degrees.

Basis for selection. Open admission. Basic skills testing, Ronald P. Carver reading test used for placement. Portfolio recommended for drafting program.

2009-2010 Annual costs. Tuition/fees (projected): $18,140. Books/supplies: $1,050. Personal expenses: $1,440.

Financial aid. Non-need-based: Scholarships awarded for academics. **Additional information:** Tuition at time of first enrollment guaranteed all students for 2 years.

Application procedures. Admission: No deadline. $25 fee. Admission notification on a rolling basis. Must reply by May 1 or within 4 week(s) if notified thereafter. **Financial aid:** Priority date 6/1; no closing date. FAFSA, institutional form required. Applicants notified on a rolling basis starting 6/15.

Academics. Special study options: Accelerated study, cooperative education, distance learning, double major, ESL, internships, student-designed major. **Credit/placement by examination:** AP, CLEP, institutional tests. 51 credit hours maximum toward associate degree. **Support services:** Learning center, pre-admission summer program, reduced course load, remedial instruction, study skills assistance, tutoring, writing center.

Majors. Business: General. **Communications technology:** Recording arts. **Computer sciences:** General, computer science, information technology, systems analysis. **Engineering:** Architectural, manufacturing, mechanical. **Engineering technology:** Electrical, manufacturing. **Visual/performing arts:** Interior design.

Computing on campus. 50 workstations in library, computer center. Online course registration, online library, wireless network available.

Student life. Freshman orientation: Mandatory. Preregistration for classes offered. **Activities:** Radio station, student newspaper, TV station, international student club.

Student services. Career counseling, student employment services, financial aid counseling, personal counseling, placement for graduates, veterans' counselor.

Contact. E-mail: neit@neit.edu
Phone: (401) 467-7744 Toll-free number: (800) 736-7744 ext. 3357
Fax: (401) 738-5122
Mark Blondin, Director of Admissions, New England Institute of Technology, 2500 Post Road, Warwick, RI 02886-2286

Providence College
Providence, Rhode Island **CB member**
www.providence.edu **CB code: 3693**

- Private 4-year liberal arts college affiliated with Roman Catholic Church
- Residential campus in small city
- 3,931 degree-seeking undergraduates: 56% women, 2% African American, 3% Asian American, 3% Hispanic American, 1% international
- 464 degree-seeking graduate students
- 45% of applicants admitted
- Application essay required
- 86% graduate within 6 years

General. Founded in 1917. Regionally accredited. In addition to its traditional undergraduate college, Providence College has a community-oriented evening school that caters to part-time students. **Degrees:** 984 bachelor's, 6 associate awarded; master's offered. **ROTC:** Army. **Location:** 50 miles from Boston, 180 miles from New York City. **Calendar:** Semester, limited summer session. **Full-time faculty:** 295 total; 92% have terminal degrees, 9% minority, 35% women. **Part-time faculty:** 92 total; 37% have terminal degrees, 8% minority, 52% women. **Class size:** 50% < 20, 46% 20-39, less than 1% 40-49, 3% 50-99, less than 1% >100.

Freshman class profile. 8,844 applied, 4,010 admitted, 988 enrolled.

Mid 50% test scores		**GPA 2.0-2.99:**	6%
SAT critical reading:	530-630	**Rank in top quarter:**	80%
SAT math:	540-640	**Rank in top tenth:**	44%
SAT writing:	550-650	**End year in good standing:**	95%
ACT composite:	23-28	**Return as sophomores:**	92%
GPA 3.75 or higher:	24%	**Out-of-state:**	88%
GPA 3.50-3.74:	24%	**Live on campus:**	97%
GPA 3.0-3.49:	46%	**International:**	2%

Basis for selection. GED not accepted. Emphasis placed on scholastic ability, motivation, character, and seriousness of purpose. Recommendations and essay considered. Strength of curriculum and grades are the most important factors. Standardized tests scores are optional. Prospective students who choose not to submit standardized test scores will receive full consideration, without penalty, for admission. Audition recommended for music programs; portfolio recommended for art programs. **Homeschooled:** Statement describing homeschool structure and mission, transcript of courses and grades, state high school equivalency certificate, letter of recommendation (nonparent) required. **Learning Disabled:** Students must provide documentation of disability. Accommodations are then made as deemed appropriate.

High school preparation. College-preparatory program required. Required and recommended units include English 4, mathematics 4, social studies 2, history 2, science 3-4 (laboratory 2) and foreign language 3.

2008-2009 Annual costs. Tuition/fees: $31,379. Room/board: $10,810. Books/supplies: $800. Personal expenses: $1,500.

2008-2009 Financial aid. Need-based: 730 full-time freshmen applied for aid; 501 were judged to have need; 501 of these received aid. Average need met was 76%. Average scholarship/grant was $15,100; average loan $4,135. 70% of total undergraduate aid awarded as scholarships/grants, 30% as loans/jobs. **Non-need-based:** Awarded to 674 full-time undergraduates,

including 183 freshmen. Scholarships awarded for academics, athletics, minority status, ROTC.

Application procedures. Admission: Closing date 1/15 (postmark date). $55 fee, may be waived for applicants with need. Admission notification 4/1. Must reply by 5/1. **Financial aid:** Closing date 2/1. FAFSA, CSS PROFILE required. Applicants notified by 4/1; must reply by 5/1.

Academics. Special study options: Combined bachelor's/graduate degree, cross-registration, distance learning, double major, dual enrollment of high school students, honors, independent study, internships, liberal arts/career combination, student-designed major, study abroad, teacher certification program, Washington semester. **Credit/placement by examination:** AP, CLEP, IB, SAT, ACT, institutional tests. International Baccalaureate credit restricted to 5-7 higher level exams. **Support services:** Learning center, reduced course load, study skills assistance, tutoring, writing center.

Majors. Area/ethnic studies: American, women's. **Biology:** General, biochemistry. **Business:** Accounting, business admin, finance, labor relations, marketing, organizational behavior. **Computer sciences:** Computer science. **Education:** Mathematics, music, secondary, special. **Engineering:** Physics, systems. **Foreign languages:** French, Italian, Spanish. **Health:** Health care admin. **History:** General. **Interdisciplinary:** Global studies. **Liberal arts:** Arts/sciences, humanities. **Math:** General. **Philosophy/religion:** Philosophy. **Physical sciences:** Chemistry. **Psychology:** General. **Public administration:** Community org/advocacy, social work. **Social sciences:** General, economics, political science, sociology. **Theology:** Theology. **Visual/performing arts:** General, art history/conservation, ceramics, drawing, painting, photography, sculpture, studio arts.

Most popular majors. Biology 7%, business/marketing 29%, education 9%, English 6%, history 6%, social sciences 14%.

Computing on campus. 278 workstations in dormitories, library, computer center, student center. Dormitories wired for high-speed internet access and linked to campus network. Commuter students can connect to campus network. Online course registration, online library, helpline, repair service, student web hosting, wireless network available.

Student life. Freshman orientation: Mandatory. Preregistration for classes offered. 2-day session held in the summer, involves both parents and students. **Housing:** Guaranteed on-campus for freshmen. Coed dorms, single-sex dorms, special housing for disabled, wellness housing available. $200 nonrefundable deposit, deadline 5/1. **Activities:** Bands, campus ministries, choral groups, dance, drama, international student organizations, literary magazine, music ensembles, musical theater, radio station, student government, student newspaper, TV station, Afro-American society, Big Brothers and Sisters, Pastoral Service Organization, PC Pals, Best Buddies, College Democrats, College Republicans, Amigos Unidos, Asian American Club.

Athletics. NCAA. **Intercollegiate:** Basketball, cross-country, diving, field hockey W, ice hockey, lacrosse M, soccer, softball W, swimming, tennis W, track and field, volleyball W. **Intramural:** Basketball, field hockey W, football (non-tackle), ice hockey, lacrosse, racquetball, soccer, softball, tennis, volleyball. **Team name:** Friars.

Student services. Adult student services, alcohol/substance abuse counseling, chaplain/spiritual director, career counseling, services for economically disadvantaged, student employment services, financial aid counseling, health services, minority student services, personal counseling, placement for graduates. **Physically disabled:** Services for visually, hearing impaired.

Contact. E-mail: pcadmiss@providence.edu
Phone: (401) 865-2535 Toll-free number: (800) 721-6444
Fax: (401) 865-2826
Christopher Lydon, Associate Vice President for Admissions and Enrollment Planning, Providence College, Harkins Hall 222, 1 Cunningham Square, Providence, RI 02918-0001

Rhode Island College

Providence, Rhode Island — **CB member**
www.ric.edu — **CB code: 3724**

- Public 4-year liberal arts college
- Commuter campus in small city
- 7,192 degree-seeking undergraduates: 25% part-time, 68% women, 6% African American, 2% Asian American, 7% Hispanic American
- 761 degree-seeking graduate students
- 71% of applicants admitted
- SAT or ACT with writing, application essay required
- 46% graduate within 6 years

General. Founded in 1854. Regionally accredited. **Degrees:** 1,246 bachelor's awarded; master's, doctoral offered. **ROTC:** Army. **Location:** 4 miles from downtown Providence. **Calendar:** Semester, extensive summer session. **Full-time faculty:** 305 total; 90% have terminal degrees, 11% minority, 54% women. **Part-time faculty:** 400 total; 55% women. **Class size:** 39% < 20, 61% 20-39, less than 1% 50-99, less than 1% >100. **Special facilities:** Center for the performing arts.

Freshman class profile. 4,028 applied, 2,865 admitted, 1,190 enrolled.

Mid 50% test scores			
SAT critical reading:	420-530	Rank in top quarter:	36%
SAT math:	420-530	Rank in top tenth:	11%
SAT writing:	430-530	Return as sophomores:	77%
ACT composite:	17-21	Out-of-state:	20%
		Live on campus:	46%

Basis for selection. High school academic record and class rank most important, followed by test scores, essay, references. TOEFL required for all applicants who are not native speakers of English. SAT scores required of non-native speakers of English who have been in the United States for more than five years. Interview available but not required; audition required for music performance; portfolio required for bachelor of fine arts. **Homeschooled:** Must submit GED scores unless their home school curriculum is provided by an accredited agency.

High school preparation. College-preparatory program required. 18 units required. Required units include English 4, mathematics 3, social studies 2, science 2 (laboratory 2), foreign language 2, academic electives 4.5. .5 unit in the arts (music, art, dance, theatre) required. Biology and either chemistry or physics are required lab sciences. 2 years of the same foreign language required. Algebra I, II and geometry required. All units must be college-preparatory.

2008-2009 Annual costs. Tuition/fees: $5,771; $14,482 out-of-state. Permanent residents of Massachusetts and Connecticut who live in selected communities within a 50-mile radius of Providence are eligible for Rhode Island's in-state tuition plus 50%. Room/board: $8,390. Books/supplies: $900. Personal expenses: $1,000.

2008-2009 Financial aid. Need-based: 971 full-time freshmen applied for aid; 683 were judged to have need; 673 of these received aid. Average need met was 27%. Average scholarship/grant was $6,485; average loan $3,221. 45% of total undergraduate aid awarded as scholarships/grants, 55% as loans/jobs. **Non-need-based:** Awarded to 220 full-time undergraduates, including 86 freshmen. Scholarships awarded for academics, alumni affiliation, art, music/drama.

Application procedures. Admission: Closing date 5/1 (postmark date). $50 fee, may be waived for applicants with need. Admission notification on a rolling basis beginning on or about 12/15. Must reply by May 1 or within 2 week(s) if notified thereafter. **Financial aid:** Priority date 3/1; no closing date. FAFSA, institutional form required. Applicants notified on a rolling basis starting 3/15; must reply within 3 week(s) of notification.

Academics. Special study options: Combined bachelor's/graduate degree, double major, dual enrollment of high school students, ESL, exchange student, honors, independent study, internships, student-designed major, study abroad, teacher certification program. **Credit/placement by examination:** AP, CLEP, SAT, ACT, institutional tests. **Support services:** Learning center, pre-admission summer program, reduced course load, remedial instruction, study skills assistance, tutoring, writing center.

Majors. Area/ethnic studies: African-American, Latin American, women's. **Biology:** General. **Business:** General, accounting, business admin, finance, labor studies, management information systems, managerial economics, marketing. **Communications:** General. **Computer sciences:** General, computer science. **Education:** Art, biology, chemistry, early childhood, elementary, English, foreign languages, French, geography, health, history, mathematics, multi-level teacher, music, physical, physics, science, secondary, social science, social studies, Spanish, special, technology/industrial arts, voc/tech. **Foreign languages:** French, Spanish. **Health:** Clinical lab science, nursing (RN), predental, premedicine, preveterinary, substance abuse counseling. **History:** General. **Legal studies:** Prelaw. **Liberal arts:** Arts/sciences. **Math:** General. **Philosophy/religion:** Philosophy. **Physical sciences:** Chemistry, physics. **Protective services:** Criminal justice. **Psychology:** General. **Public administration:** General, social work. **Social sciences:** General, anthropology, economics, geography, political science, sociology. **Visual/performing arts:** Art history/conservation, dance, dramatic, film/cinema, music performance, studio arts.

Most popular majors. Business/marketing 14%, communications/journalism 6%, education 25%, health sciences 10%, psychology 11%, visual/performing arts 8%.

Computing on campus. 675 workstations in library, computer center, student center. Dormitories wired for high-speed internet access and linked to campus network. Commuter students can connect to campus network. Online course registration, online library, helpline, repair service, student web hosting, wireless network available.

Student life. **Freshman orientation:** Available, $85 fee. Preregistration for classes offered. Held throughout July in 2-day cycles. Some single days are available. **Housing:** Guaranteed on-campus for freshmen. Coed dorms, single-sex dorms, special housing for disabled available. $214 partly refundable deposit, deadline 5/1. **Activities:** Bands, campus ministries, choral groups, dance, drama, film society, international student organizations, literary magazine, music ensembles, musical theater, radio station, student government, student newspaper, symphony orchestra, Catholic and Protestant religious organizations, Amnesty International, Cape Verdean student association, Habitat for Humanity, Intra-Varsity Student Fellowship, Latin American student association, Muslim students, RIC Angels RIC Republicans, Harambee, NAACP.

Athletics. NCAA. **Intercollegiate:** Baseball M, basketball, cross-country, golf M, gymnastics W, lacrosse W, soccer, softball W, tennis, track and field, volleyball W, wrestling M. **Intramural:** Basketball, football (non-tackle) M, gymnastics, softball, tennis, volleyball. **Team name:** Anchormen, Anchorwomen.

Student services. Adult student services, alcohol/substance abuse counseling, chaplain/spiritual director, career counseling, student employment services, financial aid counseling, health services, minority student services, on-campus daycare, personal counseling, placement for graduates, veterans' counselor, women's services. **Physically disabled:** Services for visually, speech, hearing impaired. **Learning disabled:** Comprehensive services available.

Contact. E-mail: admissions@ric.edu
Phone: (401) 456-8234 Toll-free number: (800) 669-5760
Fax: (401) 456-8817
Holly Shadoian, Director of Admissions, Rhode Island College, 600 Mount Pleasant Avenue, Providence, RI 02908

Rhode Island School of Design

Providence, Rhode Island — **CB member**
www.risd.edu — **CB code: 3726**

- Private 4-year visual arts college
- Residential campus in small city
- 1,926 degree-seeking undergraduates
- 29% of applicants admitted
- SAT or ACT with writing, application essay required

General. Founded in 1877. Regionally accredited. **Degrees:** 453 bachelor's awarded; master's offered. **Location:** 52 miles from Boston, 180 miles from New York City. **Calendar:** 4-1-4, limited summer session. **Full-time faculty:** 146 total. **Part-time faculty:** 357 total. **Special facilities:** Fine art and design museum, extensive photograph and clipping collections, slide collection, recreational farm on Narragansett Bay, nature laboratory.

Freshman class profile. 3,148 applied, 923 admitted, 438 enrolled.

Mid 50% test scores		**Rank in top quarter:**	58%
SAT critical reading:	540-660	**Rank in top tenth:**	23%
SAT math:	570-680	**Out-of-state:**	96%
SAT writing:	550-670	**Live on campus:**	98%
ACT composite:	22-29		

Basis for selection. Academic history, visual portfolio and 3 required drawings most important parts of application. Portfolio required for all applicants. **Homeschooled:** Proof of high school equivalent/GED required.

High school preparation. Architecture, interior architecture, landscape architecture, and industrial design applicants must have 2 algebra, .5 trigonometry, 1 science.

2009-2010 Annual costs. Tuition/fees: $36,659. Room/board: $10,846. Books/supplies: $2,600. Personal expenses: $2,415.

Application procedures. **Admission:** Closing date 2/15 (receipt date). $60 fee, may be waived for applicants with need. Admission notification 4/1. Must reply by 5/1. **Financial aid:** Closing date 2/15. FAFSA, CSS PROFILE required. Applicants notified by 4/1; must reply by 5/1.

Academics. **Special study options:** Cross-registration, double major, exchange student, independent study, internships, study abroad, teacher certification program. **Credit/placement by examination:** AP, CLEP, IB. **Support services:** Remedial instruction, tutoring, writing center.

Majors. **Architecture:** Architecture, interior, landscape. **Visual/performing arts:** Ceramics, cinematography, fashion design, fiber arts, graphic design, illustration, industrial design, metal/jewelry, painting, photography, printmaking, sculpture, studio arts.

Most popular majors. Architecture 9%, visual/performing arts 91%.

Computing on campus. 425 workstations in dormitories, library, computer center, student center. Dormitories wired for high-speed internet access and linked to campus network. Commuter students can connect to campus network. Online course registration, helpline, repair service, student web hosting, wireless network available.

Student life. **Freshman orientation:** Mandatory. **Housing:** Guaranteed on-campus for freshmen. Coed dorms, apartments, wellness housing available. $175 nonrefundable deposit, deadline 5/1. **Activities:** Dance, drama, film society, literary magazine, student government, student newspaper, all major religions represented on campus, professional societies, clubs.

Athletics. **Intramural:** Baseball M, basketball, ice hockey, soccer, softball.

Student services. Alcohol/substance abuse counseling, chaplain/spiritual director, career counseling, financial aid counseling, health services, legal services, minority student services, personal counseling, placement for graduates. **Physically disabled:** Services for hearing impaired.

Contact. E-mail: admissions@risd.edu
Phone: (401) 454-6300 Toll-free number: (800) 364-7473
Fax: (401) 454-6309
Edward Newhall, Director of Admissions, Rhode Island School of Design, Two College Street, Providence, RI 02903-2791

Roger Williams University

Bristol, Rhode Island — **CB member**
www.rwu.edu — **CB code: 3729**

- Private 4-year university and liberal arts college
- Residential campus in large town
- 4,297 degree-seeking undergraduates: 13% part-time, 48% women, 2% African American, 1% Asian American, 2% Hispanic American, 2% international
- 777 degree-seeking graduate students
- 61% of applicants admitted
- SAT or ACT (ACT writing recommended), application essay required
- 56% graduate within 6 years; 13% enter graduate study

General. Founded in 1956. Regionally accredited. Certificate and associate programs offered only in School of Continuing Studies in Providence and Bristol. **Degrees:** 871 bachelor's, 14 associate awarded; master's, first professional offered. **ROTC:** Army. **Location:** 18 miles from Providence, 10 miles from Newport. **Calendar:** Semester, limited summer session. **Full-time faculty:** 210 total; 84% have terminal degrees, 14% minority, 40% women. **Part-time faculty:** 374 total; 37% have terminal degrees, 6% minority, 39% women. **Class size:** 58% < 20, 42% 20-39, less than 1% 40-49, less than 1% 50-99. **Special facilities:** Marine and natural sciences building with marine biology wetlab.

Freshman class profile. 8,561 applied, 5,235 admitted, 954 enrolled.

Mid 50% test scores		**GPA 2.0-2.99:**	29%
SAT critical reading:	500-590	**Rank in top quarter:**	38%
SAT math:	520-600	**Rank in top tenth:**	14%
SAT writing:	500-590	**Return as sophomores:**	82%
ACT composite:	21-25	**Out-of-state:**	91%
GPA 3.75 or higher:	14%	**Live on campus:**	96%
GPA 3.50-3.74:	14%	**International:**	3%
GPA 3.0-3.49:	43%		

Basis for selection. High school record, standardized test scores, essay, extracurricular activities and achievements most important. Teacher or counselor recommendations considered. Audition required for dance; portfolio required for art, architecture programs. **Homeschooled:** State high school equivalency certificate required. Students must submit portfolio of their work.

High school preparation. College-preparatory program required. 22 units required; 26 recommended. Required and recommended units include English 4, mathematics 3-4, social studies 2-3, history 2-3, science 2-4 (laboratory 2), foreign language 2 and academic electives 2-3. Specific subject requirements vary with intended major.

2008-2009 Annual costs. Tuition/fees: $27,718. Tuition differential for architecture program. Room/board: $11,880. Books/supplies: $900. Personal expenses: $794.

2008-2009 Financial aid. **Need-based:** 724 full-time freshmen applied for aid; 547 were judged to have need; 543 of these received aid. Average need met was 88%. Average scholarship/grant was $5,769; average loan

$3,834. 54% of total undergraduate aid awarded as scholarships/grants, 46% as loans/jobs. **Non-need-based:** Awarded to 1,596 full-time undergraduates, including 573 freshmen. Scholarships awarded for academics, ROTC.

Application procedures. **Admission:** Closing date 2/1. $50 fee. Application must be submitted online. Admission notification on a rolling basis beginning on or about 3/15. Must reply by 5/1. **Financial aid:** Priority date 1/1, closing date 2/1. FAFSA, CSS PROFILE required. Applicants notified on a rolling basis starting 3/20; must reply by 5/1.

Academics. All students graduate with two areas of specialization: one in their major and a second in a liberal arts discipline; most students may complete two majors. **Special study options:** Combined bachelor's/graduate degree, cooperative education, distance learning, double major, dual enrollment of high school students, ESL, exchange student, external degree, honors, independent study, internships, liberal arts/career combination, semester at sea, student-designed major, study abroad, teacher certification program, Washington semester, weekend college. **Credit/placement by examination:** AP, CLEP, IB, SAT, institutional tests. 15 credit hours maximum toward associate degree, 30 toward bachelor's. Students can test out of no more than 25% of the credits required for a degree. **Support services:** Learning center, reduced course load, study skills assistance, tutoring, writing center.

Honors college/program. Applicants must have minimum SAT score of 1250 (exclusive of Writing) and a 3.3 GPA (1300/ 3.3 for Architecture and Marine Biology). Application deadline February 1.

Majors. **Architecture:** Architecture, history/criticism. **Area/ethnic studies:** American. **Biology:** General, marine. **Business:** Accounting, business admin, finance, international, management information systems, marketing. **Communications:** Journalism, media studies. **Communications technology:** Graphics. **Computer sciences:** General, computer science. **Conservation:** General. **Construction:** Site management. **Education:** Elementary, secondary. **Engineering:** General. **Foreign languages:** General. **History:** General. **Interdisciplinary:** Historic preservation. **Legal studies:** General, paralegal. **Math:** General. **Philosophy/religion:** Philosophy. **Physical sciences:** Chemistry. **Protective services:** Law enforcement admin. **Psychology:** General. **Public administration:** General. **Social sciences:** Anthropology, economics, political science, sociology. **Visual/performing arts:** Art history/conservation, dance, dramatic, graphic design, studio arts.

Most popular majors. Architecture 6%, biology 6%, business/marketing 17%, communications/journalism 7%, education 6%, engineering/engineering technologies 8%, psychology 10%, security/protective services 13%.

Computing on campus. 540 workstations in dormitories, library, computer center. Dormitories wired for high-speed internet access and linked to campus network. Commuter students can connect to campus network. Online course registration, online library, helpline, repair service, wireless network available.

Student life. **Freshman orientation:** Mandatory. Preregistration for classes offered. 2-day program with overnight stay on campus during summer; separate orientations for transfer and international students. **Housing:** Guaranteed on-campus for freshmen. Coed dorms, special housing for disabled, apartments, wellness housing available. $350 fully refundable deposit, deadline 5/1. Special interest academic and honors housing available. **Activities:** Choral groups, dance, drama, film society, international student organizations, literary magazine, Model UN, musical theater, radio station, student government, student newspaper, Hillel, Inter-Varsity Christian Fellowship, multicultural student union, College Democrats, College Republicans, environmental and animal rights club, Model UN, Best Buddies of Rhode Island, Habitat for Humanity, student volunteer association.

Athletics. NCAA. **Intercollegiate:** Baseball M, basketball, cross-country, diving, equestrian, lacrosse, sailing, soccer, softball W, swimming, tennis, volleyball W, wrestling M. **Intramural:** Basketball, field hockey, football (non-tackle), golf, racquetball, skiing, soccer, softball, squash, tennis, volleyball, water polo. **Team name:** Hawks.

Student services. Chaplain/spiritual director, career counseling, student employment services, financial aid counseling, health services, minority student services, personal counseling, women's services. **Physically disabled:** Services for visually, hearing impaired.

Contact. E-mail: admit@rwu.edu
Phone: (401) 254-3500 Toll-free number: (800) 458-7144 ext. 3500
Fax: (401) 254-3557
Didier Bouvet, Dean of Undergraduate Admissions, Roger Williams University, 1 Old Ferry Rd, Bristol, RI 02809-2921

Salve Regina University

Newport, Rhode Island — **CB member**
www.salve.edu — **CB code: 3759**

- Private 4-year university and liberal arts college affiliated with Roman Catholic Church
- Residential campus in large town
- 2,078 degree-seeking undergraduates: 4% part-time, 69% women, 1% African American, 1% Asian American, 3% Hispanic American, 1% international
- 437 degree-seeking graduate students
- 59% of applicants admitted
- SAT or ACT (ACT writing optional), application essay required
- 69% graduate within 6 years; 20% enter graduate study

General. Founded in 1934. Regionally accredited. Affiliated with Religious Sisters of Mercy. **Degrees:** 474 bachelor's awarded; master's, doctoral offered. **ROTC:** Army. **Location:** 30 miles from Providence. **Calendar:** Semester, limited summer session. **Full-time faculty:** 119 total; 78% have terminal degrees, 8% minority, 54% women. **Part-time faculty:** 136 total; 29% have terminal degrees, 6% minority, 54% women. **Class size:** 53% < 20, 47% 20-39, less than 1% 40-49. **Special facilities:** International relations and public policy center.

Freshman class profile. 5,937 applied, 3,484 admitted, 560 enrolled.

Mid 50% test scores		**GPA 2.0-2.99:**	17%
SAT critical reading:	510-580	**Rank in top quarter:**	56%
SAT math:	510-590	**Rank in top tenth:**	20%
SAT writing:	510-600	**End year in good standing:**	98%
ACT composite:	22-25	**Return as sophomores:**	73%
GPA 3.75 or higher:	17%	**Out-of-state:**	89%
GPA 3.50-3.74:	22%	**Live on campus:**	99%
GPA 3.0-3.49:	44%		

Basis for selection. High school achievement most important, followed by rank in top half of high school class, test scores, recommendations, essay, activities, interview. Special consideration given to applicants from minority and low-income families. SAT or TOEFL required for international applicants. Audition and portfolio considered. **Homeschooled:** Statement describing homeschool structure and mission, transcript of courses and grades, letter of recommendation (nonparent) required. Require two recommendations, one of which must be academic. Course syllabus required for each course; results of SAT or ACT examinations; portfolio of academic accomplishments including a reading list, course descriptions and list of extracurricular/community involvement.

High school preparation. College-preparatory program required. 16 units required. Required units include English 4, mathematics 3, social studies 1, science 2 (laboratory 2), foreign language 2 and academic electives 4. Additional course work may be required of students who have not completed recommended units. Social studies includes history.

2008-2009 Annual costs. Tuition/fees: $31,500. Required fees include a one-time laptop fee of $2,350 for all first-year students. Room/board: $10,700. Books/supplies: $900. Personal expenses: $1,000.

2008-2009 Financial aid. **Non-need-based:** Scholarships awarded for academics, ROTC.

Application procedures. **Admission:** Priority date 2/1; no deadline. $50 fee, may be waived for applicants with need. Must reply by May 1 or within 2 week(s) if notified thereafter. **Financial aid:** Priority date 3/1; no closing date. FAFSA, CSS PROFILE required. Applicants notified by 4/1; must reply by 4/15 or within 2 week(s) of notification.

Academics. Credit may be awarded for learning associated with life experience. **Special study options:** Accelerated study, combined bachelor's/graduate degree, distance learning, double major, dual enrollment of high school students, ESL, honors, independent study, internships, liberal arts/career combination, semester at sea, study abroad, teacher certification program, Washington semester. **Credit/placement by examination:** AP, CLEP, IB, SAT, ACT, institutional tests. **Support services:** Learning center, reduced course load, study skills assistance, tutoring, writing center.

Majors. **Area/ethnic studies:** American. **Biology:** General. **Business:** Accounting, business admin, finance, management science, market research. **Computer sciences:** Information systems. **Education:** Biology, drama/dance, early childhood, elementary, English, French, history, mathematics, music, Spanish, special. **Foreign languages:** French, Spanish. **Health:** Nursing (RN). **History:** American, European. **Interdisciplinary:** Historic preservation. **Liberal arts:** Arts/sciences. **Math:** General. **Philosophy/religion:** Philosophy, religion. **Physical sciences:** Chemistry. **Protective services:** Law enforcement admin. **Psychology:** General. **Public administration:** Social work. **Social sciences:** Economics, political science, sociology. **Visual/ performing arts:** Art history/conservation, ceramics, dramatic, graphic design, painting, photography, studio arts. **Other:** Interactive communication technology.

Most popular majors. Business/marketing 23%, education 16%, health sciences 13%, psychology 7%, security/protective services 10%.

Computing on campus. PC or laptop required. 300 workstations in library, computer center, student center. Dormitories wired for high-speed internet access and linked to campus network. Commuter students can connect to campus network. Online course registration, online library, helpline, repair service, student web hosting, wireless network available.

Student life. **Freshman orientation:** Mandatory, $300 fee. Preregistration for classes offered. 2-day sessions during June and July for full-time freshmen; separate sessions for international and transfer students. **Housing:** Guaranteed on-campus for freshmen. Coed dorms, single-sex dorms, special housing for disabled, apartments, wellness housing available. $500 nonrefundable deposit, deadline 5/1. Off-campus housing available to upperclassmen. **Activities:** Bands, campus ministries, choral groups, dance, drama, film society, international student organizations, literary magazine, music ensembles, Model UN, radio station, student government, student newspaper, Artist's Guild, Artist's Sanctuary, Circle K, environmental club, Student Outdoor Adventures, Volunteers Interested in Researching and Guiding, Women's Issues Now, Stagefright Theater Company.

Athletics. NCAA. **Intercollegiate:** Baseball M, basketball, cross-country M, field hockey W, football (tackle) M, ice hockey, lacrosse, soccer, softball W, tennis, track and field W, volleyball W. **Intramural:** Basketball, field hockey W, football (non-tackle) W, football (tackle) M, racquetball, soccer, softball, tennis, track and field W, volleyball, weight lifting. **Team name:** Seahawks.

Student services. Chaplain/spiritual director, career counseling, financial aid counseling, health services, minority student services, personal counseling, veterans' counselor. **Physically disabled:** Services for visually, hearing impaired.

Contact. E-mail: sruadmis@salve.edu
Phone: (401) 341-2908 Toll-free number: (888) 467-2583
Fax: (401) 848-2823
Colleen Emerson, Dean of Undergraduate Admissions, Salve Regina University, 100 Ochre Point Avenue, Newport, RI 02840-4192

University of Rhode Island

Kingston, Rhode Island — **CB member**
www.uri.edu — **CB code: 3919**

- Public 4-year university
- Commuter campus in small town
- 12,520 degree-seeking undergraduates: 11% part-time, 56% women, 5% African American, 3% Asian American, 5% Hispanic American
- 2,446 degree-seeking graduate students
- 77% of applicants admitted
- SAT or ACT (ACT writing recommended), application essay required
- 58% graduate within 6 years

General. Founded in 1892. Regionally accredited. College of Continuing Education in Providence offers credit-bearing courses for degree and nondegree part-time students. **Degrees:** 2,201 bachelor's awarded; master's, doctoral, first professional offered. **ROTC:** Army. **Location:** 30 miles from Providence. **Calendar:** Semester, extensive summer session. **Full-time faculty:** 683 total; 89% have terminal degrees, 14% minority, 42% women. **Part-time faculty:** 16 total; 69% have terminal degrees, 19% minority, 56% women. **Class size:** 34% < 20, 51% 20-39, 6% 40-49, 5% 50-99, 4% >100. **Special facilities:** Center for robotics research, animal science farm, planetarium, Narragansett Bay Campus for Marine Sciences, American historic textiles museum, aquaculture center, fisheries and marine technology laboratory, biotechnology center, human performance laboratory.

Freshman class profile. 15,887 applied, 12,184 admitted, 3,191 enrolled.

Mid 50% test scores		Out-of-state:	39%
SAT critical reading:	480-570	Live on campus:	91%
SAT math:	500-590	Fraternities:	14%
Return as sophomores:	80%	Sororities:	13%

Basis for selection. School record primary, test scores secondary; extracurricular activities considered. Economically and socially disadvantaged students from Rhode Island admitted through special program for talent development.

High school preparation. College-preparatory program required. 18 units required. Required units include English 4, mathematics 3, social studies 2, science 2 (laboratory 1), foreign language 2 and academic electives 5.

2008-2009 Annual costs. Tuition/fees: $8,678; $24,776 out-of-state. Room/ board: $8,828. Books/supplies: $1,200. Personal expenses: $1,350.

2008-2009 Financial aid. **Need-based:** 2,485 full-time freshmen applied for aid; 1,958 were judged to have need; 1,591 of these received aid. Average need met was 57%. Average scholarship/grant was $6,563; average loan $5,905. 50% of total undergraduate aid awarded as scholarships/grants, 50% as loans/jobs. **Non-need-based:** Awarded to 1,000 full-time undergraduates, including 312 freshmen. Scholarships awarded for academics, alumni affiliation, art, athletics, music/drama, ROTC.

Application procedures. **Admission:** Closing date 2/1. $65 fee, may be waived for applicants with need. Admission notification 3/31. Admission notification on a rolling basis beginning on or about 12/1. Must reply by May 1 or within 2 week(s) if notified thereafter. **Financial aid:** Priority date 3/1; no closing date. FAFSA required. Applicants notified on a rolling basis starting 3/31; must reply by 5/1.

Academics. **Special study options:** Combined bachelor's/graduate degree, distance learning, double major, dual enrollment of high school students, exchange student, honors, independent study, internships, semester at sea, study abroad, teacher certification program, Washington semester, weekend college. **Credit/placement by examination:** AP, CLEP, IB, SAT, ACT, institutional tests. **Support services:** Learning center, pre-admission summer program, reduced course load, remedial instruction, study skills assistance, tutoring, writing center.

Honors college/program. Students in top 10% of their high school class.

Majors. **Agriculture:** Animal sciences, turf management. **Architecture:** Landscape. **Area/ethnic studies:** African-American, Latin American, women's. **Biology:** General, marine, microbiology, zoology. **Business:** General, accounting, apparel, business admin, finance, international, marketing. **Communications:** General, journalism, public relations. **Computer sciences:** General. **Conservation:** Environmental studies, fisheries, management/ policy, water/wetlands/marine, wildlife. **Education:** Elementary, music, physical, secondary. **Engineering:** Biomedical, chemical, civil, computer, electrical, industrial, mechanical, ocean. **Family/consumer sciences:** Clothing/ textiles, family studies, food/nutrition. **Foreign languages:** Classics, comparative lit, French, German, Italian, Spanish. **Health:** Clinical lab science, communication disorders, dietetics, health care admin, nursing (RN), pharmacy assistant. **History:** General. **Math:** General. **Philosophy/religion:** Philosophy. **Physical sciences:** Chemistry, geology, oceanography, physics. **Psychology:** General. **Public administration:** Policy analysis. **Social sciences:** Anthropology, econometrics, economics, political science, sociology. **Visual/ performing arts:** Art history/conservation, cinematography, dramatic, music performance, music theory/composition, studio arts. **Other:** Applied sociology, Kinesiology, Urban horticulture.

Most popular majors. Biology 6%, business/marketing 17%, communications/journalism 10%, education 8%, engineering/engineering technologies 8%, health sciences 9%, personal/culinary services 8%, psychology 6%, social sciences 7%.

Computing on campus. Dormitories wired for high-speed internet access and linked to campus network. Commuter students can connect to campus network. Online course registration, online library, helpline, repair service, wireless network available.

Student life. **Freshman orientation:** Available, $150 fee. Preregistration for classes offered. Two-day program in June and July. **Housing:** Guaranteed on-campus for freshmen. Coed dorms, special housing for disabled, apartments, cooperative housing, fraternity/sorority housing, wellness housing available. $200 partly refundable deposit, deadline 5/1. Learning communities for undecided majors, honors program, health sciences, engineering, college environment and health sciences majors and nursing. **Activities:** Bands, campus ministries, choral groups, dance, drama, film society, international student organizations, literary magazine, music ensembles, musical theater, radio station, student government, student newspaper, TV station, student senate, student entertainment committee, Good Cent Cigar (newspaper), Latin American student association, NAACP, Uhuru SASA, gaming club, WRIU radio, recreation club sports council, Interfraternity/ Panhellenic Council.

Athletics. NCAA. **Intercollegiate:** Baseball M, basketball, cheerleading, cross-country, diving W, football (tackle) M, golf M, rowing (crew) W, soccer, softball W, swimming W, tennis W, track and field, volleyball W. **Team name:** Rams.

Student services. Adult student services, alcohol/substance abuse counseling, chaplain/spiritual director, career counseling, student employment services, financial aid counseling, health services, legal services, minority student services, on-campus daycare, personal counseling, placement for graduates, veterans' counselor, women's services. **Physically disabled:** Services for visually, speech, hearing impaired. **Learning disabled:** Comprehensive services available.

Contact. E-mail: admission@uri.edu
Phone: (401) 874-7000 Fax: (401) 874-5523
Cynthia Bonn, Dean of Admission, University of Rhode Island, 14 Upper College Road, Kingston, RI 02881-1322

South Carolina

Allen University

Columbia, South Carolina
www.allenuniversity.edu **CB code: 5006**

- Private 4-year university and liberal arts college affiliated with African Methodist Episcopal Church
- Residential campus in large city
- 727 degree-seeking undergraduates: 1% part-time, 54% women

General. Founded in 1870. Regionally accredited. **Degrees:** 45 bachelor's awarded. **ROTC:** Army. **Location:** 112 miles from Charleston, 72 miles from Charlotte, North Carolina. **Calendar:** Semester, limited summer session. **Full-time faculty:** 27 total; 59% have terminal degrees, 70% minority, 48% women. **Part-time faculty:** 24 total; 25% have terminal degrees, 83% minority, 71% women.

Freshman class profile.

GPA 3.75 or higher:	1%	**GPA 2.0-2.99:**	61%
GPA 3.50-3.74:	2%	**Return as sophomores:**	49%
GPA 3.0-3.49:	21%		

Basis for selection. Open admission. Applicants are reviewed by the admission committee. The decision is provided to the applicant in writing. Interview, campus visit recommended. **Homeschooled:** Statement describing homeschool structure and mission, transcript of courses and grades, state high school equivalency certificate, interview, letter of recommendation (nonparent) required.

High school preparation. College-preparatory program recommended. Recommended units include English 4, mathematics 4, social studies 3, history 3, science 3, foreign language 1 and computer science 1.

2008-2009 Annual costs. Tuition/fees: $9,884. Room/board: $5,240. Books/supplies: $800.

2008-2009 Financial aid. Non-need-based: Scholarships awarded for academics, athletics, music/drama, ROTC.

Application procedures. Admission: Priority date 6/30; deadline 7/31. No application fee. Admission notification on a rolling basis. Must reply by May 1 or within 2 week(s) if notified thereafter. **Financial aid:** Priority date 4/15, closing date 7/20. FAFSA required. Applicants notified on a rolling basis starting 4/1; must reply within 2 week(s) of notification.

Academics. Special study options: Cooperative education, honors, independent study, internships, teacher certification program, weekend college. Nontraditional program for returning students. **Credit/placement by examination:** CLEP, institutional tests. 3 credit hours maximum toward bachelor's degree. **Support services:** Learning center, pre-admission summer program, reduced course load, study skills assistance, tutoring, writing center.

Majors. Biology: General. **Business:** Business admin. **Math:** General. **Philosophy/religion:** Religion. **Physical sciences:** Chemistry. **Social sciences:** General.

Computing on campus. Dormitories linked to campus network. Commuter students can connect to campus network. Online course registration, online library, helpline, wireless network available.

Student life. Freshman orientation: Mandatory. Preregistration for classes offered. Week-long session. Students complete financial aid forms and receive dorm assignments. **Housing:** Guaranteed on-campus for freshmen. Single-sex dorms, apartments available. $50 nonrefundable deposit, deadline 7/31. **Activities:** Campus ministries, choral groups, dance, international student organizations, student government, social science club, NAACP.

Athletics. Intercollegiate: Basketball, cross-country M, track and field M, volleyball W. **Team name:** Yellow Jackets.

Student services. Adult student services, chaplain/spiritual director, career counseling, student employment services, financial aid counseling, health services, personal counseling, placement for graduates.

Contact. Phone: (803) 376-5735 Toll-free number: (877) 625-5368
Fax: (803) 758-2704
Donna Foster, Director of Admissions, Allen University, 1530 Harden Street, Columbia, SC 29204

Anderson University

Anderson, South Carolina **CB member**
www.andersonuniversity.edu **CB code: 5008**

- Private 4-year liberal arts and teachers college affiliated with Southern Baptist Convention
- Residential campus in large town
- 1,971 degree-seeking undergraduates: 24% part-time, 66% women
- 51 degree-seeking graduate students
- 78% of applicants admitted
- SAT or ACT (ACT writing optional) required
- 48% graduate within 6 years

General. Founded in 1911. Regionally accredited. **Degrees:** 243 bachelor's awarded; master's offered. **ROTC:** Army, Air Force. **Location:** 32 miles from Greenville, 100 miles from Atlanta. **Calendar:** Semester, limited summer session. **Full-time faculty:** 76 total; 66% have terminal degrees, 8% minority, 45% women. **Part-time faculty:** 75 total; 24% have terminal degrees, 4% minority, 45% women. **Class size:** 57% < 20, 42% 20-39, less than 1% 40-49, less than 1% 50-99. **Special facilities:** Fine arts center cultural program, on-campus audio recording studio, electronic classrooms.

Freshman class profile. 1,296 applied, 1,009 admitted, 394 enrolled.

Mid 50% test scores		**GPA 2.0-2.99:**	20%
SAT critical reading:	410-560	**Rank in top quarter:**	50%
SAT math:	460-560	**Rank in top tenth:**	28%
SAT writing:	450-570	**Return as sophomores:**	62%
ACT composite:	18-24	**Out-of-state:**	5%
GPA 3.75 or higher:	21%	**Live on campus:**	86%
GPA 3.50-3.74:	23%	**International:**	4%
GPA 3.0-3.49:	35%		

Basis for selection. High school achievement record, test scores important; recommendations considered. Minimum high school GPA of 2.5 and SAT (exclusive of Writing) combined score of 1000 preferred. Each applicant considered individually. Applicants not meeting these guidelines may be admitted into developmental studies program. Recommendations, further grades or interview may be required for academically weak applicants. Interview recommended for some; audition required for art, music, theater programs. **Learning Disabled:** Applicants with diagnosed learning disabilities must meet regular requirements and supply summary of recent (within 1 year of enrollment) diagnostic testing.

High school preparation. College-preparatory program recommended. 20 units required. Required and recommended units include English 4, mathematics 3-4, social studies 2, history 2, science 3-4 (laboratory 2), foreign language 2 and academic electives 4.

2008-2009 Annual costs. Tuition/fees: $18,700. Room/board: $7,300. Books/supplies: $1,650. Personal expenses: $2,450.

Financial aid. Non-need-based: Scholarships awarded for academics, alumni affiliation, art, athletics, leadership, minority status, music/drama, religious affiliation, state residency.

Application procedures. Admission: No deadline. $25 fee, may be waived for applicants with need. Admission notification on a rolling basis beginning on or about 9/1. **Financial aid:** Priority date 3/1, closing date 6/30. FAFSA required. Applicants notified on a rolling basis starting 3/15; must reply within 2 week(s) of notification.

Academics. Special study options: Accelerated study, cooperative education, distance learning, double major, dual enrollment of high school students, honors, independent study, internships, liberal arts/career combination, study abroad, teacher certification program, Washington semester. **Credit/placement by examination:** AP, CLEP, IB, institutional tests. 24 credit hours maximum toward bachelor's degree. **Support services:** Learning center, reduced course load, remedial instruction, study skills assistance, tutoring, writing center.

Majors. Biology: General. **Business:** General, business admin, finance, human resources, marketing, retailing. **Communications:** General. **Education:** Art, early childhood, elementary, English, history, mathematics, music, physical, special. **Foreign languages:** Spanish. **History:** General. **Math:** General. **Parks/recreation:** Exercise sciences. **Philosophy/religion:** Christian, religion. **Protective services:** Law enforcement admin. **Psychology:**

General. **Public administration:** Human services. **Theology:** Sacred music. **Visual/performing arts:** Art, dramatic, interior design, music performance. **Other:** Christian ministry, Pre-engineering.

Most popular majors. Business/marketing 34%, education 25%, visual/performing arts 16%.

Computing on campus. 130 workstations in library, computer center, student center. Dormitories wired for high-speed internet access and linked to campus network. Commuter students can connect to campus network. Online course registration, online library, helpline, wireless network available.

Student life. Freshman orientation: Mandatory. Preregistration for classes offered. 2 orientation sessions held during summer. **Housing:** Guaranteed on-campus for freshmen. Single-sex dorms, apartments, wellness housing available. $250 fully refundable deposit, deadline 5/1. **Activities:** Bands, campus ministries, choral groups, dance, drama, literary magazine, music ensembles, musical theater, student government, student newspaper, symphony orchestra, Gamma Beta Phi, campus activities board, Fellowship of Christian Athletes, Minorities for Change, student alumni council, Reformed University Fellowship, Young Life.

Athletics. NCAA. **Intercollegiate:** Baseball M, basketball, cheerleading M, cross-country, golf, soccer, softball W, tennis, track and field, volleyball W, wrestling M. **Intramural:** Basketball, football (non-tackle), racquetball, softball, table tennis, tennis, volleyball, weight lifting M. **Team name:** Trojans.

Student services. Adult student services, chaplain/spiritual director, career counseling, student employment services, financial aid counseling, health services, on-campus daycare, personal counseling, placement for graduates. **Physically disabled:** Services for visually impaired.

Contact. E-mail: admissions@andersonuniversity.edu
Phone: (864) 231-2030 Toll-free number: (800) 542-3594
Fax: (864) 231-2033
Pam Bryant, Director of Admissions, Anderson University, 316 Boulevard, Anderson, SC 29621-4002

Benedict College
Columbia, South Carolina — **CB member**
www.benedict.edu — **CB code: 5056**

- Private 4-year liberal arts college affiliated with American Baptist Churches in the USA
- Residential campus in very large city
- 2,883 degree-seeking undergraduates: 4% part-time, 50% women, 98% African American, 1% Hispanic American

General. Founded in 1870. Regionally accredited. Benedict College is a Historically Black Institution. **Degrees:** 342 bachelor's awarded. **ROTC:** Army, Air Force. **Location:** 110 miles from Greenville, 120 miles from Charleston. **Calendar:** Semester, limited summer session. **Full-time faculty:** 121 total; 63% have terminal degrees, 92% minority, 56% women. **Part-time faculty:** 34 total; 94% minority, 62% women. **Class size:** 49% < 20, 33% 20-39, 12% 40-49, 6% 50-99.

Freshman class profile. 4,907 applied, 4,907 admitted, 888 enrolled.

Mid 50% test scores		**GPA 2.0-2.99:**	51%
SAT critical reading:	320-430	**Rank in top quarter:**	15%
SAT math:	320-430	**Rank in top tenth:**	5%
ACT composite:	13-17	**Return as sophomores:**	59%
GPA 3.75 or higher:	4%	**Out-of-state:**	52%
GPA 3.50-3.74:	6%	**Live on campus:**	93%
GPA 3.0-3.49:	19%		

Basis for selection. Open admission.

High school preparation. College-preparatory program recommended. 20 units recommended. Recommended units include English 4, mathematics 3, social studies 3 and science 2.

2008-2009 Annual costs. Tuition/fees: $14,570. Room/board: $6,702. Books/supplies: $1,000. Personal expenses: $1,400.

Application procedures. Admission: No deadline. $25 fee. Admission notification on a rolling basis. **Financial aid:** Priority date 4/15; no closing date. FAFSA required. Applicants notified on a rolling basis starting 4/15.

Academics. Special study options: Accelerated study, double major, dual enrollment of high school students, external degree, honors, internships, teacher certification program, weekend college. **Credit/placement by examination:** AP, CLEP, institutional tests. 24 credit hours maximum toward bachelor's degree. **Support services:** Learning center, pre-admission summer program, reduced course load, remedial instruction, study skills assistance, tutoring, writing center.

Majors. Biology: General. **Business:** Accounting, business admin. **Computer sciences:** General, computer science. **Conservation:** Environmental science. **Education:** Early childhood, elementary. **Engineering technology:** Electrical. **Family/consumer sciences:** Family studies. **History:** General. **Math:** General. **Parks/recreation:** Health/fitness. **Physical sciences:** Chemistry, physics. **Public administration:** Social work. **Social sciences:** Economics, political science. **Visual/performing arts:** Art, multimedia.

Most popular majors. Biology 10%, business/marketing 20%, communications/journalism 7%, family/consumer sciences 9%, health sciences 9%, liberal arts 6%, psychology 6%, public administration/social services 6%, security/protective services 10%.

Computing on campus. 385 workstations in dormitories, library, computer center, student center. Dormitories wired for high-speed internet access and linked to campus network. Commuter students can connect to campus network. Online library, helpline, repair service, wireless network available.

Student life. Freshman orientation: Mandatory. Preregistration for classes offered. **Housing:** Guaranteed on-campus for freshmen. Single-sex dorms available. **Activities:** Bands, choral groups, dance, drama, music ensembles, radio station, student government, student newspaper, Gordon-Jenkins Theological Association.

Athletics. NAIA. **Intercollegiate:** Baseball M, basketball, cross-country, football (tackle) M, golf, soccer M, softball, tennis, track and field, volleyball W, wrestling M. **Intramural:** Baseball M, basketball, softball W, volleyball W. **Team name:** Tigers.

Student services. Adult student services, chaplain/spiritual director, career counseling, student employment services, financial aid counseling, health services, minority student services, on-campus daycare, personal counseling, placement for graduates, veterans' counselor.

Contact. E-mail: admissions@benedict.edu
Phone: (803) 705-4491 Toll-free number: (800) 868-6598
Fax: (803) 253-5167
Phyllis Thompson, Director of Admissions, Benedict College, 1600 Harden Street, Columbia, SC 29204

Bob Jones University
Greenville, South Carolina
www.bju.edu

- Private 4-year Bible and liberal arts college
- Small city

General. Regionally accredited. **Calendar:** Semester. **Full-time faculty:** 259 total. **Part-time faculty:** 75 total.

Freshman class profile. 1,051 enrolled.

Basis for selection. Open admission.

2008-2009 Annual costs. Tuition/fees: $11,425.

Academics. Credit/placement by examination: CLEP.

Majors. Business: Accounting. **Education:** Elementary. **Health:** Nursing (RN). **Liberal arts:** Humanities. **Theology:** Bible.

Contact. E-mail: admissions@bju.edu
Toll-free number: (800) 252-6363
Gary Deedrick, Director of Admissions, Bob Jones University, 1700 Wade Hampton Boulevard, Greenville, SC 29614

Charleston Southern University
Charleston, South Carolina
www.csuniv.edu — **CB code: 5079**

- Private 4-year university and liberal arts college affiliated with Southern Baptist Convention
- Commuter campus in large city
- 2,761 degree-seeking undergraduates
- 62% of applicants admitted
- SAT or ACT with writing required

General. Founded in 1964. Regionally accredited. **Degrees:** 437 bachelor's awarded; master's offered. **ROTC:** Air Force. **Location:** 15 miles from downtown. **Calendar:** 4-1-4. **Full-time faculty:** 126 total. **Part-time faculty:** 83 total. **Class size:** 46% < 20, 44% 20-39, 5% 40-49, 5% 50-99. **Special facilities:** Earthquake research center.

Freshman class profile. 2,986 applied, 1,839 admitted, 612 enrolled.

Mid 50% test scores			
SAT critical reading:	440-600	GPA 3.0-3.49:	31%
SAT math:	450-550	GPA 2.0-2.99:	27%
ACT composite:	18-22	Rank in top quarter:	52%
GPA 3.75 or higher:	25%	Rank in top tenth:	21%
GPA 3.50-3.74:	15%	Out-of-state:	23%
		Live on campus:	73%

Basis for selection. School achievement record, academic coursework, test scores, GPA most important. Interview and recommendations considered. Students may be required to take institutional math test for acceptance and/or placement. Essay, interview recommended for all; audition recommended for music programs. **Learning Disabled:** Special needs allowances require documentation and interview with Director of Special Needs.

High school preparation. 23 units required. Required and recommended units include English 4, mathematics 3-4, social studies 2, history 2, science 3 (laboratory 2) and foreign language 2.

2008-2009 Annual costs. Tuition/fees: $18,678. Room/board: $7,178. Books/supplies: $1,050.

2007-2008 Financial aid. **Non-need-based:** Scholarships awarded for academics, athletics, religious affiliation, ROTC.

Application procedures. **Admission:** No deadline. $40 fee, may be waived for applicants with need. Admission notification on a rolling basis beginning on or about 9/1. **Financial aid:** Priority date 4/15; no closing date. FAFSA required. Applicants notified on a rolling basis starting 3/1; must reply within 2 week(s) of notification.

Academics. **Special study options:** Accelerated study, combined bachelor's/graduate degree, cooperative education, cross-registration, distance learning, double major, dual enrollment of high school students, honors, internships, study abroad, teacher certification program. **Credit/placement by examination:** AP, CLEP, IB, SAT, ACT, institutional tests. 30 credit hours maximum toward associate degree, 30 toward bachelor's. **Support services:** Learning center, remedial instruction, study skills assistance, tutoring, writing center.

Majors. **Biology:** General, biochemistry. **Business:** Accounting, business admin, finance, management information systems, marketing. **Computer sciences:** Computer science. **Education:** Early childhood, elementary, English, mathematics, multi-level teacher, music, physical, science, social studies, Spanish. **Foreign languages:** Spanish. **Health:** Athletic training, music therapy, nursing (RN). **History:** General, American, European. **Liberal arts:** Humanities. **Math:** General, applied. **Parks/recreation:** Health/fitness. **Philosophy/religion:** Religion. **Physical sciences:** Chemistry. **Protective services:** Criminal justice. **Psychology:** General. **Social sciences:** General, economics, political science, sociology. **Theology:** Sacred music, youth ministry. **Visual/performing arts:** Music performance, voice/opera. **Other:** Biological and biomedical sciences, Business administration, management and operations, Dramatic/theatre arts and stagecraft, Science technologies/technicians.

Most popular majors. Biology 9%, business/marketing 23%, education 10%, health sciences 7%, psychology 10%, security/protective services 6%, social sciences 8%, visual/performing arts 6%.

Computing on campus. 150 workstations in dormitories, library, computer center, student center. Dormitories wired for high-speed internet access. Commuter students can connect to campus network. Online library, helpline, student web hosting, wireless network available.

Student life. **Freshman orientation:** Available. Preregistration for classes offered. **Policies:** Religious observance required. **Housing:** Guaranteed on-campus for freshmen. Single-sex dorms available. $200 fully refundable deposit, deadline 8/15. **Activities:** Bands, choral groups, dance, drama, international student organizations, literary magazine, music ensembles, musical theater, student government, student newspaper, College Republicans, Young Democrats, Afro-American society, Baptist Student Union, Fellowship of Christian Athletes, Campus Crusade, future teachers society.

Athletics. NCAA. **Intercollegiate:** Baseball M, basketball, cross-country, football (tackle) M, golf, soccer, softball W, tennis, track and field, volleyball W. **Intramural:** Basketball, soccer, softball, volleyball. **Team name:** Buccaneer.

Student services. Adult student services, chaplain/spiritual director, career counseling, student employment services, financial aid counseling, health services, personal counseling, placement for graduates, veterans' counselor. **Physically disabled:** Services for visually, speech, hearing impaired.

Contact. E-mail: enroll@csuniv.edu
Phone: (843) 863-7050 Toll-free number: (800) 947-7474
Fax: (843) 863-7070
Jim Rhoton, Director of Admissions, Charleston Southern University, 9200 University Boulevard, Charleston, SC 29423-8087

The Citadel

Charleston, South Carolina — **CB member**
www.citadel.edu — **CB code: 5108**

- Public 4-year military college
- Residential campus in large city
- 2,241 degree-seeking undergraduates: 3% part-time, 7% women, 7% African American, 3% Asian American, 4% Hispanic American, 1% Native American, 1% international
- 784 degree-seeking graduate students
- 75% of applicants admitted
- SAT or ACT with writing required
- 65% graduate within 6 years

General. Founded in 1842. Regionally accredited. **Degrees:** 467 bachelor's awarded; master's offered. **ROTC:** Army, Naval, Air Force. **Location:** 110 miles from Columbia; 120 miles from Savannah, Georgia. **Calendar:** Semester, extensive summer session. **Full-time faculty:** 173 total; 94% have terminal degrees, 12% minority, 28% women. **Part-time faculty:** 79 total; 37% have terminal degrees, 6% minority, 46% women. **Class size:** 43% < 20, 50% 20-39, 4% 40-49, 3% 50-99. **Special facilities:** Archives museum, beach house, boating center.

Freshman class profile. 2,024 applied, 1,521 admitted, 607 enrolled.

Mid 50% test scores		GPA 2.0-2.99:	24%
SAT critical reading:	500-590	Rank in top quarter:	34%
SAT math:	510-600	Rank in top tenth:	11%
ACT composite:	19-22	Return as sophomores:	84%
GPA 3.75 or higher:	23%	Out-of-state:	59%
GPA 3.50-3.74:	18%	Live on campus:	100%
GPA 3.0-3.49:	35%	International:	1%

Basis for selection. Admissions based on class rank, test scores, GPA, alumni recommendations, extracurricular activities. Interview recommended.

High school preparation. College-preparatory program required. 20 units required. Required and recommended units include English 4, mathematics 3-4, social studies 2, history 1, science 3 (laboratory 3), foreign language 2 and academic electives 4. One physical education or ROTC required.

2008-2009 Annual costs. Tuition/fees: $8,428; $21,031 out-of-state. Students in Corps of Cadets required to pay $1,089 in fees which include laundry and dry cleaning charges and infirmary fees. Freshmen also pay $5,630 deposit and upperclassmen pay $1,750 deposit for uniforms, books, and supplies. Room/board: $5,750.

2008-2009 Financial aid. **Need-based:** 475 full-time freshmen applied for aid; 339 were judged to have need; 327 of these received aid. Average need met was 71%. Average scholarship/grant was $15,220; average loan $3,453. 59% of total undergraduate aid awarded as scholarships/grants, 41% as loans/jobs. **Non-need-based:** Awarded to 769 full-time undergraduates, including 223 freshmen. Scholarships awarded for academics, athletics, leadership, ROTC, state residency.

Application procedures. **Admission:** No deadline. $40 fee, may be waived for applicants with need. Admission notification on a rolling basis beginning on or about 7/15. **Financial aid:** Priority date 2/28; no closing date. FAFSA required. Applicants notified on a rolling basis starting 4/1; must reply by 5/1 or within 2 week(s) of notification.

Academics. 4 years of ROTC required. **Special study options:** Cooperative education, double major, ESL, honors, independent study, internships, study abroad, teacher certification program. **Credit/placement by examination:** AP, CLEP, institutional tests. **Support services:** Learning center, preadmission summer program, study skills assistance, tutoring, writing center.

Majors. **Biology:** General. **Business:** Business admin. **Computer sciences:** General. **Education:** Physical, secondary. **Engineering:** Civil, electrical. **Foreign languages:** General. **History:** General. **Math:** General. **Physical sciences:** Chemistry, physics. **Protective services:** Law enforcement admin. **Psychology:** General. **Social sciences:** Political science.

Most popular majors. Business/marketing 32%, education 8%, engineering/engineering technologies 15%, history 8%, security/protective services 14%, social sciences 9%.

Computing on campus. 350 workstations in dormitories, library, computer center. Dormitories linked to campus network. Commuter students can connect to campus network. Online course registration, online library, helpline, repair service, wireless network available.

Student life. Freshman orientation: Mandatory. Preregistration for classes offered. **Housing:** Guaranteed on-campus for all undergraduates. Coed dorms available. **Activities:** Bands, campus ministries, choral groups, drama, literary magazine, music ensembles, student government, student newspaper, African American Society, American Society of Civil Engineers, Association for Computing Machinery, Alpha Phi Omega, Summerall Guards, African Methodist Episcopal, Baptist Student Union, Campus Crusade for Christ, Knights of Columbus, Army Aviator Association of America.

Athletics. NCAA. **Intercollegiate:** Baseball M, basketball M, cross-country, football (tackle) M, golf W, rifle, soccer W, tennis M, track and field, volleyball W, wrestling M. **Intramural:** Badminton, basketball, diving, football (non-tackle), handball, racquetball, rifle, soccer, softball, swimming, table tennis, tennis, track and field, triathlon, volleyball, water polo, weight lifting, wrestling. **Team name:** Bulldogs.

Student services. Alcohol/substance abuse counseling, chaplain/spiritual director, career counseling, student employment services, financial aid counseling, health services, minority student services, personal counseling, placement for graduates, veterans' counselor.

Contact. E-mail: admissions@citadel.edu
Phone: (843) 953-5230 Toll-free number: (800) 868-1842
Fax: (843) 953-7036
John Powell, Director of Admissions, The Citadel, 171 Moultrie Street, Charleston, SC 29409

Claflin University

Orangeburg, South Carolina — **CB member**
www.claflin.edu — **CB code: 5109**

- Private 4-year liberal arts college affiliated with United Methodist Church
- Residential campus in large town
- 1,657 degree-seeking undergraduates: 2% part-time, 68% women, 94% African American, 3% international
- 83 degree-seeking graduate students
- 36% of applicants admitted
- SAT or ACT (ACT writing optional) required
- 51% graduate within 6 years

General. Founded in 1869. Regionally accredited. **Degrees:** 273 bachelor's awarded; master's offered. **ROTC:** Army. **Location:** 45 miles from Columbia. **Calendar:** Semester, limited summer session. **Full-time faculty:** 104 total; 75% have terminal degrees, 71% minority, 44% women. **Part-time faculty:** 42 total. **Class size:** 53% < 20, 42% 20-39, 5% 40-49. **Special facilities:** Center for excellence in science and math, center for excellence in mass communication, nuclear magnetic resonance, leadership development center, museum, internet radio, biotechnology center.

Freshman class profile. 4,008 applied, 1,441 admitted, 465 enrolled.

Mid 50% test scores		**Rank in top quarter:**	51%
SAT critical reading:	410-500	**Rank in top tenth:**	11%
SAT math:	390-490	**Return as sophomores:**	68%
GPA 3.75 or higher:	15%	**Out-of-state:**	24%
GPA 3.50-3.74:	10%	**Live on campus:**	90%
GPA 3.0-3.49:	32%	**International:**	2%
GPA 2.0-2.99:	42%		

Basis for selection. School achievement record, test scores, recommendation of high school officials, personal background, experience, character traits, educational objectives important. Audition required; essay, interview, portfolio recommended.

High school preparation. 20 units required. Required units include English 4, mathematics 3, social studies 2, history 1, (laboratory 2) and academic electives 7. Physical education.

2008-2009 Annual costs. Tuition/fees: $12,768. Room/board: $6,806. Books/supplies: $1,200. Personal expenses: $1,600.

2008-2009 Financial aid. Need-based: 432 full-time freshmen applied for aid; 415 were judged to have need; 415 of these received aid. Average need met was 73%. Average scholarship/grant was $12,640; average loan $6,871. 57% of total undergraduate aid awarded as scholarships/grants, 43% as loans/jobs.

Application procedures. Admission: Closing date 8/1. $20 fee, may be waived for applicants with need. Admission notification on a rolling basis beginning on or about 10/1. **Financial aid:** Priority date 4/15; no closing date. FAFSA, institutional form required. Applicants notified on a rolling basis starting 5/15; must reply within 2 week(s) of notification.

Academics. Special study options: Accelerated study, combined bachelor's/graduate degree, cooperative education, cross-registration, double major, dual enrollment of high school students, honors, independent study, internships, liberal arts/career combination, study abroad, teacher certification program, weekend college. **Credit/placement by examination:** AP, CLEP, institutional tests. 18 credit hours maximum toward bachelor's degree. **Support services:** Learning center, pre-admission summer program, reduced course load, remedial instruction, tutoring, writing center.

Honors college/program. 30 to 35 students admitted annually based on academic achievement, leadership, and SAT scores.

Majors. Area/ethnic studies: African-American, American. **Biology:** General, biochemistry, bioinformatics, biotechnology. **Business:** Business admin, management information systems, marketing, organizational behavior. **Communications:** Media studies. **Computer sciences:** Computer science. **Conservation:** Environmental science. **Education:** Art, early childhood, elementary, English, mathematics, middle, music. **Engineering:** Software. **History:** General. **Math:** General. **Parks/recreation:** Health/fitness, sports admin. **Philosophy/religion:** Philosophy, religion. **Physical sciences:** Chemistry. **Protective services:** Law enforcement admin. **Social sciences:** Sociology. **Visual/performing arts:** Art, studio arts.

Most popular majors. Biology 8%, business/marketing 31%, communications/journalism 7%, security/protective services 16%, social sciences 19%.

Computing on campus. 500 workstations in dormitories, library, computer center, student center. Dormitories wired for high-speed internet access and linked to campus network. Commuter students can connect to campus network. Online course registration, online library, repair service, wireless network available.

Student life. Freshman orientation: Mandatory. Preregistration for classes offered. **Housing:** Guaranteed on-campus for freshmen. Single-sex dorms available. $50 deposit, deadline 4/15. **Activities:** Bands, drama, film society, literary magazine, music ensembles, radio station, student government, student newspaper, TV station, Alpha Kappa Mu, Oxford Club, literature, art and film society, Phi Beta Lambda, Esquire XIII, Students in Free Enterprise, NAACP.

Athletics. NCAA. **Intercollegiate:** Baseball M, basketball, cross-country, softball W, track and field, volleyball W. **Intramural:** Basketball, softball W, volleyball W. **Team name:** Panthers.

Student services. Adult student services, chaplain/spiritual director, career counseling, student employment services, financial aid counseling, health services, minority student services, personal counseling, placement for graduates, veterans' counselor.

Contact. E-mail: abrooks@claflin.edu
Phone: (803) 535-5404 Toll-free number: (800) 922-1276
Fax: (803) 535-5387
Anthony Brooks, Assistant Vice President for Enrollment Management, Claflin University, 400 Magnolia Street, Orangeburg, SC 29115

Clemson University

Clemson, South Carolina — **CB member**
www.clemson.edu — **CB code: 5111**

- Public 4-year university and agricultural college
- Residential campus in large town
- 14,624 degree-seeking undergraduates: 6% part-time, 46% women
- 3,177 degree-seeking graduate students
- 54% of applicants admitted
- SAT or ACT with writing required
- 79% graduate within 6 years

General. Founded in 1889. Regionally accredited. **Degrees:** 3,075 bachelor's awarded; master's, doctoral offered. **ROTC:** Army, Air Force. **Location:** 17 miles from Anderson. **Calendar:** Semester, extensive summer session. **Full-time faculty:** 1,106 total; 85% have terminal degrees, 15% minority, 34% women. **Part-time faculty:** 171 total; 50% have terminal degrees, 7% minority, 39% women. **Class size:** 49% < 20, 32% 20-39, 8% 40-49, 8% 50-99, 3% >100. **Special facilities:** Planetarium, agricultural and forestry experimental facilities, geology museum, state botanical gardens, center for sustainable living, John C. Calhoun historical site and home, performing arts center.

Freshman class profile. 15,542 applied, 8,355 admitted, 2,927 enrolled.

Mid 50% test scores		Rank in top quarter:	81%
SAT critical reading:	550-640	Rank in top tenth:	50%
SAT math:	590-680	Return as sophomores:	92%
ACT composite:	25-30	Out-of-state:	35%
GPA 3.75 or higher:	79%	Live on campus:	98%
GPA 3.50-3.74:	10%	Fraternities:	14%
GPA 3.0-3.49:	10%	Sororities:	27%
GPA 2.0-2.99:	1%		

Basis for selection. Admission competitive and based largely on high school curriculum, performance in that curriculum, peer comparison, SAT or ACT scores, and choice of major. Campus visit recommended for all. Interview, portfolio recommended for architecture and for art applicants. Audition required for performing arts program. **Homeschooled:** Include copies of all secondary school transcripts and course descriptions of any courses different from those traditionally offered in public school settings.

High school preparation. College-preparatory program required. 19 units required. Required and recommended units include English 4, mathematics 3-4, social studies 3-4, history 1-2, science 3 (laboratory 3-4), foreign language 3-4 and academic electives 2. Also require physical education or ROTC. 3 foreign language units must be in same language.

2008-2009 Annual costs. Tuition/fees: $11,108; $24,130 out-of-state. Laptop computer required of all entering new students. This cost has been estimated at $1600. Room/board: $6,556. Books/supplies: $900. Personal expenses: $1,920.

2007-2008 Financial aid. Need-based: 1,800 full-time freshmen applied for aid; 1,240 were judged to have need; 1,213 of these received aid. Average need met was 74%. Average scholarship/grant was $4,416; average loan $3,696. 40% of total undergraduate aid awarded as scholarships/grants, 60% as loans/jobs. **Non-need-based:** Awarded to 6,035 full-time undergraduates, including 1,803 freshmen. Scholarships awarded for academics, art, athletics, leadership, minority status, music/drama, ROTC, state residency.

Application procedures. Admission: Priority date 12/1; deadline 5/1 (postmark date). $60 fee, may be waived for applicants with need. Admission notification on a rolling basis beginning on or about 2/15. Must reply by 5/1. Scholarship candidates notified on rolling basis, beginning on or about October 1 for fall admission. Preferred application date of December 1. Those who apply by that date, and whose application file is complete, will receive an admission decision on or about February 15. **Financial aid:** Priority date 4/1; no closing date. FAFSA required. Applicants notified on a rolling basis starting 4/1; must reply within 3 week(s) of notification.

Academics. Special study options: Combined bachelor's/graduate degree, cooperative education, distance learning, double major, dual enrollment of high school students, exchange student, honors, independent study, internships, study abroad, teacher certification program, Washington semester. **Credit/placement by examination:** AP, CLEP, IB, institutional tests. Challenge examinations offered by each academic department. **Support services:** Learning center, pre-admission summer program, study skills assistance, tutoring, writing center.

Honors college/program. Less than 10 percent of freshman class invited to enroll. Minimum peer comparison must show student in top 3 percent of graduating secondary school class.

Majors. Agriculture: Agronomy, animal sciences, aquaculture, business, economics, food science, horticultural science, horticulture, plant sciences. **Architecture:** Architecture, landscape. **Biology:** General, biochemistry, biomedical sciences, botany, entomology, genetics, microbiology, plant pathology, zoology. **Business:** General, accounting, construction management, finance, marketing, operations. **Computer sciences:** General, information systems. **Conservation:** General, forest management, forest sciences. **Education:** Agricultural, early childhood, elementary, mathematics, middle, science, secondary, special, technology/industrial arts. **Engineering:** Agricultural, biomedical, ceramic, chemical, civil, computer, electrical, industrial, mechanical. **Foreign languages:** General, Spanish. **Health:** Clinical lab science, nursing (RN), predental, premedicine, prepharmacy, preveterinary. **History:** General. **Interdisciplinary:** Nutrition sciences. **Math:** General. **Parks/recreation:** Facilities management. **Philosophy/religion:** Philosophy. **Physical sciences:** Chemistry, geology, physics. **Psychology:** General. **Social sciences:** Economics, political science, sociology. **Visual/performing arts:** Art, industrial design.

Most popular majors. Biology 6%, business/marketing 22%, education 9%, engineering/engineering technologies 13%, health sciences 7%, social sciences 9%.

Computing on campus. PC or laptop required. 875 workstations in library, computer center. Dormitories wired for high-speed internet access and linked to campus network. Commuter students can connect to campus network. Online course registration, online library, helpline, repair service, student web hosting, wireless network available.

Student life. Freshman orientation: Mandatory, $55 fee. Preregistration for classes offered. One and 1/2-day sessions held 8 times during June and July. Students must complete online mathematics placement exam prior to participating in orientation. **Policies:** All students required to submit proof of legal presence in the United States. **Housing:** Guaranteed on-campus for all undergraduates. Coed dorms, single-sex dorms, special housing for disabled, apartments, fraternity/sorority housing, wellness housing available. $50 nonrefundable deposit. Housing guaranteed so long as continuing in on-campus housing. **Activities:** Bands, choral groups, dance, drama, international student organizations, literary magazine, music ensembles, musical theater, radio station, student government, student newspaper, symphony orchestra, TV station, religious organizations, Young Democrats, Young Republicans, minority awareness organizations, Blue Key, Alpha Phi Omega, Mortarboard, Hillel, Fellowship of Christian Athletes.

Athletics. NCAA. **Intercollegiate:** Baseball M, basketball, cross-country, diving, football (tackle) M, golf M, rowing (crew) W, soccer, swimming, tennis, track and field, volleyball W. **Intramural:** Basketball, diving, fencing, field hockey W, football (non-tackle), golf, racquetball, soccer, softball, table tennis, tennis, track and field, volleyball. **Team name:** Tigers.

Student services. Alcohol/substance abuse counseling, chaplain/spiritual director, career counseling, student employment services, financial aid counseling, health services, minority student services, personal counseling, placement for graduates, veterans' counselor. **Physically disabled:** Services for visually, speech, hearing impaired.

Contact. E-mail: cuadmissions@clemson.edu
Phone: (864) 656-2287 Fax: (864) 656-2464
Robert Barkley, Director of Admissions, Clemson University, 105 Sikes Hall, Clemson, SC 29634-5124

Coastal Carolina University

Conway, South Carolina — **CB member**
www.coastal.edu — **CB code: 5837**

- Public 4-year university
- Commuter campus in small city
- 7,322 degree-seeking undergraduates: 6% part-time, 53% women, 13% African American, 1% Asian American, 2% Hispanic American, 1% Native American, 1% international
- 231 degree-seeking graduate students
- 69% of applicants admitted
- SAT or ACT (ACT writing optional) required
- 46% graduate within 6 years

General. Founded in 1954. Regionally accredited. Barrier-reef island used for marine science field studies and research. **Degrees:** 1,076 bachelor's awarded; master's offered. **ROTC:** Army. **Location:** 9 miles from Myrtle Beach. **Calendar:** Semester, extensive summer session. **Full-time faculty:** 299 total; 79% have terminal degrees, 10% minority, 42% women. **Part-time faculty:** 262 total; 28% have terminal degrees, 10% minority, 58% women. **Class size:** 32% < 20, 52% 20-39, 11% 40-49, 5% 50-99, less than 1% >100.

Freshman class profile. 7,514 applied, 5,215 admitted, 1,655 enrolled.

Mid 50% test scores		Rank in top quarter:	34%
SAT critical reading:	460-540	Rank in top tenth:	9%
SAT math:	480-560	End year in good standing:	75%
ACT composite:	20-23	Return as sophomores:	71%
GPA 3.75 or higher:	24%	Out-of-state:	54%
GPA 3.50-3.74:	17%	Live on campus:	85%
GPA 3.0-3.49:	32%	Fraternities:	6%
GPA 2.0-2.99:	27%	Sororities:	5%

Basis for selection. Secondary school record and test scores most important; class rank important. Applicants whose native language is not English must take TOEFL. Tests are not required for applicants 22 years or older. Interview recommended for all. **Homeschooled:** Transcript of courses and grades required. Copy of declaration of intent to home school as filed with local board of education. **Learning Disabled:** To become eligible for support services, students with disabilities must provide documentation of disability to Service for Students with Disabilities Office.

High school preparation. College-preparatory program required. 20 units required. Required and recommended units include English 4, mathematics 3-4, social studies 2, history 1, science 3 (laboratory 3), foreign language 2, computer science 1, visual/performing arts 1 and academic electives 4. 1 unit of physical education or ROTC.

2008-2009 Annual costs. Tuition/fees: $8,650; $18,090 out-of-state. Room/board: $7,080.

2007-2008 Financial aid. Need-based: 1,382 full-time freshmen applied for aid; 1,006 were judged to have need; 984 of these received aid. Average need met was 53%. Average scholarship/grant was $4,016; average loan $6,861. 34% of total undergraduate aid awarded as scholarships/grants, 66% as loans/jobs. **Non-need-based:** Awarded to 2,745 full-time undergraduates, including 936 freshmen. Scholarships awarded for academics, art, athletics, leadership, music/drama, state residency.

Application procedures. Admission: Closing date 8/15. $45 fee, may be waived for applicants with need. Admission notification on a rolling basis beginning on or about 9/15. Must reply by May 1 or within 2 week(s) if notified thereafter. **Financial aid:** Priority date 3/1; no closing date. FAFSA required. Applicants notified on a rolling basis starting 3/1; must reply by 5/15.

Academics. Professional golf management option in marketing program, accredited by PGA. PGM and international tourism management options in management program. CPA/CMA option in accounting. **Special study options:** Accelerated study, combined bachelor's/graduate degree, cooperative education, distance learning, double major, dual enrollment of high school students, honors, independent study, internships, liberal arts/career combination, student-designed major, study abroad, teacher certification program. 3-2 engineering program with Clemson University. **Credit/placement by examination:** AP, CLEP, IB, SAT, institutional tests. Credit by examination must be obtained prior to reaching senior classification (90 credit hours). Will not be awarded for courses previously audited, or courses that have been previously failed. Cannot be used to raise a grade previously earned in a college course. **Support services:** Learning center, reduced course load, tutoring, writing center.

Majors. Biology: General. **Business:** Accounting, business admin, finance, managerial economics, marketing, resort management. **Communications:** General. **Computer sciences:** General. **Education:** Early childhood, elementary, middle, physical, special. **Foreign languages:** Spanish. **Health:** Public health ed. **History:** General. **Liberal arts:** Arts/sciences. **Math:** Applied. **Parks/recreation:** Exercise sciences, sports admin. **Philosophy/religion:** Philosophy. **Physical sciences:** Chemistry, physics. **Psychology:** General. **Social sciences:** Political science, sociology. **Visual/performing arts:** Dramatic, studio arts.

Most popular majors. Biology 11%, business/marketing 32%, education 12%, health sciences 6%, psychology 6%, social sciences 7%.

Computing on campus. 600 workstations in dormitories, library, computer center, student center. Dormitories wired for high-speed internet access and linked to campus network. Commuter students can connect to campus network. Online course registration, online library, helpline, student web hosting, wireless network available.

Student life. Freshman orientation: Mandatory, $90 fee. Preregistration for classes offered. 2-day programs. **Housing:** Coed dorms, special housing for disabled available. $150 partly refundable deposit, deadline 8/15. **Activities:** Bands, campus ministries, choral groups, dance, drama, international student organizations, literary magazine, music ensembles, musical theater, student government, student newspaper, Reformed University Fellowship, African American association, gospel choir, Society for Advancement of Management, Students Taking Active Responsibility, physical education club.

Athletics. NCAA. **Intercollegiate:** Baseball M, basketball, cheerleading, cross-country, football (tackle) M, golf, soccer, softball W, tennis, track and field, volleyball W. **Intramural:** Basketball, football (non-tackle), soccer, softball, volleyball, water polo. **Team name:** Chanticleers.

Student services. Adult student services, alcohol/substance abuse counseling, career counseling, student employment services, financial aid counseling, health services, minority student services, personal counseling, placement for graduates, veterans' counselor, women's services. **Physically disabled:** Services for visually, speech, hearing impaired.

Contact. E-mail: admissions@coastal.edu
Phone: (843) 349-2026 Toll-free number: (800) 277-7000
Fax: (843) 349-2127
Judy Vogt, Vice President for Enrollment Services, Coastal Carolina University, PO Box 261954, Conway, SC 29528-6054

Coker College

Hartsville, South Carolina — **CB member**
www.coker.edu — **CB code: 5112**

- Private 4-year liberal arts college
- Residential campus in large town

General. Founded in 1908. Regionally accredited. **Location:** 70 miles from Columbia, 80 miles from Charlotte, North Carolina. **Calendar:** Semester.

Annual costs/financial aid. Tuition/fees (2008-2009): $19,272. Room/board: $6,008. Books/supplies: $1,200. Personal expenses: $1,000. Need-based financial aid available to full-time and part-time students.

Contact. Phone: (843) 383-8050
Director of Admissions, 300 East College Avenue, Hartsville, SC 29550

College of Charleston

Charleston, South Carolina — **CB member**
www.cofc.edu — **CB code: 5113**

- Public 4-year liberal arts college
- Residential campus in large city
- 9,415 degree-seeking undergraduates: 5% part-time, 64% women, 5% African American, 2% Asian American, 2% Hispanic American, 1% international
- 498 degree-seeking graduate students
- 64% of applicants admitted
- SAT or ACT (ACT writing optional), application essay required
- 64% graduate within 6 years

General. Founded in 1770. Regionally accredited. **Degrees:** 2,287 bachelor's awarded; master's offered. **ROTC:** Air Force. **Calendar:** Semester, limited summer session. **Full-time faculty:** 523 total; 87% have terminal degrees, 10% minority, 43% women. **Part-time faculty:** 375 total; 33% have terminal degrees, 8% minority, 59% women. **Class size:** 34% < 20, 59% 20-39, 4% 40-49, 3% 50-99, less than 1% >100. **Special facilities:** Communications museum, early childhood development center, observatory, marine science laboratory, sculpture studio, sailing center, African-American history and culture research center, bilingual legal interpreting center, media and technology studio, center for entrepreneurship.

Freshman class profile. 9,964 applied, 6,401 admitted, 1,956 enrolled.

Mid 50% test scores		**GPA 2.0-2.99:**	1%
SAT critical reading:	570-650	**Rank in top quarter:**	62%
SAT math:	570-650	**Rank in top tenth:**	26%
ACT composite:	23-26	**Return as sophomores:**	80%
GPA 3.75 or higher:	56%	**Out-of-state:**	43%
GPA 3.50-3.74:	20%	**Live on campus:**	92%
GPA 3.0-3.49:	23%		

Basis for selection. School grades, class rank, curriculum most important, then test scores. Recommendations and activities helpful in borderline cases. Personal essay optional. Writing portion of ACT required only if student does not also submit SAT (with mandatory Writing component). Interview recommended for all. **Homeschooled:** Students should indicate which school district syllabus was followed during home schooling.

High school preparation. College-preparatory program required. 20 units required. Required and recommended units include English 4, mathematics 3-4, social studies 3, history 2, science 3-4 (laboratory 3), foreign language 3 and academic electives 4. Mathematics requirement includes 2 algebra. Social science recommendation .5 economics and .5 government. 2 units of same foreign language, 1 additional unit of advanced mathematics, computer science, world history, world geography, or Western civilization required.

2008-2009 Annual costs. Tuition/fees: $8,400; $20,418 out-of-state. Room/board: $8,999. Books/supplies: $1,123. Personal expenses: $1,573.

2007-2008 Financial aid. Need-based: 1,257 full-time freshmen applied for aid; 829 were judged to have need; 796 of these received aid. Average need met was 65%. Average scholarship/grant was $2,815; average loan $3,424. 44% of total undergraduate aid awarded as scholarships/grants, 56% as loans/jobs. **Non-need-based:** Awarded to 2,817 full-time undergraduates, including 888 freshmen. Scholarships awarded for academics, alumni affiliation, art, athletics, music/drama.

Application procedures. Admission: Priority date 11/1; deadline 4/1. $50 fee, may be waived for applicants with need. Notification sent by mid April. Must reply by 5/1. March 1 application date recommended for residence hall students. Admissions deposit refundable until May 1 for fall semester, December 1 for spring semester. Written notice required. **Financial aid:** Priority date 3/15; no closing date. FAFSA required. Applicants notified on a rolling basis starting 4/10; must reply within 8 week(s) of notification.

Academics. Special study options: Accelerated study, combined bachelor's/graduate degree, cooperative education, cross-registration, double major, dual enrollment of high school students, ESL, exchange student, honors, independent study, internships, liberal arts/career combination, semester at sea, study abroad, teacher certification program. Internships and courses in conjunction with Spoleto US (international arts festival); 3-2 engineering program with Case Western Reserve University, Clemson University, University of South Carolina; marine engineering option with University of Michigan. **Credit/placement by examination:** AP, CLEP, IB, SAT, institutional tests. 30 credit hours maximum toward bachelor's degree. **Support services:** Learning center, pre-admission summer program, reduced course load, study skills assistance, tutoring, writing center.

Majors. **Area/ethnic studies:** Latin American. **Biology:** General, biochemistry, marine. **Business:** Accounting, business admin, hospitality admin, international. **Communications:** General. **Computer sciences:** General, information systems. **Education:** Early childhood, elementary, middle, physical, special. **Foreign languages:** Classics, French, German, Spanish. **Health:** Athletic training, predental, premedicine. **History:** General. **Interdisciplinary:** Historic preservation. **Math:** General. **Philosophy/religion:** Philosophy, religion. **Physical sciences:** Astronomy, astrophysics, chemistry, geology, physics. **Psychology:** General. **Social sciences:** Anthropology, economics, political science, sociology, urban studies. **Visual/performing arts:** Art history/conservation, arts management, dramatic, studio arts. **Other:** Discovery informatics.

Most popular majors. Biology 8%, business/marketing 22%, communications/journalism 12%, education 8%, psychology 8%, social sciences 12%, visual/performing arts 9%.

Computing on campus. 2,500 workstations in dormitories, library, computer center, student center. Dormitories wired for high-speed internet access and linked to campus network. Commuter students can connect to campus network. Online course registration, helpline, wireless network available.

Student life. **Freshman orientation:** Mandatory. Preregistration for classes offered. **Housing:** Coed dorms, single-sex dorms, fraternity/sorority housing available. $200 fully refundable deposit, deadline 5/1. Restored old Charleston houses used as residence halls, some with kitchen facilities in suite. **Activities:** Bands, campus ministries, choral groups, dance, drama, international student organizations, literary magazine, music ensembles, musical theater, radio station, student government, student newspaper, symphony orchestra, over 100 organizations available.

Athletics. NCAA. **Intercollegiate:** Baseball M, basketball, cross-country, diving, equestrian W, golf, sailing, soccer, softball W, swimming, tennis, track and field W, volleyball W. **Intramural:** Badminton, basketball, equestrian W, fencing, football (tackle), racquetball, rowing (crew), rugby W, soccer, softball, tennis, volleyball, weight lifting. **Team name:** Cougars.

Student services. Adult student services, alcohol/substance abuse counseling, chaplain/spiritual director, career counseling, student employment services, financial aid counseling, health services, legal services, minority student services, on-campus daycare, personal counseling, placement for graduates, veterans' counselor. **Physically disabled:** Services for visually, speech, hearing impaired.

Contact. E-mail: admissions@cofc.edu
Phone: (843) 953-5670 Fax: (843) 953-6322
Suzette Stille, Director of Admission, College of Charleston, Office of Admissions and Adult Student Services, Charleston, SC 29424-0001

Columbia College

Columbia, South Carolina — **CB member**
www.columbiacollegesc.edu — **CB code: 5117**

- Private 4-year liberal arts college for women affiliated with United Methodist Church
- Residential campus in large city
- 1,225 degree-seeking undergraduates: 21% part-time, 97% women, 44% African American, 2% Asian American, 2% Hispanic American, 1% Native American
- 213 degree-seeking graduate students
- 76% of applicants admitted
- SAT or ACT with writing required
- 47% graduate within 6 years

General. Founded in 1854. Regionally accredited. **Degrees:** 221 bachelor's awarded; master's offered. **ROTC:** Army. **Location:** 70 miles from Charlotte, North Carolina. **Calendar:** Semester, limited summer session. **Full-time faculty:** 87 total; 75% have terminal degrees, 12% minority, 68% women. **Part-time faculty:** 76 total; 26% have terminal degrees, 14% minority, 67% women. **Class size:** 81% < 20, 19% 20-39, less than 1% 40-49. **Special facilities:** Leadership center for women.

Freshman class profile. 1,078 applied, 822 admitted, 280 enrolled.

Mid 50% test scores		**GPA 2.0-2.99:**	16%
SAT critical reading:	450-570	**Rank in top quarter:**	45%
SAT math:	450-550	**Rank in top tenth:**	19%
SAT writing:	440-560	**End year in good standing:**	65%
ACT composite:	18-24	**Return as sophomores:**	62%
GPA 3.75 or higher:	38%	**Out-of-state:**	12%
GPA 3.50-3.74:	13%	**Live on campus:**	87%
GPA 3.0-3.49:	33%		

Basis for selection. School record, test scores, recommendations most important. Audition recommended for dance, music programs; portfolio recommended for art programs; essay, interview recommended for borderline applicants.

High school preparation. 16 units recommended. Recommended units include English 4, mathematics 3, social studies 2, history 1, science 2 (laboratory 2), foreign language 2 and academic electives 2. 2.5 units in music, dance, art also recommended.

2008-2009 Annual costs. Tuition/fees: $23,030. Room/board: $6,450. Books/supplies: $800. Personal expenses: $2,750.

2007-2008 Financial aid. **Non-need-based:** Scholarships awarded for academics, alumni affiliation, art, athletics, leadership, music/drama.

Application procedures. **Admission:** No deadline. $25 fee, may be waived for applicants with need, free for online applicants. Admission notification on a rolling basis beginning on or about 10/1. Must reply by May 1 or within 4 week(s) if notified thereafter. **Financial aid:** Priority date 4/1; no closing date. FAFSA required. Applicants notified on a rolling basis starting 3/15; must reply within 2 week(s) of notification.

Academics. **Special study options:** Double major, dual enrollment of high school students, exchange student, honors, independent study, internships, student-designed major, study abroad, teacher certification program, Washington semester. **Credit/placement by examination:** AP, CLEP, IB, SAT, ACT, institutional tests. **Support services:** Learning center, reduced course load, remedial instruction, study skills assistance, tutoring, writing center.

Majors. **Biology:** General. **Business:** Accounting, business admin. **Communications:** General, journalism. **Computer sciences:** General. **Education:** Drama/dance, early childhood, elementary, middle, music, special. **Family/consumer sciences:** Family studies. **Foreign languages:** French, Spanish. **Health:** Speech pathology. **History:** General. **Liberal arts:** Arts/sciences. **Math:** General. **Philosophy/religion:** Religion. **Physical sciences:** Chemistry. **Psychology:** General. **Public administration:** Social work. **Social sciences:** General, political science. **Theology:** Religious ed. **Visual/performing arts:** Art, dance, music performance, piano/organ, studio arts, voice/opera.

Most popular majors. Business/marketing 15%, communications/journalism 6%, education 18%, English 9%, family/consumer sciences 6%, health sciences 6%, psychology 6%, public administration/social services 8%, visual/performing arts 6%.

Computing on campus. 165 workstations in dormitories, library, computer center, student center. Dormitories wired for high-speed internet access and linked to campus network. Online course registration, online library, helpline, repair service, wireless network available.

Student life. **Freshman orientation:** Available, $150 fee. Preregistration for classes offered. One-day program in June. 4-day program in August where students participate in community service project. **Policies:** All students required to live on campus during first 2 years unless living with parent or guardian. All residence halls nonsmoking. Chapel requirements in place for first-year, sophomore, and junior students. Religious observance required. **Housing:** Guaranteed on-campus for freshmen. Wellness housing available. $100 deposit, deadline 5/1. **Activities:** Concert band, choral groups, dance, drama, international student organizations, literary magazine, music ensembles, musical theater, student government, student newspaper, Young Republicans, Young Democrats, CC Serves, Sister to Sista, African-American student association, NAACP.

Athletics. NAIA. **Intercollegiate:** Basketball W, soccer W, softball W, tennis W, volleyball W. **Team name:** Koalas.

Student services. Adult student services, chaplain/spiritual director, career counseling, student employment services, financial aid counseling, health services, personal counseling, placement for graduates, veterans' counselor.

Contact. E-mail: admissions@colacoll.edu
Phone: (803) 786-3871 Toll-free number: (800) 277-1301
Fax: (803) 786-3674
Ron White, Vice President of Enrollment Management, Columbia College, 1301 Columbia College Drive, Columbia, SC 29203

Columbia International University

Columbia, South Carolina
www.ciu.edu **CB code: 5116**

- Private 4-year university and Bible college affiliated with multidenominational/evangelical churches
- Residential campus in small city
- 455 degree-seeking undergraduates
- 85% of applicants admitted
- SAT or ACT (ACT writing optional), application essay required

General. Founded in 1923. Regionally accredited; also accredited by ABHE, ATS. **Degrees:** 118 bachelor's awarded; master's, doctoral, first professional offered. **Location:** 75 miles from Charlotte, North Carolina, 225 miles from Atlanta. **Calendar:** Semester, limited summer session. **Full-time faculty:** 25 total. **Part-time faculty:** 26 total. **Class size:** 76% < 20, 15% 20-39, 2% 40-49, 4% 50-99, 3% >100. **Special facilities:** Prayer towers.

Freshman class profile. 216 applied, 183 admitted, 85 enrolled.

Mid 50% test scores			
SAT critical reading:	510-620	GPA 3.0-3.49:	20%
SAT math:	480-600	GPA 2.0-2.99:	19%
ACT composite:	20-25	Rank in top quarter:	47%
GPA 3.75 or higher:	47%	Rank in top tenth:	23%
GPA 3.50-3.74:	10%	Out-of-state:	50%
		Live on campus:	84%

Basis for selection. School achievement, recommendations, test scores, essay, school and community activities, religious commitment important. Audition required for church music program. **Homeschooled:** Transcripts should include GPA.

High school preparation. Recommended units include English 4, mathematics 2, social studies 2, science 1 and foreign language 2. Thorough background in English grammar and composition required.

2008-2009 Annual costs. Tuition/fees: $16,270. Room/board: $5,800. Books/supplies: $700. Personal expenses: $2,000.

2008-2009 Financial aid. Non-need-based: Scholarships awarded for academics, leadership, state residency. **Additional information:** Spouse scholarship program; special short quarter scholarships for missionaries on furlough.

Application procedures. Admission: Priority date 5/1; deadline 8/1 (postmark date). $45 fee, may be waived for applicants with need. Admission notification on a rolling basis. **Financial aid:** Priority date 1/31; no closing date. FAFSA, institutional form required. Applicants notified on a rolling basis starting 12/18; must reply within 4 week(s) of notification.

Academics. Special study options: Combined bachelor's/graduate degree, cross-registration, distance learning, double major, independent study, internships, liberal arts/career combination, study abroad, teacher certification program. **Credit/placement by examination:** AP, CLEP, IB. 15 credit hours maximum toward associate degree, 30 toward bachelor's. **Support services:** Learning center, reduced course load, remedial instruction, study skills assistance, tutoring.

Majors. Area/ethnic studies: Near/Middle Eastern. **Business:** Nonprofit/public. **Communications:** General. **Education:** Multi-level teacher. **Foreign languages:** Biblical. **Interdisciplinary:** Intercultural. **Liberal arts:** Humanities. **Psychology:** General. **Theology:** Bible, pastoral counseling, religious ed, sacred music, youth ministry.

Most popular majors. Communications/journalism 9%, education 6%, interdisciplinary studies 12%, liberal arts 27%, psychology 14%, theological studies 24%.

Computing on campus. 46 workstations in library, computer center. Dormitories wired for high-speed internet access and linked to campus network. Online course registration, online library, helpline, repair service available.

Student life. Freshman orientation: Mandatory, $40 fee. Preregistration for classes offered. 3 sessions held prior to start of fall semester; 1 session held 3 days prior to start of spring semester. **Policies:** Standards of Christian living are outlined in the Biblical Standards Handbook. Religious observance required. **Housing:** Guaranteed on-campus for all undergraduates. Single-sex dorms available. $100 partly refundable deposit. Mobile home park available for married students. **Activities:** Concert band, choral groups, drama, music ensembles, radio station, student government, student newspaper, symphony orchestra, student missions connection, African-American Fellowship, student senate, student union, grad life council.

Athletics. Intramural: Basketball, football (non-tackle), soccer M, softball, table tennis, volleyball.

Student services. Chaplain/spiritual director, career counseling, student employment services, financial aid counseling, health services, personal counseling, placement for graduates, veterans' counselor. **Physically disabled:** Services for visually, hearing impaired. **Learning disabled:** Comprehensive services available.

Contact. E-mail: yesciu@ciu.edu
Phone: (803) 754-4100 ext. 5024 Toll-free number: (800) 777-2227
Fax: (803) 786-4209
Michelle MacGregor, Director of Admissions, Columbia International University, PO Box 3122, Columbia, SC 29230-3122

Converse College

Spartanburg, South Carolina **CB member**
www.converse.edu **CB code: 5121**

- Private 4-year music and liberal arts college for women
- Residential campus in small city
- 725 degree-seeking undergraduates: 12% part-time, 100% women, 14% African American, 2% Asian American, 3% Hispanic American, 2% international
- 1,333 degree-seeking graduate students
- 62% of applicants admitted
- SAT or ACT (ACT writing optional), application essay required
- 65% graduate within 6 years; 27% enter graduate study

General. Founded in 1889. Regionally accredited. Men admitted to graduate programs. **Degrees:** 192 bachelor's awarded; master's offered. **ROTC:** Army. **Location:** 25 miles from Greenville, 70 miles from Charlotte, North Carolina. **Calendar:** 4-1-4, limited summer session. **Full-time faculty:** 87 total; 88% have terminal degrees, 7% minority, 53% women. **Part-time faculty:** 5 total; 40% minority, 60% women. **Class size:** 88% < 20, 12% 20-39. **Special facilities:** Science facility, music library, music and performing arts auditorium.

Freshman class profile. 1,153 applied, 717 admitted, 190 enrolled.

Mid 50% test scores			
SAT critical reading:	510-610	GPA 2.0-2.99:	5%
SAT math:	480-590	Rank in top quarter:	60%
ACT composite:	20-26	Rank in top tenth:	22%
GPA 3.75 or higher:	62%	Return as sophomores:	76%
GPA 3.50-3.74:	17%	Out-of-state:	44%
GPA 3.0-3.49:	16%	Live on campus:	90%
		International:	1%

Basis for selection. School record, class rank, test scores, extracurricular activities, school recommendation considered. Interview recommended for all; audition required for music programs. **Homeschooled:** Statement describing homeschool structure and mission, interview, letter of recommendation (nonparent) required.

High school preparation. College-preparatory program recommended. 24 units recommended. Recommended units include English 4, mathematics 3, social studies 2, history 2, science 3 (laboratory 2), foreign language 2 and academic electives 8.

2008-2009 Annual costs. Tuition/fees: $24,500. Special fees for laboratory, studio art, computer programming, and other courses requiring special materials. Room/board: $7,550. Books/supplies: $750. Personal expenses: $1,500.

2008-2009 Financial aid. Need-based: 145 full-time freshmen applied for aid; 129 were judged to have need; 129 of these received aid. Average need met was 89%. Average scholarship/grant was $20,454; average loan $4,509. 73% of total undergraduate aid awarded as scholarships/grants, 27% as loans/jobs. **Non-need-based:** Scholarships awarded for academics, alumni affiliation, art, athletics, leadership, music/drama, ROTC, state residency.

Application procedures. Admission: Priority date 4/1; no deadline. No application fee. Admission notification on a rolling basis beginning on or about 10/1. Must reply by May 1 or within 2 week(s) if notified thereafter. **Financial aid:** Closing date 3/15. FAFSA required. Applicants notified on a rolling basis starting 3/1; must reply by 5/1 or within 2 week(s) of notification.

Academics. **Special study options:** Combined bachelor's/graduate degree, cross-registration, double major, ESL, honors, independent study, internships, liberal arts/career combination, student-designed major, study abroad, teacher certification program. Women's leadership program. **Credit/placement by examination:** AP, CLEP, IB, SAT, ACT, institutional tests. 30 credit hours maximum toward bachelor's degree. **Support services:** Learning center, remedial instruction, study skills assistance, tutoring, writing center.

Majors. **Biology:** General, biochemistry. **Business:** Accounting, finance, international, managerial economics, marketing, training/development. **Computer sciences:** General. **Education:** General, Deaf/hearing impaired, early childhood, elementary, special. **Foreign languages:** General, French, Spanish. **Health:** Art therapy, music therapy. **History:** General. **Math:** General. **Philosophy/religion:** Religion. **Physical sciences:** Chemistry. **Psychology:** General. **Social sciences:** Economics, political science. **Visual/performing arts:** Art, art history/conservation, dramatic, interior design, music history, music pedagogy, music performance, music theory/composition, piano/organ, stringed instruments, studio arts, theater arts management, voice/opera.

Most popular majors. Biology 8%, business/marketing 11%, education 19%, English 6%, history 6%, psychology 10%, visual/performing arts 24%.

Computing on campus. 75 workstations in dormitories, library, computer center, student center. Dormitories wired for high-speed internet access and linked to campus network. Commuter students can connect to campus network. Online library, helpline, repair service, wireless network available.

Student life. **Freshman orientation:** Mandatory. Preregistration for classes offered. 3-day program. **Policies:** Strong honor tradition based on mutual trust and responsibility. **Housing:** Guaranteed on-campus for all undergraduates. Wellness housing available. $300 nonrefundable deposit, deadline 5/1. **Activities:** Concert band, campus ministries, choral groups, dance, drama, international student organizations, literary magazine, music ensembles, Model UN, musical theater, opera, student government, student newspaper, symphony orchestra, Student Christian Association, student activities committee, Young Republicans, community service organizations, honor organizations, student volunteer services.

Athletics. NCAA. **Intercollegiate:** Basketball W, cross-country W, equestrian W, lacrosse W, soccer W, swimming W, tennis W, volleyball W. **Intramural:** Archery W, basketball W, football (non-tackle) W, soccer W, softball W, swimming W, synchronized swimming W, volleyball W. **Team name:** Valkyries.

Student services. Adult student services, alcohol/substance abuse counseling, chaplain/spiritual director, career counseling, student employment services, financial aid counseling, health services, personal counseling, placement for graduates. **Physically disabled:** Services for hearing impaired.

Contact. E-mail: admissions@converse.edu
Phone: (864) 596-9040 Toll-free number: (800) 766-1125
Fax: (864) 596-9225
April Lewis, Director of Admissions, Converse College, 580 East Main Street, Spartanburg, SC 29302-0006

Erskine College

Due West, South Carolina — **CB member**
www.erskine.edu — **CB code: 5188**

- Private 4-year liberal arts and seminary college affiliated with Associate Reformed Presbyterian Church
- Residential campus in rural community
- 563 degree-seeking undergraduates: 54% women, 6% African American, 2% international
- 256 degree-seeking graduate students
- 59% of applicants admitted
- SAT or ACT (ACT writing optional), application essay required
- 58% graduate within 6 years

General. Founded in 1839. Regionally accredited. Affiliated with Erskine Theological Seminary. **Degrees:** 135 bachelor's awarded; master's, doctoral, first professional offered. **Location:** 18 miles from Anderson, 45 miles from Greenville. **Calendar:** 4-1-4, limited summer session. **Full-time faculty:** 42 total; 86% have terminal degrees, 5% minority, 38% women. **Part-time faculty:** 26 total; 35% have terminal degrees, 4% minority, 23% women. **Class size:** 72% < 20, 27% 20-39, less than 1% 40-49. **Special facilities:** Arts center.

Freshman class profile. 895 applied, 528 admitted, 163 enrolled.

Mid 50% test scores		**GPA 2.0-2.99:**	9%
SAT critical reading:	470-600	**Rank in top quarter:**	54%
SAT math:	490-600	**Rank in top tenth:**	32%
SAT writing:	470-580	**End year in good standing:**	80%
ACT composite:	20-26	**Return as sophomores:**	77%
GPA 3.75 or higher:	32%	**Out-of-state:**	22%
GPA 3.50-3.74:	19%	**Live on campus:**	98%
GPA 3.0-3.49:	40%	**International:**	2%

Basis for selection. High school transcript, testings and personal qualities considered in admissions decisions. Rigor of coursework most important. Grades, class rank, test scores, extracurricular activites, and essay very important. Interview required for academically weak; audition required for music. **Homeschooled:** High school diploma, GED, or college preparatory diploma certification required. Applicants must also submit portfolio of all high school work and 2 recommendations.

High school preparation. College-preparatory program required. 14 units required. Required and recommended units include English 4, mathematics 2-4, social studies 2, science 3 (laboratory 2) and foreign language 2. Biology, chemistry, physics, history highly recommended. Preference given to students with more than minimum preparation.

2008-2009 Annual costs. Tuition/fees: $23,165. Room/board: $7,961. Books/supplies: $1,250.

2007-2008 Financial aid. **Need-based:** 155 full-time freshmen applied for aid; 149 were judged to have need; 149 of these received aid. 78% of total undergraduate aid awarded as scholarships/grants, 22% as loans/jobs. **Non-need-based:** Awarded to 920 full-time undergraduates, including 173 freshmen. Scholarships awarded for academics, alumni affiliation, art, athletics, leadership, minority status, music/drama, religious affiliation, state residency. **Additional information:** Filing deadline 5/1 for institutional form, 6/30 for state form.

Application procedures. **Admission:** No deadline. $25 fee, may be waived for applicants with need, free for online applicants. Admission notification on a rolling basis beginning on or about 11/15. **Financial aid:** Priority date 4/1; no closing date. FAFSA, institutional form required. Applicants notified on a rolling basis starting 12/15; must reply within 2 week(s) of notification.

Academics. **Special study options:** Double major, independent study, internships, study abroad, teacher certification program. **Credit/placement by examination:** AP, CLEP, IB, institutional tests. 18 credit hours maximum toward bachelor's degree. **Support services:** Pre-admission summer program, tutoring, writing center.

Majors. **Area/ethnic studies:** American. **Biology:** General. **Business:** Business admin. **Education:** Early childhood, elementary, physical, secondary, social studies, special. **Foreign languages:** French, Spanish. **Health:** Athletic training, clinical lab technology. **History:** General. **Math:** General. **Parks/recreation:** General, health/fitness, sports admin. **Philosophy/religion:** Philosophy, religion. **Physical sciences:** Chemistry, physics. **Psychology:** General. **Social sciences:** Political science. **Theology:** Religious ed. **Visual/performing arts:** Art.

Most popular majors. Biology 16%, business/marketing 15%, education 12%, English 8%, foreign language 9%, parks/recreation 8%, philosophy/religious studies 9%, physical sciences 8%.

Computing on campus. Dormitories wired for high-speed internet access and linked to campus network. Commuter students can connect to campus network. Helpline, repair service, student web hosting, wireless network available.

Student life. **Freshman orientation:** Mandatory. Preregistration for classes offered. Week-long orientation in August held 1 week prior to first day of classes. **Policies:** Religious observance required. **Housing:** Guaranteed on-campus for all undergraduates. Single-sex dorms, wellness housing available. $300 deposit. **Activities:** Bands, campus ministries, choral groups, dance, drama, literary magazine, music ensembles, musical theater, radio station, student government, student newspaper, national honor societies for academics, drama, and leadership, association of minority students, denominational organizations, judicial council, Fellowship of Christian Athletes, Habitat for Humanity, council for exceptional children.

Athletics. NCAA. **Intercollegiate:** Baseball M, basketball, cross-country, soccer, softball W, tennis. **Intramural:** Basketball, football (non-tackle) W, football (tackle) M, racquetball, soccer, softball, tennis, volleyball. **Team name:** Flying Fleet.

Student services. Adult student services, chaplain/spiritual director, career counseling, financial aid counseling, health services, personal counseling, placement for graduates.

Contact. E-mail: admissions@erskine.edu
Phone: (864) 379-8838 Toll-free number: (800) 241-8721
Fax: (864) 379-2167
Woody O'Cain, Vice President for Enrollment, Erskine College, PO Box 338, Due West, SC 29639-0176

Francis Marion University
Florence, South Carolina — **CB member**
www.fmarion.edu — **CB code: 5442**

- Public 4-year university and liberal arts college
- Commuter campus in small city
- 3,185 degree-seeking undergraduates: 4% part-time, 66% women, 45% African American, 1% Asian American, 1% Hispanic American, 1% Native American, 1% international
- 221 degree-seeking graduate students
- 62% of applicants admitted
- SAT or ACT (ACT writing optional) required
- 39% graduate within 6 years

General. Founded in 1970. Regionally accredited. **Degrees:** 501 bachelor's awarded; master's offered. **Location:** 7 miles from downtown, 80 miles from Columbia. **Calendar:** Semester, limited summer session. **Full-time faculty:** 204 total; 80% have terminal degrees, 9% minority, 42% women. **Part-time faculty:** 52 total; 38% have terminal degrees, 6% minority, 65% women. **Class size:** 48% < 20, 46% 20-39, 4% 40-49, 3% 50-99. **Special facilities:** Planetarium, observatory, arboretum, hewn timber cabins.

Freshman class profile. 2,689 applied, 1,657 admitted, 681 enrolled.

Mid 50% test scores			
SAT critical reading:	420-520	Rank in top quarter:	37%
SAT math:	420-530	Rank in top tenth:	11%
SAT writing:	400-500	End year in good standing:	68%
ACT composite:	18-21	Return as sophomores:	67%
GPA 3.75 or higher:	26%	Out-of-state:	4%
GPA 3.50-3.74:	16%	Live on campus:	67%
GPA 3.0-3.49:	35%	International:	1%
GPA 2.0-2.99:	23%	Fraternities:	6%
		Sororities:	10%

Basis for selection. Combination of standardized test scores and high school GPA important. Borderline cases may be admitted provisionally. Proficiency in math and English required. **Learning Disabled:** Accommodations provided with documentation.

High school preparation. 20 units required. Required and recommended units include English 4, mathematics 3-4, social studies 3, history 1, science 3 (laboratory 3), foreign language 2 and academic electives 4. Social studies should include 1 history; 2 units of same foreign language required.

2008-2009 Annual costs. Tuition/fees: $7,632; $14,979 out-of-state. Room/board: $6,024. Books/supplies: $1,133. Personal expenses: $2,519.

2008-2009 Financial aid. Need-based: 582 full-time freshmen applied for aid; 517 were judged to have need; 501 of these received aid. 39% of total undergraduate aid awarded as scholarships/grants, 61% as loans/jobs. **Non-need-based:** Awarded to 1,705 full-time undergraduates, including 264 freshmen. Scholarships awarded for academics, music/drama.

Application procedures. Admission: No deadline. $30 fee, may be waived for applicants with need. Application must be submitted on paper. Admission notification on a rolling basis beginning on or about 9/1. April 1 reply date for dormitory students. **Financial aid:** Priority date 3/1; no closing date. FAFSA required. Applicants notified on a rolling basis starting 4/15.

Academics. Special study options: Double major, dual enrollment of high school students, honors, independent study, internships, study abroad, teacher certification program, Washington semester. **Credit/placement by examination:** AP, CLEP, institutional tests. **Support services:** Reduced course load, tutoring, writing center.

Majors. Biology: General. **Business:** Accounting, business admin, finance, management information systems, managerial economics, marketing. **Communications:** Media studies. **Computer sciences:** General. **Education:** Art, early childhood, elementary, English, history, mathematics, secondary, social studies. **Foreign languages:** French, German, Spanish. **Health:** Nursing (RN). **History:** General. **Liberal arts:** Arts/sciences. **Math:** General. **Physical sciences:** Chemistry, physics. **Psychology:** General. **Social sciences:** Economics, international relations, political science, sociology. **Visual/performing arts:** Art, dramatic.

Most popular majors. Biology 11%, business/marketing 25%, communications/journalism 7%, education 13%, health sciences 7%, psychology 8%, social sciences 9%.

Computing on campus. 551 workstations in dormitories, library, computer center, student center. Dormitories wired for high-speed internet access. Online course registration, online library available.

Student life. Freshman orientation: Mandatory, $46 fee. Preregistration for classes offered. Held in summer for fall term. Session in January for spring. **Housing:** Single-sex dorms, special housing for disabled, apartments, wellness housing available. $250 deposit. **Activities:** Jazz band, campus ministries, choral groups, drama, literary magazine, music ensembles, student government, student newspaper, TV station, College Democrats, Young Republicans, NAACP, Rotaract, minority student association, psychology club, education club, First Fellowship.

Athletics. NCAA. **Intercollegiate:** Baseball M, basketball, cross-country, golf M, soccer, softball W, tennis, track and field, volleyball W. **Intramural:** Basketball, bowling, football (non-tackle), golf, racquetball, soccer, softball, table tennis, tennis, track and field, volleyball. **Team name:** Patriots.

Student services. Adult student services, chaplain/spiritual director, career counseling, student employment services, health services, minority student services, personal counseling, placement for graduates, veterans' counselor. **Physically disabled:** Services for visually, speech, hearing impaired.

Contact. E-mail: admission@fmarion.edu
Phone: (843) 661-1231 Toll-free number: (800) 368-7551
Fax: (843) 661-4635
James Schlimmer, Director of Admissions, Francis Marion University, PO Box 100547, Florence, SC 29502-0547

Furman University
Greenville, South Carolina — **CB member**
www.furman.edu — **CB code: 5222**

- Private 4-year liberal arts college
- Residential campus in small city
- 2,771 degree-seeking undergraduates: 4% part-time, 57% women, 7% African American, 3% Asian American, 2% Hispanic American, 2% international
- 102 degree-seeking graduate students
- 57% of applicants admitted
- Application essay required
- 85% graduate within 6 years; 41% enter graduate study

General. Founded in 1826. Regionally accredited. Abundant internship and collaborative research opportunities. **Degrees:** 651 bachelor's awarded; master's offered. **ROTC:** Army. **Location:** 100 miles from Charlotte, North Carolina, 140 miles from Atlanta. **Calendar:** Semester, extensive summer session. **Full-time faculty:** 231 total; 96% have terminal degrees, 13% minority, 32% women. **Part-time faculty:** 43 total; 56% have terminal degrees, 65% women. **Class size:** 59% < 20, 40% 20-39, less than 1% 40-49. **Special facilities:** Observatory, center for engaged learning, center for international education, center for collaborative learning and communication.

Freshman class profile. 4,414 applied, 2,531 admitted, 753 enrolled.

Mid 50% test scores			
SAT critical reading:	590-690	Rank in top quarter:	87%
SAT math:	590-680	Rank in top tenth:	59%
SAT writing:	580-680	Return as sophomores:	92%
ACT composite:	26-30	Out-of-state:	68%
GPA 3.75 or higher:	42%	Live on campus:	98%
GPA 3.50-3.74:	20%	International:	2%
GPA 3.0-3.49:	29%	Fraternities:	39%
GPA 2.0-2.99:	9%	Sororities:	48%

Basis for selection. High school record including courses taken and grades most important, then SAT or ACT scores. Special talents such as fine arts, athletic ability, writing ability considered. Special consideration given to children of alumni and minorities. SAT or ACT recommended. If ACT or SAT score is not submitted, the student must submit either AP, SAT Subject Test or IB scores in both Math and English. Audition required for music scholarship applicants; portfolio required for art scholarship applicants. **Homeschooled:** SAT Subject Tests including math, subject of student's choice recommended. Interview strongly recommended.

High school preparation. College-preparatory program recommended. 14 units required; 18 recommended. Required and recommended units include English 4, mathematics 3-4, social studies 3-4, science 2-3 (laboratory 2-3) and foreign language 2-3.

2009-2010 Annual costs. Tuition/fees: $36,656. Room/board: $9,170. Books/supplies: $850. Personal expenses: $805.

2008-2009 Financial aid. **Need-based:** 456 full-time freshmen applied for aid; 315 were judged to have need; 315 of these received aid. Average need met was 85%. Average scholarship/grant was $23,709; average loan $4,102. 78% of total undergraduate aid awarded as scholarships/grants, 22% as loans/jobs. **Non-need-based:** Scholarships awarded for academics, alumni affiliation, art, athletics, leadership, music/drama, religious affiliation, ROTC, state residency. **Additional information:** 5-point comprehensive education financing plan includes financial aid packaging, money management counseling, debt management counseling, outside scholarship coordination, summer job-match program.

Application procedures. **Admission:** Closing date 1/15 (postmark date). $50 fee, may be waived for applicants with need, free for online applicants. Admission notification 3/15. Must reply by 5/1. **Financial aid:** Closing date 1/15. FAFSA, institutional form, CSS PROFILE required. Applicants notified by 3/15; must reply by 5/1.

Academics. Strong emphasis on research, internships and other opportunities for engaged, hands-on learning. **Special study options:** Combined bachelor's/graduate degree, double major, independent study, internships, student-designed major, study abroad, teacher certification program, United Nations semester, Washington semester. Undergraduate research program, 3-2 engineering with Auburn University, Clemson University, Georgia Institute of Technology, North Carolina State, Washington University in St. Louis, 3-2 forestry program with Duke University, 3-1 dentistry and medicine programs with any accredited medical or dental school, 3-2 nursing, pharmacy, physical therapy, and physician assistant programs with any accredited medical school. **Credit/placement by examination:** AP, CLEP, IB, institutional tests. **Support services:** Learning center, reduced course load, study skills assistance, tutoring, writing center.

Majors. **Area/ethnic studies:** Asian. **Biology:** General. **Business:** Accounting, business admin, management information systems. **Communications:** General. **Computer sciences:** Computer science. **Conservation:** Environmental studies. **Education:** General, music. **Foreign languages:** Ancient Greek, French, German, Latin, Spanish. **Health:** Predental, premedicine, prenursing, prepharmacy, preveterinary. **History:** General. **Interdisciplinary:** Math/computer science. **Legal studies:** Prelaw. **Liberal arts:** Arts/sciences. **Math:** General. **Parks/recreation:** Health/fitness. **Philosophy/religion:** Philosophy, religion. **Physical sciences:** Chemistry, geology, physics. **Psychology:** General. **Social sciences:** Economics, political science, sociology, urban studies. **Theology:** Sacred music. **Visual/performing arts:** Art, dramatic, music history, music performance, music theory/composition. **Other:** Mathematics economics.

Most popular majors. Business/marketing 9%, communications/journalism 8%, foreign language 8%, history 8%, philosophy/religious studies 7%, physical sciences 6%, social sciences 21%, visual/performing arts 7%.

Computing on campus. 450 workstations in library, computer center, student center. Dormitories wired for high-speed internet access and linked to campus network. Commuter students can connect to campus network. Online course registration, helpline, student web hosting, wireless network available.

Student life. **Freshman orientation:** Mandatory. Preregistration for classes offered. 4-day session including academic placement testing, advisory services, entertainment, and recreation. **Housing:** Guaranteed on-campus for freshmen. Coed dorms, single-sex dorms, apartments, wellness housing available. $400 nonrefundable deposit, deadline 5/1. Lakeside cottages and environmentally equipped eco-cottage also available. **Activities:** Bands, campus ministries, choral groups, dance, drama, film society, international student organizations, literary magazine, music ensembles, musical theater, opera, radio station, student government, student newspaper, symphony orchestra, TV station, Collegiate Educational Service Corps, Young Democrats, College Republicans, Student League for Black Culture, Fellowship of Christian Athletes, Council for Exceptional Children, Habitat for Humanity, arts students league, Amnesty International.

Athletics. NCAA. **Intercollegiate:** Baseball M, basketball, cheerleading, cross-country, football (tackle) M, golf, soccer, softball W, tennis, track and field, volleyball W. **Intramural:** Basketball, bowling, cross-country, football (non-tackle), golf, handball, racquetball, rowing (crew), soccer, softball, swimming, tennis, track and field, volleyball. **Team name:** Paladins.

Student services. Adult student services, alcohol/substance abuse counseling, chaplain/spiritual director, career counseling, student employment services, financial aid counseling, health services, minority student services, personal counseling, placement for graduates, veterans' counselor, women's services. **Physically disabled:** Services for visually, hearing impaired.

Contact. E-mail: admissions@furman.edu
Phone: (864) 294-2034 Fax: (864) 294-2018
Brad Pochard, Director of Admissions, Furman University, 3300 Poinsett Highway, Greenville, SC 29613

ITT Technical Institute: Greenville

Greenville, South Carolina
www.itt-tech.edu **CB code: 2708**

- For-profit 4-year technical college
- Commuter campus in large city

General. Accredited by ACICS. **Calendar:** Quarter.

Contact. Phone: (864) 288-0777
Director of Recruitment, 6 Independence Pointe, Greenville, SC 29615

Lander University

Greenwood, South Carolina **CB member**
www.lander.edu **CB code: 5363**

- Public 4-year liberal arts and teachers college
- Residential campus in large town
- 2,493 degree-seeking undergraduates: 9% part-time, 65% women, 27% African American, 1% Asian American, 1% Hispanic American, 1% Native American, 3% international
- 41 degree-seeking graduate students
- SAT or ACT (ACT writing optional) required
- 44% graduate within 6 years

General. Founded in 1872. Regionally accredited. **Degrees:** 404 bachelor's awarded; master's offered. **ROTC:** Army. **Location:** 55 miles from Greenville, 75 miles from Columbia. **Calendar:** Semester, limited summer session. **Full-time faculty:** 137 total; 62% have terminal degrees, 7% minority, 48% women. **Part-time faculty:** 85 total; 18% have terminal degrees, 6% minority, 59% women. **Class size:** 51% < 20, 43% 20-39, 4% 40-49, 2% 50-99.

Freshman class profile. 2,105 applied, 992 admitted, 555 enrolled.

Mid 50% test scores		**GPA 2.0-2.99:**	15%
SAT critical reading:	420-520	**Rank in top quarter:**	39%
SAT math:	430-550	**Rank in top tenth:**	12%
ACT composite:	18-22	**Return as sophomores:**	68%
GPA 3.75 or higher:	37%	**Out-of-state:**	4%
GPA 3.50-3.74:	17%	**Live on campus:**	80%
GPA 3.0-3.49:	31%	**International:**	2%

Basis for selection. Open admission, but selective for some programs. Test scores, class rank, curriculum, high school GPA important. Out-of-state students must rank in top half of high school class. Selectivity of students may be based on transcripts and GED score. Audition required for music programs; interview recommended for art, music programs; portfolio recommended for art programs.

High school preparation. 20 units recommended. Recommended units include English 4, mathematics 3, social studies 2, history 1, science 3 (laboratory 3), foreign language 2 and academic electives 4. One unit physical education or ROTC also recommended.

2008-2009 Annual costs. Tuition/fees: $8,540; $16,000 out-of-state. Room/board: $6,642. Books/supplies: $840. Personal expenses: $2,520.

2007-2008 Financial aid. **Non-need-based:** Scholarships awarded for academics, art, athletics, leadership, music/drama.

Application procedures. **Admission:** No deadline. $35 fee, may be waived for applicants with need. Admission notification on a rolling basis. **Financial aid:** Priority date 4/15; no closing date. FAFSA required. Applicants notified on a rolling basis starting 4/15; must reply within 4 week(s) of notification.

Academics. **Special study options:** Combined bachelor's/graduate degree, cooperative education, distance learning, double major, dual enrollment of high school students, honors, independent study, internships, liberal arts/career combination, student-designed major, study abroad, teacher certification program. Dual degree in engineering with Clemson University, nursing (RN to BSN completion) offered online, MBA and M.Ed. in counseling/school administration from Clemson University offered on campus. **Credit/placement by examination:** AP, CLEP, IB, institutional tests. 30 credit hours maximum toward bachelor's degree. **Support services:** Learning center, pre-admission summer program, reduced course load, remedial instruction, study skills assistance, tutoring, writing center.

Majors. **Biology:** General. **Business:** Business admin. **Computer sciences:** General. **Conservation:** Environmental science. **Education:** Early childhood, elementary, physical, secondary, special. **Foreign languages:** Spanish. **Health:** Athletic training, nursing (RN). **History:** General. **Liberal arts:** Arts/sciences, humanities. **Math:** General. **Parks/recreation:** Exercise sciences. **Physical sciences:** Chemistry. **Psychology:** General. **Social sciences:** Political science, sociology. **Visual/performing arts:** Art.

Most popular majors. Business/marketing 25%, education 13%, health sciences 9%, parks/recreation 8%, psychology 10%, social sciences 12%.

Computing on campus. PC or laptop required. 233 workstations in library, computer center. Dormitories linked to campus network. Commuter students can connect to campus network. Online course registration, online library, helpline, repair service, wireless network available.

Student life. **Freshman orientation:** Mandatory. Preregistration for classes offered. **Housing:** Coed dorms, single-sex dorms available. $175 partly refundable deposit, deadline 4/15. **Activities:** Bands, choral groups, dance, drama, literary magazine, music ensembles, student government, student newspaper, Baptist Student Union, Bible study, Young Democrats, College Republicans, Minorities on the Move, Blue Key and Alpha Kappa Gamma (honor societies).

Athletics. NCAA. **Intercollegiate:** Baseball M, basketball, cross-country W, golf M, soccer, softball W, tennis, volleyball W. **Intramural:** Basketball, football (non-tackle), golf, soccer, softball, volleyball. **Team name:** Bearcats.

Student services. Adult student services, alcohol/substance abuse counseling, career counseling, student employment services, financial aid counseling, health services, minority student services, personal counseling, placement for graduates, veterans' counselor. **Physically disabled:** Services for visually, speech, hearing impaired. **Learning disabled:** Comprehensive services available.

Contact. E-mail: admissions@lander.edu
Phone: (864) 388-8307 Fax: (864) 388-8125
Jennifer Mathis, Director of Admissions, Lander University, Stanley Avenue, Greenwood, SC 29649-2099

Limestone College
Gaffney, South Carolina
www.limestone.edu **CB code: 5366**

- Private 4-year liberal arts college
- Residential campus in large town
- 742 degree-seeking undergraduates: 2% part-time, 43% women, 19% African American, 2% Hispanic American, 5% international
- 56% of applicants admitted
- SAT or ACT (ACT writing optional) required
- 37% graduate within 6 years

General. Founded in 1845. Regionally accredited. Evening classes located at 8 sites throughout South Carolina. **Degrees:** 126 bachelor's, 3 associate awarded. **ROTC:** Army. **Location:** 25 miles from Spartanburg. **Calendar:** Semester, extensive summer session. **Full-time faculty:** 57 total; 72% have terminal degrees, 5% minority, 42% women. **Part-time faculty:** 8 total; 12% minority, 62% women. **Class size:** 66% < 20, 33% 20-39, 2% 40-49. **Special facilities:** Computer graphics art lab.

Freshman class profile. 1,249 applied, 705 admitted, 171 enrolled.

Mid 50% test scores			
SAT critical reading:	450-520	Rank in top quarter:	14%
SAT math:	460-540	Rank in top tenth:	3%
ACT composite:	17-20	End year in good standing:	76%
GPA 3.75 or higher:	16%	Return as sophomores:	54%
GPA 3.50-3.74:	9%	Out-of-state:	41%
GPA 3.0-3.49:	29%	Live on campus:	83%
GPA 2.0-2.99:	42%	International:	7%

Basis for selection. SAT combined score of 890 (exclusive of Writing) and GPA of 2.0. Admissions committee must approve all applicants who do not meet these standards. SAT requirement waived for freshmen 21 or older or in military service. The SAT or ACT requirement is waived for students admitted into the PALS (Program for Alternative Learning Styles) Program. Interview required for lower-ranking applicants; recommended for all others. Audition required of first-time, first-year freshmen for music, music education, theater programs; portfolio required for art education, studio art programs; essay required for honors program. **Learning Disabled:** Documentation required to be eligible for Program for Alternative Learning Styles (PALS).

High school preparation. 12 units required. Required units include English 4, mathematics 3, social studies 3, science 2 (laboratory 2).

2009-2010 Annual costs. Tuition/fees (projected): $18,300. Room/board: $6,800. Books/supplies: $1,870. Personal expenses: $1,640.

2008-2009 Financial aid. **Need-based:** Average need met was 68%. Average scholarship/grant was $12,036; average loan $3,022. 57% of total undergraduate aid awarded as scholarships/grants, 43% as loans/jobs. **Non-need-based:** Scholarships awarded for academics, alumni affiliation, art, athletics, job skills, leadership, music/drama, religious affiliation, ROTC, state residency.

Application procedures. **Admission:** Priority date 8/1; deadline 8/26 (receipt date). $25 fee, may be waived for applicants with need, free for online applicants. Admission notification on a rolling basis beginning on or about 6/1. **Financial aid:** Priority date 2/1; no closing date. FAFSA required. Applicants notified on a rolling basis starting 1/15; must reply within 3 week(s) of notification.

Academics. **Special study options:** Accelerated study, distance learning, double major, honors, independent study, internships, liberal arts/career combination, student-designed major, teacher certification program. **Credit/placement by examination:** AP, CLEP, institutional tests. 15 credit hours maximum toward associate degree, 30 toward bachelor's. **Support services:** Learning center, reduced course load, remedial instruction, study skills assistance, tutoring, writing center.

Majors. **Biology:** General. **Business:** Accounting, business admin, e-commerce, managerial economics, marketing, training/development. **Computer sciences:** General, computer science, database management, programming, security, system admin, web page design, webmaster. **Education:** General, elementary, English, mathematics, music, physical, secondary. **Health:** Athletic training, predental, premedicine, prenursing, prepharmacy, preveterinary. **History:** General. **Legal studies:** Prelaw. **Liberal arts:** Arts/sciences. **Math:** General. **Parks/recreation:** Exercise sciences, health/fitness, sports admin. **Physical sciences:** Chemistry. **Protective services:** Law enforcement admin. **Psychology:** General. **Public administration:** Social work. **Social sciences:** Economics. **Visual/performing arts:** Dramatic, graphic design, jazz, studio arts. **Other:** Pre-Chiropractic.

Most popular majors. Business/marketing 22%, education 34%, parks/recreation 10%, security/protective services 11%.

Computing on campus. 112 workstations in library, computer center. Dormitories wired for high-speed internet access and linked to campus network. Commuter students can connect to campus network. Online library, helpline, repair service, wireless network available.

Student life. **Freshman orientation:** Mandatory. Preregistration for classes offered. 5 days prior to start of semester. **Policies:** Alcohol-free campus. Students must live on campus unless age 21, or have attained 90 credit hours, or live with immediate family within 50 miles of campus. **Housing:** Guaranteed on-campus for freshmen. Single-sex dorms, wellness housing available. $50 fully refundable deposit. Off-campus apartments available. **Activities:** Bands, campus ministries, choral groups, drama, international student organizations, literary magazine, music ensembles, musical theater, student government, Fellowship of Christian Athletes, student alumni leadership council, Student Organization of Social Workers, Students in Free Enterprise, Christian Education and Leadership Program, Chi Alpha Sigma, outdoor recreation education club, international business club, Joyful Saints gospel choir.

Athletics. NCAA. **Intercollegiate:** Baseball M, basketball, cross-country, field hockey W, golf, lacrosse, soccer, softball W, swimming, tennis, track and field, volleyball, wrestling M. **Intramural:** Basketball, bowling, softball, table tennis, tennis, volleyball. **Team name:** Saints.

Student services. Adult student services, alcohol/substance abuse counseling, chaplain/spiritual director, career counseling, student employment services, financial aid counseling, health services, personal counseling, placement for graduates, veterans' counselor. **Learning disabled:** Comprehensive services available.

Contact. E-mail: cphenicie@limestone.edu
Phone: (864) 488-4554 Toll-free number: (800) 795-7151 ext. 4554
Fax: (864) 487-8706
Chris Phenicie, Vice President for Enrollment Services, Limestone College, 1115 College Drive, Gaffney, SC 29340-3799

Medical University of South Carolina
Charleston, South Carolina
www.musc.edu **CB code: 5407**

- Public two-year upper-division university
- Commuter campus in large city
- Test scores, application essay required

General. Founded in 1824. Regionally accredited. Upper division/graduate academic health center consisting of six colleges: dental medicine, graduate studies, health professions, medicine, nursing, and pharmacy. College offers only three undergraduate degrees. **Degrees:** 173 bachelor's awarded; master's, doctoral, first professional offered. **Location:** 350 miles from Atlanta. **Calendar:** Semester, limited summer session. **Full-time faculty:** 141 total; 88% have terminal degrees, 6% minority, 56% women. **Part-time faculty:** 95 total; 46% have terminal degrees, 10% minority, 67% women. **Class size:** 47% < 20, 47% 40-49, 7% 50-99. **Special facilities:** Historical medical library, dental museum, pharmacy museum.

Student profile. 316 degree-seeking undergraduates, 2,212 graduate students. 100% entered as juniors. 35% transferred from two-year, 65% transferred from four-year institutions.

Out-of-state:	10%	**25 or older:**	65%

Basis for selection. College transcript, application essay, standardized test scores required. Admissions policies and dates are established by each of the six MUSC colleges due to varied nature of their academic programs. Transfer accepted as juniors.

Financial aid. Non-need-based: Scholarships awarded for academics, alumni affiliation, minority status, state residency.

Application procedures. Admission: $75 fee. Application must be submitted online. All admission policies and dates vary by academic program and college. **Financial aid:** FAFSA, institutional form required.

Academics. Offers a limited undergraduate degree program (3 majors). **Special study options:** Cross-registration, distance learning. **Credit/placement by examination:** AP, CLEP, institutional tests.

Majors. Health: Health care admin, nursing (RN), perfusion technology.

Computing on campus. 300 workstations in library. Commuter students can connect to campus network. Online library, helpline, student web hosting available.

Student life. Activities: Literary magazine, student government, Christian Medical Society, campus crusade, student union, community help initiative, South Carolina health initiative, minority student union, Student National Medical Association.

Athletics. Intramural: Basketball, football (non-tackle), softball, volleyball.

Student services. Alcohol/substance abuse counseling, chaplain/spiritual director, services for economically disadvantaged, financial aid counseling, health services, legal services, minority student services, personal counseling, veterans' counselor.

Contact. E-mail: oesadmis@musc.edu
Phone: (843) 792-5396 Fax: (843) 792-6615
George Ohlandt, Director of Admissions, Medical University of South Carolina, 41 Bee Street, Charleston, SC 29425

Morris College
Sumter, South Carolina **CB member**
www.morris.edu **CB code: 5418**

- Private 4-year liberal arts college affiliated with Baptist faith
- Residential campus in large town
- 920 degree-seeking undergraduates: 3% part-time, 58% women, 100% African American
- 89% of applicants admitted
- 32% graduate within 6 years; 10% enter graduate study

General. Founded in 1908. Regionally accredited. **Degrees:** 106 bachelor's awarded. **ROTC:** Army. **Location:** 45 miles from Columbia, 110 miles from Charlotte, North Carolina. **Calendar:** Semester, limited summer session. **Full-time faculty:** 44 total; 73% have terminal degrees, 64% minority, 43% women. **Part-time faculty:** 20 total; 40% have terminal degrees, 60% minority, 40% women. **Class size:** 56% < 20, 39% 20-39, 5% 40-49, less than 1% 50-99. **Special facilities:** Radio station/training lab, electronic learning lab, television production studio.

Freshman class profile. 2,060 applied, 1,828 admitted, 293 enrolled.

GPA 3.75 or higher:	4%	**Rank in top tenth:**	3%
GPA 3.50-3.74:	3%	**Return as sophomores:**	51%
GPA 3.0-3.49:	12%	**Out-of-state:**	23%
GPA 2.0-2.99:	58%	**Live on campus:**	88%
Rank in top quarter:	10%		

Basis for selection. High school record most important. Students with less than 2.0 high school GPA may be admitted on probation but limited to 13-credit-hour load during each of first 2 semesters and required to participate in tutorial and study sessions. SAT or ACT scores must be submitted for all degree-seeking students, except foreign students. Scores are used for informational purposes only. Interview recommended.

High school preparation. 24 units required. Required and recommended units include English 4, mathematics 4, social studies 2, history 1, science 3, foreign language 1-2 and academic electives 7. 1 physical education or ROTC, 1 computer science.

2008-2009 Annual costs. Tuition/fees: $9,621. Room/board: $4,258. Books/supplies: $1,500. Personal expenses: $1,200.

2007-2008 Financial aid. All financial aid based on need. 295 full-time freshmen applied for aid; 285 were judged to have need; 285 of these received aid. Average need met was 85%. Average scholarship/grant was $4,310; average loan $3,500. 55% of total undergraduate aid awarded as scholarships/grants, 45% as loans/jobs.

Application procedures. Admission: Priority date 7/1; no deadline. $20 fee, may be waived for applicants with need. Application must be submitted on paper. Admission notification on a rolling basis beginning on or about 11/1. **Financial aid:** Priority date 3/30; no closing date. FAFSA, institutional form required. Applicants notified on a rolling basis starting 6/1; must reply within 2 week(s) of notification.

Academics. Special study options: Accelerated study, combined bachelor's/graduate degree, cooperative education, double major, honors, internships, liberal arts/career combination, teacher certification program. Adult Degree Program in Organizational Management offered through evening courses; students must be at least 25 years old and have earned 60 credit hours. **Credit/placement by examination:** AP, CLEP. 30 credit hours maximum toward bachelor's degree. **Support services:** Learning center, reduced course load, remedial instruction, study skills assistance, tutoring, writing center.

Majors. Biology: General. **Business:** Business admin, operations. **Communications:** Media studies. **Education:** Biology, early childhood, elementary, English, mathematics, social studies. **Health:** Community health services. **History:** General. **Liberal arts:** Arts/sciences. **Math:** General. **Parks/recreation:** Facilities management. **Protective services:** Law enforcement admin. **Social sciences:** Political science, sociology. **Theology:** Religious ed, theology.

Most popular majors. Biology 10%, business/marketing 28%, communications/journalism 11%, health sciences 12%, parks/recreation 12%, security/protective services 6%, social sciences 12%.

Computing on campus. 252 workstations in dormitories, library, computer center. Dormitories wired for high-speed internet access and linked to campus network. Wireless network available.

Student life. Freshman orientation: Mandatory. Preregistration for classes offered. Held during first week of fall and spring semesters. **Policies:** College promotes drug-free, alcohol-free campus. Cigarette smoking prohibited in all buildings. **Housing:** Guaranteed on-campus for freshmen. Single-sex dorms available. $100 fully refundable deposit, deadline 8/1. **Activities:** Pep band, campus ministries, choral groups, dance, drama, radio station, student government, student newspaper, Baptist Student Union, NAACP, Alpha Phi Omega, Durham Ministerial Union, National Association of Blacks in Criminal Justice.

Athletics. NAIA. **Intercollegiate:** Baseball M, basketball, cheerleading, cross-country, golf M, softball W, tennis, track and field, volleyball W. **Intramural:** Basketball, football (non-tackle), table tennis. **Team name:** Hornets.

Student services. Adult student services, alcohol/substance abuse counseling, chaplain/spiritual director, career counseling, student employment services, financial aid counseling, health services, personal counseling, placement for graduates, veterans' counselor.

Contact. E-mail: dcalhoun@morris.edu
Phone: (803) 934-3225 Toll-free number: (866) 853-1345
Fax: (803) 773-8241
Deborah Calhoun, Director of Admission and Records, Morris College, 100 West College Street, Sumter, SC 29150-3599

Newberry College

Newberry, South Carolina — **CB member**
www.newberry.edu — **CB code: 5493**

- Private 4-year liberal arts college affiliated with Evangelical Lutheran Church in America
- Residential campus in small city
- 964 degree-seeking undergraduates: 1% part-time, 41% women, 24% African American, 1% Asian American, 2% Hispanic American, 4% international
- 91% of applicants admitted
- SAT or ACT required
- 40% graduate within 6 years

General. Founded in 1856. Regionally accredited. **Degrees:** 135 bachelor's awarded. **ROTC:** Army. **Location:** 40 miles from Columbia. **Calendar:** Semester, limited summer session. **Full-time faculty:** 53 total; 72% have terminal degrees, 6% minority, 47% women. **Part-time faculty:** 31 total; 13% have terminal degrees, 3% minority, 42% women. **Class size:** 58% < 20, 40% 20-39, 2% 40-49.

Freshman class profile. 762 applied, 694 admitted, 302 enrolled.

Mid 50% test scores		**Return as sophomores:**	62%
SAT critical reading:	430-530	**Out-of-state:**	20%
SAT math:	440-540	**Live on campus:**	90%
ACT composite:	17-20	**International:**	3%
Rank in top quarter:	22%	**Fraternities:**	14%
Rank in top tenth:	6%	**Sororities:**	26%

Basis for selection. High school record and test scores important; recommendations and interview considered. Interview recommended for all; audition required for drama, music programs; portfolio required for art. **Homeschooled:** Submit transcripts from HS or home school association. If unavailable, submit major essays and course descriptions. References necessary from primary instructor and another source.

High school preparation. 15 units required. Required units include English 4, mathematics 3, social studies 2, history 1, science 2 (laboratory 2), foreign language 2 and academic electives 1.

2008-2009 Annual costs. Tuition/fees: $21,560. Room/board: $7,400. Books/supplies: $1,480. Personal expenses: $1,800.

2007-2008 Financial aid. Need-based: 71% of total undergraduate aid awarded as scholarships/grants, 29% as loans/jobs. **Non-need-based:** Scholarships awarded for academics, alumni affiliation, athletics, leadership, music/drama, religious affiliation, ROTC, state residency.

Application procedures. Admission: Priority date 1/30; no deadline. $30 fee, may be waived for applicants with need. Admission notification on a rolling basis beginning on or about 9/15. Must reply by May 1 or within 3 week(s) if notified thereafter. **Financial aid:** Priority date 3/15; no closing date. FAFSA, institutional form required. Applicants notified on a rolling basis starting 3/1; must reply by 5/1 or within 2 week(s) of notification.

Academics. Special study options: Double major, dual enrollment of high school students, ESL, external degree, honors, independent study, internships, liberal arts/career combination, student-designed major, study abroad, teacher certification program, weekend college. Medical Technology Dual Degree Program with Palmetto Baptist Medical Center. Forest and Environmental Management Dual Degree Program with Duke University. **Credit/placement by examination:** AP, CLEP, IB, institutional tests. 30 credit hours maximum toward bachelor's degree. Sophomore standing available by earning 24 credit hours based on AP exam scores. **Support services:** Learning center, reduced course load, remedial instruction, tutoring, writing center.

Majors. Biology: General. **Business:** Business admin. **Communications:** General. **Education:** General, early childhood, elementary, music, physical. **History:** General. **Interdisciplinary:** Global studies. **Legal studies:** Prelaw. **Liberal arts:** Arts/sciences, humanities. **Math:** General. **Parks/recreation:** General, sports admin. **Philosophy/religion:** Philosophy, religion. **Physical sciences:** Chemistry. **Psychology:** General. **Social sciences:** International relations, political science, sociology. **Theology:** Sacred music. **Visual/performing arts:** Art, dramatic, music history, music performance, music theory/composition.

Most popular majors. Biology 9%, business/marketing 20%, communications/journalism 10%, education 10%, parks/recreation 17%, psychology 9%, social sciences 8%.

Computing on campus. PC or laptop required. 12 workstations in library. Dormitories wired for high-speed internet access and linked to campus network. Commuter students can connect to campus network. Online course registration, online library, helpline, repair service, student web hosting, wireless network available.

Student life. Freshman orientation: Mandatory, $100 fee. Preregistration for classes offered. 2-day event. Students stay overnight on campus. **Housing:** Guaranteed on-campus for freshmen. Coed dorms, single-sex dorms available. $100 nonrefundable deposit. **Activities:** Bands, campus ministries, choral groups, drama, literary magazine, music ensembles, musical theater, radio station, student government, student newspaper, TV station, Lutheran Student Movement, Baptist student union, Young Republicans, Intervarsity Fellowship of Christian Athletes, Students Organized for Community Service, South Carolina State Student Legislature.

Athletics. NCAA. **Intercollegiate:** Baseball M, basketball, cheerleading M, cross-country, football (tackle) M, golf, soccer, softball W, tennis, volleyball W, wrestling M. **Intramural:** Basketball, softball, volleyball W.

Student services. Alcohol/substance abuse counseling, chaplain/spiritual director, career counseling, student employment services, financial aid counseling, health services, personal counseling, placement for graduates.

Contact. E-mail: admissions@newberry.edu
Phone: (803) 321-5127 Toll-free number: (800) 845-4955 ext. 5127
Fax: (803) 321-5138
Amanda Richardson, Director of Admissions, Newberry College, 2100 College Street, Newberry, SC 29108

North Greenville University

Tigerville, South Carolina
www.ngu.edu — **CB code: 5498**

- Private 4-year liberal arts college affiliated with Southern Baptist Convention
- Residential campus in rural community
- 1,916 degree-seeking undergraduates: 4% part-time, 50% women
- 109 graduate students
- 60% of applicants admitted
- SAT or ACT (ACT writing optional) required
- 45% graduate within 6 years

General. Founded in 1891. Regionally accredited. Off-site recreation and learning center for Outdoor Leadership major. **Degrees:** 319 bachelor's, 6 associate awarded; master's offered. **ROTC:** Army. **Location:** 18 miles from Greenville; 54 miles from Asheville, North Carolina. **Calendar:** Semester, limited summer session. **Full-time faculty:** 116 total; 67% have terminal degrees, 9% minority, 32% women. **Part-time faculty:** 41 total; 12% have terminal degrees, 2% minority, 44% women. **Class size:** 58% < 20, 41% 20-39, less than 1% 40-49, less than 1% 50-99. **Special facilities:** Bible museum.

Freshman class profile. 1,477 applied, 884 admitted, 516 enrolled.

Mid 50% test scores		**GPA 2.0-2.99:**	25%
SAT critical reading:	500-690	**Rank in top quarter:**	38%
SAT math:	480-640	**Rank in top tenth:**	13%
ACT composite:	21-29	**Return as sophomores:**	75%
GPA 3.75 or higher:	24%	**Out-of-state:**	21%
GPA 3.50-3.74:	17%	**Live on campus:**	86%
GPA 3.0-3.49:	32%		

Basis for selection. High school record, standardized test scores, class rank most important. Require 2 of the following: SAT 820 (exclusive of Writing); ACT 16; GPA 2.0; class rank top 60 percent. Computerized Placement Test required for those with SAT verbal and math scores below 500. Portfolio recommended for all; audition required for music, theater programs; essay required for English-deficient; interview recommended for music, theater programs. **Learning Disabled:** Meet with Director of Disability Services.

High school preparation. 12 units required; 18 recommended. Required and recommended units include English 4, mathematics 2-3, social studies 1, history 1, science 2-3 (laboratory 1), foreign language 2, computer science 1, visual/performing arts 1 and academic electives 2.

2008-2009 Annual costs. Tuition/fees: $11,680. Room/board: $6,720. Books/supplies: $1,000. Personal expenses: $2,000.

Financial aid. All financial aid based on need.

Application procedures. **Admission:** Priority date 6/1; deadline 8/26. $25 fee, may be waived for applicants with need. Admission notification on a rolling basis. **Financial aid:** Priority date 6/1, closing date 6/30. FAFSA required. Applicants notified on a rolling basis starting 8/1; must reply within 2 week(s) of notification.

Academics. **Special study options:** Cross-registration, double major, dual enrollment of high school students, ESL, honors, independent study, internships, student-designed major, teacher certification program. **Credit/placement by examination:** AP, CLEP, IB, institutional tests. 16 credit hours maximum toward associate degree, 30 toward bachelor's. CLEP and other exam credits cannot exceed 25 percent of hours needed for degree. **Support services:** Learning center, reduced course load, remedial instruction, study skills assistance, tutoring, writing center.

Majors. **Biology:** General. **Business:** General, accounting, business admin, international, marketing. **Communications:** General, journalism, media studies, radio/tv. **Education:** Biology, early childhood, elementary, English, music, social studies. **Health:** Predental, premedicine, prepharmacy. **History:** General. **Interdisciplinary:** Accounting/computer science. **Legal studies:** Prelaw. **Liberal arts:** Arts/sciences. **Math:** General. **Parks/recreation:** General, sports admin. **Physical sciences:** Chemistry. **Psychology:** General. **Social sciences:** Economics. **Theology:** Bible, missionary, sacred music, youth ministry. **Visual/performing arts:** Dramatic, music history, music performance, piano/organ, studio arts, theater arts management, voice/opera. **Other:** Health promotion and wellness.

Most popular majors. Business/marketing 23%, communications/journalism 10%, education 13%, liberal arts 11%, parks/recreation 7%, theological studies 13%.

Computing on campus. 75 workstations in library, computer center, student center. Dormitories wired for high-speed internet access. Commuter students can connect to campus network. Online library, helpline, wireless network available.

Student life. **Freshman orientation:** Mandatory. Preregistration for classes offered. Held in August. **Policies:** Religious observance required. **Housing:** Guaranteed on-campus for all undergraduates. Single-sex dorms, special housing for disabled, apartments, wellness housing available. $100 deposit, deadline 8/26. **Activities:** Bands, campus ministries, choral groups, drama, literary magazine, music ensembles, radio station, student government, student newspaper, symphony orchestra, Baptist student union, athletic ministries, Etude music society, Fellowship of Christians in Service, College Republicans.

Athletics. NCAA, NCCAA. **Intercollegiate:** Baseball M, basketball, cheerleading, cross-country, football (tackle) M, golf M, soccer, softball W, tennis, volleyball W. **Intramural:** Basketball, football (non-tackle) M, softball, table tennis, tennis, volleyball. **Team name:** Crusaders.

Student services. Chaplain/spiritual director, career counseling, student employment services, financial aid counseling, health services, on-campus daycare, personal counseling, placement for graduates. **Physically disabled:** Services for visually impaired.

Contact. E-mail: admissions@ngu.edu
Phone: (864) 977-7001 Toll-free number: (800) 468-6642
Fax: (864) 977-7177
Keli Sewell, Vice President for Admissions and Financial Aid, North Greenville University, PO Box 1892, Tigerville, SC 29688-1892

Presbyterian College

Clinton, South Carolina — **CB member**
www.presby.edu — **CB code: 5540**

- Private 4-year liberal arts college affiliated with Presbyterian Church (USA)
- Residential campus in small town
- 1,140 degree-seeking undergraduates: 1% part-time, 48% women, 8% African American, 1% Asian American, 1% Hispanic American, 1% international
- 69% of applicants admitted
- SAT or ACT (ACT writing optional), application essay required
- 73% graduate within 6 years; 30% enter graduate study

General. Founded in 1880. Regionally accredited. **Degrees:** 247 bachelor's awarded. **ROTC:** Army. **Location:** 40 miles from Greenville, 35 miles from Spartanburg. **Calendar:** Semester, limited summer session. **Full-time faculty:** 89 total; 90% have terminal degrees, 6% minority, 33% women. **Part-time faculty:** 26 total; 31% have terminal degrees, 12% minority, 50% women. **Class size:** 62% < 20, 38% 20-39, less than 1% 50-99. **Special facilities:** Scanning electron and transmission microscopes, ecological research center, Southeastern Center for Intercultural Studies.

Freshman class profile. 1,403 applied, 962 admitted, 324 enrolled.

Mid 50% test scores		**Rank in top quarter:**	66%
SAT critical reading:	500-630	**Rank in top tenth:**	35%
SAT math:	520-640	**End year in good standing:**	91%
ACT composite:	22-27	**Return as sophomores:**	84%
GPA 3.75 or higher:	35%	**Out-of-state:**	36%
GPA 3.50-3.74:	17%	**Live on campus:**	99%
GPA 3.0-3.49:	23%	**International:**	1%
GPA 2.0-2.99:	25%		

Basis for selection. Rigor of high school curriculum most important, followed by test scores, high school GPA, and high school recommendation. Extracurricular involvement and interview considered in some cases. Interview recommended. **Homeschooled:** Transcript of courses and grades, state high school equivalency certificate required.

High school preparation. College-preparatory program required. 18 units required. Required and recommended units include English 4, mathematics 4, social studies 2, history 2, science 2-4 (laboratory 2), foreign language 2-3 and academic electives 2. 2 or more units of laboratory science recommended for science majors.

2008-2009 Annual costs. Tuition/fees: $27,902. Room/board: $8,064.

2008-2009 Financial aid. **Non-need-based:** Scholarships awarded for academics, alumni affiliation, athletics, job skills, leadership, minority status, music/drama, religious affiliation, ROTC.

Application procedures. **Admission:** Priority date 2/1; deadline 6/30 (postmark date). $40 fee, may be waived for applicants with need. Admission notification 3/15. Must reply by 5/1. **Financial aid:** Priority date 3/15, closing date 6/30. FAFSA required. Applicants notified by 3/1; Applicants notified on a rolling basis starting 4/1; must reply by 5/1.

Academics. **Special study options:** Combined bachelor's/graduate degree, double major, dual enrollment of high school students, exchange student, honors, independent study, internships, liberal arts/career combination, semester at sea, study abroad, teacher certification program, Washington semester. 3-2 environmental science program, 3-2 engineering program, religious educational program, dual degrees offered with Auburn University (AL), Clemson University, Vanderbilt University (TN). **Credit/placement by examination:** AP, CLEP, IB, SAT, ACT, institutional tests. 40 credit hours maximum toward bachelor's degree. **Support services:** Preadmission summer program, reduced course load, study skills assistance, tutoring, writing center.

Majors. **Biology:** General. **Business:** Accounting, business admin. **Computer sciences:** Computer science. **Education:** Early childhood, middle, music, special. **Foreign languages:** General, French, German, Spanish. **History:** General. **Math:** General. **Philosophy/religion:** Philosophy, religion. **Physical sciences:** Chemistry, physics. **Psychology:** General. **Social sciences:** Economics, political science, sociology. **Theology:** Sacred music. **Visual/performing arts:** Art, art history/conservation, dramatic, music performance, studio arts. **Other:** Medical Physics, Religious Education.

Most popular majors. Biology 16%, business/marketing 23%, education 6%, history 12%, philosophy/religious studies 7%, psychology 7%, social sciences 11%, visual/performing arts 6%.

Computing on campus. 120 workstations in dormitories, library, computer center, student center. Dormitories wired for high-speed internet access and linked to campus network. Commuter students can connect to campus network. Online course registration, online library, helpline, student web hosting, wireless network available.

Student life. **Freshman orientation:** Mandatory, $100 fee. Preregistration for classes offered. Orientation includes registration, placement testing and organization fair. **Policies:** Honor code governs conduct inside and outside classroom, on and off campus. Cultural Enrichment Program requires students to attend 40 on-campus cultural events as part of graduation requirement. **Housing:** Guaranteed on-campus for all undergraduates. Coed dorms, single-sex dorms, apartments, fraternity/sorority housing, wellness housing available. $400 nonrefundable deposit, deadline 5/1. All full-time students, except those commuting daily from family's residence, required to live on campus. Sorority housing not available. **Activities:** Bands, campus ministries, choral groups, dance, drama, international student organizations, literary magazine, music ensembles, musical theater, opera, radio station, student government, student newspaper, symphony orchestra, volunteer organizations, multicultural student union, Young Democrats and Republicans, interdenominational organizations, Habitat for Humanity, Amnesty International, Fellowship of Christian Athletes.

Athletics. NCAA. **Intercollegiate:** Baseball M, basketball, cheerleading, cross-country, football (tackle) M, golf, lacrosse, soccer, softball W, tennis, volleyball W. **Intramural:** Basketball, football (non-tackle), golf, soccer, softball, tennis, volleyball. **Team name:** Blue Hose.

Student services. Chaplain/spiritual director, career counseling, student employment services, financial aid counseling, health services, minority student services, personal counseling, placement for graduates.

Contact. E-mail: admissions@presby.edu
Phone: (864) 833-8230 Toll-free number: (800) 960-7583
Fax: (864) 833-8195
Leni Patterson, Dean of Admissions and Financial Aid, Presbyterian College, 503 South Broad Street, Clinton, SC 29325

South Carolina State University

Orangeburg, South Carolina — **CB member**
www.scsu.edu — **CB code: 5618**

- Public 4-year university
- Residential campus in large town
- 4,075 degree-seeking undergraduates: 9% part-time, 54% women, 96% African American
- 652 degree-seeking graduate students
- 75% of applicants admitted
- SAT or ACT (ACT writing optional) required
- 45% graduate within 6 years

General. Founded in 1896. Regionally accredited. **Degrees:** 554 bachelor's awarded; master's, doctoral offered. **ROTC:** Army, Air Force. **Location:** 40 miles from Columbia, 70 miles from Charleston. **Calendar:** Semester, limited summer session. **Full-time faculty:** 228 total; 84% have terminal degrees, 72% minority, 42% women. **Part-time faculty:** 74 total; 10% have terminal degrees, 73% minority, 45% women. **Special facilities:** Planetarium.

Freshman class profile. 4,204 applied, 3,169 admitted, 966 enrolled.

Mid 50% test scores		**GPA 2.0-2.99:**	53%
SAT critical reading:	370-470	**Rank in top quarter:**	23%
SAT math:	370-470	**Rank in top tenth:**	7%
ACT composite:	15-18	**End year in good standing:**	73%
GPA 3.75 or higher:	9%	**Return as sophomores:**	63%
GPA 3.50-3.74:	7%	**Out-of-state:**	30%
GPA 3.0-3.49:	24%		

Basis for selection. Admission decisions based primarily on high school record, class rank, and standardized test scores. Audition required for music education program; portfolio required for art education program. **Learning Disabled:** Student must submit documentation, which is sent to Student Health Services Center--Disabled Student Support Services.

High school preparation. 20 units required. Required units include English 4, mathematics 3, social studies 3, science 3 (laboratory 3), foreign language 2 and academic electives 4. 1 physical education or ROTC required.

2008-2009 Annual costs. Tuition/fees: $7,806; $15,298 out-of-state. Room/board: $8,392. Books/supplies: $1,200. Personal expenses: $3,150.

2007-2008 Financial aid. **Need-based:** Average scholarship/grant was $4,363; average loan $3,227. **Non-need-based:** Scholarships awarded for academics, athletics, ROTC.

Application procedures. **Admission:** Closing date 7/31 (postmark date). $25 fee, may be waived for applicants with need. Admission notification on a rolling basis. **Financial aid:** Closing date 5/1. FAFSA required. Applicants notified on a rolling basis starting 4/15; must reply by 7/1 or within 2 week(s) of notification.

Academics. **Special study options:** Cooperative education, cross-registration, distance learning, double major, dual enrollment of high school students, exchange student, honors, internships, liberal arts/career combination, study abroad, teacher certification program, Washington semester. **Credit/placement by examination:** AP, CLEP, institutional tests. 30 credit hours maximum toward bachelor's degree. **Support services:** Learning center, remedial instruction, tutoring, writing center.

Majors. **Agriculture:** Agribusiness operations. **Biology:** General. **Business:** Accounting, business admin, managerial economics, marketing. **Computer sciences:** General. **Education:** Art, business, early childhood, elementary, family/consumer sciences, middle, music, physical, special, technology/industrial arts. **Engineering:** Nuclear. **Engineering technology:** Civil, electrical, industrial, mechanical. **Family/consumer sciences:** General, food/nutrition. **Foreign languages:** General. **Health:** Audiology/speech pathology, nursing (RN). **History:** General. **Math:** General. **Parks/recreation:** Health/fitness. **Physical sciences:** Chemistry, physics. **Protective services:** Law enforcement admin. **Psychology:** General. **Public administration:** Social work. **Social sciences:** General, political science, sociology. **Visual/performing arts:** Dramatic, music management, music performance, studio arts.

Most popular majors. Biology 9%, business/marketing 19%, education 14%, engineering/engineering technologies 6%, family/consumer sciences 12%, public administration/social services 6%.

Computing on campus. 300 workstations in dormitories, library, computer center, student center. Dormitories wired for high-speed internet access and linked to campus network. Commuter students can connect to campus network. Online course registration, online library, helpline, repair service, wireless network available.

Student life. **Freshman orientation:** Available. Preregistration for classes offered. **Housing:** Guaranteed on-campus for freshmen. Single-sex dorms, apartments available. $25 deposit. **Activities:** Bands, choral groups, dance, drama, music ensembles, radio station, student government, student newspaper.

Athletics. NCAA. **Intercollegiate:** Basketball, bowling W, cross-country, football (tackle) M, golf, soccer W, softball W, tennis, track and field, volleyball W. **Intramural:** Basketball, softball. **Team name:** Bulldogs.

Student services. Adult student services, career counseling, health services, personal counseling, placement for graduates, veterans' counselor. **Physically disabled:** Services for speech, hearing impaired.

Contact. E-mail: admissions@scsu.edu
Phone: (803) 536-7185 Toll-free number: (800) 260-5956
Fax: (803) 536-8990
Antonio Boyle, Assistant Vice President of Enrollment Management and Director of Admissions, South Carolina State University, 300 College Street NE, Orangeburg, SC 29117

South University: Columbia

Columbia, South Carolina
www.southuniversity.edu — **CB code: 5097**

- For-profit 4-year university
- Commuter campus in small city
- 774 degree-seeking undergraduates: 35% part-time, 80% women
- 264 graduate students

General. Founded in 1935. Regionally accredited. **Degrees:** 39 bachelor's, 50 associate awarded; master's offered. **Location:** 5 miles from downtown. **Calendar:** Quarter, extensive summer session. **Full-time faculty:** 27 total. **Part-time faculty:** 26 total.

Freshman class profile. 85 applied, 50 admitted, 26 enrolled.

Basis for selection. Open admission, but selective for some programs. Special requirements for pharmacy, nursing, physician assistant studies programs (Savannah campus of South University). SAT or ACT may be submitted in place of required institutional tests for placement. Score report due by September 15. **Homeschooled:** Transcript of courses and grades required.

2008-2009 Annual costs. Tuition/fees: $13,035.

Financial aid. All financial aid based on need.

Application procedures. **Admission:** No deadline. $50 fee, may be waived for applicants with need. Admission notification on a rolling basis. **Financial aid:** Priority date 5/30; no closing date. FAFSA required. Applicants notified on a rolling basis starting 5/30.

Academics. **Special study options:** Cooperative education, distance learning, double major, internships, weekend college. **Credit/placement by examination:** AP, CLEP, institutional tests. **Support services:** Reduced course load, remedial instruction, study skills assistance, tutoring, writing center.

Majors. **Business:** Business admin. **Computer sciences:** Information technology. **Health:** Nursing (RN). **Legal studies:** General. **Protective services:** Corrections, juvenile corrections, law enforcement admin, police science.

Computing on campus. 40 workstations in library, computer center. Commuter students can connect to campus network. Online library, helpline, wireless network available.

Student life. Freshman orientation: Mandatory. Preregistration for classes offered. **Activities:** Literary magazine.

Student services. Adult student services, career counseling, student employment services, financial aid counseling, personal counseling, placement for graduates, veterans' counselor. **Physically disabled:** Services for visually, speech, hearing impaired.

Contact. Phone: (803) 799-9082 Toll-free number: (866) 629-3031
Fax: (803) 799-9038
Trisha Wade, Director of Admissions, South University: Columbia, 9 Science Court, Columbia, SC 29203

Southern Methodist College
Orangeburg, South Carolina
www.smcollege.edu

- Private 4-year Bible college
- Large town
- 27 degree-seeking undergraduates

General. Regionally accredited. **Calendar:** Semester. **Full-time faculty:** 5 total. **Part-time faculty:** 4 total.

Freshman class profile. 5 enrolled.

2008-2009 Annual costs. Tuition/fees: $7,432.

Academics. Credit/placement by examination: CLEP.

Majors. Theology: Bible.

Contact. E-mail: smcinfo@smcollege.edu
Phone: (803) 268-1322
Richard Blank, Director of Admissions, Southern Methodist College, 541 Broughton St., Orangeburg, SC 29115

Southern Wesleyan University
Central, South Carolina
www.swu.edu **CB code: 5896**

- Private 4-year university and liberal arts college affiliated with Wesleyan Church
- Commuter campus in small town
- 1,616 degree-seeking undergraduates: 63% women, 30% African American, 2% Hispanic American, 1% Native American, 1% international
- 760 degree-seeking graduate students
- 89% of applicants admitted
- SAT or ACT (ACT writing optional), application essay required
- 41% graduate within 6 years

General. Founded in 1906. Regionally accredited. **Degrees:** 177 bachelor's, 72 associate awarded; master's offered. **ROTC:** Army, Air Force. **Location:** 25 miles from Greenville. **Calendar:** Semester, limited summer session. **Full-time faculty:** 49 total; 78% have terminal degrees, 8% minority, 26% women. **Part-time faculty:** 197 total; 34% have terminal degrees, 14% minority, 40% women. **Class size:** 83% < 20, 17% 20-39, less than 1% 40-49. **Special facilities:** Electron microscope facility.

Freshman class profile. 655 applied, 583 admitted, 142 enrolled.

Mid 50% test scores		**GPA 2.0-2.99:**	15%
SAT critical reading:	460-550	**Rank in top quarter:**	30%
SAT math:	450-550	**Rank in top tenth:**	8%
SAT writing:	430-530	**Return as sophomores:**	64%
ACT composite:	18-22	**Out-of-state:**	35%
GPA 3.75 or higher:	40%	**Live on campus:**	80%
GPA 3.50-3.74:	23%	**International:**	1%
GPA 3.0-3.49:	22%		

Basis for selection. GPA, class rank, test scores, and religious commitment important. Recommendations considered. Students admitted conditionally if combined SAT score is less than 800 (exclusive of Writing) or high school GPA is less than 2.3, and rank in bottom half of class. Students admitted conditionally take limited number of course hours and are on academic warning. Audition required for music; interview recommended for applicants with special physical, emotional problems.

High school preparation. College-preparatory program recommended. 10 units required. Required units include English 4, mathematics 2, social studies 2 and science 2.

2009-2010 Annual costs. Tuition/fees (projected): $18,700. Room/board: $7,800. Books/supplies: $950. Personal expenses: $1,000.

2008-2009 Financial aid. Need-based: Average need met was 75%. Average scholarship/grant was $12,621; average loan $3,145. 55% of total undergraduate aid awarded as scholarships/grants, 45% as loans/jobs. **Non-need-based:** Scholarships awarded for academics, athletics, music/drama.

Application procedures. Admission: Closing date 8/1 (postmark date). $25 fee, may be waived for applicants with need. Admission notification on a rolling basis beginning on or about 10/1. Must reply by 5/1. **Financial aid:** Priority date 3/31, closing date 6/30. FAFSA, institutional form required. Applicants notified on a rolling basis starting 2/1; must reply within 2 week(s) of notification.

Academics. Special study options: Cooperative education, cross-registration, distance learning, double major, dual enrollment of high school students, external degree, honors, independent study, internships, liberal arts/career combination, student-designed major, study abroad, teacher certification program, Washington semester. **Credit/placement by examination:** AP, CLEP, SAT, ACT, institutional tests. 48 credit hours maximum toward associate degree, 68 toward bachelor's. **Support services:** Learning center, reduced course load, remedial instruction, study skills assistance, tutoring, writing center.

Majors. Biology: General. **Business:** Accounting, business admin, e-commerce, human resources. **Communications:** General. **Computer sciences:** General, computer forensics. **Education:** Biology, early childhood, elementary, emotionally handicapped, English, learning disabled, mathematics, mentally handicapped, music, physical, special. **Health:** Medical radiologic technology/radiation therapy, predental, premedicine, prenursing. **History:** General. **Math:** General. **Parks/recreation:** General, sports admin. **Philosophy/religion:** Religion. **Physical sciences:** Chemistry. **Protective services:** Criminal justice, forensics. **Psychology:** General. **Public administration:** Human services. **Social sciences:** General.

Most popular majors. Business/marketing 67%, education 11%.

Computing on campus. 256 workstations in dormitories, library, computer center. Dormitories wired for high-speed internet access and linked to campus network. Commuter students can connect to campus network. Online course registration, online library, helpline, repair service, student web hosting, wireless network available.

Student life. Freshman orientation: Mandatory. Preregistration for classes offered. Held at the beginning of fall and spring semesters. **Policies:** Students must agree to abide by lifestyle expectations of university. Religious observance required. **Housing:** Guaranteed on-campus for all undergraduates. Coed dorms, single-sex dorms, special housing for disabled, apartments, wellness housing available. $200 fully refundable deposit. **Activities:** Bands, choral groups, drama, literary magazine, music ensembles, musical theater, student government, Christian Service Organization, Student Missions Fellowship, Rotaract, Fellowship of Christian Athletes, student activities board, Habitat for Humanity.

Athletics. NAIA, NCCAA. **Intercollegiate:** Baseball M, basketball, cross-country, golf M, soccer, softball W, volleyball W. **Intramural:** Basketball, football (non-tackle), soccer, softball, table tennis, tennis, volleyball. **Team name:** Warriors.

Student services. Adult student services, alcohol/substance abuse counseling, chaplain/spiritual director, career counseling, financial aid counseling, health services, minority student services, personal counseling. **Physically disabled:** Services for visually, hearing impaired.

Contact. E-mail: admissions@swu.edu
Phone: (864) 644-5550 Toll-free number: (800) 282-8798
Fax: (864) 644-5972
Amanda Young, Director of Admissions, Southern Wesleyan University, PO Box 1020, Central, SC 29630-1020

University of South Carolina
Columbia, South Carolina **CB member**
www.sc.edu **CB code: 5818**

- Public 4-year university
- Residential campus in small city

- 19,458 degree-seeking undergraduates: 7% part-time, 55% women, 12% African American, 3% Asian American, 2% Hispanic American, 1% international
- 7,241 degree-seeking graduate students
- 58% of applicants admitted
- SAT or ACT with writing required
- 67% graduate within 6 years

General. Founded in 1801. Regionally accredited. **Degrees:** 3,828 bachelor's, 11 associate awarded; master's, doctoral, first professional offered. **ROTC:** Army, Naval, Air Force. **Location:** 70 miles from Charlotte, North Carolina. **Calendar:** Semester, extensive summer session. **Full-time faculty:** 1,201 total; 83% have terminal degrees, 9% minority, 40% women. **Part-time faculty:** 508 total; 38% have terminal degrees, 8% minority, 46% women. **Class size:** 46% < 20, 38% 20-39, 6% 40-49, 8% 50-99, 3% >100. **Special facilities:** Observatory, arboretum, green dorm with learning center focusing on sustainability.

Freshman class profile. 17,018 applied, 9,954 admitted, 3,859 enrolled.

Mid 50% test scores		**Rank in top quarter:**	69%
SAT critical reading:	540-640	**Rank in top tenth:**	30%
SAT math:	550-650	**Return as sophomores:**	87%
ACT composite:	24-28	**Out-of-state:**	38%
GPA 3.75 or higher:	61%	**Live on campus:**	94%
GPA 3.50-3.74:	16%	**International:**	1%
GPA 3.0-3.49:	20%	**Fraternities:**	4%
GPA 2.0-2.99:	3%	**Sororities:**	6%

Basis for selection. Admission based on high school curriculum, grades in required high school courses, SAT and ACT scores. **Learning Disabled:** Diagnostic tests required for learning disabled students.

High school preparation. College-preparatory program required. 19 units required. Required units include English 4, mathematics 3, social studies 2, history 1, science 3 (laboratory 3), foreign language 2 and academic electives 4. One unit of physical education or ROTC required.

2008-2009 Annual costs. Tuition/fees: $8,838; $22,908 out-of-state. Health professions (pharmacy, health, nursing), law and medical professions have higher undergraduate and graduate fees. Room/board: $6,652. Books/supplies: $900. Personal expenses: $2,420.

2008-2009 Financial aid. **Need-based:** 2,541 full-time freshmen applied for aid; 1,528 were judged to have need; 1,522 of these received aid. Average need met was 75%. Average scholarship/grant was $4,368; average loan $2,401. 53% of total undergraduate aid awarded as scholarships/grants, 47% as loans/jobs. **Non-need-based:** Scholarships awarded for academics, alumni affiliation, art, athletics, job skills, leadership, minority status, music/drama, religious affiliation, ROTC, state residency.

Application procedures. **Admission:** Closing date 12/1. $50 fee, may be waived for applicants with need. Application must be submitted on paper. Admission notification on a rolling basis beginning on or about 3/15. Must reply by May 1 or within 2 week(s) if notified thereafter. **Financial aid:** Priority date 4/1; no closing date. FAFSA required. Applicants notified on a rolling basis starting 4/1.

Academics. One-month May term focusing on specialized topics. **Special study options:** Accelerated study, combined bachelor's/graduate degree, cooperative education, cross-registration, distance learning, double major, dual enrollment of high school students, ESL, exchange student, external degree, honors, independent study, internships, student-designed major, study abroad, teacher certification program, weekend college. Alternative Spring Break, Dobson Volunteer Service Program, International Program for Students, Undergraduate Research. **Credit/placement by examination:** AP, CLEP, IB, institutional tests. Maximum number of semester hours of credit by examination allowed varies according to degree and program of study. **Support services:** Learning center, reduced course load, study skills assistance, tutoring, writing center.

Honors college/program. To be competitive for admission, students must have an SAT score of at least 1300 (exclusive of Writing) and a high school GPA of at least 3.5. 600 are admitted to yield a freshman class of 275. Academic program consists of 115-125 honors classes per semester across most disciplines and levels.

Majors. **Area/ethnic studies:** African-American, European, Latin American, women's. **Biology:** General, marine. **Business:** Accounting, business admin, finance, hospitality admin, insurance, management science, managerial economics, marketing, office management, real estate, retailing. **Communications:** Advertising, broadcast journalism, journalism, media studies, public relations. **Computer sciences:** General. **Education:** Art, early childhood, physical. **Engineering:** Biomedical, chemical, civil, computer, electrical, mechanical. **Foreign languages:** Classics, French, German, Italian, Russian, Spanish. **Health:** Cardiovascular technology, nursing (RN). **History:** General. **Liberal arts:** Arts/sciences. **Math:** General, statistics. **Parks/recreation:** Exercise sciences, sports admin. **Philosophy/religion:** Philosophy, religion. **Physical sciences:** Chemistry, geology, geophysics, physics. **Protective services:** Law enforcement admin. **Psychology:** Experimental. **Social sciences:** Anthropology, economics, geography, international relations, political science, sociology. **Visual/performing arts:** Art history/conservation, dance, dramatic, film/cinema, studio arts. **Other:** Business & technology education, Technology Support and Training Management, Visual Communications.

Most popular majors. Biology 6%, business/marketing 25%, communications/journalism 9%, education 6%, parks/recreation 6%, social sciences 10%, visual/performing arts 7%.

Computing on campus. 2,800 workstations in dormitories, library, computer center, student center. Dormitories wired for high-speed internet access and linked to campus network. Commuter students can connect to campus network. Online course registration, online library, helpline, wireless network available.

Student life. **Freshman orientation:** Available, $60 fee. Preregistration for classes offered. Parents may also attend to view campus for $20 fee. **Housing:** Guaranteed on-campus for freshmen. Coed dorms, single-sex dorms, special housing for disabled, apartments, fraternity/sorority housing, wellness housing available. $145 deposit, deadline 5/1. Honors (undergraduate) and wellness housing, Preston Residential College, communities for premedical, engineering, athletic, teaching fellows, global, and environmentally friendly available. **Activities:** Bands, campus ministries, choral groups, dance, drama, film society, international student organizations, literary magazine, music ensembles, Model UN, musical theater, opera, radio station, student government, student newspaper, symphony orchestra, TV station, Baptist Collegiate Ministry, University Ambassadors, Association of African American Students, Habitat for Humanity, Dance Marathon, cultural exchange association, orientation leaders association, Hill of the Lord, BGLSA.

Athletics. NCAA. **Intercollegiate:** Baseball M, basketball, cross-country W, diving, equestrian W, football (tackle) M, golf, soccer, softball W, swimming, tennis, track and field, volleyball W. **Intramural:** Badminton, basketball, bowling, golf, racquetball, soccer, softball, swimming, table tennis, tennis, volleyball, weight lifting. **Team name:** Fighting Gamecocks.

Student services. Adult student services, alcohol/substance abuse counseling, career counseling, services for economically disadvantaged, student employment services, financial aid counseling, health services, minority student services, personal counseling, placement for graduates, veterans' counselor. **Physically disabled:** Services for visually, speech, hearing impaired. **Learning disabled:** Comprehensive services available.

Contact. E-mail: admissions-ugrad@sc.edu
Phone: (803) 777-7700 Toll-free number: (800) 868-5872
Fax: (803) 777-0101
Scott Verzyl, Director of Undergraduate Admissions, University of South Carolina, Office of Undergraduate Admissions, Columbia, SC 29208

University of South Carolina at Aiken

Aiken, South Carolina — **CB member**
www.usca.edu — **CB code: 5840**

- Public 4-year university and liberal arts college
- Commuter campus in large town
- 2,813 degree-seeking undergraduates: 15% part-time, 66% women
- 49 degree-seeking graduate students
- 38% of applicants admitted
- SAT or ACT (ACT writing recommended) required
- 39% graduate within 6 years

General. Founded in 1961. Regionally accredited. **Degrees:** 502 bachelor's awarded; master's offered. **Location:** 55 miles from Columbia, 15 miles from Augusta, Georgia. **Calendar:** Semester, limited summer session. **Full-time faculty:** 151 total; 7% minority, 49% women. **Part-time faculty:** 72 total; 8% minority, 54% women. **Class size:** 57% < 20, 43% 20-39, less than 1% 40-49. **Special facilities:** Fine arts center, science center, natatorium, planetarium, convocation center.

Freshman class profile. 2,358 applied, 898 admitted, 594 enrolled.

Mid 50% test scores		**GPA 2.0-2.99:**	14%
SAT critical reading:	440-530	**Rank in top quarter:**	41%
SAT math:	440-540	**Rank in top tenth:**	13%
SAT writing:	430-510	**Return as sophomores:**	69%
ACT composite:	18-22	**Out-of-state:**	9%
GPA 3.75 or higher:	36%	**Live on campus:**	54%
GPA 3.50-3.74:	16%	**Fraternities:**	5%
GPA 3.0-3.49:	34%	**Sororities:**	9%

Basis for selection. Test scores, high school core GPA important. Admission based on course selection, standardized test scores and a predicted college GPA. Audition, essay, interview, portfolio recommended.

High school preparation. 21 units required. Required units include English 4, mathematics 4, social studies 2, history 1, science 3 (laboratory 3), foreign language 2, computer science 1, visual/performing arts 1 and academic electives 4. Physical education or ROTC of 1 unit; elective college preparatory credits must come from 3 different fields.

2008-2009 Annual costs. Tuition/fees: $7,582; $14,946 out-of-state. Room/board: $6,250. Books/supplies: $1,080. Personal expenses: $1,690.

2007-2008 Financial aid. Need-based: 520 full-time freshmen applied for aid; 281 were judged to have need; 237 of these received aid. Average need met was 61%. Average scholarship/grant was $1,310; average loan $3,330. 35% of total undergraduate aid awarded as scholarships/grants, 65% as loans/jobs. **Non-need-based:** Awarded to 663 full-time undergraduates, including 140 freshmen. Scholarships awarded for academics, alumni affiliation, art, athletics, leadership, minority status, music/drama, state residency.

Application procedures. Admission: Priority date 7/1; deadline 8/1 (postmark date). $45 fee, may be waived for applicants with need. Admission notification on a rolling basis beginning on or about 9/1. Must reply by May 1 or within 3 week(s) if notified thereafter. **Financial aid:** Priority date 3/15; no closing date. FAFSA required. Applicants notified on a rolling basis starting 11/1; must reply within 2 week(s) of notification.

Academics. Special study options: Cooperative education, distance learning, double major, dual enrollment of high school students, ESL, honors, independent study, internships, study abroad, teacher certification program. **Credit/placement by examination:** AP, CLEP, IB, institutional tests. 30 credit hours maximum toward bachelor's degree. **Support services:** Learning center, study skills assistance, tutoring, writing center.

Majors. Biology: General. **Business:** General. **Communications:** General. **Education:** General, early childhood, elementary, English, mathematics, middle, music, science, secondary, social science, social studies, special. **Health:** Nursing (RN). **History:** General. **Interdisciplinary:** Math/computer science. **Math:** Applied. **Parks/recreation:** Exercise sciences. **Physical sciences:** Chemistry. **Psychology:** General. **Social sciences:** Political science, sociology. **Visual/performing arts:** Studio arts.

Most popular majors. Biology 6%, business/marketing 28%, communications/journalism 7%, education 10%, health sciences 13%, parks/recreation 6%, psychology 6%, social sciences 12%.

Computing on campus. 802 workstations in dormitories, library, computer center, student center. Dormitories wired for high-speed internet access and linked to campus network. Commuter students can connect to campus network. Online course registration, helpline, wireless network available.

Student life. Freshman orientation: Mandatory, $75 fee. Preregistration for classes offered. Held in June, July, and August. June and July orientations offer registration. **Housing:** Coed dorms, special housing for disabled, apartments, wellness housing available. $25 partly refundable deposit. **Activities:** Bands, campus ministries, dance, drama, international student organizations, music ensembles, musical theater, student government, student newspaper, symphony orchestra, Campus Crusade for Christ, honor societies, Association for Women's Issues, Pacer Union Board, High Adventure Club, African American Students' Alliance, Community Action Board, College Republicans.

Athletics. NCAA. **Intercollegiate:** Baseball M, basketball, cheerleading, cross-country W, golf M, soccer, softball W, tennis, volleyball W. **Intramural:** Badminton, baseball M, basketball, bowling, golf, soccer, softball, table tennis, tennis, volleyball. **Team name:** Pacers.

Student services. Adult student services, alcohol/substance abuse counseling, career counseling, student employment services, financial aid counseling, health services, minority student services, on-campus daycare, personal counseling, placement for graduates, veterans' counselor. **Physically disabled:** Services for visually, speech, hearing impaired.

Contact. E-mail: admit@usca.edu
Phone: (803) 641-3366 Toll-free number: (888) 969-8722
Fax: (803) 641-3727
Andrew Hendrix, Director of Admissions, University of South Carolina at Aiken, 471 University Parkway, Aiken, SC 29801-6399

University of South Carolina at Beaufort

Bluffton, South Carolina — **CB member**
www.uscb.edu — **CB code: 5845**

- Public 4-year university and liberal arts college
- Commuter campus in large town
- 1,313 degree-seeking undergraduates: 25% part-time, 59% women, 15% African American, 1% Asian American, 4% Hispanic American, 1% Native American, 1% international
- SAT or ACT (ACT writing optional) required

General. Founded in 1959. Regionally accredited. South Campus located at Gateway to Hilton Head, North Campus located in Historic Beaufort. **Degrees:** 138 bachelor's, 24 associate awarded. **Location:** 72 miles from Charleston, 42 miles from Savannah, Georgia. **Calendar:** Semester, limited summer session. **Full-time faculty:** 53 total; 77% have terminal degrees, 15% minority, 40% women. **Part-time faculty:** 62 total; 40% have terminal degrees. **Class size:** 59% < 20, 38% 20-39, 2% 40-49, less than 1% 50-99. **Special facilities:** Performing arts center.

Freshman class profile.

Mid 50% test scores		**Return as sophomores:**	57%
SAT critical reading:	430-540	**Out-of-state:**	20%
SAT math:	420-540	**Live on campus:**	40%
ACT composite:	17-21	**International:**	2%

Basis for selection. Test scores, rigor of secondary school record important; academic GPA considered.

High school preparation. 20 units required. Required units include English 4, mathematics 3, social studies 2, history 1, science 3 (laboratory 3), foreign language 2 and academic electives 5. Electives must be from 3 areas. Computer Science course recommended. 1 PE or ROTC required.

2008-2009 Annual costs. Tuition/fees: $7,134; $14,710 out-of-state. Books/supplies: $975. Personal expenses: $1,512.

2008-2009 Financial aid. Non-need-based: Scholarships awarded for academics, state residency.

Application procedures. Admission: No deadline. $40 fee, may be waived for applicants with need. Admission notification on a rolling basis beginning on or about 2/1. Students may submit application through CollegeNET. **Financial aid:** Priority date 4/15; no closing date. FAFSA required. Applicants notified on a rolling basis starting 5/31; must reply within 2 week(s) of notification.

Academics. Special study options: Cooperative education, distance learning, dual enrollment of high school students, independent study, internships, student-designed major, study abroad, teacher certification program. **Credit/placement by examination:** AP, CLEP, institutional tests. 15 credit hours maximum toward associate degree, 30 toward bachelor's. **Support services:** Learning center, reduced course load, study skills assistance, tutoring, writing center.

Majors. Biology: General. **Business:** Business admin, hospitality admin. **Education:** Early childhood. **Foreign languages:** Spanish. **Health:** Nursing (RN). **History:** General. **Liberal arts:** Arts/sciences. **Psychology:** General. **Social sciences:** General.

Most popular majors. Business/marketing 38%, education 10%, English 9%, liberal arts 7%, psychology 12%, social sciences 17%.

Computing on campus. 114 workstations in library, computer center. Dormitories wired for high-speed internet access. Online course registration, online library available.

Student life. Freshman orientation: Mandatory. Preregistration for classes offered. **Housing:** Special housing for disabled, apartments, wellness housing available. **Activities:** Drama, literary magazine, musical theater, student government, student newspaper, African American student association, Christian student fellowship, business club, veterans association, education club, Gamma Beta Phi honor society, psychology/sociology/anthropology club.

Athletics. NAIA. **Intercollegiate:** Baseball M, cross-country, golf. **Intramural:** Football (non-tackle), soccer. **Team name:** Sand Sharks.

Student services. Career counseling, services for economically disadvantaged, student employment services, financial aid counseling, personal counseling, veterans' counselor.

Contact. E-mail: jofferyb@uscb.edu
Phone: (843) 208-8000 Toll-free number: (877) 885-5271
Fax: (843) 208-8290
Joffery Blair, Director of Admissions, University of South Carolina at Beaufort, One University Boulevard, Bluffton, SC 29909

University of South Carolina Upstate

Spartanburg, South Carolina
www.uscupstate.edu **CB code: 5850**

- Public 4-year university
- Commuter campus in small city
- 4,754 degree-seeking undergraduates: 13% part-time, 65% women, 25% African American, 2% Asian American, 3% Hispanic American, 2% international
- 5 degree-seeking graduate students
- 66% of applicants admitted
- SAT or ACT (ACT writing optional) required
- 38% graduate within 6 years

General. Founded in 1967. Regionally accredited. **Degrees:** 927 bachelor's awarded; master's offered. **ROTC:** Army. **Location:** 30 miles from Greenville, 70 miles from Charlotte, North Carolina. **Calendar:** Semester, extensive summer session. **Full-time faculty:** 235 total; 68% have terminal degrees, 15% minority, 57% women. **Part-time faculty:** 176 total; 22% have terminal degrees, 10% minority, 55% women. **Class size:** 56% < 20, 42% 20-39, 1% 40-49, less than 1% 50-99. **Special facilities:** Art Studies, film, theater, recital hall, language laboratory, center for international studies and language services, audiovisual production center, digital lab; centers for interdisciplinary studies, watershed ecology center.

Freshman class profile. 2,505 applied, 1,649 admitted, 727 enrolled.

Mid 50% test scores		**Rank in top quarter:**	41%
SAT critical reading:	440-530	**Rank in top tenth:**	14%
SAT math:	450-540	**Return as sophomores:**	65%
SAT writing:	430-520	**Out-of-state:**	6%
ACT composite:	19-22	**Live on campus:**	53%
GPA 3.75 or higher:	38%	**International:**	3%
GPA 3.50-3.74:	17%	**Fraternities:**	1%
GPA 3.0-3.49:	29%	**Sororities:**	1%
GPA 2.0-2.99:	16%		

Basis for selection. Cumulative average of C or better in preparatory courses and minimum 850 SAT (exclusive of Writing), or 18 ACT required. Higher grades may offset lower SAT/ACT scores, and higher SAT/ACT scores may offset lower grades. Interviews recommended.

High school preparation. College-preparatory program required. 20 units required; 22 recommended. Required and recommended units include English 4, mathematics 3-4, social studies 2, history 1, science 3 (laboratory 3), foreign language 2-3 and academic electives 4. Students who graduated from high school between 1988-2000 must meet above requirements. However, these students need 2 rather than 3 laboratory sciences and 1 rather than 4 electives.

2008-2009 Annual costs. Tuition/fees: $8,512; $16,854 out-of-state. Room/board: $6,400. Books/supplies: $1,000. Personal expenses: $200.

2007-2008 Financial aid. Need-based: 666 full-time freshmen applied for aid; 503 were judged to have need; 500 of these received aid. Average need met was 67%. Average scholarship/grant was $4,139; average loan $3,064. 40% of total undergraduate aid awarded as scholarships/grants, 60% as loans/jobs. **Non-need-based:** Awarded to 1,522 full-time undergraduates, including 571 freshmen. Scholarships awarded for academics, athletics, minority status, ROTC, state residency. **Additional information:** Out-of-state students who are recipients of financial aid may qualify for out-of-state fee waiver. Educational benefits available to veterans and children of deceased/disabled veterans.

Application procedures. Admission: Priority date 8/15; no deadline. $40 fee, may be waived for applicants with need. Admission notification on a rolling basis beginning on or about 9/15. **Financial aid:** Priority date 3/1, closing date 7/15. FAFSA, institutional form required. Applicants notified on a rolling basis starting 5/1; must reply within 2 week(s) of notification.

Academics. Special study options: Accelerated study, cross-registration, distance learning, double major, ESL, exchange student, honors, independent study, internships, liberal arts/career combination, student-designed major, study abroad, teacher certification program, Washington semester. **Credit/placement by examination:** AP, CLEP, IB, institutional tests. 30 credit hours maximum toward bachelor's degree. Credit also awarded for: American College Testing Program, Defense Activity for Nontraditional Education Support, Institution Credit by Examination, Military Service School Credit, Credit for Non-collegiate Programs, and Correspondence Course Credits. **Support services:** Learning center, reduced course load, remedial instruction, study skills assistance, tutoring, writing center.

Majors. Biology: General. **Business:** Business admin. **Communications:** General. **Computer sciences:** General, information systems. **Education:** Early childhood, elementary, physical, secondary, special. **Engineering technology:** Industrial management. **Foreign languages:** Spanish. **Health:** Nursing (RN). **History:** General. **Interdisciplinary:** Accounting/computer science. **Liberal arts:** Arts/sciences. **Math:** General, applied. **Physical sciences:** Chemistry. **Protective services:** Criminal justice. **Psychology:** General. **Social sciences:** Political science, sociology. **Visual/performing arts:** Commercial/advertising art, design.

Most popular majors. Business/marketing 16%, education 16%, health sciences 26%, liberal arts 9%, psychology 8%.

Computing on campus. 600 workstations in dormitories, library, computer center, student center. Dormitories wired for high-speed internet access and linked to campus network. Commuter students can connect to campus network. Online course registration, online library, helpline, repair service, student web hosting, wireless network available.

Student life. Freshman orientation: Available. Preregistration for classes offered. **Housing:** Coed dorms, apartments, wellness housing available. $135 fully refundable deposit, deadline 6/1. **Activities:** Jazz band, campus ministries, choral groups, dance, drama, international student organizations, literary magazine, music ensembles, student government, student newspaper, African-American Association, Baptist student union, Campus Crusade for Christ, College Republicans, Young Democrats, student education association, campus activity board, Association for the Education of Young Children, environmental club, Amnesty International.

Athletics. NCAA. **Intercollegiate:** Baseball M, basketball, cheerleading, cross-country, golf, soccer, softball W, tennis, track and field, volleyball W. **Intramural:** Basketball, bowling, football (non-tackle), soccer, softball, table tennis, tennis, track and field, volleyball. **Team name:** Spartans.

Student services. Adult student services, alcohol/substance abuse counseling, chaplain/spiritual director, career counseling, services for economically disadvantaged, student employment services, financial aid counseling, health services, minority student services, on-campus daycare, personal counseling, placement for graduates, veterans' counselor, women's services. **Physically disabled:** Services for visually, speech, hearing impaired. **Learning disabled:** Comprehensive services available.

Contact. E-mail: dstewart@uscupstate.edu
Phone: (864) 503-5246 Toll-free number: (800) 277-8727
Fax: (864) 503-5727
Donette Stewart, Assistant Vice Chancellor for Enrollment Services, University of South Carolina Upstate, 800 University Way, Spartanburg, SC 29303

Voorhees College

Denmark, South Carolina
www.voorhees.edu **CB code: 5863**

- Private 4-year liberal arts college affiliated with Episcopal Church
- Residential campus in small town

General. Founded in 1897. Regionally accredited. **Location:** 50 miles from Columbia and Augusta, Georgia. **Calendar:** Semester.

Annual costs/financial aid. Tuition/fees (2008-2009): $9,284. Room/board: $5,946. Books/supplies: $600. Personal expenses: $1,365. Need-based financial aid available to full-time and part-time students.

Contact. Phone: (803) 780-1031
Dean, Enrollment Management, 213 Wiggins Road, Denmark, SC 29042

W.L. Bonner Bible College

Columbia, South Carolina
www.wlbonnercollege.org

- Private 4-year Bible college
- Small city

General. Accredited by ABHE. **Calendar:** Semester.

Annual costs/financial aid. Tuition/fees (2008-2009): $7,720. Room: $2,240.

Contact. Phone: (803) 754-3950
Registrar, 4430 Argent Court, Columbia, SC 29203

Winthrop University
Rock Hill, South Carolina — **CB member**
www.winthrop.edu — **CB code: 5910**

- Public 4-year university
- Residential campus in small city
- 4,801 degree-seeking undergraduates: 7% part-time, 68% women, 27% African American, 2% Asian American, 2% Hispanic American, 1% Native American, 2% international
- 1,005 degree-seeking graduate students
- 68% of applicants admitted
- SAT or ACT (ACT writing optional) required
- 61% graduate within 6 years

General. Founded in 1886. Regionally accredited. **Degrees:** 930 bachelor's awarded; master's offered. **ROTC:** Army. **Location:** 20 miles from Charlotte, North Carolina. **Calendar:** Semester, extensive summer session. **Full-time faculty:** 282 total; 82% have terminal degrees, 12% minority, 49% women. **Part-time faculty:** 277 total; 21% have terminal degrees, 11% minority, 59% women. **Class size:** 40% < 20, 48% 20-39, 9% 40-49, 4% 50-99. **Special facilities:** Nursery laboratory, music conservatory.

Freshman class profile. 4,062 applied, 2,776 admitted, 1,049 enrolled.

Mid 50% test scores			
SAT critical reading:	470-580	Rank in top quarter:	46%
SAT math:	490-590	Rank in top tenth:	17%
ACT composite:	20-25	Return as sophomores:	71%
GPA 3.75 or higher:	49%	Out-of-state:	13%
GPA 3.50-3.74:	18%	Live on campus:	89%
GPA 3.0-3.49:	29%	International:	2%
GPA 2.0-2.99:	4%	Sororities:	3%

Basis for selection. School achievement record, test scores, counselor recommendations important, school and community activities considered. Essay, interview recommended for all; audition recommended for dance, music, theater programs.

High school preparation. 20 units required. Required units include English 4, mathematics 3, social studies 2, history 1, science 3 (laboratory 3), foreign language 2 and academic electives 4. Physical education or ROTC required.

2008-2009 Annual costs. Tuition/fees: $11,060; $20,610 out-of-state. Room/board: $6,140. Books/supplies: $750. Personal expenses: $1,236.

2007-2008 Financial aid. **Need-based:** 61% of total undergraduate aid awarded as scholarships/grants, 39% as loans/jobs. **Non-need-based:** Scholarships awarded for academics, art, athletics, music/drama, state residency. **Additional information:** Academic scholarships from $1,500 to full tuition and board awarded to approximately one-third of entering freshman class each year.

Application procedures. **Admission:** Closing date 5/1. $40 fee, may be waived for applicants with need. Application must be submitted on paper. Admission notification on a rolling basis beginning on or about 10/21. Must reply by May 1 or within 3 week(s) if notified thereafter. 8 monthly notification dates for fall between October and May on the 21st of the month. **Financial aid:** Priority date 3/1; no closing date. FAFSA required. Applicants notified on a rolling basis starting 4/1; must reply within 2 week(s) of notification.

Academics. **Special study options:** Cooperative education, cross-registration, distance learning, double major, exchange student, honors, independent study, internships, study abroad, teacher certification program, United Nations semester. **Credit/placement by examination:** AP, CLEP, IB, SAT, ACT, institutional tests. 30 credit hours maximum toward bachelor's degree. **Support services:** Pre-admission summer program, study skills assistance, tutoring, writing center.

Majors. **Biology:** General. **Business:** Business admin, e-commerce. **Communications:** Journalism, public relations. **Computer sciences:** General. **Education:** Early childhood, elementary, middle, music, physical, special. **Family/consumer sciences:** Food/nutrition. **Foreign languages:** General. **Health:** Clinical lab science, communication disorders. **History:** General. **Math:** General. **Parks/recreation:** Sports admin. **Philosophy/religion:** Philosophy, religion. **Physical sciences:** Chemistry. **Psychology:** General. **Public administration:** Social work. **Social sciences:** Political science, sociology. **Visual/performing arts:** Art, art history/conservation, dance, dramatic, studio arts.

Most popular majors. Business/marketing 21%, communications/journalism 6%, education 25%, psychology 8%, social sciences 6%, visual/performing arts 13%.

Computing on campus. 584 workstations in dormitories, library, computer center, student center. Dormitories wired for high-speed internet access and linked to campus network. Commuter students can connect to campus network. Online course registration, helpline, student web hosting, wireless network available.

Student life. **Freshman orientation:** Available. 3-day session in June. **Policies:** First and second year students are required to live on campus unless living with parents within 50 miles. **Housing:** Guaranteed on-campus for freshmen. Coed dorms, single-sex dorms, special housing for disabled, apartments, fraternity/sorority housing, wellness housing available. $100 deposit. **Activities:** Bands, campus ministries, choral groups, dance, drama, international student organizations, literary magazine, music ensembles, Model UN, musical theater, radio station, student government, student newspaper, symphony orchestra, TV station, 115 clubs and organizations.

Athletics. NCAA. **Intercollegiate:** Baseball M, basketball, cross-country, golf, soccer, softball W, tennis, track and field, volleyball W. **Intramural:** Badminton, basketball, cross-country, fencing, football (non-tackle), football (tackle) M, golf, handball, racquetball, soccer, softball, swimming, table tennis, tennis, volleyball. **Team name:** Eagles.

Student services. Adult student services, alcohol/substance abuse counseling, career counseling, student employment services, financial aid counseling, health services, minority student services, personal counseling, placement for graduates, veterans' counselor.

Contact. E-mail: admissions@winthrop.edu
Phone: (803) 323-2191 Toll-free number: (800) 763-0230
Fax: (803) 323-2137
Debi Barber, Director of Admissions, Winthrop University, 701 Oakland Avenue, Rock Hill, SC 29733

Wofford College
Spartanburg, South Carolina — **CB member**
www.wofford.edu — **CB code: 5912**

- Private 4-year liberal arts college affiliated with United Methodist Church
- Residential campus in small city
- 1,377 degree-seeking undergraduates: 1% part-time, 48% women, 6% African American, 3% Asian American, 2% Hispanic American, 1% international
- 59% of applicants admitted
- SAT or ACT with writing, application essay required
- 83% graduate within 6 years; 47% enter graduate study

General. Founded in 1854. Regionally accredited. Opportunities for summer research "Community of Scholars," studies abroad, service learning, and environmental studies. **Degrees:** 299 bachelor's awarded. **ROTC:** Army. **Location:** 70 miles from Charlotte, North Carolina, 180 miles from Atlanta. **Calendar:** 4-1-4, limited summer session. **Full-time faculty:** 113 total; 94% have terminal degrees, 8% minority, 39% women. **Part-time faculty:** 32 total; 34% have terminal degrees, 6% minority, 41% women. **Class size:** 59% < 20, 39% 20-39, 1% 40-49, 1% 50-99. **Special facilities:** National arboretum, South Carolina Methodist Archives.

Freshman class profile. 2,278 applied, 1,342 admitted, 415 enrolled.

Mid 50% test scores			
SAT critical reading:	560-660	Rank in top quarter:	77%
SAT math:	570-680	Rank in top tenth:	56%
SAT writing:	560-660	End year in good standing:	98%
ACT composite:	22-27	Return as sophomores:	91%
GPA 3.75 or higher:	68%	Out-of-state:	45%
GPA 3.50-3.74:	12%	Live on campus:	98%
GPA 3.0-3.49:	17%	International:	1%
GPA 2.0-2.99:	3%	Fraternities:	46%
		Sororities:	54%

Basis for selection. High school record, including AP courses, most important. Test scores important. School recommendation, leadership, extracurricular activities considered. Interview recommended. **Learning Disabled:** Prospective students with learning disabilities consult with the Dean of Health Services.

High school preparation. College-preparatory program recommended. 20 units recommended. Recommended units include English 4, mathematics 4, social studies 2, history 1, (laboratory 3), foreign language 3, computer science 1, visual/performing arts 1 and academic electives 1.

2009-2010 Annual costs. Tuition/fees: $30,280. Room/board: $8,480. Books/supplies: $1,050. Personal expenses: $1,232.

2008-2009 Financial aid. Need-based: 293 full-time freshmen applied for aid; 216 were judged to have need; 216 of these received aid. Average need met was 88%. Average scholarship/grant was $25,295; average loan $3,655. 82% of total undergraduate aid awarded as scholarships/grants, 18% as loans/jobs. **Non-need-based:** Awarded to 747 full-time undergraduates, including 214 freshmen. Scholarships awarded for academics, athletics, leadership, music/drama, religious affiliation, ROTC, state residency.

Application procedures. Admission: Closing date 2/1 (postmark date). $35 fee, may be waived for applicants with need. Application must be submitted online. Admission notification 3/15. Must reply by 5/1. Must be admitted by December 15 to be eligible for Wofford Scholars (academic merit scholarship) program. **Financial aid:** Priority date 3/15; no closing date. FAFSA required. Applicants notified on a rolling basis starting 3/31; must reply by 5/1.

Academics. January interim program devoted to internships, foreign travel, independent study, and other nontraditional academic pursuits. **Special study options:** Accelerated study, combined bachelor's/graduate degree, cross-registration, double major, dual enrollment of high school students, independent study, internships, liberal arts/career combination, student-designed major, study abroad, teacher certification program, Washington semester. **Credit/placement by examination:** AP, CLEP, IB. 30 credit hours maximum toward bachelor's degree. **Support services:** Tutoring, writing center.

Majors. Biology: General. **Business:** Accounting, finance, international, managerial economics. **Computer sciences:** General, computer science. **Conservation:** Environmental studies. **Foreign languages:** Chinese, French, German, Spanish. **History:** General. **Liberal arts:** Arts/sciences. **Math:** General. **Philosophy/religion:** Philosophy, religion. **Physical sciences:** Chemistry, physics. **Psychology:** General. **Social sciences:** Economics, sociology, U.S. government. **Visual/performing arts:** Art history/conservation, theater design.

Most popular majors. Biology 19%, business/marketing 33%, English 6%, foreign language 9%, social sciences 12%.

Computing on campus. 250 workstations in library, computer center, student center. Dormitories wired for high-speed internet access and linked to campus network. Commuter students can connect to campus network. Online course registration, online library, helpline, student web hosting, wireless network available.

Student life. Freshman orientation: Mandatory. Preregistration for classes offered. **Policies:** Honor code and honor council. Students not living with immediate family member must secure permission to live off-campus. **Housing:** Guaranteed on-campus for all undergraduates. Coed dorms, apartments, wellness housing available. $300 nonrefundable deposit, deadline 5/1. **Activities:** Bands, campus ministries, choral groups, dance, drama, literary magazine, music ensembles, student government, student newspaper, Fellowship of Christian Athletes, Baptist Collegiate Ministry, Association of African-American Students, student volunteer services, Wesley Fellowship, College Republicans, College Democrats, Lion's Club, Rotaract Club.

Athletics. NCAA. **Intercollegiate:** Baseball M, basketball, cross-country, football (tackle) M, golf, rifle, soccer, tennis, track and field, volleyball W. **Intramural:** Basketball, football (non-tackle), soccer, softball, volleyball. **Team name:** Terriers.

Student services. Alcohol/substance abuse counseling, chaplain/spiritual director, career counseling, student employment services, financial aid counseling, health services, minority student services, personal counseling, placement for graduates. **Physically disabled:** Services for visually, speech, hearing impaired.

Contact. E-mail: admission@wofford.edu
Phone: (864) 597-4130 Fax: (864) 597-4147
Jennifer Mauran, Director of Admission, Wofford College, 429 North Church Street, Spartanburg, SC 29303-3663

South Dakota

Augustana College

Sioux Falls, South Dakota
www.augie.edu
CB member
CB code: 6015

- Private 4-year liberal arts college affiliated with Evangelical Lutheran Church in America
- Residential campus in small city
- 1,701 degree-seeking undergraduates: 4% part-time, 64% women, 1% African American, 1% Asian American, 2% international
- 21 degree-seeking graduate students
- 81% of applicants admitted
- SAT or ACT (ACT writing optional), application essay required
- 68% graduate within 6 years; 21% enter graduate study

General. Founded in 1860. Regionally accredited. **Degrees:** 387 bachelor's awarded; master's offered. **Location:** 160 miles from Omaha, Nebraska, 230 miles from Minneapolis-St. Paul. **Calendar:** 4-1-4, limited summer session. **Full-time faculty:** 119 total; 78% have terminal degrees, 4% minority, 44% women. **Part-time faculty:** 55 total; 62% women. **Class size:** 51% < 20, 46% 20-39, 2% 40-49, 1% 50-99. **Special facilities:** Western studies museum and archives, archeology lab, liturgical art center, prairie garden, ASL laboratory, art gallery, model classroom.

Freshman class profile. 1,186 applied, 966 admitted, 438 enrolled.

Mid 50% test scores		**GPA 2.0-2.99:**	7%
SAT critical reading:	520-610	**Rank in top quarter:**	62%
SAT math:	500-620	**Rank in top tenth:**	28%
SAT writing:	500-660	**End year in good standing:**	78%
ACT composite:	22-28	**Return as sophomores:**	78%
GPA 3.75 or higher:	47%	**Out-of-state:**	61%
GPA 3.50-3.74:	23%	**Live on campus:**	97%
GPA 3.0-3.49:	22%	**International:**	3%

Basis for selection. High school transcript, test scores, 1 recommendation, and writing sample required. Minimum requirements: 20 ACT (or equivalent SAT), 2.75 GPA, class rank at 50% or higher. Interview recommended for all; supplementary essay questions/materials required for students who do not meet minimum admission requirements.

High school preparation. 16 units recommended. Recommended units include English 4, mathematics 4, social studies 3, science 3 (laboratory 2) and foreign language 2. 1 unit fine arts and 1/2 unit computer science also recommended.

2008-2009 Annual costs. Tuition/fees: $22,452. Room/board: $5,920. Books/supplies: $800. Personal expenses: $800.

2008-2009 Financial aid. Non-need-based: Scholarships awarded for academics, alumni affiliation, art, athletics, leadership, minority status, music/drama, religious affiliation, state residency.

Application procedures. Admission: Priority date 1/15; no deadline. No application fee. Admission notification on a rolling basis beginning on or about 10/1. Must reply by May 1 or within 3 week(s) if notified thereafter. **Financial aid:** Priority date 3/1; no closing date. FAFSA required. Applicants notified on a rolling basis starting 3/15; must reply within 3 week(s) of notification.

Academics. Special study options: Combined bachelor's/graduate degree, cooperative education, cross-registration, double major, dual enrollment of high school students, exchange student, external degree, honors, independent study, internships, liberal arts/career combination, study abroad, teacher certification program, urban semester, Washington semester. **Credit/placement by examination:** AP, CLEP, IB, SAT, ACT, institutional tests. 32 credit hours maximum toward bachelor's degree. **Support services:** Learning center, pre-admission summer program, reduced course load, remedial instruction, study skills assistance, tutoring, writing center.

Majors. Biology: General. **Business:** General, accounting, business admin, communications, management information systems. **Communications:** General, journalism. **Computer sciences:** Computer science. **Education:** Art, biology, Deaf/hearing impaired, elementary, emotionally handicapped, English, French, German, history, learning disabled, mathematics, mentally handicapped, multicultural, music, physical, physically handicapped, physics, psychology, secondary, social studies, Spanish, special, speech, speech impaired. **Engineering:** Physics. **Foreign languages:** General, American Sign Language, French, German, sign language interpretation, Spanish. **Health:** Athletic training, audiology/speech pathology, clinical lab science, clinical lab technology, communication disorders, nursing (RN), predental, premedicine, prepharmacy, preveterinary. **History:** General. **Interdisciplinary:** Global studies. **Math:** General. **Parks/recreation:** Exercise sciences, health/fitness, sports admin. **Philosophy/religion:** Philosophy, religion. **Physical sciences:** Chemistry, physics. **Protective services:** Forensics. **Psychology:** General. **Social sciences:** Anthropology, economics, political science, sociology. **Theology:** Sacred music. **Visual/performing arts:** Art, dramatic.

Most popular majors. Biology 7%, business/marketing 19%, education 18%, health sciences 13%, psychology 6%, social sciences 10%.

Computing on campus. 255 workstations in dormitories, library, computer center, student center. Dormitories wired for high-speed internet access and linked to campus network. Commuter students can connect to campus network. Online course registration, online library, helpline, repair service, wireless network available.

Student life. Freshman orientation: Mandatory. Preregistration for classes offered. Begins on move-in day and extends through first week of class. **Housing:** Guaranteed on-campus for all undergraduates. Coed dorms, special housing for disabled, apartments, wellness housing available. $100 fully refundable deposit. **Activities:** Bands, campus ministries, choral groups, dance, drama, literary magazine, music ensembles, musical theater, radio station, student government, student newspaper, symphony orchestra, Lutheran-ELCA congregation, Fellowship of Christian Athletes, Circle K, Augie Democrats, College Republicans, Augie Green, Catholics in Action, Augustana Coalition for Social Justice, Young Life, Colleges Against Cancer.

Athletics. NCAA. **Intercollegiate:** Baseball M, basketball, cheerleading M, cross-country, football (tackle) M, golf, soccer W, softball W, tennis, track and field, volleyball W, wrestling M. **Intramural:** Basketball, football (non-tackle), golf, racquetball, soccer, softball, triathlon, volleyball. **Team name:** Vikings.

Student services. Adult student services, alcohol/substance abuse counseling, chaplain/spiritual director, career counseling, student employment services, financial aid counseling, health services, on-campus daycare, personal counseling, placement for graduates, veterans' counselor. **Physically disabled:** Services for visually, hearing impaired.

Contact. E-mail: admission@augie.edu
Phone: (605) 274-5516 Toll-free number: (800) 727-2844
Fax: (605) 274-5518
Nancy Davidson, Vice President for Enrollment, Augustana College, 2001 South Summit Avenue, Sioux Falls, SD 57197-9990

Black Hills State University

Spearfish, South Dakota
www.bhsu.edu
CB code: 6042

- Public 4-year liberal arts and teachers college
- Commuter campus in large town
- 3,139 degree-seeking undergraduates: 20% part-time, 63% women, 1% African American, 1% Asian American, 2% Hispanic American, 4% Native American, 1% international
- 150 degree-seeking graduate students
- 95% of applicants admitted
- SAT or ACT (ACT writing optional) required

General. Founded in 1883. Regionally accredited. Evening degree program available at Ellsworth Air Force Base campus in Rapid City. **Degrees:** 394 bachelor's, 32 associate awarded; master's offered. **ROTC:** Army. **Location:** 45 miles from Rapid City. **Calendar:** Semester, extensive summer session. **Full-time faculty:** 117 total; 71% have terminal degrees, 8% minority, 39% women. **Part-time faculty:** 73 total; 34% have terminal degrees, 6% minority, 48% women. **Class size:** 39% < 20, 50% 20-39, 5% 40-49, 4% 50-99, less than 1% >100.

Freshman class profile. 1,205 applied, 1,150 admitted, 583 enrolled.

Mid 50% test scores		**Rank in top tenth:**	9%
ACT composite:	18-23	**End year in good standing:**	58%
GPA 3.75 or higher:	13%	**Return as sophomores:**	56%
GPA 3.50-3.74:	14%	**Out-of-state:**	23%
GPA 3.0-3.49:	32%	**Live on campus:**	67%
GPA 2.0-2.99:	36%	**International:**	1%
Rank in top quarter:	28%		

Basis for selection. For bachelor's degree programs, minimum ACT composite score of 18 or class rank in top 60% (in-state applicants), top half (out-of-state applicants), or minimum GPA 2.6 in required courses. Portfolio recommended.

High school preparation. College-preparatory program recommended. 14 units required. Required units include English 4, mathematics 3, social studies 3, science 3 (laboratory 3) and visual/performing arts 1.

2008-2009 Annual costs. Tuition/fees: $5,877; $7,197 out-of-state. Reciprocity agreements reduce tuition for some out-of-state students . Room/board: $5,438. Books/supplies: $1,000. Personal expenses: $1,500.

2007-2008 Financial aid. All financial aid based on need.

Application procedures. Admission: Closing date 7/15. $20 fee. Admission notification on a rolling basis. **Financial aid:** Closing date 2/15. FAFSA required. Applicants notified on a rolling basis starting 5/15; must reply within 3 week(s) of notification.

Academics. Special study options: Cooperative education, distance learning, double major, dual enrollment of high school students, honors, independent study, internships, study abroad, teacher certification program. **Credit/placement by examination:** AP, CLEP, SAT, ACT, institutional tests. 32 credit hours maximum toward bachelor's degree. **Support services:** Learning center, remedial instruction, study skills assistance, tutoring, writing center.

Majors. Area/ethnic studies: Native American. **Biology:** General. **Business:** Accounting, business admin, entrepreneurial studies, human resources, marketing, office management, tourism/travel. **Communications:** Media studies. **Education:** Art, biology, business, chemistry, elementary, English, foreign languages, history, kindergarten/preschool, mathematics, middle, music, physical, science, social science, special, speech, technology/industrial arts. **Engineering technology:** Industrial. **Foreign languages:** Spanish. **Health:** Facilities admin. **History:** General. **Math:** General. **Parks/recreation:** General, exercise sciences, sports admin. **Physical sciences:** General, chemistry. **Psychology:** General. **Public administration:** Community org/advocacy. **Social sciences:** General, political science, sociology. **Visual/performing arts:** Art, commercial/advertising art.

Most popular majors. Business/marketing 21%, communications/journalism 8%, education 23%, parks/recreation 6%, psychology 6%, public administration/social services 11%.

Computing on campus. 500 workstations in dormitories, library, student center. Dormitories wired for high-speed internet access and linked to campus network. Commuter students can connect to campus network. Online course registration, online library, helpline, wireless network available.

Student life. Freshman orientation: Available. Preregistration for classes offered. **Housing:** Guaranteed on-campus for freshmen. Coed dorms, single-sex dorms, apartments available. $100 deposit. Married student housing. **Activities:** Bands, campus ministries, choral groups, drama, international student organizations, music ensembles, musical theater, radio station, student government, student newspaper, symphony orchestra, TV station, Native American Special Services, Inter-Greek Council, United Ministry, Veterans Club, Young Democrats, Young Republicans.

Athletics. NAIA. **Intercollegiate:** Basketball, cross-country, football (tackle) M, golf W, softball W, track and field, volleyball W. **Intramural:** Archery, badminton, basketball, bowling, golf, skiing, soccer, softball, swimming, table tennis, tennis, volleyball. **Team name:** Yellow Jackets.

Student services. Chaplain/spiritual director, career counseling, student employment services, financial aid counseling, health services, on-campus daycare, personal counseling, placement for graduates, veterans' counselor. **Physically disabled:** Services for visually, speech, hearing impaired.

Contact. E-mail: admissions@bhsu.edu
Phone: (605) 642-6343 Toll-free number: (800) 255-2478
Fax: (605) 642-6022
Beth Azevedo, Director of Admissions, Black Hills State University, University Street Box 9502, Spearfish, SD 57799-9502

Dakota State University

Madison, South Dakota
www.dsu.edu **CB code: 6247**

- Public 4-year university
- Residential campus in small town
- 1,450 degree-seeking undergraduates: 24% part-time, 49% women
- 229 degree-seeking graduate students
- 96% of applicants admitted
- SAT or ACT (ACT writing optional) required
- 48% graduate within 6 years

General. Founded in 1881. Regionally accredited. All degree-seeking undergraduates participate in the Wireless Mobile Computing Initiative. Students are provided with: a TabletPC, licensed software installed, ubiquitous access to wireless network, repair components not covered by warranty or accidental damage protection plan, and access to licensed software installed on Citrix servers - support of graphics/math/analytical applications. Students are assessed a fee each semester for these services. **Degrees:** 222 bachelor's, 47 associate awarded; master's, doctoral offered. **ROTC:** Army, Air Force. **Location:** 45 miles from Sioux Falls. **Calendar:** Semester, limited summer session. **Full-time faculty:** 89 total; 71% have terminal degrees, 3% minority, 36% women. **Part-time faculty:** 32 total; 25% have terminal degrees, 50% women. **Class size:** 64% < 20, 33% 20-39, less than 1% 40-49, 2% 50-99, less than 1% >100. **Special facilities:** State museum, technology building.

Freshman class profile. 509 applied, 490 admitted, 257 enrolled.

Mid 50% test scores		**GPA 2.0-2.99:**	40%
ACT composite:	18-24	**Rank in top quarter:**	21%
GPA 3.75 or higher:	14%	**Rank in top tenth:**	7%
GPA 3.50-3.74:	14%	**Out-of-state:**	25%
GPA 3.0-3.49:	30%	**Live on campus:**	89%

Basis for selection. All students must be either in top 60% of class or have minimum ACT composite scores of 18, or have high school minimum GPA of 2.6 in core courses. Underqualified applicants considered. **Home-schooled:** State high school equivalency certificate required.

High school preparation. Recommended units include English 4, mathematics 3, social studies 3, science 3 (laboratory 3). 1 fine arts required, 0.5 computer studies.

2008-2009 Annual costs. Tuition/fees: $6,497; $7,817 out-of-state. Reciprocity agreements reduce tuition for some out-of-state students. Room/board: $4,681. Books/supplies: $900. Personal expenses: $2,291.

2007-2008 Financial aid. Need-based: 225 full-time freshmen applied for aid; 169 were judged to have need; 169 of these received aid. Average need met was 85%. Average scholarship/grant was $3,317; average loan $4,028. 27% of total undergraduate aid awarded as scholarships/grants, 73% as loans/jobs. **Non-need-based:** Awarded to 657 full-time undergraduates, including 198 freshmen. Scholarships awarded for academics, alumni affiliation, art, athletics, leadership, minority status, music/drama, state residency. **Additional information:** Application deadline for grants and scholarships March 1. No deadline for loan and job applications.

Application procedures. Admission: No deadline. $20 fee. Admission notification on a rolling basis. **Financial aid:** Priority date 3/1; no closing date. FAFSA required. Applicants notified on a rolling basis starting 4/1; must reply within 2 week(s) of notification.

Academics. Health information management degree, master of science in information systems, master of science in educational technology, and master of science in information assurance offered online. **Special study options:** Cooperative education, cross-registration, distance learning, double major, dual enrollment of high school students, ESL, honors, independent study, internships, teacher certification program. **Credit/placement by examination:** AP, CLEP, IB, SAT, ACT, institutional tests. 16 credit hours maximum toward associate degree, 32 toward bachelor's. **Support services:** Learning center, reduced course load, remedial instruction, study skills assistance, tutoring, writing center.

Majors. Biology: General. **Business:** Accounting, business admin, finance, marketing. **Computer sciences:** General, computer graphics, information systems, security. **Education:** Biology, business, computer, elementary, English, mathematics, physical. **Health:** Medical records admin, respiratory therapy technology. **Parks/recreation:** Exercise sciences. **Physical sciences:** General. **Science technology:** Chemical. **Other:** Biology for information systems, Elementary education/special learning behavior, English for information systems, Mathematics for information systems.

Most popular majors. Business/marketing 25%, computer/information sciences 41%, education 18%, parks/recreation 7%.

Computing on campus. PC or laptop required. 6 workstations in dormitories, library, computer center, student center. Dormitories wired for high-speed internet access and linked to campus network. Commuter students can connect to campus network. Online course registration, online library, helpline, student web hosting, wireless network available.

Student life. Freshman orientation: Mandatory. Preregistration for classes offered. **Policies:** Alcohol/drug free campus. Two year live in requirement, residence halls are in 24/7 lockdown for student safety. Students living in residence halls are required to have meal plan. **Housing:** Guaranteed on-campus for freshmen. Coed dorms, single-sex dorms, apartments, wellness housing available. $50 fully refundable deposit. **Activities:** Bands, choral groups, dance, drama, international student organizations, literary magazine, music ensembles, musical theater, radio station, student government, student newspaper, InterVarsity Christian Fellowship, Colleges against Cancer.

Athletics. NAIA. **Intercollegiate:** Baseball M, basketball, cheerleading, cross-country, football (tackle) M, softball W, track and field, volleyball W. **Intramural:** Basketball, football (non-tackle), racquetball, softball, table tennis, tennis, volleyball. **Team name:** Trojans.

Student services. Alcohol/substance abuse counseling, chaplain/spiritual director, career counseling, student employment services, financial aid counseling, health services, minority student services, personal counseling, placement for graduates, veterans' counselor. **Physically disabled:** Services for visually, speech, hearing impaired.

Contact. E-mail: yourfuture@dsu.edu
Phone: (605) 256-5139 Toll-free number: (888) 378-9988
Fax: (605) 256-5020
Amy Crissinger, Director of Admission, Dakota State University, 820 North Washington Avenue, Madison, SD 57042

Dakota Wesleyan University
Mitchell, South Dakota
www.dwu.edu **CB code: 6155**

- Private 4-year university and liberal arts college affiliated with United Methodist Church
- Commuter campus in large town
- 682 degree-seeking undergraduates: 7% part-time, 59% women
- 24 degree-seeking graduate students

General. Founded in 1885. Regionally accredited. **Degrees:** 102 bachelor's, 66 associate awarded; master's offered. **Location:** 70 miles from Sioux Falls. **Calendar:** Semester, limited summer session. **Full-time faculty:** 44 total; 66% have terminal degrees, 52% women. **Part-time faculty:** 35 total; 26% have terminal degrees, 51% women. **Class size:** 72% < 20, 26% 20-39, 1% 40-49, 1% 50-99. **Special facilities:** Observatory.

Freshman class profile. 523 applied, 391 admitted, 162 enrolled.

Mid 50% test scores			
SAT critical reading:	340-520	GPA 3.0-3.49:	37%
SAT math:	400-540	GPA 2.0-2.99:	29%
ACT composite:	18-25	End year in good standing:	90%
GPA 3.75 or higher:	16%	Return as sophomores:	58%
GPA 3.50-3.74:	17%	Out-of-state:	47%
		Live on campus:	87%

Basis for selection. Open admission, but selective for some programs. High school record, test scores, school activities, personal interview considered. Recommendations and personal interview used for marginal students. **Homeschooled:** Transcript of courses and grades required. Meeting with an admissions counselor and placement testing when appropriate. Would also like to see scores on ACT or SAT. **Learning Disabled:** For special assistance, documentation of student's learning disability required.

High school preparation. Recommended units include English 4, mathematics 4, social studies 4, history 3, science 3 (laboratory 1) and foreign language 2.

2008-2009 Annual costs. Tuition/fees: $18,500. Room/board: $5,550. Books/supplies: $800. Personal expenses: $1,200.

2008-2009 Financial aid. Need-based: 150 full-time freshmen applied for aid; 139 were judged to have need; 139 of these received aid. Average need met was 60%. 53% of total undergraduate aid awarded as scholarships/grants, 47% as loans/jobs. **Non-need-based:** Awarded to 234 full-time undergraduates, including 60 freshmen. Scholarships awarded for academics, alumni affiliation, art, athletics, leadership, minority status, music/drama, religious affiliation.

Application procedures. Admission: Closing date 8/25 (receipt date). $25 fee, may be waived for applicants with need. Admission notification on a rolling basis. **Financial aid:** Priority date 4/15; no closing date. FAFSA required. Applicants notified on a rolling basis starting 3/1; must reply within 2 week(s) of notification.

Academics. Special study options: Cross-registration, distance learning, double major, dual enrollment of high school students, exchange student, honors, independent study, internships, student-designed major, study abroad, teacher certification program, Washington semester. **Credit/placement by examination:** AP, CLEP, IB, institutional tests. 12 credit hours maximum toward associate degree, 63 toward bachelor's. **Support services:** Learning center, pre-admission summer program, reduced course load, remedial instruction, study skills assistance, tutoring, writing center.

Majors. Biology: General. **Business:** General, accounting. **Communications:** General, journalism. **Computer sciences:** Web page design. **Conservation:** Wildlife. **Education:** General, art, biology, business, elementary, English, mathematics, music, physical, science, social science, social studies, special. **Health:** Athletic training, predental, premedicine, prepharmacy, preveterinary. **History:** General. **Interdisciplinary:** Behavioral sciences. **Legal studies:** Prelaw. **Math:** General. **Parks/recreation:** Exercise sciences, sports admin. **Philosophy/religion:** Religion. **Protective services:** Criminal justice. **Psychology:** General. **Public administration:** Human services. **Social sciences:** General, sociology. **Theology:** Sacred music. **Visual/performing arts:** Art, dramatic. **Other:** Public Service and Leadership.

Most popular majors. Biology 7%, business/marketing 17%, education 20%, English 6%, health sciences 16%, psychology 7%, public administration/social services 6%, security/protective services 11%.

Computing on campus. 85 workstations in dormitories, library, computer center, student center. Dormitories wired for high-speed internet access and linked to campus network. Commuter students can connect to campus network. Online library, helpline, repair service, student web hosting, wireless network available.

Student life. Freshman orientation: Mandatory. Preregistration for classes offered. 2 days, the weekend before fall classes begin. In spring, held first day of finalization. **Housing:** Guaranteed on-campus for freshmen. Coed dorms, single-sex dorms, apartments, wellness housing available. Honor housing available for upperclassmen; ADA rooms and apartments available. **Activities:** Concert band, choral groups, drama, literary magazine, music ensembles, student government, student newspaper, Variety of religious, ethnic, minority, political, and service groups.

Athletics. NAIA. **Intercollegiate:** Baseball M, basketball, cheerleading, cross-country, football (tackle) M, golf, soccer, softball W, track and field, volleyball W, wrestling M. **Intramural:** Basketball, softball, volleyball, weight lifting. **Team name:** Tigers.

Student services. Adult student services, alcohol/substance abuse counseling, chaplain/spiritual director, career counseling, services for economically disadvantaged, student employment services, financial aid counseling, health services, minority student services, on-campus daycare, personal counseling, placement for graduates. **Physically disabled:** Services for visually, hearing impaired.

Contact. E-mail: admissions@dwu.edu
Phone: (605) 995-2650 Toll-free number: (800) 333-8506
Fax: (605) 995-2699
Melissa Herr-Valburg, Director of Admissions, Dakota Wesleyan University, 1200 West University Avenue, Mitchell, SD 57301-4398

Mount Marty College
Yankton, South Dakota
www.mtmc.edu **CB code: 6416**

- Private 4-year liberal arts college affiliated with Roman Catholic Church
- Residential campus in large town
- 825 degree-seeking undergraduates: 28% part-time, 63% women
- 134 graduate students
- 54% graduate within 6 years; 10% enter graduate study

General. Founded in 1936. Regionally accredited. **Degrees:** 169 bachelor's, 26 associate awarded; master's offered. **ROTC:** Army. **Location:** 75 miles from Sioux Falls, 60 miles from Sioux City, Iowa. **Calendar:** Semester, limited summer session. **Full-time faculty:** 46 total; 70% have terminal degrees, 2% minority, 41% women. **Part-time faculty:** 35 total; 20% have terminal degrees, 20% women. **Class size:** 80% < 20, 19% 20-39, less than 1% 40-49, less than 1% 50-99, less than 1% >100.

Freshman class profile. 375 applied, 293 admitted, 161 enrolled.

Mid 50% test scores			
SAT critical reading:	400-570	End year in good standing:	75%
SAT math:	410-610	Return as sophomores:	75%
SAT writing:	430-490	Out-of-state:	60%
ACT composite:	19-24	Live on campus:	95%

Basis for selection. Open admission, but selective for some programs. Academic record, test scores, GPA very important. Minimum 2.0 GPA and 18 ACT required for admission consideration. Interview recommended for all; audition required for scholarship recipients, music and theater programs. **Learning Disabled:** Students requesting disability services must submit letter requesting services and documentation to support diagnosed disability.

2008-2009 Annual costs. Tuition/fees: $18,250. Room/board: $5,210. Books/supplies: $920. Personal expenses: $1,704.

2008-2009 Financial aid. Non-need-based: Scholarships awarded for academics, art, athletics, leadership, music/drama, religious affiliation. **Additional information:** Prestige scholarships application deadline 2/1.

Application procedures. Admission: Closing date 8/30 (receipt date). $35 fee, may be waived for applicants with need. Admission notification on a rolling basis. **Financial aid:** Priority date 3/1; no closing date. FAFSA, institutional form required. Applicants notified on a rolling basis starting 3/15; must reply within 2 week(s) of notification.

Academics. Special study options: Accelerated study, double major, dual enrollment of high school students, honors, independent study, internships, liberal arts/career combination, student-designed major, teacher certification program. **Credit/placement by examination:** AP, CLEP, IB, institutional tests. 88 credit hours maximum toward associate degree, 24 toward bachelor's. **Support services:** Learning center, reduced course load, remedial instruction, study skills assistance, tutoring, writing center.

Majors. Biology: General. **Business:** Accounting, business admin. **Communications:** Digital media. **Computer sciences:** Computer science, information technology, programming. **Education:** Biology, chemistry, elementary, English, health, history, mathematics, middle, music, physical, science, secondary, social science, special. **Health:** Clinical lab science, medical radiologic technology/radiation therapy, nursing (RN). **History:** General. **Liberal arts:** Arts/sciences. **Math:** General. **Parks/recreation:** Facilities management. **Philosophy/religion:** Religion. **Physical sciences:** Chemistry. **Protective services:** Criminal justice, forensics. **Psychology:** General. **Social sciences:** General. **Visual/performing arts:** Dramatic. **Other:** Exercise and wellness, Forensic accounting, IT management.

Most popular majors. Business/marketing 15%, education 17%, health sciences 23%, liberal arts 10%, social sciences 12%.

Computing on campus. PC or laptop required. 53 workstations in dormitories, library, computer center, student center. Dormitories wired for high-speed internet access and linked to campus network. Commuter students can connect to campus network. Online library, helpline, repair service, wireless network available.

Student life. Freshman orientation: Mandatory. Preregistration for classes offered. 3-day intensive orientation prior to beginning of fall semester. Orientation programs throughout academic year. **Policies:** Alcohol, tobacco and drug-free campus. Unmarried undergraduates under 21 required to live in college housing unless living with family. **Housing:** Guaranteed on-campus for freshmen. Single-sex dorms, special housing for disabled, wellness housing available. $50 partly refundable deposit. **Activities:** Bands, campus ministries, choral groups, drama, literary magazine, music ensembles, musical theater, student government, student newspaper, outreach team, Habitat for Humanity, education club, nursing club, English club.

Athletics. NAIA. **Intercollegiate:** Baseball M, basketball, cross-country, soccer, softball W, track and field, volleyball W. **Intramural:** Basketball. **Team name:** Lancers.

Student services. Adult student services, alcohol/substance abuse counseling, chaplain/spiritual director, career counseling, student employment services, financial aid counseling, health services, on-campus daycare, personal counseling, placement for graduates, veterans' counselor. **Learning disabled:** Comprehensive services available.

Contact. E-mail: mmcadmit@mtmc.edu
Phone: (800) 658-4552 Toll-free number: (800) 658-4552
Fax: (605) 668-1607
Brandi Tschumper, Vice President of Enrollment Management, Mount Marty College, 1105 West Eighth Street, Yankton, SD 57078

National American University: Rapid City

Rapid City, South Dakota
www.national.edu **CB code: 6464**

- For-profit 4-year business and technical college
- Residential campus in small city
- 475 degree-seeking undergraduates

General. Founded in 1941. Regionally accredited. **Degrees:** 292 bachelor's, 68 associate awarded; master's offered. **ROTC:** Army. **Location:** 400 miles from Denver. **Calendar:** Quarter, extensive summer session. **Full-time faculty:** 13 total; 23% have terminal degrees, 46% women. **Part-time faculty:** 34 total; 15% have terminal degrees, 53% women. **Special facilities:** Animal health laboratories, athletic training facility.

Basis for selection. Open admission, but selective for some programs. All students required to complete university assessment testing prior to enrollment. Selective admission to equine management program; essay required. TOEFL and/or TWE used for placement. Interview recommended for all. **Homeschooled:** Completion of GED or accredited high school correspondence required.

High school preparation. Algebra helpful for computer technology. Science recommended for health program.

2008-2009 Annual costs. Books/supplies: $400.

Financial aid. All financial aid based on need.

Application procedures. Admission: No deadline. $25 fee. Admission notification on a rolling basis. **Financial aid:** No deadline. FAFSA, institutional form required. Applicants notified on a rolling basis; must reply within 4 week(s) of notification.

Academics. Applied management program for students with associate degree in health or technical fields who desire to continue education in management. **Special study options:** Accelerated study, cooperative education, distance learning, double major, independent study, internships, liberal arts/career combination. **Credit/placement by examination:** AP, CLEP, IB, institutional tests. **Support services:** Learning center, reduced course load, remedial instruction, tutoring.

Majors. Agriculture: Animal training. **Business:** Accounting, business admin, management information systems, marketing, personal/financial services. **Computer sciences:** General, LAN/WAN management, programming, systems analysis, web page design, webmaster. **Health:** Athletic training, facilities admin. **Legal studies:** Paralegal, prelaw.

Most popular majors. Business/marketing 38%, computer/information sciences 7%, legal studies 6%.

Computing on campus. 77 workstations in dormitories, library, computer center. Wireless network available.

Student life. Freshman orientation: Mandatory. Preregistration for classes offered. **Housing:** Coed dorms available. $100 deposit. **Activities:** Student government, student newspaper.

Athletics. Team name: Mavericks.

Student services. Career counseling, student employment services, financial aid counseling, personal counseling, placement for graduates, veterans' counselor.

Contact. E-mail: rcadmissions@national.edu
Phone: (605) 394-4800 Toll-free number: (800) 209-0490
Fax: (605) 394-4871
Wanda Redlin, director of Enrollment Management, National American University: Rapid City, 321 Kansas City Street, Rapid City, SD 57701

Northern State University

Aberdeen, South Dakota
www.northern.edu **CB code: 6487**

- Public 4-year university and liberal arts college
- Residential campus in large town
- 1,946 degree-seeking undergraduates: 11% part-time, 56% women
- 132 degree-seeking graduate students
- 92% of applicants admitted
- ACT (writing optional) required
- 46% graduate within 6 years; 13% enter graduate study

General. Founded in 1901. Regionally accredited. Technology proficiency certification available for all degree programs. Emphasis on distance delivery technology in all degree programs, especially in all levels of teacher preparation. **Degrees:** 253 bachelor's, 14 associate awarded; master's offered. **Location:** 285 miles from Minneapolis-St. Paul. **Calendar:** Semester, limited summer session. **Full-time faculty:** 91 total; 85% have terminal degrees, 10% minority, 34% women. **Class size:** 42% < 20, 46% 20-39, 9% 40-49, 3% 50-99, less than 1% >100. **Special facilities:** E-learning center, center of excellence for international business.

Freshman class profile. 915 applied, 841 admitted, 400 enrolled.

Mid 50% test scores		**Out-of-state:**	18%
ACT composite:	18-24	**International:**	2%
Return as sophomores:	68%		

Basis for selection. Applicants to 4-year programs must meet following: GPA in required courses or rank in top 60% of graduating class. Minimum ACT composite score of 18. Minimum GPA 2.6. Applicants lacking required high school units admitted provisionally. Equivalent work must be completed within 2 years. Interview recommended for borderline applicants; portfolio recommended for art program.

High school preparation. 13 units required. Required units include English 4, mathematics 3, social studies 3, science 3 (laboratory 3). Mathematics units must be algebra or above; .5 fine arts required.

2008-2009 Annual costs. Tuition/fees: $5,712; $7,032 out-of-state. Reciprocity agreements reduce tuition for some out-of-state students. Room/board: $4,486. Books/supplies: $900. Personal expenses: $1,650.

2008-2009 Financial aid. Non-need-based: Scholarships awarded for academics, art, athletics, leadership, minority status, music/drama, state residency.

Application procedures. Admission: No deadline. $20 fee. Admission notification on a rolling basis. **Financial aid:** Priority date 3/1; no closing date. FAFSA required. Applicants notified by 4/15; must reply within 2 week(s) of notification.

Academics. Special study options: Accelerated study, cooperative education, cross-registration, distance learning, double major, dual enrollment of high school students, ESL, exchange student, external degree, honors, independent study, internships, liberal arts/career combination, student-designed major, study abroad, teacher certification program, Washington semester, weekend college. **Credit/placement by examination:** AP, CLEP, IB, institutional tests. 32 credit hours maximum toward bachelor's degree. **Support services:** Learning center, pre-admission summer program, reduced course load, remedial instruction, study skills assistance, tutoring, writing center.

Majors. Biology: General, ecology. **Business:** General, accounting, banking/financial services, business admin, finance, international, management information systems, marketing, office/clerical. **Computer sciences:** General. **Education:** General, art, business, early childhood, elementary, English, foreign languages, history, mathematics, multi-level teacher, music, physical, science, social science, special, speech. **Foreign languages:** French, German, Spanish. **Health:** Audiology/hearing, audiology/speech pathology, clinical lab science, speech pathology. **History:** General. **Math:** General. **Parks/recreation:** Health/fitness, sports admin. **Physical sciences:** Chemistry. **Psychology:** General. **Public administration:** Community org/advocacy, social work. **Social sciences:** Economics, political science, sociology. **Visual/performing arts:** Art.

Computing on campus. 900 workstations in dormitories, library, computer center, student center. Dormitories wired for high-speed internet access and linked to campus network. Commuter students can connect to campus network. Online course registration, online library, helpline, repair service, student web hosting, wireless network available.

Student life. Freshman orientation: Mandatory. Preregistration for classes offered. **Housing:** Coed dorms, single-sex dorms, special housing for disabled, apartments available. $50 deposit. Married graduate student housing available for summer session as well. **Activities:** Bands, choral groups, dance, drama, literary magazine, music ensembles, musical theater, student government, student newspaper, symphony orchestra, TV station, over 100 student organizations.

Athletics. NCAA. **Intercollegiate:** Baseball M, basketball, cheerleading, cross-country, football (tackle) M, golf, rugby, soccer W, softball W, swimming W, tennis, track and field, volleyball W, wrestling M. **Intramural:** Badminton, baseball M, basketball, field hockey W, softball, swimming, table tennis, tennis, volleyball, weight lifting. **Team name:** Wolves.

Student services. Adult student services, alcohol/substance abuse counseling, chaplain/spiritual director, career counseling, services for economically disadvantaged, student employment services, financial aid counseling, health services, legal services, minority student services, on-campus daycare, personal counseling, placement for graduates, veterans' counselor, women's services. **Physically disabled:** Services for visually, speech, hearing impaired. **Learning disabled:** Comprehensive services available.

Contact. E-mail: admissions1@northern.edu
Phone: (605) 626-2544 Toll-free number: (800) 678-5330
Fax: (605) 626-2587
Allan Vogel, Director of Admissions, Northern State University, 1200 South Jay Street, Aberdeen, SD 57401-7198

Oglala Lakota College
Kyle, South Dakota
www.olc.edu **CB code: 1430**

- Public 4-year liberal arts and teachers college
- Commuter campus in small town
- 1,551 degree-seeking undergraduates: 50% part-time, 78% women
- 51 degree-seeking graduate students

General. Founded in 1971. Regionally accredited. Tribal College and a founding member of the American Indian Higher Education Consortium. **Degrees:** 38 bachelor's, 97 associate awarded; master's offered. **Location:** 90 miles from Rapid City, on Pine Ridge Indian Reservation. **Calendar:** Semester, extensive summer session. **Full-time faculty:** 66 total; 12% have terminal degrees, 35% minority, 70% women. **Part-time faculty:** 89 total; 26% have terminal degrees, 29% minority, 36% women.

Basis for selection. Open admission. Testing for placement.

2009-2010 Annual costs. Tuition/fees (projected): $2,900. Above rates for Native Americans. Non-Native American students pay tuition rate of $2,940 and $98 per credit hour. Books/supplies: $260. Personal expenses: $450.

2007-2008 Financial aid. Need-based: 99% of total undergraduate aid awarded as scholarships/grants, 1% as loans/jobs. **Additional information:** Deadline for applications for Bureau of Indian Affairs Higher Education Grants, is March 15; applicants notified early summer.

Application procedures. Admission: No deadline. No application fee. Application must be submitted on paper. **Financial aid:** No deadline. Applicants notified on a rolling basis.

Academics. College is one of 2 tribally chartered, fully accredited institutions in the United States. **Special study options:** Distance learning, double major, independent study, internships, liberal arts/career combination, teacher certification program. **Credit/placement by examination:** CLEP, institutional tests. 13 credit hours maximum toward bachelor's degree. **Support services:** Learning center, reduced course load, remedial instruction, tutoring.

Majors. Area/ethnic studies: Native American. **Business:** Accounting, business admin, management information systems. **Computer sciences:** General. **Conservation:** General. **Education:** Elementary. **History:** General. **Liberal arts:** Arts/sciences. **Public administration:** Human services, social work. **Social sciences:** Sociology. **Other:** Life science.

Computing on campus. 175 workstations in library, student center. Dormitories wired for high-speed internet access. Wireless network available.

Student life. Freshman orientation: Available. Preregistration for classes offered. **Housing:** Coed dorms available. **Activities:** Student government, student newspaper, TV station.

Athletics. NJCAA. **Intercollegiate:** Basketball, cross-country, volleyball. **Team name:** Brave Hearts.

Student services. Career counseling, personal counseling.

Contact. Phone: (605) 455-6000 Fax: (605) 455-2787
Leslie Mesteth, Registrar, Oglala Lakota College, Box 490, Kyle, SD 57752-0490

Presentation College
Aberdeen, South Dakota
www.presentation.edu **CB code: 6582**

- Private 4-year business and health science college affiliated with Roman Catholic Church
- Commuter campus in large town
- 504 degree-seeking undergraduates
- 61% of applicants admitted
- SAT or ACT (ACT writing optional) required

General. Founded in 1951. Regionally accredited. **Degrees:** 131 bachelor's, 33 associate awarded. **Location:** 200 miles from Sioux Falls, 280 miles from Minneapolis-St. Paul. **Calendar:** Semester, extensive summer session. **Full-time faculty:** 37 total. **Part-time faculty:** 50 total.

Freshman class profile. 259 applied, 158 admitted, 83 enrolled.

Mid 50% test scores		GPA 3.0-3.49:	29%
ACT composite:	17-22	GPA 2.0-2.99:	33%
GPA 3.75 or higher:	18%	Out-of-state:	19%
GPA 3.50-3.74:	10%	Live on campus:	90%

Basis for selection. Academic GPA very important, followed by rigor of secondary school record and standardized test scores. Minimum ACT composite of 18 or combined SAT score of 860 (exclusive of Writing). ACT required for admission to radiologic technology program. COMPASS assessment used for math placement. TOEFL required for ESL students. **Homeschooled:** Official transcript from local schooling guild, detailed course descriptions, and textbooks used required. Letter of academic recommendation from primary educator also required.

High school preparation. 16 units recommended. Recommended units include English 4, mathematics 3, social studies 2 and science 2. CPR certificate required of nursing and allied health applicants.

2008-2009 Annual costs. Tuition/fees: $13,951. Room/board: $4,875. Books/supplies: $1,300. Personal expenses: $620.

Application procedures. Admission: Priority date 4/1; deadline 9/1 (receipt date). $25 fee. Admission notification on a rolling basis. **Financial aid:** Priority date 4/1; no closing date. FAFSA required. Applicants notified on a rolling basis starting 5/1; must reply within 2 week(s) of notification.

Academics. Special study options: Distance learning, double major, dual enrollment of high school students, external degree, internships, liberal arts/career combination. **Credit/placement by examination:** CLEP, ACT, institutional tests. 15 credit hours maximum toward associate degree, 30 toward bachelor's. **Support services:** Learning center, reduced course load, remedial instruction, study skills assistance, tutoring.

Majors. Business: Business admin. **Communications:** General. **Health:** Health care admin, medical radiologic technology/radiation therapy, nursing (RN). **Parks/recreation:** General. **Public administration:** Social work.

Computing on campus. 180 workstations in dormitories, library, computer center. Dormitories wired for high-speed internet access and linked to campus network.

Student life. Freshman orientation: Mandatory. Preregistration for classes offered. **Housing:** Coed dorms available. $250 deposit, deadline 7/15. **Activities:** Drama, student government, student newspaper, Native American club.

Athletics. NAIA. **Intercollegiate:** Baseball M, basketball, cross-country, golf, soccer, softball W, volleyball W. **Intramural:** Basketball, volleyball W. **Team name:** Saints.

Student services. Adult student services, career counseling, student employment services, health services, personal counseling, placement for graduates, veterans' counselor.

Contact. E-mail: admit@presentation.edu
Phone: (605) 229-8492 Toll-free number: (800) 437-6060
Fax: (605) 229-8425
JoEllen Lindner, Vice President for Enrollment and Student Retention Services, Presentation College, 1500 North Main Street, Aberdeen, SD 57401

Sinte Gleska University

Mission, South Dakota
www.sintegleska.edu/ **CB code: 7328**

- Public 4-year university and liberal arts college
- Commuter campus in rural community

General. Founded in 1970. Regionally accredited. **Location:** 90 miles from Pierre, 240 miles from Sioux Falls. **Calendar:** Semester.

Annual costs/financial aid. Books/supplies: $500. Personal expenses: $500. Need-based financial aid available to full-time and part-time students.

Contact. Phone: (605) 747-2263
Registrar, Box 105, Mission, SD 57555

South Dakota School of Mines and Technology

Rapid City, South Dakota
www.sdsmt.edu **CB code: 6652**

- Public 4-year university and engineering college
- Commuter campus in small city
- 1,564 degree-seeking undergraduates: 12% part-time, 23% women, 1% African American, 1% Asian American, 1% Hispanic American, 2% Native American, 1% international
- 234 degree-seeking graduate students
- 83% of applicants admitted
- SAT or ACT (ACT writing optional) required
- 36% graduate within 6 years

General. Founded in 1885. Regionally accredited. **Degrees:** 250 bachelor's, 9 associate awarded; master's, doctoral offered. **ROTC:** Army. **Location:** 222 miles from Cheyenne, Wyoming. **Calendar:** Semester, limited summer session. **Full-time faculty:** 135 total; 81% have terminal degrees, 13% minority, 20% women. **Part-time faculty:** 10 total; 10% have terminal degrees, 10% minority, 50% women. **Class size:** 43% < 20, 45% 20-39, 7% 40-49, 4% 50-99, less than 1% >100. **Special facilities:** Geology/paleontology museum, engineering/mining experiment station, atmospheric science institute, CAMP-center for advanced manufacturing and production, advanced materials processing and joining lab, analytical characterization and testing laboratory, additive manufacturing laboratory, center for accelerated applications at the nanoscale, center for bioenergy.

Freshman class profile. 891 applied, 737 admitted, 317 enrolled.

Mid 50% test scores		Rank in top quarter:	57%
SAT critical reading:	470-630	Rank in top tenth:	22%
SAT math:	570-680	Return as sophomores:	76%
ACT composite:	24-28	Out-of-state:	42%
GPA 3.75 or higher:	38%	Live on campus:	82%
GPA 3.50-3.74:	22%	International:	3%
GPA 3.0-3.49:	27%	Fraternities:	19%
GPA 2.0-2.99:	13%	Sororities:	23%

Basis for selection. Test scores, GPA or class rank very important. ACT Math and English scores and/or COMPASS math and English placement tests are used for initial student placement. **Homeschooled:** Must have completed the GED with a combined score of 225 and a minimum of 40 on each test (paper based); or 2250 combined score and minimum of 410 on each test (computer based); or submit ACT/SAT scores and be reviewed by admissions review committee.

High school preparation. College-preparatory program recommended. 20 units required. Required units include English 4, mathematics 4, social studies 3, science 4 (laboratory 3) and foreign language 2. One year of fine arts is required. 1/2 unit of computer science is required. Basic keyboarding skills, experience in using computer word processing, database and spreadsheet packages, internet skills required.

2008-2009 Annual costs. Tuition/fees: $6,040; $7,360 out-of-state. Reciprocity agreements reduce tuition for some out-of-state students. Room/board: $4,400. Books/supplies: $1,200. Personal expenses: $1,650.

2007-2008 Financial aid. Need-based: 328 full-time freshmen applied for aid; 188 were judged to have need; 187 of these received aid. Average need met was 76%. Average scholarship/grant was $3,510; average loan $2,993. 34% of total undergraduate aid awarded as scholarships/grants, 66% as loans/jobs. **Non-need-based:** Awarded to 605 full-time undergraduates, including 219 freshmen. Scholarships awarded for academics, athletics, leadership, ROTC. **Additional information:** Closing date for scholarship applications February 1.

Application procedures. Admission: No deadline. $20 fee. Admission notification on a rolling basis beginning on or about 11/1. **Financial aid:** Priority date 3/15; no closing date. FAFSA required. Applicants notified on a rolling basis starting 5/1; must reply within 3 week(s) of notification.

Academics. Leading institution in friction stir-welding technology. Undergraduate teams compete in solar vehicle, ChemE Car, unmanned aero vehicle, SAE aero design, ASCE concrete canoe and bridge, SAE Formula SAE, SAE Mini Baja, ASME human-powered vehicle, SAE clean snowmobile challenge and SAMPE Composites national competitions. **Special study options:** Cooperative education, cross-registration, distance learning, dual enrollment of high school students, ESL, independent study, internships, liberal arts/career combination, study abroad. Web-based technical management MS program. **Credit/placement by examination:** AP, CLEP, IB, SAT, ACT, institutional tests. 18 credit hours maximum toward associate degree, 36 toward bachelor's. **Support services:** Learning center, reduced course load, remedial instruction, study skills assistance, tutoring.

Majors. Computer sciences: Computer science. **Engineering:** Chemical, civil, computer, electrical, environmental, geological, industrial, mechanical, metallurgical, mining. **Interdisciplinary:** Science/society. **Math:** General. **Physical sciences:** Atmospheric science, chemistry, geology, physics. **Other:** Business applications in science and technology.

Most popular majors. Computer/information sciences 6%, engineering/engineering technologies 72%, interdisciplinary studies 11%, physical sciences 8%.

Computing on campus. PC or laptop required. 210 workstations in dormitories, library, computer center, student center. Dormitories wired for high-speed internet access and linked to campus network. Commuter students can connect to campus network. Online course registration, online library, helpline, repair service, student web hosting, wireless network available.

Student life. Freshman orientation: Available. Preregistration for classes offered. Held in April and May. Adventure weekends for various groups in summer including special one for athletes and special welcome week activities the first week of school in the fall semester. **Housing:** Guaranteed on-campus for freshmen. Coed dorms, special housing for disabled, apartments, fraternity/sorority housing, wellness housing available. $100 nonrefundable deposit, deadline 8/15. **Activities:** Bands, campus ministries, choral groups, dance, drama, international student organizations, music ensembles, radio station, student government, student newspaper, Circle K, College Republicans, College Democrats, American Indian Science & Engineering Society, Habitat for Humanity, Muslim student association, Intervarsity Christian Fellowship.

Athletics. NAIA. **Intercollegiate:** Basketball, cross-country, football (tackle) M, golf, track and field, volleyball W. **Intramural:** Basketball, golf, racquetball, skiing, softball, swimming, track and field, volleyball. **Team name:** Hardrockers.

Student services. Adult student services, alcohol/substance abuse counseling, chaplain/spiritual director, career counseling, student employment services, financial aid counseling, health services, minority student services, on-campus daycare, personal counseling, placement for graduates, veterans' counselor, women's services. **Physically disabled:** Services for visually, speech, hearing impaired.

Contact. E-mail: admissions@sdsmt.edu
Phone: (605) 394-2414 Toll-free number: (877) 877-6044
Fax: (605) 394-1979
Charles Claymore, Associate Director/Senior Recruiter, South Dakota School of Mines and Technology, 501 East St. Joseph Street, Rapid City, SD 57701

South Dakota State University

Brookings, South Dakota
www.sdstate.edu **CB code: 6653**

- Public 4-year university
- Commuter campus in large town
- 9,516 degree-seeking undergraduates: 13% part-time, 51% women, 1% African American, 1% Asian American, 1% Hispanic American, 2% Native American, 1% international
- 1,463 graduate students
- 93% of applicants admitted
- SAT or ACT (ACT writing optional) required
- 54% graduate within 6 years

General. Founded in 1881. Regionally accredited. **Degrees:** 1,735 bachelor's, 16 associate awarded; master's, doctoral, first professional offered. **ROTC:** Army, Air Force. **Location:** 50 miles from Sioux Falls. **Calendar:** Semester, limited summer session. **Full-time faculty:** 478 total; 77% have terminal degrees, 14% minority, 44% women. **Part-time faculty:** 193 total; 23% have terminal degrees, 4% minority, 67% women. **Class size:** 30% < 20, 49% 20-39, 8% 40-49, 9% 50-99, 3% >100. **Special facilities:** Water resources research center, agricultural experiment station, cooperative extension service, Northern Great Plains biostress center, agricultural heritage museum, animal disease research and diagnostic laboratory, entrepreneur institute, GIS center of excellence, innovation research park, performing arts center.

Freshman class profile. 3,961 applied, 3,688 admitted, 2,101 enrolled.

Mid 50% test scores		**Rank in top quarter:**	39%
ACT composite:	20-25	**Rank in top tenth:**	16%
GPA 3.75 or higher:	27%	**Return as sophomores:**	77%
GPA 3.50-3.74:	19%	**Out-of-state:**	33%
GPA 3.0-3.49:	30%	**Live on campus:**	97%
GPA 2.0-2.99:	23%	**International:**	1%

Basis for selection. School achievement record and test scores most important. ACT not required of first-time freshmen over 24. **Home-schooled:** Transcript of courses and grades required. Must take ACT and receive scores of 18 Comp, 18 English, 20 Math, 17 Social Studies/Reasoning, and 17 Science Reasoning.

High school preparation. College-preparatory program required. 14 units required. Required units include English 4, mathematics 3, social studies 3, science 3 (laboratory 3), computer science 1 and visual/performing arts 1. 1 fine arts required for students graduating from SD high school. Will accept noncredit fine arts activities in out-of-state schools that do not require it.

2008-2009 Annual costs. Tuition/fees: $5,786; $7,128 out-of-state. Reduced out-of-state tuition for Minnesota students. Room/board: $5,423. Books/supplies: $1,014. Personal expenses: $2,024.

2008-2009 Financial aid. Need-based: 1,692 full-time freshmen applied for aid; 1,421 were judged to have need; 1,421 of these received aid. Average need met was 89%. Average scholarship/grant was $4,144; average loan $4,432. 32% of total undergraduate aid awarded as scholarships/grants, 68% as loans/jobs. **Non-need-based:** Awarded to 7,613 full-time undergraduates, including 1,671 freshmen. Scholarships awarded for academics, art, athletics, job skills, leadership, minority status, music/drama, ROTC, state residency.

Application procedures. Admission: No deadline. $20 fee. Admission notification on a rolling basis. **Financial aid:** Priority date 3/11; no closing date. FAFSA required. Applicants notified on a rolling basis starting 4/1; must reply within 3 week(s) of notification.

Academics. Evening, weekend and other condensed degree-awarding classes available at Sioux Falls Center for Public Higher Education. **Special study options:** Accelerated study, combined bachelor's/graduate degree, cooperative education, cross-registration, distance learning, double major, dual enrollment of high school students, exchange student, honors, independent study, internships, liberal arts/career combination, study abroad, teacher certification program. **Credit/placement by examination:** AP, CLEP, IB, ACT, institutional tests. 16 credit hours maximum toward associate degree, 32 toward bachelor's. **Support services:** Pre-admission summer program, reduced course load, remedial instruction, study skills assistance, tutoring, writing center.

Majors. Agriculture: General, agribusiness operations, agronomy, animal sciences, dairy, economics, horticulture, landscaping, mechanization, range science. **Biology:** General, biochemistry, microbiology. **Business:** Entrepreneurial studies, hotel/motel admin. **Communications:** Journalism. **Computer sciences:** General. **Conservation:** Management/policy, wildlife. **Education:** Agricultural, early childhood, music, secondary, voc/tech. **Engineering:** Agricultural, civil, electrical, mechanical, physics, software. **Engineering technology:** Construction, electrical, industrial management, industrial safety, manufacturing. **Family/consumer sciences:** Apparel marketing, consumer economics, family resources, family studies, food/nutrition. **Foreign languages:** French, German, Spanish. **Health:** Athletic training, clinical lab science, nursing (RN), pharmaceutical sciences. **History:** General. **Interdisciplinary:** Global studies. **Liberal arts:** Arts/sciences. **Math:** General. **Parks/recreation:** Facilities management, health/fitness. **Physical sciences:** Chemistry, physics. **Psychology:** General. **Social sciences:** Economics, geography, political science, sociology. **Transportation:** Aviation, aviation management, flight instructor. **Visual/performing arts:** General, graphic design, interior design, music management. **Other:** Health promotion.

Most popular majors. Agriculture 12%, biology 6%, engineering/engineering technologies 14%, health sciences 22%, social sciences 10%.

Computing on campus. 692 workstations in dormitories, library, computer center, student center. Dormitories wired for high-speed internet access and linked to campus network. Commuter students can connect to campus network. Online course registration, online library, helpline, repair service, wireless network available.

Student life. Freshman orientation: Mandatory. Preregistration for classes offered. 2-day programs in June, one-day programs later in the summer. **Policies:** Students out of high school for less than 2 years required to live in campus housing unless living with family. **Housing:** Guaranteed on-campus for freshmen. Coed dorms, special housing for disabled, apartments, fraternity/sorority housing, wellness housing available. $50 fully refundable deposit. Limited single rooms with optional meal plan available for upperclassmen. **Activities:** Bands, choral groups, dance, drama, literary magazine, music ensembles, musical theater, radio station, student government, student newspaper, symphony orchestra, University Program Council, Golden Key International Honor Society, Campus Crusade for Christ, Fellowship of Christian Athletes, Native American club, Circle K International, Black Student Alliance, geography club.

Athletics. NCAA. **Intercollegiate:** Baseball M, basketball, cross-country, equestrian W, football (tackle) M, golf, soccer W, softball W, swimming, tennis, track and field, volleyball W, wrestling M. **Intramural:** Badminton, basketball, football (non-tackle), golf, racquetball, soccer W, softball, swimming, table tennis, track and field, volleyball, wrestling M. **Team name:** Jackrabbits.

Student services. Adult student services, alcohol/substance abuse counseling, chaplain/spiritual director, career counseling, services for economically disadvantaged, student employment services, financial aid counseling,

health services, legal services, minority student services, personal counseling, placement for graduates, veterans' counselor. **Physically disabled:** Services for visually, speech, hearing impaired.

Contact. E-mail: SDSU.Admissions@sdstate.edu
Phone: (605) 688-4121 Toll-free number: (800) 952-3541
Fax: (605) 688-6891
Tracy Welsh, Director of Admissions and High School Relations, South Dakota State University, Box 2201 SAD 200, Brookings, SD 57007-0649

University of Sioux Falls

Sioux Falls, South Dakota
www.usiouxfalls.edu **CB code: 6651**

- Private 4-year university and liberal arts college affiliated with American Baptist Churches in the USA
- Residential campus in small city
- 1,243 degree-seeking undergraduates: 19% part-time, 53% women
- 321 degree-seeking graduate students
- 97% of applicants admitted
- SAT or ACT (ACT writing optional) required

General. Founded in 1883. Regionally accredited. **Degrees:** 297 bachelor's, 1 associate awarded; master's offered. **Location:** 180 miles from Omaha, Nebraska. **Calendar:** 4-1-4, limited summer session. **Full-time faculty:** 65 total. **Part-time faculty:** 75 total. **Class size:** 58% < 20, 32% 20-39, 5% 40-49, 5% 50-99, less than 1% >100.

Freshman class profile. 759 applied, 738 admitted, 286 enrolled.

Mid 50% test scores			
SAT critical reading:	390-480	ACT composite:	16-26
SAT math:	430-470	Out-of-state:	40%
		Live on campus:	83%

Basis for selection. ACT or SAT Scores, high school and post-secondary GPAs, and class rank within graduating class important when determining acceptance. Audition required for music, theater programs; portfolio recommended for art program. **Homeschooled:** Statement describing homeschool structure and mission, transcript of courses and grades required.

High school preparation. Recommended units include English 4, mathematics 3, social studies 3, history 3, science 2 and computer science 1.

2009-2010 Annual costs. Tuition/fees: $20,290. Room/board: $5,920. Books/supplies: $1,000. Personal expenses: $2,000.

2007-2008 Financial aid. Need-based: 64% of total undergraduate aid awarded as scholarships/grants, 36% as loans/jobs. **Non-need-based:** Scholarships awarded for academics, alumni affiliation, art, athletics, job skills, leadership, music/drama, religious affiliation, state residency.

Application procedures. Admission: No deadline. $25 fee, may be waived for applicants with need. Admission notification on a rolling basis. **Financial aid:** Priority date 3/1; no closing date. FAFSA required. Applicants notified on a rolling basis starting 3/1; must reply within 2 week(s) of notification.

Academics. Degree completion program offered for adults 25 and older with 64 hours previous college education. **Special study options:** Accelerated study, cross-registration, distance learning, double major, dual enrollment of high school students, honors, independent study, internships, liberal arts/career combination, student-designed major, study abroad, teacher certification program, Washington semester. **Credit/placement by examination:** AP, CLEP, IB, SAT, ACT, institutional tests. 16 credit hours maximum toward bachelor's degree. **Support services:** Learning center, preadmission summer program, reduced course load, remedial instruction, study skills assistance, tutoring, writing center.

Majors. Biology: General. **Business:** Accounting, business admin, hospitality admin, organizational behavior. **Communications:** Journalism. **Computer sciences:** General, computer science. **Education:** Art, elementary, health, multi-level teacher, music. **Foreign languages:** Spanish. **History:** General. **Liberal arts:** Arts/sciences. **Math:** General, applied. **Parks/recreation:** Exercise sciences. **Philosophy/religion:** Religion. **Physical sciences:** Chemistry. **Protective services:** Criminal justice, police science. **Psychology:** General. **Public administration:** Social work. **Social sciences:** General, political science, sociology. **Theology:** Theology. **Visual/performing arts:** Art, dramatic.

Most popular majors. Biology 6%, business/marketing 49%, education 18%.

Computing on campus. 75 workstations in dormitories, library, computer center, student center. Dormitories wired for high-speed internet access and linked to campus network. Commuter students can connect to campus network. Online library, helpline, repair service, student web hosting, wireless network available.

Student life. Freshman orientation: Available. Preregistration for classes offered. Held 2 days immediately preceding fall semester. **Policies:** No alcohol at university-sponsored events. Freshmen and sophomores required to live in college housing unless over 20 years of age or given permission by director of residence life. **Housing:** Coed dorms, single-sex dorms, apartments available. $100 deposit. **Activities:** Bands, choral groups, dance, drama, music ensembles, musical theater, opera, radio station, student government, student newspaper, symphony orchestra, TV station, nontraditional student association, student volunteer groups, religious organizations, Fellowship of Christian Athletes.

Athletics. NAIA. **Intercollegiate:** Baseball M, basketball, cheerleading M, cross-country, football (tackle) M, golf, soccer, softball W, tennis, track and field, volleyball W, wrestling M. **Intramural:** Basketball, golf, soccer, softball, table tennis, tennis, volleyball. **Team name:** Cougars.

Student services. Adult student services, alcohol/substance abuse counseling, chaplain/spiritual director, career counseling, student employment services, financial aid counseling, health services, personal counseling, placement for graduates, veterans' counselor, women's services. **Physically disabled:** Services for hearing impaired.

Contact. E-mail: admissions@usiouxfalls.edu
Phone: (605) 331-6600 Toll-free number: (800) 888-1047
Fax: (605) 331-6615
Amanda Anderson, Director of Admissions and Academic Advising, University of Sioux Falls, 1101 West 22nd Street, Sioux Falls, SD 57105-1699

University of South Dakota

Vermillion, South Dakota **CB member**
www.usd.edu **CB code: 6881**

- Public 4-year university
- Residential campus in large town
- 6,036 degree-seeking undergraduates: 27% part-time, 63% women, 2% African American, 1% Asian American, 1% Hispanic American, 2% Native American
- 2,059 degree-seeking graduate students
- 83% of applicants admitted
- SAT or ACT (ACT writing optional), interview required
- 47% graduate within 6 years; 48% enter graduate study

General. Founded in 1862. Regionally accredited. **Degrees:** 939 bachelor's, 284 associate awarded; master's, doctoral, first professional offered. **ROTC:** Army. **Location:** 55 miles from Sioux Falls, 35 miles from Sioux City, Iowa. **Calendar:** Semester, extensive summer session. **Full-time faculty:** 385 total; 79% have terminal degrees, 11% minority, 45% women. **Part-time faculty:** 22 total; 4% have terminal degrees, 54% women. **Class size:** 44% < 20, 42% 20-39, 8% 40-49, 4% 50-99, 3% >100. **Special facilities:** Center for instructional design and delivery, center for disabilities, governmental research bureau, state data center, federal technical procurement center, geological survey, archaeology lab, speech and hearing center, disaster mental health institute.

Freshman class profile. 3,349 applied, 2,778 admitted, 1,168 enrolled.

Mid 50% test scores		Rank in top tenth:	11%
SAT critical reading:	470-660	End year in good standing:	83%
SAT math:	480-610	Return as sophomores:	76%
ACT composite:	20-25	Out-of-state:	29%
GPA 3.75 or higher:	23%	Live on campus:	82%
GPA 3.50-3.74:	17%	International:	1%
GPA 3.0-3.49:	32%	Fraternities:	20%
GPA 2.0-2.99:	27%	Sororities:	12%
Rank in top quarter:	35%		

Basis for selection. Admission in good standing granted with 2.0 GPA or higher in required courses or 2.6 overall, rank in top 60% of class, or ACT composite score of 20 or above. Interview recommended for dental hygiene, nursing, physician assistant programs; audition recommended for music, theater programs; portfolio recommended for art progam. **Homeschooled:** State high school equivalency certificate required.

High school preparation. College-preparatory program required. 14 units required; 18 recommended. Required and recommended units include English 4, mathematics 3-4, social studies 3, science 3-4 (laboratory 3) and foreign language 2. 1 fine arts required.

2008-2009 Annual costs. Tuition/fees: $5,828; $7,148 out-of-state. Reciprocity agreement in place for Minnesota residents. Reduced tuition for Iowa residents. Room/board: $5,442. Books/supplies: $900. Personal expenses: $2,000.

2007-2008 Financial aid. **Need-based:** 900 full-time freshmen applied for aid; 601 were judged to have need; 521 of these received aid. Average need met was 76%. Average scholarship/grant was $4,189; average loan $3,408. 32% of total undergraduate aid awarded as scholarships/grants, 68% as loans/jobs. **Non-need-based:** Awarded to 2,090 full-time undergraduates, including 623 freshmen. Scholarships awarded for academics, art, athletics, leadership, minority status, music/drama, ROTC.

Application procedures. **Admission:** No deadline. $20 fee. Admission notification on a rolling basis beginning on or about 9/20. February 15 closing date for application to dental hygiene and nursing programs. **Financial aid:** Priority date 3/15; no closing date. FAFSA required. Applicants notified on a rolling basis starting 5/5.

Academics. **Special study options:** Accelerated study, combined bachelor's/graduate degree, cross-registration, distance learning, double major, dual enrollment of high school students, ESL, exchange student, external degree, honors, independent study, internships, liberal arts/career combination, student-designed major, study abroad, teacher certification program. **Credit/placement by examination:** AP, CLEP, institutional tests. 30 credit hours maximum toward bachelor's degree. **Support services:** Pre-admission summer program, reduced course load, remedial instruction, tutoring.

Honors college/program. University Honors Program open to students in all majors who displayed potential for honors work in high school through good grades, college preparatory curriculum, high ACT scores, and participation in school and community activities.

Majors. **Area/ethnic studies:** Native American. **Biology:** General. **Business:** Accounting, business admin, finance, managerial economics. **Communications:** General, journalism, media studies. **Computer sciences:** General. **Education:** Biology, chemistry, drama/dance, early childhood, elementary, English, foreign languages, French, German, history, kindergarten/preschool, mathematics, music, physical, physics, science, social science, Spanish, special, speech. **Foreign languages:** French, German, Spanish. **Health:** Communication disorders, dental hygiene, health services admin, substance abuse counseling. **History:** General. **Interdisciplinary:** Global studies. **Liberal arts:** Arts/sciences. **Math:** General. **Parks/recreation:** General. **Philosophy/religion:** Philosophy. **Physical sciences:** Chemistry, geology, physics. **Protective services:** Criminal justice. **Psychology:** General. **Public administration:** Social work. **Social sciences:** Anthropology, economics, political science, sociology. **Visual/performing arts:** Art, arts management, dramatic, music performance, studio arts.

Most popular majors. Business/marketing 21%, communications/journalism 6%, education 14%, health sciences 11%, psychology 12%, security/protective services 6%, social sciences 8%.

Computing on campus. 885 workstations in dormitories, library, student center. Dormitories wired for high-speed internet access and linked to campus network. Commuter students can connect to campus network. Online course registration, online library, helpline, repair service, student web hosting, wireless network available.

Student life. **Freshman orientation:** Mandatory. Preregistration for classes offered. **Policies:** Students required to live in residence halls for first 2 years unless living in fraternity or sorority housing, or commuting from home. **Housing:** Guaranteed on-campus for freshmen. Coed dorms, special housing for disabled, apartments, fraternity/sorority housing, wellness housing available. $100 partly refundable deposit, deadline 9/1. Apartments available for students with dependent children. **Activities:** Bands, choral groups, dance, drama, international student organizations, literary magazine, music ensembles, musical theater, opera, radio station, student government, student newspaper, symphony orchestra, TV station, Young Democrats, College Republicans, Campus Crusade for Christ, Chinese student association, gay/lesbian/bisexual alliance, Habitat for Humanity, nontraditional student association, political science league.

Athletics. NCAA. **Intercollegiate:** Basketball, cross-country, diving, football (tackle) M, golf, soccer W, softball W, swimming, tennis W, track and field. **Intramural:** Badminton, basketball, bowling, cross-country, football (non-tackle), golf, racquetball, soccer, softball, swimming, table tennis, tennis, track and field, volleyball. **Team name:** Coyotes.

Student services. Adult student services, alcohol/substance abuse counseling, chaplain/spiritual director, career counseling, services for economically disadvantaged, student employment services, financial aid counseling, health services, legal services, minority student services, on-campus daycare, personal counseling, placement for graduates, veterans' counselor. **Physically disabled:** Services for visually, speech, hearing impaired.

Contact. E-mail: admission@usd.edu
Phone: (605) 677-5434 Toll-free number: (877) 269-6837
Fax: (605) 677-6753
Stephanie Moser, Director, University of South Dakota, 414 East Clark Street, Vermillion, SD 57069-2390

Four-Year Colleges

Tennessee

American Baptist College of ABT Seminary
Nashville, Tennessee
www.abcnash.edu **CB code: 2401**

- Private 4-year Bible college affiliated with Baptist faith
- Commuter campus in very large city

General. Founded in 1924. Accredited by ABHE. **Calendar:** Semester.

Annual costs/financial aid. Books/supplies: $440. Need-based financial aid available for full-time students.

Contact. Phone: (615) 256-1463
Director of Enrollment Management, 1800 Baptist World Center Drive, Nashville, TN 37207

Aquinas College
Nashville, Tennessee **CB member**
www.aquinascollege.edu **CB code: 7318**

- Private 4-year nursing and liberal arts college affiliated with Roman Catholic Church
- Commuter campus in very large city
- 821 degree-seeking undergraduates
- 70% of applicants admitted

General. Founded in 1961. Regionally accredited. **Degrees:** 60 bachelor's, 115 associate awarded. **Location:** 1 mile from downtown, 195 miles from Knoxville. **Calendar:** Semester, limited summer session. **Full-time faculty:** 25 total. **Part-time faculty:** 60 total.

Freshman class profile. 233 applied, 162 admitted, 52 enrolled.

Mid 50% test scores			
SAT critical reading:	560-660	SAT writing:	490-620
SAT math:	460-600	ACT composite:	18-25

Basis for selection. School achievement record, test scores important. **Homeschooled:** Transcript of courses and grades required. Must provide copy of transcript from accredited home school agency along with official ACT Report.

High school preparation. 20 units recommended. Recommended units include English 4, mathematics 3, social studies 3, science 3, foreign language 2 and academic electives 5.

2008-2009 Annual costs. Tuition/fees: $15,850. Additional $50 per-credit hour for nursing classes. Additional required fees for nursing and teacher education programs. Books/supplies: $1,000. Personal expenses: $1,500.

2008-2009 Financial aid. Non-need-based: Scholarships awarded for academics, alumni affiliation, leadership, religious affiliation.

Application procedures. Admission: Priority date 3/1; no deadline. $25 fee, may be waived for applicants with need. Admission notification on a rolling basis. **Financial aid:** Priority date 3/1; no closing date. FAFSA required. Applicants notified on a rolling basis starting 3/1; must reply within 2 week(s) of notification.

Academics. Special study options: Accelerated study, independent study, liberal arts/career combination, teacher certification program. **Credit/placement by examination:** AP, CLEP, SAT, ACT, institutional tests. 30 credit hours maximum toward associate degree, 30 toward bachelor's. **Support services:** Learning center, reduced course load, remedial instruction, study skills assistance, tutoring, writing center.

Majors. Business: Business admin, management information systems. **Education:** Elementary. **Health:** Nursing (RN). **Liberal arts:** Arts/sciences.

Computing on campus. 50 workstations in library, computer center. Online library, helpline available.

Student life. Freshman orientation: Mandatory. **Policies:** Drug-free/alcohol-free campus. **Activities:** Campus ministries, choral groups, student government, Phi Beta Lambda, Delta Epsilon Sigma, Association of Student Nurses, Association for Supervision and Curriculum Development student chapter, student affairs council, Frassati Society, Sigma Beta Delta.

Athletics. Intramural: Football (non-tackle), softball, volleyball. **Team name:** Cavaliers.

Student services. Chaplain/spiritual director, financial aid counseling.

Contact. E-mail: admissions@aquinascollege.edu
Phone: (615) 297-7545 ext. 460 Toll-free number: (800) 649-9956
Fax: (615) 279-3893
Connie Hansom, Director of Admissions, Aquinas College, 4210 Harding Road, Nashville, TN 37205-2086

Austin Peay State University
Clarksville, Tennessee **CB member**
www.apsu.edu **CB code: 1028**

- Public 4-year university and liberal arts college
- Commuter campus in small city
- 8,403 degree-seeking undergraduates: 23% part-time, 62% women, 18% African American, 2% Asian American, 4% Hispanic American, 1% Native American, 1% international
- 818 degree-seeking graduate students
- 88% of applicants admitted
- 33% graduate within 6 years

General. Founded in 1927. Regionally accredited. **Degrees:** 1,168 bachelor's, 109 associate awarded; master's offered. **ROTC:** Army, Air Force. **Location:** 45 miles from Nashville. **Calendar:** Semester, limited summer session. **Full-time faculty:** 302 total; 13% minority, 44% women. **Part-time faculty:** 209 total; 10% minority, 57% women. **Class size:** 41% < 20, 48% 20-39, 6% 40-49, 4% 50-99, less than 1% >100. **Special facilities:** Zoological museum.

Freshman class profile. 2,865 applied, 2,520 admitted, 1,471 enrolled.

Mid 50% test scores			
SAT critical reading:	460-510	Rank in top quarter:	39%
SAT math:	450-490	Rank in top tenth:	14%
ACT composite:	19-24	Return as sophomores:	68%
GPA 3.75 or higher:	13%	Out-of-state:	12%
GPA 3.50-3.74:	13%	Live on campus:	42%
GPA 3.0-3.49:	36%	International:	1%
GPA 2.0-2.99:	34%	Fraternities:	4%
		Sororities:	3%

Basis for selection. Rigor of secondary school record, GPA, standardized test scores very important. Four available admission categories: Unconditional, Conditional, Admission by Exception, or Admission by Alternative Standards. ACT/SAT is required for all first time freshman applicants under age 21, except for active duty military. All first time freshman applicants 21 years of age and older, except for active duty military, must submit official COMPASS assessment scores prior to admission. **Learning Disabled:** Students with learning disabilities are admitted as regular students.

High school preparation. 14 units required. Required units include English 4, mathematics 3, social studies 1, history 1, science 2 (laboratory 1) and foreign language 2. Mathematics units should be algebra I and II, 1 geometry or advanced mathematics. Social science units should be 1 social studies, 1 US history. Foreign language units must be in 1 language. 1 visual and/or performing arts also required.

2008-2009 Annual costs. Tuition/fees: $5,526; $16,418 out-of-state. Room/board: $5,870. Books/supplies: $1,404. Personal expenses: $1,575.

2007-2008 Financial aid. Need-based: 47% of total undergraduate aid awarded as scholarships/grants, 53% as loans/jobs. **Non-need-based:** Scholarships awarded for academics, art, athletics, leadership, music/drama, ROTC, state residency.

Application procedures. Admission: Closing date 7/25. $15 fee. Admission notification on a rolling basis. **Financial aid:** Priority date 3/1; no closing date. FAFSA required. Applicants notified on a rolling basis starting 5/1.

Academics. Special study options: Accelerated study, cooperative education, distance learning, double major, dual enrollment of high school students, ESL, honors, independent study, internships, study abroad, teacher certification program. Service Members Opportunity College (associate and bachelor's degrees). **Credit/placement by examination:** AP, CLEP, SAT, ACT, institutional tests. 32 credit hours maximum toward associate degree,

64 toward bachelor's. **Support services:** Learning center, remedial instruction, study skills assistance, tutoring, writing center.

Honors college/program. Rank in the top 10% of high school class, have a minimum ACT composite score of 26, and have a commendable high school record.

Majors. Agriculture: General. **Biology:** General. **Business:** General, nonprofit/public. **Communications:** Media studies. **Computer sciences:** General. **Education:** Health, special. **Engineering technology:** General. **Foreign languages:** General, Spanish. **Health:** Clinical lab science, medical radiologic technology/radiation therapy, nursing (RN). **History:** General. **Liberal arts:** Arts/sciences. **Math:** General. **Parks/recreation:** Health/fitness. **Philosophy/religion:** Philosophy. **Physical sciences:** Chemistry, geology, physics. **Protective services:** Law enforcement admin. **Psychology:** General. **Public administration:** Social work. **Social sciences:** Political science, sociology. **Visual/performing arts:** Art.

Most popular majors. Business/marketing 21%, health sciences 10%, interdisciplinary studies 7%, liberal arts 8%, psychology 6%.

Computing on campus. 760 workstations in dormitories, library, computer center, student center. Dormitories wired for high-speed internet access and linked to campus network. Commuter students can connect to campus network. Online course registration, online library, helpline, wireless network available.

Student life. Freshman orientation: Mandatory, $60 fee. Preregistration for classes offered. **Policies:** Alcohol not permitted on campus. **Housing:** Coed dorms, single-sex dorms, special housing for disabled, apartments, fraternity/sorority housing available. $200 fully refundable deposit, deadline 8/15. **Activities:** Bands, campus ministries, choral groups, dance, drama, literary magazine, music ensembles, musical theater, radio station, student government, student newspaper, TV station, Wesley Foundation, Room In the Inn, Student Organization to Advance Renewable Energy, student art league.

Athletics. NCAA. **Intercollegiate:** Baseball M, basketball, cross-country, football (tackle) M, golf, rifle W, soccer W, softball W, tennis, track and field W, volleyball W. **Intramural:** Basketball, football (non-tackle), racquetball, soccer, table tennis, volleyball. **Team name:** Governors.

Student services. Adult student services, alcohol/substance abuse counseling, career counseling, student employment services, financial aid counseling, health services, on-campus daycare, personal counseling, veterans' counselor. **Physically disabled:** Services for visually, speech, hearing impaired.

Contact. E-mail: admissions@apsu.edu
Phone: (931) 221-7661 Toll-free number: (800) 844-2778
Fax: (931) 221-6168
Ryan Forsythe, Director of Admissions, Austin Peay State University, PO Box 4548, Clarksville, TN 37044

Baptist College of Health Sciences
Memphis, Tennessee
www.bchs.edu

- Private 4-year health science and nursing college affiliated with Baptist faith
- Commuter campus in very large city
- 928 degree-seeking undergraduates: 40% part-time, 87% women, 30% African American, 2% Asian American, 2% Hispanic American
- 18% of applicants admitted
- SAT or ACT (ACT writing optional) required
- 34% graduate within 6 years

General. Regionally accredited. **Degrees:** 201 bachelor's awarded. **Calendar:** Trimester, limited summer session. **Full-time faculty:** 60 total. **Part-time faculty:** 37 total. **Class size:** 59% < 20, 38% 20-39, 3% 40-49, less than 1% 50-99.

Freshman class profile. 391 applied, 70 admitted, 70 enrolled.

GPA 3.75 or higher:	21%	**GPA 2.0-2.99:**	8%
GPA 3.50-3.74:	17%	**End year in good standing:**	88%
GPA 3.0-3.49:	54%	**Return as sophomores:**	61%

Basis for selection. GED not accepted. Standardized test scores, GPA, rigor of secondary school record, recommendations very important. **Homeschooled:** Transcript of courses and grades, letter of recommendation (nonparent) required. Transcript must be from an accredited home school agency showing GPA, high school graduation date, and all courses and grades. **Learning Disabled:** With proper documentation, students may be allowed to take the entrance exam with pencil and paper instead of on computer.

High school preparation. College-preparatory program required. 10 units required; 15 recommended. Required and recommended units include English 4, mathematics 2, social studies 1, history 1, science 2 (laboratory 2), foreign language 2 and academic electives 1.

2008-2009 Annual costs. Tuition/fees: $9,070.

2007-2008 Financial aid. Need-based: 41% of total undergraduate aid awarded as scholarships/grants, 59% as loans/jobs.

Application procedures. Admission: Priority date 2/15; deadline 6/1 (postmark date). $25 fee, may be waived for applicants with need. Admission notification on a rolling basis beginning on or about 6/1. Must reply by 7/1.

Academics. Credit/placement by examination: AP, CLEP, institutional tests. 15 credit hours maximum toward bachelor's degree. **Support services:** Learning center, tutoring.

Majors. Health: Health care admin, medical radiologic technology/radiation therapy, nuclear medical technology, nursing (RN), radiologic technology/medical imaging, respiratory therapy technology, sonography.

Computing on campus. Dormitories linked to campus network. Commuter students can connect to campus network. Online course registration, helpline, wireless network available.

Student life. Freshman orientation: Mandatory. Preregistration for classes offered. **Housing:** Coed dorms, wellness housing available. $100 fully refundable deposit. **Activities:** Campus ministries, student government.

Student services. Chaplain/spiritual director, financial aid counseling, health services, personal counseling.

Contact. E-mail: admissions@bchs.edu
Phone: (901) 575-2247 Toll-free number: (866) 575-2247
Fax: (901) 572-2461
Lissa Morgan, Manager, Admissions, Baptist College of Health Sciences, 1003 Monroe Avenue, Memphis, TN 38104

Belmont University
Nashville, Tennessee
www.belmont.edu — **CB code: 1058**

- Private 4-year university
- Residential campus in very large city
- 4,131 degree-seeking undergraduates: 7% part-time, 58% women, 4% African American, 2% Asian American, 2% Hispanic American, 1% international
- 801 degree-seeking graduate students
- 63% of applicants admitted
- SAT or ACT (ACT writing optional), interview required
- 67% graduate within 6 years; 17% enter graduate study

General. Founded in 1951. Regionally accredited. **Degrees:** 915 bachelor's awarded; master's, doctoral offered. **ROTC:** Army, Naval, Air Force. **Location:** 2 miles from downtown. **Calendar:** Semester, limited summer session. **Full-time faculty:** 263 total; 78% have terminal degrees, 5% minority, 51% women. **Part-time faculty:** 326 total; 23% have terminal degrees, 4% minority, 52% women. **Class size:** 50% < 20, 49% 20-39, less than 1% 40-49, less than 1% 50-99. **Special facilities:** 22-track recording studio, Studio B on Music Row, 140-year-old antebellum mansion.

Freshman class profile. 3,060 applied, 1,918 admitted, 932 enrolled.

Mid 50% test scores		**Rank in top tenth:**	36%
SAT critical reading:	540-630	**End year in good standing:**	89%
SAT math:	530-630	**Return as sophomores:**	81%
ACT composite:	23-28	**Out-of-state:**	39%
GPA 3.75 or higher:	34%	**Live on campus:**	94%
GPA 3.50-3.74:	22%	**International:**	1%
GPA 3.0-3.49:	36%	**Fraternities:**	3%
GPA 2.0-2.99:	8%	**Sororities:**	5%
Rank in top quarter:	70%		

Basis for selection. Admissions based on test scores, course selection, GPA, class rank, recommendations, leadership activity. Interview required for music business; audition required for music programs.

High school preparation. College-preparatory program required. 18 units required. Required and recommended units include English 4, mathematics 3-4, social studies 2, science 2-3, foreign language 2 and academic electives 5.

2008-2009 Annual costs. Tuition/fees: $21,110. Room/board: $8,200. Books/supplies: $1,300. Personal expenses: $1,600.

2007-2008 Financial aid. Need-based: 704 full-time freshmen applied for aid; 391 were judged to have need; 391 of these received aid. Average need met was 78%. Average scholarship/grant was $4,678; average loan $3,377. 30% of total undergraduate aid awarded as scholarships/grants, 70% as loans/jobs. **Non-need-based:** Awarded to 1,549 full-time undergraduates, including 435 freshmen. Scholarships awarded for academics, art, athletics, leadership, music/drama, religious affiliation, state residency.

Application procedures. Admission: Priority date 12/1; deadline 8/1. $50 fee. Admission notification on a rolling basis beginning on or about 9/1. Must reply by May 1 or within 2 week(s) if notified thereafter. **Financial aid:** Priority date 3/1; no closing date. FAFSA required. Applicants notified on a rolling basis starting 3/15; must reply by 5/1 or within 2 week(s) of notification.

Academics. Special study options: Accelerated study, combined bachelor's/graduate degree, cooperative education, distance learning, double major, dual enrollment of high school students, ESL, honors, independent study, internships, liberal arts/career combination, student-designed major, study abroad, teacher certification program, Washington semester. **Credit/placement by examination:** AP, CLEP, IB, SAT, ACT, institutional tests. 24 credit hours maximum toward bachelor's degree. **Support services:** Learning center, pre-admission summer program, reduced course load, tutoring, writing center.

Majors. Biology: General, environmental, molecular, molecular biochemistry. **Business:** General, accounting, entrepreneurial studies, finance, hospitality admin, management information systems, management science, managerial economics, marketing. **Communications:** General, broadcast journalism, journalism, media studies, public relations. **Computer sciences:** Computer science, information systems. **Education:** General, art, biology, chemistry, early childhood, elementary, English, French, health, health occupations, history, mathematics, middle, music, physical, physics, science, secondary, social science, social studies, Spanish. **Family/consumer sciences:** Child care. **Foreign languages:** French, German, Spanish. **Health:** Nursing (RN). **History:** General. **Liberal arts:** Arts/sciences. **Math:** General. **Parks/recreation:** Exercise sciences, health/fitness. **Philosophy/religion:** Philosophy, religion. **Physical sciences:** Chemistry, physics. **Psychology:** General. **Public administration:** Social work. **Social sciences:** Economics, political science, sociology. **Theology:** Sacred music. **Visual/performing arts:** Art, commercial/advertising art, dramatic, music management, music pedagogy, music performance, music theory/composition, piano/organ, voice/opera.

Most popular majors. Business/marketing 18%, health sciences 11%, liberal arts 6%, visual/performing arts 37%.

Computing on campus. 500 workstations in dormitories, library, computer center, student center. Dormitories wired for high-speed internet access and linked to campus network. Commuter students can connect to campus network. Online course registration, online library, helpline, wireless network available.

Student life. Freshman orientation: Mandatory, $60 fee. Preregistration for classes offered. 2-day program in summer or 4-day program in fall before classes start. **Housing:** Guaranteed on-campus for freshmen. Single-sex dorms, apartments, wellness housing available. $100 nonrefundable deposit, deadline 5/1. **Activities:** Bands, campus ministries, choral groups, dance, drama, international student organizations, literary magazine, music ensembles, musical theater, opera, radio station, student government, student newspaper, symphony orchestra, TV station, Baptist student union, Christian music society, Campus Crusade for Christ, Fellowship of Christian Athletes, Black Student Alliance.

Athletics. NCAA. **Intercollegiate:** Baseball M, basketball, cross-country, golf, soccer, softball W, tennis, track and field, volleyball W. **Intramural:** Basketball, bowling, golf M, racquetball, softball, table tennis, tennis, volleyball. **Team name:** Bruins.

Student services. Adult student services, alcohol/substance abuse counseling, chaplain/spiritual director, career counseling, student employment services, financial aid counseling, health services, minority student services, personal counseling, placement for graduates, veterans' counselor.

Contact. E-mail: buadmission@mail.belmont.edu
Phone: (615) 460-6785 Fax: (615) 460-5434
Kathy Baugher, Dean of Enrollment Services, Belmont University, 1900 Belmont Boulevard, Nashville, TN 37212-3757

Bethel College

McKenzie, Tennessee
www.bethel-college.edu **CB code: 1063**

- Private 4-year liberal arts college affiliated with Presbyterian Church (USA)
- Residential campus in small town
- 2,126 degree-seeking undergraduates: 17% part-time, 59% women, 33% African American, 1% Hispanic American, 2% international
- 282 degree-seeking graduate students
- 56% of applicants admitted
- SAT or ACT (ACT writing optional) required
- 30% graduate within 6 years

General. Founded in 1842. Regionally accredited. Students are provided with a laptop computer upon full-time registration. **Degrees:** 372 bachelor's awarded; master's offered. **Location:** 115 miles from Nashville, 120 miles from Memphis. **Calendar:** Semester, limited summer session. **Full-time faculty:** 84 total; 8% minority, 46% women. **Part-time faculty:** 144 total; 13% minority, 46% women. **Class size:** 72% < 20, 28% 20-39, less than 1% 40-49, less than 1% 50-99. **Special facilities:** Wildlife agency research laboratory.

Freshman class profile. 869 applied, 487 admitted, 260 enrolled.

Mid 50% test scores			
SAT critical reading:	420-470	Return as sophomores:	62%
SAT math:	390-500	Out-of-state:	7%
ACT composite:	17-21	Live on campus:	32%
		International:	3%

Basis for selection. Counselor recommendation, interview considered for academically marginal applicants. High school GPA and academic units considered. **Homeschooled:** ACT of 19 or above and passing score on GED required.

High school preparation. College-preparatory program recommended. Required units include English 4, mathematics 2, social studies 2 and science 2.

2008-2009 Annual costs. Tuition/fees: $12,242. Room/board: $6,926. Books/supplies: $1,000. Personal expenses: $1,750.

2008-2009 Financial aid. Need-based: 55% of total undergraduate aid awarded as scholarships/grants, 45% as loans/jobs. **Non-need-based:** Scholarships awarded for academics, athletics, music/drama, religious affiliation, state residency.

Application procedures. Admission: Priority date 2/3; no deadline. $30 fee. Admission notification on a rolling basis. **Financial aid:** Priority date 3/3, closing date 6/30. FAFSA, institutional form required. Applicants notified on a rolling basis starting 3/1.

Academics. Special study options: Accelerated study, combined bachelor's/graduate degree, double major, honors, independent study, internships, student-designed major, teacher certification program, weekend college. **Credit/placement by examination:** AP, CLEP, SAT, ACT, institutional tests. 30 credit hours maximum toward bachelor's degree. Accepts CLEP, DANTES, institutional exams for credit. **Support services:** Remedial instruction, study skills assistance, tutoring.

Majors. Biology: General. **Business:** Accounting/business management, business admin, management information systems. **Education:** Elementary, music, physical, special. **Health:** Nursing (RN), premedicine, prepharmacy. **History:** General. **Math:** General. **Philosophy/religion:** Christian. **Physical sciences:** Chemistry. **Psychology:** General. **Public administration:** Human services. **Social sciences:** Sociology. **Visual/performing arts:** Dramatic, music management.

Most popular majors. Business/marketing 78%, education 7%.

Computing on campus. PC or laptop required. 650 workstations in dormitories, library. Dormitories wired for high-speed internet access and linked to campus network. Commuter students can connect to campus network. Online library, helpline, repair service, wireless network available.

Student life. Freshman orientation: Mandatory. Preregistration for classes offered. One-day held in June, July, August on Saturdays. Week-long sessions held the week prior to the start of fall classes. **Housing:** Guaranteed on-campus for freshmen. Coed dorms, single-sex dorms, apartments available. $175 nonrefundable deposit, deadline 8/18. **Activities:** Bands, choral groups, drama, music ensembles, musical theater, student government, Fellowship of Christian Athletes, honor societies, American Chemical Society, Student TN Education Association, art club, Students in Free Enterprise, Arete, Campus Crusade for Christ, Relay for Life.

Athletics. NAIA. **Intercollegiate:** Baseball M, basketball, cheerleading, cross-country, football (tackle) M, golf, soccer, softball W, tennis, track and field, volleyball W. **Intramural:** Basketball, football (non-tackle), softball, swimming, table tennis, volleyball W. **Team name:** Wildcats.

Student services. Adult student services, alcohol/substance abuse counseling, chaplain/spiritual director, career counseling, student employment services, financial aid counseling, personal counseling, veterans' counselor.

Contact. E-mail: admissions@bethel-college.edu
Phone: (731) 352-4030 Fax: (731) 352-4069
Tina Hodges, Enrollment Director of Admissions and Financial Aid, Bethel College, 325 Cherry Avenue, McKenzie, TN 38201

Bryan College

Dayton, Tennessee
www.bryan.edu **CB code: 1908**

- Private 4-year liberal arts college affiliated with interdenominational tradition
- Residential campus in small town

General. Founded in 1930. Regionally accredited. **Location:** 40 miles from Chattanooga. **Calendar:** Semester.

Annual costs/financial aid. Tuition/fees (2008-2009): $17,020. Room/board: $5,095. Books/supplies: $1,000. Personal expenses: $1,000. Need-based financial aid available to full-time and part-time students.

Contact. Phone: (423) 775-7204
Director of Enrollment Management, PO Box 7000, Dayton, TN 37321-7000

Carson-Newman College

Jefferson City, Tennessee **CB member**
www.cn.edu **CB code: 1102**

- Private 4-year liberal arts college affiliated with Southern Baptist Convention
- Residential campus in small town
- 1,808 degree-seeking undergraduates: 6% part-time, 58% women, 8% African American, 1% Asian American, 1% Hispanic American, 3% international
- 209 degree-seeking graduate students
- 71% of applicants admitted
- SAT or ACT required
- 52% graduate within 6 years

General. Founded in 1851. Regionally accredited. **Degrees:** 348 bachelor's awarded; master's offered. **ROTC:** Army, Air Force. **Location:** 30 miles from Knoxville. **Calendar:** Semester, extensive summer session. **Full-time faculty:** 132 total; 76% have terminal degrees. **Part-time faculty:** 81 total. **Class size:** 59% < 20, 38% 20-39, 2% 40-49, less than 1% 50-99. **Special facilities:** Appalachia museum.

Freshman class profile. 2,815 applied, 2,012 admitted, 444 enrolled.

Mid 50% test scores		**Rank in top tenth:**	27%
ACT composite:	20-25	**Return as sophomores:**	67%
GPA 3.0-3.49:	68%	**Out-of-state:**	32%
GPA 2.0-2.99:	30%	**Live on campus:**	90%
Rank in top quarter:	47%	**International:**	2%

Basis for selection. Minimum 2.5 high school GPA, minimum ACT composite score of 19 or SAT combined score of 920 (exclusive of Writing), school and community activities, and recommendations important. Rank in top half of class considered. Essay required for marginal students; audition required for music; portfolio required for art; interview recommended for academically weak.

High school preparation. 20 units required. Required and recommended units include English 4, mathematics 2-3, social studies 3, history 2, science 2 (laboratory 1) and foreign language 2.

2009-2010 Annual costs. Tuition/fees: $18,702. Room/board: $5,608. Books/supplies: $1,088. Personal expenses: $1,921.

2008-2009 Financial aid. Need-based: 426 full-time freshmen applied for aid; 353 were judged to have need; 353 of these received aid. Average need met was 79%. Average scholarship/grant was $12,838; average loan $2,757. 65% of total undergraduate aid awarded as scholarships/grants, 35% as loans/jobs. **Non-need-based:** Awarded to 1,695 full-time undergraduates, including 446 freshmen. Scholarships awarded for academics, art, athletics, leadership, minority status, music/drama, religious affiliation, ROTC.

Application procedures. Admission: Priority date 12/31; deadline 8/1. $25 fee, may be waived for applicants with need. Admission notification on a rolling basis. Must reply by May 1 or within 4 week(s) if notified thereafter. **Financial aid:** Priority date 4/1; no closing date. FAFSA, institutional form required. Applicants notified on a rolling basis starting 2/1; must reply within 2 week(s) of notification.

Academics. 3-year pre-engineering programs available. **Special study options:** Accelerated study, double major, dual enrollment of high school students, ESL, exchange student, honors, independent study, internships, liberal arts/career combination, student-designed major, study abroad, teacher certification program, Washington semester, weekend college. **Credit/placement by examination:** AP, CLEP, institutional tests. 32 credit hours maximum toward associate degree, 32 toward bachelor's. **Support services:** Learning center, pre-admission summer program, reduced course load, remedial instruction, tutoring.

Majors. Biology: General. **Business:** General, accounting, business admin, managerial economics, small business admin. **Communications:** General, journalism. **Computer sciences:** General. **Education:** General, early childhood, elementary, family/consumer sciences, music, physical, secondary, special. **Family/consumer sciences:** Clothing/textiles, family/community services, food/nutrition. **Foreign languages:** French, German, Spanish. **Health:** Athletic training, health care admin, nursing (RN), predental, premedicine, prepharmacy. **History:** General. **Liberal arts:** Arts/sciences. **Math:** General. **Parks/recreation:** General, exercise sciences, health/fitness. **Philosophy/religion:** Philosophy, religion. **Physical sciences:** Applied physics, chemistry, physics. **Psychology:** General. **Social sciences:** Economics, international economics, political science, sociology. **Theology:** Sacred music, theology. **Visual/performing arts:** General, art, drawing, interior design, music performance, music theory/composition, painting, photography.

Most popular majors. Business/marketing 13%, communications/journalism 6%, education 19%, health sciences 21%, psychology 6%, social sciences 6%.

Computing on campus. 100 workstations in dormitories, library, computer center.

Student life. Freshman orientation: Available. Preregistration for classes offered. **Policies:** Religious observance required. **Housing:** Guaranteed on-campus for freshmen. Single-sex dorms, apartments available. $50 deposit, deadline 8/1. Honors house available. **Activities:** Bands, choral groups, dance, drama, film society, literary magazine, music ensembles, musical theater, radio station, student government, student newspaper, TV station, Baptist Student Union, Fellowship of Christian Athletes, honor societies, Appalachian Outreach, Bonners Scholars Community Service.

Athletics. NCAA. **Intercollegiate:** Baseball M, basketball, cross-country, football (tackle) M, golf M, soccer, softball W, tennis, track and field, volleyball W, wrestling M. **Intramural:** Badminton, basketball, bowling, golf, racquetball, soccer, softball, swimming, table tennis, tennis, volleyball. **Team name:** Eagles.

Student services. Adult student services, career counseling, health services, personal counseling, placement for graduates, veterans' counselor. **Physically disabled:** Services for visually, hearing impaired.

Contact. E-mail: mredding@cn.edu
Phone: (865) 471-3223 Fax: (865) 471-3502
Melanie Redding, Director of Admissions, Carson-Newman College, 1646 Russell Avenue, Jefferson City, TN 37760

Christian Brothers University

Memphis, Tennessee **CB member**
www.cbu.edu **CB code: 1121**

- Private 4-year university affiliated with Roman Catholic Church
- Commuter campus in very large city
- 1,404 degree-seeking undergraduates: 14% part-time, 55% women, 32% African American, 5% Asian American, 3% Hispanic American, 2% international
- 442 degree-seeking graduate students
- 59% of applicants admitted
- SAT or ACT (ACT writing optional), application essay required

General. Founded in 1871. Regionally accredited. **Degrees:** 260 bachelor's awarded; master's offered. **ROTC:** Army, Naval, Air Force. **Location:** 200 miles from Nashville, 150 miles from Little Rock, Arkansas. **Calendar:** Semester, limited summer session. **Full-time faculty:** 96 total; 88%

have terminal degrees, 16% minority, 33% women. **Part-time faculty:** 69 total; 42% have terminal degrees, 14% minority, 54% women. **Class size:** 69% < 20, 30% 20-39, less than 1% 40-49. **Special facilities:** Center for life sciences.

Freshman class profile. 1,634 applied, 972 admitted, 308 enrolled.

Mid 50% test scores		**GPA 2.0-2.99:**	11%
SAT critical reading:	470-590	**Rank in top quarter:**	73%
SAT math:	500-610	**Rank in top tenth:**	40%
ACT composite:	22-27	**Out-of-state:**	22%
GPA 3.75 or higher:	50%	**Live on campus:**	60%
GPA 3.50-3.74:	22%	**Fraternities:**	24%
GPA 3.0-3.49:	17%	**Sororities:**	22%

Basis for selection. Graduation from approved secondary school or GED equivalent, GPA of 2.0 and rank in upper 2/3 of graduating class, and satisfactory test scores required. SAT and ACT scores are used for math placement. Audition required for some programs; interview recommended for all. **Homeschooled:** Must have standardized test scores.

High school preparation. Recommended units include English 4, mathematics 4 and science 4. College-preparatory program required of engineering applicants.

2008-2009 Annual costs. Tuition/fees: $22,600. Room/board: $6,050.

2007-2008 Financial aid. Need-based: 296 full-time freshmen applied for aid; 229 were judged to have need; 229 of these received aid. Average need met was 93%. Average scholarship/grant was $6,626; average loan $3,271. 52% of total undergraduate aid awarded as scholarships/grants, 48% as loans/jobs. **Non-need-based:** Awarded to 1,128 full-time undergraduates, including 333 freshmen. Scholarships awarded for academics, alumni affiliation, athletics, music/drama, state residency. **Additional information:** ROTC scholarships available to qualified applicants.

Application procedures. Admission: Priority date 12/1; no deadline. $25 fee, may be waived for applicants with need. Admission notification on a rolling basis beginning on or about 12/1. Must reply by May 1 or within 3 week(s) if notified thereafter. **Financial aid:** Priority date 2/15; no closing date. FAFSA required. Applicants notified on a rolling basis starting 3/1; must reply within 2 week(s) of notification.

Academics. Special study options: Accelerated study, double major, dual enrollment of high school students, exchange student, honors, independent study, internships, liberal arts/career combination, study abroad, teacher certification program. **Credit/placement by examination:** AP, CLEP, IB, SAT, ACT, institutional tests. 30 credit hours maximum toward bachelor's degree. **Support services:** Pre-admission summer program, reduced course load, tutoring, writing center.

Majors. Biology: General, biomedical sciences. **Business:** General, business admin. **Computer sciences:** Computer science. **Education:** Biology, chemistry, elementary, English, history, mathematics, physics, secondary. **Engineering:** Chemical, civil, computer, electrical, mechanical, physics. **History:** General. **Interdisciplinary:** Biological/physical sciences, intercultural, math/computer science, natural sciences. **Liberal arts:** Arts/sciences. **Math:** General. **Philosophy/religion:** Philosophy, religion. **Physical sciences:** General, chemistry, physics. **Psychology:** General. **Visual/performing arts:** Studio arts.

Most popular majors. Biology 7%, business/marketing 40%, education 6%, engineering/engineering technologies 13%, physical sciences 8%, psychology 19%.

Computing on campus. 310 workstations in dormitories, library, computer center, student center. Dormitories wired for high-speed internet access and linked to campus network. Commuter students can connect to campus network. Online course registration, online library, helpline, wireless network available.

Student life. Freshman orientation: Mandatory. Preregistration for classes offered. Held Friday through Monday before classes begin in fall. Spring orientation held the morning on the day before classes begin. **Housing:** Guaranteed on-campus for freshmen. Single-sex dorms, apartments available. $300 nonrefundable deposit, deadline 5/1. Juniors and seniors may live in on-campus apartments. All Freshmen and Sophomores whose permanent address is beyond a 30 mile radius are required to live on campus. **Activities:** Choral groups, drama, literary magazine, musical theater, student government, Black Student Association, The Chosen Generation, Intercultural Club, Lasallian Collegians, Student Peace Association, Up 'Til Dawn.

Athletics. NCAA. **Intercollegiate:** Baseball M, basketball, cross-country, golf, soccer, softball W, tennis, volleyball W. **Intramural:** Basketball, bowling, football (non-tackle), soccer, softball, swimming, tennis, volleyball. **Team name:** Buccaneers.

Student services. Adult student services, alcohol/substance abuse counseling, chaplain/spiritual director, career counseling, student employment services, financial aid counseling, health services, minority student services, personal counseling, placement for graduates.

Contact. E-mail: admissions@cbu.edu
Phone: (901) 321-3205 Toll-free number: (800) 288-7576
Fax: (901) 321-3202
Tracey Dysart-Ford, Dean of Admissions, Christian Brothers University, 650 East Parkway South, Memphis, TN 38104-5519

Crichton College
Memphis, Tennessee
www.crichton.edu **CB code: 1782**

- Private 4-year liberal arts college affiliated with nondenominational tradition
- Commuter campus in very large city
- 912 degree-seeking undergraduates: 21% part-time, 67% women, 71% African American, 3% Hispanic American, 2% international
- 96 degree-seeking graduate students
- 15% of applicants admitted
- SAT or ACT (ACT writing optional), application essay required

General. Founded in 1941. Regionally accredited. **Degrees:** 124 bachelor's awarded. **Location:** 7 miles from downtown. **Calendar:** Semester, limited summer session. **Full-time faculty:** 29 total; 45% have terminal degrees, 31% minority, 45% women. **Part-time faculty:** 65 total; 22% have terminal degrees, 38% women. **Class size:** 82% < 20, 18% 20-39, less than 1% 50-99.

Freshman class profile. 1,457 applied, 224 admitted, 103 enrolled.

Mid 50% test scores		**GPA 2.0-2.99:**	55%
ACT composite:	15-20	**End year in good standing:**	69%
GPA 3.75 or higher:	3%	**Return as sophomores:**	42%
GPA 3.50-3.74:	3%	**Out-of-state:**	17%
GPA 3.0-3.49:	17%	**Live on campus:**	30%

Basis for selection. School achievement record, test scores, interview, references, and class rank considered. Minimum ACT composite score of 19 or minimum of 900 on SAT (combined math and critical reading) required for regular admission. **Homeschooled:** Transcript of courses and grades required. The home school must be accredited or affiliated with an accredited institution in order to be considered for acceptance. **Learning Disabled:** Student is responsible for disclosing information regarding nature of the disability and must register with the Office of Student Success and provide current documentation of the qualified disability.

High school preparation. College-preparatory program recommended. 14 units required. Required units include English 4, mathematics 3, social studies 3, science 3 and academic electives 1.

2008-2009 Annual costs. Tuition/fees: $12,120. Room/board: $8,332. Books/supplies: $1,032. Personal expenses: $3,588.

2007-2008 Financial aid. Need-based: Average scholarship/grant was $1,438; average loan $1,708. 49% of total undergraduate aid awarded as scholarships/grants, 51% as loans/jobs. **Non-need-based:** Scholarships awarded for academics, alumni affiliation, athletics, leadership, music/drama, religious affiliation.

Application procedures. Admission: Priority date 1/1; no deadline. $25 fee, may be waived for applicants with need. Admission notification on a rolling basis. **Financial aid:** Priority date 3/15; no closing date. FAFSA, institutional form required. Applicants notified on a rolling basis starting 3/1; must reply within 2 week(s) of notification.

Academics. Special study options: Accelerated study, distance learning, double major, dual enrollment of high school students, independent study, internships, liberal arts/career combination, student-designed major, study abroad, teacher certification program. **Credit/placement by examination:** AP, CLEP, IB, SAT, ACT, institutional tests. 30 credit hours maximum toward bachelor's degree. **Support services:** Learning center, pre-admission summer program, reduced course load, remedial instruction, study skills assistance, tutoring, writing center.

Majors. Biology: General, biomedical sciences. **Business:** Business admin. **Education:** General, biology, business, chemistry, elementary, English, history, mathematics, middle, psychology. **History:** General. **Legal studies:** Prelaw. **Liberal arts:** Arts/sciences. **Psychology:** General. **Theology:** Bible.

Most popular majors. Business/marketing 44%, education 18%, liberal arts 20%, psychology 6%, theological studies 7%.

Computing on campus. 34 workstations in library, computer center. Dormitories wired for high-speed internet access and linked to campus network. Commuter students can connect to campus network. Online library, helpline, repair service, wireless network available.

Student life. Freshman orientation: Mandatory, $40 fee. Preregistration for classes offered. 2-day program. **Policies:** Religious observance required. **Housing:** Special housing for disabled, apartments, wellness housing available. $150 fully refundable deposit, deadline 8/15. **Activities:** Campus ministries, choral groups, dance, drama, international student organizations, musical theater, student government, Christian Responsibility to Engage our World (Community Service), Crichton Christian Fellowship, Campus Crusade for Christ, InterVarsity.

Athletics. NAIA. **Intercollegiate:** Baseball M, basketball M, cross-country, golf, soccer, softball W, volleyball W. **Team name:** Comets.

Student services. Adult student services, chaplain/spiritual director, career counseling, student employment services, financial aid counseling, personal counseling, placement for graduates.

Contact. E-mail: admissions@crichton.edu
Phone: (901) 320-9797 Toll-free number: (800) 960-9777
Fax: (901) 320-9791
Robert Thompson, Vice President Admissions, Crichton College, 255 North Highland, Memphis, TN 38111-1375

Cumberland University

Lebanon, Tennessee
www.cumberland.edu **CB code: 1146**

- Private 4-year university and liberal arts college
- Commuter campus in large town
- 998 degree-seeking undergraduates: 10% part-time, 54% women, 11% African American, 1% Asian American, 2% Hispanic American, 1% Native American, 4% international
- 296 degree-seeking graduate students
- 59% of applicants admitted
- ACT (writing optional), application essay required
- 38% graduate within 6 years; 19% enter graduate study

General. Founded in 1842. Regionally accredited. **Degrees:** 195 bachelor's, 2 associate awarded; master's offered. **ROTC:** Army. **Location:** 30 miles from Nashville. **Calendar:** Semester, limited summer session. **Full-time faculty:** 44 total; 84% have terminal degrees, 4% minority, 41% women. **Part-time faculty:** 73 total; 16% have terminal degrees, 6% minority, 45% women. **Class size:** 56% < 20, 34% 20-39, 6% 40-49, 4% 50-99.

Freshman class profile. 592 applied, 348 admitted, 196 enrolled.

Mid 50% test scores		**Rank in top tenth:**	19%
SAT critical reading:	440-540	**End year in good standing:**	54%
SAT math:	450-540	**Return as sophomores:**	55%
ACT composite:	19-23	**Out-of-state:**	12%
GPA 3.75 or higher:	20%	**Live on campus:**	60%
GPA 3.50-3.74:	14%	**International:**	3%
GPA 3.0-3.49:	31%	**Fraternities:**	19%
GPA 2.0-2.99:	34%	**Sororities:**	12%
Rank in top quarter:	38%		

Basis for selection. High school academic record and standardized test scores most important. Audition, portfolio required for some programs; interview recommended for academically weak. **Homeschooled:** Transcript of courses and grades required.

High school preparation. 16 units required; 19 recommended. Required and recommended units include English 4, mathematics 3-4, social studies 2, history 2, science 3 (laboratory 1-2) and foreign language 2.

2009-2010 Annual costs. Tuition/fees (projected): $17,430. Room/board: $6,350. Books/supplies: $1,260. Personal expenses: $2,545.

2008-2009 Financial aid. Non-need-based: Scholarships awarded for academics, art, athletics, music/drama.

Application procedures. Admission: Priority date 2/15; no deadline. $25 fee, may be waived for applicants with need. Admission notification on a rolling basis beginning on or about 3/1. Permission of high school principal or guidance counselor required for early admission. Housing deposit refundable before August 1. **Financial aid:** Priority date 2/1; no closing date. FAFSA, institutional form required. Applicants notified on a rolling basis starting 5/1; must reply within 2 week(s) of notification.

Academics. Selection of major or minor not required. **Special study options:** Accelerated study, combined bachelor's/graduate degree, cooperative education, distance learning, double major, dual enrollment of high school students, honors, independent study, internships, liberal arts/career combination, teacher certification program. **Credit/placement by examination:** AP, CLEP, ACT, institutional tests. 30 credit hours maximum toward bachelor's degree. **Support services:** Learning center, pre-admission summer program, reduced course load, remedial instruction, study skills assistance, tutoring, writing center.

Majors. Area/ethnic studies: American. **Biology:** General. **Business:** General, accounting, management science. **Education:** General, biology, early childhood, elementary, English, history, mathematics, middle, multi-level teacher, music, physical, secondary, social science, special. **Health:** Nursing (RN), predental, premedicine, prepharmacy, preveterinary. **History:** General. **Legal studies:** Prelaw. **Liberal arts:** Arts/sciences. **Math:** General. **Parks/recreation:** Health/fitness, sports admin. **Protective services:** Criminal justice. **Psychology:** General. **Public administration:** General. **Social sciences:** General, political science, sociology. **Visual/performing arts:** Studio arts.

Most popular majors. Business/marketing 19%, education 24%, health sciences 28%, security/protective services 8%.

Computing on campus. 60 workstations in library, computer center. Dormitories linked to campus network. Commuter students can connect to campus network. Online library, helpline, repair service, wireless network available.

Student life. Freshman orientation: Mandatory. Preregistration for classes offered. Held on August 27 and 28, 1-1/2 days long. **Housing:** Single-sex dorms, apartments, wellness housing available. $200 deposit, deadline 8/1. **Activities:** Bands, campus ministries, choral groups, dance, drama, music ensembles, musical theater, radio station, student government, student newspaper, Fellowship of Christian Athletes, African American student association, Campus Crusade for Christ, Champions for Christ.

Athletics. NAIA. **Intercollegiate:** Baseball M, basketball, cheerleading, cross-country, football (tackle) M, golf, soccer, softball W, tennis, volleyball W, wrestling M. **Intramural:** Basketball, bowling, football (non-tackle) M, softball, table tennis, volleyball. **Team name:** Bulldogs.

Student services. Adult student services, chaplain/spiritual director, career counseling, student employment services, financial aid counseling, health services, personal counseling, placement for graduates. **Physically disabled:** Services for visually impaired.

Contact. E-mail: admissions@cumberland.edu
Phone: (615) 444-2562 Toll-free number: (800) 467-0562
Fax: (615) 444-2569
Beatrice LaChance, Director of Admissions and Student Financial Services, Cumberland University, One Cumberland Square, Lebanon, TN 37087

DeVry University: Memphis

Memphis, Tennessee
www.devry.edu

- For-profit 4-year business and technical college
- Very large city
- 68 degree-seeking undergraduates: 57% part-time, 63% women, 72% African American, 4% Asian American, 3% Hispanic American
- 67 degree-seeking graduate students

General. Regionally accredited. **Degrees:** 1 bachelor's awarded; master's offered. **Calendar:** Semester. **Part-time faculty:** 32 total; 47% minority, 41% women.

Basis for selection. Academic GPA important. Test scores, class rank condidered. SAT/ACT tests considered but not required for admission. If applicant chooses not to submit either, he/she must take DeVry-administered admissions test.

2008-2009 Annual costs. Tuition/fees: $13,930. Books/supplies: $1,300. Personal expenses: $5,082.

2007-2008 Financial aid. Non-need-based: Scholarships awarded for academics.

Application procedures. Admission: No deadline. $50 fee. Admission notification on a rolling basis. **Financial aid:** No deadline. FAFSA required. Applicants notified on a rolling basis.

Academics. Special study options: Accelerated study, distance learning. **Credit/placement by examination:** CLEP.

Majors. Business: Business admin. **Other:** Technical management.

Contact. DeVry University: Memphis, 6401 Poplar Avenue, Ste. 600, Memphis, TN 38119

East Tennessee State University

Johnson City, Tennessee — CB member
www.etsu.edu — CB code: 1198

- Public 4-year university
- Commuter campus in small city
- 10,654 degree-seeking undergraduates
- 90% of applicants admitted
- SAT or ACT (ACT writing optional) required

General. Founded in 1911. Regionally accredited. Additional campuses in Kingsport, Bristol, and Greeneville. Paramedical center, College of Medicine, College of Pharmacy, pre-professional programs. **Degrees:** 1,694 bachelor's awarded; master's, doctoral, first professional offered. **ROTC:** Army. **Location:** 90 miles from Knoxville, 60 miles from Asheville, North Carolina. **Calendar:** Semester, extensive summer session. **Full-time faculty:** 514 total. **Part-time faculty:** 296 total. **Class size:** 44% < 20, 40% 20-39, 7% 40-49, 7% 50-99, 2% >100. **Special facilities:** Appalachian archives, planetarium, observatory, arboretum.

Freshman class profile. 4,612 applied, 4,151 admitted, 1,968 enrolled.

Mid 50% test scores		**GPA 2.0-2.99:**	25%
SAT critical reading:	440-560	**Rank in top quarter:**	42%
SAT math:	440-560	**Rank in top tenth:**	17%
SAT writing:	420-550	**Out-of-state:**	14%
ACT composite:	20-25	**Live on campus:**	53%
GPA 3.75 or higher:	25%	**Fraternities:**	5%
GPA 3.50-3.74:	17%	**Sororities:**	5%
GPA 3.0-3.49:	32%		

Basis for selection. Completion of 14 specific high school units required by state. Minimum 2.3 GPA or ACT composite score of 19 or comparable SAT score required. Those with ACT composite scores below 19 or Math or English scores below 19 complete the appropriate assessment (COMPASS). Interview recommended for dental hygiene, health-related professions, nursing, physical therapy programs; audition required for music; portfolio recommended for art. **Homeschooled:** Transcript of courses and grades required.

High school preparation. 14 units required; 16 recommended. Required and recommended units include English 4, mathematics 3-4, social studies 1, history 1, science 2-3 (laboratory 1), foreign language 2 and visual/performing arts 1.

2008-2009 Annual costs. Tuition/fees: $5,201; $16,093 out-of-state. Room/board: $5,278. Books/supplies: $1,008. Personal expenses: $2,718.

2008-2009 Financial aid. Non-need-based: Scholarships awarded for academics, alumni affiliation, art, athletics, job skills, leadership, minority status, music/drama, religious affiliation, ROTC, state residency. **Additional information:** Housing costs payable by installment.

Application procedures. Admission: Priority date 7/1; deadline 7/15. $15 fee, may be waived for applicants with need. Admission notification on a rolling basis. **Financial aid:** Priority date 4/15; no closing date. FAFSA required. Applicants notified on a rolling basis starting 4/15; must reply within 2 week(s) of notification.

Academics. Special study options: Accelerated study, combined bachelor's/graduate degree, cooperative education, distance learning, double major, dual enrollment of high school students, exchange student, honors, independent study, internships, study abroad, teacher certification program. **Credit/placement by examination:** AP, CLEP, IB, SAT, ACT, institutional tests. **Support services:** Learning center, reduced course load, study skills assistance, tutoring.

Honors college/program. Honors program selects 20 new freshmen each year for specifically designed courses. Requires minimum 29 ACT or comparable SAT, 3.5 high school GPA.

Majors. Biology: General. **Business:** Accounting, business admin, finance, managerial economics, marketing. **Communications:** Media studies. **Communications technology:** Animation/special effects. **Computer sciences:** General. **Education:** Special. **Engineering technology:** General, surveying. **Family/consumer sciences:** General, child development, family studies. **Foreign languages:** General. **Health:** Dental hygiene, environmental health, health services, nursing (RN). **History:** General. **Liberal arts:** Arts/sciences. **Math:** General. **Parks/recreation:** Health/fitness, sports admin. **Philosophy/religion:** Philosophy. **Physical sciences:** Chemistry, physics. **Protective services:** Law enforcement admin. **Psychology:** General. **Public administration:** Social work. **Social sciences:** Economics, geography, political science, sociology. **Visual/performing arts:** Art.

Most popular majors. Business/marketing 15%, family/consumer sciences 6%, health sciences 19%, interdisciplinary studies 7%, liberal arts 8%.

Computing on campus. 1,400 workstations in dormitories, library, computer center, student center. Dormitories wired for high-speed internet access and linked to campus network. Commuter students can connect to campus network. Online course registration, online library, helpline, repair service, student web hosting, wireless network available.

Student life. Freshman orientation: Mandatory. Preregistration for classes offered. 5 sessions during summer for 1-2 days. **Housing:** Coed dorms, single-sex dorms, special housing for disabled, apartments, fraternity/sorority housing, wellness housing available. $100 fully refundable deposit. **Activities:** Bands, campus ministries, choral groups, drama, international student organizations, literary magazine, music ensembles, radio station, student government, student newspaper, TV station, Baptist Student Union, Campus Crusade, Catholic Center, Christian Student Fellowship, Fellowship of Christian Athletes, Real Life Fellowship, Wesley Foundation, Black Affairs Association.

Athletics. NCAA. **Intercollegiate:** Baseball M, basketball, cross-country, golf, soccer, softball W, tennis, track and field, volleyball W. **Intramural:** Basketball, cross-country, football (non-tackle), golf, handball, racquetball, softball, tennis, volleyball W, weight lifting M. **Team name:** Buccaneers.

Student services. Adult student services, alcohol/substance abuse counseling, chaplain/spiritual director, career counseling, services for economically disadvantaged, student employment services, financial aid counseling, health services, legal services, minority student services, on-campus daycare, personal counseling, placement for graduates, veterans' counselor, women's services. **Physically disabled:** Services for visually, speech, hearing impaired.

Contact. E-mail: go2etsu@etsu.edu
Phone: (423) 439-4213 Toll-free number: (800) 462-3878
Fax: (423) 439-4630
Michael Pitts, Director of Admissions, East Tennessee State University, ETSU Box 70731, Johnson City, TN 37614

Fisk University

Nashville, Tennessee — CB member
www.fisk.edu — CB code: 1224

- Private 4-year liberal arts college affiliated with United Church of Christ
- Residential campus in very large city
- 683 degree-seeking undergraduates: 4% part-time, 68% women, 82% African American, 1% Asian American, 12% international
- 41 degree-seeking graduate students
- 53% of applicants admitted
- SAT or ACT with writing, interview required
- 53% graduate within 6 years; 25% enter graduate study

General. Founded in 1866. Regionally accredited. **Degrees:** 128 bachelor's awarded; master's offered. **ROTC:** Army, Naval. **Location:** 216 miles from Memphis, 225 miles from Atlanta. **Calendar:** Semester, limited summer session. **Full-time faculty:** 56 total; 75% have terminal degrees, 71% minority, 46% women. **Part-time faculty:** 30 total; 17% have terminal degrees, 83% minority, 33% women. **Class size:** 74% < 20, 23% 20-39, 1% 40-49, 1% 50-99.

Freshman class profile. 917 applied, 484 admitted, 115 enrolled.

Mid 50% test scores		**Rank in top quarter:**	40%
SAT critical reading:	430-560	**Rank in top tenth:**	17%
SAT math:	420-540	**End year in good standing:**	71%
ACT composite:	18-22	**Return as sophomores:**	76%
GPA 3.75 or higher:	13%	**Out-of-state:**	70%
GPA 3.50-3.74:	15%	**Live on campus:**	92%
GPA 3.0-3.49:	28%	**International:**	6%
GPA 2.0-2.99:	44%		

Basis for selection. School achievement record, class rank, test scores, recommendations, activities important. Essay recommended for all; audition recommended for music. Interview required for scholarship nominees and must take place prior to 2/15.

High school preparation. 20 units recommended. Recommended units include English 4, mathematics 3, social studies 3, history 1, science 1, foreign language 1 and academic electives 6. 1 algebra and 1 geometry recommended.

2008-2009 Annual costs. Tuition/fees: $16,240. Room/board: $7,725. Books/supplies: $1,600. Personal expenses: $2,000.

2008-2009 Financial aid. All financial aid based on need.

Application procedures. Admission: Priority date 2/15; deadline 3/1 (receipt date). $50 fee, may be waived for applicants with need. Application must be submitted on paper. Admission notification on a rolling basis. Must reply by May 1 or within 2 week(s) if notified thereafter. **Financial aid:** Priority date 3/1, closing date 7/1. FAFSA required. Applicants notified on a rolling basis starting 4/1; must reply within 2 week(s) of notification.

Academics. Special study options: Combined bachelor's/graduate degree, cooperative education, cross-registration, double major, dual enrollment of high school students, exchange student, honors, independent study, internships, liberal arts/career combination, student-designed major, study abroad, teacher certification program. 2-2 program with Rush-Presbyterian-St. Luke's Medical Center in nursing, dual degree in science and engineering, dual degree in engineering and natural sciences in 5 years, 3-3 program with Howard University for Doctor of Pharmacy, 5-year MBA program with Vanderbilt University, 7-year MD, PhD, DDS programs with Meharry Medical College. **Credit/placement by examination:** AP, CLEP, IB, SAT, ACT, institutional tests. 30 credit hours maximum toward bachelor's degree. **Support services:** Learning center, pre-admission summer program, tutoring, writing center.

Majors. Biology: General. **Business:** Business admin. **Computer sciences:** Computer science. **Education:** Music, special. **Foreign languages:** Spanish. **Health:** Nursing (RN), premedicine. **History:** General. **Math:** General. **Physical sciences:** Chemistry, physics. **Psychology:** General. **Social sciences:** Political science, sociology. **Visual/performing arts:** Art, dramatic, music performance. **Other:** Religious and philosophical studies.

Most popular majors. Biology 10%, business/marketing 16%, English 6%, physical sciences 6%, psychology 25%, social sciences 16%.

Computing on campus. 100 workstations in dormitories, library, computer center. Dormitories wired for high-speed internet access and linked to campus network. Online course registration, helpline, student web hosting, wireless network available.

Student life. Freshman orientation: Available. Preregistration for classes offered. 3-5 day orientation held 1 week before classes. **Policies:** All students required to live on-campus, with few exceptions. All freshmen have curfew of 12:00 am. **Housing:** Guaranteed on-campus for all undergraduates. Single-sex dorms, special housing for disabled available. $100 deposit, deadline 7/15. **Activities:** Jazz band, campus ministries, choral groups, dance, drama, literary magazine, music ensembles, radio station, student government, student newspaper, TV station, Baptist student union, Muslim student association, Nation of Islam, Carribean student union, African student association, race relations students' organization.

Athletics. NCAA. **Intercollegiate:** Baseball M, basketball, cross-country, soccer, softball W, tennis, track and field, volleyball W. **Intramural:** Badminton, basketball, football (non-tackle) M, football (tackle) M, softball, volleyball. **Team name:** Bulldogs.

Student services. Career counseling, student employment services, financial aid counseling, health services, personal counseling, placement for graduates.

Contact. E-mail: admit@fisk.edu
Phone: (615) 329-8665 Toll-free number: (888) 702-0022
Fax: (615) 329-8774
Keith Chandler, Dean of Admissions, Fisk University, 1000 17th Avenue North, Nashville, TN 37208-3051

Free Will Baptist Bible College

Nashville, Tennessee
www.fwbbc.edu **CB code: 1232**

- Private 4-year Bible and teachers college affiliated with Free Will Baptists
- Residential campus in very large city
- 269 degree-seeking undergraduates: 22% part-time, 50% women, 6% African American, 1% Hispanic American, 1% Native American, 1% international
- 43% graduate within 6 years; 1% enter graduate study

General. Founded in 1942. Regionally accredited; also accredited by ABHE. **Degrees:** 66 bachelor's, 5 associate awarded. **ROTC:** Army, Air Force. **Location:** 3 miles from downtown. **Calendar:** Semester, limited summer session. **Full-time faculty:** 21 total; 33% have terminal degrees, 33% women. **Part-time faculty:** 24 total; 62% have terminal degrees, 12% minority, 38% women. **Class size:** 87% < 20, 12% 20-39, 1% 40-49.

Freshman class profile. 164 applied, 164 admitted, 65 enrolled.

Mid 50% test scores		**GPA 2.0-2.99:**	23%
ACT composite:	18-25	**Return as sophomores:**	68%
GPA 3.75 or higher:	38%	**Out-of-state:**	62%
GPA 3.50-3.74:	14%	**Live on campus:**	87%
GPA 3.0-3.49:	25%		

Basis for selection. Open admission. Applicants without high school diploma or GED must pass GED prior to receiving degree.

High school preparation. 22 units recommended. Recommended units include English 4, mathematics 4, social studies 3, history 2, science 4, foreign language 3 and academic electives 2.

2008-2009 Annual costs. Tuition/fees: $13,086. Room/board: $5,358. Books/supplies: $600. Personal expenses: $820.

2007-2008 Financial aid. Need-based: 34% of total undergraduate aid awarded as scholarships/grants, 66% as loans/jobs. **Non-need-based:** Scholarships awarded for academics, art, music/drama.

Application procedures. Admission: Priority date 4/15; no deadline. $35 fee. Admission notification on a rolling basis. **Financial aid:** Priority date 4/15; no closing date. FAFSA, institutional form required. Applicants notified on a rolling basis starting 7/1; must reply within 2 week(s) of notification.

Academics. Special study options: Distance learning, double major, dual enrollment of high school students, independent study, internships, teacher certification program. **Credit/placement by examination:** AP, CLEP, IB, institutional tests. 16 credit hours maximum toward bachelor's degree. **Support services:** Reduced course load, remedial instruction, tutoring.

Majors. Business: Business admin. **Education:** Early childhood, elementary, music, physical, secondary. **History:** General. **Parks/recreation:** Exercise sciences. **Psychology:** General. **Theology:** Bible, missionary, religious ed, theology.

Most popular majors. Business/marketing 16%, education 18%, psychology 7%, theological studies 47%.

Computing on campus. 42 workstations in library, computer center, student center. Commuter students can connect to campus network. Online library, repair service, wireless network available.

Student life. Freshman orientation: Mandatory. Preregistration for classes offered. **Policies:** Religious observance required. **Housing:** Single-sex dorms, apartments available. $100 deposit, deadline 8/1. Single students required to live on campus unless living with parents or close relatives. **Activities:** Campus ministries, choral groups, drama, music ensembles, musical theater, student government, ministerial and missionary organizations, Christian service assignments, organization for business students, literary societies.

Athletics. NCCAA. **Intercollegiate:** Baseball M, basketball, volleyball W. **Intramural:** Basketball, softball, table tennis M, tennis, volleyball. **Team name:** Flames.

Student services. Career counseling, student employment services, financial aid counseling, personal counseling, placement for graduates, veterans' counselor.

Contact. E-mail: recruit@fwbbc.edu
Phone: (615) 844-5000 Toll-free number: (800) 763-9222
Fax: (615) 269-6028
Jeff Caudill, Director of Enrollment Services, Free Will Baptist Bible College, 3606 West End Avenue, Nashville, TN 37205-2403

Freed-Hardeman University

Henderson, Tennessee **CB member**
www.fhu.edu **CB code: 1230**

- Private 4-year university and liberal arts college affiliated with Church of Christ
- Residential campus in small town

- 1,534 degree-seeking undergraduates: 8% part-time, 55% women, 4% African American, 1% Hispanic American, 1% Native American, 2% international
- 527 graduate students
- 56% of applicants admitted
- SAT or ACT (ACT writing recommended) required
- 53% graduate within 6 years

General. Founded in 1869. Regionally accredited. Henderson Church of Christ facilities adjacent to campus. Campus in Verviers, Belgium. **Degrees:** 341 bachelor's, 18 associate awarded; master's, first professional offered. **Location:** 15 miles from Jackson, 85 miles from Memphis. **Calendar:** Semester, limited summer session. **Full-time faculty:** 106 total; 67% have terminal degrees, 4% minority, 30% women. **Part-time faculty:** 45 total; 36% have terminal degrees, 4% minority, 44% women. **Class size:** 50% < 20, 41% 20-39, 6% 40-49, 3% 50-99.

Freshman class profile. 1,231 applied, 687 admitted, 405 enrolled.

Mid 50% test scores			
SAT critical reading:	510-630	GPA 2.0-2.99:	22%
SAT math:	440-590	Rank in top quarter:	54%
ACT composite:	20-26	Rank in top tenth:	26%
GPA 3.75 or higher:	37%	Return as sophomores:	75%
GPA 3.50-3.74:	17%	Out-of-state:	50%
GPA 3.0-3.49:	24%	Live on campus:	90%
		International:	2%

Basis for selection. Admissions based on school achievement record, test scores, references. Applicants without minimum test score or high school GPA may be admitted with restrictions after further evaluation. **Homeschooled:** Applicants expected to take ACT or SAT.

High school preparation. 20 units recommended. Recommended units include English 4, mathematics 2, social studies 2, science 2 and academic electives 10. Additional science and mathematics courses recommended.

2008-2009 Annual costs. Tuition/fees: $14,060. Room/board: $6,970. Books/supplies: $1,800. Personal expenses: $2,080.

2008-2009 Financial aid. Non-need-based: Scholarships awarded for academics, art, athletics, leadership, minority status, music/drama, state residency.

Application procedures. Admission: No deadline. No application fee. Admission notification on a rolling basis. Housing deposit refundable up to 30 days prior to term. **Financial aid:** Priority date 3/1; no closing date. FAFSA required. Applicants notified on a rolling basis starting 3/1; must reply within 4 week(s) of notification.

Academics. Students enrolled for 12 or more undergraduate hours must register for Bible class. **Special study options:** Accelerated study, combined bachelor's/graduate degree, cooperative education, cross-registration, distance learning, double major, dual enrollment of high school students, honors, independent study, internships, liberal arts/career combination, student-designed major, study abroad, teacher certification program. 3-2 engineering, Honors College, study abroad programs in Belgium and Italy. **Credit/placement by examination:** AP, CLEP, IB, SAT, ACT; institutional tests. 33 credit hours maximum toward bachelor's degree. **Support services:** Learning center, reduced course load, remedial instruction, study skills assistance, tutoring.

Honors college/program. Approximately 5% of freshmen class admitted to honors course work as result of competitive application process.

Majors. Biology: General, biochemistry. **Business:** Accounting, business admin, finance, human resources, management information systems, marketing. **Communications:** General, journalism, media studies, public relations. **Computer sciences:** General. **Education:** Art, biology, curriculum, early childhood, elementary, English, history, mathematics, middle, multi-level teacher, music, physical, science, secondary, special. **Family/consumer sciences:** Family studies. **Health:** Health care admin. **History:** General. **Liberal arts:** Arts/sciences. **Math:** General. **Parks/recreation:** Exercise sciences. **Philosophy/religion:** Philosophy. **Physical sciences:** General, chemistry. **Protective services:** Criminal justice. **Psychology:** General. **Public administration:** Social work. **Social sciences:** General. **Theology:** Bible, missionary, theology. **Visual/performing arts:** Acting, art, design, interior design, theater design.

Most popular majors. Biology 6%, business/marketing 16%, communications/journalism 7%, family/consumer sciences 8%, interdisciplinary studies 10%, public administration/social services 6%, theological studies 13%, visual/performing arts 7%.

Computing on campus. 238 workstations in dormitories, library, computer center, student center. Dormitories wired for high-speed internet access and linked to campus network. Commuter students can connect to campus network. Online course registration, online library, helpline, repair service, wireless network available.

Student life. Freshman orientation: Mandatory. Preregistration for classes offered. 4 days prior to start of classes in August. **Policies:** Daily chapel is mandatory. Nightly curfew. Religious observance required. **Housing:** Guaranteed on-campus for freshmen. Single-sex dorms, apartments, wellness housing available. Some student-teacher housing for education majors. **Activities:** Bands, choral groups, drama, international student organizations, music ensembles, musical theater, radio station, student government, student newspaper, TV station, evangelism forum, preachers club, student-alumni association, university student ambassadors, university program council, youth workers club, Impact Team, Young Republicans, Young Democrats.

Athletics. NAIA. **Intercollegiate:** Baseball M, basketball, cheerleading W, soccer, softball W, volleyball W. **Intramural:** Badminton, basketball, cross-country, football (non-tackle), racquetball, soccer, softball, table tennis, tennis, volleyball. **Team name:** Lions.

Student services. Alcohol/substance abuse counseling, chaplain/spiritual director, career counseling, student employment services, financial aid counseling, health services, on-campus daycare, personal counseling, placement for graduates, veterans' counselor. **Physically disabled:** Services for visually, hearing impaired.

Contact. E-mail: admissions@fhu.edu
Phone: (731) 989-6651 Toll-free number: (800) 630-3480
Fax: (731) 989-6047
Belinda Anderson, Director of Admissions, Freed-Hardeman University, 158 East Main Street, Henderson, TN 38340

International Academy of Design and Technology: Nashville

Nashville, Tennessee
www.iadtnashville.com

- For-profit 4-year branch campus and visual arts college
- Commuter campus in very large city
- 643 degree-seeking undergraduates

General. Accredited by ACICS. **Degrees:** 20 bachelor's, 70 associate awarded. **Calendar:** Quarter, extensive summer session. **Full-time faculty:** 9 total. **Part-time faculty:** 43 total.

Basis for selection. Open admission.

2008-2009 Annual costs. Tuition/fees: $15,875. Books/supplies: $1,800.

2008-2009 Financial aid. Need-based: 32% of total undergraduate aid awarded as scholarships/grants, 68% as loans/jobs.

Application procedures. Admission: No deadline. $50 fee. **Financial aid:** No deadline.

Academics. Credit/placement by examination: CLEP.

Majors. Business: Fashion. **Visual/performing arts:** Fashion design, graphic design, interior design.

Computing on campus. Online library available.

Student life. Freshman orientation: Available.

Student services. Student employment services, financial aid counseling, placement for graduates.

Contact. E-mail: admissions@iadtnashville.com
Phone: (866) 302-4238
Sonya Flanagan-Ensign, Director of Admissions, International Academy of Design and Technology: Nashville, 1 Bridgestone Park, Nashville, TN 37214

ITT Technical Institute: Knoxville

Knoxville, Tennessee
www.itt-tech.edu **CB code: 7139**

- For-profit 4-year technical college
- Commuter campus in small city

General. Accredited by ACICS. **Calendar:** Quarter.

Contact. Phone: (865) 671-2800
Director of Recruitment, 10208 Technology Drive, Knoxville, TN 37932

ITT Technical Institute: Memphis

Cordova, Tennessee
www.itt-tech.edu **CB code: 2731**

- For-profit 4-year technical college
- Commuter campus in very large city

General. Accredited by ACICS. **Calendar:** Quarter.

Contact. Phone: (901) 762-0556
Director of Recruitment, 7260 Goodlett Farms Parkway, Cordova, TN 38016

ITT Technical Institute: Nashville

Nashville, Tennessee
www.itt-tech.edu **CB code: 7025**

- For-profit 4-year technical college
- Commuter campus in very large city

General. Accredited by ACICS. **Calendar:** Quarter.

Contact. Phone: (615) 889-8700
Director of Recruitment, 2845 Elm Hill Pike, Nashville, TN 37214

Johnson Bible College

Knoxville, Tennessee
www.jbc.edu **CB code: 1345**

- Private 4-year Bible college affiliated with Christian Church
- Residential campus in large city
- 664 degree-seeking undergraduates: 3% part-time, 49% women
- 116 graduate students
- SAT or ACT (ACT writing recommended), application essay required
- 67% graduate within 6 years

General. Founded in 1893. Regionally accredited; also accredited by ABHE. **Degrees:** 115 bachelor's, 20 associate awarded; master's offered. **Location:** 7 miles from Knoxville. **Calendar:** Semester, limited summer session. **Full-time faculty:** 29 total. **Part-time faculty:** 36 total. **Class size:** 38% < 20, 31% 20-39, 13% 40-49, 19% 50-99.

Freshman class profile.

Mid 50% test scores		**GPA 3.50-3.74:**	17%
SAT critical reading:	460-590	**GPA 3.0-3.49:**	30%
SAT math:	480-590	**GPA 2.0-2.99:**	28%
SAT writing:	460-570	**Rank in top quarter:**	46%
ACT composite:	19-26	**Rank in top tenth:**	20%
GPA 3.75 or higher:	25%	**Live on campus:**	96%

Basis for selection. High school transcript and 3 references, 1 from minister required. Combination of high school percentile rank and ACT score determines initial admission criteria. Interview recommended.

High school preparation. 16 units required. Required units include academic electives 4. 12 of the 16 units must be content courses such as English, history, mathematics, foreign language, and science.

2008-2009 Annual costs. Tuition/fees: $7,780. Room/board: $4,890. Books/supplies: $900. Personal expenses: $2,060.

2008-2009 Financial aid. Non-need-based: Scholarships awarded for academics, leadership, minority status, music/drama, religious affiliation, state residency.

Application procedures. Admission: Closing date 7/1 (receipt date). $35 fee. Admission notification 9/1. Admission notification on a rolling basis. **Financial aid:** Priority date 5/1, closing date 8/1. FAFSA, institutional form required. Applicants notified on a rolling basis starting 4/30; must reply within 2 week(s) of notification.

Academics. All degree programs have major in Bible. Double majors in Bible and music, Bible and teacher education, Bible and counseling, Bible and preaching, Bible and youth ministry/preaching offered. **Special study options:** Accelerated study, combined bachelor's/graduate degree, cooperative education, distance learning, double major, ESL, honors, independent study, internships, teacher certification program. **Credit/placement by examination:** AP, CLEP, institutional tests. 32 credit hours maximum toward bachelor's degree. **Support services:** Learning center, remedial instruction, study skills assistance, tutoring.

Majors. Theology: Bible, sacred music.

Most popular majors. Education 13%, philosophy/religious studies 87%.

Computing on campus. 50 workstations in library, computer center. Dormitories linked to campus network. Commuter students can connect to campus network. Helpline, student web hosting, wireless network available.

Student life. Freshman orientation: Mandatory. Preregistration for classes offered. Weekend preceeding first semester. **Policies:** Religious observance required. **Housing:** Single-sex dorms, apartments, wellness housing available. $100 deposit, deadline 8/1. Mobile homes, duplex houses, available for family housing. **Activities:** Jazz band, campus ministries, choral groups, drama, literary magazine, music ensembles, musical theater, radio station, student government.

Athletics. NCCAA. **Intercollegiate:** Baseball M, basketball, soccer, volleyball W. **Intramural:** Basketball, softball, tennis, volleyball.

Student services. Alcohol/substance abuse counseling, chaplain/spiritual director, career counseling, student employment services, financial aid counseling, health services, on-campus daycare, personal counseling, placement for graduates. **Physically disabled:** Services for visually impaired.

Contact. E-mail: twingfield@jbc.edu
Phone: (865) 251-2233 Toll-free number: (800) 827-2122
Fax: (865) 251-2336
Tim Wingfield, Director of Admissions, Johnson Bible College, 7900 Johnson Drive, Knoxville, TN 37998-0001

King College

Bristol, Tennessee **CB member**
www.king.edu **CB code: 1371**

- Private 4-year nursing and liberal arts college affiliated with Presbyterian Church (USA)
- Residential campus in large town
- 1,320 degree-seeking undergraduates: 2% part-time, 65% women, 2% African American, 2% Hispanic American, 3% international
- 261 degree-seeking graduate students
- 63% of applicants admitted
- SAT or ACT (ACT writing optional), application essay required
- 53% graduate within 6 years

General. Founded in 1867. Regionally accredited. Christian values emphasized. **Degrees:** 368 bachelor's awarded; master's offered. **ROTC:** Army. **Location:** 110 miles from Knoxville, 95 miles from Asheville, North Carolina. **Calendar:** Semester, limited summer session. **Full-time faculty:** 66 total; 77% have terminal degrees, 3% minority, 52% women. **Part-time faculty:** 89 total; 29% have terminal degrees, 57% women. **Class size:** 62% < 20, 35% 20-39, 2% 40-49, less than 1% 50-99. **Special facilities:** Observatory, nuclear physics laboratory.

Freshman class profile. 898 applied, 562 admitted, 187 enrolled.

Mid 50% test scores		**GPA 2.0-2.99:**	21%
SAT critical reading:	450-540	**Rank in top quarter:**	49%
SAT math:	440-550	**Rank in top tenth:**	28%
ACT composite:	19-24	**Return as sophomores:**	70%
GPA 3.75 or higher:	25%	**Out-of-state:**	40%
GPA 3.50-3.74:	24%	**Live on campus:**	81%
GPA 3.0-3.49:	29%	**International:**	3%

Basis for selection. Qualified applicants should have a minimum of a 2.4/4.0 GPA and a minimum ACT or SAT composite score of 19 or 890 (exclusive of Writing). Those who do not present this pattern may be conditionally accepted with permission from the Admissions Committee. SAT or ACT scores must be received by the 1st day of fall classes for fall-term admission. SAT Writing scores are used for finanaical aid eligibility purposes only. Interview recommended.

High school preparation. 19 units required. Required units include English 4, mathematics 3, social studies 2, history 2, science 1 (laboratory 1), foreign language 2, computer science 1 and academic electives 4. 2 Algebra (Algebra I and II); one unit of Geometry; 1 Natural Science required.

2008-2009 Annual costs. Tuition/fees: $20,582. Room/board: $6,900. Books/supplies: $800.

2008-2009 Financial aid. Need-based: 173 full-time freshmen applied for aid; 147 were judged to have need; 147 of these received aid. Average need met was 84%. Average scholarship/grant was $16,000; average loan $4,239. 65% of total undergraduate aid awarded as scholarships/grants, 35%

as loans/jobs. **Non-need-based:** Awarded to 446 full-time undergraduates, including 80 freshmen. Scholarships awarded for academics, art, athletics, music/drama.

Application procedures. Admission: No deadline. $20 fee, may be waived for applicants with need, free for online applicants. Admission notification on a rolling basis. Refund available in full until May 1. **Financial aid:** Priority date 3/1; no closing date. FAFSA required. Applicants notified on a rolling basis starting 4/1; must reply within 2 week(s) of notification.

Academics. Special study options: Accelerated study, combined bachelor's/graduate degree, cross-registration, double major, dual enrollment of high school students, ESL, exchange student, honors, independent study, internships, student-designed major, study abroad, teacher certification program, Washington semester. **Credit/placement by examination:** AP, CLEP, SAT, ACT, institutional tests. 30 credit hours maximum toward bachelor's degree. **Support services:** Learning center, reduced course load, remedial instruction, study skills assistance, tutoring, writing center.

Honors college/program. Current students may be invited to join the Jack E. Snider Honors Center by invitation from a faculty member. Prospective students will meet entrance exam requirements.

Majors. Area/ethnic studies: American. **Biology:** General, biochemistry, biophysics. **Business:** Accounting, business admin, management information systems. **Communications:** Digital media. **Education:** Music. **Engineering:** General. **Foreign languages:** General, French, Spanish. **Health:** Athletic training, clinical lab science, nursing (RN). **History:** General. **Math:** General. **Parks/recreation:** Health/fitness. **Philosophy/religion:** Religion. **Physical sciences:** Chemistry, physics. **Psychology:** General. **Social sciences:** Economics, political science. **Theology:** Bible, youth ministry. **Visual/performing arts:** General. **Other:** Applied science.

Most popular majors. Biology 6%, business/marketing 33%, health sciences 41%.

Computing on campus. PC or laptop required. 88 workstations in library, computer center, student center. Dormitories wired for high-speed internet access and linked to campus network. Commuter students can connect to campus network. Online library, helpline, repair service, wireless network available.

Student life. Freshman orientation: Available. Preregistration for classes offered. **Policies:** Traditional undergraduate students participate in Chapel and Convocation series as a part of their service requirements necessary to fulfill degree requirements. Religious observance required. **Housing:** Guaranteed on-campus for all undergraduates. Single-sex dorms, special housing for disabled, apartments available. $50 fully refundable deposit. **Activities:** Bands, campus ministries, choral groups, dance, drama, international student organizations, music ensembles, musical theater, student government, student newspaper, Fellowship of Christian Athletes, Young Life Leadership, Student Life and Activities Committee at King, Students in Free Enterprise, King College Republicans, World Christian Fellowship, literary society.

Athletics. NAIA. **Intercollegiate:** Baseball M, basketball, cheerleading, cross-country, golf, soccer, softball W, tennis, track and field, volleyball W, wrestling M. **Intramural:** Badminton, basketball, cross-country, football (non-tackle), golf, soccer, softball W, table tennis, track and field, volleyball. **Team name:** Tornado.

Student services. Adult student services, chaplain/spiritual director, career counseling, student employment services, financial aid counseling, health services, personal counseling, placement for graduates.

Contact. E-mail: admissions@king.edu
Phone: (423) 652-4861 Toll-free number: (800) 362-0014
Fax: (423) 652-4727
Melinda Clark, Vice President of Enrollment Management, King College, 1350 King College Road, Bristol, TN 37620-2699

Lambuth University

Jackson, Tennessee
www.lambuth.edu **CB code: 1394**

- Private 4-year university and liberal arts college affiliated with United Methodist Church
- Residential campus in small city
- 765 degree-seeking undergraduates: 2% part-time, 47% women
- 62% of applicants admitted
- SAT or ACT (ACT writing optional), application essay required
- 40% graduate within 6 years; 21% enter graduate study

General. Founded in 1843. Regionally accredited. **Degrees:** 123 bachelor's awarded. **ROTC:** Army. **Location:** 80 miles from Memphis, 120 miles from Nashville. **Calendar:** Semester, limited summer session. **Full-time faculty:** 50 total; 80% have terminal degrees, 2% minority, 42% women. **Part-time faculty:** 47 total; 15% have terminal degrees, 6% minority, 36% women. **Class size:** 74% < 20, 24% 20-39, less than 1% 40-49, less than 1% 50-99, less than 1% >100. **Special facilities:** Planetarium, art and interior design complex, biological field station, education curriculum lab.

Freshman class profile. 679 applied, 421 admitted, 205 enrolled.

Mid 50% test scores		**GPA 2.0-2.99:**	30%
SAT critical reading:	440-570	**Rank in top quarter:**	42%
SAT math:	460-570	**Rank in top tenth:**	21%
ACT composite:	20-25	**End year in good standing:**	94%
GPA 3.75 or higher:	21%	**Return as sophomores:**	60%
GPA 3.50-3.74:	15%	**Out-of-state:**	17%
GPA 3.0-3.49:	33%	**Live on campus:**	82%

Basis for selection. High school comprehensive record, test scores important. Applicants whose native language is not English need to provide evidence of English proficiency by results of TOEFL or results of ACT or SAT. Other approved English proficiency tests may be considered. Audition required for drama, music programs; portfolio recommended for art program; tryouts required for athletes. **Learning Disabled:** Appropriate documentation supporting request for accommodations must be provided to director of student disabilities.

High school preparation. 14 units recommended. Recommended units include English 4, mathematics 3, social studies 2, history 1, science 3 and foreign language 1.

2008-2009 Annual costs. Tuition/fees: $17,450. Room/board: $7,570. Books/supplies: $1,200. Personal expenses: $2,000.

2008-2009 Financial aid. Need-based: 204 full-time freshmen applied for aid; 166 were judged to have need; 164 of these received aid. Average need met was 77%. Average scholarship/grant was $13,752; average loan $3,909. 73% of total undergraduate aid awarded as scholarships/grants, 27% as loans/jobs. **Non-need-based:** Awarded to 299 full-time undergraduates, including 87 freshmen. Scholarships awarded for academics, alumni affiliation, art, athletics, job skills, leadership, music/drama, religious affiliation, state residency. **Additional information:** Part-time students eligible for federal and state aid, but not institutional aid.

Application procedures. Admission: No deadline. $25 fee, may be waived for applicants with need. Admission notification on a rolling basis beginning on or about 10/1. Must reply by May 1 or within 2 week(s) if notified thereafter. **Financial aid:** Priority date 2/15; no closing date. FAFSA required. Applicants notified on a rolling basis starting 3/1; must reply by 5/1 or within 2 week(s) of notification.

Academics. Math and science study halls are held three nights during the week and are led by professors and peer tutors. **Special study options:** Combined bachelor's/graduate degree, cross-registration, double major, ESL, honors, independent study, internships, liberal arts/career combination, student-designed major, study abroad, teacher certification program, Washington semester. Legislative internships at state and national level. **Credit/placement by examination:** AP, CLEP, IB, SAT, ACT. 32 credit hours maximum toward bachelor's degree. **Support services:** Learning center, reduced course load, remedial instruction, study skills assistance, tutoring.

Majors. Biology: General. **Business:** General, accounting, accounting/business management, business admin, fashion, international, management information systems, managerial economics, marketing. **Communications:** General. **Computer sciences:** General. **Conservation:** Environmental science. **Education:** General, art, biology, business, chemistry, Deaf/hearing impaired, developmentally delayed, elementary, English, health, history, mathematics, mentally handicapped, middle, multiple handicapped, music, physical, secondary, special, speech impaired. **Family/consumer sciences:** General, clothing/textiles, food/nutrition. **Foreign languages:** General, French, Germanic, Spanish. **Health:** Communication disorders. **History:** General. **Interdisciplinary:** Global studies. **Legal studies:** Prelaw. **Liberal arts:** Arts/sciences. **Math:** General. **Parks/recreation:** Facilities management, health/fitness, sports admin. **Philosophy/religion:** Philosophy, religion. **Physical sciences:** Chemistry. **Protective services:** Law enforcement admin. **Psychology:** General. **Public administration:** Social work. **Social sciences:** International relations, political science, sociology. **Theology:** Sacred music. **Visual/performing arts:** General, art, art history/conservation, design, dramatic, interior design, music performance, piano/organ, studio arts, voice/opera.

Most popular majors. Biology 7%, business/marketing 13%, communications/journalism 8%, education 6%, parks/recreation 16%, psychology 8%, social sciences 9%, visual/performing arts 7%.

Computing on campus. 100 workstations in dormitories, library, computer center, student center. Dormitories wired for high-speed internet access and linked to campus network. Commuter students can connect to campus network. Online library, helpline, repair service, wireless network available.

Student life. **Freshman orientation:** Mandatory, $55 fee. Preregistration for classes offered. Held each summer and one-session several days prior to the beginning of classes. **Policies:** No alcohol regardless of age, no drug paraphernalia, hazing, fireworks, or firearms. **Housing:** Guaranteed on-campus for freshmen. Coed dorms, single-sex dorms, special housing for disabled, apartments, fraternity/sorority housing, wellness housing available. $100 nonrefundable deposit, deadline 5/1. **Activities:** Bands, campus ministries, choral groups, dance, drama, international student organizations, literary magazine, music ensembles, Model UN, musical theater, student government, student newspaper, Black Student Union, Alpha Omega, Gamma Beta Phi, Fellowship of Christian Athletes, Best Buddies, Phi Sigma Eta, Religious Life Council, Companions in Christ, Discipleship/Accountability groups.

Athletics. NAIA. **Intercollegiate:** Baseball M, basketball, football (tackle) M, golf, soccer, softball W, tennis. **Intramural:** Basketball, football (non-tackle), softball, table tennis. **Team name:** Eagles.

Student services. Chaplain/spiritual director, career counseling, student employment services, financial aid counseling, health services, personal counseling, placement for graduates, veterans' counselor. **Physically disabled:** Services for visually, speech, hearing impaired.

Contact. E-mail: admit@lambuth.edu
Phone: (731) 425-3223 Toll-free number: (800) 526-2884
Fax: (731) 425-3496
James Bekkering, Vice President for Enrollment, Lambuth University, 705 Lambuth Boulevard, Jackson, TN 38301-5296

Lane College
Jackson, Tennessee
www.lanecollege.edu **CB code: 1395**

- Private 4-year liberal arts college affiliated with Christian Methodist Episcopal Church
- Residential campus in small city
- 1,982 degree-seeking undergraduates: 2% part-time, 52% women, 99% African American
- 35% of applicants admitted
- SAT or ACT (ACT writing optional) required
- 25% graduate within 6 years

General. Founded in 1882. Regionally accredited. **Degrees:** 175 bachelor's awarded. **Location:** 80 miles from Memphis, 126 miles from Nashville. **Calendar:** Semester, limited summer session. **Full-time faculty:** 82 total. **Part-time faculty:** 14 total. **Class size:** 30% < 20, 69% 20-39, less than 1% 40-49, less than 1% 50-99.

Freshman class profile. 4,350 applied, 1,507 admitted, 625 enrolled.

GPA 3.75 or higher:	1%	**Rank in top tenth:**	28%
GPA 3.50-3.74:	2%	**Return as sophomores:**	67%
GPA 3.0-3.49:	10%	**Out-of-state:**	43%
GPA 2.0-2.99:	62%	**Live on campus:**	97%
Rank in top quarter:	53%		

Basis for selection. School achievement record and recommendations most important. TOEFL required to establish language proficiency.

High school preparation. 16 units recommended. Recommended units include English 4, mathematics 2, social studies 2, science 2 and foreign language 2.

2008-2009 Annual costs. Tuition/fees: $7,770. Room/board: $5,250. Books/supplies: $1,000. Personal expenses: $675.

2007-2008 Financial aid. **Need-based:** 588 full-time freshmen applied for aid; 540 were judged to have need; 481 of these received aid. Average need met was 1%. Average scholarship/grant was $879. 50% of total undergraduate aid awarded as scholarships/grants, 50% as loans/jobs. **Non-need-based:** Awarded to 134 full-time undergraduates, including 96 freshmen. Scholarships awarded for academics, athletics, religious affiliation.

Application procedures. **Admission:** Priority date 7/1; deadline 8/1 (postmark date). No application fee. Admission notification on a rolling basis beginning on or about 2/1. Must reply by May 1 or within 2 week(s) if notified thereafter. **Financial aid:** Priority date 3/1; no closing date. FAFSA required. Applicants notified on a rolling basis starting 3/31; must reply within 2 week(s) of notification.

Academics. **Special study options:** Accelerated study, independent study, internships, study abroad, teacher certification program. **Credit/placement by examination:** AP, CLEP. **Support services:** Study skills assistance, tutoring, writing center.

Majors. **Biology:** General. **Business:** Business admin. **Communications:** General. **Computer sciences:** General. **Education:** Physical. **Foreign languages:** French. **History:** General. **Math:** General. **Philosophy/religion:** Religion. **Physical sciences:** Chemistry, physics. **Protective services:** Criminal justice. **Social sciences:** Sociology.

Most popular majors. Biology 13%, business/marketing 21%, communications/journalism 9%, education 7%, interdisciplinary studies 9%, security/protective services 15%, social sciences 14%.

Computing on campus. 470 workstations in library, computer center. Dormitories wired for high-speed internet access and linked to campus network. Online library, helpline, wireless network available.

Student life. **Freshman orientation:** Mandatory. Preregistration for classes offered. Held during weekend in July. **Policies:** Religious observance required. **Housing:** Guaranteed on-campus for all undergraduates. Single-sex dorms available. $50 nonrefundable deposit. **Activities:** Bands, campus ministries, choral groups, dance, drama, music ensembles, student government, student newspaper, Student Ministerial Alliance, Student Christian Association, Pre-Alumni Council.

Athletics. NCAA. **Intercollegiate:** Baseball M, basketball, cross-country, football (tackle) M, softball W, tennis, track and field, volleyball W. **Intramural:** Badminton, basketball, softball, swimming, table tennis, volleyball. **Team name:** Dragons.

Student services. Alcohol/substance abuse counseling, chaplain/spiritual director, career counseling, services for economically disadvantaged, student employment services, financial aid counseling, health services, personal counseling, placement for graduates, veterans' counselor.

Contact. E-mail: ebrown@lanecollege.edu
Phone: (731) 426-7533 Toll-free number: (800) 960-7533
Fax: (731) 426-7559
Evelyn Brown, Director of Admissions, Lane College, 545 Lane Avenue, Jackson, TN 38301-4598

Lee University
Cleveland, Tennessee
www.leeuniversity.edu **CB code: 1401**

- Private 4-year university and liberal arts college affiliated with Church of God
- Residential campus in large town
- 3,689 degree-seeking undergraduates: 9% part-time, 56% women, 4% African American, 1% Asian American, 3% Hispanic American, 6% international
- 238 degree-seeking graduate students
- 64% of applicants admitted
- SAT or ACT (ACT writing optional) required
- 52% graduate within 6 years

General. Founded in 1918. Regionally accredited. **Degrees:** 577 bachelor's awarded; master's offered. **Location:** 20 miles from Chattanooga, 75 miles from Knoxville. **Calendar:** Semester, limited summer session. **Full-time faculty:** 153 total; 78% have terminal degrees, 14% minority, 33% women. **Part-time faculty:** 174 total; 26% have terminal degrees, 12% minority, 42% women. **Class size:** 57% < 20, 32% 20-39, 6% 40-49, 5% 50-99, less than 1% >100.

Freshman class profile. 1,674 applied, 1,071 admitted, 860 enrolled.

Mid 50% test scores		**GPA 2.0-2.99:**	20%
SAT critical reading:	480-590	**Rank in top quarter:**	47%
SAT math:	460-580	**Rank in top tenth:**	25%
ACT composite:	20-27	**Return as sophomores:**	72%
GPA 3.75 or higher:	33%	**Out-of-state:**	64%
GPA 3.50-3.74:	19%	**Live on campus:**	96%
GPA 3.0-3.49:	27%	**International:**	4%

Basis for selection. School achievement record and test scores considered. Students with 16 college semester hours, 24 for TN residents, are not required to provide test scores. Audition required for music program. **Homeschooled:** Must have high school transcript with date of graduation and 17 on ACT or 860 on SAT (exclusive of Writing).

High school preparation. College-preparatory program recommended. 13 units required; 14 recommended. Required and recommended units include English 4, mathematics 3, social studies 2, history 1, science 2, foreign language 1 and computer science 1.

2009-2010 Annual costs. Tuition/fees: $11,660. Room/board: $5,650. Books/supplies: $900. Personal expenses: $1,610.

2008-2009 Financial aid. Need-based: 702 full-time freshmen applied for aid; 539 were judged to have need; 522 of these received aid. Average need met was 65%. Average scholarship/grant was $7,968; average loan $3,701. 48% of total undergraduate aid awarded as scholarships/grants, 52% as loans/jobs. **Non-need-based:** Awarded to 1,153 full-time undergraduates, including 385 freshmen. Scholarships awarded for academics, alumni affiliation, athletics, leadership, minority status, music/drama, religious affiliation, state residency.

Application procedures. Admission: Closing date 9/1 (receipt date). $25 fee. Admission notification on a rolling basis beginning on or about 9/1. **Financial aid:** Priority date 3/15; no closing date. FAFSA required. Applicants notified on a rolling basis starting 2/1; must reply within 3 week(s) of notification.

Academics. Special study options: Distance learning, double major, dual enrollment of high school students, ESL, exchange student, external degree, honors, independent study, internships, liberal arts/career combination, study abroad, teacher certification program, Washington semester. **Credit/placement by examination:** AP, CLEP, IB, SAT, ACT, institutional tests. 32 credit hours maximum toward bachelor's degree. **Support services:** Learning center, pre-admission summer program, reduced course load, remedial instruction, tutoring, writing center.

Majors. Biology: General, biochemistry, environmental. **Business:** Accounting, business admin. **Communications:** General, advertising, digital media, journalism, public relations. **Computer sciences:** General. **Education:** General, biology, business, early childhood, elementary, English, foreign languages, health, history, mathematics, music, physical, psychology, secondary, Spanish, special. **Family/consumer sciences:** Family studies. **Foreign languages:** French, Spanish. **Health:** Athletic training, health services. **History:** General. **Math:** General. **Parks/recreation:** Health/fitness. **Physical sciences:** Chemistry. **Psychology:** General. **Social sciences:** Anthropology, political science, sociology. **Theology:** Bible, missionary, pastoral counseling, preministerial, religious ed, sacred music, theology, youth ministry. **Visual/performing arts:** Dramatic, music management, music performance. **Other:** Missiology/Intercultural Studies.

Most popular majors. Business/marketing 13%, communications/journalism 15%, education 18%, psychology 12%, theological studies 15%.

Computing on campus. 470 workstations in dormitories, library, computer center, student center. Dormitories wired for high-speed internet access and linked to campus network. Online library, helpline, wireless network available.

Student life. Freshman orientation: Mandatory. Preregistration for classes offered. New student and parent orientation held weekend before classes begin. **Policies:** Religious observance required. **Housing:** Guaranteed on-campus for freshmen. Single-sex dorms, apartments, wellness housing available. $200 fully refundable deposit, deadline 9/1. University leases apartments and houses for students. **Activities:** Bands, campus ministries, choral groups, drama, international student organizations, literary magazine, music ensembles, Model UN, musical theater, opera, student government, student newspaper, symphony orchestra, Greek councils, student leadership council, Collegiate Sertoma, Married Students Fellowship, Pioneers for Christ, Fellowship of Christian Athletes, Missions Alive, Deaf Ministry Association.

Athletics. NAIA, NCCAA. **Intercollegiate:** Baseball M, basketball, cross-country, golf M, soccer, softball W, tennis, volleyball W. **Intramural:** Basketball, bowling, football (non-tackle) M, racquetball, soccer, softball, table tennis, tennis, volleyball. **Team name:** Flames.

Student services. Alcohol/substance abuse counseling, chaplain/spiritual director, career counseling, student employment services, financial aid counseling, health services, personal counseling, placement for graduates, veterans' counselor.

Contact. E-mail: admissions@leeuniversity.edu
Phone: (423) 614-8500 Toll-free number: (800) 533-9930
Fax: (423) 614-8533
Phil Cook, Assistant Vice President for Enrollment, Lee University, 1120 North Ocoee Street, Cleveland, TN 37320-3450

LeMoyne-Owen College

Memphis, Tennessee
www.loc.edu
CB member
CB code: 1403

- Private 4-year liberal arts college affiliated with United Church of Christ and Tennessee Baptist Convention
- Commuter campus in very large city
- 658 degree-seeking undergraduates
- 48% of applicants admitted
- SAT or ACT (ACT writing recommended) required

General. Founded in 1862. Regionally accredited. **Degrees:** 99 bachelor's awarded. **ROTC:** Army, Air Force. **Calendar:** Semester, extensive summer session. **Full-time faculty:** 53 total. **Part-time faculty:** 35 total. **Class size:** 82% < 20, 18% 20-39, less than 1% 40-49.

Freshman class profile. 446 applied, 214 admitted, 78 enrolled.

Mid 50% test scores		Out-of-state:	5%
ACT composite:	14-18	Live on campus:	10%

Basis for selection. High school transcript, test scores, letter of recommendation, and interview important. Special consideration given to children of alumni. Essay, interview recommended.

High school preparation. 15 units required. Required units include English 4, mathematics 3, history 2, science 3, foreign language 2 and academic electives 1.

2008-2009 Annual costs. Tuition/fees: $10,318. Room/board: $4,852. Books/supplies: $750. Personal expenses: $1,800.

2007-2008 Financial aid. Non-need-based: Scholarships awarded for academics, athletics, music/drama.

Application procedures. Admission: Closing date 4/15. $25 fee, may be waived for applicants with need. Admission notification on a rolling basis. Must reply by May 1 or within 2 week(s) if notified thereafter. **Financial aid:** Priority date 4/15; no closing date. FAFSA required. Applicants notified on a rolling basis starting 4/1.

Academics. Special study options: Accelerated study, cooperative education, cross-registration, distance learning, double major, dual enrollment of high school students, exchange student, honors, internships, liberal arts/career combination, student-designed major, study abroad, teacher certification program, weekend college. **Credit/placement by examination:** AP, CLEP, IB, ACT, institutional tests. 24 credit hours maximum toward bachelor's degree. **Support services:** Learning center, pre-admission summer program, reduced course load, remedial instruction, tutoring.

Majors. Biology: General. **Business:** Business admin. **Computer sciences:** Computer science, information technology. **Education:** Early childhood, English, mathematics, science, social studies, special. **History:** General. **Liberal arts:** Humanities. **Math:** General. **Physical sciences:** Chemistry. **Protective services:** Police science. **Public administration:** Social work. **Social sciences:** General, political science, sociology. **Visual/performing arts:** Art.

Most popular majors. Biology 8%, business/marketing 39%, education 19%, security/protective services 11%.

Computing on campus. 223 workstations in library, computer center. Helpline, repair service available.

Student life. Freshman orientation: Mandatory. Preregistration for classes offered. **Housing:** Single-sex dorms, wellness housing available. $100 deposit. **Activities:** Jazz band, choral groups, dance, drama, music ensembles, student government, student newspaper, NAACP, Social Work Club, Students for Free Enterprise, Pre-Alumni Council, National Student Business Organization.

Athletics. NCAA. **Intercollegiate:** Baseball M, basketball, cross-country, golf, soccer, softball W, tennis, volleyball W. **Intramural:** Basketball. **Team name:** Magicians.

Student services. Adult student services, career counseling, student employment services, health services, personal counseling, placement for graduates, veterans' counselor.

Contact. E-mail: admission@loc.edu
Phone: (901) 435-1500 Fax: (901) 435-1524
June Chinn-Jointer, Director of Admissions/Recruitment, LeMoyne-Owen College, 807 Walker Avenue, Memphis, TN 38126

Lincoln Memorial University

Harrogate, Tennessee
www.lmunet.edu
CB member
CB code: 1408

- Private 4-year university and liberal arts college
- Commuter campus in small town

- 1,336 degree-seeking undergraduates: 14% part-time, 70% women
- 1,936 degree-seeking graduate students

General. Founded in 1897. Regionally accredited. **Degrees:** 140 bachelor's, 163 associate awarded; master's, first professional offered. **Location:** 50 miles from Knoxville. **Calendar:** Semester, limited summer session. **Full-time faculty:** 119 total; 2% minority, 49% women. **Part-time faculty:** 96 total; 52% women. **Special facilities:** Abraham Lincoln Library and Museum, Cumberland Mountain Research Center.

Freshman class profile.

Mid 50% test scores			
SAT critical reading:	420-530	ACT composite:	18-23
SAT math:	430-570	Fraternities:	10%
		Sororities:	10%

Basis for selection. Academic record, ACT or SAT, recommendations, interviews for some programs. Specialized programs often have admission requirements in addition to those of the general university. In some programs, specialized admission tests also required. Interviews and essays help candidates seeking academic or talent related scholarships. **Homeschooled:** Must submit SAT or ACT scores.

High school preparation. 16 units required. Required units include English 4, mathematics 3, social studies 1, history 1, science 2, foreign language 2 and visual/performing arts 1.

2008-2009 Annual costs. Tuition/fees: $15,120. Room/board: $5,580.

Financial aid. Non-need-based: Scholarships awarded for academics, athletics, music/drama, state residency.

Application procedures. Admission: Priority date 3/1; no deadline. $25 fee, may be waived for applicants with need, free for online applicants. Admission notification on a rolling basis beginning on or about 9/1. **Financial aid:** Priority date 4/1; no closing date. FAFSA required. Applicants notified on a rolling basis starting 4/15; must reply within 3 week(s) of notification.

Academics. Special study options: Double major, ESL, independent study, internships, liberal arts/career combination, teacher certification program. **Credit/placement by examination:** AP, CLEP, IB, ACT, institutional tests. 16 credit hours maximum toward associate degree, 32 toward bachelor's. **Support services:** Learning center, reduced course load, remedial instruction, study skills assistance, tutoring.

Majors. Area/ethnic studies: American. **Biology:** General. **Business:** General, accounting, business admin, management science, managerial economics, office/clerical. **Communications:** General, broadcast journalism. **Computer sciences:** General. **Conservation:** General, fisheries, wildlife. **Education:** General, art, biology, business, chemistry, early childhood, elementary, English, health, history, mathematics, middle, physical, science, secondary, social science, social studies. **Health:** Athletic training, clinical lab science, clinical lab technology, nursing (RN), predental, premedicine, prepharmacy, preveterinary, veterinary technology/assistant. **History:** General. **Legal studies:** Prelaw. **Liberal arts:** Arts/sciences. **Math:** General. **Parks/recreation:** Health/fitness. **Physical sciences:** Chemistry. **Psychology:** General. **Public administration:** Social work. **Social sciences:** General. **Visual/performing arts:** General, art.

Computing on campus. 150 workstations in library, computer center. Dormitories wired for high-speed internet access and linked to campus network. Commuter students can connect to campus network. Online library available.

Student life. Freshman orientation: Mandatory. Preregistration for classes offered. 4 sessions over summer proceeding fall semester. **Housing:** Guaranteed on-campus for all undergraduates. Coed dorms, single-sex dorms, apartments available. $100 deposit, deadline 8/1. **Activities:** Choral groups, drama, literary magazine, radio station, student government, student newspaper, TV station, Baptist Student Union, Wesley Foundation.

Athletics. NCAA. **Intercollegiate:** Baseball M, basketball, cheerleading, cross-country, golf, soccer, softball W, tennis, volleyball W. **Intramural:** Basketball, soccer M, softball, table tennis, volleyball. **Team name:** Railsplitters.

Student services. Alcohol/substance abuse counseling, career counseling, financial aid counseling, on-campus daycare, personal counseling, placement for graduates, veterans' counselor.

Contact. E-mail: admissions@lmunet.edu
Phone: (423) 869-3611 ext. 6280 Toll-free
number: (800) 325-0900 ext. 6280 Fax: (423) 869-6250
Conrad Daniels, Dean of Admissions, Lincoln Memorial University, 6965 Cumberland Gap Parkway, Harrogate, TN 37752-1901

Lipscomb University
Nashville, Tennessee
www.lipscomb.edu **CB code: 1161**

- Private 4-year Bible and liberal arts college affiliated with Church of Christ
- Residential campus in very large city
- 2,384 degree-seeking undergraduates: 7% part-time, 57% women, 5% African American, 2% Asian American, 2% Hispanic American, 3% international
- 607 degree-seeking graduate students
- 75% of applicants admitted
- SAT or ACT (ACT writing recommended), interview required
- 63% graduate within 6 years

General. Founded in 1891. Regionally accredited. **Degrees:** 490 bachelor's awarded; master's, first professional offered. **ROTC:** Army, Air Force. **Location:** 4 miles from downtown. **Calendar:** Semester, extensive summer session. **Full-time faculty:** 117 total; 88% have terminal degrees, 2% minority, 29% women. **Part-time faculty:** 197 total; 43% have terminal degrees, 8% minority, 41% women. **Class size:** 54% < 20, 36% 20-39, 3% 40-49, 7% 50-99, less than 1% >100.

Freshman class profile. 2,028 applied, 1,513 admitted, 658 enrolled.

Mid 50% test scores			
SAT critical reading:	490-600	Rank in top quarter:	48%
SAT math:	490-610	Rank in top tenth:	24%
ACT composite:	21-26	End year in good standing:	85%
GPA 3.75 or higher:	34%	Return as sophomores:	77%
GPA 3.50-3.74:	15%	Out-of-state:	38%
GPA 3.0-3.49:	31%	Live on campus:	84%
GPA 2.0-2.99:	20%	International:	6%

Basis for selection. School achievement record, test scores, educational and personal references required. Strong moral character desired. Audition required for music; portfolio required for art; interview recommended for art, honors, music programs.

High school preparation. College-preparatory program recommended. 14 units required. Required units include English 4, mathematics 2, social studies 2, science 2, foreign language 2 and academic electives 2. Math units preferably Algebra I, II. Foreign language units in the same language. 2 academic electives should be selected from natural sciences, mathematics, foreign languages, or social sciences.

2008-2009 Annual costs. Tuition/fees: $18,580. Room/board: $7,400. Books/supplies: $1,000. Personal expenses: $1,250.

2008-2009 Financial aid. Need-based: 652 full-time freshmen applied for aid; 402 were judged to have need; 402 of these received aid. Average need met was 65%. Average scholarship/grant was $5,568; average loan $3,638. 60% of total undergraduate aid awarded as scholarships/grants, 40% as loans/jobs. **Non-need-based:** Awarded to 1,667 full-time undergraduates, including 686 freshmen. Scholarships awarded for academics, alumni affiliation, art, athletics, leadership, minority status, music/drama, religious affiliation, state residency.

Application procedures. Admission: Priority date 10/31; no deadline. $25 fee, may be waived for applicants with need. Admission notification on a rolling basis beginning on or about 8/15. **Financial aid:** Priority date 3/1; no closing date. FAFSA required. Applicants notified on a rolling basis starting 2/15.

Academics. Special study options: Combined bachelor's/graduate degree, cross-registration, distance learning, double major, dual enrollment of high school students, honors, independent study, internships, study abroad, teacher certification program, weekend college. **Credit/placement by examination:** AP, CLEP, IB, SAT, ACT, institutional tests. 30 credit hours maximum toward bachelor's degree. **Support services:** Learning center, pre-admission summer program, reduced course load, remedial instruction, study skills assistance, tutoring, writing center.

Majors. Area/ethnic studies: American. **Biology:** General, biochemistry. **Business:** Accounting, business admin, fashion, human resources, international, management information systems, managerial economics, marketing. **Communications:** Journalism, media studies, organizational, public relations. **Computer sciences:** Computer science, information technology. **Conservation:** Environmental science. **Education:** Art, biology, chemistry, drama/dance, elementary, English, ESL, French, German, history, mathematics, music, physical, physics, Spanish. **Engineering:** Computer, mechanical, mechanics, science. **Family/consumer sciences:** General, clothing/textiles, family systems, institutional food production. **Foreign languages:**

French, German, Spanish. **Health:** Athletic training, dietetics, nursing (RN), predental, premedicine, prenursing, prepharmacy, preveterinary. **History:** General. **Interdisciplinary:** Peace/conflict. **Legal studies:** General, prelaw. **Math:** General. **Parks/recreation:** Exercise sciences. **Philosophy/religion:** Philosophy. **Physical sciences:** Chemistry, physics. **Psychology:** General. **Public administration:** General, social work. **Social sciences:** Political science, urban studies. **Theology:** Bible, missionary, youth ministry. **Visual/performing arts:** Commercial/advertising art, dramatic, music performance, music theory/composition, piano/organ, studio arts, voice/opera. **Other:** Pre-engineering.

Most popular majors. Business/marketing 28%, education 10%, health sciences 9%, psychology 8%, theological studies 7%.

Computing on campus. 203 workstations in dormitories, library, computer center, student center. Dormitories wired for high-speed internet access and linked to campus network. Commuter students can connect to campus network. Online course registration, helpline, repair service, wireless network available.

Student life. Freshman orientation: Mandatory, $110 fee. Preregistration for classes offered. **Policies:** Daily chapel service and Bible studies required. Out-of-town undergraduates required to live on campus, except for seniors, students over age of 21, married students. Religious observance required. **Housing:** Single-sex dorms, apartments available. $125 fully refundable deposit. **Activities:** Bands, campus ministries, choral groups, drama, international student organizations, literary magazine, music ensembles, musical theater, radio station, student government, student newspaper, College Republicans, Young Democrats, honorary societies, multicultural association, Circle K, Fellowship of Christian Athletes, Youth Encouragement Services, men and women's service clubs, homeless ministry, DAC (ministry to the hearing impaired).

Athletics. NCAA. **Intercollegiate:** Baseball M, basketball, cross-country, golf, soccer, softball W, tennis, track and field, volleyball W. **Intramural:** Badminton, basketball, football (non-tackle), racquetball, soccer, softball, tennis, volleyball. **Team name:** Bisons.

Student services. Adult student services, chaplain/spiritual director, career counseling, student employment services, financial aid counseling, health services, minority student services, personal counseling, placement for graduates. **Physically disabled:** Services for visually, speech, hearing impaired.

Contact. E-mail: admissions@lipscomb.edu
Phone: (615) 966-1776 Toll-free number: (877) 582-4766
Fax: (615) 966-1804
Ricky Holaway, Director of Admissions, Lipscomb University, One University Park Drive, Nashville, TN 37204-3951

Martin Methodist College
Pulaski, Tennessee
www.martinmethodist.edu **CB code: 1449**

- Private 4-year liberal arts college affiliated with United Methodist Church
- Residential campus in small town
- 892 degree-seeking undergraduates: 18% part-time, 62% women
- 55% graduate within 6 years; 10% enter graduate study

General. Founded in 1870. Regionally accredited. **Degrees:** 104 bachelor's, 15 associate awarded. **Location:** 70 miles from Nashville, 40 miles from Huntsville, Alabama. **Calendar:** Semester, limited summer session. **Full-time faculty:** 40 total; 58% have terminal degrees, 40% women. **Part-time faculty:** 33 total; 24% have terminal degrees, 39% women. **Class size:** 78% < 20, 21% 20-39, less than 1% 40-49.

Freshman class profile. 554 applied, 233 admitted, 229 enrolled.

Mid 50% test scores		**GPA 3.0-3.49:**	34%
SAT critical reading:	430-520	**GPA 2.0-2.99:**	28%
SAT math:	410-460	**End year in good standing:**	89%
ACT composite:	17-23	**Return as sophomores:**	90%
GPA 3.75 or higher:	15%	**Out-of-state:**	13%
GPA 3.50-3.74:	19%	**Live on campus:**	46%

Basis for selection. Open admission, but selective for some programs. High school record, interview, test scores important. Minimum 2.0 GPA, 18 ACT, or rank in upper 50% of class. Must meet 2 of these 3 criteria for admission or apply for "special circumstances" admission status. Students whose academic record or test scores do not qualify them for admission can be conditionally admitted and offered full enrollment if they complete a semester with a 2.0 GPA. Audition recommended for music; portfolio recommended for art.

High school preparation. 13 units required. Required and recommended units include English 4, mathematics 2-3, social studies 2, history 1, science 2 (laboratory 2), foreign language 2, computer science 1 and academic electives 4.

2008-2009 Annual costs. Tuition/fees: $17,626. Room/board: $6,800. Books/supplies: $750. Personal expenses: $1,200.

2007-2008 Financial aid. Non-need-based: Scholarships awarded for academics, art, athletics, leadership, music/drama, religious affiliation, state residency.

Application procedures. Admission: Priority date 5/1; deadline 8/1 (postmark date). $30 fee. Admission notification on a rolling basis. **Financial aid:** No deadline. FAFSA, institutional form required. Applicants notified on a rolling basis starting 3/1; must reply within 2 week(s) of notification.

Academics. Special study options: Dual enrollment of high school students, ESL, honors, independent study, study abroad. **Credit/placement by examination:** AP, CLEP. 30 credit hours maximum toward associate degree. **Support services:** Learning center, pre-admission summer program, reduced course load, remedial instruction, study skills assistance, tutoring, writing center.

Majors. Biology: General. **Business:** General, accounting, business admin. **Education:** Elementary, middle, secondary. **Health:** Nursing (RN). **History:** General. **Parks/recreation:** Sports admin. **Philosophy/religion:** Religion. **Psychology:** General. **Public administration:** Human services. **Other:** Criminal justice, History and political science, Sport management.

Most popular majors. Biology 10%, business/marketing 15%, education 13%, liberal arts 13%, social sciences 22%.

Computing on campus. 150 workstations in library, computer center. Dormitories wired for high-speed internet access and linked to campus network. Commuter students can connect to campus network. Online course registration, online library, helpline, wireless network available.

Student life. Freshman orientation: Mandatory. Preregistration for classes offered. 3 days prior to other students coming on campus. **Housing:** Guaranteed on-campus for all undergraduates. Single-sex dorms, apartments available. $125 fully refundable deposit, deadline 6/1. **Activities:** Campus ministries, choral groups, drama, international student organizations, music ensembles, student government, student newspaper, student Christian association, black student union, Fellowship of Christian Athletes.

Athletics. NAIA, NJCAA. **Intercollegiate:** Baseball M, basketball, bowling, cheerleading M, golf, soccer, softball W, tennis, volleyball W. **Intramural:** Basketball, football (non-tackle), racquetball, softball, swimming, table tennis, volleyball. **Team name:** RedHawks.

Student services. Adult student services, chaplain/spiritual director, career counseling, student employment services, financial aid counseling, personal counseling, placement for graduates, veterans' counselor.

Contact. E-mail: lsmith2@martinmethodist.edu
Phone: (931) 363-9868 Toll-free number: (800) 467-1273
Fax: (931) 363-9803
Lisa Smith, Director of Admissions, Martin Methodist College, 433 West Madison, Pulaski, TN 38478-2799

Maryville College
Maryville, Tennessee **CB member**
www.maryvillecollege.edu **CB code: 1454**

- Private 4-year liberal arts college affiliated with Presbyterian Church (USA)
- Residential campus in small city
- 1,114 degree-seeking undergraduates: 2% part-time, 55% women, 5% African American, 1% Asian American, 2% Hispanic American, 4% international
- 75% of applicants admitted
- SAT or ACT (ACT writing optional) required
- 51% graduate within 6 years; 16% enter graduate study

General. Founded in 1819. Regionally accredited. **Degrees:** 222 bachelor's awarded. **Location:** 15 miles from Knoxville. **Calendar:** 4-1-4, limited summer session. **Full-time faculty:** 79 total; 85% have terminal degrees, 6% minority, 54% women. **Part-time faculty:** 42 total; 26% have terminal degrees, 10% minority, 45% women. **Class size:** 73% < 20, 27% 20-39, less than 1% 40-49. **Special facilities:** Science center, fine arts center, Mountain Challenge outdoor program, college woods with ropes courses, equestrian center.

Freshman class profile. 1,621 applied, 1,217 admitted, 297 enrolled.

Mid 50% test scores		GPA 2.0-2.99:	9%
SAT critical reading:	470-630	Rank in top quarter:	65%
SAT math:	480-610	Rank in top tenth:	34%
SAT writing:	450-610	End year in good standing:	85%
ACT composite:	21-28	Return as sophomores:	67%
GPA 3.75 or higher:	39%	Out-of-state:	23%
GPA 3.50-3.74:	21%	Live on campus:	87%
GPA 3.0-3.49:	31%		

Basis for selection. Students are admitted based on academic criteria, extracurricular involvement, and personal achievement, without regard to financial need. Successful students typically follow strong college preparatory curriculums in high school and rank in the top 25% of their classes. International students who score at least 525 on TOEFL or 80 on Michigan Test eligible to enroll full time. Others may enroll in limited number of college level courses until they complete international students' orientation. Writing samples are encouraged for assistance in admissions decisions. Essay, interview recommended for all; audition required for music; portfolio recommended for art. **Homeschooled:** Pursue rigorous curriculum that includes strong emphasis on writing and reasoning.

High school preparation. 15 units required. Required and recommended units include English 4, mathematics 3, social studies 2, history 1, science 2 (laboratory 1), foreign language 2 and academic electives 1.

2008-2009 Annual costs. Tuition/fees: $26,947. Room/board: $8,240. Books/supplies: $880. Personal expenses: $930.

2008-2009 Financial aid. Need-based: 259 full-time freshmen applied for aid; 259 were judged to have need; 259 of these received aid. Average need met was 91%. Average scholarship/grant was $20,692; average loan $3,158. 75% of total undergraduate aid awarded as scholarships/grants, 25% as loans/jobs. **Non-need-based:** Awarded to 428 full-time undergraduates, including 119 freshmen. Scholarships awarded for academics, art, leadership, minority status, music/drama, religious affiliation, state residency.

Application procedures. Admission: Priority date 1/15; no deadline. No application fee. Admission notification on a rolling basis beginning on or about 10/1. Must reply by May 1 or within 2 week(s) if notified thereafter. Required enrollment deposit of $200 includes housing deposit, refundable before May 1. **Financial aid:** Priority date 3/1; no closing date. FAFSA required. Applicants notified on a rolling basis starting 3/15; must reply within 4 week(s) of notification.

Academics. All students complete 6 credit-hour research project and comprehensive examination in their major area of study. **Special study options:** Combined bachelor's/graduate degree, double major, ESL, honors, independent study, internships, liberal arts/career combination, student-designed major, study abroad, teacher certification program, Washington semester. **Credit/placement by examination:** AP, CLEP, IB, institutional tests. 32 credit hours maximum toward bachelor's degree. Students may petition individual departments for credit by examination. **Support services:** Learning center, reduced course load, remedial instruction, study skills assistance, tutoring, writing center.

Majors. Biology: General, biochemistry. **Business:** Business admin, international. **Computer sciences:** General. **Conservation:** Environmental studies. **Education:** General, biology, chemistry, English, ESL, health, history, mathematics, music, physical, social science, social studies, Spanish. **Engineering:** General. **Foreign languages:** American Sign Language, sign language interpretation, Spanish. **Health:** Nursing (RN), predental, premedicine, prenursing, prepharmacy, preveterinary. **History:** General. **Interdisciplinary:** Math/computer science. **Math:** General. **Parks/recreation:** General, health/fitness. **Philosophy/religion:** Philosophy, religion. **Physical sciences:** Chemical physics, chemistry. **Psychology:** General. **Social sciences:** Economics, international relations, political science, sociology. **Visual/performing arts:** Art, dramatic, music performance, studio arts.

Most popular majors. Biology 8%, business/marketing 24%, education 20%, English 6%, psychology 8%, social sciences 10%, visual/performing arts 6%.

Computing on campus. 265 workstations in library, computer center. Dormitories wired for high-speed internet access and linked to campus network. Commuter students can connect to campus network. Online course registration, online library, helpline, repair service, wireless network available.

Student life. Freshman orientation: Mandatory, $25 fee. Preregistration for classes offered. Includes Mountain Challenge component. Begins several days before registration. Optional 3-day wilderness experience. **Housing:** Guaranteed on-campus for all undergraduates. Coed dorms, single-sex dorms, special housing for disabled, apartments, wellness housing available. $200 fully refundable deposit, deadline 5/1. **Activities:** Bands, campus ministries, choral groups, dance, drama, film society, international student organizations, literary magazine, music ensembles, Model UN, student government, student newspaper, symphony orchestra, Habitat for Humanity, Literary Corps, Fellowship of Christian Athletes, MC Wellness Council, Student Programming Board, Black student association.

Athletics. NCAA. **Intercollegiate:** Baseball M, basketball, cross-country, equestrian, football (tackle) M, soccer, softball W, tennis, volleyball W. **Intramural:** Archery, badminton, baseball M, basketball, bowling, football (non-tackle), golf, racquetball, rugby, skiing, soccer, softball, swimming, table tennis, tennis, track and field, volleyball, water polo. **Team name:** Scots.

Student services. Adult student services, alcohol/substance abuse counseling, chaplain/spiritual director, career counseling, student employment services, financial aid counseling, health services, minority student services, personal counseling, placement for graduates. **Physically disabled:** Services for visually, speech, hearing impaired.

Contact. E-mail: admissions@maryvillecollege.edu
Phone: (865) 981-8092 Toll-free number: (800) 597-2687
Fax: (865) 981-8005
Bill Sliwa, Vice President for Enrollment Management, Maryville College, 502 East Lamar Alexander Parkway, Maryville, TN 37804-5907

Memphis College of Art
Memphis, Tennessee
www.mca.edu **CB code: 1511**

- Private 4-year visual arts college
- Residential campus in very large city
- 320 degree-seeking undergraduates: 6% part-time, 57% women, 19% African American, 2% Asian American, 3% Hispanic American, 2% international
- 81 degree-seeking graduate students
- 52% of applicants admitted
- SAT or ACT (ACT writing optional) required
- 40% graduate within 6 years; 10% enter graduate study

General. Founded in 1936. Regionally accredited. Situated in 324-acre city park with bicycle trails and golf course. Students have access to Memphis Brooks Museum of Art and Overton Park Zoo. Consortium with four other colleges provides greater selection of liberal studies classes. Mobility program with 30+ other independent colleges of art around the country and in Canada available. **Degrees:** 46 bachelor's awarded; master's offered. **Location:** 500 miles from New Orleans, 700 miles from Dallas. **Calendar:** Semester, limited summer session. **Full-time faculty:** 21 total; 81% have terminal degrees, 10% minority, 48% women. **Part-time faculty:** 24 total; 54% have terminal degrees, 58% women. **Class size:** 87% < 20, 13% 20-39. **Special facilities:** 5 campus galleries for faculty, student and visiting artist exhibitions.

Freshman class profile. 664 applied, 342 admitted, 101 enrolled.

Mid 50% test scores		GPA 2.0-2.99:	36%
ACT composite:	19-25	Return as sophomores:	66%
GPA 3.75 or higher:	18%	Out-of-state:	68%
GPA 3.50-3.74:	19%	Live on campus:	75%
GPA 3.0-3.49:	27%	International:	1%

Basis for selection. Art portfolio, high school transcript, test scores required; letter of recommendation from art teacher and essay considered, but not required. Portfolio required; essay, interview recommended for all.

High school preparation. College-preparatory program recommended. Portfolio should include 10 to 20 pieces of work, originals or slides, with focus on direct observational drawing.

2008-2009 Annual costs. Tuition/fees: $21,560. Room/board: $7,600. Books/supplies: $1,600. Personal expenses: $1,490.

2008-2009 Financial aid. Non-need-based: Scholarships awarded for academics, art. **Additional information:** Students considered for institutional resources through admissions application process.

Application procedures. Admission: Priority date 3/31; no deadline. $25 fee, may be waived for applicants with need. Admission notification on a rolling basis beginning on or about 11/15. Must reply by May 1 or within 3 week(s) if notified thereafter. **Financial aid:** Priority date 3/1; no closing date. FAFSA required. Applicants notified on a rolling basis starting 3/15; must reply within 3 week(s) of notification.

Academics. Special study options: Combined bachelor's/graduate degree, cross-registration, double major, exchange student, independent study, internships, New York semester, study abroad. New York Studio Exchange Program. Mobility semester exchange at 30+ independent art colleges across the country (AICAD consortium). **Credit/placement by examination:** AP, CLEP, IB, SAT, ACT, institutional tests. 15 credit hours maximum toward bachelor's degree. **Support services:** Reduced course load, remedial instruction, study skills assistance, tutoring, writing center.

Majors. Computer sciences: Computer graphics. **Visual/performing arts:** Art, commercial/advertising art, design, drawing, graphic design, illustration, metal/jewelry, multimedia, painting, photography, printmaking, sculpture, studio arts.

Computing on campus. 200 workstations in dormitories, library, computer center. Dormitories wired for high-speed internet access. Wireless network available.

Student life. Freshman orientation: Mandatory. Preregistration for classes offered. 4-day session and parent sessions. **Policies:** Considerable assistance available in matching roommates and helping students find affordable housing within walking distance. **Housing:** Coed dorms, apartments, wellness housing available. $300 deposit. . **Activities:** International student organizations, student government, student newspaper, photography club, student alliance, multicultural student association.

Student services. Adult student services, career counseling, student employment services, financial aid counseling, personal counseling, placement for graduates, veterans' counselor.

Contact. E-mail: info@mca.edu
Phone: (901) 272-5151 Toll-free number: (800) 727-1088
Fax: (901) 272-5158
Annette Moore, Director of Admissions, Memphis College of Art, 1930 Poplar Avenue, Memphis, TN 38104-2764

Middle Tennessee State University

Murfreesboro, Tennessee — **CB member**
www.mtsu.edu — **CB code: 1466**

- Public 4-year university
- Commuter campus in small city
- 21,252 degree-seeking undergraduates: 15% part-time, 52% women, 15% African American, 3% Asian American, 2% Hispanic American
- 2,620 degree-seeking graduate students
- 65% of applicants admitted
- SAT or ACT (ACT writing optional) required

General. Founded in 1911. Regionally accredited. **Degrees:** 3,547 bachelor's awarded; master's, doctoral offered. **ROTC:** Army. **Location:** 32 miles from Nashville. **Calendar:** Semester, extensive summer session. **Full-time faculty:** 931 total; 4% have terminal degrees, 16% minority, 44% women. **Part-time faculty:** 336 total; less than 1% have terminal degrees, 10% minority, 53% women. **Special facilities:** 3 recording studios, observatory, flight simulators, weather center, electronic music laboratory, digital audio edit laboratory, satellite mapping equipment, seismograph, 3 television studios, electronic newsroom, Centers for Historic Preservation and Popular Music.

Freshman class profile. 9,583 applied, 6,202 admitted, 3,456 enrolled.

Mid 50% test scores			
SAT critical reading:	450-580	Rank in top tenth:	12%
SAT math:	450-580	Out-of-state:	1%
ACT composite:	19-24	Live on campus:	60%
Rank in top quarter:	29%	Fraternities:	7%
		Sororities:	7%

Basis for selection. Must meet high school curriculum requirements and have 3.0 high school GPA or ACT composite score of 22 or a combination of a 19 ACT and a 2.7 GPA. Personal statement required of students who do not meet standard requirements.

High school preparation. College-preparatory program recommended. 14 units required. Required units include English 4, mathematics 3, social studies 1, history 1, science 2 (laboratory 1), foreign language 2 and visual/performing arts 1. Foreign language units must be in single language. Mathematics units must include algebra I and II, geometry or other advanced mathematics. 1 US history, 1 global studies also required.

2008-2009 Annual costs. Tuition/fees: $5,700; $16,592 out-of-state. Room/board: $6,453. Books/supplies: $1,000. Personal expenses: $1,400.

2008-2009 Financial aid. Non-need-based: Scholarships awarded for academics, alumni affiliation, art, athletics, job skills, leadership, minority status, music/drama, religious affiliation, ROTC, state residency. **Additional information:** Application filing deadline for scholarships February 15.

Application procedures. Admission: Closing date 7/1 (postmark date). $25 fee. Admission notification on a rolling basis. **Financial aid:** Priority date 5/1; no closing date. FAFSA required. Applicants notified on a rolling basis starting 4/15; must reply within 2 week(s) of notification.

Academics. Special study options: Cooperative education, distance learning, double major, dual enrollment of high school students, honors, independent study, internships, study abroad, teacher certification program. Academic basic skills. **Credit/placement by examination:** AP, CLEP, IB, SAT, ACT, institutional tests. 66 credit hours maximum toward bachelor's degree. Up to 66 semester hours from correspondence study, credit-by-examination, credit for service-related experience, and flight training may be counted toward degree. **Support services:** Learning center, preadmission summer program, reduced course load, remedial instruction, study skills assistance, tutoring, writing center.

Honors college/program. Must have minimum ACT composite score of 26 (1170 SAT, exclusive of Writing) and 3.0 GPA or 3.5 GPA and ACT of 22 (950 SAT); returning or transfer students must have overall college GPA of 3.0 or higher.

Majors. Agriculture: Agribusiness operations, animal sciences, plant sciences, soil science. **Biology:** General. **Business:** Accounting, business admin, finance, management information systems, managerial economics, marketing, office management, purchasing, sales/distribution. **Communications:** Media studies. **Computer sciences:** General, computer science. **Education:** Art, business, early childhood, health, kindergarten/preschool, sales/marketing, special, technology/industrial arts. **Engineering technology:** General, architectural, environmental, industrial, industrial management. **Family/consumer sciences:** Clothing/textiles, family resources, food/nutrition. **Foreign languages:** General. **Health:** Athletic training, nursing (RN). **History:** General. **Interdisciplinary:** Biological/physical sciences. **Liberal arts:** Arts/sciences. **Math:** General. **Parks/recreation:** Facilities management, health/fitness. **Philosophy/religion:** Philosophy. **Physical sciences:** Chemistry, geology, physics. **Protective services:** Law enforcement admin. **Psychology:** General. **Public administration:** Social work. **Social sciences:** Anthropology, economics, international relations, political science, sociology. **Transportation:** Aviation. **Visual/performing arts:** Art, art history/conservation, dramatic, interior design, music management.

Most popular majors. Business/marketing 19%, communications/journalism 8%, interdisciplinary studies 8%, liberal arts 6%, visual/performing arts 12%.

Computing on campus. 2,300 workstations in dormitories, library, computer center, student center. Dormitories wired for high-speed internet access and linked to campus network. Commuter students can connect to campus network. Online course registration, online library, helpline, wireless network available.

Student life. Freshman orientation: Mandatory, $45 fee. Preregistration for classes offered. Held from mid-June to mid-July. **Policies:** Parents notified when student under age of 21 found responsible for use and/or possession of drugs or alcohol. **Housing:** Coed dorms, single-sex dorms, special housing for disabled, apartments, cooperative housing, fraternity/sorority housing available. $200 partly refundable deposit. **Activities:** Bands, campus ministries, choral groups, dance, drama, international student organizations, literary magazine, music ensembles, Model UN, musical theater, opera, radio station, student government, student newspaper, symphony orchestra, TV station, Golden Key National Honor Society, African American student association, Fellowship of Christian Athletes, Collegiate Women International, Citizens for Action, Baptist Student Union, Aerospace Maintenance Club, agricultural council, Student Tennessee Education Association.

Athletics. NCAA. **Intercollegiate:** Baseball M, basketball, cross-country, football (tackle) M, golf, soccer W, softball W, tennis, track and field, volleyball W. **Intramural:** Basketball M, boxing M, equestrian, football (tackle) M, racquetball, rugby M, soccer, softball, swimming, tennis, volleyball. **Team name:** Blue Raiders.

Student services. Adult student services, chaplain/spiritual director, career counseling, student employment services, financial aid counseling, health services, minority student services, on-campus daycare, personal counseling, placement for graduates, veterans' counselor, women's services. **Physically disabled:** Services for visually, speech, hearing impaired.

Contact. E-mail: admissions@mtsu.edu
Phone: (615) 898-2111 Fax: (615) 898-5478
Lynn Palmer, Director of Admissions, Middle Tennessee State University, 1301 East Main Street, Murfreesboro, TN 37132

Milligan College
Milligan College, Utah
www.milligan.edu **CB code: 1469**

- Private 4-year liberal arts college affiliated with Christian Churches/Churches of Christ
- Residential campus in small city
- 837 degree-seeking undergraduates: 3% part-time, 62% women
- 219 degree-seeking graduate students
- 74% of applicants admitted
- SAT or ACT (ACT writing optional), application essay required
- 69% graduate within 6 years

General. Founded in 1866. Regionally accredited. Weekly chapels, convocation programs, vespers. **Degrees:** 204 bachelor's awarded; master's offered. **ROTC:** Army. **Location:** 3 miles from Johnson City. **Calendar:** Semester, limited summer session. **Full-time faculty:** 66 total; 80% have terminal degrees, 3% minority, 50% women. **Part-time faculty:** 46 total; 28% have terminal degrees, 48% women. **Class size:** 68% < 20, 30% 20-39, less than 1% 40-49, less than 1% 50-99, less than 1% >100.

Freshman class profile. 580 applied, 431 admitted, 176 enrolled.

Mid 50% test scores		**GPA 2.0-2.99:**	14%
SAT critical reading:	500-600	**Rank in top quarter:**	63%
SAT math:	460-600	**Rank in top tenth:**	25%
SAT writing:	460-580	**Return as sophomores:**	71%
ACT composite:	20-25	**Out-of-state:**	37%
GPA 3.75 or higher:	40%	**Live on campus:**	85%
GPA 3.50-3.74:	17%	**International:**	1%
GPA 3.0-3.49:	29%		

Basis for selection. Academic work, test scores, and references from minister or church leader and high school principal or counselor required for admission. Audition required for music; interview recommended in some instances.

High school preparation. 17 units recommended. Recommended units include English 4, mathematics 3, social studies 2, history 3, science 3 and foreign language 2.

2008-2009 Annual costs. Tuition/fees: $20,560. Room/board: $5,850. Books/supplies: $750. Personal expenses: $1,132.

2008-2009 Financial aid. Need-based: Average need met was 85%. Average scholarship/grant was $13,884; average loan $3,348. 65% of total undergraduate aid awarded as scholarships/grants, 35% as loans/jobs. **Non-need-based:** Scholarships awarded for academics, alumni affiliation, art, athletics, job skills, minority status, music/drama, religious affiliation, state residency.

Application procedures. Admission: Priority date 4/1; deadline 8/1 (postmark date). $30 fee, may be waived for applicants with need. Admission notification on a rolling basis beginning on or about 10/1. Must reply by May 1 or within 2 week(s) if notified thereafter. Housing deposit is refundable until May 1. **Financial aid:** Priority date 3/1; no closing date. FAFSA required. Applicants notified on a rolling basis starting 3/15; must reply within 2 week(s) of notification.

Academics. Special study options: Cross-registration, double major, independent study, internships, study abroad, teacher certification program, Washington semester. American Studies Program in Washington, DC; Australia Studies Center; China Studies Program; Contemporary Music Center in Martha's Vineyard; Latin American Studies Program in Costa Rica; Los Angeles Film Studies Center; Middle East Studies Program in Egypt; Russian Studies Program; Scholars' Semester in Oxford; Uganda Studies Program; Summer Institute of Journalism in Washington, DC; Oxford Summer Programme. **Credit/placement by examination:** AP, CLEP, IB, SAT, ACT, institutional tests. 32 credit hours maximum toward bachelor's degree. Students may not receive credit by examination upon achieving a total of 64 credit hours. **Support services:** Reduced course load, remedial instruction, study skills assistance, tutoring, writing center.

Majors. Biology: General. **Business:** Accounting, business admin. **Communications:** General. **Computer sciences:** General. **Education:** General, early childhood, music. **Health:** Nursing (RN). **History:** General. **Liberal arts:** Humanities. **Math:** General. **Parks/recreation:** Health/fitness. **Physical sciences:** Chemistry. **Psychology:** General. **Public administration:** Human services. **Social sciences:** Sociology. **Theology:** Bible. **Visual/performing arts:** General.

Most popular majors. Business/marketing 17%, education 24%, health sciences 14%, visual/performing arts 7%.

Computing on campus. 102 workstations in library, computer center. Dormitories wired for high-speed internet access and linked to campus network. Commuter students can connect to campus network. Online library, helpline, repair service, student web hosting, wireless network available.

Student life. Freshman orientation: Available, $10 fee. Preregistration for classes offered. Weekend sessions available in April or June for students and parents. Abbreviated version offered weekend prior to first day of fall classes. **Policies:** Smoking and alcoholic beverages are not permitted on campus. Students must live in college housing unless married or living with members of immediate family. Religious observance required. **Housing:** Guaranteed on-campus for all undergraduates. Single-sex dorms, apartments, wellness housing available. $200 nonrefundable deposit, deadline 8/15. **Activities:** Bands, choral groups, drama, literary magazine, music ensembles, musical theater, radio station, student government, student newspaper, symphony orchestra, Fellowship of Christian Athletes, missions club, service seekers, student government association, College Republicans, Habitat for Humanity, political awareness group, Roteract.

Athletics. NAIA. **Intercollegiate:** Baseball M, basketball, cross-country, golf M, soccer, softball W, swimming, tennis, track and field, volleyball W. **Intramural:** Basketball, football (non-tackle), softball, table tennis, tennis, volleyball. **Team name:** Buffaloes.

Student services. Adult student services, chaplain/spiritual director, career counseling, financial aid counseling, health services, minority student services, personal counseling, placement for graduates.

Contact. E-mail: admissions@milligan.edu
Phone: (423) 461-8730 Toll-free number: (800) 262-8337
Fax: (423) 461-8982
Tracy Brinn, Director of Enrollment Management, Milligan College, Box 210, Milligan College, TN 37682

O'More College of Design
Franklin, Tennessee
www.omorecollege.edu **CB code: 1545**

- Private 4-year visual arts college
- Commuter campus in large town
- 200 degree-seeking undergraduates
- 43% of applicants admitted
- SAT or ACT (ACT writing optional) required

General. Founded in 1970. Accredited by ACCSCT. Interior design program accredited by Council for Interior Design Accreditation. **Degrees:** 48 bachelor's awarded. **Location:** 15 miles from Nashville. **Calendar:** Semester, limited summer session. **Full-time faculty:** 14 total. **Part-time faculty:** 33 total.

Freshman class profile. 122 applied, 52 admitted, 35 enrolled.

Mid 50% test scores		**GPA 3.50-3.74:**	8%
SAT critical reading:	560-680	**GPA 3.0-3.49:**	48%
SAT math:	450-620	**GPA 2.0-2.99:**	16%
ACT composite:	20-25	**Out-of-state:**	8%
GPA 3.75 or higher:	24%		

Basis for selection. High school record most important. Test scores, grades given equal weight. Portfolio or departmental home exam may be required. Portfolio of artwork is recommended for students not admitted automatically on the basis of his or her grades or test scores. If student does not have portfolio and does not meet admittance criteria on basis of academic record alone, the student will need to contact chair of department to which he or she seeks admittance for instructions on completing department's home exam.

High school preparation. 18 units recommended. Recommended units include English 4, mathematics 3, social studies 1, history 2, science 3, foreign language 2 and academic electives 3. Art, mechanical drawing, and design courses are recommended.

2008-2009 Annual costs. Tuition/fees: $17,280. Books/supplies: $750.

2008-2009 Financial aid. All financial aid based on need. 52% of total undergraduate aid awarded as scholarships/grants, 48% as loans/jobs.

Application procedures. Admission: Closing date 8/1 (postmark date). $50 fee, may be waived for applicants with need. Admission notification on a rolling basis. **Financial aid:** Priority date 4/1; no closing date. FAFSA required. Applicants notified on a rolling basis starting 8/1.

Academics. Special study options: Dual enrollment of high school students, internships, liberal arts/career combination, study abroad. Students may pick a minor at Belmont University. Annual study-abroad program in Ireland, and one every third year in Italy. **Credit/placement by examination:** AP, CLEP, institutional tests. 9 credit hours maximum toward bachelor's degree.

Majors. Business: Fashion. **Visual/performing arts:** Commercial/advertising art, interior design.

Computing on campus. PC or laptop required. 25 workstations in library, computer center, student center. Student web hosting, wireless network available.

Student life. Freshman orientation: Mandatory. Preregistration for classes offered. **Activities:** Student government, student chapter of American Society of Interior Designers, O'More Fashion Merchandisers Association, Student Government Association, American Institute of Graphic Arts, International Interior Design Association.

Student services. Career counseling.

Contact. E-mail: admissions@omorecollege.edu
Phone: (615) 794-4254 Fax: (615) 790-1662
Christopher Lee, Dean of Enrollment, O'More College of Design, 423 South Margin Street, Franklin, TN 37064-0908

Rhodes College
Memphis, Tennessee
www.rhodes.edu
CB member
CB code: 1730

- Private 4-year liberal arts college affiliated with Presbyterian Church (USA)
- Residential campus in very large city
- 1,649 degree-seeking undergraduates: 58% women, 7% African American, 5% Asian American, 2% Hispanic American, 2% international
- 9 degree-seeking graduate students
- 50% of applicants admitted
- SAT or ACT (ACT writing optional), application essay required
- 73% graduate within 6 years; 39% enter graduate study

General. Founded in 1848. Regionally accredited. **Degrees:** 404 bachelor's awarded; master's offered. **ROTC:** Army, Air Force. **Location:** 4 miles from downtown. **Calendar:** Semester. **Full-time faculty:** 158 total; 94% have terminal degrees, 11% minority, 44% women. **Part-time faculty:** 34 total; 59% have terminal degrees, 18% minority, 41% women. **Class size:** 73% < 20, 25% 20-39, 1% 40-49, less than 1% 50-99. **Special facilities:** Arboretum, scanning electron microscope, rooftop observatory, cell culture facility, nuclear magnetic resonance instrument.

Freshman class profile. 3,747 applied, 1,868 admitted, 477 enrolled.

Mid 50% test scores			
SAT critical reading:	580-680	Rank in top quarter:	82%
SAT math:	580-670	Rank in top tenth:	52%
ACT composite:	26-30	Return as sophomores:	85%
GPA 3.75 or higher:	53%	Out-of-state:	77%
GPA 3.50-3.74:	18%	Live on campus:	97%
GPA 3.0-3.49:	22%	International:	3%
GPA 2.0-2.99:	7%	Fraternities:	46%
		Sororities:	53%

Basis for selection. Academic record, standardized test scores, class rank, recommendations, essay, school and community activities important. Applications sought from international students, minorities, and children of alumni. Interview recommended. **Homeschooled:** Applicants must submit two SAT Subject Tests other than mathematics or literature in addition to usual requirements.

High school preparation. 16 units required. Required units include English 4, mathematics 3, social studies 2, science 2 (laboratory 2), foreign language 2 and academic electives 3.

2008-2009 Annual costs. Tuition/fees: $32,446. Room/board: $7,842. Books/supplies: $1,020. Personal expenses: $1,350.

2008-2009 Financial aid. Need-based: Average need met was 89%. Average scholarship/grant was $19,705; average loan $2,424. 80% of total undergraduate aid awarded as scholarships/grants, 20% as loans/jobs. **Non-need-based:** Scholarships awarded for academics, art, minority status, music/drama, religious affiliation. **Additional information:** Auditions required for theater and music achievement awards and art achievement awards. Interviews recommended for merit scholarships.

Application procedures. Admission: Priority date 1/15; no deadline. $45 fee, may be waived for applicants with need, free for online applicants. Admission notification 3/1. Must reply by 5/1. Notification of admissions decision for Bellingrath Scholarship applicants by 03/15; must reply by 05/01. **Financial aid:** Closing date 3/1. FAFSA, CSS PROFILE required. Must reply by 5/1.

Academics. Expense-paid summer internships in businesses abroad. Model United Nations program, opportunities for participation in computer-simulated international negotiating, mock trial program. **Special study options:** Combined bachelor's/graduate degree, cooperative education, cross-registration, double major, dual enrollment of high school students, exchange student, honors, independent study, internships, liberal arts/career combination, student-designed major, study abroad, Washington semester. **Credit/placement by examination:** AP, CLEP, IB, institutional tests. 28 credit hours maximum toward bachelor's degree. **Support services:** Tutoring, writing center.

Majors. Area/ethnic studies: Latin American, Russian/Slavic. **Biology:** General, Biochemistry/biophysics and molecular biology. **Business:** Business admin, managerial economics. **Computer sciences:** Computer science. **Foreign languages:** Classics, French, German, modern Greek, Russian, Spanish. **History:** General. **Math:** General. **Philosophy/religion:** Philosophy, religion. **Physical sciences:** Chemistry, physics. **Psychology:** General. **Social sciences:** Anthropology, economics, international relations, political science, sociology, urban studies. **Visual/performing arts:** Art, dramatic.

Most popular majors. Biology 17%, business/marketing 9%, English 8%, history 9%, philosophy/religious studies 6%, psychology 11%, social sciences 24%.

Computing on campus. 220 workstations in library, computer center, student center. Dormitories wired for high-speed internet access and linked to campus network. Commuter students can connect to campus network. Online course registration, online library, helpline, repair service, wireless network available.

Student life. Freshman orientation: Mandatory, $110 fee. Preregistration for classes offered. 2-day summer program. **Policies:** Student-run honor system central to campus life. **Housing:** Guaranteed on-campus for freshmen. Coed dorms, single-sex dorms, apartments, wellness housing available. Special interest townhouses. **Activities:** Bands, campus ministries, choral groups, dance, drama, film society, international student organizations, literary magazine, music ensembles, Model UN, musical theater, radio station, student government, student newspaper, symphony orchestra, TV station, Black Student Association, Kinney (social service), Inter-Varsity Christian Fellowship, International House, Habitat for Humanity, Interfaith Circle, Diversity Group, College Democrats, College Republicans.

Athletics. NCAA. **Intercollegiate:** Baseball M, basketball, cross-country, field hockey W, football (tackle) M, golf, soccer, softball W, swimming, tennis, track and field, volleyball W. **Intramural:** Basketball, football (non-tackle), football (tackle), racquetball, soccer, squash M, table tennis, tennis, volleyball. **Team name:** Lynx.

Student services. Alcohol/substance abuse counseling, chaplain/spiritual director, career counseling, student employment services, financial aid counseling, health services, minority student services, personal counseling, placement for graduates, women's services. **Physically disabled:** Services for visually, speech, hearing impaired.

Contact. E-mail: adminfo@rhodes.edu
Phone: (901) 843-3700 Toll-free number: (800) 844-5969
Fax: (901) 843-3631
David Wottle, Dean of Admissions and Financial Aid, Rhodes College, 2000 North Parkway, Memphis, TN 38112

South College
Knoxville, Tennessee
www.southcollegetn.edu
CB code: 0711

- For-profit 4-year liberal arts college
- Commuter campus in small city
- 725 degree-seeking undergraduates
- SAT or ACT (ACT writing optional), interview required

General. Founded in 1882. Regionally accredited. **Degrees:** 37 bachelor's, 54 associate awarded. **Location:** Downtown. **Calendar:** Quarter, extensive summer session. **Full-time faculty:** 75 total. **Part-time faculty:** 25 total.

Basis for selection. CPTS examination required. CPAt can be submitted in place of SAT/ACT.

2008-2009 Annual costs. Tuition/fees: $14,925. Reported annual costs are for programs in physical therapy assistance, radiography, health science.

Costs of other programs vary by program. Books/supplies: $1,300. Personal expenses: $1,200.

2007-2008 Financial aid. All financial aid based on need.

Application procedures. Admission: No deadline. $50 fee. Admission notification on a rolling basis. **Financial aid:** No deadline. FAFSA, institutional form required. Applicants notified on a rolling basis.

Academics. Special study options: Accelerated study, double major, dual enrollment of high school students, internships, teacher certification program. **Credit/placement by examination:** CLEP, institutional tests. **Support services:** Learning center, reduced course load, study skills assistance, tutoring, writing center.

Majors. Business: Business admin. **Legal studies:** General.

Computing on campus. 85 workstations in library, computer center. Online library, wireless network available.

Student life. Freshman orientation: Mandatory. Preregistration for classes offered. **Activities:** Literary magazine, student government, student newspaper, Collegiate Secretaries International, paralegal association, student affairs advisory council, business club, students of medical assisting, movie club, community service club.

Student services. Career counseling, student employment services, financial aid counseling, placement for graduates, veterans' counselor.

Contact. E-mail: admissions@southcollegetn.edu
Phone: (865) 251-1800 Fax: (865) 470-8737
Walter Hosea, Admissions Director, South College, 3904 Lonas Drive, Knoxville, TN 37909

Southern Adventist University

Collegedale, Tennessee
www.southern.edu **CB code: 1727**

- Private 4-year university and liberal arts college affiliated with Seventh-day Adventists
- Residential campus in small town
- 2,430 degree-seeking undergraduates
- 70% of applicants admitted
- SAT or ACT (ACT writing optional) required

General. Founded in 1892. Regionally accredited. **Degrees:** 302 bachelor's, 131 associate awarded; master's offered. **Location:** 18 miles from Chattanooga. **Calendar:** Semester, limited summer session. **Full-time faculty:** 139 total; 66% have terminal degrees, 14% minority, 39% women. **Part-time faculty:** 124 total; 36% have terminal degrees, 8% minority, 42% women. **Special facilities:** Civil War collection, Lincoln collection, Anton Memorial Organ.

Freshman class profile. 1,510 applied, 1,056 admitted, 540 enrolled.

Mid 50% test scores		**GPA 3.0-3.49:**	28%
SAT math:	450-570	**GPA 2.0-2.99:**	20%
ACT composite:	19-25	**Out-of-state:**	76%
GPA 3.75 or higher:	32%	**Live on campus:**	89%
GPA 3.50-3.74:	20%		

Basis for selection. School achievement record and test scores are important. Interview recommended for all; audition required for music, gymnastics programs. **Homeschooled:** Transcript of courses and grades required. Home school organization must be academically accredited or student must take GED. Portfolio required and must include a copy of an original research paper and written statement reflecting on value student received from the home school experience.

High school preparation. College-preparatory program recommended. 18 units required; 24 recommended. Required and recommended units include English 3-4, mathematics 2-3, social studies 1, history 1-2, science 2-3, foreign language 2 and academic electives 9. One unit chemistry (2.0 GPA or better) required for nursing majors. 2 units foreign language required for BA program applicants. Computer competency strongly recommended.

2008-2009 Annual costs. Tuition/fees: $16,560. Room/board: $4,900. Books/supplies: $1,000. Personal expenses: $2,000.

2008-2009 Financial aid. Need-based: Average need met was 85%. Average scholarship/grant was $10,115; average loan $4,688. **Non-need-based:** Scholarships awarded for academics, alumni affiliation, art, leadership, music/drama.

Application procedures. Admission: Closing date 9/8 (receipt date). $25 fee, may be waived for applicants with need. Admission notification on a rolling basis. Must reply by 9/8. **Financial aid:** Priority date 3/1; no closing date. FAFSA required. Applicants notified on a rolling basis starting 2/15; must reply within 2 week(s) of notification.

Academics. Special study options: Combined bachelor's/graduate degree, double major, dual enrollment of high school students, ESL, honors, independent study, internships, study abroad, teacher certification program. **Credit/placement by examination:** AP, CLEP, SAT, ACT, institutional tests. 12 credit hours maximum toward bachelor's degree. **Support services:** Learning center, reduced course load, remedial instruction, study skills assistance, tutoring, writing center.

Majors. Biology: General, biochemistry, biophysics. **Business:** Accounting, business admin, finance, human resources, international, management information systems, management science, marketing, nonprofit/public. **Communications:** Advertising, broadcast journalism, journalism, media studies, public relations. **Communications technology:** General. **Computer sciences:** Computer science, programming. **Education:** Art, biology, chemistry, elementary, English, French, history, mathematics, music, physical, physics, Spanish. **Family/consumer sciences:** Family systems. **Foreign languages:** General, French, Spanish. **Health:** Art therapy, clinical lab science, health care admin, nursing (RN). **History:** General, European. **Math:** General. **Parks/recreation:** Exercise sciences, sports admin. **Philosophy/religion:** Religion. **Physical sciences:** Chemistry, physics. **Psychology:** General. **Public administration:** Social work. **Social sciences:** Archaeology. **Theology:** Missionary, pastoral counseling, religious ed, theology. **Visual/performing arts:** Art, cinematography, commercial/advertising art, music performance, music theory/composition, photography. **Other:** Outdoor education.

Most popular majors. Biology 9%, business/marketing 17%, communications/journalism 7%, education 8%, health sciences 18%, theological studies 6%, visual/performing arts 9%.

Computing on campus. 200 workstations in dormitories, library, computer center. Dormitories wired for high-speed internet access and linked to campus network. Commuter students can connect to campus network. Online course registration, online library, helpline, repair service, student web hosting, wireless network available.

Student life. Freshman orientation: Mandatory. Preregistration for classes offered. Orientation prior to registration for fall term. Includes exams and instruction in course planning as well as social occasions for students to meet faculty and fellow students. **Policies:** Alcohol and drug free. Religious observance required. **Housing:** Guaranteed on-campus for all undergraduates. Single-sex dorms, apartments available. $250 fully refundable deposit, deadline 7/15. **Activities:** Bands, campus ministries, choral groups, drama, film society, music ensembles, radio station, student government, student newspaper, symphony orchestra, TV station, African club, Black Christian Union, Partners at Wellness, Association of South East Asian Nation Students.

Athletics. Intramural: Badminton, basketball, racquetball, soccer, softball, table tennis, tennis, volleyball.

Student services. Chaplain/spiritual director, career counseling, student employment services, financial aid counseling, health services, personal counseling, placement for graduates, veterans' counselor.

Contact. E-mail: admissions@southern.edu
Phone: (423) 236-2844 Toll-free number: (800) 768-8437
Fax: (423) 236-1844
Marc Grundy, Director of Admissions, Southern Adventist University, Box 370, Collegedale, TN 37315-0370

Tennessee State University

Nashville, Tennessee **CB member**
www.tnstate.edu **CB code: 1803**

- Public 4-year university
- Residential campus in very large city
- 6,284 degree-seeking undergraduates: 19% part-time, 64% women, 81% African American, 1% Asian American, 1% Hispanic American
- 1,574 degree-seeking graduate students
- 67% of applicants admitted
- SAT or ACT with writing required

General. Founded in 1912. Regionally accredited. **Degrees:** 967 bachelor's, 144 associate awarded; master's, doctoral offered. **ROTC:** Air Force. **Location:** 115 miles from Chattanooga, 195 miles from Memphis. **Calendar:** Semester, limited summer session. **Full-time faculty:** 434 total; 80% have terminal degrees, 61% minority, 43% women. **Part-time faculty:** 167

total; 40% have terminal degrees, 48% minority, 52% women. **Class size:** 45% < 20, 49% 20-39, 4% 40-49, 3% 50-99, less than 1% >100.

Freshman class profile. 1,591 applied, 1,060 admitted, 1,041 enrolled.

Mid 50% test scores		**GPA 3.0-3.49:**	32%
SAT critical reading:	400-500	**GPA 2.0-2.99:**	54%
SAT math:	410-500	**End year in good standing:**	81%
ACT composite:	17-21	**Out-of-state:**	42%
GPA 3.75 or higher:	5%	**Live on campus:**	75%
GPA 3.50-3.74:	8%		

Basis for selection. School achievement record, test scores important. Interview required for health sciences, nursing, physical therapy programs. **Homeschooled:** State high school equivalency certificate required.

High school preparation. 14 units required. Required units include English 4, mathematics 3, social studies 2, science 2 (laboratory 1) and foreign language 2. One unit visual and/or performing arts recommended.

2008-2009 Annual costs. Tuition/fees: $5,102; $15,994 out-of-state. Room/board: $5,282. Books/supplies: $1,200. Personal expenses: $3,500.

2007-2008 Financial aid. Non-need-based: Scholarships awarded for academics.

Application procedures. Admission: Closing date 8/1. $25 fee. Application must be submitted on paper. Admission notification on a rolling basis. **Financial aid:** Priority date 4/1; no closing date. FAFSA required. Applicants notified on a rolling basis starting 4/15; must reply within 3 week(s) of notification.

Academics. Special study options: Combined bachelor's/graduate degree, cooperative education, cross-registration, distance learning, double major, ESL, exchange student, honors, independent study, internships, liberal arts/career combination, study abroad, teacher certification program. **Credit/placement by examination:** AP, CLEP, SAT, ACT, institutional tests. 33 credit hours maximum toward bachelor's degree. **Support services:** Learning center, remedial instruction, study skills assistance, tutoring, writing center.

Majors. Agriculture: Animal sciences. **Architecture:** Architecture. **Biology:** General, biochemistry. **Business:** Accounting, administrative services, business admin, managerial economics. **Communications:** General, journalism. **Computer sciences:** Computer science. **Education:** General, early childhood, physical, secondary, special. **Engineering:** General, architectural, civil, electrical. **Family/consumer sciences:** General, clothing/textiles, family studies, food/nutrition. **Foreign languages:** French, Spanish. **Health:** Audiology/speech pathology, dental hygiene, health care admin, medical records admin. **History:** General. **Interdisciplinary:** Biological/physical sciences. **Liberal arts:** Arts/sciences. **Math:** General. **Physical sciences:** Chemistry, physics. **Protective services:** Criminal justice. **Psychology:** General. **Public administration:** Social work. **Social sciences:** General, political science, sociology, urban studies. **Visual/performing arts:** Art history/conservation, dramatic.

Most popular majors. Business/marketing 19%, communications/journalism 7%, education 6%, health sciences 14%, liberal arts 19%, psychology 7%.

Computing on campus. 450 workstations in dormitories, library, computer center, student center. Dormitories wired for high-speed internet access and linked to campus network. Commuter students can connect to campus network. Online course registration, online library, helpline, repair service, student web hosting, wireless network available.

Student life. Freshman orientation: Mandatory. Preregistration for classes offered. **Housing:** Coed dorms, single-sex dorms, apartments available. $100 fully refundable deposit, deadline 4/1. **Activities:** Bands, choral groups, dance, drama, film society, international student organizations, music ensembles, musical theater, radio station, student government, student newspaper, TV station, religious organizations, honor organization, literary organization.

Athletics. NCAA. **Intercollegiate:** Baseball M, basketball, cheerleading, cross-country, football (tackle) M, golf, softball W, tennis, track and field, volleyball W. **Intramural:** Basketball, bowling, racquetball, tennis, track and field, volleyball. **Team name:** Tigers.

Student services. Career counseling, student employment services, financial aid counseling, health services, minority student services, on-campus daycare, personal counseling, placement for graduates, veterans' counselor, women's services. **Physically disabled:** Services for visually, speech, hearing impaired.

Contact. E-mail: ctaylor@tnstate.edu
Phone: (615) 963-5101 Fax: (615) 963-5108
Michael Freeman, Vice President of Student Affairs, Tennessee State University, 3500 John A. Merritt Boulevard, Nashville, TN 37209-1561

Tennessee Technological University

Cookeville, Tennessee — **CB member**
www.tntech.edu — **CB code: 1804**

- Public 4-year university
- Residential campus in large town
- 8,102 degree-seeking undergraduates: 8% part-time, 47% women, 3% African American, 1% Asian American, 1% Hispanic American, 2% international
- 1,549 degree-seeking graduate students
- 91% of applicants admitted
- SAT or ACT (ACT writing recommended) required

General. Founded in 1915. Regionally accredited. **Degrees:** 1,450 bachelor's awarded; master's, doctoral offered. **ROTC:** Army, Air Force. **Location:** 80 miles from Nashville, 100 miles from Knoxville. **Calendar:** Semester, extensive summer session. **Full-time faculty:** 386 total; 72% have terminal degrees, 14% minority, 38% women. **Part-time faculty:** 262 total; 22% have terminal degrees, 5% minority, 64% women. **Class size:** 42% < 20, 43% 20-39, 7% 40-49, 6% 50-99, 2% >100. **Special facilities:** Center for crafts, cooperative fishery research unit, agricultural pavilion, center for energy systems research, center for manufacturing research, center for the management, utilization and protection of water resources, childcare resource center.

Freshman class profile. 3,499 applied, 3,185 admitted, 1,677 enrolled.

Mid 50% test scores		**Rank in top quarter:**	54%
SAT critical reading:	470-620	**Rank in top tenth:**	24%
SAT math:	510-650	**Return as sophomores:**	73%
ACT composite:	20-26	**Out-of-state:**	4%
GPA 3.75 or higher:	26%	**Live on campus:**	67%
GPA 3.50-3.74:	17%	**International:**	1%
GPA 3.0-3.49:	31%	**Fraternities:**	10%
GPA 2.0-2.99:	26%	**Sororities:**	10%

Basis for selection. High school classes, GPA and test scores very important. Additional requirements for engineering, computer science, nursing and pre-professional majors. Interview recommended for all; audition recommended for music; portfolio recommended for arts, crafts. **Homeschooled:** Must have same core units as high school curriculum, 2.50 GPA and 19 ACT; GED required otherwise.

High school preparation. 14 units required. Required units include English 4, mathematics 3, social studies 1, history 1, science 2 (laboratory 1) and foreign language 2. Mathematics units must include algebra I and II and geometry or advanced mathematics course. Science units must be biology, chemistry, or physics with laboratories (can include physical sciences). Foreign language units must be in single language. 1 US history, 1 unit visual and/or performing arts also required. Social studies must be either world, ancient, modern, or European history, or world geography.

2008-2009 Annual costs. Tuition/fees: $5,244; $16,136 out-of-state. Room/board: $6,634. Books/supplies: $780. Personal expenses: $840.

2007-2008 Financial aid. Non-need-based: Scholarships awarded for academics, alumni affiliation, art, athletics, leadership, minority status, music/drama, ROTC, state residency. **Additional information:** Tuition and/or fee waivers available for children of Tennessee public school teachers.

Application procedures. Admission: Priority date 5/1; deadline 8/1 (postmark date). $15 fee, may be waived for applicants with need. Admission notification on a rolling basis. **Financial aid:** Priority date 3/15; no closing date. FAFSA required. Applicants notified on a rolling basis starting 3/15; must reply within 2 week(s) of notification.

Academics. Special study options: Accelerated study, cooperative education, distance learning, double major, dual enrollment of high school students, ESL, honors, independent study, internships, liberal arts/career combination, study abroad, teacher certification program. **Credit/placement by examination:** AP, CLEP, IB, institutional tests. 33 credit hours maximum toward bachelor's degree. **Support services:** Learning center, pre-admission summer program, reduced course load, remedial instruction, study skills assistance, tutoring, writing center.

Majors. Agriculture: Agribusiness operations, agronomy, animal sciences, horticultural science, horticulture, landscaping, nursery operations, soil science. **Biology:** General, biochemistry. **Business:** General, accounting, finance, labor relations, management science, managerial economics, operations. **Communications:** General, journalism. **Communications technology:** General. **Computer sciences:** General, computer science, web page design. **Conservation:** General, fisheries, wildlife. **Education:** General, agricultural, early childhood, English, health, music, physical, secondary, special. **Engineering:** Chemical, civil, computer, electrical, industrial, mechanical. **Engineering technology:** Manufacturing. **Family/consumer sciences:** General, clothing/textiles, family/community services, food/nutrition, housing. **Foreign languages:** French, German, Spanish. **Health:** Nursing (RN), predental, premedicine, prepharmacy, preveterinary. **History:** General. **Math:** General. **Parks/recreation:** Health/fitness. **Physical sciences:** Chemistry, geology, physics. **Psychology:** General. **Social sciences:** Economics, political science, sociology. **Visual/performing arts:** Ceramics, drawing, fiber arts, music performance, painting, sculpture, studio arts.

Most popular majors. Business/marketing 18%, education 20%, engineering/engineering technologies 18%.

Computing on campus. 600 workstations in dormitories, library, computer center. Dormitories wired for high-speed internet access and linked to campus network. Commuter students can connect to campus network. Online course registration, online library, helpline, wireless network available.

Student life. Freshman orientation: Mandatory, $45 fee. Preregistration for classes offered. **Housing:** Guaranteed on-campus for freshmen. Coed dorms, single-sex dorms, special housing for disabled, apartments, fraternity/sorority housing available. $50 deposit. **Activities:** Bands, choral groups, dance, drama, literary magazine, music ensembles, musical theater, opera, radio station, student government, student newspaper, symphony orchestra, TV station, over 190 organizations.

Athletics. NCAA. **Intercollegiate:** Baseball M, basketball, cheerleading, cross-country, football (tackle) M, golf, rifle, soccer W, softball W, tennis, track and field W, volleyball W. **Intramural:** Basketball, bowling, golf M, handball, racquetball, rugby M, soccer, softball, tennis, volleyball, wrestling M. **Team name:** Golden Eagles.

Student services. Alcohol/substance abuse counseling, career counseling, student employment services, financial aid counseling, health services, minority student services, on-campus daycare, personal counseling, placement for graduates, veterans' counselor, women's services. **Physically disabled:** Services for visually, speech, hearing impaired. **Learning disabled:** Comprehensive services available.

Contact. E-mail: admissions@tntech.edu
Phone: (931) 372-3888 Toll-free number: (800) 255-8881
Fax: (931) 372-6250
Vanessa Palmer, Admissions, Tennessee Technological University, Office of Admissions, Cookeville, TN 38505-0001

Tennessee Temple University

Chattanooga, Tennessee
www.tntemple.edu **CB code: 1818**

- Private 4-year university and Bible college affiliated with Baptist faith
- Residential campus in small city
- 505 undergraduates
- 24% of applicants admitted
- SAT or ACT with writing, application essay required

General. Founded in 1946. **Degrees:** 74 bachelor's, 4 associate awarded; master's, doctoral, first professional offered. **Location:** 120 miles from Atlanta. **Calendar:** Semester, limited summer session. **Full-time faculty:** 25 total. **Part-time faculty:** 20 total. **Class size:** 77% < 20, 17% 20-39, 4% 40-49, less than 1% 50-99, less than 1% >100.

Freshman class profile. 683 applied, 167 admitted, 140 enrolled.

Mid 50% test scores		**ACT composite:**	15-25
SAT critical reading:	350-610	**Out-of-state:**	26%
SAT math:	340-530	**Live on campus:**	72%

Basis for selection. Test scores, one personal reference, one pastoral reference and a written personal testimony about applicant's faith are required. **Homeschooled:** Relevant experiences that may indicate and support ability to succeed in college work may be substituted for high school diploma or GED. Students should submit a transcript and other supporting information, such as course or curriculum descriptions, grades, graduation date, and the signatures of the instructor. Students should submit official transcripts from other secondary or post secondary institutions attended. Students must submit official scores from the ACT Enhanced Test or SAT Test.

High school preparation. 10 units required; 15 recommended. Required and recommended units include English 4, mathematics 2-3, social studies 2-3, science 2-3 and foreign language 2. Computer fundamentals recommended.

2008-2009 Annual costs. Tuition/fees: $10,662. Room/board: $5,930. Books/supplies: $700. Personal expenses: $850.

Financial aid. Non-need-based: Scholarships awarded for academics, alumni affiliation, athletics, leadership, music/drama, state residency.

Application procedures. Admission: Priority date 3/31; deadline 8/1 (receipt date). $35 fee, may be waived for applicants with need. Admission notification on a rolling basis. **Financial aid:** Priority date 3/31; no closing date. FAFSA required. Applicants notified on a rolling basis starting 2/15; must reply within 2 week(s) of notification.

Academics. Special study options: Distance learning, double major, dual enrollment of high school students, external degree, independent study, internships, liberal arts/career combination, teacher certification program, Washington semester. **Credit/placement by examination:** AP, CLEP, IB, institutional tests. 16 credit hours maximum toward associate degree, 32 toward bachelor's. **Support services:** Reduced course load, remedial instruction, study skills assistance, tutoring, writing center.

Majors. Biology: General. **Business:** General, administrative services, business admin, office management. **Computer sciences:** Computer science. **Education:** Biology, Deaf/hearing impaired, elementary, English, history, mathematics, music, science, secondary, speech. **Health:** Premedicine. **History:** General. **Legal studies:** Prelaw. **Liberal arts:** Arts/sciences. **Math:** General. **Physical sciences:** General. **Psychology:** General. **Social sciences:** Political science. **Theology:** Bible, missionary, religious ed, sacred music, theology.

Computing on campus. 105 workstations in dormitories, library, computer center. Dormitories wired for high-speed internet access and linked to campus network. Commuter students can connect to campus network. Wireless network available.

Student life. Freshman orientation: Mandatory, $25 fee. Held 2-3 days prior to beginning of classes. **Policies:** Religious observance required. **Housing:** Guaranteed on-campus for all undergraduates. Single-sex dorms, apartments available. $100 deposit, deadline 5/31. **Activities:** Choral groups, drama, music ensembles, radio station, student government, student newspaper, Student Missions Fellowship, Student Preachers Fellowship.

Athletics. NCCAA. **Intercollegiate:** Baseball M, basketball, soccer M, volleyball W. **Intramural:** Basketball, football (tackle) M, soccer, softball, table tennis, tennis, volleyball, wrestling M. **Team name:** Crusaders.

Student services. Chaplain/spiritual director, student employment services, financial aid counseling, personal counseling, placement for graduates, veterans' counselor. **Physically disabled:** Services for visually, hearing impaired.

Contact. E-mail: ttuinfo@tntemple.edu
Phone: (423) 493-4371 Toll-free number: (800) 553-4050
Fax: (423) 493-4497
Diana Knowles, Director of Enrollment Services, Tennessee Temple University, 1815 Union Avenue, Chattanooga, TN 37404

Tennessee Wesleyan College

Athens, Tennessee
www.twcnet.edu **CB code: 1805**

- Private 4-year liberal arts and teachers college affiliated with United Methodist Church
- Commuter campus in large town
- 979 degree-seeking undergraduates: 14% part-time, 61% women, 4% African American, 1% Asian American, 2% Hispanic American
- 84% of applicants admitted
- SAT or ACT (ACT writing optional) required
- 79% graduate within 6 years

General. Founded in 1857. Regionally accredited. Baccalaureate programs in nursing and evening business school through Knoxville campus. **Degrees:** 216 bachelor's awarded. **ROTC:** Army, Naval, Air Force. **Location:** 50 miles from Chattanooga and Knoxville. **Calendar:** Semester, extensive summer session. **Full-time faculty:** 44 total. **Part-time faculty:** 44 total. **Class size:** 65% < 20, 28% 20-39, 4% 40-49, 2% 50-99.

Freshman class profile. 629 applied, 530 admitted, 261 enrolled.

Mid 50% test scores			
SAT critical reading:	430-570	GPA 3.0-3.49:	28%
SAT math:	480-560	GPA 2.0-2.99:	32%
ACT composite:	19-24	Rank in top quarter:	43%
GPA 3.75 or higher:	21%	Rank in top tenth:	18%
GPA 3.50-3.74:	18%	Out-of-state:	12%
		Live on campus:	65%

Basis for selection. Test scores, school records, recommendations and GPA very important. ACT/SAT not required if student has GED. Essay recommended for all; interview recommended for academically weak; audition required for music and theater.

High school preparation. College-preparatory program recommended. 10 units recommended. Recommended units include English 4, mathematics 2, social studies 1, history 1 and science 2.

2008-2009 Annual costs. Tuition/fees: $17,050. Room/board: $5,830. Books/supplies: $1,000. Personal expenses: $2,000.

2007-2008 Financial aid. **Need-based:** 374 full-time freshmen applied for aid; 309 were judged to have need; 305 of these received aid. Average need met was 75%. Average scholarship/grant was $12,625; average loan $3,205. 69% of total undergraduate aid awarded as scholarships/grants, 31% as loans/jobs. **Non-need-based:** Awarded to 467 full-time undergraduates, including 173 freshmen. Scholarships awarded for academics, alumni affiliation, athletics, job skills, minority status, music/drama, religious affiliation.

Application procedures. **Admission:** Closing date 8/15 (receipt date). $25 fee, may be waived for applicants with need. Admission notification on a rolling basis beginning on or about 9/1. **Financial aid:** No deadline. FAFSA, institutional form required. Applicants notified on a rolling basis starting 2/15; must reply within 2 week(s) of notification.

Academics. Study abroad opportunities available for students wishing to extend their learning globally. **Special study options:** Accelerated study, double major, exchange student, honors, independent study, internships, student-designed major, study abroad, teacher certification program. Member of the Private College Consortium for International Studies (semester in London program). **Credit/placement by examination:** AP, CLEP, IB, SAT, ACT, institutional tests. 12 credit hours maximum toward bachelor's degree. **Support services:** Learning center, reduced course load, remedial instruction, study skills assistance, tutoring, writing center.

Majors. **Area/ethnic studies:** American. **Biology:** General. **Business:** Accounting, business admin, finance, human resources. **Computer sciences:** General. **Conservation:** Environmental studies. **Education:** Early childhood, elementary, multi-level teacher, secondary. **Health:** Nursing (RN), predental, premedicine, prenursing, prepharmacy, preveterinary. **History:** General. **Interdisciplinary:** Behavioral sciences, global studies, intercultural. **Legal studies:** Prelaw. **Math:** General. **Parks/recreation:** Health/fitness, sports admin. **Philosophy/religion:** Christian. **Physical sciences:** Chemistry. **Psychology:** General. **Public administration:** Human services. **Theology:** Preministerial. **Other:** Pre-physical therapy.

Most popular majors. Business/marketing 25%, education 26%, health sciences 20%, interdisciplinary studies 6%, parks/recreation 7%.

Computing on campus. 133 workstations in dormitories, library, computer center, student center. Dormitories wired for high-speed internet access and linked to campus network. Online library, wireless network available.

Student life. **Freshman orientation:** Mandatory. Preregistration for classes offered. Held in August. **Policies:** All students required to live on-campus unless residing with relative within commuting distance, married, or have children. Visitation hours in dorms by opposite sex restricted. No alcohol allowed on campus. Religious observance required. **Housing:** Guaranteed on-campus for freshmen. Single-sex dorms, apartments, wellness housing available. **Activities:** Concert band, campus ministries, choral groups, drama, literary magazine, music ensembles, student government, student newspaper, Circle K, Hackberry and Oak Society, National Student Nurses Association, student activities board, Education Angels, Fellowship of Christian Athletes, Wesleyan Christian Fellowship, College Democrats.

Athletics. NAIA. **Intercollegiate:** Baseball M, basketball, cross-country, golf, soccer, softball W, tennis, volleyball W. **Team name:** Bulldogs.

Student services. Adult student services, alcohol/substance abuse counseling, chaplain/spiritual director, career counseling, student employment services, financial aid counseling, personal counseling, placement for graduates, veterans' counselor. **Physically disabled:** Services for visually, hearing impaired.

Contact. E-mail: admissions@twcnet.edu
Phone: (423) 745-7504 Toll-free number: (800) 742-5892
Fax: (423) 745-9335
Stan Harrison, Vice President Enrollment Management and Director of Athletics, Tennessee Wesleyan College, 204 East College Street, Athens, TN 37371-0040

Trevecca Nazarene University

Nashville, Tennessee
www.trevecca.edu **CB code: 1809**

- Private 4-year university and liberal arts college affiliated with Church of the Nazarene
- Residential campus in very large city
- 1,182 degree-seeking undergraduates: 7% part-time, 56% women, 9% African American, 2% Asian American, 2% Hispanic American, 1% Native American, 2% international
- 1,075 degree-seeking graduate students
- 69% of applicants admitted
- SAT or ACT (ACT writing optional) required
- 49% graduate within 6 years

General. Founded in 1901. Regionally accredited. **Degrees:** 334 bachelor's awarded; master's, doctoral offered. **ROTC:** Army. **Location:** 200 miles from Memphis, 175 miles from Knoxville. **Calendar:** Semester, limited summer session. **Full-time faculty:** 80 total; 80% have terminal degrees, 9% minority, 31% women. **Part-time faculty:** 121 total; 43% have terminal degrees, 2% minority, 45% women. **Class size:** 67% < 20, 28% 20-39, 3% 40-49, 2% 50-99, less than 1% >100.

Freshman class profile. 816 applied, 559 admitted, 234 enrolled.

Mid 50% test scores			
SAT critical reading:	450-580	GPA 2.0-2.99:	32%
SAT math:	440-580	Rank in top quarter:	38%
ACT composite:	19-25	Rank in top tenth:	18%
GPA 3.75 or higher:	21%	Return as sophomores:	69%
GPA 3.50-3.74:	14%	Out-of-state:	48%
GPA 3.0-3.49:	32%	Live on campus:	87%
		International:	3%

Basis for selection. Freshmen required to meet one of two conditions: a minimum 18 ACT composite (860 SAT composite, exclusive of Writing) or 2.5 high school GPA based on 4.0 scale. **Homeschooled:** Transcript with all subjects and grades should be provided by the correspondence-school based organization or the parent depending on the method of homeschooling. **Learning Disabled:** Contact Disability Services in the Academic Support Center for information concerning documentation of disability and services available.

High school preparation. College-preparatory program recommended. 15 units recommended. Recommended units include English 4, mathematics 2, social studies 1, history 1, science 1, foreign language 2 and academic electives 4.

2008-2009 Annual costs. Tuition/fees: $16,288. Room/board: $7,134.

2007-2008 Financial aid. **Need-based:** 34% of total undergraduate aid awarded as scholarships/grants, 66% as loans/jobs. **Non-need-based:** Scholarships awarded for academics, alumni affiliation, athletics, leadership, minority status, religious affiliation.

Application procedures. **Admission:** Priority date 4/1; no deadline. $25 fee. Admission notification on a rolling basis. Enrollment deposit of $200 due by May 1. Refundable if notification received by May 1. **Financial aid:** Priority date 3/1; no closing date. FAFSA required. Applicants notified on a rolling basis starting 3/1.

Academics. **Special study options:** Double major, internships, study abroad, teacher certification program. Adult degree completion program. **Credit/placement by examination:** AP, CLEP, IB, SAT, ACT. 22 credit hours maximum toward associate degree, 45 toward bachelor's. Credit awarded after one semester and tuition paid. **Support services:** Learning center, remedial instruction, study skills assistance, tutoring.

Majors. **Biology:** General. **Business:** Accounting, business admin, e-commerce, management information systems, marketing. **Communications:** General, media studies, organizational. **Computer sciences:** Information technology, web page design. **Education:** Biology, business, chemistry, drama/dance, elementary, English, history, mathematics, music, physical, physics, secondary, special, speech. **Health:** Clinical lab science, nursing (RN). **History:** General. **Interdisciplinary:** Behavioral sciences. **Math:** General. **Parks/recreation:** Exercise sciences, sports admin. **Philosophy/**

religion: Religion. **Physical sciences:** Chemistry, physics. **Protective services:** Law enforcement admin. **Psychology:** General. **Public administration:** Social work. **Social sciences:** General. **Theology:** Sacred music. **Visual/performing arts:** Dramatic, music management. **Other:** Christian ministries, Financial mathematics, History/political science, Interpersonal communications, Mathematical biology, Professional accountancy.

Most popular majors. Business/marketing 56%, education 8%, philosophy/religious studies 7%, visual/performing arts 6%.

Computing on campus. 200 workstations in dormitories, library, computer center, student center. Dormitories linked to campus network. Commuter students can connect to campus network. Wireless network available.

Student life. Freshman orientation: Mandatory. Preregistration for classes offered. **Policies:** Religious observance required. **Housing:** Single-sex dorms, apartments available. **Activities:** Bands, campus ministries, choral groups, drama, literary magazine, music ensembles, musical theater, radio station, student government, student newspaper, symphony orchestra, TV station, Mission Club, Trevecca Ministerial Association, Phi Beta Lambda.

Athletics. NAIA. **Intercollegiate:** Baseball M, basketball, golf, soccer, softball W, volleyball W. **Intramural:** Badminton, basketball, football (tackle) M, golf, racquetball, softball, table tennis, track and field, volleyball. **Team name:** Trojans.

Student services. Chaplain/spiritual director, career counseling, student employment services, financial aid counseling, health services, personal counseling, placement for graduates.

Contact. E-mail: admissions_und@trevecca.edu
Phone: (615) 248-1320 Toll-free number: (888) 210-4868
Fax: (615) 248-7406
Michael Cantrell, Director of Admissions, Trevecca Nazarene University, 333 Murfreesboro Road, Nashville, TN 37210

Tusculum College

Greeneville, Tennessee — **CB member**
www.tusculum.edu — **CB code: 1812**

- Private 4-year liberal arts college affiliated with Presbyterian Church (USA)
- Residential campus in large town
- 2,070 degree-seeking undergraduates: 1% part-time, 62% women, 11% African American, 2% Hispanic American, 2% international
- 171 degree-seeking graduate students
- 74% of applicants admitted
- SAT or ACT (ACT writing optional), application essay required
- 39% graduate within 6 years; 12% enter graduate study

General. Founded in 1794. Regionally accredited. Strong civic arts focus and service-learning curriculum. **Degrees:** 599 bachelor's awarded; master's offered. **Location:** 70 miles from Knoxville, 30 miles from Johnson City. **Calendar:** Differs by program, limited summer session. **Full-time faculty:** 73 total; 66% have terminal degrees, 51% women. **Part-time faculty:** 130 total. **Class size:** 65% < 20, 35% 20-39.

Freshman class profile. 1,871 applied, 1,381 admitted, 289 enrolled.

Mid 50% test scores			
SAT critical reading:	430-520	Return as sophomores:	61%
SAT math:	430-540	Out-of-state:	33%
ACT composite:	19-24	Live on campus:	71%
		International:	2%

Basis for selection. Admissions based on secondary school record and standardized test scores. Essay also important. Math and English placement tests may be required based on ACT or SAT scores. Interview recommended.

High school preparation. College-preparatory program recommended. 12 units required. Required units include English 4, mathematics 3, social studies 3 and science 2.

2008-2009 Annual costs. Tuition/fees: $18,870. Room/board: $7,120. Books/supplies: $960. Personal expenses: $1,400.

Financial aid. Non-need-based: Scholarships awarded for academics, athletics, leadership, religious affiliation, state residency.

Application procedures. Admission: No deadline. No application fee. Admission notification on a rolling basis. **Financial aid:** Closing date 2/15. FAFSA required. Applicants notified on a rolling basis starting 3/1; must reply within 3 week(s) of notification.

Academics. Semesters are comprised of 4 blocks, each 3 1/2 weeks long. Students take one course per block. Students and faculty can concentrate on one course at a time. Intensive 16-month professional studies program designed for non-traditional students also offered. **Special study options:** Accelerated study, double major, honors, independent study, internships, student-designed major, study abroad, teacher certification program. **Credit/placement by examination:** AP, CLEP, institutional tests, 30 credit hours maximum toward bachelor's degree. **Support services:** Learning center, pre-admission summer program, study skills assistance, tutoring, writing center.

Majors. Biology: General. **Business:** Accounting, business admin, entrepreneurial studies. **Communications:** Journalism. **Conservation:** General, environmental studies. **Education:** Art, biology, business, early childhood, elementary, English, health, history, mathematics, middle, physical, psychology, secondary, special. **Health:** Athletic training, clinical lab science, premedicine, prepharmacy. **History:** General. **Interdisciplinary:** Museum. **Legal studies:** Prelaw. **Math:** General. **Parks/recreation:** Health/fitness, sports admin. **Psychology:** General. **Social sciences:** Political science. **Visual/performing arts:** General.

Most popular majors. Business/marketing 55%, education 34%.

Computing on campus. 160 workstations in library, computer center, student center. Dormitories wired for high-speed internet access and linked to campus network. Commuter students can connect to campus network. Online library, helpline, repair service available.

Student life. Freshman orientation: Mandatory. Preregistration for classes offered. **Housing:** Guaranteed on-campus for freshmen. Single-sex dorms, apartments available. $200 nonrefundable deposit, deadline 6/1. **Activities:** Choral groups, drama, literary magazine, radio station, student government, student newspaper, TV station, Bonwandi, Campus Activities Board, Fellowship of Christian Athletes.

Athletics. NCAA. **Intercollegiate:** Baseball M, basketball, cheerleading M, cross-country, football (tackle) M, golf, soccer, softball W, tennis, volleyball W. **Intramural:** Basketball, football (tackle), soccer, softball, table tennis, tennis, volleyball. **Team name:** Pioneers.

Student services. Adult student services, alcohol/substance abuse counseling, chaplain/spiritual director, career counseling, financial aid counseling, health services, personal counseling, placement for graduates, veterans' counselor.

Contact. E-mail: mripley@tusculum.edu
Phone: (423) 636-7300 Toll-free number: (800) 729-0256
Fax: (423) 638-7166
Melissa Ripley, Director of Admissions, Tusculum College, 60 Shiloh Road, Greeneville, TN 37743

Union University

Jackson, Tennessee
www.uu.edu — **CB code: 1826**

- Private 4-year university and liberal arts college affiliated with Southern Baptist Convention
- Residential campus in small city
- 2,275 degree-seeking undergraduates: 11% part-time, 60% women
- 1,003 degree-seeking graduate students
- 82% of applicants admitted

General. Founded in 1823. Regionally accredited. **Degrees:** 459 bachelor's, 2 associate awarded; master's, doctoral, first professional offered. **Location:** 80 miles from Memphis, 120 miles from Nashville. **Calendar:** Semester, extensive summer session. **Full-time faculty:** 177 total; 83% have terminal degrees, 6% minority, 44% women. **Part-time faculty:** 8 total; 25% minority, 75% women. **Class size:** 64% < 20, 32% 20-39, 4% 40-49, less than 1% 50-99, less than 1% >100. **Special facilities:** Aquatic center, creative communications center.

Freshman class profile. 1,164 applied, 953 admitted, 444 enrolled.

Mid 50% test scores		GPA 2.0-2.99:	8%
SAT critical reading:	510-650	Rank in top quarter:	60%
SAT math:	510-640	Rank in top tenth:	35%
ACT composite:	21-29	Out-of-state:	36%
GPA 3.75 or higher:	52%	Live on campus:	86%
GPA 3.50-3.74:	20%	Fraternities:	8%
GPA 3.0-3.49:	20%	Sororities:	16%

Basis for selection. School achievement, recommendations, special talents, test scores important. Minimum 22 ACT or 1030 SAT (exclusive of Writing), top 50% of high school class, and 2.5 GPA required. Interview recommended for all; audition required for music; portfolio recommended for art, communications. Essay required for academic and leadership scholarships. **Homeschooled:** If a class rank is unavailable, students may be admitted without conditions provided they meet minimum ACT/SAT scores and GPA requirements.

High school preparation. College-preparatory program required. 15 units required; 22 recommended. Required and recommended units include English 4, mathematics 3-4, social studies 2, history 1-2, science 3-4 (laboratory 2), foreign language 1-2, computer science 1, visual/performing arts 1 and academic electives 1-4.

2008-2009 Annual costs. Tuition/fees: $19,610. Room/board: $7,200. Books/supplies: $1,000. Personal expenses: $3,200.

2008-2009 Financial aid. **Need-based:** Average need met was 80%. Average scholarship/grant was $5,503; average loan $3,754. 63% of total undergraduate aid awarded as scholarships/grants, 37% as loans/jobs. **Non-need-based:** Scholarships awarded for academics, alumni affiliation, art, athletics, leadership, minority status, music/drama, religious affiliation, state residency.

Application procedures. **Admission:** Priority date 12/1; deadline 8/1 (postmark date). $35 fee, may be waived for applicants with need. Admission notification on a rolling basis beginning on or about 10/1. Must reply by May 1 or within 2 week(s) if notified thereafter. **Financial aid:** Priority date 2/15, closing date 3/1. FAFSA, institutional form required. Applicants notified on a rolling basis starting 2/15; must reply by 5/1 or within 2 week(s) of notification.

Academics. **Special study options:** Accelerated study, combined bachelor's/graduate degree, cooperative education, cross-registration, distance learning, double major, dual enrollment of high school students, ESL, exchange student, honors, independent study, internships, study abroad, teacher certification program, Washington semester. **Credit/placement by examination:** CLEP, IB, institutional tests. 32 credit hours maximum toward bachelor's degree. **Support services:** Learning center, pre-admission summer program, reduced course load, remedial instruction, study skills assistance, tutoring, writing center.

Majors. **Biology:** General, cellular/molecular, conservation, zoology. **Business:** Accounting, business admin, international, managerial economics, marketing. **Communications:** General, advertising, broadcast journalism, digital media, journalism, public relations. **Computer sciences:** Computer science, web page design. **Education:** General, art, biology, business, chemistry, early childhood special, elementary, English, ESL, foreign languages, French, history, kindergarten/preschool, mathematics, middle, music, physical, science, secondary, Spanish, special. **Engineering:** Electrical, mechanical, physics. **Family/consumer sciences:** Family systems. **Foreign languages:** French, Spanish. **Health:** Athletic training, clinical lab science, nursing (RN). **History:** General. **Interdisciplinary:** Intercultural. **Math:** General. **Parks/recreation:** Exercise sciences, sports admin. **Philosophy/religion:** Christian, ethics, philosophy, religion. **Physical sciences:** General, chemical physics, chemistry, physics. **Psychology:** General. **Public administration:** Social work. **Social sciences:** Economics, political science, sociology. **Theology:** Sacred music, theology, youth ministry. **Visual/performing arts:** Dramatic, music performance, music theory/composition, studio arts.

Most popular majors. Business/marketing 8%, education 9%, health sciences 30%, interdisciplinary studies 15%, public administration/social services 7%.

Computing on campus. 300 workstations in dormitories, library, computer center, student center. Dormitories wired for high-speed internet access and linked to campus network. Commuter students can connect to campus network. Online course registration, online library, helpline, repair service, wireless network available.

Student life. **Freshman orientation:** Available, $70 fee. Preregistration for classes offered. Held 4 days before classes begin for freshmen and transfer students. **Policies:** Full-time resident students required to attend 14 chapel services per semester. Smoke and alcohol-free campus. Religious observance required. **Housing:** Guaranteed on-campus for all undergraduates. Single-sex dorms, special housing for disabled, apartments available. $100 nonrefundable deposit, deadline 5/1. **Activities:** Bands, campus ministries, choral groups, drama, film society, international student organizations, literary magazine, music ensembles, student government, student newspaper, Fellowship of Christian Athletes, Ministerial Association, student activity council, Mu Kappa, honors student association, Tennessee Intercollegiate State Legislature, LIFE Groups, Klemata.

Athletics. NAIA. **Intercollegiate:** Baseball M, basketball, cheerleading M, cross-country, golf M, soccer, softball W, tennis, volleyball W. **Intramural:** Basketball, cheerleading W, cross-country, football (non-tackle), golf, racquetball, softball, swimming, table tennis, tennis, volleyball, weight lifting. **Team name:** Bulldogs.

Student services. Adult student services, alcohol/substance abuse counseling, chaplain/spiritual director, career counseling, student employment services, financial aid counseling, health services, personal counseling, placement for graduates, veterans' counselor. **Physically disabled:** Services for visually, speech, hearing impaired.

Contact. E-mail: info@uu.edu
Phone: (731) 661-5000 Toll-free number: (800) 338-6466
Fax: (731) 661-5017
Rich Grimm, Vice President for Enrollment Services, Union University, 1050 Union University Drive, Jackson, TN 38305-3697

University of Memphis

Memphis, Tennessee
www.memphis.edu **CB code: 1459**

- Public 4-year university
- Commuter campus in very large city
- 15,116 degree-seeking undergraduates: 22% part-time, 62% women, 39% African American, 2% Asian American, 2% Hispanic American, 2% international
- 3,546 degree-seeking graduate students
- 67% of applicants admitted
- SAT or ACT (ACT writing optional) required
- 39% graduate within 6 years

General. Founded in 1912. Regionally accredited. **Degrees:** 2,456 bachelor's awarded; master's, doctoral, first professional offered. **ROTC:** Army, Naval, Air Force. **Location:** 10 miles from downtown. **Calendar:** Semester, extensive summer session. **Full-time faculty:** 851 total; 74% have terminal degrees, 20% minority, 40% women. **Part-time faculty:** 533 total; 32% have terminal degrees, 20% minority, 54% women. **Class size:** 39% < 20, 47% 20-39, 5% 40-49, 7% 50-99, 2% >100. **Special facilities:** Institute of Egyptian art and archaeology, speech and hearing center, earthquake research and information center, technology institute, Chucalissa Indian village and museum, Confucius institute.

Freshman class profile. 5,361 applied, 3,591 admitted, 1,989 enrolled.

Mid 50% test scores			
SAT critical reading:	440-590	GPA 2.0-2.99:	36%
SAT math:	440-590	Rank in top quarter:	42%
SAT writing:	440-570	Rank in top tenth:	17%
ACT composite:	19-24	Return as sophomores:	75%
GPA 3.75 or higher:	18%	Out-of-state:	10%
GPA 3.50-3.74:	13%	Live on campus:	47%
GPA 3.0-3.49:	32%	International:	2%

Basis for selection. High school GPA and test scores are important. An Admissions Index will be calculated for each applicant by first multiplying the cumulative high school GPA by 30 and then adding the ACT composite score. The admission of first-time freshmen is competitive based on the calculated index, and also includes an evaluation of the high school curriculum completed. Interview required for university college; audition required for music; portfolio required for fine arts. **Homeschooled:** Transcript of courses and grades required. Applicants must comply with state law by submitting proof of registration with the local education agency.

High school preparation. Required units include English 4, mathematics 3, social studies 2, history 1, science 2 (laboratory 1), foreign language 2 and visual/performing arts 1.

2008-2009 Annual costs. Tuition/fees: $6,128; $17,714 out-of-state. Room/board: $5,660. Books/supplies: $1,100. Personal expenses: $2,393.

2008-2009 Financial aid. **Need-based:** 1,849 full-time freshmen applied for aid; 1,354 were judged to have need; 1,135 of these received aid. Average need met was 79%. Average scholarship/grant was $5,759; average loan $1,667. 50% of total undergraduate aid awarded as scholarships/grants, 50% as loans/jobs. **Non-need-based:** Awarded to 7,209 full-time undergraduates, including 1,600 freshmen. Scholarships awarded for academics, alumni affiliation, art, athletics, leadership, minority status, music/drama, ROTC, state residency.

Application procedures. **Admission:** Closing date 7/1 (postmark date). $25 fee. Admission notification on a rolling basis. Must meet registration deadline. **Financial aid:** Priority date 3/1, closing date 6/1. FAFSA required. Applicants notified on a rolling basis starting 3/1; must reply within 2 week(s) of notification.

Academics. University enables students to create non-traditional degrees. **Special study options:** Accelerated study, combined bachelor's/graduate degree, cooperative education, cross-registration, distance learning, double major, dual enrollment of high school students, ESL, exchange student, external degree, honors, independent study, internships, liberal arts/career combination, student-designed major, study abroad, teacher certification program. **Credit/placement by examination:** AP, CLEP, IB, SAT, ACT, institutional tests. 24 credit hours maximum toward bachelor's degree. Number of credits awarded decided by individual departments. **Support services:** Learning center, pre-admission summer program, reduced course load, remedial instruction, study skills assistance, tutoring, writing center.

Honors college/program. ACT of 27 or higher or a combined SAT score of 1200 or more (exclusive of Writing); 3.5 cumulative high school GPA.

Majors. Architecture: Architecture, environmental design. **Area/ethnic studies:** African-American. **Biology:** General, bacteriology. **Business:** Accounting, business admin, finance, hospitality admin, hotel/motel admin, international, logistics, management information systems, managerial economics, marketing, real estate, resort management, sales/distribution, selling. **Communications:** Journalism, media studies. **Computer sciences:** Computer science. **Education:** Elementary, multi-level teacher, physical, special. **Engineering:** Biomedical, civil, computer, electrical, mechanical. **Engineering technology:** Computer, electrical, manufacturing. **Family/consumer sciences:** Family studies. **Foreign languages:** General. **Health:** Nursing (RN). **History:** General. **Liberal arts:** Arts/sciences. **Math:** General. **Parks/recreation:** Exercise sciences, sports admin. **Philosophy/religion:** Philosophy. **Physical sciences:** Chemistry, geology, physics. **Protective services:** Law enforcement admin. **Psychology:** General. **Public administration:** Social work. **Social sciences:** Anthropology, economics, geography, international relations, political science, sociology. **Visual/performing arts:** Art, art history/conservation, dramatic, music management.

Most popular majors. Business/marketing 20%, communications/journalism 6%, education 9%, health sciences 7%, interdisciplinary studies 11%, liberal arts 7%, social sciences 6%.

Computing on campus. 2,000 workstations in dormitories, library, computer center, student center. Dormitories wired for high-speed internet access and linked to campus network. Commuter students can connect to campus network. Online course registration, online library, helpline, repair service, wireless network available.

Student life. Freshman orientation: Mandatory. Preregistration for classes offered. One or 2-day sessions, evening program for adult students. Fees vary by program. **Housing:** Coed dorms, single-sex dorms, special housing for disabled, apartments, fraternity/sorority housing available. **Activities:** Bands, choral groups, dance, drama, literary magazine, music ensembles, musical theater, opera, radio station, student government, student newspaper, symphony orchestra.

Athletics. NCAA. **Intercollegiate:** Baseball M, basketball, cross-country, football (tackle) M, golf, rifle, soccer, softball W, tennis, track and field, volleyball W. **Intramural:** Basketball, bowling, cross-country, football (non-tackle), golf, racquetball, soccer, softball, table tennis, tennis, volleyball. **Team name:** Tigers.

Student services. Adult student services, career counseling, student employment services, health services, minority student services, on-campus daycare, personal counseling, placement for graduates, veterans' counselor, women's services. **Physically disabled:** Services for visually, speech, hearing impaired.

Contact. E-mail: recruitment@memphis.edu
Phone: (901) 678-2111 Toll-free number: (800) 669-2678
Fax: (901) 678-3053
Gloria Moore, Associate Director of Admissions, University of Memphis, 101 Wilder Tower, Memphis, TN 38152

University of Tennessee Health Science Center

Memphis, Tennessee
www.utmem.edu — **CB code: 1850**

- Public two-year upper-division university and health science college
- Commuter campus in very large city
- Test scores, application essay, interview required

General. Founded in 1911. Regionally accredited. **Degrees:** 106 bachelor's awarded; master's, doctoral, first professional offered. **Location:** 220 miles from Nashville, 299 miles from St. Louis, Missouri. **Calendar:** Semester, limited summer session. **Full-time faculty:** 1,033 total; 11% minority, 51% women. **Part-time faculty:** 227 total; 6% minority, 49% women. **Special facilities:** Computer laboratories, special laboratories for nursing, pharmacy, allied health, and dentistry instruction, simulated patients.

Student profile. 289 degree-seeking undergraduates, 2,660 degree-seeking graduate students. 58% entered as juniors, 42% entered as seniors. 58% transferred from two-year, 42% transferred from four-year institutions.

Women:	90%	**Out-of-state:**	16%
Part-time:	20%	**25 or older:**	50%

Basis for selection. High school transcript, college transcript, application essay, interview, standardized test scores required. Students must have minimum 2 years of college and meet minimum requirements. Admissions based on GPA, test scores, consistency in achievement, course load and content, recommendations, extracurricular performance, motivation and goals, preprofessional evaluation, interview if required by program. Minimum GPA requirements and application closing dates vary by program. Transfer accepted as juniors, seniors.

2008-2009 Annual costs. Tuition/fees: $5,652; $12,902 out-of-state. Above cost are for bachelor's program in nursing. Other programs vary by cost. Books/supplies: $1,182.

Financial aid. Need-based: Average need met was 68%. 7% of total undergraduate aid awarded as scholarships/grants, 93% as loans/jobs. **Non-need-based:** Scholarships awarded for academics, leadership, minority status, state residency. **Additional information:** Scholarships available to defray out-of-state portion of fees charged to out-of-state minority students.

Application procedures. Admission: $50 fee, may be waived for applicants with need. Must reply by 6/1. **Financial aid:** No deadline. Applicants notified on a rolling basis starting 5/1; must reply within 2 weeks of notification. FAFSA required.

Academics. Special study options: Accelerated study, combined bachelor's/graduate degree, cooperative education, cross-registration, distance learning, double major, exchange student, independent study, internships. **Credit/placement by examination:** CLEP.

Honors college/program. Varies for each undergraduate program.

Majors. Health: Clinical lab science, cytotechnology, dental hygiene, medical records admin, nursing (RN).

Computing on campus. 100 workstations in library, computer center. Commuter students can connect to campus network. Online library, helpline, repair service, student web hosting, wireless network available.

Student life. Housing: Coed dorms, wellness housing available. $50 fully refundable deposit. **Activities:** International student organizations, student government, student newspaper, Baptist Student Union, United Methodist Fellowship, Catholic Student Association, Black Student Association.

Athletics. Intramural: Badminton, basketball, bowling, golf, handball, racquetball, soccer, softball, squash, swimming, table tennis, tennis, volleyball, water polo.

Student services. Adult student services, alcohol/substance abuse counseling, career counseling, services for economically disadvantaged, student employment services, financial aid counseling, health services, legal services, minority student services, personal counseling, placement for graduates, veterans' counselor. **Physically disabled:** Services for visually, speech, hearing impaired. **Learning disabled:** Comprehensive services available.

Contact. E-mail: etaylor@utmem.edu
Phone: (901) 448-5562 Fax: (901) 448-7772
Eunice Taylor, Registrar, University of Tennessee Health Science Center, 800 Madison Avenue, Memphis, TN 38163

University of Tennessee: Chattanooga

Chattanooga, Tennessee
www.utc.edu — **CB code: 1831**

- Public 4-year university
- Commuter campus in large city
- 8,232 degree-seeking undergraduates: 11% part-time, 56% women, 17% African American, 2% Asian American, 2% Hispanic American, 1% international
- 1,346 degree-seeking graduate students
- 79% of applicants admitted
- SAT or ACT (ACT writing optional) required
- 40% graduate within 6 years

General. Founded in 1886. Regionally accredited. **Degrees:** 1,326 bachelor's awarded; master's, doctoral offered. **ROTC:** Army. **Location:** 130

miles from Nashville, 118 miles from Atlanta. **Calendar:** Semester, extensive summer session. **Full-time faculty:** 402 total; 68% have terminal degrees, 18% minority, 46% women. **Part-time faculty:** 288 total; 22% have terminal degrees, 18% minority, 52% women. **Class size:** 42% < 20, 49% 20-39, 8% 40-49, 1% 50-99, less than 1% >100. **Special facilities:** 2 art galleries, theater, observatory.

Freshman class profile. 5,849 applied, 4,606 admitted, 2,083 enrolled.

Mid 50% test scores		**GPA 2.0-2.99:**	35%
ACT composite:	20-24	**Return as sophomores:**	62%
GPA 3.75 or higher:	16%	**Out-of-state:**	6%
GPA 3.50-3.74:	15%	**International:**	1%
GPA 3.0-3.49:	34%		

Basis for selection. High school curriculum and GPA very important. Either: 2.75 GPA and a minimum 17 ACT composite (830 SAT composite); or 21 ACT composite (990 SAT composite) and a minimum 2.0 high school GPA (4.0 scale). Test scores, special talents, recommendations, essay or personal statement considered. Essay recommended. **Homeschooled:** Transcript of courses and grades required. Entrance requirements for home schooled students: 2.75 HS GPA; 21 ACT or 980 SAT (excluding writing). **Learning Disabled:** Admissions process is the same for all prospective students. Once students with any disability are accepted, they may then choose to register for services with the Office for Students with Disabilities.

High school preparation. 14 units required; 15 recommended. Required and recommended units include English 4, mathematics 3, social studies 1, history 1, science 2-4 (laboratory 2), foreign language 2 and visual/performing arts 1. Math units must include algebra I and II, and geometry. Foreign language units must be in same language. History unit should be US history. Social studies unit should be world history, European history or world geography.

2008-2009 Annual costs. Tuition/fees: $5,310; $15,870 out-of-state. Room/board: $6,983. Books/supplies: $1,000. Personal expenses: $1,402.

2008-2009 Financial aid. Need-based: 1,974 full-time freshmen applied for aid; 1,181 were judged to have need; 1,168 of these received aid. Average need met was 86%. Average scholarship/grant was $4,270; average loan $3,803. 46% of total undergraduate aid awarded as scholarships/grants, 54% as loans/jobs. **Non-need-based:** Awarded to 3,733 full-time undergraduates, including 1,306 freshmen. Scholarships awarded for academics, alumni affiliation, art, athletics, job skills, leadership, minority status, music/drama, religious affiliation, ROTC, state residency.

Application procedures. Admission: Closing date 8/1. $30 fee, may be waived for applicants with need. Admission notification on a rolling basis. **Financial aid:** Priority date 4/1; no closing date. FAFSA, institutional form required. Applicants notified on a rolling basis starting 3/1; must reply within 6 week(s) of notification.

Academics. Special study options: Combined bachelor's/graduate degree, cooperative education, cross-registration, distance learning, double major, dual enrollment of high school students, ESL, honors, independent study, internships, study abroad, teacher certification program. Cooperative program in criminal justice with Cleveland State Community College. **Credit/placement by examination:** AP, CLEP, SAT, ACT, institutional tests. 24 credit hours maximum toward bachelor's degree. May only be used for elective credit hours. **Support services:** Learning center, pre-admission summer program, reduced course load, remedial instruction, study skills assistance, tutoring, writing center.

Honors college/program. Application, teacher evaluations, essay, official high school transcript, and ACT or SAT scores. About 45 applicants receive invitations to join each year.

Majors. Biology: General. **Business:** Business admin. **Communications:** General. **Computer sciences:** Computer science. **Conservation:** Environmental science. **Education:** Art, early childhood, English, foreign languages, mathematics, middle, music, science, social studies, special. **Engineering:** General, electrical, mechanical. **Engineering technology:** Industrial management. **Family/consumer sciences:** General. **Foreign languages:** General. **Health:** Clinical lab science, nursing (RN). **History:** General. **Legal studies:** Paralegal. **Liberal arts:** Humanities. **Math:** General, applied. **Parks/recreation:** Exercise sciences. **Physical sciences:** Chemistry, geology, physics. **Protective services:** Law enforcement admin. **Psychology:** General. **Public administration:** Community org/advocacy, social work. **Social sciences:** General, economics, political science, sociology. **Visual/performing arts:** Art, dramatic, interior design. **Other:** Philosophy and religion, Sociology and anthropology.

Most popular majors. Biology 6%, business/marketing 24%, education 6%, family/consumer sciences 11%, psychology 8%, social sciences 6%.

Computing on campus. 1,200 workstations in library, computer center, student center. Dormitories wired for high-speed internet access and linked to campus network. Commuter students can connect to campus network. Online course registration, online library, helpline, repair service, wireless network available.

Student life. Freshman orientation: Mandatory, $65 fee. Preregistration for classes offered. Held in summer, 2 days, at 7 different times. **Housing:** Coed dorms, apartments, fraternity/sorority housing, wellness housing available. $75 partly refundable deposit. **Activities:** Bands, campus ministries, choral groups, dance, drama, film society, international student organizations, music ensembles, radio station, student government, student newspaper, symphony orchestra, several religious, political, ethnic, and social service organizations.

Athletics. NCAA. **Intercollegiate:** Basketball, cross-country, football (tackle) M, golf, rowing (crew), soccer W, softball W, tennis, track and field, volleyball W, wrestling M. **Intramural:** Archery, badminton, basketball, bowling, fencing, football (non-tackle), golf, racquetball, soccer, softball W, swimming, table tennis, tennis, track and field, volleyball, weight lifting, wrestling M. **Team name:** Mocs.

Student services. Adult student services, chaplain/spiritual director, career counseling, student employment services, financial aid counseling, health services, minority student services, on-campus daycare, personal counseling, placement for graduates, veterans' counselor, women's services. **Physically disabled:** Services for visually, speech, hearing impaired. **Learning disabled:** Comprehensive services available.

Contact. E-mail: yancy-freeman@utc.edu
Phone: (423) 425-4662 Toll-free number: (800) 882-6627
Fax: (423) 425-4157
Yancy Freeman, Director of Student Recruitment and Admissions, University of Tennessee: Chattanooga, 615 McCallie Avenue, Chattanooga, TN 37403

University of Tennessee: Knoxville

Knoxville, Tennessee — **CB member**
www.utk.edu — **CB code: 1843**

- Public 4-year university
- Residential campus in large city
- 21,378 degree-seeking undergraduates: 5% part-time, 50% women, 8% African American, 3% Asian American, 2% Hispanic American, 1% international
- 8,367 degree-seeking graduate students
- 65% of applicants admitted
- SAT or ACT (ACT writing optional) required
- 60% graduate within 6 years

General. Founded in 1794. Regionally accredited. **Degrees:** 3,655 bachelor's awarded; master's, doctoral, first professional offered. **ROTC:** Army, Air Force. **Location:** 224 miles from Atlanta, 178 miles from Nashville. **Calendar:** Semester, extensive summer session. **Full-time faculty:** 1,562 total; 83% have terminal degrees, 13% minority, 39% women. **Part-time faculty:** 130 total; 67% have terminal degrees, 12% minority, 35% women. **Class size:** 30% < 20, 57% 20-39, 5% 40-49, 5% 50-99, 3% >100. **Special facilities:** 2 theaters, science/engineering research facility, international house, Olympic track, baseball stadium.

Freshman class profile. 13,894 applied, 8,999 admitted, 4,215 enrolled.

Mid 50% test scores		**Rank in top quarter:**	71%
SAT critical reading:	530-630	**Rank in top tenth:**	41%
SAT math:	540-640	**Return as sophomores:**	84%
ACT composite:	24-29	**Out-of-state:**	13%
GPA 3.75 or higher:	56%	**Live on campus:**	95%
GPA 3.50-3.74:	15%	**International:**	1%
GPA 3.0-3.49:	22%	**Fraternities:**	22%
GPA 2.0-2.99:	7%	**Sororities:**	25%

Basis for selection. Admission based on high school grades in core academic subjects and standardized test scores. Other factors that indicate future academic success considered, as are special talents, student statement, extracurricular leadership, community involvement, class rank, and background. Essay not required but preferred; portfolio required for architecture and interior design; audition required for music.

High school preparation. College-preparatory program required. 14 units required. Required units include English 4, mathematics 3, social studies 1, history 1, science 2 (laboratory 1), foreign language 2 and visual/performing arts 1. Social science units must be 1 U.S. history and either world history, European history, or world geography. Mathematics units must include algebra I, algebra II, and 1 unit of either geometry, trigonometry, advanced mathematics, or calculus.

2008-2009 Annual costs. Tuition/fees: $6,250; $18,908 out-of-state. Out-of-state students pay additional required fees of $300. Room/board: $6,888. Books/supplies: $1,326. Personal expenses: $3,104.

2008-2009 Financial aid. All financial aid based on need. 3,966 full-time freshmen applied for aid; 1,990 were judged to have need; 1,967 of these received aid. Average need met was 79%. Average scholarship/grant was $2,746; average loan $3,708. 51% of total undergraduate aid awarded as scholarships/grants, 49% as loans/jobs. **Additional information:** Application priority date for scholarships 2/1.

Application procedures. Admission: Closing date 12/1 (postmark date). $30 fee, may be waived for applicants with need. Priority applicants notified in January. Regular applicants notified in March. Must reply by 5/1. **Financial aid:** Priority date 3/1; no closing date. FAFSA required. Applicants notified on a rolling basis starting 3/15; must reply within 3 week(s) of notification.

Academics. Special study options: Combined bachelor's/graduate degree, cooperative education, distance learning, double major, dual enrollment of high school students, ESL, exchange student, external degree, honors, independent study, internships, liberal arts/career combination, student-designed major, study abroad, teacher certification program. **Credit/placement by examination:** AP, CLEP, IB, institutional tests. Departmental proficiency available. Up to 50 hours of credit awarded for International Baccalaureate. **Support services:** Learning center, study skills assistance, tutoring, writing center.

Majors. Agriculture: Animal sciences, economics, food science, ornamental horticulture, plant sciences, soil chem/physics. **Architecture:** Architecture. **Area/ethnic studies:** African-American, American, Asian, Latin American, Russian/Slavic, women's. **Biology:** General. **Business:** General, accounting, business admin, finance, hotel/motel admin, human resources, logistics, managerial economics, marketing, tourism/travel. **Communications:** Advertising, journalism, public relations. **Computer sciences:** Computer science. **Conservation:** Forestry, wildlife. **Education:** Agricultural, art, Deaf/hearing impaired, music, special. **Engineering:** Aerospace, agricultural, biomedical, chemical, civil, computer, electrical, industrial, materials, materials science, mechanical, nuclear, physics, science. **Family/consumer sciences:** Consumer economics, family studies, food/nutrition. **Foreign languages:** Ancient Greek, classics, comparative lit, French, German, Italian, Latin, Portuguese, Russian, Spanish. **Health:** Audiology/hearing, clinical lab science, nursing (RN), occupational health nursing, predental, premedicine, prepharmacy, preveterinary, speech pathology. **History:** General. **Interdisciplinary:** Medieval/Renaissance. **Legal studies:** Prelaw. **Math:** General, statistics. **Parks/recreation:** General, exercise sciences, sports admin. **Philosophy/religion:** Philosophy, religion. **Physical sciences:** Chemistry, geology, physics. **Psychology:** General. **Public administration:** General. **Social sciences:** Anthropology, economics, geography, political science, sociology. **Visual/performing arts:** Art, art history/conservation, commercial/advertising art, dramatic, interior design, music theory/composition, piano/organ, studio arts, voice/opera. **Other:** Journalism and electronic media.

Most popular majors. Business/marketing 18%, communications/journalism 10%, engineering/engineering technologies 8%, psychology 10%, social sciences 12%.

Computing on campus. 1,000 workstations in dormitories, library, computer center, student center. Dormitories wired for high-speed internet access and linked to campus network. Commuter students can connect to campus network. Online course registration, online library, helpline, repair service, student web hosting, wireless network available.

Student life. Freshman orientation: Mandatory, $99 fee. Preregistration for classes offered. 2 days. Parents may attend orientation for $35 per parent; does not include housing. **Policies:** Freshmen must live on campus unless residing with parent or legal guardian. **Housing:** Guaranteed on-campus for freshmen. Coed dorms, single-sex dorms, special housing for disabled, apartments, fraternity/sorority housing available. $100 fully refundable deposit. Transfer student floors available. **Activities:** Bands, campus ministries, choral groups, dance, drama, film society, international student organizations, literary magazine, music ensembles, Model UN, musical theater, opera, radio station, student government, student newspaper, symphony orchestra, TV station, Black cultural center, student political, ethnic, social, and service organizations, women's center, various denomination student unions.

Athletics. NCAA. **Intercollegiate:** Baseball M, basketball, cricket, cross-country, diving, football (tackle) M, golf, rowing (crew) W, soccer W, softball W, swimming, tennis, track and field, volleyball W. **Intramural:** Badminton, basketball, bowling, cross-country, field hockey, golf, racquetball, skin diving, soccer, softball, swimming, table tennis, tennis, track and field, volleyball. **Team name:** Volunteers.

Student services. Adult student services, alcohol/substance abuse counseling, chaplain/spiritual director, career counseling, student employment services, financial aid counseling, health services, minority student services, on-campus daycare, personal counseling, placement for graduates, veterans' counselor, women's services. **Physically disabled:** Services for visually, speech, hearing impaired.

Contact. E-mail: admissions@utk.edu
Phone: (865) 974-2184 Fax: (865) 974-1182
Nancy McGlasson, Director of Admissions, University of Tennessee: Knoxville, 320 Student Services Building, Knoxville, TN 37996-0230

University of Tennessee: Martin

Martin, Tennessee
www.utm.edu **CB code: 1844**

- Public 4-year university
- Commuter campus in small town
- 6,090 degree-seeking undergraduates: 10% part-time, 57% women, 15% African American, 1% Asian American, 1% Hispanic American, 2% international
- 369 degree-seeking graduate students
- 75% of applicants admitted
- SAT or ACT (ACT writing optional) required
- 49% graduate within 6 years; 18% enter graduate study

General. Founded in 1927. Regionally accredited. Sponsors only collegiate rodeo team in Tennessee; coordinates online education for UT system. **Degrees:** 998 bachelor's awarded; master's offered. **ROTC:** Army. **Location:** 125 miles from Memphis, 150 miles from Nashville. **Calendar:** Semester, extensive summer session. **Full-time faculty:** 263 total; 77% have terminal degrees, 8% minority, 44% women. **Part-time faculty:** 262 total; 24% have terminal degrees, 4% minority, 54% women. **Class size:** 51% < 20, 37% 20-39, 5% 40-49, 7% 50-99, less than 1% >100. **Special facilities:** Center for global studies and international education, four off-campus educational centers, four compressed video classrooms, network of compressed video classes across the state, teacher resource center, 680-acre agriculture, natural resources teaching, demonstration complex, teaching/research facility resort.

Freshman class profile. 3,283 applied, 2,478 admitted, 1,392 enrolled.

Mid 50% test scores		**End year in good standing:**	72%
ACT composite:	20-25	**Return as sophomores:**	71%
GPA 3.75 or higher:	27%	**Out-of-state:**	4%
GPA 3.50-3.74:	17%	**Live on campus:**	70%
GPA 3.0-3.49:	36%	**International:**	2%
GPA 2.0-2.99:	20%	**Fraternities:**	23%
Rank in top quarter:	53%	**Sororities:**	12%
Rank in top tenth:	26%		

Basis for selection. High School GPA of 2.85 and minimum ACT composite score of 18, or GPA of 2.50 and minimum ACT score of 21. Students not meeting regular admission requirements may be considered for conditional admission. **Homeschooled:** 21 ACT and 2.85 GPA.

High school preparation. College-preparatory program required. 14 units required. Required units include English 4, mathematics 3, history 2, science 2 (laboratory 1) and foreign language 2. 1 visual and performing arts.

2008-2009 Annual costs. Tuition/fees: $5,255; $15,897 out-of-state. Room/board: $4,606. Books/supplies: $1,200. Personal expenses: $2,240.

2008-2009 Financial aid. All financial aid based on need. 1,320 full-time freshmen applied for aid; 909 were judged to have need; 902 of these received aid. Average need met was 83%. Average scholarship/grant was $5,774; average loan $2,693. 59% of total undergraduate aid awarded as scholarships/grants, 41% as loans/jobs.

Application procedures. Admission: Priority date 2/1; deadline 8/1. $30 fee. Admission notification on a rolling basis beginning on or about 9/1. **Financial aid:** Priority date 3/1; no closing date. FAFSA required. Applicants notified on a rolling basis starting 4/1.

Academics. Special study options: Accelerated study, cooperative education, cross-registration, distance learning, double major, dual enrollment of high school students, ESL, exchange student, honors, independent study, internships, student-designed major, study abroad, teacher certification program. 3-1 pharmacy program, 3-1 veterinary medicine program, 3-1 dentistry program, 3-1 medicine program, 3-1 optometry program, 3-1 podiatry program, 3-1 chiropractory program. **Credit/placement by examination:** AP, CLEP, SAT, ACT, institutional tests. 30 credit hours maximum toward bachelor's degree. **Support services:** Learning center, remedial instruction, study skills assistance, tutoring, writing center.

Majors. Agriculture: General. **Biology:** General. **Business:** Accounting, business admin, finance, management information systems, managerial economics, marketing. **Communications:** General. **Computer sciences:** Computer science. **Conservation:** Management/policy. **Education:** Biology, business, chemistry, English, French, geography, German, history, mathematics, Spanish, special. **Engineering:** General. **Family/consumer sciences:** General. **Foreign languages:** French, Spanish. **Health:** Health services, nursing (RN). **History:** General. **Math:** General. **Parks/recreation:** Health/fitness. **Philosophy/religion:** Philosophy. **Physical sciences:** Chemistry, geology. **Protective services:** Law enforcement admin. **Psychology:** General. **Public administration:** Social work. **Social sciences:** International relations, political science, sociology. **Visual/performing arts:** General.

Most popular majors. Agriculture 6%, business/marketing 20%, health sciences 6%, interdisciplinary studies 23%.

Computing on campus. 234 workstations in dormitories, library, student center. Dormitories wired for high-speed internet access and linked to campus network. Commuter students can connect to campus network. Online course registration, online library, helpline, repair service, student web hosting, wireless network available.

Student life. Freshman orientation: Available, $165 fee. Preregistration for classes offered. 4-day program held in August. **Policies:** Freshmen must live on campus. **Housing:** Guaranteed on-campus for freshmen. Coed dorms, single-sex dorms, special housing for disabled, apartments, fraternity/sorority housing available. $100 fully refundable deposit, deadline 8/1. **Activities:** Bands, campus ministries, choral groups, dance, drama, international student organizations, literary magazine, music ensembles, opera, radio station, student government, student newspaper, TV station, Chi Alpha Christian Fellowship, Interfaith Student Center, Rotaract, Free Thinkers Club, Fellowship of Christian Athletes, College Democrats, College Republicans, Reformed University Fellowship, Japanese Animation Research Society.

Athletics. NCAA. **Intercollegiate:** Baseball M, basketball, cheerleading M, cross-country, equestrian W, football (tackle) M, golf M, rifle, rodeo, soccer W, softball W, tennis, volleyball W. **Intramural:** Cross-country, football (non-tackle), golf, soccer, tennis, volleyball. **Team name:** Skyhawks.

Student services. Adult student services, alcohol/substance abuse counseling, chaplain/spiritual director, career counseling, services for economically disadvantaged, student employment services, financial aid counseling, health services, minority student services, on-campus daycare, personal counseling, placement for graduates, veterans' counselor, women's services. **Physically disabled:** Services for visually, speech, hearing impaired. **Learning disabled:** Comprehensive services available.

Contact. E-mail: admitme@utm.edu
Phone: (731) 881-7020 Toll-free number: (800) 829-8861
Fax: (731) 881-7029
Judy Rayburn, Director of Admissions, University of Tennessee: Martin, 200 Hall Moody Administration Building, Martin, TN 38238

University of the South

Sewanee, Tennessee
www.sewanee.edu

CB member
CB code: 1842

- Private 4-year university affiliated with Episcopal Church
- Residential campus in rural community
- 1,464 degree-seeking undergraduates: 53% women, 4% African American, 3% Asian American, 3% Hispanic American, 1% Native American, 2% international
- 76 degree-seeking graduate students
- 64% of applicants admitted
- Application essay required
- 77% graduate within 6 years

General. Founded in 1857. Regionally accredited; also accredited by ATS. **Degrees:** 382 bachelor's awarded; master's, doctoral, first professional offered. **Location:** 45 miles from Chattanooga, 57 miles from Huntsville. **Calendar:** Semester, limited summer session. **Full-time faculty:** 132 total; 90% have terminal degrees, 11% minority, 37% women. **Part-time faculty:** 39 total; 77% have terminal degrees, 3% minority, 38% women. **Class size:** 71% < 20, 27% 20-39, 1% 40-49, less than 1% 50-99. **Special facilities:** Landscape analysis lab, observatory, materials analysis laboratory with electron microscopy, 13,000- acre wooded campus, hiking and horseback riding trails, climbing.

Freshman class profile. 2,488 applied, 1,593 admitted, 410 enrolled.

Mid 50% test scores			
SAT critical reading:	570-680	Rank in top quarter:	67%
SAT math:	580-680	Rank in top tenth:	49%
ACT composite:	26-30	Return as sophomores:	88%
GPA 3.75 or higher:	42%	Out-of-state:	78%
GPA 3.50-3.74:	19%	Live on campus:	100%
GPA 3.0-3.49:	30%	International:	2%
GPA 2.0-2.99:	9%	Fraternities:	65%
		Sororities:	71%

Basis for selection. GED not accepted. School achievement record, recommendations, extracurricular activities, test scores, essay important. Children of alumni and minority applicants given special consideration. SAT or ACT recommended. Interview recommended.

High school preparation. College-preparatory program required. 13 units required; 20 recommended. Required and recommended units include English 4, mathematics 3-4, social studies 1-2, history 1-2, science 2-4 (laboratory 2-3) and foreign language 2-4.

2009-2010 Annual costs. Tuition/fees: $34,172. Room/board: $9,760. Books/supplies: $800. Personal expenses: $900.

2008-2009 Financial aid. Need-based: 234 full-time freshmen applied for aid; 161 were judged to have need; 160 of these received aid. Average need met was 98%. Average scholarship/grant was $25,676; average loan $3,759. 83% of total undergraduate aid awarded as scholarships/grants, 17% as loans/jobs. **Non-need-based:** Awarded to 339 full-time undergraduates, including 95 freshmen. Scholarships awarded for academics, minority status, religious affiliation.

Application procedures. Admission: Closing date 2/1 (postmark date). $45 fee, may be waived for applicants with need, free for online applicants. Admission notification 4/1. Must reply by 5/1. Must reply by May 1 or within 2 week(s) if notified thereafter. **Financial aid:** Priority date 3/1; no closing date. FAFSA, institutional form required. Applicants notified by 4/1; must reply within 4 week(s) of notification.

Academics. Special study options: Double major, independent study, internships, semester at sea, student-designed major, study abroad, teacher certification program, Washington semester. Oak Ridge semester in experimental science, summer science program on St. Catherines Island, Georgia. **Credit/placement by examination:** AP, CLEP, IB, SAT, ACT, institutional tests. 60 credit hours maximum toward bachelor's degree. **Support services:** Tutoring.

Majors. Area/ethnic studies: American, Asian, French, German, Russian/Slavic. **Biology:** General, biochemistry. **Computer sciences:** General, computer science. **Conservation:** Environmental studies, forestry, management/policy. **Foreign languages:** Ancient Greek, comparative lit, French, German, Latin, modern Greek, Russian, Spanish. **History:** General. **Interdisciplinary:** Global studies, math/computer science, medieval/Renaissance. **Math:** General. **Philosophy/religion:** Philosophy, religion. **Physical sciences:** Chemistry, geology, physics. **Psychology:** General. **Social sciences:** Anthropology, economics, political science. **Visual/performing arts:** General, art history/conservation, studio arts.

Most popular majors. Biology 6%, English 12%, foreign language 10%, history 12%, philosophy/religious studies 7%, psychology 7%, social sciences 22%, visual/performing arts 9%.

Computing on campus. 200 workstations in dormitories, library, computer center. Dormitories wired for high-speed internet access and linked to campus network. Commuter students can connect to campus network. Online course registration, online library, helpline, repair service, student web hosting, wireless network available.

Student life. Freshman orientation: Mandatory. Preregistration for classes offered. Several days before the college opens in the fall. Students dine with the faculty advisor, sign the Honor Code, and participate in discussions of the summer reading. **Policies:** Student-administered honor code strictly observed. **Housing:** Guaranteed on-campus for freshmen. Coed dorms, single-sex dorms, special housing for disabled, apartments, fraternity/sorority housing, wellness housing available. $300 nonrefundable deposit, deadline 5/1. **Activities:** Jazz band, campus ministries, choral groups, dance, drama, film society, international student organizations, literary magazine, music ensembles, Model UN, musical theater, radio station, student government, student newspaper, symphony orchestra, tutoring center for disadvantaged youth, religious organizations, Big Brother-Big Sister program.

Athletics. NCAA. **Intercollegiate:** Baseball M, basketball, cross-country, diving, equestrian, fencing, field hockey W, football (tackle) M, golf, lacrosse, rowing (crew), rugby M, skiing, soccer, softball W, swimming, tennis, track and field, volleyball W. **Intramural:** Basketball, cross-country, diving, golf, handball, racquetball, skin diving, soccer, softball, swimming, table tennis, tennis, track and field, volleyball, wrestling M. **Team name:** Tigers.

Student services. Chaplain/spiritual director, career counseling, student employment services, health services, minority student services, on-campus daycare, personal counseling, placement for graduates, women's services. **Physically disabled:** Services for visually, hearing impaired.

Contact. E-mail: admiss@sewanee.edu
Phone: (931) 598-1238 Toll-free number: (800) 522-2234
Fax: (931) 538-3248
David Lesesne, Dean of Admission, University of the South, Office of Admission, Sewanee, TN 37383-1000

Vanderbilt University

Nashville, Tennessee **CB member**
www.vanderbilt.edu **CB code: 1871**

- Private 4-year university
- Residential campus in very large city
- 6,598 degree-seeking undergraduates: 52% women, 9% African American, 7% Asian American, 6% Hispanic American, 3% international
- 5,341 degree-seeking graduate students
- 25% of applicants admitted
- SAT or ACT with writing, application essay required
- 89% graduate within 6 years; 37% enter graduate study

General. Founded in 1873. Regionally accredited. **Degrees:** 1,542 bachelor's awarded; master's, doctoral, first professional offered. **ROTC:** Army, Naval, Air Force. **Location:** 240 miles from Atlanta, 300 miles from St. Louis. **Calendar:** Semester, limited summer session. **Full-time faculty:** 866 total; 97% have terminal degrees, 15% minority, 34% women. **Class size:** 64% < 20, 26% 20-39, 3% 40-49, 4% 50-99, 2% >100. **Special facilities:** Observatory, electron microscopes, television news archive, national arboretum, video productions, Black cultural center, women's center, cinema and art museum.

Freshman class profile. 16,944 applied, 4,292 admitted, 1,569 enrolled.

Mid 50% test scores			
SAT critical reading:	650-740	Rank in top quarter:	97%
SAT math:	680-760	Rank in top tenth:	84%
SAT writing:	650-730	Return as sophomores:	97%
ACT composite:	30-33	Out-of-state:	84%
GPA 3.75 or higher:	55%	Live on campus:	100%
GPA 3.50-3.74:	24%	International:	5%
GPA 3.0-3.49:	20%	Fraternities:	42%
GPA 2.0-2.99:	1%	Sororities:	53%

Basis for selection. Academic achievement, recommendation, essay, test scores, activities important. SAT Subject Tests recommended. Recommend SAT Subject tests and ACT exams but not required for admission. Audition required for music program. **Homeschooled:** Statement describing homeschool structure and mission required.

High school preparation. College-preparatory program required. 18 units required; 21 recommended. Required and recommended units include English 4, mathematics 3-4, social studies 2-3, history 1, science 3-4 (laboratory 2-3), foreign language 2 and academic electives 3. Additional unit in mathematics and 2 in science recommended for engineering applicants. Blair School of Music does not require 2 units of science. School of Engineering recommends 2 years of language. Peabody College of Education & Human Development does not require language. Blair, Engineering, and Peabody require 1 year of history.

2008-2009 Annual costs. Tuition/fees: $37,005. Room/board: $12,028. Books/supplies: $1,208. Personal expenses: $2,062.

2008-2009 Financial aid. Need-based: 788 full-time freshmen applied for aid; 660 were judged to have need; 659 of these received aid. Average need met was 100%. Average scholarship/grant was $31,711; average loan $2,899. 87% of total undergraduate aid awarded as scholarships/grants, 13% as loans/jobs. **Non-need-based:** Awarded to 2,379 full-time undergraduates, including 636 freshmen. Scholarships awarded for academics, athletics, leadership, minority status, music/drama, ROTC, state residency. **Additional information:** Financial aid packages for incoming students do not include need-based loans. Need-based loans replaced with increased amounts of scholarship and/or grant assistance.

Application procedures. Admission: Closing date 1/3 (postmark date). $50 fee, may be waived for applicants with need. Admission notification 4/1. Must reply by 5/1. **Financial aid:** Priority date 2/1; no closing date. FAFSA, CSS PROFILE required. Applicants notified on a rolling basis starting 4/1; must reply by 5/1.

Academics. All undergraduates take portion of coursework in College of Arts and Science. **Special study options:** Accelerated study, combined bachelor's/graduate degree, cooperative education, cross-registration, distance learning, double major, dual enrollment of high school students, ESL, honors, independent study, internships, student-designed major, study abroad, teacher certification program, Washington semester. **Credit/placement by examination:** AP, CLEP, IB, institutional tests. 30 credit hours maximum toward bachelor's degree. **Support services:** Learning center, study skills assistance, tutoring, writing center.

Majors. Area/ethnic studies: African-American, American, Central/Eastern European, East Asian, European, German, Latin American, regional, Russian/Slavic, Spanish/Iberian, Western European, women's. **Biology:** General, molecular. **Communications:** General. **Computer sciences:** Computer science. **Education:** General, early childhood, elementary, secondary, special. **Engineering:** Biomedical, chemical, civil, computer. **Foreign languages:** Classics, French, German, Romance, Russian, Spanish. **History:** General. **Interdisciplinary:** Classical/archaeology, cognitive science, natural sciences, neuroscience, science/society. **Math:** General. **Philosophy/religion:** Judaic, philosophy, religion. **Physical sciences:** Chemistry, geology, physics. **Psychology:** General. **Social sciences:** General, anthropology, applied economics, economics, international economic development, political science, sociology, urban studies. **Visual/performing arts:** Art, art history/conservation, dramatic, film/cinema, music performance, music theory/composition, piano/organ, stringed instruments, studio arts, voice/opera. **Other:** Language and literacy studies.

Most popular majors. Engineering/engineering technologies 15%, foreign language 7%, interdisciplinary studies 7%, psychology 6%, social sciences 32%.

Computing on campus. 400 workstations in library, computer center, student center. Dormitories wired for high-speed internet access and linked to campus network. Commuter students can connect to campus network. Online course registration, online library, helpline, repair service, student web hosting, wireless network available.

Student life. Freshman orientation: Mandatory. Preregistration for classes offered. **Housing:** Guaranteed on-campus for freshmen. Coed dorms, single-sex dorms, special housing for disabled, apartments, wellness housing available. **Activities:** Bands, campus ministries, choral groups, dance, drama, film society, literary magazine, music ensembles, Model UN, musical theater, opera, radio station, student government, student newspaper, symphony orchestra, TV station, over 400 clubs and organizations.

Athletics. NCAA. **Intercollegiate:** Baseball M, basketball, bowling W, cheerleading, cross-country, football (tackle) M, golf, lacrosse W, soccer W, swimming W, tennis, track and field W. **Intramural:** Badminton, basketball, bowling, football (non-tackle), golf, racquetball, soccer, softball, squash, swimming, table tennis, tennis, track and field, volleyball, water polo, wrestling. **Team name:** Commodores.

Student services. Alcohol/substance abuse counseling, chaplain/spiritual director, career counseling, student employment services, financial aid counseling, health services, minority student services, on-campus daycare, personal counseling, placement for graduates, women's services. **Physically disabled:** Services for visually, speech, hearing impaired.

Contact. E-mail: admissions@vanderbilt.edu
Phone: (615) 322-2561 Toll-free number: (800) 288-0432
Fax: (615) 343-7765
John Gaines, Director, Enrollment Management, Vanderbilt University, 2305 West End Avenue, Nashville, TN 37203-1727

Visible School - Music and Worship Arts College

Lakeland, Tennessee
www.visibleschool.com

- Private 3-year Bible and performing arts college affiliated with Christian Church
- Very large city
- 91 degree-seeking undergraduates
- SAT or ACT (ACT writing optional), application essay, interview required

General. Candidate for regional accreditation. VISIBLE SCHOOL is a small community of musicians, music business professionals and producers. We provide excellent hands-on training for our students who want to be worship leaders, recording artists, touring musicians, record producers, managers, etc. All the while receiving practical ministry training and discipleship. **Degrees:** 9 bachelor's awarded. **Location:** 4 miles east of Memphis, TN. **Calendar:** Semester, limited summer session. **Full-time faculty:** 18 total. **Part-time faculty:** 2 total.

Basis for selection. Students must have a personal relationship with Jesus Christ, having had a salvation experience. Require ACT score of 18; SAT combined score (reading and math) 750; SAT combined score (reading, math, writing) 1500. Students applying to the Modern Music Ministry program must also complete an audition.

2008-2009 Annual costs. Tuition/fees: $15,800. Room only: $3,400.

Application procedures. Admission: No deadline.

Academics. Credit/placement by examination: CLEP.

Majors. Communications: Digital media. **Theology:** Theology. **Visual/performing arts:** Music management, music performance.

Contact. E-mail: seeyourself@visibleschool.com
Phone: (901) 381-3939 ext. 206 Toll-free number: (877) 558-4742
Fax: (901) 377-0544
Heather Isaac, Admissions Coordinator, Visible School - Music and Worship Arts College, 9817 Huff n Puff Road, Lakeland, TN 38002

Watkins College of Art, Design and Film
Nashville, Tennessee
www.watkins.edu

- Private 4-year visual arts college
- Very large city
- 385 degree-seeking undergraduates

General. Candidate for regional accreditation. **Calendar:** Semester. **Full-time faculty:** 19 total. **Part-time faculty:** 26 total.

Freshman class profile. 57 enrolled.

2009-2010 Annual costs. Tuition/fees (projected): $17,700.

Application procedures. Admission: Closing date 7/15.

Academics. Credit/placement by examination: CLEP.

Majors. Visual/performing arts: Art, film/cinema, graphic design, interior design, photography, studio arts.

Contact. E-mail: admissions@watkins.edu
Phone: (615) 383-4848
Linda Schwab, Director of Admissions, Watkins College of Art, Design and Film, 2298 Rosa L. Parks Boulevard, Nashville, TN 37228

Williamson Christian College
Franklin, Tennessee
www.williamsoncc.edu

- Private 4-year liberal arts college affiliated with interdenominational tradition
- Commuter campus in small city
- 80 degree-seeking undergraduates

General. Accredited by ABHE. Accelerated degree completion programs available for working adults. **Degrees:** 9 bachelor's awarded. **Location:** 15 miles from downtown. **Calendar:** Semester, limited summer session. **Full-time faculty:** 5 total. **Part-time faculty:** 25 total. **Class size:** 100% < 20.

Basis for selection. Open admission, but selective for some programs.

2008-2009 Annual costs. Tuition/fees: $9,540. Books/supplies: $800. Personal expenses: $3,800.

Application procedures. Admission: No deadline. $25 fee. Application must be submitted on paper. Admission notification on a rolling basis. **Financial aid:** No deadline.

Academics. Special study options: Accelerated study, distance learning, liberal arts/career combination, weekend college. **Credit/placement by examination:** AP, CLEP. 15 credit hours maximum toward associate degree, 32 toward bachelor's.

Majors. Business: Nonprofit/public. **Philosophy/religion:** Religion.

Most popular majors. Business/marketing 50%, philosophy/religious studies 50%.

Computing on campus. 3 workstations in computer center. Wireless network available.

Student life. Freshman orientation: Mandatory. Preregistration for classes offered. **Activities:** Student government, student newspaper.

Student services. Adult student services, chaplain/spiritual director, financial aid counseling, personal counseling.

Contact. E-mail: chris@williamsoncc.edu
Phone: (615) 771-7821 Fax: (615) 771-7810
Steve Smith, Director of Admissions, Williamson Christian College, 200 Seaboard Lane, Franklin, TN 37067

Texas

Abilene Christian University

Abilene, Texas **CB member**
www.acu.edu **CB code: 6001**

- Private 4-year university affiliated with Church of Christ
- Residential campus in small city
- 3,845 degree-seeking undergraduates: 6% part-time, 54% women, 8% African American, 1% Asian American, 6% Hispanic American, 1% Native American, 4% international
- 763 degree-seeking graduate students
- 47% of applicants admitted
- SAT or ACT (ACT writing recommended) required
- 58% graduate within 6 years

General. Founded in 1906. Regionally accredited. **Degrees:** 851 bachelor's, 3 associate awarded; master's, doctoral, first professional offered. **Location:** 180 miles from Dallas. **Calendar:** Semester, limited summer session. **Full-time faculty:** 227 total; 82% have terminal degrees, 10% minority, 34% women. **Part-time faculty:** 140 total; 34% have terminal degrees, 3% minority, 33% women. **Class size:** 47% < 20, 40% 20-39, 6% 40-49, 5% 50-99, less than 1% >100. **Special facilities:** Museum of university's history, Center for Restoration Studies, Voice Institute, demonstration farm and ranch, observatory.

Freshman class profile. 3,897 applied, 1,820 admitted, 971 enrolled.

Mid 50% test scores		**GPA 2.0-2.99:**	12%
SAT critical reading:	490-610	**Rank in top quarter:**	53%
SAT math:	490-620	**Rank in top tenth:**	23%
ACT composite:	21-27	**Return as sophomores:**	74%
GPA 3.75 or higher:	31%	**Out-of-state:**	14%
GPA 3.50-3.74:	32%	**Live on campus:**	96%
GPA 3.0-3.49:	24%	**International:**	2%

Basis for selection. Rank in top half of class and/or 960 SAT (exclusive of Writing) or 20 ACT required. Interview, portfolio recommended for all; audition required for debate, forensics, music, theater programs. **Homeschooled:** Transcript of courses and grades required.

High school preparation. College-preparatory program required. 12 units recommended. Recommended units include English 4, mathematics 3, science 3 (laboratory 2) and foreign language 2.

2008-2009 Annual costs. Tuition/fees: $18,855. Room/board: $7,236. Books/supplies: $1,150. Personal expenses: $1,794.

2007-2008 Financial aid. Need-based: 753 full-time freshmen applied for aid; 596 were judged to have need; 596 of these received aid. Average need met was 76%. Average scholarship/grant was $10,998; average loan $3,378. 66% of total undergraduate aid awarded as scholarships/grants, 34% as loans/jobs. **Non-need-based:** Awarded to 2,723 full-time undergraduates, including 674 freshmen. Scholarships awarded for academics, art, athletics, leadership, minority status, music/drama, religious affiliation, state residency. **Additional information:** Early estimate service available.

Application procedures. Admission: Priority date 2/1; deadline 8/1 (postmark date). $50 fee. Admission notification on a rolling basis beginning on or about 8/1. Admitted students planning on enrolling should confirm the offer by submitting $250 enrollment deposit (non-refundable after May 1), along with letter of intent to the Admissions Office. Enrollment deposit is a pre-payment toward your total bill. **Financial aid:** Priority date 3/1; no closing date. FAFSA, institutional form required. Applicants notified on a rolling basis starting 4/1.

Academics. Special study options: Combined bachelor's/graduate degree, cross-registration, distance learning, double major, dual enrollment of high school students, ESL, honors, independent study, internships, student-designed major, study abroad, teacher certification program. Campus abroad programs in England, Mexico, Uruguay; pass/fail grading option. **Credit/placement by examination:** AP, CLEP, IB, SAT, ACT, institutional tests. 15 credit hours maximum toward associate degree, 30 toward bachelor's. **Support services:** Pre-admission summer program, reduced course load, remedial instruction, study skills assistance, tutoring, writing center.

Majors. Agriculture: Agribusiness operations, animal sciences. **Biology:** General, biochemistry. **Business:** Accounting, business admin, finance, information resources management, management information systems, marketing. **Communications:** General, advertising, digital media, journalism, public relations. **Computer sciences:** Computer science, information technology. **Conservation:** Environmental science. **Education:** Art, biology, elementary, English, foreign languages, history, mathematics, middle, music, physical, science, secondary, social studies, special. **Engineering:** Science. **Family/consumer sciences:** Family studies. **Foreign languages:** Spanish. **Health:** Clinical lab science, dietetics, nursing (RN), ophthalmic lab technology, predental, premedicine, prepharmacy, preveterinary, speech pathology. **History:** General. **Interdisciplinary:** Global studies. **Legal studies:** Prelaw. **Liberal arts:** Arts/sciences. **Math:** General. **Parks/recreation:** Health/fitness, sports admin. **Physical sciences:** Chemistry, physics. **Protective services:** Law enforcement admin. **Psychology:** General. **Public administration:** Social work. **Social sciences:** Political science, sociology. **Theology:** Bible, missionary, preministerial, youth ministry. **Visual/performing arts:** Dramatic, graphic design, interior design, piano/organ, studio arts, voice/opera. **Other:** Ministry.

Most popular majors. Business/marketing 25%, communications/journalism 10%, education 11%, health sciences 6%, interdisciplinary studies 10%, visual/performing arts 6%.

Computing on campus. 650 workstations in dormitories, library, computer center. Dormitories wired for high-speed internet access and linked to campus network. Commuter students can connect to campus network. Online course registration, online library, helpline, student web hosting, wireless network available.

Student life. Freshman orientation: Mandatory, $115 fee. Preregistration for classes offered. Overnight program, held twice in summer; includes assessment testing and registration. **Policies:** Religious observance required. **Housing:** Guaranteed on-campus for freshmen. Single-sex dorms, special housing for disabled, apartments available. **Activities:** Bands, campus ministries, choral groups, drama, international student organizations, literary magazine, music ensembles, musical theater, opera, radio station, student government, student newspaper, symphony orchestra, TV station, student association, Seekers of the Word, international student association, campus activities team, Hispanos Unidos, College Democrats, African Missions Fellowship, Essence of Ebony, mission student committee, College Republicans.

Athletics. NCAA. **Intercollegiate:** Baseball M, basketball, cross-country, football (tackle) M, golf M, soccer W, softball W, tennis, track and field, volleyball W. **Intramural:** Badminton, basketball, bowling, cross-country, football (non-tackle), racquetball, soccer, softball, table tennis, tennis, track and field, volleyball, water polo M. **Team name:** Wildcats.

Student services. Adult student services, alcohol/substance abuse counseling, chaplain/spiritual director, career counseling, student employment services, financial aid counseling, health services, minority student services, personal counseling, placement for graduates, veterans' counselor. **Physically disabled:** Services for visually, speech, hearing impaired.

Contact. E-mail: info@admissions.acu.edu
Phone: (325) 674-2650 Toll-free number: (800) 460-6228 ext. 2650
Fax: (325) 674-2130
Hayley Webb, Director of Admissions, Abilene Christian University, ACU Box 29000, Abilene, TX 79699

Amberton University

Garland, Texas
www.amberton.edu **CB code: 6140**

- Private 4-year university affiliated with nondenominational tradition
- Commuter campus in small city
- 447 degree-seeking undergraduates
- 1,115 graduate students

General. Founded in 1971. Regionally accredited. Upper level and graduate institution designed for adult students. Must have previous college and be over 21 years old to attend. **Degrees:** 105 bachelor's awarded; master's offered. **Location:** 12 miles from downtown Dallas. **Calendar:** Four 10-week sessions. Extensive summer session. **Full-time faculty:** 15 total; 93% have terminal degrees. **Part-time faculty:** 60 total; 92% have terminal degrees.

Basis for selection. All students required to have previously completed college work. No first-time freshmen. Must be at least 21 years of age.

2008-2009 Annual costs. Tuition/fees: $6,750. Books/supplies: $500.

Application procedures. Admission: No deadline. No application fee. Application must be submitted on paper. Admission notification on a rolling basis. Amberton enrolls no first-time freshman students. **Financial aid:** No deadline.

Academics. Special study options: Distance learning, independent study, weekend college. **Credit/placement by examination:** CLEP. 30 credit hours maximum toward bachelor's degree.

Majors. Business: General, accounting, business admin. **Liberal arts:** Arts/sciences.

Most popular majors. Business/marketing 90%, liberal arts 10%.

Computing on campus. 25 workstations in library, computer center. Online library available.

Student services. Adult student services, career counseling, personal counseling, placement for graduates, veterans' counselor.

Contact. E-mail: advisor@amberton.edu
Phone: (972) 279-6511 Fax: (972) 279-9773
Don Hebbard, Academic Dean, Amberton University, 1700 Eastgate Drive, Garland, TX 75041-5595

Angelo State University

San Angelo, Texas — **CB member**
www.angelo.edu — **CB code: 6644**

- Public 4-year university
- Residential campus in small city
- 5,512 degree-seeking undergraduates: 14% part-time, 54% women
- 448 degree-seeking graduate students
- 97% of applicants admitted
- SAT or ACT (ACT writing optional) required

General. Founded in 1928. Regionally accredited. **Degrees:** 780 bachelor's, 61 associate awarded; master's offered. **ROTC:** Air Force. **Location:** 215 miles from San Antonio, 200 miles from Austin. **Calendar:** Semester, extensive summer session. **Full-time faculty:** 241 total; 73% have terminal degrees, 15% minority, 44% women. **Part-time faculty:** 95 total; 17% have terminal degrees, 16% minority, 52% women. **Class size:** 24% < 20, 51% 20-39, 14% 40-49, 10% 50-99, 1% >100. **Special facilities:** Planetarium, management, instruction, and research center for agriculture, food safety and product development laboratory, West Texas collection, natural history collections.

Freshman class profile. 3,010 applied, 2,934 admitted, 1,467 enrolled.

Mid 50% test scores			
SAT critical reading:	410-520	Rank in top tenth:	12%
SAT math:	420-550	Out-of-state:	3%
SAT writing:	400-510	Live on campus:	74%
ACT composite:	17-22	Fraternities:	3%
Rank in top quarter:	35%	Sororities:	4%

Basis for selection. Applicants must graduate from accredited high school and satisfactorily complete recommended high school program or advanced college-prep curriculum, or rank in top half of high school class. If ranked in third quarter, must have 23 ACT or 1030 SAT (exclusive of Writing). If ranked in fourth quarter, must have 30 ACT or 1270 SAT. **Homeschooled:** Transcript of courses and grades required. Recommend that students have completed the equivalent of a high school curriculum.

High school preparation. 23 units recommended. Recommended units include English 4, mathematics 3, social studies 3, science 3 and foreign language 2. One computer science recommended.

2008-2009 Annual costs. Tuition/fees: $5,411; $13,841 out-of-state. Fifty percent of freshmen dorms are private rooms and higher rates apply. Room/board: $6,612. Books/supplies: $1,000.

2007-2008 Financial aid. Need-based: 1,240 full-time freshmen applied for aid; 974 were judged to have need; 941 of these received aid. Average scholarship/grant was $2,095. 55% of total undergraduate aid awarded as scholarships/grants, 45% as loans/jobs. **Non-need-based:** Awarded to 7,257 full-time undergraduates, including 1,212 freshmen. Scholarships awarded for academics, athletics, leadership, music/drama, ROTC, state residency. **Additional information:** The Blue and Gold Guarantee provides full tuition and mandatory fees for first-time Texas resident freshmen from families with adjusted gross income of $40,000 or less. Must be Pell eligible.

Application procedures. Admission: Closing date 8/15 (postmark date). $25 fee. Admission notification on a rolling basis. **Financial aid:** Priority date 4/1; no closing date. FAFSA required. Applicants notified on a rolling basis starting 4/1; must reply within 30 week(s) of notification.

Academics. Special study options: Combined bachelor's/graduate degree, distance learning, double major, dual enrollment of high school students, honors, independent study, internships, study abroad, teacher certification program. 4+1 programs in various fields with Texas Tech University allowing recipients of ASU bachelor's degree to earn a master's degree in related field in one year at TTU. 3-2 engineering-physics and 3-2 agriculture-education programs with Texas A&M and University of Texas El Paso. **Credit/placement by examination:** AP, CLEP, SAT, ACT. Unlimited credits by examination provided student meets hours required in residence. **Support services:** Learning center, reduced course load, remedial instruction, tutoring, writing center.

Honors college/program. Students admitted must have a 3.25 GPA in coursework done at ASU. If enrolling from high school the student must be in the top 10% of their graduating class and have scored a 27 on the ACT or a 1200 on the SAT (exclusive of Writing). Some classes are strictly honors students only. Normal grade level classes can be given honors credit by contract. The student must meet with the professor before the semester and discuss what additional coursework will make it qualify for honors credit.

Majors. Agriculture: Animal husbandry, animal sciences. **Biology:** General, biochemistry, ecology, evolutionary. **Business:** Accounting, business admin, finance, international, management information systems, marketing, real estate. **Communications:** General, journalism. **Computer sciences:** General. **Conservation:** Management/policy. **Family/consumer sciences:** Child development. **Foreign languages:** French, German, Spanish. **Health:** Athletic training, clinical lab science, nursing (RN). **History:** General. **Math:** General. **Parks/recreation:** Health/fitness. **Physical sciences:** Applied physics, chemistry, physics. **Protective services:** Criminal justice. **Psychology:** General. **Social sciences:** Political science, sociology. **Visual/performing arts:** Art, dramatic, studio arts.

Most popular majors. Business/marketing 25%, communications/journalism 8%, health sciences 6%, interdisciplinary studies 13%, parks/recreation 13%, psychology 8%.

Computing on campus. 700 workstations in dormitories, library, computer center, student center. Dormitories wired for high-speed internet access and linked to campus network. Commuter students can connect to campus network. Online course registration, online library, helpline, student web hosting, wireless network available.

Student life. Freshman orientation: Available, $25 fee. Preregistration for classes offered. Sessions offered several times during the summer. **Policies:** Single undergraduates with 12-60 semester credit hours of college-level work who do not live with parents are required to reside in University-owned housing. **Housing:** Coed dorms, single-sex dorms, special housing for disabled, apartments, wellness housing available. $100 fully refundable deposit. **Activities:** Bands, campus ministries, choral groups, dance, drama, film society, international student organizations, literary magazine, music ensembles, musical theater, radio station, student government, student newspaper, TV station, Association of Mexican-American Students, Baptist Student Union, Black Organization Striving for Success, Block and Bridle, College Republicans, Newman Center, Nontraditional Student Organization, Residence Hall Association, Young Democrats.

Athletics. NCAA. **Intercollegiate:** Baseball M, basketball, cross-country, football (tackle) M, golf W, soccer W, softball W, track and field, volleyball W. **Intramural:** Badminton, basketball, football (non-tackle), golf, racquetball, soccer, softball, swimming, table tennis, tennis, track and field, volleyball. **Team name:** Rams.

Student services. Adult student services, alcohol/substance abuse counseling, chaplain/spiritual director, career counseling, services for economically disadvantaged, student employment services, financial aid counseling, health services, minority student services, personal counseling, placement for graduates, veterans' counselor. **Physically disabled:** Services for visually, hearing impaired.

Contact. E-mail: admissions@angelo.edu
Phone: (325) 942-2185 Toll-free number: (800) 946-8627
Fax: (325) 942-2078
Frederic Dietz, Director of Admissions, Angelo State University, ASU Station #11014, San Angelo, TX 76909-1014

Arlington Baptist College

Arlington, Texas
www.abconline.edu — **CB code: 6039**

- Private 4-year Bible and teachers college affiliated with Baptist faith
- Residential campus in very large city

- 138 degree-seeking undergraduates: 22% part-time, 53% women, 7% African American, 1% Asian American, 4% Hispanic American, 4% international
- Application essay required

General. Founded in 1939. Accredited by ABHE. **Degrees:** 34 bachelor's awarded. **Location:** 10 miles from Fort Worth, 25 miles from Dallas. **Calendar:** Semester, limited summer session. **Full-time faculty:** 8 total; 12% minority, 50% women. **Part-time faculty:** 10 total; 30% have terminal degrees, 10% minority, 10% women. **Class size:** 91% < 20, 9% 20-39.

Freshman class profile. 20 applied, 20 admitted, 11 enrolled.

GPA 3.75 or higher:	16%	**Rank in top tenth:**	17%
GPA 3.50-3.74:	17%	**End year in good standing:**	75%
GPA 3.0-3.49:	50%	**Return as sophomores:**	68%
GPA 2.0-2.99:	17%	**Out-of-state:**	9%
Rank in top quarter:	33%	**Live on campus:**	45%

Basis for selection. Open admission. Interview recommended for all; audition required for music. **Homeschooled:** Transcript of courses and grades, interview required. Advised to obtain GED.

High school preparation. 16 units recommended. Recommended units include English 3, mathematics 2, social studies 3, history 3 and science 1.

2008-2009 Annual costs. Tuition/fees: $6,740. Room/board: $4,200. Books/supplies: $750. Personal expenses: $720.

2007-2008 Financial aid. All financial aid based on need. 15 full-time freshmen applied for aid; 15 were judged to have need; 15 of these received aid. Average need met was 80%. Average scholarship/grant was $1,537; average loan $2,223. 36% of total undergraduate aid awarded as scholarships/grants, 64% as loans/jobs.

Application procedures. **Admission:** Priority date 8/1; no deadline. $15 fee, may be waived for applicants with need. Application must be submitted on paper. Admission notification on a rolling basis. **Financial aid:** Closing date 8/15. FAFSA required. Applicants notified on a rolling basis.

Academics. **Special study options:** Distance learning, double major, dual enrollment of high school students, external degree, teacher certification program. **Credit/placement by examination:** AP, CLEP, institutional tests. 30 credit hours maximum toward bachelor's degree. **Support services:** Reduced course load, remedial instruction.

Majors. **Education:** General, elementary, English, kindergarten/preschool, middle, multi-level teacher, music, science, secondary, social studies. **Philosophy/religion:** Religion. **Psychology:** Counseling. **Theology:** Bible, missionary, pastoral counseling, religious ed, sacred music, youth ministry.

Most popular majors. Education 27%, theological studies 33%.

Computing on campus. 17 workstations in library, computer center. Wireless network available.

Student life. **Freshman orientation:** Mandatory. Preregistration for classes offered. Orientation includes placement testing. **Policies:** Religious observance required. **Housing:** Guaranteed on-campus for freshmen. Single-sex dorms, wellness housing available. $25 nonrefundable deposit. **Activities:** Campus ministries, choral groups, music ensembles, student government, student missionary association, student preachers' fellowship, youth majors organization.

Athletics. **Intercollegiate:** Baseball M, basketball, volleyball W. **Team name:** Patriots.

Student services. Chaplain/spiritual director, career counseling, student employment services, financial aid counseling, personal counseling, placement for graduates, veterans' counselor.

Contact. E-mail: jtaylor@abconline.org
Phone: (817) 461-8741 ext. 105 Fax: (817) 274-1138
Janie Taylor, Registrar, Arlington Baptist College, 3001 West Division, Arlington, TX 76012

Art Institute of Dallas

Dallas, Texas
www.aid.edu — **CB code: 2680**

- For-profit 4-year visual arts college
- Very large city
- 1,897 degree-seeking undergraduates

General. Regionally accredited. **Degrees:** 118 bachelor's, 186 associate awarded. **Calendar:** Quarter. **Full-time faculty:** 60 total. **Part-time faculty:** 41 total.

Basis for selection. Open admission, but selective for some programs. Some animation, art and design associate degree programs may require portfolio evaluation.

2008-2009 Annual costs. Total program costs vary by program: bachelor's programs $84,012-$88,530; associate programs $49,332-$52,075. Personal expenses: $2,880.

Application procedures. **Admission:** No deadline. $50 fee. Admission notification on a rolling basis. **Financial aid:** FAFSA required. Applicants notified on a rolling basis.

Academics. **Credit/placement by examination:** CLEP.

Majors. **Visual/performing arts:** Studio arts.

Contact. E-mail: cwilliams@aii.edu
Phone: (214) 692-8080 Toll-free number: (800) 275-4243
Myrna Little, Director of Admissions, Art Institute of Dallas, Two North Park, 8080 Park Lane, Dallas, TX 75231

Art Institute of Houston

Houston, Texas
www.artinstitutes.edu/houston — **CB code: 8271**

- For-profit 4-year culinary school and visual arts college
- Very large city
- 1,936 degree-seeking undergraduates

General. Regionally accredited. **Degrees:** 202 bachelor's, 165 associate awarded. **Calendar:** Quarter. **Full-time faculty:** 61 total. **Part-time faculty:** 41 total.

Basis for selection. Based on high school record or GED and personal interview with admissions representative; test scores optional but may be considered if submitted. Observes TASP guidelines. ASSET or COMPASS testing may be required. Remediation may be required if test scores fall below required ranges; some remediation available on campus.

2008-2009 Annual costs. Tuition and fees vary by program.

Application procedures. **Admission:** No deadline. $50 fee. Admission notification on a rolling basis. **Financial aid:** Priority date 3/1; no closing date. FAFSA, institutional form required.

Academics. **Special study options:** Distance learning, honors, internships, study abroad. **Credit/placement by examination:** CLEP.

Majors. **Visual/performing arts:** Graphic design, interior design.

Contact. E-mail: aihadm@aii.edu
Phone: (713) 623-2040 Toll-free number: (800) 275-4244
Fax: (713) 966-2797
Susanne Behrens, Director of Admission, Art Institute of Houston, 1900 Yorktown, Houston, TX 77056-4115

Austin College

Sherman, Texas — **CB member**
www.austincollege.edu — **CB code: 6016**

- Private 4-year liberal arts and teachers college affiliated with Presbyterian Church (USA)
- Residential campus in small city
- 1,253 degree-seeking undergraduates: 55% women, 2% African American, 16% Asian American, 9% Hispanic American, 1% Native American, 2% international
- 29 degree-seeking graduate students
- 78% of applicants admitted
- SAT or ACT with writing, application essay required
- 78% graduate within 6 years; 24% enter graduate study

General. Founded in 1849. Regionally accredited. **Degrees:** 335 bachelor's awarded; master's offered. **Location:** 60 miles from Dallas. **Calendar:** 4-1-4, limited summer session. **Full-time faculty:** 94 total; 93% have terminal degrees, 10% minority, 32% women. **Part-time faculty:** 32 total; 25% have terminal degrees, 19% minority, 47% women. **Class size:** 65% < 20, 30% 20-39, 3% 40-49, 2% 50-99. **Special facilities:** Environmental research areas totaling 174 acres, lake recreation area, tissue culture facility for study of cellular molecular interactions of eukaryotic cells, high performance numeric and graphics computing facility for advanced scientific computing and 3-D graphics.

Freshman class profile. 1,525 applied, 1,182 admitted, 319 enrolled.

Mid 50% test scores		**Rank in top quarter:**	67%
SAT critical reading:	560-660	**Rank in top tenth:**	36%
SAT math:	570-670	**End year in good standing:**	79%
SAT writing:	550-660	**Return as sophomores:**	80%
ACT composite:	23-29	**Out-of-state:**	7%
GPA 3.75 or higher:	23%	**Live on campus:**	96%
GPA 3.50-3.74:	26%	**International:**	2%
GPA 3.0-3.49:	40%	**Fraternities:**	12%
GPA 2.0-2.99:	11%	**Sororities:**	24%

Basis for selection. Academic transcript record, test scores, recommendations, extracurricular involvement, essay important. Interview considered. Interview recommended for all; audition recommended for music, theater (required for scholarship consideration); portfolio recommended for art (required for scholarship consideration).

High school preparation. College-preparatory program recommended. Required and recommended units include English 4, mathematics 3-4, social studies 2-3, science 3-4 (laboratory 2-3), foreign language 2-3, visual/performing arts 1-2 and academic electives 1.

2009-2010 Annual costs. Tuition/fees: $27,875. Room/board: $9,090. Books/supplies: $1,000. Personal expenses: $750.

2008-2009 Financial aid. **Need-based:** 253 full-time freshmen applied for aid; 204 were judged to have need; 204 of these received aid. Average need met was 99%. Average scholarship/grant was $19,197; average loan $5,130. 68% of total undergraduate aid awarded as scholarships/grants, 32% as loans/jobs. **Non-need-based:** Awarded to 681 full-time undergraduates, including 192 freshmen. Scholarships awarded for academics, alumni affiliation, art, leadership, music/drama, religious affiliation, state residency.

Application procedures. **Admission:** Priority date 1/15; deadline 5/1 (postmark date). $35 fee, may be waived for applicants with need, free for online applicants. Must reply by 5/1. **Financial aid:** Priority date 4/1; no closing date. FAFSA required. Applicants notified on a rolling basis starting 3/1; must reply by 5/1.

Academics. **Special study options:** Double major, exchange student, honors, independent study, internships, liberal arts/career combination, student-designed major, study abroad, teacher certification program, Washington semester. 3-2 dual degree engineering program with University of Texas Dallas, Washington University in St. Louis, Columbia University, Texas A&M University. **Credit/placement by examination:** AP, CLEP, IB, institutional tests. **Support services:** Learning center, study skills assistance, tutoring.

Majors. **Area/ethnic studies:** American, Latin American. **Biology:** General, biochemistry. **Business:** General. **Communications:** General. **Computer sciences:** Computer science. **Conservation:** Environmental studies. **Foreign languages:** Classics, French, German, Latin, Spanish. **History:** General. **Math:** General. **Philosophy/religion:** Philosophy, religion. **Physical sciences:** Chemistry, physics. **Psychology:** General. **Social sciences:** Economics, international economics, international relations, political science, sociology. **Visual/performing arts:** Art.

Most popular majors. Biology 8%, business/marketing 12%, English 7%, foreign language 8%, history 6%, psychology 15%, social sciences 16%, visual/performing arts 6%.

Computing on campus. 160 workstations in dormitories, library, computer center, student center. Dormitories wired for high-speed internet access and linked to campus network. Commuter students can connect to campus network. Online library, helpline, student web hosting, wireless network available.

Student life. **Freshman orientation:** Mandatory. Preregistration for classes offered. Held the weekend prior to the first day of classes. **Housing:** Guaranteed on-campus for all undergraduates. Coed dorms, single-sex dorms, apartments available. Language emphasis residence, suite-style housing for upper-level students with private bedroom, common area, kitchenette. **Activities:** Bands, campus ministries, choral groups, dance, drama, international student organizations, literary magazine, music ensembles, Model UN, musical theater, student government, student newspaper, symphony orchestra, Alpha Phi Omega, Intervarsity Christian Fellowship, Black Expressions, Young Democrats, Service Station, Los Amigos, Habitat for Humanity, Activators, Amnesty International.

Athletics. NCAA. **Intercollegiate:** Baseball M, basketball, football (tackle) M, soccer, softball W, swimming, tennis, volleyball W. **Intramural:** Basketball, football (non-tackle), soccer, softball, volleyball. **Team name:** Roos.

Student services. Chaplain/spiritual director, career counseling, student employment services, financial aid counseling, health services, personal counseling.

Contact. E-mail: admission@austincollege.edu
Phone: (903) 813-3000 Toll-free number: (800) 526-4276
Fax: (903) 813-3198
Nan Davis, Vice President for Institutional Enrollment, Austin College, 900 North Grand Avenue, Suite 6N, Sherman, TX 75090-4400

Austin Graduate School of Theology

Austin, Texas
www.austingrad.edu **CB code: 4969**

- Private two-year upper-division Bible and seminary college affiliated with Church of Christ
- Commuter campus in large city
- Application essay required

General. Founded in 1917. Regionally accredited. **Degrees:** 7 bachelor's awarded; master's offered. **Location:** 80 miles from San Antonio, 150 miles from Houston. **Calendar:** Semester, limited summer session. **Full-time faculty:** 4 total; 100% have terminal degrees. **Part-time faculty:** 7 total; 71% have terminal degrees, 14% minority. **Class size:** 90% < 20, 10% 20-39.

Student profile. 22 degree-seeking undergraduates, 37 degree-seeking graduate students.

Women:	36%	**Hispanic American:**	9%
African American:	36%	**Part-time:**	91%
Asian American:	9%		

Basis for selection. Open admission. College transcript, application essay required. Transcript, GPA, recommendations required. High school transcript, test scores required for applicants with fewer than 35 hours. Transfer accepted as sophomores, juniors, seniors.

2008-2009 Annual costs. Tuition/fees: $7,500. Books/supplies: $500. Personal expenses: $1,963.

Financial aid. **Need-based:** 7 applied for aid; 7 were judged to have need; 7 of these received aid. 62% of total undergraduate aid awarded as scholarships/grants; 38% as loans/jobs. **Non-need-based:** Awarded to 3 undergraduates. Scholarships awarded for academics, leadership. **Additional information:** Generous scholarships for students taking at least 12 hours. Federal work study program available. Institutional work study program (need-based) available.

Application procedures. **Admission:** Priority date 6/1. No application fee. Application must be submitted on paper. **Financial aid:** No deadline. FAFSA, institutional form required.

Academics. **Special study options:** Dual enrollment of high school students, liberal arts/career combination. Liberal arts/career combination program in religion; combined bachelor's/graduate program in ministry. **Credit/placement by examination:** AP, CLEP. 18 credit hours maximum toward bachelor's degree.

Majors. **Theology:** Bible, theology.

Computing on campus. 8 workstations in library, computer center, student center. Online library available.

Student life. **Policies:** Religious observance required. **Activities:** Student government.

Student services. Financial aid counseling, personal counseling.

Contact. E-mail: admissions@austingrad.edu
Phone: (512) 476-2772 ext. 103 Toll-free number: (866) 287-4723
Fax: (512) 476-3919
Celeste Scarborough, Registrar, Austin Graduate School of Theology, 7640 Guadalupe Street, Austin, TX 78752-1333

Baptist Missionary Association Theological Seminary

Jacksonville, Texas
www.bmats.edu **CB code: 7042**

- Private 4-year Bible and seminary college affiliated with Baptist faith
- Commuter campus in large town
- 58 degree-seeking undergraduates

General. Founded in 1955. Regionally accredited. **Degrees:** 11 bachelor's, 1 associate awarded; master's, first professional offered. **Location:** 120 miles from Dallas. **Calendar:** Semester, limited summer session. **Full-time faculty:** 5 total; 100% have terminal degrees. **Part-time faculty:** 4 total; 100% have terminal degrees.

Freshman class profile. 20 applied, 18 admitted, 18 enrolled.

Basis for selection. Open admission, but selective for some programs. Essay or personal statement very important. Religious commitment, interview, recommendations, school and community activities important.

2008-2009 Annual costs. Tuition/fees: $3,310. Room/board: $2,400.

Application procedures. Admission: No deadline. $35 fee.

Academics. Special study options: Internships. **Credit/placement by examination:** CLEP.

Majors. Philosophy/religion: Religion. **Theology:** Theology.

Computing on campus. 2 workstations in library.

Student life. Activities: Student government.

Student services. Career counseling, personal counseling.

Contact. E-mail: bmatsem@bmats.edu
Phone: (903) 586-2501 Fax: (903) 586-0378
Philip Attebery, Dean/Registrar, Baptist Missionary Association Theological Seminary, 1530 East Pine Street, Jacksonville, TX 75766

Baptist University of the Americas

San Antonio, Texas
www.bua.edu

- Private 4-year university and Bible college affiliated with Baptist General Convention of Texas
- Commuter campus in very large city
- 175 degree-seeking undergraduates

General. Accredited by ABHE. Baptist University of the Americas trains cross-culturally students in Biblical/Theological Studies and Ministry Studies, at a higher education academic level, from a Hispanic context. **Degrees:** 30 bachelor's, 4 associate awarded. **Calendar:** Semester, limited summer session. **Full-time faculty:** 8 total. **Part-time faculty:** 17 total.

Freshman class profile. 23 applied, 23 admitted, 23 enrolled.

Basis for selection. Open admission. Observes THEA requirements.

2008-2009 Annual costs. Tuition/fees: $4,490. Books/supplies: $1,740.

Application procedures. Admission: No deadline. $25 fee. **Financial aid:** No deadline.

Academics. Credit/placement by examination: CLEP.

Majors. Theology: Bible, theology.

Student life. Freshman orientation: Available, $25 fee. **Housing:** $200 deposit.

Contact. E-mail: mranjel@bua.edu
Phone: (210) 924-4338
Mary Ranjel, Director of Admissions, Baptist University of the Americas, 8019 South Pan Am Expressway, San Antonio, TX 78224

Baylor University

Waco, Texas — **CB member**
www.baylor.edu — **CB code: 6032**

- Private 4-year university affiliated with Baptist faith
- Residential campus in small city
- 12,105 degree-seeking undergraduates: 2% part-time, 58% women, 7% African American, 7% Asian American, 11% Hispanic American, 1% Native American, 2% international
- 2,366 degree-seeking graduate students
- 51% of applicants admitted
- SAT or ACT with writing, application essay required
- 73% graduate within 6 years

General. Founded in 1845. Regionally accredited. **Degrees:** 2,445 bachelor's awarded; master's, doctoral, first professional offered. **ROTC:** Army, Air Force. **Location:** 100 miles from Dallas-Fort Worth, 100 miles from Austin. **Calendar:** Semester, extensive summer session. **Full-time faculty:** 823 total; 80% have terminal degrees, 9% minority, 37% women. **Part-time faculty:** 273 total; 7% minority, 50% women. **Class size:** 44% < 20, 39% 20-39, 7% 40-49, 7% 50-99, 3% >100. **Special facilities:** Museum of natural science, Texas collection library, Armstrong Browning library.

Freshman class profile. 25,501 applied, 13,096 admitted, 3,062 enrolled.

Mid 50% test scores		**Rank in top tenth:**	41%
SAT critical reading:	540-650	**End year in good standing:**	91%
SAT math:	560-660	**Return as sophomores:**	86%
SAT writing:	530-630	**Out-of-state:**	18%
ACT composite:	23-28	**Live on campus:**	99%
Rank in top quarter:	72%	**International:**	1%

Basis for selection. Competitive high school performance and competitive scores on ACT or SAT most important; above-average achievement and potential expected. Audition required for music and theater programs; interview recommended for marginal achievers; portfolio recommended for art. **Homeschooled:** Transcript of courses and grades required. If applicant graduated from home school not officially recognized by state in which school is located, applicant must be 17 before first day of class unless GED certificate submitted prior to registration.

High school preparation. College-preparatory program required. Required units include English 4, mathematics 3, social studies 1, history 1, science 3 (laboratory 2) and foreign language 2.

2009-2010 Annual costs. Tuition/fees: $27,910. Cited cost includes room rate of $4,240 per year for community bath and 16-meal plan. Other room types are higher. Room/board: $7,971. Books/supplies: $1,398. Personal expenses: $1,890.

2008-2009 Financial aid. Need-based: 2,130 full-time freshmen applied for aid; 1,670 were judged to have need; 1,669 of these received aid. Average need met was 69%. Average scholarship/grant was $15,395; average loan $2,636. 58% of total undergraduate aid awarded as scholarships/grants, 42% as loans/jobs. **Non-need-based:** Awarded to 9,050 full-time undergraduates, including 2,832 freshmen. Scholarships awarded for academics, art, athletics, job skills, leadership, music/drama, ROTC.

Application procedures. Admission: No deadline. $50 fee, may be waived for applicants with need. Application must be submitted online. Must reply by May 1 or within 2 week(s) if notified thereafter. Notification of admission decision by 1/15 for 11/1 applications and by 3/15 for 2/1 applications; after 3/15 on space available basis. $300 enrollment deposit required by May 1. **Financial aid:** Priority date 1/15, closing date 8/15. FAFSA required. Applicants notified on a rolling basis starting 3/1; must reply by 5/1 or within 2 week(s) of notification.

Academics. Online support (website advising resources and tutoring) is available when success center is closed. **Special study options:** Accelerated study, combined bachelor's/graduate degree, double major, honors, internships, student-designed major, study abroad, teacher certification program. Architecture program with Washington University, forestry with Duke University. **Credit/placement by examination:** AP, CLEP, IB, institutional tests. 60 credit hours maximum toward bachelor's degree. **Support services:** Learning center, pre-admission summer program, reduced course load, remedial instruction, study skills assistance, tutoring, writing center.

Honors college/program. All highly qualified and highly motivated students are eligible to apply to join the Honors program as freshmen. While not required, applicants are helped by having SAT or ACT scores at least in the average range set by prior years' Honors freshmen. The cohort entering the program in 2007-2008 averaged around 1350 on the SAT (Math plus Critical Reading) and/or over 31 (Composite) on the ACT.

Majors. Architecture: Architecture. **Area/ethnic studies:** American, Asian, Latin American, Slavic. **Biology:** General, biochemistry, bioinformatics, exercise physiology. **Business:** General, accounting, business admin, entrepreneurial studies, fashion, finance, financial planning, human resources, insurance, international, logistics, management information systems, managerial economics, marketing, real estate, sales/distribution. **Communications:** General, digital media, journalism. **Computer sciences:** Computer science. **Conservation:** Environmental science, environmental studies, forestry. **Education:** General, early childhood, elementary, English, health occupations, mathematics, music, physical, science, social studies, special. **Engineering:** General, electrical, mechanical. **Family/consumer sciences:** General, family studies, human nutrition. **Foreign languages:** Ancient Greek, Biblical, classics, French, German, Latin, linguistics, Russian, Spanish. **Health:** Athletic training, clinical lab science, communication disorders, nursing (RN), predental, premedicine, prenursing. **History:** General. **Interdisciplinary:** Museum, neuroscience. **Liberal arts:** Humanities. **Math:** General, applied, statistics. **Parks/recreation:** Health/fitness. **Philosophy/religion:** Philosophy, religion. **Physical sciences:** Chemistry, geology, geophysics, physics. **Psychology:** General. **Public administration:** General, social work. **Social sciences:** Anthropology, geography, international relations, political science, sociology. **Theology:** Sacred music. **Transportation:** Airline/commercial pilot. **Visual/performing arts:** Acting, art history/conservation, dramatic, fashion design, interior design, music history, music pedagogy, music performance, music theory/composition, studio arts, theater design. **Other:** Media business, Recreation.

Most popular majors. Biology 9%, business/marketing 25%, communications/journalism 10%, education 6%, health sciences 10%, social sciences 7%.

Computing on campus. 1,668 workstations in dormitories, library, computer center, student center. Dormitories wired for high-speed internet access and linked to campus network. Commuter students can connect to campus network. Online course registration, online library, helpline, repair service, student web hosting, wireless network available.

Student life. Freshman orientation: Mandatory. Preregistration for classes offered. 10 2-day sessions primarily in June. **Policies:** All students required to participate in chapel-forum for 2 semesters. **Housing:** Guaranteed on-campus for freshmen. Single-sex dorms, special housing for disabled, apartments, wellness housing available. Brooks Residential College, Honors Residential College, Engineering and Computer Science living-learning center, Outdoor Adventure living-learning center, Leadership living-learning center. **Activities:** Bands, campus ministries, choral groups, dance, drama, film society, international student organizations, literary magazine, music ensembles, Model UN, musical theater, opera, radio station, student government, student newspaper, symphony orchestra, TV station, Campus Crusade for Christ, College Republicans, Young Democrats, association of black students, Hispanic student association, Asian student association, Habitat for Humanity, Alpha Phi Omega, Baylor Chamber of Commerce.

Athletics. NCAA. **Intercollegiate:** Baseball M, basketball, cross-country, equestrian W, football (tackle) M, golf, soccer W, softball W, tennis, track and field, volleyball W. **Intramural:** Basketball, bowling, cross-country, equestrian, football (non-tackle), golf, lacrosse, racquetball, soccer, softball, swimming, table tennis, tennis, track and field, volleyball, weight lifting. **Team name:** Bears.

Student services. Chaplain/spiritual director, career counseling, student employment services, financial aid counseling, health services, legal services, personal counseling, placement for graduates. **Physically disabled:** Services for visually, speech, hearing impaired.

Contact. E-mail: admissions@baylor.edu
Phone: (254) 710-3435 Toll-free number: (800) 229-5678
Fax: (254) 710-3436
Jennifer Carron, Director of Admissions Services, Baylor University, One Bear Place #97056, Waco, TX 76798-7056

College of Biblical Studies-Houston
Houston, Texas
www.cbshouston.edu **CB code: 3946**

- Private 4-year Bible college
- Commuter campus in very large city
- 1,234 undergraduates

General. Accredited by ABHE. Multidenominational Christian Bible college. **Degrees:** 116 bachelor's, 25 associate awarded. **Calendar:** Trimester, extensive summer session. **Full-time faculty:** 10 total. **Part-time faculty:** 43 total.

Basis for selection. Open admission, but selective for some programs. ASSET testing may be required for associate or baccalaureate level programs. **Homeschooled:** State high school equivalency certificate required.

2008-2009 Annual costs. Tuition/fees: $4,890. Books/supplies: $900. Personal expenses: $2,766.

Application procedures. Admission: No deadline. $20 fee. Admission notification on a rolling basis. **Financial aid:** No deadline.

Academics. Special study options: Accelerated study, dual enrollment of high school students, ESL, independent study. **Credit/placement by examination:** CLEP, institutional tests. **Support services:** Learning center, remedial instruction.

Majors. Theology: Bible, preministerial.

Computing on campus. 14 workstations in library.

Student life. Freshman orientation: Mandatory. Preregistration for classes offered. 2 sessions lasting 2 hours held week before classes begin; new students requested to attend 1 session. **Policies:** Religious observance required. **Activities:** Student government.

Student services. Adult student services, career counseling, financial aid counseling.

Contact. E-mail: cbs@cbshouston.edu
Phone: (713) 785-5995 Fax: (713) 785-5998
Lydia Love, Director of Admission, College of Biblical Studies-Houston, 7000 Regency Square Boulevard, #110, Houston, TX 77036-3211

College of Saint Thomas More
Fort Worth, Texas
www.cstm.edu **CB code: 0169**

- Private 4-year liberal arts college affiliated with Roman Catholic Church
- Residential campus in very large city
- 31 degree-seeking undergraduates: 35% part-time, 29% women, 3% African American, 13% Hispanic American
- 100% of applicants admitted
- SAT or ACT (ACT writing optional), application essay, interview required
- 75% graduate within 6 years; 75% enter graduate study

General. Regionally accredited. **Degrees:** 5 bachelor's, 2 associate awarded. **ROTC:** Army, Air Force. **Location:** 5 miles from downtown. **Calendar:** Semester, limited summer session. **Full-time faculty:** 4 total; 100% have terminal degrees, 25% women. **Part-time faculty:** 5 total; 40% have terminal degrees, 20% women. **Class size:** 100% < 20.

Freshman class profile. 4 applied, 4 admitted, 4 enrolled.

End year in good standing:	90%	**Live on campus:**	90%
Return as sophomores:	100%		

Basis for selection. Secondary school record, essay, interview, test scores important; 2 letters of recommendation required. **Homeschooled:** Transcript of courses and grades, interview, letter of recommendation (nonparent) required.

High school preparation. College-preparatory program recommended.

2008-2009 Annual costs. Tuition/fees: $12,150. Student housing includes use of private kitchen. Room only: $4,050. Books/supplies: $500. Personal expenses: $1,000.

2007-2008 Financial aid. Need-based: 70% of total undergraduate aid awarded as scholarships/grants, 30% as loans/jobs. **Non-need-based:** Scholarships awarded for academics.

Application procedures. Admission: No deadline. $35 fee. Application must be submitted on paper. Admission notification on a rolling basis. **Financial aid:** Closing date 7/1. FAFSA required. Applicants notified on a rolling basis starting 1/1.

Academics. Three inter-term courses that are part of the curriculum are presented in Rome, Greece, and Oxford, England. Rome is offered freshmen year, Greece after the sophomore year, and Oxford in the senior year. **Special study options:** Dual enrollment of high school students, study abroad. **Credit/placement by examination:** CLEP. **Support services:** Remedial instruction, study skills assistance, tutoring, writing center.

Majors. Liberal arts: Arts/sciences.

Computing on campus. 10 workstations in library, student center. Dormitories wired for high-speed internet access and linked to campus network. Online library, wireless network available.

Student life. Freshman orientation: Mandatory. Preregistration for classes offered. **Housing:** Guaranteed on-campus for freshmen. Apartments available. $200 fully refundable deposit. **Activities:** Student government, Chapel of Christ the Teacher, Adoration, Culture Society.

Student services. Alcohol/substance abuse counseling, chaplain/spiritual director, career counseling, financial aid counseling, personal counseling.

Contact. E-mail: tcooper@cstm.edu
Phone: (817) 923-8459 Toll-free number: (800) 583-6489
Fax: (817) 924-3206
Travis Cooper, Registrar, College of Saint Thomas More, 3020 Lubbock Avenue, Fort Worth, TX 76109

Concordia University Texas

Austin, Texas
www.concordia.edu **CB code: 6127**

- Private 4-year university and liberal arts college affiliated with Lutheran Church - Missouri Synod
- Commuter campus in very large city
- 1,169 degree-seeking undergraduates: 23% part-time, 57% women, 11% African American, 2% Asian American, 18% Hispanic American, 1% Native American
- 1,089 degree-seeking graduate students
- 66% of applicants admitted
- SAT or ACT (ACT writing optional) required
- 32% graduate within 6 years

General. Founded in 1926. Regionally accredited. **Degrees:** 199 bachelor's, 16 associate awarded; master's offered. **ROTC:** Army, Air Force. **Calendar:** Semester, extensive summer session. **Full-time faculty:** 58 total; 71% have terminal degrees, 9% minority, 31% women. **Part-time faculty:** 307 total; 38% have terminal degrees, 8% minority, 16% women. **Class size:** 80% < 20, 20% 20-39.

Freshman class profile. 817 applied, 539 admitted, 234 enrolled.

Mid 50% test scores		**GPA 3.0-3.49:**	34%
SAT critical reading:	440-550	**GPA 2.0-2.99:**	31%
SAT math:	450-550	**Rank in top quarter:**	32%
SAT writing:	430-530	**Rank in top tenth:**	10%
ACT composite:	18-23	**Return as sophomores:**	55%
GPA 3.75 or higher:	18%	**Out-of-state:**	5%
GPA 3.50-3.74:	15%	**Live on campus:**	90%

Basis for selection. School achievement record, test scores, and 2.5 GPA important. Interview recommended for academically weak.

High school preparation. Basic college preparatory program recommended.

2008-2009 Annual costs. Tuition/fees: $20,490. Room/board: $7,800. Books/supplies: $1,200. Personal expenses: $1,195.

2007-2008 Financial aid. Need-based: 82 full-time freshmen applied for aid; 59 were judged to have need; 56 of these received aid. Average need met was 79%. Average scholarship/grant was $10,644; average loan $5,626. 67% of total undergraduate aid awarded as scholarships/grants, 33% as loans/jobs. **Non-need-based:** Awarded to 172 full-time undergraduates, including 37 freshmen. Scholarships awarded for academics, alumni affiliation, leadership, music/drama, religious affiliation.

Application procedures. Admission: Priority date 5/1; no deadline. $25 fee, may be waived for applicants with need. Admission notification on a rolling basis beginning on or about 8/15. Reply by August 15 if dormitory applicant. **Financial aid:** No deadline. FAFSA, institutional form required. Applicants notified on a rolling basis starting 2/15; must reply within 2 week(s) of notification.

Academics. Special study options: Accelerated study, combined bachelor's/graduate degree, double major, independent study, liberal arts/career combination, study abroad. Simultaneous enrollment with other institutions of Concordia University System for two semesters. **Credit/placement by examination:** AP, CLEP, IB, SAT, ACT, institutional tests. 15 credit hours maximum toward associate degree, 30 toward bachelor's. **Support services:** Reduced course load, remedial instruction, tutoring.

Majors. Biology: General. **Business:** General, business admin, training/development. **Communications:** General. **Computer sciences:** Computer science. **Conservation:** Environmental studies. **Education:** Elementary, secondary. **Health:** Health care admin. **History:** General. **Legal studies:** Prelaw. **Liberal arts:** Arts/sciences. **Math:** General. **Parks/recreation:** Exercise sciences. **Philosophy/religion:** Religion. **Protective services:** Law enforcement admin. **Social sciences:** General. **Theology:** Religious ed, sacred music. **Visual/performing arts:** Conducting, piano/organ.

Most popular majors. Business/marketing 44%, education 13%, social sciences 17%.

Computing on campus. 45 workstations in library, computer center. Dormitories wired for high-speed internet access and linked to campus network. Commuter students can connect to campus network. Helpline, student web hosting available.

Student life. Freshman orientation: Mandatory. **Housing:** Guaranteed on-campus for freshmen. Coed dorms available. $200 nonrefundable deposit, deadline 7/1. **Activities:** Bands, campus ministries, choral groups, drama, literary magazine, music ensembles, radio station, student government, student newspaper, Sisters in Christ, Lutheran Student Fellowship, Lutheran Women's Missionary League, Pro Life, College Republicans, Pre-Sem Club (pre-seminary students), Fellowship of Christian Athletes, students active for the environment, writer's guild.

Athletics. NCAA. **Intercollegiate:** Baseball M, basketball, cross-country, golf, soccer, softball W, tennis, volleyball W. **Intramural:** Badminton, basketball, bowling, handball, racquetball, softball, table tennis, tennis, volleyball. **Team name:** Tornadoes.

Student services. Adult student services, alcohol/substance abuse counseling, chaplain/spiritual director, career counseling, student employment services, financial aid counseling, personal counseling, placement for graduates, veterans' counselor.

Contact. E-mail: admissions@concordia.edu
Phone: (512) 313-3000 Toll-free number: (800) 865-4282
Fax: (512) 313-3999
Kristi Kirk, Associate Director of Admissions, Concordia University Texas, 11400 Concordia University Drive, Austin, TX 78726

Criswell College

Dallas, Texas
www.criswell.edu **CB code: 0794**

- Private 4-year Bible and seminary college affiliated with Southern Baptist Convention
- Commuter campus in very large city

General. Founded in 1970. Regionally accredited. **Calendar:** Semester.

Annual costs/financial aid. Tuition/fees (2008-2009): $6,502. Books/supplies: $600.

Contact. Phone: (214) 818-1305
Academic and Enrollment Services, 4010 Gaston Avenue, Dallas, TX 75246-1537

Dallas Baptist University

Dallas, Texas **CB member**
www.dbu.edu **CB code: 6159**

- Private 4-year university affiliated with Baptist faith
- Commuter campus in very large city
- 3,575 degree-seeking undergraduates: 38% part-time, 58% women, 18% African American, 2% Asian American, 9% Hispanic American, 1% Native American, 8% international
- 1,722 degree-seeking graduate students
- 47% of applicants admitted
- SAT or ACT with writing, application essay required
- 50% graduate within 6 years

General. Founded in 1898. Regionally accredited. **Degrees:** 811 bachelor's awarded; master's, doctoral offered. **ROTC:** Army, Air Force. **Location:** 13 miles from downtown, 29 miles from Fort Worth. **Calendar:** 4-1-4, extensive summer session. **Full-time faculty:** 121 total; 72% have terminal degrees, 14% minority, 40% women. **Part-time faculty:** 402 total; 33% have terminal degrees, 8% minority, 45% women. **Class size:** 65% < 20, 30% 20-39, 2% 40-49, 3% 50-99, less than 1% >100.

Freshman class profile. 1,305 applied, 618 admitted, 350 enrolled.

Mid 50% test scores		**GPA 2.0-2.99:**	11%
SAT critical reading:	470-590	**Rank in top quarter:**	40%
SAT math:	480-590	**Rank in top tenth:**	18%
ACT composite:	19-24	**Return as sophomores:**	71%
GPA 3.75 or higher:	35%	**Out-of-state:**	7%
GPA 3.50-3.74:	20%	**Live on campus:**	96%
GPA 3.0-3.49:	34%		

Basis for selection. All factors considered for admission, including test scores, class rank, essay and GPA. Interview recommended. **Home-schooled:** Transcript of courses and grades required. If student is not in accredited program, GED required.

High school preparation. College-preparatory program recommended. 16 units recommended. Recommended units include English 4, mathematics 3, social studies 3, history 2, science 2 and foreign language 2.

2008-2009 Annual costs. Tuition/fees: $16,440. Room/board: $5,409. Books/supplies: $1,800. Personal expenses: $1,602.

2008-2009 Financial aid. Need-based: 335 full-time freshmen applied for aid; 217 were judged to have need; 216 of these received aid. Average need met was 86%. Average scholarship/grant was $3,046; average loan $3,023. 44% of total undergraduate aid awarded as scholarships/grants, 56% as loans/jobs. **Non-need-based:** Awarded to 1,548 full-time undergraduates, including 326 freshmen. Scholarships awarded for academics, athletics, job skills, leadership, music/drama, religious affiliation.

Application procedures. Admission: Priority date 1/15; no deadline. $25 fee. Admission notification on a rolling basis. **Financial aid:** Priority date 3/6, closing date 5/1. FAFSA, institutional form required. Applicants notified on a rolling basis starting 2/1.

Academics. Special study options: Accelerated study, combined bachelor's/graduate degree, distance learning, double major, dual enrollment of high school students, ESL, honors, independent study, internships, study abroad, teacher certification program, Washington semester, weekend college. **Credit/placement by examination:** AP, CLEP, IB, SAT, ACT, institutional tests. Credit by examination not counted toward residency hours. Credits recorded on permanent record after student has completed minimum of 12 hours in residence. **Support services:** Learning center, pre-admission summer program, remedial instruction, study skills assistance, tutoring, writing center.

Majors. Biology: General. **Business:** General, accounting, business admin, finance, management information systems, managerial economics, marketing. **Communications:** General. **Computer sciences:** General, computer science. **Education:** General, early childhood, elementary, music, physical, science, secondary. **Health:** Health care admin. **History:** General. **Liberal arts:** Arts/sciences. **Math:** General. **Philosophy/religion:** Philosophy. **Protective services:** Criminal justice. **Psychology:** General. **Social sciences:** Political science, sociology. **Theology:** Bible, pastoral counseling, religious ed, sacred music. **Visual/performing arts:** Art, music theory/composition, piano/organ, voice/opera.

Computing on campus. 220 workstations in dormitories, library, computer center, student center. Dormitories wired for high-speed internet access and linked to campus network. Commuter students can connect to campus network. Online library, helpline, wireless network available.

Student life. Freshman orientation: Available. Preregistration for classes offered. **Policies:** Religious observance required. **Housing:** Single-sex dorms, special housing for disabled, apartments, wellness housing available. $100 fully refundable deposit. **Activities:** Campus ministries, choral groups, drama, international student organizations, music ensembles, musical theater, opera, student government, College Republicans, Spanish-speaking students association, Chinese student association, Ministerial Alliance, Japanese student association, Korean student association.

Athletics. NCAA, NCCAA. **Intercollegiate:** Baseball M, cross-country, golf, soccer, tennis, track and field, volleyball W. **Intramural:** Badminton, basketball, football (non-tackle), golf M, softball, table tennis, tennis, volleyball. **Team name:** Patriots.

Student services. Adult student services, alcohol/substance abuse counseling, chaplain/spiritual director, career counseling, student employment services, financial aid counseling, health services, personal counseling, placement for graduates, veterans' counselor. **Physically disabled:** Services for visually, speech, hearing impaired.

Contact. E-mail: admiss@dbu.edu
Phone: (214) 333-5360 Toll-free number: (800) 460-1328
Fax: (214) 333-5447
Bobby Soto, Director of Undergraduate Admissions, Dallas Baptist University, 3000 Mountain Creek Parkway, Dallas, TX 75211-9299

Dallas Christian College

Dallas, Texas
www.dallas.edu **CB code: 0792**

- Private 4-year Bible college affiliated with nondenominational tradition
- Commuter campus in very large city
- 301 degree-seeking undergraduates: 37% part-time, 45% women, 18% African American, 1% Asian American, 11% Hispanic American, 3% Native American
- 14 degree-seeking graduate students
- 18% of applicants admitted
- SAT or ACT (ACT writing recommended), application essay required
- 41% graduate within 6 years; 56% enter graduate study

General. Founded in 1950. Accredited by ABHE. Special program for adult, nontraditional students. **Degrees:** 52 bachelor's, 1 associate awarded. **Location:** 10 miles from downtown. **Calendar:** 4-1-4, limited summer session. **Full-time faculty:** 8 total; 50% have terminal degrees, 25% women. **Part-time faculty:** 48 total; 23% have terminal degrees, 10% minority, 17% women.

Freshman class profile. 309 applied, 57 admitted, 31 enrolled.

Mid 50% test scores		**GPA 2.0-2.99:**	20%
SAT critical reading:	390-500	**Rank in top quarter:**	40%
SAT math:	340-530	**Rank in top tenth:**	2%
SAT writing:	400-540	**End year in good standing:**	84%
ACT composite:	17-22	**Return as sophomores:**	48%
GPA 3.75 or higher:	11%	**Out-of-state:**	17%
GPA 3.50-3.74:	28%	**Live on campus:**	98%
GPA 3.0-3.49:	41%		

Basis for selection. School record and recommendation, followed by test scores. Class rank also important. Interview recommended.

High school preparation. College-preparatory program recommended.

2008-2009 Annual costs. Tuition/fees: $10,170. Room/board: $6,250. Books/supplies: $600.

2008-2009 Financial aid. Non-need-based: Scholarships awarded for leadership, music/drama.

Application procedures. Admission: Priority date 7/1; deadline 7/15 (postmark date). $40 fee, may be waived for applicants with need. Admission notification on a rolling basis. Must reply by 8/15. **Financial aid:** Closing date 4/15. FAFSA, institutional form required. Applicants notified on a rolling basis; must reply within 2 week(s) of notification.

Academics. Special study options: Combined bachelor's/graduate degree, distance learning, double major, dual enrollment of high school students, independent study, internships, liberal arts/career combination, teacher certification program. Evening degree-seeking program for adults. **Credit/placement by examination:** AP, CLEP, IB, SAT, ACT, institutional tests. 15 credit hours maximum toward associate degree, 30 toward bachelor's. **Support services:** Reduced course load, remedial instruction, study skills assistance, tutoring.

Majors. Business: Business admin. **Education:** General, early childhood, elementary, English, history, multi-level teacher, music, secondary. **Interdisciplinary:** Intercultural. **Liberal arts:** Arts/sciences. **Psychology:** General. **Theology:** Bible, religious ed, sacred music, theology.

Most popular majors. Business/marketing 23%, education 8%, theological studies 66%.

Computing on campus. 16 workstations in library, student center. Dormitories wired for high-speed internet access. Commuter students can connect to campus network. Online library, helpline, wireless network available.

Student life. Freshman orientation: Mandatory, $100 fee. Preregistration for classes offered. Held 3 days prior to registration. **Policies:** All resident students and those taking 6 hours or more required to attend campus chapel services 2 times a week. **Housing:** Guaranteed on-campus for all undergraduates. Single-sex dorms, wellness housing available. $150 deposit, deadline 8/10. **Activities:** Pep band, campus ministries, choral groups, drama, music ensembles, student government, student newspaper.

Athletics. NCCAA. **Intercollegiate:** Basketball, soccer, volleyball W. **Intramural:** Football (non-tackle), soccer, table tennis, volleyball. **Team name:** Crusaders.

Student services. Adult student services, chaplain/spiritual director, student employment services, financial aid counseling, personal counseling, placement for graduates.

Contact. E-mail: dcc@dallas.edu
Phone: (972) 241-3371 ext. 161 Toll-free number: (800) 688-1029
Fax: (972) 241-8021
Ted Smith, Director of Enrollment Management, Dallas Christian College, 2700 Christian Parkway, Dallas, TX 75234-7299

DeVry University: Houston
Houston, Texas
www.devry.edu **CB code: 4132**

- For-profit 4-year university
- Commuter campus in very large city
- 1,095 degree-seeking undergraduates: 48% part-time, 45% women, 37% African American, 6% Asian American, 36% Hispanic American, 1% international
- 186 degree-seeking graduate students

General. **Degrees:** 104 bachelor's, 41 associate awarded; master's offered. **Calendar:** Semester. **Full-time faculty:** 23 total; 39% minority, 30% women. **Part-time faculty:** 151 total; 50% minority, 43% women.

Freshman class profile.

Out-of-state:	1%	**International:**	1%

Basis for selection. Interview, high school GPA, and test scores most important. DeVry-administered admissions tests may be submitted in place of SAT/ACT.

2008-2009 Annual costs. Tuition/fees: $14,130. Books/supplies: $1,300. Personal expenses: $5,082.

2007-2008 Financial aid. **Non-need-based:** Scholarships awarded for academics.

Application procedures. **Admission:** No deadline. $50 fee. Admission notification on a rolling basis. **Financial aid:** No deadline. FAFSA required. Applicants notified on a rolling basis.

Academics. **Special study options:** Accelerated study, distance learning. **Credit/placement by examination:** CLEP.

Majors. **Business:** Business admin. **Computer sciences:** Networking, systems analysis. **Engineering technology:** Biomedical, computer, electrical. **Other:** Technical management.

Most popular majors. Business/marketing 96%.

Contact. Phone: (713) 973-3000 Fax: (713) 896-7650
DeVry University: Houston, 11125 Equity Drive, Houston, TX 77041-8217

DeVry University: Irving
Dallas, Texas **CB member**
www.devry.edu **CB code: 6180**

- For-profit 4-year university
- Commuter campus in small city
- 1,582 degree-seeking undergraduates: 54% part-time, 29% women, 29% African American, 4% Asian American, 22% Hispanic American, 1% Native American
- 220 degree-seeking graduate students
- Interview required

General. Founded in 1969. Regionally accredited. **Degrees:** 189 bachelor's, 49 associate awarded; master's offered. **Location:** 12 miles from Dallas. **Calendar:** Semester, extensive summer session. **Full-time faculty:** 43 total; 28% minority, 40% women. **Part-time faculty:** 99 total; 30% minority, 41% women.

Basis for selection. Applicants must have a high school diploma or equivalent or a degree from an accredited postsecondary institution, demonstrating proficiency in basic college-level skills through SAT or ACT scores or institution-administered placement examinations, and be at least 17 years of age on the first day of classes. New students may enter at beginning of any semester. CPT also accepted.

2008-2009 Annual costs. Tuition/fees: $14,130. Books/supplies: $1,300. Personal expenses: $5,082.

2007-2008 Financial aid. All financial aid based on need.

Application procedures. **Admission:** No deadline. $50 fee. Admission notification on a rolling basis. **Financial aid:** No deadline. FAFSA required. Applicants notified on a rolling basis.

Academics. **Special study options:** Accelerated study, distance learning. **Credit/placement by examination:** CLEP, institutional tests. No more than 35% of credit toward graduation requirement accepted. **Support services:** Learning center, remedial instruction, tutoring.

Majors. **Biology:** Bioinformatics. **Business:** Business admin. **Computer sciences:** Networking, systems analysis. **Engineering:** Software. **Engineering technology:** Biomedical, computer, electrical. **Other:** Technical management.

Most popular majors. Business/marketing 65%, computer/information sciences 24%, engineering/engineering technologies 11%.

Computing on campus. 450 workstations in library, computer center. Online course registration, online library, helpline available.

Student life. **Freshman orientation:** Mandatory. **Activities:** Student newspaper, Association of Information Technology Professionals, campus Bible study, Christian Students Fellowship, Habitat for Humanity, Institute of Electrical and Electronics Engineers, Institute of Management Accountants, minority student union, National Society of Black Engineers, Society of Women Engineers, Telecommunications Management and Associations, Society of Hispanic Professionals Engineers, gamers.

Athletics. **Intramural:** Basketball, football (tackle) M, volleyball.

Student services. Career counseling, student employment services, financial aid counseling, placement for graduates, veterans' counselor. **Physically disabled:** Services for visually, hearing impaired.

Contact. E-mail: cwilliams@mail.dal.devry.edu
Phone: (972) 929-5777 Toll-free number: (800) 633-3879
Fax: (972) 929-2860
Chad Williams, Director of Admissions, DeVry University: Irving, 4800 Regent Boulevard, Dallas, TX 75063-2439

East Texas Baptist University
Marshall, Texas
www.etbu.edu **CB code: 6187**

- Private 4-year university and liberal arts college affiliated with Baptist faith
- Residential campus in large town
- 1,134 degree-seeking undergraduates: 4% part-time, 51% women, 18% African American, 1% Asian American, 6% Hispanic American, 2% Native American, 1% international
- 55% of applicants admitted
- SAT or ACT (ACT writing optional) required
- 39% graduate within 6 years

General. Founded in 1912. Regionally accredited. **Degrees:** 258 bachelor's awarded. **Location:** 35 miles from Shreveport, Louisiana, 20 miles from Longview. **Calendar:** Semester, extensive summer session. **Full-time faculty:** 64 total; 83% have terminal degrees, 6% minority, 34% women. **Part-time faculty:** 31 total; 19% have terminal degrees, 6% minority, 48% women. **Class size:** 50% < 20, 42% 20-39, 7% 40-49, 1% 50-99. **Special facilities:** Caddo Lake international wetlands.

Freshman class profile. 970 applied, 532 admitted, 295 enrolled.

Mid 50% test scores		**Rank in top quarter:**	46%
SAT critical reading:	420-530	**Rank in top tenth:**	18%
SAT math:	450-550	**End year in good standing:**	86%
ACT composite:	18-23	**Return as sophomores:**	56%
GPA 3.75 or higher:	21%	**Out-of-state:**	9%
GPA 3.50-3.74:	22%	**Live on campus:**	96%
GPA 3.0-3.49:	38%	**International:**	1%
GPA 2.0-2.99:	19%		

Basis for selection. School achievement record and test scores most important. Evidence of good character also important. Applicants should be in top 40% of class. Interview recommended for academically deficient; audition recommended for music, speech, theater arts programs. **Learning Disabled:** Student should provide documentation of learning disability to Office of Student Services, which verifies documentation and assists in acquiring reasonable accommodations.

High school preparation. College-preparatory program recommended. 22 units recommended. Recommended units include English 4, mathematics 3, social studies 2.5, science 2 and academic electives 1. 0.5 economics, 1.5 physical education, 0.5 health education, 1 technology applications, 0.5 speech.

2009-2010 Annual costs. Tuition/fees: $17,180. Room/board: $5,164. Books/supplies: $892. Personal expenses: $1,448.

2007-2008 Financial aid. **Need-based:** 294 full-time freshmen applied for aid; 252 were judged to have need; 252 of these received aid. Average need met was 61%. Average scholarship/grant was $7,156; average loan $2,966. 56% of total undergraduate aid awarded as scholarships/grants, 44% as loans/jobs. **Non-need-based:** Awarded to 993 full-time undergraduates, including 277 freshmen. Scholarships awarded for academics, alumni affiliation, leadership, music/drama, religious affiliation.

Application procedures. **Admission:** Closing date 8/24 (receipt date). $25 fee, may be waived for applicants with need. Admission notification on a rolling basis beginning on or about 9/1. **Financial aid:** Priority date 6/1; no closing date. FAFSA, institutional form required. Applicants notified on a rolling basis starting 1/15; must reply within 3 week(s) of notification.

Academics. **Special study options:** Accelerated study, cross-registration, distance learning, double major, dual enrollment of high school students, exchange student, honors, independent study, internships, liberal arts/career combination, student-designed major, study abroad, teacher certification program, Washington semester. **Credit/placement by examination:** AP, CLEP, IB, SAT, ACT, institutional tests. 30 credit hours maximum toward bachelor's degree. ACT is used for mathematics placement. Departmental examinations administered on request upon approval of department chair. **Support services:** Reduced course load, study skills assistance, tutoring, writing center.

Majors. **Biology:** General. **Business:** General. **Communications:** Media studies. **Education:** General, biology, chemistry, drama/dance, elementary, English, history, mathematics, music, physical, social studies, Spanish, speech. **Foreign languages:** Spanish. **Health:** Athletic training, nursing (RN). **History:** General. **Interdisciplinary:** Global studies. **Liberal arts:** Arts/sciences. **Math:** General. **Parks/recreation:** Health/fitness. **Philosophy/religion:** Religion. **Physical sciences:** Chemistry. **Psychology:** General. **Social sciences:** Sociology. **Theology:** Bible, missionary, pastoral counseling, religious ed, sacred music, youth ministry. **Visual/performing arts:** Dramatic, piano/organ, voice/opera. **Other:** University studies.

Most popular majors. Business/marketing 14%, education 22%, health sciences 12%, interdisciplinary studies 8%, psychology 7%, theological studies 6%.

Computing on campus. 206 workstations in dormitories, library, computer center, student center. Dormitories wired for high-speed internet access and linked to campus network. Commuter students can connect to campus network. Online course registration, online library, helpline, repair service, wireless network available.

Student life. **Freshman orientation:** Available. Preregistration for classes offered. 5 days of activities, lectures, seminar sessions, community service activities. **Policies:** Required chapel attendance, graded curfew, weekly clean room check. Religious observance required. **Housing:** Guaranteed on-campus for all undergraduates. Single-sex dorms, apartments, wellness housing available. $100 fully refundable deposit. **Activities:** Bands, campus ministries, choral groups, drama, international student organizations, literary magazine, music ensembles, Model UN, musical theater, student government, student newspaper, symphony orchestra, Fellowship of Christian Athletes, political awareness society, Delta Pi Theta, Pi Sigma, Sigma Sigma Epsilon, Delta Chi Rho.

Athletics. NCAA. **Intercollegiate:** Baseball M, basketball, cross-country, football (tackle) M, soccer, softball W, volleyball W. **Intramural:** Basketball, football (non-tackle), racquetball, soccer, softball, volleyball. **Team name:** Tigers.

Student services. Adult student services, chaplain/spiritual director, student employment services, financial aid counseling, health services, personal counseling, placement for graduates, veterans' counselor.

Contact. E-mail: admissions@etbu.edu
Phone: (903) 923-2000 Toll-free number: (800) 804-3828
Fax: (903) 923-2001
Melissa Fitts, Director of Admissions, East Texas Baptist University, 1209 North Grove, Marshall, TX 75670-1498

Hardin-Simmons University

Abilene, Texas **CB member**
www.hsutx.edu **CB code: 6268**

- Private 4-year university affiliated with Baptist faith
- Residential campus in small city
- 1,914 degree-seeking undergraduates: 9% part-time, 58% women, 5% African American, 1% Asian American, 10% Hispanic American, 1% Native American, 1% international
- 453 degree-seeking graduate students
- 35% of applicants admitted
- SAT or ACT with writing required
- 50% graduate within 6 years; 44% enter graduate study

General. Founded in 1891. Regionally accredited. Part of 3-member consortium (with Abilene Christian University and McMurry University) comprising Abilene Intercollegiate School of Nursing. **Degrees:** 380 bachelor's awarded; master's, doctoral, first professional offered. **Location:** 150 miles from Fort Worth. **Calendar:** Semester, extensive summer session. **Full-time faculty:** 134 total; 77% have terminal degrees, 2% minority, 35% women. **Part-time faculty:** 64 total; 19% have terminal degrees, 3% minority, 52% women. **Class size:** 62% < 20, 35% 20-39, 3% 40-49, less than 1% 50-99. **Special facilities:** Rare and fine book room, observatory.

Freshman class profile. 1,816 applied, 633 admitted, 471 enrolled.

Mid 50% test scores		**GPA 2.0-2.99:**	9%
SAT critical reading:	450-560	**Rank in top quarter:**	56%
SAT math:	470-570	**Rank in top tenth:**	24%
SAT writing:	440-550	**End year in good standing:**	79%
ACT composite:	19-25	**Return as sophomores:**	66%
GPA 3.75 or higher:	54%	**Out-of-state:**	5%
GPA 3.50-3.74:	18%	**Live on campus:**	91%
GPA 3.0-3.49:	19%	**International:**	1%

Basis for selection. Applicants admitted on basis of acceptable combination of test scores and prior academic record. Special cases considered individually. Non-native speakers of English require score of 550 on TOEFL, unless transferring 24 or more credits. Audition required for music program; interview recommended for special cases. Written essay, interview, and separate application required for honors program. **Homeschooled:** GED scores required only if applicant plans to apply for federal need-based financial aid. **Learning Disabled:** There are no special admission requirements for students with disabilities. Once accepted, there is an application process to the Office for Students with Disabilities.

High school preparation. College-preparatory program recommended. 16 units required. Required units include English 3, mathematics 2, social studies 2, science 2 and academic electives 7. Math must include algebra I and above.

2009-2010 Annual costs. Tuition/fees: $19,790. Room/board: $5,788. Books/supplies: $800. Personal expenses: $1,476.

2008-2009 Financial aid. **Need-based:** 463 full-time freshmen applied for aid; 322 were judged to have need; 322 of these received aid. Average need met was 65%. Average scholarship/grant was $5,814; average loan $3,132. 42% of total undergraduate aid awarded as scholarships/grants, 58% as loans/jobs. **Non-need-based:** Awarded to 1,174 full-time undergraduates, including 344 freshmen. Scholarships awarded for academics, art, job skills, leadership, music/drama, religious affiliation.

Application procedures. **Admission:** No deadline. $50 fee, may be waived for applicants with need. Admission notification on a rolling basis beginning on or about 9/1. **Financial aid:** Priority date 3/1; no closing date. FAFSA required. Applicants notified on a rolling basis starting 2/1; must reply within 2 week(s) of notification.

Academics. **Special study options:** Accelerated study, cross-registration, distance learning, double major, dual enrollment of high school students, honors, independent study, internships, New York semester, study abroad, teacher certification program, United Nations semester, Washington semester. **Credit/placement by examination:** AP, CLEP, SAT, ACT, institutional tests. 32 credit hours maximum toward bachelor's degree. Maximum 14 hours in any one discipline. **Support services:** Pre-admission summer program, reduced course load, remedial instruction, study skills assistance, tutoring, writing center.

Majors. **Agriculture:** Agronomy, animal sciences, business. **Biology:** General, Biochemistry/biophysics and molecular biology. **Business:** Accounting, business admin, finance, management information systems, management science, marketing. **Communications:** General, broadcast journalism, media studies, public relations, radio/tv. **Computer sciences:** Programming. **Conservation:** Environmental science. **Education:** Art, business, computer, drama/dance, early childhood, English, history, mathematics, music, physical, reading, science, social studies, Spanish, speech. **Foreign languages:** Spanish. **Health:** Athletic training, audiology/speech pathology, nursing (RN), predental, premedicine. **History:** General. **Legal studies:** Prelaw. **Math:** General. **Parks/recreation:** Exercise sciences, health/fitness. **Philosophy/religion:** Philosophy. **Physical sciences:** Chemistry, geology, physics. **Protective services:** Criminal justice. **Psychology:** General. **Public administration:** Social work. **Social sciences:** Economics, political science, sociology. **Theology:** Bible, missionary, preministerial, sacred music, theology, youth ministry. **Visual/performing arts:** Dramatic, graphic design, music history, music management, music performance, music theory/composition, piano/organ, stringed instruments, studio arts, voice/opera.

Most popular majors. Business/marketing 17%, education 21%, health sciences 11%, parks/recreation 11%.

Computing on campus. 225 workstations in dormitories, library, computer center, student center. Dormitories wired for high-speed internet access and linked to campus network. Online library, helpline, wireless network available.

Student life. Freshman orientation: Available, $10 fee. Preregistration for classes offered. Held Tuesday through Sunday the week before classes begin. **Policies:** Single, undergraduate students under 21 who have not completed 60 credit hours and are not living at home required to live in residence halls. Religious observance required. **Housing:** Guaranteed on-campus for freshmen. Single-sex dorms, special housing for disabled, apartments, wellness housing available. $100 fully refundable deposit. Single and duplex housing available with priority given to families. **Activities:** Bands, campus ministries, choral groups, drama, international student organizations, literary magazine, music ensembles, Model UN, musical theater, opera, student government, student newspaper, symphony orchestra, unity group, student foundation, black student fellowship, moot court team, Latin American club, United Mexican American Students, social work club, criminal justice club, Students in Free Enterprise, Collegiates for Racial Harmony.

Athletics. NCAA. **Intercollegiate:** Baseball M, basketball, cheerleading, cross-country, football (tackle) M, golf, soccer, softball W, tennis, track and field, volleyball W. **Intramural:** Badminton, basketball, bowling, football (non-tackle), football (tackle), golf, handball, racquetball, soccer, softball, tennis, volleyball. **Team name:** Cowboys/Cowgirls.

Student services. Chaplain/spiritual director, career counseling, student employment services, financial aid counseling, health services, personal counseling, placement for graduates, veterans' counselor. **Physically disabled:** Services for visually, speech, hearing impaired.

Contact. E-mail: enroll@hsutx.edu
Phone: (325) 670-1206 Toll-free number: (877) 464-7889
Fax: (325) 671-2115
Vicki House, Director of Admissions and Recruiting, Hardin-Simmons University, PO Box 16050, Abilene, TX 79698-0001

Houston Baptist University

Houston, Texas — **CB member**
www.hbu.edu — **CB code: 6282**

- Private 4-year university and liberal arts college affiliated with Baptist faith
- Commuter campus in very large city
- 2,177 degree-seeking undergraduates: 13% part-time, 65% women, 21% African American, 14% Asian American, 20% Hispanic American, 5% international
- 341 degree-seeking graduate students
- 49% of applicants admitted
- SAT or ACT (ACT writing recommended), application essay required
- 45% graduate within 6 years

General. Founded in 1960. Regionally accredited. **Degrees:** 333 bachelor's, 5 associate awarded; master's offered. **ROTC:** Army, Naval, Air Force. **Location:** 10 miles from downtown. **Calendar:** Semester, extensive summer session. **Full-time faculty:** 140 total; 79% have terminal degrees, 16% minority, 51% women. **Part-time faculty:** 132 total; 45% have terminal degrees, 24% minority, 54% women. **Class size:** 61% < 20, 35% 20-39, 2% 40-49, 2% 50-99. **Special facilities:** Morris Cultural Arts Center, Museum of American Architecture and Decorative Arts, Bible in America Museum, Museum of Southern History.

Freshman class profile. 6,243 applied, 3,040 admitted, 560 enrolled.

Mid 50% test scores		**Rank in top tenth:**	26%
SAT critical reading:	470-570	**Return as sophomores:**	71%
SAT math:	480-590	**Out-of-state:**	3%
SAT writing:	460-570	**Live on campus:**	52%
ACT composite:	20-24	**International:**	3%
Rank in top quarter:	56%	**Sororities:**	1%

Basis for selection. School achievement record, test scores, recommendations, class rank, special talents, and skills most important. Audition required for music majors; portfolio required for art majors; interview recommended for academically weak students.

High school preparation. College-preparatory program recommended. 14 units required; 24 recommended. Required and recommended units include English 4, mathematics 3, social studies 4, history 2, science 3, foreign language 2, computer science 1, visual/performing arts 1, academic electives 3.5. 2 physical education/health, 0.5 speech.

2009-2010 Annual costs. Tuition/fees (projected): $20,830. Tuition is flat rate for fall and spring for undergraduates taking 12-18 hours per semester. Room/board: $6,975. Books/supplies: $1,230. Personal expenses: $1,825.

2008-2009 Financial aid. Need-based: 451 full-time freshmen applied for aid; 393 were judged to have need; 392 of these received aid. Average need met was 75%. Average scholarship/grant was $5,765; average loan $3,622. 58% of total undergraduate aid awarded as scholarships/grants, 42% as loans/jobs. **Non-need-based:** Awarded to 1,412 full-time undergraduates, including 569 freshmen. Scholarships awarded for academics, alumni affiliation, art, athletics, music/drama, religious affiliation, ROTC.

Application procedures. Admission: No deadline. No application fee. Admission notification on a rolling basis. **Financial aid:** Priority date 3/1, closing date 4/15. FAFSA required. Applicants notified on a rolling basis starting 3/10.

Academics. Special study options: Accelerated study, combined bachelor's/graduate degree, double major, honors, internships, study abroad, teacher certification program. **Credit/placement by examination:** AP, CLEP, IB, SAT, ACT, institutional tests. CLEP credit limited to students with 63 or fewer credit hours. **Support services:** Reduced course load, remedial instruction, tutoring, writing center.

Majors. Biology: General, molecular. **Business:** General, accounting, business admin, entrepreneurial studies, finance, information resources management, management information systems, managerial economics, marketing. **Communications:** General, media studies. **Education:** Art, early childhood, English, mathematics, middle, music, physical, science, secondary, social studies. **Family/consumer sciences:** Child development. **Foreign languages:** Biblical, French, Spanish. **Health:** Nursing (RN). **History:** General. **Interdisciplinary:** Accounting/computer science. **Math:** General. **Parks/recreation:** Exercise sciences, health/fitness. **Philosophy/religion:** Christian. **Physical sciences:** Chemistry, physics. **Psychology:** General. **Public administration:** Policy analysis. **Social sciences:** Economics, political science, sociology. **Theology:** Pastoral counseling, sacred music. **Visual/performing arts:** Music performance, music theory/composition, studio arts.

Most popular majors. Biology 12%, business/marketing 31%, education 9%, psychology 10%.

Computing on campus. 95 workstations in dormitories, library, computer center. Dormitories wired for high-speed internet access and linked to campus network. Commuter students can connect to campus network. Online course registration, online library, helpline, repair service, wireless network available.

Student life. Freshman orientation: Available. Preregistration for classes offered. 2-and-a-half-day camp held off campus. **Policies:** Spiritual Life Program graduation requirement for all undergraduate students. **Housing:** Guaranteed on-campus for freshmen. Single-sex dorms, apartments available. $200 partly refundable deposit. **Activities:** Bands, campus ministries, choral groups, drama, international student organizations, music ensembles, student government, student newspaper, symphony orchestra, Christian Life on Campus, Psi Chi, Nursing Association, international club, Black Student Fellowship, Toastmasters, Digital Eon, Vietnamese Student Association, Indian Student Association, Sisters for the Lord, Brothers Under Christ.

Athletics. NCAA. **Intercollegiate:** Baseball M, basketball, cheerleading, cross-country, golf, soccer, softball W, track and field, volleyball W. **Intramural:** Badminton, basketball, bowling, football (non-tackle), softball, table tennis, tennis, volleyball. **Team name:** Huskies.

Student services. Adult student services, alcohol/substance abuse counseling, chaplain/spiritual director, career counseling, student employment services, financial aid counseling, health services, personal counseling, placement for graduates, women's services. **Physically disabled:** Services for visually, speech, hearing impaired.

Contact. E-mail: admissions@hbu.edu
Phone: (281) 649-3211 Toll-free number: (800) 969-3210
Fax: (281) 649-3217
Ed Borges, Director of Admissions, Houston Baptist University, 7502 Fondren Road, Houston, TX 77074-3298

Howard Payne University

Brownwood, Texas
www.hputx.edu — **CB code: 6278**

- Private 4-year liberal arts and teachers college affiliated with Baptist faith
- Residential campus in large town
- 1,173 degree-seeking undergraduates: 11% part-time, 49% women, 7% African American, 1% Asian American, 14% Hispanic American, 1% Native American, 1% international

- 17 degree-seeking graduate students
- 50% of applicants admitted
- SAT or ACT with writing, application essay, interview required
- 35% graduate within 6 years

General. Founded in 1889. Regionally accredited. **Degrees:** 219 bachelor's, 4 associate awarded; master's offered. **Location:** 150 miles from Dallas, 77 miles from Abilene. **Calendar:** Semester, limited summer session. **Full-time faculty:** 76 total; 58% have terminal degrees, 3% minority, 33% women. **Part-time faculty:** 70 total; 10% have terminal degrees, 14% minority, 36% women. **Class size:** 74% < 20, 25% 20-39, less than 1% 40-49, less than 1% 50-99. **Special facilities:** General Douglas MacArthur Academy of Freedom.

Freshman class profile. 858 applied, 432 admitted, 308 enrolled.

Mid 50% test scores			
SAT critical reading:	440-540	Rank in top tenth:	16%
SAT math:	440-550	End year in good standing:	55%
ACT composite:	18-23	Return as sophomores:	57%
GPA 3.75 or higher:	14%	Out-of-state:	2%
GPA 3.50-3.74:	32%	Live on campus:	91%
GPA 3.0-3.49:	53%	International:	3%
GPA 2.0-2.99:	1%	Fraternities:	15%
Rank in top quarter:	37%	Sororities:	15%

Basis for selection. Students who are academically successful at Howard Payne generally present the following high school credentials: average GPA of 3.5 on 4.0 scale, top 50% class rank, ACT composite score of 21 and above or SAT 1 score of 1000 and above (exclusive of Writing). ACT/SAT scores used to exempt students from placement tests in English, math, or reading. Interview required for academic program applicants, required for competitive merit scholarship, and recommended for all others. Interview may be required by admissions committee. Audition required for music program. **Homeschooled:** Letter of recommendation (nonparent) required. **Learning Disabled:** HPU does not have a special program for students with differences, but if a student meets requirements for admission, and has a documented learning difference, appropriate accommodations will be initiated by Student Success Services.

High school preparation. College-preparatory program required. 16 units required. Required and recommended units include English 4, mathematics 3, social studies 2, history 2, science 3 and foreign language 2.

2008-2009 Annual costs. Tuition/fees: $17,400. Room/board: $5,051. Books/supplies: $1,000. Personal expenses: $1,500.

2007-2008 Financial aid. Need-based: 227 full-time freshmen applied for aid; 201 were judged to have need; 201 of these received aid. Average need met was 80%. Average scholarship/grant was $9,156; average loan $2,794. 51% of total undergraduate aid awarded as scholarships/grants, 49% as loans/jobs. **Non-need-based:** Awarded to 262 full-time undergraduates, including 59 freshmen. Scholarships awarded for academics, alumni affiliation, art, music/drama.

Application procedures. Admission: Priority date 3/15; no deadline. $25 fee. Admission notification on a rolling basis. **Financial aid:** Priority date 3/15; no closing date. FAFSA, institutional form required. Applicants notified on a rolling basis starting 2/1; must reply within 2 week(s) of notification.

Academics. Special study options: Accelerated study, cooperative education, distance learning, double major, dual enrollment of high school students, ESL, honors, independent study, internships, liberal arts/career combination, study abroad, teacher certification program. Extension classes in El Paso, Corpus Christi, Harlingen, Ft. Worth, Midland. **Credit/placement by examination:** AP, CLEP, SAT, ACT, institutional tests. 30 credit hours maximum toward bachelor's degree. **Support services:** Reduced course load, remedial instruction, study skills assistance, tutoring, writing center.

Majors. Biology: General. **Business:** General, accounting, business admin, finance, marketing. **Communications:** General, public relations. **Communications technology:** Graphics, radio/tv. **Computer sciences:** Information systems. **Education:** General, art, biology, business, chemistry, drama/dance, elementary, English, history, mathematics, multi-level teacher, music, physical, science, secondary, social science, Spanish, speech. **Foreign languages:** Biblical, Spanish. **Health:** Athletic training, premedicine. **History:** General. **Interdisciplinary:** Intercultural. **Legal studies:** Prelaw. **Liberal arts:** Arts/sciences. **Math:** General. **Parks/recreation:** General, exercise sciences, health/fitness, sports admin. **Philosophy/religion:** Philosophy, religion. **Physical sciences:** Chemistry. **Protective services:** Police science. **Psychology:** General. **Public administration:** Social work. **Social sciences:** General, political science, sociology. **Theology:** Bible, religious ed, sacred music, theology, youth ministry. **Visual/performing arts:** Art, dramatic, music performance, piano/organ, stringed instruments, studio arts, voice/opera.

Most popular majors. Business/marketing 14%, communications/journalism 8%, education 17%, psychology 12%, security/protective services 7%, theological studies 12%.

Computing on campus. 260 workstations in dormitories, library, computer center, student center. Dormitories wired for high-speed internet access and linked to campus network. Online library, helpline, wireless network available.

Student life. Freshman orientation: Available, $50 fee. Preregistration for classes offered. Held the weekend before fall semester classes begin. **Policies:** Religious observance required. **Housing:** Guaranteed on-campus for freshmen. Single-sex dorms, apartments, wellness housing available. $100 nonrefundable deposit, deadline 8/1. **Activities:** Bands, campus ministries, choral groups, dance, drama, literary magazine, music ensembles, musical theater, opera, radio station, student government, student newspaper, student foundation, ministerial alliance, Fellowship of Christian Athletes.

Athletics. NCAA. **Intercollegiate:** Baseball M, basketball, cheerleading, football (tackle) M, soccer, softball W, tennis, volleyball W. **Intramural:** Basketball, football (non-tackle), softball, table tennis, tennis, volleyball. **Team name:** Yellow Jackets.

Student services. Adult student services, chaplain/spiritual director, career counseling, student employment services, financial aid counseling, health services, personal counseling, placement for graduates.

Contact. E-mail: enroll@hputx.edu
Phone: (325) 649-8020 Toll-free number: (800) 880-4478
Fax: (325) 649-8901
Trudy Mohre, Director of Admission, Howard Payne University, 1000 Fisk Street, Brownwood, TX 76801-2794

Huston-Tillotson University

Austin, Texas — **CB member**
www.htu.edu — **CB code: 6280**

- Private 4-year business and liberal arts college affiliated with United Church of Christ and United Methodist Church
- Residential campus in very large city
- 721 degree-seeking undergraduates: 6% part-time, 49% women, 79% African American, 11% Hispanic American, 3% international
- 60 degree-seeking graduate students
- 56% of applicants admitted
- SAT or ACT (ACT writing optional) required

General. Founded in 1876. Regionally accredited. **Degrees:** 93 bachelor's awarded. **ROTC:** Army. **Location:** Downtown. **Calendar:** Semester, extensive summer session. **Full-time faculty:** 38 total; 47% women. **Part-time faculty:** 32 total; 38% women. **Class size:** 63% < 20, 35% 20-39, 1% 40-49, less than 1% 50-99.

Freshman class profile. 743 applied, 413 admitted, 179 enrolled.

Mid 50% test scores			
SAT critical reading:	360-460	GPA 2.0-2.99:	62%
SAT math:	350-500	Rank in top quarter:	23%
ACT composite:	14-18	Rank in top tenth:	12%
GPA 3.75 or higher:	5%	Return as sophomores:	49%
GPA 3.50-3.74:	8%	Out-of-state:	9%
GPA 3.0-3.49:	23%	Live on campus:	58%
		International:	4%

Basis for selection. School achievement record important. Test scores and interview considered.

High school preparation. College-preparatory program recommended. 22 units required. Required and recommended units include English 4, mathematics 3, social studies 3, science 2, foreign language 2 and computer science 1. Health, physical education.

2008-2009 Annual costs. Tuition/fees: $11,184. Room/board: $6,400. Books/supplies: $800. Personal expenses: $2,252.

2007-2008 Financial aid. Non-need-based: Scholarships awarded for academics, alumni affiliation, art, athletics, job skills, leadership, minority status, music/drama, religious affiliation, state residency.

Application procedures. Admission: Priority date 3/1; deadline 7/1. $25 fee, may be waived for applicants with need. Admission notification on a rolling basis beginning on or about 1/1. **Financial aid:** Priority date 3/15; no closing date. FAFSA, institutional form required. Applicants notified on a rolling basis starting 4/1; must reply within 4 week(s) of notification.

Academics. **Special study options:** Cooperative education, cross-registration, distance learning, double major, dual enrollment of high school students, external degree, honors, independent study, internships, liberal arts/career combination, study abroad, teacher certification program. 3-2 engineering program with Prairie View A&M University. **Credit/placement by examination:** AP, CLEP, SAT, ACT, institutional tests. 15 credit hours maximum toward bachelor's degree. **Support services:** Learning center, remedial instruction, tutoring, writing center.

Majors. **Biology:** General. **Business:** Accounting, business admin, international, marketing. **Computer sciences:** General, computer science. **Education:** General, physical. **History:** General. **Liberal arts:** Arts/sciences. **Math:** General. **Physical sciences:** Chemistry. **Protective services:** Criminal justice. **Psychology:** General. **Social sciences:** General, political science, sociology.

Computing on campus. 400 workstations in dormitories, library, computer center, student center. Dormitories wired for high-speed internet access and linked to campus network. Commuter students can connect to campus network. Online library, helpline, wireless network available.

Student life. **Freshman orientation:** Mandatory. Preregistration for classes offered. **Housing:** Guaranteed on-campus for all undergraduates. Single-sex dorms, wellness housing available. **Activities:** Jazz band, campus ministries, choral groups, dance, drama, film society, international student organizations, literary magazine, music ensembles, Model UN, student government.

Athletics. NAIA. **Intercollegiate:** Baseball M, basketball, golf, soccer M, track and field, volleyball W. **Intramural:** Basketball, soccer M, softball, table tennis, volleyball. **Team name:** Rams.

Student services. Adult student services, career counseling, student employment services, financial aid counseling, health services, personal counseling, placement for graduates, veterans' counselor. **Physically disabled:** Services for visually, hearing impaired.

Contact. E-mail: slstinson@htu.edu
Phone: (512) 505-3028 Toll-free number: (877) 505-3028
Fax: (512) 505-3192
Shakitha Stinson, Director of Admission, Huston-Tillotson University, 900 Chicon Street, Austin, TX 78702-2795

Jarvis Christian College

Hawkins, Texas
www.jarvis.edu **CB code: 6319**

- Private 4-year liberal arts and teachers college affiliated with Christian Church (Disciples of Christ)
- Residential campus in rural community
- 695 degree-seeking undergraduates: 54% women, 99% African American

General. Founded in 1912. Regionally accredited. **Degrees:** 65 bachelor's awarded. **Location:** 100 miles from Dallas; 100 miles from Shreveport, Louisiana. **Calendar:** Semester, limited summer session. **Full-time faculty:** 35 total; 40% have terminal degrees, 51% minority, 43% women. **Part-time faculty:** 7 total; 29% have terminal degrees, 43% minority, 43% women. **Class size:** 40% < 20, 54% 20-39, 5% 40-49, 1% >100. **Special facilities:** Observatory, natatorium, archives of black Christian church (Disciples of Christ).

Freshman class profile. 309 applied, 309 admitted, 149 enrolled.

GPA 3.75 or higher:	3%	**GPA 2.0-2.99:**	57%
GPA 3.50-3.74:	5%	**Out-of-state:**	13%
GPA 3.0-3.49:	34%	**Live on campus:**	93%

Basis for selection. Open admission. **Homeschooled:** State high school equivalency certificate required.

High school preparation. 16 units recommended. Recommended units include English 3, mathematics 2, social studies 3, science 1 and academic electives 7.

2008-2009 Annual costs. Tuition/fees: $8,208. Room/board: $5,078. Books/supplies: $800. Personal expenses: $950.

2007-2008 Financial aid. All financial aid based on need. 144 full-time freshmen applied for aid; 144 were judged to have need; 144 of these received aid. Average loan was $144. 64% of total undergraduate aid awarded as scholarships/grants, 36% as loans/jobs. **Additional information:** High school transcript required for scholarship consideration.

Application procedures. **Admission:** No deadline. $25 fee, may be waived for applicants with need. Admission notification on a rolling basis beginning on or about 4/1. **Financial aid:** Priority date 6/30, closing date 1/3. FAFSA required. Applicants notified on a rolling basis starting 5/1; must reply within 2 week(s) of notification.

Academics. **Special study options:** Accelerated study, combined bachelor's/graduate degree, cooperative education, cross-registration, distance learning, double major, dual enrollment of high school students, ESL, honors, internships, liberal arts/career combination, student-designed major, teacher certification program, Washington semester. **Credit/placement by examination:** AP, CLEP, IB, institutional tests. 18 credit hours maximum toward bachelor's degree. **Support services:** Learning center, reduced course load, remedial instruction, study skills assistance, tutoring, writing center.

Majors. **Biology:** General. **Business:** Business admin. **Communications:** Journalism. **Computer sciences:** General. **Education:** General, biology, business, early childhood, elementary, English, history, mathematics, middle, physical, reading, secondary, special. **Health:** Premedicine. **History:** General. **Math:** General. **Philosophy/religion:** Religion. **Physical sciences:** Chemistry. **Protective services:** Criminal justice. **Social sciences:** Sociology.

Most popular majors. Business/marketing 22%, education 11%, interdisciplinary studies 29%, security/protective services 22%.

Computing on campus. 359 workstations in dormitories, library, computer center. Dormitories wired for high-speed internet access and linked to campus network. Commuter students can connect to campus network. Online library, helpline, repair service, wireless network available.

Student life. **Freshman orientation:** Mandatory. Preregistration for classes offered. **Policies:** Religious services available, regardless of denomination. Religious observance required. **Housing:** Guaranteed on-campus for all undergraduates. Coed dorms, single-sex dorms, special housing for disabled, apartments, wellness housing available. $100 nonrefundable deposit, deadline 8/1. Single parents housing available on limited basis. **Activities:** Bands, choral groups, music ensembles, student government, student ministers' association, United Campus Christian Fellowship, pre-law club, National Society of Black Accountants, Student National Educational Association, Students in Free Enterprise, Phi Beta Lambda English Club, college church.

Athletics. NAIA. **Intercollegiate:** Baseball M, basketball, cheerleading, volleyball W. **Intramural:** Baseball M, basketball, football (non-tackle), football (tackle) M, golf, soccer, softball, swimming, table tennis, tennis, volleyball, weight lifting, wrestling M. **Team name:** Bulldogs.

Student services. Alcohol/substance abuse counseling, chaplain/spiritual director, career counseling, services for economically disadvantaged, student employment services, financial aid counseling, health services, personal counseling, placement for graduates, veterans' counselor. **Physically disabled:** Services for visually, speech, hearing impaired.

Contact. E-mail: felecia_tyiska@jarvis.edu
Phone: (903) 769-5734 Fax: (903) 769-1282
Felecia Tyiska, Director of Admissions, Jarvis Christian College, PO Box 1470, Hawkins, TX 75765-1470

Lamar University

Beaumont, Texas **CB member**
www.lamar.edu **CB code: 6360**

- Public 4-year university
- Commuter campus in small city
- 8,429 degree-seeking undergraduates: 25% part-time, 60% women, 28% African American, 3% Asian American, 7% Hispanic American, 1% Native American, 1% international
- 1,412 degree-seeking graduate students
- 88% of applicants admitted
- SAT or ACT required
- 31% graduate within 6 years

General. Founded in 1923. Regionally accredited. **Degrees:** 1,215 bachelor's, 30 associate awarded; master's, doctoral offered. **Location:** 75 miles from Houston. **Calendar:** Semester, limited summer session. **Full-time faculty:** 392 total; 66% have terminal degrees, 17% minority, 44% women. **Part-time faculty:** 128 total; 27% have terminal degrees, 12% minority, 48% women. **Class size:** 34% < 20, 46% 20-39, 11% 40-49, 7% 50-99, less than 1% >100. **Special facilities:** Texas Hazardous Waste Research Center, Spindletop/Gladys City Museum, Gulf Coast Hazardous Substance Research Center.

Freshman class profile. 3,873 applied, 3,403 admitted, 1,461 enrolled.

Mid 50% test scores		End year in good standing:	80%
SAT critical reading:	400-510	Return as sophomores:	65%
SAT math:	400-520	Out-of-state:	2%
SAT writing:	390-490	Live on campus:	45%
ACT composite:	16-21	International:	1%
Rank in top quarter:	37%	Fraternities:	5%
Rank in top tenth:	13%	Sororities:	3%

Basis for selection. Admission decision based on high school class rank, SAT scores, and completion of 14 high school units of college preparatory courses. SAT Subject Tests recommended for students with strong academic background. Interview required of students accepted with GED tests and required for early entry. **Homeschooled:** Transcript of courses and grades required. Must submit SAT and meet state TASP testing requirements.

High school preparation. 15 units required. Required and recommended units include English 4, mathematics 3, social studies 3, science 2, foreign language 2 and academic electives 3.

2008-2009 Annual costs. Tuition/fees: $6,014; $14,444 out-of-state. Room/board: $6,290. Books/supplies: $2,870. Personal expenses: $4,152.

2008-2009 Financial aid. All financial aid based on need. 1,009 full-time freshmen applied for aid; 636 were judged to have need; 636 of these received aid. Average need met was 51%. 53% of total undergraduate aid awarded as scholarships/grants, 47% as loans/jobs.

Application procedures. Admission: Closing date 8/1. $25 fee. Admission notification on a rolling basis. **Financial aid:** Priority date 4/1; no closing date. FAFSA, institutional form required. Applicants notified on a rolling basis starting 4/1; must reply within 2 week(s) of notification.

Academics. Special study options: Accelerated study, cooperative education, distance learning, double major, dual enrollment of high school students, ESL, honors, independent study, internships, study abroad, teacher certification program. **Credit/placement by examination:** AP, CLEP, institutional tests. 15 credit hours maximum toward associate degree, 30 toward bachelor's. **Support services:** Learning center, pre-admission summer program, reduced course load, remedial instruction, study skills assistance, tutoring, writing center.

Majors. Architecture: Interior. **Biology:** General, marine. **Business:** General, accounting, business admin, finance, human resources, management information systems, managerial economics, marketing, office management, sales/distribution. **Communications:** General, advertising. **Computer sciences:** General. **Conservation:** General, environmental studies. **Education:** Art, Deaf/hearing impaired, early childhood, elementary, family/consumer sciences, health, mathematics, music, physical, school counseling, science, secondary, social studies, special. **Engineering:** General, chemical, civil, electrical, environmental, industrial, mechanical. **Engineering technology:** Industrial, industrial management. **Family/consumer sciences:** General, clothing/textiles, family/community services, food/nutrition. **Foreign languages:** French, Spanish. **Health:** Audiology/speech pathology, clinical lab science, nursing (RN). **History:** General. **Liberal arts:** Arts/sciences. **Math:** General, applied. **Parks/recreation:** Health/fitness. **Physical sciences:** Chemistry, geology, physics, planetary. **Protective services:** Criminal justice. **Psychology:** General. **Public administration:** Social work. **Social sciences:** Economics, political science, sociology. **Visual/performing arts:** Art, commercial/advertising art, dance, dramatic, voice/opera.

Most popular majors. Business/marketing 21%, engineering/engineering technologies 9%, health sciences 12%, interdisciplinary studies 15%, liberal arts 11%.

Computing on campus. 644 workstations in dormitories, library, computer center, student center. Dormitories wired for high-speed internet access and linked to campus network. Commuter students can connect to campus network. Online course registration, online library, helpline, repair service, student web hosting, wireless network available.

Student life. Freshman orientation: Available, $10 fee. Preregistration for classes offered. One-day program available June-August. **Housing:** Guaranteed on-campus for freshmen. Coed dorms, single-sex dorms, special housing for disabled, wellness housing available. $150 deposit, deadline 8/1. **Activities:** Bands, choral groups, dance, drama, film society, literary magazine, music ensembles, musical theater, opera, radio station, student government, student newspaper, symphony orchestra, TV station, Catholic student union, Church of Latter-day Saints, Episcopal Center, Church of Christ Student Center, Wesley Foundation, Vietnamese student organization.

Athletics. NCAA. **Intercollegiate:** Baseball M, basketball, cross-country, golf, soccer W, tennis, track and field, volleyball W. **Intramural:** Badminton, basketball, cross-country, racquetball, soccer, softball, swimming, table tennis, tennis, track and field, volleyball, weight lifting. **Team name:** Cardinals.

Student services. Adult student services, career counseling, student employment services, health services, on-campus daycare, personal counseling, placement for graduates, veterans' counselor. **Physically disabled:** Services for visually, speech, hearing impaired.

Contact. E-mail: admissions@hal.lamar.edu
Phone: (409) 880-8888 Fax: (409) 880-8463
James Rush, Director of Academic Services, Lamar University, Box 10009, Beaumont, TX 77705

LeTourneau University
Longview, Texas
www.letu.edu **CB code: 6365**

- Private 4-year university affiliated with nondenominational tradition
- Residential campus in small city
- 3,296 degree-seeking undergraduates: 8% part-time, 56% women, 20% African American, 1% Asian American, 8% Hispanic American, 1% international
- 291 degree-seeking graduate students
- 66% of applicants admitted
- SAT or ACT (ACT writing optional), application essay required

General. Founded in 1946. Regionally accredited. Centers in Tyler, Dallas, Houston, Austin, and Bedford. **Degrees:** 648 bachelor's, 3 associate awarded; master's offered. **Location:** 120 miles from Dallas, 60 miles from Shreveport, Louisiana. **Calendar:** Semester, limited summer session. **Full-time faculty:** 74 total; 74% have terminal degrees, 11% minority, 18% women. **Part-time faculty:** 277 total; 34% have terminal degrees, 14% minority, 46% women. **Class size:** 87% < 20, 11% 20-39, less than 1% 40-49, less than 1% 50-99. **Special facilities:** Microprocessor and robotics laboratory, CAD laboratory, scanning electronic microscope, dynamic simulation laboratory, fleet of nine up-to-date airplanes, biomedical engineering laboratory with motion analysis system.

Freshman class profile. 970 applied, 642 admitted, 322 enrolled.

Mid 50% test scores		GPA 2.0-2.99:	8%
SAT critical reading:	520-650	Rank in top quarter:	59%
SAT math:	540-660	Rank in top tenth:	30%
SAT writing:	490-620	Return as sophomores:	75%
ACT composite:	22-29	Out-of-state:	54%
GPA 3.75 or higher:	41%	Live on campus:	92%
GPA 3.50-3.74:	27%	International:	1%
GPA 3.0-3.49:	24%		

Basis for selection. Applicants should rank in top half of high school graduating class, have minimum ACT of 20 or minimum SAT of 950 (exclusive of Writing), and GPA of 2.5. Interview recommended. **Homeschooled:** Require SAT or ACT, transcript; recommend GED and detailed summary of curriculum used.

High school preparation. College-preparatory program recommended. 16 units required. Required and recommended units include English 4, mathematics 3, social studies 2, history 1, science 3 (laboratory 3), foreign language 1 and academic electives 2. 4 math (including trigonometry) recommended for engineering applicants.

2008-2009 Annual costs. Tuition/fees: $19,140. Tuition for 1-6 hours is $344 per credit, for 7-11 hours is $756 per credit. Room/board: $7,500. Books/supplies: $1,300. Personal expenses: $1,050.

2007-2008 Financial aid. Non-need-based: Scholarships awarded for academics, leadership.

Application procedures. Admission: Priority date 12/31; deadline 8/1. $25 fee, may be waived for applicants with need. Admission notification on a rolling basis beginning on or about 9/15. **Financial aid:** Priority date 2/15; no closing date. FAFSA required. Applicants notified on a rolling basis starting 3/1; must reply within 3 week(s) of notification.

Academics. Peer advisers, student resource center, CARE committee, freshman year experience course available. **Special study options:** Accelerated study, cooperative education, distance learning, double major, dual enrollment of high school students, honors, independent study, internships, study abroad, teacher certification program, weekend college. **Credit/placement by examination:** AP, CLEP, IB, SAT, ACT, institutional tests. Credit must be established by end of student's first year at school. **Support services:** Reduced course load, remedial instruction, tutoring.

Majors. Biology: General. **Business:** General, accounting, business admin, finance, human resources, international, management information systems, marketing, operations. **Computer sciences:** General, computer science, information systems. **Education:** Business, computer, elementary, English, history, mathematics, middle, multi-level teacher, physical, science, secondary, social studies. **Engineering:** General, biomedical, computer, electrical, mechanical. **Engineering technology:** Aerospace, computer, electrical, mechanical. **Health:** Predental, premedicine, prepharmacy, preveterinary. **History:** General. **Interdisciplinary:** Math/computer science. **Legal studies:** Prelaw. **Math:** General. **Mechanic/repair:** Aircraft, aircraft powerplant. **Parks/recreation:** Exercise sciences, sports admin. **Physical sciences:** Chemistry, physical chemistry. **Psychology:** General. **Social sciences:** Political science. **Theology:** Bible. **Transportation:** Airline/commercial pilot, aviation, aviation management.

Most popular majors. Business/marketing 13%, education 8%, engineering/engineering technologies 29%, trade and industry 18%.

Computing on campus. 200 workstations in library, computer center. Dormitories wired for high-speed internet access and linked to campus network. Commuter students can connect to campus network. Online library, helpline, wireless network available.

Student life. **Freshman orientation:** Mandatory, $65 fee. Preregistration for classes offered. 3-day event for students and parents held before classes start. **Policies:** Religious observance required. **Housing:** Guaranteed on-campus for all undergraduates. Single-sex dorms, special housing for disabled, apartments available. $100 deposit, deadline 5/1. Residential societies available. **Activities:** Jazz band, campus ministries, choral groups, drama, film society, international student organizations, literary magazine, music ensembles, musical theater, student government, student newspaper, international student organization, Fellowship of Christian Athletes, Student Foundation, Habitat for Humanity, summer missions, married student fellowship, student ministries, 2 CARE Council.

Athletics. NCAA, NCCAA. **Intercollegiate:** Baseball M, basketball, golf, soccer, softball W, tennis, volleyball W. **Intramural:** Badminton, basketball, cross-country, football (non-tackle), golf, racquetball, soccer, softball, swimming, table tennis, tennis, volleyball. **Team name:** YellowJackets.

Student services. Chaplain/spiritual director, career counseling, student employment services, financial aid counseling, health services, personal counseling, placement for graduates, veterans' counselor. **Physically disabled:** Services for visually, speech, hearing impaired.

Contact. E-mail: admissions@letu.edu
Phone: (903) 233-4300 Toll-free number: (800) 759-8811
Fax: (903) 233-4301
James Townsend, Director of Admissions, LeTourneau University, PO Box 7001, Longview, TX 75607-7001

Lubbock Christian University

Lubbock, Texas
www.lcu.edu **CB code: 6378**

- Private 4-year university and liberal arts college affiliated with Church of Christ
- Commuter campus in small city
- 1,564 degree-seeking undergraduates: 18% part-time, 58% women, 5% African American, 16% Hispanic American, 1% international
- 304 degree-seeking graduate students
- 67% of applicants admitted
- SAT or ACT (ACT writing recommended) required
- 43% graduate within 6 years

General. Founded in 1957. Regionally accredited. **Degrees:** 351 bachelor's, 1 associate awarded; master's offered. **ROTC:** Army. **Location:** 300 miles from Dallas; 325 miles from Albuquerque, New Mexico. **Calendar:** Semester, limited summer session. **Full-time faculty:** 86 total; 70% have terminal degrees, 5% minority, 43% women. **Part-time faculty:** 81 total; 27% have terminal degrees, 12% minority, 56% women. **Class size:** 61% < 20, 31% 20-39, 2% 40-49, 6% 50-99. **Special facilities:** 2 farms totaling 450 acres.

Freshman class profile. 1,099 applied, 733 admitted, 273 enrolled.

Mid 50% test scores		**GPA 2.0-2.99:**	12%
SAT critical reading:	430-560	**Rank in top quarter:**	49%
SAT math:	440-530	**Rank in top tenth:**	17%
SAT writing:	440-570	**Return as sophomores:**	65%
ACT composite:	18-23	**Out-of-state:**	13%
GPA 3.75 or higher:	41%	**Live on campus:**	72%
GPA 3.50-3.74:	27%	**Fraternities:**	8%
GPA 3.0-3.49:	19%	**Sororities:**	14%

Basis for selection. Standardized test scores and secondary academic record considered. **Homeschooled:** Transcript of courses and grades required. **Learning Disabled:** Applicants accepted for admission who claim disabilities must provide evidence of disabilities to Disability Coordinator.

High school preparation. College-preparatory program recommended. 23 units recommended. Recommended units include English 4, mathematics 3, social studies 2, history 2, science 3 (laboratory 2), foreign language 2, computer science 1 and academic electives 4.

2008-2009 Annual costs. Tuition/fees: $14,700. Room/board: $4,850. Books/supplies: $1,100. Personal expenses: $2,054.

2007-2008 Financial aid. **Need-based:** 222 full-time freshmen applied for aid; 192 were judged to have need; 192 of these received aid. Average need met was 74%. Average scholarship/grant was $7,949; average loan $3,465. 43% of total undergraduate aid awarded as scholarships/grants, 57% as loans/jobs. **Non-need-based:** Awarded to 357 full-time undergraduates, including 99 freshmen. Scholarships awarded for academics, athletics, job skills, leadership, music/drama.

Application procedures. **Admission:** Closing date 8/15 (receipt date). $25 fee, may be waived for applicants with need. Admission notification on a rolling basis. **Financial aid:** Priority date 6/1; no closing date. FAFSA, institutional form required. Applicants notified on a rolling basis starting 3/1.

Academics. Computer use integrated into the curriculum. **Special study options:** Distance learning, double major, honors, independent study, internships, liberal arts/career combination, student-designed major, study abroad, teacher certification program. **Credit/placement by examination:** AP, CLEP, IB, SAT, ACT, institutional tests. 45 credit hours maximum toward bachelor's degree. **Support services:** Learning center, pre-admission summer program, reduced course load, remedial instruction, study skills assistance, tutoring.

Majors. **Agriculture:** General, animal sciences, business, plant sciences. **Biology:** General. **Business:** Accounting, business admin, finance, management information systems, marketing. **Communications:** General, organizational. **Education:** Agricultural, art, biology, business, chemistry, computer, early childhood, elementary, English, history, mathematics, multi-level teacher, music, physical, science, secondary, social studies, Spanish, special, speech. **Engineering:** General. **Family/consumer sciences:** Work/family studies. **Health:** Athletic training, nursing (RN), predental, premedicine, prenursing, prepharmacy, preveterinary. **Liberal arts:** Humanities. **Math:** General. **Parks/recreation:** Exercise sciences, health/fitness, sports admin. **Physical sciences:** Chemistry. **Protective services:** Law enforcement admin. **Psychology:** General. **Public administration:** Social work. **Theology:** Bible, missionary, sacred music, youth ministry. **Visual/performing arts:** Design.

Most popular majors. Business/marketing 27%, education 14%, health sciences 13%, public administration/social services 7%, theological studies 7%.

Computing on campus. 235 workstations in dormitories, library, computer center, student center. Dormitories wired for high-speed internet access and linked to campus network. Commuter students can connect to campus network. Online course registration, online library, helpline, repair service, wireless network available.

Student life. **Freshman orientation:** Available, $145 fee. Preregistration for classes offered. Week-long orientation held the week before fall semester begins. **Policies:** Chapel attendance required for full-time students age 24 or under. Religious observance required. **Housing:** Guaranteed on-campus for freshmen. Single-sex dorms, special housing for disabled, apartments, wellness housing available. $90 nonrefundable deposit, deadline 8/15. **Activities:** Jazz band, campus ministries, choral groups, drama, international student organizations, music ensembles, musical theater, student government, student newspaper, Best Friends, Missions Club, Fellowship of Christian Athletes, Students in Free Enterprise, Social Work Outreach Association, social clubs, Organization of Latin American Students.

Athletics. NAIA. **Intercollegiate:** Baseball M, basketball, golf, softball W, volleyball W. **Intramural:** Badminton, basketball, bowling, football (non-tackle), soccer, softball, table tennis, tennis, volleyball. **Team name:** Chaparrals.

Student services. Adult student services, alcohol/substance abuse counseling, chaplain/spiritual director, career counseling, student employment services, financial aid counseling, health services, personal counseling, placement for graduates, veterans' counselor.

Contact. E-mail: admissions@lcu.edu
Phone: (806) 720-7151 Toll-free number: (800) 933-7601 ext. 7151
Fax: (806) 720-7162
Charlie Webb, Director of Admissions, Lubbock Christian University, 5601 19th Street, Lubbock, TX 79407

McMurry University
Abilene, Texas **CB member**
www.mcm.edu **CB code: 6402**

- Private 4-year university and liberal arts college affiliated with United Methodist Church
- Residential campus in small city
- 1,383 degree-seeking undergraduates: 13% part-time, 50% women, 15% African American, 1% Asian American, 15% Hispanic American, 1% Native American, 1% international
- 58% of applicants admitted
- SAT or ACT (ACT writing recommended), application essay required
- 41% graduate within 6 years; 30% enter graduate study

General. Founded in 1923. Regionally accredited. Three-week May term available; additional off-campus extension at Dyess Air Force Base; part of 3-member consortium providing collegiate nursing education in Texas. **Degrees:** 226 bachelor's awarded. **Location:** 155 miles from Fort Worth, 220 miles from Austin. **Calendar:** Semester, extensive summer session. **Full-time faculty:** 80 total; 80% have terminal degrees, 8% minority, 34% women. **Part-time faculty:** 44 total; 25% have terminal degrees, 46% women. **Class size:** 61% < 20, 38% 20-39, less than 1% 40-49, 1% 50-99. **Special facilities:** Buffalo Gap historical village.

Freshman class profile. 1,448 applied, 834 admitted, 332 enrolled.

Mid 50% test scores		**GPA 2.0-2.99:**	24%
SAT critical reading:	410-530	**Rank in top quarter:**	39%
SAT math:	420-540	**Rank in top tenth:**	12%
ACT composite:	17-23	**End year in good standing:**	79%
GPA 3.75 or higher:	31%	**Return as sophomores:**	57%
GPA 3.50-3.74:	13%	**Out-of-state:**	4%
GPA 3.0-3.49:	32%	**Live on campus:**	88%

Basis for selection. Applicants evaluated on basis of ACT or SAT scores, high school rank and GPA, academic preparation, and extracurricular activities; character considered. Interview recommended for all; audition required for music, theater programs; portfolio required for art; interview required for admission to Honors Program. **Learning Disabled:** Appropriate documentation required for students seeking special accommodations.

High school preparation. College-preparatory program recommended. 14 units required; 16 recommended. Required and recommended units include English 4, mathematics 3, social studies 4, science 3 and foreign language 2. 2 units of foreign language strongly recommended; those who enroll with fewer than 2 units required to take 8 hours of foreign language.

2008-2009 Annual costs. Tuition/fees: $18,135. Room/board: $6,657. Books/supplies: $1,200. Personal expenses: $1,800.

2008-2009 Financial aid. Need-based: 313 full-time freshmen applied for aid; 282 were judged to have need; 282 of these received aid. Average need met was 92%. Average scholarship/grant was $11,389; average loan $3,165. 68% of total undergraduate aid awarded as scholarships/grants, 32% as loans/jobs. **Non-need-based:** Awarded to 716 full-time undergraduates, including 485 freshmen. Scholarships awarded for academics, alumni affiliation, art, music/drama, religious affiliation.

Application procedures. Admission: Priority date 3/15; deadline 8/15 (receipt date). $20 fee, may be waived for applicants with need. Admission notification on a rolling basis beginning on or about 9/1. Must reply by May 1 or within 2 week(s) if notified thereafter. **Financial aid:** Priority date 3/15; no closing date. FAFSA required. Applicants notified on a rolling basis starting 2/1; must reply within 3 week(s) of notification.

Academics. Students receive credit for both nontraditional and traditional courses on and off campus during 3-week May term. Opportunities for bachelor's degree after early admission to dental, medical, or veterinary school. **Special study options:** Accelerated study, combined bachelor's/graduate degree, cross-registration, double major, dual enrollment of high school students, honors, independent study, internships, liberal arts/career combination, student-designed major, study abroad, teacher certification program. Engineering with Texas A&M University. **Credit/placement by examination:** AP, CLEP, IB, SAT, ACT, institutional tests. 45 credit hours maximum toward bachelor's degree. Special examinations may be given, upon approval of necessary department, for credit in areas not covered by AP or CLEP. **Support services:** Learning center, reduced course load, remedial instruction, study skills assistance, tutoring, writing center.

Majors. Biology: General, biochemistry, biomedical sciences. **Business:** General, accounting, business admin, finance, management information systems, marketing. **Computer sciences:** General. **Education:** Art, biology, computer, early childhood, elementary, English, history, mathematics, middle, physical, secondary, Spanish. **Foreign languages:** Spanish. **Health:** Athletic training, nursing (RN). **History:** General. **Math:** General. **Parks/recreation:** Exercise sciences. **Philosophy/religion:** Religion. **Physical sciences:** Chemistry, physics. **Psychology:** General. **Social sciences:** Political science, sociology. **Visual/performing arts:** Dramatic, graphic design, studio arts. **Other:** Multi-/Interdisciplinary studies.

Most popular majors. Biology 6%, business/marketing 17%, education 21%, health sciences 10%, psychology 8%, social sciences 9%, visual/performing arts 9%.

Computing on campus. PC or laptop required. 248 workstations in library, computer center, student center. Dormitories wired for high-speed internet access and linked to campus network. Commuter students can connect to campus network. Online library, helpline, student web hosting, wireless network available.

Student life. Freshman orientation: Available, $150 fee. Preregistration for classes offered. Summer weekend orientation plus 4-day orientation before first week of classes. **Housing:** Guaranteed on-campus for all undergraduates. Coed dorms, single-sex dorms, special housing for disabled, apartments, wellness housing available. $150 partly refundable deposit, deadline 5/1. **Activities:** Bands, campus ministries, choral groups, drama, literary magazine, music ensembles, Model UN, musical theater, student government, student newspaper, Alpha Phi Omega, Fellowship of Christian Athletes, Religious Life, Servant Leadership, Kappa Delta Sigma, Student Ambassador Board, Zeta Phi Beta, campus activities board.

Athletics. NCAA. **Intercollegiate:** Baseball M, basketball, cheerleading, cross-country, diving, football (tackle) M, golf, soccer, swimming, tennis, track and field, volleyball W. **Intramural:** Basketball, football (non-tackle), golf, racquetball, soccer, softball, tennis, volleyball.

Student services. Alcohol/substance abuse counseling, chaplain/spiritual director, career counseling, student employment services, financial aid counseling, health services, personal counseling, placement for graduates, veterans' counselor.

Contact. E-mail: admissions@mcm.edu
Phone: (325) 793-4700 Toll-free number: (800) 460-2392
Fax: (325) 793-4701
Dave Voskuil, Vice President for Enrollment Management, McMurry University, South 14th and Sayles Boulevard, Abilene, TX 79697-0001

Midwestern State University
Wichita Falls, Texas **CB member**
www.mwsu.edu **CB code: 6408**

- Public 4-year university and liberal arts college
- Commuter campus in small city
- 5,360 degree-seeking undergraduates: 26% part-time, 57% women, 14% African American, 4% Asian American, 10% Hispanic American, 1% Native American, 6% international
- 690 degree-seeking graduate students
- 53% of applicants admitted
- SAT or ACT with writing required

General. Founded in 1922. Regionally accredited. **Degrees:** 974 bachelor's, 38 associate awarded; master's offered. **ROTC:** Air Force. **Location:** 130 miles from Dallas-Fort Worth. **Calendar:** Semester, extensive summer session. **Full-time faculty:** 214 total; 72% have terminal degrees, 13% minority, 47% women. **Part-time faculty:** 143 total; 24% have terminal degrees, 8% minority, 51% women. **Class size:** 34% < 20, 46% 20-39, 9% 40-49, 10% 50-99, less than 1% >100. **Special facilities:** Kurzweil reading machine for the blind, greenhouse, 2 biologic study properties.

Freshman class profile. 2,517 applied, 1,345 admitted, 667 enrolled.

Mid 50% test scores		**Rank in top quarter:**	38%
SAT critical reading:	450-530	**Rank in top tenth:**	11%
SAT math:	460-560	**Return as sophomores:**	71%
SAT writing:	430-540	**Out-of-state:**	5%
ACT composite:	19-23	**Live on campus:**	50%
GPA 3.75 or higher:	31%	**International:**	4%
GPA 3.50-3.74:	18%	**Fraternities:**	10%
GPA 3.0-3.49:	29%	**Sororities:**	17%
GPA 2.0-2.99:	21%		

Basis for selection. For unconditional admission, students must graduate from accredited high school, meet requirements, submit official transcripts and ACT/SAT scores. Entrance exams determined by class rank. Texas public universities require THEA test score on file prior to enrollment unless student exempt. Audition required for applied music program.

High school preparation. College-preparatory program recommended. 15 units required. Required units include English 4, mathematics 3, science 2 and academic electives 6.

2008-2009 Annual costs. Tuition/fees: $5,918; $6,818 out-of-state. Room/board: $5,600. Books/supplies: $1,200. Personal expenses: $1,379.

2008-2009 Financial aid. **Need-based:** 453 full-time freshmen applied for aid; 301 were judged to have need; 300 of these received aid. Average need met was 75%. Average scholarship/grant was $6,178; average loan $5,783. 40% of total undergraduate aid awarded as scholarships/grants, 60% as loans/jobs. **Non-need-based:** Awarded to 1,279 full-time undergraduates, including 264 freshmen. Scholarships awarded for academics, alumni affiliation, art, athletics, leadership, music/drama. **Additional information:** Employees offered educational incentive plan in which tuition reimbursed provided employee meets stated criteria. Additionally, dependents and children of faculty and staff may receive scholarship to defer local tuition and fees.

Application procedures. **Admission:** Priority date 7/1; deadline 8/7 (receipt date). $25 fee. Admission notification on a rolling basis beginning on or about 9/1. **Financial aid:** Priority date 5/1; no closing date. FAFSA required. Applicants notified on a rolling basis starting 4/1; must reply within 4 week(s) of notification.

Academics. **Special study options:** Combined bachelor's/graduate degree, distance learning, double major, dual enrollment of high school students, ESL, honors, independent study, internships, liberal arts/career combination, study abroad, teacher certification program. Study abroad in England, France, Spain, and Mexico. **Credit/placement by examination:** AP, CLEP, IB, SAT, ACT, institutional tests. 26 credit hours maximum toward associate degree, 60 toward bachelor's. **Support services:** Learning center, reduced course load, remedial instruction, study skills assistance, tutoring, writing center.

Majors. **Biology:** General. **Business:** General, accounting, business admin, finance, international, management information systems, marketing. **Communications:** Media studies. **Computer sciences:** General. **Conservation:** Environmental science. **Education:** Bilingual, early childhood, English. **Engineering:** General, mechanical. **Engineering technology:** Manufacturing. **Foreign languages:** Spanish. **Health:** Athletic training, clinical lab science, dental hygiene, nursing (RN), predental, premedicine, prepharmacy, preveterinary, radiologic technology/medical imaging, respiratory therapy technology. **History:** General. **Interdisciplinary:** Global studies. **Legal studies:** Prelaw. **Liberal arts:** Humanities. **Math:** General. **Parks/recreation:** Exercise sciences, facilities management, health/fitness. **Physical sciences:** General, chemistry, geology, physics. **Protective services:** Criminal justice. **Psychology:** General. **Public administration:** Social work. **Social sciences:** Economics, political science, sociology. **Visual/performing arts:** Art, dramatic, studio arts.

Most popular majors. Business/marketing 17%, education 8%, health sciences 24%, interdisciplinary studies 16%.

Computing on campus. 429 workstations in dormitories, library, computer center, student center. Dormitories wired for high-speed internet access and linked to campus network. Commuter students can connect to campus network. Online course registration, online library, wireless network available.

Student life. **Freshman orientation:** Mandatory. Preregistration for classes offered. Parents and family welcome to attend orientation events. **Housing:** Guaranteed on-campus for freshmen. Coed dorms, single-sex dorms, special housing for disabled, apartments, wellness housing available. $100 fully refundable deposit. Cooperative housing units for honors students and biology students. **Activities:** Bands, campus ministries, choral groups, dance, drama, film society, international student organizations, literary magazine, music ensembles, student government, student newspaper, TV station, Methodist student foundation, Baptist student center, Student Ambassadors, black student union, organization of Hispanic students, University Democrats, College Republicans, Amnesty International.

Athletics. NCAA. **Intercollegiate:** Basketball, cross-country W, football (tackle) M, rowing (crew) W, soccer, softball W, tennis, volleyball W. **Intramural:** Archery, badminton, basketball, bowling, football (non-tackle), football (tackle) M, golf, soccer, softball, table tennis, tennis, volleyball. **Team name:** Mustangs.

Student services. Alcohol/substance abuse counseling, career counseling, student employment services, financial aid counseling, health services, personal counseling, placement for graduates, veterans' counselor. **Physically disabled:** Services for visually, speech, hearing impaired.

Contact. E-mail: admissions@mwsu.edu
Phone: (940) 397-4334 Toll-free number: (800) 842-1922
Fax: (940) 397-4672
Barbara Merkle, Director of Admissions, Midwestern State University, 3410 Taft Boulevard, Wichita Falls, TX 76308-2099

Northwood University: Texas
Cedar Hill, Texas
www.northwood.edu **CB code: 6499**

- Private 4-year university and business college
- Residential campus in large town
- 461 degree-seeking undergraduates: 5% part-time, 46% women, 15% African American, 4% Asian American, 30% Hispanic American, 2% Native American, 7% international
- 55% of applicants admitted
- SAT or ACT (ACT writing optional), application essay required
- 30% graduate within 6 years

General. Founded in 1966. Regionally accredited. Specialty university offering only business degrees in professional management; 3 residential campuses in Michigan, Florida, and Texas; 40 program centers; library center in Maine. **Degrees:** 111 bachelor's, 90 associate awarded. **Location:** 18 miles from Dallas, 28 miles from Fort Worth. **Calendar:** Quarter, limited summer session. **Full-time faculty:** 26 total; 19% have terminal degrees, 12% minority, 31% women. **Part-time faculty:** 13 total; 15% have terminal degrees, 8% minority, 31% women. **Class size:** 63% < 20, 35% 20-39, 2% 40-49.

Freshman class profile. 503 applied, 277 admitted, 99 enrolled.

Mid 50% test scores		**GPA 2.0-2.99:**	13%
SAT critical reading:	410-540	**Rank in top quarter:**	36%
SAT math:	430-540	**Rank in top tenth:**	12%
SAT writing:	400-510	**End year in good standing:**	74%
ACT composite:	18-22	**Return as sophomores:**	60%
GPA 3.75 or higher:	8%	**Out-of-state:**	5%
GPA 3.50-3.74:	19%	**Live on campus:**	45%
GPA 3.0-3.49:	60%	**International:**	1%

Basis for selection. Minimum GPA of 2.0 and strong interest in business or related field. Test scores considered. Students with lower GPA possibly admitted on probation. Interview recommended. **Homeschooled:** Transcript of courses and grades, state high school equivalency certificate required.

High school preparation. College-preparatory program recommended. 17 units recommended. Recommended units include English 4, mathematics 3, social studies 3, science 3 (laboratory 2), foreign language 1 and computer science 1.

2008-2009 Annual costs. Tuition/fees: $18,468. Room/board: $7,506. Books/supplies: $1,404. Personal expenses: $1,395.

2008-2009 Financial aid. **Need-based:** 80 full-time freshmen applied for aid; 73 were judged to have need; 73 of these received aid. Average need met was 64%. Average scholarship/grant was $6,098; average loan $3,344. 54% of total undergraduate aid awarded as scholarships/grants, 46% as loans/jobs. **Non-need-based:** Awarded to 186 full-time undergraduates, including 31 freshmen. Scholarships awarded for academics, alumni affiliation, athletics, leadership, minority status, state residency.

Application procedures. **Admission:** No deadline. $25 fee, may be waived for applicants with need, free for online applicants. Admission notification on a rolling basis. **Financial aid:** No deadline. FAFSA required. Applicants notified on a rolling basis starting 3/1.

Academics. **Special study options:** Accelerated study, distance learning, double major, dual enrollment of high school students, external degree, honors, independent study, internships, student-designed major, study abroad. **Credit/placement by examination:** AP, CLEP, IB, SAT, ACT, institutional tests. 12 credit hours maximum toward associate degree, 12 toward bachelor's. **Support services:** Learning center, reduced course load, remedial instruction, study skills assistance, tutoring, writing center.

Majors. **Business:** Accounting, banking/financial services, business admin, entrepreneurial studies, fashion, hotel/motel admin, international, management information systems, marketing, vehicle parts marketing. **Communications:** Advertising. **Computer sciences:** General. **Parks/recreation:** Sports admin.

Most popular majors. Business/marketing 91%.

Computing on campus. 50 workstations in library, computer center. Dormitories wired for high-speed internet access and linked to campus network. Commuter students can connect to campus network. Online course registration, online library, helpline, student web hosting, wireless network available.

Student life. **Freshman orientation:** Mandatory, $125 fee. Preregistration for classes offered. 5 days in early September. **Housing:** Guaranteed on-campus for freshmen. Single-sex dorms, apartments, wellness housing available. $100 fully refundable deposit, deadline 8/1. **Activities:** Choral groups, dance, drama, literary magazine, student government, student newspaper, Christian Fellowship.

Athletics. NAIA. **Intercollegiate:** Baseball M, cross-country, golf, soccer, softball W, track and field. **Intramural:** Basketball, volleyball. **Team name:** Knights.

Student services. Adult student services, career counseling, student employment services, financial aid counseling, health services, personal counseling, placement for graduates.

Contact. E-mail: txadmit@northwood.edu
Phone: (972) 293-5400 Toll-free number: (800) 927-9663
Fax: (972) 291-3824
Sylvia Correa, Director of Admissions, Northwood University: Texas, 1114 West FM 1382, Cedar Hill, TX 75104

Our Lady of the Lake University of San Antonio

San Antonio, Texas — **CB member**
www.ollusa.edu — **CB code: 6550**

- Private 4-year university affiliated with Roman Catholic Church
- Commuter campus in very large city
- 1,546 degree-seeking undergraduates: 26% part-time, 73% women, 7% African American, 1% Asian American, 72% Hispanic American
- 1,073 degree-seeking graduate students
- 51% of applicants admitted
- SAT or ACT (ACT writing optional) required
- 37% graduate within 6 years

General. Founded in 1895. Regionally accredited. **Degrees:** 318 bachelor's awarded; master's, doctoral offered. **ROTC:** Army, Air Force. **Location:** 4 miles from downtown, 80 miles from Austin. **Calendar:** Semester, limited summer session. **Full-time faculty:** 111 total; 74% have terminal degrees, 44% minority, 59% women. **Part-time faculty:** 135 total; 37% minority, 42% women. **Class size:** 78% < 20, 22% 20-39, less than 1% 40-49. **Special facilities:** International center, international folk culture center, speech and hearing clinic, community counseling center, elementary school, child development center, center for social work research, center for women in church and society.

Freshman class profile. 2,054 applied, 1,057 admitted, 306 enrolled.

Mid 50% test scores		**Rank in top quarter:**	54%
SAT critical reading:	420-510	**Rank in top tenth:**	20%
SAT math:	430-520	**End year in good standing:**	66%
ACT composite:	17-21	**Return as sophomores:**	53%
GPA 3.75 or higher:	11%	**Out-of-state:**	1%
GPA 3.50-3.74:	31%	**Live on campus:**	64%
GPA 3.0-3.49:	40%	**International:**	1%
GPA 2.0-2.99:	17%		

Basis for selection. High school academic record and test scores important. **Homeschooled:** Transcript of courses and grades required.

High school preparation. College-preparatory program recommended. 16 units required. Required and recommended units include English 4, mathematics 2-3, social studies 3, science 2 (laboratory 2), foreign language 3 and academic electives 3.

2008-2009 Annual costs. Tuition/fees: $20,232. Room/board: $6,238. Books/supplies: $1,200. Personal expenses: $1,850.

2008-2009 Financial aid. Need-based: 47% of total undergraduate aid awarded as scholarships/grants, 53% as loans/jobs. **Non-need-based:** Scholarships awarded for academics, alumni affiliation, art, music/drama.

Application procedures. Admission: Priority date 5/1; deadline 7/15 (receipt date). $25 fee, may be waived for applicants with need. Admission notification on a rolling basis. **Financial aid:** Priority date 2/28; no closing date. FAFSA required. Applicants notified on a rolling basis starting 4/1; must reply within 2 week(s) of notification.

Academics. Special study options: Combined bachelor's/graduate degree, cooperative education, cross-registration, distance learning, double major, dual enrollment of high school students, ESL, honors, independent study, internships, liberal arts/career combination, study abroad, teacher certification program, weekend college. Service learning. **Credit/placement by examination:** AP, CLEP, IB, institutional tests. No limit to number of credit hours that may be awarded through CLEP or that may be counted towards bachelor's degree. **Support services:** Learning center, pre-admission summer program, reduced course load, remedial instruction, study skills assistance, tutoring.

Majors. Biology: General. **Business:** Accounting, business admin, human resources, marketing, nonprofit/public. **Communications:** General, broadcast journalism, journalism, public relations. **Computer sciences:** General. **Education:** Kindergarten/preschool, special, speech impaired. **Family/consumer sciences:** Business. **Foreign languages:** Spanish. **Health:** Speech pathology. **History:** General. **Interdisciplinary:** Natural sciences. **Liberal arts:** Arts/sciences. **Math:** General. **Philosophy/religion:** Philosophy, religion. **Physical sciences:** Chemistry. **Protective services:** Criminal justice. **Psychology:** General. **Public administration:** Social work. **Social sciences:** General, political science, sociology. **Visual/performing arts:** Art, dramatic.

Most popular majors. Business/marketing 19%, education 19%, family/consumer sciences 6%, liberal arts 7%, psychology 11%, public administration/social services 8%, social sciences 8%.

Computing on campus. 208 workstations in dormitories, library, computer center, student center. Dormitories wired for high-speed internet access and linked to campus network. Commuter students can connect to campus network. Online course registration, online library, helpline, repair service, wireless network available.

Student life. Freshman orientation: Mandatory, $50 fee. Preregistration for classes offered. Overnight program, 4 times during the spring and summer. Familiarity with faculty, staff, campus, and assessment testing. Parent participation encouraged. **Housing:** Guaranteed on-campus for freshmen. Coed dorms, single-sex dorms, special housing for disabled, wellness housing available. $100 fully refundable deposit, deadline 8/1. **Activities:** Jazz band, campus ministries, choral groups, dance, drama, music ensembles, musical theater, student government, student newspaper, symphony orchestra, TV station, religious organizations, black and Hispanic clubs, service clubs.

Athletics. NAIA. **Intercollegiate:** Soccer, volleyball W. **Intramural:** Basketball, football (non-tackle), golf, racquetball, soccer W, softball, swimming, tennis, volleyball M. **Team name:** Saints.

Student services. Adult student services, alcohol/substance abuse counseling, chaplain/spiritual director, career counseling, student employment services, financial aid counseling, health services, personal counseling, placement for graduates, veterans' counselor, women's services. **Physically disabled:** Services for visually, speech, hearing impaired.

Contact. E-mail: admission@lake.ollusa.edu
Phone: (210) 434-6711 ext. 2314 Toll-free number: (800) 436-6558
Fax: (210) 431-4036
Michael Acosta, Vice President, Enrollment Management, Our Lady of the Lake University of San Antonio, 411 Southwest 24th Street, San Antonio, TX 78207-4689

Paul Quinn College

Dallas, Texas
www.pqc.edu — **CB code: 6577**

- Private 4-year liberal arts college affiliated with African Methodist Episcopal Church
- Residential campus in very large city

General. Founded in 1872. Regionally accredited. **Location:** 12 miles from Dallas. **Calendar:** Semester.

Annual costs/financial aid. Tuition/fees (2008-2009): $9,980. Room/board: $5,170. Books/supplies: $1,000. Personal expenses: $500.

Contact. Phone: (214) 302-3575
Director of Admissions, 3837 Simpson Stuart Road, Dallas, TX 75241

Prairie View A&M University

Prairie View, Texas — **CB member**
www.pvamu.edu — **CB code: 6580**

- Public 4-year university
- Commuter campus in small town
- 6,178 degree-seeking undergraduates: 8% part-time, 57% women, 89% African American, 2% Asian American, 4% Hispanic American, 1% international
- 1,925 degree-seeking graduate students
- 71% of applicants admitted

- SAT or ACT (ACT writing optional) required
- 36% graduate within 6 years

General. Founded in 1876. Regionally accredited. Historically black college. **Degrees:** 787 bachelor's awarded; master's, doctoral offered. **ROTC:** Army, Naval. **Location:** 45 miles from Houston. **Calendar:** Semester, extensive summer session. **Full-time faculty:** 369 total; 78% minority, 38% women. **Part-time faculty:** 131 total; 63% minority, 56% women. **Class size:** 27% < 20, 58% 20-39, 8% 40-49, 7% 50-99, less than 1% >100. **Special facilities:** Nuclear magnetic resonance spectrometric differentiator, scanning calorimeter, high pressure liquid chromatograph, solid state engineering laboratory, computer-aided design and drafting laboratory, center for learning and teaching effectiveness, international dairy goat research center, cooperative agricultural research center, solar observatory.

Freshman class profile. 5,879 applied, 4,170 admitted, 1,580 enrolled.

Mid 50% test scores		**GPA 3.0-3.49:**	33%
SAT critical reading:	370-460	**GPA 2.0-2.99:**	57%
SAT math:	380-480	**Rank in top quarter:**	25%
ACT composite:	15-19	**Rank in top tenth:**	7%
GPA 3.75 or higher:	2%	**Return as sophomores:**	75%
GPA 3.50-3.74:	7%		

Basis for selection. Score on institution's entrance examination, personal qualities, high school GPA important. Students may be admitted conditionally if grades or test scores are below minimum requirement.

High school preparation. 16 units required; 18 recommended. Required and recommended units include English 4, mathematics 3-4, social studies 2, science 3, foreign language 2 and academic electives 4. Recommend 1 computer science.

2009-2010 Annual costs. Tuition/fees: $7,199; $15,689 out-of-state. Room/board: $7,445. Books/supplies: $1,200. Personal expenses: $5,000.

2008-2009 Financial aid. Need-based: 53% of total undergraduate aid awarded as scholarships/grants, 47% as loans/jobs. **Non-need-based:** Scholarships awarded for academics, athletics, ROTC.

Application procedures. Admission: Closing date 6/1 (postmark date). $25 fee, may be waived for applicants with need. Admission notification on a rolling basis. **Financial aid:** Closing date 3/15. FAFSA, institutional form required. Applicants notified by 6/1; must reply by 8/1.

Academics. Special study options: Accelerated study, combined bachelor's/graduate degree, cooperative education, cross-registration, distance learning, double major, dual enrollment of high school students, exchange student, external degree, honors, independent study, internships, liberal arts/career combination, study abroad, teacher certification program, weekend college. **Credit/placement by examination:** AP, CLEP. 30 credit hours maximum toward bachelor's degree. **Support services:** Learning center, preadmission summer program, reduced course load, remedial instruction, tutoring.

Majors. Agriculture: General. **Architecture:** Architecture. **Biology:** General. **Business:** Accounting, business admin, finance, management information systems. **Communications:** General. **Computer sciences:** General. **Engineering:** Chemical, civil, computer, electrical, mechanical. **Engineering technology:** Computer, construction, drafting, electrical, industrial. **Family/consumer sciences:** Food/nutrition. **Foreign languages:** Spanish. **Health:** Clinical lab science, health services, nursing (RN). **History:** General. **Math:** General. **Parks/recreation:** Health/fitness. **Physical sciences:** Chemistry, physics. **Protective services:** Criminal justice. **Psychology:** General. **Public administration:** Social work. **Social sciences:** Political science, sociology. **Visual/performing arts:** Dramatic, music performance, piano/organ, voice/opera.

Most popular majors. Agriculture 6%, architecture 6%, biology 8%, business/marketing 7%, communications/journalism 7%, education 8%, health sciences 11%, interdisciplinary studies 8%, legal studies 8%, psychology 6%, security/protective services 9%.

Computing on campus. 500 workstations in dormitories, library, computer center, student center. Dormitories wired for high-speed internet access and linked to campus network. Commuter students can connect to campus network. Online library, helpline, wireless network available.

Student life. Freshman orientation: Mandatory, $60 fee. Preregistration for classes offered. 1 day for Phase 1; 3 days for Phase 2. **Housing:** Guaranteed on-campus for freshmen. Coed dorms, special housing for disabled, apartments available. $150 fully refundable deposit. **Activities:** Bands, choral groups, dance, drama, international student organizations, literary magazine, music ensembles, musical theater, radio station, student government, student newspaper, symphony orchestra, College Republicans, Spanish-speaking students association, Baptist student ministry, Chinese student association, ministerial alliance, Japanese student association, Korean student association.

Athletics. NAIA, NCAA. **Intercollegiate:** Baseball M, basketball, bowling W, cross-country, football (tackle) M, golf, soccer W, softball W, tennis, track and field, volleyball W. **Intramural:** Basketball, bowling W, football (tackle) M, golf, soccer W, softball, tennis, track and field, volleyball W. **Team name:** Panthers.

Student services. Adult student services, alcohol/substance abuse counseling, chaplain/spiritual director, career counseling, student employment services, financial aid counseling, health services, personal counseling, placement for graduates, veterans' counselor. **Physically disabled:** Services for hearing impaired.

Contact. E-mail: admissions@pvamu.edu
Phone: (936) 261-1000
Mary Gooch, Assistant Director Admissions, Prairie View A&M University, PO Box 519, MS 1009, Prairie View, TX 77446-0519

Rice University

Houston, Texas — **CB member**
www.rice.edu — **CB code: 6609**

- Private 4-year university
- Residential campus in very large city
- 3,102 degree-seeking undergraduates: 1% part-time, 48% women, 7% African American, 21% Asian American, 12% Hispanic American, 6% international
- 2,237 degree-seeking graduate students
- 23% of applicants admitted
- SAT and SAT Subject Tests or ACT with writing, application essay required
- 93% graduate within 6 years

General. Founded in 1891. Regionally accredited. Every student member of one of 9 residential colleges. **Degrees:** 978 bachelor's awarded; master's, doctoral offered. **ROTC:** Army, Naval, Air Force. **Location:** 3 miles from downtown Houston. **Calendar:** Semester, limited summer session. **Full-time faculty:** 598 total; 97% have terminal degrees, 18% minority, 29% women. **Part-time faculty:** 143 total; 77% have terminal degrees, 10% minority, 40% women. **Class size:** 65% < 20, 23% 20-39, 4% 40-49, 6% 50-99, 2% >100. **Special facilities:** Art gallery, wetland center for biochemical research, nanotechnology lab, center for study of languages and culture, civil engineering lab, concert hall with grand organ, institute for public policy, observatory, digital media center.

Freshman class profile. 9,813 applied, 2,255 admitted, 789 enrolled.

Mid 50% test scores		**Rank in top tenth:**	85%
SAT critical reading:	650-750	**Return as sophomores:**	97%
SAT math:	670-780	**Out-of-state:**	44%
SAT writing:	640-750	**Live on campus:**	98%
ACT composite:	30-34	**International:**	8%
Rank in top quarter:	94%		

Basis for selection. High school course selection and performance, test scores, teacher and counselor recommendations, extracurricular activity, and application answers/essay most important. If student submits SAT Reasoning, two SAT Subject Tests are also required (recommend subject tests be in subjects related to student's area of interest). If student submits ACT with Writing, then no SAT Subject Tests are required. Audition required for music; portfolio required for architecture. Interview recommended for all freshman applicants. **Homeschooled:** Statement describing homeschool structure and mission, letter of recommendation (nonparent) required.

High school preparation. College-preparatory program required. 16 units required; 20 recommended. Required and recommended units include English 4, mathematics 3-4, social studies 2, science 2-4 (laboratory 2-3), foreign language 2-4 and academic electives 3. Trigonometry (pre-calculus), physics, and chemistry required of engineering and natural science majors, although 2nd year of chemistry or biology may replace physics requirement.

2008-2009 Annual costs. Tuition/fees: $30,486. Room/board: $10,750. Books/supplies: $800. Personal expenses: $1,550.

2008-2009 Financial aid. Need-based: 679 full-time freshmen applied for aid; 275 were judged to have need; 275 of these received aid. Average need met was 100%. Average scholarship/grant was $28,392; average loan $896. 90% of total undergraduate aid awarded as scholarships/grants, 10%

as loans/jobs. **Non-need-based:** Awarded to 1,011 full-time undergraduates, including 192 freshmen. Scholarships awarded for academics, art, athletics, leadership, minority status, music/drama, ROTC, state residency.

Application procedures. **Admission:** Closing date 1/2 (postmark date). $60 fee, may be waived for applicants with need. Admission notification 4/1. Must reply by May 1 or within 2 week(s) if notified thereafter. Early decision housing deposit due by 1/1. **Financial aid:** Priority date 3/1; no closing date. FAFSA, CSS PROFILE required. Applicants notified by 4/1; must reply by 5/1.

Academics. **Special study options:** Combined bachelor's/graduate degree, cross-registration, double major, dual enrollment of high school students, ESL, exchange student, honors, independent study, internships, liberal arts/career combination, student-designed major, study abroad, teacher certification program. 8-year guaranteed medical school program with Baylor College of Medicine for 15 entering freshmen. **Credit/placement by examination:** AP, CLEP, IB, institutional tests. **Support services:** Study skills assistance, tutoring.

Majors. **Architecture:** Architecture. **Area/ethnic studies:** Asian, German, Hispanic-American/Latino/Chicano, Latin American, Slavic, women's. **Biology:** General, biochemistry, ecology, evolutionary. **Business:** Business admin. **Computer sciences:** Computer science. **Engineering:** Biomedical, chemical, civil, computer, electrical, environmental, materials, mechanical. **Foreign languages:** Ancient Greek, classics, French, German, Latin, linguistics, Slavic, Spanish. **History:** General. **Interdisciplinary:** Classical/archaeology, cognitive science, medieval/Renaissance. **Math:** General, applied, statistics. **Parks/recreation:** Exercise sciences. **Philosophy/religion:** Philosophy, religion. **Physical sciences:** Astronomy, astrophysics, chemical physics, chemistry, geology, geophysics, physical chemistry, physics. **Psychology:** General. **Public administration:** Policy analysis. **Social sciences:** General, anthropology, economics, political science, sociology. **Visual/performing arts:** General, art, art history/conservation, music history, music performance, music theory/composition, studio arts.

Most popular majors. Biology 9%, engineering/engineering technologies 15%, English 6%, psychology 6%, social sciences 17%.

Computing on campus. 523 workstations in dormitories, library, computer center, student center. Dormitories wired for high-speed internet access and linked to campus network. Commuter students can connect to campus network. Online course registration, online library, helpline, student web hosting, wireless network available.

Student life. **Freshman orientation:** Mandatory, $250 fee. Held the week before start of classes. **Policies:** Academic honor code. All undergraduates are granted membership in one of 9 residential college communities and maintains that affiliation for their entire college career. Each college is self governing and designed to facilitate student and faculty networking, leadership development, pre-major advising, and social interaction. **Housing:** Guaranteed on-campus for freshmen. Coed dorms, special housing for disabled available. $100 deposit, deadline 5/1. **Activities:** Bands, campus ministries, choral groups, dance, drama, film society, international student organizations, literary magazine, music ensembles, Model UN, musical theater, opera, radio station, student government, student newspaper, symphony orchestra, TV station, Hispanic student association, Hillel, Black student association, Young Democrats, Young Republicans, Chinese student association, Baptist Student Union, Catholic student center, student volunteer program.

Athletics. NCAA. **Intercollegiate:** Baseball M, basketball, cheerleading, cross-country, fencing M, field hockey W, football (tackle) M, golf M, lacrosse, rowing (crew), rugby M, soccer, softball W, swimming W, tennis, track and field, volleyball W. **Intramural:** Badminton, basketball, football (non-tackle), racquetball, softball, swimming, table tennis, tennis, track and field, volleyball. **Team name:** Owls.

Student services. Alcohol/substance abuse counseling, chaplain/spiritual director, career counseling, student employment services, financial aid counseling, health services, minority student services, personal counseling, placement for graduates, women's services. **Physically disabled:** Services for visually, speech, hearing impaired.

Contact. E-mail: admission@rice.edu
Phone: (713) 348-7423 Toll-free number: (800) 527-6957
Fax: (713) 348-5952
Keith Todd, Director of Admission, Rice University, 6100 Main Street, Houston, TX 77251-1892

St. Edward's University

Austin, Texas — **CB member**
www.gotostedwards.com — **CB code: 6619**

- Private 4-year university and liberal arts college affiliated with Roman Catholic Church
- Residential campus in very large city
- 4,341 degree-seeking undergraduates: 21% part-time, 60% women, 5% African American, 2% Asian American, 31% Hispanic American, 1% Native American, 2% international
- 925 degree-seeking graduate students
- 64% of applicants admitted
- SAT or ACT with writing, application essay required
- 62% graduate within 6 years

General. Founded in 1885. Regionally accredited. **Degrees:** 921 bachelor's awarded; master's offered. **ROTC:** Army, Air Force. **Location:** 80 miles from San Antonio, 180 miles from Dallas. **Calendar:** Semester, limited summer session. **Full-time faculty:** 186 total; 89% have terminal degrees, 9% minority, 47% women. **Part-time faculty:** 308 total; 49% have terminal degrees, 16% minority, 50% women. **Class size:** 52% < 20, 48% 20-39, less than 1% 40-49. **Special facilities:** Fine arts facility with photography laboratory, theater, chapel, natural sciences center including laboratories, classrooms and seminar rooms, interdisciplinary research laboratory at Wild Basin Wilderness Preserve, living-learning communities.

Freshman class profile. 2,766 applied, 1,762 admitted, 741 enrolled.

Mid 50% test scores			
SAT critical reading:	520-620	Rank in top tenth:	17%
SAT math:	510-610	End year in good standing:	92%
SAT writing:	510-600	Return as sophomores:	84%
ACT composite:	21-27	Out-of-state:	7%
Rank in top quarter:	51%	Live on campus:	91%
		International:	2%

Basis for selection. Grades and curriculum, rank in top half of class, test scores in top 50th percentile nationally most important. Extracurricular leadership and service, essay, letter of recommendation also considered. **Homeschooled:** Transcript of courses and grades required. Assessment done on individual basis. **Learning Disabled:** Students may submit learning disability documentation with admission application, if they so choose.

High school preparation. College-preparatory program recommended. 14 units required; 20 recommended. Required and recommended units include English 4, mathematics 3-4, social studies 1, history 2-3, science 2-3 (laboratory 2-3), foreign language 2-3, computer science 1 and academic electives 1.

2009-2010 Annual costs. Tuition/fees: $24,440. Room/board: $8,496. Books/supplies: $1,100. Personal expenses: $2,394.

2008-2009 Financial aid. **Need-based:** 586 full-time freshmen applied for aid; 475 were judged to have need; 475 of these received aid. Average need met was 75%. Average scholarship/grant was $12,160; average loan $3,232. 71% of total undergraduate aid awarded as scholarships/grants, 29% as loans/jobs. **Non-need-based:** Awarded to 1,665 full-time undergraduates, including 454 freshmen. Scholarships awarded for academics, art, athletics, leadership, music/drama, state residency.

Application procedures. **Admission:** Priority date 2/1; deadline 5/1 (postmark date). $45 fee, may be waived for applicants with need. Admission notification on a rolling basis beginning on or about 11/1. Must reply by May 1 or within 2 week(s) if notified thereafter. Applicants seeking scholarship consideration must apply by February 1. **Financial aid:** Priority date 3/1, closing date 4/15. FAFSA required. Applicants notified on a rolling basis starting 1/15; must reply by 5/1 or within 2 week(s) of notification.

Academics. **Special study options:** Double major, honors, independent study, internships, semester at sea, student-designed major, study abroad, teacher certification program. **Credit/placement by examination:** AP, CLEP, IB, SAT, ACT, institutional tests. 90 credit hours maximum toward bachelor's degree. **Support services:** Learning center, reduced course load, remedial instruction, study skills assistance, tutoring, writing center.

Majors. **Area/ethnic studies:** Latin American. **Biology:** General, biochemistry, bioinformatics. **Business:** Accounting, accounting technology, business admin, entrepreneurial studies, finance, international, marketing. **Communications:** Digital media, media studies. **Computer sciences:** General, computer science. **Conservation:** Environmental studies. **Education:** Art, biology, chemistry, drama/dance, history, mathematics, multi-level teacher, physical, social studies, Spanish. **Foreign languages:** Spanish. **History:** General. **Interdisciplinary:** Global studies. **Liberal arts:** Arts/sciences. **Math:** General. **Parks/recreation:** Exercise sciences. **Philosophy/religion:** Philosophy. **Physical sciences:** Chemistry. **Protective services:** Criminal justice, forensics. **Psychology:** General. **Public administration:** Social work. **Social sciences:** Criminology, economics, political science, sociology. **Theology:** Religious ed, theology. **Visual/performing arts:** Art, dramatic, graphic design, photography. **Other:** Environmental chemistry.

Most popular majors. Business/marketing 31%, communications/journalism 12%, psychology 8%, social sciences 10%, visual/performing arts 8%.

Computing on campus. 678 workstations in dormitories, library, computer center, student center. Dormitories wired for high-speed internet access and linked to campus network. Commuter students can connect to campus network. Online course registration, online library, helpline, student web hosting, wireless network available.

Student life. **Freshman orientation:** Mandatory, $150 fee. Preregistration for classes offered. 2-day sessions held 6 times during summer. **Policies:** Student organizations must receive annual university recognition through office of student life. **Housing:** Guaranteed on-campus for freshmen. Coed dorms, single-sex dorms, special housing for disabled, apartments available. $150 nonrefundable deposit, deadline 5/1. Community-style living in casitas/casas available. Two living-learning communities: Global Understanding and Service/Social Justice. **Activities:** Jazz band, campus ministries, choral groups, dance, drama, film society, international student organizations, literary magazine, music ensembles, Model UN, musical theater, student government, student newspaper, symphony orchestra, TV station, 90 student organizations on campus.

Athletics. NCAA. **Intercollegiate:** Baseball M, basketball, cross-country, golf, soccer, softball W, tennis, volleyball W. **Intramural:** Basketball, football (non-tackle), soccer, softball, volleyball. **Team name:** Hilltoppers.

Student services. Adult student services, alcohol/substance abuse counseling, chaplain/spiritual director, career counseling, student employment services, financial aid counseling, health services, personal counseling, placement for graduates, veterans' counselor. **Physically disabled:** Services for visually, speech, hearing impaired.

Contact. E-mail: seu.admit@stedwards.edu
Phone: (512) 448-8500 Toll-free number: (800) 555-0164
Fax: (512) 464-8877
Tracy Manier, Associate VP & Dean of Undergraduate Admission, St. Edward's University, 3001 South Congress Avenue, Austin, TX 78704-6489

St. Mary's University

San Antonio, Texas — **CB member**
www.stmarytx.edu — **CB code: 6637**

- Private 4-year university affiliated with Roman Catholic Church
- Residential campus in very large city
- 2,360 degree-seeking undergraduates: 7% part-time, 60% women, 4% African American, 3% Asian American, 69% Hispanic American, 4% international
- 1,517 degree-seeking graduate students
- 63% of applicants admitted
- SAT or ACT (ACT writing recommended), application essay required
- 59% graduate within 6 years

General. Founded in 1852. Regionally accredited. **Degrees:** 434 bachelor's awarded; master's, doctoral, first professional offered. **ROTC:** Army, Air Force. **Location:** 5 miles from downtown. **Calendar:** Semester, limited summer session. **Full-time faculty:** 192 total; 93% have terminal degrees, 24% minority, 38% women. **Part-time faculty:** 159 total; 60% have terminal degrees, 28% minority, 42% women. **Class size:** 60% < 20, 39% 20-39, less than 1% 40-49.

Freshman class profile. 2,390 applied, 1,513 admitted, 537 enrolled.

Mid 50% test scores		**GPA 2.0-2.99:**	12%
SAT critical reading:	470-570	**Rank in top quarter:**	66%
SAT math:	480-580	**Rank in top tenth:**	37%
SAT writing:	450-560	**End year in good standing:**	85%
ACT composite:	20-25	**Return as sophomores:**	77%
GPA 3.75 or higher:	23%	**Out-of-state:**	3%
GPA 3.50-3.74:	30%	**Live on campus:**	76%
GPA 3.0-3.49:	34%	**International:**	4%

Basis for selection. Recommendations, talent/ability, character/personal qualities very important. Secondary school record, class rank, standardized test scores, essay and volunteer work important. Interviews, extracurricular activities, alumni/ae relation, religious affiliation or commitment, and work experience considered.

High school preparation. College-preparatory program recommended. 19 units recommended. Recommended units include English 4, mathematics 3, social studies 3, science 3, foreign language 2 and academic electives 1. Applicants to science and engineering program should complete 4 units of math and 3 units of lab science.

2008-2009 Annual costs. Tuition/fees: $21,156. Notebook computer $1,000. Room/board: $6,892. Books/supplies: $2,300. Personal expenses: $2,154.

2007-2008 Financial aid. **Need-based:** 508 full-time freshmen applied for aid; 445 were judged to have need; 445 of these received aid. Average need met was 83%. Average scholarship/grant was $15,952; average loan $4,315. 62% of total undergraduate aid awarded as scholarships/grants, 38% as loans/jobs. **Non-need-based:** Awarded to 480 full-time undergraduates, including 153 freshmen. Scholarships awarded for academics, alumni affiliation, athletics, leadership, music/drama, ROTC.

Application procedures. **Admission:** Priority date 1/15; no deadline. $30 fee, may be waived for applicants with need, free for online applicants. Admission notification on a rolling basis beginning on or about 10/20. Must reply by May 1 or within 2 week(s) if notified thereafter. **Financial aid:** Priority date 2/15; no closing date. FAFSA required. Applicants notified on a rolling basis starting 3/1; must reply by 5/1 or within 2 week(s) of notification.

Academics. Writing across the curriculum program requires students in all undergraduate programs to take writing-intensive courses. **Special study options:** Combined bachelor's/graduate degree, cross-registration, distance learning, double major, dual enrollment of high school students, ESL, exchange student, honors, independent study, internships, liberal arts/career combination, study abroad, teacher certification program, Washington semester. Evening studies program. **Credit/placement by examination:** AP, CLEP, SAT, ACT, institutional tests. 30 credit hours maximum toward bachelor's degree. **Support services:** Learning center, pre-admission summer program, reduced course load, remedial instruction, study skills assistance, tutoring, writing center.

Majors. **Biology:** General, biochemistry. **Business:** General, accounting, business admin, entrepreneurial studies, finance, human resources, international, management information systems, marketing. **Communications:** General. **Computer sciences:** General, computer science. **Education:** General. **Engineering:** Computer, electrical, industrial, science. **Engineering technology:** Industrial management. **Foreign languages:** French, Spanish. **History:** General. **Liberal arts:** Arts/sciences. **Math:** General. **Parks/recreation:** Exercise sciences. **Philosophy/religion:** Philosophy. **Physical sciences:** Chemistry, geology, physics. **Protective services:** Criminal justice. **Psychology:** General. **Social sciences:** Economics, international relations, political science, sociology. **Theology:** Theology. **Other:** Multinational organization studies.

Most popular majors. Biology 15%, business/marketing 27%, communications/journalism 6%, public administration/social services 7%, social sciences 11%.

Computing on campus. PC or laptop required. 100 workstations in dormitories, library, computer center, student center. Dormitories wired for high-speed internet access and linked to campus network. Commuter students can connect to campus network. Online course registration, online library, helpline, repair service, wireless network available.

Student life. **Freshman orientation:** Mandatory, $130 fee. Preregistration for classes offered. 2-day program offered twice in June and once in August. Parallel program for parents. June program offers campus accommodations for students and parents. Transfer student orientation is a 1-day program, held once in May and once in August. **Housing:** Guaranteed on-campus for freshmen. Coed dorms, single-sex dorms available. $100 nonrefundable deposit, deadline 5/1. Nontraditional residence halls for students 22 years old or above available. **Activities:** Bands, campus ministries, choral groups, dance, drama, international student organizations, literary magazine, music ensembles, musical theater, student government, student newspaper, Circle K, Amnesty International, Black student union, College Democrats, Habitat for Humanity, League of United Latin American Citizens, Youth for a United World, Environmental Conservation Organization, Mexican student association, Alpha Phi Omega.

Athletics. NCAA. **Intercollegiate:** Baseball M, basketball, cheerleading, cross-country W, golf, soccer, softball W, tennis, volleyball W. **Intramural:** Basketball, football (tackle), racquetball, soccer, softball, table tennis, tennis, volleyball. **Team name:** Rattlers.

Student services. Adult student services, alcohol/substance abuse counseling, chaplain/spiritual director, career counseling, student employment services, financial aid counseling, health services, personal counseling, placement for graduates, veterans' counselor. **Physically disabled:** Services for visually, speech, hearing impaired.

Contact. E-mail: uadm@stmarytx.edu
Phone: (210) 436-3126 Toll-free number: (800) 367-7868
Fax: (210) 431-6742
Chadd Bridwell, Director of Admission, St. Mary's University, One Camino Santa Maria, San Antonio, TX 78228-8503

Sam Houston State University

Huntsville, Texas **CB member**
www.shsu.edu **CB code: 6643**

- Public 4-year university
- Residential campus in large town
- 14,303 degree-seeking undergraduates: 16% part-time, 57% women, 15% African American, 1% Asian American, 13% Hispanic American, 1% Native American, 1% international
- 2,349 degree-seeking graduate students
- 53% of applicants admitted
- SAT or ACT (ACT writing optional) required

General. Founded in 1879. Regionally accredited. **Degrees:** 2,696 bachelor's awarded; master's, doctoral offered. **ROTC:** Army. **Location:** 69 miles from Houston, 170 miles from Dallas. **Calendar:** Semester, extensive summer session. **Full-time faculty:** 646 total; 69% have terminal degrees, 18% minority, 43% women. **Part-time faculty:** 285 total; 27% have terminal degrees, 16% minority, 58% women. **Class size:** 31% < 20, 50% 20-39, 9% 40-49, 8% 50-99, 2% >100. **Special facilities:** Sam Houston Memorial Museum, Huntsville State Park, Sam Houston Statue and Visitors Center.

Freshman class profile. 9,193 applied, 4,856 admitted, 2,143 enrolled.

Mid 50% test scores			
SAT critical reading:	450-540	Rank in top tenth:	15%
SAT math:	460-560	Return as sophomores:	72%
ACT composite:	19-23	Out-of-state:	1%
Rank in top quarter:	29%	Live on campus:	83%

Basis for selection. Test scores, school achievement records very important. Students graduating in top quarter of accredited high school exempt from test requirements.

High school preparation. College-preparatory program recommended. 22 units required; 26 recommended. Required and recommended units include English 4, mathematics 3-4, social studies 2.5-3.5, history 2.5-3.5, science 2-4 (laboratory 1), foreign language 2, computer science 1, visual/performing arts 1 and academic electives 1.

2008-2009 Annual costs. Tuition/fees: $5,910; $14,250 out-of-state. Room/board: $6,046. Books/supplies: $1,038. Personal expenses: $1,816.

2007-2008 Financial aid. Need-based: 47% of total undergraduate aid awarded as scholarships/grants, 53% as loans/jobs. **Non-need-based:** Scholarships awarded for academics, athletics, ROTC.

Application procedures. Admission: Priority date 6/15; deadline 8/1 (postmark date). $40 fee, may be waived for applicants with need. Admission notification on a rolling basis beginning on or about 9/1. **Financial aid:** Priority date 3/31, closing date 5/31. FAFSA, institutional form required. Applicants notified on a rolling basis starting 5/1; must reply within 4 week(s) of notification.

Academics. Special study options: Combined bachelor's/graduate degree, distance learning, double major, dual enrollment of high school students, ESL, honors, independent study, internships, liberal arts/career combination, study abroad, teacher certification program, weekend college. **Credit/placement by examination:** AP, CLEP, IB, SAT, ACT, institutional tests. 30 credit hours maximum toward bachelor's degree. **Support services:** Learning center, pre-admission summer program, reduced course load, remedial instruction, study skills assistance, tutoring, writing center.

Majors. Agriculture: General, agribusiness operations, animal sciences, horticultural science, mechanization. **Architecture:** Interior. **Biology:** General. **Business:** General, accounting, banking/financial services, business admin, fashion, finance, human resources, international, managerial economics, marketing, operations. **Communications:** Advertising, journalism, media studies, public relations, radio/tv. **Communications technology:** Animation/special effects. **Computer sciences:** General. **Conservation:** Environmental science. **Engineering technology:** Construction, drafting, electrical, industrial, manufacturing. **Family/consumer sciences:** General, food/nutrition, institutional food production. **Foreign languages:** French, Spanish. **Health:** Health services, music therapy. **History:** General. **Interdisciplinary:** Biological/physical sciences. **Math:** General. **Parks/recreation:** Health/fitness. **Philosophy/religion:** Philosophy. **Physical sciences:** Chemistry, geology, physics. **Protective services:** Corrections, criminal justice. **Psychology:** General. **Social sciences:** Geography, political science, sociology. **Visual/performing arts:** Art, commercial/advertising art, dance, dramatic, music performance, photography, studio arts. **Other:** Academic studies, Forensic chemistry, Victim studies.

Most popular majors. Business/marketing 25%, interdisciplinary studies 13%, psychology 6%, security/protective services 18%.

Computing on campus. 552 workstations in library, computer center, student center. Dormitories wired for high-speed internet access and linked to campus network. Commuter students can connect to campus network. Online course registration, online library, helpline, repair service, student web hosting, wireless network available.

Student life. Freshman orientation: Available, $125 fee. Preregistration for classes offered. Overnight program throughout summer and before classes commence. Parent participation. **Housing:** Guaranteed on-campus for freshmen. Coed dorms, single-sex dorms, apartments, fraternity/sorority housing available. $200 deposit. Non-traditional student house for juniors, seniors, graduates, and students 24+ years of age; honors house; first-year living/learning community. **Activities:** Bands, campus ministries, choral groups, dance, drama, international student organizations, music ensembles, musical theater, radio station, student government, student newspaper, symphony orchestra, TV station, Democratic and Republican student associations, Baptist student ministry, Church of Christ student center, Lutheran student center, Hillel, Muslim students association, student Pagan association, ROTARACT, Habitat for Humanity, Wesley Foundation.

Athletics. NCAA. **Intercollegiate:** Baseball M, basketball, cross-country, equestrian, football (tackle) M, golf, rifle, rodeo, soccer, softball W, tennis, track and field, volleyball W. **Intramural:** Baseball M, basketball, bowling, diving, football (tackle) M, golf, gymnastics W, handball, lacrosse M, racquetball, rugby M, soccer, softball W, swimming, tennis, volleyball, water polo. **Team name:** Bearkats.

Student services. Alcohol/substance abuse counseling, career counseling, student employment services, financial aid counseling, health services, legal services, minority student services, on-campus daycare, personal counseling, placement for graduates, veterans' counselor. **Physically disabled:** Services for visually impaired.

Contact. E-mail: admissions@shsu.edu
Phone: (936) 294-1828 Toll-free number: (866) 232-7528
Fax: (936) 294-3758
Trevor Thorn, Director of Admissions, Sam Houston State University, Box 2418, Huntsville, TX 77341-2418

Schreiner University

Kerrville, Texas **CB member**
www.schreiner.edu **CB code: 6647**

- Private 4-year liberal arts college affiliated with Presbyterian Church (USA)
- Residential campus in large town
- 940 degree-seeking undergraduates: 4% part-time, 57% women, 4% African American, 1% Asian American, 21% Hispanic American, 1% Native American
- 19 degree-seeking graduate students
- 59% of applicants admitted
- SAT or ACT with writing required
- 42% graduate within 6 years

General. Founded in 1923. Regionally accredited. **Degrees:** 137 bachelor's, 1 associate awarded; master's offered. **Location:** 60 miles from San Antonio, 80 miles from Austin. **Calendar:** Semester, limited summer session. **Full-time faculty:** 58 total; 71% have terminal degrees, 10% minority, 47% women. **Part-time faculty:** 43 total; 28% have terminal degrees, 7% minority, 46% women. **Class size:** 66% < 20, 34% 20-39.

Freshman class profile. 1,028 applied, 607 admitted, 266 enrolled.

Mid 50% test scores		GPA 3.0-3.49:	45%
SAT critical reading:	440-550	Rank in top quarter:	36%
SAT math:	440-550	Rank in top tenth:	11%
SAT writing:	430-540	Return as sophomores:	63%
ACT composite:	18-24	Out-of-state:	1%
GPA 3.75 or higher:	14%	Live on campus:	84%
GPA 3.50-3.74:	41%		

Basis for selection. High school courses taken, grades, class rank, extracurricular activities, test scores, recommendations, interviews considered. Students admitted to Learning Support Services program not required to take SAT or ACT. Interview recommended for all; essay required for applicants not meeting certain admissions standards; portfolio recommended for fine arts.

High school preparation. College-preparatory program recommended. 24 units recommended. Recommended units include English 4, mathematics 3, social studies 2, history 2, science 3 (laboratory 2), foreign language 2, computer science 1 and visual/performing arts 1.

2008-2009 Annual costs. Tuition/fees: $17,892. Room/board: $8,822. Books/supplies: $1,000. Personal expenses: $1,000.

2007-2008 Financial aid. **Need-based:** 245 full-time freshmen applied for aid; 202 were judged to have need; 202 of these received aid. Average need met was 71%. Average scholarship/grant was $10,133; average loan $2,768. 65% of total undergraduate aid awarded as scholarships/grants, 35% as loans/jobs. **Non-need-based:** Awarded to 258 full-time undergraduates, including 102 freshmen. Scholarships awarded for academics, art, leadership, music/drama, religious affiliation.

Application procedures. **Admission:** Priority date 5/1; deadline 8/1. $25 fee, may be waived for applicants with need. Admission notification on a rolling basis. Must reply by 5/1. **Financial aid:** No deadline. FAFSA required. Applicants notified on a rolling basis starting 2/8; must reply within 2 week(s) of notification.

Academics. **Special study options:** Accelerated study, double major, dual enrollment of high school students, honors, independent study, internships, liberal arts/career combination, student-designed major, study abroad, teacher certification program, weekend college. **Credit/placement by examination:** AP, CLEP, IB, SAT, ACT, institutional tests. **Support services:** Learning center, reduced course load, remedial instruction, study skills assistance, tutoring, writing center.

Majors. **Biology:** General, biochemistry. **Business:** General, accounting, management information systems. **Education:** General, biology, early childhood, elementary, English, history, mathematics, middle, music, physical, secondary. **Engineering:** General. **Health:** Predental. **History:** General. **Interdisciplinary:** Accounting/computer science. **Legal studies:** Prelaw. **Liberal arts:** Arts/sciences, humanities. **Math:** General. **Parks/recreation:** Exercise sciences. **Philosophy/religion:** Religion. **Physical sciences:** Chemistry. **Psychology:** General. **Social sciences:** Political science. **Visual/performing arts:** Dramatic, graphic design.

Most popular majors. Biology 10%, business/marketing 25%, education 16%, parks/recreation 8%, psychology 14%.

Computing on campus. 103 workstations in dormitories, library, computer center, student center. Dormitories wired for high-speed internet access and linked to campus network. Commuter students can connect to campus network. Online library, repair service, student web hosting, wireless network available.

Student life. **Freshman orientation:** Mandatory. Preregistration for classes offered. Overnight program prior to start of classes. **Housing:** Guaranteed on-campus for all undergraduates. Coed dorms, special housing for disabled, apartments available. $100 nonrefundable deposit, deadline 5/1. **Activities:** Pep band, campus ministries, choral groups, dance, drama, literary magazine, music ensembles, musical theater, student government, student newspaper, symphony orchestra, community outreach program, Best Buddies, BACCHUS (Boosting Alcohol Consciousness Concerning the Health of University Students), Celtic Cross, Episcopal-Lutheran Association, Fellowship of Christian Athletes, Young Catholic Adults, Young Republicans.

Athletics. NCAA. **Intercollegiate:** Baseball M, basketball, cheerleading M, golf, soccer, softball W, tennis, volleyball W. **Intramural:** Basketball, football (non-tackle), football (tackle), golf, racquetball, soccer, swimming, table tennis, tennis, volleyball. **Team name:** Mountaineers.

Student services. Adult student services, chaplain/spiritual director, career counseling, student employment services, health services, personal counseling, placement for graduates. **Physically disabled:** Services for visually, speech, hearing impaired. **Learning disabled:** Comprehensive services available.

Contact. E-mail: admissions@schreiner.edu
Phone: (830) 792-7217 Toll-free number: (800) 343-4919
Fax: (830) 792-7226
Sandra Speed, Director of Admissions, Schreiner University, 2100 Memorial Boulevard, Kerrville, TX 78028-5697

Southern Methodist University

Dallas, Texas — **CB member**
www.smu.edu — **CB code: 6660**

- Private 4-year university affiliated with United Methodist Church
- Residential campus in large town
- 6,172 degree-seeking undergraduates: 4% part-time, 53% women, 5% African American, 6% Asian American, 8% Hispanic American, 1% Native American, 6% international
- 4,395 degree-seeking graduate students
- 50% of applicants admitted
- SAT or ACT (ACT writing optional), application essay required
- 74% graduate within 6 years

General. Founded in 1911. Regionally accredited. Courses are also offered at SMU-in-Legacy in Plano and SMU-in-Taos in New Mexico. **Degrees:** 1,533 bachelor's awarded; master's, doctoral, first professional offered. **ROTC:** Army, Air Force. **Location:** 5 miles from downtown. **Calendar:** Semester, limited summer session. **Full-time faculty:** 656 total; 84% have terminal degrees, 17% minority, 35% women. **Part-time faculty:** 378 total; 47% have terminal degrees, 8% minority, 39% women. **Class size:** 58% < 20, 27% 20-39, 8% 40-49, 6% 50-99, 1% >100. **Special facilities:** Film/video archives, New Mexico archeological dig of 13th century Indian pueblo, institute for the study of Earth and man, seismological observatory, electron microscopy laboratory, paleontology museum, business information center.

Freshman class profile. 8,270 applied, 4,113 admitted, 1,398 enrolled.

Mid 50% test scores		**GPA 2.0-2.99:**	9%
SAT critical reading:	560-660	**Rank in top quarter:**	73%
SAT math:	590-680	**Rank in top tenth:**	42%
SAT writing:	560-660	**Return as sophomores:**	89%
ACT composite:	25-30	**Out-of-state:**	56%
GPA 3.75 or higher:	40%	**Live on campus:**	95%
GPA 3.50-3.74:	23%	**International:**	5%
GPA 3.0-3.49:	28%		

Basis for selection. GED not accepted. Students evaluated comprehensively. High school curriculum, GPA, test scores, school/community activities, recommendations, and essay important. Special talents considered. Interview recommended for all; audition required for performing arts; portfolio recommended for studio art. **Homeschooled:** SAT Subject Tests required.

High school preparation. 15 units required. Required and recommended units include English 4, mathematics 3-4, social studies 1-2, history 2-3, science 3-4 (laboratory 2-3) and foreign language 2-3.

2008-2009 Annual costs. Tuition/fees: $33,170. Room/board: $11,875. Books/supplies: $800. Personal expenses: $1,100.

2008-2009 Financial aid. **Need-based:** 638 full-time freshmen applied for aid; 445 were judged to have need; 445 of these received aid. Average need met was 88%. Average scholarship/grant was $17,383; average loan $2,481. 77% of total undergraduate aid awarded as scholarships/grants, 23% as loans/jobs. **Non-need-based:** Awarded to 3,608 full-time undergraduates, including 995 freshmen. Scholarships awarded for academics, art, athletics, leadership, music/drama, religious affiliation, ROTC, state residency.

Application procedures. **Admission:** Priority date 1/15; deadline 3/15 (postmark date). $60 fee, may be waived for applicants with need. Admission notification on a rolling basis beginning on or about 12/31. Must reply by 5/1. **Financial aid:** Priority date 2/15; no closing date. FAFSA, CSS PROFILE required. Applicants notified on a rolling basis starting 3/15.

Academics. **Special study options:** Accelerated study, combined bachelor's/graduate degree, cooperative education, distance learning, double major, ESL, exchange student, honors, independent study, internships, student-designed major, study abroad, teacher certification program, Washington semester. **Credit/placement by examination:** AP, CLEP, IB, SAT, ACT, institutional tests. No limit on number of AP credits that may be counted toward bachelor's degree. Maximum of 8 hours of International Baccalaureate credits may be counted toward bachelor's degree. **Support services:** Learning center, pre-admission summer program, remedial instruction, study skills assistance, tutoring, writing center.

Majors. **Area/ethnic studies:** African-American, European, German, Hispanic-American/Latino/Chicano, Italian, Latin American. **Biology:** General, biochemistry. **Business:** General, accounting, business admin, finance, financial planning, management information systems, management science, marketing, organizational behavior, real estate. **Communications:** Advertising, journalism, media studies, public relations, radio/tv. **Computer sciences:** Computer science, information systems. **Conservation:** Environmental science. **Education:** Music. **Engineering:** Civil, computer, electrical, environmental, mechanical. **Engineering technology:** Industrial management. **Foreign languages:** General, French, German, Italian, Russian, Spanish. **Health:** Music therapy. **History:** General. **Interdisciplinary:** Medieval/Renaissance. **Liberal arts:** Humanities. **Math:** General, statistics. **Philosophy/religion:** Philosophy, religion. **Physical sciences:** Chemistry, geology, geophysics, physics. **Psychology:** General. **Public administration:** Policy analysis. **Social sciences:** General, anthropology, applied economics, econometrics, economics, international relations, political science, sociology. **Visual/performing arts:** Art, art history/conservation, dance, dramatic, film/cinema, music performance, music theory/composition, piano/organ, studio arts, voice/opera.

Most popular majors. Business/marketing 24%, communications/journalism 12%, psychology 7%, social sciences 19%, visual/performing arts 8%.

Computing on campus. 758 workstations in dormitories, library, computer center, student center. Dormitories wired for high-speed internet access and linked to campus network. Commuter students can connect to campus network. Online course registration, online library, helpline, repair service, student web hosting, wireless network available.

Student life. Freshman orientation: Mandatory. **Housing:** Guaranteed on-campus for freshmen. Coed dorms, apartments, fraternity/sorority housing, wellness housing available. $200 nonrefundable deposit, deadline 5/15. **Activities:** Bands, campus ministries, choral groups, dance, drama, film society, international student organizations, literary magazine, music ensembles, musical theater, opera, radio station, student government, student newspaper, symphony orchestra, over 130 groups available.

Athletics. NCAA. **Intercollegiate:** Basketball, cross-country W, diving, equestrian W, football (tackle) M, golf, rowing (crew) W, soccer, swimming, tennis, track and field W, volleyball W. **Intramural:** Basketball, bowling, golf, racquetball, soccer, softball, swimming, table tennis, tennis, volleyball. **Team name:** Mustangs.

Student services. Adult student services, alcohol/substance abuse counseling, chaplain/spiritual director, career counseling, student employment services, financial aid counseling, health services, on-campus daycare, personal counseling, placement for graduates, veterans' counselor, women's services. **Physically disabled:** Services for visually, speech, hearing impaired.

Contact. E-mail: enrol_serv@smu.edu
Phone: (214) 768-3417 Toll-free number: (800) 323-0672
Fax: (214) 768-0202
Ron Moss, Executive Director of Enrollment Services, Southern Methodist University, PO Box 750181, Dallas, TX 75275-0181

Southwestern Adventist University

Keene, Texas
www.swau.edu **CB code: 6671**

- Private 4-year university and liberal arts college affiliated with Seventh-day Adventists
- Residential campus in small town
- 728 degree-seeking undergraduates
- 50% of applicants admitted

General. Founded in 1893. Regionally accredited. **Degrees:** 103 bachelor's, 31 associate awarded; master's offered. **Location:** 55 miles from Dallas, 25 miles from Fort Worth. **Calendar:** Semester, limited summer session. **Full-time faculty:** 54 total; 39% women. **Part-time faculty:** 74 total; 38% women. **Class size:** 65% < 20, 24% 20-39, 9% 40-49, 2% 50-99, less than 1% >100. **Special facilities:** Observatory, museum of student life.

Freshman class profile. 759 applied, 376 admitted, 112 enrolled.

Mid 50% test scores			
SAT critical reading:	440-560	ACT composite:	19-24
SAT math:	420-540	Out-of-state:	44%
		Live on campus:	35%

Basis for selection. Secondary school record, test scores important. Additional requirements for nursing and education programs. SAT or ACT recommended. SAT preferred for placement. **Homeschooled:** A state high school equivalency certificate is accepted instead of a high school diploma or GED.

High school preparation. Recommended units include English 4, mathematics 2, social studies 2.5, science 2 and foreign language 2.

2008-2009 Annual costs. Tuition/fees: $15,236. Room/board: $6,742. Books/supplies: $936. Personal expenses: $1,244.

Financial aid. Non-need-based: Scholarships awarded for academics, leadership, music/drama.

Application procedures. Admission: Closing date 8/31. No application fee. Admission notification on a rolling basis. **Financial aid:** Priority date 3/15; no closing date. FAFSA, institutional form required. Applicants notified on a rolling basis starting 4/15.

Academics. Special study options: Accelerated study, combined bachelor's/graduate degree, cooperative education, cross-registration, distance learning, double major, ESL, external degree, honors, independent study, internships, liberal arts/career combination, student-designed major, study abroad, teacher certification program. **Credit/placement by examination:** AP, CLEP, IB, institutional tests. **Support services:** Reduced course load, remedial instruction, tutoring, writing center.

Majors. Biology: General, biostatistics. **Business:** Accounting, administrative services, business admin, communications, international, management information systems, management science, office management. **Communications:** General, broadcast journalism, journalism. **Computer sciences:** General, computer science, information systems. **Education:** Business, elementary. **Health:** Clinical lab technology, health care admin, medical secretary, nursing (RN). **History:** General. **Math:** General, applied. **Parks/recreation:** Health/fitness. **Philosophy/religion:** Religion. **Physical sciences:** Chemistry, theoretical physics. **Protective services:** Criminal justice. **Psychology:** General. **Social sciences:** General, international relations. **Theology:** Theology.

Most popular majors. Business/marketing 13%, education 24%, liberal arts 9%, psychology 10%, theological studies 11%.

Computing on campus. 150 workstations in library, computer center. Dormitories wired for high-speed internet access and linked to campus network. Commuter students can connect to campus network. Helpline, repair service, student web hosting, wireless network available.

Student life. Freshman orientation: Mandatory. Preregistration for classes offered. Held the week prior to fall registration. **Housing:** Guaranteed on-campus for all undergraduates. Single-sex dorms, apartments available. $100 fully refundable deposit, deadline 8/31. **Activities:** Concert band, campus ministries, choral groups, drama, international student organizations, music ensembles, musical theater, radio station, student government, student newspaper, symphony orchestra, TV station.

Athletics. Intramural: Baseball M, basketball, gymnastics, soccer M, volleyball W.

Student services. Adult student services, career counseling, student employment services, financial aid counseling, health services, personal counseling, placement for graduates, veterans' counselor.

Contact. E-mail: admissions@swau.edu
Phone: (817) 202-6252 Toll-free number: (800) 433-2240
Fax: (817) 556-4744
Steve Stafford, Enrollment and Marketing Vice President, Southwestern Adventist University, Box 567, Keene, TX 76059

Southwestern Assemblies of God University

Waxahachie, Texas
www.sagu.edu **CB code: 6669**

- Private 4-year university and Bible college affiliated with Assemblies of God
- Residential campus in large town
- 1,545 degree-seeking undergraduates: 23% part-time, 48% women
- 273 degree-seeking graduate students
- SAT or ACT (ACT writing optional), application essay required

General. Founded in 1927. Regionally accredited. **Degrees:** 238 bachelor's, 51 associate awarded; master's offered. **ROTC:** Army. **Location:** 20 miles from Dallas. **Calendar:** Semester, limited summer session. **Full-time faculty:** 62 total; 53% have terminal degrees, 8% minority, 31% women. **Part-time faculty:** 73 total; 14% have terminal degrees, 7% minority, 36% women.

Freshman class profile.

Mid 50% test scores			
SAT critical reading:	420-520	ACT composite:	16-23
SAT math:	410-510	Out-of-state:	45%
		Live on campus:	80%

Basis for selection. Minister's reference and 1 personal reference required. Interview recommended. **Learning Disabled:** Enrollment with the Achievement Center indicated.

2008-2009 Annual costs. Tuition/fees: $12,850. Room/board: $5,282. Books/supplies: $612. Personal expenses: $1,479.

2007-2008 Financial aid. Need-based: 207 full-time freshmen applied for aid; 182 were judged to have need; 182 of these received aid. Average need met was 59%. Average scholarship/grant was $7,151; average loan $3,549. 47% of total undergraduate aid awarded as scholarships/grants, 53% as loans/jobs. **Non-need-based:** Awarded to 171 full-time undergraduates, including 73 freshmen.

Application procedures. Admission: Priority date 7/1; no deadline. $35 fee. Admission notification on a rolling basis beginning on or about 3/1.

Financial aid: Priority date 3/1, closing date 6/1. FAFSA required. Applicants notified on a rolling basis starting 6/1; must reply within 2 week(s) of notification.

Academics. Special study options: Distance learning, double major, dual enrollment of high school students, external degree, independent study, internships, teacher certification program. **Credit/placement by examination:** AP, CLEP, institutional tests. 15 credit hours maximum toward associate degree, 30 toward bachelor's. **Support services:** Learning center, reduced course load, remedial instruction, tutoring.

Majors. Business: General, accounting, business admin, marketing. **Education:** Early childhood, elementary, English, music, reading, secondary, social studies. **Health:** Clinical pastoral counseling. **History:** General. **Philosophy/religion:** Christian. **Theology:** Bible, missionary, pastoral counseling, religious ed, sacred music, youth ministry. **Visual/performing arts:** Music performance, piano/organ, voice/opera.

Computing on campus. 45 workstations in dormitories, library, computer center. Dormitories wired for high-speed internet access and linked to campus network. Online library, repair service, wireless network available.

Student life. Freshman orientation: Mandatory. Preregistration for classes offered. **Policies:** Dress code observed. Religious observance required. **Housing:** Guaranteed on-campus for freshmen. Coed dorms, single-sex dorms, apartments available. Unmarried students 23 and under required to live in college housing unless alternative arrangements agreed to upon enrollment. **Activities:** Bands, campus ministries, choral groups, drama, music ensembles, musical theater, student government, student newspaper, prayer groups, ministry labs.

Athletics. NAIA, NCCAA. **Intercollegiate:** Baseball M, basketball, cheerleading, football (tackle) M, soccer M, volleyball W. **Intramural:** Basketball, football (non-tackle) W, racquetball, softball, table tennis, volleyball. **Team name:** Lions.

Student services. Adult student services, chaplain/spiritual director, career counseling, student employment services, financial aid counseling, health services, personal counseling, placement for graduates, veterans' counselor.

Contact. E-mail: admissions@sagu.edu
Phone: (972) 937-7248 Toll-free number: (888) 937-7248
Fax: (972) 923-0006
Pat Thompson, Admissions Counselor, Southwestern Assemblies of God University, 1200 Sycamore Street, Waxahachie, TX 75165

Southwestern Baptist Theological Seminary

Fort Worth, Texas
www.swbts.edu

- Private 4-year Bible and seminary college
- Very large city

General. Regionally accredited. **Calendar:** Semester.

Annual costs/financial aid. Tuition/fees (projected): $6,866.

Contact. Phone: (800) 792-8701
PO Box 22000, Fort Worth, TX 76122

Southwestern Christian College

Terrell, Texas
www.swcc.edu CB code: 6705

- Private 4-year Bible and liberal arts college affiliated with Church of Christ
- Residential campus in large town

General. Founded in 1949. Regionally accredited. **Location:** 30 miles from Dallas. **Calendar:** Semester.

Annual costs/financial aid. Tuition/fees (2008-2009): $6,182. Room/board: $4,132. Books/supplies: $460. Personal expenses: $400.

Contact. Phone: (972) 524-3341
Director of Admissions, Box 10, Terrell, TX 75160

Southwestern University

Georgetown, Texas CB member
www.southwestern.edu CB code: 6674

- Private 4-year liberal arts college affiliated with United Methodist Church
- Residential campus in large town
- 1,259 degree-seeking undergraduates: 1% part-time, 61% women, 3% African American, 5% Asian American, 15% Hispanic American, 1% Native American
- 65% of applicants admitted
- SAT or ACT with writing, application essay required
- 76% graduate within 6 years; 25% enter graduate study

General. Founded in 1840. Regionally accredited. **Degrees:** 305 bachelor's awarded. **Location:** 28 miles from Austin. **Calendar:** Semester, limited summer session. **Full-time faculty:** 121 total; 97% have terminal degrees, 12% minority, 48% women. **Part-time faculty:** 49 total; 55% have terminal degrees, 8% minority, 51% women. **Class size:** 79% < 20, 21% 20-39, less than 1% 50-99.

Freshman class profile. 1,923 applied, 1,258 admitted, 349 enrolled.

Mid 50% test scores		**End year in good standing:**	87%
SAT critical reading:	550-670	**Return as sophomores:**	84%
SAT math:	560-660	**Out-of-state:**	8%
ACT composite:	24-29	**Live on campus:**	100%
Rank in top quarter:	77%	**Fraternities:**	30%
Rank in top tenth:	51%	**Sororities:**	26%

Basis for selection. School record, class rank, recommendations, test scores, essay most important. Audition required for music, theater programs; portfolio required for art program.

High school preparation. College-preparatory program required. 17 units required; 20 recommended. Required and recommended units include English 4, mathematics 4, social studies 2-3, history 1-2, science 3-4 (laboratory 2-3), foreign language 2-3 and academic electives 1.

2008-2009 Annual costs. Tuition/fees: $27,940. Room/board: $8,380. Books/supplies: $1,000. Personal expenses: $900.

2008-2009 Financial aid. Need-based: 265 full-time freshmen applied for aid; 205 were judged to have need; 202 of these received aid. Average need met was 87%. Average scholarship/grant was $20,783; average loan $4,951. 66% of total undergraduate aid awarded as scholarships/grants, 34% as loans/jobs. **Non-need-based:** Awarded to 822 full-time undergraduates, including 246 freshmen. Scholarships awarded for academics, art, minority status, music/drama, religious affiliation.

Application procedures. Admission: Closing date 2/15 (postmark date). $40 fee, may be waived for applicants with need. Admission notification 4/1. Must reply by 5/1. Applicants accepted after 2/15 if space allows. **Financial aid:** Priority date 3/1; no closing date. FAFSA required. Applicants notified on a rolling basis starting 3/1; must reply by 5/1 or within 2 week(s) of notification.

Academics. Students must demonstrate computer skills and grasp of major through capstone project, course, or examination prior to graduation. **Special study options:** Combined bachelor's/graduate degree, double major, honors, independent study, internships, liberal arts/career combination, New York semester, student-designed major, study abroad, teacher certification program, Washington semester. **Credit/placement by examination:** AP, CLEP, IB, institutional tests. **Support services:** Reduced course load, study skills assistance, tutoring, writing center.

Majors. Area/ethnic studies: American, Latin American, women's. **Biology:** General, animal behavior, biochemistry. **Business:** General, accounting. **Communications:** General, media studies. **Computer sciences:** General. **Conservation:** Environmental studies. **Education:** General, elementary, music, physical, science, social studies. **Foreign languages:** Chinese, classics, French, German, Latin, Spanish. **Health:** Athletic training. **History:** General. **Math:** General. **Philosophy/religion:** Philosophy, religion. **Physical sciences:** General, chemistry, physics. **Psychology:** General. **Social sciences:** Anthropology, economics, international relations, political science, sociology. **Visual/performing arts:** Art, art history/conservation, dramatic, music history, music performance, music theory/composition, musicology.

Most popular majors. Biology 9%, business/marketing 13%, communications/journalism 10%, education 6%, English 7%, psychology 8%, social sciences 16%, visual/performing arts 10%.

Computing on campus. 410 workstations in dormitories, library, computer center, student center. Dormitories wired for high-speed internet access and linked to campus network. Online course registration, online library, helpline, repair service, student web hosting, wireless network available.

Student life. **Freshman orientation:** Mandatory. **Housing:** Guaranteed on-campus for freshmen. Coed dorms, single-sex dorms, special housing for disabled, apartments, fraternity/sorority housing available. $250 nonrefundable deposit, deadline 5/14. **Activities:** Bands, choral groups, dance, drama, film society, literary magazine, music ensembles, musical theater, student government, student newspaper, Alpha Phi Omega, Ebony, Mexican American student association, political science society, international club, Equal Voice For Women's Perspective.

Athletics. NCAA. **Intercollegiate:** Baseball M, basketball, cross-country, diving, golf, soccer, softball W, swimming, tennis, track and field, volleyball W. **Team name:** Bucs/Pirates.

Student services. Alcohol/substance abuse counseling, chaplain/spiritual director, career counseling, student employment services, financial aid counseling, health services, minority student services, personal counseling, placement for graduates. **Physically disabled:** Services for hearing impaired.

Contact. E-mail: admission@southwestern.edu
Phone: (512) 863-1200 Toll-free number: (800) 252-3166
Fax: (512) 863-9601
Tom Oliver, Vice President Enrollment Services, Southwestern University, 1001 East University Avenue, Georgetown, TX 78626

Stephen F. Austin State University

Nacogdoches, Texas — **CB member**
www.sfasu.edu — **CB code: 6682**

- Public 4-year university
- Residential campus in large town
- 10,404 degree-seeking undergraduates: 13% part-time, 60% women, 21% African American, 1% Asian American, 9% Hispanic American, 1% Native American, 1% international
- 1,274 degree-seeking graduate students
- 72% of applicants admitted
- SAT or ACT with writing required
- 39% graduate within 6 years

General. Founded in 1923. Regionally accredited. **Degrees:** 1,783 bachelor's awarded; master's, doctoral offered. **ROTC:** Army. **Location:** 140 miles from Houston, 70 miles from Longview. **Calendar:** Semester, extensive summer session. **Full-time faculty:** 477 total; 71% have terminal degrees, 8% minority, 45% women. **Part-time faculty:** 174 total; 36% have terminal degrees, 5% minority, 55% women. **Class size:** 30% < 20, 51% 20-39, 11% 40-49, 6% 50-99, 2% >100. **Special facilities:** Computerized observatory; experimental forest; on-campus arboretum; beef, poultry and swine research facilities; biotechnology/environmental science research center; Stone Fort museum; agricultural pond; forest resources institute; geographic information systems lab; regional geospatial service center.

Freshman class profile. 7,810 applied, 5,657 admitted, 2,354 enrolled.

Mid 50% test scores		**Out-of-state:**	2%
SAT math:	440-560	**Live on campus:**	89%
ACT composite:	18-23	**International:**	1%
Rank in top quarter:	43%	**Fraternities:**	14%
Rank in top tenth:	14%	**Sororities:**	11%
Return as sophomores:	63%		

Basis for selection. Applicants must complete prescribed high school preparation and submit official high school transcript and SAT or ACT scores. No minimum score required for those ranking in top quartile; those in second quartile must have composite score (exclusive of Writing) of 850 SAT, 18 ACT; third quartile 1050 SAT, 23 ACT; fourth quartile 1250 SAT, 28 ACT. Applicants not meeting rank-in-class and test requirements reviewed on individual basis. SAT or ACT scores must be received by last day of registration for fall term admission. **Homeschooled:** Applicants assessed on individual basis; those whose academic background indicates probability of success may be admitted.

High school preparation. 12 units required; 18 recommended. Required and recommended units include English 4, mathematics 3, social studies 3, science 3 and foreign language 2. 1 fine arts, 1 computer science, 1 government/economics recommended.

2009-2010 Annual costs. Tuition/fees (projected): $6,432; $14,862 out-of-state. Room/board: $7,022. Books/supplies: $1,020. Personal expenses: $1,593.

2007-2008 Financial aid. **Need-based:** 1,570 full-time freshmen applied for aid; 1,148 were judged to have need; 1,132 of these received aid. Average need met was 87%. Average scholarship/grant was $3,186; average loan $3,115. 45% of total undergraduate aid awarded as scholarships/grants, 55% as loans/jobs. **Non-need-based:** Awarded to 2,048 full-time undergraduates, including 551 freshmen. Scholarships awarded for academics, alumni affiliation, athletics, leadership, music/drama, state residency.

Application procedures. **Admission:** No deadline. $35 fee, may be waived for applicants with need. Admission notification on a rolling basis beginning on or about 9/1. **Financial aid:** Priority date 4/1; no closing date. FAFSA, institutional form required. Applicants notified on a rolling basis starting 4/10; must reply within 3 week(s) of notification.

Academics. **Special study options:** Accelerated study, combined bachelor's/graduate degree, distance learning, double major, dual enrollment of high school students, honors, independent study, internships, liberal arts/career combination, student-designed major, study abroad, teacher certification program. **Credit/placement by examination:** AP, CLEP, IB, institutional tests. 32 credit hours maximum toward bachelor's degree. **Support services:** Learning center, pre-admission summer program, reduced course load, remedial instruction, study skills assistance, tutoring, writing center.

Majors. **Agriculture:** General, agribusiness operations, agronomy, animal sciences, horticultural science, horticulture, mechanization, poultry, production. **Architecture:** Interior. **Biology:** General, biochemistry. **Business:** General, accounting, business admin, fashion, finance, hospitality admin, international, managerial economics, marketing, office management, special products marketing. **Communications:** General, journalism, radio/tv. **Computer sciences:** General, data processing, information technology. **Conservation:** Environmental science, forest management, forestry, wildlife. **Family/consumer sciences:** General, family studies, food/nutrition. **Foreign languages:** French, Spanish. **Health:** Audiology/hearing, audiology/speech pathology, clinical lab science, health services, nursing (RN). **History:** General. **Interdisciplinary:** Gerontology. **Legal studies:** Paralegal. **Liberal arts:** Arts/sciences, humanities. **Math:** General. **Parks/recreation:** Facilities management, health/fitness. **Philosophy/religion:** Philosophy. **Physical sciences:** Chemistry, geology, physics. **Protective services:** Corrections, criminal justice, police science. **Psychology:** General. **Public administration:** General, social work. **Social sciences:** General, economics, geography, political science, sociology. **Visual/performing arts:** Art, art history/conservation, dance, dramatic, music performance. **Other:** Applied arts & sciences, Orientation & mobility.

Most popular majors. Business/marketing 19%, health sciences 10%, interdisciplinary studies 18%, parks/recreation 6%, visual/performing arts 8%.

Computing on campus. 1,000 workstations in dormitories, library, computer center, student center. Dormitories wired for high-speed internet access and linked to campus network. Commuter students can connect to campus network. Online course registration, online library, helpline, repair service, student web hosting, wireless network available.

Student life. **Freshman orientation:** Available, $130 fee. Preregistration for classes offered. Five 3-day sessions held each summer for students and parents. **Housing:** Guaranteed on-campus for freshmen. Coed dorms, single-sex dorms, special housing for disabled, apartments, fraternity/sorority housing, wellness housing available. $100 fully refundable deposit, deadline 4/9. Students must live in college housing until 60 semester hours completed. Off-campus housing permitted if student is 21 or older, married, commutes from permanent address of parent or relative, or enrolls for 8 hours or less. **Activities:** Bands, campus ministries, choral groups, dance, drama, film society, international student organizations, literary magazine, music ensembles, musical theater, opera, radio station, student government, student newspaper, symphony orchestra, TV station, African American student association, Canterbury Episcopal student association, Campus Crusade for Christ, Jewish Student Fellowship, Habitat for Humanity, SFA Democrats, Young Republicans, social services.

Athletics. NCAA. **Intercollegiate:** Baseball M, basketball, cross-country, equestrian W, football (tackle) M, golf M, soccer W, softball W, tennis W, track and field, volleyball W. **Intramural:** Badminton, baseball M, basketball, cross-country, gymnastics, lacrosse M, racquetball, rodeo, rugby, soccer M, softball, table tennis, tennis, volleyball, water polo, wrestling M. **Team name:** Lumberjacks/Ladyjacks.

Student services. Adult student services, alcohol/substance abuse counseling, career counseling, student employment services, financial aid counseling, health services, legal services, minority student services, on-campus daycare, personal counseling, placement for graduates, veterans' counselor. **Physically disabled:** Services for visually, speech, hearing impaired.

Contact. E-mail: admissions@sfasu.edu
Phone: (936) 468-2504 Fax: (936) 468-3849
Monique Cossich, Executive Director of Enrollment Management, Stephen F. Austin State University, Box 13051, SFA Station, Nacogdoches, TX 75962-3051

Sul Ross State University

Alpine, Texas — **CB member**
www.sulross.edu — **CB code: 6685**

- Public 4-year university
- Residential campus in small town
- 1,978 degree-seeking undergraduates: 35% part-time, 57% women, 5% African American, 1% Asian American, 62% Hispanic American, 1% Native American, 1% international
- 750 degree-seeking graduate students
- SAT or ACT (ACT writing optional) required

General. Founded in 1917. Regionally accredited. Off-campus upper-level and graduate programs also available at Rio Grande College in Del Rio, Eagle Pass, and Uvalde. **Degrees:** 361 bachelor's, 14 associate awarded; master's offered. **Location:** 140 miles from Odessa, 220 miles from El Paso. **Calendar:** Semester, limited summer session. **Full-time faculty:** 106 total. **Part-time faculty:** 28 total. **Class size:** 61% < 20, 33% 20-39, 4% 40-49, 3% 50-99. **Special facilities:** Center for Big Bend studies, materials characterization laboratory.

Freshman class profile.

Mid 50% test scores			
SAT critical reading:	390-500	Out-of-state:	3%
SAT math:	390-490	Live on campus:	74%
ACT composite:	15-20	International:	1%

Basis for selection. Students must meet one of following criteria: ACT score of 20, SAT score of 800 (exclusive of Writing), or rank in top half of graduating class. Probational admission for all other applicants.

High school preparation. 16 units required; 25.5 recommended. Required and recommended units include English 4, mathematics 3-4, social studies 2, history 1-2, science 2-4 (laboratory 2), foreign language 3, academic electives 2.5. 1 fine art, 1 computer science required.

2008-2009 Annual costs. Tuition/fees: $5,058; $13,398 out-of-state. Room/board: $6,190. Books/supplies: $1,110. Personal expenses: $1,872.

Financial aid. Non-need-based: Scholarships awarded for academics, alumni affiliation, leadership.

Application procedures. Admission: Priority date 3/1; no deadline. $25 fee, may be waived for applicants with need. Admission notification on a rolling basis. **Financial aid:** Priority date 5/1; no closing date. FAFSA, institutional form required. Applicants notified on a rolling basis starting 5/1; must reply within 2 week(s) of notification.

Academics. Special study options: Distance learning, honors, internships, teacher certification program. **Credit/placement by examination:** AP, CLEP, institutional tests. 30 credit hours maximum toward bachelor's degree. **Support services:** Learning center, pre-admission summer program, reduced course load, remedial instruction, study skills assistance, tutoring, writing center.

Majors. Agriculture: Agribusiness operations, animal health, animal sciences, equestrian studies, food science, range science. **Biology:** General. **Business:** General, accounting, administrative services, business admin, finance, marketing, office management. **Communications:** General. **Computer sciences:** General. **Conservation:** General, management/policy, wildlife. **Education:** Elementary. **Foreign languages:** Spanish. **History:** General. **Math:** General. **Parks/recreation:** Health/fitness. **Physical sciences:** Chemistry, geology. **Protective services:** Criminal justice. **Psychology:** General. **Social sciences:** General, political science. **Visual/performing arts:** Art, dramatic.

Computing on campus. 200 workstations in library, computer center. Dormitories wired for high-speed internet access and linked to campus network. Commuter students can connect to campus network. Online library, helpline, repair service, wireless network available.

Student life. Freshman orientation: Available, $100 fee. Preregistration for classes offered. **Housing:** Guaranteed on-campus for freshmen. Coed dorms, single-sex dorms, special housing for disabled, apartments available. $100 deposit, deadline 8/1. Students not living with parents must live on campus until they reach 20 years of age and complete 45 semester credit hours. **Activities:** Bands, choral groups, dance, drama, literary magazine, music ensembles, musical theater, radio station, student government, student newspaper, Wesley Foundation, Newman Club, Baptist Student Union, Fellowship of Christian Athletes, Spanish club, rodeo club, black student association, international student association, nontraditional student association.

Athletics. NCAA. **Intercollegiate:** Baseball M, basketball, cross-country, football (tackle) M, softball W, tennis, track and field, volleyball W. **Intramural:** Basketball, football (non-tackle), racquetball, soccer, softball, tennis, volleyball, water polo, weight lifting. **Team name:** Lobos.

Student services. Alcohol/substance abuse counseling, chaplain/spiritual director, career counseling, student employment services, financial aid counseling, health services, on-campus daycare, personal counseling, placement for graduates, veterans' counselor. **Physically disabled:** Services for visually, hearing impaired.

Contact. E-mail: admissions@sulross.edu
Phone: (432) 837-8053 Toll-free number: (888) 722-7778
Fax: (432) 837-8431
Gregory Schwab, Associate VP for Enrollment Management, Sul Ross State University, Box C-114, Alpine, TX 79832

Tarleton State University

Stephenville, Texas — **CB member**
www.tarleton.edu — **CB code: 6817**

- Public 4-year university
- Residential campus in large town
- 7,860 degree-seeking undergraduates: 25% part-time, 57% women, 9% African American, 1% Asian American, 10% Hispanic American, 1% Native American, 1% international
- 1,747 degree-seeking graduate students
- 52% of applicants admitted
- SAT or ACT with writing required
- 52% graduate within 6 years

General. Founded in 1899. Regionally accredited. Graduate courses available at several off-campus locations within 150-mile radius. Upper level/graduate program offered at Tarleton University System Center in Killeen. Educational program for prison inmates offered in Gatesville on Fort Hood Military Post. **Degrees:** 1,705 bachelor's, 6 associate awarded; master's, doctoral offered. **ROTC:** Army. **Location:** 65 miles from Fort Worth. **Calendar:** Semester, extensive summer session. **Full-time faculty:** 343 total; 66% have terminal degrees, 11% minority, 47% women. **Part-time faculty:** 242 total; 6% have terminal degrees, 10% minority, 44% women. **Class size:** 43% < 20, 45% 20-39, 5% 40-49, 6% 50-99, less than 1% >100. **Special facilities:** University farm and equine center, planetarium.

Freshman class profile. 4,010 applied, 2,085 admitted, 1,246 enrolled.

Mid 50% test scores			
SAT critical reading:	420-520	Rank in top tenth:	11%
SAT math:	440-540	Return as sophomores:	66%
SAT writing:	420-510	Out-of-state:	1%
ACT composite:	18-23	Live on campus:	73%
Rank in top quarter:	35%	Fraternities:	8%
		Sororities:	7%

Basis for selection. Unconditional admission requires 930 combined SAT (exclusive of Writing) or 20 ACT. Rank in top quarter of class ensures unconditional admission if student has taken 4 years English and 3 years math. **Homeschooled:** Must provide proof of curriculum completed from an agency or teacher. **Learning Disabled:** Contact Director of Disability Services for appropriate accommodation.

High school preparation. College-preparatory program recommended. 19 units required. Required and recommended units include English 4, mathematics 3, social studies 2, history 1, science 2-3 (laboratory 2), foreign language 2 and academic electives 2-4.

2008-2009 Annual costs. Tuition/fees: $5,565; $13,995 out-of-state. Freshmen pay additional $100 first-year experience fee, first semester only. All undergraduates: distance learning fee additional $40 per credit hour. Room/board: $6,984. Books/supplies: $1,050.

2007-2008 Financial aid. Need-based: 963 full-time freshmen applied for aid; 849 were judged to have need; 625 of these received aid. Average need met was 76%. Average scholarship/grant was $4,278; average loan $2,969. 49% of total undergraduate aid awarded as scholarships/grants, 51% as loans/jobs. **Non-need-based:** Awarded to 2,812 full-time undergraduates, including 700 freshmen. Scholarships awarded for academics, alumni affiliation, art, athletics, leadership, music/drama, ROTC.

Application procedures. Admission: Priority date 7/1; deadline 8/1 (receipt date). $30 fee. Admission notification on a rolling basis beginning on or about 2/1. Early acceptance available to applicants who rank in top 10% of class; notification on rolling basis beginning January 1. **Financial aid:** Priority date 4/1, closing date 10/15. FAFSA required. Applicants notified on a rolling basis starting 2/1; must reply within 2 week(s) of notification.

Academics. Special study options: Accelerated study, distance learning, double major, dual enrollment of high school students, honors, internships, study abroad, teacher certification program. Specialized bachelor of applied arts and science degree for students with practical work experience in field of study; cooperative doctoral program in educational administration offered in partnership with Texas A&M University-Commerce; 2-2 engineering with Texas A&M University and University of Texas Arlington. **Credit/placement by examination:** AP, CLEP, SAT, ACT, institutional tests. Students can earn the majority of credits toward their degree by examination. **Support services:** Learning center, pre-admission summer program, reduced course load, remedial instruction, study skills assistance, tutoring, writing center.

Majors. Agriculture: General, agribusiness operations, agronomy, animal husbandry, animal sciences, business, economics, livestock, mechanization, ornamental horticulture, supplies. **Biology:** General, zoology. **Business:** General, accounting, business admin, finance, human resources, management information systems, marketing, office management. **Communications:** General. **Computer sciences:** General. **Conservation:** Wildlife. **Education:** Computer, science. **Engineering:** Environmental, physics. **Engineering technology:** General, industrial, manufacturing. **Family/consumer sciences:** General. **Foreign languages:** Spanish. **Health:** Clinical lab science, nursing (RN). **History:** General. **Liberal arts:** Arts/sciences. **Math:** General. **Parks/recreation:** Health/fitness. **Physical sciences:** Chemistry, geology, hydrology, physics. **Protective services:** Criminal justice. **Psychology:** General. **Public administration:** Social work. **Social sciences:** Economics, political science, sociology. **Transportation:** Airline/commercial pilot, aviation management. **Visual/performing arts:** Dramatic, music performance, studio arts.

Most popular majors. Agriculture 11%, business/marketing 28%, interdisciplinary studies 12%, parks/recreation 9%.

Computing on campus. 1,600 workstations in dormitories, library, computer center, student center. Dormitories wired for high-speed internet access and linked to campus network. Commuter students can connect to campus network. Online course registration, online library, helpline, repair service, student web hosting, wireless network available.

Student life. Freshman orientation: Mandatory, $100 fee. Preregistration for classes offered. Held multiple times during the summer. **Housing:** Guaranteed on-campus for freshmen. Coed dorms, single-sex dorms, apartments, wellness housing available. $100 fully refundable deposit. **Activities:** Bands, campus ministries, choral groups, dance, drama, international student organizations, literary magazine, music ensembles, musical theater, radio station, student government, student newspaper, symphony orchestra, Los Tejanos, Chinese student association, progressive united black student organization, student social work association, Alpha Phi Omega, Circle K, Fellowship of Christian Athletes, Fellowship of Christian Cowboys, College Republicans, Young Democrats.

Athletics. NCAA. **Intercollegiate:** Baseball M, basketball, cheerleading, cross-country, football (tackle) M, golf W, rodeo, softball W, tennis W, track and field, volleyball W. **Intramural:** Archery, basketball, football (non-tackle) M, football (tackle), golf, racquetball, rodeo, soccer, softball, table tennis, tennis, volleyball. **Team name:** Texans.

Student services. Adult student services, alcohol/substance abuse counseling, chaplain/spiritual director, career counseling, student employment services, financial aid counseling, health services, legal services, minority student services, on-campus daycare, personal counseling, placement for graduates, veterans' counselor. **Physically disabled:** Services for visually, speech, hearing impaired.

Contact. E-mail: uadm@tarleton.edu
Phone: (254) 968-9125 Toll-free number: (800) 687-8236
Fax: (254) 968-9951
Cindy Hess, Director of Admissions, Tarleton State University, Box T-0030, Stephenville, TX 76402

Texas A&M International University

Laredo, Texas — **CB member**
www.tamiu.edu — **CB code: 0359**

- Public 4-year university
- Commuter campus in small city
- 4,734 degree-seeking undergraduates
- 60% of applicants admitted
- SAT or ACT (ACT writing recommended) required

General. Founded in 1969. Regionally accredited. **Degrees:** 684 bachelor's awarded; master's, doctoral offered. **Location:** 150 miles from San Antonio and Corpus Christi. **Calendar:** Semester, extensive summer session. **Full-time faculty:** 229 total. **Part-time faculty:** 100 total. **Class size:** 39% < 20, 46% 20-39, 6% 40-49, 8% 50-99, less than 1% >100. **Special facilities:** Planetarium.

Freshman class profile. 2,590 applied, 1,549 admitted, 710 enrolled.

Mid 50% test scores			
SAT critical reading:	380-490	GPA 3.50-3.74:	42%
SAT math:	410-500	GPA 3.0-3.49:	26%
SAT writing:	380-480	GPA 2.0-2.99:	3%
ACT composite:	15-20	Rank in top quarter:	54%
GPA 3.75 or higher:	27%	Rank in top tenth:	22%

Basis for selection. Students in top half of graduating class admitted with no minimum ACT or SAT score. Students in bottom half need minimum score of 860 on SAT (exclusive of Writing) or 18 on ACT.

High school preparation. Required and recommended units include English 4, mathematics 3, history 3, science 2, foreign language 2 and academic electives 2. 1 computer technology, 1 fine arts recommended.

2008-2009 Annual costs. Tuition/fees: $5,417; $13,757 out-of-state. Room/board: $6,750.

2007-2008 Financial aid. Need-based: 62% of total undergraduate aid awarded as scholarships/grants, 38% as loans/jobs. **Non-need-based:** Scholarships awarded for academics.

Application procedures. Admission: Closing date 7/1. No application fee. Admission notification on a rolling basis beginning on or about 11/1. **Financial aid:** Priority date 3/15; no closing date. FAFSA, institutional form required. Applicants notified on a rolling basis starting 7/15; must reply within 2 week(s) of notification.

Academics. Special study options: Cooperative education, cross-registration, double major, dual enrollment of high school students, ESL, honors, independent study, internships, liberal arts/career combination, study abroad, teacher certification program. **Credit/placement by examination:** AP, CLEP, IB, institutional tests. 33 credit hours maximum toward bachelor's degree. **Support services:** Learning center, pre-admission summer program, reduced course load, remedial instruction, study skills assistance, tutoring, writing center.

Majors. Area/ethnic studies: Latin American. **Biology:** General. **Business:** Accounting, business admin, finance, management information systems, managerial economics, marketing. **Communications:** General. **Conservation:** General. **Education:** Bilingual, biology, early childhood, elementary, English, history, mathematics, reading, social studies, Spanish, special. **Foreign languages:** Spanish. **Health:** Nursing (RN), preop/surgical nursing. **History:** General. **Math:** General. **Parks/recreation:** Health/fitness. **Physical sciences:** Chemistry. **Protective services:** Criminal justice. **Psychology:** General. **Public administration:** Social work. **Social sciences:** General, political science, sociology, urban studies.

Most popular majors. Business/marketing 27%, interdisciplinary studies 28%, psychology 8%, security/protective services 8%.

Computing on campus. 200 workstations in dormitories, library, computer center. Dormitories wired for high-speed internet access and linked to campus network. Commuter students can connect to campus network.

Student life. Freshman orientation: Available, $30 fee. Preregistration for classes offered. Day program offered in May, June, July and August. **Housing:** Apartments available. On-campus housing, not owned by college (private contractor) available. **Activities:** Concert band, choral groups, dance, drama, literary magazine, music ensembles, student government, student newspaper, Student Ambassadors, Association of International Students, Tau Sigma Chi (criminal justice), High Twisters, Ballet Folklorico, Student System Group, Student Finance Society.

Athletics. Intramural: Baseball, basketball, soccer, table tennis, volleyball, weight lifting. **Team name:** Dust Devils.

Student services. Career counseling, services for economically disadvantaged, student employment services, financial aid counseling, health services, personal counseling, placement for graduates, veterans' counselor. **Physically disabled:** Services for visually, speech, hearing impaired.

Contact. E-mail: enroll@tamiu.edu
Phone: (956) 326-2200 Fax: (956) 326-2199
Rosa Dickinson, Director of Admissions, Texas A&M International University, 5201 University Boulevard, Laredo, TX 78041-1900

Texas A&M University

College Station, Texas **CB member**
www.tamu.edu **CB code: 6003**

- Public 4-year university
- Residential campus in small city
- 38,341 degree-seeking undergraduates: 8% part-time, 48% women, 3% African American, 5% Asian American, 14% Hispanic American, 1% Native American, 1% international
- 9,379 degree-seeking graduate students
- 70% of applicants admitted
- SAT or ACT with writing, application essay required
- 78% graduate within 6 years

General. Founded in 1876. Regionally accredited. **Degrees:** 8,117 bachelor's awarded; master's, doctoral, first professional offered. **ROTC:** Army, Naval, Air Force. **Location:** 90 miles from Houston, 100 miles from Austin. **Calendar:** Semester, extensive summer session. **Full-time faculty:** 2,234 total; 90% have terminal degrees, 22% minority, 30% women. **Part-time faculty:** 603 total; 67% have terminal degrees, 25% minority, 36% women. **Class size:** 22% < 20, 48% 20-39, 8% 40-49, 13% 50-99, 10% >100. **Special facilities:** Reactor, cyclotron, observatory, agriculture research property, 18-hole golf course, supercomputer center, oceanographic research vessel, Italian study center, George H. W. Bush Presidential Library and Museum.

Freshman class profile. 20,887 applied, 14,640 admitted, 8,093 enrolled.

Mid 50% test scores			
SAT critical reading:	520-630	Rank in top tenth:	54%
SAT math:	560-670	Return as sophomores:	92%
SAT writing:	500-610	Out-of-state:	3%
ACT composite:	23-29	Live on campus:	66%
Rank in top quarter:	86%	International:	1%

Basis for selection. Automatic admission to applicants in top 10% of Texas high school class (with completed application), as specified by state law. Strong senior year course schedule recommended. Test scores required of all applicants but not used for admission of applicants from top 10% of any Texas high school class. **Learning Disabled:** Must provide documentation of disability from qualified professional licensed or certified to diagnose disability.

High school preparation. College-preparatory program required. 17.5 units required; 18.5 recommended. Required and recommended units include English 4, mathematics 3.5, social studies 2, history 1, science 3 (laboratory 2) and foreign language 2. 1 unit computer usage required.

2008-2009 Annual costs. Tuition/fees: $7,844; $22,184 out-of-state. Room/board: $8,000. Books/supplies: $1,200. Personal expenses: $2,187.

2007-2008 Financial aid. Need-based: 4,843 full-time freshmen applied for aid; 2,874 were judged to have need; 2,815 of these received aid. Average need met was 89%. Average scholarship/grant was $9,951; average loan $3,874. 63% of total undergraduate aid awarded as scholarships/grants, 37% as loans/jobs. **Non-need-based:** Awarded to 6,311 full-time undergraduates, including 1,503 freshmen. Scholarships awarded for academics, alumni affiliation, art, athletics, job skills, leadership, music/drama, ROTC, state residency. **Additional information:** Short-term loans available. Out-of-state students awarded academic scholarships of $1,000 or more are eligible for waiver of out-of-state tuition.

Application procedures. Admission: Priority date 12/1; deadline 1/15 (receipt date). $60 fee, may be waived for applicants with need. Admission notification on a rolling basis beginning on or about 4/1. Must reply by 5/1. Housing deposit due at time of application. **Financial aid:** Priority date 3/31; no closing date. FAFSA required. Applicants notified on a rolling basis starting 3/15; must reply within 4 week(s) of notification.

Academics. Core curriculum requirements in foreign language and computer science may be satisfied by selected high school courses. **Special study options:** Accelerated study, combined bachelor's/graduate degree, cooperative education, distance learning, double major, dual enrollment of high school students, ESL, honors, independent study, internships, liberal arts/career combination, study abroad, teacher certification program. Exchange programs in architecture with Instituto Tecnologico y de Estudios Superiores de Monterrey, King's College London (England), University of Lancaster (England), Denmark's international study program, Ruhr University Bochum (Germany), University of Lausanne (Switzerland). **Credit/placement by examination:** AP, CLEP, IB, institutional tests. **Support services:** Learning center, pre-admission summer program, remedial instruction, tutoring, writing center.

Majors. Agriculture: General, agribusiness operations, agronomy, animal husbandry, animal sciences, aquaculture, business, communications, dairy, economics, farm/ranch, food science, horticultural science, horticulture, ornamental horticulture, plant protection, plant sciences, poultry, production, range science, soil science, supplies, turf management. **Architecture:** Architecture, environmental design, landscape. **Area/ethnic studies:** American. **Biology:** General, biochemistry, biomedical sciences, botany, cellular/molecular, entomology, environmental, microbiology, molecular genetics, zoology. **Business:** Accounting, finance, management science, marketing, sales/distribution, tourism promotion, tourism/travel. **Communications:** Digital media, journalism. **Computer sciences:** Computer science. **Conservation:** General, environmental science, environmental studies, forest management, forestry, management/policy, urban forestry, wildlife. **Engineering:** Aerospace, agricultural, biomedical, chemical, civil, computer, electrical, geological, industrial, mechanical, nuclear, ocean, petroleum. **Engineering technology:** General, construction, electrical, manufacturing. **Family/consumer sciences:** Food/nutrition. **Foreign languages:** Classics, French, German, Russian, Spanish. **Health:** Community health services, preveterinary. **History:** General. **Interdisciplinary:** Global studies. **Math:** General, applied. **Parks/recreation:** General, facilities management, health/fitness. **Philosophy/religion:** Philosophy. **Physical sciences:** Atmospheric science, chemistry, geology, geophysics, physics. **Protective services:** Forensics. **Psychology:** General. **Public administration:** Community org/advocacy. **Social sciences:** Anthropology, cartography, economics, geography, political science, sociology. **Visual/performing arts:** Dramatic.

Most popular majors. Agriculture 13%, biology 9%, business/marketing 16%, engineering/engineering technologies 16%, English 6%, interdisciplinary studies 9%, social sciences 8%.

Computing on campus. 1,321 workstations in dormitories, library, computer center, student center. Dormitories wired for high-speed internet access and linked to campus network. Commuter students can connect to campus network. Online course registration, online library, helpline, repair service, student web hosting, wireless network available.

Student life. Freshman orientation: Mandatory, $35 fee. Preregistration for classes offered. 2 1/2 day program throughout the summer. **Housing:** Coed dorms, single-sex dorms, special housing for disabled, apartments, fraternity/sorority housing, wellness housing available. $300 fully refundable deposit. Campus housing guaranteed to members of Corps of Cadets and recipients of major 4-year endowed academic scholarships. Freshman honors dorm available. **Activities:** Bands, campus ministries, choral groups, dance, drama, film society, literary magazine, music ensembles, musical theater, radio station, student government, student newspaper, symphony orchestra, TV station, Black awareness committee, committee for the awareness of Mexican American culture, student Y association, student conference on national affairs, social service organizations, College Republicans, Aggie Democrats, political forum, Aggies for Christ, Corps of Cadets.

Athletics. NCAA. **Intercollegiate:** Archery W, baseball M, basketball, cross-country, diving, equestrian W, football (tackle) M, golf, soccer W, softball W, swimming, tennis, track and field, volleyball W. **Intramural:** Archery, badminton, basketball, bowling, diving, golf, lacrosse, racquetball, rodeo, soccer, softball, squash, swimming, table tennis, track and field, volleyball. **Team name:** Aggies.

Student services. Alcohol/substance abuse counseling, career counseling, student employment services, financial aid counseling, health services, legal services, minority student services, on-campus daycare, personal counseling, placement for graduates, veterans' counselor, women's services. **Physically disabled:** Services for visually, speech, hearing impaired.

Contact. E-mail: admissions@tamu.edu
Phone: (979) 845-3741 Fax: (979) 458-1808
Scott McDonald, Director of Admissions, Texas A&M University, PO Box 30014, College Station, TX 77842-3014

Texas A&M University-Baylor College of Dentistry

Dallas, Texas
www.bcd.tamhsc.edu **CB code: 6059**

- Public two-year upper-division health science college
- Commuter campus in very large city
- 26% of applicants admitted
- Application essay, interview required

General. Founded in 1905. Regionally accredited. **Degrees:** 30 bachelor's awarded; master's, doctoral, first professional offered. **Articulation:** Agreement with Collin Community College District. **Calendar:** Semester. **Full-time faculty:** 121 total; 100% have terminal degrees, 11% minority, 37% women. **Part-time faculty:** 123 total; 100% have terminal degrees, 9% minority, 28% women.

Student profile. 61 degree-seeking undergraduates, 507 degree-seeking graduate students. 120 applied as first time-transfer students, 31 admitted, 31 enrolled. 60% transferred from two-year, 40% transferred from four-year institutions.

Women:	98%	**Native American:**	2%
Asian American:	23%	**Out-of-state:**	4%
Hispanic American:	15%	**25 or older:**	25%

Basis for selection. High school transcript, college transcript, application essay, interview required. School achievement most important. Essay, interview, and recommendations highly considered. Transfer accepted as juniors.

2008-2009 Annual costs. Tuition/fees: $5,660; $15,495 out-of-state. Personal expenses: $2,850.

Financial aid. Need-based: 62 applied for aid; 57 were judged to have need; 52 of these received aid. Average need met was 43%. 50% of total undergraduate aid awarded as scholarships/grants, 50% as loans/jobs. **Non-need-based:** Scholarships awarded for academics.

Application procedures. Admission: Priority date 12/31. $35 fee. **Financial aid:** FAFSA, institutional form required.

Academics. Participation in research activities under faculty sponsorship and annual research fellowships awarded by college offered. **Special study options:** Combined bachelor's/graduate degree, internships. **Credit/placement by examination:** CLEP.

Majors. Health: Dental hygiene.

Computing on campus. 25 workstations in library, computer center. Commuter students can connect to campus network. Online library, helpline, wireless network available.

Student life. Housing: Baylor Medical Center nursing dormitory housing available. **Activities:** Student government.

Student services. Student employment services, financial aid counseling, health services, personal counseling.

Contact. Phone: (214) 828-8230 Fax: (214) 828-8346
Barbara Miller, Director, Texas A&M University-Baylor College of Dentistry, PO Box 660677, Dallas, TX 75266-0677

Texas A&M University-Commerce

Commerce, Texas — **CB member**
www.tamu-commerce.edu — **CB code: 6188**

- Public 4-year university
- Commuter campus in small town
- 4,990 degree-seeking undergraduates: 27% part-time, 63% women, 19% African American, 2% Asian American, 10% Hispanic American, 1% Native American, 1% international
- 3,828 degree-seeking graduate students
- 51% of applicants admitted
- SAT or ACT with writing required
- 40% graduate within 6 years; 15% enter graduate study

General. Founded in 1889. Regionally accredited. **Degrees:** 1,469 bachelor's awarded; master's, doctoral offered. **Location:** 60 miles southeast of Dallas. **Calendar:** Semester, extensive summer session. **Full-time faculty:** 285 total; 66% have terminal degrees, 6% minority, 36% women. **Part-time faculty:** 175 total; 27% have terminal degrees, 65% women. **Class size:** 47% < 20, 44% 20-39, 5% 40-49, 4% 50-99, less than 1% >100. **Special facilities:** Instructional university farm, planetarium.

Freshman class profile. 3,057 applied, 1,552 admitted, 568 enrolled.

Mid 50% test scores		**GPA 2.0-2.99:**	32%
SAT critical reading:	440-550	**Rank in top quarter:**	46%
SAT math:	430-550	**Rank in top tenth:**	20%
ACT composite:	18-23	**End year in good standing:**	67%
GPA 3.75 or higher:	18%	**Return as sophomores:**	64%
GPA 3.50-3.74:	16%	**Out-of-state:**	2%
GPA 3.0-3.49:	33%		

Basis for selection. ACT or SAT scores most important, followed by high school grades and class rank. Students admitted with 20 ACT or 920 SAT (exclusive of Writing). TASP scores may exempt student from SAT or ACT tests. If student is TASP remedial, must take TASP within first semester of enrolling. Portfolio required for advertising art program; audition recommended for music program. **Homeschooled:** Must earn GED and be at least 18 years of age.

High school preparation. 12 units required. Required and recommended units include English 4, mathematics 3, science 2 and foreign language 2. 2.5 hours history/social studies required.

2008-2009 Annual costs. Tuition/fees: $5,130; $13,380 out-of-state. Room/board: $6,650. Books/supplies: $1,200. Personal expenses: $1,700.

2007-2008 Financial aid. Need-based: 474 full-time freshmen applied for aid; 354 were judged to have need; 351 of these received aid. Average need met was 65%. Average scholarship/grant was $6,012; average loan $2,122. 40% of total undergraduate aid awarded as scholarships/grants, 60% as loans/jobs. **Non-need-based:** Awarded to 463 full-time undergraduates, including 122 freshmen. Scholarships awarded for academics, art, athletics, leadership, music/drama. **Additional information:** Work-study also available for full-time students.

Application procedures. Admission: Closing date 8/1 (postmark date). $25 fee ($50 out-of-state). Admission notification on a rolling basis beginning on or about 10/1. High school seniors may enroll part-time before graduation with consent of high school principal if they meet requirements. **Financial aid:** Priority date 4/1; no closing date. FAFSA required. Applicants notified on a rolling basis starting 4/1; must reply within 2 week(s) of notification.

Academics. Special study options: Combined bachelor's/graduate degree, cooperative education, distance learning, double major, dual enrollment of high school students, external degree, honors, independent study, internships, liberal arts/career combination, study abroad, teacher certification program, weekend college. **Credit/placement by examination:** AP, CLEP, IB, SAT, ACT, institutional tests. 6 credit hours maximum toward bachelor's degree. **Support services:** Learning center, pre-admission summer program, remedial instruction, study skills assistance, tutoring, writing center.

Majors. Agriculture: Animal sciences, communications, economics, food science, plant sciences, soil science. **Biology:** General, cell/histology. **Business:** General, accounting, business admin, human resources, management information systems, managerial economics, marketing, office management, office/clerical, operations, public finance. **Communications:** General, advertising, broadcast journalism, digital media, journalism, public relations. **Communications technology:** Graphic/printing. **Computer sciences:** General, computer science, information systems. **Conservation:** General, environmental studies, wildlife. **Construction:** Maintenance. **Education:** Bilingual, biology, chemistry, driver/safety, early childhood, elementary, middle, multi-level teacher, physical, special. **Engineering:** Operations research. **Engineering technology:** Construction, manufacturing. **Foreign languages:** German, Spanish. **Health:** Athletic training, health care admin, medical records admin, predental, premedicine, prepharmacy, preveterinary. **History:** General. **Interdisciplinary:** Biological/physical sciences. **Legal studies:** Legal secretary, paralegal, prelaw. **Liberal arts:** Arts/sciences, library science. **Math:** General. **Parks/recreation:** Health/fitness. **Physical sciences:** Chemistry, geology, organic chemistry, physics, planetary. **Protective services:** Criminal justice, law enforcement admin. **Psychology:** General. **Public administration:** Social work. **Social sciences:** General, anthropology, criminology, economics, geography, political science, sociology. **Theology:** Preministerial. **Visual/performing arts:** General, art, arts management, ceramics, commercial photography, commercial/advertising art, design, dramatic, industrial design, metal/jewelry, music history, music pedagogy, music performance, music theory/composition, musicology, painting, photography, piano/organ, printmaking, sculpture, voice/opera.

Computing on campus. 1,500 workstations in dormitories, library, computer center, student center. Dormitories wired for high-speed internet access and linked to campus network. Commuter students can connect to campus network. Online course registration, online library, helpline, repair service, wireless network available.

Student life. Freshman orientation: Mandatory, $100 fee. Preregistration for classes offered. Held throughout summer; includes advising, assessment testing, and parental involvement. **Housing:** Coed dorms, single-sex dorms, special housing for disabled, apartments, fraternity/sorority housing, wellness housing available. $100 deposit, deadline 7/1. Shared freshman experience housing available. **Activities:** Bands, choral groups, dance, drama, film society, literary magazine, music ensembles, musical theater, opera, radio station, student government, student newspaper, symphony orchestra, TV station, Baptist student union, Church of Christ Bible chair, Newman Club, university Christian center, Young Democrats, association cultural de Hispanos-Americanos, Chinese student association, Muslim society, NAACP, Thai students association, Alpha Phi Omega.

Athletics. NCAA. **Intercollegiate:** Basketball, cross-country, football (tackle) M, golf, soccer W, track and field, volleyball W. **Intramural:** Archery, badminton, baseball M, basketball, bowling, cross-country, golf, racquetball, softball, swimming, table tennis, tennis, track and field, volleyball. **Team name:** Lions.

Student services. Alcohol/substance abuse counseling, chaplain/ spiritual director, career counseling, student employment services, financial aid counseling, health services, legal services, on-campus daycare, personal counseling, placement for graduates, veterans' counselor. **Physically disabled:** Services for visually, speech, hearing impaired.

Contact. E-mail: jody_todhunterl@tamu-commerce.edu
Phone: (903) 886-5081 Toll-free number: (888) 886-2682
Fax: (903) 468-6080
Hope Young, Director of Admissions, Texas A&M University-Commerce, Box 3011, Commerce, TX 75429-3011

Texas A&M University-Corpus Christi

Corpus Christi, Texas **CB member**
www.tamucc.edu **CB code: 0366**

- Public 4-year university
- Commuter campus in large city
- 7,249 degree-seeking undergraduates: 21% part-time, 60% women
- 1,758 degree-seeking graduate students
- 62% of applicants admitted
- SAT or ACT required

General. Founded in 1947. Regionally accredited. **Degrees:** 1,340 bachelor's awarded; master's, doctoral offered. **ROTC:** Army. **Location:** 150 miles from San Antonio, 200 miles from Houston. **Calendar:** Semester, extensive summer session. **Full-time faculty:** 324 total; 30% minority, 46% women. **Part-time faculty:** 215 total; 39% minority, 52% women. **Class size:** 25% < 20, 51% 20-39, 8% 40-49, 13% 50-99, 2% >100. **Special facilities:** National spill control school, institute for surveying and science, center for coastal studies, center for environmental studies and services, early childhood development center, South Texas Institute for the Arts.

Freshman class profile. 6,174 applied, 3,826 admitted, 1,230 enrolled.

Mid 50% test scores			
SAT critical reading:	420-520	ACT composite:	19-23
SAT math:	400-520	Out-of-state:	2%

Basis for selection. High school GPA, class rank, and course work most important. Test scores, school and community leadership activities, special talents also considered. Minimum 900 SAT (exclusive of Writing), required. Applicants not meeting minimum requirements may apply to admission committee for special consideration. Local placement exams in reading, writing and math required of all first-time freshmen.

High school preparation. 15 units required. Required units include English 4, mathematics 3, social studies 3, science 3 and foreign language 2.

2008-2009 Annual costs. Tuition/fees: $5,737; $14,167 out-of-state. Room/ board: $8,709. Books/supplies: $840. Personal expenses: $1,245.

2007-2008 Financial aid. **Need-based:** 43% of total undergraduate aid awarded as scholarships/grants, 57% as loans/jobs. **Non-need-based:** Scholarships awarded for academics, art, athletics, music/drama.

Application procedures. **Admission:** Closing date 7/1 (receipt date). $20 fee. Admission notification on a rolling basis. **Financial aid:** Closing date 4/1. FAFSA, institutional form required. Applicants notified on a rolling basis starting 5/1; must reply within 2 week(s) of notification.

Academics. **Special study options:** Cooperative education, distance learning, double major, dual enrollment of high school students, ESL, independent study, internships, teacher certification program. **Credit/placement by examination:** CLEP, IB, institutional tests. DANTES, ACT, PEP accepted. **Support services:** Learning center, remedial instruction, study skills assistance, tutoring, writing center.

Majors. **Biology:** General. **Business:** Accounting, business admin, finance, management information systems, marketing. **Communications:** General. **Computer sciences:** General, information systems. **Conservation:** General. **Engineering:** Mechanical. **Engineering technology:** Surveying. **Foreign languages:** Spanish. **Health:** Clinical lab science. **History:** General. **Math:** General. **Parks/recreation:** Health/fitness. **Physical sciences:** Chemistry, geology. **Psychology:** General. **Social sciences:** Political science, sociology. **Visual/performing arts:** General, studio arts.

Most popular majors. Biology 7%, business/marketing 22%, communications/journalism 8%, education 15%, health sciences 17%, legal studies 6%, psychology 8%.

Computing on campus. 500 workstations in library, computer center. Commuter students can connect to campus network. Helpline, repair service available.

Student life. **Freshman orientation:** Available. Preregistration for classes offered. Program held various times in summer before fall entry. **Policies:** No alcohol on campus except by adult students in their own apartments. **Housing:** Guaranteed on-campus for freshmen. Coed dorms, apartments available. $150 deposit. **Activities:** Bands, choral groups, dance, drama, film society, literary magazine, music ensembles, musical theater, opera, student government, student newspaper, symphony orchestra, Baptist Student Union, Newman Club, Friends Meeting, LDS Students Association, Amigos, computer science club, African-American Cultural Society.

Athletics. NCAA. **Intercollegiate:** Baseball, basketball, cross-country, golf W, softball W, swimming W, tennis, track and field, volleyball W. **Intramural:** Badminton, baseball M, basketball, cross-country, golf, gymnastics, handball, racquetball, sailing, soccer, softball, swimming, table tennis, tennis, track and field, volleyball. **Team name:** Islanders.

Student services. Alcohol/substance abuse counseling, chaplain/ spiritual director, career counseling, student employment services, financial aid counseling, health services, personal counseling, placement for graduates, veterans' counselor. **Physically disabled:** Services for visually, speech, hearing impaired.

Contact. E-mail: admiss@tamucc.edu
Phone: (361) 825-2624 Toll-free number: (800) 482-6822
Fax: (361) 825-5887
J. Christopher Fleming, Director of Admissions, Texas A&M University-Corpus Christi, 6300 Ocean Drive, Corpus Christi, TX 78412

Texas A&M University-Galveston

Galveston, Texas **CB member**
www.tamug.edu **CB code: 6835**

- Public 4-year university and branch campus college
- Residential campus in small city
- 1,566 degree-seeking undergraduates: 10% part-time, 40% women, 3% African American, 2% Asian American, 12% Hispanic American, 1% Native American, 1% international
- 46 degree-seeking graduate students
- 91% of applicants admitted
- SAT or ACT (ACT writing optional), application essay required
- 46% graduate within 6 years; 35% enter graduate study

General. Founded in 1962. Regionally accredited. Institution houses Texas Maritime Academy, 1 of 5 seacoast maritime academies in the U.S. preparing graduates for licensing as officers in the Merchant Marine. **Degrees:** 258 bachelor's awarded; master's offered. **ROTC:** Naval. **Location:** 50 miles from Houston. **Calendar:** Semester, limited summer session. **Full-time faculty:** 93 total; 69% have terminal degrees, 19% minority, 28% women. **Part-time faculty:** 77 total; 27% have terminal degrees, 14% minority, 35% women. **Class size:** 67% < 20, 23% 20-39, 4% 40-49, 4% 50-99, 2% >100. **Special facilities:** Fleet of research and training boats, 300-acre wetlands on west Galveston Bay, wetlands research center, ship bridge simulator.

Freshman class profile. 1,236 applied, 1,128 admitted, 518 enrolled.

Mid 50% test scores			
SAT critical reading:	460-590	Rank in top tenth:	11%
SAT math:	490-600	End year in good standing:	78%
ACT composite:	20-25	Return as sophomores:	66%
Rank in top quarter:	40%	Out-of-state:	14%
		Live on campus:	75%

Basis for selection. School achievement record and test scores most important. Adverse circumstances, leadership, exceptional talents, course selections, and references reviewed on individual basis. **Homeschooled:** Transcript of courses and grades, letter of recommendation (nonparent) required.

High school preparation. 13 units required; 19 recommended. Required and recommended units include English 4, mathematics 3-4, social studies 3, science 3-4 (laboratory 2) and foreign language 3. 1 unit computer literacy required. Science courses must be selected from biology, chemistry or physics.

2008-2009 Annual costs. Tuition/fees: $6,528; $14,958 out-of-state. Room/ board: $5,758. Books/supplies: $1,381. Personal expenses: $1,960.

2007-2008 Financial aid. **Need-based:** 272 full-time freshmen applied for aid; 233 were judged to have need; 219 of these received aid. Average need met was 14%. Average scholarship/grant was $4,898; average loan $2,789. 44% of total undergraduate aid awarded as scholarships/grants, 56%

as loans/jobs. **Non-need-based:** Awarded to 162 full-time undergraduates, including 42 freshmen. Scholarships awarded for academics, state residency.

Application procedures. **Admission:** No deadline. $45 fee, may be waived for applicants with need. Admission notification on a rolling basis. **Financial aid:** Priority date 4/1; no closing date. FAFSA required. Applicants notified on a rolling basis starting 3/15; must reply within 3 week(s) of notification.

Academics. All academic programs are ocean-related. USCG ship officer's license may be earned through license option program. **Special study options:** Accelerated study, combined bachelor's/graduate degree, cooperative education, double major, dual enrollment of high school students, independent study, internships, liberal arts/career combination, semester at sea, study abroad, teacher certification program. Merchant marine licensing program available with marine biology, marine science, marine transportation, and marine engineering technology degrees. **Credit/placement by examination:** AP, CLEP, IB, institutional tests. **Support services:** Learning center, pre-admission summer program, remedial instruction, study skills assistance, tutoring.

Majors. **Agriculture:** Aquaculture. **Biology:** General, aquatic, biomedical sciences, botany, marine, zoology. **Business:** Business admin, international, international finance, tourism/travel, transportation. **Conservation:** General, fisheries. **Education:** Biology, science. **Engineering:** Marine, ocean, systems. **Engineering technology:** Mechanical. **Interdisciplinary:** Biological/physical sciences. **Liberal arts:** Arts/sciences. **Parks/recreation:** General. **Physical sciences:** General, geology, hydrology, oceanography. **Transportation:** General, commercial fishing, maritime/Merchant Marine.

Most popular majors. Biology 31%, business/marketing 21%, engineering/engineering technologies 13%, interdisciplinary studies 7%, natural resources/environmental science 11%, trade and industry 12%.

Computing on campus. 130 workstations in dormitories, library, computer center. Dormitories wired for high-speed internet access and linked to campus network. Commuter students can connect to campus network. Helpline, repair service available.

Student life. **Freshman orientation:** Mandatory, $50 fee. Preregistration for classes offered. 4 days in June and August. **Housing:** Coed dorms, single-sex dorms, special housing for disabled, apartments, wellness housing available. $250 fully refundable deposit. **Activities:** Choral groups, dance, drama, literary magazine, student government, student newspaper, Circle K, Campus Crusade for Christ, emergency care team, outdoor and environmental conservation, Catholic student association, SEED (Students Encouraging Ethnic Diversity), Wesley Foundation.

Athletics. **Intercollegiate:** Rowing (crew), sailing. **Intramural:** Basketball, football (non-tackle), racquetball, soccer, softball, tennis, volleyball, water polo. **Team name:** Aggies.

Student services. Alcohol/substance abuse counseling, chaplain/spiritual director, career counseling, student employment services, financial aid counseling, health services, minority student services, personal counseling, placement for graduates, veterans' counselor. **Physically disabled:** Services for hearing impaired.

Contact. E-mail: seaaggie@tamug.edu
Phone: (409) 740-4414 Toll-free number: (877) 322-4443
Fax: (409) 740-4731
Cheryl Moon, Executive Director of Enrollment Services, Texas A&M University-Galveston, PO Box 1675, Galveston, TX 77553-1675

Texas A&M University-Kingsville

Kingsville, Texas — **CB member**
www.tamuk.edu — **CB code: 6822**

- Public 4-year university
- Commuter campus in large town
- 5,512 degree-seeking undergraduates
- 1,592 graduate students

General. Founded in 1925. Regionally accredited. **Degrees:** 915 bachelor's awarded; master's, doctoral offered. **ROTC:** Army. **Location:** 40 miles from Corpus Christi, 250 miles from Houston. **Calendar:** Semester, extensive summer session. **Full-time faculty:** 270 total. **Part-time faculty:** 149 total. **Class size:** 41% < 20, 51% 20-39, 5% 40-49, 2% 50-99, less than 1% >100. **Special facilities:** Equine facilities, observatory, college-operated farms, research center for citrus.

Freshman class profile.

Mid 50% test scores			
SAT critical reading:	410-520	Out-of-state:	1%
SAT math:	410-540	Live on campus:	60%
ACT composite:	16-21	Fraternities:	2%
		Sororities:	2%

Basis for selection. Open admission, but selective for some programs. Audition required, portfolio recommended for music program.

High school preparation. 24 units recommended. Recommended units include English 4, mathematics 3, social studies 4, history 3, science 3, foreign language 3 and academic electives 3. One fine arts, 1 computer recommended.

2008-2009 Annual costs. Tuition/fees: $5,424; $13,854 out-of-state. Room/board: $4,874. Books/supplies: $614. Personal expenses: $2,108.

Financial aid. **Non-need-based:** Scholarships awarded for academics, leadership.

Application procedures. **Admission:** No deadline. $15 fee, may be waived for applicants with need. Admission notification on a rolling basis. **Financial aid:** FAFSA required. Applicants notified on a rolling basis.

Academics. **Special study options:** Cooperative education, distance learning, double major, ESL, honors, internships, study abroad, teacher certification program. **Credit/placement by examination:** AP, CLEP.

Majors. **Agriculture:** Agribusiness operations, animal sciences, business, food science, plant sciences, range science. **Architecture:** Interior. **Biology:** General. **Business:** General, accounting, finance, international, management information systems, management science, managerial economics. **Communications:** General. **Conservation:** Wildlife. **Education:** General, agricultural, art, bilingual, elementary, family/consumer sciences, health, music, physical, secondary. **Engineering:** Chemical, civil, computer, electrical, mechanical, petroleum. **Engineering technology:** Industrial management. **Family/consumer sciences:** General, clothing/textiles, family studies, food/nutrition. **Foreign languages:** Spanish. **Health:** Speech pathology. **History:** General. **Math:** General. **Physical sciences:** Chemistry, geology, physics. **Psychology:** General. **Social sciences:** Anthropology, political science, sociology. **Visual/performing arts:** Dramatic, interior design, studio arts.

Student life. **Freshman orientation:** Mandatory. **Housing:** Guaranteed on-campus for freshmen. Coed dorms, single-sex dorms, apartments available. **Activities:** Bands, choral groups, dance, drama, music ensembles, musical theater, radio station, student government, student newspaper, TV station, Muslim student association, Baptist student associates, black student union, La Barraca Tejana, American Society of Women Engineers, Society of Hispanic Professional Engineers, pre-law society.

Athletics. NCAA. **Intercollegiate:** Baseball M, basketball, cross-country, football (tackle) M, softball W, tennis, track and field, volleyball W. **Intramural:** Archery, bowling, equestrian, golf, racquetball, softball, volleyball.

Student services. Adult student services, career counseling, student employment services, health services, on-campus daycare, personal counseling, placement for graduates, veterans' counselor. **Physically disabled:** Services for visually, speech, hearing impaired.

Contact. E-mail: ksossrx@tamuk.edu
Phone: (361) 593-2315 Toll-free number: (800) 687-6000
Fax: (361) 593-2195
Laura Knippers, Director of Admissions and Registrar, Texas A&M University-Kingsville, MSC 105, Kingsville, TX 78363-8201

Texas A&M University-Texarkana

Texarkana, Texas
www.tamut.edu — **CB code: 6206**

- Public two-year upper-division university
- Commuter campus in small city
- 97% of applicants admitted
- Test scores required

General. Founded in 1971. Regionally accredited. **Degrees:** 334 bachelor's awarded; master's offered. **Articulation:** Agreements with Texarkana College, Northeast Texas Community College, Panola College, Paris Junior College, Cossatot College, Rich Mountain College, University of Arkansas Community College at Hope. **Location:** 180 miles from Dallas, 145 miles from Little Rock, Arkansas. **Calendar:** Semester, limited summer session. **Full-time faculty:** 59 total; 15% minority, 41% women. **Part-time faculty:** 70 total; 11% minority, 64% women.

Student profile. 1,030 degree-seeking undergraduates, 479 degree-seeking graduate students. 351 applied as first time-transfer students, 340 admitted, 270 enrolled.

Women:	71%	**Out-of-state:**	25%
Part-time:	61%	**25 or older:**	60%

Basis for selection. Open admission. College transcript, standardized test scores required. Minimum 2.0 GPA for 75 hours or more; 1.75 GPA for less than 75 hours; must satisfy Texas Success Initiative. Transfer accepted as sophomores, juniors, seniors.

2008-2009 Annual costs. Tuition/fees: $4,235; $12,665 out-of-state. Books/supplies: $1,160. Personal expenses: $1,648.

Financial aid. Need-based: 57% of total undergraduate aid awarded as scholarships/grants, 43% as loans/jobs. **Non-need-based:** Scholarships awarded for academics, leadership, state residency.

Application procedures. Admission: Rolling admission. No application fee. **Financial aid:** Applicants notified on a rolling basis; must reply within 10 weeks of notification. Must have completed minimum of 54 semester hours of transferable college credit to apply for financial aid. Notified applicants must reply within 45 days from date of award letter. Exceptions made on individual basis. April 1 financial aid deadline for scholarships.

Academics. Special study options: Combined bachelor's/graduate degree, cross-registration, distance learning, dual enrollment of high school students, independent study, internships, liberal arts/career combination, student-designed major, teacher certification program. **Credit/placement by examination:** AP, CLEP, IB, institutional tests. BAAS degree limits credit by exam to 18 semester credit hours. **Support services:** Tutoring, writing center.

Majors. Biology: General. **Business:** General, accounting, business admin, finance, human resources, international, management information systems, marketing. **Communications:** Media studies. **Computer sciences:** General. **Engineering:** Electrical. **Health:** Nursing (RN). **History:** General. **Math:** General. **Protective services:** Criminal justice. **Psychology:** General. **Social sciences:** Political science.

Most popular majors. Business/marketing 19%, interdisciplinary studies 42%, liberal arts 10%, psychology 7%.

Computing on campus. 119 workstations in library, computer center. Commuter students can connect to campus network. Online library, wireless network available.

Student life. Activities: Student government, student newspaper, multicultural association.

Student services. Career counseling, student employment services, financial aid counseling, personal counseling, placement for graduates, veterans' counselor. **Physically disabled:** Services for visually, hearing impaired.

Contact. E-mail: admissions@tamut.edu
Phone: (903) 223-3069 Fax: (903) 223-3140
Patricia Black, Director of Admissions and Registrar, Texas A&M University-Texarkana, 2600 North Robinson Road, Texarkana, TX 75505-5518

Texas Christian University

Fort Worth, Texas — **CB member**
www.tcu.edu — **CB code: 6820**

- Private 4-year university affiliated with Christian Church (Disciples of Christ)
- Residential campus in very large city
- 7,369 degree-seeking undergraduates: 4% part-time, 59% women, 5% African American, 3% Asian American, 8% Hispanic American, 5% international
- 1,210 degree-seeking graduate students
- 50% of applicants admitted
- SAT or ACT (ACT writing recommended), application essay required
- 69% graduate within 6 years

General. Founded in 1873. Regionally accredited. Two comprehensive leadership programs offered. Leadership center, information and resources related to leadership development and training. **Degrees:** 1,592 bachelor's awarded; master's, doctoral offered. **ROTC:** Army, Air Force. **Location:** 3 miles from downtown, 29 miles from Dallas. **Calendar:** Semester, limited summer session. **Full-time faculty:** 506 total; 83% have terminal degrees, 12% minority, 41% women. **Part-time faculty:** 305 total; 26% have terminal degrees, 8% minority, 49% women. **Class size:** 48% < 20, 37% 20-39, 9% 40-49, 4% 50-99, 2% >100. **Special facilities:** Geological center for remote sensing, nuclear magnetic resonance facility, observatory, film library, performance complex, behavioral research institute, meteorite collection, lab school, speech and hearing clinic.

Freshman class profile. 12,212 applied, 6,157 admitted, 1,630 enrolled.

Mid 50% test scores		**End year in good standing:**	88%
SAT critical reading:	520-630	**Return as sophomores:**	86%
SAT math:	540-640	**Out-of-state:**	24%
SAT writing:	530-640	**Live on campus:**	93%
ACT composite:	23-28	**International:**	3%
Rank in top quarter:	63%	**Fraternities:**	39%
Rank in top tenth:	32%	**Sororities:**	42%

Basis for selection. GED not accepted. Academic credentials most important; talents, leadership potential, and applicant's determination to make difference considered. Audition, portfolio required for fine arts students; interview recommended for all. **Homeschooled:** Interview with admissions officer recommended, additional weight may be placed on SAT/ACT scores in admissions process.

High school preparation. 17 units required; 24 recommended. Required and recommended units include English 4, mathematics 3-4, social studies 3-4, science 3-4, foreign language 2-4 and academic electives 2-4.

2009-2010 Annual costs. Tuition/fees: $28,298. Room/board: $9,800. Books/supplies: $880. Personal expenses: $1,500.

2008-2009 Financial aid. Need-based: 764 full-time freshmen applied for aid; 555 were judged to have need; 553 of these received aid. Average need met was 75%. Average scholarship/grant was $16,065; average loan $3,885. 63% of total undergraduate aid awarded as scholarships/grants, 37% as loans/jobs. **Non-need-based:** Awarded to 2,389 full-time undergraduates, including 567 freshmen. Scholarships awarded for academics, alumni affiliation, art, minority status, music/drama, religious affiliation, ROTC, state residency.

Application procedures. Admission: Priority date 11/1; deadline 2/15 (postmark date). $40 fee, may be waived for applicants with need. Admission notification 4/1. Admission notification on a rolling basis. Must reply by 5/1. **Financial aid:** Closing date 5/1. FAFSA required. Applicants notified on a rolling basis starting 3/15; must reply by 5/1 or within 2 week(s) of notification.

Academics. Premajor option and accompanying special academic advising for entering students unsure of major; can be used for up to 4 semesters. **Special study options:** Accelerated study, combined bachelor's/graduate degree, cross-registration, distance learning, double major, ESL, honors, independent study, internships, liberal arts/career combination, semester at sea, study abroad, teacher certification program, Washington semester. **Credit/placement by examination:** AP, CLEP, IB, institutional tests. **Support services:** Study skills assistance, tutoring, writing center.

Majors. Biology: General, biochemistry. **Business:** Accounting, business admin, e-commerce, fashion, finance, international, international finance, international marketing, management science, marketing, real estate. **Communications:** General, advertising, broadcast journalism, journalism, radio/tv. **Computer sciences:** General, information technology. **Conservation:** Environmental science. **Education:** Art, Deaf/hearing impaired, early childhood, English, mathematics, music, physical, science, secondary, social studies. **Engineering:** General. **Foreign languages:** French, German, Japanese, Spanish. **Health:** Athletic training, dietetics, movement therapy, nursing (RN), speech pathology. **History:** General. **Interdisciplinary:** Neuroscience. **Liberal arts:** Arts/sciences. **Math:** General. **Parks/recreation:** Health/fitness. **Personal/culinary services:** Food service. **Philosophy/religion:** Philosophy, religion. **Physical sciences:** Chemistry, geology, physics. **Protective services:** Criminal justice. **Psychology:** General. **Public administration:** Social work. **Social sciences:** Anthropology, economics, geography, international economics, international relations, political science, sociology. **Theology:** Sacred music. **Visual/performing arts:** Acting, art history/conservation, ballet, ceramics, dance, directing/producing, dramatic, film/cinema, graphic design, interior design, music performance, music theory/composition, painting, photography, piano/organ, printmaking, sculpture, studio arts, theater design. **Other:** Writing.

Most popular majors. Business/marketing 24%, communications/journalism 19%, education 7%, health sciences 13%, social sciences 7%, visual/performing arts 7%.

Computing on campus. Dormitories wired for high-speed internet access and linked to campus network. Commuter students can connect to campus network. Online course registration, online library, helpline, repair service, wireless network available.

Student life. **Freshman orientation:** Mandatory, $115 fee. Preregistration for classes offered. 2 or 3 day program for students and parents. **Housing:** Guaranteed on-campus for freshmen. Coed dorms, single-sex dorms, apartments, fraternity/sorority housing, wellness housing available. $250 partly refundable deposit, deadline 5/1. Designated rooms available for ADA needs. **Activities:** Bands, campus ministries, choral groups, dance, drama, international student organizations, literary magazine, music ensembles, Model UN, musical theater, opera, radio station, student government, student newspaper, TV station, over 200 social, religious, service, academic, and pre-professional organizations.

Athletics. NCAA. **Intercollegiate:** Baseball M, basketball, cross-country, diving, equestrian W, football (tackle) M, golf, rifle W, soccer W, swimming, tennis, track and field, volleyball W. **Team name:** Horned Frogs.

Student services. Adult student services, alcohol/substance abuse counseling, chaplain/spiritual director, career counseling, student employment services, financial aid counseling, health services, minority student services, personal counseling, placement for graduates, veterans' counselor, women's services. **Physically disabled:** Services for visually, speech, hearing impaired.

Contact. E-mail: frogmail@tcu.edu
Phone: (817) 257-7490 Toll-free number: (800) 828-3764
Fax: (817) 257-7268
Raymond Brown, Dean of Admissions, Texas Christian University, TCU Box 297013, Fort Worth, TX 76129

Texas College
Tyler, Texas
www.texascollege.edu **CB code: 6821**

- Private 4-year liberal arts college affiliated with Christian Methodist Episcopal Church
- Residential campus in small city
- 705 degree-seeking undergraduates: 6% part-time, 41% women, 84% African American, 11% Hispanic American
- 31 degree-seeking graduate students

General. Founded in 1894. Regionally accredited. Charter member college of the United Negro College Fund. **Degrees:** 82 bachelor's, 1 associate awarded. **Location:** 90 miles from Dallas, 100 miles from Shreveport, Louisiana. **Calendar:** Semester, limited summer session. **Full-time faculty:** 35 total; 43% have terminal degrees, 69% minority, 40% women. **Part-time faculty:** 16 total; 19% have terminal degrees, 81% minority, 44% women. **Class size:** 65% < 20, 15% 20-39, 5% 40-49, 14% 50-99, less than 1% >100.

Freshman class profile. 188 enrolled.

Return as sophomores:	44%	**Out-of-state:**	27%

Basis for selection. Open admission. Students who do not meet the minimum 2.0 GPA requirement may enroll in the 2-year Associate in Arts general studies program. After completing this program the student may petition to enroll in the baccalaureate degree program. SAT/ACT recommended for scholarships and placement. **Homeschooled:** Must submit notarized copy of home school transcript showing date of graduation and course requirements that meet the state of Texas graduation requirements as approved by the State Board of Education. **Learning Disabled:** Students who need special assistance should provide documentation of the disability to the Records/Registrar's Office and report the need for assistance for any type of disability to the Office of Academic Affairs. Other referrals for assistance may be suggested.

High school preparation. 16 units required. Required units include English 4, mathematics 2, social studies 2, science 2 and academic electives 6.

2009-2010 Annual costs. Tuition/fees: $9,228. Room/board: $6,600. Books/supplies: $2,300.

Application procedures. **Admission:** No deadline. $20 fee, may be waived for applicants with need. Admission notification on a rolling basis. **Financial aid:** Priority date 6/1; no closing date.

Academics. **Special study options:** Accelerated study, distance learning, double major, dual enrollment of high school students, independent study, internships, teacher certification program. **Credit/placement by examination:** AP, CLEP, institutional tests. 32 credit hours maximum toward bachelor's degree. **Support services:** Learning center, reduced course load, remedial instruction, study skills assistance, tutoring.

Majors. **Biology:** General. **Business:** Business admin. **Computer sciences:** General. **Education:** Art, biology, elementary, history, mathematics, middle, music, physical. **History:** General. **Liberal arts:** Arts/sciences. **Math:** General. **Parks/recreation:** Health/fitness. **Philosophy/religion:** Religion. **Protective services:** Law enforcement admin. **Public administration:** Social work. **Social sciences:** Political science, sociology. **Visual/performing arts:** Studio arts.

Most popular majors. Biology 10%, business/marketing 45%, parks/recreation 9%, public administration/social services 7%, social sciences 15%.

Computing on campus. 200 workstations in dormitories, library, computer center. Dormitories wired for high-speed internet access and linked to campus network. Commuter students can connect to campus network. Online library, helpline, repair service, student web hosting, wireless network available.

Student life. **Freshman orientation:** Mandatory. Preregistration for classes offered. Held 2-3 days prior to first day of classes each semester. **Policies:** Students required to attend chapel weekly. Religious observance required. **Housing:** Guaranteed on-campus for freshmen. Single-sex dorms, wellness housing available. $150 nonrefundable deposit. **Activities:** Bands, choral groups, dance, music ensembles, student government, Young Adults for Christ, Fellowship of Christian Athletes, Pre-alumni Council, Omega Psi Phi, Delta Sigma Theta, Alpha Kappa Alpha.

Athletics. NAIA. **Intercollegiate:** Baseball M, basketball, cheerleading, football (tackle) M, soccer, softball W, track and field, volleyball W. **Intramural:** Basketball, football (non-tackle), soccer, softball W, volleyball W. **Team name:** Steers.

Student services. Adult student services, alcohol/substance abuse counseling, chaplain/spiritual director, career counseling, student employment services, financial aid counseling, health services, on-campus daycare, personal counseling.

Contact. E-mail: chanks@texascollege.edu
Phone: (903) 593-8311 ext. 2297 Toll-free number: (800) 306-6299
Fax: (903) 526-7879
Charles Hanks, Director of Admissions, Texas College, 2404 North Grand Avenue, Tyler, TX 75712-4500

Texas Lutheran University
Seguin, Texas **CB member**
www.tlu.edu **CB code: 6823**

- Private 4-year university and liberal arts college affiliated with Evangelical Lutheran Church in America
- Residential campus in large town
- 1,400 degree-seeking undergraduates: 3% part-time, 51% women, 10% African American, 1% Asian American, 20% Hispanic American, 1% international
- 73% of applicants admitted
- SAT or ACT (ACT writing optional), application essay required
- 52% graduate within 6 years

General. Founded in 1891. Regionally accredited. **Degrees:** 250 bachelor's awarded. **ROTC:** Army, Air Force. **Location:** 30 miles from San Antonio, 55 miles from Austin. **Calendar:** Semester, limited summer session. **Full-time faculty:** 69 total; 77% have terminal degrees, 13% minority, 41% women. **Part-time faculty:** 66 total; 46% have terminal degrees, 12% minority, 46% women. **Class size:** 55% < 20, 41% 20-39, 4% 40-49, less than 1% 50-99. **Special facilities:** Biology field station, Mexican-American study center, life enrichment center, geological museum.

Freshman class profile. 1,103 applied, 809 admitted, 396 enrolled.

Mid 50% test scores		**GPA 2.0-2.99:**	24%
SAT critical reading:	430-550	**Rank in top quarter:**	46%
SAT math:	460-570	**Rank in top tenth:**	16%
SAT writing:	420-530	**Return as sophomores:**	72%
ACT composite:	18-24	**Out-of-state:**	3%
GPA 3.75 or higher:	33%	**Live on campus:**	93%
GPA 3.50-3.74:	15%	**International:**	1%
GPA 3.0-3.49:	27%		

Basis for selection. Quality of academic curriculum pursued and class rank most important. Academic record and test scores also important. Interview recommended. **Homeschooled:** Transcript of courses and grades, letter of recommendation (nonparent) required. Greater emphasis placed on SAT or ACT scores.

High school preparation. College-preparatory program recommended. 17 units required; 23 recommended. Required and recommended units include English 4, mathematics 3-4, social studies 3-4, history 2, science 3-4 (laboratory 2), foreign language 2-3, computer science 1 and academic electives 1.

2008-2009 Annual costs. Tuition/fees: $20,970. Room/board: $6,600. Books/supplies: $740. Personal expenses: $1,100.

2008-2009 Financial aid. **Need-based:** 391 full-time freshmen applied for aid; 302 were judged to have need; 302 of these received aid. Average need met was 46%. Average scholarship/grant was $13,912; average loan $4,109. 63% of total undergraduate aid awarded as scholarships/grants, 37% as loans/jobs. **Non-need-based:** Awarded to 102 full-time undergraduates, including 52 freshmen. Scholarships awarded for academics, alumni affiliation, leadership, music/drama, religious affiliation.

Application procedures. **Admission:** Priority date 5/1; deadline 8/1 (postmark date). $25 fee, may be waived for applicants with need. Admission notification on a rolling basis beginning on or about 10/1. **Financial aid:** Priority date 3/1; no closing date. FAFSA required. Applicants notified on a rolling basis starting 3/1; must reply within 2 week(s) of notification.

Academics. **Special study options:** Combined bachelor's/graduate degree, double major, dual enrollment of high school students, honors, independent study, internships, liberal arts/career combination, study abroad, teacher certification program, Washington semester. International studies curriculum, dual BS program in applied science and engineering in conjunction with Texas state institutions. **Credit/placement by examination:** AP, CLEP, IB, institutional tests. 30 credit hours maximum toward bachelor's degree. **Support services:** Study skills assistance, tutoring, writing center.

Majors. **Biology:** General, molecular. **Business:** General, accounting, business admin. **Communications:** General. **Computer sciences:** General, computer science, information systems. **Education:** Elementary, English, history, mathematics, middle, multi-level teacher, music, physical, reading, social studies. **Foreign languages:** Spanish. **Health:** Athletic training. **History:** General, public archives. **Math:** General. **Parks/recreation:** Exercise sciences, health/fitness, sports admin. **Philosophy/religion:** Philosophy. **Physical sciences:** Chemistry, physics. **Psychology:** General. **Social sciences:** Economics, political science, sociology. **Theology:** Preministerial, youth ministry. **Visual/performing arts:** General, art, dramatic, music history, music performance. **Other:** Pre-engineering/applied science.

Most popular majors. Biology 11%, business/marketing 22%, education 10%, parks/recreation 13%, physical sciences 6%, psychology 11%, visual/performing arts 6%.

Computing on campus. 216 workstations in dormitories, library, computer center, student center. Dormitories wired for high-speed internet access and linked to campus network. Commuter students can connect to campus network. Online library, helpline, wireless network available.

Student life. **Freshman orientation:** Mandatory. Preregistration for classes offered. Held 2 days prior to start of fall semester. **Housing:** Guaranteed on-campus for freshmen. Coed dorms, single-sex dorms, apartments available. $200 fully refundable deposit, deadline 8/1. **Activities:** Bands, campus ministries, choral groups, dance, drama, literary magazine, music ensembles, musical theater, student government, student newspaper, symphony orchestra, black student union, Mexican American student association, Young Democrats, College Republicans, Fellowship of Christian Athletes, Students Make a Difference, Lutheran student movement, Canterbury, Catholic student organization, international student association.

Athletics. NCAA. **Intercollegiate:** Baseball M, basketball, cross-country W, football (tackle) M, golf, soccer, softball W, tennis, track and field W, volleyball W. **Intramural:** Basketball, bowling, football (non-tackle), handball, racquetball, softball, swimming, tennis, volleyball. **Team name:** Bulldogs.

Student services. Alcohol/substance abuse counseling, chaplain/spiritual director, career counseling, student employment services, financial aid counseling, health services, personal counseling, placement for graduates, veterans' counselor.

Contact. E-mail: admissions@tlu.edu
Phone: (830) 372-8050 Toll-free number: (800) 771-8521
Fax: (830) 372-8096
Dale Gaubatz, Director of Admissions, Texas Lutheran University, 1000 West Court Street, Seguin, TX 78155-5999

Texas Southern University

Houston, Texas — **CB member**
www.tsu.edu — **CB code: 6824**

- Public 4-year university
- Commuter campus in very large city
- 7,132 degree-seeking undergraduates: 19% part-time, 58% women, 90% African American, 2% Asian American, 3% Hispanic American, 3% international
- 1,970 degree-seeking graduate students

General. Founded in 1947. Regionally accredited. **Degrees:** 807 bachelor's awarded; master's, doctoral, first professional offered. **ROTC:** Army. **Location:** 2 miles from downtown. **Calendar:** Semester, extensive summer session. **Full-time faculty:** 380 total; 87% minority, 42% women. **Part-time faculty:** 225 total; 91% minority, 52% women. **Class size:** 36% < 20, 44% 20-39, 12% 40-49, 8% 50-99, less than 1% >100. **Special facilities:** University museum.

Freshman class profile. 6,092 applied, 6,007 admitted, 1,347 enrolled.

Mid 50% test scores		**Rank in top quarter:**	21%
SAT critical reading:	320-430	**Rank in top tenth:**	5%
SAT math:	330-430	**End year in good standing:**	41%
SAT writing:	340-430	**Return as sophomores:**	59%
ACT composite:	14-17	**Out-of-state:**	20%
GPA 3.75 or higher:	2%	**Live on campus:**	21%
GPA 3.50-3.74:	5%	**International:**	1%
GPA 3.0-3.49:	26%	**Fraternities:**	3%
GPA 2.0-2.99:	58%	**Sororities:**	1%

Basis for selection. Open admission, but selective for some programs. Special requirements for pharmacy, law, accounting, marketing, and computer science programs. For selective programs high school achievement, interview, essay important; test scores, individual abilities, high school activities considered.

High school preparation. College-preparatory program recommended. Recommended units include English 4, mathematics 3, social studies 4, science 2, foreign language 2 and academic electives 6.

2008-2009 Annual costs. Tuition/fees: $6,401; $14,831 out-of-state. Books/supplies: $1,228. Personal expenses: $1,629.

2007-2008 Financial aid. All financial aid based on need.

Application procedures. **Admission:** Priority date 7/31; deadline 8/15 (postmark date). $42 fee, may be waived for applicants with need. Admission notification on a rolling basis. Must reply by 7/31. **Financial aid:** Priority date 5/1; no closing date. FAFSA required. Applicants notified on a rolling basis starting 6/1.

Academics. **Special study options:** Cooperative education, distance learning, double major, ESL, honors, internships, teacher certification program, weekend college. **Credit/placement by examination:** CLEP, institutional tests. **Support services:** Learning center, pre-admission summer program, remedial instruction, study skills assistance, tutoring.

Majors. **Biology:** General. **Business:** Accounting, banking/financial services, business admin, management information systems, marketing, operations. **Communications:** General, journalism, radio/tv. **Communications technology:** Recording arts. **Computer sciences:** General. **Conservation:** Environmental studies. **Education:** Health, physical. **Engineering technology:** Civil, electrical, industrial. **Family/consumer sciences:** General, child development, food/nutrition. **Foreign languages:** French, Spanish. **Health:** Clinical lab science, dietetics, environmental health, health care admin, health services, medical records admin, nursing (RN), prepharmacy, respiratory therapy technology. **History:** General. **Math:** General. **Parks/recreation:** Health/fitness. **Physical sciences:** Chemistry, physics. **Protective services:** Law enforcement admin. **Psychology:** General. **Public administration:** General, social work. **Social sciences:** Economics, political science, sociology. **Transportation:** Aviation, aviation management. **Visual/performing arts:** Dramatic, fashion design, studio arts.

Most popular majors. Biology 8%, business/marketing 28%, communications/journalism 7%, health sciences 11%, interdisciplinary studies 6%, psychology 6%, security/protective services 7%.

Computing on campus. 500 workstations in library, computer center, student center. Dormitories wired for high-speed internet access and linked to campus network. Online course registration, online library, wireless network available.

Student life. **Freshman orientation:** Mandatory. Preregistration for classes offered. Two-day orientation held every semester during registration week. First-time freshmen and transfer students participate in seminars, meet with academic advisors, complete course selection/registration, and take placement test. **Housing:** Guaranteed on-campus for freshmen. Single-sex dorms, apartments available. $300 deposit, deadline 6/1. **Activities:** Bands, choral groups, drama, film society, music ensembles, musical theater, opera, radio station, student government, student newspaper, symphony orchestra, TV station, Alpha Phi Omega, Campus Crusade for Christ, health information management association, sociology club, political science club, student psychological club, NAACP.

Athletics. NCAA. **Intercollegiate:** Baseball M, basketball, bowling W, cross-country, football (tackle) M, golf, soccer W, softball W, tennis, track and field, volleyball W. **Intramural:** Basketball, bowling W, cheerleading, softball W, tennis, track and field, volleyball W. **Team name:** Tigers.

Student services. Alcohol/substance abuse counseling, chaplain/spiritual director, career counseling, student employment services, financial aid counseling, health services, on-campus daycare, personal counseling, placement for graduates, veterans' counselor. **Physically disabled:** Services for speech impaired.

Contact. E-mail: admissions@tsu.edu
Phone: (713) 313-7472 Toll-free number: (866) 878-4968
Fax: (713) 313-7851
Brian Armstrong, Director of Recruitment and Retention, Texas Southern University, 3100 Cleburne Street, Houston, TX 77004

Texas State University: San Marcos

San Marcos, Texas — **CB member**
www.txstate.edu — **CB code: 6667**

- Public 4-year university
- Commuter campus in large town
- 24,810 degree-seeking undergraduates: 19% part-time, 55% women, 5% African American, 2% Asian American, 23% Hispanic American, 1% Native American, 1% international
- 3,746 degree-seeking graduate students
- 74% of applicants admitted
- SAT or ACT with writing, application essay required
- 54% graduate within 6 years; 20% enter graduate study

General. Founded in 1899. Regionally accredited. **Degrees:** 4,991 bachelor's awarded; master's, doctoral, first professional offered. **ROTC:** Army, Air Force. **Location:** 30 miles from Austin, 49 miles from San Antonio. **Calendar:** Semester, extensive summer session. **Full-time faculty:** 963 total; 77% have terminal degrees, 20% minority, 45% women. **Part-time faculty:** 408 total; 32% have terminal degrees, 9% minority, 56% women. **Class size:** 17% < 20, 56% 20-39, 9% 40-49, 12% 50-99, 7% >100. **Special facilities:** Ranch, natural spring with unique aquatic plants and animals, Southwestern writers collection (original manuscripts), observatory with 17-inch telescope, archaeological forensic laboratory, clean room microchip production lab.

Freshman class profile. 11,435 applied, 8,494 admitted, 3,260 enrolled.

Mid 50% test scores			
SAT critical reading:	470-570	Rank in top tenth:	13%
SAT math:	490-590	End year in good standing:	75%
SAT writing:	460-560	Return as sophomores:	78%
ACT composite:	21-25	Out-of-state:	1%
Rank in top quarter:	53%	Live on campus:	87%

Basis for selection. Applicants who rank in top 10% of high school class have no minimum test score requirements. Otherwise score requirements are as follows: rank in next 15%, 920 SAT or 20 ACT; rank in second quarter, 1010 SAT, 22 ACT; rank in third quarter, 1180 SAT, 26 ACT; rank in bottom quarter, 1270 SAT, 29 ACT. (SAT scores exclusive of Writing). SAT Subject Tests required for placement in certain higher level courses, but not used in the admissions decision. The Office of Admission collects data from the writing sections of the ACT and SAT as supplemental information. Audition required for music program. **Homeschooled:** Transcript of courses and grades required. Minimum 26 ACT or 1180 SAT (exclusive of Writing) and admissions essay.

High school preparation. College-preparatory program required. 24 units required; 26 recommended. Required and recommended units include English 4, mathematics 3-4, social studies 3.5, science 3-4 (laboratory 2), foreign language 2-3, computer science 1, visual/performing arts 1, academic electives 3.5. 1.5 physical education, 0.5 economics, 0.5 speech required, 0.5 health education required.

2008-2009 Annual costs. Tuition/fees: $6,994; $15,424 out-of-state. Room/board: $6,012. Books/supplies: $1,000. Personal expenses: $2,550.

2008-2009 Financial aid. Need-based: 2,229 full-time freshmen applied for aid; 1,538 were judged to have need; 1,468 of these received aid. Average need met was 70%. Average scholarship/grant was $6,280; average loan $3,173. 51% of total undergraduate aid awarded as scholarships/grants, 49% as loans/jobs. **Non-need-based:** Awarded to 2,026 full-time undergraduates, including 662 freshmen. Scholarships awarded for academics, art, athletics, leadership, music/drama, ROTC, state residency. **Additional information:** To be eligible for the Bobcat Promise program you must be an entering first-time freshmen (transfer students are not eligible), be a Texas resident, have a family adjusted gross income of $25,000 or less, be enrolled full-time and complete at least 30 credit hours during each academic year (fall and spring semester), and submit a completed FAFSA no later than April 1.

Application procedures. Admission: Closing date 5/1 (receipt date). $60 fee, may be waived for applicants with need. Admission notification on a rolling basis beginning on or about 9/1. All applicants to the McCoy College of Business must have their application in by March 15 for Summer and Fall Admission and October 15 for Spring admission. Applicants to the Department of Communication Design must have application in by March 15 for fall admission and October 15 for Spring admission. **Financial aid:** Priority date 4/1; no closing date. FAFSA required. Applicants notified on a rolling basis starting 5/1; must reply within 3 week(s) of notification.

Academics. Special study options: Accelerated study, combined bachelor's/graduate degree, distance learning, double major, dual enrollment of high school students, ESL, exchange student, honors, independent study, internships, study abroad, teacher certification program, Washington semester, weekend college. **Credit/placement by examination:** AP, CLEP, IB, institutional tests. Credit hours earned by exam do not count as credit earned in residence. **Support services:** Learning center, remedial instruction, study skills assistance, tutoring, writing center.

Majors. Agriculture: General, agribusiness operations, animal sciences. **Architecture:** Urban/community planning. **Area/ethnic studies:** American, Asian, European, Near/Middle Eastern, Russian/Slavic. **Biology:** General, animal physiology, aquatic, biochemistry, botany, microbiology, wildlife, zoology. **Business:** Accounting, business admin, fashion, finance, management information systems, managerial economics, marketing. **Communications:** Advertising, journalism, media studies, public relations, radio/tv. **Communications technology:** Desktop publishing, recording arts. **Computer sciences:** General. **Conservation:** Environmental science, water/wetlands/marine. **Engineering:** General, electrical, industrial, manufacturing. **Engineering technology:** General, construction, industrial, manufacturing. **Family/consumer sciences:** General, family studies, food/nutrition. **Foreign languages:** French, German, Spanish. **Health:** Athletic training, audiology/speech pathology, clinical lab science, health care admin, health services, medical radiologic technology/radiation therapy, medical records admin, respiratory therapy technology. **History:** General. **Interdisciplinary:** Biological/physical sciences, global studies. **Math:** General, applied. **Parks/recreation:** Facilities management, health/fitness, sports admin. **Philosophy/religion:** Philosophy. **Physical sciences:** Chemistry, physics. **Protective services:** Corrections, criminal justice, police science. **Psychology:** General. **Public administration:** General, social work. **Social sciences:** Anthropology, cartography, economics, geography, international relations, political science, sociology. **Visual/performing arts:** Art, dance, dramatic, graphic design, interior design, jazz, music performance, studio arts.

Most popular majors. Business/marketing 20%, communications/journalism 7%, English 6%, interdisciplinary studies 13%, parks/recreation 7%, psychology 6%, social sciences 7%, visual/performing arts 8%.

Computing on campus. 1,480 workstations in dormitories, library, computer center, student center. Dormitories wired for high-speed internet access and linked to campus network. Commuter students can connect to campus network. Online course registration, helpline, repair service, student web hosting, wireless network available.

Student life. Freshman orientation: Mandatory, $25 fee. Preregistration for classes offered. 2-day program combined with welcome week prior to start of semester. **Policies:** All unmarried students under 21 with fewer than 56 credit hours must live in university housing. **Housing:** Guaranteed on-campus for freshmen. Coed dorms, single-sex dorms, apartments, fraternity/sorority housing available. $300 partly refundable deposit. **Activities:** Bands, campus ministries, choral groups, dance, drama, film society, international student organizations, literary magazine, music ensembles, Model UN, musical theater, opera, radio station, student government, student newspaper, symphony orchestra, nearly 300 social, service, religious, political, and professional organizations.

Athletics. NCAA. **Intercollegiate:** Baseball M, basketball, cheerleading, cross-country, football (tackle) M, golf, soccer W, softball W, tennis W, track and field, volleyball W. **Intramural:** Basketball, bowling, football (non-tackle), golf, racquetball, soccer, softball, tennis, volleyball. **Team name:** Bobcats.

Student services. Adult student services, alcohol/substance abuse counseling, chaplain/spiritual director, career counseling, student employment services, financial aid counseling, health services, legal services, minority student services, personal counseling, placement for graduates, veterans' counselor. **Physically disabled:** Services for visually, speech, hearing impaired.

Contact. E-mail: admissions@txstate.edu
Phone: (512) 245-2364 Fax: (512) 245-8044
Stephanie Anderson, Director of Admissions, Texas State University: San Marcos, 429 North Guadalupe Street, San Marcos, TX 78666-5709

Texas Tech University

Lubbock, Texas — **CB member**
www.ttu.edu — **CB code: 6827**

- Public 4-year university
- Commuter campus in small city
- 23,080 degree-seeking undergraduates: 8% part-time, 44% women, 4% African American, 3% Asian American, 14% Hispanic American, 1% Native American, 1% international
- 5,093 degree-seeking graduate students
- 72% of applicants admitted
- SAT or ACT (ACT writing optional) required
- 57% graduate within 6 years

General. Founded in 1923. Regionally accredited. **Degrees:** 4,838 bachelor's awarded; master's, doctoral, first professional offered. **ROTC:** Army, Air Force. **Location:** 348 miles from Dallas, 321 miles from Albuquerque, New Mexico. **Calendar:** Semester, extensive summer session. **Full-time faculty:** 1,099 total; 87% have terminal degrees, 16% minority, 36% women. **Part-time faculty:** 81 total; 46% have terminal degrees, 7% minority, 52% women. **Class size:** 25% < 20, 42% 20-39, 12% 40-49, 13% 50-99, 8% >100. **Special facilities:** Museum, national ranching heritage center, special collections library, archaeological dig/state park, international cultural center, international textile research center, science research laboratory, arid and semi-arid land studies center, seismological observatory, child development research center, institutes for environmental and human health, Vietnam center, Moody planetarium.

Freshman class profile. 16,143 applied, 11,643 admitted, 4,385 enrolled.

Mid 50% test scores			
SAT critical reading:	490-590	End year in good standing:	80%
SAT math:	520-620	Return as sophomores:	80%
SAT writing:	460-570	Out-of-state:	4%
ACT composite:	22-26	Live on campus:	90%
Rank in top quarter:	52%	International:	1%
Rank in top tenth:	21%	Fraternities:	16%
		Sororities:	23%

Basis for selection. Class rank and test scores considered first, and students meeting the following score requirements (exclusive of Writing) eligible for unconditional admission: class rank in top 10%, no minimum test scores; rank in next 15%, with 1140 SAT or 25 ACT; rank in second quarter, with 1230 SAT or 28 ACT; rank in lower half, with 1270 SAT or 29 ACT. Applicants who do not meet assured admission criteria will have records reviewed in holistic manner. Auditions and portfolios required for admission to some programs.

High school preparation. College-preparatory program recommended. 11 units required. Required units include English 4, mathematics 3, science 2 (laboratory 2) and foreign language 2.

2008-2009 Annual costs. Tuition/fees: $6,783; $15,213 out-of-state. Students from adjacent counties in New Mexico and Oklahoma pay in-state tuition rates; students from all other counties in New Mexico and Oklahoma pay reduced out-of-state tuition rates. Room/board: $7,310. Books/supplies: $900. Personal expenses: $1,890.

2007-2008 Financial aid. **Non-need-based:** Scholarships awarded for academics, art, athletics, job skills, leadership, music/drama, ROTC.

Application procedures. **Admission:** Closing date 5/1 (receipt date). $50 fee, may be waived for applicants with need. Admission notification on a rolling basis. **Financial aid:** Priority date 4/15; no closing date. FAFSA required. Applicants notified on a rolling basis; must reply within 2 week(s) of notification.

Academics. **Special study options:** Accelerated study, combined bachelor's/graduate degree, cooperative education, distance learning, double major, dual enrollment of high school students, ESL, external degree, honors, independent study, internships, liberal arts/career combination, semester at sea, student-designed major, study abroad, teacher certification program. **Credit/placement by examination:** AP, CLEP, IB, SAT, ACT, institutional tests. **Support services:** Learning center, pre-admission summer program, remedial instruction, study skills assistance, tutoring, writing center.

Honors college/program. Requires separate application, minimum 1200 SAT (exclusive of Writing) or 26 ACT, or top 10% class rank, essays, 2 teacher recommendations. 317 freshmen admitted. Average SAT score: 1299; total enrollment 883. Two tracks offered to students: nondegree program working with all colleges and majors to provide honors academic, co-curricular and social program; and interdisciplinary degree program for bachelor of arts degree in natural history and humanities or Honors Arts and Letters.

Majors. **Agriculture:** General, agronomy, animal sciences, business, communications, economics, food science, horticulture, range science. **Architecture:** Architecture, interior, landscape. **Area/ethnic studies:** Latin American, Russian/Slavic. **Biology:** General, biochemistry, cellular/molecular, microbiology, zoology. **Business:** General, accounting, business admin, fashion, finance, hotel/motel admin, international, management information systems, marketing. **Communications:** Advertising, journalism, photojournalism, public relations, radio/tv. **Computer sciences:** General. **Conservation:** General, fisheries, wildlife. **Engineering:** General, chemical, civil, computer, electrical, environmental, industrial, mechanical, petroleum, physics. **Engineering technology:** General, architectural, electrical, mechanical. **Family/consumer sciences:** General, child development, clothing/textiles, family resources, family studies, family systems, family/community services, food/nutrition. **Foreign languages:** Classics, French, German, Spanish. **Health:** Dietetics, health services. **History:** General. **Interdisciplinary:** Biological/physical sciences. **Liberal arts:** Arts/sciences. **Math:** General. **Parks/recreation:** Health/fitness. **Philosophy/religion:** Philosophy. **Physical sciences:** Chemistry, geology, geophysics, physics. **Psychology:** General. **Public administration:** Social work. **Social sciences:** Anthropology, economics, geography, political science, sociology. **Visual/performing arts:** Acting, art, art history/conservation, dance, dramatic, fashion design, graphic design, music performance, music theory/composition, studio arts, theater design. **Other:** Energy commerce.

Most popular majors. Business/marketing 24%, communications/journalism 6%, engineering/engineering technologies 9%, family/consumer sciences 11%.

Computing on campus. 3,000 workstations in dormitories, library, computer center, student center. Dormitories wired for high-speed internet access and linked to campus network. Commuter students can connect to campus network. Online course registration, online library, helpline, repair service, student web hosting, wireless network available.

Student life. **Freshman orientation:** Mandatory, $150 fee. Preregistration for classes offered. Three-day sessions held in January, April, May, June and July. **Policies:** Freshmen required to live on campus. **Housing:** Guaranteed on-campus for freshmen. Coed dorms, single-sex dorms, special housing for disabled, apartments, wellness housing available. $50 nonrefundable deposit, deadline 5/1. Special interest housing: honors, intensive study, learning communities, upperclass-graduate areas. **Activities:** Bands, campus ministries, choral groups, dance, drama, international student organizations, music ensembles, musical theater, radio station, student government, student newspaper, symphony orchestra, TV station, College Republicans, Wesley Foundation, Black Student Association, Hispanic Law Student Association, Alpha Phi Omega, Women's Service Organization, University Democrats, Campus Crusade for Christ.

Athletics. NCAA. **Intercollegiate:** Baseball M, basketball, cross-country, football (tackle) M, golf, soccer W, softball W, tennis, track and field, volleyball W. **Intramural:** Badminton, baseball, basketball, bowling, football (non-tackle), golf, racquetball, soccer, softball, swimming, table tennis, tennis, volleyball, weight lifting M. **Team name:** Red Raiders/ Lady Raiders.

Student services. Alcohol/substance abuse counseling, career counseling, student employment services, financial aid counseling, health services, legal services, personal counseling, placement for graduates, veterans' counselor. **Physically disabled:** Services for visually, speech, hearing impaired. **Learning disabled:** Comprehensive services available.

Contact. E-mail: admissions@ttu.edu
Phone: (806) 742-1480 Fax: (806) 742-0062
Ethan Logan, Managing Director of Undergraduate Recruitment and Admissions, Texas Tech University, Box 45005, Lubbock, TX 79409-5005

Texas Tech University Health Sciences Center

Lubbock, Texas
www.ttuhsc.edu — **CB code: 3423**

- Public two-year upper-division university
- Commuter campus in small city
- Application essay required

General. Founded in 1969. Regionally accredited. **Degrees:** 479 bachelor's awarded; master's, doctoral, first professional offered. **Calendar:** Semester, limited summer session. **Full-time faculty:** 745 total; 80% have terminal degrees, 14% minority, 43% women. **Part-time faculty:** 77 total; 79% have terminal degrees, 10% minority, 36% women. **Class size:** 58% < 20, 30% 20-39, 4% 40-49, 6% 50-99, 2% >100.

Student profile. 723 degree-seeking undergraduates, 2,181 degree-seeking graduate students.

Women:	83%	**International:**	1%
African American:	9%	**Part-time:**	12%
Asian American:	3%	**Out-of-state:**	5%
Hispanic American:	13%	**25 or older:**	38%
Native American:	1%		

Basis for selection. College transcript, application essay required. Transfer accepted as juniors.

2008-2009 Annual costs. Tuition and fees vary for each of the programs within the five schools: Allied Health, Medicine, Nursing, Pharmacy and the Graduate School of Biomedical Sciences. Books/supplies: $1,119. Personal expenses: $3,651.

Financial aid. Need-based: 39% of total undergraduate aid awarded as scholarships/grants, 61% as loans/jobs. **Non-need-based:** Scholarships awarded for academics.

Application procedures. Admission: $40 fee. **Financial aid:** No deadline. Applicants notified on a rolling basis.

Academics. Special study options: Combined bachelor's/graduate degree, distance learning. **Credit/placement by examination:** CLEP.

Majors. Health: Clinical lab science, communication disorders, health care admin, health services, nursing (RN).

Computing on campus. PC or laptop required. 160 workstations in library. Commuter students can connect to campus network. Online library, wireless network available.

Student services. Physically disabled: Services for visually, speech, hearing impaired.

Contact. Phone: (806) 743-2300
Texas Tech University Health Sciences Center, 3601 Fourth Street, Lubbock, TX 79430

Texas Wesleyan University
Fort Worth, Texas
www.txwes.edu **CB code: 6828**

- Private 4-year university affiliated with United Methodist Church
- Commuter campus in large city
- 1,488 degree-seeking undergraduates: 24% part-time, 67% women, 21% African American, 1% Asian American, 21% Hispanic American, 1% Native American, 2% international
- 1,494 degree-seeking graduate students
- 58% of applicants admitted
- SAT or ACT (ACT writing optional) required

General. Founded in 1890. Regionally accredited. **Degrees:** 300 bachelor's awarded; master's, doctoral, first professional offered. **ROTC:** Army, Air Force. **Location:** 2 miles from downtown. **Calendar:** Semester, limited summer session. **Full-time faculty:** 155 total; 12% minority, 49% women. **Part-time faculty:** 111 total; 7% minority, 49% women. **Class size:** 62% < 20, 36% 20-39, 1% 40-49, less than 1% 50-99.

Freshman class profile. 754 applied, 434 admitted, 206 enrolled.

Mid 50% test scores		**GPA 2.0-2.99:**	24%
SAT critical reading:	440-530	**Rank in top quarter:**	48%
SAT math:	440-530	**Rank in top tenth:**	18%
SAT writing:	420-520	**Return as sophomores:**	63%
ACT composite:	18-22	**Out-of-state:**	1%
GPA 3.50-3.74:	46%	**Live on campus:**	48%
GPA 3.0-3.49:	30%	**International:**	2%

Basis for selection. Regular freshmen admission requires minimum 2.5 high school GPA, 19 ACT or 920 SAT combined score (exclusive of Writing), top 50% ranking in senior class. **Homeschooled:** Transcript of courses and grades required.

High school preparation. College-preparatory program recommended. 20 units recommended. Recommended units include English 4, mathematics 4, social studies 3, science 3, foreign language 1 and academic electives 7.

2008-2009 Annual costs. Tuition/fees: $16,730. Room/board: $6,100. Books/supplies: $1,020. Personal expenses: $1,863.

2007-2008 Financial aid. All financial aid based on need. 169 full-time freshmen applied for aid; 147 were judged to have need; 147 of these received aid. Average need met was 59%. Average scholarship/grant was $9,011; average loan $2,500. 66% of total undergraduate aid awarded as scholarships/grants, 34% as loans/jobs.

Application procedures. Admission: No deadline. $25 fee, may be waived for applicants with need. Admission notification on a rolling basis. **Financial aid:** Priority date 3/15; no closing date. FAFSA required. Applicants notified on a rolling basis starting 3/15.

Academics. Special study options: Accelerated study, combined bachelor's/graduate degree, distance learning, double major, dual enrollment of high school students, ESL, exchange student, independent study, internships, liberal arts/career combination, study abroad, teacher certification program, weekend college. **Credit/placement by examination:** AP, CLEP, institutional tests. 30 credit hours maximum toward bachelor's degree. **Support services:** Learning center, pre-admission summer program, reduced course load, remedial instruction, study skills assistance, tutoring, writing center.

Majors. Biology: General, biochemistry. **Business:** Accounting, business admin, finance, international marketing, management science, office technology. **Communications:** General, journalism, public relations, radio/tv. **Computer sciences:** General, computer science, information systems. **Education:** General, bilingual, biology, business, chemistry, early childhood, elementary, English, history, mathematics, multi-level teacher, music, physical, reading, secondary, social science, social studies, Spanish. **Foreign languages:** Spanish. **Health:** Athletic training, predental, premedicine. **History:** General. **Legal studies:** Paralegal, prelaw. **Math:** General. **Parks/recreation:** Facilities management, health/fitness. **Philosophy/religion:** Religion. **Physical sciences:** Chemistry. **Psychology:** General. **Social sciences:** General, political science. **Theology:** Religious ed. **Visual/performing arts:** General, art, dramatic. **Other:** Criminal justice, Liberal studies.

Computing on campus. 306 workstations in library, computer center. Dormitories wired for high-speed internet access and linked to campus network. Online library, wireless network available.

Student life. Freshman orientation: Mandatory. Preregistration for classes offered. **Policies:** Resident chaplain on staff. **Housing:** Coed dorms, single-sex dorms, apartments, fraternity/sorority housing, wellness housing available. $150 partly refundable deposit. **Activities:** Bands, choral groups, dance, drama, international student organizations, literary magazine, music ensembles, musical theater, opera, student government, student newspaper, Methodist and Baptist student unions, Student Foundation, Alpha Phi Omega, Fellowship of Christian Athletes.

Athletics. NAIA. **Intercollegiate:** Baseball M, basketball, golf M, soccer, softball W, table tennis M, volleyball W. **Intramural:** Badminton, basketball, bowling, diving, golf M, soccer, softball, swimming, table tennis, tennis W, volleyball. **Team name:** Rams.

Student services. Adult student services, alcohol/substance abuse counseling, chaplain/spiritual director, career counseling, student employment services, financial aid counseling, health services, personal counseling, placement for graduates, veterans' counselor.

Contact. E-mail: admission@txwes.edu
Phone: (817) 531-4422 Toll-free number: (800) 580-8980
Fax: (817) 531-7515
Holly Kiser, Director of Freshman Admissions, Texas Wesleyan University, 1201 Wesleyan Street, Fort Worth, TX 76105-1536

Texas Woman's University
Denton, Texas **CB member**
www.twu.edu **CB code: 6826**

- Public 4-year university
- Residential campus in small city
- 7,389 degree-seeking undergraduates: 31% part-time, 93% women, 21% African American, 8% Asian American, 18% Hispanic American, 1% Native American, 2% international
- 4,577 degree-seeking graduate students
- 56% of applicants admitted

- SAT or ACT (ACT writing optional) required
- 44% graduate within 6 years

General. Founded in 1901. Regionally accredited. Primarily women's university. **Degrees:** 1,446 bachelor's awarded; master's, doctoral offered. **ROTC:** Army, Air Force. **Location:** 35 miles from Dallas and Fort Worth. **Calendar:** Semester, extensive summer session. **Full-time faculty:** 306 total; 17% minority, 71% women. **Part-time faculty:** 443 total; 13% minority, 74% women. **Class size:** 48% < 20, 42% 20-39, 4% 40-49, 5% 50-99, less than 1% >100. **Special facilities:** Art collection, Little Chapel-in-the-Woods, Texas Women's Hall of Fame, Texas First Ladies Historic Costume Collection, Woman's Collection, Women Airforce Service Pilots, botanical gardens, Gertrude Gibson Guest House, Clarabel Tanner Collection of Children's Book Art, cookbook collection.

Freshman class profile. 3,649 applied, 2,047 admitted, 798 enrolled.

Mid 50% test scores		**Rank in top quarter:**	47%
SAT critical reading:	440-560	**Rank in top tenth:**	18%
SAT math:	440-560	**End year in good standing:**	79%
ACT composite:	19-24	**Return as sophomores:**	71%
GPA 3.75 or higher:	22%	**Out-of-state:**	1%
GPA 3.50-3.74:	15%	**Live on campus:**	77%
GPA 3.0-3.49:	38%	**Sororities:**	3%
GPA 2.0-2.99:	25%		

Basis for selection. School achievement record and test scores most important: Texas Academic Skills Program, SAT of 950 (exclusive of Writing) or ACT of 20. Interview and audition required for drama and music programs; interview required and portfolio recommended for art program.

High school preparation. 22 units required. Required units include English 4, mathematics 3, social studies 2, science 2 and academic electives 11.

2008-2009 Annual costs. Tuition/fees: $6,540; $14,880 out-of-state. Room/board: $5,846. Books/supplies: $960. Personal expenses: $1,890.

Application procedures. Admission: Priority date 2/1; deadline 7/1 (receipt date). $30 fee, may be waived for applicants with need. Admission notification on a rolling basis beginning on or about 3/1. **Financial aid:** Priority date 4/1; no closing date. FAFSA, institutional form required. Applicants notified on a rolling basis starting 3/1; must reply within 2 week(s) of notification.

Academics. Special study options: Accelerated study, combined bachelor's/graduate degree, cooperative education, cross-registration, distance learning, double major, dual enrollment of high school students, honors, independent study, internships, liberal arts/career combination, study abroad, teacher certification program, weekend college. **Credit/placement by examination:** AP, CLEP, SAT, ACT, institutional tests. 30 credit hours maximum toward bachelor's degree. **Support services:** Learning center, preadmission summer program, reduced course load, remedial instruction, study skills assistance, tutoring, writing center.

Majors. Biology: General, biochemistry, zoology. **Business:** Accounting, administrative services, business admin, fashion, finance, marketing. **Computer sciences:** General. **Family/consumer sciences:** General, child development, family studies, food/nutrition. **Health:** Clinical lab science, dental hygiene, dietetics, health services, music therapy, nursing (RN). **History:** General. **Interdisciplinary:** Nutrition sciences. **Legal studies:** Paralegal. **Math:** General. **Parks/recreation:** Health/fitness. **Physical sciences:** Chemistry. **Protective services:** Criminal justice. **Psychology:** General. **Public administration:** Social work. **Social sciences:** Political science, sociology. **Visual/performing arts:** Art, dance, dramatic, fashion design. **Other:** Interdisciplinary studies.

Most popular majors. Business/marketing 6%, family/consumer sciences 6%, health sciences 36%, interdisciplinary studies 11%, liberal arts 9%, psychology 6%.

Computing on campus. 1,000 workstations in dormitories, library, computer center, student center. Dormitories linked to campus network. Commuter students can connect to campus network. Online course registration, helpline available.

Student life. Freshman orientation: Mandatory, $25 fee. Preregistration for classes offered. Two-day event. **Housing:** Guaranteed on-campus for all undergraduates. Coed dorms, single-sex dorms, special housing for disabled, apartments, cooperative housing, fraternity/sorority housing, wellness housing available. $125 partly refundable deposit. Family housing, honors students housing. **Activities:** Jazz band, campus ministries, choral groups, dance, drama, international student organizations, music ensembles, musical theater, opera, student government, student newspaper, Alpha Theta Omega, LULAC, multicultural African organization, NAACP, Alpha Kappa Alpha Sorority, Delta Sigma Theta Sorority, Zeta Phi Beta Sorority, Golden Key international honor society.

Athletics. NCAA. **Intercollegiate:** Basketball W, gymnastics W, soccer W, softball W, volleyball W. **Intramural:** Basketball, football (non-tackle), golf, racquetball, soccer, softball, swimming, table tennis M, tennis, volleyball, weight lifting. **Team name:** Pioneers.

Student services. Adult student services, alcohol/substance abuse counseling, career counseling, student employment services, financial aid counseling, health services, minority student services, personal counseling, placement for graduates, veterans' counselor, women's services. **Physically disabled:** Services for visually, speech, hearing impaired.

Contact. E-mail: admissions@twu.edu
Phone: (940) 898-3188 Toll-free number: (866) 809-6130
Fax: (940) 898-3081
Erma Nieto, Director of Admissions, Texas Woman's University, Box 425589, Denton, TX 76204-5589

Trinity University

San Antonio, Texas — **CB member**
www.trinity.edu — **CB code: 6831**

- Private 4-year liberal arts college affiliated with Presbyterian Church (USA)
- Residential campus in very large city
- 2,475 degree-seeking undergraduates: 1% part-time, 53% women, 4% African American, 7% Asian American, 11% Hispanic American, 1% Native American, 6% international
- 213 degree-seeking graduate students
- 58% of applicants admitted
- SAT or ACT (ACT writing optional), application essay required
- 81% graduate within 6 years

General. Founded in 1869. Regionally accredited. **Degrees:** 544 bachelor's awarded; master's offered. **ROTC:** Air Force. **Location:** 3 miles from downtown. **Calendar:** Semester, limited summer session. **Full-time faculty:** 248 total; 100% have terminal degrees, 12% minority, 37% women. **Part-time faculty:** 75 total. **Class size:** 57% < 20, 38% 20-39, 3% 40-49, 1% 50-99, less than 1% >100.

Freshman class profile. 3,754 applied, 2,186 admitted, 656 enrolled.

Mid 50% test scores		**Rank in top quarter:**	85%
SAT critical reading:	600-690	**Rank in top tenth:**	53%
SAT math:	610-690	**End year in good standing:**	90%
ACT composite:	27-31	**Return as sophomores:**	90%
GPA 3.75 or higher:	37%	**Out-of-state:**	28%
GPA 3.50-3.74:	23%	**Live on campus:**	100%
GPA 3.0-3.49:	32%	**International:**	6%
GPA 2.0-2.99:	8%		

Basis for selection. GPA, high school rank, test scores, essay, interview, recommendations, extracurricular involvement, and achievement important. **Homeschooled:** At least 3 SAT Subject Tests recommended, including natural science and foreign language.

High school preparation. 15 units required; 19 recommended. Required and recommended units include English 4, mathematics 3, social studies 3, science 3 (laboratory 2-3), foreign language 2-3 and academic electives 3.

2008-2009 Annual costs. Tuition/fees: $27,699. Room/board: $8,822. Books/supplies: $950. Personal expenses: $1,050.

2008-2009 Financial aid. Need-based: 394 full-time freshmen applied for aid; 263 were judged to have need; 263 of these received aid. Average need met was 95%. Average scholarship/grant was $17,299; average loan $4,746. 73% of total undergraduate aid awarded as scholarships/grants, 27% as loans/jobs. **Non-need-based:** Awarded to 1,292 full-time undergraduates, including 357 freshmen. Scholarships awarded for academics, leadership, music/drama.

Application procedures. Admission: Closing date 2/1 (postmark date). $50 fee, may be waived for applicants with need, free for online applicants. Admission notification 4/1. Admission notification on a rolling basis. Must reply by 5/1. **Financial aid:** Priority date 2/1, closing date 4/1. FAFSA required. Must reply by 5/1 or within 4 week(s) of notification.

Academics. **Special study options:** Accelerated study, combined bachelor's/graduate degree, double major, honors, independent study, internships, liberal arts/career combination, New York semester, semester at sea, student-designed major, study abroad, teacher certification program, United Nations semester, urban semester, Washington semester. **Credit/placement by examination:** AP, CLEP, IB, institutional tests. 36 credit hours maximum toward bachelor's degree. **Support services:** Writing center.

Majors. **Area/ethnic studies:** Asian, European, Latin American. **Biology:** General, biochemistry. **Business:** Accounting, business admin, finance, international, management science, marketing. **Communications:** General. **Computer sciences:** General. **Education:** Elementary. **Engineering:** Science. **Foreign languages:** Chinese, classics, French, German, Russian, Spanish. **History:** General. **Math:** General. **Philosophy/religion:** Philosophy, religion. **Physical sciences:** Chemistry, geology, physics. **Psychology:** General. **Social sciences:** Anthropology, economics, political science, sociology, urban studies. **Visual/performing arts:** Art, art history/conservation, dramatic, music performance, music theory/composition, theater design, voice/opera.

Most popular majors. Business/marketing 23%, communications/journalism 8%, English 6%, foreign language 10%, social sciences 14%.

Computing on campus. 400 workstations in library, computer center, student center. Dormitories wired for high-speed internet access and linked to campus network. Commuter students can connect to campus network. Online course registration, online library, helpline, student web hosting, wireless network available.

Student life. **Freshman orientation:** Available. **Housing:** Guaranteed on-campus for freshmen. Coed dorms, wellness housing available. $500 nonrefundable deposit, deadline 5/1. **Activities:** Bands, campus ministries, choral groups, dance, drama, film society, literary magazine, music ensembles, Model UN, musical theater, opera, radio station, student government, student newspaper, symphony orchestra, TV station, Phi Beta Kappa, academic honor societies, activities council, Young Democrats, Young Republicans, association of student representatives, Alpha Phi Omega, religious organizations, minority student organizations (Trinity Multicultural Network).

Athletics. NCAA. **Intercollegiate:** Baseball M, basketball, cross-country, diving, football (tackle) M, golf, soccer, softball W, swimming, tennis, track and field, volleyball W. **Intramural:** Basketball, cross-country, football (non-tackle), racquetball, soccer, softball, swimming, table tennis, tennis, volleyball, wrestling. **Team name:** Tigers.

Student services. Chaplain/spiritual director, career counseling, student employment services, financial aid counseling, health services, personal counseling, placement for graduates, veterans' counselor. **Physically disabled:** Services for visually, hearing impaired.

Contact. E-mail: admissions@trinity.edu
Phone: (210) 999-7207 Toll-free number: (800) 874-6489
Fax: (210) 999-8164
Christopher Ellertson, Dean of Admissions and Financial Aid, Trinity University, One Trinity Place, San Antonio, TX 78212-7200

University of Dallas

Irving, Texas — **CB member**
www.udallas.edu — **CB code: 6868**

- Private 4-year university and liberal arts college affiliated with Roman Catholic Church
- Residential campus in small city
- 1,289 degree-seeking undergraduates: 2% part-time, 52% women, 1% African American, 5% Asian American, 16% Hispanic American, 2% international
- 1,576 degree-seeking graduate students
- 91% of applicants admitted
- SAT or ACT with writing, application essay required
- 57% graduate within 6 years; 37% enter graduate study

General. Founded in 1956. Regionally accredited. Additional campus in Rome, Italy. **Degrees:** 227 bachelor's awarded; master's, doctoral offered. **ROTC:** Army, Air Force. **Location:** 5 miles from Dallas. **Calendar:** Semester, limited summer session. **Full-time faculty:** 127 total; 91% have terminal degrees, 7% minority, 28% women. **Part-time faculty:** 104 total; 36% have terminal degrees, 5% minority, 28% women. **Class size:** 52% < 20, 43% 20-39, 4% 40-49, 2% 50-99, less than 1% >100.

Freshman class profile. 1,060 applied, 965 admitted, 342 enrolled.

Mid 50% test scores		**GPA 2.0-2.99:**	5%
SAT critical reading:	550-680	**Rank in top quarter:**	63%
SAT math:	550-650	**Rank in top tenth:**	29%
SAT writing:	530-670	**End year in good standing:**	85%
ACT composite:	24-29	**Return as sophomores:**	80%
GPA 3.75 or higher:	48%	**Out-of-state:**	57%
GPA 3.50-3.74:	25%	**Live on campus:**	92%
GPA 3.0-3.49:	22%	**International:**	3%

Basis for selection. Sufficient academic preparation and ability to do the work required along with evidence of good character. Critical writing and composition skills important. Interview recommended for academically marginal; audition recommended for theater program; portfolio recommended for art program.

High school preparation. College-preparatory program recommended. Recommended units include English 4, mathematics 4, social studies 4, history 4, science 3 (laboratory 3), foreign language 2 and visual/performing arts 2.

2008-2009 Annual costs. Tuition/fees: $24,770. Room/board: $7,885. Books/supplies: $1,500. Personal expenses: $1,500.

2007-2008 Financial aid. **Need-based:** 292 full-time freshmen applied for aid; 237 were judged to have need; 237 of these received aid. Average need met was 84%. Average scholarship/grant was $15,925; average loan $4,325. 76% of total undergraduate aid awarded as scholarships/grants, 24% as loans/jobs. **Non-need-based:** Awarded to 525 full-time undergraduates, including 148 freshmen. Scholarships awarded for academics, art, leadership, music/drama.

Application procedures. **Admission:** Priority date 1/15; deadline 8/1 (postmark date). $40 fee, may be waived for applicants with need. Admission notification on a rolling basis beginning on or about 2/1. Must reply by May 1 or within 4 week(s) if notified thereafter. **Financial aid:** Priority date 3/1, closing date 7/1. FAFSA required. Applicants notified on a rolling basis starting 3/1; must reply by 5/1 or within 2 week(s) of notification.

Academics. 80% of undergraduates spend semester of sophomore year at university's campus in Rome, Italy. Optional credit-bearing intersession available. **Special study options:** Combined bachelor's/graduate degree, double major, dual enrollment of high school students, independent study, internships, liberal arts/career combination, student-designed major, study abroad, teacher certification program. Intensive honors chemistry summer program for entering freshmen. **Credit/placement by examination:** AP, CLEP, IB, institutional tests. 32 credit hours maximum toward bachelor's degree. **Support services:** Pre-admission summer program, reduced course load, tutoring, writing center.

Majors. **Biology:** General, biochemistry. **Business:** Business admin. **Education:** General, elementary. **Foreign languages:** Classics, French, German, Spanish. **History:** General. **Math:** General. **Philosophy/religion:** Philosophy. **Physical sciences:** Chemistry, physics. **Psychology:** General. **Social sciences:** Economics, political science. **Theology:** Preministerial, theology. **Visual/performing arts:** Art history/conservation, ceramics, dramatic, painting, printmaking, sculpture.

Most popular majors. Biology 6%, business/marketing 13%, English 13%, foreign language 7%, history 10%, psychology 7%, social sciences 16%, theological studies 10%, visual/performing arts 6%.

Computing on campus. 125 workstations in library, computer center, student center. Dormitories wired for high-speed internet access and linked to campus network. Commuter students can connect to campus network. Online library, helpline, wireless network available.

Student life. **Freshman orientation:** Mandatory. One-day program prior to fall semester. **Housing:** Guaranteed on-campus for freshmen. Coed dorms, single-sex dorms, apartments available. $100 fully refundable deposit, deadline 8/1. **Activities:** Campus ministries, choral groups, dance, drama, film society, international student organizations, literary magazine, music ensembles, musical theater, radio station, student government, student newspaper, Best Buddies, Society of St. Vincent de Paul, Alpha Phi Omega, Crusaders for Life, Asian student organization, Latin American student association.

Athletics. NCAA. **Intercollegiate:** Baseball M, basketball, cross-country, golf M, lacrosse W, soccer, softball W, tennis W, track and field, volleyball W. **Intramural:** Basketball M, football (non-tackle), soccer, softball, volleyball. **Team name:** Crusaders.

Student services. Chaplain/spiritual director, career counseling, student employment services, financial aid counseling, health services, personal counseling, placement for graduates. **Physically disabled:** Services for visually impaired.

Contact. E-mail: ugadmis@udallas.edu
Phone: (972) 721-5266 Toll-free number: (800) 628-6999
Fax: (972) 721-5017
John Plotts, Dean of Enrollment, University of Dallas, 1845 East Northgate Drive, Irving, TX 75062-4736

University of Houston

Houston, Texas **CB member**
www.uh.edu **CB code: 6870**

- Public 4-year university
- Commuter campus in very large city
- 27,602 degree-seeking undergraduates: 26% part-time, 51% women, 15% African American, 22% Asian American, 23% Hispanic American, 4% international
- 7,304 degree-seeking graduate students
- 79% of applicants admitted
- SAT or ACT with writing required
- 42% graduate within 6 years

General. Founded in 1927. Regionally accredited. Research university with highly diverse student population. **Degrees:** 4,759 bachelor's awarded; master's, doctoral, first professional offered. **ROTC:** Army, Naval, Air Force. **Location:** 3 miles from downtown. **Calendar:** Semester, extensive summer session. **Full-time faculty:** 1,229 total; 88% have terminal degrees, 21% minority, 34% women. **Part-time faculty:** 544 total; 48% have terminal degrees, 19% minority, 42% women. **Class size:** 31% < 20, 37% 20-39, 8% 40-49, 15% 50-99, 9% >100. **Special facilities:** Theater complex, observatory, opera house, underground satellite center, wellness and recreation center, art museum.

Freshman class profile. 11,542 applied, 9,093 admitted, 3,797 enrolled.

Mid 50% test scores		**Rank in top tenth:**	21%
SAT critical reading:	460-570	**End year in good standing:**	91%
SAT math:	490-600	**Return as sophomores:**	79%
ACT composite:	19-24	**Out-of-state:**	3%
GPA 3.75 or higher:	17%	**Live on campus:**	25%
GPA 3.50-3.74:	23%	**International:**	4%
GPA 3.0-3.49:	38%	**Fraternities:**	2%
GPA 2.0-2.99:	21%	**Sororities:**	3%
Rank in top quarter:	30%		

Basis for selection. Freshmen applicants ranked in top 20% of class are automatically accepted. Applicants in next 30% with minimum score of 1000 SAT (exclusive of Writing) or 21 ACT will be admitted. After that, applicants individually reviewed. Audition required for music program; essay recommended for honors college and individual review. **Homeschooled:** State high school equivalency certificate required. Must submit minimum SAT score of 1180 (exclusive of Writing) and transcript (can be created by parent). In order to qualify for financial aid, must pass GED exam. SAT not recognized by financial aid department. **Learning Disabled:** Intake appointment with counselor scheduled upon receipt of required documentation indicating that disability substantially limits some major life activity.

High school preparation. College-preparatory program recommended. Recommended units include English 4, mathematics 3, social studies 3, science 2 and foreign language 2.

2008-2009 Annual costs. Tuition/fees: $8,167; $16,597 out-of-state. Room/board: $6,935. Books/supplies: $1,100. Personal expenses: $3,074.

2008-2009 Financial aid. Need-based: 2,546 full-time freshmen applied for aid; 2,091 were judged to have need; 2,007 of these received aid. Average need met was 74%. Average scholarship/grant was $7,481; average loan $5,031. 39% of total undergraduate aid awarded as scholarships/grants, 61% as loans/jobs. **Non-need-based:** Awarded to 1,361 full-time undergraduates, including 445 freshmen. Scholarships awarded for academics, alumni affiliation, art, athletics, job skills, leadership, music/drama, ROTC, state residency.

Application procedures. Admission: Priority date 1/15; deadline 4/1 (postmark date). $50 fee ($75 out-of-state), may be waived for applicants with need. Admission notification on a rolling basis. **Financial aid:** Priority date 4/1; no closing date. FAFSA required. Applicants notified on a rolling basis starting 5/1; must reply within 4 week(s) of notification.

Academics. Special study options: Accelerated study, combined bachelor's/graduate degree, cooperative education, cross-registration, distance learning, double major, dual enrollment of high school students, ESL, exchange student, honors, independent study, internships, study abroad, teacher certification program, Washington semester, weekend college. Academic enrichment programs, certification programs and affiliated studies. **Credit/placement by examination:** AP, CLEP, IB, institutional tests. **Support services:** Learning center, reduced course load, remedial instruction, study skills assistance, tutoring, writing center.

Honors college/program. All students are encouraged to apply. The Honors College Admissions Committee considers the high school and/or academic record, extracurricular activities, test scores, and essay of each applicant. No specific requirements for admission, however the average Honors student is in the top 10 percent of high school class with an SAT score of 1270 or above.

Majors. Architecture: Architecture, environmental design, interior. **Area/ethnic studies:** German, Russian/Slavic. **Biology:** General, biochemistry, biophysics. **Business:** Accounting, communications, entrepreneurial studies, finance, human resources, management information systems, managerial economics, marketing, merchandising, operations, organizational behavior, personal/financial services, sales/distribution, statistics. **Communications:** General, journalism, public relations, radio/tv. **Computer sciences:** General, information systems, systems analysis. **Education:** Health, physical, trade/industrial. **Engineering:** Chemical, civil, computer, electrical, mechanical. **Engineering technology:** Architectural, civil, construction, electrical, industrial, industrial management, manufacturing. **Family/consumer sciences:** General, business, family studies, food/nutrition. **Foreign languages:** Classics, French, German, Italian, Latin, Spanish. **Health:** Audiology/speech pathology, clinical lab science, communication disorders, kinesiotherapy, nuclear medical technology, optician, prepharmacy. **History:** General. **Math:** General, applied. **Parks/recreation:** Exercise sciences, health/fitness, sports admin. **Philosophy/religion:** Philosophy. **Physical sciences:** Chemistry, geology, geophysics, physics, planetary. **Psychology:** General. **Social sciences:** Anthropology, economics, political science, sociology, urban studies. **Visual/performing arts:** Art, art history/conservation, ceramics, commercial/advertising art, dance, dramatic, graphic design, industrial design, interior design, metal/jewelry, music performance, music theory/composition, painting, photography, printmaking, sculpture, studio arts.

Most popular majors. Business/marketing 31%, communications/journalism 6%, engineering/engineering technologies 10%, psychology 8%, social sciences 8%.

Computing on campus. 625 workstations in library, computer center, student center. Dormitories wired for high-speed internet access and linked to campus network. Commuter students can connect to campus network. Online course registration, online library, helpline, repair service, student web hosting, wireless network available.

Student life. Freshman orientation: Mandatory, $90 fee. Preregistration for classes offered. Two-day conferences include advising, phone registration, placement testing, textbook orders. Held late spring and through the summer. **Policies:** Have to be enrolled or affiliated with the University of Houston - main campus. Can't house sexual offenders. **Housing:** Coed dorms, special housing for disabled, apartments, fraternity/sorority housing available. $300 partly refundable deposit. **Activities:** Bands, campus ministries, choral groups, dance, drama, film society, international student organizations, literary magazine, music ensembles, musical theater, opera, radio station, student government, student newspaper, symphony orchestra, TV station, Asian student association, Hispanic student association, Habitat for Humanity, Hillel, College Republicans/Democrats, NAACP, Green Party, Indian student association, Muslim students association, Bahai student association.

Athletics. NCAA. **Intercollegiate:** Baseball M, basketball, cross-country, diving W, football (tackle) M, golf M, soccer W, softball W, swimming W, tennis W, track and field, volleyball W. **Intramural:** Badminton, basketball, bowling, cross-country, diving, football (tackle) M, golf, racquetball, soccer, softball, swimming, table tennis, tennis, track and field, volleyball, water polo. **Team name:** Cougars.

Student services. Adult student services, chaplain/spiritual director, career counseling, student employment services, financial aid counseling, health services, on-campus daycare, personal counseling, placement for graduates, veterans' counselor, women's services. **Physically disabled:** Services for visually, speech, hearing impaired.

Contact. E-mail: admissions@uh.edu
Phone: (713) 743-1010 Fax: (713) 743-9633
Djuana Young, Director of Admissions, University of Houston, 122 E. Cullen Building, Houston, TX 77204-2023

University of Houston-Clear Lake

Houston, Texas **CB member**
www.uhcl.edu **CB code: 6916**

- Public two-year upper-division university
- Commuter campus in very large city
- 73% of applicants admitted

General. Founded in 1971. Regionally accredited. Upper level university for undergraduates. Located 3 miles from NASA. **Degrees:** 1,247 bachelor's awarded; master's, doctoral offered. **Articulation:** Agreements with all community colleges in Houston metropolitan area, Houston CC, Lone Star CC, San Jacinto College, Galveston College, Alvin CC, Lee College, College of the Mainland, Wharton County Junior College. **Location:** 21 miles from Houston. **Calendar:** Semester, limited summer session. **Full-time faculty:** 196 total; 100% have terminal degrees, 28% minority, 41% women. **Part-time faculty:** 320 total; 96% have terminal degrees, 16% minority, 61% women. **Class size:** 44% < 20, 48% 20-39, 5% 40-49, 3% 50-99.

Student profile. 3,912 degree-seeking undergraduates, 3,607 graduate students. 1,787 applied as first time-transfer students, 1,299 admitted, 1,016 enrolled. 82% entered as juniors, 18% entered as seniors.

Women:	69%	**Live on campus:**	1%
Part-time:	51%	**25 or older:**	62%

Basis for selection. College transcript required. Students with 54 hours of credit with grades 2.0 or better (exclusive of remedial or development or repeated courses) from regionally accredited institution will be admitted. Students must also have completed college algebra or higher mathematics course and have passing scores on THEA. Students must be eligible to return to last institution attended. Transfer accepted as juniors, seniors.

2008-2009 Annual costs. Tuition/fees: $5,532; $14,442 out-of-state. Room only: $10,308.

Financial aid. Need-based: 1,601 applied for aid; 1,567 were judged to have need; 1,561 of these received aid. Average need met was 42%. 41% of total undergraduate aid awarded as scholarships/grants, 59% as loans/jobs. **Non-need-based:** Awarded to 65 undergraduates. Scholarships awarded for state residency.

Application procedures. Admission: Rolling admission. $35 fee. **Financial aid:** No deadline. Applicants notified on a rolling basis starting 5/15; must reply within 4 weeks of notification. FAFSA, institutional form required.

Academics. Special study options: Combined bachelor's/graduate degree, cooperative education, distance learning, double major, dual enrollment of high school students, independent study, internships, student-designed major, study abroad, teacher certification program, weekend college. **Credit/placement by examination:** AP, CLEP. 18 credit hours maximum toward bachelor's degree. No more than 3 hours in history and government may be earned through CLEP.

Majors. Biology: General. **Business:** General, accounting, business admin, finance, management information systems, marketing. **Communications:** General. **Computer sciences:** General, computer science. **Conservation:** General, environmental science, environmental studies. **Education:** General. **Engineering:** Computer. **Health:** Health care admin. **History:** General. **Interdisciplinary:** Behavioral sciences, math/computer science. **Legal studies:** Prelaw. **Liberal arts:** Arts/sciences, humanities. **Math:** General. **Parks/recreation:** Health/fitness. **Physical sciences:** Chemistry. **Psychology:** General. **Public administration:** Policy analysis, social work. **Social sciences:** Anthropology, criminology, geography, political science, sociology. **Visual/performing arts:** Art.

Computing on campus. 715 workstations in library, computer center, student center. Commuter students can connect to campus network. Online library, helpline, wireless network available.

Student life. Housing: Limited apartments on campus. **Activities:** Campus ministries, film society, international student organizations, literary magazine, student government, student newspaper, Black student association, Chinese Christian student fellowship, Hispanic advancement in culture and education, student organization for Native American studies, student council for exceptional children, clinical psychology club, Muslim student association.

Student services. Alcohol/substance abuse counseling, career counseling, student employment services, financial aid counseling, health services, minority student services, personal counseling, placement for graduates, veterans' counselor, women's services. **Physically disabled:** Services for visually, speech, hearing impaired.

Contact. E-mail: admissions@uhcl.edu
Phone: (281) 283-2500 Fax: (281) 283-2522
Rauchelle Jones, Director of Admissions, University of Houston-Clear Lake, 2700 Bay Area Boulevard, Houston, TX 77058-1098

University of Houston-Downtown

Houston, Texas — CB member
www.uhd.edu — CB code: 6922

- Public 4-year university
- Commuter campus in very large city
- 12,134 degree-seeking undergraduates: 52% part-time, 61% women, 28% African American, 10% Asian American, 37% Hispanic American, 3% international
- 149 degree-seeking graduate students

General. Founded in 1974. Regionally accredited. Distance education locations in the surrounding area at these locations: Katy (Cinco Ranch), The Woodlands, Kingwood, and Cypress. **Degrees:** 2,002 bachelor's awarded; master's offered. **ROTC:** Army, Air Force. **Calendar:** Semester, limited summer session. **Full-time faculty:** 306 total; 82% have terminal degrees, 32% minority, 47% women. **Part-time faculty:** 263 total; 31% have terminal degrees, 38% minority, 48% women. **Class size:** 26% < 20, 60% 20-39, 10% 40-49, 3% 50-99, less than 1% >100.

Freshman class profile. 2,050 applied, 2,044 admitted, 990 enrolled.

Return as sophomores:	58%	**Fraternities:**	1%
Out-of-state:	1%	**Sororities:**	1%
International:	3%		

Basis for selection. Open admission. **Homeschooled:** Transcript of courses and grades required.

High school preparation. College-preparatory program recommended. 27.5 units recommended. Recommended units include English 4, mathematics 3, social studies 3.5, science 3, foreign language 3, visual/performing arts 1 and academic electives 1. 9 units recommended in speech, technology applications, health education, economics, and physical education.

2008-2009 Annual costs. Tuition/fees: $5,000; $13,430 out-of-state. Books/supplies: $1,076. Personal expenses: $3,800.

2008-2009 Financial aid. Need-based: 566 full-time freshmen applied for aid; 526 were judged to have need; 514 of these received aid. Average need met was 59%. Average scholarship/grant was $7,134; average loan $3,254. 37% of total undergraduate aid awarded as scholarships/grants, 63% as loans/jobs. **Non-need-based:** Awarded to 383 full-time undergraduates, including 214 freshmen. Scholarships awarded for academics, leadership.

Application procedures. Admission: Closing date 7/15 (postmark date). $35 fee, may be waived for applicants with need. Application must be submitted online. Notified within 3-5 business days after all items received. **Financial aid:** Priority date 4/1; no closing date. FAFSA required. Applicants notified on a rolling basis starting 4/15; must reply within 4 week(s) of notification.

Academics. Special study options: Distance learning, dual enrollment of high school students, ESL, honors, independent study, internships, study abroad, teacher certification program, weekend college. **Credit/placement by examination:** AP, CLEP, institutional tests. 24 credit hours maximum toward bachelor's degree. **Support services:** Learning center, reduced course load, remedial instruction, study skills assistance, tutoring, writing center.

Majors. Biology: General, microbiology. **Business:** General, accounting, business admin, finance, international, management information systems, marketing, purchasing. **Computer sciences:** General. **Engineering technology:** Civil, computer, industrial safety, mechanical, occupational safety. **Foreign languages:** Spanish. **History:** General. **Interdisciplinary:** Biological/physical sciences. **Liberal arts:** Arts/sciences, humanities. **Math:** General, applied. **Philosophy/religion:** Philosophy. **Physical sciences:** Chemistry. **Protective services:** Criminal justice. **Psychology:** General. **Public administration:** Social work. **Social sciences:** General, political science, sociology. **Visual/performing arts:** General. **Other:** Industrial chemistry, Interdisciplinary studies, education.

Most popular majors. Business/marketing 41%, interdisciplinary studies 9%, liberal arts 20%, psychology 7%, security/protective services 7%.

Computing on campus. 1,266 workstations in library, computer center, student center. Commuter students can connect to campus network. Online course registration, online library, helpline, student web hosting, wireless network available.

Student life. Freshman orientation: Mandatory, $80 fee. Preregistration for classes offered. 2-day program in which students and parents can find out more about UHD and its enrollment process, test and meet with advisors to enroll. Offered throughout the summer, May-July. **Policies:** Students must have at least a 2.5 GPA to be an officer in a student organization and at least a 2.0 GPA to be a member of a student organization. **Activities:** Campus ministries, drama, international student organizations, literary magazine, student government, student newspaper, African student association, Black Student Alliance, Christ Over Our Life, College Democrats, Friends of Central America student association, League of United Latin American Citizens, Muslim student association, NAACP, Caribbean students association, Kingdom Connection.

Athletics. Intramural: Badminton, basketball, bowling, football (non-tackle), soccer, softball, tennis, volleyball, weight lifting. **Team name:** Gator.

Student services. Alcohol/substance abuse counseling, career counseling, student employment services, financial aid counseling, health services, legal services, personal counseling, placement for graduates, veterans' counselor. **Physically disabled:** Services for visually, hearing impaired.

Contact. E-mail: uhdadmit@uhd.edu
Phone: (713) 221-8522 Fax: (713) 221-8257
Jose Cantu, Director of Admissions and Recruitment, University of Houston-Downtown, One Main Street, Suite 350-S, Houston, TX 77002

University of Houston-Victoria

Victoria, Texas
www.uhv.edu **CB code: 6917**

- Public two-year upper-division university
- Commuter campus in small city
- 95% of applicants admitted
- Test scores required

General. Founded in 1973. Regionally accredited. **Degrees:** 390 bachelor's awarded; master's offered. **Articulation:** Agreements with Bee County College, Victoria College, Wharton County Junior College, Blinn College. **Location:** 100 miles from Houston and San Antonio. **Calendar:** Semester, limited summer session. **Full-time faculty:** 88 total; 96% have terminal degrees, 36% minority, 43% women. **Part-time faculty:** 88 total; 40% have terminal degrees, 24% minority, 56% women.

Student profile. 1,569 degree-seeking undergraduates, 1,528 degree-seeking graduate students. 709 applied as first time-transfer students, 671 admitted, 325 enrolled. 90% entered as juniors, 10% entered as seniors.

Women:	73%	**Native American:**	1%
African American:	11%	**Part-time:**	63%
Asian American:	6%	**Out-of-state:**	1%
Hispanic American:	22%	**25 or older:**	66%

Basis for selection. College transcript, standardized test scores required. Minimum of 54 semester hours in non-remedial college-level coursework from an institution accredited by one of the recognized regional accrediting associations is required for unconditional admission. Student must have earned minimum 2.0 (A-4.0) GPA and have passed all parts (reading, writing and mathematics) of TASP/THEA exam. Transfer accepted as juniors, seniors.

2008-2009 Annual costs. Tuition/fees: $5,220; $13,650 out-of-state.

Financial aid. Non-need-based: Scholarships awarded for academics, athletics, leadership, state residency. **Additional information:** Short-term loans available at registration.

Application procedures. Admission: Rolling admission. No application fee. Application must be submitted online. **Financial aid:** No deadline. Applicants notified on a rolling basis; must reply within 3 weeks of notification. FAFSA required.

Academics. Online course support. **Special study options:** Distance learning, double major, honors, independent study, internships, study abroad, teacher certification program. **Credit/placement by examination:** CLEP.

Majors. Biology: General. **Business:** General, accounting, business admin, marketing. **Communications:** General. **Computer sciences:** General, information systems. **Education:** General. **Health:** Nursing (RN). **History:** General. **Math:** General. **Protective services:** Law enforcement admin. **Psychology:** General.

Most popular majors. Business/marketing 9%, education 32%, health sciences 15%, psychology 9%.

Computing on campus. 250 workstations in library, computer center, student center. Commuter students can connect to campus network. Online library, helpline, repair service, wireless network available.

Student life. Activities: International student organizations, student government, student newspaper.

Athletics. NAIA. **Intercollegiate:** Baseball M, softball W. **Team name:** Jaguares.

Student services. Career counseling, student employment services, financial aid counseling, placement for graduates, veterans' counselor. **Physically disabled:** Services for visually, hearing impaired.

Contact. E-mail: admission@uhv.edu
Phone: (361) 570-4110 Toll-free number: (877) 970-4848 ext. 110
Fax: (361) 570-4114
Trudy Wortham, Director of Admissions, University of Houston-Victoria, 3007 North Ben Wilson, Victoria, TX 77901-4450

University of Mary Hardin-Baylor

Belton, Texas **CB member**
www.umhb.edu **CB code: 6396**

- Private 4-year university affiliated with Baptist faith
- Residential campus in large town
- 2,502 degree-seeking undergraduates: 12% part-time, 63% women, 12% African American, 2% Asian American, 13% Hispanic American, 1% Native American, 1% international
- 199 degree-seeking graduate students
- 43% of applicants admitted
- SAT or ACT with writing required
- 43% graduate within 6 years

General. Founded in 1845. Regionally accredited. Information, counseling, and administrative services, as well as limited number of undergraduate and graduate level evening courses, offered at Fort Hood. Affiliated with Baptist General Convention of Texas. **Degrees:** 470 bachelor's awarded; master's, doctoral offered. **ROTC:** Air Force. **Location:** 60 miles from Austin. **Calendar:** Semester, limited summer session. **Full-time faculty:** 143 total; 63% have terminal degrees, 11% minority, 54% women. **Part-time faculty:** 95 total; 8% have terminal degrees, 5% minority, 41% women. **Class size:** 54% < 20, 40% 20-39, 6% 40-49, less than 1% 50-99.

Freshman class profile. 3,703 applied, 1,585 admitted, 479 enrolled.

Mid 50% test scores			
SAT critical reading:	410-620	**End year in good standing:**	80%
SAT math:	420-620	**Return as sophomores:**	63%
SAT writing:	400-610	**Out-of-state:**	1%
ACT composite:	18-27	**Live on campus:**	90%

Basis for selection. School achievement record and test scores important. Must either rank in top 10% of graduating class; rank in the top half of class and score 950 SAT or 20 ACT; or rank in lower half of class and score 990 SAT or 21 ACT (all SAT scores exclusive of Writing). Academically deficient students may be accepted on individual basis by approval of admissions committee. Interview recommended for academically marginal; audition recommended for music. **Homeschooled:** Transcript of courses and grades required. Admission based on ACT or SAT test scores.

High school preparation. College-preparatory program recommended. 22 units required. Required units include English 4, mathematics 3, social studies 2.5.

2009-2010 Annual costs. Tuition/fees: $20,650. Room/board: $5,350. Books/supplies: $1,200. Personal expenses: $1,702.

2008-2009 Financial aid. Need-based: 393 full-time freshmen applied for aid; 312 were judged to have need; 312 of these received aid. Average need met was 64%. Average scholarship/grant was $8,888; average loan $3,911. 65% of total undergraduate aid awarded as scholarships/grants, 35% as loans/jobs. **Non-need-based:** Awarded to 314 full-time undergraduates, including 118 freshmen. Scholarships awarded for academics, art, leadership, music/drama, religious affiliation.

Application procedures. Admission: No deadline. $35 fee, may be waived for applicants with need. Admission notification on a rolling basis. Must reply by May 1 or within 2 week(s) if notified thereafter. **Financial aid:** Priority date 3/1; no closing date. FAFSA required. Applicants notified on a rolling basis starting 2/1; must reply within 2 week(s) of notification.

Academics. Special study options: Accelerated study, combined bachelor's/graduate degree, double major, dual enrollment of high school students, ESL, honors, independent study, internships, study abroad, teacher certification program. Servicemember Opportunity Colleges (SOC) programs, military degree completion programs, tuition exchange program with other participating universities. **Credit/placement by examination:** AP, CLEP, IB, institutional tests. 31 credit hours maximum toward bachelor's degree. No more than one-fourth of total credit hours required for degree may be earned through credit by examination. **Support services:** Learning center, pre-admission summer program, reduced course load, remedial instruction, study skills assistance, tutoring.

Majors. **Area/ethnic studies:** American. **Biology:** Biomedical sciences. **Business:** General, accounting, business admin, finance, management information systems, marketing. **Communications:** General. **Computer sciences:** General, computer graphics, computer science, information systems. **Education:** Chemistry, elementary, English, mathematics, music, physical, science, social studies, special. **Foreign languages:** Spanish. **Health:** Athletic training, clinical lab science, nursing (RN). **History:** General. **Math:** General. **Parks/recreation:** General, sports admin. **Philosophy/religion:** Christian, religion. **Physical sciences:** Chemistry. **Protective services:** Law enforcement admin. **Psychology:** General. **Public administration:** Social work. **Social sciences:** Political science, sociology. **Theology:** Bible, pastoral counseling, sacred music, theology. **Visual/performing arts:** Dramatic, music performance, music theory/composition, studio arts.

Most popular majors. Business/marketing 14%, education 15%, health sciences 15%, liberal arts 9%, psychology 8%.

Computing on campus. 275 workstations in dormitories, library, computer center, student center. Dormitories wired for high-speed internet access and linked to campus network. Online course registration, online library, helpline, wireless network available.

Student life. **Freshman orientation:** Available, $30 fee. Preregistration for classes offered. One-day orientation in summer for students and parents. Full-week orientation for students only before start of classes. **Policies:** Religious observance required. **Housing:** Guaranteed on-campus for freshmen. Single-sex dorms, special housing for disabled, apartments, wellness housing available. $300 partly refundable deposit. **Activities:** Bands, campus ministries, choral groups, drama, international student organizations, literary magazine, music ensembles, musical theater, opera, student government, student newspaper, symphony orchestra, Catholic student organization, College Democrats, College Republicans, Crusaders for Christ, Fellowship of Christian Athletes, Focus (community-wide worship), Habitat for Humanity.

Athletics. NCAA. **Intercollegiate:** Baseball M, basketball, football (tackle) M, golf, soccer, softball W, tennis, volleyball W. **Intramural:** Basketball, football (non-tackle), golf, soccer, softball, table tennis, volleyball, weight lifting. **Team name:** Crusaders.

Student services. Alcohol/substance abuse counseling, chaplain/spiritual director, career counseling, student employment services, financial aid counseling, health services, personal counseling, placement for graduates, veterans' counselor. **Physically disabled:** Services for visually, speech, hearing impaired.

Contact. E-mail: admissions@umhb.edu
Phone: (254) 295-4520 Toll-free number: (800) 727-8642 ext. 4520
Fax: (254) 295-5049
Robbin Steen, Director of Admissions and Recruiting, University of Mary Hardin-Baylor, 900 College Street, Belton, TX 76513

University of North Texas

Denton, Texas — **CB member**
www.unt.edu — **CB code: 6481**

- Public 4-year university and liberal arts college
- Residential campus in small city
- 27,779 degree-seeking undergraduates: 22% part-time, 54% women, 14% African American, 6% Asian American, 13% Hispanic American, 1% Native American, 2% international
- 6,919 degree-seeking graduate students
- 64% of applicants admitted
- SAT or ACT (ACT writing recommended) required
- 45% graduate within 6 years

General. Founded in 1890. Regionally accredited. **Degrees:** 5,200 bachelor's awarded; master's, doctoral offered. **ROTC:** Army, Air Force. **Location:** 35 miles from Dallas and Fort Worth. **Calendar:** Semester, extensive summer session. **Full-time faculty:** 1,005 total; 81% have terminal degrees, 24% minority, 38% women. **Part-time faculty:** 430 total; 3% have terminal degrees, 36% minority, 53% women. **Class size:** 29% < 20, 39% 20-39, 11% 40-49, 11% 50-99, 10% >100. **Special facilities:** Laser, observatory, accelerators, environmental science facility, planetarium.

Freshman class profile. 13,150 applied, 8,411 admitted, 3,613 enrolled.

Mid 50% test scores			
SAT critical reading:	490-600	End year in good standing:	72%
SAT math:	500-610	Return as sophomores:	76%
ACT composite:	21-26	Out-of-state:	3%
Rank in top quarter:	44%	Live on campus:	83%
Rank in top tenth:	19%	International:	2%

Basis for selection. It is recommended that students apply well in advance of stated application deadlines. School achievement record most important. Test score minimums vary with class rank: top 10% no minimum. On an individual basis, UNT may admit high school students to the freshman class after completion of the junior year of high school. To be considered, students must be ranked in the top quarter of their class, have a strong B average, completed 3 units of English and 2 units each of solid mathematics, social sciences and natural sciences, present minimum combined SAT (critical reading + math) score of 1180 or ACT composite of 26, submit letters from high school counselor or principal recommending early admission, submit a letter from parents or guardians stating they approve, and arrange an interview in the Office of Admissions. Audition required for music program. **Homeschooled:** Statement describing homeschool structure and mission, transcript of courses and grades required. An interview, essay and letters of recommendation may be required after a review of the application.

High school preparation. 24 units required. Required units include English 4, mathematics 4, social studies 2, history 2, science 3, foreign language 3, academic electives 2.5. 0.5 health, 1.5 physical education, 0.5-1 computer sciences, 1 fine arts recommended.

2008-2009 Annual costs. Tuition/fees: $6,767; $15,107 out-of-state. Room/board: $6,026.

2007-2008 Financial aid. **Need-based:** 2,414 full-time freshmen applied for aid; 1,578 were judged to have need; 1,553 of these received aid. Average need met was 79%. Average scholarship/grant was $5,830; average loan $2,815. 40% of total undergraduate aid awarded as scholarships/grants, 60% as loans/jobs. **Non-need-based:** Awarded to 4,130 full-time undergraduates, including 987 freshmen. Scholarships awarded for academics.

Application procedures. **Admission:** Priority date 6/15; deadline 8/17 (postmark date). $40 fee, may be waived for applicants with need. Admission notification on a rolling basis beginning on or about 10/1. **Financial aid:** Priority date 4/15; no closing date. FAFSA required. Applicants notified on a rolling basis starting 4/1.

Academics. **Special study options:** Accelerated study, combined bachelor's/graduate degree, cooperative education, cross-registration, distance learning, double major, dual enrollment of high school students, ESL, exchange student, external degree, honors, independent study, internships, study abroad, teacher certification program, weekend college. **Credit/placement by examination:** AP, CLEP, IB, institutional tests. **Support services:** Learning center, pre-admission summer program, remedial instruction, study skills assistance, tutoring, writing center.

Majors. **Architecture:** Interior. **Biology:** General, biochemistry. **Business:** General, accounting, banking/financial services, e-commerce, fashion, financial planning, hospitality admin, insurance, logistics, management information systems, managerial economics, marketing, operations, organizational behavior, real estate, sales/distribution, special products marketing. **Communications:** Broadcast journalism, journalism, radio/tv. **Computer sciences:** General, information systems. **Engineering:** Computer, electrical, materials science, mechanical. **Engineering technology:** Construction, electrical, manufacturing, mechanical. **Family/consumer sciences:** Family studies. **Foreign languages:** French, German, Spanish. **Health:** Audiology/speech pathology, clinical lab science, cytotechnology, health services, vocational rehab counseling. **History:** General. **Interdisciplinary:** Behavioral sciences, gerontology, global studies. **Math:** General. **Parks/recreation:** Facilities management, health/fitness. **Philosophy/religion:** Philosophy. **Physical sciences:** Chemistry, physics. **Protective services:** Criminal justice. **Psychology:** General. **Public administration:** General, social work. **Science technology:** Nuclear power. **Social sciences:** General, anthropology, economics, geography, political science, sociology. **Visual/performing arts:** Art, art history/conservation, commercial/advertising art, dance, dramatic, fashion design, jazz, music history, music performance, music theory/composition, studio arts. **Other:** Applied technology and performance improvement, Engineering physics, Rehabilitation studies.

Most popular majors. Business/marketing 19%, education 16%, social sciences 10%, visual/performing arts 8%.

Computing on campus. 705 workstations in dormitories, library, computer center, student center. Dormitories wired for high-speed internet access and linked to campus network. Commuter students can connect to campus network. Online course registration, online library, helpline, student web hosting, wireless network available.

Student life. **Freshman orientation:** Mandatory, $144 fee. Preregistration for classes offered. Nine sessions during June and July; includes overnight stay in one of the resident halls. **Housing:** Guaranteed on-campus for freshmen. Coed dorms, single-sex dorms, special housing for disabled, apartments, fraternity/sorority housing, wellness housing available. $400 fully refundable deposit. **Activities:** Bands, choral groups, dance, drama, film society, international student organizations, literary magazine, music ensembles, musical theater, opera, radio station, student government, student newspaper, symphony orchestra, TV station, honorary societies; religious, ethnic, and social service organizations.

Athletics. NCAA. **Intercollegiate:** Basketball, cross-country, diving W, football (tackle) M, golf, soccer W, softball, swimming W, tennis W, track and field, volleyball W. **Intramural:** Basketball, bowling, football (non-tackle), golf, racquetball, soccer, softball, table tennis, tennis, volleyball. **Team name:** Mean Green.

Student services. Adult student services, alcohol/substance abuse counseling, career counseling, student employment services, financial aid counseling, health services, legal services, minority student services, on-campus daycare, personal counseling, placement for graduates, veterans' counselor, women's services. **Physically disabled:** Services for visually, speech, hearing impaired.

Contact. E-mail: undergrad@unt.edu
Phone: (940) 565-2681 Toll-free number: (800) 868-8211
Fax: (940) 565-2408
Rebecca Lothringer, Director of Admissions, University of North Texas, 1401 West Prairie, Suite 309, Denton, TX 76203-5017

University of St. Thomas

Houston, Texas — **CB member**
www.stthom.edu — **CB code: 6880**

- Private 4-year university and liberal arts college affiliated with Roman Catholic Church
- Commuter campus in very large city
- 1,657 degree-seeking undergraduates: 23% part-time, 59% women, 5% African American, 11% Asian American, 34% Hispanic American, 1% Native American, 5% international
- 1,029 degree-seeking graduate students
- 81% of applicants admitted
- SAT or ACT with writing required
- 47% graduate within 6 years

General. Founded in 1947. Regionally accredited. **Degrees:** 346 bachelor's awarded; master's, doctoral, first professional offered. **ROTC:** Army, Air Force. **Location:** 3 miles from downtown. **Calendar:** Semester, limited summer session. **Full-time faculty:** 135 total; 13% minority, 33% women. **Part-time faculty:** 138 total; 12% minority, 49% women. **Class size:** 62% < 20, 38% 20-39, less than 1% 40-49, less than 1% 50-99. **Special facilities:** Chapel of St. Basil, archaeology gallery.

Freshman class profile. 810 applied, 654 admitted, 298 enrolled.

Mid 50% test scores		**GPA 2.0-2.99:**	15%
SAT critical reading:	500-620	**Rank in top quarter:**	58%
SAT math:	520-610	**Rank in top tenth:**	30%
SAT writing:	500-620	**End year in good standing:**	83%
ACT composite:	22-28	**Return as sophomores:**	72%
GPA 3.75 or higher:	35%	**Out-of-state:**	3%
GPA 3.50-3.74:	21%	**Live on campus:**	68%
GPA 3.0-3.49:	29%	**International:**	4%

Basis for selection. School achievement record, test scores, and graded essay most important. Cumulative high school GPA of 2.5 or higher in a minimum of 18 college preparatory units required, as well as minimum 1020 SAT (exclusive of Writing) or 22 ACT. High school class rank in the upper 50% required, if high school attended ranks graduates. Audition required for applied music, drama, voice programs; portfolio required for art program.

High school preparation. College-preparatory program recommended. 18 units required. Required units include English 4, mathematics 3, social studies 2, history 1, science 3 (laboratory 2), foreign language 2 and academic electives 3.

2008-2009 Annual costs. Tuition/fees: $20,510. Room/board: $7,700.

2008-2009 Financial aid. **Need-based:** 205 full-time freshmen applied for aid; 162 were judged to have need; 160 of these received aid. Average need met was 78%. Average scholarship/grant was $13,251; average loan $3,521. 74% of total undergraduate aid awarded as scholarships/grants, 26% as loans/jobs. **Non-need-based:** Awarded to 466 full-time undergraduates, including 159 freshmen. Scholarships awarded for academics, athletics.

Application procedures. **Admission:** No deadline. $25 fee, may be waived for applicants with need. Admission notification on a rolling basis beginning on or about 9/15. Must reply by May 1 or within 2 week(s) if notified thereafter. **Financial aid:** No deadline. FAFSA required. Applicants notified on a rolling basis starting 3/22; must reply within 2 week(s) of notification.

Academics. **Special study options:** Combined bachelor's/graduate degree, distance learning, double major, honors, independent study, internships, study abroad. First-year experiences, learning communities, service learning, senior capstone or culminating academic experiences, undergraduate research/creative projects. **Credit/placement by examination:** AP, CLEP, IB, SAT, ACT, institutional tests. 30 credit hours maximum toward bachelor's degree. Validation of credit by examination contingent upon completion of at least 24 semester hours in residence at institution. **Support services:** Learning center, reduced course load, remedial instruction, study skills assistance, tutoring, writing center.

Majors. **Biology:** General, bioinformatics. **Business:** Accounting, business admin, finance, marketing. **Communications:** General. **Conservation:** Environmental science, environmental studies. **Education:** General, elementary, music, secondary. **Foreign languages:** French, Spanish. **History:** General. **Liberal arts:** Arts/sciences. **Math:** General. **Philosophy/religion:** Philosophy. **Physical sciences:** Chemistry. **Psychology:** General. **Social sciences:** International relations, political science. **Theology:** Pastoral counseling, theology. **Visual/performing arts:** Dramatic, studio arts.

Most popular majors. Business/marketing 25%, communications/journalism 7%, liberal arts 20%, psychology 8%, social sciences 11%.

Computing on campus. 156 workstations in dormitories, library, computer center, student center. Dormitories wired for high-speed internet access. Online library, helpline, wireless network available.

Student life. **Freshman orientation:** Available. Preregistration for classes offered. Held in August and January. **Housing:** Coed dorms available. $300 fully refundable deposit. Pets allowed in dorm rooms. Houses and living-learning center available. **Activities:** Jazz band, campus ministries, choral groups, drama, international student organizations, literary magazine, music ensembles, musical theater, student government, student newspaper, Al-Nadi Cultural Society, Black student union, Chinese student association, Defense for Darfur, Fairy Godmother Project, Filipino student association, Student Organization of Latinos, Vietnamese student association, American Red Cross.

Athletics. NAIA. **Intercollegiate:** Soccer M, volleyball W. **Intramural:** Basketball, bowling, football (non-tackle), racquetball, table tennis, tennis, volleyball. **Team name:** Celts.

Student services. Adult student services, chaplain/spiritual director, career counseling, student employment services, financial aid counseling, health services, personal counseling, placement for graduates.

Contact. E-mail: admissions@stthom.edu
Phone: (713) 525-3500 Toll-free number: (800) 856-8565
Fax: (713) 525-3558
David Melton, Assistant Vice President of University Admissions, University of St. Thomas, 3800 Montrose Boulevard, Houston, TX 77006-4626

University of Texas at Arlington

Arlington, Texas — **CB member**
www.uta.edu — **CB code: 6013**

- Public 4-year university
- Commuter campus in large city
- 18,586 degree-seeking undergraduates: 30% part-time, 52% women, 15% African American, 12% Asian American, 18% Hispanic American, 1% Native American, 4% international
- 5,772 degree-seeking graduate students
- 76% of applicants admitted
- SAT or ACT with writing required
- 38% graduate within 6 years

General. Founded in 1895. Regionally accredited. **Degrees:** 3,835 bachelor's awarded; master's, doctoral offered. **ROTC:** Army, Air Force. **Location:** 15 miles from Dallas and Fort Worth. **Calendar:** 4-1-4-1 January and May terms. Extensive summer session. **Full-time faculty:** 832 total; less than 1% have terminal degrees, 25% minority, 38% women. **Part-time faculty:** 344 total; 15% have terminal degrees, 14% minority, 52% women.

Class size: 28% < 20, 40% 20-39, 8% 40-49, 19% 50-99, 5% >100. **Special facilities:** Robotics center, observatory, planetarium, maps collection, minority cultures collection, cartographic history library, library of Texana and Mexican War material, 3 art galleries, Nursing Smart Hospital, Mavericks Activities Center, studio art center, civil engineering research lab building, workforce development center, amphibian and reptile diversity research center.

Freshman class profile. 5,533 applied, 4,215 admitted, 2,300 enrolled.

Mid 50% test scores		**Return as sophomores:**	61%
SAT critical reading:	460-570	**Out-of-state:**	3%
SAT math:	490-610	**Live on campus:**	71%
ACT composite:	19-24	**International:**	3%
Rank in top quarter:	59%	**Fraternities:**	11%
Rank in top tenth:	19%	**Sororities:**	7%
End year in good standing:	87%		

Basis for selection. GED not accepted. Admission based on test scores and high school rank. Fourth quarter of high school class must be approved by director of admissions or associate director. SAT or ACT math scores used for placement for students majoring in architecture, engineering, biology, biochemistry, chemistry, math, physics and students majoring in the BS geology or BS psychology program. Interview recommended for academically weak; audition recommended for music; portfolio recommended for art, architecture programs. **Homeschooled:** Transcript of courses and grades, letter of recommendation (nonparent) required.

High school preparation. College-preparatory program required. 20 units required. Required and recommended units include English 4, mathematics 3-4, social studies 3-4, science 3, foreign language 2-3 and academic electives 5. 1 computing proficiency, 1 fine arts, 1 music/theater art, 1.5 physical education, .5 health recommended.

2008-2009 Annual costs. Tuition/fees: $7,780; $16,210 out-of-state. Room/board: $5,916. Books/supplies: $882. Personal expenses: $1,450.

Application procedures. Admission: Priority date 6/1; no deadline. $35 fee ($50 out-of-state), may be waived for applicants with need. Notified 3-7 days after application completed. **Financial aid:** Priority date 5/15; no closing date. FAFSA required. Applicants notified on a rolling basis starting 4/1; must reply within 3 week(s) of notification.

Academics. Special study options: Combined bachelor's/graduate degree, cross-registration, distance learning, double major, dual enrollment of high school students, ESL, honors, independent study, internships, student-designed major, study abroad, teacher certification program. **Credit/placement by examination:** AP, CLEP, IB, institutional tests. Credit by exam does not count as credit earned in residence. **Support services:** Learning center, reduced course load, remedial instruction, study skills assistance, tutoring, writing center.

Majors. Architecture: Architecture, interior. **Biology:** General, biochemistry, microbiology. **Business:** Accounting, banking/financial services, business admin, international, management information systems, managerial economics, marketing, real estate. **Communications:** Advertising, digital media, journalism, public relations, radio/tv. **Computer sciences:** Computer science. **Engineering:** General, aerospace, civil, computer, electrical, industrial, mechanical, software. **Family/consumer sciences:** Child development. **Foreign languages:** General, French, German, Russian, Spanish. **Health:** Athletic training, clinical lab science, nursing (RN). **History:** General. **Math:** General. **Parks/recreation:** Health/fitness. **Philosophy/religion:** Philosophy. **Physical sciences:** Chemistry, geology, physics. **Protective services:** Criminal justice. **Psychology:** General. **Public administration:** Social work. **Social sciences:** Anthropology, economics, political science, sociology. **Visual/performing arts:** Art, art history/conservation, dramatic, studio arts. **Other:** Multi-Interdisciplinary studies.

Most popular majors. Biology 8%, business/marketing 24%, communications/journalism 6%, engineering/engineering technologies 8%, health sciences 8%, interdisciplinary studies 12%.

Computing on campus. 1,000 workstations in dormitories, library, computer center, student center. Dormitories wired for high-speed internet access and linked to campus network. Commuter students can connect to campus network. Online course registration, online library, helpline, student web hosting, wireless network available.

Student life. Freshman orientation: Mandatory. Preregistration for classes offered. One-and-a-half-day sessions held in June, July, August. Students stay in residence halls. **Housing:** Coed dorms, single-sex dorms, apartments, fraternity/sorority housing available. $350 partly refundable deposit. Priority given to students with dependent children. **Activities:** Bands, campus ministries, choral groups, dance, drama, film society, international student organizations, literary magazine, music ensembles, opera, radio station, student government, student newspaper, symphony orchestra, University Democrats, Baptist student ministry, international students organization, association of Mexican American students, Vietnamese student association, Wesley Foundation, Mavericks for Christ, Business Beta Gamana Sigma, College Republicans, Business Delta Sigma Pi.

Athletics. NCAA. **Intercollegiate:** Baseball M, basketball, cross-country, golf M, softball W, tennis, track and field, volleyball W. **Intramural:** Badminton, basketball, bowling, golf, racquetball, soccer, softball, table tennis, tennis, track and field, volleyball. **Team name:** Mavericks.

Student services. Alcohol/substance abuse counseling, chaplain/spiritual director, career counseling, services for economically disadvantaged, student employment services, financial aid counseling, health services, legal services, minority student services, on-campus daycare, personal counseling, placement for graduates, veterans' counselor. **Physically disabled:** Services for visually, hearing impaired.

Contact. E-mail: admissions@uta.edu
Phone: (817) 272-6287 Fax: (817) 272-3435
Hans Gatterdam, Executive Director of Admissions, Records and Registration, University of Texas at Arlington, Box 19111, Arlington, TX 76019

University of Texas at Austin

Austin, Texas — **CB member**
www.utexas.edu — **CB code: 6882**

- Public 4-year university
- Commuter campus in very large city
- 36,711 degree-seeking undergraduates: 6% part-time, 52% women, 5% African American, 18% Asian American, 18% Hispanic American, 4% international
- 12,594 degree-seeking graduate students
- 44% of applicants admitted
- SAT or ACT with writing, application essay required
- 78% graduate within 6 years

General. Founded in 1883. Regionally accredited. **Degrees:** 8,669 bachelor's awarded; master's, doctoral, first professional offered. **ROTC:** Army, Naval, Air Force. **Location:** 70 miles from San Antonio, 163 miles from Houston. **Calendar:** Semester, extensive summer session. **Full-time faculty:** 2,687 total; 88% have terminal degrees, 19% minority, 37% women. **Part-time faculty:** 296 total; 63% have terminal degrees, 16% minority, 45% women. **Class size:** 36% < 20, 34% 20-39, 6% 40-49, 15% 50-99, 8% >100. **Special facilities:** Humanities and scientific research centers, observatory, marine science institute, fusion reactor, presidential library and museum, performing arts center, museum of natural history, museum of art.

Freshman class profile. 29,501 applied, 12,843 admitted, 6,718 enrolled.

Mid 50% test scores		**End year in good standing:**	91%
SAT critical reading:	540-660	**Return as sophomores:**	91%
SAT math:	570-690	**Out-of-state:**	5%
SAT writing:	540-670	**Live on campus:**	59%
ACT composite:	24-30	**International:**	3%
Rank in top quarter:	95%	**Fraternities:**	14%
Rank in top tenth:	75%	**Sororities:**	17%

Basis for selection. Applicants from top 10% of class from accredited Texas high school automatically admitted with completed application. Off-campus coordinated admission program available for Texans who complete all required high school units and apply immediately upon high school graduation, but are not otherwise eligible for regular admission. Audition required, interview recommended for music program; interview recommended for art, liberal arts honors program.

High school preparation. College-preparatory program recommended. 15.5 units required; 20 recommended. Required and recommended units include English 4, mathematics 3-4, social studies 3, science 2-4 (laboratory 2-3), foreign language 2-3, academic electives 1.5. .5 fine arts elective strongly recommended.

2008-2009 Annual costs. Tuition/fees: $8,532; $27,760 out-of-state. Room/board: $9,246. Books/supplies: $818. Personal expenses: $2,354.

2008-2009 Financial aid. Need-based: 4,800 full-time freshmen applied for aid; 4,000 were judged to have need; 4,000 of these received aid. Average need met was 82%. Average scholarship/grant was $6,500; average loan $3,900. 58% of total undergraduate aid awarded as scholarships/grants, 42% as loans/jobs. **Non-need-based:** Awarded to 10,000 full-time undergraduates, including 1,250 freshmen. Scholarships awarded for academics, art, athletics, leadership, music/drama, ROTC, state residency. **Additional information:** In general, Texas resident students from families earning less than $40,000 will be awarded grant/scholarship aid (from federal, state, institutional and private sources) to cover tuition costs.

Application procedures. Admission: Closing date 12/15 (receipt date). $60 fee, may be waived for applicants with need. Admission notification 4/1. Admission notification on a rolling basis beginning on or about 10/15. Must reply by May 1 or within 2 week(s) if notified thereafter. **Financial aid:** Priority date 4/1; no closing date. FAFSA required. Applicants notified on a rolling basis starting 3/15.

Academics. Special study options: Accelerated study, combined bachelor's/graduate degree, cooperative education, distance learning, double major, dual enrollment of high school students, ESL, honors, independent study, internships, liberal arts/career combination, student-designed major, study abroad, teacher certification program, Washington semester. **Credit/placement by examination:** AP, CLEP, IB, institutional tests. **Support services:** Learning center, reduced course load, remedial instruction, study skills assistance, tutoring, writing center.

Majors. Architecture: Architecture. **Area/ethnic studies:** American, Asian, European, Latin American, Near/Middle Eastern, Russian/Slavic, women's. **Biology:** General, biochemistry. **Business:** General, accounting, business admin, finance, logistics, management information systems, marketing. **Communications:** General, advertising, journalism, public relations, radio/tv. **Communications technology:** Recording arts. **Computer sciences:** General. **Engineering:** Aerospace, architectural, biomedical, chemical, civil, electrical, mechanical, petroleum. **Family/consumer sciences:** General, clothing/textiles, family studies, food/nutrition. **Foreign languages:** Ancient Greek, Arabic, classics, Czech, East Asian, French, German, Hebrew, Italian, Latin, linguistics, Persian, Portuguese, Russian, Scandinavian, Semitic, Spanish, Turkish. **Health:** Athletic training, clinical lab science, communication disorders, health services, nursing (RN). **History:** General. **Interdisciplinary:** Ancient studies, biological/physical sciences, math/computer science. **Liberal arts:** Arts/sciences, humanities. **Math:** General. **Parks/recreation:** Health/fitness, sports admin. **Philosophy/religion:** Islamic, Judaic, philosophy, religion. **Physical sciences:** Astronomy, chemistry, geology, geophysics, hydrology, physics. **Psychology:** General. **Public administration:** Social work. **Social sciences:** Anthropology, archaeology, economics, geography, political science, sociology, urban studies. **Visual/performing arts:** General, art, art history/conservation, dance, design, dramatic, interior design, jazz, music history, music management, music performance, music theory/composition, studio arts. **Other:** Geosystems engineering and hydrogeology, Petroleum land management, Youth and community studies.

Most popular majors. Biology 8%, business/marketing 13%, communications/journalism 13%, engineering/engineering technologies 11%, social sciences 13%.

Computing on campus. 500 workstations in dormitories, library, computer center, student center. Dormitories wired for high-speed internet access and linked to campus network. Commuter students can connect to campus network. Online course registration, online library, helpline, repair service, student web hosting, wireless network available.

Student life. Freshman orientation: Available, $105 fee. **Housing:** Coed dorms, single-sex dorms, apartments available. $300 fully refundable deposit. Honors residence, living-learning centers available for first-time freshmen. **Activities:** Bands, campus ministries, choral groups, dance, drama, film society, international student organizations, literary magazine, music ensembles, musical theater, opera, radio station, student government, student newspaper, symphony orchestra, TV station, wide variety of religious, political, ethnic, and social service organizations.

Athletics. NCAA. **Intercollegiate:** Baseball M, basketball, cross-country, diving, football (tackle) M, golf, rowing (crew) W, soccer W, softball W, swimming, tennis, track and field, volleyball W. **Intramural:** Badminton, basketball, bowling, football (non-tackle), golf, handball, racquetball, soccer, softball, squash, swimming, table tennis, tennis, track and field, volleyball, weight lifting. **Team name:** Longhorns.

Student services. Adult student services, alcohol/substance abuse counseling, career counseling, services for economically disadvantaged, student employment services, financial aid counseling, health services, legal services, minority student services, on-campus daycare, personal counseling, placement for graduates, veterans' counselor, women's services. **Physically disabled:** Services for visually, speech, hearing impaired. **Learning disabled:** Comprehensive services available.

Contact. Phone: (512) 475-7399 Fax: (512) 475-7478
Bruce Walker, Vice Provost and Director of Admissions, University of Texas at Austin, PO Box 8058, Austin, TX 78713-8058

University of Texas at Brownsville - Texas Southmost College

Brownsville, Texas — **CB member**
www.utb.edu — **CB code: 6825**

- Public 4-year university and community college
- Commuter campus in small city
- 10,145 degree-seeking undergraduates: 47% part-time, 60% women, 90% Hispanic American, 4% international
- 849 degree-seeking graduate students

General. Founded in 1977. Regionally accredited. **Degrees:** 918 bachelor's, 867 associate awarded; master's, doctoral offered. **ROTC:** Army. **Location:** 150 miles from Corpus Christi. **Calendar:** Semester, extensive summer session. **Full-time faculty:** 384 total. **Part-time faculty:** 247 total. **Class size:** 64% < 20, 30% 20-39, 2% 40-49, 4% 50-99, less than 1% >100.

Freshman class profile. 3,174 applied, 3,174 admitted, 1,797 enrolled.

GPA 3.75 or higher:	11%	**Rank in top tenth:**	10%
GPA 3.50-3.74:	6%	**Return as sophomores:**	68%
GPA 3.0-3.49:	17%	**Out-of-state:**	1%
GPA 2.0-2.99:	45%	**Live on campus:**	1%
Rank in top quarter:	27%	**International:**	4%

Basis for selection. Open admission, but selective for some programs. Special requirements for nursing and allied health programs.

High school preparation. College-preparatory program recommended.

2008-2009 Annual costs. Tuition/fees: $5,258; $13,688 out-of-state. Books/supplies: $615. Personal expenses: $2,523.

2007-2008 Financial aid. Need-based: 59% of total undergraduate aid awarded as scholarships/grants, 41% as loans/jobs.

Application procedures. Admission: Priority date 3/1; deadline 7/1 (receipt date). No application fee. Admission notification on a rolling basis. **Financial aid:** Priority date 3/1, closing date 8/15. FAFSA required. Applicants notified on a rolling basis; must reply within 4 week(s) of notification.

Academics. Special study options: Cooperative education, cross-registration, distance learning, double major, dual enrollment of high school students, ESL, independent study, internships, liberal arts/career combination, study abroad, teacher certification program. **Credit/placement by examination:** AP, CLEP, IB, institutional tests. **Support services:** Learning center, pre-admission summer program, reduced course load, remedial instruction, study skills assistance, tutoring, writing center.

Majors. Biology: General. **Business:** General, accounting, business admin, entrepreneurial studies, finance, international, marketing. **Communications:** General. **Computer sciences:** General, information systems. **Conservation:** Environmental science. **Engineering:** Physics. **Engineering technology:** Electrical, industrial, manufacturing, mechanical. **Foreign languages:** Spanish. **Health:** Health services, nursing (RN). **History:** General. **Liberal arts:** Arts/sciences. **Math:** General. **Parks/recreation:** Health/fitness. **Physical sciences:** Chemistry, physics. **Protective services:** Corrections, law enforcement admin. **Psychology:** General. **Public administration:** General. **Social sciences:** Political science, sociology. **Visual/performing arts:** Art.

Most popular majors. Biology 6%, business/marketing 16%, interdisciplinary studies 27%, parks/recreation 6%, security/protective services 9%.

Computing on campus. 650 workstations in dormitories, library, computer center. Dormitories wired for high-speed internet access and linked to campus network. Commuter students can connect to campus network. Online course registration, online library, helpline, repair service, student web hosting, wireless network available.

Student life. Freshman orientation: Mandatory, $50 fee. Preregistration for classes offered. **Housing:** Coed dorms, wellness housing available. **Activities:** Jazz band, campus ministries, choral groups, dance, international student organizations, music ensembles, student government, student newspaper.

Athletics. NAIA. **Intercollegiate:** Baseball M, golf, soccer, volleyball W. **Team name:** Scorpions.

Student services. Adult student services, career counseling, services for economically disadvantaged, student employment services, financial aid counseling, health services, minority student services, on-campus daycare, personal counseling, placement for graduates, veterans' counselor. **Physically disabled:** Services for visually, speech, hearing impaired.

Contact. E-mail: admissions@utb.edu
Phone: (956) 882-8295 Toll-free number: (800) 850-0160
Fax: (956) 882-7810
Rene Villarreal, Director of Admissions, University of Texas at Brownsville - Texas Southmost College, 80 Fort Brown, Brownsville, TX 78520

University of Texas at Dallas

Richardson, Texas **CB member**
www.utdallas.edu **CB code: 6897**

- Public 4-year university
- Commuter campus in very large city
- 9,202 degree-seeking undergraduates: 25% part-time, 46% women, 8% African American, 21% Asian American, 11% Hispanic American, 1% Native American, 4% international
- 5,015 degree-seeking graduate students
- 54% of applicants admitted
- SAT or ACT with writing required
- 59% graduate within 6 years

General. Founded in 1969. Regionally accredited. Established internships in industrial practice positions with over 200 advanced technology firms located near the university. **Degrees:** 2,384 bachelor's awarded; master's, doctoral offered. **ROTC:** Army, Air Force. **Location:** 18 miles from downtown Dallas. **Calendar:** Semester, extensive summer session. **Full-time faculty:** 515 total; 92% have terminal degrees, 28% minority, 26% women. **Part-time faculty:** 257 total; 46% have terminal degrees, 18% minority, 53% women. **Class size:** 28% < 20, 35% 20-39, 11% 40-49, 20% 50-99, 6% >100. **Special facilities:** Geological information library, history of aviation library, rare book library, philatelic research library, center for communications disorders, Holocaust collection, translation library.

Freshman class profile. 4,916 applied, 2,639 admitted, 1,118 enrolled.

Mid 50% test scores			
SAT critical reading:	550-670	Rank in top quarter:	72%
SAT math:	590-700	Rank in top tenth:	42%
SAT writing:	530-650	End year in good standing:	82%
ACT composite:	24-30	Return as sophomores:	83%
GPA 3.75 or higher:	35%	Out-of-state:	5%
GPA 3.50-3.74:	33%	Live on campus:	63%
GPA 3.0-3.49:	29%	International:	3%
GPA 2.0-2.99:	3%	Fraternities:	6%
		Sororities:	9%

Basis for selection. 1140 SAT (exclusive of Writing) or 25 ACT, rank in top 25% of class, completion of required high school course work required for automatic admission. All others reviewed for admission. In-state high school students finishing in top 10% of class automatically admitted to state public universities. Texas Higher Education Assessment test required for some based on high school performance.

High school preparation. College-preparatory program required. 18 units required; 24 recommended. Required and recommended units include English 4, mathematics 3.5-4, social studies 3-4, science 3 (laboratory 3), foreign language 2-3, computer science 1, visual/performing arts .5-1, academic electives 1.5-2.5. 0.5 health, 1.5 physical education recommended.

2008-2009 Annual costs. Tuition/fees: $9,850; $21,000 out-of-state. Room/board: $6,828. Books/supplies: $1,200. Personal expenses: $1,929.

2008-2009 Financial aid. Need-based: 612 full-time freshmen applied for aid; 495 were judged to have need; 495 of these received aid. Average need met was 81%. Average scholarship/grant was $7,336; average loan $3,228. 35% of total undergraduate aid awarded as scholarships/grants, 65% as loans/jobs. **Non-need-based:** Awarded to 2,537 full-time undergraduates, including 632 freshmen. Scholarships awarded for academics.

Application procedures. Admission: Closing date 7/1 (postmark date). $50 fee, may be waived for applicants with need. Admission notification on a rolling basis. **Financial aid:** Priority date 3/31, closing date 4/12. FAFSA required. Applicants notified on a rolling basis starting 3/1; must reply within 2 week(s) of notification.

Academics. Special study options: Accelerated study, combined bachelor's/graduate degree, cooperative education, cross-registration, distance learning, double major, dual enrollment of high school students, honors, independent study, internships, student-designed major, study abroad, teacher certification program, Washington semester, weekend college. 3-2 engineering and 2-2 transfer programs. **Credit/placement by examination:** AP, CLEP, IB, institutional tests. 30 credit hours maximum toward bachelor's degree. No limit on lower-level courses, 6 hours limit on upper-level courses. SAT Subject Tests in Math Levels I and II accepted for advanced placement.

Support services: Learning center, pre-admission summer program, reduced course load, remedial instruction, study skills assistance, tutoring, writing center.

Majors. Area/ethnic studies: American, women's. **Biology:** General, biochemistry, molecular. **Business:** General, accounting, finance. **Computer sciences:** General. **Engineering:** Computer, electrical, software. **Foreign languages:** Comparative lit. **Health:** Audiology/speech pathology. **History:** General. **Interdisciplinary:** Cognitive science, neuroscience. **Liberal arts:** Arts/sciences. **Math:** General, applied, statistics. **Physical sciences:** Chemistry, geology, physics. **Psychology:** General. **Public administration:** General. **Social sciences:** Criminology, economics, geography, political science, sociology. **Visual/performing arts:** General, studio arts. **Other:** Interdisciplinary studies.

Most popular majors. Biology 8%, business/marketing 31%, engineering/engineering technologies 7%, interdisciplinary studies 14%, psychology 9%, social sciences 10%.

Computing on campus. 630 workstations in library, computer center. Dormitories linked to campus network. Commuter students can connect to campus network. Online course registration, online library, helpline, wireless network available.

Student life. Freshman orientation: Available, $100 fee. Preregistration for classes offered. Family 1-day sessions and student 2-day sessions held in April, July and August. **Housing:** Apartments available. $100 partly refundable deposit, deadline 6/30. Pets allowed in dorm rooms. Living-learning communities for freshmen. **Activities:** Dance, drama, radio station, student government, student newspaper, College Republicans, campus Hispanic association, African American student alliance, Friendship Association of Chinese Students and Visiting Scholars, Indian students association, multicultural association, Campus Crusade for Christ, Muslim students association, Pacific Asian student association.

Athletics. NCAA. **Intercollegiate:** Baseball M, basketball, cross-country, golf, soccer, softball W, tennis, volleyball W. **Intramural:** Basketball, cheerleading, football (non-tackle), racquetball, squash, volleyball. **Team name:** Comets.

Student services. Alcohol/substance abuse counseling, career counseling, student employment services, financial aid counseling, health services, legal services, minority student services, on-campus daycare, personal counseling, placement for graduates, veterans' counselor, women's services. **Physically disabled:** Services for visually, speech, hearing impaired.

Contact. E-mail: interest@utdallas.edu
Phone: (972) 883-2270 Toll-free number: (800) 889-2443
Fax: (972) 883-2599
Curt Eley, VP of Enrollment Management, University of Texas at Dallas, Office of Enrollment Services, Richardson, TX 75083-0688

University of Texas at El Paso

El Paso, Texas **CB member**
www.utep.edu **CB code: 6829**

- Public 4-year university
- Commuter campus in very large city
- 16,976 degree-seeking undergraduates
- 99% of applicants admitted

General. Founded in 1913. Regionally accredited. Bilingual community, programs, and student body. Located within 100 yards of Mexico. **Degrees:** 2,631 bachelor's awarded; master's, doctoral offered. **ROTC:** Army, Air Force. **Calendar:** Semester, extensive summer session. **Full-time faculty:** 681 total. **Part-time faculty:** 496 total. **Class size:** 31% < 20, 49% 20-39, 8% 40-49, 9% 50-99, 3% >100. **Special facilities:** Solar energy facility.

Freshman class profile. 5,548 applied, 5,492 admitted, 2,555 enrolled.

Mid 50% test scores			
SAT critical reading:	410-520	Rank in top quarter:	43%
SAT math:	420-530	Rank in top tenth:	18%
ACT composite:	16-21	Out-of-state:	3%

Basis for selection. Minimum GED score of 45, or top half of high school class with 20 ACT or 920 SAT (exclusive of Writing). Provisional admission for in-state residents not meeting these criteria. For students in top quarter of high school class, any score acceptable. SAT or ACT, when required, may be used for counseling. Credit may be given for selected SAT Subject Tests.

High school preparation. 21 units recommended. Recommended units include English 4, mathematics 3, social studies 2, history 2, science 3 and foreign language 2. 1 additional math for science and engineering majors.

2008-2009 Annual costs. Tuition/fees: $5,924; $14,354 out-of-state. Mexican citizens who show need may qualify for in-state tuition. Reported room-only cost based on double-occupancy apartment at $485 per month for nine months. Optional a la carte meal plan. Room only: $4,365. Books/supplies: $900. Personal expenses: $1,780.

2007-2008 Financial aid. **Need-based:** 43% of total undergraduate aid awarded as scholarships/grants, 57% as loans/jobs. **Non-need-based:** Scholarships awarded for academics, alumni affiliation, art, athletics, job skills, leadership, minority status, music/drama, religious affiliation, ROTC, state residency. **Additional information:** Emergency loans available.

Application procedures. **Admission:** Priority date 5/1; deadline 7/31 (postmark date). No application fee. Admission notification on a rolling basis. Notification of early action applicants when admission file is complete. **Financial aid:** Closing date 3/15. FAFSA, institutional form required. Applicants notified by 6/30; must reply within 2 week(s) of notification.

Academics. **Special study options:** Accelerated study, combined bachelor's/graduate degree, cooperative education, cross-registration, distance learning, double major, dual enrollment of high school students, ESL, exchange student, honors, independent study, internships, study abroad, teacher certification program, weekend college. **Credit/placement by examination:** AP, CLEP, IB, SAT, institutional tests. **Support services:** Learning center, pre-admission summer program, reduced course load, remedial instruction, study skills assistance, tutoring, writing center.

Majors. **Area/ethnic studies:** Hispanic-American/Latino/Chicano, Latin American. **Biology:** General, microbiology. **Business:** General, accounting, business admin, finance, management information systems, managerial economics, marketing, operations. **Communications:** General, advertising, journalism, media studies, public relations. **Computer sciences:** General. **Conservation:** Environmental science. **Education:** General, elementary, middle, special. **Engineering:** General, civil, electrical, industrial, mechanical, metallurgical. **Foreign languages:** Comparative lit, French, German, linguistics, Spanish. **Health:** Audiology/speech pathology, clinical lab science, community health services, health services, nursing (RN). **History:** General. **Interdisciplinary:** Biological/physical sciences. **Liberal arts:** Arts/sciences. **Math:** General, applied, statistics. **Parks/recreation:** Health/fitness. **Philosophy/religion:** Philosophy. **Physical sciences:** General, chemistry, geology, geophysics, physics. **Protective services:** Criminal justice. **Psychology:** General. **Public administration:** Social work. **Social sciences:** Anthropology, political science, sociology. **Visual/performing arts:** Art, ceramics, dance, dramatic, drawing, graphic design, metal/jewelry, music performance, music theory/composition, painting, piano/organ, printmaking, sculpture, studio arts, voice/opera.

Most popular majors. Biology 6%, business/marketing 17%, engineering/engineering technologies 9%, health sciences 9%, interdisciplinary studies 29%.

Computing on campus. 2,500 workstations in library, computer center, student center. Dormitories wired for high-speed internet access. Commuter students can connect to campus network. Online course registration, online library, helpline, student web hosting, wireless network available.

Student life. **Freshman orientation:** Available. Preregistration for classes offered. 3-5 day program. **Housing:** Special housing for disabled, apartments available. **Activities:** Bands, choral groups, dance, drama, film society, literary magazine, music ensembles, musical theater, opera, radio station, student government, student newspaper, symphony orchestra, black student coalition, Mexican student organizations, Society of Hispanic Professional Engineers.

Athletics. NCAA. **Intercollegiate:** Basketball, cross-country, football (tackle) M, golf, rifle, soccer W, softball W, tennis, track and field, volleyball W. **Intramural:** Badminton, baseball M, basketball, bowling, fencing, football (tackle) M, golf, gymnastics, handball, racquetball, skiing, soccer, softball, squash, swimming, table tennis, tennis, track and field, volleyball, water polo, wrestling M. **Team name:** Miners.

Student services. Alcohol/substance abuse counseling, chaplain/spiritual director, career counseling, student employment services, financial aid counseling, health services, on-campus daycare, personal counseling, placement for graduates, veterans' counselor, women's services. **Physically disabled:** Services for visually, speech, hearing impaired.

Contact. E-mail: futureminer@utep.edu
Phone: (915) 747-5890 Fax: (915) 747-8893
Luisa Havens, Director of Admissions, University of Texas at El Paso, 500 West University Avenue, El Paso, TX 79968-0510

University of Texas at San Antonio

San Antonio, Texas — **CB member**
www.utsa.edu — **CB code: 6919**

- Public 4-year university
- Commuter campus in very large city
- 24,308 degree-seeking undergraduates: 20% part-time, 51% women, 8% African American, 7% Asian American, 43% Hispanic American, 2% international
- 3,765 graduate students
- 88% of applicants admitted
- SAT or ACT with writing required
- 30% graduate within 6 years

General. Founded in 1969. Regionally accredited. Second campus in downtown area. **Degrees:** 3,553 bachelor's awarded; master's, doctoral offered. **ROTC:** Army, Air Force. **Location:** 15 miles from downtown. **Calendar:** Semester, limited summer session. **Full-time faculty:** 976 total; 67% have terminal degrees, 35% minority, 41% women. **Part-time faculty:** 248 total; 45% have terminal degrees, 32% minority, 44% women. **Class size:** 27% < 20, 41% 20-39, 10% 40-49, 14% 50-99, 9% >100. **Special facilities:** Institute of Texan cultures, center for archaeological research, neuroscience research center, center for water research, center for lasers and materials science, center for economic development, culture and policy institute, institute for music research, center for professional excellence.

Freshman class profile. 12,442 applied, 10,949 admitted, 4,858 enrolled.

Mid 50% test scores			
SAT critical reading:	450-560	Return as sophomores:	59%
SAT math:	470-580	Out-of-state:	1%
SAT writing:	430-540	Live on campus:	43%
ACT composite:	19-24	International:	2%
Rank in top quarter:	36%	Fraternities:	2%
Rank in top tenth:	11%	Sororities:	1%

Basis for selection. Texas residents who graduate in top 10% of high school graduating class admitted, regardless of ACT or SAT scores. Those not in top 10% must meet appropriate ACT or SAT scores based on class rank. If test score/rank criteria not met, additional factors may be taken into consideration. Out-of-state applicants must graduate in top half of graduating class in addition to meeting corresponding ACT or SAT score requirements. **Homeschooled:** Conditional admissions decision based on SAT score over 970 (exclusive of Writing) plus high school educational record (courses taken and grades earned) signed and dated by person responsible for conducting educational program. Upon high school graduation, final high school record indicating graduation date signed and dated by responsible educator must be submitted.

High school preparation. College-preparatory program recommended. 16.5 units recommended. Recommended units include English 4, mathematics 3, social studies 3.5, science 3, foreign language 2 and visual/performing arts 1. 1 or more fine arts recommended.

2008-2009 Annual costs. Tuition/fees: $7,100; $15,530 out-of-state. Room/board: $7,821. Books/supplies: $1,000. Personal expenses: $2,202.

2007-2008 Financial aid. **Need-based:** 3,638 full-time freshmen applied for aid; 2,510 were judged to have need; 2,387 of these received aid. Average need met was 60%. Average scholarship/grant was $6,317; average loan $3,176. 45% of total undergraduate aid awarded as scholarships/grants, 55% as loans/jobs. **Non-need-based:** Awarded to 2,933 full-time undergraduates, including 1,095 freshmen. Scholarships awarded for academics, alumni affiliation, art, athletics, job skills, leadership, music/drama, ROTC, state residency.

Application procedures. **Admission:** Priority date 5/1; deadline 7/1 (receipt date). $40 fee, may be waived for applicants with need. Admission notification 9/1. Admission notification on a rolling basis. **Financial aid:** Priority date 3/31; no closing date. FAFSA, institutional form required. Applicants notified on a rolling basis starting 4/1; must reply within 4 week(s) of notification.

Academics. Freshman Initiative includes learning communities and freshman seminar program, enhancing academic services for new students in order to increase retention and success in college. **Special study options:** Accelerated study, cooperative education, distance learning, double major, dual enrollment of high school students, ESL, exchange student, honors, independent study, internships, study abroad, teacher certification program. 2-2 programs with Alamo Community College District, Southwest Texas Junior College, Laredo Junior College, Victoria College, Del Mar College, Coastal Bend Community College, Austin Community College; telecampus agreement with UT System. **Credit/placement by examination:** AP, CLEP, institutional tests. Some departments have limits on number of credits earned by examination. **Support services:** Learning center, pre-admission summer program, remedial instruction, study skills assistance, tutoring, writing center.

Majors. **Architecture:** Architecture, interior. **Area/ethnic studies:** American, Hispanic-American/Latino/Chicano. **Biology:** General. **Business:** General, accounting, actuarial science, business admin, finance, human resources, international, management information systems, management science, managerial economics, marketing, operations, sales/distribution, tourism/travel. **Communications:** General, media studies, public relations. **Computer sciences:** General, security. **Conservation:** Environmental science. **Engineering:** Civil, electrical, mechanical. **Foreign languages:** Classics, French, German, Spanish. **Health:** Clinical lab science, health services. **History:** General. **Interdisciplinary:** Biological/physical sciences. **Liberal arts:** Humanities. **Math:** General, statistics. **Parks/recreation:** Health/fitness. **Philosophy/religion:** Philosophy. **Physical sciences:** General, chemistry, geology, physics. **Protective services:** Criminal justice. **Psychology:** General. **Social sciences:** General, anthropology, geography, political science, sociology. **Visual/performing arts:** Art, art history/conservation, music management, music performance, music theory/composition, studio arts.

Most popular majors. Biology 10%, business/marketing 27%, engineering/engineering technologies 6%, interdisciplinary studies 13%, psychology 7%, social sciences 6%.

Computing on campus. 550 workstations in dormitories, library, computer center, student center. Dormitories wired for high-speed internet access and linked to campus network. Commuter students can connect to campus network. Online course registration, online library, helpline, repair service, student web hosting, wireless network available.

Student life. **Freshman orientation:** Mandatory, $55 fee. Preregistration for classes offered. One-day sessions held throughout the year; optional 2-day camp held in August. **Housing:** Coed dorms, apartments available. $200 nonrefundable deposit. **Activities:** Bands, campus ministries, choral groups, dance, drama, international student organizations, literary magazine, music ensembles, opera, student government, student newspaper, symphony orchestra, IDS student association, pre-med society, Golden Key national honor society, Intervarsity Christian Fellowship, S/B Alpha Chi national honor society, Catholic student association, Mortar Board national college senior honor society, Texas Association of Chicanos in Higher Education.

Athletics. NCAA. **Intercollegiate:** Baseball M, basketball, cross-country, golf, soccer W, softball W, tennis, track and field, volleyball W. **Intramural:** Badminton, basketball, bowling, football (non-tackle), golf, racquetball, soccer, softball, table tennis, tennis, volleyball, weight lifting. **Team name:** Roadrunners.

Student services. Career counseling, student employment services, financial aid counseling, health services, personal counseling, placement for graduates, veterans' counselor. **Physically disabled:** Services for visually, speech, hearing impaired.

Contact. E-mail: prospects@utsa.edu
Phone: (210) 458-8000 Toll-free number: (800) 669-0919
Fax: (210) 458-2001
George Norton, Director of Admissions, University of Texas at San Antonio, One UTSA Circle, San Antonio, TX 78249-0617

University of Texas at Tyler

Tyler, Texas — **CB member**
www.uttyler.edu — **CB code: 0389**

- Public 4-year university
- Commuter campus in small city
- 4,958 degree-seeking undergraduates: 23% part-time, 59% women, 10% African American, 2% Asian American, 7% Hispanic American, 1% Native American, 1% international
- 946 degree-seeking graduate students
- 80% of applicants admitted
- SAT or ACT (ACT writing optional) required

General. Founded in 1971. Regionally accredited. Off-campus sites at Palestine and Longview. Internet courses and telecampus available. **Degrees:** 1,029 bachelor's awarded; master's, doctoral offered. **Location:** 80 miles from Dallas. **Calendar:** Semester, limited summer session. **Full-time faculty:** 267 total; 72% have terminal degrees, 13% minority, 52% women. **Part-time faculty:** 132 total; 26% have terminal degrees, 4% minority, 48% women. **Class size:** 35% < 20, 44% 20-39, 7% 40-49, 12% 50-99, 2% >100. **Special facilities:** Desktop manufacturing lab, computer-based virtual lab instruments.

Freshman class profile. 1,411 applied, 1,129 admitted, 581 enrolled.

Mid 50% test scores			
SAT critical reading:	490-590	Return as sophomores:	65%
SAT math:	470-580	Out-of-state:	3%
SAT writing:	470-570	Live on campus:	68%
ACT composite:	20-25	Fraternities:	4%
		Sororities:	7%

Basis for selection. Top 10% accepted automatically, others admitted based on ACT/SAT scores and high school preparation.

High school preparation. College-preparatory program recommended. Required and recommended units include English 4, mathematics 3-4, social studies 3, science 3 (laboratory 1-3) and foreign language 2. Math requirement must be algebra I and higher. 4 mathematics recommended for science, engineering, and other technical fields.

2008-2009 Annual costs. Tuition/fees: $5,742; $14,172 out-of-state. Room/board: $7,510. Books/supplies: $900. Personal expenses: $1,148.

2007-2008 Financial aid. **Non-need-based:** Scholarships awarded for academics, art, music/drama. **Additional information:** Apply early for all programs.

Application procedures. **Admission:** No deadline. $25 fee, may be waived for applicants with need. Admission notification on a rolling basis beginning on or about 9/1. Must reply by May 1 or within 4 week(s) if notified thereafter. **Financial aid:** Priority date 4/1; no closing date. FAFSA, institutional form required. Applicants notified on a rolling basis starting 4/15; must reply within 2 week(s) of notification.

Academics. **Special study options:** Cooperative education, distance learning, double major, independent study, internships, student-designed major, study abroad, teacher certification program. **Credit/placement by examination:** AP, CLEP, IB, SAT, ACT, institutional tests. AP, CLEP and International Baccalaureate awarded transfer credit with no maximum limit. **Support services:** Learning center, remedial instruction, study skills assistance, tutoring, writing center.

Honors college/program. New Honors Program starting in Fall 2009, approximately 15-20 students. Must have a minimum score of 28 ACT or 1860 SAT. Essay required.

Majors. **Biology:** General. **Business:** Accounting, business admin, construction management, finance, managerial economics, marketing, sales/distribution, training/development. **Communications:** Journalism. **Computer sciences:** General. **Engineering:** Civil, electrical, mechanical. **Engineering technology:** General, industrial, occupational safety. **Foreign languages:** General, Spanish. **Health:** Clinical lab science, community health services, nursing (RN). **History:** General. **Math:** General. **Parks/recreation:** Health/fitness. **Physical sciences:** Chemistry. **Protective services:** Criminal justice. **Psychology:** General. **Social sciences:** Political science, sociology. **Visual/performing arts:** Art.

Most popular majors. Business/marketing 22%, engineering/engineering technologies 7%, English 6%, health sciences 23%, interdisciplinary studies 12%, psychology 7%.

Computing on campus. 175 workstations in dormitories, library, computer center, student center. Dormitories wired for high-speed internet access and linked to campus network. Commuter students can connect to campus network. Online course registration, online library, wireless network available.

Student life. **Freshman orientation:** Mandatory, $35 fee. Preregistration for classes offered. One-day orientation in summer for students and parents. **Housing:** Coed dorms, apartments available. **Activities:** Bands, campus ministries, choral groups, international student organizations, literary magazine, music ensembles, Model UN, musical theater, opera, student government, student newspaper, Bible study fellowship, University Democrats, student government association, Nurses Christian Fellowship, international student organization, Wesley Foundation Student Fellowship, Baptist student ministry, Patriots Special Olympics Texas Volunteers (Patriots SOTX), University Mothers Against Drunk Driving (UMADD), Indian student association.

Athletics. NCAA. **Intercollegiate:** Baseball M, basketball, cheerleading, cross-country, golf, soccer, softball W, tennis, track and field, volleyball W. **Intramural:** Baseball M, basketball, bowling, football (non-tackle), football (tackle), golf, racquetball, soccer, softball, table tennis, tennis, volleyball. **Team name:** Patriots.

Student services. Adult student services, alcohol/substance abuse counseling, career counseling, student employment services, financial aid counseling, health services, personal counseling, veterans' counselor. **Physically disabled:** Services for visually, speech, hearing impaired.

Contact. E-mail: admissions@mail.uttyl.edu
Phone: (903) 566-7202 Toll-free number: (800) 888-9537
Fax: (903) 566-7068
Sarah Bowdin, Director of Admissions, University of Texas at Tyler, 3900 University Boulevard, Tyler, TX 75799

University of Texas Health Science Center at Houston

Houston, Texas
www.uth.tmc.edu **CB code: 6888**

- Public two-year upper-division university and health science college
- Commuter campus in very large city

General. Founded in 1972. Regionally accredited. **Location:** 5 miles from downtown. **Calendar:** Semester.

Annual costs/financial aid. Tuition/fees (2008-2009): $4,595; $16,145 out-of-state. Cost above are for RN-BSN nursing program. Nursing program students must attend for full calendar year (fall, spring, summer semesters). Books/supplies: $1,050. Need-based financial aid available to full-time and part-time students.

Contact. Phone: (713) 500-3361
Associate Registrar, Box 20036, Houston, TX 77225

University of Texas Health Science Center at San Antonio

San Antonio, Texas **CB member**
www.uthscsa.edu **CB code: 6908**

- Public two-year upper-division university and health science college
- Commuter campus in very large city

General. Founded in 1969. Regionally accredited. Located in South Texas Medical Center. **Degrees:** 326 bachelor's awarded; master's, doctoral, first professional offered. **Location:** 10 miles from downtown. **Calendar:** Semester, limited summer session. **Full-time faculty:** 1,154 total. **Part-time faculty:** 355 total.

Student profile. 773 degree-seeking undergraduates, 2,255 degree-seeking graduate students. 99% entered as juniors, 1% entered as seniors.

Women:	71%	**Out-of-state:**	13%
Part-time:	26%		

Basis for selection. High school transcript, college transcript required. Admission varies with each program. In many cases, academic records and interview required. Application closing and priority dates vary with each program. Transfer accepted as juniors.

2008-2009 Annual costs. Tuition/fees: $6,083; $16,252 out-of-state. Tuition and fees vary by program. Books/supplies: $850. Personal expenses: $1,100.

Financial aid. Additional information: Students strongly advised to provide parental information on need analysis form regardless of dependency status.

Application procedures. Admission: $45 fee. Application must be submitted online. Application fees vary from $10 to $55 depending on program. **Financial aid:** FAFSA, institutional form required.

Academics. Special study options: Combined bachelor's/graduate degree, cross-registration, distance learning, internships. PharmD program with University of Texas-Austin; joint degree Health Professions program with University of Texas-San Antonio. **Credit/placement by examination:** CLEP, institutional tests.

Majors. Health: Clinical lab science, dental hygiene, dental lab technology, nursing (RN), physician assistant, respiratory therapy technology.

Computing on campus. 50 workstations in library. Commuter students can connect to campus network. Helpline, wireless network available.

Student life. Activities: Student government, student newspaper, Texas Association of Mexican-American Medical Students, Latin-American Nursing Student Association, Diversified Dental Students.

Athletics. Intramural: Baseball M, basketball, softball, tennis, volleyball.

Student services. Adult student services, alcohol/substance abuse counseling, financial aid counseling, health services, personal counseling, veterans' counselor.

Contact. E-mail: registrars@uthscsa.edu
Phone: (210) 567-2621 Fax: (210) 567-2685
Amy McGilvray, Registrar, University of Texas Health Science Center at San Antonio, 7703 Floyd Curl Drive, San Antonio, TX 78229-3900

University of Texas Medical Branch at Galveston

Galveston, Texas
www.utmb.edu **CB code: 6887**

- Public two-year upper-division health science and nursing college
- Commuter campus in small city

General. Founded in 1881. Regionally accredited. **Degrees:** 279 bachelor's awarded; master's, doctoral, first professional offered. **Location:** 50 miles from Houston. **Calendar:** Semester, limited summer session.

Student profile. 470 degree-seeking undergraduates, 1,868 degree-seeking graduate students.

Women:	80%	**International:**	2%
African American:	16%	**Part-time:**	43%
Asian American:	14%	**Out-of-state:**	1%
Hispanic American:	13%	**25 or older:**	56%

Basis for selection. College transcript required. Students with 60 hours from accredited college or university considered. Nonresident enrollment limited by legislature to not more than 10% of any class. Transfer decisions based on competitive comparison of transcripts, allied health experience, departmental testing, and personal interviews. Specific prerequisites and application closing dates vary by program. Transfer accepted as juniors, seniors.

2008-2009 Annual costs. Tuition/fees: $5,443; $13,873 out-of-state. Tuition and fees vary by program.

Financial aid. Non-need-based: Scholarships awarded for academics, minority status, state residency.

Application procedures. Admission: Rolling admission. $30 fee. Application closing dates vary with school and program. **Financial aid:** FAFSA required.

Academics. Special study options: Distance learning, independent study, internships. **Credit/placement by examination:** CLEP, IB. 30 credit hours maximum toward bachelor's degree.

Majors. Health: Clinical lab science, nursing (RN), respiratory therapy technology.

Computing on campus. Dormitories wired for high-speed internet access and linked to campus network. Commuter students can connect to campus network. Online library, helpline, repair service, wireless network available.

Student life. Housing: Coed dorms, apartments, fraternity/sorority housing available. **Activities:** Campus ministries, international student organizations, student government, student newspaper, Wesley Foundation, Newman Center, sports clubs, Christian Medical and Dental Society, Jewish student and faculty organization, multicultural awareness council, student national medical association, Texas Association of Latin American Medical Students.

Athletics. Intramural: Basketball, football (non-tackle), soccer, softball, volleyball.

Student services. Alcohol/substance abuse counseling, chaplain/spiritual director, career counseling, student employment services, financial aid counseling, health services, legal services, on-campus daycare, personal counseling, veterans' counselor, women's services. **Physically disabled:** Services for visually, speech, hearing impaired.

Contact. E-mail: enrollment.services@utmb.edu
Phone: (409) 772-1215 Fax: (409) 772-4466
Vicki Brewer, Registrar, University of Texas Medical Branch at Galveston, 301 University Boulevard, Galveston, TX 77555-1305

Four-Year Colleges

University of Texas of the Permian Basin

Odessa, Texas
www.utpb.edu
CB member
CB code: 0448

- Public 4-year university
- Commuter campus in small city
- 2,489 degree-seeking undergraduates: 26% part-time, 60% women, 5% African American, 1% Asian American, 41% Hispanic American, 1% Native American, 1% international
- 750 degree-seeking graduate students
- 90% of applicants admitted
- SAT or ACT (ACT writing optional) required
- 30% graduate within 6 years

General. Founded in 1969. Regionally accredited. **Degrees:** 494 bachelor's awarded; master's offered. **Location:** 150 miles from Lubbock, 350 miles from Dallas. **Calendar:** Semester, extensive summer session. **Full-time faculty:** 107 total; 82% have terminal degrees, 24% minority, 50% women. **Part-time faculty:** 116 total; 33% have terminal degrees, 8% minority, 51% women. **Class size:** 44% < 20, 42% 20-39, 6% 40-49, 7% 50-99, less than 1% >100.

Freshman class profile. 775 applied, 701 admitted, 366 enrolled.

Mid 50% test scores		**Rank in top tenth:**	23%
SAT critical reading:	440-550	**Out-of-state:**	7%
SAT math:	460-570	**Live on campus:**	46%
ACT composite:	18-23	**International:**	2%
Rank in top quarter:	54%		

Basis for selection. Secondary school record, class rank, test scores important. Foreign students whose native language is not English must take TOEFL. Requirement may be waived for non-English speakers transferring from a U.S. college or high school. Essay not required but considered if provided. **Homeschooled:** No additional requirements. Home-schooled students reviewed on an individual basis. **Learning Disabled:** No special requirements but must meet minimum admission standards.

High school preparation. College-preparatory program recommended. 24 units required. Required units include English 4, mathematics 3, social studies 3.5, science 3 (laboratory 3), foreign language 2, computer science 1, visual/performing arts 1, academic electives 3.5.

2008-2009 Annual costs. Tuition/fees: $4,934; $13,364 out-of-state. New Mexico residents living in areas contiguous to Texas border pay in-district rate. Books/supplies: $900. Personal expenses: $3,368.

2007-2008 Financial aid. Need-based: 267 full-time freshmen applied for aid; 201 were judged to have need; 201 of these received aid. Average need met was 69%. Average scholarship/grant was $5,161; average loan $2,605. 67% of total undergraduate aid awarded as scholarships/grants, 33% as loans/jobs. **Non-need-based:** Awarded to 1,024 full-time undergraduates, including 355 freshmen. Scholarships awarded for academics, art, athletics, music/drama.

Application procedures. Admission: Closing date 7/15 (postmark date). No application fee. Admission notification on a rolling basis. **Financial aid:** Priority date 5/1, closing date 7/15. FAFSA required. Applicants notified on a rolling basis starting 6/1; must reply within 2 week(s) of notification.

Academics. Special study options: Distance learning, double major, dual enrollment of high school students, ESL, honors, independent study, internships, teacher certification program, weekend college. **Credit/placement by examination:** CLEP, SAT, ACT, institutional tests. 28 credit hours maximum toward bachelor's degree. Credit/placement awarded on AP or CLEP exams, special exams administered by School of Business. **Support services:** Learning center, remedial instruction, study skills assistance, tutoring, writing center.

Majors. Biology: General. **Business:** Accounting, business admin, finance, managerial economics, marketing. **Communications:** General. **Computer sciences:** General, information systems. **Conservation:** Environmental studies. **Engineering technology:** Industrial. **Family/consumer sciences:** Family studies. **Foreign languages:** Spanish. **Health:** Athletic training. **History:** General. **Interdisciplinary:** Biological/physical sciences. **Liberal arts:** Humanities. **Math:** General. **Parks/recreation:** Health/fitness. **Physical sciences:** Chemistry, geology. **Protective services:** Criminal justice. **Psychology:** General. **Public administration:** Social work. **Social sciences:** Criminology, political science, sociology. **Visual/performing arts:** Art. **Other:** Leadership studies.

Most popular majors. Business/marketing 21%, English 6%, family/consumer sciences 11%, psychology 10%, social sciences 9%.

Computing on campus. 170 workstations in dormitories, library, computer center. Dormitories wired for high-speed internet access and linked to campus network. Commuter students can connect to campus network. Online course registration, online library, helpline, wireless network available.

Student life. Freshman orientation: Mandatory, $75 fee. Preregistration for classes offered. Choice of 3 separate 3-day sessions in June, July, August, includes some meals and lodging for out-of-town students; 1-day orientation in January for students entering in Spring; 1-day express orientation in August available. **Housing:** Coed dorms, apartments available. $150 fully refundable deposit, deadline 7/15. Family housing units. **Activities:** Bands, campus ministries, choral groups, dance, drama, international student organizations, literary magazine, music ensembles, radio station, student government, student newspaper, symphony orchestra, Baptist student ministries, Black leadership conference, Catholic student organization, international students club, Young Democrats, Young Republicans.

Athletics. NCAA. **Intercollegiate:** Baseball M, basketball, cheerleading, cross-country, soccer, softball W, swimming, volleyball W. **Intramural:** Basketball, bowling, football (non-tackle), table tennis, tennis, volleyball. **Team name:** Falcons.

Student services. Adult student services, alcohol/substance abuse counseling, career counseling, services for economically disadvantaged, student employment services, financial aid counseling, health services, minority student services, personal counseling.

Contact. E-mail: admissions@utpb.edu
Phone: (432) 552-2605 Toll-free number: (866) 552-8872
Fax: (432) 552-3605
Scott Smiley, Director of Admissions, University of Texas of the Permian Basin, 4901 East University, Odessa, TX 79762

University of Texas Southwestern Medical Center at Dallas

Dallas, Texas
www.utsouthwestern.edu
CB code: 0273

- Public two-year upper-division university and health science college
- Commuter campus in very large city
- 26% of applicants admitted
- Application essay required

General. Founded in 1943. Regionally accredited. Four teaching hospitals adjoin campus. **Degrees:** 47 bachelor's awarded; master's, doctoral, first professional offered. **Articulation:** Agreements with Dallas County Community College District, Collin County Community College, Tarrant County College District. **Location:** 3 miles from downtown. **Calendar:** Semester, limited summer session. **Full-time faculty:** 1,539 total. **Part-time faculty:** 425 total. **Class size:** 88% < 20, 12% 20-39.

Student profile. 103 degree-seeking undergraduates, 2,355 degree-seeking graduate students. 57 applied as first time-transfer students, 15 admitted, 13 enrolled. 92% entered as juniors, 8% entered as seniors.

Women:	78%	**International:**	11%
African American:	13%	**Part-time:**	8%
Asian American:	8%	**Out-of-state:**	13%
Hispanic American:	6%	**25 or older:**	53%

Basis for selection. College transcript, application essay required. Application closing dates vary by program. No limit on transferable credits. Students must complete prescribed professional curriculum and be Texas Core Curriculum complete. Transfer accepted as juniors, seniors.

2008-2009 Annual costs. Tuition/fees: $4,190; $12,530 out-of-state. Tuition and fees are based on Allied Health program. Books/supplies: $775.

Financial aid. Need-based: 84 applied for aid; 84 were judged to have need; 75 of these received aid. Average need met was 84%. 22% of total undergraduate aid awarded as scholarships/grants, 78% as loans/jobs. **Non-need-based:** Awarded to 5 undergraduates.

Application procedures. Admission: Rolling admission. $10 fee. **Financial aid:** Priority date 3/1. Applicants notified on a rolling basis starting 4/1; must reply within 3 weeks of notification.

Academics. Special study options: Cross-registration, distance learning, independent study, internships. **Credit/placement by examination:** CLEP, institutional tests. Credit granted in English, government and history via advanced standing exams. Cannot exceed 3 semester hours in each subject.

Majors. Health: Clinical lab science, dietetics, orthotics/prosthetics.

Computing on campus. 150 workstations in library, computer center. Commuter students can connect to campus network. Online library, helpline available.

Student life. Activities: Student Dietetic Association, student membership in American Physical Therapy Association, American Academy of Physician Assistants, American Dietetic Association, American Society for Medical Technology, National Rehabilitation Association, American Society of Allied Health Professions.

Athletics. Intramural: Basketball, golf, softball, table tennis, tennis, volleyball.

Student services. Career counseling, financial aid counseling, health services, personal counseling, placement for graduates, veterans' counselor.

Contact. E-mail: admissions@utsouthwestern.edu
Phone: (214) 648-5617 Fax: (214) 648-3289
Anne McLane, Associate Director of Admissions, University of Texas Southwestern Medical Center at Dallas, 5323 Harry Hines Boulevard, Dallas, TX 75390-9162

University of Texas: Pan American

Edinburg, Texas — **CB member**
www.utpa.edu — **CB code: 6570**

- Public 4-year university
- Commuter campus in small city
- 15,064 degree-seeking undergraduates: 25% part-time, 58% women, 1% African American, 1% Asian American, 88% Hispanic American, 5% international
- 2,198 degree-seeking graduate students
- 85% of applicants admitted
- SAT or ACT (ACT writing optional) required
- 36% graduate within 6 years

General. Founded in 1927. Regionally accredited. Hispanic-serving institution. **Degrees:** 2,420 bachelor's awarded; master's, doctoral offered. **ROTC:** Army. **Location:** 250 miles from San Antonio, 300 miles from Austin. **Calendar:** Semester, extensive summer session. **Full-time faculty:** 665 total; 40% minority, 40% women. **Part-time faculty:** 177 total; 60% minority, 49% women. **Class size:** 20% < 20, 48% 20-39, 12% 40-49, 18% 50-99, 2% >100. **Special facilities:** Coastal studies laboratory on South Padre Island.

Freshman class profile. 5,235 applied, 4,457 admitted, 2,662 enrolled.

Mid 50% test scores		**Return as sophomores:**	72%
SAT critical reading:	410-510	**Out-of-state:**	1%
SAT math:	420-530	**Live on campus:**	9%
ACT composite:	17-21	**International:**	3%
Rank in top quarter:	49%	**Fraternities:**	3%
Rank in top tenth:	19%	**Sororities:**	2%

Basis for selection. For regular admission, rank in top quartile of class or acceptable ACT/SAT scores required. Students who do not meet criteria for regular or clear admission placed in PEP (Provisional Enrollment Program).

High school preparation. 24 units required. Required units include English 4, mathematics 3, social studies 3.5, science 3, foreign language 2, academic electives 3.5. .5 economics, .5 health education, 1 fine arts, .5 speech, 1 technology required, 1.5 physical education required.

2008-2009 Annual costs. Tuition/fees: $5,125; $13,555 out-of-state. Mexican citizens may be eligible for in-state tuition rates. Room/board: $4,900. Books/supplies: $1,000. Personal expenses: $1,800.

2007-2008 Financial aid. Need-based: 2,109 full-time freshmen applied for aid; 2,022 were judged to have need; 1,984 of these received aid. Average need met was 72%. Average scholarship/grant was $9,057; average loan $1,868. 69% of total undergraduate aid awarded as scholarships/grants, 31% as loans/jobs. **Non-need-based:** Awarded to 812 full-time undergraduates, including 182 freshmen. Scholarships awarded for academics, alumni affiliation, art, athletics, leadership, music/drama, ROTC, state residency.

Application procedures. Admission: Priority date 2/1; deadline 8/11 (receipt date). No application fee. Admission notification on a rolling basis. **Financial aid:** Closing date 3/1. FAFSA required. Applicants notified on a rolling basis starting 3/15; must reply within 2 week(s) of notification.

Academics. Special study options: Accelerated study, combined bachelor's/graduate degree, cooperative education, distance learning, double major, dual enrollment of high school students, ESL, exchange student, honors, independent study, internships, study abroad, teacher certification program, weekend college. Concurrent enrollment (high school students taking limited number of college classes either on campus or through distance learning). **Credit/placement by examination:** AP, CLEP, IB, institutional tests. 45 credit hours maximum toward bachelor's degree. **Support services:** Learning center, pre-admission summer program, remedial instruction, study skills assistance, tutoring, writing center.

Majors. Area/ethnic studies: American, Hispanic-American/Latino/Chicano. **Biology:** General. **Business:** Accounting, business admin, finance, international, management information systems, marketing. **Communications:** General, journalism. **Computer sciences:** General, computer science. **Engineering:** Electrical, industrial, manufacturing, mechanical. **Foreign languages:** French, Spanish. **Health:** Audiology/speech pathology, clinical lab science, dietetics, health services, nursing (RN), physician assistant, substance abuse counseling, vocational rehab counseling. **History:** General. **Legal studies:** Prelaw. **Math:** General. **Parks/recreation:** Health/fitness. **Philosophy/religion:** Philosophy. **Physical sciences:** Chemistry, physics. **Protective services:** Law enforcement admin. **Psychology:** General. **Public administration:** Social work. **Social sciences:** General, anthropology, economics, political science, sociology. **Visual/performing arts:** Dance, dramatic, studio arts. **Other:** Applied arts and sciences, Deaf studies.

Most popular majors. Biology 7%, business/marketing 18%, English 7%, health sciences 11%, interdisciplinary studies 13%, security/protective services 6%.

Computing on campus. 900 workstations in dormitories, library, computer center. Dormitories wired for high-speed internet access and linked to campus network. Commuter students can connect to campus network. Online course registration, online library, helpline, student web hosting, wireless network available.

Student life. Freshman orientation: Mandatory, $15 fee. Preregistration for classes offered. Several 1-day sessions held prior to beginning of semester. **Housing:** Coed dorms, single-sex dorms, apartments, wellness housing available. $75 fully refundable deposit. **Activities:** Bands, campus ministries, choral groups, dance, drama, international student organizations, music ensembles, musical theater, student government, student newspaper, symphony orchestra, Episcopal Canterbury Association, Latter-day Saints student association, Baha'i association, Baptist student union, Campus Crusade for Christ, Fellowship of Christian Athletes, Asian American students association, Society of Hispanic Professional Engineers.

Athletics. NCAA. **Intercollegiate:** Baseball M, basketball, cross-country, golf, tennis, track and field, volleyball W. **Intramural:** Badminton, basketball, bowling, cheerleading, football (non-tackle), golf, racquetball, soccer, softball, tennis, volleyball. **Team name:** Broncs/Lady Broncs.

Student services. Alcohol/substance abuse counseling, career counseling, services for economically disadvantaged, student employment services, financial aid counseling, health services, on-campus daycare, personal counseling, placement for graduates, veterans' counselor, women's services. **Physically disabled:** Services for visually, speech, hearing impaired.

Contact. E-mail: admissions@utpa.edu
Phone: (956) 381-2201 Toll-free number: (866) 441-8872
Fax: (956) 381-2212
Magdalena Hinojosa, Dean of Admissions & Enrollment Services, University of Texas: Pan American, 1201 West University Drive, Edinburg, TX 78541-2999

University of the Incarnate Word

San Antonio, Texas — **CB member**
www.uiw.edu — **CB code: 6303**

- Private 4-year university and liberal arts college affiliated with Roman Catholic Church
- Commuter campus in very large city
- 5,071 degree-seeking undergraduates: 35% part-time, 66% women, 7% African American, 2% Asian American, 58% Hispanic American, 2% international
- 1,248 degree-seeking graduate students
- 67% of applicants admitted
- SAT or ACT (ACT writing optional) required
- 38% graduate within 6 years

General. Founded in 1881. Regionally accredited. Off-campus courses available at Northeast Campus, San Antonio College, Delmar Campus, Incarnate Word High School, Northwest Campus, and online. **Degrees:** 802 bachelor's, 10 associate awarded; master's, doctoral, first professional offered. **ROTC:** Army, Air Force. **Location:** 5 miles from downtown. **Calendar:**

Semester, extensive summer session. **Full-time faculty:** 200 total; 63% have terminal degrees, 28% minority, 54% women. **Part-time faculty:** 358 total; 19% have terminal degrees, 30% minority, 51% women. **Class size:** 54% < 20, 44% 20-39, 1% 40-49, less than 1% 50-99.

Freshman class profile. 3,390 applied, 2,267 admitted, 888 enrolled.

Mid 50% test scores		**GPA 2.0-2.99:**	6%
SAT critical reading:	420-530	**Rank in top quarter:**	48%
SAT math:	430-540	**Rank in top tenth:**	20%
SAT writing:	420-520	**End year in good standing:**	64%
ACT composite:	17-22	**Return as sophomores:**	63%
GPA 3.75 or higher:	23%	**Out-of-state:**	2%
GPA 3.50-3.74:	28%	**Live on campus:**	52%
GPA 3.0-3.49:	42%	**International:**	2%

Basis for selection. Test scores and school achievement record most important. Interview helpful. Rolling policy for submission of test scores. Interview recommended for academically weak. **Homeschooled:** Statement describing homeschool structure and mission, transcript of courses and grades, state high school equivalency certificate, letter of recommendation (nonparent) required. Interview and testing may be necessary for some students.

High school preparation. College-preparatory program required. 16 units required; 18 recommended. Required and recommended units include English 4, mathematics 3-4, social studies 3-4, science 3, foreign language 2 and visual/performing arts 1.

2009-2010 Annual costs. Tuition/fees: $21,290. Room/board: $8,780. Books/supplies: $1,200. Personal expenses: $1,590.

2008-2009 Financial aid. Need-based: 868 full-time freshmen applied for aid; 685 were judged to have need; 685 of these received aid. Average need met was 65%. Average scholarship/grant was $7,132; average loan $3,550. 52% of total undergraduate aid awarded as scholarships/grants, 48% as loans/jobs. **Non-need-based:** Awarded to 2,428 full-time undergraduates, including 882 freshmen. Scholarships awarded for academics, alumni affiliation, art, athletics, leadership, music/drama, religious affiliation, ROTC, state residency. **Additional information:** Students encouraged to pursue outside scholarship programs.

Application procedures. Admission: Priority date 2/1; no deadline. $20 fee, may be waived for applicants with need. Notification approximately 2 weeks following submission. Must reply by May 1 or within 4 week(s) if notified thereafter. **Financial aid:** Priority date 4/1; no closing date. FAFSA required. Applicants notified on a rolling basis starting 2/15; must reply within 2 week(s) of notification.

Academics. Special study options: Accelerated study, combined bachelor's/graduate degree, cross-registration, distance learning, double major, dual enrollment of high school students, ESL, honors, independent study, internships, student-designed major, study abroad, teacher certification program, weekend college. **Credit/placement by examination:** AP, CLEP, SAT, ACT, institutional tests. 30 credit hours maximum toward bachelor's degree. **Support services:** Learning center, reduced course load, remedial instruction, study skills assistance, tutoring, writing center.

Honors college/program. Incoming freshman for the fall semester should submit an application to the university, have a minimum high school GPA of 3.5, and combined SAT score (Verbal, Math and Writing) of 1800 and/or a combined ACT score (English, Reading and Math) of 87 (27 Composite). Applicants also need an essay, teacher recommendation, and interview. Students enroll in advanced courses, participate in one mission trip, a travel or study abroad experience, additional professional development experiences, and complete a senior project.

Majors. Biology: General. **Business:** Business admin, human resources, organizational behavior. **Communications:** General. **Computer sciences:** General. **Conservation:** Environmental science. **Education:** Elementary, music. **Family/consumer sciences:** Child development. **Foreign languages:** Spanish. **Health:** Athletic training, music therapy, nuclear medical technology, nursing (RN). **History:** General. **Interdisciplinary:** Nutrition sciences. **Liberal arts:** Arts/sciences. **Math:** General. **Parks/recreation:** Exercise sciences. **Philosophy/religion:** Philosophy, religion. **Physical sciences:** Chemistry, meteorology. **Psychology:** General. **Social sciences:** Political science, sociology. **Visual/performing arts:** Art, design, dramatic, interior design. **Other:** Computer graphic arts, Cultural studies, Engineering management, Fashion management.

Most popular majors. Business/marketing 45%, education 8%, health sciences 13%, liberal arts 6%, visual/performing arts 7%.

Computing on campus. PC or laptop required. 175 workstations in library, computer center. Dormitories wired for high-speed internet access and linked to campus network. Commuter students can connect to campus network. Online course registration, online library, helpline, repair service, wireless network available.

Student life. Freshman orientation: Mandatory, $200 fee. Preregistration for classes offered. Overnight program for out-of-towners and 1-day session for local students. Parents encouraged to participate. **Housing:** Guaranteed on-campus for freshmen. Coed dorms, single-sex dorms, special housing for disabled, apartments available. $225 fully refundable deposit. **Activities:** Jazz band, campus ministries, choral groups, dance, drama, international student organizations, literary magazine, music ensembles, musical theater, radio station, student government, student newspaper, symphony orchestra, Hispanic student association, Black student association, international student association, Student Ambassadors, Pi Sigma Alpha, Phi Alpha Delta, Catholic Daughters Association, Alpha Phi Omega, ethics club, Christian Pharmacy Fellowship International.

Athletics. NCAA. **Intercollegiate:** Baseball M, basketball, cross-country, golf, soccer, softball W, swimming, tennis, track and field, volleyball W. **Intramural:** Basketball, football (non-tackle), racquetball, soccer, softball, tennis, volleyball, water polo. **Team name:** Cardinals.

Student services. Adult student services, alcohol/substance abuse counseling, chaplain/spiritual director, career counseling, services for economically disadvantaged, student employment services, financial aid counseling, health services, personal counseling. **Physically disabled:** Services for visually, speech, hearing impaired. **Learning disabled:** Comprehensive services available.

Contact. E-mail: admis@uiwtx.edu
Phone: (210) 829-6005 Toll-free number: (800) 749-9673
Fax: (210) 829-3921
Andrea Cyterski-Acosta, Dean of Enrollment, University of the Incarnate Word, 4301 Broadway, San Antonio, TX 78209-6397

Wayland Baptist University

Plainview, Texas — **CB member**
www.wbu.edu — **CB code: 6930**

- Private 4-year university and liberal arts college affiliated with Southern Baptist Convention
- Residential campus in large town
- 891 degree-seeking undergraduates: 14% part-time, 53% women, 6% African American, 1% Asian American, 22% Hispanic American, 1% Native American, 3% international
- 222 degree-seeking graduate students
- 99% of applicants admitted
- SAT or ACT (ACT writing optional) required
- 39% graduate within 6 years

General. Founded in 1908. Regionally accredited. Off-campus sites in Amarillo, Lubbock, San Antonio, Wichita Falls, Alaska, Arizona, Hawaii, Oklahoma, New Mexico. **Degrees:** 151 bachelor's, 2 associate awarded; master's offered. **ROTC:** Army, Air Force. **Location:** 50 miles from Lubbock, 70 miles from Amarillo. **Calendar:** Semester, limited summer session. **Full-time faculty:** 80 total; 76% have terminal degrees, 5% minority, 31% women. **Part-time faculty:** 40 total; 10% have terminal degrees, 2% minority, 38% women. **Class size:** 75% < 20, 25% 20-39, less than 1% 40-49. **Special facilities:** Museum of the Llano Estacado.

Freshman class profile. 286 applied, 284 admitted, 205 enrolled.

Mid 50% test scores		**Rank in top quarter:**	37%
SAT critical reading:	400-510	**Rank in top tenth:**	14%
SAT math:	410-550	**Return as sophomores:**	66%
SAT writing:	400-510	**Out-of-state:**	14%
ACT composite:	17-22	**Live on campus:**	80%
GPA 3.75 or higher:	35%	**International:**	3%
GPA 3.50-3.74:	15%	**Fraternities:**	2%
GPA 3.0-3.49:	20%	**Sororities:**	1%
GPA 2.0-2.99:	28%		

Basis for selection. Regular freshman admission based on combination of class rank and on either the ACT composite or SAT score. Interview, audition recommended.

High school preparation. 9 units required. Required and recommended units include English 3, mathematics 2-3, social studies 2 and science 2-3.

2008-2009 Annual costs. Tuition/fees: $12,000. Room/board: $3,691. Books/supplies: $1,200. Personal expenses: $1,732.

2008-2009 Financial aid. Need-based: 161 full-time freshmen applied for aid; 156 were judged to have need; 150 of these received aid. Average need met was 68%. Average scholarship/grant was $6,286; average loan $2,846. 50% of total undergraduate aid awarded as scholarships/grants, 50% as loans/jobs. **Non-need-based:** Awarded to 254 full-time undergraduates,

including 77 freshmen. Scholarships awarded for academics, alumni affiliation, art, athletics, job skills, leadership, minority status, music/drama, religious affiliation, state residency.

Application procedures. Admission: Priority date 8/1; no deadline. $35 fee. Admission notification on a rolling basis beginning on or about 3/1. **Financial aid:** Priority date 5/1; no closing date. FAFSA, institutional form required. Applicants notified on a rolling basis starting 2/15; must reply within 3 week(s) of notification.

Academics. Special study options: Accelerated study, distance learning, double major, dual enrollment of high school students, external degree, honors, internships, teacher certification program. **Credit/placement by examination:** AP, CLEP, IB, SAT, ACT, institutional tests. 30 credit hours maximum toward bachelor's degree. **Support services:** Learning center, reduced course load, remedial instruction, study skills assistance, tutoring, writing center.

Majors. Biology: General, molecular. **Business:** Business admin. **Communications:** General, media studies. **Education:** Business, elementary, English, music, physical, technology/industrial arts, trade/industrial. **Foreign languages:** Spanish. **Health:** Nursing (RN). **History:** General. **Math:** General. **Philosophy/religion:** Christian. **Physical sciences:** General, chemistry. **Protective services:** Criminal justice. **Psychology:** General. **Public administration:** Human services. **Social sciences:** Political science, sociology. **Theology:** Religious ed, sacred music. **Visual/performing arts:** Art, dramatic.

Most popular majors. Biology 7%, business/marketing 27%, education 23%, psychology 7%, public administration/social services 7%.

Computing on campus. 227 workstations in library, computer center. Dormitories linked to campus network. Commuter students can connect to campus network. Helpline, wireless network available.

Student life. Freshman orientation: Mandatory, $15 fee. Preregistration for classes offered. Entry seminar course designed to help students succeed academically, socially, and spiritually. Taken during initial term of enrollment. **Policies:** Religious observance required. **Housing:** Guaranteed on-campus for freshmen. Single-sex dorms, apartments available. $100 fully refundable deposit. **Activities:** Bands, campus ministries, choral groups, drama, music ensembles, musical theater, radio station, student government, student newspaper, TV station, Over 20 religious, service, and special interest organizations available.

Athletics. NAIA. **Intercollegiate:** Baseball M, basketball, cheerleading, cross-country, golf, soccer, track and field, volleyball W. **Intramural:** Basketball, football (non-tackle), softball, volleyball. **Team name:** Pioneers, Flying Queens.

Student services. Chaplain/spiritual director, career counseling, student employment services, financial aid counseling, health services, personal counseling, placement for graduates.

Contact. E-mail: admityou@wbu.edu
Phone: (806) 291-3500 Toll-free number: (800) 588-1928
Fax: (806) 291-1960
Debbie Stennett, Director of Admissions, Wayland Baptist University, 1900 West Seventh Street, CMB #712, Plainview, TX 79072

West Texas A&M University

Canyon, Texas — **CB member**
www.wtamu.edu — **CB code: 6938**

- Public 4-year university
- Residential campus in large town
- 6,051 degree-seeking undergraduates: 23% part-time, 55% women, 5% African American, 2% Asian American, 19% Hispanic American, 1% Native American, 1% international
- 1,297 degree-seeking graduate students
- SAT or ACT (ACT writing optional) required
- 42% graduate within 6 years

General. Founded in 1909. Regionally accredited. **Degrees:** 1,188 bachelor's awarded; master's, doctoral offered. **Location:** 17 miles from Amarillo. **Calendar:** Semester, limited summer session. **Full-time faculty:** 252 total; 68% have terminal degrees, 6% minority, 44% women. **Part-time faculty:** 90 total; 14% have terminal degrees, 7% minority, 63% women. **Class size:** 32% < 20, 50% 20-39, 7% 40-49, 11% 50-99, less than 1% >100. **Special facilities:** 24,000-acre farm and ranch, alternative energy institute, Texas' largest historical museum, event center.

Freshman class profile.

Mid 50% test scores			
SAT critical reading:	440-580	Rank in top tenth:	15%
SAT math:	440-560	Return as sophomores:	64%
ACT composite:	18-23	Out-of-state:	7%
Rank in top quarter:	49%	International:	1%

Basis for selection. Freshman applicants must be in top half of graduating class, have minimum 950 SAT (exclusive of Writing) or 20 ACT, or attend a summer provisional term. Texas Success Initiative Testing required of all incoming students before entrance. Audition required for music program; portfolio recommended for art, theater programs.

High school preparation. 24 units required. Required and recommended units include English 4, mathematics 3, social studies 3.5, science 3 and foreign language 2.

2008-2009 Annual costs. Tuition/fees: $5,312; $13,652 out-of-state. Out-of-district students from border counties pay in-state tuition. Tuition reduction plan available to students from border states. Room/board: $5,710. Books/supplies: $900. Personal expenses: $1,668.

2008-2009 Financial aid. Non-need-based: Scholarships awarded for academics, art, athletics, leadership, music/drama, state residency. **Additional information:** Scholarship deadline February 1.

Application procedures. Admission: Priority date 7/20; no deadline. $25 fee, may be waived for applicants with need. Admission notification on a rolling basis. **Financial aid:** Priority date 4/15; no closing date. FAFSA required. Applicants notified on a rolling basis starting 3/1; must reply within 2 week(s) of notification.

Academics. Special study options: Combined bachelor's/graduate degree, cooperative education, distance learning, double major, ESL, honors, independent study, internships, liberal arts/career combination, study abroad, teacher certification program, Washington semester. **Credit/placement by examination:** AP, CLEP, IB, institutional tests. Only 6 of a student's last 30 hours can come from CLEP. **Support services:** Learning center, remedial instruction, study skills assistance, tutoring, writing center.

Majors. Agriculture: General, agribusiness operations, animal sciences, business, equestrian studies, plant protection, plant sciences. **Biology:** General, biotechnology. **Business:** General, accounting, business admin, finance, management information systems, managerial economics, marketing. **Communications:** Advertising, broadcast journalism, journalism. **Computer sciences:** General. **Conservation:** Environmental science, wildlife. **Engineering:** Mechanical. **Engineering technology:** Industrial. **Foreign languages:** Spanish. **Health:** Athletic training, clinical lab science, communication disorders, music therapy, nursing (RN). **History:** General. **Legal studies:** Prelaw. **Math:** General. **Parks/recreation:** Health/fitness. **Physical sciences:** Chemistry, geology, physics. **Protective services:** Law enforcement admin. **Psychology:** General. **Public administration:** General, social work. **Social sciences:** General, economics, geography, political science, sociology. **Visual/performing arts:** Art, dance, dramatic, graphic design, music performance, music theory/composition, studio arts.

Most popular majors. Agriculture 7%, business/marketing 14%, health sciences 11%, interdisciplinary studies 16%, liberal arts 16%, visual/performing arts 6%.

Computing on campus. 1,800 workstations in dormitories, library, computer center, student center. Dormitories wired for high-speed internet access and linked to campus network. Commuter students can connect to campus network. Online course registration, online library, helpline, student web hosting, wireless network available.

Student life. Freshman orientation: Available, $50 fee. Preregistration for classes offered. 2-day summer orientation and preregistration and 3-day orientation before school starts. **Policies:** Students with fewer than 60 semester hours accumulated, enrolled in 9 or more semester hours, and under 21 on first day of class each semester required to live in university residence halls. **Housing:** Guaranteed on-campus for all undergraduates. Coed dorms, single-sex dorms, special housing for disabled, fraternity/sorority housing available. $100 fully refundable deposit. Honors hall for students in honors program available. **Activities:** Bands, campus ministries, choral groups, dance, drama, international student organizations, literary magazine, music ensembles, musical theater, opera, radio station, student government, student newspaper, symphony orchestra, Chinese student association, Hispanic association, agriculture organizations, Students in Free Enterprise, preprofessional organizations, Black students association, College Republicans, Catholic student association.

Athletics. NCAA. **Intercollegiate:** Baseball M, basketball, cross-country, equestrian W, football (tackle) M, golf, soccer, softball W, volleyball W.

Intramural: Archery, badminton, basketball, bowling, football (non-tackle), golf, racquetball, rodeo, soccer, softball, swimming, table tennis, tennis, volleyball. **Team name:** Buffaloes.

Student services. Alcohol/substance abuse counseling, career counseling, services for economically disadvantaged, student employment services, financial aid counseling, health services, on-campus daycare, personal counseling, placement for graduates, veterans' counselor. **Physically disabled:** Services for visually, speech, hearing impaired.

Contact. E-mail: admissions@mail.wtamu.edu
Phone: (806) 651-2020 Toll-free number: (800) 999-8268
Fax: (806) 651-5268
Shawn Thomas, Director of Admissions, West Texas A&M University, 2501 Fourth Avenue, WTAMU Box 60907, Canyon, TX 79016-0001

Wiley College

Marshall, Texas — **CB member**
www.wileyc.edu — **CB code: 6940**

- Private 4-year liberal arts college affiliated with United Methodist Church
- Residential campus in large town
- 947 degree-seeking undergraduates

General. Founded in 1873. Regionally accredited. **Degrees:** 155 bachelor's, 1 associate awarded. **Location:** 40 miles from Shreveport, Louisiana, 150 miles from Dallas. **Calendar:** Semester, extensive summer session. **Full-time faculty:** 58 total. **Part-time faculty:** 16 total. **Class size:** 60% < 20, 35% 20-39, 3% 40-49, 2% 50-99. **Special facilities:** Nature trail.

Freshman class profile.

Mid 50% test scores			
SAT critical reading:	320-430	Rank in top quarter:	15%
SAT math:	320-430	Rank in top tenth:	3%
ACT composite:	13-17	Out-of-state:	38%
		Live on campus:	90%

Basis for selection. Open admission, but selective for some programs.

High school preparation. 16 units recommended. Recommended units include English 4, mathematics 2, social studies 2, science 2 and academic electives 6.

2008-2009 Annual costs. Tuition/fees: $9,970. Reported tuition includes cost of books. Room/board: $5,620. Books/supplies: $1,320. Personal expenses: $1,002.

Financial aid. All financial aid based on need.

Application procedures. Admission: No deadline. $25 fee. Admission notification on a rolling basis. **Financial aid:** No deadline. FAFSA, institutional form required. Applicants notified on a rolling basis.

Academics. Special study options: Accelerated study, cross-registration, distance learning, double major, dual enrollment of high school students, honors, independent study, internships, liberal arts/career combination, study abroad, teacher certification program, weekend college. **Credit/placement by examination:** AP, CLEP, institutional tests. **Support services:** Learning center, reduced course load, remedial instruction, study skills assistance, tutoring.

Majors. Biology: General. **Business:** Accounting, business admin, operations. **Communications:** Journalism. **Computer sciences:** Computer science. **Education:** Elementary, physical, secondary. **History:** General. **Math:** General. **Physical sciences:** Chemistry. **Protective services:** Law enforcement admin. **Social sciences:** Sociology.

Most popular majors. Business/marketing 66%, education 6%.

Computing on campus. 177 workstations in dormitories, library, computer center. Dormitories wired for high-speed internet access and linked to campus network. Commuter students can connect to campus network. Online course registration, online library, helpline, wireless network available.

Student life. Freshman orientation: Mandatory. Preregistration for classes offered. **Policies:** Religious observance required. **Housing:** Single-sex dorms, wellness housing available. $50 deposit. **Activities:** Choral groups, drama, music ensembles, radio station, student government, student newspaper, national service fraternity, interdenominational student movement, religion majors club.

Athletics. NAIA. **Intercollegiate:** Baseball M, basketball, cross-country, softball W, track and field, volleyball W. **Intramural:** Baseball M, basketball, cheerleading, softball, table tennis, tennis, track and field, volleyball, weight lifting M. **Team name:** Wildcats.

Student services. Adult student services, chaplain/spiritual director, career counseling, services for economically disadvantaged, student employment services, financial aid counseling, health services, personal counseling, placement for graduates, veterans' counselor.

Contact. E-mail: admissions@wileyc.edu
Phone: (903) 927-3311 Toll-free number: (800) 658-6889
Fax: (903) 927-3366
Alvena Jones, Director of Admissions and Recruitment, Wiley College, 711 Wiley Avenue, Marshall, TX 75670

Utah

Brigham Young University

Provo, Utah — **CB member**
www.byu.edu — **CB code: 4019**

- Private 4-year university affiliated with Church of Jesus Christ of Latter-day Saints
- Residential campus in small city
- 30,912 degree-seeking undergraduates: 9% part-time, 49% women, 4% Asian American, 4% Hispanic American, 1% Native American, 2% international
- 3,332 degree-seeking graduate students
- 69% of applicants admitted
- ACT (writing recommended), application essay, interview required
- 79% graduate within 6 years

General. Founded in 1875. Regionally accredited. Additional educational center in Salt Lake City. **Degrees:** 6,995 bachelor's awarded; master's, doctoral, first professional offered. **ROTC:** Army, Air Force. **Location:** 45 miles from Salt Lake City. **Calendar:** Semester, limited summer session. **Full-time faculty:** 1,326 total; 84% have terminal degrees, 6% minority, 21% women. **Part-time faculty:** 455 total; 25% have terminal degrees, 7% minority, 64% women. **Class size:** 47% < 20, 37% 20-39, 5% 40-49, 7% 50-99, 3% >100. **Special facilities:** Aquatic ecology laboratory, science and anthropological museums, veterinary pathology laboratory, fine arts museum, reading and writing laboratories, math and language computer laboratories, supercomputer.

Freshman class profile. 10,081 applied, 6,983 admitted, 5,440 enrolled.

Mid 50% test scores			
SAT critical reading:	550-660	GPA 2.0-2.99:	1%
SAT math:	570-680	Rank in top quarter:	83%
ACT composite:	25-30	Rank in top tenth:	49%
GPA 3.75 or higher:	62%	Return as sophomores:	83%
GPA 3.50-3.74:	24%	Out-of-state:	67%
GPA 3.0-3.49:	13%	Live on campus:	76%
		International:	1%

Basis for selection. School achievement record, test scores, endorsements and recommendations important. Students must maintain ideals and standards in harmony with The Church of Jesus Christ of Latter-Day Saints. Interview is ecclesiastical. **Learning Disabled:** Untimed ACT accepted.

High school preparation. Required and recommended units include English 4, mathematics 3-4, history 2, science 2-3 (laboratory 2-3), foreign language 2-4, computer science 1 and visual/performing arts 1. 2 units of literature/writing required.

2009-2010 Annual costs. Tuition/fees: $4,290. Tuition is $8,580 for nonmembers of The Church of Jesus Christ of Latter-day Saints. Undergraduate per-credit-hour charge $440 for nonmembers. Room/board: $6,840. Books/supplies: $1,000. Personal expenses: $1,961.

2008-2009 Financial aid. Need-based: 1,975 full-time freshmen applied for aid; 1,238 were judged to have need; 1,021 of these received aid. Average need met was 24%. Average scholarship/grant was $1,770; average loan $1,046. 67% of total undergraduate aid awarded as scholarships/grants, 33% as loans/jobs. **Non-need-based:** Scholarships awarded for academics, art, athletics, leadership, minority status, music/drama, religious affiliation, ROTC, state residency. **Additional information:** Students notified of scholarships on or about April 20th.

Application procedures. Admission: Closing date 2/1 (receipt date). $30 fee, may be waived for applicants with need. Admission notification on a rolling basis. **Financial aid:** Priority date 4/15; no closing date. FAFSA required. Applicants notified on a rolling basis starting 4/1.

Academics. Special study options: Accelerated study, combined bachelor's/graduate degree, cooperative education, cross-registration, distance learning, double major, ESL, external degree, honors, independent study, internships, liberal arts/career combination, study abroad, teacher certification program, Washington semester. **Credit/placement by examination:** AP, CLEP, IB, ACT, institutional tests. **Support services:** Learning center, pre-admission summer program, reduced course load, remedial instruction, study skills assistance, tutoring, writing center.

Majors. Agriculture: Crop production, food processing, food science, landscaping. **Area/ethnic studies:** American, Asian, European, German, Latin American. **Biology:** General, biochemistry, bioinformatics, biophysics, biostatistics, biotechnology, botany, conservation, exercise physiology, microbiology, molecular, physiology, wildlife. **Business:** General, accounting, actuarial science, business admin, construction management, entrepreneurial studies, finance, financial planning, information resources management, logistics, management information systems, managerial economics, marketing, organizational behavior, statistics. **Communications:** General, advertising, journalism. **Communications technology:** Animation/special effects. **Computer sciences:** Computer science, information technology. **Conservation:** Environmental science, wildlife. **Education:** Biology, chemistry, drama/dance, early childhood, elementary, English, family/consumer sciences, French, German, health, history, Latin, mathematics, music, physical, physics, science, social science, Spanish, special, technology/industrial arts. **Engineering:** Chemical, civil, computer, electrical, manufacturing, mechanical. **Family/consumer sciences:** General, facilities/event planning, family studies, family systems. **Foreign languages:** General, ancient Greek, Arabic, Biblical, Chinese, classics, comparative lit, French, German, Germanic, Italian, Japanese, Korean, Latin, linguistics, Portuguese, Russian, Spanish, translation. **Health:** Athletic training, audiology/speech pathology, clinical lab science, dietetics, nursing (RN), public health ed, recreational therapy. **History:** General. **Interdisciplinary:** Biological/physical sciences, neuroscience, nutrition sciences. **Liberal arts:** Humanities. **Math:** General, statistics. **Parks/recreation:** General, health/fitness. **Philosophy/religion:** Philosophy. **Physical sciences:** Applied physics, astronomy, chemistry, geology, hydrology, physics. **Psychology:** General. **Public administration:** Social work. **Social sciences:** Anthropology, archaeology, cartography, economics, geography, international relations, political science, sociology. **Visual/performing arts:** Acting, art, art history/conservation, ballet, dance, design, dramatic, film/cinema, graphic design, illustration, industrial design, jazz, music history, music performance, music theory/composition, photography, piano/organ, stringed instruments, studio arts, voice/opera. **Other:** Family history; genealogy, Geography: urban, rural, and environmental planning emphasis, Integrative biology, Media music studies.

Most popular majors. Biology 10%, business/marketing 16%, education 10%, family/consumer sciences 6%, foreign language 6%, social sciences 10%.

Computing on campus. 2,000 workstations in dormitories, library, computer center, student center. Dormitories wired for high-speed internet access and linked to campus network. Commuter students can connect to campus network. Online course registration, online library, helpline, repair service, student web hosting, wireless network available.

Student life. Freshman orientation: Available. Preregistration for classes offered. **Policies:** Honor code enforced. Religious observance required. **Housing:** Single-sex dorms, special housing for disabled, apartments, wellness housing available. $100 fully refundable deposit. Language houses available. **Activities:** Bands, choral groups, dance, drama, film society, literary magazine, music ensembles, musical theater, opera, radio station, student government, student newspaper, symphony orchestra, TV station, College Republicans, College Democrats, African American club, black student union, Latin American student association, international student association, Intercollegiate Knights, Circle-K International, Southeast Asian club, Baptist student union.

Athletics. NCAA. **Intercollegiate:** Baseball M, basketball, cheerleading, cross-country, diving, football (tackle) M, golf, gymnastics W, soccer W, softball W, swimming, tennis, track and field, volleyball. **Intramural:** Badminton, basketball, football (non-tackle), football (tackle), golf, racquetball, soccer, softball, tennis, volleyball, water polo, wrestling M. **Team name:** Cougars.

Student services. Chaplain/spiritual director, career counseling, services for economically disadvantaged, student employment services, financial aid counseling, health services, minority student services, personal counseling, placement for graduates, veterans' counselor, women's services. **Physically disabled:** Services for visually, speech, hearing impaired.

Contact. E-mail: admissions@byu.edu
Phone: (801) 422-2507 Fax: (801) 422-0005
Tom Gourley, Director of Admissions, Brigham Young University, A-41ASB, BYU, Provo, UT 84602

DeVry University: Sandy

Sandy, Utah

- For-profit 4-year business and technical college
- Small city
- 52 degree-seeking undergraduates: 77% part-time, 42% women, 4% Asian American, 8% Hispanic American
- 41 degree-seeking graduate students

General. Regionally accredited. **Degrees:** 8 bachelor's awarded; master's offered. **Calendar:** Semester. **Part-time faculty:** 18 total; 6% minority, 39% women.

Basis for selection. Applicants must have high school diploma or equivalent, or degree from accredited post-secondary institution, demonstrate proficiency in basic college-level skills through SAT or ACT scores or institution-administered placement examinations, and be at least 17 years of age. DeVry-administered admissions test required if SAT or ACT test scores are not submitted.

2008-2009 Annual costs. Tuition/fees: $13,930. Books/supplies: $1,300. Personal expenses: $5,082.

2007-2008 Financial aid. **Non-need-based:** Scholarships awarded for academics.

Application procedures. **Admission:** No deadline. $50 fee. Admission notification on a rolling basis. **Financial aid:** No deadline. FAFSA required. Applicants notified on a rolling basis.

Academics. **Special study options:** Accelerated study, distance learning. **Credit/placement by examination:** CLEP.

Majors. **Business:** Business admin. **Computer sciences:** Networking, systems analysis.

Contact. DeVry University: Sandy, 9350 South 150 East, Suite 420, Sandy, UT 84070

Dixie State College of Utah

St. George, Utah
new.dixie.edu CB code: 4283

- Public 4-year liberal arts college
- Commuter campus in small city
- 5,193 degree-seeking undergraduates: 35% part-time, 51% women, 1% African American, 2% Asian American, 5% Hispanic American, 1% Native American

General. Founded in 1911. Regionally accredited. **Degrees:** 150 bachelor's, 741 associate awarded. **ROTC:** Army. **Location:** 305 miles from Salt Lake City, 121 miles from Las Vegas. **Calendar:** Semester, limited summer session. **Full-time faculty:** 140 total; 51% have terminal degrees, 6% minority, 42% women. **Part-time faculty:** 192 total; 4% have terminal degrees, 53% women. **Class size:** 39% < 20, 47% 20-39, 11% 40-49, 3% 50-99, less than 1% >100.

Freshman class profile. 3,152 applied, 2,184 admitted, 1,431 enrolled.

Mid 50% test scores			
SAT critical reading:	420-520	GPA 3.0-3.49:	30%
SAT math:	430-540	GPA 2.0-2.99:	30%
SAT writing:	390-510	Rank in top quarter:	26%
ACT composite:	18-23	Rank in top tenth:	9%
GPA 3.75 or higher:	19%	Return as sophomores:	57%
GPA 3.50-3.74:	18%	Out-of-state:	3%
		International:	1%

Basis for selection. Open admission, but selective for some programs. Some health occupation programs have prerequisites. Applicants for bachelor's degrees in elementary education, business administration, CIT, and nursing must have associate degree or advance standing. Some courses use test scores combined with high school GPA as prerequisite. CPT (computerized placement test) or COMPASS may be taken in lieu of ACT/SAT. **Homeschooled:** Copy of formal letter of release from high school counselor or secondary school district that states the student is no longer required to attend secondary school required. Statement from student certifying that they have completed the equivalent of a high school diploma required.

High school preparation. College-preparatory program recommended. 16 units recommended. Recommended units include English 4, mathematics 4, history 3, science 2 (laboratory 1) and foreign language 2. One computer literacy unit recommended.

2008-2009 Annual costs. Tuition/fees: $2,893; $10,063 out-of-state. Room/board: $3,498. Books/supplies: $1,150. Personal expenses: $2,854.

2007-2008 Financial aid. **Need-based:** 522 full-time freshmen applied for aid; 420 were judged to have need; 406 of these received aid. Average need met was 44%. Average scholarship/grant was $3,994; average loan $2,838. 57% of total undergraduate aid awarded as scholarships/grants, 43% as loans/jobs. **Non-need-based:** Awarded to 1,909 full-time undergraduates, including 742 freshmen. Scholarships awarded for academics, alumni affiliation, art, athletics, leadership, minority status, music/drama, religious affiliation. **Additional information:** SunFirst Bank Scholarship for communications students; Daniels Fund Scholarship for non-traditional students based on need.

Application procedures. **Admission:** Priority date 2/15; no deadline. $35 fee. Admission notification on a rolling basis. Students who have received approval for early release from high school must provide copy of formal letter or release from high school counselor, as well as written authorization from parent or legal guardian. **Financial aid:** Priority date 3/1, closing date 5/1. FAFSA required. Applicants notified on a rolling basis starting 3/1; must reply within 2 week(s) of notification.

Academics. Bachelor's and master's degree course work from Utah's 4-year universities presented over distance-learning media and on-campus instruction. Four-year programs in business administration, computer technology, communications media, elementary education, biology, English and nursing offered on campus. **Special study options:** Accelerated study, cooperative education, distance learning, dual enrollment of high school students, ESL, honors, independent study, internships, student-designed major, study abroad, teacher certification program. **Credit/placement by examination:** AP, CLEP. 30 credit hours maximum toward associate degree, 30 toward bachelor's. **Support services:** Learning center, remedial instruction, study skills assistance, tutoring, writing center.

Majors. **Biology:** General. **Business:** Accounting, business admin. **Communications:** General. **Computer sciences:** General. **Education:** Biology, elementary, English, science. **Health:** Dental hygiene, nursing (RN). **Transportation:** Aviation management. **Other:** Integrated studies.

Most popular majors. Business/marketing 39%, communications/journalism 9%, computer/information sciences 13%, education 27%, health sciences 7%.

Computing on campus. 400 workstations in dormitories, library, computer center, student center. Dormitories wired for high-speed internet access and linked to campus network. Commuter students can connect to campus network. Online course registration, online library, helpline, repair service, wireless network available.

Student life. **Freshman orientation:** Mandatory. Preregistration for classes offered. Four-hour program held in summer. **Policies:** Stringent drug and alcohol policies. **Housing:** Coed dorms, single-sex dorms, apartments, wellness housing available. $75 fully refundable deposit. **Activities:** Bands, campus ministries, choral groups, dance, drama, international student organizations, literary magazine, music ensembles, musical theater, radio station, student government, student newspaper, symphony orchestra, TV station, international club, religious groups, Native American club, Polynesian club, political clubs, diversity club, Phi Beta Lambda.

Athletics. NCAA. **Intercollegiate:** Baseball M, basketball, cross-country, football (tackle) M, golf M, soccer, softball W, tennis W, volleyball W. **Intramural:** Badminton, basketball, bowling, football (non-tackle), golf, racquetball, soccer, softball, swimming, tennis, volleyball, water polo, weight lifting, wrestling M.

Student services. Adult student services, alcohol/substance abuse counseling, career counseling, services for economically disadvantaged, student employment services, financial aid counseling, health services, minority student services, personal counseling, placement for graduates, veterans' counselor. **Physically disabled:** Services for visually, speech, hearing impaired.

Contact. Phone: (435) 652-7708 Toll-free number: (888) 462-3494
Fax: (435) 656-4005
Brandon Boulter, Director of Admissions, Dixie State College of Utah, 225 South 700 East, St. George, UT 84770-3876

Independence University

Salt Lake City, Utah
www.independence.edu

- For-profit 4-year health science college
- Commuter campus in small city
- 1,200 full-time, degree-seeking undergraduates

General. Founded in 1975. Accredited by DETC. Primarily serves home-study students. **Degrees:** 36 bachelor's, 121 associate awarded; master's offered. **Calendar:** Continuous. **Full-time faculty:** 10 total. **Part-time faculty:** 100 total.

Basis for selection. Open admission.

Financial aid. **Additional information:** Financial aid available for resident students only, not correspondence students.

Application procedures. **Admission:** No deadline. $50 fee. Admission notification on a rolling basis. **Financial aid:** No deadline. FAFSA required.

Academics. **Special study options:** Distance learning, liberal arts/career combination. **Credit/placement by examination:** CLEP. 30 credit hours maximum toward associate degree, 30 toward bachelor's. **Support services:** Tutoring.

Majors. **Business:** General, accounting, marketing. **Health:** Health care admin.

Most popular majors. Business/marketing 11%, health sciences 89%.

Student life. **Activities:** Student newspaper.

Student services. Adult student services.

Contact. E-mail: admissns@cchs.edu
Phone: (800) 972-5149 Toll-free number: (800) 972-5149
Independence University, 5295 South Commerce Drive Suite G-50, Salt Lake City, UT 84107

ITT Technical Institute: Murray

Murray, Utah
www.itt-tech.edu **CB code: 3601**

- For-profit 4-year technical college
- Commuter campus in small city

General. Founded in 1984. Accredited by ACICS. **Location:** 10 miles from Salt Lake City. **Calendar:** Quarter.

Contact. Phone: (801) 263-3313
Director of Recruitment, 920 West LeVoy Drive, Murray, UT 84123

Neumont University

South Jordan, Utah
www.neumont.edu **CB code: 4516**

- For-profit 4-year engineering and technical college
- Residential campus in very large city
- 267 degree-seeking undergraduates
- SAT or ACT (ACT writing optional), application essay, interview required

General. Accredited by ACICS. **Degrees:** 88 bachelor's awarded; master's offered. **Location:** 20 miles from Salt Lake City. **Calendar:** Quarter, extensive summer session. **Full-time faculty:** 17 total. **Part-time faculty:** 25 total.

Freshman class profile.

Return as sophomores:	64%	**Live on campus:**	50%
Out-of-state:	50%		

Basis for selection. High school GPA, SAT and/or ACT scores, specific computer experience, and interest and motivation for the program considered in admissions process. **Homeschooled:** State high school equivalency certificate required.

2009-2010 Annual costs. Tuition/fees (projected): $28,935. Room/board: $1,272.

Application procedures. **Admission:** No deadline. $35 fee, may be waived for applicants with need. Admission notification on a rolling basis. **Financial aid:** No deadline.

Academics. **Special study options:** Accelerated study, internships. **Credit/placement by examination:** AP, CLEP. **Support services:** Remedial instruction, study skills assistance, tutoring.

Majors. **Computer sciences:** Computer science.

Computing on campus. PC or laptop required. Commuter students can connect to campus network. Online library, helpline, repair service, student web hosting, wireless network available.

Student life. **Freshman orientation:** Mandatory. Preregistration for classes offered. **Housing:** Guaranteed on-campus for all undergraduates. Apartments available. $275 deposit. **Activities:** Student government.

Student services. Career counseling, financial aid counseling, placement for graduates.

Contact. E-mail: admissions@neumont.edu
Phone: (801) 302-2800 Toll-free number: (888) 638-6668
Fax: (801) 302-2880
Charlie Parker, Dean of Admissions, Neumont University, 10701 South River Front Parkway, Suite 300, South Jordan, UT 84095

Southern Utah University

Cedar City, Utah **CB member**
www.suu.edu **CB code: 4092**

- Public 4-year university
- Residential campus in large town
- 5,434 degree-seeking undergraduates: 12% part-time, 57% women, 1% African American, 2% Asian American, 4% Hispanic American, 2% Native American, 1% international
- 732 degree-seeking graduate students
- 72% of applicants admitted
- SAT or ACT (ACT writing optional) required
- 39% graduate within 6 years

General. Founded in 1897. Regionally accredited. **Degrees:** 880 bachelor's, 209 associate awarded; master's offered. **ROTC:** Army. **Location:** 265 miles from Salt Lake City, 160 miles from Las Vegas. **Calendar:** Semester, extensive summer session. **Full-time faculty:** 229 total; 76% have terminal degrees, 13% minority, 32% women. **Part-time faculty:** 95 total; 28% have terminal degrees, 13% minority, 50% women. **Class size:** 44% < 20, 43% 20-39, 6% 40-49, 6% 50-99, 2% >100. **Special facilities:** Natural life museum, observatory, Shakespearean theater.

Freshman class profile. 3,282 applied, 2,359 admitted, 1,244 enrolled.

Mid 50% test scores		**GPA 2.0-2.99:**	15%
SAT critical reading:	450-580	**Rank in top quarter:**	54%
SAT math:	440-580	**Rank in top tenth:**	29%
ACT composite:	18-25	**Out-of-state:**	19%
GPA 3.75 or higher:	33%	**Live on campus:**	41%
GPA 3.50-3.74:	22%	**Fraternities:**	4%
GPA 3.0-3.49:	30%	**Sororities:**	4%

Basis for selection. Admission based on GPA and ACT/SAT scores.

High school preparation. College-preparatory program recommended. Recommended units include English 4, mathematics 3, social studies 3, science 3 (laboratory 1) and foreign language 2. 1 unit of social studies must be U.S. history and government; 2 math units must be elementary algebra or above; English units should have a composition and literature emphasis.

2008-2009 Annual costs. Tuition/fees: $4,028; $12,086 out-of-state. Room/board: $5,238.

2007-2008 Financial aid. **Need-based:** 743 full-time freshmen applied for aid; 591 were judged to have need; 586 of these received aid. Average need met was 64%. Average scholarship/grant was $4,450; average loan $3,141. 47% of total undergraduate aid awarded as scholarships/grants, 53% as loans/jobs. **Non-need-based:** Awarded to 2,859 full-time undergraduates, including 1,034 freshmen. Scholarships awarded for academics, alumni affiliation, art, athletics, job skills, leadership, minority status, music/drama, state residency.

Application procedures. **Admission:** Closing date 8/1. $40 fee. Admission notification on a rolling basis. **Financial aid:** No deadline. FAFSA, institutional form required. Applicants notified on a rolling basis starting 11/1.

Academics. **Special study options:** Combined bachelor's/graduate degree, cooperative education, distance learning, double major, ESL, honors, independent study, internships, liberal arts/career combination, teacher certification program, weekend college. **Credit/placement by examination:** AP, CLEP, ACT. 25 credit hours maximum toward associate degree, 25 toward bachelor's. **Support services:** Learning center, pre-admission summer program, reduced course load, remedial instruction, study skills assistance, tutoring, writing center.

Majors. **Agriculture:** General, business. **Biology:** General. **Business:** Accounting, business admin, finance, hospitality admin, management information systems, managerial economics, marketing. **Communications:** General. **Computer sciences:** General, computer science. **Conservation:** Forestry.

Construction: Site management. **Education:** General, art, biology, business, chemistry, drama/dance, elementary, English, family/consumer sciences, foreign languages, French, German, history, learning disabled, mathematics, music, physical, science, secondary, social science, Spanish, special, speech, technology/industrial arts, trade/industrial. **Engineering:** General, science. **Engineering technology:** General. **Family/consumer sciences:** General, human nutrition. **Foreign languages:** French, German. **Health:** Athletic training, nursing (RN), premedicine, prepharmacy, preveterinary. **History:** General. **Legal studies:** Prelaw. **Math:** General. **Parks/recreation:** General. **Philosophy/religion:** Philosophy. **Physical sciences:** Geology. **Protective services:** Police science. **Psychology:** General. **Social sciences:** General, economics, political science, sociology. **Visual/performing arts:** Art, commercial/advertising art, dance, dramatic, music performance, studio arts. **Other:** Pre-medical technology.

Most popular majors. Biology 6%, business/marketing 16%, communications/journalism 6%, education 20%, health sciences 10%, psychology 8%, visual/performing arts 6%.

Computing on campus. 300 workstations in dormitories, library, computer center. Dormitories wired for high-speed internet access and linked to campus network. Commuter students can connect to campus network. Online library, helpline, wireless network available.

Student life. Freshman orientation: Mandatory. Preregistration for classes offered. One-day program held throughout summer. Parents welcome and encouraged to attend. **Housing:** Coed dorms, single-sex dorms, special housing for disabled, apartments, fraternity/sorority housing available. $200 fully refundable deposit. **Activities:** Bands, choral groups, dance, drama, literary magazine, music ensembles, musical theater, opera, radio station, student government, student newspaper, symphony orchestra, TV station, intercultural club, LDSSA, Newman Club, Campus Christian Fellowship, College Republicans, College Democrats.

Athletics. NAIA, NCAA. **Intercollegiate:** Badminton, baseball M, basketball, cross-country, football (tackle) M, golf M, gymnastics W, rodeo, soccer W, softball W, tennis W, track and field. **Intramural:** Badminton, basketball, golf, soccer, tennis, volleyball. **Team name:** Thunderbirds.

Student services. Career counseling, student employment services, health services, minority student services, personal counseling, placement for graduates, veterans' counselor. **Physically disabled:** Services for speech impaired.

Contact. E-mail: adminfo@suu.edu
Phone: (435) 586-7740 Fax: (435) 865-8223
Stephen Allen, Director of Admissions, Southern Utah University, 351 West Center Street, Cedar City, UT 84720

Stevens-Henager College: Logan

Logan, Utah
www.stevenshenager.edu

- For-profit 4-year business and technical college
- Large town

General. Accredited by ACCSCT. **Calendar:** Continuous.

Contact. Phone: (435) 713-4777
755 South Highway 89-91, Logan, UT 84321

Stevens-Henager College: Murray

Salt Lake City, Utah
www.stevenshenager.edu

- For-profit 4-year business and health science college
- Commuter campus in large town
- 670 degree-seeking undergraduates
- Interview required

General. Accredited by ACCSCT. **Degrees:** 65 bachelor's, 95 associate awarded; master's offered. **Location:** 5 Miles from Salt Lake City. **Calendar:** Continuous. **Full-time faculty:** 9 total. **Part-time faculty:** 20 total.

Basis for selection. Open admission, but selective for some programs. Consideration given to secondary school record, GPA, recommendations, test scores, interview, residency and level of interest. **Homeschooled:** State high school equivalency certificate required.

2008-2009 Annual costs. Tuition for academic year varies by program from $15,000 - $16,500.

2008-2009 Financial aid. Additional information: Financial aid application must be completed prior to enrollment.

Application procedures. Admission: No deadline. No application fee. Admission notification on a rolling basis. **Financial aid:** No deadline.

Academics. Credit/placement by examination: CLEP.

Majors. Business: Accounting technology, business admin. **Computer sciences:** General. **Health:** Health care admin.

Computing on campus. Commuter students can connect to campus network. Online library available.

Student life. Freshman orientation: Mandatory.

Student services. Adult student services, career counseling, financial aid counseling, placement for graduates.

Contact. Phone: (800) 622-2640 Fax: (801) 262-7660
Ken Reynolds, Admissions Director, Stevens-Henager College: Murray, 383 West Vine Street, Salt Lake City, UT 84123

Stevens-Henager College: Ogden

Ogden, Utah
www.stevenshenager.edu **CB code: 4751**

- For-profit 4-year liberal arts college
- Commuter campus in small city
- 395 degree-seeking undergraduates
- 5 graduate students
- Interview required

General. Accredited by ACCSCT. **Degrees:** 48 bachelor's, 54 associate awarded. **Location:** 35 miles from Salt Lake City. **Calendar:** Continuous. **Full-time faculty:** 15 total. **Part-time faculty:** 15 total.

Basis for selection. Open admission, but selective for some programs. Special requirements for surgical technology program.

High school preparation. Recommended units include history 4.

2008-2009 Annual costs. Tuition/fees: $19,933. Tuition and fees vary by program. Personal expenses: $4,000.

Application procedures. Admission: No deadline. No application fee. Application must be submitted on paper. Admission notification on a rolling basis.

Academics. Special study options: Accelerated study, cooperative education, distance learning, liberal arts/career combination. **Credit/placement by examination:** AP, CLEP. **Support services:** Tutoring.

Majors. Business: Accounting, business admin. **Computer sciences:** General. **Health:** Health care admin.

Computing on campus. 15 workstations in library, computer center. Commuter students can connect to campus network. Online library available.

Student life. Freshman orientation: Mandatory. **Housing:** Single-sex dorms available. $100 deposit.

Student services. Financial aid counseling, placement for graduates.

Contact. Phone: (801) 394-7791 Fax: (801) 621-0853
Cynthia Williams, Director of Admissions, Stevens-Henager College: Ogden, 1890 South 1350 West, Ogden, UT 84401

Stevens-Henager College: Orem

Orem, Utah
www.stevenshenager.edu

- For-profit 4-year business and health science college
- Large city
- 600 degree-seeking undergraduates

General. Founded in 1891. Accredited by ACCSCT. **Degrees:** 100 bachelor's, 100 associate awarded; master's offered. **Location:** 35 miles from Salt Lake City. **Calendar:** Continuous. **Full-time faculty:** 10 total. **Part-time faculty:** 20 total. **Special facilities:** Job placement.

Freshman class profile.

Out-of-state:	10%	**Live on campus:**	16%

Basis for selection. Open admission.

2008-2009 Annual costs. Personal expenses: $2,123.

Application procedures. Admission: No deadline. No application fee. Admission notification on a rolling basis. **Financial aid:** No deadline. Applicants notified on a rolling basis; must reply within 3 week(s) of notification.

Academics. Special study options: Accelerated study, dual enrollment of high school students, ESL, independent study, internships. **Credit/placement by examination:** AP, CLEP, institutional tests. **Support services:** Reduced course load, tutoring.

Majors. Business: Accounting, business admin.

Computing on campus. 26 workstations in library, computer center.

Student life. Freshman orientation: Mandatory. **Housing:** Single-sex dorms available. **Activities:** Student government, Future Business Leaders Association, Latter-day Saints student association.

Student services. Career counseling, student employment services, personal counseling, placement for graduates.

Contact. E-mail: jhafen@sfcn.org
Phone: (801) 375-5455 Fax: (801) 375-9836
Daniel Write, Director of Admissions, Stevens-Henager College: Orem, 1476 South Sand Hill Road, Orem, UT 84058

University of Utah

Salt Lake City, Utah — **CB member**
www.utah.edu — **CB code: 4853**

- Public 4-year university
- Commuter campus in very large city
- 20,475 degree-seeking undergraduates: 30% part-time, 45% women, 1% African American, 6% Asian American, 5% Hispanic American, 1% Native American, 3% international
- 6,685 degree-seeking graduate students
- 81% of applicants admitted
- SAT or ACT (ACT writing optional) required
- 51% graduate within 6 years

General. Founded in 1850. Regionally accredited. **Degrees:** 4,882 bachelor's awarded; master's, doctoral, first professional offered. **ROTC:** Army, Naval, Air Force. **Location:** 2 miles from downtown. **Calendar:** Semester, limited summer session. **Full-time faculty:** 1,276 total; 82% have terminal degrees, 11% minority, 40% women. **Part-time faculty:** 651 total; 34% have terminal degrees, 6% minority, 43% women. **Class size:** 45% < 20, 34% 20-39, 6% 40-49, 11% 50-99, 4% >100. **Special facilities:** Arboretum, fine arts museum, natural history museum, architecture exhibition hall, Olympic Cauldron Park, cancer research institute.

Freshman class profile. 7,234 applied, 5,868 admitted, 2,995 enrolled.

Mid 50% test scores		**Rank in top quarter:**	49%
SAT critical reading:	490-610	**Rank in top tenth:**	29%
SAT math:	500-640	**End year in good standing:**	88%
SAT writing:	470-610	**Return as sophomores:**	83%
ACT composite:	21-27	**Out-of-state:**	30%
GPA 3.75 or higher:	37%	**Live on campus:**	35%
GPA 3.50-3.74:	20%	**International:**	3%
GPA 3.0-3.49:	32%	**Fraternities:**	2%
GPA 2.0-2.99:	11%	**Sororities:**	4%

Basis for selection. High school course requirements, admissions index using high school GPA and test scores important. Recommendations and extracurricular activities considered. Audition required for dance, drama, music programs; portfolio required for art program. **Homeschooled:** 23 ACT or 1060 SAT (exclusive of Writing), high school transcript, 550 GED required. Students who graduate from non-accredited high school with test score in upper quartile (25 ACT, 1140 SAT), with no individual score below freshman class average, will not be required to take GED. **Learning Disabled:** Disclosure of learning disabilities not required; Center for Disability Services assists students with disabilities in the admission process.

High school preparation. 16 units required. Required units include English 4, mathematics 2, history 1, science 3 (laboratory 2), foreign language 2 and academic electives 4. 4 units from at least 2 of the following: history, English, math beyond algebra, laboratory science, foreign language, social science, fine arts.

2008-2009 Annual costs. Tuition/fees: $5,285; $16,601 out-of-state. Room/board: $5,972. Books/supplies: $1,080. Personal expenses: $4,032.

2008-2009 Financial aid. Need-based: 1,033 full-time freshmen applied for aid; 715 were judged to have need; 707 of these received aid. Average need met was 57%. Average scholarship/grant was $5,896; average loan $4,050. 36% of total undergraduate aid awarded as scholarships/grants, 64% as loans/jobs. **Non-need-based:** Awarded to 885 full-time undergraduates, including 265 freshmen. Scholarships awarded for academics, alumni affiliation, art, athletics, leadership, minority status, music/drama, ROTC, state residency.

Application procedures. Admission: Priority date 2/15; deadline 4/1 (postmark date). $35 fee. Admission notification on a rolling basis. **Financial aid:** Closing date 3/15. FAFSA, institutional form required. Applicants notified on a rolling basis starting 4/15; must reply within 6 week(s) of notification.

Academics. Special study options: Accelerated study, combined bachelor's/graduate degree, cooperative education, distance learning, double major, ESL, exchange student, honors, independent study, internships, liberal arts/career combination, student-designed major, study abroad, teacher certification program, Washington semester. **Credit/placement by examination:** AP, CLEP, IB, SAT, ACT, institutional tests. 32 credit hours maximum toward bachelor's degree. **Support services:** Learning center, pre-admission summer program, reduced course load, remedial instruction, study skills assistance, tutoring, writing center.

Majors. Architecture: Architecture. **Area/ethnic studies:** Asian, Near/Middle Eastern, women's. **Biology:** General, cell/histology. **Business:** General, accounting, business admin, entrepreneurial studies, finance, management information systems, marketing. **Communications:** General, media studies. **Computer sciences:** Computer science. **Conservation:** Environmental science, environmental studies. **Education:** Art, biology, chemistry, drama/dance, elementary, English, foreign languages, French, geography, German, health, history, mathematics, multi-level teacher, music, psychology, science, social science, social studies, Spanish, special, speech. **Engineering:** General, biomedical, chemical, civil, computer, electrical, geological, materials, mechanical, metallurgical, mining. **Family/consumer sciences:** Consumer economics, family resources, family studies. **Foreign languages:** Arabic, Chinese, classics, French, German, Hebrew, Japanese, linguistics, Persian, Russian, Spanish. **Health:** Audiology/speech pathology, clinical lab science, health services, nursing (RN), public health ed. **History:** General. **Interdisciplinary:** Global studies. **Liberal arts:** Humanities. **Math:** General. **Parks/recreation:** General, exercise sciences, health/fitness. **Philosophy/religion:** Philosophy. **Physical sciences:** General, chemistry, geology, geophysics, meteorology, physics. **Psychology:** General. **Public administration:** Social work. **Social sciences:** General, anthropology, economics, geography, political science, sociology, urban studies. **Visual/performing arts:** General, art, art history/conservation, ballet, dance, dramatic, film/cinema. **Other:** Pharmacy.

Most popular majors. Business/marketing 12%, communications/journalism 9%, engineering/engineering technologies 6%, health sciences 8%, social sciences 19%, visual/performing arts 6%.

Computing on campus. 8,800 workstations in dormitories, library, computer center, student center. Dormitories wired for high-speed internet access and linked to campus network. Commuter students can connect to campus network. Online course registration, online library, helpline, repair service, student web hosting, wireless network available.

Student life. Freshman orientation: Mandatory. Preregistration for classes offered. One-day, 2-day, and 4-day programs offered before fall semester. Late orientations offered in August and mini-orientations held the first day of class. Some orientation options have fees. **Housing:** Single-sex dorms, special housing for disabled, apartments, fraternity/sorority housing, wellness housing available. $100 partly refundable deposit, deadline 3/28. Limited visitation, 24-hour quiet housing available. **Activities:** Bands, choral groups, dance, drama, film society, literary magazine, music ensembles, musical theater, opera, radio station, student government, student newspaper, symphony orchestra, TV station, political and religious groups, ethnic clubs, outdoor clubs, community service organization.

Athletics. NCAA. **Intercollegiate:** Baseball M, basketball, cheerleading, cross-country W, diving, football (tackle) M, golf M, gymnastics W, skiing, soccer W, softball W, swimming, tennis, track and field W, volleyball W. **Intramural:** Fencing, lacrosse, racquetball, rugby M, soccer M, volleyball M, water polo M. **Team name:** Utes.

Student services. Adult student services, alcohol/substance abuse counseling, chaplain/spiritual director, career counseling, student employment services, financial aid counseling, health services, minority student services, on-campus daycare, personal counseling, placement for graduates, veterans' counselor, women's services. **Physically disabled:** Services for visually, speech, hearing impaired.

Contact. E-mail: admissions@sa.utah.edu
Phone: (801) 581-7281 Fax: (801) 585-7864
Timothy Ebner, Associate Vice President of Enrollment Management, University of Utah, 201 South 1460 East, Room 250 S, Salt Lake City, UT 84112-9057

Utah State University

Logan, Utah **CB member**
www.usu.edu **CB code: 4857**

- Public 4-year university
- Residential campus in small city
- 13,251 degree-seeking undergraduates: 16% part-time, 49% women, 1% African American, 2% Asian American, 3% Hispanic American, 1% Native American, 4% international
- 1,607 degree-seeking graduate students
- 97% of applicants admitted
- SAT or ACT (ACT writing optional) required

General. Founded in 1888. Regionally accredited. **Degrees:** 2,844 bachelor's, 15 associate awarded; master's, doctoral offered. **ROTC:** Army, Air Force. **Location:** 80 miles from Salt Lake City. **Calendar:** Semester, extensive summer session. **Full-time faculty:** 744 total; 86% have terminal degrees, 6% minority, 32% women. **Part-time faculty:** 201 total; 6% minority, 53% women. **Class size:** 38% < 20, 38% 20-39, 8% 40-49, 10% 50-99, 6% >100. **Special facilities:** Agricultural experiment stations, water research laboratory, space shuttle experiments, forestry research facility, botanical gardens, teaching greenhouse, research park, laboratory school, off-campus theater performance lab, anthropology museum.

Freshman class profile. 5,951 applied, 5,799 admitted, 2,762 enrolled.

Mid 50% test scores		**GPA 2.0-2.99:**	12%
SAT critical reading:	470-600	**Rank in top quarter:**	49%
SAT math:	470-610	**Rank in top tenth:**	23%
ACT composite:	21-27	**Out-of-state:**	21%
GPA 3.75 or higher:	41%	**International:**	2%
GPA 3.50-3.74:	22%	**Fraternities:**	2%
GPA 3.0-3.49:	25%	**Sororities:**	2%

Basis for selection. High school record, test scores most important. Audition required for music; portfolio required for art. **Homeschooled:** Early entry policy applies: junior equivalent, letters of approval. **Learning Disabled:** Recent documentation/diagnosis required for special consideration.

High school preparation. College-preparatory program required. Required and recommended units include English 4, mathematics 3, history 1, science 3 (laboratory 1), foreign language 2 and academic electives 4. Some social studies electives required.

2008-2009 Annual costs. Tuition/fees: $4,445; $12,951 out-of-state. Room/board: $4,650. Books/supplies: $1,150. Personal expenses: $2,100.

2008-2009 Financial aid. **Need-based:** 1,211 full-time freshmen applied for aid; 872 were judged to have need; 854 of these received aid. Average need met was 68%. Average scholarship/grant was $3,850; average loan $3,300. 51% of total undergraduate aid awarded as scholarships/grants, 49% as loans/jobs. **Non-need-based:** Awarded to 2,716 full-time undergraduates, including 638 freshmen. Scholarships awarded for academics, alumni affiliation, art, athletics, leadership, minority status, music/drama, religious affiliation, ROTC.

Application procedures. **Admission:** Priority date 4/1; no deadline. $40 fee. Admission notification on a rolling basis. **Financial aid:** No deadline. FAFSA required. Applicants notified on a rolling basis starting 4/1; must reply within 4 week(s) of notification.

Academics. **Special study options:** Accelerated study, cooperative education, cross-registration, distance learning, double major, dual enrollment of high school students, ESL, exchange student, honors, independent study, internships, liberal arts/career combination, student-designed major, study abroad, teacher certification program, weekend college. **Credit/placement by examination:** AP, CLEP, IB, SAT, ACT, institutional tests. 16 credits of lower division course work per language. **Support services:** Learning center, pre-admission summer program, reduced course load, remedial instruction, study skills assistance, tutoring, writing center.

Majors. **Agriculture:** Agronomy, animal sciences, business, dairy, economics, equipment technology, food science, horticultural science, ornamental horticulture, range science, soil science. **Architecture:** Landscape. **Area/ethnic studies:** American, Asian. **Biology:** General, botany, ecology, entomology, zoology. **Business:** General, accounting, administrative services, business admin, fashion, finance, human resources, marketing, operations. **Communications:** Journalism. **Computer sciences:** General, information systems. **Conservation:** Forestry, wildlife. **Education:** Agricultural, biology, business, chemistry, early childhood, elementary, family/consumer sciences, health, mathematics, multi-level teacher, music, physical, physics, sales/marketing, science, secondary, social studies, special, technology/industrial arts, voc/tech. **Engineering:** General, aerospace, agricultural, civil, computer, electrical, environmental, mechanical. **Engineering technology:** Electrical. **Family/consumer sciences:** Clothing/textiles, family studies, food/nutrition, housing. **Foreign languages:** French, German, Spanish. **Health:** Audiology/speech pathology, clinical lab science, music therapy, predental, premedicine, preveterinary. **History:** General. **Legal studies:** Prelaw. **Liberal arts:** Arts/sciences. **Math:** General, statistics. **Mechanic/repair:** Aircraft. **Parks/recreation:** General, facilities management. **Philosophy/religion:** Philosophy. **Physical sciences:** Chemistry, geology, hydrology, physics. **Psychology:** General. **Public administration:** Social work. **Social sciences:** Anthropology, economics, geography, political science, sociology. **Visual/performing arts:** Art, dance, dramatic, interior design.

Most popular majors. Business/marketing 17%, education 16%, engineering/engineering technologies 8%, interdisciplinary studies 7%, social sciences 6%.

Computing on campus. 910 workstations in dormitories, library, computer center, student center. Dormitories wired for high-speed internet access and linked to campus network. Commuter students can connect to campus network. Online course registration, helpline, repair service, student web hosting available.

Student life. **Freshman orientation:** Mandatory, $25 fee. Preregistration for classes offered. Half-day, 1-, 2- and 4-day sessions available in June and July. **Housing:** Coed dorms, single-sex dorms, special housing for disabled, apartments, fraternity/sorority housing, wellness housing available. $150 partly refundable deposit, deadline 3/15. Mobile home park available. **Activities:** Bands, choral groups, drama, music ensembles, musical theater, opera, radio station, student government, student newspaper, symphony orchestra, TV station, Latter-day Saints, Catholic, Lutheran, Baptist student organizations; Crusade for Christ; Christian Fellowship; black student union; Hispanic student union; Native American student union; Polynesian student union; Asian American student union.

Athletics. NCAA. **Intercollegiate:** Basketball, cross-country, football (tackle) M, golf M, gymnastics W, soccer W, softball W, tennis, track and field, volleyball W. **Intramural:** Badminton, basketball, cross-country, football (non-tackle), golf, racquetball, soccer, softball, table tennis, tennis, triathlon, volleyball. **Team name:** Aggies.

Student services. Adult student services, alcohol/substance abuse counseling, career counseling, student employment services, financial aid counseling, health services, minority student services, on-campus daycare, personal counseling, placement for graduates, veterans' counselor, women's services. **Physically disabled:** Services for visually, speech, hearing impaired.

Contact. E-mail: admit@usu.edu
Phone: (435) 797-1079 Toll-free number: (800) 488-8108
Fax: (435) 797-3708
Jenn Putnam, Director of Admissions, Utah State University, 0160 Old Main Hill, Logan, UT 84322-0160

Utah Valley University

Orem, Utah
www.uvu.edu **CB code: 4870**

- Public 4-year university and technical college
- Commuter campus in small city
- 21,857 degree-seeking undergraduates: 43% part-time, 42% women, 1% African American, 3% Asian American, 6% Hispanic American, 1% Native American, 2% international
- 20 degree-seeking graduate students

General. Founded in 1941. Regionally accredited. Access to libraries at Brigham Young University. **Degrees:** 1,532 bachelor's, 1,716 associate awarded; master's offered. **ROTC:** Army, Air Force. **Location:** 45 miles from Salt Lake City. **Calendar:** Semester, limited summer session. **Full-time faculty:** 482 total; 10% minority, 34% women. **Part-time faculty:** 995 total; 4% minority, 28% women. **Class size:** 42% < 20, 48% 20-39, 4% 40-49, 5% 50-99, less than 1% >100. **Special facilities:** Provo airport campus.

Freshman class profile. 5,192 applied, 5,192 admitted, 3,697 enrolled.

Mid 50% test scores			
SAT critical reading:	420-540	GPA 3.0-3.49:	31%
SAT math:	410-580	GPA 2.0-2.99:	28%
SAT writing:	410-530	Rank in top quarter:	28%
ACT composite:	18-23	Rank in top tenth:	9%
GPA 3.75 or higher:	19%	Return as sophomores:	43%
GPA 3.50-3.74:	18%	Out-of-state:	15%
		International:	2%

Basis for selection. Open admission. Students admitted without ACT/SAT scores, but all students under 21 must complete ACT/SAT prior to registration for placement. ACT/SAT score minimums (19 ACT English and Math, 500 SAT Verbal and Math) required or must take New Student Assessment prior to being cleared for registrations. **Homeschooled:** State high school equivalency certificate required. **Learning Disabled:** Students with learning disabilities may apply for reasonable accommodations and assistance through the Accessibility Services Department.

2008-2009 Annual costs. Tuition/fees: $3,752; $11,514 out-of-state. Books/supplies: $1,562. Personal expenses: $2,914.

2008-2009 Financial aid. Need-based: 1,161 full-time freshmen applied for aid; 1,003 were judged to have need; 888 of these received aid. Average need met was 64%. Average scholarship/grant was $4,104; average loan $3,397. 32% of total undergraduate aid awarded as scholarships/grants, 68% as loans/jobs. **Non-need-based:** Awarded to 226 full-time undergraduates, including 49 freshmen. Scholarships awarded for academics, alumni affiliation, art, athletics, job skills, leadership, minority status, music/drama, religious affiliation, ROTC, state residency.

Application procedures. Admission: Closing date 8/15. $35 fee, may be waived for applicants with need. Admission notification on a rolling basis. **Financial aid:** Priority date 5/1; no closing date. FAFSA, institutional form required. Applicants notified on a rolling basis starting 5/15; must reply within 2 week(s) of notification.

Academics. Special study options: Cooperative education, distance learning, double major, dual enrollment of high school students, ESL, honors, independent study, internships, student-designed major, study abroad, teacher certification program, weekend college. Evening school, internet programs. **Credit/placement by examination:** AP, CLEP, IB, SAT, ACT, institutional tests. 16 credit hours maximum toward associate degree, 16 toward bachelor's. No more than 25% of credits applied toward associate degree, diploma, or certificate may be awarded through challenge credit. **Support services:** Learning center, reduced course load, remedial instruction, study skills assistance, tutoring, writing center.

Majors. Biology: General, biotechnology. **Business:** Accounting, business admin, hospitality admin, operations. **Communications:** General. **Computer sciences:** General, computer science, data processing, web page design. **Education:** Biology, business, chemistry, drama/dance, early childhood, elementary, English, health, history, kindergarten/preschool, mathematics, music, physical, science, Spanish. **Foreign languages:** American Sign Language, Spanish. **Health:** Community health, nursing (RN). **History:** General. **Legal studies:** Paralegal. **Math:** General. **Parks/recreation:** Health/fitness. **Philosophy/religion:** Philosophy. **Physical sciences:** Chemistry, physics. **Protective services:** Fire services admin, forensics, law enforcement admin. **Psychology:** General. **Social sciences:** Economics, political science. **Transportation:** Airline/commercial pilot. **Visual/performing arts:** Dance, design, dramatic.

Most popular majors. Business/marketing 27%, computer/information sciences 7%, education 16%, psychology 12%, trade and industry 9%.

Computing on campus. 1,000 workstations in library, computer center, student center. Commuter students can connect to campus network. Online course registration, online library, helpline, repair service, wireless network available.

Student life. Freshman orientation: Mandatory. Three-day adventure session in mountain setting with river rafting, rock climbing. On-campus session also available. **Activities:** Bands, choral groups, dance, drama, international student organizations, literary magazine, music ensembles, musical theater, student government, student newspaper, symphony orchestra, TV station, Baptist student union, black student union, German club, international student council, Japan club, Latin American club, Latter-day Saint student association, multi-cultural voices, Native Sun, Russian club.

Athletics. NCAA. **Intercollegiate:** Baseball M, basketball, cross-country, golf, soccer W, softball W, track and field, volleyball W, wrestling M. **Intramural:** Football (tackle). **Team name:** Wolverines.

Student services. Adult student services, alcohol/substance abuse counseling, career counseling, services for economically disadvantaged, student employment services, financial aid counseling, health services, legal services, minority student services, on-campus daycare, personal counseling, placement for graduates, veterans' counselor, women's services. **Physically disabled:** Services for visually, speech, hearing impaired.

Contact. E-mail: info@uvsc.edu
Phone: (801) 863-8466 Fax: (801) 225-4677
Liz Childs, Director of Admissions, Utah Valley University, 800 West University Parkway, Orem, UT 84058-5999

Weber State University

Ogden, Utah — **CB member**
www.weber.edu — **CB code: 4941**

- Public 4-year university
- Commuter campus in small city
- 16,831 degree-seeking undergraduates: 44% part-time, 51% women, 1% African American, 3% Asian American, 5% Hispanic American, 1% Native American, 1% international
- 518 degree-seeking graduate students
- 41% graduate within 6 years

General. Founded in 1889. Regionally accredited. **Degrees:** 1,881 bachelor's, 1,677 associate awarded; master's offered. **ROTC:** Army, Naval, Air Force. **Location:** 35 miles from Salt Lake City. **Calendar:** Semester, extensive summer session. **Full-time faculty:** 460 total; 85% have terminal degrees, 10% minority, 41% women. **Part-time faculty:** 436 total. **Class size:** 58% < 20, 34% 20-39, 3% 40-49, 4% 50-99, less than 1% >100. **Special facilities:** Museum of natural history, planetarium, aerospace technology center.

Freshman class profile. 4,297 applied, 4,297 admitted, 2,439 enrolled.

Mid 50% test scores			
ACT composite:	18-24	Return as sophomores:	70%
GPA 3.75 or higher:	21%	Out-of-state:	2%
GPA 3.50-3.74:	17%	Live on campus:	4%
GPA 3.0-3.49:	29%	International:	2%
GPA 2.0-2.99:	28%	Fraternities:	1%
		Sororities:	1%

Basis for selection. Open admission, but selective for some programs. Special requirements for nursing, dental health, health professions.

High school preparation. College-preparatory program recommended. 15 units recommended. Recommended units include English 4, mathematics 2, history 1, science 2, foreign language 2 and academic electives 4. 4 additional courses recommended, at least 2 of which should be from the following: history, English, math beyond algebra, laboratory science, fine arts and computer science.

2008-2009 Annual costs. Tuition/fees: $3,850; $11,157 out-of-state. Room/board: $7,578. Books/supplies: $1,200. Personal expenses: $2,892.

2007-2008 Financial aid. All financial aid based on need. 648 full-time freshmen applied for aid; 540 were judged to have need; 474 of these received aid. Average need met was 41%. Average scholarship/grant was $3,121; average loan $2,906. 44% of total undergraduate aid awarded as scholarships/grants, 56% as loans/jobs.

Application procedures. Admission: Closing date 8/21. $45 fee. Admission notification on a rolling basis. **Financial aid:** Priority date 3/1; no closing date. FAFSA, institutional form required. Applicants notified on a rolling basis starting 3/15; must reply within 2 week(s) of notification.

Academics. Students apply for upper-division courses in junior year. **Special study options:** Accelerated study, cooperative education, distance learning, double major, dual enrollment of high school students, ESL, exchange student, external degree, honors, independent study, internships, New York semester, semester at sea, student-designed major, study abroad, teacher certification program, United Nations semester, Washington semester. First-year experience. **Credit/placement by examination:** AP, CLEP, IB, institutional tests. 30 credit hours maximum toward bachelor's degree. **Support services:** Learning center, pre-admission summer program, reduced course load, remedial instruction, study skills assistance, tutoring, writing center.

Majors. Area/ethnic studies: African-American, Hispanic-American/Latino/Chicano, Native American. **Biology:** Bacteriology, botany, zoology. **Business:** Accounting, administrative services, business admin, finance, human resources, logistics, management information systems, managerial economics, marketing, office management. **Communications:** Broadcast journalism, journalism, public relations. **Computer sciences:** General, computer science, information systems, networking. **Construction:** Maintenance. **Education:** Art, bilingual, biology, business, chemistry, drama/dance, early childhood, elementary, English, French, German, history, mathematics, music, physical, physics, science, secondary, social science, social studies, Spanish. **Engineering technology:** Electrical. **Family/consumer sciences:** Family studies. **Foreign languages:** French, German, Spanish. **Health:** Athletic training, clinical lab science, dental hygiene, health care admin, medical radiologic technology/radiation therapy, nuclear medical technology, nursing (RN), respiratory therapy technology, sonography. **History:** General. **Interdisciplinary:** Gerontology. **Liberal arts:** Arts/sciences. **Math:** General, applied. **Military:** General. **Parks/recreation:** Exercise sciences, health/fitness. **Physical sciences:** Chemistry, geology, physics. **Protective services:** Corrections, criminal justice, police science. **Psychology:** General. **Public administration:** Social work. **Social sciences:** Economics, geography, political science, sociology. **Visual/performing arts:** General, art, commercial/advertising art, dance, design, dramatic, music performance, photography, piano/organ, studio arts, voice/opera.

Most popular majors. Business/marketing 18%, education 11%, health sciences 21%, security/protective services 6%.

Computing on campus. 558 workstations in dormitories, library, computer center, student center. Dormitories wired for high-speed internet access and linked to campus network. Commuter students can connect to campus network. Online course registration, online library, helpline, repair service, student web hosting, wireless network available.

Student life. Freshman orientation: Available. Preregistration for classes offered. Student and parent orientations offered by appointment. **Housing:** Single-sex dorms, special housing for disabled, apartments, wellness housing available. $175 partly refundable deposit, deadline 8/1. **Activities:** Bands, choral groups, dance, drama, film society, literary magazine, music ensembles, musical theater, opera, radio station, student government, student newspaper, symphony orchestra, TV station, Latter-day Saint Student Association, Newman Center, Black Scholars United, international student association, physically challenged student association.

Athletics. NCAA. **Intercollegiate:** Basketball, cross-country, football (tackle) M, golf, soccer W, tennis, track and field, volleyball W. **Intramural:** Baseball M, basketball, bowling, racquetball, soccer, softball, tennis, track and field, volleyball. **Team name:** Wildcats.

Student services. Adult student services, alcohol/substance abuse counseling, chaplain/spiritual director, career counseling, services for economically disadvantaged, student employment services, financial aid counseling, health services, legal services, minority student services, on-campus daycare, personal counseling, placement for graduates, veterans' counselor, women's services. **Physically disabled:** Services for visually, speech, hearing impaired.

Contact. E-mail: admissions@weber.edu
Phone: (801) 626-6744 Toll-free number: (800) 848-7770
Fax: (801) 626-6747
Christopher Rivera, Director of Admissions, Weber State University, 1137 University Circle, Ogden, UT 84408-1137

Western Governors University

Salt Lake City, Utah
www.wgu.edu

- Private 4-year virtual college
- Very large city
- 8,344 degree-seeking undergraduates: 59% women
- 1,953 degree-seeking graduate students
- 38% graduate within 6 years

General. Candidate for regional accreditation; also accredited by DETC. Programs are online-only. Degrees awarded after students demonstrate competency (through tests and assignments) in all required subjects; they are not based on credit hours. Mentors work with students to develop academic plans, monitor progress, and provide learning resources as needed. Tuition paid for 6-month terms. **Degrees:** 730 bachelor's, 5 associate awarded; master's offered. **Calendar:** Continuous, extensive summer session. **Full-time faculty:** 246 total; 22% minority, 67% women. **Part-time faculty:** 4 total; 75% women.

Basis for selection. Open admission.

2008-2009 Annual costs. Tuition/fees: $5,870. Tuition is based on 2 six month terms. BSN program tuition is $6,500.

Financial aid. Non-need-based: Scholarships awarded for academics.

Application procedures. Admission: No deadline. $65 fee, may be waived for applicants with need. Admission notification on a rolling basis.

Academics. All students have access to online communities that contain learning resources and academic mentors in their field of study. Academic model is competency-based; there are learning resources, not courses available. **Special study options:** Accelerated study, distance learning, teacher certification program. **Credit/placement by examination:** CLEP. **Support services:** Learning center, tutoring.

Majors. Business: Accounting, business admin, finance, human resources, management information systems, marketing. **Computer sciences:** General, information technology, LAN/WAN management, security, system admin. **Education:** Biology, chemistry, elementary, kindergarten/preschool, mathematics, science, secondary, social science, special. **Health:** Medical informatics, nursing (RN).

Student life. Freshman orientation: Available.

Student services. Career counseling, financial aid counseling, veterans' counselor.

Contact. E-mail: info@wgu.edu
Phone: (801) 274-3280 Toll-free number: (877) 435-7948
Fax: (801) 274-3305
Eddie Rios, Director of Enrollment, Western Governors University, 4001 South 700 East, Suite 700, Salt Lake City, UT 84107

Westminster College

Salt Lake City, Utah
www.westminstercollege.edu **CB code: 4948**

- Private 4-year liberal arts college
- Commuter campus in very large city
- 2,104 degree-seeking undergraduates: 8% part-time, 56% women, 1% African American, 3% Asian American, 6% Hispanic American, 1% international
- 721 degree-seeking graduate students
- 81% of applicants admitted
- SAT or ACT (ACT writing recommended), application essay required
- 55% graduate within 6 years; 20% enter graduate study

General. Founded in 1875. Regionally accredited. Curriculum combines professional and liberal arts study. **Degrees:** 402 bachelor's awarded; master's offered. **ROTC:** Army, Naval, Air Force. **Location:** 6 miles from downtown. **Calendar:** 4-1-4, limited summer session. **Full-time faculty:** 132 total; 70% have terminal degrees, 2% minority, 47% women. **Part-time faculty:** 166 total; 25% have terminal degrees, 58% women. **Class size:** 61% < 20, 38% 20-39, 2% 40-49. **Special facilities:** Meade Lx200 telescope, elevated soccer/lacrosse field.

Freshman class profile. 1,348 applied, 1,097 admitted, 449 enrolled.

Mid 50% test scores			
SAT critical reading:	500-610	Rank in top quarter:	55%
SAT math:	510-630	Rank in top tenth:	26%
ACT composite:	21-27	End year in good standing:	91%
GPA 3.75 or higher:	33%	Return as sophomores:	78%
GPA 3.50-3.74:	20%	Out-of-state:	33%
GPA 3.0-3.49:	31%	Live on campus:	64%
GPA 2.0-2.99:	16%	International:	2%

Basis for selection. Academic performance and GPA important. Interviews recommended.

High school preparation. College-preparatory program recommended. Required and recommended units include English 4, mathematics 2-3, social studies 2, history 1, science 3, foreign language 2-3 and academic electives 2-3.

2008-2009 Annual costs. Tuition/fees: $23,790. Room/board: $6,672. Books/supplies: $1,200. Personal expenses: $1,225.

2008-2009 Financial aid. Need-based: 316 full-time freshmen applied for aid; 242 were judged to have need; 242 of these received aid. Average need met was 87%. Average scholarship/grant was $14,306; average loan $4,077. 55% of total undergraduate aid awarded as scholarships/grants, 45% as loans/jobs. **Non-need-based:** Awarded to 810 full-time undergraduates, including 234 freshmen. Scholarships awarded for academics, alumni affiliation, art, athletics, leadership, minority status, music/drama, religious affiliation, ROTC.

Application procedures. Admission: Priority date 4/15; no deadline. $40 fee, may be waived for applicants with need. Admission notification on a rolling basis beginning on or about 9/1. Must reply by May 1 or within 3 week(s) if notified thereafter. **Financial aid:** Priority date 4/15; no closing date. FAFSA required. Applicants notified on a rolling basis starting 3/15; must reply by 5/1 or within 3 week(s) of notification.

Academics. Special study options: Accelerated study, combined bachelor's/graduate degree, cooperative education, distance learning, double major, dual enrollment of high school students, honors, independent study, internships, liberal arts/career combination, semester at sea, student-designed major, study abroad, teacher certification program, weekend college. **Credit/placement by examination:** AP, CLEP, IB, SAT, ACT, institutional tests. 40 credit hours maximum toward bachelor's degree. **Support services:** Remedial instruction, study skills assistance, tutoring, writing center.

Honors college/program. Admission by invitation; 35 freshman admitted per year.

Majors. Biology: General. **Business:** General, accounting, business admin, entrepreneurial studies, finance, human resources, information resources management, international, management information systems, management science, managerial economics, marketing. **Communications:** General. **Computer sciences:** Computer science. **Conservation:** Environmental studies. **Education:** General, early childhood, elementary, secondary, special. **Health:** Nursing (RN). **History:** General. **Math:** General. **Philosophy/religion:** Philosophy. **Physical sciences:** Chemistry, physics. **Protective services:** Criminal justice. **Psychology:** General. **Social sciences:** General, political science, sociology. **Transportation:** Aviation, aviation management. **Visual/performing arts:** Art, arts management.

Most popular majors. Business/marketing 32%, education 6%, health sciences 19%, psychology 6%.

Computing on campus. 412 workstations in dormitories, library, computer center, student center. Dormitories wired for high-speed internet access and linked to campus network. Commuter students can connect to campus network. Online course registration, online library, helpline, student web hosting, wireless network available.

Student life. Freshman orientation: Mandatory. Preregistration for classes offered. **Housing:** Guaranteed on-campus for freshmen. Coed dorms, single-sex dorms, apartments available. $200 nonrefundable deposit, deadline 6/1. **Activities:** Jazz band, campus ministries, choral groups, dance, drama, film society, international student organizations, literary magazine, music ensembles, musical theater, student government, student newspaper, symphony orchestra, College Democrats, College Republicans, Habitat for Humanity, Earth Effort, Latter-day Saint student association, Native American club, volunteer club, pride club.

Athletics. NAIA. **Intercollegiate:** Basketball, cross-country, golf, lacrosse, skiing, soccer, volleyball W. **Intramural:** Basketball, football (non-tackle), volleyball. **Team name:** Griffins.

Student services. Alcohol/substance abuse counseling, chaplain/spiritual director, career counseling, student employment services, financial aid counseling, health services, minority student services, personal counseling, placement for graduates, veterans' counselor. **Physically disabled:** Services for visually, speech, hearing impaired.

Contact. E-mail: admission@westminstercollege.edu
Phone: (801) 832-2200 Toll-free number: (800) 748-4753
Fax: (801) 832-3101
Darlene Dilley, Director of Undergraduate Admissions, Westminster College, 1840 South 1300 East, Salt Lake City, UT 84105

Vermont

Bennington College

Bennington, Vermont
www.bennington.edu

CB member
CB code: 3080

- Private 4-year liberal arts college
- Residential campus in large town
- 618 degree-seeking undergraduates: 1% part-time, 66% women, 2% African American, 2% Asian American, 3% Hispanic American, 4% international
- 134 degree-seeking graduate students
- 62% of applicants admitted
- Application essay required
- 61% graduate within 6 years

General. Founded in 1932. Regionally accredited. **Degrees:** 145 bachelor's awarded; master's offered. **Location:** 40 miles from Albany, New York; 150 miles from Boston. **Calendar:** 14-week fall and spring terms; 7-week winter field work term. **Full-time faculty:** 62 total; 73% have terminal degrees, 14% minority, 44% women. **Part-time faculty:** 30 total; 37% have terminal degrees, 13% minority, 27% women. **Class size:** 84% < 20, 14% 20-39, less than 1% 40-49, less than 1% 50-99, less than 1% >100. **Special facilities:** Observatory, greenhouse, digital arts lab, architecture, drawing, painting, printmaking, and sculpture studios, ceramics studio and kilns, color and black-and-white photography darkrooms, film and video editing studio, fully equipped professional theaters, scripts library, dance studios and archives, electronic music and sound recording studios, music practice rooms, music library.

Freshman class profile. 1,057 applied, 651 admitted, 190 enrolled.

Mid 50% test scores		**GPA 2.0-2.99:**	15%
SAT critical reading:	620-720	**Rank in top quarter:**	80%
SAT math:	560-660	**Rank in top tenth:**	31%
SAT writing:	650-770	**End year in good standing:**	96%
ACT composite:	24-28	**Return as sophomores:**	89%
GPA 3.75 or higher:	26%	**Out-of-state:**	98%
GPA 3.50-3.74:	28%	**Live on campus:**	100%
GPA 3.0-3.49:	31%	**International:**	5%

Basis for selection. Strength of applicant's academic record and extracurricular activities, quality of ideas expressed in application, and support of teachers and guidance counselor in discussing student's performance in school. The Test of English as a Foreign Language (TOEFL) or SAT is required for international students. Interviews strongly encouraged. Portfolio reviews not offered or required, but supplemental materials to application welcome. **Homeschooled:** Statement describing homeschool structure and mission, state high school equivalency certificate, letter of recommendation (nonparent) required. Documentation of academic work, course descriptions, reading list required. Strongly encourage standardized test, SAT or ACT.

High school preparation. College-preparatory program recommended. 21 units recommended. Recommended units include English 4, mathematics 4, social studies 4, history 4, science 3 and foreign language 2.

2008-2009 Annual costs. Tuition/fees: $38,270. Room/board: $10,680.

2008-2009 Financial aid. Need-based: 135 full-time freshmen applied for aid; 118 were judged to have need; 115 of these received aid. Average need met was 80%. Average scholarship/grant was $26,395; average loan $2,980. 81% of total undergraduate aid awarded as scholarships/grants, 19% as loans/jobs. **Non-need-based:** Awarded to 62 full-time undergraduates, including 25 freshmen. Scholarships awarded for academics. **Additional information:** All applicants for undergraduate admission considered for scholarships based on quality of overall application.

Application procedures. Admission: Closing date 1/5 (postmark date). $60 fee, may be waived for applicants with need. Admission notification 4/1. Must reply by May 1 or within 2 week(s) if notified thereafter. **Financial aid:** Priority date 3/1; no closing date. FAFSA, institutional form required. CSS PROFILE required of early decision applicants only. Applicants notified by 4/1; must reply by 5/1 or within 2 week(s) of notification.

Academics. Internships and field work required. **Special study options:** Accelerated study, combined bachelor's/graduate degree, cross-registration, double major, ESL, independent study, internships, student-designed major, study abroad, teacher certification program. Annual 7-week winter internship / field work period; postbaccalaureate program for medical or allied health school graduate programs. **Credit/placement by examination:** AP, CLEP, IB. **Support services:** Reduced course load, study skills assistance, tutoring, writing center.

Majors. Architecture: Architecture. **Area/ethnic studies:** American, Asian, European, gay/lesbian, Latin American, women's. **Biology:** General, botany, cellular/molecular, ecology, environmental, evolutionary, zoology. **Communications:** Journalism. **Communications technology:** Animation/special effects. **Computer sciences:** General, computer science. **Conservation:** Environmental science, environmental studies. **Education:** General, early childhood, elementary, middle, secondary. **Family/consumer sciences:** Child development. **Foreign languages:** General, Chinese, French, Germanic, Italian, Japanese, Spanish. **Health:** Premedicine. **History:** General, American, European. **Interdisciplinary:** Global studies, math/computer science, peace/conflict. **Legal studies:** Prelaw. **Liberal arts:** Arts/sciences, humanities. **Math:** General. **Philosophy/religion:** Judaic, philosophy. **Physical sciences:** General, astronomy, chemistry, physics. **Psychology:** General, social. **Social sciences:** General, anthropology, international relations, political science, sociology, U.S. government. **Visual/performing arts:** General, acting, art history/conservation, ceramics, cinematography, dance, design, directing/producing, dramatic, drawing, film/cinema, jazz, multimedia, music history, music performance, music theory/composition, musicology, painting, photography, piano/organ, play/screenwriting, printmaking, sculpture, stringed instruments, studio arts, theater design, theater history, voice/opera.

Most popular majors. English 12%, foreign language 9%, liberal arts 6%, social sciences 6%, visual/performing arts 51%.

Computing on campus. 100 workstations in library, computer center, student center. Dormitories wired for high-speed internet access and linked to campus network. Commuter students can connect to campus network. Online library, helpline, repair service, wireless network available.

Student life. Freshman orientation: Available. Preregistration for classes offered. 6-day orientation program prior to start of fall classes. International students have 1 extra day. Students may also participate in pre-orientation service or camping trips run by Outing Club. **Housing:** Guaranteed on-campus for all undergraduates. Coed dorms, special housing for disabled, cooperative housing available. **Activities:** Jazz band, choral groups, dance, drama, film society, international student organizations, literary magazine, musical theater, opera, student government, student newspaper.

Athletics. Intramural: Badminton, basketball, bowling, skiing, soccer, softball, table tennis, tennis, volleyball.

Student services. Alcohol/substance abuse counseling, career counseling, student employment services, financial aid counseling, health services, minority student services, on-campus daycare, personal counseling, placement for graduates, women's services. **Physically disabled:** Services for hearing impaired.

Contact. E-mail: admissions@bennington.edu
Phone: (802) 440-4312 Toll-free number: (800) 833-6845
Fax: (802) 440-4320
Ken Himmelman, Dean of Admissions and Financial Aid, Bennington College, One College Drive, Bennington, VT 05201-6003

Burlington College

Burlington, Vermont
www.burlington.edu

CB code: 1119

- Private 4-year liberal arts college
- Residential campus in small city
- 157 degree-seeking undergraduates: 31% part-time, 47% women, 3% African American, 3% Asian American, 2% Hispanic American, 1% Native American, 2% international
- 54% of applicants admitted
- Application essay required

General. Founded in 1972. Regionally accredited. **Degrees:** 37 bachelor's, 3 associate awarded. **Location:** 90 miles from Montreal, 160 miles from Boston. **Calendar:** Semester, limited summer session. **Full-time faculty:** 9 total; 22% have terminal degrees, 44% women. **Part-time faculty:** 55 total; 31% have terminal degrees, 47% women. **Class size:** 99% < 20, 1% 20-39. **Special facilities:** Film and video editing labs.

Freshman class profile. 93 applied, 50 admitted, 21 enrolled.

End year in good standing:	56%	**Live on campus:**	80%
Return as sophomores:	39%	**International:**	5%
Out-of-state:	80%		

Basis for selection. Application essay and interview very important, followed by recommendations, GPA, and test scores. Writing samples needed for distance learning independent degree program. Two letters of recommendation for all programs. SAT or ACT scores not required, but students must take assessments for math, writing, and computer literacy. **Homeschooled:** Portfolio-style transcripts accepted.

High school preparation. College-preparatory program recommended. 24 units recommended. Recommended units include English 4, mathematics 3, social studies 4, history 3, science 3 (laboratory 1), foreign language 2 and academic electives 4.

2008-2009 Annual costs. Tuition/fees: $19,640. Room only: $6,095. Books/supplies: $990. Personal expenses: $1,800.

2008-2009 Financial aid. **Need-based:** Average need met was 56%. Average scholarship/grant was $6,496; average loan $4,786. 32% of total undergraduate aid awarded as scholarships/grants, 68% as loans/jobs. **Non-need-based:** Scholarships awarded for academics, leadership.

Application procedures. **Admission:** No deadline. $50 fee, may be waived for applicants with need. Admission notification on a rolling basis. Must confirm by registration period. Application fee may be deferred until enrollment for qualified financial aid applicants. **Financial aid:** No deadline. FAFSA required. Applicants notified on a rolling basis starting 3/15.

Academics. **Special study options:** Cross-registration, distance learning, double major, dual enrollment of high school students, external degree, independent study, internships, liberal arts/career combination, student-designed major, study abroad. **Credit/placement by examination:** AP, CLEP, IB, institutional tests. 45 credit hours maximum toward associate degree, 90 toward bachelor's. **Support services:** Reduced course load, study skills assistance, tutoring, writing center.

Majors. **Area/ethnic studies:** Latin American. **Legal studies:** General. **Psychology:** General. **Public administration:** Human services. **Visual/performing arts:** Film/cinema, photography, studio arts. **Other:** Gender Studies, Transpersonal Psychology.

Most popular majors. English 11%, interdisciplinary studies 24%, legal studies 8%, psychology 24%, public administration/social services 11%, visual/performing arts 19%.

Computing on campus. 20 workstations in library, computer center, student center. Dormitories wired for high-speed internet access. Commuter students can connect to campus network. Online library, wireless network available.

Student life. **Freshman orientation:** Mandatory, $150 fee. Preregistration for classes offered. **Housing:** Apartments, cooperative housing available. **Activities:** Drama, film society, literary magazine, student government, student newspaper, The Institute for Civic Engagement, The Recon Soiree, Burlington College Community Garden.

Student services. Adult student services, career counseling, financial aid counseling, legal services, personal counseling. **Physically disabled:** Services for hearing impaired.

Contact. E-mail: admissions@burlington.edu
Phone: (802) 862-9616 ext. 104 Toll-free number: (800) 862-9616 ext. 104
Fax: (802) 660-4331
Laryn Runco, Admissions Director, Burlington College, 95 North Avenue, Burlington, VT 05401

Castleton State College

Castleton, Vermont — **CB member**
www.castleton.edu — **CB code: 3765**

- Public 4-year liberal arts college
- Residential campus in small town
- 1,891 degree-seeking undergraduates: 8% part-time, 54% women
- 43 degree-seeking graduate students
- 68% of applicants admitted
- SAT or ACT with writing, application essay required
- 48% graduate within 6 years

General. Founded in 1787. Regionally accredited. **Degrees:** 281 bachelor's, 64 associate awarded; master's offered. **ROTC:** Army. **Location:** 12 miles from Rutland. **Calendar:** Semester, limited summer session. **Full-time faculty:** 88 total; 93% have terminal degrees, 6% minority, 46% women. **Part-time faculty:** 127 total; 22% have terminal degrees, 39% women. **Class size:** 72% < 20, 26% 20-39, less than 1% 40-49, 1% 50-99, less than 1% >100. **Special facilities:** Medical society museum, outdoor classroom.

Freshman class profile. 2,190 applied, 1,497 admitted, 475 enrolled.

Mid 50% test scores		**GPA 3.0-3.49:**	29%
SAT critical reading:	440-530	**GPA 2.0-2.99:**	62%
SAT math:	450-550	**Rank in top quarter:**	15%
SAT writing:	430-530	**Rank in top tenth:**	3%
ACT composite:	18-22	**Return as sophomores:**	71%
GPA 3.75 or higher:	3%	**Out-of-state:**	42%
GPA 3.50-3.74:	6%	**Live on campus:**	84%

Basis for selection. School achievement record, test scores, essay, recommendations, class rank very important. Interview recommended for all; audition recommended for music.

High school preparation. College-preparatory program required. 14 units required; 16 recommended. Required and recommended units include English 4, mathematics 3-4, social studies 3-4, history 3, science 3-4 (laboratory 2) and foreign language 2.

2008-2009 Annual costs. Tuition/fees: $8,284; $16,948 out-of-state. New England Board of Higher Education rate for students from other New England states: 150% of Vermont resident tuition. Available to degree candidates in academic areas not offered by educational institutions in their home states. Room/board: $7,510. Books/supplies: $800. Personal expenses: $600.

2007-2008 Financial aid. **Non-need-based:** Scholarships awarded for academics, alumni affiliation, art, leadership, music/drama, state residency.

Application procedures. **Admission:** No deadline. $35 fee, may be waived for applicants with need. Admission notification on a rolling basis beginning on or about 12/1. **Financial aid:** Priority date 2/15; no closing date. FAFSA required. Applicants notified on a rolling basis starting 1/1; must reply by 5/1 or within 2 week(s) of notification.

Academics. **Special study options:** Combined bachelor's/graduate degree, cooperative education, cross-registration, double major, dual enrollment of high school students, honors, independent study, internships, liberal arts/career combination, student-designed major, study abroad, teacher certification program. 5-year MBA with Clarkson University, 7-year physical therapy with Sage Graduate School, 6-year occupational therapy with Sage Graduate School. **Credit/placement by examination:** AP, CLEP, SAT, ACT, institutional tests. 30 credit hours maximum toward associate degree, 60 toward bachelor's. **Support services:** Learning center, reduced course load, remedial instruction, study skills assistance, tutoring, writing center.

Majors. **Biology:** General. **Business:** General, accounting, business admin, management science, marketing. **Communications:** Digital media, journalism, media studies. **Computer sciences:** General. **Conservation:** Environmental science. **Education:** Art, biology, chemistry, drama/dance, elementary, English, foreign languages, history, mathematics, middle, music, physical, physics, science, secondary, social science, social studies, Spanish. **Foreign languages:** Spanish. **Health:** Athletic training. **History:** General. **Interdisciplinary:** Biological/physical sciences, math/computer science, natural sciences. **Math:** General, statistics. **Parks/recreation:** Exercise sciences, health/fitness, sports admin. **Philosophy/religion:** Philosophy. **Physical sciences:** Geology. **Protective services:** Criminal justice. **Psychology:** General. **Public administration:** Social work. **Social sciences:** General, criminology, sociology. **Visual/performing arts:** General, art, dramatic.

Most popular majors. Business/marketing 22%, communications/journalism 9%, parks/recreation 10%, psychology 8%, social sciences 8%, visual/performing arts 9%.

Computing on campus. 225 workstations in dormitories, library, computer center. Dormitories wired for high-speed internet access and linked to campus network. Commuter students can connect to campus network. Repair service, wireless network available.

Student life. **Freshman orientation:** Mandatory. Preregistration for classes offered. 2 and a half day program. **Housing:** Guaranteed on-campus for freshmen. Coed dorms, wellness housing available. $100 nonrefundable deposit, deadline 5/1. **Activities:** Jazz band, choral groups, dance, drama, literary magazine, music ensembles, musical theater, radio station, student government, student newspaper, TV station, Christian fellowships, political discussion group, Spanish club, social issues club, community service club, women's issues group.

Athletics. NCAA. **Intercollegiate:** Baseball M, basketball, cross-country, field hockey W, golf M, ice hockey, lacrosse, skiing, soccer, softball W, tennis, volleyball W. **Intramural:** Basketball, football (non-tackle), racquetball, soccer, softball, swimming, table tennis, tennis, volleyball. **Team name:** Spartans.

Student services. Adult student services, alcohol/substance abuse counseling, career counseling, services for economically disadvantaged, student employment services, financial aid counseling, health services, personal counseling, placement for graduates.

Contact. E-mail: info@castleton.edu
Phone: (802) 468-1213 Toll-free number: (800) 639-8521
Fax: (802) 468-1476
Maurice Ouimet, Director of Admissions, Castleton State College, Seminary Street, Castleton, VT 05735

Champlain College

Burlington, Vermont — **CB member**
www.champlain.edu — **CB code: 3291**

- Private 4-year business and liberal arts college
- Residential campus in small city
- 2,618 degree-seeking undergraduates: 20% part-time, 43% women, 1% African American, 2% Asian American, 1% Hispanic American
- 139 degree-seeking graduate students
- 74% of applicants admitted
- SAT or ACT (ACT writing optional), application essay required
- 72% graduate within 6 years; 8% enter graduate study

General. Founded in 1878. Regionally accredited. **Degrees:** 414 bachelor's, 77 associate awarded; master's offered. **ROTC:** Army. **Location:** 200 miles from Boston, 90 miles from Montreal. **Calendar:** Semester, limited summer session. **Full-time faculty:** 88 total; 51% have terminal degrees, 2% minority, 39% women. **Part-time faculty:** 219 total; 24% have terminal degrees, 3% minority, 42% women. **Class size:** 50% < 20, 50% 20-39.

Freshman class profile. 2,978 applied, 2,189 admitted, 614 enrolled.

Mid 50% test scores			
SAT critical reading:	500-600	Rank in top tenth:	10%
SAT math:	510-600	End year in good standing:	75%
ACT composite:	20-26	Return as sophomores:	75%
Rank in top quarter:	31%	Out-of-state:	73%
		Live on campus:	90%

Basis for selection. GPA, level of difficulty of high school curriculum, essay, interview, counselor recommendations most important. Waiting list for Radiography and Electronic Gaming and Interactive Design programs only. Interview strongly recommended. **Homeschooled:** GED or 2 SAT Subject Tests required.

High school preparation. 20 units required. Required and recommended units include English 4, mathematics 3-4, social studies 2, history 4, science 3-4 (laboratory 2-3), foreign language 2 and academic electives 4.

2008-2009 Annual costs. Tuition/fees: $24,355. Room/board: $11,210. Books/supplies: $600. Personal expenses: $600.

2008-2009 Financial aid. Non-need-based: Scholarships awarded for academics, leadership.

Application procedures. Admission: Closing date 1/31. $50 fee, may be waived for applicants with need, free for online applicants. Admission notification on a rolling basis beginning on or about 3/25. Must reply by 5/1. Housing deposit refundable prior to 5/1 only. **Financial aid:** Closing date 3/1. FAFSA required. Applicants notified by 3/19; must reply by 5/1.

Academics. 96% of majors include required internship. **Special study options:** Accelerated study, combined bachelor's/graduate degree, cooperative education, cross-registration, distance learning, double major, honors, independent study, internships, liberal arts/career combination, study abroad, teacher certification program. Clinical internships at Fletcher Allen Medical Center. **Credit/placement by examination:** AP, CLEP, IB, institutional tests. 30 credit hours maximum toward associate degree, 75 toward bachelor's. **Support services:** Reduced course load, study skills assistance, tutoring, writing center.

Majors. Business: General, accounting, accounting/business management, accounting/finance, business admin, communications, e-commerce, hospitality admin, hospitality/recreation, hotel/motel admin, human resources, international, marketing, organizational behavior, restaurant/food services, small business admin, tourism promotion, tourism/travel, travel services. **Communications:** Digital media, journalism, media studies, organizational, public relations. **Communications technology:** Animation/special effects, graphics. **Computer sciences:** General, computer graphics, computer science, information systems, LAN/WAN management, networking, security, system admin, systems analysis, web page design, webmaster. **Education:** General, early childhood, elementary, kindergarten/preschool, middle, secondary. **Engineering:** Software. **Family/consumer sciences:** Family/community services. **Legal studies:** Paralegal, prelaw. **Liberal arts:** Arts/sciences. **Personal/culinary services:** Restaurant/catering. **Protective services:** Criminal justice, forensics, law enforcement admin, security management, security services. **Psychology:** General. **Public administration:** Human services, social work. **Visual/performing arts:** Cinematography, design, graphic design, multimedia.

Most popular majors. Business/marketing 37%, communications/journalism 8%, computer/information sciences 17%, education 6%, security/protective services 6%, visual/performing arts 14%.

Computing on campus. 260 workstations in library, computer center, student center. Dormitories wired for high-speed internet access and linked to campus network. Commuter students can connect to campus network. Online course registration, online library, helpline, wireless network available.

Student life. Freshman orientation: Available, $60 fee. Preregistration for classes offered. 4-day program. **Policies:** No alcohol permitted on campus. **Housing:** Guaranteed on-campus for freshmen. Coed dorms, single-sex dorms, wellness housing available. $150 nonrefundable deposit, deadline 5/1. **Activities:** Choral groups, dance, drama, international student organizations, literary magazine, musical theater, radio station, student government, student newspaper, cultural diversity committee, GET REAL community service, outing club, Champlain Heritage Society, Reader's Exchange, flash animation club, Intercollegiate Writers Exchange.

Athletics. Intramural: Basketball, bowling, golf, ice hockey, skiing, soccer, volleyball.

Student services. Adult student services, alcohol/substance abuse counseling, career counseling, student employment services, financial aid counseling, health services, minority student services, personal counseling, placement for graduates. **Physically disabled:** Services for visually, hearing impaired.

Contact. E-mail: admission@champlain.edu
Phone: (802) 860-2727 Toll-free number: (800) 570-5858
Fax: (802) 860-2767
Mary Kennedy, Vice President for Enrollment, Champlain College, 163 South Willard Street, Burlington, VT 05402-0670

College of St. Joseph in Vermont

Rutland, Vermont — **CB member**
www.csj.edu — **CB code: 3297**

- Private 4-year liberal arts and teachers college affiliated with Roman Catholic Church
- Residential campus in large town
- 202 degree-seeking undergraduates: 24% part-time, 54% women, 7% African American, 4% Hispanic American, 1% Native American
- 158 degree-seeking graduate students
- 88% of applicants admitted
- SAT or ACT (ACT writing optional), application essay required
- 45% graduate within 6 years

General. Founded in 1950. Regionally accredited. **Degrees:** 59 bachelor's, 16 associate awarded; master's offered. **Location:** 70 miles from Burlington, 100 miles from Albany, New York. **Calendar:** Semester, extensive summer session. **Full-time faculty:** 15 total; 47% have terminal degrees, 7% minority, 27% women. **Part-time faculty:** 45 total; 20% have terminal degrees, 4% minority, 40% women. **Class size:** 94% < 20, 6% 20-39. **Special facilities:** Photography and ceramics studios.

Freshman class profile. 100 applied, 88 admitted, 46 enrolled.

Mid 50% test scores			
SAT critical reading:	380-480	GPA 2.0-2.99:	49%
SAT math:	390-490	Rank in top quarter:	11%
ACT composite:	15-20	End year in good standing:	66%
GPA 3.75 or higher:	2%	Return as sophomores:	57%
GPA 3.50-3.74:	5%	Out-of-state:	35%
GPA 3.0-3.49:	40%	Live on campus:	67%

Basis for selection. Decisions based on high school course selection, minimum 2.0 out of 4.0 high school GPA in college preparatory coursework, 2 academic letters of recommendation, essay, ACT or SAT scores; and extracurricular activities are considered. CSJ only accepts the GED for students age 22 and over. Interview recommended. **Homeschooled:** Transcript of courses and grades, interview, letter of recommendation (nonparent) required.

High school preparation. College-preparatory program recommended. 16 units required. Required and recommended units include English 4, mathematics 3, history 3, science 2, foreign language 2 and academic electives 5.

2008-2009 Annual costs. Tuition/fees: $16,790. Room/board: $8,150. Books/supplies: $1,000. Personal expenses: $1,350.

2008-2009 Financial aid. **Need-based:** Average need met was 77%. Average scholarship/grant was $11,115; average loan $3,876. 51% of total undergraduate aid awarded as scholarships/grants, 49% as loans/jobs. **Non-need-based:** Scholarships awarded for academics. **Additional information:** Instructors at local Catholic schools are granted a tuition reduction.

Application procedures. **Admission:** Priority date 3/1; no deadline. $25 fee, may be waived for applicants with need. Admission notification on a rolling basis. Must reply by May 1 or within 2 week(s) if notified thereafter. **Financial aid:** Priority date 3/1; no closing date. FAFSA, institutional form required. Applicants notified on a rolling basis starting 3/15.

Academics. Experiential educational options including internships available. **Special study options:** Accelerated study, double major, dual enrollment of high school students, internships, liberal arts/career combination, teacher certification program. **Credit/placement by examination:** AP, CLEP, IB, SAT, ACT, institutional tests. 12 credit hours maximum toward associate degree, 12 toward bachelor's. **Support services:** Learning center, reduced course load, study skills assistance, tutoring, writing center.

Majors. **Business:** Accounting, business admin, operations. **Education:** Elementary, English, history, multi-level teacher, secondary, social studies. **Health:** Radiologic technology/medical imaging. **History:** General. **Interdisciplinary:** Behavioral sciences. **Liberal arts:** Arts/sciences. **Parks/recreation:** Sports admin. **Protective services:** Law enforcement admin. **Psychology:** General. **Other:** Alcohol and substance abuse counseling, Child and family services, Professional studies - health sciences.

Most popular majors. Business/marketing 34%, education 14%, liberal arts 17%, psychology 25%.

Computing on campus. 34 workstations in library, computer center, student center. Dormitories wired for high-speed internet access and linked to campus network. Commuter students can connect to campus network. Online library, repair service, wireless network available.

Student life. **Freshman orientation:** Mandatory, $125 fee. Preregistration for classes offered. 5-day orientation before upperclassmen move into dorms. **Housing:** Guaranteed on-campus for all undergraduates. Single-sex dorms available. $200 nonrefundable deposit, deadline 5/1. Some single rooms available and graduate housing available. **Activities:** Campus ministries, choral groups, dance, literary magazine, student government, student ambassadors, human services club, education club, honor societies.

Athletics. NAIA. **Intercollegiate:** Baseball M, basketball, soccer, softball W. **Intramural:** Weight lifting. **Team name:** Fighting Saints.

Student services. Adult student services, alcohol/substance abuse counseling, chaplain/spiritual director, career counseling, student employment services, financial aid counseling, personal counseling, placement for graduates, veterans' counselor. **Physically disabled:** Services for visually, speech, hearing impaired.

Contact. E-mail: admissions@csj.edu
Phone: (802) 773-5900 ext. 3286 Toll-free number: (877) 270-9998
Fax: (802) 776-5258
Susan Englese, Dean of Admissions, College of St. Joseph in Vermont, 71 Clement Road, Rutland, VT 05701-3899

Goddard College

Plainfield, Vermont
www.goddard.edu **CB code: 3416**

- Private 4-year liberal arts college
- Commuter campus in rural community
- 243 degree-seeking undergraduates: 70% women, 3% African American, 6% Hispanic American, 1% Native American
- 479 degree-seeking graduate students
- 100% of applicants admitted
- Application essay, interview required

General. Founded in 1938. Regionally accredited. **Degrees:** 62 bachelor's awarded; master's offered. **Location:** 10 miles from Montpelier, 45 miles from Burlington. **Calendar:** Semester. **Full-time faculty:** 5 total; 60% women. **Part-time faculty:** 107 total; 71% women.

Basis for selection. Academic potential, maturity, ability to work independently, personal statement, interview most important; additional writing sample may be needed. Portfolios recommended when appropriate. **Homeschooled:** State high school equivalency certificate required. GED recommended.

2008-2009 Annual costs. Annual tuition for low-residency Bachelor of Arts is $11,504, for Bachelor of Fine Arts in creative writing $12,554. Tuition is slightly higher for graduate programs, and varies by program. Students attend one week on campus each semester; room and board is $1,088 per year for the Vermont campus, and marginally higher for our Washington state location (only the MFA programs are offered on the West Coast). Books/supplies: $600.

2007-2008 Financial aid. **Need-based:** 9 full-time freshmen applied for aid; 8 were judged to have need; 8 of these received aid. Average need met was 40%. Average scholarship/grant was $4,376; average loan $4,232. 27% of total undergraduate aid awarded as scholarships/grants, 73% as loans/jobs. **Non-need-based:** Scholarships awarded for academics, art, job skills, leadership, music/drama, state residency.

Application procedures. **Admission:** $40 fee, may be waived for applicants with need. Admission notification on a rolling basis. **Financial aid:** No deadline. FAFSA required. Applicants notified on a rolling basis starting 4/15; must reply within 4 week(s) of notification.

Academics. Written evaluations replace grades. Individually designed majors at bachelor's and master's levels. Students design programs of study in collaboration with faculty mentor. Students on campus for 8 days at beginning of each semester and then work from home following study plan designed in collaboration with advisor. **Special study options:** Distance learning, external degree, independent study, internships, student-designed major, study abroad, teacher certification program. Guided-independent study programs convenient for working adults; students required to be on site twice a year for eight days each time. Students design their own curriculum in collaboration with faculty and spend the rest of the semester studying at home or elsewhere. MFA in Creative Writing and MFA in Interdisciplinary Arts offered in Port Townsend, WA as well as Plainfield, VT. **Credit/placement by examination:** AP, CLEP, IB. 30 credit hours maximum toward bachelor's degree. **Support services:** Study skills assistance.

Majors. **Area/ethnic studies:** African-American, American, European, gay/lesbian, Latin American, Native American, Near/Middle Eastern, women's. **Biology:** General, ecology. **Business:** Business admin. **Conservation:** Environmental studies. **Education:** General, art, early childhood, elementary, English, foundations, history, middle, secondary, social studies. **Health:** Aromatherapy, community health, community health services, environmental health, health services, herbalism, movement therapy, polarity therapy, public health ed, Reiki, somatic bodywork. **History:** General. **Interdisciplinary:** Global studies, intercultural, nutrition sciences, peace/conflict. **Liberal arts:** Arts/sciences, humanities. **Philosophy/religion:** Judaic, philosophy, religion. **Psychology:** General. **Public administration:** Community org/advocacy, social work. **Social sciences:** General. **Visual/performing arts:** General, crafts, dramatic, multimedia, play/screenwriting, studio arts.

Computing on campus. PC or laptop required. 100 workstations in library, computer center, student center. Dormitories wired for high-speed internet access and linked to campus network. Commuter students can connect to campus network. Online library, helpline, wireless network available.

Student life. **Freshman orientation:** Mandatory, $125 fee. Held day before registration. **Policies:** Dogs are not allowed on campus, with the exception of service dogs. **Housing:** Coed dorms, wellness housing available. $250 nonrefundable deposit. Housing available 8 days per semester. **Activities:** Radio station, student government.

Student services. Financial aid counseling.

Contact. E-mail: admissions@goddard.edu
Phone: (802) 454-8311 ext. 243 Toll-free number: (800) 906-8312
Fax: (802) 454-1029
Lucinda Garthwaite, Special Assistant to the President, Goddard College, Goddard College Admissions, Plainfield, VT 05667

Green Mountain College

Poultney, Vermont **CB member**
www.greenmtn.edu **CB code: 3418**

- Private 4-year liberal arts college affiliated with United Methodist Church
- Residential campus in small town

- 767 degree-seeking undergraduates: 2% part-time, 51% women, 3% African American, 1% Asian American, 2% Hispanic American, 1% Native American
- 86 degree-seeking graduate students
- 70% of applicants admitted
- Application essay required
- 30% graduate within 6 years

General. Founded in 1834. Regionally accredited. **Degrees:** 127 bachelor's awarded; master's offered. **Location:** 20 miles from Rutland, 35 miles from Killington. **Calendar:** Differs by program. **Full-time faculty:** 49 total; 90% have terminal degrees, 4% minority, 29% women. **Part-time faculty:** 33 total; 24% have terminal degrees, 46% women. **Class size:** 54% < 20, 46% 20-39. **Special facilities:** Student-operated organically managed farm, ropes course, 80-acre nature preserve, collection of Welsh artifacts and literature, collection of early American decoration, art collection.

Freshman class profile. 1,431 applied, 1,008 admitted, 221 enrolled.

Out-of-state:	85%	**Live on campus:**	96%

Basis for selection. Academic achievement, recommendations, interview, essay, test scores or Insight portfolio submission, personal statement, school and community activities important. Tests are required for home-schooled students, students with a GED, and students attending high schools outside of the U.S. Interview recommended; audition recommended for theater or music; portfolio recommended for art. **Homeschooled:** Statement describing homeschool structure and mission, transcript of courses and grades, state high school equivalency certificate, letter of recommendation (nonparent) required. Applicants advised to develop thorough portfolio of all work completed. Students highly encouraged to interview on campus.

High school preparation. College-preparatory program recommended. 21 units required. Required and recommended units include English 4, mathematics 3-4, social studies 3, history 1-2, science 3-4 (laboratory 2), foreign language 2-3 and academic electives 5.

2008-2009 Annual costs. Tuition/fees: $25,838. Room/board: $9,522. Books/supplies: $1,100. Personal expenses: $770.

2008-2009 Financial aid. Need-based: 179 full-time freshmen applied for aid; 150 were judged to have need; 150 of these received aid. Average need met was 68%. Average scholarship/grant was $14,969; average loan $3,942. 65% of total undergraduate aid awarded as scholarships/grants, 35% as loans/jobs. **Non-need-based:** Awarded to 157 full-time undergraduates, including 55 freshmen. Scholarships awarded for academics, alumni affiliation, art, leadership, music/drama, religious affiliation. **Additional information:** Service/recognition awards available to all students.

Application procedures. Admission: Priority date 3/1; no deadline. $30 fee, may be waived for applicants with need, free for online applicants. Admission notification on a rolling basis beginning on or about 9/1. Must reply by May 1 or within 2 week(s) if notified thereafter. **Financial aid:** Priority date 3/1; no closing date. FAFSA required. CSS PROFILE is recommended to receive an earlier financial aid package. Applicants notified on a rolling basis starting 11/1; must reply by 5/1 or within 4 week(s) of notification.

Academics. Environmental core curriculum. **Special study options:** Accelerated study, double major, ESL, exchange student, honors, independent study, internships, liberal arts/career combination, student-designed major, study abroad, teacher certification program. Exchange programs at Aberystwyth University (Wales), Hannam University (Korea), Nogoya University (Japan). Credit granted for programs of National Outdoor Leadership School. Member of Eco-League Consortium; students can spend up to 2 semesters at one of 5 other schools: Alaska Pacific University, Antioch University, College of the Atlantic, Northand College, Prescott College. **Credit/placement by examination:** AP, CLEP, IB, SAT, ACT, institutional tests. **Support services:** Learning center, pre-admission summer program, reduced course load, remedial instruction, study skills assistance, tutoring, writing center.

Majors. Biology: General. **Business:** Business admin, hospitality admin, hospitality/recreation, resort management. **Communications:** General, journalism. **Conservation:** General, environmental studies, management/policy. **Education:** Art, elementary, English, middle, secondary, social studies, special. **History:** General. **Liberal arts:** Arts/sciences. **Parks/recreation:** General, facilities management. **Philosophy/religion:** Philosophy. **Psychology:** General. **Social sciences:** Anthropology, sociology. **Visual/performing arts:** Art, studio arts. **Other:** Environmental Management.

Computing on campus. 60 workstations in dormitories, library, computer center, student center. Dormitories wired for high-speed internet access and linked to campus network. Commuter students can connect to campus network. Online course registration, online library, helpline, wireless network available.

Student life. Freshman orientation: Mandatory, $100 fee. Preregistration for classes offered. Orientation held week before classes begin in August and January. Students also may opt to come to campus on specified days during summer. **Housing:** Guaranteed on-campus for all undergraduates. Coed dorms, wellness housing available. **Activities:** Bands, choral groups, drama, film society, literary magazine, music ensembles, radio station, student government, student newspaper, outdoor adventure programs, Poultney Partners Mentoring Program, environmental volunteer and research groups, African American Culture Club, diversity club, UNICEF.

Athletics. NCAA. **Intercollegiate:** Basketball, cross-country, golf M, lacrosse, skiing, soccer, softball W, tennis, volleyball W. **Intramural:** Basketball, football (non-tackle), skiing, soccer, softball, table tennis, tennis, volleyball. **Team name:** Eagles.

Student services. Alcohol/substance abuse counseling, chaplain/spiritual director, career counseling, student employment services, financial aid counseling, health services, personal counseling, placement for graduates.

Contact. E-mail: admiss@greenmtn.edu
Phone: (802) 287-8207 Toll-free number: (800) 776-6675
Fax: (802) 287-8099
Sandra Bartholomew, Dean of Enrollment Management, Green Mountain College, One Brennan Circle, Poultney, VT 05764

Johnson State College

Johnson, Vermont — **CB member**
www.jsc.edu — **CB code: 3766**

- Public 4-year liberal arts college
- Residential campus in rural community
- 1,520 degree-seeking undergraduates: 31% part-time, 59% women
- 266 graduate students
- 82% of applicants admitted
- SAT or ACT (ACT writing optional), application essay required

General. Founded in 1828. Regionally accredited. Special tuition rate for New England residents who apply to selected fields of study. **Degrees:** 284 bachelor's, 14 associate awarded; master's offered. **ROTC:** Army. **Location:** 50 miles from Burlington, 90 miles from Montreal. **Calendar:** Semester, limited summer session. **Full-time faculty:** 56 total; 71% have terminal degrees, 30% women. **Part-time faculty:** 87 total; 16% have terminal degrees, 54% women. **Class size:** 72% < 20, 28% 20-39. **Special facilities:** 1,000-acre nature preserve, visual arts center, human performance laboratory, interactive multimedia math, science laboratory, recording studio, community service learning center, Vermont interactive television site, snowboard park.

Freshman class profile. 1,034 applied, 845 admitted, 316 enrolled.

Mid 50% test scores			
SAT critical reading:	430-550	**ACT composite:**	20-28
SAT math:	430-550	**Out-of-state:**	29%
		Live on campus:	90%

Basis for selection. High school transcript, GPA, SAT or ACT scores, class rank, recommendations, and essay are important. Tests are not required for any student who have graduated from high school for at least a year or for students taking the GED. Interview recommended. **Homeschooled:** Transcript of courses and grades, state high school equivalency certificate, letter of recommendation (nonparent) required. SAT required. Applicants encouraged to complete GED or other state certified achievement test to demonstrate aptitude.

High school preparation. 9 units required; 15 recommended. Required and recommended units include English 4, mathematics 3-4, social studies 2, history 2, science 2-3 (laboratory 1-2) and foreign language 1. Mathematics units to include algebra I, geometry and algebra II.

2008-2009 Annual costs. Tuition/fees: $8,184; $16,848 out-of-state. New England Board of Higher Education rate for students from other New England states: 150% of Vermont resident tuition. Available to degree candidates in academic areas not offered by educational institutions in their home states. Room/board: $7,510. Books/supplies: $1,000. Personal expenses: $650.

2008-2009 Financial aid. Non-need-based: Scholarships awarded for academics.

Application procedures. Admission: Priority date 3/1; no deadline. $35 fee, may be waived for applicants with need, free for online applicants. Admission notification on a rolling basis beginning on or about 12/1. Must reply by May 1 or within 2 week(s) if notified thereafter. **Financial aid:** Priority date 3/1; no closing date. FAFSA required. Applicants notified on a rolling basis starting 4/1; must reply within 3 week(s) of notification.

Academics. Transition program for students who show potential academic success but may be unprepared academically and/or socially. **Special study options:** Accelerated study, cross-registration, distance learning, double major, dual enrollment of high school students, ESL, exchange student, external degree, independent study, internships, study abroad, teacher certification program. **Credit/placement by examination:** AP, CLEP, institutional tests. **Support services:** Learning center, pre-admission summer program, reduced course load, remedial instruction, study skills assistance, tutoring, writing center.

Majors. Biology: General, cell/histology, molecular. **Business:** General, business admin, hospitality admin, tourism/travel. **Communications:** Journalism. **Conservation:** General, environmental studies, management/policy. **Education:** General, art, biology, drama/dance, elementary, English, history, mathematics, middle, multi-level teacher, music, physical, science, secondary, social science, social studies. **Foreign languages:** Comparative lit. **Health:** Athletic training, premedicine. **History:** General. **Liberal arts:** Arts/sciences. **Math:** General. **Parks/recreation:** General, exercise sciences, health/fitness, sports admin. **Psychology:** General. **Social sciences:** General, anthropology, political science, sociology. **Visual/performing arts:** General, art, dance, dramatic, jazz, music history, music performance, music theory/composition, piano/organ, studio arts, theater design, voice/opera. **Other:** Wellness and alternative medicine.

Most popular majors. Business/marketing 13%, education 15%, history 6%, liberal arts 21%, psychology 17%, visual/performing arts 11%.

Computing on campus. 131 workstations in library, computer center. Dormitories wired for high-speed internet access and linked to campus network. Commuter students can connect to campus network. Online course registration, helpline, wireless network available.

Student life. Freshman orientation: Mandatory, $189 fee. Preregistration for classes offered. Held prior to start of semester. **Housing:** Guaranteed on-campus for all undergraduates. Coed dorms, apartments, wellness housing available. $300 nonrefundable deposit, deadline 5/1. **Activities:** Bands, choral groups, dance, drama, film society, international student organizations, literary magazine, music ensembles, musical theater, radio station, student government, student newspaper, Behavioral science club, Christian Fellowship Club, Diversity committee, Political Awareness club, Little Brother/Little Sister, Habitat for Humanity, Native American club, Students Enriching and Responding Through Volunteer Efforts, Earth Awareness club.

Athletics. NCAA. **Intercollegiate:** Basketball, cross-country, golf M, lacrosse M, soccer, softball W, tennis, volleyball W. **Intramural:** Badminton, basketball, bowling, cross-country, golf, lacrosse, racquetball, rugby, soccer, softball, swimming, table tennis, tennis, volleyball, water polo, weight lifting. **Team name:** Badgers.

Student services. Adult student services, alcohol/substance abuse counseling, career counseling, services for economically disadvantaged, student employment services, financial aid counseling, health services, on-campus daycare, personal counseling, placement for graduates, women's services. **Physically disabled:** Services for visually, hearing impaired.

Contact. E-mail: jscadmissions@jsc.edu
Phone: (802) 635-1219 Toll-free number: (800) 635-2356
Fax: (802) 635-1230
Penny Howrigan, Associate Dean of Enrollment Services, Johnson State College, 337 College Hill, Johnson, VT 05656

Lyndon State College

Lyndonville, Vermont — **CB member**
www.lyndonstate.edu — **CB code: 3767**

- Public 4-year liberal arts and teachers college
- Residential campus in small town
- 1,391 degree-seeking undergraduates
- Application essay, interview required

General. Founded in 1911. Regionally accredited. **Degrees:** 183 bachelor's, 17 associate awarded; master's offered. **ROTC:** Air Force. **Location:** 10 miles from St. Johnsbury, 85 miles from Burlington. **Calendar:** Semester, limited summer session. **Full-time faculty:** 58 total; 91% have terminal degrees, 40% women. **Part-time faculty:** 109 total; 43% have terminal degrees, 2% minority, 44% women. **Class size:** 75% < 20, 25% 20-39, less than 1% 40-49. **Special facilities:** Meteorology laboratory and observation deck, ropes course.

Freshman class profile.

Mid 50% test scores			
SAT critical reading:	400-510	ACT composite:	18-21
SAT math:	400-510	Out-of-state:	58%
SAT writing:	400-500	Live on campus:	65%

Basis for selection. SAT optional. School record, GPA, recommendations and test scores most important. SAT or ACT recommended. **Homeschooled:** Transcript of courses and grades, interview, letter of recommendation (nonparent) required. **Learning Disabled:** Required to meet with our Learning Specialist and provide documentation of disability.

High school preparation. College-preparatory program recommended. Required and recommended units include English 4, mathematics 3-4, social studies 2, history 1, science 2-4 (laboratory 2) and foreign language 2. Physics and pre-calc for meteorology and computer science recommended.

2008-2009 Annual costs. Tuition/fees: $8,284; $16,948 out-of-state. New England Board of Higher Education rate for students from other New England states: 150% of Vermont resident tuition. Available to degree candidates in academic areas not offered by educational institutions in their home states. Room/board: $7,510. Books/supplies: $600. Personal expenses: $900.

2007-2008 Financial aid. Non-need-based: Scholarships awarded for academics, leadership.

Application procedures. Admission: Priority date 5/1; no deadline. $37 fee, may be waived for applicants with need. Admission notification on a rolling basis beginning on or about 11/1. Must reply by May 1 or within 2 week(s) if notified thereafter. **Financial aid:** Priority date 2/1; no closing date. FAFSA required. Applicants notified on a rolling basis starting 4/1; must reply within 2 week(s) of notification.

Academics. Special study options: Accelerated study, combined bachelor's/graduate degree, cooperative education, distance learning, double major, dual enrollment of high school students, ESL, honors, internships, liberal arts/career combination, student-designed major, study abroad, teacher certification program. **Credit/placement by examination:** AP, CLEP, IB, institutional tests. 60 credit hours maximum toward bachelor's degree. **Support services:** Learning center, reduced course load, remedial instruction, study skills assistance, tutoring, writing center.

Majors. Business: Accounting, accounting/business management, accounting/finance, business admin, entrepreneurial studies, finance, marketing, resort management, small business admin. **Communications:** General, broadcast journalism, journalism, media studies, photojournalism, radio/tv. **Communications technology:** General. **Computer sciences:** General. **Conservation:** Environmental science. **Education:** General, early childhood, elementary, English, physical, science, social science, special. **Health:** Athletic training, prenursing. **Interdisciplinary:** Biological/physical sciences, global studies, natural sciences. **Liberal arts:** Arts/sciences. **Math:** General. **Parks/recreation:** Exercise sciences, facilities management, health/fitness, sports admin. **Philosophy/religion:** Philosophy. **Physical sciences:** Atmospheric science, meteorology. **Psychology:** General. **Public administration:** Human services. **Social sciences:** General. **Visual/performing arts:** General, commercial/advertising art, design, graphic design, illustration, music management, music performance. **Other:** English: journalism and writing, Exercise science, Meteorology: military track, Mountain recreation management, Music business and industry, Philosophy and film, Sustainability studies.

Most popular majors. Business/marketing 13%, communications/journalism 7%, communication technologies 11%, parks/recreation 13%, physical sciences 10%, psychology 7%, public administration/social services 14%, visual/performing arts 7%.

Computing on campus. 50 workstations in library, computer center. Dormitories wired for high-speed internet access and linked to campus network. Commuter students can connect to campus network. Online course registration, online library, helpline, repair service, wireless network available.

Student life. Freshman orientation: Mandatory. Preregistration for classes offered. **Policies:** All students under 23 years of age must live on campus unless residing with parents or must live within 45-mile commuting distance. Exceptions are made on a case-by-case basis. **Housing:** Guaranteed on-campus for freshmen. Coed dorms, single-sex dorms, special housing for disabled, wellness housing available. $100 deposit, deadline 5/1. **Activities:** Jazz band, choral groups, dance, drama, literary magazine, music ensembles, radio station, student government, student newspaper, symphony orchestra, TV station, American Meteorological Society (student chapter), community service learning group, alternative spring break.

Athletics. NAIA. **Intercollegiate:** Baseball M, basketball, cross-country, ice hockey, soccer, softball W, tennis. **Intramural:** Basketball, cross-country, handball, ice hockey, lacrosse, racquetball, rugby, soccer, softball, squash, swimming, table tennis, tennis, track and field, volleyball, water polo M, weight lifting. **Team name:** Hornets.

Student services. Alcohol/substance abuse counseling, career counseling, student employment services, financial aid counseling, health services, personal counseling, placement for graduates, veterans' counselor. **Physically disabled:** Services for visually, hearing impaired.

Contact. E-mail: admissions@lyndonstate.edu
Phone: (802) 626-6413 Toll-free number: (800) 225-1998
Fax: (802) 626-6335
Patricia Krahnke, Dean of Admissions/Marketing, Lyndon State College, 1001 College Road, Lyndonville, VT 05851

Marlboro College

Marlboro, Vermont — **CB member**
www.marlboro.edu — **CB code: 3509**

- Private 4-year liberal arts college
- Residential campus in rural community
- 328 degree-seeking undergraduates: 2% part-time, 50% women
- 1 degree-seeking graduate students
- 64% of applicants admitted
- Application essay required

General. Founded in 1946. Regionally accredited. **Degrees:** 74 bachelor's awarded; master's offered. **Location:** 12 miles from Brattleboro, 70 miles from Albany, New York. **Calendar:** Semester. **Full-time faculty:** 37 total; 89% have terminal degrees, 5% minority, 46% women. **Part-time faculty:** 2 total; 50% have terminal degrees, 50% minority. **Special facilities:** Aviary, observatory, darkroom, theater 3/4 round, robotics lab, DNA lab, nature preserve, organic campus farm.

Freshman class profile. 447 applied, 287 admitted, 102 enrolled.

Mid 50% test scores			
SAT critical reading:	590-690	ACT composite:	24-32
SAT math:	510-650	Out-of-state:	90%
		Live on campus:	98%

Basis for selection. Academic ability, intellectual potential, writing skills, demonstrated leadership qualities, and potential to offer contribution to college community most important considerations. Selected applicants may be required to interview at discretion of admission committee. All transter applicants are required to interview. **Homeschooled:** Statement describing homeschool structure and mission, letter of recommendation (nonparent) required. Provide documentation of home school curriculum and projects. List of textbooks preferred. Writing sample required. **Learning Disabled:** Additional documentation may be required.

High school preparation. Recommended units include English 4, mathematics 3, social studies 2, history 2, science 3 (laboratory 3), foreign language 3 and academic electives 5. Advanced electives in area of interest and in performing and/or visual arts also recommended.

2009-2010 Annual costs. Tuition/fees: $33,660. Room/board: $9,220. Books/supplies: $1,000. Personal expenses: $150.

2008-2009 Financial aid. Need-based: 66% of total undergraduate aid awarded as scholarships/grants, 34% as loans/jobs. **Non-need-based:** Scholarships awarded for academics, leadership.

Application procedures. Admission: Priority date 3/1; no deadline. $50 fee, may be waived for applicants with need. Admission notification on a rolling basis beginning on or about 12/15. Must reply by May 1 or within 2 week(s) if notified thereafter. **Financial aid:** Closing date 3/1. FAFSA required. Applicants notified on a rolling basis starting 2/15; must reply by 5/1 or within 2 week(s) of notification.

Academics. Students self-design field of study, often interdisciplinary in nature. They work closely with faculty to determine concentration and have formal review in senior year by internal and external faculty. **Special study options:** Double major, dual enrollment of high school students, independent study, internships, student-designed major, study abroad. World Studies Program: opportunity to integrate study-abroad experience and/or internship in undergraduate course of study. **Credit/placement by examination:** AP, CLEP, IB, institutional tests. **Support services:** Learning center, reduced course load, study skills assistance, tutoring, writing center.

Majors. Area/ethnic studies: American, Asian, Central/Eastern European, East Asian, European, Latin American, Near/Middle Eastern, Russian/Slavic, South Asian, Southeast Asian, Western European. **Biology:** General, biochemistry, botany, cell/histology, ecology, genetics, molecular, plant physiology. **Computer sciences:** General, computer science. **Conservation:** General, environmental studies. **Foreign languages:** General, comparative lit, linguistics, Spanish, translation. **History:** General. **Interdisciplinary:** Biological/physical sciences, global studies, math/computer science, peace/conflict. **Legal studies:** Prelaw. **Liberal arts:** Arts/sciences. **Math:** General. **Philosophy/religion:** Philosophy, religion. **Physical sciences:** Astronomy, chemistry, organic chemistry, physics, theoretical physics. **Psychology:** General. **Social sciences:** General, anthropology, economics, political science, sociology. **Visual/performing arts:** General, art, art history/conservation, ceramics, cinematography, dance, dramatic, drawing, film/cinema, music history, painting, photography, play/screenwriting, sculpture, studio arts, theater design, theater history.

Computing on campus. 45 workstations in dormitories, library, computer center. Dormitories wired for high-speed internet access and linked to campus network. Commuter students can connect to campus network. Online library, helpline, student web hosting, wireless network available.

Student life. Freshman orientation: Mandatory. 5-day program in late August, option to go on pre-orientation outdoor trips during week prior to on-campus orientation and student enrollment. **Policies:** Self-governing community based on old-fashioned, historical New England-style town meeting. Students, faculty, and staff have equal vote. Elected community court enforces bylaws. **Housing:** Guaranteed on-campus for freshmen. Coed dorms, single-sex dorms, apartments, wellness housing available. $400 nonrefundable deposit, deadline 5/1. **Activities:** Dance, drama, film society, literary magazine, music ensembles, musical theater, student government, student newspaper, Amnesty International, animal rights, gay/lesbian and bisexual group, Committee on Environmental Quality, fire and safety commission.

Athletics. Intercollegiate: Soccer. **Intramural:** Basketball, fencing, soccer, softball, swimming, table tennis, volleyball. **Team name:** Fighting Dead Trees.

Student services. Alcohol/substance abuse counseling, career counseling, financial aid counseling, health services, personal counseling. **Physically disabled:** Services for visually impaired.

Contact. E-mail: admissions@marlboro.edu
Phone: (802) 258-9236 Toll-free number: (800) 343-0049
Fax: (802) 451-7555
Doug Swartz, Dean of Enrollment and Financial Aid, Marlboro College, PO Box A, Marlboro, VT 05344-0300

Middlebury College

Middlebury, Vermont — **CB member**
www.middlebury.edu — **CB code: 3526**

- Private 4-year liberal arts college
- Residential campus in small town
- 2,422 degree-seeking undergraduates: 50% women, 3% African American, 9% Asian American, 6% Hispanic American, 1% Native American, 10% international
- 17% of applicants admitted
- SAT and SAT Subject Tests or ACT (ACT writing optional), application essay required
- 93% graduate within 6 years

General. Founded in 1800. Regionally accredited. Affiliated with Monterey Institute of International Studies. **Degrees:** 636 bachelor's awarded; master's, doctoral offered. **ROTC:** Army. **Location:** 200 miles from Boston, 250 miles from New York City. **Calendar:** 4-1-4, limited summer session. **Full-time faculty:** 249 total; 94% have terminal degrees, 12% minority, 39% women. **Part-time faculty:** 62 total; 68% have terminal degrees, 13% minority, 50% women. **Class size:** 70% < 20, 23% 20-39, 5% 40-49, 2% 50-99. **Special facilities:** Observatory, fine arts center, downhill and cross country ski areas, interactive language laboratories, 18-hole golf course.

Freshman class profile. 7,823 applied, 1,316 admitted, 576 enrolled.

Mid 50% test scores			
SAT critical reading:	630-740	Rank in top tenth:	86%
SAT math:	640-740	Return as sophomores:	95%
SAT writing:	640-740	Out-of-state:	95%
ACT composite:	29-33	Live on campus:	100%
Rank in top quarter:	93%	International:	12%

Basis for selection. School record most important (including course selection and course load), followed by class rank, extracurricular activities, letters of recommendation, and test scores. Requirement may be met by submitting ACT, SAT, or 3 exams in different areas of study, which may be selected from SAT Subject Tests, AP exams, or International Baccalaureate exams.

High school preparation. Recommended units include English 4, mathematics 4, social studies 3, science 3 (laboratory 3) and foreign language 4. Music, art, or drama recommended.

2009-2010 Annual costs. Comprehensive fee: $50,780. Books/supplies: $750. Personal expenses: $1,000.

2007-2008 Financial aid. All financial aid based on need. 390 full-time freshmen applied for aid; 308 were judged to have need; 308 of these received aid. Average need met was 100%. Average scholarship/grant was $31,446; average loan $3,231. 89% of total undergraduate aid awarded as scholarships/grants, 11% as loans/jobs. **Additional information:** College maintains need-blind admissions policy and meets full demonstrated financial need of students who qualify for admission, to degree resources permit.

Application procedures. Admission: Closing date 1/1 (postmark date). $65 fee, may be waived for applicants with need. Admission notification 4/1. Must reply by 5/1. **Financial aid:** Priority date 11/15, closing date 2/1. FAFSA, institutional form, CSS PROFILE required. Applicants notified by 4/1; must reply by 5/1.

Academics. Special study options: Accelerated study, double major, exchange student, honors, independent study, internships, semester at sea, student-designed major, study abroad, teacher certification program, Washington semester. Williams College-Mystic Seaport Program in American Maritime Studies, Oxford University summer program, independent scholar program, exchange programs with Berea College and Swarthmore College, 3-year international major. **Credit/placement by examination:** AP, CLEP, IB, institutional tests. **Support services:** Learning center, pre-admission summer program, reduced course load, study skills assistance, tutoring, writing center.

Majors. Area/ethnic studies: African, American, Central/Eastern European, East Asian, European, Latin American, Near/Middle Eastern, Russian/Slavic, Southeast Asian, women's. **Biology:** General, biochemistry, molecular. **Computer sciences:** Computer science. **Conservation:** Environmental studies. **Foreign languages:** Chinese, classics, French, German, Italian, Japanese, Russian, Spanish. **History:** General. **Interdisciplinary:** Neuroscience. **Liberal arts:** Arts/sciences. **Math:** General. **Philosophy/religion:** Philosophy, religion. **Physical sciences:** Chemistry, geology, physics. **Psychology:** General. **Social sciences:** Economics, geography, international relations, political science, sociology. **Visual/performing arts:** Art history/conservation, cinematography, dance, dramatic, studio arts.

Most popular majors. Area/ethnic studies 9%, English 11%, foreign language 7%, history 6%, natural resources/environmental science 6%, psychology 6%, social sciences 30%, visual/performing arts 10%.

Computing on campus. 494 workstations in dormitories, library, computer center, student center. Dormitories wired for high-speed internet access and linked to campus network. Commuter students can connect to campus network. Online course registration, online library, helpline, repair service, student web hosting, wireless network available.

Student life. Freshman orientation: Mandatory. Elective portion of orientation carries cost of $150. **Housing:** Guaranteed on-campus for all undergraduates. Coed dorms, special housing for disabled, apartments, wellness housing available. $200 deposit, deadline 5/1. Multicultural, environmental, foreign language, and 5 social houses available. Commons System organizes residence halls into 5 groups, each with own budget, government, faculty, and staff associates. **Activities:** Jazz band, choral groups, dance, drama, film society, international student organizations, literary magazine, music ensembles, musical theater, radio station, student government, student newspaper, symphony orchestra, African-American Alliance, Alianza Latinoamerica y Caribena, Asian students organization, environmental quality, Hillel, Gay Lesbian Bisexual Alliance, mountain club, volunteer service program, women's organization.

Athletics. NCAA. **Intercollegiate:** Baseball M, basketball, cross-country, diving, field hockey W, football (tackle) M, golf, ice hockey, lacrosse, skiing, soccer, softball W, squash W, swimming, tennis, track and field, volleyball W. **Intramural:** Badminton, basketball, cross-country, diving, football (non-tackle), golf, ice hockey, lacrosse, skiing, soccer, softball, squash W, swimming, table tennis, tennis, triathlon, volleyball. **Team name:** Panthers.

Student services. Alcohol/substance abuse counseling, chaplain/spiritual director, career counseling, student employment services, financial aid counseling, health services, minority student services, personal counseling, placement for graduates, women's services. **Physically disabled:** Services for visually, speech, hearing impaired.

Contact. E-mail: admissions@middlebury.edu
Phone: (802) 443-3000 Fax: (802) 443-0258
Robert Clagett, Dean of Admissions, Middlebury College, The Emma Willard House, Middlebury, VT 05753-6002

Norwich University

Northfield, Vermont — **CB member**
www.norwich.edu — **CB code: 3669**

- Private 4-year university and military college
- Residential campus in small town
- 2,148 degree-seeking undergraduates
- SAT or ACT (ACT writing optional) required

General. Founded in 1819. Regionally accredited. Oldest private military college in U.S. Adult programs, baccalaureate and masters, are self-designed, individually mentored programs. Both military and civilian students accepted. **Degrees:** 414 bachelor's awarded; master's offered. **ROTC:** Army, Naval, Air Force. **Location:** 50 miles from Burlington, 180 miles from Boston. **Calendar:** Semester, limited summer session. **Full-time faculty:** 125 total. **Part-time faculty:** 137 total. **Special facilities:** Museum.

Freshman class profile.

Mid 50% test scores		**ACT composite:**	19-24
SAT critical reading:	470-600	**Out-of-state:**	80%
SAT math:	480-600	**Live on campus:**	98%

Basis for selection. High school record, recommendations, activities, honors, awards, test scores important. Class rank considered in admissions decisions and will be criterion for financial aid awarding.

High school preparation. 18 units recommended. Recommended units include English 4, mathematics 3, social studies 2, science 1 and foreign language 2.

2008-2009 Annual costs. Tuition/fees: $26,064. Military students pay an additional $1,550 per year for cadet uniform for first and second years. Room/board: $9,032. Books/supplies: $1,000.

Financial aid. Non-need-based: Scholarships awarded for academics, leadership, music/drama, ROTC. **Additional information:** Winners of ROTC scholarships receive full room and board; must maintain 2.75 GPA. Renewable up to 4 years.

Application procedures. Admission: Priority date 5/1; no deadline. $35 fee, may be waived for applicants with need. Admission notification on a rolling basis beginning on or about 11/30. Must reply by May 1 or within 3 week(s) if notified thereafter. **Financial aid:** Priority date 3/1; no closing date. FAFSA, institutional form, CSS PROFILE required. Applicants notified on a rolling basis starting 12/15.

Academics. Special study options: Accelerated study, combined bachelor's/graduate degree, distance learning, double major, external degree, honors, independent study, internships, liberal arts/career combination, student-designed major, study abroad, teacher certification program. **Credit/placement by examination:** AP, CLEP, IB, institutional tests. 12 credit hours maximum toward bachelor's degree. **Support services:** Learning center, pre-admission summer program, reduced course load, remedial instruction, tutoring.

Majors. Architecture: Architecture. **Biology:** General, biochemistry, biomedical sciences. **Business:** Accounting, business admin. **Communications:** General. **Computer sciences:** General, computer science. **Conservation:** General. **Education:** Physical. **Engineering:** Civil, electrical, mechanical. **Health:** Athletic training. **History:** General. **Interdisciplinary:** Peace/conflict. **Legal studies:** Prelaw. **Liberal arts:** Arts/sciences. **Math:** General. **Physical sciences:** Chemistry, geology, physics. **Protective services:** Criminal justice. **Psychology:** General. **Social sciences:** Economics, international relations, political science.

Computing on campus. 150 workstations in library, computer center. Dormitories linked to campus network. Commuter students can connect to campus network. Online library, helpline, repair service, wireless network available.

Student life. Freshman orientation: Available, $10 fee. Preregistration for classes offered. Wednesday through Sunday, including 1-day cruise dinner. **Policies:** ROTC participants must live in dormitories. **Housing:** Guaranteed on-campus for freshmen. Coed dorms available. $250 deposit, deadline 5/1. **Activities:** Bands, choral groups, drama, international student organizations, literary magazine, music ensembles, musical theater, radio station, student government, student newspaper, symphony orchestra, Arnold Air Society, Special Operations Company Association of the United States Army, Norwich University Volunteer Organization, Norwich Christian Fellowship, ambulance rescue squad, Young Republicans, Square and Compass.

Athletics. NCAA. **Intercollegiate:** Baseball M, basketball, cross-country, diving, football (tackle) M, golf, ice hockey, lacrosse, rifle, rugby, soccer, softball W, swimming, wrestling M. **Intramural:** Basketball, cross-country, fencing, football (tackle) M, ice hockey, lacrosse M, racquetball, skiing, soccer, softball, tennis, track and field, volleyball. **Team name:** Cadets.

Student services. Adult student services, chaplain/spiritual director, career counseling, student employment services, financial aid counseling, health services, personal counseling, placement for graduates, veterans' counselor.

Contact. E-mail: nuadm@norwich.edu
Phone: (802) 485-2002 Toll-free number: (800) 468-6679
Fax: (802) 485-2002
Karen McGrath, Dean of Enrollment, Norwich University, 158 Harmon Drive, Northfield, VT 05663

St. Michael's College

Colchester, Vermont — **CB member**
www.smcvt.edu — **CB code: 3757**

- Private 4-year liberal arts college affiliated with Roman Catholic Church
- Residential campus in large town
- 1,980 degree-seeking undergraduates: 1% part-time, 53% women, 1% African American, 1% Asian American, 1% Hispanic American, 1% international
- 261 degree-seeking graduate students
- 69% of applicants admitted
- SAT or ACT with writing, application essay required
- 81% graduate within 6 years; 18% enter graduate study

General. Founded in 1904. Regionally accredited. **Degrees:** 441 bachelor's awarded; master's offered. **ROTC:** Army, Air Force. **Location:** 3 miles from Burlington, 95 miles from Montreal, Canada. **Calendar:** Semester, limited summer session. **Full-time faculty:** 154 total; 85% have terminal degrees, 7% minority, 45% women. **Part-time faculty:** 55 total; 42% have terminal degrees, 4% minority, 54% women. **Class size:** 57% < 20, 41% 20-39, less than 1% 40-49, less than 1% 50-99, less than 1% >100. **Special facilities:** Observatory.

Freshman class profile. 3,618 applied, 2,489 admitted, 551 enrolled.

Mid 50% test scores		**GPA 2.0-2.99:**	23%
SAT critical reading:	520-620	**Rank in top quarter:**	52%
SAT math:	520-610	**Rank in top tenth:**	24%
SAT writing:	530-620	**End year in good standing:**	92%
ACT composite:	22-26	**Return as sophomores:**	86%
GPA 3.75 or higher:	33%	**Out-of-state:**	85%
GPA 3.50-3.74:	17%	**Live on campus:**	98%
GPA 3.0-3.49:	27%	**International:**	1%

Basis for selection. Curriculum, high school performance and test scores are important considerations. Application essay, recommendations, and activities also important. College administers its own language placement tests during academic orientation prior to beginning of each semester. SAT Subject Tests are not required for admission, can be utilized by the College for language placement if available. **Homeschooled:** Statement describing homeschool structure and mission, transcript of courses and grades, state high school equivalency certificate required. Standardized tests (SAT or ACT) take on additional emphasis.

High school preparation. College-preparatory program required. 16 units required; 20 recommended. Required and recommended units include English 4, mathematics 3-4, social studies 3-4, science 3-4 (laboratory 2-3) and foreign language 3-4. Physics, mathematics, chemistry, biology emphasized for science applicants. History courses fulfill social studies requirement.

2008-2009 Annual costs. Tuition/fees: $31,940. Room/board: $7,960. Books/supplies: $1,200. Personal expenses: $450.

2008-2009 Financial aid. Need-based: 414 full-time freshmen applied for aid; 319 were judged to have need; 319 of these received aid. Average need met was 76%. Average scholarship/grant was $14,273; average loan $4,658. 69% of total undergraduate aid awarded as scholarships/grants, 31% as loans/jobs. **Non-need-based:** Awarded to 704 full-time undergraduates, including 259 freshmen. Scholarships awarded for academics, athletics, ROTC.

Application procedures. Admission: Priority date 11/1; deadline 2/1 (postmark date). $50 fee, may be waived for applicants with need. Admission notification 4/1. Must reply by May 1 or within 2 week(s) if notified thereafter. 2 Early Action deadlines: November 1 and December 1. Corresponding Early Action notification of admission decision dates January 1 and February 1. **Financial aid:** Priority date 3/15; no closing date. FAFSA required. Applicants notified on a rolling basis starting 2/1; must reply by 5/1 or within 2 week(s) of notification.

Academics. All students must achieve second-language proficiency. **Special study options:** Combined bachelor's/graduate degree, cross-registration, distance learning, double major, ESL, honors, independent study, internships, liberal arts/career combination, semester at sea, student-designed major, study abroad, teacher certification program, Washington semester. 3-2 engineering with University of Vermont and Clarkson University, 4-1 MBA with Clarkson University, international exchange student program. **Credit/placement by examination:** AP, CLEP, IB, institutional tests. 30 credit hours maximum toward bachelor's degree. **Support services:** Learning center, reduced course load, study skills assistance, tutoring, writing center.

Majors. Area/ethnic studies: American. **Biology:** General, biochemistry. **Business:** Accounting, business admin. **Communications:** Journalism. **Computer sciences:** Computer science, information systems. **Conservation:** Environmental science. **Education:** Art, elementary. **Engineering:** General. **Foreign languages:** General, classics, French, Latin, Spanish. **History:** General. **Math:** General. **Philosophy/religion:** Philosophy, religion. **Physical sciences:** General, chemistry, physics. **Psychology:** General. **Social sciences:** Anthropology, economics, political science, sociology. **Visual/performing arts:** Art, dramatic, studio arts. **Other:** Gender Studies.

Most popular majors. Biology 7%, business/marketing 22%, communications/journalism 6%, English 9%, history 6%, psychology 11%, social sciences 12%, visual/performing arts 7%.

Computing on campus. 375 workstations in dormitories, library, computer center, student center. Dormitories wired for high-speed internet access and linked to campus network. Commuter students can connect to campus network. Online course registration, online library, helpline, student web hosting, wireless network available.

Student life. Freshman orientation: Mandatory. Preregistration for classes offered. One-day academic orientation held in July. Off-campus weekend experience during summer offered to all new students. **Policies:** Limited number of parking permits available for first-time, first-year students to have cars on campus during spring semester. **Housing:** Guaranteed on-campus for all undergraduates. Coed dorms, single-sex dorms, special housing for disabled, apartments, wellness housing available. $500 nonrefundable deposit, deadline 5/1. **Activities:** Bands, campus ministries, choral groups, dance, drama, international student organizations, literary magazine, music ensembles, musical theater, radio station, student government, student newspaper, fire and rescue squad, Mobilization of Volunteer Efforts, Martin Luther King Society, Diversity Coalition, Green Up SMC/environmental club, Alianza Society, peace and justice club, Student Global AIDS Campaign.

Athletics. NCAA. **Intercollegiate:** Baseball M, basketball, cross-country, diving, field hockey W, golf M, ice hockey, lacrosse, skiing, soccer, softball W, swimming, tennis, volleyball W. **Intramural:** Badminton, basketball, bowling, football (non-tackle), ice hockey, racquetball, soccer, softball, squash, table tennis, volleyball. **Team name:** Purple Knights.

Student services. Alcohol/substance abuse counseling, chaplain/spiritual director, career counseling, student employment services, financial aid counseling, health services, minority student services, on-campus daycare, personal counseling, placement for graduates, veterans' counselor, women's services. **Physically disabled:** Services for visually, speech, hearing impaired.

Contact. E-mail: admission@smcvt.edu
Phone: (802) 654-3000 Toll-free number: (800) 762-8000
Fax: (802) 654-2906
Jacqueline Murphy, Director of Admissions, St. Michael's College, One Winooski Park, Colchester, VT 05439

Southern Vermont College

Bennington, Vermont — **CB member**
www.svc.edu — **CB code: 3796**

- Private 4-year liberal arts college
- Residential campus in large town
- 444 degree-seeking undergraduates: 13% part-time, 61% women, 6% African American, 1% Asian American, 4% Hispanic American, 1% international
- 64% of applicants admitted
- SAT or ACT (ACT writing recommended), application essay required
- 38% graduate within 6 years

General. Founded in 1926. Regionally accredited. **Degrees:** 55 bachelor's, 39 associate awarded. **Location:** 40 miles from Albany, NY; 90 miles from Springfield, MA. **Calendar:** Semester, limited summer session. **Full-time faculty:** 19 total; 47% women. **Part-time faculty:** 29 total. **Class size:** 71% < 20, 29% 20-39. **Special facilities:** 25 miles of trails, 2 natural ponds, 27-room Edwardian mansion.

Freshman class profile. 673 applied, 434 admitted, 189 enrolled.

Mid 50% test scores		Rank in top quarter:	4%
SAT critical reading:	420-500	End year in good standing:	85%
SAT math:	400-500	Return as sophomores:	67%
ACT composite:	15-21	Out-of-state:	76%
GPA 3.50-3.74:	2%	Live on campus:	92%
GPA 3.0-3.49:	30%	International:	1%
GPA 2.0-2.99:	67%		

Basis for selection. Potential for academic achievement most important. Test scores, interview, personal references important. None of admissions criteria intended as absolute cut-offs, but students failing to meet these standards must demonstrate potential for academic success in other ways. Interview strongly recommended. **Homeschooled:** Statement describing homeschool structure and mission, transcript of courses and grades required. **Learning Disabled:** Documentation of LD.

High school preparation. College-preparatory program recommended. Required and recommended units include English 4, mathematics 3, social studies 4, history 4, science 3, foreign language 2 and academic electives 4.

2008-2009 Annual costs. Tuition/fees: $18,160. Health insurance, if applicable, $650 per year. Room/board: $8,500.

2008-2009 Financial aid. Non-need-based: Scholarships awarded for academics, leadership.

Application procedures. Admission: No deadline. $30 fee, may be waived for applicants with need, free for online applicants. Admission notification on a rolling basis beginning on or about 12/1. Must reply by May 1 or within 2 week(s) if notified thereafter. . **Financial aid:** No deadline. FAFSA required. Applicants notified on a rolling basis.

Academics. Students can receive free walk-in tutoring, individualized tutoring, study group sessions, workshops for skill review, proofreading, and note-taking. Disabilities Support Program. **Special study options:** Combined bachelor's/graduate degree, cross-registration, double major, independent study, internships, liberal arts/career combination. **Credit/placement by examination:** CLEP, SAT, ACT. **Support services:** Learning center, reduced course load, remedial instruction, study skills assistance, tutoring, writing center.

Majors. Business: Business admin, entrepreneurial studies, nonprofit/public. **Communications:** General. **Health:** Nursing (RN). **Legal studies:** Prelaw. **Liberal arts:** Arts/sciences. **Protective services:** Police science. **Psychology:** General. **Other:** History and politics, Liberal arts/management.

Most popular majors. Business/marketing 17%, communications/journalism 13%, English 6%, health sciences 17%, liberal arts 6%, psychology 10%, science technologies 15%, security/protective services 17%.

Computing on campus. 43 workstations in library, computer center. Dormitories wired for high-speed internet access and linked to campus network. Commuter students can connect to campus network. Online course registration, online library, repair service, student web hosting, wireless network available.

Student life. Freshman orientation: Mandatory. 4-day experience held with 3-part theme: academics, student life, outdoor recreation. Outdoor component parallels what students encounter during first semester: learning to adapt to unfamiliar environment. **Housing:** Guaranteed on-campus for freshmen. Coed dorms, wellness housing available. $200 deposit. **Activities:** Drama, international student organizations, literary magazine, student government, student newspaper, criminal justice club, Everyone's Earth, community action program.

Athletics. NCAA. **Intercollegiate:** Baseball M, basketball, cross-country, rugby, soccer, softball W, volleyball. **Intramural:** Basketball, ice hockey, skiing, soccer, tennis, volleyball. **Team name:** Mountaineers.

Student services. Adult student services, alcohol/substance abuse counseling, career counseling, student employment services, financial aid counseling, health services, personal counseling, placement for graduates. **Physically disabled:** Services for visually, hearing impaired.

Contact. E-mail: admissions@svc.edu
Phone: (802) 447-6304 Toll-free number: (800) 378-2782
Fax: (802) 447-6313
Grant Thatcher, Director of Admissions, Southern Vermont College, 982 Mansion Drive, Bennington, VT 05201

Sterling College

Craftsbury Common, Vermont — **CB member**
www.sterlingcollege.edu — **CB code: 3752**

- Private 4-year liberal arts college
- Residential campus in rural community
- 98 degree-seeking undergraduates: 4% part-time, 43% women, 1% Asian American, 1% Hispanic American
- 78% of applicants admitted
- Application essay required

General. Founded in 1958. Regionally accredited. Global Field Studies in Labrador, Scotland, Newfoundland, Iceland, Canada, Japan, India, Belize, and Scandinavian countries. Member of National Work Colleges Consortium. Special accreditation through the Association of Experiential Educators. Comprehensive environmental internship program. **Degrees:** 17 bachelor's, 2 associate awarded. **Location:** 40 miles from Montpelier, 70 miles from Burlington. **Calendar:** Semester, limited summer session. **Full-time faculty:** 16 total; 25% have terminal degrees, 50% women. **Part-time faculty:** 14 total; 36% have terminal degrees, 7% minority, 36% women. **Class size:** 100% < 20. **Special facilities:** Managed woodlots, diverse livestock farm, cross-country ski trails, back-country recreation, solar and wind powered barns, organic gardens, greenhouse, 32-foot climbing wall, low and high ropes challenge course, sugar house, 300-acre educational Bear Swamp (boreal forest and muskeg).

Freshman class profile. 104 applied, 81 admitted, 27 enrolled.

GPA 3.75 or higher:	8%	Rank in top quarter:	21%
GPA 3.50-3.74:	4%	Rank in top tenth:	11%
GPA 3.0-3.49:	34%	Out-of-state:	78%
GPA 2.0-2.99:	54%	Live on campus:	100%

Basis for selection. Demonstrated interest in programs, motivation, interview, academic record, recommendations important; test scores considered if submitted. Admissions interview is highly recommended. **Homeschooled:** Transcript of courses and grades required. Portfolio of educational and life experience may be submitted in lieu of diploma or equivalency. Students must meet home school requirements for their particular state of residence.

High school preparation. Required and recommended units include English 4, mathematics 3-4, social studies 2, history 2, science 2-3 (laboratory 2-3) and foreign language 2.

2008-2009 Annual costs. Tuition/fees: $21,655. Students receive $1,550 tuition and book credit in exchange for work done on campus. Room/board: $7,192. Books/supplies: $800. Personal expenses: $700.

2008-2009 Financial aid. Non-need-based: Scholarships awarded for academics, leadership, state residency.

Application procedures. Admission: Priority date 2/15; deadline 4/1 (postmark date). $35 fee, may be waived for applicants with need. Admission notification 4/1. Must reply by May 1 or within 2 week(s) if notified thereafter. **Financial aid:** Priority date 3/15; no closing date. FAFSA, institutional form required. Applicants notified on a rolling basis starting 2/1; must reply by 5/1 or within 2 week(s) of notification.

Academics. Special study options: Double major, dual enrollment of high school students, exchange student, independent study, internships, semester at sea, student-designed major, study abroad, urban semester. 2-week Global Field Studies. **Credit/placement by examination:** AP, CLEP, institutional tests. **Support services:** Learning center, reduced course load, remedial instruction, study skills assistance, tutoring, writing center.

Majors. Agriculture: General. **Biology:** Conservation, ecology, environmental, wildlife. **Conservation:** General, environmental studies, forest management, forestry, water/wetlands/marine, wildlife. **Education:** Agricultural, curriculum. **Liberal arts:** Arts/sciences. **Parks/recreation:** General. **Other:** Circumpolar studies/northern studies, Environmental education.

Most popular majors. Agriculture 18%, area/ethnic studies 12%, liberal arts 29%, natural resources/environmental science 18%, parks/recreation 23%.

Computing on campus. 20 workstations in library, computer center, student center. Dormitories wired for high-speed internet access and linked to campus network. Commuter students can connect to campus network. Online library, helpline, repair service, wireless network available.

Student life. Freshman orientation: Mandatory. All entering freshmen participate in series of adventure challenge and academic activities. **Housing:** Guaranteed on-campus for all undergraduates. Coed dorms, apartments, wellness housing available. Pets allowed in dorm rooms. **Activities:** Choral groups, drama, film society, music ensembles, student government.

Athletics. **Intramural:** Archery, badminton, baseball, basketball, bowling, boxing, cross-country, equestrian, fencing, ice hockey, rifle, skiing, soccer, softball, swimming, table tennis, volleyball, weight lifting.

Student services. Adult student services, alcohol/substance abuse counseling, career counseling, student employment services, financial aid counseling, health services, personal counseling, placement for graduates, veterans' counselor.

Contact. E-mail: admissions@sterlingcollege.edu
Phone: (802) 586-7711 ext. 2 Toll-free number: (800) 648-3591 ext. 2
Fax: (802) 586-2596
Gwyn Harris, Director of Admissions, Sterling College, PO Box 72, Craftsbury Common, VT 05827-0072

University of Vermont

Burlington, Vermont — **CB member**
www.uvm.edu — **CB code: 3920**

- Public 4-year university
- Residential campus in large town
- 9,867 degree-seeking undergraduates: 4% part-time, 56% women, 1% African American, 2% Asian American, 2% Hispanic American, 1% international
- 1,837 degree-seeking graduate students
- 65% of applicants admitted
- SAT or ACT with writing, application essay required
- 71% graduate within 6 years; 25% enter graduate study

General. Founded in 1791. Regionally accredited. **Degrees:** 2,004 bachelor's awarded; master's, doctoral, first professional offered. **ROTC:** Army. **Location:** 225 miles from Boston, 100 miles from Montreal. **Calendar:** Semester, extensive summer session. **Full-time faculty:** 609 total; 84% have terminal degrees, 14% minority, 42% women. **Part-time faculty:** 156 total; 30% have terminal degrees, 4% minority, 58% women. **Class size:** 48% < 20, 35% 20-39, 6% 40-49, 7% 50-99, 5% >100. **Special facilities:** Horse farm, dairy farm, geology museum, natural areas, science center, research vessel on Lake Champlain, ecosystem science laboratory on Lake Champlain, art and anthropology museum, maple research facility.

Freshman class profile. 21,062 applied, 13,651 admitted, 2,468 enrolled.

Mid 50% test scores		**Rank in top tenth:**	29%
SAT critical reading:	540-640	**End year in good standing:**	90%
SAT math:	550-650	**Return as sophomores:**	86%
SAT writing:	540-640	**Out-of-state:**	74%
ACT composite:	23-28	**Live on campus:**	97%
Rank in top quarter:	72%	**International:**	1%

Basis for selection. School achievement record of primary importance; test scores also important. Essay, extracurricular activities considered. Letter of recommendation required. Special consideration to Vermont residents, children of alumni, minority students, and foreign students. Informational interview recommended. Music applicants must present audition tape or CD. **Homeschooled:** Transcript of courses and grades, state high school equivalency certificate, letter of recommendation (nonparent) required. Applicants must provide proof of completion of minimum entrance requirements and completion of GED.

High school preparation. College-preparatory program required. 16 units required. Required units include English 4, mathematics 3, social studies 3, science 2 (laboratory 1) and foreign language 2. Additional mathematics and/or science units required in engineering, business, health science programs.

2008-2009 Annual costs. Tuition/fees: $12,844; $29,682 out-of-state. Room/board: $8,534. Books/supplies: $990. Personal expenses: $1,202.

2007-2008 Financial aid. **Need-based:** 1,753 full-time freshmen applied for aid; 1,297 were judged to have need; 1,295 of these received aid. Average need met was 81%. Average scholarship/grant was $12,311; average loan $5,760. 70% of total undergraduate aid awarded as scholarships/grants, 30% as loans/jobs. **Non-need-based:** Awarded to 2,083 full-time undergraduates, including 864 freshmen. Scholarships awarded for academics, art, athletics, ROTC.

Application procedures. **Admission:** Closing date 1/15 (postmark date). $45 fee, may be waived for applicants with need. Admission notification 3/31. Must reply by May 1 or within 3 week(s) if notified thereafter. Waitlist admits have 2 days to reply. Early action candidates may have final decision deferred until completion of fall semester review. **Financial aid:** Priority date 2/10; no closing date. FAFSA required. Applicants notified on a rolling basis starting 3/15; must reply within 4 week(s) of notification.

Academics. **Special study options:** Combined bachelor's/graduate degree, cooperative education, cross-registration, distance learning, double major, dual enrollment of high school students, exchange student, honors, independent study, internships, liberal arts/career combination, student-designed major, study abroad, teacher certification program, Washington semester. Evening university option in several programs, limited English as a second language. **Credit/placement by examination:** AP, CLEP, IB, institutional tests. Half of major and half of minor requirements must be completed in residence. **Support services:** Learning center, pre-admission summer program, reduced course load, study skills assistance, tutoring, writing center.

Honors college/program. All first-year applicants automatically considered for Honors College. Admission considerations include excellent SAT and/or ACT scores, high school rank, challenging high school course work, and an ability to overcome obstacles; about 100 admitted each year.

Majors. **Agriculture:** General, agronomy, animal sciences, horticultural science. **Area/ethnic studies:** Asian, Canadian, European, Italian, Latin American, Russian/Slavic, women's. **Biology:** General, biochemistry, biomedical sciences, botany, microbiology, molecular, wildlife, zoology. **Business:** Business admin, entrepreneurial studies. **Communications:** Advertising, public relations. **Computer sciences:** Computer science, systems analysis. **Conservation:** General, environmental science, environmental studies, forestry. **Education:** General, art, early childhood, early childhood special, elementary, English, family/consumer sciences, foreign languages, mathematics, middle, music, physical, science, secondary, social studies. **Engineering:** Civil, electrical, environmental, industrial, mechanical. **Family/consumer sciences:** Family studies. **Foreign languages:** Ancient Greek, Chinese, classics, French, German, Japanese, Latin, Russian, Spanish. **Health:** Athletic training, clinical lab science, communication disorders, dietetics, medical radiologic technology/radiation therapy, nuclear medical technology, nursing (RN). **History:** General. **Interdisciplinary:** Nutrition sciences. **Liberal arts:** Arts/sciences. **Math:** General, statistics. **Parks/recreation:** Exercise sciences, facilities management. **Philosophy/religion:** Philosophy, religion. **Physical sciences:** Chemistry, geology, physics. **Psychology:** General. **Public administration:** Social work. **Social sciences:** Anthropology, economics, geography, international economic development, political science, sociology. **Visual/performing arts:** Art history/conservation, dramatic, film/cinema, music performance, studio arts.

Most popular majors. Business/marketing 10%, education 7%, English 7%, health sciences 8%, natural resources/environmental science 6%, psychology 8%, social sciences 19%, visual/performing arts 6%.

Computing on campus. 685 workstations in dormitories, library, computer center, student center. Dormitories wired for high-speed internet access and linked to campus network. Commuter students can connect to campus network. Online course registration, online library, helpline, repair service, wireless network available.

Student life. **Freshman orientation:** Mandatory. Preregistration for classes offered. 2-day sessions offered at various times in June. For those who cannot attend in June, a session is offered prior to the start of the fall term in August. **Policies:** Student code of conduct. **Housing:** Guaranteed on-campus for freshmen. Coed dorms, apartments, fraternity/sorority housing, wellness housing available. **Activities:** Bands, campus ministries, choral groups, dance, drama, film society, international student organizations, literary magazine, music ensembles, musical theater, radio station, student government, student newspaper, TV station, Hillel, black student union, Asian American student union, gay/lesbian/bisexual/transgender alliance, Alianza Latina, Catholic center, Volunteers in Action, Vermont student environmental program.

Athletics. NCAA. **Intercollegiate:** Baseball M, basketball, cross-country, diving W, field hockey W, ice hockey, lacrosse, skiing, soccer, softball W, swimming W, track and field. **Intramural:** Badminton, basketball, bowling, cheerleading, equestrian, fencing, football (non-tackle), ice hockey, racquetball, rowing (crew), soccer, softball, table tennis, tennis, volleyball, water polo. **Team name:** Catamounts.

Student services. Alcohol/substance abuse counseling, chaplain/spiritual director, career counseling, services for economically disadvantaged, student employment services, financial aid counseling, health services, minority student services, on-campus daycare, personal counseling, placement for graduates, veterans' counselor, women's services. **Physically disabled:** Services for visually, speech, hearing impaired. **Learning disabled:** Comprehensive services available.

Contact. E-mail: admissions@uvm.edu
Phone: (802) 656-3370 Fax: (802) 656-8611
Beth Wiser, Director of Admissions, University of Vermont, 194 South Prospect Street, Burlington, VT 05401-3596

Vermont Technical College
Randolph Center, Vermont **CB member**
www.vtc.edu **CB code: 3941**

- Public 4-year technical college
- Residential campus in small town
- 1,454 degree-seeking undergraduates: 16% part-time, 41% women, 1% African American, 2% Asian American, 1% Hispanic American, 1% Native American, 1% international
- 62% of applicants admitted
- 49% graduate within 6 years; 2% enter graduate study

General. Founded in 1866. Regionally accredited. Some classes offered on Vermont Interactive Television and broadcast to 12 locations in Vermont. Vermont Academy of Science and Technology enrolls high school seniors who excel in math/science to complete last year of high school and first year of college simultaneously. **Degrees:** 59 bachelor's, 307 associate awarded. **ROTC:** Army. **Location:** 20 miles from Montpelier, 50 miles from Burlington. **Calendar:** Semester, limited summer session. **Full-time faculty:** 79 total; 70% have terminal degrees, 40% women. **Part-time faculty:** 150 total; 27% have terminal degrees, 57% women. **Class size:** 64% < 20, 34% 20-39, 2% 40-49, less than 1% 50-99. **Special facilities:** 500-acre farmstead and orchard, lighted ski hill.

Freshman class profile. 945 applied, 590 admitted, 293 enrolled.

Mid 50% test scores		**GPA 2.0-2.99:**	42%
SAT critical reading:	410-530	**Rank in top quarter:**	21%
SAT math:	450-570	**Rank in top tenth:**	6%
SAT writing:	400-510	**End year in good standing:**	69%
GPA 3.75 or higher:	6%	**Return as sophomores:**	78%
GPA 3.50-3.74:	10%	**Out-of-state:**	18%
GPA 3.0-3.49:	40%	**Live on campus:**	75%

Basis for selection. School achievement record most important, followed by test scores, recommendations, interview. Interview and essay required for veterinary applicants. Entrance exam required for nursing applicants. Veterinary technology, dental hygiene, and nursing programs highly selective. SAT or ACT not required of nursing applicants or non-traditional students. Interview is required in some cases, but always strongly encouraged. Post-application essay is required during placement testing. **Homeschooled:** Statement describing homeschool structure and mission required. May choose affiliated Vermont Academy of Science and Technology to get high school diploma and first year of college simultaneously.

High school preparation. 16 units required. Required and recommended units include English 4, mathematics 3-4, social studies 2, history 2, science 2-3 (laboratory 1-2), foreign language 2 and academic electives 2.

2008-2009 Annual costs. Tuition/fees: $9,984; $18,408 out-of-state. New England Board of Higher Education rate for students from other New England states: 150% of Vermont resident tuition. Available to degree candidates in academic areas not offered by educational institutions in their home states. Room/board: $7,510. Books/supplies: $1,000. Personal expenses: $650.

2007-2008 Financial aid. Need-based: 260 full-time freshmen applied for aid; 225 were judged to have need; 224 of these received aid. Average need met was 72%. Average scholarship/grant was $5,305; average loan $2,840. 42% of total undergraduate aid awarded as scholarships/grants, 58% as loans/jobs. **Non-need-based:** Awarded to 30 full-time undergraduates, including 12 freshmen. Scholarships awarded for academics.

Application procedures. Admission: Priority date 3/1; no deadline. $37 fee, may be waived for applicants with need. Admission notification on a rolling basis beginning on or about 12/15. Must reply by May 1 or within 4 week(s) if notified thereafter. Nursing, Dental Hygiene and Veterinary Technology applicants may not defer their acceptance. **Financial aid:** Priority date 3/1; no closing date. FAFSA required. Applicants notified on a rolling basis starting 3/15; must reply within 2 week(s) of notification.

Academics. 3-year preparatory program options for students planning engineering programs. **Special study options:** Accelerated study, distance learning, double major, dual enrollment of high school students, ESL, honors, independent study, internships. Vermont Academy of Science and Technology program combines senior year of high school and first year of college. **Credit/placement by examination:** CLEP, institutional tests. 36 credit hours maximum toward associate degree, 60 toward bachelor's. **Support services:** Learning center, pre-admission summer program, reduced course load, remedial instruction, study skills assistance, tutoring, writing center.

Majors. Business: General, business admin. **Computer sciences:** General, information technology, LAN/WAN management, networking, programming, security, system admin, web page design, webmaster. **Engineering technology:** Architectural, computer, construction, electrical. **Health:** Dental hygiene. **Other:** Sustainable design and technology/green technology.

Most popular majors. Architecture 15%, business/marketing 49%, engineering/engineering technologies 36%.

Computing on campus. 250 workstations in dormitories, library, computer center. Dormitories wired for high-speed internet access and linked to campus network. Commuter students can connect to campus network. Online library, helpline, repair service, student web hosting, wireless network available.

Student life. Freshman orientation: Mandatory, $100 fee. Preregistration for classes offered. 2 days prior to start of classes. **Housing:** Coed dorms, special housing for disabled, wellness housing available. $100 deposit, deadline 6/1. Williston Campus has townhouse style residence halls. **Activities:** International student organizations, radio station, student government, student newspaper, TV station, national student chapters of: American Institute of Architects, American Society of Civil Engineers, Institute of Electrical and Electronic Engineers, Society of Manufacturing Engineers, Society of Women Engineers, National Association of Veterinary Technicians, Women Issues Christian Fellowship, Phi Theta Kappa, Tau Alpha Pi.

Athletics. NAIA, USCAA. **Intercollegiate:** Baseball M, basketball, cross-country, golf, soccer, softball W. **Intramural:** Basketball, football (non-tackle), golf, racquetball, skiing, soccer, softball, swimming, table tennis, tennis, volleyball, water polo. **Team name:** Knights.

Student services. Alcohol/substance abuse counseling, career counseling, services for economically disadvantaged, student employment services, financial aid counseling, health services, minority student services, personal counseling, placement for graduates, veterans' counselor, women's services. **Physically disabled:** Services for visually, hearing impaired.

Contact. E-mail: admissions@vtc.edu
Phone: (802) 728-1242 Toll-free number: (800) 442-8821
Fax: (802) 728-1390
Dwight Cross, Assistant Dean of Enrollment, Vermont Technical College, PO Box 500, Randolph Center, VT 05061-0500

Woodbury Institute of Champlain College
Montpelier, Vermont
www.woodbury-college.edu **CB code: 2600**

- Private 4-year technical and career college
- Commuter campus in small town

General. Regionally accredited. **Location:** 38 miles from Burlington. **Calendar:** Trimester.

Annual costs/financial aid. Tuition/fees (2008-2009): $16,845. Books/supplies: $600. Personal expenses: $2,400. Need-based financial aid available to full-time and part-time students.

Contact. Phone: (802) 229-0516 ext. 232
Director of Admissions, 660 Elm Street, Montpelier, VT 05602

Virginia

Art Institute of Washington

Arlington, Virginia
www.aiw.artinstitutes.edu **CB code: 3836**

- For-profit 4-year culinary school and visual arts college
- Commuter campus in small city
- 914 degree-seeking undergraduates: 44% women
- Application essay, interview required

General. Regionally accredited. **Degrees:** 121 bachelor's, 41 associate awarded. **Location:** One mile from Washington, DC. **Calendar:** Quarter, extensive summer session. **Full-time faculty:** 60 total. **Part-time faculty:** 71 total.

Basis for selection. Secondary school record, essay, placement test scores, interview most important; portfolio also considered. Students may take math and English placement test at the college, free of charge, in lieu of SAT or ACT. **Homeschooled:** Transcript of courses and grades required.

2008-2009 Annual costs. Tuition/fees: $21,744. Room only: $9,246.

Application procedures. Admission: No deadline. $50 fee. Admission notification on a rolling basis. **Financial aid:** FAFSA, institutional form required.

Academics. Special study options: Accelerated study, independent study, internships, study abroad. **Credit/placement by examination:** AP, CLEP, IB, SAT, ACT. **Support services:** Learning center, pre-admission summer program, reduced course load, remedial instruction, study skills assistance, tutoring, writing center.

Majors. Communications: Advertising, digital media. **Communications technology:** Animation/special effects, graphics, recording arts. **Computer sciences:** Web page design. **Personal/culinary services:** Baking, chef training, culinary arts, restaurant/catering. **Visual/performing arts:** Graphic design, interior design.

Computing on campus. Online course registration, online library, student web hosting, wireless network available.

Student life. Freshman orientation: Mandatory. Preregistration for classes offered. **Housing:** Coed dorms available. $250 partly refundable deposit. **Activities:** Radio station.

Student services. Adult student services, alcohol/substance abuse counseling, career counseling, student employment services, financial aid counseling. **Physically disabled:** Services for visually, speech, hearing impaired. **Learning disabled:** Comprehensive services available.

Contact. E-mail: aiwadm@aii.edu
Phone: (703) 358-9550 Fax: (703) 358-9759
Sara Cruley, Director of Admissions, Art Institute of Washington, 1820 North Fort Myer Drive, Arlington, VA 22209-1802

Averett University

Danville, Virginia **CB member**
www.averett.edu **CB code: 5017**

- Private 4-year university and liberal arts college
- Residential campus in small city
- 774 degree-seeking undergraduates: 3% part-time, 45% women, 30% African American, 1% Asian American, 3% Hispanic American, 1% Native American, 3% international
- 29 degree-seeking graduate students
- 88% of applicants admitted
- SAT or ACT (ACT writing optional) required
- 44% graduate within 6 years

General. Founded in 1859. Regionally accredited. **Degrees:** 153 bachelor's awarded; master's offered. **Location:** 45 miles from Greensboro, North Carolina, 150 miles from Richmond. **Calendar:** Semester, limited summer session. **Full-time faculty:** 47 total; 66% have terminal degrees, 4% minority, 45% women. **Part-time faculty:** 47 total; 26% have terminal degrees, 4% minority, 55% women. **Class size:** 76% < 20, 24% 20-39. **Special facilities:** 100-acre equestrian center, flight center.

Freshman class profile. 1,214 applied, 1,074 admitted, 248 enrolled.

Mid 50% test scores			
SAT critical reading:	410-490	Rank in top quarter:	22%
SAT math:	420-510	Rank in top tenth:	9%
ACT composite:	15-20	End year in good standing:	92%
GPA 3.75 or higher:	11%	Return as sophomores:	65%
GPA 3.50-3.74:	8%	Out-of-state:	47%
GPA 3.0-3.49:	27%	Live on campus:	80%
GPA 2.0-2.99:	53%	Fraternities:	13%
		Sororities:	7%

Basis for selection. Rigor of secondary school record and GPA very important; standardized test scores important. Recommendations, essay, interview, extracurricular activities, talent/ability/alumni/ae relation, volunteer work, work experience and level of interest all considered. Auditions required for music program; portfolios for art recommended. Essay recommended. **Homeschooled:** Transcript of courses and grades, state high school equivalency certificate required. **Learning Disabled:** Documentation of neuropsychological or comprehensive psychoeducational evaluation required for access to learning disabled services. Minimum SAT requirements may be waived.

High school preparation. College-preparatory program required. 16 units required; 25 recommended. Required and recommended units include English 4, mathematics 3-4, social studies 3-4, history 3, science 3-4 (laboratory 3), foreign language 3, computer science 2, visual/performing arts 1 and academic electives 3.

2008-2009 Annual costs. Tuition/fees: $21,300. Room/board: $7,390.

2007-2008 Financial aid. Need-based: 228 full-time freshmen applied for aid; 207 were judged to have need; 206 of these received aid. Average need met was 76%. Average scholarship/grant was $10,326; average loan $4,966. 65% of total undergraduate aid awarded as scholarships/grants, 35% as loans/jobs. **Non-need-based:** Awarded to 227 full-time undergraduates, including 56 freshmen. Scholarships awarded for academics, alumni affiliation, art, leadership, minority status, music/drama, state residency.

Application procedures. Admission: Priority date 5/1; deadline 7/15 (receipt date). No application fee. Admission notification on a rolling basis. Must reply by May 1 or within 2 week(s) if notified thereafter. Deferred admission is up to 1 year. **Financial aid:** Priority date 4/1; no closing date. FAFSA required. Applicants notified on a rolling basis starting 2/15; must reply within 2 week(s) of notification.

Academics. Special study options: Accelerated study, cooperative education, cross-registration, double major, dual enrollment of high school students, exchange student, honors, independent study, internships, student-designed major, study abroad, teacher certification program, Washington semester. Undergraduates may take graduate level classes. **Credit/placement by examination:** AP, CLEP, SAT, ACT, institutional tests. 27 credit hours maximum toward associate degree, 90 toward bachelor's. **Support services:** Learning center, reduced course load, remedial instruction, study skills assistance, tutoring, writing center.

Majors. Agriculture: Equestrian studies. **Biology:** General, ecology. **Business:** Accounting, business admin, finance, management science, marketing. **Communications:** Journalism. **Computer sciences:** Information systems. **Conservation:** Environmental science. **Education:** Art, biology, chemistry, English, health, mathematics, multi-level teacher, social studies. **Health:** Athletic training, clinical lab science, medical radiologic technology/radiation therapy, premedicine. **History:** General. **Interdisciplinary:** Biological/physical sciences. **Legal studies:** Prelaw. **Liberal arts:** Arts/sciences. **Math:** General. **Parks/recreation:** Health/fitness, sports admin. **Philosophy/religion:** Religion. **Physical sciences:** Chemistry. **Protective services:** Law enforcement admin. **Psychology:** Clinical, cognitive, industrial, psychobiology. **Social sciences:** Political science, sociology. **Transportation:** Airline/commercial pilot, aviation, aviation management. **Visual/performing arts:** Art, dramatic, theater history. **Other:** Criminal justice/aerospace management, Wellness/sports medicine.

Most popular majors. Business/marketing 10%, computer/information sciences 6%, education 15%, health sciences 8%, liberal arts 9%, parks/recreation 14%, security/protective services 9%.

Computing on campus. 150 workstations in library, computer center, student center. Dormitories wired for high-speed internet access. Online course registration, online library, helpline, student web hosting, wireless network available.

Student life. Freshman orientation: Mandatory, $50 fee. Preregistration for classes offered. 11-day orientation; begins on Saturday and lasts until classes start. **Policies:** No alcohol on campus, no smoking in dorms. **Housing:** Guaranteed on-campus for all undergraduates. Coed dorms, single-sex dorms, apartments available. $400 deposit, deadline 5/1. Coed housing by floor or suite. **Activities:** Campus ministries, choral groups, drama, international student organizations, literary magazine, Model UN, musical theater, student government, student newspaper, Alpha Beta Rho, Brothers and Sisters in Christ, campus activities board, Christian Student Union, Fellowship of Christian Athletes, multicultural student association, Phi Sigma Sigma, Phi Kappa Phi.

Athletics. NCAA. **Intercollegiate:** Baseball M, basketball, cross-country, equestrian, football (tackle) M, golf M, lacrosse W, soccer, softball W, tennis, volleyball W. **Intramural:** Basketball, cheerleading, football (non-tackle) M, softball. **Team name:** Cougars.

Student services. Adult student services, alcohol/substance abuse counseling, career counseling, student employment services, financial aid counseling, personal counseling, placement for graduates, veterans' counselor. **Physically disabled:** Services for visually, speech, hearing impaired.

Contact. E-mail: admit@averett.edu
Phone: (434) 791-4996 Toll-free number: (800) 283-7388
Fax: (434) 797-2784
Kathie Tune, Dean of Admissions, Averett University, 420 West Main Street, Danville, VA 24541

Bluefield College
Bluefield, Virginia
www.bluefield.edu **CB code: 5063**

- Private 4-year liberal arts college affiliated with Baptist faith
- Residential campus in small town
- 730 degree-seeking undergraduates: 17% part-time, 60% women, 17% African American, 1% Asian American, 2% Hispanic American
- 53% of applicants admitted
- SAT or ACT (ACT writing optional) required
- 38% graduate within 6 years; 13% enter graduate study

General. Founded in 1920. Regionally accredited. **Degrees:** 298 bachelor's awarded. **Location:** 90 miles from Roanoke. **Calendar:** Semester, limited summer session. **Full-time faculty:** 37 total; 65% have terminal degrees, 3% minority, 40% women. **Part-time faculty:** 59 total; 42% have terminal degrees, 5% minority, 39% women. **Class size:** 87% < 20, 13% 20-39.

Freshman class profile. 477 applied, 252 admitted, 88 enrolled.

Mid 50% test scores		**End year in good standing:**	78%
SAT critical reading:	420-520	**Return as sophomores:**	63%
SAT math:	420-530	**Out-of-state:**	19%
ACT composite:	17-20	**Live on campus:**	67%
GPA 3.75 or higher:	23%	**International:**	1%
GPA 3.50-3.74:	14%	**Fraternities:**	7%
GPA 3.0-3.49:	30%	**Sororities:**	10%
GPA 2.0-2.99:	33%		

Basis for selection. Students must have minimum 2.0 GPA, 18 ACT or SAT equivalent. **Homeschooled:** Must supply written description and transcript of home school curriculum.

High school preparation. 22 units required. Required units include English 4, mathematics 3, social studies 3, science 3 (laboratory 1) and academic electives 6. 2 units of health and physical education; 1 unit of fine arts.

2009-2010 Annual costs. Tuition/fees: $17,900. Room/board: $6,826. Books/supplies: $1,100. Personal expenses: $1,500.

2008-2009 Financial aid. **Need-based:** Average need met was 82%. Average scholarship/grant was $11,959; average loan $3,110. 48% of total undergraduate aid awarded as scholarships/grants, 52% as loans/jobs. **Non-need-based:** Scholarships awarded for academics, alumni affiliation, art, athletics, music/drama, religious affiliation, state residency.

Application procedures. **Admission:** Closing date 8/1 (postmark date). $30 fee, may be waived for applicants with need, free for online applicants. Admission notification on a rolling basis beginning on or about 9/1. Must reply by May 1 or within 3 week(s) if notified thereafter. **Financial aid:** Priority date 3/15; no closing date. FAFSA required. Applicants notified on a rolling basis starting 3/1; must reply within 3 week(s) of notification.

Academics. **Special study options:** Double major, honors, internships, liberal arts/career combination, study abroad, teacher certification program. **Credit/placement by examination:** AP, CLEP, IB, SAT, ACT, institutional tests. 30 credit hours maximum toward bachelor's degree. **Support services:** Learning center, reduced course load, remedial instruction, study skills assistance, tutoring, writing center.

Majors. **Biology:** General, exercise physiology. **Business:** Business admin. **Communications:** General. **Communications technology:** Graphics. **Computer sciences:** Information technology. **Education:** General, art, biology, business, chemistry, elementary, English, health, history, mathematics, middle, multi-level teacher, music, physical, reading, secondary, social studies. **History:** General. **Interdisciplinary:** Behavioral sciences. **Liberal arts:** Arts/sciences. **Math:** General. **Parks/recreation:** Exercise sciences. **Philosophy/religion:** Christian. **Physical sciences:** Chemistry. **Protective services:** Forensics, law enforcement admin, police science. **Psychology:** General. **Social sciences:** General. **Theology:** Bible, preministerial, sacred music, theology, youth ministry. **Visual/performing arts:** Art, design, dramatic, music performance, piano/organ, voice/opera.

Most popular majors. Business/marketing 39%, psychology 25%, security/protective services 22%.

Computing on campus. 100 workstations in dormitories, library, computer center, student center. Dormitories wired for high-speed internet access and linked to campus network. Commuter students can connect to campus network. Online library, wireless network available.

Student life. **Freshman orientation:** Available. Preregistration for classes offered. Held in June or July. **Policies:** Weekly convocation attendance required. Limited visitation hours in dormitories. Religious observance required. **Housing:** Guaranteed on-campus for freshmen. Coed dorms, single-sex dorms, apartments, wellness housing available. $100 fully refundable deposit. **Activities:** Jazz band, campus ministries, choral groups, drama, film society, literary magazine, music ensembles, musical theater, opera, student government, student newspaper, Fellowship of Christian Athletes, Alpha Delta, Phi Mu Delta, Kappa Psi Omicron, Sigma Alpha Alpha.

Athletics. NAIA. **Intercollegiate:** Baseball M, basketball, cross-country, golf M, soccer, softball W, tennis, volleyball W. **Intramural:** Badminton, basketball, bowling, football (non-tackle), softball, table tennis, tennis, volleyball. **Team name:** Rams.

Student services. Adult student services, chaplain/spiritual director, career counseling, financial aid counseling, health services, personal counseling, placement for graduates, veterans' counselor.

Contact. E-mail: admissions@bluefield.edu
Phone: (276) 326-4602 Toll-free number: (800) 872-0175
Fax: (276) 326-4288
George Campbell, Director of Traditional Admissions, Bluefield College, 3000 College Drive, Bluefield, VA 24605

Bridgewater College
Bridgewater, Virginia **CB member**
www.bridgewater.edu **CB code: 5069**

- Private 4-year liberal arts college affiliated with Church of the Brethren
- Residential campus in small town
- 1,490 degree-seeking undergraduates: 1% part-time, 58% women, 7% African American, 1% Asian American, 2% Hispanic American, 1% Native American, 1% international
- 83% of applicants admitted
- SAT or ACT (ACT writing optional) required
- 59% graduate within 6 years

General. Founded in 1880. Regionally accredited. **Degrees:** 377 bachelor's awarded. **Location:** 8 miles from Harrisonburg, 130 miles from Washington, DC. **Calendar:** 4-1-4, limited summer session. **Full-time faculty:** 93 total; 81% have terminal degrees, 1% minority, 37% women. **Part-time faculty:** 38 total; 29% have terminal degrees, 5% minority, 58% women. **Class size:** 58% < 20, 39% 20-39, 3% 40-49, less than 1% 50-99. **Special facilities:** 75-acre equestrian center for equestrian competitions and boarding of College- and student-owned horses.

Freshman class profile. 2,769 applied, 2,285 admitted, 488 enrolled.

Mid 50% test scores		GPA 2.0-2.99:	15%
SAT critical reading:	460-570	Rank in top quarter:	48%
SAT math:	460-570	Rank in top tenth:	16%
SAT writing:	460-560	Return as sophomores:	73%
ACT composite:	19-24	Out-of-state:	19%
GPA 3.75 or higher:	26%	Live on campus:	92%
GPA 3.50-3.74:	20%	International:	1%
GPA 3.0-3.49:	39%		

Basis for selection. High school GPA most important, followed by test scores and letters of recommendation. Prefer applicants in top half of high school class. Consider those in bottom half with strong compensating qualities. Interview required for some, recommended for all. **Homeschooled:** GED required for students applying for Title IV financial aid.

High school preparation. College-preparatory program recommended. 15 units required; 22 recommended. Required and recommended units include English 4, mathematics 3-4, science 2-4 (laboratory 2), foreign language 3 and academic electives 4. Social studies and history: 2 required, 3 recommended.

2009-2010 Annual costs. Tuition/fees: $24,500. Room/board: $9,900. Books/supplies: $1,050. Personal expenses: $1,080.

2008-2009 Financial aid. Need-based: 451 full-time freshmen applied for aid; 378 were judged to have need; 378 of these received aid. Average need met was 77%. Average scholarship/grant was $17,739; average loan $4,575. 70% of total undergraduate aid awarded as scholarships/grants, 30% as loans/jobs. **Non-need-based:** Awarded to 1,364 full-time undergraduates, including 482 freshmen. Scholarships awarded for academics, music/drama, religious affiliation.

Application procedures. Admission: No deadline. $30 fee, may be waived for applicants with need, free for online applicants. Admission notification on a rolling basis beginning on or about 9/1. Must reply by May 1 or within 2 week(s) if notified thereafter. **Financial aid:** Priority date 3/1; no closing date. FAFSA required. Applicants notified on a rolling basis starting 3/16; must reply within 2 week(s) of notification.

Academics. Special study options: Combined bachelor's/graduate degree, double major, honors, independent study, internships, liberal arts/career combination, study abroad, teacher certification program, Washington semester. 3-2 engineering with George Washington University (BA/BA) and 3-2 engineering with Virginia Tech (BA/BA), 3-2 forestry with Duke University (BA/MS), 3-2 nursing with Vanderbilt University (BA/MN), 3-2 physical therapy with George Washington University (BA/MPT), 3-4 physical therapy with Shenandoah University (BA/DPT), 3-4 veterinary medicine with Virginia Tech (BA/DVM). **Credit/placement by examination:** AP, CLEP, IB, institutional tests. **Support services:** Reduced course load, study skills assistance, tutoring, writing center.

Majors. Biology: General. **Business:** Business admin, management information systems. **Communications:** Media studies. **Computer sciences:** Computer science. **Conservation:** Environmental science. **Education:** Physical. **Family/consumer sciences:** General, food/nutrition. **Foreign languages:** French, Spanish. **Health:** Athletic training, clinical lab science. **History:** General. **Liberal arts:** Arts/sciences. **Math:** General. **Parks/recreation:** Exercise sciences, health/fitness. **Philosophy/religion:** Philosophy, religion. **Physical sciences:** Chemistry, physics. **Psychology:** General. **Social sciences:** Economics, international relations, political science, sociology. **Visual/performing arts:** Music history, studio arts.

Most popular majors. Biology 10%, business/marketing 19%, communications/journalism 10%, education 9%, family/consumer sciences 7%, parks/recreation 11%, psychology 6%, social sciences 7%.

Computing on campus. Dormitories wired for high-speed internet access and linked to campus network. Commuter students can connect to campus network. Online course registration, online library, helpline, repair service, student web hosting, wireless network available.

Student life. Freshman orientation: Mandatory. Preregistration for classes offered. Students may choose from 2 spring 2-day sessions. One-day summer session also available. Further orientation activities 2 days preceding classes. Parents included in spring and summer orientations. **Policies:** Alcoholic beverages not permitted on campus. Co-ed visitation hours. Smoking and other tobacco products permitted only in designated areas minimum of 20 feet from residence hall. Unmarried students under age 23 must live on campus unless living with parents. **Housing:** Guaranteed on-campus for all undergraduates. Single-sex dorms, special housing for disabled, apartments, wellness housing available. **Activities:** Bands, campus ministries, choral groups, dance, drama, international student organizations, literary magazine, music ensembles, musical theater, radio station, student government, student newspaper, Believers Strongly United, Brethren Student Movement, Campus Crusade for Christ, Catholic Campus Ministry, College Republicans, Young Democrats, Black Student Association, Fellowship of Christian Athletes, Invisible Children Club, Habitat for Humanity.

Athletics. NCAA. **Intercollegiate:** Baseball M, basketball, cross-country, equestrian, field hockey W, football (tackle) M, golf M, lacrosse W, soccer, softball W, swimming W, tennis, track and field, volleyball W. **Intramural:** Badminton, basketball, bowling, football (non-tackle), golf, racquetball, soccer, softball, table tennis, tennis, volleyball. **Team name:** Eagles.

Student services. Chaplain/spiritual director, career counseling, student employment services, financial aid counseling, health services, minority student services, personal counseling, placement for graduates. **Physically disabled:** Services for visually impaired.

Contact. E-mail: admissions@bridgewater.edu
Phone: (540) 828-5375 Toll-free number: (800) 759-8328
Fax: (540) 828-5481
Linda Stout, Director of Enrollment Operations, Bridgewater College, 402 East College Street, Bridgewater, VA 22812-1599

Catholic Distance University
Hamilton, Virginia
www.cdu.edu

- Private two-year upper-division virtual university
- Rural community

General. Accredited by DETC. **Calendar:** Differs by program.

Annual costs/financial aid. Tuition/fees (2008-2009): $7,140.

Contact. Phone: (540) 338-2700 ext. 710
Director of Admissions, 120 East Colonial Highway, Hamilton, VA 20158-9012

Christendom College
Front Royal, Virginia
www.christendom.edu **CB code: 5691**

- Private 4-year liberal arts college affiliated with Roman Catholic Church
- Residential campus in large town
- 421 degree-seeking undergraduates: 1% part-time, 54% women, 2% Asian American, 2% Hispanic American, 4% international
- 53 degree-seeking graduate students
- 88% of applicants admitted
- SAT or ACT (ACT writing optional), application essay required
- 72% graduate within 6 years

General. Founded in 1977. Regionally accredited. **Degrees:** 95 bachelor's, 2 associate awarded; master's offered. **Location:** 70 miles from Washington, DC. **Calendar:** Semester, limited summer session. **Full-time faculty:** 20 total. **Part-time faculty:** 21 total.

Freshman class profile. 271 applied, 239 admitted, 124 enrolled.

Mid 50% test scores		GPA 2.0-2.99:	7%
SAT critical reading:	570-700	Rank in top quarter:	63%
SAT math:	520-630	Rank in top tenth:	40%
SAT writing:	560-690	End year in good standing:	100%
ACT composite:	23-28	Return as sophomores:	89%
GPA 3.75 or higher:	31%	Out-of-state:	85%
GPA 3.50-3.74:	31%	Live on campus:	98%
GPA 3.0-3.49:	31%		

Basis for selection. Secondary school record, essay, test scores, class rank, GPA, recommendations important. Applicants can present additional material and explain scores, evaluations, etc. which they believe do not adequately reflect their abilities. Interview recommended. **Homeschooled:** Transcript forms required (available from college).

High school preparation. 14 units recommended. Recommended units include English 4, mathematics 2, social studies 1, history 2, science 2, foreign language 2 and academic electives 1.

2008-2009 Annual costs. Tuition/fees: $18,806. Room/board: $6,688. Books/supplies: $500. Personal expenses: $300.

2008-2009 Financial aid. Need-based: 76 full-time freshmen applied for aid; 61 were judged to have need; 61 of these received aid. Average

need met was 90%. Average scholarship/grant was $6,565; average loan $5,719. 54% of total undergraduate aid awarded as scholarships/grants, 46% as loans/jobs. **Non-need-based:** Awarded to 147 full-time undergraduates, including 54 freshmen. Scholarships awarded for academics, alumni affiliation. **Additional information:** Christendom accepts no direct federal aid, nor does it participate in indirect programs of federal aid.

Application procedures. Admission: Priority date 3/1; no deadline. $25 fee. Admission notification on a rolling basis. **Financial aid:** Priority date 4/1, closing date 6/1. Institutional form required. Applicants notified on a rolling basis starting 2/1; must reply within 4 week(s) of notification.

Academics. Special study options: Double major, honors, independent study, internships, study abroad. Junior semester in Rome. **Credit/placement by examination:** AP, CLEP, institutional tests. **Support services:** Pre-admission summer program, reduced course load, writing center.

Majors. Foreign languages: Classics. **History:** General. **Philosophy/religion:** Philosophy. **Social sciences:** Political science.

Computing on campus. 70 workstations in library. Online course registration available.

Student life. Freshman orientation: Mandatory. Preregistration for classes offered. Orientation held weekend before school starts. **Policies:** Although no student is required to participate, college encourages religious activities. **Housing:** Guaranteed on-campus for all undergraduates. Single-sex dorms, wellness housing available. $250 deposit, deadline 3/15. **Activities:** Campus ministries, choral groups, dance, drama, film society, literary magazine, musical theater, student government, student newspaper, Legion of Mary, Shield of Roses, St. Genesius Society, Holy Rood Guild, College Republicans, works of mercy group.

Athletics. USCAA. **Intercollegiate:** Baseball M, basketball, rugby M, soccer, volleyball W. **Intramural:** Basketball, boxing M, cross-country, fencing, football (non-tackle), golf, handball, racquetball, skiing, soccer, softball, table tennis, tennis, volleyball. **Team name:** Crusaders.

Student services. Chaplain/spiritual director, career counseling, financial aid counseling, health services, personal counseling, placement for graduates.

Contact. E-mail: admissions@christendom.edu
Phone: (540) 636-2900 Toll-free number: (800) 877-5456
Fax: (540) 636-1655
Thomas McFadden, Director of Admissions, Christendom College, 134 Christendom Drive, Front Royal, VA 22630

Christopher Newport University

Newport News, Virginia — **CB member**
www.cnu.edu — **CB code: 5128**

- Public 4-year university and liberal arts college
- Residential campus in small city
- 4,746 degree-seeking undergraduates: 3% part-time, 55% women, 8% African American, 3% Asian American, 3% Hispanic American, 1% Native American
- 131 degree-seeking graduate students
- 56% of applicants admitted
- Application essay required
- 49% graduate within 6 years

General. Founded in 1960. Regionally accredited. **Degrees:** 837 bachelor's awarded; master's offered. **ROTC:** Army. **Location:** 20 miles from Norfolk, 70 miles from Richmond. **Calendar:** Semester, limited summer session. **Full-time faculty:** 239 total; 84% have terminal degrees, 13% minority, 46% women. **Part-time faculty:** 125 total; 26% have terminal degrees, 12% minority, 42% women. **Class size:** 42% < 20, 51% 20-39, 5% 40-49, 2% 50-99, less than 1% >100. **Special facilities:** Mariner's museum, center for the arts.

Freshman class profile. 7,174 applied, 3,984 admitted, 1,137 enrolled.

Mid 50% test scores			
SAT critical reading:	540-630	GPA 2.0-2.99:	3%
SAT math:	550-630	Rank in top quarter:	58%
ACT composite:	22-26	Rank in top tenth:	20%
GPA 3.75 or higher:	27%	End year in good standing:	85%
GPA 3.50-3.74:	34%	Return as sophomores:	80%
GPA 3.0-3.49:	36%	Out-of-state:	7%
		Live on campus:	94%

Basis for selection. Minimum 3.0 GPA, rank in top half of class. Type of diploma and difficulty of classes taken considered. Test scores required for freshman applicants who graduated from high school within past 2 years unless they achieve a 3.5 or better GPA (on a 4.0 scale) with a strong academic curriculum. Audition required for music; interview recommended for marginal; portfolio recommended for art. **Homeschooled:** Applicants should submit copy of high school transcript and descriptions, along with ACT or SAT score.

High school preparation. College-preparatory program required. 23 units required. Required and recommended units include English 4, mathematics 4, history 3-4, science 3-4 and foreign language 3-4.

2008-2009 Annual costs. Tuition/fees: $7,550; $14,932 out-of-state. Room/board: $8,900. Books/supplies: $870. Personal expenses: $2,011.

2008-2009 Financial aid. Need-based: 822 full-time freshmen applied for aid; 468 were judged to have need; 460 of these received aid. Average need met was 75%. Average scholarship/grant was $5,096; average loan $3,100. 49% of total undergraduate aid awarded as scholarships/grants, 51% as loans/jobs. **Non-need-based:** Awarded to 730 full-time undergraduates, including 302 freshmen. Scholarships awarded for academics, art, leadership, music/drama, state residency.

Application procedures. Admission: Closing date 3/1 (receipt date). $45 fee, may be waived for applicants with need. Admission notification on a rolling basis beginning on or about 12/1. Must reply by May 1 or within 2 week(s) if notified thereafter. **Financial aid:** Priority date 3/1; no closing date. FAFSA required. Applicants notified on a rolling basis starting 2/21; must reply within 3 week(s) of notification.

Academics. Special programs for Leadership, Honors and freshman learning communities. **Special study options:** Cross-registration, double major, dual enrollment of high school students, honors, independent study, internships, student-designed major, study abroad. Member of Virginia Tidewater Consortium, Freshman Learning Communities. **Credit/placement by examination:** AP, CLEP, IB, institutional tests. **Support services:** Study skills assistance, tutoring, writing center.

Majors. Biology: General. **Business:** Accounting, business admin, finance, managerial economics, marketing. **Communications:** General. **Computer sciences:** Computer science, information systems. **Conservation:** Environmental studies. **Engineering:** Computer. **Foreign languages:** French, German, Spanish. **History:** General. **Math:** General. **Philosophy/religion:** Philosophy. **Physical sciences:** Chemistry, physics. **Psychology:** General. **Public administration:** Social work. **Social sciences:** Political science, sociology. **Visual/performing arts:** Dramatic, music performance, studio arts.

Most popular majors. Biology 9%, business/marketing 21%, communications/journalism 10%, English 7%, history 8%, psychology 10%, social sciences 19%, visual/performing arts 7%.

Computing on campus. 330 workstations in dormitories, library, computer center, student center. Dormitories wired for high-speed internet access and linked to campus network. Commuter students can connect to campus network. Online course registration, online library, helpline, student web hosting, wireless network available.

Student life. Freshman orientation: Mandatory, $250 fee. Preregistration for classes offered. 2 programs required: 1.5-day program with overnight stay in residence halls, offered June-July, and welcome week program prior to start of classes in fall. **Policies:** Alcohol not permitted in residence halls; 1st and 2nd year students required to live on campus unless they reside with their parents or legal guardians in Gloucester, Hampton, Isle of Wight, James City County, Matthews County, Newport News, Poquoson, Williamsburg or York County (of Virginia). **Housing:** Guaranteed on-campus for freshmen. Coed dorms, apartments, fraternity/sorority housing, wellness housing available. $250 partly refundable deposit, deadline 5/1. Learning communities available. **Activities:** Bands, campus ministries, choral groups, dance, drama, international student organizations, literary magazine, music ensembles, Model UN, musical theater, opera, radio station, student government, student newspaper, symphony orchestra, TV station, Baptist Student Union, Intervarsity Christian Fellowship, Lutheran student association, various honor societies, Young Life.

Athletics. NCAA. **Intercollegiate:** Baseball M, basketball, cheerleading, cross-country, equestrian, field hockey W, football (tackle) M, golf M, lacrosse, sailing, soccer, softball W, tennis, track and field, volleyball W. **Intramural:** Badminton, basketball, football (non-tackle) M, soccer, softball, tennis, volleyball. **Team name:** Captains.

Student services. Chaplain/spiritual director, career counseling, student employment services, financial aid counseling, health services, minority student services, personal counseling, placement for graduates, veterans' counselor. **Physically disabled:** Services for visually, speech, hearing impaired.

Contact. E-mail: admit@cnu.edu
Phone: (757) 594-7015 Toll-free number: (800) 333-4268
Fax: (757) 594-7333
Patricia Patten, Dean of Admissions, Christopher Newport University, 1 University Place, Newport News, VA 23606-2998

College of William and Mary

Williamsburg, Virginia **CB member**
www.wm.edu **CB code: 5115**

- Public 4-year university
- Residential campus in large town
- 5,811 degree-seeking undergraduates: 1% part-time, 55% women, 7% African American, 8% Asian American, 6% Hispanic American, 1% Native American, 2% international
- 1,961 degree-seeking graduate students
- 34% of applicants admitted
- SAT or ACT (ACT writing optional), application essay required

General. Founded in 1693. Regionally accredited. **Degrees:** 1,454 bachelor's awarded; master's, doctoral, first professional offered. **ROTC:** Army. **Location:** 50 miles from Richmond, 50 miles from Norfolk. **Calendar:** Semester, limited summer session. **Full-time faculty:** 628 total; 89% have terminal degrees, 10% minority, 37% women. **Part-time faculty:** 173 total; 40% have terminal degrees, 9% minority, 42% women. **Special facilities:** Observatory, continuous beam accelerator, 3 interdisciplinary centers in humanities, international studies, writing resources, marine science institute, materials processes research center, public policy research center.

Freshman class profile. 11,636 applied, 3,966 admitted, 1,387 enrolled.

Mid 50% test scores		**Rank in top quarter:**	97%
SAT critical reading:	630-730	**Rank in top tenth:**	79%
SAT math:	620-710	**Return as sophomores:**	94%
SAT writing:	610-720	**Out-of-state:**	36%
ACT composite:	27-32	**Live on campus:**	100%
GPA 3.75 or higher:	78%	**International:**	3%
GPA 3.50-3.74:	16%	**Fraternities:**	18%
GPA 3.0-3.49:	6%	**Sororities:**	19%

Basis for selection. Academic preparation most important, with particular emphasis on course selection and grades, test scores, special talents and abilities. Special consideration given to children of alumni. Preference given to Virginia residents. Diverse backgrounds, special abilities, unique interests and experiences preferred. Applications evaluated on own merits without specific course requirements. Advanced placement, honors, accelerated courses strongly weighed in evaluation process.

High school preparation. College-preparatory program recommended. Recommended units include English 4, mathematics 4, social studies 4, science 4 (laboratory 3) and foreign language 4.

2008-2009 Annual costs. Tuition/fees: $10,246; $29,116 out-of-state. Room/board: $8,030.

2008-2009 Financial aid. Need-based: 814 full-time freshmen applied for aid; 393 were judged to have need; 393 of these received aid. Average need met was 82%. Average scholarship/grant was $13,088; average loan $2,690. 74% of total undergraduate aid awarded as scholarships/grants, 26% as loans/jobs. **Non-need-based:** Awarded to 1,137 full-time undergraduates, including 279 freshmen. Scholarships awarded for academics, athletics, leadership, ROTC.

Application procedures. Admission: Closing date 1/1 (postmark date). $60 fee, may be waived for applicants with need. Admission notification 4/1. Must reply by 5/1. **Financial aid:** Priority date 2/15; no closing date. FAFSA required. Applicants notified on a rolling basis starting 3/15; must reply by 5/1 or within 2 week(s) of notification.

Academics. Special study options: Accelerated study, combined bachelor's/graduate degree, double major, dual enrollment of high school students, exchange student, honors, independent study, internships, student-designed major, study abroad, teacher certification program, Washington semester. **Credit/placement by examination:** AP, CLEP, IB, institutional tests. **Support services:** Pre-admission summer program, reduced course load, study skills assistance, tutoring, writing center.

Majors. Area/ethnic studies: African-American, American, women's. **Biology:** General. **Business:** Business admin. **Computer sciences:** General. **Conservation:** Environmental studies. **Foreign languages:** Chinese, classics, French, German, linguistics, Spanish. **History:** General. **Interdisciplinary:** Medieval/Renaissance, neuroscience. **Math:** General. **Parks/recreation:** Exercise sciences. **Philosophy/religion:** Philosophy, religion. **Physical sciences:** Chemistry, geology, physics. **Psychology:** General. **Public administration:** Policy analysis. **Social sciences:** Anthropology, economics, international relations, political science, sociology. **Visual/performing arts:** Art, dramatic. **Other:** Literary and cultural studies.

Most popular majors. Biology 6%, business/marketing 12%, English 7%, history 8%, interdisciplinary studies 10%, psychology 9%, social sciences 23%.

Computing on campus. PC or laptop required. 350 workstations in dormitories, library, computer center, student center. Dormitories wired for high-speed internet access and linked to campus network. Commuter students can connect to campus network. Online course registration, online library, helpline, repair service, student web hosting, wireless network available.

Student life. Freshman orientation: Mandatory, $144 fee. Preregistration for classes offered. 5-day program immediately preceding fall semester. **Policies:** Honor system in effect. **Housing:** Guaranteed on-campus for freshmen. Coed dorms, single-sex dorms, special housing for disabled, apartments, fraternity/sorority housing available. $350 nonrefundable deposit, deadline 5/1. **Activities:** Bands, campus ministries, choral groups, dance, drama, film society, international student organizations, literary magazine, music ensembles, Model UN, musical theater, opera, radio station, student government, student newspaper, symphony orchestra, TV station, College Republicans, Young Democrats, Black Student Organization, Asian Student Council, Hispanic Cultural Organization, College Partnership for Kids, Student Environmental Action Coalition, AIDS Tanzania, Global Village Project.

Athletics. NCAA. **Intercollegiate:** Baseball M, basketball, cross-country, diving, field hockey W, football (tackle) M, golf, gymnastics, lacrosse W, soccer, swimming, tennis, track and field, volleyball W. **Intramural:** Badminton, basketball, golf, racquetball, soccer, softball, table tennis, tennis, volleyball, wrestling M. **Team name:** Tribe.

Student services. Alcohol/substance abuse counseling, career counseling, financial aid counseling, health services, legal services, minority student services, on-campus daycare, personal counseling, placement for graduates. **Physically disabled:** Services for visually, hearing impaired.

Contact. E-mail: admission@wm.edu
Phone: (757) 221-4223 Fax: (757) 221-1242
Henry Broaddus, Dean of Admissions, College of William and Mary, PO Box 8795, Williamsburg, VA 23187-8795

DeVry University: Arlington

Arlington, Virginia
www.devry.edu **CB code: 3813**

- For-profit 4-year university
- Commuter campus in very large city
- 593 degree-seeking undergraduates: 46% part-time, 26% women, 56% African American, 4% Asian American, 11% Hispanic American, 1% Native American, 1% international
- 113 degree-seeking graduate students
- Interview required

General. Degrees: 76 bachelor's, 3 associate awarded; master's offered. **Calendar:** Semester, extensive summer session. **Full-time faculty:** 15 total; 47% minority, 27% women. **Part-time faculty:** 84 total; 39% minority, 37% women.

Freshman class profile.

Out-of-state:	67%	**International:**	1%

Basis for selection. Applicant must have high school diploma or equivalent, degree from an accredited postsecondary institution, or submit acceptable test scores and be at least 17 years of age. CPT also accepted.

High school preparation. Required units include mathematics 1. Math unit must be algebra or higher.

2008-2009 Annual costs. Tuition/fees: $14,390. Books/supplies: $1,300. Personal expenses: $3,152.

2007-2008 Financial aid. All financial aid based on need.

Application procedures. Admission: No deadline. $50 fee. Admission notification on a rolling basis. **Financial aid:** No deadline. FAFSA required. Applicants notified on a rolling basis.

Academics. Special study options: Accelerated study, cooperative education, distance learning. **Credit/placement by examination:** CLEP. **Support services:** Learning center, remedial instruction, tutoring.

Majors. Business: Business admin. **Computer sciences:** Networking, systems analysis, web page design. **Engineering:** Software. **Other:** Technical management.

Most popular majors. Business/marketing 57%, computer/information sciences 25%, engineering/engineering technologies 18%.

Computing on campus. Online course registration, online library, helpline available.

Student life. Freshman orientation: Mandatory. **Activities:** Linux users' group.

Athletics. Intramural: Basketball, volleyball.

Student services. Career counseling, student employment services, financial aid counseling, placement for graduates, veterans' counselor. **Physically disabled:** Services for visually, hearing impaired.

Contact. E-mail: admissions@crys.devry.edu
Phone: (703) 414-4100 Toll-free number: (866) 338-7932
Fax: (703) 414-4040
Bob Pavlovics, Director of Admissions, DeVry University: Arlington, 2450 Crystal Drive, Arlington, VA 22202

Eastern Mennonite University

Harrisonburg, Virginia — **CB member**
www.emu.edu — **CB code: 5181**

- Private 4-year university and liberal arts college affiliated with Mennonite Church
- Residential campus in large town
- 951 degree-seeking undergraduates: 1% part-time, 63% women, 7% African American, 1% Asian American, 4% Hispanic American, 3% international
- 337 degree-seeking graduate students
- 69% of applicants admitted
- SAT or ACT with writing required
- 64% graduate within 6 years

General. Founded in 1917. Regionally accredited. **Degrees:** 280 bachelor's, 17 associate awarded; master's, first professional offered. **Location:** 110 miles from Richmond, 110 miles from Washington, DC. **Calendar:** Semester, limited summer session. **Full-time faculty:** 114 total; 68% have terminal degrees, 4% minority, 51% women. **Part-time faculty:** 48 total; 44% have terminal degrees, 6% minority, 29% women. **Class size:** 66% < 20, 29% 20-39, 3% 40-49, 2% 50-99. **Special facilities:** Museum of natural history, arboretum, student-run coffee shop.

Freshman class profile. 717 applied, 493 admitted, 184 enrolled.

Mid 50% test scores			
SAT critical reading:	460-600	GPA 2.0-2.99:	21%
SAT math:	460-600	Rank in top quarter:	39%
SAT writing:	440-570	Rank in top tenth:	17%
ACT composite:	19-25	Return as sophomores:	80%
GPA 3.75 or higher:	38%	Out-of-state:	50%
GPA 3.50-3.74:	15%	Live on campus:	92%
GPA 3.0-3.49:	25%	International:	1%

Basis for selection. 2.2 high school GPA required. SAT score of 920 (exclusive of Writing) or ACT minimum composite score of 20 required. Conditional admission possible for motivated applicants who fail to reach minimum admissions requirements. Interviews recommended. **Homeschooled:** Detailed record of coursework completed for grades 9-12, SAT or ACT required. **Learning Disabled:** Interview recommended for learning disabled; meet with academic support center personnel.

High school preparation. College-preparatory program recommended. 21 units recommended. Recommended units include English 4, mathematics 3, social studies 3, science 3 (laboratory 3), foreign language 2 and academic electives 6.

2008-2009 Annual costs. Tuition/fees: $23,180. Room/board: $7,200. Books/supplies: $1,000. Personal expenses: $920.

2008-2009 Financial aid. Non-need-based: Scholarships awarded for academics, alumni affiliation, art, leadership, religious affiliation, state residency.

Application procedures. Admission: No deadline. $25 fee, may be waived for applicants with need. Admission notification on a rolling basis. **Financial aid:** Priority date 3/1; no closing date. FAFSA required. Applicants notified on a rolling basis starting 3/1; must reply within 4 week(s) of notification.

Academics. Missions programs available. Cross-cultural education component required in 3-week or 3-month assignments to locations around the world. **Special study options:** Distance learning, double major, ESL, honors, independent study, internships, liberal arts/career combination, study abroad, teacher certification program, Washington semester. **Credit/placement by examination:** AP, CLEP, IB, SAT, ACT, institutional tests. **Support services:** Learning center, reduced course load, remedial instruction, study skills assistance, tutoring, writing center.

Majors. Biology: General, biochemistry. **Business:** Accounting, business admin, international, organizational behavior. **Communications:** General, digital media. **Computer sciences:** Computer science. **Conservation:** Environmental science. **Education:** Physical. **Foreign languages:** French, Spanish. **Health:** Clinical lab science, nursing (RN), predental, premedicine, preveterinary. **History:** General. **Interdisciplinary:** Peace/conflict. **Liberal arts:** Arts/sciences. **Math:** General. **Parks/recreation:** Sports admin. **Physical sciences:** Chemistry. **Psychology:** General. **Public administration:** Social work. **Social sciences:** General, economics, international economic development, sociology. **Theology:** Bible, preministerial, theology. **Visual/performing arts:** Art, dramatic, photography. **Other:** Camping, Recreation, and Outdoor Ministries, Congregational and Youth Ministries, Philosophy and Theology.

Most popular majors. Business/marketing 20%, education 9%, health sciences 25%, liberal arts 14%.

Computing on campus. 100 workstations in library, computer center, student center. Dormitories wired for high-speed internet access and linked to campus network. Commuter students can connect to campus network. Online library, helpline, student web hosting, wireless network available.

Student life. Freshman orientation: Mandatory. Preregistration for classes offered. One-week orientation begins 5 days before fall semester. **Policies:** Alcohol and drug use by students prohibited. Chapel attendance expected. Students must sign and adhere to Community Lifestyle Commitment. Emphasis on justice and peacemaking. **Housing:** Guaranteed on-campus for freshmen. Coed dorms, single-sex dorms, special housing for disabled, apartments, wellness housing available. Intentional communities available. **Activities:** Bands, campus ministries, choral groups, dance, drama, film society, international student organizations, literary magazine, music ensembles, musical theater, student government, student newspaper, symphony orchestra, Young People's Christian Association, Peace Fellowship, Black student union, Latino student alliance, Earth Keepers, Social Work is People, A Safe Place, Alpha Omega Steppers For Christ.

Athletics. NCAA. **Intercollegiate:** Baseball M, basketball, cross-country, field hockey W, soccer, softball W, track and field, volleyball. **Intramural:** Basketball, football (tackle) M, golf, soccer, table tennis, tennis, volleyball. **Team name:** Royals.

Student services. Adult student services, alcohol/substance abuse counseling, chaplain/spiritual director, career counseling, student employment services, financial aid counseling, health services, minority student services, personal counseling, placement for graduates. **Physically disabled:** Services for visually, speech, hearing impaired.

Contact. E-mail: admiss@emu.edu
Phone: (540) 432-4118 Toll-free number: (800) 368-2665
Fax: (540) 432-4444
Stephanie Shafer, Director of Admissions, Eastern Mennonite University, 1200 Park Road, Harrisonburg, VA 22802-2462

ECPI College of Technology: Newport News

Newport News, Virginia
www.ecpi.edu

- For-profit 4-year business and technical college
- Very large city
- 1,249 degree-seeking undergraduates

General. Regionally accredited. **Degrees:** 50 bachelor's, 1,760 associate awarded. **Calendar:** Continuous. **Full-time faculty:** 35 total. **Part-time faculty:** 47 total.

2008-2009 Annual costs. Tuition/fees: $10,650.

Application procedures. Admission: No deadline. $100 fee.

Academics. Credit/placement by examination: CLEP.

Majors. Computer sciences: Security.

Contact. John Olson, Director of Admissions, ECPI College of Technology: Newport News, 1001 Omni Boulevard Suite 105, Newport News, VA 23662

ECPI College of Technology: Virginia Beach

Virginia Beach, Virginia
www.ecpi.edu **CB code: 7140**

- For-profit 4-year health science and technical college
- Commuter campus in very large city
- 6,000 degree-seeking undergraduates
- Interview required

General. Founded in 1966. Regionally accredited. **Degrees:** 54 bachelor's, 1,764 associate awarded. **Calendar:** Continuous, extensive summer session. **Full-time faculty:** 300 total. **Part-time faculty:** 200 total. **Class size:** 80% < 20, 20% 20-39.

Basis for selection. Requirements include interview and program specific admissions test. No special considerations given. SAT or ACT recommended. **Learning Disabled:** Consideration may be given on case-by-case basis.

High school preparation. Recommended units include English 4, mathematics 2, social studies 2, history 2 and science 2.

2008-2009 Annual costs. Tuition/fees: $10,650. Personal expenses: $1,710.

Financial aid. Non-need-based: Scholarships awarded for academics.

Application procedures. Admission: No deadline. $75 fee. Admission notification on a rolling basis. **Financial aid:** No deadline. Institutional form required. Applicants notified on a rolling basis.

Academics. Special study options: Accelerated study, cooperative education, distance learning, double major, dual enrollment of high school students, independent study, internships. **Credit/placement by examination:** AP, CLEP, ACT, institutional tests. 18 credit hours maximum toward associate degree, 33 toward bachelor's. **Support services:** Learning center, remedial instruction, study skills assistance, tutoring, writing center.

Majors. Computer sciences: General.

Computing on campus. 2,800 workstations in library, computer center, student center. Commuter students can connect to campus network. Online course registration, online library, helpline, wireless network available.

Student life. Freshman orientation: Mandatory. Preregistration for classes offered. Half-day orientation held day prior to each term start. **Housing:** Wellness housing available. Student housing assistance provided at Virginia Beach campus. **Activities:** Student government, student newspaper, student electronic technicians association, information technology exchange, accounting society, International Association of Administrative Professionals, Phi Theta Kappa.

Student services. Adult student services, alcohol/substance abuse counseling, career counseling, services for economically disadvantaged, student employment services, financial aid counseling, personal counseling, placement for graduates, veterans' counselor.

Contact. Phone: (757) 671-7171 Toll-free number: (800) 986-1200
Fax: (757) 671-8661
Jeff Marcus, Director of Admissions, ECPI College of Technology: Virginia Beach, 5555 Greenwich Road, Suite 300, Virginia Beach, VA 23462-6542

ECPI Technical College: Glen Allen

Glen Allen, Virginia
www.ecpitech.edu

- For-profit 4-year technical college
- Commuter campus in large town

General. Accredited by ACCSCT. **Calendar:** Semester.

Annual costs/financial aid. Tuition/fees (2008-2009): $10,650.

Contact. Phone: (804) 934-0100
Admissions, 4305 Cox Road, Glen Allen, VA 23060

Emory & Henry College

Emory, Virginia **CB member**
www.ehc.edu **CB code: 5185**

- Private 4-year liberal arts college affiliated with United Methodist Church
- Residential campus in rural community
- 886 degree-seeking undergraduates: 2% part-time, 48% women, 6% African American, 1% Asian American, 1% Hispanic American, 1% Native American, 1% international
- 37 degree-seeking graduate students
- 72% of applicants admitted
- SAT or ACT (ACT writing recommended) required
- 55% graduate within 6 years

General. Founded in 1836. Regionally accredited. Partnership with Barter Theatre (state theater of Virginia), extensive Lyceum/cultural program, annual ScienceFest. **Degrees:** 216 bachelor's awarded; master's offered. **Location:** 25 miles from Bristol. **Calendar:** Semester, limited summer session. **Full-time faculty:** 76 total; 82% have terminal degrees, 5% minority, 40% women. **Part-time faculty:** 44 total; 14% have terminal degrees, 39% women. **Class size:** 75% < 20, 24% 20-39, less than 1% 40-49. **Special facilities:** Observatory, 1912 art depot, outdoor leadership center, disc golf course, golf course.

Freshman class profile. 1,131 applied, 817 admitted, 304 enrolled.

Mid 50% test scores			
SAT critical reading:	450-580	GPA 3.0-3.49:	37%
SAT math:	430-560	GPA 2.0-2.99:	22%
SAT writing:	430-540	Rank in top quarter:	41%
ACT composite:	19-25	Rank in top tenth:	14%
GPA 3.75 or higher:	24%	Out-of-state:	37%
GPA 3.50-3.74:	17%	Live on campus:	89%
		International:	1%

Basis for selection. School achievement record, test scores, involvement in extracurricular and community activities, class rank, recommendations used. Audition required for preprofessional degrees in acting, directing, musical theater, and design/production. Auditions required for performance and teacher preparation tracks within music program. Portfolio recommended for art program.

High school preparation. College-preparatory program required. 15 units required. Required units include English 4, mathematics 3, social studies 2, science 2 (laboratory 2), foreign language 2 and visual/performing arts 1. 1 fine arts recommended.

2008-2009 Annual costs. Tuition/fees: $23,860. Room/board: $7,980. Books/supplies: $800. Personal expenses: $1,000.

2008-2009 Financial aid. Need-based: 226 full-time freshmen applied for aid; 198 were judged to have need; 198 of these received aid. Average need met was 90%. Average scholarship/grant was $20,518; average loan $3,436. 82% of total undergraduate aid awarded as scholarships/grants, 18% as loans/jobs. **Non-need-based:** Awarded to 232 full-time undergraduates, including 54 freshmen. Scholarships awarded for academics, art, music/drama, religious affiliation, state residency. **Additional information:** Virginia residents eligible for additional in-state tuition grants.

Application procedures. Admission: No deadline. $30 fee, may be waived for applicants with need, free for online applicants. Admission notification on a rolling basis beginning on or about 8/1. **Financial aid:** Priority date 4/15; no closing date. FAFSA required. Applicants notified on a rolling basis starting 3/1; must reply by 6/15.

Academics. Special study options: Combined bachelor's/graduate degree, cooperative education, distance learning, double major, dual enrollment of high school students, honors, independent study, internships, liberal arts/career combination, student-designed major, study abroad, teacher certification program. **Credit/placement by examination:** AP, CLEP, IB, SAT, ACT, institutional tests. **Support services:** Learning center, pre-admission summer program, reduced course load, study skills assistance, tutoring, writing center.

Majors. Area/ethnic studies: East Asian, European, French, Near/Middle Eastern, Spanish/Iberian. **Biology:** General. **Business:** Accounting, business admin, international. **Communications:** General. **Computer sciences:** General, computer science. **Conservation:** Environmental science, environmental studies. **Education:** Art, biology, business, chemistry, English, French, physical, Spanish. **Foreign languages:** French, Spanish. **Health:** Athletic training, prepharmacy, preveterinary. **History:** General, public archives. **Legal studies:** Prelaw. **Math:** General. **Parks/recreation:** Health/fitness, sports admin. **Philosophy/religion:** Philosophy, religion. **Physical sciences:** Chemistry, physics. **Psychology:** General. **Public administration:** Community org/advocacy. **Social sciences:** Anthropology, economics, geography, political science, sociology, U.S. government. **Visual/performing arts:** Acting, art, directing/producing, dramatic, graphic design, music performance. **Other:** Pre-health.

Most popular majors. Biology 9%, business/marketing 9%, education 10%, psychology 9%, social sciences 14%, visual/performing arts 7%.

Computing on campus. 202 workstations in dormitories, library, computer center, student center. Dormitories wired for high-speed internet access and linked to campus network. Commuter students can connect to campus network. Online library, helpline, wireless network available.

Student life. **Freshman orientation:** Mandatory. Preregistration for classes offered. Orientation occurs before registration. Students participate in community service activity and attend fine arts event following weekend as part of extended orientation. **Housing:** Guaranteed on-campus for all undergraduates. Coed dorms, single-sex dorms, special housing for disabled, wellness housing available. $400 fully refundable deposit, deadline 8/1. **Activities:** Pep band, campus ministries, choral groups, drama, literary magazine, music ensembles, musical theater, radio station, student government, student newspaper, TV station, Young Democrats, Young Republicans, Alpha Phi Omega, Fellowship of Christian Athletes, outdoor leadership program, Habitat for Humanity, Campus Christian Fellowship, multicultural student association.

Athletics. NCAA. **Intercollegiate:** Baseball M, basketball, cheerleading M, cross-country, football (tackle) M, golf M, soccer, softball W, swimming W, tennis, volleyball W. **Intramural:** Badminton, basketball, football (non-tackle), golf, soccer, softball, swimming, table tennis, tennis, volleyball. **Team name:** Wasps.

Student services. Alcohol/substance abuse counseling, chaplain/spiritual director, career counseling, student employment services, financial aid counseling, health services, on-campus daycare, personal counseling, placement for graduates, veterans' counselor. **Physically disabled:** Services for visually, hearing impaired. **Learning disabled:** Comprehensive services available.

Contact. E-mail: ehadmiss@ehc.edu
Phone: (276) 944-6133 Toll-free number: (800) 848-5493
Fax: (276) 944-6935
David Hawsey, Vice President of Enrollment Management, Emory & Henry College, Box 10, Emory, VA 24327

Ferrum College

Ferrum, Virginia — **CB member**
www.ferrum.edu — **CB code: 5213**

- Private 4-year liberal arts college affiliated with United Methodist Church
- Residential campus in rural community
- 1,367 degree-seeking undergraduates: 1% part-time, 46% women, 28% African American, 1% Asian American, 3% Hispanic American, 1% international
- 78% of applicants admitted
- SAT or ACT (ACT writing optional) required
- 30% graduate within 6 years

General. Founded in 1913. Regionally accredited. **Degrees:** 137 bachelor's awarded. **Location:** 35 miles from Roanoke, 65 miles from Greensboro, North Carolina. **Calendar:** Semester, limited summer session. **Full-time faculty:** 73 total; 75% have terminal degrees, 44% women. **Part-time faculty:** 48 total; 8% have terminal degrees. **Class size:** 48% < 20, 52% 20-39, less than 1% 40-49. **Special facilities:** Farm museum, state center for Blue Ridge folklore, forest and agricultural acreage used as outdoor labs in science, high and low ropes courses, dinner theater.

Freshman class profile. 2,371 applied, 1,842 admitted, 587 enrolled.

Mid 50% test scores		**GPA 3.0-3.49:**	21%
SAT critical reading:	400-480	**GPA 2.0-2.99:**	62%
SAT math:	390-490	**Rank in top quarter:**	13%
ACT composite:	16-20	**Rank in top tenth:**	4%
GPA 3.75 or higher:	4%	**Return as sophomores:**	55%
GPA 3.50-3.74:	4%	**International:**	1%

Basis for selection. High school record most important, followed by test scores, counselor recommendations, areas of intended college study, and extracurricular activities. Essay and interview recommended. **Home-schooled:** Transcript of courses and grades required. **Learning Disabled:** Submit current disability documentation to Director of Disability Services.

High school preparation. College-preparatory program recommended. 22 units required; 24 recommended. Required and recommended units include English 4, mathematics 3, social studies 3, science 2 (laboratory 1), foreign language 2 and academic electives 2.

2008-2009 Annual costs. Tuition/fees: $22,545. Room/board: $7,300. Books/supplies: $900. Personal expenses: $1,300.

2008-2009 Financial aid. **Need-based:** 568 full-time freshmen applied for aid; 509 were judged to have need; 509 of these received aid. Average need met was 98%. Average scholarship/grant was $11,542; average loan $3,228. 66% of total undergraduate aid awarded as scholarships/grants, 34% as loans/jobs. **Non-need-based:** Awarded to 1,140 full-time undergraduates, including 530 freshmen. Scholarships awarded for academics, leadership, religious affiliation, state residency.

Application procedures. **Admission:** $25 fee, may be waived for applicants with need. Admission notification on a rolling basis beginning on or about 9/16. Must reply by May 1 or within 4 week(s) if notified thereafter. Must reply no later than 30 days after receiving official acceptance letter. **Financial aid:** Priority date 3/1; no closing date. FAFSA required. Applicants notified on a rolling basis starting 1/10.

Academics. Field experiences and internships emphasized. Academic services/support available fall and spring academic semesters. **Special study options:** Double major, dual enrollment of high school students, exchange student, honors, independent study, internships, liberal arts/career combination, student-designed major, study abroad, teacher certification program. **Credit/placement by examination:** AP, CLEP, IB, institutional tests. 12 credit hours maximum toward bachelor's degree. **Support services:** Learning center, pre-admission summer program, reduced course load, remedial instruction, study skills assistance, tutoring, writing center.

Majors. **Agriculture:** Business, horticultural science. **Biology:** General. **Business:** Accounting, business admin, finance, management information systems, marketing. **Computer sciences:** Information systems. **Conservation:** Environmental science. **Education:** General. **Foreign languages:** Russian, Spanish. **Health:** Clinical lab science, health services. **History:** General. **Liberal arts:** Arts/sciences. **Math:** General. **Parks/recreation:** General, health/fitness, sports admin. **Philosophy/religion:** Philosophy, religion. **Physical sciences:** Chemistry. **Protective services:** Criminal justice. **Psychology:** General. **Public administration:** Social work. **Social sciences:** General, international relations, political science. **Visual/performing arts:** General, art, dramatic.

Computing on campus. PC or laptop required. 600 workstations in dormitories, library, computer center, student center. Dormitories wired for high-speed internet access and linked to campus network. Commuter students can connect to campus network. Online course registration, online library, helpline, repair service, student web hosting, wireless network available.

Student life. **Freshman orientation:** Mandatory. Preregistration for classes offered. 2-day student orientation held immediately prior to fall semester. **Policies:** All housing substance-free; no alcohol or tobacco products allowed. **Housing:** Guaranteed on-campus for all undergraduates. Coed dorms, single-sex dorms, apartments available. **Activities:** Jazz band, campus ministries, choral groups, dance, drama, literary magazine, music ensembles, Model UN, musical theater, radio station, student government, student newspaper, Environmental Action Coalition, Big Buddy/Little Buddy, African American student association, Bonner Scholars, Student Christian Fellowship, Kappa Delta Chi, Habitat for Humanity, Colleges Against Cancer, Alpha Phi Omega.

Athletics. NCAA. **Intercollegiate:** Baseball M, basketball, cheerleading, cross-country, football (tackle) M, golf M, lacrosse W, soccer, softball W, tennis, volleyball W. **Intramural:** Basketball, bowling, football (non-tackle), racquetball, soccer, softball, swimming, table tennis, tennis, volleyball. **Team name:** Panthers.

Student services. Adult student services, alcohol/substance abuse counseling, chaplain/spiritual director, career counseling, student employment services, financial aid counseling, health services, minority student services, personal counseling, placement for graduates, veterans' counselor.

Contact. E-mail: admissions@ferrum.edu
Phone: (540) 365-4290 Toll-free number: (800) 868-9797
Fax: (540) 365-4266
Gilda Woods, Director of Admissions, Ferrum College, Spilman-Daniel House, Ferrum, VA 24088

George Mason University

Fairfax, Virginia — **CB member**
www.gmu.edu — **CB code: 5827**

- Public 4-year university
- Residential campus in large town
- 18,240 degree-seeking undergraduates: 22% part-time, 53% women, 7% African American, 16% Asian American, 6% Hispanic American, 3% international
- 10,027 degree-seeking graduate students
- 63% of applicants admitted

- Application essay required
- 60% graduate within 6 years

General. Founded in 1972. Regionally accredited. **Degrees:** 3,809 bachelor's awarded; master's, doctoral, first professional offered. **ROTC:** Army, Naval, Air Force. **Location:** 15 miles from Washington, DC. **Calendar:** Semester, extensive summer session. **Full-time faculty:** 1,123 total; 92% have terminal degrees, 18% minority, 41% women. **Part-time faculty:** 950 total; 16% minority, 49% women. **Class size:** 35% < 20, 42% 20-39, 9% 40-49, 11% 50-99, 3% >100. **Special facilities:** Library of Congress Federal Theater Project collection, center for the arts, astronomy observatory, National Zoo's conservation and research center.

Freshman class profile. 12,943 applied, 8,112 admitted, 2,558 enrolled.

Mid 50% test scores		**Rank in top tenth:**	18%
SAT critical reading:	500-600	**End year in good standing:**	82%
SAT math:	520-610	**Return as sophomores:**	84%
ACT composite:	22-26	**Out-of-state:**	21%
GPA 3.75 or higher:	21%	**Live on campus:**	70%
GPA 3.50-3.74:	24%	**International:**	2%
GPA 3.0-3.49:	50%	**Fraternities:**	6%
GPA 2.0-2.99:	5%	**Sororities:**	3%
Rank in top quarter:	52%		

Basis for selection. Test scores, class rank, academic record with emphasis on courses taken, and GPA are most important. Special talents and abilities and counselor recommendations are also important. SAT and SAT Subject Tests or ACT recommended. Writing tests are not used in the admissions process at Mason. Score optional (allows applicants to be considered without submitting test scores). Candidates will submit academic credentials that exhibit the following: A minimum GPA of 3.5; strong preformance in a challenging academic curriculum; estimated class rank in the top 20 percent of high school class; and evidence of strong leadership skills. Audition required for dance and music applicants. Portfolio required for art and visual technology BFA applicants.

High school preparation. College-preparatory program required. 18 units required; 24 recommended. Required and recommended units include English 4, mathematics 3-4, social studies 3-4, science 3-4 (laboratory 3-4), foreign language 2-3 and academic electives 3-5. Additional mathematics and science units required for engineering, mathematics, and computer science applicants.

2008-2009 Annual costs. Tuition/fees: $7,512; $22,476 out-of-state. Room/board: $7,360. Books/supplies: $900. Personal expenses: $1,440.

2007-2008 Financial aid. **Need-based:** 1,460 full-time freshmen applied for aid; 931 were judged to have need; 889 of these received aid. Average need met was 71%. Average scholarship/grant was $5,835; average loan $3,393. 44% of total undergraduate aid awarded as scholarships/grants, 56% as loans/jobs. **Non-need-based:** Awarded to 1,453 full-time undergraduates, including 401 freshmen. Scholarships awarded for academics, athletics, minority status, music/drama, ROTC, state residency.

Application procedures. **Admission:** Priority date 12/1; deadline 1/15 (postmark date). $70 fee, may be waived for applicants with need. Admission notification 4/1. Must reply by May 1 or within 3 week(s) if notified thereafter. **Financial aid:** Priority date 3/1; no closing date. FAFSA required. Applicants notified by 4/1; Applicants notified on a rolling basis starting 4/1; must reply within 3 week(s) of notification.

Academics. **Special study options:** Accelerated study, combined bachelor's/graduate degree, cooperative education, cross-registration, distance learning, double major, dual enrollment of high school students, ESL, exchange student, external degree, honors, independent study, internships, liberal arts/career combination, student-designed major, study abroad, teacher certification program. **Credit/placement by examination:** AP, CLEP, IB, institutional tests. 30 credit hours maximum toward bachelor's degree. **Support services:** Learning center, study skills assistance, tutoring, writing center.

Majors. **Area/ethnic studies:** Latin American, Russian/Slavic. **Biology:** General. **Business:** Accounting, business admin, finance, marketing. **Computer sciences:** General. **Education:** Health, physical. **Engineering:** Civil, computer, electrical, systems. **Foreign languages:** General. **Health:** Athletic training, clinical lab science, nursing (RN). **History:** General. **Interdisciplinary:** Math/computer science, neuroscience, peace/conflict. **Liberal arts:** Arts/sciences. **Math:** General. **Parks/recreation:** General, health/fitness. **Philosophy/religion:** Philosophy, religion. **Physical sciences:** Astronomy, chemistry, geology, physics. **Protective services:** Police science. **Psychology:** General. **Public administration:** General, social work. **Social sciences:** Anthropology, economics, geography, international relations, political science, sociology. **Visual/performing arts:** General, art, cinematography, dance, dramatic, music performance. **Other:** Decision science and operations management, Electronics and communications engineering, Global and environmental change, Health science, Integrative studies, Tourism and events management.

Most popular majors. Business/marketing 20%, engineering/engineering technologies 8%, English 10%, health sciences 7%, psychology 8%, social sciences 13%, visual/performing arts 6%.

Computing on campus. 1,500 workstations in dormitories, library, computer center, student center. Dormitories wired for high-speed internet access and linked to campus network. Commuter students can connect to campus network. Online course registration, online library, helpline, repair service, student web hosting, wireless network available.

Student life. **Freshman orientation:** Mandatory, $160 fee. Preregistration for classes offered. Held at the beginning of the fall and spring semesters. **Housing:** Guaranteed on-campus for freshmen. Coed dorms, single-sex dorms, special housing for disabled, apartments, wellness housing available. $300 nonrefundable deposit, deadline 5/1. **Activities:** Bands, campus ministries, choral groups, dance, drama, film society, international student organizations, literary magazine, music ensembles, musical theater, opera, radio station, student government, student newspaper, symphony orchestra, TV station, Campus Crusade for Christ, Baha'i Student Association, Afghan student association, Jewish student association, Muslim student association, African student association, Students for Justice in Palestine, Alpha Phi Omega, Circle K International, UgandaHELP.

Athletics. NCAA. **Intercollegiate:** Baseball M, basketball, cross-country, diving, golf M, lacrosse W, rowing (crew) W, soccer, softball W, swimming, tennis, track and field, volleyball, wrestling M. **Intramural:** Basketball, soccer, tennis, volleyball. **Team name:** Patriots.

Student services. Alcohol/substance abuse counseling, chaplain/spiritual director, career counseling, student employment services, financial aid counseling, health services, minority student services, on-campus daycare, personal counseling, placement for graduates, veterans' counselor, women's services. **Physically disabled:** Services for visually, hearing impaired.

Contact. E-mail: admissions@gmu.edu
Phone: (703) 993-2400 Fax: (703) 993-4622
Andrew Flagel, Associate Vice President, Enrollment Development / Dean of Admissions, George Mason University, 4400 University Drive, MSN 3A4, Fairfax, VA 22030-4444

Hampden-Sydney College

Hampden-Sydney, Virginia — **CB member**
www.hsc.edu — **CB code: 5291**

- Private 4-year liberal arts college for men affiliated with Presbyterian Church (USA)
- Residential campus in rural community
- 1,120 degree-seeking undergraduates
- 64% of applicants admitted
- SAT or ACT with writing, application essay required
- 62% graduate within 6 years; 20% enter graduate study

General. Founded in 1776. Regionally accredited. **Degrees:** 229 bachelor's awarded. **ROTC:** Army. **Location:** 60 miles from Richmond, 69 miles from Charlottesville. **Calendar:** Semester, limited summer session. **Full-time faculty:** 97 total; 82% have terminal degrees, 7% minority, 28% women. **Part-time faculty:** 24 total; 46% have terminal degrees, 4% minority, 33% women. **Class size:** 68% < 20, 32% 20-39. **Special facilities:** International communications center, observatory, college operated museum, Athlete Hall of Fame museum, hiking trails.

Freshman class profile. 1,553 applied, 987 admitted, 314 enrolled.

Mid 50% test scores		**GPA 2.0-2.99:**	35%
SAT critical reading:	500-610	**End year in good standing:**	92%
SAT math:	520-610	**Return as sophomores:**	79%
SAT writing:	480-590	**Out-of-state:**	26%
ACT composite:	20-26	**Live on campus:**	100%
GPA 3.75 or higher:	19%	**International:**	2%
GPA 3.50-3.74:	13%	**Fraternities:**	34%
GPA 3.0-3.49:	33%		

Basis for selection. High school academic record, recommendations, test scores, extracurricular activities, essay most important. SAT Subject Tests recommended. SAT Subject Test in Math Level 1 recommended. Interview recommended. **Homeschooled:** Letter of recommendation (nonparent) required. Curriculum statement required.

High school preparation. College-preparatory program recommended. 16 units required. Required and recommended units include English 4, mathematics 3-4, social studies 1, history 1, science 2-3 (laboratory 1), foreign language 2-3 and academic electives 3.

2008-2009 Annual costs. Tuition/fees: $29,366. Room/board: $9,228. Books/supplies: $1,100. Personal expenses: $1,200.

2008-2009 Financial aid. **Need-based:** 216 full-time freshmen applied for aid; 168 were judged to have need; 167 of these received aid. Average need met was 85%. Average scholarship/grant was $18,714; average loan $3,847. 74% of total undergraduate aid awarded as scholarships/grants, 26% as loans/jobs. **Non-need-based:** Awarded to 658 full-time undergraduates, including 198 freshmen. Scholarships awarded for academics, leadership, religious affiliation, ROTC, state residency.

Application procedures. **Admission:** Closing date 3/1 (postmark date). $30 fee, may be waived for applicants with need, free for online applicants. Admission notification 4/15. Must reply by 5/1. **Financial aid:** Priority date 3/1; no closing date. FAFSA, CSS PROFILE required. Applicants notified on a rolling basis starting 2/1; must reply by 5/1 or within 2 week(s) of notification.

Academics. Public service concentration for men interested in government involves classwork and internship followed by paper presented and defended publicly. **Special study options:** Combined bachelor's/graduate degree, cross-registration, double major, dual enrollment of high school students, exchange student, honors, independent study, internships, semester at sea, study abroad, Washington semester. Appalachian semester, junior year exchange program with members of Virginia consortium. **Credit/placement by examination:** AP, CLEP, IB, SAT, ACT, institutional tests. **Support services:** Reduced course load, study skills assistance, tutoring, writing center.

Majors. **Biology:** General, biochemistry, biophysics. **Business:** Managerial economics. **Computer sciences:** Computer science. **Foreign languages:** Ancient Greek, classics, French, German, Latin, Spanish. **History:** General. **Interdisciplinary:** Math/computer science. **Liberal arts:** Humanities. **Math:** General, applied. **Philosophy/religion:** Philosophy, religion. **Physical sciences:** Chemistry, physics. **Psychology:** General. **Social sciences:** Econometrics, economics, international relations, political science. **Visual/performing arts:** Studio arts.

Computing on campus. 98 workstations in dormitories, library, computer center. Dormitories wired for high-speed internet access and linked to campus network. Commuter students can connect to campus network. Online course registration, online library, helpline, repair service, wireless network available.

Student life. **Freshman orientation:** Mandatory, $150 fee. Preregistration for classes offered. 4-day program before start of classes. **Policies:** All entering freshman participate in a presentation and discussion regarding the HSC Honor Code. **Housing:** Guaranteed on-campus for all undergraduates. Apartments, fraternity/sorority housing available. $300 deposit, deadline 5/1. **Activities:** Pep band, campus ministries, choral groups, drama, film society, international student organizations, literary magazine, music ensembles, radio station, student government, student newspaper, Inter-Varsity Christian Fellowship, Republican Society, volunteer fire department, Good Men and Good Citizens (community service), Student Environmental Action Coalition, museum board, Fellowship of Christian Athletes, Minority Student Union, Young Democrats.

Athletics. NCAA. **Intercollegiate:** Baseball M, basketball M, cross-country M, football (tackle) M, golf M, lacrosse M, soccer M, tennis M. **Intramural:** Basketball M, racquetball M, rugby M, soccer M, softball M, volleyball M. **Team name:** Tigers.

Student services. Alcohol/substance abuse counseling, chaplain/spiritual director, career counseling, student employment services, financial aid counseling, health services, minority student services, personal counseling, placement for graduates.

Contact. E-mail: hsapp@hsc.edu
Phone: (434) 223-6120 Toll-free number: (800) 755-0733
Fax: (434) 223-6346
Anita Garland, Dean of Admissions, Hampden-Sydney College, Box 667, Hampden-Sydney, VA 23943

Hampton University

Hampton, Virginia — **CB member**
www.hamptonu.edu — **CB code: 5292**

- Private 4-year university
- Residential campus in small city
- 4,689 degree-seeking undergraduates: 5% part-time, 64% women
- 453 graduate students
- SAT or ACT, application essay required

General. Founded in 1868. Regionally accredited. **Degrees:** 988 bachelor's, 2 associate awarded; master's, doctoral, first professional offered. **ROTC:** Army, Naval. **Location:** 10 miles from Norfolk. **Calendar:** Semester, extensive summer session. **Full-time faculty:** 325 total. **Part-time faculty:** 125 total. **Class size:** 51% < 20, 38% 20-39, 7% 40-49, 4% 50-99, less than 1% >100. **Special facilities:** African American literature and history collection, university archives, North American Indian, African, Oceanic and Black American art collections.

Freshman class profile.

Mid 50% test scores		**GPA 3.0-3.49:**	41%
SAT critical reading:	470-620	**GPA 2.0-2.99:**	40%
SAT math:	470-580	**Out-of-state:**	68%
ACT composite:	17-26	**Live on campus:**	71%
GPA 3.75 or higher:	2%	**Fraternities:**	5%
GPA 3.50-3.74:	17%	**Sororities:**	4%

Basis for selection. Academic record, rank in top half of graduating class, personal references, intended major, test scores and personal statement important. Extracurricular activities, essay, school recommendation considered. Audition required for music. **Homeschooled:** Transcript of courses and grades required. Must present secondary school record if it exists, GED test scores, verification by state/regional official, SAT or ACT results.

High school preparation. 17 units required. Required and recommended units include English 4, mathematics 3, social studies 2, science 2 (laboratory 2), foreign language 2 and academic electives 6. One chemistry, biology with lab, algebra I and II, geometry required.

2008-2009 Annual costs. Tuition/fees: $16,392. Room/board: $7,440. Books/supplies: $750. Personal expenses: $1,103.

2008-2009 Financial aid. **Non-need-based:** Scholarships awarded for academics, athletics, leadership, music/drama, ROTC.

Application procedures. **Admission:** Priority date 12/1; deadline 3/1 (postmark date). $35 fee. Admission notification on a rolling basis beginning on or about 12/15. Must reply by 5/1. **Financial aid:** Priority date 3/1; no closing date. FAFSA required. Applicants notified on a rolling basis starting 4/15; must reply within 2 week(s) of notification.

Academics. Students who have completed one semester with minimum 3.2 GPA may apply to honors program. Academic skills workshops held throughout year available for all students. Students may take courses at other Tidewater consortium schools. **Special study options:** Accelerated study, combined bachelor's/graduate degree, cooperative education, cross-registration, distance learning, double major, dual enrollment of high school students, honors, independent study, internships, study abroad, teacher certification program. Grad level programs for undergraduates, coop programs in arts, business, education, engineering, social/behavioral science. **Credit/placement by examination:** AP, CLEP, IB, institutional tests. 30 credit hours maximum toward bachelor's degree. **Support services:** Learning center, pre-admission summer program, reduced course load, remedial instruction, tutoring, writing center.

Majors. **Architecture:** Architecture. **Biology:** General, marine, molecular. **Business:** Accounting, banking/financial services, business admin, finance, management information systems, managerial economics, marketing. **Communications:** Advertising, broadcast journalism, journalism, media studies, public relations. **Computer sciences:** General, computer science, networking. **Conservation:** Environmental science. **Education:** General, health, physical, special. **Engineering:** General, chemical, computer, electrical. **Foreign languages:** Spanish. **Health:** Audiology/speech pathology, communication disorders, nursing (RN). **History:** General. **Legal studies:** Paralegal, prelaw. **Liberal arts:** Arts/sciences. **Math:** General. **Parks/recreation:** General, facilities management, sports admin. **Physical sciences:** Chemistry, physics. **Protective services:** Fire services admin, law enforcement admin. **Psychology:** General. **Social sciences:** Political science, sociology. **Theology:** Theology. **Transportation:** Aviation management. **Visual/performing arts:** Art, commercial/advertising art, dramatic, music performance.

Computing on campus. 1,500 workstations in dormitories, library, computer center, student center. Dormitories wired for high-speed internet access and linked to campus network. Commuter students can connect to campus network. Online course registration, online library, helpline, repair service, student web hosting, wireless network available.

Student life. **Freshman orientation:** Mandatory. Preregistration for classes offered. One-week orientation held in August. **Housing:** Guaranteed on-campus for freshmen. Coed dorms, single-sex dorms, wellness housing available. $500 deposit, deadline 5/1. **Activities:** Bands, choral groups, dance, drama, international student organizations, music ensembles, musical theater, opera, radio station, student government, student newspaper, symphony orchestra, TV station, Christian student association, Big Brothers/Big Sisters, political science/pre-law club, Women in Communications, Muslim student fellowship, service learning and leadership organizations, National Leadership of Black Journalists.

Athletics. NCAA. **Intercollegiate:** Basketball, bowling W, cheerleading M, cross-country, football (tackle) M, golf, sailing, softball W, tennis, track and field, volleyball W. **Intramural:** Basketball, bowling W, softball W, swimming. **Team name:** Pirates.

Student services. Chaplain/spiritual director, career counseling, services for economically disadvantaged, student employment services, financial aid counseling, health services, on-campus daycare, personal counseling, placement for graduates, veterans' counselor. **Physically disabled:** Services for visually, speech, hearing impaired.

Contact. E-mail: admit@hamptonu.edu
Phone: (757) 727-5328 Toll-free number: (800) 624-3328
Fax: (757) 727-5095
Angela Boyd, Director of Admissions, Hampton University, Office of Admissions, Hampton, VA 23668

Hollins University

Roanoke, Virginia — **CB member**
www.hollins.edu — **CB code: 5294**

- Private 4-year university and liberal arts college for women
- Residential campus in small city
- 785 degree-seeking undergraduates: 5% part-time, 100% women, 8% African American, 2% Asian American, 3% Hispanic American, 1% Native American, 5% international
- 233 degree-seeking graduate students
- 87% of applicants admitted
- SAT or ACT (ACT writing optional), application essay required
- 61% graduate within 6 years

General. Founded in 1842. Regionally accredited. **Degrees:** 181 bachelor's awarded; master's offered. **Location:** 175 miles from Richmond, 250 miles from Washington, DC. **Calendar:** 4-1-4, limited summer session. **Full-time faculty:** 73 total; 96% have terminal degrees, 10% minority, 49% women. **Part-time faculty:** 35 total; 43% have terminal degrees, 6% minority, 69% women. **Class size:** 84% < 20, 15% 20-39, less than 1% 40-49. **Special facilities:** Electron microscope facilities, EEG and biofeedback equipment, research facilities for chromatography, spectrophotometry, electrochemistry, gas kinetics, centrifugation.

Freshman class profile. 658 applied, 573 admitted, 209 enrolled.

Mid 50% test scores		GPA 2.0-2.99:	18%
SAT critical reading:	540-650	Rank in top quarter:	59%
SAT math:	490-590	Rank in top tenth:	30%
GPA 3.75 or higher:	39%	Return as sophomores:	74%
GPA 3.50-3.74:	15%	Live on campus:	94%
GPA 3.0-3.49:	28%	International:	5%

Basis for selection. School achievement record, school recommendation, and test scores very important. Essay, talent/ability important. Interview, class rank, character, alumni relation, extracurricular activities, volunteer work, work experience considered. Interview recommended. **Homeschooled:** Applicants encouraged to take 3 SAT Subject Tests.

High school preparation. College-preparatory program recommended. 16 units required. Required units include English 4, mathematics 3, social studies 3, science 3 and foreign language 3.

2008-2009 Annual costs. Tuition/fees: $27,055. Room/board: $9,650. Books/supplies: $800. Personal expenses: $850.

2008-2009 Financial aid. Non-need-based: Scholarships awarded for academics, alumni affiliation, art, leadership, music/drama, state residency.

Application procedures. Admission: Priority date 2/1; no deadline. $35 fee, may be waived for applicants with need. Admission notification on a rolling basis beginning on or about 12/15. Must reply by May 1 or within 2 week(s) if notified thereafter. **Financial aid:** Priority date 2/15; no closing date. FAFSA required. Applicants notified on a rolling basis starting 3/1; must reply by 5/1.

Academics. Special study options: Accelerated study, combined bachelor's/graduate degree, cooperative education, cross-registration, double major, dual enrollment of high school students, exchange student, independent study, internships, liberal arts/career combination, student-designed major, study abroad, teacher certification program. Numerous college exchange programs, 5- and 6-year dual degree programs in engineering with Washington University in St. Louis and Virginia Tech, Louis D. Rubin, Jr., Semester in Creative Writing. **Credit/placement by examination:** AP, CLEP, IB, institutional tests. **Support services:** Tutoring, writing center.

Majors. Area/ethnic studies: Women's. **Biology:** General, environmental. **Business:** General. **Communications:** General. **Conservation:** Environmental studies. **Foreign languages:** Classics, French, German, Spanish. **History:** General. **Interdisciplinary:** Global studies. **Math:** General. **Philosophy/religion:** Philosophy, religion. **Physical sciences:** Chemistry, physics. **Psychology:** General. **Social sciences:** Economics, political science, sociology. **Visual/performing arts:** Art history/conservation, dance, dramatic, studio arts.

Most popular majors. Biology 7%, business/marketing 7%, communications/journalism 7%, English 17%, psychology 7%, social sciences 13%, visual/performing arts 21%.

Computing on campus. 100 workstations in dormitories, library, computer center, student center. Dormitories wired for high-speed internet access and linked to campus network. Commuter students can connect to campus network. Online course registration, online library, helpline, wireless network available.

Student life. Freshman orientation: Mandatory. 5-day program includes mini-classes and community service. **Housing:** Guaranteed on-campus for all undergraduates. Special housing for disabled, apartments, wellness housing available. $400 nonrefundable deposit. Special interest housing. **Activities:** Choral groups, dance, drama, film society, literary magazine, music ensembles, Model UN, musical theater, student government, student newspaper, TV station, religious life association, Black student alliance, College Democrats, College Republicans, Colleges Against Cancer, Student Health Advisory Board, Students Helping Achieve Rewarding Experiences, Mujeres Unidas, Circle K.

Athletics. NCAA. **Intercollegiate:** Basketball W, equestrian W, field hockey W, golf W, lacrosse W, soccer W, swimming W, tennis W, volleyball W.

Student services. Adult student services, alcohol/substance abuse counseling, chaplain/spiritual director, career counseling, student employment services, financial aid counseling, health services, minority student services, personal counseling, placement for graduates, women's services. **Physically disabled:** Services for visually, hearing impaired.

Contact. E-mail: huadm@hollins.edu
Phone: (540) 362-6401 Toll-free number: (800) 456-9595
Fax: (540) 362-6218
Rebecca Eckstein, Dean of Admissions, Hollins University, PO Box 9707, Roanoke, VA 24020-1707

ITT Technical Institute: Chantilly

Chantilly, Virginia
CB code: 4086

- For-profit 4-year technical college
- Commuter campus in large town

General. Accredited by ACICS. **Calendar:** Quarter.

Contact. Phone: (703) 263-2541
Director of Recruitment, 14420 Albemarle Point Place, Chantilly, VA 20151

ITT Technical Institute: Norfolk

Norfolk, Virginia
www.itt-tech.edu — **CB code: 2737**

- For-profit 4-year technical college
- Commuter campus in large city

General. Accredited by ACICS. **Location:** 81 miles from Richmond, 145 miles from Washington, DC. **Calendar:** Quarter.

Contact. Phone: (757) 466-1260
Director of Recruitment, 863 Glenrock Road, Norfolk, VA 23502

ITT Technical Institute: Richmond

Richmond, Virginia
www.itt-tech.edu — **CB code: 2748**

- For-profit 4-year technical college
- Commuter campus in small city

General. Accredited by ACICS. **Location:** 98 miles from Washington, DC. **Calendar:** Quarter.

Contact. Phone: (804) 330-4992
Director of Recruitment, 300 Gateway Centre Parkway, Richmond, VA 23235

ITT Technical Institute: Springfield
Springfield, Virginia

- For-profit 4-year technical college
- Commuter campus in large town

General. Accredited by ACICS. **Calendar:** Quarter.

Contact. Phone: (703) 440-9535
Director of Recruitment, 7300 Boston Boulevard, Springfield, VA 22153

James Madison University
Harrisonburg, Virginia **CB member**
www.jmu.edu **CB code: 5392**

- Public 4-year university
- Residential campus in large town
- 16,648 degree-seeking undergraduates: 3% part-time, 60% women, 4% African American, 5% Asian American, 2% Hispanic American, 1% international
- 1,241 degree-seeking graduate students
- 65% of applicants admitted
- SAT or ACT (ACT writing optional) required
- 82% graduate within 6 years; 23% enter graduate study

General. Founded in 1908. Regionally accredited. **Degrees:** 3,504 bachelor's awarded; master's, doctoral offered. **ROTC:** Army, Air Force. **Location:** 123 miles from Washington, DC. **Calendar:** Semester, extensive summer session. **Full-time faculty:** 897 total; 78% have terminal degrees, 8% minority, 46% women. **Part-time faculty:** 406 total; 23% have terminal degrees, 3% minority, 50% women. **Class size:** 35% < 20, 45% 20-39, 7% 40-49, 9% 50-99, 4% >100. **Special facilities:** Arboretum, observatory, planetarium, mineral museum, science on a sphere (SOS).

Freshman class profile. 19,245 applied, 12,522 admitted, 3,957 enrolled.

Mid 50% test scores			
SAT critical reading:	520-620	Rank in top quarter:	73%
SAT math:	540-630	Rank in top tenth:	29%
SAT writing:	520-620	End year in good standing:	90%
ACT composite:	22-26	Return as sophomores:	91%
GPA 3.75 or higher:	44%	Out-of-state:	33%
GPA 3.50-3.74:	27%	Live on campus:	99%
GPA 3.0-3.49:	27%	International:	1%
GPA 2.0-2.99:	2%	Fraternities:	6%
		Sororities:	6%

Basis for selection. Rigor of high school curriculum, as shown by the quantity and quality of courses, most important. Class rank or GPA, test scores, extracurricular activities, special skills or talents important. Counselor recommendation considered. Applicants with solid achievement in 5 or more academic courses in each of 4 years of high school have decided advantage in admissions process. Audition required for dance, music, theater programs; portfolio and interview required for art. Nursing, justice studies, media arts and design, political science, psychology, and social work students must apply to their applicable departments in addition to applying for undergraduate admission. **Homeschooled:** Statement describing homeschool structure and mission required.

High school preparation. College-preparatory program recommended. Required and recommended units include English 4, mathematics 4, social studies 3-4, science 3-4 (laboratory 3-4) and foreign language 3. 3 of same foreign language recommended, or 2 of one language and 2 of another. Social studies may include units in history. History and social studies "units required" and "units recommended" are combined for the two subjects.

2008-2009 Annual costs. Tuition/fees: $6,964; $18,458 out-of-state. Room/board: $7,458. Books/supplies: $876. Personal expenses: $1,866.

2008-2009 Financial aid. **Need-based:** 2,916 full-time freshmen applied for aid; 1,447 were judged to have need; 1,214 of these received aid. Average need met was 45%. Average scholarship/grant was $7,046; average loan $3,488. 51% of total undergraduate aid awarded as scholarships/grants, 49% as loans/jobs. **Non-need-based:** Awarded to 1,655 full-time undergraduates, including 678 freshmen. Scholarships awarded for academics, alumni affiliation, art, athletics, leadership, minority status, music/drama, state residency.

Application procedures. **Admission:** Priority date 11/1; deadline 1/15 (postmark date). $40 fee, may be waived for applicants with need. Admission notification 4/1. Must reply by 5/1. **Financial aid:** Priority date 3/1; no closing date. FAFSA required. Applicants notified on a rolling basis starting 4/1; must reply within 4 week(s) of notification.

Academics. **Special study options:** Accelerated study, combined bachelor's/graduate degree, distance learning, double major, honors, independent study, internships, study abroad, teacher certification program, Washington semester. Continuing education programs offered on campus. **Credit/placement by examination:** AP, CLEP, IB, institutional tests. Students enrolled in the BIS program earn up to 30 credits toward their bachelor's degrees through non-traditional means, such as prior learning experience and CLEP exams. Eight non-traditional credits, considered earned credits, the remainder treated as transfer credits when calculating the minimum credits earned at the university in order to obtain a degree from JMU. **Support services:** Learning center, study skills assistance, tutoring, writing center.

Majors. **Biology:** General, biotechnology. **Business:** Accounting, business admin, finance, hospitality admin, international, managerial economics, marketing. **Communications:** General. **Computer sciences:** General, information systems. **Engineering:** General. **Family/consumer sciences:** Food/nutrition. **Foreign languages:** General. **Health:** Athletic training, community health services, health care admin, nursing (RN), speech pathology. **History:** General. **Interdisciplinary:** Science/society, systems science. **Liberal arts:** Arts/sciences. **Math:** General. **Parks/recreation:** Health/fitness. **Physical sciences:** Chemistry, geology, physics. **Psychology:** General. **Public administration:** General, social work. **Social sciences:** General, anthropology, economics, geography, international relations, political science, sociology. **Visual/performing arts:** Art, art history/conservation, dramatic, music performance. **Other:** Justice studies, Philosophy and religion, Quantitative finance.

Most popular majors. Business/marketing 23%, communications/journalism 8%, health sciences 11%, liberal arts 6%, psychology 6%, social sciences 10%, visual/performing arts 6%.

Computing on campus. 1,583 workstations in dormitories, library, computer center, student center. Dormitories wired for high-speed internet access and linked to campus network. Commuter students can connect to campus network. Online course registration, online library, helpline, repair service, student web hosting, wireless network available.

Student life. **Freshman orientation:** Mandatory, $150 fee. Preregistration for classes offered. One-day orientation in June or July, plus 5-day program in August prior to the beginning of classes. **Housing:** Guaranteed on-campus for freshmen. Coed dorms, apartments, fraternity/sorority housing, wellness housing available. Fraternities located off campus. **Activities:** Bands, campus ministries, choral groups, dance, drama, international student organizations, literary magazine, music ensembles, musical theater, opera, radio station, student government, student newspaper, symphony orchestra, 283 student organizations and clubs.

Athletics. NCAA. **Intercollegiate:** Baseball M, basketball, cheerleading, cross-country W, diving W, field hockey W, football (tackle) M, golf, lacrosse W, soccer, softball W, swimming W, tennis, track and field W, volleyball W. **Intramural:** Basketball, bowling, football (non-tackle), golf, racquetball, soccer, softball, table tennis, tennis, volleyball. **Team name:** Dukes.

Student services. Adult student services, alcohol/substance abuse counseling, chaplain/spiritual director, career counseling, student employment services, financial aid counseling, health services, minority student services, personal counseling, placement for graduates. **Physically disabled:** Services for visually, speech, hearing impaired.

Contact. E-mail: admissions@jmu.edu
Phone: (540) 568-5681 Fax: (540) 568-3332
Michael Walsh, Director of Admissions, James Madison University, Sonner Hall, MSC 0101, Harrisonburg, VA 22807

Jefferson College of Health Sciences
Roanoke, Virginia
www.jchs.edu **CB code: 5099**

- Private 4-year health science and nursing college
- Commuter campus in large city
- 899 degree-seeking undergraduates: 31% part-time, 83% women, 12% African American, 2% Asian American, 1% Hispanic American
- 88 degree-seeking graduate students
- 48% of applicants admitted

- SAT or ACT (ACT writing recommended) required
- 73% graduate within 6 years; 21% enter graduate study

General. Founded in 1982. Regionally accredited. Access to educational seminars broadcast live by American Hospital Association, Hospital Satellite network, and other networks. One of 50 demonstration centers nationwide for interactive video in nursing education. As part of the Carilion system, JCHS has access to Carilion Clinic resources, including the medical library. **Degrees:** 72 bachelor's, 183 associate awarded; master's offered. **Calendar:** Semester, limited summer session. **Full-time faculty:** 70 total; 33% have terminal degrees, 64% women. **Part-time faculty:** 52 total; 19% have terminal degrees, 65% women. **Class size:** 58% < 20, 39% 20-39, 3% 40-49.

Freshman class profile. 609 applied, 295 admitted, 73 enrolled.

Mid 50% test scores			
SAT critical reading:	420-530	GPA 3.0-3.49:	41%
SAT math:	430-510	GPA 2.0-2.99:	24%
SAT writing:	430-500	End year in good standing:	89%
ACT composite:	18-23	Return as sophomores:	79%
GPA 3.75 or higher:	16%	Out-of-state:	6%
GPA 3.50-3.74:	19%	Live on campus:	36%

Basis for selection. Certification required for some programs. Emergency health sciences program requires emergency medical technician ambulance certification prior to entering program. SAT/ACT test scores are not required if applicant has been out of high school for three years or more.

High school preparation. 16 units required. Required and recommended units include English 4, mathematics 2-3 and science 2-4.

2008-2009 Annual costs. Tuition/fees: $16,275. Room/board: $7,010. Books/supplies: $1,150. Personal expenses: $2,576.

2007-2008 Financial aid. **Need-based:** 80 full-time freshmen applied for aid; 71 were judged to have need; 71 of these received aid. Average need met was 40%. Average scholarship/grant was $3,213; average loan $3,626. 18% of total undergraduate aid awarded as scholarships/grants, 82% as loans/jobs. **Non-need-based:** Awarded to 635 full-time undergraduates, including 84 freshmen. Scholarships awarded for academics.

Application procedures. **Admission:** No deadline. $35 fee, may be waived for applicants with need, free for online applicants. Admission notification on a rolling basis. Must reply by May 1 or within 2 week(s) if notified thereafter. **Financial aid:** No deadline. FAFSA, institutional form required. Applicants notified on a rolling basis; must reply within 2 week(s) of notification.

Academics. **Special study options:** Accelerated study, cross-registration, distance learning, double major, dual enrollment of high school students, independent study, internships, liberal arts/career combination. **Credit/placement by examination:** AP, CLEP, IB, SAT, ACT, institutional tests. Maximum of 18 credit hours may be satisfied by CLEP/DANTES examinations. **Support services:** Learning center, pre-admission summer program, study skills assistance, tutoring.

Majors. **Biology:** Biomedical sciences. **Health:** Athletic training, health care admin, nursing (RN), physician assistant, premedicine, prenursing, prepharmacy. **Parks/recreation:** Exercise sciences. **Psychology:** Medical.

Most popular majors. Biology 13%, health sciences 88%.

Computing on campus. 56 workstations in library, computer center. Dormitories wired for high-speed internet access. Online library, helpline, repair service available.

Student life. **Freshman orientation:** Mandatory. Preregistration for classes offered. One-day orientation held multiple times during summer. **Housing:** Coed dorms available. $250 nonrefundable deposit. **Activities:** Campus ministries, choral groups, student government, student newspaper, student nurse association, student occupational therapy association, student physical therapy assistant assembly, Good Samaritan Club, Habitat for Humanity, Hands of Healing.

Athletics. **Team name:** Blue Healers.

Student services. Adult student services, career counseling, student employment services, financial aid counseling, health services, personal counseling, placement for graduates. **Physically disabled:** Services for visually impaired.

Contact. E-mail: jmckeon@jchs.edu
Phone: (540) 985-8483 Toll-free number: (888) 985-8483
Fax: (540) 985-9773
Judith McKeon, Director of Admissions, Jefferson College of Health Sciences, Box 13186, Roanoke, VA 24031-3186

Liberty University

Lynchburg, Virginia — **CB member**
www.liberty.edu — **CB code: 5385**

- Private 4-year university affiliated with Baptist faith
- Residential campus in small city
- 21,506 degree-seeking undergraduates: 32% part-time, 52% women, 12% African American, 1% Asian American, 3% Hispanic American, 1% Native American, 3% international
- 11,814 degree-seeking graduate students
- 96% of applicants admitted
- SAT or ACT (ACT writing optional), application essay required
- 51% graduate within 6 years

General. Founded in 1971. Regionally accredited. **Degrees:** 2,499 bachelor's, 171 associate awarded; master's, doctoral, first professional offered. **ROTC:** Army, Air Force. **Location:** 120 miles from Richmond, 150 miles from Raleigh, North Carolina. **Calendar:** Semester, limited summer session. **Full-time faculty:** 394 total. **Part-time faculty:** 188 total. **Class size:** 36% < 20, 50% 20-39, 3% 40-49, 6% 50-99, 5% >100. **Special facilities:** Ice rink, running and hiking trails, paintball fields, indoor soccer complex, snowflex ski and snowboard hill.

Freshman class profile. 7,123 applied, 6,850 admitted, 2,979 enrolled.

Mid 50% test scores			
SAT critical reading:	430-540	GPA 2.0-2.99:	41%
SAT math:	420-530	Rank in top quarter:	23%
ACT composite:	18-23	Rank in top tenth:	5%
GPA 3.75 or higher:	12%	Return as sophomores:	73%
GPA 3.50-3.74:	14%	Out-of-state:	64%
GPA 3.0-3.49:	31%	Live on campus:	67%
		International:	7%

Basis for selection. Secondary school record, standardized test scores, and essay most important. Applicants who fail to meet the minimum required GPA may be admitted on academic warning status and will be limited to 13 semester hours of coursework. TOEFL required for international students.

High school preparation. College-preparatory program required. 17 units recommended. Recommended units include English 4, mathematics 3, social studies 2, science 2 (laboratory 2), foreign language 2 and academic electives 4.

2009-2010 Annual costs. Tuition/fees (projected): $17,742. Room/board: $5,996. Books/supplies: $1,400. Personal expenses: $1,400.

2008-2009 Financial aid. **Non-need-based:** Scholarships awarded for academics, alumni affiliation, athletics, leadership, music/drama, religious affiliation, ROTC, state residency.

Application procedures. **Admission:** Priority date 6/30; no deadline. $40 fee, may be waived for applicants with need. Admission notification on a rolling basis. Must reply by May 1 or within 2 week(s) if notified thereafter. **Financial aid:** Closing date 3/1. FAFSA required. Applicants notified on a rolling basis starting 3/15; must reply within 3 week(s) of notification.

Academics. **Special study options:** Accelerated study, cooperative education, distance learning, double major, dual enrollment of high school students, ESL, external degree, honors, independent study, internships, student-designed major, teacher certification program, weekend college. Associate school of the Institute of Holy Land Studies in Jerusalem. **Credit/placement by examination:** AP, CLEP, IB, SAT, ACT, institutional tests. 30 credit hours maximum toward bachelor's degree. **Support services:** Learning center, reduced course load, remedial instruction, study skills assistance, tutoring.

Majors. **Biology:** General, biochemistry. **Business:** General, accounting, management information systems. **Communications:** General. **Computer sciences:** General, web page design. **Education:** ESL. **Engineering:** Computer, electrical, industrial, software, systems. **Family/consumer sciences:** General, clothing/textiles. **Foreign languages:** Spanish. **Health:** Athletic training, community health, nursing (RN), public health ed. **History:** General. **Liberal arts:** Arts/sciences. **Math:** General. **Parks/recreation:** Exercise sciences, health/fitness, sports admin. **Philosophy/religion:** Philosophy, religion. **Protective services:** Criminal justice. **Psychology:** General. **Social sciences:** General, political science. **Theology:** Bible, missionary, pastoral counseling, sacred music, youth ministry. **Transportation:** Aviation. **Visual/performing arts:** Design, dramatic.

Most popular majors. Business/marketing 17%, communications/journalism 6%, health sciences 7%, interdisciplinary studies 14%, philosophy/religious studies 20%, psychology 13%.

Computing on campus. 406 workstations in library, computer center, student center. Dormitories wired for high-speed internet access and linked to campus network. Commuter students can connect to campus network. Online course registration, online library, helpline, repair service, wireless network available.

Student life. Freshman orientation: Mandatory. Preregistration for classes offered. **Policies:** All students involved in Christian or community service. **Housing:** Guaranteed on-campus for all undergraduates. Single-sex dorms, special housing for disabled, apartments, wellness housing available. $250 nonrefundable deposit. Students required to live on campus unless living with parents, over age 21, or married. **Activities:** Bands, campus ministries, choral groups, drama, music ensembles, musical theater, opera, radio station, student government, student newspaper, TV station, Circle K, Youthquest, Light Ministries, Fellowship of Christian Athletes, Students Teaching Elementary School, College Republicans, Campus SERVE.

Athletics. NCAA. **Intercollegiate:** Baseball M, basketball, cheerleading, cross-country, football (tackle) M, golf M, soccer, softball W, tennis, track and field, volleyball W. **Intramural:** Basketball, football (non-tackle), soccer, softball, tennis, volleyball. **Team name:** Flames.

Student services. Chaplain/spiritual director, career counseling, student employment services, financial aid counseling, health services, minority student services, personal counseling, placement for graduates, veterans' counselor, women's services. **Physically disabled:** Services for hearing impaired.

Contact. E-mail: admissions@liberty.edu
Phone: (434) 582-5985 Toll-free number: (800) 543-5317
Fax: (800) 542-2311
Paul Clark, Director of Residential Admissions, Liberty University, 1971 University Boulevard, Lynchburg, VA 24502

Longwood University

Farmville, Virginia — **CB member**
www.longwood.edu — **CB code: 5368**

- Public 4-year university
- Residential campus in small town
- 3,971 degree-seeking undergraduates: 4% part-time, 66% women, 6% African American, 2% Asian American, 2% Hispanic American, 1% Native American
- 437 degree-seeking graduate students
- 69% of applicants admitted
- SAT or ACT (ACT writing optional), application essay required
- 65% graduate within 6 years

General. Founded in 1839. Regionally accredited. **Degrees:** 746 bachelor's awarded; master's offered. **ROTC:** Army. **Location:** 65 miles from Richmond, 60 miles from Charlottesville. **Calendar:** Semester, limited summer session. **Full-time faculty:** 211 total; 6% minority, 49% women. **Part-time faculty:** 76 total; 13% minority, 57% women. **Class size:** 46% < 20, 48% 20-39, 4% 40-49, 1% 50-99. **Special facilities:** Golf course, flora collection, visual arts center, greenhouse.

Freshman class profile. 4,197 applied, 2,879 admitted, 1,049 enrolled.

Mid 50% test scores		**GPA 2.0-2.99:**	19%
SAT critical reading:	490-570	**Rank in top quarter:**	39%
SAT math:	480-570	**Rank in top tenth:**	11%
ACT composite:	21-23	**Return as sophomores:**	79%
GPA 3.75 or higher:	15%	**Out-of-state:**	4%
GPA 3.50-3.74:	17%	**Live on campus:**	98%
GPA 3.0-3.49:	49%		

Basis for selection. Rank in top half of class, combined SAT score (exclusive of Writing) of 1000 minimum and GPA of 2.7 minimum in college preparatory courses required. Extracurricular activities and recommendations also considered. Early Action consideration, applicants must have 3.0 GPA and 1000 on SAT (exclusive of Writing). Modern language majors required to take SAT subject test in intended language of study for placement. Audition required for music. **Homeschooled:** Statement describing homeschool structure and mission, letter of recommendation (nonparent) required. Applications reviewed on case-by-case basis.

High school preparation. College-preparatory program required. 24 units required. Required and recommended units include English 4, mathematics 3-4, social studies 2, history 2, science 3-4 (laboratory 2-3), foreign language 2-4 and visual/performing arts 1.

2008-2009 Annual costs. Tuition/fees: $8,502; $17,114 out-of-state. Required laptop computer for first year students $1,700. Room/board: $6,856. Books/supplies: $800. Personal expenses: $1,200.

2007-2008 Financial aid. Need-based: 579 full-time freshmen applied for aid; 434 were judged to have need; 434 of these received aid. Average need met was 64%. Average scholarship/grant was $5,201; average loan $3,297. 46% of total undergraduate aid awarded as scholarships/grants, 54% as loans/jobs. **Non-need-based:** Awarded to 145 full-time undergraduates, including 39 freshmen. Scholarships awarded for academics, alumni affiliation, art, athletics, leadership, music/drama, ROTC, state residency.

Application procedures. Admission: Priority date 3/1; no deadline. $40 fee, may be waived for applicants with need. Admission notification on a rolling basis beginning on or about 1/15. Must reply by May 1 or within 1 week(s) if notified thereafter. **Financial aid:** Priority date 3/1; no closing date. FAFSA required. Applicants notified on a rolling basis starting 4/1; must reply within 4 week(s) of notification.

Academics. Special study options: Accelerated study, combined bachelor's/graduate degree, cross-registration, distance learning, double major, dual enrollment of high school students, honors, independent study, internships, study abroad, teacher certification program. Summer field programs in archaeology and botany. **Credit/placement by examination:** AP, CLEP, IB, institutional tests. **Support services:** Learning center, reduced course load, study skills assistance, tutoring, writing center.

Majors. Biology: General. **Business:** General, accounting, business admin, finance, management information systems, management science, marketing, retailing. **Communications:** General. **Computer sciences:** General, computer science. **Education:** General, art, biology, business, chemistry, early childhood, elementary, English, French, German, health, history, mathematics, middle, multi-level teacher, music, physical, physics, science, social studies, Spanish, special, speech impaired. **Foreign languages:** French, German, Spanish. **Health:** Athletic training, nursing (RN), predental, premedicine, prepharmacy, preveterinary, recreational therapy. **History:** General, public archives. **Legal studies:** Prelaw. **Liberal arts:** Arts/sciences. **Math:** General. **Parks/recreation:** Exercise sciences, health/fitness. **Physical sciences:** Chemistry, physics. **Protective services:** Criminal justice. **Psychology:** General. **Public administration:** Social work. **Social sciences:** Anthropology, criminology, economics, political science, sociology. **Visual/performing arts:** General, art, art history/conservation, commercial/advertising art, dramatic, music performance, studio arts.

Most popular majors. Business/marketing 19%, liberal arts 22%, parks/recreation 6%, psychology 7%, social sciences 8%, visual/performing arts 8%.

Computing on campus. PC or laptop required. 197 workstations in dormitories, library, computer center, student center. Dormitories wired for high-speed internet access and linked to campus network. Commuter students can connect to campus network. Online course registration, online library, helpline, repair service, student web hosting, wireless network available.

Student life. Freshman orientation: Mandatory, $75 fee. Preregistration for classes offered. One-day orientation held during spring and summer. **Housing:** Guaranteed on-campus for freshmen. Coed dorms, single-sex dorms, special housing for disabled, apartments, fraternity/sorority housing, wellness housing available. $400 nonrefundable deposit, deadline 5/1. Honor student housing available. **Activities:** Bands, campus ministries, choral groups, dance, drama, international student organizations, literary magazine, music ensembles, radio station, student government, student newspaper, College Democrats, unity alliance, interfraternity council, Habitat for Humanity, Alpha Phi Omega, Students Educating for Active Leadership, College Republicans, Peer Helpers, Big Sibling Program.

Athletics. NCAA. **Intercollegiate:** Baseball M, basketball, cheerleading, cross-country, field hockey W, golf, soccer, softball W, tennis. **Intramural:** Basketball, bowling, football (non-tackle), soccer, softball, tennis, volleyball. **Team name:** Lancers.

Student services. Adult student services, alcohol/substance abuse counseling, career counseling, student employment services, financial aid counseling, health services, minority student services, personal counseling, placement for graduates, women's services. **Physically disabled:** Services for visually, speech, hearing impaired.

Contact. E-mail: admissions@longwood.edu
Phone: (434) 395-2060 Toll-free number: (800) 281-4677 ext. 2
Fax: (434) 395-2332
Robert Chonko, Dean of Admissions, Longwood University, 201 High Street, Farmville, VA 23909-1898

Lynchburg College

Lynchburg, Virginia **CB member**
www.lynchburg.edu **CB code: 5372**

- Private 4-year liberal arts college affiliated with Christian Church (Disciples of Christ)
- Residential campus in small city
- 2,091 degree-seeking undergraduates: 4% part-time, 59% women, 7% African American, 1% Asian American, 3% Hispanic American, 1% Native American, 1% international
- 299 degree-seeking graduate students
- 68% of applicants admitted
- SAT or ACT (ACT writing optional) required
- 59% graduate within 6 years; 18% enter graduate study

General. Founded in 1903. Regionally accredited. **Degrees:** 427 bachelor's awarded; master's offered. **ROTC:** Army. **Location:** 180 miles from Washington, DC, 60 miles from Roanoke. **Calendar:** Semester, extensive summer session. **Full-time faculty:** 160 total; 81% have terminal degrees, 6% minority, 48% women. **Part-time faculty:** 77 total; 20% have terminal degrees, 5% minority, 49% women. **Class size:** 60% < 20, 40% 20-39, less than 1% 40-49. **Special facilities:** Nature study center, center for media development, geographic information system labs, forensic cadaver lab, astronomical observatory.

Freshman class profile. 4,501 applied, 3,055 admitted, 594 enrolled.

Mid 50% test scores		**GPA 2.0-2.99:**	41%
SAT critical reading:	460-560	**Rank in top quarter:**	33%
SAT math:	450-570	**Rank in top tenth:**	11%
SAT writing:	460-560	**End year in good standing:**	79%
ACT composite:	18-23	**Return as sophomores:**	75%
GPA 3.75 or higher:	15%	**Out-of-state:**	41%
GPA 3.50-3.74:	12%	**Live on campus:**	95%
GPA 3.0-3.49:	32%	**International:**	1%

Basis for selection. School record, test scores, school and community involvement, recommendation, academic quality of secondary school attended, essay, interview important. Audition recommended for music, theater arts programs; portfolio recommended for studio art. Essay or personal statement strongly encouraged, but not formally required. **Learning Disabled:** Documentation must be received no later than 45 days prior to the first day of class.

High school preparation. College-preparatory program required. 16 units required; 20 recommended. Required and recommended units include English 4, mathematics 3-4, social studies 2, history 2, science 3-4 (laboratory 2) and foreign language 2-3.

2009-2010 Annual costs. Tuition/fees (projected): $28,105. Room/board: $7,570. Books/supplies: $750. Personal expenses: $800.

2008-2009 Financial aid. Need-based: 479 full-time freshmen applied for aid; 382 were judged to have need; 382 of these received aid. Average need met was 82%. Average scholarship/grant was $16,846; average loan $2,889. 74% of total undergraduate aid awarded as scholarships/grants, 26% as loans/jobs. **Non-need-based:** Awarded to 765 full-time undergraduates, including 237 freshmen. Scholarships awarded for academics, leadership, music/drama, religious affiliation.

Application procedures. Admission: No deadline. $30 fee, may be waived for applicants with need, free for online applicants. Admission notification on a rolling basis beginning on or about 9/1. Must reply by May 1 or within 2 week(s) if notified thereafter. **Financial aid:** Priority date 3/1; no closing date. FAFSA required. Applicants notified on a rolling basis starting 3/15; must reply by 5/1 or within 2 week(s) of notification.

Academics. Special study options: Accelerated study, cross-registration, double major, dual enrollment of high school students, honors, independent study, internships, study abroad, teacher certification program. **Credit/placement by examination:** AP, CLEP, IB, institutional tests. **Support services:** Study skills assistance, tutoring, writing center.

Majors. Biology: General, ecology, exercise physiology. **Business:** Accounting, business admin, international, marketing. **Communications:** General. **Computer sciences:** General. **Conservation:** Environmental science. **Education:** Elementary, health, physical. **Family/consumer sciences:** Family studies. **Foreign languages:** Comparative lit, French, Spanish. **Health:** Athletic training, nursing (RN). **History:** General. **Math:** General. **Parks/recreation:** Health/fitness, sports admin. **Philosophy/religion:** Philosophy, religion. **Physical sciences:** Chemistry, physics. **Psychology:** General. **Social sciences:** Economics, international relations, political science, sociology. **Visual/performing arts:** Art, dramatic.

Most popular majors. Biology 7%, business/marketing 13%, communications/journalism 12%, education 13%, health sciences 11%, psychology 6%, social sciences 10%.

Computing on campus. Dormitories wired for high-speed internet access and linked to campus network. Online library, repair service, wireless network available.

Student life. Freshman orientation: Mandatory. Preregistration for classes offered. Held during summer for fall semester students and in January for spring semester students. Separate but concurrent orientation programs available to parents and other guests of new students. **Policies:** Honor system promoted and adhered to. **Housing:** Guaranteed on-campus for all undergraduates. Coed dorms, single-sex dorms, special housing for disabled, apartments, fraternity/sorority housing, wellness housing available. $200 nonrefundable deposit, deadline 5/1. College-owned townhomes, houses, and special interest houses available. **Activities:** Bands, campus ministries, choral groups, dance, drama, film society, international student organizations, literary magazine, music ensembles, Model UN, musical theater, student government, student newspaper, symphony orchestra, over 50 clubs and organizations.

Athletics. NCAA. **Intercollegiate:** Baseball M, basketball, cheerleading M, cross-country, equestrian, field hockey W, golf M, lacrosse, soccer, softball W, tennis, track and field, volleyball W. **Intramural:** Basketball, field hockey W, football (non-tackle), lacrosse M, soccer, softball, volleyball. **Team name:** Hornets.

Student services. Adult student services, chaplain/spiritual director, career counseling, student employment services, financial aid counseling, health services, minority student services, personal counseling. **Physically disabled:** Services for visually, hearing impaired.

Contact. E-mail: admissions@lynchburg.edu
Phone: (434) 544-8300 Toll-free number: (800) 426-8101 ext. 8300
Fax: (434) 544-8653
Sharon Walters-Bower, Director of Recruitment, Lynchburg College, 1501 Lakeside Drive, Lynchburg, VA 24501-3199

Mary Baldwin College

Staunton, Virginia **CB member**
www.mbc.edu **CB code: 5397**

- Private 4-year liberal arts college for women affiliated with Presbyterian Church (USA)
- Residential campus in large town
- 1,390 degree-seeking undergraduates: 26% part-time, 95% women, 19% African American, 2% Asian American, 4% Hispanic American, 1% Native American, 1% international
- 201 degree-seeking graduate students
- 70% of applicants admitted
- SAT or ACT (ACT writing optional), interview required
- 51% graduate within 6 years; 20% enter graduate study

General. Founded in 1842. Regionally accredited. Bachelor's degree available for younger women (13-15) in program for exceptionally gifted. Adult degree program available on main campus and at several satellite campuses throughout Virginia. Men admitted to adult program. The Virginia Women's Institute for Leadership program. **Degrees:** 243 bachelor's awarded; master's offered. **ROTC:** Army, Naval, Air Force. **Location:** 100 miles from Richmond, 150 miles from Washington, DC. **Calendar:** 4-1-4, limited summer session. **Full-time faculty:** 77 total; 97% have terminal degrees, 9% minority, 51% women. **Part-time faculty:** 66 total; 18% minority, 62% women. **Class size:** 66% < 20, 34% 20-39. **Special facilities:** Electron microscope, gas chromatoscope.

Freshman class profile. 1,784 applied, 1,256 admitted, 271 enrolled.

Mid 50% test scores		**GPA 2.0-2.99:**	34%
SAT critical reading:	460-600	**Rank in top quarter:**	39%
SAT math:	430-560	**Rank in top tenth:**	13%
SAT writing:	430-580	**End year in good standing:**	88%
ACT composite:	18-23	**Return as sophomores:**	65%
GPA 3.75 or higher:	25%	**Out-of-state:**	32%
GPA 3.50-3.74:	15%	**Live on campus:**	91%
GPA 3.0-3.49:	26%		

Basis for selection. School achievement record most important; test scores, involvement in school or civic groups also important; recommendations considered; 3.0 GPA recommended. Portfolio recommended for art majors.

High school preparation. Required and recommended units include English 4, mathematics 3, social studies 3, science 2 (laboratory 1), foreign language 2-3 and academic electives 2. Higher requirements for Virginia Women's Institute for Leadership.

2008-2009 Annual costs. Tuition/fees: $23,645. Room/board: $6,730. Books/supplies: $900. Personal expenses: $915.

2007-2008 Financial aid. Need-based: 223 full-time freshmen applied for aid; 197 were judged to have need; 197 of these received aid. Average need met was 91%. Average scholarship/grant was $11,175; average loan $2,548. 73% of total undergraduate aid awarded as scholarships/grants, 27% as loans/jobs. **Non-need-based:** Awarded to 1,006 full-time undergraduates, including 241 freshmen. Scholarships awarded for academics, leadership, state residency.

Application procedures. Admission: No deadline. $35 fee, may be waived for applicants with need. Admission notification on a rolling basis beginning on or about 9/1. Regular admission notification within 48 hours of receipt of all necessary materials. It is recommended for International Students to get applications in by June 1 to allow time to get a visa. **Financial aid:** Priority date 5/15; no closing date. FAFSA required. Applicants notified on a rolling basis starting 2/1; must reply by 5/1.

Academics. Students complete requirements in experiential education, international education, women's studies. May term offers opportunity for individualized programming, externships, study abroad. Institute combines academics, physical training and leadership development in rigorous 4-year bachelor's program. **Special study options:** Accelerated study, combined bachelor's/graduate degree, cooperative education, cross-registration, distance learning, double major, dual enrollment of high school students, ESL, exchange student, external degree, honors, independent study, internships, liberal arts/career combination, semester at sea, student-designed major, study abroad, teacher certification program. Summer exchange program with Doshisha Women's College in Kyoto, Japan. **Credit/placement by examination:** AP, CLEP, IB, institutional tests. 25% of required credits may be counted toward bachelor's degree. **Support services:** Learning center, reduced course load, study skills assistance, tutoring, writing center.

Honors college/program. Minimum SAT score of 1150 (exclusive of Writing) or ACT score of 25, minimum 3.5 high school GPA, essay, interview required for admission. About 36 freshmen admitted.

Majors. Area/ethnic studies: Asian. **Biology:** General, biochemistry. **Business:** Business admin. **Communications:** General. **Computer sciences:** General. **Foreign languages:** French, Spanish. **Health:** Clinical lab science, health care admin. **History:** General. **Math:** General, applied. **Philosophy/religion:** Philosophy, religion. **Physical sciences:** Chemistry, physics. **Psychology:** General. **Social sciences:** Economics, international relations, political science, sociology. **Visual/performing arts:** Art, arts management, dramatic.

Most popular majors. Business/marketing 8%, education 14%, history 9%, psychology 12%, social sciences 16%, visual/performing arts 15%.

Computing on campus. 244 workstations in dormitories, library, computer center. Dormitories wired for high-speed internet access and linked to campus network. Commuter students can connect to campus network. Online course registration, online library, helpline, repair service, wireless network available.

Student life. Freshman orientation: Mandatory. Preregistration for classes offered. **Policies:** College prohibits drinking under age 21. Honor code observed. **Housing:** Guaranteed on-campus for all undergraduates. Apartments, wellness housing available. $300 partly refundable deposit. **Activities:** Marching band, choral groups, dance, drama, film society, literary magazine, music ensembles, musical theater, radio station, student government, student newspaper, TV station, Circle K, Habitat for Humanity, College Republicans, College Democrats, Black Student Alliance, Latinas Unidas, Christian Student Union, Campus Crusade for Christ, Anointed Voices of Praise Gospel Choir.

Athletics. NCAA. **Intercollegiate:** Basketball W, cross-country W, field hockey W, soccer W, softball W, swimming W, tennis W, volleyball W. **Team name:** Squirrels.

Student services. Adult student services, chaplain/spiritual director, career counseling, student employment services, health services, minority student services, personal counseling, placement for graduates, women's services. **Physically disabled:** Services for visually, hearing impaired.

Contact. E-mail: admit@mbc.edu
Phone: (540) 887-7019 Toll-free number: (800) 468-2262
Fax: (540) 887-7279
Lisa Branson, Associate Vice President for Enrollment Management, Mary Baldwin College, Office of Admissions, Staunton, VA 24401

Marymount University

Arlington, Virginia — **CB member**
www.marymount.edu — **CB code: 5405**

- Private 4-year university affiliated with Roman Catholic Church
- Residential campus in small city
- 2,162 degree-seeking undergraduates: 14% part-time, 74% women, 15% African American, 9% Asian American, 12% Hispanic American, 7% international
- 1,279 degree-seeking graduate students
- 84% of applicants admitted
- SAT or ACT (ACT writing optional) required
- 51% graduate within 6 years; 35% enter graduate study

General. Founded in 1950. Regionally accredited. Courses taught in three sites: Marymount's main campus, the Ballston Center in Arlington, VA, and Reston Center in Reston, VA. Classes available in government sites including Office of Naval Research and Navy Federal Credit Union. **Degrees:** 550 bachelor's awarded; master's, doctoral offered. **ROTC:** Army. **Location:** 7 miles from Washington, DC. **Calendar:** Semester, extensive summer session. **Full-time faculty:** 138 total; 88% have terminal degrees, 4% minority, 72% women. **Part-time faculty:** 185 total; 45% have terminal degrees, 4% minority, 58% women. **Class size:** 47% < 20, 52% 20-39, 1% 40-49, less than 1% 50-99.

Freshman class profile. 1,766 applied, 1,489 admitted, 411 enrolled.

Mid 50% test scores		**GPA 2.0-2.99:**	50%
SAT critical reading:	440-540	**Rank in top quarter:**	49%
SAT math:	440-540	**Rank in top tenth:**	38%
SAT writing:	440-540	**End year in good standing:**	78%
ACT composite:	19-23	**Return as sophomores:**	73%
GPA 3.75 or higher:	9%	**Out-of-state:**	48%
GPA 3.50-3.74:	9%	**Live on campus:**	69%
GPA 3.0-3.49:	32%	**International:**	4%

Basis for selection. GPA in academic courses and test scores most important. Class rank, recommendations from guidance counselors and teachers also important. Essay, interview recommended.

High school preparation. College-preparatory program required. 15 units required. Required and recommended units include English 4, mathematics 3, social studies 3, science 2 and foreign language 3.

2008-2009 Annual costs. Tuition/fees: $21,528. Room/board: $9,190. Books/supplies: $800. Personal expenses: $900.

2008-2009 Financial aid. Need-based: 332 full-time freshmen applied for aid; 271 were judged to have need; 270 of these received aid. Average need met was 72%. Average scholarship/grant was $5,108; average loan $3,612. 46% of total undergraduate aid awarded as scholarships/grants, 54% as loans/jobs. **Non-need-based:** Awarded to 1,322 full-time undergraduates, including 387 freshmen. Scholarships awarded for academics, alumni affiliation, leadership, ROTC, state residency.

Application procedures. Admission: Priority date 5/1; no deadline. $40 fee, may be waived for applicants with need. Admission notification on a rolling basis. Must reply by May 1 or within 3 week(s) if notified thereafter. **Financial aid:** Priority date 3/1; no closing date. FAFSA required. Applicants notified on a rolling basis starting 3/15; must reply within 2 week(s) of notification.

Academics. All undergraduates complete internship before graduation. **Special study options:** Accelerated study, combined bachelor's/graduate degree, cross-registration, distance learning, double major, ESL, honors, independent study, internships, student-designed major, study abroad, teacher certification program. Member of the Consortium of Universities of the Washington DC metropolitan area. **Credit/placement by examination:** AP, CLEP, IB, institutional tests. 30 credit hours maximum toward bachelor's degree. Credit for prior work/life experience available through Portfolio Assessment and Credit by Examination program. **Support services:** Learning center, reduced course load, tutoring.

Honors college/program. Admission competitive and limited to 20 students each year. Minimum high school or college GPA of 3.5, minimum composite SAT score of 1200 (exclusive of Writing) or ACT score of 26, minimum TOEFL score of 617 (paper), 260 (computer), or 105 (internet) for international students, and strong background in English composition and literature.

Majors. Biology: General, cellular/molecular. **Business:** Business admin, fashion, human resources. **Communications:** General. **Computer sciences:** Information systems. **Health:** Nursing (RN). **History:** General. **Liberal arts:** Arts/sciences. **Math:** General. **Parks/recreation:** Exercise sciences. **Philosophy/religion:** Philosophy, religion. **Protective services:** Criminal justice. **Psychology:** General. **Social sciences:** Criminology, economics, political science, sociology. **Visual/performing arts:** Fashion design, graphic design, interior design, studio arts.

Most popular majors. Business/marketing 19%, health sciences 27%, liberal arts 6%, psychology 9%, social sciences 7%, visual/performing arts 16%.

Computing on campus. 270 workstations in dormitories, library, computer center. Dormitories wired for high-speed internet access and linked to campus network. Commuter students can connect to campus network. Online course registration, online library, helpline, wireless network available.

Student life. Freshman orientation: Mandatory. Preregistration for classes offered. 3 weekend sessions in summer. **Housing:** Guaranteed on-campus for freshmen. Coed dorms, single-sex dorms available. $300 nonrefundable deposit, deadline 5/1. **Activities:** Campus ministries, choral groups, dance, drama, international student organizations, literary magazine, student government, student newspaper, Black student alliance, Circle K, College Democrats/College Republicans, Latino student association, international club, Muslim student association, Students in Free Enterprise.

Athletics. NCAA. **Intercollegiate:** Basketball, cross-country, golf M, lacrosse, soccer, swimming, volleyball W. **Intramural:** Basketball, football (non-tackle), golf M, soccer, softball, swimming, volleyball, water polo, weight lifting. **Team name:** Saints.

Student services. Alcohol/substance abuse counseling, chaplain/spiritual director, career counseling, student employment services, financial aid counseling, health services, personal counseling. **Physically disabled:** Services for visually, speech, hearing impaired.

Contact. E-mail: admissions@marymount.edu
Phone: (703) 284-1500 Toll-free number: (800) 548-7638
Fax: (703) 522-0349
Chris Domes, Vice President for Enrollment and Student Services, Marymount University, 2807 North Glebe Road, Arlington, VA 22207-4299

National College: Roanoke Valley

Roanoke, Virginia
www.national-college.edu **CB code: 5502**

- For-profit 4-year business college
- Commuter campus in large city
- 615 degree-seeking undergraduates
- Interview required

General. Founded in 1886. Accredited by ACICS. **Degrees:** 22 bachelor's, 83 associate awarded; master's offered. **Calendar:** Quarter, limited summer session. **Full-time faculty:** 15 total. **Part-time faculty:** 41 total.

Basis for selection. Open admission.

2008-2009 Annual costs. Tuition/fees: $9,585.

Financial aid. All financial aid based on need.

Application procedures. Admission: Closing date 9/1 (receipt date). $30 fee, may be waived for applicants with need. Admission notification on a rolling basis. **Financial aid:** No deadline. FAFSA required. Applicants notified on a rolling basis.

Academics. Special study options: Double major, internships. **Credit/placement by examination:** CLEP, institutional tests. **Support services:** Tutoring.

Majors. Business: Accounting, business admin.

Computing on campus. 35 workstations in library, computer center.

Student life. Freshman orientation: Mandatory. Preregistration for classes offered. **Housing:** Coed dorms available. Hotel accommodations available. **Activities:** Student government.

Student services. Career counseling, financial aid counseling, placement for graduates.

Contact. Phone: (540) 986-1800 Fax: (540) 444-4198
Larry Steele, Vice President of Admissions, National College: Roanoke Valley, PO Box 6400, Roanoke, VA 24017-0400

Norfolk State University

Norfolk, Virginia **CB member**
www.nsu.edu **CB code: 5864**

- Public 4-year university
- Commuter campus in small city
- 5,582 degree-seeking undergraduates: 16% part-time, 63% women, 89% African American, 1% Asian American, 2% Hispanic American, 1% international
- 607 degree-seeking graduate students
- SAT or ACT (ACT writing optional) required

General. Founded in 1935. Regionally accredited. **Degrees:** 737 bachelor's, 54 associate awarded; master's, doctoral offered. **ROTC:** Army, Naval. **Location:** 5 miles from downtown. **Calendar:** Semester, extensive summer session. **Full-time faculty:** 272 total; 70% have terminal degrees, 72% minority, 48% women. **Part-time faculty:** 105 total. **Class size:** 54% < 20, 38% 20-39, 6% 40-49, 2% 50-99. **Special facilities:** Planetarium, crystal laboratory, laser laboratory, nuclear magnetic resonance laboratory, institute for service learning, literacy center for entrepreneurial studies, center for materials research, institute for minorities in applied sciences, assistive technology laboratory.

Freshman class profile.

Mid 50% test scores			
SAT critical reading:	370-460	GPA 2.0-2.99:	72%
SAT math:	360-460	Rank in top quarter:	25%
ACT composite:	16-19	Rank in top tenth:	7%
GPA 3.75 or higher:	4%	Out-of-state:	27%
GPA 3.50-3.74:	4%	Live on campus:	75%
GPA 3.0-3.49:	20%	Fraternities:	10%
		Sororities:	10%

Basis for selection. Combination of academic preparation, aptitude, achievements, and motivation predict a reasonable probability of success are most important. Interview recommended for electronics, engineering, nursing programs; audition recommended for music; portfolio recommended for art. **Homeschooled:** Transcript of courses and grades required.

High school preparation. 22 units required. Required units include English 4, mathematics 3, history 3, science 3 and academic electives 9. 2 science required for nursing applicants: 1 chemistry, 1 biology, 2 high school math (1 algebra), 2 science required for business applicants. 1 geometry, 2 algebra recommended for mathematics applicants. 2 mathematics must include algebra for computer science applicants.

2008-2009 Annual costs. Tuition/fees: $5,560; $16,807 out-of-state. Room/board: $7,116. Books/supplies: $1,000. Personal expenses: $1,400.

2008-2009 Financial aid. Non-need-based: Scholarships awarded for academics, alumni affiliation, athletics, leadership, music/drama, ROTC, state residency.

Application procedures. Admission: Closing date 5/31 (postmark date). $25 fee, may be waived for applicants with need. Admission notification on a rolling basis. Must reply by May 1 or within 2 week(s) if notified thereafter. **Financial aid:** Priority date 5/31; no closing date. FAFSA required. Applicants notified on a rolling basis starting 4/1; must reply within 2 week(s) of notification.

Academics. Special study options: Combined bachelor's/graduate degree, cooperative education, cross-registration, distance learning, double major, dual enrollment of high school students, ESL, honors, independent study, internships, liberal arts/career combination, teacher certification program. **Credit/placement by examination:** AP, CLEP, SAT, ACT, institutional tests. No limit on number of credits university will accept, as long as student passes exam and has departmental approval. **Support services:** Learning center, reduced course load, study skills assistance, tutoring, writing center.

Majors. Biology: General. **Business:** General, accounting, hospitality admin. **Communications:** Journalism, media studies. **Computer sciences:** General. **Education:** Business, kindergarten/preschool, special, trade/industrial. **Engineering:** Electrical. **Engineering technology:** CAD/CADD, computer, construction, electrical. **Health:** Clinical lab science, health care admin, medical records admin, nursing (RN). **History:** General. **Math:** General. **Parks/recreation:** Exercise sciences. **Physical sciences:** Chemistry, optics, physics. **Psychology:** General. **Public administration:** Social work. **Social sciences:** Political science, sociology. **Visual/performing arts:** Art.

Computing on campus. 1,028 workstations in dormitories, library, computer center. Dormitories linked to campus network. Online library, helpline available.

Student life. Freshman orientation: Mandatory. Preregistration for classes offered. Held during June, July and August. **Housing:** Single-sex dorms, special housing for disabled, wellness housing available. $300 nonrefundable deposit, deadline 5/31. **Activities:** Bands, choral groups, dance, drama, music ensembles, radio station, student government, student newspaper, symphony orchestra, TV station, Beta Psi Club, Omega Psi Phi, Alpha Kappa Alpha, Delta Sigma Theta, Alpha Delta Mu, Young Democrats, Young Republicans, Alpha Phi Alpha, Kappa Alpha Psi.

Athletics. NCAA. **Intercollegiate:** Baseball M, basketball, bowling W, cross-country, football (tackle) M, softball W, tennis, track and field, volleyball W. **Intramural:** Basketball, bowling, cheerleading, football (non-tackle) M, soccer M, softball, swimming, table tennis, tennis, volleyball. **Team name:** Spartans.

Student services. Adult student services, alcohol/substance abuse counseling, chaplain/spiritual director, career counseling, student employment services, financial aid counseling, health services, on-campus daycare, personal counseling, placement for graduates, veterans' counselor, women's services. **Physically disabled:** Services for visually, speech, hearing impaired.

Contact. E-mail: admissions@nsu.edu
Phone: (757) 823-8396 Fax: (757) 823-2078
Michelle Marable, Director of Admissions, Norfolk State University, 700 Park Avenue, Norfolk, VA 23504

Old Dominion University

Norfolk, Virginia — **CB member**
www.odu.edu — **CB code: 5126**

- Public 4-year university
- Commuter campus in small city
- 16,971 degree-seeking undergraduates: 25% part-time, 56% women, 23% African American, 6% Asian American, 4% Hispanic American, 1% Native American, 2% international
- 4,055 degree-seeking graduate students
- 72% of applicants admitted
- SAT or ACT with writing required
- 47% graduate within 6 years

General. Founded in 1930. Regionally accredited. 4 regional Centers of Higher Education, distance learning network TELETECHNET, includes more than 40 sites across Virginia, Georgia, Illinois, Arizona, Washington, the Bahamas and the District of Columbia, along with U.S. Navy ships at sea. **Degrees:** 2,883 bachelor's awarded; master's, doctoral offered. **ROTC:** Army, Naval. **Location:** 2 miles from downtown, 200 miles from Washington, DC. **Calendar:** Semester, extensive summer session. **Full-time faculty:** 700 total; 79% have terminal degrees, 22% minority, 40% women. **Part-time faculty:** 448 total; 15% minority, 57% women. **Class size:** 35% < 20, 43% 20-39, 9% 40-49, 8% 50-99, 5% >100. **Special facilities:** Student art gallery, centers for urban research/service, economic education and child study centers, laser optics lab, planetarium, robotics lab, sub-/super-sonic wind tunnels, marine science research vessel, random wave pool.

Freshman class profile. 9,484 applied, 6,800 admitted, 2,812 enrolled.

Mid 50% test scores			
SAT critical reading:	480-570	Rank in top quarter:	39%
SAT math:	490-590	Rank in top tenth:	12%
SAT writing:	470-570	End year in good standing:	77%
ACT composite:	18-23	Return as sophomores:	80%
GPA 3.75 or higher:	13%	Out-of-state:	7.5%
GPA 3.50-3.74:	17%	Live on campus:	66%
GPA 3.0-3.49:	45%	International:	2%
GPA 2.0-2.99:	25%	Fraternities:	5%
		Sororities:	5%

Basis for selection. Students who submit acceptable GPA and SAT/ACT scores are admitted. Those who do not meet acceptable GPA or SAT scores are reviewed by admissions committee. Committee looks at grades in core curriculum courses, student essay, student activity, resume/letters of recommendation, high school attended, IB and AP courses taken, etc. Audition required for music; portfolio required for art. **Homeschooled:** Scores from SAT or ACT must be submitted. GED not required. Students not attending program that requires regular curriculum review and submission of test scores to local school board must submit Stanford 9 results. **Learning Disabled:** Documentation of disabilities must be submitted before receiving services from Office of Disability Services.

High school preparation. College-preparatory program recommended. 16 units required. Required units include English 4, mathematics 3, social studies 3, science 3 and foreign language 3.

2008-2009 Annual costs. Tuition/fees: $6,918; $18,588 out-of-state. Room/board: $7,100. Books/supplies: $1,000. Personal expenses: $1,875.

2008-2009 Financial aid. Need-based: 2,105 full-time freshmen applied for aid; 1,849 were judged to have need; 1,689 of these received aid. Average need met was 85%. Average scholarship/grant was $4,578; average loan $3,370. 49% of total undergraduate aid awarded as scholarships/grants, 51% as loans/jobs. **Non-need-based:** Awarded to 2,239 full-time undergraduates, including 864 freshmen. Scholarships awarded for academics, alumni affiliation, art, athletics, leadership, music/drama, ROTC, state residency.

Application procedures. Admission: Priority date 12/1; deadline 3/15 (receipt date). $40 fee, may be waived for applicants with need. Admission notification on a rolling basis beginning on or about 1/15. Students are required to submit following: $40 application fee, high school transcripts, application, SAT or ACT scores, 1-3 letters of recommendation, one essay, one student activity resume. **Financial aid:** Priority date 2/15, closing date 3/15. FAFSA required. Applicants notified on a rolling basis starting 2/1; must reply within 2 week(s) of notification.

Academics. Guaranteed work or internship experience for credit in all fields of study. **Special study options:** Accelerated study, combined bachelor's/graduate degree, cooperative education, cross-registration, distance learning, double major, dual enrollment of high school students, ESL, exchange student, honors, independent study, internships, liberal arts/career combination, student-designed major, study abroad, teacher certification program, weekend college. Experiential learning. **Credit/placement by examination:** AP, CLEP, IB, institutional tests. 60 credit hours maximum toward bachelor's degree. Work life credits awarded through certification or department evaluations. Essay required to receive CLEP credit in Analysis and Interpretation of Literature, and Western Civilization I and II. **Support services:** Learning center, pre-admission summer program, reduced course load, study skills assistance, tutoring, writing center.

Majors. Area/ethnic studies: African-American, Asian, women's. **Biology:** General, biochemistry, marine. **Business:** Accounting, business admin, finance, international, management information systems, managerial economics, marketing. **Communications:** General. **Computer sciences:** General. **Education:** Art, biology, chemistry, drama/dance, English, foreign languages, French, geography, German, history, mathematics, music, physical, physics, sales/marketing, Spanish, technology/industrial arts. **Engineering:** Civil, computer, electrical, environmental, mechanical. **Engineering technology:** General, civil, computer, electrical, mechanical, nuclear. **Foreign languages:** General, French, German, Spanish. **Health:** Audiology/speech pathology, clinical lab science, community health services, cytotechnology, dental hygiene, environmental health, health services, nuclear medical technology, nursing (RN), ophthalmic technology. **History:** General. **Math:** General. **Parks/recreation:** Exercise sciences, facilities management, sports admin. **Philosophy/religion:** Philosophy. **Physical sciences:** Chemistry, geology, oceanography, physics. **Psychology:** General. **Social sciences:** Criminology, economics, geography, international relations, political science, sociology. **Visual/performing arts:** Acting, art, art history/conservation, dance, dramatic, graphic design, music performance, studio arts. **Other:** Maritime and supply chain management.

Most popular majors. Business/marketing 18%, education 6%, engineering/engineering technologies 11%, English 9%, health sciences 16%, interdisciplinary studies 8%, psychology 6%, social sciences 11%.

Computing on campus. 2,035 workstations in library, computer center, student center. Dormitories wired for high-speed internet access and linked to campus network. Commuter students can connect to campus network. Online course registration, online library, helpline, repair service, wireless network available.

Student life. Freshman orientation: Mandatory, $100 fee. Preregistration for classes offered. **Policies:** All student sponsored dances are restricted to ODU students only. Students must agree to hazing policy and can agree to FERPA when they sign up on-line for their organizations. **Housing:** Coed dorms, special housing for disabled, apartments available. $150 fully refundable deposit, deadline 5/1. **Activities:** Bands, choral groups, dance, drama, international student organizations, music ensembles, Model UN, musical theater, radio station, student government, student newspaper, TV station, College Democrats, College Republicans, Baptist Student Union, Black Student Alliance, African Caribbean Association, Catholic Campus Ministry, Intervarsity Christian Fellowship, Chi Alpha Christian Fellowship, Filipino American student association, Asian Pacific American student association.

Athletics. NCAA. **Intercollegiate:** Baseball M, basketball, diving, field hockey W, football (tackle) M, golf, lacrosse W, rowing (crew) W, sailing, soccer, tennis, wrestling M. **Intramural:** Badminton, basketball, bowling, cross-country, football (non-tackle), golf, racquetball, sailing, soccer, softball, table tennis, tennis, volleyball. **Team name:** Monarchs.

Student services. Adult student services, alcohol/substance abuse counseling, chaplain/spiritual director, career counseling, services for economically disadvantaged, student employment services, financial aid counseling, health services, minority student services, on-campus daycare, personal counseling, placement for graduates, veterans' counselor, women's services. **Physically disabled:** Services for visually, speech, hearing impaired. **Learning disabled:** Comprehensive services available.

Contact. E-mail: admit@odu.edu
Phone: (757) 683-3685 Toll-free number: (800) 348-7926
Fax: (757) 683-3255
Lakeisha Phelps, Director of Admissions, Old Dominion University, 108 Rollins Hall, 5115 Hampton Boulevard, Norfolk, VA 23529

Patrick Henry College
Purcellville, Virginia
www.phc.edu **CB code: 2804**

- Private 4-year liberal arts college affiliated with non-denominational Christian
- Residential campus in small town
- 327 degree-seeking undergraduates: 7% part-time, 46% women
- SAT or ACT (ACT writing optional), application essay, interview required

General. Regionally accredited. **Degrees:** 47 bachelor's awarded. **Location:** 50 miles from Washington, DC. **Calendar:** Semester, limited summer session. **Full-time faculty:** 20 total; 95% have terminal degrees. **Part-time faculty:** 22 total; 59% have terminal degrees. **Class size:** 60% < 20, 39% 20-39, 1% 40-49.

Freshman class profile.

Mid 50% test scores			
SAT critical reading:	650-760	GPA 3.75 or higher:	78%
SAT math:	550-670	GPA 3.50-3.74:	9%
SAT writing:	610-700	GPA 3.0-3.49:	9%
ACT composite:	24-32	GPA 2.0-2.99:	4%
		Return as sophomores:	80%

Basis for selection. School record, GPA, recommendations, test scores, essay, interview, character, and religious commitment very important. Reading List.

High school preparation. College-preparatory program required. 18 units required. Required units include English 4, mathematics 3, history 2, science 2, foreign language 1 and academic electives 5. 1 course of government is required.

2008-2009 Annual costs. Tuition/fees: $18,500. Room/board: $6,600.

2008-2009 Financial aid. Need-based: 29% of total undergraduate aid awarded as scholarships/grants, 71% as loans/jobs. **Non-need-based:** Scholarships awarded for academics, leadership, music/drama, state residency.

Application procedures. Admission: Priority date 11/1; deadline 6/15 (postmark date). $40 fee, may be waived for applicants with need. Admission notification on a rolling basis beginning on or about 10/1. Must reply by 7/15. **Financial aid:** Priority date 2/1, closing date 6/15. Institutional form required. Required for students seeking need-based aid. Applicants notified on a rolling basis starting 4/1; must reply by 5/1.

Academics. Special study options: Distance learning, internships, liberal arts/career combination. **Credit/placement by examination:** AP, CLEP, institutional tests. Credits from the Program on Non-Collegiate Sponsored Instruction, Dantes Subject Standardized Tests, and International Baccalaureate are evaluated on a case by case basis. **Support services:** Tutoring.

Majors. Communications: Journalism. **History:** General. **Liberal arts:** Arts/sciences. **Social sciences:** Political science.

Most popular majors. Communications/journalism 12%, English 7%, social sciences 70%.

Computing on campus. PC or laptop required. Dormitories wired for high-speed internet access and linked to campus network. Online course registration, online library, helpline available.

Student life. Freshman orientation: Mandatory. Held for four days prior to beginning of fall classes. **Policies:** PHC students are accountable to uphold public legal standards, biblical standards, and to the College's community standards. We have a redemptive approach to discipline. Religious observance required. **Housing:** Single-sex dorms available. $250 fully refundable deposit, deadline 7/15. **Activities:** Campus ministries, choral groups, drama, film society, literary magazine, music ensembles, Model UN, student government, student newspaper, College Republicans, International Justice Mission, College Democrats, Libertas Society, Sans Frontieres, the Alexis de Tocqueville Society, Community Involvement Commission, Generation Joshua.

Athletics. Intercollegiate: Basketball, soccer. **Intramural:** Football (non-tackle) M, softball, tennis, volleyball. **Team name:** The Sentinels.

Student services. Chaplain/spiritual director, career counseling, financial aid counseling, personal counseling. **Physically disabled:** Services for visually impaired.

Contact. E-mail: admissions@phc.edu
Phone: (888) 338-1776 ext. 8881 Fax: (540) 338-9808
Rebekah Knable, Director of Admissions, Patrick Henry College, One Patrick Henry Circle, Purcellville, VA 20132-3197

Potomac College
Herndon, Virginia
www.potomac.edu

- For-profit 4-year business college
- Residential campus in large town

General. Location: 30 miles from Washington, DC. **Calendar:** Continuous.

Annual costs/financial aid. Tuition/fees (2008-2009): $13,480. Upper division tuition and fees vary.

Contact. Phone: (703) 709-5875
Admissions Director, 1029 Herndon Parkway, Herndon, VA 20170

Radford University
Radford, Virginia
www.radford.edu **CB member** **CB code: 5565**

- Public 4-year university
- Residential campus in large town
- 8,107 degree-seeking undergraduates: 4% part-time, 57% women, 6% African American, 2% Asian American, 3% Hispanic American, 1% international
- 870 degree-seeking graduate students
- 74% of applicants admitted
- SAT or ACT (ACT writing optional) required
- 60% graduate within 6 years

General. Founded in 1910. Regionally accredited. **Degrees:** 1,825 bachelor's awarded; master's, doctoral offered. **ROTC:** Army. **Location:** 36 miles from Roanoke. **Calendar:** Semester, limited summer session. **Full-time faculty:** 400 total; 84% have terminal degrees, 10% minority, 47% women. **Part-time faculty:** 231 total; 5% have terminal degrees, 9% minority, 54% women. **Class size:** 33% < 20, 54% 20-39, 9% 40-49, 3% 50-99, less than 1% >100. **Special facilities:** Center for visual and performing arts.

Freshman class profile. 7,819 applied, 5,768 admitted, 1,875 enrolled.

Mid 50% test scores			
SAT critical reading:	460-550	GPA 2.0-2.99:	39%
SAT math:	460-550	Rank in top quarter:	25%
ACT composite:	19-23	Rank in top tenth:	6%
GPA 3.75 or higher:	9%	Return as sophomores:	78%
GPA 3.50-3.74:	10%	Out-of-state:	8%
GPA 3.0-3.49:	42%	Live on campus:	96%

Basis for selection. High school records, including grades, strength of academic program, and performance trend: standardized test scores, optional student essay, and evidence of interest and motivation as indicated in supplied materials. **Homeschooled:** Recommended SAT subject tests, Math and English. If curriculum is not supported by a recognized home school organization, the student may need to supply course decriptions (including text book information, where appropriate.).

High school preparation. College-preparatory program recommended. 24 units recommended. Recommended units include English 4, mathematics 4, social studies 2, history 2, science 4 (laboratory 3), foreign language 3 and academic electives 5. Pre-nursing students should complete units in both biology and chemistry.

2008-2009 Annual costs. Tuition/fees: $6,536; $15,550 out-of-state. Room/board: $6,716. Books/supplies: $877. Personal expenses: $1,600.

2007-2008 Financial aid. Need-based: 1,144 full-time freshmen applied for aid; 645 were judged to have need; 613 of these received aid. Average need met was 78%. Average scholarship/grant was $6,025; average loan $3,119. 86% of total undergraduate aid awarded as scholarships/grants, 14% as loans/jobs. **Non-need-based:** Awarded to 1,010 full-time undergraduates, including 298 freshmen. Scholarships awarded for academics, art, athletics, leadership, music/drama, ROTC. **Additional information:** Student's need and grades considered. Top consideration given to those with greatest need and who apply by deadline.

Application procedures. Admission: Closing date 2/1 (postmark date). $50 fee, may be waived for applicants with need. Admission notification 3/20. Must reply by 5/1. **Financial aid:** Priority date 3/1; no closing date. FAFSA required. Applicants notified on a rolling basis starting 4/15; must reply within 4 week(s) of notification.

Academics. Special study options: Accelerated study, cross-registration, distance learning, double major, dual enrollment of high school students, honors, independent study, internships, student-designed major, study abroad, teacher certification program. **Credit/placement by examination:** AP, CLEP, IB. **Support services:** Learning center, study skills assistance, tutoring, writing center.

Majors. Biology: General. **Business:** Accounting, business admin, finance, marketing. **Communications:** General, journalism. **Computer sciences:** Computer science, information systems. **Education:** Health, physical. **Family/consumer sciences:** Food/nutrition. **Foreign languages:** General. **Health:** Nursing (RN). **History:** General. **Math:** General. **Parks/recreation:** General. **Physical sciences:** Chemistry, geology, physics. **Protective services:** Criminal justice. **Psychology:** General. **Public administration:** Social work. **Social sciences:** General, anthropology, economics, geography, political science, sociology. **Visual/performing arts:** Art, dance, design, dramatic, studio arts.

Most popular majors. Business/marketing 20%, communications/journalism 10%, health sciences 8%, interdisciplinary studies 13%, psychology 6%, security/protective services 7%, social sciences 6%, visual/performing arts 8%.

Computing on campus. 762 workstations in dormitories, library, computer center, student center. Dormitories wired for high-speed internet access and linked to campus network. Commuter students can connect to campus network. Online course registration, online library, helpline, repair service, student web hosting, wireless network available.

Student life. Freshman orientation: Available, $275 fee. Preregistration for classes offered. 5 2-day sessions in June or August. **Policies:** Honor code enforced. **Housing:** Guaranteed on-campus for freshmen. Coed dorms, special housing for disabled, apartments, wellness housing available. $200 nonrefundable deposit, deadline 5/1. **Activities:** Bands, campus ministries, choral groups, dance, drama, international student organizations, literary magazine, music ensembles, musical theater, radio station, student government, student newspaper, TV station, College Republicans, Young Democrats, International Student Advisory Council, Black Student Advisory Council, Young Men of Standards, Young Women of Power and Purpose, Habitat for Humanity, American Red Cross, Campus Crusade for Christ, Catholic student organization.

Athletics. NCAA. **Intercollegiate:** Baseball M, basketball, cross-country, diving W, field hockey W, golf, soccer, softball W, swimming W, tennis, track and field, volleyball W. **Intramural:** Basketball, bowling, cross-country, football (non-tackle), racquetball, soccer, softball, table tennis, tennis, volleyball, weight lifting. **Team name:** Highlanders.

Student services. Adult student services, alcohol/substance abuse counseling, chaplain/spiritual director, career counseling, services for economically disadvantaged, student employment services, financial aid counseling, health services, minority student services, personal counseling, placement for graduates, veterans' counselor, women's services. **Physically disabled:** Services for visually, speech, hearing impaired.

Contact. E-mail: admissions@radford.edu
Phone: (540) 831-5371 Fax: (540) 831-5038
Radford University, 209 Martin Hall, Radford, VA 24142

Randolph College

Lynchburg, Virginia — **CB member**
www.randolphcollege.edu — **CB code: 5567**

- Private 4-year liberal arts college affiliated with United Methodist Church
- Residential campus in small city
- 549 degree-seeking undergraduates: 1% part-time, 82% women, 9% African American, 3% Asian American, 7% Hispanic American, 1% Native American, 12% international
- 6 degree-seeking graduate students
- 84% of applicants admitted
- SAT or ACT (ACT writing optional), application essay required
- 67% graduate within 6 years; 27% enter graduate study

General. Founded in 1891. Regionally accredited. **Degrees:** 154 bachelor's awarded; master's offered. **Location:** 60 miles from Roanoke and Charlottesville. **Calendar:** Semester, limited summer session. **Full-time faculty:** 66 total; 92% have terminal degrees, 11% minority, 46% women. **Part-time faculty:** 22 total; 46% have terminal degrees, 64% women. **Class size:** 88% < 20, 12% 20-39. **Special facilities:** Observatory, 3 nature preserves, botanical garden, 100-acre equestrian center, museum of American art, science and mathematics resource center, learning resources center, writing lab, new artificial turf field and track facility.

Freshman class profile. 1,585 applied, 1,329 admitted, 144 enrolled.

Mid 50% test scores		**GPA 2.0-2.99:**	20%
SAT critical reading:	500-630	**Rank in top quarter:**	60%
SAT math:	490-600	**Rank in top tenth:**	20%
ACT composite:	21-29	**Return as sophomores:**	70%
GPA 3.75 or higher:	19%	**Out-of-state:**	48%
GPA 3.50-3.74:	19%	**Live on campus:**	97%
GPA 3.0-3.49:	42%	**International:**	6%

Basis for selection. Rigor of high school curriculum and achievement most important, followed by teacher and counselor recommendations, test scores, activities, personal achievement. International students may submit SAT or ACT in lieu of TOEFL. Interview recommended. Essay submission may be essay written on topic of applicant's choice, copy of graded essay written by applicant in 11th or 12th grade, or SAT/ACT writing component. **Learning Disabled:** Submit documentation to Director of the Learning Resources Center, who will work in consultation with Office of the Dean of the College and faculty to determine reasonable and appropriate accommodations.

High school preparation. College-preparatory program required. 16 units required. Required and recommended units include English 4, mathematics 3, history 2, science 2 (laboratory 2), foreign language 3-4 and academic electives 1-2. 3 years of one foreign language recommended, but applicants may offer 2 units of each of 2 languages instead. Student must have successfully completed or be enrolled in algebra II senior year in order for application to be considered.

2008-2009 Annual costs. Tuition/fees: $27,890. Room and board charges include free use of laundry facilities. Room/board: $9,310. Books/supplies: $800. Personal expenses: $1,000.

2008-2009 Financial aid. Need-based: 133 full-time freshmen applied for aid; 111 were judged to have need; 110 of these received aid. Average need met was 85%. Average scholarship/grant was $16,917; average loan $6,653. 67% of total undergraduate aid awarded as scholarships/grants, 33% as loans/jobs. **Non-need-based:** Awarded to 273 full-time undergraduates, including 67 freshmen. Scholarships awarded for academics, alumni affiliation, art, leadership, minority status, music/drama, religious affiliation, state residency.

Application procedures. Admission: Priority date 12/1; deadline 4/1 (postmark date). $50 fee, may be waived for applicants with need. Admission notification 4/15. Must reply by May 1 or within 2 week(s) if notified thereafter. **Financial aid:** Priority date 3/1; no closing date. FAFSA required. Applicants notified on a rolling basis starting 3/1; must reply by 5/1 or within 2 week(s) of notification.

Academics. Honor system includes self-scheduled examinations. **Special study options:** Accelerated study, combined bachelor's/graduate degree, cross-registration, double major, dual enrollment of high school students, exchange student, honors, independent study, internships, liberal arts/career combination, student-designed major, study abroad, teacher certification program, Washington semester. 7-college exchange with Washington and Lee University, Hollins University, Hampden-Sydney College, Mary Baldwin College, Sweet Briar College, Randolph-Macon College; junior year abroad program at University of Reading, England; affiliate abroad programs in Greece, France, Denmark, Japan, Italy, Ireland, Mexico, Spain; assistance with non-affiliated abroad programs; Marine Biological Laboratory Semester in Environmental Science; American Culture program (1-semester program including study on-site at key locations in and near Virginia), Tri-College Consortium with Lynchburg College and Sweet Briar College. **Credit/placement by examination:** AP, CLEP, IB, SAT, ACT, institutional tests. Applicants with scores at or above 50th percentile awarded credit for CLEP subject examinations in subject areas offered by college. However, subject tests in foreign languages granted credit only if they represent achievement beyond that of previous high school or college preparation. **Support services:** Learning center, reduced course load, study skills assistance, tutoring, writing center.

Majors. Biology: General. **Business:** General. **Communications:** General. **Conservation:** Environmental studies. **Engineering:** Physics. **Foreign languages:** Ancient Greek, classics, French, Latin, Spanish. **Health:** Health services. **History:** General. **Interdisciplinary:** Global studies, museum. **Math:** General. **Philosophy/religion:** Philosophy, religion. **Physical sciences:** Chemistry, physics. **Psychology:** General. **Social sciences:** Economics, political science, sociology. **Visual/performing arts:** Art history/conservation, dance, dramatic, music history, music performance, music theory/composition, studio arts.

Most popular majors. Biology 12%, English 8%, foreign language 6%, psychology 8%, social sciences 25%, visual/performing arts 14%.

Computing on campus. 155 workstations in dormitories, library, computer center, student center. Dormitories wired for high-speed internet access and linked to campus network. Commuter students can connect to campus network. Online course registration, online library, helpline, student web hosting, wireless network available.

Student life. **Freshman orientation:** Mandatory, $150 fee. Preregistration for classes offered. 5 days before start of classes. **Policies:** The Honor code is fundamental to the conduct and governance of the College. **Housing:** Guaranteed on-campus for all undergraduates. Coed dorms, single-sex dorms, wellness housing available. $300 nonrefundable deposit, deadline 5/1. **Activities:** Campus ministries, choral groups, dance, drama, film society, international student organizations, literary magazine, music ensembles, Model UN, radio station, student government, student newspaper, Young Democrats, College Republicans, Amnesty International, Club Asia, Catholic Students Association, Black Students Alliance, Circle K, IVCF, Pan World Club.

Athletics. NCAA. **Intercollegiate:** Basketball, cross-country, equestrian, lacrosse, soccer, softball W, swimming W, tennis, volleyball W. **Intramural:** Basketball, softball, table tennis, tennis, volleyball. **Team name:** Wildcats.

Student services. Adult student services, alcohol/substance abuse counseling, chaplain/spiritual director, career counseling, student employment services, financial aid counseling, health services, minority student services, personal counseling, placement for graduates, women's services. **Physically disabled:** Services for visually, hearing impaired.

Contact. E-mail: admissions@randolphcollege.edu
Phone: (434) 947-8100 Toll-free number: (800) 745-7692
Fax: (434) 947-8996
John White, Dean of Admissions and Student Financial Services, Randolph College, 2500 Rivermont Avenue, Lynchburg, VA 24503-1555

Randolph-Macon College

Ashland, Virginia — **CB member**
www.rmc.edu — **CB code: 5566**

- Private 4-year liberal arts college affiliated with United Methodist Church
- Residential campus in small town
- 1,178 degree-seeking undergraduates: 1% part-time, 53% women, 11% African American, 2% Asian American, 3% Hispanic American, 1% Native American, 2% international
- 58% of applicants admitted
- SAT or ACT (ACT writing recommended), application essay required
- 65% graduate within 6 years; 41% enter graduate study

General. Founded in 1830. Regionally accredited. **Degrees:** 242 bachelor's awarded. **ROTC:** Army. **Location:** 15 miles from Richmond, 90 miles from Washington, DC. **Calendar:** 4-1-4, limited summer session. **Full-time faculty:** 93 total; 92% have terminal degrees, 6% minority, 41% women. **Part-time faculty:** 74 total; 39% have terminal degrees, 3% minority, 50% women. **Class size:** 66% < 20, 33% 20-39, less than 1% 50-99. **Special facilities:** Observatory with 12-inch reflecting telescope and 3-meter radio telescope, 6 historic buildings, greenhouse.

Freshman class profile. 3,502 applied, 2,034 admitted, 362 enrolled.

Mid 50% test scores		**Rank in top quarter:**	49%
SAT critical reading:	500-590	**Rank in top tenth:**	20%
SAT math:	490-590	**End year in good standing:**	86%
SAT writing:	490-580	**Return as sophomores:**	77%
GPA 3.75 or higher:	22%	**Out-of-state:**	37%
GPA 3.50-3.74:	17%	**Live on campus:**	96%
GPA 3.0-3.49:	33%	**International:**	3%
GPA 2.0-2.99:	28%		

Basis for selection. School achievement record, class rank, and test scores most important. Personal recommendations, leadership skills and participation considered. Interview recommended. **Homeschooled:** Statement describing homeschool structure and mission, transcript of courses and grades, letter of recommendation (nonparent) required. **Learning Disabled:** Students with learning disabilities encouraged to meet with director of disability support services.

High school preparation. College-preparatory program required. 16 units required; 22 recommended. Required and recommended units include English 4, mathematics 3-4, social studies 1-2, history 2, science 3-4 (laboratory 2-4), foreign language 2-4 and academic electives 1-2.

2008-2009 Annual costs. Tuition/fees: $28,355. Room/board: $8,610. Books/supplies: $1,000. Personal expenses: $720.

2008-2009 Financial aid. **Need-based:** 249 full-time freshmen applied for aid; 240 were judged to have need; 240 of these received aid. Average need met was 85%. Average scholarship/grant was $18,143; average loan $4,385. 74% of total undergraduate aid awarded as scholarships/grants, 26% as loans/jobs. **Non-need-based:** Awarded to 568 full-time undergraduates, including 170 freshmen. Scholarships awarded for academics, alumni affiliation, minority status, religious affiliation, state residency.

Application procedures. **Admission:** Priority date 2/1; deadline 3/1 (postmark date). $30 fee, may be waived for applicants with need, free for online applicants. Admission notification 4/1. Must reply by May 1 or within 2 week(s) if notified thereafter. Applications accepted after March 1 on space-available basis. **Financial aid:** Priority date 2/1, closing date 3/1. FAFSA required. Applicants notified by 3/15; must reply by 5/1 or within 2 week(s) of notification.

Academics. Comprehensive liberal arts core curriculum. All students must complete an internship, study abroad, or original research project for graduation. Interdisciplinary First-Year Experience for all freshmen. **Special study options:** Accelerated study, combined bachelor's/graduate degree, cross-registration, double major, dual enrollment of high school students, exchange student, honors, independent study, internships, liberal arts/career combination, study abroad, teacher certification program, United Nations semester, Washington semester. Member of Seven College consortium, 3-2 program in engineering with Columbia University and University of Virginia, 3-2 in forestry with Duke University, 4-1 in accounting with Virginia Commonwealth University. **Credit/placement by examination:** AP, CLEP, IB, institutional tests. 75 credit hours maximum toward bachelor's degree. At least one-half major course of study must be completed at Randolph-Macon College. **Support services:** Learning center, reduced course load, study skills assistance, tutoring, writing center.

Majors. **Area/ethnic studies:** Women's. **Biology:** General. **Business:** Accounting, managerial economics. **Computer sciences:** General. **Conservation:** Environmental studies. **Foreign languages:** Ancient Greek, classics, French, German, Latin, Spanish. **History:** General. **Interdisciplinary:** Global studies. **Math:** General. **Philosophy/religion:** Philosophy, religion. **Physical sciences:** Chemistry, physics. **Psychology:** General. **Social sciences:** Economics, political science, sociology. **Visual/performing arts:** Art history/conservation, arts management, dramatic, studio arts.

Most popular majors. Biology 7%, business/marketing 20%, English 11%, history 7%, psychology 9%, social sciences 24%.

Computing on campus. 350 workstations in library, computer center, student center. Dormitories wired for high-speed internet access and linked to campus network. Commuter students can connect to campus network. Online course registration, online library, helpline, repair service, student web hosting, wireless network available.

Student life. **Freshman orientation:** Mandatory, $100 fee. Preregistration for classes offered. 4-day program held for students and parents prior to start of fall classes. **Housing:** Guaranteed on-campus for all undergraduates. Coed dorms, single-sex dorms, special housing for disabled, apartments, fraternity/sorority housing, wellness housing available. Honors house, special interest housing available. **Activities:** Bands, choral groups, dance, drama, film society, literary magazine, musical theater, radio station, student government, student newspaper, TV station, over 100 clubs and organizations.

Athletics. NCAA. **Intercollegiate:** Baseball M, basketball, field hockey W, football (tackle) M, golf M, lacrosse, soccer, softball W, swimming W, tennis, volleyball W. **Intramural:** Basketball, football (non-tackle), lacrosse, racquetball, rugby, soccer, softball, table tennis, tennis, volleyball. **Team name:** Yellow Jackets.

Student services. Alcohol/substance abuse counseling, chaplain/spiritual director, career counseling, student employment services, financial aid counseling, health services, minority student services, personal counseling, placement for graduates, women's services. **Physically disabled:** Services for visually, speech, hearing impaired.

Contact. E-mail: admissions@rmc.edu
Phone: (804) 752-7305 Toll-free number: (800) 888-1762
Fax: (804) 752-4707
Steven Nape, Dean of Admissions and Financial Aid, Randolph-Macon College, PO Box 5005, Ashland, VA 23005-5505

Regent University
Virginia Beach, Virginia
www.regent.edu **CB code: 4452**

- Private 4-year university affiliated with interdenominational tradition
- Commuter campus in large city
- 1,458 degree-seeking undergraduates: 43% part-time, 68% women, 25% African American, 2% Asian American, 6% Hispanic American, 1% Native American, 1% international
- 2,798 degree-seeking graduate students
- 88% of applicants admitted
- SAT or ACT (ACT writing optional), application essay required

General. Founded in 1977. Regionally accredited. **Degrees:** 203 bachelor's awarded; master's, doctoral, first professional offered. **ROTC:** Army. **Location:** 8 miles from Norfolk. **Calendar:** Semester, extensive summer session. **Full-time faculty:** 179 total; 20% minority, 33% women. **Part-time faculty:** 397 total; 18% minority, 48% women. **Class size:** 66% < 20, 34% 20-39. **Special facilities:** Communication and performing arts center.

Freshman class profile. 684 applied, 599 admitted, 214 enrolled.

Mid 50% test scores		**GPA 3.0-3.49:**	25%
SAT critical reading:	470-600	**GPA 2.0-2.99:**	39%
SAT math:	450-550	**End year in good standing:**	76%
SAT writing:	460-590	**Return as sophomores:**	75%
ACT composite:	20-25	**Out-of-state:**	62%
GPA 3.75 or higher:	16%	**Live on campus:**	11%
GPA 3.50-3.74:	14%		

Basis for selection. GPA, test scores, response to an essay question all required along with application. **Homeschooled:** Transcript of courses and grades required.

High school preparation. Recommended units include English 4, mathematics 3, social studies 3, science 3 and foreign language 3.

2009-2010 Annual costs. Tuition/fees: $13,950. Room only: $5,625. Books/supplies: $598. Personal expenses: $6,606.

2007-2008 Financial aid. Need-based: Average need met was 49%. Average scholarship/grant was $5,253; average loan $2,178. 34% of total undergraduate aid awarded as scholarships/grants, 66% as loans/jobs. **Non-need-based:** Scholarships awarded for academics, leadership.

Application procedures. Admission: Closing date 8/3 (receipt date). $50 fee. Admission notification on a rolling basis. Must reply by 8/15. **Financial aid:** Priority date 3/15; no closing date. FAFSA, institutional form required. Applicants notified on a rolling basis starting 3/1; must reply within 2 week(s) of notification.

Academics. Special study options: Combined bachelor's/graduate degree, distance learning, double major, dual enrollment of high school students, internships, study abroad, teacher certification program, Washington semester. **Credit/placement by examination:** AP, CLEP, IB. 30 credit hours maximum toward bachelor's degree. **Support services:** Remedial instruction, study skills assistance, tutoring, writing center.

Majors. Business: Business admin, international, organizational behavior. **Communications:** General, journalism. **Communications technology:** Animation/special effects. **Education:** General. **Philosophy/religion:** Religion. **Psychology:** General. **Social sciences:** Political science. **Visual/performing arts:** Cinematography, theater arts management.

Most popular majors. Business/marketing 28%, communications/journalism 13%, interdisciplinary studies 8%, philosophy/religious studies 18%, psychology 29%.

Computing on campus. 130 workstations in library, computer center, student center. Dormitories wired for high-speed internet access and linked to campus network. Online course registration, online library, helpline, wireless network available.

Student life. Freshman orientation: Mandatory. Preregistration for classes offered. **Housing:** Apartments available. **Activities:** Concert band, campus ministries, choral groups, dance, drama, international student organizations, student government, student newspaper, Association of Black Psychologists, College Republicans, Undergraduate Student Advisory Council, Newman Club, Regent Students for Life, Students in Free Enterprise, Student Alumni Association, Student Advisory Leadership Team.

Athletics. Intramural: Basketball, soccer, volleyball.

Student services. Chaplain/spiritual director, career counseling, financial aid counseling.

Contact. E-mail: admissions@regent.edu
Phone: (757) 352-4127 Toll-free number: (800) 373-5504
Fax: (757) 352-4381
Ken Baker, Director of Admissions, Regent University, 1000 Regent University Drive, SC 218, Virginia Beach, VA 23464-9800

Roanoke College
Salem, Virginia **CB member**
www.roanoke.edu **CB code: 5571**

- Private 4-year liberal arts college affiliated with Evangelical Lutheran Church in America
- Residential campus in large town
- 1,947 degree-seeking undergraduates: 2% part-time, 55% women, 3% African American, 1% Asian American, 3% Hispanic American, 1% international
- 70% of applicants admitted
- SAT or ACT (ACT writing optional) required
- 61% graduate within 6 years; 20% enter graduate study

General. Founded in 1842. Regionally accredited. **Degrees:** 429 bachelor's awarded. **Location:** 7 miles from Roanoke. **Calendar:** Semester, extensive summer session. **Full-time faculty:** 153 total; 81% have terminal degrees, 10% minority, 48% women. **Part-time faculty:** 37 total; 24% have terminal degrees, 3% minority, 51% women. **Class size:** 60% < 20, 39% 20-39, less than 1% 40-49. **Special facilities:** Fine arts center with 3 galleries, multimedia classrooms, greenhouse, nuclear magnetic resonance equipment, center for community research, center for church and society, center for teaching and learning.

Freshman class profile. 3,579 applied, 2,500 admitted, 529 enrolled.

Mid 50% test scores		**Rank in top quarter:**	53%
SAT critical reading:	500-600	**Rank in top tenth:**	22%
SAT math:	510-600	**Return as sophomores:**	77%
SAT writing:	470-570	**Out-of-state:**	51%
GPA 3.75 or higher:	23%	**Live on campus:**	93%
GPA 3.50-3.74:	13%	**International:**	2%
GPA 3.0-3.49:	34%	**Fraternities:**	15%
GPA 2.0-2.99:	30%	**Sororities:**	13%

Basis for selection. School achievement record and class rank most important. Essay, interview recommended for all; audition recommended for music; portfolio recommended for graphic arts. **Homeschooled:** Transcript of courses and grades required. **Learning Disabled:** Documentation of learning disability needed for special services after enrollment.

High school preparation. College-preparatory program recommended. 18 units required. Required and recommended units include English 4, mathematics 3, social studies 2, science 2 (laboratory 2), foreign language 4 and academic electives 5. Mathematics must include algebra II.

2008-2009 Annual costs. Tuition/fees: $27,935. Room/board: $9,285. Books/supplies: $1,000. Personal expenses: $1,000.

2008-2009 Financial aid. Need-based: 411 full-time freshmen applied for aid; 335 were judged to have need; 335 of these received aid. Average need met was 88.5%. Average scholarship/grant was $19,390; average loan $3,958. 68% of total undergraduate aid awarded as scholarships/grants, 32% as loans/jobs. **Non-need-based:** Awarded to 1,863 full-time undergraduates, including 508 freshmen. Scholarships awarded for academics, minority status, music/drama, religious affiliation.

Application procedures. Admission: Closing date 3/15 (postmark date). $33 fee, may be waived for applicants with need, free for online applicants. Admission notification 4/1. Must reply by May 1 or within 2 week(s) if notified thereafter. **Financial aid:** Priority date 3/1; no closing date. FAFSA required. Applicants notified on a rolling basis starting 11/1; must reply within 2 week(s) of notification.

Academics. Special study options: Accelerated study, combined bachelor's/graduate degree, cross-registration, double major, dual enrollment of high school students, ESL, honors, independent study, internships, liberal arts/career combination, study abroad, teacher certification program, Washington semester. **Credit/placement by examination:** AP, CLEP, IB, institutional tests. 27 credit hours maximum toward bachelor's degree. **Support services:** Learning center, reduced course load, study skills assistance, tutoring, writing center.

Majors. **Biology:** General, biochemistry. **Business:** Business admin. **Computer sciences:** General, computer science, information systems. **Conservation:** Environmental science, management/policy. **Education:** Physical. **Foreign languages:** French, Spanish. **Health:** Athletic training, clinical lab science. **History:** General. **Math:** General. **Parks/recreation:** Health/fitness. **Philosophy/religion:** Philosophy, religion. **Physical sciences:** Chemistry, physics. **Protective services:** Criminal justice. **Psychology:** General. **Social sciences:** Economics, international relations, political science, sociology. **Theology:** Theology. **Visual/performing arts:** Art, art history/conservation, dramatic.

Most popular majors. Biology 8%, business/marketing 25%, English 7%, history 8%, parks/recreation 6%, psychology 9%, social sciences 16%, visual/performing arts 6%.

Computing on campus. 185 workstations in library, computer center, student center. Dormitories wired for high-speed internet access and linked to campus network. Commuter students can connect to campus network. Online course registration, online library, helpline, repair service, student web hosting, wireless network available.

Student life. **Freshman orientation:** Mandatory, $125 fee. Preregistration for classes offered. **Housing:** Guaranteed on-campus for freshmen. Coed dorms, single-sex dorms, apartments, fraternity/sorority housing, wellness housing available. $300 deposit, deadline 5/1. **Activities:** Bands, campus ministries, choral groups, dance, drama, film society, literary magazine, music ensembles, Model UN, musical theater, radio station, student government, student newspaper, Alpha Phi Omega, Earthbound, Fellowship of Christian Athletes, Habitat for Humanity, Lutheran Student Movement, Baptist Student Union, Shades of Maroon.

Athletics. NCAA. **Intercollegiate:** Baseball M, basketball, cross-country, field hockey W, golf M, lacrosse, soccer, softball W, tennis, track and field, volleyball W. **Intramural:** Badminton, baseball M, basketball, field hockey W, football (non-tackle), golf W, racquetball, soccer, softball, table tennis, tennis, volleyball. **Team name:** Maroons.

Student services. Adult student services, alcohol/substance abuse counseling, chaplain/spiritual director, career counseling, student employment services, financial aid counseling, health services, minority student services, personal counseling, placement for graduates.

Contact. E-mail: admissions@roanoke.edu
Phone: (540) 375-2270 Toll-free number: (800) 388-2276
Fax: (540) 375-2267
Brenda Poggendorf, Vice President of Enrollment Management, Roanoke College, 221 College Lane, Salem, VA 24153-3794

St. Paul's College

Lawrenceville, Virginia
www.saintpauls.edu
CB member
CB code: 5604

- Private 4-year liberal arts college affiliated with Episcopal Church
- Residential campus in small town
- 642 degree-seeking undergraduates: 3% part-time, 49% women, 97% African American, 1% Hispanic American
- 98% of applicants admitted
- SAT or ACT (ACT writing optional), application essay required

General. Founded in 1888. Regionally accredited. **Degrees:** 125 bachelor's awarded. **ROTC:** Army. **Location:** 80 miles from Richmond. **Calendar:** Semester, limited summer session. **Full-time faculty:** 28 total; 61% have terminal degrees, 75% minority, 39% women. **Part-time faculty:** 10 total; 70% minority, 50% women. **Class size:** 65% < 20, 26% 20-39, 8% 40-49, 1% 50-99, less than 1% >100.

Freshman class profile. 508 applied, 496 admitted, 200 enrolled.

Mid 50% test scores		**GPA 2.0-2.99:**	57%
SAT critical reading:	320-410	**Rank in top quarter:**	10%
SAT math:	310-400	**Rank in top tenth:**	3%
SAT writing:	320-390	**End year in good standing:**	53%
ACT composite:	13-17	**Return as sophomores:**	45%
GPA 3.75 or higher:	1%	**Out-of-state:**	24%
GPA 3.50-3.74:	1%	**Live on campus:**	93%
GPA 3.0-3.49:	7%	**International:**	1%

Basis for selection. School achievement record most important. School recommendations considered. Rank in top half of class important. 3.0 GPA recommended. Interview recommended.

High school preparation. 10 units required. Required units include English 4, mathematics 2, social studies 2 and science 2.

2008-2009 Annual costs. Tuition/fees: $13,210. Room/board: $6,640. Books/supplies: $1,500. Personal expenses: $2,730.

2007-2008 Financial aid. **Non-need-based:** Scholarships awarded for academics, athletics, leadership, ROTC.

Application procedures. **Admission:** No deadline. $20 fee, may be waived for applicants with need. Admission notification on a rolling basis. Must reply by May 1 or within 2 week(s) if notified thereafter. **Financial aid:** No deadline. FAFSA required. Applicants notified on a rolling basis starting 1/15; must reply by 7/1 or within 4 week(s) of notification.

Academics. **Special study options:** Accelerated study, cooperative education, cross-registration, double major, exchange student, honors, independent study, internships, teacher certification program. Organizational Management Program for adults 25 and older. **Credit/placement by examination:** AP, CLEP, institutional tests. 24 credit hours maximum toward bachelor's degree. **Support services:** Learning center, pre-admission summer program, reduced course load, remedial instruction, tutoring.

Majors. **Biology:** General, marine. **Business:** Accounting, administrative services, business admin, management information systems, operations. **Computer sciences:** General. **Conservation:** General. **Education:** Business. **Math:** General. **Philosophy/religion:** Philosophy, religion. **Protective services:** Criminal justice. **Social sciences:** General, political science, sociology.

Most popular majors. Business/marketing 76%.

Computing on campus. 100 workstations in dormitories, library, computer center, student center. Dormitories wired for high-speed internet access and linked to campus network. Commuter students can connect to campus network. Helpline, repair service, wireless network available.

Student life. **Freshman orientation:** Mandatory. Preregistration for classes offered. **Housing:** Single-sex dorms available. $50 nonrefundable deposit. **Activities:** Pep band, choral groups, dance, student government, Altar Guild, veterans club, Canterbury club, NAACP, single parent support system.

Athletics. NCAA. **Intercollegiate:** Baseball M, basketball, bowling, cross-country, football (tackle) M, golf, softball W, tennis, track and field, volleyball W. **Intramural:** Basketball, softball, volleyball. **Team name:** Tigers.

Student services. Adult student services, career counseling, student employment services, financial aid counseling, health services, on-campus daycare, personal counseling, placement for graduates, veterans' counselor.

Contact. E-mail: admissions@saintpauls.edu
Phone: (434) 848-3111 Toll-free number: (800) 678-7071
Fax: (434) 848-1846
Rosemary Lewis, Director of Admissions, St. Paul's College, 115 College Drive, Lawrenceville, VA 23868

Sanford-Brown College: Vienna

Vienna, Virginia
www.gibbsva.edu
CB code: 5655

- For-profit 4-year business and technical college
- Large city

General. Accredited by ACICS. **Calendar:** Quarter.

Contact. Phone: (703) 556-8888
1980 Gallows Road, Vienna, VA 22182

Shenandoah University

Winchester, Virginia
www.su.edu
CB member
CB code: 5613

- Private 4-year university affiliated with United Methodist Church
- Residential campus in small city
- 1,671 degree-seeking undergraduates: 5% part-time, 56% women
- 1,517 degree-seeking graduate students
- 87% of applicants admitted
- SAT or ACT (ACT writing optional) required
- 46% graduate within 6 years

General. Founded in 1875. Regionally accredited. **Degrees:** 314 bachelor's, 7 associate awarded; master's, doctoral, first professional offered. **Location:** 100 miles from Baltimore, 75 miles from Washington, DC. **Calendar:** Semester, limited summer session. **Full-time faculty:** 211 total; 77% have terminal degrees, 12% minority, 52% women. **Part-time faculty:** 175

total; 34% have terminal degrees, 12% minority, 64% women. **Special facilities:** Arts and media centers, conservatory, recording studio.

Freshman class profile. 1,279 applied, 1,109 admitted, 402 enrolled.

Mid 50% test scores		**GPA 3.0-3.49:**	28%
SAT critical reading:	440-570	**GPA 2.0-2.99:**	35%
SAT math:	440-570	**Return as sophomores:**	70%
ACT composite:	18-23	**Live on campus:**	95%
GPA 3.75 or higher:	22%	**International:**	1%
GPA 3.50-3.74:	14%		

Basis for selection. Applicants evaluated on basis of GPA and standardized test scores along with recommendation. Audition required for Conservatory applicants. Nursing applicants must take ATI Test of Essential Academic Skills. In-house English proficiency tests administered. Interview recommended for all; audition required for dance, music, and theater programs. **Homeschooled:** Transcript of courses and grades, letter of recommendation (nonparent) required. May request GED score. Applicants must submit written documentation of local school district approval of the homeschool arrangement if available.

High school preparation. College-preparatory program recommended. 15 units required. Required units include English 4, mathematics 3, social studies 2, science 2 (laboratory 1) and foreign language 2.

2009-2010 Annual costs. Tuition/fees (projected): $24,150. Room/board: $8,600. Books/supplies: $1,000. Personal expenses: $1,500.

2008-2009 Financial aid. Need-based: 336 full-time freshmen applied for aid; 336 were judged to have need; 336 of these received aid. Average need met was 86%. Average scholarship/grant was $8,000; average loan $3,500. **Non-need-based:** Awarded to 1,115 full-time undergraduates, including 348 freshmen. Scholarships awarded for academics, job skills, music/drama, religious affiliation, state residency.

Application procedures. Admission: Priority date 3/1; deadline 8/29. $30 fee, may be waived for applicants with need. Admission notification on a rolling basis beginning on or about 10/1. Must reply by May 1 or within 2 week(s) if notified thereafter. **Financial aid:** Closing date 3/15. FAFSA required. Applicants notified on a rolling basis starting 3/15; must reply within 2 week(s) of notification.

Academics. Special study options: Accelerated study, combined bachelor's/graduate degree, distance learning, double major, dual enrollment of high school students, ESL, internships, study abroad, teacher certification program, weekend college. **Credit/placement by examination:** AP, CLEP, IB, SAT, ACT, institutional tests. AP placement grade may be higher for exams taken in student's major. CEEB, CLEP, academic department exams used. **Support services:** Learning center, reduced course load, remedial instruction, study skills assistance, tutoring, writing center.

Majors. Area/ethnic studies: American. **Biology:** General. **Business:** Business admin. **Communications:** General. **Education:** Drama/dance, music, physical. **Foreign languages:** Spanish. **Health:** Music therapy, nursing (RN), respiratory therapy technology. **History:** General. **Liberal arts:** Arts/sciences. **Math:** General. **Philosophy/religion:** Religion. **Physical sciences:** Chemistry. **Protective services:** Law enforcement admin. **Psychology:** General. **Public administration:** General. **Social sciences:** Sociology. **Visual/performing arts:** General, acting, arts management, dance, dramatic, music performance, music theory/composition, piano/organ, theater design.

Most popular majors. Biology 7%, business/marketing 11%, education 9%, health sciences 30%, visual/performing arts 17%.

Computing on campus. 175 workstations in dormitories, library, computer center, student center. Dormitories wired for high-speed internet access and linked to campus network. Commuter students can connect to campus network. Online course registration, online library, helpline, repair service, wireless network available.

Student life. Freshman orientation: Mandatory. Preregistration for classes offered. One week; week before start of classes. **Policies:** All first and second year undergraduate students required to live in on-campus housing. **Housing:** Guaranteed on-campus for freshmen. Coed dorms, special housing for disabled, wellness housing available. $100 nonrefundable deposit, deadline 7/1. **Activities:** Bands, choral groups, dance, drama, literary magazine, music ensembles, musical theater, opera, student government, student newspaper, symphony orchestra, TV station, Circle K, Alpha Chi Honor Society, Alpha Lambda Delta, freshman honor society, nursing honor society, Christian Pharmacists Fellowship International, Omicron Delta Kappa, College Democrats, College Republicans.

Athletics. NCAA. **Intercollegiate:** Baseball M, basketball, cross-country, field hockey W, football (tackle) M, golf M, lacrosse, soccer, softball W, tennis. **Team name:** Hornets.

Student services. Adult student services, alcohol/substance abuse counseling, chaplain/spiritual director, career counseling, student employment services, financial aid counseling, health services, minority student services, personal counseling, placement for graduates, veterans' counselor. **Physically disabled:** Services for visually, speech, hearing impaired.

Contact. E-mail: admit@su.edu
Phone: (540) 665-4581 Toll-free number: (800) 432-2266
Fax: (540) 665-4627
David Anthony, Dean of Admissions, Shenandoah University, 1460 University Drive, Winchester, VA 22601-5195

Southern Virginia University

Buena Vista, Virginia — **CB member**
www.svu.edu — **CB code: 5625**

- Private 4-year liberal arts college affiliated with Church of Jesus Christ of Latter-day Saints
- Residential campus in small town
- 683 degree-seeking undergraduates: 3% part-time, 55% women, 3% African American, 2% Asian American, 3% Hispanic American, 1% Native American, 2% international
- 98% of applicants admitted
- SAT or ACT (ACT writing optional) required

General. International students must pay a $255 administration fee. **Degrees:** 113 bachelor's awarded. **ROTC:** Army. **Location:** 60 miles from Roanoke, 60 miles from Charlottesville. **Calendar:** Semester, limited summer session. **Full-time faculty:** 36 total; 67% have terminal degrees, 8% minority, 42% women. **Part-time faculty:** 32 total; 16% have terminal degrees, 34% women. **Class size:** 66% < 20, 32% 20-39, 1% 50-99, less than 1% >100.

Freshman class profile. 624 applied, 610 admitted, 244 enrolled.

Mid 50% test scores		**GPA 3.0-3.49:**	35%
SAT critical reading:	450-580	**GPA 2.0-2.99:**	28%
SAT math:	440-560	**Rank in top quarter:**	36%
SAT writing:	450-560	**Rank in top tenth:**	14%
ACT composite:	19-25	**Out-of-state:**	81%
GPA 3.75 or higher:	17%	**Live on campus:**	88%
GPA 3.50-3.74:	19%		

Basis for selection. GPA, test scores, interview, religious affiliation or commitment all important. **Homeschooled:** Transcript of courses and grades required.

High school preparation. Recommended units include English 4, mathematics 2, social studies 2, history 2, science 2 (laboratory 2), foreign language 2 and academic electives 1.

2008-2009 Annual costs. Tuition/fees: $16,500. International students pay a $255 administration fee. Room/board: $5,500. Books/supplies: $1,000. Personal expenses: $400.

2007-2008 Financial aid. Non-need-based: Scholarships awarded for academics, art, athletics, leadership, music/drama.

Application procedures. Admission: Closing date 7/31. $35 fee, may be waived for applicants with need. **Financial aid:** FAFSA required. Applicants notified on a rolling basis starting 2/1; must reply by 5/1 or within 3 week(s) of notification.

Academics. Special study options: Double major, independent study, internships, liberal arts/career combination, study abroad. **Credit/placement by examination:** AP, CLEP, IB, SAT, ACT, institutional tests. **Support services:** Learning center, remedial instruction, study skills assistance, tutoring.

Majors. Biology: General. **Business:** Business admin. **Computer sciences:** General. **Family/consumer sciences:** Family systems. **Foreign languages:** Spanish. **History:** General. **Liberal arts:** Arts/sciences. **Philosophy/religion:** Philosophy. **Visual/performing arts:** Art, dramatic.

Most popular majors. Business/marketing 29%, English 7%, liberal arts 18%, parks/recreation 7%, visual/performing arts 14%.

Computing on campus. 46 workstations in library, computer center. Dormitories wired for high-speed internet access and linked to campus network. Commuter students can connect to campus network. Online course registration, online library, helpline, repair service, wireless network available.

Student life. **Freshman orientation:** Mandatory. Preregistration for classes offered. **Policies:** Students are responsible for familiarizing themselves with and abiding by the honor code, the dress and grooming standards, and the residential living policies. Most housing is wheelchair accessible. **Housing:** Guaranteed on-campus for freshmen. Single-sex dorms, apartments, wellness housing available. $250 fully refundable deposit, deadline 9/6. **Activities:** Bands, campus ministries, choral groups, dance, drama, international student organizations, literary magazine, music ensembles, musical theater, student government, student newspaper, symphony orchestra.

Athletics. NAIA, USCAA. **Intercollegiate:** Baseball M, basketball M, cheerleading, cross-country, football (tackle) M, golf, soccer, softball W, tennis, track and field, volleyball W, wrestling M. **Team name:** Knights.

Student services. Chaplain/spiritual director, career counseling, financial aid counseling, health services, personal counseling.

Contact. E-mail: admissions@svu.edu
Phone: (540) 261-2756 Toll-free number: (800) 229-8420
Jody Mask, Dean of Admissions, Southern Virginia University, One University Hill Drive, Buena Vista, VA 24416

Stratford University: Falls Church

Falls Church, Virginia
www.stratford.edu
CB code: 3778

- For-profit 4-year university and career college
- Commuter campus in small city
- 860 degree-seeking undergraduates
- Interview required

General. Accredited by ACICS. **Degrees:** 35 bachelor's, 89 associate awarded; master's offered. **Location:** 12 Miles from the District of Columbia. **Calendar:** Quarter, extensive summer session. **Special facilities:** Complete kitchen laboratory facilities.

Basis for selection. Open admission. **Homeschooled:** Transcript of courses and grades, state high school equivalency certificate, interview required.

2008-2009 Annual costs. Tuition/fees: $14,625.

Application procedures. **Admission:** No deadline. $50 fee. Admission notification on a rolling basis.

Academics. **Special study options:** Accelerated study, distance learning, external degree, independent study, internships. **Credit/placement by examination:** CLEP. **Support services:** Remedial instruction, study skills assistance, tutoring.

Majors. **Business:** General, business admin, hospitality admin, management information systems. **Computer sciences:** General, computer graphics, information technology, networking. **Personal/culinary services:** Restaurant/catering.

Most popular majors. Business/marketing 17%, computer/information sciences 83%.

Computing on campus. Online course registration, online library available.

Student life. **Freshman orientation:** Mandatory. **Activities:** Student newspaper.

Student services. Adult student services, placement for graduates, veterans' counselor.

Contact. E-mail: admissions@stratford.edu
Phone: (703) 821-8570 Toll-free number: (800) 444-0804
Safia Habib, Director of Admissions, Stratford University: Falls Church, 7777 Leesburg Pike, Falls Church, VA 22043

Stratford University: Woodbridge

Woodbridge, Virginia
www.stratford.edu

- For-profit 4-year university
- Large town

General. Accredited by ACICS. **Calendar:** Quarter.

Annual costs/financial aid. Tuition/fees (2008-2009): $14,625.

Contact. Phone: (703) 897-1982
Director of Admissions, 13576 Minnieville Road, Woodbridge, VA 22192

Sweet Briar College

Sweet Briar, Virginia
www.sbc.edu
CB member
CB code: 5634

- Private 4-year liberal arts college for women
- Residential campus in rural community
- 647 degree-seeking undergraduates: 1% part-time, 100% women, 3% African American, 1% Asian American, 3% Hispanic American, 1% Native American, 1% international
- 15 degree-seeking graduate students
- 83% of applicants admitted
- SAT or ACT (ACT writing optional), application essay required
- 72% graduate within 6 years; 30% enter graduate study

General. Founded in 1901. Regionally accredited. **Degrees:** 130 bachelor's awarded; master's offered. **Location:** 12 miles from Lynchburg, 166 miles from Washington, DC. **Calendar:** Semester, limited summer session. **Full-time faculty:** 65 total; 100% have terminal degrees, 5% minority, 49% women. **Part-time faculty:** 36 total; 8% minority, 67% women. **Special facilities:** Indoor and outdoor riding facilities, three nature sanctuaries, art barn, college-run nursery school and kindergarten for student teaching, observatory, environmental education and nature center.

Freshman class profile. 629 applied, 520 admitted, 198 enrolled.

Mid 50% test scores		**Rank in top quarter:**	53%
SAT critical reading:	510-630	**Rank in top tenth:**	28%
SAT math:	470-600	**End year in good standing:**	80%
ACT composite:	20-26	**Return as sophomores:**	71%
GPA 3.75 or higher:	39%	**Out-of-state:**	56%
GPA 3.50-3.74:	14%	**Live on campus:**	95%
GPA 3.0-3.49:	26%	**International:**	2%
GPA 2.0-2.99:	21%		

Basis for selection. High school curriculum and grades are of primary importance, followed by school and teacher recommendations, test scores, and writing ability as demonstrated by essay or personal statement. Interview, extracurricular activities, and personal characteristics are also considered. **Learning Disabled:** Applicant must submit written request for accommodated admissions review to Office of Admissions and enclose appropriate documentation with request.

High school preparation. College-preparatory program required. 16 units required; 20 recommended. Required and recommended units include English 4, mathematics 3-4, social studies 3-4, science 3-4 (laboratory 2-3) and foreign language 2-4. Mathematics preparation must be at least through Algebra II. Foreign language must include 2 consecutive years of same language.

2008-2009 Annual costs. Tuition/fees: $26,995. Room/board: $10,160. Books/supplies: $900. Personal expenses: $950.

2008-2009 Financial aid. **Need-based:** 152 full-time freshmen applied for aid; 127 were judged to have need; 127 of these received aid. Average need met was 71%. Average scholarship/grant was $13,427; average loan $4,295. 72% of total undergraduate aid awarded as scholarships/grants, 28% as loans/jobs. **Non-need-based:** Awarded to 498 full-time undergraduates, including 128 freshmen. Scholarships awarded for academics, art, leadership, music/drama, state residency.

Application procedures. **Admission:** Closing date 2/1 (postmark date). $40 fee, may be waived for applicants with need. Admission notification 3/15. Must reply by 5/1. **Financial aid:** Priority date 2/15; no closing date. FAFSA required. Applicants notified on a rolling basis starting 3/1; must reply by 5/1 or within 2 week(s) of notification.

Academics. General Education Program: students complete requirements that involve communication and quantitative reasoning skills; rationale for broad liberal arts background; emphasis on internships; regular progress self-assessments. Summer research program provides opportunities for high-level work with faculty. **Special study options:** Accelerated study, combined bachelor's/graduate degree, cross-registration, double major, dual enrollment of high school students, exchange student, honors, independent study, internships, liberal arts/career combination, student-designed major, study abroad, teacher certification program, Washington semester. **Credit/placement by examination:** AP, CLEP, IB, institutional tests. Exemption from 1 or more of degree requirements and/or admission to advanced courses may be granted on basis of Advanced Placement Exams, International Baccalaureate Program, transfer credit, or, in some cases, placement tests taken at college. **Support services:** Learning center, study skills assistance, tutoring, writing center.

Majors. Area/ethnic studies: German, Italian. **Biology:** General. **Business:** General. **Computer sciences:** Computer science. **Conservation:** Environmental science, environmental studies. **Engineering:** Science. **Engineering technology:** Industrial management. **Foreign languages:** General, classics, French, German, Spanish. **History:** General. **Liberal arts:** Arts/sciences. **Math:** General. **Philosophy/religion:** Philosophy, religion. **Physical sciences:** Chemistry, physics, theoretical physics. **Psychology:** General. **Social sciences:** Anthropology, archaeology, economics, international relations, political science, sociology. **Visual/performing arts:** Art history/conservation, dance, dramatic, studio arts. **Other:** Biochemistry and molecular biology, Multi/interdisciplinary studies.

Most popular majors. Biology 11%, business/marketing 7%, English 6%, history 6%, liberal arts 6%, psychology 7%, social sciences 18%, visual/performing arts 11%.

Computing on campus. 117 workstations in library, computer center. Dormitories wired for high-speed internet access and linked to campus network. Commuter students can connect to campus network. Online course registration, online library, helpline, repair service, student web hosting, wireless network available.

Student life. Freshman orientation: Mandatory. Preregistration for classes offered. Begins on a Saturday in August through the following Thursday, which is the official beginning of classes. **Policies:** Self-governing student body; honor system observed. **Housing:** Guaranteed on-campus for all undergraduates. Wellness housing available. $500 deposit, deadline 5/1. **Activities:** Campus ministries, choral groups, dance, drama, film society, literary magazine, music ensembles, musical theater, radio station, student government, student newspaper, symphony orchestra, TV station, Campus Christian Fellowship, campus spirituality coalition, College Republicans, College Democrats, Circle K, Habitat for Humanity, student environmental organization, Vixen PAWS, Newman Club.

Athletics. NCAA. **Intercollegiate:** Field hockey W, lacrosse W, soccer W, softball W, swimming W, tennis W, volleyball W. **Team name:** Vixens.

Student services. Alcohol/substance abuse counseling, chaplain/spiritual director, career counseling, student employment services, financial aid counseling, health services, personal counseling, placement for graduates, women's services. **Physically disabled:** Services for hearing impaired.

Contact. E-mail: admissions@sbc.edu
Phone: (434) 381-6142 Toll-free number: (800) 381-6142
Fax: (434) 381-6152
Ken Huus, Dean of Admissions, Sweet Briar College, PO Box B, Sweet Briar, VA 24595

University of Management and Technology
Arlington, Virginia
www.umtweb.edu

- For-profit 4-year business and engineering college
- Very large city

General. Accredited by DETC. **Calendar:** Continuous.

Contact. Phone: (703) 516-0035
1901 N Fort Myer Drive/Suite 700, Arlington, VA 22209

University of Mary Washington
Fredericksburg, Virginia — **CB member**
www.umw.edu — **CB code: 5398**

- Public 4-year university and liberal arts college
- Residential campus in small city
- 4,070 degree-seeking undergraduates: 12% part-time, 66% women, 4% African American, 4% Asian American, 4% Hispanic American
- 712 degree-seeking graduate students
- 71% of applicants admitted
- SAT or ACT (ACT writing optional), application essay required
- 76% graduate within 6 years

General. Founded in 1908. Regionally accredited. Stafford location offering bachelor's degree-completion program and master's degrees. **Degrees:** 1,011 bachelor's awarded; master's offered. **ROTC:** Army. **Location:** 50 miles from Richmond, 50 miles from Washington, DC. **Calendar:** Semester, limited summer session. **Full-time faculty:** 246 total; 98% have terminal degrees, 13% minority, 46% women. **Part-time faculty:** 131 total; 8% minority, 53% women. **Class size:** 49% < 20, 44% 20-39, 4% 40-49, 3% 50-99, less than 1% >100. **Special facilities:** Center for historic preservation, James Monroe museum and memorial library, Gari Melchers home and studio, center for Asian studies.

Freshman class profile. 4,600 applied, 3,258 admitted, 917 enrolled.

Mid 50% test scores		**GPA 3.0-3.49:**	35%
SAT critical reading:	550-650	**GPA 2.0-2.99:**	7%
SAT math:	540-620	**Return as sophomores:**	83%
SAT writing:	540-640	**Out-of-state:**	27%
ACT composite:	24-28	**Live on campus:**	95%
GPA 3.75 or higher:	33%	**International:**	1%
GPA 3.50-3.74:	25%		

Basis for selection. Rigor of high school program most important, followed by GPA, standardized test scores, activities, essays, recommendations. SAT Subject Tests recommended including mathematics, writing, and one subject of student's choice. Music majors encouraged to audition. **Homeschooled:** Students strongly advised to take 3 SAT Subject Tests: math and 2 other subject areas of choice.

High school preparation. College-preparatory program recommended. 15 units required; 20 recommended. Required and recommended units include English 4, mathematics 3-4, social studies 2, history 1-2, science 3-4 (laboratory 3-4) and foreign language 2-4.

2008-2009 Annual costs. Tuition/fees: $6,694; $17,861 out-of-state. Room/board: $7,846. Books/supplies: $1,000. Personal expenses: $1,500.

2008-2009 Financial aid. Need-based: 590 full-time freshmen applied for aid; 250 were judged to have need; 220 of these received aid. Average need met was 50%. Average scholarship/grant was $5,600; average loan $2,600. 48% of total undergraduate aid awarded as scholarships/grants, 52% as loans/jobs. **Non-need-based:** Awarded to 420 full-time undergraduates, including 185 freshmen. Scholarships awarded for academics, alumni affiliation, art, leadership, music/drama, state residency.

Application procedures. Admission: Priority date 1/15; deadline 2/1 (postmark date). $50 fee, may be waived for applicants with need. Admission notification 4/1. Admission notification on a rolling basis. Must reply by 5/1. Applicants for regular admission who complete application by 1/15 eligible for honor admission (early notification, non-binding). **Financial aid:** Priority date 3/1, closing date 5/31. FAFSA, institutional form required. Applicants notified by 4/15; must reply by 5/1 or within 2 week(s) of notification.

Academics. College provides grants for undergraduate research program enabling students to work individually with faculty members. **Special study options:** Accelerated study, combined bachelor's/graduate degree, double major, independent study, internships, semester at sea, student-designed major, study abroad, teacher certification program, Washington semester. **Credit/placement by examination:** AP, CLEP, IB, institutional tests. Credit from CLEP scores applicable to adult degree; limited to to BA/BS degree program. **Support services:** Pre-admission summer program, study skills assistance, tutoring, writing center.

Majors. Area/ethnic studies: American. **Biology:** General. **Business:** Business admin. **Computer sciences:** General. **Foreign languages:** General, classics. **History:** General. **Interdisciplinary:** Historic preservation. **Liberal arts:** Arts/sciences. **Math:** General. **Philosophy/religion:** Philosophy, religion. **Physical sciences:** Chemistry, physics. **Psychology:** General. **Social sciences:** Anthropology, economics, geography, international relations, political science, sociology. **Visual/performing arts:** General, art history/conservation.

Most popular majors. Biology 8%, business/marketing 14%, English 11%, interdisciplinary studies 9%, liberal arts 8%, psychology 8%, social sciences 15%.

Computing on campus. 306 workstations in library, computer center, student center. Dormitories wired for high-speed internet access and linked to campus network. Commuter students can connect to campus network. Online course registration, online library, helpline, repair service, wireless network available.

Student life. Freshman orientation: Mandatory. Preregistration for classes offered. 5-day freshmen/transfer orientation held in August prior to start of classes. **Policies:** Honor system. **Housing:** Guaranteed on-campus for freshmen. Coed dorms, single-sex dorms, special housing for disabled, apartments, wellness housing available. $200 nonrefundable deposit, deadline 5/1. **Activities:** Bands, campus ministries, choral groups, dance, drama, film society, international student organizations, literary magazine, music ensembles, Model UN, musical theater, opera, radio station, student government, student newspaper, symphony orchestra, Amnesty International, Baptist Student Union, Catholic Student Union, Hillel, Hispanic student association, Asian student association, Young Democrats, Campus Christian Community, College Republicans.

Athletics. NCAA. **Intercollegiate:** Baseball M, basketball, cross-country, equestrian, field hockey W, lacrosse, rowing (crew), soccer, softball W, swimming, tennis, track and field, volleyball W. **Intramural:** Basketball, bowling, football (non-tackle), golf, handball, soccer, softball, volleyball, water polo. **Team name:** Eagles.

Student services. Adult student services, chaplain/spiritual director, career counseling, services for economically disadvantaged, student employment services, financial aid counseling, health services, minority student services, personal counseling, placement for graduates, veterans' counselor, women's services. **Physically disabled:** Services for visually, speech, hearing impaired.

Contact. E-mail: admit@umw.edu
Phone: (540) 654-2000 Toll-free number: (800) 468-5614
Fax: (540) 654-1857
Martin Wilder, Vice President for Enrollment and Communications, University of Mary Washington, 1301 College Avenue, Fredericksburg, VA 22401-5300

University of Richmond

University of Richmond, Virginia — **CB member**
www.richmond.edu — **CB code: 5569**

- Private 4-year university and liberal arts college
- Residential campus in very large city
- 2,689 degree-seeking undergraduates: 1% part-time, 51% women, 6% African American, 4% Asian American, 3% Hispanic American, 5% international
- 649 degree-seeking graduate students
- 32% of applicants admitted
- SAT or ACT (ACT writing optional), application essay required
- 87% graduate within 6 years

General. Founded in 1830. Regionally accredited. **Degrees:** 794 bachelor's, 4 associate awarded; master's, first professional offered. **ROTC:** Army. **Location:** 6 miles from Richmond, 100 miles from Washington, DC. **Calendar:** Semester, limited summer session. **Full-time faculty:** 322 total; 84% have terminal degrees, 12% minority, 41% women. **Part-time faculty:** 45 total; 62% have terminal degrees, 4% minority, 58% women. **Class size:** 71% < 20, 29% 20-39. **Special facilities:** Greenhouse, electron microscope, radionuclide complex, print study center, natural sciences museum, neuroscience research laboratory, music technology laboratory, art technology laboratory, foundry, herbarium, computer connection to the Jefferson Lab's particle accelerator.

Freshman class profile. 7,970 applied, 2,525 admitted, 738 enrolled.

Mid 50% test scores			
SAT critical reading:	580-680	Return as sophomores:	91%
SAT math:	590-680	Out-of-state:	83%
SAT writing:	590-690	Live on campus:	98%
ACT composite:	26-30	International:	7%

Basis for selection. High school transcript, test scores, essay, GPA, character/personal qualities and letter of reference. Campus visits recommended; interviews not offered. SAT Subject Tests in foreign languages may be used for placement, but not required. January SAT and SAT Subject Test date and February ACT test date are last acceptable testing dates for fall admission. Character statement required. **Homeschooled:** Statement describing homeschool structure and mission, interview required. Applicant must submit narrative description of home schooling environment. 2 SAT Subject Tests in history and natural science strongly recommended.

High school preparation. 16 units required; 20 recommended. Required and recommended units include English 4, mathematics 3-4, history 2-4, science 2-4 (laboratory 2-4) and foreign language 2-4.

2008-2009 Annual costs. Tuition/fees: $38,850. Room/board: $8,200. Books/supplies: $1,050. Personal expenses: $990.

2008-2009 Financial aid. Need-based: 412 full-time freshmen applied for aid; 308 were judged to have need; 308 of these received aid. Average need met was 100%. Average scholarship/grant was $31,626; average loan $2,961. 92% of total undergraduate aid awarded as scholarships/grants, 8% as loans/jobs. **Non-need-based:** Scholarships awarded for academics, art, athletics, leadership, minority status, music/drama, ROTC. **Additional information:** VA residents whose family income is $40,000 or less and who qualify for need-based aid will receive grant assistance equal to full tuition, room and board. Early decision: Financial aid package estimated using historical data; applicant still required to submit all financial aid forms.

Application procedures. Admission: Closing date 1/15 (postmark date). $50 fee, may be waived for applicants with need. Admission notification 4/1. Admission notification on a rolling basis. Must reply by May 1 or within 2 week(s) if notified thereafter. **Financial aid:** Closing date 2/15. FAFSA, institutional form required. Applicants notified by 4/1; must reply within 4 week(s) of notification.

Academics. Special study options: Accelerated study, cross-registration, distance learning, double major, ESL, exchange student, external degree, honors, independent study, internships, student-designed major, study abroad, teacher certification program, Washington semester. 86 different study abroad programs in over 30 different countries. **Credit/placement by examination:** AP, CLEP, IB, institutional tests. 30 credit hours maximum toward bachelor's degree. School of Continuing Studies follows different guidelines and credit granting procedures. **Support services:** Learning center, study skills assistance, tutoring, writing center.

Majors. Area/ethnic studies: African, American, Asian, European, German, Latin American, Russian/Slavic, women's. **Biology:** General, molecular biochemistry. **Business:** Accounting, business admin, human resources, organizational behavior. **Communications:** Journalism. **Computer sciences:** General, information technology. **Conservation:** Environmental studies. **Foreign languages:** Ancient Greek, French, Latin, Spanish. **History:** General. **Interdisciplinary:** Ancient studies, cognitive science. **Liberal arts:** Humanities. **Math:** General. **Philosophy/religion:** Philosophy, religion. **Physical sciences:** Chemistry, physics. **Protective services:** Criminal justice. **Psychology:** General. **Public administration:** Human services. **Social sciences:** Anthropology, economics, international economics, international relations, political science, sociology. **Visual/performing arts:** Art history/conservation, dramatic, studio arts. **Other:** Mathematical Economics.

Most popular majors. Biology 7%, business/marketing 32%, English 9%, psychology 6%, social sciences 18%.

Computing on campus. 900 workstations in dormitories, library, computer center, student center. Dormitories wired for high-speed internet access and linked to campus network. Commuter students can connect to campus network. Online course registration, online library, helpline, repair service, student web hosting, wireless network available.

Student life. Freshman orientation: Mandatory. 3 days before upperclassmen arrive in the fall. **Policies:** Undergraduate students become members of residential colleges: Richmond College (men) and Westhampton College (women). Classes and extracurricular activities co-educational. Separate student governments, honor/judicial councils and deans. **Housing:** Coed dorms, single-sex dorms, special housing for disabled, apartments, wellness housing available. $300 nonrefundable deposit, deadline 5/1. **Activities:** Bands, campus ministries, choral groups, dance, drama, film society, international student organizations, literary magazine, music ensembles, Model UN, musical theater, radio station, student government, student newspaper, symphony orchestra, over 200 organizations.

Athletics. NCAA. **Intercollegiate:** Baseball M, basketball, cross-country, diving W, field hockey W, football (tackle) M, golf, lacrosse W, soccer, swimming W, tennis, track and field. **Intramural:** Badminton, basketball, golf, handball, racquetball, soccer, softball, squash, swimming, synchronized swimming W, table tennis, tennis, volleyball, water polo M, wrestling M. **Team name:** Spiders.

Student services. Alcohol/substance abuse counseling, chaplain/spiritual director, career counseling, student employment services, financial aid counseling, health services, minority student services, personal counseling, placement for graduates, veterans' counselor. **Physically disabled:** Services for visually, speech, hearing impaired.

Contact. E-mail: admissions@richmond.edu
Phone: (804) 289-8640 Toll-free number: (800) 700-1662
Fax: (804) 287-6003
Pamela Spence, Dean of Admissions, University of Richmond, 28 Westhampton Way, University of Richmond, VA 23173

University of Virginia

Charlottesville, Virginia — **CB member**
www.virginia.edu — **CB code: 5820**

- Public 4-year university
- Residential campus in small city

- 13,869 degree-seeking undergraduates: 2% part-time, 56% women, 9% African American, 11% Asian American, 4% Hispanic American, 5% international
- 6,511 degree-seeking graduate students
- 37% of applicants admitted
- SAT or ACT with writing, application essay required

General. Founded in 1819. Regionally accredited. **Degrees:** 3,526 bachelor's awarded; master's, doctoral, first professional offered. **ROTC:** Army, Naval, Air Force. **Location:** 70 miles from Richmond, 120 miles from Washington, DC. **Calendar:** Semester, extensive summer session. **Full-time faculty:** 1,267 total; 92% have terminal degrees, 12% minority, 34% women. **Part-time faculty:** 77 total; 70% have terminal degrees, 5% minority, 47% women. **Class size:** 50% < 20, 30% 20-39, 6% 40-49, 8% 50-99, 6% >100. **Special facilities:** Observatory, center for biological timing, experimental farm.

Freshman class profile. 18,363 applied, 6,735 admitted, 3,256 enrolled.

Mid 50% test scores			
SAT critical reading:	600-710	GPA 2.0-2.99:	1%
SAT math:	620-730	Rank in top quarter:	98%
SAT writing:	610-720	Rank in top tenth:	88%
ACT composite:	27-32	End year in good standing:	97%
GPA 3.75 or higher:	88%	Return as sophomores:	97%
GPA 3.50-3.74:	8%	Out-of-state:	33%
GPA 3.0-3.49:	3%	Live on campus:	100%
		International:	6%

Basis for selection. School achievement record, class rank, test scores most important. Extracurricular activities and interests, quality of writing, recommendation also important. Special consideration for minorities, children of alumni, and in-state students. School diploma may be waived for especially qualified applicants. Following international tests accepted: International Baccalaureate, German Abitur, British AICE, French Baccalaureate, Swiss Federal Maturity Certificate. SAT Subject Tests recommended. SAT scores accepted for tests taken in January, but not reported by January 31.

High school preparation. College-preparatory program required. 16 units required. Required and recommended units include English 4, mathematics 4-5, social studies 1-4, science 2-4 and foreign language 2-5. 3 units of science (1 chemistry, 1 physics) required if applying to the School of Engineering and Applied Science.

2008-2009 Annual costs. Tuition/fees: $9,505; $29,798 out-of-state. Room/board: $7,820.

2008-2009 Financial aid. Need-based: 1,972 full-time freshmen applied for aid; 875 were judged to have need; 875 of these received aid. Average need met was 100%. Average scholarship/grant was $13,449; average loan $4,331. 79% of total undergraduate aid awarded as scholarships/grants, 21% as loans/jobs. **Non-need-based:** Awarded to 2,442 full-time undergraduates, including 665 freshmen. Scholarships awarded for academics, athletics, leadership, minority status, music/drama, state residency.

Application procedures. Admission: Closing date 1/2 (receipt date). $60 fee, may be waived for applicants with need. Admission notification 4/1. Must reply by May 1 or within 2 week(s) if notified thereafter. Deferred admission maximum postponement is one year. **Financial aid:** Priority date 3/1; no closing date. FAFSA, institutional form required. Applicants notified by 4/1; must reply by 5/1.

Academics. Special study options: Accelerated study, combined bachelor's/graduate degree, cooperative education, double major, ESL, exchange student, honors, independent study, internships, liberal arts/career combination, semester at sea, student-designed major, study abroad, teacher certification program. Jefferson, Echols, Rodman, and College Science Scholar programs for highest-achieving high school students. January Term. **Credit/placement by examination:** AP, CLEP, IB, institutional tests. **Support services:** Learning center, pre-admission summer program, reduced course load, study skills assistance, tutoring, writing center.

Majors. Architecture: Architecture, history/criticism, urban/community planning. **Area/ethnic studies:** African-American, Latin American. **Biology:** General. **Business:** General. **Computer sciences:** General. **Conservation:** Environmental science. **Engineering:** General, aerospace, biomedical, chemical, civil, computer, electrical, mechanical, systems. **Foreign languages:** Classics, comparative lit, French, German, Italian, Slavic, Spanish. **Health:** Audiology/speech pathology, nursing (RN). **History:** General. **Liberal arts:** Arts/sciences. **Math:** General. **Parks/recreation:** Exercise sciences. **Philosophy/religion:** Philosophy, religion. **Physical sciences:** Astronomy, chemistry, physics. **Psychology:** General. **Social sciences:** Anthropology, economics, international relations, political science, sociology. **Visual/performing arts:** Art, dramatic.

Most popular majors. Biology 6%, business/marketing 8%, engineering/engineering technologies 10%, English 6%, foreign language 6%, history 6%, liberal arts 7%, psychology 8%, social sciences 23%.

Computing on campus. Dormitories wired for high-speed internet access and linked to campus network. Commuter students can connect to campus network. Online course registration, online library, helpline, repair service, student web hosting, wireless network available.

Student life. Freshman orientation: Mandatory, $190 fee. Preregistration for classes offered. 2-day program held in July; August session held for international students. **Housing:** Guaranteed on-campus for freshmen. Coed dorms, apartments, fraternity/sorority housing available. 5 residential colleges available. **Activities:** Bands, choral groups, dance, drama, film society, international student organizations, literary magazine, music ensembles, Model UN, musical theater, opera, radio station, student government, student newspaper, symphony orchestra, TV station, community service group, Black Student Alliance, general clubs and religious organizations, political organizations, service fraternities and sororities, debating union.

Athletics. NCAA. **Intercollegiate:** Baseball M, basketball, cross-country, diving, field hockey W, football (tackle) M, golf, lacrosse, rowing (crew) W, soccer, softball W, swimming, tennis, track and field, volleyball W, wrestling M. **Intramural:** Basketball, field hockey W, football (non-tackle), golf, racquetball, rowing (crew), soccer, softball, tennis, volleyball, water polo. **Team name:** Cavaliers.

Student services. Alcohol/substance abuse counseling, career counseling, student employment services, financial aid counseling, health services, legal services, minority student services, on-campus daycare, personal counseling, placement for graduates, veterans' counselor, women's services. **Physically disabled:** Services for visually, speech, hearing impaired.

Contact. E-mail: undergradadmission@virginia.edu
Phone: (434) 982-3200 Fax: (434) 924-3587
Gregory Roberts, Dean of Admission, University of Virginia, Box 400160, Charlottesville, VA 22904-4160

University of Virginia's College at Wise

Wise, Virginia — **CB member**
www.uvawise.edu — **CB code: 5124**

- Public 4-year liberal arts college
- Commuter campus in small town
- 1,612 degree-seeking undergraduates: 11% part-time, 50% women, 10% African American, 1% Asian American, 2% Hispanic American
- 76% of applicants admitted
- SAT or ACT (ACT writing recommended) required
- 48% graduate within 6 years

General. Founded in 1954. Regionally accredited. **Degrees:** 308 bachelor's awarded. **Location:** 60 miles from Bristol. **Calendar:** Semester, limited summer session. **Full-time faculty:** 94 total; 72% have terminal degrees, 8% minority, 38% women. **Part-time faculty:** 72 total; 14% have terminal degrees, 3% minority, 58% women. **Class size:** 60% < 20, 35% 20-39, 3% 40-49, less than 1% 50-99, less than 1% >100. **Special facilities:** Observatory, scanning electron microscope, oral communication center, nursing assessment stations.

Freshman class profile. 1,293 applied, 977 admitted, 427 enrolled.

Mid 50% test scores			
SAT critical reading:	420-520	GPA 2.0-2.99:	52%
SAT math:	420-530	Rank in top quarter:	37%
SAT writing:	400-510	Rank in top tenth:	14%
ACT composite:	17-21	Return as sophomores:	65%
GPA 3.75 or higher:	18%	Out-of-state:	6%
GPA 3.50-3.74:	7%	Live on campus:	75%
GPA 3.0-3.49:	22%	Fraternities:	5%
		Sororities:	2%

Basis for selection. Applications reviewed on rolling basis. Emphasis given to academic courses and grades earned in those courses. Interview required for marginal applicants.

High school preparation. 18 units required. Required units include English 4, mathematics 3, social studies 1, history 1, science 2 (laboratory 2), foreign language 2 and academic electives 5. 1 American history, 1 world history required.

2008-2009 Annual costs. Tuition/fees: $6,439; $18,213 out-of-state. Room/board: $7,350. Books/supplies: $756. Personal expenses: $1,182.

2008-2009 Financial aid. Need-based: 349 full-time freshmen applied for aid; 272 were judged to have need; 272 of these received aid. Average

need met was 94%. Average scholarship/grant was $5,837; average loan $2,180. 65% of total undergraduate aid awarded as scholarships/grants, 35% as loans/jobs. **Non-need-based:** Awarded to 1,032 full-time undergraduates, including 391 freshmen. Scholarships awarded for academics, alumni affiliation, art, athletics, job skills, leadership, music/drama, religious affiliation, state residency.

Application procedures. Admission: Priority date 12/1; deadline 8/15 (postmark date). $25 fee, may be waived for applicants with need. Admission notification 8/20. Admission notification on a rolling basis beginning on or about 8/15. Must reply by May 1 or within 2 week(s) if notified thereafter. Early action notification on a rolling basis. **Financial aid:** Priority date 4/1; no closing date. FAFSA required. Applicants notified on a rolling basis starting 2/15; must reply within 4 week(s) of notification.

Academics. Special study options: Accelerated study, cooperative education, distance learning, double major, dual enrollment of high school students, honors, independent study, internships, liberal arts/career combination, student-designed major, study abroad, teacher certification program. **Credit/placement by examination:** AP, CLEP, IB, institutional tests. **Support services:** Learning center, reduced course load, remedial instruction, study skills assistance, tutoring, writing center.

Majors. Biology: General. **Business:** Accounting, business admin, management information systems. **Communications:** General. **Computer sciences:** Computer science. **Conservation:** Environmental studies. **Engineering technology:** Software. **Foreign languages:** General, French, Spanish. **Health:** Clinical lab science, nursing (RN). **History:** General. **Liberal arts:** Arts/sciences. **Math:** General. **Physical sciences:** Chemistry. **Protective services:** Criminal justice. **Psychology:** General. **Public administration:** General. **Social sciences:** Economics, political science, sociology. **Visual/performing arts:** Art, dramatic.

Most popular majors. Biology 6%, business/marketing 23%, history 10%, liberal arts 16%, psychology 8%, social sciences 14%.

Computing on campus. 300 workstations in dormitories, library, computer center. Dormitories wired for high-speed internet access and linked to campus network. Commuter students can connect to campus network. Helpline, repair service, student web hosting available.

Student life. Freshman orientation: Mandatory, $45 fee. Preregistration for classes offered. 2-day program held for students and parents. Dormitory space available (free for students, $35 per night for parents). **Housing:** Coed dorms, single-sex dorms, special housing for disabled, apartments available. $150 deposit, deadline 5/1. **Activities:** Concert band, choral groups, dance, drama, international student organizations, literary magazine, music ensembles, musical theater, radio station, student government, student newspaper, TV station, Young Republicans, Young Democrats, multicultural alliance, honors societies, professional organizations, student activities board, Baptist Student Union, Wesley Foundation.

Athletics. NAIA. **Intercollegiate:** Baseball M, basketball, cross-country, football (tackle) M, golf M, softball W, tennis, track and field, volleyball W. **Intramural:** Badminton, basketball, football (non-tackle), racquetball, soccer, softball, table tennis, tennis, volleyball, water polo. **Team name:** Cavaliers.

Student services. Alcohol/substance abuse counseling, chaplain/spiritual director, career counseling, services for economically disadvantaged, student employment services, financial aid counseling, health services, minority student services, personal counseling, placement for graduates. **Physically disabled:** Services for visually, speech, hearing impaired.

Contact. E-mail: admissions@uvawise.edu
Phone: (276) 328-0102 Toll-free number: (888) 282-9324
Fax: (276) 328-0251
Russell Necessary, Vice Chancellor of Enrollment Management, University of Virginia's College at Wise, 1 College Avenue, Wise, VA 24293-4412

Virginia Baptist College
Fredericksburg, Virginia
www.vbc.edu

- Private 4-year Bible college
- Large city
- 95 degree-seeking undergraduates

General. Regionally accredited. **Calendar:** Semester. **Full-time faculty:** 4 total. **Part-time faculty:** 18 total.

Freshman class profile. 12 enrolled.

2008-2009 Annual costs. Tuition/fees: $3,645.

Academics. Credit/placement by examination: CLEP.

Majors. Other: Ministry.

Contact. E-mail: office@vbc.edu
Phone: (540) 785-5440
Wayne Scott, Director of Admissions, Virginia Baptist College, 4105 Plank Road, Fredericksburg, VA 22407

Virginia Commonwealth University
Richmond, Virginia — **CB member**
www.vcu.edu — **CB code: 5570**

- Public 4-year university
- Commuter campus in small city
- 20,993 degree-seeking undergraduates: 13% part-time, 58% women, 20% African American, 11% Asian American, 4% Hispanic American, 1% Native American, 3% international
- 7,267 degree-seeking graduate students
- 58% of applicants admitted
- SAT or ACT (ACT writing optional), application essay required
- 49% graduate within 6 years

General. Founded in 1838. Regionally accredited. **Degrees:** 3,572 bachelor's awarded; master's, doctoral, first professional offered. **ROTC:** Army. **Location:** 100 miles from Washington, DC. **Calendar:** Semester, extensive summer session. **Full-time faculty:** 1,927 total; 19% minority, 42% women. **Part-time faculty:** 1,161 total; 14% minority, 51% women. **Class size:** 41% < 20, 41% 20-39, 5% 40-49, 6% 50-99, 6% >100. **Special facilities:** School of engineering clean rooms.

Freshman class profile. 17,489 applied, 10,193 admitted, 3,724 enrolled.

Mid 50% test scores		**Rank in top quarter:**	46%
SAT critical reading:	490-600	**Rank in top tenth:**	17%
SAT math:	480-590	**End year in good standing:**	78%
SAT writing:	480-580	**Return as sophomores:**	85%
ACT composite:	19-25	**Out-of-state:**	9%
GPA 3.75 or higher:	21%	**Live on campus:**	77%
GPA 3.50-3.74:	15%	**International:**	3%
GPA 3.0-3.49:	43%	**Fraternities:**	5%
GPA 2.0-2.99:	21%	**Sororities:**	5%

Basis for selection. Strength of the high school transcript, grades and test scores important. Some programs review additional material such as art portfolios or auditions. **Homeschooled:** Transcript of courses and grades required.

High school preparation. College-preparatory program recommended. 20 units required; 24 recommended. Required and recommended units include English 4, mathematics 3-4, social studies 1, history 2-3, science 3-4 (laboratory 1), foreign language 2-3, visual/performing arts 1 and academic electives 5-4.

2008-2009 Annual costs. Tuition/fees: $6,779; $19,556 out-of-state. Room/board: $7,914. Books/supplies: $2,400. Personal expenses: $3,260.

2007-2008 Financial aid. Need-based: 2,526 full-time freshmen applied for aid; 1,713 were judged to have need; 1,713 of these received aid. Average need met was 69%. Average scholarship/grant was $5,166; average loan $39,650. 41% of total undergraduate aid awarded as scholarships/grants, 59% as loans/jobs. **Non-need-based:** Awarded to 2,474 full-time undergraduates, including 1,030 freshmen. Scholarships awarded for academics, alumni affiliation, art, athletics, leadership, music/drama.

Application procedures. Admission: Priority date 2/1; no deadline. $40 fee, may be waived for applicants with need. Admission notification on a rolling basis beginning on or about 12/1. Must reply by May 1 or within 4 week(s) if notified thereafter. **Financial aid:** Priority date 3/1; no closing date. FAFSA required. Applicants notified on a rolling basis starting 4/1; must reply within 2 week(s) of notification.

Academics. Special study options: Accelerated study, combined bachelor's/graduate degree, cooperative education, distance learning, double major, dual enrollment of high school students, ESL, exchange student, honors, independent study, internships, liberal arts/career combination, student-designed major, study abroad, teacher certification program. **Credit/placement by examination:** AP, CLEP, IB, institutional tests. **Support services:** Learning center, reduced course load, study skills assistance, tutoring, writing center.

Honors college/program. Open to qualified entering freshmen and continuing students who demonstrate excellence after enrolling at VCU, and transfer students who have shown similar ability at other institutions. Entering students with combined SAT scores of at least 1910 who rank in the upper 15% of their graduating class and have a 3.5 or higher unweighted high school GPA or are the recipients of a VCU Presidential Scholarship are eligible. Number of freshmen admitted in 2008 is 143. To graduate with the distinction of University Honors, students must: complete the honors core curriculum, maintain a 3.5 cumulative GPA, present a dossier documenting how he/she has become a well-educated individual to the dean and the Honors council in the penultimate semester of the student's academic work.

Majors. **Area/ethnic studies:** African-American, women's. **Biology:** General, bioinformatics. **Business:** Accounting, business admin, managerial economics, marketing. **Communications:** Media studies. **Computer sciences:** General, information systems. **Conservation:** Environmental studies. **Education:** Art, health. **Engineering:** Biomedical, chemical, computer, electrical, mechanical. **Foreign languages:** General. **Health:** Clinical lab science, dental hygiene, nursing (RN), radiologic technology/medical imaging. **History:** General. **Interdisciplinary:** Biological/physical sciences. **Math:** General. **Parks/recreation:** General. **Philosophy/religion:** Philosophy, religion. **Physical sciences:** Chemistry, physics. **Protective services:** Forensics, law enforcement admin. **Psychology:** General. **Public administration:** Social work. **Social sciences:** Anthropology, political science, sociology, urban studies. **Visual/performing arts:** Art history/conservation, cinematography, crafts, dance, dramatic, fashion design, graphic design, illustration, interior design, music performance, painting, photography, sculpture. **Other:** Emergency management/homeland security, Financial technology, Interdisciplinary studies, International studies.

Most popular majors. Business/marketing 14%, health sciences 11%, psychology 10%, security/protective services 8%, social sciences 6%, visual/performing arts 14%.

Computing on campus. PC or laptop required. 2,000 workstations in dormitories, library, computer center, student center. Dormitories wired for high-speed internet access and linked to campus network. Commuter students can connect to campus network. Online course registration, online library, helpline, repair service, student web hosting, wireless network available.

Student life. **Freshman orientation:** Mandatory, $40 fee. Preregistration for classes offered. **Housing:** Coed dorms, special housing for disabled, apartments available. $250 fully refundable deposit. **Activities:** Bands, campus ministries, choral groups, dance, drama, film society, international student organizations, literary magazine, music ensembles, Model UN, musical theater, radio station, student government, student newspaper, symphony orchestra, TV station, Alternative Spring Break, Alpha Phi Omega Service Fraternity, Intervarsity Christian Fellowship, Muslim students association, Reformed University Fellowship, College Republicans, Young Democrats, Tiranga Indian National Dance, Filipino Americans Coming Together, Black Caucus.

Athletics. NAIA, NCAA. **Intercollegiate:** Baseball M, basketball, cross-country, field hockey W, golf M, soccer, tennis, track and field, volleyball W. **Intramural:** Badminton, basketball, football (non-tackle), racquetball, soccer, softball, table tennis, tennis, volleyball. **Team name:** Rams.

Student services. Adult student services, alcohol/substance abuse counseling, career counseling, student employment services, financial aid counseling, health services, on-campus daycare, personal counseling, placement for graduates, veterans' counselor. **Physically disabled:** Services for visually, speech, hearing impaired.

Contact. E-mail: ugrad@vcu.edu
Phone: (804) 828-1222 Toll-free number: (800) 841-3638
Fax: (804) 828-1899
Sybil Halloran, Director of Admissions, Virginia Commonwealth University, Box 842526, Richmond, VA 23284-2526

Virginia Intermont College

Bristol, Virginia
www.vic.edu **CB code: 5857**

- Private 4-year liberal arts college affiliated with Baptist faith
- Residential campus in small city
- 549 degree-seeking undergraduates: 6% African American, 1% Hispanic American, 1% international
- 64% of applicants admitted
- SAT or ACT (ACT writing recommended) required
- 42% graduate within 6 years; 7% enter graduate study

General. Founded in 1884. Regionally accredited. Evening and weekend college available for working adults; limited majors available. **Degrees:** 184 bachelor's, 1 associate awarded. **Location:** 144 miles from Roanoke, 114 miles from Knoxville, Tennessee. **Calendar:** Semester, limited summer session. **Full-time faculty:** 39 total; 80% have terminal degrees, 5% minority, 44% women. **Part-time faculty:** 42 total; 40% have terminal degrees, 2% minority, 57% women. **Class size:** 96% <20, 4% 20-39, less than 1% 40-49. **Special facilities:** 120-acre riding center with 2 indoor riding arenas.

Freshman class profile. 902 applied, 574 admitted, 126 enrolled.

Mid 50% test scores		**GPA 2.0-2.99:**	17%
SAT critical reading:	400-550	**Rank in top quarter:**	40%
SAT math:	400-540	**Rank in top tenth:**	20%
ACT composite:	17-24	**End year in good standing:**	71%
GPA 3.75 or higher:	23%	**Out-of-state:**	58%
GPA 3.50-3.74:	20%	**Live on campus:**	47%
GPA 3.0-3.49:	40%		

Basis for selection. School achievement record, SAT or ACT scores, school and community activities important. Essay, interview recommended for all; audition recommended for dance, equine studies, performing arts; portfolio recommended for art, photography. **Homeschooled:** Transcript of courses and grades, state high school equivalency certificate required. **Learning Disabled:** Students admitted conditionally, restricted to 12 credit hours in first semester.

High school preparation. College-preparatory program recommended. 16 units required. Required units include English 4, mathematics 2, social studies 2, science 2 (laboratory 1) and academic electives 5.

2008-2009 Annual costs. Tuition/fees: $22,260. Room/board: $6,820. Books/supplies: $1,000. Personal expenses: $2,190.

2007-2008 Financial aid. **Need-based:** 70 full-time freshmen applied for aid; 59 were judged to have need; 59 of these received aid. Average need met was 58%. Average scholarship/grant was $99,413; average loan $3,247. 50% of total undergraduate aid awarded as scholarships/grants, 50% as loans/jobs. **Non-need-based:** Awarded to 161 full-time undergraduates, including 53 freshmen. Scholarships awarded for art, athletics, music/drama, religious affiliation, state residency.

Application procedures. **Admission:** No deadline. $25 fee, may be waived for applicants with need. Admission notification on a rolling basis. **Financial aid:** Priority date 3/1, closing date 6/1. FAFSA required. Applicants notified on a rolling basis starting 2/15; must reply within 3 week(s) of notification.

Academics. **Special study options:** Accelerated study, cross-registration, distance learning, double major, dual enrollment of high school students, honors, independent study, internships, teacher certification program. **Credit/placement by examination:** AP, CLEP, IB, institutional tests. No maximums for prior work or credit by examination; no cumulative restrictions imposed upon hours earned toward elective credits. Students must complete at least one half of major and take minimum of 25% of classes at school to meet minimum residency requirement. **Support services:** Learning center, reduced course load, study skills assistance, tutoring, writing center.

Majors. **Agriculture:** Equestrian studies. **Biology:** General. **Business:** Business admin, international, marketing. **Computer sciences:** General. **Conservation:** Environmental studies. **Education:** General, art, biology, elementary, English, physical, secondary, social studies, special. **Health:** Premedicine, preveterinary. **History:** General. **Legal studies:** General, paralegal, prelaw. **Liberal arts:** Arts/sciences. **Parks/recreation:** Health/fitness, sports admin. **Philosophy/religion:** Religion. **Protective services:** Law enforcement admin. **Psychology:** General. **Public administration:** General, social work. **Social sciences:** Political science. **Visual/performing arts:** Art, dance, dramatic, photography.

Most popular majors. Agriculture 13%, business/marketing 12%, education 40%, parks/recreation 7%, public administration/social services 6%, visual/performing arts 9%.

Computing on campus. 100 workstations in dormitories, library, computer center. Dormitories wired for high-speed internet access and linked to campus network. Commuter students can connect to campus network. Online course registration, online library, helpline, wireless network available.

Student life. **Freshman orientation:** Mandatory. Preregistration for classes offered. **Policies:** Alcohol and tobacco use prohibited on campus. No open flame items or cooking appliances other than microwave ovens. (Juniors and seniors may live off campus, but all other students under 21 years of age not living with parents must live on campus.). **Housing:** Guaranteed on-campus for all undergraduates. Coed dorms, single-sex dorms, apartments, wellness housing available. $200 partly refundable deposit. **Activities:** Campus ministries, choral groups, dance, drama, international student organizations, music ensembles, musical theater, student government, Christian student union, Cardinal Key, social work action group, Fellowship of Christian Athletes, Alpha Phi Omega.

Athletics. NAIA. **Intercollegiate:** Baseball M, basketball, cheerleading M, equestrian, golf M, soccer, softball W, volleyball W. **Intramural:** Basketball, football (non-tackle), golf, softball, table tennis, volleyball. **Team name:** Cobras.

Student services. Adult student services, alcohol/substance abuse counseling, chaplain/spiritual director, career counseling, student employment services, financial aid counseling, health services, minority student services, personal counseling, placement for graduates. **Physically disabled:** Services for visually, hearing impaired.

Contact. E-mail: viadmit@vic.edu
Phone: (276) 466-7856 Toll-free number: (800) 451-1842
Fax: (276) 466-7855
Tony England, Vice President of Enrollment, Virginia Intermont College, 1013 Moore Street, Bristol, VA 24201

Virginia Military Institute

Lexington, Virginia
www.vmi.edu
CB member
CB code: 5858

- Public 4-year liberal arts and military college
- Residential campus in small town
- 1,428 degree-seeking undergraduates: 8% women, 6% African American, 4% Asian American, 4% Hispanic American, 2% international
- 54% of applicants admitted
- SAT or ACT (ACT writing optional) required
- 68% graduate within 6 years

General. Founded in 1839. Regionally accredited. Mandatory ROTC classes and optional commissioning in the Army, Air Force, Navy, or Marines. **Degrees:** 280 bachelor's awarded. **ROTC:** Army, Naval, Air Force. **Location:** 55 miles from Roanoke, 140 miles from Richmond. **Calendar:** Semester, limited summer session. **Full-time faculty:** 130 total; 90% have terminal degrees, 6% minority, 18% women. **Part-time faculty:** 42 total; 38% have terminal degrees, 10% minority, 33% women. **Class size:** 73% < 20, 27% 20-39. **Special facilities:** Historical museums, research library, observatory, particle accelerator.

Freshman class profile. 1,600 applied, 858 admitted, 412 enrolled.

Mid 50% test scores			
SAT critical reading:	510-620	GPA 2.0-2.99:	22%
SAT math:	530-620	Rank in top quarter:	40%
SAT writing:	480-590	Rank in top tenth:	10%
ACT composite:	21-26	Return as sophomores:	87%
GPA 3.75 or higher:	18%	Out-of-state:	41%
GPA 3.50-3.74:	18%	Live on campus:	100%
GPA 3.0-3.49:	42%	International:	2%

Basis for selection. GED not accepted. Admissions based on secondary school record, class rank, standardized test scores, character, and personal qualities. Interview, extracurricular activities, state residency, minority status, and volunteer work also important. **Homeschooled:** Require transcript with list of texts used or group affiliation.

High school preparation. College-preparatory program required. Required and recommended units include English 4, mathematics 3-4, science 3 (laboratory 3) and foreign language 3-4.

2008-2009 Annual costs. Tuition/fees: $10,556; $27,454 out-of-state. Room/board: $6,444. Books/supplies: $775. Personal expenses: $1,500.

2007-2008 Financial aid. Need-based: 283 full-time freshmen applied for aid; 195 were judged to have need; 195 of these received aid. Average need met was 91%. Average scholarship/grant was $8,398; average loan $3,358. 80% of total undergraduate aid awarded as scholarships/grants, 20% as loans/jobs. **Non-need-based:** Awarded to 469 full-time undergraduates, including 159 freshmen. Scholarships awarded for academics, athletics, leadership, music/drama, ROTC.

Application procedures. Admission: Closing date 2/15 (postmark date). $35 fee, may be waived for applicants with need. Admission notification on a rolling basis beginning on or about 1/1. Must reply by 5/1. Must reply by May 1 or within 2 week(s) if notified thereafter. **Financial aid:** Priority date 3/1; no closing date. FAFSA, institutional form required. Applicants notified on a rolling basis starting 3/15; must reply by 5/1.

Academics. Special study options: Accelerated study, double major, exchange student, honors, independent study, internships, study abroad, teacher certification program. Summer Transition program: Optional for incoming freshmen. **Credit/placement by examination:** AP, CLEP, IB, institutional tests. No policy, but it is unlikely any student would receive more than 36 hours credit. **Support services:** Learning center, pre-admission summer program, study skills assistance, tutoring, writing center.

Majors. Biology: General. **Computer sciences:** Computer science. **Engineering:** Civil, electrical, mechanical. **Foreign languages:** General. **History:** General. **Interdisciplinary:** Global studies. **Math:** General. **Physical sciences:** Chemistry, physics. **Psychology:** General. **Social sciences:** Economics.

Most popular majors. Biology 6%, engineering/engineering technologies 27%, history 20%, psychology 7%, social sciences 31%.

Computing on campus. PC or laptop required. 200 workstations in library, computer center. Dormitories wired for high-speed internet access and linked to campus network. Online course registration, online library, helpline, repair service, wireless network available.

Student life. Freshman orientation: Mandatory. 8 days before beginning of fall classes. Optional month-long summer orientation program coincides with summer academic session, and participants can complete 1 freshman course. **Policies:** Student-run honor system integral part of institution. **Housing:** Guaranteed on-campus for all undergraduates. Barracks house 3-5 students per room. **Activities:** Bands, choral groups, drama, literary magazine, music ensembles, musical theater, student government, student newspaper, more than 50 clubs and student organizations available.

Athletics. NCAA. **Intercollegiate:** Baseball M, basketball M, cross-country, diving M, football (tackle) M, golf M, lacrosse M, rifle M, soccer, swimming, tennis M, track and field, wrestling M. **Intramural:** Basketball, football (non-tackle), soccer, softball. **Team name:** Keydets.

Student services. Alcohol/substance abuse counseling, chaplain/spiritual director, career counseling, student employment services, financial aid counseling, health services, personal counseling, placement for graduates.

Contact. E-mail: admissions@vmi.edu
Phone: (540) 464-7211 Toll-free number: (800) 767-4207
Fax: (540) 464-7746
Col. Vernon Beitzel, Director of Admissions, Virginia Military Institute, VMI Office of Admissions, Lexington, VA 24450-9967

Virginia Polytechnic Institute and State University

Blacksburg, Virginia
www.vt.edu
CB member
CB code: 5859

- Public 4-year university
- Residential campus in large town
- 23,447 degree-seeking undergraduates: 2% part-time, 43% women, 4% African American, 8% Asian American, 3% Hispanic American, 2% international
- 7,160 degree-seeking graduate students
- 65% of applicants admitted
- SAT or ACT with writing required
- 79% graduate within 6 years

General. Founded in 1872. Regionally accredited. Option of enrolling as member of cadet corps. **Degrees:** 5,049 bachelor's, 33 associate awarded; master's, doctoral, first professional offered. **ROTC:** Army, Naval, Air Force. **Location:** 38 miles from Roanoke. **Calendar:** Semester, limited summer session. **Full-time faculty:** 1,369 total; 90% have terminal degrees, 15% minority, 31% women. **Part-time faculty:** 229 total; 8% minority, 42% women. **Class size:** 24% < 20, 43% 20-39, 11% 40-49, 13% 50-99, 9% >100. **Special facilities:** Natural history, geology and art museums, observatory, wind tunnel, Black cultural center, digital music center, robotics laboratory, multimedia laboratory, media center, women's center, math emporium, advanced communications/information technology center, teaching forest.

Freshman class profile. 20,615 applied, 13,485 admitted, 5,460 enrolled.

Mid 50% test scores			
SAT critical reading:	540-630	Rank in top quarter:	81%
SAT math:	570-670	Rank in top tenth:	42%
SAT writing:	530-630	Return as sophomores:	91%
GPA 3.75 or higher:	54%	Out-of-state:	32%
GPA 3.50-3.74:	28%	Live on campus:	99%
GPA 3.0-3.49:	16%	International:	2%
GPA 2.0-2.99:	2%	Fraternities:	9%
		Sororities:	22%

Basis for selection. High school course work, grades, test scores most important. Prospective students encouraged to pursue rigorous preparatory course of study through senior year. Students from other than accredited schools must take, in addition to SAT (including mandatory Writing component) or ACT (including Writing component), SAT Subject Tests in Math (Level Ic or IIc) and second area of study to be chosen by applicant. SAT Subject Tests may not be required if student has dual-enrollment or AP credit. Audition required for music. **Homeschooled:** Transcript of courses and grades required. Must submit standardized test scores; statement describing homeschool structure and mission recommended but not required.

High school preparation. 18 units required. Required and recommended units include English 4, mathematics 3-4, social studies 1, history 1, science 2-3 (laboratory 2), foreign language 3 and academic electives 4. Preference given to applicants with mathematics beyond Algebra II. 4 mathematics required for general engineering, biochemistry, chemistry, computer science, math, physics and statistics. 3 science including physics required for engineering and recommended for all science-related majors.

2008-2009 Annual costs. Tuition/fees: $8,198; $20,655 out-of-state. Room/board: $5,476. Books/supplies: $1,080. Personal expenses: $1,500.

2007-2008 Financial aid. **Need-based:** 3,687 full-time freshmen applied for aid; 2,211 were judged to have need; 1,819 of these received aid. Average need met was 64%. Average scholarship/grant was $6,924; average loan $3,917. 54% of total undergraduate aid awarded as scholarships/grants, 46% as loans/jobs. **Non-need-based:** Awarded to 3,706 full-time undergraduates, including 1,145 freshmen. Scholarships awarded for art, athletics, ROTC.

Application procedures. **Admission:** Closing date 1/15 (postmark date). $50 fee, may be waived for applicants with need. Admission notification 4/1. Must reply by 5/1. $400 matriculation deposit required. **Financial aid:** Priority date 3/11; no closing date. FAFSA required. Applicants notified on a rolling basis starting 3/30; must reply by 5/1 or within 4 week(s) of notification.

Academics. **Special study options:** Accelerated study, combined bachelor's/graduate degree, cooperative education, distance learning, double major, dual enrollment of high school students, ESL, honors, independent study, internships, study abroad, teacher certification program, Washington semester. **Credit/placement by examination:** AP, CLEP, IB, institutional tests. 12 credit hours maximum toward associate degree, 12 toward bachelor's. **Support services:** Learning center, pre-admission summer program, study skills assistance, tutoring, writing center.

Majors. **Agriculture:** General, agronomy, animal sciences, dairy, economics, food science, horticultural science. **Architecture:** Architecture, landscape. **Biology:** General, biochemistry. **Business:** Accounting, business admin, construction management, finance, hospitality admin, management science, managerial economics, marketing. **Communications:** General. **Computer sciences:** General. **Conservation:** Environmental science, environmental studies, forestry. **Education:** Secondary. **Engineering:** Aerospace, agricultural, chemical, civil, computer, construction, electrical, industrial, materials, mechanical, mechanics, mining. **Family/consumer sciences:** Business, family studies, food/nutrition. **Foreign languages:** General. **History:** General. **Interdisciplinary:** Science/society. **Liberal arts:** Arts/sciences. **Math:** General, statistics. **Philosophy/religion:** Philosophy. **Physical sciences:** Chemistry, geology, physics. **Psychology:** General. **Public administration:** Policy analysis. **Social sciences:** Economics, geography, international relations, political science, sociology. **Visual/performing arts:** Art, dramatic, industrial design, interior design.

Most popular majors. Biology 7%, business/marketing 20%, engineering/engineering technologies 21%, family/consumer sciences 8%, social sciences 8%.

Computing on campus. PC or laptop required. 1,000 workstations in dormitories, library, computer center. Dormitories wired for high-speed internet access and linked to campus network. Commuter students can connect to campus network. Online course registration, online library, helpline, repair service, student web hosting, wireless network available.

Student life. **Freshman orientation:** Available, $140 fee. Preregistration for classes offered. Day and a half long program held in July. **Policies:** Freshmen required to live on campus, unless living with parents or close relatives, married, veteran, or at least 21 years old. Honor system in force. **Housing:** Guaranteed on-campus for freshmen. Coed dorms, single-sex dorms, special housing for disabled, fraternity/sorority housing, wellness housing available. Cadets live in cadet residence halls. Foreign language hall and academic success hall available. **Activities:** Bands, choral groups, dance, drama, literary magazine, music ensembles, musical theater, radio station, student government, student newspaper, 400 clubs and organizations available.

Athletics. NCAA. **Intercollegiate:** Baseball M, basketball, cheerleading, cross-country, diving, football (tackle) M, golf M, lacrosse W, soccer, softball W, swimming, tennis, track and field, volleyball W, wrestling M. **Intramural:** Basketball, bowling, football (non-tackle), golf, racquetball, soccer, softball, squash, swimming, table tennis, tennis, volleyball, water polo. **Team name:** Hokies.

Student services. Alcohol/substance abuse counseling, chaplain/spiritual director, career counseling, student employment services, financial aid counseling, health services, legal services, minority student services, personal counseling, placement for graduates, veterans' counselor, women's services. **Physically disabled:** Services for visually, hearing impaired.

Contact. E-mail: vtadmiss@vt.edu
Phone: (540) 231-6267 Fax: (540) 231-3242
Mildred Johnson, Director of Undergraduate Admissions, Virginia Polytechnic Institute and State University, 201 Burruss Hall, Blacksburg, VA 24061-0202

Virginia State University

Petersburg, Virginia — **CB member**
www.vsu.edu — **CB code: 5860**

- Public 4-year university
- Residential campus in large town
- 4,420 degree-seeking undergraduates: 7% part-time, 61% women, 94% African American
- 409 degree-seeking graduate students
- 65% of applicants admitted
- SAT or ACT (ACT writing optional) required
- 43% graduate within 6 years

General. Founded in 1882. Regionally accredited. **Degrees:** 599 bachelor's, 14 associate awarded; master's, doctoral offered. **ROTC:** Army. **Location:** 25 miles from Richmond. **Calendar:** Semester, limited summer session. **Full-time faculty:** 254 total; 42% women. **Part-time faculty:** 105 total; 76% minority, 45% women.

Freshman class profile. 6,823 applied, 4,403 admitted, 1,324 enrolled.

Mid 50% test scores		**GPA 2.0-2.99:**	66%
SAT critical reading:	400-470	**Rank in top quarter:**	23%
SAT math:	390-470	**Rank in top tenth:**	7%
SAT writing:	380-460	**Return as sophomores:**	68%
GPA 3.75 or higher:	4%	**Out-of-state:**	41%
GPA 3.50-3.74:	6%	**Live on campus:**	89%
GPA 3.0-3.49:	24%		

Basis for selection. School achievement record most important; recommendation required. Essay recommended for all; audition required for music; portfolio recommended for art.

High school preparation. 11 units required. Required and recommended units include English 4, mathematics 3, social studies 2, science 2 (laboratory 1) and foreign language 2. Mathematics requirement must include algebra I.

2008-2009 Annual costs. Tuition/fees: $5,903; $14,018 out-of-state. Out of state students pay an additional fee. Room/board: $7,710. Books/supplies: $900. Personal expenses: $675.

2007-2008 Financial aid. **Non-need-based:** Scholarships awarded for academics, alumni affiliation, art, athletics, job skills, leadership, music/drama, religious affiliation, ROTC. **Additional information:** Strongly recommend that students apply for scholarship assistance through federal, state, local and private agencies.

Application procedures. **Admission:** Priority date 3/31; deadline 5/1 (postmark date). $25 fee, may be waived for applicants with need. Admission notification on a rolling basis. Must reply by May 1 or within 2 week(s) if notified thereafter. **Financial aid:** Priority date 3/31, closing date 5/1. FAFSA, institutional form required. Applicants notified on a rolling basis starting 5/1; must reply within 2 week(s) of notification.

Academics. **Special study options:** Cooperative education, double major, dual enrollment of high school students, exchange student, honors, independent study, internships, teacher certification program. **Credit/placement by examination:** AP, CLEP, institutional tests. 12 credit hours maximum toward bachelor's degree. **Support services:** Study skills assistance, tutoring, writing center.

Majors. **Agriculture:** General. **Biology:** General. **Business:** Accounting, business admin, hospitality admin, managerial economics, marketing. **Communications:** Media studies. **Computer sciences:** Computer science, information technology. **Education:** Business, physical, trade/industrial. **Engineering:** Computer, manufacturing. **Engineering technology:** General, electrical, mechanical. **Family/consumer sciences:** Communication. **History:** General. **Liberal arts:** Arts/sciences. **Math:** General. **Physical sciences:** Chemistry, physics. **Protective services:** Criminal justice. **Psychology:** General. **Public administration:** General, social work. **Social sciences:** Political science, sociology. **Visual/performing arts:** General, music performance.

Most popular majors. Business/marketing 22%, communications/journalism 9%, education 9%, psychology 8%, security/protective services 11%, social sciences 6%.

Computing on campus. 750 workstations in dormitories, library, student center. Dormitories wired for high-speed internet access and linked to campus network. Commuter students can connect to campus network. Online course registration, online library, helpline, repair service available.

Student life. Freshman orientation: Mandatory, $75 fee. Preregistration for classes offered. Two-day orientation held at various times in the summer. **Housing:** Guaranteed on-campus for freshmen. Coed dorms, single-sex dorms, apartments, wellness housing available. $150 deposit. **Activities:** Bands, campus ministries, choral groups, dance, drama, literary magazine, music ensembles, radio station, student government, student newspaper, TV station, NAACP, Black Students Against Drugs, Muslim student organization, peer mediators, Betterment of Brothers and Sisters, Caribbean students association, Institute for Leadership Development.

Athletics. NCAA. **Intercollegiate:** Baseball M, basketball, bowling W, cheerleading, cross-country, football (tackle) M, golf, softball W, tennis, track and field, volleyball W. **Intramural:** Basketball, football (tackle) M, swimming, table tennis, tennis, track and field, volleyball W. **Team name:** Trojans.

Student services. Alcohol/substance abuse counseling, chaplain/spiritual director, career counseling, services for economically disadvantaged, student employment services, financial aid counseling, health services, personal counseling, placement for graduates, veterans' counselor. **Physically disabled:** Services for visually, hearing impaired.

Contact. E-mail: admiss@vsu.edu
Phone: (804) 524-5902 Toll-free number: (800) 871-7611
Fax: (804) 524-5055
Irene Logan, Director of Admissions, Virginia State University, One Hayden Drive, Petersburg, VA 23806

Virginia Union University
Richmond, Virginia
www.vuu.edu
CB member
CB code: 5862

- Private 4-year university and liberal arts college affiliated with Baptist faith
- Residential campus in small city
- 1,073 degree-seeking undergraduates: 3% part-time, 52% women
- 378 degree-seeking graduate students
- 70% of applicants admitted
- SAT or ACT (ACT writing recommended) required

General. Founded in 1865. Regionally accredited. **Degrees:** 187 bachelor's awarded; master's, doctoral, first professional offered. **ROTC:** Army. **Location:** 90 miles from Norfolk, 100 miles from Washington, DC. **Calendar:** Semester, limited summer session. **Full-time faculty:** 64 total. **Part-time faculty:** 34 total. **Special facilities:** Police academy, learning resource center.

Freshman class profile. 2,674 applied, 1,872 admitted, 346 enrolled.

Mid 50% test scores		GPA 2.0-2.99:	70%
SAT critical reading:	350-420	Rank in top quarter:	12%
SAT math:	320-410	Rank in top tenth:	4%
ACT composite:	13-17	End year in good standing:	72%
GPA 3.75 or higher:	2%	Return as sophomores:	52%
GPA 3.50-3.74:	2%	Out-of-state:	46%
GPA 3.0-3.49:	8%	Live on campus:	79%

Basis for selection. Secondary school record, test scores, extracurricular activities most important. Essay, interview, and talent or ability also important. Essay recommended for all. Interview recommended for academically weak. Audition required for band, choir, music, university players.

High school preparation. 16 units required. Required units include English 4, mathematics 3, social studies 2, science 2, foreign language 2 and academic electives 3.

2009-2010 Annual costs. Tuition/fees: $13,662. Room/board: $6,328. Books/supplies: $1,080. Personal expenses: $1,750.

2008-2009 Financial aid. Non-need-based: Scholarships awarded for academics, athletics, ROTC, state residency.

Application procedures. Admission: Priority date 6/30; no deadline. $25 fee, may be waived for applicants with need. Admission notification on a rolling basis. **Financial aid:** Priority date 4/27; no closing date. FAFSA required. Applicants notified on a rolling basis starting 5/1; must reply within 2 week(s) of notification.

Academics. Special study options: Cooperative education, honors, independent study, internships, liberal arts/career combination, teacher certification program, weekend college. **Credit/placement by examination:** AP, CLEP, IB, institutional tests. 18 credit hours maximum toward bachelor's degree. **Support services:** Learning center, reduced course load, remedial instruction, tutoring, writing center.

Majors. Biology: General. **Business:** Accounting, business admin, finance, management information systems, sales/distribution. **Communications:** Journalism. **Computer sciences:** General. **Education:** Multi-level teacher. **History:** General. **Interdisciplinary:** Natural sciences. **Math:** General. **Philosophy/religion:** Religion. **Physical sciences:** Chemistry. **Psychology:** General. **Public administration:** Social work. **Social sciences:** Political science, sociology. **Visual/performing arts:** Art, dramatic, music theory/composition, piano/organ, voice/opera.

Most popular majors. Business/marketing 14%, education 9%, psychology 8%, social sciences 11%, theological studies 42%.

Computing on campus. PC or laptop required. 148 workstations in library, computer center. Dormitories linked to campus network. Online course registration, wireless network available.

Student life. Freshman orientation: Mandatory. Preregistration for classes offered. **Housing:** Coed dorms, single-sex dorms available. $250 deposit, deadline 7/1. **Activities:** Bands, campus ministries, choral groups, dance, drama, music ensembles, musical theater, opera, student government, student newspaper, social work club, sociology club, student education association, Ministers Alliance.

Athletics. NCAA. **Intercollegiate:** Basketball, bowling W, cross-country, football (tackle) M, golf, softball W, tennis, track and field, volleyball W. **Intramural:** Basketball, football (non-tackle) M, softball, table tennis. **Team name:** Panthers.

Student services. Career counseling, student employment services, health services, personal counseling, placement for graduates.

Contact. E-mail: admissions@vuu.edu
Phone: (804) 342-3570 Toll-free number: (800) 368-3227
Fax: (804) 342-3511
Delores Scott, Vice President of Student Affairs, Virginia Union University, 1500 North Lombardy Street, Richmond, VA 23220

Virginia University of Lynchburg
Lynchburg, Virginia
www.vul.edu

- Private 4-year liberal arts and seminary college
- Commuter campus in small city
- 129 degree-seeking undergraduates

General. Regionally accredited. **Degrees:** 26 bachelor's, 7 associate awarded; master's, doctoral, first professional offered. **Calendar:** Semester, limited summer session. **Full-time faculty:** 10 total; 100% have terminal degrees, 100% minority, 40% women. **Part-time faculty:** 72 total; 49% have terminal degrees, 90% minority, 42% women.

Basis for selection. Open admission. **Homeschooled:** Transcript of courses and grades, state high school equivalency certificate required.

2008-2009 Annual costs. Tuition/fees: $5,300. Books/supplies: $500.

Application procedures. Admission: No deadline. $25 fee, may be waived for applicants with need. Application must be submitted on paper. Admission notification on a rolling basis.

Academics. Special study options: Distance learning, external degree. **Credit/placement by examination:** AP, CLEP, IB, institutional tests. **Support services:** Learning center, remedial instruction, tutoring, writing center.

Majors. Business: Business admin, management science. **Philosophy/religion:** Religion. **Social sciences:** Sociology.

Computing on campus. 10 workstations in library, computer center. Dormitories wired for high-speed internet access and linked to campus network. Commuter students can connect to campus network. Online library, helpline, wireless network available.

Student life. **Freshman orientation:** Mandatory. Preregistration for classes offered. **Housing:** Coed dorms available. **Activities:** Campus ministries, choral groups, student government.

Student services. Adult student services, career counseling, financial aid counseling, veterans' counselor.

Contact. E-mail: cglass@vul.edu
Phone: (434) 528-5276 Fax: (434) 528-4257
Cheryl Glass, Director of Admissions, Virginia University of Lynchburg, 2058 Garfield Avenue, Lynchburg, VA 24501-6417

Virginia Wesleyan College

Norfolk, Virginia — **CB member**
www.vwc.edu — **CB code: 5867**

- Private 4-year liberal arts college affiliated with United Methodist Church
- Residential campus in large city
- 1,326 degree-seeking undergraduates: 13% part-time, 62% women, 19% African American, 2% Asian American, 4% Hispanic American, 1% international
- 77% of applicants admitted
- SAT or ACT (ACT writing optional), application essay required
- 44% graduate within 6 years; 25% enter graduate study

General. Founded in 1961. Regionally accredited. **Degrees:** 279 bachelor's awarded. **ROTC:** Army. **Location:** 8 miles from downtown. **Calendar:** 4-1-4, limited summer session. **Full-time faculty:** 85 total; 88% have terminal degrees, 9% minority, 41% women. **Part-time faculty:** 64 total; 2% have terminal degrees, 9% minority, 58% women. **Class size:** 76% < 20, 24% 20-39. **Special facilities:** 46 foot research vessel, center for sacred music, greenhouse, center for study of religious freedom, 142-acre woodlands, 36 foot rock climbing wall.

Freshman class profile. 1,447 applied, 1,114 admitted, 329 enrolled.

Mid 50% test scores		**GPA 2.0-2.99:**	43%
SAT critical reading:	450-550	**Rank in top quarter:**	36%
SAT math:	450-550	**Rank in top tenth:**	14%
ACT composite:	17-25	**End year in good standing:**	83%
GPA 3.75 or higher:	12%	**Return as sophomores:**	65%
GPA 3.50-3.74:	14%	**Out-of-state:**	28%
GPA 3.0-3.49:	29%	**Live on campus:**	79%

Basis for selection. Above average grades in solid college-preparatory curriculum, SAT scores, campus interview, personal statement, extracurricular activities important. **Homeschooled:** Transcript of courses and grades required. **Learning Disabled:** Interview with Student Disabilities Coordinator, Appropriate Documentation dated within past 3-5 years.

High school preparation. College-preparatory program recommended. 12 units required; 16 recommended. Required and recommended units include English 4, mathematics 3, history 1, science 2 (laboratory 2), foreign language 2, computer science 1 and academic electives 4.

2008-2009 Annual costs. Tuition/fees: $26,438. Room/board: $7,100. Books/supplies: $900. Personal expenses: $1,800.

2007-2008 Financial aid. **Need-based:** 327 full-time freshmen applied for aid; 286 were judged to have need; 286 of these received aid. Average need met was 77%. Average scholarship/grant was $4,005; average loan $3,950. 29% of total undergraduate aid awarded as scholarships/grants, 71% as loans/jobs. **Non-need-based:** Awarded to 1,180 full-time undergraduates, including 357 freshmen. Scholarships awarded for academics, alumni affiliation, leadership, religious affiliation, ROTC, state residency.

Application procedures. **Admission:** Priority date 3/1; no deadline. $40 fee, may be waived for applicants with need. Admission notification on a rolling basis beginning on or about 9/15. Must reply by May 1 or within 2 week(s) if notified thereafter. **Financial aid:** Priority date 3/1; no closing date. FAFSA required. Applicants notified on a rolling basis starting 2/15; must reply by 5/1 or within 2 week(s) of notification.

Academics. **Special study options:** Accelerated study, cross-registration, double major, honors, independent study, internships, liberal arts/career combination, student-designed major, study abroad, teacher certification program. Externships; 4-year competitive honors program integrates liberal arts and experiential learning. **Credit/placement by examination:** AP, CLEP, IB, institutional tests. 30 credit hours maximum toward bachelor's degree. **Support services:** Learning center, reduced course load, remedial instruction, study skills assistance, tutoring, writing center.

Majors. **Area/ethnic studies:** Women's. **Biology:** General. **Business:** Business admin. **Communications:** General. **Computer sciences:** Computer science. **Conservation:** Environmental studies. **Education:** Art. **Foreign languages:** General, French, German, Spanish. **Health:** Predental, premedicine, prepharmacy, preveterinary. **History:** General. **Interdisciplinary:** Global studies, math/computer science, natural sciences. **Liberal arts:** Arts/sciences, humanities. **Math:** General. **Parks/recreation:** General. **Philosophy/religion:** Philosophy, religion. **Physical sciences:** Chemistry. **Protective services:** Criminal justice. **Psychology:** General. **Public administration:** Human services. **Social sciences:** General, international relations, political science, sociology. **Visual/performing arts:** Art, dramatic, theater history.

Most popular majors. Business/marketing 19%, communications/journalism 6%, education 6%, interdisciplinary studies 6%, parks/recreation 9%, security/protective services 11%, social sciences 11%.

Computing on campus. 99 workstations in library, computer center, student center. Dormitories wired for high-speed internet access and linked to campus network. Online course registration, online library, helpline, repair service, student web hosting, wireless network available.

Student life. **Freshman orientation:** Mandatory, $225 fee. Preregistration for classes offered. 2-day event scheduled twice in July; multi-day academic-related orientation in August. **Housing:** Guaranteed on-campus for freshmen. Coed dorms, single-sex dorms, special housing for disabled, apartments, fraternity/sorority housing, wellness housing available. $300 nonrefundable deposit, deadline 5/1. Pets allowed in dorm rooms. **Activities:** Campus ministries, choral groups, dance, drama, international student organizations, literary magazine, Model UN, musical theater, radio station, student government, student newspaper, Political Science Association, Habitat for Humanity, Black student Union, Holy Fire, Honors & Scholars, Campus Kaleidoscope, SALSA, Activities Council.

Athletics. NCAA. **Intercollegiate:** Baseball M, basketball, cheerleading M, cross-country, field hockey W, golf M, lacrosse, soccer, softball W, tennis, track and field, volleyball W. **Intramural:** Basketball, field hockey W, football (non-tackle), racquetball, soccer, table tennis, volleyball. **Team name:** Marlins.

Student services. Adult student services, alcohol/substance abuse counseling, chaplain/spiritual director, career counseling, student employment services, financial aid counseling, health services, minority student services, personal counseling, veterans' counselor, women's services. **Physically disabled:** Services for visually, hearing impaired.

Contact. E-mail: admissions@vwc.edu
Phone: (757) 455-3208 Toll-free number: (800) 737-8684
Fax: (757) 461-5238
Richard Hinshaw, Vice President for Enrollment Management and Dean of Admissions, Virginia Wesleyan College, 1584 Wesleyan Drive, Norfolk, VA 23502-5599

Washington and Lee University

Lexington, Virginia — **CB member**
www.wlu.edu — **CB code: 5887**

- Private 4-year university and liberal arts college
- Residential campus in small town
- 1,749 degree-seeking undergraduates: 50% women, 4% African American, 3% Asian American, 2% Hispanic American, 4% international
- 403 graduate students
- 17% of applicants admitted
- SAT or ACT with writing, SAT Subject Tests, application essay required
- 90% graduate within 6 years; 27% enter graduate study

General. Founded in 1749. Regionally accredited. Front campus and Lee Chapel designated as National Historic Landmark. **Degrees:** 449 bachelor's awarded; master's, first professional offered. **ROTC:** Army. **Location:** 50 miles from Roanoke, 60 miles from Charlottesville. **Calendar:** 4-4-2. **Full-time faculty:** 204 total; 97% have terminal degrees, 9% minority, 35% women. **Part-time faculty:** 101 total; 12% minority, 40% women. **Class size:** 72% < 20, 28% 20-39, less than 1% 40-49, less than 1% 50-99. **Special facilities:** Asian export pottery center, Asian art pavilion, performing arts center, university special collections, multimedia center, archaeology museum.

Freshman class profile. 6,386 applied, 1,074 admitted, 454 enrolled.

Mid 50% test scores		End year in good standing:	99%
SAT critical reading:	660-740	Return as sophomores:	94%
SAT math:	660-740	Out-of-state:	85%
SAT writing:	660-730	Live on campus:	100%
ACT composite:	28-31	International:	4%
Rank in top quarter:	99%	Fraternities:	82%
Rank in top tenth:	84%	Sororities:	78%

Basis for selection. School achievement record most important, followed closely by test scores, school and community activities, recommendations and personal qualities. Special consideration given to children of alumni and applicants from minorities and low-income families. 2 unrelated SAT Subject Tests required. Interview recommended. **Homeschooled:** Recommend taking 5 SAT Subject Tests in unrelated fields, interview with admissions officer. Require documentation of reading lists and syllabi.

High school preparation. 16 units required. Required and recommended units include English 4, mathematics 3-4, social studies 1, history 1-2, science 1-3 (laboratory 1), foreign language 3 and academic electives 4.

2008-2009 Annual costs. Tuition/fees: $37,412. Room/board: $9,400. Books/supplies: $1,650. Personal expenses: $1,778.

2008-2009 Financial aid. Need-based: 244 full-time freshmen applied for aid; 177 were judged to have need; 177 of these received aid. Average need met was 99%. Average scholarship/grant was $27,989; average loan $3,101. 89% of total undergraduate aid awarded as scholarships/grants, 11% as loans/jobs. **Non-need-based:** Awarded to 728 full-time undergraduates, including 157 freshmen. Scholarships awarded for academics.

Application procedures. Admission: Closing date 1/15 (postmark date). $50 fee, may be waived for applicants with need. Admission notification 4/1. Admission notification on a rolling basis. Must reply by 5/1. **Financial aid:** Priority date 2/1, closing date 3/1. FAFSA, CSS PROFILE required. Applicants notified by 4/1; must reply by 5/1.

Academics. Special study options: Combined bachelor's/graduate degree, double major, exchange student, honors, independent study, internships, liberal arts/career combination, student-designed major, study abroad, teacher certification program, Washington semester. Member Seven College Consortium, professional ethics seminars in business, law, medicine, journalism. **Credit/placement by examination:** AP, CLEP, IB, SAT, ACT, institutional tests. **Support services:** Study skills assistance, tutoring, writing center.

Majors. Area/ethnic studies: East Asian, Russian/Slavic. **Biology:** General, biochemistry. **Business:** Accounting, business admin. **Communications:** Journalism. **Computer sciences:** General. **Conservation:** Environmental science. **Engineering:** Chemical, physics. **Foreign languages:** General, classics, East Asian, French, German, Romance, Spanish. **History:** General. **Interdisciplinary:** Medieval/Renaissance, neuroscience. **Math:** General. **Philosophy/religion:** Philosophy, religion. **Physical sciences:** Chemistry, geology, physics. **Psychology:** General. **Public administration:** Policy analysis. **Social sciences:** Anthropology, archaeology, economics, political science, sociology. **Visual/performing arts:** Art history/conservation, dramatic, studio arts.

Most popular majors. Biology 7%, business/marketing 20%, English 6%, foreign language 7%, history 7%, social sciences 23%, visual/performing arts 6%.

Computing on campus. 410 workstations in dormitories, library, computer center, student center. Dormitories wired for high-speed internet access and linked to campus network. Commuter students can connect to campus network. Online course registration, online library, helpline, repair service, wireless network available.

Student life. Freshman orientation: Mandatory. Preregistration for classes offered. 4 days prior to beginning of fall term. **Policies:** Student-run honor system, observed with single sanction. **Housing:** Guaranteed on-campus for freshmen. Coed dorms, apartments, fraternity/sorority housing available. $150 nonrefundable deposit, deadline 5/1. Outing Club House, Spanish House, Chavis House available. **Activities:** Bands, choral groups, dance, drama, film society, international student organizations, literary magazine, music ensembles, radio station, student government, student newspaper, symphony orchestra, TV station, Alpha Phi Omega, Christian fellowship, service league, Hillel, Habitat for Humanity, minority student association, outing club.

Athletics. NCAA. **Intercollegiate:** Baseball M, basketball, cross-country, equestrian W, field hockey W, football (tackle) M, golf M, lacrosse, soccer, swimming, tennis, track and field, volleyball W, wrestling M. **Intramural:** Badminton, basketball, football (non-tackle), soccer, softball, swimming, table tennis, tennis, volleyball, water polo, wrestling M. **Team name:** Generals.

Student services. Alcohol/substance abuse counseling, chaplain/spiritual director, career counseling, student employment services, health services, personal counseling, placement for graduates. **Physically disabled:** Services for visually, hearing impaired.

Contact. E-mail: admissions@wlu.edu
Phone: (540) 458-8710 Fax: (540) 458-8062
William Hartog, Dean of Admissions and Financial Aid, Washington and Lee University, 204 West Washington Street, Lexington, VA 24450-2116

World College
Virginia Beach, Virginia
www.cie-wc.edu
CB code: 3970

- For-profit 4-year technical college
- Large city
- 461 degree-seeking undergraduates

General. Accredited by DETC. Affiliated with Cleveland Institute of Electronics. **Degrees:** 14 bachelor's awarded. **Calendar:** Continuous. **Full-time faculty:** 6 total. **Part-time faculty:** 75 total.

Basis for selection. Open admission, but selective for some programs.

2008-2009 Annual costs. Tuition/fees: $3,540. Books/supplies: $1,600.

Application procedures. Admission: No deadline. No application fee. Admission notification on a rolling basis.

Academics. Special study options: Accelerated study, distance learning, independent study. **Credit/placement by examination:** CLEP.

Majors. Computer sciences: Security. **Engineering technology:** Electrical.

Computing on campus. PC or laptop required.

Contact. E-mail: instruct@cie-wc.edu
Phone: (800) 696-7532 Toll-free number: (800) 696-7532
World College, Lake Shore Plaza, 5193 Shore Drive, Suite 105, Virginia Beach, VA 23455-2500

Washington

Antioch University Seattle

Seattle, Washington
www.antiochsea.edu **CB code: 3070**

- Private two-year upper-division university and liberal arts college
- Commuter campus in very large city
- Application essay, interview required

General. Founded in 1976. Regionally accredited. Individualized degree programs offered on both graduate and undergraduate levels. **Degrees:** 56 bachelor's awarded; master's, doctoral offered. **Calendar:** Quarter, extensive summer session. **Full-time faculty:** 40 total. **Part-time faculty:** 30 total.

Student profile. 250 degree-seeking undergraduates, 800 graduate students.

Basis for selection. High school transcript, college transcript, application essay, interview required. Transfer accepted as juniors, seniors.

2008-2009 Annual costs. Tuition/fees: $21,435. For BA with Teacher Prep program, $20,025 per year, $445 per credit hour. Books/supplies: $918. Personal expenses: $555.

Financial aid. Need-based: 44% of total undergraduate aid awarded as scholarships/grants, 56% as loans/jobs.

Application procedures. Admission: Rolling admission. $50 fee, may be waived for applicants with need. **Financial aid:** Applicants notified on a rolling basis starting 5/1; must reply within 2 weeks of notification. FAFSA required.

Academics. Bachelor's program is a completion program only. Students generally transfer in with at least 90 credits. **Special study options:** Accelerated study, cross-registration, dual enrollment of high school students, independent study, student-designed major, study abroad, teacher certification program, weekend college. **Credit/placement by examination:** CLEP.

Majors. Liberal arts: Arts/sciences.

Computing on campus. 16 workstations in library, computer center. Commuter students can connect to campus network. Online library, wireless network available.

Student life. Activities: Literary magazine, student government, student newspaper.

Student services. Career counseling, financial aid counseling, personal counseling, veterans' counselor. **Physically disabled:** Services for visually impaired.

Contact. E-mail: admissions@antiochsea.edu
Phone: (206) 441-5352 ext. 5201 Toll-free number: (888) 268-4477
Fax: (206) 441-3307
Doug Arnold, Director of Admissions, Antioch University Seattle, 2326 Sixth Avenue, Seattle, WA 98121-1814

Art Institute of Seattle

Seattle, Washington
www.ais.edu **CB code: 4805**

- For-profit 4-year visual arts and technical college
- Commuter campus in very large city
- 2,234 degree-seeking undergraduates: 34% part-time, 51% women, 5% African American, 12% Asian American, 6% Hispanic American, 1% Native American, 6% international
- Application essay, interview required

General. Founded in 1982. Regionally accredited. **Degrees:** 163 bachelor's, 303 associate awarded. **Location:** Downtown. **Calendar:** Quarter, extensive summer session. **Full-time faculty:** 59 total; 22% have terminal degrees, 8% minority, 32% women. **Part-time faculty:** 81 total; 10% have terminal degrees, 21% minority, 40% women. **Class size:** 45% < 20, 54% 20-39, 1% 40-49. **Special facilities:** Gallery with rotating art/design shows.

Freshman class profile. 926 applied, 886 admitted, 709 enrolled.

Out-of-state:	37%	**International:**	1%
Live on campus:	20%		

Basis for selection. Open admission, but selective for some programs. Secondary school record, essay, interview most important; recommendations, academic records, test scores required. Some programs require a portfolio. **Learning Disabled:** Admissions notifies counselors of students who disclose learning disabilities and special needs. Counselor determines eligibility.

2008-2009 Annual costs. Tuition/fees: $20,385. Room/board: $10,080. Books/supplies: $975. Personal expenses: $2,265.

2008-2009 Financial aid. Need-based: 26% of total undergraduate aid awarded as scholarships/grants, 74% as loans/jobs. **Non-need-based:** Scholarships awarded for academics, art.

Application procedures. Admission: No deadline. $50 fee. Admission notification on a rolling basis. **Financial aid:** Priority date 4/15; no closing date. FAFSA required. Applicants notified on a rolling basis; must reply within 4 week(s) of notification.

Academics. Special study options: Distance learning, ESL, independent study, internships, study abroad. **Credit/placement by examination:** AP, CLEP, IB, institutional tests. 6 credit hours maximum toward associate degree, 6 toward bachelor's. Course waived by proficiency exam; credit does not count toward degree. **Support services:** Learning center, reduced course load, remedial instruction, study skills assistance, tutoring.

Majors. Computer sciences: Web page design. **Visual/performing arts:** General, cinematography, fashion design, graphic design, interior design. **Other:** Fashion marketing.

Computing on campus. 494 workstations in library, computer center, student center. Dormitories wired for high-speed internet access. Online course registration, online library, helpline, student web hosting, wireless network available.

Student life. Freshman orientation: Available. Preregistration for classes offered. 1- to 4-day program held 1 week before start of the quarter. **Housing:** Guaranteed on-campus for all undergraduates. Coed dorms available. $200 deposit. AIS housing located 1 mile from campus. Students share 1 bedroom and studio apartments in secured apartment complexes. **Activities:** Student government, student newspaper.

Athletics. Intramural: Soccer, softball.

Student services. Adult student services, career counseling, student employment services, financial aid counseling, personal counseling, placement for graduates, veterans' counselor. **Physically disabled:** Services for visually, speech, hearing impaired.

Contact. E-mail: aisadm@aii.edu
Phone: (206) 448-6600 Toll-free number: (800) 275-2471
Fax: (206) 269-0275
Brian Cicero, Director of Admissions, Art Institute of Seattle, 2323 Elliott Avenue, Seattle, WA 98121-1622

Bastyr University

Kenmore, Washington
www.bastyr.edu **CB code: 0181**

- Private two-year upper-division university and health science college
- Commuter campus in small city
- Application essay required

General. Founded in 1978. Regionally accredited. **Degrees:** 83 bachelor's awarded; master's, doctoral, first professional offered. **Location:** 16 miles from Seattle. **Calendar:** Quarter, limited summer session. **Full-time faculty:** 46 total; 78% have terminal degrees, 17% minority, 59% women. **Part-time faculty:** 81 total; 86% have terminal degrees, 15% minority, 59% women. **Special facilities:** Gourmet vegetarian cafeteria, research center, natural health sciences library and bookstore, medicinal herb and culinary garden, reflexology path.

Student profile. 201 degree-seeking undergraduates, 768 degree-seeking graduate students. 100% entered as juniors. 75% transferred from two-year, 25% transferred from four-year institutions.

Women:	84%	**Part-time:**	16%
African American:	1%	**Out-of-state:**	13%
Asian American:	5%	**Live on campus:**	5%
Hispanic American:	6%	**25 or older:**	63%
International:	4%		

Basis for selection. College transcript, application essay required. Transfer accepted as juniors, seniors.

2008-2009 Annual costs. Tuition/fees: $17,790. Room/board: $4,100. Books/supplies: $1,125.

Financial aid. Need-based: Average need met was 50%. 73% of total undergraduate aid awarded as scholarships/grants, 27% as loans/jobs. **Non-need-based:** Scholarships awarded for academics.

Application procedures. Admission: Priority date 3/15. $60 fee. **Financial aid:** Priority date 5/1, no deadline. Applicants notified on a rolling basis; must reply within 3 weeks of notification. FAFSA, institutional form required.

Academics. Special study options: Double major, internships. Selected tracks within major. **Credit/placement by examination:** AP, CLEP.

Majors. Health: Acupuncture, Chinese medicine/herbology, herbalism. **Interdisciplinary:** Nutrition sciences. **Parks/recreation:** Exercise sciences. **Psychology:** General.

Computing on campus. 53 workstations in library, computer center. Dormitories wired for high-speed internet access and linked to campus network. Online library, helpline, wireless network available.

Student life. Housing: Coed dorms, wellness housing available. **Activities:** Student government, student newspaper, Student Physicians for Social Responsibility, Herbal Ways, Nature Cure Club, Africana student association, Christian Fellowship, pediatrics club, Student Nutrition Association, Tai Chi club, yoga club, Voice for Queer Natural Health.

Athletics. Intramural: Basketball, soccer.

Student services. Career counseling, financial aid counseling, health services, on-campus daycare, personal counseling, placement for graduates. **Physically disabled:** Services for visually impaired.

Contact. E-mail: admissions@bastyr.edu
Phone: (425) 602-3330 Fax: (425) 602-3090
Ted Olsen, Director of Admissions, Bastyr University, 14500 Juanita Drive, NE, Kenmore, WA 98028

Central Washington University

Ellensburg, Washington — **CB member**
www.cwu.edu — **CB code: 4044**

- Public 4-year university
- Residential campus in large town
- 9,688 degree-seeking undergraduates: 11% part-time, 51% women, 3% African American, 7% Asian American, 8% Hispanic American, 3% Native American, 2% international
- 409 degree-seeking graduate students
- 79% of applicants admitted
- SAT or ACT (ACT writing optional) required
- 56% graduate within 6 years

General. Founded in 1890. Regionally accredited. **Degrees:** 2,485 bachelor's awarded; master's offered. **ROTC:** Army, Air Force. **Location:** 105 miles from Seattle. **Calendar:** Quarter, limited summer session. **Full-time faculty:** 432 total; 12% minority, 39% women. **Part-time faculty:** 169 total; 5% minority, 55% women. **Class size:** 39% < 20, 47% 20-39, 8% 40-49, 6% 50-99, less than 1% >100. **Special facilities:** Chimpanzee and Human Communication Institute, geodesy lab, data analysis center, education technology center, Northwest Native American and Circum-Pacific artifacts museum.

Freshman class profile. 5,013 applied, 3,968 admitted, 1,570 enrolled.

Mid 50% test scores		**GPA 2.0-2.99:**	37%
SAT critical reading:	440-540	**Rank in top quarter:**	23%
SAT math:	440-550	**Rank in top tenth:**	4%
ACT composite:	18-23	**Out-of-state:**	5%
GPA 3.75 or higher:	10%	**Live on campus:**	97%
GPA 3.50-3.74:	13%	**International:**	1%
GPA 3.0-3.49:	40%		

Basis for selection. Admission generally based on weighted combination of test scores and GPA. Interview, essay, and recommendations required for students whose grades or test scores do not reflect their potential for success. Additional academic support provided within alternate admission program. **Homeschooled:** Must submit transcripts for any periods enrolled in secondary school, submit ACT or SAT scores, write substantial essay about applicant's preparation for college and how schooling meets or parallels core requirements.

High school preparation. College-preparatory program required. 15 units required; 17 recommended. Required and recommended units include English 4, mathematics 3, social studies 3, science 2-3 (laboratory 1-2) and foreign language 2. One year of a performing or fine art or additional year of study in any main subject area is also required. Coursework in U.S. history and U.S. government recommended and will count toward social studies requirements.

2008-2009 Annual costs. Tuition/fees: $5,540; $15,411 out-of-state. Room/board: $8,052. Books/supplies: $924. Personal expenses: $1,683.

2007-2008 Financial aid. Non-need-based: Scholarships awarded for academics, alumni affiliation, art, athletics, job skills, leadership, minority status, music/drama, religious affiliation, ROTC, state residency.

Application procedures. Admission: Priority date 10/1; no deadline. $55 fee, may be waived for applicants with need. Admission notification on a rolling basis beginning on or about 11/1. **Financial aid:** Priority date 3/1; no closing date. FAFSA required. Applicants notified on a rolling basis starting 4/15; must reply within 4 week(s) of notification.

Academics. Extended degree programs at locations in Yakima, Wenatchee, and greater Seattle area. **Special study options:** Cooperative education, distance learning, double major, dual enrollment of high school students, ESL, exchange student, honors, independent study, internships, liberal arts/career combination, student-designed major, study abroad, teacher certification program. **Credit/placement by examination:** AP, CLEP, IB, SAT, ACT, institutional tests. 45 credit hours maximum toward bachelor's degree. **Support services:** Learning center, reduced course load, remedial instruction, study skills assistance, tutoring, writing center.

Honors college/program. General education program emphasizes history, philosophy, literature. Applicants should score in upper 10 percent on SAT and ACT Verbal Composite and Quantitative Composite. 3.0 GPA required. 25 freshmen generally admitted.

Majors. Area/ethnic studies: Asian. **Biology:** General. **Business:** Accounting, business admin, construction management, fashion, office management. **Communications:** General, journalism, public relations. **Computer sciences:** General. **Education:** Art, biology, business, chemistry, drama/dance, early childhood, elementary, English, family/consumer sciences, foreign languages, French, German, health, history, mathematics, music, physical, science, social science, Spanish, special, technology/industrial arts, trade/industrial. **Engineering technology:** Construction, electrical, industrial, mechanical. **Family/consumer sciences:** General, food/nutrition. **Foreign languages:** Chinese, French, German, Japanese, Russian, Spanish. **Health:** Occupational health. **History:** General. **Interdisciplinary:** Gerontology. **Math:** General. **Parks/recreation:** General, sports admin. **Philosophy/religion:** Philosophy, religion. **Physical sciences:** Chemistry, geology, physics, planetary. **Protective services:** Criminal justice. **Psychology:** General. **Public administration:** Human services, policy analysis. **Social sciences:** General, anthropology, economics, geography, political science, sociology. **Transportation:** Aviation. **Visual/performing arts:** Art, commercial/advertising art, dramatic, music management, music performance, music theory/composition, piano/organ, stringed instruments, studio arts, voice/opera.

Most popular majors. Business/marketing 25%, education 21%, security/protective services 7%, social sciences 10%.

Computing on campus. 700 workstations in dormitories, library, computer center, student center. Dormitories wired for high-speed internet access and linked to campus network. Commuter students can connect to campus network. Online course registration, online library, helpline, student web hosting, wireless network available.

Student life. Freshman orientation: Mandatory. Preregistration for classes offered. 2-day introduction to campus held for students and parents. **Housing:** Guaranteed on-campus for freshmen. Coed dorms, single-sex dorms, special housing for disabled, apartments available. $200 partly refundable deposit, deadline 6/1. Academic interests, upperclassmen, over 21 housing available. **Activities:** Bands, campus ministries, choral groups, dance, drama, film society, international student organizations, literary magazine, music ensembles, musical theater, opera, radio station, student government, student newspaper, symphony orchestra, TV station, religious, political, ethnic, minority student organizations, professional societies, major field clubs available.

Athletics. NAIA, NCAA. **Intercollegiate:** Baseball M, basketball, cheerleading, cross-country, football (tackle) M, soccer W, softball W, track and field, volleyball W. **Intramural:** Badminton, basketball, football (non-tackle), soccer, softball, tennis, volleyball. **Team name:** Wildcats.

Student services. Adult student services, alcohol/substance abuse counseling, chaplain/spiritual director, career counseling, services for economically disadvantaged, student employment services, financial aid counseling, health services, minority student services, on-campus daycare, personal counseling, placement for graduates, veterans' counselor, women's services. **Physically disabled:** Services for visually, speech, hearing impaired.

Contact. E-mail: cwuadmis@cwu.edu
Phone: (509) 963-1211 Toll-free number: (866) 298-4968
Fax: (509) 963-3022
Lisa Garcia-Hanson, Director of Admissions, Central Washington University, 400 East University Way, Ellensburg, WA 98926-7463

City University of Seattle

Bellevue, Washington
www.cityu.edu **CB code: 4042**

- Private two-year upper-division university
- Commuter campus in very large city

General. Founded in 1973. Regionally accredited. University maintains satellite sites in Renton, Everett, North Seattle, Tacoma, and Vancouver, Washington; Victoria, Vancouver, Edmonton, and Calgary, Canada; Trencin and Bratislava, Slovakia; Prague, Czech Republic; Sophia and Pratvetz, Bulgaria; Athens, Greece; Zurich, Switzerland; and Beijing, China; partnerships in Queensland, Australia and Santiago, Chile. **Degrees:** 587 bachelor's, 37 associate awarded; master's offered. **Location:** 12 miles from Seattle. **Calendar:** Quarter, extensive summer session. **Full-time faculty:** 25 total. **Part-time faculty:** 1,231 total. **Class size:** 95% < 20, 5% 20-39.

Student profile. 1,268 degree-seeking undergraduates, 2,057 degree-seeking graduate students.

Women:	62%	**International:**	5%
African American:	4%	**Part-time:**	43%
Asian American:	5%	**Out-of-state:**	15%
Hispanic American:	3%	**25 or older:**	81%
Native American:	1%		

Basis for selection. Open admission. High school transcript, college transcript required. Based on course content equivalency and grade point average. Transfer accepted as sophomores, juniors, seniors.

2008-2009 Annual costs. Tuition/fees: $14,580. Books/supplies: $860.

Financial aid. Non-need-based: Scholarships awarded for academics. **Additional information:** All degree programs approved for veteran's administration education benefits.

Application procedures. Admission: Rolling admission. $50 fee. **Financial aid:** FAFSA, institutional form required.

Academics. Online tutoring service available to all registered students at all times. **Special study options:** Accelerated study, distance learning, double major, dual enrollment of high school students, ESL, external degree, internships, student-designed major, study abroad, teacher certification program, weekend college. **Credit/placement by examination:** CLEP, IB. 45 credit hours maximum toward associate degree, 90 toward bachelor's. **Support services:** Reduced course load, tutoring.

Majors. Business: Accounting, business admin, international, management information systems, marketing. **Communications:** General. **Computer sciences:** Programming. **Education:** Elementary, middle, special. **Liberal arts:** Arts/sciences. **Psychology:** General.

Most popular majors. Business/marketing 64%, computer/information sciences 7%, education 20%.

Computing on campus. PC or laptop required. 150 workstations in library, computer center. Commuter students can connect to campus network. Online course registration, online library, helpline, wireless network available.

Student services. Adult student services, career counseling, financial aid counseling, personal counseling, veterans' counselor. **Physically disabled:** Services for visually, hearing impaired.

Contact. E-mail: info@cityu.edu
Phone: (425) 637-1010 Toll-free number: (888) 422-4898
Fax: (425) 709-5361
Melissa Mecham, Vice President Admissions/Student Affairs, City University of Seattle, 11900 NE First Street, Bellevue, WA 98005

Cornish College of the Arts

Seattle, Washington
www.cornish.edu **CB code: 0058**

- Private 4-year visual arts and performing arts college
- Commuter campus in very large city
- 814 degree-seeking undergraduates
- 69% of applicants admitted
- Application essay required

General. Founded in 1914. Regionally accredited. **Degrees:** 144 bachelor's awarded. **Calendar:** Semester, limited summer session. **Full-time faculty:** 55 total. **Part-time faculty:** 95 total. **Class size:** 87% < 20, 13% 20-39. **Special facilities:** Electronic music laboratory, experimental books laboratory, music listening center, costumemaking facilities, video editing facilities.

Freshman class profile. 886 applied, 611 admitted, 308 enrolled.

Basis for selection. Portfolio (for visual artists) or audition (for performing artists), academic achievement history, creative ability, and artistic goals considered. SAT or ACT recommended. Interview recommended for all; audition required for dance, music, theater; portfolio required for art, design, performance production. Alternative audition and portfolio arrangements for long-distance applicants. **Homeschooled:** Transcript of courses and grades, state high school equivalency certificate required.

High school preparation. Required and recommended units include English 4, mathematics 2-4, social studies 3, science 2-4 (laboratory 1) and foreign language 2.

2008-2009 Annual costs. Tuition/fees: $26,100. Design majors required to have laptop computer and Adobe software, estimated cost $3,000. Books/supplies: $1,800. Personal expenses: $2,000.

2008-2009 Financial aid. Non-need-based: Scholarships awarded for academics.

Application procedures. Admission: Priority date 3/1; deadline 8/15 (receipt date). $35 fee, may be waived for applicants with need. Admission notification on a rolling basis beginning on or about 1/1. Must reply by May 1 or within 2 week(s) if notified thereafter. **Financial aid:** Priority date 2/15; no closing date. FAFSA, institutional form required. Applicants notified on a rolling basis starting 4/15; must reply by 5/1 or within 2 week(s) of notification.

Academics. Special study options: Cooperative education, independent study, internships, study abroad. **Credit/placement by examination:** AP, CLEP, institutional tests. 30 credit hours maximum toward bachelor's degree. A total of 30 credits through a combination of prior work experience and credit by exam allowed. **Support services:** Remedial instruction, study skills assistance, tutoring, writing center.

Majors. Visual/performing arts: General, acting, art, cinematography, commercial/advertising art, dance, design, directing/producing, dramatic, drawing, graphic design, illustration, interior design, jazz, music performance, music theory/composition, painting, photography, piano/organ, play/screenwriting, printmaking, sculpture, stringed instruments, studio arts, theater design, voice/opera.

Computing on campus. 91 workstations in library, computer center, student center. Online library, helpline, wireless network available.

Student life. Freshman orientation: Mandatory, $175 fee. Preregistration for classes offered. Begins one week before class starts each fall. Students will meet the Chair of their department and register for classes. **Activities:** Bands, choral groups, dance, drama, film society, literary magazine, music ensembles, musical theater, opera, student government, student newspaper, art history club, Birds and Whistles, Black student alliance, bowling club, digital illustration club, Inform the Misinformed Campaign/Corporate Watchdogs, movie club, Salt and Light (Bible study), sports/intramural club.

Student services. Adult student services, alcohol/substance abuse counseling, career counseling, student employment services, financial aid counseling, personal counseling, placement for graduates. **Physically disabled:** Services for visually impaired.

Contact. E-mail: admissions@cornish.edu
Phone: (206) 726-5016 Toll-free number: (800) 726-2787
Fax: (206) 720-1011
Sharron Starling, Director of Admissions, Cornish College of the Arts, 1000 Lenora Street, Seattle, WA 98121

DeVry University: Federal Way

Federal Way, Washington
www.devry.edu **CB code: 3696**

- For-profit 4-year university
- Commuter campus in large city
- 657 degree-seeking undergraduates: 37% part-time, 28% women, 11% African American, 12% Asian American, 7% Hispanic American, 1% Native American, 1% international
- 108 degree-seeking graduate students
- Interview required

General. Degrees: 126 bachelor's, 12 associate awarded; master's offered. **ROTC:** Army. **Calendar:** Semester, extensive summer session. **Full-time faculty:** 20 total; 30% minority, 20% women. **Part-time faculty:** 39 total; 3% minority, 31% women.

Basis for selection. Applicants must have high school diploma or equivalent, or a degree from an accredited postsecondary institution. Must demonstrate proficiency in basic college level skills through test scores and/or institutionally-administered placement exams, and be at least 17 years of age on the first day of classes. New students may enter at the beginning of any semester. CPT also accepted.

High school preparation. Required units include mathematics 1. Math unit must be algebra or higher.

2008-2009 Annual costs. Tuition/fees: $14,800. Books/supplies: $1,300. Personal expenses: $5,082.

2007-2008 Financial aid. All financial aid based on need.

Application procedures. Admission: No deadline. $50 fee. Admission notification on a rolling basis. **Financial aid:** No deadline. FAFSA required. Applicants notified on a rolling basis.

Academics. Special study options: Accelerated study, distance learning. **Credit/placement by examination:** CLEP. **Support services:** Learning center, remedial instruction, tutoring.

Majors. Business: General, business admin. **Computer sciences:** Information technology, security, systems analysis, web page design. **Engineering technology:** Biomedical, computer, electrical.

Most popular majors. Business/marketing 60%, computer/information sciences 27%, engineering/engineering technologies 14%.

Computing on campus. 335 workstations in library, computer center. Online course registration, online library, helpline available.

Student life. Freshman orientation: Mandatory. **Housing:** Private apartments, student-plan housing, private rooms. **Activities:** Student government, student newspaper, alternative sports, business & technology club, gaming, robotics, Institution of Electrical and Electronic Engineers, network gaming.

Student services. Career counseling, student employment services, financial aid counseling, placement for graduates, veterans' counselor. **Physically disabled:** Services for visually, hearing impaired.

Contact. E-mail: admissions@sea.devry.edu
Phone: (253) 943-2810 Toll-free number: (877) 923-3879
Fax: (253) 943-3291
Fred Pressel, Director of Admissions, DeVry University: Federal Way, 3600 South 344th Way, Federal Way, WA 98001-9558

DigiPen Institute of Technology

Redmond, Washington
www.digipen.edu **CB code: 4138**

- For-profit 4-year visual arts and engineering college
- Residential campus in large town
- 825 degree-seeking undergraduates
- 42 graduate students
- Application essay required

General. Accredited by ACCSCT. Comprised of two campuses: main campus and the art campus. **Degrees:** 103 bachelor's awarded; master's offered. **Location:** 20 miles from downtown Seattle. **Calendar:** Semester, limited summer session. **Full-time faculty:** 41 total; 27% women. **Part-time faculty:** 26 total; 15% women. **Class size:** 45% < 20, 35% 20-39, 8% 40-49, 13% 50-99.

Freshman class profile.

Mid 50% test scores			
SAT critical reading:	540-670	SAT writing:	480-600
SAT math:	560-680	ACT composite:	25-30
		Out-of-state:	61%

Basis for selection. Applicants must submit official transcripts, test scores, recommendation letters, a personal statement, and an art portfolio when applying to the animation program. Non-native English speakers must provide a minimum TOEFL iBT score of 80. Applicants who have already graduated from high school and have at least one year of full-time college experience are not required to submit SAT/ACT scores. Portfolios of 10-20 pieces of work required for BFA program applicants. Art portfolio and supplemental pieces required for the Game Design degrees. **Homeschooled:** State high school equivalency certificate required. Applicants who have completed an accredited high school curriculum may submit official transcripts as proof of their high school equivalence. Applicants who did not complete an accredited program must take an official high school equivalence test, such as the GED, and submit those scores. **Learning Disabled:** Students desiring special needs should contact the Disability Support Services Coordinator to arrange accommodations.

High school preparation. College-preparatory program recommended. Recommended units include English 4, mathematics 4, science 4, computer science 1 and visual/performing arts 1. Applicants for the BFA program are recommended to take as many art classes as possible and BS applicants are encouraged to take classes in computer science and physics.

2008-2009 Annual costs. Full-time tuition for academic year (based on 20 hours per term), $19,040; required fees, $160; per-credit-hour charge, $476. Full-time tuition for non-resident aliens for academic year (based on 20 hours per term), $24,840; per-credit-hour charge, $621. Books/supplies: $972.

Financial aid. Non-need-based: Scholarships awarded for job skills, leadership, minority status. **Additional information:** Many aid programs are on a first-come, first-serve basis.

Application procedures. Admission: Priority date 2/1; no deadline. $35 fee, may be waived for applicants with need. Admission notification on a rolling basis. Applicants must respond by the date listed on their individual acceptance letters. **Financial aid:** Priority date 4/15; no closing date. FAFSA, institutional form required. Applicants notified on a rolling basis starting 1/1; must reply within 4 week(s) of notification.

Academics. Special study options: Accelerated study, independent study, internships. **Credit/placement by examination:** AP, CLEP, IB, institutional tests. **Support services:** Reduced course load, study skills assistance, tutoring.

Majors. Computer sciences: Applications programming. **Engineering:** Computer hardware. **Visual/performing arts:** Design, multimedia.

Computing on campus. Online course registration, helpline, wireless network available.

Student life. Freshman orientation: Mandatory. Preregistration for classes offered. 3-4 day orientation is held the week before classes begin. **Housing:** All housing is off campus. Most students live in co-ed situations with 2-4 students in an apartment; housing options near campus. Most students relocate to Redmond, WA. DigiPen offers resources for acquiring housing and finding roommates. **Activities:** International student organizations, student government.

Student services. Career counseling, student employment services, financial aid counseling, personal counseling, veterans' counselor. **Physically disabled:** Services for hearing impaired.

Contact. E-mail: admissions@digipen.edu
Phone: (425) 558-0299 Toll-free number: (866) 478-5236
Fax: (425) 558-0378
Angela Kugler, Director of Admissions, DigiPen Institute of Technology, 5001-150th Avenue Northeast, Redmond, WA 98052

Eastern Washington University

Cheney, Washington — **CB member**
www.ewu.edu — **CB code: 4301**

- Public 4-year university
- Commuter campus in large town
- 9,485 degree-seeking undergraduates: 13% part-time, 56% women, 4% African American, 4% Asian American, 8% Hispanic American, 2% Native American, 2% international
- 1,324 degree-seeking graduate students
- 83% of applicants admitted
- SAT or ACT with writing required
- 48% graduate within 6 years

General. Founded in 1882. Regionally accredited. **Degrees:** 2,015 bachelor's awarded; master's, doctoral offered. **ROTC:** Army. **Location:** 17 miles from Spokane, 200 miles from Seattle. **Calendar:** Quarter, extensive summer session. **Full-time faculty:** 440 total; 97% have terminal degrees, 11% minority, 46% women. **Part-time faculty:** 225 total; 6% minority, 60% women. **Class size:** 39% < 20, 43% 20-39, 8% 40-49, 10% 50-99, less than 1% >100. **Special facilities:** Planetarium, 17,000-acre national wildlife refuge, on-campus elementary school, anthropology museum, laboratory for ecological studies, photography and print gallery, children's center, English language institute, state crime lab.

Freshman class profile. 3,713 applied, 3,076 admitted, 1,518 enrolled.

Mid 50% test scores		**GPA 3.50-3.74:**	15%
SAT critical reading:	420-530	**GPA 3.0-3.49:**	39%
SAT math:	430-540	**GPA 2.0-2.99:**	34%
SAT writing:	410-520	**Return as sophomores:**	72%
ACT composite:	17-23	**Out-of-state:**	9%
GPA 3.75 or higher:	12%	**International:**	1%

Basis for selection. Admission based on index combining GPA, test scores and requisite high school core curriculum. Essay and special review considered for applicants who do not meet these standards. Limited number enrolled below index and core requirements. Letters of recommendation from teachers and/or counselors encouraged. Interview or essay required for returning adult applicants and high school students below admission index. **Homeschooled:** Must show evidence of completing required core courses.

High school preparation. College-preparatory program required. 15 units required. Required units include English 4, mathematics 3, social studies 3, science 2 (laboratory 1), foreign language 2 and visual/performing arts 1. Math requirement includes algebra, geometry, and trigonometry or advanced algebra. One year fine arts or core elective required. Foreign language requirement includes 2 years in 1 foreign language (American Sign Language accepted).

2008-2009 Annual costs. Tuition/fees: $5,216; $13,889 out-of-state. Prepaid tuition plan available to Washington state residents. Room/board: $6,756. Books/supplies: $1,305. Personal expenses: $2,163.

2007-2008 Financial aid. **Need-based:** 1,015 full-time freshmen applied for aid; 719 were judged to have need; 693 of these received aid. Average need met was 90%. Average scholarship/grant was $5,199; average loan $2,180. 49% of total undergraduate aid awarded as scholarships/grants, 51% as loans/jobs. **Non-need-based:** Awarded to 1,365 full-time undergraduates, including 420 freshmen. Scholarships awarded for academics, alumni affiliation, athletics, ROTC. **Additional information:** The High Demand Scholarship program helps low income students pursue "high demand" careers.

Application procedures. **Admission:** Priority date 3/1; deadline 8/15. $50 fee, may be waived for applicants with need. Admission notification on a rolling basis beginning on or about 11/1. Must reply by May 1 or within 4 week(s) if notified thereafter. Application deadline is 10 days prior to start of quarter. **Financial aid:** Priority date 4/1; no closing date. FAFSA required. Applicants notified on a rolling basis starting 4/1; must reply within 4 week(s) of notification.

Academics. Extensive internship opportunities available. **Special study options:** Distance learning, double major, ESL, honors, independent study, internships, student-designed major, study abroad, teacher certification program. Nursing consortium with Washington State University, Whitworth College, Gonzaga University. Dual degree program: Master's of Social Work (EWU) and Law (Gonzaga). **Credit/placement by examination:** AP, CLEP, IB, SAT, ACT, institutional tests. 45 credit hours maximum toward bachelor's degree. **Support services:** Learning center, pre-admission summer program, remedial instruction, study skills assistance, tutoring, writing center.

Majors. **Architecture:** Urban/community planning. **Area/ethnic studies:** Women's. **Biology:** General. **Business:** Accounting, business admin, finance, management information systems, managerial economics, marketing. **Communications:** General, journalism. **Communications technology:** Graphics. **Computer sciences:** General. **Conservation:** Environmental science. **Education:** Art, biology, business, chemistry, early childhood, early childhood special, English, French, health, mathematics, music, physics, reading, science, social studies, Spanish, special. **Engineering:** Electrical. **Engineering technology:** Computer, mechanical. **Family/consumer sciences:** Child development. **Foreign languages:** French, Spanish. **Health:** Athletic training, community health services, dental hygiene, health care admin, nursing (RN), public health ed, recreational therapy, speech pathology. **History:** General. **Liberal arts:** Humanities. **Math:** General. **Military:** General. **Parks/recreation:** General, exercise sciences, facilities management, health/fitness. **Philosophy/religion:** Philosophy. **Physical sciences:** Chemistry, geology, physics. **Psychology:** General, developmental. **Public administration:** Social work. **Social sciences:** Anthropology, criminology, economics, geography, international relations, political science, sociology. **Visual/performing arts:** Art history/conservation, cinematography, dramatic, graphic design, studio arts. **Other:** Interdisciplinary studies, Technology.

Most popular majors. Biology 6%, business/marketing 21%, education 11%, health sciences 10%, interdisciplinary studies 7%, social sciences 8%.

Computing on campus. 226 workstations in dormitories, library, computer center, student center. Dormitories wired for high-speed internet access and linked to campus network. Commuter students can connect to campus network. Online course registration, online library, helpline, student web hosting, wireless network available.

Student life. **Freshman orientation:** Available. Preregistration for classes offered. One-day sessions in summer plus a 3-day program prior to start of classes with advising, student activities, enrollment services. **Policies:** Student conduct code, academic integrity policy, alcohol/substance use and abuse policy. **Housing:** Coed dorms, special housing for disabled, apartments, fraternity/sorority housing, wellness housing available. $250 nonrefundable deposit, deadline 5/1. **Activities:** Bands, campus ministries, choral groups, dance, drama, film society, international student organizations, literary magazine, music ensembles, Model UN, musical theater, radio station, student government, student newspaper, symphony orchestra, Native American student association; Chinese student association; R.A.I.C.E.S. (Reconociendo A La Identidad con Educacion y Sociedad); Black Student Union; United Ministries; international affairs club; Mind, Body, and Soul; Eastern Environmental; debate club.

Athletics. NCAA. **Intercollegiate:** Basketball, cheerleading, cross-country, football (tackle) M, golf W, soccer W, tennis, track and field, volleyball W. **Intramural:** Badminton, basketball, bowling, cross-country, football (tackle), golf, racquetball, soccer, softball, tennis, triathlon, volleyball. **Team name:** Eagles.

Student services. Alcohol/substance abuse counseling, career counseling, student employment services, financial aid counseling, health services, minority student services, on-campus daycare, personal counseling, placement for graduates, veterans' counselor, women's services. **Physically disabled:** Services for visually, speech, hearing impaired.

Contact. E-mail: admissions@mail.ewu.edu
Phone: (509) 359-2397 Fax: (509) 359-6692
Shannon Carr, Director of Admissions, Eastern Washington University, 101 Sutton Hall, Cheney, WA 99004-2447

Evergreen State College

Olympia, Washington — **CB member**
www.evergreen.edu — **CB code: 4292**

- Public 4-year liberal arts college
- Commuter campus in small city
- 4,228 degree-seeking undergraduates: 7% part-time, 55% women, 5% African American, 5% Asian American, 5% Hispanic American, 3% Native American, 1% international
- 311 degree-seeking graduate students
- 94% of applicants admitted
- SAT or ACT (ACT writing optional) required
- 58% graduate within 6 years

General. Founded in 1967. Regionally accredited. **Degrees:** 1,077 bachelor's awarded; master's offered. **Location:** 6 miles from downtown, 60 miles from Seattle. **Calendar:** Quarter, limited summer session. **Full-time faculty:** 164 total; 90% have terminal degrees, 24% minority, 50% women. **Part-time faculty:** 79 total; 47% have terminal degrees, 13% minority, 52% women. **Class size:** 33% < 20, 38% 20-39, 17% 40-49, 12% 50-99. **Special facilities:** Organic farm and community gardens, Longhouse Education and Cultural Center, animation and design studio, ceramics studio, metal shop, wood shop, photography studios and darkrooms, 3,000 feet of waterfront property on Puget Sound.

Freshman class profile. 1,989 applied, 1,876 admitted, 665 enrolled.

Mid 50% test scores		**GPA 2.0-2.99:**	44%
SAT critical reading:	530-660	**Rank in top quarter:**	22%
SAT math:	470-600	**Rank in top tenth:**	9%
ACT composite:	22-27	**Return as sophomores:**	70%
GPA 3.75 or higher:	6%	**Out-of-state:**	49%
GPA 3.50-3.74:	13%	**Live on campus:**	79%
GPA 3.0-3.49:	36%	**International:**	1%

Basis for selection. School achievement record, test scores, strength of curriculum taken in high school, personal statement, and understanding of interdisciplinary study. Official TOEFL test scores are required for most students whose native language is not English. Essay recommended. Interviews optional (by appointment for non-residents.). **Homeschooled:** Transcript of courses and grades required.

High school preparation. 15 units required. Required units include English 4, mathematics 3, social studies 3, science 2 (laboratory 1), foreign language 2 and academic electives 1. One fine, visual, or performing arts elective or other college prep elective from the areas above required.

2008-2009 Annual costs. Tuition/fees: $5,329; $16,189 out-of-state. Room/board: $8,052. Books/supplies: $900. Personal expenses: $1,890.

2007-2008 Financial aid. Need-based: 430 full-time freshmen applied for aid; 289 were judged to have need; 271 of these received aid. Average need met was 76%. Average scholarship/grant was $6,009; average loan $3,480. 58% of total undergraduate aid awarded as scholarships/grants, 42% as loans/jobs. **Non-need-based:** Awarded to 388 full-time undergraduates, including 168 freshmen. Scholarships awarded for academics, art, athletics, state residency. **Additional information:** Application deadline for merit and cultural diversity scholarships February 1. Minority students may apply for tuition and fee waiver scholarships; amount of award equal to in-state tuition and fees. To meet priority deadline for required financial aid forms, official results of FAFSA must be received by March 15.

Application procedures. Admission: Priority date 3/1; no deadline. $50 fee, may be waived for applicants with need. Admission notification on a rolling basis beginning on or about 12/1. Must reply by May 1 or within 4 week(s) if notified thereafter. **Financial aid:** Priority date 3/15; no closing date. FAFSA, institutional form required. Applicants notified on a rolling basis starting 4/1; must reply within 8 week(s) of notification.

Academics. Special study options: Accelerated study, double major, exchange student, independent study, internships, student-designed major, study abroad, teacher certification program, weekend college. **Credit/placement by examination:** AP, CLEP, IB. 135 credit hours maximum toward bachelor's degree. **Support services:** Learning center, reduced course load, study skills assistance, tutoring, writing center.

Majors. Agriculture: General. **Area/ethnic studies:** Native American. **Biology:** General. **Business:** Business admin. **Communications:** General, journalism. **Computer sciences:** General. **Conservation:** General, environmental science, environmental studies. **Education:** General. **Foreign languages:** General, classics, linguistics. **Health:** Health services. **History:** General. **Interdisciplinary:** Biological/physical sciences, global studies, intercultural, natural sciences. **Liberal arts:** Arts/sciences, humanities. **Math:** Probability. **Philosophy/religion:** Philosophy, religion. **Physical sciences:** General. **Psychology:** General. **Public administration:** General. **Social sciences:** General, political science, sociology. **Visual/performing arts:** General, art, cinematography, dramatic, film/cinema, multimedia, studio arts.

Most popular majors. Interdisciplinary studies 14%, liberal arts 86%.

Computing on campus. 375 workstations in dormitories, library, computer center. Dormitories wired for high-speed internet access and linked to campus network. Commuter students can connect to campus network. Online course registration, online library, helpline, student web hosting, wireless network available.

Student life. Freshman orientation: Mandatory. Preregistration for classes offered. Week-long orientation offers academic and social events to familiarize students with teaching, learning, and resources at campus. **Housing:** Guaranteed on-campus for freshmen. Coed dorms, special housing for disabled, apartments, wellness housing available. $250 fully refundable deposit, deadline 7/15. Freshmen halls, freshmen quiet, community action, sustainability, apartment-style quiet available. **Activities:** Pep band, choral groups, dance, drama, film society, literary magazine, music ensembles, radio station, student government, student newspaper, TV station, Developing Ecological Agricultural Practices, Evergreen Queer Alliance, Women of Color Coalition, Common Bread, MEChA, Women's resource center, political information center, Students at Evergreen for Ecological Design, Geoduck Union.

Athletics. NAIA. **Intercollegiate:** Basketball, cross-country, soccer, track and field, volleyball W. **Intramural:** Badminton, basketball, racquetball, soccer, softball, tennis. **Team name:** Geoducks.

Student services. Adult student services, alcohol/substance abuse counseling, career counseling, services for economically disadvantaged, student employment services, financial aid counseling, health services, minority student services, on-campus daycare, personal counseling, placement for graduates, veterans' counselor, women's services. **Physically disabled:** Services for visually, speech, hearing impaired.

Contact. E-mail: admissions@evergreen.edu
Phone: (360) 867-6170 Fax: (360) 867-5114
Doug Scrima, Director of Admissions, Evergreen State College, 2700 Evergreen Parkway NW, Olympia, WA 98505

Faith Evangelical Seminary

Tacoma, Washington
www.faithseminary.edu

- Private 4-year seminary college
- Large city
- 60 degree-seeking undergraduates

General. Regionally accredited. **Degrees:** 12 bachelor's awarded; master's, doctoral, first professional offered. **Calendar:** Quarter, limited summer session. **Full-time faculty:** 9 total. **Part-time faculty:** 4 total.

Freshman class profile. 27 enrolled.

Basis for selection. Open admission, but selective for some programs.

2008-2009 Annual costs. Tuition/fees: $6,210.

Application procedures. Admission: No deadline. $40 fee. **Financial aid:** Closing date 8/15.

Academics. Credit/placement by examination: CLEP.

Majors. Philosophy/religion: Religion. **Theology:** Theology.

Contact. E-mail: admissions@faithseminary.edu
Phone: (888) 777-7675 ext. 21
Eric Rice, Director of Admissions, Faith Evangelical Seminary, 3504 North Pearl Street, Tacoma, WA 98407

Gonzaga University

Spokane, Washington **CB member**
www.gonzaga.edu **CB code: 4330**

- Private 4-year university and liberal arts college affiliated with Roman Catholic Church
- Residential campus in large city
- 4,442 degree-seeking undergraduates: 2% part-time, 53% women, 1% African American, 5% Asian American, 4% Hispanic American, 1% Native American, 2% international
- 2,577 degree-seeking graduate students
- 78% of applicants admitted
- SAT or ACT (ACT writing optional), application essay required
- 80% graduate within 6 years

General. Founded in 1887. Regionally accredited. **Degrees:** 994 bachelor's awarded; master's, doctoral, first professional offered. **ROTC:** Army. **Location:** 300 miles from Seattle. **Calendar:** Semester, extensive summer session. **Full-time faculty:** 372 total; 84% have terminal degrees, 12% minority, 37% women. **Part-time faculty:** 342 total. **Class size:** 45% < 20, 50% 20-39, 3% 40-49, 2% 50-99. **Special facilities:** 2 electron microscopes.

Freshman class profile. 5,026 applied, 3,921 admitted, 1,107 enrolled.

Mid 50% test scores		**Rank in top quarter:**	69%
SAT critical reading:	540-630	**Rank in top tenth:**	36%
SAT math:	550-650	**End year in good standing:**	95%
ACT composite:	24-29	**Return as sophomores:**	92%
GPA 3.75 or higher:	45%	**Out-of-state:**	51%
GPA 3.50-3.74:	23%	**Live on campus:**	95%
GPA 3.0-3.49:	28%	**International:**	1%
GPA 2.0-2.99:	4%		

Basis for selection. GED not accepted. Academic achievement, scholastic aptitude, personal characteristics important. GPA below 3.0 reevaluated to include only grades in academic subjects. Course content and test scores important. Interview recommended for all; audition recommended for music. **Homeschooled:** Test scores, interview by admissions representative required.

High school preparation. College-preparatory program required. Required and recommended units include English 4, mathematics 3-4, social studies 2-3, history 2-3, science 3-4 (laboratory 3-4), foreign language 3-4 and academic electives 3. Algebra, geometry, trigonometry required of engineering applicants. Of 6 additional electives 4 must be from subjects mentioned and the arts.

2008-2009 Annual costs. Tuition/fees: $28,262. Room/board: $7,860. Books/supplies: $750. Personal expenses: $1,700.

2007-2008 Financial aid. Need-based: 836 full-time freshmen applied for aid; 567 were judged to have need; 567 of these received aid. Average need met was 88%. Average scholarship/grant was $12,464; average loan $4,890. 65% of total undergraduate aid awarded as scholarships/grants, 35% as loans/jobs. **Non-need-based:** Awarded to 2,577 full-time undergraduates, including 534 freshmen. Scholarships awarded for academics, alumni affiliation, athletics, leadership, minority status, music/drama, ROTC.

Application procedures. Admission: Closing date 2/1 (postmark date). $50 fee, may be waived for applicants with need. Admission notification 3/15. Must reply by 5/1. **Financial aid:** Priority date 2/1, closing date 6/30. FAFSA required. Applicants notified on a rolling basis starting 3/1; must reply by 5/1 or within 3 week(s) of notification.

Academics. Special study options: Accelerated study, combined bachelor's/graduate degree, double major, ESL, exchange student, honors, independent study, internships, semester at sea, study abroad, teacher certification program, Washington semester, weekend college. **Credit/placement by examination:** AP, CLEP, IB, SAT, ACT. 32 credit hours maximum toward bachelor's degree. **Support services:** Pre-admission summer program, study skills assistance, writing center.

Majors. Area/ethnic studies: Asian, European, Latin American, women's. **Biology:** General, biochemistry. **Business:** Accounting, banking/financial services, business admin, international, management information systems, managerial economics. **Communications:** Broadcast journalism, journalism, public relations. **Computer sciences:** Computer science. **Education:** Music, physical, special. **Engineering:** General, civil, computer, electrical, mechanical. **Foreign languages:** Comparative lit, French, Italian, Spanish. **Health:** Preop/surgical nursing. **History:** General. **Liberal arts:** Arts/sciences. **Math:** General. **Parks/recreation:** Sports admin. **Philosophy/religion:** Philosophy, religion. **Physical sciences:** Chemistry, physics. **Protective services:** Criminal justice. **Psychology:** General. **Social sciences:** Economics, international relations, political science, sociology. **Visual/performing arts:** Dramatic, music performance, studio arts.

Most popular majors. Business/marketing 26%, communications/journalism 9%, engineering/engineering technologies 10%, health sciences 6%, history 6%, psychology 7%, social sciences 10%.

Computing on campus. 560 workstations in library, computer center. Dormitories wired for high-speed internet access and linked to campus network. Commuter students can connect to campus network. Online course registration, online library, helpline, repair service, student web hosting, wireless network available.

Student life. Freshman orientation: Mandatory, $60 fee. Preregistration for classes offered. **Housing:** Guaranteed on-campus for freshmen. Coed dorms, single-sex dorms, special housing for disabled, apartments, wellness housing available. $200 fully refundable deposit, deadline 5/1. International students, freshmen and sophomores under 21 must live on campus, unless living at home. **Activities:** Bands, campus ministries, choral groups, dance, drama, international student organizations, literary magazine, music ensembles, radio station, student government, student newspaper, symphony orchestra, TV station, 102 student clubs and service organizations.

Athletics. NCAA. **Intercollegiate:** Baseball M, basketball, cross-country, golf, rowing (crew), soccer, tennis, track and field, volleyball W. **Intramural:** Badminton, basketball, racquetball, soccer, softball, tennis, volleyball, weight lifting, wrestling M. **Team name:** Bulldogs.

Student services. Adult student services, alcohol/substance abuse counseling, chaplain/spiritual director, career counseling, student employment services, financial aid counseling, health services, minority student services, personal counseling, veterans' counselor. **Physically disabled:** Services for visually, speech, hearing impaired.

Contact. E-mail: mcculloh@gu.gonzaga.edu
Phone: (509) 313-6572 Toll-free number: (800) 322-2584
Fax: (509) 313-5780
Julie McCulloh, Dean of Admissions, Gonzaga University, 502 East Boone Avenue, Spokane, WA 99258-0001

Heritage University
Toppenish, Washington
www.heritage.edu **CB code: 4344**

- Private 4-year liberal arts and teachers college affiliated with interdenominational tradition
- Commuter campus in small town
- 745 degree-seeking undergraduates

General. Founded in 1982. Regionally accredited. **Degrees:** 109 bachelor's, 16 associate awarded; master's offered. **Location:** 165 miles from Seattle, 20 miles from Yakima. **Calendar:** Semester, limited summer session. **Full-time faculty:** 45 total. **Part-time faculty:** 142 total. **Class size:** 76% < 20, 24% 20-39. **Special facilities:** Solar telescope, portable planetarium.

Freshman class profile. 243 applied, 156 admitted, 73 enrolled.

Basis for selection. Open admission. All students take institutional placement test. **Homeschooled:** State high school equivalency certificate required.

High school preparation. Recommended units include English 3, mathematics 2, history 3, science 1 (laboratory 1) and academic electives 4.

2008-2009 Annual costs. Tuition/fees: $12,205. Books/supplies: $1,155. Personal expenses: $2,984.

2007-2008 Financial aid. Need-based: 58% of total undergraduate aid awarded as scholarships/grants, 42% as loans/jobs. **Non-need-based:** Scholarships awarded for academics, leadership, minority status.

Application procedures. Admission: Priority date 4/15; no deadline. No application fee. Application must be submitted on paper. Admission notification on a rolling basis. **Financial aid:** Priority date 2/10; no closing date. FAFSA, institutional form required. Applicants notified on a rolling basis; must reply within 2 week(s) of notification.

Academics. Special study options: Cooperative education, distance learning, double major, dual enrollment of high school students, ESL, honors, independent study, internships, liberal arts/career combination, student-designed major, teacher certification program. **Credit/placement by examination:** AP, CLEP, institutional tests. 14 credit hours maximum toward associate degree, 30 toward bachelor's. **Support services:** Learning center, reduced course load, remedial instruction, study skills assistance, tutoring, writing center.

Majors. Agriculture: Horticulture. **Area/ethnic studies:** American. **Biology:** General. **Business:** General, accounting, business admin, entrepreneurial studies, human resources, marketing. **Computer sciences:** General. **Conservation:** General, environmental science. **Education:** General, bilingual, biology, chemistry, computer, early childhood, elementary, English, ESL, history, mathematics, middle, reading, science, secondary, Spanish, special. **Health:** Health care admin. **Interdisciplinary:** Math/computer science, natural sciences. **Math:** General. **Physical sciences:** General, chemistry. **Psychology:** General. **Public administration:** Social work.

Most popular majors. Business/marketing 7%, computer/information sciences 6%, education 53%, public administration/social services 16%.

Computing on campus. 160 workstations in library, computer center. Commuter students can connect to campus network. Online library, wireless network available.

Student life. Freshman orientation: Available. Preregistration for classes offered. Typically held one day during the week before classes start for the fall and spring semesters. **Activities:** Dance, drama, literary magazine, music ensembles, student government, student newspaper, Native American, Heritage Community Volunteers in Action, Heritage Educators Association, social work club, Nursing students club.

Student services. Adult student services, career counseling, services for economically disadvantaged, student employment services, financial aid counseling, on-campus daycare, personal counseling, placement for graduates, veterans' counselor.

Contact. E-mail: admissions@heritage.edu
Phone: (509) 865-8508 Toll-free number: (888) 272-6190
Fax: (509) 865-8659
MIguel Puente, Director of Admissions, Heritage University, 3240 Fort Road, Toppenish, WA 98948-9599

International Academy of Design and Technology: Seattle

Seattle, Washington
www.iadtseattle.com

- For-profit 4-year university
- Very large city
- 511 degree-seeking undergraduates

General. Accredited by ACICS. **Degrees:** 58 bachelor's, 28 associate awarded. **Calendar:** Quarter. **Full-time faculty:** 10 total. **Part-time faculty:** 41 total.

Freshman class profile. 116 applied, 116 admitted, 107 enrolled.

Basis for selection. Open admission.

2008-2009 Annual costs. Tuition/fees: $16,200.

2007-2008 Financial aid. Need-based: 25% of total undergraduate aid awarded as scholarships/grants, 75% as loans/jobs.

Application procedures. Admission: No deadline. $50 fee. **Financial aid:** No deadline.

Academics. Credit/placement by examination: CLEP.

Majors. Visual/performing arts: Fashion design, graphic design, interior design.

Contact. Phone: (888) 424-8111
Lynette Rickman, Director of Admissions, International Academy of Design and Technology: Seattle, 645 Andover Park West, Seattle, WA 98188

ITT Technical Institute: Everett

Everett, Washington
www.itt-tech.edu **CB code: 2697**

- For-profit 4-year technical college
- Commuter campus in large town

General. Accredited by ACICS. **Calendar:** Quarter.

Contact. Phone: (425) 485-0303
Director of Recruitment, 1615 75th Street, S.W., Everett, WA 98203

ITT Technical Institute: Seattle

Seattle, Washington
www.itt-tech.edu **CB code: 3599**

- For-profit 4-year technical college
- Commuter campus in very large city

General. Founded in 1932. Accredited by ACICS. **Location:** 12 miles from downtown. **Calendar:** Quarter.

Contact. Phone: (206) 244-3300
Director of Recruitment, 12720 Gateway Drive, Suite 100, Seattle, WA 98168

ITT Technical Institute: Spokane

Spokane Valley, Washington
www.itt-tech.edu **CB code: 7027**

- For-profit 4-year technical college
- Commuter campus in small city

General. Accredited by ACICS. **Location:** 5 miles from downtown. **Calendar:** Quarter.

Contact. Phone: (509) 926-2900
Director of Recruitment, 13518 East Indiana Avenue, Spokane Valley, WA 99216

Northwest College of Art

Poulsbo, Washington
www.nca.edu **CB code: 2432**

- For-profit 4-year visual arts college
- Commuter campus in small town
- 91 full-time, degree-seeking undergraduates
- Application essay, interview required

General. Founded in 1982. Accredited by ACCSCT. **Degrees:** 28 bachelor's awarded. **Location:** 30 miles from Seattle, 60 miles from Tacoma. **Calendar:** Semester, extensive summer session. **Part-time faculty:** 15 total; 27% have terminal degrees, 40% women. **Class size:** 98% < 20, 2% 20-39.

Basis for selection. Requirements include minimum 2.5 GPA, 2 interviews, 3 letters of recommendation, 2-3 page typed essay, portfolio. TOEFL test required for international students from non-English speaking countries. SAT required for students with a GED. Portfolio required and a second essay is required if your grade point is below 2.0. **Homeschooled:** GED required except when homeschool programs show proof of school or program accreditation.

2009-2010 Annual costs. Tuition/fees (projected): $16,200. Books/supplies: $2,700.

Financial aid. Non-need-based: Scholarships awarded for academics, art, state residency.

Application procedures. Admission: Priority date 3/1; deadline 6/1 (postmark date). $50 fee. Application must be submitted on paper. Admission notification on a rolling basis. **Financial aid:** Priority date 3/1, closing date 6/1. FAFSA required. Applicants notified on a rolling basis.

Academics. Special study options: Double major, internships. **Credit/placement by examination:** AP, CLEP.

Majors. Visual/performing arts: Design, studio arts.

Computing on campus. Wireless network available.

Student life. Freshman orientation: Mandatory, $15 fee. Preregistration for classes offered.

Student services. Adult student services, career counseling, student employment services, financial aid counseling, personal counseling, placement for graduates.

Contact. E-mail: Mstoddard@nca.edu
Phone: (360) 779-9993 Toll-free number: (800) 769-2787
Fax: (360) 779-9933
Mark Stoddard, Northwest College of Art, Northwest College of Art, 16301 Creative Drive NE, Poulsbo, WA 98370-8651

Northwest University

Kirkland, Washington
www.northwestu.edu **CB code: 4541**

- Private 4-year university and liberal arts college affiliated with Assemblies of God
- Residential campus in small city
- 1,094 degree-seeking undergraduates: 14% part-time, 61% women
- 176 degree-seeking graduate students
- 77% of applicants admitted
- SAT or ACT (ACT writing optional), application essay required

General. Founded in 1934. Regionally accredited. **Degrees:** 250 bachelor's, 9 associate awarded; master's offered. **ROTC:** Army. **Location:** 10 miles from Seattle. **Calendar:** Semester, limited summer session. **Full-time faculty:** 55 total. **Part-time faculty:** 53 total.

Freshman class profile. 477 applied, 368 admitted, 169 enrolled.

Mid 50% test scores			
SAT critical reading:	460-600	GPA 3.75 or higher:	23%
SAT math:	440-560	GPA 3.50-3.74:	18%
SAT writing:	450-580	GPA 3.0-3.49:	32%
ACT composite:	18-26	GPA 2.0-2.99:	27%
		Out-of-state:	18%

Basis for selection. Entire application reviewed: includes essay, references, transcript, SAT or ACT. GPA of 2.3 required: those with GPA below 2.3 but greater than 2.0 admitted on academic probation if space available. TOEFL (minimum score 500) required for non-native speakers of English. Audition recommended for music and drama scholarships. **Learning Disabled:** Interview with Director of Student Success.

High school preparation. 16 units recommended. Recommended units include English 4, mathematics 3, social studies 2, history 2, science 2, foreign language 2 and academic electives 3.

2008-2009 Annual costs. Tuition/fees: $20,790. Room/board: $6,578. Books/supplies: $900. Personal expenses: $1,600.

2008-2009 Financial aid. Need-based: 57% of total undergraduate aid awarded as scholarships/grants, 43% as loans/jobs. **Non-need-based:** Scholarships awarded for academics, art, athletics, leadership, music/drama, religious affiliation.

Application procedures. Admission: Priority date 3/1; deadline 8/1 (postmark date). $30 fee, may be waived for applicants with need. Admission notification on a rolling basis beginning on or about 10/1. **Financial aid:** Priority date 3/1, closing date 8/1. FAFSA, institutional form required. Applicants notified by 3/31; Applicants notified on a rolling basis starting 3/3; must reply within 4 week(s) of notification.

Academics. Special study options: Accelerated study, double major, dual enrollment of high school students, ESL, independent study, internships, student-designed major, study abroad, teacher certification program, Washington semester. **Credit/placement by examination:** AP, CLEP, IB, SAT, ACT, institutional tests. 30 credit hours maximum toward associate degree, 30 toward bachelor's. **Support services:** Learning center, reduced course load, remedial instruction, study skills assistance, tutoring, writing center.

Majors. Biology: General. **Business:** Business admin. **Communications:** General, media studies, organizational. **Conservation:** Environmental science. **Education:** Elementary, middle, secondary. **Health:** Nursing (RN), premedicine. **History:** General. **Math:** General. **Philosophy/religion:** Philosophy. **Psychology:** General. **Social sciences:** Political science. **Theology:** Bible, missionary, pastoral counseling, sacred music, theology, youth ministry. **Other:** Communications/drama.

Most popular majors. Business/marketing 25%, communications/journalism 6%, education 10%, health sciences 13%, psychology 8%, theological studies 21%.

Computing on campus. 135 workstations in dormitories, library, computer center, student center. Dormitories wired for high-speed internet access and linked to campus network. Commuter students can connect to campus network. Online course registration, online library, helpline, repair service, student web hosting, wireless network available.

Student life. Freshman orientation: Mandatory. Held end of August, one week before start of classes. **Policies:** Religious observance required. **Housing:** Guaranteed on-campus for all undergraduates. Single-sex dorms, apartments available. $300 fully refundable deposit, deadline 5/1. **Activities:** Bands, choral groups, drama, music ensembles, musical theater, radio station, student government, student newspaper, community outreach groups, Psi Chi Honor Society (psychology), Association of International Students, Environmental Stewardship Club, Students in Free Enterprise.

Athletics. NAIA, NCCAA. **Intercollegiate:** Basketball, cross-country, soccer, track and field, volleyball W. **Intramural:** Football (non-tackle). **Team name:** Eagles.

Student services. Adult student services, alcohol/substance abuse counseling, chaplain/spiritual director, career counseling, student employment services, financial aid counseling, health services, personal counseling, veterans' counselor. **Physically disabled:** Services for visually impaired.

Contact. E-mail: admissions@northwestu.edu
Phone: (425) 889-5231 Toll-free number: (800) 669-3781
Fax: (425) 889-5224
Rose-mary Smith, Assistant Vice President, Enrollment, Northwest University, 5520 108th Avenue, NE, Kirkland, WA 98083-0579

Pacific Lutheran University

Tacoma, Washington — **CB member**
www.plu.edu — **CB code: 4597**

- Private 4-year university affiliated with Evangelical Lutheran Church in America
- Residential campus in large city
- 3,265 degree-seeking undergraduates: 4% part-time, 63% women, 2% African American, 6% Asian American, 2% Hispanic American, 1% Native American, 5% international
- 321 degree-seeking graduate students
- 75% of applicants admitted
- SAT or ACT (ACT writing optional), application essay required
- 70% graduate within 6 years

General. Founded in 1890. Regionally accredited. **Degrees:** 797 bachelor's awarded; master's offered. **ROTC:** Army. **Location:** 7 miles from Tacoma, 30 miles from Seattle. **Calendar:** 4-1-4, extensive summer session. **Full-time faculty:** 240 total; 82% have terminal degrees, 12% minority, 47% women. **Part-time faculty:** 15 total; 73% have terminal degrees, 7% minority, 53% women. **Class size:** 28% < 20, 66% 20-39, 4% 40-49, 2% 50-99, less than 1% >100. **Special facilities:** Herbarium, invertebrate and vertebrate museums, greenhouse, field station and boat equipped for studies of Puget Sound, Scandinavian cultural center, observatory, performing arts center.

Freshman class profile. 2,555 applied, 1,914 admitted, 716 enrolled.

Mid 50% test scores			
SAT critical reading:	490-630	GPA 3.0-3.49:	23%
SAT math:	500-620	GPA 2.0-2.99:	10%
SAT writing:	490-600	Rank in top quarter:	66%
ACT composite:	22-28	Rank in top tenth:	32%
GPA 3.75 or higher:	45%	Out-of-state:	29%
GPA 3.50-3.74:	22%	Live on campus:	90%
		International:	1%

Basis for selection. Grades, test scores, essay, recommendations, service, leadership. Admission on rolling basis until class is full. Interview recommended for borderline, exceptional; audition required for music, forensics, theater; portfolio recommended for art. **Homeschooled:** Must provide proof of high-school equivalency.

High school preparation. College-preparatory program required. 17 units recommended. Required and recommended units include English 4, mathematics 2-3, social studies 2, science 2 (laboratory 2), foreign language 2, visual/performing arts 1 and academic electives 3. Computer science, speech, debate, music also recommended. 2 years visual or performing arts recommended.

2008-2009 Annual costs. Tuition/fees: $26,800. Room/board: $8,200. Books/supplies: $924. Personal expenses: $2,094.

2008-2009 Financial aid. Need-based: 641 full-time freshmen applied for aid; 524 were judged to have need; 520 of these received aid. Average need met was 91%. Average scholarship/grant was $16,508; average loan $6,318. 60% of total undergraduate aid awarded as scholarships/grants, 40% as loans/jobs. **Non-need-based:** Awarded to 2,389 full-time undergraduates, including 580 freshmen. Scholarships awarded for academics, alumni affiliation, art, leadership, music/drama, religious affiliation, ROTC.

Application procedures. Admission: Priority date 2/1; no deadline. $40 fee, may be waived for applicants with need, free for online applicants. Admission notification on a rolling basis beginning on or about 10/1. Must reply by May 1 or within 2 week(s) if notified thereafter. Housing deposit is refundable only through May 1. **Financial aid:** Priority date 1/31; no closing date. FAFSA required. Applicants notified on a rolling basis starting 3/15; must reply by 5/1 or within 4 week(s) of notification.

Academics. Freshman year program includes topic-oriented writing and critical conversation classes. **Special study options:** Combined bachelor's/graduate degree, cooperative education, cross-registration, double major, dual enrollment of high school students, ESL, exchange student, honors, independent study, internships, liberal arts/career combination, student-designed major, study abroad, teacher certification program. **Credit/placement by examination:** AP, CLEP, IB, institutional tests. 30 credit hours maximum toward bachelor's degree. **Support services:** Pre-admission summer program, reduced course load, study skills assistance, tutoring, writing center.

Majors. Area/ethnic studies: Scandinavian, women's. **Biology:** General. **Business:** Business admin. **Communications:** General. **Computer sciences:** Computer science. **Conservation:** Environmental science. **Education:** Elementary, secondary. **Engineering:** Computer, science. **Foreign languages:** Chinese, classics, French, German, Norwegian, Spanish. **Health:** Nursing (RN). **History:** General. **Interdisciplinary:** Global studies. **Math:**

General. **Parks/recreation:** General, health/fitness. **Philosophy/religion:** Philosophy, religion. **Physical sciences:** Chemistry, geology, physics. **Psychology:** General. **Public administration:** Social work. **Social sciences:** Anthropology, economics, political science, sociology. **Visual/performing arts:** Art, studio arts, theater arts management.

Most popular majors. Biology 8%, business/marketing 14%, communications/journalism 6%, education 7%, English 6%, health sciences 10%, psychology 6%, social sciences 11%.

Computing on campus. 250 workstations in library, student center. Dormitories wired for high-speed internet access and linked to campus network. Commuter students can connect to campus network. Helpline, student web hosting available.

Student life. Freshman orientation: Available. Preregistration for classes offered. **Policies:** All single, full-time students must live in university housing, unless student lives at home with parent or legal guardian, is 20 years of age or older on or before a specific college-designated date, or has achieved junior status. **Housing:** Guaranteed on-campus for all undergraduates. Coed dorms, single-sex dorms, special housing for disabled, apartments available. $200 deposit, deadline 5/1. **Activities:** Bands, campus ministries, choral groups, dance, drama, film society, international student organizations, literary magazine, music ensembles, musical theater, opera, radio station, student government, student newspaper, symphony orchestra, TV station, Intervarsity Christian Fellowship, Advocates for Social Justice, Asian & Pacific Islanders club, B.L.A.C.K. at PLU, environmental action, Puentes, social work organization, Amnesty International, Habitat for Humanity, Young Life.

Athletics. NCAA. **Intercollegiate:** Baseball M, basketball, cheerleading, cross-country, football (tackle) M, golf, rowing (crew), soccer, softball W, swimming, tennis, track and field, volleyball W. **Intramural:** Badminton, basketball, bowling, cross-country, football (non-tackle), golf, handball, racquetball, soccer, softball, squash, table tennis, tennis, track and field, volleyball. **Team name:** Lutes.

Student services. Adult student services, chaplain/spiritual director, career counseling, student employment services, financial aid counseling, health services, minority student services, personal counseling, placement for graduates, veterans' counselor, women's services. **Physically disabled:** Services for visually, speech, hearing impaired.

Contact. E-mail: admission@plu.edu
Phone: (253) 535-7151 Toll-free number: (800) 274-6758
Fax: (253) 536-5136
Karl Stumo, Dean of Admission and Financial Aid, Pacific Lutheran University, Office of Admissions, Tacoma, WA 98447-0003

Saint Martin's University

Lacey, Washington
www.stmartin.edu
CB member
CB code: 4674

- Private 4-year university affiliated with Roman Catholic Church
- Residential campus in large town
- 1,296 degree-seeking undergraduates: 20% part-time, 55% women, 7% African American, 11% Asian American, 6% Hispanic American, 2% Native American, 6% international
- 272 degree-seeking graduate students
- 84% of applicants admitted
- SAT or ACT with writing, application essay required
- 54% graduate within 6 years

General. Founded in 1895. Regionally accredited. Saint Martin's Abbey, located on campus, is the home of the Benedictine monks. **Degrees:** 303 bachelor's awarded; master's offered. **ROTC:** Army, Air Force. **Location:** 3 miles from Olympia, 60 miles from Seattle. **Calendar:** Semester, limited summer session. **Full-time faculty:** 79 total; 76% have terminal degrees, 13% minority, 35% women. **Part-time faculty:** 119 total; 25% have terminal degrees, 8% minority, 44% women. **Class size:** 65% < 20, 26% 20-39, 2% 40-49, 6% 50-99, 1% >100.

Freshman class profile. 624 applied, 522 admitted, 204 enrolled.

Mid 50% test scores		**GPA 2.0-2.99:**	34%
SAT critical reading:	420-550	**Rank in top quarter:**	41%
SAT math:	430-570	**Rank in top tenth:**	15%
SAT writing:	410-540	**End year in good standing:**	84%
ACT composite:	17-23	**Return as sophomores:**	72%
GPA 3.75 or higher:	18%	**Out-of-state:**	13%
GPA 3.50-3.74:	17%	**Live on campus:**	72%
GPA 3.0-3.49:	31%		

Basis for selection. School achievement record most important. Test scores important. 3.0 GPA required for regular admittance. Interview recommended. **Homeschooled:** Statement describing homeschool structure and mission, transcript of courses and grades required. **Learning Disabled:** Students with disabilities initiate contact with the Office of Disability Support Services.

High school preparation. College-preparatory program recommended. 18 units recommended. Recommended units include English 4, mathematics 3, social studies 2, science 3 (laboratory 1), foreign language 2 and academic electives 3.

2008-2009 Annual costs. Tuition/fees: $24,110. Room/board: $8,040. Books/supplies: $1,000. Personal expenses: $1,000.

2007-2008 Financial aid. Need-based: 197 full-time freshmen applied for aid; 168 were judged to have need; 168 of these received aid. Average need met was 81%. Average scholarship/grant was $16,068; average loan $3,147. 64% of total undergraduate aid awarded as scholarships/grants, 36% as loans/jobs. **Non-need-based:** Awarded to 263 full-time undergraduates, including 83 freshmen. Scholarships awarded for academics, ROTC.

Application procedures. Admission: Priority date 3/1; no deadline. $35 fee, may be waived for applicants with need. Admission notification on a rolling basis beginning on or about 10/1. Must reply by May 1 or within 3 week(s) if notified thereafter. **Financial aid:** Priority date 3/1; no closing date. FAFSA required. Applicants notified on a rolling basis starting 2/15.

Academics. Special study options: Distance learning, double major, ESL, exchange student, independent study, internships, study abroad, teacher certification program, Washington semester. **Credit/placement by examination:** AP, CLEP, IB, institutional tests. 32 credit hours maximum toward associate degree, 64 toward bachelor's. **Support services:** Learning center, pre-admission summer program, reduced course load, remedial instruction, study skills assistance, tutoring, writing center.

Majors. Biology: General. **Business:** Accounting, business admin. **Computer sciences:** General, computer science. **Education:** Elementary, special. **Engineering:** Civil, mechanical. **Health:** Predental, premedicine, prepharmacy, preveterinary. **History:** General. **Liberal arts:** Humanities. **Math:** General. **Philosophy/religion:** Philosophy, religion. **Physical sciences:** Chemistry. **Protective services:** Criminal justice. **Psychology:** General. **Public administration:** Community org/advocacy. **Social sciences:** Political science, sociology. **Visual/performing arts:** Dramatic.

Most popular majors. Biology 8%, business/marketing 34%, education 7%, engineering/engineering technologies 9%, psychology 13%, security/protective services 7%, social sciences 6%.

Computing on campus. 80 workstations in library, computer center. Dormitories wired for high-speed internet access and linked to campus network. Commuter students can connect to campus network. Online library, helpline, repair service, wireless network available.

Student life. Freshman orientation: Mandatory, $150 fee. Preregistration for classes offered. Freshmen orientation program begins on the Thursday before school starts in the fall. **Policies:** Alcohol possession, consumption, possession by means of consumption (if under the age of 21) and the sale of alcoholic beverages is prohibited in or around University-owned or University-controlled property. **Housing:** Guaranteed on-campus for freshmen. Coed dorms, special housing for disabled, apartments available. $200 fully refundable deposit, deadline 7/1. **Activities:** Bands, campus ministries, choral groups, dance, drama, international student organizations, Model UN, musical theater, student government, student newspaper, Circle K, Hawaiian club, international club, Non-traditional students group, social action club, College Republicans, Gay/Straight Alliance, Young Democrats, Saint for Life.

Athletics. NCAA. **Intercollegiate:** Baseball M, basketball, cross-country, golf, soccer, softball W, track and field, volleyball W. **Intramural:** Basketball, bowling, soccer, softball, tennis, volleyball. **Team name:** Saints.

Student services. Adult student services, alcohol/substance abuse counseling, chaplain/spiritual director, career counseling, financial aid counseling, health services, personal counseling, veterans' counselor. **Physically disabled:** Services for visually, hearing impaired.

Contact. E-mail: admissions@stmartin.edu
Phone: (360) 438-4311 Toll-free number: (800) 368-8803
Fax: (360) 412-6189
Eric Pedersen, Dean, Enrollment and Financial Aid, Saint Martin's University, 5300 Pacific Avenue SE, Lacey, WA 98503-7500

Seattle Pacific University

Seattle, Washington — **CB member**
www.spu.edu — **CB code: 4694**

- Private 4-year university affiliated with Free Methodist Church of North America
- Residential campus in very large city
- 2,985 degree-seeking undergraduates: 5% part-time, 67% women, 2% African American, 7% Asian American, 3% Hispanic American, 1% Native American, 1% international
- 853 degree-seeking graduate students
- 88% of applicants admitted
- SAT or ACT (ACT writing optional), application essay required
- 64% graduate within 6 years

General. Founded in 1891. Regionally accredited. **Degrees:** 734 bachelor's awarded; master's, doctoral offered. **ROTC:** Army, Naval, Air Force. **Location:** 3 miles from downtown. **Calendar:** Quarter, limited summer session. **Full-time faculty:** 190 total; 85% have terminal degrees, 8% minority, 40% women. **Part-time faculty:** 157 total; 10% have terminal degrees, 4% minority, 57% women. **Class size:** 54% < 20, 33% 20-39, 8% 40-49, 5% 50-99, less than 1% >100. **Special facilities:** 2 island campuses used for biological studies.

Freshman class profile. 2,049 applied, 1,808 admitted, 713 enrolled.

Mid 50% test scores		**GPA 3.50-3.74:**	22%
SAT critical reading:	530-640	**GPA 3.0-3.49:**	32%
SAT math:	520-620	**GPA 2.0-2.99:**	3%
SAT writing:	520-610	**Return as sophomores:**	82%
ACT composite:	21-28	**Out-of-state:**	54%
GPA 3.75 or higher:	43%	**Live on campus:**	97%

Basis for selection. Admission decisions based primarily based on grades, grade trend, test scores, essays, letters of recommendation and extracurricular activities. Audition required for music, performing art workshop; portfolio required for fine art scholarship. **Homeschooled:** Copy of reading list and information regarding the curriculum used in home school program. **Learning Disabled:** Contact Disability Support Services in the Center for Learning at 206-281-2272 to make arrangements for an interview to determine the level of assistance needed. Students required to provide documentation of the nature of the disability.

High school preparation. College-preparatory program recommended. Required units include English 4, mathematics 3, history 2, science 3 and foreign language 3.

2008-2009 Annual costs. Tuition/fees: $26,817. Room/board: $8,454. Books/supplies: $924. Personal expenses: $1,863.

2008-2009 Financial aid. Need-based: 585 full-time freshmen applied for aid; 457 were judged to have need; 456 of these received aid. Average need met was 84%. Average scholarship/grant was $21,236; average loan $5,479. 63% of total undergraduate aid awarded as scholarships/grants, 37% as loans/jobs. **Non-need-based:** Awarded to 853 full-time undergraduates, including 222 freshmen. Scholarships awarded for academics, alumni affiliation, art, athletics, leadership, minority status, music/drama, religious affiliation, ROTC.

Application procedures. Admission: Closing date 2/1 (postmark date). $45 fee, may be waived for applicants with need. Admission notification 3/1. Admission notification on a rolling basis. Must reply by May 1 or within 2 week(s) if notified thereafter. **Financial aid:** Priority date 2/1; no closing date. FAFSA required. Applicants notified on a rolling basis starting 3/11; must reply by 5/1 or within 30 week(s) of notification.

Academics. Special study options: Distance learning, double major, exchange student, external degree, honors, independent study, internships, liberal arts/career combination, student-designed major, study abroad, teacher certification program, Washington semester. **Credit/placement by examination:** AP, CLEP, IB, SAT, ACT, institutional tests. 45 credit hours maximum toward bachelor's degree. **Support services:** Learning center, reduced course load, remedial instruction, study skills assistance, tutoring, writing center.

Majors. Area/ethnic studies: European, Latin American. **Biology:** General, biochemistry. **Business:** Accounting. **Communications:** General. **Computer sciences:** Computer science. **Education:** Art, English, mathematics, music, science, social science, special. **Engineering:** Computer, electrical, science. **Family/consumer sciences:** Clothing/textiles, food/nutrition. **Foreign languages:** Classics, French, German, Latin, Russian, Spanish. **Health:** Nursing (RN). **History:** General. **Legal studies:** Prelaw. **Liberal arts:** Arts/sciences. **Math:** General, computational. **Parks/recreation:** Exercise sciences. **Philosophy/religion:** Philosophy. **Physical sciences:** Chemistry, physics. **Psychology:** General. **Social sciences:** Economics, political science, sociology. **Theology:** Religious ed. **Visual/performing arts:** General, art, dramatic, interior design. **Other:** Global development studies.

Most popular majors. Biology 7%, business/marketing 15%, communications/journalism 8%, family/consumer sciences 7%, health sciences 8%, psychology 9%, social sciences 7%, theological studies 6%, visual/performing arts 10%.

Computing on campus. 150 workstations in dormitories, library, computer center, student center. Dormitories wired for high-speed internet access and linked to campus network. Commuter students can connect to campus network. Online course registration, online library, helpline, repair service, wireless network available.

Student life. Freshman orientation: Mandatory. Preregistration for classes offered. **Policies:** Religious observance required. **Housing:** Coed dorms, special housing for disabled, apartments available. $300 fully refundable deposit, deadline 6/1. **Activities:** Bands, campus ministries, choral groups, drama, literary magazine, music ensembles, musical theater, radio station, student government, student newspaper, symphony orchestra, more than 25 clubs and organizations.

Athletics. NCAA. **Intercollegiate:** Basketball, cross-country, gymnastics W, rowing (crew), soccer, track and field, volleyball W. **Intramural:** Badminton, basketball, bowling, cross-country, football (tackle) M, golf, skiing, soccer, softball, swimming, table tennis, tennis, track and field, volleyball, wrestling M. **Team name:** Falcons.

Student services. Adult student services, chaplain/spiritual director, career counseling, student employment services, financial aid counseling, health services, minority student services, personal counseling, placement for graduates, veterans' counselor. **Physically disabled:** Services for visually, hearing impaired.

Contact. E-mail: admissions@spu.edu
Phone: (206) 281-2021 Toll-free number: (800) 366-3344
Fax: (206) 281-2669
Jobe Korb-Nice, Director of Undergraduate Admissions, Seattle Pacific University, 3307 Third Avenue West, Suite 115, Seattle, WA 98119-1997

Seattle University

Seattle, Washington — **CB member**
www.seattleu.edu — **CB code: 4695**

- Private 4-year university affiliated with Roman Catholic Church
- Residential campus in very large city
- 4,168 degree-seeking undergraduates: 5% part-time, 61% women, 6% African American, 19% Asian American, 8% Hispanic American, 1% Native American, 8% international
- 3,320 degree-seeking graduate students
- 65% of applicants admitted
- SAT or ACT (ACT writing optional), application essay required
- 71% graduate within 6 years

General. Founded in 1891. Regionally accredited. Courses also offered at Bellevue Campus. **Degrees:** 1,128 bachelor's awarded; master's, doctoral, first professional offered. **ROTC:** Army, Naval, Air Force. **Location:** One mile from downtown. **Calendar:** Quarter, extensive summer session. **Full-time faculty:** 437 total; 76% have terminal degrees, 14% minority, 47% women. **Part-time faculty:** 216 total; 56% have terminal degrees, 3% minority, 49% women. **Class size:** 55% < 20, 42% 20-39, 2% 40-49, 1% 50-99. **Special facilities:** Design center (where engineering students work with major companies in the area), observatory.

Freshman class profile. 4,999 applied, 3,266 admitted, 888 enrolled.

Mid 50% test scores		**GPA 2.0-2.99:**	4%
SAT critical reading:	520-640	**Rank in top quarter:**	63%
SAT math:	530-630	**Rank in top tenth:**	32%
SAT writing:	510-620	**Return as sophomores:**	87%
ACT composite:	23-28	**Out-of-state:**	51%
GPA 3.75 or higher:	33%	**Live on campus:**	93%
GPA 3.50-3.74:	24%	**International:**	3%
GPA 3.0-3.49:	39%		

Basis for selection. 2.75 GPA minimum, higher for some programs. Secondary school record, recommendations, test scores most important. Essay, school, community activities also important. Applicants must submit one test with writing component. ACT writing component is required if applicant does not submit SAT Reasoning scores. Interview recommended for marginal students.

High school preparation. 16 units required. Required and recommended units include English 4, mathematics 3-4, science 2-3 (laboratory 2), foreign language 2 and academic electives 3.

2008-2009 Annual costs. Tuition/fees: $28,260. $200 enrollment deposit, $95 matriculation fee required. $95 per-credit-hour charge for credit by examination. $95 per-credit-hour charge for validation of field experience. Room/board: $8,340. Books/supplies: $945. Personal expenses: $1,878.

2008-2009 Financial aid. Non-need-based: Scholarships awarded for academics, alumni affiliation, athletics, leadership, minority status, music/drama, ROTC, state residency.

Application procedures. Admission: Priority date 1/15; no deadline. $45 fee, may be waived for applicants with need. Admission notification on a rolling basis beginning on or about 2/6. Must reply by May 1 or within 4 week(s) if notified thereafter. **Financial aid:** Priority date 1/15; no closing date. FAFSA required. Applicants notified on a rolling basis starting 3/21; must reply by 5/1 or within 2 week(s) of notification.

Academics. Special study options: Cooperative education, cross-registration, double major, honors, independent study, internships, liberal arts/career combination, student-designed major, study abroad, teacher certification program. **Credit/placement by examination:** AP, CLEP, IB, institutional tests. 45 credit hours maximum toward bachelor's degree. Special arrangements for nursing majors who take NLN exams. 50 credits maximum. **Support services:** Learning center, pre-admission summer program, reduced course load, study skills assistance, tutoring, writing center.

Majors. Area/ethnic studies: Asian, women's. **Biology:** General, biochemistry. **Business:** General, accounting, business admin, e-commerce, finance, international, managerial economics, marketing. **Communications:** Journalism, media studies, public relations. **Computer sciences:** Computer science. **Conservation:** General. **Engineering:** Civil, electrical, mechanical. **Foreign languages:** General, French, Spanish. **Health:** Clinical lab science, medical records admin, nurse practitioner, nursing (RN), public health nursing, sonography. **History:** General. **Interdisciplinary:** Global studies. **Liberal arts:** Arts/sciences, humanities. **Math:** General. **Philosophy/religion:** Philosophy, religion. **Physical sciences:** General, chemistry, physics. **Protective services:** Criminal justice, criminalistics. **Psychology:** General. **Public administration:** General, social work. **Social sciences:** Economics, political science, sociology. **Visual/performing arts:** General, art history/conservation, dramatic.

Most popular majors. Business/marketing 21%, English 6%, health sciences 14%, liberal arts 7%, psychology 6%, social sciences 7%.

Computing on campus. 401 workstations in dormitories, library, computer center, student center. Dormitories wired for high-speed internet access and linked to campus network. Commuter students can connect to campus network. Helpline, student web hosting, wireless network available.

Student life. Freshman orientation: Mandatory. Preregistration for classes offered. 3 days prior to start of classes. **Housing:** Guaranteed on-campus for freshmen. Coed dorms, apartments, wellness housing available. $300 nonrefundable deposit, deadline 5/1. Single-gender floors available. **Activities:** Bands, campus ministries, choral groups, dance, drama, international student organizations, literary magazine, music ensembles, musical theater, radio station, student government, student newspaper, 65 clubs available.

Athletics. NCAA. **Intercollegiate:** Baseball M, basketball, cross-country, golf, soccer, softball W, swimming, tennis, track and field, volleyball W. **Intramural:** Basketball, football (non-tackle), soccer, softball, tennis, volleyball. **Team name:** Redhawks.

Student services. Adult student services, alcohol/substance abuse counseling, chaplain/spiritual director, career counseling, student employment services, financial aid counseling, health services, minority student services, personal counseling, placement for graduates, veterans' counselor, women's services. **Physically disabled:** Services for visually, speech, hearing impaired.

Contact. E-mail: admissions@seattleu.edu
Phone: (206) 296-2000 Toll-free number: (800) 426-7123
Fax: (206) 296-5656
Michael McKeon, Dean of Admissions, Seattle University, 901 12th Avenue, Seattle, WA 98122-4340

Trinity Lutheran College

Everett, Washington
www.tlc.edu
CB code: 4408

- Private 4-year Bible and liberal arts college affiliated with Lutheran Church
- Residential campus in small city
- 100 degree-seeking undergraduates
- 27% of applicants admitted
- SAT or ACT (ACT writing optional) required

General. Founded in 1944. Regionally accredited. All students participate in off-campus service learning practicums. **Degrees:** 21 bachelor's awarded. **Location:** 30 miles from Seattle. **Calendar:** 4-1-4. **Full-time faculty:** 13 total. **Part-time faculty:** 18 total. **Special facilities:** Children, youth and family resource center; preschool and Christian school.

Freshman class profile. 151 applied, 41 admitted, 32 enrolled.

Basis for selection. High school GPA, test scores,1 recommendation. Interview considered. **Homeschooled:** Statement describing homeschool structure and mission, transcript of courses and grades, letter of recommendation (nonparent) required.

High school preparation. Recommended units include English 3, mathematics 2, history 2, science 2 and foreign language 1.

2008-2009 Annual costs. Tuition/fees: $19,425. Room/board: $6,501. Books/supplies: $642. Personal expenses: $1,818.

2008-2009 Financial aid. Non-need-based: Scholarships awarded for academics, alumni affiliation, art, leadership, music/drama.

Application procedures. Admission: Priority date 2/1; no deadline. $25 fee, may be waived for applicants with need, free for online applicants. Admission notification on a rolling basis beginning on or about 10/1. Must reply by May 1 or within 2 week(s) if notified thereafter. **Financial aid:** Priority date 3/1; no closing date. FAFSA, institutional form required. Applicants notified on a rolling basis starting 3/15; must reply within 2 week(s) of notification.

Academics. Special study options: Combined bachelor's/graduate degree, cooperative education, dual enrollment of high school students, independent study, internships, liberal arts/career combination, student-designed major, study abroad, urban semester. Study trips to Holy Lands, Italy, Greece, Africa. **Credit/placement by examination:** AP, CLEP, IB, institutional tests. 8 credit hours maximum toward associate degree, 8 toward bachelor's. **Support services:** Reduced course load, remedial instruction, study skills assistance, tutoring, writing center.

Majors. Business: Business admin, nonprofit/public. **Communications:** Media studies. **Education:** Early childhood, elementary. **Philosophy/religion:** Christian, religion. **Psychology:** General. **Public administration:** Social work. **Theology:** Bible, missionary, sacred music, theology, youth ministry.

Computing on campus. 15 workstations in dormitories, library, computer center, student center. Dormitories wired for high-speed internet access and linked to campus network. Commuter students can connect to campus network. Online library, helpline, wireless network available.

Student life. Freshman orientation: Mandatory. Preregistration for classes offered. **Housing:** Guaranteed on-campus for all undergraduates. Single-sex dorms, special housing for disabled, apartments, wellness housing available. $75 partly refundable deposit, deadline 5/1. **Activities:** Choral groups, drama, music ensembles, musical theater, student government, student newspaper, Student learning practicums, Global Concerns Mission, Worship Commission, Environmental Commission.

Athletics. Intramural: Basketball, football (non-tackle), soccer, softball, table tennis, tennis, volleyball. **Team name:** Eagles.

Student services. Adult student services, chaplain/spiritual director, career counseling, student employment services, financial aid counseling, health services, personal counseling, placement for graduates. **Physically disabled:** Services for visually impaired.

Contact. E-mail: admissions@tlc.edu
Phone: (425) 249-4800 Toll-free number: (800) 843-5659
Fax: (425) 249-4801
Pamela Renn, Director of Enrollment, Trinity Lutheran College, 2802 Wetmore Avenue, Everett, WA 98201

University of Puget Sound

Tacoma, Washington
www.ups.edu
CB member
CB code: 4067

- Private 4-year university and liberal arts college
- Residential campus in small city
- 2,566 degree-seeking undergraduates: 1% part-time, 58% women, 3% African American, 9% Asian American, 4% Hispanic American, 1% Native American

- 263 degree-seeking graduate students
- 65% of applicants admitted
- SAT or ACT (ACT writing recommended), application essay required
- 76% graduate within 6 years; 26% enter graduate study

General. Founded in 1888. Regionally accredited. **Degrees:** 611 bachelor's awarded; master's, first professional offered. **ROTC:** Army. **Location:** 35 miles from Seattle, 28 miles from Olympia. **Calendar:** Semester, limited summer session. **Full-time faculty:** 228 total; 89% have terminal degrees, 9% minority, 46% women. **Part-time faculty:** 51 total; 33% have terminal degrees, 6% minority, 59% women. **Class size:** 58% < 20, 40% 20-39, 2% 40-49, less than 1% 50-99. **Special facilities:** Natural history museum, arboretum, x-ray laboratory, electron microscope lab, observatory, concert hall, sculpture building, greenhouse, sedimentology lab, rock and mineral collection, exercise science lab, physiology labs.

Freshman class profile. 5,580 applied, 3,646 admitted, 676 enrolled.

Mid 50% test scores			
SAT critical reading:	570-680	GPA 2.0-2.99:	9%
SAT math:	570-670	Rank in top quarter:	75%
SAT writing:	560-660	Rank in top tenth:	39%
ACT composite:	25-29	End year in good standing:	94%
GPA 3.75 or higher:	35%	Return as sophomores:	85%
GPA 3.50-3.74:	22%	Out-of-state:	80%
GPA 3.0-3.49:	34%	Live on campus:	98%
		International:	1%

Basis for selection. High school record most important followed by test scores. Writing ability as demonstrated through the essay and short answer questions. Recommendations and activities important. If applicants have taken both SAT and ACT, they should submit all scores. Interview recommended for all; audition required for music; portfolio recommended for art; audition recommended for theater. **Homeschooled:** Applicants should show work in writing, critical reading, mathematics, history; and social, physical, and natural sciences. Foreign language recommended.

High school preparation. College-preparatory program recommended. 19 units recommended. Recommended units include English 4, mathematics 4, social studies 3, history 3, science 4 (laboratory 4), foreign language 3 and visual/performing arts 1. One fine, visual or performing art recommended.

2008-2009 Annual costs. Tuition/fees: $33,975. Room/board: $8,760. Books/supplies: $1,000. Personal expenses: $1,800.

2008-2009 Financial aid. Need-based: 461 full-time freshmen applied for aid; 369 were judged to have need; 369 of these received aid. Average need met was 84%. Average scholarship/grant was $21,649; average loan $4,701. 66% of total undergraduate aid awarded as scholarships/grants, 34% as loans/jobs. **Non-need-based:** Awarded to 745 full-time undergraduates, including 211 freshmen. Scholarships awarded for academics, alumni affiliation, art, leadership, music/drama, religious affiliation. **Additional information:** Cooperative education allows qualified upperclassmen to alternate semesters of full-time study and full-time work.

Application procedures. Admission: Closing date 1/15 (postmark date). $50 fee, may be waived for applicants with need. Admission notification 4/1. Must reply by May 1 or within 2 week(s) if notified thereafter. **Financial aid:** Priority date 2/1; no closing date. FAFSA required. Students applying for Early Decision must complete the CSS PROFILE for notification of need-based financial aid eligibility. Applicants notified on a rolling basis starting 3/15; must reply by 5/1 or within 2 week(s) of notification.

Academics. All students complete core curriculum, including courses in writing and rhetoric, scholarly and creative inquiry, fine arts, humanistic, mathematical, natural scientific and social scientific approaches, and a connections course intended to develop an understanding of the interrelationship of fields of knowledge. **Special study options:** Combined bachelor's/graduate degree, cooperative education, double major, honors, independent study, internships, student-designed major, study abroad, teacher certification program. Institution also offers community service opportunities, forensics & debate, diversity & leadership training, multiple speaker/lecturer programs, year of study in Asia, 3-2 engineering program, business leadership program. **Credit/placement by examination:** AP, CLEP, IB, institutional tests. **Support services:** Learning center, reduced course load, study skills assistance, tutoring, writing center.

Majors. Area/ethnic studies: Asian. **Biology:** General, biochemistry, cellular/molecular. **Business:** Business admin. **Communications:** General. **Computer sciences:** General, computer science. **Education:** Music. **Foreign languages:** Classics, French, German, Spanish. **History:** General. **Interdisciplinary:** Natural sciences, science/society. **Math:** General. **Parks/recreation:** Exercise sciences. **Philosophy/religion:** Philosophy, religion. **Physical sciences:** Chemistry, geology, physics. **Psychology:** General. **Social sciences:** Economics, international economics, political science, sociology. **Visual/performing arts:** Art, dramatic, music management, music performance.

Most popular majors. Biology 7%, business/marketing 17%, English 6%, foreign language 8%, psychology 9%, social sciences 18%, visual/performing arts 7%.

Computing on campus. 324 workstations in dormitories, library, computer center, student center. Dormitories wired for high-speed internet access and linked to campus network. Commuter students can connect to campus network. Online course registration, online library, helpline, repair service, student web hosting, wireless network available.

Student life. Freshman orientation: Available. 9-day introduction to academic life and campus community. **Housing:** Guaranteed on-campus for freshmen. Coed dorms, single-sex dorms, special housing for disabled, fraternity/sorority housing, wellness housing available. $200 nonrefundable deposit, deadline 5/1. 56 university-owned homes on campus. **Activities:** Bands, choral groups, dance, drama, film society, literary magazine, music ensembles, musical theater, opera, radio station, student government, student newspaper, symphony orchestra, Black student union, Hui-o-Hawaii, Circle K, Jewish student organization, Bisexuals, Gays, Lesbians, and Allies for Diversity, Pacific American student union, Students for Peace and Justice, First Nations, Habitat for Humanity, film and theatre society.

Athletics. NCAA. **Intercollegiate:** Baseball M, basketball, cheerleading, cross-country, football (tackle) M, golf, lacrosse W, rowing (crew), soccer, softball W, swimming, tennis, track and field, volleyball W. **Intramural:** Basketball, football (non-tackle), soccer, softball, tennis, volleyball. **Team name:** Loggers.

Student services. Alcohol/substance abuse counseling, chaplain/spiritual director, career counseling, services for economically disadvantaged, student employment services, financial aid counseling, health services, legal services, minority student services, personal counseling, placement for graduates. **Physically disabled:** Services for visually, speech, hearing impaired.

Contact. E-mail: admission@ups.edu
Phone: (253) 879-3211 Toll-free number: (800) 396-7191
Fax: (253) 879-3993
George Mills, Vice President for Enrollment, University of Puget Sound, 1500 North Warner Street, Tacoma, WA 98416-1062

University of Washington

Seattle, Washington — **CB member**
www.washington.edu — **CB code: 4854**

- Public 4-year university
- Residential campus in very large city
- 27,365 degree-seeking undergraduates: 9% part-time, 52% women, 3% African American, 28% Asian American, 6% Hispanic American, 1% Native American, 5% international
- 12,120 degree-seeking graduate students
- 61% of applicants admitted
- SAT or ACT with writing, application essay required

General. Founded in 1861. Regionally accredited. **Degrees:** 6,961 bachelor's awarded; master's, doctoral, first professional offered. **ROTC:** Army, Naval, Air Force. **Location:** 5 miles from downtown. **Calendar:** Quarter, extensive summer session. **Full-time faculty:** 2,640 total; 89% have terminal degrees, 17% minority, 36% women. **Part-time faculty:** 656 total; 83% have terminal degrees, 14% minority, 47% women. **Class size:** 35% < 20, 40% 20-39, 8% 40-49, 9% 50-99, 7% >100. **Special facilities:** Arboretum, observatory, anthropological museum, applied physics laboratory, planetarium.

Freshman class profile. 20,224 applied, 12,327 admitted, 5,719 enrolled.

Mid 50% test scores			
SAT critical reading:	530-650	GPA 2.0-2.99:	1%
SAT math:	570-680	Rank in top quarter:	97%
SAT writing:	530-640	Rank in top tenth:	86%
ACT composite:	24-29	Out-of-state:	16%
GPA 3.75 or higher:	54%	Live on campus:	63%
GPA 3.50-3.74:	31%	International:	6%
GPA 3.0-3.49:	14%	Fraternities:	10%
		Sororities:	9%

Basis for selection. Applicants evaluated and ranked on completion of core subject requirements, grades and test scores and supplemental factors including personal statement, completion of substantial number of courses beyond minimum, grades in college-preparatory courses, enrollment in AP or honors courses, cultural diversity and documented evidence of exceptional artistic talent. Auditions required for admission to performing arts programs. Application interviews not available, only informational appointments. **Homeschooled:** Each applicant is reviewed case-by-case. To confirm successful completion of certain core subject requirements or levels, applicants may be asked to provide additional documentation or placement testing information. **Learning Disabled:** Applicants with documented disabilities not expected to disclose them at time of application, but welcome do so in the applicant's own written materials, or via relevant documentation or letters. Students encouraged to first speak with an admissions counselor.

High school preparation. 15 units required; 20 recommended. Required and recommended units include English 4, mathematics 3-4, social studies 3-4, history 1, science 2-3 (laboratory 1-3), foreign language 2-3, computer science 1, visual/performing arts .5-1. One semester (.5) elective from required subjects list and .5 fine arts course.

2008-2009 Annual costs. Tuition/fees: $6,802; $23,219 out-of-state. Room/board: $8,640. Books/supplies: $1,008. Personal expenses: $2,265.

2008-2009 Financial aid. **Non-need-based:** Scholarships awarded for academics, alumni affiliation, art, athletics, leadership, music/drama, ROTC. **Additional information:** Tuition not due until third week of term.

Application procedures. **Admission:** Priority date 12/1; deadline 1/15 (postmark date). $50 fee, may be waived for applicants with need. Admission notification 4/15. Admission notification on a rolling basis beginning on or about 12/1. Must reply by 5/1. Applications accepted after closing date on space-available basis. **Financial aid:** Priority date 2/28; no closing date. FAFSA required. Applicants notified by 3/31; must reply within 3 week(s) of notification.

Academics. **Special study options:** Combined bachelor's/graduate degree, cooperative education, distance learning, double major, ESL, exchange student, honors, independent study, internships, student-designed major, study abroad, teacher certification program, Washington semester. Quarter at Friday Harbor Laboratories, San Juan Islands. **Credit/placement by examination:** AP, CLEP, IB, institutional tests. 90 credit hours maximum toward bachelor's degree. **Support services:** Learning center, pre-admission summer program, reduced course load, remedial instruction, study skills assistance, tutoring, writing center.

Majors. **Architecture:** Architecture, landscape, urban/community planning. **Area/ethnic studies:** African, African-American, Asian, Asian-American, Canadian, Central/Eastern European, Chinese, European, French, German, Hispanic-American/Latino/Chicano, Italian, Japanese, Korean, Latin American, Native American, Near/Middle Eastern, Russian/Slavic, Scandinavian, Slavic, South Asian, Southeast Asian, women's. **Biology:** General, bacteriology, biochemistry, botany, ecology, marine, microbiology, zoology. **Business:** Accounting, business admin, construction management, finance, human resources, international, management information systems, organizational behavior. **Communications:** General. **Computer sciences:** General, computer science, information systems, information technology. **Conservation:** General, fisheries, forest resources, forestry, wildlife. **Education:** Music. **Engineering:** General, aerospace, biomedical, ceramic, chemical, civil, computer, electrical, environmental, forest, industrial, materials, materials science, mechanical, metallurgical. **Foreign languages:** Ancient Greek, Arabic, Chinese, classics, comparative lit, Danish, East Asian, French, German, Germanic, Hebrew, Italian, Japanese, Korean, Latin, linguistics, Norwegian, Russian, Scandinavian, South Asian, Southeast Asian, Spanish, Swedish, Turkish, Ukrainian. **Health:** Audiology/speech pathology, clinical lab science, dental hygiene, environmental health, nursing (RN), orthotics/prosthetics, physician assistant. **History:** General. **Interdisciplinary:** Peace/conflict. **Liberal arts:** Arts/sciences. **Math:** General, applied. **Philosophy/religion:** Judaic, philosophy, religion. **Physical sciences:** Astronomy, astrophysics, atmospheric science, chemistry, geology, oceanography, physics, planetary. **Psychology:** General. **Public administration:** Social work. **Social sciences:** General, anthropology, economics, geography, international relations, political science, sociology. **Visual/performing arts:** Art, art history/conservation, ceramics, commercial/advertising art, dance, dramatic, fiber arts, industrial design, metal/jewelry, music history, music performance, music theory/composition, musicology, painting, photography, piano/organ, printmaking, sculpture, stringed instruments, voice/opera.

Most popular majors. Biology 10%, business/marketing 10%, communications/journalism 6%, engineering/engineering technologies 9%, psychology 6%, social sciences 19%.

Computing on campus. 1,500 workstations in dormitories, library, computer center, student center. Dormitories wired for high-speed internet access and linked to campus network. Commuter students can connect to campus network. Online course registration, online library, helpline, repair service, student web hosting, wireless network available.

Student life. **Freshman orientation:** Mandatory, $250 fee. Preregistration for classes offered. Advising and registration throughout the summer. **Housing:** Guaranteed on-campus for freshmen. Coed dorms, special housing for disabled, apartments, cooperative housing, fraternity/sorority housing, wellness housing available. $500 nonrefundable deposit, deadline 5/1. Special interest houses available. **Activities:** Bands, campus ministries, choral groups, dance, drama, film society, international student organizations, literary magazine, music ensembles, Model UN, musical theater, opera, radio station, student government, student newspaper, symphony orchestra, TV station, over 500 student organizations.

Athletics. NCAA. **Intercollegiate:** Baseball M, basketball, cheerleading, cross-country, football (tackle) M, golf, gymnastics W, rowing (crew), soccer, softball W, swimming, tennis, track and field, volleyball W. **Intramural:** Basketball, bowling, football (non-tackle), racquetball, rowing (crew), soccer, softball, swimming, tennis, volleyball. **Team name:** Huskies.

Student services. Alcohol/substance abuse counseling, career counseling, services for economically disadvantaged, student employment services, financial aid counseling, health services, legal services, minority student services, on-campus daycare, personal counseling, placement for graduates, veterans' counselor, women's services. **Physically disabled:** Services for visually, speech, hearing impaired.

Contact. Phone: (206) 543-9686 Fax: (206) 685-3655
Philip Ballinger, Director of Admissions, University of Washington, 1410 Northeast Campus Parkway, Box 355852, Seattle, WA 98195-5852

University of Washington Bothell

Bothell, Washington
www.uwb.edu **CB code: 4467**

- Public 4-year university
- Commuter campus in large town
- 1,912 degree-seeking undergraduates
- 341 graduate students
- SAT or ACT with writing, application essay required

General. **Degrees:** 560 bachelor's awarded; master's offered. **Location:** 25 miles from Seattle. **Calendar:** Quarter, limited summer session. **Full-time faculty:** 80 total; 98% have terminal degrees, 46% women. **Part-time faculty:** 36 total; 100% have terminal degrees, 50% women. **Class size:** 31% < 20, 53% 20-39, 11% 40-49, 4% 50-99. **Special facilities:** 58 acres of wetlands.

Freshman class profile.

Mid 50% test scores			
SAT critical reading:	460-560	SAT writing:	450-550
SAT math:	490-590	ACT composite:	20-24
		Out-of-state:	3%

Basis for selection. GPA, test scores, academic rigor, essays most important. Non-resident alien applicants must report scores from one of the following: TOEFL, the University of Washington-administered Michigan Language Test (MLT) or the International English Language Testing System (IELTS).

High school preparation. Required and recommended units include English 4, mathematics 3-4, social studies 3, science 2-3 (laboratory 1) and foreign language 2.

2008-2009 Annual costs. Tuition/fees: $6,673; $23,090 out-of-state. Books/supplies: $1,008. Personal expenses: $2,265.

Financial aid. **Non-need-based:** Scholarships awarded for academics, alumni affiliation, art, athletics, leadership, music/drama, ROTC.

Application procedures. **Admission:** Closing date 1/15 (postmark date). $50 fee, may be waived for applicants with need. Admission notification on a rolling basis beginning on or about 11/1. Must reply by May 1 or within 3 week(s) if notified thereafter. **Financial aid:** Priority date 2/28; no closing date. FAFSA required. Applicants notified by 3/31.

Academics. **Special study options:** Combined bachelor's/graduate degree, double major, dual enrollment of high school students, internships, study abroad, teacher certification program. **Credit/placement by examination:** AP, CLEP, institutional tests. **Support services:** Learning center, pre-admission summer program, reduced course load, study skills assistance, writing center.

Majors. **Biology:** General. **Business:** Accounting/finance, business admin. **Communications:** Media studies. **Computer sciences:** General. **Conservation:** Environmental science. **Engineering:** Electrical. **Health:** Nursing assistant. **Interdisciplinary:** Intercultural, science/society. **Psychology:** Community. **Other:** American studies, Applied computing, Global studies.

Most popular majors. Business/marketing 38%, computer/information sciences 10%, health sciences 17%, interdisciplinary studies 35%.

Computing on campus. 1,000 workstations in library, computer center, student center. Commuter students can connect to campus network. Online course registration, online library, helpline, student web hosting, wireless network available.

Student life. Freshman orientation: Mandatory. **Housing:** Housing coordinator to assist students with housing. **Activities:** International student organizations, Model UN, student government, student newspaper.

Athletics. Intramural: Basketball, football (non-tackle), soccer, softball, tennis, volleyball. **Team name:** Huskies.

Student services. Career counseling, student employment services, financial aid counseling, personal counseling, veterans' counselor. **Physically disabled:** Services for visually, speech, hearing impaired. **Learning disabled:** Comprehensive services available.

Contact. E-mail: admissions@uwb.edu
Phone: (425) 352-5000 Toll-free number: (800) 736-6650
Fax: (425) 352-5455
Jill Orcutt, Director of Admissions, University of Washington Bothell, 18115 Campus Way Northeast, Bothell, WA 98011-8246

University of Washington Tacoma

Tacoma, Washington
www.tacoma.washington.edu **CB member**

- Public 4-year university and branch campus college
- Commuter campus in small city
- 2,400 degree-seeking undergraduates: 25% part-time, 60% women, 7% African American, 17% Asian American, 7% Hispanic American, 1% Native American, 1% international
- 515 degree-seeking graduate students
- 92% of applicants admitted
- SAT or ACT (ACT writing optional), application essay required

General. Regionally accredited. **Degrees:** 658 bachelor's awarded; master's offered. **Calendar:** Quarter, limited summer session. **Full-time faculty:** 124 total; 94% have terminal degrees, 53% women. **Part-time faculty:** 31 total; 55% women. **Class size:** 33% < 20, 53% 20-39, 12% 40-49, 2% 50-99.

Freshman class profile. 521 applied, 477 admitted, 222 enrolled.

Mid 50% test scores		**GPA 3.0-3.49:**	40%
SAT critical reading:	420-560	**GPA 2.0-2.99:**	35%
SAT math:	430-560	**End year in good standing:**	65%
SAT writing:	420-540	**Return as sophomores:**	68%
ACT composite:	16-26	**Out-of-state:**	3%
GPA 3.75 or higher:	12%	**Live on campus:**	5%
GPA 3.50-3.74:	13%		

Basis for selection. Admissions based on school achievement record, including quality of test scores. **Homeschooled:** Transcript of courses and grades required.

High school preparation. College-preparatory program required. 16 units required. Required units include English 4, mathematics 3, social studies 3, science 2 (laboratory 1), foreign language 2, visual/performing arts .5, academic electives 0.5.

Application procedures. Admission: Priority date 3/1; deadline 8/1 (receipt date). $50 fee, may be waived for applicants with need. Application must be submitted online. Admission notification on a rolling basis beginning on or about 11/1. Must reply by May 1 or within 2 week(s) if notified thereafter.

Academics. Special study options: Cross-registration, double major, dual enrollment of high school students, honors, independent study, internships, semester at sea, student-designed major, study abroad, teacher certification program. **Credit/placement by examination:** AP, CLEP, IB, institutional tests. 90 credit hours maximum toward bachelor's degree. **Support services:** Learning center, pre-admission summer program, study skills assistance, tutoring, writing center.

Majors. Area/ethnic studies: American, Asian, Hispanic-American/Latino/Chicano. **Business:** General, accounting, business admin, finance, international, marketing. **Communications:** General. **Computer sciences:** General, security, systems analysis. **Conservation:** Environmental science, environmental studies. **Health:** Nursing (RN). **History:** Public archives. **Interdisciplinary:** Intercultural. **Liberal arts:** Arts/sciences. **Psychology:** General. **Public administration:** Social work. **Social sciences:** International relations, political science, urban studies. **Other:** Ethnic, gender and labor studies, Politics and value, Self and society.

Most popular majors. Business/marketing 26%, computer/information sciences 7%, health sciences 7%, interdisciplinary studies 49%.

Computing on campus. 138 workstations in library, computer center, student center. Commuter students can connect to campus network. Online course registration, online library, helpline, student web hosting, wireless network available.

Student life. Freshman orientation: Mandatory. Preregistration for classes offered. **Housing:** Special housing for disabled, apartments available. $150 nonrefundable deposit, deadline 6/1. **Activities:** Campus ministries, literary magazine, student government, student newspaper.

Athletics. Team name: Huskies.

Student services. Alcohol/substance abuse counseling, career counseling, financial aid counseling, minority student services, personal counseling, veterans' counselor. **Physically disabled:** Services for visually, speech, hearing impaired.

Contact. E-mail: uwtinfo@u.washington.edu
Phone: (253) 692-4400 Toll-free number: (800) 736-7750
Fax: (253) 692-4414
Derek Levy, Director of Admission and Enrollment Services, University of Washington Tacoma, Campus Box 358400, Tacoma, WA 98402-3100

Walla Walla University

College Place, Washington
www.wallawalla.edu **CB code: 4940**

- Private 4-year university and liberal arts college affiliated with Seventh-day Adventists
- Residential campus in large town
- 1,555 degree-seeking undergraduates: 6% part-time, 48% women, 3% African American, 6% Asian American, 10% Hispanic American, 1% Native American, 1% international
- 237 degree-seeking graduate students
- 98% of applicants admitted
- SAT or ACT (ACT writing optional) required

General. Founded in 1892. Regionally accredited. Branch campus in Portland, Oregon, for final two years of nursing program. Summer biology courses offered at marine research facility near Anacortes. Graduate social work program in Billings and Missoula, Montana. **Degrees:** 293 bachelor's, 6 associate awarded; master's offered. **Location:** 270 miles from Seattle, 250 miles from Portland, Oregon. **Calendar:** Quarter, extensive summer session. **Full-time faculty:** 117 total; 71% have terminal degrees, 5% minority, 36% women. **Part-time faculty:** 88 total; 19% have terminal degrees, 9% minority, 58% women. **Class size:** 67% < 20, 24% 20-39, 5% 40-49, 3% 50-99, less than 1% >100. **Special facilities:** Marine biological research facility, observatory.

Freshman class profile. 505 applied, 496 admitted, 315 enrolled.

Return as sophomores:	69%	**Live on campus:**	90%
Out-of-state:	38%	**International:**	2%

Basis for selection. Must have a combined 2.0 high school GPA. If entering with GED must have an average score of 500 or higher and each test must be 450 or higher. Official TOEFL scores required for prospective students whose first language is not English. ACT recommended. Audition recommended. **Homeschooled:** May be admitted by acceptable score on ACT test, GED test, or transcript from accredited home school organization.

High school preparation. College-preparatory program recommended. 11 units required; 16 recommended. Required and recommended units include English 4, mathematics 3-4, social studies 1, history 2, science 2-3 (laboratory 2) and foreign language 2. Mathematics units must be algebra and geometry. 2 laboratory units recommended.

2008-2009 Annual costs. Tuition/fees: $21,936. Room/board: $4,320. Books/supplies: $1,014. Personal expenses: $1,746.

2007-2008 Financial aid. Need-based: 328 full-time freshmen applied for aid; 239 were judged to have need; 239 of these received aid. Average need met was 90%. Average scholarship/grant was $6,219; average loan $5,950. 52% of total undergraduate aid awarded as scholarships/grants, 48%

as loans/jobs. **Non-need-based:** Awarded to 1,012 full-time undergraduates, including 311 freshmen. Scholarships awarded for academics, leadership, music/drama.

Application procedures. Admission: No deadline. $40 fee, may be waived for applicants with need. Admission notification on a rolling basis beginning on or about 9/25. **Financial aid:** Priority date 4/30; no closing date. FAFSA, institutional form required. Applicants notified on a rolling basis starting 3/15.

Academics. Special study options: Combined bachelor's/graduate degree, cooperative education, distance learning, double major, honors, independent study, internships, liberal arts/career combination, study abroad, teacher certification program. **Credit/placement by examination:** AP, CLEP, IB, SAT, ACT, institutional tests. 12 credit hours maximum toward associate degree, 24 toward bachelor's. **Support services:** Learning center, pre-admission summer program, reduced course load, remedial instruction, study skills assistance, tutoring, writing center.

Majors. Biology: General, biochemistry, biophysics. **Business:** Accounting, business admin, finance, human resources, international, management science. **Communications:** General, journalism, media studies. **Communications technology:** Graphic/printing. **Computer sciences:** General, computer graphics, computer science, data processing, information systems. **Education:** General, business, elementary, music, physical, special, voc/tech. **Engineering:** General, biomedical, civil, computer, electrical, mechanical. **Foreign languages:** French, German, Spanish. **Health:** Nursing (RN). **History:** General. **Liberal arts:** Arts/sciences. **Math:** General. **Mechanic/repair:** Automotive. **Philosophy/religion:** Religion. **Physical sciences:** Chemistry, physics. **Psychology:** General. **Public administration:** Social work. **Social sciences:** Sociology. **Theology:** Theology. **Visual/performing arts:** Art, music performance.

Most popular majors. Biology 8%, business/marketing 17%, communications/journalism 7%, education 6%, engineering/engineering technologies 12%, health sciences 19%.

Computing on campus. 105 workstations in dormitories, library, computer center. Dormitories wired for high-speed internet access and linked to campus network. Commuter students can connect to campus network. Online course registration, online library, helpline, repair service, student web hosting, wireless network available.

Student life. Freshman orientation: Mandatory. Preregistration for classes offered. Held during week before classes begin. **Policies:** Chapel requirement once a week; worship policy for resident students. Religious observance required. **Housing:** Guaranteed on-campus for all undergraduates. Single-sex dorms, special housing for disabled, apartments, wellness housing available. **Activities:** Concert band, campus ministries, choral groups, drama, international student organizations, music ensembles, radio station, student government, student newspaper, symphony orchestra, TV station, student entrepreneur group, student missionary groups, drama, foreign student organizations, academic department clubs, service clubs, music groups.

Athletics. NCCAA. **Intercollegiate:** Basketball, golf, ice hockey M, soccer M, softball W, volleyball. **Intramural:** Badminton, basketball, football (non-tackle), racquetball, soccer, softball, table tennis, tennis, volleyball. **Team name:** Wolves.

Student services. Chaplain/spiritual director, career counseling, student employment services, financial aid counseling, health services, minority student services, on-campus daycare, personal counseling, placement for graduates, veterans' counselor. **Physically disabled:** Services for visually, speech, hearing impaired.

Contact. E-mail: info@wallawalla.edu
Phone: (509) 527-2327 Toll-free number: (800) 541-8900
Fax: (509) 527-2397
Dallas Weis, Vice President for Admissions and Marketing, Walla Walla University, 204 South College Avenue, College Place, WA 99324-3000

Washington State University

Pullman, Washington — **CB member**
www.wsu.edu — **CB code: 4705**

- Public 4-year university
- Residential campus in large town
- 20,690 degree-seeking undergraduates: 13% part-time, 52% women, 2% African American, 6% Asian American, 5% Hispanic American, 1% Native American, 3% international
- 4,056 degree-seeking graduate students
- 72% of applicants admitted
- SAT or ACT (ACT writing optional) required
- 67% graduate within 6 years; 38% enter graduate study

General. Founded in 1890. Regionally accredited. Regional campuses in Spokane, Tri-Cities, Vancouver, and Distance Degree Programs (online degree). **Degrees:** 4,818 bachelor's awarded; master's, doctoral, first professional offered. **ROTC:** Army, Naval, Air Force. **Location:** 80 miles from Spokane. **Calendar:** Semester, extensive summer session. **Full-time faculty:** 1,204 total; 90% have terminal degrees, 12% minority, 39% women. **Part-time faculty:** 456 total; 50% have terminal degrees, 6% minority, 51% women. **Class size:** 41% < 20, 34% 20-39, 8% 40-49, 12% 50-99, 6% >100. **Special facilities:** Anthropology museum, art museum, creamery, ecological reserve, geological collections, historic textiles and costume collection, entomological collection, natural history museum, observatory, planetarium, herbarium and mycological herbarium, soil monolith collection, veterinary anatomy teaching museum, laboratory for atmospheric research, laboratory for biotechnology and bioanalysis, electron microscopy center, environmental research center, geoanalytical laboratory, nuclear radiation center, social and economic sciences research center, state of Washington water research center, center for spectroscopy, music recording studio, center for teaching, learning and technology, vet teaching hospital.

Freshman class profile. 11,983 applied, 8,677 admitted, 3,710 enrolled.

Mid 50% test scores		**Rank in top tenth:**	44%
SAT critical reading:	490-600	**End year in good standing:**	83%
SAT math:	510-610	**Return as sophomores:**	82%
ACT composite:	21-26	**Out-of-state:**	11%
GPA 3.75 or higher:	26%	**Live on campus:**	99%
GPA 3.50-3.74:	23%	**International:**	2%
GPA 3.0-3.49:	42%	**Fraternities:**	16%
GPA 2.0-2.99:	9%	**Sororities:**	25%
Rank in top quarter:	61%		

Basis for selection. Combination of high school GPA and SAT or ACT scores, completion of course work, and personal statement. Special circumstances, community activities and recommendations considered in some cases. An appeal process is available for those denied admission. **Homeschooled:** Transcript of courses and grades required. Official transcripts from GED exam or an academic resume that provides documentation of all subjects studied, or proof that the home based instruction fulfills our core requirements must be provided. **Learning Disabled:** Upon acceptance a student can opt to notify Disability Services of desire to have assistance with disability.

High school preparation. 17 units required; 18 recommended. Required and recommended units include English 4, mathematics 3-4, social studies 3, science 2 (laboratory 1), foreign language 2, visual/performing arts 1 and academic electives 1. Mathematics units must include one year each, algebra, geometry, and advanced algebra. Foreign language must be 2 years of single language (Native American or American Sign Language are accepted). One unit fine/performing arts or additional academic elective.

2008-2009 Annual costs. Tuition/fees: $7,565; $18,601 out-of-state. Room/board: $8,482. Books/supplies: $936. Personal expenses: $2,108.

2007-2008 Financial aid. Need-based: 2,404 full-time freshmen applied for aid; 1,460 were judged to have need; 1,455 of these received aid. Average need met was 84%. Average scholarship/grant was $6,334; average loan $3,528. 54% of total undergraduate aid awarded as scholarships/grants, 46% as loans/jobs. **Non-need-based:** Awarded to 4,532 full-time undergraduates, including 1,738 freshmen. Scholarships awarded for academics, alumni affiliation, art, athletics, job skills, leadership, minority status, music/drama, religious affiliation, ROTC, state residency.

Application procedures. Admission: Priority date 1/31; no deadline. $50 fee, may be waived for applicants with need. Admission notification on a rolling basis beginning on or about 11/1. Must reply by May 1 or within 2 week(s) if notified thereafter. Applications accepted after May 1 and later, if space is still available. **Financial aid:** Priority date 3/1; no closing date. FAFSA required. Applicants notified on a rolling basis starting 4/15.

Academics. Special study options: Accelerated study, combined bachelor's/graduate degree, cross-registration, distance learning, double major, dual enrollment of high school students, ESL, exchange student, honors, independent study, internships, liberal arts/career combination, semester at sea, student-designed major, study abroad, teacher certification program. **Credit/placement by examination:** AP, CLEP, IB, SAT, ACT, institutional tests. 60 credit hours maximum toward bachelor's degree. **Support services:** Learning center, pre-admission summer program, reduced course load, study skills assistance, tutoring, writing center.

Honors college/program. Acceptance into the Honors College is competitive, and spaces are limited. Selection is based on GPA and SAT/ACT scores, essay responses, strength of high school curriculum, Running Start credits, AP/IP programs, honors courses, 2 letters of recommendation, one from a math or science teacher and one from an English teacher, and overall motivation, organizational skills, and a desire for challenge.

Majors. **Agriculture:** General, agronomy, animal sciences, business, communications, crop production, economics, horticultural science, mechanization, plant protection, products processing, soil science. **Architecture:** Architecture, landscape. **Area/ethnic studies:** American, Asian, women's. **Biology:** General, biochemistry, biomedical sciences, biotechnology, entomology, genetics, microbiology, molecular genetics, zoology. **Business:** General, accounting, business admin, construction management, e-commerce, entrepreneurial studies, finance, hospitality admin, human resources, insurance, international, management information systems, management science, managerial economics, marketing, real estate. **Communications:** Digital media, media studies. **Computer sciences:** General, computer science. **Conservation:** General, environmental science, forestry, wildlife. **Education:** General, agricultural, bilingual, biology, chemistry, early childhood, elementary, English, ESL, family/consumer sciences, foreign languages, French, German, health, history, kindergarten/preschool, mathematics, multi-level teacher, music, physical, physics, reading, science, secondary, social studies, Spanish, special. **Engineering:** Agricultural, biomedical, chemical, civil, computer, electrical, manufacturing, materials, mechanical. **Family/consumer sciences:** General, clothing/textiles, family studies, food/nutrition, human nutrition. **Foreign languages:** General, French, German, linguistics, Russian, Spanish. **Health:** Athletic training, audiology/speech pathology, nursing (RN), premedicine. **History:** General. **Interdisciplinary:** Biological/physical sciences, global studies, neuroscience. **Legal studies:** Prelaw. **Liberal arts:** Arts/sciences, humanities. **Math:** General, applied. **Parks/recreation:** General, exercise sciences, sports admin. **Philosophy/religion:** Philosophy, religion. **Physical sciences:** General, chemistry, geology, physics. **Protective services:** Police science. **Psychology:** General. **Public administration:** Policy analysis. **Social sciences:** General, anthropology, economics, political science, sociology. **Visual/performing arts:** Art, dramatic, interior design, music performance, music theory/composition, studio arts.

Most popular majors. Business/marketing 18%, communications/journalism 8%, engineering/engineering technologies 6%, health sciences 8%, psychology 6%, social sciences 15%.

Computing on campus. 2,500 workstations in dormitories, library, computer center, student center. Dormitories wired for high-speed internet access and linked to campus network. Commuter students can connect to campus network. Online course registration, online library, helpline, student web hosting, wireless network available.

Student life. **Freshman orientation:** Mandatory, $227 fee. Preregistration for classes offered. Three-day (two-day for transfer students) orientation and registration program offered to new students and their families throughout the year depending on enrolled semester start date. **Housing:** Guaranteed on-campus for freshmen. Coed dorms, single-sex dorms, special housing for disabled, apartments, fraternity/sorority housing, wellness housing available. $550 partly refundable deposit, deadline 6/1. Single undergraduate freshmen under 20 required to live on campus. **Activities:** Bands, campus ministries, choral groups, dance, drama, film society, international student organizations, literary magazine, music ensembles, Model UN, musical theater, opera, radio station, student government, student newspaper, symphony orchestra, TV station.

Athletics. NCAA. **Intercollegiate:** Baseball M, basketball, cross-country, football (tackle) M, golf, rowing (crew) W, soccer W, swimming W, tennis W, track and field, volleyball W. **Intramural:** Badminton, basketball, football (non-tackle), golf, racquetball, soccer, softball, tennis, volleyball. **Team name:** Cougars.

Student services. Adult student services, alcohol/substance abuse counseling, chaplain/spiritual director, career counseling, student employment services, financial aid counseling, health services, legal services, minority student services, on-campus daycare, personal counseling, placement for graduates, veterans' counselor, women's services. **Physically disabled:** Services for visually, speech, hearing impaired.

Contact. E-mail: admiss2@wsu.edu
Phone: (509) 335-5586 Toll-free number: (888) 468-6978
Fax: (509) 335-4902
Wendy Peterson, Director of Admissions, Washington State University, 370 Lighty Student Services Bldg, Pullman, WA 99164-1067

Western Washington University

Bellingham, Washington — **CB member**
www.wwu.edu — **CB code: 4947**

- Public 4-year university
- Residential campus in small city
- 13,236 degree-seeking undergraduates: 8% part-time, 55% women, 3% African American, 9% Asian American, 4% Hispanic American, 3% Native American, 1% international
- 1,214 graduate students
- 71% of applicants admitted
- SAT or ACT (ACT writing optional), application essay required

General. Founded in 1893. Regionally accredited. **Degrees:** 3,079 bachelor's awarded; master's offered. **Location:** 90 miles from Seattle. **Calendar:** Quarter, extensive summer session. **Full-time faculty:** 511 total; 88% have terminal degrees, 14% minority, 41% women. **Part-time faculty:** 221 total; 38% have terminal degrees, 10% minority, 56% women. **Class size:** 53% < 20, 33% 20-39, 4% 40-49, 8% 50-99, 2% >100. **Special facilities:** Wind tunnel, electron microscope, neutron generator laboratory, planetarium, air pollution laboratory, motor vehicle research laboratory, electronic music studio, 11-acre recreational park on lake, marine laboratory, integrated laboratory network.

Freshman class profile. 9,518 applied, 6,750 admitted, 2,697 enrolled.

Mid 50% test scores		**GPA 3.0-3.49:**	42%
SAT critical reading:	490-610	**GPA 2.0-2.99:**	6%
SAT math:	500-610	**Rank in top quarter:**	61%
SAT writing:	480-590	**Rank in top tenth:**	26%
ACT composite:	21-26	**End year in good standing:**	84%
GPA 3.75 or higher:	23%	**Out-of-state:**	9%
GPA 3.50-3.74:	29%	**Live on campus:**	92%

Basis for selection. Academic achievement most significant factor. Curriculum rigor (level and difficulty of courses), grade trends, school, community activities, special talent, multicultural experience, personal circumstances considered. All students encouraged to take courses beyond minimums. Consideration given to motivation, achievements outside of classroom, multicultural experience, and attributes that will enhance institution's learning community. Audition recommended for music; portfolio required for art.

High school preparation. College-preparatory program required. 16 units required. Required units include English 4, mathematics 3, social studies 3, science 2 (laboratory 1), foreign language 2, visual/performing arts .5, academic electives 0.5. Mathematics requirement includes 2 algebra. Sciences include 1 algebra-based chemistry or physics. Foreign language should be in 1 language. .5 fine arts and .5 academic elective required.

2008-2009 Annual costs. Tuition/fees: $5,535; $17,166 out-of-state. Room/board: $7,446. Books/supplies: $924. Personal expenses: $1,854.

2008-2009 Financial aid. **Need-based:** 1,908 full-time freshmen applied for aid; 988 were judged to have need; 941 of these received aid. Average need met was 89%. Average scholarship/grant was $7,159; average loan $3,197. 54% of total undergraduate aid awarded as scholarships/grants, 46% as loans/jobs. **Non-need-based:** Awarded to 490 full-time undergraduates, including 110 freshmen. Scholarships awarded for academics, alumni affiliation, art, athletics, job skills, leadership, minority status, music/drama, state residency. **Additional information:** Short-term student loans ranging from $100 to $1,000 available on a quarterly basis.

Application procedures. **Admission:** Closing date 3/1 (postmark date). $50 fee, may be waived for applicants with need. Admission notification on a rolling basis beginning on or about 11/1. Must reply by May 1 or within 2 week(s) if notified thereafter. **Financial aid:** Priority date 2/15; no closing date. FAFSA required. Applicants notified on a rolling basis starting 3/20; must reply within 3 week(s) of notification.

Academics. **Special study options:** Distance learning, double major, ESL, exchange student, honors, independent study, internships, student-designed major, study abroad, teacher certification program. **Credit/placement by examination:** AP, CLEP, IB, institutional tests. 135 credit hours maximum toward bachelor's degree. **Support services:** Learning center, study skills assistance, tutoring, writing center.

Majors. **Area/ethnic studies:** American, Canadian, East Asian. **Biology:** General, biochemistry, botany, cell/histology, cellular/molecular, ecology, evolutionary, marine, zoology. **Business:** Accounting, business admin, finance, human resources, international, management information systems, marketing, operations. **Communications:** General, journalism. **Computer sciences:** General. **Conservation:** Environmental science, environmental studies. **Education:** Art, biology, chemistry, drama/dance, elementary, English, German, history, mathematics, music, physical, science, social science, social studies, Spanish, special, speech, technology/industrial arts. **Engineering technology:** Electrical, industrial, manufacturing, plastics. **Family/consumer sciences:** Child development. **Foreign languages:** General, French, German, linguistics, Spanish. **Health:** Audiology/speech pathology, community health services. **History:** General. **Interdisciplinary:** Accounting/computer science, biological/physical sciences. **Liberal arts:** Humanities. **Math:** General, applied. **Parks/recreation:** General, health/fitness. **Philosophy/religion:** Philosophy. **Physical sciences:** Chemistry, geology, geophysics, physics. **Psychology:** General, developmental. **Public administration:** Human services. **Social sciences:** Anthropology, archaeology, economics, geography, political science, sociology. **Visual/performing arts:** General, art,

art history/conservation, ceramics, commercial/advertising art, dance, design, dramatic, drawing, fiber arts, graphic design, industrial design, multimedia, music history, music performance, music theory/composition, painting, photography, printmaking, sculpture.

Most popular majors. Business/marketing 15%, English 6%, psychology 6%, social sciences 13%, visual/performing arts 6%.

Computing on campus. 2,479 workstations in dormitories, library, computer center, student center. Dormitories wired for high-speed internet access and linked to campus network. Commuter students can connect to campus network. Online course registration, online library, helpline, repair service, student web hosting, wireless network available.

Student life. **Freshman orientation:** Available. Preregistration for classes offered. 6 programs offered for students and family members, early-mid August. Program 1-2 days, based on housing needs. **Housing:** Coed dorms, special housing for disabled, apartments, wellness housing available. $200 partly refundable deposit, deadline 6/15. Multicultural floors, honors, quiet floors, freshman interest groups available. **Activities:** Bands, campus ministries, choral groups, dance, drama, film society, international student organizations, literary magazine, music ensembles, musical theater, opera, radio station, student government, student newspaper, symphony orchestra, TV station, Campus Christian Fellowship, veteran's outreach center, volunteer services and resources, international student club, The Inn (nondenominational), ethnic student center, Mecha, Circle K, American Red Cross chapter.

Athletics. NCAA. **Intercollegiate:** Basketball, cross-country, football (tackle) M, golf, rowing (crew), soccer, softball W, track and field, volleyball W. **Intramural:** Basketball, football (non-tackle), golf, racquetball, soccer, softball, table tennis, tennis, volleyball. **Team name:** Vikings.

Student services. Adult student services, alcohol/substance abuse counseling, chaplain/spiritual director, career counseling, student employment services, financial aid counseling, health services, minority student services, on-campus daycare, personal counseling, placement for graduates, veterans' counselor. **Physically disabled:** Services for visually, speech, hearing impaired.

Contact. E-mail: admit@wwu.edu
Phone: (360) 650-3440 Fax: (360) 650-7369
Karen Copetas, Director of Admissions and Enrollment Planning, Western Washington University, 516 High Street, Bellingham, WA 98225-9009

Whitman College

Walla Walla, Washington — **CB member**
www.whitman.edu — **CB code: 4951**

- Private 4-year liberal arts college
- Residential campus in large town
- 1,430 degree-seeking undergraduates: 1% part-time, 55% women, 2% African American, 10% Asian American, 6% Hispanic American, 1% Native American, 3% international
- 46% of applicants admitted
- SAT or ACT with writing, application essay required
- 92% graduate within 6 years

General. Founded in 1883. Regionally accredited. **Degrees:** 381 bachelor's awarded. **Location:** 150 miles from Spokane, 235 miles from Portland, Oregon. **Calendar:** Semester. **Full-time faculty:** 129 total; 94% have terminal degrees, 16% minority, 43% women. **Part-time faculty:** 55 total; 47% have terminal degrees, 2% minority, 46% women. **Class size:** 74% < 20, 24% 20-39, 2% 40-49, less than 1% 50-99. **Special facilities:** Asian art collection, natural history museum, planetarium, 2 electron microscopes, outdoor observatory, indoor and outdoor rock-climbing walls, outdoor sculpture walk, organic garden.

Freshman class profile. 3,096 applied, 1,417 admitted, 401 enrolled.

Mid 50% test scores			
SAT critical reading:	630-730	Rank in top tenth:	71%
SAT math:	610-700	End year in good standing:	100%
SAT writing:	620-710	Return as sophomores:	93%
ACT composite:	28-32	Out-of-state:	60%
GPA 3.75 or higher:	72%	Live on campus:	100%
GPA 3.50-3.74:	20%	International:	2%
GPA 3.0-3.49:	8%	Fraternities:	34%
Rank in top quarter:	94%	Sororities:	28%

Basis for selection. Scholastic record, quality of written expression, and level of motivation are very important. Evidence of talent, imagination, creativity, leadership, responsibility, and maturity are also considered. Writing for all students. TOEFL, ELPT, or APIEL accepted as language proficiency exams. Interview recommended.

High school preparation. College-preparatory program recommended. 16 units recommended. Recommended units include English 4, mathematics 4, social studies 2, history 2, science 3 (laboratory 2), foreign language 2 and visual/performing arts 1.

2008-2009 Annual costs. Tuition/fees: $35,192. Room/board: $8,820. Books/supplies: $1,400.

2008-2009 Financial aid. **Need-based:** 267 full-time freshmen applied for aid; 192 were judged to have need; 192 of these received aid. Average need met was 96%. Average scholarship/grant was $23,309; average loan $4,088. 81% of total undergraduate aid awarded as scholarships/grants, 19% as loans/jobs. **Non-need-based:** Scholarships awarded for academics, art, leadership, minority status, music/drama, religious affiliation, state residency.

Application procedures. **Admission:** Priority date 11/15; deadline 1/15 (postmark date). $50 fee, may be waived for applicants with need. Admission notification 4/1. Must reply by May 1 or within 2 week(s) if notified thereafter. **Financial aid:** Priority date 11/15, closing date 2/1. FAFSA, CSS PROFILE required. Applicants notified on a rolling basis starting 12/22; must reply within 2 week(s) of notification.

Academics. Library open 24 hours, seven days a week during academic year. **Special study options:** Accelerated study, combined bachelor's/graduate degree, cooperative education, cross-registration, double major, dual enrollment of high school students, exchange student, honors, independent study, liberal arts/career combination, student-designed major, study abroad, urban semester, Washington semester. Study abroad opportunities in over 20 countries; Whitman-In-China allows recent graduates to spend a year teaching English in one of 3 Chinese universities; 3-2 engineering and computer science programs with California Institute of Technology, Columbia University (NY), Duke University (NC), Washington University (MO) and University of Washington; 3-2 oceanography and biology or geology program with University of Washington; 3-3 law program with Columbia University; 3-2 program with Monterey Institute of International Studies; 4-1 program with Bank Street College of Education; undergraduate research conference; semester in the West field study. **Credit/placement by examination:** AP, CLEP, IB, institutional tests. 30 credit hours maximum toward bachelor's degree. **Support services:** Learning center, reduced course load, study skills assistance, tutoring, writing center.

Majors. **Area/ethnic studies:** Asian, Latin American. **Biology:** General, Biochemistry/biophysics and molecular biology. **Conservation:** Environmental studies. **Foreign languages:** Classics, French, German, Spanish. **History:** General. **Math:** General. **Philosophy/religion:** Philosophy, religion. **Physical sciences:** Astronomy, chemistry, geology, physics. **Psychology:** General. **Social sciences:** Anthropology, economics, political science, sociology. **Visual/performing arts:** Art history/conservation, dramatic, film/cinema, studio arts. **Other:** Race and ethnic studies.

Most popular majors. Biology 13%, English 9%, history 6%, philosophy/religious studies 7%, physical sciences 10%, psychology 10%, social sciences 21%, visual/performing arts 9%.

Computing on campus. 410 workstations in dormitories, library, computer center, student center. Dormitories wired for high-speed internet access and linked to campus network. Commuter students can connect to campus network. Online library, helpline, student web hosting available.

Student life. **Freshman orientation:** Available. **Housing:** Guaranteed on-campus for freshmen. Coed dorms, single-sex dorms, apartments, fraternity/sorority housing available. $300 nonrefundable deposit, deadline 5/1. German, French, Spanish, Japanese language houses. Asian Studies, multiethnic, environmental, fine arts, community service, writing, global awareness houses available, college-owned rentals. **Activities:** Bands, campus ministries, choral groups, dance, drama, film society, international student organizations, literary magazine, music ensembles, Model UN, musical theater, radio station, student government, student newspaper, symphony orchestra, multi-ethnic cultural association, community service, political organizations, environmental groups, sexual-assault prevention educators.

Athletics. NCAA. **Intercollegiate:** Baseball M, basketball, cross-country, golf, skiing, soccer, swimming, tennis, volleyball W. **Intramural:** Basketball, bowling, football (non-tackle), soccer, tennis, triathlon, volleyball. **Team name:** Missionaries.

Student services. Adult student services, alcohol/substance abuse counseling, career counseling, student employment services, financial aid counseling, health services, minority student services, on-campus daycare, personal counseling, placement for graduates, veterans' counselor, women's services. **Physically disabled:** Services for visually, speech, hearing impaired.

Contact. E-mail: admission@whitman.edu
Phone: (509) 527-5176 Toll-free number: (877) 462-9448
Fax: (509) 527-4967
Tony Cabasco, Dean of Admission and Financial Aid, Whitman College, 345 Boyer Avenue, Walla Walla, WA 99362-2046

Whitworth University

Spokane, Washington — **CB member**
www.whitworth.edu — **CB code: 4953**

- Private 4-year liberal arts college affiliated with Presbyterian Church (USA)
- Residential campus in large city
- 2,365 degree-seeking undergraduates: 12% part-time, 58% women, 2% African American, 3% Asian American, 3% Hispanic American, 1% Native American, 1% international
- 236 degree-seeking graduate students
- 51% of applicants admitted
- Application essay required
- 77% graduate within 6 years

General. Founded in 1890. Regionally accredited. **Degrees:** 549 bachelor's awarded; master's offered. **ROTC:** Army. **Location:** 6 miles from downtown, 280 miles from Seattle. **Calendar:** 4-1-4, limited summer session. **Full-time faculty:** 126 total; 75% have terminal degrees, 6% minority, 41% women. **Part-time faculty:** 169 total; 10% minority. **Class size:** 58% < 20, 35% 20-39, 4% 40-49, 2% 50-99, less than 1% >100.

Freshman class profile. 5,472 applied, 2,802 admitted, 546 enrolled.

Mid 50% test scores			
SAT critical reading:	550-660	GPA 3.0-3.49:	19%
SAT math:	550-650	GPA 2.0-2.99:	4%
SAT writing:	540-630	End year in good standing:	87%
ACT composite:	25-29	Return as sophomores:	86%
GPA 3.75 or higher:	55%	Out-of-state:	40%
GPA 3.50-3.74:	22%	Live on campus:	96%
		International:	3%

Basis for selection. School achievement, extracurricular activities, recommendations most important. SAT or ACT recommended. Interview recommended.

High school preparation. College-preparatory program recommended. 18 units recommended. Recommended units include English 4, mathematics 3, social studies 3, history 3, science 3 (laboratory 2) and foreign language 2.

2008-2009 Annual costs. Tuition/fees: $27,420. Room/board: $7,700. Books/supplies: $912. Personal expenses: $1,682.

2008-2009 Financial aid. **Need-based:** 442 full-time freshmen applied for aid; 353 were judged to have need; 353 of these received aid. Average need met was 86%. Average scholarship/grant was $17,899; average loan $4,173. 66% of total undergraduate aid awarded as scholarships/grants, 34% as loans/jobs. **Non-need-based:** Awarded to 752 full-time undergraduates, including 212 freshmen. Scholarships awarded for academics, art, music/drama, ROTC.

Application procedures. **Admission:** Closing date 3/1 (postmark date). No application fee. Admission notification on a rolling basis beginning on or about 12/20. Must reply by 5/1. **Financial aid:** Priority date 3/1; no closing date. FAFSA required. Applicants notified on a rolling basis starting 3/1; must reply by 5/1 or within 4 week(s) of notification.

Academics. **Special study options:** Accelerated study, cross-registration, distance learning, double major, dual enrollment of high school students, ESL, independent study, internships, student-designed major, study abroad, teacher certification program, Washington semester. 3-2 engineering programs. **Credit/placement by examination:** AP, CLEP, IB, SAT, ACT, institutional tests. 32 credit hours maximum toward bachelor's degree. **Support services:** Learning center, reduced course load, study skills assistance, tutoring, writing center.

Majors. **Area/ethnic studies:** American. **Biology:** General. **Business:** Accounting, business admin, international, marketing. **Communications:** General, journalism. **Computer sciences:** General, computer science. **Education:** General, biology, chemistry, elementary, ESL, French, history, mathematics, middle, multi-level teacher, music, physical, physics, secondary, Spanish, special, speech. **Engineering:** General. **Foreign languages:** French, Spanish. **Health:** Athletic training, nursing (RN). **History:** General. **Interdisciplinary:** Peace/conflict. **Liberal arts:** Arts/sciences. **Math:** General, applied. **Parks/recreation:** Health/fitness. **Philosophy/religion:** Philosophy. **Physical sciences:** Chemistry, physics. **Psychology:** General. **Social sciences:** General, economics, international relations, political science, sociology. **Theology:** Theology. **Visual/performing arts:** General, art, jazz, music performance, piano/organ, theater history, voice/opera.

Most popular majors. Biology 6%, business/marketing 22%, communications/journalism 6%, education 10%, English 6%, liberal arts 6%, social sciences 7%.

Computing on campus. 150 workstations in library, computer center, student center. Dormitories wired for high-speed internet access and linked to campus network. Commuter students can connect to campus network. Online course registration, helpline, repair service available.

Student life. **Freshman orientation:** Mandatory. Preregistration for classes offered. **Housing:** Guaranteed on-campus for freshmen. Coed dorms, single-sex dorms, special housing for disabled, apartments available. $100 partly refundable deposit, deadline 5/1. **Activities:** Bands, campus ministries, choral groups, dance, drama, international student organizations, literary magazine, music ensembles, Model UN, musical theater, radio station, student government, student newspaper, symphony orchestra, Black Student Union, Fellowship of Christian Athletes, international club, Hawaiian club, political activist club, Native American club, Amnesty International, Habitat for Humanity, Asian American club, Circle-K International.

Athletics. NCAA. **Intercollegiate:** Baseball M, basketball, cross-country, football (tackle) M, golf, soccer, softball W, swimming, tennis, track and field, volleyball W. **Intramural:** Basketball, soccer, softball, table tennis, tennis, volleyball. **Team name:** Pirates.

Student services. Adult student services, chaplain/spiritual director, career counseling, student employment services, financial aid counseling, health services, minority student services, personal counseling, placement for graduates, veterans' counselor. **Physically disabled:** Services for visually, speech, hearing impaired.

Contact. E-mail: admissions@whitworth.edu
Phone: (509) 777-4786 Toll-free number: (800) 533-4668
Fax: (509) 777-3758
Fred Pfursich, Vice President, Admissions and Financial Aid, Whitworth University, 300 West Hawthorne Road, Spokane, WA 99251-0002

West Virginia

Alderson-Broaddus College
Philippi, West Virginia
www.ab.edu **CB code: 5005**

- Private 4-year liberal arts college affiliated with American Baptist Churches in the USA
- Residential campus in small town
- 591 degree-seeking undergraduates: 5% part-time, 67% women, 5% African American, 2% Asian American, 2% Hispanic American, 2% international
- 129 degree-seeking graduate students
- 70% of applicants admitted
- SAT and SAT Subject Tests or ACT (ACT writing optional) required
- 44% graduate within 6 years; 12% enter graduate study

General. Founded in 1871. Regionally accredited. **Degrees:** 144 bachelor's, 13 associate awarded; master's offered. **Location:** 100 miles from Charleston, 125 miles from Pittsburgh. **Calendar:** Semester, limited summer session. **Full-time faculty:** 61 total; 46% have terminal degrees, 10% minority, 54% women. **Part-time faculty:** 26 total; 27% have terminal degrees, 50% women. **Class size:** 79% < 20, 17% 20-39, 2% 40-49, 2% 50-99. **Special facilities:** Gross anatomy laboratory, hydro-therapy pool.

Freshman class profile. 637 applied, 445 admitted, 157 enrolled.

Mid 50% test scores			
SAT critical reading:	420-530	GPA 2.0-2.99:	26%
SAT math:	430-520	Rank in top quarter:	49%
SAT writing:	420-520	Rank in top tenth:	25%
ACT composite:	19-23	End year in good standing:	90%
GPA 3.75 or higher:	28%	Return as sophomores:	64%
GPA 3.50-3.74:	19%	Out-of-state:	14%
GPA 3.0-3.49:	26%	Live on campus:	77%
		International:	3%

Basis for selection. High school record, rank in top half of class, test scores, interview very important. Physician's assistant and nursing applicants should have strong background in science. Interview required for physician's assistant applicants, recommended for all others. Audition required for music. **Homeschooled:** Results from Iowa Tests required.

High school preparation. College-preparatory program recommended. 10 units required; 15 recommended. Required and recommended units include English 4, mathematics 3, social studies 2, history 2, science 3 (laboratory 3) and foreign language 1.

2008-2009 Annual costs. Tuition/fees: $21,020. Room/board: $6,798. Books/supplies: $800. Personal expenses: $1,500.

2007-2008 Financial aid. Need-based: 151 full-time freshmen applied for aid; 143 were judged to have need; 143 of these received aid. Average need met was 82%. Average scholarship/grant was $14,743; average loan $4,272. 58% of total undergraduate aid awarded as scholarships/grants, 42% as loans/jobs. **Non-need-based:** Awarded to 103 full-time undergraduates, including 27 freshmen. Scholarships awarded for academics, athletics, music/drama.

Application procedures. Admission: No deadline. $25 fee, may be waived for applicants with need. Admission notification on a rolling basis. **Financial aid:** Priority date 3/1; no closing date. FAFSA required. Applicants notified on a rolling basis starting 2/15; must reply within 2 week(s) of notification.

Academics. Special study options: Double major, honors, independent study, internships, liberal arts/career combination, study abroad, teacher certification program. Business department offers on-line certificate program. **Credit/placement by examination:** AP, CLEP, SAT, ACT, institutional tests. 40 credit hours maximum toward associate degree, 60 toward bachelor's. **Support services:** Learning center, reduced course load, remedial instruction, study skills assistance, tutoring.

Majors. Biology: General. **Business:** Accounting, business admin, marketing, nonprofit/public. **Communications:** General. **Computer sciences:** Computer science. **Conservation:** Environmental science. **Education:** Elementary, music, physical, secondary. **Family/consumer sciences:** Family systems. **Health:** Health services, medical radiologic technology/radiation therapy, nursing (RN), recreational therapy. **History:** General. **Interdisciplinary:** Natural sciences. **Liberal arts:** Arts/sciences. **Math:** Applied. **Parks/recreation:** Facilities management, sports admin. **Philosophy/religion:** Christian. **Physical sciences:** Chemistry. **Psychology:** General. **Social sciences:** Political science. **Visual/performing arts:** Music performance, studio arts.

Most popular majors. Biology 10%, business/marketing 8%, education 8%, health sciences 47%.

Computing on campus. 100 workstations in dormitories, library, student center. Dormitories wired for high-speed internet access and linked to campus network. Commuter students can connect to campus network. Online library, helpline, student web hosting, wireless network available.

Student life. Freshman orientation: Available. Preregistration for classes offered. Held Saturday prior to start of fall classes. **Policies:** Participation in campus activities stressed. Voluntary weekly chapel service offered. **Housing:** Guaranteed on-campus for all undergraduates. Coed dorms, single-sex dorms, special housing for disabled, apartments, wellness housing available. $100 fully refundable deposit. **Activities:** Bands, campus ministries, choral groups, dance, drama, literary magazine, music ensembles, musical theater, opera, radio station, student government, student newspaper, TV station, A-B Collegiate 4-H, association of women's studies, College Players, Fellowship of Christian Athletes, Students in Free Enterprise, Students Learning in Community Education, A-B mission team.

Athletics. NCAA. **Intercollegiate:** Baseball M, basketball, cross-country, soccer, softball W, track and field, volleyball W. **Intramural:** Basketball, bowling, football (non-tackle), golf, racquetball, soccer, softball W, tennis, volleyball. **Team name:** Battlers.

Student services. Adult student services, alcohol/substance abuse counseling, chaplain/spiritual director, career counseling, financial aid counseling, health services, personal counseling, placement for graduates, veterans' counselor. **Physically disabled:** Services for visually, hearing impaired.

Contact. E-mail: admissions@ab.edu
Phone: (304) 457-6256 Toll-free number: (800) 263-1549
Fax: (304) 457-6239
Kimberly Klaus, Director of Admissions, Alderson-Broaddus College, 101 College Hill Drive, Philippi, WV 26416

American Public University System
Charles Town, West Virginia
www.apus.edu

- For-profit 4-year virtual university
- Small town
- 29,008 degree-seeking undergraduates
- 9,092 graduate students

General. Accredited by DETC. Regionally and nationally accredited online institution serving military and public service communities through the American Military University and American Public University. **Degrees:** 1,041 bachelor's, 237 associate awarded; master's offered. **Location:** Online university. **Calendar:** Continuous. **Full-time faculty:** 165 total. **Part-time faculty:** 461 total.

Basis for selection. Open admission.

2008-2009 Annual costs. Tuition/fees: $7,500. Distance learning only. Personal expenses: $1,840.

Financial aid. Additional information: Students should complete a Federal Student Aid Intent Form and register for classes at least 37 days prior to start to allow sufficient time for financial aid process.

Application procedures. Admission: No deadline. No application fee. Application must be submitted online. Admission notification on a rolling basis. **Financial aid:** No deadline. FAFSA, institutional form required. Applicants notified on a rolling basis; must reply within 14 week(s) of notification.

Academics. Credit/placement by examination: CLEP. **Support services:** Remedial instruction, study skills assistance, tutoring.

Majors. Area/ethnic studies: African-American, Asian, Near/Middle Eastern. **Business:** Business admin, hospitality admin, marketing. **Computer sciences:** Information technology. **Conservation:** Environmental studies. **Family/consumer sciences:** Child development, family systems. **History:** General. **Legal studies:** General. **Parks/recreation:** Sports admin. **Philosophy/religion:** Philosophy, religion. **Protective services:** Emergency management/homeland security, fire services admin, law enforcement admin, security management. **Psychology:** General. **Social sciences:** International relations, political science, sociology. **Transportation:** Aviation. **Other:** International peace and conflict resolution, Military history, Transportation and logistics management.

Most popular majors. Business/marketing 23%, military 20%, security/protective services 27%, social sciences 6%.

Computing on campus. PC or laptop required. Online library available.

Student life. Freshman orientation: Mandatory. Preregistration for classes offered.

Contact. E-mail: info@apus.edu
Phone: (877) 468-6268 Toll-free number: (877) 468-6268
Fax: (304) 724-3787
Terry Grant, Director of Admissions, American Public University System, 111 West Congress Street, Charles Town, WV 25414

Appalachian Bible College
Bradley, West Virginia
www.abc.edu **CB code: 7305**

- Private 4-year Bible college affiliated with nondenominational tradition
- Residential campus in rural community
- 217 degree-seeking undergraduates
- 71% of applicants admitted
- SAT or ACT (ACT writing optional), application essay required

General. Founded in 1950. Regionally accredited; also accredited by ABHE. **Degrees:** 41 bachelor's, 12 associate awarded; master's offered. **Location:** 5 miles from Beckley. **Calendar:** Semester, limited summer session. **Full-time faculty:** 10 total. **Part-time faculty:** 5 total.

Freshman class profile. 112 applied, 80 admitted, 68 enrolled.

Mid 50% test scores			
SAT critical reading:	440-610	ACT composite:	19-26
SAT math:	430-580	Out-of-state:	64%
		Live on campus:	89%

Basis for selection. Profession of Jesus Christ as Savior, essential agreement with doctrinal statement of college, approved character very important. Minimum 2.0 GPA, test scores, achievement and potential in English also considered. If no scores are submitted, student must test on first available test date after enrollment and must take developmental English. Interview recommended. **Homeschooled:** Must provide accurate record of curriculum used, subjects studied, grades earned for grade levels 9-12.

High school preparation. Recommended units include English 4, mathematics 3, social studies 3, history 3, science 3, foreign language 1 and academic electives 4.

2008-2009 Annual costs. Tuition/fees: $9,880. Room/board: $5,160. Books/supplies: $1,200. Personal expenses: $1,162.

2007-2008 Financial aid. All financial aid based on need. 74% of total undergraduate aid awarded as scholarships/grants, 26% as loans/jobs.

Application procedures. Admission: No deadline. $20 fee, may be waived for applicants with need. Admission notification on a rolling basis. **Financial aid:** Closing date 6/15. FAFSA, institutional form required. Applicants notified on a rolling basis starting 6/15; must reply by 8/1 or within 4 week(s) of notification.

Academics. Special study options: Cooperative education, dual enrollment of high school students, independent study, internships, teacher certification program. **Credit/placement by examination:** AP, CLEP, SAT, ACT, institutional tests. 29 credit hours maximum toward bachelor's degree. **Support services:** Reduced course load, remedial instruction, study skills assistance, tutoring.

Majors. Theology: Bible.

Computing on campus. 10 workstations in library. Dormitories wired for high-speed internet access and linked to campus network. Commuter students can connect to campus network. Online library, repair service available.

Student life. Freshman orientation: Mandatory. Preregistration for classes offered. Held for 3 days immediately prior to beginning of semester. **Policies:** Chapel held three times a week. Annual Spiritual Life Conference, Distinguished Christian Lecture Series, Bible and missions conferences. Religious observance required. **Housing:** Single-sex dorms, apartments, wellness housing available. $25 nonrefundable deposit. **Activities:** Choral groups, drama, music ensembles, student government.

Athletics. NCCAA. **Intercollegiate:** Basketball, soccer M, volleyball W. **Intramural:** Basketball, soccer M, table tennis, tennis, volleyball. **Team name:** Warriors.

Student services. Career counseling, financial aid counseling, health services, personal counseling, placement for graduates, veterans' counselor.

Contact. E-mail: admissions@abc.edu
Phone: (304) 877-6428 ext. 3213 Toll-free number: (800) 678-9222
Fax: (304) 877-5082
Scott Ross, Director of Admissions, Appalachian Bible College, PO Box ABC, Bradley, WV 25818-1353

Bethany College
Bethany, West Virginia **CB member**
www.bethanywv.edu **CB code: 5060**

- Private 4-year liberal arts college affiliated with Christian Church (Disciples of Christ)
- Residential campus in rural community
- 804 degree-seeking undergraduates: 53% women
- 94% of applicants admitted
- SAT or ACT (ACT writing recommended), application essay required
- 55% graduate within 6 years; 37% enter graduate study

General. Founded in 1840. Regionally accredited. **Degrees:** 167 bachelor's awarded. **Location:** 14 miles from Wheeling, 40 miles from Pittsburgh. **Calendar:** 4-1-4. **Full-time faculty:** 53 total; 70% have terminal degrees, 9% minority, 40% women. **Part-time faculty:** 21 total; 19% have terminal degrees, 62% women. **Class size:** 76% < 20, 21% 20-39, 3% 40-49, less than 1% 50-99.

Freshman class profile. 1,237 applied, 1,164 admitted, 263 enrolled.

Mid 50% test scores			
SAT critical reading:	420-530	GPA 2.0-2.99:	47%
SAT math:	420-530	Rank in top quarter:	26%
ACT composite:	18-24	Rank in top tenth:	7%
GPA 3.75 or higher:	11%	End year in good standing:	70%
GPA 3.50-3.74:	11%	Return as sophomores:	70%
GPA 3.0-3.49:	28%	Live on campus:	98%

Basis for selection. Rank in top half of graduating class, test scores, interview, activities, and recommendations important. Interviews strongly recommended, but not required. **Homeschooled:** Statement describing homeschool structure and mission required. **Learning Disabled:** Students with learning disabilities must apply by February 15 for priority consideration in limited-enrollment learning disabled program. Students should submit official diagnosis of learning disability after acceptance.

High school preparation. College-preparatory program recommended. 15 units required. Required and recommended units include English 4, mathematics 3, social studies 3, science 3 (laboratory 1), foreign language 2 and academic electives 2.

2008-2009 Annual costs. Tuition/fees: $18,695. Room/board: $8,160. Books/supplies: $1,000. Personal expenses: $900.

2008-2009 Financial aid. Need-based: Average scholarship/grant was $10,050; average loan $4,500. 78% of total undergraduate aid awarded as scholarships/grants, 22% as loans/jobs. **Non-need-based:** Scholarships awarded for academics, alumni affiliation, art, leadership, music/drama, religious affiliation, state residency. **Additional information:** Scholarships available for travel program.

Application procedures. Admission: Priority date 4/1; no deadline. $25 fee, may be waived for applicants with need, free for online applicants. Admission notification on a rolling basis beginning on or about 10/1. Must reply by May 1 or within 3 week(s) if notified thereafter. **Financial aid:** Priority date 3/1; no closing date. FAFSA required. Applicants notified on a rolling basis starting 1/15.

Academics. Special study options: Accelerated study, combined bachelor's/graduate degree, distance learning, double major, dual enrollment of high school students, ESL, independent study, internships, liberal arts/career combination, student-designed major, study abroad, teacher certification program, United Nations semester, Washington semester. **Credit/placement by examination:** AP, CLEP, IB, SAT, ACT, institutional tests. 80 credit hours maximum toward bachelor's degree. **Support services:** Learning center, pre-admission summer program, remedial instruction, study skills assistance, tutoring, writing center.

Majors. **Biology:** General, biochemistry. **Business:** General, accounting, finance, international, international finance. **Communications:** General, advertising, broadcast journalism, journalism, public relations, radio/tv. **Communications technology:** Graphics. **Computer sciences:** General, computer science. **Conservation:** Environmental studies. **Education:** General, art, biology, chemistry, elementary, English, foreign languages, French, German, history, learning disabled, mathematics, multi-level teacher, multiple handicapped, physical, secondary, social studies, Spanish, special. **Foreign languages:** French, German, Spanish. **History:** General. **Interdisciplinary:** Biological/physical sciences, global studies, math/computer science. **Math:** General. **Parks/recreation:** Health/fitness, sports admin. **Philosophy/religion:** Philosophy, religion. **Physical sciences:** Chemistry, physics. **Psychology:** General. **Public administration:** Social work. **Social sciences:** Economics, international relations, political science. **Visual/performing arts:** General, art, design, dramatic, studio arts.

Most popular majors. Communications/journalism 13%, education 20%, interdisciplinary studies 10%, psychology 10%, visual/performing arts 6%.

Computing on campus. 145 workstations in dormitories, library, computer center, student center. Dormitories wired for high-speed internet access and linked to campus network. Commuter students can connect to campus network. Online library, helpline, repair service, student web hosting, wireless network available.

Student life. **Freshman orientation:** Mandatory, $100 fee. Preregistration for classes offered. Sessions held during the summer and prior to start of Fall classes. **Housing:** Guaranteed on-campus for all undergraduates. Coed dorms, single-sex dorms, special housing for disabled, apartments, fraternity/sorority housing available. **Activities:** Bands, choral groups, dance, drama, film society, international student organizations, literary magazine, music ensembles, Model UN, musical theater, radio station, student government, student newspaper, TV station, community service organization, ecumenical religious organization, multicultural students club, advertising club, social work club, Amnesty International, Coalition for Christian Outreach, Circle K, equestrian club.

Athletics. NCAA. **Intercollegiate:** Baseball M, basketball, cheerleading, cross-country, diving, football (tackle) M, golf M, soccer, softball W, swimming, tennis, track and field, volleyball W. **Intramural:** Basketball, football (non-tackle) M, handball, racquetball, soccer, softball, swimming, tennis, volleyball. **Team name:** Bison.

Student services. Alcohol/substance abuse counseling, chaplain/spiritual director, career counseling, student employment services, financial aid counseling, health services, minority student services, personal counseling, placement for graduates, women's services. **Physically disabled:** Services for visually, speech, hearing impaired. **Learning disabled:** Comprehensive services available.

Contact. E-mail: kdayich@bethanywv.edu
Phone: (304) 829-7611 Toll-free number: (800) 922-7611
Fax: (304) 829-7142
Karina Dayich, Director of Admission, Bethany College, Office of Admission, Bethany, WV 26032-0428

Bluefield State College
Bluefield, West Virginia
www.bluefieldstate.edu **CB code: 5064**

- Public 4-year liberal arts and technical college
- Commuter campus in large town
- 1,790 degree-seeking undergraduates: 16% part-time, 60% women, 12% African American, 1% Hispanic American, 3% international
- 83% of applicants admitted
- SAT or ACT with writing required

General. Founded in 1895. Regionally accredited. Off-campus locations at Lewisburg, Welch, and Beckley. **Degrees:** 219 bachelor's, 85 associate awarded. **Location:** 100 miles from Charleston; 100 miles from Roanoke, Virginia. **Calendar:** Semester, limited summer session. **Full-time faculty:** 76 total; 54% have terminal degrees, 10% minority, 49% women. **Part-time faculty:** 74 total; 12% have terminal degrees, 4% minority, 47% women. **Class size:** 61% < 20, 35% 20-39, 3% 40-49, less than 1% 50-99. **Special facilities:** Instructional technology center.

Freshman class profile. 463 applied, 384 admitted, 302 enrolled.

Mid 50% test scores		**GPA 2.0-2.99:**	25%
SAT critical reading:	410-510	**End year in good standing:**	58%
SAT math:	420-530	**Return as sophomores:**	60%
ACT composite:	16-21	**Out-of-state:**	15%
GPA 3.75 or higher:	16%	**Fraternities:**	1%
GPA 3.50-3.74:	21%	**Sororities:**	1%
GPA 3.0-3.49:	36%		

Basis for selection. 2.5 GPA, college preparatory program, test scores required for applicants to health, teacher education, humanities, social science and business administration programs. High school requirements not necessary for associate's program.

High school preparation. College-preparatory program recommended. 17 units required. Required units include English 4, mathematics 4, social studies 3, history 1, science 3 (laboratory 2), foreign language 2 and visual/performing arts 1.

2008-2009 Annual costs. Tuition/fees: $4,272; $8,568 out-of-state. Tuition for students residing in border counties is $6,288. Books/supplies: $1,600. Personal expenses: $2,840.

2008-2009 Financial aid. **Need-based:** Average need met was 70%. Average scholarship/grant was $3,400; average loan $3,500. 56% of total undergraduate aid awarded as scholarships/grants, 44% as loans/jobs. **Non-need-based:** Scholarships awarded for academics, alumni affiliation, art, athletics, job skills, leadership, minority status, music/drama, state residency.

Application procedures. **Admission:** No deadline. No application fee. Admission notification on a rolling basis. **Financial aid:** Closing date 3/1. FAFSA, institutional form required. Applicants notified by 5/1.

Academics. **Special study options:** Distance learning, honors, internships, liberal arts/career combination, student-designed major, teacher certification program. **Credit/placement by examination:** AP, CLEP, IB, ACT, institutional tests. **Support services:** Learning center, pre-admission summer program, reduced course load, remedial instruction, study skills assistance, tutoring, writing center.

Majors. **Business:** Accounting, business admin. **Computer sciences:** General. **Education:** Elementary. **Engineering technology:** Architectural, civil, electrical, mechanical, mining. **Health:** Nursing (RN), radiologic technology/medical imaging. **Interdisciplinary:** Biological/physical sciences. **Liberal arts:** Arts/sciences, humanities. **Protective services:** Criminal justice. **Social sciences:** General.

Most popular majors. Business/marketing 18%, education 14%, engineering/engineering technologies 12%, health sciences 8%, liberal arts 20%, security/protective services 7%, social sciences 13%.

Computing on campus. 370 workstations in library, computer center. Online library, helpline, student web hosting, wireless network available.

Student life. **Freshman orientation:** Available. Preregistration for classes offered. One day in July or August. **Housing:** Off-campus housing services provided. **Activities:** Campus ministries, choral groups, international student organizations, Model UN, radio station, student government, student newspaper, Minorities on the Move, student nurses association.

Athletics. NCAA. **Intercollegiate:** Baseball M, basketball, cheerleading, cross-country, golf M, softball W, tennis, volleyball W. **Intramural:** Badminton, basketball, bowling, football (non-tackle) M, golf, racquetball, softball, swimming, table tennis, tennis, volleyball. **Team name:** Big Blues.

Student services. Career counseling, student employment services, financial aid counseling, health services, minority student services, personal counseling, placement for graduates, veterans' counselor. **Physically disabled:** Services for visually, speech, hearing impaired.

Contact. E-mail: bscadmit@bluefieldstate.edu
Phone: (304) 327-4065 Toll-free number: (800) 654-7798
Fax: (304) 325-7747
Kenny Mandeville, Director of Admissions, Bluefield State College, 219 Rock Street, Bluefield, WV 24701

Concord University
Athens, West Virginia **CB member**
www.concord.edu **CB code: 5120**

- Public 4-year university and liberal arts college
- Residential campus in small town

- 2,384 full-time, degree-seeking undergraduates
- 97 graduate students
- 75% of applicants admitted
- SAT or ACT (ACT writing optional) required

General. Founded in 1872. Regionally accredited. **Degrees:** 355 bachelor's, 2 associate awarded; master's offered. **Location:** 5 miles from Princeton, 80 miles from Charleston. **Calendar:** Semester, extensive summer session. **Full-time faculty:** 104 total; 61% have terminal degrees, 44% women. **Part-time faculty:** 88 total; 16% have terminal degrees, 54% women. **Class size:** 60% < 20, 32% 20-39, 5% 40-49, 3% 50-99, less than 1% >100. **Special facilities:** Southern West Virginia technology center.

Freshman class profile. 2,489 applied, 1,877 admitted, 882 enrolled.

Mid 50% test scores			
SAT critical reading:	310-610	SAT writing:	310-610
SAT math:	300-620	ACT composite:	17-28

Basis for selection. 2.0 GPA and 810 SAT (exclusive of Writing) required. **Homeschooled:** Statement describing homeschool structure and mission, transcript of courses and grades required.

High school preparation. Required units include English 4, mathematics 3, social studies 2, history 1, science 1 (laboratory 2). Math courses must include algebra I and another higher level course. Social science requirement includes 1 US history.

2008-2009 Annual costs. Tuition/fees: $4,578; $10,170 out-of-state. Room and board may be paid in 2 installments each semester: 60% at registration, 40% six weeks later. Room/board: $6,530. Books/supplies: $1,500. Personal expenses: $2,169.

2007-2008 Financial aid. Non-need-based: Scholarships awarded for academics, alumni affiliation, art, athletics, job skills, leadership, minority status, music/drama, state residency. **Additional information:** March 1 priority deadline for state forms. April 15 priority deadline for FAFSA.

Application procedures. Admission: No deadline. No application fee. Admission notification on a rolling basis beginning on or about 9/1. **Financial aid:** FAFSA, institutional form required. Applicants notified on a rolling basis starting 3/1; must reply within 2 week(s) of notification.

Academics. Special study options: Cooperative education, distance learning, double major, dual enrollment of high school students, ESL, honors, internships, liberal arts/career combination, student-designed major, study abroad, teacher certification program. English as a second language program for foreign students, mentoring programs for pre-law and pre-med students. **Credit/placement by examination:** AP, CLEP, SAT, ACT, institutional tests. **Support services:** Learning center, reduced course load, remedial instruction, study skills assistance, tutoring, writing center.

Majors. Biology: General, genetics. **Business:** General, accounting, business admin, finance, hospitality admin, hospitality/recreation, hotel/motel admin, human resources, managerial economics, marketing, resort management, restaurant/food services, tourism promotion, tourism/travel. **Communications:** General, advertising, broadcast journalism, journalism, public relations. **Computer sciences:** General, computer science. **Education:** General, art, biology, business, chemistry, early childhood, elementary, English, health, learning disabled, mathematics, mentally handicapped, music, physical, science, social studies, speech. **Health:** Athletic training, clinical lab science, predental, premedicine, prepharmacy, preveterinary. **History:** General. **Interdisciplinary:** Global studies. **Legal studies:** Prelaw. **Liberal arts:** Arts/sciences, library science. **Math:** General. **Parks/recreation:** General, facilities management, health/fitness, sports admin. **Personal/culinary services:** Restaurant/catering. **Physical sciences:** Chemistry, geology. **Psychology:** General. **Public administration:** General, social work. **Social sciences:** Geography, political science, sociology. **Visual/performing arts:** Art, commercial/advertising art, dramatic, graphic design, studio arts.

Most popular majors. Biology 7%, business/marketing 25%, education 27%, liberal arts 9%, social sciences 7%.

Computing on campus. 250 workstations in dormitories, library, computer center, student center. Dormitories wired for high-speed internet access. Online library, helpline, repair service, wireless network available.

Student life. Freshman orientation: Mandatory, $40 fee. Preregistration for classes offered. **Housing:** Guaranteed on-campus for all undergraduates. Coed dorms, single-sex dorms, special housing for disabled, apartments, fraternity/sorority housing, wellness housing available. $50 deposit. **Activities:** Bands, choral groups, dance, drama, film society, literary magazine, music ensembles, radio station, student government, student newspaper, TV station, over 50 clubs and organizations.

Athletics. NCAA. **Intercollegiate:** Baseball M, basketball, cross-country, football (tackle) M, golf, soccer, softball W, tennis, track and field, volleyball W. **Intramural:** Archery, badminton, basketball, bowling, football (tackle) M, golf, handball, racquetball, soccer W, softball, swimming, tennis, track and field, volleyball, water polo. **Team name:** Mountain Lions.

Student services. Career counseling, student employment services, financial aid counseling, health services, on-campus daycare, personal counseling, placement for graduates, veterans' counselor. **Learning disabled:** Comprehensive services available.

Contact. E-mail: admissions@concord.edu
Phone: (304) 384-5248 Toll-free number: (888) 384-5249
Fax: (304) 384-3218
Kent Gamble, Director of Enrollment, Concord University, PO Box 1000, Athens, WV 24712-1000

Davis and Elkins College

Elkins, West Virginia — **CB member**
www.davisandelkins.edu — **CB code: 5151**

- Private 4-year liberal arts college affiliated with Presbyterian Church (USA)
- Residential campus in small town
- 531 degree-seeking undergraduates: 4% part-time, 62% women, 5% African American, 1% Hispanic American, 1% Native American, 6% international
- 80% of applicants admitted
- SAT or ACT (ACT writing optional) required
- 48% graduate within 6 years; 13% enter graduate study

General. Founded in 1904. Regionally accredited. **Degrees:** 122 bachelor's, 60 associate awarded. **Location:** 130 miles from Pittsburgh; 200 miles from Washington, DC. **Calendar:** 4-1-4, extensive summer session. **Full-time faculty:** 37 total; 89% have terminal degrees, 11% minority, 51% women. **Part-time faculty:** 26 total; 19% have terminal degrees, 50% women. **Class size:** 75% < 20, 22% 20-39, 3% 40-49, 1% 50-99. **Special facilities:** Pearl S. Buck collection, observatory, greenhouse, planetarium, 8 buildings on the national historic registry.

Freshman class profile. 430 applied, 346 admitted, 126 enrolled.

Mid 50% test scores			
SAT critical reading:	380-490	Rank in top quarter:	26%
SAT math:	390-490	Rank in top tenth:	7%
SAT writing:	390-490	End year in good standing:	66%
ACT composite:	18-23	Return as sophomores:	67%
GPA 3.75 or higher:	13%	Out-of-state:	44%
GPA 3.50-3.74:	10%	Live on campus:	79%
GPA 3.0-3.49:	25%	International:	13%
GPA 2.0-2.99:	46%	Fraternities:	2%
		Sororities:	50%

Basis for selection. Admission based on school achievement record, 2.0 GPA, test scores, and extracurricular activities. Recommended interview also important. Tests are required for admission and must be submitted before application can be evaluated. Essay, academic/personal recommendations recommended for all applicants; audition required for musicians and theater students; portfolio required for art students. **Homeschooled:** Transcript of courses and grades required. **Learning Disabled:** Must complete a separate application for the Supported Learning Program.

High school preparation. College-preparatory program recommended. 15 units required. Required and recommended units include English 4, mathematics 3-4, social studies 3-4, science 3-4 (laboratory 1-2), foreign language 1-2 and academic electives 4. Math units must include Algebra I or Algebra II, and Geometry.

2008-2009 Annual costs. Tuition/fees: $20,060. Room/board: $6,700. Books/supplies: $800. Personal expenses: $1,500.

2008-2009 Financial aid. Need-based: 107 full-time freshmen applied for aid; 95 were judged to have need; 95 of these received aid. Average need met was 79%. Average scholarship/grant was $4,563; average loan $4,538. 43% of total undergraduate aid awarded as scholarships/grants, 57% as loans/jobs. **Non-need-based:** Awarded to 543 full-time undergraduates, including 130 freshmen. Scholarships awarded for academics, alumni affiliation, art, athletics, leadership, minority status, music/drama, religious affiliation.

Application procedures. Admission: Priority date 5/1; no deadline. No application fee. Admission notification on a rolling basis beginning on or about 9/30. **Financial aid:** Priority date 3/1; no closing date. FAFSA required. Applicants notified on a rolling basis starting 5/1; must reply within 2 week(s) of notification.

Academics. **Special study options:** Combined bachelor's/graduate degree, cooperative education, cross-registration, distance learning, double major, dual enrollment of high school students, external degree, honors, independent study, internships, liberal arts/career combination, student-designed major, study abroad, teacher certification program, Washington semester. **Credit/placement by examination:** AP, CLEP, IB, institutional tests. **Support services:** Learning center, reduced course load, remedial instruction, study skills assistance, tutoring, writing center.

Majors. **Biology:** General. **Business:** Accounting, business admin, hospitality admin, international, international marketing, management information systems, marketing. **Computer sciences:** Computer science, information systems. **Conservation:** Environmental science. **Education:** Business, drama/dance, elementary, mathematics, music, physical. **Foreign languages:** Spanish. **History:** General. **Math:** General. **Parks/recreation:** General, exercise sciences, sports admin. **Philosophy/religion:** Religion. **Physical sciences:** Chemistry. **Psychology:** General. **Social sciences:** Criminology, economics, political science, sociology. **Theology:** Religious ed. **Visual/performing arts:** Dramatic, theater design. **Other:** Biology and environmental sciences, Pre-forestry.

Most popular majors. Business/marketing 30%, education 8%, English 6%, history 8%, parks/recreation 8%, psychology 10%, social sciences 10%, theological studies 7%.

Computing on campus. 81 workstations in library, computer center, student center. Dormitories wired for high-speed internet access and linked to campus network. Commuter students can connect to campus network. Helpline, repair service, wireless network available.

Student life. **Freshman orientation:** Mandatory. Preregistration for classes offered. Various options available. **Housing:** Guaranteed on-campus for all undergraduates. Coed dorms, single-sex dorms, fraternity/sorority housing, wellness housing available. **Activities:** Bands, choral groups, drama, international student organizations, literary magazine, music ensembles, musical theater, radio station, student government, student newspaper, black student assembly, Common Ground, Food For Thought.

Athletics. NCAA. **Intercollegiate:** Baseball M, basketball, cross-country, golf M, skiing, soccer, softball W, volleyball W. **Intramural:** Basketball, soccer, tennis, volleyball. **Team name:** Senators.

Student services. Alcohol/substance abuse counseling, chaplain/spiritual director, career counseling, student employment services, financial aid counseling, health services, personal counseling, placement for graduates, veterans' counselor. **Learning disabled:** Comprehensive services available.

Contact. E-mail: admiss@davisandelkins.edu
Phone: (304) 637-1230 Toll-free number: (800) 624-3157 ext. 1230
Fax: (304) 637-1800
Kevin Wilson, Vice President for Enrollment Management, Davis and Elkins College, 100 Campus Drive, Elkins, WV 26241-3996

Fairmont State University
Fairmont, West Virginia
www.fairmontstate.edu **CB code: 5211**

- Public 4-year university and technical college
- Commuter campus in large town
- 4,046 degree-seeking undergraduates: 13% part-time, 55% women, 4% African American, 1% Asian American, 1% Hispanic American, 2% international
- 381 degree-seeking graduate students
- 88% of applicants admitted
- SAT or ACT required

General. Founded in 1865. Regionally accredited. **Degrees:** 672 bachelor's, 79 associate awarded; master's offered. **ROTC:** Army, Air Force. **Location:** 90 miles from Pittsburgh. **Calendar:** Semester, limited summer session. **Full-time faculty:** 165 total; 72% have terminal degrees, 9% minority, 47% women. **Part-time faculty:** 169 total; 32% have terminal degrees, 8% minority, 56% women. **Class size:** 48% < 20, 42% 20-39, 3% 40-49, 6% 50-99, 2% >100. **Special facilities:** Student life center, folk-life center.

Freshman class profile. 3,072 applied, 2,690 admitted, 771 enrolled.

Mid 50% test scores		**Rank in top quarter:**	30%
SAT critical reading:	410-530	**Rank in top tenth:**	9%
SAT math:	420-540	**Return as sophomores:**	67%
ACT composite:	18-23	**Out-of-state:**	10%
GPA 3.75 or higher:	11%	**Live on campus:**	51%
GPA 3.50-3.74:	16%	**International:**	5%
GPA 3.0-3.49:	34%	**Fraternities:**	3%
GPA 2.0-2.99:	38%	**Sororities:**	2%

Basis for selection. 2.5 GPA and 17 ACT or 830 SAT (exclusive of Writing) required for bachelor's programs. For associate degree programs, SAT or ACT required for placement but not admission. **Homeschooled:** GED required.

High school preparation. 24 units required; 26 recommended. Required and recommended units include English 4, mathematics 3, social studies 2, history 1, science 3 (laboratory 2), foreign language 2 and academic electives 11. 1 unit U.S. history required. Math must include algebra and at least 1 higher unit. 2 units lab science required for biology, chemistry, and physics majors.

2008-2009 Annual costs. Tuition/fees: $4,804; $10,370 out-of-state. Room/board: $7,020. Books/supplies: $1,000. Personal expenses: $1,500.

2007-2008 Financial aid. All financial aid based on need. 579 full-time freshmen applied for aid; 417 were judged to have need; 405 of these received aid. Average scholarship/grant was $8,985; average loan $2,887. 48% of total undergraduate aid awarded as scholarships/grants, 52% as loans/jobs.

Application procedures. **Admission:** Priority date 3/1; deadline 8/15 (postmark date). No application fee. Admission notification on a rolling basis beginning on or about 10/1. **Financial aid:** Closing date 3/1. FAFSA required. Applicants notified on a rolling basis starting 4/1; must reply within 2 week(s) of notification.

Academics. **Special study options:** Cooperative education, distance learning, double major, dual enrollment of high school students, ESL, exchange student, honors, internships, liberal arts/career combination, study abroad, teacher certification program, Washington semester, weekend college. **Credit/placement by examination:** AP, CLEP, IB, institutional tests. 28 credit hours maximum toward bachelor's degree. **Support services:** Learning center, reduced course load, remedial instruction, study skills assistance, tutoring.

Majors. **Biology:** General. **Business:** General, accounting, banking/financial services, business admin, management information systems, management science, office management. **Communications:** General. **Communications technology:** Graphic/printing. **Computer sciences:** General, computer science. **Education:** General, art, biology, business, chemistry, early childhood, elementary, emotionally handicapped, English, family/consumer sciences, gifted/talented, history, mathematics, mentally handicapped, middle, music, physical, physics, science, secondary, social studies, speech, technology/industrial arts, trade/industrial. **Engineering technology:** Aerospace, architectural, civil, construction, drafting, electrical, mechanical, occupational safety. **Family/consumer sciences:** General. **Foreign languages:** French, Spanish. **Health:** Health care admin, nursing (RN). **History:** General. **Math:** General. **Parks/recreation:** Exercise sciences, health/fitness. **Physical sciences:** Chemistry. **Protective services:** Criminal justice, forensics, law enforcement admin. **Psychology:** General. **Social sciences:** Political science, sociology. **Transportation:** Aviation, aviation management. **Visual/performing arts:** Commercial/advertising art, dramatic.

Most popular majors. Business/marketing 24%, education 20%, engineering/engineering technologies 9%, liberal arts 7%, psychology 8%, security/protective services 9%.

Computing on campus. 950 workstations in dormitories, library, computer center, student center. Dormitories wired for high-speed internet access and linked to campus network. Commuter students can connect to campus network. Online library, helpline, student web hosting, wireless network available.

Student life. **Freshman orientation:** Available. Preregistration for classes offered. Held 2 days in fall, 1 day in spring. **Policies:** Alcohol not allowed. **Housing:** Guaranteed on-campus for freshmen. Coed dorms, single-sex dorms, apartments available. $200 fully refundable deposit, deadline 6/15. **Activities:** Bands, campus ministries, choral groups, dance, drama, literary magazine, music ensembles, musical theater, student government, student newspaper, symphony orchestra, black student union, Circle K, disabled students society, international relations society, society of non-traditional students.

Athletics. NCAA. **Intercollegiate:** Baseball M, basketball, cheerleading M, cross-country, football (tackle) M, golf, softball W, swimming, tennis, volleyball W. **Intramural:** Archery, badminton W, basketball, bowling, cross-country, field hockey W, football (tackle) M, golf, gymnastics, racquetball, softball, swimming, table tennis, tennis, track and field, volleyball, wrestling M. **Team name:** Falcons.

Student services. Adult student services, career counseling, student employment services, financial aid counseling, health services, on-campus daycare, personal counseling, placement for graduates, veterans' counselor. **Physically disabled:** Services for visually, hearing impaired.

Contact. E-mail: admit@fairmontstate.edu
Phone: (304) 367-4892 Toll-free number: (800) 641-5678
Fax: (304) 367-4789
Steve Leadman, Executive Director of Enrollment Services, Fairmont State University, 1201 Locust Avenue, Fairmont, WV 26554-2470

Glenville State College

Glenville, West Virginia — **CB member**
www.glenville.edu — **CB code: 5254**

- Public 4-year liberal arts and teachers college
- Commuter campus in rural community
- 1,180 degree-seeking undergraduates: 5% part-time, 48% women
- 60% of applicants admitted
- SAT or ACT (ACT writing optional) required
- 39% graduate within 6 years; 29% enter graduate study

General. Founded in 1872. Regionally accredited. **Degrees:** 188 bachelor's, 30 associate awarded. **Location:** 87 miles from Charleston, 86 miles from Morgantown. **Calendar:** Semester, limited summer session. **Full-time faculty:** 59 total; 56% have terminal degrees, 5% minority, 39% women. **Part-time faculty:** 34 total; 15% have terminal degrees, 3% minority, 44% women. **Class size:** 56% < 20, 40% 20-39, 3% 40-49, 2% 50-99. **Special facilities:** Law enforcement teaching and training center, nature trail.

Freshman class profile. 1,043 applied, 629 admitted, 303 enrolled.

Mid 50% test scores		**GPA 2.0-2.99:**	51%
SAT critical reading:	340-490	**Rank in top quarter:**	21%
SAT math:	350-480	**Rank in top tenth:**	5%
ACT composite:	20-	**End year in good standing:**	60%
GPA 3.75 or higher:	7%	**Return as sophomores:**	72%
GPA 3.50-3.74:	7%	**Out-of-state:**	24%
GPA 3.0-3.49:	24%	**Live on campus:**	43%

Basis for selection. Students must have graduated from accredited high school with 2.0 GPA or 17 ACT/820 SAT (exclusive of Writing). Associate degree programs open to all students who have graduated from high school or hold a GED. Students who want to pursue bachelor's degree, but do not meet the requirements may enter a 2-year program and later transfer into bachelor's degree program. Audition required for music education only. **Homeschooled:** GED required. **Learning Disabled:** Students must provide documentation of their disability to the disabilities coordinator to receive services.

High school preparation. 28 units required. Required units include English 4, mathematics 4, social studies 3, science 3 (laboratory 2), foreign language 2, visual/performing arts 1 and academic electives 15. 3 of the math units must be algebra I or higher. Social studies should include US history. English should include courses in grammar, composition, and literature.

2008-2009 Annual costs. Tuition/fees: $4,486; $10,738 out-of-state. Room/board: $6,250. Books/supplies: $1,000. Personal expenses: $2,140.

2007-2008 Financial aid. Need-based: 270 full-time freshmen applied for aid; 239 were judged to have need; 235 of these received aid. Average need met was 72%. Average scholarship/grant was $5,027; average loan $2,983. 54% of total undergraduate aid awarded as scholarships/grants, 46% as loans/jobs. **Non-need-based:** Awarded to 516 full-time undergraduates, including 169 freshmen. Scholarships awarded for academics, athletics, music/drama, state residency.

Application procedures. Admission: No deadline. $10 fee, may be waived for applicants with need. Admission notification on a rolling basis. **Financial aid:** Priority date 2/1; no closing date. FAFSA required. Applicants notified on a rolling basis starting 4/1; must reply within 2 week(s) of notification.

Academics. Students can receive credit for employment, military, and/or life experience in Regents Bachelor of Arts program (designed for nontraditional students). **Special study options:** Accelerated study, cooperative education, distance learning, double major, dual enrollment of high school students, honors, internships, student-designed major, study abroad, teacher certification program, Washington semester. **Credit/placement by examination:** AP, CLEP, SAT, ACT, institutional tests. Unlimited number of hours of credit may be counted for degree. **Support services:** Remedial instruction, study skills assistance, tutoring, writing center.

Majors. Biology: General. **Business:** General, business admin. **Conservation:** Management/policy. **Education:** Elementary, kindergarten/preschool, secondary, special. **History:** General. **Physical sciences:** Chemistry. **Social sciences:** General. **Visual/performing arts:** Music performance. **Other:** Multi/Interdisciplinary studies.

Most popular majors. Business/marketing 17%, education 32%, liberal arts 11%, natural resources/environmental science 13%, social sciences 19%.

Computing on campus. 183 workstations in library, computer center, student center. Dormitories wired for high-speed internet access and linked to campus network. Commuter students can connect to campus network. Online course registration, online library, helpline, repair service, wireless network available.

Student life. Freshman orientation: Mandatory, $100 fee. Preregistration for classes offered. **Policies:** All unmarried students who have earned less than 58 credit hours required to reside on campus. Alcoholic beverages and controlled substances not permitted on campus. All students required to adhere to Student Code of Conduct. Community service required of student organizations. **Housing:** Guaranteed on-campus for freshmen. Single-sex dorms, special housing for disabled, apartments, wellness housing available. $75 partly refundable deposit, deadline 4/1. **Activities:** Bands, choral groups, drama, literary magazine, music ensembles, student government, student newspaper, Fellowship of Christian Athletes, environmental organization, students in free enterprise, Student National Education Association, student athlete advisory committee, student awareness organization, Music Educators National Conference, Kappa Delta Pi.

Athletics. NCAA. **Intercollegiate:** Basketball, cross-country, football (tackle) M, golf, softball W, track and field, volleyball W. **Intramural:** Basketball, fencing, football (non-tackle), softball, table tennis, tennis, track and field, volleyball, weight lifting, wrestling. **Team name:** Pioneers.

Student services. Adult student services, alcohol/substance abuse counseling, career counseling, services for economically disadvantaged, student employment services, financial aid counseling, health services, personal counseling, placement for graduates, veterans' counselor. **Physically disabled:** Services for visually, speech, hearing impaired.

Contact. E-mail: admissions@glenville.edu
Phone: (304) 462-4128 Toll-free number: (800) 924-2010
Fax: (304) 462-8619
Donald Chapman, Vice President for Enrollment Services, Glenville State College, Office of Enrollment Services, Glenville, WV 26351-1292

Marshall University

Huntington, West Virginia — **CB member**
www.marshall.edu — **CB code: 5396**

- Public 4-year university
- Commuter campus in small city
- 8,758 degree-seeking undergraduates: 12% part-time, 56% women, 6% African American, 1% Asian American, 1% Hispanic American, 1% international
- 3,442 degree-seeking graduate students
- 83% of applicants admitted
- SAT or ACT (ACT writing optional) required
- 42% graduate within 6 years

General. Founded in 1837. Regionally accredited. **Degrees:** 1,450 bachelor's, 100 associate awarded; master's, doctoral, first professional offered. **ROTC:** Army. **Location:** 126 miles from Lexington, Kentucky; 160 miles from Columbus, Ohio. **Calendar:** Semester, limited summer session. **Full-time faculty:** 470 total; 79% have terminal degrees, 13% minority, 42% women. **Part-time faculty:** 227 total; 9% have terminal degrees, 6% minority, 48% women. **Class size:** 43% < 20, 46% 20-39, 7% 40-49, 4% 50-99, less than 1% >100. **Special facilities:** Confederate history collection, superconducting nuclear magnetic resonance spectrometer.

Freshman class profile. 2,409 applied, 2,006 admitted, 1,686 enrolled.

Mid 50% test scores			
SAT critical reading:	450-560	GPA 3.50-3.74:	17%
SAT math:	440-560	GPA 3.0-3.49:	28%
SAT writing:	440-550	GPA 2.0-2.99:	26%
ACT composite:	19-25	Return as sophomores:	71%
GPA 3.75 or higher:	27%	Out-of-state:	28%

Basis for selection. Full admission requires 2.0 GPA and 19 ACT/910 SAT (exclusive of Writing). Conditional admission granted with below 2.0 GPA or the above scores, on a limited, first-come, first-served basis. Programs and colleges may have different requirements for admissions. Audition required for music majors; interview recommended for academically weak, learning disabled; portfolio recommended. **Homeschooled:** Applicants should apply early and have home schooling well documented.

High school preparation. 20 units required. Required units include English 4, mathematics 4, social studies 3, science 3 (laboratory 3), foreign language 2 and visual/performing arts 1.

2008-2009 Annual costs. Tuition/fees: $4,598; $11,702 out-of-state. Room/board: $7,210. Books/supplies: $1,000. Personal expenses: $2,540.

2008-2009 Financial aid. **Need-based:** 1,061 full-time freshmen applied for aid; 756 were judged to have need; 750 of these received aid. Average need met was 58%. Average scholarship/grant was $5,243; average loan $5,635. 37% of total undergraduate aid awarded as scholarships/grants, 63% as loans/jobs. **Non-need-based:** Awarded to 3,235 full-time undergraduates, including 820 freshmen. Scholarships awarded for academics, art, athletics, minority status, music/drama, ROTC, state residency.

Application procedures. **Admission:** No deadline. $30 fee, may be waived for applicants with need. Admission notification on a rolling basis beginning on or about 9/1. **Financial aid:** Priority date 3/1; no closing date. FAFSA required. Applicants notified on a rolling basis starting 5/1; must reply within 2 week(s) of notification.

Academics. **Special study options:** Accelerated study, combined bachelor's/graduate degree, cooperative education, cross-registration, distance learning, double major, dual enrollment of high school students, ESL, exchange student, honors, independent study, internships, study abroad, teacher certification program, Washington semester. 2-2 preengineering program, 3-2 program in forestry with Duke University. **Credit/placement by examination:** AP, CLEP, IB, institutional tests. **Support services:** Learning center, pre-admission summer program, reduced course load, remedial instruction, study skills assistance, tutoring, writing center.

Majors. **Biology:** General. **Business:** Accounting, business admin, finance, management information systems, managerial economics, marketing. **Communications:** Journalism. **Computer sciences:** General. **Conservation:** Environmental science. **Education:** Elementary, physical, school counseling, secondary. **Engineering:** General. **Engineering technology:** Occupational safety. **Family/consumer sciences:** General. **Foreign languages:** General. **Health:** Clinical lab science, cytotechnology, dietetics, nursing (RN), respiratory therapy technology, speech pathology. **History:** General. **Interdisciplinary:** Systems science. **Liberal arts:** Humanities. **Math:** General. **Parks/recreation:** Facilities management. **Physical sciences:** Chemistry, geology, physics. **Protective services:** Criminal justice. **Psychology:** General. **Public administration:** Social work. **Social sciences:** Economics, geography, international relations, political science, sociology. **Visual/performing arts:** Art, fashion design.

Most popular majors. Business/marketing 19%, education 18%, health sciences 8%, liberal arts 16%, psychology 7%.

Computing on campus. 1,461 workstations in dormitories, library, computer center, student center. Dormitories wired for high-speed internet access and linked to campus network. Commuter students can connect to campus network. Online course registration, online library, helpline, student web hosting available.

Student life. **Freshman orientation:** Available. Preregistration for classes offered. One-day programs in June, July, August. **Housing:** Guaranteed on-campus for freshmen. Coed dorms, single-sex dorms, special housing for disabled, apartments available. $200 deposit. **Activities:** Bands, campus ministries, choral groups, drama, international student organizations, literary magazine, music ensembles, musical theater, opera, radio station, student government, student newspaper, symphony orchestra, TV station, Black United Students, College Republicans, Lambda Society, Habitat for Humanity, student organization for alumni relations.

Athletics. NCAA. **Intercollegiate:** Baseball M, basketball, cross-country, football (tackle) M, golf, soccer, softball W, swimming W, tennis W, track and field, volleyball W. **Intramural:** Basketball, bowling, football (tackle), golf, racquetball, soccer, softball, swimming, tennis, track and field, volleyball. **Team name:** Thundering Herd.

Student services. Adult student services, alcohol/substance abuse counseling, chaplain/spiritual director, career counseling, student employment services, health services, minority student services, on-campus daycare, personal counseling, placement for graduates, veterans' counselor, women's services. **Physically disabled:** Services for visually, speech, hearing impaired.

Contact. E-mail: admissions@marshall.edu
Phone: (304) 696-3160 Toll-free number: (800) 642-3499
Fax: (304) 696-3135
Tammy Johnson, Director of Admissions, Marshall University, One John Marshall Drive, Huntington, WV 25755

Mountain State University

Beckley, West Virginia — **CB member**
www.mountainstate.edu — **CB code: 5054**

- Private 4-year university and health science college
- Commuter campus in large town
- 4,266 degree-seeking undergraduates: 25% part-time, 66% women, 11% African American, 2% Asian American, 2% Hispanic American, 8% international
- 730 degree-seeking graduate students

General. Founded in 1933. Regionally accredited. **Degrees:** 719 bachelor's, 178 associate awarded; master's offered. **Location:** 55 miles from Charleston. **Calendar:** Semester, limited summer session. **Full-time faculty:** 104 total; 27% have terminal degrees, 9% minority, 68% women. **Part-time faculty:** 348 total; 19% have terminal degrees, 6% minority, 52% women. **Class size:** 75% < 20, 24% 20-39, less than 1% 40-49, less than 1% 50-99. **Special facilities:** YMCA, medicinal botanical garden, greenhouse.

Freshman class profile. 1,867 applied, 1,867 admitted, 565 enrolled.

Mid 50% test scores			
SAT critical reading:	-700	Rank in top quarter:	20%
SAT math:	300-600	Rank in top tenth:	7%
SAT writing:	-700	End year in good standing:	41%
ACT composite:	17-23	Return as sophomores:	46%
GPA 3.75 or higher:	13%	Out-of-state:	21%
GPA 3.50-3.74:	8%	Live on campus:	7%
GPA 3.0-3.49:	31%	International:	17%
GPA 2.0-2.99:	40%	Fraternities:	1%

Basis for selection. Open admission, but selective for some programs. Special requirements for health science programs. ACT/SAT scores required for nursing and physician's assistant programs. **Homeschooled:** Provide official academic records.

High school preparation. College-preparatory program recommended. 15 units recommended. Recommended units include English 4, mathematics 2, social studies 3, history 2, science 2 (laboratory 2).

2008-2009 Annual costs. Tuition/fees: $8,400. Certain programs require additional costs: health science and culinary/hospitality are $320 per credit hour. Room/board: $6,116. Books/supplies: $1,300. Personal expenses: $3,000.

2007-2008 Financial aid. **Need-based:** 258 full-time freshmen applied for aid; 222 were judged to have need; 222 of these received aid. Average need met was 39%. Average scholarship/grant was $3,336; average loan $3,378. 40% of total undergraduate aid awarded as scholarships/grants, 60% as loans/jobs. **Non-need-based:** Awarded to 103 full-time undergraduates, including 27 freshmen. Scholarships awarded for academics, alumni affiliation, athletics, leadership, minority status.

Application procedures. **Admission:** No deadline. $25 fee, may be waived for applicants with need. Admission notification on a rolling basis. **Financial aid:** No deadline. FAFSA required. Applicants notified on a rolling basis starting 4/1.

Academics. **Special study options:** Accelerated study, combined bachelor's/graduate degree, cooperative education, cross-registration, distance learning, double major, dual enrollment of high school students, ESL, independent study, internships, liberal arts/career combination, student-designed major, weekend college. Degree completion program, credit for prior learning (challenge exam and portfolio assessment). **Credit/placement by examination:** AP, CLEP, IB, institutional tests. 32 credit hours maximum toward associate degree, 64 toward bachelor's. CLEP, DANTES and Challenge exams available. **Support services:** Learning center, reduced course load, remedial instruction, study skills assistance, tutoring, writing center.

Majors. Biology: General. **Business:** General, accounting, business admin, e-commerce, entrepreneurial studies, financial planning, hospitality admin, hospitality/recreation, human resources, international, logistics, management science, marketing, nonprofit/public, office management, organizational behavior, tourism/travel. **Communications:** Media studies. **Computer sciences:** Computer science, information systems, LAN/WAN management, networking, webmaster. **Conservation:** General, environmental studies. **Health:** Health care admin, health services, nursing (RN), occupational health, premedicine, public health ed, respiratory therapy assistant, respiratory therapy technology, sonography. **Interdisciplinary:** Accounting/computer science, behavioral sciences, biological/physical sciences, math/computer science. **Legal studies:** General. **Liberal arts:** Arts/sciences, humanities, library science. **Personal/culinary services:** Chef training. **Philosophy/religion:** Religion. **Physical sciences:** General. **Protective services:** Correctional facilities, corrections, criminal justice, emergency management/homeland security, forensics, law enforcement admin, security management. **Psychology:** General. **Public administration:** Social work. **Transportation:** Aviation management. **Other:** Health education and wellness, Organizational leadership.

Most popular majors. Business/marketing 28%, health sciences 36%, interdisciplinary studies 9%, security/protective services 20%.

Computing on campus. 90 workstations in library, computer center. Dormitories wired for high-speed internet access and linked to campus network. Commuter students can connect to campus network. Online course registration, online library, helpline, repair service, student web hosting, wireless network available.

Student life. Freshman orientation: Available. Preregistration for classes offered. One-day orientation during summer. Special sessions for parents. **Housing:** Guaranteed on-campus for freshmen. Coed dorms, wellness housing available. $150 fully refundable deposit. Handicapped-accessible dorms, off-campus housing for athletes available. **Activities:** Pep band, choral groups, drama, international student organizations, student government, student newspaper, Christian student organization, American Association of Medical Assistants, criminal justice association, forensic club, legal club, student association for respiratory care, student nursing association, Students in Free Enterprise, student social work organization.

Athletics. NAIA. **Intercollegiate:** Basketball M, cheerleading, soccer, softball W, volleyball W. **Intramural:** Basketball, football (non-tackle), football (tackle), soccer, softball, table tennis, volleyball. **Team name:** Cougars.

Student services. Adult student services, alcohol/substance abuse counseling, career counseling, student employment services, financial aid counseling, health services, on-campus daycare, personal counseling, placement for graduates, veterans' counselor.

Contact. E-mail: gomsu@mountainstate.edu
Phone: (304) 929-1433 Toll-free number: (800) 766-6067
Fax: (304) 253-3463
Tammy Toney, Director of the Admissions Process, Mountain State University, 609 South Kanawha Street, Beckley, WV 25802-9003

Ohio Valley University

Vienna, West Virginia
www.ovu.edu **CB code: 5519**

- Private 4-year university and liberal arts college affiliated with Church of Christ
- Residential campus in small city
- 491 degree-seeking undergraduates: 9% part-time, 53% women, 5% African American, 4% Hispanic American, 9% international
- 54% of applicants admitted
- SAT or ACT (ACT writing optional) required
- 48% graduate within 6 years

General. Founded in 1960. Regionally accredited. **Degrees:** 122 bachelor's, 14 associate awarded; master's offered. **Location:** 95 miles from Columbus, 120 miles from Pittsburgh. **Calendar:** Semester, limited summer session. **Full-time faculty:** 25 total; 44% have terminal degrees, 4% minority, 40% women. **Part-time faculty:** 56 total; 16% have terminal degrees, 38% women. **Class size:** 78% < 20, 22% 20-39.

Freshman class profile. 445 applied, 240 admitted, 114 enrolled.

Mid 50% test scores		**GPA 2.0-2.99:**	38%
SAT critical reading:	430-570	**Rank in top quarter:**	34%
SAT math:	450-570	**Rank in top tenth:**	18%
SAT writing:	430-530	**End year in good standing:**	87%
ACT composite:	18-24	**Return as sophomores:**	61%
GPA 3.75 or higher:	23%	**Out-of-state:**	12%
GPA 3.50-3.74:	11%	**Live on campus:**	90%
GPA 3.0-3.49:	26%	**International:**	3%

Basis for selection. School achievement record, test scores and reference considered. Essay, interview recommended.

High school preparation. 12 units recommended. Recommended units include English 3, mathematics 3, social studies 2, history 1, science 3 (laboratory 1).

2008-2009 Annual costs. Tuition/fees: $16,120. Room/board: $6,324. Books/supplies: $1,000. Personal expenses: $800.

2008-2009 Financial aid. Need-based: Average need met was 67%. Average scholarship/grant was $7,972; average loan $3,044. 50% of total undergraduate aid awarded as scholarships/grants, 50% as loans/jobs. **Non-need-based:** Scholarships awarded for academics, alumni affiliation, athletics, job skills, leadership, music/drama.

Application procedures. Admission: No deadline. $20 fee, may be waived for applicants with need. Admission notification on a rolling basis. **Financial aid:** Priority date 2/15; no closing date. FAFSA required. Applicants notified on a rolling basis starting 3/15; must reply within 4 week(s) of notification.

Academics. Bible course required of full-time students each semester. **Special study options:** Cooperative education, double major, dual enrollment of high school students, ESL, honors, independent study, internships, student-designed major, teacher certification program, weekend college. Degree completion programs and special certifications. **Credit/placement by examination:** AP, CLEP, IB, SAT, ACT, institutional tests. 30 credit hours maximum toward associate degree, 30 toward bachelor's. Challenge course testing. **Support services:** Learning center, pre-admission summer program, reduced course load, remedial instruction, study skills assistance, tutoring.

Majors. Business: Accounting, business admin, human resources, nonprofit/public. **Computer sciences:** Information technology. **Education:** General, elementary, English, mathematics, multi-level teacher, physical, science, secondary, social studies. **Liberal arts:** Arts/sciences. **Philosophy/religion:** Religion. **Psychology:** General. **Theology:** Bible.

Most popular majors. Business/marketing 46%, education 21%, interdisciplinary studies 7%, psychology 14%, theological studies 6%.

Computing on campus. 44 workstations in dormitories, library, computer center. Dormitories wired for high-speed internet access and linked to campus network. Commuter students can connect to campus network. Online library, repair service, wireless network available.

Student life. Freshman orientation: Mandatory. Preregistration for classes offered. **Policies:** Chapel/assembly attendance required 3 times a week. Religious observance required. **Housing:** Guaranteed on-campus for all undergraduates. Single-sex dorms, apartments, wellness housing available. $150 deposit, deadline 8/20. **Activities:** Bands, choral groups, drama, literary magazine, music ensembles, musical theater, student government, student newspaper, symphony orchestra, prospective ministers and prospective missionaries clubs, women's club, Diversity at the University club.

Athletics. NCAA. **Intercollegiate:** Baseball M, basketball, cross-country, golf, soccer, softball W, volleyball W. **Intramural:** Basketball, bowling, cross-country, football (non-tackle), soccer, softball, table tennis, track and field, volleyball. **Team name:** Fighting Scots.

Student services. Adult student services, alcohol/substance abuse counseling, chaplain/spiritual director, career counseling, student employment services, financial aid counseling, health services, minority student services, personal counseling, placement for graduates.

Contact. E-mail: admissions@ovu.edu
Phone: (304) 865-6200 Toll-free number: (877) 446-8668
Fax: (304) 865-6175
Amy Bortell, Director of Admissions, Ohio Valley University, One Campus View Drive, Vienna, WV 26105

Salem International University
Salem, West Virginia
www.salemu.edu **CB code: 5608**

- For-profit 4-year university and liberal arts college
- Residential campus in rural community
- 442 degree-seeking undergraduates: 52% women, 13% African American, 2% Asian American, 3% Hispanic American, 10% international
- 167 degree-seeking graduate students

General. Founded in 1888. Regionally accredited. **Degrees:** 46 bachelor's awarded; master's offered. **Location:** 12 miles from Clarksburg, 125 miles from Pittsburgh. **Calendar:** Semester, limited summer session. **Full-time faculty:** 13 total; 46% have terminal degrees, 8% minority, 23% women. **Part-time faculty:** 3 total; 67% women. **Class size:** 77% < 20, 17% 20-39, 6% 40-49.

Freshman class profile.

Out-of-state:	46%	**Fraternities:**	5%
Live on campus:	90%	**Sororities:**	8%
International:	10%		

Basis for selection. School achievement record, test scores, counselor recommendations most important. SAT or ACT recommended. Essay, interview recommended. **Homeschooled:** State high school equivalency certificate required.

High school preparation. 16 units recommended. Recommended units include English 4, mathematics 2, social studies 3, science 2 and foreign language 2.

2008-2009 Annual costs. Tuition/fees: $14,100. Room/board: $6,600. Books/supplies: $660. Personal expenses: $320.

2007-2008 Financial aid. Non-need-based: Scholarships awarded for academics.

Application procedures. Admission: No deadline. $25 fee, may be waived for applicants with need. Admission notification on a rolling basis. **Financial aid:** Priority date 4/15; no closing date. FAFSA required. Applicants notified on a rolling basis starting 2/15; must reply within 4 week(s) of notification.

Academics. In keeping with college's mission to foster global awareness, all students required to complete international core curriculum. **Special study options:** Accelerated study, distance learning, double major, dual enrollment of high school students, independent study, internships, liberal arts/career combination, student-designed major, study abroad, teacher certification program, Washington semester. **Credit/placement by examination:** AP, CLEP, IB, institutional tests. 24 credit hours maximum toward bachelor's degree. **Support services:** Learning center, reduced course load, remedial instruction, study skills assistance, tutoring, writing center.

Majors. Biology: General. **Business:** Business admin. **Computer sciences:** General, computer science. **Education:** General, multi-level teacher, secondary. **Liberal arts:** Arts/sciences. **Protective services:** Criminal justice.

Most popular majors. Business/marketing 44%, computer/information sciences 26%, liberal arts 13%.

Computing on campus. 50 workstations in library, computer center. Dormitories wired for high-speed internet access and linked to campus network. Commuter students can connect to campus network. Online library, helpline, wireless network available.

Student life. Freshman orientation: Available, $30 fee. Preregistration for classes offered. Program includes introduction to international aspects of college. Special orientation for international students with U.S. life-skills training. **Policies:** Unless local resident, freshmen and sophomores required to live on-campus. **Housing:** Guaranteed on-campus for all undergraduates. Coed dorms, single-sex dorms, wellness housing available. $50 fully refundable deposit. Private rooms subject to availability. **Activities:** Choral groups, international student organizations, student government, student newspaper, Gamma Beta Phi honor society, Alpha Phi Omega fraternity service organization, Campus Crusade for Christ, Rainbow Alliance, international woman's alliance, Christian Student Fellowship, Indian student association, Chinese student association.

Athletics. NCAA. **Intercollegiate:** Baseball M, basketball, golf, soccer, softball W, tennis M, volleyball W, water polo. **Intramural:** Basketball, football (non-tackle), racquetball, skiing M, soccer, swimming, table tennis, tennis, volleyball. **Team name:** Tigers.

Student services. Services for economically disadvantaged, financial aid counseling.

Contact. E-mail: admissions@salemu.edu
Phone: (888) 235-5024 Toll-free number: (888) 235-5024
Fax: (304) 326-1592
Gina Cossey, Vice President, Recruiting and Marketing, Salem International University, 223 West Main Street, Salem, WV 26426

Shepherd University
Shepherdstown, West Virginia **CB member**
www.shepherd.edu **CB code: 5615**

- Public 4-year university
- Commuter campus in small town
- 3,554 degree-seeking undergraduates: 11% part-time, 58% women, 6% African American, 2% Asian American, 2% Hispanic American, 1% Native American, 1% international
- 141 degree-seeking graduate students
- 75% of applicants admitted
- SAT or ACT (ACT writing recommended) required
- 39% graduate within 6 years; 28% enter graduate study

General. Founded in 1871. Regionally accredited. **Degrees:** 642 bachelor's awarded; master's offered. **ROTC:** Air Force. **Location:** 8 miles from Martinsburg; 70 miles from Washington, DC. **Calendar:** Semester, extensive summer session. **Full-time faculty:** 119 total; 79% have terminal degrees, 13% minority, 45% women. **Part-time faculty:** 208 total; 31% have terminal degrees, 5% minority, 47% women. **Class size:** 42% < 20, 54% 20-39, 2% 40-49, 1% 50-99. **Special facilities:** Creative arts center with computer-controlled theater, recital hall with concert grand piano, recording studio, nursery school, 3 theaters, Civil War center, observatory, center for legislative studies, nursing building.

Freshman class profile. 2,067 applied, 1,547 admitted, 707 enrolled.

Mid 50% test scores		**GPA 3.0-3.49:**	29%
SAT critical reading:	460-560	**GPA 2.0-2.99:**	43%
SAT math:	450-550	**End year in good standing:**	62%
ACT composite:	19-24	**Return as sophomores:**	65%
GPA 3.75 or higher:	17%	**Out-of-state:**	42%
GPA 3.50-3.74:	10%	**Live on campus:**	39%

Basis for selection. 2.0 GPA and 19 ACT/910 SAT (exclusive of Writing) required. Essays and recommendations optional but important. Interview required for honors program and nursing applicants; recommended for others. Audition required for music; portfolio required for art majors. **Homeschooled:** Portfolio of completed work required.

High school preparation. College-preparatory program recommended. 21 units required. Required units include English 4, mathematics 4, social studies 3, history 1, science 3 (laboratory 3), foreign language 2, visual/performing arts 1 and academic electives 6. History unit must include US history; science unit must include biology. All science courses must be college preparatory laboratory sciences.

2008-2009 Annual costs. Tuition/fees: $4,898; $12,812 out-of-state. Room/board: $6,938. Books/supplies: $1,100. Personal expenses: $1,000.

2008-2009 Financial aid. Need-based: 621 full-time freshmen applied for aid; 364 were judged to have need; 352 of these received aid. Average need met was 91%. Average scholarship/grant was $4,306; average loan $3,383. 45% of total undergraduate aid awarded as scholarships/grants, 55% as loans/jobs. **Non-need-based:** Awarded to 1,242 full-time undergraduates, including 354 freshmen. Scholarships awarded for academics, art, athletics, job skills, leadership, minority status, music/drama, state residency.

Application procedures. Admission: Priority date 2/1; no deadline. $45 fee, may be waived for applicants with need. Admission notification on a rolling basis beginning on or about 9/1. Must reply by May 1 or within 3 week(s) if notified thereafter. **Financial aid:** Priority date 3/1; no closing date. FAFSA required. Applicants notified on a rolling basis starting 3/15; must reply within 3 week(s) of notification.

Academics. Special study options: Cooperative education, double major, honors, independent study, internships, liberal arts/career combination, study abroad, teacher certification program, Washington semester. **Credit/placement by examination:** AP, CLEP, IB, SAT, ACT, institutional tests. 32 credit hours maximum toward bachelor's degree. No limit for students pursuing Regents' Bachelor of Arts degree. **Support services:** Learning center, reduced course load, remedial instruction, study skills assistance, tutoring, writing center.

Majors. **Biology:** General. **Business:** Accounting, business admin. **Communications:** General. **Computer sciences:** General, applications programming. **Conservation:** General, environmental studies. **Education:** Elementary, secondary. **Family/consumer sciences:** General. **Foreign languages:** Spanish. **Health:** Nursing (RN). **History:** General. **Math:** General. **Parks/recreation:** General. **Physical sciences:** Chemistry. **Psychology:** General. **Public administration:** Social work. **Social sciences:** Economics, political science, sociology. **Visual/performing arts:** Art.

Most popular majors. Business/marketing 13%, education 13%, health sciences 7%, liberal arts 16%, parks/recreation 9%, social sciences 7%, visual/performing arts 7%.

Computing on campus. 370 workstations in library, computer center, student center. Dormitories wired for high-speed internet access and linked to campus network. Commuter students can connect to campus network. Online course registration, helpline, student web hosting, wireless network available.

Student life. **Freshman orientation:** Mandatory, $75 fee. Preregistration for classes offered. Two-day sessions held in June and July for students and parents. August orientation conducted on the Thursday and/or Friday and Saturday prior to the first day of classes. **Housing:** Guaranteed on-campus for all undergraduates. Coed dorms, apartments, wellness housing available. $200 partly refundable deposit, deadline 6/1. Honors housing available. **Activities:** Bands, campus ministries, choral groups, dance, drama, international student organizations, literary magazine, music ensembles, musical theater, radio station, student government, student newspaper, symphony orchestra, College Republicans, College Democrats, Christians in Action, NAACP, United Brothers, Shepherd Greens, Allies, Sistaz, Student Community Services.

Athletics. NCAA. **Intercollegiate:** Baseball M, basketball, football (tackle) M, golf M, lacrosse W, soccer, softball W, tennis, volleyball W. **Intramural:** Basketball, bowling, football (non-tackle), racquetball, soccer, softball, swimming, table tennis, tennis, volleyball, water polo, weight lifting, wrestling. **Team name:** Rams.

Student services. Adult student services, alcohol/substance abuse counseling, career counseling, student employment services, financial aid counseling, health services, minority student services, personal counseling, placement for graduates, veterans' counselor. **Physically disabled:** Services for visually, speech, hearing impaired.

Contact. E-mail: admissions@shepherd.edu
Phone: (304) 876-5212 Toll-free number: (800) 344-5231 ext. 5212
Fax: (304) 876-5165
Randall Friend, Director of Admissions, Shepherd University, PO Box 5000, Shepherdstown, WV 25443-5000

University of Charleston

Charleston, West Virginia **CB member**
www.ucwv.edu **CB code: 5419**

- Private 4-year university and liberal arts college
- Residential campus in small city
- 1,102 degree-seeking undergraduates: 2% part-time, 58% women, 7% African American, 1% Asian American, 1% Hispanic American, 10% international
- 309 degree-seeking graduate students
- 66% of applicants admitted
- SAT or ACT (ACT writing optional) required
- 44% graduate within 6 years

General. Founded in 1888. Regionally accredited. **Degrees:** 147 bachelor's, 26 associate awarded; master's, first professional offered. **ROTC:** Army. **Location:** 200 miles from Pittsburgh; 200 miles from Charlotte, North Carolina. **Calendar:** Semester, limited summer session. **Full-time faculty:** 100 total; 55% have terminal degrees, 10% minority, 60% women. **Part-time faculty:** 42 total; 17% have terminal degrees, 57% women. **Class size:** 70% < 20, 29% 20-39, less than 1% 40-49, less than 1% 50-99. **Special facilities:** Sports medicine clinic, clinics at nearby hospital, entrepreneurship center.

Freshman class profile. 1,647 applied, 1,092 admitted, 311 enrolled.

Mid 50% test scores			
SAT critical reading:	430-530	**Rank in top quarter:**	43%
SAT math:	440-580	**Rank in top tenth:**	25%
ACT composite:	19-25	**Return as sophomores:**	71%
GPA 3.75 or higher:	31%	**Out-of-state:**	46%
GPA 3.50-3.74:	13%	**Live on campus:**	78%
GPA 3.0-3.49:	28%	**Fraternities:**	2%
GPA 2.0-2.99:	27%	**Sororities:**	6%

Basis for selection. School achievement record and courses taken most important. Test scores, school recommendation, school and community activities, class rank, and interview also considered. GPA recomputed to reflect performance in academic subjects only. Essay, interview, portfolio recommended for all; audition required for music. **Homeschooled:** If part of diploma-granting organization, list of coursework completed and level of performance required. Otherwise, detailed portfolio required and essay, 3 letters of reference, on-campus interview recommended. **Learning Disabled:** Documentation from professional within last 2 years required.

High school preparation. 16 units recommended. Recommended units include English 4, mathematics 3, social studies 3, history 2, science 3 and foreign language 1. Chemistry, algebra required for 4-year nursing program.

2008-2009 Annual costs. Tuition/fees: $23,150. Tuition for pharmacy students: $25,224. Room/board: $8,325. Books/supplies: $1,000. Personal expenses: $500.

2007-2008 Financial aid. **Need-based:** 199 full-time freshmen applied for aid; 178 were judged to have need; 178 of these received aid. Average need met was 80%. Average scholarship/grant was $4,500; average loan $6,900. 54% of total undergraduate aid awarded as scholarships/grants, 46% as loans/jobs. **Non-need-based:** Awarded to 359 full-time undergraduates, including 164 freshmen. Scholarships awarded for academics, alumni affiliation, art, athletics, leadership, music/drama, ROTC.

Application procedures. **Admission:** Priority date 5/1; no deadline. $25 fee, may be waived for applicants with need, free for online applicants. Admission notification on a rolling basis. For most health science programs, application deadline is January 15, early decision recommended. **Financial aid:** Priority date 3/1; no closing date. FAFSA required. Applicants notified on a rolling basis starting 3/1; must reply by 5/1 or within 4 week(s) of notification.

Academics. Students can fulfill course requirements at their own pace. **Special study options:** Accelerated study, combined bachelor's/graduate degree, cooperative education, double major, dual enrollment of high school students, ESL, exchange student, independent study, internships, liberal arts/career combination, student-designed major, study abroad, teacher certification program, Washington semester. **Credit/placement by examination:** AP, CLEP, IB, SAT, ACT, institutional tests. 30 credit hours maximum toward associate degree, 60 toward bachelor's. **Support services:** Learning center, reduced course load, remedial instruction, study skills assistance, tutoring, writing center.

Majors. **Biology:** General. **Business:** Accounting, business admin, finance. **Communications:** Media studies. **Education:** General, biology, elementary, English, health, physical, science, secondary, social studies, special. **Health:** Athletic training, nursing (RN), predental, premedicine, prepharmacy, preveterinary, radiologic technology/medical imaging. **Parks/recreation:** Sports admin. **Physical sciences:** Chemistry. **Psychology:** General. **Public administration:** Policy analysis. **Visual/performing arts:** Art, interior design.

Most popular majors. Biology 13%, business/marketing 23%, communications/journalism 9%, education 7%, health sciences 24%, parks/recreation 6%, social sciences 7%.

Computing on campus. 65 workstations in dormitories, library, computer center, student center. Dormitories wired for high-speed internet access and linked to campus network. Commuter students can connect to campus network. Online library, helpline, student web hosting, wireless network available.

Student life. **Freshman orientation:** Mandatory. Preregistration for classes offered. **Policies:** On-campus housing required for dependent freshmen and sophomores not living with parents or legal guardian in local area. **Housing:** Guaranteed on-campus for freshmen. Coed dorms, special housing for disabled, wellness housing available. $100 fully refundable deposit. Single rooms and suites available. **Activities:** Pep band, campus ministries, choral groups, drama, international student organizations, musical theater, student government, student newspaper, honorary fraternities, Fellowship Christian Athletes, Young Republicans, College Democrats.

Athletics. NCAA. **Intercollegiate:** Baseball M, basketball, cheerleading, cross-country, football (tackle) M, golf M, rowing (crew) W, soccer, softball

W, tennis, track and field W, volleyball W. **Intramural:** Basketball, bowling, football (non-tackle) M, tennis, volleyball. **Team name:** Golden Eagles.

Student services. Career counseling, student employment services, financial aid counseling, personal counseling, placement for graduates.

Contact. E-mail: admissions@ucwv.edu
Phone: (304) 357-4750 Toll-free number: (800) 995-4682
Fax: (304) 357-4781
Alan Liebrecht, Vice President for Enrollment, University of Charleston, 2300 MacCorkle Avenue, SE, Charleston, WV 25304

West Liberty State College

West Liberty, West Virginia
www.westliberty.edu **CB code: 5901**

- Public 4-year liberal arts college
- Residential campus in rural community
- 2,307 degree-seeking undergraduates: 6% part-time, 56% women
- 18 graduate students
- 80% of applicants admitted
- SAT or ACT with writing required
- 44% graduate within 6 years

General. Founded in 1837. Regionally accredited. **Degrees:** 374 bachelor's, 31 associate awarded. **ROTC:** Army. **Location:** 10 miles from Wheeling, 50 miles from Pittsburgh. **Calendar:** Semester, limited summer session. **Full-time faculty:** 103 total; 53% have terminal degrees, 4% minority, 39% women. **Part-time faculty:** 66 total; 61% women. **Class size:** 46% < 20, 46% 20-39, 7% 40-49, less than 1% 50-99. **Special facilities:** Media arts center, rare book room, rare sheet music collection.

Freshman class profile. 1,785 applied, 1,432 admitted, 552 enrolled.

Mid 50% test scores			
SAT critical reading:	390-480	Rank in top quarter:	30%
SAT math:	400-470	Rank in top tenth:	9%
ACT composite:	17-23	Return as sophomores:	67%
GPA 3.75 or higher:	15%	Out-of-state:	9%
GPA 3.50-3.74:	14%	Live on campus:	82%
GPA 3.0-3.49:	32%	Fraternities:	2%
GPA 2.0-2.99:	39%	Sororities:	2%

Basis for selection. 2.0 GPA or 17 ACT or 810 SAT (exclusive of Writing) required. Audition required for music education; portfolio recommended for art.

High school preparation. College-preparatory program required. 15 units required. Required and recommended units include English 4, mathematics 3, social studies 2, history 1, science 3 (laboratory 2) and foreign language 2. Math must be algebra I and higher. Social science must include American history.

2008-2009 Annual costs. Tuition/fees: $4,464; $10,896 out-of-state. Tuition for students residing in border counties is $8,896. Room/board: $6,282. Books/supplies: $1,000. Personal expenses: $1,000.

2008-2009 Financial aid. Need-based: Average scholarship/grant was $4,308; average loan $3,374. **Non-need-based:** Scholarships awarded for academics, alumni affiliation, art, athletics, leadership, music/drama. **Additional information:** Non-need based student employment available at food service, college union, bookstore, and tutoring office. Resident assistant and campus security jobs also available.

Application procedures. Admission: No deadline. No application fee. Admission notification on a rolling basis beginning on or about 9/1. **Financial aid:** Priority date 3/1; no closing date. FAFSA required. Applicants notified on a rolling basis starting 2/15; must reply within 2 week(s) of notification.

Academics. Freshman experience course available. **Special study options:** Accelerated study, distance learning, double major, dual enrollment of high school students, external degree, honors, independent study, internships, liberal arts/career combination, student-designed major, study abroad, teacher certification program, Washington semester. **Credit/placement by examination:** AP, CLEP, SAT, ACT, institutional tests. **Support services:** Reduced course load, remedial instruction, tutoring.

Majors. Biology: General, bacteriology, biotechnology. **Business:** General, accounting, banking/financial services, business admin, managerial economics, tourism promotion, tourism/travel. **Communications:** General. **Computer sciences:** Information systems. **Education:** Art, biology, chemistry, early childhood, elementary, English, health, mathematics, mentally handicapped, music, physical, science, secondary, social science, special. **Health:** Clinical lab science, dental hygiene. **History:** General. **Liberal arts:** Arts/sciences. **Math:** General. **Parks/recreation:** Exercise sciences. **Physical sciences:** Chemistry. **Protective services:** Criminal justice. **Psychology:** General. **Social sciences:** General, political science, sociology. **Visual/performing arts:** Commercial/advertising art.

Most popular majors. Business/marketing 24%, education 22%, health sciences 10%, liberal arts 15%, security/protective services 9%.

Computing on campus. 300 workstations in dormitories, library, computer center, student center. Dormitories wired for high-speed internet access and linked to campus network. Commuter students can connect to campus network. Online course registration, helpline, repair service available.

Student life. Freshman orientation: Mandatory, $30 fee. Preregistration for classes offered. Held Friday through Sunday before first day of classes. **Housing:** Guaranteed on-campus for all undergraduates. Coed dorms, single-sex dorms, special housing for disabled, apartments available. $100 fully refundable deposit, deadline 6/1. Honors residence for students who meet criteria. **Activities:** Bands, choral groups, drama, international student organizations, literary magazine, music ensembles, musical theater, radio station, student government, student newspaper, TV station, Amnesty International, Students for Life, B-Pride, Electric Square, non-traditional student support group, Students in Free Enterprise, Students for Unity and Understanding.

Athletics. NCAA. **Intercollegiate:** Baseball M, basketball, cross-country, football (tackle) M, golf, softball W, tennis, track and field, volleyball W, wrestling M. **Intramural:** Basketball, golf, handball M, racquetball, softball, table tennis, tennis, volleyball. **Team name:** Hilltoppers.

Student services. Alcohol/substance abuse counseling, chaplain/spiritual director, career counseling, student employment services, financial aid counseling, health services, minority student services, personal counseling, placement for graduates, veterans' counselor. **Physically disabled:** Services for visually, hearing impaired.

Contact. E-mail: wladmsn1@wlsc.edu
Phone: (304) 336-8076 Toll-free number: (800) 732-6204
Fax: (304) 336-8403
Brenda King, Director of Admissions & Recruitment, West Liberty State College, Box 295, West Liberty, WV 26074-0295

West Virginia State University

Institute, West Virginia **CB member**
www.wvstateu.edu **CB code: 5903**

- Public 4-year liberal arts and teachers college
- Commuter campus in small town
- 2,961 degree-seeking undergraduates
- 56% of applicants admitted
- SAT or ACT with writing required

General. Founded in 1891. Regionally accredited. **Degrees:** 442 bachelor's awarded; master's offered. **ROTC:** Army. **Location:** 8 miles from Charleston. **Calendar:** Semester, limited summer session. **Full-time faculty:** 118 total. **Part-time faculty:** 83 total.

Freshman class profile. 1,719 applied, 971 admitted, 390 enrolled.

Mid 50% test scores			
		SAT writing:	330-390
SAT critical reading:	340-430	ACT composite:	16-21
SAT math:	330-450	Out-of-state:	20%

Basis for selection. School achievement record and test scores considered for 4-year programs. Open admission for community college component. Interview recommended for academically weak applicants to regents bachelor of arts programs. **Homeschooled:** Must provide detailed description of home school curriculum.

High school preparation. 14 units required. Required units include English 4, mathematics 2, social studies 3, science 3 (laboratory 2) and foreign language 2.

2008-2009 Annual costs. Tuition/fees: $4,466; $10,466 out-of-state. Room/board: $6,020. Books/supplies: $948. Personal expenses: $2,951.

Financial aid. Non-need-based: Scholarships awarded for academics, athletics, ROTC, state residency.

Application procedures. Admission: No deadline. No application fee. Admission notification on a rolling basis. **Financial aid:** Priority date 3/1, closing date 6/15. FAFSA required. Applicants notified on a rolling basis starting 2/15; must reply within 2 week(s) of notification.

Academics. **Special study options:** Cooperative education, cross-registration, distance learning, double major, dual enrollment of high school students, external degree, honors, internships, teacher certification program, weekend college. Nontraditional life experience degree program. **Credit/placement by examination:** AP, CLEP, IB, institutional tests. **Support services:** Learning center, reduced course load, remedial instruction, study skills assistance, tutoring.

Majors. **Biology:** General. **Business:** General, accounting, banking/financial services, business admin. **Communications:** General. **Computer sciences:** Computer science. **Education:** General, art, early childhood, elementary, English, gifted/talented, health, mathematics, mentally handicapped, middle, music, physical, science, secondary, social studies, special. **Health:** Recreational therapy. **History:** General. **Liberal arts:** Arts/sciences. **Math:** General, applied. **Parks/recreation:** Facilities management. **Physical sciences:** Chemistry, physics. **Protective services:** Criminal justice, police science. **Psychology:** General. **Public administration:** Social work. **Social sciences:** Economics, political science, sociology. **Visual/performing arts:** Ceramics, commercial/advertising art, drawing, fiber arts, painting, photography, printmaking, sculpture, studio arts.

Computing on campus. 200 workstations in dormitories, library, computer center, student center. Dormitories linked to campus network. Commuter students can connect to campus network. Helpline available.

Student life. **Freshman orientation:** Mandatory. Preregistration for classes offered. **Housing:** Guaranteed on-campus for freshmen. Single-sex dorms, apartments available. **Activities:** Bands, choral groups, drama, film society, literary magazine, music ensembles, radio station, student government, student newspaper, TV station, DNA science club, pre-alumni club, College Students for Christ, NAACP, access awareness council, Fellowship for Christian Athletes, poetry workshop.

Athletics. NCAA. **Intercollegiate:** Baseball M, basketball, football (tackle) M, golf, softball W, tennis, track and field, volleyball W. **Intramural:** Basketball, bowling, football (tackle) M, softball, swimming, tennis, volleyball. **Team name:** Yellow Jackets.

Student services. Career counseling, student employment services, health services, on-campus daycare, personal counseling, placement for graduates, veterans' counselor. **Physically disabled:** Services for visually, speech, hearing impaired.

Contact. E-mail: admission@wvstateu.edu
Phone: (304) 766-3221 Toll-free number: (800) 987-2112
Fax: (304) 766-4104
Tryreno Sowell, Director, West Virginia State University, Campus Box 197, Institute, WV 25112-1000

West Virginia University

Morgantown, West Virginia — **CB member**
www.wvu.edu — **CB code: 5904**

- Public 4-year university
- Residential campus in small city
- 21,930 degree-seeking undergraduates: 6% part-time, 45% women, 3% African American, 2% Asian American, 2% Hispanic American, 2% international
- 6,910 degree-seeking graduate students
- 88% of applicants admitted
- SAT or ACT (ACT writing optional) required
- 55% graduate within 6 years

General. Founded in 1867. Regionally accredited. Regional centers at Charleston, Clarksburg, Parkersburg, Potomac State College in Keyser, Shepherdstown, WVU Institute of Technology, and West Liberty. Health Sciences Center operates division in Charleston. **Degrees:** 3,790 bachelor's awarded; master's, doctoral, first professional offered. **ROTC:** Army, Air Force. **Location:** 70 miles from Pittsburgh, 200 miles from Baltimore. **Calendar:** Semester, extensive summer session. **Full-time faculty:** 876 total; 80% have terminal degrees, 12% minority, 38% women. **Part-time faculty:** 312 total; 32% have terminal degrees, 3% minority, 53% women. **Class size:** 45% < 20, 32% 20-39, 7% 40-49, 10% 50-99, 6% >100. **Special facilities:** Personal rapid transit system, arboretum, planetarium, herbarium, pharmacy museum, 2 art galleries, 7 experimental farms, 3 forests, software development center, mineral and energy resources museum, black culture and research center.

Freshman class profile. 15,094 applied, 13,232 admitted, 5,135 enrolled.

Mid 50% test scores			
SAT critical reading:	470-560	**Rank in top quarter:**	44%
SAT math:	480-580	**Rank in top tenth:**	19%
ACT composite:	21-26	**Return as sophomores:**	81%
GPA 3.75 or higher:	25%	**Out-of-state:**	53%
GPA 3.50-3.74:	16%	**Live on campus:**	84%
GPA 3.0-3.49:	32%	**International:**	1%
GPA 2.0-2.99:	27%	**Fraternities:**	10%
		Sororities:	12%

Basis for selection. High school GPA and SAT/ACT scores most important. 2.0 GPA and 910 SAT (exclusive of Writing) or 19 ACT required of state residents. 2.5 GPA and 990 SAT or 21 ACT required of nonresidents. Applicants with high GPA, high test scores, or special talents (athletics or the arts) who do not meet all admissions criteria may be considered on individual basis. Up to 5% of each incoming class may be admitted under this special policy. Interview required for dental hygiene; audition required for drama, music; portfolio required for art. Essay required for some programs. **Homeschooled:** Typed manuscript of completed courses required, including content of courses, measurement of student assessment, grades, and number of credits earned for each course. Description should be separated by year of study and be signed by the person who administrated the curriculum.

High school preparation. 17 units required. Required units include English 4, mathematics 4, social studies 3, science 3 (laboratory 3), foreign language 2 and visual/performing arts 1.

2008-2009 Annual costs. Tuition/fees: $5,100; $15,770 out-of-state. Room/board: $7,434. Books/supplies: $1,160. Personal expenses: $970.

2008-2009 Financial aid. **Need-based:** 4,033 full-time freshmen applied for aid; 3,186 were judged to have need; 2,107 of these received aid. Average need met was 72%. Average scholarship/grant was $4,082; average loan $3,738. 45% of total undergraduate aid awarded as scholarships/grants, 55% as loans/jobs. **Non-need-based:** Awarded to 10,535 full-time undergraduates, including 1,313 freshmen. Scholarships awarded for academics, alumni affiliation, art, athletics, job skills, leadership, minority status, music/drama, state residency. **Additional information:** February 1 closing date for freshman scholarships.

Application procedures. **Admission:** Priority date 3/1; deadline 8/1. $25 fee ($40 out-of-state), may be waived for applicants with need. Admission notification on a rolling basis beginning on or about 9/15. **Financial aid:** Closing date 3/1. FAFSA required. Applicants notified on a rolling basis starting 3/15; must reply within 4 week(s) of notification.

Academics. **Special study options:** Accelerated study, combined bachelor's/graduate degree, cooperative education, distance learning, double major, ESL, exchange student, external degree, honors, independent study, internships, semester at sea, student-designed major, study abroad, teacher certification program, Washington semester. **Credit/placement by examination:** AP, CLEP, IB, SAT, ACT, institutional tests. 38 credit hours maximum toward bachelor's degree. **Support services:** Learning center, pre-admission summer program, reduced course load, remedial instruction, study skills assistance, tutoring, writing center.

Majors. **Agriculture:** Agronomy, animal sciences, business, economics, horticultural science, plant sciences, soil science. **Architecture:** Landscape. **Biology:** General, biochemistry, exercise physiology. **Business:** Accounting, business admin, finance, management information systems, managerial economics, marketing. **Communications:** General, advertising, broadcast journalism, journalism, media studies, public relations. **Computer sciences:** Computer science. **Conservation:** Forest management, wildlife, wood science. **Education:** Agricultural, physical. **Engineering:** Aerospace, chemical, civil, computer, electrical, industrial, mechanical, mining, petroleum. **Family/consumer sciences:** General, child development, clothing/textiles, family/community services, food/nutrition. **Foreign languages:** General. **Health:** Athletic training, audiology/speech pathology, clinical lab science, dental hygiene, nursing (RN), prenursing, prepharmacy. **History:** General. **Liberal arts:** Arts/sciences. **Math:** General. **Parks/recreation:** Exercise sciences, facilities management, health/fitness, sports admin. **Philosophy/religion:** Philosophy. **Physical sciences:** Chemistry, geology, physics. **Protective services:** Criminalistics, forensics. **Psychology:** General. **Public administration:** Social work. **Social sciences:** Economics, geography, political science, sociology. **Visual/performing arts:** General, art, art history/conservation, dramatic, theater history. **Other:** Biometric systems, Multidisciplinary.

Most popular majors. Biology 6%, business/marketing 13%, communications/journalism 10%, engineering/engineering technologies 10%, health sciences 8%, liberal arts 6%, social sciences 8%.

Computing on campus. 2,500 workstations in dormitories, library, computer center, student center. Dormitories wired for high-speed internet access and linked to campus network. Commuter students can connect to campus network. Online course registration, online library, helpline, repair service, student web hosting, wireless network available.

Student life. **Freshman orientation:** Available, $45 fee. Preregistration for classes offered. Held during summer; several options ranging in length and fees. **Policies:** Anti-hazing, affirmative action and nondiscrimination policies. Mandatory freshmen housing program places faculty residence hall leaders adjacent to residence halls. **Housing:** Guaranteed on-campus for freshmen. Coed dorms, single-sex dorms, special housing for disabled, apartments, fraternity/sorority housing, wellness housing available. $200 partly refundable deposit, deadline 5/1. Special interest floors available. **Activities:** Bands, campus ministries, choral groups, dance, drama, international student organizations, literary magazine, music ensembles, musical theater, radio station, student government, student newspaper, symphony orchestra, TV station, Sierra student coalition, Hillel House, Zeta Delat Phi, Circle K, Campus Crusade for Christ, College Republicans, Muslim student association.

Athletics. NCAA. **Intercollegiate:** Baseball M, basketball, cross-country W, diving, football (tackle) M, gymnastics W, rifle, rowing (crew) W, soccer, swimming, tennis W, track and field W, volleyball W, wrestling M. **Intramural:** Badminton, basketball, bowling, football (non-tackle), racquetball, soccer, tennis W, volleyball. **Team name:** Mountaineers.

Student services. Adult student services, alcohol/substance abuse counseling, chaplain/spiritual director, career counseling, services for economically disadvantaged, student employment services, financial aid counseling, health services, legal services, minority student services, personal counseling, placement for graduates, veterans' counselor, women's services. **Physically disabled:** Services for visually, speech, hearing impaired.

Contact. E-mail: go2wvu@mail.wvu.edu
Phone: (304) 293-2121 Toll-free number: (800) 344-9881
Fax: (304) 293-3080
Marlynn Potts, Director of Admissions and Records, West Virginia University, Admissions and Records Office, Morgantown, WV 26506-6009

West Virginia University at Parkersburg

Parkersburg, West Virginia
www.wvup.edu **CB code: 5932**

- Public 4-year community college
- Commuter campus in large town
- 3,174 degree-seeking undergraduates: 30% part-time, 63% women, 1% African American, 1% Asian American, 1% Hispanic American
- 36% graduate within 6 years; 15% enter graduate study

General. Founded in 1971. Regionally accredited. Regional campus of West Virginia University. **Degrees:** 200 bachelor's, 352 associate awarded. **Location:** 80 miles from Charleston; 110 miles from Columbus, Ohio. **Calendar:** Semester, limited summer session. **Full-time faculty:** 88 total; 16% have terminal degrees, 3% minority, 52% women. **Part-time faculty:** 163 total; 4% have terminal degrees, 1% minority, 45% women. **Class size:** 56% < 20, 40% 20-39, 2% 40-49, 1% 50-99.

Freshman class profile. 614 applied, 614 admitted, 614 enrolled.

Mid 50% test scores		**GPA 2.0-2.99:**	46%
ACT composite:	16-21	**End year in good standing:**	72%
GPA 3.75 or higher:	8%	**Return as sophomores:**	57%
GPA 3.50-3.74:	9%	**Out-of-state:**	1%
GPA 3.0-3.49:	30%		

Basis for selection. Open admission, but selective for some programs. Special requirements for nursing, surgical technology, paramedic science and bachelor's degree programs. SAT or ACT (ACT preferred) required but not used in admission decisions. Interview required for nursing program.

High school preparation. 16 units recommended. Recommended units include English 4, mathematics 3, social studies 4, science 3 (laboratory 2). Social studies recommendations may be fulfilled with history units.

2008-2009 Annual costs. Tuition/fees: $1,912; $6,766 out-of-state. Books/supplies: $1,000. Personal expenses: $1,400.

2008-2009 Financial aid. **Need-based:** 470 full-time freshmen applied for aid; 440 were judged to have need; 440 of these received aid. Average need met was 80%. Average scholarship/grant was $5,450; average loan $3,050. 97% of total undergraduate aid awarded as scholarships/grants, 3% as loans/jobs. **Non-need-based:** Awarded to 709 full-time undergraduates, including 268 freshmen. Scholarships awarded for academics, state residency.

Application procedures. **Admission:** No deadline. No application fee. Admission notification on a rolling basis. **Financial aid:** Priority date 3/1; no closing date. FAFSA required. Applicants notified on a rolling basis; must reply within 2 week(s) of notification.

Academics. **Special study options:** Combined bachelor's/graduate degree, cooperative education, cross-registration, distance learning, dual enrollment of high school students, ESL, external degree, honors, independent study, internships, teacher certification program. **Credit/placement by examination:** AP, CLEP, institutional tests. **Support services:** Learning center, reduced course load, remedial instruction, study skills assistance, tutoring.

Majors. **Business:** Business admin. **Education:** Elementary. **Engineering technology:** Industrial management.

Most popular majors. Business/marketing 19%, education 20%, liberal arts 56%.

Computing on campus. 435 workstations in library, computer center. Online course registration, wireless network available.

Student life. **Freshman orientation:** Available. Preregistration for classes offered. Held several weeks prior to the start of classes. **Activities:** Choral groups, drama, student government, student newspaper, Campus Christian Fellowship, criminal justice organization, social service organization.

Athletics. **Intramural:** Basketball, bowling, softball, table tennis, volleyball.

Student services. Adult student services, career counseling, services for economically disadvantaged, student employment services, financial aid counseling, health services, on-campus daycare, personal counseling, placement for graduates, veterans' counselor. **Physically disabled:** Services for visually, speech, hearing impaired.

Contact. E-mail: info@mail.wvup.edu
Phone: (304) 424-8220 Fax: (304) 424-8332
Leslie Sims, Registrar, West Virginia University at Parkersburg, 300 Campus Drive, Parkersburg, WV 26104-8647

West Virginia University Institute of Technology

Montgomery, West Virginia
www.wvutech.edu **CB code: 5902**

- Public 4-year engineering and technical college
- Commuter campus in small town
- 1,040 full-time, degree-seeking undergraduates
- 46% of applicants admitted
- SAT or ACT with writing required

General. Founded in 1895. Regionally accredited. **Degrees:** 206 bachelor's awarded; master's offered. **ROTC:** Army. **Location:** 30 miles from Charleston. **Calendar:** Semester, limited summer session. **Full-time faculty:** 119 total. **Part-time faculty:** 57 total. **Class size:** 64% < 20, 31% 20-39, 3% 40-49, 2% 50-99, less than 1% >100. **Special facilities:** Hiking trail.

Freshman class profile. 1,143 applied, 523 admitted, 237 enrolled.

Mid 50% test scores		**SAT writing:**	380-500
SAT critical reading:	380-500	**ACT composite:**	18-24
SAT math:	380-500	**Live on campus:**	23%

Basis for selection. School achievement record and test scores important. Out-of-state applicants must rank in top three-quarters of class or have 820 SAT (exclusive of Writing) or 17 ACT. Higher requirements for both in-state and out-of-state engineering applicants. Selective admission to dental hygiene, respiratory therapy and surgical technology; open admissions to most other associate degree programs. For associate degree programs, SAT/ACT required for placement but not admission. Interview recommended for engineering. **Homeschooled:** Students may be required to take GED exam.

High school preparation. 17 units required. Required and recommended units include English 4, mathematics 2, social studies 3, history 3, science 2 (laboratory 2). 2 algebra, 1 plane geometry, 1 advanced math required of engineering majors. 1 algebra, 1 chemistry, 1 biology required of dental hygiene majors. 2 laboratory sciences, including chemistry, 2 higher mathematics required for nursing program.

2008-2009 Annual costs. Tuition/fees: $4,964; $12,748 out-of-state. Room/board: $6,544. Books/supplies: $800. Personal expenses: $1,600.

Financial aid. **Additional information:** Room and board may be deferred for up to 60 days. First 50% due in 30 days.

Application procedures. **Admission:** Closing date 8/15. No application fee. Admission notification on a rolling basis. Must reply by May 1 or within 2 week(s) if notified thereafter. **Financial aid:** Priority date 2/1, closing date 4/1. FAFSA, institutional form required. Applicants notified on a rolling basis; must reply within 3 week(s) of notification.

Academics. Special study options: Combined bachelor's/graduate degree, cooperative education, distance learning, double major, dual enrollment of high school students, external degree, internships, liberal arts/career combination, student-designed major. Cooperative programs in engineering and business. **Credit/placement by examination:** AP, CLEP, institutional tests. 90 credit hours maximum toward bachelor's degree. **Support services:** Learning center, pre-admission summer program, reduced course load, remedial instruction, tutoring.

Majors. Biology: General. **Business:** General, business admin. **Computer sciences:** General, computer science, programming. **Education:** Physical. **Engineering:** Chemical, civil, electrical, mechanical. **Engineering technology:** Electrical. **History:** General. **Math:** General. **Physical sciences:** Chemistry.

Computing on campus. 500 workstations in dormitories, library, computer center, student center. Dormitories wired for high-speed internet access and linked to campus network. Online library, helpline, wireless network available.

Student life. Freshman orientation: Available, $25 fee. Preregistration for classes offered. **Housing:** Guaranteed on-campus for all undergraduates. Coed dorms, single-sex dorms, fraternity/sorority housing available. $100 deposit. **Activities:** Bands, choral groups, drama, music ensembles, student government, student newspaper, Christian student union, Alpha Phi Omega service fraternity.

Athletics. NCAA. **Intercollegiate:** Baseball M, basketball, football (tackle) M, golf M, soccer W, softball W, tennis, volleyball W. **Intramural:** Badminton, basketball, handball, racquetball, rowing (crew), softball, swimming, table tennis, tennis, volleyball, water polo, wrestling M. **Team name:** Golden Bears.

Student services. Adult student services, career counseling, student employment services, financial aid counseling, health services, on-campus daycare, personal counseling, placement for graduates, veterans' counselor. **Physically disabled:** Services for speech impaired.

Contact. E-mail: admissions@wvutech.edu
Phone: (304) 442-3167 Toll-free number: (888) 554-8324
Fax: (304) 442-3097
Donna Varney, Director of Admissions, West Virginia University Institute of Technology, 405 Fayette Pike, Montgomery, WV 25136-2436

West Virginia Wesleyan College

Buckhannon, West Virginia
www.wvwc.edu **CB code: 5905**

- Private 4-year liberal arts college affiliated with United Methodist Church
- Residential campus in small town
- 1,226 full-time, degree-seeking undergraduates
- 72% of applicants admitted
- SAT or ACT (ACT writing optional) required

General. Founded in 1890. Regionally accredited. **Degrees:** 227 bachelor's awarded; master's offered. **Location:** 115 miles from Charleston, 135 miles from Pittsburgh. **Calendar:** Semester, limited summer session. **Full-time faculty:** 76 total. **Part-time faculty:** 80 total. **Class size:** 63% < 20, 35% 20-39, 2% 40-49, less than 1% 50-99. **Special facilities:** Planetarium, botany museum, herbarium, greenhouse.

Freshman class profile. 1,428 applied, 1,029 admitted, 382 enrolled.

Mid 50% test scores		**GPA 3.0-3.49:**	26%
SAT critical reading:	430-540	**GPA 2.0-2.99:**	29%
SAT math:	430-550	**Rank in top quarter:**	57%
SAT writing:	410-550	**Rank in top tenth:**	29%
ACT composite:	20-26	**Out-of-state:**	39%
GPA 3.75 or higher:	27%	**Live on campus:**	90%
GPA 3.50-3.74:	17%		

Basis for selection. School achievement record and test scores required. Essay, interview recommended for all; audition recommended for drama, music; portfolio recommended for art. **Homeschooled:** Transcript of courses and grades, state high school equivalency certificate required.

High school preparation. 15 units recommended. Recommended units include English 4, mathematics 2, social studies 2, history 2, science 2 (laboratory 2), foreign language 1, computer science 1 and visual/performing arts 1.

2008-2009 Annual costs. Tuition/fees: $22,880. Room/board: $6,470. Books/supplies: $2,500. Personal expenses: $2,500.

2008-2009 Financial aid. Need-based: 353 full-time freshmen applied for aid; 310 were judged to have need; 310 of these received aid. Average need met was 85%. Average scholarship/grant was $18,351; average loan $3,791. 81% of total undergraduate aid awarded as scholarships/grants, 19% as loans/jobs. **Non-need-based:** Awarded to 817 full-time undergraduates, including 237 freshmen. Scholarships awarded for academics, alumni affiliation, art, athletics, leadership, music/drama, religious affiliation, state residency.

Application procedures. Admission: Priority date 5/1; no deadline. $35 fee, may be waived for applicants with need, free for online applicants. Admission notification on a rolling basis beginning on or about 9/15. Must reply by May 1 or within 5 week(s) if notified thereafter. **Financial aid:** Priority date 3/1; no closing date. FAFSA required. Applicants notified on a rolling basis starting 3/15; must reply within 4 week(s) of notification.

Academics. Special study options: Combined bachelor's/graduate degree, double major, ESL, exchange student, honors, independent study, internships, liberal arts/career combination, student-designed major, study abroad, teacher certification program, Washington semester. **Credit/placement by examination:** AP, CLEP, IB, SAT, ACT, institutional tests. 60 credit hours maximum toward bachelor's degree. **Support services:** Learning center, reduced course load, remedial instruction, study skills assistance, tutoring, writing center.

Majors. Biology: General. **Business:** Accounting, business admin, finance, international, managerial economics, marketing. **Communications:** General, public relations. **Computer sciences:** General, computer science, information systems. **Conservation:** Environmental science. **Education:** General, art, biology, chemistry, elementary, English, health, history, kindergarten/preschool, learning disabled, mathematics, music, physical, science, secondary, social studies, special. **Engineering:** General. **Health:** Athletic training, predental, premedicine, prepharmacy, preveterinary. **History:** General. **Legal studies:** Prelaw. **Math:** General. **Parks/recreation:** Exercise sciences, health/fitness. **Philosophy/religion:** Philosophy, religion. **Physical sciences:** Chemistry, physics. **Protective services:** Law enforcement admin. **Psychology:** General. **Social sciences:** Economics, international relations, political science, sociology. **Theology:** Religious ed. **Visual/performing arts:** Art, arts management, ceramics, dramatic, drawing, graphic design, painting, studio arts, theater arts management.

Most popular majors. Biology 6%, business/marketing 20%, communications/journalism 6%, education 13%, health sciences 8%, social sciences 9%.

Computing on campus. PC or laptop required. Dormitories wired for high-speed internet access and linked to campus network. Commuter students can connect to campus network. Online library, helpline, repair service, wireless network available.

Student life. Freshman orientation: Mandatory, $200 fee. Preregistration for classes offered. Held weekend before fall class registration; provides programs for new students and parents. **Policies:** Full-time students required to live on campus unless married, living with parents, or have received written permission from the Housing Committee to live off campus. **Housing:** Guaranteed on-campus for all undergraduates. Coed dorms, single-sex dorms, special housing for disabled, apartments, fraternity/sorority housing, wellness housing available. $200 deposit. **Activities:** Bands, campus ministries, choral groups, dance, drama, international student organizations, literary magazine, music ensembles, musical theater, radio station, student government, student newspaper, TV station, Christian life council, Fellowship of Christian Athletes, Alpha Phi Omega service fraternity, black student union, College Republicans, Young Democrats, green club, Wesleyan service corps.

Athletics. NCAA. **Intercollegiate:** Baseball M, basketball, cross-country, football (tackle) M, golf, soccer, softball W, swimming, tennis, track and field, volleyball W. **Intramural:** Basketball, football (non-tackle), racquetball, softball, table tennis, volleyball, water polo M. **Team name:** Bobcats.

Student services. Alcohol/substance abuse counseling, chaplain/spiritual director, career counseling, financial aid counseling, health services, minority student services, personal counseling, placement for graduates. **Physically disabled:** Services for visually, speech, hearing impaired.

Contact. E-mail: admission@wvwc.edu
Phone: (304) 473-8510 Toll-free number: (800) 722-9933
Fax: (304) 473-8108
John Waltz, Director of Admission, West Virginia Wesleyan College, 59 College Avenue, Buckhannon, WV 26201-2998

Wheeling Jesuit University

Wheeling, West Virginia — **CB member**
www.wju.edu — **CB code: 5906**

- Private 4-year university and liberal arts college affiliated with Roman Catholic Church
- Residential campus in small city
- 971 degree-seeking undergraduates: 12% part-time, 61% women, 2% African American, 1% Asian American, 2% Hispanic American, 3% international
- 240 degree-seeking graduate students
- 66% of applicants admitted
- SAT or ACT (ACT writing optional), application essay required
- 64% graduate within 6 years

General. Founded in 1954. Regionally accredited. **Degrees:** 248 bachelor's awarded; master's, doctoral offered. **Location:** 55 miles from Pittsburgh; 125 miles from Columbus, Ohio. **Calendar:** Semester, limited summer session. **Full-time faculty:** 73 total; 68% have terminal degrees, 10% minority, 41% women. **Part-time faculty:** 52 total; 27% have terminal degrees, 2% minority, 58% women. **Class size:** 68% < 20, 32% 20-39, less than 1% 40-49. **Special facilities:** NASA Classroom of the Future.

Freshman class profile. 1,188 applied, 788 admitted, 185 enrolled.

Mid 50% test scores			
SAT critical reading:	450-550	Rank in top quarter:	55%
SAT math:	450-550	Rank in top tenth:	21%
ACT composite:	20-25	End year in good standing:	85%
GPA 3.75 or higher:	31%	Return as sophomores:	70%
GPA 3.50-3.74:	26%	Out-of-state:	60%
GPA 3.0-3.49:	25%	Live on campus:	80%
GPA 2.0-2.99:	18%	International:	3%

Basis for selection. High school GPA, quality of courses taken, and test scores most important. Some exception made to minimum when warranted by high school record. Personal recommendations and extracurricular activities important. In-state and out-of-state applicants treated equally. Interview recommended. **Learning Disabled:** Students need to submit written documentation of disability.

High school preparation. 15 units required. Required and recommended units include English 4, mathematics 2, social studies 2, history 2, science 1 (laboratory 1), foreign language 2 and academic electives 6. Applicants for programs in natural sciences should have 1 biology and 1 chemistry. Applicants preparing for future study in physical therapy doctorate program should have 3 years of college preparatory math and 3 years of lab science, including physics.

2008-2009 Annual costs. Tuition/fees: $24,390. Room/board: $7,650. Books/supplies: $800. Personal expenses: $600.

2008-2009 Financial aid. Need-based: 171 full-time freshmen applied for aid; 144 were judged to have need; 144 of these received aid. Average need met was 96%. Average scholarship/grant was $6,718; average loan $4,018. 51% of total undergraduate aid awarded as scholarships/grants, 49% as loans/jobs. **Non-need-based:** Awarded to 823 full-time undergraduates, including 197 freshmen. Scholarships awarded for academics, alumni affiliation, athletics, leadership, music/drama.

Application procedures. Admission: No deadline. $25 fee, may be waived for applicants with need, free for online applicants. Admission notification on a rolling basis beginning on or about 9/1. Must reply by May 1 or within 2 week(s) if notified thereafter. **Financial aid:** Priority date 2/15; no closing date. FAFSA required. Applicants notified on a rolling basis starting 3/15; must reply within 2 week(s) of notification.

Academics. Special study options: Combined bachelor's/graduate degree, distance learning, double major, ESL, honors, independent study, internships, liberal arts/career combination, semester at sea, student-designed major, study abroad, teacher certification program, United Nations semester, Washington semester. **Credit/placement by examination:** AP, CLEP, SAT, ACT. 30 credit hours maximum toward bachelor's degree. **Support services:** Learning center, remedial instruction, study skills assistance, tutoring, writing center.

Majors. Biology: General. **Business:** Accounting, business admin, international. **Computer sciences:** Computer science. **Education:** Science. **Foreign languages:** French, Spanish. **Health:** Health care admin, nuclear medical technology, respiratory therapy technology. **History:** General. **Liberal arts:** Arts/sciences. **Math:** General. **Philosophy/religion:** Philosophy. **Physical sciences:** Chemistry, physics. **Protective services:** Criminal justice. **Psychology:** General. **Social sciences:** International relations, political science. **Theology:** Theology. **Other:** Political and economic philosophy.

Computing on campus. 243 workstations in dormitories, library, computer center, student center. Dormitories wired for high-speed internet access and linked to campus network. Commuter students can connect to campus network. Online library, helpline, wireless network available.

Student life. Freshman orientation: Available. Preregistration for classes offered. Three-day orientation held prior to beginning of fall semester. **Housing:** Guaranteed on-campus for all undergraduates. Coed dorms, single-sex dorms, apartments available. $100 fully refundable deposit. **Activities:** Pep band, campus ministries, choral groups, dance, drama, international student organizations, literary magazine, student government, student newspaper, TV station, social service outreach organization, academic clubs, leadership development group.

Athletics. NCAA. **Intercollegiate:** Baseball M, basketball, cheerleading, cross-country, golf, lacrosse M, soccer, softball W, swimming, track and field, volleyball W. **Intramural:** Basketball, soccer, softball, tennis, volleyball. **Team name:** Cardinals.

Student services. Adult student services, alcohol/substance abuse counseling, chaplain/spiritual director, career counseling, student employment services, financial aid counseling, health services, minority student services, personal counseling, placement for graduates, veterans' counselor.

Contact. E-mail: admiss@wju.edu
Phone: (304) 243-2359 Toll-free number: (800) 624-6992
Fax: (304) 243-2397
Denny Bardos, Dean of Enrollment, Wheeling Jesuit University, 316 Washington Avenue, Wheeling, WV 26003-6295

Wisconsin

Alverno College

Milwaukee, Wisconsin — **CB member**
www.alverno.edu — **CB code: 1012**

- Private 4-year liberal arts college for women affiliated with Roman Catholic Church
- Commuter campus in very large city
- 2,303 degree-seeking undergraduates: 26% part-time, 100% women, 17% African American, 5% Asian American, 13% Hispanic American, 1% Native American, 1% international
- 306 degree-seeking graduate students
- 89% of applicants admitted
- SAT or ACT (ACT writing optional), application essay required
- 39% graduate within 6 years; 10% enter graduate study

General. Founded in 1887. Regionally accredited. **Degrees:** 246 bachelor's, 4 associate awarded; master's offered. **ROTC:** Army, Air Force. **Location:** 5 miles from downtown. **Calendar:** Semester, limited summer session. **Full-time faculty:** 113 total; 90% have terminal degrees, 6% minority, 76% women. **Part-time faculty:** 136 total; 61% have terminal degrees, 11% minority, 84% women. **Class size:** 55% < 20, 45% 20-39, less than 1% 40-49. **Special facilities:** Multimedia productions facility, independent science research areas, native prairie, clinical nursing resource center.

Freshman class profile. 560 applied, 496 admitted, 267 enrolled.

Mid 50% test scores		**GPA 2.0-2.99:**	45%
ACT composite:	17-22	**Return as sophomores:**	73%
GPA 3.75 or higher:	8%	**Out-of-state:**	4%
GPA 3.50-3.74:	9%	**Live on campus:**	33%
GPA 3.0-3.49:	33%	**Sororities:**	2%

Basis for selection. Review of high school transcripts including GPA, academic units completed, standardized test scores, essay, Communication Placement Assessment results. Audition required for music therapy; portfolio required for studio art. **Homeschooled:** Letter of recommendation (nonparent) required. Portfolio of work required.

High school preparation. College-preparatory program required. 17 units required. Required and recommended units include English 4, mathematics 3, social studies 3, science 3, foreign language 2 and academic electives 4.

2008-2009 Annual costs. Tuition/fees: $18,161. Tuition and fees may vary by program. Room/board: $6,336. Books/supplies: $1,050. Personal expenses: $1,760.

2008-2009 Financial aid. **Need-based:** 235 full-time freshmen applied for aid; 200 were judged to have need; 200 of these received aid. Average scholarship/grant was $14,559; average loan $2,939. 63% of total undergraduate aid awarded as scholarships/grants, 37% as loans/jobs. **Non-need-based:** Awarded to 1,234 full-time undergraduates, including 215 freshmen. Scholarships awarded for academics, alumni affiliation, leadership.

Application procedures. **Admission:** No deadline. $20 fee, may be waived for applicants with need, free for online applicants. Admission notification on a rolling basis beginning on or about 9/1. Must reply by May 1 or within 2 week(s) if notified thereafter. **Financial aid:** Priority date 3/15; no closing date. FAFSA, institutional form required. Applicants notified on a rolling basis starting 3/15; must reply within 2 week(s) of notification.

Academics. Required internships in all majors provide research opportunities through federal government, local organizations and businesses. Students in every major area spend from 8 to 12 hours per week for one semester in field internship. Students also have opportunities to do service learning through individual courses. Degrees with honor awarded based on outstanding achievement and application of learning in service to others. **Special study options:** Double major, independent study, internships, semester at sea, student-designed major, study abroad, teacher certification program, Washington semester, weekend college. **Credit/placement by examination:** AP, CLEP, IB, institutional tests. **Support services:** Learning center, pre-admission summer program, reduced course load, remedial instruction, study skills assistance, tutoring, writing center.

Majors. **Biology:** General, molecular. **Business:** Business admin, international. **Communications:** General. **Computer sciences:** General. **Conservation:** Environmental science. **Education:** General, art, elementary, English, middle, music, science, social studies. **Health:** Art therapy, music therapy, nursing (RN). **History:** General. **Liberal arts:** Arts/sciences. **Math:** General. **Philosophy/religion:** Philosophy, religion. **Physical sciences:** Chemistry. **Psychology:** General. **Public administration:** Community org/advocacy. **Social sciences:** General, international relations, political science, sociology. **Visual/performing arts:** Art. **Other:** Business administration/management and operations, Communication management and technology, Interactive media design, Multi/Interdisciplinary studies.

Most popular majors. Business/marketing 17%, communications/journalism 7%, education 6%, health sciences 44%, psychology 7%.

Computing on campus. 557 workstations in dormitories, library, computer center. Dormitories wired for high-speed internet access and linked to campus network. Commuter students can connect to campus network. Online library, student web hosting, wireless network available.

Student life. **Freshman orientation:** Mandatory. Preregistration for classes offered. Overnight program held during the summer. **Housing:** $100 partly refundable deposit. Smoke-free areas available, semi-apartment living within residence halls available to older students. **Activities:** Campus ministries, choral groups, dance, drama, international student organizations, literary magazine, music ensembles, student newspaper, College Democrats, College Republicans, Student Education Organization, Association for Women in Communications, Circle K, Hispanic Women of Alverno, Pre-professional Women of Alverno, Student Nurses Association, Students in Free Enterprise, Women of Asian Ethnicity.

Athletics. NCAA. **Intercollegiate:** Basketball W, cross-country W, soccer W, softball W, tennis W, volleyball W. **Intramural:** Basketball W, volleyball W. **Team name:** Alverno Inferno.

Student services. Adult student services, chaplain/spiritual director, career counseling, financial aid counseling, health services, on-campus daycare, personal counseling. **Physically disabled:** Services for visually, speech, hearing impaired.

Contact. E-mail: admissions@alverno.edu
Phone: (414) 382-6101 Toll-free number: (800) 933-3401
Fax: (414) 382-6055
Dianna Gaebler, Executive Director of Admissions, Alverno College, 3400 South 43rd Street, Milwaukee, WI 53234-3922

Bellin College of Nursing

Green Bay, Wisconsin
www.bcon.edu — **CB code: 1046**

- Private 4-year nursing college
- Commuter campus in small city

General. Founded in 1909. Regionally accredited. **Location:** 120 miles from Milwaukee. **Calendar:** Semester.

Annual costs/financial aid. Tuition/fees (2008-2009): $17,939. Books/supplies: $875. Personal expenses: $665. Need-based financial aid available to full-time and part-time students.

Contact. Phone: (920) 433-5803 ext. 5803
Director of Admissions, PO Box 23400, Green Bay, WI 54305-3400

Beloit College

Beloit, Wisconsin — **CB member**
www.beloit.edu — **CB code: 1059**

- Private 4-year liberal arts college
- Residential campus in large town
- 1,297 degree-seeking undergraduates: 57% women, 4% African American, 3% Asian American, 3% Hispanic American, 5% international
- 63% of applicants admitted
- SAT or ACT (ACT writing optional), application essay required
- 78% graduate within 6 years

General. Founded in 1846. Regionally accredited. **Degrees:** 311 bachelor's awarded. **Location:** 60 miles from Madison, 90 miles from Chicago. **Calendar:** Semester, limited summer session. **Full-time faculty:** 124 total; 96% have terminal degrees, 12% minority, 48% women. **Part-time faculty:** 9 total; 44% have terminal degrees, 22% minority, 22% women. **Class size:** 70% < 20, 30% 20-39. **Special facilities:** LEED-certified science center, anthropology museum, art museum, observatory, 2 nature preserves, social science research laboratory, immunology laboratory, 2 electron microscopes, superconducting NMR, ICAP spectrometer, marketing research center, center for entrepreneurial leadership.

Freshman class profile. 2,248 applied, 1,412 admitted, 337 enrolled.

Mid 50% test scores			
SAT critical reading:	570-700	Rank in top quarter:	71%
SAT math:	560-690	Rank in top tenth:	40%
ACT composite:	25-30	End year in good standing:	97%
GPA 3.75 or higher:	25%	Return as sophomores:	89%
GPA 3.50-3.74:	22%	Out-of-state:	80%
GPA 3.0-3.49:	37%	Live on campus:	100%
GPA 2.0-2.99:	16%	International:	6%

Basis for selection. Rigor of high school curriculum and high school record are most important. Test scores, recommendations, essays, interviews, extracurricular activities also very important. Interview recommended. **Homeschooled:** Letter of recommendation (nonparent) required.

High school preparation. Recommended units include English 4, mathematics 4, social studies 4, science 3 and foreign language 2.

2008-2009 Annual costs. Tuition/fees: $31,540. Room/board: $6,696. Books/supplies: $400. Personal expenses: $900.

2008-2009 Financial aid. Need-based: 278 full-time freshmen applied for aid; 223 were judged to have need; 223 of these received aid. Average need met was 99%. Average scholarship/grant was $21,253; average loan $3,160. 67% of total undergraduate aid awarded as scholarships/grants, 33% as loans/jobs. **Non-need-based:** Awarded to 352 full-time undergraduates, including 90 freshmen. Scholarships awarded for academics, leadership, minority status, music/drama.

Application procedures. Admission: Priority date 1/15; no deadline. $35 fee, may be waived for applicants with need. Admission notification on a rolling basis beginning on or about 2/15. Must reply by May 1 or within 2 week(s) if notified thereafter. **Financial aid:** Closing date 3/1. FAFSA, institutional form required. Applicants notified on a rolling basis starting 4/1; must reply by 5/1 or within 2 week(s) of notification.

Academics. Heavy emphasis placed on international education, interdisciplinary study, and experiential learning. **Special study options:** Combined bachelor's/graduate degree, double major, ESL, exchange student, independent study, internships, liberal arts/career combination, student-designed major, study abroad, teacher certification program, urban semester, Washington semester. Field schools in archeology and geology, Center for Language Studies, intensive summer foreign language program, reserved admission to Medical College of Wisconsin. 3-2 programs in engineering, nursing, med tech and forestry. **Credit/placement by examination:** AP, CLEP, IB. 32 credit hours maximum toward bachelor's degree. **Support services:** Learning center, study skills assistance, tutoring, writing center.

Majors. Area/ethnic studies: Women's. **Biology:** General, biochemistry, cellular/molecular, environmental, molecular. **Business:** Business admin, managerial economics. **Computer sciences:** Computer science. **Conservation:** Environmental science, forestry. **Education:** General, art, science. **Engineering:** General. **Foreign languages:** General, classics, comparative lit, East Asian, French, German, Russian, Spanish. **Health:** Nursing (RN). **History:** General. **Interdisciplinary:** Science/society. **Liberal arts:** Arts/sciences. **Math:** General. **Philosophy/religion:** Philosophy, religion. **Physical sciences:** Chemistry, geology, physics. **Psychology:** General. **Social sciences:** Anthropology, economics, international relations, political science, sociology. **Visual/performing arts:** Art history/conservation, dance, dramatic. **Other:** Health and Society.

Most popular majors. Biology 7%, education 6%, English 13%, foreign language 13%, physical sciences 6%, psychology 6%, social sciences 26%, visual/performing arts 11%.

Computing on campus. 270 workstations in dormitories, library, computer center, student center. Dormitories wired for high-speed internet access and linked to campus network. Commuter students can connect to campus network. Helpline, student web hosting, wireless network available.

Student life. Freshman orientation: Mandatory. Preregistration for classes offered. First year initiatives begins 10 days before start of fall semester. **Housing:** Guaranteed on-campus for all undergraduates. Coed dorms, single-sex dorms, apartments, cooperative housing, fraternity/sorority housing, wellness housing available. Residence hall system is student managed. Special-interest housing available to students that have completed at least one semester. **Activities:** Jazz band, campus ministries, choral groups, dance, drama, film society, international student organizations, literary magazine, music ensembles, musical theater, radio station, student government, student newspaper, symphony orchestra, TV station, volunteer community tutoring service, women's center program, Gay Alliance, Young Republicans, Young Democrats, Science Fiction and Fantasy Association, Voces Latinas, Black Students United.

Athletics. NCAA. **Intercollegiate:** Baseball M, basketball, cross-country, diving, football (tackle) M, golf, soccer, softball W, swimming, tennis, track and field, volleyball W. **Intramural:** Basketball, fencing, handball, ice hockey M, racquetball, rugby M, sailing, soccer, softball, swimming, tennis, volleyball, water polo. **Team name:** Bucs.

Student services. Chaplain/spiritual director, career counseling, services for economically disadvantaged, student employment services, financial aid counseling, health services, minority student services, on-campus daycare, personal counseling, placement for graduates, women's services. **Physically disabled:** Services for visually, hearing impaired.

Contact. E-mail: admiss@beloit.edu
Phone: (608) 363-2500 Toll-free number: (800) 923-5648
Fax: (608) 363-2075
Nancy Benedict, Vice President of Enrollment Services, Beloit College, 700 College Street, Beloit, WI 53511-5595

Cardinal Stritch University

Milwaukee, Wisconsin
www.stritch.edu **CB code: 1100**

- Private 4-year university affiliated with Roman Catholic Church
- Commuter campus in very large city
- 3,060 undergraduates
- 3,179 graduate students
- 90% of applicants admitted
- SAT or ACT (ACT writing optional), application essay required

General. Founded in 1937. Regionally accredited. **Degrees:** 563 bachelor's, 235 associate awarded; master's, doctoral offered. **Location:** 7 miles from downtown, 85 miles from Chicago. **Calendar:** Semester, limited summer session. **Full-time faculty:** 100 total. **Part-time faculty:** 360 total. **Class size:** 97% < 20, 3% 20-39, less than 1% 40-49, less than 1% 50-99.

Freshman class profile. 947 applied, 857 admitted, 215 enrolled.

Mid 50% test scores			
SAT critical reading:	450-530	ACT composite:	19-24
SAT math:	480-570	Out-of-state:	20%
		Live on campus:	63%

Basis for selection. High school GPA of 2.0, minimum ACT test score of 20 or SAT combined score of 840 (exclusive of Writing). Interview, activities, recommendations considered. Conditional admission available to applicants not meeting all admissions criteria. Institutional tests used for admission of academically weak students. Interview recommended for all; portfolio recommended for art; audition recommended for music and theatre.

High school preparation. College-preparatory program recommended. 16 units required; 18 recommended. Required and recommended units include English 4, mathematics 2-3, social studies 1, history 1, science 2-3, foreign language 2 and academic electives 4.

2008-2009 Annual costs. Tuition/fees: $20,510. Additional $55 per credit for the nursing program. Room/board: $6,020. Books/supplies: $500. Personal expenses: $1,200.

Financial aid. Non-need-based: Scholarships awarded for academics, art, athletics, music/drama.

Application procedures. Admission: Priority date 4/1; no deadline. $25 fee, may be waived for applicants with need, free for online applicants. Admission notification on a rolling basis beginning on or about 9/1. **Financial aid:** Priority date 4/15; no closing date. FAFSA, institutional form required. Applicants notified on a rolling basis starting 3/1; must reply within 3 week(s) of notification.

Academics. Special study options: Accelerated study, distance learning, double major, exchange student, independent study, internships, student-designed major, study abroad, teacher certification program. **Credit/placement by examination:** AP, CLEP, IB, institutional tests. 30 credit hours maximum toward associate degree, 60 toward bachelor's. **Support services:** Learning center, reduced course load, remedial instruction, study skills assistance, tutoring, writing center.

Majors. Biology: General. **Business:** General, accounting, business admin, international, management information systems. **Communications:** General. **Computer sciences:** Computer science. **Education:** General, special.

Foreign languages: Spanish. **Health:** Nursing (RN). **History:** General. **Interdisciplinary:** Math/computer science. **Legal studies:** Prelaw. **Math:** General. **Parks/recreation:** Sports admin. **Philosophy/religion:** Religion. **Physical sciences:** Chemistry. **Psychology:** General. **Social sciences:** General, political science, sociology. **Theology:** Pastoral counseling, youth ministry. **Visual/performing arts:** Art, commercial/advertising art, dramatic, music performance, photography, studio arts.

Most popular majors. Business/marketing 75%, education 6%.

Computing on campus. 236 workstations in dormitories, library, computer center, student center. Dormitories wired for high-speed internet access and linked to campus network. Commuter students can connect to campus network. Online library, helpline, wireless network available.

Student life. Freshman orientation: Mandatory. Preregistration for classes offered. One week long program prior to first week of classes. **Housing:** Coed dorms available. $50 fully refundable deposit. **Activities:** Bands, campus ministries, choral groups, dance, drama, literary magazine, music ensembles, Model UN, musical theater, radio station, student government, student newspaper, Students for Political Awareness, multicultural committee, Asian club, Black student union, United Latino Organization, Fellowship of Christian Students, service corps, peer helpers.

Athletics. NAIA. **Intercollegiate:** Baseball M, basketball, cross-country, soccer, softball W, volleyball. **Intramural:** Basketball, volleyball. **Team name:** Wolves.

Student services. Adult student services, alcohol/substance abuse counseling, chaplain/spiritual director, career counseling, student employment services, financial aid counseling, health services, personal counseling, placement for graduates, veterans' counselor. **Physically disabled:** Services for hearing impaired.

Contact. E-mail: admityou@stritch.edu
Phone: (414) 410-4040 Toll-free number: (800) 347-8822 ext. 4040
Fax: (414) 410-4058
Kirk Messer, Director of Admission, Cardinal Stritch University, 6801 North Yates Road, Box 516, Milwaukee, WI 53217-7516

Carroll University
Waukesha, Wisconsin
www.carrollu.edu **CB code: 1101**

- Private 4-year liberal arts college affiliated with Presbyterian Church (USA)
- Residential campus in small city
- 2,947 degree-seeking undergraduates: 15% part-time, 67% women
- 484 degree-seeking graduate students
- 73% of applicants admitted
- 53% graduate within 6 years

General. Founded in 1846. Regionally accredited. **Degrees:** 489 bachelor's awarded; master's, doctoral, first professional offered. **ROTC:** Army, Air Force. **Location:** 15 miles from Milwaukee. **Calendar:** Semester, extensive summer session. **Full-time faculty:** 121 total; 63% have terminal degrees, 2% minority, 46% women. **Part-time faculty:** 168 total; 17% have terminal degrees, 65% women. **Class size:** 54% < 20, 40% 20-39, 3% 40-49, 3% 50-99. **Special facilities:** Scientific study and conservancy, class 1 trout stream, wetland and upland habitats.

Freshman class profile. 2,906 applied, 2,113 admitted, 742 enrolled.

Mid 50% test scores		**Rank in top tenth:**	18%
ACT composite:	20-25	**End year in good standing:**	79%
GPA 3.75 or higher:	22%	**Return as sophomores:**	74%
GPA 3.50-3.74:	22%	**Out-of-state:**	24%
GPA 3.0-3.49:	34%	**Live on campus:**	86%
GPA 2.0-2.99:	22%	**Fraternities:**	4%
Rank in top quarter:	50%	**Sororities:**	9%

Basis for selection. School achievement record most important, followed by test scores. Recommendations, essay, interview considered. Essay, interview recommended for all; audition recommended for music, theater; portfolio recommended for art. **Homeschooled:** Transcript of courses and grades required.

High school preparation. 17 units recommended. Recommended units include English 4, mathematics 4, social studies 3, history 3, science 3 (laboratory 2).

2008-2009 Annual costs. Tuition/fees: $21,926. Room/board: $6,694. Books/supplies: $1,060. Personal expenses: $1,291.

2008-2009 Financial aid. Need-based: 609 full-time freshmen applied for aid; 513 were judged to have need; 513 of these received aid. Average need met was 100%. Average scholarship/grant was $13,249; average loan $2,459. 71% of total undergraduate aid awarded as scholarships/grants, 29% as loans/jobs. **Non-need-based:** Awarded to 2,270 full-time undergraduates, including 602 freshmen. Scholarships awarded for academics, alumni affiliation, art, leadership, music/drama, ROTC.

Application procedures. Admission: Priority date 3/15; no deadline. No application fee. Admission notification on a rolling basis beginning on or about 8/11. **Financial aid:** No deadline. FAFSA required. Applicants notified on a rolling basis starting 2/15; must reply by 5/1 or within 2 week(s) of notification.

Academics. Education majors must maintain 2.75 GPA in major and teaching minors. Nursing students must maintain 2.75 GPA. Six majors available for pre-physical therapy programs. **Special study options:** Combined bachelor's/graduate degree, distance learning, double major, exchange student, honors, independent study, internships, liberal arts/career combination, student-designed major, study abroad, teacher certification program, United Nations semester, Washington semester. **Credit/placement by examination:** AP, CLEP, IB, institutional tests. 24 credit hours maximum toward bachelor's degree. **Support services:** Learning center, pre-admission summer program, reduced course load, study skills assistance, tutoring, writing center.

Majors. Area/ethnic studies: European. **Biology:** General, animal behavior, biochemistry. **Business:** Accounting, actuarial science, business admin, finance, human resources, management information systems, marketing, organizational behavior, small business admin. **Communications:** General, journalism, organizational, public relations. **Communications technology:** Graphics, printing management. **Computer sciences:** General, information systems. **Conservation:** General, environmental science. **Education:** General, art, biology, chemistry, early childhood, elementary, English, foreign languages, geography, health, history, mathematics, middle, music, physical, psychology, science, social science, social studies, Spanish. **Engineering:** Physics, software. **Foreign languages:** Spanish. **Health:** Athletic training, clinical lab science, nursing (RN), predental, premedicine, prepharmacy, preveterinary, radiologic technology/medical imaging. **History:** General, European. **Interdisciplinary:** Global studies. **Math:** General, applied. **Parks/recreation:** Exercise sciences, facilities management, health/fitness. **Philosophy/religion:** Religion. **Physical sciences:** Applied physics, chemistry. **Protective services:** Criminal justice, forensics. **Psychology:** General. **Social sciences:** Political science, sociology. **Visual/performing arts:** Art, commercial/advertising art, dramatic, photography, studio arts. **Other:** Philosophy, politics, and economics.

Most popular majors. Biology 6%, business/marketing 16%, education 10%, health sciences 24%, psychology 11%, social sciences 8%.

Computing on campus. 250 workstations in dormitories, library, computer center, student center. Dormitories wired for high-speed internet access and linked to campus network. Commuter students can connect to campus network. Online library, helpline, student web hosting, wireless network available.

Student life. Freshman orientation: Mandatory, $140 fee. Preregistration for classes offered. **Housing:** Guaranteed on-campus for freshmen. Coed dorms, single-sex dorms, apartments available. $200 nonrefundable deposit. **Activities:** Bands, campus ministries, choral groups, dance, drama, international student organizations, literary magazine, music ensembles, radio station, student government, student newspaper, Bible study group, Intervarsity Christian Fellowship, Fellowship of Christian Athletes, Black student union, Queers & Allies, Questions & Answers, international experience club, Latin American student organization, Carroll University Republicans, College Democrats.

Athletics. NCAA. **Intercollegiate:** Baseball M, basketball, cross-country, football (tackle) M, golf, soccer, swimming, tennis, track and field, volleyball W. **Intramural:** Basketball, bowling, cheerleading, football (non-tackle), soccer, tennis, volleyball. **Team name:** Pioneers.

Student services. Adult student services, chaplain/spiritual director, career counseling, student employment services, financial aid counseling, health services, minority student services, personal counseling, placement for graduates. **Physically disabled:** Services for visually, hearing impaired.

Contact. E-mail: ccinfo@carrollu.edu
Phone: (262) 524-7220 Toll-free number: (800) 227-7655
Fax: (262) 951-3037
Jim Wiseman, Vice President for Enrollment, Carroll University, 100 North East Avenue, Waukesha, WI 53186-9988

Carthage College
Kenosha, Wisconsin **CB member**
www.carthage.edu **CB code: 1103**

- Private 4-year liberal arts college affiliated with Evangelical Lutheran Church in America
- Residential campus in small city

- 2,372 degree-seeking undergraduates
- 76% of applicants admitted
- SAT or ACT (ACT writing optional) required

General. Founded in 1847. Regionally accredited. **Degrees:** 439 bachelor's awarded; master's offered. **ROTC:** Army, Air Force. **Location:** 60 miles from Chicago, 30 miles from Milwaukee. **Calendar:** 4-1-4, limited summer session. **Full-time faculty:** 137 total. **Part-time faculty:** 85 total. **Class size:** 54% < 20, 45% 20-39, 1% 40-49. **Special facilities:** Planetarium, paleontology institute, center for children's literature, undergraduate science research laboratory, computer/mathematics research laboratory, greenhouse, arboretum, Audubon sanctuary, geographic information systems (GIS) lab, 24-hour cyber-cafe.

Freshman class profile. 5,496 applied, 4,204 admitted, 753 enrolled.

Mid 50% test scores		**GPA 3.50-3.74:**	18%
SAT critical reading:	490-610	**GPA 3.0-3.49:**	29%
SAT math:	480-630	**GPA 2.0-2.99:**	31%
ACT composite:	20-27	**Out-of-state:**	72%
GPA 3.75 or higher:	22%		

Basis for selection. High school GPA (calculated based on academic courses) and test scores most important. Interview recommended; audition recommended for music and theater. **Homeschooled:** Transcript of courses and grades required.

High school preparation. 18 units recommended. Recommended units include English 4, mathematics 3, social studies 3, science 3 (laboratory 2), foreign language 2 and academic electives 3.

2008-2009 Annual costs. Tuition/fees: $26,500. Room/board: $7,500. Books/supplies: $1,200. Personal expenses: $1,500.

2008-2009 Financial aid. **Non-need-based:** Scholarships awarded for academics, alumni affiliation, art, leadership, minority status, music/drama, religious affiliation.

Application procedures. **Admission:** Closing date 5/1. $25 fee, may be waived for applicants with need. Admission notification on a rolling basis. Must reply by May 1 or within 2 week(s) if notified thereafter. **Financial aid:** Priority date 2/15; no closing date. FAFSA required. Applicants notified on a rolling basis starting 3/1.

Academics. All students take the Heritage Seminar Series, a 2-course combination of oral and written communication skills and cross-cultural studies. Students must also complete a Carthage symposium and a senior thesis in their major. **Special study options:** Accelerated study, combined bachelor's/graduate degree, cross-registration, double major, dual enrollment of high school students, honors, independent study, internships, liberal arts/career combination, student-designed major, study abroad, teacher certification program, Washington semester. **Credit/placement by examination:** AP, CLEP, IB, institutional tests. 32 credit hours maximum toward bachelor's degree. **Support services:** Pre-admission summer program, reduced course load, study skills assistance, tutoring, writing center.

Majors. **Area/ethnic studies:** Asian. **Biology:** General. **Business:** Accounting, business admin, management information systems, marketing. **Communications:** Public relations. **Communications technology:** Graphics. **Computer sciences:** Computer science. **Conservation:** Environmental science. **Education:** Elementary, physical, special. **Foreign languages:** Classics, French, German, Spanish. **Health:** Athletic training. **History:** General. **Interdisciplinary:** Neuroscience. **Liberal arts:** Humanities. **Math:** General. **Parks/recreation:** Exercise sciences. **Philosophy/religion:** Philosophy, religion. **Physical sciences:** Chemistry, physics. **Protective services:** Correctional facilities, police science. **Psychology:** General. **Public administration:** Social work. **Social sciences:** General, economics, geography, international economics, political science, sociology. **Visual/performing arts:** Art history/conservation, dramatic, studio arts, theater design. **Other:** Communications and media studies.

Most popular majors. Business/marketing 23%, education 9%, social sciences 7%, visual/performing arts 7%.

Computing on campus. 275 workstations in dormitories, library, computer center, student center. Dormitories wired for high-speed internet access and linked to campus network. Commuter students can connect to campus network. Online library, helpline, repair service, student web hosting, wireless network available.

Student life. **Freshman orientation:** Mandatory. Preregistration for classes offered. Held for a few days immediately prior to start of fall classes. **Housing:** Guaranteed on-campus for freshmen. Coed dorms, single-sex dorms, apartments, fraternity/sorority housing, wellness housing available. $300 deposit, deadline 5/1. **Activities:** Bands, campus ministries, choral groups, dance, drama, film society, international student organizations, literary magazine, music ensembles, Model UN, musical theater, opera, radio station, student government, student newspaper, symphony orchestra, Black Student Union, International Friendship Society, United Women of Color, Carthage Christian Fellowship, Latinos Unidos, Circle K International, College Republicans, Young Democrats.

Athletics. NCAA. **Intercollegiate:** Baseball M, basketball, cross-country, football (tackle) M, golf, lacrosse, soccer, softball W, swimming, tennis, track and field, volleyball, water polo W. **Intramural:** Basketball, football (non-tackle), racquetball, soccer, softball, volleyball. **Team name:** Red Men, Lady Reds.

Student services. Adult student services, alcohol/substance abuse counseling, chaplain/spiritual director, career counseling, student employment services, financial aid counseling, health services, personal counseling, placement for graduates, veterans' counselor.

Contact. E-mail: admissions@carthage.edu
Phone: (262) 551-6000 Toll-free number: (800) 351-4058
Fax: (262) 551-5762
Bradley Andrews, Vice President for Enrollment and Student Life, Carthage College, 2001 Alford Park Drive, Kenosha, WI 53140-1994

Columbia College of Nursing

Milwaukee, Wisconsin
www.ccon.edu **CB code: 3409**

- Private 4-year nursing college
- Commuter campus in very large city
- 215 degree-seeking undergraduates

General. Founded in 1901. Regionally accredited. Joint bachelor's degree in nursing awarded with Mount Mary College. **Degrees:** 60 bachelor's awarded. **Location:** 90 miles from Chicago, 70 miles from Madison. **Calendar:** Semester, limited summer session. **Full-time faculty:** 16 total; 12% have terminal degrees, 6% minority, 88% women. **Part-time faculty:** 2 total; 100% women. **Class size:** 23% < 20, 15% 20-39, 38% 40-49, 23% 50-99.

Basis for selection. Admission to Mount Mary college required. Admission to nursing major occurs in sophomore year. 2.8 GPA and all prerequisites required.

High school preparation. 3 units required. Required and recommended units include English 4, mathematics 1-2, science 2-3 and foreign language 2. Algebra required. Chemistry, biology required as science units.

2009-2010 Annual costs. Tuition/fees (projected): $20,500. Room/board: $5,600. Books/supplies: $734. Personal expenses: $1,234.

2008-2009 Financial aid. **Non-need-based:** Scholarships awarded for academics. **Additional information:** Students must apply to and meet financial aid requirements of Mount Mary College.

Application procedures. **Admission:** Closing date 3/1 (receipt date). Admission notification on a rolling basis. **Financial aid:** No deadline. FAFSA required. Applicants notified on a rolling basis starting 2/15; must reply by 5/1 or within 2 week(s) of notification.

Academics. Students generally complete first 2 years on Mt. Mary campus and last 2 years on Columbia campus. **Special study options:** Accelerated study, combined bachelor's/graduate degree, double major, ESL, honors, independent study, study abroad. Cultural immersion options. **Credit/placement by examination:** CLEP. **Support services:** Learning center, remedial instruction, study skills assistance, tutoring, writing center.

Majors. **Health:** Nursing (RN).

Computing on campus. 20 workstations in library, computer center. Online library, helpline available.

Student life. **Freshman orientation:** Mandatory. **Housing:** Guaranteed on-campus for freshmen. Coed dorms, apartments, wellness housing available. **Activities:** Student newspaper, student nursing organization, nursing honor society.

Student services. Alcohol/substance abuse counseling, chaplain/spiritual director, career counseling, financial aid counseling, health services, minority student services, personal counseling, placement for graduates.

Contact. E-mail: admiss@mtmary.edu
Phone: (414) 256-1219 Toll-free number: (800) 321-6265
Fax: (414) 256-0180
Brooke Konapacki, Dean of Enrollment, Mount Mary College, Columbia College of Nursing, Mount Mary College Enrollment Office, Milwaukee, WI 53222-4597

Concordia University Wisconsin
Mequon, Wisconsin
www.cuw.edu **CB code: 1139**

- Private 4-year university and liberal arts college affiliated with Lutheran Church - Missouri Synod
- Residential campus in large town
- 3,408 degree-seeking undergraduates: 45% part-time, 64% women, 13% African American, 1% Asian American, 2% Hispanic American, 1% Native American, 1% international
- 2,576 degree-seeking graduate students
- 64% of applicants admitted
- ACT (writing optional) required
- 70% graduate within 6 years

General. Founded in 1881. Regionally accredited. **Degrees:** 583 bachelor's, 12 associate awarded; master's, doctoral offered. **Location:** 15 miles from Milwaukee. **Calendar:** 4-1-4, limited summer session. **Full-time faculty:** 99 total; 68% have terminal degrees, 6% minority, 44% women. **Part-time faculty:** 146 total; 15% have terminal degrees, 14% minority, 66% women. **Class size:** 57% < 20, 40% 20-39, 2% 40-49, less than 1% 50-99. **Special facilities:** Access to Lake Michigan.

Freshman class profile. 1,772 applied, 1,130 admitted, 405 enrolled.

Mid 50% test scores		**Rank in top quarter:**	41%
ACT composite:	20-26	**Rank in top tenth:**	19%
GPA 3.75 or higher:	27%	**Return as sophomores:**	80%
GPA 3.50-3.74:	18%	**Out-of-state:**	33%
GPA 3.0-3.49:	33%	**Live on campus:**	92%
GPA 2.0-2.99:	21%	**International:**	1%

Basis for selection. School achievement record and test scores important. Essay, interview recommended; audition recommended for music.

High school preparation. College-preparatory program recommended. 16 units required. Required and recommended units include English 3-4, mathematics 2-3, social studies 2, science 2, foreign language 2 and academic electives 5. Two liberal arts required.

2008-2009 Annual costs. Tuition/fees: $19,990. Room/board: $7,500. Books/supplies: $1,100. Personal expenses: $1,950.

2008-2009 Financial aid. Need-based: 409 full-time freshmen applied for aid; 352 were judged to have need; 352 of these received aid. Average need met was 80%. Average scholarship/grant was $12,172; average loan $5,082. 58% of total undergraduate aid awarded as scholarships/grants, 42% as loans/jobs. **Non-need-based:** Awarded to 688 full-time undergraduates, including 200 freshmen. Scholarships awarded for academics, minority status, music/drama, religious affiliation.

Application procedures. Admission: Priority date 5/1; deadline 8/15. $35 fee, may be waived for applicants with need, free for online applicants. Admission notification on a rolling basis beginning on or about 10/15. **Financial aid:** Priority date 4/1; no closing date. FAFSA required. Applicants notified on a rolling basis starting 2/15; must reply within 3 week(s) of notification.

Academics. Special study options: Accelerated study, combined bachelor's/graduate degree, cross-registration, distance learning, double major, dual enrollment of high school students, ESL, exchange student, independent study, internships, liberal arts/career combination, student-designed major, study abroad, teacher certification program, weekend college. Cooperative programs with Cardinal Stritch University, Marquette University, and Milwaukee Institute of Art and Design. **Credit/placement by examination:** AP, CLEP, IB, ACT, institutional tests. 15 credit hours maximum toward associate degree, 30 toward bachelor's. **Support services:** Learning center, reduced course load, remedial instruction, tutoring, writing center.

Majors. Biology: General, exercise physiology. **Business:** General, accounting, actuarial science, business admin, finance, international finance, marketing. **Communications:** General, broadcast journalism, digital media, media studies. **Computer sciences:** General. **Conservation:** Environmental studies. **Education:** General, art, biology, business, early childhood, elementary, English, health, history, kindergarten/preschool, mathematics, middle, multi-level teacher, music, physical, science, secondary, social science, social studies, Spanish. **Foreign languages:** Biblical, German, Spanish. **Health:** Athletic training, clinical/medical social work, health services, medical radiologic technology/radiation therapy, nursing (RN). **History:** General. **Legal studies:** Prelaw. **Liberal arts:** Arts/sciences, humanities. **Math:** General. **Philosophy/religion:** Religion. **Protective services:** Criminal justice. **Psychology:** General. **Public administration:** Social work. **Social sciences:** Economics. **Theology:** Bible, missionary, pastoral counseling, preministerial, religious ed, sacred music, theology, youth ministry. **Visual/performing arts:** Art, commercial/advertising art, graphic design, illustration, interior design, music performance, photography, piano/organ. **Other:** Business communication, Rehabilitative science.

Most popular majors. Business/marketing 38%, education 12%, health sciences 16%, security/protective services 10%, theological studies 7%.

Computing on campus. 200 workstations in dormitories, library, computer center, student center. Dormitories wired for high-speed internet access and linked to campus network. Commuter students can connect to campus network. Online library, helpline, repair service available.

Student life. Freshman orientation: Available. Preregistration for classes offered. Held before start of fall semester, includes sessions for parents. **Policies:** Lutheran church services available every Sunday. Chapel services held daily. **Housing:** Single-sex dorms, wellness housing available. $160 deposit, deadline 4/15. **Activities:** Bands, campus ministries, choral groups, dance, drama, international student organizations, music ensembles, musical theater, radio station, student government, student newspaper, Jeremiah Project, Servant Events.

Athletics. NCAA. **Intercollegiate:** Baseball M, basketball, cross-country, football (tackle) M, golf, soccer, softball W, tennis, track and field, volleyball, wrestling M. **Intramural:** Basketball, soccer, softball, table tennis, tennis, volleyball. **Team name:** Falcons.

Student services. Adult student services, alcohol/substance abuse counseling, chaplain/spiritual director, career counseling, student employment services, financial aid counseling, health services, minority student services, personal counseling, placement for graduates, veterans' counselor. **Physically disabled:** Services for hearing impaired.

Contact. E-mail: admission@cuw.edu
Phone: (262) 243-5700 Toll-free number: (888) 628-9472
Fax: (262) 243-4545
Kenneth Gaschk, Vice President of Enrollment Services, Concordia University Wisconsin, 12800 North Lake Shore Drive, Mequon, WI 53097

DeVry University: Milwaukee
Milwaukee, Wisconsin
www.devry.edu

- For-profit 4-year university
- Commuter campus in very large city
- 119 degree-seeking undergraduates: 66% part-time, 55% women, 46% African American, 5% Asian American, 9% Hispanic American, 1% Native American
- 96 degree-seeking graduate students
- Interview required

General. Degrees: 7 bachelor's awarded; master's offered. **Calendar:** Semester. **Full-time faculty:** 1 total; 100% women. **Part-time faculty:** 1 total.

Basis for selection. Interview important.

2008-2009 Annual costs. Tuition/fees: $13,930. Books/supplies: $1,300. Personal expenses: $5,082.

2007-2008 Financial aid. Non-need-based: Scholarships awarded for academics.

Application procedures. Admission: No deadline. $50 fee. Admission notification on a rolling basis. **Financial aid:** No deadline. FAFSA required. Applicants notified on a rolling basis.

Academics. Special study options: Accelerated study, distance learning. **Credit/placement by examination:** CLEP.

Majors. Business: Business admin. **Computer sciences:** General, systems analysis. **Other:** Technical management.

Contact. Phone: (414) 278-7677
DeVry University: Milwaukee, 100 East Wisconsin Avenue, Suite 2550, Milwaukee, WI 53202

Four-Year Colleges

Edgewood College

Madison, Wisconsin **CB member**
www.edgewood.edu **CB code: 1202**

- Private 4-year liberal arts college affiliated with Roman Catholic Church
- Commuter campus in small city
- 1,880 degree-seeking undergraduates: 17% part-time, 70% women, 3% African American, 2% Asian American, 3% Hispanic American, 2% international
- 332 degree-seeking graduate students
- Application essay required
- 47% graduate within 6 years

General. Founded in 1927. Regionally accredited. **Degrees:** 380 bachelor's awarded; master's, doctoral offered. **ROTC:** Army. **Location:** 82 miles from Milwaukee, 140 miles from Chicago. **Calendar:** Semester, limited summer session. **Full-time faculty:** 99 total; 10% minority, 48% women. **Part-time faculty:** 189 total; 8% minority, 60% women. **Class size:** 78% < 20, 21% 20-39, less than 1% 40-49, less than 1% 50-99. **Special facilities:** Science center, biological research station, nursery school.

Freshman class profile. 1,244 applied, 982 admitted, 300 enrolled.

Mid 50% test scores		**GPA 2.0-2.99:**	21%
SAT critical reading:	470-590	**Rank in top quarter:**	36%
SAT math:	460-560	**Rank in top tenth:**	13%
ACT composite:	20-25	**Return as sophomores:**	76%
GPA 3.75 or higher:	19%	**Out-of-state:**	10%
GPA 3.50-3.74:	19%	**Live on campus:**	84%
GPA 3.0-3.49:	41%	**International:**	1%

Basis for selection. Open admission, but selective for some programs. High school transcript and test scores most important. Recommendation.

High school preparation. College-preparatory program recommended. 16 units required. Required units include English 4, mathematics 2, social studies 2, history 1, science 2 (laboratory 1) and foreign language 2.

2008-2009 Annual costs. Tuition/fees: $20,040. Room/board: $6,692. Books/supplies: $800. Personal expenses: $2,235.

2007-2008 Financial aid. Need-based: 263 full-time freshmen applied for aid; 220 were judged to have need; 220 of these received aid. Average need met was 82%. Average scholarship/grant was $10,597; average loan $4,092. 50% of total undergraduate aid awarded as scholarships/grants, 50% as loans/jobs. **Non-need-based:** Awarded to 376 full-time undergraduates, including 85 freshmen. Scholarships awarded for academics, alumni affiliation, art, leadership, music/drama, religious affiliation. **Additional information:** Auditions required for music scholarships, portfolios required for fine arts scholarships, essays required for a number of institutional scholarships, including AHANA Student Advancement Award, Alumni Association Scholarship, O'Connor Memorial Scholarship.

Application procedures. Admission: Priority date 3/1; deadline 8/26 (receipt date). $25 fee, may be waived for applicants with need. Admission notification on a rolling basis beginning on or about 9/15. **Financial aid:** Priority date 3/1; no closing date. FAFSA, institutional form required. Applicants notified on a rolling basis starting 3/15; must reply within 2 week(s) of notification.

Academics. Special study options: Accelerated study, double major, dual enrollment of high school students, honors, independent study, internships, liberal arts/career combination, student-designed major, study abroad, teacher certification program. **Credit/placement by examination:** AP, CLEP, IB, institutional tests. 30 credit hours maximum toward associate degree, 60 toward bachelor's. **Support services:** Learning center, reduced course load, remedial instruction, study skills assistance, tutoring, writing center.

Majors. Area/ethnic studies: Women's. **Biology:** General. **Business:** General, accounting, business admin, management information systems. **Communications:** General. **Computer sciences:** General. **Education:** Art, biology, business, chemistry, early childhood, early childhood special, elementary, English, French, history, mathematics, music, science, Spanish, special. **Foreign languages:** French, Spanish. **Health:** Art therapy, cytotechnology, nursing (RN). **History:** General. **Interdisciplinary:** Natural sciences. **Math:** General. **Philosophy/religion:** Religion. **Physical sciences:** Chemistry. **Protective services:** Criminal justice. **Psychology:** General. **Social sciences:** Economics, international relations, political science, sociology. **Theology:** Religious ed. **Visual/performing arts:** General, art, graphic design. **Other:** Multi-/interdisciplinary studies.

Most popular majors. Biology 6%, business/marketing 18%, communications/journalism 6%, education 20%, health sciences 22%, psychology 7%, social sciences 8%.

Computing on campus. 100 workstations in dormitories, library, computer center, student center. Dormitories wired for high-speed internet access and linked to campus network. Commuter students can connect to campus network. Online course registration, online library, helpline available.

Student life. Freshman orientation: Available. Preregistration for classes offered. 3-day program held in fall. **Housing:** Coed dorms, single-sex dorms, special housing for disabled, apartments available. $150 fully refundable deposit. Student leadership house. **Activities:** Bands, campus ministries, choral groups, dance, drama, international student organizations, literary magazine, music ensembles, musical theater, student government, student newspaper, symphony orchestra, student business association, student nurse association, Amnesty International, Habitat for Humanity.

Athletics. NCAA. **Intercollegiate:** Baseball M, basketball, cross-country, golf, soccer, softball W, tennis, volleyball W. **Intramural:** Basketball, bowling, diving, skiing, softball, swimming, table tennis, volleyball, weight lifting. **Team name:** Eagles.

Student services. Chaplain/spiritual director, career counseling, student employment services, financial aid counseling, health services, minority student services, personal counseling, placement for graduates, veterans' counselor.

Contact. E-mail: admissions@edgewood.edu
Phone: (608) 663-2294 Toll-free number: (800) 444-4861 ext. 2294
Fax: (608) 663-2214
Christine Benedict, Director of Undergraduate Admissions, Edgewood College, 1000 Edgewood College Drive, Madison, WI 53711-1997

Herzing College

Madison, Wisconsin
www.herzing.edu/madison **CB code: 0388**

- For-profit 3-year business and career college
- Commuter campus in small city
- 840 degree-seeking undergraduates
- Interview required

General. Founded in 1948. Regionally accredited. **Degrees:** 84 bachelor's, 106 associate awarded. **Location:** 90 miles from Milwaukee, 150 miles from Chicago. **Calendar:** Continuous, extensive summer session. **Full-time faculty:** 25 total. **Part-time faculty:** 21 total.

Basis for selection. Open admission, but selective for some programs. Interview and placement test required prior to acceptance. Application process varies by program. **Homeschooled:** State high school equivalency certificate required. **Learning Disabled:** Must provide documentation to admissions advisor prior to starting classes.

2008-2009 Annual costs. Tuition/fees: $11,200. Tuition is $350 per credit hour for most on-campus courses; $390 for on-line courses. Book use included in tuition. Personal expenses: $3,213.

Application procedures. Admission: No deadline. No application fee. Application must be submitted on paper. Admission notification on a rolling basis. **Financial aid:** No deadline. FAFSA, institutional form required. Applicants notified on a rolling basis.

Academics. Bachelors degree may be acquired in 3 years, associate degree in 1 year, 8 months. **Special study options:** Combined bachelor's/graduate degree, cooperative education, distance learning, honors, independent study, internships, liberal arts/career combination, study abroad. **Credit/placement by examination:** AP, CLEP, institutional tests. **Support services:** Learning center, reduced course load, remedial instruction, study skills assistance, tutoring, writing center.

Majors. BACHELOR'S. Business: Accounting, accounting/business management, accounting/finance, business admin, finance, human resources, office management, office technology, office/clerical. **Communications technology:** Animation/special effects. **Computer sciences:** General, applications programming, computer graphics, computer science, information systems, information technology, LAN/WAN management, networking, programming. **Engineering:** Software. **Engineering technology:** Architectural drafting, CAD/CADD, civil, civil drafting, computer, computer hardware, computer systems, drafting, electrical, electrical drafting, mechanical drafting, software, telecommunications. **Health:** Facilities admin, health care admin, medical records admin, medical records technology, office admin, ward clerk, ward supervisor. **Legal studies:** General. **Mechanic/repair:** Communications systems, computer, electronics/electrical, industrial electronics. **Protective services:** Emergency management/homeland security. **Visual/**

performing arts: Graphic design. **Other:** Electronics engineering technology. **ASSOCIATE. Business:** Accounting/business management, business admin, office management, office technology, office/clerical. **Communications technology:** Animation/special effects. **Computer sciences:** General, applications programming, computer graphics, computer science, information systems, information technology, LAN/WAN management, networking, programming. **Engineering:** Software. **Engineering technology:** Architectural drafting, CAD/CADD, civil, civil drafting, computer, computer hardware, computer systems, drafting, electrical, electrical drafting, mechanical drafting, software, telecommunications. **Health:** Insurance coding, insurance specialist, medical records admin, nursing (RN), office admin, office assistant, office computer specialist, receptionist. **Legal studies:** General, paralegal. **Mechanic/repair:** Communications systems, computer, electronics/ electrical, industrial electronics. **Visual/performing arts:** Graphic design. **Other:** Electronics engineering technology.

Computing on campus. 450 workstations in library, computer center, student center. Commuter students can connect to campus network. Online library, helpline, repair service, wireless network available.

Student life. Freshman orientation: Mandatory. **Activities:** Student government, student newspaper.

Student services. Adult student services, career counseling, student employment services, financial aid counseling, personal counseling, placement for graduates. **Physically disabled:** Services for visually, speech, hearing impaired.

Contact. E-mail: info@msn.herzing.edu
Phone: (608) 249-6611 Toll-free number: (800) 582-1227
Fax: (608) 249-8593
Matthew Schneider, Director of Admissions, Herzing College, 5218 East Terrace Drive, Madison, WI 53718.

ITT Technical Institute: Green Bay

Green Bay, Wisconsin
www.itt-tech.edu

- For-profit 4-year technical college
- Small city

General. Accredited by ACICS. **Calendar:** Trimester.

Contact. Phone: (920) 662-9000
Director of Recruitment, 470 Security Boulevard, Green Bay, WI 54313

ITT Technical Institute: Greenfield

Greenfield, Wisconsin
www.itt-tech.edu **CB code: 2706**

- For-profit 4-year technical college
- Commuter campus in large town

General. Accredited by ACICS. **Calendar:** Quarter.

Contact. Phone: (414) 282-9494
Director of Recruitment, 6300 West Layton Avenue, Greenfield, WI 53220-4612

Lakeland College

Sheboygan, Wisconsin
www.lakeland.edu **CB code: 1393**

- Private 4-year liberal arts college affiliated with United Church of Christ
- Residential campus in small city
- 2,839 degree-seeking undergraduates
- 919 graduate students
- 90% of applicants admitted
- SAT or ACT (ACT writing recommended) required

General. Founded in 1862. Regionally accredited. Evening, online, and graduate classes offered for nontraditional students at 7 in-state sites. Associate program available at Tokyo, Japan campus. **Degrees:** 618 bachelor's, 24 associate awarded; master's offered. **Location:** 60 miles from Milwaukee, 60 miles from Green Bay. **Calendar:** 4-4-1. Limited summer session. **Full-time faculty:** 57 total. **Part-time faculty:** 307 total. **Class size:** 69% < 20, 30% 20-39, 1% 40-49.

Freshman class profile. 918 applied, 826 admitted, 210 enrolled.

Mid 50% test scores		**Rank in top quarter:**	24%
ACT composite:	18-23	**Rank in top tenth:**	8%
GPA 3.75 or higher:	10%	**Out-of-state:**	15%
GPA 3.50-3.74:	9%	**Live on campus:**	90%
GPA 3.0-3.49:	29%	**Fraternities:**	3%
GPA 2.0-2.99:	49%	**Sororities:**	3%

Basis for selection. Applicants with 19 ACT, 2.0 GPA and rank in the top half of class admitted. Essays are recommended. **Homeschooled:** Transcript of courses and grades, state high school equivalency certificate required.

High school preparation. Recommended units include English 4, mathematics 2, social studies 2, history 2, science 2, foreign language 2 and academic electives 2.

2008-2009 Annual costs. Tuition/fees: $18,435. Room/board: $6,360. Books/supplies: $900. Personal expenses: $750.

2008-2009 Financial aid. Non-need-based: Scholarships awarded for academics.

Application procedures. Admission: No deadline. $20 fee, may be waived for applicants with need. Admission notification on a rolling basis. **Financial aid:** Priority date 3/31, closing date 7/1. FAFSA, institutional form required. Applicants notified on a rolling basis starting 2/1; must reply within 2 week(s) of notification.

Academics. Applicants whose test scores reflect weakness in basic skills must take basic skills courses in freshman year. **Special study options:** Combined bachelor's/graduate degree, cooperative education, distance learning, double major, dual enrollment of high school students, ESL, honors, independent study, internships, liberal arts/career combination, study abroad, teacher certification program. Engineering program with University of Wisconsin-Madison, nursing program with Bellin College of Nursing. **Credit/ placement by examination:** AP, CLEP, IB, institutional tests. 30 credit hours maximum toward bachelor's degree. **Support services:** Learning center, reduced course load, remedial instruction, study skills assistance, tutoring, writing center.

Majors. Biology: General, biochemistry. **Business:** Accounting, business admin, international, marketing, nonprofit/public, resort management. **Computer sciences:** Computer science. **Education:** Elementary, kindergarten/ preschool, middle, secondary. **Foreign languages:** German, Spanish. **History:** General. **Math:** General. **Philosophy/religion:** Religion. **Physical sciences:** Chemistry. **Protective services:** Law enforcement admin. **Psychology:** General. **Social sciences:** Sociology. **Visual/performing arts:** Art.

Most popular majors. Business/marketing 68%, computer/information sciences 19%, education 11%.

Computing on campus. 218 workstations in dormitories, library, computer center, student center. Dormitories wired for high-speed internet access and linked to campus network. Commuter students can connect to campus network. Online course registration, online library, helpline, wireless network available.

Student life. Freshman orientation: Mandatory. Preregistration for classes offered. **Housing:** Guaranteed on-campus for freshmen. Coed dorms, single-sex dorms, special housing for disabled, apartments available. $50 deposit. Honor apartments and apartments for students with senior standing available. **Activities:** Concert band, choral groups, drama, international student organizations, music ensembles, student government, student newspaper, campus activities board, black student union, Mortar Board, global students association, business fraternity, Inter-Greek Council.

Athletics. NCAA. **Intercollegiate:** Baseball M, basketball, cross-country, football (tackle) M, golf, soccer, softball W, tennis, track and field, volleyball W, wrestling M. **Team name:** Muskies.

Student services. Alcohol/substance abuse counseling, chaplain/ spiritual director, career counseling, services for economically disadvantaged, student employment services, financial aid counseling, health services, on-campus daycare, personal counseling, placement for graduates, veterans' counselor. **Physically disabled:** Services for visually impaired.

Contact. E-mail: admissions@lakeland.edu
Phone: (920) 565-1217 Toll-free number: (800) 242-3347
Fax: (920) 565-1206
Nathan Dehne, Vice President of Enrollment Management, Lakeland College, Box 359, Sheboygan, WI 53082-0359

Four-Year Colleges

Lawrence University

Appleton, Wisconsin **CB member**
www.lawrence.edu **CB code: 1398**

- Private 4-year music and liberal arts college
- Residential campus in small city
- 1,452 degree-seeking undergraduates: 3% part-time, 54% women, 2% African American, 3% Asian American, 2% Hispanic American, 8% international
- 59% of applicants admitted
- Application essay required
- 76% graduate within 6 years; 17% enter graduate study

General. Founded in 1847. Regionally accredited. **Degrees:** 371 bachelor's awarded. **Location:** 100 miles from Milwaukee, 30 miles from Green Bay. **Calendar:** Trimester. **Full-time faculty:** 155 total; 96% have terminal degrees, 11% minority, 39% women. **Part-time faculty:** 31 total; 39% have terminal degrees, 6% minority, 36% women. **Class size:** 73% < 20, 21% 20-39, 4% 40-49, 2% 50-99, less than 1% >100. **Special facilities:** Laser physics laboratory, 250 MHz nuclear magnetic resonance spectrometer, physics/computational graphics laboratory, Bjorklunden-425 acre lakefront retreat center.

Freshman class profile. 2,618 applied, 1,539 admitted, 382 enrolled.

Mid 50% test scores		**GPA 2.0-2.99:**	5%
SAT critical reading:	590-720	**Rank in top quarter:**	73%
SAT math:	610-720	**Rank in top tenth:**	41%
SAT writing:	610-690	**Return as sophomores:**	85%
ACT composite:	27-31	**Out-of-state:**	69%
GPA 3.75 or higher:	50%	**Live on campus:**	99%
GPA 3.50-3.74:	24%	**International:**	9%
GPA 3.0-3.49:	21%		

Basis for selection. GED not accepted. Strength of curriculum, school achievement record most important. Recommendations, out-of-class activities, test scores considered. Music applicants judged on musicianship, teacher's recommendations, and academic ability. Interview recommended; portfolio recommended for studio art. Audition required for conservatory of music study. **Homeschooled:** Require some standardized test results, evidence of coursework completed and level of performance, letters of recommendation, and GED if applicable.

High school preparation. College-preparatory program recommended. 16 units required. Required and recommended units include English 4, mathematics 3, social studies 2, history 2, science 3 and foreign language 2. Strong musical preparation required of music applicants.

2008-2009 Annual costs. Tuition/fees: $33,264. Room/board: $6,957. Books/supplies: $675. Personal expenses: $1,005.

2008-2009 Financial aid. Need-based: 281 full-time freshmen applied for aid; 258 were judged to have need; 258 of these received aid. Average need met was 93%. Average scholarship/grant was $19,410; average loan $5,290. 75% of total undergraduate aid awarded as scholarships/grants, 25% as loans/jobs. **Non-need-based:** Awarded to 346 full-time undergraduates, including 90 freshmen. Scholarships awarded for academics, alumni affiliation, minority status, music/drama. **Additional information:** The first $1,000 (aggregate) of independently-sponsored scholarships received by a needy student will reduce student's loan or work-study commitment. Half of scholarships in excess of $1,000 will offset loan or work-study and the other half will reduce institutional need-based grant funding.

Application procedures. Admission: Closing date 1/15 (postmark date). $40 fee, may be waived for applicants with need. Admission notification 4/1. Must reply by 5/1. **Financial aid:** Priority date 3/15; no closing date. FAFSA, institutional form required. Applicants notified on a rolling basis starting 3/1; must reply by 5/1 or within 2 week(s) of notification.

Academics. As an adjunct to a major, students may pursue 1 interdisciplinary area of study: biomedical ethics, international studies, neuroscience, or cognitive science. **Special study options:** Combined bachelor's/graduate degree, double major, independent study, internships, student-designed major, study abroad, teacher certification program, urban semester, Washington semester. Study abroad programs in 27 countries; marine biology term, Oak Ridge science semester; urban semester in Chicago; Newberry Library Program in humanities; environmental studies and forestry programs with Duke University; occupational therapy program with Washington University, St. Louis. **Credit/placement by examination:** AP, CLEP, IB, institutional tests. 30 credit hours maximum toward bachelor's degree. Course credit awarded for scores of at least 5 on International Baccalaureate examinations. **Support services:** Learning center, reduced course load, study skills assistance, tutoring, writing center.

Majors. Area/ethnic studies: Chinese, East Asian, Japanese, Russian/Slavic. **Biology:** General, biochemistry. **Computer sciences:** General. **Conservation:** Environmental studies. **Education:** Music. **Foreign languages:** Ancient Greek, Chinese, classics, East Asian, French, German, Japanese, Latin, linguistics, Russian, Spanish. **History:** General. **Interdisciplinary:** Cognitive science, global studies, math/computer science, natural sciences, neuroscience. **Math:** General. **Philosophy/religion:** Philosophy, religion. **Physical sciences:** Chemistry, geology, physics. **Psychology:** General. **Social sciences:** Anthropology, economics, political science. **Visual/performing arts:** Art, art history/conservation, dramatic, music performance, music theory/composition, studio arts.

Most popular majors. Biology 7%, English 8%, foreign language 9%, history 6%, interdisciplinary studies 9%, physical sciences 6%, psychology 8%, social sciences 12%, visual/performing arts 21%.

Computing on campus. 354 workstations in dormitories, library, computer center. Dormitories wired for high-speed internet access and linked to campus network. Commuter students can connect to campus network. Online course registration, online library, helpline, repair service, wireless network available.

Student life. Freshman orientation: Mandatory. Preregistration for classes offered. 5 days prior to start of fall classes. **Policies:** Honor code in effect. **Housing:** Guaranteed on-campus for all undergraduates. Coed dorms, single-sex dorms, apartments, wellness housing available. Apartment-style units available to upperclass students. All single students are required to live in university residence halls for 4 years. **Activities:** Bands, campus ministries, choral groups, dance, drama, film society, international student organizations, literary magazine, music ensembles, musical theater, opera, radio station, student government, student newspaper, symphony orchestra, Chavurah, Lawrence Christian Fellowship, Black organization of students, Latin American student organization, social service groups, political and academic clubs, professional sororities and fraternities.

Athletics. NCAA. **Intercollegiate:** Baseball M, basketball, cross-country, diving, fencing, football (tackle) M, golf M, ice hockey M, soccer, softball W, swimming, tennis, track and field, volleyball W, wrestling M. **Intramural:** Badminton, basketball, bowling, fencing, football (non-tackle), golf, handball, racquetball, soccer, softball, squash, table tennis, tennis, volleyball, water polo. **Team name:** Vikings.

Student services. Alcohol/substance abuse counseling, career counseling, student employment services, financial aid counseling, health services, minority student services, personal counseling, placement for graduates. **Physically disabled:** Services for visually, speech, hearing impaired.

Contact. E-mail: excel@lawrence.edu
Phone: (920) 832-6500 Toll-free number: (800) 227-0982
Fax: (920) 832-6782
Steven Syverson, Vice President for Enrollment Management, Lawrence University, Box 599, Appleton, WI 54912-0599

Maranatha Baptist Bible College

Watertown, Wisconsin
www.mbbc.edu **CB code: 2732**

- Private 4-year Bible college affiliated with Baptist faith
- Residential campus in large town
- 800 degree-seeking undergraduates: 4% part-time, 55% women, 1% African American, 1% Asian American, 2% Hispanic American, 1% international
- 40 degree-seeking graduate students
- 66% of applicants admitted
- SAT or ACT (ACT writing optional), application essay required
- 48% graduate within 6 years; 18% enter graduate study

General. Founded in 1968. Regionally accredited. **Degrees:** 119 bachelor's, 13 associate awarded; master's offered. **ROTC:** Army, Air Force. **Location:** 45 miles from Milwaukee, 38 miles from Madison. **Calendar:** Semester, limited summer session. **Full-time faculty:** 46 total; 30% have terminal degrees, 6% minority, 30% women. **Part-time faculty:** 32 total; 19% have terminal degrees, 3% minority, 41% women. **Class size:** 56% < 20, 33% 20-39, 4% 40-49, 5% 50-99, 2% >100.

Freshman class profile. 311 applied, 204 admitted, 194 enrolled.

Mid 50% test scores		**Return as sophomores:**	70%
ACT composite:	20-25	**Out-of-state:**	76%
End year in good standing:	91%	**Live on campus:**	76%

Basis for selection. Recommendations, religious commitment most important. Secondary school record, test scores, character also important. Class rank, essay considered. At-risk students placed on admissions probation. Audition required for fine arts.

High school preparation. College-preparatory program recommended. 18 units recommended. Recommended units include English 4, mathematics 3, social studies 3, history 3, science 3 and foreign language 2. Two units of physical education and one unit of word processing recommended.

2008-2009 Annual costs. Tuition/fees: $10,560. Room/board: $5,800. Books/supplies: $840. Personal expenses: $1,890.

2007-2008 Financial aid. **Non-need-based:** Scholarships awarded for academics.

Application procedures. **Admission:** No deadline. $50 fee. Admission notification on a rolling basis. **Financial aid:** Priority date 3/1; no closing date. FAFSA required. Applicants notified on a rolling basis starting 2/1; must reply within 2 week(s) of notification.

Academics. Hands-on ministerial work available. **Special study options:** Distance learning, double major, independent study, internships, liberal arts/career combination, study abroad, teacher certification program. **Credit/placement by examination:** AP, CLEP, ACT, institutional tests. 12 credit hours maximum toward associate degree, 12 toward bachelor's. Only 6 credits may be counted in any one field of study. **Support services:** Reduced course load, remedial instruction, study skills assistance, tutoring, writing center.

Majors. **Area/ethnic studies:** Women's. **Biology:** General. **Business:** Accounting/business management, business admin, management information systems, marketing, office management. **Education:** General, business, early childhood, elementary, English, history, mathematics, music, physical, science, secondary, social studies. **Health:** Nursing (RN). **Liberal arts:** Humanities. **Theology:** Bible, missionary, pastoral counseling, sacred music, youth ministry. **Visual/performing arts:** Music pedagogy, music performance, piano/organ.

Most popular majors. Business/marketing 19%, education 26%, liberal arts 13%, theological studies 27%, visual/performing arts 8%.

Computing on campus. 120 workstations in dormitories, library, computer center. Dormitories wired for high-speed internet access and linked to campus network. Online library, repair service, student web hosting, wireless network available.

Student life. **Freshman orientation:** Mandatory. Preregistration for classes offered. Held Saturday through Monday before classes begin. **Policies:** Religious observance required. **Housing:** Guaranteed on-campus for all undergraduates. Single-sex dorms, wellness housing available. $175 nonrefundable deposit. **Activities:** Bands, campus ministries, choral groups, drama, music ensembles, musical theater, student government, symphony orchestra.

Athletics. NCAA, NCCAA. **Intercollegiate:** Baseball M, basketball, cross-country, football (tackle) M, soccer, softball W, volleyball W, wrestling M. **Intramural:** Basketball, soccer W, volleyball. **Team name:** Crusaders.

Student services. Chaplain/spiritual director, career counseling, financial aid counseling, health services, on-campus daycare, personal counseling, placement for graduates, veterans' counselor.

Contact. E-mail: admissions@mbbc.edu
Phone: (920) 261-9300 Toll-free number: (800) 611-1947
Fax: (920) 261-9109
James Harrison, Director of Admissions, Maranatha Baptist Bible College, 745 West Main Street, Watertown, WI 53094

Marian University

Fond du Lac, Wisconsin — **CB member**
www.marianuniversity.edu — **CB code: 1443**

- Private 4-year university and liberal arts college affiliated with Roman Catholic Church
- Residential campus in large town
- 1,903 degree-seeking undergraduates: 27% part-time, 75% women, 5% African American, 1% Asian American, 2% Hispanic American, 1% Native American, 1% international
- 703 degree-seeking graduate students
- 86% of applicants admitted
- SAT or ACT (ACT writing optional) required
- 41% graduate within 6 years; 11% enter graduate study

General. Founded in 1936. Regionally accredited. Offsite center for law enforcement training. **Degrees:** 392 bachelor's awarded; master's, doctoral offered. **ROTC:** Army. **Location:** 60 miles from Milwaukee, 65 miles from Green Bay. **Calendar:** Semester, extensive summer session. **Full-time faculty:** 83 total; 60% have terminal degrees, 6% minority, 55% women. **Part-time faculty:** 221 total; 10% have terminal degrees, 9% minority, 58% women. **Class size:** 73% < 20, 27% 20-39, less than 1% 50-99.

Freshman class profile. 843 applied, 727 admitted, 289 enrolled.

Mid 50% test scores		**Rank in top tenth:**	9%
ACT composite:	18-22	**Return as sophomores:**	71%
GPA 3.75 or higher:	10%	**Out-of-state:**	9%
GPA 3.50-3.74:	14%	**Live on campus:**	74%
GPA 3.0-3.49:	32%	**Fraternities:**	4%
GPA 2.0-2.99:	39%	**Sororities:**	6%
Rank in top quarter:	30%		

Basis for selection. School achievement record most important, followed by test scores. Applicants must meet 2 of following 3 criteria: 2.0 GPA, top half of class, 18 ACT. Special admissions procedures required for nursing and education divisions. If admission criteria not met, students may be admitted on provisional basis. Interview, audition recommended.

High school preparation. College-preparatory program required. Required and recommended units include English 4, mathematics 2-3, history 1, science 1-2 (laboratory 1) and foreign language 2. Biology and chemistry prerequisite for nursing program.

2008-2009 Annual costs. Tuition/fees: $19,925. Room/board: $5,380. Books/supplies: $700. Personal expenses: $1,420.

2008-2009 Financial aid. **Need-based:** 281 full-time freshmen applied for aid; 257 were judged to have need; 257 of these received aid. Average need met was 92%. Average scholarship/grant was $11,440; average loan $5,288. 55% of total undergraduate aid awarded as scholarships/grants, 45% as loans/jobs. **Non-need-based:** Awarded to 1,140 full-time undergraduates, including 259 freshmen. Scholarships awarded for academics, ROTC, state residency.

Application procedures. **Admission:** Priority date 4/1; no deadline. $20 fee, may be waived for applicants with need. Admission notification on a rolling basis. Must reply by May 1 or within 4 week(s) if notified thereafter. **Financial aid:** Priority date 3/1; no closing date. FAFSA, institutional form required. Applicants notified on a rolling basis starting 3/1; must reply within 4 week(s) of notification.

Academics. **Special study options:** Accelerated study, cooperative education, distance learning, double major, dual enrollment of high school students, honors, independent study, internships, liberal arts/career combination, student-designed major, study abroad, teacher certification program. Accelerated programs for adults in business, nursing, operation management, radiologic technology, organizational communication, administration of justice. **Credit/placement by examination:** AP, CLEP, IB, institutional tests. 30 credit hours maximum toward bachelor's degree. Writing sample required for placement and counseling. **Support services:** Learning center, pre-admission summer program, reduced course load, remedial instruction, study skills assistance, tutoring, writing center.

Honors college/program. Unrestricted admissions with 25 ACT, 3.5 GPA, positive recommendation, application essay.

Majors. **Biology:** General. **Business:** General, accounting, business admin, finance, human resources, marketing, operations. **Communications:** General, organizational. **Computer sciences:** Information technology. **Education:** General, art, biology, chemistry, early childhood, elementary, English, history, mathematics, music, science, secondary, social studies, Spanish. **Foreign languages:** Spanish. **Health:** Cytotechnology, nursing (RN), radiologic technology/medical imaging. **History:** General. **Liberal arts:** Arts/sciences. **Math:** General. **Parks/recreation:** Sports admin. **Physical sciences:** Chemistry. **Protective services:** Law enforcement admin. **Psychology:** General. **Public administration:** Social work. **Social sciences:** Political science. **Visual/performing arts:** Graphic design, music management, studio arts.

Most popular majors. Business/marketing 29%, education 9%, health sciences 28%, security/protective services 10%.

Computing on campus. 400 workstations in dormitories, library, computer center, student center. Dormitories wired for high-speed internet access and linked to campus network. Commuter students can connect to campus network. Online course registration, online library, helpline, repair service, wireless network available.

Student life. **Freshman orientation:** Mandatory. Preregistration for classes offered. **Policies:** Emphasis on community volunteer activity. Service transcript available for graduates. **Housing:** Guaranteed on-campus for all undergraduates. Coed dorms, special housing for disabled, apartments, fraternity/

sorority housing, wellness housing available. $100 nonrefundable deposit. Townhouses, penthouses and residential suites available. **Activities:** Bands, campus ministries, choral groups, dance, drama, international student organizations, literary magazine, music ensembles, Model UN, student government, student newspaper, symphony orchestra, environmental club, social justice committee, African American student union, Association Latina, math and science association.

Athletics. NCAA. **Intercollegiate:** Baseball M, basketball, cross-country, golf, ice hockey M, soccer, softball W, tennis, volleyball W. **Intramural:** Badminton, basketball, bowling, football (non-tackle) M, skiing, softball M, tennis, volleyball. **Team name:** Sabres.

Student services. Adult student services, alcohol/substance abuse counseling, chaplain/spiritual director, career counseling, services for economically disadvantaged, student employment services, financial aid counseling, health services, minority student services, on-campus daycare, personal counseling, placement for graduates, women's services. **Physically disabled:** Services for visually, speech, hearing impaired.

Contact. E-mail: admissions@marianuniversity.edu
Phone: (920) 923-7650 Toll-free number: (800) 262-7426
Fax: (920) 923-8755
Stacey Akey, Vice President for Enrollment and Marketing, Marian University, 45 South National Avenue, Fond du Lac, WI 54935-4699

Marquette University

Milwaukee, Wisconsin — **CB member**
www.marquette.edu — **CB code: 1448**

- Private 4-year university affiliated with Roman Catholic Church
- Residential campus in very large city
- 7,821 degree-seeking undergraduates: 3% part-time, 53% women, 5% African American, 4% Asian American, 6% Hispanic American, 2% international
- 3,429 degree-seeking graduate students
- 65% of applicants admitted
- SAT or ACT (ACT writing recommended), application essay required
- 76% graduate within 6 years

General. Founded in 1881. Regionally accredited. **Degrees:** 1,766 bachelor's awarded; master's, doctoral, first professional offered. **ROTC:** Army, Naval, Air Force. **Location:** Downtown. **Calendar:** Semester, extensive summer session. **Full-time faculty:** 622 total; 89% have terminal degrees, 15% minority, 38% women. **Part-time faculty:** 474 total; 46% have terminal degrees, 10% minority, 42% women. **Class size:** 39% < 20, 42% 20-39, 8% 40-49, 8% 50-99, 4% >100. **Special facilities:** 15th century St. Joan of Arc chapel.

Freshman class profile. 15,206 applied, 9,907 admitted, 1,950 enrolled.

Mid 50% test scores			
SAT critical reading:	520-630	**Rank in top tenth:**	36%
SAT math:	540-650	**Return as sophomores:**	89%
SAT writing:	530-630	**Out-of-state:**	60%
ACT composite:	24-29	**Live on campus:**	93%
Rank in top quarter:	65%	**International:**	1%

Basis for selection. High school course selection, trend of performance, test scores and class rank most important. Essay, leadership, community service and extracurricular activities considered. **Homeschooled:** Provide detailed list of curriculum and bibliography. Personal interview may be required.

High school preparation. 16 units required; 22 recommended. Required and recommended units include English 4, mathematics 2-4, social studies 2-3, science 2-3 (laboratory 2-3), foreign language 2 and academic electives 2-5. Algebra, geometry, and intermediate algebra required for arts & sciences, business administration and health sciences. Algebra and geometry required for nursing. 3 years of science recommended for premedical, predental and science majors. Students interested in international business strongly urged to complete 4 units of single foreign language.

2009-2010 Annual costs. Tuition/fees (projected): $29,096. Required fees include cost of UPASS, which allows unlimited use of Milwaukee County Bus System. Room/board: $9,288. Books/supplies: $900. Personal expenses: $1,350.

2008-2009 Financial aid. Need-based: 1,540 full-time freshmen applied for aid; 1,185 were judged to have need; 1,180 of these received aid. Average need met was 84%. Average scholarship/grant was $16,448; average loan $4,504. 59% of total undergraduate aid awarded as scholarships/grants, 41% as loans/jobs. **Non-need-based:** Awarded to 2,075 full-time undergraduates, including 556 freshmen. Scholarships awarded for academics, athletics, leadership, music/drama, ROTC.

Application procedures. Admission: Closing date 12/1 (postmark date). $30 fee, may be waived for applicants with need, free for online applicants. Admission notification 1/31. Admission notification on a rolling basis. Must reply by May 1 or within 2 week(s) if notified thereafter. Application closing date for physical therapy and athletic training programs is 12/1 for direct admits. **Financial aid:** Priority date 2/1; no closing date. FAFSA required. Applicants notified on a rolling basis starting 3/20; must reply by 5/1 or within 3 week(s) of notification.

Academics. Special study options: Accelerated study, combined bachelor's/graduate degree, cooperative education, cross-registration, double major, dual enrollment of high school students, honors, internships, student-designed major, study abroad, teacher certification program, Washington semester, weekend college. **Credit/placement by examination:** AP, CLEP, IB, institutional tests. 30 credit hours maximum toward bachelor's degree. **Support services:** Learning center, pre-admission summer program, reduced course load, study skills assistance, tutoring, writing center.

Majors. Area/ethnic studies: African-American, women's. **Biology:** General, biochemistry, molecular. **Business:** Accounting, accounting technology, business admin, e-commerce, finance, human resources, international, management information systems, managerial economics, marketing. **Communications:** General, advertising, broadcast journalism, journalism, media studies, public relations. **Computer sciences:** Computer science, information systems. **Education:** Elementary, English, foreign languages, mathematics, middle, science, secondary, social science, social studies. **Engineering:** General, biomedical, civil, computer, construction, electrical, environmental, manufacturing, mechanical. **Foreign languages:** Classics, French, German, Spanish. **Health:** Athletic training, audiology/speech pathology, clinical lab technology, nursing (RN), predental, premedicine. **History:** General. **Interdisciplinary:** Global studies, intercultural, math/computer science. **Legal studies:** Prelaw. **Math:** General, computational, statistics. **Parks/recreation:** Exercise sciences. **Philosophy/religion:** Philosophy, religion. **Physical sciences:** Chemistry, physics. **Psychology:** General. **Social sciences:** General, anthropology, criminology, economics, international relations, political science, sociology. **Visual/performing arts:** Dramatic.

Most popular majors. Biology 8%, business/marketing 22%, communications/journalism 12%, education 6%, engineering/engineering technologies 9%, health sciences 10%, social sciences 10%.

Computing on campus. 1,200 workstations in dormitories, library, computer center, student center. Dormitories wired for high-speed internet access and linked to campus network. Commuter students can connect to campus network. Online course registration, online library, helpline, student web hosting, wireless network available.

Student life. Freshman orientation: Available. Preregistration for classes offered. 4 day session held week before classes begin in fall; June program also available. **Policies:** Written policies concerning racial and sexual harassment, alcohol, drugs and safety. Students provided materials detailing policies and programs. **Housing:** Guaranteed on-campus for freshmen. Coed dorms, single-sex dorms, special housing for disabled, apartments, cooperative housing, fraternity/sorority housing, wellness housing available. $200 nonrefundable deposit, deadline 5/1. Special housing for engineering, nursing, and honor students. **Activities:** Bands, campus ministries, choral groups, dance, drama, international student organizations, literary magazine, music ensembles, Model UN, musical theater, opera, radio station, student government, student newspaper, symphony orchestra, TV station, JUSTICE, College Republicans, College Democrats, Campus Crusade for Christ, Intervarsity, Latin American student organization.

Athletics. NCAA. **Intercollegiate:** Basketball, cheerleading, cross-country, golf M, soccer, tennis, track and field, volleyball W. **Intramural:** Badminton, basketball, football (tackle), golf, racquetball, soccer, softball, squash, tennis, track and field, volleyball, water polo, weight lifting. **Team name:** Golden Eagles.

Student services. Adult student services, alcohol/substance abuse counseling, chaplain/spiritual director, career counseling, services for economically disadvantaged, student employment services, financial aid counseling, health services, minority student services, on-campus daycare, personal counseling, placement for graduates. **Physically disabled:** Services for visually, speech, hearing impaired.

Contact. E-mail: admissions@marquette.edu
Phone: (414) 288-7302 Toll-free number: (800) 222-6544
Fax: (414) 288-3764
Robert Blust, Dean of Undergraduate Admissions, Marquette University, PO Box 1881, Milwaukee, WI 53201-1881

Milwaukee Institute of Art & Design

Milwaukee, Wisconsin
www.miad.edu **CB code: 1506**

- Private 4-year visual arts college
- Commuter campus in very large city
- 666 degree-seeking undergraduates
- 75% of applicants admitted
- Application essay, interview required

General. Founded in 1974. Regionally accredited. **Degrees:** 123 bachelor's awarded. **Location:** 90 miles from Chicago. **Calendar:** Semester, limited summer session. **Full-time faculty:** 34 total. **Part-time faculty:** 90 total. **Class size:** 87% < 20, 13% 20-39, less than 1% 40-49. **Special facilities:** Design center, advertising and design museum, gallery of industrial design, Riverwalk (public art project), art galleries, foundry, 3-D lab.

Freshman class profile. 548 applied, 412 admitted, 177 enrolled.

GPA 3.75 or higher:	9%	**Rank in top quarter:**	25%
GPA 3.50-3.74:	14%	**Rank in top tenth:**	6%
GPA 3.0-3.49:	32%	**Out-of-state:**	46%
GPA 2.0-2.99:	43%	**Live on campus:**	65%

Basis for selection. Portfolio and interview most important. 3.0 GPA in high school art curriculum recommended. Portfolio of 15-20 pieces of artwork required. **Homeschooled:** Transcript of courses and grades required.

High school preparation. 4 years high school visual art study highly recommended.

2008-2009 Annual costs. Tuition/fees: $25,400. Room/board: $7,400. Books/supplies: $1,828. Personal expenses: $1,624.

2007-2008 Financial aid. Non-need-based: Scholarships awarded for academics, art, leadership.

Application procedures. Admission: Priority date 2/15; no deadline. $25 fee, may be waived for applicants with need. Admission notification on a rolling basis beginning on or about 5/1. Must reply by May 1 or within 2 week(s) if notified thereafter. **Financial aid:** Priority date 3/1; no closing date. FAFSA required. Applicants notified on a rolling basis starting 4/1; must reply by 5/1 or within 4 week(s) of notification.

Academics. Special study options: Double major, exchange student, independent study, internships, liberal arts/career combination, New York semester, study abroad. **Credit/placement by examination:** AP, CLEP. **Support services:** Learning center, reduced course load, remedial instruction, study skills assistance, tutoring, writing center.

Majors. Visual/performing arts: Commercial/advertising art, drawing, industrial design, interior design, painting, photography, printmaking, sculpture.

Computing on campus. 175 workstations in library, computer center, student center. Commuter students can connect to campus network. Wireless network available.

Student life. Freshman orientation: Mandatory. Held before each semester for 2 days. **Housing:** Coed dorms available. $175 nonrefundable deposit, deadline 5/1. **Activities:** Drama, literary magazine, student government, minority student organization, Interior Design Society of America, National Industrial Design Society, student activities committee.

Student services. Alcohol/substance abuse counseling, career counseling, student employment services, financial aid counseling, health services, minority student services, personal counseling, placement for graduates, veterans' counselor.

Contact. E-mail: admissions@miad.edu
Phone: (414) 291-8070 Toll-free number: (888) 749-6423
Fax: (414) 291-8077
Mark Fetherson, Director of Admissions, Milwaukee Institute of Art & Design, 273 East Erie Street, Milwaukee, WI 53202

Milwaukee School of Engineering

Milwaukee, Wisconsin **CB member**
www.msoe.edu **CB code: 1476**

- Private 4-year university
- Residential campus in very large city
- 2,418 degree-seeking undergraduates: 10% part-time, 18% women, 4% African American, 3% Asian American, 2% Hispanic American, 2% international
- 204 degree-seeking graduate students
- 70% of applicants admitted
- SAT or ACT (ACT writing optional) required
- 55% graduate within 6 years; 24% enter graduate study

General. Founded in 1903. Regionally accredited. **Degrees:** 373 bachelor's awarded; master's offered. **ROTC:** Army, Naval, Air Force. **Location:** 72 miles from Chicago. **Calendar:** Quarter, limited summer session. **Full-time faculty:** 130 total; 72% have terminal degrees, 10% minority, 26% women. **Part-time faculty:** 129 total; 26% have terminal degrees, 13% minority, 29% women. **Class size:** 44% < 20, 55% 20-39, less than 1% 50-99. **Special facilities:** Museum, teaching and research laboratories for fluid power motion control, construction engineering, energy systems, rapid prototyping, software development, health and wellness facility with indoor ice hockey arena.

Freshman class profile. 2,279 applied, 1,595 admitted, 645 enrolled.

Mid 50% test scores		**End year in good standing:**	75%
SAT critical reading:	530-640	**Return as sophomores:**	74%
SAT math:	590-680	**Out-of-state:**	38%
ACT composite:	23-28	**Live on campus:**	83%
GPA 3.75 or higher:	30%	**International:**	1%
GPA 3.50-3.74:	22%	**Fraternities:**	4%
GPA 3.0-3.49:	33%	**Sororities:**	8%
GPA 2.0-2.99:	15%		

Basis for selection. Admissions based on secondary school record and standardized test scores. **Homeschooled:** Transcript of courses and grades required. **Learning Disabled:** Untimed standardized tests required.

High school preparation. College-preparatory program recommended. 10 units required. Required and recommended units include English 4, mathematics 4, science 2 (laboratory 2). For business and technical communication, math units should include 1 algebra. For biomedical engineering, science units should include 1 biological science.

2009-2010 Annual costs. Tuition/fees (projected): $28,665. $1,140 technology package required for all full-time first-year students. Includes laptop computer, software, Internet, insurance and repairs, upgrade every two years, wireless access, training and support, and compatibility computing throughout campus. Room/board: $7,164. Books/supplies: $1,500. Personal expenses: $3,140.

2007-2008 Financial aid. Need-based: 514 full-time freshmen applied for aid; 458 were judged to have need; 457 of these received aid. Average need met was 67%. Average scholarship/grant was $14,511; average loan $2,304. 67% of total undergraduate aid awarded as scholarships/grants, 33% as loans/jobs. **Non-need-based:** Awarded to 506 full-time undergraduates, including 139 freshmen. Scholarships awarded for academics, ROTC.

Application procedures. Admission: Priority date 2/1; no deadline. $25 fee, may be waived for applicants with need, free for online applicants. Admission notification on a rolling basis beginning on or about 10/1. **Financial aid:** Priority date 3/15; no closing date. FAFSA required. Applicants notified on a rolling basis starting 3/1; must reply within 2 week(s) of notification.

Academics. Average of 600 hours of laboratory experience for each program. **Special study options:** Accelerated study, combined bachelor's/graduate degree, distance learning, double major, dual enrollment of high school students, ESL, internships, study abroad. Bachelor of Science in business, mechanical engineering, and in electrical engineering with Lubeck University of Applied Sciences, Germany; exchange program with Czech Technical University, bachelor's or master's option in an engineering discipline and master's in environmental engineering. **Credit/placement by examination:** AP, CLEP, IB, SAT, ACT. **Support services:** Learning center, pre-admission summer program, reduced course load, study skills assistance, tutoring, writing center.

Majors. Business: General, business admin, construction management, international, management information systems. **Communications:** General. **Engineering:** General, architectural, biomedical, computer, electrical, industrial, mechanical, software. **Engineering technology:** Electrical, mechanical. **Health:** Nursing (RN).

Most popular majors. Business/marketing 20%, engineering/engineering technologies 66%, health sciences 13%.

Computing on campus. PC or laptop required. 150 workstations in dormitories, library, computer center, student center. Dormitories wired for

high-speed internet access and linked to campus network. Commuter students can connect to campus network. Online course registration, online library, helpline, repair service, student web hosting, wireless network available.

Student life. **Freshman orientation:** Available. Preregistration for classes offered. 3-4 day program prior to start of classes. **Policies:** Smoke-free campus and residential facilities. **Housing:** Guaranteed on-campus for all undergraduates. Coed dorms, special housing for disabled, wellness housing available. $75 nonrefundable deposit, deadline 6/1. **Activities:** Bands, campus ministries, dance, drama, international student organizations, literary magazine, radio station, student government, symphony orchestra, residence hall association, Circle-K, Society of Hispanic Professional Engineers, National Society of Black Engineers, National Student Nurses Association, campus volunteer services, Mont Pelleriu Colloquim.

Athletics. NCAA. **Intercollegiate:** Baseball M, basketball, cheerleading, cross-country, golf, ice hockey M, rowing (crew) M, soccer, softball W, tennis, track and field, volleyball, wrestling M. **Intramural:** Basketball, football (non-tackle), soccer, softball, volleyball. **Team name:** Raiders.

Student services. Alcohol/substance abuse counseling, career counseling, services for economically disadvantaged, student employment services, financial aid counseling, health services, personal counseling, placement for graduates, veterans' counselor, women's services. **Physically disabled:** Services for visually, speech, hearing impaired. **Learning disabled:** Comprehensive services available.

Contact. E-mail: explore@msoe.edu
Phone: (414) 277-6763 Toll-free number: (800) 332-6763
Fax: (414) 277-7475
Dana Grennier, Director, Admission, Milwaukee School of Engineering, 1025 North Broadway, Milwaukee, WI 53202-3109

Mount Mary College

Milwaukee, Wisconsin
www.mtmary.edu **CB code: 1490**

- Private 4-year liberal arts college for women affiliated with Roman Catholic Church
- Commuter campus in very large city
- 1,226 degree-seeking undergraduates: 29% part-time, 98% women, 19% African American, 4% Asian American, 7% Hispanic American, 1% Native American, 1% international
- 402 degree-seeking graduate students
- 58% of applicants admitted
- SAT or ACT (ACT writing optional) required
- 37% graduate within 6 years

General. Founded in 1913. Regionally accredited. Open to all faiths. Small number of men admitted as part-time non-degree-seeking students and for joint nursing students with Columbia College of Nursing. **Degrees:** 220 bachelor's awarded; master's offered. **ROTC:** Army, Naval. **Location:** 7 miles from Downtown. **Calendar:** Semester, limited summer session. **Full-time faculty:** 67 total; 61% have terminal degrees, 4% minority, 85% women. **Part-time faculty:** 146 total; 23% have terminal degrees, 78% women. **Class size:** 81% < 20, 18% 20-39, less than 1% 40-49, less than 1% 50-99. **Special facilities:** Historic costume collection, labyrinth.

Freshman class profile. 608 applied, 354 admitted, 131 enrolled.

Mid 50% test scores		**Rank in top tenth:**	12%
ACT composite:	17-22	**End year in good standing:**	85%
GPA 3.75 or higher:	11%	**Return as sophomores:**	68%
GPA 3.50-3.74:	12%	**Out-of-state:**	6%
GPA 3.0-3.49:	27%	**Live on campus:**	52%
GPA 2.0-2.99:	46%	**International:**	1%
Rank in top quarter:	45%		

Basis for selection. Academic record, test scores and supplemental information are reviewed. Class rank, core curriculum, test scores and GPA important. Interview recommended and essay required for students who do not meet direct admission requirements. **Homeschooled:** Transcript of courses and grades required. **Learning Disabled:** Students encouraged to talk with Disabilities Coordinator, at least one semester prior to enrollment, to determine if reasonable accommodations can be made.

High school preparation. College-preparatory program recommended. 16 units required. Required and recommended units include English 4, mathematics 2-3, social studies 2, history 2, science 2 (laboratory 2), foreign language 2 and academic electives 2.

2009-2010 Annual costs. Tuition/fees: $20,736. Room/board: $7,280.

2008-2009 Financial aid. **Need-based:** 159 full-time freshmen applied for aid; 142 were judged to have need; 138 of these received aid. Average need met was 64%. Average scholarship/grant was $10,894; average loan $3,517. 54% of total undergraduate aid awarded as scholarships/grants, 46% as loans/jobs. **Non-need-based:** Awarded to 139 full-time undergraduates, including 27 freshmen. Scholarships awarded for academics, alumni affiliation, art, leadership, music/drama.

Application procedures. **Admission:** No deadline. $25 fee, may be waived for applicants with need, free for online applicants. Admission notification on a rolling basis beginning on or about 9/15. **Financial aid:** Priority date 3/1; no closing date. FAFSA required. Applicants notified on a rolling basis starting 3/1; must reply within 2 week(s) of notification.

Academics. **Special study options:** Accelerated study, combined bachelor's/graduate degree, double major, honors, independent study, internships, liberal arts/career combination, student-designed major, study abroad, teacher certification program. **Credit/placement by examination:** AP, CLEP, IB, ACT, institutional tests. Maximum of 24 credits earned through a combination of credit exams, credit from life experience, directed and independent study. **Support services:** Learning center, reduced course load, remedial instruction, study skills assistance, tutoring.

Majors. **Biology:** General. **Business:** Accounting, business admin, fashion, marketing. **Communications:** General, public relations. **Education:** General, art, biology, business, chemistry, early childhood, elementary, English, foreign languages, French, history, mathematics, music, science, secondary, social studies, Spanish. **Foreign languages:** French, Spanish. **Health:** Art therapy, dietetics, nursing (RN), predental, premedicine, preveterinary. **History:** General. **Interdisciplinary:** Behavioral sciences, biological/physical sciences. **Legal studies:** Prelaw. **Math:** General. **Philosophy/religion:** Philosophy, religion. **Physical sciences:** Chemistry. **Protective services:** Criminal justice. **Psychology:** General. **Public administration:** Social work. **Social sciences:** General, international relations. **Theology:** Religious ed. **Visual/performing arts:** Art, commercial/advertising art, fashion design, interior design.

Most popular majors. Business/marketing 16%, health sciences 32%, visual/performing arts 15%.

Computing on campus. 313 workstations in dormitories, library, computer center, student center. Dormitories wired for high-speed internet access and linked to campus network. Commuter students can connect to campus network. Online course registration, online library, helpline, wireless network available.

Student life. **Freshman orientation:** Mandatory. Preregistration for classes offered. **Policies:** No overnight male visitation. **Housing:** Guaranteed on-campus for freshmen. $100 nonrefundable deposit, deadline 5/1. **Activities:** Campus ministries, choral groups, dance, international student organizations, literary magazine, music ensembles, Model UN, student government, student newspaper, commuter council, hall council, gospel choir, programming and activities council, department-affiliated clubs.

Athletics. NCAA. **Intercollegiate:** Basketball W, cross-country W, soccer W, softball W, tennis W, volleyball W. **Intramural:** Basketball W, bowling W, cross-country W, golf W, skiing W, soccer W, swimming W, tennis W, track and field W, volleyball W. **Team name:** Blue Angels.

Student services. Adult student services, chaplain/spiritual director, career counseling, student employment services, financial aid counseling, minority student services, on-campus daycare, personal counseling. **Physically disabled:** Services for visually impaired.

Contact. E-mail: admiss@mtmary.edu
Phone: (414) 256-1219 Toll-free number: (800) 321-6265
Fax: (414) 256-0180
Amy Dobson, Dean of Enrollment, Mount Mary College, 2900 North Menomonee River Parkway, Milwaukee, WI 53222-4597

Northland Baptist Bible College

Dunbar, Wisconsin
www.nbbc.edu

- Private 4-year Bible college
- Rural community
- 545 degree-seeking undergraduates

General. Regionally accredited. **Calendar:** Semester. **Full-time faculty:** 27 total. **Part-time faculty:** 12 total.

Freshman class profile. 138 enrolled.

2008-2009 Annual costs. Tuition/fees: $5,740.

Application procedures. Financial aid: Priority date 8/31; no closing date.

Academics. Credit/placement by examination: CLEP.

Majors. Education: Elementary, mathematics, speech. **History:** General. **Theology:** Bible. **Other:** Church ministries, Cross-cultural studies.

Contact. E-mail: admissions@nbbc.edu
Phone: (715) 324-6900 ext. 3100
Mike Glanzer, Director of Admissions, Northland Baptist Bible College, W10085 Pike Plains Road, Dunbar, WI 54119

Northland College

Ashland, Wisconsin — **CB member**
www.northland.edu — **CB code: 1561**

- Private 4-year liberal arts college affiliated with United Church of Christ
- Residential campus in small town
- 624 degree-seeking undergraduates: 4% part-time, 53% women, 2% African American, 1% Asian American, 2% Hispanic American, 3% Native American, 3% international
- 74% of applicants admitted
- SAT or ACT (ACT writing optional), application essay required
- 98% graduate within 6 years

General. Founded in 1892. Regionally accredited. **Degrees:** 135 bachelor's awarded. **Location:** 220 miles from Minneapolis-St. Paul, 65 miles from Duluth, Minnesota. **Calendar:** 4-1-4, limited summer session. **Full-time faculty:** 39 total; 82% have terminal degrees, 10% minority, 23% women. **Part-time faculty:** 44 total; 25% have terminal degrees, 16% minority, 39% women. **Class size:** 71% < 20, 29% 20-39. **Special facilities:** Field stations for natural science courses, atmospheric and environmental satellite links.

Freshman class profile. 634 applied, 470 admitted, 133 enrolled.

Mid 50% test scores		**GPA 2.0-2.99:**	29%
SAT critical reading:	530-620	**Rank in top quarter:**	39%
SAT math:	440-600	**Rank in top tenth:**	21%
ACT composite:	21-27	**Return as sophomores:**	76%
GPA 3.75 or higher:	22%	**Out-of-state:**	53.1%
GPA 3.50-3.74:	13%	**Live on campus:**	99%
GPA 3.0-3.49:	35%	**International:**	5%

Basis for selection. High school curriculum evaluation, class rank, guidance counselor recommendation, GPA, and test scores considered. Audition, portfolio recommended; interview required for borderline applicants.

High school preparation. College-preparatory program recommended. 18 units required; 21 recommended. Required and recommended units include English 4, mathematics 3, social studies 3, science 3 (laboratory 2), foreign language 2 and academic electives 3-4.

2008-2009 Annual costs. Tuition/fees: $23,101. Room/board: $6,440. Books/supplies: $800. Personal expenses: $1,600.

2008-2009 Financial aid. Need-based: 123 full-time freshmen applied for aid; 104 were judged to have need; 104 of these received aid. Average need met was 91%. Average scholarship/grant was $15,341; average loan $3,982. 71% of total undergraduate aid awarded as scholarships/grants, 29% as loans/jobs. **Non-need-based:** Awarded to 122 full-time undergraduates, including 27 freshmen. Scholarships awarded for academics, alumni affiliation, art, job skills, leadership, minority status, music/drama, religious affiliation, state residency.

Application procedures. Admission: Priority date 12/1; no deadline. $25 fee, may be waived for applicants with need, free for online applicants. Admission notification on a rolling basis beginning on or about 9/1. Must reply by May 1 or within 2 week(s) if notified thereafter. **Financial aid:** Priority date 4/15; no closing date. FAFSA required. Applicants notified on a rolling basis starting 3/1; must reply by 5/1 or within 4 week(s) of notification.

Academics. Accelerated evening degree completion business program offered; classes meet one night a week over 16-month period. Accelerated Bachelor of Nursing for students who have an earned RN. **Special study options:** Combined bachelor's/graduate degree, double major, exchange student, honors, independent study, internships, student-designed major, study abroad, teacher certification program. 3-2 cooperative degree programs in engineering with Michigan Technological University and Washington University. Member of the Ecoleague exchange consortium with Alaska Pacific University, Green Mountain College, Prescott College, and College of the Atlantic. **Credit/placement by examination:** AP, CLEP, IB, SAT, ACT, institutional tests. 30 credit hours maximum toward bachelor's degree. **Support services:** Learning center, reduced course load, study skills assistance, tutoring, writing center.

Majors. Area/ethnic studies: Native American. **Biology:** General, aquatic, conservation, ecology, environmental, wildlife. **Business:** Business admin, management science. **Conservation:** Fisheries, management/policy, wildlife. **Education:** General, elementary, multi-level teacher, secondary. **Engineering:** General. **Health:** Health care admin, predental, premedicine, prepharmacy, preveterinary, recreational therapy. **History:** General. **Interdisciplinary:** Behavioral sciences, biological/physical sciences, global studies, math/computer science, natural sciences. **Legal studies:** Prelaw. **Liberal arts:** Humanities. **Math:** General. **Philosophy/religion:** Religion. **Physical sciences:** General, atmospheric science, chemistry, geology, hydrology, meteorology. **Psychology:** General, environmental. **Public administration:** General, community org/advocacy, policy analysis. **Social sciences:** General, sociology. **Theology:** Preministerial. **Visual/performing arts:** Art, music history, studio arts. **Other:** Ecopsychology, Environmental geosciences, Fisheries biology, Humanity and nature studies, Management and leadership, Outdoor education, Social justice, Sustainable community development, Writing.

Most popular majors. Biology 16%, business/marketing 8%, education 18%, English 7%, health sciences 7%, interdisciplinary studies 12%, natural resources/environmental science 12%, social sciences 6%.

Computing on campus. 125 workstations in dormitories, library, computer center, student center. Dormitories wired for high-speed internet access and linked to campus network. Commuter students can connect to campus network. Online course registration, online library, helpline, repair service, wireless network available.

Student life. Freshman orientation: Mandatory. Preregistration for classes offered. Outdoor orientation or North County orientation. **Housing:** Guaranteed on-campus for freshmen. Coed dorms, single-sex dorms, apartments, cooperative housing, wellness housing available. $200 nonrefundable deposit. **Activities:** Bands, choral groups, dance, drama, international student organizations, music ensembles, radio station, student government, student newspaper, symphony orchestra, Native American Council, veterans organization, environmental group, ecology club.

Athletics. NAIA, NCAA. **Intercollegiate:** Baseball M, basketball, cross-country, ice hockey M, soccer, softball W, volleyball W. **Intramural:** Archery, badminton, basketball, football (non-tackle), ice hockey, racquetball, rugby, skiing, soccer, softball, table tennis, tennis, volleyball. **Team name:** Lumberjacks, Lumberjills.

Student services. Adult student services, alcohol/substance abuse counseling, chaplain/spiritual director, career counseling, services for economically disadvantaged, student employment services, financial aid counseling, health services, minority student services, personal counseling, placement for graduates, women's services. **Physically disabled:** Services for visually, hearing impaired.

Contact. E-mail: admit@northland.edu
Phone: (715) 682-1224 Toll-free number: (800) 753-1840
Fax: (715) 682-1258
Susan Greenwald, Director of Admission, Northland College, 1411 Ellis Avenue, Ashland, WI 54806

Ripon College

Ripon, Wisconsin — **CB member**
www.ripon.edu — **CB code: 1664**

- Private 4-year liberal arts college
- Residential campus in small town
- 1,037 degree-seeking undergraduates: 52% women, 2% African American, 1% Asian American, 3% Hispanic American, 1% Native American, 2% international
- 79% of applicants admitted
- SAT or ACT (ACT writing optional), application essay required
- 70% graduate within 6 years; 35% enter graduate study

General. Founded in 1851. Regionally accredited. **Degrees:** 187 bachelor's awarded. **ROTC:** Army. **Location:** 80 miles from Milwaukee, 80 miles from Madison. **Calendar:** Semester. **Full-time faculty:** 56 total; 95% have terminal degrees, 9% minority, 45% women. **Part-time faculty:** 36 total; 42% have terminal degrees, 39% women. **Class size:** 58% < 20, 37% 20-39, 2% 40-49, 2% 50-99. **Special facilities:** Woodland preservation area with outdoor classroom.

Freshman class profile. 1,081 applied, 853 admitted, 284 enrolled.

Mid 50% test scores			
SAT critical reading:	460-610	Rank in top tenth:	26%
SAT math:	500-630	End year in good standing:	94%
ACT composite:	20-27	Return as sophomores:	85%
GPA 3.75 or higher:	25%	Out-of-state:	29%
GPA 3.50-3.74:	18%	Live on campus:	98%
GPA 3.0-3.49:	35%	International:	3%
GPA 2.0-2.99:	21%	Fraternities:	27%
Rank in top quarter:	50%	Sororities:	17%

Basis for selection. School achievement record, interview, class rank, test scores, recommendations, extracurricular or community activities important. **Homeschooled:** Transcript of courses and grades required.

High school preparation. College-preparatory program recommended. 17 units required. Required and recommended units include English 4, mathematics 2-4, social studies 2-4, science 2-4 and foreign language 2. Math must include 1 algebra and geometry. 7 units chosen from additional units in math, science, social science, foreign language.

2008-2009 Annual costs. Tuition/fees: $24,245. Room/board: $6,770. Books/supplies: $1,000. Personal expenses: $800.

2008-2009 Financial aid. Need-based: 257 full-time freshmen applied for aid; 223 were judged to have need; 223 of these received aid. Average need met was 95%. Average scholarship/grant was $17,033; average loan $4,551. 74% of total undergraduate aid awarded as scholarships/grants, 26% as loans/jobs. **Non-need-based:** Awarded to 343 full-time undergraduates, including 103 freshmen. Scholarships awarded for academics, alumni affiliation, art, leadership, minority status, music/drama, religious affiliation, ROTC, state residency.

Application procedures. Admission: Priority date 3/15; no deadline. $30 fee, may be waived for applicants with need. Admission notification on a rolling basis beginning on or about 9/15. Must reply by May 1 or within 2 week(s) if notified thereafter. **Financial aid:** Priority date 3/1; no closing date. FAFSA required. Applicants notified on a rolling basis starting 3/1; must reply within 2 week(s) of notification.

Academics. Special study options: Accelerated study, combined bachelor's/graduate degree, double major, exchange student, internships, liberal arts/career combination, student-designed major, study abroad, teacher certification program, urban semester, Washington semester. Domestic and international off-campus study programs. **Credit/placement by examination:** AP, CLEP, IB. Amount of credit and placement for AP exams subject to departmental approval. **Support services:** Learning center, study skills assistance, tutoring.

Majors. Area/ethnic studies: Latin American, women's. **Biology:** General, biochemistry. **Business:** Business admin. **Communications:** General. **Computer sciences:** Computer science. **Conservation:** Environmental studies. **Education:** General. **Foreign languages:** General, classics, French, German, Spanish. **Health:** Predental, premedicine, prenursing, prepharmacy, preveterinary. **History:** General. **Interdisciplinary:** Biopsychology, global studies. **Legal studies:** Prelaw. **Math:** General. **Parks/recreation:** Exercise sciences. **Philosophy/religion:** Philosophy, religion. **Physical sciences:** General, chemistry, physics. **Psychology:** General. **Social sciences:** Anthropology, economics, political science, sociology. **Visual/performing arts:** Art, art history/conservation, dramatic.

Most popular majors. Biology 6%, business/marketing 17%, English 8%, history 11%, interdisciplinary studies 9%, psychology 9%, social sciences 11%, visual/performing arts 7%.

Computing on campus. 150 workstations in dormitories, library, computer center. Dormitories wired for high-speed internet access and linked to campus network. Commuter students can connect to campus network. Helpline, student web hosting available.

Student life. Freshman orientation: Mandatory, $45 fee. Preregistration for classes offered. 2-day overnight orientation held in late June for students and family. **Housing:** Guaranteed on-campus for all undergraduates. Coed dorms, single-sex dorms, fraternity/sorority housing, wellness housing available. $200 nonrefundable deposit, deadline 8/15. **Activities:** Bands, choral groups, dance, drama, film society, international student organizations, literary magazine, music ensembles, musical theater, radio station, student government, student newspaper, symphony orchestra, Christian Fellowship, Big Brother/Big Sister, multicultural club, romance language club, environmental group, Feminists for Equality, College Democrats, College Republicans.

Athletics. NCAA. **Intercollegiate:** Baseball M, basketball, cross-country, diving, football (tackle) M, golf, soccer, softball W, swimming, tennis, track and field, volleyball W. **Intramural:** Basketball, bowling, fencing, football (non-tackle), golf, racquetball, soccer, softball, table tennis, tennis, volleyball, water polo. **Team name:** Red Hawks.

Student services. Career counseling, student employment services, financial aid counseling, health services, personal counseling, placement for graduates.

Contact. E-mail: adminfo@ripon.edu
Phone: (920) 748-8114 Toll-free number: (800) 947-4766
Fax: (920) 748-8335
Leigh Mlodzik, Director of Admission, Ripon College, 300 Seward Street, Ripon, WI 54971-0248

St. Norbert College

De Pere, Wisconsin — **CB member**
www.snc.edu — **CB code: 1706**

- Private 4-year liberal arts college affiliated with Roman Catholic Church
- Residential campus in large town
- 2,036 degree-seeking undergraduates: 1% part-time, 56% women, 1% African American, 1% Asian American, 2% Hispanic American, 1% Native American, 3% international
- 32 degree-seeking graduate students
- 81% of applicants admitted
- SAT or ACT (ACT writing optional) required
- 74% graduate within 6 years; 11% enter graduate study

General. Founded in 1898. Regionally accredited. Study abroad strongly supported, and students are allowed to apply all of their financial aid to their study abroad program costs; student/faculty collaborative research. **Degrees:** 440 bachelor's awarded; master's offered. **ROTC:** Army. **Location:** 5 miles from Green Bay. **Calendar:** Semester, limited summer session. **Full-time faculty:** 132 total; 86% have terminal degrees, 6% minority, 42% women. **Part-time faculty:** 48 total; 35% have terminal degrees, 2% minority, 44% women. **Class size:** 46% < 20, 54% 20-39, less than 1% 40-49. **Special facilities:** Marina, on-campus hotel and conference center, fine and performing arts centers, art galleries, center for international education, peace and justice center, center for leadership and service, children's center, women's center, men's center, prayer and reflection spaces, survey center, center for Norbertine studies.

Freshman class profile. 2,116 applied, 1,717 admitted, 533 enrolled.

Mid 50% test scores			
ACT composite:	22-27	Rank in top quarter:	58%
GPA 3.75 or higher:	36%	Rank in top tenth:	27%
GPA 3.50-3.74:	19%	Return as sophomores:	84%
GPA 3.0-3.49:	29%	Out-of-state:	36%
GPA 2.0-2.99:	16%	Live on campus:	98%
		International:	4%

Basis for selection. High school record, rigor of courses, and grades earned important. Preference given to students successfully completing challenging courses. Counselor and teacher recommendations, community service considered. Students not in college preparatory programs may be offered admission if test results, class rank, and grades demonstrate aptitude for college work. Essay, interview recommended for all; audition recommended for music. **Learning Disabled:** Students should submit documentation of specific disability to receive proper level of support from institution.

High school preparation. College-preparatory program recommended. 16 units recommended. Recommended units include English 4, mathematics 3, social studies 3, history 3, science 3 (laboratory 3) and foreign language 2. As many college-prep elective units as possible.

2008-2009 Annual costs. Tuition/fees: $25,926. Room/board: $6,781. Books/supplies: $900. Personal expenses: $750.

2007-2008 Financial aid. Need-based: 439 full-time freshmen applied for aid; 361 were judged to have need; 361 of these received aid. Average need met was 85%. Average scholarship/grant was $14,378; average loan $3,904. 59% of total undergraduate aid awarded as scholarships/grants, 41% as loans/jobs. **Non-need-based:** Awarded to 661 full-time undergraduates, including 166 freshmen. Scholarships awarded for academics, art, leadership, minority status, music/drama, ROTC, state residency.

Application procedures. Admission: Priority date 4/1; no deadline. $25 fee, may be waived for applicants with need. Admission notification on a rolling basis beginning on or about 9/15. Must reply by May 1 or within 3 week(s) if notified thereafter. **Financial aid:** Priority date 3/15; no closing date. FAFSA required. Applicants notified on a rolling basis starting 3/15; must reply within 2 week(s) of notification.

Academics. **Special study options:** Double major, ESL, honors, independent study, internships, student-designed major, study abroad, teacher certification program, Washington semester. Foundation for International Education (London) Internship. **Credit/placement by examination:** AP, CLEP, IB, institutional tests. **Support services:** Learning center, reduced course load, remedial instruction, study skills assistance, tutoring, writing center.

Majors. **Biology:** General, biochemistry. **Business:** General, accounting, business admin, finance, human resources, international, management information systems, marketing. **Communications:** General, media studies. **Computer sciences:** Computer graphics, computer science. **Conservation:** Environmental science. **Education:** Early childhood, elementary, music. **Foreign languages:** French, German, Spanish. **Health:** Predental, premedicine, prenursing, prepharmacy, preveterinary. **History:** General. **Interdisciplinary:** Biological/physical sciences. **Legal studies:** Prelaw. **Liberal arts:** Humanities. **Math:** General. **Philosophy/religion:** Philosophy, religion. **Physical sciences:** Chemistry, geology, physics. **Psychology:** General. **Social sciences:** Economics, international economics, international relations, political science, sociology. **Theology:** Religious ed. **Visual/performing arts:** Art, commercial/advertising art, dramatic, graphic design.

Most popular majors. Biology 6%, business/marketing 24%, communications/journalism 8%, education 17%, social sciences 13%.

Computing on campus. 233 workstations in dormitories, library, computer center, student center. Dormitories wired for high-speed internet access and linked to campus network. Commuter students can connect to campus network. Online course registration, online library, helpline, repair service, wireless network available.

Student life. **Freshman orientation:** Mandatory. Preregistration for classes offered. 2-day summer program for students and parents. **Housing:** Guaranteed on-campus for all undergraduates. Coed dorms, single-sex dorms, special housing for disabled, apartments, wellness housing available. $100 nonrefundable deposit, deadline 5/1. Townhouses and college-owned houses near campus. **Activities:** Bands, campus ministries, choral groups, drama, film society, international student organizations, literary magazine, music ensembles, musical theater, radio station, student government, student newspaper, TV station, ballroom club, Beyond Borders, Campus Crusade for Christ, College Democrats and Republicans, environmental club, Graphos, Habitat for Humanity, pre-health science club, Rainbow Alliance, Students in Free Enterprise.

Athletics. NCAA. **Intercollegiate:** Baseball M, basketball, cross-country, football (tackle) M, golf, ice hockey M, soccer, softball W, swimming W, tennis, track and field, volleyball W. **Intramural:** Basketball, football (non-tackle), softball, volleyball. **Team name:** Green Knights.

Student services. Alcohol/substance abuse counseling, chaplain/spiritual director, career counseling, student employment services, financial aid counseling, health services, minority student services, on-campus daycare, personal counseling, placement for graduates, veterans' counselor, women's services. **Physically disabled:** Services for visually, speech, hearing impaired.

Contact. E-mail: admit@snc.edu
Phone: (920) 403-3005 Toll-free number: (800) 236-4878
Fax: (920) 403-4072
Bridget O'Connor, Enrollment Management and Communications, St. Norbert College, 100 Grant Street, De Pere, WI 54115-2099

Sanford-Brown College: Milwaukee

West Allis, Wisconsin
www.sbcmilwaukee.com

- For-profit 4-year business and health science college
- Commuter campus in small city

General. Accredited by ACICS. **Calendar:** Continuous.

Annual costs/financial aid. Criminal Justice Associate and Bachelor degree $3750 per term (12 credits), Business Associate and Bachelor degree $3250 per term (12 credits), Medical Assistant Associate degree $3250 per term (12 credits), Medical Assistant diploma program $2750 per term (12 credits), Medical Coding and Billing diploma program $2750 per term (12 credits).

Contact. Phone: (414) 771-2200
6737 West Washington Street, Suite 2355, West Allis, WI 53214

Silver Lake College

Manitowoc, Wisconsin
www.sl.edu **CB code: 1300**

- Private 4-year business and liberal arts college affiliated with Roman Catholic Church
- Commuter campus in large town
- 384 degree-seeking undergraduates
- 47% of applicants admitted
- SAT or ACT (ACT writing optional) required

General. Founded in 1935. Regionally accredited. **Degrees:** 76 bachelor's awarded; master's offered. **Location:** 80 miles from Milwaukee, 30 miles from Green Bay. **Calendar:** Semester, extensive summer session. **Full-time faculty:** 41 total. **Part-time faculty:** 80 total. **Class size:** 97% < 20, 3% 20-39. **Special facilities:** Nature preserve.

Freshman class profile. 243 applied, 115 admitted, 33 enrolled.

Mid 50% test scores		**GPA 2.0-2.99:**	39%
ACT composite:	16-22	**Rank in top quarter:**	21%
GPA 3.75 or higher:	14%	**Out-of-state:**	10%
GPA 3.50-3.74:	11%	**Live on campus:**	70%
GPA 3.0-3.49:	33%		

Basis for selection. Admission based on formula of GPA x ACT x 10. Those below 300 will be denied admission, 301-449 granted provisional admission, and 450 and above accepted. Audition required, interview recommended for music; portfolio, interview recommended for art. **Home-schooled:** Transcript of courses and grades required. **Learning Disabled:** Provide IEP information to Director of Learning Resources.

High school preparation. 21 units required. Required and recommended units include English 4, mathematics 2, social studies 2, history 2, science 2 (laboratory 2), foreign language 1 and academic electives 8.

2008-2009 Annual costs. Tuition/fees: $19,194. Room/board: $7,150. Books/supplies: $890. Personal expenses: $1,200.

2008-2009 Financial aid. **Need-based:** 45% of total undergraduate aid awarded as scholarships/grants, 55% as loans/jobs. **Non-need-based:** Scholarships awarded for academics, art, athletics, leadership, music/drama, religious affiliation, state residency.

Application procedures. **Admission:** Priority date 8/1; no deadline. $35 fee, may be waived for applicants with need, free for online applicants. Admission notification on a rolling basis beginning on or about 9/1. **Financial aid:** Priority date 3/15; no closing date. FAFSA required. Applicants notified on a rolling basis starting 3/15; must reply within 2 week(s) of notification.

Academics. **Special study options:** Accelerated study, combined bachelor's/graduate degree, distance learning, double major, dual enrollment of high school students, independent study, internships, liberal arts/career combination, student-designed major, teacher certification program. **Credit/placement by examination:** AP, CLEP, IB, SAT, ACT, institutional tests. 30 credit hours maximum toward associate degree, 60 toward bachelor's. **Support services:** Learning center, reduced course load, remedial instruction, study skills assistance, tutoring.

Majors. **Biology:** General. **Business:** Accounting, business admin, human resources. **Computer sciences:** Computer science, information systems. **Education:** Art, early childhood, elementary, learning disabled, mentally handicapped, music. **History:** General. **Math:** General. **Psychology:** General. **Public administration:** General. **Theology:** Theology. **Visual/performing arts:** Art.

Most popular majors. Business/marketing 55%, education 21%, psychology 9%.

Computing on campus. 40 workstations in library, computer center, student center. Commuter students can connect to campus network. Online course registration, online library, wireless network available.

Student life. **Freshman orientation:** Mandatory. Preregistration for classes offered. **Housing:** Apartments, wellness housing available. $100 nonrefundable deposit, deadline 8/1. Men's and women's housing available, located off campus. **Activities:** Jazz band, campus ministries, choral groups, dance, literary magazine, music ensembles, student government, student newspaper, student forum, student Wisconsin Education Association, student Wisconsin Early Childhood Association, student council for exceptional children, music educators national conference for students.

Athletics. USCAA. **Intercollegiate:** Basketball, cross-country, golf. **Intramural:** Table tennis, volleyball. **Team name:** Lakers.

Student services. Adult student services, alcohol/substance abuse counseling, chaplain/spiritual director, career counseling, student employment services, financial aid counseling, health services, personal counseling, placement for graduates.

Contact. E-mail: admslc@silver.sl.edu
Phone: (920) 686-6175 Toll-free number: (800) 236-4752 ext. 175
Fax: (920) 684-7082
Jane Bishop, Dean of Enrollment Management, Silver Lake College, 2406 South Alverno Road, Manitowoc, WI 54220-9319

University of Wisconsin-Eau Claire

Eau Claire, Wisconsin
www.uwec.edu **CB code: 1913**

- Public 4-year university
- Residential campus in small city
- 10,215 degree-seeking undergraduates: 5% part-time, 59% women, 1% African American, 3% Asian American, 1% Hispanic American, 1% Native American, 1% international
- 448 degree-seeking graduate students
- 64% of applicants admitted
- SAT or ACT (ACT writing optional) required
- 61% graduate within 6 years; 9% enter graduate study

General. Founded in 1916. Regionally accredited. **Degrees:** 1,836 bachelor's, 6 associate awarded; master's offered. **ROTC:** Army. **Location:** 90 miles from Minneapolis-St. Paul. **Calendar:** Semester, extensive summer session. **Full-time faculty:** 412 total; 82% have terminal degrees, 10% minority, 45% women. **Part-time faculty:** 141 total; 25% have terminal degrees, 3% minority, 78% women. **Class size:** 29% < 20, 50% 20-39, 9% 40-49, 10% 50-99, 2% >100. **Special facilities:** Bird museum, human development center, planetarium, natural preserve, ropes course, material sciences center, clinical simulation skills Lab, 200 kev transmission electron microscope, x-ray photoelectron spectroscopy system, scanning tunneling microscope, scanning electron microscope with energy dispersive x-ray microanalysis, x-ray fluorescence spectrometer, x-ray diffractometer, high resolution inductively coupled plasma mass spectrometer.

Freshman class profile. 8,060 applied, 5,194 admitted, 2,058 enrolled.

Mid 50% test scores		**Rank in top tenth:**	27%
SAT critical reading:	500-640	**End year in good standing:**	90%
SAT math:	550-650	**Return as sophomores:**	83%
SAT writing:	490-620	**Out-of-state:**	24%
ACT composite:	23-26	**Live on campus:**	94%
Rank in top quarter:	59%	**International:**	1%

Basis for selection. Applicants must present required combination of rank and test scores. Special consideration to disadvantaged, veterans, and minority applicants. Applicants with rank in top 50% and/or ACT score of 23 or better given first priority. Some applicants not admitted to the fall semester may be considered for admission to the following spring semester. Wisconsin residents required to take ACT; non-residents may submit SAT. Audition required for music programs.

High school preparation. 17 units required. Required units include English 4, mathematics 3, social studies 3, science 3, foreign language 2 and academic electives 2. 3 units English must be composition and/or literature. One of the 3 social studies units must be world or US history.

2008-2009 Annual costs. Tuition/fees: $6,203; $13,777 out-of-state. Minnesota reciprocity tuition: $270 per credit hour. Room/board: $5,210. Books/supplies: $460. Personal expenses: $1,800.

2007-2008 Financial aid. Need-based: 1,555 full-time freshmen applied for aid; 872 were judged to have need; 866 of these received aid. Average need met was 94%. Average scholarship/grant was $4,764; average loan $4,264. 35% of total undergraduate aid awarded as scholarships/grants, 65% as loans/jobs. **Non-need-based:** Awarded to 891 full-time undergraduates, including 341 freshmen. Scholarships awarded for academics, art, leadership, minority status, music/drama, state residency.

Application procedures. Admission: Priority date 12/1; no deadline. $35 fee, may be waived for applicants with need. Admission notification on a rolling basis beginning on or about 9/15. Closing and priority dates vary. **Financial aid:** Priority date 4/15; no closing date. FAFSA required. Applicants notified on a rolling basis starting 4/15.

Academics. Baccalaureate degree includes service-learning requirement, freshman seminars, capstone courses, internships in most majors, and opportunities for students to collaborate with faculty on research and scholarly projects. **Special study options:** Accelerated study, cooperative education, distance learning, double major, dual enrollment of high school students, ESL, exchange student, external degree, honors, independent study, internships, study abroad, teacher certification program. Program with University of Wisconsin-STOUT in early childhood education. **Credit/placement by examination:** AP, CLEP, IB, ACT, institutional tests. 15 credit hours maximum toward associate degree, 30 toward bachelor's. **Support services:** Learning center, pre-admission summer program, reduced course load, remedial instruction, study skills assistance, tutoring, writing center.

Majors. Area/ethnic studies: Latin American, Native American, women's. **Biology:** General, molecular. **Business:** Accounting, business admin, finance, information resources management, marketing. **Communications:** General, journalism, media studies. **Computer sciences:** General. **Education:** Elementary, science, social studies, special. **Foreign languages:** French, Germanic, Spanish. **Health:** Athletic training, communication disorders, community health, health care admin, music therapy, nursing (RN). **History:** General. **Math:** General. **Parks/recreation:** Exercise sciences. **Philosophy/religion:** Philosophy, religion. **Physical sciences:** Chemistry, geology, physics. **Protective services:** Criminal justice. **Psychology:** General. **Public administration:** Social work. **Social sciences:** Economics, geography, political science, sociology. **Visual/performing arts:** Art, dramatic. **Other:** Chemistry with business emphasis, Physics-math.

Most popular majors. Business/marketing 21%, communications/journalism 8%, education 8%, health sciences 12%, parks/recreation 6%, psychology 6%, security/protective services 6%, social sciences 6%.

Computing on campus. 1,150 workstations in dormitories, library, computer center, student center. Dormitories wired for high-speed internet access and linked to campus network. Commuter students can connect to campus network. Online course registration, online library, helpline, wireless network available.

Student life. Freshman orientation: Mandatory, $100 fee. Preregistration for classes offered. **Housing:** Guaranteed on-campus for freshmen. Coed dorms, single-sex dorms, apartments available. $75 fully refundable deposit. **Activities:** Bands, campus ministries, choral groups, dance, drama, film society, international student organizations, literary magazine, music ensembles, Model UN, musical theater, opera, radio station, student government, student newspaper, symphony orchestra, TV station, College Republicans, College Democrats, Newman Student Association, ecumenical religious center student association, Alpha Phi Omega service fraternity, Mortar Board, Black student organization, Native American student organization, Hmong student association.

Athletics. NCAA. **Intercollegiate:** Basketball, cross-country, diving, football (tackle) M, golf, gymnastics W, ice hockey, soccer W, softball W, swimming, tennis, track and field, volleyball W, wrestling M. **Intramural:** Badminton, baseball M, basketball, bowling, diving, football (tackle), golf, ice hockey, racquetball, rugby, skiing, soccer, softball, swimming, table tennis, tennis, volleyball, water polo M, weight lifting. **Team name:** Blugolds.

Student services. Adult student services, alcohol/substance abuse counseling, chaplain/spiritual director, career counseling, services for economically disadvantaged, student employment services, financial aid counseling, health services, legal services, minority student services, on-campus daycare, personal counseling, placement for graduates, veterans' counselor, women's services. **Physically disabled:** Services for visually, speech, hearing impaired.

Contact. E-mail: admissions@uwec.edu
Phone: (715) 836-5415 Fax: (715) 836-2409
Kristina Anderson, Executive Director, Enrollment Services & Admissions, University of Wisconsin-Eau Claire, 112 Schofield Hall, Eau Claire, WI 54701

University of Wisconsin-Green Bay

Green Bay, Wisconsin **CB member**
www.uwgb.edu **CB code: 1859**

- Public 4-year university and liberal arts college
- Residential campus in small city
- 5,726 degree-seeking undergraduates: 18% part-time, 65% women, 1% African American, 3% Asian American, 2% Hispanic American, 2% Native American, 1% international
- 162 degree-seeking graduate students
- 72% of applicants admitted
- SAT or ACT (ACT writing optional) required
- 56% graduate within 6 years; 17% enter graduate study

General. Founded in 1965. Regionally accredited. **Degrees:** 984 bachelor's, 3 associate awarded; master's offered. **ROTC:** Army. **Location:** 80 miles from Milwaukee. **Calendar:** Semester, limited summer session. **Full-time faculty:** 188 total; 86% have terminal degrees, 14% minority, 42% women. **Part-time faculty:** 146 total; 16% have terminal degrees, 4% minority, 56% women. **Class size:** 28% < 20, 44% 20-39, 12% 40-49, 11%

50-99, 4% >100. **Special facilities:** Natural history museum, herbarium, 290-acre arboretum, performing arts center.

Freshman class profile. 3,669 applied, 2,632 admitted, 1,017 enrolled.

Mid 50% test scores		End year in good standing:	82%
ACT composite:	20-25	Return as sophomores:	73%
GPA 3.75 or higher:	17%	Out-of-state:	5%
GPA 3.50-3.74:	15%	Live on campus:	80%
GPA 3.0-3.49:	43%	Fraternities:	1%
GPA 2.0-2.99:	25%	Sororities:	1%

Basis for selection. ACT score, high school GPA and extracurricular or community involvement very important. Priority given to students with 23 ACT or 3.25 GPA. Students not meeting standard admission requirements (17 ACT and 2.25 GPA) may be considered on individual basis. ACT requirement may be waived for international students at application. ACT reports should be supplied prior to receiving admission. Interview may be requested of borderline applicants; audition required for music. **Homeschooled:** Transcript of courses and grades required.

High school preparation. College-preparatory program required. 17 units required; 19 recommended. Required and recommended units include English 4, mathematics 3, social studies 3, science 3 (laboratory 1), foreign language 2 and academic electives 4. Math must include algebra or more advanced course. 2 of the 4 required academic electives must be from English, math, science, social studies, or foreign language.

2008-2009 Annual costs. Tuition/fees: $6,308; $13,881 out-of-state. Room/board: $5,460. Books/supplies: $800. Personal expenses: $1,960.

2008-2009 Financial aid. Need-based: 869 full-time freshmen applied for aid; 586 were judged to have need; 563 of these received aid. Average need met was 86%. Average scholarship/grant was $5,278; average loan $3,876. 45% of total undergraduate aid awarded as scholarships/grants, 55% as loans/jobs. **Non-need-based:** Awarded to 1,315 full-time undergraduates, including 270 freshmen. Scholarships awarded for academics, art, athletics, leadership, minority status, music/drama. **Additional information:** Auditions required for music and theater scholarships. Tuition is waived for children of Wisconsin soldiers and policemen who were slain in the line of duty. Tuition is also waived for all veterans.

Application procedures. Admission: Priority date 4/15; no deadline. $44 fee, may be waived for applicants with need. Admission notification on a rolling basis beginning on or about 9/15. **Financial aid:** Priority date 4/1; no closing date. FAFSA required. Applicants notified on a rolling basis starting 1/1; must reply within 3 week(s) of notification.

Academics. Minimum credit hours required in major for bachelor's degree varies depending on field. Teacher certification available in conjunction with bachelor's degree. **Special study options:** Combined bachelor's/graduate degree, distance learning, double major, dual enrollment of high school students, exchange student, external degree, independent study, internships, liberal arts/career combination, student-designed major, study abroad, teacher certification program. **Credit/placement by examination:** AP, CLEP, IB, ACT, institutional tests. 47 credit hours maximum toward associate degree, 93 toward bachelor's. **Support services:** Pre-admission summer program, reduced course load, remedial instruction, study skills assistance, tutoring, writing center.

Majors. Area/ethnic studies: Native American, women's. **Biology:** General. **Business:** Accounting, business admin. **Communications:** General. **Computer sciences:** Computer science, information systems. **Conservation:** Environmental science, environmental studies. **Education:** Elementary. **Foreign languages:** French, German, Spanish. **Health:** Nursing (RN). **History:** General. **Interdisciplinary:** Biological/physical sciences. **Liberal arts:** Arts/sciences, humanities. **Math:** General. **Philosophy/religion:** Philosophy. **Physical sciences:** Chemistry, physics. **Psychology:** General. **Public administration:** General, social work. **Social sciences:** Economics, political science, sociology, urban studies. **Visual/performing arts:** General, art, dramatic.

Most popular majors. Biology 10%, business/marketing 17%, communications/journalism 6%, education 6%, psychology 18%, public administration/social services 6%, social sciences 7%, visual/performing arts 7%.

Computing on campus. 600 workstations in dormitories, library, computer center, student center. Dormitories wired for high-speed internet access and linked to campus network. Commuter students can connect to campus network. Online course registration, online library, helpline, repair service, wireless network available.

Student life. Freshman orientation: Available, $200 fee. Preregistration for classes offered. Held the week before fall classes begin. **Housing:** Coed dorms, apartments, wellness housing available. $225 fully refundable deposit. Suite-style apartments with private bathrooms. **Activities:** Bands, choral groups, dance, drama, film society, literary magazine, music ensembles, Model UN, musical theater, radio station, student government, student newspaper, TV station, College Republicans, College Democrats, Habitat for Humanity, Circle K, Ten Percent Society, Athletes in Action, American Marketing Association, psychology and human development club, student government association, Wisconsin Education Assocation Council.

Athletics. NCAA. **Intercollegiate:** Basketball, cheerleading, cross-country, diving, golf, skiing, soccer, softball W, swimming, tennis, volleyball W. **Intramural:** Basketball, football (non-tackle), golf, racquetball, soccer, softball, tennis, volleyball. **Team name:** Phoenix.

Student services. Adult student services, alcohol/substance abuse counseling, career counseling, student employment services, financial aid counseling, health services, minority student services, personal counseling, placement for graduates, veterans' counselor. **Physically disabled:** Services for visually, hearing impaired.

Contact. E-mail: admissions@uwgb.edu
Phone: (920) 465-2111 Fax: (920) 465-5754
Pam Harvey-Jacobs, Director of Admissions, University of Wisconsin-Green Bay, 2420 Nicolet Drive, Green Bay, WI 54311-7001

University of Wisconsin-La Crosse

La Crosse, Wisconsin — **CB member**
www.uwlax.edu — **CB code: 1914**

- Public 4-year university
- Residential campus in small city
- 8,426 degree-seeking undergraduates: 4% part-time, 58% women, 1% African American, 4% Asian American, 2% Hispanic American, 1% Native American, 2% international
- 1,152 degree-seeking graduate students
- 66% of applicants admitted
- SAT or ACT (ACT writing optional) required
- 66% graduate within 6 years; 23% enter graduate study

General. Founded in 1909. Regionally accredited. **Degrees:** 1,543 bachelor's, 6 associate awarded; master's, first professional offered. **ROTC:** Army. **Location:** 140 miles from Madison, 160 miles from Minneapolis-St. Paul. **Calendar:** Semester, limited summer session. **Full-time faculty:** 351 total; 80% have terminal degrees, 10% minority, 40% women. **Part-time faculty:** 156 total; 26% have terminal degrees, 4% minority, 54% women. **Class size:** 35% < 20, 48% 20-39, 8% 40-49, 7% 50-99, 1% >100. **Special facilities:** Greenhouse, planetarium, nuclear radiation laboratory, river studies center, archaeology center.

Freshman class profile. 6,875 applied, 4,563 admitted, 1,784 enrolled.

Mid 50% test scores		Return as sophomores:	87%
SAT critical reading:	500-600	Out-of-state:	16%
SAT math:	490-610	Live on campus:	94%
ACT composite:	23-27	International:	2%
Rank in top quarter:	79%	Fraternities:	1%
Rank in top tenth:	32%	Sororities:	1%
End year in good standing:	93%		

Basis for selection. Applicants should rank in top 25% of class, minimum ACT composite score of 23 (or rank in upper 30% of class with score of 26), and complete a rigorous college prep curriculum. Interviews not required, but may be considered in admission decision. Auditions may be required for some scholarships. Portfolios and essays may be included with application and will be considered in admission decision. **Homeschooled:** Interview may be required. **Learning Disabled:** Information regarding a learning disability may be considered in admission decision.

High school preparation. College-preparatory program required. 17 units required; 21 recommended. Required and recommended units include English 4, mathematics 3-4, social studies 3-4, science 3-4 (laboratory 2), foreign language 3 and academic electives 4.

2008-2009 Annual costs. Tuition/fees: $6,647; $14,220 out-of-state. Room/board: $5,420. Books/supplies: $300. Personal expenses: $2,000.

2007-2008 Financial aid. Need-based: 1,228 full-time freshmen applied for aid; 669 were judged to have need; 608 of these received aid. Average need met was 79%. Average scholarship/grant was $5,493; average loan $3,087. 35% of total undergraduate aid awarded as scholarships/grants, 65% as loans/jobs. **Non-need-based:** Awarded to 489 full-time undergraduates, including 129 freshmen. Scholarships awarded for academics, alumni affiliation, art, minority status, music/drama, ROTC, state residency.

Application procedures. Admission: Priority date 2/1; no deadline. $44 fee, may be waived for applicants with need. Admission notification on a

rolling basis beginning on or about 9/15. **Financial aid:** Priority date 3/15; no closing date. FAFSA, institutional form required. Applicants notified on a rolling basis starting 4/1.

Academics. **Special study options:** Cooperative education, cross-registration, distance learning, double major, dual enrollment of high school students, ESL, honors, independent study, internships, liberal arts/career combination, study abroad, teacher certification program. **Credit/placement by examination:** AP, CLEP, IB, SAT, ACT, institutional tests. 16 credit hours maximum toward associate degree, 32 toward bachelor's. **Support services:** Learning center, pre-admission summer program, reduced course load, remedial instruction, study skills assistance, tutoring, writing center.

Majors. **Biology:** General, biochemistry, microbiology. **Business:** Accounting, business admin, finance, international, management information systems, marketing. **Communications:** General. **Computer sciences:** General. **Education:** Elementary, health, science, social studies. **Foreign languages:** French, German, Spanish. **Health:** Athletic training, clinical lab science, community health, nuclear medical technology, physician assistant, recreational therapy. **History:** General. **Math:** General. **Parks/recreation:** Exercise sciences, facilities management. **Philosophy/religion:** Philosophy. **Physical sciences:** Chemistry, physics. **Psychology:** General. **Social sciences:** Archaeology, economics, geography, political science, sociology. **Visual/performing arts:** Art, dramatic.

Most popular majors. Biology 13%, business/marketing 21%, communications/journalism 6%, education 15%, health sciences 8%, psychology 9%, social sciences 10%.

Computing on campus. 600 workstations in dormitories, library, computer center, student center. Dormitories wired for high-speed internet access and linked to campus network. Commuter students can connect to campus network. Online course registration, online library, helpline, wireless network available.

Student life. **Freshman orientation:** Available, $60 fee. Preregistration for classes offered. Held week prior to classes. **Housing:** Coed dorms, special housing for disabled, fraternity/sorority housing, wellness housing available. $75 nonrefundable deposit, deadline 5/1. First Year Experience housing available. **Activities:** Bands, campus ministries, choral groups, dance, drama, international student organizations, literary magazine, music ensembles, musical theater, radio station, student government, student newspaper, symphony orchestra, TV station, Black Students Unity, Native American Council, Hispanic student organization, Asian association, Amnesty International, Newman Club, hall councils, Intervarsity Christian Fellowship, Campus Crusade.

Athletics. NAIA, NCAA. **Intercollegiate:** Baseball M, basketball, cross-country, diving, football (tackle) M, gymnastics W, soccer W, softball W, swimming, tennis, track and field, volleyball W, wrestling M. **Intramural:** Badminton, basketball, football (non-tackle), golf M, racquetball, soccer, softball, tennis, volleyball. **Team name:** Eagles.

Student services. Adult student services, alcohol/substance abuse counseling, chaplain/spiritual director, career counseling, services for economically disadvantaged, student employment services, financial aid counseling, health services, legal services, minority student services, on-campus daycare, personal counseling, placement for graduates, veterans' counselor, women's services. **Physically disabled:** Services for visually, speech, hearing impaired.

Contact. E-mail: admissions@uwlax.edu
Phone: (608) 785-8939 Fax: (608) 785-8940
Kathryn Kiefer, Associate Director of Admissions, University of Wisconsin-La Crosse, 1725 State Street, 115 Graff Main Hall, La Crosse, WI 54601

University of Wisconsin-Madison

Madison, Wisconsin — **CB member**
www.wisc.edu — **CB code: 1846**

- Public 4-year university
- Residential campus in small city
- 29,153 degree-seeking undergraduates: 5% part-time, 52% women, 3% African American, 6% Asian American, 4% Hispanic American, 1% Native American, 5% international
- 11,280 degree-seeking graduate students
- 53% of applicants admitted
- SAT or ACT with writing, application essay required
- 82% graduate within 6 years

General. Founded in 1849. Regionally accredited. **Degrees:** 6,376 bachelor's awarded; master's, doctoral, first professional offered. **ROTC:** Army, Naval, Air Force. **Location:** 90 miles from Milwaukee, 150 miles from Chicago. **Calendar:** Semester, extensive summer session. **Full-time faculty:** 2,388 total; 91% have terminal degrees, 16% minority, 34% women. **Part-time faculty:** 512 total; 62% have terminal degrees, 8% minority, 48% women. **Class size:** 44% < 20, 32% 20-39, 5% 40-49, 10% 50-99, 10% >100. **Special facilities:** Teaching nuclear reactor, observatory, botanical gardens, arboretum, museums.

Freshman class profile. 25,478 applied, 13,438 admitted, 5,774 enrolled.

Mid 50% test scores			
SAT critical reading:	540-670	Rank in top quarter:	93%
SAT math:	620-730	Rank in top tenth:	58%
SAT writing:	570-670	Return as sophomores:	94%
ACT composite:	26-30	Out-of-state:	36%
GPA 3.75 or higher:	55%	Live on campus:	88%
GPA 3.50-3.74:	23%	International:	6%
GPA 3.0-3.49:	18%	Fraternities:	9%
GPA 2.0-2.99:	4%	Sororities:	8%

Basis for selection. Secondary school record including level of challenge relative to high school offerings, evidence of either increasing or consistent level of academic challenge and performance, course grades, class rank, ACT or SAT test scores. Also consider application statement (essay), recommendations, extracurricular activities and personal characteristics. Audition required for music; portfolio recommended for fine arts.

High school preparation. 17 units required; 20 recommended. Required and recommended units include English 4, mathematics 3-4, social studies 3-4, science 3-4, foreign language 2-4 and academic electives 2. Math units must include 1 each algebra and geometry, plus 1 year advanced math. Computer science or statistics will not fulfill math requirement. Applicants strongly advised to present academic credentials well in excess of minimum units.

2008-2009 Annual costs. Tuition/fees: $7,568; $21,818 out-of-state. Room/board: $7,700.

2007-2008 Financial aid. **Need-based:** 3,498 full-time freshmen applied for aid; 1,911 were judged to have need; 1,906 of these received aid. Average need met was 78%. Average scholarship/grant was $3,287; average loan $4,385. 37% of total undergraduate aid awarded as scholarships/grants, 63% as loans/jobs. **Non-need-based:** Awarded to 8,753 full-time undergraduates, including 2,977 freshmen. Scholarships awarded for academics, alumni affiliation, art, athletics, job skills, leadership, minority status, music/drama, religious affiliation, ROTC, state residency.

Application procedures. **Admission:** Closing date 2/1 (postmark date). $44 fee, may be waived for applicants with need. Admission notification on a rolling basis beginning on or about 10/1. Must reply by May 1 or within 3 week(s) if notified thereafter. **Financial aid:** No deadline. FAFSA, institutional form required. Applicants notified on a rolling basis starting 4/1; must reply within 9 week(s) of notification.

Academics. **Special study options:** Accelerated study, combined bachelor's/graduate degree, cooperative education, distance learning, double major, dual enrollment of high school students, ESL, honors, independent study, internships, liberal arts/career combination, student-designed major, study abroad, teacher certification program. **Credit/placement by examination:** AP, CLEP, IB, institutional tests. **Support services:** Learning center, pre-admission summer program, reduced course load, remedial instruction, study skills assistance, tutoring, writing center.

Majors. **Agriculture:** Agronomy, animal sciences, business, communications, dairy, economics, food science, horticultural science, poultry, soil science. **Area/ethnic studies:** African-American, Asian, Latin American, Scandinavian, South Asian, women's. **Biology:** General, bacteriology, biochemistry, botany, conservation, entomology, genetics, microbiology, molecular, pharmacology/toxicology, plant pathology, zoology. **Business:** General, accounting, actuarial science, business admin, finance, insurance, international, management information systems, marketing, operations, real estate. **Communications:** General, journalism. **Computer sciences:** General. **Conservation:** Forest sciences, wildlife. **Education:** Agricultural, art, elementary, family/consumer sciences, music, social studies, special. **Engineering:** Agricultural, biomedical, chemical, civil, computer, electrical, geological, industrial, marine, materials, mechanical, mechanics, nuclear, physics. **Family/consumer sciences:** General, clothing/textiles, communication, consumer economics, family studies, merchandising. **Foreign languages:** Ancient Greek, Chinese, classics, comparative lit, French, Germanic, Hebrew, Italian, Japanese, Latin, linguistics, Polish, Portuguese, Romance, Russian, Spanish. **Health:** Audiology/speech pathology, clinical lab science, communication disorders, nursing (RN), physician assistant, vocational rehab counseling. **History:** General, science/technology. **Interdisciplinary:** Behavioral sciences, global studies. **Legal studies:** General. **Math:** General, applied, statistics. **Parks/recreation:** Exercise sciences, facilities management. **Philosophy/religion:**

Philosophy, religion. **Physical sciences:** Astronomy, astrophysics, atmospheric science, chemistry, geology, geophysics, physics, planetary. **Protective services:** Criminal justice. **Psychology:** General. **Public administration:** Social work. **Social sciences:** Anthropology, cartography, economics, geography, political science, sociology. **Visual/performing arts:** Art, art history/conservation, ceramics, cinematography, commercial/advertising art, conducting, dance, design, dramatic, fashion design, fiber arts, film/cinema, interior design, jazz, metal/jewelry, music history, music performance, music theory/composition, painting, piano/organ, printmaking, sculpture, theater design, voice/opera.

Most popular majors. Biology 12%, business/marketing 9%, communications/journalism 6%, engineering/engineering technologies 9%, social sciences 14%.

Computing on campus. 3,350 workstations in dormitories, library, computer center, student center. Dormitories wired for high-speed internet access and linked to campus network. Commuter students can connect to campus network. Online course registration, online library, helpline, repair service, student web hosting, wireless network available.

Student life. Freshman orientation: Mandatory, $85 fee. Preregistration for classes offered. **Housing:** Coed dorms, single-sex dorms, apartments, cooperative housing, fraternity/sorority housing, wellness housing available. $50 nonrefundable deposit. Residential learning communities available. **Activities:** Bands, choral groups, dance, drama, film society, international student organizations, literary magazine, music ensembles, musical theater, opera, radio station, student government, student newspaper, symphony orchestra, TV station.

Athletics. NCAA. **Intercollegiate:** Basketball, cheerleading, cross-country, football (tackle) M, golf, ice hockey, rowing (crew), soccer, softball W, swimming, tennis, track and field, volleyball W, wrestling M. **Team name:** Badgers.

Student services. Adult student services, alcohol/substance abuse counseling, career counseling, services for economically disadvantaged, student employment services, financial aid counseling, health services, minority student services, personal counseling, placement for graduates, veterans' counselor, women's services. **Physically disabled:** Services for visually, speech, hearing impaired.

Contact. E-mail: onwisconsin@admissions.wisc.edu
Phone: (608) 262-3961 Fax: (608) 262-7706
Steve Amundson, Director of Admissions, University of Wisconsin-Madison, Armory & Gymnasium, Madison, WI 53706-1481

University of Wisconsin-Milwaukee

Milwaukee, Wisconsin — **CB member**
www.uwm.edu — **CB code: 1473**

- Public 4-year university
- Commuter campus in very large city
- 22,909 degree-seeking undergraduates: 13% part-time, 51% women, 7% African American, 5% Asian American, 4% Hispanic American, 1% Native American, 1% international
- 4,413 degree-seeking graduate students
- 79% of applicants admitted
- SAT or ACT (ACT writing optional) required

General. Founded in 1956. Regionally accredited. **Degrees:** 3,612 bachelor's awarded; master's, doctoral offered. **ROTC:** Army, Air Force. **Location:** 90 miles from Chicago. **Calendar:** Semester, extensive summer session. **Full-time faculty:** 762 total; 28% minority, 40% women. **Part-time faculty:** 62 total; 18% minority, 48% women. **Class size:** 44% < 20, 30% 20-39, 8% 40-49, 10% 50-99, 9% >100. **Special facilities:** Planetarium, geological museum, American Geological Society Collection.

Freshman class profile. 11,917 applied, 9,437 admitted, 4,050 enrolled.

Mid 50% test scores			
SAT critical reading:	470-590	GPA 3.0-3.49:	36%
SAT math:	470-640	GPA 2.0-2.99:	40%
SAT writing:	460-580	Rank in top quarter:	25%
ACT composite:	20-24	Rank in top tenth:	7%
GPA 3.75 or higher:	9%	Out-of-state:	6%
GPA 3.50-3.74:	13%	Live on campus:	61%
		International:	1%

Basis for selection. High school academic record and class rank (top half) important. If applicant ranks in lower half of class, minimum 21 ACT required. ACT (or equivalent SAT score) for out-of-state residents required. Additional requirements for architecture. Students who do not meet standard admission requirements may apply through Academic Opportunity Program Office. SAT and ACT may be accepted for foreign students in lieu of other criteria. Some applicants must also take placement tests in chemistry and/or foreign language. Audition required for dance, music, theater.

High school preparation. College-preparatory program required. 17 units required; 20 recommended. Required and recommended units include English 4, mathematics 3, social studies 3, science 3 (laboratory 1), foreign language 2 and academic electives 2. Math includes algebra, geometry, and beyond.

2008-2009 Annual costs. Tuition/fees: $7,309; $17,038 out-of-state. Minnesota reciprocity tuition: $343 per credit hour. Room/board: $7,870. Books/supplies: $950. Personal expenses: $1,600.

2008-2009 Financial aid. Need-based: 3,131 full-time freshmen applied for aid; 2,382 were judged to have need; 2,246 of these received aid. Average need met was 53%. Average scholarship/grant was $6,190; average loan $3,704. 41% of total undergraduate aid awarded as scholarships/grants, 59% as loans/jobs. **Non-need-based:** Awarded to 1,847 full-time undergraduates, including 501 freshmen. Scholarships awarded for academics, art, athletics.

Application procedures. Admission: Closing date 7/1. $44 fee, may be waived for applicants with need. Admission notification on a rolling basis beginning on or about 9/15. **Financial aid:** Priority date 3/1; no closing date. FAFSA required. Applicants notified on a rolling basis starting 3/1.

Academics. Special study options: Accelerated study, cooperative education, cross-registration, distance learning, double major, dual enrollment of high school students, ESL, external degree, honors, independent study, internships, liberal arts/career combination, student-designed major, study abroad, teacher certification program, United Nations semester, Washington semester. **Credit/placement by examination:** AP, CLEP, institutional tests. **Support services:** Learning center, pre-admission summer program, reduced course load, remedial instruction, tutoring, writing center.

Majors. Architecture: Architecture. **Area/ethnic studies:** African-American, women's. **Biology:** General, biochemistry, conservation, microbiology. **Business:** Accounting, actuarial science, finance, human resources, management information systems, marketing, operations, real estate, training/development. **Communications:** General, journalism, media studies. **Computer sciences:** General, computer science. **Conservation:** Environmental science. **Education:** General, art, music. **Engineering:** Civil, computer, electrical, manufacturing, materials, mechanical. **Foreign languages:** Classics, comparative lit, French, German, Hebrew, Italian, linguistics, Russian, Spanish. **Health:** Clinical lab science, communication disorders, facilities admin, nursing (RN), predental, premedicine, prepharmacy, preveterinary, recreational therapy. **History:** General. **Interdisciplinary:** Global studies. **Legal studies:** Prelaw. **Math:** General, applied. **Parks/recreation:** General, exercise sciences. **Philosophy/religion:** Judaic, philosophy, religion. **Physical sciences:** Atmospheric physics, chemistry, geology, physics. **Protective services:** Criminal justice. **Psychology:** General. **Public administration:** Social work. **Social sciences:** General, anthropology, economics, geography, political science, sociology, urban studies. **Visual/performing arts:** Art, art history/conservation, dance, dramatic, film/cinema, multimedia.

Most popular majors. Business/marketing 24%, communications/journalism 7%, education 10%, health sciences 9%, social sciences 7%, visual/performing arts 7%.

Computing on campus. 1,255 workstations in dormitories, library, computer center, student center. Dormitories wired for high-speed internet access and linked to campus network. Commuter students can connect to campus network. Online course registration, online library, helpline, repair service, student web hosting, wireless network available.

Student life. Housing: Coed dorms, special housing for disabled, apartments available. $300 partly refundable deposit. **Activities:** Bands, choral groups, dance, drama, film society, literary magazine, music ensembles, musical theater, radio station, student government, student newspaper, symphony orchestra.

Athletics. NCAA. **Intercollegiate:** Baseball M, basketball, cross-country, diving, soccer, swimming, tennis, track and field, volleyball. **Intramural:** Badminton, baseball M, basketball, bowling, diving, fencing, football (tackle) M, golf, handball, racquetball, rugby, sailing, skiing, soccer, softball, swimming, tennis, volleyball, water polo, wrestling M. **Team name:** Panthers.

Student services. Adult student services, career counseling, student employment services, health services, on-campus daycare, personal counseling, placement for graduates, veterans' counselor. **Physically disabled:** Services for visually, speech, hearing impaired.

Contact. E-mail: uwmlook@uwm.edu
Phone: (414) 229-2222 Fax: (414) 229-6940
Beth Weckmueller, Executive Director of Enrollment Services and Registrar, University of Wisconsin-Milwaukee, Box 749, Milwaukee, WI 53201

University of Wisconsin-Oshkosh

Oshkosh, Wisconsin
www.uwosh.edu
CB member
CB code: 1916

- Public 4-year university
- Residential campus in small city
- 10,078 degree-seeking undergraduates: 12% part-time, 58% women, 1% African American, 3% Asian American, 2% Hispanic American, 1% Native American, 1% international
- 1,032 degree-seeking graduate students
- 81% of applicants admitted
- ACT (writing optional) required
- 46% graduate within 6 years

General. Founded in 1871. Regionally accredited. **Degrees:** 1,789 bachelor's awarded; master's offered. **ROTC:** Army. **Location:** 90 miles from Milwaukee. **Calendar:** Semester, limited summer session. **Full-time faculty:** 386 total; 81% have terminal degrees, 10% minority, 45% women. **Part-time faculty:** 213 total; 24% have terminal degrees, 5% minority, 63% women. **Class size:** 36% < 20, 53% 20-39, 2% 40-49, 6% 50-99, 3% >100. **Special facilities:** Planetarium.

Freshman class profile. 5,329 applied, 4,297 admitted, 1,842 enrolled.

Mid 50% test scores		**Rank in top tenth:**	10%
ACT composite:	20-24	**End year in good standing:**	85%
GPA 3.75 or higher:	13%	**Return as sophomores:**	76%
GPA 3.50-3.74:	16%	**Out-of-state:**	3%
GPA 3.0-3.49:	45%	**Live on campus:**	85%
GPA 2.0-2.99:	26%	**Fraternities:**	6%
Rank in top quarter:	37%	**Sororities:**	5%

Basis for selection. Students must rank in top half of high school class or have 22 ACT if rank is in third quartile. Out-of-state applicants may submit SAT scores. Interview recommended for all; audition required for music.

High school preparation. College-preparatory program required. 17 units required. Required and recommended units include English 4, mathematics 3-4, social studies 3, science 3-4 (laboratory 3-4), foreign language 2 and academic electives 4. Social studies must include 1 history.

2008-2009 Annual costs. Tuition/fees: $6,037; $13,610 out-of-state. Minnesota reciprocity tuition: $230 per credit hour. Room/board: $5,510. Books/supplies: $800. Personal expenses: $2,214.

2007-2008 Financial aid. Non-need-based: Scholarships awarded for academics, alumni affiliation, art, leadership, minority status, music/drama, state residency.

Application procedures. Admission: No deadline. $44 fee, may be waived for applicants with need. Admission notification on a rolling basis. **Financial aid:** Priority date 3/15; no closing date. FAFSA required. Applicants notified on a rolling basis starting 4/15; must reply within 2 week(s) of notification.

Academics. Special study options: Accelerated study, cooperative education, cross-registration, distance learning, double major, dual enrollment of high school students, ESL, exchange student, honors, independent study, internships, liberal arts/career combination, student-designed major, study abroad, teacher certification program, weekend college. **Credit/placement by examination:** AP, CLEP, IB, institutional tests. 32 credit hours maximum toward bachelor's degree. **Support services:** Learning center, preadmission summer program, reduced course load, study skills assistance, tutoring, writing center.

Majors. Biology: General, bacteriology. **Business:** Accounting, finance, human resources, management information systems, operations. **Communications:** General, broadcast journalism, journalism. **Computer sciences:** Computer science. **Education:** Elementary, emotionally handicapped, learning disabled, mentally handicapped, music, physical, science, secondary, social science, special. **Foreign languages:** French, German, Spanish. **Health:** Clinical lab technology, nursing (RN), predental, premedicine, prepharmacy, preveterinary. **History:** General. **Legal studies:** Prelaw. **Liberal arts:** Arts/sciences. **Math:** General. **Philosophy/religion:** Philosophy, religion. **Physical sciences:** Chemistry, geology, physics. **Psychology:** General. **Public administration:** Human services, social work. **Social sciences:** Anthropology, economics, geography, political science, sociology, urban studies. **Visual/performing arts:** Art, cinematography, dramatic, studio arts.

Most popular majors. Business/marketing 19%, communications/journalism 8%, education 17%, health sciences 12%, social sciences 8%.

Computing on campus. 475 workstations in dormitories, library, computer center, student center. Dormitories wired for high-speed internet access and linked to campus network. Commuter students can connect to campus network. Online course registration, helpline, wireless network available.

Student life. Freshman orientation: Available. Preregistration for classes offered. **Policies:** Select group of freshmen take part in residential college experience for more individualized instruction. **Housing:** Guaranteed on-campus for freshmen. Coed dorms, single-sex dorms available. $125 deposit, deadline 6/15. **Activities:** Bands, campus ministries, choral groups, dance, drama, film society, literary magazine, music ensembles, Model UN, musical theater, opera, radio station, student government, student newspaper, symphony orchestra, TV station, black student union, Asian student association, American Indian student association, Hispanic Cultures United, InterVarsity Christian Fellowship, Athletes in Action, community involvement program, Habitat for Humanity.

Athletics. NCAA. **Intercollegiate:** Baseball M, basketball, cross-country, diving, football (tackle) M, golf W, gymnastics W, rifle, soccer, softball W, swimming, tennis, track and field, volleyball W, wrestling M. **Intramural:** Basketball, racquetball, skiing, soccer, softball, volleyball. **Team name:** Titans.

Student services. Adult student services, alcohol/substance abuse counseling, career counseling, services for economically disadvantaged, student employment services, financial aid counseling, health services, minority student services, on-campus daycare, personal counseling, placement for graduates, veterans' counselor, women's services. **Physically disabled:** Services for visually, speech, hearing impaired.

Contact. E-mail: oshadmuw@uwosh.edu
Phone: (920) 424-0202 Fax: (920) 424-1098
Jill Endries, Director of Admissions, University of Wisconsin-Oshkosh, 800 Algoma Boulevard, Oshkosh, WI 54901-8602

University of Wisconsin-Parkside

Kenosha, Wisconsin
www.uwp.edu
CB member
CB code: 1860

- Public 4-year university
- Commuter campus in small city
- 4,757 degree-seeking undergraduates: 23% part-time, 54% women, 11% African American, 3% Asian American, 8% Hispanic American, 1% Native American
- 96 degree-seeking graduate students
- 79% of applicants admitted
- 32% graduate within 6 years

General. Founded in 1968. Regionally accredited. **Degrees:** 656 bachelor's awarded; master's offered. **ROTC:** Army. **Location:** 30 miles from Milwaukee, 60 miles from Chicago. **Calendar:** Semester, extensive summer session. **Full-time faculty:** 174 total; 73% have terminal degrees, 23% minority, 44% women. **Part-time faculty:** 100 total; 22% have terminal degrees, 11% minority, 45% women. **Class size:** 52% < 20, 35% 20-39, 6% 40-49, 7% 50-99, less than 1% >100. **Special facilities:** Communication arts building.

Freshman class profile. 2,421 applied, 1,904 admitted, 928 enrolled.

Mid 50% test scores		**Out-of-state:**	8%
ACT composite:	18-22	**Live on campus:**	37%
Rank in top quarter:	28%	**International:**	1%
Rank in top tenth:	7%	**Fraternities:**	2%
Return as sophomores:	63%	**Sororities:**	2%

Basis for selection. Rank in top half of graduating class with specified distribution of high school units for standard admission. Students can be admitted on conditional status if in top 65% of class or with 18 ACT. Scores also used for placement in English and math courses. Audition required for theater, recommended for music; portfolio recommended for art. **Homeschooled:** Applicants reviewed on an individual basis.

High school preparation. College-preparatory program required. 17 units required; 19 recommended. Required and recommended units include English 4, mathematics 3-4, social studies 3-4, science 3-4 (laboratory 1-2), foreign language 2, visual/performing arts 2 and academic electives 2.

2008-2009 Annual costs. Tuition/fees: $6,070; $13,908 out-of-state. Minnesota Reciprocity tuition and fees: $6,510 full-time; $230 per credit hour. Room/board: $5,986. Books/supplies: $800. Personal expenses: $1,564.

2007-2008 Financial aid. Need-based: 665 full-time freshmen applied for aid; 533 were judged to have need; 510 of these received aid. Average scholarship/grant was $5,725. 53% of total undergraduate aid awarded as scholarships/grants, 47% as loans/jobs. **Non-need-based:** Awarded to 435 full-time undergraduates, including 131 freshmen. Scholarships awarded for academics, art, athletics, minority status, music/drama, state residency.

Application procedures. Admission: Priority date 3/1; deadline 8/1 (postmark date). $44 fee, may be waived for applicants with need. Admission notification on a rolling basis beginning on or about 9/15. **Financial aid:** Priority date 3/15; no closing date. FAFSA required. Applicants notified on a rolling basis starting 4/1; must reply within 2 week(s) of notification.

Academics. Special study options: Accelerated study, distance learning, double major, dual enrollment of high school students, exchange student, honors, independent study, internships, liberal arts/career combination, study abroad, teacher certification program, weekend college. Cooperative nursing program with University of Wisconsin-Milwaukee. **Credit/placement by examination:** AP, CLEP, IB, SAT, ACT, institutional tests. 30 credit hours maximum toward bachelor's degree. Retroactive credit policy for foreign language study. **Support services:** Learning center, reduced course load, remedial instruction, study skills assistance, tutoring, writing center.

Majors. Area/ethnic studies: French, German. **Biology:** General, molecular. **Business:** General, accounting, business admin, finance, human resources, management information systems. **Communications:** General. **Computer sciences:** Computer science. **Foreign languages:** French, German, Spanish. **Health:** Predental, premedicine, preveterinary. **History:** General. **Interdisciplinary:** Math/computer science. **Legal studies:** Prelaw. **Liberal arts:** Arts/sciences. **Math:** General. **Parks/recreation:** Sports admin. **Philosophy/religion:** Philosophy. **Physical sciences:** Chemistry, geology, physics. **Protective services:** Criminal justice. **Psychology:** General. **Social sciences:** Economics, geography, political science, sociology. **Visual/performing arts:** Art, dramatic.

Most popular majors. Biology 7%, business/marketing 20%, communications/journalism 8%, English 8%, parks/recreation 8%, psychology 9%, public administration/social services 11%, science technologies 8%, visual/performing arts 7%.

Computing on campus. 225 workstations in dormitories, library, computer center, student center. Dormitories wired for high-speed internet access and linked to campus network. Commuter students can connect to campus network. Online course registration, online library, helpline, student web hosting, wireless network available.

Student life. Freshman orientation: Mandatory, $52 fee. Preregistration for classes offered. Day-long session offered several times throughout summer before fall semester. **Housing:** Coed dorms, special housing for disabled, apartments, wellness housing available. $50 fully refundable deposit. **Activities:** Bands, choral groups, dance, drama, international student organizations, literary magazine, music ensembles, musical theater, radio station, student government, student newspaper, symphony orchestra, Campus Crusade for Christ, Intervarsity Christian Fellowship, Parkside Ethnic Organization, Amnesty International, Black Student Union, activities board.

Athletics. NCAA. **Intercollegiate:** Baseball M, basketball, cross-country, golf M, soccer, softball W, track and field, volleyball W, wrestling M. **Intramural:** Basketball, racquetball, soccer, softball, table tennis, tennis, volleyball. **Team name:** Rangers.

Student services. Adult student services, alcohol/substance abuse counseling, career counseling, services for economically disadvantaged, student employment services, financial aid counseling, health services, minority student services, on-campus daycare, personal counseling, placement for graduates, veterans' counselor, women's services. **Physically disabled:** Services for visually, speech, hearing impaired.

Contact. E-mail: matthew.jensen@uwp.edu
Phone: (262) 595-2355 Fax: (262) 595-2008
Matthew Jensen, Director of Admissions, University of Wisconsin-Parkside, PO Box 2000, Kenosha, WI 53141-2000

University of Wisconsin-Platteville

Platteville, Wisconsin — **CB member**
www.uwplatt.edu — **CB code: 1917**

- Public 4-year university
- Residential campus in large town
- 6,435 degree-seeking undergraduates: 9% part-time, 36% women, 2% African American, 1% Asian American, 1% Hispanic American, 1% Native American
- 609 degree-seeking graduate students
- 85% of applicants admitted
- SAT or ACT (ACT writing optional) required
- 54% graduate within 6 years

General. Founded in 1866. Regionally accredited. **Degrees:** 980 bachelor's, 1 associate awarded; master's offered. **Location:** 25 miles from Dubuque, Iowa, 75 miles from Madison. **Calendar:** Semester, limited summer session. **Full-time faculty:** 290 total. **Part-time faculty:** 85 total. **Class size:** 32% < 20, 53% 20-39, 9% 40-49, 4% 50-99, 1% >100.

Freshman class profile. 3,600 applied, 3,047 admitted, 1,465 enrolled.

Mid 50% test scores		**Return as sophomores:**	75%
ACT composite:	20-25	**Out-of-state:**	19%
Rank in top quarter:	33%	**Live on campus:**	92%
Rank in top tenth:	9%		

Basis for selection. School record, class rank, and test scores most important. Competency Based Admission requirements. Audition required for music scholarships.

High school preparation. 17 units required. Required units include English 4, mathematics 3, social studies 3, science 3 (laboratory 2) and academic electives 4. 3 units natural science (2 from biology, chemistry, or physics), 3 units algebra I, geometry, algebra II, or higher.

2008-2009 Annual costs. Tuition/fees: $6,147; $13,720 out-of-state. Minnesota reciprocity tuition: $230 per credit hour. Room/board: $5,466. Books/supplies: $300. Personal expenses: $1,170.

Financial aid. All financial aid based on need.

Application procedures. Admission: Priority date 1/1; no deadline. $35 fee, may be waived for applicants with need. Admission notification on a rolling basis beginning on or about 9/15. **Financial aid:** Priority date 3/15; no closing date. FAFSA required. Applicants notified on a rolling basis starting 6/1; must reply within 2 week(s) of notification.

Academics. Tri-State Initiative offers Illinois and Iowa students a discounted out-of-state rate for attending UWP in select majors. **Special study options:** Combined bachelor's/graduate degree, cooperative education, distance learning, double major, dual enrollment of high school students, ESL, exchange student, external degree, honors, independent study, internships, liberal arts/career combination, student-designed major, study abroad, teacher certification program. **Credit/placement by examination:** AP, CLEP, institutional tests. 30 credit hours maximum toward bachelor's degree. **Support services:** Learning center, study skills assistance, tutoring, writing center.

Majors. Agriculture: Agribusiness operations, agronomy, animal sciences, economics. **Biology:** General. **Business:** General, accounting, business admin, entrepreneurial studies, finance, human resources, investments/securities, organizational behavior. **Communications:** General. **Computer sciences:** Computer science. **Conservation:** General. **Construction:** Maintenance. **Education:** Agricultural, art, biology, chemistry, early childhood, elementary, English, German, history, mathematics, science, social science, social studies, Spanish, speech, technology/industrial arts, voc/tech. **Engineering:** Civil, electrical, mechanical, physics. **Foreign languages:** German, Spanish. **History:** General. **Math:** General. **Parks/recreation:** Health/fitness. **Philosophy/religion:** Philosophy. **Physical sciences:** Chemistry. **Protective services:** Law enforcement admin. **Psychology:** General. **Social sciences:** General, economics, geography, political science, sociology. **Visual/performing arts:** Art, commercial/advertising art, dramatic.

Most popular majors. Agriculture 8%, business/marketing 15%, education 12%, engineering/engineering technologies 32%, security/protective services 9%.

Computing on campus. 483 workstations in dormitories, library, computer center. Dormitories wired for high-speed internet access and linked to campus network. Commuter students can connect to campus network. Online course registration, online library, helpline, repair service, student web hosting available.

Student life. Freshman orientation: Available. **Housing:** Guaranteed on-campus for freshmen. Coed dorms available. $100 partly refundable deposit. **Activities:** Bands, campus ministries, choral groups, drama, international student organizations, literary magazine, music ensembles, musical theater, radio station, student government, student newspaper, symphony orchestra, TV station, black student union, ASIA student group, Hmong club, inter-tribal council, Young Democrats, College Republicans, Circle K.

Athletics. NCAA. **Intercollegiate:** Baseball M, basketball, cross-country, football (tackle) M, golf W, soccer, softball W, track and field, volleyball W, wrestling M. **Intramural:** Basketball, bowling, football (tackle), racquetball, soccer, softball, tennis, volleyball, water polo. **Team name:** Pioneers.

Student services. Adult student services, alcohol/substance abuse counseling, chaplain/spiritual director, career counseling, student employment services, financial aid counseling, health services, minority student services, on-campus daycare, personal counseling, placement for graduates, veterans' counselor, women's services. **Physically disabled:** Services for visually, speech, hearing impaired.

Contact. E-mail: admit@uwplatt.edu
Phone: (608) 342-1125 Toll-free number: (800) 362-5515
Fax: (608) 342-1122
Angela Udelhofen, Dean of Admissions and Enrollment Management, University of Wisconsin-Platteville, One University Plaza, Platteville, WI 53818

University of Wisconsin-River Falls

River Falls, Wisconsin
www.uwrf.edu **CB code: 1918**

- Public 4-year university and liberal arts college
- Residential campus in large town
- 6,050 degree-seeking undergraduates
- 490 graduate students
- 91% of applicants admitted
- ACT (writing optional), application essay required
- 58% graduate within 6 years

General. Founded in 1874. Regionally accredited. **Degrees:** 1,079 bachelor's awarded; master's offered. **ROTC:** Army. **Location:** 30 miles from Minneapolis-St. Paul. **Calendar:** Semester, limited summer session. **Full-time faculty:** 236 total; 89% have terminal degrees, 42% women. **Part-time faculty:** 149 total. **Class size:** 33% < 20, 52% 20-39, 10% 40-49, 5% 50-99, less than 1% >100. **Special facilities:** 2 laboratory farms, 20-inch reflecting telescope, USDA-approved food science laboratory, computerized greenhouse, 42-foot rapelling and climbing wall, indoor track and field house, ice arena, electron microscope, observatory, education regional archive collection.

Freshman class profile. 2,886 applied, 2,630 admitted, 1,287 enrolled.

Mid 50% test scores		**Out-of-state:**	54%
ACT composite:	19-24	**Live on campus:**	90%
Rank in top quarter:	33%	**Fraternities:**	5%
Rank in top tenth:	12%	**Sororities:**	5%
Return as sophomores:	74%		

Basis for selection. Rank in top 40% of class with 18 ACT, or rank in top 60% with 22 ACT. Minority student applications given special consideration. Elementary education applicants must rank in the top 40% of class and 24 ACT.

High school preparation. 17 units required. Required and recommended units include English 4, mathematics 3-4, social studies 3-4, science 3-4, foreign language 1 and academic electives 4. Vocational agriculture units also recommended for applicants to College of Agriculture. Wisconsin residents who receive GED must also complete Wisconsin high school equivalency diploma.

2008-2009 Annual costs. Tuition/fees: $6,220; $13,793 out-of-state. Minnesota reciprocity tuition and fees: $6,591 full-time, $230 per credit hour. Room/board: $5,106. Books/supplies: $330. Personal expenses: $1,800.

2008-2009 Financial aid. All financial aid based on need.

Application procedures. Admission: Priority date 2/1; no deadline. $35 fee, may be waived for applicants with need. Admission notification on a rolling basis beginning on or about 9/15. Late applicants considered on individual basis through appeal procedure. **Financial aid:** Priority date 3/15; no closing date. FAFSA required. Applicants notified on a rolling basis starting 4/1; must reply within 4 week(s) of notification.

Academics. Special study options: Accelerated study, combined bachelor's/graduate degree, cooperative education, cross-registration, distance learning, double major, dual enrollment of high school students, ESL, exchange student, honors, independent study, internships, liberal arts/career combination, student-designed major, study abroad, teacher certification program. **Credit/placement by examination:** AP, CLEP, IB, ACT, institutional tests. 27 credit hours maximum toward bachelor's degree. Placement in English, foreign languages, and math based on university system placement exams. **Support services:** Learning center, reduced course load, remedial instruction, study skills assistance, tutoring, writing center.

Majors. Agriculture: General, agronomy, animal sciences, business, crop production, dairy, dairy husbandry, equestrian studies, equine science, equipment technology, food science, greenhouse operations, horticultural science, horticulture, landscaping, products processing, soil science. **Biology:** General, biochemistry, biotechnology. **Business:** Accounting, business admin. **Communications:** General, journalism. **Computer sciences:** General. **Conservation:** General, environmental science, management/policy. **Education:** Agricultural, art, elementary, ESL, music, physical, speech impaired. **Foreign languages:** French, German, Spanish. **Health:** Communication disorders. **History:** General. **Interdisciplinary:** Biological/physical sciences, global studies. **Math:** General. **Physical sciences:** Chemistry, geology, organic chemistry, physics, planetary, polymer chemistry. **Psychology:** General. **Public administration:** Social work. **Social sciences:** General, economics, geography, political science, sociology. **Visual/performing arts:** Art, studio arts.

Most popular majors. Agriculture 16%, biology 8%, business/marketing 20%, education 20%, psychology 8%, science technologies 10%.

Computing on campus. 700 workstations in dormitories, library, computer center, student center. Dormitories wired for high-speed internet access and linked to campus network. Commuter students can connect to campus network. Online course registration, online library, helpline, repair service, student web hosting, wireless network available.

Student life. Freshman orientation: Mandatory. Preregistration for classes offered. Held weekend prior to classes starting. **Policies:** Freshmen and sophomores must live in residence halls unless they reside with parents. **Housing:** Guaranteed on-campus for freshmen. Coed dorms, single-sex dorms, apartments, fraternity/sorority housing, wellness housing available. $125 partly refundable deposit. **Activities:** Bands, campus ministries, choral groups, dance, drama, international student organizations, literary magazine, music ensembles, musical theater, radio station, student government, student newspaper, symphony orchestra, TV station, African American Alliance, Hispanic Student Coalition, Native American Council, Hmong student association, Habitat for Humanity, Fellowship of Christian Athletes, Young Democrats, Young Republicans, Young Life, Intervarsity Christian Fellowship.

Athletics. NCAA. **Intercollegiate:** Basketball, cross-country, diving, football (tackle) M, golf W, ice hockey, soccer W, softball W, swimming, tennis W, track and field, volleyball W. **Intramural:** Badminton, basketball, bowling, cheerleading, football (non-tackle), golf, handball, ice hockey, racquetball, softball, swimming, tennis, volleyball, water polo. **Team name:** Falcons.

Student services. Adult student services, alcohol/substance abuse counseling, chaplain/spiritual director, career counseling, services for economically disadvantaged, student employment services, financial aid counseling, health services, minority student services, on-campus daycare, personal counseling, placement for graduates, veterans' counselor, women's services. **Physically disabled:** Services for visually, speech, hearing impaired.

Contact. E-mail: admit@uwrf.edu
Phone: (715) 425-3500 Fax: (715) 425-0676
Mark Meydam, Director of Admission, University of Wisconsin-River Falls, 410 South 3rd Street, River Falls, WI 54022-5001

University of Wisconsin-Stevens Point

Stevens Point, Wisconsin **CB member**
www.uwsp.edu **CB code: 1919**

- Public 4-year university
- Residential campus in large town
- 8,558 degree-seeking undergraduates: 4% part-time, 53% women, 1% African American, 2% Asian American, 1% Hispanic American, 1% Native American, 2% international
- 254 degree-seeking graduate students
- 74% of applicants admitted
- SAT or ACT (ACT writing optional) required
- 95% graduate within 6 years

General. Founded in 1894. Regionally accredited. **Degrees:** 1,583 bachelor's, 14 associate awarded; master's, doctoral offered. **ROTC:** Army. **Location:** 110 miles from Madison, 240 miles from Chicago. **Calendar:** Semester, extensive summer session. **Full-time faculty:** 399 total; 78% have terminal degrees, 6% minority, 43% women. **Part-time faculty:** 53 total; 38% have terminal degrees, 6% minority, 51% women. **Class size:** 29% < 20, 50% 20-39, 7% 40-49, 10% 50-99, 4% >100. **Special facilities:** Natural history museum, planetarium and observatory, nature preserve, Foucault pendulum, electron microscope, 1,000-acre natural resources summer camp, fire science center, multicultural center.

Freshman class profile. 5,423 applied, 3,991 admitted, 1,618 enrolled.

Mid 50% test scores		**GPA 2.0-2.99:**	13%
SAT critical reading:	440-610	**Rank in top quarter:**	47%
SAT math:	460-610	**Rank in top tenth:**	15%
SAT writing:	440-640	**Return as sophomores:**	75%
ACT composite:	21-25	**Out-of-state:**	9%
GPA 3.75 or higher:	22%	**Live on campus:**	89%
GPA 3.50-3.74:	22%	**International:**	2%
GPA 3.0-3.49:	43%		

Basis for selection. Applicants must rank in top 25% of high school class or have 21 ACT/990 SAT (exclusive of Writing) and rank in top 50% of class or have 3.25 GPA. Campus visit recommended.

High school preparation. College-preparatory program required. 17 units required. Required and recommended units include English 4, mathematics 3, social studies 3-4, science 3-4 and foreign language 2. Additional 2 units from English, math, social sciences, sciences, or foreign language and 2 units from above areas or fine arts, computer science, or other academic areas.

2008-2009 Annual costs. Tuition/fees: $6,200; $13,773 out-of-state. Minnesota reciprocity tuition and fees: $6,638 full-year or $230 per credit hour. Room/board: $5,180. Books/supplies: $450. Personal expenses: $1,775.

2007-2008 Financial aid. Need-based: 1,272 full-time freshmen applied for aid; 809 were judged to have need; 754 of these received aid. Average scholarship/grant was $5,761; average loan $3,661. 37% of total undergraduate aid awarded as scholarships/grants, 63% as loans/jobs. **Non-need-based:** Awarded to 1,081 full-time undergraduates, including 200 freshmen. Scholarships awarded for academics, alumni affiliation, art, music/drama, ROTC. **Additional information:** Tuition discounts offered to qualified residents from other states.

Application procedures. Admission: No deadline. $44 fee, may be waived for applicants with need. Admission notification on a rolling basis beginning on or about 9/15. **Financial aid:** Priority date 5/15, closing date 6/15. FAFSA required. Applicants notified on a rolling basis starting 5/1; must reply within 4 week(s) of notification.

Academics. Special study options: Accelerated study, cooperative education, distance learning, double major, dual enrollment of high school students, ESL, independent study, internships, student-designed major, study abroad, teacher certification program. Cooperative program with University of Wisconsin: Eau Claire and St. Joseph's Hospital; collaborative degree program with University of Wisconsin-Marshfield, University of Wisconsin-Marathon and University of Wisconsin-Marinette. **Credit/placement by examination:** AP, CLEP, IB, institutional tests. 16 credit hours maximum toward associate degree, 32 toward bachelor's. **Support services:** Learning center, pre-admission summer program, reduced course load, remedial instruction, study skills assistance, tutoring, writing center.

Majors. Agriculture: Soil science. **Architecture:** Interior. **Biology:** General. **Business:** Accounting, business admin. **Communications:** General. **Computer sciences:** General, web page design. **Conservation:** General, fisheries, forestry, water/wetlands/marine, wildlife, wood science. **Education:** Early childhood, elementary, family/consumer sciences, music, physical, secondary. **Foreign languages:** French, German, Spanish. **Health:** Athletic training, audiology/speech pathology, clinical lab science. **History:** General. **Interdisciplinary:** Biological/physical sciences. **Liberal arts:** Arts/sciences. **Math:** General. **Parks/recreation:** Health/fitness. **Philosophy/religion:** Philosophy. **Physical sciences:** Chemistry, physics. **Psychology:** General. **Public administration:** General. **Social sciences:** General, economics, geography, political science, sociology. **Visual/performing arts:** General, art, arts management, dance, dramatic, interior design, music history, music performance.

Most popular majors. Biology 8%, business/marketing 8%, communications/journalism 6%, education 11%, natural resources/environmental science 12%, psychology 6%, social sciences 11%, visual/performing arts 8%.

Computing on campus. 634 workstations in dormitories, library, computer center, student center. Dormitories wired for high-speed internet access and linked to campus network. Commuter students can connect to campus network. Online course registration, online library, helpline, student web hosting, wireless network available.

Student life. Freshman orientation: Mandatory, $35 fee. **Policies:** Nonsmoking policy for all campus buildings. **Housing:** Coed dorms, single-sex dorms, wellness housing available. $125 partly refundable deposit. **Activities:** Bands, campus ministries, choral groups, dance, drama, film society, international student organizations, literary magazine, music ensembles, Model UN, musical theater, radio station, student government, student newspaper, symphony orchestra, TV station, American Indians Reaching for Opportunities, black student union, College Republicans, College Democrats, Lutheran Collegians, Association for Community Tasks, Newman Catholic student association, Habitat for Humanity, gay-straight alliance.

Athletics. NCAA. **Intercollegiate:** Baseball M, basketball, cross-country, diving, football (tackle) M, golf W, ice hockey, soccer W, softball W, swimming, tennis W, track and field, volleyball W, wrestling M. **Intramural:** Badminton, basketball, football (non-tackle), football (tackle) M, golf, ice hockey, racquetball, soccer, softball, tennis, volleyball. **Team name:** Pointers.

Student services. Adult student services, alcohol/substance abuse counseling, career counseling, services for economically disadvantaged, student employment services, financial aid counseling, health services, minority student services, on-campus daycare, personal counseling, placement for graduates, veterans' counselor, women's services. **Physically disabled:** Services for visually, speech, hearing impaired.

Contact. E-mail: admiss@uwsp.edu
Phone: (715) 346-2441 Fax: (715) 346-3296
Catherine Glennon, Director of Admissions, University of Wisconsin-Stevens Point, Student Services Center, Stevens Point, WI 54481

University of Wisconsin-Stout

Menomonie, Wisconsin
www.uwstout.edu **CB code: 1740**

- Public 4-year university
- Residential campus in large town
- 7,666 degree-seeking undergraduates: 11% part-time, 48% women, 1% African American, 3% Asian American, 1% Hispanic American, 1% Native American, 1% international
- 753 degree-seeking graduate students
- 56% of applicants admitted
- SAT or ACT (ACT writing optional) required

General. Founded in 1891. Regionally accredited. **Degrees:** 1,451 bachelor's awarded; master's offered. **ROTC:** Army, Air Force. **Location:** 60 miles from Minneapolis-St. Paul. **Calendar:** 4-1-4, limited summer session. **Full-time faculty:** 335 total; 75% have terminal degrees, 12% minority, 44% women. **Part-time faculty:** 85 total; 35% have terminal degrees, 2% minority, 54% women. **Class size:** 34% < 20, 57% 20-39, 4% 40-49, 4% 50-99, 1% >100. **Special facilities:** Teleproduction center, technology transfer institute, vocational rehabilitation institute.

Freshman class profile. 3,938 applied, 2,214 admitted, 1,631 enrolled.

Mid 50% test scores		**Rank in top tenth:**	6%
ACT composite:	19-23	**Return as sophomores:**	72%
GPA 3.75 or higher:	9%	**Out-of-state:**	36%
GPA 3.50-3.74:	15%	**Live on campus:**	95%
GPA 3.0-3.49:	42%	**Fraternities:**	5%
GPA 2.0-2.99:	34%	**Sororities:**	12%
Rank in top quarter:	23%		

Basis for selection. Rank in top half of high school class or 22 ACT required. Rolling admissions with limited enrollment in all programs. Art-graphic design deadline of November 1; not all qualified applicants will be admitted. Applied science and manufacturing engineering require upper 40% of class or 22 ACT, along with 22 ACT-Math score. **Learning Disabled:** Current IEP may be submitted with application.

High school preparation. College-preparatory program required. Required and recommended units include English 4, mathematics 3, social studies 3, science 3, foreign language 2 and academic electives 4. Electives in English, math, social sciences, and sciences, technology business, fine art, family & consumer education, sciences.

2008-2009 Annual costs. Tuition/fees: $7,584; $15,330 out-of-state. Laptop computer included in the cost of tuition. Room/board: $5,170. Books/supplies: $343. Personal expenses: $1,810.

2008-2009 Financial aid. Need-based: 1,310 full-time freshmen applied for aid; 812 were judged to have need; 809 of these received aid. Average need met was 87%. Average scholarship/grant was $5,933; average loan $3,491. 37% of total undergraduate aid awarded as scholarships/grants, 63% as loans/jobs. **Non-need-based:** Awarded to 960 full-time undergraduates, including 381 freshmen. Scholarships awarded for academics.

Application procedures. Admission: Priority date 1/1; no deadline. $44 fee, may be waived for applicants with need. Admission notification on a

rolling basis beginning on or about 9/15. Enrollment limited. Early application recommended. **Financial aid:** Priority date 3/15; no closing date. FAFSA required. Applicants notified on a rolling basis starting 4/1; must reply within 4 week(s) of notification.

Academics. **Special study options:** Accelerated study, cooperative education, cross-registration, distance learning, double major, dual enrollment of high school students, exchange student, external degree, honors, independent study, internships, study abroad, teacher certification program. **Credit/placement by examination:** AP, CLEP, IB, ACT, institutional tests. **Support services:** Learning center, pre-admission summer program, reduced course load, remedial instruction, study skills assistance, tutoring, writing center.

Majors. **Business:** Business admin, customer service, hospitality admin, operations, sales/distribution. **Communications technology:** Printing management. **Computer sciences:** Networking. **Education:** Art, early childhood, family/consumer sciences, mentally handicapped, sales/marketing, technology/industrial arts, voc/tech. **Engineering:** Computer, manufacturing, polymer. **Engineering technology:** General, construction. **Family/consumer sciences:** Clothing/textiles, family studies, institutional food production. **Health:** Dietetics, vocational rehab counseling. **Math:** Applied. **Psychology:** General. **Other:** Applied Science, Art, Information and Communications Technology, Packaging.

Most popular majors. Business/marketing 42%, education 14%, engineering/engineering technologies 10%, family/consumer sciences 7%, visual/performing arts 10%.

Computing on campus. 590 workstations in dormitories, library, computer center, student center. Dormitories wired for high-speed internet access and linked to campus network. Commuter students can connect to campus network. Online course registration, helpline, repair service, student web hosting, wireless network available.

Student life. **Freshman orientation:** Available. One-day program with additional activities week immediately before classes begin. **Housing:** Guaranteed on-campus for freshmen. Coed dorms, special housing for disabled, apartments, wellness housing available. $125 partly refundable deposit. **Activities:** Bands, campus ministries, choral groups, dance, drama, film society, international student organizations, literary magazine, music ensembles, Model UN, musical theater, radio station, student government, student newspaper, black student union, Hmong Stout student organization, Lutheran student fellowship, College Democrats, College Republicans, Chi Alpha Christians in Action, single parent association, Club Los Hispanos.

Athletics. NCAA. **Intercollegiate:** Baseball M, basketball, cross-country, football (tackle) M, gymnastics W, ice hockey M, soccer W, softball W, tennis W, track and field, volleyball W. **Intramural:** Baseball M, basketball, golf, ice hockey, racquetball, soccer, softball, volleyball. **Team name:** Blue Devils.

Student services. Chaplain/spiritual director, career counseling, student employment services, health services, on-campus daycare, personal counseling, placement for graduates, veterans' counselor. **Physically disabled:** Services for visually, speech, hearing impaired.

Contact. E-mail: admissions@uwstout.edu
Phone: (715) 232-1411 Toll-free number: (800) 447-8688
Fax: (715) 232-1667
Cindy Gilberts, Executive Director of Enrollment Services, University of Wisconsin-Stout, 1 Clocktower Plaza, Menomonie, WI 54751

University of Wisconsin-Superior

Superior, Wisconsin
www.uwsuper.edu **CB code: 1920**

- Public 4-year university and liberal arts college
- Commuter campus in small city
- 2,353 degree-seeking undergraduates: 17% part-time, 57% women, 1% African American, 1% Asian American, 1% Hispanic American, 4% Native American, 4% international
- 205 degree-seeking graduate students
- 70% of applicants admitted
- SAT or ACT (ACT writing optional) required

General. Founded in 1893. Regionally accredited. **Degrees:** 468 bachelor's, 6 associate awarded; master's offered. **ROTC:** Air Force. **Location:** 2 miles from Duluth, Minnesota, 150 miles from Minneapolis-St. Paul. **Calendar:** Semester, limited summer session. **Full-time faculty:** 122 total; 75% have terminal degrees, 10% minority, 45% women. **Part-time faculty:** 65 total; 26% have terminal degrees, 11% minority, 46% women. **Class size:** 55% < 20, 39% 20-39, 2% 40-49, 3% 50-99, less than 1% >100. **Special facilities:** Observatory, wetlands, research vessel on Lake Superior.

Freshman class profile. 921 applied, 643 admitted, 312 enrolled.

Mid 50% test scores		**Out-of-state:**	41%
ACT composite:	20-24	**Live on campus:**	60%
Rank in top quarter:	39%	**International:**	8%
Rank in top tenth:	14%	**Sororities:**	5%

Basis for selection. Admissions based on secondary school record and class rank. Standardized test scores also important. Essay, audition, portfolio, interview recommended. **Homeschooled:** Statement describing homeschool structure and mission, transcript of courses and grades required.

High school preparation. 17 units required. Required and recommended units include English 4, mathematics 3-4, social studies 3-4, science 3-4, foreign language 2 and academic electives 4.

2008-2009 Annual costs. Tuition/fees: $6,360; $13,933 out-of-state. Room/board: $5,158. Books/supplies: $860. Personal expenses: $1,890.

2008-2009 Financial aid. **Need-based:** 216 full-time freshmen applied for aid; 165 were judged to have need; 163 of these received aid. Average scholarship/grant was $5,786; average loan $2,892. 43% of total undergraduate aid awarded as scholarships/grants, 57% as loans/jobs. **Non-need-based:** Awarded to 351 full-time undergraduates, including 85 freshmen. Scholarships awarded for academics, alumni affiliation, art, leadership, minority status, music/drama, ROTC, state residency. **Additional information:** Tuition Assistance Program (TAP) available to non-resident students on limited basis.

Application procedures. **Admission:** Priority date 4/1; no deadline. $44 fee, may be waived for applicants with need. Admission notification on a rolling basis beginning on or about 10/1. Must reply by May 1 or within 4 week(s) if notified thereafter. **Financial aid:** Priority date 4/1; no closing date. FAFSA required. Applicants notified on a rolling basis starting 3/15; must reply by 5/1 or within 4 week(s) of notification.

Academics. Post-bachelor's certificates offered in early childhood education, counseling, and secondary education. Post-master's certificate offered in library science. **Special study options:** Combined bachelor's/graduate degree, cooperative education, cross-registration, distance learning, double major, dual enrollment of high school students, ESL, exchange student, external degree, independent study, internships, liberal arts/career combination, student-designed major, study abroad, teacher certification program. Engineering with University of Wisconsin-Madison and Michigan Technological University, Forestry with Michigan Technological University. **Credit/placement by examination:** AP, CLEP, IB, ACT, institutional tests. 32 credit hours maximum toward associate degree, 32 toward bachelor's. **Support services:** Learning center, pre-admission summer program, reduced course load, remedial instruction, study skills assistance, tutoring, writing center.

Majors. **Biology:** General, aquatic, botany, cell/histology, ecology, environmental, molecular. **Business:** General, accounting, business admin, finance, international, management information systems, marketing. **Communications:** General, broadcast journalism, journalism, media studies. **Computer sciences:** Computer science. **Education:** Art, biology, chemistry, elementary, English, history, mathematics, multi-level teacher, music, physical, science, social science, social studies. **Health:** Art therapy. **History:** General. **Interdisciplinary:** Biological/physical sciences. **Legal studies:** General, prelaw. **Liberal arts:** Arts/sciences. **Math:** General. **Physical sciences:** Chemistry. **Protective services:** Criminal justice, police science. **Psychology:** General. **Public administration:** General, policy analysis, social work. **Social sciences:** General, economics, political science, sociology. **Transportation:** General. **Visual/performing arts:** General, art, art history/conservation, dramatic, music performance, studio arts.

Most popular majors. Biology 8%, business/marketing 21%, communications/journalism 9%, education 15%, interdisciplinary studies 10%, public administration/social services 7%, social sciences 7%, visual/performing arts 8%.

Computing on campus. 340 workstations in dormitories, library, computer center, student center. Dormitories wired for high-speed internet access and linked to campus network. Commuter students can connect to campus network. Online course registration, online library, helpline, repair service, student web hosting, wireless network available.

Student life. **Freshman orientation:** Mandatory, $93 fee. Preregistration for classes offered. Sessions held in spring and summer; 2 1/2 day program just prior to classes beginning. **Housing:** Guaranteed on-campus for freshmen. Coed dorms, single-sex dorms, special housing for disabled, wellness housing available. $125 partly refundable deposit, deadline 7/1. Suites available in nontraditional residence halls for married students. Single parents have access to student residences. **Activities:** Bands, choral groups, dance, drama, international student organizations, music ensembles, radio station, student government, student newspaper, symphony orchestra, TV station, criminal justice association, black student union, College Democrats, social work student association, College Republicans, intervarsity Christian fellowship.

Athletics. NCAA. **Intercollegiate:** Baseball M, basketball, cross-country, golf W, ice hockey, soccer, softball W, track and field, volleyball W. **Intramural:** Badminton, basketball, bowling, cheerleading, football (non-tackle), golf, ice hockey, racquetball, rifle, skiing, soccer, softball, swimming, table tennis, tennis, volleyball. **Team name:** Yellowjackets.

Student services. Adult student services, alcohol/substance abuse counseling, chaplain/spiritual director, career counseling, services for economically disadvantaged, student employment services, financial aid counseling, health services, minority student services, on-campus daycare, personal counseling, placement for graduates, veterans' counselor, women's services. **Physically disabled:** Services for visually, hearing impaired.

Contact. E-mail: admissions@uwsuper.edu
Phone: (715) 394-8230 Fax: (715) 394-8407
Tonya Roth, Director of Admission, University of Wisconsin-Superior, Belknap and Catlin, PO Box 2000, Superior, WI 54880

University of Wisconsin-Whitewater

Whitewater, Wisconsin
www.uww.edu **CB code: 1921**

- Public 4-year university
- Residential campus in large town
- 9,452 degree-seeking undergraduates: 7% part-time, 49% women, 5% African American, 2% Asian American, 2% Hispanic American, 1% Native American, 1% international
- 1,341 graduate students
- 73% of applicants admitted
- 55% graduate within 6 years

General. Founded in 1868. Regionally accredited. **Degrees:** 1,705 bachelor's, 16 associate awarded; master's offered. **ROTC:** Army, Air Force. **Location:** 40 miles from Madison, 50 miles from Milwaukee. **Calendar:** Semester, extensive summer session. **Full-time faculty:** 383 total; 84% have terminal degrees, 19% minority, 44% women. **Part-time faculty:** 121 total; 35% have terminal degrees, 9% minority, 49% women. **Class size:** 35% < 20, 50% 20-39, 10% 40-49, 4% 50-99, less than 1% >100. **Special facilities:** Observatory, nature preserve and recreation area, weather station.

Freshman class profile. 6,805 applied, 4,975 admitted, 2,140 enrolled.

Mid 50% test scores		**Rank in top quarter:**	31%
SAT critical reading:	470-610	**Rank in top tenth:**	9%
SAT math:	480-600	**Return as sophomores:**	76%
ACT composite:	20-24	**Out-of-state:**	7%
GPA 3.75 or higher:	11%	**Live on campus:**	90%
GPA 3.50-3.74:	18%	**International:**	1%
GPA 3.0-3.49:	42%	**Fraternities:**	7%
GPA 2.0-2.99:	29%	**Sororities:**	6%

Basis for selection. College prep curriculum and rank in top 40% of high school class important. SAT or ACT recommended. Audition required for music; portfolio recommended for art. **Homeschooled:** Transcript of courses and grades required. **Learning Disabled:** Disability should be referenced in essay and include review by Center for Students with Disabilities. Medical documentation may be requested.

High school preparation. 17 units required; 20 recommended. Required and recommended units include English 4, mathematics 3-4, social studies 3-4, science 3-4 (laboratory 1), foreign language 2 and academic electives 4.

2008-2009 Annual costs. Tuition/fees: $6,162; $13,736 out-of-state. Room/board: $4,790. Books/supplies: $170. Personal expenses: $400.

2008-2009 Financial aid. **Non-need-based:** Scholarships awarded for academics, alumni affiliation, art, leadership, minority status, music/drama, ROTC, state residency.

Application procedures. **Admission:** Priority date 1/1; deadline 5/1 (postmark date). $44 fee, may be waived for applicants with need. Admission notification on a rolling basis beginning on or about 9/15. **Financial aid:** Priority date 3/15; no closing date. FAFSA required. Applicants notified on a rolling basis starting 4/1; must reply within 3 week(s) of notification.

Academics. **Special study options:** Accelerated study, combined bachelor's/graduate degree, cooperative education, cross-registration, distance learning, double major, dual enrollment of high school students, ESL, exchange student, external degree, honors, independent study, internships, liberal arts/career combination, student-designed major, study abroad, teacher certification program, weekend college. **Credit/placement by examination:** AP, CLEP, IB, SAT, ACT, institutional tests. 30 credit hours maximum toward associate degree, 60 toward bachelor's. **Support services:** Learning center, pre-admission summer program, reduced course load, remedial instruction, study skills assistance, tutoring, writing center.

Majors. **Area/ethnic studies:** Women's. **Biology:** General. **Business:** General, accounting, business admin, finance, human resources, managerial economics, marketing, nonprofit/public, office/clerical, operations. **Communications:** General, broadcast journalism, journalism. **Computer sciences:** General, information technology, systems analysis, web page design. **Education:** General, art, biology, business, chemistry, computer, drama/dance, early childhood, elementary, English, French, German, history, learning disabled, mathematics, music, physical, sales/marketing, science, secondary, social science, social studies, Spanish, special, speech. **Engineering technology:** Occupational safety. **Foreign languages:** French, German, Spanish. **Health:** Speech pathology. **History:** General. **Interdisciplinary:** Global studies. **Legal studies:** Prelaw. **Liberal arts:** Arts/sciences. **Math:** General. **Physical sciences:** Chemistry, physics. **Psychology:** General. **Public administration:** General, policy analysis, social work. **Social sciences:** General, economics, geography, political science, sociology. **Visual/performing arts:** Art, art history/conservation, dance, dramatic, music theory/composition, theater arts management, theater history. **Other:** Integrated Science/Business.

Most popular majors. Business/marketing 28%, communications/journalism 10%, education 17%, public administration/social services 6%, social sciences 9%.

Computing on campus. 1,373 workstations in dormitories, library, computer center, student center. Dormitories wired for high-speed internet access and linked to campus network. Commuter students can connect to campus network. Online course registration, online library, helpline, repair service, student web hosting, wireless network available.

Student life. **Freshman orientation:** Mandatory, $75 fee. Preregistration for classes offered. Full-day program held in summer. **Housing:** Guaranteed on-campus for freshmen. Coed dorms, single-sex dorms, special housing for disabled, wellness housing available. $125 partly refundable deposit. **Activities:** Bands, choral groups, dance, drama, literary magazine, music ensembles, musical theater, opera, radio station, student government, student newspaper, symphony orchestra, TV station, Campus Crusade for Christ, Diamond Way Buddhist, College Democrats, College Republicans, Arabic club, Black Student Union, Adopt-A-School Program, America Reads.

Athletics. NCAA. **Intercollegiate:** Baseball M, basketball, bowling W, cross-country, diving, football (tackle) M, golf W, gymnastics W, soccer, softball W, swimming, tennis, track and field, volleyball W, wrestling M. **Intramural:** Badminton, basketball, bowling, football (non-tackle), golf, racquetball, soccer, softball, table tennis, tennis, volleyball. **Team name:** Warhawks.

Student services. Adult student services, alcohol/substance abuse counseling, chaplain/spiritual director, career counseling, services for economically disadvantaged, student employment services, financial aid counseling, health services, legal services, minority student services, on-campus daycare, personal counseling, placement for graduates, veterans' counselor, women's services. **Physically disabled:** Services for visually, speech, hearing impaired. **Learning disabled:** Comprehensive services available.

Contact. E-mail: uwwadmit@uww.edu
Phone: (262) 472-1440 Fax: (262) 472-1515
Stephen McKellips, Director of Admissions, University of Wisconsin-Whitewater, 800 West Main Street, Whitewater, WI 53190-1790

Viterbo University

La Crosse, Wisconsin **CB member**
www.viterbo.edu **CB code: 1878**

- Private 4-year university and liberal arts college affiliated with Roman Catholic Church
- Residential campus in small city
- 1,997 degree-seeking undergraduates: 24% part-time, 72% women, 1% African American, 2% Asian American, 1% Hispanic American, 1% Native American, 1% international
- 460 degree-seeking graduate students
- 86% of applicants admitted
- ACT (writing optional) required
- 45% graduate within 6 years; 12% enter graduate study

General. Founded in 1890. Regionally accredited. **Degrees:** 391 bachelor's, 5 associate awarded; master's offered. **ROTC:** Army. **Location:** 150 miles from Minneapolis-St. Paul, 150 miles from Madison. **Calendar:** Semester, limited summer session. **Full-time faculty:** 107 total; 59% have terminal degrees, 5% minority, 57% women. **Part-time faculty:** 125 total; 25% have terminal degrees, 3% minority, 62% women. **Class size:** 64%

< 20, 34% 20-39, 1% 40-49, 1% 50-99. **Special facilities:** Center for ethics, science and technology; fine arts center; center for recreation and education in conjunction with Boys and Girls Club of America.

Freshman class profile. 1,294 applied, 1,110 admitted, 365 enrolled.

Mid 50% test scores		**Rank in top tenth:**	14%
ACT composite:	20-24	**End year in good standing:**	83%
GPA 3.75 or higher:	26%	**Return as sophomores:**	69%
GPA 3.50-3.74:	15%	**Out-of-state:**	25%
GPA 3.0-3.49:	32%	**Live on campus:**	93%
GPA 2.0-2.99:	26%	**International:**	2%
Rank in top quarter:	39%		

Basis for selection. High school GPA and ACT score most important, then placement testing. Auditions and portfolio reviews required for students applying to School of Fine Arts (music, theater, art, dance). Interview required for students not meeting admission requirements. **Homeschooled:** Transcript of courses and grades required. **Learning Disabled:** All students encouraged to file ADA petition for reasonable accommodations, preferably 8 weeks prior to start of classes.

High school preparation. College-preparatory program recommended. 16 units required; 19 recommended. Required and recommended units include English 3-4, mathematics 2, social studies 2, history 2, science 2 (laboratory 2), foreign language 2 and academic electives 5. Chemistry required for nursing, dietetics, natural sciences, allied health preprofessional students. Portfolios or auditions required for fine arts students.

2009-2010 Annual costs. Tuition/fees (projected): $20,160. Additional fees for some fine arts, dietetics, science courses, and nursing clinicals. Room/board: $7,510. Books/supplies: $850. Personal expenses: $1,800.

Financial aid. Non-need-based: Scholarships awarded for academics, alumni affiliation, art, athletics, leadership, minority status, music/drama, ROTC.

Application procedures. Admission: Priority date 8/1; no deadline. $25 fee, may be waived for applicants with need, free for online applicants. Admission notification on a rolling basis. Must reply by May 1 or within 2 week(s) if notified thereafter. **Financial aid:** Priority date 3/15; no closing date. FAFSA, institutional form required. Applicants notified on a rolling basis starting 4/1; must reply within 3 week(s) of notification.

Academics. Learning Center offers individual and small group tutoring in all subject areas daily. Library services available daily, on weekends and evenings. **Special study options:** Accelerated study, combined bachelor's/graduate degree, cross-registration, distance learning, double major, dual enrollment of high school students, honors, independent study, internships, liberal arts/career combination, student-designed major, study abroad, teacher certification program, urban semester, Washington semester, weekend college. Weekend college is basically at Master's level. **Credit/placement by examination:** AP, CLEP, IB, ACT, institutional tests. 30 credit hours maximum toward bachelor's degree. 16 hours awarded for military services. **Support services:** Learning center, reduced course load, remedial instruction, study skills assistance, tutoring, writing center.

Majors. Biology: General, biochemistry. **Business:** Accounting, business admin, management information systems, marketing. **Computer sciences:** General. **Education:** Art, biology, business, chemistry, drama/dance, elementary, English, mathematics, music, science, secondary, social studies, Spanish, technology/industrial arts. **Foreign languages:** Spanish. **Health:** Dietetics, nursing (RN). **Interdisciplinary:** Biological/physical sciences, natural sciences. **Liberal arts:** Arts/sciences. **Math:** General. **Philosophy/religion:** Religion. **Physical sciences:** Chemistry. **Protective services:** Criminal justice. **Psychology:** General. **Public administration:** Social work. **Social sciences:** General, sociology. **Visual/performing arts:** General, art, arts management, design, dramatic, graphic design, music pedagogy, music performance, studio arts. **Other:** English and theatre arts, Individualized learning, Ministry, Organizational management, Religious studies/philosophy.

Most popular majors. Business/marketing 21%, education 10%, health sciences 37%, interdisciplinary studies 8%, visual/performing arts 6%.

Computing on campus. 396 workstations in dormitories, library, computer center, student center. Dormitories wired for high-speed internet access and linked to campus network. Commuter students can connect to campus network. Online course registration, online library, helpline, wireless network available.

Student life. Freshman orientation: Mandatory. Preregistration for classes offered. One-day program offered 4 times in the summer for incoming freshmen and parents. **Policies:** Standards of conduct, sexual harassment code, anti-hazing initiation policy, academic honesty policy, academic due process, campus security policy, residence hall terms and conditions, alcohol and drug policy, student event policies. **Housing:** Guaranteed on-campus for freshmen. Coed dorms, apartments, wellness housing available. $100 fully refundable deposit, deadline 8/1. **Activities:** Pep band, campus ministries, choral groups, dance, drama, international student organizations, literary magazine, music ensembles, musical theater, opera, student government, student newspaper, Connect, Students in Free Enterprise, Circle K, student nurses association, education club, Sigma Pi Delta, CREW, Global Rhythms, psychology club.

Athletics. NAIA. **Intercollegiate:** Baseball M, basketball, bowling, cross-country, golf, soccer, softball W, volleyball W. **Intramural:** Badminton, basketball, bowling, cross-country, golf, handball, racquetball, rugby M, skiing, soccer, softball, table tennis, tennis, volleyball. **Team name:** V-Hawks.

Student services. Adult student services, alcohol/substance abuse counseling, chaplain/spiritual director, career counseling, services for economically disadvantaged, student employment services, financial aid counseling, health services, personal counseling, placement for graduates, veterans' counselor, women's services. **Physically disabled:** Services for visually, hearing impaired.

Contact. E-mail: admission@viterbo.edu
Phone: (608) 796-3010 Toll-free number: (800) 848-3726
Fax: (608) 796-3020
Roland Nelson, Vice President for Enrollment, Viterbo University, 900 Viterbo Drive, La Crosse, WI 54601-8804

Wisconsin Lutheran College

Milwaukee, Wisconsin
www.wlc.edu **CB code: 1513**

- Private 4-year liberal arts college affiliated with Wisconsin Evangelical Lutheran Synod
- Residential campus in very large city
- 755 undergraduates
- 76% of applicants admitted
- SAT or ACT (ACT writing optional) required

General. Founded in 1973. Regionally accredited. Challenging academic program in a conservative Christian environment. **Degrees:** 130 bachelor's awarded. **ROTC:** Army, Naval, Air Force. **Calendar:** Semester, limited summer session. **Full-time faculty:** 58 total. **Part-time faculty:** 42 total.

Freshman class profile. 646 applied, 493 admitted, 225 enrolled.

Mid 50% test scores	**ACT composite:**	21-26

Basis for selection. Test scores, class rank, GPA most important. Interview recommended for some; audition required for music scholarships.

High school preparation. 16 units required; 20 recommended. Required and recommended units include English 4, mathematics 3-4, history 2, science 2-3 (laboratory 1-2), foreign language 2-4 and academic electives 3. Mathematics or science majors should complete 4 units of mathematics and 3-4 units of appropriate science courses.

2008-2009 Annual costs. Tuition/fees: $20,560. Room/board: $7,300. Books/supplies: $700. Personal expenses: $1,440.

Financial aid. Non-need-based: Scholarships awarded for academics, art, leadership, minority status, music/drama, state residency.

Application procedures. Admission: Priority date 3/1; no deadline. $20 fee, may be waived for applicants with need, free for online applicants. Admission notification on a rolling basis beginning on or about 9/1. Must reply by May 1 or within 2 week(s) if notified thereafter. **Financial aid:** Priority date 3/1; no closing date. FAFSA, institutional form required. Applicants notified on a rolling basis starting 3/15; must reply within 2 week(s) of notification.

Academics. Special graduation requirements include freshman seminar. **Special study options:** Double major, dual enrollment of high school students, independent study, internships, student-designed major, study abroad, teacher certification program. **Credit/placement by examination:** AP, CLEP, institutional tests. **Support services:** Learning center, reduced course load, study skills assistance, tutoring, writing center.

Majors. Biology: General, biochemistry. **Business:** Managerial economics. **Communications:** General. **Education:** Elementary. **Foreign languages:** Spanish. **History:** General. **Math:** General. **Physical sciences:** Chemistry. **Psychology:** General. **Social sciences:** General, political science. **Theology:** Theology. **Visual/performing arts:** Art, dramatic.

Computing on campus. 200 workstations in dormitories, library, computer center, student center. Dormitories wired for high-speed internet access and linked to campus network. Commuter students can connect to campus network. Online library, helpline, repair service, wireless network available.

Student life. **Freshman orientation:** Mandatory. Preregistration for classes offered. 2-day program held week before start of fall semester. **Policies:** Drug free campus program. No alcohol on campus. Smoking permitted outside only. **Housing:** Guaranteed on-campus for all undergraduates. Single-sex dorms, apartments available. $100 deposit, deadline 5/1. All traditional age, unmarried students less than 5 years out of high school must live in college housing. Upperclassmen eligible for college apartments. **Activities:** Bands, choral groups, dance, drama, music ensembles, student government, student newspaper.

Athletics. NCAA. **Intercollegiate:** Baseball M, basketball, cross-country, football (tackle) M, golf, soccer, softball W, tennis W, track and field, volleyball W. **Intramural:** Basketball, football (tackle), softball, volleyball. **Team name:** Warriors.

Student services. Adult student services, chaplain/spiritual director, career counseling, student employment services, financial aid counseling, health services, personal counseling, placement for graduates. **Physically disabled:** Services for visually, hearing impaired.

Contact. E-mail: admissions@wlc.edu
Phone: (414) 443-8811 Toll-free number: (888) 947-5884
Fax: (414) 443-8514
Craig Swiontek, Director of Admissions, Wisconsin Lutheran College, 8800 West Bluemound Road, Milwaukee, WI 53226-4699

Wyoming

University of Wyoming

Laramie, Wyoming
www.uwyo.edu

CB member
CB code: 4855

- Public 4-year university
- Residential campus in large town
- 9,304 degree-seeking undergraduates: 15% part-time, 52% women, 1% African American, 1% Asian American, 4% Hispanic American, 1% Native American, 3% international
- 2,200 degree-seeking graduate students
- 96% of applicants admitted
- SAT or ACT (ACT writing optional) required
- 57% graduate within 6 years; 26% enter graduate study

General. Founded in 1886. Regionally accredited. Undergraduate and graduate degree programs offered in Casper. Extension classes available in off-campus locations throughout the state. Online classes offered nationally. **Degrees:** 1,786 bachelor's awarded; master's, doctoral, first professional offered. **ROTC:** Army, Air Force. **Location:** 45 miles from Cheyenne, 130 miles from Denver. **Calendar:** Semester, extensive summer session. **Full-time faculty:** 715 total; 84% have terminal degrees, 8% minority, 36% women. **Part-time faculty:** 52 total; 44% have terminal degrees, 4% minority, 58% women. **Class size:** 42% < 20, 43% 20-39, 6% 40-49, 4% 50-99, 4% >100. **Special facilities:** Museums (art, geological, anthropology, entomology), range herbarium, Rocky Mountain herbarium/mycological herbarium, spatial data and visualization center, botany conservatory, zoological center, learning resource center, meteorological station, Grand Teton National Park research center, planetarium, veterinary laboratory, materials characterization lab, biological research facility, on-site elementary school, infrared telescope observatory, survey research center, institute of environment/ natural resources, fishery and wildlife research unit, American heritage center, insect galleries.

Freshman class profile. 3,581 applied, 3,443 admitted, 1,693 enrolled.

Mid 50% test scores		**Rank in top tenth:**	23%
SAT critical reading:	470-610	**End year in good standing:**	74%
SAT math:	500-640	**Return as sophomores:**	73%
ACT composite:	21-27	**Out-of-state:**	54%
GPA 3.75 or higher:	35%	**Live on campus:**	88%
GPA 3.50-3.74:	19%	**International:**	3%
GPA 3.0-3.49:	29%	**Fraternities:**	7%
GPA 2.0-2.99:	17%	**Sororities:**	10%
Rank in top quarter:	51%		

Basis for selection. GPA, ACT or SAT scores and completion of 13 required units in pre-college curriculum most important. Test scores not required for non-degree-seeking students. **Homeschooled:** Credit evaluation form completed by homeschool instructor required. **Learning Disabled:** Must apply and present documentation of disability.

High school preparation. College-preparatory program required. 13 units required; 19 recommended. Required and recommended units include English 4, mathematics 3-4, science 3-4 (laboratory 3) and foreign language 2. 3 cultural context electives required. Select from behavioral or social sciences; visual or performing arts; humanities or earth/space sciences.

2009-2010 Annual costs. Tuition/fees: $3,686; $11,606 out-of-state. International students must pay an additional $40 fee per semester. Room/board: $8,006. Books/supplies: $1,200. Personal expenses: $2,200.

2007-2008 Financial aid. Need-based: 1,205 full-time freshmen applied for aid; 711 were judged to have need; 693 of these received aid. Average need met was 35%. Average scholarship/grant was $3,085; average loan $2,816. 41% of total undergraduate aid awarded as scholarships/grants, 59% as loans/jobs. **Non-need-based:** Awarded to 3,780 full-time undergraduates, including 774 freshmen. Scholarships awarded for academics, alumni affiliation, art, athletics, leadership, minority status, music/drama, religious affiliation, ROTC, state residency.

Application procedures. Admission: Priority date 3/1; deadline 8/10 (postmark date). $40 fee, may be waived for applicants with need. Admission notification on a rolling basis. Early application recommended for students seeking financial aid and university housing preferences. **Financial aid:** Priority date 2/1; no closing date. FAFSA required. Applicants notified by 3/15; Applicants notified on a rolling basis starting 3/15; must reply within 3 week(s) of notification.

Academics. Remedial instruction offered on campus through Laramie County Community College. **Special study options:** Accelerated study, distance learning, double major, ESL, exchange student, external degree, honors, independent study, internships, semester at sea, student-designed major, study abroad, Washington semester. **Credit/placement by examination:** AP, CLEP, IB, SAT, ACT, institutional tests. Unlimited hours of credit examination may be counted toward a bachelor's degree. Individual departments may also allow additional tests on case-by-case basis. **Support services:** Learning center, pre-admission summer program, reduced course load, study skills assistance, tutoring, writing center.

Majors. Agriculture: Agribusiness operations, animal sciences, communications, range science. **Area/ethnic studies:** American, women's. **Biology:** General, botany, microbiology, molecular, physiology, wildlife, zoology. **Business:** Accounting, business admin, finance, management science, managerial economics, marketing. **Communications:** General, journalism. **Computer sciences:** Computer science. **Conservation:** Environmental studies. **Education:** Agricultural, elementary, music, physical, secondary, special, technology/industrial arts, trade/industrial. **Engineering:** Architectural, chemical, civil, computer, electrical, mechanical, petroleum. **Family/consumer sciences:** General. **Foreign languages:** French, German, Russian, Spanish. **Health:** Audiology/speech pathology, dental hygiene, health services, nursing (RN). **History:** General. **Liberal arts:** Humanities. **Math:** General, statistics. **Parks/recreation:** Exercise sciences. **Philosophy/religion:** Philosophy. **Physical sciences:** General, chemistry, geology, physics. **Protective services:** Criminal justice. **Psychology:** General. **Public administration:** Social work. **Social sciences:** General, anthropology, geography, international relations, political science, sociology. **Visual/performing arts:** Art, dramatic, music performance.

Most popular majors. Agriculture 7%, biology 6%, business/marketing 13%, education 14%, engineering/engineering technologies 9%, health sciences 7%, social sciences 8%.

Computing on campus. 885 workstations in dormitories, library, computer center, student center. Dormitories wired for high-speed internet access and linked to campus network. Commuter students can connect to campus network. Online course registration, online library, helpline, student web hosting, wireless network available.

Student life. Freshman orientation: Available, $60 fee. Preregistration for classes offered. One 2-day session in May; 8 in June. **Policies:** New freshmen subject to live-in policy. **Housing:** Guaranteed on-campus for all undergraduates. Coed dorms, special housing for disabled, apartments, fraternity/sorority housing available. $100 partly refundable deposit. **Activities:** Bands, campus ministries, choral groups, dance, drama, international student organizations, literary magazine, music ensembles, Model UN, musical theater, opera, radio station, student government, student newspaper, symphony orchestra, TV station, black student leaders, local church organizations, College Republicans, Rocky Mountain Democrats, Fellowship of Christian Athletes, Amnesty International, lesbian/gay/bisexual/transgendered association, Movimiento Estudiantil Chicanos de Atzlan, student health advisory council.

Athletics. NCAA. **Intercollegiate:** Basketball, cross-country, diving, football (tackle) M, golf, soccer W, swimming, tennis W, track and field, volleyball W, wrestling M. **Intramural:** Badminton, basketball, bowling, football (non-tackle), golf, racquetball, soccer, softball, swimming, table tennis, tennis, track and field, volleyball, water polo, wrestling M. **Team name:** Cowboys, Cowgirls.

Student services. Adult student services, alcohol/substance abuse counseling, career counseling, services for economically disadvantaged, student employment services, financial aid counseling, health services, legal services, minority student services, on-campus daycare, personal counseling, placement for graduates, veterans' counselor, women's services. **Physically disabled:** Services for visually, speech, hearing impaired. **Learning disabled:** Comprehensive services available.

Contact. E-mail: why-wyo@uwyo.edu
Phone: (307) 766-5160 Toll-free number: (800) 342-5996
Fax: (307) 766-4042
Noah Buckley, Director of Admissions, University of Wyoming, 1000 East University Avenue/Department 3435, Laramie, WY 82071

Guam

University of Guam
Mangilao, Guam
www.uog.edu **CB code: 0959**

- Public 4-year university
- Large town
- 3,000 degree-seeking undergraduates

General. Founded in 1952. Regionally accredited. **Degrees:** 275 bachelor's, 4 associate awarded; master's offered. **ROTC:** Army. **Calendar:** Semester, limited summer session. **Full-time faculty:** 182 total. **Part-time faculty:** 69 total. **Special facilities:** University-operated athletic center, planetarium, marine lab, Pacific and Micronesian library resources.

Freshman class profile. 597 enrolled.

Basis for selection. Open admission, but selective for some programs.

2008-2009 Annual costs. Books/supplies: $705. Personal expenses: $1,830.

2007-2008 Financial aid. Need-based: 93% of total undergraduate aid awarded as scholarships/grants, 7% as loans/jobs.

Application procedures. Admission: $49 fee. Admission notification on a rolling basis. **Financial aid:** Priority date 4/15; no closing date. FAFSA required. Applicants notified on a rolling basis starting 6/1; must reply within 2 week(s) of notification.

Academics. Special study options: Double major, internships. **Credit/placement by examination:** CLEP, institutional tests. **Support services:** Reduced course load, remedial instruction, tutoring.

Majors. Biology: General. **Business:** Accounting, business admin, finance, international. **Communications:** General. **Computer sciences:** General. **Education:** Bilingual, early childhood, elementary, physical, secondary, special. **Family/consumer sciences:** General. **Health:** Nursing (RN). **History:** General. **Math:** General. **Physical sciences:** Chemistry. **Protective services:** Criminal justice. **Psychology:** General. **Public administration:** General, social work. **Social sciences:** Anthropology, economics, political science, sociology. **Visual/performing arts:** Art.

Computing on campus. Dormitories linked to campus network. Commuter students can connect to campus network. Wireless network available.

Student life. Housing: Single-sex dorms available. **Activities:** Choral groups, dance, drama, musical theater, student government, student newspaper.

Athletics. Intercollegiate: Archery, badminton, baseball M, basketball, bowling, boxing M, cross-country, diving, equestrian, fencing, field hockey W, football (tackle) M, golf, gymnastics, handball, ice hockey, lacrosse, racquetball, rifle, rowing (crew), rugby, sailing, skiing, soccer, softball, squash, swimming, table tennis, tennis, track and field, volleyball, water polo, wrestling M. **Intramural:** Archery, badminton, baseball M, basketball, bowling, boxing M, cross-country, diving, equestrian, fencing, field hockey W, football (tackle) M, golf, gymnastics, handball, ice hockey, lacrosse, racquetball, rifle, rowing (crew), rugby, sailing, skiing, skin diving, soccer, softball, squash, swimming, table tennis, tennis, track and field, volleyball, water polo, wrestling M. **Team name:** Tritons.

Student services. Student employment services, health services, on-campus daycare, personal counseling, placement for graduates.

Contact. E-mail: admitme@uog.edu
Phone: (671) 735-2201
Remedios Cristobal, Registrar, University of Guam, UOG Station, Mangilao, GU 96923

Virgin Islands, U.S.

University of the Virgin Islands
St. Thomas, Virgin Islands, U.S. **CB member**
www.uvi.edu **CB code: 0879**

- Public 4-year university
- Commuter campus in small city
- 2,083 degree-seeking undergraduates: 34% part-time, 73% women, 75% African American, 7% Hispanic American, 7% international
- 161 degree-seeking graduate students
- 68% of applicants admitted
- SAT or ACT (ACT writing optional) required
- 32% graduate within 6 years

General. Founded in 1962. Regionally accredited. Additional campus on St. Croix. Housing available on St. Thomas and St. Croix. **Degrees:** 193 bachelor's, 69 associate awarded; master's offered. **ROTC:** Army. **Location:** 45 miles from San Juan, Puerto Rico. **Calendar:** Semester, limited summer session. **Full-time faculty:** 103 total; 66% have terminal degrees, 57% minority, 42% women. **Part-time faculty:** 111 total; 19% have terminal degrees, 81% minority, 57% women. **Class size:** 76% < 20, 23% 20-39, less than 1% 40-49, less than 1% 50-99. **Special facilities:** Outdoor amphitheater, Caribbean collection, African art collection.

Freshman class profile. 1,236 applied, 839 admitted, 596 enrolled.

Mid 50% test scores		**GPA 2.0-2.99:**	67%
SAT critical reading:	340-450	**Rank in top quarter:**	30%
SAT math:	320-430	**Rank in top tenth:**	12%
SAT writing:	350-450	**End year in good standing:**	95%
ACT composite:	13-19	**Return as sophomores:**	73%
GPA 3.75 or higher:	4%	**Out-of-state:**	4%
GPA 3.50-3.74:	5%	**International:**	8%
GPA 3.0-3.49:	20%		

Basis for selection. Secondary school record very important. Must have at least a 2.0 GPA. Nursing Aptitude Test required of nursing applicants.

High school preparation. 11 units required. Required units include English 4, mathematics 2, social studies 2, science 2 and foreign language 1.

2009-2010 Annual costs. Tuition/fees: $4,100; $11,300 out-of-state. Room/board: $8,420. Books/supplies: $1,500. Personal expenses: $1,800.

2007-2008 Financial aid. Need-based: 304 full-time freshmen applied for aid; 286 were judged to have need; 271 of these received aid. Average scholarship/grant was $3,870; average loan $2,875. 71% of total undergraduate aid awarded as scholarships/grants, 29% as loans/jobs. **Non-need-based:** Awarded to 226 full-time undergraduates, including 150 freshmen. Scholarships awarded for academics, art, athletics.

Application procedures. Admission: Priority date 2/1; deadline 4/30 (postmark date). $30 fee. Admission notification on a rolling basis. Must reply by 6/30. **Financial aid:** Closing date 3/1. FAFSA required. Applicants notified on a rolling basis starting 4/1; must reply within 2 week(s) of notification.

Academics. Special study options: Combined bachelor's/graduate degree, distance learning, exchange student, external degree, independent study, internships. **Credit/placement by examination:** AP, CLEP, SAT, ACT, institutional tests. **Support services:** Learning center, pre-admission summer program, reduced course load, remedial instruction, study skills assistance, tutoring, writing center.

Majors. Biology: General, marine. **Business:** Accounting, business admin. **Computer sciences:** Computer science. **Education:** Elementary, music. **Health:** Nursing (RN). **Liberal arts:** Arts/sciences. **Math:** General. **Physical sciences:** Chemistry. **Protective services:** Police science. **Psychology:** General. **Social sciences:** General.

Most popular majors. Biology 8%, business/marketing 46%, education 10%, psychology 6%.

Computing on campus. 150 workstations in library, computer center, student center. Dormitories linked to campus network. Online course registration, helpline, wireless network available.

Student life. Freshman orientation: Mandatory, $90 fee. One-week orientation activities held on both campuses. **Housing:** Single-sex dorms available. $100 partly refundable deposit, deadline 6/1. **Activities:** Jazz band, choral groups, drama, music ensembles, student government, student newspaper, political clubs, president's club, Future Business Leaders of America, explorer's club, Virgin Islands student association, British Virgin Islands student association, Baptist Student Union, environment association, peer health educators.

Athletics. NCAA. **Intercollegiate:** Basketball, cross-country, tennis, volleyball. **Intramural:** Archery, badminton, basketball, fencing, golf, gymnastics, racquetball, softball, swimming, table tennis, tennis, track and field, volleyball. **Team name:** Bucs.

Student services. Career counseling, student employment services, financial aid counseling, health services, personal counseling, placement for graduates. **Physically disabled:** Services for visually, speech, hearing impaired.

Contact. E-mail: admissions@uvi.edu
Phone: (340) 693-1150 Fax: (340) 693-1155
Edward Alexander, Director of Admissions, University of the Virgin Islands, No. 2 John Brewers Bay, St. Thomas, VI 00802-9990

Northern Mariana Islands

Northern Marianas College

Saipan, Northern Mariana Islands
www.nmcnet.edu **CB code: 0781**

- Public two-year upper-division community and liberal arts college
- Commuter campus in large town

General. Founded in 1981. Regionally accredited. **Degrees:** 28 bachelor's, 81 associate awarded. **ROTC:** Army. **Location:** 150 miles from Guam, 3,000 miles from Hawaii. **Calendar:** Semester, limited summer session. **Full-time faculty:** 27 total. **Part-time faculty:** 26 total. **Special facilities:** Commonwealth of the Northern Marianas Archives.

Student profile. 709 degree-seeking undergraduates.

Basis for selection. Open admission. College transcript required. Transfer accepted as sophomores.

2008-2009 Annual costs. Books/supplies: $1,500. Personal expenses: $900.

Application procedures. Admission: Rolling admission. $25 fee ($50 out-of-state). **Financial aid:** FAFSA required.

Academics. Special study options: Cooperative education, cross-registration, distance learning, ESL, independent study, internships, teacher certification program. **Credit/placement by examination:** CLEP, institutional tests. **Support services:** Learning center, remedial instruction, tutoring.

Majors. Education: Elementary.

Computing on campus. 40 workstations in computer center.

Student life. Activities: Radio station, student government.

Athletics. Intramural: Baseball, basketball M, softball, table tennis, volleyball. **Team name:** Proa.

Student services. Career counseling, student employment services, financial aid counseling, personal counseling, veterans' counselor. **Physically disabled:** Services for visually, speech, hearing impaired.

Contact. Phone: (670) 234-3690 ext. 1528 Fax: (670) 235-4967
Rosaline Cepeda, Director of Admissions and Records, Northern Marianas College, PO Box 501250, Saipan, MP 96950

Bolivia

Universidad Privada Boliviana

Cochabamba, Bolivia
www.upb.edu **CB code: 0856**

- Private 4-year university, business and engineering college
- Very large city

General. Founded in 1992. **Location:** 4 miles from Cochabamba City. **Calendar:** Semester.

Annual costs/financial aid. Books/supplies: $400.

Contact. Phone: (4) 426-8287 ext. 255
Director of Admissions, Km 6.5 camimo antiguo a Quillacollo Casilla: 3967, Cochabamba, BO

Canada

Acadia University

Wolfville, Canada
www.acadiau.ca **CB code: 0901**

- Public 4-year university
- Residential campus in small town
- 2,864 degree-seeking undergraduates: 3% part-time, 56% women
- 390 graduate students
- SAT required

General. Regionally accredited. **Degrees:** 778 bachelor's awarded; master's, first professional offered. **Location:** 60 miles from Halifax. **Calendar:** Semester, limited summer session. **Full-time faculty:** 211 total. **Part-time faculty:** 37 total. **Special facilities:** Environmental science center and botanical gardens.

Basis for selection. GED not accepted. Academic record and recommendations most important. Class rank and standardized test scores also important. **Homeschooled:** Applicants considered on a case-by-case basis.

High school preparation. Required and recommended units include English 3, mathematics 2, history 2 and science 2.

2008-2009 Annual costs. Costs reported in Canadian dollars: $13,754 annually for tuition/fees for international students and $7,467 annually for Canadian students (non-Nova Scotia residents); $7,771 for room & board; $800 health/dental insurance fee for non-Canadian international students, $309 for Canadian students. Books/supplies: $1,300.

Financial aid. Non-need-based: Scholarships awarded for academics, athletics.

Application procedures. Admission: Priority date 3/1; no deadline. $25 fee, may be waived for applicants with need. Admission notification on a rolling basis beginning on or about 10/1.

Academics. Acadia Advantage program integrates technology into the undergraduate curriculum. **Special study options:** Combined bachelor's/graduate degree, cooperative education, distance learning, double major, ESL, exchange student, honors, independent study, internships, liberal arts/career combination, semester at sea, study abroad, teacher certification program. **Credit/placement by examination:** AP, CLEP, IB. **Support services:** Remedial instruction, study skills assistance, tutoring, writing center.

Majors. Area/ethnic studies: Canadian. **Biology:** General. **Business:** General. **Computer sciences:** General. **Conservation:** Environmental science.

Education: General. **Family/consumer sciences:** Food/nutrition. **Foreign languages:** General. **History:** General. **Math:** General. **Parks/recreation:** General, exercise sciences. **Philosophy/religion:** Philosophy. **Physical sciences:** Chemistry, geology, physics. **Psychology:** General. **Social sciences:** Economics, political science, sociology. **Theology:** Theology. **Visual/performing arts:** Dramatic.

Most popular majors. Biology 7%, business/marketing 18%, education 18%, history 7%, parks/recreation 10%, psychology 6%, social sciences 13%.

Computing on campus. PC or laptop required. Dormitories wired for high-speed internet access and linked to campus network. Commuter students can connect to campus network. Online course registration, online library, helpline, repair service, student web hosting, wireless network available.

Student life. Freshman orientation: Available. Preregistration for classes offered. **Housing:** Guaranteed on-campus for all undergraduates. Coed dorms, single-sex dorms, special housing for disabled, wellness housing available. $100 deposit. **Activities:** Bands, choral groups, dance, drama, literary magazine, music ensembles, musical theater, opera, radio station, student government, student newspaper, symphony orchestra.

Athletics. Intercollegiate: Basketball, cross-country W, football (tackle) M, ice hockey M, rugby W, soccer, volleyball W. **Intramural:** Badminton, baseball, basketball, cheerleading, football (non-tackle) M, football (tackle) M, ice hockey, rugby, soccer, softball, track and field, volleyball. **Team name:** Axemen/Axewomen.

Student services. Chaplain/spiritual director, career counseling, student employment services, financial aid counseling, health services, legal services, minority student services, personal counseling, women's services. **Physically disabled:** Services for visually, hearing impaired.

Contact. E-mail: admissions@acadiau.ca
Phone: (902) 585-1016 Fax: (902) 585-1081
Anne Scott, Manager of Admissions, Acadia University, University Hall, Room 126, Wolfville, CN

McGill University

Montreal, Canada — **CB member**
www.mcgill.ca — **CB code: 0935**

- Public 4-year university
- Commuter campus in very large city
- 20,831 degree-seeking undergraduates: 12% part-time, 59% women, 17% international
- 8,737 degree-seeking graduate students
- 54% of applicants admitted
- 85% graduate within 6 years

General. Founded in 1821. In addition to main campus, McGill maintains Macdonald Campus (20 miles west of downtown Montreal campus), which occupies 1,600 acres on western tip of island. **Degrees:** 4,584 bachelor's awarded; master's, doctoral, first professional offered. **Location:** Main campus located at the foot of Mount Royal, in the heart of downtown Montreal. The Macdonald campus is situated on the western tip of the island of Montreal, in Saint Anne de Bellevue. **Calendar:** Semester, limited summer session. **Full-time faculty:** 1,689 total; 95% have terminal degrees, 29% women. **Part-time faculty:** 867 total; 41% have terminal degrees, 48% women. **Class size:** 35% < 20, 27% 20-39, 7% 40-49, 20% 50-99, 11% >100. **Special facilities:** Museum of Canadian history, museum of natural history, entomological museum and research laboratory, ecomuseum, Canadian architecture collection, arboretum, nature reserve, herbarium, Canadian history archives, arctic research station, subarctic research station, sound recording studio.

Freshman class profile. 21,242 applied, 11,380 admitted, 5,035 enrolled.

Mid 50% test scores		**GPA 3.0-3.49:**	49%
SAT critical reading:	640-740	**GPA 2.0-2.99:**	1%
SAT math:	650-720	**Return as sophomores:**	93%
SAT writing:	650-730	**Out-of-state:**	43%
ACT composite:	29-32	**Live on campus:**	51%
GPA 3.75 or higher:	12%	**International:**	18%
GPA 3.50-3.74:	38%		

Basis for selection. GED not accepted. School achievement record, grades in prerequisite courses, test scores most important. Advanced Placement (AP) results, class rank, recommendations also considered. Generally, minimum of 3.3 high school GPA required. For demonstration of English proficiency, TOEFL, Michigan, IELTS or APIEL acceptable. SAT I and II or ACT required for U.S. students, optional for Canadian. Audition required of music majors. Portfolio required of architecture majors. Language tests required for TESL education programs. **Homeschooled:** Statement describing homeschool structure and mission, transcript of courses and grades, letter of recommendation (nonparent) required. Description should include comprehensive list of all texts (and editions) studied, personal statement from applicant and separate statement from home educator. In some cases, further information and/or interview(s) with admissions officer, associate dean, or program director may be required. **Learning Disabled:** No special admission requirements, no specific allowances. Students not asked questions about disabilities in admissions application. Students free to add extenuating circumstances information with application.

High school preparation. College-preparatory program required. 15 units recommended. Recommended units include English 4, mathematics 4, social studies 1, history 1, science 3 (laboratory 3) and foreign language 3. 15-20 total recommended academic units; 3 or more combined recommended units for social studies and history. High school requirements vary according to program.

2008-2009 Annual costs. Costs reported in Canadian dollars. Full-time tuition for Quebec residents $1,868, for other Canadian students $5,378, for international students $13,965 to $15,420 depending on program. Required fees start at $1,425 and range upward depending on program. Room and board $8,996 to $12,948. Per-credit-hour charges for Quebec residents $62, for other Canadian students $179, for international students $467 to $514 depending on program. Compulsory health insurance for international students $639 (single), $1,794 (dependent), and $3,408 (family). Books and supplies $1,000 and transportation (public transit system) $407. Other expenses estimated at $2,000. Books/supplies: $1,000. Personal expenses: $2,000.

2007-2008 Financial aid. All financial aid based on need. 38% of total undergraduate aid awarded as scholarships/grants, 62% as loans/jobs. **Additional information:** McGill offers awards ranging in value from $3,000 renewable to $10,000 renewable and based on outstanding academic achievement or combination of outstanding academic achievement and leadership qualities. Finalists for scholarships valued at over $5,000 may be interviewed. Students who meet following eligibility conditions may apply for entrance awards: must be entering a university for the first time to undertake full-time undergraduate degree program; must be in top 5% of class based on last 2 years of full-time studies.

Application procedures. Admission: Closing date 1/15 (postmark date). $85 fee. Admission notification on a rolling basis beginning on or about 1/30. Must reply by May 1 or within 3 week(s) if notified thereafter. Reply by dates are later for CEGEP and Canadian high schools. Closing dates for transfer students are January 15 for international students, May 1 for Canadian students, and June 15 for Quebec students. **Financial aid:** Closing date 6/30. Institutional form required. Applicants notified on a rolling basis starting 3/1; must reply within 4 week(s) of notification.

Academics. Students permitted to submit papers and exams in French. **Special study options:** Accelerated study, combined bachelor's/graduate degree, cooperative education, cross-registration, distance learning, double major, ESL, exchange student, honors, independent study, internships, study abroad, teacher certification program, Washington semester. **Credit/placement by examination:** AP, CLEP, IB, institutional tests. 30 credit hours maximum toward bachelor's degree. Maximum 30 AP credits on 120-credit program. **Support services:** Pre-admission summer program, reduced course load, remedial instruction, study skills assistance, tutoring.

Majors. Agriculture: General, agronomy, animal sciences, business, economics, food science, horticulture, plant sciences, soil science. **Architecture:** Architecture. **Area/ethnic studies:** African, Canadian, Caribbean, East Asian, German, Hispanic-American/Latino/Chicano, Italian, Latin American, Near/Middle Eastern, regional, Russian/Slavic, Spanish/Iberian, women's. **Biology:** General, anatomy, animal behavior, aquatic, bacteriology, biochemistry, biomedical sciences, botany, cell/histology, cellular/anatomical, ecology, environmental, genetics, marine, microbiology, molecular, neuroanatomy, physiology, wildlife, zoology. **Business:** General, accounting, accounting/finance, entrepreneurial studies, finance, human resources, international, international finance, labor relations, management science, managerial economics, marketing, operations, organizational behavior. **Computer sciences:** General, computer science. **Conservation:** General, economics, environmental science, environmental studies, management/policy, wildlife. **Education:** General, bilingual, biology, chemistry, early childhood, elementary, English, ESL, French, geography, health, history, mathematics, music, physical, physics, science, secondary, social science, social studies. **Engineering:** Agricultural, chemical, civil, computer, electrical, materials, mechanical, metallurgical, mining, software. **Family/consumer sciences:** Food/nutrition, human nutrition. **Foreign languages:** Classics, East Asian, French, German, Italian, linguistics, Russian, Spanish, translation. **Health:** Nursing (RN). **History:** General, Asian, Canadian history, European. **Interdisciplinary:** Biological/physical sciences, cognitive science, math/

computer science, natural sciences, nutrition sciences. **Legal studies:** General. **Liberal arts:** Humanities. **Math:** General, applied, probability, statistics. **Parks/recreation:** Exercise sciences, health/fitness. **Philosophy/religion:** Judaic, philosophy, religion. **Physical sciences:** Analytical chemistry, atmospheric physics, atmospheric science, chemistry, geology, geophysics, hydrology, inorganic chemistry, organic chemistry, physics, planetary. **Psychology:** General. **Public administration:** Social work. **Social sciences:** Anthropology, economics, geography, international economic development, political science, sociology, urban studies. **Theology:** Religious ed, sacred music, theology. **Visual/performing arts:** Art history/conservation, dramatic, jazz, music history, music pedagogy, music performance, music theory/composition, piano/organ, stringed instruments, voice/opera.

Most popular majors. Biology 11%, business/marketing 13%, education 7%, engineering/engineering technologies 8%, health sciences 8%, psychology 6%, social sciences 17%.

Computing on campus. 3,730 workstations in dormitories, library, computer center, student center. Dormitories wired for high-speed internet access and linked to campus network. Commuter students can connect to campus network. Online course registration, online library, helpline, repair service, wireless network available.

Student life. **Freshman orientation:** Available. One-day campus-wide orientation session held at end of August; new students meet administrators, senior students from their programs. **Housing:** Guaranteed on-campus for freshmen. Coed dorms, single-sex dorms, special housing for disabled, apartments, wellness housing available. $1,500 partly refundable deposit, deadline 6/15. Shared facilities housing, which is similar to cooperative housing; however, chores and costs not shared among the students. **Activities:** Bands, choral groups, dance, drama, film society, international student organizations, literary magazine, music ensembles, musical theater, opera, radio station, student government, student newspaper, symphony orchestra, TV station, over 100 clubs, service groups, and independent student organizations with interests that include sports, social activities, religion and politics.

Athletics. **Intercollegiate:** Badminton, baseball M, basketball, cheerleading, cross-country, fencing, field hockey W, football (tackle) M, golf, ice hockey, lacrosse, rowing (crew), rugby, sailing, skiing, soccer, squash, swimming, synchronized swimming W, tennis, track and field, volleyball, wrestling. **Intramural:** Badminton, basketball, football (non-tackle), ice hockey, soccer, squash, table tennis, tennis, volleyball. **Team name:** Redmen, Martlets.

Student services. Adult student services, alcohol/substance abuse counseling, chaplain/spiritual director, career counseling, services for economically disadvantaged, student employment services, financial aid counseling, health services, legal services, minority student services, on-campus daycare, personal counseling, placement for graduates, women's services. **Physically disabled:** Services for visually, speech, hearing impaired.

Contact. E-mail: admissions@mcgill.ca
Phone: (514) 398-3910 Fax: (514) 398-4193
Kim Bartlett, Director, Admissions and Recruitment, McGill University, 845 Sherbrooke Street West, Montreal, CN H3A-2T5

Memorial University of Newfoundland

St. John's, Newfoundland, Canada — **CB member**
www.mun.ca — **CB code: 0885**

- Public 4-year university
- Commuter campus in small city
- 14,429 degree-seeking undergraduates: 15% part-time, 61% women
- 2,626 graduate students

General. Founded in 1925. Additional campus (Sir Wilfred Grenfell College) in Corner Brook, Newfoundland; campus in Harlow, England. **Degrees:** 2,597 bachelor's awarded; master's, doctoral, first professional offered. **Location:** Located in St. John's. **Calendar:** Trimester, limited summer session. **Full-time faculty:** 1,151 total; 33% women. **Part-time faculty:** 45 total; 22% women. **Special facilities:** Center for cold ocean resources engineering, botanical gardens, archaeology unit, ocean sciences center, flume tank, center for fisheries innovation, marine simulator.

Basis for selection. GED not accepted. School achievement in a university preparatory high school program most important. Non-native speakers of English must submit TOEFL, Michigan Test of English Proficiency (minimum score of 85), or other acceptable test, unless graduating from English-language high school. Interviews, auditions, and essay required of music, theater, and visual arts majors. Portfolio required of visual arts majors.

High school preparation. 16 units required. Required units include English 3, mathematics 3, social studies 1, science 2, foreign language 1 and academic electives 6.

2008-2009 Annual costs. Costs reported in Canadian dollars. Annual tuition for Canadians $2,550; for non-Canadians $8,800. Required fees $200. Room and board $6,138. Books/supplies: $700.

Application procedures. **Admission:** Closing date 3/1 (receipt date). $40 fee. Admission notification on a rolling basis beginning on or about 4/30. Application fee $40 CAD for in-province residents, $80 CAD for out-of-province and international students. Housing deposit $200 CAD. **Financial aid:** Priority date 3/15; no closing date.

Academics. 3-year diplomas in fisheries and nautical science available from Marine Institute. **Special study options:** Accelerated study, cooperative education, distance learning, double major, ESL, exchange student, honors, internships, liberal arts/career combination, study abroad, teacher certification program. **Credit/placement by examination:** AP, CLEP, IB. **Support services:** Learning center, reduced course load, remedial instruction, study skills assistance, tutoring, writing center.

Majors. **Area/ethnic studies:** Canadian, regional, Russian/Slavic, women's. **Biology:** General, bacteriology, biochemistry, cell/histology, ecology, entomology, marine, parasitology. **Business:** Business admin, marketing. **Computer sciences:** General, computer science. **Conservation:** General, environmental studies, forestry. **Education:** General, adult/continuing, bilingual, biology, chemistry, curriculum, early childhood, elementary, French, history, music, physical, physics, reading, science, secondary, social science, social studies, special. **Engineering:** General, civil, electrical, marine, mechanical, ocean. **Foreign languages:** Classics, French, German, linguistics, Spanish. **Health:** Preop/surgical nursing. **History:** General. **Interdisciplinary:** Math/computer science, medieval/Renaissance, neuroscience, nutrition sciences. **Liberal arts:** Arts/sciences, humanities. **Math:** General, applied, statistics. **Parks/recreation:** General, facilities management. **Philosophy/religion:** Philosophy, religion. **Physical sciences:** Chemistry, geology, oceanography, physics. **Psychology:** General. **Social sciences:** Anthropology, archaeology, demography, economics, geography, political science, sociology. **Visual/performing arts:** General, dramatic, music history, music performance, music theory/composition, studio arts, theater design.

Most popular majors. Biology 6%, business/marketing 12%, education 21%, engineering/engineering technologies 6%, health sciences 11%, science technologies 7%.

Computing on campus. 850 workstations in dormitories, library, computer center. Dormitories wired for high-speed internet access and linked to campus network. Commuter students can connect to campus network. Online course registration, helpline, repair service, student web hosting, wireless network available.

Student life. **Freshman orientation:** Mandatory. Held a few days prior to start of classes. **Housing:** Coed dorms, single-sex dorms, special housing for disabled, apartments available. $500 nonrefundable deposit, deadline 5/31. **Activities:** Bands, choral groups, dance, drama, international student organizations, literary magazine, music ensembles, musical theater, radio station, student government, student newspaper, symphony orchestra, numerous clubs and societies available.

Athletics. **Intercollegiate:** Basketball, cross-country, diving, fencing, field hockey W, soccer, swimming, volleyball. **Intramural:** Badminton, basketball, boxing, cheerleading, cross-country, diving, fencing, field hockey W, ice hockey M, judo, racquetball, rifle, soccer, softball, squash, swimming, table tennis, tennis, volleyball, water polo, weight lifting M, wrestling. **Team name:** Seahawks.

Student services. Chaplain/spiritual director, career counseling, student employment services, health services, on-campus daycare, personal counseling, placement for graduates, women's services. **Physically disabled:** Services for visually, speech, hearing impaired.

Contact. E-mail: admissions@mun.ca
Phone: (709) 737-4431 Fax: (709) 737-4893
Glenn Collins, Registrar, Memorial University of Newfoundland, Memorial University of Newfoundland, Admissions Office-Arts and Admin. Bldg, St. John's, Newfoundland, Canada, CN A1C-S7

Simon Fraser University

Burnaby, Canada — **CB member**
www.sfu.ca — **CB code: 0999**

- Public 4-year university
- Commuter campus in very large city
- 22,816 degree-seeking undergraduates
- 64% of applicants admitted
- SAT or ACT (ACT writing recommended) required

General. Founded in 1965. Regionally accredited. Harbour Centre campus in downtown Vancouver; Surrey campus in Surrey, British Columbia. **Degrees:** 4,160 bachelor's awarded; master's, doctoral offered. **Location:** 9 miles from Vancouver, British Columbia. **Calendar:** Trimester, extensive summer session. **Full-time faculty:** 937 total; 87% have terminal degrees, 34% women. **Class size:** 24% < 20, 35% 20-39, 12% 40-49, 14% 50-99, 15% >100. **Special facilities:** Climbing wall, child care facility, hyperbaric chamber, underwater laboratory, combative room, apiary, archaeology museum.

Freshman class profile. 16,498 applied, 10,610 admitted, 5,226 enrolled.

Basis for selection. GED not accepted. Senior academic courses, test scores, and advanced academic course work (International Baccalaureate, Advanced Placement, honors, etc.). Successful applicants normally require GPA of 2.80 or above (3.00 for programs in the Faculty of Business Administration) and SAT score of 1550 or higher (ACT 22). Academic background, GPA and test scores most important. Canadian residents not required to submit SAT or ACT. Audition/interview may be required for school of contemporary arts. Applicants may submit personal information profile and at least one letter of reference. **Homeschooled:** Transcript of courses and grades required. Applicants must meet state high school graduation requirements.

High school preparation. 13 units required. Required units include English 4, mathematics 3, social studies 1, history 1, science 2 and foreign language 2.

Financial aid. Non-need-based: Scholarships awarded for academics, art, athletics, leadership, minority status, music/drama, state residency.

Application procedures. Admission: Priority date 2/28; deadline 4/30 (receipt date). $45 fee ($100 out-of-state). Application must be submitted online. Admission notification 6/30. Admission notification on a rolling basis beginning on or about 1/25. Must reply by May 1 or within 3 week(s) if notified thereafter. Application fee of $100 (Canadian) if academic records originate outside of Canada. **Financial aid:** Priority date 7/1, closing date 11/15. Institutional form required.

Academics. Special study options: Cooperative education, distance learning, double major, exchange student, honors, independent study, study abroad, teacher certification program. Dual degree program with Zhejiang University in China. **Credit/placement by examination:** AP, CLEP, IB. 60 credit hours maximum toward bachelor's degree. **Support services:** Learning center, study skills assistance, writing center.

Majors. Area/ethnic studies: Canadian, women's. **Biology:** General, biochemistry, molecular. **Business:** Accounting/business management, actuarial science, business admin, entrepreneurial studies, finance, management information systems, management science, marketing. **Communications:** General, digital media. **Computer sciences:** General, information systems, programming. **Conservation:** General, environmental science, environmental studies. **Education:** General. **Engineering:** Science. **Foreign languages:** French, linguistics. **Health:** International public health. **History:** General. **Interdisciplinary:** Cognitive science, math/computer science, systems science. **Liberal arts:** Arts/sciences. **Math:** General, applied, statistics. **Parks/recreation:** Exercise sciences. **Philosophy/religion:** Philosophy. **Physical sciences:** Chemical physics, chemistry, geology, physics, planetary, theoretical physics. **Psychology:** General. **Social sciences:** Anthropology, archaeology, criminology, economics, geography, political science, sociology. **Visual/performing arts:** General, cinematography, dance, design, dramatic.

Most popular majors. Biology 6%, business/marketing 14%, communications/journalism 7%, education 12%, physical sciences 6%, psychology 6%, social sciences 23%.

Computing on campus. 900 workstations in library, computer center, student center. Dormitories wired for high-speed internet access. Commuter students can connect to campus network. Online course registration, helpline, repair service, student web hosting, wireless network available.

Student life. Freshman orientation: Available, $20 fee. Depending on type of program, 1 or 2 days. **Housing:** Coed dorms, single-sex dorms, special housing for disabled, apartments available. $450 nonrefundable deposit. **Activities:** Dance, drama, film society, international student organizations, radio station, student government, student newspaper, First Nations student center, center for students with disabilities, crisis line, public interest research group, women's center, interfaith center, harassment resolution office, Canadian Federation of Students, student society.

Athletics. NAIA. **Intercollegiate:** Basketball, cross-country, diving, field hockey W, football (tackle) M, soccer, softball W, swimming, track and field, volleyball W, wrestling. **Intramural:** Badminton, basketball, football (non-tackle), soccer, softball, tennis, volleyball. **Team name:** The Clan.

Student services. Alcohol/substance abuse counseling, chaplain/spiritual director, career counseling, financial aid counseling, health services, legal services, minority student services, on-campus daycare, personal counseling, women's services. **Physically disabled:** Services for visually, speech, hearing impaired.

Contact. E-mail: undergraduate-admissions@sfu.ca
Phone: (778) 782-3397 Fax: (778) 782-4969
Mehran Kiai, Director of Enrollment Services, Simon Fraser University, 8888 University Drive, Burnaby, CN

University of Alberta

Edmonton, Canada — **CB member**
www.ualberta.ca — **CB code: 0963**

- Public 4-year university
- Commuter campus in very large city
- 29,188 degree-seeking undergraduates
- 6,695 graduate students

General. Founded in 1906. Regionally accredited. **Degrees:** 5,711 bachelor's awarded; master's, doctoral, first professional offered. **Location:** 180 miles from Calgary. **Calendar:** Semester, extensive summer session. **Full-time faculty:** 2,291 total. **Part-time faculty:** 623 total. **Special facilities:** Fine arts center, botanical gardens, research farm (including several agricultural research stations), field mission scanning electron microscope, professional development center, National Institute for Nanotechnology, heart institute.

Basis for selection. GED not accepted. Admission is based on completion of five appropriate Grade 12 subjects (faculty/program specific), including English. Applicant must present a competitive average for admission, with a minimum grade of 50% in each subject. Competitive averages range from 70-85%. SAT Subject Tests recommended. Auditions, portfolios, letters of intent/essays or interviews are required for several programs; however, admission to most programs is based solely on academic merit.

High school preparation. 3 units required. Required and recommended units include English 3, mathematics 3, social studies 3, history 3, science 3 (laboratory 3), foreign language 3 and academic electives 3. Specific course requirements vary depending on program.

2008-2009 Annual costs. Undergraduate tuition and required fees (most degree programs), Canadian citizens and permanent residents: $5,600; non-Canadian citizens: $17,700. Standard double-occupancy on-campus room: $2,432; board (19 meals per week): $3,990. Figures, which cover expenses for full academic year, are in Canadian dollars. Books/supplies: $1,200. Personal expenses: $1,000.

2007-2008 Financial aid. Additional information: American students may use U.S. federal aid and student loans towards university tuition, but must apply for that aid in United States prior to attending university.

Application procedures. Admission: Closing date 5/1 (postmark date). $115 fee. Admission notification on a rolling basis beginning on or about 7/1. Must reply by 8/15. **Financial aid:** Closing date 5/1. Institutional form required. Applicants notified on a rolling basis; must reply by 8/15.

Academics. Special study options: Combined bachelor's/graduate degree, cooperative education, distance learning, double major, ESL, exchange student, honors, internships, student-designed major, study abroad, teacher certification program. **Credit/placement by examination:** AP, CLEP, IB. **Support services:** Learning center, pre-admission summer program, reduced course load, remedial instruction, study skills assistance, tutoring, writing center.

Majors. Agriculture: General, animal sciences, business, crop production, economics, food science, horticultural science. **Area/ethnic studies:** African, Central/Eastern European, East Asian, Latin American, Near/Middle Eastern, Scandinavian, Southeast Asian, women's. **Biology:** General, animal physiology, biochemistry, bioinformatics, botany, cell/histology, environmental, microbiology, molecular genetics, neurobiology/physiology, pharmacology, physiology, plant molecular, zoology. **Business:** General, accounting, actuarial science, business admin, communications, entrepreneurial studies, finance, human resources, international, international finance, management information systems, marketing, operations, organizational behavior, retailing, sales/distribution. **Computer sciences:** Computer science, programming. **Conservation:** General, forestry, wildlife. **Education:** Agricultural, art, biology, comparative, computer, drama/dance, early childhood, English, ESL, foreign languages, French, mathematics, middle, music, physical, physics, science, social studies, special, trade/industrial. **Engineering:** General, chemical, civil, computer, electrical, materials, mechanical, mechanics, mining, petroleum, physics, software. **Family/consumer sciences:** Clothing/

textiles, family/community services, food/nutrition. **Foreign languages:** General, Chinese, classics, French, German, Italian, Japanese, Latin, linguistics, modern Greek, Romance, Scandinavian, Spanish. **Health:** Athletic training, clinical lab technology, dental hygiene, hematology, nursing (RN), occupational therapy assistant, predental, premedicine, preop/surgical nursing, prepharmacy, preveterinary. **History:** General. **Legal studies:** General. **Math:** General, computational, statistics. **Parks/recreation:** General, exercise sciences, sports admin. **Philosophy/religion:** Philosophy, religion. **Physical sciences:** Atmospheric science, chemistry, physics. **Protective services:** Criminal justice. **Psychology:** General. **Social sciences:** Anthropology, criminology, economics, geography, international relations, political science, sociology. **Visual/performing arts:** Dramatic, film/cinema, metal/jewelry, music history, music theory/composition, printmaking, studio arts, theater design.

Computing on campus. 1,300 workstations in dormitories, library, computer center, student center. Dormitories wired for high-speed internet access and linked to campus network. Commuter students can connect to campus network. Online course registration, online library, helpline, wireless network available.

Student life. **Freshman orientation:** Available. Preregistration for classes offered. Two-day program includes peer advice presentations and campus tour. **Housing:** Coed dorms, single-sex dorms, special housing for disabled, apartments, fraternity/sorority housing available. $150 deposit. **Activities:** Bands, choral groups, dance, drama, film society, literary magazine, music ensembles, musical theater, opera, radio station, student government, student newspaper, symphony orchestra, more than 300 clubs available.

Athletics. **Intercollegiate:** Basketball, cross-country, field hockey W, football (tackle) M, golf, gymnastics, ice hockey, rugby W, soccer, swimming, tennis, track and field, volleyball, wrestling. **Intramural:** Archery M, badminton, baseball, basketball, bowling, cross-country, diving, football (non-tackle) M, football (tackle) M, golf, gymnastics, ice hockey, judo, racquetball, rugby, skiing, soccer, softball, squash, swimming, table tennis, tennis, track and field, triathlon, volleyball, water polo, wrestling. **Team name:** Golden Bears, Pandas.

Student services. Adult student services, alcohol/substance abuse counseling, chaplain/spiritual director, career counseling, services for economically disadvantaged, student employment services, financial aid counseling, health services, legal services, minority student services, on-campus daycare, personal counseling, placement for graduates, women's services. **Physically disabled:** Services for visually, speech, hearing impaired. **Learning disabled:** Comprehensive services available.

Contact. Phone: (780) 492-3113 Fax: (780) 492-7172
Pat Dalton, Associate Registrar and Director of Enrollment Management, University of Alberta, Administration Building, Room 120, Edmonton, CN T6G 2-M7

University of British Columbia

Vancouver, Canada **CB member**
www.ubc.ca **CB code: 0965**

- Public 4-year university
- Commuter campus in very large city
- 27,443 degree-seeking undergraduates: 16% part-time, 54% women
- 14,716 graduate students
- 41% of applicants admitted
- 77% graduate within 6 years

General. Founded in 1915. UBC comprises 18 faculties, 14 schools and 3 colleges across two major campuses (UBC Vancouver & UBC Okanagan) and two satellite campuses. Undergraduate students may study abroad at any one of 155 partner institutions in 42 countries. **Degrees:** 5,755 bachelor's awarded; master's, doctoral, first professional offered. **Location:** 6 miles from downtown Vancouver (Vancouver campus), 5 miles from downtown Kelowna (Okanagan campus). **Calendar:** Semester, limited summer session. **Full-time faculty:** 2,547 total; 66% have terminal degrees, 33% women. **Class size:** 34% < 20, 30% 20-39, 9% 40-49, 14% 50-99, 12% >100. **Special facilities:** Museum of anthropology (Canada's largest teaching museum), museum of geological sciences, botany collection and herbarium, botanical garden, Japanese garden, two astronomical observatories, performing arts centre, global issues centre, winter sports centre (venue for events of the 2010 Olympic Winter Games), world's largest cyclotron.

Freshman class profile. 21,120 applied, 8,699 admitted, 4,272 enrolled.

Basis for selection. GED not accepted. Admission competitive, with academic averages most important. Minimum requirement is strong B+ average; for science and engineering-based programs, strong A average likely to be required. Evaluation of those from American curriculum will be made on best 8 academic courses from junior and senior years. Applicants schooled outside of Canada encouraged to submit a Broader Based Admission package (including personal statement, references, and special academic and extracurricular achievements). Applicants must also meet specific program requirements. Additional criteria may be considered for secondary-school applicants who have studied outside Canada for at least 1 year before applying. Encourages applications from students completing enriched secondary school programs such as International Baccalaureate (IB), Advanced Placement (AP), General Certificate of Education (GCE), and French Baccalaureate. Generous first-year credit offered to students with high academic achievement in these programs. Standardized achievement test results must be submitted by applicants following US curriculum. Exceptions may be granted for countries where tests not available. Minimum scores for admissions consideration: combined SAT score of 1500, or ACT Composite score of 24 (plus 8 on the Writing section). Interviews generally not required. Exceptions at UBC Vancouver are applications to School of Music (interview, audition, and/or portfolio required) and School of Business (supplemental application demonstrating documented leadership and accomplishment required). At UBC Okanagan application to Fine Arts program requires portfolio and letter of intent.

High school preparation. College-preparatory program required. 19 units required. Required units include English 4, mathematics 3 and academic electives 12.

2008-2009 Annual costs. UBC Tuition fees are assessed per credit. Tuition for international students (those who are not Canadian citizens or permanent residents) is currently (2008-09) $644 per credit for most programs. Tuition for Canadian citizens is $142 per credit for most programs. Tuition fees are reviewed annually, and are subject to increases for cost-of-living and other education service costs. Student fees vary according to program, but are generally $650 to $750, which includes a transit pass for all local public transit. On-campus room and board varies according to accommodation selected, but costs an average of $7,500 per academic year. Amounts shown are in Canadian dollars. Books/supplies: $1,500.

2007-2008 Financial aid. **Non-need-based:** Scholarships awarded for academics, athletics. **Additional information:** Need-based financial aid from public funds is available only to Canadian citizens or permanent residents of Canada. Need-based financial aid to international students is limited.

Application procedures. **Admission:** Closing date 2/28. $60 fee ($100 out-of-state). Admission notification on a rolling basis beginning on or about 1/30. Students applying for on-campus student housing must accept offer of admission by May 31 in order to retain offer of housing placement. Students not required to accept admission offers by May 1; applicants receive admissions decision by May 1 deadline, provided they submit all required supporting documents by March 31. **Financial aid:** Closing date 2/15. Institutional form required. Applicants notified by 4/14.

Academics. Several cross-disciplinary options available in first-year study. Undergraduate students encouraged to engage in research projects supported by annual Undergraduate Research Conference. **Special study options:** Combined bachelor's/graduate degree, cooperative education, cross-registration, distance learning, double major, dual enrollment of high school students, ESL, exchange student, honors, internships, liberal arts/career combination, student-designed major, study abroad, teacher certification program. **Credit/placement by examination:** AP, CLEP, IB. **Support services:** Learning center, pre-admission summer program, reduced course load, study skills assistance, tutoring, writing center.

Majors. **Agriculture:** General, agronomy, animal sciences, aquaculture, economics, food processing, food science, horticultural science, plant sciences, soil science. **Architecture:** Environmental design. **Area/ethnic studies:** Asian, Canadian, Central/Eastern European, East Asian, European, German, Hispanic-American/Latino/Chicano, Italian, Latin American, Russian/Slavic, Slavic, South Asian, Southeast Asian, Western European, women's. **Biology:** General, anatomy, animal physiology, bacteriology, biochemistry, biophysics, biotechnology, cell/histology, conservation, ecology, environmental, epidemiology, evolutionary, genetics, molecular, molecular biochemistry, pathology, pharmacology/toxicology, physiology, reproductive. **Business:** General, accounting, business admin, finance, human resources, international, international finance, international marketing, investments/securities, labor relations, management information systems, management science, managerial economics, marketing, operations, real estate, transportation. **Computer sciences:** General, a.i./robotics, computer science. **Conservation:** General, economics, environmental science, environmental studies, forest management, forest resources, forest sciences, forestry, management/policy, wood science. **Education:** General, elementary, middle, multi-level teacher, Native American, physical, secondary. **Engineering:** General, biomedical, chemical, civil, computer, electrical, environmental, forest, geological, materials, materials science, mechanical, mechanics, metallurgical, mining, operations research, physics, software. **Family/consumer sciences:** General, family/community services, food/nutrition, human nutrition. **Foreign languages:** Chinese, classics, French, German, Germanic, Italian, Japanese, Korean, Latin, linguistics, Native American, Portuguese, Romance, Slavic, South Asian, Spanish, Urdu. **Health:** Athletic training, clinical lab assistant, community health, dental hygiene, nurse midwife, nursing (RN), occupational health, preveterinary. **History:** General. **Interdisciplinary:** Ancient studies, biological/physical sciences, classical/archaeology, cognitive science, medieval/Renaissance, neuroscience, nutrition sciences. **Legal studies:** General. **Math:** General, applied, statistics. **Parks/recreation:** Exercise sciences, facilities management, health/fitness, sports admin. **Philosophy/religion:** Philosophy, religion. **Physical sciences:** Astronomy, atmospheric science, chemistry, geology, geophysics, oceanography, physics, planetary, theoretical physics. **Psychology:** General. **Public administration:** Social work. **Science technology:** Biological. **Social sciences:** Anthropology, archaeology, Canadian government, economics, geography, international relations, political science, sociology. **Transportation:** General. **Visual/performing arts:** General, art, art history/conservation, cinematography, conducting, dramatic, film/cinema, music history, music performance, music theory/composition, musicology, piano/organ, stringed instruments, theater arts management, theater design, voice/opera.

Computing on campus. Dormitories wired for high-speed internet access and linked to campus network. Commuter students can connect to campus network. Online course registration, online library, helpline, repair service, wireless network available.

Student life. **Freshman orientation:** Available. Preregistration for classes offered. 3 different orientation programs: GALA International Orientation, 3-day event held during week before start of winter term; Parents Orientation, on Sunday before start of term; IMAGINE UBC (Vancouver) and CREATE (UBC Okanagan), official welcome and orientation experience, on first day of winter term. **Housing:** Guaranteed on-campus for freshmen. Coed dorms, single-sex dorms, apartments, fraternity/sorority housing available. $700 partly refundable deposit, deadline 5/1. Cultural houses in partnership with universities in Japan, Korea, and Mexico available. **Activities:** Bands, choral groups, dance, drama, film society, international student organizations, literary magazine, music ensembles, musical theater, opera, radio station, student government, student newspaper, symphony orchestra, TV station, over 250 clubs, societies, and other groups.

Athletics. NAIA. **Intercollegiate:** Baseball M, basketball, cross-country, field hockey, football (tackle) M, golf, ice hockey, rowing (crew), rugby, soccer, swimming, track and field, volleyball. **Intramural:** Badminton, basketball, cheerleading, cross-country, football (non-tackle), ice hockey, judo, racquetball, skiing, soccer, softball, squash, swimming, tennis, triathlon, volleyball, water polo, wrestling M. **Team name:** Thunderbirds.

Student services. Alcohol/substance abuse counseling, career counseling, student employment services, financial aid counseling, health services, minority student services, on-campus daycare, personal counseling, placement for graduates, women's services. **Physically disabled:** Services for visually, speech, hearing impaired.

Contact. Phone: (604) 822-8999 Toll-free number: (877) 272-1422
Fax: (604) 822-9858
Denise Lauritano, Assistant Registrar, International Undergraduate Admissions, University of British Columbia, 2016 - 1874 East Mall, Vancouver, CN

University of Manitoba

Winnipeg, Canada — **CB member**
www.umanitoba.ca — **CB code: 0973**

- Public 4-year university
- Commuter campus in very large city
- 22,628 degree-seeking undergraduates

General. Founded in 1877. **Degrees:** 4,811 bachelor's awarded; master's, doctoral, first professional offered. **Location:** 10 miles from downtown Winnipeg. **Calendar:** Semester, limited summer session. **Full-time faculty:** 1,700 total. **Part-time faculty:** 1,600 total. **Special facilities:** Planetarium.

Basis for selection. Open admission, but selective for some programs.

High school preparation. 28 units required.

Application procedures. **Admission:** $90 fee.

Academics. **Special study options:** Combined bachelor's/graduate degree, cooperative education, distance learning, double major, ESL, honors, independent study, internships, liberal arts/career combination, study abroad, teacher certification program, weekend college. **Credit/placement by examination:** CLEP, IB. 30 credit hours maximum toward bachelor's degree. **Support services:** Learning center, reduced course load, study skills assistance.

Majors. **Agriculture:** General, agribusiness operations, agronomy, animal health, animal nutrition, animal sciences, business, dairy, economics, farm/ranch, food science, horticultural science, ornamental horticulture, plant breeding, plant protection, plant sciences, poultry, soil science. **Architecture:** Environmental design. **Area/ethnic studies:** Asian, Canadian, Central/Eastern European, Latin American, Near/Middle Eastern, Russian/Slavic, women's. **Biology:** Bacteriology, biochemistry, botany, cell/histology, ecology, entomology, genetics, molecular, pathology, pharmacology, plant pathology, plant physiology, zoology. **Business:** Accounting, actuarial science, business admin, finance, international, labor relations, market research. **Computer sciences:** General, computer science, data processing, information systems, programming, systems analysis. **Conservation:** General, environmental studies. **Education:** General, adult ed admin, business, curriculum, early childhood, elementary, ESL, family/consumer sciences, foundations, instructional media, leadership, middle, multi-level teacher, music, physical, secondary, special, technology/industrial arts. **Engineering:** General, agricultural, civil, computer, electrical, materials science, mechanical. **Family/consumer sciences:** General, clothing/textiles, family/community services, food/nutrition. **Foreign languages:** Biblical, classics, comparative lit, French, German, Hebrew, Italian, linguistics, modern Greek, Russian, Spanish. **Health:** Athletic training, dental hygiene, nursing (RN), occupational therapy, physical therapy. **History:** General. **Interdisciplinary:** Behavioral sciences, gerontology, global studies, math/computer science, medieval/Renaissance, nutrition sciences. **Legal studies:** General. **Math:** General, applied, statistics. **Parks/recreation:** General, exercise sciences, health/fitness, sports admin. **Philosophy/religion:** Judaic, philosophy, religion. **Physical sciences:** Astronomy, chemistry, geology, physics. **Psychology:** General, clinical, counseling, educational. **Public administration:** General, social work. **Social sciences:** Anthropology, criminology, economics, geography, political science, sociology. **Visual/performing arts:** Art, art history/conservation, commercial/advertising art, dramatic, film/cinema, interior design, music history, music performance, music theory/composition, piano/organ, studio arts, theater history, voice/opera.

Computing on campus. 392 workstations in library, computer center. Commuter students can connect to campus network. Online course registration, online library, helpline, repair service, student web hosting available.

Student life. **Freshman orientation:** Mandatory. **Activities:** Bands, choral groups, dance, drama, music ensembles, radio station, student government, student newspaper, symphony orchestra.

Athletics. **Intercollegiate:** Basketball, cross-country, diving, field hockey W, football (tackle) M, gymnastics, ice hockey, skiing, swimming, synchronized swimming W, tennis, track and field, volleyball, weight lifting M, wrestling. **Intramural:** Archery, basketball, cross-country, diving, field hockey W, football (non-tackle) M, handball, ice hockey, judo M, racquetball, soccer, squash, swimming, tennis, volleyball. **Team name:** Bisons.

Student services. Adult student services, alcohol/substance abuse counseling, chaplain/spiritual director, career counseling, student employment services, financial aid counseling, health services, legal services, on-campus daycare, personal counseling, placement for graduates. **Physically disabled:** Services for visually, speech, hearing impaired.

Contact. E-mail: admissions@umanitoba.ca
Phone: (204) 474-8808 Fax: (204) 474-7554
Iris Reece-Tougas, Director of Admissions, University of Manitoba, 424 University Centre, Winnipeg, CN R3T 2-N2

University of Toronto

Toronto, Canada
www.utoronto.ca/ — **CB member**

- Public 4-year university
- Commuter campus in very large city
- 50,817 degree-seeking undergraduates: 10% part-time, 55% women
- 19,100 degree-seeking graduate students
- SAT or ACT with writing, SAT Subject Tests, application essay required
- 74% graduate within 6 years

General. **Degrees:** 9,469 bachelor's awarded; master's, doctoral, first professional offered. **Location:** 95 miles from Buffalo, NY. **Calendar:** Semester, limited summer session. **Full-time faculty:** 2,719 total. **Part-time faculty:** 288 total. **Special facilities:** Greenhouses, observatory, university-operated art galleries and theaters, teaching hospitals, 150-acre farm.

Freshman class profile. 60,776 applied, 44,269 admitted, 12,349 enrolled.

Basis for selection. Typically, applicants who are competitive for admission to the University of Toronto are among the top third of their class. Only those applicants who have attained a high level of academic achievement in these qualifications and who present credits to satisfy any prerequisites of specific courses or programs in which they intend to enroll will be admitted. The Faculty of Arts and Science St. George campus, University of Toronto Mississauga, University of Toronto Scarborough, the Faculty of Music, and the Faculty of Physical Education and Health/Kinesiology will consider applications from students in the USA and other countries who have completed or who are completing 12th grade in an accredited high school; such applicants must present high scores in SAT Reasoning or ACT examinations including the Writing Test component and at least three SAT Subject Tests or AP/IB subjects appropriate to their proposed area of study. Scores below 500 in any part of the SAT Reasoning or SAT Subject Tests are not acceptable. Many programs require higher scores. Students seeking admission to science or business/commerce programs are strongly advised to complete AP Calculus (AB or BC) or IB Mathematics (HL or SL or Math Methods with Calculus option). Student profiles required for some programs. **Homeschooled:** Statement describing homeschool structure and mission, transcript of courses and grades required. Application should include course outlines, textbooks and method of evaluation used, samples of written work, relevant details of any independent evaluations or assessments; results of standardized tests may also be considered. **Learning Disabled:** Students can send a letter with supporting documentation.

2008-2009 Annual costs. Costs reported in Canadian dollars. Tuition fees vary between programs. Books/supplies: $1,000.

Financial aid. All financial aid based on need.

Application procedures. Admission: Closing date 3/1 (receipt date). $105 fee. Admission notification 5/1. Admission notification on a rolling basis beginning on or about 3/1. Must reply by 5/28. Application deadlines vary by program.

Academics. Special study options: Combined bachelor's/graduate degree, cooperative education, double major, ESL, exchange student, honors, independent study, internships, student-designed major, study abroad, teacher certification program. **Credit/placement by examination:** AP, CLEP, IB, SAT, ACT, institutional tests. **Support services:** Learning center, preadmission summer program, reduced course load, study skills assistance, tutoring, writing center.

Majors. Architecture: Architecture, environmental design, history/criticism, urban/community planning. **Area/ethnic studies:** African, African-American, American, Asian, Canadian, Caribbean, Central/Eastern European, Chinese, East Asian, European, French, gay/lesbian, German, Italian, Latin American, Native American, Near/Middle Eastern, Polish, Russian/Slavic, Slavic, Spanish/Iberian, Ukraine, women's. **Biology:** General, animal physiology, biochemistry, Biochemistry/biophysics and molecular biology, bioinformatics, biophysics, biotechnology, botany, cellular/anatomical, conservation, ecology, environmental, genetics, molecular, molecular biochemistry, molecular biophysics, molecular pharmacology, pharmacology, pharmacology/toxicology, toxicology, zoology. **Business:** General. **Communications:** General, digital media, health, journalism, media studies. **Communications technology:** General. **Computer sciences:** General, a.i./robotics, computer science, information systems, information technology, programming, systems analysis. **Conservation:** General, environmental science, environmental studies, forestry. **Education:** General, elementary, middle, multi-level teacher, secondary. **Engineering:** General, aerospace, agricultural, biomedical, chemical, civil, computer, environmental, industrial, materials, mechanical, physics, science. **Foreign languages:** Ancient Greek, Biblical, Celtic, classics, Czech, French, German, Germanic, Hebrew, Italian, Latin, linguistics, Polish, Portuguese, Russian, Serbo-Croatian, Slavic, Slovak, South Asian, Southeast Asian, Spanish, Ukrainian. **Health:** EMT paramedic, ethics, pharmaceutical sciences, predental, premedicine, prepharmacy. **History:** General, European, science/technology. **Interdisciplinary:** Accounting/computer science, ancient studies, behavioral sciences, biological/physical sciences, classical/archaeology, cognitive science, global studies, intercultural, math/computer science, medieval/Renaissance, neuroscience, nutrition sciences, peace/conflict. **Legal studies:** Prelaw. **Liberal arts:** Arts/sciences, humanities. **Math:** General, probability, statistics. **Parks/recreation:** Exercise sciences, health/fitness. **Philosophy/religion:** Buddhist, Christian, ethics, Judaic, logic, philosophy, religion. **Physical sciences:** General, applied physics, astronomy, astrophysics, chemistry, forensic chemistry, paleontology, physics, planetary. **Psychology:** General, forensic. **Social sciences:** Anthropology, archaeology, Canadian government, criminology, economics, geography, international economic development, international economics, international relations, physical anthropology, political science, sociology, U.S. government, urban studies. **Theology:** Religious ed, theology. **Visual/performing arts:** General, art, art history/conservation, dramatic, film/cinema, jazz, music history, music performance, music theory/composition, stringed instruments, studio arts, voice/opera. **Other:** Estonian studies.

Computing on campus. Dormitories wired for high-speed internet access and linked to campus network. Commuter students can connect to campus network. Online course registration, online library, helpline, repair service, student web hosting, wireless network available.

Student life. Freshman orientation: Available. Usually held the week before classes begin. Cost varies. **Housing:** Guaranteed on-campus for freshmen. Coed dorms, single-sex dorms, special housing for disabled, apartments, cooperative housing, wellness housing available. $600 nonrefundable deposit, deadline 6/15. **Activities:** Bands, campus ministries, choral groups, dance, drama, film society, international student organizations, literary magazine, music ensembles, Model UN, musical theater, opera, radio station, student government, student newspaper, symphony orchestra, TV station.

Athletics. Intercollegiate: Badminton, baseball M, basketball, cross-country, fencing, field hockey W, football (non-tackle) M, football (tackle) M, golf, ice hockey, lacrosse, rowing (crew), rugby M, skiing, soccer, softball W, swimming, synchronized swimming W, tennis, track and field, volleyball, water polo, wrestling M. **Intramural:** Badminton, baseball M, basketball, cross-country, fencing, field hockey W, football (non-tackle) M, football (tackle) M, golf, ice hockey, lacrosse, rowing (crew) M, rugby M, skiing, soccer, softball W, swimming, tennis, track and field, volleyball, water polo, wrestling M. **Team name:** Varsity Blues.

Student services. Adult student services, alcohol/substance abuse counseling, chaplain/spiritual director, career counseling, services for economically disadvantaged, student employment services, financial aid counseling, health services, legal services, minority student services, on-campus daycare, personal counseling, placement for graduates, women's services. **Physically disabled:** Services for visually, speech, hearing impaired. **Learning disabled:** Comprehensive services available.

Contact. E-mail: admissions.help@utoronto.ca
Phone: (416) 978-8345 Fax: (416) 978-7022
University of Toronto, 315 Bloor Street West, Toronto, CN

Egypt

American University in Cairo

Cairo, Egypt
www.aucegypt.edu
CB member
CB code: 0903

- Private 4-year university
- Commuter campus in very large city
- 4,530 degree-seeking undergraduates: 10% part-time, 52% women
- 1,047 degree-seeking graduate students
- 54% of applicants admitted
- Application essay required
- 80% graduate within 6 years

General. Founded in 1919. Regionally accredited. Language of instruction is English; 75% of degree-seeking students must be of Egyptian nationality. **Degrees:** 688 bachelor's awarded; master's offered. **Location:** 40 kilometers from downtown. **Calendar:** Semester, extensive summer session. **Full-time faculty:** 374 total; 66% have terminal degrees, 50% women. **Part-time faculty:** 303 total; 60% have terminal degrees, 55% women. **Class size:** 59% < 20, 36% 20-39, 5% 40-49, less than 1% 50-99.

Freshman class profile. 2,476 applied, 1,328 admitted, 1,059 enrolled.

Mid 50% test scores		**GPA 3.50-3.74:**	14%
SAT critical reading:	420-510	**GPA 3.0-3.49:**	28%
SAT math:	500-620	**GPA 2.0-2.99:**	26%
SAT writing:	490-570	**Return as sophomores:**	93%
GPA 3.75 or higher:	32%		

Basis for selection. Applicants from the United States expected to have completed college preparatory (academic) high school program and submit 1000 SAT (exclusive of Writing). Arab students must take Thanawiya 'Amma; minimum score of 75% required. CE/GCSE/IGCSE certificates will also be considered for admission. SAT Subject Tests required for applicants who have graduated from American-style high schools with less than 3 semesters in residence. **Homeschooled:** Statement describing homeschool structure and mission, transcript of courses and grades, state high school equivalency certificate required.

High school preparation. Recommended units include English 3, mathematics 3, social studies 3, science 2 and foreign language 2. One unit fine arts recommended.

2008-2009 Annual costs. Books/supplies: $700. Personal expenses: $2,200.

2007-2008 Financial aid. Non-need-based: Scholarships awarded for academics, art, athletics, leadership, music/drama, state residency.

Application procedures. Admission: Priority date 3/1; deadline 5/15 (receipt date). $50 fee. Admission notification on a rolling basis beginning on or about 7/20. **Financial aid:** Closing date 5/15. Institutional form required. Applicants notified by 8/15.

Academics. Special study options: Double major, ESL, independent study, liberal arts/career combination, study abroad. **Credit/placement by examination:** CLEP, IB, SAT, institutional tests. **Support services:** Learning center, reduced course load, remedial instruction, study skills assistance, writing center.

Majors. Area/ethnic studies: Near/Middle Eastern. **Biology:** General. **Business:** Accounting, actuarial science, business admin. **Communications:** Journalism, media studies. **Computer sciences:** General. **Engineering:** Architectural, computer, construction, electrical, mechanical, petroleum. **Foreign languages:** Arabic, comparative lit. **History:** General, Asian. **Math:** General. **Philosophy/religion:** Philosophy. **Physical sciences:** Chemistry, physics. **Psychology:** General. **Social sciences:** Anthropology, archaeology, economics, political science, sociology. **Visual/performing arts:** Art, dramatic.

Most popular majors. Business/marketing 30%, communications/journalism 22%, computer/information sciences 6%, engineering/engineering technologies 18%, social sciences 13%.

Computing on campus. 687 workstations in dormitories, library, computer center. Dormitories wired for high-speed internet access and linked to campus network. Commuter students can connect to campus network. Online course registration, online library, helpline, repair service available.

Student life. Freshman orientation: Available. Held in August for 3 days. **Policies:** Non-smoking campus. **Housing:** Single-sex dorms, apartments available. $300 nonrefundable deposit, deadline 9/1. 255 spaces available for students in rented hotels facilities. **Activities:** Choral groups, dance, drama, film society, literary magazine, music ensembles, Model UN, radio station, student government, student newspaper, African students association, community service society, Model United Nations, Model Arab League.

Athletics. Intercollegiate: Basketball, boxing M, diving, equestrian, fencing, gymnastics, handball, judo, rowing (crew), rugby M, soccer, squash, swimming, table tennis, tennis, track and field, volleyball, water polo M, wrestling M. **Intramural:** Badminton, basketball, skin diving, soccer, swimming, table tennis, tennis, volleyball, weight lifting M.

Student services. Adult student services, career counseling, student employment services, health services, on-campus daycare, personal counseling, placement for graduates.

Contact. E-mail: diskaros@aucnyo.edu
Phone: (212) 730-8800 ext. 223 Fax: (212) 730-1600
Ghada Hazem, Director of Admissions, American University in Cairo, 420 Fifth Avenue, Third Floor, New York, NY 10018-2729

France

American University of Paris

Paris, France
www.aup.edu **CB code: 0866**

- Private 4-year university and liberal arts college
- Commuter campus in very large city
- 728 degree-seeking undergraduates: 5% part-time, 67% women
- 94 degree-seeking graduate students
- 72% of applicants admitted
- Application essay required
- 57% graduate within 6 years

General. Founded in 1962. Regionally accredited. **Degrees:** 164 bachelor's awarded; master's offered. **Calendar:** Semester, extensive summer session. **Full-time faculty:** 64 total; 80% have terminal degrees, 42% women. **Part-time faculty:** 66 total; 44% women. **Class size:** 55% < 20, 45% 20-39.

Freshman class profile. 662 applied, 477 admitted, 224 enrolled.

Mid 50% test scores		SAT math:	520-640
SAT critical reading:	550-660	Return as sophomores:	71%

Basis for selection. Applicants evaluated on basis of academic performance. Most important sources of information about academic achievements include academic transcripts of all secondary and/or university-level coursework, as well as applicable test scores such as SAT, ACT, and national exams. Non-English speakers are required to take TOEFL or TOEIC or IELTS. **Homeschooled:** Statement describing homeschool structure and mission, transcript of courses and grades, state high school equivalency certificate, interview, letter of recommendation (nonparent) required.

High school preparation. 18 units recommended. Recommended units include English 4, mathematics 3, social studies 3, history 2, science 2 (laboratory 1) and foreign language 3.

2008-2009 Annual costs. Full-time tuition for academic year: 23,000 euros; housing costs vary, and all accommodations are off-campus. Books/supplies: $1,200.

2007-2008 Financial aid. Need-based: 89% of total undergraduate aid awarded as scholarships/grants, 11% as loans/jobs. **Non-need-based:** Scholarships awarded for academics.

Application procedures. Admission: Closing date 3/15 (postmark date). $65 fee. Application must be submitted online. Admission notification on a rolling basis. Must reply by May 1 or within 2 week(s) if notified thereafter. **Financial aid:** No deadline. FAFSA, institutional form required.

Academics. Special study options: Cooperative education, cross-registration, double major, exchange student, honors, independent study, internships, study abroad. **Credit/placement by examination:** AP, CLEP, IB, institutional tests. 30 credit hours maximum toward bachelor's degree. **Support services:** Reduced course load, study skills assistance, tutoring, writing center.

Majors. Area/ethnic studies: European, French. **Business:** Finance, international. **Communications:** General. **Computer sciences:** General. **Foreign languages:** General, comparative lit, French. **History:** General. **Psychology:** General. **Social sciences:** Economics, international relations. **Visual/performing arts:** Art history/conservation, film/cinema.

Most popular majors. Business/marketing 28%, communications/journalism 22%, social sciences 33%, visual/performing arts 7%.

Computing on campus. 120 workstations in library, computer center, student center. Commuter students can connect to campus network. Online course registration, online library, helpline, wireless network available.

Student life. Freshman orientation: Mandatory, $500 fee. Held week before classes begin. Students assisted in housing process, receive academic advising, attend workshops on living in Paris. **Housing:** $550 nonrefundable deposit, deadline 5/1. **Activities:** Choral groups, dance, drama, film society, literary magazine, music ensembles, musical theater, radio station, student government, student newspaper.

Student services. Career counseling, financial aid counseling, personal counseling.

Contact. E-mail: usoffice@aup.edu
Phone: (303) 757-6333 Fax: (303) 757-6444
Paul Beel, Director of Admissions, American University of Paris, 950 South Cherry Street, Suite 210, Denver, CO 80246

Parsons Paris School of Design

Paris, France
www.parsons-paris.com **CB member**

- Private 4-year visual arts and business college
- Commuter campus in very large city
- 94 degree-seeking undergraduates: 86% women
- 90% of applicants admitted
- Application essay required

General. While the legal structure of the school is that of an independent organization, the academic program of Parsons Paris is coordinated with that of Parsons The New School for Design in New York. **Degrees:** 14 bachelor's awarded. **Calendar:** Semester, limited summer session. **Full-time faculty:** 2 total; 50% women. **Part-time faculty:** 70 total; 54% women.

Freshman class profile. 141 applied, 127 admitted, 69 enrolled.

Out-of-state:	100%	Live on campus:	5%

Basis for selection. A large part of the Admissions Committee's decision is based upon evaluation of the portfolio and home exam. A prospective student's potential for artistic achievement is one of the most important criteria in evaluating candidates for admission. Portfolio of art work and home assignment.

2008-2009 Financial aid. Need-based: Average need met was 15%. Average scholarship/grant was $2,000.

Application procedures. Admission: Closing date 7/1. $75 fee. **Financial aid:** Closing date 5/1.

Academics. Special study options: Accelerated study, ESL, independent study, internships, study abroad. **Credit/placement by examination:** AP, CLEP, IB. 18 credit hours maximum toward bachelor's degree. **Support services:** Pre-admission summer program, writing center.

Majors. Visual/performing arts: Design, fashion design, illustration, photography, studio arts.

Computing on campus. 40 workstations in computer center. Wireless network available.

Student life. Freshman orientation: Mandatory. **Housing:** Coed dorms available.

Contact. E-mail: admissions@parsons-paris.com
Sara Krauskopf, Director of Admissions, Parsons Paris School of Design, 14 rue Letellier, Paris, FR

Germany

University of Karlsruhe

Karlsruhe, Germany — **CB member**
www.university-karlsruhe.de — **CB code: 3592**

- Public 3-year university
- Small city
- 17,493 undergraduates
- Application essay, interview required

General. Partnerships with industry; special internship arrangement and placement for graduates. **Calendar:** Semester, limited summer session. **Full-time faculty:** 300 total.

Basis for selection. GED not accepted. SAT or ACT recommended. **Homeschooled:** Statement describing homeschool structure and mission, transcript of courses and grades, state high school equivalency certificate, interview, letter of recommendation (nonparent) required. SAT is not mandatory, yet applicants might enhance their chances by adding this element to their application package. **Learning Disabled:** Successful completion of entrance examination prior to official enrollment.

High school preparation. Required units include mathematics 4, science 4 and computer science 4.

Application procedures. Admission: Priority date 4/15; deadline 7/15 (receipt date). No application fee. Admission notification 6/1. Admission notification on a rolling basis beginning on or about 3/1. Must reply by 7/31. Must reply by May 1 or within 4 week(s) if notified thereafter. Complete application file should be submitted by June 1st. After review of file, candidate is invited for interview; letters of admission are usually sent within four weeks following interview. The final enrollment decision is based on entrance examination. A preparatory course is offered starting mid-August of each year.

Academics. Special study options: Double major, dual enrollment of high school students, exchange student, internships, study abroad. **Credit/placement by examination:** CLEP, institutional tests. **Support services:** Pre-admission summer program, study skills assistance, tutoring, writing center.

Majors. Architecture: Architecture. **Biology:** General. **Communications:** Journalism. **Computer sciences:** General, information technology. **Engineering:** Electrical, mechanical. **Physical sciences:** Chemistry, geology, physics. **Social sciences:** Economics.

Computing on campus. PC or laptop required. 20 workstations in computer center. Dormitories wired for high-speed internet access and linked to campus network. Wireless network available.

Student life. Freshman orientation: Available. **Housing:** $400 fully refundable deposit, deadline 8/15.

Contact. E-mail: kappes@id.uni-karlsruhe.de
Phone: (721) 608-7880
Birgitta Kappes, Admissions Director, University of Karlsruhe, Schlossplatz 19, Karlsruhe, GE

Guatemala

Universidad del Valle de Guatemala

Guatemala City, Guatemala — **CB member**
www.uvg.edu.gt — **CB code: 3875**

- Private 5-year university and engineering college
- Commuter campus in very large city

General. Calendar: Semester.

Annual costs/financial aid. Need-based financial aid available to full-time and part-time students.

Contact. Phone: (502) 364-0336 ext. 453
Secretaria General, 18 Avenida 11-95 zona 15, Vista Hermosa III, Guatemala City, GT 01015

Lebanon

American University of Beirut

Beirut, Lebanon — **CB member**
www.aub.edu.lb — **CB code: 0902**

- Private 4-year university
- Commuter campus in very large city
- 6,009 degree-seeking undergraduates: 2% part-time, 48% women
- 1,306 degree-seeking graduate students
- 68% of applicants admitted
- SAT required
- 82% graduate within 6 years; 16% enter graduate study

General. Regionally accredited. Most students are from the Arab world. **Degrees:** 1,366 bachelor's awarded; master's, doctoral, first professional offered. **Location:** In Beirut City. **Calendar:** Semester, extensive summer session. **Full-time faculty:** 419 total; 82% have terminal degrees, 38% women. **Part-time faculty:** 277 total; 48% have terminal degrees, 45% women. **Class size:** 29% < 20, 56% 20-39, 5% 40-49, 7% 50-99, 3% >100. **Special facilities:** Archaeological museum, geological museum, rare biological collection.

Freshman class profile. 3,394 applied, 2,314 admitted, 1,497 enrolled.

Mid 50% test scores			
SAT critical reading:	430-530	GPA 2.0-2.99:	40%
SAT math:	560-670	Rank in top quarter:	56%
SAT writing:	450-550	Rank in top tenth:	31%
GPA 3.75 or higher:	5%	End year in good standing:	89%
GPA 3.50-3.74:	11%	Return as sophomores:	93%
GPA 3.0-3.49:	32%	Live on campus:	19%

Basis for selection. Admission based on composite scores: 50% SAT (25% verbal, 25% math) and 50% standardized school grades. Holders of Lebanese, French and International Baccalaureate, among other regional governmental secondary diplomas, will be admittted directly into the sophomore class. SAT must be taken before January of the year preceding admissions. **Homeschooled:** State high school equivalency certificate required. Most applicants must take 3 SAT Subject Tests.

2009-2010 Annual costs. Tuition/fees (projected): $12,495. Room only: $2,924. Books/supplies: $300. Personal expenses: $100.

2007-2008 Financial aid. Need-based: Average scholarship/grant was $3,313. 83% of total undergraduate aid awarded as scholarships/grants, 17% as loans/jobs. **Non-need-based:** Scholarships awarded for academics.

Application procedures. Admission: Priority date 11/30; deadline 1/15 (receipt date). $50 fee. Admission notification on a rolling basis beginning on or about 4/30. Must reply by 6/30. Early action applicants must have a minimum SAT and must have been in top 40th percentile of their class for the past two years. **Financial aid:** Closing date 2/4. Institutional form required. Applicants notified by 6/15.

Academics. Special study options: Cross-registration, ESL, exchange student, honors, independent study, internships, liberal arts/career combination, study abroad, teacher certification program. **Credit/placement by examination:** AP, CLEP, IB, SAT, institutional tests. **Support services:** Learning center, remedial instruction, study skills assistance, tutoring, writing center.

Majors. Agriculture: General, food science, landscaping. **Architecture:** Architecture. **Biology:** General. **Business:** Business admin. **Computer sciences:** Computer science. **Education:** Elementary. **Engineering:** Civil, computer, electrical, mechanical, petroleum. **Foreign languages:** Arabic. **Health:** Clinical lab technology, dietetics, environmental health, nursing (RN). **History:** General. **Math:** General, statistics. **Philosophy/religion:** Philosophy. **Physical sciences:** Chemistry, geology, physics. **Psychology:** General. **Public administration:** General. **Social sciences:** Anthropology, archaeology, economics, political science, sociology. **Visual/performing arts:** Art history/conservation, graphic design, studio arts.

Most popular majors. Biology 12%, business/marketing 27%, engineering/engineering technologies 15%, health sciences 6%, social sciences 8%.

Computing on campus. 835 workstations in dormitories, library, computer center, student center. Dormitories wired for high-speed internet access and linked to campus network. Commuter students can connect to campus network. Online course registration, online library, helpline, repair service, student web hosting, wireless network available.

Student life. Freshman orientation: Mandatory. Preregistration for classes offered. Week-long program held in September, one week before classes begin. **Policies:** Student code of conduct; violations may be of an academic or non-academic nature. Designated smoking areas. **Housing:** Guaranteed on-campus for freshmen. Single-sex dorms, wellness housing available. $100 fully refundable deposit, deadline 8/8. **Activities:** Choral groups, dance, drama, film society, international student organizations, music ensembles, Model UN, student government, student newspaper, Gulf club, Palestinian cultural club, Syrian cultural club, Jordanian cultural club, Lebanese Armenian heritage club, Lebanese Red Cross club, human rights and peace club, special support club for special people, women's rights club, debate club.

Athletics. Intercollegiate: Basketball, cross-country, handball, rugby M, skiing, soccer, squash, swimming, table tennis, tennis, track and field, triathlon, volleyball, water polo M. **Intramural:** Basketball, cross-country, handball, soccer, squash, swimming, table tennis, tennis, volleyball, weight lifting.

Student services. Alcohol/substance abuse counseling, career counseling, student employment services, financial aid counseling, health services, personal counseling, placement for graduates. **Physically disabled:** Services for visually, hearing impaired.

Contact. E-mail: admissions@aub.edu.lb
Phone: (961) 137-4374 ext. 2590 Fax: (961) 175-0775
Salim Kanaan, Director of Admissions, American University of Beirut, PO Box 11-0236, Beirut, LB

Mexico

Instituto Tecnologico Autonomo de Mexico

Mexico City, Mexico — **CB member**
www.itam.mx — **CB code: 7144**

- Private 4-year university, business and engineering college
- Residential campus in very large city
- 4,793 degree-seeking undergraduates

General. Degrees: 526 bachelor's awarded; master's, doctoral, first professional offered. **Calendar:** Semester, limited summer session. **Full-time faculty:** 476 total. **Part-time faculty:** 454 total.

Basis for selection. Open admission. High school records and admission test mandatory. **Homeschooled:** Complete high school diploma, minimum GPA, and admission test.

2008-2009 Annual costs. Undergraduates pay approximately 127,027 Mexican pesos for academic year.

Application procedures. Admission: No deadline. $54 fee, may be waived for applicants with need. Application must be submitted on paper. Admission notification on a rolling basis.

Academics. Special study options: Combined bachelor's/graduate degree, double major, ESL, exchange student, liberal arts/career combination, study abroad. **Credit/placement by examination:** AP, CLEP, IB, institutional tests. **Support services:** Study skills assistance, tutoring, writing center.

Majors. Business: Accounting, accounting/business management, actuarial science, business admin. **Communications:** Digital media. **Communications technology:** Computer typography. **Computer sciences:** General. **Engineering:** Computer. **Engineering technology:** General. **Interdisciplinary:** Science/society. **Legal studies:** General, prelaw. **Math:** Applied. **Social sciences:** Economics, international relations, political science.

Computing on campus. 140 workstations in library, computer center. Commuter students can connect to campus network. Online library, wireless network available.

Student life. Freshman orientation: Available. **Activities:** Concert band, choral groups, dance, drama, international student organizations, literary magazine, music ensembles, Model UN, radio station, student government, student newspaper.

Athletics. Intercollegiate: Baseball M, basketball, soccer, volleyball. **Team name:** Dragones.

Student services. Student employment services, health services, legal services.

Contact. E-mail: admisiones@itam.mx
Phone: (5) 556-284156 Toll-free number: (55) 018-00000 ext. 4826
Fax: (5) 554-904655
Cynthia Figueroa, Director of Admissions, Instituto Tecnologico Autonomo de Mexico, Rio Hondo 1, Colonia Progreso Tizapan, Mexico City, MX

Instituto Tecnologico y de Estudios Superiores de Occidente

Tlaquepaque, Mexico — **CB member**
www.iteso.mx — **CB code: 7145**

- Private 4-year university, business and engineering college affiliated with Roman Catholic Church
- Commuter campus in very large city

General. Location: In metropolitan Guadalajara. **Calendar:** Semester.

Annual costs/financial aid. Tuition ranges from 880 to 904 Mexican pesos per credit hour.

Contact. Phone: (52) 333-6693535
Chief of the Admission Office, AP 31-175, Zapopan, MX 45090

Universidad Anahuac

Huixquilucan, Mexico **CB member**
www.anahuac.mx **CB code: 7146**

- Private 6-year university affiliated with Roman Catholic Church
- Commuter campus in small city
- SAT, interview required

General. Founded in 1964. **Location:** 5 miles from Mexico City. **Calendar:** Semester, limited summer session. **Full-time faculty:** 191 total. **Part-time faculty:** 770 total.

Basis for selection. GED not accepted. Admission decisions based on careful consideration of all factors in process of personal attention to each applicant and not on numerical factors alone. Recommend that U.S. mainland applicants take the PAA, SAT.

High school preparation. 13 units required. Required units include English 2, mathematics 2, social studies 1, history 2, science 2, foreign language 3 and academic electives 1.

2008-2009 Annual costs. Books/supplies: $200. Personal expenses: $550.

2008-2009 Financial aid. All financial aid based on need.

Application procedures. Admission: Closing date 7/31. $99 fee. Application must be submitted on paper. Admission notification on a rolling basis. Must reply by 7/31. **Financial aid:** Priority date 7/20; no closing date. Institutional form required. Applicants notified on a rolling basis starting 8/13; must reply within 2 week(s) of notification.

Academics. Special study options: Cooperative education, double major, ESL, exchange student, study abroad, teacher certification program. **Credit/placement by examination:** CLEP, SAT. **Support services:** Learning center, pre-admission summer program, reduced course load, remedial instruction, study skills assistance, tutoring.

Majors. Architecture: Architecture. **Business:** Accounting, actuarial science, business admin, international, international marketing, tourism/travel. **Communications:** General, advertising, public relations. **Communications technology:** General. **Computer sciences:** Data processing, information systems. **Engineering:** Civil, electrical, mechanics, systems. **Engineering technology:** Electrical, industrial management. **Family/consumer sciences:** General. **Legal studies:** General. **Personal/culinary services:** General, culinary arts. **Psychology:** General. **Social sciences:** Economics.

Computing on campus. 500 workstations in library, computer center, student center. Online course registration, online library, helpline, wireless network available.

Student life. Freshman orientation: Available. **Housing:** Host families provide housing for international and out-of-state students. **Activities:** Bands, campus ministries, choral groups, dance, drama, music ensembles, musical theater, opera, radio station, student government, student newspaper, Anahuac Challenge, Anahuac for Mexico, Anahuac Social Action, Anahuac Social Foundation, Center for Integral Community Development, Perpetual Adoration Society, Red Cross, Youth Weekend Mission Program.

Athletics. Intercollegiate: Baseball M, basketball M, cheerleading M, diving, judo, soccer, swimming, tennis, volleyball. **Intramural:** Cheerleading W, diving, judo, soccer, swimming, tennis, volleyball.

Student services. Chaplain/spiritual director, career counseling, financial aid counseling, health services, personal counseling, placement for graduates.

Contact. E-mail: pbertha@anahuac.mx
Phone: (555) 627-0210 ext. 8458 Toll-free number: (800) 508-9800
Fax: (555) 596-1938
Bertha Perez Vera, Director of Admissions, Universidad Anahuac, Av. Lomas Anahuac #46., Huixquilucan, MX

Universidad Autonoma de Aguascalientes

Aguascalientes, Mexico **CB member**
www.uaa.mx **CB code: 7147**

- Public 4-year university
- Residential campus in very large city

General. Founded in 1974. Regionally accredited. **Location:** 319 miles from Mexico City. **Calendar:** Semester.

Annual costs/financial aid. Need-based financial aid available for full-time students.

Contact. Phone: (449) 910-7422
Jefe de Departamento de Control Escolar, Av. Universidad No. 940, Aguascalientes, MX

Universidad Autonoma de Coahuila

Saltillo, Mexico **CB member**
www.uadec.mx **CB code: 7148**

- Public 4-year university
- Very large city

General. Calendar: Semester.

Contact. Phone: (844) 4-3-81729
Rector, Boulevard V. Carranza y Gonzalez, 25280 Saltillo, Coahuila, Mexico, MX

Universidad de Monterrey

San Pedro Garza Garcia, Mexico
www.udem.edu.mx **CB member**

- Private 4-year university affiliated with Roman Catholic Church
- Residential campus in very large city
- SAT, application essay, interview required

General. Calendar: Semester, limited summer session.

Basis for selection. Open admission, but selective for some programs. GED not accepted. High school record and standardized test scores most important. Minimum PAA score of 1000, with neither portion below 450. English, computer tests required. **Homeschooled:** Interview required.

High school preparation. PAA score of 1000 required, plus tests in English and computer literacy. Interview required for psychology, law, medical programs. Essay required of prospective law students.

Application procedures. Admission: Closing date 8/1. $120 fee, may be waived for applicants with need. Admission notification on a rolling basis.

Academics. Special study options: Business administration cooperative program in partnership with Athabasca University (Canada). **Credit/placement by examination:** CLEP.

Majors. Architecture: Architecture. **Business:** General, accounting, international, international finance, international marketing. **Communications:** General. **Computer sciences:** Information technology. **Education:** General. **Engineering:** Computer, industrial, mechanical, systems. **Liberal arts:** Humanities. **Psychology:** General. **Public administration:** General. **Social sciences:** General, economics, international relations, political science. **Visual/performing arts:** General, graphic design, industrial design.

Computing on campus. Online course registration, online library, wireless network available.

Student life. Activities: Choral groups, dance, drama, radio station, student newspaper, Misiones al sur de Nuevo Leon (Galeana, Iturbide y Aramberri), Pasa tiempo con ni?os especiales, Sobrevive (Campamento extremo), Misiones solidarias, UDEM en el campo, UDEM en la Tarahumara, Misiones en Schoenstatt, Voluntariado, Misiones en Familia, Misiones para profesionistas.

Contact. E-mail: admisiones@udem.edu.mx
Phone: (81) 821-51010 Fax: (81) 821-51013
Ana Cantu Lozano, Dean of Admissions, Universidad de Monterrey, Avenida Ignacio Morones Prieto, 4500 Pte., San Pedro Garza Garcia, NL, MX 66238

Monaco

International University of Monaco
Monte-Carlo, Monaco
www.monaco.edu

- For-profit 4-year university and business college
- Commuter campus in small city
- 138 full-time, degree-seeking undergraduates
- 107 graduate students
- Application essay required

General. IUM comprises more than 50 nationalities among its students and faculty and has received top rankings for student diversity. **Degrees:** 42 bachelor's awarded; master's, doctoral offered. **Location:** 12 miles from Nice, France. **Calendar:** Trimester, limited summer session. **Full-time faculty:** 36 total. **Part-time faculty:** 21 total. **Special facilities:** Principality of Monaco features high-quality sports facilities, museums and other leisure activities.

Basis for selection. IUM seeks to enroll students from wide range of backgrounds and nationalities. Students who show clear commitment to international education (may be demonstrated by travel experience or languages spoken) and leadership potential given priority. Students should also have high level of math preparation as degree programs require excellent quantitative skills. **Homeschooled:** Interview, letter of recommendation (nonparent) required.

High school preparation. Recommended units include mathematics 4 and foreign language 4.

2008-2009 Annual costs. Flat fee for all nationalities of 12,800 euros per academic year, over 3 years. One-time enrollment fee of 1,500 (euros) for freshmen. Housing costs range from 500 to 950 (euros) per month. If students live and pay rent in France, it is possible to receive housing subsidy from French government (approximately 120 euros per month). Books/supplies: $1,000.

2008-2009 Financial aid. **Non-need-based:** Scholarships awarded for academics, leadership.

Application procedures. **Admission:** Priority date 1/2; deadline 6/15 (postmark date). $150 fee. Application must be submitted on paper. Admission notification on a rolling basis. Admission must be accepted within 14 days of receiving offer.

Academics. One-on-one personalized academic counseling session with academic adviser before each term; high faculty to student ratio (1:8); small class size (fewer than 15 students per class). **Special study options:** Accelerated study, ESL, exchange student, internships, study abroad. **Credit/placement by examination:** CLEP. **Support services:** Reduced course load, study skills assistance, tutoring.

Majors. **Business:** Business admin.

Computing on campus. 100 workstations in library, computer center, student center. Commuter students can connect to campus network. Online library, helpline, repair service, wireless network available.

Student life. **Freshman orientation:** Mandatory. Preregistration for classes offered. Orientation held each year at Club Med, Opio, France. Students taken by bus to resort for intensive 3-day teambuilding session. **Housing:** Apartments available. **Activities:** Student government.

Athletics. **Intramural:** Basketball, golf, sailing, soccer, tennis.

Student services. Career counseling, student employment services, placement for graduates.

Contact. E-mail: info@monaco.edu
Phone: (377) 979-86994 Fax: (377) 920-52830
Leila Bello, Director of Admissions, International University of Monaco, Admissions, Monte-Carlo, MC

Republic of Korea

Yonsei University
Seoul, Republic of Korea — **CB member**
www.yonsei.ac.kr/eng/ — **CB code: 9893**

- Private 4-year university
- Commuter campus in very large city
- 25,353 degree-seeking undergraduates
- 8,867 graduate students
- 14% of applicants admitted
- Application essay, interview required

General. **ROTC:** Army. **Calendar:** Semester, limited summer session. **Full-time faculty:** 1,725 total. **Part-time faculty:** 2,137 total.

Freshman class profile. 30,018 applied, 4,186 admitted, 3,895 enrolled.

Mid 50% test scores		SAT math:	720-790
SAT critical reading:	640-750	SAT writing:	660-730

Basis for selection. Admission based on two stages: (1) high school and junior high school academic performance, foreign language proficiency certification, teachers' recommendations, personal statement, and other application information; (2) candidates selected from 1st stage in admission process will proceed to interview, and each candidate will be scored for interview evaluation. Final admission granted to top scoring candidates based on combined scores from 1st and 2nd rounds of selection process. **Homeschooled:** State high school equivalency certificate required.

2008-2009 Annual costs. Per-semester charges: $3,172 (tuition), $1,643 (on-campus room/board); books and miscellaneous expenses, $710.

Application procedures. **Admission:** Closing date 5/15 (postmark date). $200 fee.

Academics. **Special study options:** Accelerated study, combined bachelor's/graduate degree, cooperative education, cross-registration, double major, dual enrollment of high school students, study abroad, teacher certification program. **Credit/placement by examination:** AP, CLEP, institutional tests. **Support services:** Learning center, pre-admission summer program, study skills assistance, tutoring, writing center.

Majors. **Architecture:** Architecture, urban/community planning. **Biology:** General, biochemistry. **Business:** General. **Communications:** Media studies. **Computer sciences:** General, information technology. **Education:** General. **Engineering:** Ceramic, chemical, civil, computer, electrical, metallurgical. **Engineering technology:** Electrical. **Foreign languages:** Chinese, French, German, Korean, Russian. **Health:** Nursing (RN), predental, premedicine. **History:** General. **Legal studies:** General. **Liberal arts:** Library science. **Math:** General, statistics. **Philosophy/religion:** Philosophy. **Physical sciences:** Chemistry. **Psychology:** General. **Public administration:** General. **Social sciences:** Economics. **Theology:** Theology.

Computing on campus. 1,050 workstations in dormitories, library, computer center, student center. Dormitories wired for high-speed internet access. Commuter students can connect to campus network. Online course registration, online library, helpline, repair service, student web hosting, wireless network available.

Student life. **Freshman orientation:** Available. **Housing:** Coed dorms available. **Activities:** Bands, campus ministries, choral groups, dance, drama, film society, international student organizations, literary magazine, music ensembles, Model UN, musical theater, opera, radio station, student government, student newspaper, symphony orchestra, TV station.

Student services. Chaplain/spiritual director, career counseling, services for economically disadvantaged, student employment services, financial aid counseling, health services, minority student services, personal counseling, placement for graduates, women's services. **Physically disabled:** Services for visually, speech, hearing impaired. **Learning disabled:** Comprehensive services available.

Contact. E-mail: ysadms@yonsei.ac.kr
Phone: (822) 212-34131 Fax: (822) 364-2364
Eun-kyung Kim, Admissions Officer, Yonsei University, 262 Seongsanno, Seodaemun-gu, Seoul, KR

Singapore

Singapore Management University

Singapore, Singapore **CB member**
www.smu.edu.sg **CB code: 3873**

- Private 4-year university
- Very large city
- 5,720 degree-seeking undergraduates
- SAT or ACT with writing required

General. **Degrees:** 1,063 bachelor's awarded; master's, doctoral offered. **Calendar:** Semester. **Full-time faculty:** 233 total. **Part-time faculty:** 262 total.

Freshman class profile. 1,660 enrolled.

Basis for selection. Holistic selection approach based on academic record, co-curricular activities, SAT scores, and admissions interview for short-listed applicants; application fee is $15 (Singapore dollars).

2008-2009 Annual costs. Full tuition and fees for Law and non-Law programs are $27,900 (Singapore dollars) per year. Successfully enrolled students are eligible for tuition grant offered by Singapore government that provides qualified students with a subsidy worth on average 50% of full tuition and fees. Subsidized tuition and fees for international students admitted into a non-Law program are $13,700 (Singapore dollars) per year; $15,080 (Singapore dollars) per year for Law program. Students who opt for this tuition grant will be bonded to work in any Singapore-registered company for three years upon graduation.

Application procedures. **Admission:** Closing date 4/8. Admission notification 7/1. Admission notification on a rolling basis beginning on or about 5/1. **Financial aid:** No deadline.

Academics. **Special study options:** Cooperative education, double major, exchange student, honors, internships, study abroad. **Credit/placement by examination:** CLEP.

Majors. **Business:** Accounting, business admin, communications, finance, marketing, operations, organizational behavior. **Computer sciences:** Information systems. **Legal studies:** General. **Psychology:** General. **Social sciences:** General, economics, political science, sociology.

Student life. **Activities:** Bands, choral groups, dance, drama, film society, literary magazine, music ensembles, musical theater, radio station, student government, student newspaper, symphony orchestra.

Athletics. **Intramural:** Archery, badminton, basketball, bowling, cricket, cross-country, fencing, football (non-tackle), golf, handball, judo, rugby, sailing, soccer M, squash, swimming, table tennis, tennis, track and field, volleyball, water polo.

Student services. Personal counseling.

Contact. E-mail: admissions@smu.edu.sg
Phone: (65) 682-80305 Fax: (65) 682-80303
Alan Goh, Director of Undergraduate Admissions, Singapore Management University, 81 Victoria Street, Singapore, SG 25975

Switzerland

Franklin College: Switzerland

Lugano, Switzerland **CB member**
www.fc.edu **CB code: 0922**

- Private 4-year liberal arts college
- Residential campus in small city
- 416 degree-seeking undergraduates: 1% part-time, 65% women
- 71% of applicants admitted
- SAT or ACT with writing, application essay required
- 58% graduate within 6 years

General. Founded in 1969. Regionally accredited. Undergraduate degree programs are accredited in United States and in Switzerland. Instruction in English. Students from 50 nations. **Degrees:** 62 bachelor's, 2 associate awarded. **Location:** 60 miles from Milan, Italy; 80 miles from Lucerne. **Calendar:** Semester, extensive summer session. **Full-time faculty:** 24 total; 79% have terminal degrees, 29% women. **Part-time faculty:** 33 total; 27% have terminal degrees, 61% women. **Class size:** 72% < 20, 28% 20-39.

Freshman class profile. 612 applied, 434 admitted, 139 enrolled.

Mid 50% test scores			
SAT critical reading:	560-660	**GPA 3.50-3.74:**	19%
SAT math:	520-640	**GPA 3.0-3.49:**	31%
SAT writing:	530-650	**GPA 2.0-2.99:**	35%
ACT composite:	24-29	**End year in good standing:**	93%
GPA 3.75 or higher:	15%	**Return as sophomores:**	75%
		Live on campus:	99%

Basis for selection. High school academic record, recommendations, extracurricular participation most important. Essay, test scores, interview also important. TOEFL required for students whose first language is not English. SAT Subject Tests recommended. Essay and personal statement required. Interview recommended for all. **Homeschooled:** Statement describing homeschool structure and mission, letter of recommendation (nonparent) required.

High school preparation. College-preparatory program required. 19 units recommended. Recommended units include English 4, mathematics 3, social studies 1, history 3, science 3, foreign language 3 and academic electives 2. Electives include computer science, art, music.

2008-2009 Annual costs. Tuition/fees: $33,100. Room/board: $11,500. Books/supplies: $1,500. Personal expenses: $1,450.

2007-2008 Financial aid. All financial aid based on need.

Application procedures. **Admission:** Priority date 3/15; no deadline. $90 fee. Admission notification on a rolling basis beginning on or about 12/15. Must reply by May 1 or within 2 week(s) if notified thereafter. **Financial aid:** Priority date 2/15, closing date 3/30. FAFSA, institutional form required. CSS PROFILE preferred. Applicants notified on a rolling basis starting 2/15; must reply by 5/1 or within 3 week(s) of notification.

Academics. 2-week credit-bearing academic travel program required each semester. **Special study options:** Double major, ESL, exchange student, honors, independent study, internships, semester at sea, study abroad, Washington semester. Sophomore and junior year abroad programs with cooperating colleges/universities. **Credit/placement by examination:** AP, CLEP, IB, institutional tests. 15 credit hours maximum toward associate degree, 30 toward bachelor's. **Support services:** Reduced course load, study skills assistance, tutoring, writing center.

Majors. **Area/ethnic studies:** European. **Conservation:** Environmental science. **Foreign languages:** General, French, Italian. **History:** General. **Social sciences:** International economics, international relations. **Visual/performing arts:** General, art history/conservation. **Other:** Communications and media studies, Creative writing and literature, French studies, International management.

Most popular majors. Business/marketing 36%, communications/journalism 24%, social sciences 21%, visual/performing arts 6%.

Computing on campus. 57 workstations in library, computer center, student center. Dormitories wired for high-speed internet access and linked to campus network. Commuter students can connect to campus network. Online library, repair service, student web hosting, wireless network available.

Student life. **Freshman orientation:** Mandatory, $265 fee. **Policies:** All students live within the Lugano community; 55% from United States. **Housing:** Guaranteed on-campus for freshmen. Coed dorms, single-sex dorms, apartments, wellness housing available. $315 partly refundable deposit, deadline 6/15. College-owned and leased apartments on and adjacent to campus and in Lugano; freshmen and sophomores must live in college housing. **Activities:** Dance, drama, literary magazine, student government, student newspaper, international business club, language clubs, numerous sports clubs, international relations club, cultural clubs, booster club, film society, Amnesty International, Far Lawn Club.

Athletics. **Intramural:** Basketball, soccer, tennis, volleyball. **Team name:** Falcons.

Student services. Alcohol/substance abuse counseling, career counseling, student employment services, financial aid counseling, health services, personal counseling, placement for graduates, women's services.

Contact. E-mail: info@fc.edu
Phone: (718) 335-6800 Fax: (718) 335-6733
Karen Ballard, Director of Admissions, Franklin College: Switzerland, 420 Lexington Avenue, Suite 2746, New York, NY 10170

United Arab Emirates

American University in Dubai

Dubai, United Arab Emirates **CB member**
www.aud.edu **CB code: 2688**

- Private 4-year university
- Commuter campus in very large city
- 2,480 degree-seeking undergraduates: 15% part-time, 45% women
- 119 degree-seeking graduate students
- 90% of applicants admitted
- Application essay required

General. Regionally accredited. **Degrees:** 392 bachelor's awarded; master's offered. **Calendar:** Semester, extensive summer session. **Full-time faculty:** 96 total; 27% women. **Part-time faculty:** 82 total; 65% women.

Freshman class profile. 865 applied, 780 admitted, 493 enrolled.

Basis for selection. GED not accepted. Applications reviewed on a rolling basis. Students will be notified of their admissions status within two weeks after applying. Students can take math placement test or submit acceptable SAT score. All engineering applicants must take SAT; combined score of 1090 (exclusive of Writing) required for admissions to the program. **Learning Disabled:** Student should declare disability upon applying. Student services provides support on a case by case basis.

2008-2009 Annual costs. Tuition/fees: $16,082. Room only: $4,658. Books/supplies: $600.

2008-2009 Financial aid. Non-need-based: Scholarships awarded for academics, athletics.

Application procedures. Admission: Closing date 8/20. $50 fee. Application must be submitted on paper. Admission notification on a rolling basis.

Academics. Special study options: Combined bachelor's/graduate degree, ESL, internships, study abroad. **Credit/placement by examination:** AP, CLEP, IB, SAT, institutional tests. **Support services:** Pre-admission summer program, reduced course load, remedial instruction, study skills assistance, tutoring, writing center.

Majors. Business: General, accounting, banking/financial services, e-commerce, management science, marketing. **Communications:** Media studies. **Communications technology:** Graphics. **Computer sciences:** Information technology. **Engineering:** Civil, computer, electrical. **Visual/performing arts:** Commercial/advertising art, graphic design, illustration, interior design, photography.

Computing on campus. 65 workstations in library, computer center. Dormitories wired for high-speed internet access. Commuter students can connect to campus network. Online library, helpline, repair service, wireless network available.

Student life. Freshman orientation: Mandatory. **Policies:** Dress code; no alcohol and no drugs on campus. **Housing:** Single-sex dorms, special housing for disabled, wellness housing available. $680 nonrefundable deposit, deadline 6/2. **Activities:** Dance, drama, international student organizations, student government, student newspaper, African cultural club, Egyptian cultural club, Indian cultural club, Khaleej student association, Lebanese student association, Palestinian student association, Pakistani student association, Syrian and Islamic awareness club.

Athletics. Intercollegiate: Basketball, soccer, swimming, tennis, track and field, volleyball. **Intramural:** Soccer, table tennis, volleyball, water polo.

Student services. Alcohol/substance abuse counseling, career counseling, student employment services, health services, on-campus daycare, personal counseling, placement for graduates. **Physically disabled:** Services for visually, speech, hearing impaired.

Contact. E-mail: admissions@aud.edu
Phone: (4) 399-9000 Fax: (4) 399-8899
Carol Maalouf, Director of Admissions, American University in Dubai, PO Box 28282, Dubai, AE

United Kingdom

Richmond, The American International University in London

Richmond-upon-Thames, United Kingdom **CB member**
www.richmond.ac.uk **CB code: 0823**

- Private 4-year university and liberal arts college
- Residential campus in very large city
- 703 degree-seeking undergraduates: 1% part-time, 61% women
- 7 degree-seeking graduate students
- Application essay required
- 51% graduate within 6 years; 72% enter graduate study

General. Founded in 1972. Regionally accredited. International student body with over 110 countries represented. Students spend their first two years on the Richmond Hill campus and the second two on the Kensington campus in London. Study centers in Florence and Rome, Italy. Degrees accredited in the both the US and the UK. **Degrees:** 133 bachelor's awarded; master's offered. **Calendar:** Semester, extensive summer session. **Full-time faculty:** 43 total. **Part-time faculty:** 69 total. **Class size:** 68% < 20, 32% 20-39, less than 1% 40-49. **Special facilities:** The Richmond Hill campus is next to Richmond Park, the largest of the Royal Parks and Europe's largest urban walled park.

Freshman class profile. 1,400 applied, 980 admitted, 400 enrolled.

End year in good standing:	90%	**Out-of-state:**	100%
Return as sophomores:	74%	**Live on campus:**	86%

Basis for selection. Open admission, but selective for some programs. School achievement record most important. Letters of recommendation and personal statement considered. SAT/ACT scores also considered but not required. SAT or ACT recommended. Interviews and campus visits are recommended but not required.

High school preparation. College-preparatory program recommended. 19 units required. Required and recommended units include English 4, mathematics 3-4, social studies 1, history 1, science 3-4 (laboratory 1), foreign language 2-3, computer science 1, visual/performing arts 1 and academic electives 2-4.

2008-2009 Annual costs. Tuition/fees: $27,000. Room/board: $12,900. Books/supplies: $600. Personal expenses: $4,500.

2008-2009 Financial aid. Non-need-based: Scholarships awarded for academics. **Additional information:** U.S. government loan programs available for eligible U.S. citizens/students.

Application procedures. Admission: Priority date 3/1; no deadline. $50 fee, may be waived for applicants with need. Admission notification on a rolling basis. Must reply by May 1 or within 4 week(s) if notified thereafter. **Financial aid:** Priority date 3/15, closing date 8/1. FAFSA required. Applicants notified on a rolling basis starting 3/1; must reply by 5/1 or within 4 week(s) of notification.

Academics. English language development programs for non-native English speakers. **Special study options:** Combined bachelor's/graduate degree, cross-registration, double major, ESL, independent study, internships, liberal arts/career combination, study abroad. Joint engineering program with George Washington University. **Credit/placement by examination:** AP, CLEP, IB, institutional tests. **Support services:** Reduced course load, remedial instruction, study skills assistance, tutoring, writing center.

Majors. **Business:** Finance, international, marketing. **Communications:** Media studies. **Computer sciences:** General. **Engineering:** General, computer. **History:** General. **Liberal arts:** Arts/sciences. **Psychology:** General. **Social sciences:** Economics, international relations, political science. **Visual/performing arts:** Design, studio arts.

Most popular majors. Business/marketing 35%, communications/journalism 20%, computer/information sciences 9%, psychology 6%, social sciences 18%, visual/performing arts 6%.

Computing on campus. 333 workstations in dormitories, library, computer center, student center. Dormitories wired for high-speed internet access and linked to campus network. Commuter students can connect to campus network. Online course registration, online library, helpline, student web hosting, wireless network available.

Student life. **Freshman orientation:** Mandatory. Preregistration for classes offered. **Housing:** Guaranteed on-campus for all undergraduates. Coed dorms, single-sex dorms, special housing for disabled, apartments, wellness housing available. $1,000 nonrefundable deposit, deadline 5/1. **Activities:** Bands, choral groups, dance, drama, film society, international student organizations, literary magazine, music ensembles, Model UN, musical theater, student government, student newspaper, Community Outreach Club, Amnesty International, Pan-African Club, Middle Eastern Society, Literary Society, International Night, Student Ambassadors, Kuwaiti United, History/Politics Society, Royal United Services Institute for Defense and Security Studies (RUSI for Richmond University).

Athletics. **Team name:** Roebucks.

Student services. Alcohol/substance abuse counseling, career counseling, student employment services, financial aid counseling, health services, minority student services, personal counseling, placement for graduates.

Contact. E-mail: enroll@richmond.ac.uk
Phone: (617) 450-5617 Fax: (617) 450-5601
Nicholas Atkinson, Director, US Office of Admissions, Richmond, The American International University in London, 343 Congress Street, Suite 3100, Boston, MA 02210-1214

Two-year colleges

Alabama

Alabama Southern Community College
Monroeville, Alabama
www.ascc.edu **CB code: 1644**

- Public 2-year community and junior college
- Commuter campus in small town

General. Founded in 1965. Regionally accredited. Institution has 3 campuses and 3 centers. **Enrollment:** 1,300 degree-seeking undergraduates. **Degrees:** 141 associate awarded. **Location:** 85 miles from Mobile. **Calendar:** Semester, extensive summer session. **Full-time faculty:** 45 total. **Part-time faculty:** 70 total. **Special facilities:** Nature trail.

Basis for selection. Open admission.

2008-2009 Annual costs. Tuition/fees: $2,700; $4,830 out-of-state. Per-credit charge: $71 in-state; $142 out-of-state. Books/supplies: $750.

Application procedures. Admission: No deadline. No application fee. Admission notification on a rolling basis. **Financial aid:** Priority date 7/15; no closing date. FAFSA required. Applicants notified on a rolling basis; must reply within 4 week(s) of notification.

Academics. Special study options: Accelerated study, dual enrollment of high school students, honors, independent study. Degrees in allied health available through University of Alabama at Birmingham, registered nurse program through Jefferson Davis State Junior College. **Credit/placement by examination:** CLEP, institutional tests. 30 credit hours maximum toward associate degree. **Support services:** GED preparation and test center, learning center, pre-admission summer program, reduced course load, remedial instruction, tutoring.

Majors. Business: General, administrative services. **Computer sciences:** General. **Engineering:** Electrical. **Engineering technology:** Electrical. **Health:** Licensed practical nurse, nursing (RN), nursing assistant. **Liberal arts:** Arts/sciences. **Mechanic/repair:** Electronics/electrical, industrial. **Personal/culinary services:** Cosmetic. **Protective services:** Firefighting.

Computing on campus. 9 workstations in library, computer center.

Student life. Freshman orientation: Mandatory. Preregistration for classes offered. **Activities:** Bands, choral groups, student government, student newspaper, Baptist student union, Circle K, ethnic student society, Phi Theta Kappa, Phi Beta Lambda, Baptist campus ministry, Students in Free Enterprise.

Athletics. NJCAA. **Intercollegiate:** Baseball M, basketball M. **Intramural:** Basketball M, softball, table tennis, tennis, volleyball. **Team name:** Eagles.

Student services. Adult student services, career counseling, personal counseling, placement for graduates, veterans' counselor.

Contact. Phone: (251) 575-3156 Fax: (251) 575-5238
Ann Clánton, Dean of Students, Alabama Southern Community College, Box 2000, Monroeville, AL 36461

Bevill State Community College
Sumiton, Alabama
www.bscc.edu **CB code: 0723**

- Public 2-year community college
- Commuter campus in small town

General. Founded in 1969. Regionally accredited. Additional campuses in Fayette, Hamilton, and Jasper. Learning site in Carrollton. **Enrollment:** 3,899 degree-seeking undergraduates. **Degrees:** 468 associate awarded. **Location:** 25 miles from Birmingham. **Calendar:** Semester, limited summer session. **Full-time faculty:** 121 total. **Part-time faculty:** 182 total. **Special facilities:** Observatory, simulated underground mine, museum.

Student profile. Among degree-seeking undergraduates, 43% enrolled in a transfer program, 57% enrolled in a vocational program, 928 enrolled as first-time, first-year students, 1,763 transferred in from other institutions.

Transfer out. Colleges most students transferred to 2008: University of Alabama, Auburn University, University of North Alabama, University of Alabama Birmingham, University of Montevallo.

Basis for selection. Open admission, but selective for some programs. Admission to nursing programs competitive and limited. High school diploma not required in some technical programs. COMPASS required for placement unless applicant has 480 SAT verbal and 526 SAT math, or 20 ACT. **Adult students:** COMPASS placement testing required unless student is senior citizen or non-award seeking major taking classes for vocational reasons. **Homeschooled:** State high school equivalency certificate required.

2008-2009 Annual costs. Tuition/fees: $2,730; $4,860 out-of-state. Per-credit charge: $71 in-state; $142 out-of-state. Room only: $1,350. Books/supplies: $1,200. Personal expenses: $1,400.

2007-2008 Financial aid. Need-based: Need-based aid available for part-time students. **Non-need-based:** Scholarships awarded for academics, athletics, leadership, music/drama.

Application procedures. Admission: No deadline. No application fee. Admission notification on a rolling basis beginning on or about 7/1. **Financial aid:** Priority date 5/1; no closing date. FAFSA required. Applicants notified on a rolling basis starting 7/1.

Academics. Special study options: Accelerated study, cooperative education, distance learning, dual enrollment of high school students, ESL, honors, weekend college. License preparation in nursing, paramedic, physical therapy, real estate. **Credit/placement by examination:** AP, CLEP, institutional tests. Only 25% of program credits can be awarded through non-traditional means. **Support services:** GED preparation and test center, learning center, reduced course load, remedial instruction, tutoring, writing center.

Majors. Business: Administrative services. **Computer sciences:** General, computer science. **Construction:** Electrician. **Engineering technology:** Drafting, heat/ac/refrig. **Family/consumer sciences:** Child care. **Health:** EMT paramedic, nursing (RN). **Legal studies:** Paralegal. **Liberal arts:** Arts/sciences. **Mechanic/repair:** Industrial electronics. **Personal/culinary services:** Cosmetic. **Production:** Tool and die.

Computing on campus. 1,200 workstations in library, computer center, student center. Dormitories wired for high-speed internet access and linked to campus network. Commuter students can connect to campus network. Online course registration, online library, helpline, wireless network available.

Student life. Freshman orientation: Mandatory, $30 fee. Preregistration for classes offered. **Housing:** Coed dorms, wellness housing available. Housing for student athletes available. **Activities:** Bands, campus ministries, choral groups, dance, drama, music ensembles, student government, student newspaper.

Athletics. NJCAA. **Intercollegiate:** Baseball M, basketball, cheerleading, cross-country W, softball W, volleyball W. **Intramural:** Basketball, bowling, boxing, football (non-tackle), softball, table tennis. **Team name:** Bears.

Student services. Chaplain/spiritual director, career counseling, services for economically disadvantaged, student employment services, financial aid counseling, on-campus daycare, placement for graduates. **Physically disabled:** Services for visually, speech, hearing impaired. **Transfer:** Transfer adviser, college fairs on campus for students transferring to 4-year colleges.

Contact. E-mail: sbarton@bscc.edu
Phone: (205) 648-3271 ext. 5400 Toll-free number: (800) 648-3271 ext. 5400 Fax: (205) 648-3311
Melissa Stowe, Assistant to the Dean of Student Services, Bevill State Community College, Box 800, Sumiton, AL 35148

Bishop State Community College

Mobile, Alabama
www.bishop.edu **CB code: 1517**

- Public 2-year community college
- Commuter campus in small city

General. Founded in 1963. Regionally accredited. 4 off-campus sites for technical and health-related programs. **Enrollment:** 2,820 degree-seeking undergraduates. **Degrees:** 268 associate awarded. **ROTC:** Army, Air Force. **Calendar:** Semester, limited summer session. **Full-time faculty:** 115 total. **Part-time faculty:** 20 total. **Partnerships:** Training for business and industry, JTPA Assessment Center, formal partnership with Mobile County public school system.

Basis for selection. Open admission.

2008-2009 Annual costs. Tuition/fees: $2,700; $4,830 out-of-state. Per-credit charge: $71 in-state; $142 out-of-state. Books/supplies: $700. Personal expenses: $1,033.

Financial aid. Non-need-based: Scholarships awarded for academics, athletics.

Application procedures. Admission: No deadline. No application fee. Admission notification on a rolling basis. **Financial aid:** Priority date 4/1; no closing date. FAFSA, institutional form required. Applicants notified on a rolling basis; must reply within 2 week(s) of notification.

Academics. Students must complete 112 credit hours for graduation from technical programs. **Special study options:** Accelerated study, cooperative education, cross-registration, dual enrollment of high school students, honors, internships, weekend college. Degree programs available in allied health through University of Alabama at Birmingham. License preparation in nursing. **Credit/placement by examination:** CLEP. **Support services:** Learning center, pre-admission summer program, reduced course load, remedial instruction, tutoring.

Majors. Business: Accounting, administrative services, business admin. **Computer sciences:** General. **Education:** General. **Engineering technology:** Civil, drafting. **Health:** Medical records technology, nursing (RN), physical therapy assistant. **Liberal arts:** Arts/sciences. **Mechanic/repair:** Electronics/electrical. **Personal/culinary services:** Culinary arts, mortuary science. **Protective services:** Fire services admin, law enforcement admin.

Computing on campus. 71 workstations in library, computer center.

Student life. Freshman orientation: Available. **Activities:** Bands, choral groups, dance, drama, music ensembles, radio station, student government, student newspaper, social service organization, Baptist student union, Young Democrats.

Athletics. NJCAA. **Intercollegiate:** Baseball M, basketball, softball W. **Team name:** Wildcats.

Student services. Adult student services, career counseling, student employment services, health services, on-campus daycare, personal counseling, placement for graduates, veterans' counselor. **Physically disabled:** Services for visually, speech, hearing impaired. **Transfer:** Transfer adviser for students transferring to 4-year colleges.

Contact. Phone: (251) 405-7000 Fax: (251) 438-5403
Wanda Daniels, Director of Admissions, Bishop State Community College, 351 North Broad Street, Mobile, AL 36603-5898

Calhoun Community College

Decatur, Alabama **CB member**
www.calhoun.edu **CB code: 1356**

- Public 2-year community and junior college
- Commuter campus in small city

General. Founded in 1963. Regionally accredited. Satellite campuses at Research Park in Huntsville and at Redstone Arsenal. **Enrollment:** 9,750 degree-seeking undergraduates. **Degrees:** 615 associate awarded. **Location:** 20 miles from Huntsville. **Calendar:** Semester, limited summer session. **Full-time faculty:** 129 total. **Part-time faculty:** 289 total. **Partnerships:** Formal partnership with Boeing.

Transfer out. Colleges most students transferred to 2008: Athens State University, University of North Alabama, Wallace State Community College, Auburn University, University of Alabama.

Basis for selection. Open admission, but selective for some programs. SAT/ACT scores used for placement. Students from unaccredited high schools are required to have a minimum ACT score of 16 or SAT score of 790 (exclusive of Writing). Selective admission to nursing program. Portfolio recommended for art majors. **Homeschooled:** Must have ACT score of at least 16, SAT score of 790 (exclusive of Writing), successfully complete GED or high school graduation examination.

High school preparation. 26 units recommended. Recommended units include English 4, mathematics 4, social studies 4, science 4, foreign language 2 and academic electives 10. In-state high school graduates must pass state high school competency examination.

2008-2009 Annual costs. Tuition/fees: $2,850; $4,980 out-of-state. Per-credit charge: $71 in-state; $142 out-of-state. Books/supplies: $1,500. Personal expenses: $1,000.

Financial aid. Need-based: Work-study available for part-time students. **Non-need-based:** Scholarships awarded for academics.

Application procedures. Admission: No deadline. No application fee. Admission notification on a rolling basis. **Financial aid:** Priority date 5/1; no closing date. FAFSA, institutional form required. Applicants notified on a rolling basis starting 7/1; must reply within 2 week(s) of notification.

Academics. Numerous courses available online and by videocassette. **Special study options:** Accelerated study, distance learning, dual enrollment of high school students, liberal arts/career combination, weekend college. License preparation in dental hygiene, nursing, paramedic, real estate. **Credit/placement by examination:** AP, CLEP, institutional tests. 30 credit hours maximum toward associate degree. AP Exam credit limited to 18 semester hours. **Support services:** GED preparation and test center, reduced course load, remedial instruction, tutoring, writing center.

Majors. Agriculture: General. **Biology:** General. **Business:** Accounting, business admin. **Communications technology:** General, photo/film/video. **Computer sciences:** General, applications programming, computer graphics, programming. **Construction:** Electrician. **Education:** General, secondary. **Engineering technology:** Aerospace, drafting, heat/ac/refrig. **Family/consumer sciences:** Child care, child development. **Health:** Cytogenetics, dental assistant, EMT paramedic, nursing (RN), predental, premedicine, prenursing, prepharmacy, preveterinary. **History:** General. **Legal studies:** Paralegal, prelaw. **Liberal arts:** Arts/sciences. **Math:** General. **Mechanic/repair:** Heating/ac/refrig. **Parks/recreation:** Health/fitness. **Physical sciences:** Chemistry. **Production:** Machine tool, tool and die. **Social sciences:** General. **Transportation:** Aviation. **Visual/performing arts:** Commercial/advertising art, photography, theater arts management. **Other:** Aerospace technology, Family financial planning and counseling, Missile and munitions technology, Music industry communications.

Most popular majors. Business/marketing 22%, computer/information sciences 6%, education 10%, health sciences 25%, liberal arts 22%, military 14%.

Computing on campus. 166 workstations in library, student center. Commuter students can connect to campus network. Online course registration, wireless network available.

Student life. Freshman orientation: Mandatory, $95 fee. Preregistration for classes offered. Class held the first semester of attendance. **Activities:** Jazz band, choral groups, drama, music ensembles, student government, student newspaper, TV station, BACCHUS/SADD, campus ministries, black students alliance club, criminal justice club, Native American club, Phi Theta Kappa, Allied Health Students Association, The Centurians.

Athletics. NJCAA. **Intercollegiate:** Baseball M, softball W. **Intramural:** Basketball, volleyball. **Team name:** Warhawks.

Student services. Career counseling, financial aid counseling, minority student services, on-campus daycare, veterans' counselor. **Transfer:** Transfer adviser, college fairs on campus for students transferring to 4-year colleges.

Contact. E-mail: sjl@calhoun.edu
Phone: (256) 306-2593 Toll-free number: (800) 626-3628
Fax: (256) 306-2941
Rob Steinmetz, Associate Dean of Enrollment Management, Calhoun Community College, Box 2216, Decatur, AL 35609-2216

Central Alabama Community College

Childersburg, Alabama
www.cacc.cc.al.us **CB code: 0715**

- Public 2-year community college
- Commuter campus in large town

General. Founded in 1965. Regionally accredited. 2 campuses: Childersburg, predominantly for technical courses, and Alexander City, predominantly for transfer courses. **Enrollment:** 2,200 degree-seeking undergraduates. **Degrees:** 214 associate awarded. **Location:** 50 miles from Montgomery, 35 miles from Birmingham. **Calendar:** Semester, extensive summer session. **Full-time faculty:** 60 total. **Part-time faculty:** 70 total. **Special facilities:** Wildlife museum, wellness center, pioneer village.

Student profile.

Out-of-state:	1%	25 or older:	39%

Basis for selection. Open admission, but selective for some programs. Graduates of non-accredited high schools and certain nursing applicants may be required to take SAT or ACT.

2008-2009 Annual costs. Tuition/fees: $2,700; $4,830 out-of-state. Per-credit charge: $71 in-state; $142 out-of-state. Books/supplies: $300. Personal expenses: $500.

Financial aid. Non-need-based: Scholarships awarded for academics, athletics, state residency.

Application procedures. Admission: Closing date 8/21. No application fee. Admission notification on a rolling basis. **Financial aid:** Priority date 7/15; no closing date. FAFSA, institutional form required. Applicants notified on a rolling basis.

Academics. Special study options: Cooperative education, dual enrollment of high school students, independent study. **Credit/placement by examination:** CLEP, institutional tests. 48 credit hours maximum toward associate degree. **Support services:** GED preparation and test center, learning center, remedial instruction, study skills assistance, tutoring.

Majors. Agriculture: Business. **Business:** General, administrative services, business admin, management information systems. **Computer sciences:** General. **Education:** General. **Engineering:** General. **Engineering technology:** Drafting, electrical. **Health:** Clinical lab science, EMT paramedic, health services, medical assistant, medical radiologic technology/radiation therapy, medical records technology, occupational therapy assistant, physical therapy assistant, respiratory therapy technology. **Liberal arts:** Arts/sciences. **Protective services:** Criminal justice, firefighting, police science.

Computing on campus. 45 workstations in library, computer center, student center.

Student life. Freshman orientation: Mandatory. **Activities:** Jazz band, choral groups, dance, drama, radio station, student government.

Athletics. NJCAA. **Intercollegiate:** Baseball M, golf M, softball W, tennis, volleyball W. **Team name:** Trojans.

Student services. Career counseling, personal counseling, veterans' counselor. **Transfer:** Pre-admission transcript evaluation for new students. Transfer adviser, college fairs on campus for students transferring to 4-year colleges.

Contact. Phone: (256) 215-4255 Toll-free number: (800) 643-2657
Amanda Harkins, Dean of Students, Central Alabama Community College, 34091 US Highway 280 South, Childersburg, AL 35044

Chattahoochee Valley Community College

Phenix City, Alabama
www.cv.edu **CB code: 1187**

- Public 2-year community college
- Commuter campus in small city

General. Founded in 1974. Regionally accredited. **Enrollment:** 1,925 degree-seeking undergraduates. **Degrees:** 187 associate awarded. **ROTC:** Army. **Location:** 5 miles from Columbus, Georgia. **Calendar:** Semester, extensive summer session. **Full-time faculty:** 31 total. **Part-time faculty:** 98 total.

Transfer out. Colleges most students transferred to 2008: Columbus State University, Auburn University, Columbus Technical College, Southern Union State Community College, Troy State University.

Basis for selection. Open admission, but selective for some programs. SAT and ACT considered if submitted. ASSET waived for students submitting appropriate ACT/SAT scores. Additional requirements for health occupation programs. **Homeschooled:** State high school equivalency certificate required. Program must be accreditated by state or federal department of education.

2008-2009 Annual costs. Tuition/fees: $2,700; $4,830 out-of-state. Per-credit charge: $71 in-state; $142 out-of-state. Books/supplies: $800. Personal expenses: $750.

2007-2008 Financial aid. Need-based: 59% of total undergraduate aid awarded as scholarships/grants, 41% as loans/jobs. Need-based aid available for part-time students. Work-study available nights, weekends and for part-time students. **Non-need-based:** Scholarships awarded for academics, art, athletics, leadership, music/drama.

Application procedures. Admission: Priority date 7/15; no deadline. No application fee. Admission notification on a rolling basis. **Financial aid:** Priority date 7/1; no closing date. FAFSA required. Applicants notified on a rolling basis; must reply within 1 week(s) of notification.

Academics. Special study options: Accelerated study, distance learning, dual enrollment of high school students, honors, independent study, liberal arts/career combination. License preparation in nursing. **Credit/placement by examination:** CLEP, institutional tests. 18 credit hours maximum toward associate degree. **Support services:** GED test center, learning center, reduced course load, remedial instruction.

Majors. Biology: General. **Business:** Accounting, administrative services, business admin. **Computer sciences:** General, data processing. **Conservation:** Forestry. **Education:** Business, elementary, physical, secondary. **Engineering:** General. **Health:** Medical records technology, nursing (RN). **Liberal arts:** Arts/sciences. **Math:** General. **Parks/recreation:** Health/fitness. **Physical sciences:** Chemistry, physics. **Protective services:** Criminal justice, firefighting. **Visual/performing arts:** Art history/conservation, dramatic.

Computing on campus. 150 workstations in library, computer center. Online library available.

Student life. Freshman orientation: Available. Preregistration for classes offered. **Activities:** Choral groups, drama, music ensembles, musical theater, student government, student newspaper.

Athletics. NJCAA. **Intercollegiate:** Baseball M, basketball, softball W. **Team name:** Pirates.

Student services. Adult student services, career counseling, personal counseling, placement for graduates, veterans' counselor. **Physically disabled:** Services for visually, hearing impaired.

Contact. Phone: (334) 291-4900 ext. 4929 Fax: (334) 291-4994
David Hodge, Dean of Student and Administrative Services, Chattahoochee Valley Community College, 2602 College Drive, Phenix City, AL 36869

Community College of the Air Force

Maxwell-Gunter AFB, Alabama **CB member**
www.au.af.mil/au/ccaf **CB code: 1175**

- Public 2-year community and technical college
- Commuter campus in small city
- Interview required

General. Founded in 1972. Regionally accredited. Multicampus, worldwide, for United States Air Force enlisted personnel. Administrative offices at Maxwell Air Force Base. Primary campuses are technical training centers located at 5 Air Force bases in 3 states. Other campuses include USAF PME Centers, USAF Command Sponsored Schools, and Field Training Detachments. **Enrollment:** 321,775 degree-seeking undergraduates. **Degrees:** 18,091 associate awarded. **Location:** 160 miles from Atlanta, 90 miles from Birmingham. **Calendar:** Continuous, extensive summer session. **Full-time faculty:** 5,800 total.

Basis for selection. Open admission. All USAF enlisted personnel automatically registered upon completion of basic military training and assignment to an Air Force career field. All applicants must take the Armed Services Vocational Aptitude Battery.

High school preparation. 16 units recommended. Recommended units include English 4, mathematics 3, social studies 3, science 2 and foreign language 2.

2008-2009 Annual costs. Students pay no tuition or fees.

Financial aid. Additional information: Air Force Tuition Assistance program available for general and technical education courses taken at civilian colleges and universities. Pays 75% of tuition costs.

Application procedures. Admission: No deadline. No application fee. Admission notification on a rolling basis. **Financial aid:** No deadline.

Academics. Special study options: Accelerated study, distance learning, independent study, internships, liberal arts/career combination. License preparation in aviation, physical therapy, radiology. **Credit/placement by examination:** AP, CLEP, institutional tests. 30 credit hours maximum toward associate degree. **Support services:** Reduced course load, remedial instruction, tutoring.

Majors. Business: Human resources, management information systems, office management, operations, purchasing. **Communications:** Public relations. **Communications technology:** General. **Computer sciences:** General, networking. **Education:** Technology/industrial arts. **Engineering technology:** Construction, electrical. **Health:** Cardiovascular technology, dental assistant, dental lab technology, health care admin, health services, histologic assistant, medical assistant, nuclear medical technology, ophthalmic lab technology, pharmacy assistant, physical therapy assistant, radiologic technology/medical imaging, sonography, surgical technology. **History:** General. **Interdisciplinary:** Nutrition sciences. **Legal studies:** Paralegal. **Mechanic/repair:** Aircraft, electronics/electrical, heating/ac/refrig, industrial. **Military:** General. **Parks/recreation:** General. **Physical sciences:** Atmospheric science. **Protective services:** Criminal justice, fire safety technology. **Public administration:** Social work. **Transportation:** General, air traffic control, aviation, aviation management.

Student life. Policies: Air Force bases provide housing, student services, activities, and athletics. **Housing:** Coed dorms, single-sex dorms, apartments available.

Athletics. Intramural: Badminton, baseball M, basketball, bowling, boxing M, cross-country, golf, handball, racquetball, rifle, soccer M, softball, squash, swimming, table tennis, tennis, track and field, volleyball, weight lifting.

Student services. Adult student services, alcohol/substance abuse counseling, career counseling, financial aid counseling, health services, legal services, on-campus daycare, personal counseling, veterans' counselor. **Transfer:** Transfer center, transfer adviser, college fairs on campus for students transferring to 4-year colleges.

Contact. E-mail: registrar.ccaf@maxwell.af.mil
Phone: (334) 953-2794 Fax: (334) 953-5231
Terry Amatuzzi, Director of Admissions, Community College of the Air Force, 100 South Turner Boulevard, Maxwell-Gunter AFB, AL 36114-3011

Enterprise-Ozark Community College

Enterprise, Alabama
www.eocc.edu **CB code: 1213**

- Public 2-year community college
- Commuter campus in large town

General. Founded in 1963. Regionally accredited. Courses offered at Enterprise, Ozark, Fort Rucker, and Mobile. **Enrollment:** 2,284 undergraduates. **Degrees:** 208 associate awarded. **Location:** 85 miles from Montgomery. **Calendar:** Semester, limited summer session. **Full-time faculty:** 59 total; 7% have terminal degrees, 34% minority, 36% women. **Part-time faculty:** 75 total; 27% minority, 37% women.

Student profile. 65% enrolled in a transfer program, 15% enrolled in a vocational program.

Transfer out. Colleges most students transferred to 2008: Troy State University, Troy State University at Dothan, Auburn University.

Basis for selection. Open admission. **Homeschooled:** If sponsoring organization is not accredited, then the student must either take Alabama High School Exit Exam and pass all five parts or take the ACT scoring at least a 16.

High school preparation. 28 units recommended. Recommended units include English 4, mathematics 4, social studies 4 and science 4.

2008-2009 Annual costs. Tuition/fees: $2,700; $4,830 out-of-state. Per-credit charge: $71 in-state; $142 out-of-state. Books/supplies: $500. Personal expenses: $500.

Financial aid. Need-based: Work-study available for part-time students. **Non-need-based:** Scholarships awarded for academics, art, athletics, leadership, music/drama, state residency.

Application procedures. Admission: No deadline. No application fee. Application must be submitted on paper. Admission notification on a rolling basis. **Financial aid:** Priority date 6/15; no closing date. FAFSA, institutional form required. Applicants notified on a rolling basis starting 7/1; must reply within 2 week(s) of notification.

Academics. FAA aviation certified program. **Special study options:** Distance learning, dual enrollment of high school students, ESL, honors, internships, weekend college. License preparation in aviation, paramedic. **Credit/placement by examination:** AP, CLEP, institutional tests. 30 credit hours maximum toward associate degree. **Support services:** GED preparation and test center, learning center, remedial instruction, tutoring.

Majors. Business: Administrative services, business admin, management information systems, office management, real estate. **Computer sciences:** General. **Health:** EMT paramedic, medical assistant, medical records technology. **Legal studies:** Paralegal. **Liberal arts:** Arts/sciences. **Mechanic/repair:** Aircraft, avionics.

Computing on campus. 125 workstations in library, computer center, student center. Commuter students can connect to campus network. Online course registration, online library, helpline available.

Student life. Freshman orientation: Mandatory, $10 fee. Preregistration for classes offered. **Activities:** Concert band, choral groups, dance, drama, literary magazine, music ensembles, student government, student newspaper, scholastic honorary fraternity, African American organizations.

Athletics. NJCAA. **Intercollegiate:** Baseball M, basketball, softball W. **Team name:** Boll Weevils.

Student services. Adult student services, career counseling, student employment services, financial aid counseling, on-campus daycare, personal counseling, placement for graduates, veterans' counselor, women's services. **Physically disabled:** Services for visually, speech, hearing impaired. **Transfer:** Transfer adviser, college fairs on campus for students transferring to 4-year colleges.

Contact. Phone: (334) 347-2623 ext. 2234 Fax: (334) 347-5569
M. Gary Deas, Associate Dean of Students/Registrar, Enterprise-Ozark Community College, Box 1300, Enterprise, AL 36331

Faulkner State Community College

Bay Minette, Alabama
www.faulknerstate.edu **CB code: 1939**

- Public 2-year community college
- Commuter campus in large town

General. Founded in 1965. Regionally accredited. Branch campuses in Fairhope and Gulf Shores. **Enrollment:** 3,507 degree-seeking undergraduates. **Degrees:** 260 associate awarded. **Location:** 35 miles from Mobile. **Calendar:** Semester, extensive summer session. **Full-time faculty:** 71 total. **Part-time faculty:** 123 total.

Transfer out. Colleges most students transferred to 2008: University of Alabama, Auburn University, University of South Alabama.

Basis for selection. Open admission, but selective for some programs. Students applying for dental assisting program must take and pass Health Occupations Aptitude exam. Audition recommended for music majors, portfolio for art majors. **Homeschooled:** If school is non-accredited, 16 ACT or GED required.

2008-2009 Annual costs. Tuition/fees: $2,790; $4,920 out-of-state. Per-credit charge: $71 in-state; $142 out-of-state. Room/board: $4,050. Books/supplies: $450. Personal expenses: $800.

Application procedures. Admission: No deadline. No application fee. Admission notification on a rolling basis. **Financial aid:** Priority date 7/1, closing date 8/1. FAFSA, institutional form required. Applicants notified on a rolling basis starting 8/1.

Academics. Special study options: Accelerated study, cooperative education, distance learning, double major, dual enrollment of high school students, honors, independent study, internships. **Credit/placement by examination:** CLEP. 20 credit hours maximum toward associate degree. **Support**

services: GED preparation and test center, learning center, remedial instruction, tutoring.

Majors. Agriculture: General, business, landscaping. **Biology:** General. **Business:** Administrative services, business admin, finance, hospitality admin, office technology. **Communications:** Journalism. **Computer sciences:** General, computer graphics, systems analysis. **Conservation:** Forestry. **Education:** Business, early childhood, elementary, physical. **Engineering technology:** Hazardous materials. **Family/consumer sciences:** General. **Health:** Clinical lab science, clinical lab technology, dental assistant, EMT paramedic, medical secretary, predental, premedicine, prenursing, prepharmacy, preveterinary. **Legal studies:** Court reporting, legal secretary, paralegal. **Liberal arts:** Arts/sciences. **Math:** General. **Parks/recreation:** Facilities management. **Personal/culinary services:** Culinary arts. **Physical sciences:** Chemistry. **Social sciences:** General. **Visual/performing arts:** General, art, commercial/advertising art, studio arts.

Computing on campus. 16 workstations in library, computer center.

Student life. Freshman orientation: Available. **Housing:** Single-sex dorms available. $35 deposit. **Activities:** Jazz band, choral groups, drama, music ensembles, student government, student newspaper, Pow-wow leadership, Phi Beta Lambda, Baptist campus ministries, Phi Theta Kappa, Psi Beta, association of computational machinery.

Athletics. NJCAA. **Intercollegiate:** Baseball M, basketball, cheerleading, golf, softball W, tennis, volleyball. **Intramural:** Basketball M, bowling, racquetball, softball, volleyball W. **Team name:** Sun Chiefs.

Student services. Career counseling, student employment services, health services, personal counseling, placement for graduates, veterans' counselor. **Physically disabled:** Services for visually impaired. **Transfer:** Transfer adviser for students transferring to 4-year colleges.

Contact. E-mail: pduck@faulknerstate.edu
Phone: (251) 580-2111 Toll-free number: (800) 231-3752
Fax: (251) 580-2285
Betty Shefield, Director of Admissions, Faulkner State Community College, 1900 Highway 31 South, Bay Minette, AL 36507

Gadsden State Community College

Gadsden, Alabama
www.gadsdenstate.edu **CB code: 1262**

- Public 2-year community and technical college
- Commuter campus in large town

General. Founded in 1985. Regionally accredited. Off-campus sites include Ayers Campus, McClellan Campus and Cherokee County Center. **Enrollment:** 4,467 degree-seeking undergraduates; 989 non-degree-seeking students. **Degrees:** 476 associate awarded. **ROTC:** Army. **Location:** 60 miles from Birmingham. **Calendar:** Semester, extensive summer session. **Full-time faculty:** 151 total; 9% have terminal degrees, 57% women. **Part-time faculty:** 116 total; 9% have terminal degrees, 50% women. **Special facilities:** Advanced technology center, language institute, aquaculture education, cadaver lab.

Student profile. Among degree-seeking undergraduates, 1,175 enrolled as first-time, first-year students.

Part-time:	43%	**25 or older:**	30%
Out-of-state:	2%	**Live on campus:**	4%
Women:	64%		

Transfer out. Colleges most students transferred to 2008: Jacksonville State University, Auburn University, University of Alabama, University of Alabama at Birmingham, University of Alabama at Huntsville.

Basis for selection. Open admission, but selective for some programs. Special requirements for health-related programs. Career Program Assessment Test required for some programs. Interview recommended for computer technology, court reporting, and most health science majors. **Homeschooled:** Transcript of courses and grades required. 16 ACT or 790 SAT required.

High school preparation. 27 units recommended. Recommended units include English 4, mathematics 4, social studies 4, science 4 (laboratory 2) and academic electives 9. Electives must include .5 unit computer, .5 unit of fine arts.

2008-2009 Annual costs. Tuition/fees: $2,700; $4,830 out-of-state. Per-credit charge: $71 in-state; $142 out-of-state. Room/board: $3,200. Books/supplies: $800. Personal expenses: $825.

2007-2008 Financial aid. Need-based: Average scholarship/grant was $1,975. 95% of total undergraduate aid awarded as scholarships/grants, 5% as loans/jobs. Need-based aid available for part-time students. Work-study available for part-time students. **Non-need-based:** Scholarships awarded for academics, alumni affiliation, art, athletics, job skills, leadership, minority status, music/drama, state residency.

Application procedures. Admission: No deadline. No application fee. Admission notification on a rolling basis. **Financial aid:** Priority date 4/15; no closing date. FAFSA, institutional form required. Applicants notified on a rolling basis starting 6/10.

Academics. Special study options: Accelerated study, cooperative education, cross-registration, distance learning, dual enrollment of high school students, ESL, honors, independent study, internships, weekend college. License preparation in nursing, paramedic, radiology. **Credit/placement by examination:** CLEP, institutional tests. 20 credit hours maximum toward associate degree. **Support services:** GED preparation and test center, remedial instruction, study skills assistance, tutoring, writing center.

Majors. Agriculture: General. **Area/ethnic studies:** American. **Biology:** General. **Business:** Accounting technology, administrative services, business admin, sales/distribution. **Communications:** General. **Communications technology:** General, graphics. **Computer sciences:** General, computer science, information systems, information technology, LAN/WAN management, networking, programming. **Conservation:** Forestry. **Education:** General, early childhood, elementary, kindergarten/preschool, mathematics. **Engineering:** General. **Engineering technology:** Civil, civil drafting, computer systems, electrical, heat/ac/refrig, industrial, mechanical, mechanical drafting, telecommunications. **Family/consumer sciences:** Child development. **Health:** Clinical lab assistant, clinical lab technology, EMT paramedic, medical radiologic technology/radiation therapy, medical records technology, nursing (RN), predental, premedicine, prenursing, prepharmacy, preveterinary, substance abuse counseling. **History:** General. **Legal studies:** Court reporting, paralegal, prelaw. **Liberal arts:** Arts/sciences. **Math:** General. **Mechanic/repair:** Electronics/electrical, heating/ac/refrig, industrial. **Parks/recreation:** Health/fitness. **Philosophy/religion:** Religion. **Physical sciences:** Chemistry. **Protective services:** Law enforcement admin. **Psychology:** General. **Social sciences:** Sociology. **Visual/performing arts:** Art.

Computing on campus. 250 workstations in library, computer center, student center. Dormitories wired for high-speed internet access. Online course registration, online library available.

Student life. Freshman orientation: Mandatory, $90 fee. Preregistration for classes offered. **Housing:** Coed dorms, wellness housing available. **Activities:** Bands, choral groups, dance, drama, student government, Circle-K, international club, Baptist student union, Phi Beta Lambda.

Athletics. NJCAA. **Intercollegiate:** Baseball M, basketball, cross-country W, golf M, softball W, volleyball W. **Team name:** Cardinals.

Student services. Adult student services, career counseling, services for economically disadvantaged, student employment services, personal counseling, placement for graduates, veterans' counselor. **Physically disabled:** Services for visually, speech, hearing impaired. **Transfer:** Pre-admission transcript evaluation for new students. Transfer adviser, college fairs on campus for students transferring to 4-year colleges.

Contact. E-mail: info@gadsdenstate.edu
Phone: (256) 549-8210 Toll-free number: (800) 226-5563
Fax: (256) 549-8205
Teresa Rhea, Associate Dean of Student Services and Registrar, Gadsden State Community College, 1001 George Wallace Drive, Gadsden, AL 35902-0227

George C. Wallace Community College at Dothan

Dothan, Alabama
www.wallace.edu **CB code: 1264**

- Public 2-year community college
- Commuter campus in small city

General. Founded in 1949. Regionally accredited. Additional campuses in Eufaula and Ft. Rucker. **Enrollment:** 1,835 degree-seeking undergraduates. **Degrees:** 485 associate awarded. **Calendar:** Semester, extensive summer session. **Full-time faculty:** 127 total; 11% minority, 61% women. **Part-time faculty:** 101 total; 14% minority, 63% women.

Student profile.

Out-of-state:	4%	**25 or older:**	43%

Transfer out. **Colleges most students transferred to 2008:** University of Alabama, Auburn University, University of Alabama at Birmingham.

Basis for selection. Open admission, but selective for some programs. Additional requirements for allied health and nursing programs. National League for Nursing examination required for nursing applicants. Interview required of nursing majors.

2008-2009 Annual costs. Tuition/fees: $2,700; $4,830 out-of-state. Per-credit charge: $71 in-state; $142 out-of-state. Books/supplies: $1,900. Personal expenses: $666.

Financial aid. **Need-based:** Work-study available for part-time students. **Non-need-based:** Scholarships awarded for academics, athletics, leadership.

Application procedures. **Admission:** No deadline. No application fee. Admission notification on a rolling basis. **Financial aid:** Priority date 5/1; no closing date. FAFSA required. Applicants notified on a rolling basis.

Academics. **Special study options:** Accelerated study, cooperative education, cross-registration, distance learning, dual enrollment of high school students, ESL, honors. License preparation in nursing, paramedic, physical therapy, radiology. **Credit/placement by examination:** AP, CLEP, institutional tests. 48 credit hours maximum toward associate degree. **Support services:** GED preparation and test center, learning center, pre-admission summer program, remedial instruction, study skills assistance, tutoring.

Majors. **Business:** Administrative services. **Computer sciences:** General. **Construction:** Electrician. **Engineering technology:** Drafting. **Health:** EMT paramedic, medical assistant, medical radiologic technology/radiation therapy, respiratory therapy technology. **Liberal arts:** Arts/sciences. **Mechanic/repair:** Electronics/electrical.

Student life. **Freshman orientation:** Mandatory. Preregistration for classes offered. **Activities:** Jazz band, choral groups, drama, music ensembles, student government, student newspaper, Association of Student Practical Nursing, Diplomats, Elite club, National Vocational-Technical Honor Society, Phi Theta Kappa, Phi Beta Lambda, Respiratory Therapy Association for Better Breathing.

Athletics. NJCAA. **Intercollegiate:** Baseball M, softball W. **Team name:** Govs (M), Lady Govs (W).

Student services. Adult student services, career counseling, services for economically disadvantaged, student employment services, financial aid counseling, personal counseling, placement for graduates, veterans' counselor. **Learning disabled:** Comprehensive services available. **Transfer:** Transfer adviser, college fairs on campus for students transferring to 4-year colleges.

Contact. E-mail: bbarnes@wallace.edu
Phone: (334) 983-3521 Toll-free number: (800) 543-2426
Fax: (334) 983-6066
Brenda Barnes, Assistant Dean of Student Affairs, George C. Wallace Community College at Dothan, 1141 Wallace Drive, Dothan, AL 36303-0943

George C. Wallace State Community College at Selma

Selma, Alabama
www.wccs.edu **CB code: 3146**

- Public 2-year community and technical college
- Commuter campus in large town

General. Founded in 1963. Regionally accredited. **Enrollment:** 1,800 undergraduates. **Degrees:** 245 associate awarded. **Location:** 50 miles from Montgomery, 90 miles from Birmingham. **Calendar:** Semester, extensive summer session. **Full-time faculty:** 42 total. **Part-time faculty:** 58 total.

Basis for selection. Open admission, but selective for some programs. Generic/mobility (RN) nursing candidates need 20 ACT. Practical (LPN) nursing candidates need 18 ACT, or 41 on the Nursing Entrance Test.

2008-2009 Annual costs. Tuition/fees: $2,700; $4,830 out-of-state. Per-credit charge: $71 in-state; $142 out-of-state. Books/supplies: $690. Personal expenses: $976.

2007-2008 Financial aid. **Non-need-based:** Scholarships awarded for academics, athletics.

Application procedures. **Admission:** Priority date 8/21; no deadline. No application fee. Admission notification on a rolling basis. **Financial aid:** Priority date 6/1; no closing date. FAFSA required. Applicants notified on a rolling basis starting 6/15.

Academics. **Special study options:** Accelerated study, double major, dual enrollment of high school students. **Credit/placement by examination:** CLEP, institutional tests. 30 credit hours maximum toward associate degree. **Support services:** GED preparation and test center, learning center, reduced course load, remedial instruction, study skills assistance, tutoring.

Majors. **Business:** Administrative services, business admin. **Computer sciences:** General. **Engineering technology:** Drafting. **Health:** Nursing (RN). **Liberal arts:** Arts/sciences. **Mechanic/repair:** General.

Student life. **Freshman orientation:** Available. Preregistration for classes offered. **Activities:** Student government, Baptist student union, Phi Theta Kappa, Fellowship of Christian Athletes.

Athletics. NJCAA. **Intercollegiate:** Baseball M, basketball, softball W. **Intramural:** Baseball M, basketball, softball. **Team name:** Patriots.

Student services. Career counseling, student employment services, personal counseling, placement for graduates, veterans' counselor. **Physically disabled:** Services for visually, speech, hearing impaired. **Transfer:** Transfer adviser, college fairs on campus for students transferring to 4-year colleges.

Contact. Phone: (334) 876-9295 Fax: (334) 876-9300
Donitha Griffin, Dean of Students, George C. Wallace State Community College at Selma, PO Box 2530, Selma, AL 36702-2530

Jefferson Davis Community College

Brewton, Alabama
www.jdcc.edu **CB code: 1355**

- Public 2-year nursing and community college
- Commuter campus in small town

General. Founded in 1965. Regionally accredited. **Enrollment:** 1,099 degree-seeking undergraduates. **Degrees:** 150 associate awarded. **Location:** 60 miles from Pensacola, Florida. **Calendar:** Semester, limited summer session. **Full-time faculty:** 41 total. **Part-time faculty:** 38 total. **Class size:** 63% < 20, 37% 20-39. **Special facilities:** Museum, golf course, telecommunications center.

Student profile.

Out-of-state:	8%	**Live on campus:**	6%
25 or older:	48%		

Basis for selection. Open admission, but selective for some programs. Special admissions requirements for nursing program. **Homeschooled:** 16 ACT required.

High school preparation. 24 units recommended. Recommended units include English 4, mathematics 4, social studies 4, science 4 and academic electives 8.

2008-2009 Annual costs. Tuition/fees: $2,700; $4,830 out-of-state. Per-credit charge: $71 in-state; $142 out-of-state. Room only: $1,866. Books/supplies: $800. Personal expenses: $400.

2007-2008 Financial aid. **Need-based:** 89% of total undergraduate aid awarded as scholarships/grants, 11% as loans/jobs. Need-based aid available for part-time students. Work-study available nights and for part-time students. **Non-need-based:** Scholarships awarded for academics, athletics, leadership.

Application procedures. **Admission:** No deadline. No application fee. Admission notification on a rolling basis. **Financial aid:** Priority date 5/8; no closing date. FAFSA required. Applicants notified on a rolling basis; must reply within 2 week(s) of notification.

Academics. **Special study options:** Cooperative education, distance learning, dual enrollment of high school students, ESL, honors, independent study. Bachelor's degree programs available on campus. License preparation in nursing, paramedic. **Credit/placement by examination:** AP, CLEP. **Support services:** GED preparation and test center, learning center, remedial instruction, study skills assistance, tutoring.

Majors. **Business:** Administrative services. **Engineering technology:** Drafting. **Health:** Nursing (RN). **Liberal arts:** Arts/sciences.

Most popular majors. Health sciences 34%, liberal arts 60%.

Computing on campus. 420 workstations in library, computer center. Online course registration, wireless network available.

Student life. Freshman orientation: Mandatory. Preregistration for classes offered. Held during summer. **Housing:** Coed dorms, wellness housing available. $150 partly refundable deposit. **Activities:** Campus ministries, student government, student newspaper, Baptist student union, Phi Theta Kappa, Phi Beta Lambda, Psi Beta.

Athletics. NJCAA. **Intercollegiate:** Baseball M, basketball M, softball W, volleyball W. **Team name:** Warhawks.

Student services. Adult student services, chaplain/spiritual director, career counseling, services for economically disadvantaged, financial aid counseling, personal counseling, veterans' counselor. **Physically disabled:** Services for visually impaired. **Transfer:** Pre-admission transcript evaluation for new students. Transfer adviser, college fairs on campus for students transferring to 4-year colleges.

Contact. Phone: (251) 809-1594 Fax: (251) 809-1593
Robin Sessions, Registrar, Jefferson Davis Community College, PO Box 958, Brewton, AL 36427

Jefferson State Community College

Birmingham, Alabama
www.jeffstateonline.com **CB code: 1352**

- Public 2-year community college
- Commuter campus in very large city

General. Founded in 1963. Regionally accredited. **Enrollment:** 6,404 degree-seeking undergraduates; 1,540 non-degree-seeking students. **Degrees:** 693 associate awarded. **ROTC:** Army, Air Force. **Location:** 12 miles from downtown. **Calendar:** Semester, extensive summer session. **Full-time faculty:** 150 total; 17% have terminal degrees, 19% minority, 69% women. **Part-time faculty:** 294 total; 14% have terminal degrees, 22% minority, 56% women. **Class size:** 60% < 20, 37% 20-39, 3% 40-49, less than 1% 50-99. **Special facilities:** Learning success center, nature trail.

Student profile. Among degree-seeking undergraduates, 50% enrolled in a transfer program, 50% enrolled in a vocational program, 1,336 enrolled as first-time, first-year students, 734 transferred in from other institutions.

Part-time:	55%	**Asian American:**	2%
Out-of-state:	5%	**Hispanic American:**	2%
Women:	63%	**International:**	1%
African American:	20%	**25 or older:**	48%

Transfer out. Colleges most students transferred to 2008: University of Alabama at Birmingham, University of Alabama, Auburn University.

Basis for selection. Open admission, but selective for some programs. Special requirements for allied health programs. Students registering for 5 or more hours of credit must take ACT ASSET or ACT COMPASS prior to registration. Placement test exemptions given for students who have completed college level math or English courses, or students who have equivalent ACT scores. Applicants from non-accredited high schools admitted with high school diploma and 16 ACT or equivalent SAT score. **Homeschooled:** Must have 16 ACT or pass Alabama Public High School Graduation Exam.

High school preparation. Recommended units include English 4, mathematics 4, social studies 2, science 3 and foreign language 2.

2008-2009 Annual costs. Tuition/fees: $3,060; $5,190 out-of-state. Per-credit charge: $71 in-state; $142 out-of-state. Books/supplies: $1,404. Personal expenses: $3,908.

2007-2008 Financial aid. Need-based: Need-based aid available for part-time students. Work-study available nights and for part-time students. **Non-need-based:** Scholarships awarded for academics, art, athletics, leadership, music/drama. **Additional information:** Any Alabama resident over age 60 may attend classes tuition free, on a space available basis.

Application procedures. Admission: No deadline. No application fee. Admission notification on a rolling basis. **Financial aid:** Priority date 5/1; no closing date. FAFSA, institutional form required. Applicants notified on a rolling basis starting 6/1.

Academics. Special study options: Accelerated study, distance learning, dual enrollment of high school students, ESL, honors, independent study, internships. License preparation in nursing, paramedic, radiology, real estate. **Credit/placement by examination:** AP, CLEP, IB, institutional tests. 20 credit hours maximum toward associate degree. **Support services:** GED preparation and test center, learning center, reduced course load, remedial instruction, study skills assistance, tutoring.

Majors. Agriculture: Business. **Business:** General, accounting technology, administrative services, banking/financial services, hospitality admin. **Communications technology:** Radio/tv. **Computer sciences:** General. **Engineering technology:** General, construction, manufacturing. **Family/consumer sciences:** Child care. **Health:** Clinical lab technology, EMT paramedic, medical radiologic technology/radiation therapy, nursing (RN), physical therapy assistant, veterinary technology/assistant. **Liberal arts:** Arts/sciences. **Personal/culinary services:** Mortuary science. **Protective services:** Fire services admin, police science.

Most popular majors. Business/marketing 13%, health sciences 44%, liberal arts 23%.

Computing on campus. 293 workstations in library, computer center. Commuter students can connect to campus network. Online course registration, online library, helpline available.

Student life. Freshman orientation: Available. Preregistration for classes offered. **Activities:** Campus ministries, choral groups, drama, literary magazine, music ensembles, musical theater, radio station, student government, student newspaper, senior adult student club, African American society, BACCHUS, Students in Free Enterprise, ambassadors.

Athletics. NJCAA. **Intercollegiate:** Baseball M, softball W. **Intramural:** Basketball, football (non-tackle), softball, volleyball. **Team name:** Pioneers.

Student services. Adult student services, career counseling, student employment services, financial aid counseling, placement for graduates, veterans' counselor, women's services. **Physically disabled:** Services for visually, speech, hearing impaired. **Transfer:** Transfer adviser, college fairs on campus for students transferring to 4-year colleges.

Contact. E-mail: help@jeffstateonline.com
Phone: (205) 856-7704 Toll-free number: (800) 239-5900
Fax: (205) 856-6070
Lillian Owens, Director, Admissions & Retention, Jefferson State Community College, 2601 Carson Road, Birmingham, AL 35215-3098

Lawson State Community College

Birmingham, Alabama **CB member**
www.lawsonstate.edu **CB code: 1933**

- Public 2-year community college
- Commuter campus in small city

General. Founded in 1949. Regionally accredited. **Enrollment:** 3,609 degree-seeking undergraduates. **Degrees:** 200 associate awarded. **Calendar:** Semester, limited summer session. **Full-time faculty:** 100 total. **Part-time faculty:** 121 total. **Class size:** 100% >100.

Student profile. Among degree-seeking undergraduates, 931 enrolled as first-time, first-year students, 535 transferred in from other institutions.

Part-time:	47%	**Women:**	65%
Out-of-state:	1%	**Live on campus:**	2%

Transfer out. Colleges most students transferred to 2008: Miles College, University of Alabama at Birmingham, Alabama A&M University, Alabama State University, Jefferson State Community College.

Basis for selection. Open admission, but selective for some programs. Advanced placement option for licensed practical nurses (LPN) and nursing education. Nursing students must pass nursing entrance exam or have 20 ACT or comparable SAT.

2008-2009 Annual costs. Tuition/fees: $3,000; $5,130 out-of-state. Per-credit charge: $71 in-state; $142 out-of-state. Books/supplies: $1,390. Personal expenses: $920.

2008-2009 Financial aid. All financial aid based on need. 96% of total undergraduate aid awarded as scholarships/grants, 4% as loans/jobs. Need-based aid available for part-time students. Work-study available nights and for part-time students.

Application procedures. Admission: No deadline. No application fee. Admission notification on a rolling basis. **Financial aid:** Priority date 6/1; no closing date. FAFSA required. Applicants notified on a rolling basis starting 8/1; must reply within 2 week(s) of notification.

Academics. Special study options: Accelerated study, double major, dual enrollment of high school students, internships, liberal arts/career combination, student-designed major. License preparation in dental hygiene, nursing, real estate. **Credit/placement by examination:** AP, CLEP, institutional tests. **Support services:** GED preparation and test center, learning center, reduced course load, remedial instruction, tutoring.

Majors. Business: Accounting, administrative services, business admin, office management, office technology, operations. **Computer sciences:** Computer science. **Construction:** General. **Engineering:** Electrical. **Engineering technology:** Architectural, automotive, construction, drafting, electrical, mechanical drafting. **Health:** Medical secretary, nursing (RN). **Legal studies:** Legal secretary, prelaw. **Liberal arts:** Arts/sciences. **Mechanic/repair:** Auto body. **Protective services:** Criminal justice. **Public administration:** Social work.

Most popular majors. Business/marketing 19%, computer/information sciences 9%, engineering/engineering technologies 10%, health sciences 17%, liberal arts 33%.

Computing on campus. 447 workstations in dormitories, library, computer center, student center. Dormitories linked to campus network. Online course registration, online library available.

Student life. Freshman orientation: Mandatory. Preregistration for classes offered. **Housing:** Coed dorms available. **Activities:** Jazz band, choral groups, dance, drama, music ensembles, radio station, student government, scholars bowl team, Sophist club.

Athletics. NJCAA. **Intercollegiate:** Baseball M, basketball, track and field M, volleyball W. **Intramural:** Baseball M, basketball. **Team name:** Cougars.

Student services. Adult student services, career counseling, services for economically disadvantaged, student employment services, financial aid counseling, health services, on-campus daycare, personal counseling, placement for graduates, veterans' counselor. **Physically disabled:** Services for hearing impaired. **Transfer:** College fairs on campus for students transferring to 4-year colleges.

Contact. E-mail: jshelley@lawsonstate.edu
Phone: (205) 929-6309 Fax: (205) 923-7106
Jeff Shelley, Director of Admissions, Lawson State Community College, 3060 Wilson Road SW, Birmingham, AL 35221-1717

Lurleen B. Wallace Community College

Andalusia, Alabama
www.lbwcc.edu **CB code: 1429**

- Public 2-year junior college
- Commuter campus in small town

General. Founded in 1969. Regionally accredited. Additional campuses in Opp and Greenville. **Enrollment:** 1,698 degree-seeking undergraduates. **Degrees:** 191 associate awarded. **Location:** 90 miles from Montgomery. **Calendar:** Semester, limited summer session. **Full-time faculty:** 51 total. **Part-time faculty:** 45 total. **Special facilities:** Nature trail.

Transfer out. Colleges most students transferred to 2008: Troy State University, Auburn University, Auburn University in Montgomery.

Basis for selection. Open admission. COMPASS required for placement unless student scores 20 or higher in math and English on ACT.

2008-2009 Annual costs. Tuition/fees: $2,700; $4,830 out-of-state. Per-credit charge: $71 in-state; $142 out-of-state. Books/supplies: $450. Personal expenses: $600.

2007-2008 Financial aid. Non-need-based: Scholarships awarded for academics, art, athletics, leadership, music/drama, state residency.

Application procedures. Admission: No deadline. No application fee. Admission notification on a rolling basis. **Financial aid:** Priority date 5/1; no closing date. Applicants notified on a rolling basis starting 7/1; must reply within 2 week(s) of notification.

Academics. Special study options: Accelerated study, cooperative education, dual enrollment of high school students, honors. License preparation in paramedic. **Credit/placement by examination:** CLEP, institutional tests. 30 credit hours maximum toward associate degree. **Support services:** GED preparation and test center, learning center, reduced course load, remedial instruction, tutoring.

Majors. Conservation: Forest resources. **Health:** EMT paramedic. **Liberal arts:** Arts/sciences.

Most popular majors. Liberal arts 87%.

Computing on campus. 50 workstations in computer center.

Student life. Freshman orientation: Available, $10 fee. **Activities:** Jazz band, choral groups, drama, music ensembles, musical theater, student government, student newspaper, Collegiate Civitan club, Circle-K, Christian student union, adult re-entry club.

Athletics. NJCAA. **Intercollegiate:** Baseball M, basketball, cross-country, softball W. **Team name:** Saints.

Student services. Career counseling, student employment services, personal counseling, placement for graduates, veterans' counselor. **Transfer:** Transfer adviser, college fairs on campus for students transferring to 4-year colleges.

Contact. Phone: (334) 222-6591 ext. 271 Fax: (334) 222-0136
Mackie Stephens, Director of Admissions, Lurleen B. Wallace Community College, Box 1418, Andalusia, AL 36420-1418

Marion Military Institute

Marion, Alabama
www.marionmilitary.edu **CB code: 1447**

- Public 2-year junior and military college
- Residential campus in small town
- SAT or ACT (ACT writing optional) required

General. Founded in 1842. Regionally accredited. **Enrollment:** 398 degree-seeking undergraduates; 56 non-degree-seeking students. **Degrees:** 86 associate awarded. **ROTC:** Army, Air Force. **Location:** 70 miles from Birmingham, 52 miles from Tuscaloosa. **Calendar:** Semester. **Full-time faculty:** 20 total. **Part-time faculty:** 4 total. **Class size:** 48% < 20, 37% 20-39, 6% 40-49, 6% 50-99, 3% >100. **Special facilities:** Alabama Military Hall of Honor, golf course, bird sanctuary.

Student profile. Among degree-seeking undergraduates, 273 enrolled as first-time, first-year students, 17 transferred in from other institutions.

Out-of-state:	62%	**Hispanic American:**	6%
Women:	17%	**Native American:**	1%
African American:	22%	**Live on campus:**	100%
Asian American:	3%		

Transfer out. 75% of students enrolled in the transfer program go on to 4-year colleges. **Colleges most students transferred to 2008:** University of Alabama, Auburn University, University of Alabama in Huntsville, Oregon State University-Cascades.

Basis for selection. Academic record, recommendations, test scores, character and personal qualities important. Extracurricular activities and alumni relation also important. Interview recommended. **Homeschooled:** Applicants must have been enrolled in approved programs.

High school preparation. 25 units required. Required and recommended units include English 4, mathematics 4, social studies 1, history 3, science 4, foreign language 2 and academic electives 8.

2008-2009 Annual costs. Tuition/fees: $8,570; $14,570 out-of-state. Per-credit charge: $200 in-state; $400 out-of-state. Required fees include one-time uniform fee of $1,850 and accident insurance of $150 per academic year. Room/board: $3,450.

2007-2008 Financial aid. Need-based: Need-based aid available for part-time students.

Application procedures. Admission: Closing date 8/15 (receipt date). $40 fee, may be waived for applicants with need. Admission notification on a rolling basis. Must reply by 8/15. **Financial aid:** No deadline. FAFSA required. Applicants notified on a rolling basis starting 6/15; must reply within 6 week(s) of notification.

Academics. Special preparation for national service academies. **Special study options:** Cross-registration, dual enrollment of high school students, ESL. Students have option to participate in precision drill team, orienteering team, and United States Army Ranger-type training. **Credit/placement by examination:** AP, CLEP, SAT, ACT, institutional tests. **Support services:** Reduced course load, remedial instruction, study skills assistance, tutoring.

Majors. Liberal arts: Arts/sciences.

Computing on campus. 50 workstations in library, computer center. Dormitories wired for high-speed internet access. Online library, helpline, wireless network available.

Student life. Freshman orientation: Mandatory. Preregistration for classes offered. **Policies:** Structured military school environment. Students must live on campus. **Housing:** Guaranteed on-campus for all undergraduates. Single-sex dorms, wellness housing available. $200 nonrefundable deposit, deadline 8/15. **Activities:** Bands, choral groups, drama, music ensembles, musical theater, student government, Normandy Society.

Athletics. NJCAA. **Intercollegiate:** Baseball M, basketball M, cheerleading, softball W, tennis. **Intramural:** Basketball, cross-country, football (non-tackle), golf, racquetball, rifle, swimming, track and field, volleyball, weight lifting. **Team name:** Tigers.

Student services. Chaplain/spiritual director, career counseling, student employment services, financial aid counseling, health services, personal counseling, veterans' counselor. **Transfer:** Transfer adviser for students transferring to 4-year colleges.

Contact. E-mail: admissions@marionmilitary.edu
Phone: (334) 683-2305 Toll-free number: (800) 664-1842
Fax: (334) 683-2383
SGM. Dennis Hastings, Director of Enrollment Management, Marion Military Institute, 1101 Washington Street, Marion, AL 36756-0420

Northeast Alabama Community College

Rainsville, Alabama
www.nacc.edu **CB code: 1576**

- Public 2-year community college
- Commuter campus in rural community

General. Founded in 1963. Regionally accredited. **Enrollment:** 2,050 degree-seeking undergraduates. **Degrees:** 313 associate awarded. **Location:** 55 miles from Huntsville, 110 miles from Birmingham. **Calendar:** Semester, extensive summer session. **Full-time faculty:** 45 total. **Special facilities:** Community theater, lakeside walking trail.

Transfer out. Colleges most students transferred to 2008: Jacksonville State University, University of Alabama at Huntsville, Athens State University, University of Alabama, Auburn University.

Basis for selection. Open admission, but selective for some programs. **Homeschooled:** Transcript of courses and grades required. 16 ACT required. **Learning Disabled:** Students who may require accommodations encouraged to communicate with Disability Services.

High school preparation. 24 units recommended. Recommended units include English 4, mathematics 4, social studies 2, history 2, science 4 (laboratory 2), foreign language 2 and academic electives 4.

2008-2009 Annual costs. Tuition/fees: $2,850; $4,980 out-of-state. Per-credit charge: $71 in-state; $142 out-of-state. In-state costs apply to on-campus or distance-learning courses. Out-of-state distance-learning students pay $5,400 for academic year (or $180 per-credit-hour). Personal expenses: $1,500.

Financial aid. Need-based: Need-based aid available for part-time students. Work-study available for part-time students. **Non-need-based:** Scholarships awarded for academics, art, leadership, minority status, music/drama.

Application procedures. Admission: No deadline. No application fee. Admission notification on a rolling basis. **Financial aid:** No deadline. FAFSA required. Applicants notified on a rolling basis.

Academics. Special study options: Accelerated study, distance learning, dual enrollment of high school students, ESL. 2-year degree programs in allied health available requiring 1 year study at Wallace State Community College at Hanceville. Bachelor's degree programs available on campus. License preparation in nursing, paramedic. **Credit/placement by examination:** AP, CLEP, institutional tests. 16 credit hours maximum toward associate degree. **Support services:** GED preparation and test center, learning center, remedial instruction, study skills assistance, tutoring, writing center.

Majors. Business: General, administrative services, banking/financial services, business admin, office management. **Computer sciences:** General, computer science. **Engineering technology:** CAD/CADD, electrical. **Health:** EMT paramedic, nursing (RN). **Legal studies:** Paralegal.

Computing on campus. 400 workstations in library, computer center. Commuter students can connect to campus network. Online course registration, online library, helpline, wireless network available.

Student life. Freshman orientation: Available. Preregistration for classes offered. Groups of 100 meet for an afternoon. **Activities:** Bands, campus ministries, choral groups, dance, drama, literary magazine, music ensembles, musical theater, student government.

Athletics. Intramural: Basketball. **Team name:** Mustangs.

Student services. Career counseling, student employment services, financial aid counseling, personal counseling, placement for graduates, veterans' counselor. **Physically disabled:** Services for visually, speech, hearing impaired. **Transfer:** Pre-admission transcript evaluation for new students. Transfer adviser, college fairs on campus for students transferring to 4-year colleges.

Contact. E-mail: nibletttt@nacc.edu
Phone: (256) 228-6001 ext. 222 Fax: (256) 638-6043
Tonie Niblett, Dean of Student Services, Northeast Alabama Community College, Admissions Office, NACC, Rainsville, AL 35986-0159

Northwest-Shoals Community College

Muscle Shoals, Alabama
www.nwscc.edu **CB code: 0188**

- Public 2-year community and technical college
- Commuter campus in large town

General. Founded in 1966. Regionally accredited. Two campuses: Phil Campbell and Muscle Shoals. **Enrollment:** 4,055 degree-seeking undergraduates. **Degrees:** 288 associate awarded. **ROTC:** Army. **Location:** 120 miles from Birmingham; 134 miles from Memphis, Tennessee. **Calendar:** Semester, extensive summer session. **Full-time faculty:** 92 total; 6% have terminal degrees, 8% minority, 51% women. **Part-time faculty:** 157 total; 2% have terminal degrees, 11% minority, 52% women. **Class size:** 43% < 20, 37% 20-39, 20% 50-99.

Student profile. Among degree-seeking undergraduates, 41% enrolled in a transfer program, 44% enrolled in a vocational program.

Out-of-state:	1%	**Native American:**	1%
African American:	11%	**25 or older:**	35%
Asian American:	1%	**Live on campus:**	2%
Hispanic American:	1%		

Transfer out. Colleges most students transferred to 2008: University of North Alabama, University of Alabama, Athens State University, University of Alabama at Huntsville.

Basis for selection. Open admission, but selective for some programs. Additional requirements for health occupation programs. **Homeschooled:** Equivalent number of required units for graduation and 16 ACT or 790 SAT (exclusive of Writing) required.

High school preparation. 22 units recommended. Recommended units include English 4, mathematics 2, social studies 3 and science 4.

2008-2009 Annual costs. Tuition/fees: $2,880; $5,010 out-of-state. Per-credit charge: $71 in-state; $142 out-of-state. Room only: $1,600. Books/supplies: $1,190.

2007-2008 Financial aid. Need-based: 51% of total undergraduate aid awarded as scholarships/grants, 49% as loans/jobs. Need-based aid available for part-time students. Work-study available nights, weekends and for part-time students. **Non-need-based:** Scholarships awarded for academics, art, athletics, leadership, minority status, music/drama.

Application procedures. Admission: No deadline. No application fee. Admission notification on a rolling basis. **Financial aid:** Priority date 4/1, closing date 8/1. FAFSA, institutional form required. Applicants notified on a rolling basis; must reply within 2 week(s) of notification.

Academics. Special study options: Accelerated study, cooperative education, cross-registration, distance learning, dual enrollment of high school students, honors, independent study, internships, liberal arts/career combination, weekend college. License preparation in nursing, paramedic. **Credit/placement by examination:** AP, CLEP, institutional tests. 30 credit hours maximum toward associate degree. **Support services:** GED preparation and test center, learning center, pre-admission summer program, remedial instruction, tutoring.

Majors. Agriculture: Business. **Business:** Accounting technology, administrative services. **Computer sciences:** General, applications programming, information systems, information technology, programming. **Conservation:** Environmental studies, forestry. **Engineering technology:** Drafting, environmental. **Health:** EMT paramedic, nursing (RN). **Liberal arts:** Arts/sciences. **Protective services:** Police science.

Most popular majors. Business/marketing 9%, health sciences 24%, interdisciplinary studies 7%, liberal arts 41%.

Computing on campus. 650 workstations in library, computer center, student center. Online course registration, online library, helpline, repair service, wireless network available.

Student life. Freshman orientation: Mandatory, $10 fee. Preregistration for classes offered. Program includes components for developing research skills and good study habits. Occupational students also receive orientation to work ethics and workplace readiness. **Housing:** Coed dorms, wellness housing available. $75 fully refundable deposit. **Activities:** Bands, campus ministries, choral groups, music ensembles, student government, Phi Theta Kappa, Ambassadors, Fellowship of Christian Athletes, Music Educators National Conference, student government association, college bowl team, science club, American Society of Heating, Refrigerating and Air Conditioning Engineers.

Athletics. NJCAA. **Intercollegiate:** Baseball M, basketball, cheerleading, softball W, volleyball W. **Intramural:** Basketball, table tennis. **Team name:** Patriots.

Student services. Career counseling, student employment services, financial aid counseling, on-campus daycare, personal counseling, placement for graduates, veterans' counselor. **Physically disabled:** Services for visually, speech, hearing impaired. **Transfer:** Pre-admission transcript evaluation for new students. Transfer adviser, college fairs on campus for students transferring to 4-year colleges.

Contact. Phone: (256) 331-5363 Fax: (256) 331-5366
Karen Berryhill, Vice President for Student Development Services, Northwest-Shoals Community College, PO Box 2545, Muscle Shoals, AL 35662

Prince Institute of Professional Studies

Montgomery, Alabama
www.princeinstitute.edu **CB code: 3450**

- For-profit 2-year technical college
- Commuter campus in large city
- Interview required

General. Accredited by ACICS. **Enrollment:** 59 undergraduates. **Degrees:** 7 associate awarded. **Calendar:** Quarter, extensive summer session. **Full-time faculty:** 10 total. **Part-time faculty:** 5 total.

Basis for selection. Open admission.

2008-2009 Annual costs. Tuition/fees: $6,895. Per-credit charge: $183. Books/supplies: $2,000. Personal expenses: $1,674.

2008-2009 Financial aid. All financial aid based on need. Need-based aid available for part-time students.

Application procedures. Admission: No deadline. $125 fee. Applications must be received before class start. **Financial aid:** No deadline. FAFSA required.

Academics. Special study options: Distance learning. **Credit/placement by examination:** CLEP.

Majors. Computer sciences: Information systems. **Health:** Medical transcription. **Legal studies:** Court reporting.

Student life. Freshman orientation: Available. Preregistration for classes offered.

Contact. E-mail: shill@princeinstitute.edu
Phone: (334) 271-1670 ext. 209 Toll-free number: (877) 853-5569
Fax: (334) 271-1671
Sherry Hill, Admissions Director, Prince Institute of Professional Studies, 7735 Atlanta Highway, Montgomery, AL 36117-4231

Remington College: Mobile

Mobile, Alabama
www.remingtoncollege.edu **CB code: 3157**

- Private 2-year technical college
- Commuter campus in large city

General. Accredited by ACCSCT. **Enrollment:** 145 degree-seeking undergraduates. **Degrees:** 56 associate awarded. **Calendar:** Quarter, extensive summer session. **Full-time faculty:** 30 total. **Part-time faculty:** 15 total.

Basis for selection. Open admission. **Homeschooled:** Must take CDAT Test.

2008-2009 Annual costs. Associate degree programs annual tuition $19,950. 8-month diploma program full tuition $13,900. Bachelor degree programs annual tuition $16,950. There is a one-time $50 application fee. Tuition includes books and supplies.

2007-2008 Financial aid. All financial aid based on need. Work-study available nights.

Application procedures. Admission: No deadline. $50 fee. **Financial aid:** FAFSA required.

Academics. Special study options: Cooperative education, distance learning, honors, liberal arts/career combination. Bachelor's degree programs available on campus. **Credit/placement by examination:** CLEP. **Support services:** Tutoring.

Majors. Computer sciences: System admin. **Protective services:** Law enforcement admin. **Other:** Computer and network administration, Electronics and computer technology.

Computing on campus. PC or laptop required. Helpline, repair service available.

Student life. Freshman orientation: Available. Preregistration for classes offered. Held the week before class for 2 1/2 hours.

Student services. Career counseling, financial aid counseling, placement for graduates. **Transfer:** Pre-admission transcript evaluation for new students.

Contact. Phone: (251) 343-8200 Toll-free number: (800) 866-0850
Fax: (251) 343-8200
David Helveston, Director of Admissions, Remington College: Mobile, 828 Downtowner Loop West, Mobile, AL 36609-5404

Shelton State Community College

Tuscaloosa, Alabama
www.sheltonstate.edu **CB code: 3338**

- Public 2-year community and technical college
- Commuter campus in small city

General. Founded in 1963. Regionally accredited. Designated as Alabama's Community College of the Fine Arts; includes C.A. Fredd campus, a Historically Black College. **Enrollment:** 5,350 degree-seeking undergraduates. **Degrees:** 250 associate awarded. **ROTC:** Army, Air Force. **Location:** 60 miles from Birmingham. **Calendar:** Semester, extensive summer session. **Full-time faculty:** 78 total; 13% have terminal degrees, 19% minority, 58% women. **Part-time faculty:** 168 total; 5% have terminal degrees, 23% minority, 59% women. **Class size:** 42% < 20, 48% 20-39, 10% 40-49, less than 1% 50-99. **Special facilities:** Observatories, wellness center, community theatre.

Student profile.

Out-of-state:	5%	**25 or older:**	32%

Transfer out. Colleges most students transferred to 2008: University of Alabama, Auburn University, Stillman College, University of Alabama at Birmingham.

Basis for selection. Open admission. COMPASS test required of all first-time freshmen for placement unless students have taken ACT.

2008-2009 Annual costs. Tuition/fees: $2,700; $4,830 out-of-state. Per-credit charge: $71 in-state; $142 out-of-state. Books/supplies: $750. Personal expenses: $200.

Financial aid. All financial aid based on need. Need-based aid available for part-time students. Work-study available nights.

Application procedures. Admission: No deadline. No application fee. Admission notification on a rolling basis. **Financial aid:** Priority date 6/30; no closing date. FAFSA required. Applicants notified on a rolling basis starting 7/30.

Academics. Special study options: Accelerated study, distance learning, double major, dual enrollment of high school students, honors, liberal arts/career combination. License preparation in nursing, real estate. **Credit/placement by examination:** AP, CLEP, IB, institutional tests. 20 credit hours maximum toward associate degree. **Support services:** GED preparation and test center, learning center, reduced course load, remedial instruction, study skills assistance, tutoring.

Majors. **Architecture:** Technology. **Business:** Administrative services. **Construction:** Electrician. **Education:** General, music, secondary. **Engineering:** General. **Engineering technology:** Drafting, heat/ac/refrig. **Health:** Nursing (RN), respiratory therapy technology. **Liberal arts:** Arts/sciences. **Math:** General. **Mechanic/repair:** Industrial electronics. **Production:** General, tool and die. **Public administration:** Social work. **Visual/performing arts:** Studio arts.

Most popular majors. Business/marketing 25%, health sciences 26%, liberal arts 33%, trade and industry 11%.

Computing on campus. 300 workstations in library, computer center. Commuter students can connect to campus network. Online course registration, wireless network available.

Student life. **Freshman orientation:** Mandatory. Preregistration for classes offered. **Activities:** Jazz band, choral groups, dance, drama, music ensembles, musical theater, student government, student newspaper, Phi Theta Kappa, Circle K.

Athletics. NJCAA. **Intercollegiate:** Baseball M, basketball, cheerleading, soccer W, softball W. **Team name:** Buccaneers.

Student services. Career counseling, student employment services, financial aid counseling, personal counseling, placement for graduates, veterans' counselor. **Transfer:** College fairs on campus for students transferring to 4-year colleges.

Contact. E-mail: admissions@sheltonstate.edu
Phone: (205) 391-2214 Fax: (205) 391-3910
Tommy Taylor, Dean of Student Services, Shelton State Community College, 9500 Old Greensboro Road, Tuscaloosa, AL 35405-8522

Snead State Community College

Boaz, Alabama
www.snead.edu **CB code: 1721**

- Public 2-year community college
- Commuter campus in small town

General. Founded in 1898. Regionally accredited. Upper-level courses offered on campus through Athens State University and distance learning. **Enrollment:** 2,249 degree-seeking undergraduates. **Degrees:** 237 associate awarded. **Location:** 65 miles from Birmingham. **Calendar:** Semester, extensive summer session. **Full-time faculty:** 34 total. **Part-time faculty:** 60 total. **Special facilities:** Museum, state diagnostic lab. **Partnerships:** Partnership with Marshall County Tech Prep Consortium (grant writer and fiscal agent for eight secondary schools).

Student profile.

Out-of-state:	2%	**Live on campus:**	4%
25 or older:	33%		

Transfer out. **Colleges most students transferred to 2008:** Jacksonville State University, Auburn University, University of Alabama, University of Alabama at Birmingham, University of Alabama in Huntsville.

Basis for selection. Open admission, but selective for some programs. Nursing students must submit application package. 16 ACT or equivalent SAT required for high school graduates from non-accredited schools and for those receiving occupational diplomas.

High school preparation. 24 units recommended. Recommended units include English 4, mathematics 4, social studies 4, science 4, foreign language 2 and academic electives 8. Half unit fine arts, 1/2 computer applications, 5 1/2 electives recommended.

2008-2009 Annual costs. Tuition/fees: $2,820; $4,950 out-of-state. Per-credit charge: $71 in-state; $142 out-of-state. Room/board: $3,290. Books/supplies: $1,050. Personal expenses: $1,200.

Financial aid. **Need-based:** Need-based aid available for part-time students. Work-study available nights and for part-time students. **Non-need-based:** Scholarships awarded for academics, alumni affiliation, art, athletics, leadership, music/drama.

Application procedures. **Admission:** Closing date 8/14 (postmark date). No application fee. Application must be submitted on paper. Admission notification on a rolling basis. **Financial aid:** Priority date 4/15; no closing date. FAFSA required. Applicants notified on a rolling basis starting 4/15.

Academics. **Special study options:** Accelerated study, distance learning, dual enrollment of high school students, independent study, internships, student-designed major. **Credit/placement by examination:** AP, CLEP, institutional tests. 20 credit hours maximum toward associate degree. **Support services:** GED preparation and test center, learning center, remedial instruction, study skills assistance, tutoring, writing center.

Majors. **Business:** Administrative services. **Computer sciences:** General. **Engineering:** General. **Engineering technology:** General. **Family/consumer sciences:** Child care. **Health:** Nursing (RN). **Liberal arts:** Arts/sciences. **Personal/culinary services:** Cosmetic.

Computing on campus. 350 workstations in library, computer center, student center. Online course registration, online library available.

Student life. **Freshman orientation:** Available, $94 fee. Preregistration for classes offered. Orientation offered on 2 consecutive Fridays or Saturdays. **Housing:** Coed dorms available. $25 deposit. **Activities:** Jazz band, choral groups, music ensembles, student government, student newspaper, Baptist campus ministry, Ambassadors, agricultural organization, Phi Beta Lambda, Phi Theta Kappa, student government association, College Republicans, Civitans.

Athletics. NJCAA. **Intercollegiate:** Baseball M, basketball, softball W, tennis W. **Intramural:** Basketball, softball, table tennis, volleyball. **Team name:** Parsons.

Student services. Chaplain/spiritual director, career counseling, services for economically disadvantaged, student employment services, financial aid counseling, personal counseling, placement for graduates, veterans' counselor. **Physically disabled:** Services for visually, speech, hearing impaired. **Transfer:** Pre-admission transcript evaluation for new students. Transfer center, transfer adviser, college fairs on campus for students transferring to 4-year colleges.

Contact. E-mail: mbuchanan@snead.edu
Phone: (256) 593-5120 ext. 207 Fax: (256) 593-7180
Amanda Harbison, Admissions and Records Director, Snead State Community College, PO Box 734, Boaz, AL 35957-0734

Southern Union State Community College

Wadley, Alabama
www.suscc.edu **CB code: 1728**

- Public 2-year community and technical college
- Commuter campus in small city

General. Founded in 1963. Regionally accredited. Additional campuses in Opelika and Valley. **Enrollment:** 4,810 degree-seeking undergraduates. **Degrees:** 420 associate awarded. **Location:** 90 miles from Atlanta, 90 miles from Birmingham. **Calendar:** Semester, extensive summer session. **Full-time faculty:** 85 total. **Part-time faculty:** 240 total.

Student profile.

Out-of-state:	20%	**Live on campus:**	4%
25 or older:	25%		

Basis for selection. Open admission, but selective for some programs. Criteria for some health sciences programs include test scores.

2008-2009 Annual costs. Tuition/fees: $2,700; $4,830 out-of-state. Per-credit charge: $71 in-state; $142 out-of-state. Room/board: $3,200. Books/supplies: $400. Personal expenses: $1,100.

Financial aid. **Need-based:** Need-based aid available for part-time students.

Application procedures. **Admission:** No deadline. No application fee. Admission notification on a rolling basis. **Financial aid:** Priority date 7/1; no closing date. FAFSA required. Applicants notified on a rolling basis.

Academics. **Special study options:** Accelerated study, distance learning, dual enrollment of high school students. License preparation in nursing, paramedic, radiology. **Credit/placement by examination:** CLEP. **Support services:** GED preparation and test center, remedial instruction, tutoring.

Majors. **Biology:** General. **Business:** Accounting, office management. **Communications:** General. **Computer sciences:** General. **Construction:** Carpentry. **Education:** Physical. **Engineering technology:** Drafting. **Health:** EMT paramedic, insurance coding, nursing (RN), radiologic technology/medical imaging. **Mechanic/repair:** Heating/ac/refrig. **Physical sciences:** Chemistry. **Social sciences:** General.

Student life. **Freshman orientation:** Available. Preregistration for classes offered. Held during June and July. **Housing:** Single-sex dorms, wellness housing available. **Activities:** Choral groups, dance, drama, musical theater, student government, student newspaper, student government association, association of radiologic students, Baptist campus ministries, global environmental organization of students, music club, letterman's club, National Student Nurses' Association, Phi Beta Lambda, Phi Theta Kappa, Southern Union Players.

Athletics. NJCAA. **Intercollegiate:** Baseball M, basketball, cheerleading, cross-country, softball W, volleyball W. **Team name:** Bisons.

Student services. Adult student services, career counseling, financial aid counseling.

Contact. E-mail: cstringfellow@suscc.edu
Phone: (256) 395-2211 Fax: (256) 395-2215
Catherine Stringfellow, Registrar, Southern Union State Community College, 750 Roberts Street, Wadley, AL 36276

Virginia College at Mobile

Mobile, Alabama
www.vc.edu/mobile

- For-profit 2-year technical college
- Commuter campus in large city

General. Accredited by ACICS. **Enrollment:** 162 full-time, degree-seeking students. **Degrees:** 32 associate awarded. **Calendar:** Continuous.

Basis for selection. Open admission, but selective for some programs.

2008-2009 Annual costs. Students taking 13-16 hours pay $4,320 per quarter; additional fees vary according to program of study.

Application procedures. **Admission:** No deadline. Admission notification on a rolling basis.

Academics. **Special study options:** Accelerated study, independent study. **Credit/placement by examination:** CLEP.

Contact. Phone: (251) 343-7227 Toll-free number: (888) 208-6932
Fax: (251) 343-7287
Mary Anaya, Director of Admissions, Virginia College at Mobile, 2970 Cottage Hill Road, Mobile, AL 36606

Virginia College at Montgomery

Montgomery, Alabama
www.vc.edu

- For-profit 2-year health science and career college
- Large city

General. Regionally accredited; also accredited by ACICS. **Calendar:** Quarter. **Full-time faculty:** 12 total. **Part-time faculty:** 16 total.

Application procedures. **Financial aid:** Closing date 9/30.

Academics. **Credit/placement by examination:** CLEP.

Majors. **Business:** Administrative services. **Health:** Massage therapy, office admin, surgical technology. **Personal/culinary services:** Salon management.

Contact. Phone: (334) 277-3390
Virginia College at Montgomery, 6200 Atlanta Highway, Montgomery, AL 36117

Wallace State Community College at Hanceville

Hanceville, Alabama
www.wallacestate.edu **CB code: 0528**

- Public 2-year health science and community college
- Commuter campus in rural community

General. Founded in 1966. Regionally accredited. **Enrollment:** 3,078 full-time, degree-seeking students. **Degrees:** 904 associate awarded. **Location:** 35 miles from Birmingham, 50 miles from Huntsville. **Calendar:** Semester, limited summer session. **Full-time faculty:** 125 total. **Part-time faculty:** 150 total. **Special facilities:** Extensive genealogy collection, recording studio, nature trail, college-operated museum.

Transfer out. **Colleges most students transferred to 2008:** Athens State College, University of Alabama, University of Alabama in Huntsville, University of Alabama at Birmingham, Auburn University.

Basis for selection. Open admission, but selective for some programs. ACT required of applicants to certain allied health programs. National League for Nursing, Pre-Nursing and Guidance Examination required for nursing applicants. Interview recommended for health program applicants; auditions recommended for music education majors.

2008-2009 Annual costs. Tuition/fees: $2,700; $4,830 out-of-state. Per-credit charge: $71 in-state; $142 out-of-state. Room only-Dorms $1,550; House $1,100. Room only: $1,450. Books/supplies: $700. Personal expenses: $2,650.

Financial aid. All financial aid based on need. Need-based aid available for part-time students. Work-study available nights.

Application procedures. **Admission:** No deadline. No application fee. Admission notification on a rolling basis beginning on or about 7/15. **Financial aid:** Priority date 5/1; no closing date. FAFSA required. Applicants notified on a rolling basis starting 7/15; must reply within 2 week(s) of notification.

Academics. **Special study options:** Accelerated study, cooperative education, distance learning, double major, dual enrollment of high school students, internships, weekend college. Bachelor's degree programs available on campus. License preparation in aviation, dental hygiene, nursing, occupational therapy, paramedic, physical therapy, radiology, real estate. **Credit/placement by examination:** AP, CLEP, institutional tests. 26 credit hours maximum toward associate degree. **Support services:** GED preparation and test center, learning center, reduced course load, remedial instruction, study skills assistance, tutoring.

Majors. **Agriculture:** Agribusiness operations. **Business:** General, accounting, banking/financial services, fashion, insurance, labor relations, office management, office/clerical, sales/distribution. **Computer sciences:** Data processing, programming. **Education:** General. **Engineering:** General, electrical. **Engineering technology:** Drafting. **Family/consumer sciences:** Child care, food/nutrition, institutional food production. **Health:** Athletic training, clinical lab technology, dental assistant, dental hygiene, EMT paramedic, health services, medical assistant, medical radiologic technology/radiation therapy, medical records technology, nursing (RN), occupational therapy assistant, physical therapy assistant, respiratory therapy technology, sonography, substance abuse counseling. **Legal studies:** Legal secretary, paralegal, prelaw. **Liberal arts:** Arts/sciences. **Mechanic/repair:** Auto body, automotive, diesel, electronics/electrical, heating/ac/refrig. **Parks/recreation:** Facilities management. **Production:** Woodworking. **Protective services:** Police science. **Visual/performing arts:** Art, fashion design, interior design.

Most popular majors. Business/marketing 6%, health sciences 61%, liberal arts 17%.

Computing on campus. 65 workstations in library, computer center. Commuter students can connect to campus network. Online course registration, online library, helpline, wireless network available.

Student life. **Freshman orientation:** Available. Preregistration for classes offered. **Housing:** Single-sex dorms, wellness housing available. $200 deposit. **Activities:** Bands, choral groups, drama, music ensembles, student government, student newspaper, Baptist campus ministry.

Athletics. NJCAA. **Intercollegiate:** Baseball M, basketball, cross-country, golf M, soccer M, softball W, track and field M, volleyball. **Intramural:** Badminton, basketball, softball, tennis, track and field, volleyball. **Team name:** Lions.

Student services. Chaplain/spiritual director, career counseling, student employment services, financial aid counseling, placement for graduates, veterans' counselor. **Physically disabled:** Services for visually, speech, hearing impaired. **Transfer:** Transfer adviser, college fairs on campus for students transferring to 4-year colleges.

Contact. Phone: (256) 352-8236 Toll-free number: (866) 350-9722
Fax: (256) 352-8129
Linda Sperling, Director of Admissions/Registrar, Wallace State Community College at Hanceville, PO Box 2000, Hanceville, AL 35077-2000

Alaska

Ilisagvik College

Barrow, Alaska
www.ilisagvik.cc **CB code: 0469**

- Public 2-year tribal community college
- Commuter campus in rural community

General. **Enrollment:** 90 degree-seeking undergraduates. **Degrees:** 12 associate awarded. **Location:** 500 miles from Fairbanks. **Calendar:** Semester, limited summer session. **Full-time faculty:** 12 total. **Part-time faculty:** 17 total.

Basis for selection. Open admission.

2008-2009 Annual costs. Tuition/fees: $1,590; $3,030 out-of-state. Per-credit charge: $60 in-state; $120 out-of-state. Room/board: $10,600.

Application procedures. **Admission:** No deadline. No application fee. Application must be submitted on paper. **Financial aid:** No deadline.

Academics. Many Inupiat Eskimo traditional courses offered. **Special study options:** Dual enrollment of high school students, ESL, independent study. **Credit/placement by examination:** CLEP. 12 credit hours maximum toward associate degree. **Support services:** GED preparation and test center, remedial instruction, tutoring.

Majors. **Business:** Management science. **Construction:** General.

Computing on campus. Commuter students can connect to campus network. Helpline, wireless network available.

Student life. **Freshman orientation:** Available. **Housing:** Coed dorms, apartments available. **Activities:** Student government.

Student services. Financial aid counseling, personal counseling.

Contact. E-mail: dararath@ilisagvik.cc
Phone: (907) 852-1763 Toll-free number: (907) 478-7337 ext. 1784
Fax: (907) 852-1784
Dararath Cahoon, Registrar, Ilisagvik College, 100 Stevenson Road, Barrow, AK 99723

Prince William Sound Community College

Valdez, Alaska
www.pwscc.edu **CB code: 4636**

- Public 2-year community college
- Commuter campus in small town

General. Founded in 1978. Regionally accredited. Service area of 44,000 square miles. Full schedule of courses plus live video and audio conferencing for students in remote areas. Off-campus centers at Cordova and Glennallen offer credit-bearing courses. **Enrollment:** 155 degree-seeking undergraduates. **Degrees:** 13 associate awarded. **Location:** 300 miles from Anchorage. **Calendar:** Semester, limited summer session. **Full-time faculty:** 7 total. **Part-time faculty:** 50 total. **Class size:** 94% < 20, 5% 20-39, less than 1% 40-49, less than 1% 50-99, less than 1% >100. **Special facilities:** Alaska native museum.

Transfer out. **Colleges most students transferred to 2008:** University of Alaska-Anchorage.

Basis for selection. Open admission. **Homeschooled:** Statement describing homeschool structure and mission required.

2008-2009 Annual costs. Tuition/fees: $3,840. Per-credit charge: $116. Room/board: $4,730. Books/supplies: $600.

Financial aid. **Need-based:** Need-based aid available for part-time students. **Non-need-based:** Scholarships awarded for state residency.

Application procedures. **Admission:** No deadline. $25 fee. Application must be submitted on paper. Admission notification on a rolling basis. **Financial aid:** Priority date 6/30; no closing date. FAFSA required. Applicants notified on a rolling basis.

Academics. **Special study options:** Distance learning, double major, dual enrollment of high school students, ESL, external degree, honors, independent study, internships. Bachelor's degree programs available on campus. **Credit/placement by examination:** AP, CLEP, IB, institutional tests. **Support services:** GED preparation and test center, learning center, reduced course load, remedial instruction, study skills assistance, tutoring.

Majors. **Business:** Office management. **Engineering technology:** Electrical. **Liberal arts:** Arts/sciences.

Computing on campus. 50 workstations in dormitories, library, computer center. Online library, helpline available.

Student life. **Freshman orientation:** Available. Preregistration for classes offered. **Housing:** Coed dorms, apartments, wellness housing available. $200 deposit. **Activities:** Drama, film society, student government.

Student services. Adult student services, career counseling, financial aid counseling, veterans' counselor. **Transfer:** Transfer adviser, college fairs on campus for students transferring to 4-year colleges.

Contact. E-mail: sfoster@pwscc.edu
Phone: (907) 834-1632 Toll-free number: (800) 478-8800
Fax: (907) 834-1635
Shannon Foster, Director of Admissions, Prince William Sound Community College, Box 97, Valdez, AK 99686

Arizona

Two-Year Colleges

Anthem College

Phoenix, Arizona
www.hightechinstitute.edu **CB code: 3170**

- For-profit 2-year technical college
- Commuter campus in very large city
- Interview required

General. Accredited by ACCSCT. **Enrollment:** 5,745 degree-seeking undergraduates. **Degrees:** 149 bachelor's, 1,328 associate awarded. **Calendar:** Continuous, extensive summer session. **Full-time faculty:** 55 total.

Basis for selection. Open admission. **Homeschooled:** Transcript of courses and grades, state high school equivalency certificate, interview required.

2008-2009 Annual costs. Costs for diploma programs range from $12,150 to $25,850. Fees, books, uniforms and tools included. Personal expenses: $205.

Financial aid. All financial aid based on need.

Application procedures. Admission: No deadline. $50 fee. Application must be submitted on paper. Admission notification on a rolling basis. **Financial aid:** No deadline.

Academics. Special study options: Distance learning. Bachelor's degree programs available on campus. **Credit/placement by examination:** CLEP, institutional tests. **Support services:** GED preparation, study skills assistance, tutoring.

Majors. Business: Business admin. **Computer sciences:** Security, web page design. **Engineering:** General, electrical. **Engineering technology:** Drafting. **Health:** Insurance specialist, office computer specialist. **Protective services:** Police science.

Most popular majors. Computer/information sciences 73%, health sciences 27%.

Computing on campus. 2 workstations in library, computer center. Commuter students can connect to campus network. Online course registration, online library, helpline available.

Student life. Freshman orientation: Mandatory.

Student services. Financial aid counseling, placement for graduates. **Transfer:** Pre-admission transcript evaluation for new students.

Contact. Phone: (602) 279-9700 Toll-free number: (800) 832-4011
Fax: (602) 279-2999
Todd Rash, Director of Marketing, Anthem College, 1515 East Indian School Road, Phoenix, AZ 85014-4901

Arizona Automotive Institute

Glendale, Arizona
www.aai.edu **CB code: 2127**

- For-profit 2-year technical college
- Commuter campus in small city

General. Founded in 1967. Accredited by ACCSCT. **Enrollment:** 625 degree-seeking undergraduates. **Degrees:** 300 associate awarded. **Location:** 3 miles from Phoenix. **Calendar:** Quarter, extensive summer session. **Full-time faculty:** 25 total. **Part-time faculty:** 5 total.

Student profile.

Out-of-state:	36%	**25 or older:**	25%

Basis for selection. Open admission. Interview highly recommended.

2008-2009 Annual costs. Total cost of associate degree program is $27,412 including tuition, books, uniforms, supplies, tools. Cost of diploma is $18,308.

Application procedures. Admission: No deadline. $100 fee. Admission notification on a rolling basis. **Financial aid:** No deadline. FAFSA, institutional form required. Applicants notified on a rolling basis.

Academics. Special study options: Double major. **Credit/placement by examination:** CLEP. **Support services:** Tutoring.

Majors. Mechanic/repair: Automotive, diesel.

Computing on campus. 15 workstations in computer center.

Student life. Freshman orientation: Available. Preregistration for classes offered. **Housing:** Apartments available.

Athletics. Intramural: Basketball M, bowling, football (tackle) M, softball, volleyball.

Student services. Career counseling, student employment services, personal counseling, placement for graduates, veterans' counselor.

Contact. E-mail: info@azautoinst.com
Phone: (623) 934-7273 Toll-free number: (800) 528-0717
Fax: (623) 930-4948
Deborah Armstrong, Director of Admissions, Arizona Automotive Institute, 6829 North 46th Avenue, Glendale, AZ 85301

Arizona Western College

Yuma, Arizona **CB member**
www.azwestern.edu **CB code: 4013**

- Public 2-year community college
- Commuter campus in small city

General. Founded in 1963. Regionally accredited. Satellite sites in Parker, San Luis-Somerton, Wellton. Campus shared with Northern Arizona University, which offers completion of bachelor's, master's and doctoral programs. **Enrollment:** 6,690 degree-seeking undergraduates; 790 non-degree-seeking students. **Degrees:** 651 associate awarded. **Location:** 7 miles from Yuma. **Calendar:** Semester, limited summer session. **Full-time faculty:** 110 total. **Part-time faculty:** 234 total. **Class size:** 54% < 20, 45% 20-39, less than 1% 40-49, less than 1% 50-99, less than 1% >100. **Partnerships:** Formal partnerships with Yuma Educational Consortium and Yuma Regional Medical Center.

Student profile. Among degree-seeking undergraduates, 64% enrolled in a transfer program, 35% enrolled in a vocational program, 4% already have a bachelor's degree or higher, 1,126 enrolled as first-time, first-year students.

Part-time:	66%	**Hispanic American:**	57%
Out-of-state:	14%	**Native American:**	1%
Women:	60%	**International:**	12%
African American:	3%	**25 or older:**	31%
Asian American:	2%		

Transfer out. 33% of students enrolled in the transfer program go on to 4-year colleges. **Colleges most students transferred to 2008:** Northern Arizona University at Yuma, Arizona State University, University of Arizona.

Basis for selection. Open admission, but selective for some programs. Out-of-state applicants screened for social or disciplinary problems. Special requirements for nursing program.

2008-2009 Annual costs. Tuition/fees: $1,680; $6,240 out-of-state. Per-credit charge: $56 in-state; $208 out-of-state. Room/board: $4,898. Books/supplies: $1,269. Personal expenses: $2,962.

2008-2009 Financial aid. Need-based: Need-based aid available for part-time students. Work-study available nights, weekends and for part-time students. **Non-need-based:** Scholarships awarded for academics, athletics.

Application procedures. Admission: No deadline. No application fee. Admission notification on a rolling basis. **Financial aid:** Priority date 4/1; no closing date. FAFSA, institutional form required. Applicants notified on a rolling basis starting 5/1.

Academics. Special study options: Accelerated study, cooperative education, distance learning, dual enrollment of high school students, ESL, honors, independent study, internships, study abroad, teacher certification program, weekend college. License preparation in nursing, occupational therapy, paramedic, radiology. **Credit/placement by examination:** AP, CLEP, IB, institutional tests. 24 credit hours maximum toward associate degree. **Support services:** GED preparation, learning center, reduced course load, remedial instruction, study skills assistance, tutoring, writing center.

Majors. **Agriculture:** General, plant sciences. **Biology:** General. **Business:** General, business admin, hospitality admin, management science, marketing, office management. **Communications:** General, radio/tv. **Communications technology:** Radio/tv. **Computer sciences:** General, computer graphics, data entry. **Conservation:** Environmental science. **Education:** General, secondary. **Engineering:** General. **Engineering technology:** CAD/CADD, industrial, water quality. **Family/consumer sciences:** General, child development. **Foreign languages:** Spanish. **Health:** EMT paramedic, health services, massage therapy, nursing (RN), nursing admin, radiologic technology/medical imaging. **History:** General. **Math:** General. **Mechanic/repair:** Automotive, electronics/electrical, heating/ac/refrig. **Parks/recreation:** Health/fitness. **Personal/culinary services:** Restaurant/catering. **Philosophy/religion:** Philosophy. **Physical sciences:** Chemistry, oceanography, physics. **Production:** Welding. **Protective services:** Firefighting, law enforcement admin, police science. **Public administration:** Human services. **Social sciences:** General, political science. **Visual/performing arts:** Dramatic, multimedia, studio arts.

Most popular majors. Business/marketing 15%, health sciences 14%, liberal arts 35%, security/protective services 8%.

Computing on campus. 270 workstations in dormitories, library, computer center, student center. Dormitories wired for high-speed internet access and linked to campus network. Commuter students can connect to campus network. Online course registration, online library, helpline, repair service, student web hosting, wireless network available.

Student life. **Freshman orientation:** Available. Preregistration for classes offered. **Housing:** Guaranteed on-campus for all undergraduates. Coed dorms, single-sex dorms, special housing for disabled, wellness housing available. $100 nonrefundable deposit. **Activities:** Bands, choral groups, dance, drama, literary magazine, music ensembles, radio station, student government, student newspaper, TV station, AACHE, Phi Theta Kappa, Native American club, Hispanic students club, international students club.

Athletics. NJCAA. **Intercollegiate:** Baseball M, basketball, football (tackle) M, soccer M, softball W, volleyball W. **Team name:** Matadors.

Student services. Adult student services, career counseling, services for economically disadvantaged, student employment services, financial aid counseling, health services, minority student services, on-campus daycare, personal counseling, placement for graduates, veterans' counselor, women's services. **Physically disabled:** Services for visually, hearing impaired. **Transfer:** Pre-admission transcript evaluation for new students. Transfer center, transfer adviser, college fairs on campus for students transferring to 4-year colleges.

Contact. E-mail: veronica.garcia@azwestern.edu
Phone: (928) 317-6000 Toll-free number: (888) 293-0392
Fax: (928) 344-7543
Bryan Doak, Associate Dean of Enrollment Services, Arizona Western College, PO Box 929, Yuma, AZ 85366-0929

Bryman School

Phoenix, Arizona
www.brymanschool.edu **CB code: 3040**

- For-profit 2-year health science college
- Very large city

General. Accredited by ACCSCT. **Enrollment:** 1,080 degree-seeking undergraduates. **Degrees:** 234 associate awarded. **Calendar:** Continuous. **Full-time faculty:** 60 total.

Basis for selection. Open admission. Wonderlic exam required for placement.

2008-2009 Annual costs. Diploma programs range from $10,750 to $21,950 ($9,050 to $19,850 for agency) and $22,950 to $26,250 for degree ($18,100 to $22,000 for agency). Registration fee of $50.00. Books/supplies: $642. Personal expenses: $3,360.

Application procedures. **Admission:** No deadline. No application fee. Admission notification on a rolling basis.

Academics. **Credit/placement by examination:** CLEP.

Majors. **Health:** Insurance coding, insurance specialist.

Student life. **Freshman orientation:** Mandatory.

Contact. Phone: (602) 274-4300 Toll-free number: (800) 987-0110
Cecilia Gomez, Director of Admissions, Bryman School, 2250 West Peoria Ave, Phoenix, AZ 85029-4919

Central Arizona College

Coolidge, Arizona
www.centralaz.edu **CB code: 4122**

- Public 2-year community college
- Commuter campus in rural community

General. Founded in 1962. Regionally accredited. **Enrollment:** 1,300 full-time, degree-seeking students. **Degrees:** 287 associate awarded. **Location:** 45 miles from Phoenix. **Calendar:** Semester, limited summer session. **Full-time faculty:** 97 total. **Part-time faculty:** 256 total. **Special facilities:** Observatory. **Partnerships:** Formal partnership with CAVIT.

Student profile.

Out-of-state:	2%	**Live on campus:**	4%
25 or older:	65%		

Transfer out. **Colleges most students transferred to 2008:** Arizona State University, Northern Arizona University, University of Arizona.

Basis for selection. Open admission, but selective for some programs. Special requirements for nursing programs. **Learning Disabled:** Student must register disability and present appropriate documentation.

2008-2009 Annual costs. Tuition/fees: $1,705; $7,501 out-of-state. Per-credit charge: $60 in-state; $120 out-of-state. Room/board: $4,645. Books/supplies: $1,050. Personal expenses: $1,350.

Financial aid. **Need-based:** Need-based aid available for part-time students. Work-study available nights, weekends and for part-time students.

Application procedures. **Admission:** No deadline. No application fee. Admission notification on a rolling basis. **Financial aid:** Priority date 5/1, closing date 7/15. FAFSA required. Must reply within 3 week(s) of notification.

Academics. **Special study options:** Distance learning, dual enrollment of high school students, ESL, honors, independent study, liberal arts/career combination, student-designed major. Bachelor's degree programs available on campus. License preparation in nursing, radiology, real estate. **Credit/placement by examination:** AP, CLEP, institutional tests. 30 credit hours maximum toward associate degree. **Support services:** GED preparation and test center, learning center, pre-admission summer program, reduced course load, remedial instruction, study skills assistance, tutoring, writing center.

Majors. **Agriculture:** Business. **Biology:** General. **Business:** General, accounting, administrative services, business admin, hospitality/recreation, management information systems, office technology. **Communications:** Journalism. **Computer sciences:** General, applications programming, data processing, programming. **Education:** General, early childhood, elementary, multi-level teacher, special. **Engineering:** General, civil, mechanical, mechanics. **Engineering technology:** Electrical, industrial management, manufacturing. **Family/consumer sciences:** Family studies. **Health:** EMT paramedic, medical assistant, medical secretary, medical transcription, nursing (RN), pharmacy assistant, preveterinary. **Interdisciplinary:** Biological/physical sciences. **Legal studies:** Legal secretary. **Liberal arts:** Arts/sciences, humanities. **Math:** General. **Mechanic/repair:** Automotive, diesel, industrial. **Parks/recreation:** Exercise sciences. **Personal/culinary services:** Culinary arts. **Physical sciences:** Chemistry. **Protective services:** Corrections, criminal justice, firefighting. **Psychology:** General. **Social sciences:** General, criminology. **Visual/performing arts:** General, art, dramatic.

Computing on campus. 500 workstations in dormitories, library, computer center, student center. Dormitories wired for high-speed internet access. Commuter students can connect to campus network. Online course registration, helpline, wireless network available.

Student life. **Freshman orientation:** Available. Preregistration for classes offered. **Policies:** Student code of conduct must be followed. **Housing:** Coed dorms, special housing for disabled, wellness housing available. $100 fully refundable deposit. **Activities:** Bands, choral groups, drama, music ensembles, musical theater, student government, student newspaper, Phi Theta Kappa/Lamba, art club, Playmasters, Campus Crusade For Christ, international club, Native American club, rodeo club, We Can Do It club, Student Nurses Association of Arizona.

Athletics. NJCAA. **Intercollegiate:** Baseball M, basketball, cross-country, rodeo, softball W, track and field. **Team name:** Vaqueros.

Student services. Adult student services, alcohol/substance abuse counseling, career counseling, student employment services, financial aid counseling, on-campus daycare, personal counseling, placement for graduates. **Physically disabled:** Services for visually, hearing impaired. **Transfer:** Reentry adviser, pre-admission transcript evaluation for new students. Transfer center, transfer adviser, college fairs on campus for students transferring to 4-year colleges.

Contact. E-mail: admissions@centralaz.edu
Phone: (520) 494-5260 Toll-free number: (800) 237-9814
Fax: (520) 494-5083
James Moore, Director of Admission and Records, Central Arizona College, 8470 North Overfield Road, Coolidge, AZ 85228-9778

Chandler-Gilbert Community College: Pecos

Chandler, Arizona
www.cgc.maricopa.edu **CB code: 0535**

- Public 2-year community college
- Commuter campus in small city

General. Regionally accredited. Additional campuses in Sun Lakes and Williams. **Enrollment:** 1,776 degree-seeking undergraduates; 8,501 non-degree-seeking students. **Degrees:** 342 associate awarded. **Location:** 20 miles from Phoenix. **Calendar:** Semester, limited summer session. **Full-time faculty:** 116 total. **Part-time faculty:** 340 total. **Class size:** 44% < 20, 47% 20-39, 9% 40-49, less than 1% 50-99.

Student profile. Among degree-seeking undergraduates, 75% enrolled in a transfer program, 18% enrolled in a vocational program, 4% already have a bachelor's degree or higher, 599 enrolled as first-time, first-year students.

Part-time:	58%	**Hispanic American:**	18%
Out-of-state:	5%	**Native American:**	2%
Women:	60%	**25 or older:**	28%
African American:	5%	**Live on campus:**	2%
Asian American:	4%		

Transfer out. Colleges most students transferred to 2008: Arziona State University, Northern Arizona University, University of Arizona.

Basis for selection. Open admission.

2008-2009 Annual costs. Tuition/fees: $2,145; $8,595 out-of-state. Per-credit charge: $71 in-state; $286 out-of-state. Books/supplies: $1,064. Personal expenses: $4,878.

2008-2009 Financial aid. Need-based: Work-study available nights, weekends and for part-time students.

Application procedures. Admission: No deadline. No application fee.

Academics. Special study options: Distance learning, dual enrollment of high school students, ESL, honors, independent study, teacher certification program, weekend college. License preparation in aviation, nursing. **Credit/placement by examination:** AP, CLEP, IB, institutional tests. 30 credit hours maximum toward associate degree. **Support services:** Learning center, reduced course load, remedial instruction, study skills assistance, tutoring, writing center.

Majors. Business: General, accounting, nonprofit/public, office technology, retailing. **Computer sciences:** General, computer science, data entry, information technology, networking, system admin, vendor certification. **Education:** Elementary. **Health:** Clinical nutrition, dietetic technician, massage therapy, nursing assistant. **Transportation:** Aviation. **Visual/performing arts:** Music management. **Other:** Automated manufacturing systems.

Most popular majors. Computer/information sciences 7%, education 10%, history 7%, liberal arts 63%, physical sciences 9%.

Computing on campus. 140 workstations in library, computer center. Commuter students can connect to campus network. Online course registration, online library, wireless network available.

Student life. Freshman orientation: Available. Preregistration for classes offered. One-day sessions held at beginning of term; choice of weekend day and weeknight evening. **Housing:** Coed dorms available. Student housing for CGCC students available on-campus only at Williams campus in cooperation with Arizona State University Polytechnic. CGCC students attending any of the college's campuses can apply for student housing at the Williams campus. **Activities:** Bands, choral groups, dance, drama, music ensembles, musical theater, student government, political science organization, Christians in Action, Latter Day Saints student association, intercultural exchange club, Wall Street club, Phi Theta Kappa, black student union, Hispanic student organization.

Athletics. NJCAA. **Intercollegiate:** Baseball M, basketball, golf, soccer, softball W, volleyball W. **Team name:** Coyotes.

Student services. Adult student services, alcohol/substance abuse counseling, career counseling, services for economically disadvantaged, student employment services, financial aid counseling, personal counseling, placement for graduates, veterans' counselor. **Physically disabled:** Services for visually, speech, hearing impaired. **Transfer:** Pre-admission transcript evaluation for new students. Transfer center, transfer adviser, college fairs on campus for students transferring to 4-year colleges.

Contact. Phone: (480) 732-7320
Douglas Bullock, Dean Enrollment Services, Chandler-Gilbert Community College: Pecos, 2626 East Pecos Road, Chandler, AZ 85225

Chandler-Gilbert Community College: Sun Lakes Education Center

Sun Lakes, Arizona
www.cgc.maricopa.edu **CB code: 3826**

- Public 2-year community college
- Commuter campus in small town

General. Regionally accredited. **Location:** 25 miles from Phoenix. **Calendar:** Semester.

Annual costs/financial aid. Tuition/fees (2008-2009): $2,145; $8,595 out-of-state. Books/supplies: $1,064. Personal expenses: $4,878.

Contact. Phone: (480) 857-5500
Supervisor of Admissions Records and Registration, 25105 South Alma School Road, Sun Lakes, AZ 85248-7158

Chandler-Gilbert Community College: Williams Campus

Mesa, Arizona
www.cgc.maricopa.edu **CB code: 3827**

- Public 2-year community college
- Commuter campus in large city

General. Regionally accredited. **Location:** 33 miles from Phoenix. **Calendar:** Semester.

Annual costs/financial aid. Tuition/fees (2008-2009): $2,145; $8,595 out-of-state. Books/supplies: $1,064. Personal expenses: $4,878.

Contact. Phone: (480) 732-7320
Supervisor of Admissions, Records and Registration, 2626 East Pecos Road, Chandler, AZ 85225-2499

Cochise College

Douglas, Arizona **CB member**
www.cochise.edu **CB code: 4097**

- Public 2-year community college
- Commuter campus in large town

General. Founded in 1962. Regionally accredited. Courses offered at 2 campuses; 4 extended learning centers located in 2 counties and online. **Enrollment:** 2,879 degree-seeking undergraduates; 1,256 non-degree-seeking students. **Degrees:** 990 associate awarded. **Location:** 120 miles from Tucson. **Calendar:** Semester, limited summer session. **Full-time faculty:** 93 total; 4% have terminal degrees, 16% minority, 43% women. **Part-time faculty:** 227 total; 7% have terminal degrees, 20% minority, 50% women. **Class size:** 85% < 20, 14% 20-39, less than 1% 40-49, less than 1% 50-99. **Special facilities:** Asian art collection, college airport.

Student profile. Among degree-seeking undergraduates, 34% enrolled in a transfer program, 66% enrolled in a vocational program, 495 enrolled as first-time, first-year students, 1,263 transferred in from other institutions.

Part-time:	68%	**Asian American:**	3%
Out-of-state:	11%	**Hispanic American:**	38%
Women:	59%	**25 or older:**	54%
African American:	6%	**Live on campus:**	2%

Transfer out. Colleges most students transferred to 2008: University of Phoenix, Wayland Baptist University-External Campus, Northern Arizona University, Arizona State University, Western International University.

Basis for selection. Open admission, but selective for some programs. Special requirements for air transportation (professional pilot, aviation maintenance) and nursing programs; interview required. Walk-in admission available.

2008-2009 Annual costs. Tuition/fees: $1,540; $7,330 out-of-state. Room/board: $4,380. Books/supplies: $1,000. Personal expenses: $1,350.

2007-2008 Financial aid. **Need-based:** 329 full-time freshmen applied for aid; 274 were judged to have need; 266 of these received aid. Average scholarship/grant was $2,801; average loan $2,722. 72% of total undergraduate aid awarded as scholarships/grants, 28% as loans/jobs. Need-based aid available for part-time students. Work-study available for part-time students. **Non-need-based:** Awarded to 227 full-time undergraduates, including 87 freshmen. Scholarships awarded for academics, athletics.

Application procedures. **Admission:** No deadline. No application fee. Admission notification on a rolling basis. **Financial aid:** Closing date 4/15. FAFSA, institutional form required. Applicants notified on a rolling basis starting 6/15; must reply within 2 week(s) of notification.

Academics. **Special study options:** Cooperative education, distance learning, dual enrollment of high school students, ESL, honors, independent study, internships, teacher certification program. License preparation in aviation, nursing, paramedic, real estate. **Credit/placement by examination:** AP, CLEP, institutional tests. 30 credit hours maximum toward associate degree. Student must complete at least one Cochise College course before credit may be granted for CLEP/DANTES. **Support services:** GED preparation and test center, learning center, pre-admission summer program, reduced course load, remedial instruction, tutoring, writing center.

Majors. **Agriculture:** Business. **Biology:** General. **Business:** Administrative services, business admin. **Communications:** General, journalism. **Computer sciences:** Computer science, data processing, information systems, networking, programming, security. **Construction:** General. **Education:** Art, biology, chemistry, early childhood, English, foreign languages, history, mathematics, music, physical. **Engineering:** Manufacturing. **Engineering technology:** Electrical. **Family/consumer sciences:** Family studies. **Foreign languages:** General, sign language interpretation, translation. **Health:** EMT paramedic, health services, nursing (RN), prenursing. **History:** General. **Liberal arts:** Humanities. **Math:** General. **Mechanic/repair:** Aircraft, automotive, avionics. **Military:** General. **Parks/recreation:** Health/fitness. **Personal/culinary services:** Chef training. **Physical sciences:** Chemistry, physics. **Production:** Welding. **Protective services:** Fire safety technology, police science. **Psychology:** General. **Public administration:** Human services. **Social sciences:** Anthropology, economics, geography, political science, sociology. **Transportation:** Airline/commercial pilot. **Visual/performing arts:** General, art.

Most popular majors. Liberal arts 14%, military 60%.

Computing on campus. 571 workstations in dormitories, library, computer center. Dormitories wired for high-speed internet access. Online course registration, online library, wireless network available.

Student life. **Freshman orientation:** Available. Preregistration for classes offered. **Housing:** Single-sex dorms, apartments available. $100 partly refundable deposit. **Activities:** Choral groups, drama, film society, literary magazine, music ensembles, student government, animal science club, armed forces communications and electronics association, Cineaste circle film club, math and computer sciences club, Phi Theta Kappa honor society, prepharmacy club, residence hall association, social concerns club, Spanish club.

Athletics. NJCAA. **Intercollegiate:** Baseball M, basketball, rodeo, soccer W. **Team name:** Apaches.

Student services. Career counseling, student employment services, financial aid counseling, health services, personal counseling, placement for graduates, veterans' counselor. **Physically disabled:** Services for visually, hearing impaired. **Transfer:** Transfer adviser, college fairs on campus for students transferring to 4-year colleges.

Contact. E-mail: admissions@cochise.edu
Phone: (520) 515-5412 Toll-free number: (800) 593-9567
Fax: (520) 515-5452
Debbie Quick, Director of Admissions, Cochise College, 901 North Colombo Avenue, Sierra Vista, AZ 85635

Coconino County Community College

Flagstaff, Arizona — **CB member**
www.coconino.edu — **CB code: 1712**

- Public 2-year community college
- Commuter campus in small city

General. Regionally accredited. **Enrollment:** 2,854 degree-seeking undergraduates; 897 non-degree-seeking students. **Degrees:** 188 associate awarded. **ROTC:** Army, Air Force. **Location:** 140 miles from Phoenix. **Calendar:** Semester, limited summer session. **Full-time faculty:** 38 total; 55% women. **Part-time faculty:** 220 total; 52% women. **Special facilities:** Community garden, wind turbine, green building, telescope.

Student profile. Among degree-seeking undergraduates, 54% enrolled in a transfer program, 16% enrolled in a vocational program, 3% already have a bachelor's degree or higher, 903 enrolled as first-time, first-year students, 455 transferred in from other institutions.

Part-time:	73%	**Women:**	57%
Out-of-state:	2%	**25 or older:**	39%

Transfer out. 48% of students enrolled in the transfer program go on to 4-year colleges. **Colleges most students transferred to 2008:** Northern Arizona University, Arizona State University, University of Arizona.

Basis for selection. Open admission, but selective for some programs. Special requirements for nursing program.

2008-2009 Annual costs. Tuition/fees: $1,800; $7,680 out-of-state. Per-credit charge: $75 in-state; $320 out-of-state. Books/supplies: $968. Personal expenses: $3,222.

Application procedures. **Admission:** No deadline. No application fee. Application must be submitted on paper. Admission notification on a rolling basis. **Financial aid:** Priority date 4/15, closing date 6/30.

Academics. Writing center, learning center and tutoring available. **Special study options:** Distance learning, dual enrollment of high school students, honors, internships. License preparation in nursing, paramedic, real estate. **Credit/placement by examination:** CLEP. **Support services:** GED preparation and test center, learning center, remedial instruction, study skills assistance, tutoring, writing center.

Majors. **Architecture:** Technology. **Business:** General, accounting, business admin, construction management, finance, hospitality admin, marketing. **Computer sciences:** System admin. **Conservation:** Environmental science. **Construction:** Carpentry. **Education:** General, early childhood, elementary. **Engineering:** General. **Engineering technology:** Architectural drafting, CAD/CADD, computer systems, construction, software, solar energy. **Health:** Medical secretary, nursing assistant. **Interdisciplinary:** Biological/physical sciences. **Legal studies:** Paralegal. **Protective services:** Criminal justice, firefighting. **Psychology:** General. **Public administration:** Social work. **Social sciences:** Anthropology, sociology. **Visual/performing arts:** Art. **Other:** Colorado plateau studies.

Most popular majors. Business/marketing 6%, health sciences 15%, history 49%.

Computing on campus. 100 workstations in library, computer center, student center. Online course registration, online library, helpline available.

Student life. **Freshman orientation:** Available. Preregistration for classes offered. **Housing:** Some dorm opportunities may be available through Northern Arizona University. **Activities:** Jazz band, dance, symphony orchestra.

Athletics. **Team name:** Comets.

Student services. Adult student services, career counseling, financial aid counseling, on-campus daycare, veterans' counselor. **Physically disabled:** Services for visually, speech, hearing impaired. **Transfer:** Pre-admission transcript evaluation for new students. Transfer adviser, college fairs on campus for students transferring to 4-year colleges.

Contact. E-mail: admissions®istration@coconino.edu
Phone: (928) 527-1222 ext. 4299 Toll-free number: (800) 350-7122 ext. 4299 Fax: (928) 226-4110
Liz Gallegos, Registrar/Director for Admissions, Coconino County Community College, 2800 South Lone Tree Road, Flagstaff, AZ 86001

Dine College

Tsaile, Arizona — **CB member**
www.dinecollege.edu — **CB code: 4550**

- Public 2-year community college
- Residential campus in rural community

General. Founded in 1968. Regionally accredited. The first tribally controlled community college in the United States; chartered by the Navajo Nation. **Enrollment:** 550 full-time, degree-seeking students. **Degrees:** 232

associate awarded. **Location:** 55 miles from Window Rock. **Calendar:** Semester, limited summer session. **Full-time faculty:** 61 total; 43% women. **Part-time faculty:** 73 total; 48% women. **Special facilities:** Museum.

Student profile.

Out-of-state:	15%	**Live on campus:**	20%
25 or older:	49%		

Transfer out. Colleges most students transferred to 2008: Northern Arizona University, Arizona State University, Fort Lewis College, University of Arizona, University of New Mexico.

Basis for selection. Open admission. **Homeschooled:** Statement describing homeschool structure and mission, transcript of courses and grades, state high school equivalency certificate required.

2008-2009 Annual costs. Tuition/fees: $850. Per-credit charge: $30. Room/board: $3,764. Books/supplies: $950. Personal expenses: $2,500.

2007-2008 Financial aid. All financial aid based on need. Need-based aid available for part-time students.

Application procedures. Admission: No deadline. $20 fee. Application must be submitted on paper. Admission notification on a rolling basis. **Financial aid:** Priority date 4/15; no closing date. FAFSA, institutional form required. Applicants notified on a rolling basis starting 5/1; must reply within 4 week(s) of notification.

Academics. Special study options: Cooperative education, distance learning, double major, independent study. **Credit/placement by examination:** CLEP, institutional tests. 12 credit hours maximum toward associate degree. **Support services:** Learning center, pre-admission summer program, remedial instruction, tutoring.

Majors. Area/ethnic studies: Native American. **Biology:** General. **Business:** Administrative services, business admin, office/clerical. **Computer sciences:** General, computer science. **Conservation:** Environmental science. **Education:** General. **Foreign languages:** Native American. **Health:** Public health ed. **Liberal arts:** Arts/sciences. **Psychology:** General. **Social sciences:** General. **Visual/performing arts:** Studio arts. **Other:** Pre-Engineering.

Computing on campus. 104 workstations in dormitories, library, computer center, student center. Dormitories wired for high-speed internet access and linked to campus network. Online library, helpline, repair service, wireless network available.

Student life. Freshman orientation: Available. Preregistration for classes offered. **Housing:** Coed dorms, single-sex dorms, wellness housing available. **Activities:** Student government, Red Dawn Indian club.

Athletics. NJCAA. **Intercollegiate:** Archery, cross-country, rodeo. **Intramural:** Archery, cross-country, rodeo. **Team name:** Warrior.

Student services. Alcohol/substance abuse counseling, career counseling, personal counseling, veterans' counselor. **Transfer:** Pre-admission transcript evaluation for new students. Transfer adviser, college fairs on campus for students transferring to 4-year colleges.

Contact. Phone: (928) 724-6630 Fax: (928) 724-3349
Louise Litzin, Registrar, Dine College, Box 67, Tsaile, AZ 86556

Eastern Arizona College

Thatcher, Arizona
www.eac.edu **CB code: 4297**

- Public 2-year community college
- Commuter campus in large town

General. Founded in 1888. Regionally accredited. Near archaeological sites. Several continuing education centers within 165 miles of campus. **Enrollment:** 4,224 degree-seeking undergraduates; 2,332 non-degree-seeking students. **Degrees:** 309 associate awarded. **Location:** 160 miles from Phoenix, 130 miles from Tucson. **Calendar:** Semester, limited summer session. **Full-time faculty:** 96 total; 12% have terminal degrees, 14% minority, 34% women. **Part-time faculty:** 227 total; 2% have terminal degrees, 16% minority, 58% women. **Class size:** 79% < 20, 18% 20-39, 1% 40-49, 2% 50-99, less than 1% >100. **Special facilities:** Observatory, golf course, wilderness area. **Partnerships:** Formal partnerships with local high schools allow high school students to obtain degrees in areas such as office technology and drafting.

Student profile. Among degree-seeking undergraduates, 68% enrolled in a transfer program, 32% enrolled in a vocational program, 1,401 enrolled as first-time, first-year students, 40 transferred in from other institutions.

Part-time:	58%	**Hispanic American:**	19%
Out-of-state:	5%	**Native American:**	10%
Women:	56%	**International:**	1%
African American:	3%	**25 or older:**	51%
Asian American:	2%	**Live on campus:**	6%

Basis for selection. Open admission, but selective for some programs. Special requirements for nursing and several paramedical programs.

High school preparation. 15 units recommended. Recommended units include English 4, mathematics 4, social studies 1, history 1, science 3 (laboratory 3) and foreign language 2.

2008-2009 Annual costs. Tuition/fees: $1,380; $7,440 out-of-state. Per-credit charge: $60 in-state; $120 out-of-state. Room/board: $4,703. Books/supplies: $800. Personal expenses: $1,722.

2008-2009 Financial aid. Need-based: Average need met was 43%. Average scholarship/grant was $4,137. 92% of total undergraduate aid awarded as scholarships/grants, 8% as loans/jobs. Need-based aid available for part-time students. Work-study available nights, weekends and for part-time students. **Non-need-based:** Scholarships awarded for academics, art, athletics, leadership, music/drama, state residency. **Additional information:** Limited number of tuition waivers for New Mexico residents. Unlimited number of waivers for those meeting WUE requirements.

Application procedures. Admission: No deadline. No application fee. Admission notification on a rolling basis. **Financial aid:** Priority date 3/1; no closing date. FAFSA, institutional form required. Applicants notified on a rolling basis starting 3/15.

Academics. Special study options: Cooperative education, distance learning, double major, dual enrollment of high school students, independent study. Bachelor's degree programs available on campus. License preparation in nursing, paramedic. **Credit/placement by examination:** AP, CLEP, IB, institutional tests. 48 credit hours maximum toward associate degree. **Support services:** GED preparation and test center, learning center, reduced course load, remedial instruction, study skills assistance, tutoring, writing center.

Majors. Agriculture: Agribusiness operations. **Biology:** General, environmental, wildlife. **Business:** Administrative services, business admin, entrepreneurial studies, office technology. **Computer sciences:** Information systems, system admin. **Conservation:** Forestry. **Education:** Art, business, elementary, secondary, technology/industrial arts. **Engineering technology:** Civil, drafting, mining. **Foreign languages:** General. **Health:** EMT paramedic, nursing (RN), pharmacy assistant, premedicine, prepharmacy. **History:** General. **Legal studies:** Prelaw. **Liberal arts:** Arts/sciences. **Math:** General. **Mechanic/repair:** Automotive. **Parks/recreation:** Health/fitness. **Personal/culinary services:** Cosmetic. **Physical sciences:** Chemistry, geology, physics. **Protective services:** Law enforcement admin, police science. **Psychology:** General. **Social sciences:** Anthropology, political science, sociology. **Visual/performing arts:** Art, commercial/advertising art, dramatic, studio arts.

Most popular majors. Business/marketing 9%, health sciences 21%, liberal arts 44%.

Computing on campus. 564 workstations in library, computer center. Dormitories wired for high-speed internet access and linked to campus network. Online course registration, online library, wireless network available.

Student life. Freshman orientation: Available. Preregistration for classes offered. Half-day session given the week prior to beginning of classes each semester and weekly during summer months. **Housing:** Single-sex dorms, wellness housing available. $150 fully refundable deposit. **Activities:** Bands, choral groups, dance, drama, literary magazine, music ensembles, musical theater, student government, symphony orchestra, Latter-Day-Saints student association, Newman club, drama club, Hispanic Leaders, Intertribal club, Phi Theta Kappa, Spanish Club, Gila Force, Rowdy Reptiles.

Athletics. NJCAA. **Intercollegiate:** Baseball M, basketball, football (tackle) M, golf M, softball W, tennis W, volleyball W. **Intramural:** Basketball, soccer, swimming, tennis, volleyball. **Team name:** Gila Monsters.

Student services. Adult student services, alcohol/substance abuse counseling, career counseling, services for economically disadvantaged, student employment services, financial aid counseling, minority student services, personal counseling, placement for graduates, veterans' counselor, women's services. **Physically disabled:** Services for visually, speech, hearing impaired. **Transfer:** Re-entry adviser, pre-admission transcript evaluation for new students. Transfer adviser, college fairs on campus for students transferring to 4-year colleges.

Contact. E-mail: admissions@eac.edu
Phone: (928) 428-8272 Toll-free number: (800) 678-3808
Fax: (928) 428-8462
Erik Lehmann, Admissions Counselor, Eastern Arizona College, 615 North Stadium Avenue, Thatcher, AZ 85552-0769

Estrella Mountain Community College
Avondale, Arizona
www.estrellamountain.edu **CB code: 3810**

- Public 2-year community college
- Commuter campus in small city

General. Regionally accredited. **Enrollment:** 2,156 degree-seeking undergraduates; 3,817 non-degree-seeking students. **Degrees:** 445 associate awarded. **ROTC:** Air Force. **Location:** 15 miles from Phoenix. **Calendar:** Semester, limited summer session. **Full-time faculty:** 73 total; 37% minority, 56% women. **Part-time faculty:** 200 total; 24% minority.

Student profile. Among degree-seeking undergraduates, 36% enrolled in a transfer program, 8% enrolled in a vocational program, 3% already have a bachelor's degree or higher, 460 enrolled as first-time, first-year students.

Part-time:	63%	**Women:**	63%
Out-of-state:	1%	**25 or older:**	46%

Transfer out. Colleges most students transferred to 2008: Arizona State University.

Basis for selection. Open admission.

2008-2009 Annual costs. Tuition/fees: $2,145; $8,595 out-of-state. Per-credit charge: $71 in-state; $286 out-of-state. Books/supplies: $1,104. Personal expenses: $2,718.

2007-2008 Financial aid. Need-based: Need-based aid available for part-time students. Work-study available nights and for part-time students. **Non-need-based:** Scholarships awarded for leadership.

Application procedures. Admission: Closing date 3/1. $5 fee. **Financial aid:** Priority date 4/1; no closing date. Applicants notified on a rolling basis starting 4/15.

Academics. Special study options: Accelerated study, dual enrollment of high school students, ESL, honors, independent study, weekend college. **Credit/placement by examination:** CLEP, IB. 30 credit hours maximum toward associate degree. **Support services:** GED test center, learning center, pre-admission summer program, reduced course load, remedial instruction, study skills assistance, tutoring, writing center.

Majors. Business: Business admin, hotel/motel admin, organizational behavior. **Computer sciences:** Applications programming, data entry, LAN/WAN management, vendor certification. **Education:** General, secondary, teacher assistance. **Health:** Speech-language pathology assistant. **Liberal arts:** Arts/sciences. **Personal/culinary services:** Chef training, culinary arts. **Protective services:** Criminal justice. **Psychology:** General. **Public administration:** Social work.

Computing on campus. 185 workstations in library, computer center. Online course registration, online library, helpline, wireless network available.

Student life. Freshman orientation: Available. Preregistration for classes offered. **Activities:** Literary magazine, student government.

Student services. Adult student services, alcohol/substance abuse counseling, career counseling, financial aid counseling, personal counseling, veterans' counselor. **Physically disabled:** Services for visually, speech, hearing impaired. **Transfer:** Pre-admission transcript evaluation for new students. College fairs on campus for students transferring to 4-year colleges.

Contact. Phone: (623) 935-8000 Fax: (623) 935-8870
Frank Amparo, Director of Admission and Records, Estrella Mountain Community College, 3000 North Dysart Road, Avondale, AZ 85392-1010

Everest College: Phoenix
Phoenix, Arizona
www.everest-college.com **CB code: 2172**

- For-profit 2-year junior and technical college
- Commuter campus in very large city
- Interview required

General. Founded in 1982. Regionally accredited. **Enrollment:** 2,613 degree-seeking undergraduates. **Degrees:** 16 bachelor's, 247 associate awarded. **Location:** 10 miles from downtown. **Calendar:** Quarter, extensive summer session. **Full-time faculty:** 7 total; 14% have terminal degrees, 43% minority, 71% women. **Part-time faculty:** 32 total; 12% have terminal degrees, 16% minority, 28% women. **Class size:** 79% < 20, 21% 20-39.

Student profile. Among degree-seeking undergraduates, 585 transferred in from other institutions.

Out-of-state:	5%	**25 or older:**	65%

Transfer out. Colleges most students transferred to 2008: Arizona State University, Northern Arizona University, University of Phoenix.

Basis for selection. Open admission, but selective for some programs. Interview very important for selective programs.

2008-2009 Annual costs. Full-time tuition is $11,268 for associate and bachelor degree students, except for nursing which is $14,544. Diploma program tuition averages $11,500 for entire certificate program.

Application procedures. Admission: No deadline. No application fee. Admission notification on a rolling basis. **Financial aid:** No deadline. FAFSA required. Applicants notified on a rolling basis.

Academics. Special study options: Cooperative education, distance learning, independent study, internships, weekend college. Bachelor's degree programs available on campus. License preparation in nursing. **Credit/placement by examination:** AP, CLEP, institutional tests. 68 credit hours maximum toward associate degree, 136 toward bachelor's. **Support services:** Reduced course load, remedial instruction, study skills assistance, tutoring.

Majors. Business: Accounting, business admin, office management. **Health:** Nursing (RN). **Legal studies:** Paralegal. **Protective services:** Criminal justice.

Most popular majors. Business/marketing 7%, legal studies 28%, security/protective services 65%.

Computing on campus. 120 workstations in library, computer center. Commuter students can connect to campus network. Online course registration, online library, helpline, wireless network available.

Student life. Freshman orientation: Mandatory.

Student services. Adult student services, career counseling, student employment services, financial aid counseling, personal counseling, placement for graduates, veterans' counselor. **Transfer:** Re-entry adviser, pre-admission transcript evaluation for new students. Transfer adviser for students transferring to 4-year colleges.

Contact. E-mail: jaskins@cci.edu
Phone: (602) 942-4141 Toll-free number: (888) 741-4271
Fax: (602) 943-0960
Jim Askins, Director of Admissions, Everest College: Phoenix, 10400 North 25th Avenue Suite 190, Phoenix, AZ 85021

Gateway Community College
Phoenix, Arizona
www.gatewaycc.edu **CB code: 0455**

- Public 2-year community and technical college
- Commuter campus in very large city

General. Founded in 1968. Regionally accredited. **Enrollment:** 5,810 degree-seeking undergraduates. **Degrees:** 567 associate awarded. **ROTC:** Army, Naval, Air Force. **Calendar:** Semester, extensive summer session. **Full-time faculty:** 98 total; 55% minority, 63% women. **Part-time faculty:** 266 total; 57% women. **Partnerships:** Formal partnerships with Intel, Johnson Control, Toyota, Motorola.

Student profile. Among degree-seeking undergraduates, 12% enrolled in a transfer program, 88% enrolled in a vocational program. Of all enrolled students, 10% already have a bachelor's degree or higher.

Out-of-state:	5%	**25 or older:**	80%

Transfer out. 1% of students enrolled in the transfer program go on to 4-year colleges. **Colleges most students transferred to 2008:** Arizona State University, Northern Arizona University, University of Arizona.

Basis for selection. Open admission, but selective for some programs. Special requirements for nursing and some allied health programs. General Aptitude Test Battery required of health science applicants.

2008-2009 Annual costs. Tuition/fees: $2,145; $8,085 out-of-state. Per-credit charge: $71 in-state; $269 out-of-state.

2007-2008 Financial aid. Need-based: Need-based aid available for part-time students. Work-study available nights, weekends and for part-time students. **Non-need-based:** Scholarships awarded for athletics.

Application procedures. Admission: No deadline. No application fee. Admission notification on a rolling basis. **Financial aid:** Priority date 4/15; no closing date. FAFSA, institutional form required. Applicants notified on a rolling basis starting 7/1; must reply within 4 week(s) of notification.

Academics. Special study options: Accelerated study, cooperative education, cross-registration, distance learning, double major, dual enrollment of high school students, ESL, honors, independent study, internships, liberal arts/career combination, study abroad, teacher certification program. License preparation in nursing, physical therapy, radiology. **Credit/placement by examination:** AP, CLEP, IB, institutional tests. 30 credit hours maximum toward associate degree. **Support services:** GED test center, learning center, reduced course load, remedial instruction, study skills assistance, tutoring, writing center.

Majors. Business: General, accounting, administrative services, banking/financial services, international, office management. **Computer sciences:** General, information systems, LAN/WAN management, networking, system admin, systems analysis. **Construction:** Carpentry, electrician, maintenance, masonry, pipefitting, power transmission. **Education:** General, elementary. **Engineering:** General, aerospace. **Engineering technology:** Aerospace, hazardous materials, manufacturing, occupational safety, water quality. **Health:** Health care admin, medical radiologic technology/radiation therapy, medical transcription, nuclear medical technology, nursing (RN), physical therapy assistant, respiratory therapy technology, sonography, surgical technology. **Legal studies:** Court reporting. **Liberal arts:** Arts/sciences. **Mechanic/repair:** Automotive, electronics/electrical, heating/ac/refrig. **Social sciences:** Sociology.

Most popular majors. Health sciences 67%, liberal arts 23%.

Computing on campus. 100 workstations in library, computer center, student center. Commuter students can connect to campus network. Online course registration, online library, helpline, wireless network available.

Student life. Freshman orientation: Available. Preregistration for classes offered. **Activities:** Film society, student government, student newspaper, Newman club, MEHCA, Indian tribal club, single parents association, VA club, internatilonal student club, women's club, health sciences club, business club.

Athletics. NJCAA. **Intercollegiate:** Cross-country, golf, soccer M, softball W, tennis. **Team name:** Geckos.

Student services. Adult student services, alcohol/substance abuse counseling, career counseling, services for economically disadvantaged, student employment services, financial aid counseling, minority student services, on-campus daycare, personal counseling, placement for graduates, veterans' counselor, women's services. **Physically disabled:** Services for visually, speech, hearing impaired. **Learning disabled:** Comprehensive services available. **Transfer:** Re-entry adviser, pre-admission transcript evaluation for new students. Transfer center, transfer adviser, college fairs on campus for students transferring to 4-year colleges.

Contact. E-mail: rosie.click@gwmail.maricopa.edu
Phone: (602) 286-8200 Fax: (602) 286-8072
Rosie Click, Supervisor Registration and Records, Gateway Community College, 108 North 40th Street, Phoenix, AZ 85034

Glendale Community College

Glendale, Arizona
www.gccaz.edu **CB code: 4338**

- Public 2-year community college
- Commuter campus in small city

General. Founded in 1965. Regionally accredited. Additional campus in Peoria. **Enrollment:** 5,792 degree-seeking undergraduates; 12,651 non-degree-seeking students. **Degrees:** 1,565 associate awarded. **Location:** 17 miles from Phoenix. **Calendar:** Semester, extensive summer session. **Full-time faculty:** 240 total; 15% minority, 51% women. **Part-time faculty:** 488 total; 14% minority, 48% women. **Class size:** 48% < 20, 49% 20-39, 2% 40-49, less than 1% 50-99, less than 1% >100. **Special facilities:** Performing arts center, high-technology centers, international student center. **Partnerships:** Formal partnerships with General Motors, Ford, Chrysler, Best Western, and John Deere.

Student profile. Among degree-seeking undergraduates, 31% enrolled in a transfer program, 5% already have a bachelor's degree or higher.

Part-time:	60%	**Hispanic American:**	21%
Out-of-state:	5%	**Native American:**	2%
Women:	57%	**International:**	2%
African American:	6%	**25 or older:**	49%
Asian American:	4%		

Transfer out. Colleges most students transferred to 2008: Arizona State University, Arizona State University West, University of Arizona, Grand Canyon University.

Basis for selection. Open admission, but selective for some programs. Special requirements for nursing, basic emergency medical technology, General Motors and Ford automotive programs, international students. **Home-schooled:** If under 18, special admissions required.

2008-2009 Annual costs. Tuition/fees: $2,115; $8,595 out-of-state. Per-credit charge: $71 in-state; $286 out-of-state. Books/supplies: $1,200. Personal expenses: $2,970.

2007-2008 Financial aid. Need-based: Need-based aid available for part-time students. Work-study available nights, weekends and for part-time students.

Application procedures. Admission: No deadline. No application fee. Admission notification on a rolling basis. **Financial aid:** Priority date 4/30, closing date 8/1. FAFSA required. Applicants notified on a rolling basis starting 6/1.

Academics. Special study options: Cooperative education, distance learning, dual enrollment of high school students, ESL, honors, independent study, internships, weekend college. ACE Plus (Achieving College Education), high school bridge program, intensive English program. License preparation in nursing, paramedic. **Credit/placement by examination:** AP, CLEP, institutional tests. 30 credit hours maximum toward associate degree. **Support services:** GED preparation and test center, learning center, remedial instruction, study skills assistance, tutoring, writing center.

Majors. Biology: Biotechnology. **Business:** General, accounting technology, administrative services, marketing, real estate. **Communications:** Public relations. **Communications technology:** Radio/tv. **Computer sciences:** General, data entry, networking, security, systems analysis. **Education:** Early childhood, trade/industrial. **Engineering technology:** Architectural drafting, computer, energy systems. **Health:** EMT paramedic, nursing (RN). **Interdisciplinary:** Behavioral sciences. **Mechanic/repair:** Automotive. **Parks/recreation:** Exercise sciences. **Protective services:** Criminal justice, firefighting, security services. **Visual/performing arts:** Commercial/advertising art, graphic design, music management.

Most popular majors. Business/marketing 11%, health sciences 10%, liberal arts 49%, physical sciences 8%.

Computing on campus. 1,500 workstations in library, computer center, student center. Commuter students can connect to campus network. Online course registration, online library, helpline, student web hosting, wireless network available.

Student life. Freshman orientation: Available. Preregistration for classes offered. **Activities:** Bands, choral groups, dance, drama, literary magazine, music ensembles, musical theater, opera, student government, student newspaper.

Athletics. NJCAA. **Intercollegiate:** Baseball M, basketball, cheerleading, cross-country, football (tackle) M, golf M, soccer, softball W, tennis, track and field, volleyball W. **Team name:** Gauchos.

Student services. Adult student services, chaplain/spiritual director, career counseling, student employment services, financial aid counseling, minority student services, on-campus daycare, veterans' counselor. **Physically disabled:** Services for visually, speech, hearing impaired. **Transfer:** Transfer adviser, college fairs on campus for students transferring to 4-year colleges.

Contact. E-mail: admissions.recruitment@gcmail.maricopa.edu
Phone: (623) 845-3333 Fax: (623) 845-3060
Mary Blackwell, Dean, Enrollment Services, Glendale Community College, 6000 West Olive Avenue, Glendale, AZ 85302

Golf Academy of America: Phoenix

Scottsdale, Arizona
www.golfacademy.edu **CB code: 3460**

- For-profit 2-year college of golf course management
- Small city

General. Accredited by ACICS. **Calendar:** Semester.

Annual costs/financial aid. Tuition/fees (2008-2009): $13,350. Books/supplies: $700. Personal expenses: $2,862.

Contact. Phone: (480) 905-9288
7373 North Scottsdale Road, Suite B-100, Scottsdale, AZ 85253

IIA College: Mesa

Mesa, Arizona
www.iia.edu **CB code: 3455**

- For-profit 2-year branch campus and career college
- Commuter campus in very large city
- Interview required

General. Accredited by ACICS. Additional campuses in Phoenix, Tucson, and Albuquerque. **Enrollment:** 191 degree-seeking undergraduates. **Degrees:** 20 associate awarded. **Location:** 5 miles from Phoenix. **Calendar:** Continuous, extensive summer session. **Full-time faculty:** 6 total; 33% have terminal degrees, 50% women. **Part-time faculty:** 15 total; 13% have terminal degrees, 73% women.

Student profile.

Women:	90%	**25 or older:**	57%

Basis for selection. Open admission, but selective for some programs. **Homeschooled:** Letter of Attestation required.

2009-2010 Annual costs. Tuition/fees (projected): $11,750. Tuition and fees may vary by program.

Financial aid. All financial aid based on need.

Application procedures. Admission: No deadline. $250 fee. Application must be submitted on paper. Admission notification on a rolling basis. **Financial aid:** FAFSA, institutional form required.

Academics. Special study options: Accelerated study, distance learning. Bachelor's degree programs available on campus. **Credit/placement by examination:** CLEP, institutional tests. **Support services:** GED preparation, learning center.

Majors. Business: Accounting, business admin. **Health:** Health care admin. **Legal studies:** Paralegal.

Most popular majors. Business/marketing 40%, health sciences 25%, legal studies 35%.

Computing on campus. Commuter students can connect to campus network. Online library available.

Student life. Freshman orientation: Mandatory.

Student services. Career counseling, services for economically disadvantaged, financial aid counseling, placement for graduates.

Contact. E-mail: pdabous@iia.edu
Phone: (480) 545-8755 Toll-free number: (888) 744-6340
Fax: (480) 926-1371
Patrick Dabous, Regional Director of Admissions, IIA College: Mesa, 925 South Gilbert Road, Suite 201, Mesa, AZ 85204-4448

IIA College: Phoenix

Phoenix, Arizona
www.iia.edu **CB code: 2188**

- For-profit 2-year career college
- Commuter campus in very large city
- Interview required

General. Accredited by ACICS. Additional campuses in Mesa, Tucson, and Albuquerque. **Enrollment:** 609 degree-seeking undergraduates. **Degrees:** 22 bachelor's, 112 associate awarded. **Calendar:** Continuous, extensive summer session. **Full-time faculty:** 21 total; 29% have terminal degrees, 71% women. **Part-time faculty:** 23 total; 13% have terminal degrees, 74% women.

Student profile.

Women:	91%	**25 or older:**	56%

Basis for selection. Open admission, but selective for some programs. **Homeschooled:** Letter of Attestation required.

2009-2010 Annual costs. Tuition/fees (projected): $11,750. Tuition and fees may vary by program.

Financial aid. All financial aid based on need.

Application procedures. Admission: No deadline. $250 fee. Application must be submitted on paper. Admission notification on a rolling basis. **Financial aid:** No deadline. FAFSA, institutional form required.

Academics. Special study options: Accelerated study, distance learning. Bachelor's degree programs available on campus. License preparation in nursing. **Credit/placement by examination:** CLEP, institutional tests. **Support services:** GED preparation, learning center.

Majors. Business: Accounting, business admin. **Health:** Health care admin, nursing (RN). **Legal studies:** Paralegal.

Most popular majors. Business/marketing 19%, health sciences 68%, legal studies 13%.

Computing on campus. 240 workstations in library, computer center. Commuter students can connect to campus network. Online library available.

Student life. Freshman orientation: Mandatory.

Student services. Career counseling, services for economically disadvantaged, financial aid counseling, placement for graduates. **Transfer:** Preadmission transcript evaluation for new students.

Contact. E-mail: pdabous@iia.edu
Phone: (602) 242-6265 Toll-free number: (888) 744-6340
Fax: (602) 973-2572
Patrick Dabous, Regional Director of Admissions, IIA College: Phoenix, 4240 West Bethany Home Road, Phoenix, AZ 85019-1808

IIA College: Tucson

Tucson, Arizona
www.iia.edu **CB code: 3454**

- For-profit 2-year branch campus and career college
- Commuter campus in very large city
- Interview required

General. Accredited by ACICS. Additional campuses in Phoenix, Mesa, and Albuquerque. **Enrollment:** 317 degree-seeking undergraduates. **Degrees:** 32 associate awarded. **Calendar:** Continuous, extensive summer session. **Full-time faculty:** 8 total; 25% have terminal degrees, 25% women. **Part-time faculty:** 10 total; 60% women.

Student profile.

Women:	80%	**25 or older:**	60%

Basis for selection. Open admission, but selective for some programs. **Homeschooled:** Letter of Attestation required.

2009-2010 Annual costs. Tuition/fees (projected): $11,750. Tuition and fees may vary by program.

Financial aid. All financial aid based on need. Need-based aid available for part-time students.

Application procedures. Admission: No deadline. $250 fee. Application must be submitted on paper. Admission notification on a rolling basis. **Financial aid:** No deadline. FAFSA, institutional form required.

Academics. Special study options: Accelerated study, distance learning. Bachelor's degree programs available on campus. **Credit/placement by examination:** CLEP, institutional tests. **Support services:** GED preparation, learning center.

Majors. Business: Accounting, business admin. **Health:** Health care admin. **Legal studies:** Paralegal. **Protective services:** Law enforcement admin.

Most popular majors. Business/marketing 38%, health sciences 22%, legal studies 40%.

Computing on campus. 240 workstations in library, computer center. Commuter students can connect to campus network. Online library available.

Student life. **Freshman orientation:** Mandatory.

Student services. Career counseling, services for economically disadvantaged, financial aid counseling, placement for graduates. **Transfer:** Pre-admission transcript evaluation for new students.

Contact. E-mail: pdabous@iia.edu
Phone: (520) 748-9799 Toll-free number: (888) 744-6340
Fax: (520) 748-9355
Patrick Dabous, Regional Director of Admissions, IIA College: Tucson, 5441 East 22nd Street, Suite 125, Tucson, AZ 85711-5444

Kaplan College: Phoenix

Phoenix, Arizona
www.kc-phoenix.com **CB code: 3052**

- For-profit 2-year technical college
- Residential campus in very large city
- Interview required

General. Accredited by ACICS, ACCSCT. **Enrollment:** 430 full-time, degree-seeking students. **Degrees:** 70 associate awarded. **Calendar:** Continuous. **Full-time faculty:** 40 total.

Basis for selection. Open admission, but selective for some programs. Wonderlic entrance exam required for placement.

Application procedures. **Admission:** No deadline. $25 fee.

Academics. **Credit/placement by examination:** CLEP. **Support services:** Learning center, tutoring.

Majors. **Health:** Respiratory therapy technology.

Student life. **Freshman orientation:** Mandatory.

Contact. E-mail: mcrance@kaplan.edu
Phone: (602) 548-1955 ext. 1366 Toll-free number: (877) 548-1955 ext. 1366 Fax: (602) 548-1956
Michael Crance, Director of Admissions, Kaplan College: Phoenix, 13610 North Black Canyon Highway, Suite 104, Phoenix, AZ 85029

Lamson College

Tempe, Arizona
www.lamsoncollege.com **CB code: 1899**

- For-profit 2-year junior and technical college
- Commuter campus in very large city
- Interview required

General. Founded in 1889. Accredited by ACICS. **Enrollment:** 460 full-time, degree-seeking students. **Degrees:** 41 associate awarded. **Calendar:** Quarter, extensive summer session.

Basis for selection. Open admission.

2008-2009 Annual costs. Per-credit-hour charges vary according to program: $250 to $271; cost of books and supplies ranges from $995 to $3,000, depending on program of study.

Financial aid. **Need-based:** Need-based aid available for part-time students.

Application procedures. **Admission:** No deadline. $30 fee. Application must be submitted on paper. Admission notification on a rolling basis. **Financial aid:** No deadline. FAFSA required. Applicants notified on a rolling basis.

Academics. **Special study options:** Independent study, internships. **Credit/placement by examination:** CLEP. **Support services:** Learning center, tutoring.

Majors. **Business:** Accounting, business admin. **Health:** Medical assistant. **Legal studies:** Paralegal.

Computing on campus. 73 workstations in library, computer center.

Student life. **Freshman orientation:** Mandatory.

Student services. Career counseling, student employment services, financial aid counseling, placement for graduates, veterans' counselor. **Transfer:** Pre-admission transcript evaluation for new students.

Contact. E-mail: lamsonadmissions@gryphoncolleges.edu
Phone: (480) 898-7000 Toll-free number: (800) 898-7017
Fax: (480) 967-6645
Jeff Bing, Director of Admission, Lamson College, 1126 North Scottsdale Road, Suite 17, Tempe, AZ 85281-1700

Mesa Community College

Mesa, Arizona
www.mc.maricopa.edu **CB code: 4513**

- Public 2-year community college
- Commuter campus in very large city

General. Founded in 1965. Regionally accredited. **Enrollment:** 2,660 degree-seeking undergraduates. **Degrees:** 1,639 associate awarded. **ROTC:** Army, Naval, Air Force. **Location:** 12 miles from Phoenix. **Calendar:** Semester, extensive summer session. **Full-time faculty:** 300 total. **Part-time faculty:** 900 total.

Basis for selection. Open admission, but selective for some programs. General education requirements and 2.5 GPA required for nursing, mortuary science, and fire academy programs.

2008-2009 Annual costs. Tuition/fees: $2,160; $8,610 out-of-state. Per-credit charge: $71 in-state; $286 out-of-state. Books/supplies: $500.

Financial aid. **Non-need-based:** Scholarships awarded for academics, athletics. **Additional information:** Awards available for Maricopa County residents.

Application procedures. **Admission:** No deadline. No application fee. Admission notification on a rolling basis. Diploma or GED required for applicants under 18. **Financial aid:** Priority date 5/1; no closing date. Institutional form required. Applicants notified on a rolling basis starting 7/1.

Academics. Associate of General Studies degree allows students to take half of credits in required courses, and dictate own program of electives. **Special study options:** Cooperative education, cross-registration, distance learning, dual enrollment of high school students, ESL, exchange student, honors, independent study, internships, liberal arts/career combination, student-designed major, study abroad, teacher certification program, weekend college. License preparation in dental hygiene, nursing, real estate. **Credit/placement by examination:** CLEP, IB, institutional tests. 30 credit hours maximum toward associate degree. **Support services:** GED preparation and test center, learning center, remedial instruction, study skills assistance, tutoring, writing center.

Honors college/program. Honors courses open to all students with 3.5 GPA.

Majors. **Agriculture:** Agribusiness operations, horticulture, landscaping. **Business:** Accounting, business admin, fashion, marketing, office management, office/clerical. **Communications:** Journalism. **Computer sciences:** General, applications programming, computer science, networking. **Education:** Teacher assistance. **Engineering:** General. **Engineering technology:** Architectural. **Family/consumer sciences:** Clothing/textiles, food/nutrition. **Health:** Nursing (RN). **Liberal arts:** Library assistant. **Visual/performing arts:** Interior design.

Computing on campus. 1,000 workstations in library, computer center, student center. Commuter students can connect to campus network. Online course registration, online library, helpline, repair service, student web hosting, wireless network available.

Student life. **Freshman orientation:** Available. **Housing:** Coed dorms, apartments available. Housing available at Williams campus. **Activities:** Jazz band, choral groups, dance, drama, music ensembles, musical theater, student government, student newspaper.

Athletics. NJCAA. **Intercollegiate:** Baseball M, basketball, cross-country, football (tackle) M, golf, gymnastics W, soccer, softball W, swimming M, track and field, volleyball W, wrestling M. **Intramural:** Basketball, bowling, cross-country, football (tackle) M, softball, track and field, volleyball, wrestling M. **Team name:** Thunderbirds.

Student services. Adult student services, alcohol/substance abuse counseling, career counseling, services for economically disadvantaged, student employment services, financial aid counseling, legal services, on-campus daycare, personal counseling, placement for graduates, veterans' counselor. **Physically disabled:** Services for visually, speech, hearing impaired. **Transfer:** Transfer adviser for students transferring to 4-year colleges.

Contact. E-mail: admissions@mc.maricopa.edu
Phone: (480) 461-7000 Fax: (480) 461-7805
Director of Admissions, Mesa Community College, 1833 West Southern Avenue, Mesa, AZ 85202

Mohave Community College
Kingman, Arizona
www.mohave.edu **CB code: 0443**

- Public 2-year community college
- Commuter campus in small city

General. Founded in 1971. Regionally accredited. **Enrollment:** 5,539 degree-seeking undergraduates. **Degrees:** 285 associate awarded. **Location:** 200 miles from Phoenix, 100 miles from Las Vegas. **Calendar:** Semester, limited summer session. **Full-time faculty:** 60 total. **Part-time faculty:** 328 total.

Transfer out. Colleges most students transferred to 2008: Northern Arizona University, University of Arizona, Arizona State University.

Basis for selection. Open admission, but selective for some programs. Special requirements for nursing, dental hygiene and EMT/paramedic programs.

2008-2009 Annual costs. Tuition/fees: $1,850; $5,390 out-of-state. Per-credit charge: $59 in-state; $177 out-of-state.

Financial aid. Need-based: Need-based aid available for part-time students. Work-study available nights and for part-time students.

Application procedures. Admission: No deadline. No application fee. **Financial aid:** Priority date 4/15; no closing date. FAFSA, institutional form required. Applicants notified on a rolling basis starting 5/1; must reply within 2 week(s) of notification.

Academics. Special study options: Distance learning, dual enrollment of high school students, ESL, independent study, internships, liberal arts/career combination, student-designed major. License preparation in dental hygiene, nursing, paramedic, physical therapy. **Credit/placement by examination:** CLEP, IB, institutional tests. 20 credit hours maximum toward associate degree. **Support services:** GED preparation and test center, learning center, reduced course load, remedial instruction, study skills assistance, tutoring.

Majors. Business: Administrative services, business admin. **Computer sciences:** General. **Education:** General. **Health:** Dental hygiene, nursing (RN), pharmacy assistant, physical therapy assistant, surgical technology. **Legal studies:** Paralegal. **Liberal arts:** Arts/sciences. **Mechanic/repair:** Automotive, heating/ac/refrig. **Protective services:** Firefighting, police science. **Other:** Chemical dependency therapy.

Computing on campus. 300 workstations in library, computer center. Commuter students can connect to campus network. Online course registration, online library, helpline, wireless network available.

Student life. Freshman orientation: Available. Preregistration for classes offered. **Activities:** Dance, drama, music ensembles, musical theater, student government.

Student services. Adult student services, career counseling, student employment services, financial aid counseling, veterans' counselor. **Physically disabled:** Services for visually, speech, hearing impaired. **Transfer:** Transfer adviser for students transferring to 4-year colleges.

Contact. E-mail: johwil@mohave.edu
Phone: (928) 757-0847 Toll-free number: (866) 664-2832
Fax: (928) 757-0808
John Wilson, Director of Admissions, Mohave Community College, 1971 Jagerson Avenue, Kingman, AZ 86409

Northland Pioneer College
Holbrook, Arizona
www.npc.edu **CB code: 0325**

- Public 2-year community and technical college
- Commuter campus in small town

General. Founded in 1973. Regionally accredited. 10 locations in Navajo and Apache Counties. **Enrollment:** 3,649 degree-seeking undergraduates. **Degrees:** 145 associate awarded. **Location:** 200 miles from Phoenix, 90 miles from Flagstaff. **Calendar:** Semester, limited summer session. **Full-time faculty:** 85 total; 12% have terminal degrees. **Part-time faculty:** 260 total.

Student profile.

Out-of-state:	5%	**25 or older:**	42%

Transfer out. Colleges most students transferred to 2008: Northern Arizona University, University of Arizona, Arizona State University, Western New Mexico University, Brigham Young University.

Basis for selection. Open admission, but selective for some programs. Limited admission for nursing and cosmetology.

2008-2009 Annual costs. Tuition/fees: $1,440; $7,050 out-of-state. Per-credit charge: $48 in-state; $80 out-of-state. Books/supplies: $1,200. Personal expenses: $3,260.

2007-2008 Financial aid. Need-based: 95% of total undergraduate aid awarded as scholarships/grants, 5% as loans/jobs. Need-based aid available for part-time students. Work-study available nights, weekends and for part-time students. **Non-need-based:** Scholarships awarded for academics, art, job skills, leadership, minority status, music/drama, state residency.

Application procedures. Admission: No deadline. No application fee. Admission notification on a rolling basis. **Financial aid:** Priority date 6/1; no closing date. FAFSA, institutional form required. Applicants notified on a rolling basis starting 5/15; must reply within 2 week(s) of notification.

Academics. Special study options: Cooperative education, distance learning, dual enrollment of high school students, honors, independent study, internships, liberal arts/career combination. License preparation in nursing, paramedic, real estate. **Credit/placement by examination:** AP, CLEP, IB, institutional tests. 52 credit hours maximum toward associate degree. **Support services:** GED preparation and test center, learning center, remedial instruction, study skills assistance, tutoring, writing center.

Majors. Agriculture: Turf management. **Business:** General, accounting, administrative services, business admin. **Communications technology:** General. **Computer sciences:** General, computer graphics, data processing, networking. **Construction:** General, carpentry, electrician, plumbing. **Education:** General, early childhood, elementary. **Engineering technology:** Electrical. **Family/consumer sciences:** Child care. **Health:** EMT paramedic, medical assistant, medical transcription, nursing (RN). **Interdisciplinary:** Biological/physical sciences. **Liberal arts:** Arts/sciences, library assistant. **Mechanic/repair:** Automotive, heating/ac/refrig, industrial. **Parks/recreation:** General. **Personal/culinary services:** Cosmetic. **Production:** Welding. **Protective services:** Criminal justice, firefighting. **Transportation:** Heavy/earthmoving equipment. **Other:** Power plant operations.

Computing on campus. 130 workstations in library, computer center. Commuter students can connect to campus network. Online course registration, online library, helpline, wireless network available.

Student life. Freshman orientation: Available. Preregistration for classes offered. **Activities:** Jazz band, choral groups, dance, drama, literary magazine, music ensembles, musical theater, student government, symphony orchestra, National Honor Society, Phi Theta Kappa.

Athletics. NJCAA. **Team name:** Golden Eagles.

Student services. Adult student services, career counseling, services for economically disadvantaged, student employment services, financial aid counseling, placement for graduates, veterans' counselor. **Physically disabled:** Services for visually, hearing impaired. **Transfer:** Pre-admission transcript evaluation for new students. Transfer adviser, college fairs on campus for students transferring to 4-year colleges.

Contact. E-mail: admissions@npc.edu
Phone: (928) 536-6257 Toll-free number: (800) 266-7845
Fax: (928) 524-7612
Ann Hess, Director of Marketing and Recruitment, Northland Pioneer College, PO Box 610, Holbrook, AZ 86025-0610

Paradise Valley Community College
Phoenix, Arizona **CB member**
www.pvc.maricopa.edu **CB code: 2179**

- Public 2-year community college
- Commuter campus in very large city

General. Founded in 1985. Regionally accredited. **Enrollment:** 3,290 degree-seeking undergraduates. **Degrees:** 530 associate awarded. **ROTC:** Army. **Calendar:** Semester, limited summer session. **Full-time faculty:** 98 total; 20% minority, 50% women. **Part-time faculty:** 275 total. **Special facilities:** Studio theater, performing arts center.

Student profile.

Out-of-state:	3%	**25 or older:**	50%

Transfer out. Colleges most students transferred to 2008: Arizona State University, Arizona State University West, Northern Arizona University, University of Arizona.

Basis for selection. Open admission.

2008-2009 Annual costs. Tuition/fees: $2,160; $8,610 out-of-state. Per-credit charge: $71 in-state; $286 out-of-state. Books/supplies: $700. Personal expenses: $1,185.

Financial aid. Need-based: Need-based aid available for part-time students.

Application procedures. Admission: No deadline. No application fee. Admission notification on a rolling basis. **Financial aid:** No deadline. FAFSA required. Applicants notified on a rolling basis starting 6/1.

Academics. Special study options: Accelerated study, cooperative education, cross-registration, distance learning, dual enrollment of high school students, ESL, honors, independent study, internships, teacher certification program, weekend college. License preparation in nursing, paramedic. **Credit/placement by examination:** AP, CLEP, institutional tests. 30 credit hours maximum toward associate degree. **Support services:** Learning center, remedial instruction, study skills assistance, tutoring, writing center.

Majors. Business: General, accounting, administrative services, international, office technology, office/clerical, organizational behavior. **Computer sciences:** General, word processing. **Engineering technology:** Hazardous materials. **Liberal arts:** Arts/sciences. **Visual/performing arts:** Music.

Computing on campus. 600 workstations in library, computer center, student center. Commuter students can connect to campus network. Online course registration, helpline, wireless network available.

Student life. Freshman orientation: Mandatory. **Activities:** Jazz band, choral groups, dance, drama, international student organizations, literary magazine, music ensembles, musical theater, opera, student government, student newspaper, Phi Theta Kappa, student Christian association, human service club, Returning Adults to Education, environmental club, Latter Day Saints student association, recreational outdoor club.

Athletics. NJCAA. **Intercollegiate:** Baseball M, cross-country, golf, soccer, softball W, tennis, track and field. **Team name:** Pumas.

Student services. Adult student services, alcohol/substance abuse counseling, career counseling, student employment services, financial aid counseling, minority student services, on-campus daycare, personal counseling, placement for graduates, veterans' counselor, women's services. **Physically disabled:** Services for visually, speech, hearing impaired. **Transfer:** Transfer adviser, college fairs on campus for students transferring to 4-year colleges.

Contact. Phone: (602) 787-7020 Fax: (602) 787-6625
Shirley Green, Associate Dean Student Services, Paradise Valley Community College, 18401 North 32nd Street, Phoenix, AZ 85032

Paralegal Institute
Glendale, Arizona
www.theparalegalinstitute.edu **CB code: 3888**

- For-profit 2-year virtual career college
- Very large city

General. Accredited by DETC. **Enrollment:** 315 degree-seeking undergraduates. **Degrees:** 60 associate awarded. **Calendar:** Continuous, extensive summer session. **Full-time faculty:** 2 total. **Part-time faculty:** 2 total.

Basis for selection. Open admission.

2008-2009 Annual costs. Diploma programs are $3,600; associate degree programs are $7,200.

Application procedures. Admission: No deadline. No application fee. Application must be submitted on paper.

Academics. Credit/placement by examination: CLEP.

Majors. Legal studies: Paralegal.

Student life. Freshman orientation: Available. Preregistration for classes offered.

Student services. Transfer: Pre-admission transcript evaluation for new students.

Contact. E-mail: kallen@theparalegalinstitute.edu
Phone: (602) 212-0501 Toll-free number: (800) 354-1254
Fax: (602) 212-0502
Paralegal Institute, 18275 North 59th Avenue, Suite 186 Building N, Glendale, AZ 85308

Penn Foster College
Scottsdale, Arizona
www.pennfostercollege.edu **CB code: 7313**

- For-profit 2-year virtual college
- Commuter campus in small city

General. Founded in 1975. Accredited by DETC. All courses offered via distance learning. **Enrollment:** 27,000 undergraduates. **Degrees:** 175 associate awarded. **Calendar:** Continuous. **Full-time faculty:** 23 total. **Part-time faculty:** 53 total.

Basis for selection. Open admission. **Homeschooled:** Copy of completion document from a school or copy of standardized tests required. **Learning Disabled:** Evidence of disability recommended so that accommodations can be made.

2008-2009 Annual costs. Average cost for a four-semester full associate degree program: $6,145; bachelor's degree: $11,200.

Application procedures. Admission: No deadline. $200 fee. Admission notification on a rolling basis.

Academics. Students allowed 12 months to complete semester (15-20 credit hours). **Special study options:** Distance learning, external degree, independent study. Bachelor's degree programs available on campus. **Credit/placement by examination:** CLEP. **Support services:** Remedial instruction, tutoring.

Majors. Business: General, accounting, finance, hospitality admin, marketing. **Computer sciences:** General. **Education:** Early childhood. **Engineering technology:** Civil, electrical, industrial, mechanical. **Health:** Medical records technology. **Legal studies:** Paralegal. **Protective services:** Police science.

Student life. Freshman orientation: Mandatory.

Student services. Veterans' counselor. **Transfer:** Pre-admission transcript evaluation for new students.

Contact. Phone: (800) 275-4410 Toll-free number: (800) 275-4410
Linda Smith, Manager, DP Services, Penn Foster College, 14300 North Northsight Boulevard, Suite 111, Scottsdale, AZ 85260

Phoenix College
Phoenix, Arizona
www.pc.maricopa.edu **CB code: 4606**

- Public 2-year community college
- Commuter campus in very large city

General. Founded in 1920. Regionally accredited. **Enrollment:** 2,633 full-time, degree-seeking students. **Degrees:** 967 associate awarded. **ROTC:** Army, Air Force. **Calendar:** Semester, limited summer session. **Full-time faculty:** 145 total. **Part-time faculty:** 419 total. **Class size:** 63% < 20, 35% 20-39, 1% 40-49, 1% 50-99, less than 1% >100.

Student profile.

Out-of-state:	2%	**25 or older:**	51%

Basis for selection. Open admission, but selective for some programs. ASSET, COMPASS and Celsa test scores used for placement.

2008-2009 Annual costs. Tuition/fees: $2,160; $8,610 out-of-state. Per-credit charge: $71 in-state; $286 out-of-state. Books/supplies: $700. Personal expenses: $3,654.

Financial aid. Need-based: Work-study available weekends.

Application procedures. Admission: No deadline. No application fee. Admission notification on a rolling basis. **Financial aid:** Priority date 6/30; no closing date. FAFSA required. Applicants notified on a rolling basis starting 5/1.

Academics. **Special study options:** Cooperative education, cross-registration, distance learning, dual enrollment of high school students, ESL, honors, independent study, internships, liberal arts/career combination, study abroad. License preparation in nursing. **Credit/placement by examination:** CLEP, institutional tests. 30 credit hours maximum toward associate degree. **Support services:** GED test center, learning center, reduced course load, remedial instruction, tutoring.

Honors college/program. Requires 3.0 GPA.

Majors. **Architecture:** Interior. **Business:** General, accounting, banking/financial services, business admin, management information systems, management science, marketing, tourism promotion, tourism/travel. **Communications:** General. **Computer sciences:** General, computer graphics, information systems. **Education:** General, family/consumer sciences. **Engineering:** General, software. **Engineering technology:** Civil. **Family/consumer sciences:** General, child care, institutional food production. **Foreign languages:** Sign language interpretation. **Health:** Clinical lab science, dental assistant, dental hygiene, EMT paramedic, medical records technology, medical transcription, nursing (RN), premedicine. **Legal studies:** Legal secretary, paralegal. **Liberal arts:** Arts/sciences. **Physical sciences:** Chemistry. **Protective services:** Firefighting, police science. **Visual/performing arts:** Art, commercial/advertising art, interior design.

Computing on campus. Online course registration, helpline, wireless network available.

Student life. **Freshman orientation:** Available. Preregistration for classes offered. **Activities:** Bands, choral groups, dance, drama, music ensembles, musical theater, opera, student newspaper, symphony orchestra, TV station.

Athletics. NJCAA. **Intercollegiate:** Baseball M, basketball, cross-country, football (tackle) M, golf M, soccer M, softball W, tennis, track and field, volleyball W. **Team name:** PC Bears.

Student services. Adult student services, career counseling, services for economically disadvantaged, student employment services, legal services, on-campus daycare, personal counseling, placement for graduates, veterans' counselor. **Physically disabled:** Services for visually, speech, hearing impaired. **Transfer:** Re-entry adviser, pre-admission transcript evaluation for new students. Transfer adviser, college fairs on campus for students transferring to 4-year colleges.

Contact. E-mail: info@pcmail.maricopa.edu
Phone: (602) 285-7502 Fax: (602) 285-7813
Kathy French, Director of Admissions and Records, Phoenix College, 1202 West Thomas Road, Phoenix, AZ 85013

Pima Community College

Tucson, Arizona — **CB member**
www.pima.edu — **CB code: 4623**

- Public 2-year community and technical college
- Commuter campus in very large city

General. Founded in 1966. Regionally accredited. 6 campuses, 3 centers and Public Safety Institute serve Tucson metropolitan area. **Enrollment:** 27,190 degree-seeking undergraduates. **Degrees:** 2,359 associate awarded. **ROTC:** Army, Naval, Air Force. **Location:** 120 miles from Phoenix. **Calendar:** Semester, limited summer session. **Full-time faculty:** 325 total. **Part-time faculty:** 1,157 total. **Special facilities:** Arts center.

Student profile.

Out-of-state:	5%	**25 or older:**	41%

Transfer out. **Colleges most students transferred to 2008:** University of Arizona, Arizona State University, Northern Arizona University, University of Phoenix.

Basis for selection. Open admission, but selective for some programs. Special requirements for nursing, dental hygiene, and pharmacy technology.

2008-2009 Annual costs. Tuition/fees: $1,625; $7,610 out-of-state. Per-credit charge: $50 in-state; $84 out-of-state. Books/supplies: $2,000. Personal expenses: $2,520.

Financial aid. **Need-based:** Need-based aid available for part-time students. **Non-need-based:** Scholarships awarded for academics, alumni affiliation, art, athletics, minority status, music/drama.

Application procedures. **Admission:** No deadline. No application fee. Admission notification on a rolling basis. **Financial aid:** Priority date 3/15; no closing date. FAFSA required. Applicants notified on a rolling basis starting 7/1; must reply within 2 week(s) of notification.

Academics. Upward Bound programs available. **Special study options:** Accelerated study, cooperative education, distance learning, double major, dual enrollment of high school students, ESL, honors, independent study, internships, student-designed major, teacher certification program, weekend college. License preparation in dental hygiene, nursing, radiology. **Credit/placement by examination:** AP, CLEP, institutional tests. 30 credit hours maximum toward associate degree. **Support services:** GED preparation and test center, learning center, pre-admission summer program, remedial instruction, study skills assistance, tutoring.

Majors. **Area/ethnic studies:** Native American. **Business:** Accounting, administrative services, business admin, fashion, hospitality admin, international, tourism/travel. **Communications:** Digital media, radio/tv. **Communications technology:** Animation/special effects, graphics. **Computer sciences:** General, networking, systems analysis. **Construction:** Maintenance. **Education:** General, adult/continuing, early childhood. **Engineering technology:** Architectural drafting, computer, construction, environmental, laser/optical. **Family/consumer sciences:** Child development. **Foreign languages:** Sign language interpretation. **Health:** Clinical lab technology, dental hygiene, dental lab technology, EMT paramedic, histologic assistant, massage therapy, medical records admin, medical records technology, nursing (RN), pharmacy assistant, radiologic technology/medical imaging, respiratory therapy technology, substance abuse counseling, veterinary technology/assistant. **Legal studies:** Paralegal. **Liberal arts:** Arts/sciences. **Mechanic/repair:** Aircraft powerplant, automotive, industrial electronics. **Personal/culinary services:** Restaurant/catering. **Production:** Machine shop technology, welding. **Protective services:** Criminal justice, firefighting, police science. **Social sciences:** Anthropology, archaeology, political science, sociology. **Visual/performing arts:** General, art, design, dramatic.

Most popular majors. Business/marketing 10%, health sciences 17%, liberal arts 59%.

Computing on campus. 1,500 workstations in library, computer center. Commuter students can connect to campus network. Online course registration, online library, helpline available.

Student life. **Freshman orientation:** Mandatory. Orientation programs based on majors. **Activities:** Bands, choral groups, dance, drama, literary magazine, music ensembles, student government, student newspaper, TV station, forensics activities, speech communication program, clubs for various student groups.

Athletics. NJCAA. **Intercollegiate:** Baseball M, basketball, cross-country, football (tackle) M, golf, soccer, softball W, tennis, track and field, volleyball W. **Intramural:** Badminton, baseball M, basketball, cross-country, football (non-tackle) M, golf, racquetball, tennis, track and field, volleyball. **Team name:** Aztecs.

Student services. Career counseling, student employment services, health services, minority student services, on-campus daycare, personal counseling, placement for graduates, veterans' counselor. **Physically disabled:** Services for visually, speech, hearing impaired. **Transfer:** Transfer adviser, college fairs on campus for students transferring to 4-year colleges.

Contact. E-mail: coadmit@pima.edu
Phone: (520) 206-4643 Toll-free number: (800) 860-7462
Fax: (520) 206-4790
Michael Tulino, Director and Registrar, Pima Community College, 4905B East Broadway, Tucson, AZ 85709-1120

Refrigeration School

Phoenix, Arizona
www.rsiaz.edu — **CB code: 2888**

- For-profit 2-year technical college
- Very large city
- Interview required

General. Accredited by ACCSCT. **Enrollment:** 170 full-time, degree-seeking students. **Degrees:** 25 associate awarded. **Calendar:** 3, 6 or 8 month programs. **Full-time faculty:** 12 total. **Part-time faculty:** 14 total.

Basis for selection. Open admission. **Homeschooled:** State high school equivalency certificate required.

2008-2009 Annual costs. Costs of entire programs range from $6,500 to $21,780; includes books and supplies.

Application procedures. **Admission:** No deadline. No application fee.

Academics. **Credit/placement by examination:** CLEP. **Support services:** Tutoring.

Majors. **Engineering technology:** Energy systems. **Mechanic/repair:** Heating/ac/refrig.

Computing on campus. 4 workstations in library.

Contact. Phone: (602) 275-7133 Toll-free number: (877) 477-4669
Fax: (602) 267-4805
Mary Simmons, Admissions Director, Refrigeration School, 4210 East Washington Street, Phoenix, AZ 85034-1816

Rio Salado College

Tempe, Arizona
www.riosalado.edu
CB member
CB code: 0997

- Public 2-year virtual community college
- Commuter campus in very large city

General. Founded in 1978. Regionally accredited. Access to libraries at Arizona State University and 10 Maricopa County community colleges. **Enrollment:** 4,849 degree-seeking undergraduates. **Degrees:** 405 associate awarded. **Location:** 120 miles from Tucson, 10 miles from Phoenix. **Calendar:** Semester, extensive summer session. **Full-time faculty:** 31 total. **Part-time faculty:** 997 total. **Special facilities:** Public radio stations.

Student profile.

Out-of-state:	5%	25 or older:	46%

Transfer out. Colleges most students transferred to 2008: Arizona State University, University of Arizona, Northern Arizona University.

Basis for selection. Open admission, but selective for some programs. Dental hygiene program has GPA requirements.

2008-2009 Annual costs. Tuition/fees: $2,160; $8,610 out-of-state. Per-credit charge: $71 in-state; $286 out-of-state. Books/supplies: $1,024. Personal expenses: $2,616.

2007-2008 Financial aid. All financial aid based on need. Need-based aid available for part-time students.

Application procedures. Admission: No deadline. No application fee. Admission notification on a rolling basis. **Financial aid:** Priority date 6/30; no closing date. FAFSA, institutional form required. Applicants notified on a rolling basis starting 6/30.

Academics. Agreement with Army allows military personnel to take Internet courses. Online nursing and clinical dental assisting programs. **Special study options:** Accelerated study, cooperative education, cross-registration, distance learning, double major, dual enrollment of high school students, ESL, honors, independent study, internships, liberal arts/career combination, weekend college. License preparation in dental hygiene, nursing. **Credit/placement by examination:** AP, CLEP, institutional tests. 30 credit hours maximum toward associate degree. **Support services:** GED preparation, learning center, remedial instruction, study skills assistance, tutoring, writing center.

Majors. Business: General, accounting, banking/financial services, business admin, international, office management. **Computer sciences:** General. **Engineering technology:** Water quality. **Health:** Dental hygiene, nursing assistant, substance abuse counseling. **Protective services:** Law enforcement admin. **Public administration:** General.

Computing on campus. 500 workstations in library, computer center. Commuter students can connect to campus network. Online course registration, online library, helpline, wireless network available.

Student life. Activities: Radio station, Phi Theta Kappa.

Student services. Adult student services, career counseling, student employment services, financial aid counseling, personal counseling, veterans' counselor. **Physically disabled:** Services for visually, speech, hearing impaired. **Transfer:** Re-entry adviser, pre-admission transcript evaluation for new students. Transfer adviser for students transferring to 4-year colleges.

Contact. E-mail: admissions@email.rio.maricopa.edu
Phone: (480) 517-8150 Toll-free number: (800) 729-1197
Fax: (480) 517-8199
Ruby Miller, Director of Registration and Records, Rio Salado College, 2323 West 14th Street, Tempe, AZ 85281

Scottsdale Community College

Scottsdale, Arizona
www.scottsdalecc.edu
CB code: 4755

- Public 2-year community college
- Commuter campus in small city

General. Founded in 1969. Regionally accredited. **Enrollment:** 2,729 degree-seeking undergraduates. **Degrees:** 806 associate awarded. **Location:** 10 miles from Tempe. **Calendar:** Semester, limited summer session. **Full-time faculty:** 168 total; 27% have terminal degrees, 14% minority, 49% women. **Part-time faculty:** 486 total; 7% have terminal degrees, 12% minority, 51% women. **Class size:** 57% < 20, 40% 20-39, 1% 40-49, 1% 50-99, less than 1% >100. **Special facilities:** Student-operated restaurant associated with school of culinary arts.

Student profile.

Out-of-state:	5%	25 or older:	39%

Basis for selection. Open admission.

High school preparation. 16 units recommended. Recommended units include English 4, mathematics 4, social studies 2, history 1, science 3 and foreign language 2.

2008-2009 Annual costs. Tuition/fees: $2,160; $8,610 out-of-state. Per-credit charge: $71 in-state; $286 out-of-state. Books/supplies: $848. Personal expenses: $4,194.

2007-2008 Financial aid. Non-need-based: Scholarships awarded for academics, athletics. **Additional information:** Athletic scholarships offered in rodeo. All athletic scholarships limited to county residents.

Application procedures. Admission: No deadline. No application fee. Admission notification on a rolling basis. **Financial aid:** Priority date 6/30; no closing date. FAFSA, institutional form required. Applicants notified on a rolling basis starting 4/1; must reply by 7/15 or within 3 week(s) of notification.

Academics. Special study options: Cooperative education, cross-registration, distance learning, dual enrollment of high school students, ESL, honors, internships, study abroad, teacher certification program. **Credit/placement by examination:** AP, CLEP, institutional tests. 52 credit hours maximum toward associate degree. **Support services:** Learning center, remedial instruction, tutoring, writing center.

Majors. Agriculture: Equestrian studies. **Architecture:** Environmental design. **Area/ethnic studies:** Native American. **Business:** General, accounting, administrative services, fashion, hospitality admin, international, management information systems, retailing. **Communications:** Public relations. **Communications technology:** Radio/tv. **Computer sciences:** General, information systems. **Construction:** Building inspection. **Education:** Early childhood. **Engineering technology:** Architectural drafting. **Family/consumer sciences:** Child care. **Health:** EMT paramedic, medical radiologic technology/radiation therapy, nursing (RN). **Liberal arts:** Arts/sciences. **Parks/recreation:** General. **Personal/culinary services:** Culinary arts. **Physical sciences:** General. **Protective services:** Criminal justice, firefighting, law enforcement admin. **Visual/performing arts:** General, cinematography, dance, dramatic, interior design, studio arts.

Most popular majors. Business/marketing 13%, communication technologies 7%, health sciences 20%, liberal arts 38%, visual/performing arts 7%.

Computing on campus. 998 workstations in library, computer center, student center. Commuter students can connect to campus network. Online course registration, online library, helpline, repair service, wireless network available.

Student life. Freshman orientation: Available. Preregistration for classes offered. **Activities:** Bands, choral groups, dance, drama, international student organizations, music ensembles, student government, student newspaper, symphony orchestra, TV station, American Indian honor society, black student union, Latino student association, green club, GLBT-straight alliance, Rotoract, advocacy group, international community club, student leadership club.

Athletics. NAIA, NJCAA. **Intercollegiate:** Baseball M, basketball, cross-country, football (tackle) M, golf M, soccer M, softball W, tennis, track and field, volleyball W. **Intramural:** Baseball M. **Team name:** Artichokes.

Student services. Alcohol/substance abuse counseling, career counseling, student employment services, financial aid counseling, personal counseling, placement for graduates, veterans' counselor. **Physically disabled:**

Services for visually, speech, hearing impaired. **Transfer:** Transfer adviser, college fairs on campus for students transferring to 4-year colleges.

Contact. E-mail: admissions@sccmail.maricopa.edu
Phone: (480) 423-6100 Fax: (480) 423-6200
Fran Watkins, Director of Admissions and Records, Scottsdale Community College, 9000 East Chaparral Road, Scottsdale, AZ 85256-2626

Scottsdale Culinary Institute

Scottsdale, Arizona
www.scichefs.com **CB code: 3028**

- For-profit 2-year culinary school and technical college
- Commuter campus in large city
- Application essay, interview required

General. Accredited by ACCSCT. **Enrollment:** 1,275 degree-seeking undergraduates. **Degrees:** 46 bachelor's, 542 associate awarded. **Location:** 2 miles from downtown. **Calendar:** Continuous. **Full-time faculty:** 40 total. **Part-time faculty:** 32 total.

Student profile.

Out-of-state:	55%	**25 or older:**	60%

Basis for selection. Open admission.

2008-2009 Annual costs. Tuition and fees vary by degree and by program. Total costs of programs (includes fees and books): certificate programs start at $21,350; Associate degree programs start at $35,100; Bachelor's degree programs start at $61,400. Personal expenses: $2,275.

Application procedures. Admission: No deadline. $95 fee. Admission notification on a rolling basis.

Academics. Credit/placement by examination: CLEP. **Support services:** Learning center, remedial instruction, tutoring.

Majors. Personal/culinary services: Culinary arts.

Student life. Freshman orientation: Mandatory.

Student services. Alcohol/substance abuse counseling, career counseling, financial aid counseling, placement for graduates.

Contact. E-mail: fred@scichefs.com
Phone: (480) 990-3773 Toll-free number: (800) 848-2433
Director of Admissions, Scottsdale Culinary Institute, 8100 East Camelback Road, Suite 1001, Scottsdale, AZ 85251

South Mountain Community College

Phoenix, Arizona **CB member**
www.smc.maricopa.edu **CB code: 4734**

- Public 2-year community college
- Commuter campus in very large city

General. Founded in 1979. Regionally accredited. Learning Center in Guadalupe. Arizona Agribusiness Equine Charter school located on campus. **Enrollment:** 870 degree-seeking undergraduates. **Degrees:** 241 associate awarded. **Location:** 8 miles from downtown Phoenix. **Calendar:** Semester, limited summer session. **Full-time faculty:** 54 total. **Part-time faculty:** 160 total. **Partnerships:** Formal partnership with Arizona Agribusiness Equine Charter School.

Student profile.

Out-of-state:	2%	**25 or older:**	45%

Basis for selection. Open admission.

2008-2009 Annual costs. Tuition/fees: $2,160; $8,610 out-of-state. Per-credit charge: $71 in-state; $286 out-of-state. Books/supplies: $760. Personal expenses: $1,250.

Financial aid. Need-based: Need-based aid available for part-time students. Work-study available nights, weekends and for part-time students. **Non-need-based:** Scholarships awarded for academics, athletics, minority status, music/drama.

Application procedures. Admission: No deadline. No application fee. Admission notification on a rolling basis. **Financial aid:** Priority date 5/1; no closing date. FAFSA required. Applicants notified on a rolling basis starting 5/15; must reply within 3 week(s) of notification.

Academics. Special study options: Cooperative education, cross-registration, dual enrollment of high school students, ESL, honors, independent study. **Credit/placement by examination:** CLEP, IB, institutional tests. 30 credit hours maximum toward associate degree. **Support services:** GED preparation and test center, learning center, remedial instruction, tutoring.

Majors. Biology: General. **Business:** Administrative services, business admin, international, logistics, office technology. **Computer sciences:** General, information systems, security, system admin, systems analysis. **Education:** General, early childhood, music, physical. **Engineering technology:** Software. **Family/consumer sciences:** General. **History:** General. **Liberal arts:** Arts/sciences. **Math:** General. **Physical sciences:** General, chemistry, physics. **Psychology:** General. **Social sciences:** Political science, sociology. **Visual/performing arts:** Art, music.

Most popular majors. Computer/information sciences 6%, liberal arts 83%.

Computing on campus. 125 workstations in library, computer center.

Student life. Freshman orientation: Available. **Activities:** Concert band, choral groups, dance, drama, music ensembles, student government, student newspaper, African-American unity coalition, Society of Hispanic Engineers and Scientists, Christian student club, Native American club, forensic club, music club, volunteers program, Phi Theta Kappa.

Athletics. NJCAA. **Intercollegiate:** Baseball M, basketball, golf, soccer M, softball W, tennis, volleyball W. **Team name:** Cougars.

Student services. Career counseling, student employment services, on-campus daycare, personal counseling, veterans' counselor. **Transfer:** Reentry adviser, pre-admission transcript evaluation for new students. Transfer adviser, college fairs on campus for students transferring to 4-year colleges.

Contact. Phone: (602) 243-8123 Fax: (602) 243-8199
Raul Sandoval, Associate Dean of Student Services, South Mountain Community College, 7050 South 24th Street, Phoenix, AZ 85042

Tohono O'odham Community College

Sells, Arizona
www.tocc.cc.az.us

- Public 2-year Tribal College
- Commuter campus in rural community

General. Enrollment: 100 degree-seeking undergraduates. **Degrees:** 21 associate awarded. **Location:** 60 miles from Tucson. **Calendar:** Semester, limited summer session. **Full-time faculty:** 14 total; 21% have terminal degrees. **Part-time faculty:** 15 total. **Class size:** 98% < 20, 2% 20-39.

Basis for selection. Open admission. **Homeschooled:** Transcript of courses and grades, state high school equivalency certificate required.

2008-2009 Annual costs. Tuition/fees: $1,270; $6,340 out-of-state. Per-credit charge: $42 in-state; $72 out-of-state. Books/supplies: $750.

2007-2008 Financial aid. All financial aid based on need. Need-based aid available for part-time students. Work-study available for part-time students.

Application procedures. Admission: No deadline. No application fee. **Financial aid:** No deadline. FAFSA, institutional form required. Applicants notified on a rolling basis.

Academics. Special study options: Distance learning, dual enrollment of high school students, independent study. **Credit/placement by examination:** CLEP. **Support services:** GED preparation, learning center, remedial instruction, study skills assistance, tutoring, writing center.

Majors. Agriculture: Production. **Business:** Business admin. **Computer sciences:** System admin. **Construction:** Carpentry, electrician, painting, plumbing, site management. **Education:** Early childhood special, elementary. **Liberal arts:** Arts/sciences. **Social sciences:** General.

Most popular majors. Business/marketing 17%, education 33%, interdisciplinary studies 33%, public administration/social services 17%.

Student life. Freshman orientation: Mandatory. Preregistration for classes offered. Orientation class offers information on student services and academic support services. **Activities:** Student government.

Student services. Adult student services, career counseling, student employment services, financial aid counseling, personal counseling, placement for graduates. **Transfer:** Re-entry adviser, pre-admission transcript evaluation for new students. College fairs on campus for students transferring to 4-year colleges.

Contact. E-mail: lluna@tocc.cc.az.us
Phone: (520) 383-8401 ext. 35 Fax: (520) 383-0029
Leslie Luna, Registrar, Tohono O'odham Community College, PO Box 3129, Sells, AZ 85634-3129

Universal Technical Institute
Avondale, Arizona
www.uti.edu **CB code: 2504**

- For-profit 2-year technical college
- Commuter campus in small city

General. Founded in 1965. Accredited by ACCSCT. **Enrollment:** 1,628 degree-seeking undergraduates; 9 non-degree-seeking students. **Degrees:** 1,269 associate awarded. **Location:** 17 miles from Phoenix, 11 miles from Glendale. **Calendar:** Continuous, extensive summer session. **Full-time faculty:** 75 total.

Student profile. Among degree-seeking undergraduates, 100% enrolled in a vocational program, 557 enrolled as first-time, first-year students.

Out-of-state:	65%	**Women:**	2%

Basis for selection. Open admission. **Homeschooled:** Must pass the Wonderlic Scholastic Level Exam. **Learning Disabled:** Students seeking accommodations must provide copy of IEP from high school and/or medical documentation. They must also complete paperwork requesting the accommodation and meet with the School Counselor or Student Services Director prior to starting school.

2009-2010 Annual costs. Tuition/fees: $16,015. Tuition varies by program and by campus.

Application procedures. Admission: No deadline. No application fee. Admission notification on a rolling basis. **Financial aid:** No deadline. FAFSA required.

Academics. Special study options: Accelerated study. **Credit/placement by examination:** CLEP. **Support services:** Tutoring.

Majors. Mechanic/repair: Automotive, diesel.

Computing on campus. 9 workstations in library.

Student life. Freshman orientation: Mandatory.

Student services. Career counseling, services for economically disadvantaged, student employment services, financial aid counseling, veterans' counselor. **Physically disabled:** Services for hearing impaired.

Contact. E-mail: info@uticorp.com
Phone: (623) 245-4600 Toll-free number: (800) 859-1202
Fax: (602) 245-4601
Bruce Trexler, Campus Admissions Director, Universal Technical Institute, 10695 West Pierce Street, Avondale, AZ 85323

Yavapai College
Prescott, Arizona
www.yc.edu **CB code: 4996**

- Public 2-year community college
- Commuter campus in large town

General. Founded in 1966. Regionally accredited. Classes offered at branch campus in Clarkdale and several locations in Yavapai County. **Enrollment:** 4,720 degree-seeking undergraduates. **Degrees:** 381 associate awarded. **ROTC:** Army, Air Force. **Location:** 100 miles from Phoenix. **Calendar:** Semester, limited summer session. **Full-time faculty:** 98 total; 9% minority, 45% women. **Part-time faculty:** 309 total; 16% minority, 52% women. **Special facilities:** Solar laboratory, solar greenhouse, performance hall, career technical educational center.

Student profile.

Out-of-state:	6%	**Live on campus:**	10%
25 or older:	24%		

Transfer out. Colleges most students transferred to 2008: Arizona State University, Northern Arizona University, University of Arizona, Old Dominion University.

Basis for selection. Open admission, but selective for some programs. Limited admission for registered nursing, gunsmithing, and independent filmmaking. Interview required of nursing majors. Essay for independent filmmaking.

2008-2009 Annual costs. Tuition/fees: $1,560; $8,230 out-of-state. Per-credit charge: $52 in-state; $330 out-of-state. Room/board: $4,530. Books/supplies: $1,000. Personal expenses: $1,576.

2008-2009 Financial aid. Need-based: Need-based aid available for part-time students. **Non-need-based:** Scholarships awarded for academics, athletics.

Application procedures. Admission: No deadline. No application fee. Admission notification on a rolling basis. **Financial aid:** Priority date 4/1; no closing date. FAFSA required. Applicants notified on a rolling basis.

Academics. Special study options: Accelerated study, distance learning, dual enrollment of high school students, ESL, honors, independent study, internships, liberal arts/career combination, teacher certification program, weekend college. 2-2 program with Northern Arizona University for bachelor degree in education and business, program with Old Dominion University offering bachelor degree completion. Bachelor's degree programs available on campus. License preparation in nursing, paramedic, real estate. **Credit/placement by examination:** AP, CLEP, IB, institutional tests. 30 credit hours maximum toward associate degree. **Support services:** GED preparation and test center, learning center, pre-admission summer program, reduced course load, remedial instruction, study skills assistance, tutoring, writing center.

Majors. Agriculture: Business. **Architecture:** Environmental design. **Business:** Accounting, administrative services, business admin, office management, office technology. **Computer sciences:** General. **Construction:** Maintenance. **Education:** Early childhood. **Engineering technology:** Manufacturing. **Health:** Medical secretary, nursing (RN). **Legal studies:** Legal secretary, paralegal. **Liberal arts:** Arts/sciences. **Mechanic/repair:** Automotive, gunsmithing. **Protective services:** Firefighting, law enforcement admin. **Visual/performing arts:** Commercial/advertising art, industrial design.

Computing on campus. 1,609 workstations in dormitories, library, computer center. Dormitories wired for high-speed internet access and linked to campus network. Online course registration, online library, wireless network available.

Student life. Freshman orientation: Available. Preregistration for classes offered. **Housing:** Coed dorms, special housing for disabled, wellness housing available. $150 deposit. **Activities:** Bands, choral groups, dance, drama, literary magazine, music ensembles, musical theater, student government, student newspaper, nursing association, Native American club, international student club, Hispanic club, Campus Crusade for Christ, Bahai club, PTK, Veterans' club.

Athletics. NJCAA. **Intercollegiate:** Baseball M, basketball, soccer M, volleyball W. **Team name:** Roughriders.

Student services. Adult student services, career counseling, student employment services, financial aid counseling, health services, personal counseling, placement for graduates, veterans' counselor. **Physically disabled:** Services for visually, hearing impaired. **Transfer:** College fairs on campus for students transferring to 4-year colleges.

Contact. E-mail: registration@yc.edu
Phone: (928) 445-7300 ext. 2148 Toll-free number: (800) 922-6787
Fax: (928) 776-2151
David Van Ness, Registrar, Yavapai College, 1100 East Sheldon Street, Prescott, AZ 86301

Arkansas

Arkansas Northeastern College
Blytheville, Arkansas
www.anc.edu **CB code: 1267**

- Public 2-year community college
- Commuter campus in large town

General. Founded in 1974. Regionally accredited. **Enrollment:** 1,425 degree-seeking undergraduates. **Degrees:** 202 associate awarded. **Location:** 65 miles from Memphis, Tennessee. **Calendar:** Semester, limited summer session. **Full-time faculty:** 78 total. **Part-time faculty:** 95 total. **Class size:** 66% < 20, 32% 20-39, less than 1% 40-49, 1% 50-99. **Partnerships:** Formal partnership with Tech Prep for business and technical courses.

Student profile.

Out-of-state:	18%	**25 or older:**	50%

Transfer out. Colleges most students transferred to 2008: Arkansas State University, Southeast Missouri State University.

Basis for selection. Open admission, but selective for some programs. Entrance exam required for nursing program.

High school preparation. Recommended units include English 4, mathematics 4, social studies 1, history 2, science 3 (laboratory 3).

2008-2009 Annual costs. Tuition/fees: $1,720; $2,020 out-of-district; $3,520 out-of-state. Per-credit charge: $50 in-district; $60 out-of-district; $110 out-of-state. Books/supplies: $1,000. Personal expenses: $4,307.

2007-2008 Financial aid. Need-based: 82% of total undergraduate aid awarded as scholarships/grants, 18% as loans/jobs. Need-based aid available for part-time students. Work-study available nights and for part-time students. **Non-need-based:** Scholarships awarded for academics, minority status, music/drama, state residency.

Application procedures. Admission: No deadline. No application fee. Admission notification on a rolling basis. **Financial aid:** Priority date 4/15; no closing date. FAFSA, institutional form required. Applicants notified on a rolling basis starting 5/1; must reply within 2 week(s) of notification.

Academics. Special study options: Distance learning, double major, dual enrollment of high school students, weekend college. Bachelor's degree programs available on campus. License preparation in nursing, paramedic. **Credit/placement by examination:** CLEP, institutional tests. 15 credit hours maximum toward associate degree. Placement tests required for algebra, English composition. **Support services:** GED preparation and test center, learning center, reduced course load, remedial instruction, study skills assistance, tutoring, writing center.

Majors. Agriculture: Food science, horticulture. **Business:** General, administrative services, management information systems. **Education:** Middle. **Engineering technology:** Metallurgical. **Health:** Nursing (RN). **Liberal arts:** Arts/sciences. **Mechanic/repair:** Industrial. **Protective services:** Police science.

Most popular majors. Business/marketing 12%, education 8%, health sciences 12%, liberal arts 58%.

Computing on campus. 400 workstations in library, computer center. Commuter students can connect to campus network. Online library available.

Student life. Freshman orientation: Available. Preregistration for classes offered. **Activities:** Choral groups, music ensembles, student newspaper, Cultural Diversity Association, Baptist College Ministry, Adult Student Association.

Student services. Adult student services, career counseling, services for economically disadvantaged, student employment services, financial aid counseling, on-campus daycare, personal counseling, placement for graduates, veterans' counselor. **Physically disabled:** Services for visually, speech, hearing impaired. **Transfer:** Pre-admission transcript evaluation for new students. Transfer adviser, college fairs on campus for students transferring to 4-year colleges.

Contact. E-mail: jwalters@anc.edu
Phone: (870) 762-1020 ext. 1114 Fax: (870) 763-1654
June Walters, Vice President for Student Services and Registrar, Arkansas Northeastern College, Box 1109, Blytheville, AR 72316-1109

Arkansas State University: Beebe
Beebe, Arkansas
www.asub.edu **CB code: 0782**

- Public 2-year community college
- Commuter campus in small town

General. Founded in 1927. Regionally accredited. Approved as Serviceman's Opportunity College. **Enrollment:** 3,489 degree-seeking undergraduates. **Degrees:** 481 associate awarded. **Location:** 35 miles from Little Rock. **Calendar:** Semester, extensive summer session. **Full-time faculty:** 121 total. **Part-time faculty:** 141 total.

Student profile.

Out-of-state:	1%	**Live on campus:**	4%

Basis for selection. Open admission.

High school preparation. College-preparatory program recommended. 15 units recommended. Recommended units include English 3, mathematics 1, social studies 2 and science 2.

2008-2009 Annual costs. Tuition/fees: $2,670; $4,350 out-of-state. Per-credit charge: $78 in-state; $134 out-of-state. Room/board: $2,930. Books/supplies: $800. Personal expenses: $1,900.

2007-2008 Financial aid. Need-based: 17% of total undergraduate aid awarded as scholarships/grants, 83% as loans/jobs. Need-based aid available for part-time students. Work-study available nights, weekends and for part-time students. **Non-need-based:** Scholarships awarded for academics, leadership, music/drama.

Application procedures. Admission: No deadline. No application fee. Admission notification on a rolling basis. **Financial aid:** Priority date 6/1; no closing date. FAFSA, institutional form required. Applicants notified on a rolling basis starting 6/1; must reply within 2 week(s) of notification.

Academics. Special study options: Accelerated study, double major, dual enrollment of high school students, honors, independent study. Bachelor's degree programs available on campus. **Credit/placement by examination:** CLEP. 30 credit hours maximum toward associate degree. **Support services:** Learning center, reduced course load, remedial instruction, tutoring.

Majors. Agriculture: Business. **Biology:** General, botany, zoology. **Business:** General, administrative services, business admin, office management, office technology. **Computer sciences:** General. **Education:** General, music. **Engineering technology:** Drafting, electrical. **History:** General. **Liberal arts:** Arts/sciences. **Math:** General. **Social sciences:** General, sociology.

Computing on campus. Dormitories linked to campus network. Online course registration, wireless network available.

Student life. Freshman orientation: Available. Preregistration for classes offered. **Housing:** Single-sex dorms available. $75 partly refundable deposit. **Activities:** Choral groups, drama, student government, Gamma Beta Phi.

Athletics. Intramural: Badminton, basketball, bowling, football (non-tackle), racquetball, softball, table tennis, tennis, track and field, volleyball.

Student services. Career counseling, financial aid counseling, personal counseling, veterans' counselor. **Learning disabled:** Comprehensive services available. **Transfer:** Transfer adviser, college fairs on campus for students transferring to 4-year colleges.

Contact. E-mail: rahayes@asub.edu
Phone: (501) 882-8260 Toll-free number: (800) 632-9985
Fax: (501) 882-8370
Robin Hayes, Director of Admissions, Arkansas State University: Beebe, PO Box 1000, Beebe, AR 72012-1000

Arkansas State University: Mountain Home
Mountain Home, Arkansas
www.asumh.edu **CB code: 6057**

- Public 2-year community and technical college
- Commuter campus in large town

General. **Enrollment:** 1,173 degree-seeking undergraduates; 123 non-degree-seeking students. **Degrees:** 165 associate awarded. **ROTC:** Army. **Location:** 130 miles north of Little Rock. **Calendar:** Semester, limited summer session. **Full-time faculty:** 42 total; 24% have terminal degrees, 5% minority, 64% women. **Part-time faculty:** 24 total; 4% have terminal degrees, 62% women. **Class size:** 67% < 20, 33% 20-39.

Student profile. Among degree-seeking undergraduates, 22% enrolled in a transfer program, 2% enrolled in a vocational program, 2% already have a bachelor's degree or higher, 319 enrolled as first-time, first-year students, 254 transferred in from other institutions.

Part-time:	37%	**Women:**	68%
Out-of-state:	20%	**25 or older:**	36%

Transfer out. **Colleges most students transferred to 2008:** Arkansas State University-Jonesboro, University of Central Arkansas-Conway, University of Arkansas-Fayetteville.

Basis for selection. Open admission, but selective for some programs. Additional requirements for practical nursing program, respiratory care program, and phlebotomy program. **Homeschooled:** Statement describing homeschool structure and mission, transcript of courses and grades, state high school equivalency certificate required. **Learning Disabled:** Students with learning disabilities must document them with disability coordinator.

High school preparation. College-preparatory program recommended. Recommended units include English 4, mathematics 4, social studies 3 and science 4.

2008-2009 Annual costs. Tuition/fees: $2,760; $4,410 out-of-state. Per-credit charge: $77 in-state; $132 out-of-state. Fees: $25 science lab fee; 25 welding lab fee; $35 practical nursing exam fee; $100 funeral science practicum fee; $20 per credit hour online course fee; $15 per credit hour infrastructure fee. Books/supplies: $800.

2008-2009 Financial aid. **Need-based:** Need-based aid available for part-time students. **Non-need-based:** Scholarships awarded for academics, state residency.

Application procedures. **Admission:** Closing date 8/15 (receipt date). No application fee. Application must be submitted on paper. Admission notification on a rolling basis. **Financial aid:** Priority date 7/1; no closing date. FAFSA, institutional form required. Applicants notified on a rolling basis starting 5/1; must reply within 2 week(s) of notification.

Academics. **Special study options:** Cooperative education, distance learning, dual enrollment of high school students, honors, independent study, liberal arts/career combination. License preparation in funeral sciences; AAS in Hearing Healthcare or Opticianry is online. Bachelor's degree programs available on campus. License preparation in nursing, paramedic, radiology. **Credit/placement by examination:** AP, CLEP. 15 credit hours maximum toward associate degree, 15 toward bachelor's. **Support services:** GED preparation and test center, learning center, remedial instruction, study skills assistance, tutoring, writing center.

Majors. **Business:** Administrative services. **Computer sciences:** Information systems. **Education:** Middle. **Health:** EMT paramedic, respiratory therapy technology. **Liberal arts:** Arts/sciences. **Personal/culinary services:** Mortuary science. **Production:** Welding. **Protective services:** Forensics, law enforcement admin.

Most popular majors. Computer/information sciences 17%, education 10%, health sciences 6%, legal studies 7%, liberal arts 52%, personal/culinary services 8%.

Computing on campus. 50 workstations in library, computer center, student center. Commuter students can connect to campus network. Online course registration, online library, wireless network available.

Student life. **Freshman orientation:** Available. Preregistration for classes offered. **Activities:** Campus ministries, choral groups, drama, literary magazine, student government, Circle K, criminal justice club, mortuary science club, student ambassadors, student practical nurses association, Phi Beta Lambda, Phi Delta Kappa, Phi Theta Kappa, Rotaract.

Student services. Adult student services, chaplain/spiritual director, career counseling, financial aid counseling, veterans' counselor. **Physically disabled:** Services for visually, hearing impaired. **Transfer:** Pre-admission transcript evaluation for new students. College fairs on campus for students transferring to 4-year colleges.

Contact. E-mail: rblagg@asumh.edu
Phone: (870) 508-6104 Fax: (870) 508-6287
Rosalyn Blagg, Assistant Vice Chancellor for Enrollment, Arkansas State University: Mountain Home, 1600 South College Street, Mountain Home, AR 72653

Arkansas State University: Newport
Newport, Arkansas
www.asun.edu

- Public 2-year community and liberal arts college
- Commuter campus in small town

General. **Enrollment:** 1,090 degree-seeking undergraduates. **Degrees:** 81 associate awarded. **Location:** 100 miles from Little Rock. **Calendar:** Semester, limited summer session. **Full-time faculty:** 73 total. **Part-time faculty:** 30 total.

Transfer out. **Colleges most students transferred to 2008:** University of Central Arkansas.

Basis for selection. Open admission. **Homeschooled:** Transcript of courses and grades required.

2008-2009 Annual costs. Tuition/fees: $2,400; $3,930 out-of-state. Per-credit charge: $75 in-state; $126 out-of-state.

Application procedures. **Admission:** No deadline. No application fee. Admission notification on a rolling basis.

Academics. **Special study options:** Cooperative education, distance learning, dual enrollment of high school students, independent study, internships, liberal arts/career combination, study abroad, teacher certification program. License preparation in nursing. **Credit/placement by examination:** AP, CLEP, institutional tests. 30 credit hours maximum toward associate degree. **Support services:** GED preparation and test center, learning center, remedial instruction, study skills assistance, tutoring.

Majors. **Business:** General, management information systems. **Education:** Middle. **Engineering technology:** Computer. **Health:** EMT paramedic. **Liberal arts:** Arts/sciences.

Computing on campus. Commuter students can connect to campus network. Online course registration, online library, helpline, repair service, wireless network available.

Student life. **Activities:** Drama, student government.

Student services. **Transfer:** Re-entry adviser, pre-admission transcript evaluation for new students. Transfer adviser, college fairs on campus for students transferring to 4-year colleges.

Contact. E-mail: tbyrd@asun.edu
Phone: (870) 512-7800 Toll-free number: (800) 976-1676
Fax: (870) 512-7825
Tara Byrd, Registrar/Director of Admissions, Arkansas State University: Newport, 7648 Victory Boulevard, Newport, AR 72112

Black River Technical College
Pocahontas, Arkansas
www.blackrivertech.edu **CB code: 3879**

- Public 2-year technical college
- Large town
- SAT or ACT (ACT writing optional) required

General. Regionally accredited. **Enrollment:** 1,571 degree-seeking undergraduates. **Degrees:** 158 associate awarded. **Calendar:** Semester, limited summer session. **Full-time faculty:** 59 total. **Part-time faculty:** 66 total.

Basis for selection. High school transcript and standardized test scores most important. **Homeschooled:** Transcript of courses and grades required.

2008-2009 Annual costs. Tuition/fees: $2,190; $5,550 out-of-state. Per-credit charge: $70 in-state; $182 out-of-state.

Application procedures. **Admission:** No deadline. No application fee. **Financial aid:** Priority date 4/1, closing date 6/30.

Academics. **Credit/placement by examination:** CLEP. **Support services:** Learning center, remedial instruction, tutoring.

Majors. **Business:** Accounting, business admin, management information systems. **Education:** Early childhood, elementary. **Protective services:** Criminal justice. **Social sciences:** Economics. **Visual/performing arts:** Art.

Student life. **Freshman orientation:** Mandatory. **Activities:** Choral groups, music ensembles.

Contact. E-mail: rachel.koons@blackrivertech.edu
Phone: (870) 248-4000 Fax: (870) 248-4100
Mary Anderson, Academic Advisor, Black River Technical College, Highway 304 East, Pocahontas, AR 72455

Cossatot Community College of the University of Arkansas

De Queen, Arkansas
www.cccua.edu **CB code: 3613**

- Public 2-year community college
- Commuter campus in small town

General. Regionally accredited. Off-campus sites located in Nashville and Ashdown. **Enrollment:** 1,396 degree-seeking undergraduates. **Degrees:** 96 associate awarded. **Location:** 60 miles from Texarkana. **Calendar:** Semester, limited summer session. **Full-time faculty:** 26 total. **Part-time faculty:** 51 total. **Class size:** 69% < 20, 31% 20-39. **Partnerships:** Secondary Vocational Center for local high schools.

Student profile. Among degree-seeking undergraduates, 40% enrolled in a transfer program, 24% enrolled in a vocational program.

Out-of-state:	2%	**25 or older:**	38%

Transfer out. Colleges most students transferred to 2008: Henderson State University, Texas A&M - Texarkana, Arkansas Tech University, University of Central Arkansas, Southern Arkansas University.

Basis for selection. Open admission, but selective for some programs. Admission to Nursing programs are based upon test scores and previous course grades.

High school preparation. 22 units required. Required units include English 4, mathematics 4, social studies 2, history 1, science 3 (laboratory 2), foreign language 1 and academic electives 5.

2008-2009 Annual costs. Tuition/fees: $1,710; $2,010 out-of-district; $5,310 out-of-state. Per-credit charge: $45 in-district; $55 out-of-district; $165 out-of-state. Residents of bordering out-of-state counties may qualify for in-state tuition. Books/supplies: $1,100. Personal expenses: $1,658.

2007-2008 Financial aid. Need-based: Need-based aid available for part-time students. Work-study available nights and for part-time students. **Additional information:** Active or honorably discharged military and their dependents receive tuition discounts.

Application procedures. Admission: No deadline. No application fee. Admission notification on a rolling basis. **Financial aid:** Priority date 5/1; no closing date. FAFSA, institutional form required. Applicants notified on a rolling basis starting 3/1.

Academics. Special study options: Combined bachelor's/graduate degree, cooperative education, distance learning, double major, dual enrollment of high school students, ESL, exchange student, independent study, internships, liberal arts/career combination, student-designed major. Bachelor's degree programs available on campus. License preparation in nursing. **Credit/placement by examination:** AP, CLEP, institutional tests. 15 credit hours maximum toward associate degree. **Support services:** GED preparation and test center, learning center, remedial instruction, study skills assistance, tutoring.

Majors. Business: General, management information systems. **Construction:** Carpentry. **Education:** Elementary, middle. **Family/consumer sciences:** Child care. **Health:** Medical assistant, nursing (RN). **Liberal arts:** Arts/sciences. **Mechanic/repair:** Automotive. **Protective services:** Forensics, law enforcement admin.

Most popular majors. Business/marketing 23%, liberal arts 68%.

Computing on campus. 95 workstations in library, computer center. Commuter students can connect to campus network. Online course registration, online library, helpline, wireless network available.

Student life. Freshman orientation: Available. Preregistration for classes offered. Course offered each semester. **Activities:** Student government, student newspaper, Baptist Collegiate Ministry, Phi Theta Kappa, Journalism Club, Arkansas Licensed Practical Nursing Association, Amnesty International, SkillsUSA.

Student services. Adult student services, alcohol/substance abuse counseling, career counseling, services for economically disadvantaged, student employment services, financial aid counseling, minority student services, on-campus daycare, personal counseling, placement for graduates, veterans' counselor. **Physically disabled:** Services for visually, speech, hearing impaired. **Transfer:** Pre-admission transcript evaluation for new students. Transfer adviser, college fairs on campus for students transferring to 4-year colleges.

Contact. E-mail: ncowling@cccua.edu
Phone: (870) 584-4471 Toll-free number: (800) 844-4471
Fax: (870) 642-8766
Brenda Morris, Director of Institutional Research and Registrar, Cossatot Community College of the University of Arkansas, 183 Highway 399, De Queen, AR 71832

Crowley's Ridge College

Paragould, Arkansas
www.crowleysridgecollege.edu **CB code: 6131**

- Private 2-year junior college affiliated with Church of Christ
- Commuter campus in large town

General. Regionally accredited. **Enrollment:** 136 degree-seeking undergraduates. **Degrees:** 26 associate awarded. **Location:** 23 miles from Jonesboro. **Calendar:** Semester, limited summer session. **Full-time faculty:** 10 total. **Part-time faculty:** 10 total.

Transfer out. Colleges most students transferred to 2008: Arkansas State University, Williams Baptist College, Harding University, Freed-Hardeman University.

Basis for selection. Open admission. Placement in freshman composition and algebra determined by ACT and ASSET scores. Development courses required for students with ACT score under 19.

2008-2009 Annual costs. Tuition/fees: $8,650. Per-credit charge: $245. Room/board: $5,300. Books/supplies: $550.

2008-2009 Financial aid. Need-based: Work-study available nights and weekends. **Non-need-based:** Scholarships awarded for academics, leadership, music/drama.

Application procedures. Admission: No deadline. No application fee. Admission notification on a rolling basis. **Financial aid:** No deadline. FAFSA required.

Academics. Special study options: Dual enrollment of high school students, independent study. **Credit/placement by examination:** CLEP. 34 credit hours maximum toward associate degree. **Support services:** Remedial instruction, study skills assistance, tutoring.

Majors. Education: General. **Liberal arts:** Arts/sciences. **Philosophy/religion:** Religion.

Computing on campus. 15 workstations in dormitories, library, computer center. Dormitories linked to campus network.

Student life. Freshman orientation: Available. Preregistration for classes offered. Takes place second week of August. **Policies:** Chapel attendance required. **Housing:** Guaranteed on-campus for all undergraduates. Single-sex dorms available. $100 deposit. **Activities:** Choral groups, music ensembles, student government.

Athletics. Intercollegiate: Baseball M, basketball, volleyball W. **Intramural:** Baseball M, basketball M, softball W, volleyball W. **Team name:** Pioneers.

Student services. Chaplain/spiritual director, financial aid counseling. **Transfer:** Pre-admission transcript evaluation for new students. College fairs on campus for students transferring to 4-year colleges.

Contact. E-mail: njoneshill@crowleysridgecollege.edu
Phone: (870) 236-6901 ext. 14 Toll-free number: (800) 264-1096
Fax: (870) 236-7748
Nancy Joneshill, Admissions Director, Crowley's Ridge College, 100 College Drive, Paragould, AR 72450

East Arkansas Community College

Forrest City, Arkansas
www.eacc.edu **CB code: 0847**

- Public 2-year community college
- Commuter campus in large town

General. Founded in 1973. Regionally accredited. **Enrollment:** 1,139 degree-seeking undergraduates. **Degrees:** 125 associate awarded. **Location:** 40 miles

from Memphis, Tennessee. **Calendar:** Semester, limited summer session. **Full-time faculty:** 32 total. **Part-time faculty:** 59 total.

Student profile.

Out-of-state:	1%	**25 or older:**	47%

Transfer out. Colleges most students transferred to 2008: Arkansas State University.

Basis for selection. Open admission. ASSET may be substituted for ACT or SAT for placement. Interview required of Allied Health majors. **Homeschooled:** Transcript of courses and grades, state high school equivalency certificate required.

2008-2009 Annual costs. Tuition/fees: $1,890; $2,130 out-of-district; $2,550 out-of-state. Per-credit charge: $55 in-district; $63 out-of-district; $77 out-of-state. Books/supplies: $900. Personal expenses: $1,000.

Financial aid. All financial aid based on need. Need-based aid available for part-time students.

Application procedures. Admission: No deadline. No application fee. Application must be submitted on paper. Admission notification on a rolling basis. **Financial aid:** Priority date 3/1, closing date 7/1. FAFSA required. Applicants notified on a rolling basis starting 5/15; must reply within 2 week(s) of notification.

Academics. Special study options: Cooperative education, distance learning, dual enrollment of high school students, honors, internships, liberal arts/career combination. License preparation in nursing, paramedic, radiology. **Credit/placement by examination:** AP, CLEP, institutional tests. 12 credit hours maximum toward associate degree. **Support services:** Learning center, remedial instruction, tutoring.

Majors. Agriculture: General. **Business:** Administrative services, business admin, finance, management information systems. **Computer sciences:** Web page design. **Education:** Middle. **Engineering technology:** CAD/CADD, environmental. **Family/consumer sciences:** Child care. **Health:** EMT paramedic, medical radiologic technology/radiation therapy, nursing (RN). **Mechanic/repair:** Industrial. **Protective services:** Police science.

Most popular majors. Business/marketing 11%, health sciences 28%, liberal arts 54%, security/protective services 6%.

Computing on campus. 35 workstations in library, computer center. Commuter students can connect to campus network.

Student life. Freshman orientation: Available. Preregistration for classes offered. **Activities:** Choral groups, student government, student newspaper.

Athletics. Intramural: Basketball, softball, tennis, volleyball.

Student services. Career counseling, student employment services, health services, personal counseling, placement for graduates, veterans' counselor. **Physically disabled:** Services for visually, hearing impaired. **Transfer:** Transfer adviser, college fairs on campus for students transferring to 4-year colleges.

Contact. E-mail: dadams@eacc.edu
Phone: (870) 633-4480 ext. 300 Toll-free number: (877) 797-3222
Fax: (870) 633-3840
DeAnna Adams, Director of Enrollment Management/Institutional Research, East Arkansas Community College, 1700 Newcastle Road, Forrest City, AR 72335-9598

Mid-South Community College

West Memphis, Arkansas
www.midsouthcc.edu **CB code: 3880**

- Public 2-year community and junior college
- Commuter campus in large town

General. Regionally accredited. **Enrollment:** 1,133 degree-seeking undergraduates; 671 non-degree-seeking students. **Degrees:** 65 associate awarded. **Location:** 8 miles from Memphis, Tennessee. **Calendar:** Semester, limited summer session. **Full-time faculty:** 45 total; 2% have terminal degrees, 33% minority, 42% women. **Part-time faculty:** 68 total; 6% have terminal degrees, 34% minority, 69% women. **Class size:** 77% < 20, 23% 20-39.

Student profile. Among degree-seeking undergraduates, 58% enrolled in a transfer program, 26% enrolled in a vocational program, 323 enrolled as first-time, first-year students.

Part-time:	61%	**Hispanic American:**	1%
Out-of-state:	10%	**International:**	1%
Women:	73%	**25 or older:**	53%
African American:	58%		

Transfer out. Colleges most students transferred to 2008: Arkansas State University, University of Memphis.

Basis for selection. Open admission. **Homeschooled:** Transcript of courses and grades required.

2008-2009 Annual costs. Tuition/fees: $1,950; $2,280 out-of-district; $3,930 out-of-state. Per-credit charge: $55 in-district; $66 out-of-district; $121 out-of-state. Books/supplies: $1,000. Personal expenses: $5,500.

2007-2008 Financial aid. Need-based: Need-based aid available for part-time students. Work-study available nights and for part-time students. **Non-need-based:** Scholarships awarded for academics, state residency.

Application procedures. Admission: No deadline. No application fee. Application must be submitted on paper. Admission notification on a rolling basis. **Financial aid:** No deadline. FAFSA, institutional form required. Applicants notified on a rolling basis starting 6/1; must reply within 2 week(s) of notification.

Academics. Special study options: Cooperative education, distance learning, dual enrollment of high school students, liberal arts/career combination. Bachelor's degree programs available on campus. **Credit/placement by examination:** AP, CLEP, institutional tests. 18 credit hours maximum toward associate degree. **Support services:** GED preparation and test center, learning center, reduced course load, remedial instruction, study skills assistance, tutoring, writing center.

Majors. Agriculture: General. **Business:** Office technology. **Computer sciences:** General. **Education:** Middle. **Liberal arts:** Arts/sciences. **Protective services:** Forensics, law enforcement admin.

Computing on campus. 250 workstations in library, computer center, student center. Commuter students can connect to campus network. Online course registration, online library available.

Student life. Freshman orientation: Available. Preregistration for classes offered. **Activities:** Jazz band, choral groups, student newspaper, TV station.

Student services. Adult student services, career counseling, services for economically disadvantaged, student employment services, financial aid counseling, minority student services, veterans' counselor. **Physically disabled:** Services for visually, speech, hearing impaired. **Transfer:** Transfer adviser, college fairs on campus for students transferring to 4-year colleges.

Contact. E-mail: admission@midsouthcc.edu
Phone: (870) 733-6728 Fax: (870) 733-6719
Jeremy Reece, Director of Admissions and Recruiting, Mid-South Community College, 2000 West Broadway, West Memphis, AR 72301

National Park Community College

Hot Springs, Arkansas
www.npcc.edu **CB code: 6243**

- Public 2-year liberal arts and technical college
- Commuter campus in large town

General. Founded in 1973. Regionally accredited. Located in the Hot Springs National Park. **Enrollment:** 1,529 full-time, degree-seeking students. **Degrees:** 292 associate awarded. **Location:** 53 miles from Little Rock. **Calendar:** Semester, extensive summer session. **Full-time faculty:** 62 total. **Part-time faculty:** 142 total. **Class size:** 63% < 20, 37% 20-39, less than 1% 40-49, less than 1% 50-99.

Student profile.

Out-of-state:	1%	**25 or older:**	56%

Transfer out. Colleges most students transferred to 2008: Henderson State University, Arkadelphia-University of Arkansas, University of Arkansas-Little Rock, University of Arkansas-Fayetteville.

Basis for selection. Open admission, but selective for some programs. Limited admission to allied health programs and nursing. Interview required for some health-related majors.

High school preparation. 18 units recommended. Recommended units include English 4, mathematics 4, social studies 3, history 2, science 3 (laboratory 3) and foreign language 2.

2008-2009 Annual costs. Tuition/fees: $1,925; $2,225 out-of-district; $4,145 out-of-state. Per-credit charge: $60 in-district; $70 out-of-district; $134 out-of-state. Books/supplies: $700. Personal expenses: $1,420.

Financial aid. Need-based: Need-based aid available for part-time students. Work-study available nights, weekends and for part-time students. **Non-need-based:** Scholarships awarded for academics, minority status, music/drama, state residency.

Application procedures. Admission: No deadline. No application fee. Admission notification on a rolling basis beginning on or about 3/1. **Financial aid:** Priority date 7/1; no closing date. FAFSA, institutional form required. Applicants notified on a rolling basis starting 3/1.

Academics. Special study options: Cooperative education, cross-registration, distance learning, double major, dual enrollment of high school students, honors, independent study, internships, liberal arts/career combination, student-designed major. Bachelor's degree programs available on campus. License preparation in aviation, nursing, paramedic, radiology, real estate. **Credit/placement by examination:** AP, CLEP, institutional tests. 18 credit hours maximum toward associate degree. **Support services:** Learning center, reduced course load, remedial instruction, study skills assistance, tutoring, writing center.

Majors. Business: Accounting, hospitality admin, hospitality/recreation, office management, office technology. **Computer sciences:** General, applications programming, computer graphics. **Engineering technology:** Electrical. **Health:** Clinical lab technology, EMT paramedic, medical assistant, medical radiologic technology/radiation therapy, medical records technology, medical secretary, nursing (RN). **Liberal arts:** Arts/sciences. **Parks/recreation:** General. **Visual/performing arts:** Commercial/advertising art.

Computing on campus. 470 workstations in library, computer center, student center. Online library available.

Student life. Freshman orientation: Mandatory. Preregistration for classes offered. 2-day orientation, held one week prior to beginning of classes. **Activities:** Choral groups, dance, literary magazine, music ensembles, student government, student newspaper, Baptist Student Union, Black Awareness, Association for Barrier Awareness.

Athletics. Intramural: Baseball, basketball, bowling, skin diving, softball, table tennis, tennis, volleyball.

Student services. Adult student services, career counseling, services for economically disadvantaged, student employment services, financial aid counseling, health services, personal counseling, placement for graduates, veterans' counselor. **Physically disabled:** Services for visually, speech, hearing impaired. **Learning disabled:** Comprehensive services available. **Transfer:** Pre-admission transcript evaluation for new students. Transfer adviser, college fairs on campus for students transferring to 4-year colleges.

Contact. E-mail: admissions@npcc.edu
Phone: (501) 767-4222 Toll-free number: (800) 761-1825
Fax: (501) 760-4100
Holly Garrett, Director of Admissions, National Park Community College, 101 College Drive, Hot Springs, AR 71913

North Arkansas College
Harrison, Arkansas
www.northark.edu **CB code: 1423**

- Public 2-year community and technical college
- Commuter campus in large town

General. Founded in 1974. Regionally accredited. **Enrollment:** 1,789 degree-seeking undergraduates; 383 non-degree-seeking students. **Degrees:** 215 associate awarded. **Location:** 75 miles from Fayetteville. **Calendar:** Semester, limited summer session. **Full-time faculty:** 63 total; 8% have terminal degrees, 49% women. **Part-time faculty:** 86 total; 1% minority, 58% women. **Class size:** 67% < 20, 32% 20-39, less than 1% 40-49, less than 1% 50-99. **Special facilities:** Community health resource center, lyric theater.

Student profile. Among degree-seeking undergraduates, 44% enrolled in a transfer program, 54% enrolled in a vocational program, 1% already have a bachelor's degree or higher, 485 enrolled as first-time, first-year students, 150 transferred in from other institutions.

Part-time:	28%	**Hispanic American:**	2%
Out-of-state:	5%	**Native American:**	1%
Women:	63%	**25 or older:**	41%
Asian American:	1%		

Transfer out. 48% of students enrolled in the transfer program go on to 4-year colleges. **Colleges most students transferred to 2008:** Arkansas Tech University, College of the Ozarks, University of Arkansas, University of Central Arkansas, Arkansas State University.

Basis for selection. Open admission, but selective for some programs. Allied health programs require separate application. Regarding CLEP examinations, to receive college credit, a student must score at the 50th percentile or higher, based on national norms, and may not have earned college credit nor have ever been enrolled in the course for which he/she is writing the test.

High school preparation. College-preparatory program required. 14 units recommended. Recommended units include English 4, mathematics 4, social studies 1, history 2, science 3 (laboratory 3).

2008-2009 Annual costs. Tuition/fees: $1,800; $2,460 out-of-district; $4,590 out-of-state. Per-credit charge: $60 in-district; $82 out-of-district; $153 out-of-state. Books/supplies: $902. Personal expenses: $1,897.

2007-2008 Financial aid. Need-based: Need-based aid available for part-time students. Work-study available nights and for part-time students. **Non-need-based:** Scholarships awarded for academics, athletics, state residency.

Application procedures. Admission: No deadline. No application fee. Application must be submitted on paper. Admission notification on a rolling basis. **Financial aid:** Priority date 5/1; no closing date. FAFSA, institutional form required. Applicants notified on a rolling basis starting 5/1.

Academics. Special study options: Distance learning, dual enrollment of high school students, ESL, honors, independent study, internships, student-designed major. Bachelor's degree programs available on campus. License preparation in nursing, paramedic, radiology, real estate. **Credit/placement by examination:** AP, CLEP, institutional tests. 20 credit hours maximum toward associate degree. Only one-third of the credit hours for a degree can be from Advanced Placement, CLEP, the College Now Program, Challenge Test, various other examinations, or independent studies. Credit for Advanced Placement, CLEP, or Professional Certification Examinations will not be posted to an academic record until the student has successfully completed at least 12 semester credit hours of work. **Support services:** GED preparation and test center, learning center, pre-admission summer program, remedial instruction, study skills assistance, tutoring, writing center.

Majors. Agriculture: General. **Business:** General. **Computer sciences:** General. **Education:** Multi-level teacher. **Engineering technology:** Biomedical, electrical. **Health:** Clinical lab technology, EMT paramedic, medical radiologic technology/radiation therapy, nursing (RN), surgical technology. **Liberal arts:** Arts/sciences. **Protective services:** Forensics, law enforcement admin. **Other:** General Technology.

Most popular majors. Business/marketing 13%, health sciences 36%, liberal arts 42%.

Computing on campus. 250 workstations in library, computer center. Online course registration, online library, repair service, wireless network available.

Student life. Activities: Drama, literary magazine, student government, Baptist Student Union, Future Farmers of America, Health Occupations Students of America, Phi Beta Lambda, Phi Theta Kappa, Pioneer Hands club, Rad Tech club, Skills USA, student nurses association.

Athletics. NJCAA. **Intercollegiate:** Baseball M, basketball, cheerleading M, rodeo, softball W. **Intramural:** Archery, badminton, basketball, football (non-tackle) M, golf, racquetball, softball, table tennis, tennis, volleyball, weight lifting. **Team name:** Pioneers.

Student services. Adult student services, alcohol/substance abuse counseling, career counseling, services for economically disadvantaged, student employment services, financial aid counseling, placement for graduates, veterans' counselor. **Physically disabled:** Services for visually, speech, hearing impaired. **Transfer:** Pre-admission transcript evaluation for new students. Transfer adviser, college fairs on campus for students transferring to 4-year colleges.

Contact. E-mail: charlam@northark.edu
Phone: (870) 391-3505 Toll-free number: (800) 679-6622
Fax: (870) 391-3339
Charla Jennings, Director of Enrollment Services, North Arkansas College, 1515 Pioneer Drive, Harrison, AR 72601

Northwest Arkansas Community College
Bentonville, Arkansas
www.nwacc.edu **CB code: 7101**

- Public 2-year community college
- Commuter campus in small city

General. Regionally accredited. **Enrollment:** 5,385 degree-seeking undergraduates; 1,831 non-degree-seeking students. **Degrees:** 457 associate awarded. **ROTC:** Army, Air Force. **Location:** 30 miles from Fayetteville. **Calendar:** Semester, extensive summer session. **Full-time faculty:** 108 total. **Part-time faculty:** 216 total. **Class size:** 41% < 20, 59% 20-39, less than 1% 40-49.

Student profile. Among degree-seeking undergraduates, 1,187 enrolled as first-time, first-year students, 550 transferred in from other institutions.

Part-time:	59%	**Women:**	60%
Out-of-state:	1%	**25 or older:**	20%

Transfer out. Colleges most students transferred to 2008: University of Arkansas, John Brown University.

Basis for selection. Open admission, but selective for some programs. Additional requirements for nursing, physical therapy, respiratory therapy, emergency medical technician/paramedic programs.

High school preparation. 22 units recommended. Recommended units include English 4, mathematics 3, social studies 1, history 1, science 2, foreign language 1 and academic electives 10.

2008-2009 Annual costs. Tuition/fees: $2,410; $3,460 out-of-district; $4,652 out-of-state. Per-credit charge: $63 in-district; $98 out-of-district; $138 out-of-state. Books/supplies: $973.

Financial aid. Need-based: Need-based aid available for part-time students. Work-study available nights, weekends and for part-time students. **Non-need-based:** Scholarships awarded for academics, leadership, music/drama, state residency.

Application procedures. Admission: No deadline. $10 fee. Admission notification on a rolling basis. **Financial aid:** Priority date 4/1; no closing date. FAFSA, institutional form required. Applicants notified on a rolling basis starting 4/1; must reply within 2 week(s) of notification.

Academics. Special study options: Distance learning, dual enrollment of high school students, ESL, honors, independent study, internships, liberal arts/career combination, weekend college. License preparation in nursing, paramedic, physical therapy. **Credit/placement by examination:** AP, CLEP. 15 credit hours maximum toward associate degree. **Support services:** GED preparation and test center, learning center, remedial instruction, study skills assistance, tutoring, writing center.

Majors. Business: Accounting, administrative services, banking/financial services, business admin. **Computer sciences:** General, LAN/WAN management, programming, webmaster. **Engineering:** Environmental. **Engineering technology:** Drafting, electrical. **Family/consumer sciences:** Child care. **Health:** EMT paramedic, nursing (RN), physical therapy assistant, respiratory therapy technology. **Legal studies:** Paralegal. **Liberal arts:** Arts/sciences. **Mechanic/repair:** Aircraft. **Protective services:** Firefighting, law enforcement admin. **Transportation:** Aviation. **Visual/performing arts:** Commercial/advertising art.

Most popular majors. Health sciences 19%, liberal arts 58%.

Computing on campus. 125 workstations in library, computer center, student center. Commuter students can connect to campus network. Online course registration, online library, wireless network available.

Student life. Freshman orientation: Available. Preregistration for classes offered. **Activities:** Choral groups, drama, literary magazine, music ensembles, musical theater, student government, student newspaper, symphony orchestra.

Athletics. Intramural: Archery, basketball, bowling, golf, soccer, softball, table tennis, volleyball.

Student services. Adult student services, alcohol/substance abuse counseling, career counseling, financial aid counseling, personal counseling, placement for graduates, veterans' counselor. **Transfer:** Transfer center, transfer adviser, college fairs on campus for students transferring to 4-year colleges.

Contact. E-mail: askregistration@nwacc.edu
Phone: (479) 619-4398 Toll-free number: (800) 995-6922
Fax: (479) 619-2229
Todd Kitchen, Director of Admissions, Northwest Arkansas Community College, One College Drive, Bentonville, AR 72712

Ouachita Technical College
Malvern, Arkansas
www.otcweb.edu **CB code: 3619**

- Public 2-year community and technical college
- Commuter campus in small town

General. Regionally accredited. **Enrollment:** 821 degree-seeking undergraduates; 779 non-degree-seeking students. **Degrees:** 78 associate awarded. **ROTC:** Army. **Location:** 45 miles from Little Rock. **Calendar:** Semester, limited summer session. **Full-time faculty:** 35 total. **Part-time faculty:** 70 total.

Student profile. Among degree-seeking undergraduates, 38% enrolled in a transfer program, 62% enrolled in a vocational program, 201 enrolled as first-time, first-year students, 115 transferred in from other institutions.

Part-time:	36%	**Asian American:**	1%
Out-of-state:	1%	**Hispanic American:**	1%
Women:	64%	**International:**	1%
African American:	13%	**25 or older:**	28%

Transfer out. Colleges most students transferred to 2008: Henderson State University, University of Central Arkansas.

Basis for selection. Open admission, but selective for some programs. Admission to practical nursing, registered nursing, and cosmetology programs based on test scores.

2008-2009 Annual costs. Tuition/fees: $2,150; $3,830 out-of-state. Per-credit charge: $56 in-state; $112 out-of-state. Books/supplies: $1,834. Personal expenses: $1,202.

Financial aid. Need-based: Need-based aid available for part-time students. Work-study available nights.

Application procedures. Admission: No deadline. No application fee. **Financial aid:** Closing date 6/30. FAFSA required. Applicants notified on a rolling basis starting 7/1; must reply within 6 week(s) of notification.

Academics. Associate of Arts in General Education and Associate of Applied Science in Criminal Justice offered online. **Special study options:** Distance learning, dual enrollment of high school students, independent study, internships, liberal arts/career combination. License preparation in nursing. **Credit/placement by examination:** AP, CLEP, institutional tests. **Support services:** GED preparation and test center, learning center, remedial instruction, study skills assistance, tutoring.

Majors. Business: General, business admin. **Computer sciences:** General. **Education:** Early childhood. **Family/consumer sciences:** Child care. **Health:** Nursing (RN). **Liberal arts:** Arts/sciences. **Production:** General. **Protective services:** Criminal justice, forensics.

Most popular majors. Business/marketing 18%, computer/information sciences 13%, family/consumer sciences 8%, liberal arts 42%, trade and industry 13%.

Computing on campus. 150 workstations in library, computer center. Online library, helpline, wireless network available.

Student life. Freshman orientation: Mandatory. Preregistration for classes offered. Mandatory orientation can be completed online. Optional orientation offered on-campus. **Activities:** Student government.

Student services. Adult student services, alcohol/substance abuse counseling, chaplain/spiritual director, career counseling, services for economically disadvantaged, student employment services, financial aid counseling, personal counseling, placement for graduates, veterans' counselor. **Physically disabled:** Services for visually, speech, hearing impaired. **Transfer:** Pre-admission transcript evaluation for new students. College fairs on campus for students transferring to 4-year colleges.

Contact. E-mail: info@otcweb.edu
Phone: (501) 337-5000 ext. 1118 Fax: (501) 337-9382
Linda Johnson, Registrar, Ouachita Technical College, One College Circle, Malvern, AR 72104

Ozarka College
Melbourne, Arkansas
www.ozarka.edu **CB code: 3621**

- Public 2-year community and technical college
- Commuter campus in rural community

General. Regionally accredited. **Enrollment:** 944 degree-seeking undergraduates. **Degrees:** 100 associate awarded. **Location:** 125 miles from Little Rock, 160 miles from Memphis, Tennessee. **Calendar:** Semester, limited summer session. **Full-time faculty:** 37 total. **Part-time faculty:** 50 total.

Transfer out. Colleges most students transferred to 2008: Arkansas State University, Lyon College, University of Arkansas, University of Central Arkansas, Williams Baptist College.

Basis for selection. Open admission, but selective for some programs. Admission to licensed practical nursing, Registered Nursing, and culinary arts programs based on test scores, and/or essay, interview. **Adult students:** ACT/ASSET/COMPASS/SAT are accepted for placement in math and English. **Homeschooled:** Transcript of courses and grades required.

2008-2009 Annual costs. Tuition/fees: $2,310; $5,400 out-of-state. Per-credit charge: $70 in-state; $173 out-of-state. Books/supplies: $800. Personal expenses: $1,800.

2008-2009 Financial aid. Need-based: Need-based aid available for part-time students.

Application procedures. Admission: No deadline. No application fee. Admission notification on a rolling basis. **Financial aid:** No deadline. FAFSA required. Applicants notified on a rolling basis; must reply within 2 week(s) of notification.

Academics. Special study options: Combined bachelor's/graduate degree, cooperative education, distance learning, dual enrollment of high school students, liberal arts/career combination. Bachelor's degree programs available on campus. License preparation in nursing. **Credit/placement by examination:** AP, CLEP, institutional tests. 36 credit hours maximum toward associate degree. **Support services:** GED preparation and test center, learning center, remedial instruction, study skills assistance, tutoring.

Majors. Business: Business admin, information resources management. **Education:** General, elementary, middle. **Engineering technology:** General. **Health:** Licensed practical nurse, medical transcription. **Liberal arts:** Arts/sciences. **Mechanic/repair:** Automotive. **Personal/culinary services:** Culinary arts. **Protective services:** Law enforcement admin.

Computing on campus. 175 workstations in library, computer center. Commuter students can connect to campus network. Online course registration, helpline, wireless network available.

Student life. Freshman orientation: Mandatory. **Activities:** Student government.

Athletics. Team name: Eagles.

Student services. Chaplain/spiritual director, career counseling, services for economically disadvantaged, financial aid counseling, on-campus daycare, veterans' counselor, women's services. **Transfer:** Pre-admission transcript evaluation for new students. College fairs on campus for students transferring to 4-year colleges.

Contact. E-mail: zwilkerson@ozarka.edu
Phone: (870) 368-2028 Toll-free number: (800) 821-4335 ext. 2028
Fax: (870) 368-2091
Zeda Wilkerson, Director of Admissions, Ozarka College, 218 College Drive, Melbourne, AR 72556-0010

Phillips Community College of the University of Arkansas
Helena, Arkansas
www.pccua.edu **CB code: 6583**

- Public 2-year community college
- Commuter campus in large town

General. Founded in 1965. Regionally accredited. Campuses in Helena, Phillips County, as well as Stuttgart and DeWitt in Arkansas County. **Enrollment:** 1,154 degree-seeking undergraduates; 294 non-degree-seeking students. **Degrees:** 164 associate awarded. **Location:** 117 miles from Little Rock, 70 miles from Memphis, Tennessee. **Calendar:** Semester, limited summer session. **Full-time faculty:** 79 total; 4% have terminal degrees, 16% minority, 72% women. **Part-time faculty:** 51 total; 4% have terminal degrees, 18% minority, 71% women. **Class size:** 78% < 20, 22% 20-39, less than 1% 50-99. **Special facilities:** Performing arts center.

Student profile. Among degree-seeking undergraduates, 34% enrolled in a transfer program, 22% enrolled in a vocational program, 35% already have a bachelor's degree or higher, 185 enrolled as first-time, first-year students.

Part-time:	42%	**African American:**	49%
Out-of-state:	3%	**Hispanic American:**	2%
Women:	77%	**Native American:**	1%

Basis for selection. Open admission, but selective for some programs. Additional requirements for nursing program. Interview required of applicants with no high school transcript or test scores. **Adult students:** ASSET or COMPASS test required for students taking English or math. **Homeschooled:** Transcript of courses and grades, state high school equivalency certificate required.

2008-2009 Annual costs. Tuition/fees: $2,020; $2,290 out-of-district; $3,430 out-of-state. Per-credit charge: $55 in-district; $64 out-of-district; $102 out-of-state. Books/supplies: $1,200. Personal expenses: $3,660.

2007-2008 Financial aid. All financial aid based on need. 85% of total undergraduate aid awarded as scholarships/grants, 15% as loans/jobs. Need-based aid available for part-time students. Work-study available nights and for part-time students. **Additional information:** Tuition waivers are given to firefighters and law enforcement officers.

Application procedures. Admission: No deadline. No application fee. Admission notification on a rolling basis. **Financial aid:** Priority date 4/1, closing date 6/30. FAFSA required. Applicants notified on a rolling basis starting 4/1; must reply within 2 week(s) of notification.

Academics. Special study options: Distance learning, dual enrollment of high school students, honors, independent study, internships, weekend college. Bachelor's degree programs available on campus. License preparation in nursing. **Credit/placement by examination:** CLEP, institutional tests. 30 credit hours maximum toward associate degree. **Support services:** GED preparation and test center, learning center, remedial instruction, study skills assistance, tutoring.

Majors. Biology: General. **Business:** General, business admin, office technology. **Communications technology:** Graphic/printing. **Computer sciences:** Computer science, information technology, LAN/WAN management. **Education:** General, early childhood, elementary. **Engineering:** General. **Engineering technology:** Biomedical, drafting, manufacturing. **Health:** Nursing (RN), phlebotomy. **Legal studies:** Prelaw. **Liberal arts:** Arts/sciences. **Math:** General. **Mechanic/repair:** Industrial. **Physical sciences:** Chemistry, physics. **Psychology:** General. **Social sciences:** General. **Visual/performing arts:** Printmaking.

Computing on campus. 275 workstations in library, computer center. Commuter students can connect to campus network. Online course registration, wireless network available.

Student life. Freshman orientation: Available. Preregistration for classes offered. **Activities:** Choral groups, dance, drama, musical theater, Baptist Collegiate Ministries, Phi Theta Kappa, Arkansas Licensed Practical Nurses Association, National Student Nurses Association.

Athletics. Intramural: Archery, badminton, basketball, football (non-tackle) M, golf, soccer, softball, table tennis, tennis, volleyball.

Student services. Adult student services, career counseling, services for economically disadvantaged, student employment services, financial aid counseling, personal counseling, placement for graduates, veterans' counselor. **Physically disabled:** Services for visually, hearing impaired. **Transfer:** Transfer adviser, college fairs on campus for students transferring to 4-year colleges.

Contact. E-mail: lboone@pccua.edu
Phone: (870) 338-6474 ext. 1336 Fax: (870) 338-7542
Lynn Boone, Vice Chancellor for Student Services/Registrar, Phillips Community College of the University of Arkansas, 1000 Campus Drive, Helena, AR 72342

Two-Year Colleges

Pulaski Technical College
North Little Rock, Arkansas
www.pulaskitech.edu **CB code: 3622**

- Public 2-year community and technical college
- Commuter campus in small city

General. Regionally accredited. **Enrollment:** 7,984 degree-seeking undergraduates; 1,108 non-degree-seeking students. **Degrees:** 597 associate awarded. **Location:** 4 miles from Little Rock. **Calendar:** Semester, extensive summer session. **Full-time faculty:** 144 total; 7% have terminal degrees, 7% minority, 47% women. **Part-time faculty:** 308 total; 22% minority, 62% women. **Class size:** 55% < 20, 45% 20-39.

Student profile. Among degree-seeking undergraduates, 69% enrolled in a transfer program, 31% enrolled in a vocational program, 1% already have a bachelor's degree or higher, 1,214 enrolled as first-time, first-year students, 626 transferred in from other institutions.

Part-time:	51%	**Asian American:**	1%
Out-of-state:	1%	**Hispanic American:**	2%
Women:	69%	**25 or older:**	59%
African American:	53%		

Transfer out. Colleges most students transferred to 2008: University of Arkansas at Little Rock, University of Central Arkansas.

Basis for selection. Open admission, but selective for some programs. Additional requirements for dental assisting, practical nursing, respiratory therapy, occupational therapy assistant and military technology programs. **Adult students:** COMPASS or ACT scores may be used for placement.

2008-2009 Annual costs. Tuition/fees: $2,630; $4,160 out-of-state. Per-credit charge: $77 in-state; $128 out-of-state. Books/supplies: $1,200. Personal expenses: $2,732.

2008-2009 Financial aid. Need-based: Need-based aid available for part-time students. Work-study available for part-time students.

Application procedures. Admission: No deadline. No application fee. Admission notification on a rolling basis. **Financial aid:** Priority date 5/15; no closing date. FAFSA, institutional form required. Applicants notified on a rolling basis starting 5/1; must reply within 2 week(s) of notification.

Academics. Special study options: Cooperative education, distance learning, double major, dual enrollment of high school students, external degree, internships, liberal arts/career combination, weekend college. License preparation in aviation, dental hygiene, nursing, occupational therapy. **Credit/placement by examination:** AP, CLEP, institutional tests. **Support services:** Learning center, pre-admission summer program, remedial instruction, study skills assistance, tutoring.

Majors. Business: General, hospitality admin, management information systems. **Construction:** General. **Education:** Early childhood. **Engineering technology:** Drafting, environmental, industrial, manufacturing. **Family/consumer sciences:** Child care. **Health:** Occupational therapy assistant, respiratory therapy technology. **Legal studies:** Paralegal. **Liberal arts:** Arts/sciences. **Mechanic/repair:** Aircraft powerplant, electronics/electrical, heating/ac/refrig. **Military:** General. **Personal/culinary services:** Chef training. **Protective services:** Forensics, law enforcement admin. **Transportation:** Airline/commercial pilot. **Other:** General technologies.

Most popular majors. Business/marketing 13%, liberal arts 69%.

Computing on campus. 281 workstations in library, computer center, student center. Commuter students can connect to campus network. Online course registration, online library, helpline, wireless network available.

Student life. Freshman orientation: Available. Preregistration for classes offered. Online orientation is ongoing. **Activities:** Campus ministries, choral groups, literary magazine, student government, Metro student ministries, Culture Shock, philosophy club, Student Ambassadors, Phi Theta Kappa, College Democrats, Fusion, Phi Beta Lambda.

Student services. Adult student services, career counseling, services for economically disadvantaged, student employment services, financial aid counseling, minority student services, personal counseling, veterans' counselor. **Physically disabled:** Services for visually, hearing impaired. **Learning disabled:** Comprehensive services available. **Transfer:** Transfer adviser, college fairs on campus for students transferring to 4-year colleges.

Contact. E-mail: admissions@pulaskitech.edu
Phone: (501) 812-2231 Fax: (501) 812-2316
Clark Atkins, Director of Admissions, Pulaski Technical College, 3000 West Scenic Drive, North Little Rock, AR 72118-3347

Remington College: Little Rock
Little Rock, Arkansas
www.remingtoncollege.edu

- For-profit 2-year technical college
- Commuter campus in very large city

General. Accredited by ACCSCT. **Calendar:** Quarter.

Annual costs/financial aid. Associate degree programs annual tuition $19,500 plus $50 fees. 8-month diploma program full tuition $13,900 plus $50 fees. Tuition includes textbooks and supplies.

Contact. Phone: (501) 312-0007
Director of Admissions, 19 Remington Drive, Little Rock, AR 72204

Rich Mountain Community College
Mena, Arkansas
www.rmcc.edu **CB code: 0226**

- Public 2-year community college
- Commuter campus in small town

General. Founded in 1983. Regionally accredited. **Enrollment:** 367 full-time, degree-seeking students. **Degrees:** 62 associate awarded. **Location:** 85 miles from Fort Smith, 80 miles from Hot Springs. **Calendar:** Semester, limited summer session. **Full-time faculty:** 21 total. **Part-time faculty:** 52 total.

Student profile.

Out-of-state:	25%	**25 or older:**	51%

Transfer out. Colleges most students transferred to 2008: Henderson State University, Arkansas Tech University, Westark College, Cossatot Community College.

Basis for selection. Open admission, but selective for some programs. Limited admission to licensed practical nurse program.

High school preparation. 18 units recommended. Recommended units include English 4, mathematics 3, social studies 2 and science 4.

2008-2009 Annual costs. Tuition/fees: $1,620; $2,010 out-of-district; $5,190 out-of-state. Per-credit charge: $51 in-district; $64 out-of-district; $170 out-of-state. Books/supplies: $1,000. Personal expenses: $2,974.

2007-2008 Financial aid. Need-based: Need-based aid available for part-time students. Work-study available for part-time students. **Non-need-based:** Scholarships awarded for academics.

Application procedures. Admission: No deadline. No application fee. Admission notification on a rolling basis. **Financial aid:** Priority date 7/1; no closing date. FAFSA, institutional form required. Applicants notified on a rolling basis starting 6/1; must reply within 2 week(s) of notification.

Academics. MBA, masters in education leadership offered on campus by Henderson State University. **Special study options:** Cooperative education, distance learning, dual enrollment of high school students, external degree, internships, student-designed major. License preparation in nursing. **Credit/placement by examination:** AP, CLEP, institutional tests. 30 credit hours maximum toward associate degree. **Support services:** GED preparation and test center, pre-admission summer program, remedial instruction, study skills assistance, tutoring.

Majors. Agriculture: General. **Business:** Administrative services, business admin, management information systems. **Computer sciences:** General, information systems, LAN/WAN management, programming, systems analysis. **Education:** General. **Engineering technology:** Computer hardware. **Liberal arts:** Arts/sciences. **Production:** Machine tool.

Most popular majors. Business/marketing 17%, liberal arts 78%.

Computing on campus. 73 workstations in library, computer center. Commuter students can connect to campus network.

Student life. Freshman orientation: Available. Preregistration for classes offered. **Activities:** Radio station, student government, TV station, Baptist student union.

Student services. Adult student services, career counseling, services for economically disadvantaged, financial aid counseling, personal counseling, veterans' counselor. **Physically disabled:** Services for visually, hearing impaired. **Transfer:** Pre-admission transcript evaluation for new students. Transfer adviser, college fairs on campus for students transferring to 4-year colleges.

Contact. Phone: (501) 394-7622 ext. 1410 Fax: (501) 394-2760
Tammy Young, Director of Admissions, Rich Mountain Community College, 1100 College Drive, Mena, AR 71953

South Arkansas Community College

El Dorado, Arkansas
www.southark.edu **CB code: 1550**

- Public 2-year community and junior college
- Commuter campus in large town

General. Founded in 1975. Regionally accredited. **Enrollment:** 1,525 degree-seeking undergraduates. **Degrees:** 107 associate awarded. **Location:** 115 miles from Little Rock. **Calendar:** Semester, limited summer session. **Full-time faculty:** 62 total. **Part-time faculty:** 53 total.

Transfer out. Colleges most students transferred to 2008: Southern Arkansas University, Louisiana Tech.

Basis for selection. Open admission. **Homeschooled:** Transcript of courses and grades, state high school equivalency certificate required.

High school preparation. Recommended units include English 4, mathematics 3, social studies 3 and science 4.

2008-2009 Annual costs. Tuition/fees: $2,180; $2,420 out-of-district; $4,250 out-of-state. Per-credit charge: $66 in-district; $74 out-of-district; $135 out-of-state. $25 lab fee for most courses. Books/supplies: $600. Personal expenses: $550.

2007-2008 Financial aid. Need-based: Need-based aid available for part-time students.

Application procedures. Admission: Priority date 7/31; no deadline. No application fee. Admission notification on a rolling basis. **Financial aid:** Closing date 8/1. FAFSA, institutional form required. Applicants notified on a rolling basis starting 7/1; must reply within 2 week(s) of notification.

Academics. Special study options: Dual enrollment of high school students, liberal arts/career combination. License preparation in nursing, occupational therapy, paramedic, physical therapy, radiology, real estate. **Credit/placement by examination:** AP, CLEP, IB, institutional tests. 30 credit hours maximum toward associate degree. **Support services:** GED preparation and test center, learning center, reduced course load, remedial instruction, tutoring.

Majors. Business: General, administrative services, business admin. **Communications:** Digital media. **Communications technology:** Desktop publishing. **Computer sciences:** General, applications programming, computer graphics, computer science, information technology, programming. **Conservation:** General. **Education:** General, secondary. **Family/consumer sciences:** Child care. **Health:** Clinical lab technology, EMT paramedic, medical radiologic technology/radiation therapy, nursing (RN), occupational therapy assistant, physical therapy assistant, radiologic technology/medical imaging. **Liberal arts:** Arts/sciences. **Mechanic/repair:** Automotive, industrial. **Protective services:** Police science. **Visual/performing arts:** Commercial/advertising art.

Computing on campus. 250 workstations in library, computer center, student center. Online course registration, student web hosting available.

Student life. Freshman orientation: Available. Preregistration for classes offered. **Activities:** Choral groups, literary magazine, Phi Beta Lambda, Phi Theta Kappa, student leadership group.

Athletics. Intramural: Basketball, tennis, volleyball.

Student services. Adult student services, career counseling, services for economically disadvantaged, student employment services, financial aid counseling, personal counseling, placement for graduates, veterans' counselor. **Physically disabled:** Services for visually, hearing impaired. **Transfer:** Transfer adviser, college fairs on campus for students transferring to 4-year colleges.

Contact. E-mail: registrar@southark.edu
Phone: (870) 862-8131 Toll-free number: (800) 955-2289
Fax: (870) 864-7137
Dean Inman, Director of Enrollment Services, South Arkansas Community College, Box 7010, El Dorado, AR 71731-7010

Southeast Arkansas College

Pine Bluff, Arkansas
www.seark.edu **CB code: 3624**

- Public 2-year community and technical college
- Commuter campus in small city

General. Regionally accredited. **Enrollment:** 1,605 degree-seeking undergraduates; 406 non-degree-seeking students. **Degrees:** 148 associate awarded. **Location:** 42 miles from Little Rock. **Calendar:** Semester, limited summer session. **Full-time faculty:** 58 total; 28% minority, 66% women. **Part-time faculty:** 90 total; 37% minority, 60% women. **Class size:** 79% < 20, 21% 20-39.

Student profile. Among degree-seeking undergraduates, 82% enrolled in a vocational program, 250 enrolled as first-time, first-year students, 43 transferred in from other institutions.

Part-time:	43%	**Asian American:**	1%
Women:	73%	**Hispanic American:**	1%
African American:	54%		

Transfer out. Colleges most students transferred to 2008: University of Arkansas at Pine Bluff, University of Arkansas at Monticello, University of Arkansas at Little Rock.

Basis for selection. Open admission, but selective for some programs. Additional requirements for some health programs. ACT, ASSET or COMPASS required for placement.

High school preparation. Recommended units include English 4, mathematics 2, social studies 2, history 2, science 2 and foreign language 1.

2008-2009 Annual costs. Tuition/fees: $2,290; $4,330 out-of-state. Per-credit charge: $68 in-state; $136 out-of-state. Books/supplies: $800. Personal expenses: $3,400.

Financial aid. Need-based: Need-based aid available for part-time students. Work-study available nights, weekends and for part-time students. **Non-need-based:** Scholarships awarded for academics, leadership, state residency.

Application procedures. Admission: No deadline. No application fee. **Financial aid:** Priority date 6/1; no closing date. FAFSA required. Applicants notified on a rolling basis starting 5/1; must reply within 2 week(s) of notification.

Academics. Special study options: Cooperative education, distance learning, independent study, internships. License preparation in nursing, paramedic, real estate. **Credit/placement by examination:** AP, CLEP. 15 credit hours maximum toward associate degree. Credit awarded through challenge exams. **Support services:** GED preparation and test center, learning center, remedial instruction, tutoring.

Majors. Biology: Biotechnology. **Business:** General. **Computer sciences:** General, networking, web page design, webmaster. **Engineering technology:** Drafting. **Family/consumer sciences:** Child care. **Health:** EMT paramedic, medical assistant, medical radiologic technology/radiation therapy, nursing (RN), surgical technology. **Legal studies:** Paralegal. **Liberal arts:** Arts/sciences. **Mechanic/repair:** Electronics/electrical, industrial. **Protective services:** Criminal justice, firefighting.

Most popular majors. Business/marketing 15%, computer/information sciences 9%, health sciences 27%, legal studies 6%, liberal arts 30%, trade and industry 9%.

Computing on campus. PC or laptop required. 500 workstations in library, computer center.

Student life. Freshman orientation: Available. Preregistration for classes offered. 1-hour program held Sunday afternoon before start of classes. **Activities:** Student government.

Student services. Adult student services, alcohol/substance abuse counseling, career counseling, services for economically disadvantaged, student employment services, financial aid counseling, personal counseling, placement for graduates, veterans' counselor. **Physically disabled:** Services for visually, speech, hearing impaired. **Learning disabled:** Comprehensive services available. **Transfer:** Pre-admission transcript evaluation for new students. College fairs on campus for students transferring to 4-year colleges.

Contact. E-mail: hpost@seark.edu
Phone: (870) 543-5908 Fax: (870) 543-5956
Barbara Dunn, Admissions and Enrollment Management Coordinator, Southeast Arkansas College, 1900 Hazel Street, Pine Bluff, AR 71603

Southern Arkansas University Tech

Camden, Arkansas
www.sautech.edu **CB code: 6704**

- Public 2-year community and technical college
- Commuter campus in large town

General. Founded in 1967. Regionally accredited. **Enrollment:** 871 degree-seeking undergraduates; 946 non-degree-seeking students. **Degrees:** 112 associate awarded. **Location:** 90 miles from Little Rock. **Calendar:** Semester, limited summer session. **Full-time faculty:** 29 total; 3% have terminal degrees, 7% minority, 48% women. **Part-time faculty:** 75 total; 4% have terminal degrees, 8% minority, 43% women. **Class size:** 73% < 20, 25% 20-39, 2% 40-49, less than 1% 50-99. **Special facilities:** Fire training academy, environmental science academy, law enforcement academy, career academy, business and industry center. **Partnerships:** Formal partnerships with area businesses/industries and high schools.

Student profile. Among degree-seeking undergraduates, 37% enrolled in a transfer program, 59% enrolled in a vocational program, 1% already have a bachelor's degree or higher, 237 enrolled as first-time, first-year students.

Part-time:	34%	**Hispanic American:**	1%
Out-of-state:	2%	**Native American:**	1%
Women:	51%	**International:**	1%
African American:	30%	**25 or older:**	28%
Asian American:	1%	**Live on campus:**	2%

Transfer out. 90% of students enrolled in the transfer program go on to 4-year colleges. **Colleges most students transferred to 2008:** Southern Arkansas University, Henderson State University, University of Arkansas at Monticello, University of Central Arkansas, South Arkansas Community College.

Basis for selection. Open admission, but selective for some programs. Additional application and testing for nursing program. **Homeschooled:** State high school equivalency certificate required. Applicants must take the GED test.

High school preparation. College-preparatory program recommended. 23 units recommended. Recommended units include English 4, mathematics 4, social studies 2, history 2, science 3, foreign language 2 and academic electives 6.

2008-2009 Annual costs. Tuition/fees: $3,008; $4,238 out-of-state. Per-credit charge: $80 in-state; $121 out-of-state. Books/supplies: $875. Personal expenses: $4,500.

2007-2008 Financial aid. Need-based: 71% of total undergraduate aid awarded as scholarships/grants, 29% as loans/jobs. Need-based aid available for part-time students. Work-study available nights, weekends and for part-time students. **Non-need-based:** Scholarships awarded for academics, state residency.

Application procedures. Admission: Priority date 7/15; deadline 6/1 (postmark date). No application fee. Admission notification on a rolling basis. **Financial aid:** Priority date 6/1; no closing date. FAFSA required. Applicants notified on a rolling basis starting 5/1.

Academics. Special study options: Distance learning, double major, dual enrollment of high school students, honors, independent study, internships. Articulation agreements for Nursing Assistant and Practical Nursing programs. Bachelor's degree programs available on campus. License preparation in aviation, nursing. **Credit/placement by examination:** AP, CLEP, institutional tests. 15 credit hours maximum toward associate degree. **Support services:** GED preparation and test center, learning center, pre-admission summer program, remedial instruction, study skills assistance, tutoring, writing center.

Majors. Business: Business admin, office management. **Computer sciences:** Computer science, networking, programming. **Education:** Multi-level teacher. **Engineering technology:** Computer systems, environmental, industrial. **Mechanic/repair:** Aircraft powerplant. **Protective services:** Fire services admin, firefighting. **Other:** Multimedia technology, Professional studies, Technology.

Most popular majors. Business/marketing 18%, computer/information sciences 18%, education 13%, engineering/engineering technologies 29%, liberal arts 10%.

Computing on campus. 250 workstations in library, computer center. Dormitories wired for high-speed internet access and linked to campus network. Commuter students can connect to campus network. Online course registration, online library, helpline, repair service, wireless network available.

Student life. Freshman orientation: Mandatory. Preregistration for classes offered. One-day program in late July or early August. **Housing:** Apartments, wellness housing available. $100 partly refundable deposit, deadline 7/15. Off-campus housing is available. **Activities:** Campus ministries, radio station, student government, TV station, Multi-Cultural Club, Aviation Club, IMEDIO (multimedia graphics, audio/video) CCUB, Computer Club, Electronics Club, Phi Beta Lambda, Phi Theta Kappa, SAU Tech Ambassadors, Allied Health Student Club, Student Advisers.

Athletics. Intramural: Basketball, football (non-tackle), soccer, softball, tennis, volleyball, weight lifting. **Team name:** Varmits.

Student services. Adult student services, chaplain/spiritual director, career counseling, services for economically disadvantaged, student employment services, financial aid counseling, on-campus daycare, personal counseling, placement for graduates, veterans' counselor. **Physically disabled:** Services for visually, speech, hearing impaired. **Transfer:** Re-entry adviser, pre-admission transcript evaluation for new students. Transfer center, transfer adviser, college fairs on campus for students transferring to 4-year colleges.

Contact. E-mail: bclark@sautech.edu
Phone: (870) 574-4558 Fax: (870) 574-4478
Patricia Sindle, Director, Enrollment Services, Southern Arkansas University Tech, PO Box 3499, Camden, AR 71711-1599

University of Arkansas Community College at Morrilton

Morrilton, Arkansas
www.uaccm.edu **CB code: 3881**

- Public 2-year community college
- Commuter campus in small town

General. Regionally accredited. **Enrollment:** 1,855 degree-seeking undergraduates; 60 non-degree-seeking students. **Degrees:** 169 associate awarded. **Location:** 26 miles from Russellville. **Calendar:** Semester, limited summer session. **Full-time faculty:** 56 total; 2% have terminal degrees, 52% women. **Part-time faculty:** 44 total; 7% have terminal degrees, 2% minority, 70% women.

Student profile. Among degree-seeking undergraduates, 44% enrolled in a transfer program, 56% enrolled in a vocational program, 559 enrolled as first-time, first-year students, 257 transferred in from other institutions.

Part-time:	30%	**Hispanic American:**	4%
Women:	61%	**Native American:**	1%
African American:	8%	**25 or older:**	33%
Asian American:	1%		

Transfer out. Colleges most students transferred to 2008: University of Central Arkansas, Arkansas Tech University, University of Arkansas at Fayetteville, University of Arkansas at Little Rock.

Basis for selection. ASSET or COMPASS test scores required for placement. **Homeschooled:** Transcript of courses and grades required.

2008-2009 Annual costs. Tuition/fees: $2,520; $2,730 out-of-district; $3,720 out-of-state. Per-credit charge: $67 in-district; $74 out-of-district; $107 out-of-state.

2008-2009 Financial aid. Need-based: 351 full-time freshmen applied for aid; 309 were judged to have need; 278 of these received aid. Average need met was 53%. Average scholarship/grant was $1,531; average loan $1,204. 75% of total undergraduate aid awarded as scholarships/grants, 25% as loans/jobs. Need-based aid available for part-time students. Work-study available nights and for part-time students. **Non-need-based:** Awarded to 278 full-time undergraduates, including 153 freshmen. Scholarships awarded for academics, leadership, state residency.

Application procedures. Admission: No deadline. No application fee. Admission notification on a rolling basis. **Financial aid:** Priority date 7/1; no closing date. FAFSA, institutional form, CSS PROFILE required. Applicants notified by 5/1.

Academics. Special study options: Cooperative education, distance learning, internships, liberal arts/career combination. License preparation in nursing. **Credit/placement by examination:** AP, CLEP, institutional tests. 30 credit hours maximum toward associate degree. **Support services:** GED preparation and test center, learning center, remedial instruction, study skills assistance, tutoring, writing center.

Majors. Business: General, finance. **Engineering technology:** General, computer systems, drafting, petroleum, surveying. **Family/consumer sciences:** Child development. **Health:** Nursing (RN). **Liberal arts:** Arts/sciences. **Mechanic/repair:** Auto body, automotive, heating/ac/refrig. **Protective services:** Forensics, law enforcement admin.

Student life. Freshman orientation: Available. Preregistration for classes offered. **Activities:** Choral groups, drama, student government, student newspaper.

Athletics. Intramural: Basketball, football (non-tackle), table tennis, volleyball. **Team name:** Timberwolves.

Student services. Career counseling, student employment services, financial aid counseling, on-campus daycare, placement for graduates. **Physically disabled:** Services for visually, speech, hearing impaired. **Transfer:** College fairs on campus for students transferring to 4-year colleges.

Contact. E-mail: adm@uaccm.edu
Phone: (501) 977-2053 Toll-free number: (800) 264-1094
Fax: (501) 977-2123
Susan Dewey, Director of Admissions, University of Arkansas Community College at Morrilton, 1537 University Boulevard, Morrilton, AR 72110

University of Arkansas: Community College at Batesville

Batesville, Arkansas
www.uaccb.edu **CB code: 3628**

- Public 2-year community college
- Commuter campus in small town

General. Regionally accredited. **Enrollment:** 1,333 degree-seeking undergraduates. **Degrees:** 153 associate awarded. **Location:** 90 miles from Little Rock. **Calendar:** Semester, limited summer session. **Full-time faculty:** 50 total; 10% have terminal degrees, 4% minority, 64% women. **Part-time faculty:** 57 total; 4% minority, 58% women.

Student profile. Among degree-seeking undergraduates, 82 transferred in from other institutions.

Transfer out. Colleges most students transferred to 2008: Lyon College, Arkansas State University, University of Arkansas, University of Central Arkansas, Arkansas Tech University.

Basis for selection. Open admission, but selective for some programs. Admission to nursing program based on GPA in prerequisite courses and a nursing entrance exam. **Homeschooled:** Transcript of courses and grades required.

2008-2009 Annual costs. Tuition/fees: $2,077; $2,377 out-of-district; $4,117 out-of-state. Per-credit charge: $52 in-district; $62 out-of-district; $120 out-of-state. Books/supplies: $700. Personal expenses: $2,100.

Financial aid. All financial aid based on need. Work-study available nights, weekends and for part-time students.

Application procedures. Admission: No deadline. No application fee. Application must be submitted on paper. Admission notification on a rolling basis. **Financial aid:** No deadline. FAFSA required. Applicants notified on a rolling basis starting 3/1; must reply within 2 week(s) of notification.

Academics. Special study options: Cooperative education, distance learning, dual enrollment of high school students, ESL, independent study, internships, liberal arts/career combination, weekend college. Bachelor's degree programs available on campus. License preparation in paramedic. **Credit/placement by examination:** AP, CLEP, institutional tests. **Support services:** GED preparation and test center, remedial instruction, study skills assistance, tutoring.

Majors. Business: General, accounting, administrative services, business admin. **Computer sciences:** General. **Education:** Early childhood. **Health:** EMT paramedic, nursing (RN). **Liberal arts:** Arts/sciences. **Mechanic/repair:** General, aircraft, electronics/electrical, industrial. **Protective services:** Criminal justice.

Most popular majors. Business/marketing 14%, health sciences 37%, liberal arts 38%.

Computing on campus. 25 workstations in library, computer center.

Student life. Freshman orientation: Available. Preregistration for classes offered. **Activities:** Student government, Baptist Collegiate Ministry, Young Democrats, College Republicans.

Student services. Adult student services, career counseling, services for economically disadvantaged, student employment services, financial aid counseling, personal counseling, veterans' counselor. **Physically disabled:** Services for visually, speech, hearing impaired. **Transfer:** Pre-admission transcript evaluation for new students. College fairs on campus for students transferring to 4-year colleges.

Contact. E-mail: crystal.walling@uaccb.edu
Phone: (870) 612-2000 Toll-free number: (800) 508-7878
Fax: (870) 793-4988
Sharon Gage, Admissions and Student Activities Coordinator, University of Arkansas: Community College at Batesville, Box 3350, Batesville, AR 72503

University of Arkansas: Community College at Hope

Hope, Arkansas
www.uacch.edu **CB code: 3629**

- Public 2-year community and technical college
- Commuter campus in small town

General. Regionally accredited. **Enrollment:** 964 degree-seeking undergraduates. **Degrees:** 82 associate awarded. **Location:** 30 miles from Texarkana. **Calendar:** Semester, limited summer session. **Full-time faculty:** 38 total; 5% have terminal degrees, 8% minority, 45% women. **Part-time faculty:** 23 total; 48% women.

Basis for selection. Open admission, but selective for some programs. Additional requirements for nursing, funeral services, respiratory therapy programs.

High school preparation. 15 units recommended. Recommended units include English 4, mathematics 3, social studies 1, history 2, science 3 and academic electives 2.

2008-2009 Annual costs. Tuition/fees: $1,790; $1,940 out-of-district; $3,620 out-of-state. Per-credit charge: $54 in-district; $59 out-of-district; $115 out-of-state. Books/supplies: $900. Personal expenses: $500.

2007-2008 Financial aid. Need-based: Need-based aid available for part-time students. Work-study available nights and for part-time students. **Non-need-based:** Scholarships awarded for academics.

Application procedures. Admission: No deadline. No application fee. Admission notification on a rolling basis. **Financial aid:** Priority date 7/6; no closing date. FAFSA, institutional form required. Applicants notified on a rolling basis starting 1/1; must reply within 4 week(s) of notification.

Academics. Special study options: Distance learning, double major, dual enrollment of high school students, ESL, independent study, liberal arts/career combination. Bachelor's degree programs available on campus. License preparation in nursing, paramedic. **Credit/placement by examination:** AP, CLEP, institutional tests. **Support services:** GED test center, remedial instruction, study skills assistance, tutoring.

Majors. Agriculture: General. **Business:** General. **Education:** Middle. **Family/consumer sciences:** Child care. **Health:** Respiratory therapy technology. **Legal studies:** Paralegal. **Liberal arts:** Arts/sciences. **Personal/culinary services:** Mortuary science. **Protective services:** Forensics, law enforcement admin, police science.

Most popular majors. Business/marketing 7%, health sciences 9%, legal studies 6%, liberal arts 62%, personal/culinary services 7%.

Computing on campus. 20 workstations in library. Commuter students can connect to campus network. Online course registration, online library, helpline, wireless network available.

Student life. Freshman orientation: Available. **Activities:** Jazz band, choral groups, drama, music ensembles, student government, student newspaper.

Student services. Adult student services, alcohol/substance abuse counseling, chaplain/spiritual director, career counseling, services for economically disadvantaged, student employment services, financial aid counseling, personal counseling, placement for graduates, veterans' counselor. **Physically disabled:** Services for visually, speech, hearing impaired. **Transfer:** Pre-admission transcript evaluation for new students. College fairs on campus for students transferring to 4-year colleges.

Contact. E-mail: diana.syata@uacch.edu
Phone: (870) 777-5722 Fax: (870) 722-6630
Judy Anderson, Director for Enrollment Services, University of Arkansas: Community College at Hope, 2500 South Main, Hope, AR 71802-0140

California

Allan Hancock College
Santa Maria, California
www.hancockcollege.edu **CB code: 4002**

- Public 2-year community college
- Commuter campus in small city

General. Founded in 1920. Regionally accredited. **Enrollment:** 6,481 degree-seeking undergraduates. **Degrees:** 1,173 associate awarded. **Location:** 70 miles from Santa Barbara, 175 miles from Los Angeles. **Calendar:** Semester, extensive summer session. **Full-time faculty:** 158 total. **Part-time faculty:** 450 total.

Transfer out. Colleges most students transferred to 2008: California Polytechnic State University, San Luis Obispo; UC Santa Barbara, CSU, San Diego; CSU, Northridge; CSU, Fresno.

Basis for selection. Open admission, but selective for some programs. Special requirements for allied health and drama programs. Students required to make separate application for admission to nursing, drama, police academy programs. Interviews required for allied health applicants. Auditions required for drama applicants. **Adult students:** SAT/ACT scores not required.

2008-2009 Annual costs. Tuition/fees: $647; $6,077 out-of-state. Per-credit charge: $20 in-state; $201 out-of-state. Books/supplies: $1,422. Personal expenses: $2,924.

Financial aid. All financial aid based on need. Need-based aid available for part-time students. Work-study available for part-time students.

Application procedures. Admission: No deadline. No application fee. Admission notification on a rolling basis. **Financial aid:** Priority date 5/1; no closing date. FAFSA required. Applicants notified on a rolling basis starting 6/1.

Academics. Special study options: Accelerated study, cooperative education, distance learning, double major, dual enrollment of high school students, ESL, honors, independent study, internships, liberal arts/career combination, study abroad, weekend college. Bachelor's degree programs available on campus. License preparation in dental hygiene, nursing, paramedic, real estate. **Credit/placement by examination:** AP, CLEP, institutional tests. 30 credit hours maximum toward associate degree. **Support services:** GED preparation and test center, learning center, reduced course load, remedial instruction, study skills assistance, tutoring, writing center.

Majors. Agriculture: Agribusiness operations. **Architecture:** Technology. **Biology:** General. **Business:** General, accounting, administrative services, business admin, international marketing, management information systems, management science, office technology, office/clerical. **Communications technology:** Animation/special effects, graphic/printing, graphics, photo/film/video. **Computer sciences:** General, computer science, information technology. **Conservation:** Environmental studies. **Education:** Early childhood, elementary, physical. **Engineering:** General. **Engineering technology:** General, architectural, civil, electrical, electromechanical, environmental, robotics. **Family/consumer sciences:** General, fashion consultant, housing. **Foreign languages:** Spanish. **Health:** Dental assistant, health services, licensed practical nurse, medical assistant, medical records admin, medical records technology, nursing (RN), physical therapy assistant. **Legal studies:** Legal secretary. **Liberal arts:** Arts/sciences. **Math:** General, computational. **Mechanic/repair:** General, auto body, automotive, diesel, electronics/electrical. **Parks/recreation:** General. **Personal/culinary services:** Chef training, cosmetic. **Physical sciences:** Chemistry, physics. **Protective services:** Fire safety technology. **Psychology:** General. **Public administration:** Human services. **Social sciences:** General, international relations. **Visual/performing arts:** Art, commercial photography, commercial/advertising art, dance, design, fashion design, film/cinema, interior design, photography.

Most popular majors. Health sciences 9%, liberal arts 58%, security/protective services 12%.

Computing on campus. 180 workstations in library, computer center. Online library, wireless network available.

Student life. Freshman orientation: Available. **Activities:** Bands, choral groups, dance, drama, film society, literary magazine, music ensembles, musical theater, student government, student newspaper.

Athletics. Intercollegiate: Baseball M, basketball, cross-country, football (tackle) M, golf, soccer, tennis, track and field, volleyball W. **Team name:** Bulldogs.

Student services. Adult student services, career counseling, services for economically disadvantaged, student employment services, health services, on-campus daycare, personal counseling, placement for graduates, veterans' counselor. **Physically disabled:** Services for visually, hearing impaired. **Transfer:** Pre-admission transcript evaluation for new students. Transfer center, transfer adviser, college fairs on campus for students transferring to 4-year colleges.

Contact. Phone: (805) 922-6966 ext. 3248 Fax: (805) 922-3477
Adela Esquivel-Swinson, Director, Admissions and Records, Allan Hancock College, 800 South College Drive, Santa Maria, CA 93454-6399

American Academy of Dramatic Arts: West
Los Angeles, California
www.aada.org **CB code: 7024**

- Private 2-year performing arts college
- Commuter campus in very large city
- Application essay, interview required

General. Founded in 1974. Regionally accredited. **Enrollment:** 220 degree-seeking undergraduates. **Degrees:** 20 associate awarded. **Calendar:** Semester, limited summer session. **Full-time faculty:** 1 total; 100% women. **Part-time faculty:** 27 total; 11% minority, 63% women. **Class size:** 93% < 20, 7% 20-39. **Special facilities:** Performance theater.

Student profile.

Out-of-state:	25%	**25 or older:**	20%

Basis for selection. Student attitude, seriousness of intent, and potential as professional actor as indicated by written recommendations, interview, and audition. All applicants must have full command of English language. Auditions required.

2008-2009 Annual costs. Tuition/fees: $20,000. Books/supplies: $600. Personal expenses: $1,232.

2007-2008 Financial aid. Non-need-based: Scholarships awarded for academics, music/drama.

Application procedures. Admission: No deadline. $50 fee. Admission notification on a rolling basis. SAT or ACT recommended for applicants attending directly from high school. **Financial aid:** Priority date 7/1; no closing date. Institutional form required. Applicants notified on a rolling basis starting 6/1; must reply within 3 week(s) of notification.

Academics. Select group of students invited to return for additional year of study and performance after graduation in repertory situation. **Special study options:** Cross-registration, exchange student. Students may study 1 year in each of 2 campuses (NY and CA). **Credit/placement by examination:** AP, CLEP. **Support services:** Pre-admission summer program, tutoring, writing center.

Majors. Visual/performing arts: Acting.

Computing on campus. 10 workstations in computer center.

Student life. Freshman orientation: Mandatory. **Activities:** Student government.

Student services. Alcohol/substance abuse counseling, career counseling, financial aid counseling, personal counseling, veterans' counselor.

Contact. E-mail: khigginbotham@ca.aada.org
Phone: (323) 464-2777 ext. 103 Toll-free number: (800) 222-2867
Fax: (323) 464-1250
Karen Higginbotham, Director of Admissions, American Academy of Dramatic Arts: West, 1336 N. La Brea Avenue, Los Angeles, CA 90028

American River College
Sacramento, California
www.arc.losrios.edu **CB code: 4004**

- Public 2-year community college
- Commuter campus in large city

General. Founded in 1955. Regionally accredited. **Enrollment:** 21,549 degree-seeking undergraduates. **Degrees:** 1,390 associate awarded. **Location:** 10 miles from downtown. **Calendar:** Semester, limited summer session. **Full-time faculty:** 380 total. **Part-time faculty:** 605 total.

Basis for selection. Open admission, but selective for some programs. Limited admission to nursing program. **Homeschooled:** Transcript of courses and grades, interview, letter of recommendation (nonparent) required.

2008-2009 Annual costs. Tuition/fees: $632; $6,062 out-of-state. Per-credit charge: $20 in-state; $201 out-of-state. Books/supplies: $1,440. Personal expenses: $2,210.

Financial aid. All financial aid based on need. Need-based aid available for part-time students.

Application procedures. Admission: No deadline. No application fee in-state; $181 out-of-state. Application must be submitted online. Admission notification on a rolling basis beginning on or about 7/1. **Financial aid:** Priority date 3/2; no closing date. FAFSA required. Applicants notified on a rolling basis starting 7/1; must reply within 2 week(s) of notification.

Academics. Special study options: Accelerated study, cooperative education, cross-registration, distance learning, ESL, honors, independent study, liberal arts/career combination, study abroad, weekend college. **Credit/placement by examination:** AP, CLEP, IB. 15 credit hours maximum toward associate degree. **Support services:** Learning center, pre-admission summer program, reduced course load, remedial instruction, study skills assistance, tutoring, writing center.

Majors. Architecture: Landscape. **Business:** Accounting, administrative services, fashion, hospitality/recreation, management information systems, office/clerical, real estate. **Communications:** Journalism. **Communications technology:** Graphic/printing. **Computer sciences:** General, database management, networking, programming. **Conservation:** General. **Education:** Teacher assistance. **Engineering technology:** General, biomedical, drafting, electrical. **Family/consumer sciences:** General, child care, institutional food production. **Health:** Health services, nursing (RN), respiratory therapy technology. **Interdisciplinary:** Biological/physical sciences, gerontology. **Legal studies:** Paralegal. **Liberal arts:** Arts/sciences. **Mechanic/repair:** Automotive. **Parks/recreation:** General. **Personal/culinary services:** Culinary arts, mortuary science, restaurant/catering. **Protective services:** Fire safety technology, police science. **Visual/performing arts:** Dramatic, interior design.

Computing on campus. Online course registration, helpline available.

Student life. Freshman orientation: Available. **Activities:** Bands, choral groups, dance, drama, international student organizations, literary magazine, music ensembles, Model UN, musical theater, student government, student newspaper, symphony orchestra.

Athletics. Intercollegiate: Baseball M, basketball, cross-country, football (tackle) M, golf, soccer, softball W, swimming, tennis, track and field, volleyball W, water polo M. **Team name:** Beavers.

Student services. Adult student services, career counseling, services for economically disadvantaged, student employment services, financial aid counseling, health services, minority student services, on-campus daycare, personal counseling, placement for graduates, veterans' counselor. **Physically disabled:** Services for visually, speech, hearing impaired. **Learning disabled:** Comprehensive services available.

Contact. Phone: (916) 484-8261 Fax: (916) 484-8864
Robin Neal, Dean of Enrollment Services, American River College, 4700 College Oak Drive, Sacramento, CA 95841

Antelope Valley College

Lancaster, California
www.avc.edu **CB code: 4005**

- Public 2-year community college
- Commuter campus in large city

General. Founded in 1929. Regionally accredited. Shares campus with Cal State Bakersfield. **Enrollment:** 10,505 degree-seeking undergraduates. **Degrees:** 928 associate awarded. **Location:** 50 miles from Los Angeles. **Calendar:** Semester, extensive summer session. **Full-time faculty:** 183 total. **Part-time faculty:** 397 total. **Class size:** 27% < 20, 63% 20-39, 6% 40-49, 3% 50-99, less than 1% >100. **Partnerships:** Formal partnerships with Lockheed Martin Corporation, Boeing Corporation.

Transfer out. Colleges most students transferred to 2008: California State University: Northridge, California State University: Bakersfield, University of California: Los Angeles.

Basis for selection. Open admission, but selective for some programs. High school graduate, GED or 18 years of age.

2008-2009 Annual costs. Tuition/fees: $602; $6,032 out-of-state. Per-credit charge: $20 in-state; $201 out-of-state. Books/supplies: $1,566. Personal expenses: $3,024.

Financial aid. Need-based: Need-based aid available for part-time students. Work-study available for part-time students.

Application procedures. Admission: No deadline. No application fee in-state; $175 out-of-state. Admission notification on a rolling basis. **Financial aid:** Priority date 3/2; no closing date. FAFSA, institutional form required. Applicants notified on a rolling basis starting 7/15; must reply within 2 week(s) of notification.

Academics. Special study options: Accelerated study, cooperative education, distance learning, double major, dual enrollment of high school students, ESL, honors, independent study, internships, study abroad, teacher certification program, weekend college. Bachelor's degree programs available on campus. License preparation in aviation, nursing, real estate. **Credit/placement by examination:** AP, CLEP, institutional tests. Maximum of 4 courses allowed. **Support services:** GED preparation, learning center, reduced course load, remedial instruction, study skills assistance, tutoring, writing center.

Majors. Agriculture: Landscaping, ornamental horticulture. **Biology:** General. **Business:** General, administrative services, business admin, real estate. **Communications technology:** Graphic/printing. **Computer sciences:** General, computer graphics, computer science, data processing, information systems, programming. **Education:** Teacher assistance. **Engineering:** General. **Engineering technology:** Aerospace, construction, drafting. **Family/consumer sciences:** General, child care, child development, clothing/textiles, communication, family resources, food/nutrition, home furnishings. **Foreign languages:** American Sign Language. **Health:** Medical assistant, medical secretary, nursing (RN), office assistant. **Liberal arts:** Arts/sciences. **Math:** General. **Mechanic/repair:** Aircraft, auto body, automotive, electronics/electrical. **Parks/recreation:** Health/fitness. **Production:** Welding. **Protective services:** Fire safety technology. **Visual/performing arts:** General, cinematography, interior design, multimedia, photography.

Computing on campus. 300 workstations in library, computer center, student center. Online course registration, online library available.

Student life. Freshman orientation: Available. Preregistration for classes offered. Online orientation available. **Activities:** Bands, choral groups, dance, drama, music ensembles, Model UN, musical theater, student government, student newspaper, symphony orchestra.

Athletics. NCAA. **Intercollegiate:** Baseball M, basketball, cheerleading, cross-country, football (tackle) M, golf, soccer W, softball W, track and field, volleyball W. **Team name:** Marauders.

Student services. Adult student services, career counseling, services for economically disadvantaged, student employment services, financial aid counseling, health services, minority student services, on-campus daycare, personal counseling, veterans' counselor. **Physically disabled:** Services for visually, speech, hearing impaired. **Learning disabled:** Comprehensive services available. **Transfer:** Re-entry adviser for new students. Transfer center, transfer adviser, college fairs on campus for students transferring to 4-year colleges.

Contact. Phone: (661) 722-6332 Fax: (661) 722-6531
LaDonna Trimble, Dean of Enrollment Services, Antelope Valley College, 3041 West Avenue K, Lancaster, CA 93536-5426

Art Institute of California: Los Angeles

Santa Monica, California
www.artinstitutes.edu/losangeles **CB code: 2490**

- For-profit 2-year visual arts college
- Commuter campus in small city
- Application essay, interview required

General. Accredited by ACICS. **Enrollment:** 2,179 degree-seeking undergraduates. **Degrees:** 309 bachelor's, 113 associate awarded. **Calendar:** Continuous. **Full-time faculty:** 64 total. **Part-time faculty:** 63 total. **Class size:** 57% < 20, 43% 20-39.

Basis for selection. High school record and general appropriateness of educational background to specific program applied for most important. Portfolio, interview, standardized test scores also important. SAT or ACT recommended.

Two-Year Colleges

2008-2009 Annual costs. Tuition/fees: $23,234. Per-credit charge: $483. Apartment-style housing: $2,663/quarter for 2-bedroom, $3,227/quarter for 1-bedroom unit. Books/supplies: $1,733. Personal expenses: $1,500.

2008-2009 Financial aid. Need-based: Need-based aid available for part-time students. Work-study available nights, weekends and for part-time students. **Non-need-based:** Scholarships awarded for academics.

Application procedures. Admission: No deadline. $50 fee. Admission notification on a rolling basis. **Financial aid:** No deadline. FAFSA required. Applicants notified on a rolling basis.

Academics. Special study options: Independent study, internships, study abroad. Bachelor's degree programs available on campus. **Credit/placement by examination:** AP, CLEP, SAT, ACT, institutional tests. **Support services:** Reduced course load, tutoring, writing center.

Majors. Computer sciences: Computer graphics, web page design. **Personal/culinary services:** Chef training, culinary arts, food prep. **Visual/performing arts:** Cinematography, commercial/advertising art, design, graphic design.

Computing on campus. 250 workstations in library, computer center. Student web hosting available.

Student life. Freshman orientation: Mandatory. Preregistration for classes offered. One day program before start of quarter. **Housing:** Guaranteed on-campus for all undergraduates. Apartments available. $250 deposit. **Activities:** Literary magazine, gay, lesbian, straight alliance.

Athletics. Intramural: Basketball, softball, volleyball.

Student services. Alcohol/substance abuse counseling, career counseling, student employment services, financial aid counseling, personal counseling, placement for graduates.

Contact. E-mail: ailaadm@aii.edu
Phone: (310) 752-4700 Toll-free number: (888) 646-4610
Fax: (310) 752-4708
Paul Sallenbach, Director of Admissions, Art Institute of California: Los Angeles, 2900 31st Street, Santa Monica, CA 90405-3035

Art Institute of California: Sunnyvale
Sunnyvale, California

- For-profit 2-year technical college
- Residential campus in very large city

General. Regionally accredited. **Location:** 45 miles south of San Francisco. **Calendar:** Quarter.

Annual costs/financial aid. Tuition/fees (2008-2009): $21,888. Room/board: $13,536. Books/supplies: $3,088.

Contact. Phone: (408) 962-6400
Director of Admissions, 1120 Kifer Road, Sunnyvale, CA 94086

Bakersfield College
Bakersfield, California
www.bakersfieldcollege.edu **CB code: 4015**

- Public 2-year community college
- Commuter campus in small city

General. Founded in 1913. Regionally accredited. **Enrollment:** 11,827 degree-seeking undergraduates. **Degrees:** 988 associate awarded. **Location:** 114 miles from Los Angeles. **Calendar:** Semester, limited summer session. **Full-time faculty:** 255 total. **Part-time faculty:** 250 total. **Special facilities:** Planetarium.

Basis for selection. Open admission, but selective for some programs. Nursing and other allied health programs have additional admission requirements including required coursework.

2008-2009 Annual costs. Tuition/fees: $638; $6,548 out-of-state. Per-credit charge: $20 in-state; $217 out-of-state. Books/supplies: $1,500. Personal expenses: $2,150.

Application procedures. Admission: No deadline. No application fee. **Financial aid:** Priority date 3/2; no closing date. FAFSA required. Applicants notified on a rolling basis starting 6/1; must reply within 2 week(s) of notification.

Academics. Special study options: Double major, dual enrollment of high school students. **Credit/placement by examination:** CLEP, institutional tests. 12 credit hours maximum toward associate degree. **Support services:** Learning center, pre-admission summer program, reduced course load, remedial instruction, tutoring.

Majors. Agriculture: Agribusiness operations, animal sciences, horticulture, ornamental horticulture. **Biology:** General, bacteriology. **Business:** Accounting, administrative services, business admin, management information systems, office technology, office/clerical, real estate. **Communications:** Broadcast journalism, journalism. **Communications technology:** General, graphic/printing. **Computer sciences:** Applications programming, data processing. **Conservation:** Forestry. **Construction:** Carpentry, masonry, pipefitting, power transmission. **Engineering technology:** Aerospace, drafting. **Family/consumer sciences:** General, food/nutrition, institutional food production. **Foreign languages:** German, Spanish. **Health:** Dental assistant, EMT paramedic, licensed practical nurse, medical radiologic technology/radiation therapy, nursing (RN), predental, premedicine, prepharmacy, preveterinary. **History:** General. **Legal studies:** Prelaw. **Liberal arts:** Arts/sciences. **Math:** General. **Mechanic/repair:** Automotive. **Parks/recreation:** General. **Personal/culinary services:** Culinary arts. **Philosophy/religion:** Philosophy. **Physical sciences:** Chemistry, geology, physics. **Production:** Woodworking. **Protective services:** Fire safety technology, police science. **Psychology:** General. **Social sciences:** Anthropology, criminology, economics, geography, political science, sociology. **Visual/performing arts:** Interior design, photography.

Student life. Activities: Bands, choral groups, dance, drama, literary magazine, music ensembles, radio station, student government, student newspaper.

Athletics. Intercollegiate: Baseball M, basketball, cross-country, diving, football (tackle) M, golf M, softball W, swimming, tennis, track and field, volleyball W, wrestling M. **Team name:** Renegades.

Student services. Career counseling, student employment services, health services, on-campus daycare. **Physically disabled:** Services for visually, speech, hearing impaired.

Contact. Phone: (661) 395-4301
Sue Vaughn, Director of Enrollment Services, Bakersfield College, 1801 Panorama Drive, Bakersfield, CA 93305

Barstow Community College
Barstow, California
www.barstow.edu **CB code: 4020**

- Public 2-year community college
- Commuter campus in large town

General. Founded in 1959. Regionally accredited. **Enrollment:** 1,581 degree-seeking undergraduates. **Degrees:** 393 associate awarded. **Location:** 70 miles from San Bernardino. **Calendar:** Semester, limited summer session. **Full-time faculty:** 35 total. **Part-time faculty:** 70 total.

Student profile.

Out-of-state:	10%	**25 or older:**	43%

Basis for selection. Open admission.

2008-2009 Annual costs. Tuition/fees: $600; $5,520 out-of-state. Per-credit charge: $20 in-state; $184 out-of-state.

2007-2008 Financial aid. All financial aid based on need. 98% of total undergraduate aid awarded as scholarships/grants, 2% as loans/jobs. Need-based aid available for part-time students.

Application procedures. Admission: No deadline. No application fee. Admission notification on a rolling basis. **Financial aid:** Closing date 5/22. FAFSA required. Applicants notified on a rolling basis starting 7/1.

Academics. Special study options: Accelerated study, cooperative education, distance learning, double major, dual enrollment of high school students, ESL, independent study, liberal arts/career combination. **Credit/placement by examination:** AP, CLEP, institutional tests. 30 credit hours maximum toward associate degree. **Support services:** Learning center, reduced course load, remedial instruction, study skills assistance, tutoring.

Majors. Biology: General. **Business:** General, accounting, administrative services, business admin, management information systems, managerial economics, office management, office technology, office/clerical, real estate. **Communications:** General. **Computer sciences:** General, applications programming, programming. **Education:** General, elementary, teacher assistance. **Family/consumer sciences:** Child care. **Liberal arts:** Arts/sciences. **Math:**

General. **Production:** Welding. **Protective services:** Fire safety technology, police science. **Psychology:** General. **Social sciences:** General. **Visual/performing arts:** Dramatic, studio arts.

Computing on campus. 40 workstations in library, computer center. Online course registration, online library, wireless network available.

Student life. Freshman orientation: Available. Preregistration for classes offered. **Activities:** Bands, choral groups, dance, drama, music ensembles, musical theater, student government, Christian Club, Alpha Gamma Sigma, Phi Theta Kappa.

Athletics. NJCAA. **Intercollegiate:** Baseball M, basketball M, cross-country, softball W. **Intramural:** Badminton, baseball M, basketball, bowling, soccer, softball, swimming, tennis, volleyball. **Team name:** Vikings.

Student services. Adult student services, career counseling, services for economically disadvantaged, student employment services, financial aid counseling, personal counseling, placement for graduates, veterans' counselor. **Physically disabled:** Services for visually, speech, hearing impaired. **Transfer:** Pre-admission transcript evaluation for new students. Transfer center, transfer adviser, college fairs on campus for students transferring to 4-year colleges.

Contact. E-mail: admit@barstow.edu
Phone: (760) 252-2411 Fax: (760) 252-6754
Heather Porter, Admissions, Records and Financial Aid Manager, Barstow Community College, 2700 Barstow Road, Barstow, CA 92311-9984

Berkeley City College

Berkeley, California
www.berkeleycitycollege.edu **CB code: 7711**

- Public 2-year community college
- Commuter campus in small city

General. Founded in 1974. Regionally accredited. **Enrollment:** 2,634 degree-seeking undergraduates. **Degrees:** 142 associate awarded. **Location:** 15 miles from San Francisco. **Calendar:** Semester, limited summer session. **Full-time faculty:** 49 total. **Part-time faculty:** 137 total.

Student profile.

Out-of-state:	1%	**25 or older:**	55%

Basis for selection. Open admission.

2008-2009 Annual costs. Tuition/fees: $604; $6,034 out-of-state. Per-credit charge: $20 in-state; $201 out-of-state. Books/supplies: $1,450. Personal expenses: $2,600.

Financial aid. All financial aid based on need. Need-based aid available for part-time students. Work-study available for part-time students.

Application procedures. Admission: No deadline. No application fee. Admission notification on a rolling basis. **Financial aid:** No deadline. Applicants notified on a rolling basis.

Academics. Special study options: Accelerated study, cooperative education, cross-registration, distance learning, dual enrollment of high school students, ESL, independent study, liberal arts/career combination, study abroad, weekend college. **Credit/placement by examination:** CLEP, institutional tests. 6 credit hours maximum toward associate degree. **Support services:** Learning center, reduced course load, remedial instruction, study skills assistance, tutoring, writing center.

Majors. Biology: Biotechnology. **Business:** Business admin, office/clerical, small business admin. **Computer sciences:** General. **Foreign languages:** Sign language interpretation. **Visual/performing arts:** Art.

Computing on campus. Commuter students can connect to campus network. Online course registration, online library, wireless network available.

Student life. Freshman orientation: Mandatory. Preregistration for classes offered. Assessments and orientations scheduled several times before the beginning of the semester. **Activities:** Literary magazine, student government, Phi Theta Kappa, Spanish Club, X Club, Bahai Club.

Student services. Adult student services, career counseling, services for economically disadvantaged, student employment services, financial aid counseling, veterans' counselor. **Physically disabled:** Services for visually, speech, hearing impaired. **Learning disabled:** Comprehensive services available. **Transfer:** Transfer center, transfer adviser, college fairs on campus for students transferring to 4-year colleges.

Contact. Phone: (510) 981-2805 Fax: (510) 841-7333
Loretta Newsom, Admissions and Records Specialist, Berkeley City College, 2050 Center Street, Berkeley, CA 94704

Bryan College: Los Angeles

Los Angeles, California
www.bryancollege.edu

- For-profit 2-year virtual technical college
- Very large city

General. Regionally accredited; also accredited by ACICS. **Enrollment:** 420 degree-seeking undergraduates. **Calendar:** Quarter. **Full-time faculty:** 21 total. **Part-time faculty:** 5 total.

Basis for selection. Open admission, but selective for some programs.

2008-2009 Annual costs. Tuition/fees: $3,250.

Application procedures. Admission: $100 fee, may be waived for applicants with need.

Academics. Credit/placement by examination: CLEP. **Support services:** Learning center, remedial instruction, study skills assistance, tutoring.

Majors. Health: Massage therapy.

Contact. E-mail: info@bryancollege.edu
Phone: (877) 484-8850 Fax: (213) 483-3936
Mark Evans, Director of Admissions, Bryan College: Los Angeles, 3580 Wilshire Boulevard, Suite 400, Los Angeles, CA 90010

Bryan College: Sacramento

Gold River, California
www.bryancollege.com

- For-profit 2-year technical college
- Very large city
- Interview required

General. Accredited by ACCSCT. **Enrollment:** 315 degree-seeking undergraduates. **Degrees:** 94 associate awarded. **Location:** 10 miles from downtown Sacramento. **Calendar:** Continuous, limited summer session. **Full-time faculty:** 25 total. **Part-time faculty:** 10 total.

Basis for selection. Interview, interest important.

2008-2009 Annual costs. AOS Massage: $20,508.71, AOS Massage/Fitness: $20,949.72, AOS Exercise Science: $21,097.79, AAS Court Reporting: $3,303/quarter. Price does not include books, supplies, testing.

Application procedures. Admission: No deadline. $25 fee. **Financial aid:** No deadline.

Academics. Special study options: Massage therapy students get hands-on experience in public massage clinic. Personal training students work with fitness professionals to gain field experience. **Credit/placement by examination:** CLEP.

Majors. Biology: Exercise physiology. **Health:** Massage therapy. **Legal studies:** Court reporting.

Contact. E-mail: admissions@bryancollege.com
Phone: (916) 649-2400 Toll-free number: (866) 649-2400
Fax: (916) 641-8649
Jordan Farmer, Assistant Director of Admissions, Bryan College: Sacramento, 2317 Gold Meadow Way, Gold River, CA 95670

Butte College

Oroville, California
www.butte.edu **CB code: 4226**

- Public 2-year community college
- Commuter campus in small city

General. Founded in 1966. Regionally accredited. **Enrollment:** 7,879 degree-seeking undergraduates. **Degrees:** 956 associate awarded. **Location:** 100 miles from Sacramento. **Calendar:** Semester, extensive summer session. **Full-time faculty:** 130 total. **Part-time faculty:** 470 total. **Special facilities:** 900-acre wild game refuge, nature trails.

Basis for selection. Open admission, but selective for some programs. Nursing, allied health programs have special requirements. Interviews required for allied health applicants.

2008-2009 Annual costs. Tuition/fees: $778; $6,328 out-of-state. Per-credit charge: $20 in-state; $205 out-of-state. Books/supplies: $1,324. Personal expenses: $1,954.

Application procedures. Admission: No deadline. No application fee. Admission notification on a rolling basis. **Financial aid:** Priority date 5/1; no closing date. FAFSA required. Applicants notified on a rolling basis starting 8/1.

Academics. Special study options: Cooperative education, cross-registration, distance learning, double major, dual enrollment of high school students, ESL, honors, independent study, study abroad. License preparation in nursing, paramedic, real estate. **Credit/placement by examination:** CLEP, institutional tests. 9 credit hours maximum toward associate degree. **Support services:** Learning center, remedial instruction, study skills assistance, tutoring.

Majors. Agriculture: Agronomy, animal sciences, business, horticulture, ornamental horticulture. **Business:** General, accounting, administrative services, business admin, fashion, management information systems, marketing, office technology, real estate, tourism promotion. **Communications:** Broadcast journalism, journalism. **Communications technology:** General, graphic/printing. **Computer sciences:** General, applications programming, networking. **Construction:** Maintenance. **Education:** General, bilingual, early childhood, physical. **Engineering technology:** Civil, construction, drafting, electrical. **Family/consumer sciences:** General, child care. **Health:** Cardiovascular technology, EMT paramedic, licensed practical nurse, medical assistant, medical secretary, nursing (RN), respiratory therapy technology, substance abuse counseling. **Legal studies:** Court reporting, legal secretary, paralegal, prelaw. **Liberal arts:** Arts/sciences. **Math:** General. **Mechanic/repair:** Automotive. **Parks/recreation:** Facilities management. **Personal/culinary services:** Cosmetic. **Production:** Welding. **Protective services:** Fire safety technology, police science. **Social sciences:** General. **Visual/performing arts:** Ceramics, commercial photography, commercial/advertising art, fashion design, photography, studio arts.

Computing on campus. 200 workstations in library, computer center. Wireless network available.

Student life. Activities: Bands, drama, film society, music ensembles, radio station, student government, student newspaper, symphony orchestra, TV station.

Athletics. NJCAA. **Intercollegiate:** Baseball M, basketball, cross-country, field hockey W, football (tackle) M, golf, soccer, softball W, tennis, track and field, volleyball W. **Team name:** Roadrunners.

Student services. Adult student services, career counseling, student employment services, health services, on-campus daycare, personal counseling, placement for graduates, veterans' counselor. **Physically disabled:** Services for visually, speech, hearing impaired. **Transfer:** Re-entry adviser for new students. Transfer center, transfer adviser for students transferring to 4-year colleges.

Contact. E-mail: admissions@butte.edu
Phone: (530) 895-2361 Fax: (530) 895-2411
Clinton Slaughter, Director of Admissions and Records, Butte College, 3536 Butte Campus Drive, Oroville, CA 95965

Cabrillo College
Aptos, California
www.cabrillo.edu **CB code: 4084**

- Public 2-year community college
- Commuter campus in large town

General. Founded in 1959. Regionally accredited. **Enrollment:** 7,634 degree-seeking undergraduates. **Degrees:** 849 associate awarded. **Location:** 25 miles from San Jose. **Calendar:** Semester, extensive summer session. **Full-time faculty:** 217 total. **Part-time faculty:** 403 total. **Special facilities:** Observatory, planetarium, horticulture garden.

Student profile.

Out-of-state:	2%	**25 or older:**	52%

Transfer out. Colleges most students transferred to 2008: University of California-Santa Cruz, San Jose State University, California State University-Monterey Bay.

Basis for selection. Open admission, but selective for some programs. Special prerequisite requirements for nursing, dental hygiene, and radiologic technology. International applicants have special admission requirements.

2008-2009 Annual costs. Tuition/fees: $636; $6,066 out-of-state. Per-credit charge: $20 in-state; $201 out-of-state. Books/supplies: $1,566. Personal expenses: $2,754.

2007-2008 Financial aid. Need-based: Need-based aid available for part-time students.

Application procedures. Admission: No deadline. No application fee. Admission notification on a rolling basis beginning on or about 6/1. **Financial aid:** No deadline. FAFSA, institutional form required. Applicants notified on a rolling basis starting 7/31; must reply within 3 week(s) of notification.

Academics. Special study options: Dual enrollment of high school students, honors, independent study, internships, liberal arts/career combination, study abroad. License preparation in dental hygiene, nursing, radiology. **Credit/placement by examination:** AP, CLEP, institutional tests. **Support services:** Learning center, pre-admission summer program, reduced course load, remedial instruction, tutoring.

Majors. Agriculture: Ornamental horticulture. **Area/ethnic studies:** Asian. **Biology:** General. **Business:** General, accounting, banking/financial services, business admin, construction management, entrepreneurial studies, office technology, real estate. **Communications:** Journalism. **Computer sciences:** General, data processing. **Engineering technology:** Hazardous materials, solar energy. **Family/consumer sciences:** General, child care. **Foreign languages:** General, French, German, Italian, Japanese, Spanish. **Health:** Dental hygiene, licensed practical nurse, medical assistant, medical radiologic technology/radiation therapy, nursing (RN). **History:** General. **Liberal arts:** Arts/sciences, library science. **Math:** General. **Mechanic/repair:** Industrial. **Physical sciences:** Chemistry, physics. **Protective services:** Firefighting, police science. **Psychology:** General. **Social sciences:** General, anthropology, economics, geography, political science, sociology. **Visual/performing arts:** General, art, dance, studio arts.

Computing on campus. 350 workstations in library, computer center, student center.

Student life. Freshman orientation: Available. Preregistration for classes offered. **Activities:** Bands, choral groups, dance, drama, music ensembles, musical theater, student government, student newspaper, various clubs, literacy, recreational, cultural and/or ethnic organizations.

Athletics. Intercollegiate: Baseball M, basketball, cross-country, diving, football (tackle) M, golf M, soccer M, softball W, swimming, tennis, track and field, volleyball W, water polo M. **Team name:** Seahawks.

Student services. Adult student services, career counseling, student employment services, health services, personal counseling, placement for graduates, veterans' counselor. **Physically disabled:** Services for visually, speech, hearing impaired. **Transfer:** Transfer center, transfer adviser for students transferring to 4-year colleges.

Contact. Phone: (831) 479-6201 Fax: (831) 479-5782
Masina Hunnicutt, Director of Admissions and Records, Cabrillo College, 6500 Soquel Drive, Aptos, CA 95003

California Christian College
Fresno, California
www.calchristiancollege.org

- Private 2-year Bible college
- Large city

General. Regionally accredited. **Enrollment:** 27 degree-seeking undergraduates. **Calendar:** Semester. **Full-time faculty:** 2 total. **Part-time faculty:** 10 total.

2008-2009 Annual costs. Tuition/fees: $8,650.

Academics. Credit/placement by examination: CLEP.

Majors. Other: Bible and Christian Ministry.

Contact. E-mail: cccadmissions@sbcglobal.net
Mallory Breshears, Admissions, California Christian College, 4881 East University Avenue, Fresno, CA 93703

California Culinary Academy

San Francisco, California
www.caculinary.edu **CB code: 2209**

- For-profit 2-year culinary school and career college
- Commuter campus in very large city

General. Founded in 1977. Accredited by ACCSCT. **Location:** Downtown. **Calendar:** Continuous.

Annual costs/financial aid. Tuition/fees (2008-2009): $28,000. Room: $600. Need-based financial aid available for full-time students.

Contact. Phone: (415) 771-3500
Director of Admissions, 350 Rhode Island, San Francisco, CA 94103

California School of Culinary Arts

Pasadena, California
www.csca.edu

- For-profit 2-year culinary school
- Commuter campus in very large city
- Interview required

General. Accredited by ACICS. Le Cordon Bleu college. **Enrollment:** 1,536 degree-seeking undergraduates. **Degrees:** 783 associate awarded. **Location:** 15 miles from downtown Los Angeles. **Calendar:** Continuous, extensive summer session. **Full-time faculty:** 80 total; 1% have terminal degrees, 30% minority, 38% women. **Part-time faculty:** 11 total; 36% minority, 54% women. **Special facilities:** Fine-dining restaurant and casual cafe where students gain practical work experience.

Basis for selection. Open admission. High school diploma/GED, entrance examination required. Students whose first language is not English are required to submit evidence of English Proficiency. This may be done by submitting a TOEFL test score of 500 or higher (for the CPT version, a score of 150 or higher). Entrance Test is required by state agency for diploma programs. Wonderlic SLE Exam used to comply with these regulations. **Learning Disabled:** Students requesting special needs and services required to submit Application for Auxiliary Aid request. Application must include supporting documentation as evidence of disability.

2008-2009 Annual costs. Diploma programs vary in cost. Associate of occupational studies in culinary arts program tuition: $43,950, fees $3,000. Associate of occupational students in hospitality/restaurant management tuition: $31,000, fees $4,015. Books/supplies: $1,500. Personal expenses: $1,347.

2007-2008 Financial aid. Need-based: Need-based aid available for part-time students. Work-study available nights and weekends.

Application procedures. Admission: No deadline. $75 fee. Admission notification on a rolling basis. **Financial aid:** No deadline. FAFSA required. Applicants notified on a rolling basis.

Academics. Special study options: Honors. **Credit/placement by examination:** AP, CLEP. **Support services:** Learning center, study skills assistance, tutoring.

Majors. Personal/culinary services: Chef training, restaurant/catering.

Computing on campus. 40 workstations in library, computer center, student center. Commuter students can connect to campus network. Online library available.

Student life. Freshman orientation: Mandatory. Preregistration for classes offered. **Activities:** Student newspaper.

Student services. Adult student services, career counseling, financial aid counseling, placement for graduates. **Transfer:** Re-entry adviser, pre-admission transcript evaluation for new students.

Contact. E-mail: admissionsinfo@csca.edu
Phone: (626) 229-1300 Toll-free number: (888) 900-2433
Fax: (626) 403-4835
Robert Woy, Vice President of Admissions, California School of Culinary Arts, 530 East Colorado Boulevard, Pasadena, CA 91101

Canada College

Redwood City, California
www.canadacollege.edu **CB code: 4109**

- Public 2-year community college
- Commuter campus in small city

General. Founded in 1968. Regionally accredited. **Enrollment:** 2,864 degree-seeking undergraduates. **Degrees:** 212 associate awarded. **Location:** 20 miles from San Francisco. **Calendar:** Semester, limited summer session. **Full-time faculty:** 65 total. **Part-time faculty:** 182 total.

Transfer out. Colleges most students transferred to 2008: San Francisco State, San Jose State, College of Notre de Namur, California State University-East Bay.

Basis for selection. Open admission, but selective for some programs. Special admission to radiologic technology programs.

2008-2009 Annual costs. Tuition/fees: $648; $6,378 out-of-state. Per-credit charge: $20 in-state; $211 out-of-state. Books/supplies: $1,260. Personal expenses: $2,376.

Application procedures. Admission: No deadline. No application fee. Admission notification on a rolling basis. **Financial aid:** Priority date 5/1; no closing date. FAFSA required. Applicants notified on a rolling basis starting 7/15; must reply within 2 week(s) of notification.

Academics. Special study options: Cooperative education, cross-registration, distance learning, double major, dual enrollment of high school students, ESL, independent study, internships, study abroad. Bachelor's degree programs available on campus. **Credit/placement by examination:** AP, CLEP, IB, institutional tests. 12 credit hours maximum toward associate degree. **Support services:** Learning center, reduced course load, remedial instruction, study skills assistance, tutoring, writing center.

Majors. Biology: General. **Business:** General, accounting, administrative services, banking/financial services, business admin, fashion, management information systems, management science, office technology, office/clerical, tourism/travel. **Communications:** Journalism. **Computer sciences:** General, applications programming, programming. **Education:** Early childhood. **Engineering technology:** Computer hardware. **Family/consumer sciences:** General, child care. **Foreign languages:** French, Spanish. **Health:** Medical radiologic technology/radiation therapy, ophthalmic lab technology. **History:** General. **Legal studies:** Paralegal. **Liberal arts:** Arts/sciences. **Math:** General. **Philosophy/religion:** Philosophy. **Physical sciences:** Chemistry, physics. **Psychology:** General. **Public administration:** Human services. **Social sciences:** General, anthropology, geography, political science. **Visual/performing arts:** Art, dramatic, interior design, multimedia.

Computing on campus. 300 workstations in library, computer center. Online course registration, wireless network available.

Student life. Freshman orientation: Available. Preregistration for classes offered. **Activities:** Concert band, choral groups, dance, drama, music ensembles, student government, symphony orchestra, Latin American club, Rotarians, international student club, black student union.

Athletics. NJCAA. **Intercollegiate:** Baseball M, basketball M, golf M, soccer, tennis M. **Team name:** Colts.

Student services. Adult student services, career counseling, health services, personal counseling, veterans' counselor. **Physically disabled:** Services for visually, hearing impaired. **Transfer:** Transfer center, transfer adviser, college fairs on campus for students transferring to 4-year colleges.

Contact. Phone: (650) 306-3226 Fax: (650) 306-3113
Ruth Miller, Assistant Registrar, Canada College, 4200 Farm Hill Boulevard, Redwood City, CA 94061

Cerritos College

Norwalk, California **CB member**
www.cerritos.edu **CB code: 4083**

- Public 2-year community college
- Commuter campus in large city

General. Founded in 1955. Regionally accredited. **Enrollment:** 17,600 degree-seeking undergraduates. **Degrees:** 1,417 associate awarded. **Location:** 15 miles from Los Angeles. **Calendar:** Semester, limited summer session. **Full-time faculty:** 290 total. **Part-time faculty:** 590 total. **Special facilities:** Health occupations lab.

Basis for selection. Open admission, but selective for some programs. Limited admissions to nursing program.

2008-2009 Annual costs. Tuition/fees: $648; $6,078 out-of-state. Per-credit charge: $20 in-state; $201 out-of-state. Books/supplies: $1,566. Personal expenses: $2,664.

Application procedures. **Admission:** No deadline. No application fee. Admission notification on a rolling basis. **Financial aid:** Priority date 5/8; no closing date. FAFSA required. Applicants notified on a rolling basis; must reply within 2 week(s) of notification.

Academics. **Special study options:** Cooperative education, distance learning, dual enrollment of high school students, honors. Bachelor's degree programs available on campus. License preparation in dental hygiene, nursing, physical therapy. **Credit/placement by examination:** CLEP, institutional tests. 12 credit hours maximum toward associate degree. **Support services:** Learning center, remedial instruction, tutoring.

Majors. **Agriculture:** Ornamental horticulture. **Area/ethnic studies:** Hispanic-American/Latino/Chicano. **Biology:** General, bacteriology, biomedical sciences, botany, zoology. **Business:** General, accounting, administrative services, banking/financial services, business admin, human resources, logistics, office management, office/clerical, real estate. **Communications:** Journalism. **Computer sciences:** General, applications programming, data processing, programming, systems analysis. **Conservation:** Wildlife. **Education:** Bilingual, early childhood, special, teacher assistance. **Engineering technology:** Drafting, electrical, manufacturing, plastics, robotics. **Family/consumer sciences:** General, clothing/textiles, institutional food production. **Foreign languages:** French, German, Spanish. **Health:** Dental assistant, dental hygiene, licensed practical nurse, medical assistant, medical records technology, nursing (RN), physical therapy assistant. **History:** General. **Legal studies:** Court reporting, paralegal. **Math:** General. **Mechanic/repair:** General, auto body, electronics/electrical. **Parks/recreation:** General. **Philosophy/religion:** Philosophy. **Physical sciences:** Chemistry, geology, physics, planetary. **Protective services:** Police science. **Psychology:** General. **Social sciences:** Anthropology, economics, geography, political science, sociology. **Visual/performing arts:** Art, dramatic, interior design, photography.

Computing on campus. 100 workstations in computer center.

Student life. **Activities:** Bands, choral groups, dance, drama, film society, literary magazine, music ensembles, musical theater, radio station, student government, student newspaper, symphony orchestra, Ahora, Indian club, Vietnamese club, Black Student Union.

Athletics. NJCAA. **Intercollegiate:** Baseball M, basketball, cross-country, diving, football (tackle) M, golf M, soccer M, softball W, swimming, tennis, track and field, volleyball W, water polo M, wrestling M. **Team name:** Falcons.

Student services. Adult student services, career counseling, financial aid counseling, health services, on-campus daycare, personal counseling, veterans' counselor, women's services. **Physically disabled:** Services for visually, speech, hearing impaired. **Transfer:** Transfer adviser, college fairs on campus for students transferring to 4-year colleges.

Contact. Phone: (562) 860-2451 ext. 2211 Fax: (562) 860-9680
Stephanie Murguia, Dean, Admissions and Records, Cerritos College, 11110 Alondra Boulevard, Norwalk, CA 90650

Cerro Coso Community College
Ridgecrest, California
www.cerrocoso.edu **CB code: 4027**

- Public 2-year community college
- Commuter campus in large town

General. Founded in 1973. Regionally accredited. **Enrollment:** 2,159 degree-seeking undergraduates. **Degrees:** 210 associate awarded. **Location:** 120 miles from Bakersfield. **Calendar:** Semester, limited summer session. **Full-time faculty:** 55 total; 27% have terminal degrees. **Part-time faculty:** 140 total. **Class size:** 44% < 20, 52% 20-39, 3% 40-49, 1% 50-99. **Special facilities:** Nature preserve, sculpture garden.

Student profile.

Out-of-state:	2%	**25 or older:**	63%

Basis for selection. Open admission. Interview required of nursing majors.

2008-2009 Annual costs. Tuition/fees: $600; $6,510 out-of-state. Per-credit charge: $20 in-state; $217 out-of-state. Books/supplies: $1,314. Personal expenses: $1,656.

Financial aid. **Need-based:** Need-based aid available for part-time students. Work-study available nights and for part-time students.

Application procedures. **Admission:** No deadline. No application fee. Admission notification on a rolling basis. **Financial aid:** Priority date 5/15; no closing date. FAFSA required. Applicants notified on a rolling basis starting 6/1; must reply within 2 week(s) of notification.

Academics. **Special study options:** Cooperative education, distance learning, double major, dual enrollment of high school students, ESL, honors, independent study, internships, study abroad. License preparation in nursing. **Credit/placement by examination:** AP, CLEP. 30 credit hours maximum toward associate degree. **Support services:** GED preparation and test center, learning center, remedial instruction, study skills assistance, tutoring.

Majors. **Business:** General, administrative services, business admin, office management, office technology, office/clerical. **Computer sciences:** General. **Education:** Early childhood. **Engineering technology:** General, drafting, electrical. **Family/consumer sciences:** Child care. **Health:** Licensed practical nurse. **Interdisciplinary:** Biological/physical sciences. **Liberal arts:** Arts/sciences. **Mechanic/repair:** Auto body, heating/ac/refrig. **Parks/recreation:** Facilities management. **Physical sciences:** General. **Protective services:** Fire safety technology, police science. **Social sciences:** General. **Visual/performing arts:** Art.

Most popular majors. Business/marketing 18%, computer/information sciences 6%, health sciences 6%, liberal arts 52%, social sciences 13%.

Computing on campus. Online course registration, online library available.

Student life. **Freshman orientation:** Available. **Activities:** Bands, choral groups, drama, literary magazine, student government, student newspaper, symphony orchestra.

Athletics. **Intercollegiate:** Baseball M, basketball W, softball W, volleyball W. **Team name:** Coyotes.

Student services. Career counseling, student employment services, financial aid counseling, on-campus daycare, personal counseling, placement for graduates, veterans' counselor. **Physically disabled:** Services for visually, speech, hearing impaired. **Learning disabled:** Comprehensive services available. **Transfer:** Transfer adviser, college fairs on campus for students transferring to 4-year colleges.

Contact. E-mail: jboard@cerrocoso.edu
Phone: (760) 384-6357 Fax: (760) 384-6377
Dave Cornell, Director of Admission and Records, Cerro Coso Community College, 3000 College Heights Boulevard, Ridgecrest, CA 93555-7777

Chabot College
Hayward, California
www.chabotcollege.edu **CB code: 4725**

- Public 2-year community college
- Commuter campus in large city

General. Founded in 1961. Regionally accredited. **Enrollment:** 8,752 degree-seeking undergraduates. **Degrees:** 751 associate awarded. **ROTC:** Army, Air Force. **Location:** 30 miles from San Francisco, 15 miles from Berkeley. **Calendar:** Semester, extensive summer session. **Full-time faculty:** 184 total; 28% minority. **Part-time faculty:** 338 total; 28% minority. **Special facilities:** Planetarium. **Partnerships:** Formal partnership with Lawrence Livermore National Lab.

Student profile.

Out-of-state:	1%	**25 or older:**	45%

Transfer out. **Colleges most students transferred to 2008:** CSU: East Bay, San Jose State University, UC: Berkeley, San Francisco State University, UC: Davis.

Basis for selection. Open admission, but selective for some programs. All applicants must be 18 years of age or high school graduates. Selective admission to nursing, dental hygiene, and paramedic programs.

2008-2009 Annual costs. Tuition/fees: $626; $6,026 out-of-state. Per-credit charge: $20 in-state; $200 out-of-state. Books/supplies: $1,566. Personal expenses: $2,664.

Financial aid. **Need-based:** Work-study available nights, weekends and for part-time students. **Additional information:** Tuition and/or fee waivers for low-income students.

Application procedures. **Admission:** No deadline. No application fee. Admission notification on a rolling basis. Early action available for local high school students only. **Financial aid:** Priority date 8/1; no closing date. FAFSA, institutional form required. Applicants notified on a rolling basis.

Academics. **Special study options:** Cooperative education, cross-registration, distance learning, double major, dual enrollment of high school students, ESL, independent study, internships, liberal arts/career combination, student-designed major, study abroad, weekend college. License preparation in dental hygiene, nursing, real estate. **Credit/placement by examination:** CLEP, institutional tests. 15 credit hours maximum toward associate degree. English and math tests required for placement. **Support services:** Learning center, pre-admission summer program, reduced course load, remedial instruction, study skills assistance, tutoring, writing center.

Majors. **Biology:** General. **Business:** General, accounting, administrative services, banking/financial services, logistics, management information systems, management science, office management, office technology, office/clerical, real estate, sales/distribution, tourism/travel. **Communications:** Broadcast journalism, journalism. **Communications technology:** General, radio/tv. **Computer sciences:** General, applications programming, computer science, data processing, information systems, programming. **Construction:** Maintenance, power transmission. **Education:** Early childhood, teacher assistance. **Engineering:** General. **Engineering technology:** Architectural, civil, drafting, electrical, surveying. **Family/consumer sciences:** Child care, clothing/textiles. **Foreign languages:** French, German, Italian, Portuguese, Spanish. **Health:** Clinical lab technology, dental hygiene, medical assistant, medical records admin, medical records technology, nursing (RN), predental, premedicine, prepharmacy, preveterinary. **History:** General. **Legal studies:** Court reporting, legal secretary, prelaw. **Liberal arts:** Arts/sciences, library assistant. **Math:** General. **Mechanic/repair:** Auto body, automotive, electronics/electrical. **Parks/recreation:** General. **Personal/culinary services:** General. **Philosophy/religion:** Philosophy. **Physical sciences:** Physics. **Production:** Welding. **Protective services:** Firefighting, police science. **Psychology:** General. **Social sciences:** General, criminology, geography, political science, sociology. **Transportation:** Aviation, flight attendant. **Visual/performing arts:** Art, ceramics, commercial/advertising art, dance, dramatic, drawing, music performance, painting, photography, sculpture, studio arts.

Most popular majors. Business/marketing 10%, health sciences 15%, liberal arts 50%.

Student life. **Freshman orientation:** Available. Introduction to college experience, programs, services, and registration process. **Activities:** Bands, choral groups, drama, film society, literary magazine, musical theater, radio station, student government, student newspaper, TV station, various religious, political, ethnic, and social service organizations.

Athletics. NJCAA. **Intercollegiate:** Baseball M, basketball, cross-country, football (tackle) M, golf M, soccer, softball W, swimming, tennis, track and field, volleyball W, water polo W, wrestling M. **Intramural:** Archery, badminton, basketball, bowling, handball, racquetball, soccer, softball, table tennis, tennis, volleyball. **Team name:** Gladiators.

Student services. Adult student services, career counseling, student employment services, on-campus daycare, personal counseling, placement for graduates. **Physically disabled:** Services for visually, speech, hearing impaired. **Transfer:** Re-entry adviser for new students. Transfer center, college fairs on campus for students transferring to 4-year colleges.

Contact. E-mail: jyoung@chabotcollege.edu
Phone: (510) 723-6700 Fax: (510) 723-7510
Judy Young, Registrar, Chabot College, 25555 Hesperian Boulevard, Hayward, CA 94545

Chaffey College
Rancho Cucamonga, California
www.chaffey.edu **CB code: 4046**

- Public 2-year community college
- Commuter campus in small city

General. Founded in 1883. Regionally accredited. **Enrollment:** 13,295 degree-seeking undergraduates. **Degrees:** 1,394 associate awarded. **Location:** 50 miles from Los Angeles. **Calendar:** Semester, limited summer session. **Special facilities:** Nature preserve, natural history collection, planetarium, 2 swimming pools, children's center.

Transfer out. **Colleges most students transferred to 2008:** CSU San Bernardino, California State Polytechnic University: Pomona, CSU Fullerton, University of LaVerne, Loma Linda University.

Basis for selection. Open admission. Assessment testing is recommended.

2008-2009 Annual costs. Tuition/fees: $630; $6,060 out-of-state. Per-credit charge: $20 in-state; $201 out-of-state. Books/supplies: $1,566. Personal expenses: $3,024.

Financial aid. **Need-based:** Need-based aid available for part-time students. Work-study available for part-time students. **Non-need-based:** Scholarships awarded for academics. **Additional information:** State of California Board of Governors fee waivers to qualified state residents. Criteria for eligibility: households which receive public assistance, meet state's low income guidelines, and demonstrate need as defined by Title IV programs.

Application procedures. **Admission:** No deadline. No application fee. Admission notification on a rolling basis. **Financial aid:** No deadline. FAFSA required. Applicants notified on a rolling basis starting 7/15; must reply within 2 week(s) of notification.

Academics. **Special study options:** Accelerated study, cooperative education, dual enrollment of high school students, ESL, honors, independent study, internships, liberal arts/career combination, study abroad, weekend college. License preparation in aviation, nursing. **Credit/placement by examination:** CLEP, institutional tests. **Support services:** GED preparation, learning center, remedial instruction, tutoring, writing center.

Majors. **Biology:** General. **Business:** Accounting, administrative services, business admin, fashion, office management, sales/distribution. **Communications:** General, broadcast journalism. **Computer sciences:** General, applications programming. **Conservation:** Environmental studies. **Education:** General, early childhood, physical. **Engineering:** General. **Engineering technology:** Architectural, drafting. **Family/consumer sciences:** General, child care. **Foreign languages:** French, German, Spanish. **Health:** Dental assistant, medical radiologic technology/radiation therapy, nursing (RN). **History:** General. **Interdisciplinary:** Gerontology, science/society. **Liberal arts:** Arts/sciences. **Math:** General. **Mechanic/repair:** Aircraft, auto body, automotive, electronics/electrical. **Philosophy/religion:** Philosophy, religion. **Physical sciences:** Chemistry, geology, physics, planetary. **Psychology:** General. **Social sciences:** General, anthropology, economics, geography, political science, sociology. **Visual/performing arts:** Art, commercial/advertising art, dance, design, dramatic, fashion design, graphic design, interior design, multimedia, photography, studio arts.

Computing on campus. 950 workstations in library, computer center. Repair service available.

Student life. **Freshman orientation:** Mandatory. 3-hour session covers registration procedures, fees, financial aid, programs and services, counseling, course descriptions. **Activities:** Bands, choral groups, dance, drama, film society, music ensembles, Model UN, musical theater, student government, student newspaper, multicultural organizations, Vietnamese club, MECHA, Alpha Gamma Sigma, Black Student Union, ski club, religious organizations, French club, German club, Spanish club, Lambda.

Athletics. **Intercollegiate:** Baseball M, basketball, diving, football (tackle) M, softball W, swimming, volleyball W, water polo M. **Team name:** Panthers.

Student services. Alcohol/substance abuse counseling, career counseling, services for economically disadvantaged, student employment services, financial aid counseling, health services, on-campus daycare, personal counseling, veterans' counselor. **Physically disabled:** Services for visually, speech, hearing impaired. **Transfer:** Pre-admission transcript evaluation for new students. Transfer center, transfer adviser, college fairs on campus for students transferring to 4-year colleges.

Contact. Phone: (909) 652-6600 Fax: (909) 652-6006
Cecilia Carrera, Director of Admissions, Chaffey College, 5885 Haven Avenue, Rancho Cucamonga, CA 91701-3002

Citrus College
Glendora, California
www.citruscollege.edu **CB code: 4051**

- Public 2-year community college
- Commuter campus in large town

General. Founded in 1915. Regionally accredited. **Enrollment:** 6,812 degree-seeking undergraduates. **Degrees:** 778 associate awarded. **Location:** 25 miles from Los Angeles. **Calendar:** Semester, limited summer session. **Full-time faculty:** 172 total. **Part-time faculty:** 284 total. **Special facilities:** Performing arts center, golf driving range.

Student profile.

Out-of-state:	3%	**25 or older:**	29%

Basis for selection. Open admission.

2008-2009 Annual costs. Tuition/fees: $617; $6,047 out-of-state. Per-credit charge: $20 in-state; $201 out-of-state. Books/supplies: $1,566. Personal expenses: $2,664.

2008-2009 Financial aid. Need-based: Need-based aid available for part-time students. Work-study available nights, weekends and for part-time students.

Application procedures. Admission: No deadline. No application fee. Application must be submitted on paper. Admission notification on a rolling basis. **Financial aid:** Priority date 3/1; no closing date. FAFSA required. Applicants notified on a rolling basis; must reply within 2 week(s) of notification.

Academics. Special study options: Cooperative education, distance learning, double major, dual enrollment of high school students, ESL, honors, independent study, study abroad. License preparation in nursing. **Credit/placement by examination:** AP, CLEP. 30 credit hours maximum toward associate degree. **Support services:** Learning center, remedial instruction, tutoring.

Majors. Biology: Botany, zoology. **Business:** General, management information systems, office management, office/clerical. **Computer sciences:** General, data processing. **Conservation:** Forestry. **Engineering:** General. **Engineering technology:** Drafting. **Foreign languages:** French, German, Japanese, Spanish. **Health:** Dental assistant, licensed practical nurse, medical assistant. **Interdisciplinary:** Biological/physical sciences. **Liberal arts:** Arts/sciences, library assistant, library science. **Math:** General. **Mechanic/repair:** Automotive, diesel, electronics/electrical, heating/ac/refrig. **Parks/recreation:** Health/fitness. **Personal/culinary services:** Cosmetic. **Physical sciences:** Chemistry, physics. **Protective services:** Criminal justice, law enforcement admin. **Psychology:** General. **Social sciences:** General. **Visual/performing arts:** Art, photography, studio arts.

Most popular majors. Business/marketing 17%, English 6%, interdisciplinary studies 15%, liberal arts 13%, social sciences 33%, visual/performing arts 9%.

Computing on campus. 1,100 workstations in library, computer center. Online course registration available.

Student life. Freshman orientation: Available. **Activities:** Jazz band, dance, drama, literary magazine, music ensembles, musical theater, student government, student newspaper, African American Student Alliance, European Heritage Club, Get Real Christian Fellowship, International Students Club, Latinos Unidos Student Association, Latter Day Saints Students Association, Natives of the Americas Student Association, Students United for Societal Change.

Athletics. Intercollegiate: Baseball M, basketball, cross-country, football (tackle) M, golf, soccer, softball W, swimming, tennis, track and field, volleyball W, water polo. **Team name:** Owls.

Student services. Career counseling, services for economically disadvantaged, student employment services, financial aid counseling, health services, legal services, minority student services, on-campus daycare, personal counseling, placement for graduates, veterans' counselor. **Physically disabled:** Services for visually, speech, hearing impaired.

Contact. E-mail: admissions@citruscollege.edu
Phone: (626) 914-8511 Fax: (626) 914-8613
Lois Papner, Dean of Admissions, Citrus College, 1000 West Foothill Boulevard, Glendora, CA 91741-1899

City College of San Francisco

San Francisco, California — **CB member**
www.ccsf.edu — **CB code: 4052**

- Public 2-year community college
- Commuter campus in very large city

General. Founded in 1935. Regionally accredited. **Enrollment:** 18,393 degree-seeking undergraduates. **Degrees:** 1,192 associate awarded. **ROTC:** Army. **Location:** Downtown. **Calendar:** Semester, extensive summer session. **Full-time faculty:** 741 total; 39% minority. **Part-time faculty:** 1,184 total; 34% minority. **Special facilities:** Observatory.

Student profile.

Out-of-state:	3%	**25 or older:**	65%

Transfer out. Colleges most students transferred to 2008: San Francisco State University, CSU: East Bay, San Jose State University, UC: Berkeley, UC: Davis.

Basis for selection. Open admission, but selective for some programs. If applicant lacks high school diploma or equivalent, must be 18 or older and demonstrate ability to benefit. Program for registered nursing and a few other programs have a competitive/ special admissions process. All students entering the credit program are tested for placement into English or ESL and mathematics courses. **Adult students:** SAT/ACT scores not required. Credit programs require placement tests in English or ESL and mathematics. Free noncredit classes require placement tests depending on intended course of study.

2008-2009 Annual costs. Tuition/fees: $632; $6,002 out-of-state. Per-credit charge: $20 in-state; $199 out-of-state. Books/supplies: $1,566. Personal expenses: $2,664.

Financial aid. Need-based: Work-study available nights, weekends and for part-time students. **Additional information:** Board of Governor fee waiver for low income students.

Application procedures. Admission: No deadline. No application fee. Admission notification on a rolling basis. **Financial aid:** Priority date 3/1; no closing date. FAFSA required. Applicants notified on a rolling basis starting 7/1.

Academics. Free, noncredit classes offered in some subjects. Working Adults Degree Program. Bookloan program for low-income students. Intercollegiate Speech and Debate. Learning assistance, diversity, and student success programs. **Special study options:** Accelerated study, distance learning, dual enrollment of high school students, ESL, honors, independent study, internships, liberal arts/career combination, study abroad, weekend college. Credit is available for service-learning. License preparation in dental hygiene, nursing, paramedic, radiology. **Credit/placement by examination:** AP, CLEP, institutional tests. 45 credit hours maximum toward associate degree. Various limitations and stipulations on credit by examination. **Support services:** GED preparation and test center, learning center, pre-admission summer program, remedial instruction, study skills assistance, tutoring, writing center.

Majors. Agriculture: Floriculture, landscaping, nursery operations, ornamental horticulture. **Architecture:** Environmental design, interior. **Biology:** General. **Business:** Accounting, administrative services, business admin, fashion, hospitality/recreation, human resources, management information systems, marketing, office technology, office/clerical, operations, real estate, tourism promotion, tourism/travel. **Communications:** Journalism. **Communications technology:** General, graphic/printing. **Computer sciences:** General, computer science. **Construction:** Site management. **Education:** Teacher assistance. **Engineering:** General, mechanical. **Engineering technology:** General, mechanical. **Family/consumer sciences:** Child development. **Health:** Clinical lab science, dental assistant, EMT paramedic, medical assistant, medical radiologic technology/radiation therapy, medical records admin, medical records technology, medical secretary, nursing (RN), office admin, office assistant, physician assistant, ward clerk. **Legal studies:** Legal secretary, paralegal. **Liberal arts:** Library science. **Mechanic/repair:** Aircraft. **Personal/culinary services:** Chef training, restaurant/catering. **Physical sciences:** Chemistry. **Protective services:** Fire safety technology, police science. **Transportation:** Aviation. **Visual/performing arts:** Cinematography, graphic design, interior design, photography, printmaking.

Computing on campus. 750 workstations in library, computer center, student center. Commuter students can connect to campus network. Online course registration, online library, helpline, wireless network available.

Student life. Freshman orientation: Mandatory. **Activities:** Jazz band, choral groups, dance, drama, film society, literary magazine, music ensembles, musical theater, opera, radio station, student government, student newspaper, symphony orchestra, TV station, City College Press Club; Cartoon Illustration and Art; La Raza Unida; Chinese Culture Club; Christian Fellowship Club; Le Cercle Francais; African American Changing Times; LBGTstr8 Alliance; Students Linking Education and Activism; Women of Color Organization.

Athletics. NJCAA. **Intercollegiate:** Badminton W, baseball M, basketball, cheerleading, cross-country, football (tackle) M, judo W, soccer, softball W, tennis, track and field, volleyball W. **Intramural:** Archery, badminton, baseball, basketball, cheerleading, fencing, football (non-tackle), golf, gymnastics, judo, racquetball, soccer, swimming, tennis, volleyball, weight lifting. **Team name:** Rams.

Student services. Adult student services, alcohol/substance abuse counseling, career counseling, services for economically disadvantaged, student employment services, financial aid counseling, health services, minority student services, on-campus daycare, personal counseling, placement for graduates, veterans' counselor, women's services. **Physically disabled:** Services for visually, speech, hearing impaired. **Transfer:** Transfer adviser, college fairs on campus for students transferring to 4-year colleges.

Contact. E-mail: admits@ccsf.edu
Phone: (415) 239-3285 Fax: (415) 239-3936
MaryLou Leyba-Frank, Dean of Admissions and Records, City College of San Francisco, Office of Admissions and Records E-107, San Francisco, CA 94112

Coastline Community College

Fountain Valley, California
www.coastline.edu
CB member
CB code: 0933

- Public 2-year community college
- Commuter campus in small city

General. Founded in 1976. Regionally accredited. Classes held at community-based sites during the daytime, evenings, weekends, and through extensive distance learning education. **Enrollment:** 5,520 degree-seeking undergraduates. **Degrees:** 1,769 associate awarded. **Location:** 30 miles from Los Angeles. **Calendar:** Semester, limited summer session. **Full-time faculty:** 45 total. **Part-time faculty:** 295 total. **Class size:** 45% < 20, 40% 20-39, 6% 40-49, 6% 50-99, 2% >100. **Special facilities:** Workplace preparation center.

Student profile.

Out-of-state:	1%	**25 or older:**	73%

Transfer out. Colleges most students transferred to 2008: California State University: Long Beach, University of California: Irvine, California State University: Fullerton, National University.

Basis for selection. Open admission. If submitted, SAT/ACT used for placement and counseling, in lieu of college administered English and math tests.

2008-2009 Annual costs. Tuition/fees: $658; $6,088 out-of-state. Per-credit charge: $20 in-state; $201 out-of-state. Books/supplies: $1,566. Personal expenses: $3,024.

2007-2008 Financial aid. All financial aid based on need. Need-based aid available for part-time students. **Additional information:** Board of Governor's Grant: statewide fee waiver program for students or dependents receiving HFOL/TANF, SSI, General Relief, or whose income meets set standards or who are considered eligible through Federal needs analysis.

Application procedures. Admission: No deadline. No application fee. Admission notification on a rolling basis. **Financial aid:** Priority date 3/2; no closing date. FAFSA, institutional form required. Applicants notified on a rolling basis starting 8/1; must reply within 2 week(s) of notification.

Academics. Special study options: Accelerated study, cooperative education, distance learning, dual enrollment of high school students, ESL, independent study, liberal arts/career combination, study abroad, weekend college. Midnight college via telecourse delivery. License preparation in physical therapy, real estate. **Credit/placement by examination:** AP, CLEP. 30 credit hours maximum toward associate degree. **Support services:** GED preparation, reduced course load, remedial instruction, tutoring.

Majors. Business: General, accounting, business admin, entrepreneurial studies, management science, office technology, real estate. **Computer sciences:** General. **Liberal arts:** Arts/sciences. **Mechanic/repair:** Electronics/electrical.

Computing on campus. 100 workstations in computer center.

Student life. Freshman orientation: Available. Preregistration for classes offered. **Activities:** Choral groups, dance, student government.

Student services. Career counseling, services for economically disadvantaged, student employment services, financial aid counseling, health services, personal counseling, veterans' counselor. **Physically disabled:** Services for hearing impaired. **Transfer:** Transfer center, transfer adviser, college fairs on campus for students transferring to 4-year colleges.

Contact. E-mail: jmcdonald@cccd.edu
Phone: (714) 241-6176 Fax: (714) 241-6288
Jennifer McDonald, Director of Admissions and Records, Coastline Community College, 11460 Warner Avenue, Fountain Valley, CA 92708

Coleman College: San Marcos

San Marcos, California
www.coleman.edu

- For-profit 2-year technical college
- Commuter campus in small city

General. Accredited by ACICS. Branch campus of Coleman College, La Mesa. **Enrollment:** 50 degree-seeking undergraduates. **Degrees:** 39 associate awarded. **Calendar:** Continuous. **Full-time faculty:** 6 total. **Part-time faculty:** 12 total.

Student profile. Among degree-seeking undergraduates, 81 enrolled as first-time, first-year students.

2008-2009 Annual costs. Per-credit charge: $290. Tuition $31,320 for 13-month associate degree program; costs vary by program.

Academics. Credit/placement by examination: CLEP.

Majors. Biology: Bioinformatics. **Computer sciences:** Programming. **Visual/performing arts:** Graphic design.

Contact. Phone: (760) 747-3990
Coleman College: San Marcos, 1284 West San Marcos Boulevard, Suite 110, San Marcos, CA 92069

College of Alameda

Alameda, California
alameda.peralta.edu
CB code: 4118

- Public 2-year community college
- Commuter campus in small city

General. Founded in 1970. Regionally accredited. **Enrollment:** 2,703 degree-seeking undergraduates. **Degrees:** 260 associate awarded. **Calendar:** Semester, limited summer session. **Full-time faculty:** 80 total; 15% have terminal degrees, 38% minority, 35% women. **Part-time faculty:** 120 total.

Student profile.

Out-of-state:	2%	**Hispanic American:**	12%
African American:	32%	**Native American:**	1%
Asian American:	32%	**25 or older:**	44%

Basis for selection. Open admission.

High school preparation. College-preparatory program recommended.

2008-2009 Annual costs. Tuition/fees: $604; $6,034 out-of-state. Per-credit charge: $20 in-state; $201 out-of-state. Books/supplies: $1,566. Personal expenses: $3,024.

2007-2008 Financial aid. Need-based: 94% of total undergraduate aid awarded as scholarships/grants, 6% as loans/jobs.

Application procedures. Admission: No deadline. No application fee. Admission notification on a rolling basis. **Financial aid:** Priority date 3/2; no closing date. FAFSA required. Applicants notified on a rolling basis starting 7/1; must reply within 2 week(s) of notification.

Academics. Special study options: Cooperative education, cross-registration, dual enrollment of high school students, honors, independent study, liberal arts/career combination. License preparation in aviation. **Credit/placement by examination:** CLEP, institutional tests. **Support services:** Learning center, remedial instruction, tutoring.

Majors. Area/ethnic studies: African-American. **Biology:** General. **Business:** General, accounting, administrative services, business admin, entrepreneurial studies, fashion, marketing, office/clerical. **Education:** Teacher assistance. **Foreign languages:** Spanish. **Health:** Dental assistant, health aide. **History:** General. **Liberal arts:** Arts/sciences. **Math:** General. **Mechanic/repair:** Aircraft. **Philosophy/religion:** Philosophy. **Psychology:** General. **Social sciences:** General, anthropology, economics, geography, political science, sociology, urban studies. **Transportation:** Aviation management. **Visual/performing arts:** General, studio arts.

Computing on campus. Online course registration available.

Student life. Freshman orientation: Available. **Activities:** Jazz band, choral groups, dance, drama, student government, student newspaper.

Athletics. Intercollegiate: Basketball, bowling, cross-country M, fencing, golf, soccer M, tennis, track and field, volleyball. **Intramural:** Golf, sailing, softball W. **Team name:** COUGARS.

Student services. Adult student services, career counseling, services for economically disadvantaged, student employment services, health services, on-campus daycare, personal counseling, placement for graduates, veterans' counselor. **Physically disabled:** Services for visually, speech, hearing impaired. **Transfer:** Transfer adviser, college fairs on campus for students transferring to 4-year colleges.

Contact. E-mail: admissions@peralta.edu
Phone: (510) 748-2228 Fax: (510) 748-5227
Kelly Compton, Vice President of Student Services, College of Alameda, 555 Ralph Appezzato Memorial Parkway, Alameda, CA 94501

College of Marin: Kentfield
Kentfield, California
www.marin.edu **CB code: 4061**

- Public 2-year community college
- Commuter campus in small town

General. Founded in 1926. Regionally accredited. Additional campus at Indian Valley - Novato, CA. **Enrollment:** 2,768 degree-seeking undergraduates. **Degrees:** 276 associate awarded. **Location:** 15 miles from San Francisco. **Calendar:** Semester. **Full-time faculty:** 135 total. **Part-time faculty:** 160 total.

Transfer out. Colleges most students transferred to 2008: University of California: Berkeley, San Francisco State, University of California: Davis.

Basis for selection. Open admission. Limited admissions to nursing programs. **Adult students:** SAT/ACT scores not required.

2008-2009 Annual costs. Tuition/fees: $636; $6,126 out-of-state. Per-credit charge: $20 in-state; $203 out-of-state. Books/supplies: $1,566. Personal expenses: $3,024.

Financial aid. Need-based: Need-based aid available for part-time students.

Application procedures. Admission: No deadline. No application fee. Admission notification on a rolling basis. **Financial aid:** Priority date 3/1; no closing date. FAFSA required. Applicants notified on a rolling basis starting 5/15.

Academics. Special study options: Distance learning, ESL. **Credit/placement by examination:** CLEP, institutional tests. **Support services:** Remedial instruction, study skills assistance, tutoring, writing center.

Majors. Agriculture: Landscaping, nursery operations. **Architecture:** Environmental design. **Biology:** General, environmental. **Business:** General, accounting, real estate. **Communications:** General, broadcast journalism, public relations. **Computer sciences:** General, programming, systems analysis. **Foreign languages:** General, French, Spanish. **History:** General. **Legal studies:** Court reporting. **Liberal arts:** Arts/sciences. **Math:** General. **Mechanic/repair:** Auto body. **Physical sciences:** General, chemistry, physics. **Psychology:** General. **Visual/performing arts:** Studio arts.

Student life. Activities: Student government, student newspaper.

Athletics. Intercollegiate: Baseball M, basketball, cross-country, diving, football (tackle) M, soccer, softball, squash, tennis, track and field. **Intramural:** Cross-country, softball, swimming.

Student services. Transfer: Transfer center, transfer adviser, college fairs on campus for students transferring to 4-year colleges.

Contact. Phone: (415) 485-9412
Robert Balestreri, Dean of Enrollment Services, College of Marin: Kentfield, 835 College Avenue, Kentfield, CA 94904

College of San Mateo
San Mateo, California
www.collegeofsanmateo.edu **CB code: 4070**

- Public 2-year community college
- Commuter campus in small city

General. Founded in 1922. Regionally accredited. **Enrollment:** 5,598 degree-seeking undergraduates. **Degrees:** 415 associate awarded. **ROTC:** Army, Air Force. **Location:** 15 miles from San Francisco. **Calendar:** Semester, limited summer session. **Full-time faculty:** 350 total. **Part-time faculty:** 200 total. **Special facilities:** Planetarium.

Student profile.

Out-of-state:	2%	**25 or older:**	51%

Basis for selection. Open admission, but selective for some programs. Nursing program has separate requirements.

2008-2009 Annual costs. Tuition/fees: $628; $6,358 out-of-state. Per-credit charge: $20 in-state; $211 out-of-state. Books/supplies: $1,566. Personal expenses: $2,376.

2007-2008 Financial aid. Need-based: 87% of total undergraduate aid awarded as scholarships/grants, 13% as loans/jobs.

Application procedures. Admission: No deadline. No application fee. Admission notification on a rolling basis. Completion of CSM Placement tests for English, reading and mathematics recommmended prior to counseling session. **Financial aid:** Priority date 3/2; no closing date. FAFSA, institutional form required. Applicants notified on a rolling basis starting 6/15.

Academics. Special study options: Cooperative education, cross-registration, distance learning, double major, dual enrollment of high school students, ESL, honors, independent study, liberal arts/career combination, study abroad, weekend college. License preparation in dental hygiene, nursing, real estate. **Credit/placement by examination:** AP, CLEP, IB, institutional tests. 12 credit hours maximum toward associate degree. **Support services:** Learning center, reduced course load, remedial instruction, study skills assistance, tutoring, writing center.

Majors. Agriculture: Horticulture, ornamental horticulture. **Biology:** General, biomedical sciences. **Business:** General, accounting, entrepreneurial studies, fashion, logistics, management information systems, office/clerical, real estate. **Communications:** Advertising, broadcast journalism. **Communications technology:** General. **Computer sciences:** General, web page design. **Construction:** Pipefitting. **Engineering:** General. **Engineering technology:** Drafting, electrical. **Foreign languages:** French, German, Spanish. **Health:** Dental assistant, medical assistant, nursing (RN), substance abuse counseling. **Legal studies:** Legal secretary. **Liberal arts:** Arts/sciences. **Math:** General. **Mechanic/repair:** Aircraft, heating/ac/refrig. **Personal/culinary services:** General. **Physical sciences:** Chemistry, geology, physics. **Protective services:** Fire safety technology. **Social sciences:** General. **Transportation:** Airline/commercial pilot, aviation. **Visual/performing arts:** Cinematography, commercial/advertising art, painting, photography, studio arts.

Computing on campus. 150 workstations in library, computer center, student center. Online course registration, wireless network available.

Student life. Freshman orientation: Available. **Activities:** Bands, choral groups, dance, literary magazine, radio station, student government, student newspaper, symphony orchestra, TV station, Asian student union, Christian Fellowship, ethnic studies society, international students union, Latin American student organization, Arts in Recovery, Ballet Folklorico de CSM, Earth Preservation Committee, Peace Action, Unity Among Brothers.

Athletics. NCAA. **Intercollegiate:** Baseball M, basketball W, cross-country, football (tackle) M, softball W, swimming, tennis W, track and field, water polo. **Team name:** Bulldogs.

Student services. Adult student services, alcohol/substance abuse counseling, career counseling, services for economically disadvantaged, student employment services, financial aid counseling, health services, minority student services, on-campus daycare, personal counseling, veterans' counselor. **Physically disabled:** Services for visually, speech, hearing impaired. **Learning disabled:** Comprehensive services available. **Transfer:** Pre-admission transcript evaluation for new students. Transfer center, transfer adviser, college fairs on campus for students transferring to 4-year colleges.

Contact. E-mail: villarealh@smccd.net
Phone: (650) 574-6165 Fax: (650) 574-6506
Henry Villareal, Dean of Admissions and Records, College of San Mateo, 1700 West Hillsdale Boulevard, San Mateo, CA 94402-3784

College of the Canyons
Santa Clarita, California
www.canyons.edu **CB code: 4117**

- Public 2-year community college
- Commuter campus in large city

General. Founded in 1967. Regionally accredited. **Enrollment:** 8,572 degree-seeking undergraduates. **Degrees:** 933 associate awarded. **Location:** 15 miles from Los Angeles. **Calendar:** Semester, extensive summer session. **Full-time faculty:** 196 total. **Part-time faculty:** 476 total. **Class size:** 31% < 20, 60% 20-39, 7% 40-49, 1% 50-99, less than 1% >100. **Special facilities:** Performing arts center, proscenium performing arts stage, experimental "black box" theater, university center for access to upper-division and graduate programs.

Student profile. Among degree-seeking undergraduates, 50% enrolled in a transfer program, 7% enrolled in a vocational program, 12% already have a bachelor's degree or higher, 4,674 enrolled as first-time, first-year students, 878 transferred in from other institutions.

Out-of-state:	2%	**Native American:**	1%
African American:	5%	**International:**	1%
Asian American:	10%	**25 or older:**	31%
Hispanic American:	25%		

Transfer out. **Colleges most students transferred to 2008:** California State University: Northridge, University of California: Los Angeles, San Diego State University, California State University: Long Beach, University of California: Santa Barbara.

Basis for selection. Open admission, but selective for some programs. Limited admission to nursing program. **Homeschooled:** Transcript of courses and grades required. Per state guidelines, students must be associated with program approved through Los Angeles County, or must be taught by person holding California teaching credential, or must hold a current private school affidavit filed with the State Superintendent of Public Instruction.

2008-2009 Annual costs. Tuition/fees: $612; $5,262 out-of-state. Per-credit charge: $20 in-state; $175 out-of-state. Books/supplies: $1,638. Personal expenses: $3,096.

2007-2008 Financial aid. **Need-based:** 69% of total undergraduate aid awarded as scholarships/grants, 31% as loans/jobs. Need-based aid available for part-time students. Work-study available nights, weekends and for part-time students. **Non-need-based:** Scholarships awarded for academics, alumni affiliation, art, leadership, minority status, music/drama, state residency.

Application procedures. **Admission:** No deadline. No application fee. Admission notification on a rolling basis. **Financial aid:** Closing date 3/2. FAFSA required. Applicants notified on a rolling basis starting 6/1; must reply within 4 week(s) of notification.

Academics. **Special study options:** Accelerated study, cooperative education, distance learning, dual enrollment of high school students, ESL, honors, independent study, internships, liberal arts/career combination, study abroad, weekend college. Bachelor's degree programs available on campus. License preparation in nursing, real estate. **Credit/placement by examination:** AP, CLEP, institutional tests. 18 credit hours maximum toward associate degree. Applicants must take institutional English, ESL, chemistry, and mathematics placement tests. **Support services:** GED preparation, learning center, remedial instruction, study skills assistance, tutoring.

Majors. **Agriculture:** Landscaping. **Business:** Accounting, administrative services, business admin, hotel/motel admin, real estate, sales/distribution, small business admin. **Communications:** Digital media, journalism, radio/tv. **Communications technology:** Animation/special effects. **Computer sciences:** Computer science, networking. **Construction:** Site management. **Engineering:** General. **Engineering technology:** Architectural drafting, manufacturing, surveying, water quality. **Family/consumer sciences:** Child development. **Foreign languages:** French, sign language interpretation, Spanish. **Health:** Nursing (RN). **Interdisciplinary:** Biological/physical sciences. **Legal studies:** Paralegal. **Liberal arts:** Arts/sciences, humanities, library assistant. **Math:** General. **Mechanic/repair:** Automotive. **Parks/recreation:** General, health/fitness. **Personal/culinary services:** Restaurant/catering. **Production:** Welding. **Protective services:** Firefighting, police science. **Psychology:** General. **Social sciences:** General. **Visual/performing arts:** Art, cinematography, dramatic, graphic design, interior design, multimedia, photography. **Other:** Mathematics & sciences, Music: performance/concert.

Most popular majors. Business/marketing 11%, health sciences 10%, liberal arts 47%, security/protective services 6%, social sciences 6%.

Computing on campus. 1,698 workstations in library, computer center, student center. Online course registration, online library, helpline, wireless network available.

Student life. **Freshman orientation:** Mandatory. **Activities:** Jazz band, choral groups, dance, drama, music ensembles, Model UN, musical theater, student government, student newspaper, symphony orchestra, TV station, Bible Talk, Grace on Campus, Persian club, speech & debate society, Club MESA, political science club, students for sustainability, future educators club.

Athletics. **Intercollegiate:** Baseball M, basketball, cross-country, football (tackle) M, golf, soccer, softball W, swimming, track and field, volleyball W. **Team name:** Cougars.

Student services. Adult student services, career counseling, services for economically disadvantaged, student employment services, financial aid counseling, health services, on-campus daycare, personal counseling, placement for graduates, veterans' counselor. **Physically disabled:** Services for visually, speech, hearing impaired. **Learning disabled:** Comprehensive services available. **Transfer:** Re-entry adviser, pre-admission transcript evaluation for new students. Transfer center, transfer adviser, college fairs on campus for students transferring to 4-year colleges.

Contact. E-mail: jasmine.ruys@canyons.edu
Phone: (661) 362-3280 Fax: (661) 259-8302
Jasmine Ruys, Director, Admissions, Records and Online Services, College of the Canyons, 26455 Rockwell Canyon Road, Santa Clarita, CA 91355

College of the Desert

Palm Desert, California — **CB member**
www.collegeofthedesert.edu — **CB code: 4085**

- Public 2-year community college
- Commuter campus in small city

General. Founded in 1958. Regionally accredited. **Enrollment:** 5,426 degree-seeking undergraduates. **Degrees:** 540 associate awarded. **Location:** 20 miles from Palm Springs, 120 miles from Los Angeles. **Calendar:** Semester, limited summer session. **Full-time faculty:** 106 total; 23% have terminal degrees, 17% minority, 47% women. **Part-time faculty:** 307 total; 16% have terminal degrees, 22% minority, 47% women. **Special facilities:** Performing arts center, golf institute, public safety academy.

Student profile. Among degree-seeking undergraduates, 541 enrolled as first-time, first-year students.

Out-of-state:	3%	**Native American:**	1%
African American:	4%	**International:**	4%
Asian American:	5%	**25 or older:**	40%
Hispanic American:	51%		

Basis for selection. Open admission, but selective for some programs. Separate application requirements for nursing and golf management and public safety academy. Interviews required for nursing/allied health majors. **Adult students:** SAT/ACT scores not required. **Learning Disabled:** Participation is voluntary. Interested students must meet with the appropriate Disabled Students Programs and Services counselor to apply for these programs.

2008-2009 Annual costs. Tuition/fees: $630; $5,730 out-of-state. Per-credit charge: $20 in-state; $190 out-of-state. Books/supplies: $1,566. Personal expenses: $3,024.

2007-2008 Financial aid. All financial aid based on need. 92% of total undergraduate aid awarded as scholarships/grants, 8% as loans/jobs. Need-based aid available for part-time students. Work-study available weekends and for part-time students.

Application procedures. **Admission:** Priority date 4/28; deadline 9/7 (receipt date). No application fee. Application must be submitted online. Admission notification on a rolling basis. **Financial aid:** Priority date 3/2; no closing date. FAFSA required. Applicants notified on a rolling basis starting 7/1.

Academics. **Special study options:** Cooperative education, distance learning, double major, dual enrollment of high school students, ESL, honors, independent study, liberal arts/career combination. License preparation in nursing. **Credit/placement by examination:** CLEP, institutional tests. **Support services:** GED preparation and test center, learning center, remedial instruction, study skills assistance, tutoring, writing center.

Majors. **Agriculture:** Business, ornamental horticulture, plant sciences, turf management. **Architecture:** Technology. **Biology:** General. **Business:** Business admin, construction management, hotel/motel admin, managerial economics, office management, restaurant/food services. **Communications:** General, journalism, media studies, organizational. **Computer sciences:** General, computer science. **Conservation:** General, environmental science, environmental studies. **Engineering technology:** Architectural, architectural drafting, drafting, heat/ac/refrig. **Family/consumer sciences:** Child care, food/nutrition, human nutrition. **Foreign languages:** French, German, Italian, Spanish. **Health:** Dietetic technician, licensed practical nurse, nursing (RN). **History:** General. **Interdisciplinary:** Biological/physical sciences. **Liberal arts:** Arts/sciences. **Math:** General. **Mechanic/repair:** Heating/ac/refrig. **Parks/recreation:** General, facilities management. **Personal/culinary services:** Restaurant/catering. **Philosophy/religion:** Philosophy. **Physical sciences:** Chemistry, geology, physics. **Protective services:** Fire safety technology, law enforcement admin. **Psychology:** General. **Social sciences:** General, anthropology, economics, geography, political science, sociology. **Visual/performing arts:** Acting, art, art history/conservation, dance, dramatic, drawing, graphic design, painting, photography, printmaking, studio arts, theater history.

Most popular majors. Business/marketing 55%, computer/information sciences 8%, English 11%, family/consumer sciences 10%, health sciences 97%, psychology 13%, security/protective services 17%, social sciences 18%, visual/performing arts 13%.

Computing on campus. 125 workstations in library, computer center, student center. Online course registration, online library, wireless network available.

Student life. **Freshman orientation:** Mandatory. **Activities:** Choral groups, dance, drama, international student organizations, music ensembles, musical theater, opera, student government, student newspaper.

Athletics. **Intercollegiate:** Baseball M, basketball, cheerleading, cross-country, fencing, football (tackle) M, golf, soccer M, softball W, tennis, volleyball W. **Team name:** Roadrunners.

Student services. Adult student services, career counseling, services for economically disadvantaged, student employment services, financial aid counseling, health services, minority student services, on-campus daycare, personal counseling, placement for graduates, veterans' counselor. **Physically disabled:** Services for visually, speech, hearing impaired. **Learning disabled:** Comprehensive services available. **Transfer:** Re-entry adviser, pre-admission transcript evaluation for new students. Transfer center, transfer adviser, college fairs on campus for students transferring to 4-year colleges.

Contact. Phone: (760) 773-2516 Fax: (760) 862-1379
John Loera, Dean of Enrollment Services, College of the Desert, 43-500 Monterey Avenue, Palm Desert, CA 92260

College of the Redwoods
Eureka, California
www.redwoods.edu **CB code: 4100**

- Public 2-year community college
- Commuter campus in large town

General. Founded in 1964. Regionally accredited. Centers at Fort Bragg and Crescent City; instructional sites in Hoopa, Klamath, downtown Eureka, and Arcata. **Enrollment:** 4,410 degree-seeking undergraduates. **Degrees:** 367 associate awarded. **Location:** 275 miles from San Francisco. **Calendar:** Semester, limited summer session. **Full-time faculty:** 95 total. **Part-time faculty:** 310 total. **Class size:** 19% < 20, 64% 20-39, 12% 40-49, 5% 50-99. **Special facilities:** Observatories, fish hatchery, working organic farm.

Student profile.

Out-of-state:	4%	**Live on campus:**	1%
25 or older:	43%		

Transfer out. **Colleges most students transferred to 2008:** Humboldt State University, California State University: Chico.

Basis for selection. Open admission, but selective for some programs. Admission for nursing applicants based on school record and test scores. **Homeschooled:** Must submit a copy of affidavit filed with County Office of Education.

2008-2009 Annual costs. Tuition/fees: $624; $7,794 out-of-state. Per-credit charge: $20 in-state; $259 out-of-state. Room/board: $6,284. Books/supplies: $1,566. Personal expenses: $1,476.

2008-2009 Financial aid. **Need-based:** Need-based aid available for part-time students. Work-study available for part-time students.

Application procedures. **Admission:** Priority date 8/14; no deadline. No application fee. Admission notification on a rolling basis. **Financial aid:** Priority date 4/15; no closing date. FAFSA, institutional form required. Applicants notified on a rolling basis starting 5/1; must reply within 6 week(s) of notification.

Academics. **Special study options:** Cooperative education, cross-registration, distance learning, double major, dual enrollment of high school students, ESL, honors, independent study, teacher certification program. License preparation in nursing. **Credit/placement by examination:** CLEP, institutional tests. **Support services:** GED preparation and test center, learning center, pre-admission summer program, remedial instruction, tutoring, writing center.

Majors. **Agriculture:** Agribusiness operations, animal sciences, plant sciences. **Business:** General, administrative services, hospitality admin, managerial economics, office technology, real estate. **Communications:** Journalism. **Computer sciences:** General. **Conservation:** Fisheries, forestry. **Construction:** Maintenance. **Education:** Early childhood. **Engineering:** Electrical. **Engineering technology:** Construction, drafting. **Legal studies:** Legal secretary, paralegal. **Liberal arts:** Arts/sciences. **Physical sciences:** Planetary. **Protective services:** Law enforcement admin. **Visual/performing arts:** Commercial/advertising art.

Most popular majors. Health sciences 14%, liberal arts 65%.

Computing on campus. 578 workstations in dormitories, library, computer center, student center. Dormitories wired for high-speed internet access. Online course registration, online library available.

Student life. **Freshman orientation:** Available. Preregistration for classes offered. **Housing:** Coed dorms available. Limited housing also available for police academy students. **Activities:** Jazz band, choral groups, dance, student government, student newspaper, Native American club, international students club, apologetics club, Bible study, Latter-day Saints club, veterans club, EOPS club.

Athletics. **Intercollegiate:** Baseball M, basketball, cross-country, football (tackle) M, golf M, soccer W, track and field, volleyball W. **Intramural:** Badminton, bowling, diving, golf, gymnastics, soccer, volleyball, water polo. **Team name:** Corsairs.

Student services. Career counseling, services for economically disadvantaged, student employment services, financial aid counseling, health services, on-campus daycare, personal counseling, placement for graduates, veterans' counselor. **Physically disabled:** Services for visually, speech, hearing impaired. **Transfer:** Transfer center, transfer adviser, college fairs on campus for students transferring to 4-year colleges.

Contact. E-mail: admissions@redwoods.edu
Phone: (707) 476-4200 Toll-free number: (800) 641-0400
Fax: (707) 476-4406
Kathy Goodlive, Manager, Admissions and Records, College of the Redwoods, 7351 Tompkins Hill Road, Eureka, CA 95501-9300

College of the Sequoias
Visalia, California
www.cos.edu **CB code: 4071**

- Public 2-year agricultural and community college
- Commuter campus in small city

General. Founded in 1925. Regionally accredited. Affiliated with University of California at Davis School of Veterinary Medicine in Tulare. **Enrollment:** 8,216 degree-seeking undergraduates. **Degrees:** 777 associate awarded. **ROTC:** Air Force. **Location:** 45 miles from Fresno. **Calendar:** Semester, limited summer session. **Full-time faculty:** 176 total. **Part-time faculty:** 278 total. **Special facilities:** Self-sufficient farm.

Student profile.

Out-of-state:	3%	**25 or older:**	39%

Transfer out. **Colleges most students transferred to 2008:** California State University: Fresno, California State University: Bakersfield, California Polytechnic State University: San Luis Obispo, California State University: Long Beach, California State University: Davis.

Basis for selection. Open admission, but selective for some programs. Limited admission to nursing program. Interviews required for work program, nursing majors. Auditions required for music majors.

High school preparation. College-preparatory program recommended.

2008-2009 Annual costs. Tuition/fees: $642; $6,192 out-of-state. Per-credit charge: $20 in-state; $205 out-of-state. Books/supplies: $1,566. Personal expenses: $3,024.

Application procedures. **Admission:** No deadline. No application fee. Admission notification on a rolling basis. **Financial aid:** Priority date 3/2; no closing date. FAFSA, institutional form required. Applicants notified on a rolling basis starting 6/1; must reply within 2 week(s) of notification.

Academics. **Special study options:** Distance learning, dual enrollment of high school students, ESL, honors, independent study, internships, student-designed major, study abroad, weekend college. License preparation in nursing, paramedic, physical therapy. **Credit/placement by examination:** CLEP, institutional tests. 12 credit hours maximum toward associate degree. **Support services:** Learning center, pre-admission summer program, reduced course load, remedial instruction, study skills assistance, tutoring, writing center.

Majors. **Agriculture:** Agribusiness operations, landscaping, ornamental horticulture. **Business:** General, accounting, administrative services, management information systems, office/clerical, real estate, sales/distribution. **Communications:** General, journalism. **Computer sciences:** Computer science. **Construction:** Carpentry, maintenance. **Education:** Adult/continuing, physical. **Engineering:** General. **Engineering technology:** Architectural, construction, drafting, electrical, industrial, manufacturing. **Family/consumer sciences:** General, child care. **Foreign languages:** General, French. **Health:**

Nursing (RN). **Interdisciplinary:** Biological/physical sciences. **Legal studies:** Paralegal. **Liberal arts:** Arts/sciences. **Math:** General. **Mechanic/repair:** Electronics/electrical. **Parks/recreation:** Facilities management. **Personal/culinary services:** Cosmetic. **Protective services:** Fire safety technology, law enforcement admin. **Public administration:** Human services. **Social sciences:** General. **Visual/performing arts:** Art, commercial/advertising art, dramatic, multimedia, studio arts, theater design.

Computing on campus. 325 workstations in library, computer center. Online course registration, helpline, wireless network available.

Student life. Freshman orientation: Available. Both online and in person. In person classes are held just before the beginning of each semester. **Activities:** Bands, choral groups, dance, drama, music ensembles, musical theater, student government, student newspaper, symphony orchestra.

Athletics. Intercollegiate: Baseball M, basketball, cross-country, diving, football (tackle) M, golf, soccer W, softball W, swimming, tennis, track and field, volleyball W. **Team name:** Giants.

Student services. Adult student services, alcohol/substance abuse counseling, career counseling, services for economically disadvantaged, student employment services, financial aid counseling, health services, minority student services, personal counseling, placement for graduates, veterans' counselor. **Physically disabled:** Services for visually, speech, hearing impaired. **Learning disabled:** Comprehensive services available. **Transfer:** Transfer adviser, college fairs on campus for students transferring to 4-year colleges.

Contact. Phone: (559) 730-3727 Fax: (559) 730-3894
Don Mast, Dean of Student Services, College of the Sequoias, 915 South Mooney Boulevard, Visalia, CA 93277

College of the Siskiyous

Weed, California
www.siskiyous.edu **CB code: 4087**

- Public 2-year community and junior college
- Commuter campus in small town

General. Founded in 1957. Regionally accredited. **Enrollment:** 1,424 degree-seeking undergraduates. **Degrees:** 176 associate awarded. **Location:** 285 miles from San Francisco, 80 miles from Medford, Oregon. **Calendar:** Semester, limited summer session. **Full-time faculty:** 50 total; 16% have terminal degrees, 10% minority, 36% women. **Part-time faculty:** 150 total; 8% have terminal degrees, 10% minority, 36% women. **Class size:** 57% < 20, 35% 20-39, 3% 40-49, 4% 50-99, less than 1% >100. **Special facilities:** Fire science burn tower and flashover unit, welding lab, emergency services training center, distance learning center.

Student profile. Among degree-seeking undergraduates, 51% enrolled in a transfer program, 49% enrolled in a vocational program, 5% already have a bachelor's degree or higher, 232 transferred in from other institutions.

Out-of-state:	27%	**Live on campus:**	14%
25 or older:	39%		

Transfer out. 51% of students enrolled in the transfer program go on to 4-year colleges. **Colleges most students transferred to 2008:** California State University: Chico, Southern Oregon University, University of California: Davis, Simpson University, Humboldt State University.

Basis for selection. Open admission, but selective for some programs. **Adult students:** SAT/ACT scores not required. SAT/ACT scores not required if out of high school 1 year(s) or more.

2008-2009 Annual costs. Tuition/fees: $630; $6,330 out-of-state. Per-credit charge: $20 in-state; $210 out-of-state. Oregon residents with interstate exchange program: $42 per unit (no enrollment fee). Room/board: $7,550. Books/supplies: $1,350. Personal expenses: $2,000.

2007-2008 Financial aid. All financial aid based on need. Need-based aid available for part-time students. Work-study available nights, weekends and for part-time students.

Application procedures. Admission: No deadline. No application fee. **Financial aid:** Priority date 4/30; no closing date. FAFSA required. Applicants notified on a rolling basis starting 6/1; must reply within 2 week(s) of notification.

Academics. Special study options: Cooperative education, distance learning, dual enrollment of high school students, ESL, exchange student, independent study, internships, liberal arts/career combination, student-designed major, study abroad. Bachelor's degree programs available on campus. License preparation in nursing, paramedic. **Credit/placement by examination:** AP, CLEP, institutional tests. 48 credit hours maximum toward associate degree. **Support services:** GED preparation, learning center, preadmission summer program, reduced course load, remedial instruction, study skills assistance, tutoring, writing center.

Majors. Biology: General. **Business:** General, accounting, accounting technology, administrative services, business admin, management information systems, office management, office/clerical. **Communications:** General, broadcast journalism, digital media, media studies, radio/tv. **Communications technology:** General, graphics, radio/tv. **Computer sciences:** General, applications programming, computer science, programming. **Education:** General, early childhood, early childhood special. **Engineering:** General. **Family/consumer sciences:** Child care, child development, family studies, family/community services. **Foreign languages:** Spanish. **Health:** EMT paramedic, licensed practical nurse, nursing (RN), predental, premedicine, prenursing, prepharmacy, preveterinary, substance abuse counseling. **History:** General. **Interdisciplinary:** Accounting/computer science, behavioral sciences, biological/physical sciences, natural sciences. **Legal studies:** Prelaw. **Liberal arts:** Arts/sciences, humanities. **Math:** General. **Parks/recreation:** Health/fitness. **Philosophy/religion:** Philosophy. **Physical sciences:** General, chemistry, geology, physics. **Production:** Welding. **Protective services:** Criminal justice, fire safety technology, fire services admin, firefighting, law enforcement admin, police science. **Psychology:** General. **Public administration:** Human services. **Social sciences:** General, anthropology. **Visual/performing arts:** General, acting, art, directing/producing, dramatic, graphic design, music performance, studio arts, theater arts management, voice/opera. **Other:** Alcohol and drug studies.

Most popular majors. Liberal arts 89%, security/protective services 9%.

Computing on campus. 260 workstations in dormitories, library, computer center. Dormitories wired for high-speed internet access and linked to campus network. Commuter students can connect to campus network. Online course registration, online library, helpline, repair service, wireless network available.

Student life. Freshman orientation: Available. Preregistration for classes offered. Held three months prior to the start of the semester. **Housing:** Guaranteed on-campus for freshmen. Coed dorms, wellness housing available. $100 fully refundable deposit. **Activities:** Bands, choral groups, dance, drama, international student organizations, music ensembles, musical theater, student government, student newspaper, symphony orchestra, TV station, Latino Student Union, Black Student Union, Phi Theta Kappa honor society, intercultural club, American Indian Alliance, intervarsity club, speech club, chess club, disabled student aliance, speech and forensics club.

Athletics. Intercollegiate: Baseball M, basketball, cross-country, football (tackle) M, skiing, softball W, track and field, volleyball W. **Intramural:** Badminton, basketball, bowling, boxing, golf, skiing, softball, tennis, volleyball. **Team name:** Eagles.

Student services. Adult student services, alcohol/substance abuse counseling, career counseling, services for economically disadvantaged, student employment services, financial aid counseling, health services, legal services, on-campus daycare, personal counseling, veterans' counselor. **Physically disabled:** Services for visually, speech, hearing impaired. **Learning disabled:** Comprehensive services available. **Transfer:** Re-entry adviser, pre-admission transcript evaluation for new students. Transfer center, transfer adviser, college fairs on campus for students transferring to 4-year colleges.

Contact. E-mail: registration@siskiyous.edu
Phone: (530) 938-5555 Toll-free number: (888) 397-4339
Fax: (530) 938-5367
Teresa Winkelman, Director of Admissions & Records, College of the Siskiyous, 800 College Avenue, Weed, CA 96094-2899

Columbia College

Sonora, California
www.gocolumbia.edu **CB code: 4108**

- Public 2-year community college
- Commuter campus in small town

General. Founded in 1968. Regionally accredited. **Enrollment:** 1,806 degree-seeking undergraduates. **Degrees:** 177 associate awarded. **Location:** 150 miles from Sacramento. **Calendar:** Semester, limited summer session. **Full-time faculty:** 45 total. **Part-time faculty:** 80 total. **Special facilities:** Jogging/fitness trail, arboretum, astronomy dome, seismograph, on-campus fire house.

Basis for selection. Open admission. Institution uses own assessment test for placement only.

Two-Year Colleges

2008-2009 Annual costs. Tuition/fees: $646; $6,076 out-of-state. Per-credit charge: $20 in-state; $201 out-of-state. Books/supplies: $1,638. Personal expenses: $2,514.

2008-2009 Financial aid. **Need-based:** Need-based aid available for part-time students. **Non-need-based:** Scholarships awarded for academics.

Application procedures. **Admission:** No deadline. No application fee. Admission notification on a rolling basis. Matriculation procedures required before new or returning students may register. Early application assures accommodation to new student priority registration periods. **Financial aid:** Priority date 3/2; no closing date. FAFSA, institutional form required. Applicants notified on a rolling basis starting 6/15; must reply within 2 week(s) of notification.

Academics. **Special study options:** Cooperative education, distance learning, double major, ESL, independent study, internships, liberal arts/career combination. License preparation in paramedic. **Credit/placement by examination:** AP, CLEP, institutional tests. 12 credit hours maximum toward associate degree. **Support services:** GED preparation and test center, learning center, remedial instruction, study skills assistance, tutoring, writing center.

Majors. **Biology:** General. **Business:** General, administrative services, business admin, hospitality admin. **Computer sciences:** General, programming. **Conservation:** General, forest technology, forestry, management/policy. **Family/consumer sciences:** Child development. **Interdisciplinary:** Natural sciences. **Liberal arts:** Arts/sciences. **Math:** General. **Mechanic/repair:** Automotive. **Parks/recreation:** Health/fitness. **Personal/culinary services:** Culinary arts. **Physical sciences:** Chemistry, physics, planetary. **Protective services:** Fire safety technology. **Social sciences:** General. **Visual/performing arts:** Art, photography.

Computing on campus. 60 workstations in library, computer center, student center. Online course registration, online library, wireless network available.

Student life. **Freshman orientation:** Mandatory. 1-hour session prior to registration. **Housing:** Coed dorms, special housing for disabled, apartments available. **Activities:** Bands, choral groups, dance, drama, music ensembles, student government, student newspaper, symphony orchestra.

Athletics. **Intercollegiate:** Basketball M, volleyball W. **Team name:** Claim Jumpers.

Student services. Adult student services, alcohol/substance abuse counseling, career counseling, services for economically disadvantaged, student employment services, financial aid counseling, health services, on-campus daycare, personal counseling, placement for graduates, veterans' counselor. **Physically disabled:** Services for visually, speech, hearing impaired. **Transfer:** Re-entry adviser for new students. Transfer center, transfer adviser, college fairs on campus for students transferring to 4-year colleges.

Contact. Phone: (209) 588-5231 Fax: (209) 588-5337
Kathy Smith, Director of Admissions and Records, Columbia College, 11600 Columbia College Drive, Sonora, CA 95370

Concorde Career College: Garden Grove
Garden Grove, California
www.concorde.edu

- For-profit 2-year health science and technical college
- Small city

General. Regionally accredited; also accredited by ACCSCT. **Enrollment:** 150 degree-seeking undergraduates. **Degrees:** 79 associate awarded. **Calendar:** Continuous. **Full-time faculty:** 40 total.

Basis for selection. Open admission, but selective for some programs.

2008-2009 Annual costs. Advanced Respiratory Therapy $9,778; Medical Assistant $12,293; Dental Assistant $12,014; Insurance Coding and Billing Specialist $12,034; Vocational Nurse (weekday) $29,574; Vocational Nurse (weekend) $30,569; Respiratory Therapy (A.S.) $35,513.

Academics. **Credit/placement by examination:** CLEP.

Majors. **Health:** Respiratory therapy technology.

Contact. E-mail: agueco@concorde.edu
Phone: (714) 703-1900
Cary Kaplan, Director of Admissions, Concorde Career College: Garden Grove, 12951 Euclid Street, #101, Garden Grove, CA 92840

Concorde Career College: North Hollywood
North Hollywood, California
www.concorde.edu

- For-profit 2-year health science college
- Large city

General. Accredited by ACCSCT. **Enrollment:** 142 degree-seeking undergraduates. **Degrees:** 85 associate awarded. **Calendar:** Continuous. **Full-time faculty:** 35 total. **Part-time faculty:** 15 total.

Basis for selection. Institutional exam scores important. CPAT, Wonderlic used.

2008-2009 Annual costs. Tuition/fees: $19,410. Cost quoted representative annual cost; individual cost may vary by program. Candidates are requested to speak with an admissions representative to discuss tuition.

Application procedures. **Admission:** No deadline. No application fee. Admission notification on a rolling basis.

Academics. **Credit/placement by examination:** CLEP.

Majors. **Health:** Respiratory therapy technology.

Contact. Phone: (818) 766-8151 Toll-free number: (800) 464-1212
Fax: (818) 766-1587
Concorde Career College: North Hollywood, 12412 Victory Boulevard, North Hollywood, CA 91606

Concorde Career College: San Bernardino
San Bernardino, California
www.concorde.edu

- For-profit 2-year technical college
- Small city

General. Regionally accredited. **Calendar:** Continuous.

Contact. 201 East Airport Dr., San Bernardino, CA 92408

Concorde Career College: San Diego
San Diego, California
www.concorde.edu

- For-profit 2-year health science and nursing college
- Very large city

General. Regionally accredited. **Calendar:** Differs by program.

Annual costs/financial aid. Tuition and fees vary by program from $12,836 to $34,169.

Contact. Director of Admissions, 4393 Imperial Avenue, San Diego, CA 92113

Contra Costa College
San Pablo, California
www.contracosta.edu **CB code: 4943**

- Public 2-year community college
- Large town

General. Founded in 1948. Regionally accredited. Middle College High School on-campus. 100% pass rate on NCLEX for nursing program graduates. **Enrollment:** 3,304 degree-seeking undergraduates. **Degrees:** 628 associate awarded. **ROTC:** Naval. **Location:** 20 miles from San Francisco. **Calendar:** Semester, limited summer session. **Full-time faculty:** 110 total. **Part-time faculty:** 225 total. **Special facilities:** Center for scientific excellence.

Student profile. Among degree-seeking undergraduates, 70% enrolled in a transfer program, 30% enrolled in a vocational program, 7% already have a bachelor's degree or higher.

Transfer out. **Colleges most students transferred to 2008:** California State University: East Bay, California State University: San Francisco, University of California: Davis, San Jose State University, University of California: Berkeley.

Basis for selection. Open admission.

High school preparation. College-preparatory program recommended.

2008-2009 Annual costs. Tuition/fees: $602; $6,032 out-of-state. Per-credit charge: $20 in-state; $201 out-of-state.

Application procedures. Admission: No deadline. No application fee. Admission notification on a rolling basis. **Financial aid:** Priority date 3/2; no closing date. FAFSA required. Applicants notified on a rolling basis; must reply within 2 week(s) of notification.

Academics. Special study options: Cross-registration, dual enrollment of high school students, honors, independent study. **Credit/placement by examination:** CLEP, institutional tests. 12 credit hours maximum toward associate degree. **Support services:** Learning center, remedial instruction, tutoring.

Majors. Area/ethnic studies: African-American, Hispanic-American/Latino/Chicano. **Biology:** General. **Business:** Administrative services, office/clerical, real estate. **Computer sciences:** General, applications programming. **Education:** Bilingual, teacher assistance. **Engineering:** General. **Engineering technology:** Architectural, drafting. **Family/consumer sciences:** Institutional food production. **Health:** Dental assistant, medical assistant, nursing (RN). **History:** General. **Liberal arts:** Arts/sciences. **Math:** General. **Mechanic/repair:** Auto body. **Personal/culinary services:** Cosmetic. **Physical sciences:** Chemistry, physics. **Protective services:** Police science. **Psychology:** General. **Social sciences:** Geography, sociology. **Visual/performing arts:** Dramatic, interior design.

Most popular majors. Business/marketing 11%, health sciences 20%, liberal arts 48%.

Student life. Activities: Jazz band, student newspaper, TV station.

Athletics. Intercollegiate: Baseball M, basketball, football (tackle) M, tennis, track and field. **Team name:** Comets.

Student services. Career counseling, student employment services, health services, personal counseling. **Transfer:** Re-entry adviser for new students. Transfer center, transfer adviser, college fairs on campus for students transferring to 4-year colleges.

Contact. Phone: (510) 235-7800 ext. 4210 Fax: (510) 236-6768
Frank Hernandez, Senior Dean of Student Services, Contra Costa College, 2600 Mission Bell Drive, San Pablo, CA 94806

Copper Mountain College
Joshua Tree, California
www.cmccd.edu **CB code: 3889**

- Public 2-year community college
- Commuter campus in small town

General. Regionally accredited. **Enrollment:** 1,101 degree-seeking undergraduates. **Degrees:** 287 associate awarded. **Location:** 120 miles from Los Angeles, 45 miles from Palm Springs. **Calendar:** Semester, limited summer session. **Full-time faculty:** 40 total. **Part-time faculty:** 115 total.

Transfer out. Colleges most students transferred to 2008: California State University: San Bernardino.

Basis for selection. Open admission. Limited admission to some allied health programs. **Adult students:** Accuplacer assessment tests required.

2008-2009 Annual costs. Tuition/fees: $602; $6,032 out-of-state. Per-credit charge: $20 in-state; $201 out-of-state. Books/supplies: $1,566. Personal expenses: $2,520.

2007-2008 Financial aid. Need-based: 1,016 full-time freshmen applied for aid; 600 were judged to have need; 340 of these received aid. Average loan was $3,132. Need-based aid available for part-time students.

Application procedures. Admission: No deadline. No application fee. Application must be submitted online. Admission notification on a rolling basis. **Financial aid:** Priority date 3/2; no closing date. FAFSA required.

Academics. Special study options: Distance learning, dual enrollment of high school students, ESL, independent study, study abroad. License preparation in nursing, paramedic. **Credit/placement by examination:** AP, CLEP, institutional tests. **Support services:** GED preparation and test center, remedial instruction, study skills assistance, tutoring.

Majors. Business: Business admin. **Communications:** General. **Computer sciences:** General, computer science. **Foreign languages:** Spanish. **Health:** Licensed practical nurse. **History:** General. **Liberal arts:** Arts/sciences. **Math:** General. **Mechanic/repair:** Automotive. **Philosophy/religion:** Philosophy. **Protective services:** Fire safety technology, law enforcement admin. **Psychology:** General. **Social sciences:** General, anthropology, economics, political science. **Visual/performing arts:** Art.

Computing on campus. 40 workstations in library, computer center.

Student life. Freshman orientation: Mandatory. Preregistration for classes offered. 1.5 hour group orientation offered about 16 times prior to each semester. **Activities:** Literary magazine, student government, student newspaper.

Student services. Adult student services, career counseling, services for economically disadvantaged, student employment services, financial aid counseling, veterans' counselor. **Physically disabled:** Services for visually, speech, hearing impaired. **Transfer:** Pre-admission transcript evaluation for new students. Transfer center, transfer adviser, college fairs on campus for students transferring to 4-year colleges.

Contact. Phone: (760) 366-3791 ext. 4232 Toll-free number: (866) 366-3791 ext. 4232 Fax: (760) 366-5257
Gregory Brown, Vice President of Student Services, Copper Mountain College, 6162 Rotary Way, Joshua Tree, CA 92252

Cosumnes River College
Sacramento, California
www.crc.losrios.edu **CB code: 4121**

- Public 2-year junior college
- Commuter campus in large city

General. Founded in 1970. Regionally accredited. Classes offered at Folsom Lake Center, El Dorado Center and Folsom Prison. **Enrollment:** 9,733 degree-seeking undergraduates. **Degrees:** 642 associate awarded. **Location:** 12 miles from downtown. **Calendar:** Semester, limited summer session. **Full-time faculty:** 175 total. **Part-time faculty:** 200 total.

Basis for selection. Open admission.

2008-2009 Annual costs. Tuition/fees: $632; $6,062 out-of-state. Per-credit charge: $20 in-state; $201 out-of-state. Books/supplies: $1,440. Personal expenses: $2,210.

Application procedures. Admission: No deadline. No application fee. Admission notification on a rolling basis beginning on or about 3/1. First-time students encouraged to participate in orientation and matriculation sessions. English and mathematics tests for placement recommended. **Financial aid:** Priority date 5/1; no closing date. FAFSA required. Applicants notified on a rolling basis starting 7/20; must reply within 4 week(s) of notification.

Academics. Special study options: Cooperative education, distance learning, double major, dual enrollment of high school students, ESL, honors, independent study, internships, study abroad. **Credit/placement by examination:** CLEP. 15 credit hours maximum toward associate degree. **Support services:** Learning center, reduced course load, remedial instruction, tutoring.

Majors. Agriculture: Animal sciences, business, equestrian studies, horticultural science, plant sciences. **Architecture:** Environmental design, interior, landscape. **Area/ethnic studies:** American, women's. **Business:** General, accounting, business admin, entrepreneurial studies, finance, real estate. **Communications:** Advertising, broadcast journalism, journalism, public relations. **Communications technology:** General. **Computer sciences:** Information systems, programming. **Construction:** Maintenance. **Education:** Early childhood. **Engineering technology:** Drafting. **Health:** Medical assistant, medical records technology. **Interdisciplinary:** Gerontology. **Liberal arts:** Arts/sciences. **Protective services:** Fire safety technology, law enforcement admin. **Social sciences:** Sociology. **Visual/performing arts:** Art, art history/conservation, cinematography, commercial photography, dramatic, interior design, photography, studio arts.

Most popular majors. Business/marketing 8%, health sciences 6%, liberal arts 52%, trade and industry 6%.

Student life. Activities: Bands, choral groups, drama, radio station, student government, student newspaper, TV station, African-American Students Association, Hispanic/Latino Scholars, Asian American Club, Christian Club, earth club.

Athletics. Intercollegiate: Baseball M, basketball, soccer, softball W, tennis, track and field, volleyball W. **Intramural:** Badminton, bowling, fencing, golf, racquetball, skiing, swimming, tennis, track and field, volleyball.

Student services. Adult student services, career counseling, student employment services, health services, on-campus daycare, personal counseling, placement for graduates, veterans' counselor. **Physically disabled:** Services for hearing impaired. **Transfer:** Transfer adviser for students transferring to 4-year colleges.

Contact. Phone: (916) 691-7410 Fax: (916) 691-7467
Celia Esposito-Noy, Vice President, Student Services and Enrollment Management, Cosumnes River College, 8401 Center Parkway, Sacramento, CA 95823

Crafton Hills College
Yucaipa, California
www.craftonhills.edu **CB code: 4126**

- Public 2-year community college
- Commuter campus in large town

General. Founded in 1972. Regionally accredited. **Enrollment:** 4,211 degree-seeking undergraduates. **Degrees:** 323 associate awarded. **Location:** 12 miles from San Bernardino. **Calendar:** Semester, limited summer session. **Full-time faculty:** 58 total. **Part-time faculty:** 160 total. **Special facilities:** Walking trails, child care services for preschool-aged children.

Student profile. Among degree-seeking undergraduates, 263 enrolled as first-time, first-year students.

Basis for selection. Open admission.

2008-2009 Annual costs. Tuition/fees: $642; $6,222 out-of-state. Per-credit charge: $20 in-state; $206 out-of-state. Books/supplies: $1,566. Personal expenses: $1,800.

Financial aid. All financial aid based on need. Need-based aid available for part-time students. Work-study available nights and for part-time students.

Application procedures. Admission: No deadline. No application fee. Students under 18 admitted with special permission. **Financial aid:** Priority date 4/15, closing date 6/2. FAFSA, institutional form required. Applicants notified on a rolling basis starting 7/31; must reply within 2 week(s) of notification.

Academics. Special study options: Cooperative education, cross-registration, distance learning, double major, dual enrollment of high school students, honors, study abroad. License preparation in paramedic, radiology. **Credit/placement by examination:** AP, CLEP, institutional tests. 36 credit hours maximum toward associate degree. **Support services:** Learning center, remedial instruction, study skills assistance, tutoring.

Majors. Biology: General, bacteriology. **Business:** Administrative services, business admin, marketing, office/clerical. **Computer sciences:** General, programming. **Education:** Early childhood, health occupations. **Foreign languages:** General, French, Spanish. **Health:** EMT paramedic, medical radiologic technology/radiation therapy, respiratory therapy technology. **History:** General. **Liberal arts:** Arts/sciences. **Math:** General. **Physical sciences:** Chemistry, geology, physics. **Protective services:** Firefighting, law enforcement admin. **Psychology:** General. **Social sciences:** General, anthropology, economics, geography, political science, sociology. **Visual/performing arts:** Art, dramatic.

Most popular majors. Health sciences 16%, interdisciplinary studies 48%, public administration/social services 7%, social sciences 6%.

Computing on campus. 172 workstations in library, computer center.

Student life. Freshman orientation: Mandatory. **Activities:** Jazz band, drama, music ensembles, musical theater, student government, student newspaper.

Athletics. Intercollegiate: Golf, tennis, volleyball, weight lifting.

Student services. Career counseling, student employment services, health services, on-campus daycare, personal counseling, placement for graduates, veterans' counselor. **Physically disabled:** Services for visually, speech, hearing impaired. **Transfer:** Pre-admission transcript evaluation for new students. Transfer center, transfer adviser, college fairs on campus for students transferring to 4-year colleges.

Contact. E-mail: admissions@craftonhills.edu
Phone: (909) 389-3372 Fax: (909) 389-9141
Joe Cabrales, Dean, Student Services, Student Development, Crafton Hills College, 11711 Sand Canyon Road, Yucaipa, CA 92399-1799

Cuesta College
San Luis Obispo, California
www.cuesta.org **CB code: 4101**

- Public 2-year community college
- Commuter campus in large town

General. Founded in 1964. Regionally accredited. Additional North County Campus in Paso Robles and South County Center(s) in Arroyo Grande and Nipomo. **Enrollment:** 7,440 degree-seeking undergraduates. **Degrees:** 706 associate awarded. **Location:** 200 miles from Los Angeles, 6 miles from San Luis Obispo. **Calendar:** Semester, extensive summer session. **Full-time faculty:** 145 total. **Part-time faculty:** 315 total. **Special facilities:** Adobe museum (Chumash Indian).

Student profile.

Out-of-state:	3%	**25 or older:**	33%

Transfer out. Colleges most students transferred to 2008: California Polytechnic State University: San Luis Obispo, CSU: Chico, San Francisco State University, California State Polytechnic University: Pomona.

Basis for selection. Open admission, but selective for some programs. Nursing program requires critical thinking and math assessments. Prerequisite courses evaluated. **Learning Disabled:** No special admission but must be assessed and qualified to receive services.

2008-2009 Annual costs. Tuition/fees: $668; $6,098 out-of-state. Per-credit charge: $20 in-state; $201 out-of-state. Books/supplies: $1,566. Personal expenses: $2,754.

Financial aid. Need-based: Work-study available for part-time students.

Application procedures. Admission: No deadline. No application fee. Admission notification on a rolling basis. **Financial aid:** Priority date 3/2; no closing date. FAFSA required. Applicants notified on a rolling basis starting 4/15.

Academics. Special study options: Cooperative education, distance learning, double major, ESL, honors, independent study, student-designed major, study abroad, weekend college. Bachelor's degree programs available on campus. **Credit/placement by examination:** CLEP, institutional tests. 12 credit hours maximum toward associate degree. **Support services:** Learning center, remedial instruction, study skills assistance, tutoring, writing center.

Majors. Biology: General. **Business:** General, real estate. **Communications:** General, broadcast journalism, journalism. **Computer sciences:** Computer science. **Education:** Art, early childhood, mathematics, physical, special. **Engineering:** Electrical. **Health:** Nursing (RN). **Liberal arts:** Arts/sciences, library assistant. **Math:** General. **Mechanic/repair:** Auto body. **Physical sciences:** Chemistry, physics. **Protective services:** Law enforcement admin. **Visual/performing arts:** Interior design.

Computing on campus. 300 workstations in library, computer center, student center. Online course registration, online library available.

Student life. Freshman orientation: Available. **Activities:** Jazz band, choral groups, dance, drama, music ensembles, musical theater, radio station, student government, student newspaper, TV station, Alpha Gamma Sigma (honor society).

Athletics. Intercollegiate: Baseball M, basketball, cross-country, diving, soccer W, softball W, swimming, tennis W, track and field, volleyball W, water polo, wrestling M.

Student services. Adult student services, career counseling, student employment services, financial aid counseling, health services, legal services, on-campus daycare, personal counseling, veterans' counselor. **Physically disabled:** Services for visually, speech, hearing impaired. **Transfer:** Reentry adviser for new students. Transfer center, transfer adviser, college fairs on campus for students transferring to 4-year colleges.

Contact. E-mail: admit@bass.cuesta.cc.ca.us
Phone: (805) 546-3140 Fax: (805) 546-3975
Joy Chambers, Director of Admissions and Records, Cuesta College, Box 8106, San Luis Obispo, CA 93403

Cuyamaca College
El Cajon, California
www.cuyamaca.net **CB code: 4252**

- Public 2-year community college
- Small city

General. Founded in 1978. Regionally accredited. **Enrollment:** 4,947 degree-seeking undergraduates. **Degrees:** 357 associate awarded. **ROTC:** Army, Air Force. **Location:** 18 miles from San Diego. **Calendar:** Semester, limited summer session. **Full-time faculty:** 77 total. **Part-time faculty:** 294 total. **Special facilities:** Automotive technology facility, water gardens, child care facility, museum.

Transfer out. Colleges most students transferred to 2008: San Diego State University, National University.

Basis for selection. Open admission, but selective for some programs.

2008-2009 Annual costs. Tuition/fees: $638; $6,068 out-of-state. Per-credit charge: $20 in-state; $201 out-of-state. Books/supplies: $1,500. Personal expenses: $1,500.

2007-2008 Financial aid. Need-based: Work-study available nights, weekends and for part-time students.

Application procedures. Admission: No deadline. No application fee in-state; $163 out-of-state. Admission notification on a rolling basis. **Financial aid:** Priority date 3/2; no closing date. FAFSA required. Applicants notified on a rolling basis; must reply within 2 week(s) of notification.

Academics. Special study options: Cooperative education, cross-registration, distance learning, double major, dual enrollment of high school students, ESL, honors, independent study, internships, study abroad, weekend college. License preparation in real estate. **Credit/placement by examination:** AP, CLEP, institutional tests. **Support services:** Remedial instruction, tutoring.

Majors. Agriculture: Ornamental horticulture. **Business:** Accounting, business admin, real estate. **Engineering technology:** Architectural, computer systems, drafting, electrical, surveying. **Family/consumer sciences:** Child care. **Liberal arts:** Arts/sciences.

Most popular majors. Business/marketing 15%, computer/information sciences 6%, education 7%, liberal arts 48%.

Computing on campus. Online course registration available.

Student life. Freshman orientation: Available. **Activities:** Dance, student government, student newspaper, African American student union, Christian club, Cuyamaca College Spanish club, MECHA, Phi Theta Kappa.

Athletics. Intercollegiate: Basketball, cross-country, golf M, soccer, tennis W, track and field, volleyball W. **Team name:** Coyotes.

Student services. Adult student services, career counseling, student employment services, financial aid counseling, health services, on-campus daycare, personal counseling, veterans' counselor. **Physically disabled:** Services for visually, speech, hearing impaired. **Transfer:** Pre-admission transcript evaluation for new students. Transfer center, transfer adviser, college fairs on campus for students transferring to 4-year colleges.

Contact. Phone: (619) 660-4275 Fax: (619) 660-4575
Susan Topham, Admissions Director, Cuyamaca College, 900 Rancho San Diego Parkway, El Cajon, CA 92019-4304

Cypress College
Cypress, California
www.cypresscollege.edu **CB code: 4104**

- Public 2-year community college
- Commuter campus in small city

General. Founded in 1966. Regionally accredited. **Enrollment:** 10,822 degree-seeking undergraduates. **Degrees:** 742 associate awarded. **Location:** 30 miles from Los Angeles. **Calendar:** Semester, limited summer session. **Full-time faculty:** 190 total. **Part-time faculty:** 220 total.

Student profile.

Out-of-state:	5%	**25 or older:**	44%

Transfer out. Colleges most students transferred to 2008: CSU Fullerton, CSU Long Beach.

Basis for selection. Open admission. College administered English and math placement exams used for placement.

High school preparation. College-preparatory program required.

2008-2009 Annual costs. Tuition/fees: $630; $5,700 out-of-state. Per-credit charge: $20 in-state; $189 out-of-state. Books/supplies: $1,386. Personal expenses: $1,898.

Application procedures. Admission: No deadline. No application fee. Admission notification on a rolling basis. **Financial aid:** Priority date 5/31; no closing date. FAFSA required. Applicants notified on a rolling basis starting 8/1; must reply within 2 week(s) of notification.

Academics. Special study options: Distance learning, dual enrollment of high school students, ESL, honors, independent study, internships, liberal arts/career combination, study abroad. License preparation in aviation, dental hygiene, nursing, real estate. **Credit/placement by examination:** CLEP, institutional tests. 12 credit hours maximum toward associate degree. **Support services:** Learning center, reduced course load, remedial instruction, study skills assistance, tutoring, writing center.

Majors. Area/ethnic studies: Asian, Latin American. **Business:** General, accounting, administrative services, business admin, hospitality/recreation, management information systems, management science, office technology, office/clerical, tourism promotion. **Communications:** Journalism. **Computer sciences:** General, data processing, information systems. **Conservation:** Forestry. **Education:** General, elementary, physical, secondary, technology/industrial arts. **Engineering:** General. **Family/consumer sciences:** Institutional food production. **Foreign languages:** French, German, Spanish. **Health:** Dental assistant, dental hygiene, dental lab technology, health services, medical assistant, medical radiologic technology/radiation therapy, medical records admin, medical records technology, nursing (RN), predental, premedicine, prepharmacy, preveterinary. **History:** General. **Legal studies:** Court reporting, legal secretary, prelaw. **Liberal arts:** Arts/sciences. **Math:** General. **Mechanic/repair:** Aircraft, auto body, automotive, electronics/electrical, heating/ac/refrig. **Parks/recreation:** General. **Personal/culinary services:** Culinary arts, mortuary science. **Philosophy/religion:** Philosophy. **Physical sciences:** Chemistry, geology, physics. **Psychology:** General. **Public administration:** Human services. **Social sciences:** Anthropology, economics, geography, political science, sociology. **Transportation:** Airline/commercial pilot, aviation, aviation management, flight attendant. **Visual/performing arts:** General, art, commercial/advertising art, dance, dramatic, music performance, theater design.

Computing on campus. 800 workstations in library, computer center, student center.

Student life. Freshman orientation: Available. **Activities:** Bands, choral groups, dance, drama, literary magazine, music ensembles, musical theater, student government, student newspaper.

Athletics. NJCAA. **Intercollegiate:** Baseball M, basketball, diving, golf, soccer, softball W, swimming, tennis, volleyball W, water polo, wrestling M. **Intramural:** Badminton, baseball M, basketball, softball, volleyball. **Team name:** Chargers.

Student services. Career counseling, student employment services, health services, on-campus daycare, personal counseling, veterans' counselor. **Physically disabled:** Services for visually, speech, hearing impaired. **Transfer:** Re-entry adviser, pre-admission transcript evaluation for new students. Transfer center, transfer adviser, college fairs on campus for students transferring to 4-year colleges.

Contact. E-mail: admissions@cypresscollege.edu
Phone: (714) 484-7346 Fax: (714) 484-7446
Dave Wassenaar, Dean of Admissions and Records, Cypress College, 9200 Valley View Street, Cypress, CA 90630

De Anza College
Cupertino, California
www.deanza.edu **CB code: 4286**

- Public 2-year community college
- Commuter campus in large town

General. Founded in 1967. Regionally accredited. **Enrollment:** 18,138 degree-seeking undergraduates. **Degrees:** 1,094 associate awarded. **ROTC:** Army, Air Force. **Location:** 5 miles from San Jose, 40 miles from San Francisco. **Calendar:** Quarter, extensive summer session. **Full-time faculty:** 300 total. **Part-time faculty:** 540 total. **Special facilities:** Planetarium, California history center, environmental studies area, advanced technology center.

Transfer out. Colleges most students transferred to 2008: University of California: Davis, San Jose State, San Francisco State, University of California: Berkeley, University of California: Santa Cruz.

Basis for selection. Open admission, but selective for some programs. Limited admission for nursing and physical therapist assistant applicants.

2008-2009 Annual costs. Tuition/fees: $675; $5,850 out-of-state. Per-credit charge: $13 in-state; $128 out-of-state. Books/supplies: $1,656. Personal expenses: $2,754.

Financial aid. All financial aid based on need. Need-based aid available for part-time students.

Application procedures. Admission: No deadline. No application fee. Admission notification on a rolling basis. **Financial aid:** No deadline. FAFSA required. Applicants notified on a rolling basis starting 5/15; must reply within 2 week(s) of notification.

Academics. Special study options: Cooperative education, cross-registration, distance learning, dual enrollment of high school students, ESL, honors, independent study, internships, study abroad, weekend college. License preparation in nursing. **Credit/placement by examination:** CLEP, institutional tests. 45 credit hours maximum toward associate degree. **Support services:** Learning center, pre-admission summer program, remedial instruction, tutoring.

Majors. Area/ethnic studies: African-American, Asian-American, Hispanic-American/Latino/Chicano, Latin American, Native American. **Biology:** General. **Business:** Accounting, administrative services, business admin, marketing, purchasing, real estate, taxation. **Communications:** General. **Computer sciences:** General, applications programming, computer science, programming, systems analysis. **Education:** Early childhood. **Engineering:** General, computer, electrical, mechanical. **Engineering technology:** Drafting. **Foreign languages:** French, German, Spanish. **Health:** Medical assistant, nursing (RN). **History:** General. **Legal studies:** Paralegal. **Liberal arts:** Arts/sciences. **Math:** General. **Philosophy/religion:** Philosophy. **Physical sciences:** Astronomy, chemistry, geology, physics. **Protective services:** Law enforcement admin, security services. **Psychology:** General. **Science technology:** Biological. **Social sciences:** Anthropology, economics, geography, political science, sociology. **Visual/performing arts:** Art, art history/conservation, ceramics, cinematography, commercial/advertising art, painting, photography, printmaking, sculpture.

Computing on campus. 300 workstations in library, computer center, student center. Online course registration available.

Student life. Freshman orientation: Available. Two day counseling course for new, incoming students. **Activities:** Bands, choral groups, dance, drama, literary magazine, music ensembles, student government, student newspaper, symphony orchestra, TV station.

Athletics. Intercollegiate: Baseball M, basketball, cross-country, diving, football (tackle) M, golf, soccer, softball W, swimming, tennis, track and field, volleyball, water polo M. **Intramural:** Badminton, baseball M, basketball, bowling, fencing, gymnastics, racquetball, soccer W, swimming, tennis, volleyball. **Team name:** Dons.

Student services. Adult student services, alcohol/substance abuse counseling, career counseling, services for economically disadvantaged, student employment services, financial aid counseling, health services, legal services, minority student services, on-campus daycare, personal counseling, placement for graduates, veterans' counselor. **Physically disabled:** Services for visually, speech, hearing impaired. **Transfer:** Re-entry adviser for new students. Transfer center, transfer adviser, college fairs on campus for students transferring to 4-year colleges.

Contact. E-mail: webreg@fhda.edu
Phone: (408) 864-5300 Fax: (408) 864-8329
Kathleen Moberg, Dean of Admissions and Records, De Anza College, 21250 Stevens Creek Boulevard, Cupertino, CA 95014

Deep Springs College
Dyer, Nevada
www.deepsprings.edu **CB code: 4281**

- Private 2-year liberal arts college for men
- Residential campus in rural community
- SAT or ACT (ACT writing optional), application essay, interview required

General. Founded in 1917. Regionally accredited. **Enrollment:** 26 degree-seeking undergraduates. **Degrees:** 13 associate awarded. **Location:** 45 miles from Bishop. **Calendar:** Continuous, limited summer session. **Full-time faculty:** 4 total; 75% have terminal degrees, 25% women. **Part-time faculty:** 2 total; 100% have terminal degrees. **Class size:** 100% < 20. **Special facilities:** Student-operated 2,600-acre cattle and alfalfa ranch, dairy.

Student profile. Among degree-seeking undergraduates, 2 transferred in from other institutions.

Out-of-state:	100%	**Live on campus:**	100%

Transfer out. Colleges most students transferred to 2008: Harvard University, University of Chicago, Oxford University, Stanford University, Yale University.

Basis for selection. Essays most important. School achievement record, interview, extracurricular activities, and recommendations strongly considered. Admissions process created and run by student committee. SAT Subject Tests recommended. International students who cannot take SAT or who have taken equivalent standardized test evaluated on case-by-case basis. 2-round application process: in first round, 3 essays are required. If accepted into second round, additional 4 essays and 3- to 4-day campus visit and interview required.

2008-2009 Annual costs. All students receive full scholarship covering tuition, room, and board. Books/supplies: $1,500.

Financial aid. Need-based: Work-study available nights and weekends. **Non-need-based:** Scholarships awarded for academics.

Application procedures. Admission: Closing date 11/15 (postmark date). No application fee. Admission notification 4/15. Must reply by 5/1. Approximately 40 applicants are invited to complete part II of application process between January and March. This includes a 3-day campus visit, interview, and writing 4 additional essays. Foreign students and those with economic hardship may be exempt from the visit upon request. **Financial aid:** No deadline.

Academics. Students required to take 3 classes: composition, public speaking, and summer seminar (interdisciplinary course broadly oriented around questions of political theory). **Special study options:** Independent study. **Credit/placement by examination:** CLEP.

Majors. Liberal arts: Arts/sciences.

Computing on campus. 7 workstations in library, computer center. Helpline, repair service available.

Student life. Freshman orientation: Mandatory. **Policies:** All students work on jobs running college or ranch. Student committees organize all community events as well as handle admissions, faculty hiring, public relations, and review/reinvitation process. Students also self-govern, managing community issues and each other's conduct. Student-formulated isolation and drug/alcohol policies: drugs prohibited, students prohibited from leaving valley during term, guests prohibited from visiting. **Housing:** Guaranteed on-campus for all undergraduates. Pets allowed in dorm rooms. **Activities:** Jazz band, dance, drama, film society, literary magazine, music ensembles, musical theater, radio station, student government, student newspaper.

Athletics. Intramural: Basketball M, cross-country M, equestrian M, football (non-tackle) M, football (tackle) M, rifle M, rodeo M, skiing M, soccer M, swimming M, table tennis M, track and field M, weight lifting M, wrestling M.

Student services. Career counseling, health services, personal counseling, placement for graduates. **Transfer:** Transfer adviser for students transferring to 4-year colleges.

Contact. E-mail: apcom@deepsprings.edu
Phone: (760) 872-2000 Fax: (760) 872-4466
Nathan Garrett, Chair, Applications Committee, Deep Springs College, Applications Committee, Dyer, NV 89010-9803

Diablo Valley College
Pleasant Hill, California
www.dvc.edu **CB code: 4295**

- Public 2-year community college
- Commuter campus in large town

General. Founded in 1948. Regionally accredited. College for Kids available on-campus which provides enrichment activities for fourth through ninth graders. **Enrollment:** 12,058 degree-seeking undergraduates. **Degrees:** 624 associate awarded. **ROTC:** Army, Naval. **Location:** 25 miles from San Francisco. **Calendar:** Semester, extensive summer session. **Full-time faculty:** 255 total; 36% minority, 54% women. **Part-time faculty:** 551 total; 38% minority, 52% women. **Class size:** 20% < 20, 61% 20-39, 16% 40-49, 3% 50-99, less than 1% >100. **Special facilities:** Student-run restaurant, observatory, planetarium, three art collections. **Partnerships:** Formal partnerships with Wells Fargo, Chevron, Pacific Bell, City of San Ramon, Contra Costa/Tri-Valley Telecommunication Incubator.

Student profile. Among degree-seeking undergraduates, 92% enrolled in a transfer program, 8% enrolled in a vocational program.

Out-of-state:	1%	**25 or older:**	38%

Transfer out. 53% of students enrolled in the transfer program go on to 4-year colleges. **Colleges most students transferred to 2008:** University of California: Berkeley, San Francisco State, University of California: East Bay, California State University: Sacramento, University of California: Davis.

Basis for selection. Open admission. **Adult students:** SAT/ACT scores not required. **Homeschooled:** Applicants must supply a copy of their private school affidavit.

2008-2009 Annual costs. Tuition/fees: $600; $5,700 out-of-state. Per-credit charge: $20 in-state; $190 out-of-state. Books/supplies: $1,332. Personal expenses: $2,430.

2007-2008 Financial aid. **Need-based:** 89% of total undergraduate aid awarded as scholarships/grants, 11% as loans/jobs. Need-based aid available for part-time students.

Application procedures. **Admission:** Priority date 4/1; no deadline. No application fee. Admission notification on a rolling basis beginning on or about 4/1. **Financial aid:** Priority date 3/2, closing date 5/1. FAFSA, institutional form required. Applicants notified on a rolling basis starting 6/1; must reply within 2 week(s) of notification.

Academics. The college offers a comprehensive educational program that includes courses in general education, transfer, vocational, basic skills, and life-long learning. These courses are offered in flexible formats that include different hours, days, term length, and a variety of instructional delivery methods (classroom and on-line). **Special study options:** Accelerated study, cooperative education, cross-registration, distance learning, dual enrollment of high school students, ESL, honors, independent study, internships, liberal arts/career combination, study abroad, weekend college. Study abroad programs in Florence, Italy; Salamanca, Spain; Capetown, South Africa; Ghana; and London, England. License preparation in dental hygiene. **Credit/placement by examination:** AP, CLEP, institutional tests. **Support services:** Learning center, pre-admission summer program, reduced course load, remedial instruction, study skills assistance, tutoring, writing center.

Majors. **Computer sciences:** General, computer science, networking. **Education:** Physical, special. **Health:** Athletic training. **Other:** Interdisciplinary studies.

Most popular majors. Interdisciplinary studies 88%.

Computing on campus. 1,000 workstations in library, computer center, student center. Commuter students can connect to campus network. Online course registration, online library, helpline, repair service, wireless network available.

Student life. **Freshman orientation:** Mandatory. **Policies:** No smoking except in the quad. **Activities:** Bands, choral groups, dance, drama, film society, international student organizations, literary magazine, music ensembles, musical theater, student government, student newspaper, symphony orchestra, TV station, Alpha Gamma Sigma, Asian student union, DVC Republicans, DVC Democrats, Black student union, Latino students' alliance, Muslim student association, Christians on Campus, Greater China Cultural Association, Taiwan Discovery Club.

Athletics. NJCAA. **Intercollegiate:** Baseball M, basketball, cross-country, football (tackle) M, soccer W, softball W, swimming, tennis, track and field, volleyball W, water polo. **Team name:** Vikings.

Student services. Adult student services, career counseling, services for economically disadvantaged, student employment services, financial aid counseling, on-campus daycare, personal counseling, placement for graduates, veterans' counselor, women's services. **Physically disabled:** Services for visually, speech, hearing impaired. **Learning disabled:** Comprehensive services available. **Transfer:** Re-entry adviser for new students. Transfer center, transfer adviser, college fairs on campus for students transferring to 4-year colleges.

Contact. E-mail: informationcenter@dvc.edu
Phone: (925) 685-1310 Fax: (925) 685-8085
Ileana Dorn, Director of Admissions and Records, Diablo Valley College, 321 Golf Club Road, Pleasant Hill, CA 94523

East Los Angeles College

Monterey Park, California — **CB member**
www.elac.edu — **CB code: 4296**

- Public 2-year community college
- Commuter campus in very large city

General. Founded in 1945. Regionally accredited. **Enrollment:** 11,105 degree-seeking undergraduates. **Degrees:** 1,223 associate awarded. **Location:** 7 miles from Los Angeles. **Calendar:** Semester, limited summer session. **Full-time faculty:** 264 total; 49% minority, 52% women. **Part-time faculty:** 604 total; 44% minority, 35% women. **Class size:** 30% < 20, 50% 20-39, 15% 40-49, 4% 50-99.

Student profile. Among degree-seeking undergraduates, 31% enrolled in a transfer program, 27% enrolled in a vocational program, 5% already have a bachelor's degree or higher, 2,202 enrolled as first-time, first-year students.

Out-of-state:	.4%	**Hispanic American:**	67%
African American:	2%	**International:**	9%
Asian American:	16%	**25 or older:**	43%

Transfer out. **Colleges most students transferred to 2008:** California State University: Los Angeles, California State Polytechnic University: Pomona, California State University: Long Beach, California State University: Dominguez Hills, University of California: Los Angeles.

Basis for selection. Open admission, but selective for some programs. Limited admission to nursing and allied health associate programs. Institution uses Assessment Placement Test for English and mathematics placement. Interview required for some nursing, respiratory technology majors.

2008-2009 Annual costs. Tuition/fees: $622; $6,052 out-of-state. Per-credit charge: $20 in-state; $201 out-of-state. Books/supplies: $2,316. Personal expenses: $3,024.

2007-2008 Financial aid. All financial aid based on need. 97% of total undergraduate aid awarded as scholarships/grants, 3% as loans/jobs. Need-based aid available for part-time students. Work-study available nights, weekends and for part-time students. **Additional information:** Need-based enrollment fee waivers available through a state aid program.

Application procedures. **Admission:** No deadline. No application fee. **Financial aid:** Closing date 3/2. FAFSA required.

Academics. Plan A major requires 18 credits in major; Plan B major requires 36 credits in major. **Special study options:** Accelerated study, cooperative education, cross-registration, distance learning, double major, dual enrollment of high school students, ESL, honors, independent study, study abroad, weekend college. Program for Adult College Education (PACE), ITV and Saturday classes. License preparation in nursing. **Credit/placement by examination:** AP, CLEP, institutional tests. 15 credit hours maximum toward associate degree. **Support services:** GED preparation, learning center, pre-admission summer program, reduced course load, remedial instruction, study skills assistance, tutoring, writing center.

Majors. **Architecture:** Landscape, urban/community planning. **Area/ethnic studies:** African-American. **Business:** Accounting, administrative services, business admin, international marketing, managerial economics, office technology, office/clerical, real estate, sales/distribution. **Communications:** Journalism. **Communications technology:** Animation/special effects, desktop publishing. **Computer sciences:** General, programming. **Engineering:** General, architectural, civil, electrical, mechanics. **Engineering technology:** Architectural. **Family/consumer sciences:** Child development. **Health:** Community health, electrocardiograph technology, medical assistant, nursing (RN), respiratory therapy technology. **History:** General. **Legal studies:** Legal secretary. **Liberal arts:** Arts/sciences. **Math:** General. **Mechanic/repair:** Automotive. **Parks/recreation:** Health/fitness. **Philosophy/religion:** Philosophy. **Physical sciences:** Chemistry, geology, physics. **Protective services:** Firefighting, police science. **Psychology:** General. **Social sciences:** General, anthropology, economics, geography, political science, sociology. **Visual/performing arts:** Art, dramatic, photography. **Other:** Electron microscopy.

Most popular majors. Health sciences 14%, liberal arts 67%, security/protective services 9%.

Computing on campus. 1,597 workstations in library, computer center, student center. Online course registration, online library, helpline, wireless network available.

Student life. **Freshman orientation:** Available. **Policies:** All Student Life activities conform to Title V, LACCD regulations, LACCD Board Rules, Roberts rules of order, and CA Brown Act. **Activities:** Bands, campus ministries, dance, drama, international student organizations, music ensembles, musical theater, student government, student newspaper, Associated Students Union, engineering club, French club, Asia club, Chicanos for Creative Medicine, MESA, American Society of Engineers and Architects.

Athletics. NJCAA. **Intercollegiate:** Badminton W, baseball M, basketball, cheerleading M, cross-country, football (tackle) M, soccer, softball W, track and field, volleyball W, wrestling M. **Team name:** Huskies.

Student services. Adult student services, alcohol/substance abuse counseling, career counseling, services for economically disadvantaged, student employment services, financial aid counseling, health services, minority student services, on-campus daycare, personal counseling, placement for graduates, veterans' counselor, women's services. **Physically disabled:** Services

Two-Year Colleges

for visually, hearing impaired. **Transfer:** Pre-admission transcript evaluation for new students. Transfer center, transfer adviser, college fairs on campus for students transferring to 4-year colleges.

Contact. Phone: (323) 265-8712 Fax: (323) 265-8688
Jeremy Allred, Dean of Admissions, East Los Angeles College, 1301 Avenida Cesar Chavez, Monterey Park, CA 91754

El Camino College
Torrance, California
www.elcamino.edu **CB code: 4302**

- Public 2-year community college
- Commuter campus in very large city

General. Founded in 1947. Regionally accredited. **Enrollment:** 14,100 degree-seeking undergraduates. **Degrees:** 1,103 associate awarded. **ROTC:** Army. **Location:** 15 miles from Los Angeles. **Calendar:** Semester, limited summer session. **Full-time faculty:** 333 total; 53% women. **Part-time faculty:** 650 total; 51% women. **Special facilities:** Anthropology museum, planetarium, conference center, computer/media center, child development center.

Student profile. Among degree-seeking undergraduates, 12% enrolled in a transfer program, 22% enrolled in a vocational program, 7% already have a bachelor's degree or higher, 2,995 enrolled as first-time, first-year students.

Out-of-state:	1%	**25 or older:**	36%

Transfer out. 18% of students enrolled in the transfer program go on to 4-year colleges. **Colleges most students transferred to 2008:** California State University: Long Beach, California State University: Dominguez Hills, California State University: Northridge, University of California: Los Angeles.

Basis for selection. Open admission. Allied health programs require completion of preparatory courses (anatomy, microbiology, college-level English and mathematics). Interview required for nursing, honors program, x-ray technician, respiratory care majors. **Adult students:** SAT/ACT scores not required. **Homeschooled:** Statement describing homeschool structure and mission, transcript of courses and grades, state high school equivalency certificate, letter of recommendation (nonparent) required. Home school must be registered with state of California. **Learning Disabled:** Contact Special Resources Center and provide evidence of a learning disability.

2008-2009 Annual costs. Tuition/fees: $629; $6,059 out-of-state. Per-credit charge: $20 in-state; $201 out-of-state. Books/supplies: $1,566. Personal expenses: $2,556.

2007-2008 Financial aid. Need-based: 86% of total undergraduate aid awarded as scholarships/grants, 14% as loans/jobs. Need-based aid available for part-time students. Work-study available for part-time students. **Non-need-based:** Scholarships awarded for academics, art, athletics, leadership, music/drama. **Additional information:** Students may apply for Pell grants until June 30.

Application procedures. Admission: No deadline. No application fee. Admission notification on a rolling basis beginning on or about 8/20. **Financial aid:** Priority date 3/2, closing date 6/30. FAFSA, institutional form required. Applicants notified on a rolling basis starting 7/15.

Academics. Special study options: Cooperative education, cross-registration, distance learning, double major, dual enrollment of high school students, ESL, honors, independent study, liberal arts/career combination, study abroad, weekend college. License preparation in nursing, radiology. **Credit/placement by examination:** CLEP, IB, institutional tests. 15 credit hours maximum toward associate degree. **Support services:** Learning center, remedial instruction, study skills assistance, tutoring, writing center.

Majors. Agriculture: Ornamental horticulture. **Area/ethnic studies:** African-American, American, Asian-American, Hispanic-American/Latino/Chicano, Native American. **Biology:** General, botany, zoology. **Business:** General, administrative services, business admin, office management, real estate, sales/distribution. **Communications:** Journalism. **Communications technology:** General. **Computer sciences:** General, computer science. **Construction:** Maintenance. **Education:** Early childhood. **Engineering:** General. **Engineering technology:** Architectural, construction, drafting. **Family/consumer sciences:** General. **Foreign languages:** French, German, Japanese, Spanish. **Health:** Licensed practical nurse, medical radiologic technology/radiation therapy, nursing (RN), predental, premedicine, prepharmacy, respiratory therapy technology. **History:** General. **Legal studies:** Paralegal. **Math:** General. **Mechanic/repair:** Auto body, automotive, electronics/electrical, heating/ac/refrig. **Parks/recreation:** Health/fitness. **Personal/culinary services:** Cosmetic. **Philosophy/religion:** Philosophy. **Physical sciences:** Astronomy, chemistry, geology, physics. **Protective services:** Fire safety technology, law enforcement admin, police science. **Psychology:** General. **Social sciences:** Anthropology, economics, geography, political science, sociology. **Visual/performing arts:** Art, dance, dramatic, photography, studio arts.

Most popular majors. Business/marketing 13%, health sciences 11%, liberal arts 37%, social sciences 6%.

Computing on campus. Online course registration, wireless network available.

Student life. Freshman orientation: Available. **Activities:** Bands, choral groups, dance, drama, literary magazine, music ensembles, musical theater, student government, student newspaper, symphony orchestra, approximately 60 service, special interest, activist and religious clubs.

Athletics. NJCAA. **Intercollegiate:** Badminton W, baseball M, basketball, cross-country, football (tackle) M, golf M, soccer, softball W, swimming, tennis, track and field, volleyball, water polo. **Team name:** Warriors.

Student services. Adult student services, career counseling, student employment services, health services, on-campus daycare, personal counseling, placement for graduates, veterans' counselor. **Physically disabled:** Services for visually, speech, hearing impaired. **Transfer:** Re-entry adviser, pre-admission transcript evaluation for new students. Transfer center, transfer adviser, college fairs on campus for students transferring to 4-year colleges.

Contact. E-mail: admissionshelp@elcamino.edu
Phone: (310) 660-3414 Toll-free number: (866) 352-2646
Fax: (310) 660-3818
Bill Mulrooney, Director of Admissions and Records, El Camino College, 16007 Crenshaw Boulevard, Torrance, CA 90506

El Camino College: Compton Center
Compton, California **CB member**
www.compton.edu **CB code: 4078**

- Public 2-year community college
- Commuter campus in small city

General. Founded in 1927. Regionally accredited. **Enrollment:** 2,704 degree-seeking undergraduates. **Degrees:** 106 associate awarded. **Location:** 25 miles from Los Angeles. **Calendar:** Semester, limited summer session. **Full-time faculty:** 85 total. **Part-time faculty:** 115 total.

Transfer out. Colleges most students transferred to 2008: California State University: Dominguez Hills.

Basis for selection. Open admission, but selective for some programs and for out-of-state students. If under 18, applicant must have graduated from high school and passed the California High School Certificate of Proficiency test. Selective admission to nursing programs.

2008-2009 Annual costs. Tuition/fees: $601; $6,031 out-of-state. Per-credit charge: $20 in-state; $201 out-of-state. Books/supplies: $1,566. Personal expenses: $2,556.

Application procedures. Admission: No deadline. No application fee. Admission notification on a rolling basis. **Financial aid:** Closing date 5/15. FAFSA required. Applicants notified on a rolling basis starting 5/15.

Academics. Special study options: Accelerated study, cooperative education, cross-registration, honors. **Credit/placement by examination:** CLEP, institutional tests. 12 credit hours maximum toward associate degree. **Support services:** Learning center, reduced course load, remedial instruction, tutoring.

Majors. Area/ethnic studies: Women's. **Biology:** General, bacteriology, botany. **Business:** Accounting, administrative services, banking/financial services, business admin, entrepreneurial studies, management information systems, office technology, office/clerical, real estate. **Communications:** Journalism. **Communications technology:** Graphics. **Computer sciences:** General, applications programming, data processing. **Education:** Bilingual, physical, special, teacher assistance. **Engineering:** Computer. **Engineering technology:** Construction, drafting, electrical. **Family/consumer sciences:** General, child care, clothing/textiles. **Foreign languages:** French, German, Spanish. **Health:** EMT paramedic, licensed practical nurse, medical assistant, medical radiologic technology/radiation therapy, nursing (RN), premedicine, preop/surgical nursing, respiratory therapy technology. **History:** General. **Legal studies:** Paralegal. **Liberal arts:** Arts/sciences. **Math:** General. **Mechanic/repair:** General, auto body, automotive, small engine. **Parks/recreation:** General. **Personal/culinary services:** Cosmetic. **Philosophy/religion:** Philosophy. **Physical sciences:** Astronomy, chemistry, geology, physics. **Production:** Woodworking. **Protective services:** Firefighting, police science. **Psychology:** General. **Social sciences:** General, geography, political science, sociology. **Visual/performing arts:** Art, commercial/advertising art, dance, dramatic.

Computing on campus. 35 workstations in computer center.

Student life. Activities: Bands, choral groups, dance, drama, music ensembles, musical theater, student government, student newspaper, TV station, Christian club, Moslem student association.

Athletics. Intercollegiate: Baseball M, basketball, cross-country, football (tackle) M, tennis M, track and field. **Intramural:** Basketball, tennis. **Team name:** Tartars.

Student services. Career counseling, student employment services, on-campus daycare, personal counseling, placement for graduates, veterans' counselor. **Physically disabled:** Services for visually, speech, hearing impaired. **Transfer:** Transfer adviser, college fairs on campus for students transferring to 4-year colleges.

Contact. E-mail: info@compton.edu
Phone: (310) 900-1600 ext. 2043 Fax: (310) 900-1695
Gerald Bateman, Director of Admission and Records, El Camino College: Compton Center, 1111 East Artesia Boulevard, Compton, CA 90221

Empire College
Santa Rosa, California
www.empcol.edu **CB code: 4275**

- For-profit 2-year business college
- Commuter campus in small city
- Interview required

General. Accredited by ACICS. **Enrollment:** 202 degree-seeking undergraduates; 242 non-degree-seeking students. **Degrees:** 202 associate awarded. **Location:** 55 miles from San Francisco. **Calendar:** Continuous. **Full-time faculty:** 33 total; 52% women. **Part-time faculty:** 7 total; 43% women. **Special facilities:** Law library.

Student profile. Among degree-seeking undergraduates, 202 enrolled as first-time, first-year students.

Women:	68%	**25 or older:**	55%

Transfer out. Colleges most students transferred to 2008: Santa Rosa Junior College.

Basis for selection. Open admission. Scholastic Level Exam (SLE) administered during admission process. Some programs also have typing speed requirement for entrance.

2008-2009 Annual costs. Tuition/fees: $8,625. Books/supplies: $1,700. Personal expenses: $207.

2008-2009 Financial aid. All financial aid based on need.

Application procedures. Admission: No deadline. $75 fee. Admission notification on a rolling basis. No fall term, ongoing 5-week application/entry. **Financial aid:** No deadline. FAFSA required. Applicants notified on a rolling basis.

Academics. Special study options: Accelerated study, double major, internships. **Credit/placement by examination:** CLEP. **Support services:** Tutoring.

Majors. Business: Accounting, administrative services. **Computer sciences:** Information systems. **Health:** Medical secretary. **Legal studies:** Paralegal.

Computing on campus. 450 workstations in library, computer center. Online library, student web hosting, wireless network available.

Student life. Freshman orientation: Mandatory. **Activities:** Student newspaper.

Student services. Student employment services, financial aid counseling, placement for graduates. **Transfer:** Re-entry adviser, pre-admission transcript evaluation for new students.

Contact. E-mail: dstraub@empirecollege.com
Phone: (707) 546-4000 ext. 238 Fax: (707) 546-4058
Dahnja Straub, Director of Admissions, Empire College, 3035 Cleveland Avenue, Santa Rosa, CA 95403-2100

Evergreen Valley College
San Jose, California
www.evc.edu **CB code: 4273**

- Public 2-year community and junior college
- Commuter campus in very large city

General. Founded in 1975. Regionally accredited. **Enrollment:** 5,426 degree-seeking undergraduates. **Degrees:** 411 associate awarded. **Location:** 7 miles from downtown. **Calendar:** Semester, extensive summer session. **Full-time faculty:** 127 total; 32% have terminal degrees. **Part-time faculty:** 203 total. **Special facilities:** Hiking trails, parks, observatory, natural habitat (used in natural science and biology course work), cross-country course.

Transfer out. Colleges most students transferred to 2008: San Jose State.

Basis for selection. Open admission, but selective for some programs. Limited admission for nursing and criminal justice programs. **Home-schooled:** Interview required. Must complete form R-42 and state affidavit.

2008-2009 Annual costs. Tuition/fees: $627; $6,357 out-of-state. Per-credit charge: $20 in-state; $211 out-of-state. Books/supplies: $1,566. Personal expenses: $3,024.

Application procedures. Admission: No deadline. No application fee. Admission notification on a rolling basis. **Financial aid:** Priority date 5/31; no closing date. FAFSA required. Applicants notified on a rolling basis.

Academics. Special study options: Accelerated study, cooperative education, cross-registration, distance learning, double major, dual enrollment of high school students, ESL, honors, independent study, internships, liberal arts/career combination, weekend college. License preparation in nursing, paramedic. **Credit/placement by examination:** AP, CLEP, institutional tests. 12 credit hours maximum toward associate degree. Assessment testing as prescribed by California law required for placement in English and mathematics. **Support services:** Learning center, reduced course load, remedial instruction, study skills assistance, tutoring, writing center.

Majors. Business: Administrative services, fashion, management information systems, office technology, office/clerical. **Computer sciences:** General, applications programming. **Engineering technology:** Drafting. **Health:** Nursing (RN). **Liberal arts:** Arts/sciences. **Protective services:** Police science. **Visual/performing arts:** Commercial/advertising art.

Computing on campus. 800 workstations in library, computer center, student center.

Student life. Freshman orientation: Mandatory. Preregistration for classes offered. **Activities:** Choral groups, dance, drama, literary magazine, music ensembles, musical theater, student government, student newspaper, Black Students Union, ASPIRE, Enlace, AFFIRM.

Athletics. NJCAA. **Intercollegiate:** Soccer, track and field, volleyball W, wrestling M. **Intramural:** Basketball, football (non-tackle) M. **Team name:** Hawks.

Student services. Alcohol/substance abuse counseling, career counseling, services for economically disadvantaged, student employment services, financial aid counseling, health services, minority student services, on-campus daycare, personal counseling, veterans' counselor. **Physically disabled:** Services for visually, speech, hearing impaired. **Transfer:** Transfer center, transfer adviser, college fairs on campus for students transferring to 4-year colleges.

Contact. E-mail: lynn.gulkin@evc.edu
Phone: (408) 270-6441 Fax: (408) 223-9351
Octavio Cruz, Dean of Enrollment Services, Evergreen Valley College, 3095 Yerba Buena Road, San Jose, CA 95135

Fashion Careers College
San Diego, California
www.fashioncareerscollege.com **CB code: 3494**

- Private 2-year business college
- Commuter campus in very large city
- Application essay, interview required

General. Accredited by ACICS. **Enrollment:** 74 degree-seeking undergraduates. **Degrees:** 42 associate awarded. **Calendar:** Quarter. **Part-time faculty:** 10 total; 100% women.

Basis for selection. Exam score, essay, interview important. Wonderlic test used for admission.

2008-2009 Annual costs. Tuition/fees: $17,400.

Application procedures. Admission: No deadline. $25 fee. Admission notification on a rolling basis. **Financial aid:** No deadline. FAFSA required.

Academics. Credit/placement by examination: CLEP.

Majors. Business: Fashion. **Visual/performing arts:** Fashion design.

Most popular majors. Business/marketing 50%, visual/performing arts 50%.

Computing on campus. 23 workstations in computer center. Repair service available.

Student life. Freshman orientation: Mandatory. Held 1 week before classes start.

Student services. Career counseling, financial aid counseling, placement for graduates.

Contact. E-mail: info@fashioncareerscollege.com
Phone: (619) 275-4700 Toll-free number: (888) 322-2999
Fax: (619) 275-0635
Kathleen Hammond, Director of Admission, Fashion Careers College, 1923 Morena Boulevard, San Diego, CA 92110

Fashion Institute of Design and Merchandising: Los Angeles

Los Angeles, California
www.fidm.edu
CB member
CB code: 4457

- For-profit 2-year visual arts and business college
- Commuter campus in very large city
- Application essay, interview required

General. Founded in 1969. Regionally accredited. Branch campuses in Orange County, San Francisco and San Diego. **Enrollment:** 4,651 degree-seeking undergraduates. **Degrees:** 65 bachelor's, 1,788 associate awarded. **Calendar:** Quarter, extensive summer session. **Full-time faculty:** 60 total; 23% minority, 57% women. **Part-time faculty:** 232 total; 16% minority, 62% women. **Class size:** 77% < 20, 23% 20-39. **Special facilities:** Hollywood costume collection, costume study collection and museum, textile museum, fragrance bottle collection, fashion library.

Student profile. Among degree-seeking undergraduates, 881 enrolled as first-time, first-year students, 865 transferred in from other institutions.

Part-time:	12%	**Hispanic American:**	19%
Out-of-state:	35%	**Native American:**	1%
Women:	91%	**International:**	8%
African American:	5%	**25 or older:**	32%
Asian American:	14%		

Basis for selection. High school transcripts, standardized test scores, references, portfolio or admissions project, essays, and evidence of interest in major area through work experience, high school preparation, or extracurricular activities considered. In addition to transcript evaluation, SAT and/or ACT scores are considered to determine if additional testing is required. SAT or ACT recommended. Portfolio or admissions project required. Out-of-state applicants interviewed by telephone. Projects are required of all students. International students are not required to interview. **Homeschooled:** Statement describing homeschool structure and mission, interview required. Admissions or standardized testing required.

High school preparation. College-preparatory program recommended.

2009-2010 Annual costs. Tuition/fees: $20,685. Tuition and fees may vary depending on program. Books/supplies: $2,160.

Financial aid. Non-need-based: Scholarships awarded for academics. **Additional information:** Tuition/fee expenses may be reduced by applying for admission by December 31 of year before student plans to attend.

Application procedures. Admission: No deadline. $225 fee ($375 out-of-state). Admission notification on a rolling basis. **Financial aid:** Priority date 3/1; no closing date. FAFSA, institutional form required. Applicants notified on a rolling basis starting 3/15; must reply within 3 week(s) of notification.

Academics. Faculty and staff come from related industries. Project-oriented courses give students hands-on experience. **Special study options:** Distance learning, ESL, exchange student, independent study, internships, study abroad, weekend college. **Credit/placement by examination:** AP, CLEP, IB, institutional tests. 45 credit hours maximum toward associate degree, 45 toward bachelor's. **Support services:** Learning center, reduced course load, remedial instruction, study skills assistance, tutoring, writing center.

Majors. Business: Fashion, marketing, merchandising, operations, retailing, sales/distribution. **Family/consumer sciences:** Apparel marketing, clothing/textiles, fashion consultant, merchandising, textile manufacture, textile science. **Visual/performing arts:** Design, fashion design, fiber arts, graphic design, interior design, metal/jewelry, multimedia, theater design.

Most popular majors. Visual/performing arts 12%.

Computing on campus. 400 workstations in library, computer center, student center. Commuter students can connect to campus network. Online course registration, online library, helpline, wireless network available.

Student life. Freshman orientation: Mandatory. Preregistration for classes offered. **Activities:** International student organizations, student government, student newspaper, honor society, international club, design council, ASID, Phi Theta Kappa.

Student services. Adult student services, alcohol/substance abuse counseling, career counseling, student employment services, financial aid counseling, personal counseling, placement for graduates, women's services. **Physically disabled:** Services for visually, hearing impaired. **Transfer:** Preadmission transcript evaluation for new students. Transfer center, transfer adviser for students transferring to 4-year colleges.

Contact. E-mail: admissionsdirector@fidm.edu
Phone: (213) 624-1200 Toll-free number: (800) 624-1200
Fax: (213) 624-4799
Susan Aronson, Executive Director of Admissions, Fashion Institute of Design and Merchandising: Los Angeles, 919 South Grand Avenue, Los Angeles, CA 90015-1421

Fashion Institute of Design and Merchandising: San Diego

San Diego, California
www.fidm.edu
CB code: 2949

- For-profit 2-year visual arts and business college
- Commuter campus in very large city
- Application essay, interview required

General. Regionally accredited. Other campuses in Los Angeles, Orange County, and San Francisco. **Enrollment:** 265 degree-seeking undergraduates. **Degrees:** 54 associate awarded. **Calendar:** Quarter, extensive summer session. **Full-time faculty:** 3 total; 67% women. **Part-time faculty:** 24 total; 29% minority, 88% women. **Class size:** 77% < 20, 23% 20-39. **Special facilities:** Hollywood costume study collection and museum, textile museum, historical Annette Green fragrance bottle collection, fashion library.

Student profile. Among degree-seeking undergraduates, 20% already have a bachelor's degree or higher, 93 enrolled as first-time, first-year students, 92 transferred in from other institutions.

Part-time:	9%	**Hispanic American:**	20%
Women:	94%	**International:**	2%
African American:	3%	**25 or older:**	19%
Asian American:	9%		

Basis for selection. High school transcripts, standardized test scores, references, portfolio or admissions project, essays and evidence of interest in major through work experience, high school preparation, or extracurricular activities considered. In addition to transcript evaluation, SAT and/or ACT scores are considered to determine if additional testing is required. SAT or ACT recommended. Portfolio or admissions project required of all applicants. Out-of-state applicants are interviewed by telephone. International students are not required to interview. **Homeschooled:** Transcript of courses and grades, state high school equivalency certificate, interview required. Admissions or standardized testing required.

High school preparation. College-preparatory program recommended.

2009-2010 Annual costs. Tuition/fees: $20,685. Tuition and fees vary by program. Books/supplies: $2,160.

Financial aid. Non-need-based: Scholarships awarded for academics.

Application procedures. **Admission:** No deadline. $225 fee ($375 out-of-state). Admission notification on a rolling basis. **Financial aid:** No deadline. FAFSA, institutional form required. Applicants notified on a rolling basis; must reply within 3 week(s) of notification.

Academics. Faculty and staff are recruited from industry. Project-oriented courses provide hands-on learning experiences. **Special study options:** Distance learning, ESL, exchange student, independent study, internships, study abroad, weekend college. **Credit/placement by examination:** AP, CLEP, IB, institutional tests. 15 credit hours maximum toward associate degree. **Support services:** Learning center, reduced course load, remedial instruction, study skills assistance, tutoring, writing center.

Majors. **Business:** Fashion, marketing. **Family/consumer sciences:** Apparel marketing, clothing/textiles, fashion consultant, merchandising, textile manufacture, textile science. **Visual/performing arts:** Design, fashion design, fiber arts, graphic design.

Computing on campus. 35 workstations in library, computer center, student center. Commuter students can connect to campus network. Online course registration, online library, helpline, wireless network available.

Student life. **Freshman orientation:** Mandatory. Preregistration for classes offered. **Activities:** International student organizations, honor students society, alumni association, ASID student chapter, Design Council, Phi Theta Kappa, student activities committee.

Student services. Adult student services, alcohol/substance abuse counseling, career counseling, student employment services, financial aid counseling, personal counseling, placement for graduates, women's services. **Physically disabled:** Services for visually, hearing impaired. **Transfer:** Preadmission transcript evaluation for new students. Transfer center, transfer adviser for students transferring to 4-year colleges.

Contact. E-mail: admissionsdirector@fidm.edu
Phone: (619) 235-2049 Toll-free number: (800) 243-3436
Fax: (619) 232-4322
Susan Aronson, Executive Director of Admissions, Fashion Institute of Design and Merchandising: San Diego, 350 Tenth Avenue, Third Floor, San Diego, CA 92101

Fashion Institute of Design and Merchandising: San Francisco

San Francisco, California
www.fidm.edu **CB code: 4988**

- For-profit 2-year visual arts and business college
- Commuter campus in very large city
- Application essay, interview required

General. Founded in 1969. Regionally accredited. Other campuses in Los Angeles, Orange County, and San Diego. **Enrollment:** 950 degree-seeking undergraduates. **Degrees:** 377 associate awarded. **Calendar:** Quarter, extensive summer session. **Full-time faculty:** 13 total; 8% minority, 69% women. **Part-time faculty:** 57 total; 18% minority, 68% women. **Class size:** 77% < 20, 23% 20-39. **Special facilities:** Acces to Hollywood costume collection, costume study collection and museum, textiles museum, Annette Green fragrance bottle collection, fashion library.

Student profile. Among degree-seeking undergraduates, 30% already have a bachelor's degree or higher, 211 enrolled as first-time, first-year students, 224 transferred in from other institutions.

Part-time:	13%	**Asian American:**	19%
Out-of-state:	10%	**Hispanic American:**	17%
Women:	92%	**International:**	4%
African American:	5%		

Basis for selection. Recommendations and application essay very important. Rigor of secondary school record and academic GPA important. In addition to transcript, SAT and/or ACT scores are considered to determine if additional testing is required. SAT or ACT recommended. Portfolio or admissions project is required of all candidates. Out-of-state applicants are interviewed by telephone. International students are not required to interview. **Homeschooled:** Statement describing homeschool structure and mission, interview required.

High school preparation. College-preparatory program recommended. High school transcripts, standardized test scores, references, portfolio or admissions project, essays, and evidence of interest in major through work experience, high school preparation, or extracurricular activities accepted.

2009-2010 Annual costs. Tuition/fees: $20,685. Tuition and fees vary by program. Books/supplies: $2,160.

Financial aid. **Non-need-based:** Scholarships awarded for academics.

Application procedures. **Admission:** No deadline. $225 fee ($375 out-of-state). Admission notification on a rolling basis. **Financial aid:** No deadline. FAFSA, institutional form required. Applicants notified on a rolling basis starting 3/15; must reply within 3 week(s) of notification.

Academics. Faculty and staff are recruited from industry. Project oriented courses provide hands-on learning experiences. **Special study options:** Distance learning, ESL, exchange student, independent study, internships, study abroad, weekend college. **Credit/placement by examination:** AP, CLEP, IB, institutional tests. 45 credit hours maximum toward associate degree, 45 toward bachelor's. **Support services:** Learning center, reduced course load, remedial instruction, study skills assistance, tutoring, writing center.

Majors. **Business:** Fashion. **Computer sciences:** Computer graphics, webmaster. **Family/consumer sciences:** Apparel marketing, clothing/textiles, fashion consultant, merchandising, textile manufacture, textile science. **Visual/performing arts:** Design, fashion design, fiber arts, graphic design, interior design, metal/jewelry, multimedia, theater design.

Most popular majors. Business/marketing 36%, visual/performing arts 64%.

Computing on campus. 130 workstations in library, computer center, student center. Commuter students can connect to campus network. Online course registration, online library, helpline, wireless network available.

Student life. **Freshman orientation:** Mandatory. Preregistration for classes offered. **Activities:** International student organizations, student government, student newspaper, honor society, international club, design council, ASID student chapter, Phi Theta Kappa.

Student services. Adult student services, alcohol/substance abuse counseling, career counseling, student employment services, financial aid counseling, personal counseling, placement for graduates, women's services. **Physically disabled:** Services for visually, hearing impaired. **Transfer:** Preadmission transcript evaluation for new students. Transfer center, transfer adviser for students transferring to 4-year colleges.

Contact. E-mail: admissionsdirector@fidm.edu
Phone: (415) 675-5200 Toll-free number: (800) 422-3436
Fax: (415) 394-9700
Sheryl Badalamente, Director of Admissions, Fashion Institute of Design and Merchandising: San Francisco, 55 Stockton Street, San Francisco, CA 94108-5805

Feather River College

Quincy, California
www.frc.edu **CB code: 4318**

- Public 2-year community and liberal arts college
- Residential campus in small town

General. Founded in 1968. Regionally accredited. **Enrollment:** 757 degree-seeking undergraduates. **Degrees:** 145 associate awarded. **Location:** 150 miles from Sacramento, 80 miles from Reno, Nevada. **Calendar:** Semester, limited summer session. **Full-time faculty:** 25 total. **Part-time faculty:** 85 total. **Class size:** 54% < 20, 46% 20-39. **Special facilities:** Fish hatchery, horse boarding and training facility, state wildlife preserve.

Student profile.

Out-of-state:	30%	**Live on campus:**	10%
25 or older:	35%		

Transfer out. **Colleges most students transferred to 2008:** California State University: Chico, Humboldt State University, University of Nevada: Reno, California Polytechnic State University: San Luis Obispo, University of California: Davis.

Basis for selection. Open admission. Institute's own test required of all students for placement purposes. **Learning Disabled:** Placement tests in English and Math are required for new students with no college experience.

2008-2009 Annual costs. Tuition/fees: $664; $6,124 out-of-state. Per-credit charge: $20 in-state; $202 out-of-state. Good neighbor per unit fee is $42/unit for Nevada residents. Room only: $4,208. Books/supplies: $1,386.

Financial aid. **Need-based:** Need-based aid available for part-time students. Work-study available nights, weekends and for part-time students.

Application procedures. **Admission:** No deadline. No application fee. **Financial aid:** No deadline. FAFSA required. Applicants notified on a rolling basis starting 7/30; must reply within 3 week(s) of notification.

Academics. General education/core courses are offered that satisfy all lower division requirements of California State University, University of California, and University of Nevada system. **Special study options:** Cooperative education, cross-registration, distance learning, double major, dual enrollment of high school students, ESL, honors, independent study, liberal arts/career combination. License preparation in nursing, paramedic. **Credit/placement by examination:** AP, CLEP, IB, institutional tests. 12 credit hours maximum toward associate degree. **Support services:** GED preparation and test center, learning center, reduced course load, remedial instruction, study skills assistance, tutoring.

Majors. Agriculture: Agribusiness operations, business, equestrian studies, equine science, farm/ranch. **Biology:** General, wildlife. **Business:** Business admin, office/clerical. **Computer sciences:** Computer science. **Conservation:** General, environmental studies, fisheries, forest technology, forestry, management/policy, wildlife. **Construction:** Carpentry, maintenance. **Education:** General, early childhood. **Engineering technology:** Construction. **Family/consumer sciences:** Child care. **Health:** Licensed practical nurse. **History:** General. **Liberal arts:** Arts/sciences. **Math:** General. **Parks/recreation:** Exercise sciences, health/fitness, sports admin. **Protective services:** Law enforcement admin. **Social sciences:** General, criminology. **Visual/performing arts:** Art. **Other:** Outdoor recreation leadership.

Most popular majors. Agriculture 15%, business/marketing 8%, liberal arts 70%.

Computing on campus. 120 workstations in dormitories, library, computer center, student center. Dormitories wired for high-speed internet access. Online library, wireless network available.

Student life. Freshman orientation: Mandatory, $26 fee. 2-day, 1-night orientation held in fall and spring. **Housing:** Apartments available. **Activities:** Choral groups, drama, literary magazine, musical theater, student government, Phi Theta Kappa.

Athletics. NJCAA. **Intercollegiate:** Baseball M, basketball, football (tackle) M, rodeo, soccer, softball W, volleyball W. **Intramural:** Basketball, equestrian, skiing, softball, volleyball. **Team name:** Golden Eagles.

Student services. Adult student services, career counseling, services for economically disadvantaged, student employment services, financial aid counseling, health services, on-campus daycare, personal counseling, placement for graduates, veterans' counselor. **Physically disabled:** Services for visually, speech, hearing impaired. **Transfer:** Re-entry adviser, pre-admission transcript evaluation for new students. Transfer center, transfer adviser, college fairs on campus for students transferring to 4-year colleges.

Contact. Phone: (530) 283-0202 ext. 285 Toll-free number: (800) 442-9799 ext. 285 Fax: (530) 283-3757
Tama Bolton, Registrar, Feather River College, 570 Golden Eagle Avenue, Quincy, CA 95971

Folsom Lake College
Folsom, California
www.flc.losrios.edu **CB code: 4462**

- Public 2-year community college
- Commuter campus in small city

General. Regionally accredited. **Enrollment:** 5,591 degree-seeking undergraduates. **Degrees:** 579 associate awarded. **Location:** 25 miles from Sacramento. **Calendar:** Semester, limited summer session. **Full-time faculty:** 93 total. **Part-time faculty:** 193 total. **Special facilities:** Observatory.

Transfer out. Colleges most students transferred to 2008: California State University: Sacramento, University of California: Davis.

Basis for selection. Open admission. **Adult students:** SAT/ACT scores not required.

2008-2009 Annual costs. Tuition/fees: $632; $6,062 out-of-state. Per-credit charge: $20 in-state; $201 out-of-state. Books/supplies: $1,440. Personal expenses: $2,210.

Application procedures. Admission: No deadline. No application fee.

Academics. Special study options: Distance learning, ESL, study abroad. **Credit/placement by examination:** CLEP, institutional tests. **Support services:** Remedial instruction, study skills assistance, tutoring, writing center.

Majors. Biology: General. **Business:** General, accounting, administrative services, management science, marketing, real estate, small business admin. **Communications:** General, organizational. **Computer sciences:** General. **Education:** Early childhood. **Liberal arts:** Arts/sciences. **Math:** General. **Psychology:** General. **Public administration:** Human services. **Visual/performing arts:** Art.

Computing on campus. Online course registration, online library, wireless network available.

Student life. Freshman orientation: Available. **Activities:** Jazz band, choral groups, dance, drama, international student organizations, literary magazine, music ensembles, student government.

Athletics. Team name: Falcons.

Student services. Services for economically disadvantaged, financial aid counseling, health services, on-campus daycare, veterans' counselor. **Physically disabled:** Services for visually, speech, hearing impaired. **Transfer:** Transfer center, transfer adviser, college fairs on campus for students transferring to 4-year colleges.

Contact. Phone: (916) 608-6500 Fax: (916) 608-6569
Christine Wurzer, Admissions and Records Supervisor, Folsom Lake College, 10 College Parkway, Folsom, CA 95630

Foothill College
Los Altos Hills, California
www.foothill.edu **CB code: 4315**

- Public 2-year community college
- Commuter campus in large town

General. Founded in 1958. Regionally accredited. **Enrollment:** 8,223 degree-seeking undergraduates. **Degrees:** 506 associate awarded. **ROTC:** Army, Naval, Air Force. **Calendar:** Quarter, limited summer session. **Full-time faculty:** 206 total; 58% women. **Special facilities:** Center for innovation, Japanese cultural center, observatory, bamboo garden, dental health clinic travel careers computer lab, math center.

Student profile. Among degree-seeking undergraduates, 3,065 transferred in from other institutions.

Transfer out. Colleges most students transferred to 2008: San Jose State, University of California: Berkeley, University of California: Santa Cruz, University of California: Los Angeles, University of California: Davis.

Basis for selection. Open admission, but selective for some programs. Allied health programs have special prerequisites: using point system to rank required college-level and general education classes, top 20-40 students selected for admission. Must be 2-year transfer.

2008-2009 Annual costs. Tuition/fees: $628; $5,803 out-of-state. Per-credit charge: $13 in-state; $128 out-of-state. Books/supplies: $1,656. Personal expenses: $2,754.

Financial aid. All financial aid based on need. Need-based aid available for part-time students.

Application procedures. Admission: No deadline. No application fee. Admission notification on a rolling basis. **Financial aid:** Priority date 3/30; no closing date. FAFSA, institutional form required. Applicants notified on a rolling basis; must reply within 2 week(s) of notification.

Academics. NASA Ames Research Center internships available. **Special study options:** Cooperative education, cross-registration, distance learning, ESL, exchange student, honors, independent study, internships, liberal arts/career combination, study abroad, weekend college. License preparation in dental hygiene, paramedic, radiology, real estate. **Credit/placement by examination:** AP, CLEP, institutional tests. 20 credit hours maximum toward associate degree. **Support services:** Learning center, remedial instruction, study skills assistance, tutoring, writing center.

Honors college/program. Continuing students should have minimum 3.3 cumulative GPA in 10 or more units completed at Foothill College. New students must have minimum 3.5 cumulative high school GPA or SAT total of at least 2100 or Enhanced ACT Composite of 26 or minimum 3.3 cumulative GPA in 10 or more units completed at another accredited college or university. Minimum AP English score of 3 or 2, minimum score on assessment test of ENGL Reading 93 and ENGL Writing 111 or completion of English 1A with a grade of B or better. Letter of recommendation and personal statement required.

Majors. Agriculture: Landscaping, nursery operations, ornamental horticulture. **Area/ethnic studies:** American, women's. **Biology:** General, bioinformatics, biotechnology. **Business:** Accounting, business admin, international, office technology, real estate, tourism promotion. **Communications:** General, broadcast journalism, media studies, radio/tv. **Computer sciences:**

General, computer graphics, computer science, database management, information technology, LAN/WAN management, programming. **Construction:** Electrician. **Education:** Early childhood. **Engineering:** General, software. **Engineering technology:** Biomedical, electrical. **Family/consumer sciences:** Child development. **Foreign languages:** Chinese, French, Japanese, linguistics, Spanish. **Health:** Athletic training, dental assistant, dental hygiene, medical radiologic technology/radiation therapy, pharmacy assistant, physician assistant, predental, premedicine, prepharmacy, preveterinary, radiologic technology/medical imaging, respiratory therapy assistant, respiratory therapy technology, sonography, veterinary technology/assistant. **History:** General. **Interdisciplinary:** Intercultural. **Legal studies:** Prelaw. **Liberal arts:** Arts/sciences, library assistant. **Math:** General. **Mechanic/repair:** Aircraft. **Philosophy/religion:** Philosophy. **Physical sciences:** Chemistry, geology, physics. **Psychology:** General. **Science technology:** Biological. **Social sciences:** General, anthropology, economics, geography, political science, sociology. **Visual/performing arts:** Art, art history/conservation, commercial/advertising art, dramatic, photography, studio arts, theater design. **Other:** Informatics, Viticulture & enology.

Computing on campus. 200 workstations in library, computer center, student center. Commuter students can connect to campus network. Online course registration, online library, wireless network available.

Student life. **Freshman orientation:** Available. **Activities:** Bands, choral groups, dance, drama, film society, music ensembles, musical theater, radio station, student government, student newspaper, symphony orchestra, TV station, 32 different multicultural/ethnic campus clubs.

Athletics. **Intercollegiate:** Basketball, diving, football (tackle) M, golf, soccer, softball W, swimming, tennis, volleyball W, water polo W. **Intramural:** Basketball, cheerleading, football (non-tackle), soccer, softball, volleyball. **Team name:** Owls.

Student services. Adult student services, alcohol/substance abuse counseling, career counseling, services for economically disadvantaged, student employment services, financial aid counseling, health services, legal services, minority student services, personal counseling, placement for graduates, veterans' counselor. **Physically disabled:** Services for visually, speech, hearing impaired. **Transfer:** Transfer adviser, college fairs on campus for students transferring to 4-year colleges.

Contact. Phone: (650) 949-7325 Fax: (650) 949-7048
Jerry Cellilo, Interim Dean Counseling and Matriculation, Foothill College, 12345 El Monte Road, Los Altos Hills, CA 94022

Fremont College

Cerritos, California
www.fremont.edu — **CB code: 3007**

- For-profit 2-year health science and career college
- Commuter campus in very large city
- Application essay, interview required

General. Accredited by ACCSCT. Year-round program with starts every 5 weeks. **Enrollment:** 131 degree-seeking undergraduates. **Degrees:** 25 associate awarded. **Location:** 20 miles from Los Angeles. **Calendar:** Continuous. **Full-time faculty:** 2 total. **Part-time faculty:** 10 total. **Class size:** 58% < 20, 42% 20-39.

Student profile. Among degree-seeking undergraduates, 100% enrolled in a vocational program.

Basis for selection. Open admission, but selective for some programs. High school diploma or GED and successful completion of CPAt required. **Homeschooled:** State high school equivalency certificate required.

2008-2009 Annual costs. Paralegal: $22,800. Sports therapy: $21,600. Massage Therapy: $13,600.

2007-2008 Financial aid. All financial aid based on need.

Application procedures. **Admission:** No deadline. $85 fee. **Financial aid:** FAFSA, institutional form required.

Academics. **Special study options:** Accelerated study. **Credit/placement by examination:** CLEP. **Support services:** Tutoring.

Majors. **Business:** General. **Legal studies:** Paralegal. **Parks/recreation:** Exercise sciences.

Computing on campus. PC or laptop required. 30 workstations in library, computer center.

Student life. **Freshman orientation:** Available. Preregistration for classes offered.

Student services. Financial aid counseling, placement for graduates. **Transfer:** Pre-admission transcript evaluation for new students.

Contact. E-mail: leads@fremont.edu
Phone: (562) 809-5100 Toll-free number: (877) 344-2345
Fax: (562) 809-7100
Brian Watson, Admissions Director, Fremont College, 18000 Studebaker Road, 900A, Cerritos, CA 90703-5342

Fresno City College

Fresno, California — **CB member**
www.fresnocitycollege.edu — **CB code: 4311**

- Public 2-year community and liberal arts college
- Commuter campus in large city

General. Founded in 1910. Regionally accredited. **Enrollment:** 12,583 degree-seeking undergraduates. **Degrees:** 1,386 associate awarded. **ROTC:** Army, Air Force. **Location:** 185 miles from San Francisco. **Calendar:** Semester, extensive summer session. **Full-time faculty:** 309 total; 29% minority, 47% women. **Part-time faculty:** 742 total; 22% minority, 43% women. **Class size:** 28% < 20, 59% 20-39, 7% 40-49, 4% 50-99, 3% >100. **Special facilities:** Anthropology museum, greenhouse and koi pond, high-tech laboratory for disabled students.

Student profile.

Out-of-state:	2%	**25 or older:**	39%

Transfer out. **Colleges most students transferred to 2008:** California State University: Fresno, University of Phoenix, National University, Fresno Pacific University.

Basis for selection. Open admission, but selective for some programs. Limited admission to allied health programs, police academy, and apprenticeship programs.

2008-2009 Annual costs. Tuition/fees: $630; $6,060 out-of-state. Per-credit charge: $20 in-state; $201 out-of-state. Books/supplies: $1,400. Personal expenses: $2,472.

Financial aid. All financial aid based on need. Need-based aid available for part-time students. Work-study available for part-time students. **Additional information:** Board of Governors Grant Program to offset enrollment fees based on untaxed income, low income, or calculated need. Students qualifying for program also automatically exempt from health fees. March 2 application deadline for California grants.

Application procedures. **Admission:** No deadline. No application fee. Admission notification on a rolling basis. **Financial aid:** Priority date 4/15; no closing date. FAFSA required. Applicants notified on a rolling basis starting 4/1.

Academics. **Special study options:** Accelerated study, cross-registration, distance learning, double major, dual enrollment of high school students, ESL, honors, independent study, internships, study abroad, weekend college. License preparation in dental hygiene, nursing, radiology, real estate. **Credit/placement by examination:** AP, CLEP, institutional tests. 48 credit hours maximum toward associate degree. **Support services:** Learning center, pre-admission summer program, reduced course load, remedial instruction, study skills assistance, tutoring, writing center.

Majors. **Agriculture:** General, food science. **Area/ethnic studies:** African-American, Hispanic-American/Latino/Chicano, Native American, women's. **Business:** General, accounting, administrative services, banking/financial services, business admin, fashion, insurance, office/clerical, purchasing, real estate. **Communications:** General, journalism. **Communications technology:** Graphic/printing. **Computer sciences:** General, computer science, data processing, information systems, programming. **Conservation:** General. **Construction:** Carpentry, electrician, maintenance, pipefitting, power transmission. **Education:** Bilingual, early childhood, multi-level teacher. **Engineering:** General. **Engineering technology:** Drafting. **Family/consumer sciences:** General, child care, clothing/textiles, food/nutrition, institutional food production. **Foreign languages:** General, Spanish. **Health:** Clinical lab technology, dental hygiene, medical assistant, medical radiologic technology/radiation therapy, medical records technology, medical secretary, medical transcription, nursing (RN), respiratory therapy technology, substance abuse counseling. **History:** General. **Interdisciplinary:** Biological/physical sciences. **Legal studies:** Legal secretary, paralegal. **Liberal arts:** Arts/sciences, library science. **Math:** General. **Mechanic/repair:** General, auto body, automotive, electronics/electrical, heating/ac/refrig, industrial. **Parks/recreation:** General, facilities management. **Physical sciences:** Chemistry. **Protective services:** Corrections, firefighting, law enforcement admin, police science. **Psychology:** General. **Public administration:** General, social work. **Social sciences:** General, anthropology, criminology, geography, sociology. **Transportation:** General. **Visual/performing arts:** General, art, crafts, dance, dramatic, music management, photography, piano/organ, printmaking, theater design, voice/opera.

Most popular majors. Health sciences 30%, liberal arts 55%.

Computing on campus. 400 workstations in library, computer center. Commuter students can connect to campus network. Online course registration, online library, wireless network available.

Student life. **Freshman orientation:** Available. **Activities:** Bands, choral groups, dance, drama, film society, international student organizations, literary magazine, music ensembles, musical theater, student government, student newspaper, symphony orchestra, TV station, Christian Athletes in Acting, MECHA, Pan American Association, Alpha Gamma Sigma, Phi Theta Kappa.

Athletics. NJCAA. **Intercollegiate:** Badminton, baseball M, basketball, cheerleading, cross-country, football (tackle) M, golf, soccer, softball W, tennis, track and field, volleyball W, wrestling M. **Intramural:** Basketball, football (non-tackle), soccer, softball, table tennis, volleyball, weight lifting. **Team name:** Rams.

Student services. Adult student services, career counseling, services for economically disadvantaged, student employment services, financial aid counseling, health services, minority student services, on-campus daycare, personal counseling, placement for graduates, veterans' counselor. **Physically disabled:** Services for visually, speech, hearing impaired. **Transfer:** Transfer center, transfer adviser, college fairs on campus for students transferring to 4-year colleges.

Contact. E-mail: info@scccd.com
Phone: (559) 442-4600 Toll-free number: (866) 245-3276
Fax: (559) 237-4232
John Cummings, District Dean of Admissions, Records and Institutional Research, Fresno City College, 1101 East University Avenue, Fresno, CA 93741

Fullerton College

Fullerton, California
www.fullcoll.edu **CB code: 4314**

- Public 2-year community and technical college
- Commuter campus in small city
- SAT or ACT required

General. Founded in 1913. Regionally accredited. **Enrollment:** 16,271 degree-seeking undergraduates. **Degrees:** 1,123 associate awarded. **ROTC:** Naval. **Location:** 35 miles from Los Angeles. **Calendar:** Semester, extensive summer session. **Full-time faculty:** 315 total. **Part-time faculty:** 480 total.

Basis for selection. Open admission. College-administered English, reading, and math exams used for placement.

2008-2009 Annual costs. Tuition/fees: $628; $5,698 out-of-state. Per-credit charge: $20 in-state; $189 out-of-state. Books/supplies: $648. Personal expenses: $1,818.

Application procedures. **Admission:** No deadline. No application fee. Admission notification on a rolling basis. **Financial aid:** No deadline. FAFSA required. Applicants notified on a rolling basis.

Academics. **Special study options:** Distance learning, double major, dual enrollment of high school students, ESL, honors, independent study, internships, study abroad. License preparation in real estate. **Credit/placement by examination:** AP, CLEP, institutional tests. 15 credit hours maximum toward associate degree. **Support services:** Learning center, remedial instruction, study skills assistance, tutoring, writing center.

Majors. **Agriculture:** Horticulture, nursery operations. **Architecture:** Landscape. **Area/ethnic studies:** Latin American. **Biology:** General, bacteriology, zoology. **Business:** Accounting, administrative services, business admin, fashion, international, management information systems, purchasing, real estate, tourism promotion. **Communications:** General, broadcast journalism, journalism. **Communications technology:** Graphic/printing. **Computer sciences:** General, applications programming, data processing. **Conservation:** General, fisheries, forestry. **Construction:** Carpentry, maintenance. **Education:** Business, trade/industrial. **Engineering:** General. **Engineering technology:** Drafting, electrical. **Family/consumer sciences:** General, child care, family studies. **Foreign languages:** General. **Health:** Clinical lab science, prenursing. **History:** General. **Legal studies:** Legal secretary, paralegal. **Liberal arts:** Arts/sciences, library assistant. **Math:** General. **Mechanic/repair:** Auto body. **Parks/recreation:** General. **Personal/culinary services:** Cosmetic. **Philosophy/religion:** Philosophy. **Physical sciences:** Astronomy, chemistry, geology, physics. **Protective services:** Police science. **Psychology:** General. **Social sciences:** Anthropology, economics, geography, political science, sociology. **Visual/performing arts:** General, art, commercial/advertising art, dance, design, dramatic, fashion design.

Computing on campus. 400 workstations in library, computer center. Online course registration, helpline, wireless network available.

Student life. **Activities:** Bands, choral groups, dance, drama, film society, literary magazine, music ensembles, musical theater, radio station, student government, student newspaper, symphony orchestra, TV station, volunteer bureau, Movimiento Estudiantil Chicano de Aztlan.

Athletics. **Intercollegiate:** Badminton, baseball M, basketball, cross-country, diving, football (tackle) M, golf M, gymnastics, soccer, softball W, swimming, tennis, track and field, volleyball, water polo M. **Team name:** Hornets.

Student services. Adult student services, career counseling, student employment services, health services, on-campus daycare, personal counseling, placement for graduates, veterans' counselor. **Physically disabled:** Services for visually, speech, hearing impaired. **Transfer:** Transfer adviser for students transferring to 4-year colleges.

Contact. E-mail: admissions@fullcoll.edu
Phone: (714) 992-7568
Albert Abutin, Dean, Admissions and Records, Fullerton College, 321 East Chapman Avenue, Fullerton, CA 92832-2095

Gavilan College

Gilroy, California
www.gavilan.edu **CB code: 4678**

- Public 2-year community college
- Large town

General. Founded in 1919. Regionally accredited. **Enrollment:** 3,115 degree-seeking undergraduates. **Degrees:** 260 associate awarded. **Location:** 35 miles from San Jose. **Calendar:** Semester, limited summer session. **Full-time faculty:** 71 total; 11% have terminal degrees. **Part-time faculty:** 116 total; 3% have terminal degrees. **Special facilities:** Golf course, hiking trails.

Transfer out. **Colleges most students transferred to 2008:** San Jose State, California State University: Monterey Bay, University of California: Santa Cruz.

Basis for selection. Open admission.

2008-2009 Annual costs. Tuition/fees: $642; $6,162 out-of-state. Per-credit charge: $20 in-state; $204 out-of-state. Books/supplies: $1,332. Personal expenses: $2,430.

Application procedures. **Admission:** No deadline. No application fee. Application must be submitted on paper. Admission notification on a rolling basis. **Financial aid:** Priority date 6/30; no closing date. FAFSA required. Applicants notified on a rolling basis starting 7/15; must reply within 2 week(s) of notification.

Academics. **Special study options:** Distance learning, dual enrollment of high school students, ESL, honors, independent study, internships, liberal arts/career combination, study abroad. License preparation in aviation, nursing. **Credit/placement by examination:** AP, CLEP, institutional tests. **Support services:** Learning center, reduced course load, remedial instruction, study skills assistance, tutoring, writing center.

Majors. **Biology:** General, ecology. **Business:** General. **Communications:** General, journalism. **Computer sciences:** General, computer graphics. **Foreign languages:** Spanish. **Health:** Nursing (RN). **History:** General. **Liberal arts:** Arts/sciences. **Math:** General. **Mechanic/repair:** Aircraft. **Personal/culinary services:** Cosmetic. **Philosophy/religion:** Philosophy. **Physical sciences:** Astronomy, chemistry, geology. **Protective services:** Corrections. **Psychology:** General. **Social sciences:** General, anthropology, economics, geography, political science, sociology. **Visual/performing arts:** Art, art history/conservation, dramatic, music performance, studio arts, theater design.

Most popular majors. Education 6%, health sciences 18%, liberal arts 61%, security/protective services 6%.

Computing on campus. 600 workstations in library, computer center. Wireless network available.

Student life. **Freshman orientation:** Mandatory. **Activities:** Choral groups, drama, literary magazine, music ensembles, musical theater, student government, student newspaper, symphony orchestra, TV station.

Athletics. **Intercollegiate:** Baseball M, basketball, football (tackle) M, golf, soccer W, softball W, tennis, volleyball W. **Team name:** Rams.

Student services. Adult student services, career counseling, services for economically disadvantaged, financial aid counseling, health services, on-campus daycare, personal counseling, veterans' counselor. **Physically disabled:** Services for visually, speech, hearing impaired. **Learning disabled:** Comprehensive services available. **Transfer:** Transfer center, transfer adviser, college fairs on campus for students transferring to 4-year colleges.

Contact. Phone: (408) 848-4735 Fax: (408) 848-4940
Joy Parker, Director of Admissions and Records, Gavilan College, 5055 Santa Teresa Boulevard, Gilroy, CA 95020

Glendale Community College

Glendale, California — **CB member**
www.glendale.edu — **CB code: 4327**

- Public 2-year community college
- Commuter campus in small city

General. Founded in 1927. Regionally accredited. **Enrollment:** 12,517 degree-seeking undergraduates. **Degrees:** 649 associate awarded. **Location:** 10 miles from Los Angeles. **Calendar:** Semester, extensive summer session. **Full-time faculty:** 248 total; 25% minority, 51% women. **Part-time faculty:** 536 total; 22% minority, 51% women. **Class size:** 30% < 20, 52% 20-39, 12% 40-49, 5% 50-99, less than 1% >100. **Special facilities:** Science center with planetarium, Baja California (Mexico) field station.

Student profile. Among degree-seeking undergraduates, 72% enrolled in a transfer program, 7% enrolled in a vocational program, 8% already have a bachelor's degree or higher, 2,220 enrolled as first-time, first-year students, 752 transferred in from other institutions.

Out-of-state:	1%	**Hispanic American:**	23%
African American:	3%	**International:**	22%
Asian American:	10%	**25 or older:**	41%

Transfer out. **Colleges most students transferred to 2008:** California State University: Northridge, University of California: Los Angeles, California State University: Los Angeles, University of Southern California.

Basis for selection. Open admission, but selective for some programs. Nursing program has special requirements.

2008-2009 Annual costs. Tuition/fees: $633; $6,063 out-of-state. Per-credit charge: $20 in-state; $201 out-of-state. Books/supplies: $1,566. Personal expenses: $2,340.

2007-2008 Financial aid. All financial aid based on need. Need-based aid available for part-time students. Work-study available nights, weekends and for part-time students.

Application procedures. **Admission:** Priority date 4/15; no deadline. No application fee. Admission notification on a rolling basis. **Financial aid:** Priority date 4/15; no closing date. FAFSA, institutional form required. Applicants notified on a rolling basis starting 6/15; must reply within 2 week(s) of notification.

Academics. **Special study options:** Cooperative education, distance learning, dual enrollment of high school students, ESL, honors, independent study, internships, study abroad. License preparation in aviation, nursing, real estate. **Credit/placement by examination:** AP, CLEP, institutional tests. 12 credit hours maximum toward associate degree. **Support services:** GED preparation and test center, learning center, remedial instruction, study skills assistance, tutoring, writing center.

Honors college/program. Scholars program admits academically accomplished students and offers priority transfer opportunites at UCLA, USC, Pepperdine, and others.

Majors. **Biology:** General. **Business:** General, accounting, administrative services, hospitality/recreation, office management, real estate. **Communications:** Broadcast journalism, journalism. **Computer sciences:** General. **Education:** Early childhood, multi-level teacher. **Engineering technology:** Drafting. **Family/consumer sciences:** General, child care, clothing/textiles, food/nutrition. **Foreign languages:** General, French, Spanish. **Health:** Licensed practical nurse, medical assistant, medical secretary, nursing (RN). **History:** General. **Interdisciplinary:** Biological/physical sciences. **Legal studies:** Legal secretary, paralegal. **Liberal arts:** Arts/sciences, humanities. **Math:** General. **Mechanic/repair:** Aircraft. **Parks/recreation:** General. **Personal/culinary services:** Cosmetic, culinary arts. **Philosophy/religion:** Philosophy. **Physical sciences:** Chemistry, physics. **Protective services:** Fire safety technology, law enforcement admin, police science. **Psychology:** General. **Social sciences:** General, anthropology, economics, sociology. **Visual/performing arts:** General, commercial/advertising art, dance, theater design.

Most popular majors. Business/marketing 15%, English 7%, health sciences 11%, liberal arts 52%, social sciences 6%.

Computing on campus. 1,000 workstations in library, computer center. Online course registration, helpline, repair service, wireless network available.

Student life. **Freshman orientation:** Available. **Activities:** Bands, choral groups, dance, drama, literary magazine, music ensembles, musical theater, radio station, student government, student newspaper, TV station, International Student Association, Armenian Student Association, Korean Christian Club, Organization of Latin for Higher Education, Association of Latin American Students.

Athletics. **Intercollegiate:** Baseball M, basketball, cross-country, football (tackle) M, soccer M, tennis, track and field, volleyball W. **Team name:** Vaqueros.

Student services. Adult student services, career counseling, services for economically disadvantaged, student employment services, financial aid counseling, health services, on-campus daycare, personal counseling, placement for graduates, veterans' counselor. **Physically disabled:** Services for visually, speech, hearing impaired. **Learning disabled:** Comprehensive services available. **Transfer:** Re-entry adviser for new students. Transfer center, transfer adviser, college fairs on campus for students transferring to 4-year colleges.

Contact. E-mail: info@glendale.edu
Phone: (818) 240-1000 ext. 5901 Fax: (818) 549-9436
Sharon Combs, Dean of Admissions and Records, Glendale Community College, 1500 North Verdugo Road, Glendale, CA 91208-2809

Golden West College

Huntington Beach, California
www.goldenwestcollege.edu — **CB code: 4339**

- Public 2-year community college
- Commuter campus in small city

General. Founded in 1966. Regionally accredited. **Enrollment:** 8,981 degree-seeking undergraduates. **Degrees:** 781 associate awarded. **Location:** 40 miles from Los Angeles. **Calendar:** Semester, extensive summer session. **Full-time faculty:** 190 total. **Part-time faculty:** 300 total. **Special facilities:** Outdoor amphitheatre, California native garden.

Transfer out. **Colleges most students transferred to 2008:** California State University: Long Beach, California State University: Dominguez Hills, California State University: Fullerton, University of California: Irvine, University of California: Los Angeles.

Basis for selection. Open admission, but selective for some programs. Any student at least 18 years of age eligible for admission. Limited admission to police academy and nursing program. Nursing applicants accepted on basis of prerequisite courses completed and GPA. SAT or ACT scores can be used for counseling and placement in lieu of institutional placement exams.

2008-2009 Annual costs. Tuition/fees: $632; $6,062 out-of-state. Per-credit charge: $20 in-state; $201 out-of-state. Parking fee is $30 per semester. Books/supplies: $810. Personal expenses: $1,530.

2008-2009 Financial aid. **Non-need-based:** Scholarships awarded for academics.

Application procedures. **Admission:** Priority date 4/1; no deadline. No application fee. Admission notification on a rolling basis. **Financial aid:** Priority date 6/1; no closing date. FAFSA, institutional form required. Applicants notified on a rolling basis starting 7/1; must reply within 3 week(s) of notification.

Academics. **Special study options:** Accelerated study, cooperative education, cross-registration, distance learning, double major, dual enrollment of high school students, ESL, honors, independent study, study abroad, weekend college. License preparation in nursing, real estate. **Credit/placement by examination:** AP, CLEP, institutional tests. 6 credit hours maximum toward associate degree. **Support services:** Learning center, pre-admission summer program, remedial instruction, tutoring, writing center.

Two-Year Colleges

Majors. **Agriculture:** Horticultural science. **Biology:** General. **Business:** General, accounting, administrative services, business admin, office management, office technology, office/clerical, real estate, sales/distribution. **Communications:** Broadcast journalism, journalism, public relations. **Computer sciences:** General. **Education:** Physical. **Engineering technology:** Architectural, drafting. **Foreign languages:** General, French, German, sign language interpretation, Spanish. **Health:** Nursing (RN), predental, premedicine, prepharmacy, preveterinary. **History:** General. **Interdisciplinary:** Biological/physical sciences. **Legal studies:** Legal secretary, prelaw. **Liberal arts:** Arts/sciences. **Math:** General. **Mechanic/repair:** Auto body, automotive, diesel. **Personal/culinary services:** Cosmetic. **Philosophy/religion:** Philosophy. **Physical sciences:** Astronomy, chemistry, geology. **Protective services:** Criminal justice, law enforcement admin. **Psychology:** General. **Social sciences:** General, anthropology, economics, political science, sociology. **Visual/performing arts:** Art, commercial/advertising art, dance, dramatic, music performance, music theory/composition, photography, studio arts.

Computing on campus. Online course registration, online library, wireless network available.

Student life. **Freshman orientation:** Mandatory. Preregistration for classes offered. Program held prior to enrollment. **Activities:** Bands, choral groups, dance, drama, film society, international student organizations, literary magazine, music ensembles, musical theater, radio station, student government, student newspaper, symphony orchestra, TV station, honor society, student nurses organization, cosmetology club, French club, Circle K, Women of Action.

Athletics. NJCAA. **Intercollegiate:** Baseball M, basketball, cross-country, football (tackle) M, golf M, soccer, softball W, swimming, tennis, track and field, volleyball, water polo M, wrestling M. **Team name:** Rustlers.

Student services. Adult student services, career counseling, services for economically disadvantaged, student employment services, health services, on-campus daycare, personal counseling, placement for graduates, veterans' counselor. **Physically disabled:** Services for visually, speech, hearing impaired. **Transfer:** Transfer center, transfer adviser, college fairs on campus for students transferring to 4-year colleges.

Contact. Phone: (714) 895-8306 Fax: (714) 895-8960
Shirley Donnelly, Director Enrollment Services, Golden West College, 15744 Golden West Street, Box 2748, Huntington Beach, CA 92647-2748

Golf Academy of America: San Diego

Carlsbad, California
www.golfacademy.edu **CB code: 3495**

- For-profit 2-year college of golf course management
- Small city

General. Accredited by ACICS. **Calendar:** Semester.

Annual costs/financial aid. Tuition/fees (2008-2009): $13,350. Books/supplies: $700.

Contact. Phone: (760) 734-1208
1950 Camino Vida Roble, Suite 125, Carlsbad, CA 92008

Grossmont College

El Cajon, California
www.grossmont.edu **CB code: 4334**

- Public 2-year community college
- Commuter campus in small city

General. Founded in 1961. Regionally accredited. **Enrollment:** 12,595 degree-seeking undergraduates. **Degrees:** 1,227 associate awarded. **Location:** 25 miles from San Diego. **Calendar:** Semester, extensive summer session. **Full-time faculty:** 180 total. **Part-time faculty:** 550 total.

Transfer out. **Colleges most students transferred to 2008:** San Diego State University.

Basis for selection. Open admission, but selective for some programs. Limited admission to health professions programs.

2008-2009 Annual costs. Tuition/fees: $630; $6,060 out-of-state. Per-credit charge: $20 in-state; $201 out-of-state. Books/supplies: $1,500. Personal expenses: $1,500.

2007-2008 Financial aid. All financial aid based on need. 86% of total undergraduate aid awarded as scholarships/grants, 14% as loans/jobs. Need-based aid available for part-time students. Work-study available nights, weekends and for part-time students.

Application procedures. **Admission:** Priority date 8/22; no deadline. No application fee. Admission notification on a rolling basis. **Financial aid:** Priority date 2/1; no closing date. FAFSA required. Applicants notified on a rolling basis starting 7/15; must reply within 2 week(s) of notification.

Academics. **Special study options:** Accelerated study, cross-registration, distance learning, double major, dual enrollment of high school students, ESL, independent study, internships, student-designed major, study abroad. License preparation in nursing. **Credit/placement by examination:** AP, CLEP. Students may earn a maximum of 18 units on the CLEP general examinations. **Support services:** Learning center, reduced course load, remedial instruction, tutoring, writing center.

Majors. **Area/ethnic studies:** Native American. **Biology:** General. **Business:** General, administrative services, business admin, executive assistant, hospitality admin, international, management science, marketing, sales/distribution, tourism promotion, tourism/travel. **Communications:** General, broadcast journalism, digital media, journalism. **Computer sciences:** General, applications programming, computer science, LAN/WAN management, programming, webmaster. **Family/consumer sciences:** Child care, child development. **Foreign languages:** American Sign Language, Arabic, French, German, Japanese, Russian, Spanish. **Health:** Athletic training, cardiovascular technology, nursing (RN), occupational therapy assistant, respiratory therapy technology, speech-language pathology assistant. **History:** General. **Liberal arts:** Arts/sciences. **Math:** General. **Parks/recreation:** Exercise sciences. **Personal/culinary services:** Baking, culinary arts, restaurant/catering. **Philosophy/religion:** Philosophy. **Physical sciences:** Chemistry, geology, physics. **Protective services:** Corrections, forensics, police science, security services. **Social sciences:** Economics, geography, political science. **Visual/performing arts:** Acting, art history/conservation, ceramics, cinematography, dance, drawing, jazz, painting, photography, sculpture, theater design. **Other:** Orthopedic technology.

Computing on campus. 500 workstations in library, computer center. Online course registration, wireless network available.

Student life. **Freshman orientation:** Available. **Activities:** Bands, choral groups, dance, drama, music ensembles, musical theater, radio station, student government, student newspaper, symphony orchestra.

Athletics. **Intercollegiate:** Baseball M, basketball, football (tackle) M, soccer W, softball W, swimming, tennis, volleyball, water polo. **Team name:** Griffins.

Student services. Adult student services, alcohol/substance abuse counseling, career counseling, services for economically disadvantaged, student employment services, financial aid counseling, health services, on-campus daycare, personal counseling, placement for graduates. **Physically disabled:** Services for visually, speech, hearing impaired. **Transfer:** Transfer center, transfer adviser, college fairs on campus for students transferring to 4-year colleges.

Contact. Phone: (619) 644-7186 Fax: (619) 644-7933
Brad Tiffany, Dean of Admissions and Records, Grossmont College, 8800 Grossmont College Drive, El Cajon, CA 92020

Hartnell College

Salinas, California
www.hartnell.edu **CB code: 4340**

- Public 2-year community college
- Commuter campus in small city

General. Founded in 1920. Regionally accredited. **Enrollment:** 4,092 degree-seeking undergraduates. **Degrees:** 435 associate awarded. **Location:** 110 miles from San Francisco, 65 miles from San Jose. **Calendar:** Semester, limited summer session. **Full-time faculty:** 97 total. **Part-time faculty:** 235 total.

Basis for selection. Open admission, but selective for some programs. Limited admission to nursing programs and animal health technology. Interview required for nursing, physician's assistant, animal health technician majors.

2008-2009 Annual costs. Tuition/fees: $608; $6,038 out-of-state. Per-credit charge: $20 in-state; $201 out-of-state. Books/supplies: $1,566. Personal expenses: $3,024.

2007-2008 Financial aid. **Need-based:** 96% of total undergraduate aid awarded as scholarships/grants, 4% as loans/jobs.

Application procedures. Admission: No deadline. No application fee. Admission notification on a rolling basis. **Financial aid:** Priority date 8/1; no closing date. FAFSA required. Applicants notified on a rolling basis.

Academics. Special study options: Cooperative education. **Credit/placement by examination:** CLEP. **Support services:** Learning center, remedial instruction, tutoring.

Majors. Agriculture: General, agribusiness operations. **Biology:** General. **Business:** Administrative services, banking/financial services, business admin, real estate. **Communications:** Digital media. **Computer sciences:** Information technology, programming, system admin, web page design. **Construction:** Site management. **Education:** Teacher assistance. **Engineering:** General. **Engineering technology:** General, drafting, hazardous materials, mechanical, water quality. **Family/consumer sciences:** Child development. **Health:** Clinical lab technology, dental hygiene, nursing (RN), physician assistant, substance abuse counseling, veterinary technology/assistant. **History:** General. **Liberal arts:** Arts/sciences. **Math:** General. **Mechanic/repair:** Auto body, automotive, diesel, electronics/electrical. **Physical sciences:** Chemistry, geology, physics. **Protective services:** Corrections, firefighting, law enforcement admin. **Psychology:** General. **Social sciences:** General. **Visual/performing arts:** Art, dramatic, photography.

Student life. Activities: Bands, choral groups, drama, music ensembles, musical theater, student government, student newspaper.

Athletics. Intercollegiate: Baseball M, basketball, cross-country M, football (tackle) M, soccer M.

Student services. Career counseling, student employment services, personal counseling, placement for graduates.

Contact. Phone: (831) 755-6711 Fax: (831) 759-6014
Mary Dominguez, Director of Enrollment Services, Hartnell College, 156 Homestead Avenue, Salinas, CA 93901

Heald College: Concord
Concord, California
www.heald.edu **CB code: 0235**

- Private 2-year business college
- Commuter campus in small city
- Interview required

General. Founded in 1863. Regionally accredited. **Enrollment:** 983 degree-seeking undergraduates. **Degrees:** 310 associate awarded. **Location:** 25 miles from San Francisco. **Calendar:** Quarter. **Full-time faculty:** 21 total. **Part-time faculty:** 32 total.

Basis for selection. Institutional admissions examination and personal interview. Institutionally designed test used for admissions.

2008-2009 Annual costs. Tuition/fees: $11,550. Books/supplies: $1,500.

Financial aid. All financial aid based on need. Need-based aid available for part-time students. Work-study available nights, weekends and for part-time students.

Application procedures. Admission: No deadline. No application fee. Admission notification on a rolling basis. **Financial aid:** No deadline. FAFSA required. Applicants notified on a rolling basis.

Academics. Special study options: Cooperative education, internships. **Credit/placement by examination:** CLEP. **Support services:** Learning center, remedial instruction, study skills assistance, tutoring.

Majors. Business: Business admin. **Health:** Dental assistant, office admin.

Computing on campus. Online library available.

Student services. Placement for graduates, veterans' counselor.

Contact. E-mail: info@heald.edu
Phone: (925) 288-5800 Toll-free number: (800) 755-3550
Fax: (925) 288-5896
Keith Woodman, Admissions Director, Heald College: Concord, 5130 Commercial Circle, Concord, CA 94520

Heald College: Fresno
Fresno, California
www.heald.edu **CB code: 2119**

- Private 2-year business and technical college
- Commuter campus in small city
- Interview required

General. Founded in 1863. Regionally accredited. **Enrollment:** 1,050 degree-seeking undergraduates. **Degrees:** 342 associate awarded. **Location:** 200 miles from San Francisco. **Calendar:** Quarter. **Full-time faculty:** 25 total. **Part-time faculty:** 22 total. **Class size:** 46% < 20, 54% 20-39.

Transfer out. Colleges most students transferred to 2008: California State University: Fresno, Fresno City College, National University.

Basis for selection. CPAT entrance exam.

2008-2009 Annual costs. Tuition/fees: $11,550. Books/supplies: $1,500.

Application procedures. Admission: No deadline. No application fee. Admission notification on a rolling basis. **Financial aid:** No deadline. FAFSA required. Applicants notified on a rolling basis.

Academics. Special study options: Liberal arts/career combination. **Credit/placement by examination:** CLEP. **Support services:** Tutoring.

Majors. Business: Accounting, business admin, management information systems, office technology, office/clerical. **Computer sciences:** Data processing. **Legal studies:** Legal secretary.

Student life. Freshman orientation: Mandatory.

Student services. Adult student services, career counseling, student employment services, placement for graduates.

Contact. E-mail: info@heald.edu
Phone: (559) 438-4222 Toll-free number: (800) 755-3550
Fax: (559) 438-0948
Tina Mathis, Admissions Director, Heald College: Fresno, 255 West Bullard, Fresno, CA 93704-1706

Heald College: Hayward
Hayward, California
www.heald.edu **CB code: 7106**

- Private 2-year technical college
- Commuter campus in small city

General. Regionally accredited. **Enrollment:** 829 degree-seeking undergraduates. **Degrees:** 367 associate awarded. **Calendar:** Quarter. **Full-time faculty:** 22 total. **Part-time faculty:** 31 total.

Basis for selection. Admission based on high school diploma/GED equivalent, entrance placement assessment, recommendation of admissions adviser.

2008-2009 Annual costs. Tuition/fees: $11,550. Books/supplies: $1,500.

Financial aid. All financial aid based on need. Need-based aid available for part-time students. Work-study available nights, weekends and for part-time students.

Application procedures. Admission: No deadline. No application fee. **Financial aid:** No deadline. FAFSA required.

Academics. Special study options: Cooperative education, internships. **Credit/placement by examination:** CLEP. **Support services:** Learning center, remedial instruction, study skills assistance, tutoring.

Majors. Business: Business admin. **Health:** Dental assistant, office admin.

Computing on campus. Online library available.

Student services. Career counseling, student employment services, financial aid counseling, placement for graduates.

Contact. Phone: (510) 783-2100 Toll-free number: (800) 755-3550
Fax: (510) 783-3287
Cheryl Valente, Admissions Director, Heald College: Hayward, 25500 Industrial Boulevard, Hayward, CA 94545

Heald College: Rancho Cordova
Rancho Cordova, California
www.heald.edu **CB code: 7105**

- Private 2-year technical college
- Commuter campus in large city
- Interview required

General. Regionally accredited. **Enrollment:** 566 degree-seeking undergraduates. **Degrees:** 240 associate awarded. **Calendar:** Quarter. **Full-time faculty:** 17 total. **Part-time faculty:** 28 total.

Basis for selection. Institutional admissions test and interview very important.

2008-2009 Annual costs. Tuition/fees: $11,550. Books/supplies: $1,500.

Financial aid. All financial aid based on need. Need-based aid available for part-time students. Work-study available nights, weekends and for part-time students.

Application procedures. Admission: No deadline. No application fee. **Financial aid:** No deadline. FAFSA required.

Academics. Special study options: Cooperative education, internships. **Credit/placement by examination:** CLEP. **Support services:** Learning center, remedial instruction, study skills assistance, tutoring.

Majors. Business: Accounting, hospitality admin, office technology. **Computer sciences:** Networking. **Health:** Medical secretary. **Legal studies:** Legal secretary.

Computing on campus. Online library available.

Student services. Career counseling, student employment services, financial aid counseling, placement for graduates.

Contact. E-mail: info@heald.edu
Phone: (916) 638-1616 Toll-free number: (800) 884-323
Fax: (916) 638-1580
Cindi Stevens, Director of Admissions, Heald College: Rancho Cordova, 2910 Prospect Park Drive, Rancho Cordova, CA 95670

Heald College: Roseville
Roseville, California
www.heald.edu **CB code: 4145**

- Private 2-year business and junior college
- Commuter campus in small city
- Interview required

General. Regionally accredited. **Enrollment:** 685 degree-seeking undergraduates. **Degrees:** 216 associate awarded. **Calendar:** Quarter. **Full-time faculty:** 12 total. **Part-time faculty:** 26 total. **Class size:** 66% < 20, 34% 20-39. **Special facilities:** CISCO Lab, Medical Lab.

Basis for selection. Institutional placement assessment, interview considered.

2008-2009 Annual costs. Tuition/fees: $11,550. Books/supplies: $1,500.

Financial aid. All financial aid based on need. Need-based aid available for part-time students. Work-study available nights, weekends and for part-time students.

Application procedures. Admission: No deadline. No application fee. **Financial aid:** No deadline. FAFSA required.

Academics. Special study options: Cooperative education, internships. **Credit/placement by examination:** CLEP. **Support services:** Learning center, remedial instruction, study skills assistance, tutoring.

Majors. Business: Accounting, business admin. **Computer sciences:** Security, system admin. **Health:** Health services, medical assistant, office admin. **Legal studies:** Paralegal. **Protective services:** Corrections, law enforcement admin.

Computing on campus. Online library available.

Student life. Freshman orientation: Mandatory. **Activities:** Phi Theta Kappa.

Student services. Adult student services, career counseling, student employment services, financial aid counseling, placement for graduates, veterans' counselor.

Contact. E-mail: rosevilleinfo@heald.edu
Phone: (916) 789-8600 Toll-free number: (800) 755-3550
Fax: (916) 789-8616
Vickie McDougal, Admissions Director, Heald College: Roseville, 7 Sierra Gate Plaza, Roseville, CA 95678

Heald College: Salinas
Salinas, California
www.heald.edu **CB code: 7107**

- Private 2-year business college
- Commuter campus in small city
- Interview required

General. Regionally accredited. **Enrollment:** 573 degree-seeking undergraduates. **Degrees:** 126 associate awarded. **Location:** 62 miles from San Jose. **Calendar:** Quarter. **Full-time faculty:** 13 total. **Part-time faculty:** 22 total.

Basis for selection. Entrance placement assessment, interview important.

2008-2009 Annual costs. Tuition/fees: $11,550. Books/supplies: $1,500. Personal expenses: $1,400.

Financial aid. All financial aid based on need. Need-based aid available for part-time students. Work-study available nights, weekends and for part-time students.

Application procedures. Admission: No deadline. No application fee. **Financial aid:** No deadline. FAFSA required.

Academics. Special study options: Cooperative education, internships. **Credit/placement by examination:** CLEP. **Support services:** Learning center, remedial instruction, study skills assistance, tutoring.

Majors. Business: General, accounting, administrative services. **Health:** Medical secretary. **Protective services:** Law enforcement admin.

Computing on campus. Online library available.

Student services. Career counseling, student employment services, financial aid counseling, placement for graduates.

Contact. Phone: (831) 443-1700 Toll-free number: (800) 755-3550
Fax: (831) 443-1050
Daniel Ujueta, Admissions Director, Heald College: Salinas, 1450 North Main Street, Salinas, CA 93906

Heald College: San Francisco
San Francisco, California
www.heald.edu **CB code: 7109**

- Private 2-year business college
- Commuter campus in very large city
- Interview required

General. Regionally accredited. **Enrollment:** 650 degree-seeking undergraduates. **Degrees:** 125 associate awarded. **Calendar:** Quarter. **Full-time faculty:** 15 total. **Part-time faculty:** 25 total.

Basis for selection. Admission based on high school diploma/GED equivalent, entrance placement assessment, recommendation of admissions adviser.

2008-2009 Annual costs. Tuition/fees: $11,550. Books/supplies: $1,500.

Financial aid. All financial aid based on need. Need-based aid available for part-time students. Work-study available nights, weekends and for part-time students.

Application procedures. Admission: No deadline. No application fee. **Financial aid:** No deadline. FAFSA required.

Academics. Special study options: Cooperative education, internships. **Credit/placement by examination:** CLEP. **Support services:** Learning center, remedial instruction, study skills assistance, tutoring.

Majors. Business: Business admin. **Engineering technology:** Computer. **Health:** Medical secretary.

Computing on campus. Online library available.

Student services. Career counseling, student employment services, financial aid counseling, placement for graduates.

Contact. Phone: (415) 808-3000 Toll-free number: (800) 755-3550
Fax: (418) 808-3005
Edward Lubin, Admissions Director, Heald College: San Francisco, 350 Mission Street, San Francisco, CA 94103

Heald College: San Jose

Milpitas, California
www.heald.edu **CB code: 0405**

- Private 2-year business college
- Commuter campus in very large city
- Interview required

General. Founded in 1863. Regionally accredited. **Enrollment:** 761 degree-seeking undergraduates. **Degrees:** 266 associate awarded. **Location:** 45 miles from San Francisco. **Calendar:** Quarter. **Full-time faculty:** 18 total. **Part-time faculty:** 13 total.

Basis for selection. Institutional admissions test and personal interview most important.

2008-2009 Annual costs. Tuition/fees: $11,550. Books/supplies: $1,500.

Financial aid. All financial aid based on need. Need-based aid available for part-time students. Work-study available nights, weekends and for part-time students.

Application procedures. Admission: No deadline. No application fee. Admission notification on a rolling basis. **Financial aid:** No deadline. FAFSA required. Applicants notified on a rolling basis starting 6/15; must reply within 2 week(s) of notification.

Academics. Special study options: Cooperative education, internships. **Credit/placement by examination:** CLEP, institutional tests. 45 credit hours maximum toward associate degree. **Support services:** Learning center, reduced course load, remedial instruction, tutoring.

Majors. Business: Accounting, business admin, office management. **Health:** Office admin. **Legal studies:** Legal secretary.

Computing on campus. Online library available.

Student services. Career counseling, student employment services, financial aid counseling, placement for graduates.

Contact. E-mail: sanjoseinfo@heald.edu
Phone: (408) 934-4900 Toll-free number: (800) 755-3550
Fax: (415) 934-7777
Clarence Hardiman, Director of Admissions, Heald College: San Jose, 341 Great Mall Parkway, Milpitas, CA 95035

Heald College: Stockton

Stockton, California
www.heald.edu **CB code: 7108**

- Private 2-year business college
- Large city

General. Regionally accredited. **Enrollment:** 1,095 degree-seeking undergraduates. **Degrees:** 327 associate awarded. **Calendar:** Quarter. **Full-time faculty:** 21 total. **Part-time faculty:** 37 total.

Basis for selection. Open admission. Interview, entrance placement assessment considered.

2008-2009 Annual costs. Tuition/fees: $11,550. Books/supplies: $1,500.

Financial aid. Need-based: Work-study available for part-time students.

Application procedures. Admission: No deadline. No application fee. **Financial aid:** No deadline. FAFSA required.

Academics. Credit/placement by examination: CLEP.

Majors. Business: Accounting, office technology. **Computer sciences:** Data entry, vendor certification.

Contact. Phone: (209) 473-5200 Toll-free number: (800) 755-3550
Fax: (209) 477-2739
Ezra Salas, Admissions Director, Heald College: Stockton, 1605 East March Lane, Stockton, CA 95210

Imperial Valley College

Imperial, California **CB member**
www.imperial.edu **CB code: 4358**

- Public 2-year community college
- Commuter campus in rural community

General. Founded in 1922. Regionally accredited. **Enrollment:** 5,701 degree-seeking undergraduates. **Degrees:** 538 associate awarded. **Location:** 6 miles from El Centro. **Calendar:** Semester, limited summer session. **Full-time faculty:** 156 total. **Part-time faculty:** 195 total.

Student profile. Among degree-seeking undergraduates, 1,943 enrolled as first-time, first-year students.

Transfer out. Colleges most students transferred to 2008: San Diego State University, California State Polytechnic University: Pomona, California State University: San Marcos, California State University: San Bernadino, California State University: Long Beach.

Basis for selection. Open admission, but selective for some programs. Limited admission for nursing programs.

2008-2009 Annual costs. Tuition/fees: $630; $5,820 out-of-state. Per-credit charge: $20 in-state; $193 out-of-state. Books/supplies: $1,422. Personal expenses: $2,862.

2007-2008 Financial aid. Need-based: Need-based aid available for part-time students.

Application procedures. Admission: No deadline. No application fee. Application must be submitted online. Admission notification on a rolling basis. **Financial aid:** Priority date 3/2; no closing date. FAFSA required. Applicants notified on a rolling basis.

Academics. Special study options: Accelerated study, distance learning, double major, dual enrollment of high school students, ESL, liberal arts/career combination. License preparation in nursing, paramedic, real estate. **Credit/placement by examination:** AP, CLEP, institutional tests. 25 credit hours maximum toward associate degree. **Support services:** GED test center, learning center, reduced course load, remedial instruction, study skills assistance, tutoring, writing center.

Majors. Agriculture: Business. **Business:** Administrative services, banking/financial services, business admin, office management, office technology, office/clerical, real estate. **Communications:** Journalism. **Computer sciences:** General. **Education:** Bilingual, early childhood, elementary. **Engineering:** General, agricultural. **Family/consumer sciences:** Child care. **Foreign languages:** General, French, Spanish. **Health:** Health care admin, licensed practical nurse, nursing (RN), substance abuse counseling. **Legal studies:** Paralegal. **Liberal arts:** Arts/sciences. **Math:** General. **Mechanic/repair:** General, auto body. **Parks/recreation:** Health/fitness. **Protective services:** Corrections, firefighting, law enforcement admin. **Psychology:** General. **Social sciences:** General, anthropology. **Visual/performing arts:** Art.

Computing on campus. 90 workstations in library, computer center, student center. Commuter students can connect to campus network. Online course registration, online library, helpline available.

Student life. Freshman orientation: Available. **Activities:** Jazz band, choral groups, music ensembles, student government, student newspaper, Christian club, Movimiento Estudiantil Chicano de Aztlan, Upward Bound club, French club, Spirit club, adventure club, agriculture club, business club, educational talent search club, Lamplighter's club.

Athletics. Intercollegiate: Baseball W, basketball, cheerleading, soccer, softball M, tennis, volleyball M. **Team name:** Arabs.

Student services. Adult student services, career counseling, services for economically disadvantaged, student employment services, financial aid counseling, health services, on-campus daycare, personal counseling, veterans' counselor. **Physically disabled:** Services for visually, speech, hearing impaired. **Learning disabled:** Comprehensive services available. **Transfer:** Pre-admission transcript evaluation for new students. Transfer center, transfer adviser, college fairs on campus for students transferring to 4-year colleges.

Contact. Phone: (760) 352-8320 Fax: (760) 355-2663
Kathie Westerfield, Associate Dean, Admissions & Records, Imperial Valley College, Box 158, Imperial, CA 92251-0158

Irvine Valley College
Irvine, California
www.ivc.edu **CB code: 3356**

- Public 2-year community college
- Commuter campus in small city

General. Regionally accredited. **Enrollment:** 4,818 degree-seeking undergraduates. **Degrees:** 354 associate awarded. **ROTC:** Air Force. **Location:** 50 miles from Los Angeles. **Calendar:** Semester, extensive summer session. **Full-time faculty:** 117 total. **Part-time faculty:** 597 total. **Special facilities:** Dance studio, Microsoft Office user specialist testing site, telescope, performing arts center.

Transfer out. Colleges most students transferred to 2008: University of California: Irvine, California State University: Fullerton.

Basis for selection. Open admission.

2008-2009 Annual costs. Tuition/fees: $647; $6,077 out-of-state. Per-credit charge: $20 in-state; $201 out-of-state. Books/supplies: $1,556. Personal expenses: $3,024.

2007-2008 Financial aid. All financial aid based on need. 81% of total undergraduate aid awarded as scholarships/grants, 19% as loans/jobs. Need-based aid available for part-time students. Work-study available nights and for part-time students.

Application procedures. Admission: No deadline. No application fee. Admission notification on a rolling basis. **Financial aid:** No deadline. FAFSA, institutional form required. Applicants notified on a rolling basis starting 4/30.

Academics. Special study options: Accelerated study, cooperative education, cross-registration, distance learning, double major, dual enrollment of high school students, ESL, honors, independent study, internships, study abroad, weekend college. **Credit/placement by examination:** CLEP, institutional tests. 12 credit hours maximum toward associate degree. Minimum 2.0 GPA in at least 12 units completed at IVC required to enroll in credit by examination. **Support services:** Learning center, remedial instruction, study skills assistance, tutoring, writing center.

Majors. Area/ethnic studies: Women's. **Biology:** General, ecology. **Business:** General, accounting, business admin, office management, office technology, real estate. **Communications:** Advertising. **Computer sciences:** General, applications programming, networking, programming, systems analysis. **Conservation:** General. **Education:** Early childhood, physical. **Engineering technology:** Drafting, electrical, manufacturing. **Foreign languages:** French, Spanish. **History:** General. **Liberal arts:** Arts/sciences. **Math:** General. **Parks/recreation:** Health/fitness. **Philosophy/religion:** Philosophy. **Physical sciences:** Chemistry, geology. **Protective services:** Law enforcement admin, police science. **Psychology:** General. **Social sciences:** Anthropology, economics, geography, political science, sociology. **Visual/performing arts:** General, art, dance, dramatic, photography, studio arts, theater design.

Most popular majors. Business/marketing 9%, liberal arts 77%.

Computing on campus. 250 workstations in library, computer center. Commuter students can connect to campus network. Online course registration, online library, helpline available.

Student life. Freshman orientation: Mandatory. **Housing:** Homestay referral for international students. **Activities:** Bands, choral groups, dance, drama, literary magazine, music ensembles, musical theater, student government, student newspaper, symphony orchestra, administration of justice club, Phi Theta Kappa honor society, Muslim Student Association, biology society, dance club, geology club, health sciences society, journalism club, Phi Theta Kappa, Psi Beta.

Athletics. Intercollegiate: Badminton W, baseball M, basketball, cross-country, golf, soccer, softball W, tennis, volleyball. **Intramural:** Basketball, soccer, tennis, volleyball. **Team name:** Lasers.

Student services. Adult student services, career counseling, services for economically disadvantaged, student employment services, financial aid counseling, health services, on-campus daycare, personal counseling, placement for graduates, veterans' counselor, women's services. **Physically disabled:** Services for visually, speech, hearing impaired. **Transfer:** Re-entry adviser for new students. Transfer center, transfer adviser, college fairs on campus for students transferring to 4-year colleges.

Contact. E-mail: admissions@ivc.edu
Phone: (949) 451-5461 Fax: (949) 451-5443
Arleen Elseroad, Director of Admissions, Records & Enrollment Services, Irvine Valley College, 5500 Irvine Center Drive, Irvine, CA 92618-4399

Kaplan College: Palm Springs
Palm Springs, California
www.mariccollege.edu

- For-profit 2-year health science and technical college
- Commuter campus in large town

General. Accredited by ACCSCT. **Calendar:** Continuous.

Annual costs/financial aid. Tuition varies by program from $12,576 (fees $95) to $31,656 (fees $170).

Contact. Phone: (760) 327-4562
2475 East Tahquitz Canyon Way, Palm Springs, CA 92262

Kaplan College: Panorama City
Panorama City, California
www.mariccollege.edu **CB code: 3541**

- For-profit 2-year junior and technical college
- Commuter campus in very large city
- Interview required

General. Accredited by ACICS. **Enrollment:** 40 degree-seeking undergraduates. **Degrees:** 23 associate awarded. **Location:** 15 miles from Los Angeles. **Calendar:** Continuous. **Full-time faculty:** 7 total. **Part-time faculty:** 7 total. **Class size:** 76% < 20, 24% 20-39.

Basis for selection. Open admission. **Homeschooled:** Interview required.

2008-2009 Annual costs. Tuition varies by program from $12,720 (fees $45) to $26,175 (fees $45).

Financial aid. All financial aid based on need. Work-study available nights.

Application procedures. Admission: No deadline. No application fee. Application must be submitted on paper. **Financial aid:** No deadline. FAFSA, institutional form required.

Academics. Special study options: Internships, liberal arts/career combination. **Credit/placement by examination:** AP, CLEP. **Support services:** Learning center, study skills assistance, tutoring.

Majors. Business: Accounting, accounting technology, accounting/business management, business admin, office management. **Computer sciences:** Information technology, LAN/WAN management, system admin. **Legal studies:** Court reporting, paralegal.

Most popular majors. Business/marketing 17%, computer/information sciences 35%, legal studies 46%.

Computing on campus. 20 workstations in library, computer center. Online library available.

Student life. Freshman orientation: Mandatory. **Activities:** Student newspaper.

Student services. Career counseling, student employment services, financial aid counseling, placement for graduates.

Contact. E-mail: lking@mariccollege.edu
Phone: (818) 672-3000 Toll-free number: (800) 206-0095
Fax: (818) 672-8919
Carol Kersting, Director of Admissions, Kaplan College: Panorama City, 14355 Roscoe Boulevard, Panorama City, CA 91402

Kaplan College: Sacramento
Sacramento, California
www.mariccollege.edu

- For-profit 2-year business and technical college
- Commuter campus in large city

General. Accredited by ACICS. **Calendar:** Continuous.

Annual costs/financial aid. Tuition varies by program from $12,265 (fees $400) to $22,706 (fees 145).

Contact. Phone: (916) 649-8168
Director of Admissions, 4330 Watt Avenue, Suite 400, Sacramento, CA 95821

Kaplan College: Salida
Salida, California
www.mariccollege.edu

- For-profit 2-year health science and technical college
- Commuter campus in small city

General. Accredited by ACCSCT. **Calendar:** Continuous.

Annual costs/financial aid. Tuition varies by program from $11,385 (fees $205) to $31,294 (fees $1,786).

Contact. Phone: (209) 543-7000
Director of Admissions, 5172 Kiernan Court, Salida, CA 95368

Kaplan College: San Diego
San Diego, California
www.mariccollege.edu **CB code: 3064**

- For-profit 2-year business and health science college
- Commuter campus in very large city

General. Accredited by ACCSCT. **Calendar:** Continuous.

Contact. Phone: (858) 279-4500
9055 Balboa Avenue, San Diego, CA 92123

Kaplan College: Vista
Vista, California
www.mariccollege.edu

- For-profit 2-year technical college
- Commuter campus in small city

General. Accredited by ACCSCT. **Enrollment:** 883 degree-seeking undergraduates. **Degrees:** 76 associate awarded. **Calendar:** Continuous. **Full-time faculty:** 20 total. **Part-time faculty:** 33 total.

Basis for selection. Institutional entrance exam important. High school diploma/GED required for some programs. Timed institutional examination administered onsite.

2008-2009 Annual costs. Tuition/fees: $12,476. Associate degree program costs range from $23,567-$27,620.

Application procedures. Admission: No deadline. $20 fee.

Academics. Credit/placement by examination: CLEP.

Majors. Computer sciences: LAN/WAN management. **Legal studies:** Paralegal. **Protective services:** Criminal justice.

Contact. Phone: (760) 630-1555 Fax: (760) 630-1656
Renee Codner, Director of Admissions, Kaplan College: Vista, 2022 University Drive, Vista, CA 92083

Lake Tahoe Community College
South Lake Tahoe, California
www.ltcc.edu **CB code: 4420**

- Public 2-year community college
- Commuter campus in large town

General. Founded in 1975. Regionally accredited. Located in the forest on the south shore of Lake Tahoe. **Enrollment:** 1,190 degree-seeking undergraduates. **Degrees:** 148 associate awarded. **Location:** 55 miles from Reno, Nevada, 110 miles from Sacramento. **Calendar:** Quarter, limited summer session. **Full-time faculty:** 50 total. **Part-time faculty:** 180 total. **Special facilities:** LTCC demonstration garden.

Transfer out. Colleges most students transferred to 2008: California State University, University of California, University of Nevada: Reno.

Basis for selection. Open admission. Special admission criteria apply to international students. **Learning Disabled:** Assistance is available through the Disability Resource Center.

2008-2009 Annual costs. Tuition/fees: $597; $6,447 out-of-state. Per-credit charge: $13 in-state; $143 out-of-state. Out-of-state tuition reduction plan available to Nevada residents. Books/supplies: $1,566. Personal expenses: $3,024.

Application procedures. Admission: No deadline. No application fee. Application must be submitted online. Admission notification on a rolling basis. **Financial aid:** Priority date 5/1; no closing date. FAFSA required. Applicants notified on a rolling basis starting 7/1; must reply within 2 week(s) of notification.

Academics. Special study options: Cooperative education, distance learning, double major, ESL, internships, study abroad. License preparation in real estate. **Credit/placement by examination:** AP, CLEP, institutional tests. 4 credit hours maximum toward associate degree. **Support services:** GED preparation, learning center, remedial instruction, study skills assistance, tutoring, writing center.

Majors. Business: General, accounting, administrative services, entrepreneurial studies, finance, marketing, office management, office/clerical, real estate. **Education:** Early childhood. **Foreign languages:** Spanish. **Health:** Medical assistant, medical records admin. **Interdisciplinary:** Natural sciences. **Legal studies:** Legal secretary. **Liberal arts:** Arts/sciences. **Parks/recreation:** Health/fitness. **Personal/culinary services:** Culinary arts. **Protective services:** Firefighting, law enforcement admin. **Psychology:** General. **Social sciences:** General. **Visual/performing arts:** Art, dance, dramatic, studio arts.

Computing on campus. 155 workstations in library, computer center, student center. Online course registration, online library, wireless network available.

Student life. Freshman orientation: Available. **Activities:** Choral groups, dance, drama, music ensembles, musical theater, student government, Alpha Gamma Sigma, associated student council, international club.

Student services. Career counseling, services for economically disadvantaged, student employment services, financial aid counseling, minority student services, on-campus daycare, personal counseling, placement for graduates, veterans' counselor. **Physically disabled:** Services for visually, speech, hearing impaired. **Learning disabled:** Comprehensive services available. **Transfer:** Transfer center, transfer adviser, college fairs on campus for students transferring to 4-year colleges.

Contact. E-mail: admissions@ltcc.edu
Phone: (530) 541-4660 ext. 211 Fax: (530) 542-1781
Cheri Jones, Director of Admissions & Records, Lake Tahoe Community College, One College Drive, South Lake Tahoe, CA 96150-4524

Laney College
Oakland, California
laney.peralta.edu **CB code: 4406**

- Public 2-year community college
- Commuter campus in large city

General. Founded in 1953. Regionally accredited. Vocational programs include programs with PGE and a solar program with UC Lawrence Laboratories. **Enrollment:** 4,988 degree-seeking undergraduates. **Degrees:** 453 associate awarded. **Location:** 10 miles from San Francisco. **Calendar:** Semester, extensive summer session. **Full-time faculty:** 122 total. **Part-time faculty:** 364 total. **Special facilities:** CAD laboratory.

Student profile.

Out-of-state:	2%	**25 or older:**	61%

Transfer out. Colleges most students transferred to 2008: California State University: East Bay, San Francisco State, University of California: Berkeley.

Basis for selection. Open admission.

2008-2009 Annual costs. Tuition/fees: $604; $6,034 out-of-state. Per-credit charge: $20 in-state; $201 out-of-state. Books/supplies: $648. Personal expenses: $1,620.

Application procedures. Admission: No deadline. No application fee. Admission notification on a rolling basis. **Financial aid:** Priority date 4/1; no closing date. FAFSA, institutional form required. Applicants notified on a rolling basis; must reply within 2 week(s) of notification.

Academics. **Special study options:** Cooperative education, distance learning, dual enrollment of high school students, ESL, honors, independent study, liberal arts/career combination, weekend college. **Credit/placement by examination:** CLEP, institutional tests. **Support services:** Learning center, remedial instruction, study skills assistance, tutoring.

Majors. **Area/ethnic studies:** African-American, Asian, Latin American. **Business:** General, accounting, administrative services, banking/financial services, management information systems, office technology, office/clerical, operations, sales/distribution. **Communications:** Broadcast journalism, journalism. **Communications technology:** General, graphic/printing. **Computer sciences:** General, information systems. **Construction:** Carpentry, maintenance. **Education:** General. **Engineering technology:** Architectural. **Interdisciplinary:** Biological/physical sciences. **Liberal arts:** Arts/sciences. **Math:** General. **Mechanic/repair:** Heating/ac/refrig. **Personal/culinary services:** Cosmetic, culinary arts. **Production:** Woodworking. **Social sciences:** General. **Visual/performing arts:** Art, ceramics, commercial/advertising art, dance, design, dramatic.

Computing on campus. 400 workstations in library, computer center, student center. Online course registration, online library available.

Student life. **Freshman orientation:** Mandatory. Preregistration for classes offered. **Activities:** Pep band, dance, drama, literary magazine, musical theater, student government, student newspaper, TV station.

Athletics. **Intercollegiate:** Badminton W, baseball M, basketball M, football (tackle) M, softball W, swimming, track and field W, volleyball W, water polo W. **Team name:** Eagles.

Student services. Adult student services, career counseling, services for economically disadvantaged, student employment services, financial aid counseling, health services, minority student services, on-campus daycare, personal counseling, placement for graduates. **Physically disabled:** Services for visually, speech, hearing impaired. **Transfer:** Re-entry adviser for new students. Transfer center, transfer adviser, college fairs on campus for students transferring to 4-year colleges.

Contact. E-mail: admissions@peralta.edu
Phone: (510) 464-3121 Fax: (510) 464-3240
Howard Perdue, Director of Admissions and Records, Laney College, 900 Fallon Street, Oakland, CA 94607

Las Positas College

Livermore, California
www.laspositascollege.edu **CB code: 6507**

- Public 2-year community college
- Commuter campus in small city

General. Founded in 1991. Regionally accredited. **Enrollment:** 5,593 degree-seeking undergraduates. **Degrees:** 416 associate awarded. **Location:** 43 miles from San Francsico, 39 miles from San Jose. **Calendar:** Semester, limited summer session. **Full-time faculty:** 101 total. **Part-time faculty:** 250 total.

Transfer out. **Colleges most students transferred to 2008:** California State University: East Bay.

Basis for selection. Open admission. High school diploma or GED required for student under 18 years.

2008-2009 Annual costs. Tuition/fees: $622; $6,022 out-of-state. Per-credit charge: $20 in-state; $200 out-of-state. Books/supplies: $1,566. Personal expenses: $2,664.

2007-2008 Financial aid. **Need-based:** 88% of total undergraduate aid awarded as scholarships/grants, 12% as loans/jobs.

Application procedures. **Admission:** No deadline. No application fee. Admission notification on a rolling basis. **Financial aid:** Priority date 5/1; no closing date. Institutional form required. Applicants notified on a rolling basis starting 7/1; must reply within 2 week(s) of notification.

Academics. **Special study options:** Accelerated study, distance learning, dual enrollment of high school students, ESL, independent study, internships, student-designed major. **Credit/placement by examination:** CLEP. **Support services:** Learning center, remedial instruction, tutoring.

Majors. **Agriculture:** Ornamental horticulture. **Biology:** General. **Business:** Office management, sales/distribution. **Communications technology:** Graphic/printing. **Computer sciences:** General, computer science. **Engineering technology:** Drafting. **Family/consumer sciences:** Child care. **Health:** Environmental health. **Liberal arts:** Arts/sciences. **Mechanic/repair:** Electronics/electrical. **Physical sciences:** Chemistry, physics. **Protective services:** Firefighting. **Social sciences:** General, international relations, sociology. **Visual/performing arts:** Commercial/advertising art, dramatic, interior design, studio arts.

Most popular majors. Business/marketing 26%, computer/information sciences 10%, liberal arts 55%.

Computing on campus. 285 workstations in library, computer center.

Student life. **Freshman orientation:** Available. **Activities:** Choral groups, dance, drama, literary magazine, music ensembles, musical theater, student government, student newspaper, TV station.

Athletics. **Intercollegiate:** Cross-country, soccer. **Intramural:** Basketball, bowling, fencing, handball M, racquetball, skin diving, soccer, volleyball.

Student services. Adult student services, career counseling, student employment services, financial aid counseling, health services, personal counseling, veterans' counselor. **Learning disabled:** Comprehensive services available. **Transfer:** Transfer center, transfer adviser, college fairs on campus for students transferring to 4-year colleges.

Contact. Phone: (925) 424-1000 Fax: (925) 443-0742
Sylvia Rodriguez, Registrar, Las Positas College, 3033 Collier Canyon Road, Livermore, CA 94551

Lassen Community College

Susanville, California
www.lassencollege.edu **CB code: 4383**

- Public 2-year community college
- Small town

General. Founded in 1925. Regionally accredited. **Enrollment:** 923 degree-seeking undergraduates. **Degrees:** 138 associate awarded. **Location:** 100 miles from Chico, 84 miles from Reno, Nevada. **Calendar:** Semester, limited summer session. **Full-time faculty:** 35 total. **Part-time faculty:** 68 total.

Student profile.

Out-of-state:	7%	**Live on campus:**	3%

Basis for selection. Open admission, but selective for some programs. Limited admission to nursing program.

2008-2009 Annual costs. Tuition/fees: $616; $6,106 out-of-state. Per-credit charge: $20 in-state; $203 out-of-state. Nevada residents pay $42 per-credit-hour with good neighbor policy. Room/board: $6,960. Books/supplies: $1,566. Personal expenses: $2,214.

2007-2008 Financial aid. **Need-based:** 95% of total undergraduate aid awarded as scholarships/grants, 5% as loans/jobs. **Additional information:** Board of Governors Grant: low-income California residents can have registration fees waived.

Application procedures. **Admission:** No deadline. No application fee. Admission notification on a rolling basis. Institutional placement tests recommended. **Financial aid:** Priority date 7/1; no closing date. FAFSA required. Applicants notified on a rolling basis starting 7/1; must reply within 2 week(s) of notification.

Academics. Gunsmithing and summer NRA programs offered. **Special study options:** Cooperative education, distance learning, dual enrollment of high school students, honors, independent study, internships. **Credit/placement by examination:** AP, CLEP, institutional tests. 15 credit hours maximum toward associate degree. **Support services:** Learning center, preadmission summer program, reduced course load, remedial instruction, tutoring.

Majors. **Business:** General, accounting, administrative services, business admin, management information systems, office technology, office/clerical, real estate. **Communications:** Journalism. **Computer sciences:** General, applications programming. **Construction:** Maintenance. **Education:** General, early childhood, physical. **Health:** Nursing (RN), nursing assistant. **Interdisciplinary:** Biological/physical sciences. **Liberal arts:** Arts/sciences. **Math:** General. **Mechanic/repair:** Auto body, automotive. **Protective services:** Corrections, law enforcement admin, police science. **Social sciences:** General. **Visual/performing arts:** Art.

Computing on campus. 40 workstations in computer center.

Student life. **Housing:** Coed dorms available. **Activities:** Choral groups, drama, film society, student government, student newspaper, over 20 student organizations and clubs.

Athletics. NJCAA. **Intercollegiate:** Baseball M, basketball, cross-country, golf, rifle, softball W, track and field, volleyball W, wrestling M. **Intramural:** Skiing.

Student services. Career counseling, health services, on-campus daycare, personal counseling, veterans' counselor. **Physically disabled:** Services for visually, speech, hearing impaired. **Transfer:** Transfer adviser, college fairs on campus for students transferring to 4-year colleges.

Contact. Phone: (530) 251-8808 Fax: (530) 257-8964
Registrar and Admissions Director, Lassen Community College, Box 3000, Susanville, CA 96130

Long Beach City College
Long Beach, California
www.lbcc.edu **CB code: 4388**

- Public 2-year community college
- Commuter campus in large city

General. Founded in 1927. Regionally accredited. **Enrollment:** 15,613 degree-seeking undergraduates. **Degrees:** 883 associate awarded. **Location:** 20 miles from downtown Los Angeles. **Calendar:** Semester, limited summer session. **Full-time faculty:** 356 total. **Part-time faculty:** 623 total. **Class size:** 35% < 20, 47% 20-39, 10% 40-49, 7% 50-99, 1% >100.

Student profile.

Out-of-state:	1%	**25 or older:**	51%

Transfer out. **Colleges most students transferred to 2008:** California State University: Long Beach, California State University: Dominguez Hills, California State University: Fullerton, University of California: Irvine.

Basis for selection. Open admission.

2008-2009 Annual costs. Tuition/fees: $628; $5,848 out-of-state. Per-credit charge: $20 in-state; $194 out-of-state. Books/supplies: $1,566. Personal expenses: $3,024.

Financial aid. All financial aid based on need. Need-based aid available for part-time students. Work-study available for part-time students.

Application procedures. **Admission:** No deadline. No application fee. Admission notification on a rolling basis. **Financial aid:** Priority date 5/6; no closing date. FAFSA, institutional form required. Applicants notified on a rolling basis starting 7/6; must reply within 2 week(s) of notification.

Academics. **Special study options:** Accelerated study, cooperative education, cross-registration, distance learning, dual enrollment of high school students, ESL, honors, independent study, internships, liberal arts/career combination, study abroad, weekend college. License preparation in aviation, nursing, radiology, real estate. **Credit/placement by examination:** AP, CLEP, IB, institutional tests. 40 credit hours maximum toward associate degree. Students must first complete 12 units in residence. **Support services:** GED preparation and test center, learning center, pre-admission summer program, remedial instruction, study skills assistance, tutoring, writing center.

Majors. **Agriculture:** Ornamental horticulture. **Biology:** General. **Business:** General, accounting, administrative services, business admin, fashion, hotel/motel admin, office technology, office/clerical, real estate, restaurant/food services, sales/distribution, tourism promotion, tourism/travel. **Communications:** Advertising, broadcast journalism, journalism, public relations, publishing. **Communications technology:** General, desktop publishing, graphic/printing. **Computer sciences:** Applications programming, data processing, word processing. **Construction:** Carpentry. **Education:** Teacher assistance. **Engineering:** General. **Engineering technology:** Architectural, architectural drafting, drafting, heat/ac/refrig. **Family/consumer sciences:** General, child care, child development, consumer economics, family resources, institutional food production. **Foreign languages:** General, Spanish. **Health:** Dietetic technician, licensed practical nurse, medical assistant, medical radiologic technology/radiation therapy, nursing (RN). **Legal studies:** Legal secretary. **Liberal arts:** Arts/sciences. **Math:** General. **Mechanic/repair:** General, aircraft powerplant, alternative fuel vehicle, auto body, automotive, diesel, electronics/electrical. **Parks/recreation:** Health/fitness. **Personal/culinary services:** Baking, culinary arts, restaurant/catering. **Physical sciences:** General. **Production:** Cabinetmaking/millwright, machine shop technology, machine tool, welding. **Protective services:** Fire safety technology, law enforcement admin. **Public administration:** General, human services. **Social sciences:** General. **Transportation:** Aviation. **Visual/performing arts:** Art, commercial photography, commercial/advertising art, dance, design, dramatic, drawing, fashion design, film/cinema, interior design, multimedia, printmaking, sculpture, theater design.

Most popular majors. Business/marketing 7%, health sciences 19%, liberal arts 44%, security/protective services 7%.

Computing on campus. 500 workstations in library, computer center, student center. Online course registration, online library, helpline, wireless network available.

Student life. **Freshman orientation:** Available. Preregistration for classes offered. **Activities:** Bands, campus ministries, choral groups, dance, drama, international student organizations, literary magazine, music ensembles, musical theater, radio station, student government, student newspaper, symphony orchestra, TV station, College Republicans, Students for a Democratic Society.

Athletics. NJCAA. **Intercollegiate:** Baseball M, basketball, cross-country, football (tackle) M, golf, soccer, softball W, swimming, tennis, track and field, volleyball, water polo. **Intramural:** Archery, badminton, basketball, bowling, golf, racquetball, soccer, softball, swimming, table tennis, tennis, track and field, volleyball, wrestling M. **Team name:** Vikings.

Student services. Career counseling, student employment services, health services, on-campus daycare, personal counseling, veterans' counselor. **Physically disabled:** Services for visually, speech, hearing impaired. **Transfer:** Re-entry adviser for new students. Transfer center, transfer adviser, college fairs on campus for students transferring to 4-year colleges.

Contact. Phone: (562) 938-4139 Fax: (562) 938-4858
Ross Miyashiro, Dean of Admissions and Records, Long Beach City College, 4901 East Carson Street, Long Beach, CA 90808

Los Angeles City College
Los Angeles, California
www.lacitycollege.edu **CB code: 4391**

- Public 2-year community college
- Very large city

General. Founded in 1929. Regionally accredited. **Enrollment:** 6,912 degree-seeking undergraduates. **Degrees:** 598 associate awarded. **ROTC:** Army, Naval, Air Force. **Location:** 5 miles from downtown. **Calendar:** Semester, limited summer session. **Full-time faculty:** 210 total; 35% minority, 42% women. **Part-time faculty:** 379 total; 31% minority, 48% women.

Basis for selection. Open admission. Auditions required of theater academy, music majors.

2008-2009 Annual costs. Tuition/fees: $622; $6,052 out-of-state. Per-credit charge: $20 in-state; $201 out-of-state. Books/supplies: $2,316. Personal expenses: $3,024.

2007-2008 Financial aid. All financial aid based on need. Need-based aid available for part-time students. **Additional information:** Fee waivers available for public assistance and Social Security insurance recipients; fee credits available for low income families.

Application procedures. **Admission:** Closing date 9/1. No application fee. Admission notification on a rolling basis beginning on or about 4/30. **Financial aid:** Priority date 3/2; no closing date. FAFSA required. Applicants notified by 7/6; Applicants notified on a rolling basis starting 7/6; must reply within 2 week(s) of notification.

Academics. **Special study options:** Accelerated study, cross-registration, dual enrollment of high school students, ESL, honors, independent study. License preparation in dental hygiene, nursing, radiology. **Credit/placement by examination:** CLEP, institutional tests. 15 credit hours maximum toward associate degree. **Support services:** Learning center, remedial instruction, tutoring.

Majors. **Area/ethnic studies:** African-American, Asian-American. **Biology:** General. **Business:** Accounting, administrative services, banking/financial services, business admin, entrepreneurial studies, management information systems, office technology, office/clerical, real estate, tourism promotion, tourism/travel. **Communications:** Advertising, broadcast journalism, journalism, public relations. **Communications technology:** General. **Computer sciences:** General, applications programming. **Engineering:** General, software. **Engineering technology:** Biomedical, drafting, electrical. **Family/consumer sciences:** General, child care. **Foreign languages:** Chinese, French, German, Italian, Japanese, Spanish. **Health:** Dental lab technology, health services, medical radiologic technology/radiation therapy, medical records technology, medical secretary. **Legal studies:** Legal secretary, paralegal. **Liberal arts:** Arts/sciences. **Math:** General. **Mechanic/**

Two-Year Colleges

repair: Electronics/electrical. **Physical sciences:** Chemistry, physics. **Protective services:** Police science. **Psychology:** General. **Visual/performing arts:** Art, cinematography, commercial/advertising art, dramatic, film/cinema, photography.

Computing on campus. 200 workstations in library, computer center.

Student life. Activities: Bands, choral groups, dance, drama, film society, literary magazine, music ensembles, musical theater, radio station, student government, student newspaper, TV station, religious, political, ethnic, and foreign student clubs.

Athletics. NJCAA. **Intercollegiate:** Baseball M, basketball M, cross-country, track and field. **Team name:** CUBS.

Student services. Career counseling, student employment services, health services, on-campus daycare, personal counseling, veterans' counselor. **Physically disabled:** Services for visually, speech, hearing impaired. **Transfer:** Transfer adviser, college fairs on campus for students transferring to 4-year colleges.

Contact. Phone: (323) 953-4381 Fax: (323) 953-4013
William Marmolejo, Dean of Admissions, Los Angeles City College, 855 North Vermont Avenue, Los Angeles, CA 90029-3589

Los Angeles County College of Nursing and Allied Health

Los Angeles, California
www.ladhs.org/wps/portal/CollegeOfNursing/

- Public 2-year nursing and community college
- Commuter campus in very large city

General. Clinical component of studies undertaken in cooperation with municipal medical centers in Los Angeles County. **Enrollment:** 321 degree-seeking undergraduates. **Degrees:** 118 associate awarded. **Location:** 2 miles from Los Angeles. **Calendar:** Semester, limited summer session. **Full-time faculty:** 40 total.

Basis for selection. Admissions criteria include high school diploma or equivalency, prior college experience, California Achievement Test. Geographical residency in Los Angeles County required.

High school preparation. College-preparatory program recommended.

2009-2010 Annual costs. Tuition/fees: $4,925. Per-credit charge: $240. $125 one-time fee for new students. Estimated books and supplies cost include uniform, shoes, malpractice insurance fee, second-hand watch along with textbooks and other supplies. Books/supplies: $1,419.

Application procedures. Admission: Closing date 3/1. $5 fee. Application must be submitted on paper. Admission notification 6/1. Admission notification on a rolling basis beginning on or about 5/1.

Academics. Special study options: License preparation in nursing. **Credit/placement by examination:** AP, CLEP, institutional tests.

Majors. Health: Nursing (RN).

Student life. Activities: Student government.

Contact. Phone: (323) 226-4911 Fax: (323) 226-6343
Maria Caballero, Dean, Administrative and Student Services, Los Angeles County College of Nursing and Allied Health, 1237 North Mission Road, Los Angeles, CA 90033-1084

Los Angeles Harbor College

Wilmington, California
www.lahc.edu **CB code: 4395**

- Public 2-year community college
- Commuter campus in small city

General. Founded in 1949. Regionally accredited. **Enrollment:** 4,054 degree-seeking undergraduates. **Degrees:** 589 associate awarded. **Location:** 15 miles from downtown. **Calendar:** Semester, limited summer session. **Full-time faculty:** 83 total. **Part-time faculty:** 305 total. **Special facilities:** Observatory, nature museum.

Student profile. Among degree-seeking undergraduates, 1,612 enrolled as first-time, first-year students.

Transfer out. Colleges most students transferred to 2008: California State University: Long Beach, California State University: Dominguez Hills.

Basis for selection. Open admission.

High school preparation. 10 units recommended. Recommended units include English 4, mathematics 3, science 2 (laboratory 1). Nursing program requires high school diploma with chemistry and algebra, or college equivalent.

2008-2009 Annual costs. Tuition/fees: $622; $6,052 out-of-state. Per-credit charge: $20 in-state; $201 out-of-state. Books/supplies: $1,314. Personal expenses: $2,826.

Financial aid. All financial aid based on need. Need-based aid available for part-time students. Work-study available nights, weekends and for part-time students.

Application procedures. Admission: Closing date 9/9. No application fee. Admission notification on a rolling basis. High school students accepted on part-time basis. **Financial aid:** Priority date 3/2; no closing date. FAFSA, institutional form required. Applicants notified on a rolling basis; must reply within 2 week(s) of notification.

Academics. Special study options: Accelerated study, cooperative education, cross-registration, distance learning, double major, dual enrollment of high school students, ESL, honors, independent study, liberal arts/career combination, study abroad, weekend college. License preparation in nursing, paramedic, physical therapy, real estate. **Credit/placement by examination:** AP, CLEP, IB, institutional tests. **Support services:** GED preparation, learning center, remedial instruction, study skills assistance, tutoring, writing center.

Majors. Architecture: Technology. **Business:** General, accounting, administrative services, business admin, management information systems, office management, office technology, office/clerical, real estate. **Computer sciences:** General, applications programming, data entry, information systems. **Engineering:** Electrical. **Engineering technology:** Architectural, computer systems, drafting, electrical. **Family/consumer sciences:** Child care. **Health:** Medical secretary, nursing (RN). **Legal studies:** Legal secretary. **Liberal arts:** Arts/sciences, library science. **Mechanic/repair:** Automotive, electronics/electrical. **Protective services:** Firefighting, police science. **Psychology:** General. **Visual/performing arts:** Art, interior design.

Most popular majors. Health sciences 14%, liberal arts 75%.

Computing on campus. 660 workstations in library, computer center, student center. Commuter students can connect to campus network. Online course registration, online library, wireless network available.

Student life. Activities: Bands, choral groups, dance, drama, literary magazine, music ensembles, musical theater, student government, student newspaper, TV station, Equal Opportunity Program Student Association.

Athletics. NJCAA. **Intercollegiate:** Baseball M, basketball, football (tackle) M, soccer, volleyball W. **Team name:** Seahawks.

Student services. Adult student services, career counseling, student employment services, health services, legal services, on-campus daycare, personal counseling, placement for graduates, veterans' counselor. **Physically disabled:** Services for visually, speech, hearing impaired. **Transfer:** Transfer center, transfer adviser, college fairs on campus for students transferring to 4-year colleges.

Contact. Phone: (310) 233-5090 Fax: (310) 233-4223
David Ching, Dean of Admissions and Records, Los Angeles Harbor College, 1111 Figueroa Place, Wilmington, CA 90744-2397

Los Angeles Mission College

Sylmar, California
www.lamission.edu **CB code: 4404**

- Public 2-year community college
- Large town

General. Founded in 1974. Regionally accredited. College serves nontraditional student body. **Enrollment:** 3,895 degree-seeking undergraduates. **Degrees:** 297 associate awarded. **ROTC:** Army, Air Force. **Location:** 20 miles from Los Angeles. **Calendar:** Semester, limited summer session. **Full-time faculty:** 60 total. **Part-time faculty:** 125 total.

Basis for selection. Open admission.

2008-2009 Annual costs. Tuition/fees: $612; $5,802 out-of-state. Per-credit charge: $20 in-state; $193 out-of-state.

2007-2008 Financial aid. **Need-based:** 92% of total undergraduate aid awarded as scholarships/grants, 8% as loans/jobs. **Additional information:** Board of Governors Grant available to those in receipt of AFDC, Social Security Insurance, or General Relief. If not in receipt of program, may qualify based on income.

Application procedures. **Admission:** Priority date 4/20; no deadline. No application fee. Admission notification on a rolling basis. **Financial aid:** Priority date 8/1; no closing date. FAFSA required. Applicants notified on a rolling basis starting 8/15.

Academics. Bilingual instruction available. **Special study options:** Accelerated study, cooperative education, dual enrollment of high school students, independent study. **Credit/placement by examination:** CLEP, institutional tests. 15 credit hours maximum toward associate degree. **Support services:** Learning center, remedial instruction, tutoring.

Majors. **Business:** Accounting, administrative services, business admin, management science, market research, office management, office/clerical, real estate. **Computer sciences:** General. **Education:** Teacher assistance. **Family/consumer sciences:** Clothing/textiles, food/nutrition, institutional food production. **Foreign languages:** Spanish. **Legal studies:** Paralegal. **Liberal arts:** Arts/sciences. **Math:** General. **Mechanic/repair:** Electronics/electrical. **Personal/culinary services:** Culinary arts. **Philosophy/religion:** Philosophy. **Protective services:** Criminal justice. **Psychology:** General. **Visual/performing arts:** Art, interior design.

Computing on campus. 10 workstations in library.

Student life. **Activities:** Choral groups, drama, student government.

Athletics. **Intercollegiate:** Baseball M, cross-country, golf M, soccer M.

Student services. Career counseling, on-campus daycare, personal counseling, placement for graduates, veterans' counselor. **Physically disabled:** Services for speech, hearing impaired.

Contact. Phone: (818) 364-7661
Joe Ramirez, Vice President, Los Angeles Mission College, 13356 Eldridge Avenue, Sylmar, CA 91342-3245

Los Angeles Pierce College

Woodland Hills, California — **CB member**
www.piercecollege.edu — **CB code: 4398**

- Public 2-year community college
- Commuter campus in very large city

General. Founded in 1947. Regionally accredited. **Enrollment:** 10,995 degree-seeking undergraduates. **Degrees:** 988 associate awarded. **Location:** 27 miles from downtown. **Calendar:** Semester, extensive summer session. **Full-time faculty:** 196 total. **Part-time faculty:** 531 total. **Special facilities:** Braille nature trail, life science museum, nature center, weather station, working farm, botanical garden.

Transfer out. **Colleges most students transferred to 2008:** California State University: Northridge, University of California: Los Angeles.

Basis for selection. Open admission, but selective for some programs. Limited admission to nursing and animal health technology programs. All students required to take English and math placement tests prior to course registration.

2008-2009 Annual costs. Tuition/fees: $622; $6,052 out-of-state. Per-credit charge: $20 in-state; $201 out-of-state. Books/supplies: $2,316. Personal expenses: $3,024.

Financial aid. All financial aid based on need. Need-based aid available for part-time students. Work-study available nights and weekends.

Application procedures. **Admission:** Closing date 9/10 (receipt date). No application fee. Admission notification on a rolling basis. **Financial aid:** Priority date 5/1; no closing date. FAFSA, institutional form required. Applicants notified on a rolling basis starting 8/1.

Academics. **Special study options:** Accelerated study, cooperative education, distance learning, dual enrollment of high school students, ESL, honors, student-designed major, study abroad. **Credit/placement by examination:** CLEP, institutional tests. 15 credit hours maximum toward associate degree. **Support services:** GED preparation, learning center, preadmission summer program, remedial instruction, study skills assistance, tutoring, writing center.

Majors. **Agriculture:** Animal health, animal sciences, business, equestrian studies, equine science, greenhouse operations, horticultural science, horticulture, landscaping, ornamental horticulture. **Architecture:** Technology. **Area/ethnic studies:** Latin American. **Business:** General, accounting, business admin, management science, marketing. **Communications:** Journalism, photojournalism. **Computer sciences:** General, applications programming, computer science, data processing, programming. **Conservation:** Management/policy. **Education:** Early childhood, kindergarten/preschool. **Engineering:** General. **Engineering technology:** Construction, drafting, electrical. **Foreign languages:** French, Italian, sign language interpretation, Spanish. **Health:** Nursing (RN), preveterinary, substance abuse counseling, veterinary technology/assistant. **Liberal arts:** Arts/sciences. **Mechanic/repair:** Auto body, automotive. **Social sciences:** Criminology. **Visual/performing arts:** Commercial/advertising art, dramatic, industrial design, studio arts, theater design.

Computing on campus. Commuter students can connect to campus network. Online course registration, online library, repair service available.

Student life. **Freshman orientation:** Available. Preregistration for classes offered. **Activities:** Bands, choral groups, dance, drama, international student organizations, literary magazine, music ensembles, musical theater, student government, student newspaper, symphony orchestra, Bible Fellowship, Alpha Gamma Sigma honor society, Phi Theta Kappa honor society, Phi Beta Lambda business association, Hillel, Union of African American Students, Muslim students association.

Athletics. **Intercollegiate:** Baseball M, basketball, cheerleading, diving, football (tackle) M, soccer W, softball W, swimming, tennis M, volleyball. **Team name:** Brahmas.

Student services. Adult student services, career counseling, services for economically disadvantaged, student employment services, financial aid counseling, health services, on-campus daycare, personal counseling, placement for graduates, veterans' counselor. **Physically disabled:** Services for visually, speech, hearing impaired. **Learning disabled:** Comprehensive services available. **Transfer:** Transfer center, transfer adviser, college fairs on campus for students transferring to 4-year colleges.

Contact. E-mail: pierceinfo@piercecollege.edu
Phone: (818) 719-6404 Fax: (818) 716-1087
Marco De La Garza, Dean of Admissions and Records, Los Angeles Pierce College, 6201 Winnetka Avenue, Woodland Hills, CA 91371

Los Angeles Southwest College

Los Angeles, California
www.lasc.edu — **CB code: 4409**

- Public 2-year community college
- Commuter campus in very large city

General. Founded in 1967. Regionally accredited. Awards associate degrees in 34 disciplines with occupational certificates in 47 disciplines. Offers college transfer, occupational, general education, transitional, continuing, community services and joint programs to diverse population. Campus is site of Middle College High School, enabling high school students to take college courses for credit. **Enrollment:** 2,965 degree-seeking undergraduates. **Degrees:** 397 associate awarded. **Calendar:** Semester, limited summer session. **Full-time faculty:** 81 total. **Part-time faculty:** 195 total. **Special facilities:** Career services center, art gallery.

Transfer out. **Colleges most students transferred to 2008:** Cal State University: Dominguez Hills, Los Angeles, Long Beach, Northridge, UCLA.

Basis for selection. Open admission, but selective for some programs. Limited admission to nursing and allied health programs.

2008-2009 Annual costs. Tuition/fees: $622; $6,052 out-of-state. Per-credit charge: $20 in-state; $201 out-of-state. Books/supplies: $2,316. Personal expenses: $3,024.

Financial aid. **Need-based:** Need-based aid available for part-time students. **Additional information:** Board of Governors Enrollment Fee Waiver available to students receiving AFDC, SSI/SSP, or General Assistance. May also qualify on basis of income.

Application procedures. **Admission:** No deadline. No application fee. Late registration allowed through third week of classes, if permitted by instructor. **Financial aid:** No deadline. FAFSA required. Applicants notified on a rolling basis; must reply within 2 week(s) of notification.

Academics. **Special study options:** Accelerated study, cooperative education, cross-registration, double major, dual enrollment of high school students, ESL, honors, independent study, liberal arts/career combination, study abroad, weekend college. **Credit/placement by examination:** CLEP, institutional tests. 15 credit hours maximum toward associate degree. **Support**

services: Learning center, reduced course load, remedial instruction, tutoring.

Majors. **Area/ethnic studies:** African-American. **Biology:** General, molecular. **Business:** General, accounting, administrative services, banking/financial services, business admin, insurance, management information systems, office technology, office/clerical, real estate. **Communications:** Advertising, journalism. **Communications technology:** General. **Computer sciences:** General, applications programming, computer graphics, computer science, programming. **Education:** General, early childhood, foreign languages, mathematics, music, teacher assistance. **Engineering:** General, electrical. **Engineering technology:** Drafting, electrical. **Family/consumer sciences:** Child care. **Foreign languages:** General, French, Spanish. **Health:** Clinical lab technology, nursing (RN), respiratory therapy technology. **History:** General. **Legal studies:** Paralegal. **Liberal arts:** Arts/sciences. **Math:** General. **Parks/recreation:** General. **Philosophy/religion:** Philosophy. **Physical sciences:** Chemistry, geology, physics. **Psychology:** General. **Social sciences:** Geography, political science, sociology. **Visual/performing arts:** Art, art history/conservation, commercial/advertising art, dramatic, fashion design, photography.

Computing on campus. Helpline, repair service available.

Student life. **Freshman orientation:** Available. **Activities:** Bands, choral groups, dance, drama, literary magazine, musical theater, student government, student newspaper.

Athletics. NJCAA. **Intercollegiate:** Basketball M, cross-country, football (tackle) M, tennis W, track and field. **Intramural:** Baseball M, basketball, bowling, golf, softball, tennis, track and field, volleyball. **Team name:** Cougars.

Student services. Career counseling, student employment services, on-campus daycare, personal counseling, placement for graduates. **Transfer:** Transfer adviser for students transferring to 4-year colleges.

Contact. Phone: (323) 241-5321
Deborah Odom, Admissions and Records Supervisor, Los Angeles Southwest College, 1600 West Imperial Highway, Los Angeles, CA 90047-4899

Los Angeles Trade and Technical College
Los Angeles, California
www.lattc.edu **CB code: 4400**

- Public 2-year community and technical college
- Commuter campus in very large city

General. Founded in 1925. Regionally accredited. Specialized culinary arts program; fashion, cosmetology, nursing programs. **Enrollment:** 4,473 degree-seeking undergraduates. **Degrees:** 489 associate awarded. **Calendar:** Semester, limited summer session. **Full-time faculty:** 185 total. **Part-time faculty:** 285 total. **Class size:** 46% < 20, 38% 20-39, 9% 40-49, 4% 50-99, 4% >100.

Student profile.

Out-of-state:	8%	**25 or older:**	60%

Transfer out. **Colleges most students transferred to 2008:** University of California: Los Angeles, California State University: Los Angeles, California State University: Dominguez Hills, University of Southern California.

Basis for selection. Open admission. Limited admission to nursing program. Portfolio recommended of commercial art majors.

2008-2009 Annual costs. Tuition/fees: $622; $6,052 out-of-state. Per-credit charge: $20 in-state; $201 out-of-state. Books/supplies: $2,316. Personal expenses: $3,024.

Financial aid. All financial aid based on need. Need-based aid available for part-time students. Work-study available nights, weekends and for part-time students.

Application procedures. **Admission:** No deadline. No application fee. Admission notification on a rolling basis. **Financial aid:** Priority date 5/1; no closing date. FAFSA required. Applicants notified on a rolling basis.

Academics. **Special study options:** Accelerated study, cooperative education, distance learning, dual enrollment of high school students, ESL, independent study, liberal arts/career combination, study abroad, weekend college. License preparation in nursing. **Credit/placement by examination:** CLEP, institutional tests. 15 credit hours maximum toward associate degree. **Support services:** GED preparation, learning center, pre-admission summer program, reduced course load, remedial instruction, study skills assistance, tutoring, writing center.

Majors. **Business:** General, accounting, administrative services, business admin, entrepreneurial studies, fashion, hospitality/recreation, labor relations, office/clerical, real estate. **Communications:** Journalism. **Communications technology:** General, graphic/printing. **Computer sciences:** General, computer science. **Construction:** Carpentry, electrician, maintenance, pipefitting, power transmission. **Engineering:** General. **Engineering technology:** Architectural, drafting, electrical. **Family/consumer sciences:** Clothing/textiles, institutional food production. **Health:** Health services, licensed practical nurse. **Liberal arts:** Arts/sciences. **Mechanic/repair:** Auto body, diesel, electronics/electrical, heating/ac/refrig. **Personal/culinary services:** Culinary arts. **Public administration:** Community org/advocacy. **Visual/performing arts:** Commercial/advertising art, fashion design, photography.

Most popular majors. Computer/information sciences 11%, health sciences 11%, liberal arts 34%, trade and industry 30%, visual/performing arts 8%.

Computing on campus. 550 workstations in library, computer center. Commuter students can connect to campus network. Online course registration, wireless network available.

Student life. **Freshman orientation:** Available. **Activities:** Dance, student government, student newspaper, political organizations.

Athletics. NJCAA. **Intercollegiate:** Basketball, cross-country, tennis, track and field. **Intramural:** Golf, swimming. **Team name:** Beaver.

Student services. Adult student services, career counseling, services for economically disadvantaged, student employment services, financial aid counseling, health services, minority student services, on-campus daycare, personal counseling, placement for graduates, veterans' counselor. **Physically disabled:** Services for visually, speech, hearing impaired. **Transfer:** Transfer adviser, college fairs on campus for students transferring to 4-year colleges.

Contact. Phone: (213) 763-7000
Ester Usaha, Registrar, Los Angeles Trade and Technical College, 400 West Washington Boulevard, Los Angeles, CA 90015-4181

Los Angeles Valley College
Valley Glen, California
www.lavc.edu **CB code: 5546**

- Public 2-year community college
- Commuter campus in very large city

General. Founded in 1949. Regionally accredited. **Enrollment:** 8,810 degree-seeking undergraduates. **Degrees:** 891 associate awarded. **Location:** 15 miles from downtown. **Calendar:** Semester, limited summer session. **Full-time faculty:** 240 total. **Part-time faculty:** 285 total. **Special facilities:** Planetarium.

Student profile.

Out-of-state:	2%	**25 or older:**	69%

Basis for selection. Open admission, but selective for some programs. Registered nursing program has competitive admission based on points accumulated for prerequisite courses, grades, and placement test scores. Institutional placement tests required of all students.

2008-2009 Annual costs. Tuition/fees: $624; $6,054 out-of-state. Per-credit charge: $20 in-state; $201 out-of-state. Books/supplies: $2,316. Personal expenses: $3,024.

Financial aid. All financial aid based on need. Need-based aid available for part-time students.

Application procedures. **Admission:** No deadline. No application fee. Admission notification on a rolling basis. **Financial aid:** Priority date 6/12; no closing date. FAFSA required. Applicants notified on a rolling basis.

Academics. **Special study options:** Cooperative education, dual enrollment of high school students, honors, independent study. License preparation in nursing, paramedic. **Credit/placement by examination:** AP, CLEP, IB, institutional tests. 15 credit hours maximum toward associate degree. **Support services:** Learning center, remedial instruction, study skills assistance, tutoring, writing center.

Majors. **Area/ethnic studies:** American. **Biology:** General. **Business:** General, administrative services, fashion, hospitality/recreation, management information systems, office technology, office/clerical. **Communications:** Broadcast journalism, journalism. **Computer sciences:** Applications programming, data processing. **Engineering technology:** Electrical. **Family/consumer sciences:** General. **Foreign languages:** French, German, Italian, Spanish. **Health:** Nursing (RN), respiratory therapy technology. **History:** General. **Liberal arts:** Arts/sciences. **Math:** General. **Parks/recreation:** General. **Philosophy/religion:** Philosophy. **Physical sciences:** Chemistry, geology, physics, planetary. **Protective services:** Police science. **Psychology:** General. **Social sciences:** Economics, geography, political science, sociology. **Visual/performing arts:** Art, art history/conservation, commercial/advertising art.

Computing on campus. 300 workstations in library, computer center, student center. Online course registration, wireless network available.

Student life. Freshman orientation: Available. Preregistration for classes offered. **Activities:** Bands, choral groups, dance, drama, film society, literary magazine, music ensembles, musical theater, radio station, student government, student newspaper, symphony orchestra.

Athletics. NJCAA. **Intercollegiate:** Baseball M, basketball, cross-country, diving, football (tackle) M, soccer W, softball W, swimming, track and field, water polo M. **Team name:** Monarchs.

Student services. Career counseling, student employment services, health services, on-campus daycare, personal counseling, placement for graduates, veterans' counselor. **Physically disabled:** Services for visually, speech, hearing impaired. **Learning disabled:** Comprehensive services available. **Transfer:** Transfer adviser, college fairs on campus for students transferring to 4-year colleges.

Contact. E-mail: trudgej@lavc.edu
Phone: (818) 947-2553 Fax: (818) 947-2501
Florentino Manzano, Dean of Enrollment Management, Los Angeles Valley College, 5800 Fulton Avenue, Valley Glen, CA 91401-4096

Los Medanos College

Pittsburg, California
www.losmedanos.edu **CB code: 4396**

- Public 2-year community college
- Commuter campus in small city

General. Founded in 1973. Regionally accredited. **Enrollment:** 4,818 degree-seeking undergraduates. **Degrees:** 375 associate awarded. **Location:** 45 miles from San Francisco. **Calendar:** Semester. **Full-time faculty:** 110 total. **Part-time faculty:** 288 total.

Student profile.

Out-of-state:	1%	**25 or older:**	53%

Basis for selection. Open admission.

2008-2009 Annual costs. Tuition/fees: $610; $6,040 out-of-state. Per-credit charge: $20 in-state; $201 out-of-state. Books/supplies: $1,566. Personal expenses: $2,664.

2007-2008 Financial aid. Need-based: 94% of total undergraduate aid awarded as scholarships/grants, 6% as loans/jobs.

Application procedures. Admission: No deadline. Admission notification on a rolling basis. **Financial aid:** Priority date 3/2; no closing date. FAFSA required. Applicants notified on a rolling basis starting 7/1; must reply within 2 week(s) of notification.

Academics. Special study options: Cooperative education, cross-registration, independent study, study abroad. **Credit/placement by examination:** CLEP, institutional tests. 20 credit hours maximum toward associate degree. **Support services:** Learning center, remedial instruction, tutoring.

Majors. Biology: General. **Business:** Accounting, entrepreneurial studies, labor relations, office management, real estate, tourism promotion. **Communications:** Journalism. **Family/consumer sciences:** Child care. **Health:** EMT paramedic, nursing (RN). **Liberal arts:** Arts/sciences. **Math:** General. **Mechanic/repair:** Electronics/electrical, small engine. **Physical sciences:** Chemistry. **Protective services:** Firefighting. **Psychology:** General. **Social sciences:** Anthropology, sociology. **Visual/performing arts:** Commercial/advertising art, music performance, studio arts.

Most popular majors. Business/marketing 7%, health sciences 18%, liberal arts 60%.

Computing on campus. 150 workstations in computer center.

Student life. Activities: Bands, choral groups, drama, music ensembles, student government, student newspaper.

Athletics. Intercollegiate: Baseball M, basketball, football (tackle) M, soccer M, softball W, volleyball W. **Intramural:** Basketball, softball, tennis.

Student services. Career counseling, student employment services, on-campus daycare, personal counseling, placement for graduates. **Physically disabled:** Services for visually, speech, hearing impaired. **Transfer:** Transfer adviser, college fairs on campus for students transferring to 4-year colleges.

Contact. Phone: (925) 439-2181 ext. 7500 Fax: (925) 427-6351
Robin Armour, Director of Admissions and Records, Los Medanos College, 2700 East Leland Road, Pittsburg, CA 94565

Marymount College

Rancho Palos Verdes, California **CB member**
www.marymountpv.edu **CB code: 4515**

- Private 2-year junior and liberal arts college affiliated with Roman Catholic Church
- Residential campus in large town

General. Founded in 1933. Regionally accredited. **Enrollment:** 617 degree-seeking undergraduates. **Degrees:** 142 associate awarded. **Location:** 30 miles from Los Angeles. **Calendar:** Semester, limited summer session. **Full-time faculty:** 39 total; 62% have terminal degrees, 13% minority, 51% women. **Part-time faculty:** 46 total; 17% have terminal degrees, 11% minority, 65% women. **Class size:** 64% < 20, 35% 20-39, less than 1% 40-49.

Student profile. Among degree-seeking undergraduates, 315 enrolled as first-time, first-year students.

Out-of-state:	17%	**Hispanic American:**	17%
Women:	51%	**International:**	9%
African American:	5%	**Live on campus:**	56%
Asian American:	5%		

Transfer out. 90% of students enrolled in the transfer program go on to 4-year colleges. **Colleges most students transferred to 2008:** University of Southern California, Loyola Marymount University, University of California, California State University, Chapman University.

Basis for selection. High school record, quality of academic preparation, recommendations, student's personal statement, standardized test scores all considered. SAT or ACT recommended. ACCUPLACER used for placement. Interview and essay recommended. **Homeschooled:** Transcript of courses and grades, letter of recommendation (nonparent) required. General syllabus of all coursework completed or private tutoring received, statement explaining why family chose home schooling and its advantages and disadvantages required. SAT or ACT scores and state H.S. equivalency certificate recommended.

High school preparation. College-preparatory program recommended. 14 units recommended. Recommended units include English 4, mathematics 3, social studies 2, science 2 (laboratory 1) and foreign language 2.

2009-2010 Annual costs. Tuition/fees: $24,422. Per-credit charge: $825. Room/board: $10,600. Books/supplies: $1,638. Personal expenses: $2,250.

2007-2008 Financial aid. Non-need-based: Scholarships awarded for academics.

Application procedures. Admission: Priority date 3/2; no deadline. $40 fee, may be waived for applicants with need. Admission notification on a rolling basis beginning on or about 12/1. Must reply by May 1 or within 4 week(s) if notified thereafter. **Financial aid:** Priority date 3/1; no closing date. FAFSA required. Applicants notified on a rolling basis starting 2/1; must reply by 5/1 or within 4 week(s) of notification.

Academics. Special study options: Cooperative education, dual enrollment of high school students, ESL, honors, independent study, internships, study abroad, urban semester, weekend college. **Credit/placement by examination:** AP, CLEP, IB, institutional tests. 15 credit hours maximum toward associate degree. **Support services:** Learning center, pre-admission summer program, reduced course load, remedial instruction, study skills assistance, tutoring.

Honors college/program. Admitted students are reviewed by the Honors faculty for Honors consideration. Average GPA is 3.3; SAT or ACT scores highly recommended. Approximately 30 students admitted each year. Students may earn their way into the Honors program based on academic success in their first year of college. Honors courses are designated each year. Successful Honors students may join Phi Theta Kappa Honor Society; graduates may secure PTK scholarships upon transfer.

Two-Year Colleges

Majors. **Liberal arts:** Arts/sciences.

Computing on campus. 77 workstations in library, computer center. Dormitories wired for high-speed internet access and linked to campus network. Commuter students can connect to campus network. Online library, helpline, repair service, wireless network available.

Student life. **Freshman orientation:** Mandatory, $150 fee. Preregistration for classes offered. **Housing:** Single-sex dorms, special housing for disabled, apartments available. $400 partly refundable deposit, deadline 7/1. Housing available through volunteers in the community. **Activities:** Campus ministries, choral groups, dance, drama, international student organizations, music ensembles, musical theater, radio station, student government, volunteer club, philosophy discussion club, pre-med club, student integrity council, Phi Theta Kappa, Latinos Unidos, Black Student Union, International Peers, Jewish club, campus ministry leadership team.

Athletics. NJCAA. **Intercollegiate:** Soccer. **Intramural:** Basketball, football (non-tackle), golf, softball. **Team name:** Mariners.

Student services. Adult student services, alcohol/substance abuse counseling, chaplain/spiritual director, career counseling, student employment services, financial aid counseling, health services, personal counseling. **Physically disabled:** Services for visually, hearing impaired. **Transfer:** Preadmission transcript evaluation for new students. Transfer center, transfer adviser, college fairs on campus for students transferring to 4-year colleges.

Contact. E-mail: admissions@marymountpv.edu
Phone: (310) 377-5501 ext. 311 Fax: (310) 265-0962
Barbara Layne, Dean of Enrollment Management, Marymount College, 30800 Palos Verdes Drive East, Rancho Palos Verdes, CA 90275-6299

Mendocino College

Ukiah, California
www.mendocino.edu **CB code: 4517**

- Public 2-year community college
- Commuter campus in large town

General. Founded in 1973. Regionally accredited. **Enrollment:** 2,186 degree-seeking undergraduates. **Degrees:** 290 associate awarded. **Location:** 60 miles from Santa Rosa, 110 miles from San Francisco. **Calendar:** Semester, limited summer session. **Full-time faculty:** 47 total; 19% have terminal degrees, 4% minority, 53% women. **Part-time faculty:** 241 total; 7% minority, 54% women. **Class size:** 69% < 20, 28% 20-39, 2% 40-49, 1% 50-99, less than 1% >100. **Special facilities:** Gallery and theater complex.

Student profile. Among degree-seeking undergraduates, 40% enrolled in a transfer program, 7% enrolled in a vocational program, 15% already have a bachelor's degree or higher, 200 enrolled as first-time, first-year students, 203 transferred in from other institutions.

Out-of-state:	5%	**Hispanic American:**	17%
African American:	2%	**Native American:**	7%
Asian American:	2%	**25 or older:**	60%

Transfer out. 20% of students enrolled in the transfer program go on to 4-year colleges. **Colleges most students transferred to 2008:** Sonoma State University, University of California.

Basis for selection. Open admission.

2008-2009 Annual costs. Tuition/fees: $634; $6,184 out-of-state. Per-credit charge: $20 in-state; $205 out-of-state. Books/supplies: $1,566. Personal expenses: $3,024.

2007-2008 Financial aid. **Need-based:** 207 full-time freshmen applied for aid; 196 were judged to have need; 195 of these received aid. Average scholarship/grant was $4,695; average loan $4,039. 85% of total undergraduate aid awarded as scholarships/grants, 15% as loans/jobs. Need-based aid available for part-time students. Work-study available nights and for part-time students. **Non-need-based:** Awarded to 191 full-time undergraduates, including 59 freshmen. Scholarships awarded for academics, leadership, state residency.

Application procedures. **Admission:** Priority date 5/1; no deadline. No application fee. Admission notification on a rolling basis beginning on or about 7/1. **Financial aid:** Priority date 5/31; no closing date. FAFSA required. Applicants notified on a rolling basis starting 7/1; must reply within 2 week(s) of notification.

Academics. **Special study options:** Distance learning, double major, dual enrollment of high school students, ESL, independent study, internships, student-designed major. License preparation in nursing, paramedic, real estate. **Credit/placement by examination:** AP, CLEP, institutional tests. 12 credit hours maximum toward associate degree. **Support services:** GED test center, learning center, pre-admission summer program, remedial instruction, tutoring.

Majors. **Agriculture:** Plant sciences. **Biology:** General. **Business:** General, accounting, administrative services, business admin, entrepreneurial studies. **Communications:** General. **Computer sciences:** General. **Foreign languages:** French, Spanish. **Health:** Substance abuse counseling. **Liberal arts:** Arts/sciences. **Math:** General. **Mechanic/repair:** Auto body, electronics/electrical. **Parks/recreation:** Sports admin. **Protective services:** Law enforcement admin. **Psychology:** General. **Public administration:** Human services. **Social sciences:** General. **Visual/performing arts:** Art, dramatic.

Most popular majors. Business/marketing 17%, health sciences 8%, liberal arts 55%, psychology 8%.

Computing on campus. 120 workstations in library, computer center, student center. Commuter students can connect to campus network. Online library, wireless network available.

Student life. **Freshman orientation:** Available. Preregistration for classes offered. **Activities:** Bands, choral groups, dance, drama, music ensembles, musical theater, radio station, student government, symphony orchestra.

Athletics. NJCAA. **Intercollegiate:** Baseball M, basketball, cheerleading M, football (tackle) M, soccer, softball W, track and field, volleyball W. **Intramural:** Basketball, bowling, softball, volleyball. **Team name:** Eagles.

Student services. Adult student services, career counseling, services for economically disadvantaged, student employment services, financial aid counseling, on-campus daycare, personal counseling, placement for graduates, veterans' counselor, women's services. **Physically disabled:** Services for visually, speech, hearing impaired. **Transfer:** Transfer adviser, college fairs on campus for students transferring to 4-year colleges.

Contact. Phone: (707) 468-3101 Fax: (707) 468-3120
Kristie Anderson, Director of Admissions and Records, Mendocino College, 1000 Hensley Creek/Box 3000, Ukiah, CA 95482

Merced College

Merced, California
www.mccd.edu **CB code: 4500**

- Public 2-year community college
- Commuter campus in small city

General. Founded in 1962. Regionally accredited. Off-campus centers at Los Banos. **Enrollment:** 7,211 degree-seeking undergraduates. **Degrees:** 556 associate awarded. **Location:** 50 miles from Fresno. **Calendar:** Semester, limited summer session. **Full-time faculty:** 120 total. **Part-time faculty:** 479 total.

Transfer out. **Colleges most students transferred to 2008:** CSU Stanislaus, CSU Fresno, UC Davis.

Basis for selection. Open admission. Institutional placement tests used.

2008-2009 Annual costs. Tuition/fees: $632; $6,062 out-of-state. Per-credit charge: $20 in-state; $201 out-of-state. Books/supplies: $650. Personal expenses: $1,750.

2007-2008 Financial aid. **Non-need-based:** Scholarships awarded for academics.

Application procedures. **Admission:** No deadline. No application fee. Application must be submitted on paper. Admission notification on a rolling basis. Must reply by May 1 or within 4 week(s) if notified thereafter. **Financial aid:** Priority date 6/1; no closing date. FAFSA required. Applicants notified on a rolling basis starting 1/2; must reply within 3 week(s) of notification.

Academics. **Special study options:** Cooperative education, distance learning, dual enrollment of high school students, honors, internships, study abroad. License preparation in nursing, paramedic, radiology, real estate. **Credit/placement by examination:** AP, CLEP, institutional tests. 12 credit hours maximum toward associate degree. **Support services:** Learning center, pre-admission summer program, remedial instruction, tutoring.

Majors. **Agriculture:** General, agronomy, animal sciences, business, horticulture, ornamental horticulture, soil science. **Biology:** General. **Business:** General, accounting, administrative services, business admin, merchandising, real estate. **Communications:** General, journalism. **Computer sciences:** General, information systems. **Education:** Early childhood. **Engineering:** General. **Engineering technology:** Drafting, electrical. **Family/consumer sciences:** General, child development, family studies. **Foreign**

languages: French, German, Spanish. **Health:** Health services, licensed practical nurse, medical radiologic technology/radiation therapy, medical secretary, nursing (RN), office admin, substance abuse counseling. **History:** General. **Legal studies:** Legal secretary. **Liberal arts:** Arts/sciences. **Math:** General. **Mechanic/repair:** Auto body, diesel, electronics/electrical, heating/ac/refrig, industrial. **Parks/recreation:** Health/fitness. **Philosophy/religion:** Philosophy. **Physical sciences:** General, chemistry, geology, physics. **Production:** Welding. **Protective services:** Firefighting, police science. **Psychology:** General. **Public administration:** Human services, social work. **Social sciences:** General, anthropology, archaeology, physical anthropology. **Visual/performing arts:** General, art history/conservation, dramatic, photography.

Computing on campus. 400 workstations in library, computer center. Commuter students can connect to campus network. Online library, helpline available.

Student life. Freshman orientation: Available. **Activities:** Bands, choral groups, dance, drama, international student organizations, music ensembles, musical theater, student government, student newspaper, symphony orchestra, black student union, Movimiento Estudiantil Chicano de Aztlan, Intervarsity Christian group, Rotaract.

Athletics. NJCAA. **Intercollegiate:** Baseball M, basketball, cheerleading M, cross-country, diving, football (tackle) M, golf, softball W, swimming, track and field, volleyball W, water polo. **Team name:** Blue Devils.

Student services. Alcohol/substance abuse counseling, career counseling, services for economically disadvantaged, student employment services, financial aid counseling, health services, on-campus daycare, personal counseling, placement for graduates, veterans' counselor. **Physically disabled:** Services for visually, speech, hearing impaired. **Transfer:** Transfer center, transfer adviser, college fairs on campus for students transferring to 4-year colleges.

Contact. Phone: (209) 384-6187 Fax: (209) 384-6339
Everett Lovelace, Dean of Student Services, Merced College,
Administration Building, Box 14, Merced, CA 95348

Merritt College
Oakland, California
www.merritt.edu **CB code: 4502**

- Public 2-year community college
- Large city

General. Founded in 1953. Regionally accredited. **Enrollment:** 2,544 degree-seeking undergraduates. **Degrees:** 458 associate awarded. **Location:** 15 miles from San Francisco. **Calendar:** Semester, extensive summer session. **Full-time faculty:** 90 total. **Part-time faculty:** 215 total. **Special facilities:** Anthropology museum, landscape/horticulture complex.

Student profile.

Out-of-state:	5%	**25 or older:**	60%

Basis for selection. Open admission.

2008-2009 Annual costs. Tuition/fees: $604; $6,034 out-of-state. Per-credit charge: $20 in-state; $201 out-of-state. Books/supplies: $1,450. Personal expenses: $2,600.

Financial aid. Need-based: Need-based aid available for part-time students.

Application procedures. Admission: No deadline. No application fee. Admission notification on a rolling basis. **Financial aid:** Priority date 4/1, closing date 6/30. FAFSA, institutional form required. Applicants notified on a rolling basis starting 6/1.

Academics. Special study options: Cooperative education, cross-registration, distance learning, dual enrollment of high school students, honors, independent study. **Credit/placement by examination:** CLEP, institutional tests. 15 credit hours maximum toward associate degree. **Support services:** Learning center, pre-admission summer program, reduced course load, remedial instruction, tutoring.

Majors. Agriculture: Horticultural science, landscaping. **Area/ethnic studies:** African-American. **Business:** General, real estate. **Computer sciences:** General. **Education:** General, business, early childhood. **Engineering:** Electrical. **Family/consumer sciences:** Child care, family/community services. **Foreign languages:** French, Spanish. **Health:** Licensed practical nurse, medical radiologic technology/radiation therapy, nursing (RN). **Legal studies:** Paralegal. **Liberal arts:** Arts/sciences. **Math:** General. **Parks/recreation:** General. **Public administration:** Community org/advocacy. **Social sciences:** General.

Computing on campus. 200 workstations in library, computer center, student center.

Student life. Activities: Choral groups, dance, student government, student newspaper, Merritt Christian Fellowship, LaRaza Student Union, Native American Association, Black Student Union, Asian Student Union, Ecology Action Club, Disabled Students Coalition.

Athletics. Intercollegiate: Basketball, cross-country, track and field. **Intramural:** Badminton, golf, tennis, volleyball.

Student services. Adult student services, career counseling, student employment services, health services, on-campus daycare, personal counseling, placement for graduates, veterans' counselor. **Physically disabled:** Services for visually, speech, hearing impaired. **Transfer:** Transfer adviser, college fairs on campus for students transferring to 4-year colleges.

Contact. E-mail: admissions@peralta.edu
Phone: (510) 436-2487
Howard Perdue, Dean of Admissions and Records, Merritt College, 12500 Campus Drive, Oakland, CA 94619

MiraCosta College
Oceanside, California
www.miracosta.edu **CB code: 4582**

- Public 2-year community college
- Commuter campus in large city

General. Founded in 1934. Regionally accredited. Study abroad programs in Japan, Mexico, Costa Rica and several countries in Europe. **Enrollment:** 8,834 degree-seeking undergraduates. **Degrees:** 525 associate awarded. **ROTC:** Army, Air Force. **Location:** 35 miles from San Diego. **Calendar:** Semester, limited summer session. **Full-time faculty:** 132 total; 29% minority, 52% women. **Part-time faculty:** 389 total; 17% minority, 60% women. **Class size:** 28% < 20, 62% 20-39, 8% 40-49, 1% 50-99, less than 1% >100. **Special facilities:** Bioprocessing training facility, music recording studios. **Partnerships:** Formal partnerships with Cisco Academy.

Student profile. Among degree-seeking undergraduates, 56% enrolled in a transfer program, 7% enrolled in a vocational program, 11% already have a bachelor's degree or higher, 1,682 enrolled as first-time, first-year students.

Out-of-state:	1%	**Hispanic American:**	23%
African American:	5%	**Native American:**	1%
Asian American:	8%	**International:**	2%

Transfer out. 33% of students enrolled in the transfer program go on to 4-year colleges. **Colleges most students transferred to 2008:** San Diego State University, Cal State: San Marcos, University of California: San Diego.

Basis for selection. Open admission, but selective for some programs. Must be either 18 yrs of age or high school graduate. High school students require principal and parental permission with grade level limitations. Nursing programs require special application with course and GPA requirements. Locally administered tests may be used for placement and counseling.

2008-2009 Annual costs. Tuition/fees: $644; $6,074 out-of-state. Per-credit charge: $20 in-state; $201 out-of-state. Books/supplies: $1,638. Personal expenses: $2,826.

2007-2008 Financial aid. Need-based: 14% of total undergraduate aid awarded as scholarships/grants, 86% as loans/jobs. Need-based aid available for part-time students. Work-study available nights and for part-time students. **Additional information:** Waiver of in-state fees for eligible low-income students.

Application procedures. Admission: No deadline. No application fee. Admission notification on a rolling basis. **Financial aid:** Priority date 4/9; no closing date. FAFSA, institutional form required. Applicants notified on a rolling basis; must reply within 4 week(s) of notification.

Academics. Special study options: Accelerated study, cooperative education, distance learning, double major, dual enrollment of high school students, ESL, honors, independent study, internships, liberal arts/career combination, student-designed major, study abroad, teacher certification program, weekend college. License preparation in nursing, real estate. **Credit/placement by examination:** AP, CLEP, IB, institutional tests. 15 credit hours maximum toward associate degree. **Support services:** GED preparation and test center, learning center, pre-admission summer program, reduced course load, remedial instruction, study skills assistance, tutoring, writing center.

Honors college/program. Students wanting to study at the honors level contract for an honors option in designated courses.

Majors. **Agriculture:** Business, floriculture, landscaping, nursery operations, turf management. **Architecture:** Landscape. **Biology:** General. **Business:** Accounting, administrative services, business admin, hospitality admin, office management, office/clerical, real estate, tourism/travel. **Communications:** General. **Computer sciences:** General, computer graphics, computer science, LAN/WAN management, programming. **Education:** Early childhood. **Engineering technology:** Drafting. **Family/consumer sciences:** Child care. **Foreign languages:** General, French, German, Japanese, Spanish. **Health:** Licensed practical nurse, premedicine, preveterinary. **History:** General. **Interdisciplinary:** Behavioral sciences, gerontology. **Legal studies:** Prelaw. **Liberal arts:** Arts/sciences. **Math:** General. **Mechanic/repair:** Auto body, automotive. **Personal/culinary services:** Cosmetic. **Philosophy/religion:** Philosophy. **Physical sciences:** Chemistry, geology, physics. **Protective services:** Police science. **Psychology:** General. **Science technology:** Biological. **Social sciences:** General, economics, geography, political science, sociology. **Visual/performing arts:** Art, art history/conservation, commercial/advertising art, dance, dramatic, theater design.

Most popular majors. Business/marketing 8%, liberal arts 66%.

Computing on campus. 1,000 workstations in library, computer center, student center. Online course registration, online library, student web hosting available.

Student life. **Freshman orientation:** Available. One-hour session offered 14 times prior to classes each semester, online orientations offered 24/7. **Activities:** Bands, choral groups, dance, drama, music ensembles, musical theater, student government, student newspaper, symphony orchestra, MECHA/Latina organization, Black Student Union, women's issues and studies group, Phi Theta Kappa, Future Educators, National Science club, allied health club, behavioral science club, Creative Entertainers.

Athletics. **Intercollegiate:** Basketball, soccer. **Intramural:** Basketball, soccer, softball, tennis, volleyball. **Team name:** Spartans.

Student services. Alcohol/substance abuse counseling, career counseling, services for economically disadvantaged, student employment services, financial aid counseling, health services, on-campus daycare, personal counseling, placement for graduates. **Physically disabled:** Services for visually, speech, hearing impaired. **Learning disabled:** Comprehensive services available. **Transfer:** Transfer center, transfer adviser, college fairs on campus for students transferring to 4-year colleges.

Contact. E-mail: admissions@miracosta.edu
Phone: (760) 795-6620 Toll-free number: (888) 201-8480
Fax: (760) 795-6626
Alicia Terry, Director of Admissions and Records, MiraCosta College, One Barnard Drive, Oceanside, CA 92056-3899

Mission College
Santa Clara, California
www.missioncollege.org **CB code: 7587**

- Public 2-year community college
- Small city

General. Founded in 1975. Regionally accredited. **Enrollment:** 5,155 degree-seeking undergraduates. **Degrees:** 492 associate awarded. **ROTC:** Naval, Air Force. **Location:** 8 miles from San Jose. **Calendar:** Semester, limited summer session. **Full-time faculty:** 146 total. **Part-time faculty:** 198 total.

Transfer out. **Colleges most students transferred to 2008:** San Jose State.

Basis for selection. Open admission. Limited admission to vocational nursing and allied health. Interviews required of nursing, psychiatric technician majors.

2008-2009 Annual costs. Tuition/fees: $650; $6,080 out-of-state. Per-credit charge: $20 in-state; $201 out-of-state. Books/supplies: $2,316. Personal expenses: $3,024.

Application procedures. **Admission:** No deadline. No application fee. Admission notification on a rolling basis. **Financial aid:** Priority date 5/1; no closing date. Applicants notified on a rolling basis starting 8/1; must reply within 2 week(s) of notification.

Academics. **Special study options:** Cooperative education, dual enrollment of high school students, honors, independent study, weekend college. Bachelor's degree programs available on campus. **Credit/placement by examination:** CLEP, institutional tests. 12 credit hours maximum toward associate degree. **Support services:** Learning center, remedial instruction, tutoring.

Majors. **Agriculture:** Food science. **Biology:** General. **Business:** General, accounting, administrative services, banking/financial services, business admin, management information systems, management science, office management, office/clerical, real estate. **Communications technology:** Graphic/printing. **Computer sciences:** Applications programming, computer science, information systems. **Engineering:** General. **Engineering technology:** Drafting. **Health:** Health services, licensed practical nurse, nursing (RN). **Liberal arts:** Arts/sciences. **Math:** General. **Physical sciences:** Chemistry, physics. **Protective services:** Fire safety technology. **Social sciences:** General. **Visual/performing arts:** Art, commercial/advertising art.

Student life. **Freshman orientation:** Available. **Activities:** Bands, music ensembles, musical theater, TV station.

Athletics. **Intercollegiate:** Baseball M, basketball W, soccer M, softball W, tennis. **Team name:** Saints.

Student services. Adult student services, career counseling, student employment services, health services, on-campus daycare, personal counseling, placement for graduates, veterans' counselor. **Transfer:** Transfer center, transfer adviser, college fairs on campus for students transferring to 4-year colleges.

Contact. Phone: (408) 988-2200 Fax: (408) 980-8980
Arlene Atondo, Director of Admissions, Mission College, 3000 Mission College Boulevard, Santa Clara, CA 95054-1897

Modesto Junior College
Modesto, California
www.mjc.edu **CB code: 4486**

- Public 2-year community college
- Commuter campus in small city

General. Founded in 1921. Regionally accredited. **Enrollment:** 14,518 degree-seeking undergraduates. **Degrees:** 1,275 associate awarded. **Location:** 90 miles from San Francisco. **Calendar:** Semester, limited summer session. **Full-time faculty:** 283 total. **Part-time faculty:** 251 total. **Special facilities:** Natural history museum.

Transfer out. **Colleges most students transferred to 2008:** California State University: Stanislaus, California State University: Fresno, California State University: Sacramento, University of California: Davis, University of California: San Diego.

Basis for selection. Open admission, but selective for some programs. Limited admission offered to nursing (RN), dental assisting, medical assisting, and related majors. Selective admission to fire academy.

High school preparation. Certain programs require specific courses.

2008-2009 Annual costs. Tuition/fees: $642; $6,072 out-of-state. Per-credit charge: $20 in-state; $201 out-of-state. Books/supplies: $1,566. Personal expenses: $3,024.

2008-2009 Financial aid. All financial aid based on need. Need-based aid available for part-time students. Work-study available nights, weekends and for part-time students. **Additional information:** Modesto Junior College scholarship priority deadline 12/15.

Application procedures. **Admission:** No deadline. No application fee. Admission notification on a rolling basis. **Financial aid:** Priority date 3/2; no closing date. FAFSA, institutional form required. Applicants notified on a rolling basis starting 5/1; must reply within 2 week(s) of notification.

Academics. **Special study options:** Cooperative education, distance learning, double major, dual enrollment of high school students, ESL, honors, independent study, internships, liberal arts/career combination, study abroad, weekend college. License preparation in nursing, real estate. **Credit/placement by examination:** AP, CLEP, institutional tests. 30 credit hours maximum toward associate degree. **Support services:** GED preparation, learning center, pre-admission summer program, remedial instruction, study skills assistance, tutoring, writing center.

Majors. **Agriculture:** Agronomy, animal breeding, animal sciences, business, dairy, food science, landscaping, ornamental horticulture, plant sciences, poultry, soil science, supplies. **Architecture:** Landscape, urban/community planning. **Business:** General, accounting, administrative services, business admin, fashion, finance, management information systems, marketing, real estate. **Communications:** General, broadcast journalism, journalism. **Communications technology:** Graphic/printing. **Computer sciences:** General, computer graphics, computer science, programming. **Conservation:** General, forestry, wildlife. **Construction:** Electrician, maintenance, pipefitting. **Engineering:** General, electrical. **Engineering technology:** Architectural, drafting. **Family/consumer sciences:** General, child care, clothing/textiles, family/community services, food/nutrition. **Foreign languages:** General, Spanish. **Health:** Dental assistant, medical assistant, nursing (RN), respiratory therapy technology. **Mechanic/repair:** General, auto body, automotive, electronics/electrical, heating/ac/refrig. **Parks/recreation:** General, health/fitness. **Personal/culinary services:** Culinary arts. **Protective services:** Firefighting, law enforcement admin. **Public administration:** Human services. **Social sciences:** General. **Visual/performing arts:** General, art, cinematography, commercial photography, commercial/advertising art, dramatic, fashion design, interior design, photography, studio arts.

Computing on campus. 137 workstations in library, computer center, student center. Commuter students can connect to campus network. Online course registration available.

Student life. **Freshman orientation:** Available. One hour, held during registration. **Activities:** Bands, choral groups, dance, drama, film society, international student organizations, music ensembles, musical theater, opera, radio station, student government, student newspaper, symphony orchestra, TV station, Christian Collegiate Fellowship; Able-Disabled Association; foreign, ethnic, minority student and women re-entry clubs; Young Farmers; other special interest and concern groups.

Athletics. **Intercollegiate:** Baseball M, basketball, cross-country, diving, football (tackle) M, golf, soccer, softball W, swimming, tennis, track and field, volleyball W, water polo, wrestling M. **Team name:** Pirates.

Student services. Adult student services, career counseling, services for economically disadvantaged, student employment services, financial aid counseling, health services, minority student services, on-campus daycare, personal counseling, placement for graduates, veterans' counselor. **Physically disabled:** Services for visually, speech, hearing impaired. **Learning disabled:** Comprehensive services available. **Transfer:** Re-entry adviser for new students. Transfer center, transfer adviser, college fairs on campus for students transferring to 4-year colleges.

Contact. Phone: (209) 575-6013 Fax: (209) 575-6859
Susie Agostini, Dean of Matriculation, Admissions, and Records, Modesto Junior College, 435 College Avenue, Modesto, CA 95350-5800

Monterey Peninsula College
Monterey, California
www.mpc.edu **CB code: 4490**

- Public 2-year community college
- Commuter campus in large town

General. Founded in 1947. Regionally accredited. **Enrollment:** 4,011 degree-seeking undergraduates. **Degrees:** 365 associate awarded. **Location:** 120 miles from San Francisco. **Calendar:** Semester, limited summer session. **Full-time faculty:** 120 total. **Part-time faculty:** 170 total.

Basis for selection. Open admission, but selective for some programs. Additional requirements, including interview, for dental assistant, nursing, administrative justice and police academy programs.

2008-2009 Annual costs. Tuition/fees: $662; $6,092 out-of-state. Per-credit charge: $20 in-state; $201 out-of-state. Books/supplies: $1,566. Personal expenses: $2,700.

Financial aid. **Need-based:** Need-based aid available for part-time students.

Application procedures. **Admission:** No deadline. No application fee. Admission notification on a rolling basis. **Financial aid:** Priority date 3/2; no closing date. FAFSA, institutional form required. Applicants notified on a rolling basis starting 6/1.

Academics. **Special study options:** Cooperative education, cross-registration, distance learning, double major, dual enrollment of high school students, ESL, independent study, weekend college. **Credit/placement by examination:** CLEP, institutional tests. 30 credit hours maximum toward associate degree. **Support services:** Learning center, remedial instruction, tutoring.

Majors. **Agriculture:** Ornamental horticulture. **Area/ethnic studies:** Women's. **Biology:** General. **Business:** General, accounting, business admin, hospitality admin, hospitality/recreation, international, office/clerical, real estate. **Communications:** General. **Computer sciences:** General, data processing, LAN/WAN management, programming, web page design, word processing. **Engineering technology:** Drafting. **Family/consumer sciences:** General, child development, clothing/textiles, family/community services, fashion consultant, institutional food production. **Foreign languages:** General. **Health:** Dental assistant, medical assistant, nursing (RN), predental, premedicine, prepharmacy, preveterinary. **History:** General. **Liberal arts:** Arts/sciences. **Math:** General. **Philosophy/religion:** Philosophy. **Physical sciences:** Chemistry, physics. **Protective services:** Fire safety technology, law enforcement admin. **Psychology:** General. **Social sciences:** Anthropology, economics, political science, sociology. **Visual/performing arts:** Acting, art, art history/conservation, ceramics, dance, directing/producing, dramatic, drawing, graphic design, interior design, metal/jewelry, painting, photography, printmaking, sculpture, studio arts.

Student life. **Activities:** Bands, choral groups, dance, drama, music ensembles, musical theater, opera, student government.

Athletics. NJCAA. **Intercollegiate:** Baseball M, basketball, cross-country, football (tackle) M, golf, softball W, swimming, tennis W, track and field, volleyball W. **Team name:** Lobos.

Student services. Career counseling, student employment services, health services, on-campus daycare, personal counseling. **Physically disabled:** Services for visually, speech, hearing impaired. **Transfer:** Transfer center, transfer adviser, college fairs on campus for students transferring to 4-year colleges.

Contact. Phone: (831) 646-4002 Fax: (831) 646-4015
Vera Coleman, Director of Admissions and Records, Monterey Peninsula College, 980 Fremont Street, Monterey, CA 93940-4799

Moorpark College
Moorpark, California
www.moorparkcollege.edu **CB code: 4512**

- Public 2-year community college
- Commuter campus in large town

General. Founded in 1963. Regionally accredited. **Enrollment:** 10,859 degree-seeking undergraduates. **Degrees:** 1,562 associate awarded. **Location:** 50 miles from Los Angeles. **Calendar:** Semester, limited summer session. **Full-time faculty:** 182 total. **Part-time faculty:** 403 total. **Special facilities:** Exotic animal compound and teaching zoo, observatory.

Student profile.

Out-of-state:	1%	**25 or older:**	74%

Transfer out. **Colleges most students transferred to 2008:** California State University, University of Southern California, University of California: Los Angeles, UC Santa Barbara.

Basis for selection. Open admission, but selective for some programs. Limited admission to nursing program, exotic animal training management program, radiologic technology.

2008-2009 Annual costs. Tuition/fees: $644; $6,074 out-of-state. Per-credit charge: $20 in-state; $201 out-of-state. Books/supplies: $1,566. Personal expenses: $3,024.

Application procedures. **Admission:** Priority date 7/30; no deadline. No application fee. Admission notification on a rolling basis. **Financial aid:** Priority date 5/14; no closing date. FAFSA required. Applicants notified on a rolling basis starting 6/15; must reply within 2 week(s) of notification.

Academics. **Special study options:** Cooperative education, distance learning, honors, independent study, internships, study abroad. **Credit/placement by examination:** AP, CLEP. 12 credit hours maximum toward associate degree. **Support services:** Learning center, remedial instruction, tutoring.

Majors. **Agriculture:** Animal sciences. **Biology:** General. **Business:** Accounting, administrative services, business admin, management information systems, office management, real estate. **Communications:** General, broadcast journalism. **Communications technology:** General, graphic/printing. **Computer sciences:** General, applications programming, information systems. **Engineering technology:** Electrical. **Family/consumer sciences:** General, child care, family studies. **Health:** Medical radiologic technology/radiation therapy, nursing (RN). **Liberal arts:** Arts/sciences. **Math:** General. **Physical sciences:** Chemistry, geology, physics. **Protective services:** Police science. **Social sciences:** General. **Visual/performing arts:** General, cinematography, commercial/advertising art, dramatic, interior design, photography, studio arts.

Most popular majors. Agriculture 10%, health sciences 9%, liberal arts 66%.

Computing on campus. 75 workstations in computer center. Online course registration, wireless network available.

Student life. Freshman orientation: Available. Online orientation. **Activities:** Bands, choral groups, dance, drama, film society, music ensembles, musical theater, opera, radio station, student government, student newspaper, TV station, Mexican-American club, Black student Union, Alpha Gamma Sigma, Muslim Student Association.

Athletics. Intercollegiate: Baseball M, basketball, cheerleading M, cross-country, football (tackle) M, golf M, softball W, tennis W, track and field, volleyball, wrestling M. **Team name:** Raiders.

Student services. Career counseling, services for economically disadvantaged, student employment services, financial aid counseling, health services, legal services, on-campus daycare, personal counseling, veterans' counselor. **Physically disabled:** Services for visually, speech, hearing impaired. **Transfer:** Transfer center, transfer adviser, college fairs on campus for students transferring to 4-year colleges.

Contact. E-mail: mcadmissions@vcccd.net
Phone: (805) 378-1429 Fax: (805) 378-1499
Katherine Colborn, Registrar, Moorpark College, 7075 Campus Road, Moorpark, CA 93021

Mount San Antonio College

Walnut, California
www.mtsac.edu **CB code: 4494**

- Public 2-year community college
- Commuter campus in small city

General. Founded in 1946. Regionally accredited. **Enrollment:** 21,447 degree-seeking undergraduates. **Degrees:** 2,203 associate awarded. **ROTC:** Air Force. **Location:** 30 miles from Los Angeles. **Calendar:** Semester, extensive summer session. **Full-time faculty:** 432 total. **Part-time faculty:** 893 total. **Special facilities:** Planetarium, wildlife sanctuary.

Transfer out. Colleges most students transferred to 2008: California State Polytechnic University: Pomona, California State University: Los Angeles, California State University: Fullerton.

Basis for selection. Open admission.

2008-2009 Annual costs. Tuition/fees: $664; $6,094 out-of-state. Per-credit charge: $20 in-state; $201 out-of-state. Books/supplies: $1,566. Personal expenses: $2,520.

Financial aid. All financial aid based on need. Need-based aid available for part-time students.

Application procedures. Admission: Closing date 9/5. No application fee. Admission notification on a rolling basis. **Financial aid:** Closing date 3/2. FAFSA, institutional form required. Applicants notified on a rolling basis starting 6/1; must reply within 4 week(s) of notification.

Academics. Special study options: Cooperative education, cross-registration, distance learning, dual enrollment of high school students, ESL, honors, internships, study abroad, teacher certification program, weekend college. License preparation in aviation, nursing, paramedic, radiology, real estate. **Credit/placement by examination:** CLEP. 12 credit hours maximum toward associate degree. **Support services:** GED preparation, learning center, pre-admission summer program, remedial instruction, study skills assistance, tutoring, writing center.

Majors. Agriculture: Animal sciences, business, horticulture. **Biology:** General, marine. **Business:** General, accounting, administrative services, banking/financial services, business admin, entrepreneurial studies, fashion, office/clerical, real estate. **Communications:** Advertising, broadcast journalism, journalism. **Communications technology:** General. **Computer sciences:** Data processing. **Conservation:** General, forestry. **Engineering:** General. **Engineering technology:** Architectural, drafting, electrical. **Family/consumer sciences:** General, clothing/textiles. **Foreign languages:** Sign language interpretation. **Health:** EMT paramedic, health services, medical radiologic technology/radiation therapy, medical secretary, nursing (RN), respiratory therapy technology. **Legal studies:** Paralegal. **Liberal arts:** Arts/sciences. **Mechanic/repair:** Aircraft, electronics/electrical, heating/ac/refrig. **Parks/recreation:** General, facilities management. **Protective services:** Firefighting, police science. **Transportation:** Air traffic control, aviation, flight attendant. **Visual/performing arts:** Design, interior design, photography.

Computing on campus. 600 workstations in library, computer center, student center. Commuter students can connect to campus network. Online course registration, helpline available.

Student life. Freshman orientation: Mandatory. Preregistration for classes offered. **Activities:** Bands, choral groups, dance, drama, film society, literary magazine, music ensembles, musical theater, radio station, student government, student newspaper, symphony orchestra, TV station, Asian student association, Chinese club, Black student alliance, Indo-Pak club, Democratic club, Republican club, sign language club, MECHA, Muslim student association.

Athletics. Intercollegiate: Badminton W, baseball M, basketball, cross-country, diving, football (tackle) M, golf, soccer, softball W, swimming, tennis, track and field, volleyball, water polo, wrestling M. **Team name:** Mounties.

Student services. Adult student services, alcohol/substance abuse counseling, career counseling, services for economically disadvantaged, student employment services, financial aid counseling, health services, minority student services, on-campus daycare, personal counseling, placement for graduates, veterans' counselor. **Physically disabled:** Services for visually, speech, hearing impaired. **Transfer:** Re-entry adviser, pre-admission transcript evaluation for new students. Transfer center, transfer adviser, college fairs on campus for students transferring to 4-year colleges.

Contact. Phone: (909) 594-5611 ext. 4415 Fax: (909) 468-4068
George Bradshaw, Director of Admissions and Records, Mount San Antonio College, 1100 North Grand Avenue, Walnut, CA 91789

Mount San Jacinto College

San Jacinto, California
www.msjc.edu **CB code: 4501**

- Public 2-year community college
- Commuter campus in small city

General. Founded in 1962. Regionally accredited. **Enrollment:** 8,794 degree-seeking undergraduates. **Degrees:** 1,382 associate awarded. **ROTC:** Army, Air Force. **Location:** 35 miles from Riverside, 45 miles from Palm Springs. **Calendar:** Semester, limited summer session. **Full-time faculty:** 134 total. **Part-time faculty:** 622 total. **Class size:** 38% < 20, 54% 20-39, 7% 40-49, less than 1% 50-99.

Transfer out. Colleges most students transferred to 2008: California State University: San Bernardino, University of California: Riverside, California State University: San Marcos, Azusa Pacific University.

Basis for selection. Open admission, but selective for some programs. Special requirements for nursing program. Interview required of nursing majors. Audition recommended of performing arts majors.

2008-2009 Annual costs. Tuition/fees: $600; $6,030 out-of-state. Per-credit charge: $20 in-state; $201 out-of-state. Books/supplies: $1,566. Personal expenses: $3,024.

Financial aid. All financial aid based on need. Need-based aid available for part-time students. Work-study available nights and for part-time students. **Additional information:** Board of Governors Grant Program for state residents to defray cost of enrollment fee.

Application procedures. Admission: Closing date 8/14. No application fee. Admission notification on a rolling basis beginning on or about 4/1. All students admitted, but nursing students have additional admissions policies. **Financial aid:** Priority date 3/2; no closing date. FAFSA, institutional form required. Applicants notified on a rolling basis starting 5/1; must reply within 3 week(s) of notification.

Academics. Special study options: Cooperative education, cross-registration, distance learning, double major, dual enrollment of high school students, ESL, honors, independent study, internships, weekend college. License preparation in nursing, paramedic, real estate. **Credit/placement by examination:** AP, CLEP, institutional tests. 12 credit hours maximum toward associate degree. **Support services:** Learning center, reduced course load, remedial instruction, study skills assistance, tutoring, writing center.

Majors. Agriculture: Turf management. **Business:** Business admin, real estate. **Computer sciences:** General. **Education:** Early childhood, physical. **Health:** Nursing (RN), substance abuse counseling. **Interdisciplinary:** Behavioral sciences. **Liberal arts:** Arts/sciences. **Math:** General. **Mechanic/repair:** Automotive. **Protective services:** Police science. **Social sciences:** General. **Visual/performing arts:** Art, dance, dramatic, photography.

Computing on campus. 120 workstations in library, computer center, student center. Commuter students can connect to campus network. Online course registration available.

Student life. **Freshman orientation:** Mandatory. 2-hour orientation. **Activities:** Bands, dance, drama, musical theater, student government, Campus Crusade, MECHA, Black Students Union.

Athletics. **Intercollegiate:** Baseball M, basketball, football (tackle) M, golf, soccer W, softball W, tennis, volleyball W. **Intramural:** Volleyball W. **Team name:** Eagles.

Student services. Adult student services, career counseling, services for economically disadvantaged, student employment services, financial aid counseling, on-campus daycare, personal counseling, veterans' counselor. **Physically disabled:** Services for visually, speech, hearing impaired. **Transfer:** Pre-admission transcript evaluation for new students. Transfer center, transfer adviser, college fairs on campus for students transferring to 4-year colleges.

Contact. E-mail: enrollsvcs@msjc.edu
Phone: (951) 487-3215 Fax: (951) 654-6738
Susan Loomis, Director, Enrollment Services, Mount San Jacinto College, 1499 North State Street, San Jacinto, CA 92583

MTI College
Sacramento, California
www.mticollege.edu **CB code: 3543**

- For-profit 2-year business and technical college
- Commuter campus in large city
- Interview required

General. Regionally accredited. **Enrollment:** 300 degree-seeking undergraduates. **Degrees:** 186 associate awarded. **Calendar:** Continuous, extensive summer session. **Full-time faculty:** 10 total. **Part-time faculty:** 61 total.

Transfer out. **Colleges most students transferred to 2008:** University of Phoenix, Golden Gate University.

Basis for selection. Interview, talent, ability, character and personal qualities important.

2008-2009 Annual costs. Tuition/fees: $11,025. Books/supplies: $1,386. Personal expenses: $322.

Financial aid. **Need-based:** Work-study available nights.

Application procedures. **Admission:** No deadline. $50 fee. Admission notification on a rolling basis.

Academics. **Special study options:** Cooperative education, distance learning, internships, liberal arts/career combination. **Credit/placement by examination:** CLEP, institutional tests. **Support services:** Learning center, reduced course load, remedial instruction, study skills assistance, tutoring.

Majors. **Business:** Business admin. **Computer sciences:** System admin, systems analysis. **Legal studies:** Paralegal.

Most popular majors. Business/marketing 9%, computer/information sciences 27%, legal studies 64%.

Computing on campus. 300 workstations in library, computer center.

Student life. **Freshman orientation:** Mandatory.

Student services. Adult student services, career counseling, financial aid counseling, placement for graduates, veterans' counselor. **Transfer:** Pre-admission transcript evaluation for new students. College fairs on campus for students transferring to 4-year colleges.

Contact. E-mail: webmaster@mticollege.edu
Phone: (916) 339-1500 Fax: (916) 339-0305
Eric Patterson, Director of Admissions, MTI College, 5221 Madison Avenue, Sacramento, CA 95841

Napa Valley College
Napa, California
www.napavalley.edu **CB code: 4530**

- Public 2-year community college
- Commuter campus in small city

General. Founded in 1940. Regionally accredited. **Enrollment:** 3,304 degree-seeking undergraduates. **Degrees:** 615 associate awarded. **Location:** 50 miles from San Francisco. **Calendar:** Semester, limited summer session. **Full-time faculty:** 112 total. **Part-time faculty:** 217 total. **Special facilities:** Nature preserve, working vineyard, telecommunications laboratory.

Basis for selection. Open admission, but selective for some programs. Special admission requirements for health occupations programs and athletic program applicants.

2008-2009 Annual costs. Tuition/fees: $628; $6,058 out-of-state. Per-credit charge: $20 in-state; $201 out-of-state. Books/supplies: $630. Personal expenses: $1,476.

Application procedures. **Admission:** No deadline. No application fee. Admission notification on a rolling basis. College-administered placement tests recommended for students enrolling in English or mathematics. **Financial aid:** Priority date 4/1; no closing date. FAFSA required. Applicants notified on a rolling basis starting 6/1; must reply within 3 week(s) of notification.

Academics. Culinary arts program available. **Special study options:** Cooperative education, distance learning, double major, dual enrollment of high school students, ESL, honors, independent study, internships, study abroad, weekend college. Exchange program with Tafe College, Tasmania. **Credit/placement by examination:** CLEP, institutional tests. 12 credit hours maximum toward associate degree. **Support services:** Learning center, remedial instruction, tutoring, writing center.

Majors. **Agriculture:** General. **Business:** General, accounting, administrative services, real estate. **Communications technology:** General. **Computer sciences:** General. **Conservation:** Wildlife. **Education:** General, early childhood. **Engineering technology:** Biomedical, drafting, electrical. **Health:** Health services, licensed practical nurse, nursing (RN), respiratory therapy technology. **Legal studies:** Paralegal. **Liberal arts:** Arts/sciences. **Protective services:** Police science. **Social sciences:** General.

Computing on campus. 30 workstations in library, computer center.

Student life. **Activities:** Bands, choral groups, dance, drama, music ensembles, musical theater, student government, student newspaper, symphony orchestra, various religious, ethnic, social service, and special interest organizations including International Student Club, Amnesty International, Hispano-Americano Club.

Athletics. NJCAA. **Intercollegiate:** Baseball M, basketball, diving, golf, soccer M, softball W, swimming, tennis, volleyball W. **Intramural:** Volleyball. **Team name:** Storm.

Student services. Adult student services, career counseling, student employment services, on-campus daycare, personal counseling, veterans' counselor. **Physically disabled:** Services for visually, speech, hearing impaired. **Transfer:** Re-entry adviser for new students. Transfer center, transfer adviser, college fairs on campus for students transferring to 4-year colleges.

Contact. Phone: (707) 253-3000 Fax: (707) 253-3064
Beth Hauscarriague, Director of Admissions, Napa Valley College, 2277 Napa-Vallejo Highway, Napa, CA 94558

National Polytechnic College of Science
San Diego, California
www.natpoly.edu **CB code: 1243**

- Private 2-year health science and maritime college
- Commuter campus in large city

General. Founded in 1969. Regionally accredited. **Enrollment:** 236 degree-seeking undergraduates. **Degrees:** 36 associate awarded. **Calendar:** Continuous. **Full-time faculty:** 10 total. **Part-time faculty:** 10 total.

Basis for selection. Open admission. Must be medically approved to dive. Applicants who do not have high school diploma or GED must prove their ability to benefit from program. Students expected to have mechanical aptitude and, if possible, experience in construction-related field. Interviews recommended.

2008-2009 Annual costs. Associate degree program charge (covering 12 months), $17,360; per-credit-hour charge, $280. Academic year is comprised of 30 weeks (36 quarter credits), with courses offered in five-week sessions. Undergraduate courses are scheduled, typically, for eight to ten hours per day (two days each week, five-week period). Some courses require basic supplies (e.g., wet suit, fins, weights, work boots) that are not covered by tuition; additional cost of these supplies could amount to $500 or more.

Financial aid. **Additional information:** Work-study programs available.

Two-Year Colleges

Application procedures. **Admission:** No deadline. $60 fee. Admission notification on a rolling basis. **Financial aid:** No deadline. FAFSA, institutional form required. Applicants notified on a rolling basis; must reply within 3 week(s) of notification.

Academics. Special programs prepare students for work as underwater welders, diver medical technicians, and topside/underwater nondestructive testing/inspection personnel. **Credit/placement by examination:** CLEP, institutional tests. 20 credit hours maximum toward associate degree. **Support services:** Remedial instruction, tutoring.

Majors. **Construction:** General. **Health:** Medical records technology, substance abuse counseling. **Protective services:** Emergency management/homeland security. **Transportation:** Diver. **Other:** Hyperbaric medical technology.

Student services. Career counseling, student employment services, personal counseling, placement for graduates, veterans' counselor. **Transfer:** Transfer adviser for students transferring to 4-year colleges.

Contact. E-mail: moreinfo@natpoly.edu
Phone: (858) 309-3510 Fax: (858) 309-3510
Shelly Mitchell, Director of Admissions, National Polytechnic College of Science, 3580 Aero Court, San Diego, CA 92123

Ohlone College
Fremont, California
www.ohlone.edu **CB code: 4579**

- Public 2-year community college
- Commuter campus in large city

General. Founded in 1966. Regionally accredited. **Enrollment:** 4,910 degree-seeking undergraduates. **Degrees:** 368 associate awarded. **ROTC:** Air Force. **Location:** 15 miles from San Jose, 40 miles from San Francisco. **Calendar:** Semester, extensive summer session. **Full-time faculty:** 154 total. **Part-time faculty:** 358 total. **Class size:** 54% < 20, 40% 20-39, 2% 40-49, 2% 50-99, less than 1% >100. **Special facilities:** Fine and performing arts center, business and technology center, Newark center for health sciences and technology. **Partnerships:** Formal partnerships with Sun Microsystems, Metatec Inc., Washington Hospital, Fremont Unified School District, Newark Unified School District.

Student profile. Among degree-seeking undergraduates, 47% enrolled in a transfer program, 12% enrolled in a vocational program, 16% already have a bachelor's degree or higher.

Out-of-state:	1%	**25 or older:**	45%

Transfer out. **Colleges most students transferred to 2008:** California State University: East Bay, San Jose State University, University of California: Berkeley, University of California: Davis, San Francisco State University.

Basis for selection. Open admission, but selective for some programs. Nursing, respiratory therapy and physical therapy assisting programs require basic competence in reading comprehension and English skills, basic knowledge of related sciences. All candidates who achieve minimum standards selected by lottery. High school diploma or equivalent not required if applicant is 18 years of age or older.

High school preparation. Nursing and physical therapy assisting programs require anatomy and physiology. Respiratory therapy program requires algebra and physics.

2008-2009 Annual costs. Tuition/fees: $652; $6,082 out-of-state. Per-credit charge: $20 in-state; $201 out-of-state. Books/supplies: $810. Personal expenses: $2,616.

Financial aid. **Need-based:** Need-based aid available for part-time students. Work-study available for part-time students. **Non-need-based:** Scholarships awarded for academics.

Application procedures. **Admission:** No deadline. No application fee. **Financial aid:** Priority date 7/1; no closing date. FAFSA, institutional form required. Applicants notified on a rolling basis starting 7/30; must reply within 2 week(s) of notification.

Academics. **Special study options:** Cooperative education, cross-registration, distance learning, double major, dual enrollment of high school students, ESL, independent study, internships, liberal arts/career combination, study abroad, weekend college. License preparation in nursing, physical therapy. **Credit/placement by examination:** AP, CLEP, IB, institutional tests. 10 credit hours maximum toward associate degree. **Support services:** Learning center, pre-admission summer program, reduced course load, remedial instruction, study skills assistance, tutoring, writing center.

Majors. **Biology:** General. **Business:** General, accounting, administrative services, business admin, marketing, office management, office technology, office/clerical, real estate, receptionist, small business admin. **Communications:** Broadcast journalism, digital media, journalism. **Communications technology:** Desktop publishing. **Computer sciences:** Computer graphics, information systems, LAN/WAN management, programming, system admin. **Education:** Early childhood. **Engineering technology:** CAD/CADD, electrical, electromechanical. **Family/consumer sciences:** Child care, food/nutrition, institutional food production. **Foreign languages:** American Sign Language. **Health:** Medical assistant, nursing (RN), physical therapy assistant, respiratory therapy technology. **Interdisciplinary:** Biological/physical sciences, natural sciences. **Liberal arts:** Arts/sciences. **Mechanic/repair:** Electronics/electrical. **Protective services:** Law enforcement admin. **Social sciences:** General. **Visual/performing arts:** Commercial/advertising art, graphic design, interior design, multimedia, studio arts, theater design.

Most popular majors. Biological/life sciences 21%, business/marketing 10%, health sciences 18%, liberal arts 38%.

Computing on campus. 450 workstations in library, computer center. Commuter students can connect to campus network. Online course registration, online library, helpline, wireless network available.

Student life. **Freshman orientation:** Mandatory. **Activities:** Bands, choral groups, dance, drama, literary magazine, music ensembles, musical theater, radio station, student government, student newspaper, symphony orchestra, TV station, Abundant Life Christian Fellowship, Afghan Students Association, Asian Pacific Islanders Club, Chinese Culture Club, Muslim Student Association, Alpha Gamma Sigma Honor Society, Ohlone Women Engineers and Physical Scientists, Theater and Dance Alliance.

Athletics. **Intercollegiate:** Baseball M, basketball, soccer, softball W, swimming, tennis, volleyball, water polo. **Team name:** Renegades.

Student services. Adult student services, career counseling, services for economically disadvantaged, student employment services, financial aid counseling, health services, on-campus daycare, personal counseling, placement for graduates, veterans' counselor. **Physically disabled:** Services for visually, hearing impaired. **Transfer:** Pre-admission transcript evaluation for new students. Transfer center, transfer adviser, college fairs on campus for students transferring to 4-year colleges.

Contact. E-mail: admissions@ohlone.edu
Phone: (510) 659-6100 Fax: (510) 659-7231
Christopher Williamson, Interim Director of Admissions and Records, Ohlone College, 43600 Mission Boulevard, Fremont, CA 94539-0390

Orange Coast College
Costa Mesa, California
www.orangecoastcollege.edu **CB code: 4584**

- Public 2-year community college
- Commuter campus in large city

General. Founded in 1947. Regionally accredited. **Enrollment:** 18,711 degree-seeking undergraduates. **Degrees:** 1,469 associate awarded. **Location:** 40 miles from Los Angeles. **Calendar:** Semester, extensive summer session. **Full-time faculty:** 300 total. **Part-time faculty:** 550 total. **Class size:** 28% < 20, 51% 20-39, 11% 40-49, 7% 50-99, 4% >100. **Special facilities:** Planetarium, plastination lab, sailing academy, international center, art gallery.

Student profile. Among degree-seeking undergraduates, 3,585 enrolled as first-time, first-year students.

Out-of-state:	3%	**25 or older:**	30%

Transfer out. **Colleges most students transferred to 2008:** University of California: Irvine, California State University: Fullerton, California State University: Long Beach.

Basis for selection. Open admission. **Homeschooled:** Transcript of courses and grades required.

2008-2009 Annual costs. Tuition/fees: $658; $6,088 out-of-state. Per-credit charge: $20 in-state; $201 out-of-state. Books/supplies: $1,566. Personal expenses: $3,024.

2007-2008 Financial aid. **Need-based:** Need-based aid available for part-time students. Work-study available for part-time students. **Non-need-based:** Scholarships awarded for academics.

Application procedures. **Admission:** No deadline. No application fee. Admission notification on a rolling basis. Admission opens January for summer and fall semester, September for spring semester; dates establish registration priority. **Financial aid:** Priority date 3/2, closing date 5/31. FAFSA, institutional form required. Applicants notified on a rolling basis; must reply within 2 week(s) of notification.

Academics. Student Success Center (individual tutoring, drop-in tutoring, online tutoring, and study skills assistance) and Math Center available. **Special study options:** Cooperative education, cross-registration, distance learning, ESL, honors, independent study, internships, liberal arts/career combination, student-designed major, study abroad, weekend college. License preparation in aviation, dental hygiene, paramedic, radiology, real estate. **Credit/placement by examination:** AP, CLEP, institutional tests. 12 credit hours maximum toward associate degree. **Support services:** Learning center, pre-admission summer program, reduced course load, remedial instruction, study skills assistance, tutoring, writing center.

Honors college/program. Students complete a minimum of 18 units in honors courses for program certification.

Majors. **Agriculture:** Ornamental horticulture. **Biology:** General, ecology. **Business:** General, accounting, administrative services, fashion, hospitality/recreation, international, management information systems, office technology, office/clerical. **Communications:** Advertising, broadcast journalism. **Computer sciences:** General, computer graphics, data entry, information systems. **Construction:** Maintenance, pipefitting, power transmission. **Education:** Early childhood. **Engineering technology:** Architectural, drafting, electrical. **Family/consumer sciences:** General, child care, food/nutrition. **Foreign languages:** French, German, Italian, Japanese, Spanish. **Health:** Athletic training, cardiovascular technology, dental assistant, electroencephalograph technology, medical assistant, medical radiologic technology/radiation therapy, medical records technology, respiratory therapy technology, sonography, speech-language pathology assistant. **History:** General. **Liberal arts:** Arts/sciences. **Math:** General. **Mechanic/repair:** Aircraft, electronics/electrical, heating/ac/refrig. **Parks/recreation:** Exercise sciences. **Personal/culinary services:** Culinary arts. **Philosophy/religion:** Philosophy, religion. **Physical sciences:** Astronomy, chemistry, geology, physics. **Psychology:** General. **Social sciences:** Anthropology, economics, geography, political science, sociology. **Transportation:** Aviation, flight attendant. **Visual/performing arts:** Art, cinematography, commercial/advertising art, dance, dramatic, fashion design, film/cinema, interior design, photography, studio arts.

Computing on campus. 1,500 workstations in library, computer center, student center. Online course registration, online library, helpline, wireless network available.

Student life. **Freshman orientation:** Mandatory. 3-hour sessions given year round. **Activities:** Bands, choral groups, dance, drama, film society, international student organizations, literary magazine, music ensembles, Model UN, musical theater, student government, student newspaper, symphony orchestra, Buddhists Crusade for Christ, Christian Fellowship, COPTIC, Hillel.

Athletics. **Intercollegiate:** Baseball M, basketball, cheerleading, cross-country, diving, football (tackle) M, golf M, rowing (crew), soccer, softball W, swimming, tennis, track and field, volleyball, water polo. **Team name:** Pirates.

Student services. Adult student services, alcohol/substance abuse counseling, career counseling, services for economically disadvantaged, student employment services, financial aid counseling, health services, minority student services, on-campus daycare, personal counseling, placement for graduates, veterans' counselor. **Physically disabled:** Services for visually, speech, hearing impaired. **Learning disabled:** Comprehensive services available. **Transfer:** Re-entry adviser for new students. Transfer center, transfer adviser, college fairs on campus for students transferring to 4-year colleges.

Contact. E-mail: campustours@occ.cccd.edu
Phone: (714) 432-5072
Efren Galvan, Director of Admissions & Records, Orange Coast College, 2701 Fairview Road, Costa Mesa, CA 92628-5005

Oxnard College
Oxnard, California
www.oxnardcollege.edu **CB code: 4591**

- Public 2-year community college
- Commuter campus in small city

General. Founded in 1975. Regionally accredited. **Enrollment:** 3,823 degree-seeking undergraduates. **Degrees:** 519 associate awarded. **Location:** 60 miles from Los Angeles. **Calendar:** Semester, limited summer session. **Full-time faculty:** 94 total. **Part-time faculty:** 175 total. **Special facilities:** Marine education center.

Student profile.

African American:	4%	**Native American:**	1%
Asian American:	9%	**25 or older:**	40%
Hispanic American:	63%		

Basis for selection. Open admission.

2008-2009 Annual costs. Tuition/fees: $644; $6,074 out-of-state. Per-credit charge: $20 in-state; $201 out-of-state. Books/supplies: $1,566. Personal expenses: $3,024.

Application procedures. **Admission:** No deadline. No application fee. Admission notification on a rolling basis. **Financial aid:** Closing date 3/2. FAFSA required. Applicants notified on a rolling basis; must reply within 2 week(s) of notification.

Academics. **Special study options:** Accelerated study, cross-registration, distance learning, dual enrollment of high school students, independent study, study abroad. First 2 years of bilingual (English-Spanish) teacher preparatory program. **Credit/placement by examination:** CLEP, institutional tests. 12 credit hours maximum toward associate degree. **Support services:** Learning center, remedial instruction, tutoring.

Majors. **Biology:** General, marine. **Business:** Accounting, administrative services, business admin, hotel/motel admin. **Communications:** Digital media, journalism, public relations, radio/tv. **Computer sciences:** General, information technology, networking, web page design. **Engineering technology:** Hazardous materials, heat/ac/refrig. **Family/consumer sciences:** Child development. **Foreign languages:** Sign language interpretation, Spanish. **Health:** Dental hygiene, medical records technology, substance abuse counseling. **History:** General. **Interdisciplinary:** Biological/physical sciences. **Legal studies:** Paralegal. **Liberal arts:** Arts/sciences, humanities. **Math:** General. **Mechanic/repair:** Auto body, automotive, electronics/electrical. **Personal/culinary services:** Culinary arts, restaurant/catering. **Philosophy/religion:** Philosophy. **Protective services:** Firefighting. **Psychology:** General. **Public administration:** Human services. **Social sciences:** Anthropology, economics, political science, sociology. **Visual/performing arts:** Art, drawing, sculpture.

Most popular majors. Business/marketing 13%, liberal arts 63%, security/protective services 6%.

Computing on campus. 57 workstations in library. Online course registration available.

Student life. **Freshman orientation:** Available. **Activities:** Jazz band, choral groups, drama, student government, student newspaper, TV station, Hispanic club, EconoBus club, Asian-American club, math club, MECha, Condor christian club, Chemistry Club, Art Underground.

Athletics. **Intercollegiate:** Baseball M, basketball, cross-country, soccer, softball W, track and field, volleyball W. **Team name:** Condors.

Student services. Career counseling, services for economically disadvantaged, student employment services, financial aid counseling, health services, on-campus daycare, personal counseling, veterans' counselor. **Physically disabled:** Services for visually, speech, hearing impaired. **Transfer:** Transfer center, transfer adviser, college fairs on campus for students transferring to 4-year colleges.

Contact. E-mail: ocadmissions@vcccd.edu
Phone: (805) 986-5810 Fax: (805) 986-5943
Susan Cabral, Director of Admissions, Oxnard College, 4000 South Rose Avenue, Oxnard, CA 93033

Palo Verde College
Blythe, California
www.paloverde.edu **CB code: 4603**

- Public 2-year community college
- Commuter campus in large town

General. Founded in 1947. Regionally accredited. **Enrollment:** 1,371 degree-seeking undergraduates. **Degrees:** 140 associate awarded. **Location:** 160 miles from Riverside. **Calendar:** Semester, limited summer session. **Full-time faculty:** 42 total. **Part-time faculty:** 98 total.

Transfer out. **Colleges most students transferred to 2008:** Coastline Community College, College of the Desert, Mohave Community College, Fresno Pacific College, Riverside Community College.

Basis for selection. Open admission, but selective for some programs. Limited admission to nursing program.

2008-2009 Annual costs. Tuition/fees: $600; $6,030 out-of-state. Per-credit charge: $20 in-state; $201 out-of-state. Books/supplies: $1,566. Personal expenses: $2,000.

2007-2008 Financial aid. All financial aid based on need. Need-based aid available for part-time students. Work-study available nights and for part-time students.

Application procedures. Admission: No deadline. No application fee. Application must be submitted on paper. Admission notification on a rolling basis. SAT or ACT recommended for placement. **Financial aid:** No deadline. FAFSA, institutional form required. Applicants notified on a rolling basis starting 7/1; must reply within 4 week(s) of notification.

Academics. Special study options: Cooperative education, distance learning, dual enrollment of high school students, ESL, independent study. **Credit/placement by examination:** AP, CLEP, institutional tests. 12 credit hours maximum toward associate degree. **Support services:** GED test center, learning center, remedial instruction, study skills assistance, tutoring, writing center.

Majors. Agriculture: General. **Business:** Accounting, business admin, office/clerical, real estate. **History:** General. **Liberal arts:** Arts/sciences. **Mechanic/repair:** Automotive. **Protective services:** Firefighting, law enforcement admin.

Most popular majors. Business/marketing 17%, liberal arts 79%.

Computing on campus. 125 workstations in library, computer center.

Student life. Freshman orientation: Mandatory. Preregistration for classes offered. **Activities:** Literary magazine, student government.

Athletics. Intramural: Soccer.

Student services. Career counseling, services for economically disadvantaged, student employment services, financial aid counseling, personal counseling, placement for graduates. **Physically disabled:** Services for visually, speech, hearing impaired. **Transfer:** Transfer center, transfer adviser, college fairs on campus for students transferring to 4-year colleges.

Contact. E-mail: mwalnoha@paloverde.edu
Phone: (760) 921-5500
Melinda Walnoha, Registrar, Palo Verde College, One College Drive, Blythe, CA 92225

Palomar College

San Marcos, California — **CB member**
www.palomar.edu — **CB code: 4602**

- Public 2-year community college
- Commuter campus in large town

General. Founded in 1946. Regionally accredited. Off-campus sites located throughout North County area. **Enrollment:** 15,698 degree-seeking undergraduates. **Degrees:** 1,498 associate awarded. **Location:** 40 miles from San Diego. **Calendar:** Semester, extensive summer session. **Full-time faculty:** 306 total. **Part-time faculty:** 1,050 total. **Special facilities:** Arboretum, observatory.

Basis for selection. Open admission, but selective for some programs. ASSET mathematics and English tests required for nursing applicants. **Adult students:** SAT/ACT scores not required.

2008-2009 Annual costs. Tuition/fees: $627; $5,997 out-of-state. Per-credit charge: $20 in-state; $199 out-of-state. Books/supplies: $648. Personal expenses: $1,620.

Financial aid. All financial aid based on need. Need-based aid available for part-time students. Work-study available nights and for part-time students.

Application procedures. Admission: Priority date 6/9; no deadline. No application fee. Application deadlines for nursing program April 1 for fall semester, November 1 for spring semester. **Financial aid:** Priority date 4/1; no closing date. FAFSA, institutional form required. Applicants notified on a rolling basis starting 6/1.

Academics. Special study options: Cooperative education, distance learning, dual enrollment of high school students, ESL, internships, liberal arts/career combination, study abroad, weekend college. **Credit/placement by examination:** AP, CLEP, institutional tests. 15 credit hours maximum toward associate degree. **Support services:** Learning center, pre-admission summer program, reduced course load, remedial instruction, tutoring, writing center.

Majors. Biology: General, zoology. **Business:** General, accounting, administrative services, banking/financial services, business admin, fashion, international, management science, office/clerical, operations, real estate, tourism promotion. **Communications:** Advertising, journalism. **Communications technology:** General, graphic/printing. **Computer sciences:** General, computer science, information systems. **Construction:** Carpentry, maintenance, masonry, pipefitting, power transmission. **Education:** Early childhood. **Engineering:** General. **Engineering technology:** Drafting, surveying. **Family/consumer sciences:** Child care, institutional food production. **Foreign languages:** Sign language interpretation. **Health:** Dental assistant, EMT paramedic, medical assistant, medical records admin, medical secretary, nursing (RN). **Legal studies:** Legal secretary, paralegal. **Liberal arts:** Arts/sciences, library science. **Math:** General. **Mechanic/repair:** General, auto body, diesel, electronics/electrical. **Parks/recreation:** General, facilities management, health/fitness. **Physical sciences:** Astronomy, chemistry, geology. **Production:** Woodworking. **Protective services:** Firefighting, law enforcement admin, police science, security services. **Public administration:** General. **Social sciences:** Archaeology, economics. **Transportation:** Aviation. **Visual/performing arts:** Art, ceramics, commercial/advertising art, crafts, dance, dramatic, fashion design, film/cinema, interior design, metal/jewelry, painting, photography, printmaking, sculpture.

Most popular majors. Health sciences 6%, liberal arts 61%, social sciences 7%, trade and industry 6%.

Computing on campus. 922 workstations in library, computer center, student center. Online course registration, online library, wireless network available.

Student life. Freshman orientation: Available. **Activities:** Bands, choral groups, dance, drama, literary magazine, music ensembles, musical theater, radio station, student government, student newspaper, symphony orchestra, TV station.

Athletics. NJCAA. **Intercollegiate:** Baseball M, basketball, football (tackle) M, golf M, soccer, softball W, swimming, tennis, volleyball, water polo M, wrestling M. **Intramural:** Volleyball W. **Team name:** Comets.

Student services. Career counseling, student employment services, financial aid counseling, health services, on-campus daycare, personal counseling, placement for graduates, veterans' counselor. **Physically disabled:** Services for visually, speech, hearing impaired. **Transfer:** Transfer center, transfer adviser, college fairs on campus for students transferring to 4-year colleges.

Contact. E-mail: admissions@palomar.edu
Phone: (760) 744-1150 ext. 2164 Fax: (760) 761-3536
Herman Lee, Director of Enrollment Services, Palomar College, 1140 West Mission Road, San Marcos, CA 92069-1487

Pasadena City College

Pasadena, California — **CB member**
www.pasadena.edu — **CB code: 4604**

- Public 2-year community college
- Commuter campus in small city

General. Founded in 1924. Regionally accredited. **Enrollment:** 20,489 degree-seeking undergraduates. **Degrees:** 1,624 associate awarded. **Location:** 10 miles from downtown Los Angeles. **Calendar:** Semester, limited summer session. **Full-time faculty:** 320 total; 30% have terminal degrees. **Part-time faculty:** 740 total; 14% have terminal degrees. **Class size:** 6% < 20, 66% 20-39, 25% 40-49, 2% 50-99, 1% >100. **Special facilities:** Observatory.

Student profile.

Out-of-state:	3%	**25 or older:**	36%

Transfer out. Colleges most students transferred to 2008: California State University: Los Angeles, Long Beach, Northridge; California State Polytechnic Institute: Pomona.

Basis for selection. Open admission, but selective for some programs. Admission to RN, LVN, dental hygiene programs based on test scores, interview, high school record; minimum 2.0 high school GPA required. School and College Ability Tests, SAT, ACT, or California Achievement Test scores used for admission to some programs. Interview required of dental hygiene majors. Audition required of music majors.

2008-2009 Annual costs. Tuition/fees: $628; $6,058 out-of-state. Per-credit charge: $20 in-state; $201 out-of-state. Books/supplies: $1,566. Personal expenses: $2,844.

Financial aid. All financial aid based on need.

Application procedures. Admission: Closing date 8/11. No application fee. Admission notification on a rolling basis beginning on or about 3/1. **Financial aid:** Priority date 5/13; no closing date. FAFSA required. Applicants notified on a rolling basis starting 6/1; must reply within 2 week(s) of notification.

Academics. Special study options: Accelerated study, distance learning, dual enrollment of high school students, honors, independent study, internships, liberal arts/career combination, study abroad. **Credit/placement by examination:** CLEP, institutional tests. 12 credit hours maximum toward associate degree. **Support services:** Learning center, pre-admission summer program, reduced course load, remedial instruction, study skills assistance, tutoring, writing center.

Majors. Biology: General. **Business:** General, accounting, administrative services, banking/financial services, entrepreneurial studies, fashion, hospitality/recreation, management information systems, office/clerical, real estate, sales/distribution, tourism promotion. **Communications:** General, broadcast journalism, journalism. **Communications technology:** General. **Computer sciences:** Applications programming, data processing, programming. **Construction:** Carpentry, maintenance. **Education:** Early childhood. **Engineering technology:** Drafting. **Health:** Clinical lab technology, dental assistant, dental hygiene, dental lab technology, licensed practical nurse, medical assistant, medical radiologic technology/radiation therapy, medical secretary, nursing (RN), speech-language pathology assistant. **Legal studies:** Legal secretary, paralegal. **Liberal arts:** Arts/sciences, library assistant. **Mechanic/repair:** Auto body. **Parks/recreation:** General. **Protective services:** Firefighting, police science. **Psychology:** General. **Social sciences:** General. **Visual/performing arts:** Ceramics, commercial photography, commercial/advertising art, crafts, drawing, painting, printmaking, sculpture, studio arts.

Computing on campus. 300 workstations in computer center, student center.

Student life. Freshman orientation: Available. **Activities:** Bands, choral groups, dance, drama, film society, literary magazine, music ensembles, musical theater, radio station, student government, student newspaper, symphony orchestra, TV station, wide variety of religious, political, ethnic, and social service organizations.

Athletics. Intercollegiate: Badminton W, baseball M, basketball, cross-country, football (tackle) M, soccer, softball W, swimming, tennis W, track and field, volleyball W, water polo W. **Team name:** Lancers.

Student services. Career counseling, student employment services, health services, personal counseling, placement for graduates. **Physically disabled:** Services for visually, speech, hearing impaired. **Transfer:** Transfer center, transfer adviser, college fairs on campus for students transferring to 4-year colleges.

Contact. Phone: (626) 578-7396 Fax: (626) 585-7912
Margaret Ramey, Associate Dean of Admissions and Records, Pasadena City College, 1570 East Colorado Boulevard, Pasadena, CA 91106

Platt College: Huntington Beach

Huntington Beach, California
www.plattcollege.edu — **CB code: 3004**

- For-profit 2-year visual arts and technical college
- Commuter campus in large city

General. Accredited by ACCSCT. **Calendar:** Continuous.

Annual costs/financial aid. Need-based financial aid available to full-time and part-time students.

Contact. Phone: (949) 833-2300
Admissions Director, 7755 Center Avenue, Suite 400, Huntington Beach, CA 92647

Platt College: Los Angeles

Alhambra, California
www.plattcollege.edu — **CB code: 3014**

- For-profit 2-year visual arts and technical college
- Commuter campus in very large city
- Application essay, interview required

General. Accredited by ACCSCT. **Enrollment:** 185 degree-seeking undergraduates. **Degrees:** 6 bachelor's, 27 associate awarded. **Location:** 10 miles from dowtown Los Angeles. **Calendar:** Continuous. **Full-time faculty:** 25 total. **Class size:** 85% < 20, 15% 20-39.

Transfer out. Colleges most students transferred to 2008: University of LaVerne, University of Phoenix.

Basis for selection. Must score at least 126 on CPAT for admissions. Multimedia program requires degree. MCSE program requires computer background. **Learning Disabled:** Students with learning disabilities allowed 30 extra minutes on CPAT examination.

2008-2009 Annual costs. Varies by program: associate degree cost range $26,780 (paralegal) to $28,370 (information technology).

Financial aid. Need-based: Need-based aid available for part-time students. Work-study available nights.

Application procedures. Admission: No deadline. $75 fee. Admission notification on a rolling basis. **Financial aid:** Priority date 3/2; no closing date. FAFSA, institutional form required. Applicants notified on a rolling basis starting 1/1.

Academics. Special study options: Accelerated study, cooperative education, internships. **Credit/placement by examination:** CLEP, institutional tests. 48 credit hours maximum toward associate degree. **Support services:** Tutoring.

Majors. Computer sciences: General, computer graphics. **Visual/performing arts:** General, commercial/advertising art.

Computing on campus. 60 workstations in library.

Student life. Freshman orientation: Mandatory. Preregistration for classes offered. 2-hour program on or around first day of classes.

Student services. Adult student services, career counseling, student employment services, financial aid counseling, placement for graduates. **Transfer:** Re-entry adviser, pre-admission transcript evaluation for new students. Transfer adviser for students transferring to 4-year colleges.

Contact. Phone: (626) 300-5444 Toll-free number: (866) 752-8852
Fax: (626) 300-3978
Alejandro Munoz, Director of Admissions, Platt College: Los Angeles, 1000 South Fremont Avenue A9W, Alhambra, CA 91803

Porterville College

Porterville, California
www.portervillecollege.edu — **CB code: 4608**

- Public 2-year community college
- Commuter campus in large town

General. Founded in 1927. Regionally accredited. **Enrollment:** 2,273 degree-seeking undergraduates. **Degrees:** 207 associate awarded. **Location:** 75 miles from Fresno, 50 miles from Bakersfield. **Calendar:** Semester, limited summer session. **Full-time faculty:** 80 total. **Part-time faculty:** 1,510 total. **Special facilities:** Anthropology library.

Basis for selection. Open admission.

2008-2009 Annual costs. Tuition/fees: $634; $6,544 out-of-state. Per-credit charge: $20 in-state; $217 out-of-state. Books/supplies: $1,656. Personal expenses: $1,800.

Application procedures. Admission: No deadline. No application fee. Admission notification on a rolling basis. **Financial aid:** Priority date 3/1; no closing date. FAFSA required. Applicants notified on a rolling basis; must reply within 2 week(s) of notification.

Academics. Special study options: Double major, dual enrollment of high school students. **Credit/placement by examination:** CLEP, institutional tests. 30 credit hours maximum toward associate degree. **Support services:** Learning center, reduced course load, remedial instruction, tutoring.

Majors. Biology: General. **Business:** General, administrative services, banking/financial services, business admin, office/clerical, real estate. **Computer sciences:** General. **Construction:** Carpentry. **Education:** General. **Engineering technology:** Drafting. **Family/consumer sciences:** Child care. **Health:** Licensed practical nurse. **Interdisciplinary:** Biological/physical sciences. **Liberal arts:** Arts/sciences. **Math:** General. **Mechanic/repair:** Auto body. **Physical sciences:** Chemistry. **Protective services:** Police science. **Social**

sciences: General, criminology. **Visual/performing arts:** General, commercial/advertising art, studio arts.

Computing on campus. 25 workstations in library, computer center.

Student life. Activities: Choral groups, drama, music ensembles, musical theater, student government, Mexican-American Student Association.

Athletics. NJCAA. **Intercollegiate:** Baseball M, basketball, tennis, volleyball W. **Team name:** Pirates.

Student services. Career counseling, student employment services, health services, on-campus daycare, personal counseling, placement for graduates, veterans' counselor. **Physically disabled:** Services for visually, speech, hearing impaired. **Transfer:** Transfer adviser for students transferring to 4-year colleges.

Contact. Phone: (209) 791-2220 Fax: (209) 784-4779
Virginia Gurrola, Vice President Student Services and Enrollment, Porterville College, 100 East College Avenue, Porterville, CA 93257

Professional Golfers Career College

Temecula, California
www.golfcollege.edu **CB code: 3548**

- For-profit 2-year golf academy
- Commuter campus in small city

General. Accredited by ACICS. **Enrollment:** 160 degree-seeking undergraduates. **Degrees:** 97 associate awarded. **Location:** 60 miles from San Diego. **Calendar:** Semester. **Full-time faculty:** 6 total; 33% have terminal degrees. **Part-time faculty:** 18 total; 11% women. **Special facilities:** Pro shop, video studio.

Student profile. Among degree-seeking undergraduates, 100% enrolled in a vocational program.

Women:	7%	**Hispanic American:**	6%
African American:	1%	**Native American:**	2%
Asian American:	3%	**International:**	37%

Basis for selection. Handicap of 20 or below, 3 letters of personal character reference, 1 letter of recommendation attesting to golf ability required. **Homeschooled:** Transcript of courses and grades, letter of recommendation (nonparent) required.

2009-2010 Annual costs. Tuition $5,590/semester for domestic students and $5,890/semester for international students; program lasts 4 semesters. Books/supplies: $200.

Application procedures. Admission: No deadline. $75 fee. Application must be submitted on paper. Admission notification on a rolling basis. **Financial aid:** No deadline.

Academics. Credit/placement by examination: CLEP.

Majors. Parks/recreation: Facilities management.

Computing on campus. Online library, wireless network available.

Student life. Freshman orientation: Mandatory. **Housing:** Single-sex dorms, apartments, wellness housing available. $700 nonrefundable deposit.

Student services. Alcohol/substance abuse counseling, career counseling, financial aid counseling, personal counseling, placement for graduates, veterans' counselor.

Contact. E-mail: admin@progolfed.com
Phone: (951) 719-2994 Toll-free number: (800) 877-4380
Fax: (951) 719-1643
Mark Bland, Admissions Director, Professional Golfers Career College, 26109 Ynez Road, Temecula, CA 92591

Reedley College

Reedley, California
www.reedleycollege.edu **CB code: 4655**

- Public 2-year community college
- Commuter campus in large town

General. Founded in 1926. Regionally accredited. Courses also offered at community campus sites in Madera, Clovis, Sanger, Easton, Selma, Kerman, Oakhurst, Parlier, Fowler, Orange Cove, Dinuba, Kingsburg, and Sunnyside. **Enrollment:** 7,718 degree-seeking undergraduates. **Degrees:** 653 associate awarded. **Location:** 25 miles from Fresno. **Calendar:** Semester, extensive summer session. **Full-time faculty:** 80 total. **Part-time faculty:** 190 total.

Student profile.

25 or older:	35%	**Live on campus:**	4%

Transfer out. Colleges most students transferred to 2008: California State University: Fresno, California State University: Long Beach.

Basis for selection. Open admission. **Homeschooled:** If under 18, a letter from parent required.

2008-2009 Annual costs. Tuition/fees: $632; $6,062 out-of-state. Per-credit charge: $20 in-state; $201 out-of-state. Room/board: $8,942. Books/supplies: $1,566. Personal expenses: $2,600.

Financial aid. All financial aid based on need. Need-based aid available for part-time students. Work-study available for part-time students. **Additional information:** Board of Governors fee waiver available for low-income students. Book voucher available for EOPS students.

Application procedures. Admission: No deadline. No application fee. Admission notification on a rolling basis. **Financial aid:** Priority date 3/2; no closing date. FAFSA required. Applicants notified on a rolling basis starting 3/2; must reply within 3 week(s) of notification.

Academics. Special study options: Cooperative education, cross-registration, distance learning, double major, dual enrollment of high school students, ESL, honors, independent study, study abroad, weekend college. License preparation in aviation, dental hygiene. **Credit/placement by examination:** AP, CLEP. 48 credit hours maximum toward associate degree. **Support services:** Learning center, pre-admission summer program, reduced course load, remedial instruction, study skills assistance, tutoring, writing center.

Majors. Agriculture: Business, plant sciences. **Biology:** General. **Business:** Accounting. **Computer sciences:** General, computer science, information systems. **Conservation:** Forestry. **Education:** Early childhood, physical. **Foreign languages:** General. **Health:** Dental assistant. **Liberal arts:** Arts/sciences. **Math:** General. **Social sciences:** General. **Visual/performing arts:** Art, dramatic.

Most popular majors. Interdisciplinary studies 80%.

Computing on campus. 140 workstations in dormitories, library, computer center. Dormitories wired for high-speed internet access and linked to campus network. Commuter students can connect to campus network. Online course registration, online library available.

Student life. Freshman orientation: Available. Preregistration for classes offered. **Housing:** Single-sex dorms available. $125 deposit. **Activities:** Bands, choral groups, drama, music ensembles, musical theater, student government, student newspaper, symphony orchestra.

Athletics. NJCAA. **Intercollegiate:** Baseball M, basketball, equestrian, football (tackle) M, golf, softball W, tennis, track and field, volleyball W. **Team name:** Tigers.

Student services. Adult student services, alcohol/substance abuse counseling, career counseling, services for economically disadvantaged, student employment services, financial aid counseling, health services, minority student services, on-campus daycare, personal counseling, placement for graduates, veterans' counselor, women's services. **Physically disabled:** Services for visually, speech, hearing impaired. **Transfer:** Transfer adviser, college fairs on campus for students transferring to 4-year colleges.

Contact. Phone: (559) 638-0323 Fax: (559) 638-5040
Leticia Alvarez, Admissions and Records Manager, Reedley College, 995 North Reed Avenue, Reedley, CA 93654

Rio Hondo College

Whittier, California
www.riohondo.edu **CB code: 4663**

- Public 2-year community college
- Commuter campus in small city

General. Founded in 1960. Regionally accredited. **Enrollment:** 9,040 degree-seeking undergraduates. **Degrees:** 854 associate awarded. **Location:** 15 miles

from Los Angeles. **Calendar:** Semester, extensive summer session. **Full-time faculty:** 199 total; 37% minority. **Part-time faculty:** 335 total; 31% minority. **Special facilities:** Observatory.

Transfer out. Colleges most students transferred to 2008: Cal State Los Angeles, Cal State Long Beach, Cal State Fullerton, Cal State Polytech, University of California-Los Angeles.

Basis for selection. Open admission, but selective for some programs. Nursing program has special requirements. **Learning Disabled:** Disabled Services Program available to stuents with disabilities.

2008-2009 Annual costs. Tuition/fees: $623; $5,723 out-of-state. Per-credit charge: $20 in-state; $190 out-of-state. Books/supplies: $1,566. Personal expenses: $3,024.

2007-2008 Financial aid. Need-based: Need-based aid available for part-time students.

Application procedures. Admission: No deadline. No application fee. Admission notification on a rolling basis. **Financial aid:** Priority date 7/15; no closing date. FAFSA required. Applicants notified on a rolling basis.

Academics. Special study options: Dual enrollment of high school students, honors, independent study, study abroad, weekend college. **Credit/placement by examination:** CLEP, institutional tests. 12 credit hours maximum toward associate degree. **Support services:** Learning center, remedial instruction, tutoring.

Majors. Business: Accounting, administrative services, office/clerical, real estate. **Communications technology:** General, graphic/printing. **Engineering technology:** Drafting. **Health:** Dental assistant, health services, licensed practical nurse, nursing (RN), respiratory therapy technology. **Liberal arts:** Arts/sciences, library assistant. **Mechanic/repair:** Automotive. **Protective services:** Fire safety technology, police science.

Most popular majors. Business/marketing 9%, education 12%, health sciences 13%, liberal arts 41%.

Computing on campus. Wireless network available.

Student life. Freshman orientation: Available. **Activities:** Jazz band, choral groups, dance, drama, film society, literary magazine, music ensembles, musical theater, radio station, student government, student newspaper, TV station.

Athletics. NJCAA. **Intercollegiate:** Baseball M, basketball, diving, golf, softball W, swimming, tennis, volleyball W, water polo, wrestling M. **Team name:** Roadrunners.

Student services. Career counseling, student employment services, health services, on-campus daycare, personal counseling, veterans' counselor. **Physically disabled:** Services for visually, speech, hearing impaired. **Transfer:** Transfer center, transfer adviser, college fairs on campus for students transferring to 4-year colleges.

Contact. Phone: (562) 908-3415 Fax: (562) 692-8318
Judy Pearson, Director of Admissions and Records, Rio Hondo College, 3600 Workman Mill Road, Whittier, CA 90601-1699

Riverside Community College

Riverside, California **CB member**
www.rcc.edu **CB code: 4658**

- Public 2-year community college
- Commuter campus in large city

General. Founded in 1916. Regionally accredited. **Enrollment:** 23,722 degree-seeking undergraduates. **Degrees:** 2,001 associate awarded. **ROTC:** Army, Naval, Air Force. **Location:** 60 miles from Los Angeles. **Calendar:** Semester, limited summer session. **Full-time faculty:** 347 total; 22% minority. **Part-time faculty:** 1,072 total; 30% minority. **Class size:** 49% < 20, 44% 20-39, 4% 40-49, 2% 50-99, less than 1% >100. **Special facilities:** Planetarium.

Student profile.

Out-of-state:	1%	**25 or older:**	36%

Transfer out. Colleges most students transferred to 2008: University of California: Riverside, California State University: San Bernardino.

Basis for selection. Open admission, but selective for some programs. Limited admission to nursing program.

2008-2009 Annual costs. Tuition/fees: $634; $6,064 out-of-state. Per-credit charge: $20 in-state; $201 out-of-state. Books/supplies: $1,566. Personal expenses: $2,754.

2007-2008 Financial aid. Need-based: Need-based aid available for part-time students. Work-study available nights, weekends and for part-time students. **Non-need-based:** Scholarships awarded for academics, alumni affiliation, art, leadership, minority status, music/drama, state residency.

Application procedures. Admission: No deadline. No application fee. Admission notification on a rolling basis. **Financial aid:** Priority date 3/1; no closing date. FAFSA, institutional form required. Applicants notified on a rolling basis starting 7/1.

Academics. Honor Society (Alpha Gamma Sigma) for freshmen with 3.0 GPA. **Special study options:** Cooperative education, distance learning, double major, dual enrollment of high school students, ESL, honors, internships, study abroad, weekend college. License preparation in nursing. **Credit/placement by examination:** AP, CLEP, institutional tests. 30 credit hours maximum toward associate degree. **Support services:** GED preparation, learning center, remedial instruction, study skills assistance, tutoring, writing center.

Majors. Business: General, accounting, administrative services, business admin, marketing, office technology, real estate. **Communications technology:** Graphic/printing. **Computer sciences:** General, programming. **Construction:** Maintenance. **Education:** Early childhood. **Engineering:** General. **Engineering technology:** Construction, drafting, electrical. **Family/consumer sciences:** General, food/nutrition. **Foreign languages:** Sign language interpretation. **Health:** Dental lab technology, licensed practical nurse, medical assistant, medical secretary, medical transcription, nursing (RN). **Legal studies:** Legal secretary. **Mechanic/repair:** General, auto body, automotive, heating/ac/refrig. **Personal/culinary services:** Cosmetic. **Protective services:** Fire safety technology. **Public administration:** Human services. **Social sciences:** Cartography. **Visual/performing arts:** Commercial/advertising art, photography.

Most popular majors. Health sciences 11%, interdisciplinary studies 35%, liberal arts 46%.

Computing on campus. 200 workstations in library, computer center. Online course registration, online library, helpline, repair service, wireless network available.

Student life. Freshman orientation: Available. **Housing:** No dormitories are available. **Activities:** Bands, choral groups, dance, drama, international student organizations, literary magazine, music ensembles, Model UN, musical theater, student government, student newspaper, TV station, College Democrats, MECHA, Latter-day Saints student association, multicultural advisory council, African American student union.

Athletics. Intercollegiate: Baseball M, basketball, cross-country, diving, football (tackle) M, golf, soccer, softball W, swimming, tennis, track and field, volleyball W, water polo. **Intramural:** Badminton, baseball M, basketball, bowling, golf, racquetball, soccer, tennis, volleyball. **Team name:** Tigers.

Student services. Adult student services, career counseling, services for economically disadvantaged, student employment services, financial aid counseling, health services, on-campus daycare, personal counseling, placement for graduates, veterans' counselor. **Physically disabled:** Services for visually, speech, hearing impaired. **Transfer:** Transfer center, transfer adviser, college fairs on campus for students transferring to 4-year colleges.

Contact. E-mail: webmstr@rcc.edu
Phone: (951) 222-8600 Fax: (951) 222-8028
Lorraine Anderson, District Dean, Admissions and Records, Riverside Community College, 4800 Magnolia Avenue, Riverside, CA 92506

Sacramento City College

Sacramento, California
www.scc.losrios.edu **CB code: 4670**

- Public 2-year community college
- Commuter campus in large city

General. Founded in 1916. Regionally accredited. **Enrollment:** 15,997 degree-seeking undergraduates. **Degrees:** 1,017 associate awarded. **ROTC:** Army, Naval, Air Force. **Location:** 75 miles from San Francisco. **Calendar:** Semester, extensive summer session. **Full-time faculty:** 290 total. **Part-time faculty:** 140 total. **Special facilities:** Observatory.

Student profile.

Out-of-state:	5%	25 or older:	68%

Basis for selection. Open admission.

2008-2009 Annual costs. Tuition/fees: $632; $6,062 out-of-state. Per-credit charge: $20 in-state; $201 out-of-state. Books/supplies: $1,440. Personal expenses: $2,210.

Financial aid. Need-based: Need-based aid available for part-time students. Work-study available nights, weekends and for part-time students.

Application procedures. Admission: Priority date 7/28; no deadline. No application fee. Admission notification on a rolling basis. **Financial aid:** Priority date 3/2; no closing date. FAFSA required. Applicants notified on a rolling basis starting 7/1; must reply within 2 week(s) of notification.

Academics. Special study options: Accelerated study, cooperative education, cross-registration, distance learning, double major, dual enrollment of high school students, ESL, honors, independent study, internships, study abroad, weekend college. License preparation in aviation, dental hygiene, nursing, physical therapy, real estate. **Credit/placement by examination:** CLEP, institutional tests. 15 credit hours maximum toward associate degree. **Support services:** Learning center, remedial instruction, study skills assistance, tutoring, writing center.

Majors. Area/ethnic studies: Women's. **Business:** General, accounting, administrative services, international marketing, management information systems, office/clerical, real estate. **Communications:** Journalism. **Communications technology:** Graphic/printing. **Computer sciences:** General. **Education:** Bilingual, special. **Engineering technology:** Drafting. **Family/consumer sciences:** General, child care, clothing/textiles, family/community services. **Health:** Dental assistant, dental hygiene, licensed practical nurse, medical secretary, nursing (RN), occupational therapy assistant, physical therapy assistant. **Legal studies:** Legal secretary. **Liberal arts:** Arts/sciences, library assistant. **Math:** General. **Mechanic/repair:** Aircraft, electronics/electrical, heating/ac/refrig. **Personal/culinary services:** Cosmetic. **Protective services:** Corrections, police science. **Social sciences:** General. **Visual/performing arts:** General, commercial photography, dramatic, music management, studio arts.

Computing on campus. 350 workstations in library, computer center. Online course registration available.

Student life. Freshman orientation: Available. **Activities:** Bands, choral groups, dance, drama, literary magazine, music ensembles, musical theater, student government, student newspaper, minority groups, professional associations, Bible club, gay and lesbian student alliance, special interest groups.

Athletics. Intercollegiate: Baseball M, basketball, cross-country, football (tackle) M, golf W, soccer W, softball W, swimming, tennis, track and field, volleyball W, water polo W, wrestling M. **Intramural:** Badminton, baseball M, basketball, bowling, boxing M, fencing, football (tackle) M, golf, handball, racquetball, softball, swimming, table tennis, tennis, volleyball. **Team name:** Panthers.

Student services. Adult student services, career counseling, services for economically disadvantaged, student employment services, financial aid counseling, health services, on-campus daycare, personal counseling, placement for graduates, veterans' counselor. **Physically disabled:** Services for visually, speech, hearing impaired. **Transfer:** Transfer center, transfer adviser, college fairs on campus for students transferring to 4-year colleges.

Contact. E-mail: sccaeinfo@scc.losrios.edu
Phone: (916) 558-2351 Fax: (916) 558-2190
Sam Sandusky, Dean of Admissions, Sacramento City College, 3835 Freeport Boulevard, Sacramento, CA 95822

Saddleback College
Mission Viejo, California
www.saddleback.edu **CB code: 4747**

- Public 2-year community college
- Commuter campus in small city

General. Founded in 1967. Regionally accredited. **Enrollment:** 9,466 degree-seeking undergraduates. **Degrees:** 1,120 associate awarded. **Location:** 55 miles from Los Angeles and San Diego. **Calendar:** Semester, limited summer session. **Full-time faculty:** 223 total. **Part-time faculty:** 509 total. **Special facilities:** Solar observatory, outdoor environmental laboratory, golf driving range, computer/technology centers, greenhouse.

Basis for selection. Open admission, but selective for some programs. Nursing candidates must complete core curriculum with 2.5 GPA or better before screening process. SAT/ACT recommended for placement and counseling.

High school preparation. 10 units recommended. Recommended units include English 3, mathematics 2, social studies 3 and science 2.

2008-2009 Annual costs. Tuition/fees: $628; $6,058 out-of-state. Per-credit charge: $20 in-state; $201 out-of-state. Books/supplies: $1,556. Personal expenses: $3,024.

2007-2008 Financial aid. All financial aid based on need. Need-based aid available for part-time students. Work-study available for part-time students.

Application procedures. Admission: No deadline. No application fee. Admission notification on a rolling basis. **Financial aid:** Closing date 6/30. FAFSA required. Applicants notified on a rolling basis starting 4/1.

Academics. Special study options: Cooperative education, cross-registration, distance learning, double major, dual enrollment of high school students, ESL, honors, independent study, internships, student-designed major, study abroad, weekend college. License preparation in nursing, paramedic, real estate. **Credit/placement by examination:** AP, CLEP, institutional tests. 30 credit hours maximum toward associate degree. **Support services:** Learning center, pre-admission summer program, reduced course load, remedial instruction, study skills assistance, tutoring, writing center.

Honors college/program. Overall GPA of 3.25 in all academic work required.

Majors. Agriculture: Ornamental horticulture. **Area/ethnic studies:** Women's. **Biology:** General. **Business:** General, accounting, administrative services, business admin, fashion, marketing, office management, real estate, tourism/travel. **Communications:** Broadcast journalism, journalism. **Computer sciences:** General, computer science, programming. **Conservation:** General, environmental studies. **Education:** Early childhood, family/consumer sciences, mathematics, music, physical, social science. **Engineering:** General. **Engineering technology:** Drafting. **Family/consumer sciences:** General, food/nutrition. **Foreign languages:** General, sign language interpretation. **Health:** Medical assistant, nursing (RN), surgical technology. **History:** General. **Interdisciplinary:** Natural sciences. **Legal studies:** Legal secretary, paralegal. **Liberal arts:** Arts/sciences. **Math:** General. **Parks/recreation:** Health/fitness. **Philosophy/religion:** Philosophy. **Physical sciences:** Astronomy, chemistry, geology, physics. **Psychology:** General. **Social sciences:** General, anthropology, economics, geography, international relations, political science, sociology. **Visual/performing arts:** Art, commercial photography, commercial/advertising art, dance, design, dramatic, fashion design, interior design, photography, studio arts.

Most popular majors. Business/marketing 13%, health sciences 11%, liberal arts 42%.

Computing on campus. 1,030 workstations in library, computer center, student center. Commuter students can connect to campus network. Online course registration, online library, wireless network available.

Student life. Activities: Bands, choral groups, dance, drama, literary magazine, music ensembles, musical theater, radio station, student government, student newspaper, symphony orchestra, TV station, Democratic Club, Republican Club, Christian Club, Black United Students, Hillel, Gay and Lesbian Club, Amnesty International, Muslim Student Union, environmental awareness, sign language club.

Athletics. NJCAA. **Intercollegiate:** Baseball M, basketball, cheerleading M, cross-country, diving, football (tackle) M, golf, soccer W, softball W, swimming, tennis, track and field, volleyball W, water polo. **Team name:** Gauchos.

Student services. Adult student services, alcohol/substance abuse counseling, career counseling, services for economically disadvantaged, student employment services, health services, on-campus daycare, personal counseling, placement for graduates, veterans' counselor, women's services. **Physically disabled:** Services for visually, speech, hearing impaired. **Transfer:** Re-entry adviser for new students. Transfer center, transfer adviser, college fairs on campus for students transferring to 4-year colleges.

Contact. E-mail: scadmissions@saddleback.edu
Phone: (949) 582-4555 Fax: (949) 347-8315
Jane Rosenkrans, Director, Admissions, Records and Enrollment Services, Saddleback College, 28000 Marguerite Parkway, Mission Viejo, CA 92692

Sage College
Moreno Valley, California
www.sagecollege.edu

- For-profit 2-year technical college
- Commuter campus in large city

General. Accredited by ACICS. **Enrollment:** 446 degree-seeking undergraduates. **Degrees:** 14 associate awarded. **Calendar:** Quarter. **Full-time faculty:** 13 total. **Part-time faculty:** 15 total.

Basis for selection. Satisfactory performance on institutional examination required. **Homeschooled:** State high school equivalency certificate required.

2008-2009 Annual costs. Tuition/fees: $8,050.

Application procedures. Admission: No deadline. $100 fee. Admission notification on a rolling basis.

Academics. Credit/placement by examination: CLEP.

Majors. Legal studies: Court reporting, paralegal.

Student life. Freshman orientation: Mandatory.

Student services. Career counseling, financial aid counseling, placement for graduates.

Contact. E-mail: admissions@sagecollege.edu
Phone: (951) 781-2727
Lauren Somma, Executive Director, Sage College, 12125 Day Street, Building L, Moreno Valley, CA 92557-6720

Salvation Army College for Officer Training at Crestmont

Rancho Palos Verdes, California
www.crestmont.edu **CB code: 3890**

- Private 2-year seminary college
- Residential campus in small city

General. Regionally accredited. **Calendar:** Semester.

Contact. Phone: (310) 377-0481
Director of Admissions, 30840 Hawthorne Boulevard, Rancho Palos Verdes, CA 90275

San Bernardino Valley College

San Bernardino, California
www.valleycollege.edu **CB code: 4679**

- Public 2-year community college
- Small city

General. Founded in 1926. Regionally accredited. **Enrollment:** 9,325 degree-seeking undergraduates. **Degrees:** 646 associate awarded. **Location:** 60 miles from Los Angeles. **Calendar:** Semester, limited summer session. **Full-time faculty:** 161 total. **Part-time faculty:** 391 total. **Special facilities:** Planetarium.

Basis for selection. Open admission, but selective for some programs. Special requirements for nursing program. **Homeschooled:** Transcript of courses and grades required.

2008-2009 Annual costs. Tuition/fees: $644; $6,224 out-of-state. Per-credit charge: $20 in-state; $206 out-of-state. Books/supplies: $1,566. Personal expenses: $1,800.

2007-2008 Financial aid. Need-based: 89% of total undergraduate aid awarded as scholarships/grants, 11% as loans/jobs.

Application procedures. Admission: No deadline. No application fee. **Financial aid:** Priority date 5/25; no closing date. Applicants notified on a rolling basis starting 5/1; must reply within 2 week(s) of notification.

Academics. Special study options: Cooperative education, cross-registration, distance learning, double major, dual enrollment of high school students, ESL, honors, independent study, internships, liberal arts/career combination, weekend college. Service Members Opportunity College. **Credit/placement by examination:** AP, CLEP, institutional tests. **Support services:** GED preparation, learning center, pre-admission summer program, reduced course load, remedial instruction, study skills assistance, tutoring, writing center.

Majors. Biology: General. **Business:** Accounting, business admin, real estate. **Communications:** General. **Computer sciences:** Computer science, systems analysis. **Engineering technology:** Electrical. **Liberal arts:** Arts/sciences, library science. **Math:** General. **Mechanic/repair:** Automotive, diesel, electronics/electrical, heating/ac/refrig. **Physical sciences:** Astronomy, chemistry, geology, physics. **Protective services:** Law enforcement admin. **Psychology:** General. **Public administration:** Social work. **Social sciences:** Geography. **Transportation:** Aviation management. **Visual/performing arts:** Commercial/advertising art.

Computing on campus. 180 workstations in library, computer center, student center.

Student life. Freshman orientation: Available. **Activities:** Choral groups, drama, literary magazine, music ensembles, musical theater, radio station, student government, student newspaper, TV station, Campus Crusade for Christ, Newman Club, Baptist Student Union, Movimiento Estudiantil Chicano de Aztlan, Black Student Union, Young Democrats, Young Republicans.

Athletics. NCAA. **Intercollegiate:** Baseball M, basketball, cross-country, football (tackle) M, soccer, softball W, track and field, volleyball W. **Team name:** Wolverines.

Student services. Adult student services, career counseling, services for economically disadvantaged, student employment services, financial aid counseling, health services, on-campus daycare, personal counseling, placement for graduates, veterans' counselor. **Physically disabled:** Services for visually, speech, hearing impaired. **Transfer:** Pre-admission transcript evaluation for new students.

Contact. E-mail: admissions@valleycollege.edu
Phone: (909) 384-4401
Dan Angelo, Associate Dean of Enrollment, San Bernardino Valley College, 701 South Mount Vernon Avenue, San Bernardino, CA 92410

San Diego City College

San Diego, California
www.sdccd.edu **CB code: 4681**

- Public 2-year community and junior college
- Commuter campus in very large city

General. Founded in 1914. Regionally accredited. **Enrollment:** 10,062 degree-seeking undergraduates. **Degrees:** 601 associate awarded. **ROTC:** Army, Air Force. **Location:** Downtown. **Calendar:** Semester, extensive summer session. **Full-time faculty:** 159 total; 87% minority. **Part-time faculty:** 561 total; 26% minority. **Special facilities:** Computerized independent study and learning laboratories, vocational training centers.

Student profile. Among degree-seeking undergraduates, 10% already have a bachelor's degree or higher, 6,298 transferred in from other institutions.

Out-of-state:	6%	**25 or older:**	49%

Basis for selection. Open admission. High school students seeking college admission must submit an approved application certified by parents, principal, registrar, and/or school district official.

2008-2009 Annual costs. Tuition/fees: $632; $6,002 out-of-state. Per-credit charge: $20 in-state; $199 out-of-state. Books/supplies: $1,566. Personal expenses: $3,024.

2007-2008 Financial aid. All financial aid based on need. 79% of total undergraduate aid awarded as scholarships/grants, 21% as loans/jobs. Need-based aid available for part-time students. Work-study available for part-time students.

Application procedures. Admission: No deadline. No application fee. **Financial aid:** Priority date 4/15; no closing date. FAFSA required. Applicants notified on a rolling basis starting 7/1; must reply within 4 week(s) of notification.

Academics. Special study options: Accelerated study, cooperative education, cross-registration, double major, dual enrollment of high school students, honors, independent study, internships, liberal arts/career combination, student-designed major, study abroad, teacher certification program, weekend college. **Credit/placement by examination:** AP, CLEP, institutional tests. 15 credit hours maximum toward associate degree. **Support services:** Learning center, pre-admission summer program, reduced course load, remedial instruction, study skills assistance, tutoring, writing center.

Majors. Area/ethnic studies: African, African-American, Latin American. **Biology:** General. **Business:** General, accounting, administrative services, business admin, labor relations, management information systems, management science, office technology, office/clerical, operations, purchasing, real estate, tourism promotion. **Communications:** Broadcast journalism. **Communications technology:** General. **Computer sciences:** General, applications programming, data entry, data processing, information systems, systems analysis. **Construction:** Pipefitting, power transmission. **Education:**

Bilingual. **Engineering:** General. **Engineering technology:** Drafting, electrical, manufacturing. **Family/consumer sciences:** Child care. **Foreign languages:** General, French, Italian, Spanish. **Health:** Nursing (RN), substance abuse counseling. **History:** General. **Interdisciplinary:** Behavioral sciences. **Legal studies:** Paralegal, prelaw. **Liberal arts:** Arts/sciences. **Math:** General, applied. **Mechanic/repair:** Heating/ac/refrig. **Parks/recreation:** Health/fitness. **Philosophy/religion:** Philosophy. **Physical sciences:** Chemistry, geology, physics. **Psychology:** General. **Science technology:** Biological. **Social sciences:** General, anthropology, geography, political science. **Visual/performing arts:** General, art history/conservation, commercial/advertising art, dramatic, photography, studio arts.

Most popular majors. Business/marketing 8%, health sciences 8%, interdisciplinary studies 9%, liberal arts 40%.

Computing on campus. 150 workstations in library, computer center, student center. Online course registration, online library, helpline, repair service available.

Student life. **Freshman orientation:** Available. **Activities:** Jazz band, choral groups, dance, drama, film society, musical theater, radio station, student government, student newspaper, symphony orchestra, TV station, Arabic club, Italian club, MECHA, National Society of Black Engineers, Society of Hispanic Professional Engineers, California Coalition Against Poverty, students for labor and solidarity, lesbian, gay, bisexual and transsexual student union.

Athletics. **Intercollegiate:** Baseball, basketball M, cross-country, football (tackle) M, golf, soccer, softball W, tennis, track and field, volleyball. **Intramural:** Archery, badminton, baseball M, basketball, bowling, racquetball, soccer, tennis, track and field, volleyball, weight lifting. **Team name:** Knights.

Student services. Adult student services, career counseling, student employment services, health services, on-campus daycare, personal counseling, placement for graduates, veterans' counselor. **Physically disabled:** Services for visually, speech, hearing impaired. **Transfer:** Pre-admission transcript evaluation for new students. Transfer center, transfer adviser, college fairs on campus for students transferring to 4-year colleges.

Contact. Phone: (619) 388-3475 Fax: (619) 388-3505
Lou Humphries, Student Services Supervisor II, San Diego City College, 1313 Park Boulevard, San Diego, CA 92101-4787

San Diego Mesa College

San Diego, California
www.sdmesa.edu
CB member
CB code: 4735

- Public 2-year community college
- Commuter campus in very large city

General. Founded in 1964. Regionally accredited. **Enrollment:** 13,465 degree-seeking undergraduates. **Degrees:** 982 associate awarded. **Calendar:** Semester, limited summer session. **Full-time faculty:** 320 total. **Part-time faculty:** 599 total. **Special facilities:** Anthropology museum.

Student profile.

Out-of-state:	1%	**25 or older:**	43%

Transfer out. **Colleges most students transferred to 2008:** San Diego State University, University of California: San Diego.

Basis for selection. Open admission. Students without high school diploma or equivalent admitted provisionally. **Learning Disabled:** Disabled Student Service Program (DSPS) available.

2008-2009 Annual costs. Tuition/fees: $632; $6,002 out-of-state. Per-credit charge: $20 in-state; $199 out-of-state. Books/supplies: $1,422. Personal expenses: $1,584.

Application procedures. **Admission:** No deadline. No application fee. Admission notification on a rolling basis. Applications not accepted by mail. **Financial aid:** Priority date 3/2; no closing date. FAFSA required. Applicants notified on a rolling basis starting 6/15; must reply within 3 week(s) of notification.

Academics. **Special study options:** Accelerated study, distance learning, double major, dual enrollment of high school students, honors, independent study, internships, liberal arts/career combination, student-designed major, study abroad, teacher certification program. License preparation in dental hygiene, physical therapy, real estate. **Credit/placement by examination:** CLEP, institutional tests. 15 credit hours maximum toward associate degree. Institutional test required for placement and counseling. **Support services:** Learning center, reduced course load, remedial instruction, study skills assistance, tutoring.

Majors. **Agriculture:** Animal health. **Architecture:** Landscape. **Area/ethnic studies:** African, African-American, Hispanic-American/Latino/Chicano. **Biology:** General. **Business:** General, accounting, business admin, fashion, hotel/motel admin, real estate, tourism/travel. **Computer sciences:** Programming, web page design. **Education:** Physical, sales/marketing, speech. **Engineering:** General. **Engineering technology:** Construction, water quality. **Family/consumer sciences:** Child development. **Foreign languages:** American Sign Language, French, Spanish. **Health:** Dental assistant, dental lab technology, medical assistant, medical radiologic technology/radiation therapy, physical therapy assistant. **Liberal arts:** Arts/sciences. **Math:** General. **Personal/culinary services:** Culinary arts. **Philosophy/religion:** Philosophy. **Physical sciences:** Chemistry, physics. **Psychology:** General. **Social sciences:** General, anthropology, sociology. **Visual/performing arts:** Art, dramatic, interior design, studio arts.

Most popular majors. Business/marketing 10%, liberal arts 20%.

Computing on campus. Commuter students can connect to campus network. Online library available.

Student life. **Freshman orientation:** Available. **Activities:** Concert band, choral groups, dance, drama, music ensembles, student government, student newspaper.

Athletics. **Intercollegiate:** Badminton W, baseball M, basketball, cross-country, diving, football (tackle) M, soccer, softball W, swimming, tennis, track and field, volleyball, water polo. **Team name:** Olympians.

Student services. Adult student services, career counseling, health services, on-campus daycare, personal counseling, placement for graduates, veterans' counselor. **Physically disabled:** Services for visually, speech, hearing impaired. **Transfer:** Transfer center, transfer adviser, college fairs on campus for students transferring to 4-year colleges.

Contact. E-mail: csawyer@sdccd.edu
Phone: (619) 388-2682 Fax: (619) 388-2960
Ivonne Alvarez, Director of Admissions and Records, San Diego Mesa College, 7250 Mesa College Drive, San Diego, CA 92111

San Diego Miramar College

San Diego, California
www.miramarcollege.net
CB code: 4728

- Public 2-year community college
- Commuter campus in very large city

General. Founded in 1969. Regionally accredited. **Enrollment:** 5,972 degree-seeking undergraduates. **Degrees:** 451 associate awarded. **Location:** 9 miles from downtown. **Calendar:** Semester, limited summer session. **Full-time faculty:** 91 total.

Student profile. Among degree-seeking undergraduates, 46% enrolled in a transfer program, 3% enrolled in a vocational program, 12% already have a bachelor's degree or higher.

Out-of-state:	1%	**25 or older:**	45%

Basis for selection. Open admission.

2008-2009 Annual costs. Tuition/fees: $626; $5,996 out-of-state. Per-credit charge: $20 in-state; $199 out-of-state. Books/supplies: $1,638. Personal expenses: $3,096.

2007-2008 Financial aid. **Need-based:** Need-based aid available for part-time students. Work-study available for part-time students. **Additional information:** Private scholarships available.

Application procedures. **Admission:** No deadline. No application fee. Admission notification on a rolling basis. **Financial aid:** Priority date 3/2; no closing date. FAFSA required. Applicants notified on a rolling basis; must reply within 3 week(s) of notification.

Academics. **Special study options:** Accelerated study, cross-registration, distance learning, dual enrollment of high school students, honors, independent study, weekend college. **Credit/placement by examination:** AP, CLEP. 15 credit hours maximum toward associate degree. Institutional placement tests required. **Support services:** Learning center, remedial instruction, study skills assistance, tutoring.

Majors. **Biology:** General. **Business:** Administrative services, business admin, marketing, office/clerical. **Communications:** General. **Computer sciences:** General. **Education:** Early childhood. **Family/consumer sciences:** Family studies. **Legal studies:** Paralegal. **Liberal arts:** Humanities. **Math:** General. **Mechanic/repair:** Aircraft, automotive, diesel, heavy equipment.

Parks/recreation: Health/fitness. **Physical sciences:** Chemistry, physics. **Protective services:** Corrections, firefighting, law enforcement admin. **Psychology:** General. **Social sciences:** General. **Visual/performing arts:** Studio arts. **Other:** Art/visual studies, Aviation operations-professional pilot, Business management-mortgage brokerage and banking, Military studies, Occupational/technical studies, Pre-engineering studies, World language studies.

Most popular majors. Business/marketing 14%, legal studies 6%, liberal arts 29%, security/protective services 30%.

Computing on campus. 10 workstations in library, computer center.

Student life. Activities: Student government, student newspaper, Amnesty International, Child Development Professionals, Filipino American Association, Latin American club, Miramar Associated Gaming Imagination Club (MAGIC), parent student advisory board, Phi Theta Kappa.

Athletics. Team name: Jets.

Student services. Career counseling, services for economically disadvantaged, health services, on-campus daycare, personal counseling, veterans' counselor. **Physically disabled:** Services for visually, hearing impaired. **Transfer:** Transfer adviser, college fairs on campus for students transferring to 4-year colleges.

Contact. E-mail: dstack@sdccd.edu
Phone: (619) 388-7844 Fax: (619) 388-7915
Dana Stack, Student Services Supervisor II, San Diego Miramar College, 10440 Black Mountain Road, San Diego, CA 92126-2999

San Joaquin Delta College
Stockton, California
www.deltacollege.edu **CB code: 4706**

- Public 2-year community college
- Commuter campus in large city

General. Founded in 1935. Regionally accredited. 14 off-campus sites located in service district. **Enrollment:** 8,003 degree-seeking undergraduates. **Degrees:** 2,256 associate awarded. **Location:** 45 miles from Sacramento. **Calendar:** Semester, extensive summer session. **Full-time faculty:** 217 total; 49% women. **Part-time faculty:** 439 total; 47% women. **Class size:** 48% < 20, 40% 20-39, 7% 40-49, 5% 50-99, less than 1% >100. **Special facilities:** Planetarium, electron microscopy laboratory, farm laboratory, natural resources laboratory, 3 theaters. **Partnerships:** Nissan, General Motors, Caterpillar.

Transfer out. Colleges most students transferred to 2008: California State University: Stanislaus, California State University: Sacramento, University of the Pacific, California State Polytechnic University, University of California: Davis.

Basis for selection. Open admission, but selective for some programs. Limited admission to registered nursing, psychiatric technician, licensed vocational nursing, radiological technician, and police academy programs.

2008-2009 Annual costs. Tuition/fees: $602; $6,032 out-of-state. Per-credit charge: $20 in-state; $201 out-of-state. Books/supplies: $1,566. Personal expenses: $3,024.

2007-2008 Financial aid. Need-based: 2,938 full-time freshmen applied for aid; 2,297 were judged to have need; 1,997 of these received aid. Average need met was 30%. Average scholarship/grant was $3,326; average loan $2,662. 84% of total undergraduate aid awarded as scholarships/grants, 16% as loans/jobs. Need-based aid available for part-time students. Work-study available nights, weekends and for part-time students. **Non-need-based:** Awarded to 7 full-time undergraduates, including 1 freshmen. Scholarships awarded for academics, athletics. **Additional information:** Enrollment fee waivers available for low-income California residents.

Application procedures. Admission: No deadline. No application fee. Admission notification on a rolling basis beginning on or about 6/5. **Financial aid:** Priority date 4/15; no closing date. FAFSA, institutional form required. Applicants notified on a rolling basis starting 5/1; must reply within 3 week(s) of notification.

Academics. Special study options: Cooperative education, distance learning, dual enrollment of high school students, ESL, internships, liberal arts/career combination, study abroad, weekend college. License preparation in nursing, real estate. **Credit/placement by examination:** AP, CLEP, IB, institutional tests. 15 credit hours maximum toward associate degree. All students taking more than one course must take ASSET or COMPASS for placement. AP and CLEP credit granted after 12 semester hours in residence completed. **Support services:** GED preparation, learning center, reduced course load, remedial instruction, study skills assistance, tutoring, writing center.

Majors. Agriculture: Agribusiness operations, agronomy, animal sciences, business, economics, food science, horticulture, ornamental horticulture, plant protection, plant sciences, soil science. **Architecture:** Landscape. **Biology:** General, botany, zoology. **Business:** General, accounting, administrative services, business admin, fashion, management information systems, managerial economics, office technology, office/clerical, real estate. **Communications:** Broadcast journalism, journalism. **Communications technology:** Graphic/printing. **Computer sciences:** General, computer science, data processing, database management, programming. **Conservation:** General, wildlife. **Construction:** Carpentry, maintenance, power transmission. **Engineering:** General, architectural. **Engineering technology:** Architectural, drafting, electrical, software. **Family/consumer sciences:** General, child care, food/nutrition, institutional food production. **Foreign languages:** French, German, Spanish. **Health:** EMT paramedic, medical radiologic technology/radiation therapy, mental health services, nursing (RN). **Interdisciplinary:** Natural sciences. **Legal studies:** Prelaw. **Liberal arts:** Arts/sciences. **Math:** General. **Mechanic/repair:** Heavy equipment, locksmithing. **Personal/culinary services:** Culinary arts. **Physical sciences:** Astronomy, chemistry, geology, physics. **Production:** Woodworking. **Protective services:** Fire safety technology, police science. **Psychology:** General. **Public administration:** General. **Social sciences:** General, anthropology. **Visual/performing arts:** General, crafts, fashion design, interior design, photography, studio arts.

Most popular majors. Business/marketing 9%, health sciences 8%, interdisciplinary studies 7%, liberal arts 62%.

Computing on campus. 220 workstations in library, computer center. Commuter students can connect to campus network. Online course registration, online library, helpline, wireless network available.

Student life. Freshman orientation: Available. **Activities:** Bands, choral groups, dance, drama, literary magazine, music ensembles, musical theater, radio station, student government, student newspaper, symphony orchestra, African-American Student Union, Movimiento Estudiantil Chicano de Aztlan, Vietnamese and Asian student clubs, International Student Association.

Athletics. NJCAA. **Intercollegiate:** Baseball M, basketball, cross-country, diving, football (tackle) M, golf M, soccer, softball W, swimming, tennis, track and field, volleyball W, water polo, wrestling M. **Intramural:** Baseball M, basketball, bowling, diving, fencing, golf, softball, swimming, tennis, track and field, volleyball. **Team name:** Mustangs.

Student services. Adult student services, alcohol/substance abuse counseling, career counseling, services for economically disadvantaged, student employment services, financial aid counseling, health services, legal services, minority student services, on-campus daycare, personal counseling, placement for graduates, veterans' counselor. **Physically disabled:** Services for visually, hearing impaired. **Transfer:** Re-entry adviser for new students. Transfer center, transfer adviser, college fairs on campus for students transferring to 4-year colleges.

Contact. Phone: (209) 954-5635 Fax: (209) 954-5644
Catherine Mooney, Registrar, San Joaquin Delta College, 5151 Pacific Avenue, Stockton, CA 95207-6370

San Joaquin Valley College
Visalia, California
www.sjvc.edu **CB code: 2052**

- For-profit 2-year junior college
- Commuter campus in small city
- Application essay, interview required

General. Regionally accredited. Additional campuses in Bakersfield, Fresno, Modesto, Rancho Cordova, and Rancho Cucamonga. Aviation campus located in Fresno. **Enrollment:** 820 degree-seeking undergraduates. **Degrees:** 451 associate awarded. **Calendar:** Semester, extensive summer session. **Full-time faculty:** 50 total. **Part-time faculty:** 20 total.

Basis for selection. Open admission, but selective for some programs. Selective admission to allied health programs. Various programs use either Accuplacer or Wonderlick for placement. ACCUPLACER for placement in Math and English.

2008-2009 Annual costs. Tuition/fees: $12,190. Costs may vary by program, annual tuition includes textbooks and supplies.

Application procedures. **Admission:** No deadline. No application fee. Admission notification on a rolling basis. **Financial aid:** No deadline. FAFSA, institutional form required.

Academics. **Special study options:** Independent study, internships, liberal arts/career combination. License preparation in aviation, dental hygiene, nursing. **Credit/placement by examination:** CLEP. **Support services:** Learning center, remedial instruction, study skills assistance, tutoring.

Majors. **Business:** Business admin, construction management, human resources. **Computer sciences:** Computer support specialist. **Health:** Dental assistant, dental hygiene, EMT paramedic, health care admin, insurance coding, licensed practical nurse, massage therapy, medical assistant, medical records admin, medical secretary, nursing (RN), office assistant, pharmacy assistant, physician assistant, respiratory therapy technology, surgical technology, veterinary technology/assistant. **Mechanic/repair:** Aircraft, heating/ac/refrig. **Protective services:** Corrections.

Computing on campus. 100 workstations in library, computer center.

Student life. **Freshman orientation:** Mandatory. Preregistration for classes offered. Full day on Friday prior to start of classes, continues through first week. **Activities:** Student government, student newspaper.

Student services. Adult student services, career counseling, services for economically disadvantaged, student employment services, financial aid counseling, personal counseling, placement for graduates. **Transfer:** Preadmission transcript evaluation for new students.

Contact. Phone: (559) 651-2500 Fax: (559) 651-0574
Susie Topjian, Enrollment Services Director, San Joaquin Valley College, 8400 West Mineral King Avenue, Visalia, CA 93291-9283

San Jose City College

San Jose, California
www.sjcc.edu **CB code: 4686**

- Public 2-year community college
- Commuter campus in very large city

General. Founded in 1921. Regionally accredited. **Enrollment:** 6,370 degree-seeking undergraduates. **Degrees:** 278 associate awarded. **Location:** 55 miles from San Francisco. **Calendar:** Semester, limited summer session. **Full-time faculty:** 170 total. **Part-time faculty:** 230 total. **Partnerships:** Formal partnerships with Intel (Manufacturing Technology program), Laser Electro-Optics Manufacturing Association (Laser Technology program), IntelSemiconductor (Mask Design Technology program).

Transfer out. **Colleges most students transferred to 2008:** San Jose State University, California State University: East Bay.

Basis for selection. Open admission.

2008-2009 Annual costs. Tuition/fees: $621; $6,351 out-of-state. Per-credit charge: $20 in-state; $211 out-of-state. Books/supplies: $712.

Financial aid. All financial aid based on need. **Additional information:** Board of Governors Grant (fee waivers) available to all qualified applicants.

Application procedures. **Admission:** No deadline. No application fee. **Financial aid:** Priority date 5/31; no closing date. FAFSA required. Applicants notified on a rolling basis; must reply within 4 week(s) of notification.

Academics. **Special study options:** Accelerated study, cooperative education, dual enrollment of high school students, honors, independent study, weekend college. License preparation in real estate. **Credit/placement by examination:** CLEP, IB, institutional tests. 30 credit hours maximum toward associate degree. **Support services:** Learning center, pre-admission summer program, reduced course load, remedial instruction, tutoring.

Majors. **Business:** Accounting, administrative services, banking/financial services, entrepreneurial studies, labor studies, marketing, office technology, office/clerical, real estate. **Communications technology:** General. **Computer sciences:** General, applications programming, data entry, networking, programming. **Construction:** General, power transmission. **Education:** Early childhood. **Engineering technology:** Drafting, electrical, heat/ac/refrig, laser/optical. **Health:** Dental assistant, substance abuse counseling. **Liberal arts:** Arts/sciences. **Mechanic/repair:** Electronics/electrical, heating/ac/refrig. **Personal/culinary services:** Cosmetic, hair styling. **Production:** Machine tool. **Protective services:** Law enforcement admin. **Psychology:** General. **Social sciences:** General. **Visual/performing arts:** Studio arts.

Computing on campus. 250 workstations in library, computer center. Commuter students can connect to campus network. Online course registration available.

Student life. **Freshman orientation:** Available. **Activities:** Bands, choral groups, dance, drama, music ensembles, musical theater, radio station, student government, student newspaper, symphony orchestra.

Athletics. **Intercollegiate:** Baseball M, basketball, cross-country, football (tackle) M, golf M, softball W, track and field, volleyball W. **Team name:** Jaguars.

Student services. Career counseling, services for economically disadvantaged, student employment services, health services, minority student services, on-campus daycare, personal counseling, veterans' counselor. **Physically disabled:** Services for visually, speech, hearing impaired. **Transfer:** Transfer center, transfer adviser, college fairs on campus for students transferring to 4-year colleges.

Contact. Phone: (408) 288-3700 Fax: (408) 298-1935
Carlo Santos, Director of Admissions and Records, San Jose City College, 2100 Moorpark Avenue, San Jose, CA 95128-2798

Santa Ana College

Santa Ana, California
www.sac.edu **CB code: 4689**

- Public 2-year community college
- Commuter campus in large city

General. Founded in 1915. Regionally accredited. **Enrollment:** 13,409 degree-seeking undergraduates. **Degrees:** 1,377 associate awarded. **Location:** 40 miles from Los Angeles. **Calendar:** Semester, extensive summer session. **Full-time faculty:** 260 total; 38% minority, 59% women. **Part-time faculty:** 1,098 total; 30% minority, 41% women. **Class size:** 21% < 20, 23% 20-39, 21% 40-49, 35% 50-99. **Special facilities:** Planetarium, 2 art galleries, digital media center/digital incubator.

Student profile. Among degree-seeking undergraduates, 12% already have a bachelor's degree or higher, 1,934 enrolled as first-time, first-year students, 2,625 transferred in from other institutions.

Out-of-state:	1%	**Hispanic American:**	52%
African American:	2%	**Native American:**	1%
Asian American:	15%	**25 or older:**	58%

Transfer out. **Colleges most students transferred to 2008:** California State University - Fullerton, California State University - Long Beach, California State University - Irvine.

Basis for selection. Open admission. All students 18 years and older who can benefit from instruction are admitted. **Adult students:** SAT/ACT scores not required.

2008-2009 Annual costs. Tuition/fees: $628; $6,058 out-of-state. Per-credit charge: $20 in-state; $201 out-of-state. Books/supplies: $1,500. Personal expenses: $2,928.

2007-2008 Financial aid. **Need-based:** 332 full-time freshmen applied for aid; 327 were judged to have need; 326 of these received aid. Average need met was 50%. Average scholarship/grant was $4,408; average loan $1,064. 83% of total undergraduate aid awarded as scholarships/grants, 17% as loans/jobs.

Application procedures. **Admission:** Priority date 4/1; no deadline. No application fee. Admission notification on a rolling basis. **Financial aid:** Priority date 6/30; no closing date. FAFSA required. Applicants notified on a rolling basis starting 6/1; must reply within 2 week(s) of notification.

Academics. **Special study options:** Cooperative education, distance learning, double major, dual enrollment of high school students, ESL, honors, independent study, internships, liberal arts/career combination, study abroad, weekend college. **Credit/placement by examination:** AP, CLEP, institutional tests. 30 credit hours maximum toward associate degree. **Support services:** GED preparation, learning center, pre-admission summer program, reduced course load, remedial instruction, study skills assistance, tutoring.

Majors. **Area/ethnic studies:** African-American, Hispanic-American/Latino/Chicano, women's. **Biology:** General. **Business:** Accounting, business admin, entrepreneurial studies, fashion, insurance, international, management science, marketing, real estate, tourism promotion. **Communications:** General, advertising, broadcast journalism, journalism. **Computer sciences:** General, computer science, data processing. **Education:** Early childhood. **Engineering:** General. **Engineering technology:** Drafting. **Family/consumer sciences:** Family/community services, food/nutrition. **Foreign languages:** General. **Health:** Medical assistant, nursing (RN), occupational therapy assistant, pharmacy assistant. **History:** General. **Legal studies:** Paralegal. **Liberal arts:** Arts/sciences, library science. **Math:** General. **Mechanic/repair:**

Automotive, diesel. **Parks/recreation:** Exercise sciences. **Philosophy/religion:** Philosophy. **Physical sciences:** Chemistry, geology, physics. **Production:** Welding. **Protective services:** Fire safety technology, fire services admin, firefighting, police science. **Psychology:** General. **Social sciences:** General, anthropology, economics, geography, political science, sociology. **Visual/performing arts:** General, commercial/advertising art, dance, dramatic, fashion design, photography.

Most popular majors. Business/marketing 8%, health sciences 12%, liberal arts 54%, security/protective services 10%.

Computing on campus. 66 workstations in library, computer center. Online course registration available.

Student life. **Freshman orientation:** Available. **Activities:** Bands, choral groups, dance, drama, international student organizations, literary magazine, music ensembles, musical theater, radio station, student government, student newspaper, TV station.

Athletics. NJCAA. **Intercollegiate:** Baseball M, basketball, cross-country, football (tackle) M, soccer, softball W, track and field, volleyball, water polo, wrestling M. **Team name:** Dons.

Student services. Adult student services, alcohol/substance abuse counseling, career counseling, services for economically disadvantaged, student employment services, financial aid counseling, health services, minority student services, on-campus daycare, personal counseling, veterans' counselor, women's services. **Physically disabled:** Services for visually, speech, hearing impaired. **Transfer:** Re-entry adviser, pre-admission transcript evaluation for new students. Transfer center, transfer adviser, college fairs on campus for students transferring to 4-year colleges.

Contact. E-mail: adm_records@rsccd.org
Phone: (714) 564-6042 Fax: (714) 564-6455
Mark Liang, Interim Director, Admissions and Records, Santa Ana College, 1530 West 17th Street, Santa Ana, CA 92706

Santa Barbara Business College

Santa Barbara, California
www.sbbcollege.edu

- For-profit 2-year junior and career college
- Large city
- Interview required

General. Accredited by ACICS. Campuses located in Santa Barbara, Ventura, Santa Maria, Bakersfield, Palm Desert, and On-Line. **Enrollment:** 100 degree-seeking undergraduates. **Degrees:** 95 associate awarded. **Location:** 90 miles from Los Angeles. **Calendar:** Terms begin every 10 weeks. **Full-time faculty:** 5 total. **Part-time faculty:** 10 total.

Student profile. Among degree-seeking undergraduates, 100% enrolled in a vocational program. Of all enrolled students, 5% already have a bachelor's degree or higher.

Basis for selection. Admission decisions based on Wonderlic assessment and interview to determine interest and motivation of prospective student. **Homeschooled:** Transcript of courses and grades required. Need to take ATB proctored test if unable to supply an official transcript.

2009-2010 Annual costs. Costs of full programs: medical assistant diploma, $20,658.34; medical assistant associate degree, $34,774.97; business administration associate degree, $35,133.38; massage therapy, $12,626.67; fitness trainer, $11,547.12. Tuition, fees, books, supplies, equipment included in program costs.

Application procedures. **Admission:** No deadline. $25 fee. **Financial aid:** FAFSA required. Applicants notified on a rolling basis.

Academics. **Special study options:** License preparation in nursing. **Credit/placement by examination:** CLEP. **Support services:** Remedial instruction, study skills assistance, tutoring.

Majors. **Business:** General. **Health:** Office assistant, pharmacy assistant. **Legal studies:** Paralegal. **Protective services:** Criminal justice.

Computing on campus. Online library available.

Student life. **Freshman orientation:** Mandatory.

Contact. Phone: (805) 967-9677 Fax: (805) 967-4248
Holly Ortiz, Director of Admissions, Santa Barbara Business College, 506 Chapala Street, Santa Barbara, CA 93101

Santa Barbara Business College: Bakersfield

Bakersfield, California
www.sbbcollege.edu

- For-profit 2-year junior and career college
- Large city
- Interview required

General. Accredited by ACICS. Campuses located in Santa Barbara, Ventura, Santa Maria, Bakersfield, Palm Desert, and On-Line. **Enrollment:** 480 degree-seeking undergraduates. **Degrees:** 135 associate awarded. **Calendar:** Terms begin every 10 weeks. **Full-time faculty:** 10 total. **Part-time faculty:** 20 total.

Student profile. Among degree-seeking undergraduates, 100% enrolled in a vocational program. Of all enrolled students, 5% already have a bachelor's degree or higher.

Basis for selection. Admissions decisions based on Wonderlic assessment and interview to determine interest and motivation of prospective student. **Homeschooled:** Transcript of courses and grades required. Need to take ATB proctored test if unable to supply an official transcript.

2009-2010 Annual costs. Costs for full programs: medical office systems diploma, $20,859.70; medical assistant diploma, $20,650.69; medical assistant associate degree, $34,760.18; business administration associate degree, $35,117.61; criminal justice associate degree, $32,730.10; network systems administration diploma, $21,823.16; network systems administration associate degree, $31,957.62; paralegal diploma for students with 2 or 4-year degree in field, $22,755.88; paralegal associate degree, $34,776.98; pharmacy technician diploma, $21,656.15; pharmacy technician associate degree, $31,571.96; vocational nursing, $30,107.47; fitness trainer, $11,542.47; massage therapy, $12,619.98. Tuition, fees, books, supplies, equipment included in program costs.

Application procedures. **Admission:** No deadline. $25 fee. **Financial aid:** FAFSA required. Applicants notified on a rolling basis.

Academics. **Special study options:** License preparation in nursing. **Credit/placement by examination:** CLEP. **Support services:** Remedial instruction, study skills assistance, tutoring.

Majors. **Business:** General. **Computer sciences:** LAN/WAN management. **Health:** Office assistant, pharmacy assistant. **Legal studies:** Paralegal. **Protective services:** Criminal justice.

Computing on campus. Online library available.

Student life. **Freshman orientation:** Mandatory.

Contact. Phone: (866) 749-7222
Holly Ortiz, Director of Admissions, Santa Barbara Business College: Bakersfield, 5300 California Avenue, Bakersfield, CA 93304

Santa Barbara Business College: Palm Desert

Palm Desert, California
www.sbbcollege.edu

- For-profit 2-year junior college
- Small city

General. Regionally accredited. **Calendar:** Continuous.

Contact. Phone: (866) 749-7222
75-030 Gerald Ford Drive, Building 2, Palm Desert, CA 92211

Santa Barbara Business College: Santa Maria

Santa Maria, California
www.sbbcollege.edu

- For-profit 2-year junior and career college
- Small city
- Interview required

General. Accredited by ACICS. Campuses located in Santa Barbara, Ventura, Santa Maria, Bakersfield, Palm Desert, and On-Line. **Enrollment:** 200

degree-seeking undergraduates. **Degrees:** 180 associate awarded. **Calendar:** Quarter. Terms begin every 10 weeks. **Full-time faculty:** 8 total. **Part-time faculty:** 12 total.

Basis for selection. Admissions decisions based on Wonderlic assessment and interview to determine interest and motivation of prospective student. **Homeschooled:** Transcript of courses and grades required. Need to take ATB proctored test if unable to supply an official transcript.

2009-2010 Annual costs. Costs for full programs as follows: medical office systems diploma, $20,867.93; medical assistant diploma, $20,658.34; medical assistant associate degree, $34,774.97; business administration associate degree, $35,133.38; criminal justice associate degree, $32,744.79; vocational nursing, $30,111.02; fitness trainer, $11,547.12; massage therapy, $12,626.67. Tuition, fees, books, supplies, equipment included in program costs.

Application procedures. Admission: No deadline. $25 fee. **Financial aid:** FAFSA required. Applicants notified on a rolling basis.

Academics. Special study options: License preparation in nursing. **Credit/placement by examination:** CLEP. **Support services:** Remedial instruction, study skills assistance, tutoring.

Majors. Business: General. **Health:** Office assistant, pharmacy assistant. **Legal studies:** Paralegal. **Protective services:** Criminal justice.

Computing on campus. Online library available.

Student life. Freshman orientation: Mandatory.

Contact. Phone: (866) 749-7222 Toll-free number: (866) 749-7222
Fax: (805) 346-1862
Holly Ortiz, Director of Admissions, Santa Barbara Business College: Santa Maria, 303 East Plaza Drive, Santa Maria, CA 93454

Santa Barbara Business College: Ventura

Ventura, California
www.sbbcollege.edu

- For-profit 2-year junior and career college
- Commuter campus in small city
- Interview required

General. Accredited by ACICS. Campuses located in Santa Barbara, Ventura, Santa Maria, Bakersfield, Palm Desert, and On-Line. **Enrollment:** 180 degree-seeking undergraduates. **Degrees:** 210 associate awarded. **Location:** 40 miles from Los Angeles. **Calendar:** Quarter. Terms begin every 10 weeks. **Full-time faculty:** 4 total. **Part-time faculty:** 27 total.

Basis for selection. Admission decisions based on Wonderlic assessment and interview to determine interest and motivation of prospective student. Wonderlic Basic Skills Test required. **Homeschooled:** Transcript of courses and grades required. Need to take ATB proctored test if unable to supply an official transcript.

2009-2010 Annual costs. Costs for full programs as follows: medical assistant diploma, $20,752.67; medical assistant associate degree, $34,832.38; business administration associate degree, $35,102.56; criminal justice associate degree, $32,746.55; paralegal diploma for students with 2 or 4-year degree in field, $22,790.53; paralegal associate degree, $34,809.17; fitness trainer, $11,752.81; massage therapy, $12,697.18; legal office system, $19,132.80. Tuition, fees, books, supplies, equipment included in program costs.

Application procedures. Admission: No deadline. $25 fee. **Financial aid:** FAFSA required. Applicants notified on a rolling basis.

Academics. Credit/placement by examination: CLEP. **Support services:** Learning center, remedial instruction, study skills assistance, tutoring.

Majors. Business: Business admin. **Health:** Office assistant. **Legal studies:** Paralegal. **Protective services:** Criminal justice.

Computing on campus. Online library available.

Student life. Freshman orientation: Mandatory.

Contact. Phone: (866) 749-7222 Fax: (805) 339-2994
Holly Ortiz, Director of Admissions, Santa Barbara Business College: Ventura, 4839 Market Street, Ventura, CA 93003

Santa Barbara City College

Santa Barbara, California
www.sbcc.edu **CB code: 4690**

- Public 2-year community college
- Commuter campus in small city

General. Founded in 1908. Regionally accredited. **Enrollment:** 11,298 degree-seeking undergraduates. **Degrees:** 1,423 associate awarded. **Location:** 90 miles from Los Angeles. **Calendar:** Semester, limited summer session. **Full-time faculty:** 266 total; 20% minority, 54% women. **Part-time faculty:** 553 total; 18% minority, 58% women. **Class size:** 18% < 20, 65% 20-39, 10% 40-49, 4% 50-99, 2% >100.

Student profile. Among degree-seeking undergraduates, 82% enrolled in a transfer program, 4% enrolled in a vocational program, 13% already have a bachelor's degree or higher, 2,292 enrolled as first-time, first-year students, 1,102 transferred in from other institutions.

Out-of-state:	7%	**Native American:**	1%
African American:	3%	**International:**	10%
Asian American:	5%	**25 or older:**	25%
Hispanic American:	24%		

Transfer out. Colleges most students transferred to 2008: University of California: Santa Barbara, California State University: Northridge, San Francisco State University, San Diego State University, University of California: Los Angeles.

Basis for selection. Open admission, but selective for some programs. Special requirements for hotel/restaurant/culinary, nursing, radiography, early childhood education, cosmetology, marine diving technology programs. Criteria vary by program. Interview required of nursing, hotel and restaurant management, marine technology majors. Audition required of some music and theater majors. **Adult students:** English assessment test required for placement.

2008-2009 Annual costs. Tuition/fees: $670; $6,100 out-of-state. Per-credit charge: $20 in-state; $201 out-of-state. Books/supplies: $1,566. Personal expenses: $3,024.

2008-2009 Financial aid. Need-based: Need-based aid available for part-time students. **Additional information:** California residents may qualify for Board of Governor's Financial Assistance Program, which will allow institutions to waive enrollment fee.

Application procedures. Admission: Priority date 2/1; deadline 8/21 (receipt date). No application fee. Admission notification on a rolling basis beginning on or about 3/1. **Financial aid:** No deadline. FAFSA required. Applicants notified on a rolling basis starting 5/1; must reply within 2 week(s) of notification.

Academics. Special study options: Cooperative education, cross-registration, distance learning, double major, dual enrollment of high school students, ESL, honors, independent study, internships, study abroad. License preparation in nursing, paramedic, radiology, real estate. **Credit/placement by examination:** AP, CLEP, IB, institutional tests. 12 credit hours maximum toward associate degree. **Support services:** Learning center, pre-admission summer program, reduced course load, remedial instruction, study skills assistance, tutoring, writing center.

Majors. Agriculture: Horticulture, landscaping, ornamental horticulture. **Area/ethnic studies:** African-American, Hispanic-American/Latino/Chicano, Native American. **Biology:** General. **Business:** General, accounting, accounting technology, administrative services, banking/financial services, business admin, finance, hospitality/recreation, international, marketing, office management, real estate, sales/distribution, selling, small business admin. **Communications:** General, digital media. **Communications technology:** General, computer typography. **Computer sciences:** General, computer science, data processing. **Conservation:** Environmental studies. **Education:** Early childhood, kindergarten/preschool, physical. **Engineering:** General, computer, marine. **Engineering technology:** General, automotive, biomedical, computer, drafting, electrical. **Family/consumer sciences:** Child care, institutional food production. **Foreign languages:** French, Spanish. **Health:** Athletic training, licensed practical nurse, medical radiologic technology/radiation therapy, nursing (RN), recreational therapy, sonography, substance abuse counseling. **History:** General. **Legal studies:** General. **Liberal arts:** Arts/sciences. **Math:** General. **Mechanic/repair:** Automotive, electronics/electrical. **Parks/recreation:** General, exercise sciences, health/fitness. **Personal/culinary services:** Cosmetic, culinary arts, institutional food service. **Philosophy/religion:** Philosophy. **Physical sciences:** Chemistry, geology, physics. **Protective services:** Law enforcement admin. **Psychology:** General. **Public administration:** General. **Science technology:** Biological. **Social sciences:** Anthropology, economics, geography, political science, sociology. **Transportation:** Diver. **Visual/performing arts:** Art, art history/conservation, commercial/advertising art, dramatic, film/cinema, interior design, multimedia, studio arts, theater design.

Most popular majors. Health sciences 9%, liberal arts 63%.

Computing on campus. 1,399 workstations in library, computer center, student center. Commuter students can connect to campus network. Online library, helpline, wireless network available.

Student life. **Freshman orientation:** Mandatory. Preregistration for classes offered. 2-hour on-campus or on-line orientation. **Activities:** Bands, choral groups, dance, drama, literary magazine, music ensembles, musical theater, student government, student newspaper, symphony orchestra, Black Student Union, College Republicans, EOPS, Hillel Club, Latter Day Saint Student Association, Phi Theta Kappa, Shodo Japanese Calligraphy Club, Special Abilities Club, Students Left Alliance Party, Student Sustainability Club, Vaquero Christian Fellowship.

Athletics. **Intercollegiate:** Baseball M, basketball, cross-country, football (tackle) M, golf, soccer, softball W, tennis, track and field, volleyball. **Team name:** Vaqueros.

Student services. Adult student services, alcohol/substance abuse counseling, career counseling, services for economically disadvantaged, student employment services, financial aid counseling, health services, minority student services, on-campus daycare, personal counseling, placement for graduates, veterans' counselor, women's services. **Physically disabled:** Services for visually, speech, hearing impaired. **Learning disabled:** Comprehensive services available. **Transfer:** Transfer center, transfer adviser, college fairs on campus for students transferring to 4-year colleges.

Contact. E-mail: admissions@sbcc.edu
Phone: (805) 965-0581 ext. 2200 Fax: (805) 963-7222
Allison Curtis, Director of Admissions and Records, Santa Barbara City College, 721 Cliff Drive, Santa Barbara, CA 93109-2394

Santa Monica College

Santa Monica, California — **CB member**
www.smc.edu — **CB code: 4691**

- Public 2-year community college
- Commuter campus in small city

General. Founded in 1929. Regionally accredited. Off-campus program at Santa Monica College of Design. **Enrollment:** 21,976 degree-seeking undergraduates. **Degrees:** 1,476 associate awarded. **Location:** 18 miles from Los Angeles. **Calendar:** Semester, extensive summer session. **Full-time faculty:** 308 total; 23% minority. **Part-time faculty:** 1,053 total; 12% minority. **Special facilities:** Planetarium, photo gallery, humanities center, entertainment technology academy. **Partnerships:** Formal partnerships with DreamWorks, Disney Channel, Sony, 20th Century Fox, and other entertainment industry leaders (for Academy of Entertainment Technology students).

Transfer out. **Colleges most students transferred to 2008:** University of California at Los Angeles, California State University-Northridge, University of Southern California.

Basis for selection. Open admission, but selective for some programs. Music, theater arts, entertainment technology are competitive with various requirements. Nursing program has course requirements for admission. Audition and portfolio required for music, theater arts.

2008-2009 Annual costs. Tuition/fees: $632; $5,552 out-of-state. Per-credit charge: $20 in-state; $184 out-of-state. Books/supplies: $1,566. Personal expenses: $2,664.

2007-2008 Financial aid. **Need-based:** Need-based aid available for part-time students.

Application procedures. **Admission:** No deadline. No application fee. Admission notification on a rolling basis. **Financial aid:** No deadline. FAFSA, institutional form required. Applicants notified on a rolling basis starting 7/1; must reply within 2 week(s) of notification.

Academics. **Special study options:** Accelerated study, cooperative education, distance learning, dual enrollment of high school students, ESL, honors, independent study, internships, study abroad, weekend college. License preparation in nursing. **Credit/placement by examination:** AP, CLEP, institutional tests. 30 credit hours maximum toward associate degree. Math and English placement tests required for some students. **Support services:** Learning center, pre-admission summer program, remedial instruction, study skills assistance, tutoring, writing center.

Majors. **Business:** General, accounting, business admin, entrepreneurial studies, office/clerical, real estate. **Communications:** Journalism. **Communications technology:** General. **Computer sciences:** Data processing, information systems, programming. **Construction:** Maintenance. **Engineering technology:** Architectural, drafting, electrical. **Family/consumer sciences:** General. **History:** General. **Liberal arts:** Arts/sciences. **Mechanic/repair:** Auto body. **Parks/recreation:** General. **Physical sciences:** Chemistry, geology, physics. **Protective services:** Firefighting, law enforcement admin, police science. **Social sciences:** General, political science. **Visual/performing arts:** Commercial photography, commercial/advertising art, dance, dramatic, photography, studio arts.

Computing on campus. 600 workstations in library, computer center, student center. Commuter students can connect to campus network. Helpline available.

Student life. **Freshman orientation:** Mandatory. **Activities:** Concert band, choral groups, dance, drama, literary magazine, music ensembles, musical theater, opera, radio station, student government, student newspaper.

Athletics. NJCAA. **Intercollegiate:** Basketball, cross-country M, diving, football (tackle) M, swimming, tennis, track and field, volleyball, water polo M. **Intramural:** Badminton. **Team name:** Corsairs.

Student services. Adult student services, career counseling, services for economically disadvantaged, student employment services, financial aid counseling, health services, minority student services, on-campus daycare, personal counseling, placement for graduates, veterans' counselor. **Physically disabled:** Services for visually, speech, hearing impaired. **Learning disabled:** Comprehensive services available. **Transfer:** Transfer center, transfer adviser, college fairs on campus for students transferring to 4-year colleges.

Contact. Phone: (310) 434-4380 Fax: (310) 434-3645
Kiersten Elliott, Dean of Enrollment Services, Santa Monica College, 1900 Pico Boulevard, Santa Monica, CA 90405-1628

Santa Rosa Junior College

Santa Rosa, California
www.santarosa.edu — **CB code: 4692**

- Public 2-year community college
- Commuter campus in small city

General. Founded in 1918. Regionally accredited. **Enrollment:** 12,663 degree-seeking undergraduates. **Degrees:** 1,110 associate awarded. **Location:** 55 miles from San Francisco. **Calendar:** Semester, extensive summer session. **Full-time faculty:** 303 total; 15% have terminal degrees, 14% minority, 59% women. **Part-time faculty:** 1,263 total; 9% have terminal degrees, 9% minority, 60% women. **Special facilities:** Native American art museum, college farm, summer repertory theater, planetarium.

Student profile.

Out-of-state:	2%	**25 or older:**	51%

Transfer out. **Colleges most students transferred to 2008:** Sonoma State University, San Francisco State University, University of California: Davis, California State University: Sacramento, University of California: Berkeley.

Basis for selection. Open admission, but selective for some programs. Audition recommended of music performance, some physical education, some communications majors.

2008-2009 Annual costs. Tuition/fees: $634; $6,064 out-of-state. Per-credit charge: $20 in-state; $201 out-of-state. Books/supplies: $1,566. Personal expenses: $3,024.

2007-2008 Financial aid. **Need-based:** Need-based aid available for part-time students. Work-study available nights, weekends and for part-time students. **Non-need-based:** Scholarships awarded for academics, art, leadership, music/drama. **Additional information:** California's Board of Governors Program provides fee waivers for applicants with need.

Application procedures. **Admission:** No deadline. No application fee. **Financial aid:** Priority date 3/1; no closing date. FAFSA required. Applicants notified on a rolling basis starting 4/5.

Academics. **Special study options:** Cooperative education, cross-registration, distance learning, dual enrollment of high school students, ESL, independent study, internships, liberal arts/career combination, study abroad, weekend college. License preparation in dental hygiene, nursing, paramedic, radiology, real estate. **Credit/placement by examination:** AP, CLEP, IB, institutional tests. 15 credit hours maximum toward associate degree.

Support services: GED preparation and test center, learning center, preadmission summer program, reduced course load, remedial instruction, study skills assistance, tutoring.

Majors. Agriculture: Agribusiness operations, equestrian studies, equine science. **Area/ethnic studies:** Latin American. **Biology:** General, physiology. **Business:** Business admin. **Computer sciences:** Computer science. **Conservation:** General, environmental studies. **Education:** General, early childhood. **Engineering:** General. **Engineering technology:** Civil, electrical. **Foreign languages:** American Sign Language, Spanish. **Health:** Dental assistant, dental hygiene, EMT paramedic, licensed practical nurse, medical radiologic technology/radiation therapy, mental health services, nursing (RN), nursing assistant, pharmacy assistant. **History:** General. **Interdisciplinary:** Natural sciences. **Liberal arts:** Arts/sciences. **Math:** General. **Parks/recreation:** General. **Philosophy/religion:** Philosophy. **Physical sciences:** Chemistry, physics. **Protective services:** Firefighting, police science. **Psychology:** General. **Social sciences:** Anthropology, economics, geography, political science, sociology. **Visual/performing arts:** Art, commercial/advertising art, dramatic, fashion design.

Most popular majors. Health sciences 11%, interdisciplinary studies 50%, psychology 8%, social sciences 15%.

Computing on campus. 1,750 workstations in library, computer center. Commuter students can connect to campus network. Online course registration, wireless network available.

Student life. Freshman orientation: Available. Preregistration for classes offered. **Activities:** Jazz band, choral groups, dance, drama, film society, international student organizations, music ensembles, musical theater, student government, student newspaper, symphony orchestra.

Athletics. Intercollegiate: Badminton W, baseball M, basketball, cross-country, diving, football (tackle) M, golf M, soccer, softball W, swimming, tennis, track and field, volleyball W, water polo, wrestling M. **Team name:** Bear Cubs.

Student services. Adult student services, career counseling, services for economically disadvantaged, student employment services, financial aid counseling, health services, on-campus daycare, personal counseling, placement for graduates, veterans' counselor. **Physically disabled:** Services for visually, speech, hearing impaired. **Transfer:** Re-entry adviser, pre-admission transcript evaluation for new students. Transfer center, transfer adviser, college fairs on campus for students transferring to 4-year colleges.

Contact. E-mail: admininfo@santarosa.edu
Phone: (707) 527-4685 Toll-free number: (800) 564-7752
Fax: (707) 527-4798
Diane Traversi, Director of Enrollment Services, Santa Rosa Junior College, 1501 Mendocino Avenue, Santa Rosa, CA 95401

Santiago Canyon College

Orange, California
www.sccollege.edu CB code: 2830

- Public 2-year community college
- Commuter campus in small city

General. Regionally accredited. **Enrollment:** 7,202 degree-seeking undergraduates. **Degrees:** 636 associate awarded. **Location:** 30 miles from Los Angeles. **Calendar:** Semester, extensive summer session. **Full-time faculty:** 117 total; 33% minority, 68% women. **Part-time faculty:** 375 total; 24% minority, 46% women.

Student profile. Among degree-seeking undergraduates, 7% already have a bachelor's degree or higher, 1,320 enrolled as first-time, first-year students, 206 transferred in from other institutions.

African American:	2%	Native American:	1%
Asian American:	11%	25 or older:	40%
Hispanic American:	38%		

Transfer out. Colleges most students transferred to 2008: California State University: Fullerton, California State University: Long Beach, Chapman University, University of California: Irvine.

Basis for selection. Open admission. **Adult students:** SAT/ACT scores not required. Placement tests for English, math, reading, and chemistry. **Homeschooled:** Statement describing homeschool structure and mission required. Must show private school affidavit confirmation from the California Department of Education.

2008-2009 Annual costs. Tuition/fees: $628; $6,358 out-of-state. Per-credit charge: $20 in-state; $211 out-of-state. Books/supplies: $1,500. Personal expenses: $2,300.

2007-2008 Financial aid. All financial aid based on need. Need-based aid available for part-time students.

Application procedures. Admission: No application fee. **Financial aid:** Priority date 7/1; no closing date. FAFSA, institutional form required. Applicants notified on a rolling basis starting 6/1.

Academics. Special study options: Accelerated study, cooperative education, distance learning, double major, dual enrollment of high school students, ESL, honors, weekend college. License preparation in real estate. **Credit/placement by examination:** CLEP, institutional tests. **Support services:** GED preparation and test center, learning center, remedial instruction, study skills assistance, tutoring, writing center.

Majors. Biology: General. **Business:** Accounting, business admin, managerial economics, marketing, selling, tourism/travel. **Communications:** General. **Communications technology:** Graphics, photo/film/video. **Computer sciences:** Computer science, information systems, web page design. **Construction:** Carpentry, electrician. **Engineering:** General. **Engineering technology:** Drafting. **Family/consumer sciences:** General. **Foreign languages:** General, American Sign Language, French, Italian, Spanish. **Health:** Medical assistant. **History:** General. **Legal studies:** Paralegal. **Liberal arts:** Arts/sciences, library science. **Math:** General. **Mechanic/repair:** Automotive. **Personal/culinary services:** Cosmetic. **Philosophy/religion:** Philosophy. **Physical sciences:** Chemistry, geology, hydrology, physics. **Protective services:** Fire safety technology. **Psychology:** General. **Social sciences:** General, anthropology, economics, geography, political science, sociology. **Visual/performing arts:** Art, commercial/advertising art, crafts, dance, fashion design, metal/jewelry.

Most popular majors. Liberal arts 82%.

Computing on campus. Online course registration, wireless network available.

Student life. Freshman orientation: Available. **Activities:** Bands, choral groups, dance, drama, music ensembles, student government, student newspaper, TV station.

Athletics. Intercollegiate: Cross-country, golf, soccer, track and field. **Intramural:** Softball, track and field. **Team name:** Hawks.

Student services. Adult student services, alcohol/substance abuse counseling, career counseling, services for economically disadvantaged, student employment services, financial aid counseling, health services, minority student services, on-campus daycare, personal counseling, veterans' counselor, women's services. **Physically disabled:** Services for visually, speech, hearing impaired. **Learning disabled:** Comprehensive services available. **Transfer:** Re-entry adviser, pre-admission transcript evaluation for new students. Transfer center, transfer adviser, college fairs on campus for students transferring to 4-year colleges.

Contact. Phone: (714) 628-4978 Fax: (714) 628-4723
Linda Miskovic, Associate Dean of Admissions, Santiago Canyon College, 8045 East Chapman Avenue, Orange, CA 92869

Shasta College

Redding, California
www.shastacollege.edu CB code: 4696

- Public 2-year community college
- Commuter campus in small city

General. Founded in 1948. Regionally accredited. **Enrollment:** 5,388 degree-seeking undergraduates. **Degrees:** 386 associate awarded. **Location:** 160 miles from Sacramento. **Calendar:** Semester, limited summer session. **Full-time faculty:** 130 total. **Part-time faculty:** 370 total. **Class size:** 58% < 20, 38% 20-39, 2% 40-49, 2% 50-99, less than 1% >100.

Student profile.

Out-of-state:	3%	Live on campus:	1%
25 or older:	46%		

Basis for selection. Open admission, but selective for some programs. Applicants to nursing program must be high school graduates, take National League for Nursing examination, and complete series of courses outlined in college catalog.

2008-2009 Annual costs. Tuition/fees: $675; $6,195 out-of-state. Per-credit charge: $20 in-state; $204 out-of-state. Room only: $2,610. Books/supplies: $1,566. Personal expenses: $2,000.

Financial aid. All financial aid based on need. Need-based aid available for part-time students.

Application procedures. **Admission:** No deadline. No application fee. Admission notification on a rolling basis. **Financial aid:** Priority date 3/2; no closing date. FAFSA, institutional form required. Applicants notified on a rolling basis starting 7/1.

Academics. On-campus programs leading to bachelor's degree from California State University: Chico offered. **Special study options:** Cooperative education, distance learning, double major, dual enrollment of high school students, ESL, honors, independent study, internships, weekend college. License preparation in dental hygiene, nursing, occupational therapy, paramedic, physical therapy, real estate. **Credit/placement by examination:** CLEP, institutional tests. 12 credit hours maximum toward associate degree. **Support services:** Learning center, reduced course load, remedial instruction, tutoring, writing center.

Majors. **Agriculture:** General, agribusiness operations, business, equestrian studies, ornamental horticulture. **Business:** General, accounting, administrative services, business admin, entrepreneurial studies, executive assistant, fashion, management information systems, office management, office technology, office/clerical, sales/distribution. **Communications:** General, journalism. **Computer sciences:** General, applications programming. **Construction:** Carpentry. **Education:** Early childhood, teacher assistance. **Engineering:** General, civil. **Engineering technology:** Architectural drafting, civil, construction, electrical. **Family/consumer sciences:** General, child care, institutional food production. **Health:** Nursing (RN). **Legal studies:** Legal secretary, paralegal. **Mechanic/repair:** General, aircraft, automotive, diesel, heating/ac/refrig. **Personal/culinary services:** Culinary arts. **Production:** Welding. **Protective services:** Fire safety technology, police science. **Public administration:** Human services. **Visual/performing arts:** Art, commercial/advertising art, dramatic, studio arts.

Computing on campus. 141 workstations in library, computer center. Online library available.

Student life. **Freshman orientation:** Mandatory. **Housing:** Single-sex dorms available. **Activities:** Bands, choral groups, dance, drama, literary magazine, music ensembles, musical theater, student government, student newspaper, symphony orchestra, Environmental Resources Leadership Club, LEAF, Ornamental Horticulture club, jazz choir, science club, Veteran's Club, dorm club.

Athletics. NJCAA. **Intercollegiate:** Baseball M, basketball, cross-country, football (tackle) M, golf, soccer, softball W, swimming, tennis, track and field, volleyball W, wrestling M. **Team name:** Knights.

Student services. Adult student services, career counseling, services for economically disadvantaged, student employment services, financial aid counseling, health services, minority student services, on-campus daycare, personal counseling, veterans' counselor. **Physically disabled:** Services for visually, speech, hearing impaired. **Transfer:** Transfer center, transfer adviser, college fairs on campus for students transferring to 4-year colleges.

Contact. E-mail: cryan@shastacollege.edu
Phone: (530) 225-4841 Fax: (530) 225-4995
Kevin O'Rorke, Dean of Enrollment Services, Shasta College, Box 496006, Redding, CA 96049-6006

Sierra College
Rocklin, California
www.sierracollege.edu **CB code: 4697**

- Public 2-year community college
- Commuter campus in large town

General. Founded in 1914. Regionally accredited. **Enrollment:** 13,403 degree-seeking undergraduates. **Degrees:** 2,301 associate awarded. **Location:** 25 miles from Sacramento. **Calendar:** Semester, extensive summer session. **Full-time faculty:** 219 total. **Part-time faculty:** 826 total. **Class size:** 30% <20, 58% 20-39, 10% 40-49, 2% 50-99, less than 1% >100. **Special facilities:** Nature trail, planetarium, science museum displays, learning resource center.

Student profile.

Out-of-state:	1%	Live on campus:	6%

Transfer out. **Colleges most students transferred to 2008:** California State University: Sacramento, University of California: Davis, California State University: Chico, University of California: Berkeley.

Basis for selection. Open admission.

2008-2009 Annual costs. Tuition/fees: $640; $6,070 out-of-state. Per-credit charge: $20 in-state; $201 out-of-state. Room/board: $7,090. Books/supplies: $1,556. Personal expenses: $1,638.

2008-2009 Financial aid. **Need-based:** 75% of total undergraduate aid awarded as scholarships/grants, 25% as loans/jobs. Need-based aid available for part-time students. Work-study available nights, weekends and for part-time students.

Application procedures. **Admission:** No deadline. No application fee. Applicants notified within 4 working days. **Financial aid:** Priority date 3/2; no closing date. FAFSA required. Applicants notified on a rolling basis starting 5/15.

Academics. **Special study options:** Cooperative education, cross-registration, distance learning, double major, dual enrollment of high school students, ESL, honors, independent study, internships, study abroad, weekend college. License preparation in nursing, real estate. **Credit/placement by examination:** AP, CLEP, institutional tests. 15 credit hours maximum toward associate degree. **Support services:** Learning center, remedial instruction, study skills assistance, tutoring, writing center.

Majors. **Agriculture:** General, animal husbandry, equestrian studies, horticulture. **Biology:** General. **Business:** General, accounting, administrative services, business admin, real estate, sales/distribution, small business admin. **Communications:** Digital media. **Computer sciences:** Data entry, information technology, networking, programming, system admin, web page design, webmaster. **Conservation:** Forestry. **Construction:** Carpentry, maintenance. **Education:** Early childhood, teacher assistance. **Engineering:** General. **Engineering technology:** Architectural drafting, hazardous materials, mechanical drafting. **Family/consumer sciences:** General, child care, institutional food production. **Foreign languages:** American Sign Language. **Health:** Licensed practical nurse, medical secretary, nursing (RN). **Legal studies:** Legal secretary. **Liberal arts:** Arts/sciences, library assistant, library science. **Math:** General. **Mechanic/repair:** Automotive, electronics/electrical. **Parks/recreation:** Health/fitness. **Philosophy/religion:** Philosophy. **Physical sciences:** Chemistry, geology. **Production:** Woodworking. **Protective services:** Criminal justice, fire safety technology, firefighting, police science, security services. **Visual/performing arts:** Art, music performance, photography, studio arts.

Computing on campus. 300 workstations in dormitories, library, computer center. Dormitories linked to campus network. Commuter students can connect to campus network. Online course registration, online library, wireless network available.

Student life. **Freshman orientation:** Mandatory. **Housing:** Coed dorms available. **Activities:** Concert band, choral groups, drama, music ensembles, student government, student newspaper.

Athletics. **Intercollegiate:** Baseball M, basketball, cross-country W, diving, football (tackle) M, golf, soccer W, softball W, swimming, tennis, track and field W, volleyball W, water polo W, wrestling M. **Intramural:** Archery, badminton, basketball, cheerleading W, football (non-tackle), golf, softball, tennis, volleyball. **Team name:** Wolverines.

Student services. Adult student services, alcohol/substance abuse counseling, career counseling, services for economically disadvantaged, student employment services, financial aid counseling, health services, on-campus daycare, personal counseling, veterans' counselor. **Physically disabled:** Services for visually, speech, hearing impaired. **Transfer:** Pre-admission transcript evaluation for new students. Transfer center, transfer adviser, college fairs on campus for students transferring to 4-year colleges.

Contact. Phone: (916) 781-0430 Toll-free number: (800) 242-4004
Fax: (916) 781-0403
Gail Modder, Admissions and Records Program Manager, Sierra College, 5000 Rocklin Road, Rocklin, CA 95677

Skyline College
San Bruno, California
www.skylinecollege.edu **CB code: 4746**

- Public 2-year community college
- Commuter campus in small city

General. Founded in 1969. Regionally accredited. **Enrollment:** 5,387 degree-seeking undergraduates. **Degrees:** 467 associate awarded. **Location:** 15 miles from San Francisco. **Calendar:** Semester, limited summer session. **Full-time faculty:** 105 total. **Part-time faculty:** 200 total.

Student profile. Among degree-seeking undergraduates, 17% enrolled in a transfer program, 1% enrolled in a vocational program, 14% already have a bachelor's degree or higher.

Out-of-state:	1%	25 or older:	49%

Transfer out. **Colleges most students transferred to 2008:** San Francisco State University, San Jose State University, California State University: East Bay.

Basis for selection. Open admission, but selective for some programs. Additional requirements for applicants to automotive technology, cosmetology, and respiratory therapy programs, and for participants in concurrent enrollment. SAT/ACT may be substituted for institutional placement tests. Interview required of respiratory therapy majors. Essay required of full-time international student applicants.

2008-2009 Annual costs. Tuition/fees: $628; $6,358 out-of-state. Per-credit charge: $20 in-state; $211 out-of-state. Books/supplies: $1,566. Personal expenses: $2,376.

Financial aid. **Need-based:** Need-based aid available for part-time students.

Application procedures. **Admission:** No deadline. No application fee. Admission notification on a rolling basis. **Financial aid:** Priority date 5/2; no closing date. FAFSA, institutional form required. Applicants notified on a rolling basis starting 5/1; must reply within 2 week(s) of notification.

Academics. Classes given on Sundays. **Special study options:** Cooperative education, cross-registration, dual enrollment of high school students, ESL, honors, study abroad. **Credit/placement by examination:** CLEP, institutional tests. 12 credit hours maximum toward associate degree. **Support services:** Learning center, study skills assistance, tutoring.

Majors. **Business:** Accounting, administrative services, business admin, hospitality admin, management information systems, office/clerical. **Communications technology:** General. **Computer sciences:** General, computer science, data processing, information systems, webmaster. **Education:** Early childhood. **Family/consumer sciences:** General, business. **Foreign languages:** Spanish. **Health:** Medical secretary, medical transcription, respiratory therapy technology, surgical technology. **Interdisciplinary:** Global studies. **Legal studies:** Legal secretary, paralegal. **Liberal arts:** Arts/sciences. **Math:** General. **Mechanic/repair:** Automotive. **Personal/culinary services:** Cosmetic. **Protective services:** Law enforcement admin. **Psychology:** General. **Science technology:** Biological. **Visual/performing arts:** General, art, dance.

Most popular majors. Business/marketing 13%, health sciences 11%, liberal arts 53%.

Computing on campus. 220 workstations in library, computer center, student center. Online course registration, helpline, repair service available.

Student life. **Freshman orientation:** Available. **Activities:** Bands, choral groups, dance, literary magazine, student government, student newspaper.

Athletics. NJCAA. **Intercollegiate:** Baseball M, basketball M, cross-country, soccer M, softball W, track and field, volleyball W, wrestling M. **Team name:** Trojans.

Student services. Career counseling, services for economically disadvantaged, student employment services, health services, minority student services, on-campus daycare, personal counseling, veterans' counselor, women's services. **Physically disabled:** Services for visually, speech, hearing impaired. **Transfer:** Transfer center, transfer adviser, college fairs on campus for students transferring to 4-year colleges.

Contact. E-mail: skyadmissions@smccd.edu
Phone: (650) 738-4252 Fax: (650) 738-4200
Sherri Hancock, Dean of Enrollment Services, Skyline College, 3300 College Drive, San Bruno, CA 94066-1662

Solano Community College
Fairfield, California
www.solano.edu **CB code: 4930**

- Public 2-year community college
- Commuter campus in small city

General. Founded in 1945. Regionally accredited. Classes offered in Vallejo and Vacaville. **Enrollment:** 7,552 degree-seeking undergraduates. **Degrees:** 940 associate awarded. **ROTC:** Air Force. **Location:** 11 miles from Vallejo. **Calendar:** Semester, extensive summer session. **Full-time faculty:** 174 total. **Part-time faculty:** 285 total.

Basis for selection. Open admission, but selective for some programs. Special requirements for nursing program.

2008-2009 Annual costs. Tuition/fees: $636; $6,066 out-of-state. Per-credit charge: $20 in-state; $201 out-of-state. Books/supplies: $1,566. Personal expenses: $2,664.

Application procedures. **Admission:** No deadline. No application fee. Admission notification on a rolling basis. **Financial aid:** Priority date 3/1; no closing date. FAFSA required. Applicants notified on a rolling basis starting 7/1.

Academics. **Special study options:** Cooperative education, cross-registration, distance learning, double major, dual enrollment of high school students, honors, independent study, internships, study abroad, weekend college. **Credit/placement by examination:** AP, CLEP, institutional tests. 15 credit hours maximum toward associate degree. **Support services:** Reduced course load, remedial instruction, tutoring, writing center.

Majors. **Agriculture:** Landscaping, ornamental horticulture. **Area/ethnic studies:** African-American, Asian-American, Hispanic-American/Latino/Chicano, Native American. **Biology:** General. **Business:** Accounting, administrative services, banking/financial services, business admin, office management, real estate. **Communications:** General, journalism. **Computer sciences:** General, programming. **Education:** Early childhood. **Engineering technology:** Aerospace, drafting, electrical, water quality. **Family/consumer sciences:** General. **Foreign languages:** General, French, German, Spanish. **Health:** Medical secretary, nursing (RN). **History:** General. **Interdisciplinary:** Biological/physical sciences. **Legal studies:** Legal secretary. **Liberal arts:** Arts/sciences. **Math:** General. **Mechanic/repair:** Aircraft, appliance, auto body, computer. **Parks/recreation:** Health/fitness, sports admin. **Personal/culinary services:** Cosmetic. **Physical sciences:** Chemistry, physics. **Production:** Welding. **Protective services:** Firefighting, police science. **Psychology:** General. **Public administration:** Human services. **Science technology:** Biological. **Social sciences:** General, international relations, political science. **Visual/performing arts:** Commercial photography, commercial/advertising art, dramatic, drawing, interior design, painting, sculpture, studio arts.

Computing on campus. 240 workstations in library, computer center.

Student life. **Freshman orientation:** Available. **Activities:** Bands, choral groups, drama, musical theater, student government, student newspaper, symphony orchestra, Black Student Union, women's change, veterans organization, Sierra club, student nurses, Filipino club, Democratic club, Mathematics, Engineering & Science Achievement club, Asian-Pacific Islander club.

Athletics. **Intercollegiate:** Baseball M, basketball, cross-country, diving, football (tackle) M, soccer W, softball W, swimming, track and field, volleyball W, water polo M. **Intramural:** Table tennis, tennis. **Team name:** Falcons.

Student services. Career counseling, student employment services, financial aid counseling, health services, on-campus daycare, personal counseling, placement for graduates, veterans' counselor. **Physically disabled:** Services for visually, speech, hearing impaired. **Transfer:** Transfer center for students transferring to 4-year colleges.

Contact. E-mail: admissions@solano.edu
Phone: (707) 864-7171 Fax: (707) 864-7175
Barbara Fountain, Interim Dean, Admissions and Records, Solano Community College, 4000 Suisun Valley Road, Fairfield, CA 94534-3197

South Coast College
Orange, California
www.southcoastcollege.com

- For-profit 2-year business and career college
- Small city

General. Accredited by ACICS. **Enrollment:** 350 degree-seeking undergraduates. **Degrees:** 20 associate awarded. **Location:** 20 miles from Los Angeles. **Calendar:** Quarter, extensive summer session. **Full-time faculty:** 20 total. **Part-time faculty:** 25 total. **Special facilities:** Computer training center.

Basis for selection. Open admission, but selective for some programs.

2008-2009 Annual costs. Tuition/fees: $9,450. Registration fee of $99; monthly program cost $1,050/month. Books/supplies: $700.

Application procedures. **Admission:** Closing date 3/31. $99 fee.

Academics. **Credit/placement by examination:** CLEP.

Majors. **Health:** Medical transcription. **Legal studies:** Paralegal.

Contact. E-mail: requestinfo@southcoastcollege.com
Phone: (714) 867-5009 Toll-free number: (800) 337-8366
Kevin Magner, Dean of Admissions and Marketing, South Coast College, 2011 West Chapman Avenue, Orange, CA 92868

Southwestern College

Chula Vista, California
www.swccd.edu **CB code: 4726**

- Public 2-year community college
- Commuter campus in small city

General. Founded in 1961. Regionally accredited. Medical occupation programs accredited by the National League for Nursing Accrediting Commission Inc. (NLNAC). **Enrollment:** 12,999 degree-seeking undergraduates. **Degrees:** 1,190 associate awarded. **Location:** 10 miles from San Diego. **Calendar:** Semester, extensive summer session. **Full-time faculty:** 80 total. **Part-time faculty:** 120 total. **Class size:** 36% < 20, 49% 20-39, 13% 40-49, 3% 50-99.

Student profile. Among degree-seeking undergraduates, 48% enrolled in a transfer program.

Transfer out. Colleges most students transferred to 2008: San Diego State University, University of California: San Diego.

Basis for selection. Open admission, but selective for some programs. Limited admission to nursing and dental hygiene programs.

2008-2009 Annual costs. Tuition/fees: $624; $6,054 out-of-state. Per-credit charge: $20 in-state; $201 out-of-state. Books/supplies: $1,566. Personal expenses: $2,664.

Financial aid. Need-based: Need-based aid available for part-time students. Work-study available nights, weekends and for part-time students.

Application procedures. Admission: No deadline. No application fee. Admission notification on a rolling basis. **Financial aid:** Closing date 3/2. FAFSA required. Applicants notified on a rolling basis starting 7/1.

Academics. Broad offerings of online and traditional courses. Online credit and non-credit courses available. **Special study options:** Cooperative education, cross-registration, distance learning, double major, dual enrollment of high school students, ESL, honors, independent study, internships, study abroad, weekend college. License preparation in dental hygiene, nursing, paramedic, real estate. **Credit/placement by examination:** AP, CLEP, IB, institutional tests. 15 credit hours maximum toward associate degree. In-house placement test required for some. **Support services:** Learning center, pre-admission summer program, remedial instruction, study skills assistance, tutoring, writing center.

Majors. Agriculture: Floriculture, greenhouse operations, landscaping, nursery operations, ornamental horticulture, turf management. **Architecture:** Landscape, technology. **Area/ethnic studies:** African-American, American, Asian-American, Hispanic-American/Latino/Chicano, women's. **Biology:** General, biotechnology. **Business:** Accounting, business admin, construction management, entrepreneurial studies, finance, financial planning, international, market research, office management, office/clerical, real estate, tourism promotion, tourism/travel. **Communications:** General, broadcast journalism, journalism. **Communications technology:** General, radio/tv, recording arts. **Computer sciences:** General, applications programming, computer science, information systems, information technology, networking, programming, web page design, webmaster. **Conservation:** Environmental studies. **Construction:** Building inspection, maintenance. **Education:** General, early childhood, elementary, kindergarten/preschool, physical. **Engineering:** General. **Engineering technology:** CAD/CADD, computer, drafting, occupational safety, telecommunications. **Family/consumer sciences:** Child care, child development. **Foreign languages:** French, Spanish. **Health:** Dental hygiene, EMT paramedic, insurance coding, licensed practical nurse, medical records admin, medical records technology, medical transcription, nursing (RN), prenursing, surgical technology. **History:** General. **Legal studies:** General, legal secretary, paralegal. **Liberal arts:** Arts/sciences, humanities. **Math:** General. **Mechanic/repair:** Automotive, electronics/electrical, small engine. **Parks/recreation:** General, health/fitness. **Philosophy/religion:** Philosophy. **Physical sciences:** Astronomy, chemistry, geology, physics. **Protective services:** Criminal justice, firefighting, forensics, law enforcement admin. **Psychology:** General. **Public administration:** Social work. **Social sciences:** Anthropology, economics, geography, political science, sociology. **Visual/performing arts:** Art, cinematography, dance, dramatic, graphic design, photography.

Computing on campus. 1,360 workstations in library, computer center. Online course registration, online library, helpline, student web hosting, wireless network available.

Student life. Freshman orientation: Available. Preregistration for classes offered. **Activities:** Jazz band, choral groups, dance, drama, literary magazine, music ensembles, musical theater, student government, student newspaper, over 40 student clubs and organizations available.

Athletics. Intercollegiate: Baseball M, basketball, cross-country, football (tackle) M, soccer, softball W, tennis, track and field, volleyball W, water polo. **Team name:** Jaguars.

Student services. Career counseling, services for economically disadvantaged, student employment services, financial aid counseling, health services, legal services, on-campus daycare, personal counseling, veterans' counselor, women's services. **Physically disabled:** Services for visually, speech, hearing impaired. **Transfer:** Pre-admission transcript evaluation for new students. Transfer center, transfer adviser, college fairs on campus for students transferring to 4-year colleges.

Contact. E-mail: admissions@swccd.edu
Phone: (619) 421-6700 ext. 5215 Fax: (619) 482-6489
Mia McClellan, Dean, Student Services, Southwestern College, 900 Otay Lakes Road, Chula Vista, CA 91910-7297

Taft College

Taft, California
www.taftcollege.edu **CB code: 4820**

- Public 2-year community college
- Commuter campus in small town

General. Founded in 1922. Regionally accredited. **Enrollment:** 1,684 degree-seeking undergraduates. **Degrees:** 223 associate awarded. **Location:** 35 miles from Bakersfield. **Calendar:** Semester, limited summer session. **Full-time faculty:** 40 total. **Part-time faculty:** 55 total.

Student profile. Among degree-seeking undergraduates, 427 enrolled as first-time, first-year students.

Transfer out. Colleges most students transferred to 2008: California State University: Bakersfield, California State University: Fresno, California Polytechnic State University: San Luis Obispo, University of La Verne.

Basis for selection. Open admission. **Adult students:** SAT/ACT scores not required.

2008-2009 Annual costs. Tuition/fees: $600; $6,030 out-of-state. Per-credit charge: $20 in-state; $201 out-of-state. Room/board: $3,640. Books/supplies: $1,566.

2007-2008 Financial aid. Need-based: 81% of total undergraduate aid awarded as scholarships/grants, 19% as loans/jobs. Need-based aid available for part-time students. Work-study available nights and for part-time students. **Non-need-based:** Scholarships awarded for academics.

Application procedures. Admission: No deadline. No application fee. Admission notification on a rolling basis. **Financial aid:** No deadline. FAFSA, institutional form required. Applicants notified on a rolling basis; must reply within 4 week(s) of notification.

Academics. Special study options: Distance learning, double major, ESL, independent study. License preparation in dental hygiene. **Credit/placement by examination:** AP, CLEP, institutional tests. 12 credit hours maximum toward associate degree. **Support services:** GED preparation and test center, learning center, pre-admission summer program, reduced course load, remedial instruction, study skills assistance, tutoring.

Majors. Business: General, accounting, administrative services, business admin, management information systems, office/clerical. **Communications:** Journalism. **Computer sciences:** General, computer science, information systems. **Education:** General, early childhood, physical, social science. **Engineering:** General. **Engineering technology:** Automotive, CAD/CADD, electrical, petroleum. **Health:** Dental hygiene. **Liberal arts:** Arts/sciences. **Math:** General. **Mechanic/repair:** Automotive, industrial. **Parks/recreation:** General. **Physical sciences:** General. **Protective services:** Corrections, criminal justice. **Social sciences:** General. **Visual/performing arts:** Art.

Computing on campus. 121 workstations in dormitories, library, computer center, student center. Dormitories wired for high-speed internet access. Online course registration, online library, helpline, wireless network available.

Student life. Freshman orientation: Available. Offered online or by video. **Housing:** Single-sex dorms, special housing for disabled available. $125 fully refundable deposit. **Activities:** Drama, student government, student newspaper, International club, Rotary club, MECHA club, Best Buddies.

Athletics. NJCAA. **Intercollegiate:** Baseball M, basketball W, soccer, softball W, volleyball W. **Team name:** Cougars.

Student services. Adult student services, career counseling, services for economically disadvantaged, student employment services, financial aid counseling, minority student services, on-campus daycare, personal counseling, veterans' counselor. **Physically disabled:** Services for visually, speech, hearing impaired. **Learning disabled:** Comprehensive services available. **Transfer:** Re-entry adviser for new students. Transfer center, transfer adviser, college fairs on campus for students transferring to 4-year colleges.

Contact. E-mail: hrussell@taft.org
Phone: (661) 763-7741 Toll-free number: (800) 379-6784
Fax: (661) 763-7758
Brian McKee, Registrar and Director of Admissions, Taft College, 29 Emmons Park Drive, Taft, CA 93268

Trinity Life Bible College
Sacramento, California
www.tlbc.edu

- Private 2-year Bible college
- Very large city

General. Regionally accredited. **Enrollment:** 161 full-time, degree-seeking students. **Degrees:** 11 bachelor's, 15 associate awarded. **Calendar:** Quarter. **Full-time faculty:** 5 total. **Part-time faculty:** 33 total.

2008-2009 Annual costs. Tuition/fees: $8,775.

Application procedures. Admission: Closing date 8/15.

Academics. Special study options: Bachelor's degree programs available on campus. **Credit/placement by examination:** CLEP.

Majors. Philosophy/religion: Christian. **Theology:** Preministerial.

Contact. Phone: (916) 348-4689
Kathy Clarke, Director of Records, Trinity Life Bible College, 5225 Hillsdale Boulevard, Sacramento, CA 95842

Ventura College
Ventura, California
www.venturacollege.edu **CB code: 4931**

- Public 2-year community college
- Commuter campus in small city

General. Founded in 1925. Regionally accredited. **Enrollment:** 7,041 degree-seeking undergraduates. **Degrees:** 1,003 associate awarded. **Location:** 60 miles from downtown Los Angeles. **Calendar:** Semester, limited summer session. **Full-time faculty:** 136 total. **Part-time faculty:** 386 total.

Student profile. Among degree-seeking undergraduates, 1,537 enrolled as first-time, first-year students.

African American:	3%	**Hispanic American:**	40%
Asian American:	8%	**Native American:**	2%

Basis for selection. Open admission, but selective for some programs. Limited admission to nursing program.

2008-2009 Annual costs. Tuition/fees: $642; $6,072 out-of-state. Per-credit charge: $20 in-state; $201 out-of-state. Books/supplies: $1,566. Personal expenses: $3,024.

Financial aid. Need-based: Need-based aid available for part-time students.

Application procedures. Admission: No deadline. No application fee. Admission notification on a rolling basis. **Financial aid:** Priority date 3/2; no closing date. FAFSA required. Applicants notified on a rolling basis.

Academics. Special study options: Cross-registration, distance learning, dual enrollment of high school students, ESL, independent study, study abroad. **Credit/placement by examination:** AP, CLEP, institutional tests. 12 credit hours maximum toward associate degree. **Support services:** Learning center, reduced course load, remedial instruction, tutoring.

Majors. Agriculture: Plant sciences. **Biology:** General. **Business:** General, accounting, administrative services, business admin, fashion, office management, office/clerical. **Computer sciences:** General. **Conservation:** General. **Construction:** Maintenance. **Education:** Early childhood. **Engineering:** General. **Engineering technology:** Architectural, drafting, water quality. **Family/consumer sciences:** General, child development. **Health:** EMT paramedic, medical secretary, nursing (RN). **Mechanic/repair:** Automotive. **Production:** Welding. **Protective services:** Criminal justice. **Social sciences:** International relations. **Visual/performing arts:** Ceramics, commercial/advertising art, dramatic, fashion design, photography, studio arts.

Computing on campus. Online course registration available.

Student life. Freshman orientation: Available. **Housing:** Student housing available off-campus at nearby apartments. **Activities:** Jazz band, choral groups, dance, drama, international student organizations, music ensembles, student government, student newspaper, religious, ethnic, political, special interest organizations, international student club.

Athletics. Intercollegiate: Baseball M, basketball, cheerleading, cross-country, diving, football (tackle) M, golf M, softball W, swimming, tennis, track and field, volleyball M, water polo M. **Team name:** Pirates.

Student services. Adult student services, career counseling, services for economically disadvantaged, student employment services, health services, on-campus daycare, personal counseling, placement for graduates, veterans' counselor. **Physically disabled:** Services for visually, hearing impaired. **Learning disabled:** Comprehensive services available. **Transfer:** Transfer center, transfer adviser, college fairs on campus for students transferring to 4-year colleges.

Contact. Phone: (805) 654-6457 Fax: (805) 654-6357
Susan Bricker, Registrar, Ventura College, 4667 Telegraph Road, Ventura, CA 93003

Victor Valley College
Victorville, California
www.vvc.edu **CB code: 4932**

- Public 2-year community college
- Small city

General. Founded in 1960. Regionally accredited. **Enrollment:** 4,933 degree-seeking undergraduates. **Degrees:** 990 associate awarded. **Location:** 38 from San Bernardino. **Calendar:** Semester, limited summer session. **Full-time faculty:** 132 total. **Part-time faculty:** 389 total. **Special facilities:** Planetarium, mock archaeological dig site.

Student profile.

Out-of-state:	1%	**25 or older:**	40%

Transfer out. Colleges most students transferred to 2008: California State University: San Bernardino.

Basis for selection. Open admission, but selective for some programs. **Adult students:** SAT/ACT scores not required. **Homeschooled:** Must complete concurrent enrollment form with parent signature.

2008-2009 Annual costs. Tuition/fees: $610; $6,040 out-of-state. Per-credit charge: $20 in-state; $201 out-of-state. Nevada residents may qualify for tuition reduction program as part of Good Neighbor policy. Books/supplies: $1,566. Personal expenses: $3,024.

Financial aid. Need-based: Need-based aid available for part-time students. Work-study available for part-time students. **Additional information:** Board of Governors grant pays enrollment fee in full for low-income students.

Application procedures. Admission: No deadline. No application fee. Admission notification on a rolling basis. **Financial aid:** Priority date 3/2; no closing date. FAFSA, institutional form, CSS PROFILE required. Applicants notified on a rolling basis starting 8/1; must reply within 4 week(s) of notification.

Academics. Special study options: Cooperative education, distance learning, double major, dual enrollment of high school students, ESL, honors, independent study, semester at sea, study abroad. License preparation in nursing, paramedic. **Credit/placement by examination:** CLEP, institutional tests. 32 credit hours maximum toward associate degree. **Support services:** Learning center, pre-admission summer program, reduced course load, remedial instruction, study skills assistance, tutoring, writing center.

Majors. Agriculture: Ornamental horticulture. **Business:** General, administrative services, business admin, real estate. **Construction:** Carpentry. **Health:** EMT paramedic, medical assistant, nursing (RN), respiratory therapy technology. **Liberal arts:** Arts/sciences. **Math:** General. **Mechanic/repair:** Automotive, electronics/electrical, industrial electronics. **Production:** Welding. **Protective services:** Fire safety technology, law enforcement admin. **Visual/performing arts:** Art.

Most popular majors. Business/marketing 12%, health sciences 9%, interdisciplinary studies 18%, liberal arts 48%.

Computing on campus. 350 workstations in computer center, student center. Online course registration, online library, helpline available.

Student life. Freshman orientation: Available. **Activities:** Jazz band, choral groups, dance, drama, music ensembles, musical theater, student government, student newspaper, symphony orchestra.

Athletics. NJCAA. **Intercollegiate:** Baseball M, basketball, cross-country, football (tackle) M, golf M, soccer, softball W, tennis, track and field, volleyball W, wrestling M. **Team name:** Rams.

Student services. Career counseling, services for economically disadvantaged, student employment services, financial aid counseling, health services, on-campus daycare, personal counseling, placement for graduates, veterans' counselor. **Physically disabled:** Services for visually, speech, hearing impaired. **Transfer:** Re-entry adviser, pre-admission transcript evaluation for new students. College fairs on campus for students transferring to 4-year colleges.

Contact. Phone: (760) 245-4271 ext. 2280 Fax: (760) 843-7707
Greta Moon, Director, Admissions and Records, Victor Valley College, 18422 Bear Valley Road, Victorville, CA 92392-5849

West Hills College: Coalinga

Coalinga, California
www.westhillscollege.com **CB code: 4056**

- Public 2-year community college
- Commuter campus in small town

General. Founded in 1932. Regionally accredited. 2 campuses in district: West Hills College-Coalinga, West Hills College-Lemore. **Enrollment:** 1,765 degree-seeking undergraduates. **Degrees:** 199 associate awarded. **Location:** 60 miles from Fresno. **Calendar:** Semester, limited summer session. **Full-time faculty:** 47 total; 11% minority, 49% women. **Part-time faculty:** 85 total; 20% minority, 42% women. **Class size:** 10% < 20, 90% 20-39.

Student profile. Among degree-seeking undergraduates, 25% enrolled in a transfer program, 75% enrolled in a vocational program, 491 enrolled as first-time, first-year students.

Out-of-state:	15%	**25 or older:**	48%

Transfer out. 20% of students enrolled in the transfer program go on to 4-year colleges. **Colleges most students transferred to 2008:** California State University: Fresno, California Polytechnic University, Univeristy of Phoenix, Fresno Pacific University.

Basis for selection. Open admission. K-12 students admitted with parental permission and principal of the educational insitution recommendation as special admit students. **Adult students:** SAT/ACT scores not required. **Homeschooled:** Students must petition President of College in writing for admittance.

2008-2009 Annual costs. Tuition/fees: $600; $6,030 out-of-state. Per-credit charge: $20 in-state; $201 out-of-state. Additional $250 refundable deposit for room and board plan. Room/board: $5,321. Books/supplies: $1,400.

Financial aid. Need-based: Need-based aid available for part-time students.

Application procedures. Admission: No deadline. No application fee. Application must be submitted online. Admission notification on a rolling basis. **Financial aid:** Priority date 3/2; no closing date. FAFSA required. Applicants notified on a rolling basis starting 6/1.

Academics. Special study options: Cooperative education, distance learning, dual enrollment of high school students, ESL, honors, independent study, study abroad. **Credit/placement by examination:** AP, CLEP, institutional tests. 15 credit hours maximum toward associate degree. **Support services:** GED preparation, learning center, reduced course load, remedial instruction, tutoring.

Majors. Agriculture: General, animal sciences, business. **Business:** General, accounting, administrative services, business admin, management information systems, office technology, office/clerical. **Computer sciences:** General, applications programming. **Education:** Early childhood. **Health:** Health services, psychiatric nursing. **Liberal arts:** Arts/sciences. **Protective services:** Police science. **Psychology:** General. **Social sciences:** General, criminology, geography. **Visual/performing arts:** Art, commercial/advertising art, studio arts.

Most popular majors. Business/marketing 9%, health sciences 7%, liberal arts 65%.

Computing on campus. 40 workstations in dormitories, library, computer center. Dormitories wired for high-speed internet access. Online course registration, helpline available.

Student life. Freshman orientation: Mandatory. Preregistration for classes offered. **Housing:** Single-sex dorms, wellness housing available. $500 fully refundable deposit. **Activities:** Dance, drama, musical theater, student government.

Athletics. NJCAA. **Intercollegiate:** Baseball M, basketball M, cross-country M, football (tackle) M, rodeo, softball W, volleyball W. **Team name:** Falcons.

Student services. Adult student services, career counseling, services for economically disadvantaged, student employment services, on-campus daycare, personal counseling, veterans' counselor. **Physically disabled:** Services for visually, speech, hearing impaired. **Transfer:** Pre-admission transcript evaluation for new students. Transfer center, transfer adviser, college fairs on campus for students transferring to 4-year colleges.

Contact. E-mail: sandradagnino@whccd.edu
Phone: (559) 934-2302 Toll-free number: (800) 266-1114
Fax: (559) 935-2788
Darlene Georgatos, Director of District Enrollment, West Hills College: Coalinga, 300 Cherry Lane, Coalinga, CA 93210

West Hills College: Lemoore

Lemoore, California
www.westhillscollege.com

- Public 2-year community college
- Large town

General. Candidate for regional accreditation. 2 campuses in district: West Hills College Coalinga and West Hills College Lemoore. **Enrollment:** 2,340 degree-seeking undergraduates. **Degrees:** 347 associate awarded. **Location:** 20 miles from Fresno. **Calendar:** Semester, extensive summer session. **Full-time faculty:** 47 total; 23% minority, 45% women. **Part-time faculty:** 104 total; 24% minority, 44% women. **Class size:** 4% < 20, 96% 20-39.

Student profile. Among degree-seeking undergraduates, 20% enrolled in a transfer program, 80% enrolled in a vocational program, 636 enrolled as first-time, first-year students.

Out-of-state:	15%	**25 or older:**	48%

Transfer out. 20% of students enrolled in the transfer program go on to 4-year colleges. **Colleges most students transferred to 2008:** California State University Fresno, California State University Bakersfield, California State University Chico.

Basis for selection. Open admission. K-12 students admitted with parental and pirincipal of the educational institution recommendation as special admit students required. **Adult students:** SAT/ACT scores not required. **Homeschooled:** Statement describing homeschool structure and mission required. Parent or guardian must petition the President of West Hills College Lemoore in writing.

2008-2009 Annual costs. Tuition/fees: $600; $6,030 out-of-state. Per-credit charge: $20 in-state; $201 out-of-state. Room/board: $5,321. Books/supplies: $1,400.

Application procedures. Admission: No deadline. No application fee. Application must be submitted online. Admission notification on a rolling basis.

Academics. Special study options: Cooperative education, distance learning, dual enrollment of high school students, ESL, honors, independent study. **Credit/placement by examination:** AP, CLEP, institutional tests. 15 credit hours maximum toward associate degree. **Support services:** GED preparation, learning center, reduced course load, remedial instruction, tutoring.

Majors. Biology: General. **Business:** General, business admin. **Computer sciences:** General. **Engineering:** General. **Liberal arts:** Arts/sciences, humanities. **Math:** General. **Personal/culinary services:** Restaurant/catering. **Protective services:** Law enforcement admin. **Psychology:** General. **Social sciences:** General.

Most popular majors. Business/marketing 12%, health sciences 8%, liberal arts 54%, security/protective services 13%.

Computing on campus. 60 workstations in library, computer center. Online course registration available.

Student life. **Freshman orientation:** Mandatory. Preregistration for classes offered. **Activities:** Student government, student newspaper.

Athletics. NJCAA. **Intercollegiate:** Golf, soccer, wrestling M. **Team name:** Golden Eagles.

Student services. Adult student services, career counseling, services for economically disadvantaged, student employment services, on-campus daycare, personal counseling, veterans' counselor. **Physically disabled:** Services for visually, speech, hearing impaired. **Learning disabled:** Comprehensive services available. **Transfer:** Pre-admission transcript evaluation for new students. Transfer center, transfer adviser, college fairs on campus for students transferring to 4-year colleges.

Contact. E-mail: admissions@westhillscollege.com
Phone: (559) 925-3317 Toll-free number: (800) 266-1114
Fax: (559) 925-3837
Darlene Georgatos, Director of District Enrollment, West Hills College: Lemoore, 555 College Avenue, Lemoore, CA 93245

West Los Angeles College

Culver City, California
www.wlac.edu **CB code: 4964**

- Public 2-year community college
- Commuter campus in large town

General. Founded in 1968. Regionally accredited. **Enrollment:** 4,656 degree-seeking undergraduates. **Degrees:** 338 associate awarded. **Location:** 10 miles from Civic Center. **Calendar:** Semester, limited summer session. **Full-time faculty:** 105 total. **Part-time faculty:** 200 total.

Student profile.

Out-of-state:	1%	**25 or older:**	74%

Basis for selection. Open admission.

2008-2009 Annual costs. Tuition/fees: $622; $6,052 out-of-state. Per-credit charge: $20 in-state; $201 out-of-state. Books/supplies: $2,316. Personal expenses: $3,024.

2008-2009 Financial aid. All financial aid based on need. Need-based aid available for part-time students. Work-study available for part-time students. **Additional information:** California residents may qualify for Board of Governors Grant Program.

Application procedures. **Admission:** No deadline. No application fee. Admission notification on a rolling basis. **Financial aid:** No deadline. FAFSA required. Applicants notified on a rolling basis; must reply within 4 week(s) of notification.

Academics. **Special study options:** Cooperative education, distance learning, dual enrollment of high school students, ESL, honors, independent study, student-designed major, study abroad. License preparation in aviation, dental hygiene, nursing, paramedic, real estate. **Credit/placement by examination:** CLEP, institutional tests. 15 credit hours maximum toward associate degree. **Support services:** GED preparation, learning center, reduced course load, remedial instruction, study skills assistance, tutoring, writing center.

Majors. **Biology:** General. **Business:** General, accounting, administrative services, business admin, real estate. **Engineering:** General. **Foreign languages:** French, Spanish. **Health:** Dental hygiene. **History:** General. **Legal studies:** Paralegal. **Liberal arts:** Arts/sciences. **Mechanic/repair:** Aircraft. **Parks/recreation:** Health/fitness. **Philosophy/religion:** Philosophy. **Physical sciences:** Chemistry, geology, physics. **Psychology:** General. **Social sciences:** Anthropology, economics, geography, political science, sociology. **Visual/performing arts:** Art, ceramics.

Student life. **Freshman orientation:** Available. 2 hour session prior to start of each semester. **Activities:** Bands, choral groups, dance, drama, film society, student government, student newspaper, TV station.

Athletics. **Intercollegiate:** Baseball M, basketball, cross-country, football (tackle) M, soccer W, track and field, volleyball W. **Team name:** Oilers.

Student services. Adult student services, career counseling, services for economically disadvantaged, student employment services, financial aid counseling, health services, on-campus daycare, personal counseling, placement for graduates, veterans' counselor. **Physically disabled:** Services for visually, speech, hearing impaired.

Contact. Phone: (310) 287-4501
Diana Baxter, Supervisor, Admissions & Records, West Los Angeles College, 9000 Overland Avenue, Culver City, CA 90230

West Valley College

Saratoga, California
www.westvalley.edu **CB code: 4958**

- Public 2-year community college
- Large town

General. Founded in 1963. Regionally accredited. **Enrollment:** 6,028 degree-seeking undergraduates. **Degrees:** 637 associate awarded. **ROTC:** Army, Air Force. **Location:** 13 miles from downtown San Jose. **Calendar:** Semester, limited summer session. **Full-time faculty:** 200 total. **Part-time faculty:** 250 total. **Special facilities:** Planetarium, wireless campus center.

Transfer out. **Colleges most students transferred to 2008:** University of California: Davis, San Jose State University.

Basis for selection. Open admission.

2008-2009 Annual costs. Tuition/fees: $658; $6,088 out-of-state. Per-credit charge: $20 in-state; $201 out-of-state. Books/supplies: $2,316. Personal expenses: $3,024.

Financial aid. All financial aid based on need. Need-based aid available for part-time students.

Application procedures. **Admission:** Priority date 4/21; no deadline. No application fee. Admission notification on a rolling basis. **Financial aid:** Priority date 5/31; no closing date. FAFSA required. Applicants notified on a rolling basis starting 7/1.

Academics. **Special study options:** Distance learning, double major, dual enrollment of high school students, ESL, honors, independent study, teacher certification program. **Credit/placement by examination:** CLEP, institutional tests. 12 credit hours maximum toward associate degree. **Support services:** Learning center, pre-admission summer program, remedial instruction, study skills assistance, tutoring, writing center.

Majors. **Architecture:** Landscape. **Area/ethnic studies:** Women's. **Biology:** General. **Business:** General, accounting, administrative services, business admin, fashion, office management, office technology, office/clerical, real estate. **Computer sciences:** General, programming. **Construction:** Maintenance. **Education:** Early childhood. **Engineering:** General. **Engineering technology:** Drafting, electrical. **Family/consumer sciences:** Child care. **Foreign languages:** General. **Health:** Medical assistant. **History:** General. **Legal studies:** Court reporting, paralegal. **Liberal arts:** Arts/sciences. **Math:** General. **Parks/recreation:** Facilities management. **Physical sciences:** Chemistry, geology, physics. **Protective services:** Criminal justice. **Psychology:** General. **Social sciences:** General, sociology. **Visual/performing arts:** Art, dramatic, fashion design, interior design.

Computing on campus. 150 workstations in library, computer center. Commuter students can connect to campus network. Online course registration, online library, wireless network available.

Student life. **Freshman orientation:** Available. **Activities:** Bands, choral groups, drama, music ensembles, student government, student newspaper, symphony orchestra, TV station, Vietnamese student association, Unlimited Horizons (handicapped), Descendants of Africa, Latin American student association, Alpha Gamma Sigma, Latter-Day Saints, fashion design, Puente, JC Ministries (Christian).

Athletics. **Intercollegiate:** Baseball M, basketball, cross-country, field hockey W, football (tackle) M, gymnastics W, soccer M, softball W, swimming, tennis, track and field, volleyball, water polo M, wrestling M. **Intramural:** Badminton, basketball, bowling, swimming, tennis, volleyball. **Team name:** Vikings.

Student services. Adult student services, career counseling, student employment services, health services, on-campus daycare, personal counseling, veterans' counselor. **Physically disabled:** Services for visually, speech, hearing impaired. **Transfer:** Re-entry adviser for new students. Transfer center, transfer adviser, college fairs on campus for students transferring to 4-year colleges.

Contact. Phone: (408) 741-2001 Fax: (408) 867-5033
Paula Prichett, Director of Admissions, West Valley College, 14000 Fruitvale Avenue, Saratoga, CA 95070-5698

Western Career College: Antioch

Antioch, California
www.westerncollege.edu **CB code: 3033**

- For-profit 2-year technical college
- Commuter campus in small city

General. Regionally accredited. **Calendar:** Continuous.

Annual costs/financial aid. Tuition and fees range from $16,065 to $43,175 depending on program; certificate program length 30 weeks to 2 years, associate degree slightly over 2 years.

Contact. Phone: (925) 522-7777
Director of Admissions, 2157 Country Hills Drive, Antioch, CA 94531

Western Career College: Citrus Heights
Citrus Heights, California
www.westerncollege.edu

- For-profit 2-year health science and technical college
- Very large city

General. Regionally accredited. **Calendar:** Continuous.

Academics. Credit/placement by examination: CLEP.

Majors. Health: Dental assistant, health care admin, massage therapy, office assistant, pharmacy assistant, sonography, surgical technology, veterinary technology/assistant. **Protective services:** Law enforcement admin.

Contact. Western Career College: Citrus Heights, 7301 Greenback Lane, Suite A, Citrus Heights, CA 95621

Western Career College: Pleasant Hill
Pleasant Hill, California
www.westerncollege.com **CB code: 2922**

- For-profit 2-year health science and technical college
- Commuter campus in small city

General. Regionally accredited. **Enrollment:** 150 degree-seeking undergraduates. **Degrees:** 68 associate awarded. **Calendar:** Continuous. **Full-time faculty:** 5 total. **Part-time faculty:** 53 total.

Basis for selection. CPAT examination important.

Application procedures. Admission: No deadline. $100 fee. Admission notification on a rolling basis. **Financial aid:** No deadline. Applicants notified on a rolling basis.

Academics. Credit/placement by examination: CLEP.

Majors. Health: Dental assistant, medical assistant.

Contact. Phone: (925) 609-6650 Toll-free number: (800) 584-4520
Fax: (925) 609-6666
Lashon Wells, Admissions Director/Executive Director, Western Career College: Pleasant Hill, 380 Civic Drive, Suite 300, Pleasant Hill, CA 94523

Western Career College: Sacramento
Sacramento, California
www.westerncollege.edu **CB code: 2917**

- For-profit 2-year health science and technical college
- Commuter campus in large city

General. Regionally accredited. **Calendar:** Continuous.

Annual costs/financial aid. Tuition/fees (2008-2009): $13,510. Tuition for 15-month associate science degree program: Veterinary Technology $29,336; Medical Assisting $27,534; Medical Administrative Assisting $27,837; Pharmacy Tech $24,355; Massage Therapy $27,132. Books/supplies: $448. Personal expenses: $1,686.

Contact. Phone: (800) 321-2386
7801 Folsom Blvd #210, Sacramento, CA 95826

Western Career College: San Jose
San Jose, California
www.svcollege.com

- For-profit 2-year technical college
- Commuter campus in very large city

General. Regionally accredited. **Calendar:** Continuous.

Annual costs/financial aid. ADD: tuition $16,092, fees $498; ADD-AS: tuition $24,372, fees $1,372; ASHS: tuition $11,385, fees $1,248; CJD: tuition $24,066, fees $2,052; DA: tuition $16,092, fees $290; DAD: tuition $27,477, fees $1,538; DH: tuition $51,972, fees $1,324; GD: tuition $20,115, fees $382; GDD: tuition $27,360, fees $1,256; HIT: tuition $16,092, fees $1,131; HITD: tuition $27,477, fees $2,379; MA: tuition $16,092, fees $387; MAD: tuition $27,477, fees $1,635; MT: tuition $14,751, fees $819; MTD: tuition $26,136, fees $2,067; PTD: tuition $24,066, fees $1,779; ST: tuition $32,863, fees $1,192; STD: tuition $40,108, fees $1,979; VTD: tuition $29,253, fees $1,760; VN: tuition $41,470, fees $1,203; VND: tuition $48,715, fees $1,985; VND-PreRN: tuition $60,993, fees $3,491. Registration fee $100.

Contact. Phone: (408) 360-0840
Admissions Director, 6201 San Ignacio Avenue, San Jose, CA 95119

Western Career College: San Leandro
San Leandro, California
www.westerncollege.edu **CB code: 2918**

- For-profit 2-year health science and technical college
- Commuter campus in small city

General. Regionally accredited. **Calendar:** Continuous.

Annual costs/financial aid. All programs require $100 registration fee. Associate in Criminal Justice (60 weeks): tuition, $24,066; books and uniform, $2,052. Associate in Pharmacy Technology (60 to 80 weeks): tuition, $24,066; books and uniform, $1,779. Associate in Veterinary Technology (86 weeks): tuition, $29,253; books and uniform, $1,760. Students in certificate programs have option to continue and complete associate degree. Following certificate programs are 36 weeks with tuition of $16,092: Dental Assisting (books and uniform, $290); Health Care Administration (books and uniform, $704); Health Information Technology (books and uniform, $1,131). Certificate in Medical Assisting (42 to 50 weeks): tuition, $16,092; books and uniform, $387. Certificate in Massage Therapy (34 weeks): tuition, $14,751; books and uniform, $1,214. Certificate in Vocational Nursing (67 weeks): tuition, $41,470; books and uniform, $1,605. Books/supplies: $448. Personal expenses: $1,686.

Contact. Phone: (510) 276-3888
1555 East 14th Street Suite 500, San Leandro, CA 94578

Western Career College: Stockton
Stockton, California
www.westerncollege.edu

- For-profit 2-year health science, technical and career college
- Small city

General. Regionally accredited. **Enrollment:** 160 degree-seeking undergraduates. **Degrees:** 122 associate awarded. **Location:** 40 miles from Sacramento. **Calendar:** Continuous. **Full-time faculty:** 14 total. **Part-time faculty:** 7 total.

Basis for selection. Admissions decisions are based upon high school diploma (GED or ATB) formal interview with applicant, a completed application and a passing score on an entrance exam.

2008-2009 Annual costs. All programs require $100 registration fee. Associate in Criminal Justice (60 weeks): tuition, $24,066; books and uniform, $2,052. Associate in Pharmacy Technology (60 to 80 weeks): tuition, $24,066; books and uniform, $1,779. Associate in Veterinary Technology (86 weeks): tuition, $29,253; books and uniform, $1,760. Associate in Health Science (30 weeks): tuition, $11,385; books and uniform, $1,248. Certificate in Medical assisting (36 weeks): tuition, $16,092; books and uniform, $387. Certificate in Health Care Administration (36 weeks): tuition, $16,092; books and uniform, $704. Certificate in Massage Therapy (34 weeks): tuition, $14,751; books and uniform, $819.

Application procedures. Admission: No deadline. $100 fee.

Academics. Special study options: Accelerated study. Bachelor's degree programs available on campus. **Credit/placement by examination:** CLEP. **Support services:** Learning center, tutoring.

Majors. Health: Health care admin, massage therapy, medical assistant, pharmacy assistant, veterinary technology/assistant. **Protective services:** Police science.

Computing on campus. 25 workstations in library, computer center. Online library available.

Student life. **Freshman orientation:** Mandatory. **Activities:** Student newspaper.

Contact. Anna Meli, Assistant Director of Admissions, Western Career College: Stockton, 1313 West Robinhood Drive Suite B, Stockton, CA 95207

Westwood College: Los Angeles
Los Angeles, California
www.westwood.edu

- For-profit 2-year technical college
- Very large city

General. Accredited by ACICS. **Enrollment:** 875 degree-seeking undergraduates. **Degrees:** 133 bachelor's, 7 associate awarded; master's offered. **Calendar:** 10-week terms throughout year. **Full-time faculty:** 12 total. **Part-time faculty:** 47 total.

Basis for selection. Open admission. Accuplacer required.

2008-2009 Annual costs. Tuition/fees: $14,028. Per-credit charge: $314. Books/supplies: $1,020.

Application procedures. **Admission:** No deadline. $100 fee. Admission notification on a rolling basis. **Financial aid:** FAFSA required. Applicants notified on a rolling basis.

Academics. **Credit/placement by examination:** CLEP.

Majors. **Business:** Fashion. **Computer sciences:** Programming. **Engineering:** Computer. **Visual/performing arts:** Fashion design, graphic design.

Contact. Phone: (213) 739-9999
Guy Lopatin, Director of Admissions, Westwood College: Los Angeles, 3250 Wilshire Boulevard, Suite 400, Los Angeles, CA 90010

WyoTech: Fremont
Fremont, California
www.wyotech.edu **CB code: 3030**

- For-profit 2-year technical college
- Small city
- Interview required

General. Accredited by ACCSCT. **Enrollment:** 1,077 degree-seeking undergraduates. **Degrees:** 101 associate awarded. **Calendar:** Continuous. **Full-time faculty:** 84 total.

Basis for selection. Satisfactory performance on state-mandated entrance exam required.

2009-2010 Annual costs. Tuition ranges from $13,150 to $34,190 depending on program. Tuition includes books, uniforms, training materials, and supplies. A set of tools will be loaned to the student at no additional charge. Additional $500 materials fee. On-line service fee $200 for AOS Degree programs.

Application procedures. **Admission:** No deadline. No application fee. **Financial aid:** FAFSA required.

Academics. **Credit/placement by examination:** CLEP. **Support services:** Learning center.

Majors. **Mechanic/repair:** General, heating/ac/refrig.

Contact. Phone: (510) 490-6900 Toll-free number: (800) 248-8585
Fax: (510) 490-8599
Sophy Son, Director of Admissions, WyoTech: Fremont, 200 Whitney Place, Fremont, CA 94539

WyoTech: Long Beach
Long Beach, California
www.wyotech.edu/campus/long_beach **CB code: 3162**

- For-profit 2-year health science and technical college
- Commuter campus in large city

General. Accredited by ACCSCT. **Enrollment:** 1,457 degree-seeking undergraduates. **Degrees:** 318 associate awarded. **Calendar:** Continuous. **Full-time faculty:** 62 total. **Part-time faculty:** 16 total.

Basis for selection. Institutional placement assessment examination, interview important.

2008-2009 Annual costs. Costs vary by program. Full program costs: automotive $23,900, electrical $18,400, HVAC $15,900, IET $23,700, massage therapy $15,600, medical assistant $14,000, plumbing $17,400.

Application procedures. **Admission:** No deadline. No application fee. Application fee varies by program.

Academics. **Credit/placement by examination:** CLEP.

Majors. **Construction:** Electrician.

Contact. Phone: (562) 624-9530 Toll-free number: (888) 741-4271
Fax: (562) 437-8111
Claudia Fimbres, Senior Admissions Representative, WyoTech: Long Beach, 2161 Technology Place, Long Beach, CA 90810

Yuba Community College District
Marysville, California
www.yccd.edu **CB code: 4994**

- Public 2-year community college
- Commuter campus in small city

General. Founded in 1927. Regionally accredited. **Enrollment:** 4,891 degree-seeking undergraduates. **Degrees:** 811 associate awarded. **Location:** 56 miles from Sacramento. **Calendar:** Semester, limited summer session. **Full-time faculty:** 135 total. **Part-time faculty:** 375 total. **Special facilities:** Veterinary technical training clinic, manufacturing technology facilities (factory), measurement science/scale repair training facilities. **Partnerships:** Formal partnerships with numerous local businesses.

Transfer out. **Colleges most students transferred to 2008:** California State University: Sacramento, California State University: Chico, University of California: Davis.

Basis for selection. Open admission, but selective for some programs. Limited admission to allied health programs. CPT tests recommended for counseling.

2008-2009 Annual costs. Tuition/fees: $612; $6,042 out-of-state. Per-credit charge: $20 in-state; $201 out-of-state. Books/supplies: $1,566. Personal expenses: $3,024.

Financial aid. **Need-based:** Need-based aid available for part-time students. Work-study available for part-time students. **Non-need-based:** Scholarships awarded for academics, athletics, job skills, minority status, music/drama. **Additional information:** Tuition fee waiver based on Board of Governors Grant.

Application procedures. **Admission:** No deadline. No application fee. Admission notification on a rolling basis beginning on or about 6/1. **Financial aid:** Closing date 3/1. FAFSA required. Applicants notified on a rolling basis starting 4/1.

Academics. **Special study options:** Cooperative education, distance learning, ESL. License preparation in nursing, radiology. **Credit/placement by examination:** CLEP, institutional tests. **Support services:** Learning center, remedial instruction, tutoring.

Majors. **Agriculture:** Business, landscaping, mechanization, ornamental horticulture. **Business:** Accounting, administrative services, business admin, entrepreneurial studies, human resources, taxation. **Communications:** Journalism, media studies. **Computer sciences:** General, computer science. **Education:** Early childhood, physical. **Engineering technology:** Electrical, water quality. **Family/consumer sciences:** Family/community services. **Health:** Medical radiologic technology/radiation therapy, medical transcription, nursing (RN), substance abuse counseling, veterinary technology/assistant. **History:** General. **Liberal arts:** Arts/sciences. **Math:** General. **Mechanic/repair:** General, automotive, electronics/electrical. **Personal/culinary services:** Cosmetology. **Production:** General, sheet metal. **Protective services:** Criminal justice, fire safety technology, police science. **Social sciences:** General. **Visual/performing arts:** Art, dramatic, photography, studio arts.

Most popular majors. Education 31%.

Computing on campus. 300 workstations in library.

Student life. **Freshman orientation:** Available. **Activities:** Bands, choral groups, drama, music ensembles, musical theater, student government, student newspaper, symphony orchestra, AD Nursing Students Association,

Care Club, EOP&S Club DECA/Marketing Club, Christian Students Association, Green Society, Future Teachers of America, Speech Team, Photography Guild, Veterinary Technicians Association.

Athletics. Intercollegiate: Baseball M, basketball, cross-country, football (tackle) M, soccer, softball W, tennis, track and field, volleyball W. **Team name:** 49'ers.

Student services. Adult student services, career counseling, services for economically disadvantaged, student employment services, financial aid counseling, health services, minority student services, on-campus daycare, personal counseling, placement for graduates, veterans' counselor, women's services. **Physically disabled:** Services for visually, speech, hearing impaired. **Transfer:** Transfer adviser, college fairs on campus for students transferring to 4-year colleges.

Contact. E-mail: kpope@yccd.edu
Phone: (530) 741-6720 Fax: (530) 741-6872
Connie Elder, Admissions Registrar, Yuba Community College District, 2088 North Beale Road, Marysville, CA 95901

Colorado

Aims Community College

Greeley, Colorado
www.aims.edu
CB member
CB code: 4204

- Public 2-year community college
- Commuter campus in small city

General. Founded in 1967. Regionally accredited. **Enrollment:** 3,547 degree-seeking undergraduates. **Degrees:** 565 associate awarded. **ROTC:** Air Force. **Location:** 55 miles from Denver. **Calendar:** Semester, extensive summer session. **Full-time faculty:** 93 total. **Part-time faculty:** 237 total.

Student profile.

Out-of-state:	2%	**25 or older:**	80%

Basis for selection. Open admission, but selective for some programs. Special requirements for radiologic technology, police academy and biofeedback programs based on test scores. All students must meet assessment requirement by taking computerized placement test, submitting ACT/SAT scores or showing proof of previous college experience. Interview required of radiologic technology, police academy, biofeedback majors.

2008-2009 Annual costs. Tuition/fees: $2,115; $2,925 out-of-district; $11,085 out-of-state. Per-credit charge: $55 in-district; $82 out-of-district; $354 out-of-state. Books/supplies: $600. Personal expenses: $450.

2007-2008 Financial aid. Need-based: 51% of total undergraduate aid awarded as scholarships/grants, 49% as loans/jobs.

Application procedures. Admission: No deadline. No application fee. Admission notification on a rolling basis. **Financial aid:** Priority date 4/15; no closing date. FAFSA required. Applicants notified on a rolling basis starting 6/1.

Academics. Special study options: Cooperative education, double major, dual enrollment of high school students, independent study, internships, weekend college. **Credit/placement by examination:** AP, CLEP, institutional tests. 48 credit hours maximum toward associate degree. **Support services:** Learning center, remedial instruction, tutoring.

Majors. Agriculture: General, supplies. **Business:** Accounting, administrative services, management information systems, marketing. **Communications technology:** Graphic/printing. **Engineering technology:** Electrical. **Family/consumer sciences:** Child care. **Health:** Medical radiologic technology/radiation therapy. **Liberal arts:** Arts/sciences. **Mechanic/repair:** Auto body. **Protective services:** Fire safety technology, law enforcement admin. **Transportation:** Aviation.

Computing on campus. 500 workstations in computer center, student center.

Student life. Activities: Concert band, dance, drama, literary magazine, musical theater, student government, student newspaper.

Athletics. Intramural: Basketball, volleyball.

Student services. Career counseling, student employment services, on-campus daycare, placement for graduates, veterans' counselor. **Physically disabled:** Services for visually, speech, hearing impaired. **Transfer:** Transfer adviser, college fairs on campus for students transferring to 4-year colleges.

Contact. E-mail: admissions.records@aims.edu
Phone: (970) 339-6404 Toll-free number: (800) 301-5388
Stuart Thomas, Director of Admissions, Aims Community College, 5401 West 20th Street, Greeley, CO 80632

Arapahoe Community College

Littleton, Colorado
www.arapahoe.edu
CB code: 4014

- Public 2-year community college
- Commuter campus in large town

General. Founded in 1965. Regionally accredited. **Enrollment:** 5,250 degree-seeking undergraduates; 1,966 non-degree-seeking students. **Degrees:** 506 associate awarded. **ROTC:** Army, Air Force. **Location:** 10 miles from Denver. **Calendar:** Semester, limited summer session. **Full-time faculty:** 97 total; 6% minority, 63% women. **Part-time faculty:** 369 total; 7% minority, 55% women. **Class size:** 71% < 20, 29% 20-39, less than 1% 50-99. **Partnerships:** Formal partnerships with National Cable Telecommunications Institute, Swedish Medical Center, Porter Adventist Hospital, Skyridge Medical Center.

Student profile. Among degree-seeking undergraduates, 1,002 enrolled as first-time, first-year students, 620 transferred in from other institutions.

Part-time:	68%	**Hispanic American:**	11%
Out-of-state:	7%	**Native American:**	1%
Women:	64%	**International:**	1%
African American:	4%	**25 or older:**	57%
Asian American:	3%		

Transfer out. Colleges most students transferred to 2008: University of Colorado at Denver, Colorado State University, University of Northern Colorado, Colorado School of Mines, Adams State College.

Basis for selection. Open admission, but selective for some programs. Allied health, nursing, automotive, legal assistant, and law enforcement programs require interviews and/or test scores.

2008-2009 Annual costs. Tuition/fees: $2,631; $11,455 out-of-state. Per-credit charge: $81 in-state; $375 out-of-state. In-state tuition based upon assumption of Colorado Opportunity Fund waiver of $92 per-credit-hour. Books/supplies: $850.

2007-2008 Financial aid. Need-based: Need-based aid available for part-time students. Work-study available nights, weekends and for part-time students. **Non-need-based:** Scholarships awarded for academics, leadership, state residency.

Application procedures. Admission: No deadline. No application fee. Admission notification on a rolling basis. Closing date for nursing applicants February 4. **Financial aid:** Priority date 5/1; no closing date. FAFSA, institutional form required. Applicants notified on a rolling basis starting 5/1; must reply within 3 week(s) of notification.

Academics. Special study options: Accelerated study, cooperative education, distance learning, double major, dual enrollment of high school students, ESL, independent study, internships, weekend college. License preparation in nursing, occupational therapy, paramedic, physical therapy, real estate. **Credit/placement by examination:** AP, CLEP, IB, institutional tests. No more than half of required credit can be fulfilled through credit for prior learning. **Support services:** GED preparation and test center, learning center, pre-admission summer program, reduced course load, remedial instruction, study skills assistance, tutoring, writing center.

Majors. Business: Accounting technology, administrative services, banking/financial services, hospitality admin, international, management information systems, marketing, office management, selling. **Communications technology:** General. **Computer sciences:** Data entry, LAN/WAN management, networking, web page design. **Construction:** General, building inspection. **Engineering technology:** General, architectural, computer, electrical, manufacturing. **Family/consumer sciences:** Child development. **Health:** Clinical lab technology, medical records technology, nursing (RN), occupational therapy assistant, office admin, physical therapy assistant. **Legal studies:** Paralegal. **Liberal arts:** Arts/sciences. **Mechanic/repair:** Automotive. **Parks/recreation:** Health/fitness. **Personal/culinary services:** Mortuary science. **Protective services:** Law enforcement admin. **Visual/performing arts:** Graphic design, interior design.

Most popular majors. Health sciences 23%, liberal arts 39%, personal/culinary services 6%, visual/performing arts 11%.

Computing on campus. 110 workstations in library, computer center, student center. Commuter students can connect to campus network. Online course registration, online library, helpline, wireless network available.

Student life. Freshman orientation: Mandatory. Preregistration for classes offered. **Activities:** Bands, choral groups, drama, music ensembles, student government, student newspaper, Phi Theta Kappa, Diversity Council, Ron Paul Society.

Athletics. Team name: Coyotes.

Student services. Adult student services, career counseling, services for economically disadvantaged, student employment services, financial aid counseling, minority student services, on-campus daycare, placement for graduates, veterans' counselor. **Physically disabled:** Services for visually, speech, hearing impaired. **Learning disabled:** Comprehensive services available.

Transfer: Pre-admission transcript evaluation for new students. Transfer adviser, college fairs on campus for students transferring to 4-year colleges.

Contact. E-mail: admissions@arapahoe.edu
Phone: (303) 797-5621 Fax: (303) 797-5970
Darcy Briggs-Jackson, Director of Admissions and Records, Arapahoe Community College, PO Box 9002, Littleton, CO 80160-9002

Bel-Rea Institute of Animal Technology

Denver, Colorado
www.bel-rea.com **CB code: 0928**

- For-profit 2-year technical college
- Commuter campus in very large city

General. Accredited by ACCSCT. **Enrollment:** 645 degree-seeking undergraduates. **Degrees:** 248 associate awarded. **Calendar:** Continuous. **Full-time faculty:** 25 total. **Part-time faculty:** 5 total.

Transfer out. Colleges most students transferred to 2008: University of Denver.

Basis for selection. Interview most important, followed by school achievement record. Recommendations considered. Minimum 2.5 GPA or GED required. Applicants with below 2.5 GPA or without GED must take entrance exam.

High school preparation. As much science and math as possible recommended. Algebra and chemistry recommended.

2008-2009 Annual costs. Tuition for full associate program $22,750 including fees. Books/supplies: $1,500. Personal expenses: $1,100.

Financial aid. All financial aid based on need.

Application procedures. Admission: No deadline. No application fee. Admission notification on a rolling basis. **Financial aid:** Priority date 8/31; no closing date. FAFSA required. Applicants notified on a rolling basis starting 8/15.

Academics. Students intern at college-affiliated emergency veterinary hospital. **Special study options:** Internships. **Credit/placement by examination:** CLEP. **Support services:** Reduced course load, study skills assistance, tutoring.

Majors. Health: Veterinary technology/assistant.

Computing on campus. PC or laptop required. 20 workstations in student center.

Student life. Freshman orientation: Available. **Activities:** Student government.

Student services. Career counseling, student employment services, personal counseling, placement for graduates, veterans' counselor.

Contact. E-mail: kaufman@bel-rea.com
Phone: (303) 751-8700 Toll-free number: (800) 950-8001
Fax: (303) 751-9969
Paulette Kaufman, Director, Bel-Rea Institute of Animal Technology, 1681 South Dayton Street, Denver, CO 80247

Boulder College of Massage Therapy

Boulder, Colorado
www.bcmt.org

- Private 2-year health science college
- Residential campus in small city
- Application essay, interview required

General. Accredited by ACCSCT. **Enrollment:** 185 degree-seeking undergraduates. **Degrees:** 29 associate awarded. **Location:** 30 miles from Denver. **Calendar:** Quarter, extensive summer session. **Full-time faculty:** 2 total. **Part-time faculty:** 38 total; 10% have terminal degrees. **Class size:** 97% < 20, 3% 20-39. **Special facilities:** Student massage therapy clinic, wellness bookstore, spa classroom.

Basis for selection. Open admission, but selective for some programs. Health history form required.

2008-2009 Annual costs. Program costs range from $13,700-$17,500.

Financial aid. All financial aid based on need. Need-based aid available for part-time students.

Application procedures. Admission: No deadline. $75 fee, may be waived for applicants with need. Application must be submitted on paper. Admission notification on a rolling basis. **Financial aid:** No deadline. FAFSA required.

Academics. Special study options: Honors, internships. **Credit/placement by examination:** CLEP. **Support services:** Learning center, reduced course load, study skills assistance, tutoring.

Majors. Health: Massage therapy.

Computing on campus. 10 workstations in library, computer center. Online library, wireless network available.

Student life. Freshman orientation: Mandatory. Preregistration for classes offered. Held Monday prior to start of quarter. **Activities:** Student government.

Student services. Adult student services, alcohol/substance abuse counseling, career counseling, services for economically disadvantaged, student employment services, financial aid counseling, personal counseling, placement for graduates, veterans' counselor. **Physically disabled:** Services for visually, speech, hearing impaired.

Contact. E-mail: admissions@bcmt.org
Phone: (303) 530-2100 Toll-free number: (800) 442-5131
Fax: (303) 530-2204
Director of Marketing and Admissions, Boulder College of Massage Therapy, 6255 Longbow Drive, Boulder, CO 80301

Cambridge College

Aurora, Colorado
www.cambridgecollege.com **CB code: 3201**

- For-profit 2-year technical college
- Commuter campus in small city
- Interview required

General. Accredited by ACCSCT. **Enrollment:** 585 degree-seeking undergraduates. **Degrees:** 170 associate awarded. **Calendar:** Continuous, extensive summer session. **Full-time faculty:** 35 total.

Basis for selection. Interview most important. Entrance exam required for students out of high school more than 6 months.

2008-2009 Annual costs. Tuition for associate degree programs ranges from $22,950 to $24,500 depending on program; tuition for diploma programs ranges from $11,550 to $23,550. Items such as books, uniforms and other fees are included in the total cost.

Financial aid. All financial aid based on need.

Application procedures. Admission: No deadline. $50 fee ($150 out-of-state). Admission notification on a rolling basis. **Financial aid:** No deadline. FAFSA, institutional form required. Applicants notified on a rolling basis.

Academics. Special study options: License preparation in radiology. **Credit/placement by examination:** CLEP. **Support services:** GED preparation.

Majors. Computer sciences: General. **Health:** Massage therapy, medical assistant, radiologic technology/medical imaging, surgical technology.

Student life. Freshman orientation: Mandatory.

Student services. Adult student services, career counseling, student employment services, financial aid counseling, placement for graduates.

Contact. Phone: (720) 859-7900 Toll-free number: (800) 322-4132
Fax: (303) 338-9701
Allison Sievers, Director of Admissions, Cambridge College, 350 Blackhawk Street, Aurora, CO 80011

CollegeAmerica: Denver

Denver, Colorado
www.collegeamerica.com

- For-profit 2-year technical college
- Commuter campus in very large city

General. Accredited by ACCSCT. **Calendar:** Continuous.

Annual costs/financial aid. Tuition, fees, books, and supplies: $35,300 for Associate degree programs; $62,300 for Bachelor's degree programs. Books/supplies: $101. Personal expenses: $1,000. Need-based financial aid available for full-time students.

Contact. Phone: (303) 691-9756
Director of Admissions, 1385 South Colorado Boulevard, 5th Floor, Denver, CO 80222-1912

Colorado Mountain College
Glenwood Springs, Colorado
www.coloradomtn.edu **CB code: 4112**

- Public 2-year community and liberal arts college
- Residential campus in small town

General. Founded in 1965. Regionally accredited. Total of 12 campuses. Three residential campuses are Alpine Campus in Steamboat Springs, Spring Valley Campus in Glenwood Springs, and Timberline Campus in Leadville. Commuter campuses in Aspen, Summit, Vail-Eagle Valley in Edwards, Rifle, Breckinridge, Buena Vista. **Enrollment:** 5,200 degree-seeking undergraduates. **Degrees:** 346 associate awarded. **Location:** 160 miles from Denver. **Calendar:** Semester, limited summer session. **Full-time faculty:** 80 total. **Part-time faculty:** 270 total. **Special facilities:** Outdoor education center, farm for veterinarian technician program, hot springs, climbing wall, ice wall, community theater.

Student profile.

Out-of-state:	10%	**25 or older:**	68%

Transfer out. Colleges most students transferred to 2008: University of Colorado-Boulder, Colorado State University, Mesa State University, Western State College, Fort Lewis College.

Basis for selection. Open admission, but selective for some programs. Special requirements for nursing applicants. Testing requirements for veterinary technology, photography, outdoor recreation leadership, culinary arts, paramedic, and ski area operations. SAT or ACT recommended for placement and counseling. College placement test may be used in place of SAT or ACT.

2008-2009 Annual costs. Tuition/fees: $1,550; $2,450 out-of-district; $7,250 out-of-state. Per-credit charge: $45 in-district; $75 out-of-district; $235 out-of-state. Room/board: $7,040. Books/supplies: $650. Personal expenses: $2,050.

2007-2008 Financial aid. All financial aid based on need. Need-based aid available for part-time students. Work-study available nights, weekends and for part-time students.

Application procedures. Admission: No deadline. No application fee. Application must be submitted on paper. Admission notification on a rolling basis. **Financial aid:** Priority date 3/31; no closing date. FAFSA required. Applicants notified on a rolling basis starting 5/15; must reply within 4 week(s) of notification.

Academics. Special study options: Distance learning, dual enrollment of high school students, independent study, internships, liberal arts/career combination, study abroad. License preparation in nursing. **Credit/placement by examination:** AP, CLEP, IB, institutional tests. 30 credit hours maximum toward associate degree. Also recognize and accept exam results for DANTES, Excelsior, Institutional Challenge Exams, and credit for life experiences. **Support services:** GED preparation and test center, learning center, reduced course load, remedial instruction, study skills assistance, tutoring.

Majors. Agriculture: Animal health, food processing, food science, soil science. **Biology:** General. **Business:** General, accounting, business admin, hospitality admin, hotel/motel admin, management information systems, real estate, resort management. **Communications:** Photojournalism. **Communications technology:** Animation/special effects, graphic/printing, graphics, photo/film/video. **Computer sciences:** General, applications programming, computer graphics, information technology, networking, programming. **Conservation:** General, forestry, management/policy. **Education:** General, bilingual. **Engineering:** General, mechanical. **Health:** Nursing (RN), prenursing, veterinary technology/assistant. **Interdisciplinary:** Accounting/computer science, biological/physical sciences, natural sciences, science/society. **Legal studies:** Prelaw. **Liberal arts:** Arts/sciences. **Math:** General. **Parks/recreation:** General, facilities management. **Personal/culinary services:** General, chef training, culinary arts, food prep, restaurant/catering. **Physical sciences:** Chemistry, geology. **Protective services:** Criminal justice, firefighting. **Social sciences:** General. **Visual/performing arts:** General, art, commercial photography, commercial/advertising art, design, dramatic, graphic design, photography.

Computing on campus. 30 workstations in dormitories, library, computer center, student center. Dormitories wired for high-speed internet access and linked to campus network. Online library, helpline, wireless network available.

Student life. Freshman orientation: Available. Preregistration for classes offered. Fee charged for some orientation activities. **Policies:** All students living on-campus must follow housing policies. **Housing:** Guaranteed on-campus for freshmen. Coed dorms, special housing for disabled, wellness housing available. $300 partly refundable deposit, deadline 7/1. **Activities:** Dance, drama, musical theater, student government, student newspaper.

Athletics. NJCAA. **Intercollegiate:** Skiing, soccer. **Intramural:** Basketball, cross-country, skiing, soccer, softball, volleyball. **Team name:** Eagles.

Student services. Adult student services, career counseling, student employment services, financial aid counseling, health services, personal counseling, placement for graduates, veterans' counselor. **Physically disabled:** Services for visually, speech, hearing impaired. **Transfer:** Transfer center, transfer adviser, college fairs on campus for students transferring to 4-year colleges.

Contact. E-mail: joinus@coloradomtn.edu
Phone: (970) 947-8327 Toll-free number: (800) 621-8559 ext. 8327
Fax: (970) 947-8324
Bill Sommers, Director of Pre-Enrollment Services, Collegewide, Colorado Mountain College, 831 Grand Avenue, Glenwood Springs, CO 81601

Colorado Northwestern Community College
Rangely, Colorado
www.cncc.edu **CB code: 4665**

- Public 2-year community college
- Residential campus in rural community

General. Founded in 1962. Regionally accredited. Courses also offered at campus in Craig and 3 off-campus sites in Meeker, Hayden, Oak Creek. **Enrollment:** 1,000 degree-seeking undergraduates. **Degrees:** 115 associate awarded. **Location:** 300 miles from Denver, 90 miles from Grand Junction. **Calendar:** Semester, limited summer session. **Full-time faculty:** 34 total. **Part-time faculty:** 69 total. **Class size:** 87% < 20, 13% 20-39. **Special facilities:** Flight simulator, firearms training simulator, cadaver lab.

Transfer out. Colleges most students transferred to 2008: University of Northern Colorado, Colorado State University, Mesa State College.

Basis for selection. Open admission, but selective for some programs. Selective admissions to dental hygiene and nursing. Both programs have application deadline and pre-requisite requirements. Interview required of dental hygiene majors.

High school preparation. Biological science and/or chemistry required for dental hygiene. Math/science desirable for aviation technology and aviation maintenance.

2008-2009 Annual costs. Tuition/fees: $2,648; $5,408 out-of-state. Per-credit charge: $81 in-state; $173 out-of-state. In-state tuition based upon assumption of Colorado Opportunity Fund waiver of $92 per-credit-hour. Room/board: $5,650. Books/supplies: $1,000. Personal expenses: $1,650.

2007-2008 Financial aid. Need-based: Need-based aid available for part-time students. Work-study available nights, weekends and for part-time students. **Non-need-based:** Scholarships awarded for academics, athletics, state residency.

Application procedures. Admission: No deadline. No application fee. Admission notification on a rolling basis. Application closing date for dental hygiene program 2/15. **Financial aid:** Priority date 5/1; no closing date. FAFSA, institutional form required. Applicants notified on a rolling basis starting 5/15; must reply within 4 week(s) of notification.

Academics. Special study options: Distance learning, dual enrollment of high school students, independent study, internships, student-designed major. Bachelor's degree programs available on campus. License preparation in aviation, dental hygiene, nursing. **Credit/placement by examination:** AP, CLEP, institutional tests. 30 credit hours maximum toward associate degree. **Support services:** GED preparation and test center, learning center, remedial instruction, study skills assistance, tutoring, writing center.

Majors. Business: Entrepreneurial studies, management information systems, office management. **Family/consumer sciences:** Child care. **Health:** Dental hygiene. **Legal studies:** Paralegal. **Liberal arts:** Arts/sciences. **Mechanic/repair:** Aircraft. **Protective services:** Law enforcement admin. **Transportation:** Aviation.

Computing on campus. 54 workstations in dormitories, library, computer center. Dormitories wired for high-speed internet access and linked to campus network. Online course registration, online library, wireless network available.

Student life. Freshman orientation: Mandatory, $45 fee. Preregistration for classes offered. Two sessions in July, one in August. **Housing:** Guaranteed on-campus for freshmen. Coed dorms, special housing for disabled, apartments available. $100 deposit. **Activities:** Concert band, choral groups, drama, music ensembles, musical theater, student government, student newspaper.

Athletics. NJCAA. **Intercollegiate:** Baseball M, basketball, softball W, volleyball W. **Intramural:** Basketball, football (non-tackle), golf, racquetball, soccer, softball, table tennis, volleyball. **Team name:** Spartans.

Student services. Adult student services, alcohol/substance abuse counseling, career counseling, student employment services, financial aid counseling, personal counseling, placement for graduates, veterans' counselor. **Physically disabled:** Services for visually, hearing impaired. **Transfer:** Preadmission transcript evaluation for new students. Transfer adviser, college fairs on campus for students transferring to 4-year colleges.

Contact. E-mail: lisa.lefevre@cncc.edu
Phone: (970) 675-3218 Toll-free number: (800) 562-1105
Fax: (970) 975-3343
Tresa England, Director of Student Services/Registrar, Colorado Northwestern Community College, 500 Kennedy Drive, Rangely, CO 81648

Colorado School of Healing Arts
Lakewood, Colorado
www.csha.net

- For-profit 2-year career college
- Commuter campus in small city
- Application essay, interview required

General. Accredited by ACCSCT. **Enrollment:** 196 degree-seeking undergraduates. **Degrees:** 32 associate awarded. **Location:** 7 miles from Denver. **Calendar:** Quarter, extensive summer session. **Part-time faculty:** 34 total. **Class size:** 79% < 20, 21% 20-39.

Basis for selection. Open admission. **Homeschooled:** Interview required.

2008-2009 Annual costs. Tuition/fees: $11,275. Per-credit charge: $150. Books, massage table package, materials fees, and insurance are included in required fees. Books/supplies: $1,164. Personal expenses: $300.

2007-2008 Financial aid. All financial aid based on need. Need-based aid available for part-time students.

Application procedures. Admission: No deadline. $50 fee. Application must be submitted on paper. Admission notification on a rolling basis. **Financial aid:** No deadline. FAFSA required.

Academics. Special study options: Accelerated study. **Credit/placement by examination:** CLEP. **Support services:** Learning center, tutoring.

Majors. Health: Massage therapy.

Computing on campus. 2 workstations in library.

Student life. Freshman orientation: Mandatory. Preregistration for classes offered. Four-hour program held prior to start of quarter.

Student services. Career counseling, financial aid counseling.

Contact. E-mail: maureen@csha.net
Phone: (303) 986-2320 Toll-free number: (800) 233-7114
Fax: (303) 980-6594
Patty Higginbotham, Admissions Representative, Colorado School of Healing Arts, 7655 West Mississippi, Suite 100, Lakewood, CO 80226

Colorado School of Trades
Lakewood, Colorado
www.schooloftrades.com **CB code: 3211**

- For-profit 2-year technical college
- Small city

General. Accredited by ACCSCT. **Enrollment:** 145 degree-seeking undergraduates. **Degrees:** 80 associate awarded. **Calendar:** Continuous. **Full-time faculty:** 10 total. **Part-time faculty:** 3 total.

Basis for selection. Open admission.

2008-2009 Annual costs. For gunsmithing program: tuition, $18,000; tools $3,000, miscellaneous $154. Farrier science program is no longer offered.

Application procedures. Admission: No deadline. $25 fee. Admission notification on a rolling basis. **Financial aid:** FAFSA, institutional form required.

Academics. Credit/placement by examination: CLEP.

Majors. Education: Trade/industrial. **Mechanic/repair:** General.

Contact. Phone: (303) 233-4697 Toll-free number: (800) 234-4594
Sunny Duvont-Holt, Director of Admissions, Colorado School of Trades, 1575 Hoyt Street, Lakewood, CO 80215

Community College of Aurora
Aurora, Colorado
www.ccaurora.edu **CB code: 0969**

- Public 2-year community college
- Commuter campus in large city

General. Founded in 1983. Regionally accredited. **Enrollment:** 1,285 full-time, degree-seeking students. **Degrees:** 356 associate awarded. **Calendar:** Semester, extensive summer session. **Full-time faculty:** 42 total. **Part-time faculty:** 300 total.

Student profile.

Out-of-state:	3%	**Live on campus:**	2%
25 or older:	60%		

Transfer out. Colleges most students transferred to 2008: Metropolitan State University, University of Colorado Denver, Colorado State University, University of Northern Colorado.

Basis for selection. Open admission.

2008-2009 Annual costs. Tuition/fees: $2,576; $11,400 out-of-state. Per-credit charge: $81 in-state; $375 out-of-state. In-state tuition based upon assumption of Colorado Opportunity Fund waiver of $92 per-credit-hour. Books/supplies: $400.

Financial aid. Need-based: Need-based aid available for part-time students. Work-study available nights and for part-time students.

Application procedures. Admission: No deadline. No application fee. Admission notification on a rolling basis. **Financial aid:** Priority date 6/1; no closing date. FAFSA, institutional form required. Applicants notified on a rolling basis starting 7/15.

Academics. Special study options: Cooperative education, cross-registration, distance learning, ESL, internships, study abroad, weekend college. License preparation in paramedic. **Credit/placement by examination:** CLEP, IB. 30 credit hours maximum toward associate degree. **Support services:** GED preparation, learning center, remedial instruction, tutoring.

Majors. Business: General, accounting, administrative services, banking/financial services, business admin, management information systems, marketing, office technology, sales/distribution. **Communications technology:** Graphic/printing. **Computer sciences:** General, information systems. **Construction:** Carpentry, power transmission. **Education:** Early childhood. **Engineering technology:** Drafting, electrical. **Family/consumer sciences:** Child care. **Health:** Medical secretary. **Legal studies:** Legal secretary, paralegal. **Mechanic/repair:** Heating/ac/refrig. **Personal/culinary services:** Culinary arts. **Protective services:** Criminal justice, law enforcement admin.

Computing on campus. 210 workstations in dormitories, library, computer center, student center. Dormitories wired for high-speed internet access and linked to campus network. Commuter students can connect to campus network. Online course registration, online library, repair service available.

Student life. Freshman orientation: Available. Preregistration for classes offered. **Housing:** Guaranteed on-campus for freshmen. Coed dorms available. $150 deposit. **Activities:** Dance, drama, music ensembles, musical theater, student government, student newspaper, black student alliance, Lazos Culturales, Phi Theta Kappa, Phi Alpha Omega, Campus Crusade for Christ.

Athletics. Intramural: Basketball, softball, tennis, volleyball.

Student services. Career counseling, student employment services, financial aid counseling, personal counseling, veterans' counselor. **Physically disabled:** Services for visually, speech, hearing impaired. **Transfer:** Transfer adviser, college fairs on campus for students transferring to 4-year colleges.

Contact. Phone: (303) 360-4700 Fax: (303) 361-7432
Kristen Cusack, Registrar, Community College of Aurora, 16000 East CentreTech Parkway, Aurora, CO 80011-9036

Community College of Denver
Denver, Colorado
www.ccd.edu **CB code: 4137**

- Public 2-year community college
- Commuter campus in very large city

General. Founded in 1970. Regionally accredited. Library, student center and physical education facilities shared with Metropolitan State College at Denver and University of Colorado/Health Sciences Center at Denver. **Enrollment:** 5,260 degree-seeking undergraduates; 2,986 non-degree-seeking students. **Degrees:** 432 associate awarded. **ROTC:** Army. **Calendar:** Semester, limited summer session. **Full-time faculty:** 80 total; 20% minority, 64% women. **Part-time faculty:** 314 total; 24% minority, 56% women. **Class size:** 56% < 20, 44% 20-39, less than 1% 40-49.

Student profile. Among degree-seeking undergraduates, 61% enrolled in a transfer program, 39% enrolled in a vocational program, 2,100 enrolled as first-time, first-year students.

Part-time:	68%	**Hispanic American:**	27%
Out-of-state:	5%	**Native American:**	1%
Women:	62%	**International:**	6%
African American:	16%	**25 or older:**	51%
Asian American:	6%		

Transfer out. Colleges most students transferred to 2008: Metropolitan State College of Denver, University of Colorado at Denver.

Basis for selection. Open admission, but selective for some programs. Special requirements for health occupations and computer information systems programs.

2008-2009 Annual costs. Tuition/fees: $2,942; $11,766 out-of-state. Per-credit charge: $81 in-state; $375 out-of-state. In-state tuition based upon assumption of Colorado Opportunity Fund waiver of $92 per-credit-hour. Books/supplies: $1,163. Personal expenses: $2,547.

2007-2008 Financial aid. Need-based: Need-based aid available for part-time students. **Non-need-based:** Scholarships awarded for academics, leadership, state residency.

Application procedures. Admission: Priority date 8/1; no deadline. No application fee. Admission notification on a rolling basis. **Financial aid:** Priority date 3/1; no closing date. FAFSA, institutional form required.

Academics. Special study options: Accelerated study, cooperative education, cross-registration, distance learning, double major, dual enrollment of high school students, ESL, independent study, internships, liberal arts/career combination, study abroad, weekend college. **Credit/placement by examination:** AP, CLEP, institutional tests. 45 credit hours maximum toward associate degree. **Support services:** GED preparation and test center, learning center, pre-admission summer program, reduced course load, remedial instruction, study skills assistance, tutoring, writing center.

Majors. Biology: Biomedical sciences. **Business:** Accounting technology, administrative services, business admin, management information systems. **Computer sciences:** General, applications programming. **Education:** Teacher assistance. **Engineering technology:** Drafting, heat/ac/refrig. **Family/consumer sciences:** Child development. **Health:** Dental hygiene, electroencephalograph technology, health aide, nursing (RN), radiologic technology/medical imaging, veterinary technology/assistant. **Legal studies:** Paralegal. **Liberal arts:** Arts/sciences. **Parks/recreation:** General, health/fitness. **Production:** Welding. **Protective services:** Security services. **Public administration:** Human services. **Visual/performing arts:** Graphic design.

Most popular majors. Health sciences 51%, liberal arts 44%.

Computing on campus. 1,032 workstations in library, computer center, student center. Commuter students can connect to campus network. Online course registration available.

Student life. Freshman orientation: Mandatory. **Housing:** Dormitory housing available at Lowry campus through cooperative agreement. **Activities:** Choral groups, drama, student government, student newspaper, Mexican-American student organization, African-American student organization, Amnesty International, nursing club.

Student services. Adult student services, career counseling, services for economically disadvantaged, student employment services, financial aid counseling, health services, legal services, minority student services, on-campus daycare, personal counseling, placement for graduates, veterans' counselor, women's services. **Physically disabled:** Services for visually, hearing impaired. **Transfer:** Re-entry adviser, pre-admission transcript evaluation for new students. Transfer center, transfer adviser, college fairs on campus for students transferring to 4-year colleges.

Contact. E-mail: enrollment_services@ccd.edu
Phone: (303) 556-2420 Fax: (303) 556-2431
Michael Rusk, Dean of Students, Community College of Denver, Campus Box 201, PO Box 173363, Denver, CO 80217-3363

Concorde Career College: Aurora
Aurora, Colorado
www.concorde.edu/denver

- For-profit 2-year health science college
- Large city

General. Accredited by ACCSCT. **Enrollment:** 625 degree-seeking undergraduates. **Degrees:** 117 associate awarded. **Calendar:** Continuous. **Full-time faculty:** 45 total. **Part-time faculty:** 20 total.

Basis for selection. Wonderlic and CPAT exams used.

Application procedures. Admission: No deadline. No application fee. Admission notification on a rolling basis.

Academics. Credit/placement by examination: CLEP.

Majors. Health: Medical radiologic technology/radiation therapy, nursing (RN), respiratory therapy technology.

Contact. Phone: (303) 861-1151
Jimmy Henig, Director of Admissions, Concorde Career College: Aurora, 111 North Havana Street, Aurora, CO 80010

Denver Academy of Court Reporting
Denver, Colorado
www.dacr.org **CB code: 3561**

- For-profit 2-year college of court reporting
- Large city
- Interview required

General. Accredited by ACICS. **Enrollment:** 150 degree-seeking undergraduates. **Degrees:** 7 associate awarded. **Calendar:** Quarter, extensive summer session. **Full-time faculty:** 10 total. **Part-time faculty:** 10 total.

Student profile.

Women:	87%	**25 or older:**	50%

Basis for selection. Open admission. Must meet with an admissions representative, tour the facility, and inspect the equipment used in the training program.

2008-2009 Annual costs. Tuition/fees: $7,470. Day program tuition $2,300 per quarter, evening program $2,200 per quarter. $150 enrollment fee. $190 per quarter technology fee. Books/supplies: $450.

Application procedures. Admission: No deadline. $175 fee.

Academics. **Special study options:** Internships. **Credit/placement by examination:** CLEP.

Majors. **Legal studies:** Court reporting.

Computing on campus. Online library, wireless network available.

Student life. **Freshman orientation:** Mandatory.

Student services. **Transfer:** Pre-admission transcript evaluation for new students.

Contact. E-mail: info@dacr.org
Phone: (303) 427-5292 Fax: (303) 427-5383
Director of Admissions, Denver Academy of Court Reporting, 9051 Harlan Street, Unit #20, Westminster, CO 80031

Everest College: Aurora
Aurora, Colorado
www.cci.edu **CB code: 3568**

- For-profit 2-year branch campus and technical college
- Commuter campus in large city
- Interview required

General. Accredited by ACICS. Small interactive learning environment. **Enrollment:** 65 degree-seeking undergraduates. **Degrees:** 64 associate awarded. **Location:** 15 miles from Denver. **Calendar:** Continuous, extensive summer session. **Full-time faculty:** 11 total. **Part-time faculty:** 15 total.

Transfer out. **Colleges most students transferred to 2008:** University of Phoenix, Florida Metropolitan University.

Basis for selection. Open admission. **Homeschooled:** Students without high school diploma or equivalent may enroll, but must receive specific score on admissions test. **Learning Disabled:** Must provide documentation of disability.

2008-2009 Annual costs. $352 per credit hour for all linear programs; $500 estimated cost per term for books, kits and supplies. Books/supplies: $900.

2008-2009 Financial aid. All financial aid based on need. Need-based aid available for part-time students. Work-study available nights and for part-time students.

Application procedures. **Admission:** No deadline. No application fee. Admission notification on a rolling basis. **Financial aid:** No deadline. FAFSA, institutional form required. Applicants notified on a rolling basis; must reply within 4 week(s) of notification.

Academics. **Special study options:** Accelerated study, cooperative education, distance learning, double major, honors, independent study, internships, liberal arts/career combination. **Credit/placement by examination:** AP, CLEP. 48 credit hours maximum toward associate degree. **Support services:** Learning center, reduced course load, remedial instruction, study skills assistance, tutoring.

Majors. **Business:** Accounting, business admin. **Computer sciences:** General. **Legal studies:** General, paralegal. **Protective services:** Criminal justice.

Most popular majors. Business/marketing 48%, computer/information sciences 14%, legal studies 39%.

Computing on campus. 6 workstations in library. Commuter students can connect to campus network. Online library, repair service available.

Student life. **Freshman orientation:** Mandatory. Preregistration for classes offered. **Activities:** Student newspaper.

Student services. Career counseling, student employment services, financial aid counseling, placement for graduates. **Physically disabled:** Services for speech, hearing impaired. **Transfer:** Re-entry adviser, pre-admission transcript evaluation for new students. Transfer adviser for students transferring to 4-year colleges.

Contact. E-mail: phardy@cci.edu
Phone: (303) 745-6244 Fax: (303) 745-6245
John Heckman, Director of Admissions, Everest College: Aurora, 14280 East Jewell Suite 100, Aurora, CO 80012

Everest College: Colorado Springs
Colorado Springs, Colorado
www.cci.edu **CB code: 0934**

- For-profit 2-year business and junior college
- Commuter campus in large city
- Interview required

General. Founded in 1897. Accredited by ACICS. **Enrollment:** 454 degree-seeking undergraduates. **Degrees:** 105 associate awarded. **Location:** 70 miles from Denver. **Calendar:** Quarter, extensive summer session. **Full-time faculty:** 3 total. **Part-time faculty:** 35 total.

Basis for selection. Open admission. Admissions based on high school diploma, GED, or ATB. 120 CPAt required for diploma or GED holders; 128 CPAt required for ATB candidates. 15 ACT or 700 SAT (exclusive of Writing) also accepted.

2008-2009 Annual costs. Accounting, Business Administration, Administrative Assistant, Criminal Justice and Paralegal programs are $328 per credit hour. CIS ? Networking, Programming and Web Design are $330 per credit hour. Business Accounting is $331 per credit hour. Diploma programs for Medical Assisting, Medical Administrative Assistant and Medical Billing and Coding are $13,140 (includes books) for the entire 8-month program. No additional fees. Books/supplies: $1,025.

Financial aid. **Need-based:** Need-based aid available for part-time students. Work-study available nights and for part-time students.

Application procedures. **Admission:** No deadline. No application fee. Application must be submitted on paper. Admission notification on a rolling basis. **Financial aid:** No deadline. FAFSA, institutional form required. Applicants notified on a rolling basis starting 7/1.

Academics. **Special study options:** Distance learning, double major, dual enrollment of high school students, independent study, internships, liberal arts/career combination. **Credit/placement by examination:** AP, CLEP, institutional tests. **Support services:** Tutoring.

Majors. **Business:** Accounting, business admin. **Computer sciences:** General, LAN/WAN management, networking. **Health:** Medical assistant, medical secretary. **Legal studies:** Legal secretary, paralegal. **Protective services:** Criminal justice.

Most popular majors. Business/marketing 22%, computer/information sciences 7%, health sciences 28%, legal studies 43%.

Computing on campus. PC or laptop required. 174 workstations in library, computer center.

Student life. **Freshman orientation:** Mandatory. Preregistration for classes offered. **Activities:** Student government, student newspaper.

Student services. Career counseling, student employment services, financial aid counseling, personal counseling, placement for graduates, veterans' counselor. **Transfer:** Pre-admission transcript evaluation for new students.

Contact. E-mail: afi@cci.edu
Phone: (719) 638-6580 Fax: (719) 574-4493
Don Webb, Director of Admissions, Everest College: Colorado Springs, 1815 Jet Wing Drive, Colorado Springs, CO 80916

Everest College: Denver
Denver, Colorado
www.cci.edu **CB code: 0349**

- For-profit 2-year junior college
- Commuter campus in very large city

General. Founded in 1895. Accredited by ACICS. **Location:** 7 miles from downtown. **Calendar:** Quarter.

Contact. Phone: (303) 457-2757
Director of Admissions, 9065 Grant Street, Denver, CO 80229

Front Range Community College
Westminster, Colorado
www.frontrange.edu **CB code: 4119**

- Public 2-year community college
- Commuter campus in large city

General. Founded in 1968. Regionally accredited. Additional campuses in Brighton, Boulder County, Larimer County. **Enrollment:** 12,583 degree-seeking undergraduates; 2,687 non-degree-seeking students. **Degrees:** 1,011 associate awarded. **ROTC:** Army, Air Force. **Location:** 12 miles from Denver. **Calendar:** Semester, limited summer session. **Full-time faculty:** 196 total; 3% have terminal degrees, 7% minority, 59% women. **Part-time faculty:** 739 total; 2% have terminal degrees, 6% minority, 57% women. **Class size:** 44% < 20, 56% 20-39, less than 1% 40-49. **Special facilities:** Observatories, city libraries. **Partnerships:** Formal partnerships with local workforce centers for career training or retraining.

Student profile. Among degree-seeking undergraduates, 68% enrolled in a transfer program, 32% enrolled in a vocational program, 2% already have a bachelor's degree or higher, 2,726 enrolled as first-time, first-year students, 931 transferred in from other institutions.

Part-time:	61%	**Asian American:**	4%
Out-of-state:	2%	**Hispanic American:**	12%
Women:	58%	**Native American:**	1%
African American:	2%	**25 or older:**	40%

Transfer out. Colleges most students transferred to 2008: University of Northern Colorado, University of Colorado at Denver, University of Colorado at Boulder, Metropolitan State College, Colorado State University.

Basis for selection. Open admission.

High school preparation. 13 units recommended. Recommended units include English 4, mathematics 3, history 3, science 2 (laboratory 1).

2008-2009 Annual costs. Tuition/fees: $2,715; $11,539 out-of-state. Per-credit charge: $81 in-state; $375 out-of-state. In-state tuition based upon assumption of Colorado Opportunity Fund waiver of $92 per-credit-hour. Books/supplies: $1,198.

2007-2008 Financial aid. Need-based: 40% of total undergraduate aid awarded as scholarships/grants, 60% as loans/jobs. Need-based aid available for part-time students. Work-study available nights, weekends and for part-time students. **Non-need-based:** Scholarships awarded for academics, job skills, leadership, ROTC, state residency.

Application procedures. Admission: No deadline. No application fee. Admission notification on a rolling basis. **Financial aid:** Priority date 5/1; no closing date. FAFSA, institutional form required. Applicants notified on a rolling basis starting 7/1; must reply within 3 week(s) of notification.

Academics. Special study options: Cooperative education, cross-registration, distance learning, double major, dual enrollment of high school students, ESL, honors, independent study, internships, liberal arts/career combination, study abroad, teacher certification program, weekend college. License preparation in dental hygiene, nursing, paramedic. **Credit/placement by examination:** AP, CLEP, institutional tests. 30 credit hours maximum toward associate degree. **Support services:** GED preparation and test center, learning center, remedial instruction, study skills assistance, tutoring.

Majors. Agriculture: Horticulture. **Business:** Accounting technology, hospitality admin, management information systems, office management. **Communications technology:** Animation/special effects. **Conservation:** Wildlife. **Construction:** Masonry. **Engineering technology:** Architectural, drafting, electrical, heat/ac/refrig, manufacturing. **Family/consumer sciences:** Child care. **Foreign languages:** Sign language interpretation. **Health:** Dietician assistant, EMT paramedic, nursing (RN), office assistant, veterinary technology/assistant. **Liberal arts:** Arts/sciences. **Mechanic/repair:** Automotive. **Physical sciences:** General. **Production:** Machine shop technology, welding. **Visual/performing arts:** Interior design. **Other:** Applied technology.

Most popular majors. Business/marketing 8%, health sciences 25%, liberal arts 58%.

Computing on campus. 233 workstations in library, computer center. Commuter students can connect to campus network. Online course registration, helpline, wireless network available.

Student life. Freshman orientation: Available. Preregistration for classes offered. **Activities:** Drama, international student organizations, student government, student newspaper, Interpreters for the Deaf, gay/straight alliance, Students in Free Enterprise, pharmacy tech club, international club, recycling club, Bible club.

Student services. Career counseling, student employment services, financial aid counseling, minority student services, on-campus daycare, personal counseling, veterans' counselor. **Physically disabled:** Services for visually, speech, hearing impaired. **Transfer:** Transfer center, college fairs on campus for students transferring to 4-year colleges.

Contact. Phone: (303) 404-5414 Fax: (303) 404-5150
Yolonda Espinoza, Registrar, Front Range Community College, 3645 West 112th Avenue, Westminster, CO 80031

Institute of Business & Medical Careers

Fort Collins, Colorado
www.ibmc.edu **CB code: 3566**

- For-profit 2-year technical college
- Residential campus in small city
- Application essay, interview required

General. Accredited by ACICS. Additional campuses in Greeley and Cheyenne, WY. **Enrollment:** 765 degree-seeking undergraduates. **Degrees:** 221 associate awarded. **Location:** 60 miles from Denver; 45 miles from Cheyenne, WY. **Calendar:** Continuous. **Full-time faculty:** 20 total; 15% minority, 85% women. **Part-time faculty:** 55 total; 6% minority, 73% women.

Transfer out. Colleges most students transferred to 2008: Colorado Christian University, Front Range Community College, Aims Community College.

Basis for selection. Open admission, but selective for some programs. Institutional entrance exam required for placement. **Homeschooled:** State high school equivalency certificate required.

2008-2009 Annual costs. Tuition/fees: $13,110. Per-credit charge: $285. Books/supplies: $1,400.

Application procedures. Admission: No deadline. $75 fee. Admission notification on a rolling basis.

Academics. Credit/placement by examination: AP, CLEP, institutional tests. Up to 50% of total progam credits may be obtained through transfer or test out. **Support services:** Learning center, reduced course load, study skills assistance, tutoring.

Majors. Business: Business admin.

Computing on campus. 4 workstations in library, student center. Commuter students can connect to campus network. Wireless network available.

Student life. Freshman orientation: Available.

Student services. Career counseling, student employment services, financial aid counseling, placement for graduates. **Transfer:** Pre-admission transcript evaluation for new students.

Contact. E-mail: info@ibmc.edu
Phone: (970) 223-2669 Toll-free number: (800) 495-2669
Karla Alpers, Registrar, Institute of Business & Medical Careers, 3842 South Mason Street, Fort Collins, CO 80525

IntelliTec College

Colorado Springs, Colorado
www.intelliteccollege.com **CB code: 2500**

- For-profit 2-year technical college
- Commuter campus in large city

General. Founded in 1965. Accredited by ACCSCT. **Enrollment:** 500 degree-seeking undergraduates. **Degrees:** 251 associate awarded. **Location:** 68 miles from Denver. **Calendar:** 6-week cycle. Extensive summer session. **Full-time faculty:** 22 total. **Part-time faculty:** 4 total.

Transfer out. Colleges most students transferred to 2008: Pikes Peak Community College, Denver Technical College.

Basis for selection. Open admission.

2008-2009 Annual costs. HVAC $24,177; CNSA $24,969; ATM $24,822; DAS $21,828; DMECH $22,122. Books/supplies: $1,200.

Financial aid. All financial aid based on need. Need-based aid available for part-time students. Work-study available nights.

Application procedures. Admission: No deadline. No application fee. Admission notification on a rolling basis. **Financial aid:** No deadline. FAFSA, institutional form required. Applicants notified on a rolling basis.

Academics. Special study options: Accelerated study, liberal arts/career combination. **Credit/placement by examination:** AP, CLEP. Maximum 50% of required credits may be awarded for prior work and/or life experience. Pre-admission interview required for placement into program. **Support services:** Learning center, tutoring.

Majors. **Computer sciences:** General, computer science, systems analysis. **Engineering technology:** Drafting. **Mechanic/repair:** Electronics/electrical, heating/ac/refrig.

Computing on campus. 125 workstations in library, computer center. Online library, repair service available.

Student life. **Freshman orientation:** Available. Preregistration for classes offered. **Activities:** Student newspaper.

Student services. Adult student services, career counseling, student employment services, financial aid counseling, personal counseling, placement for graduates, veterans' counselor. **Transfer:** Pre-admission transcript evaluation for new students.

Contact. E-mail: admcs@intelliteccollege.com
Phone: (719) 632-7626 Toll-free number: (800) 748-2282
Fax: (719) 632-7451
Mel Glyman, Director of Admissions, IntelliTec College, 2315 East Pikes Peak Avenue, Colorado Springs, CO 80909

IntelliTec College: Grand Junction

Grand Junction, Colorado
www.intelliteccollege.edu **CB code: 2489**

- For-profit 2-year technical college
- Commuter campus in small city
- Interview required

General. Accredited by ACCSCT. **Enrollment:** 152 degree-seeking undergraduates; 86 non-degree-seeking students. **Degrees:** 70 associate awarded. **Location:** 250 miles from Denver, 300 miles from Salt Lake City. **Calendar:** Continuous, extensive summer session. **Full-time faculty:** 20 total. **Part-time faculty:** 10 total.

Student profile. Among degree-seeking undergraduates, 64 enrolled as first-time, first-year students, 75 transferred in from other institutions.

Out-of-state:	2%	**25 or older:**	51%
Women:	70%		

Basis for selection. Open admission.

2008-2009 Annual costs. $200 per-credit-hour charge for all programs. Number of credits required for completion varies by program. Total costs for some programs include: Medical Assistant, $18,200; Massage Therapist, $14,600; Architectural/Structural Drafting, $22,200. Books/supplies: $1,500.

Financial aid. All financial aid based on need.

Application procedures. **Admission:** No deadline. No application fee. Admission notification on a rolling basis. **Financial aid:** No deadline. FAFSA required. Applicants notified on a rolling basis.

Academics. **Special study options:** Cooperative education. **Credit/placement by examination:** CLEP. **Support services:** Learning center, tutoring.

Majors. **Business:** Accounting/business management. **Engineering:** Electrical. **Engineering technology:** Architectural drafting, computer hardware, mechanical drafting, software. **Health:** Medical assistant. **Mechanic/repair:** Automotive.

Computing on campus. 64 workstations in library, computer center.

Student services. Career counseling, student employment services, placement for graduates.

Contact. Phone: (970) 245-8101 Fax: (970) 243-8074
Carol Earnshaw, Director of Admissions, IntelliTec College: Grand Junction, 772 Horizon Drive, Grand Junction, CO 81506

Kaplan College: Denver

Thornton, Colorado
www.kaplancollege.com

- For-profit 2-year technical and career college
- Very large city

General. Accredited by ACCSCT. **Enrollment:** 277 degree-seeking undergraduates. **Degrees:** 35 associate awarded. **Calendar:** Quarter, extensive summer session.

Basis for selection. Open admission, but selective for some programs.

Application procedures. **Admission:** No deadline. $20 fee. **Financial aid:** FAFSA required.

Academics. Paralegal program is ABA certified. **Special study options:** Accelerated study, independent study. **Credit/placement by examination:** CLEP. **Support services:** GED preparation, learning center, study skills assistance, tutoring.

Majors. **Legal studies:** Paralegal. **Protective services:** Law enforcement admin.

Computing on campus. 50 workstations in library, computer center.

Student life. **Freshman orientation:** Mandatory. Preregistration for classes offered.

Student services. Alcohol/substance abuse counseling, personal counseling, women's services.

Contact. Phone: (303) 295-0550 Toll-free number: (800) 848-0550
Fax: (303) 295-0102
Kristine Conlin, Executive Director, Kaplan College: Denver, 500 East 84th Avenue, Suite W-200, Thornton, CO 80229

Lamar Community College

Lamar, Colorado
www.lamarcc.edu **CB code: 4382**

- Public 2-year community college
- Commuter campus in large town

General. Founded in 1937. Regionally accredited. **Enrollment:** 612 degree-seeking undergraduates. **Degrees:** 116 associate awarded. **Location:** 117 miles from Pueblo. **Calendar:** Semester, limited summer session. **Full-time faculty:** 24 total. **Part-time faculty:** 34 total.

Student profile.

Out-of-state:	10%	**Live on campus:**	50%
25 or older:	75%		

Basis for selection. Open admission, but selective for some programs. Admission criteria for horse training management based on riding skills; admission to nursing based on test scores. Interview required of horse training and management, practical nursing majors.

2008-2009 Annual costs. Tuition/fees: $2,812; $5,572 out-of-state. Per-credit charge: $81 in-state; $173 out-of-state. In-state tuition based upon assumption of Colorado Opportunity Fund waiver of $92 per-credit-hour. Room/board: $4,995. Books/supplies: $1,163. Personal expenses: $420.

Financial aid. **Need-based:** Need-based aid available for part-time students.

Application procedures. **Admission:** No application fee. Admission notification on a rolling basis. Applicants to horse training and management and LPN nursing program encouraged to apply early. **Financial aid:** Priority date 4/1; no closing date. FAFSA, institutional form required. Applicants notified on a rolling basis starting 7/1.

Academics. **Special study options:** Cooperative education, dual enrollment of high school students, ESL, independent study, internships, student-designed major. **Credit/placement by examination:** CLEP, institutional tests. 16 credit hours maximum toward associate degree. **Support services:** Learning center, pre-admission summer program, remedial instruction, tutoring.

Majors. **Agriculture:** Agronomy, animal sciences, business, equestrian studies, range science. **Biology:** General. **Business:** General, accounting, administrative services, banking/financial services, business admin, office management. **Communications:** General. **Computer sciences:** Computer science, information systems. **Education:** General. **Family/consumer sciences:** Child care. **Health:** Medical secretary, predental, prepharmacy, preveterinary. **History:** General. **Legal studies:** Legal secretary, prelaw. **Liberal arts:** Arts/sciences. **Math:** General. **Psychology:** General. **Public administration:** Social work. **Social sciences:** General. **Visual/performing arts:** Art.

Computing on campus. 65 workstations in dormitories, library, computer center.

Student life. **Policies:** All single freshmen under age 21 not living with parent, guardian, or relatives must live in dormitory. **Housing:** Guaranteed

Two-Year Colleges

on-campus for freshmen. Coed dorms, single-sex dorms available. **Activities:** Choral groups, dance, drama, student government, student newspaper, Christian athletes, horse and rodeo club, Kosmetiques, LPN association, Phi Beta Lambda, nontraditional students club.

Athletics. NJCAA. **Intercollegiate:** Baseball M, basketball M, volleyball W. **Intramural:** Bowling, golf, softball, tennis, volleyball.

Student services. Career counseling, student employment services, personal counseling. **Transfer:** Transfer adviser, college fairs on campus for students transferring to 4-year colleges.

Contact. E-mail: admissions@lamarcc.edu
Phone: (719) 336-1590
Angela Woodward, Dean of Student Services, Lamar Community College, 2401 South Main Street, Lamar, CO 81052-3999

Lincoln College of Technology: Denver

Denver, Colorado
www.dadc.com
CB code: 3133

- For-profit 2-year technical college
- Very large city

General. Accredited by ACCSCT. **Enrollment:** 865 degree-seeking undergraduates. **Degrees:** 183 associate awarded. **Calendar:** Continuous, extensive summer session. **Full-time faculty:** 41 total. **Part-time faculty:** 1 total. **Special facilities:** Full automotive and diesel lab shops.

Basis for selection. Open admission.

2008-2009 Annual costs. Books/supplies: $360. Personal expenses: $1,967.

Application procedures. Admission: No deadline. $100 fee. Admission notification on a rolling basis.

Academics. Credit/placement by examination: CLEP.

Majors. Mechanic/repair: General, automotive, diesel.

Contact. Phone: (303) 722-5724 Toll-free number: (866) 647-3232
Director of Admissions, Lincoln College of Technology: Denver, 460 South Lipan Street, Denver, CO 80223-9366

Morgan Community College

Fort Morgan, Colorado
www.morgancc.edu
CB code: 0444

- Public 2-year community college
- Commuter campus in large town

General. Founded in 1967. Regionally accredited. **Enrollment:** 365 full-time, degree-seeking students. **Degrees:** 183 associate awarded. **Location:** 81 miles from Denver. **Calendar:** Semester, limited summer session. **Full-time faculty:** 35 total. **Part-time faculty:** 123 total. **Class size:** 69% < 20, 31% 20-39.

Student profile.

Out-of-state:	3%	**25 or older:**	46%

Basis for selection. Open admission, but selective for some programs. Special requirements for physical therapist assistant, occupational therapy assistant, and nursing programs. Interview required of allied health majors.

2008-2009 Annual costs. Tuition/fees: $2,597; $11,421 out-of-state. Per-credit charge: $81 in-state; $375 out-of-state. In-state tuition based upon assumption of Colorado Opportunity Fund waiver of $92 per-credit-hour. Books/supplies: $675.

2008-2009 Financial aid. Need-based: Need-based aid available for part-time students. Work-study available nights, weekends and for part-time students.

Application procedures. Admission: No deadline. No application fee. Admission notification on a rolling basis. **Financial aid:** Priority date 6/1; no closing date. FAFSA required. Applicants notified on a rolling basis.

Academics. Special study options: Distance learning, double major, dual enrollment of high school students, ESL, independent study, internships, liberal arts/career combination, student-designed major, teacher certification program, weekend college. License preparation in nursing, real estate. **Credit/placement by examination:** AP, CLEP, institutional tests. 31 credit hours maximum toward associate degree. **Support services:** GED preparation and test center, learning center, reduced course load, remedial instruction, study skills assistance, tutoring.

Majors. Business: General, accounting. **Computer sciences:** Webmaster. **Education:** General. **Health:** Nursing (RN), occupational therapy assistant, physical therapy assistant. **Interdisciplinary:** Biological/physical sciences. **Liberal arts:** Arts/sciences. **Mechanic/repair:** Auto body, automotive. **Visual/performing arts:** Art. **Other:** Agricultural business planning and financial records.

Computing on campus. 50 workstations in library, computer center, student center. Commuter students can connect to campus network. Online course registration available.

Student life. Activities: Student newspaper, TV station, occupational therapy association, vocational industrial collusion association, Phi Theta Kappa, science club, history club, student nursing association, Phi Beta Lambda, health occupation student organization, physical therapy association.

Student services. Career counseling. **Transfer:** Pre-admission transcript evaluation for new students.

Contact. Phone: (970) 542-3156 Fax: (970) 867-6608
Dan Marler, Director of Guidance and Placement, Morgan Community College, 920 Barlow Road, Fort Morgan, CO 80701

Northeastern Junior College

Sterling, Colorado
www.njc.edu
CB code: 4537

- Public 2-year community and junior college
- Commuter campus in large town

General. Founded in 1941. Regionally accredited. **Enrollment:** 1,421 degree-seeking undergraduates; 989 non-degree-seeking students. **Degrees:** 206 associate awarded. **Location:** 125 miles from Denver. **Calendar:** Semester, limited summer session. **Full-time faculty:** 53 total; 4% have terminal degrees, 2% minority, 55% women. **Part-time faculty:** 32 total; 69% women. **Class size:** 79% < 20, 20% 20-39, less than 1% 40-49, less than 1% 50-99. **Special facilities:** Equine center, greenhouse, college farm.

Student profile. Among degree-seeking undergraduates, 74% enrolled in a transfer program, 26% enrolled in a vocational program, 647 enrolled as first-time, first-year students, 86 transferred in from other institutions.

Part-time:	37%	**Hispanic American:**	9%
Out-of-state:	6%	**Native American:**	1%
Women:	57%	**25 or older:**	23%
African American:	5%	**Live on campus:**	33%
Asian American:	1%		

Transfer out. Colleges most students transferred to 2008: Colorado State University, University of Northern Colorado, University of Colorado, University of Wyoming, Oklahoma State University.

Basis for selection. Open admission, but selective for some programs. Qualifications for programs with limited space, such as licensed practical nursing program, set individually by department. SAT or ACT required for some technical vocational programs. Assessment required by ACCUPLACER, minimum ACT or SAT scores in subject areas, or proof of previous successful college experience. Cooperative admission program with Colorado State University. **Adult students:** Accuplacer required. **Home-schooled:** Transcript of courses and grades, state high school equivalency certificate required. **Learning Disabled:** IEP required.

High school preparation. College-preparatory program recommended.

2008-2009 Annual costs. Tuition/fees: $3,038; $9,609 out-of-state. Per-credit charge: $81 in-state; $300 out-of-state. In-state tuition based upon assumption of Colorado Opportunity Fund waiver of $92 per-credit-hour. Reduced out-of-state tuition for residents of AK, AZ, CA, HI, ID MT, NV NM, ND, OR, SD, UT, WA, WY may be available under the Western Undergraduate Exchange (WUE) program, and for residents of NE, KS, OK under the Border State Incentive (BUI). Room/board: $5,444. Books/supplies: $1,698. Personal expenses: $2,997.

2007-2008 Financial aid. Need-based: 56% of total undergraduate aid awarded as scholarships/grants, 44% as loans/jobs. Need-based aid available for part-time students. **Non-need-based:** Scholarships awarded for academics, alumni affiliation, art, athletics, job skills, leadership, music/drama, state residency. **Additional information:** Need-based financial aid available to part-time students taking 6 credits or more per semester.

Application procedures. Admission: No deadline. No application fee. Admission notification on a rolling basis. **Financial aid:** Priority date 3/1; no closing date. FAFSA, institutional form required. Applicants notified on a rolling basis starting 4/15; must reply within 3 week(s) of notification.

Academics. Special study options: Accelerated study, cooperative education, distance learning, dual enrollment of high school students, ESL, honors, independent study, internships. Bachelor's degree programs available on campus. License preparation in nursing. **Credit/placement by examination:** AP, CLEP, IB, institutional tests. 45 credit hours maximum toward associate degree. **Support services:** GED preparation and test center, learning center, remedial instruction, study skills assistance, tutoring.

Majors. Agriculture: Agribusiness operations, farm/ranch, horticulture, mechanization, ornamental horticulture, production. **Business:** Accounting technology, management information systems. **Education:** Early childhood. **Family/consumer sciences:** Child development. **Health:** EMT paramedic, nursing (RN). **Liberal arts:** Arts/sciences. **Mechanic/repair:** Automotive, diesel. **Protective services:** Law enforcement admin.

Most popular majors. Agriculture 12%, liberal arts 84%.

Computing on campus. 302 workstations in library, computer center, student center. Dormitories wired for high-speed internet access. Online course registration, helpline, student web hosting available.

Student life. Freshman orientation: Mandatory. Preregistration for classes offered. **Policies:** No drugs, no alcohol, no smoking on campus. **Housing:** Coed dorms, single-sex dorms available. $125 fully refundable deposit. Honors house available. **Activities:** Jazz band, campus ministries, choral groups, dance, drama, literary magazine, music ensembles, student government, student newspaper, campus Christian fellowship.

Athletics. NJCAA. **Intercollegiate:** Baseball M, basketball, rodeo, volleyball W. **Intramural:** Basketball, cheerleading W, football (non-tackle) M, tennis, volleyball. **Team name:** Plainswomen, Plainsmen.

Student services. Adult student services, alcohol/substance abuse counseling, career counseling, student employment services, financial aid counseling, health services, personal counseling. **Physically disabled:** Services for visually, speech, hearing impaired. **Transfer:** Pre-admission transcript evaluation for new students. Transfer adviser, college fairs on campus for students transferring to 4-year colleges.

Contact. E-mail: andy.long@njc.edu
Phone: (970) 521-6600 Toll-free number: (800) 626-4367 ext. 7000
Fax: (970) 521-6715
Andy Long, Director of Admissions, Northeastern Junior College, 100 College Avenue, Sterling, CO 80751

Otero Junior College

La Junta, Colorado
www.ojc.edu **CB code: 4588**

- Public 2-year community and junior college
- Commuter campus in small town

General. Founded in 1941. Regionally accredited. **Enrollment:** 1,350 degree-seeking undergraduates. **Degrees:** 140 associate awarded. **Location:** 60 miles from Pueblo, 100 miles from Colorado Springs. **Calendar:** Semester, limited summer session. **Full-time faculty:** 33 total. **Part-time faculty:** 24 total. **Class size:** 74% < 20, 21% 20-39, 2% 40-49, 3% 50-99. **Special facilities:** Koshare Indian kiva museum.

Student profile.

Out-of-state:	7%	**Live on campus:**	10%
25 or older:	33%		

Basis for selection. Open admission, but selective for some programs. Special admission requirements for nursing program.

2008-2009 Annual costs. Tuition/fees: $2,652; $5,412 out-of-state. Per-credit charge: $81 in-state; $173 out-of-state. In-state tuition based upon assumption of Colorado Opportunity Fund waiver of $92 per-credit-hour. Room/board: $4,926. Books/supplies: $1,100. Personal expenses: $2,500.

2008-2009 Financial aid. Need-based: Need-based aid available for part-time students. Work-study available nights, weekends and for part-time students. **Non-need-based:** Scholarships awarded for academics, athletics, state residency.

Application procedures. Admission: No deadline. No application fee. Admission notification on a rolling basis. **Financial aid:** Priority date 4/15; no closing date. FAFSA required. Applicants notified on a rolling basis starting 4/15; must reply within 2 week(s) of notification.

Academics. Special study options: Dual enrollment of high school students. Bachelor's degree programs available on campus. **Credit/placement by examination:** AP, CLEP, institutional tests. 30 credit hours maximum toward associate degree. **Support services:** GED preparation and test center, learning center, reduced course load, remedial instruction, study skills assistance, tutoring.

Majors. Biology: General. **Business:** Administrative services, business admin. **Computer sciences:** General. **Education:** General, early childhood, elementary, secondary, teacher assistance. **Health:** Medical secretary, nursing (RN), pharmacy assistant, predental, premedicine, prepharmacy, preveterinary, veterinary technology/assistant. **History:** General. **Legal studies:** Legal secretary, prelaw. **Liberal arts:** Arts/sciences. **Math:** General. **Physical sciences:** Chemistry. **Psychology:** General. **Social sciences:** Political science. **Visual/performing arts:** Dramatic.

Computing on campus. 100 workstations in library, computer center, student center. Dormitories linked to campus network.

Student life. Freshman orientation: Available. Preregistration for classes offered. **Housing:** Single-sex dorms available. **Activities:** Dance, drama, student government.

Athletics. NJCAA. **Intercollegiate:** Baseball M, basketball, golf, softball W, volleyball W. **Intramural:** Basketball, volleyball. **Team name:** Rattlers.

Student services. Career counseling, student employment services, on-campus daycare, personal counseling, placement for graduates, veterans' counselor. **Physically disabled:** Services for visually, hearing impaired. **Transfer:** Pre-admission transcript evaluation for new students. Transfer adviser, college fairs on campus for students transferring to 4-year colleges.

Contact. E-mail: jan.schiro@ojc.edu
Phone: (719) 384-6831 Fax: (719) 384-6933
Jan Schiro, Admissions Coordinator, Otero Junior College, 1802 Colorado Avenue, La Junta, CO 81050

Pikes Peak Community College

Colorado Springs, Colorado
www.ppcc.edu **CB code: 4291**

- Public 2-year community college
- Commuter campus in large city

General. Founded in 1967. Regionally accredited. **Enrollment:** 10,800 degree-seeking undergraduates. **Degrees:** 880 associate awarded. **Location:** 70 miles from Denver. **Calendar:** Semester, extensive summer session. **Full-time faculty:** 158 total. **Part-time faculty:** 508 total. **Class size:** 59% < 20, 41% 20-39, less than 1% 40-49, less than 1% 50-99, less than 1% >100. **Partnerships:** Formal partnership with Cheyenne Mountain Zoo.

Student profile.

Out-of-state:	17%	**25 or older:**	49%

Transfer out. Colleges most students transferred to 2008: University of Colorado at Colorado Springs, Colorado State University-Pueblo.

Basis for selection. Open admission.

High school preparation. College-preparatory program recommended.

2008-2009 Annual costs. Tuition/fees: $2,658; $11,482 out-of-state. Per-credit charge: $81 in-state; $375 out-of-state. In-state tuition eligible for Colorado Opportunity Fund (COF) waiver, currently $92 per credit hour. Books/supplies: $1,163. Personal expenses: $2,547.

Financial aid. Need-based: Need-based aid available for part-time students. Work-study available nights and for part-time students.

Application procedures. Admission: No deadline. No application fee. Admission notification on a rolling basis. **Financial aid:** Priority date 7/1; no closing date. FAFSA required. Applicants notified on a rolling basis starting 8/1; must reply within 2 week(s) of notification.

Academics. Special study options: Cooperative education, distance learning, double major, dual enrollment of high school students, ESL, external degree, independent study, internships, study abroad, weekend college. License preparation in nursing, paramedic, radiology, real estate. **Credit/placement by examination:** CLEP, IB, institutional tests. Students may receive up to 75% of total credits for all types of prior learning (testing, work and/or life experience). **Support services:** GED test center, learning center, remedial instruction, study skills assistance, tutoring, writing center.

Majors. Biology: General. **Business:** General, accounting, accounting technology, business admin, executive assistant, financial planning, international, management information systems, marketing. **Communications technology:** Graphics, radio/tv. **Computer sciences:** General, computer science, LAN/WAN management, networking. **Conservation:** Management/policy. **Construction:** Maintenance. **Engineering technology:** Architectural, CAD/CADD, drafting, electrical, robotics. **Family/consumer sciences:** Child development. **Foreign languages:** General, sign language interpretation. **Health:** Dental assistant, EMT paramedic, mental health services, nursing (RN), office admin, premedicine. **History:** General. **Legal studies:** Paralegal. **Liberal arts:** Arts/sciences, humanities. **Math:** General. **Mechanic/repair:** Auto body, automotive. **Personal/culinary services:** Culinary arts. **Philosophy/religion:** Philosophy. **Physical sciences:** Chemistry, geology, physics. **Production:** Machine shop technology, welding. **Protective services:** Emergency management/homeland security, fire safety technology, firefighting, law enforcement admin. **Social sciences:** Anthropology, geography, political science, sociology. **Visual/performing arts:** Dance, dramatic, interior design, music, studio arts.

Most popular majors. Health sciences 11%, liberal arts 53%, security/protective services 13%.

Computing on campus. 180 workstations in library, computer center. Commuter students can connect to campus network. Online course registration, helpline, wireless network available.

Student life. Freshman orientation: Available. **Policies:** Dormitory housing available through agreement with the University of Colorado at Colorado Springs. **Activities:** Choral groups, dance, drama, radio station, student government, student newspaper, Phi Theta Kappa.

Athletics. Team name: Aardvarks.

Student services. Adult student services, alcohol/substance abuse counseling, career counseling, services for economically disadvantaged, student employment services, financial aid counseling, on-campus daycare, personal counseling, placement for graduates, veterans' counselor. **Physically disabled:** Services for visually, speech, hearing impaired. **Learning disabled:** Comprehensive services available. **Transfer:** Re-entry adviser, preadmission transcript evaluation for new students. Transfer adviser, college fairs on campus for students transferring to 4-year colleges.

Contact. E-mail: admissions@ppcc.edu
Phone: (719) 502-3000 Toll-free number: (800) 456-6847
Jeffery Horner, Admissions, Pikes Peak Community College, 5675 South Academy Boulevard, Colorado Springs, CO 80906-5498

Pueblo Community College
Pueblo, Colorado
www.pueblocc.edu **CB code: 4634**

- Public 2-year community college
- Commuter campus in small city

General. Founded in 1933. Regionally accredited. **Enrollment:** 4,343 degree-seeking undergraduates; 1,006 non-degree-seeking students. **Degrees:** 478 associate awarded. **Location:** 50 miles from Colorado Springs, 100 miles from Denver. **Calendar:** Semester, extensive summer session. **Full-time faculty:** 85 total; 4% have terminal degrees, 21% minority, 64% women. **Part-time faculty:** 269 total; 5% have terminal degrees, 9% minority, 54% women. **Class size:** 82% < 20, 17% 20-39, less than 1% 40-49, less than 1% 50-99, less than 1% >100. **Special facilities:** Advanced technology center.

Student profile. Among degree-seeking undergraduates, 40% enrolled in a transfer program, 60% enrolled in a vocational program, 1% already have a bachelor's degree or higher, 947 enrolled as first-time, first-year students, 273 transferred in from other institutions.

Part-time:	57%	**Asian American:**	1%
Out-of-state:	3%	**Hispanic American:**	34%
Women:	66%	**Native American:**	3%
African American:	3%	**25 or older:**	57%

Transfer out. 30% of students enrolled in the transfer program go on to 4-year colleges. **Colleges most students transferred to 2008:** Colorado State University: Pueblo.

Basis for selection. Open admission, but selective for some programs. Admission to health programs based on GPA, high school courses, and test scores. ACT required of dental hygiene applicants; score report by May 1. Assessment testing required for all entering degree- and certificate-seeking students, unless ACT/SAT scores or transcripts showing successful completion of college-level English and math courses are provided. Interview required of allied health majors.

2008-2009 Annual costs. Tuition/fees: $2,700; $11,524 out-of-state. Per-credit charge: $81 in-state; $375 out-of-state. In-state tuition based upon assumption of Colorado Opportunity Fund waiver of $92 per-credit-hour. Books/supplies: $1,698.

2007-2008 Financial aid. Need-based: Average need met was 40%. Average scholarship/grant was $2,920; average loan $2,200. 45% of total undergraduate aid awarded as scholarships/grants, 55% as loans/jobs. Need-based aid available for part-time students. Work-study available for part-time students. **Non-need-based:** Awarded to 28 full-time undergraduates, including 20 freshmen. Scholarships awarded for academics, art, job skills, leadership, music/drama.

Application procedures. Admission: Priority date 8/1; no deadline. No application fee. Admission notification on a rolling basis. Foreign applicants must pay for 1 full academic year before acceptance. Application closing date for allied health programs, April 1. **Financial aid:** Priority date 3/15; no closing date. FAFSA required. Applicants notified on a rolling basis starting 4/1.

Academics. Special study options: Accelerated study, cooperative education, distance learning, double major, dual enrollment of high school students, ESL, honors, independent study, internships, liberal arts/career combination, weekend college. License preparation in aviation, dental hygiene, nursing, occupational therapy, paramedic, physical therapy, radiology, real estate. **Credit/placement by examination:** AP, CLEP, institutional tests. All but 15 hour residence requirement for either certificate or associate degree may be from credit for prior learning. **Support services:** GED preparation and test center, learning center, reduced course load, remedial instruction, study skills assistance, tutoring, writing center.

Majors. Business: Accounting, business admin, hospitality/recreation, office technology. **Communications technology:** General, animation/special effects. **Computer sciences:** General, web page design. **Engineering technology:** General, electrical, energy systems. **Family/consumer sciences:** Child development. **Health:** Dental assistant, dental hygiene, EMT paramedic, nursing (RN), occupational therapy assistant, physical therapy assistant, radiologic technology/medical imaging, respiratory therapy technology, sonography. **Liberal arts:** Arts/sciences, library assistant. **Mechanic/repair:** Aircraft, auto body, automotive. **Personal/culinary services:** Cosmetic. **Production:** Machine shop technology, welding. **Protective services:** Firefighting, law enforcement admin. **Other:** Applied technology.

Most popular majors. Business/marketing 11%, health sciences 38%, liberal arts 39%.

Computing on campus. Commuter students can connect to campus network. Online course registration, online library, helpline, wireless network available.

Student life. Freshman orientation: Available. **Activities:** Choral groups, dance, drama, student government, student newspaper, TV station.

Athletics. Team name: Panthers.

Student services. Adult student services, career counseling, financial aid counseling, health services, personal counseling, placement for graduates. **Physically disabled:** Services for visually, speech, hearing impaired. **Transfer:** Transfer center, transfer adviser, college fairs on campus for students transferring to 4-year colleges.

Contact. E-mail: admissions@pueblocc.edu
Phone: (719) 549-3010 Toll-free number: (888) 642-6017
Fax: (719) 549-3012
Maija Kurtz, Director of Admissions and Records, Pueblo Community College, 900 West Orman Avenue, Pueblo, CO 81004-1499

Red Rocks Community College
Lakewood, Colorado
www.rrcc.edu **CB code: 4130**

- Public 2-year community college
- Commuter campus in small city

General. Founded in 1969. Regionally accredited. **Enrollment:** 5,536 degree-seeking undergraduates. **Degrees:** 417 associate awarded. **ROTC:** Army. **Location:** 10 miles from Denver. **Calendar:** Semester, extensive summer session. **Full-time faculty:** 69 total; 12% have terminal degrees, 4% minority, 56% women. **Class size:** 66% < 20, 34% 20-39. **Partnerships:** Formal partnerships with Coors, Microsoft, Apple, Oracle.

Student profile. Among degree-seeking undergraduates, 500 transferred in from other institutions.

Out-of-state:	3%	**Hispanic American:**	13%
African American:	2%	**Native American:**	1%
Asian American:	3%	**25 or older:**	49%

Transfer out. Colleges most students transferred to 2008: Metropolitan State College of Denver, Regis University, Colorado School of Mines, University of Colorado at Boulder, Colorado State University.

Basis for selection. Open admission.

2008-2009 Annual costs. Tuition/fees: $2,719; $11,543 out-of-state. Per-credit charge: $81 in-state; $375 out-of-state. In-state tuition based upon assumption of Colorado Opportunity Fund waiver of $92 per-credit-hour. Books/supplies: $1,698. Personal expenses: $2,853.

2007-2008 Financial aid. Need-based: Need-based aid available for part-time students. Work-study available nights, weekends and for part-time students.

Application procedures. Admission: No deadline. No application fee. Admission notification on a rolling basis. **Financial aid:** Priority date 4/1; no closing date. FAFSA, institutional form required. Applicants notified on a rolling basis starting 6/1; must reply within 2 week(s) of notification.

Academics. Students in advanced ESL classes may begin some college-level courses early. Scholarships offered for outstanding ESL performance when funds are available. **Special study options:** Accelerated study, cross-registration, distance learning, dual enrollment of high school students, ESL, honors, independent study, internships, liberal arts/career combination, student-designed major, study abroad, teacher certification program, weekend college. License preparation in paramedic, radiology, real estate. **Credit/placement by examination:** AP, CLEP, IB, institutional tests. 45 credit hours maximum toward associate degree. **Support services:** GED preparation and test center, learning center, reduced course load, remedial instruction, study skills assistance, tutoring, writing center.

Majors. Biology: General, biotechnology. **Business:** Accounting technology, business admin, management information systems, office technology, real estate. **Computer sciences:** Webmaster. **Conservation:** Forest technology. **Construction:** General, carpentry, electrician, plumbing. **Education:** Teacher assistance. **Engineering technology:** Drafting, energy systems, heat/ac/refrig, industrial, manufacturing. **Family/consumer sciences:** Child development. **Foreign languages:** French, German, Spanish. **Health:** EMT paramedic, nursing (RN), office admin, radiologic technology/medical imaging, sonography. **Liberal arts:** Arts/sciences. **Mechanic/repair:** Auto body, automotive. **Personal/culinary services:** Chef training, cosmetic, manicurist. **Production:** Machine shop technology, welding, woodworking. **Protective services:** Emergency management/homeland security, fire safety technology, law enforcement admin. **Visual/performing arts:** Cinematography, photography, theater design. **Other:** Applied technology, Business-interdisciplinary.

Most popular majors. Health sciences 11%, liberal arts 57%, security/protective services 11%, trade and industry 10%.

Computing on campus. 175 workstations in library, computer center, student center. Online course registration, online library, wireless network available.

Student life. Freshman orientation: Available. **Activities:** Choral groups, dance, drama, literary magazine, musical theater, student government, student newspaper, Phi Theta Kappa, environment club, international club.

Student services. Adult student services, career counseling, student employment services, health services, on-campus daycare, personal counseling, placement for graduates, veterans' counselor. **Physically disabled:** Services for visually, speech, hearing impaired. **Transfer:** Transfer adviser, college fairs on campus for students transferring to 4-year colleges.

Contact. E-mail: admissions@rrcc.edu
Phone: (303) 914-6351 Fax: (303) 989-6919
Dean Rathe, Director of Enrollment Services, Red Rocks Community College, 13300 West Sixth Avenue, Lakewood, CO 80228-1255

Redstone College

Broomfield, Colorado
www.redstonecollege.com **CB code: 2230**

- For-profit 2-year technical college
- Commuter campus in small city

General. Accredited by ACCSCT. **Enrollment:** 440 degree-seeking undergraduates. **Degrees:** 226 associate awarded. **Location:** 15 miles from Denver and Boulder. **Calendar:** Continuous. **Full-time faculty:** 24 total. **Part-time faculty:** 20 total.

Basis for selection. Open admission.

2008-2009 Annual costs. Tuition for entire associate degree ranges from $30,891 to $35,000 depending on program of study.

2008-2009 Financial aid. All financial aid based on need.

Application procedures. Admission: No deadline. $100 fee. Admission notification on a rolling basis. **Financial aid:** No deadline. FAFSA required. Applicants notified on a rolling basis; must reply within 2 week(s) of notification.

Academics. Special study options: License preparation in aviation. **Credit/placement by examination:** CLEP. **Support services:** Learning center, tutoring.

Majors. Mechanic/repair: Aircraft, electronics/electrical.

Computing on campus. 8 workstations in computer center.

Student life. Housing: Apartments available.

Student services. Career counseling, student employment services, placement for graduates, veterans' counselor.

Contact. Phone: (303) 466-1714 Toll-free number: (800) 460-0592
Fax: (303) 469-3797
Cate Clark, Director of Admissions, Redstone College, 10851 West 120th Avenue, Broomfield, CO 80021-3401

Remington College: Colorado Springs

Colorado Springs, Colorado
www.remingtoncollege.com **CB code: 3565**

- For-profit 2-year technical college
- Commuter campus in very large city
- Interview required

General. Accredited by ACICS. **Enrollment:** 170 degree-seeking undergraduates. **Degrees:** 11 bachelor's, 13 associate awarded. **Location:** 60 miles from Denver. **Calendar:** Quarter, extensive summer session. **Full-time faculty:** 5 total; 60% women. **Part-time faculty:** 15 total; 20% have terminal degrees, 7% minority, 40% women. **Class size:** 100% < 20.

Basis for selection. Open admission, but selective for some programs. Non-GED or high school program applicants required to pass Wonderlic assessment.

2008-2009 Annual costs. Associate degree programs annual tuition $19,500 plus $50 fees. 8-month diploma program full tuition $13,900 plus $50 fees. Tuition includes textbooks and supplies.

2008-2009 Financial aid. All financial aid based on need. Need-based aid available for part-time students.

Application procedures. Admission: No deadline. $50 fee. Admission notification on a rolling basis. **Financial aid:** No deadline. FAFSA required. Applicants notified on a rolling basis; must reply within 3 week(s) of notification.

Academics. Special study options: Accelerated study. Bachelor's degree programs available on campus. **Credit/placement by examination:** AP, CLEP. **Support services:** Tutoring.

Majors. Computer sciences: System admin. **Protective services:** Criminal justice.

Computing on campus. 34 workstations in library, computer center. Online library, helpline, repair service available.

Student life. Freshman orientation: Mandatory. Preregistration for classes offered.

Student services. Alcohol/substance abuse counseling, career counseling, student employment services, financial aid counseling, personal counseling, placement for graduates, veterans' counselor. **Transfer:** Preadmission transcript evaluation for new students.

Contact. E-mail: larry.schafer@remingtoncollege.edu
Phone: (719) 532-1234 Toll-free number: (866) 803-0808
Fax: (719) 264-1234
Larry Schafer, Director of Recruitment, Remington College: Colorado Springs, 6050 Erin Park Drive, Colorado Springs, CO 80918

Trinidad State Junior College

Trinidad, Colorado
www.trinidadstate.edu **CB code: 4821**

- Public 2-year community and junior college
- Commuter campus in small town

General. Founded in 1925. Regionally accredited. **Enrollment:** 1,692 degree-seeking undergraduates. **Degrees:** 141 associate awarded. **Location:** 90 miles from Pueblo. **Calendar:** Semester, limited summer session. **Full-time faculty:** 59 total; 5% have terminal degrees, 58% women. **Part-time faculty:** 117 total; 5% have terminal degrees, 58% women. **Class size:** 93% < 20, 6% 20-39, less than 1% 40-49, less than 1% 50-99. **Special facilities:** Museum of anthropology and geology, gunsmithing laboratory, gun range.

Student profile. Among degree-seeking undergraduates, 61 transferred in from other institutions.

Out-of-state:	15%	**Live on campus:**	22%
25 or older:	43%		

Transfer out. Colleges most students transferred to 2008: Colorado State University, Pueblo, Adams State College, Colorado State University, Northern Colorado University.

Basis for selection. Open admission, but selective for some programs. Special requirements for nursing program. Interview recommended for nursing majors.

2008-2009 Annual costs. Tuition/fees: $2,820; $5,580 out-of-state. Per-credit charge: $81 in-state; $173 out-of-state. In-state tuition based upon assumption of Colorado Opportunity Fund waiver of $92 per-credit-hour. Room/board: $4,692. Books/supplies: $800. Personal expenses: $972.

2007-2008 Financial aid. Need-based: 70% of total undergraduate aid awarded as scholarships/grants, 30% as loans/jobs. Need-based aid available for part-time students. Work-study available nights and for part-time students. **Non-need-based:** Scholarships awarded for academics, athletics, state residency.

Application procedures. Admission: No deadline. No application fee. Admission notification on a rolling basis. **Financial aid:** Priority date 5/1; no closing date. FAFSA, institutional form required. Applicants notified on a rolling basis starting 6/15.

Academics. Special study options: Accelerated study, cooperative education, distance learning, double major, dual enrollment of high school students, ESL, independent study, liberal arts/career combination. Bachelor's degree programs available on campus. License preparation in nursing. **Credit/placement by examination:** AP, CLEP, institutional tests. 45 credit hours maximum toward associate degree. **Support services:** GED preparation and test center, learning center, pre-admission summer program, reduced course load, remedial instruction, study skills assistance, tutoring, writing center.

Majors. Biology: General. **Business:** General, accounting, business admin. **Communications:** Advertising, journalism. **Computer sciences:** General, computer science, programming, word processing. **Conservation:** General, fisheries. **Education:** General, physical, social studies. **Engineering:** General. **Engineering technology:** Civil, construction, drafting, manufacturing, occupational safety. **Family/consumer sciences:** Child care. **Foreign languages:** Spanish. **Health:** Massage therapy. **Legal studies:** Prelaw. **Liberal arts:** Arts/sciences. **Math:** General. **Mechanic/repair:** Auto body, automotive, diesel, gunsmithing. **Parks/recreation:** Health/fitness. **Personal/culinary services:** Cosmetic. **Philosophy/religion:** Philosophy. **Physical sciences:** Chemistry. **Production:** Welding. **Protective services:** Criminal justice, law enforcement admin, police science. **Psychology:** General. **Social sciences:** Criminology. **Transportation:** General. **Visual/performing arts:** Commercial/advertising art.

Most popular majors. Family/consumer sciences 8%, health sciences 26%, liberal arts 44%, trade and industry 8%.

Computing on campus. 260 workstations in dormitories, library. Dormitories wired for high-speed internet access and linked to campus network. Online course registration, wireless network available.

Student life. Freshman orientation: Available. Preregistration for classes offered. **Housing:** Single-sex dorms available. $150 partly refundable deposit. **Activities:** Pep band, campus ministries, choral groups, drama, music ensembles, student government, student newspaper, TV station, MECHA (for students of Chicano and Hispanic descent), black student alliance.

Athletics. NJCAA. **Intercollegiate:** Baseball M, basketball M, golf, softball W, volleyball W. **Intramural:** Baseball M, basketball, rifle, softball, table tennis, tennis, volleyball. **Team name:** Trojans.

Student services. Adult student services, alcohol/substance abuse counseling, career counseling, student employment services, financial aid counseling, on-campus daycare, personal counseling, placement for graduates, veterans' counselor. **Physically disabled:** Services for visually, speech, hearing impaired. **Transfer:** Transfer adviser, college fairs on campus for students transferring to 4-year colleges.

Contact. E-mail: johnny.noel@trinidadstate.edu
Phone: (719) 846-5622 Toll-free number: (800) 621-8752
Fax: (719) 846-5620
Sandra Veltri, Vice President of Student and Academic Affairs, Trinidad State Junior College, 600 Prospect Street, Trinidad, CO 81082

Connecticut

Asnuntuck Community College

Enfield, Connecticut
www.acc.commnet.edu
CB member
CB code: 3656

- Public 2-year community and technical college
- Commuter campus in large town

General. Founded in 1972. Regionally accredited. **Enrollment:** 1,122 degree-seeking undergraduates. **Degrees:** 137 associate awarded. **Location:** 15 miles from Hartford; 10 miles from Springfield, Massachusetts. **Calendar:** Semester, extensive summer session. **Full-time faculty:** 25 total. **Part-time faculty:** 90 total. **Class size:** 47% < 20, 52% 20-39, less than 1% 40-49.

Student profile.

Out-of-state:	4%	**25 or older:**	45%

Transfer out. Colleges most students transferred to 2008: Eastern Connecticut State University, Central Connecticut State University, University of Connecticut, Western New England College.

Basis for selection. Open admission.

2008-2009 Annual costs. Tuition/fees: $2,984; $8,912 out-of-state. Per-credit charge: $110 in-state; $330 out-of-state. Books/supplies: $1,200. Personal expenses: $1,338.

2007-2008 Financial aid. All financial aid based on need. 85% of total undergraduate aid awarded as scholarships/grants, 15% as loans/jobs. Need-based aid available for part-time students. Work-study available nights, weekends and for part-time students.

Application procedures. Admission: No deadline. $20 fee, may be waived for applicants with need. Admission notification on a rolling basis. **Financial aid:** Priority date 6/1; no closing date. FAFSA, institutional form required. Applicants notified on a rolling basis starting 7/1; must reply within 2 week(s) of notification.

Academics. On-line tutoring available. **Special study options:** Cooperative education, cross-registration, distance learning, double major, dual enrollment of high school students, independent study, internships, liberal arts/career combination, weekend college. License preparation in paramedic, real estate. **Credit/placement by examination:** AP, CLEP, institutional tests. 48 credit hours maximum toward associate degree. **Support services:** Learning center, remedial instruction, study skills assistance, tutoring.

Majors. Business: Accounting, business admin, office technology. **Communications technology:** General, radio/tv. **Computer sciences:** General. **Education:** Early childhood. **Engineering:** Science. **Engineering technology:** Industrial, manufacturing. **Family/consumer sciences:** Child care. **Health:** Mental health services. **Liberal arts:** Arts/sciences. **Production:** Machine tool, welding. **Protective services:** Police science. **Public administration:** Human services.

Most popular majors. Business/marketing 31%, family/consumer sciences 7%, liberal arts 47%, security/protective services 7%.

Computing on campus. 111 workstations in library, computer center. Online course registration, online library available.

Student life. Freshman orientation: Available. **Activities:** Drama, literary magazine, radio station, student government, human services club, Phi Theta Kappa.

Student services. Career counseling, student employment services, financial aid counseling, on-campus daycare, personal counseling, placement for graduates, veterans' counselor. **Physically disabled:** Services for visually, speech, hearing impaired. **Transfer:** Pre-admission transcript evaluation for new students. Transfer adviser, college fairs on campus for students transferring to 4-year colleges.

Contact. E-mail: dshaw@acc.commnet.edu
Phone: (860) 253-3010 Toll-free number: (800) 501-3967
Fax: (860) 253-3014
Donna Shaw, Director of Admissions and Marketing, Asnuntuck Community College, 170 Elm Street, Enfield, CT 06082

Briarwood College

Southington, Connecticut
www.briarwood.edu
CB code: 3121

- For-profit 2-year junior college
- Commuter campus in large town
- Application essay required

General. Founded in 1966. Regionally accredited. **Enrollment:** 702 degree-seeking undergraduates. **Degrees:** 6 bachelor's, 105 associate awarded. **Location:** 19 miles from Hartford. **Calendar:** Semester, limited summer session. **Full-time faculty:** 25 total. **Part-time faculty:** 60 total.

Student profile.

Out-of-state:	6%	**Live on campus:**	19%
25 or older:	41%		

Transfer out. Colleges most students transferred to 2008: Central Connecticut State University, Saint Joseph College, Quinnipiac College, Teikyo Post University, University of New Haven, University of Connecticut.

Basis for selection. Open admission, but selective for some programs. 8-hour observation and interview required for Occupational Therapy Assistant program. Interview, essay and 2 letters of recommendation required for Dental Hygiene program.

High school preparation. For occupational therapy assistant program, 2 math, 2 science (including 1 biological science) required.

2008-2009 Annual costs. Tuition/fees: $17,835. Per-credit charge: $570. Room only: $4,000. Books/supplies: $1,000. Personal expenses: $2,400.

Financial aid. Need-based: Need-based aid available for part-time students. Work-study available nights, weekends and for part-time students. **Non-need-based:** Scholarships awarded for academics, alumni affiliation, leadership.

Application procedures. Admission: No deadline. $30 fee, may be waived for applicants with need. Admission notification on a rolling basis beginning on or about 9/15. **Financial aid:** Priority date 4/30; no closing date. FAFSA required. Applicants notified on a rolling basis starting 3/15; must reply within 2 week(s) of notification.

Academics. Special study options: Double major, ESL, independent study, internships, liberal arts/career combination, weekend college. Bachelor's degree programs available on campus. **Credit/placement by examination:** AP, CLEP, institutional tests. 29 credit hours maximum toward associate degree. **Support services:** Learning center, pre-admission summer program, reduced course load, remedial instruction, study skills assistance, tutoring, writing center.

Majors. Business: General, accounting, administrative services, business admin, fashion, office technology, tourism/travel. **Communications:** General, broadcast journalism. **Family/consumer sciences:** Child care. **Health:** Dental assistant, dietetics, medical assistant, medical records technology, medical secretary, occupational therapy assistant. **Legal studies:** Legal secretary, paralegal. **Liberal arts:** Arts/sciences. **Personal/culinary services:** Mortuary science. **Protective services:** Criminal justice.

Computing on campus. 66 workstations in library, computer center. Dormitories wired for high-speed internet access.

Student life. Freshman orientation: Mandatory. **Housing:** Coed dorms, apartments, wellness housing available. $100 deposit. Townhouse apartments with kitchens available. **Activities:** Choral groups, radio station, student government, psychology honor society, allied health club.

Athletics. NJCAA. **Intramural:** Basketball M.

Student services. Career counseling, student employment services, financial aid counseling, health services, personal counseling, placement for graduates, veterans' counselor. **Physically disabled:** Services for visually, hearing impaired. **Transfer:** Pre-admission transcript evaluation for new students. Transfer adviser, college fairs on campus for students transferring to 4-year colleges.

Contact. E-mail: admis@briarwood.edu
Phone: (860) 628-4751 ext. 108 Toll-free number: (800) 952-2444 ext. 108
Fax: (860) 628-6444
Anthony Reich, Dean of Administration, Briarwood College, 2279 Mount Vernon Road, Southington, CT 06489-1057

Capital Community College
Hartford, Connecticut
www.ccc.commnet.edu
CB code: 3421

- Public 2-year community and technical college
- Commuter campus in small city

General. Founded in 1946. Regionally accredited. **Enrollment:** 3,422 degree-seeking undergraduates; 567 non-degree-seeking students. **Degrees:** 327 associate awarded. **ROTC:** Army, Naval, Air Force. **Calendar:** Semester, limited summer session. **Full-time faculty:** 69 total. **Part-time faculty:** 178 total. **Special facilities:** Math development center, computerized English as a Second Language lab, interactive videodisc instruction for nursing students, learning/writing center. **Partnerships:** Formal partnerships with high schools for Tech Prep program.

Student profile. Among degree-seeking undergraduates, 710 enrolled as first-time, first-year students.

Part-time:	69%	**25 or older:**	57%
Women:	74%		

Transfer out. Colleges most students transferred to 2008: University of Connecticut, Central Connecticut State University, University of Hartford, Eastern Connecticut State University.

Basis for selection. Open admission, but selective for some programs. SAT scores used to satisfy admission criteria for nursing, physical therapist assistant, and radiologic technology programs.

High school preparation. Algebra, biology, and chemistry required for nursing program. Physical therapy assistant, radiologic technology, and pre-nursing programs also have specific course requirements. Paramedic program has specific educational and training requirements.

2008-2009 Annual costs. Tuition/fees: $2,984; $8,912 out-of-state. Per-credit charge: $110 in-state; $330 out-of-state. Books/supplies: $850. Personal expenses: $1,965.

Financial aid. All financial aid based on need. Need-based aid available for part-time students. Work-study available nights, weekends and for part-time students.

Application procedures. Admission: No deadline. $20 fee, may be waived for applicants with need. Admission notification on a rolling basis. **Financial aid:** Closing date 7/15. FAFSA required. Applicants notified on a rolling basis starting 7/15; must reply within 2 week(s) of notification.

Academics. Special study options: Accelerated study, cross-registration, distance learning, double major, dual enrollment of high school students, ESL, independent study, internships, liberal arts/career combination, weekend college. Interdisciplinary summer program with Smith College. License preparation in nursing, paramedic, radiology. **Credit/placement by examination:** AP, CLEP, institutional tests. **Support services:** GED preparation, learning center, pre-admission summer program, remedial instruction, study skills assistance, tutoring, writing center.

Majors. Business: Accounting, administrative services, business admin. **Computer sciences:** General. **Education:** Early childhood. **Engineering:** Electrical. **Engineering technology:** Architectural. **Health:** EMT paramedic, medical assistant, medical radiologic technology/radiation therapy, mental health services, nursing (RN), physical therapy assistant. **Liberal arts:** Arts/sciences, library assistant. **Protective services:** Fire safety technology.

Most popular majors. Business/marketing 18%, health sciences 40%, liberal arts 26%, public administration/social services 6%.

Computing on campus. 500 workstations in library, computer center, student center. Commuter students can connect to campus network. Online course registration, online library, wireless network available.

Student life. Freshman orientation: Available. Preregistration for classes offered. Three-day program held prior to start of semester. **Policies:** Policies against drugs and alcohol, violence, weapons, and sexual harassment on campus. **Activities:** Choral groups, dance, drama, literary magazine, radio station, student government, TV station, Latin American students association, senior renewal club, early childhood club, pre-professional club, Phi Theta Kappa, nursing club, black student union, student senate.

Student services. Adult student services, chaplain/spiritual director, career counseling, services for economically disadvantaged, student employment services, financial aid counseling, minority student services, on-campus daycare, personal counseling, placement for graduates, veterans' counselor, women's services. **Physically disabled:** Services for visually, speech, hearing impaired. **Learning disabled:** Comprehensive services available. **Transfer:** College fairs on campus for students transferring to 4-year colleges.

Contact. E-mail: mball-davis@ccc.commnet.edu
Phone: (860) 906-5126 Toll-free number: (800) 894-6126
Marsha Ball-Davis, Director of Admissions, Capital Community College, 950 Main Street, Hartford, CT 06103-1207

Clemens College
Suffield, Connecticut
www.clemenscollege.edu
CB code: 3615

- For-profit 2-year culinary school and business college
- Residential campus in small town
- Application essay, interview required

General. Regionally accredited. Transfer to sister schools in Switzerland or Australia possible for second year. Students can complete degree program in 18-month accelerated format. Cost of attendance includes 6-month paid internship. **Enrollment:** 75 degree-seeking undergraduates. **Degrees:** 35 associate awarded. **Location:** 50 miles from Hartford. **Calendar:** Continuous, limited summer session. **Full-time faculty:** 7 total. **Part-time faculty:** 7 total. **Class size:** 95% < 20, 5% 20-39.

Student profile.

Out-of-state:	90%	**Live on campus:**	90%
25 or older:	40%		

Transfer out. Colleges most students transferred to 2008: University Center Cesar Ritz (Switzerland), Institut Hotelier Cesar Ritz (Switzerland).

Basis for selection. Recommendations and interview important. Visa required for international students.

2008-2009 Annual costs. Tuition/fees: $19,770. International students without health insurance are required to purchase it for $350 per 11-week term. Culinary students pay an extra $668 for cutlery and tools. Room/board: $5,690.

Financial aid. Need-based: Need-based aid available for part-time students. Work-study available nights, weekends and for part-time students. **Non-need-based:** Scholarships awarded for academics.

Application procedures. Admission: Priority date 1/15; no deadline. $40 fee, may be waived for applicants with need. Admission notification on a rolling basis. **Financial aid:** No deadline. Applicants notified on a rolling basis starting 1/1.

Academics. Special study options: Accelerated study, cooperative education, internships, liberal arts/career combination, study abroad. **Credit/placement by examination:** AP, CLEP, institutional tests. 18 credit hours maximum toward associate degree. **Support services:** Learning center, remedial instruction, study skills assistance, tutoring, writing center.

Majors. Business: Hospitality admin. **Personal/culinary services:** Culinary arts.

Computing on campus. 38 workstations in dormitories, library, computer center, student center. Dormitories wired for high-speed internet access and linked to campus network. Online library, helpline, wireless network available.

Student life. Freshman orientation: Mandatory. Preregistration for classes offered. Half of the first week devoted to orientation. **Housing:** Guaranteed on-campus for freshmen. Coed dorms, wellness housing available. $500 deposit. **Activities:** Film society, student government, Ritz Guild.

Athletics. Intramural: Basketball, soccer, table tennis, tennis, volleyball, weight lifting.

Student services. Adult student services, alcohol/substance abuse counseling, career counseling, student employment services, financial aid counseling, health services, placement for graduates. **Transfer:** Pre-admission transcript evaluation for new students.

Contact. E-mail: admissions@clemenscollege.edu
Phone: (860) 668-3515 ext. 228 Toll-free number: (800) 955-0809
Fax: (860) 668-7369
Jolie Swanson, Director of Admissions, Clemens College, 1760 Mapleton Avenue, Suffield, CT 06078

Gateway Community College
New Haven, Connecticut
www.gwcc.commnet.edu
CB member
CB code: 3425

- Public 2-year community college
- Commuter campus in small city

General. Founded in 1992. Regionally accredited. **Enrollment:** 5,140 degree-seeking undergraduates; 1,331 non-degree-seeking students. **Degrees:** 453 associate awarded. **Location:** 75 miles from New York City, 130 miles from Boston. **Calendar:** Semester, limited summer session. **Full-time faculty:** 91 total; 16% have terminal degrees, 22% minority, 57% women. **Part-time faculty:** 273 total; 19% minority, 52% women. **Class size:** 32% < 20, 66% 20-39, 3% 40-49, less than 1% 50-99. **Special facilities:** Early childhood learning center, day care center, student operated cafe, student art museum.

Student profile. Among degree-seeking undergraduates, 3% enrolled in a transfer program, 16% enrolled in a vocational program, 3% already have a bachelor's degree or higher, 1,844 enrolled as first-time, first-year students.

Part-time:	56%	**Asian American:**	4%
Out-of-state:	1%	**Hispanic American:**	14%
Women:	61%	**International:**	2%
African American:	26%	**25 or older:**	32%

Transfer out. Colleges most students transferred to 2008: Southern Connecticut State University, University of New Haven, Quinnipiac College.

Basis for selection. Open admission, but selective for some programs. Special requirements for radiology, nursing, nuclear medicine technology, diagnostic medical sonography, drug and alcohol rehabilitation counselor. Interview required of radiology, drug and alcohol counseling, nuclear medicine technology, diagnostic medical sonography, nursing majors. **Homeschooled:** Transcript of courses and grades required.

2008-2009 Annual costs. Tuition/fees: $2,984; $8,912 out-of-state. Per-credit charge: $110 in-state; $330 out-of-state. Books/supplies: $1,200. Personal expenses: $1,100.

Financial aid. All financial aid based on need. Need-based aid available for part-time students. Work-study available nights, weekends and for part-time students.

Application procedures. Admission: Priority date 6/1; deadline 9/1. $20 fee, may be waived for applicants with need. Admission notification on a rolling basis beginning on or about 2/1. **Financial aid:** No deadline. FAFSA, institutional form required. Applicants notified on a rolling basis; must reply within 2 week(s) of notification.

Academics. Special study options: Accelerated study, cross-registration, distance learning, dual enrollment of high school students, ESL, independent study, internships, liberal arts/career combination, weekend college. License preparation in nursing, radiology. **Credit/placement by examination:** AP, CLEP, institutional tests. 30 credit hours maximum toward associate degree. **Support services:** GED preparation, learning center, pre-admission summer program, reduced course load, remedial instruction, study skills assistance, tutoring, writing center.

Majors. Business: Accounting, administrative services, business admin, fashion, hotel/motel admin, office/clerical, restaurant/food services, sales/distribution. **Computer sciences:** Computer science, information systems, programming, word processing. **Conservation:** General, environmental science. **Education:** Early childhood, special. **Engineering:** Science. **Engineering technology:** Biomedical, electrical, manufacturing. **Family/consumer sciences:** Aging, food/nutrition, institutional food production. **Health:** Medical radiologic technology/radiation therapy, medical secretary, nuclear medical technology, nursing (RN), pharmacy assistant, sonography, substance abuse counseling. **Legal studies:** Legal secretary. **Liberal arts:** Arts/sciences. **Math:** General. **Mechanic/repair:** General, automotive. **Personal/culinary services:** Chef training, food prep, restaurant/catering. **Protective services:** Fire services admin. **Visual/performing arts:** Graphic design, studio arts.

Computing on campus. 650 workstations in library, computer center. Online library, helpline, wireless network available.

Student life. Freshman orientation: Available. **Activities:** Choral groups, drama, international student organizations, literary magazine, music ensembles, student government, student newspaper, Spanish-American club, math/science club, Phi Theta Kappa, art club, athletic club, veteran's club, biology club, Theater Goers, Black Student Union.

Athletics. NJCAA. **Intercollegiate:** Baseball M, basketball. **Team name:** Ravens.

Student services. Adult student services, career counseling, student employment services, financial aid counseling, health services, on-campus daycare, personal counseling, placement for graduates, veterans' counselor, women's services. **Physically disabled:** Services for visually, speech, hearing impaired. **Transfer:** Transfer adviser for students transferring to 4-year colleges.

Contact. E-mail: kshea@gwcc.commnet.edu
Phone: (203) 285-2010 Toll-free number: (800) 390-7723
Fax: (203) 285-2018
Shea Kim, Director of Admissions, Gateway Community College, 60 Sargent Drive, New Haven, CT 06511-5970

Goodwin College
East Hartford, Connecticut
www.goodwin.edu
CB member

- Private 2-year health science and career college
- Commuter campus in small city

General. Enrollment: 1,572 degree-seeking undergraduates; 17 non-degree-seeking students. **Degrees:** 163 associate awarded. **Location:** 5 miles from Hartford. **Calendar:** Semester, extensive summer session. **Full-time faculty:** 25 total; 20% minority, 76% women. **Part-time faculty:** 49 total.

Student profile. Among degree-seeking undergraduates, 293 enrolled as first-time, first-year students.

Part-time:	79%	**Women:**	87%

Transfer out. Colleges most students transferred to 2008: Manchester Community College, Capital Community College, University of Connecticut, Central Connecticut State University, Tunxis Community College.

Basis for selection. Open admission, but selective for some programs. Applicants to the nursing, respiratory therapist, and histology technician programs must have successfully completed pre-requisite courses prior to application and submit a completed application to program desired. Interviews may be required for some programs. **Homeschooled:** State high school equivalency certificate required.

2008-2009 Annual costs. Tuition/fees: $16,250. Per-credit charge: $490.

2007-2008 Financial aid. All financial aid based on need. 114 full-time freshmen applied for aid; 113 were judged to have need; 113 of these received aid. Average need met was 85%. Average scholarship/grant was $2,415; average loan $2,831. 35% of total undergraduate aid awarded as scholarships/grants, 65% as loans/jobs. Need-based aid available for part-time students. Work-study available nights and for part-time students.

Application procedures. Admission: No deadline. $50 fee, may be waived for applicants with need. Admission notification on a rolling basis. **Financial aid:** No deadline. FAFSA required. Applicants notified on a rolling basis starting 8/1.

Academics. Special study options: Cooperative education, distance learning, ESL, internships. Bachelor's degree programs available on campus. License preparation in nursing, paramedic. **Credit/placement by examination:** AP, CLEP, institutional tests. 30 credit hours maximum toward associate degree, 30 toward bachelor's. **Support services:** Learning center, pre-admission summer program, reduced course load, remedial instruction, study skills assistance, tutoring, writing center.

Majors. Business: General, administrative services, business admin, entrepreneurial studies, human resources, international, nonprofit/public. **Computer sciences:** General. **Conservation:** Environmental studies. **Education:** Early childhood, teacher assistance. **Family/consumer sciences:** Child care, child development. **Health:** Medical assistant, nursing (RN), office assistant, respiratory therapy technology. **Protective services:** Emergency management/homeland security. **Public administration:** Human services, youth services.

Most popular majors. Health sciences 80%.

Computing on campus. 100 workstations in library, computer center, student center. Online library, helpline, repair service, wireless network available.

Student life. Freshman orientation: Mandatory. Preregistration for classes offered. **Activities:** Student government, student newspaper.

Athletics. Intramural: Bowling, golf.

Student services. Adult student services, career counseling, student employment services, financial aid counseling, personal counseling, placement for graduates, veterans' counselor. **Physically disabled:** Services for visually impaired. **Transfer:** Re-entry adviser, pre-admission transcript evaluation for new students.

Contact. E-mail: dnoonan@goodwin.edu
Phone: (860) 727-6902 Toll-free number: (800) 889-3282
Fax: (860) 291-9550
Daniel Noonan, Director of Enrollment, Goodwin College, One RIverside Drive, East Hartford, CT 06118

Housatonic Community College

Bridgeport, Connecticut
www.hcc.commnet.edu
CB member
CB code: 3446

- Public 2-year community college
- Commuter campus in small city

General. Founded in 1966. Regionally accredited. **Enrollment:** 1,650 full-time, degree-seeking students. **Degrees:** 354 associate awarded. **Location:** 60 miles from Hartford, 60 miles from New York City. **Calendar:** Semester, extensive summer session. **Full-time faculty:** 73 total. **Part-time faculty:** 220 total. **Class size:** 45% < 20, 53% 20-39, 2% 40-49, less than 1% 50-99.

Basis for selection. Open admission, but selective for some programs. Special requirements for clinical lab science, physical therapist assistant, occupational therapy assistant, nursing programs. Interview required of allied health, computer program majors.

2008-2009 Annual costs. Tuition/fees: $2,984; $8,912 out-of-state. Per-credit charge: $110 in-state; $330 out-of-state. Books/supplies: $700.

2007-2008 Financial aid. All financial aid based on need. Need-based aid available for part-time students.

Application procedures. Admission: No deadline. $20 fee, may be waived for applicants with need. Admission notification on a rolling basis. Application period ends one week after start of classes. **Financial aid:** Priority date 11/1, closing date 5/1. FAFSA required. Applicants notified on a rolling basis starting 6/1.

Academics. Special study options: Cooperative education, distance learning, double major, dual enrollment of high school students, ESL, honors, independent study, internships, weekend college. **Credit/placement by examination:** CLEP, institutional tests. 30 credit hours maximum toward associate degree. New Jersey Basic Skills Placement Test and/or ACCUPLACER used for advising and placement. **Support services:** GED preparation, learning center, reduced course load, remedial instruction, study skills assistance, tutoring, writing center.

Majors. Business: General, accounting, administrative services, business admin. **Computer sciences:** General. **Education:** Early childhood. **Family/consumer sciences:** Child care. **Health:** Mental health services, nursing (RN), physical therapy assistant, substance abuse counseling. **Liberal arts:** Arts/sciences. **Mechanic/repair:** Aircraft. **Protective services:** Police science. **Public administration:** Human services. **Visual/performing arts:** Commercial/advertising art, studio arts.

Computing on campus. 140 workstations in library, computer center.

Student life. Freshman orientation: Available. Preregistration for classes offered. **Activities:** Drama, literary magazine, student government, student newspaper.

Student services. Adult student services, career counseling, services for economically disadvantaged, student employment services, financial aid counseling, health services, on-campus daycare, personal counseling, placement for graduates, veterans' counselor. **Transfer:** Transfer adviser, college fairs on campus for students transferring to 4-year colleges.

Contact. Phone: (203) 332-5100 Fax: (203) 332-5123
Deloris Curtis, Director of Admissions, Housatonic Community College, 900 Lafayette Boulevard, Bridgeport, CT 06604-4704

Manchester Community College

Manchester, Connecticut
www.mcc.commnet.edu
CB member
CB code: 3544

- Public 2-year community college
- Commuter campus in small city

General. Founded in 1963. Regionally accredited. **Enrollment:** 5,710 degree-seeking undergraduates; 939 non-degree-seeking students. **Degrees:** 614 associate awarded. **Location:** 8 miles from Hartford. **Calendar:** Semester, extensive summer session. **Full-time faculty:** 105 total; 19% minority, 60% women. **Part-time faculty:** 375 total; 28% minority, 53% women. **Class size:** 23% < 20, 71% 20-39, 6% 40-49.

Student profile. Among degree-seeking undergraduates, 1,592 enrolled as first-time, first-year students, 739 transferred in from other institutions.

Part-time:	47%	**Asian American:**	3%
Women:	53%	**Hispanic American:**	12%
African American:	14%	**25 or older:**	30%

Transfer out. Colleges most students transferred to 2008: Central Connecticut State University, University of Connecticut, Eastern Connecticut State University.

Basis for selection. Open admission, but selective for some programs. 2.0 GPA, 800 SAT (exclusive of Writing), rank in top half of class required for admission to allied health programs. Interview required of allied health, drug and alcohol rehabilitation counselor majors.

High school preparation. 2 units math and 1 unit laboratory science required of allied health applicants.

2008-2009 Annual costs. Tuition/fees: $2,984; $8,912 out-of-state. Per-credit charge: $110 in-state; $330 out-of-state. Books/supplies: $800. Personal expenses: $3,032.

2007-2008 Financial aid. Need-based: Need-based aid available for part-time students.

Application procedures. Admission: No deadline. $20 fee, may be waived for applicants with need. Admission notification on a rolling basis beginning on or about 5/1. **Financial aid:** Priority date 5/15; no closing date. FAFSA required. Applicants notified on a rolling basis starting 5/1; must reply within 2 week(s) of notification.

Academics. Special study options: Cooperative education, cross-registration, distance learning, double major, dual enrollment of high school students, ESL, independent study, internships, semester at sea, student-designed major, weekend college. License preparation in occupational therapy, paramedic. **Credit/placement by examination:** AP, CLEP, institutional tests. 45 credit hours maximum toward associate degree. **Support services:** Learning center, reduced course load, remedial instruction, study skills assistance, tutoring, writing center.

Majors. Area/ethnic studies: Women's. **Business:** Accounting, administrative services, business admin, hospitality/recreation, management information systems. **Communications:** Digital media, journalism. **Computer sciences:** Data entry, information systems, networking. **Education:** Early childhood, teacher assistance. **Engineering:** Science. **Engineering technology:** Manufacturing. **Family/consumer sciences:** Institutional food production. **Health:** Clinical lab technology, occupational therapy assistant, pharmacy assistant, physical therapy assistant, respiratory therapy technology, substance abuse counseling, surgical technology. **Legal studies:** Paralegal. **Liberal arts:** Arts/sciences. **Parks/recreation:** Exercise sciences. **Public administration:** Community org/advocacy. **Visual/performing arts:** Commercial/advertising art.

Most popular majors. Business/marketing 14%, education 11%, family/consumer sciences 15%, health sciences 11%, legal studies 7%, security/protective services 35%.

Computing on campus. 310 workstations in library, computer center. Online course registration, online library, wireless network available.

Student life. Freshman orientation: Available. **Activities:** Choral groups, dance, drama, student government, student newspaper, student organization of Latinos, African American Males Achieving Excellence, Muslim student association, Spanish club, political union, PRIDE, Phi Theta Kappa, Veterans Empowering Themselves to Succeed.

Athletics. NJCAA. **Intercollegiate:** Baseball, basketball M, soccer. **Intramural:** Softball M. **Team name:** Cougars.

Student services. Adult student services, career counseling, student employment services, health services, on-campus daycare, personal counseling, placement for graduates, veterans' counselor. **Physically disabled:** Services for visually, speech, hearing impaired. **Transfer:** Transfer adviser, college fairs on campus for students transferring to 4-year colleges.

Contact. Phone: (860) 512-3210 Fax: (860) 512-3221
Peter Harris, Director of Admissions, Manchester Community College, Great Path PO Box 1046, MS 12, Manchester, CT 06040-1046

Middlesex Community College

Middletown, Connecticut
www.mxcc.commnet.edu

CB member
CB code: 3551

- Public 2-year community college
- Commuter campus in large town

General. Founded in 1966. **Enrollment:** 1,940 degree-seeking undergraduates; 684 non-degree-seeking students. **Degrees:** 237 associate awarded. **Location:** 20 miles from Hartford and New Haven. **Calendar:** Semester, limited summer session. **Full-time faculty:** 43 total; 12% minority, 49% women. **Part-time faculty:** 122 total; 8% minority, 66% women. **Class size:** 24% < 20, 76% 20-39. **Special facilities:** Nature trails.

Student profile. Among degree-seeking undergraduates, 30% enrolled in a transfer program, 40% enrolled in a vocational program, 543 enrolled as first-time, first-year students, 202 transferred in from other institutions.

Part-time:	52%	**Asian American:**	2%
Out-of-state:	1%	**Hispanic American:**	14%
Women:	60%	**International:**	1%
African American:	11%	**25 or older:**	65%

Transfer out. 45% of students enrolled in the transfer program go on to 4-year colleges.

Basis for selection. Open admission, but selective for some programs. Special requirements for radiology technician, broadcast communications, human services, and drug and alcohol rehabilitation counselor programs. Interview recommended of mental health, radiology, drug and alcohol counseling program majors.

High school preparation. College-preparatory program recommended.

2008-2009 Annual costs. Tuition/fees: $2,984; $8,912 out-of-state. Per-credit charge: $110 in-state; $330 out-of-state. Out-of-state tuition includes fees. Books/supplies: $400. Personal expenses: $700.

Financial aid. All financial aid based on need. Need-based aid available for part-time students. Work-study available for part-time students. **Additional information:** Tuition and/or fee waiver for veterans.

Application procedures. Admission: Priority date 7/1; deadline 8/1 (postmark date). $20 fee, may be waived for applicants with need. Admission notification on a rolling basis beginning on or about 1/1. **Financial aid:** Priority date 6/1; no closing date. FAFSA, institutional form required. Applicants notified on a rolling basis starting 7/1; must reply within 2 week(s) of notification.

Academics. Special study options: Cross-registration, dual enrollment of high school students, ESL, independent study, internships, student-designed major. License preparation in radiology. **Credit/placement by examination:** CLEP, institutional tests. 48 credit hours maximum toward associate degree. **Support services:** Pre-admission summer program, reduced course load, remedial instruction, tutoring.

Majors. Business: Accounting, administrative services, business admin, marketing. **Communications:** General, broadcast journalism. **Computer sciences:** Information systems. **Conservation:** General. **Education:** Early childhood. **Health:** Medical radiologic technology/radiation therapy, medical secretary, ophthalmic lab technology, optician, substance abuse counseling. **Legal studies:** Legal secretary. **Liberal arts:** Arts/sciences. **Public administration:** Human services. **Visual/performing arts:** Metal/jewelry, studio arts.

Most popular majors. Business/marketing 30%, health sciences 25%, liberal arts 35%.

Computing on campus. Online library, helpline available.

Student life. Freshman orientation: Available. **Activities:** Concert band, drama, literary magazine, radio station, student government, student newspaper, TV station, black student alliance, national scholastic honor society, student guild, radio/TV club, Collegiate Secretaries International, Minority Opportunities in Education club, art club, human services organization.

Student services. Career counseling, student employment services, on-campus daycare, personal counseling, placement for graduates, veterans' counselor. **Physically disabled:** Services for visually, hearing impaired. **Transfer:** Transfer adviser, college fairs on campus for students transferring to 4-year colleges.

Contact. E-mail: mshabazz@mxcc.commnet.edu
Phone: (860) 343-5719 Toll-free number: (800) 818-5501
Fax: (860) 344-7488
Mensimah Shabazz, Director of Admissions, Middlesex Community College, 100 Training Hill Road, Middletown, CT 06457

Naugatuck Valley Community College

Waterbury, Connecticut
www.nvcc.commnet.edu

CB member
CB code: 3550

- Public 2-year community and technical college
- Commuter campus in small city

General. Founded in 1992. Regionally accredited. **Enrollment:** 5,086 degree-seeking undergraduates; 1,042 non-degree-seeking students. **Degrees:** 472 associate awarded. **Location:** 32 miles from Hartford. **Calendar:** Semester, limited summer session. **Full-time faculty:** 107 total; 11% minority, 57% women. **Part-time faculty:** 334 total. **Class size:** 34% < 20, 65% 20-39, less than 1% 40-49, less than 1% 50-99. **Special facilities:** Fine arts center, 2 theaters, music and dance studios, video studios, rehearsal rooms, fire sprinkler laboratory, automotive center, greenhouse laboratory, observatory, arboretum, nature trail. **Partnerships:** Formal partnership with Disney.

Student profile. Among degree-seeking undergraduates, 42% enrolled in a transfer program, 58% enrolled in a vocational program, 2% already have a bachelor's degree or higher, 1,218 enrolled as first-time, first-year students.

Part-time:	52%	**Asian American:**	3%
Women:	59%	**Hispanic American:**	15%
African American:	8%	**25 or older:**	37%

Transfer out. 13% of students enrolled in the transfer program go on to 4-year colleges. **Colleges most students transferred to 2008:** Western Connecticut State University, Southern Connecticut State University, Central Connecticut State University, University of Connecticut, Post University.

Basis for selection. Open admission, but selective for some programs. Admission to nursing, physical therapy assistant, radiology, respiratory care programs based on school achievement, recommendations, test scores, maturity of student, motivation. Levels of English Proficiency (LOEP) used for ESL population. Interview required of physical therapy majors. Audition recommended of music majors. Portfolio recommended of art majors. **Homeschooled:** Statement describing homeschool structure and mission, interview required. Placement test and interview required.

High school preparation. Recommended units include English 4, mathematics 3, social studies 2, history 2 and science 1. Most allied health programs require high school algebra, biology, chemistry. Engineering technologies require 2 years algebra, 1 year laboratory science (preferably physics or chemistry), and computer literacy.

2008-2009 Annual costs. Tuition/fees: $2,984; $8,912 out-of-state. Per-credit charge: $110 in-state; $330 out-of-state. Books/supplies: $1,200. Personal expenses: $1,486.

2007-2008 Financial aid. All financial aid based on need. Need-based aid available for part-time students. Work-study available for part-time students.

Application procedures. Admission: Priority date 6/1; no deadline. $20 fee, may be waived for applicants with need. Admission notification on a rolling basis beginning on or about 9/1. **Financial aid:** Priority date 4/1; no closing date. FAFSA required. Applicants notified on a rolling basis starting 6/1.

Academics. Composition, technical writing, literature, computer information systems, math, business law, psychology, astronomy, biology and criminal justice courses available through distance learning. **Special study options:** Cooperative education, cross-registration, distance learning, double major, dual enrollment of high school students, ESL, independent study, internships, study abroad. License preparation in aviation, nursing, physical therapy, radiology, real estate. **Credit/placement by examination:** AP, CLEP, institutional tests. 45 credit hours maximum toward associate degree. **Support services:** Learning center, reduced course load, remedial instruction, study skills assistance, tutoring, writing center.

Majors. Agriculture: Horticulture. **Business:** Accounting technology, administrative services, banking/financial services, business admin, merchandising. **Computer sciences:** General, networking, web page design. **Engineering technology:** General, CAD/CADD, electrical, energy systems, environmental, industrial management, manufacturing, mechanical, quality control. **Family/consumer sciences:** Child development, facilities/event planning, institutional food production. **Health:** Medical radiologic technology/radiation therapy, mental health services, nursing (RN), physical therapy assistant, respiratory therapy technology, substance abuse counseling. **Legal studies:** Legal secretary, paralegal. **Liberal arts:** Arts/sciences. **Mechanic/repair:** Automotive. **Protective services:** Fire safety technology, police science. **Psychology:** General. **Public administration:** Human services, social work. **Transportation:** Aviation. **Visual/performing arts:** Art, dance, dramatic, multimedia.

Two-Year Colleges

Most popular majors. Business/marketing 15%, health sciences 25%, liberal arts 25%, security/protective services 6%.

Computing on campus. 1,100 workstations in library, computer center. Commuter students can connect to campus network. Online course registration, online library, helpline, repair service, wireless network available.

Student life. **Freshman orientation:** Available. Preregistration for classes offered. **Activities:** Bands, choral groups, dance, drama, literary magazine, music ensembles, musical theater, opera, student government, student newspaper, symphony orchestra, black student union, Hispanic student union, human services club, Phi Theta Kappa, Alpha Beta Gamma, agro-bio club, student nurses clubs, book club.

Student services. Adult student services, career counseling, student employment services, financial aid counseling, health services, personal counseling, placement for graduates, veterans' counselor. **Physically disabled:** Services for visually, speech, hearing impaired. **Learning disabled:** Comprehensive services available. **Transfer:** Pre-admission transcript evaluation for new students. Transfer adviser, college fairs on campus for students transferring to 4-year colleges.

Contact. E-mail: nvcc@nvcc.commnet.edu
Phone: (203) 575-8054 Fax: (203) 596-8766
Linda Stango, Director of Admissions, Naugatuck Valley Community College, 750 Chase Parkway, Waterbury, CT 06708-3089

Northwestern Connecticut Community College

Winsted, Connecticut
www.nwcc.commnet.edu
CB member
CB code: 3652

- Public 2-year community and technical college
- Commuter campus in large town

General. Founded in 1965. Regionally accredited. **Enrollment:** 1,185 degree-seeking undergraduates; 536 non-degree-seeking students. **Degrees:** 136 associate awarded. **Location:** 25 miles from Hartford, 25 miles from Waterbury. **Calendar:** Semester, limited summer session. **Full-time faculty:** 28 total. **Part-time faculty:** 102 total. **Class size:** 54% < 20, 43% 20-39, 1% 40-49, 2% 50-99. **Special facilities:** Computer graphics multimedia laboratory.

Student profile. Among degree-seeking undergraduates, 316 enrolled as first-time, first-year students, 101 transferred in from other institutions.

Part-time:	53%	**Women:**	65%
Out-of-state:	1%	**25 or older:**	32%

Basis for selection. Open admission, but selective for some programs. Special requirements for drug and alcohol rehabilitation counseling, adventure education, physical therapy assistant, and dialysis patient care programs.

2008-2009 Annual costs. Tuition/fees: $2,984; $8,912 out-of-state. Per-credit charge: $110 in-state; $330 out-of-state. Books/supplies: $600. Personal expenses: $1,000.

Financial aid. **Non-need-based:** Scholarships awarded for academics, art, state residency.

Application procedures. **Admission:** No deadline. $20 fee, may be waived for applicants with need. Admission notification on a rolling basis. **Financial aid:** Priority date 6/1; no closing date. FAFSA required. Applicants notified on a rolling basis starting 6/1.

Academics. Career education for the deaf program offers full range of services and participation in all majors by deaf and hearing impaired students. Interpreting major prepares hearing students for National Registry test for interpreters for the deaf. **Special study options:** Cooperative education, cross-registration, distance learning, double major, dual enrollment of high school students, ESL, independent study, internships. **Credit/placement by examination:** AP, CLEP, institutional tests. 48 credit hours maximum toward associate degree. **Support services:** Learning center, reduced course load, remedial instruction, tutoring.

Majors. **Business:** Accounting, administrative services, business admin, management information systems, marketing. **Computer sciences:** Information systems, programming. **Education:** General, early childhood. **Foreign languages:** Sign language interpretation. **Health:** Medical assistant, physical therapy assistant, recreational therapy, substance abuse counseling, veterinary technology/assistant. **Interdisciplinary:** Behavioral sciences. **Legal studies:** Legal secretary. **Liberal arts:** Arts/sciences. **Math:** General. **Parks/recreation:** General, facilities management. **Protective services:** Law enforcement admin. **Public administration:** Human services. **Social sciences:** General. **Visual/performing arts:** Commercial/advertising art, design, studio arts.

Most popular majors. Business/marketing 13%, communication technologies 6%, engineering/engineering technologies 7%, family/consumer sciences 6%, health sciences 25%, liberal arts 30%, visual/performing arts 6%.

Computing on campus. 80 workstations in library, computer center.

Student life. **Housing:** Dormitory for hearing impaired and interpreting students available in Winsted. **Activities:** Literary magazine, student government, student newspaper, Spectrum, community service club, Signs of Our Times.

Student services. Career counseling, student employment services, on-campus daycare, personal counseling, veterans' counselor. **Physically disabled:** Services for hearing impaired. **Transfer:** Transfer adviser, college fairs on campus for students transferring to 4-year colleges.

Contact. E-mail: dmartineau@nwcc.commnet.edu
Phone: (860) 738-6330 Fax: (860) 379-4465
Beverly Chrzan, Director of Admissions, Northwestern Connecticut Community College, Park Place East, Winsted, CT 06098

Norwalk Community College

Norwalk, Connecticut
www.ncc.commnet.edu
CB code: 3677

- Public 2-year community and technical college
- Commuter campus in small city

General. Founded in 1961. Regionally accredited. Non-credit courses offered through continuing education department. Lifetime Learners Institute for senior citizens. **Enrollment:** 4,580 degree-seeking undergraduates; 1,686 non-degree-seeking students. **Degrees:** 388 associate awarded. **Location:** 45 miles from New York City. **Calendar:** Semester, extensive summer session. **Full-time faculty:** 100 total. **Part-time faculty:** 250 total. **Special facilities:** Theater, rotating art and cultural exhibits, culinary arts facility, early childhood education lab/preschool.

Student profile. Among degree-seeking undergraduates, 37% enrolled in a transfer program, 37% enrolled in a vocational program, 12% already have a bachelor's degree or higher, 874 enrolled as first-time, first-year students, 723 transferred in from other institutions.

Part-time:	56%	**Asian American:**	4%
Out-of-state:	1%	**Hispanic American:**	24%
Women:	62%	**International:**	4%
African American:	21%	**25 or older:**	52%

Basis for selection. Open admission, but selective for some programs. Special requirements for nursing, legal assistant, respiratory care programs.

High school preparation. Recommended units include English 4, mathematics 3 and science 2. Chemistry, biology and algebra required for nursing and respiratory therapy applicants. Nursing applicants must have taken chemistry within past 5 years.

2008-2009 Annual costs. Tuition/fees: $2,984; $8,912 out-of-state. Per-credit charge: $110 in-state; $330 out-of-state. New England Regional Student Program: $241.25 per credit-hour. Books/supplies: $1,200. Personal expenses: $1,751.

Financial aid. **Need-based:** Need-based aid available for part-time students. Work-study available for part-time students. **Non-need-based:** Scholarships awarded for academics, alumni affiliation.

Application procedures. **Admission:** No deadline. $20 fee, may be waived for applicants with need. Admission notification on a rolling basis. Applicants to nursing program should apply by February 1. **Financial aid:** Priority date 7/1; no closing date. FAFSA, institutional form required. Applicants notified on a rolling basis starting 7/1; must reply within 2 week(s) of notification.

Academics. Special 10-week sessions with longer class hours per day let students finish courses more quickly during fall and spring. **Special study options:** Cooperative education, cross-registration, double major, dual enrollment of high school students, ESL, honors, internships, liberal arts/career combination, weekend college. Early childhood education credential training program. License preparation in nursing, paramedic, real estate. **Credit/placement by examination:** AP, CLEP, IB, institutional tests. 45 credit hours maximum toward associate degree. **Support services:** Learning center, pre-admission summer program, reduced course load, remedial instruction, study skills assistance, tutoring, writing center.

Majors. Business: Accounting, business admin, finance, hospitality admin, management information systems, marketing, office management, office technology. **Communications:** Journalism. **Communications technology:** General. **Computer sciences:** General, applications programming, data processing, information systems, programming, systems analysis. **Education:** Early childhood. **Engineering:** General, architectural, science. **Engineering technology:** Architectural, construction. **Health:** Nursing (RN), recreational therapy, respiratory therapy technology. **Legal studies:** Legal secretary, paralegal. **Liberal arts:** Arts/sciences. **Math:** General. **Parks/recreation:** General. **Protective services:** Fire safety technology, fire services admin, law enforcement admin. **Public administration:** Human services. **Visual/performing arts:** Art, commercial/advertising art, studio arts.

Computing on campus. 90 workstations in library, computer center, student center. Commuter students can connect to campus network. Online library, helpline available.

Student life. Freshman orientation: Available. One-day orientation for new students before start of semester. **Activities:** Choral groups, drama, international student organizations, literary magazine, student government, student newspaper, TV station, African culture club, Hay Motivo, Phi Theta Kappa, legal assistants club, early childhood education club, French club, Haitian student association, criminal justice club.

Student services. Adult student services, career counseling, services for economically disadvantaged, student employment services, financial aid counseling, on-campus daycare, placement for graduates, veterans' counselor, women's services. **Physically disabled:** Services for visually, speech, hearing impaired. **Transfer:** Re-entry adviser, pre-admission transcript evaluation for new students. Transfer adviser, college fairs on campus for students transferring to 4-year colleges.

Contact. E-mail: admissions@ncc.commnet.edu
Phone: (203) 857-7060 Fax: (203) 857-3335
Kimberlee Csapo-Ebert, Director of Enrollment Management, Norwalk Community College, 188 Richards Avenue, Norwalk, CT 06854-1655

Quinebaug Valley Community College

Danielson, Connecticut
www.qvcc.commnet.edu
CB member
CB code: 3716

- Public 2-year community and technical college
- Commuter campus in large town

General. Founded in 1971. Regionally accredited. **Enrollment:** 1,660 degree-seeking undergraduates; 287 non-degree-seeking students. **Degrees:** 168 associate awarded. **Location:** 50 miles from Hartford; 25 miles from Providence, Rhode Island. **Calendar:** Semester, limited summer session. **Full-time faculty:** 30 total; 17% have terminal degrees, 10% minority, 57% women. **Part-time faculty:** 107 total; 11% have terminal degrees, 5% minority, 54% women. **Class size:** 45% < 20, 55% 20-39. **Special facilities:** Plastics laboratory.

Student profile. Among degree-seeking undergraduates, 30% enrolled in a transfer program, 60% enrolled in a vocational program, 1% already have a bachelor's degree or higher, 429 enrolled as first-time, first-year students, 216 transferred in from other institutions.

Part-time:	59%	**Asian American:**	1%
Out-of-state:	1%	**Hispanic American:**	11%
Women:	66%	**Native American:**	1%
African American:	3%	**25 or older:**	42%

Transfer out. Colleges most students transferred to 2008: Eastern Connecticut State University, University of Connecticut, Worcester State College.

Basis for selection. Open admission, but selective for some programs. Interview recommended. **Learning Disabled:** Meeting with Coordinator of Learning Disability Services recommended.

2008-2009 Annual costs. Tuition/fees: $2,984; $8,912 out-of-state. Per-credit charge: $110 in-state; $330 out-of-state. Books/supplies: $1,250. Personal expenses: $1,000.

2008-2009 Financial aid. All financial aid based on need. 96% of total undergraduate aid awarded as scholarships/grants, 4% as loans/jobs. Need-based aid available for part-time students. Work-study available nights, weekends and for part-time students.

Application procedures. Admission: No deadline. $20 fee, may be waived for applicants with need. Admission notification on a rolling basis. **Financial aid:** Closing date 10/1. FAFSA required. Applicants notified on a rolling basis starting 5/1.

Academics. Special study options: Distance learning, double major, dual enrollment of high school students, ESL, independent study, internships. License preparation in real estate. **Credit/placement by examination:** AP, CLEP, institutional tests. 30 credit hours maximum toward associate degree. **Support services:** Learning center, pre-admission summer program, reduced course load, remedial instruction, study skills assistance, tutoring, writing center.

Majors. Business: Accounting, administrative services, business admin, office management, office technology. **Computer sciences:** General. **Construction:** General. **Education:** Early childhood. **Engineering:** Polymer. **Engineering technology:** Biomedical, plastics. **Health:** Community health services, medical assistant. **Liberal arts:** Arts/sciences. **Mechanic/repair:** Aircraft. **Public administration:** Human services. **Visual/performing arts:** Studio arts.

Most popular majors. Business/marketing 11%, health sciences 8%, liberal arts 58%, visual/performing arts 7%.

Computing on campus. 115 workstations in library, computer center. Commuter students can connect to campus network. Online course registration, online library, helpline, wireless network available.

Student life. Freshman orientation: Available. **Activities:** Student government, medical assisting association, Phi Theta Kappa, Alpha Beta Gamma, book club.

Student services. Adult student services, career counseling, student employment services, financial aid counseling, minority student services, on-campus daycare, placement for graduates, veterans' counselor. **Physically disabled:** Services for visually, speech, hearing impaired. **Transfer:** Re-entry adviser, pre-admission transcript evaluation for new students. Transfer adviser, college fairs on campus for students transferring to 4-year colleges.

Contact. E-mail: qv_lsd@commnet.edu
Phone: (860) 412-7380 Fax: (860) 774-7768
Maria Angelos, Enrollment and Transition Counselor, Quinebaug Valley Community College, 742 Upper Maple Street, Danielson, CT 06239-1440

St. Vincent's College

Bridgeport, Connecticut
www.stvincentscollege.edu
CB code: 3789

- Private 2-year health science and junior college
- Commuter campus in small city
- SAT or ACT with writing, application essay required

General. Regionally accredited. Majority of students are adult learners. Nursing and radiography programs highly competitive; pre-programs available. **Enrollment:** 427 degree-seeking undergraduates. **Degrees:** 76 associate awarded. **Location:** 55 miles from New York City. **Calendar:** Semester, limited summer session. **Full-time faculty:** 12 total. **Part-time faculty:** 32 total.

Student profile. Among degree-seeking undergraduates, 100% enrolled in a vocational program, 84 transferred in from other institutions.

African American:	15%	**Hispanic American:**	11%
Asian American:	3%	**International:**	1%

Transfer out. Colleges most students transferred to 2008: Southern Connecticut State University.

Basis for selection. High school record and GPA most important, followed by character, talents, work and volunteer experience. **Adult students:** SAT/ACT scores not required if out of high school 1 year(s) or more. **Homeschooled:** Transcript of courses and grades, letter of recommendation (nonparent) required.

High school preparation. College-preparatory program required. 16 units required. Required units include English 4, mathematics 2, social studies 2, science 2 and academic electives 6.

2008-2009 Annual costs. Tuition/fees: $11,850. Per-credit charge: $360. Books/supplies: $1,400.

Application procedures. Admission: Priority date 5/1; deadline 8/1 (receipt date). $50 fee, may be waived for applicants with need. Admission notification on a rolling basis beginning on or about 10/1.

Academics. Special study options: Distance learning, internships. License preparation in nursing, radiology. **Credit/placement by examination:** AP, CLEP, institutional tests. 18 credit hours maximum toward associate degree. **Support services:** Learning center, pre-admission summer

program, reduced course load, remedial instruction, study skills assistance, tutoring, writing center.

Majors. Health: Cardiovascular technology, medical assistant, nursing (RN), radiologic technology/medical imaging.

Computing on campus. 40 workstations in computer center, student center. Commuter students can connect to campus network. Online library, wireless network available.

Student life. Freshman orientation: Mandatory. Held each spring and fall. **Activities:** Student government, student newspaper.

Student services. Alcohol/substance abuse counseling, chaplain/spiritual director, career counseling, student employment services, financial aid counseling, health services, personal counseling.

Contact. E-mail: admissions@stvincentscollege.edu
Phone: (203) 576-5513 Fax: (203) 576-5318
Joseph Marrone, Admissions Director, St. Vincent's College, 2800 Main Street, Bridgeport, CT 06606

Three Rivers Community College

Norwich, Connecticut
www.trcc.commnet.edu
CB member
CB code: 3558

- Public 2-year community and technical college
- Commuter campus in large town

General. Founded in 1969. Regionally accredited. **Enrollment:** 3,712 degree-seeking undergraduates; 420 non-degree-seeking students. **Degrees:** 371 associate awarded. **Location:** 45 miles from Hartford. **Calendar:** Semester, limited summer session. **Full-time faculty:** 76 total; 10% have terminal degrees, 10% minority, 54% women. **Part-time faculty:** 136 total; 51% women. **Special facilities:** Nuclear reactor simulator.

Student profile. Among degree-seeking undergraduates, 16% enrolled in a transfer program, 46% enrolled in a vocational program, 1% already have a bachelor's degree or higher, 948 enrolled as first-time, first-year students, 528 transferred in from other institutions.

Part-time:	63%	**Asian American:**	4%
Out-of-state:	1%	**Hispanic American:**	9%
Women:	59%	**Native American:**	1%
African American:	7%	**25 or older:**	45%

Transfer out. Colleges most students transferred to 2008: Eastern Connecticut State University, University of Connecticut, Central Connecticut State University, Southern Illinois University, Sacred Heart University.

Basis for selection. Open admission, but selective for some programs. Selective admission for nursing program based on successful performance on ATI-TEAS Exam, completion of prerequisite courses, and 2.7 GPA. **Adult students:** Basic skills placement tests in math and English required unless student has completed college level math and English course. **Homeschooled:** Student may take Ability to Benefit Test if standard documentation requirements are not met.

High school preparation. College-preparatory program recommended. One unit chemistry, biology, and algebra required for nursing program.

2008-2009 Annual costs. Tuition/fees: $2,984; $8,912 out-of-state. Per-credit charge: $110 in-state; $330 out-of-state. Out-of-state required fees: $992. New England state students pay $3,960 for tuition and $506 for fees. Books/supplies: $1,200. Personal expenses: $1,304.

2007-2008 Financial aid. All financial aid based on need. 293 full-time freshmen applied for aid; 286 were judged to have need; 280 of these received aid. Average need met was 53%. Average scholarship/grant was $2,011; average loan $1,971. 76% of total undergraduate aid awarded as scholarships/grants, 24% as loans/jobs. Need-based aid available for part-time students.

Application procedures. Admission: No deadline. $20 fee, may be waived for applicants with need. Admission notification on a rolling basis beginning on or about 3/30. **Financial aid:** Priority date 7/15; no closing date. FAFSA required. Applicants notified on a rolling basis; must reply within 2 week(s) of notification.

Academics. Special study options: Cooperative education, cross-registration, distance learning, double major, dual enrollment of high school students, ESL, independent study, internships, liberal arts/career combination, study abroad. License preparation in nursing. **Credit/placement by examination:** AP, CLEP, institutional tests. 45 credit hours maximum toward associate degree. **Support services:** Learning center, pre-admission summer program, reduced course load, remedial instruction, study skills assistance, tutoring, writing center.

Majors. Architecture: Technology. **Business:** Accounting, banking/financial services, business admin, hospitality admin, management information systems, office technology, restaurant/food services, tourism/travel. **Communications:** Public relations. **Computer sciences:** General, applications programming, information systems. **Conservation:** Environmental science. **Education:** Early childhood, special. **Engineering technology:** General, architectural, CAD/CADD, civil, drafting, electrical, environmental, hazardous materials, laser/optical, manufacturing, nuclear, water quality. **Family/consumer sciences:** Family studies. **Health:** Medical secretary, nursing (RN). **Interdisciplinary:** Accounting/computer science. **Liberal arts:** Arts/sciences. **Personal/culinary services:** Restaurant/catering. **Physical sciences:** General. **Protective services:** Criminal justice, fire safety technology, law enforcement admin, police science. **Public administration:** Human services. **Science technology:** Nuclear power. **Transportation:** Aviation.

Most popular majors. Business/marketing 15%, engineering/engineering technologies 10%, health sciences 20%, liberal arts 36%.

Computing on campus. 300 workstations in library, computer center. Online course registration, online library, helpline, wireless network available.

Student life. Freshman orientation: Available. **Policies:** Student government controls student activity fees. **Activities:** Drama, literary magazine, student government, student newspaper, Spanish-American association, Afro-American association, student chapters of professional organizations, gay-straight alliance, volunteer club, golf club, student nurses association, environmentalists club, senior student ambassadors, veterans organization.

Athletics. NJCAA.

Student services. Adult student services, career counseling, student employment services, financial aid counseling, on-campus daycare, veterans' counselor. **Physically disabled:** Services for visually, hearing impaired. **Transfer:** Re-entry adviser for new students. Transfer adviser, college fairs on campus for students transferring to 4-year colleges.

Contact. E-mail: admissions@trcc.commnet.edu
Phone: (860) 383-5260
Dan Zaneski, Director of Admissions, Three Rivers Community College, New London Turnpike, Norwich, CT 06360-6598

Tunxis Community College

Farmington, Connecticut
www.tunxis.commnet.edu
CB member
CB code: 3897

- Public 2-year community college
- Commuter campus in large town

General. Founded in 1970. Regionally accredited. **Enrollment:** 3,317 degree-seeking undergraduates; 1,017 non-degree-seeking students. **Degrees:** 237 associate awarded. **ROTC:** Army, Naval, Air Force. **Location:** 15 miles from Hartford. **Calendar:** Semester, limited summer session. **Full-time faculty:** 67 total. **Part-time faculty:** 186 total. **Class size:** 29% < 20, 70% 20-39, less than 1% 40-49. **Special facilities:** Early childhood center, art gallery.

Student profile. Among degree-seeking undergraduates, 825 enrolled as first-time, first-year students, 352 transferred in from other institutions.

Part-time:	49%	**Asian American:**	3%
Out-of-state:	1%	**Hispanic American:**	13%
Women:	62%	**25 or older:**	38%
African American:	6%		

Transfer out. 25% of students enrolled in the transfer program go on to 4-year colleges. **Colleges most students transferred to 2008:** Central Connecticut State University, Charter Oak College, St. Joseph College, University of Connecticut.

Basis for selection. Open admission, but selective for some programs. Special requirements for dental hygiene, drug and alcohol rehabilitation counselor, physical therapist assistant, technological studies: television operations option, dental assisting, criminal justice command institute: supervisory leadership programs, and correction pre-service certification. ESL placement test required of non-native English speakers. Interview required of dental hygiene, drug and alcohol rehabilitation counselor majors. **Homeschooled:** Placement test (ACCUPLACER) required. **Learning Disabled:** Contact Academic Support Center prior to placement testing if accommodations are necessary.

High school preparation. College-preparatory program recommended.

2008-2009 Annual costs. Tuition/fees: $2,984; $8,912 out-of-state. Per-credit charge: $110 in-state; $330 out-of-state. Books/supplies: $420. Personal expenses: $1,210.

2007-2008 Financial aid. Need-based: Need-based aid available for part-time students. Work-study available nights, weekends and for part-time students. **Non-need-based:** Scholarships awarded for academics, leadership. **Additional information:** Financial aid available to all students showing need. Part-time students encouraged to apply.

Application procedures. Admission: No deadline. $20 fee, may be waived for applicants with need. Admission notification on a rolling basis. Dental hygiene program closing date 1/1, notification by 3/1. **Financial aid:** Priority date 6/1; no closing date. FAFSA required. Applicants notified on a rolling basis starting 3/1.

Academics. Special study options: Cross-registration, distance learning, double major, dual enrollment of high school students, ESL, independent study, internships, liberal arts/career combination. License preparation in dental hygiene, physical therapy. **Credit/placement by examination:** CLEP, institutional tests. 30 credit hours maximum toward associate degree. **Support services:** Learning center, pre-admission summer program, reduced course load, remedial instruction, tutoring.

Majors. Business: Accounting, administrative services, business admin, fashion, finance, office/clerical. **Computer sciences:** Applications programming, computer graphics. **Education:** Early childhood. **Engineering:** Science. **Engineering technology:** Manufacturing. **Health:** Dental hygiene, medical secretary, substance abuse counseling. **Legal studies:** Legal secretary. **Liberal arts:** Arts/sciences. **Public administration:** Human services. **Visual/performing arts:** General, commercial/advertising art.

Computing on campus. 200 workstations in library, computer center. Commuter students can connect to campus network. Wireless network available.

Student life. Freshman orientation: Available. Preregistration for classes offered. Held once a week during the month before start of classes. **Activities:** Jazz band, literary magazine, student government, student newspaper, minority student alliance, human services club, criminal justice club, dental hygiene group.

Student services. Career counseling, student employment services, financial aid counseling, health services, minority student services, on-campus daycare, personal counseling, placement for graduates. **Physically disabled:** Services for visually impaired. **Transfer:** Transfer adviser, college fairs on campus for students transferring to 4-year colleges.

Contact. E-mail: tx-admissions@txcc.commnet.edu
Phone: (860) 255-3555 Fax: (860) 255-3559
Peter McCluskey, Director of Admissions, Tunxis Community College, 271 Scott Swamp Road, Farmington, CT 06032-3187

Delaware

Delaware College of Art and Design

Wilmington, Delaware
www.dcad.edu
CB code: 5161

- Private 2-year visual arts college
- Residential campus in large city

General. Regionally accredited. **Enrollment:** 227 degree-seeking undergraduates. **Degrees:** 65 associate awarded. **Calendar:** Semester, limited summer session. **Full-time faculty:** 7 total; 86% have terminal degrees, 29% women. **Part-time faculty:** 25 total. **Class size:** 86% < 20, 14% 20-39.

Student profile. Among degree-seeking undergraduates, 112 enrolled as first-time, first-year students.

Part-time:	7%	**Hispanic American:**	5%
Out-of-state:	54%	**International:**	4%
Women:	63%	**25 or older:**	8%
African American:	15%	**Live on campus:**	61%
Asian American:	3%		

Transfer out. 68% of students enrolled in the transfer program go on to 4-year colleges.

Basis for selection. High school record considered. Art Portfolio required. **Adult students:** SAT/ACT scores not required. **Homeschooled:** Transcript of courses and grades, state high school equivalency certificate required.

High school preparation. College-preparatory program recommended. Recommended units include English 4, mathematics 3, social studies 4, history 2, science 3, foreign language 2, computer science 2 and visual/performing arts 4.

2008-2009 Annual costs. Tuition/fees: $17,300. Room only: $6,400.

2007-2008 Financial aid. Need-based: 96 full-time freshmen applied for aid; 70 were judged to have need; 70 of these received aid. Average need met was 98%. Average scholarship/grant was $4,000; average loan $3,500. 46% of total undergraduate aid awarded as scholarships/grants, 54% as loans/jobs. **Non-need-based:** Awarded to 150 full-time undergraduates, including 80 freshmen.

Application procedures. Admission: Priority date 3/1; no deadline. $40 fee, may be waived for applicants with need. Admission notification on a rolling basis. Must reply by May 1 or within 2 week(s) if notified thereafter.

Academics. Special study options: Study abroad. **Credit/placement by examination:** AP, CLEP, institutional tests.

Majors. Communications technology: Animation/special effects. **Visual/performing arts:** Graphic design, illustration, interior design, photography, studio arts.

Most popular majors. Communication technologies 25%, visual/performing arts 75%.

Computing on campus. Dormitories wired for high-speed internet access. Wireless network available.

Student life. Freshman orientation: Mandatory. **Housing:** Coed dorms, apartments available. $350 nonrefundable deposit, deadline 5/1. Apartment-style housing with full kitchen/living room, semi-furnished.

Student services. Financial aid counseling.

Contact. E-mail: admissions@dcad.edu
Phone: (302) 622-8867 ext. 118 Fax: (302) 622-8870
Elizabeth Gatti, Director of Admissions, Delaware College of Art and Design, 600 North Market Street, Wilmington, DE 19801

Delaware Technical and Community College: Owens

Georgetown, Delaware
www.dtcc.edu
CB code: 5169

- Public 2-year community and technical college
- Commuter campus in rural community
- Interview required

General. Founded in 1967. Regionally accredited. **Enrollment:** 3,768 degree-seeking undergraduates; 578 non-degree-seeking students. **Degrees:** 363 associate awarded. **Location:** 80 miles from Wilmington. **Calendar:** Semester, limited summer session. **Full-time faculty:** 117 total. **Part-time faculty:** 201 total. **Class size:** 61% < 20, 39% 20-39, less than 1% 40-49, less than 1% 50-99. **Special facilities:** Treasures of the sea maritime exhibit.

Student profile. Among degree-seeking undergraduates, 899 enrolled as first-time, first-year students.

Part-time:	49%	**Women:**	65%
Out-of-state:	4%	**25 or older:**	40%

Basis for selection. Open admission, but selective for some programs. Interview required of health technology majors.

2008-2009 Annual costs. Tuition/fees: $2,631; $6,141 out-of-state. Per-credit charge: $98 in-state; $244 out-of-state. Books/supplies: $1,500. Personal expenses: $200.

Financial aid. All financial aid based on need. Need-based aid available for part-time students. Work-study available for part-time students.

Application procedures. Admission: No deadline. $10 fee, may be waived for applicants with need. Application must be submitted on paper. Admission notification on a rolling basis. **Financial aid:** Priority date 6/15; no closing date. FAFSA required. Applicants notified on a rolling basis; must reply within 2 week(s) of notification.

Academics. Special study options: Distance learning, double major, dual enrollment of high school students, ESL, internships. **Credit/placement by examination:** AP, CLEP, institutional tests. **Support services:** GED preparation and test center, remedial instruction, writing center.

Majors. Agriculture: Business, horticulture, poultry, production, turf management. **Biology:** General. **Business:** General, accounting, construction management, e-commerce, entrepreneurial studies, management information systems, marketing, office management, office technology. **Computer sciences:** General. **Education:** Early childhood, elementary, kindergarten/preschool, mathematics, multi-level teacher. **Engineering technology:** Aerospace, architectural, civil, computer systems, drafting, electrical, mechanical drafting, nuclear, water quality. **Health:** Clinical lab assistant, EMT paramedic, medical assistant, nursing (RN), occupational therapy assistant, physical therapy assistant, radiologic technology/medical imaging, respiratory therapy assistant, sonography, veterinary technology/assistant. **Legal studies:** Legal secretary. **Mechanic/repair:** Automotive, heating/ac/refrig. **Protective services:** Law enforcement admin, police science. **Public administration:** Human services. **Science technology:** Biological. **Visual/performing arts:** Music.

Computing on campus. 728 workstations in library, computer center, student center. Commuter students can connect to campus network. Online library, helpline, wireless network available.

Student life. Freshman orientation: Available. **Activities:** Radio station, student government, student newspaper.

Athletics. NJCAA. **Intercollegiate:** Baseball M, golf M. **Team name:** Road Runners.

Student services. Adult student services, career counseling, student employment services, financial aid counseling, personal counseling, placement for graduates, veterans' counselor. **Physically disabled:** Services for visually, hearing impaired. **Transfer:** Transfer adviser for students transferring to 4-year colleges.

Contact. E-mail: owens-info@dtcc.edu
Phone: (302) 856-5400
Claire MacDonald, Admissions Coordinator, Delaware Technical and Community College: Owens, PO Box 610, Georgetown, DE 19947

Delaware Technical and Community College: Stanton/Wilmington

Newark, Delaware
www.dtcc.edu **CB code: 5154**

- Public 2-year community and technical college
- Commuter campus in small city

General. Founded in 1967. Regionally accredited. Multi-location institution. **Enrollment:** 6,665 degree-seeking undergraduates; 644 non-degree-seeking students. **Degrees:** 542 associate awarded. **ROTC:** Air Force. **Location:** 30 miles from Philadelphia. **Calendar:** Semester, limited summer session. **Full-time faculty:** 177 total. **Part-time faculty:** 388 total. **Class size:** 74% < 20, 25% 20-39, less than 1% 40-49, less than 1% 50-99.

Student profile. Among degree-seeking undergraduates, 1,568 enrolled as first-time, first-year students, 263 transferred in from other institutions.

Part-time:	58%	**Women:**	60%
Out-of-state:	4%	**25 or older:**	42%

Basis for selection. Open admission, but selective for some programs. Admission to health technologies program restricted to state residents. Restricted admission to dental hygiene, nursing, and culinary arts programs. Interview required for all technology programs.

2008-2009 Annual costs. Tuition/fees: $2,631; $6,141 out-of-state. Per-credit charge: $98 in-state; $244 out-of-state. Books/supplies: $1,500. Personal expenses: $200.

Financial aid. All financial aid based on need. Need-based aid available for part-time students. Work-study available for part-time students.

Application procedures. Admission: No deadline. $10 fee, may be waived for applicants with need. Application must be submitted on paper. Admission notification on a rolling basis. **Financial aid:** Priority date 6/15; no closing date. FAFSA required. Applicants notified on a rolling basis; must reply within 2 week(s) of notification.

Academics. Special study options: Cooperative education, distance learning, double major, dual enrollment of high school students, ESL, internships. **Credit/placement by examination:** AP, CLEP, institutional tests. **Support services:** GED preparation and test center, learning center, pre-admission summer program, remedial instruction, study skills assistance, tutoring, writing center.

Majors. Agriculture: Business. **Biology:** General. **Business:** General, accounting, banking/financial services, business admin, construction management, customer service, hotel/motel admin, management information systems, management science, marketing, office management, office technology. **Computer sciences:** General, networking. **Education:** Early childhood, elementary, kindergarten/preschool, mathematics, multi-level teacher. **Engineering:** Operations research. **Engineering technology:** Architectural, CAD/CADD, civil drafting, computer, drafting, electrical, heat/ac/refrig, industrial management, manufacturing, mechanical, nuclear. **Health:** Cardiovascular technology, dental hygiene, electrocardiograph technology, EMT ambulance attendant, EMT paramedic, histologic technology, medical assistant, nuclear medical technology, nursing (RN), occupational therapy assistant, physical therapy assistant, radiologic technology/medical imaging, respiratory therapy assistant, sonography, substance abuse counseling. **Mechanic/repair:** Automotive. **Parks/recreation:** Exercise sciences. **Personal/culinary services:** Chef training, restaurant/catering. **Protective services:** Fire safety technology, fire services admin, firefighting, law enforcement admin, police science. **Public administration:** Human services. **Science technology:** Biological, chemical. **Visual/performing arts:** Music. **Other:** Science technologies.

Most popular majors. Business/marketing 20%, engineering/engineering technologies 9%, health sciences 46%, security/protective services 7%.

Computing on campus. 1,139 workstations in library, computer center. Commuter students can connect to campus network. Online library, helpline available.

Student life. Freshman orientation: Available. **Activities:** Student government, student newspaper.

Athletics. NJCAA. **Intercollegiate:** Basketball, soccer M, softball W. **Intramural:** Basketball, football (tackle), softball W, volleyball. **Team name:** Spirit.

Student services. Adult student services, career counseling, student employment services, health services, personal counseling, placement for graduates, veterans' counselor. **Physically disabled:** Services for visually, speech, hearing impaired.

Contact. Phone: (302) 454-3954 Fax: (302) 453-3084
Rebecca Bailey, Admissions Representative, Delaware Technical and Community College: Stanton/Wilmington, 400 Stanton-Christiana Road, Newark, DE 19713

Delaware Technical and Community College: Terry

Dover, Delaware **CB member**
www.dtcc.edu **CB code: 5201**

- Public 2-year community and technical college
- Commuter campus in large town

General. Founded in 1972. Regionally accredited. **Enrollment:** 3,062 degree-seeking undergraduates; 208 non-degree-seeking students. **Degrees:** 221 associate awarded. **Location:** 90 miles from Baltimore, 75 miles from Philadelphia. **Calendar:** Semester, limited summer session. **Full-time faculty:** 81 total. **Part-time faculty:** 160 total. **Class size:** 68% < 20, 32% 20-39.

Student profile. Among degree-seeking undergraduates, 844 enrolled as first-time, first-year students, 120 transferred in from other institutions.

Part-time:	55%	**Women:**	67%
Out-of-state:	2%	**25 or older:**	49%

Basis for selection. Open admission, but selective for some programs. Special requirements for health/nursing programs. Interview required of technology majors.

2008-2009 Annual costs. Tuition/fees: $2,631; $6,141 out-of-state. Per-credit charge: $98 in-state; $244 out-of-state. Books/supplies: $1,500. Personal expenses: $200.

Financial aid. All financial aid based on need. Need-based aid available for part-time students. Work-study available for part-time students.

Application procedures. Admission: No deadline. $10 fee, may be waived for applicants with need. Application must be submitted on paper. Admission notification on a rolling basis. **Financial aid:** Priority date 6/15; no closing date. FAFSA required. Applicants notified on a rolling basis starting 7/1; must reply within 2 week(s) of notification.

Academics. Special study options: Distance learning, double major, dual enrollment of high school students, ESL, internships. **Credit/placement by examination:** AP, CLEP, institutional tests. **Support services:** GED preparation and test center, pre-admission summer program, remedial instruction, tutoring, writing center.

Majors. Agriculture: Business. **Business:** General, accounting, business admin, construction management, e-commerce, entrepreneurial studies, hotel/motel admin, human resources, management information systems, marketing, office management, office technology. **Communications:** Digital media. **Computer sciences:** General, networking. **Education:** Early childhood, elementary, kindergarten/preschool, mathematics, multi-level teacher. **Engineering technology:** Architectural, biomedical, civil, computer, computer systems, electrical, electromechanical. **Health:** EMT paramedic, medical assistant, nursing (RN), substance abuse counseling. **Legal studies:** Legal secretary. **Personal/culinary services:** Chef training. **Protective services:** Law enforcement admin, police science. **Public administration:** Human services. **Visual/performing arts:** Commercial/advertising art, interior design, photography. **Other:** EMT management.

Most popular majors. Business/marketing 15%, engineering/engineering technologies 11%, health sciences 39%, security/protective services 7%, visual/performing arts 11%.

Computing on campus. 423 workstations in library, computer center. Commuter students can connect to campus network. Online library, helpline available.

Student life. Freshman orientation: Available. **Activities:** Student government, student newspaper.

Athletics. NJCAA. **Intercollegiate:** Lacrosse M, soccer, softball W. **Team name:** Hawks.

Student services. Adult student services, career counseling, student employment services, personal counseling, placement for graduates, veterans' counselor. **Physically disabled:** Services for visually, hearing impaired.

Contact. Phone: (302) 857-1020 Fax: (302) 739-6169
Maria Harris, Admissions Coordinator, Delaware Technical and Community College: Terry, 100 Campus Drive, Dover, DE 19901

Florida

Angley College
Deland, Florida
www.angley.edu

- For-profit 2-year technical and career college
- Commuter campus in small city
- Interview required

General. Accredited by ACICS. Free child care available. **Enrollment:** 129 degree-seeking undergraduates. **Degrees:** 12 associate awarded. **Location:** 30 miles from Orlando. **Calendar:** Quarter, extensive summer session. **Full-time faculty:** 8 total. **Part-time faculty:** 21 total. **Partnerships:** Formal partnerships with local hospitals, clinics and local businesses.

Student profile. Among degree-seeking undergraduates, 15% enrolled in a transfer program, 70% enrolled in a vocational program, 96 enrolled as first-time, first-year students.

Out-of-state:	15%	**25 or older:**	75%
Women:	76%		

Basis for selection. Completion of high school with standard high school diploma, succesful completion of college-administered admission test, and results of interview (in person or via telephone) with admissions officer important. **Homeschooled:** State high school equivalency certificate required.

2008-2009 Annual costs. Tuition/fees: $15,075. Per-credit charge: $315. Textbooks included in program cost. Books/supplies: $1,350. Personal expenses: $180.

Application procedures. Admission: No deadline. $25 fee. Admission notification on a rolling basis.

Academics. Special study options: Accelerated study, cooperative education, distance learning, double major, ESL, independent study, internships, weekend college. License preparation in aviation. **Credit/placement by examination:** AP, CLEP, SAT, ACT, institutional tests. 22.5 credit hours maximum toward associate degree, 45 toward bachelor's. **Support services:** Learning center, remedial instruction, study skills assistance, tutoring.

Majors. Health: Massage therapy, medical assistant, office assistant.

Computing on campus. 25 workstations in library, computer center. Online library, wireless network available.

Student life. Freshman orientation: Mandatory. Preregistration for classes offered. Held Saturday before each class start; lasts approximately 2 hours. **Activities:** Student government.

Student services. Adult student services, alcohol/substance abuse counseling, career counseling, financial aid counseling, on-campus daycare, personal counseling, placement for graduates, veterans' counselor. **Transfer:** Pre-admission transcript evaluation for new students.

Contact. E-mail: admissions@angley.edu
Phone: (386) 740-1215 Toll-free number: (866) 639-1215
Fax: (386) 740-2077
Don Smith, Director of Admissions, Angley College, 1700 Woodland Boulevard, Deland, FL 32720-4289

ATI Career Training Center: Ft. Lauderdale
Ft. Lauderdale, Florida
www.aticareertraining.edu **CB code: 2945**

- For-profit 2-year technical college
- Small city

General. Accredited by ACCSCT. **Calendar:** Continuous.

Annual costs/financial aid. Full program costs: $25,440 for electronics, $13,800 for medical assistant technician, $10,500 for medical administration assisting technology; $21,400 for Network Administration. Costs include all tuition, fees and supplies.

Contact. Phone: (954) 973-4760
2890 NW 62nd Street, Fort Lauderdale, FL 33309-9731

ATI Career Training Center: Oakland Park
Oakland Park, Florida
www.aticareertraining.edu **CB code: 3182**

- For-profit 2-year technical college
- Large town

General. Accredited by ACCSCT. **Calendar:** Continuous.

Annual costs/financial aid. Tuition and fees entire AC/refrigeration program $22,500 (diploma program $19,822); for entire automotive service technician program $26,980 (diploma program $24,740); for entire business administration technology program $16,280; for entire electronic systems technician $14,000.

Contact. Phone: (954) 563-5899
Director of Admission, 3501 NW 9th Avenue, Oakland Park, FL 33309

ATI College of Health
Miami, Florida
www.aticareertraining.edu **CB code: 3183**

- For-profit 2-year health science and technical college
- Very large city

General. Accredited by ACCSCT. **Calendar:** Semester.

Annual costs/financial aid. $44,520 tuition for diagnostic ultrasound program and respiratory therapist program; $31,102 for dental and health information technology. Personal expenses: $2,064. Need-based financial aid available to full-time and part-time students.

Contact. Phone: (305) 628-1000
1395 NW 167th Street, Miami, FL 33169-5745

Brevard Community College
Cocoa, Florida **CB member**
www.brevardcc.edu **CB code: 5073**

- Public 2-year community college
- Commuter campus in large town

General. Founded in 1960. Regionally accredited. Additional campuses in Cocoa, Melbourne, Palm Bay, Titusville. Aerospace technology courses taught at the Kennedy Space Center. **Enrollment:** 14,403 degree-seeking undergraduates; 1,204 non-degree-seeking students. **Degrees:** 2,112 associate awarded. **ROTC:** Army, Air Force. **Location:** 50 miles from Orlando. **Calendar:** Semester, extensive summer session. **Full-time faculty:** 215 total; 20% have terminal degrees, 11% minority, 60% women. **Part-time faculty:** 822 total; 9% minority, 51% women. **Class size:** 34% < 20, 66% 20-39, less than 1% 40-49, less than 1% 50-99. **Special facilities:** Planetarium, observatory, playhouse, WBCC-TV, performing arts center, multicultural center.

Student profile. Among degree-seeking undergraduates, 75% enrolled in a transfer program, 25% enrolled in a vocational program, 10% already have a bachelor's degree or higher, 3,136 enrolled as first-time, first-year students.

Part-time:	58%	**Women:**	58%
Out-of-state:	2%	**25 or older:**	34%

Transfer out. 75% of students enrolled in the transfer program go on to 4-year colleges. **Colleges most students transferred to 2008:** University of Central Florida.

Basis for selection. Open admission, but selective for some programs. Additional application and requirements for health science, law enforcement and corrections programs. CPT required for admission but scores not used. SAT or ACT may be submitted instead of CPT. California Achievement Tests, Stanford Test of Academic Skills, Test of Adult Basic Education required for health program applicants. **Homeschooled:** Affidavit of home school completion required. **Learning Disabled:** Students may self-disclose with Office for Students with Disabilities.

2008-2009 Annual costs. Tuition/fees: $2,280; $8,490 out-of-state. Books/supplies: $800. Personal expenses: $1,224.

2007-2008 Financial aid. Need-based: Need-based aid available for part-time students. **Non-need-based:** Scholarships awarded for academics, athletics.

Application procedures. Admission: Closing date 8/9 (receipt date). $30 fee, may be waived for applicants with need. Admission notification on a rolling basis. **Financial aid:** Priority date 4/15, closing date 6/30. FAFSA required. Applicants notified on a rolling basis starting 6/1; must reply within 2 week(s) of notification.

Academics. Special study options: Accelerated study, cooperative education, cross-registration, distance learning, double major, dual enrollment of high school students, ESL, honors, independent study, internships, study abroad, teacher certification program, weekend college. Bachelor's degree programs available on campus. License preparation in dental hygiene, nursing, paramedic, radiology, real estate. **Credit/placement by examination:** AP, CLEP, IB, institutional tests. 45 credit hours maximum toward associate degree. **Support services:** Learning center, reduced course load, remedial instruction, study skills assistance, tutoring, writing center.

Majors. Business: Administrative services, business admin, management information systems, office management. **Computer sciences:** Programming, systems analysis. **Education:** Early childhood. **Engineering:** General, computer. **Engineering technology:** Drafting, electrical. **Health:** Clinical lab technology, dental hygiene, EMT paramedic, medical radiologic technology/radiation therapy, nursing (RN). **Legal studies:** Court reporting, legal secretary, paralegal. **Protective services:** Firefighting, police science. **Visual/performing arts:** Commercial/advertising art.

Computing on campus. 1,800 workstations in library, computer center, student center. Commuter students can connect to campus network. Online course registration, online library, helpline, student web hosting, wireless network available.

Student life. Freshman orientation: Mandatory. **Activities:** Bands, choral groups, dance, drama, international student organizations, literary magazine, music ensembles, musical theater, student government, TV station, Student Nurses Association of Florida, Phi Theta Kappa, African American student association, Phi Mu Alpha.

Athletics. NJCAA. **Intercollegiate:** Baseball M, basketball, golf M, softball W, volleyball W. **Team name:** Titans.

Student services. Adult student services, career counseling, student employment services, financial aid counseling, minority student services, on-campus daycare, veterans' counselor. **Physically disabled:** Services for visually, speech, hearing impaired. **Learning disabled:** Comprehensive services available. **Transfer:** College fairs on campus for students transferring to 4-year colleges.

Contact. E-mail: Registrar@brevardcc.edu
Phone: (321) 632-1111 Toll-free number: (888) 747-2802
Fax: (321) 433-7357
Michelle Loufek, Associate Director, Collegewide Admissions, Brevard Community College, 1519 Clearlake Road, Cocoa, FL 32922-9987

Broward College

Fort Lauderdale, Florida — **CB member**
www.broward.edu — **CB code: 5074**

- Public 2-year community college
- Commuter campus in small city

General. Founded in 1959. Regionally accredited. Multilocation institution (3 main campuses and 6 centers as well as 4 overseas centers). **Enrollment:** 29,234 degree-seeking undergraduates; 4,214 non-degree-seeking students. **Degrees:** 3,833 associate awarded. **ROTC:** Army, Air Force. **Location:** 20 miles from Miami. **Calendar:** Semester, extensive summer session. **Full-time faculty:** 348 total; 35% minority, 52% women. **Part-time faculty:** 1,062 total; 38% minority, 48% women. **Class size:** 40% < 20, 57% 20-39, 1% 40-49, less than 1% 50-99, less than 1% >100. **Special facilities:** Concert hall, planetarium, golf course.

Student profile. Among degree-seeking undergraduates, 5,871 enrolled as first-time, first-year students, 1,040 transferred in from other institutions.

Part-time:	62%	**Asian American:**	4%
Out-of-state:	5%	**Hispanic American:**	29%
Women:	60%	**International:**	6%
African American:	29%	**25 or older:**	29%

Transfer out. Colleges most students transferred to 2008: Florida Atlantic University, Florida International University.

Basis for selection. Open admission, but selective for some programs. Limited access programs require secondary application process. SAT or ACT may be used for placement in lieu of Florida CPT. **Homeschooled:** Transcript of courses and grades required.

2008-2009 Annual costs. Tuition/fees: $2,245; $8,018 out-of-state. Books/supplies: $1,200. Personal expenses: $1,755.

2007-2008 Financial aid. Need-based: 72% of total undergraduate aid awarded as scholarships/grants, 28% as loans/jobs. Need-based aid available for part-time students. Work-study available nights, weekends and for part-time students. **Non-need-based:** Scholarships awarded for academics, athletics, leadership, state residency.

Application procedures. Admission: No deadline. $35 fee, may be waived for applicants with need. Admission notification on a rolling basis beginning on or about 2/15. **Financial aid:** Priority date 4/15, closing date 7/1. FAFSA, institutional form required. Applicants notified on a rolling basis starting 7/15.

Academics. Special study options: Accelerated study, cooperative education, distance learning, dual enrollment of high school students, ESL, exchange student, honors, independent study, internships, study abroad, weekend college. Bachelor's degree programs available on campus. License preparation in aviation, dental hygiene, nursing, paramedic, physical therapy, real estate. **Credit/placement by examination:** AP, CLEP, IB, institutional tests. 30 credit hours maximum toward associate degree. **Support services:** Learning center, pre-admission summer program, remedial instruction, study skills assistance, tutoring, writing center.

Majors. Architecture: Landscape. **Biology:** General. **Business:** General, accounting, business admin, finance, hospitality admin, international, international marketing, management science, office/clerical, tourism/travel. **Communications:** Broadcast journalism, journalism. **Computer sciences:** General, computer graphics, computer science, data processing, information systems, programming, systems analysis. **Conservation:** Environmental science. **Education:** General, early childhood, elementary, mathematics, music, science, special. **Engineering:** General, civil, computer, electrical, software. **Engineering technology:** Civil. **Family/consumer sciences:** Child care, food/nutrition. **Foreign languages:** General. **Health:** Athletic training, cardiovascular technology, clinical lab assistant, clinical lab technology, dental hygiene, EMT paramedic, health care admin, medical radiologic technology/radiation therapy, medical records admin, nuclear medical technology, nursing (RN), ophthalmic lab technology, physical therapy assistant, predental, premedicine, prenursing, prepharmacy, preveterinary, recreational therapy, respiratory therapy technology, sonography. **History:** General. **Legal studies:** Court reporting, legal secretary, paralegal, prelaw. **Liberal arts:** Arts/sciences. **Math:** General. **Mechanic/repair:** Automotive. **Parks/recreation:** General. **Philosophy/religion:** Religion. **Physical sciences:** Chemistry, physics. **Protective services:** Criminal justice, firefighting, security services. **Psychology:** General. **Public administration:** Social work. **Social sciences:** Anthropology, economics, geography, political science, sociology. **Transportation:** Aviation, aviation management. **Visual/performing arts:** Art, dramatic, interior design, music history.

Computing on campus. 5,143 workstations in library, computer center, student center. Commuter students can connect to campus network. Online course registration, online library, helpline, wireless network available.

Student life. Freshman orientation: Available. Preregistration for classes offered. **Activities:** Bands, choral groups, dance, drama, literary magazine, music ensembles, musical theater, opera, student government, student newspaper, symphony orchestra, Phi Theta Kappa, Phi Beta Lambda, African American student union, American Institute of Architecture Students, Catholic club, chess club, HIV peer educators, film club, French club.

Athletics. NJCAA. **Intercollegiate:** Baseball M, basketball, softball W, tennis W, volleyball W. **Team name:** Seahawks.

Student services. Adult student services, alcohol/substance abuse counseling, career counseling, student employment services, financial aid counseling, health services, on-campus daycare, personal counseling, placement for graduates, veterans' counselor. **Physically disabled:** Services for visually, speech, hearing impaired.

Contact. Phone: (954) 201-7541 Fax: (954) 201-7466
Willie Alexander, Associate Vice President for Student Affairs and Registrar, Broward College, 225 East Las Olas Boulevard, Fort Lauderdale, FL 33301

Brown Mackie College: Miami
Miami, Florida
www.cbcaec.com

- For-profit 2-year business and career college
- Very large city

General. Accredited by ACICS. **Location:** Downtown. **Calendar:** Quarter.

Annual costs/financial aid. Tuition/fees (2008-2009): $12,624.

Contact. Phone: (305) 341-6600
Director of Admissions, 1501 Biscayne Boulevard, Miami, FL 33132

Central Florida College
Winter Park, Florida
www.centralfloridacollege.edu

- For-profit 2-year technical college
- Very large city
- Interview required

General. Accredited by ACCSCT. **Enrollment:** 450 degree-seeking undergraduates. **Degrees:** 99 associate awarded. **Calendar:** Continuous, extensive summer session. **Full-time faculty:** 18 total. **Part-time faculty:** 20 total.

Basis for selection. Open admission.

Financial aid. All financial aid based on need.

Application procedures. Admission: No deadline. $50 fee. Admission notification on a rolling basis. **Financial aid:** No deadline. FAFSA required.

Academics. Special study options: Distance learning, liberal arts/career combination. **Credit/placement by examination:** CLEP. **Support services:** Study skills assistance.

Majors. Business: Accounting, business admin. **Health:** Insurance specialist, medical assistant, medical records technology. **Personal/culinary services:** Cosmetic. **Protective services:** Police science.

Most popular majors. Business/marketing 13%, health sciences 80%.

Computing on campus. 64 workstations in library, computer center. Online library available.

Contact. E-mail: admissions@centralfloridacollege.edu
Phone: (407) 843-3984
Bill Poulmear, Director, Central Florida College, 1573 West Fairbanks Avenue, Winter Park, FL 32789

Central Florida Community College
Ocala, Florida
www.cf.edu **CB code: 5127**

- Public 2-year community college
- Commuter campus in small city

General. Founded in 1957. Regionally accredited. **Enrollment:** 5,057 degree-seeking undergraduates. **Degrees:** 571 associate awarded. **Location:** 72 miles from Orlando. **Calendar:** Semester, extensive summer session. **Full-time faculty:** 125 total. **Part-time faculty:** 512 total. **Special facilities:** Art museum. **Partnerships:** Formal partnership with Emergency One Corporation.

Student profile.

Out-of-state:	1%	**25 or older:**	34%

Transfer out. Colleges most students transferred to 2008: University of Florida, University of Central Florida, Florida State University.

Basis for selection. Open admission, but selective for some programs. Special requirements for registered nursing, dental assisting, physical therapy assistant, child care, criminal justice, practical nursing, surgical technology programs.

High school preparation. Recommended units include English 4, mathematics 3, social studies 3 and science 3.

2008-2009 Annual costs. Tuition/fees: $2,314; $8,433 out-of-state. Books/supplies: $1,230. Personal expenses: $3,386.

2007-2008 Financial aid. Need-based: Need-based aid available for part-time students. **Non-need-based:** Scholarships awarded for academics, athletics, minority status, music/drama, state residency.

Application procedures. Admission: $20 fee, may be waived for applicants with need. Application must be submitted on paper. Admission notification on a rolling basis. **Financial aid:** No deadline. FAFSA required.

Academics. Special study options: Accelerated study, cooperative education, distance learning, dual enrollment of high school students, ESL, honors, independent study, internships, liberal arts/career combination, teacher certification program. Bachelor's degrees available through on-campus University Center. Corporate training available through CFCC Institute. Bachelor's degree programs available on campus. License preparation in real estate. **Credit/placement by examination:** AP, CLEP, IB, institutional tests. 21 credit hours maximum toward associate degree. ACT, SAT, CPT are authorized placement tests for community colleges in Florida. **Support services:** GED preparation and test center, learning center, pre-admission summer program, reduced course load, remedial instruction, study skills assistance, tutoring, writing center.

Majors. Agriculture: Equestrian studies, horticulture, landscaping. **Business:** Accounting, accounting technology, business admin, executive assistant, restaurant/food services. **Computer sciences:** System admin. **Education:** Early childhood, elementary. **Engineering technology:** Architectural drafting. **Health:** EMT paramedic, licensed practical nurse, medical records technology, nursing (RN), physical therapy assistant. **Legal studies:** Paralegal. **Liberal arts:** Arts/sciences. **Mechanic/repair:** Automotive. **Personal/culinary services:** Chef training. **Protective services:** Fire safety technology, law enforcement admin. **Public administration:** Human services.

Most popular majors. Business/marketing 6%, health sciences 14%, liberal arts 75%.

Computing on campus. 2,200 workstations in library, computer center, student center. Online library, helpline available.

Student life. Freshman orientation: Mandatory. Preregistration for classes offered. Program held prior to beginning of term; also available online. **Housing:** College Square Student Residence Center owned and operated by Central Florida Community College Foundation near campus. **Activities:** Bands, campus ministries, choral groups, dance, drama, literary magazine, music ensembles, musical theater, student government, student newspaper, symphony orchestra, Afro-student union, Hispanic club, Phi Theta Kappa, Community of Scholars, Brain Bowl, Phi Beta Lambda, gay/straight alliance, peer educators.

Athletics. NJCAA. **Intercollegiate:** Baseball M, basketball, softball W, tennis W. **Team name:** Patriots.

Student services. Adult student services, career counseling, services for economically disadvantaged, student employment services, financial aid counseling, on-campus daycare, personal counseling, placement for graduates, veterans' counselor. **Physically disabled:** Services for visually, speech, hearing impaired. **Transfer:** Transfer adviser, college fairs on campus for students transferring to 4-year colleges.

Contact. Phone: (352) 873-5801 Fax: (352) 873-5875
Lyn Powell, Director of Admissions, Central Florida Community College, 3001 SW College Road, Ocala, FL 34474-4415

City College: Casselberry
Casselberry, Florida

- For-profit 2-year career college
- Large town
- Interview required

General. Accredited by ACICS. **Enrollment:** 147 degree-seeking undergraduates. **Degrees:** 39 associate awarded. **Calendar:** Quarter, extensive summer session. **Full-time faculty:** 4 total. **Part-time faculty:** 19 total.

Basis for selection. Applicant must pass the college's entrance examination and interview.

2008-2009 Annual costs. Tuition/fees: $9,675. Per-credit charge: $215.

Application procedures. Admission: No deadline. $25 fee. **Financial aid:** No deadline.

Academics. Credit/placement by examination: CLEP.

Majors. Business: Business admin, marketing. **Computer sciences:** General. **Health:** Health services. **Protective services:** Security management.

Contact. Phone: (407) 831-8466 Fax: (407) 831-1147
I Cruz, Director of Admissions, City College: Casselberry, 853 State Road 436, Suite 200, Casselberry, FL 32707-5353

City College: Gainesville
Gainesville, Florida
www.citycollege.edu **CB code: 3579**

- For-profit 2-year business and health science college
- Small city

General. Accredited by ACICS. **Enrollment:** 268 degree-seeking undergraduates. **Degrees:** 4 bachelor's, 47 associate awarded. **Calendar:** Continuous.

Basis for selection. Open admission.

2009-2010 Annual costs. Tuition/fees (projected): $11,369. Books/supplies: $1,044. Personal expenses: $1,692.

Academics. Credit/placement by examination: CLEP.

Majors. Business: Business admin. **Computer sciences:** General. **Legal studies:** General.

Contact. E-mail: kbowden@citycollege.edu
Phone: (352) 335-4000 Fax: (352) 335-4303
Kim Bowden, Director of Admissions, City College: Gainesville, 2400 SW 13th Street, Gainesville, FL 32608

City College: Miami
Miami, Florida
www.citycollege.edu **CB code: 3580**

- For-profit 2-year business and health science college
- Large city

General. Accredited by ACICS. **Enrollment:** 270 degree-seeking undergraduates. **Degrees:** 16 bachelor's, 59 associate awarded. **Calendar:** Continuous. **Full-time faculty:** 4 total. **Part-time faculty:** 25 total.

Basis for selection. TABE is required. SAT or ACT considered if submitted.

2008-2009 Annual costs. Tuition/fees: $10,975.

Financial aid. All financial aid based on need. Need-based aid available for part-time students.

Application procedures. Admission: No deadline. $25 fee. Admission notification on a rolling basis. **Financial aid:** No deadline. FAFSA, institutional form required. Applicants notified on a rolling basis.

Academics. Credit/placement by examination: CLEP.

Majors. Business: Business admin.

Contact. E-mail: sespath@citycollege.edu
Phone: (305) 666-9242 Fax: (305) 666-9243
Sandy Espath, Director of Admissions, City College: Miami, 9300 South Dadeland Boulevard, Miami, FL 33156

College of Business and Technology: Flagler
Miami, Florida
www.cbt.edu

- Private 2-year junior and technical college
- Commuter campus in very large city
- Interview required

General. Accredited by ACICS. **Enrollment:** 153 degree-seeking undergraduates. **Calendar:** Semester. **Full-time faculty:** 8 total. **Part-time faculty:** 12 total.

Student profile. Among degree-seeking undergraduates, 10% enrolled in a transfer program, 60% enrolled in a vocational program, 77 enrolled as first-time, first-year students, 20 transferred in from other institutions.

Transfer out. 70% of students enrolled in the transfer program go on to 4-year colleges. **Colleges most students transferred to 2008:** Jones College, Carlos Albizu University.

Basis for selection. Open admission. **Homeschooled:** Transcript of courses and grades required.

2008-2009 Annual costs. Tuition/fees: $12,830. Per-credit charge: $360. Books/supplies: $1,350.

Financial aid. All financial aid based on need. Need-based aid available for part-time students. Work-study available nights and for part-time students.

Application procedures. Admission: No deadline. $25 fee. **Financial aid:** No deadline. FAFSA required.

Academics. Special study options: Distance learning, ESL. **Credit/placement by examination:** CLEP. **Support services:** Tutoring.

Majors. Business: Accounting, business admin. **Computer sciences:** Networking, web page design. **Health:** Medical assistant, office admin. **Mechanic/repair:** Heating/ac/refrig.

Computing on campus. PC or laptop required. 100 workstations in library. Online library, repair service, wireless network available.

Student life. Freshman orientation: Mandatory.

Student services. Career counseling, student employment services, financial aid counseling.

Contact. E-mail: admissions@cbt.edu
Phone: (305) 273-4499 ext. 2-203 Fax: (305) 485-4411
Margarita Velez, Director of Admission, College of Business and Technology: Flagler, 8230 West Flagler Street, Miami, FL 33144

College of Business and Technology: Hialeah
Hialeah, Florida
www.cbt.edu

- For-profit 2-year business and technical college
- Small city

General. Accredited by ACICS. **Calendar:** Continuous.

Annual costs/financial aid. Tuition/fees (2008-2009): $11,772.

Contact. Phone: (786) 693-8842
Admissions Director, 935 West 49th Street Suite 203, Hialeah, FL 33012-3436

College of Business and Technology: Kendall
Miami, Florida
www.cbt.edu

- Private 2-year health science and junior college
- Very large city

General. Accredited by ACICS. **Enrollment:** 75 degree-seeking undergraduates. **Degrees:** 20 associate awarded. **Calendar:** Semester. **Full-time faculty:** 12 total. **Part-time faculty:** 6 total.

Basis for selection. Open admission.

2008-2009 Annual costs. Tuition/fees: $11,772. Per-credit charge: $322.

Academics. Credit/placement by examination: CLEP.

Majors. Business: Accounting, business admin. **Computer sciences:** LAN/WAN management. **Health:** Medical assistant, office admin. **Mechanic/repair:** Heating/ac/refrig. **Visual/performing arts:** Graphic design.

Contact. E-mail: admissions@cbt.edu
Phone: (305) 273-4499
Margarita Velez, Director of Admissions, College of Business and Technology: Kendall, 8991 SW 107 Avenue, Miami, FL 33176

Daytona State College
Daytona Beach, Florida
www.daytonastate.edu **CB code: 5159**

- Public 2-year community and technical college
- Commuter campus in large city

General. Founded in 1958. Regionally accredited. **Enrollment:** 10,327 degree-seeking undergraduates; 3,054 non-degree-seeking students. **Degrees:** 34 bachelor's, 1,556 associate awarded. **ROTC:** Army, Air Force. **Location:** 90 miles from Jacksonville, 65 miles from Orlando. **Calendar:** Semester, limited summer session. **Full-time faculty:** 310 total; 85% have terminal degrees, 18% minority, 53% women. **Part-time faculty:** 812 total; 41% have terminal degrees, 16% minority, 47% women. **Special facilities:** Museum of photography.

Student profile. Among degree-seeking undergraduates, 1,851 enrolled as first-time, first-year students, 1,054 transferred in from other institutions.

Part-time:	56%	**Women:**	65%
Out-of-state:	8%	**25 or older:**	22%

Transfer out. 78% of students enrolled in the transfer program go on to 4-year colleges. **Colleges most students transferred to 2008:** University of Central Florida.

Basis for selection. Open admission, but selective for some programs. Special requirements for limited access programs including Bachelor's degree program.

2008-2009 Annual costs. Tuition/fees: $2,348; $8,830 out-of-state. Books/supplies: $800. Personal expenses: $2,624.

2007-2008 Financial aid. Need-based: 60% of total undergraduate aid awarded as scholarships/grants, 40% as loans/jobs. Need-based aid available for part-time students. Work-study available for part-time students. **Non-need-based:** Scholarships awarded for athletics, leadership, music/drama.

Application procedures. Admission: No deadline. No application fee. Admission notification on a rolling basis. **Financial aid:** No deadline. FAFSA required. Applicants notified on a rolling basis starting 2/15.

Academics. Special study options: Cooperative education, distance learning, dual enrollment of high school students, ESL, honors, independent study, internships, liberal arts/career combination, study abroad, teacher certification program, weekend college. Bachelor's degree programs available on campus. License preparation in dental hygiene, nursing, occupational therapy, paramedic, physical therapy, radiology. **Credit/placement by examination:** AP, CLEP, IB, institutional tests. 45 credit hours maximum toward associate degree, 45 toward bachelor's. **Support services:** GED preparation and test center, learning center, pre-admission summer program, remedial instruction, study skills assistance, tutoring.

Majors. Agriculture: Turf management. **Architecture:** Interior. **Biology:** General, botany, marine, microbiology, zoology. **Business:** Accounting, accounting technology, banking/financial services, business admin, executive assistant, hospitality admin, management information systems, marketing, operations. **Communications technology:** Photo/film/video. **Computer sciences:** General, applications programming, systems analysis. **Construction:** Electrician, plumbing. **Education:** General, Deaf/hearing impaired. **Engineering:** General, computer. **Engineering technology:** Aerospace, architectural, automotive, civil, computer systems, construction, drafting, electrical, manufacturing. **Health:** Clinical lab technology, dental hygiene, EMT paramedic, medical radiologic technology/radiation therapy, medical records technology, mental health services, nursing (RN), occupational therapy assistant, physical therapy assistant, respiratory therapy technology, veterinary technology/assistant. **Legal studies:** Paralegal. **Liberal arts:** Arts/sciences. **Math:** General, statistics. **Mechanic/repair:** Automotive. **Personal/culinary services:** Restaurant/catering. **Philosophy/religion:** Philosophy. **Physical sciences:** General, astronomy, chemistry, meteorology. **Protective services:** Fire safety technology, law enforcement admin. **Psychology:** General. **Public administration:** Human services, social work. **Social sciences:** Economics, geography, political science, sociology. **Visual/performing arts:** General, acting, art, commercial/advertising art, dance, graphic design, interior design, photography, studio arts. **Other:** Computer/Info tech services administration and management.

Most popular majors. Health sciences 17%, liberal arts 63%.

Computing on campus. 3,084 workstations in library, computer center, student center. Online course registration, helpline, wireless network available.

Student life. Freshman orientation: Mandatory. Preregistration for classes offered. **Housing:** Assistance in locating off-campus housing available to international students. **Activities:** Bands, campus ministries, choral groups, dance, drama, international student organizations, music ensembles, musical theater, opera, student government, student newspaper, symphony orchestra, TV station, Baptist Campus ministries, Campus Crusade for Christ, Black Student Nurses Association, Global Friends, human services paraprofessional organization, African American student union.

Athletics. NJCAA. **Intercollegiate:** Baseball M, basketball, golf W, softball W. **Intramural:** Basketball, football (tackle), soccer, table tennis, tennis, volleyball, weight lifting. **Team name:** Falcons.

Student services. Adult student services, alcohol/substance abuse counseling, career counseling, student employment services, financial aid counseling, on-campus daycare, personal counseling, placement for graduates, veterans' counselor, women's services. **Physically disabled:** Services for visually, speech, hearing impaired. **Transfer:** Transfer adviser, college fairs on campus for students transferring to 4-year colleges.

Contact. E-mail: admissions@daytonastate.edu
Phone: (386) 506-3000 ext. 3059 Fax: (386) 506-4489
Karen Sanders, Director of Admissions, Daytona State College, Daytona State College Admissions Office, Daytona Beach, FL 32114-2811

Florida Career College: Hialeah
Hialeah, Florida
www.careercollege.edu

- For-profit 2-year junior and technical college
- Commuter campus in very large city

General. Accredited by ACICS. **Calendar:** Quarter.

Annual costs/financial aid. Tuition varies by length of program and is $445 per credit hour; which leads to certificate, associate or bachelor degree. Books/supplies: $1,000.

Contact. Phone: (305) 825-3231
Director of Admissions, 3750 West 18th Avenue, Hialeah, FL 33012

Florida Career College: Miami
Miami, Florida
www.careercollege.edu **CB code: 3581**

- For-profit 2-year business and technical college
- Large city

General. Accredited by ACICS. **Calendar:** Continuous.

Annual costs/financial aid. Tuition varies by length of program and is $445 per credit hour; which leads to certificate, associate or bachelor degree.

Contact. Phone: (305) 553-6065
Director of Admission, 1321 SW 107 Avenue, Suite 201B, Miami, FL 3317-521

Florida Career College: Pembroke Pines
Pembroke Pines, Florida
www.careercollege.edu

- For-profit 2-year business and technical college
- Small city

General. Accredited by ACICS. **Calendar:** Continuous.

Annual costs/financial aid. Tuition varies by length of program and is $445 per credit hour; which leads to certificate, associate or bachelor degree.

Contact. Phone: (954) 965-7272
Director of Admission, 7891 Pines Boulevard, Pembroke Pines, FL 33024

Florida Career College: West Palm Beach
West Palm Beach, Florida

- For-profit 2-year technical college
- Commuter campus in small city

General. Accredited by ACICS. **Calendar:** Continuous.

Annual costs/financial aid. Tuition varies by length of program and is $445 per credit hour; which leads to certificate, associate or bachelor degree.

Contact. Phone: (561) 689-0550
Director of Admissions, 6065 Okeechobee Boulevard West, West Palm Beach, FL 33417

Florida College of Natural Health: Bradenton

Bradenton, Florida
www.fcnh.com **CB code: 5024**

- For-profit 2-year health science and career college
- Commuter campus in small city

General. Accredited by ACCSCT. **Enrollment:** 100 degree-seeking undergraduates. **Degrees:** 62 associate awarded. **Location:** 40 miles from Tampa. **Calendar:** Continuous, extensive summer session. **Full-time faculty:** 6 total. **Part-time faculty:** 6 total.

Basis for selection. Open admission, but selective for some programs.

2008-2009 Annual costs. Tuition/fees: $20,948. Books/supplies: $2,250. Personal expenses: $4,620.

Financial aid. All financial aid based on need.

Application procedures. Admission: No deadline. $50 fee. Admission notification on a rolling basis. **Financial aid:** No deadline. FAFSA required. Applicants notified on a rolling basis.

Academics. Credit/placement by examination: CLEP.

Majors. Health: Massage therapy.

Computing on campus. 2 workstations in library.

Student life. Freshman orientation: Mandatory.

Student services. Financial aid counseling, placement for graduates.

Contact. E-mail: sarasota@fcnh.com
Phone: (941) 744-1244 Toll-free number: (800) 966-7117
Fax: (941) 744-1242
Xavier Johnson, Admissions, Florida College of Natural Health: Bradenton, 616 67th Street Circle East, Bradenton, FL 34208

Florida College of Natural Health: Maitland

Maitland, Florida
www.fcnh.com **CB code: 5239**

- For-profit 2-year health science and junior college
- Large town

General. Accredited by ACCSCT. **Calendar:** Continuous.

Annual costs/financial aid. Tuition/fees (2008-2009): $20,948. Books/supplies: $2,250. Personal expenses: $2,464. Need-based financial aid available for full-time students.

Contact. Phone: (407) 261-0319
Director of Marketing, 2600 Lake Lucien Drive; Suite 240, Maitland, FL 32751

Florida College of Natural Health: Miami

Miami, Florida
www.fcnh.com **CB code: 5231**

- For-profit 2-year branch campus and community college
- Very large city

General. Accredited by ACCSCT. **Calendar:** Continuous.

Annual costs/financial aid. Tuition/fees (2008-2009): $20,948. Books/supplies: $2,250. Personal expenses: $2,464. Need-based financial aid available for full-time students.

Contact. Phone: (305) 597-9599
Director of Marketing, 7925 Northwest 12th Street, Suite 201, Miami, FL 33126

Florida College of Natural Health: Pompano Beach

Pompano Beach, Florida
www.fcnh.com **CB code: 5238**

- For-profit 2-year junior college
- Very large city

General. Accredited by ACCSCT. **Calendar:** Continuous.

Annual costs/financial aid. Need-based financial aid available for full-time students.

Contact. Phone: (954) 975-6400
Chief Operating Officer, 2001 West Sample Road, Suite 100, Pompano Beach, FL 33064

Florida Community College at Jacksonville

Jacksonville, Florida
www.fccj.edu **CB code: 5232**

- Public 2-year community college
- Commuter campus in very large city

General. Founded in 1963. Regionally accredited. 4 campus locations, 6 center sites, 1 online campus. **Enrollment:** 23,901 degree-seeking undergraduates; 3,053 non-degree-seeking students. **Degrees:** 2,978 associate awarded. **ROTC:** Naval. **Location:** Downtown. **Calendar:** Semester, extensive summer session. **Full-time faculty:** 375 total; 20% have terminal degrees, 17% minority, 59% women. **Part-time faculty:** 780 total; 14% have terminal degrees, 24% minority, 51% women. **Class size:** 51% < 20, 49% 20-39, less than 1% 40-49, less than 1% 50-99. **Special facilities:** Performing arts theater, computer support wing, allied health building, criminal justice center. **Partnerships:** Formal partnerships with Florida Construction Institute, Florida Home Builders Association, Navy Contracts, GM/ASEP contracts for non-credit (Education-To-Go), NE Florida Credit Union Association, Aviation Professional/Pilot Contract, Cisco Agreement with 2 schools in midwest.

Student profile. Among degree-seeking undergraduates, 91% enrolled in a transfer program, 9% enrolled in a vocational program, 4,369 enrolled as first-time, first-year students, 1,090 transferred in from other institutions.

Part-time:	68%	**Hispanic American:**	6%
Out-of-state:	2%	**Native American:**	1%
Women:	60%	**International:**	2%
African American:	29%	**25 or older:**	43%
Asian American:	4%		

Transfer out. Colleges most students transferred to 2008: University of North Florida, Jacksonville University, University of Florida, Florida State University, Central Florida University.

Basis for selection. Open admission, but selective for some programs. Special requirements for some associate of science degree programs. Some require specific application in addition to school application. SAT or ACT can be used to satisfy CPT test requirement for placement. **Homeschooled:** Transcript of courses and grades required. Student required to fill out form (home school letter). **Learning Disabled:** Medical documentation required.

High school preparation. 24 units recommended. Recommended units include English 4, mathematics 3, social studies 3, science 3 (laboratory 2), foreign language 2 and academic electives 9. One algebra strongly recommended. 3 social studies recommended: include .5 U.S. government, .5 economics, 1 U.S. history, 1 world history.

2008-2009 Annual costs. Tuition/fees: $2,226; $8,418 out-of-state. Books/supplies: $900. Personal expenses: $812.

2008-2009 Financial aid. Need-based: Need-based aid available for part-time students. Work-study available nights, weekends and for part-time students. **Non-need-based:** Scholarships awarded for academics, alumni affiliation, art, athletics, job skills, leadership, minority status, music/drama.

Application procedures. Admission: Priority date 8/1; no deadline. $15 fee. Admission notification on a rolling basis. **Financial aid:** Priority date 8/1; no closing date. FAFSA, institutional form required. Applicants notified by 7/1.

Academics. Special study options: Accelerated study, cooperative education, cross-registration, distance learning, double major, dual enrollment of high school students, ESL, exchange student, external degree, honors, independent study, internships, liberal arts/career combination, study abroad, teacher certification program, weekend college. Bachelor's degree programs available on campus. License preparation in aviation, dental hygiene, nursing, paramedic, physical therapy, radiology, real estate. **Credit/placement by examination:** AP, CLEP, institutional tests. 45 credit hours maximum toward associate degree. **Support services:** GED preparation and test center, learning center, reduced course load, remedial instruction, study skills assistance, tutoring.

Majors. Architecture: Environmental design, interior. **Biology:** Biomedical sciences. **Business:** Accounting, administrative services, banking/financial services, business admin, fashion, financial planning, hospitality admin, insurance, management information systems, office management, office technology, sales/distribution, tourism/travel. **Communications technology:** Graphic/printing. **Computer sciences:** General, applications programming, computer graphics, data processing, information systems, networking, programming, systems analysis. **Construction:** Maintenance. **Education:** Elementary. **Engineering:** General, civil, computer. **Engineering technology:** Architectural, biomedical, civil, construction, drafting, electrical. **Family/consumer sciences:** Clothing/textiles. **Foreign languages:** Sign language interpretation. **Health:** Clinical lab technology, dental hygiene, EMT paramedic, medical radiologic technology/radiation therapy, medical records technology, medical secretary, nursing (RN), physical therapy assistant, respiratory therapy technology, sonography, substance abuse counseling. **Legal studies:** Paralegal. **Mechanic/repair:** Automotive. **Military:** General. **Personal/culinary services:** Culinary arts, mortuary science. **Protective services:** Criminal justice, fire safety technology, fire services admin, firefighting, law enforcement admin. **Public administration:** Human services. **Transportation:** Air traffic control, aviation, aviation management. **Visual/performing arts:** General, cinematography, commercial/advertising art, design, dramatic, interior design, theater design.

Computing on campus. 2,500 workstations in library, computer center, student center. Commuter students can connect to campus network. Online course registration, online library, helpline, repair service, student web hosting, wireless network available.

Student life. Freshman orientation: Mandatory. Preregistration for classes offered. Program is for degree seeking students only. **Housing:** Housing assistance available to qualified Talent Grant students. **Activities:** Bands, choral groups, dance, drama, international student organizations, literary magazine, music ensembles, musical theater, radio station, student government, student newspaper, TV station, forensic team, brain bowl team, Phi Theta Kappa.

Athletics. NJCAA. **Intercollegiate:** Baseball M, basketball, softball W, tennis W, volleyball W. **Intramural:** Badminton, basketball, bowling, football (non-tackle), golf, soccer, softball, table tennis, tennis, volleyball. **Team name:** Stars.

Student services. Adult student services, career counseling, services for economically disadvantaged, student employment services, financial aid counseling, minority student services, on-campus daycare, personal counseling, placement for graduates, veterans' counselor, women's services. **Physically disabled:** Services for visually, speech, hearing impaired. **Transfer:** Transfer adviser, college fairs on campus for students transferring to 4-year colleges.

Contact. E-mail: info@fccj.edu
Phone: (904) 632-3100 Fax: (904) 632-5105
Rosalind Harris, Associate Director of Admissions, Florida Community College at Jacksonville, 501 West State Street, Jacksonville, FL 32202

Florida Keys Community College
Key West, Florida
www.fkcc.edu **CB code: 5236**

- Public 2-year nursing and community college
- Commuter campus in large town

General. Founded in 1965. Regionally accredited. 2-year AA and AS programs offered at the main campus in Key West, Coral Shores and Marathon branch campuses. **Enrollment:** 1,000 degree-seeking undergraduates; 455 non-degree-seeking students. **Degrees:** 150 associate awarded. **Location:** 154 miles from Miami. **Calendar:** Semester, limited summer session. **Full-time faculty:** 26 total. **Part-time faculty:** 111 total. **Special facilities:** Fine arts center and theater, marine propulsion technology center, welding lab, aquatic center, diving program underwater education complex, ceramics studio.

Student profile. Among degree-seeking undergraduates, 14% enrolled in a transfer program, 102 enrolled as first-time, first-year students.

Part-time:	73%	**Women:**	59%
Out-of-state:	2%	**25 or older:**	55%

Transfer out. Colleges most students transferred to 2008: University of Central Florida, Florida International University, University of Florida, Florida State University, St. Leo's College.

Basis for selection. Open admission, but selective for some programs. Special application, placement examination, physical examination, and interview required for nursing technology applicants. Admission based on objective points system.

High school preparation. College-preparatory program recommended. Recommended units include English 4, mathematics 3, social studies 3 and science 3.

2008-2009 Annual costs. Tuition/fees: $2,385; $8,980 out-of-state. Books/supplies: $2,300. Personal expenses: $1,000.

Financial aid. Need-based: Need-based aid available for part-time students. Work-study available for part-time students. **Non-need-based:** Scholarships awarded for academics, art, leadership, minority status.

Application procedures. Admission: No deadline. $20 fee. Admission notification on a rolling basis. **Financial aid:** Priority date 5/1; no closing date. FAFSA, institutional form required. Applicants notified on a rolling basis starting 6/15; must reply within 2 week(s) of notification.

Academics. Special study options: Distance learning, double major, dual enrollment of high school students, ESL, independent study, semester at sea, teacher certification program. Bachelor's degree programs available on campus. License preparation in nursing, paramedic, real estate. **Credit/placement by examination:** AP, CLEP, IB, institutional tests. 45 credit hours maximum toward associate degree. Students taking Florida College Entry Level Placement Test prior to registering do not need SAT or ACT. **Support services:** Learning center, reduced course load, remedial instruction, tutoring.

Majors. Biology: Marine. **Business:** Business admin. **Computer sciences:** General, programming. **Health:** Nursing (RN). **Mechanic/repair:** Marine. **Public administration:** General. **Transportation:** Diver, maritime/Merchant Marine.

Computing on campus. 25 workstations in library, computer center.

Student life. Freshman orientation: Available. Preregistration for classes offered. **Activities:** Choral groups, student government, student newspaper, nurses pinning club, Florida nurses student association, Mud-Pi ceramics club, Phi Theta Kappa, cyber league, photo guild club, wreckers club, propmasters club.

Athletics. Team name: Wreckers.

Student services. Adult student services, career counseling, student employment services, financial aid counseling, placement for graduates, veterans' counselor. **Physically disabled:** Services for visually, speech, hearing impaired. **Transfer:** Pre-admission transcript evaluation for new students. Transfer adviser, college fairs on campus for students transferring to 4-year colleges.

Contact. E-mail: cheryl.malsheimer@fkcc.edu
Phone: (305) 809-3188 Fax: (305) 292-5155
Cheryl Malsheimer, Director of Enrollment Services, Florida Keys Community College, 5901 College Road, Key West, FL 33040

Florida National College
Hialeah, Florida
www.fnc.edu **CB code: 2057**

- For-profit 2-year liberal arts college
- Commuter campus in very large city

General. Regionally accredited. **Enrollment:** 2,387 degree-seeking undergraduates; 13 non-degree-seeking students. **Degrees:** 337 associate awarded. **Location:** 12 miles from Miami. **Calendar:** Semester. **Full-time faculty:** 35 total; 34% have terminal degrees, 51% women. **Part-time faculty:** 48 total; 33% have terminal degrees, 56% women. **Class size:** 100% 20-39.

Student profile. Among degree-seeking undergraduates, 613 enrolled as first-time, first-year students.

Part-time:	27%	**25 or older:**	65%
Women:	68%		

Transfer out. 18% of students enrolled in the transfer program go on to 4-year colleges. **Colleges most students transferred to 2008:** Nova Southeastern University, Florida International University, American Intercontinental University, Miami Institute of Psychology.

Basis for selection. Open admission, but selective for some programs.

2008-2009 Annual costs. Tuition/fees: $12,594. Per-credit charge: $400. Books/supplies: $1,000.

2007-2008 Financial aid. All financial aid based on need. 522 full-time freshmen applied for aid; 516 were judged to have need; 516 of these received aid. Need-based aid available for part-time students.

Application procedures. Admission: No deadline. No application fee. Admission notification on a rolling basis beginning on or about 7/15. **Financial aid:** No deadline. FAFSA, institutional form required.

Academics. Special study options: Cooperative education, dual enrollment of high school students, ESL, student-designed major. **Credit/placement by examination:** AP, CLEP, institutional tests. 9 credit hours maximum toward associate degree. **Support services:** GED preparation, reduced course load, remedial instruction, tutoring.

Majors. Business: Accounting, business admin, tourism promotion, tourism/travel. **Computer sciences:** General, programming, system admin, web page design. **Education:** General. **Engineering technology:** Computer hardware. **Health:** Dental lab technology, medical assistant. **Legal studies:** Paralegal. **Protective services:** Criminal justice.

Most popular majors. Business/marketing 24%, computer/information sciences 8%, health sciences 47%, legal studies 14%.

Student life. Freshman orientation: Available. **Activities:** Student government, student newspaper.

Student services. Career counseling, student employment services, financial aid counseling, personal counseling.

Contact. E-mail: admissions@fnc.edu
Phone: (305) 821-3333 Fax: (305) 362-0595
Guillermo Araya, Admissions Coodinator, Florida National College, 4425 West 20th Avenue, Hialeah, FL 33012

Florida Technical College: Auburndale

Lakeland, Florida
www.flatech.edu **CB code: 3432**

- For-profit 2-year business and junior college
- Large town

General. Accredited by ACICS. **Calendar:** Continuous.

Annual costs/financial aid. Need-based financial aid available to full-time and part-time students.

Contact. Phone: (863) 967-8822
School Director, 4715 South Florida Avenue, Lakeland, FL 33813

Florida Technical College: Deland

Deland, Florida
www.flatech.edu **CB code: 3589**

- For-profit 2-year junior and technical college
- Small city
- Interview required

General. Accredited by ACICS. **Enrollment:** 188 degree-seeking undergraduates; 208 non-degree-seeking students. **Degrees:** 121 associate awarded. **Location:** 30 miles from Orlando, 20 miles from Daytona Beach. **Calendar:** Quarter, extensive summer session. **Full-time faculty:** 17 total; 24% have terminal degrees, 59% minority, 29% women. **Part-time faculty:** 2 total. **Class size:** 90% < 20, 10% 20-39. **Partnerships:** Formal partnerships with Microsoft, Pearson Vue testing center, NCCT testing center.

Basis for selection. Open admission.

Financial aid. All financial aid based on need. Need-based aid available for part-time students. Work-study available nights and for part-time students.

Application procedures. Admission: No deadline. $25 fee. Admission notification on a rolling basis. **Financial aid:** No deadline. FAFSA required. Applicants notified on a rolling basis.

Academics. Credit/placement by examination: CLEP, IB, institutional tests. Credit by examination will be charged $50 per quarter credit not covered by financial aid. Tests must be passed with 70% or higher percentile. May not test out of lab-based classes.

Majors. Business: Business admin. **Computer sciences:** General, networking, programming, systems analysis. **Engineering technology:** Drafting. **Health:** Medical assistant, medical secretary, office admin. **Legal studies:** Paralegal. **Protective services:** Police science.

Computing on campus. 90 workstations in library, computer center. Online library, wireless network available.

Student life. Freshman orientation: Mandatory.

Student services. Career counseling, financial aid counseling, placement for graduates. **Transfer:** Pre-admission transcript evaluation for new students.

Contact. Phone: (386) 734-3303 Toll-free number: (888) 724-6441
Fax: (386) 734-5150
Kirstin Reesman, Director of Admissions, Florida Technical College: Deland, 1199 South Woodland Boulevard, Deland, FL 32720

Florida Technical College: Jacksonville

Jacksonville, Florida
www.flatech.edu **CB code: 3590**

- For-profit 2-year technical college
- Very large city

General. Accredited by ACICS. **Calendar:** Continuous.

Contact. Phone: (904) 724-2229
Campus Director, 8711 Lone Star Road, Jacksonville, FL 32211

Florida Technical College: Orlando

Orlando, Florida
www.flatech.edu **CB code: 3588**

- For-profit 2-year junior and technical college
- Commuter campus in large city
- Interview required

General. Accredited by ACICS. **Enrollment:** 435 degree-seeking undergraduates. **Degrees:** 89 associate awarded. **Location:** 13 miles from downtown. **Calendar:** Continuous, extensive summer session. **Full-time faculty:** 12 total; 42% have terminal degrees, 25% minority, 42% women. **Part-time faculty:** 6 total; 50% have terminal degrees, 50% minority, 83% women.

Basis for selection. Open admission.

2008-2009 Financial aid. All financial aid based on need. Need-based aid available for part-time students.

Application procedures. Admission: No deadline. $25 fee, may be waived for applicants with need. Application must be submitted on paper. Admission notification on a rolling basis. **Financial aid:** No deadline. FAFSA required. Applicants notified on a rolling basis.

Academics. Special study options: Independent study. **Credit/placement by examination:** CLEP, institutional tests. **Support services:** Tutoring.

Majors. Business: Business admin. **Computer sciences:** Networking, programming, web page design. **Engineering technology:** Drafting. **Health:** Medical assistant, medical secretary. **Mechanic/repair:** Computer. **Protective services:** Law enforcement admin.

Computing on campus. 100 workstations in library, computer center. Online library, wireless network available.

Student life. Freshman orientation: Mandatory.

Student services. Career counseling, student employment services, financial aid counseling, placement for graduates.

Contact. E-mail: dboothe@flatech.edu
Phone: (407) 447-7300 Toll-free number: (888) 678-2929
Fax: (407) 447-7301
Dane Boothe, Director, Florida Technical College: Orlando, 12689 Challenger Parkway, #130, Orlando, FL 32826-2707

Full Sail University
Winter Park, Florida
www.fullsail.edu **CB code: 3164**

- For-profit 2-year visual arts and technical college
- Commuter campus in very large city

General. Accredited by ACCSCT. **Enrollment:** 6,717 degree-seeking undergraduates. **Degrees:** 3,956 bachelor's, 1,620 associate awarded; master's offered. **Location:** 8 miles from Orlando. **Calendar:** Continuous. **Full-time faculty:** 673 total. **Part-time faculty:** 18 total. **Special facilities:** Recording studios, production suites, sound stages.

Student profile.

Out-of-state:	75%	**25 or older:**	20%

Basis for selection. Open admission, but selective for some programs. Applicants for game design and development bachelor's degree program must have A average in Algebra II. Geometry, physics and programming experience also recommended. **Homeschooled:** Diplomas recognized if applicant's state board of education recognizes them. **Learning Disabled:** Require documentation, not more than 3 years old, describing learning disabilities.

2008-2009 Annual costs. Degree programs leading to an associate and bachelor range from $34,775 - $72,775. Includes books and supplies.

Financial aid. Need-based: Work-study available nights and weekends.

Application procedures. Admission: No deadline. $150 fee. Admission notification on a rolling basis. **Financial aid:** No deadline. FAFSA required. Applicants notified on a rolling basis; must reply within 2 week(s) of notification.

Academics. Cognitive development course offered at no charge. Tutoring offered through federal work study program. **Special study options:** Accelerated study, combined bachelor's/graduate degree, cooperative education, internships. Bachelor's degree programs available on campus. **Credit/placement by examination:** AP, CLEP, institutional tests. Students may take test-out exam in each course for which credit is being sought. If credit earned, tuition and program hours reduced accordingly. Minimum of 25% of degree program's semester hours or equivalent must be earned in residence to receive degree. **Support services:** Study skills assistance, tutoring, writing center.

Majors. Communications technology: Recording arts. **Computer sciences:** Web page design. **Other:** Show production and touring.

Computing on campus. 56 workstations in library, computer center. Online library, wireless network available.

Student life. Freshman orientation: Mandatory. **Policies:** Alcohol and drug free facility.

Student services. Financial aid counseling, placement for graduates.

Contact. E-mail: admissions@fullsail.com
Phone: (407) 679-6333 Toll-free number: (800) 226-7625
MaryBeth Plank-Mezo, Vice President of Admissions, Full Sail University, 3300 University Boulevard, Winter Park, FL 32792-7429

Golf Academy of America: Orlando
Altamonte Springs, Florida
www.golfacademy.edu

- For-profit 2-year community college
- Large town

General. Accredited by ACICS. **Calendar:** Semester.

Annual costs/financial aid. Tuition/fees (2008-2009): $13,580. Books/supplies: $700.

Contact. Phone: (480) 905-9288
7373 North Scottsdale Road, Suite B-100, Scottsdale, AZ 85253

Gulf Coast College
Tampa, Florida
www.gulfcoastcollege.edu **CB code: 3448**

- For-profit 2-year technical college
- Large city

General. Accredited by ACICS. **Enrollment:** 102 degree-seeking undergraduates. **Degrees:** 20 associate awarded. **Calendar:** Quarter.

2008-2009 Annual costs. Tuition/fees: $11,852. Reported tuition and fees reflect Nursing program; other degrees vary by program. Books/supplies: $1,200. Personal expenses: $1,863.

Academics. Credit/placement by examination: CLEP.

Majors. Business: Business admin. **Computer sciences:** General.

Contact. Phone: (813) 620-1446
Mike Dalgotta, Director of Admissions, Gulf Coast College, 3910 U.S. Highway 301 North, Suite 200, Tampa, FL 33619-1290

Gulf Coast Community College
Panama City, Florida
www.gulfcoast.edu **CB code: 5271**

- Public 2-year community college
- Commuter campus in small city

General. Founded in 1957. Regionally accredited. **Enrollment:** 4,551 degree-seeking undergraduates; 1,334 non-degree-seeking students. **Degrees:** 785 associate awarded. **Location:** 100 miles from Tallahassee, 100 miles from Pensacola. **Calendar:** Semester, limited summer session. **Full-time faculty:** 120 total. **Part-time faculty:** 375 total. **Partnerships:** Formal partnerships with local businesses.

Student profile. Among degree-seeking undergraduates, 800 enrolled as first-time, first-year students.

Part-time:	54%	**Women:**	57%
Out-of-state:	6%	**25 or older:**	42%

Transfer out. Colleges most students transferred to 2008: Florida State University, University of Florida, University of Central Florida, University of West Florida.

Basis for selection. Open admission, but selective for some programs. Admission to health science programs determined through high school transcripts, placement test performance and other admissions criteria. Interview required of allied health applicants. Audition recommended for music majors. **Homeschooled:** Home School Affidavit must be submitted with parent's signature and notarized.

High school preparation. 13 units recommended. Recommended units include English 4, mathematics 3, social studies 3 and science 3.

2008-2009 Annual costs. Tuition/fees: $2,221; $7,949 out-of-state. Books/supplies: $800. Personal expenses: $1,500.

Financial aid. Need-based: Need-based aid available for part-time students. Work-study available nights, weekends and for part-time students. **Non-need-based:** Scholarships awarded for academics, athletics, job skills, leadership, minority status, music/drama, state residency.

Application procedures. Admission: No deadline. No application fee. Admission notification on a rolling basis. Application deadline for nursing program February 28; dental hygiene April 1; EMT and paramedic June 1; radiography May 15; physical therapist assistant April 1; surgical technology October 21. **Financial aid:** Priority date 4/1, closing date 7/1. FAFSA required. Applicants notified on a rolling basis starting 7/1.

Academics. Special study options: Accelerated study, cooperative education, distance learning, dual enrollment of high school students, ESL, honors, independent study, internships, teacher certification program, weekend college. License preparation in dental hygiene, nursing, paramedic, physical therapy, radiology, real estate. **Credit/placement by examination:** AP, CLEP, IB, institutional tests. 45 credit hours maximum toward associate degree. **Support services:** GED preparation, learning center, reduced course load, remedial instruction, study skills assistance, tutoring.

Majors. Agriculture: Landscaping, ornamental horticulture. **Biology:** General, marine. **Business:** Accounting, banking/financial services, business admin, communications, marketing, office/clerical, real estate. **Communications:** General, advertising, broadcast journalism, journalism, public relations. **Computer sciences:** General, applications programming, computer science, programming, systems analysis. **Conservation:** General, forestry. **Education:** Biology, chemistry, elementary, family/consumer sciences, health, mathematics, physics, sales/marketing, science, social studies, special. **Engineering:** General, electrical, marine. **Engineering technology:** Architectural, civil, construction, electrical. **Family/consumer sciences:** General, institutional food production. **Foreign languages:** General, translation. **Health:** Dental hygiene, EMT paramedic, health services, medical radiologic technology/radiation therapy, medical records admin, nursing (RN), optician, physical therapy assistant, physics/radiologic health, predental, premedicine, prepharmacy, preveterinary, respiratory therapy technology. **History:** General. **Legal studies:** General, paralegal, prelaw. **Liberal arts:** Arts/sciences, library science. **Math:** General. **Parks/recreation:** General, health/fitness. **Personal/culinary services:** Culinary arts. **Philosophy/religion:** Philosophy, religion. **Physical sciences:** Atmospheric science, chemistry, geology, oceanography, physics. **Protective services:** Criminal justice, fire safety technology, firefighting, law enforcement admin. **Psychology:** General. **Public administration:** Human services, social work. **Social sciences:** Anthropology, archaeology, criminology, economics, political science, sociology. **Visual/performing arts:** Art, dramatic.

Computing on campus. 560 workstations in library, computer center. Commuter students can connect to campus network. Online course registration, online library, helpline, wireless network available.

Student life. Freshman orientation: Available. Preregistration for classes offered. Orientation programs also available on the Internet. **Activities:** Bands, campus ministries, choral groups, dance, drama, international student organizations, literary magazine, music ensembles, musical theater, radio station, student government, student newspaper, African-American student union.

Athletics. NJCAA. **Intercollegiate:** Baseball M, basketball, softball W, volleyball W. **Intramural:** Basketball. **Team name:** Commodores.

Student services. Adult student services, career counseling, services for economically disadvantaged, student employment services, financial aid counseling, minority student services, personal counseling, veterans' counselor, women's services. **Physically disabled:** Services for visually, speech, hearing impaired. **Learning disabled:** Comprehensive services available. **Transfer:** Pre-admission transcript evaluation for new students. Transfer adviser, college fairs on campus for students transferring to 4-year colleges.

Contact. Phone: (850) 872-3892 Toll-free number: (800) 311-3685
Fax: (850) 913-3308
Sharon Todd, Director of Enrollment Services, Gulf Coast Community College, 5230 West Highway 98, Panama City, FL 32401-1041

Herzing College
Winter Park, Florida
www.herzing.edu **CB code: 3438**

- For-profit 2-year business and health science college
- Commuter campus in very large city
- Interview required

General. Regionally accredited. **Enrollment:** 187 degree-seeking undergraduates. **Degrees:** 7 bachelor's, 18 associate awarded. **Calendar:** Semester, extensive summer session. **Full-time faculty:** 15 total. **Part-time faculty:** 10 total.

Basis for selection. Open admission, but selective for some programs. Entrance test and evaluation for all applicants. SAT or ACT considered if submitted.

2008-2009 Annual costs. Tuition/fees: $12,150. Per-credit charge: $380. Reported annual tuition is representative. Actual costs vary by program.

2007-2008 Financial aid. Need-based: 15% of total undergraduate aid awarded as scholarships/grants, 85% as loans/jobs.

Application procedures. Admission: No deadline. No application fee. Admission notification on a rolling basis.

Academics. Special study options: Distance learning. Bachelor's degree programs available on campus. **Credit/placement by examination:** AP, CLEP, IB, institutional tests. 52 credit hours maximum toward associate degree, 97 toward bachelor's. **Support services:** Reduced course load, remedial instruction, study skills assistance, tutoring.

Majors. Business: General, business admin. **Computer sciences:** Information technology, LAN/WAN management, programming. **Health:** Insurance coding, insurance specialist, nursing (RN). **Legal studies:** Paralegal.

Computing on campus. 120 workstations in library, computer center. Online library, wireless network available.

Student life. Freshman orientation: Mandatory. Preregistration for classes offered.

Student services. Adult student services, student employment services, financial aid counseling. **Transfer:** Pre-admission transcript evaluation for new students.

Contact. E-mail: info@orl.herzing.edu
Phone: (407) 478-0500 Toll-free number: (800) 574-4446
Fax: (401) 418-0501
Tessie Uranga, Director of Admissions, Herzing College, 1595 South Semoran Boulevard, Suite 1501, Winter Park, FL 32792-5509

High-Tech Institute
Orlando, Florida
www.hightechinstitute.edu

- For-profit 2-year health science and technical college
- Commuter campus in large city

General. Accredited by ACCSCT. **Calendar:** Continuous.

Contact. Phone: (407) 893-7400
Admissions Director, 3710 Maguire Boulevard, Orlando, FL 32803

Hillsborough Community College
Tampa, Florida **CB member**
www.hccfl.edu **CB code: 5304**

- Public 2-year community college
- Commuter campus in large city

General. Founded in 1968. Regionally accredited. **Enrollment:** 18,651 degree-seeking undergraduates; 5,386 non-degree-seeking students. **Degrees:** 2,193 associate awarded. **ROTC:** Army. **Calendar:** Semester, limited summer session. **Full-time faculty:** 279 total; 24% have terminal degrees, 21% minority, 55% women. **Part-time faculty:** 993 total; 9% have terminal degrees, 23% minority, 47% women. **Class size:** 22% < 20, 76% 20-39, 1% 40-49, less than 1% 50-99. **Special facilities:** Environmental study centers (English Creek, Cockroach Bay, Upper Tampa Bay Park), Florida studies center.

Student profile. Among degree-seeking undergraduates, 67% enrolled in a transfer program, 33% enrolled in a vocational program, 4,046 enrolled as first-time, first-year students, 571 transferred in from other institutions.

Part-time:	58%	**Asian American:**	4%
Out-of-state:	8%	**Hispanic American:**	23%
Women:	56%	**International:**	2%
African American:	19%	**25 or older:**	35%

Transfer out. Colleges most students transferred to 2008: University of South Florida, University of Central Florida, University of Florida, Florida State University, Florida Gulf Coast University.

Basis for selection. Open admission, but selective for some programs. Limited access programs in certain health programs. Degree-seeking students must provide assessment/placement scores from CPT, FCELPT, ACT, or SAT prior to registering for classes. Test scores may be no more than two years old. **Homeschooled:** Applicants who completed a home education program must provide a signed affidavit affirming completion to the appropriate campus Office of Admissions, Registration and Records. **Learning Disabled:** Students should contact an HCC coordinator of services for students with disabilities to discuss documentation guidelines. Students should process at least one month prior to the start of the semester.

High school preparation. 24 units recommended. Recommended units include English 4, mathematics 3, science 3, foreign language 2 and academic electives 8.

2008-2009 Annual costs. Tuition/fees: $2,348; $8,451 out-of-state. Books/supplies: $1,950. Personal expenses: $2,676.

2007-2008 Financial aid. Need-based: 86% of total undergraduate aid awarded as scholarships/grants, 14% as loans/jobs. Need-based aid available for part-time students. Work-study available nights, weekends and for part-time students. **Non-need-based:** Scholarships awarded for academics, art, athletics, minority status, music/drama.

Application procedures. **Admission:** No deadline. $20 fee, may be waived for applicants with need. Admission notification on a rolling basis. **Financial aid:** Priority date 5/15, closing date 6/30. FAFSA, institutional form required. Applicants notified on a rolling basis.

Academics. **Special study options:** Accelerated study, cross-registration, distance learning, double major, dual enrollment of high school students, ESL, honors, independent study, internships, liberal arts/career combination, study abroad, teacher certification program, weekend college. License preparation in dental hygiene, nursing, paramedic. **Credit/placement by examination:** AP, CLEP, IB, institutional tests. Approval required. **Support services:** GED preparation, learning center, remedial instruction, study skills assistance, tutoring, writing center.

Majors. **Agriculture:** Aquaculture, landscaping. **Business:** Accounting technology, business admin, executive assistant, hospitality admin, management information systems, operations, restaurant/food services. **Computer sciences:** Applications programming, systems analysis. **Education:** Deaf/hearing impaired. **Engineering technology:** Architectural, biomedical, computer systems, electrical, environmental, industrial management, manufacturing. **Family/consumer sciences:** Child care. **Health:** Dental hygiene, dietician assistant, EMT paramedic, medical radiologic technology/radiation therapy, mental health services, nuclear medical technology, nursing (RN), optician, optometric assistant, respiratory therapy technology, sonography, veterinary technology/assistant. **Legal studies:** Paralegal. **Liberal arts:** Arts/sciences. **Personal/culinary services:** Restaurant/catering. **Protective services:** Fire safety technology, law enforcement admin. **Visual/performing arts:** Cinematography. **Other:** Computer/information technology services administration and management, Environmental control technologies / technicians.

Most popular majors. Health sciences 17%, liberal arts 75%.

Computing on campus. 2,014 workstations in library, computer center, student center. Dormitories wired for high-speed internet access. Commuter students can connect to campus network. Online course registration, online library, helpline, wireless network available.

Student life. **Freshman orientation:** Mandatory. Preregistration for classes offered. Held 2 hours prior to registration. **Housing:** Apartments available. **Activities:** Bands, choral groups, dance, drama, literary magazine, music ensembles, radio station, student government, student newspaper, African-American student union, American Sign Language club, aquaculture club, Arete club, Association of Professional Scholastic Opticians, College Republicans, computer club, Democrats, dive club.

Athletics. NJCAA. **Intercollegiate:** Baseball M, basketball, softball W, tennis W, volleyball W. **Team name:** Hawks.

Student services. Career counseling, services for economically disadvantaged, student employment services, financial aid counseling, on-campus daycare. **Physically disabled:** Services for visually, speech, hearing impaired. **Learning disabled:** Comprehensive services available. **Transfer:** Transfer center, transfer adviser, college fairs on campus for students transferring to 4-year colleges.

Contact. E-mail: dmarr@hccfl.edu
Phone: (813) 253-7004 Toll-free number: (866) 253-7077
Fax: (813) 253-7196
Hillsborough Community College, Box 31127, Tampa, FL 33631-3127

Indian River State College

Fort Pierce, Florida
www.ircc.edu
CB member
CB code: 5322

- Public 2-year community college
- Commuter campus in small city

General. Founded in 1960. Regionally accredited. Branch campuses in Vero Beach, Stuart, Okeechobee, Port St. Lucie; Criminal Justice Academy, Marine Center in Fort Pierce. **Enrollment:** 9,464 degree-seeking undergraduates. **Degrees:** 1,508 associate awarded. **Location:** 65 miles from West Palm Beach. **Calendar:** Semester, limited summer session. **Full-time faculty:** 202 total. **Part-time faculty:** 750 total. **Special facilities:** Olympic-size pool complex, fine arts center, planetarium.

Student profile.

Out-of-state:	2%	**25 or older:**	42%

Transfer out. **Colleges most students transferred to 2008:** University of Central Florida, University of South Florida, University of Florida, Florida State University, Florida Atlantic University.

Basis for selection. Open admission, but selective for some programs. Testing and academic records determine admission to health science programs. SAT or ACT recommended for placement.

High school preparation. 24 units recommended. Recommended units include English 4, mathematics 3, social studies 3, history 2, science 3, foreign language 2 and academic electives 7.

2008-2009 Annual costs. Tuition/fees: $2,242; $8,332 out-of-state. Books/supplies: $700. Personal expenses: $856.

2007-2008 Financial aid. **Need-based:** 78% of total undergraduate aid awarded as scholarships/grants, 22% as loans/jobs. Need-based aid available for part-time students. Work-study available for part-time students. **Non-need-based:** Scholarships awarded for academics, athletics, minority status, music/drama, state residency.

Application procedures. **Admission:** No deadline. No application fee. Admission notification on a rolling basis. **Financial aid:** Priority date 7/18; no closing date. FAFSA, institutional form reqdired. Applicants notified on a rolling basis starting 5/15.

Academics. **Special study options:** Accelerated study, distance learning, dual enrollment of high school students, weekend college. License preparation in paramedic, real estate. **Credit/placement by examination:** AP, CLEP, IB, institutional tests. 45 credit hours maximum toward associate degree. Degree-seeking students must achieve state-designated cutoff scores on placement test to enter college-level programs, or complete sequence of developmental courses. **Support services:** GED preparation and test center, learning center, pre-admission summer program, reduced course load, remedial instruction, study skills assistance, tutoring.

Majors. **Agriculture:** Business technology, turf management. **Biology:** General. **Business:** Accounting, administrative services, business admin, hospitality admin, management information systems, office management, sales/distribution. **Communications:** Public relations. **Communications technology:** Graphic/printing. **Computer sciences:** General, applications programming, computer graphics, information technology, programming, systems analysis, web page design. **Conservation:** Environmental studies. **Education:** General, early childhood, elementary, secondary. **Engineering:** General. **Engineering technology:** Architectural drafting, civil, construction, electrical. **Foreign languages:** General. **Health:** Clinical lab technology, dental hygiene, dental lab technology, EMT paramedic, medical radiologic technology/radiation therapy, medical records admin, medical records technology, medical transcription, nursing (RN), physical therapy assistant, predental, premedicine, prepharmacy, preveterinary, respiratory therapy technology. **History:** General. **Legal studies:** Legal secretary, paralegal, prelaw. **Liberal arts:** Arts/sciences, library assistant. **Math:** General. **Mechanic/repair:** Automotive, heating/ac/refrig. **Personal/culinary services:** Restaurant/catering. **Philosophy/religion:** Philosophy. **Physical sciences:** Chemistry, physics. **Protective services:** Criminal justice, fire safety technology. **Psychology:** General. **Public administration:** Human services. **Social sciences:** Anthropology, economics, political science, sociology. **Visual/performing arts:** Art, commercial/advertising art, dance, dramatic, interior design.

Computing on campus. Online course registration, online library available.

Student life. **Freshman orientation:** Available. **Housing:** Apartments available. **Activities:** Bands, choral groups, dance, drama, international student organizations, literary magazine, music ensembles, musical theater, radio station, student government, symphony orchestra, Distributive Education Clubs of America, Vocational International Clubs of America, cultural exchange club, human services club, ambassador club, Bacchus Club, Phi Beta Lambda.

Athletics. NJCAA. **Intercollegiate:** Baseball M, basketball, cheerleading W, diving, softball W, swimming, volleyball W. **Team name:** Pioneers.

Student services. Alcohol/substance abuse counseling, career counseling, services for economically disadvantaged, student employment services, financial aid counseling, health services, minority student services, on-campus daycare, placement for graduates, veterans' counselor, women's services. **Physically disabled:** Services for visually, speech, hearing impaired. **Transfer:** Transfer adviser, college fairs on campus for students transferring to 4-year colleges.

Contact. Phone: (772) 462-4740 Toll-free number: (866) 866-4722
Fax: (772) 462-4699
Karen Chapdelaine, Director of Admissions, Indian River State College, 3209 Virginia Avenue, Fort Pierce, FL 34981-5596

Keiser Career College: Greenacres

Greenacres, Florida

- For-profit 2-year business and health science college
- Commuter campus in small city

General. Accredited by ACCSCT. **Calendar:** Continuous.

Contact. Phone: (561) 433-2330
6812 Forest Hill Boulevard, Greenacres, FL 33413

Keiser Career College: Miami Lakes
Miami Lakes, Florida

- For-profit 2-year business and health science college
- Commuter campus in large town

General. Accredited by ACCSCT. **Calendar:** Continuous.

Contact. Phone: (305) 820-5003
17395 NW 59th Avenue, Miami Lakes, FL 33015

Keiser University
Ft. Lauderdale, Florida
www.keiseruniversity.edu **CB code: 7004**

- For-profit 2-year business and health science college
- Commuter campus in large city

General. Founded in 1977. Regionally accredited. **Location:** 35 miles from Miami. **Calendar:** Semester.

Annual costs/financial aid. Need-based financial aid available to full-time and part-time students.

Contact. Phone: (954) 776-4456
Director of Admissions, 1500 Northwest 49th Street, Fort Lauderdale, FL 33309

Key College
Dania Beach, Florida
www.keycollege.edu **CB code: 3577**

- For-profit 2-year business and technical college
- Commuter campus in very large city
- Interview required

General. Accredited by ACICS. **Enrollment:** 175 degree-seeking undergraduates. **Degrees:** 11 associate awarded. **Calendar:** Quarter, extensive summer session. **Full-time faculty:** 6 total. **Part-time faculty:** 11 total.

Student profile.

Out-of-state:	6%	**25 or older:**	67%

Basis for selection. Open admission, but selective for some programs. Entrance exam required. Career Placement Assessment Test (CPAT) used in institution's admissions procedures; SAT or ACT scores may be submitted in lieu of CPAT. **Homeschooled:** State high school equivalency certificate required.

2008-2009 Annual costs. Tuition/fees: $9,210. Books/supplies: $1,050.

Financial aid. Need-based: Work-study available nights and for part-time students. **Additional information:** Federal Supplemental Educational Opportunities Grant (FSEOG), PELL grant, FFEL (federal loan program) available; direct loans offered.

Application procedures. Admission: No deadline. $35 fee. Application must be submitted on paper. Admission notification on a rolling basis. **Financial aid:** No deadline.

Academics. Credit/placement by examination: CLEP, institutional tests. **Support services:** Remedial instruction, study skills assistance.

Majors. Engineering technology: Drafting. **Legal studies:** Court reporting, paralegal.

Computing on campus. 65 workstations in library, computer center.

Student life. Freshman orientation: Mandatory. Held one week prior to beginning of classes for approximately 3 hours. **Activities:** Student newspaper.

Student services. Career counseling, financial aid counseling, personal counseling, veterans' counselor.

Contact. E-mail: admissions@keycollege.edu
Phone: (954) 923-4440 Toll-free number: (800) 581-8292
Fax: (954) 583-9458
Sandra Gabriel, Director of Admissions, Key College, 225 Dania Beach Boulevard, Dania Beach, FL 33004

Lake City Community College
Lake City, Florida **CB member**
www.lakecitycc.edu **CB code: 5377**

- Public 2-year community college
- Commuter campus in large town

General. Founded in 1947. Regionally accredited. **Enrollment:** 2,753 degree-seeking undergraduates. **Degrees:** 323 associate awarded. **Location:** 60 miles from Jacksonville, 45 miles from Gainesville. **Calendar:** Semester, limited summer session. **Full-time faculty:** 55 total. **Part-time faculty:** 110 total. **Special facilities:** Performing arts center, arboretum.

Student profile.

Out-of-state:	3%	**Live on campus:**	1%
25 or older:	30%		

Basis for selection. Open admission, but selective for some programs. Selective to allied health programs. Locally administered CPT test may be used in place of SAT or ACT. Interview recommended for most allied health programs and all golf course operations programs.

High school preparation. 13 units recommended. Recommended units include English 4, mathematics 3, social studies 3 and science 3. Applicants to forest management should have good mathematics background.

2008-2009 Annual costs. Tuition/fees: $2,237; $8,522 out-of-state. Books/supplies: $800. Personal expenses: $750.

Financial aid. Need-based: Need-based aid available for part-time students. Work-study available for part-time students. **Non-need-based:** Scholarships awarded for academics, athletics.

Application procedures. Admission: Priority date 8/1; no deadline. $15 fee. Application must be submitted on paper. Admission notification on a rolling basis. Some technical programs reach maximum enrollment and are closed prior to August 1. **Financial aid:** Priority date 6/1; no closing date. FAFSA, institutional form required. Applicants notified on a rolling basis starting 6/1; must reply within 2 week(s) of notification.

Academics. Special study options: Accelerated study, cooperative education, distance learning, dual enrollment of high school students, exchange student, independent study, internships, study abroad, teacher certification program, weekend college. Bachelor's degree programs available on campus. License preparation in nursing, paramedic, physical therapy. **Credit/placement by examination:** CLEP, IB, institutional tests. 30 credit hours maximum toward associate degree. **Support services:** GED preparation and test center, learning center, reduced course load, remedial instruction, study skills assistance, tutoring.

Majors. Agriculture: Agribusiness operations, landscaping. **Architecture:** Landscape. **Business:** General, administrative services, business admin, office/clerical. **Communications:** General. **Computer sciences:** General, information systems, programming. **Education:** General. **Health:** Clinical lab technology, EMT paramedic, nursing (RN), physical therapy assistant. **Legal studies:** Prelaw. **Liberal arts:** Arts/sciences. **Math:** General. **Parks/recreation:** Facilities management. **Protective services:** Criminal justice. **Social sciences:** Criminology.

Computing on campus. 320 workstations in library, computer center. Online library available.

Student life. Freshman orientation: Available. **Housing:** Coed dorms available. $100 deposit. **Activities:** Bands, choral groups, dance, drama, literary magazine, music ensembles, student government, TV station, Florida Turf Grass Association, Florida Student Nurses Association, Phi Theta Kappa, Baptist Student Union, Granger Hall Council, medical lab technology club, physical therapy assistant club, Practical Nurses Association.

Athletics. NJCAA. **Intercollegiate:** Baseball M, golf W, softball W. **Intramural:** Basketball, racquetball, softball, table tennis, volleyball. **Team name:** Timberwolves.

Student services. Alcohol/substance abuse counseling, career counseling, student employment services, financial aid counseling, personal counseling, veterans' counselor. **Physically disabled:** Services for visually, speech, hearing impaired. **Transfer:** Transfer adviser, college fairs on campus for students transferring to 4-year colleges.

Contact. E-mail: admissions@lakecitycc.edu
Phone: (386) 754-4287 Fax: (386) 754-4787
Vince Rice, Director, Lake City Community College, 149 SE College Place, Lake City, FL 32025-8703

Lake-Sumter Community College
Leesburg, Florida
www.lscc.edu **CB code: 5376**

- Public 2-year community college
- Commuter campus in small city

General. Founded in 1962. Regionally accredited. **Enrollment:** 3,274 degree-seeking undergraduates; 633 non-degree-seeking students. **Degrees:** 473 associate awarded. **Location:** 35 miles from Orlando. **Calendar:** Semester, limited summer session. **Full-time faculty:** 70 total; 21% have terminal degrees, 6% minority, 67% women. **Part-time faculty:** 558 total; 12% have terminal degrees, 21% minority, 54% women. **Class size:** 46% < 20, 53% 20-39, 1% 40-49, less than 1% 50-99. **Special facilities:** Wellness facilities.

Student profile. Among degree-seeking undergraduates, 78% enrolled in a transfer program, 22% enrolled in a vocational program, 687 enrolled as first-time, first-year students, 305 transferred in from other institutions.

Part-time:	63%	**Women:**	66%
Out-of-state:	1%	**25 or older:**	31%

Transfer out. Colleges most students transferred to 2008: University of Central Florida, University of Florida, Florida State University, University of South Florida.

Basis for selection. Open admission, but selective for some programs. Special requirements for nursing program. **Homeschooled:** In lieu of a high school diploma or GED, a home-schooled affidavit will be accepted.

2008-2009 Annual costs. Tuition/fees: $2,326; $8,743 out-of-state. Books/supplies: $874. Personal expenses: $2,051.

2008-2009 Financial aid. Need-based: 91 full-time freshmen applied for aid; 91 were judged to have need; 91 of these received aid. Average scholarship/grant was $1,594. Need-based aid available for part-time students. Work-study available nights and for part-time students. **Non-need-based:** Scholarships awarded for academics, art, athletics, leadership, minority status, music/drama, state residency.

Application procedures. Admission: No deadline. $25 fee. Application must be submitted on paper. Admission notification on a rolling basis. **Financial aid:** Priority date 4/15; no closing date. FAFSA, institutional form required. Applicants notified on a rolling basis starting 7/1.

Academics. Special study options: Cooperative education, distance learning, dual enrollment of high school students, independent study, liberal arts/career combination, teacher certification program. Bachelor's degree programs available on campus. License preparation in nursing, real estate. **Credit/placement by examination:** AP, CLEP, institutional tests. 45 credit hours maximum toward associate degree. **Support services:** Learning center, reduced course load, remedial instruction, study skills assistance, tutoring, writing center.

Majors. Business: Business admin, executive assistant. **Computer sciences:** Applications programming, systems analysis. **Education:** Early childhood. **Engineering technology:** Computer systems, electrical. **Health:** EMT paramedic, medical records technology, nursing (RN). **Legal studies:** Paralegal. **Liberal arts:** Arts/sciences. **Parks/recreation:** Sports admin. **Protective services:** Fire safety technology, firefighting, law enforcement admin. **Visual/performing arts:** Commercial/advertising art. **Other:** Sports medicine.

Most popular majors. Liberal arts 77%.

Computing on campus. 647 workstations in library, computer center, student center. Commuter students can connect to campus network. Online course registration, online library, wireless network available.

Student life. Freshman orientation: Mandatory. Both day and evening sessions are scheduled as well as online orientation. **Activities:** Bands, campus ministries, choral groups, drama, literary magazine, music ensembles, student government, student newspaper, symphony orchestra, College Democrats, College Republicans, environmental society, Fellowship of Christian Athletes, Health Explorers, Spanish club.

Athletics. NJCAA. **Intercollegiate:** Baseball M, softball W, volleyball W. **Intramural:** Basketball, football (non-tackle), table tennis, tennis, volleyball. **Team name:** Lakers.

Student services. Adult student services, alcohol/substance abuse counseling, career counseling, services for economically disadvantaged, student employment services, financial aid counseling, minority student services, personal counseling, placement for graduates, veterans' counselor, women's services. **Physically disabled:** Services for visually, speech, hearing impaired. **Transfer:** Pre-admission transcript evaluation for new students. Transfer adviser, college fairs on campus for students transferring to 4-year colleges.

Contact. E-mail: admissinquiry@lscc.edu
Phone: (352) 323-3665 Fax: (352) 365-3553
Mark Swearingen, Director, Admissions/ Registrar, Lake-Sumter Community College, 9501 U.S. Highway 441, Leesburg, FL 34788-8751

Le Cordon Bleu College of Culinary Arts: Miami
Hollywood, Florida
www.miamiculinary.com

- For-profit 2-year culinary school
- Small city

General. Accredited by ACCSCT. **Calendar:** Continuous.

Contact. Phone: (954) 438-8882
3221 Enterprise Way, Miramar, FL 33025

Lincoln College of Technology: West Palm Beach
West Palm Beach, Florida
www.newenglandtech.com **CB code: 0529**

- For-profit 2-year technical college
- Commuter campus in small city

General. Founded in 1982. Accredited by ACICS. **Location:** 75 miles from Miami. **Calendar:** Quarter.

Annual costs/financial aid. Need-based financial aid available for full-time students.

Contact. Phone: (561) 842-8324
Admissions Director, 2410 Metrocentre Boulevard, West Palm Beach, FL 33407

Manatee Community College
Bradenton, Florida **CB member**
www.mccfl.edu **CB code: 5427**

- Public 2-year community college
- Commuter campus in small city

General. Founded in 1957. Regionally accredited. **Enrollment:** 9,157 degree-seeking undergraduates; 1,149 non-degree-seeking students. **Degrees:** 1,659 associate awarded. **Location:** 40 miles from Tampa, 20 miles from St. Petersburg. **Calendar:** Semester, extensive summer session. **Full-time faculty:** 151 total; 24% have terminal degrees, 13% minority, 61% women. **Part-time faculty:** 266 total; 6% have terminal degrees, 10% minority, 51% women.

Student profile. Among degree-seeking undergraduates, 59% enrolled in a transfer program, 41% enrolled in a vocational program, 1,870 enrolled as first-time, first-year students.

Part-time:	50%	**Women:**	62%
Out-of-state:	2%	**25 or older:**	37%

Basis for selection. Open admission, but selective for some programs. Limited enrollment in health programs. Interview recommended for nursing, radiologic technology, respiratory therapy, occupational therapy assistant, physical therapist assistant, dental hygiene majors.

High school preparation. Recommended units include English 4, mathematics 3, social studies 2, history 1, science 3 and foreign language 2.

2008-2009 Annual costs. Tuition/fees: $2,348; $8,830 out-of-state. Books/supplies: $1,202. Personal expenses: $1,910.

2008-2009 Financial aid. **Need-based:** 890 full-time freshmen applied for aid; 695 were judged to have need; 695 of these received aid. Average scholarship/grant was $2,650. Need-based aid available for part-time students. Work-study available nights, weekends and for part-time students. **Non-need-based:** Scholarships awarded for academics, art, athletics, music/drama, state residency.

Application procedures. **Admission:** No deadline. No application fee. Admission notification on a rolling basis. **Financial aid:** Priority date 6/1, closing date 7/28. FAFSA required. Applicants notified on a rolling basis starting 3/15.

Academics. **Special study options:** Accelerated study, cooperative education, distance learning, dual enrollment of high school students, honors, independent study, teacher certification program. License preparation in dental hygiene, nursing, occupational therapy, physical therapy, radiology. **Credit/placement by examination:** AP, CLEP. 30 credit hours maximum toward associate degree. SAT, ACT or CPT (Florida Placement Test) used for placement only. **Support services:** GED preparation, learning center, remedial instruction, study skills assistance, tutoring.

Majors. **Area/ethnic studies:** African, African-American, American, Latin American, women's. **Biology:** General, bacteriology, marine. **Business:** General, accounting, administrative services, business admin. **Communications:** General, advertising, broadcast journalism, digital media, journalism, media studies, public relations, radio/tv. **Communications technology:** Radio/tv. **Computer sciences:** General, information systems, networking, programming, systems analysis. **Education:** General, biology, chemistry, early childhood, elementary, foreign languages, health, kindergarten/preschool, mathematics, music, physics, science, secondary, social studies, trade/industrial. **Engineering:** General, civil, computer, science. **Engineering technology:** Automotive, civil, construction, drafting, electrical. **Foreign languages:** French, German, Spanish. **Health:** Clinical lab science, clinical lab technology, community health services, dental hygiene, health care admin, medical radiologic technology/radiation therapy, nuclear medical technology, nursing (RN), occupational therapy assistant, physical therapy assistant, respiratory therapy technology, veterinary technology/assistant. **History:** General. **Legal studies:** General, paralegal, prelaw. **Liberal arts:** Arts/sciences, humanities. **Math:** General. **Parks/recreation:** Sports admin. **Personal/culinary services:** General. **Philosophy/religion:** Philosophy, religion. **Physical sciences:** Atmospheric science, chemistry, physics. **Protective services:** Criminal justice, firefighting. **Psychology:** General. **Public administration:** General, social work. **Social sciences:** General, economics. **Visual/performing arts:** General, art, art history/conservation, commercial/advertising art, dramatic, fashion design, jazz, music theory/composition, studio arts, theater history.

Most popular majors. Health sciences 14%, liberal arts 76%.

Computing on campus. 2,275 workstations in library, computer center. Online course registration, online library, helpline, repair service, wireless network available.

Student life. **Freshman orientation:** Mandatory. Preregistration for classes offered. **Activities:** Bands, drama, film society, literary magazine, music ensembles, musical theater, opera, student government, student newspaper, symphony orchestra, African-American Student Union, multicultural student club, art club, student Bible club, Manasota Geographic and Anthropological Society, American Chemical Society, student film club, Hispanic-American club.

Athletics. NJCAA. **Intercollegiate:** Baseball M, basketball M, softball W, volleyball W. **Intramural:** Basketball, golf, soccer, softball, volleyball, weight lifting. **Team name:** Lancers.

Student services. Chaplain/spiritual director, career counseling, student employment services, financial aid counseling, health services, personal counseling, placement for graduates, veterans' counselor. **Physically disabled:** Services for visually, speech, hearing impaired. **Transfer:** Transfer adviser for students transferring to 4-year colleges.

Contact. E-mail: admissions@mccfl.edu
Phone: (941) 752-5031 Fax: (941) 727-6380
Marilynn Lewy, Registrar, Manatee Community College, Box 1849, Bradenton, FL 34206-1849

Miami Dade College

Miami, Florida — **CB member**
www.mdc.edu/main/ — **CB code: 5458**

- Public 2-year community college
- Commuter campus in very large city

General. Founded in 1959. Regionally accredited. Multilocation institution consisting of campuses and outreach centers. **Enrollment:** 49,147 degree-seeking undergraduates; 8,075 non-degree-seeking students. **Degrees:** 94 bachelor's, 6,823 associate awarded. **ROTC:** Army, Air Force. **Calendar:** Semester, limited summer session. **Full-time faculty:** 698 total; 26% have terminal degrees, 60% minority, 53% women. **Part-time faculty:** 1,397 total; 15% have terminal degrees, 65% minority, 46% women. **Class size:** 20% < 20, 66% 20-39, 12% 40-49, 1% 50-99, less than 1% >100. **Special facilities:** Environmental demonstration center, bilingual center, greenhouse, fire science tower, fire science burn building, emerging technologies center of the Americas, center for the environment, horticulture center, firearms demonstration lab, earth science museum, studio theater, human patient simulator lab, flight simulator lab, child care labs. **Partnerships:** Formal partnerships with Florida Power and Light.

Student profile. Among degree-seeking undergraduates, 73% enrolled in a transfer program, 27% enrolled in a vocational program, 1% already have a bachelor's degree or higher, 9,717 enrolled as first-time, first-year students, 1,413 transferred in from other institutions.

Part-time:	60%	**Asian American:**	1%
Out-of-state:	6%	**Hispanic American:**	69%
Women:	60%	**International:**	3%
African American:	17%	**25 or older:**	37%

Transfer out. 82% of students enrolled in the transfer program go on to 4-year colleges. **Colleges most students transferred to 2008:** Florida International University.

Basis for selection. Open admission, but selective for some programs. Special requirements for visual and performing arts, honors, allied health, bachelor's in education, bachelor of applied science with major in public safety management, and bachelor's in nursing. Audition required of performing arts majors. Portfolio required of visual arts majors. **Learning Disabled:** The Office of ACCESS (Disability Services) provides, arranges and coordinates accommodations for students with documented disabilities.

High school preparation. 24 units recommended. 18 credits with a 3-year high school option or 24 credits with a 4-year high school option.

2008-2009 Annual costs. Tuition/fees: $2,348; $8,469 out-of-state.

2008-2009 Financial aid. **Need-based:** Average need met was 67%. Average scholarship/grant was $1,313; average loan $483. 79% of total undergraduate aid awarded as scholarships/grants, 21% as loans/jobs. Need-based aid available for part-time students. Work-study available nights, weekends and for part-time students. **Non-need-based:** Scholarships awarded for academics, art, athletics, music/drama, state residency.

Application procedures. **Admission:** No deadline. $20 fee. Admission notification on a rolling basis. **Financial aid:** Priority date 3/15, closing date 6/30. FAFSA required. Applicants notified on a rolling basis starting 5/15.

Academics. **Special study options:** Accelerated study, cooperative education, cross-registration, distance learning, dual enrollment of high school students, ESL, honors, independent study, internships, study abroad, teacher certification program, weekend college. Bachelor's degree programs available on campus. License preparation in aviation, dental hygiene, nursing, paramedic, physical therapy, radiology, real estate. **Credit/placement by examination:** AP, CLEP, IB, institutional tests. 45 credit hours maximum toward associate degree, 45 toward bachelor's. **Support services:** GED preparation, learning center, reduced course load, remedial instruction, study skills assistance, tutoring, writing center.

Majors. **Agriculture:** Agribusiness operations, landscaping. **Area/ethnic studies:** American, Asian, Latin American. **Biology:** General. **Business:** Accounting, administrative services, banking/financial services, business admin, management science, office management, office/clerical, real estate, tourism promotion, tourism/travel. **Communications:** Broadcast journalism, journalism. **Communications technology:** General, animation/special effects, graphic/printing, graphics. **Computer sciences:** General, applications programming, information systems, information technology, web page design. **Conservation:** Environmental science, forestry. **Construction:** Maintenance. **Education:** Early childhood, elementary, mathematics, physical, science, secondary, special, technology/industrial arts. **Engineering:** Architectural, civil, electrical. **Engineering technology:** Architectural, civil, electrical, electrical drafting. **Family/consumer sciences:** Child development, food/nutrition. **Foreign languages:** General, sign language interpretation, translation. **Health:** Clinical lab technology, dental hygiene, EMT paramedic, histologic technology, medical assistant, medical radiologic technology/radiation therapy, medical records admin, medical secretary, midwifery, nursing (RN), optician, predental, premedicine, prepharmacy, preveterinary, respiratory therapy technology, veterinary technology/assistant. **History:** General. **Legal studies:** Court reporting, legal secretary, paralegal, prelaw. **Liberal arts:** Arts/sciences. **Math:** General. **Mechanic/repair:** Heating/ac/refrig, industrial. **Parks/recreation:** Exercise sciences. **Personal/culinary**

services: Mortuary science. **Philosophy/religion:** Philosophy, religion. **Physical sciences:** Atmospheric science, chemistry, geology, physics. **Protective services:** Criminal justice, fire services admin. **Psychology:** General. **Public administration:** General, human services, social work. **Social sciences:** Anthropology, economics, international relations, political science, sociology. **Transportation:** Aviation, aviation management. **Visual/performing arts:** Cinematography, commercial/advertising art, dance, dramatic, studio arts.

Most popular majors. Health sciences 12%, liberal arts 79%.

Computing on campus. 8,000 workstations in library, computer center. Commuter students can connect to campus network. Online course registration, online library, helpline, wireless network available.

Student life. **Freshman orientation:** Available. **Activities:** Bands, campus ministries, choral groups, dance, drama, film society, international student organizations, literary magazine, music ensembles, Model UN, musical theater, radio station, student government, student newspaper, TV station, Newman Club, Chabad Jewish Student Union, African Student Union, Phi Beta Lambda, Phi Theta Kappa, Spirit of Faith, Haitian Boukan Club, Catholic Ministries, Miami Dade Students for Peace.

Athletics. NJCAA. **Intercollegiate:** Baseball M, basketball, softball W, volleyball W. **Intramural:** Basketball, soccer, softball, table tennis, tennis. **Team name:** Sharks.

Student services. Adult student services, career counseling, services for economically disadvantaged, student employment services, financial aid counseling, on-campus daycare, personal counseling, placement for graduates, veterans' counselor. **Physically disabled:** Services for visually, speech, hearing impaired. **Transfer:** Transfer center, transfer adviser, college fairs on campus for students transferring to 4-year colleges.

Contact. Phone: (305) 237-2222 Fax: (305) 237-2964
Dulce Beltran, College Director, Admissions and Registration Services, Miami Dade College, 11011 SW 104th Street, Miami, FL 33176-3393

North Florida Community College

Madison, Florida
www.nfcc.edu **CB code: 5503**

- Public 2-year community college
- Commuter campus in rural community

General. Founded in 1958. Regionally accredited. **Enrollment:** 820 degree-seeking undergraduates. **Degrees:** 229 associate awarded. **Location:** 56 miles from Tallahassee. **Calendar:** Semester, limited summer session. **Full-time faculty:** 37 total. **Part-time faculty:** 1 total. **Special facilities:** Nature center.

Transfer out. **Colleges most students transferred to 2008:** Florida State University, Florida A&M University, Valdosta State University, University of Florida.

Basis for selection. Open admission, but selective for some programs. Limited enrollment for nursing, criminal justice, EMT. Background checks completed by Florida Department of Law Enforcement. Florida College Entry-Level Placement Tests required for all students. Students with satisfactory ACT or SAT scores are exempt from taking FCELPT. **Homeschooled:** Statement describing homeschool structure and mission required. Submit affidavit stating that home education complies with Florida law. **Learning Disabled:** Disabilities must have documentation.

High school preparation. 24 units recommended. Recommended units include English 4, mathematics 4, social studies 3, science 2 (laboratory 1) and foreign language 2. Algebra 1 recommended.

2008-2009 Annual costs. Tuition/fees: $2,190; $7,734 out-of-state. Books/supplies: $500. Personal expenses: $475.

2007-2008 Financial aid. All financial aid based on need. Need-based aid available for part-time students. Work-study available nights, weekends and for part-time students.

Application procedures. **Admission:** Priority date 7/1; no deadline. $20 fee, may be waived for applicants with need. Application must be submitted on paper. Admission notification on a rolling basis. **Financial aid:** Priority date 5/15; no closing date. FAFSA required. Applicants notified on a rolling basis starting 6/20; must reply within 2 week(s) of notification.

Academics. **Special study options:** Accelerated study, distance learning, dual enrollment of high school students, independent study, teacher certification program. Bachelor's degree programs available on campus. License preparation in nursing, paramedic, real estate. **Credit/placement by examination:** AP, CLEP, IB, institutional tests. 45 credit hours maximum toward associate degree. **Support services:** GED preparation and test center, reduced course load, remedial instruction, study skills assistance, tutoring, writing center.

Majors. **Health:** Nursing assistant. **Liberal arts:** Arts/sciences.

Computing on campus. 65 workstations in library, computer center, student center. Online course registration, online library, wireless network available.

Student life. **Freshman orientation:** Available. **Activities:** Jazz band, choral groups, drama, music ensembles, musical theater, student government, student newspaper, environmental awareness group, African-American Association, veterans club, ASL.

Athletics. NJCAA. **Intercollegiate:** Baseball M, basketball W, softball W. **Team name:** Sentinels.

Student services. Adult student services, career counseling, student employment services, health services, personal counseling, placement for graduates, veterans' counselor. **Physically disabled:** Services for hearing impaired. **Transfer:** Pre-admission transcript evaluation for new students. Transfer adviser, college fairs on campus for students transferring to 4-year colleges.

Contact. Phone: (850) 973-1622 Toll-free number: (866) 937-6322
Fax: (850) 973-1697
Mary Wheeler, Dean of Enrollment Services, North Florida Community College, 325 NW Turner Davis Drive, Madison, FL 32340

North Florida Institute: Orange Park

Orange Park, Florida

- For-profit 2-year business and health science college
- Large city
- Interview required

General. Accredited by ACICS. **Enrollment:** 529 degree-seeking undergraduates. **Degrees:** 93 associate awarded. **Calendar:** Differs by program.

Basis for selection. Open admission. Interview required to discuss the school's programs in relation to the prospective student's career preferences, training needs, and individual motivation.

Application procedures. **Admission:** $67 fee.

Academics. **Credit/placement by examination:** CLEP.

Majors. **Business:** Business admin. **Health:** Management/clinical assistant. **Other:** Surgical technician.

Contact. Phone: (904) 269-7086
North Florida Institute: Orange Park, 560 Wells Road, Orange Park, FL 32073

Orlando Culinary Academy

Orlando, Florida
www.orlandoculinary.com

- For-profit 2-year culinary school
- Very large city

General. Accredited by ACICS. **Location:** Downtown. **Calendar:** Continuous.

Contact. Phone: (407) 888-4000
8511 Commodity Circle, Suite 100, Orlando, FL 32819

Palm Beach Community College

Lake Worth, Florida **CB member**
www.pbcc.edu **CB code: 5531**

- Public 2-year community college
- Commuter campus in large town

General. Founded in 1933. Regionally accredited. Multilocation institution with 4 campuses, numerous other locations throughout service area. **Enrollment:** 19,428 degree-seeking undergraduates; 5,694 non-degree-seeking students. **Degrees:** 2,060 associate awarded. **Location:** 30 miles from Fort Lauderdale. **Calendar:** Semester, limited summer session. **Full-time faculty:** 235 total; 25% minority, 57% women. **Part-time faculty:** 972 total; 21% minority, 41% women. **Special facilities:** Performing arts centers at 3 campuses.

Student profile. Among degree-seeking undergraduates, 4,110 enrolled as first-time, first-year students, 1,006 transferred in from other institutions.

Part-time:	58%	**Asian American:**	3%
Out-of-state:	6%	**Hispanic American:**	19%
Women:	59%	**International:**	2%
African American:	23%	**25 or older:**	40%

Transfer out. Colleges most students transferred to 2008: Florida Atlantic University, University of Florida, Florida State University, University of South Florida.

Basis for selection. Open admission, but selective for some programs. Special requirements for dental, nursing, dietetic, occupational therapy assistant programs. Admission to paramedic, radiography, respiratory care programs based on test scores and GPA. SAT or ACT required for admission to nursing and dental programs. CPT, SAT or ACT used for placement for all incoming freshmen. Interview required for nursing, dental, radiography, respiratory care, paramedic majors. Audition required of music majors. **Home-schooled:** Home education program affidavit required.

High school preparation. Special requirements for health program applicants.

2008-2009 Annual costs. Tuition/fees: $2,250; $8,101 out-of-state. Books/supplies: $1,000. Personal expenses: $400.

2008-2009 Financial aid. Need-based: 77% of total undergraduate aid awarded as scholarships/grants, 23% as loans/jobs. Work-study available nights, weekends and for part-time students. **Non-need-based:** Scholarships awarded for academics, alumni affiliation, athletics, leadership, state residency.

Application procedures. Admission: Closing date 8/23. $20 fee. Admission notification on a rolling basis beginning on or about 3/1. **Financial aid:** Priority date 7/1; no closing date. FAFSA, institutional form required. Applicants notified on a rolling basis; must reply within 2 week(s) of notification.

Academics. Center for Personalized Instruction offers full assistance in all academic areas for students. **Special study options:** Cooperative education, distance learning, double major, dual enrollment of high school students, ESL, honors, independent study, internships, study abroad, weekend college. License preparation in aviation, dental hygiene, nursing, paramedic, radiology, real estate. **Credit/placement by examination:** AP, CLEP, IB, institutional tests. 45 credit hours maximum toward associate degree. **Support services:** Learning center, pre-admission summer program, reduced course load, remedial instruction, study skills assistance, tutoring, writing center.

Majors. Agriculture: Ornamental horticulture. **Architecture:** Interior. **Biology:** General, zoology. **Business:** General, accounting, business admin, finance, hospitality admin, management information systems, marketing, sales/distribution. **Communications:** Broadcast journalism, journalism. **Communications technology:** Graphic/printing. **Computer sciences:** General, applications programming, information systems, programming, systems analysis. **Construction:** Maintenance. **Education:** Art, early childhood, elementary, health, health occupations, music, physical, sales/marketing, science, secondary, social science, voc/tech. **Engineering:** General, electrical. **Engineering technology:** Construction, drafting, electrical, industrial management, surveying. **Family/consumer sciences:** General, child care. **Health:** Clinical lab technology, dental hygiene, dietetics, EMT paramedic, health services, massage therapy, medical radiologic technology/radiation therapy, nursing (RN), occupational therapy assistant, premedicine, respiratory therapy technology. **History:** General. **Interdisciplinary:** Biological/physical sciences. **Legal studies:** Paralegal. **Liberal arts:** Arts/sciences. **Math:** General. **Mechanic/repair:** Automotive, marine. **Parks/recreation:** General, health/fitness. **Philosophy/religion:** Philosophy. **Physical sciences:** Chemistry, physics. **Protective services:** Fire services admin, firefighting. **Psychology:** General. **Public administration:** Human services, social work. **Social sciences:** General, anthropology, geography, international relations, political science, sociology. **Transportation:** Aviation. **Visual/performing arts:** General, art history/conservation, cinematography, commercial/advertising art, dance, dramatic, interior design, jazz, photography, studio arts.

Most popular majors. Biological/life sciences 10%, health sciences 10%, liberal arts 75%.

Computing on campus. 1,500 workstations in library, computer center. Online course registration, online library, helpline, wireless network available.

Student life. Freshman orientation: Mandatory. Preregistration for classes offered. **Activities:** Bands, choral groups, dance, drama, literary magazine, music ensembles, musical theater, student government, student newspaper, black student union, Students for International Understanding, ASPIRA, Christian Fellowship, Community Earth, Kiskeya Club.

Athletics. NJCAA. **Intercollegiate:** Baseball M, basketball, softball W, volleyball W. **Intramural:** Basketball, softball, volleyball. **Team name:** Panthers.

Student services. Career counseling, student employment services, personal counseling, placement for graduates, veterans' counselor. **Physically disabled:** Services for visually, speech, hearing impaired. **Transfer:** Transfer adviser, college fairs on campus for students transferring to 4-year colleges.

Contact. E-mail: muellere@pbcc.edu
Phone: (561) 868-3300 Fax: (561) 868-3584
Edward Mueller, District Registrar, Palm Beach Community College, 4200 Congress Avenue, Lake Worth, FL 33461

Pasco-Hernando Community College
New Port Richey, Florida
www.phcc.edu **CB code: 5562**

- Public 2-year community college
- Commuter campus in large town

General. Founded in 1972. Regionally accredited. District covers counties of Pasco and Hernando; 4 college locations. Distance learning courses are offered for a variety of courses. **Enrollment:** 7,747 degree-seeking undergraduates. **Degrees:** 861 associate awarded. **ROTC:** Army, Naval. **Location:** 35 miles from Tampa. **Calendar:** Semester, limited summer session. **Full-time faculty:** 103 total. **Part-time faculty:** 257 total.

Student profile.

Out-of-state:	1%	**25 or older:**	35%

Transfer out. Colleges most students transferred to 2008: University of South Florida, St. Leo University, University of Florida, University of Central Florida, St. Petersburg College.

Basis for selection. Open admission, but selective for some programs. Special requirements for nursing, paramedic, dental, radiography. Most placement based on Florida College Entry Level Placement Test (FCELPT), which is administered locally. **Learning Disabled:** Completed no-fee application and appropriate documentation to Office of Disabilities Services required.

High school preparation. 24 units recommended. Recommended units include English 4, mathematics 3, social studies 3, science 3 and foreign language 2.

2008-2009 Annual costs. Tuition/fees: $2,225; $8,397 out-of-state. Books/supplies: $1,100. Personal expenses: $1,850.

Financial aid. Need-based: Need-based aid available for part-time students. Work-study available nights, weekends and for part-time students. **Non-need-based:** Scholarships awarded for academics, athletics, minority status. **Additional information:** Childcare assistance grants available to eligible students.

Application procedures. Admission: No deadline. $25 fee. Admission notification on a rolling basis. **Financial aid:** Priority date 4/1; no closing date. FAFSA required. Applicants notified on a rolling basis starting 3/1.

Academics. License preparation in radiography. **Special study options:** Accelerated study, cross-registration, distance learning, double major, dual enrollment of high school students, ESL, honors, independent study, internships, weekend college. Bachelor's degree programs available on campus. License preparation in dental hygiene, nursing, paramedic, radiology. **Credit/placement by examination:** AP, CLEP, IB, institutional tests. 45 credit hours maximum toward associate degree. **Support services:** GED preparation and test center, learning center, reduced course load, remedial instruction, study skills assistance, tutoring.

Majors. Business: Business admin, marketing, office management. **Computer sciences:** Applications programming, information technology, networking, programming, systems analysis, vendor certification. **Health:** Dental hygiene, EMT paramedic, nursing (RN), radiologic technology/medical imaging. **Legal studies:** Paralegal. **Liberal arts:** Arts/sciences. **Protective services:** Law enforcement admin. **Public administration:** Human services.

Most popular majors. Computer/information sciences 6%, health sciences 20%, liberal arts 66%.

Computing on campus. 1,595 workstations in library, computer center. Online course registration, online library available.

Student life. Freshman orientation: Mandatory. Three- to 4-hour program held on variety of days and nights. **Activities:** Choral groups, drama, literary magazine, music ensembles, student government, human services club, student nursing club, writers' club, Phi Beta Lambda, Phi Theta Kappa, Delta Epsilon Chi, Psi Beta, STRIKE, computer club.

Athletics. NJCAA. **Intercollegiate:** Baseball M, basketball M, softball W, tennis W, volleyball W. **Team name:** Conquistadors.

Student services. Career counseling, services for economically disadvantaged, financial aid counseling, minority student services, on-campus daycare, personal counseling, placement for graduates, veterans' counselor. **Physically disabled:** Services for visually, speech, hearing impaired. **Transfer:** College fairs on campus for students transferring to 4-year colleges.

Contact. E-mail: bullard@phcc.edu
Phone: (727) 816-3261 Toll-free number: (877) 879-7422
Fax: (727) 816-3389
Debra Bullard, Director of Admissions and Student Records, Pasco-Hernando Community College, 10230 Ridge Road, New Port Richey, FL 34654-5199

Pensacola Junior College

Pensacola, Florida — **CB member**
www.pjc.edu — **CB code: 5535**

- Public 2-year community college
- Commuter campus in small city

General. Founded in 1948. Regionally accredited. Additional campuses: Milton, Warrington, Downtown Center, South Santa Rosa Campus. **Enrollment:** 7,944 degree-seeking undergraduates. **Degrees:** 1,530 associate awarded. **ROTC:** Army. **Location:** 60 miles from Mobile, Alabama. **Calendar:** Semester, extensive summer session. **Full-time faculty:** 209 total. **Part-time faculty:** 703 total. **Special facilities:** Science and space theater.

Student profile.

Out-of-state:	2%	**25 or older:**	50%

Basis for selection. Open admission, but selective for some programs. Special requirements for health programs. Florida Entry Level Placement Test must be taken for admission; student may submit SAT or ACT in its place. Scores used for placement only. **Homeschooled:** State high school equivalency certificate required.

High school preparation. 24 units recommended. Recommended units include English 4, mathematics 3, social studies 3, science 3, foreign language 2 and academic electives 11. College preparatory program required for associate of arts program: 13 academic units including 4 English, 3 science, 3 mathematics, and 3 social science.

2008-2009 Annual costs. Tuition/fees: $2,245; $8,177 out-of-state. Books/supplies: $1,100. Personal expenses: $1,170.

Financial aid. Non-need-based: Scholarships awarded for academics, athletics, state residency.

Application procedures. Admission: No deadline. $30 fee. Admission notification on a rolling basis. **Financial aid:** Priority date 4/1; no closing date. FAFSA, institutional form required. Applicants notified on a rolling basis starting 7/1; must reply within 2 week(s) of notification.

Academics. Special study options: Accelerated study, cooperative education, cross-registration, distance learning, double major, dual enrollment of high school students, ESL, honors, independent study, internships, study abroad, weekend college. License preparation in dental hygiene, nursing, paramedic, radiology. **Credit/placement by examination:** AP, CLEP, IB, institutional tests. 39 credit hours maximum toward associate degree. **Support services:** GED preparation and test center, learning center, reduced course load, remedial instruction, study skills assistance, tutoring, writing center.

Majors. Agriculture: General, ornamental horticulture. **Biology:** General, biochemistry, botany, zoology. **Business:** General, accounting, administrative services, banking/financial services, business admin, hospitality/recreation, management information systems, management science, office management. **Communications:** General, journalism. **Communications technology:** General. **Computer sciences:** General, computer science, information systems, programming. **Conservation:** Forest resources, forestry, management/policy. **Construction:** Maintenance. **Education:** General, art, early childhood, elementary, music, physical, special. **Engineering:** General, civil, computer, electrical. **Engineering technology:** Civil, construction, electrical, hazardous materials, manufacturing. **Family/consumer sciences:** Advocacy, child care, food/nutrition, institutional food production. **Health:** Dental hygiene, EMT paramedic, health care admin, medical radiologic technology/radiation therapy, medical records admin, nursing (RN), physical therapy assistant, predental, premedicine, prenursing, prepharmacy, preveterinary, sonography. **History:** General. **Legal studies:** Legal secretary, paralegal, prelaw. **Liberal arts:** Arts/sciences. **Math:** General. **Mechanic/repair:** Automotive. **Personal/culinary services:** Culinary arts. **Philosophy/religion:** Philosophy, religion. **Physical sciences:** Chemistry, geology, physics. **Protective services:** Firefighting, law enforcement admin. **Psychology:** General. **Science technology:** Chemical. **Social sciences:** Sociology. **Visual/performing arts:** Art, commercial/advertising art, dramatic.

Computing on campus. 1,500 workstations in library, computer center. Online course registration, wireless network available.

Student life. Freshman orientation: Mandatory. **Activities:** Bands, campus ministries, choral groups, dance, drama, international student organizations, literary magazine, music ensembles, musical theater, student government, student newspaper, symphony orchestra, TV station, Florida African-American Student Association, Wesley Foundation, Phi Theta Kappa, Campus Activities Board, Students for Multi-Cultural Society.

Athletics. NJCAA. **Intercollegiate:** Baseball M, basketball, cheerleading, softball W, volleyball W. **Intramural:** Archery, badminton, basketball, bowling, racquetball, skin diving, soccer, softball W, table tennis, tennis, volleyball, water polo, weight lifting. **Team name:** Pirates.

Student services. Adult student services, alcohol/substance abuse counseling, chaplain/spiritual director, career counseling, services for economically disadvantaged, student employment services, financial aid counseling, health services, minority student services, on-campus daycare, personal counseling, placement for graduates, veterans' counselor, women's services. **Physically disabled:** Services for visually, speech, hearing impaired. **Transfer:** Pre-admission transcript evaluation for new students. Transfer adviser, college fairs on campus for students transferring to 4-year colleges.

Contact. Phone: (850) 484-1601 Toll-free number: (888) 897-3605
Fax: (850) 484-1829
Martha Caughey, Director Admissions and Registrar, Pensacola Junior College, 1000 College Boulevard, Pensacola, FL 32504-8998

Polk Community College

Winter Haven, Florida — **CB member**
www.polk.edu — **CB code: 5548**

- Public 2-year community college
- Commuter campus in large town

General. Founded in 1963. Regionally accredited. Branch campus in Lakeland shared with University of South Florida. **Enrollment:** 6,718 degree-seeking undergraduates; 1,798 non-degree-seeking students. **Degrees:** 948 associate awarded. **ROTC:** Army. **Location:** 60 miles from Tampa, 60 miles from Orlando. **Calendar:** Semester, extensive summer session. **Full-time faculty:** 151 total; 17% have terminal degrees, 22% minority, 58% women. **Part-time faculty:** 294 total; 6% have terminal degrees, 20% minority, 51% women. **Class size:** 38% < 20, 62% 20-39, less than 1% 40-49, less than 1% 50-99.

Student profile. Among degree-seeking undergraduates, 71% enrolled in a transfer program, 29% enrolled in a vocational program, 1,388 enrolled as first-time, first-year students, 443 transferred in from other institutions.

Part-time:	63%	**Asian American:**	3%
Out-of-state:	1%	**Hispanic American:**	11%
Women:	63%	**International:**	1%
African American:	16%	**25 or older:**	40%

Transfer out. Colleges most students transferred to 2008: University of South Florida, University of Central Florida, University of Florida, Florida A&M, Florida State University.

Basis for selection. Open admission, but selective for some programs. Limited access to nursing, radiology, physical therapy assistant, occupational therapy assistant, repiratory therapy, paramedic programs, cardiovascular tech, medical sonography. Audition recommended for theater, music majors. Portfolio recommended for graphic arts majors. **Homeschooled:** Adheres to FLDOE policy and Florida state statute: affidavit signed by guardian attesting to home school applicant completion required in place of high school diploma. **Learning Disabled:** Students needing classroom accommodations must provide documentation as required.

High school preparation. Recommended units include English 4, mathematics 4, social studies 3, science 3 and foreign language 2.

2008-2009 Annual costs. Tuition/fees: $2,235; $8,237 out-of-state. Books/supplies: $1,200. Personal expenses: $1,500.

Financial aid. Need-based: Need-based aid available for part-time students. Work-study available nights, weekends and for part-time students. **Non-need-based:** Scholarships awarded for academics, athletics, leadership, state residency.

Application procedures. Admission: No deadline. $20 fee, may be waived for applicants with need. Admission notification on a rolling basis. **Financial aid:** Priority date 5/15; no closing date. FAFSA required. Applicants notified on a rolling basis.

Academics. Special study options: Accelerated study, cross-registration, distance learning, double major, dual enrollment of high school students, ESL, honors, independent study, internships. License preparation in nursing, occupational therapy, paramedic, physical therapy, radiology. **Credit/placement by examination:** AP, CLEP, IB. 45 credit hours maximum toward associate degree. **Support services:** Learning center, reduced course load, remedial instruction, study skills assistance, tutoring.

Honors college/program. High school graduates with 3.5 GPA may apply for honors program and designated courses.

Majors. Business: Accounting, administrative services, banking/financial services, business admin, marketing, office management, office/clerical. **Computer sciences:** General, computer graphics, information systems, programming. **Construction:** Power transmission. **Education:** General. **Engineering technology:** Electrical. **Family/consumer sciences:** Child care. **Health:** Cardiovascular technology, EMT paramedic, medical records admin, medical records technology, nursing (RN), occupational therapy assistant, physical therapy assistant, respiratory therapy technology, sonography. **Liberal arts:** Arts/sciences. **Mechanic/repair:** Computer. **Protective services:** Criminal justice, firefighting, police science. **Visual/performing arts:** Cinematography.

Most popular majors. Health sciences 23%, liberal arts 69%.

Computing on campus. 775 workstations in library, computer center, student center. Online course registration available.

Student life. Freshman orientation: Available. Preregistration for classes offered. **Activities:** Bands, choral groups, drama, music ensembles, musical theater, student government.

Athletics. NJCAA. **Intercollegiate:** Baseball M, basketball M, soccer W, softball W, volleyball W. **Intramural:** Basketball, bowling, football (non-tackle), table tennis, volleyball. **Team name:** Vikings.

Student services. Adult student services, career counseling, services for economically disadvantaged, student employment services, financial aid counseling. **Physically disabled:** Services for visually, speech, hearing impaired. **Transfer:** Re-entry adviser for new students. Transfer adviser, college fairs on campus for students transferring to 4-year colleges.

Contact. E-mail: studentservices@polk.edu
Phone: (863) 297-1010 ext. 5225 Fax: (863) 297-1060
Kathy Bucklew, Registrar, Polk Community College, 999 Avenue H NE, Winter Haven, FL 33881-4299

Professional Golfers Career College: Orlando

Winter Garden, Florida
www.golfcollege.edu

- For-profit 2-year branch campus college
- Commuter campus in very large city

General. Accredited by ACICS. **Enrollment:** 204 degree-seeking undergraduates. **Degrees:** 87 associate awarded. **Location:** 16 miles from Orlando. **Calendar:** Semester. **Full-time faculty:** 2 total. **Part-time faculty:** 13 total; 8% women. **Special facilities:** Pro shop, video studio.

Student profile. Among degree-seeking undergraduates, 100% enrolled in a vocational program.

Basis for selection. Character/personal qualities and level of applicant's interest very important. **Homeschooled:** Letter of recommendation (nonparent) required.

2009-2010 Annual costs. Tuition/fees (projected): $5,590.

Application procedures. Admission: No deadline. $75 fee. Application must be submitted on paper. Admission notification on a rolling basis.

Academics. Credit/placement by examination: CLEP, institutional tests.

Majors. Parks/recreation: Facilities management.

Computing on campus. 12 workstations in computer center. Online library available.

Student life. Freshman orientation: Mandatory.

Student services. Alcohol/substance abuse counseling, career counseling, financial aid counseling, personal counseling, placement for graduates, veterans' counselor.

Contact. E-mail: admin@golfcollege.edu
Phone: (866) 407-7422 Toll-free number: (866) 407-7422
Fax: (407) 905-2241
David Wood, Admissions Director, Professional Golfers Career College: Orlando, PO Box 892319, Temecula, CA 92589-2319

Saint Johns River Community College

Palatka, Florida
www.sjrcc.edu **CB code: 5641**

- Public 2-year community college
- Commuter campus in large town

General. Founded in 1957. Regionally accredited. **Enrollment:** 4,025 degree-seeking undergraduates. **Degrees:** 619 associate awarded. **Location:** 55 miles from Jacksonville and Daytona Beach. **Calendar:** Trimester, limited summer session. **Full-time faculty:** 106 total. **Part-time faculty:** 153 total.

Basis for selection. Open admission, but selective for some programs. Interview, audition, and portfolio required of applicants to Florida School of Arts program.

High school preparation. 24 units recommended. Recommended units include English 4, mathematics 3, social studies 3 and science 3.

2008-2009 Annual costs. Tuition/fees: $2,340; $8,794 out-of-state. Books/supplies: $752. Personal expenses: $87.

2007-2008 Financial aid. Need-based: Need-based aid available for part-time students.

Application procedures. Admission: Priority date 7/15; no deadline. $30 fee. Admission notification on a rolling basis. **Financial aid:** Priority date 5/15; no closing date. FAFSA required. Applicants notified on a rolling basis.

Academics. Special study options: Dual enrollment of high school students. **Credit/placement by examination:** AP, CLEP. 45 credit hours maximum toward associate degree. **Support services:** Remedial instruction, tutoring.

Majors. Business: Accounting, accounting technology, administrative services, business admin. **Computer sciences:** Programming, systems analysis. **Engineering technology:** Electrical. **Health:** EMT paramedic. **Liberal arts:** Arts/sciences. **Protective services:** Fire safety technology. **Visual/performing arts:** General.

Student life. Activities: Student government, student newspaper, Black Student Union, Circle-K, Compass Club, future educators, Phi Beta Lamba, Mathematical Association of America.

Athletics. NJCAA. **Intercollegiate:** Baseball M, basketball M, softball W. **Intramural:** Table tennis.

Student services. Career counseling, personal counseling, placement for graduates, veterans' counselor. **Physically disabled:** Services for speech impaired.

Contact. Phone: (386) 312-4030 Fax: (386) 312-4048
O'Neal Williams, Admission and Records, Saint Johns River Community College, 5001 St. Johns Avenue, Palatka, FL 32177-3897

St. Petersburg College

St. Petersburg, Florida **CB member**
www.spcollege.edu **CB code: 5606**

- Public 2-year community college
- Commuter campus in large city

General. Founded in 1927. Regionally accredited. Campuses include Clearwater, Seminole, St. Petersburg, Tarpon Springs. Health education center in Pinellas Park. Criminal justice/computer complex in St. Petersburg. Corporate training and Cisco at the Epicenter. Downtown and midtown centers. **Enrollment:** 19,535 degree-seeking undergraduates; 7,124 non-degree-seeking students. **Degrees:** 589 bachelor's, 2,835 associate awarded. **Location:** 20 miles from Tampa. **Calendar:** Semester, extensive summer session. **Full-time faculty:** 309 total; 35% have terminal degrees, 15% minority, 56% women. **Part-time faculty:** 1,361 total; 29% minority, 48% women. **Special facilities:** Observatory, planetarium, firing range, college-operated museums, nature preserves.

Student profile. Among degree-seeking undergraduates, 3,315 enrolled as first-time, first-year students.

Part-time:	65%	**Asian American:**	3%
Out-of-state:	4%	**Hispanic American:**	6%
Women:	61%	**International:**	1%
African American:	12%	**25 or older:**	46%

Basis for selection. Open admission, but selective for some programs. Limited enrollment to health-related programs. Florida CPT required for all degree-seeking students. Interview recommended for allied health applicants. **Homeschooled:** Transcript of courses and grades, state high school equivalency certificate required.

2008-2009 Annual costs. Tuition/fees: $2,337; $8,412 out-of-state. Books/supplies: $1,600. Personal expenses: $3,612.

Financial aid. Need-based: Need-based aid available for part-time students. Work-study available nights, weekends and for part-time students. **Non-need-based:** Scholarships awarded for academics, art, athletics, minority status, music/drama.

Application procedures. Admission: No deadline. $40 fee. Admission notification on a rolling basis. **Financial aid:** Priority date 4/15; no closing date. FAFSA required. Applicants notified on a rolling basis starting 5/15; must reply within 2 week(s) of notification.

Academics. Special study options: Accelerated study, cooperative education, cross-registration, distance learning, dual enrollment of high school students, ESL, exchange student, honors, independent study, internships, liberal arts/career combination, study abroad, teacher certification program, weekend college. 2-year associate degree program in business and computer science for deaf students. License preparation in dental hygiene, nursing, paramedic, physical therapy, radiology. **Credit/placement by examination:** AP, CLEP, IB, institutional tests. 45 credit hours maximum toward associate degree, 45 toward bachelor's. Florida CPT required for placement. **Support services:** GED preparation, learning center, reduced course load, remedial instruction, study skills assistance, tutoring.

Majors. Business: Accounting technology, banking/financial services, business admin, hospitality admin, marketing. **Computer sciences:** Networking, programming, system admin, web page design, webmaster. **Education:** Early childhood. **Engineering technology:** General, architectural drafting, computer, drafting, electrical, industrial, manufacturing. **Foreign languages:** Sign language interpretation. **Health:** Clinical lab technology, dental hygiene, EMT paramedic, maternal/child health nursing, medical records admin, nursing (RN), physical therapy assistant, radiologic technology/medical imaging, respiratory therapy technology, substance abuse counseling, veterinary technology/assistant. **Legal studies:** Paralegal. **Liberal arts:** Arts/sciences. **Mechanic/repair:** Aircraft. **Parks/recreation:** General. **Personal/culinary services:** Mortuary science. **Protective services:** Fire safety technology, firefighting, forensics, law enforcement admin, security services. **Public administration:** Human services. **Other:** Computer information, Securtiy protection service.

Most popular majors. Health sciences 20%, liberal arts 72%.

Computing on campus. 4,543 workstations in library, computer center, student center. Commuter students can connect to campus network. Online course registration, online library, helpline, student web hosting, wireless network available.

Student life. Freshman orientation: Mandatory. Preregistration for classes offered. **Activities:** Jazz band, choral groups, dance, drama, film society, international student organizations, music ensembles, student government, student newspaper, Phi Theta Kappa, Harambee black culture club, ethics club, math and science Club, American Sign Language club, Rotary club, College Deomocrats Club, College Republicans Club, Digital Artists in Motion club, Hospitality club.

Athletics. NJCAA. **Intercollegiate:** Baseball M, basketball, softball W, tennis W, volleyball. **Intramural:** Basketball, bowling, golf, table tennis, tennis, volleyball W, water polo M. **Team name:** Titans.

Student services. Career counseling, services for economically disadvantaged, student employment services, financial aid counseling, health services, minority student services, personal counseling, placement for graduates, veterans' counselor, women's services. **Physically disabled:** Services for visually, speech, hearing impaired. **Transfer:** College fairs on campus for students transferring to 4-year colleges.

Contact. Phone: (727) 341-4792
Susan Fell, Director of Admissions and Records, St. Petersburg College, Box 13489, St. Petersburg, FL 33733-3489

Sanford-Brown Institute: Jacksonville

Jacksonville, Florida
www.sbjacksonville.com

- For-profit 2-year health science college
- Commuter campus in large city

General. Accredited by ACICS. **Calendar:** Continuous.

Contact. Phone: (904) 363-6221
Director of Admissions, 10255 Fortune Parkway, Suite 501, Jacksonville, FL 32256

Sanford-Brown Institute: Tampa

Tampa, Florida
www.sbtampa.com

- For-profit 2-year health science and community college
- Large city

General. Accredited by ACICS. **Calendar:** Continuous.

Contact. Phone: (813) 621-0072
Director of Admissions, 5701 East Hillsboro Avenue, Tampa, FL 33610

Santa Fe College

Gainesville, Florida — **CB member**
www.sfcc.edu — **CB code: 5653**

- Public 2-year community college
- Commuter campus in small city

General. Founded in 1965. Regionally accredited. Branch campuses located in Gainesville and in Starke. **Enrollment:** 8,066 full-time, degree-seeking students. **Degrees:** 2,309 associate awarded. **ROTC:** Army, Air Force. **Location:** 80 miles from Jacksonville, 110 miles from Orlando. **Calendar:** Semester, extensive summer session. **Full-time faculty:** 244 total. **Part-time faculty:** 423 total. **Class size:** 43% < 20, 56% 20-39, 1% 40-49, less than 1% 50-99. **Special facilities:** Teaching zoo, plantarium.

Basis for selection. Open admission, but selective for some programs. Nursing program requires 5 prerequisite courses. Radiologic Technology and Dental Hygiene applicants selected by Admissions Committee. Radiation Therapy students must have X-ray or Nuclear Medicine license and experience. Computerized Placement Tests may be submitted in place of SAT or ACT.

High school preparation. Recommended units include foreign language 2.

2008-2009 Annual costs. Tuition/fees: $2,274; $8,462 out-of-state. Required fees for out-of-state students taking 30 semester hours: $1,285. Books/supplies: $700. Personal expenses: $1,008.

Financial aid. Need-based: Need-based aid available for part-time students. **Non-need-based:** Scholarships awarded for academics, art, athletics, leadership, minority status, music/drama, state residency.

Application procedures. Admission: No deadline. No application fee. Admission notification on a rolling basis. High school diploma not required of applicants to most vocational programs. **Financial aid:** Priority date 3/15, closing date 6/30. FAFSA required. Applicants notified by 8/1.

Academics. Special study options: Cooperative education, cross-registration, distance learning, dual enrollment of high school students, ESL, honors, independent study, internships, study abroad, teacher certification program, weekend college. License preparation in aviation, dental hygiene, nursing, paramedic, radiology, real estate. **Credit/placement by examination:** AP, CLEP, IB, institutional tests. 30 credit hours maximum toward associate degree. **Support services:** GED preparation, learning center, remedial instruction, tutoring, writing center.

Majors. Business: Accounting, administrative services, banking/financial services, business admin, fashion, marketing, office technology, office/clerical. **Computer sciences:** Data processing, programming. **Construction:** Maintenance. **Education:** Early childhood. **Engineering technology:** Drafting, electrical. **Family/consumer sciences:** Child care. **Health:** Dental hygiene, EMT paramedic, medical radiologic technology/radiation therapy, medical secretary, nuclear medical technology, nursing (RN), predental, premedicine, prepharmacy, respiratory therapy technology. **Legal studies:** Legal secretary, paralegal. **Liberal arts:** Arts/sciences. **Parks/recreation:** Exercise sciences, facilities management. **Physical sciences:** Astronomy, chemistry. **Protective services:** Fire safety technology, police science. **Social sciences:** Anthropology. **Visual/performing arts:** Commercial/advertising art, fashion design. **Other:** Biotechnology laboratory technology, Emergency medical services, Graphic design technolgy.

Most popular majors. Health sciences 10%, liberal arts 77%.

Computing on campus. Commuter students can connect to campus network. Online course registration, helpline, repair service available.

Student life. Freshman orientation: Available. **Policies:** All students are expected to abide by the college's student conduct code. **Activities:** Jazz band, choral groups, dance, drama, international student organizations, literary magazine, music ensembles, Model UN, musical theater, student government, student newspaper, Campus Advent, Christians on Campus, Black Student Union, Hispanic Org of Latino Activities, International Student Cultural Association, Democratic Saints, Republican Club, Students for Environmental Harmony, Phi Theta Kappa, Circle K International.

Athletics. NJCAA. **Intercollegiate:** Baseball M, basketball, softball W. **Intramural:** Basketball, football (non-tackle), golf, racquetball, soccer, volleyball, weight lifting. **Team name:** Saints.

Student services. Adult student services, alcohol/substance abuse counseling, career counseling, services for economically disadvantaged, student employment services, financial aid counseling, health services, legal services, minority student services, on-campus daycare, personal counseling, placement for graduates, veterans' counselor, women's services. **Physically disabled:** Services for visually, speech, hearing impaired. **Transfer:** Transfer adviser for students transferring to 4-year colleges.

Contact. E-mail: information@sfcc.edu
Phone: (352) 395-7322 Fax: (352) 395-5581
Michael Hutley, Director of Enrollment Services, Santa Fe College, 3000 NW 83rd Street, R-112, Gainesville, FL 32606

Seminole Community College

Sanford, Florida
www.scc-fl.edu **CB code: 5662**

- Public 2-year community college
- Commuter campus in large town

General. Founded in 1965. Regionally accredited. **Enrollment:** 11,705 degree-seeking undergraduates; 1,759 non-degree-seeking students. **Degrees:** 1,406 associate awarded. **Location:** 21 miles from Orlando. **Calendar:** Semester, limited summer session. **Full-time faculty:** 197 total; 85% have terminal degrees, 18% minority, 62% women. **Part-time faculty:** 551 total; 20% minority, 52% women. **Class size:** 24% < 20, 74% 20-39, 2% 40-49, less than 1% 50-99, less than 1% >100. **Special facilities:** Planetarium. **Partnerships:** Formal partnerships with Siemens/Stromberg, local businesses.

Student profile. Among degree-seeking undergraduates, 2,493 enrolled as first-time, first-year students.

Part-time:	53%	**Women:**	57%
Out-of-state:	3%	**25 or older:**	48%

Basis for selection. Open admission, but selective for some programs. Limited access to associate of science degrees including nursing, physical therapy, and respiratory care. College credit entry students need ACT or SAT scores less than 2 years old for placement, or must take state placement test. Interview recommended for respiratory therapy, nursing, and physical therapy majors. **Homeschooled:** Transcript of courses and grades required. Affidavit of home school completion required.

High school preparation. 24 units required. Required units include English 4, mathematics 4, social studies 3, science 3 and academic electives 10.

2008-2009 Annual costs. Tuition/fees: $2,434; $8,596 out-of-state. Books/supplies: $1,200. Personal expenses: $900.

2007-2008 Financial aid. Need-based: 43% of total undergraduate aid awarded as scholarships/grants, 57% as loans/jobs. Need-based aid available for part-time students. Work-study available for part-time students. **Non-need-based:** Scholarships awarded for academics, art, athletics, leadership, minority status, music/drama, state residency.

Application procedures. Admission: Closing date 9/21 (postmark date). No application fee. Admission notification on a rolling basis beginning on or about 9/1. **Financial aid:** No deadline. FAFSA required. Applicants notified on a rolling basis starting 4/1.

Academics. Special study options: Accelerated study, cooperative education, cross-registration, distance learning, dual enrollment of high school students, ESL, honors, independent study, study abroad, teacher certification program, weekend college. **Credit/placement by examination:** AP, CLEP, IB, institutional tests. 45 credit hours maximum toward associate degree. **Support services:** GED preparation and test center, learning center, reduced course load, remedial instruction, study skills assistance, tutoring.

Majors. Architecture: Interior. **Business:** Accounting technology, administrative services, banking/financial services, business admin, office management. **Communications:** General. **Communications technology:** General. **Computer sciences:** General, applications programming, computer graphics, computer science, data processing, information systems, networking, programming, systems analysis. **Education:** Kindergarten/preschool. **Engineering:** Electrical, software. **Engineering technology:** Architectural, construction, electrical. **Family/consumer sciences:** Child care. **Health:** EMT paramedic, medical secretary, nursing (RN), physical therapy assistant, respiratory therapy technology. **Legal studies:** Legal secretary, paralegal. **Liberal arts:** Arts/sciences. **Mechanic/repair:** Automotive. **Protective services:** Fire safety technology, firefighting, law enforcement admin. **Visual/performing arts:** Commercial/advertising art, interior design.

Most popular majors. Health sciences 14%, liberal arts 73%.

Computing on campus. 100 workstations in library, computer center. Commuter students can connect to campus network. Online course registration, online library, student web hosting, wireless network available.

Student life. Freshman orientation: Mandatory. Preregistration for classes offered. **Activities:** Bands, choral groups, drama, film society, international student organizations, literary magazine, music ensembles, musical theater, student government, student newspaper, symphony orchestra, African American cultural forum, College Republicans, disabled student association, Hispanic student associations, Muslim student association, Unity Organization, Fellowship of Christian Athletes, Latter-day Saint student association.

Athletics. NJCAA. **Intercollegiate:** Baseball M, basketball, golf W, softball W. **Team name:** Raider.

Student services. Adult student services, alcohol/substance abuse counseling, career counseling, services for economically disadvantaged, student employment services, financial aid counseling, minority student services, personal counseling, placement for graduates, veterans' counselor. **Physically disabled:** Services for visually, speech, hearing impaired. **Transfer:** Transfer adviser for students transferring to 4-year colleges.

Contact. E-mail: admissions@scc-fl.edu
Phone: (407) 708-2580 Fax: (407) 708-2395
Pamela Mennechey, Director of Admissions, Seminole Community College, 100 Weldon Boulevard, Sanford, FL 32773-6199

South Florida Community College

Avon Park, Florida **CB member**
www.southflorida.edu **CB code: 5666**

- Public 2-year community and technical college
- Commuter campus in small town

General. Founded in 1965. Regionally accredited. **Enrollment:** 2,328 degree-seeking undergraduates; 589 non-degree-seeking students. **Degrees:** 142 associate awarded. **ROTC:** Army. **Location:** 90 miles from Orlando. **Calendar:** Semester, limited summer session. **Full-time faculty:** 62 total; 23% have terminal degrees, 5% minority, 50% women. **Part-time faculty:** 165 total; 6% have terminal degrees, 23% minority, 53% women. **Class size:** 65% < 20, 33% 20-39, less than 1% 40-49, less than 1% 50-99, less than 1% >100. **Special facilities:** Museum of Florida art and culture, nature walk.

Two-Year Colleges

Student profile. Among degree-seeking undergraduates, 63% enrolled in a transfer program, 33% enrolled in a vocational program, 853 enrolled as first-time, first-year students, 204 transferred in from other institutions.

Part-time:	63%	**25 or older:**	27%
Out-of-state:	3%	**Live on campus:**	2%
Women:	61%		

Basis for selection. Open admission, but selective for some programs. Some programs have test and prerequisite requirements. Interview recommended for selected programs. **Homeschooled:** Students must meet with registrar prior to admission. **Learning Disabled:** Recommend students seek assistance from campus disabilities specialist.

High school preparation. College-preparatory program recommended. 24 units recommended. Recommended units include English 4, mathematics 4, social studies 1, history 2, science 3 (laboratory 2) and academic electives 1.

2008-2009 Annual costs. Tuition/fees: $2,281; $8,589 out-of-state. Books/supplies: $895. Personal expenses: $1,023.

2007-2008 Financial aid. Need-based: Need-based aid available for part-time students. Work-study available for part-time students. **Non-need-based:** Scholarships awarded for academics, athletics, leadership, minority status, music/drama, state residency.

Application procedures. Admission: No deadline. No application fee. Admission notification on a rolling basis. **Financial aid:** Priority date 3/15; no closing date. FAFSA required. Applicants notified on a rolling basis starting 4/1.

Academics. Special study options: Accelerated study, cooperative education, distance learning, double major, dual enrollment of high school students, ESL, external degree, honors, independent study, internships, teacher certification program. Bachelor's degree programs available on campus. License preparation in dental hygiene, nursing, paramedic, radiology. **Credit/placement by examination:** AP, CLEP, IB, institutional tests. 30 credit hours maximum toward associate degree. **Support services:** GED preparation and test center, learning center, reduced course load, remedial instruction, study skills assistance, tutoring, writing center.

Majors. Agriculture: General, agribusiness operations, horticultural science, ornamental horticulture. **Business:** Accounting, administrative services, business admin, hospitality admin. **Computer sciences:** LAN/WAN management, programming. **Construction:** General, power transmission. **Education:** Teacher assistance. **Engineering technology:** Biomedical, computer hardware, drafting, electrical, industrial. **Family/consumer sciences:** Child care. **Health:** Dental hygiene, EMT paramedic, medical secretary, nursing (RN), radiologic technology/medical imaging. **Liberal arts:** Arts/sciences. **Protective services:** Firefighting, law enforcement admin.

Most popular majors. Health sciences 13%, liberal arts 77%.

Computing on campus. 100 workstations in library, computer center, student center. Online course registration, online library, wireless network available.

Student life. Freshman orientation: Mandatory. Preregistration for classes offered. Online video with review quiz. **Housing:** Coed dorms, wellness housing available. **Activities:** Campus ministries, dance, drama, international student organizations, music ensembles, student government, student newspaper, Adventist social club, African American association.

Athletics. NJCAA. **Intercollegiate:** Softball W, volleyball W. **Intramural:** Baseball M. **Team name:** Panthers.

Student services. Adult student services, career counseling, services for economically disadvantaged, student employment services, financial aid counseling, minority student services, personal counseling, placement for graduates, veterans' counselor, women's services. **Physically disabled:** Services for visually, speech, hearing impaired. **Transfer:** Transfer adviser, college fairs on campus for students transferring to 4-year colleges.

Contact. E-mail: deborah.fuschetti@southflorida.edu
Phone: (863) 453-6661 ext. 7405 Fax: (863) 453-2365
Deborah Fuschetti, Registrar, South Florida Community College, 600 West College Drive, Avon Park, FL 33825

Southwest Florida College

Ft. Myers, Florida
www.swfc.edu **CB code: 3445**

- Private 2-year career college
- Commuter campus in large city

General. Accredited by ACICS. Learning site in Estero, Florida. **Enrollment:** 1,737 degree-seeking undergraduates; 17 non-degree-seeking students. **Degrees:** 18 bachelor's, 412 associate awarded. **Location:** 130 miles from Tampa. **Calendar:** Quarter, extensive summer session. **Full-time faculty:** 32 total; 6% have terminal degrees, 6% minority, 56% women. **Part-time faculty:** 90 total; 12% have terminal degrees, 27% minority, 50% women. **Class size:** 71% < 20, 27% 20-39, 2% 40-49.

Student profile. Among degree-seeking undergraduates, 409 enrolled as first-time, first-year students, 111 transferred in from other institutions.

Part-time:	16%	**Hispanic American:**	20%
Women:	73%	**Native American:**	1%
African American:	17%	**International:**	7%
Asian American:	1%	**25 or older:**	54%

Transfer out. Colleges most students transferred to 2008: International College.

Basis for selection. Open admission, but selective for some programs. Surgical Technology requires an interview with the Program Manager prior to acceptance; students placing extraordinarily low on placement assessment may not be accepted. Interviews required for some programs.

2009-2010 Annual costs. Tuition/fees (projected): $10,800. Per-credit charge: $275. Required fees do not include lab or online fees. Books/supplies: $1,110. Personal expenses: $1,815.

Financial aid. Need-based: Need-based aid available for part-time students. Work-study available nights and for part-time students.

Application procedures. Admission: No deadline. $25 fee. Application must be submitted on paper. Admission notification on a rolling basis. **Financial aid:** No deadline. FAFSA required. Applicants notified on a rolling basis.

Academics. Online academic assistance availabe to students enrolled in online courses. **Special study options:** Cooperative education, distance learning, double major, internships, liberal arts/career combination. Bachelor's degree programs available on campus. **Credit/placement by examination:** AP, CLEP, institutional tests. 24 credit hours maximum toward associate degree, 48 toward bachelor's. **Support services:** Learning center, reduced course load, remedial instruction, study skills assistance, tutoring, writing center.

Majors. Business: Accounting, business admin, hospitality admin. **Computer sciences:** General, computer graphics, security, system admin, webmaster. **Education:** Early childhood. **Engineering:** Computer. **Engineering technology:** Drafting. **Health:** Medical assistant, medical records technology, surgical technology. **Legal studies:** Paralegal. **Protective services:** Criminal justice. **Visual/performing arts:** Interior design.

Most popular majors. Architecture 8%, business/marketing 12%, computer/information sciences 7%, education 6%, engineering/engineering technologies 7%, health sciences 41%, security/protective services 9%.

Computing on campus. 194 workstations in library, computer center, student center. Online library, wireless network available.

Student life. Freshman orientation: Mandatory. Preregistration for classes offered. Held the week before classes begin and lasts 1-2 hours. **Activities:** Student newspaper.

Student services. Adult student services, career counseling, services for economically disadvantaged, student employment services, financial aid counseling, placement for graduates. **Physically disabled:** Services for visually, speech, hearing impaired. **Learning disabled:** Comprehensive services available. **Transfer:** Pre-admission transcript evaluation for new students.

Contact. E-mail: kreynolds@swfc.edu
Phone: (239) 939-4766 Toll-free number: (866) 793-2669
Fax: (239) 936-4040
Ken Reynolds, Regional Vice President of Enrollment Management, Southwest Florida College, 1685 Medical Lane, Ft. Myers, FL 33907-1108

Southwest Florida College: Tampa

Tampa, Florida
www.swfc.edu

- Private 2-year branch campus and junior college
- Commuter campus in very large city

General. Accredited by ACICS. **Location:** 15 miles from downtown. **Calendar:** Quarter.

Contact. Phone: (813) 630-4401
Vice President of Admissions, 3910 Riga Boulevard, Tampa, FL 33619

Stenotype Institute: Jacksonville
Jacksonville, Florida
www.thestenotypeinstitute.com

- For-profit 2-year business and community college
- Very large city

General. Accredited by ACICS. **Calendar:** Continuous.

Contact. Phone: (904) 398-4141
Director Of Admissions, 3986 Boulevard Center Drive, Jacksonville, FL 32207

Stenotype Institute: Orlando
Orlando, Florida

- Private 2-year technical college
- Very large city

General. Accredited by ACICS. **Calendar:** Semester.

Contact. Phone: (407) 816-5573
1636 West Oakridge Road, Orlando, FL 32809

Tallahassee Community College
Tallahassee, Florida **CB member**
www.tcc.fl.edu **CB code: 5794**

- Public 2-year community college
- Commuter campus in small city

General. Founded in 1965. Regionally accredited. **Enrollment:** 12,775 degree-seeking undergraduates. **Degrees:** 2,036 associate awarded. **ROTC:** Army, Naval, Air Force. **Location:** 230 miles from Tampa, 200 miles from Pensacola. **Calendar:** Semester, extensive summer session. **Full-time faculty:** 179 total. **Part-time faculty:** 610 total. **Class size:** 20% < 20, 60% 20-39, 15% 40-49, 6% 50-99.

Transfer out. Colleges most students transferred to 2008: Florida State University.

Basis for selection. Open admission, but selective for some programs. Special requirements for nursing, dental hygiene, emergency medical technology, radiologic technology and respiratory therapy programs. Each program requires specific course prerequisites or test scores or required GPA in addition to letters of recommendation. SAT/ACT may substitute for Florida CPT for placement. Placement test score required of degree-seeking applicants before enrolling in classes. **Homeschooled:** Present affidavit verifying completion of high school requirements. **Learning Disabled:** If service or accommodations are needed, documentation required.

2008-2009 Annual costs. Tuition/fees: $2,086; $7,523 out-of-state. Books/supplies: $800. Personal expenses: $1,800.

2007-2008 Financial aid. Need-based: 46% of total undergraduate aid awarded as scholarships/grants, 54% as loans/jobs. Need-based aid available for part-time students. **Non-need-based:** Scholarships awarded for academics, art, athletics, leadership, music/drama, state residency.

Application procedures. Admission: Closing date 8/1 (receipt date). No application fee. Admission notification on a rolling basis. Separate application procedure for health programs. **Financial aid:** Priority date 5/1; no closing date. FAFSA, institutional form required. Applicants notified on a rolling basis starting 5/15.

Academics. Special study options: Cooperative education, cross-registration, distance learning, double major, dual enrollment of high school students, ESL, honors, independent study, liberal arts/career combination, study abroad. Bachelor's degree programs available on campus. License preparation in dental hygiene, nursing, paramedic, real estate. **Credit/placement by examination:** AP, CLEP, IB, institutional tests. 45 credit hours maximum toward associate degree. **Support services:** GED preparation, learning center, pre-admission summer program, reduced course load, remedial instruction, study skills assistance, tutoring, writing center.

Majors. Business: General, accounting, administrative services, banking/financial services, business admin, management information systems, sales/distribution. **Computer sciences:** Computer graphics, networking, programming. **Construction:** Maintenance. **Education:** Early childhood, health. **Engineering:** General, civil, software. **Engineering technology:** Civil, construction, drafting, industrial management. **Health:** Dental hygiene, EMT paramedic, medical radiologic technology/radiation therapy, nursing (RN), respiratory therapy technology. **Legal studies:** Paralegal. **Liberal arts:** Arts/sciences. **Parks/recreation:** Facilities management. **Protective services:** Criminal justice, law enforcement admin. **Public administration:** General. **Social sciences:** General. **Visual/performing arts:** General, commercial/advertising art, film/cinema.

Most popular majors. Health sciences 6%, liberal arts 88%.

Computing on campus. 1,733 workstations in library, computer center, student center. Commuter students can connect to campus network. Online course registration, online library, helpline, wireless network available.

Student life. Freshman orientation: Mandatory. Preregistration for classes offered. All-day event held few days prior to start of term; includes small group meetings and advising. Online orientation also available. **Activities:** Bands, campus ministries, choral groups, dance, drama, international student organizations, literary magazine, music ensembles, musical theater, student government, student newspaper, TV station, Phi Theta Kappa, Black Student Union, Returning Adults Valuing Education, Future Educators of America, students interested in legal careers, College Democrats, BACCHUS, student environmental action coalition.

Athletics. NJCAA. **Intercollegiate:** Baseball M, basketball, softball W. **Intramural:** Basketball, golf, soccer, softball, table tennis, tennis. **Team name:** Eagles.

Student services. Adult student services, career counseling, services for economically disadvantaged, financial aid counseling, minority student services, on-campus daycare, personal counseling, placement for graduates, veterans' counselor. **Physically disabled:** Services for visually, speech, hearing impaired. **Transfer:** Transfer adviser, college fairs on campus for students transferring to 4-year colleges.

Contact. E-mail: enrollment@tcc.fl.edu
Phone: (850) 201-8555 Fax: (850) 201-8474
Katherine Nerona-Balog, Director, Enrollment Services and Testing, Tallahassee Community College, 444 Appleyard Drive, Tallahassee, FL 32304

Valencia Community College
Orlando, Florida **CB member**
www.valenciacc.edu **CB code: 5869**

- Public 2-year community college
- Commuter campus in very large city

General. Founded in 1967. Regionally accredited. **Enrollment:** 29,020 degree-seeking undergraduates; 6,440 non-degree-seeking students. **Degrees:** 4,256 associate awarded. **ROTC:** Army. **Location:** 90 miles from Tampa, 145 miles from Jacksonville. **Calendar:** Semester, extensive summer session. **Full-time faculty:** 351 total; 27% have terminal degrees, 22% minority, 56% women. **Part-time faculty:** 1,136 total; 12% have terminal degrees, 23% minority, 51% women. **Class size:** 22% < 20, 76% 20-39, 1% 40-49, less than 1% 50-99, less than 1% >100.

Student profile. Among degree-seeking undergraduates, 21% enrolled in a transfer program, 79% enrolled in a vocational program, 6,509 enrolled as first-time, first-year students, 2,146 transferred in from other institutions.

Part-time:	50%	**Asian American:**	5%
Out-of-state:	3%	**Hispanic American:**	27%
Women:	57%	**International:**	3%
African American:	16%	**25 or older:**	25%

Transfer out. 45% of students enrolled in the transfer program go on to 4-year colleges. **Colleges most students transferred to 2008:** University of Central Florida.

Basis for selection. Open admission, but selective for some programs. Special requirements for the criminal justice institute programs, A.A. pre-major dance performance, film production technology program, and health sciences programs. **Homeschooled:** Home school diplomas accepted with official Home School Verification Affidavit.

High school preparation. College-preparatory program recommended. Recommended units include English 4, mathematics 3, social studies 3 and science 3.

2008-2009 Annual costs. Tuition/fees: $2,335; $8,782 out-of-state. Books/supplies: $1,061. Personal expenses: $4,639.

Two-Year Colleges

Financial aid. **Need-based:** Need-based aid available for part-time students. Work-study available nights and for part-time students.

Application procedures. **Admission:** Closing date 8/1 (postmark date). $35 fee. Admission notification on a rolling basis beginning on or about 3/31. **Financial aid:** Closing date 5/15. FAFSA required. Applicants notified on a rolling basis starting 4/2; must reply within 2 week(s) of notification.

Academics. **Special study options:** Cooperative education, distance learning, double major, dual enrollment of high school students, ESL, honors, independent study, internships, student-designed major, study abroad, weekend college. License preparation in dental hygiene, nursing, paramedic, physical therapy, radiology, real estate. **Credit/placement by examination:** AP, CLEP, IB, institutional tests. 45 credit hours maximum toward associate degree. Less than 75 percent of a program's hours may be met with credit by examination and/or other acceleration mechanisms. **Support services:** Learning center, remedial instruction, study skills assistance, tutoring, writing center.

Majors. **Agriculture:** Horticultural science, landscaping. **Architecture:** Technology. **Biology:** General, marine. **Business:** Accounting, accounting technology, business admin, entrepreneurial studies, finance, hospitality admin, human resources, management information systems, marketing, real estate, restaurant/food services, small business admin. **Communications:** Digital media, journalism, public relations. **Computer sciences:** General, computer science, information technology, programming, systems analysis, webmaster. **Construction:** General. **Education:** General, early childhood. **Engineering:** General. **Engineering technology:** General, CAD/CADD, civil, drafting, electrical. **Family/consumer sciences:** Institutional food production. **Foreign languages:** French, Portuguese, Spanish. **Health:** Cardiovascular technology, dental hygiene, EMT paramedic, insurance coding, medical records admin, medical records technology, medical secretary, nursing (RN), radiologic technology/medical imaging, respiratory therapy assistant, respiratory therapy technology, sonography. **History:** General. **Legal studies:** Paralegal. **Liberal arts:** Arts/sciences, humanities. **Math:** General. **Personal/culinary services:** Baking, culinary arts, restaurant/catering. **Philosophy/religion:** Philosophy. **Physical sciences:** Chemistry. **Protective services:** Fire safety technology, law enforcement admin, police science. **Psychology:** General. **Social sciences:** General, economics, political science, sociology. **Visual/performing arts:** Art, dance, graphic design, theater design.

Most popular majors. Health sciences 10%, liberal arts 78%.

Computing on campus. 2,500 workstations in library, computer center, student center. Commuter students can connect to campus network. Online course registration, online library, helpline, wireless network available.

Student life. **Freshman orientation:** Mandatory. Preregistration for classes offered. 2-hour program. **Activities:** Bands, choral groups, dance, drama, international student organizations, literary magazine, music ensembles, musical theater, student government, student newspaper, symphony orchestra, African American cultural society, Brain Bowl, Latin American student organization, student nurses association, Valencia Volunteers, Phi Beta Lambda, Earth Club, Muslim student organization, Black high achievers club.

Student services. Career counseling, student employment services, financial aid counseling, health services, personal counseling, placement for graduates, veterans' counselor. **Physically disabled:** Services for visually, hearing impaired. **Transfer:** College fairs on campus for students transferring to 4-year colleges.

Contact. Phone: (407) 582-1507 Fax: (407) 582-1403
Renee Simpson, Director of Admissions and Records, Valencia Community College, PO Box 3028, Orlando, FL 32802-3028

Virginia College at Pensacola

Pensacola, Florida
www.vc.edu/pensacola

- For-profit 2-year business and health science college
- Commuter campus in small city

General. Accredited by ACICS. **Enrollment:** 181 degree-seeking undergraduates. **Degrees:** 50 associate awarded. **Calendar:** Quarter, extensive summer session. **Full-time faculty:** 15 total. **Part-time faculty:** 40 total.

Basis for selection. Open admission.

2008-2009 Annual costs. Tuition/fees: $10,872.

Application procedures. **Admission:** $100 fee.

Academics. **Credit/placement by examination:** CLEP. **Support services:** Learning center, remedial instruction, tutoring.

Majors. **Business:** Accounting/business management, business admin, fashion, retailing. **Personal/culinary services:** General.

Computing on campus. 80 workstations in library, computer center. Online library available.

Contact. E-mail: hrobbins@vc.edu
Phone: (850) 436-8444 Toll-free number: (888) 208-6932
Fax: (850) 436-4838
Heather Robbins, Director of Admissions, Virginia College at Pensacola, 19 West Garden Street, Pensacola, FL 32502

Georgia

Abraham Baldwin Agricultural College

Tifton, Georgia — **CB member**
www.abac.edu — **CB code: 5001**

- Public 2-year agricultural and community college
- Commuter campus in large town

General. Founded in 1924. Regionally accredited. **Enrollment:** 3,626 degree-seeking undergraduates; 39 non-degree-seeking students. **Degrees:** 426 associate awarded. **Location:** 100 miles from Macon, 50 miles from Albany. **Calendar:** Semester. **Full-time faculty:** 98 total; 31% have terminal degrees, 12% minority, 53% women. **Part-time faculty:** 54 total; 20% have terminal degrees, 2% minority, 65% women. **Class size:** 25% < 20, 65% 20-39, 9% 40-49, less than 1% 50-99. **Special facilities:** 200-acre farm.

Student profile. Among degree-seeking undergraduates, 1,401 enrolled as first-time, first-year students.

Part-time:	30%	**Asian American:**	1%
Out-of-state:	3%	**Hispanic American:**	2%
Women:	54%	**25 or older:**	20%
African American:	20%	**Live on campus:**	32%

Basis for selection. 1.8 GPA, 330 SAT verbal and 310 SAT math or 12 ACT English and 14 ACT math necessary to obtain required Freshman Index of 1830. College-preparatory program not required for students pursuing AAS degree. Interview recommended for nursing majors.

High school preparation. College-preparatory program recommended. 16 units required. Required units include English 4, mathematics 4, social studies 3, science 3 (laboratory 2) and foreign language 2.

2008-2009 Annual costs. Tuition/fees: $2,496; $8,498 out-of-state. Per-credit charge: $84 in-state; $333 out-of-state. Room/board: $6,060. Books/supplies: $775. Personal expenses: $1,500.

Application procedures. Admission: Closing date 8/1. $20 fee, may be waived for applicants with need. Admission notification on a rolling basis. **Financial aid:** Priority date 5/1; no closing date. FAFSA, institutional form required. Applicants notified on a rolling basis starting 5/15; must reply within 2 week(s) of notification.

Academics. Special study options: Accelerated study, distance learning, double major, dual enrollment of high school students, external degree, honors, independent study, internships, study abroad. **Credit/placement by examination:** AP, CLEP, institutional tests. **Support services:** Learning center, remedial instruction, tutoring, writing center.

Majors. Agriculture: Animal sciences, business, ornamental horticulture, plant sciences, poultry, turf management. **Biology:** General. **Business:** Accounting, business admin, fashion, hospitality admin, office technology, office/clerical. **Communications:** General, journalism, media studies. **Computer sciences:** General, applications programming, computer science, data processing, information technology, web page design. **Conservation:** Forest management, forest technology, forestry, wildlife. **Education:** General, early childhood. **Engineering:** General, agricultural. **Family/consumer sciences:** General, child care. **Foreign languages:** General. **Health:** Athletic training, dental hygiene, medical records technology, predental, premedicine, prepharmacy. **History:** General. **Legal studies:** Prelaw. **Liberal arts:** Arts/sciences. **Math:** General. **Parks/recreation:** Facilities management, health/fitness. **Physical sciences:** Chemistry, physics. **Protective services:** Police science. **Psychology:** General. **Public administration:** Human services. **Social sciences:** General, sociology. **Visual/performing arts:** General, studio arts.

Most popular majors. Agriculture 10%, health sciences 20%, liberal arts 59%.

Computing on campus. 100 workstations in library. Dormitories wired for high-speed internet access. Commuter students can connect to campus network. Online course registration, wireless network available.

Student life. Freshman orientation: Mandatory, $40 fee. **Housing:** Coed dorms, apartments available. $235 nonrefundable deposit. **Activities:** Bands, campus ministries, choral groups, drama, literary magazine, radio station, student government, student newspaper.

Athletics. NJCAA. **Intercollegiate:** Baseball M, golf M, rodeo, soccer W, softball W, tennis, volleyball W. **Intramural:** Badminton W, basketball, bowling, football (non-tackle) M, softball, tennis, volleyball.

Student services. Adult student services, career counseling, student employment services, health services, personal counseling, placement for graduates, veterans' counselor. **Transfer:** Transfer adviser, college fairs on campus for students transferring to 4-year colleges.

Contact. E-mail: admissions@abac.edu
Phone: (229) 391-5004 Toll-free number: (800) 733-3653
Fax: (229) 391-5002
Debra McCrary, Director of Admissions and Registrar, Abraham Baldwin Agricultural College, ABAC 4, 2802 Moore Highway, Tifton, GA 31793-2601

Albany Technical College

Albany, Georgia
www.albanytech.edu — **CB code: 3921**

- Public 2-year technical college
- Commuter campus in small city

General. Regionally accredited. Hands-on environment. **Enrollment:** 2,699 degree-seeking undergraduates; 305 non-degree-seeking students. **Degrees:** 104 associate awarded. **Location:** 225 miles from Atlanta. **Calendar:** Quarter, extensive summer session. **Full-time faculty:** 91 total.

Student profile. Among degree-seeking undergraduates, 482 enrolled as first-time, first-year students.

Part-time:	38%	**African American:**	71%
Women:	62%		

Transfer out. Colleges most students transferred to 2008: Albany State University.

Basis for selection. Open admission, but selective for some programs. Selective admission to health technology programs. ACT or SAT may be accepted in lieu of COMPASS or ASSET for placement.

High school preparation. College-preparatory program recommended. 22 units recommended. Recommended units include English 4, mathematics 3, social studies 3, science 3, foreign language 1 and academic electives 3. 4 tech prep, 1 health science recommended.

2008-2009 Annual costs. Tuition/fees: $1,539; $2,835 out-of-state. Per-credit charge: $36 in-state; $72 out-of-state. Books/supplies: $1,260.

2008-2009 Financial aid. Need-based: 71% of total undergraduate aid awarded as scholarships/grants, 29% as loans/jobs. Need-based aid available for part-time students. Work-study available nights and for part-time students. **Non-need-based:** Scholarships awarded for academics, state residency.

Application procedures. Admission: Closing date 10/1 (postmark date). $15 fee, may be waived for applicants with need. Admission notification on a rolling basis beginning on or about 8/1. **Financial aid:** No deadline. FAFSA required. Applicants notified on a rolling basis starting 5/1.

Academics. Special study options: Distance learning, dual enrollment of high school students, weekend college. License preparation in nursing, paramedic, radiology. **Credit/placement by examination:** AP, CLEP, institutional tests. **Support services:** GED preparation and test center, remedial instruction, tutoring.

Majors. Business: Sales/distribution. **Computer sciences:** Data processing, networking. **Conservation:** Forestry. **Construction:** Carpentry. **Education:** Early childhood. **Engineering technology:** Drafting. **Health:** Pharmacy assistant. **Mechanic/repair:** Electronics/electrical, industrial. **Personal/culinary services:** Chef training. **Protective services:** Criminal justice.

Most popular majors. Business/marketing 36%, computer/information sciences 16%, education 10%, health sciences 13%, security/protective services 17%, trade and industry 7%.

Computing on campus. Online library available.

Student life. Freshman orientation: Available. Preregistration for classes offered. Students contact advisor to register for classes. Advisor registers students via Internet. **Activities:** Choral groups, student government.

Athletics. Intercollegiate: Basketball M. **Team name:** Titans.

Student services. Adult student services, career counseling, services for economically disadvantaged, student employment services, financial aid counseling, on-campus daycare, personal counseling, placement for graduates, veterans' counselor. **Physically disabled:** Services for visually, speech, hearing impaired. **Transfer:** Pre-admission transcript evaluation for new students.

Contact. Phone: (229) 430-3520 Fax: (229) 430-6180
Director of Admissions, Albany Technical College, 1704 South Slappy Boulevard, Albany, GA 31701-3514

Andrew College
Cuthbert, Georgia
www.andrewcollege.edu **CB code: 5009**

- Private 2-year junior and liberal arts college affiliated with United Methodist Church
- Residential campus in small town
- SAT or ACT (ACT writing recommended) required

General. Founded in 1854. Regionally accredited. **Enrollment:** 266 degree-seeking undergraduates. **Degrees:** 40 associate awarded. **Location:** 60 miles from Columbus, 40 miles from Albany. **Calendar:** Semester, limited summer session. **Full-time faculty:** 21 total. **Part-time faculty:** 5 total. **Class size:** 75% < 20, 25% 20-39.

Student profile. Among degree-seeking undergraduates, 155 enrolled as first-time, first-year students.

Part-time:	2%	**Asian American:**	1%
Women:	49%	**Hispanic American:**	3%
African American:	40%	**International:**	8%

Transfer out. Colleges most students transferred to 2008: Georgia Southwestern State University, Valdosta State University, Georgia Southern University, Columbus State University, Troy State University.

Basis for selection. High school academic record, test scores, school and community activities important. Essay recommended. Interview required of the academically weak. Audition required of music majors. Portfolio recommended for art majors. **Homeschooled:** Transcript of courses and grades required.

High school preparation. 18 units recommended.

2008-2009 Annual costs. Tuition/fees: $10,976. Room/board: $6,894. Books/supplies: $600. Personal expenses: $1,200.

Financial aid. Need-based: Need-based aid available for part-time students. **Non-need-based:** Scholarships awarded for academics, art, athletics, leadership, music/drama, religious affiliation, state residency.

Application procedures. Admission: Priority date 6/1; deadline 8/1 (receipt date). $20 fee, may be waived for applicants with need. Admission notification on a rolling basis. **Financial aid:** Priority date 4/1, closing date 8/1. FAFSA, institutional form required. Applicants notified on a rolling basis starting 4/15.

Academics. Special study options: Double major, dual enrollment of high school students, ESL, honors. **Credit/placement by examination:** AP, CLEP, SAT, ACT, institutional tests. 24 credit hours maximum toward associate degree. **Support services:** Learning center, pre-admission summer program, remedial instruction, study skills assistance, tutoring.

Majors. Agriculture: General. **Business:** General. **Communications:** General, journalism. **Computer sciences:** Computer science. **Conservation:** Forestry. **Education:** General. **Engineering:** General. **Health:** Athletic training, predental, premedicine, prenursing, prepharmacy, preveterinary. **History:** General. **Legal studies:** Prelaw. **Liberal arts:** Arts/sciences. **Math:** General. **Parks/recreation:** Health/fitness. **Physical sciences:** General. **Psychology:** General. **Social sciences:** General, sociology. **Visual/performing arts:** General, dramatic.

Computing on campus. 100 workstations in dormitories, library, computer center, student center. Dormitories wired for high-speed internet access and linked to campus network. Commuter students can connect to campus network. Online library, repair service, wireless network available.

Student life. Freshman orientation: Mandatory. Preregistration for classes offered. Selected weekends during summer and beginning of fall term, 3-4 days. **Policies:** No alcohol/illegal drugs allowed on campus. **Housing:** Guaranteed on-campus for all undergraduates. Coed dorms, single-sex dorms available. **Activities:** Choral groups, drama, international student organizations, literary magazine, music ensembles, musical theater, student government, student newspaper, Baptist Student Union, Wesley Fellowship, Unity, community service group, interdenominational Christian group.

Athletics. NJCAA. **Intercollegiate:** Baseball M, basketball W, cross-country, golf, soccer, softball W. **Intramural:** Archery, badminton, basketball, cheerleading W, cross-country, football (non-tackle) M, golf, racquetball, soccer, softball, swimming, table tennis, tennis, volleyball, weight lifting. **Team name:** Tigers.

Student services. Alcohol/substance abuse counseling, chaplain/spiritual director, career counseling, services for economically disadvantaged, financial aid counseling, health services, veterans' counselor. **Transfer:** Transfer adviser, college fairs on campus for students transferring to 4-year colleges.

Contact. E-mail: admissions@andrewcollege.edu
Phone: (800) 664-9250 Toll-free number: (800) 664-9250
Fax: (229) 732-2176
Bridgett Kurkowski, Director of Admissions and Financial Aid, Andrew College, 501 College Street, Cuthbert, GA 39840-1395

Ashworth University
Norcross, Georgia
www.ashworthcollege.edu **CB code: 3912**

- For-profit 2-year community college
- Very large city

General. Accredited by DETC. **Enrollment:** 3,200 degree-seeking undergraduates. **Degrees:** 400 associate awarded; master's offered. **Calendar:** Semester. **Full-time faculty:** 20 total. **Part-time faculty:** 70 total.

Basis for selection. Open admission.

2008-2009 Annual costs. All inclusive undergraduate program is $1200 per semester (5 courses). Students enrolling in a full program will complete 4 semesters.

Academics. Credit/placement by examination: CLEP.

Majors. Business: Accounting, business admin, finance, human resources, marketing. **Construction:** Site management. **Education:** Early childhood. **Health:** Health care admin. **Legal studies:** Paralegal. **Protective services:** Criminal justice, security management. **Psychology:** General.

Contact. E-mail: info@ashworthcollege.com
Phone: (770) 729-8400 Toll-free number: (800) 223-4542
Fax: (770) 729-9389
Renee Mason, Registrar, Ashworth University, 430 Technology Parkway, Norcross, GA 30092-3406

Athens Technical College
Athens, Georgia
www.athenstech.edu **CB code: 0462**

- Public 2-year technical college
- Commuter campus in small city

General. Founded in 1959. Regionally accredited. **Enrollment:** 3,592 degree-seeking undergraduates; 545 non-degree-seeking students. **Degrees:** 265 associate awarded. **Location:** 65 miles from Atlanta. **Calendar:** Quarter, extensive summer session. **Full-time faculty:** 81 total. **Part-time faculty:** 208 total. **Class size:** 61% < 20, 36% 20-39, 1% 40-49, 2% 50-99.

Student profile. Among degree-seeking undergraduates, 570 enrolled as first-time, first-year students.

Part-time:	60%	**Asian American:**	6%
Women:	67%	**Hispanic American:**	2%
African American:	22%		

Transfer out. Colleges most students transferred to 2008: University of Georgia.

Basis for selection. Open admission, but selective for some programs. Special requirements for radiology, respiratory therapy, nursing, physical therapy assistant, dental hygiene, surgical technology, veterinary technology dental assisting, medical assisting, practical nursing and diagnostic medical sonography. School record, recommendations, standardized test scores, essay, and interview required or recommended depending on program. COMPASS and ASSET tests required for placement, but under certain conditions ACT or SAT scores may be accepted. Interview required of radiology, respiratory therapy, nursing, physical therapy assistant, dental assisting, and dental hygiene majors. **Homeschooled:** Must provide documentation of designated home study program activities.

High school preparation. College-preparatory program recommended. 22 units recommended. Recommended units include English 4, mathematics 3, social studies 3, science 3, foreign language 1 and academic electives 3. 4 tech prep and 1 health science recommended.

2008-2009 Annual costs. Tuition/fees: $1,539; $2,835 out-of-state. Per-credit charge: $36 in-state; $72 out-of-state. Books/supplies: $800. Personal expenses: $1,000.

2007-2008 Financial aid. Need-based: Need-based aid available for part-time students. Work-study available for part-time students. **Non-need-based:** Scholarships awarded for academics, leadership.

Application procedures. Admission: Priority date 8/1; no deadline. $20 fee. Admission notification on a rolling basis. February 1 deadline for applicants to nursing and dental hygiene programs. March 1 deadline for dental assistance program. April 1 deadline for radiography, surgical technology, diagnostic medical sonography, nursing accelerated, and veterinary technology programs. May 1 deadline for physical therapist assistant, and practical nursing programs. July 1 deadline for respiratory therapy. August 1 deadline for medical assistance program. **Financial aid:** No deadline. FAFSA required. Applicants notified on a rolling basis starting 6/15; must reply within 2 week(s) of notification.

Academics. Special study options: Distance learning, dual enrollment of high school students, weekend college. License preparation in real estate. **Credit/placement by examination:** AP, CLEP, institutional tests. **Support services:** GED preparation and test center, learning center, reduced course load, remedial instruction, study skills assistance, tutoring.

Majors. Biology: Biotechnology. **Business:** Accounting technology, administrative services, sales/distribution, travel services. **Computer sciences:** Applications programming, data processing, networking, programming. **Education:** Early childhood. **Health:** Dental assistant, dental hygiene, nursing (RN), physical therapy assistant, radiologic technology/medical imaging, respiratory therapy technology, sonography, veterinary technology/assistant. **Legal studies:** Paralegal. **Protective services:** Law enforcement admin. **Public administration:** Social work. **Science technology:** Biological. **Visual/performing arts:** Interior design.

Most popular majors. Business/marketing 20%, computer/information sciences 12%, education 10%, health sciences 44%.

Computing on campus. 346 workstations in computer center. Commuter students can connect to campus network. Online course registration, online library, wireless network available.

Student life. Freshman orientation: Mandatory. Preregistration for classes offered. **Activities:** Student government.

Student services. Adult student services, career counseling, student employment services, financial aid counseling, personal counseling, placement for graduates, veterans' counselor. **Physically disabled:** Services for visually, speech, hearing impaired. **Transfer:** Transfer adviser for students transferring to 4-year colleges.

Contact. E-mail: admissions@athenstech.edu
Phone: (706) 355-5005 Fax: (706) 369-5756
Yancey Gulley, Vice President for Student Affairs, Athens Technical College, 800 US Highway 29 North, Athens, GA 30601-1500

Atlanta Metropolitan College

Atlanta, Georgia — **CB member**
www.atlm.edu — **CB code: 5725**

- Public 2-year junior college
- Commuter campus in very large city

General. Founded in 1974. Regionally accredited. **Enrollment:** 2,144 degree-seeking undergraduates; 97 non-degree-seeking students. **Degrees:** 173 associate awarded. **Location:** 4 miles from downtown. **Calendar:** Semester, extensive summer session. **Full-time faculty:** 50 total; 44% have terminal degrees, 88% minority, 44% women. **Part-time faculty:** 67 total; 22% have terminal degrees, 97% minority, 64% women.

Student profile. Among degree-seeking undergraduates, 485 enrolled as first-time, first-year students.

Part-time:	44%	**25 or older:**	26%
Out-of-state:	6%	**Live on campus:**	1%
Women:	66%		

Basis for selection. Applicants who have followed college preparatory curriculum must have 2.0 GPA. Applicants who have followed technology/career curriculum must have 2.2 GPA. All applicants must meet immunization requirements. Applicants with 430 SAT verbal or 17 ACT English and completion of college preparatory curriculum in English exempt from taking COMPASS Placement Test in English and Reading. Applicants with 400 SAT math or 17 ACT math and completion of college preparatory curriculum in math exempt from taking COMPASS Placement Test in math. **Homeschooled:** Transcript of courses and grades required.

High school preparation. 16 units required. Required units include English 4, mathematics 4, social studies 1, history 2, science 3 (laboratory 2) and foreign language 2.

2008-2009 Annual costs. Tuition/fees: $2,148; $7,650 out-of-state. Per-credit charge: $77 in-state; $306 out-of-state. Books/supplies: $1,300.

2007-2008 Financial aid. All financial aid based on need. Need-based aid available for part-time students. Work-study available nights, weekends and for part-time students.

Application procedures. Admission: Priority date 7/15; no deadline. $20 fee. Admission notification on a rolling basis. **Financial aid:** Closing date 6/1. FAFSA required. Applicants notified on a rolling basis; must reply by 6/30.

Academics. Academic and technological workshops provided. Tutorial services available in math, physics, chemistry, English, reading, accounting, and general science. **Special study options:** Combined bachelor's/graduate degree, distance learning, dual enrollment of high school students, ESL, external degree, honors, independent study, study abroad, weekend college. **Credit/placement by examination:** AP, CLEP. **Support services:** Learning center, remedial instruction, study skills assistance, tutoring, writing center.

Majors. Area/ethnic studies: African-American. **Biology:** General. **Business:** Business admin, office management. **Communications:** General. **Computer sciences:** General, computer science. **Education:** Multi-level teacher. **Engineering technology:** General. **Foreign languages:** General. **Health:** Medical records admin. **History:** General. **Math:** General. **Parks/recreation:** Health/fitness. **Physical sciences:** Chemistry, physics. **Protective services:** Law enforcement admin. **Psychology:** General. **Public administration:** Social work. **Social sciences:** Political science. **Visual/performing arts:** Art.

Most popular majors. Liberal arts 94%.

Computing on campus. 580 workstations in library, computer center, student center. Commuter students can connect to campus network. Online course registration, online library, helpline, repair service, wireless network available.

Student life. Freshman orientation: Mandatory. Preregistration for classes offered. 1 daytime and 1 evening session held each semester. **Housing:** Off-campus housing available for college athletes only. **Activities:** Choral groups, dance, drama, international student organizations, student government, student newspaper.

Athletics. NJCAA. **Intercollegiate:** Basketball. **Team name:** Red-Eyed Panthers.

Student services. Adult student services, career counseling, services for economically disadvantaged, financial aid counseling, minority student services, personal counseling, veterans' counselor. **Physically disabled:** Services for visually, speech, hearing impaired. **Learning disabled:** Comprehensive services available. **Transfer:** Pre-admission transcript evaluation for new students. College fairs on campus for students transferring to 4-year colleges.

Contact. E-mail: areid@atlm.edu
Phone: (404) 756-4004 Fax: (404) 756-4407
Audrey Reid, Director of Admissions, Atlanta Metropolitan College, 1630 Metropolitan Parkway, SW, Atlanta, GA 30310-4498

Atlanta Technical College

Atlanta, Georgia
www.atlantatech.org — **CB code: 5030**

- Public 2-year community and technical college
- Commuter campus in very large city

General. Regionally accredited. **Enrollment:** 3,026 degree-seeking undergraduates; 282 non-degree-seeking students. **Degrees:** 44 associate awarded. **Location:** 2 miles from downtown. **Calendar:** Quarter. **Full-time faculty:** 86 total. **Part-time faculty:** 102 total.

Two-Year Colleges

Student profile. Among degree-seeking undergraduates, 739 enrolled as first-time, first-year students.

Part-time:	48%	**Asian American:**	1%
Women:	59%	**Hispanic American:**	1%
African American:	92%	**25 or older:**	51%

Basis for selection. Open admission, but selective for some programs. Requirements vary by program for selective admission majors. ACT or SAT may be accepted in lieu of COMPASS or ASSET for placement. **Homeschooled:** Letter from superintendent's ofice confirming compliance with Georgia/DTAE policies and attendance and final exit exam scores from accredited national testing program required.

High school preparation. College-preparatory program recommended. 22 units recommended. Recommended units include English 4, mathematics 3, social studies 3, science 3, foreign language 1 and academic electives 3. 4 tech prep and 1 health science recommended.

2008-2009 Annual costs. Tuition/fees: $1,542; $2,838 out-of-state. Per-credit charge: $36 in-state; $72 out-of-state. Books/supplies: $1,200. Personal expenses: $900.

2008-2009 Financial aid. Need-based: Need-based aid available for part-time students. Work-study available nights and for part-time students.

Application procedures. Admission: Priority date 9/8; deadline 9/22 (receipt date). $20 fee. Admission notification on a rolling basis. **Financial aid:** Priority date 3/1; no closing date. Applicants notified on a rolling basis starting 4/15.

Academics. Special study options: Distance learning, dual enrollment of high school students, ESL, weekend college. License preparation in aviation, nursing, paramedic, real estate. **Credit/placement by examination:** AP, CLEP, IB, institutional tests. **Support services:** GED test center, learning center, tutoring.

Majors. Computer sciences: General. **Legal studies:** Paralegal. **Visual/performing arts:** Music.

Most popular majors. Business/marketing 18%, computer/information sciences 11%, education 52%, legal studies 18%.

Computing on campus. 55 workstations in library, computer center. Online library, wireless network available.

Student life. Freshman orientation: Mandatory. Preregistration for classes offered.

Student services. On-campus daycare.

Contact. Phone: (404) 225-4447 Fax: (404) 225-4721
Vory Billups, Director of Admissions, Atlanta Technical College, 1560 Metropolitan Parkway, SW, Atlanta, GA 30310-4446

Augusta Technical College

Augusta, Georgia
www.augustatech.edu **CB code: 2620**

- Public 2-year technical college
- Commuter campus in large city

General. Founded in 1961. Regionally accredited. Additional campuses in Thomson and Waynesboro. **Enrollment:** 4,261 degree-seeking undergraduates; 444 non-degree-seeking students. **Degrees:** 286 associate awarded. **Location:** 145 miles from Atlanta, 75 miles from Columbia, South Carolina. **Calendar:** Quarter, extensive summer session. **Full-time faculty:** 136 total. **Part-time faculty:** 240 total.

Student profile. Among degree-seeking undergraduates, 793 enrolled as first-time, first-year students.

Part-time:	48%	**Asian American:**	2%
Women:	62%	**Hispanic American:**	2%
African American:	53%		

Basis for selection. Open admission, but selective for some programs. Admission to cardiovascular technology, respiratory therapy care, occupational therapy assistant, radiologic technology, and practical nursing competitive. These programs use combination of factors including all or some of the following: required college courses, placement exam scores, interviews, essays, and GPA. ACT or SAT may be accepted in lieu of COMPASS or ASSET for placement.

High school preparation. College-preparatory program recommended. 22 units recommended. Recommended units include English 4, mathematics 3, social studies 3, science 3, foreign language 1 and academic electives 3. Highly recommended that math units include algebra and trigonometry. 4 tech prep and 1 health science recommended.

2008-2009 Annual costs. Tuition/fees: $1,542; $2,838 out-of-state. Per-credit charge: $36 in-state; $72 out-of-state. Books/supplies: $450.

Financial aid. Non-need-based: Scholarships awarded for state residency.

Application procedures. Admission: No deadline. $15 fee, may be waived for applicants with need. Application deadlines exist for competitive healthcare programs and vary by major. **Financial aid:** No deadline. FAFSA, institutional form required. Must reply within 2 week(s) of notification.

Academics. Special study options: Distance learning, dual enrollment of high school students, weekend college. **Credit/placement by examination:** CLEP, institutional tests. **Support services:** GED preparation and test center, learning center, reduced course load, remedial instruction, tutoring.

Majors. Business: Accounting, administrative services, sales/distribution. **Computer sciences:** Applications programming. **Engineering technology:** Electrical. **Health:** Cardiovascular technology, clinical lab technology, EMT paramedic, pharmacy assistant, respiratory therapy technology.

Most popular majors. Business/marketing 27%, computer/information sciences 15%, education 11%, health sciences 21%, security/protective services 10%.

Computing on campus. Commuter students can connect to campus network. Online course registration, online library available.

Student life. Freshman orientation: Available. Preregistration for classes offered. **Activities:** Student government.

Student services. Career counseling, student employment services, financial aid counseling, on-campus daycare, placement for graduates, veterans' counselor. **Physically disabled:** Services for visually, speech, hearing impaired. **Transfer:** Pre-admission transcript evaluation for new students.

Contact. Phone: (706) 771-4028 Fax: (706) 771-4034
Brian Roberts, Director of Admissions, Augusta Technical College, 3200 Augusta Tech Drive, Augusta, GA 30906

Bainbridge College

Bainbridge, Georgia
www.bainbridge.edu **CB code: 5062**

- Public 2-year community and technical college
- Commuter campus in large town
- SAT or ACT required

General. Founded in 1973. Regionally accredited. **Enrollment:** 3,050 degree-seeking undergraduates. **Degrees:** 185 associate awarded. **Location:** 43 miles from Tallahassee, Florida. **Calendar:** Semester, limited summer session. **Full-time faculty:** 73 total; 22% have terminal degrees, 11% minority, 58% women. **Part-time faculty:** 126 total; 11% have terminal degrees, 14% minority, 57% women. **Class size:** 60% < 20, 39% 20-39, less than 1% 50-99. **Special facilities:** Nature trail.

Student profile. Among degree-seeking undergraduates, 40% enrolled in a transfer program, 60% enrolled in a vocational program, 1% already have a bachelor's degree or higher, 530 enrolled as first-time, first-year students, 141 transferred in from other institutions.

Part-time:	59%	**Women:**	70%
Out-of-state:	1%	**25 or older:**	38%

Transfer out. 75% of students enrolled in the transfer program go on to 4-year colleges. **Colleges most students transferred to 2008:** Valdosta State University, Albany State University, Georgia Southwestern University.

Basis for selection. 330 SAT verbal/13 ACT English, 310 SAT math/14 ACT math, or 1.8 GPA required. College preparatory curriculum required for associate of arts degree-seeking students. Limited number admitted who do not meet admission standards. **Adult students:** SAT/ACT scores not required. Compass test required. **Homeschooled:** Acceptable scores on COMPASS placement test required.

High school preparation. College-preparatory program recommended. 16 units required. Required units include English 4, mathematics 4, social studies 3, science 3 and foreign language 2. Tech Prep students exempt from foreign language requirement.

2008-2009 Annual costs. Tuition/fees: $2,326; $7,828 out-of-state. Per-credit charge: $77 in-state; $306 out-of-state. Books/supplies: $600. Personal expenses: $450.

2007-2008 Financial aid. All financial aid based on need. 99% of total undergraduate aid awarded as scholarships/grants, 1% as loans/jobs. Need-based aid available for part-time students. **Additional information:** 30-day loans available for tuition and fees.

Application procedures. Admission: Closing date 8/10 (receipt date). No application fee. Admission notification on a rolling basis. **Financial aid:** Priority date 6/1, closing date 8/1. FAFSA, institutional form required. Applicants notified on a rolling basis starting 6/1; must reply within 2 week(s) of notification.

Academics. Special study options: Distance learning, double major, dual enrollment of high school students, honors, independent study, internships, study abroad, weekend college. 2-year registered nursing program. Bachelor's degree programs available on campus. License preparation in nursing, real estate. **Credit/placement by examination:** AP, CLEP, institutional tests. 18 credit hours maximum toward associate degree. **Support services:** GED preparation, learning center, reduced course load, remedial instruction, study skills assistance, tutoring.

Majors. Business: General, accounting, administrative services, management information systems, marketing. **Communications:** General. **Computer sciences:** General. **Construction:** Electrician. **Education:** General, early childhood, health, middle, physical, secondary. **Engineering technology:** Drafting, electrical. **Foreign languages:** General. **Health:** Nursing (RN). **History:** General. **Math:** General. **Mechanic/repair:** Industrial. **Protective services:** Law enforcement admin. **Psychology:** General. **Social sciences:** Political science.

Most popular majors. Business/marketing 29%, liberal arts 61%.

Computing on campus. 295 workstations in library, computer center, student center. Online course registration, online library, wireless network available.

Student life. Freshman orientation: Mandatory. Preregistration for classes offered. Held prior to the semester; on-line orientation. **Activities:** Concert band, choral groups, drama, music ensembles, student government, student newspaper, Delta club, service organizations, Phi Theta Kappa, Sigma Kappa Delta.

Athletics. Intramural: Basketball M, football (non-tackle), softball, table tennis, tennis, volleyball.

Student services. Adult student services, career counseling, services for economically disadvantaged, student employment services, financial aid counseling, minority student services, personal counseling, placement for graduates, veterans' counselor. **Physically disabled:** Services for visually, speech, hearing impaired. **Transfer:** Transfer adviser, college fairs on campus for students transferring to 4-year colleges.

Contact. E-mail: csnyder@bainbridge.edu
Phone: (229) 248-2504 Fax: (229) 248-2623
Connie Snyder, Director of Admissions and Records, Bainbridge College, 2500 East Shotwell Street, Bainbridge, GA 39818-0990

Brown Mackie College: Atlanta
Atlanta, Georgia

- For-profit 2-year business, health science and technical college
- Very large city

General. Accredited by ACICS. **Enrollment:** 600 degree-seeking undergraduates. **Degrees:** 66 associate awarded. **Calendar:** Quarter. **Full-time faculty:** 7 total. **Part-time faculty:** 7 total.

Basis for selection. Open admission.

Academics. Credit/placement by examination: CLEP.

Majors. Business: Accounting, business admin. **Health:** Medical assistant, occupational therapy assistant, surgical technology. **Legal studies:** Paralegal.

Contact. E-mail: jthee@brownmackie.edu
Phone: (770) 638-0121 Toll-free number: (888) 301-3670
Jonelle Thee, Enrollment Manager, Brown Mackie College: Atlanta, 6600 Peachtree Dunwoody NE, Atlanta, GA 30328

Central Georgia Technical College
Macon, Georgia
www.cgtcollege.edu **CB code: 1709**

- Public 2-year community and technical college
- Commuter campus in small city

General. Regionally accredited. **Enrollment:** 5,308 degree-seeking undergraduates; 280 non-degree-seeking students. **Degrees:** 212 associate awarded. **Location:** 80 miles from Atlanta. **Calendar:** Quarter, extensive summer session. **Full-time faculty:** 109 total. **Part-time faculty:** 375 total. **Class size:** 87% < 20, 13% 20-39, less than 1% 40-49. **Partnerships:** Formal partnerships with Cisco and local industries.

Student profile. Among degree-seeking undergraduates, 919 enrolled as first-time, first-year students.

Part-time:	49%	**Asian American:**	1%
Out-of-state:	1%	**Hispanic American:**	1%
Women:	67%	**25 or older:**	35%
African American:	58%		

Basis for selection. Open admission, but selective for some programs. Requirements vary according to program of study. ACT or SAT may be accepted in lieu of COMPASS or ASSET for placement.

High school preparation. College-preparatory program recommended. 22 units recommended. Recommended units include English 4, mathematics 3, social studies 3, science 3, foreign language 1 and academic electives 3. 4 tech prep and 1 health science recommended.

2008-2009 Annual costs. Tuition/fees: $1,539; $2,835 out-of-state. Per-credit charge: $36 in-state; $72 out-of-state. Books/supplies: $750.

2007-2008 Financial aid. Need-based: Need-based aid available for part-time students.

Application procedures. Admission: $15 fee, may be waived for applicants with need. Admission notification on a rolling basis. Application closing date is one month prior to first day of attendance. **Financial aid:** Closing date 7/14. FAFSA, institutional form required.

Academics. Special study options: Distance learning, dual enrollment of high school students, weekend college. License preparation in dental hygiene, nursing, paramedic, radiology, real estate. **Credit/placement by examination:** CLEP, institutional tests. Dependent on approval by department/program. **Support services:** GED preparation and test center, reduced course load, remedial instruction, study skills assistance, tutoring, writing center.

Majors. Business: Accounting technology, administrative services, logistics, operations. **Computer sciences:** Data processing, networking, web page design. **Education:** Early childhood. **Engineering technology:** Drafting. **Health:** Clinical lab technology, dental hygiene, medical assistant. **Protective services:** Criminal justice.

Most popular majors. Business/marketing 30%, computer/information sciences 11%, education 10%, health sciences 31%, security/protective services 8%.

Computing on campus. 400 workstations in library, computer center. Commuter students can connect to campus network. Online course registration, online library, helpline, repair service, wireless network available.

Student life. Freshman orientation: Mandatory. Preregistration for classes offered. Held prior to each quarterly registration period. **Activities:** Student government.

Student services. Adult student services, career counseling, services for economically disadvantaged, financial aid counseling, on-campus daycare, placement for graduates, veterans' counselor. **Physically disabled:** Services for visually, speech, hearing impaired. **Transfer:** College fairs on campus for students transferring to 4-year colleges.

Contact. E-mail: info@cgtcollege.org
Phone: (478) 757-3403 Fax: (478) 757-3454
Tammy Carter, Director of Admissions, Central Georgia Technical College, 3300 Macon Tech Drive, Macon, GA 31206

Chattahoochee Technical College
Marietta, Georgia
www.chattcollege.com **CB code: 5441**

- Public 2-year technical college
- Commuter campus in large city

Two-Year Colleges

General. Founded in 1961. Regionally accredited. **Enrollment:** 4,597 degree-seeking undergraduates; 1,016 non-degree-seeking students. **Degrees:** 320 associate awarded. **Location:** 20 miles from Atlanta. **Calendar:** Quarter, extensive summer session. **Full-time faculty:** 61 total. **Part-time faculty:** 201 total.

Student profile. Among degree-seeking undergraduates, 1,167 enrolled as first-time, first-year students.

Part-time:	52%	**Asian American:**	2%
Women:	58%	**Hispanic American:**	5%
African American:	39%	**International:**	2%

Basis for selection. Open admission, but selective for some programs. Special requirements for allied health programs. ACT or SAT may be accepted in lieu of COMPASS or ASSET for placement.

High school preparation. College-preparatory program recommended. 22 units recommended. Recommended units include English 4, mathematics 3, social studies 3, science 3, foreign language 1 and academic electives 3. 4 tech prep and 1 health science recommended.

2008-2009 Annual costs. Tuition/fees: $1,560; $2,856 out-of-state. Per-credit charge: $36 in-state; $72 out-of-state. Books/supplies: $1,020. Personal expenses: $1,300.

2007-2008 Financial aid. Need-based: 97% of total undergraduate aid awarded as scholarships/grants, 3% as loans/jobs. Need-based aid available for part-time students. Work-study available nights, weekends and for part-time students. **Non-need-based:** Scholarships awarded for state residency.

Application procedures. Admission: Closing date 9/8. $15 fee. Admission notification on a rolling basis. **Financial aid:** Priority date 7/15; no closing date. FAFSA, institutional form required. Applicants notified on a rolling basis starting 6/15.

Academics. Special study options: Distance learning, dual enrollment of high school students, weekend college. License preparation in nursing. **Credit/placement by examination:** CLEP, institutional tests. 15 credit hours maximum toward associate degree. **Support services:** Learning center, reduced course load, remedial instruction, study skills assistance, tutoring.

Majors. Business: General, accounting, administrative services, marketing, office management. **Computer sciences:** General, applications programming. **Engineering technology:** Electrical. **Family/consumer sciences:** Child care. **Mechanic/repair:** Automotive. **Personal/culinary services:** Culinary arts. **Protective services:** Criminal justice.

Most popular majors. Business/marketing 44%, communication technologies 8%, computer/information sciences 10%, education 9%, engineering/engineering technologies 12%, security/protective services 8%.

Computing on campus. 857 workstations in library, computer center, student center. Commuter students can connect to campus network. Online course registration, repair service available.

Student life. Activities: Student government.

Student services. Career counseling, student employment services, personal counseling, placement for graduates, veterans' counselor. **Physically disabled:** Services for visually, hearing impaired. **Transfer:** Pre-admission transcript evaluation for new students. College fairs on campus for students transferring to 4-year colleges.

Contact. E-mail: info@chattcollege.com
Phone: (770) 528-4565 Fax: (770) 528-4580
John Parton, Director of Admissions, Chattahoochee Technical College, 980 South Cobb Drive, Marietta, GA 30060-3300

College of Coastal Georgia

Brunswick, Georgia — **CB member**
www.ccga.edu — **CB code: 5078**

- Public 2-year junior college
- Commuter campus in large town

General. Founded in 1961. Regionally accredited. Students may take courses at Camden Center in Kingsland, Georgia. **Enrollment:** 2,794 degree-seeking undergraduates; 138 non-degree-seeking students. **Degrees:** 125 associate awarded. **Location:** 70 miles from Savannah, 60 miles from Jacksonville, Florida. **Calendar:** Semester, limited summer session. **Full-time faculty:** 64 total; 19% have terminal degrees, 9% minority, 42% women. **Part-time faculty:** 60 total; 15% have terminal degrees, 12% minority, 45% women. **Class size:** 49% < 20, 48% 20-39, 3% 40-49, less than 1% 50-99.

Student profile. Among degree-seeking undergraduates, 843 enrolled as first-time, first-year students.

Part-time:	63%	**Women:**	65%
Out-of-state:	6%	**25 or older:**	40%

Transfer out. Colleges most students transferred to 2008: Armstrong Atlantic State University, Georgia Southern University.

Basis for selection. Open admission, but selective for some programs. Additional requirements for registered nursing and health science programs. Tests are not required, but will be used to exempt students from placement testing. **Homeschooled:** Statement describing homeschool structure and mission, transcript of courses and grades, letter of recommendation (nonparent) required. Must take SAT or ACT and score at the average of last year's freshman class. **Learning Disabled:** Students must go through an accreditation process with system agency on learning disabilities to receive accommodations.

High school preparation. College-preparatory program recommended. 16 units recommended. Recommended units include English 4, mathematics 4, social studies 3, science 2 (laboratory 1) and foreign language 2.

2008-2009 Annual costs. Tuition/fees: $2,050; $7,552 out-of-state. Per-credit charge: $77 in-state; $306 out-of-state. Guaranteed tuition plan locks tuition rate for up to 3 years. Cost will vary among students. Books/supplies: $600. Personal expenses: $500.

2007-2008 Financial aid. Need-based: Need-based aid available for part-time students. Work-study available nights, weekends and for part-time students. **Non-need-based:** Scholarships awarded for academics, athletics, leadership, state residency.

Application procedures. Admission: Closing date 7/15. $20 fee, may be waived for applicants with need. Admission notification on a rolling basis. **Financial aid:** Priority date 5/1; no closing date. FAFSA required. Applicants notified on a rolling basis starting 7/1.

Academics. Special study options: Accelerated study, cooperative education, distance learning, dual enrollment of high school students, independent study, liberal arts/career combination, study abroad, teacher certification program. Bachelor's degree programs available on campus. License preparation in real estate. **Credit/placement by examination:** AP, CLEP, IB, institutional tests. 24 credit hours maximum toward associate degree, 24 toward bachelor's. **Support services:** Learning center, reduced course load, remedial instruction, study skills assistance, tutoring.

Majors. Agriculture: Agribusiness operations. **Biology:** General. **Business:** Accounting. **Communications:** General. **Computer sciences:** Computer science. **Education:** General, elementary, middle, secondary, special. **Engineering:** General. **Foreign languages:** General. **Health:** Clinical lab technology, medical radiologic technology/radiation therapy, nursing (RN). **History:** General. **Legal studies:** Prelaw. **Liberal arts:** Arts/sciences. **Math:** General. **Parks/recreation:** General. **Personal/culinary services:** Restaurant/catering. **Physical sciences:** Chemistry, physics. **Protective services:** Law enforcement admin. **Psychology:** General. **Social sciences:** Sociology. **Visual/performing arts:** Art.

Most popular majors. Health sciences 39%, liberal arts 61%.

Computing on campus. 300 workstations in library, computer center, student center. Commuter students can connect to campus network. Online course registration, online library, helpline, repair service, wireless network available.

Student life. Freshman orientation: Mandatory. Preregistration for classes offered. **Activities:** Literary magazine, student government, student newspaper, minority club, Baptist student union.

Athletics. NJCAA. **Intercollegiate:** Basketball M, softball W. **Intramural:** Basketball, bowling, cheerleading W, cross-country, golf, softball, table tennis, tennis, volleyball. **Team name:** Mariners.

Student services. Adult student services, career counseling, services for economically disadvantaged, student employment services, financial aid counseling, minority student services, personal counseling, placement for graduates, veterans' counselor. **Physically disabled:** Services for visually, speech, hearing impaired. **Transfer:** College fairs on campus for students transferring to 4-year colleges.

Contact. E-mail: admiss@ccga.edu
Phone: (912) 279-5730 Toll-free number: (800) 675-7235
Fax: (912) 262-3072
Lisa Lesseig, Registrar/Director of Admissions, College of Coastal Georgia, 3700 Altama Avenue, Brunswick, GA 31520

Columbus Technical College
Columbus, Georgia
www.columbustech.org **CB code: 7005**

- Public 2-year technical college
- Commuter campus in small city
- Interview required

General. Founded in 1961. Regionally accredited. **Enrollment:** 3,621 degree-seeking undergraduates; 66 non-degree-seeking students. **Degrees:** 272 associate awarded. **Location:** 110 miles from Atlanta, 86 miles from Albany. **Calendar:** Quarter, extensive summer session. **Full-time faculty:** 77 total. **Part-time faculty:** 153 total.

Student profile. Among degree-seeking undergraduates, 659 enrolled as first-time, first-year students.

Part-time:	57%	**Asian American:**	2%
Women:	67%	**Hispanic American:**	3%
African American:	44%	**Native American:**	1%

Basis for selection. Open admission, but selective for some programs. Special requirements for health programs. ACT or SAT may be accepted in lieu of COMPASS or ASSET for placement.

High school preparation. College-preparatory program recommended. 22 units recommended. Recommended units include English 4, mathematics 3, social studies 3, science 3, foreign language 1 and academic electives 3. 4 tech prep and 1 health science recommended.

2008-2009 Annual costs. Tuition/fees: $1,539; $2,835 out-of-state. Per-credit charge: $36 in-state; $72 out-of-state. Books/supplies: $1,600. Personal expenses: $1,100.

Financial aid. Need-based: Need-based aid available for part-time students.

Application procedures. Admission: Closing date 9/16. $25 fee. Notification before registration date. **Financial aid:** No deadline. FAFSA required. Applicants notified on a rolling basis.

Academics. Special study options: Distance learning, dual enrollment of high school students, honors, internships, weekend college. License preparation in dental hygiene, nursing, paramedic, radiology, real estate. **Credit/placement by examination:** AP, CLEP. **Support services:** Learning center, remedial instruction, study skills assistance, tutoring.

Majors. Agriculture: Horticultural science. **Business:** Accounting, administrative services, business admin. **Education:** Early childhood. **Engineering technology:** Electrical. **Health:** Cardiovascular technology, dental hygiene, nursing (RN), surgical technology. **Mechanic/repair:** Automotive, industrial.

Most popular majors. Business/marketing 27%, computer/information sciences 27%, health sciences 31%.

Computing on campus. 40 workstations in library, computer center. Online library available.

Student life. Freshman orientation: Mandatory. Preregistration for classes offered. Three-hour orientation held day before start of classes. **Activities:** Student government.

Student services. Career counseling, student employment services, financial aid counseling, personal counseling, placement for graduates, veterans' counselor. **Physically disabled:** Services for speech, hearing impaired.

Contact. Phone: (706) 649-1800 Fax: (404) 649-1885
Nicole Kennedy, Director of Admissions, Columbus Technical College, 928 Manchester Expressway, Columbus, GA 31904

Coosa Valley Technical College
Rome, Georgia
www.coosavalleytech.edu

- Public 2-year technical college
- Large town

General. Regionally accredited. **Enrollment:** 2,642 degree-seeking undergraduates. **Calendar:** Quarter. **Full-time faculty:** 225 total. **Part-time faculty:** 150 total.

Basis for selection. Open admission, but selective for some programs.

Application procedures. Admission: Closing date 9/20. **Financial aid:** Closing date 9/1.

Academics. Credit/placement by examination: CLEP.

Majors. Business: Marketing. **Health:** Management/clinical assistant. **Protective services:** Law enforcement admin.

Contact. E-mail: dmcburnett@coosavalleytech.edu
Phone: (706) 295-6702
David McBurnett, Director of Admissions and Student Placement, Coosa Valley Technical College, One Maurice Culberson Drive, Rome, GA 30161

Darton College
Albany, Georgia **CB member**
www.darton.edu **CB code: 5026**

- Public 2-year community college
- Commuter campus in small city

General. Founded in 1963. Regionally accredited. **Enrollment:** 4,528 degree-seeking undergraduates; 491 non-degree-seeking students. **Degrees:** 547 associate awarded. **Location:** 175 miles from Atlanta. **Calendar:** Semester, extensive summer session. **Full-time faculty:** 112 total; 16% minority, 67% women. **Part-time faculty:** 162 total; 17% minority, 54% women. **Class size:** 56% < 20, 41% 20-39, 2% 40-49, less than 1% 50-99, less than 1% >100. **Special facilities:** 50-foot Carolina tower and climbing wall, nature trail.

Student profile. Among degree-seeking undergraduates, 51% enrolled in a transfer program, 49% enrolled in a vocational program, 1,197 enrolled as first-time, first-year students.

Part-time:	50%	**Asian American:**	1%
Out-of-state:	5%	**Hispanic American:**	1%
Women:	71%	**International:**	1%
African American:	43%	**25 or older:**	49%

Transfer out. Colleges most students transferred to 2008: Georgia Southwestern State University, Albany State University, Florida State University, Valdosta State University.

Basis for selection. Traditional students must have 2.0 college prep GPA or 2.2 tech prep GPA. 1.8 GPA required for programs of less than 12 credit hours. Interview, portfolios and essays considered when students do not meet minimum admission requirements but show promise. **Homeschooled:** Transcript of courses and grades required.

High school preparation. College-preparatory program required. 16 units required. Required units include English 4, mathematics 4, social studies 3, science 3 and foreign language 2.

2008-2009 Annual costs. Tuition/fees: $2,412; $7,914 out-of-state. Per-credit charge: $77 in-state; $306 out-of-state. Books/supplies: $1,100. Personal expenses: $1,200.

2007-2008 Financial aid. Need-based: Need-based aid available for part-time students. Work-study available nights, weekends and for part-time students. **Non-need-based:** Scholarships awarded for academics, alumni affiliation, art, athletics, music/drama, state residency. **Additional information:** Auditions, portfolios, essays, extracurricular activities impact scholarship decisions.

Application procedures. Admission: Priority date 8/1; no deadline. $20 fee. Admission notification on a rolling basis. Applications must be received 10 days prior to registration. **Financial aid:** No deadline. FAFSA, institutional form required. Applicants notified on a rolling basis; must reply within 3 week(s) of notification.

Academics. Career and transfer programs available. **Special study options:** Cooperative education, cross-registration, distance learning, double major, dual enrollment of high school students, ESL, honors, independent study, liberal arts/career combination, study abroad, weekend college. License preparation in dental hygiene, nursing, occupational therapy, paramedic, physical therapy. **Credit/placement by examination:** AP, CLEP, IB, SAT, ACT, institutional tests. 18 hours in residence required. **Support services:** Learning center, reduced course load, remedial instruction, study skills assistance, tutoring, writing center.

Majors. Agriculture: General. **Biology:** General, biomedical sciences. **Business:** Accounting, administrative services, business admin, entrepreneurial studies, office management. **Communications:** Journalism. **Computer sciences:** General, computer science, information systems, networking. **Conservation:** Environmental studies, forestry. **Education:** General, art, business, early childhood, English, foreign languages, mathematics, middle, multi-level teacher, music, social science, speech. **Engineering technology:** General.

Foreign languages: General. **Health:** Cardiovascular technology, clinical lab science, community health services, dental hygiene, EMT paramedic, histologic assistant, licensed practical nurse, medical radiologic technology/radiation therapy, medical records admin, medical records technology, mental health services, nuclear medical technology, nursing (RN), occupational therapy assistant, office admin, physical therapy assistant, predental, premedicine, prepharmacy, preveterinary, respiratory therapy assistant, respiratory therapy technology, sonography. **History:** General. **Legal studies:** Paralegal. **Liberal arts:** Humanities. **Math:** General. **Parks/recreation:** General, exercise sciences, health/fitness, sports admin. **Philosophy/religion:** Philosophy. **Physical sciences:** Chemistry, physics. **Protective services:** Criminal justice, forensics. **Psychology:** General. **Public administration:** Human services, social work. **Social sciences:** Anthropology, economics, geography, political science, sociology. **Visual/performing arts:** Art, dramatic. **Other:** Pre-engineering.

Most popular majors. Business/marketing 10%, education 11%, health sciences 53%.

Computing on campus. 400 workstations in library, computer center. Commuter students can connect to campus network. Online course registration, online library, helpline, wireless network available.

Student life. **Freshman orientation:** Available. Preregistration for classes offered. Held every semester, required of all students enrolled in learning support classes. **Activities:** Bands, choral groups, dance, drama, international student organizations, literary magazine, music ensembles, musical theater, student government, student newspaper, symphony orchestra, Cultural Exchange Club, Democratic Independent Republican Team (DIRT).

Athletics. NJCAA. **Intercollegiate:** Baseball M, basketball W, golf M, soccer, softball W, swimming, wrestling M. **Intramural:** Basketball, bowling, football (non-tackle), golf, softball, table tennis, tennis, volleyball. **Team name:** Cavaliers.

Student services. Alcohol/substance abuse counseling, career counseling, student employment services, financial aid counseling, minority student services, personal counseling, placement for graduates, veterans' counselor. **Physically disabled:** Services for visually, speech, hearing impaired. **Transfer:** Pre-admission transcript evaluation for new students. Transfer adviser, college fairs on campus for students transferring to 4-year colleges.

Contact. E-mail: info@darton.edu
Phone: (229) 317-6740 Toll-free number: (866) 775-1214
Fax: (229) 317-6607
Susan Bowen, Director of Admission, Darton College, 2400 Gillionville Road, Albany, GA 31707-3098

DeKalb Technical College

Clarkston, Georgia
www.dekalbtech.edu **CB code: 3226**

- Public 2-year technical college
- Commuter campus in large city

General. Founded in 1961. Regionally accredited. Second campus located in Covington. **Enrollment:** 3,805 degree-seeking undergraduates; 191 non-degree-seeking students. **Degrees:** 237 associate awarded. **Location:** 17 miles from Atlanta. **Calendar:** Quarter, extensive summer session. **Full-time faculty:** 101 total; 5% have terminal degrees, 38% minority, 52% women. **Part-time faculty:** 423 total; 2% have terminal degrees, 48% minority, 66% women. **Class size:** 88% < 20, 12% 20-39. **Special facilities:** Conference center. **Partnerships:** Formal partnerships wtih MARTA; Fulton County Government; DeKalb, Rockdale, Newton, Morgan County Schools; Decatur City Schools.

Student profile. Among degree-seeking undergraduates, 746 enrolled as first-time, first-year students.

Part-time:	60%	**Asian American:**	3%
Women:	63%	**Hispanic American:**	2%
African American:	75%	**25 or older:**	40%

Transfer out. **Colleges most students transferred to 2008:** Georgia State University, Southern Polytechnic State University, DeVry University, Clayton College and State University, Georgia Perimeter College.

Basis for selection. Open admission, but selective for some programs. Limited admission to health technologies programs. ACT or SAT may be accepted in lieu of COMPASS or ASSET for placement. Interview recommended.

High school preparation. College-preparatory program recommended. 22 units recommended. Recommended units include English 4, mathematics 3, social studies 3, science 3, foreign language 1 and academic electives 3. 4 tech prep and 1 health science recommended.

2008-2009 Annual costs. Tuition/fees: $1,587; $2,883 out-of-state. Per-credit charge: $36 in-state; $72 out-of-state. Truck driving and flight technology are higher cost programs. Books/supplies: $1,200. Personal expenses: $900.

2008-2009 Financial aid. **Need-based:** Need-based aid available for part-time students. Work-study available nights, weekends and for part-time students.

Application procedures. **Admission:** Closing date 8/22 (receipt date). $20 fee. Application must be submitted on paper. Admission notification on a rolling basis. **Financial aid:** Priority date 7/15, closing date 8/20. FAFSA required. Applicants notified on a rolling basis starting 6/1.

Academics. **Special study options:** Distance learning, dual enrollment of high school students. License preparation in nursing, paramedic, real estate. **Credit/placement by examination:** AP, CLEP, institutional tests. 35 credit hours maximum toward associate degree. **Support services:** GED preparation and test center, learning center, reduced course load, remedial instruction, study skills assistance, tutoring.

Majors. **Business:** Accounting, business admin, marketing. **Computer sciences:** General, programming. **Engineering:** Computer, electrical. **Engineering technology:** Electrical, instrumentation. **Health:** Ophthalmic lab technology, optician. **Mechanic/repair:** Automotive.

Most popular majors. Business/marketing 41%, computer/information sciences 13%, education 10%, health sciences 6%, legal studies 14%, security/protective services 6%, trade and industry 7%.

Computing on campus. 500 workstations in computer center. Online course registration, online library available.

Student life. **Freshman orientation:** Available. **Activities:** Student government, student newspaper, Delta Epsilon Chi, Collegiate Secretaries International, Noon Net-Working of New Connections, Phi Beta Lambda, Student Optical Society, Licensed Practical Nurses Association, Vocational Industrial Clubs of America, Epsilon Delta Phi Honorary Society, Phi Theta Kappa Honor Society.

Student services. Adult student services, career counseling, services for economically disadvantaged, student employment services, financial aid counseling, minority student services, placement for graduates, veterans' counselor, women's services. **Physically disabled:** Services for visually, speech, hearing impaired. **Transfer:** Pre-admission transcript evaluation for new students.

Contact. E-mail: admissionsclark@dekalbtech.org
Phone: (404) 297-9522 ext. 1602 Toll-free
number: (877) 780-3032 ext. 1602 Fax: (404) 294-3424
Terry Richardson, Coordinator of Admissions and Special Services, DeKalb Technical College, 495 North Indian Creek Drive, Clarkston, GA 30021-2397

East Georgia College

Swainsboro, Georgia **CB member**
www.ega.edu **CB code: 5200**

- Public 2-year community and junior college
- Commuter campus in small town

General. Founded in 1973. Regionally accredited. **Enrollment:** 2,555 degree-seeking undergraduates. **Degrees:** 122 associate awarded. **ROTC:** Army. **Location:** 85 miles from Savannah and Augusta. **Calendar:** Semester, limited summer session. **Full-time faculty:** 47 total; 36% have terminal degrees, 11% minority, 32% women. **Part-time faculty:** 49 total; 14% have terminal degrees, 14% minority, 53% women. **Class size:** 18% < 20, 76% 20-39, 5% 40-49, less than 1% >100. **Special facilities:** Outdoor exercise trail, fitness center, community learning center.

Student profile. Among degree-seeking undergraduates, 25 transferred in from other institutions.

Out-of-state:	2%	**25 or older:**	20%

Transfer out. **Colleges most students transferred to 2008:** Georgia Southern University.

Basis for selection. Graduation from accredited or approved high school or GED, 16 college prep curriculum units, Compass test scores, and 2.0

GPA required. **Homeschooled:** Students who complete an accredited home school program, whose accrediting agency is approved by the Unversity of Georgia, considered for admissions if admissions requirements for recent high school graduates are met. Graduates of non-accredited programs must take the GED.

High school preparation. 16 units required. Required and recommended units include English 4, mathematics 4, social studies 3, science 3 and foreign language 2.

2008-2009 Annual costs. Tuition/fees: $2,010; $7,512 out-of-state. Per-credit charge: $77 in-state; $306 out-of-state. Books/supplies: $1,200. Personal expenses: $1,200.

Financial aid. Need-based: Need-based aid available for part-time students. **Non-need-based:** Scholarships awarded for academics, leadership, state residency.

Application procedures. Admission: No deadline. $20 fee, may be waived for applicants with need. Admission notification on a rolling basis beginning on or about 2/1. **Financial aid:** Priority date 6/15; no closing date. FAFSA, institutional form required. Applicants notified on a rolling basis starting 6/15; must reply within 2 week(s) of notification.

Academics. Special study options: Distance learning, double major, dual enrollment of high school students, honors, independent study, study abroad. Bachelor's degree programs available on campus. License preparation in nursing. **Credit/placement by examination:** AP, CLEP, IB, institutional tests. 30 credit hours maximum toward associate degree. **Support services:** Learning center, reduced course load, remedial instruction, study skills assistance, tutoring, writing center.

Majors. Agriculture: General. **Biology:** General. **Business:** Business admin. **Computer sciences:** Computer science. **Education:** General, business, multi-level teacher. **Family/consumer sciences:** General. **Foreign languages:** Translation. **Health:** Prenursing. **History:** General. **Liberal arts:** Arts/sciences. **Math:** General. **Parks/recreation:** General, exercise sciences, health/fitness. **Physical sciences:** Chemistry, geology. **Protective services:** Criminal justice. **Psychology:** General. **Social sciences:** Anthropology, criminology, political science, sociology. **Visual/performing arts:** Art.

Computing on campus. 271 workstations in library, computer center, student center. Commuter students can connect to campus network. Online course registration, online library, helpline, wireless network available.

Student life. Freshman orientation: Mandatory. Preregistration for classes offered. Combined 1-day orientation and registration event. **Policies:** Substance-free campus. **Activities:** Campus ministries, choral groups, drama, international student organizations, literary magazine, student government, student newspaper, Afro-American union, Earth Club, Students in Free Enterprise, Student Professional Association of Georgia Educators, art club, Circle K, Non-Traditonal Club, ECHO Club, nursing club, Pursuit Club.

Athletics. Intercollegiate: Wrestling M. **Intramural:** Basketball, football (non-tackle) M, softball, table tennis, tennis, volleyball. **Team name:** Bobcats.

Student services. Adult student services, career counseling, financial aid counseling, minority student services, personal counseling, veterans' counselor. **Physically disabled:** Services for visually, hearing impaired. **Transfer:** Pre-admission transcript evaluation for new students. Transfer adviser, college fairs on campus for students transferring to 4-year colleges.

Contact. E-mail: kjones@ega.edu
Phone: (478) 289-2017 Fax: (478) 289-2140
Karen Jones, Director of Admissions, East Georgia College, 131 College Circle, Swainsboro, GA 30401-2699

Everest Institute
Atlanta, Georgia
www.georgia-med.com

- For-profit 2-year health science college
- Very large city

General. Accredited by ACCSCT. **Enrollment:** 600 degree-seeking undergraduates. **Degrees:** 41 associate awarded. **Calendar:** Continuous. **Full-time faculty:** 13 total. **Part-time faculty:** 12 total.

Basis for selection. Admission based on secondary school record and institutional testing.

Academics. Credit/placement by examination: CLEP.

Majors. Health: Respiratory therapy assistant.

Contact. Phone: (404) 327-8787
Everest Institute, 1706 Northeast Expressway, Atlanta, GA 30329

Gainesville State College
Gainesville, Georgia
www.gsc.edu **CB code: 5273**

- Public 2-year junior college
- Commuter campus in large town

General. Founded in 1964. Regionally accredited. **Enrollment:** 8,035 degree-seeking undergraduates. **Degrees:** 25 bachelor's, 647 associate awarded. **Location:** 45 miles from Atlanta, 40 miles from Athens. **Calendar:** Semester, extensive summer session. **Full-time faculty:** 194 total. **Part-time faculty:** 207 total. **Class size:** 21% < 20, 79% 20-39, less than 1% 40-49, less than 1% 50-99.

Student profile. Among degree-seeking undergraduates, 639 transferred in from other institutions.

Transfer out. Colleges most students transferred to 2008: North Georgia College and State University, University of Georgia, Brenau University, Georgia State University, Georgia Institute of Technology.

Basis for selection. 2.0 GPA required for applicants with college prep curriculum diploma; 2.2 GPA required for applicants with technical prep curriculum diploma. SAT or ACT scores may be used for placement test screening and/or academic advising.

High school preparation. College-preparatory program recommended. 16 units required. Required units include English 4, mathematics 4, social studies 3, science 3 (laboratory 3) and foreign language 2.

2008-2009 Annual costs. Tuition/fees: $2,324; $8,306 out-of-state. Per-credit charge: $84 in-state; $333 out-of-state. Books/supplies: $630. Personal expenses: $1,000.

2007-2008 Financial aid. Need-based: 55% of total undergraduate aid awarded as scholarships/grants, 45% as loans/jobs. Need-based aid available for part-time students. Work-study available nights, weekends and for part-time students. **Non-need-based:** Scholarships awarded for academics, art, leadership, music/drama.

Application procedures. Admission: Closing date 7/1 (postmark date). $25 fee, may be waived for applicants with need. Admission notification on a rolling basis. **Financial aid:** Priority date 6/1; no closing date. FAFSA required. Applicants notified on a rolling basis starting 5/1; must reply within 2 week(s) of notification.

Academics. Special study options: Distance learning, dual enrollment of high school students, ESL, honors, study abroad, teacher certification program. Bachelor's degree programs available on campus. License preparation in dental hygiene, paramedic. **Credit/placement by examination:** AP, CLEP, SAT, ACT, institutional tests. 30 credit hours maximum toward associate degree. **Support services:** Learning center, remedial instruction, study skills assistance, tutoring, writing center.

Majors. Agriculture: General, business. **Business:** General, accounting, administrative services, business admin. **Communications:** Journalism. **Computer sciences:** General. **Conservation:** Forestry. **Education:** General, art, early childhood, elementary, mathematics, music, physical, science, secondary, social science. **Engineering:** General. **Engineering technology:** Electrical. **Family/consumer sciences:** Child care. **Health:** Dental hygiene, EMT paramedic. **History:** General. **Legal studies:** Paralegal. **Liberal arts:** Arts/sciences. **Math:** General. **Physical sciences:** Chemistry, geology, physics. **Protective services:** Criminal justice. **Psychology:** General. **Public administration:** Social work. **Social sciences:** Anthropology, political science, sociology. **Visual/performing arts:** Dramatic, music performance, studio arts.

Computing on campus. 1,000 workstations in library, computer center, student center. Commuter students can connect to campus network. Online course registration, online library, helpline, student web hosting, wireless network available.

Student life. Freshman orientation: Mandatory. Preregistration for classes offered. **Activities:** Bands, choral groups, drama, film society, international student organizations, literary magazine, music ensembles, musical theater, student government, student newspaper.

Athletics. Intramural: Basketball, bowling, football (non-tackle), golf, softball, tennis, volleyball.

Student services. Adult student services, alcohol/substance abuse counseling, career counseling, student employment services, financial aid counseling, minority student services, personal counseling, placement for graduates, veterans' counselor. **Physically disabled:** Services for visually, speech, hearing impaired. **Transfer:** Transfer adviser, college fairs on campus for students transferring to 4-year colleges.

Contact. E-mail: admissions@gsc.edu
Phone: (678) 717-3641 Fax: (678) 717-3643
Mack Palmour, Director of Admissions, Gainesville State College, PO Box 1358, Gainesville, GA 30503

Georgia Highlands College

Rome, Georgia
www.highlands.edu
'CB member
CB code: 5237

- Public 2-year community and liberal arts college
- Commuter campus in small city

General. Founded in 1968. Regionally accredited. Classes offered at Cartersville, Marietta, Paulding County, and Rome. **Enrollment:** 4,700 degree-seeking undergraduates. **Degrees:** 390 associate awarded. **Location:** 75 miles from Atlanta. **Calendar:** Semester, limited summer session. **Full-time faculty:** 85 total. **Part-time faculty:** 110 total. **Special facilities:** Observatory, wetlands preserve.

Student profile. Among degree-seeking undergraduates, 9% enrolled in a transfer program, 1,206 enrolled as first-time, first-year students.

Part-time:	43%	**Asian American:**	2%
Women:	62%	**Hispanic American:**	4%
African American:	11%	**25 or older:**	22%

Transfer out. Colleges most students transferred to 2008: Kennesaw State University, State University of West Georgia, Berry College, Shorter College, University of Georgia.

Basis for selection. 2.0 college prep or 2.2 technical prep GPA required. SAT or ACT required for admissions into nursing and dental hygiene programs. SAT or ACT can be used to exempt COMPASS placement examinations. **Homeschooled:** Statement describing homeschool structure and mission, transcript of courses and grades, state high school equivalency certificate required. Must submit SAT scores that are equal to or greater than last year's freshman class average and provide completed home school college prep curriculum evaluation form; portfolio required. **Learning Disabled:** Foreign language college preparatory curriculum may be waived through Georgia Board of Regents Center of Learning Disabilities.

High school preparation. College-preparatory program recommended. 16 units recommended. Recommended units include English 4, mathematics 4, social studies 3, science 3 (laboratory 2) and foreign language 2. College preparatory program required for students planning to transfer to 4-year school.

2008-2009 Annual costs. Tuition/fees: $2,056; $7,558 out-of-state. Per-credit charge: $77 in-state; $306 out-of-state. Books/supplies: $750. Personal expenses: $550.

2007-2008 Financial aid. Need-based: Need-based aid available for part-time students. Work-study available nights and for part-time students. **Non-need-based:** Scholarships awarded for academics, art.

Application procedures. Admission: Priority date 7/1; no deadline. $20 fee, may be waived for applicants with need. Admission notification on a rolling basis beginning on or about 1/2. **Financial aid:** Closing date 4/1. FAFSA required. Applicants notified on a rolling basis starting 4/1; must reply within 2 week(s) of notification.

Academics. All classrooms and many common areas wired for computer usage. **Special study options:** Accelerated study, cooperative education, distance learning, double major, dual enrollment of high school students, independent study, liberal arts/career combination, study abroad. License preparation in dental hygiene, nursing. **Credit/placement by examination:** AP, CLEP, SAT, ACT, institutional tests. **Support services:** Learning center, remedial instruction, study skills assistance, tutoring, writing center.

Majors. Agriculture: Horticultural science, landscaping. **Biology:** General. **Business:** General, administrative services, hospitality/recreation. **Communications:** General, journalism. **Computer sciences:** General. **Education:** General, multi-level teacher. **Foreign languages:** Sign language interpretation. **Health:** Dental hygiene, EMT paramedic, health services, medical radiologic technology/radiation therapy, medical records admin, nursing (RN), premedicine, prepharmacy, preveterinary, respiratory therapy technology. **Legal studies:** Paralegal. **Liberal arts:** Arts/sciences. **Math:** General. **Mechanic/repair:** Auto body. **Physical sciences:** Chemistry. **Protective services:** Police science. **Psychology:** General. **Social sciences:** General, urban studies.

Most popular majors. Business/marketing 17%, education 28%, health sciences 30%, liberal arts 8%.

Computing on campus. Commuter students can connect to campus network. Online library, helpline, repair service, wireless network available.

Student life. Freshman orientation: Mandatory. **Policies:** Access program tracks all student involvement in school and community activities. Transcripts available for resume use or when transferring to another institution. **Housing:** Housing available through Southern Poly Tech University for Marietta Campus. **Activities:** Literary magazine, student government, student newspaper, TV station, Baptist student union, College Bowl Team, volunteer opportunity center, black student awareness, Insiders, Phi Theta Kappa.

Athletics. Intramural: Archery, badminton, basketball, bowling, field hockey W, football (tackle) M, golf, sailing, skiing, soccer, softball, table tennis, tennis, volleyball, wrestling M. **Team name:** Chargers.

Student services. Adult student services, alcohol/substance abuse counseling, career counseling, student employment services, financial aid counseling, minority student services, personal counseling, placement for graduates, veterans' counselor. **Physically disabled:** Services for visually, speech, hearing impaired. **Transfer:** Re-entry adviser, pre-admission transcript evaluation for new students. College fairs on campus for students transferring to 4-year colleges.

Contact. E-mail: admitme@highlands.edu
Phone: (706) 295-6339 Toll-free number: (800) 332-2406 ext. 6339
Fax: (706) 295-6341
Todd Jones, Director of Admissions, Georgia Highlands College, 3175 Cedartown Highway, Rome, GA 30161

Georgia Military College

Milledgeville, Georgia
www.gmc.cc.ga.us
CB code: 5249

- Public 2-year community and military college
- Commuter campus in large town

General. Founded in 1879. Regionally accredited. Multiple location institution. **Enrollment:** 5,047 degree-seeking undergraduates; 319 non-degree-seeking students. **Degrees:** 514 associate awarded. **ROTC:** Army. **Location:** 90 miles from Atlanta, 30 miles from Macon. **Calendar:** Quarter, limited summer session. **Full-time faculty:** 101 total; 15% have terminal degrees, 14% minority, 50% women. **Part-time faculty:** 265 total; 14% have terminal degrees, 24% minority, 59% women. **Class size:** 70% < 20, 30% 20-39.

Student profile. Among degree-seeking undergraduates, 3,123 enrolled as first-time, first-year students.

Part-time:	26%	**Hispanic American:**	2%
Out-of-state:	4%	**Native American:**	1%
Women:	63%	**25 or older:**	31%
African American:	40%	**Live on campus:**	2%
Asian American:	2%		

Basis for selection. Open admission, but selective for some programs. ROTC applicants for early commissioning must have 920 SAT (exclusive of Writing) or 19 ACT and 2.0 GPA. Interview recommended for ROTC cadets. **Homeschooled:** Transcript of courses and grades required. List of courses completed and bibliography of textbooks and/or assigned readings required. Must submit writing sample or show successful GED completion.

2008-2009 Annual costs. Tuition/fees: $6,300. Per-credit charge: $102. Tuition and fees for cadet students: $12,150 with $1,150 additional for uniforms. Room/board: $5,535. Books/supplies: $1,275. Personal expenses: $600.

2007-2008 Financial aid. Need-based: Need-based aid available for part-time students. Work-study available nights and for part-time students. **Non-need-based:** Scholarships awarded for athletics, leadership, ROTC, state residency. **Additional information:** Institutional aid offered to those enrolled in Cadet Corps who reside on campus.

Application procedures. Admission: Priority date 8/1; deadline 9/1 (receipt date). $35 fee, may be waived for applicants with need. Admission notification on a rolling basis. August 1 closing date for cadets. Students interested in attending ROTC Basic Camp must apply by May 1. **Financial aid:** No deadline. FAFSA required. Applicants notified on a rolling basis starting 3/1.

Academics. **Special study options:** Cross-registration, double major, external degree, independent study. **Credit/placement by examination:** AP, CLEP, institutional tests. 45 credit hours maximum toward associate degree. **Support services:** Learning center, reduced course load, remedial instruction, study skills assistance, tutoring.

Majors. **Business:** Business admin, logistics. **Computer sciences:** General. **Education:** General, early childhood, kindergarten/preschool, secondary. **Family/consumer sciences:** Family studies. **Health:** Health services, prenursing, public health ed. **History:** General. **Mechanic/repair:** Aircraft powerplant. **Protective services:** Emergency management/homeland security, law enforcement admin. **Psychology:** General. **Social sciences:** General, international relations.

Most popular majors. Business/marketing 18%, education 10%, health sciences 12%.

Computing on campus. 403 workstations in dormitories, library, computer center, student center. Dormitories wired for high-speed internet access and linked to campus network. Online library available.

Student life. **Freshman orientation:** Available. Preregistration for classes offered. Two summer orientation sessions, college athlete session, early commissioning session, state service scholarship session available. **Policies:** Resident programs only available to members of Corps of Cadets. **Housing:** Single-sex dorms, wellness housing available. $75 fully refundable deposit, deadline 9/1. **Activities:** Marching band, choral groups, drama, literary magazine, student government, student newspaper, Circle-K, Phi Theta Kappa, Alpha Phi Omega, Ranger Challenge, drill team, drama club, officer Christians' fellowship, business club, math club, debate/speech organization.

Athletics. NJCAA. **Intercollegiate:** Cross-country, football (tackle) M, golf, rifle, soccer, track and field. **Intramural:** Badminton, basketball, bowling, golf, softball, volleyball. **Team name:** Bulldogs.

Student services. Alcohol/substance abuse counseling, career counseling, financial aid counseling, health services, personal counseling, veterans' counselor. **Physically disabled:** Services for visually, speech, hearing impaired.

Contact. E-mail: admissionsinfo@gmc.cc.ga.us
Phone: (478) 445-2707 Toll-free number: (800) 342-0413
Fax: (478) 445-2688
Donna Findley, Director of Admissions and Enrollments, Georgia Military College, 201 East Greene Street, Milledgeville, GA 31061

Georgia Perimeter College

Clarkston, Georgia — **CB member**
www.gpc.edu — **CB code: 5711**

- Public 2-year junior and liberal arts college
- Commuter campus in very large city

General. Founded in 1964. Regionally accredited. Additional campuses in Alpharetta, Dunwoody, Decatur, Newton, and online. **Enrollment:** 21,036 degree-seeking undergraduates; 1,772 non-degree-seeking students. **Degrees:** 1,610 associate awarded. **Calendar:** Semester, extensive summer session. **Full-time faculty:** 338 total; 36% have terminal degrees, 30% minority, 60% women. **Part-time faculty:** 824 total; 25% have terminal degrees, 43% minority, 54% women. **Class size:** 24% < 20, 72% 20-39, 2% 40-49, less than 1% 50-99, less than 1% >100. **Special facilities:** Botanical gardens.

Student profile. Among degree-seeking undergraduates, 98% enrolled in a transfer program, 2% enrolled in a vocational program, 1% already have a bachelor's degree or higher, 4,630 enrolled as first-time, first-year students, 1,347 transferred in from other institutions.

Part-time:	54%	**Asian American:**	8%
Out-of-state:	10%	**Hispanic American:**	5%
Women:	61%	**International:**	5%
African American:	41%	**25 or older:**	31%

Transfer out. **Colleges most students transferred to 2008:** Georgia State University, University of Georgia.

Basis for selection. Admission based on high school GPA. Any college preparatory curriculum deficiencies must be satisfied by placement testing or substituting college coursework. COMPASS used for placement in English, reading, and math. SAT or ACT scores used as supplements to COMPASS results for English and reading. Satisfactory SAT or ACT scores may exempt some students from English and reading placement testing. SAT/ACT scores required of joint enrollment students. Interview required of nursing and dental hygiene majors. **Homeschooled:** Transcript of courses and grades required. A detailed portfolio must be submitted. SAT/ACT scores required.

High school preparation. 16 units required. Required units include English 4, mathematics 4, social studies 3, science 3 (laboratory 2) and foreign language 2.

2008-2009 Annual costs. Tuition/fees: $2,322; $7,824 out-of-state. Per-credit charge: $77 in-state; $306 out-of-state. Books/supplies: $1,400. Personal expenses: $1,200.

2007-2008 Financial aid. **Need-based:** Need-based aid available for part-time students. Work-study available nights, weekends and for part-time students.

Application procedures. **Admission:** Closing date 7/1 (postmark date). $20 fee, may be waived for applicants with need. Admission notification on a rolling basis. **Financial aid:** Closing date 6/1. FAFSA required. Applicants notified on a rolling basis; must reply within 3 week(s) of notification.

Academics. **Special study options:** Accelerated study, distance learning, double major, ESL, honors, liberal arts/career combination, study abroad, weekend college. Bachelor's degree programs available on campus. License preparation in dental hygiene, nursing. **Credit/placement by examination:** AP, CLEP, IB, SAT, ACT, institutional tests. 21 credit hours maximum toward associate degree. **Support services:** Learning center, remedial instruction, study skills assistance, tutoring, writing center.

Majors. **Biology:** General. **Business:** Business admin. **Communications:** General, journalism. **Computer sciences:** Computer science. **Education:** General, health, physical. **Engineering:** General. **Foreign languages:** General, sign language interpretation. **Health:** Dental hygiene, nursing (RN), predental, premedicine, prepharmacy. **History:** General. **Liberal arts:** Library science. **Math:** General. **Philosophy/religion:** Philosophy. **Physical sciences:** Chemistry, geology, physics. **Protective services:** Fire services admin, law enforcement admin. **Psychology:** General. **Social sciences:** Anthropology, political science, sociology. **Visual/performing arts:** Art, dramatic, film/cinema.

Most popular majors. Business/marketing 36%, education 14%, health sciences 12%, liberal arts 9%, psychology 8%, social sciences 7%.

Computing on campus. Commuter students can connect to campus network. Online course registration, online library, helpline, wireless network available.

Student life. **Freshman orientation:** Mandatory. Preregistration for classes offered. 6 hour program. **Activities:** Bands, choral groups, drama, international student organizations, literary magazine, music ensembles, Model UN, musical theater, student government, student newspaper, symphony orchestra, Campus Crusade for Christ, Muslim student association, math club, drama club, computer club.

Athletics. NJCAA. **Intercollegiate:** Baseball M, basketball, soccer, softball W, tennis. **Team name:** Jaguars.

Student services. Adult student services, career counseling, services for economically disadvantaged, financial aid counseling, minority student services, personal counseling, veterans' counselor. **Physically disabled:** Services for visually, hearing impaired. **Transfer:** Transfer adviser, college fairs on campus for students transferring to 4-year colleges.

Contact. Phone: (678) 891-3250 Toll-free number: (888) 696-2780
Fax: (404) 299-4574
Douglas Ruch, College Registrar, Georgia Perimeter College, 555 North Indian Creek Drive, Clarkston, GA 30021-2361

Gordon College

Barnesville, Georgia — **CB member**
www.gdn.edu — **CB code: 5256**

- Public 2-year junior college
- Commuter campus in small town

General. Founded in 1852. Regionally accredited. **Enrollment:** 3,794 degree-seeking undergraduates; 61 non-degree-seeking students. **Degrees:** 415 associate awarded. **Location:** 60 miles from Atlanta. **Calendar:** Semester, limited summer session. **Full-time faculty:** 102 total; 17% minority, 51% women. **Part-time faculty:** 83 total; 12% minority, 60% women. **Class size:** 14% < 20, 84% 20-39, 1% 40-49, less than 1% 50-99. **Special facilities:** Georgia book collection, performance theater, indoor pool, ropes course, walking trail, amphitheatre.

Two-Year Colleges

Student profile. Among degree-seeking undergraduates, 1,259 enrolled as first-time, first-year students.

Part-time:	30%	**25 or older:**	19%
Out-of-state:	1%	**Live on campus:**	26%
Women:	66%		

Transfer out. Colleges most students transferred to 2008: Clayton State University, Georgia State University, Griffin Technical College, University of Georgia, University of West Georgia.

Basis for selection. Test scores and GPA considered. Additional requirements for associate degree in nursing and bachelor's of science in education. SAT or ACT, SAT Subject Tests recommended. Interview required for nursing program. Applicants may be asked to interview for admission to B.S. in Education program. **Adult students:** COMPASS placement test used if applicant presents SAT/ACT scores lower than minimum required or if applicant lacks scores. **Homeschooled:** Statement describing homeschool structure and mission required. Portfolio demonstrating completion of college prep curriculum required. Include the following for each course: course descriptions, list of assignments, work samples and grades, and list of educational resources (textbooks and other materials).

High school preparation. College-preparatory program recommended. 16 units recommended. Recommended units include English 4, mathematics 4, social studies 3, science 3 (laboratory 2) and foreign language 2. Foreign language units must be in same language.

2008-2009 Annual costs. Tuition/fees: $2,362; $8,344 out-of-state. Per-credit charge: $84 in-state; $333 out-of-state. Room/board: $4,560. Books/supplies: $950. Personal expenses: $903.

2007-2008 Financial aid. Need-based: Need-based aid available for part-time students. Work-study available nights, weekends and for part-time students. **Non-need-based:** Scholarships awarded for academics, athletics, music/drama, state residency.

Application procedures. Admission: No deadline. $20 fee. Admission notification on a rolling basis. **Financial aid:** Priority date 5/1; no closing date. FAFSA, institutional form required. Applicants notified on a rolling basis starting 5/1.

Academics. Special study options: Distance learning, dual enrollment of high school students, ESL, honors, liberal arts/career combination, study abroad. Bachelor's degree programs available on campus. **Credit/placement by examination:** AP, CLEP, IB, SAT, ACT, institutional tests. 42 credit hours maximum toward associate degree.

Majors. Biology: General. **Business:** Business admin. **Communications:** General. **Computer sciences:** Computer science, information systems. **Conservation:** Environmental science, forestry. **Education:** Multi-level teacher. **Foreign languages:** General. **Health:** Dental hygiene, medical records admin, nuclear medical technology, nursing (RN), physician assistant, prepharmacy, radiologic technology/medical imaging, respiratory therapy assistant, sonography. **History:** General. **Math:** General. **Parks/recreation:** Health/fitness. **Physical sciences:** General, astronomy, chemistry, physics. **Protective services:** Criminal justice. **Psychology:** General. **Public administration:** Social work. **Social sciences:** Political science, sociology. **Visual/performing arts:** Art, dramatic. **Other:** Pre-occupational therapy.

Most popular majors. Business/marketing 19%, education 18%, health sciences 31%, psychology 9%, social sciences 7%.

Computing on campus. 242 workstations in dormitories, library, computer center, student center. Dormitories wired for high-speed internet access and linked to campus network. Commuter students can connect to campus network. Online course registration, online library, student web hosting, wireless network available.

Student life. Freshman orientation: Mandatory. Preregistration for classes offered. Approximately 5-6 hours in length; held twice prior to start of semester, for students and parents. **Housing:** Coed dorms, single-sex dorms, apartments, wellness housing available. $250 partly refundable deposit, deadline 7/1. **Activities:** Bands, campus ministries, choral groups, dance, drama, international student organizations, literary magazine, music ensembles, musical theater, student government, student newspaper, Baptist Collegiate Ministries, Gordon Christian Fellowship, Association of Nursing Students, art club, education association, Driftwood literary club, Phi Theta Kappa (honor society), science club, history club.

Athletics. NJCAA. **Intercollegiate:** Baseball M, basketball M, cheerleading M, cross-country, soccer, softball W, tennis W. **Intramural:** Basketball M, football (non-tackle), soccer, softball, table tennis. **Team name:** Highlanders.

Student services. Alcohol/substance abuse counseling, career counseling, student employment services, financial aid counseling, health services, minority student services, personal counseling, veterans' counselor. **Physically disabled:** Services for visually, speech, hearing impaired. **Transfer:** College fairs on campus for students transferring to 4-year colleges.

Contact. E-mail: admissions@gdn.edu
Phone: (678) 359-5021 Toll-free number: (800) 282-6504
Fax: (770) 358-5080
Lisa Shiveler, Director of Admissions, Gordon College, 419 College Drive, Barnesville, GA 30204

Griffin Technical College

Griffin, Georgia
www.griffintech.edu — **CB code: 5670**

- Public 2-year technical college
- Small city

General. Regionally accredited. **Enrollment:** 3,859 degree-seeking undergraduates; 315 non-degree-seeking students. **Degrees:** 221 associate awarded. **Calendar:** Quarter. **Full-time faculty:** 68 total. **Part-time faculty:** 172 total.

Student profile. Among degree-seeking undergraduates, 866 enrolled as first-time, first-year students.

Part-time:	52%	**Asian American:**	1%
Women:	68%	**Hispanic American:**	2%
African American:	39%		

Basis for selection. Open admission, but selective for some programs. Admission criteria vary by program. Must take admissions test if you have not taken the ACT, SAT, CPE, COMPASS or ASSET within the last five years.

High school preparation. College-preparatory program recommended. 22 units recommended. Recommended units include English 4, mathematics 3, social studies 3, science 3, foreign language 1 and academic electives 3. 4 tech prep, 1 science recommended.

2008-2009 Annual costs. Tuition/fees: $1,539; $2,835 out-of-state. Per-credit charge: $36 in-state; $72 out-of-state. Books/supplies: $150. Personal expenses: $587.

Application procedures. Admission: No deadline. $15 fee. **Financial aid:** FAFSA, institutional form required. Applicants notified on a rolling basis.

Academics. Special study options: Distance learning, double major, dual enrollment of high school students, weekend college. **Credit/placement by examination:** CLEP. **Support services:** GED preparation and test center.

Majors. Business: Accounting, administrative services, business admin, management science. **Computer sciences:** General, information systems. **Engineering technology:** Electrical. **Health:** Radiologic technology/medical imaging. **Protective services:** Law enforcement admin.

Most popular majors. Business/marketing 22%, computer/information sciences 16%, education 9%, health sciences 26%, security/protective services 14%, trade and industry 6%.

Contact. Phone: (770) 228-7348 Fax: (770) 229-3227
Xenia Johns, Director of Admissions, Griffin Technical College, 501 Varsity Road, Griffin, GA 30223

Gupton Jones College of Funeral Service

Decatur, Georgia
www.gupton-jones.edu — **CB code: 6200**

- Private 2-year technical college
- Commuter campus in very large city

General. Founded in 1920. Accredited by American Board of Funeral Service Education. **Enrollment:** 135 degree-seeking undergraduates. **Degrees:** 85 associate awarded. **Location:** 18 miles from Atlanta. **Calendar:** Quarter. **Full-time faculty:** 7 total; 29% women. **Part-time faculty:** 1 total; 100% women.

Student profile. Among degree-seeking undergraduates, 75 enrolled as first-time, first-year students.

Out-of-state:	65%	**25 or older:**	50%
Women:	47%		

Basis for selection. Open admission.

2008-2009 Annual costs. Tuition/fees: $9,000. Per-credit charge: $200. Tuition costs include all textbooks and supplies needed. Personal expenses: $500.

Financial aid. All financial aid based on need. Need-based aid available for part-time students.

Application procedures. Admission: No deadline. $50 fee. Admission notification on a rolling basis. **Financial aid:** No deadline. FAFSA required. Applicants notified on a rolling basis.

Academics. Special study options: Distance learning. Distance learning for General Studies courses only. **Credit/placement by examination:** CLEP.

Majors. Personal/culinary services: Embalming, funeral direction, mortuary science.

Computing on campus. 23 workstations in library, computer center.

Student life. Freshman orientation: Mandatory. Preregistration for classes offered.

Student services. Career counseling, student employment services, personal counseling, placement for graduates.

Contact. E-mail: gjcfs@mindspring.com
Phone: (770) 593-2257 Fax: (770) 593-1891
Patty Hutcheson, President, Gupton Jones College of Funeral Service, 5141 Snapfinger Woods Drive, Decatur, GA 30035

Gwinnett College

Lilburn, Georgia
www.gwinnettcollege.edu

- For-profit 2-year junior and career college
- Commuter campus in large city

General. Accredited by ACICS. 3 locations near Atlanta (Lilburn, Sandy Springs, Marietta) and one in Raleigh, North Carolina. **Enrollment:** 360 degree-seeking undergraduates. **Degrees:** 60 associate awarded. **Location:** 20 miles from Atlanta. **Calendar:** Quarter, extensive summer session. **Full-time faculty:** 7 total. **Part-time faculty:** 35 total.

Transfer out. Colleges most students transferred to 2008: DeVry University, Argosy University, University of Phoenix, Colorado Tech Online, Strayer University.

Basis for selection. Open admission, but selective for some programs. Aptitude testing required for some programs. **Homeschooled:** Transcript of courses and grades required.

2009-2010 Annual costs. Tuition/fees: $8,725.

2008-2009 Financial aid. Need-based: Need-based aid available for part-time students.

Application procedures. Admission: No deadline. No application fee. Application must be submitted on paper. **Financial aid:** FAFSA required.

Academics. Special study options: Combined bachelor's/graduate degree, double major, internships. **Credit/placement by examination:** CLEP. **Support services:** Reduced course load.

Majors. Business: Business admin. **Computer sciences:** Information technology. **Health:** Medical assistant, medical secretary. **Legal studies:** Paralegal.

Computing on campus. PC or laptop required. 100 workstations in library, computer center. Wireless network available.

Student services. Adult student services, financial aid counseling, placement for graduates. **Transfer:** Re-entry adviser, pre-admission transcript evaluation for new students.

Contact. E-mail: admissions@gwinnettcollege.edu
Phone: (770) 381-7200 Fax: (770) 381-0454
Lee Cates, Director of Admissions, Gwinnett College, 4230 Highway 29, Lilburn, GA 30047

Gwinnett Technical College

Lawrenceville, Georgia — **CB member**
www.gwinnetttech.edu — **CB code: 5168**

- Public 2-year technical college
- Commuter campus in large town

General. Founded in 1984. Regionally accredited. Internships available with several manufacturers and companies, including Toyota, Nissan, Chrysler, and General Motors. **Enrollment:** 5,120 degree-seeking undergraduates; 263 non-degree-seeking students. **Degrees:** 329 associate awarded. **Location:** 25 miles from Atlanta. **Calendar:** Quarter, extensive summer session. **Full-time faculty:** 71 total. **Part-time faculty:** 135 total. **Class size:** 46% < 20, 51% 20-39, 2% 40-49, less than 1% 50-99. **Special facilities:** Media center, studio, seminar room containing microcomputers and multimedia compilers.

Student profile. Among degree-seeking undergraduates, 846 enrolled as first-time, first-year students.

Part-time:	53%	**Asian American:**	7%
Women:	56%	**Hispanic American:**	7%
African American:	28%		

Basis for selection. Open admission, but selective for some programs. Selection criteria vary by program. Competitive screening process for some health science programs. ACT or SAT may be accepted in lieu of COMPASS or ASSET for placement. Interview required of carpentry, automotive, machine tools, drafting majors and health science program applicants.

High school preparation. College-preparatory program recommended. 22 units recommended. Recommended units include English 4, mathematics 3, social studies 3, science 3, foreign language 1 and academic electives 3. 4 tech prep, 1 health science recommended.

2008-2009 Annual costs. Tuition/fees: $1,605; $2,901 out-of-state. Per-credit charge: $36 in-state; $72 out-of-state. Books/supplies: $1,600. Personal expenses: $2,800.

2008-2009 Financial aid. Need-based: Need-based aid available for part-time students.

Application procedures. Admission: Closing date 8/15. $20 fee. Admission notification on a rolling basis. Application closing date of 1/15 for some health sciences programs. **Financial aid:** Closing date 7/1. FAFSA required.

Academics. Special study options: Distance learning, dual enrollment of high school students, ESL, weekend college. License preparation in dental hygiene, nursing, paramedic, physical therapy, radiology, real estate. **Credit/placement by examination:** AP, CLEP, institutional tests. **Support services:** GED preparation and test center, learning center, remedial instruction, study skills assistance, tutoring, writing center.

Majors. Biology: Biotechnology. **Business:** Accounting, administrative services, construction management, fashion, human resources, marketing, office management, office technology, restaurant/food services, tourism/travel. **Computer sciences:** LAN/WAN management, programming, security, web page design. **Construction:** General, site management. **Engineering technology:** Drafting. **Health:** Dental lab technology, EMT paramedic, health services, medical radiologic technology/radiation therapy, radiologic technology/medical imaging, respiratory therapy technology, veterinary technology/assistant. **Mechanic/repair:** Automotive. **Personal/culinary services:** Culinary arts. **Production:** Woodworking. **Protective services:** Firefighting, police science. **Visual/performing arts:** Commercial photography, interior design, photography.

Most popular majors. Business/marketing 33%, computer/information sciences 18%, health sciences 21%, visual/performing arts 7%.

Computing on campus. 120 workstations in library, computer center, student center. Commuter students can connect to campus network. Online course registration, helpline, repair service, wireless network available.

Student life. Freshman orientation: Mandatory. Preregistration for classes offered. One-hour mandatory session, four 30-minute breakout sessions on advisement, financial aid, registration, and online classes. **Activities:** Student government, student newspaper.

Student services. Adult student services, career counseling, student employment services, financial aid counseling, placement for graduates, veterans' counselor. **Physically disabled:** Services for visually, speech, hearing impaired.

Contact. Phone: (770) 962-7580 ext. 6616 Fax: (770) 685-1267
Florance Halloran, Director of Admissions, Gwinnett Technical College, 5150 Sugarloaf Parkway, Lawrenceville, GA 30243

High-Tech Institute
Marietta, Georgia
www.high-techinstitute.com

- For-profit 2-year technical college
- Commuter campus in very large city

General. Accredited by ACCSCT. **Calendar:** Continuous.

Contact. Phone: (770) 988-9877
Director of Admissions, 1090 Northchase Parkway, Marietta, GA 30067

ITT Technical Institute: Kennesaw
Kennesaw, Georgia

- For-profit 2-year business and technical college
- Large town

General. Accredited by ACICS. **Calendar:** Quarter.

Contact. 1000 Cobb Place Boulevard NW, Kennesaw, GA 30144

Le Cordon Bleu College of Culinary Arts
Tucker, Georgia
www.atlantaculinary.com

- For-profit 2-year branch campus and technical college
- Commuter campus in very large city
- Interview required

General. Accredited by ACCSCT. **Enrollment:** 1,035 degree-seeking undergraduates. **Degrees:** 436 associate awarded. **Location:** 10 miles from Atlanta. **Calendar:** Continuous. **Full-time faculty:** 38 total. **Part-time faculty:** 2 total.

Basis for selection. Open admission. Documentation of high school graduation or GED only requirement.

2008-2009 Annual costs. Total cost of accelerated 15-month associate degree program including tuition, books, toolkit, uniforms $39,500. Total cost of 12-month certificate program in patisserie and baking $20,425.

Application procedures. Admission: No deadline. $50 fee. Application must be submitted on paper. Admission notification on a rolling basis.

Academics. Credit/placement by examination: AP, CLEP. **Support services:** Study skills assistance, tutoring.

Majors. Personal/culinary services: Culinary arts.

Computing on campus. Online library available.

Student life. Freshman orientation: Mandatory.

Student services. Adult student services, career counseling, student employment services, financial aid counseling, placement for graduates. **Transfer:** Re-entry adviser for new students.

Contact. Phone: (770) 938-4711 Toll-free number: (866) 315-2433
Fax: (773) 938-4571
Terri Holte, Vice President of Admissions, Le Cordon Bleu College of Culinary Arts, 1927 Lakeside Parkway, Tucker, GA 30084

Middle Georgia College
Cochran, Georgia
www.mgc.edu **CB code: 5411**

- Public 2-year junior college
- Commuter campus in small town

General. Founded in 1884. Regionally accredited. **Enrollment:** 3,111 degree-seeking undergraduates. **Degrees:** 349 associate awarded. **Location:** 39 miles from Macon. **Calendar:** Semester, limited summer session. **Full-time faculty:** 113 total. **Part-time faculty:** 54 total. **Class size:** 38% < 20, 59% 20-39, less than 1% 40-49, 2% 50-99.

Student profile.

Out-of-state:	6%	**Live on campus:**	30%
25 or older:	25%		

Transfer out. Colleges most students transferred to 2008: Georgia College and State University, Macon College, Valdosta State University, Georgia Military College.

Basis for selection. Students graduating with college prep diploma must have 2.0 academic core GPA. Students graduating with tech prep/vocational/general diploma must have 2.2 academic core GPA. Students with college preparatory deficiencies may submit SAT Subject Tests scores in the area of deficiencies. Interview and essay required for applicants to Georgia Academy of Mathematics, Engineering, and Science Program. **Homeschooled:** Transcript of courses and grades required. Students must submit homeschooled application and obtain 920 SAT (exclusive of writing) or 19 ACT.

High school preparation. 13 units required; 16 recommended. Required and recommended units include English 4, mathematics 3-4, social studies 1, history 2, science 3 (laboratory 2) and foreign language 2.

2008-2009 Annual costs. Tuition/fees: $2,368; $8,350 out-of-state. Per-credit charge: $84 in-state; $333 out-of-state. Room/board: $4,800. Books/supplies: $800. Personal expenses: $600.

2007-2008 Financial aid. Need-based: Need-based aid available for part-time students. Work-study available nights, weekends and for part-time students. **Non-need-based:** Scholarships awarded for academics, alumni affiliation, art, athletics, job skills, leadership, minority status, music/drama, state residency.

Application procedures. Admission: Closing date 7/20 (receipt date). $20 fee, may be waived for applicants with need. Admission notification on a rolling basis. **Financial aid:** Priority date 4/1; no closing date. FAFSA required. Applicants notified on a rolling basis starting 5/1.

Academics. Special study options: Accelerated study, cooperative education, distance learning, double major, exchange student, honors, independent study, study abroad, weekend college. Weekend college at Dublin campus only; Georgia Academy of Mathematics, Engineering and Science is 2-year residential joint enrollment program for gifted high school juniors and seniors to pursue associate degree utilizing dual credits. Bachelor's degree programs available on campus. **Credit/placement by examination:** AP, CLEP, institutional tests. 30 credit hours maximum toward associate degree. **Support services:** Learning center, remedial instruction, study skills assistance, tutoring, writing center.

Majors. Agriculture: General. **Architecture:** Environmental design. **Biology:** General. **Business:** Accounting, business admin, human resources, merchandising, office technology, sales/distribution. **Communications:** Journalism. **Computer sciences:** General, applications programming, computer science, data entry, information technology, programming. **Conservation:** Forestry. **Education:** Early childhood, elementary, health, middle, secondary, special. **Engineering:** General, civil, computer, electrical. **Engineering technology:** Aerospace, civil, computer, drafting, manufacturing, surveying. **Family/consumer sciences:** Family studies. **Foreign languages:** General. **Health:** Dental assistant, dental hygiene, licensed practical nurse, medical assistant, medical radiologic technology/radiation therapy, medical records admin, medical records technology, nursing (RN), occupational therapy assistant, pharmacy assistant, physical therapy assistant, predental, premedicine, prenursing, prepharmacy, preveterinary, respiratory therapy technology, surgical technology. **History:** General. **Legal studies:** Prelaw. **Liberal arts:** Arts/sciences. **Math:** General. **Mechanic/repair:** Aircraft, auto body, automotive, electronics/electrical, heating/ac/refrig, industrial. **Parks/recreation:** General, health/fitness. **Physical sciences:** Chemistry, geology, physics. **Protective services:** Criminal justice, police science. **Psychology:** General. **Public administration:** General, social work. **Social sciences:** Economics, political science, sociology. **Visual/performing arts:** Art, dramatic.

Most popular majors. Health sciences 24%, liberal arts 67%.

Computing on campus. 464 workstations in dormitories, library. Dormitories wired for high-speed internet access and linked to campus network. Commuter students can connect to campus network. Online course registration, online library, helpline available.

Student life. Freshman orientation: Available, $15 fee. Preregistration for classes offered. Spring and summer, 1-day orientation. **Policies:** Alcohol not allowed on campus. Students must live with their immediate families or live in college housing unless given permission to live off-campus. **Housing:** Guaranteed on-campus for all undergraduates. Single-sex dorms, wellness housing available. $100 deposit, deadline 7/1. **Activities:** Campus ministries, choral groups, dance, drama, literary magazine, music ensembles, musical theater, student government, student newspaper, Baptist student union, Wesley Foundation, minority alliance club, Rotaract, cultural relations club, Young Republicans, Young Democrats, Fellowship of Christian Athletes.

Athletics. NJCAA. **Intercollegiate:** Baseball M, basketball, cross-country, soccer, softball W. **Intramural:** Badminton, basketball, football (tackle), golf, handball M, rifle M, softball, tennis, volleyball, weight lifting. **Team name:** Warriors.

Student services. Adult student services, alcohol/substance abuse counseling, career counseling, services for economically disadvantaged, student employment services, financial aid counseling, health services, minority student services, personal counseling, veterans' counselor, women's services. **Physically disabled:** Services for visually, hearing impaired. **Learning disabled:** Comprehensive services available. **Transfer:** College fairs on campus for students transferring to 4-year colleges.

Contact. E-mail: admissions@mgc.edu
Phone: (478) 934-3103 Fax: (478) 934-3403
Jennifer Brannon, Director of Admissions, Middle Georgia College, 1100 Second Street SE, Cochran, GA 31014

Middle Georgia Technical College
Warner Robins, Georgia
www.middlegatech.edu **CB code: 5035**

- Public 2-year technical college
- Commuter campus in small city

General. Regionally accredited. **Enrollment:** 2,553 degree-seeking undergraduates; 302 non-degree-seeking students. **Degrees:** 77 associate awarded. **Location:** 105 miles from Atlanta. **Calendar:** Quarter, extensive summer session. **Full-time faculty:** 110 total. **Part-time faculty:** 125 total.

Student profile. Among degree-seeking undergraduates, 3% already have a bachelor's degree or higher, 913 enrolled as first-time, first-year students.

Part-time:	48%	**Asian American:**	1%
Women:	55%	**Hispanic American:**	2%
African American:	36%		

Basis for selection. Open admission, but selective for some programs. Special requirements for allied health programs. Under certain conditions, ACT or SAT may be accepted for placement.

High school preparation. College-preparatory program recommended. 22 units recommended. Recommended units include English 4, mathematics 3, social studies 3, science 3, foreign language 1 and academic electives 3. 4 tech prep and 1 health science recommended.

2008-2009 Annual costs. Tuition/fees: $1,539; $2,835 out-of-state. Per-credit charge: $36 in-state; $72 out-of-state.

Application procedures. Admission: No deadline. $15 fee. **Financial aid:** FAFSA required.

Academics. Associate of Applied Technology degrees are terminal degrees. Courses cannot be transferred to a higher degree level. **Special study options:** Distance learning, dual enrollment of high school students, weekend college. License preparation in aviation, dental hygiene, radiology. **Credit/placement by examination:** AP, CLEP. **Support services:** GED preparation and test center, learning center, remedial instruction, tutoring.

Majors. Business: Accounting technology, marketing, office technology, office/clerical. **Computer sciences:** Computer support specialist, LAN/WAN management. **Engineering technology:** CAD/CADD, electrical. **Health:** Dental hygiene, radiologic technology/medical imaging. **Legal studies:** Paralegal. **Protective services:** Law enforcement admin. **Other:** Criminal justice.

Most popular majors. Business/marketing 43%, computer/information sciences 14%, education 8%, health sciences 18%, trade and industry 14%.

Student life. Freshman orientation: Mandatory.

Athletics. Team name: Titans.

Student services. Career counseling, financial aid counseling.

Contact. E-mail: info@middlegatech.edu
Phone: (478) 988-6850 Toll-free number: (800) 474-1031
Fax: (478) 988-6947
Dann Webb, Director of Admissions, Middle Georgia Technical College, 80 Cohen Walker Drive, Warner Robins, GA 31088

North Georgia Technical College
Clarkesville, Georgia
www.northgatech.edu

- Public 2-year community and technical college
- Commuter campus in large town

General. Regionally accredited. **Enrollment:** 2,036 degree-seeking undergraduates; 55 non-degree-seeking students. **Degrees:** 83 associate awarded. **Calendar:** Quarter, extensive summer session. **Full-time faculty:** 68 total. **Part-time faculty:** 121 total.

Student profile. Among degree-seeking undergraduates, 100% enrolled in a vocational program, 1% already have a bachelor's degree or higher, 584 enrolled as first-time, first-year students.

Part-time:	40%	**Asian American:**	1%
Out-of-state:	2%	**Hispanic American:**	1%
Women:	59%	**25 or older:**	42%
African American:	5%	**Live on campus:**	9%

Basis for selection. Open admission, but selective for some programs. ACT or SAT may be accepted in lieu of COMPASS or ASSET for placement. **Homeschooled:** Statement describing homeschool structure and mission, transcript of courses and grades required. **Learning Disabled:** Documentation of IEP required.

High school preparation. College-preparatory program recommended. 22 units recommended. Recommended units include English 4, mathematics 3, social studies 3, science 3, foreign language 1 and academic electives 3. 4 tech prep and 1 health science recommended.

2008-2009 Annual costs. Tuition/fees: $1,566; $2,862 out-of-state. Per-credit charge: $36 in-state; $72 out-of-state. Higher per-credit-hour charges for some programs. Cost of complete CDL program: $2,914. Books/supplies: $935.

Financial aid. Need-based: Need-based aid available for part-time students. Work-study available nights, weekends and for part-time students.

Application procedures. Admission: No deadline. $15 fee ($72 out-of-state).

Academics. Special study options: Distance learning, dual enrollment of high school students, internships, weekend college. License preparation in nursing, paramedic, real estate. **Credit/placement by examination:** CLEP, institutional tests. 50 credit hours maximum toward associate degree. **Support services:** GED preparation and test center, learning center, remedial instruction, tutoring.

Majors. Agriculture: Turf management. **Business:** Accounting, business admin, office technology. **Computer sciences:** Networking. **Conservation:** Environmental science. **Engineering technology:** Environmental, heat/ac/refrig, industrial. **Health:** Clinical lab technology. **Mechanic/repair:** Heating/ac/refrig. **Personal/culinary services:** Chef training. **Protective services:** Law enforcement admin. **Other:** Computer information systems, Environmental horticulture.

Most popular majors. Agriculture 6%, business/marketing 42%, computer/information sciences 12%, engineering/engineering technologies 7%, health sciences 8%, personal/culinary services 7%, security/protective services 10%, trade and industry 7%.

Computing on campus. Dormitories wired for high-speed internet access and linked to campus network. Commuter students can connect to campus network. Online course registration, online library, wireless network available.

Student life. Freshman orientation: Mandatory. **Housing:** Coed dorms available.

Athletics. Intramural: Basketball, football (tackle), softball. **Team name:** Eagles.

Contact. E-mail: amitchell@northgatech.edu
Phone: (706) 754-7724 Fax: (706) 754-7777
Amanda Mitchell, Director of Admissions, North Georgia Technical College, 1500 Highway 197 North, Clarkesville, GA 30523

Two-Year Colleges

North Metro Technical College
Acworth, Georgia
www.northmetrotech.edu **CB code: 5508**

- Public 2-year technical college
- Large town

General. Regionally accredited. **Enrollment:** 2,350 degree-seeking undergraduates; 162 non-degree-seeking students. **Degrees:** 40 associate awarded. **Calendar:** Quarter. **Full-time faculty:** 34 total. **Part-time faculty:** 76 total.

Student profile. Among degree-seeking undergraduates, 546 enrolled as first-time, first-year students.

Part-time:	54%	**Asian American:**	1%
Women:	61%	**Hispanic American:**	4%
African American:	19%		

Basis for selection. Open admission, but selective for some programs. ACT or SAT may be accepted in lieu of COMPASS or ASSET for placement.

High school preparation. College-preparatory program recommended. 22 units recommended. Recommended units include English 4, mathematics 3, social studies 3, science 3, foreign language 1 and academic electives 3. 4 tech prep and 1 health science recommended.

2008-2009 Annual costs. Tuition/fees: $1,539; $2,835 out-of-state.

Application procedures. Admission: No deadline. $15 fee.

Academics. Special study options: Distance learning, dual enrollment of high school students, weekend college. License preparation in nursing, paramedic, physical therapy, radiology. **Credit/placement by examination:** CLEP. **Support services:** GED preparation and test center, learning center, remedial instruction, study skills assistance, tutoring.

Majors. Computer sciences: General. **Health:** Health services.

Most popular majors. Agriculture 10%, business/marketing 40%, computer/information sciences 8%, education 18%, trade and industry 13%, visual/performing arts 10%.

Contact. E-mail: info@northmetrotech.edu
Phone: (770) 975-4162 Fax: (770) 975-4084
Missy Cusack, Director of Admissions, North Metro Technical College, 5198 Ross Road, Acworth, GA 30102

Northwestern Technical College
Rock Spring, Georgia
www.northwesterntech.edu **CB code: 2860**

- Public 2-year technical college
- Commuter campus in small town

General. Regionally accredited. Offers clinical and in-service work with industry and medical services prior to graduation. **Enrollment:** 1,576 degree-seeking undergraduates; 752 non-degree-seeking students. **Degrees:** 167 associate awarded. **Calendar:** Quarter, limited summer session. **Full-time faculty:** 50 total. **Part-time faculty:** 61 total. **Class size:** 71% < 20, 28% 20-39, less than 1% 40-49.

Student profile. Among degree-seeking undergraduates, 88% enrolled in a vocational program, 2% already have a bachelor's degree or higher, 328 enrolled as first-time, first-year students.

Part-time:	48%	**Hispanic American:**	2%
Women:	60%	**Native American:**	1%
African American:	5%	**25 or older:**	52%

Basis for selection. Open admission, but selective for some programs. Special requirements for nursing, emergency medical technician, licensed practical nursing, medical assistant, occupational therapy assistant, and surgical technology programs. ACT or SAT may be accepted in lieu of COMPASS or ASSET for placement. Some medical survey programs may require interview or essay/personal statement.

High school preparation. College-preparatory program recommended. 22 units recommended. Recommended units include English 4, mathematics 3, social studies 3, science 3, foreign language 1 and academic electives 3. 4 tech prep and 1 health science recommended.

2008-2009 Annual costs. Tuition/fees: $1,539; $2,835 out-of-state. Per-credit charge: $36 in-state; $72 out-of-state. Truck driving and flight technology are higher cost programs. Books/supplies: $900.

Financial aid. Need-based: Need-based aid available for part-time students.

Application procedures. Admission: Priority date 8/15; no deadline. $15 fee. Admission notification on a rolling basis. **Financial aid:** No deadline. FAFSA, institutional form required.

Academics. Online tutoring available anytime. **Special study options:** Distance learning, dual enrollment of high school students, liberal arts/career combination, weekend college. License preparation in nursing, occupational therapy. **Credit/placement by examination:** CLEP, institutional tests. **Support services:** GED preparation and test center, remedial instruction, study skills assistance, tutoring, writing center.

Majors. Architecture: Technology. **Business:** Accounting, business admin, executive assistant, office/clerical. **Communications:** Organizational. **Computer sciences:** General, data entry, data processing, information systems, information technology, LAN/WAN management, networking, programming, web page design, webmaster, word processing. **Education:** Early childhood. **Engineering technology:** Architectural, computer systems, drafting, electrical, industrial, mechanical drafting. **Health:** Cardiovascular technology, medical assistant, nursing (RN), occupational therapy assistant, pharmacy assistant, surgical technology. **Protective services:** Law enforcement admin, police science.

Most popular majors. Business/marketing 24%, computer/information sciences 9%, education 17%, health sciences 34%, security/protective services 9%.

Computing on campus. 300 workstations in library, computer center. Online course registration, helpline, wireless network available.

Student life. Freshman orientation: Mandatory. Preregistration for classes offered. **Activities:** Drama, student government, student newspaper.

Athletics. Team name: Mustangs.

Student services. Adult student services, career counseling, services for economically disadvantaged, student employment services, financial aid counseling, placement for graduates, veterans' counselor, women's services. **Physically disabled:** Services for visually, speech, hearing impaired.

Contact. Phone: (706) 764-3514 Toll-free number: (800) 735-5726
Fax: (706) 764-3707
Stuart Phillips, Director of Admissions and Career Counseling, Northwestern Technical College, 265 Bicentennial Trail, Rock Spring, GA 30739

Oxford College of Emory University
Oxford, Georgia **CB member**
www.oxford.emory.edu **CB code: 5186**

- Private 2-year branch campus and liberal arts college affiliated with United Methodist Church
- Residential campus in large town
- SAT or ACT with writing, application essay required

General. Founded in 1836. Regionally accredited. One of nine schools within Emory University. Students who successfully complete two years at Oxford automatically continue to Emory College to complete bachelor's degree. Selective continuation to Emory School of Business and Emory School of Nursing is also available. **Enrollment:** 753 degree-seeking undergraduates. **Degrees:** 315 associate awarded. **Location:** 38 miles from Atlanta. **Calendar:** Semester, extensive summer session. **Full-time faculty:** 58 total; 81% have terminal degrees, 12% minority, 53% women. **Part-time faculty:** 12 total; 17% have terminal degrees, 33% women. **Class size:** 54% < 20, 46% 20-39. **Special facilities:** Center for international studies, two hospitals, regional primate center, Center for Disease Control.

Student profile. Among degree-seeking undergraduates, 424 enrolled as first-time, first-year students, 3 transferred in from other institutions.

Women:	58%	**Hispanic American:**	5%
African American:	16%	**International:**	5%
Asian American:	27%		

Transfer out. 100% of students enrolled in the transfer program go on to 4-year colleges.

Basis for selection. GED not accepted. High school curriculum and transcript most important, standardized test scores, letters of recommendation, extracurricular activities, and essays also important. **Adult students:** SAT/ACT scores not required if out of high school 1 year(s) or more. **Homeschooled:** Transcript of courses and grades, state high school equivalency certificate required. 3 SAT Subject Tests, including Math, required.

High school preparation. College-preparatory program required. 16 units recommended. Recommended units include English 4, mathematics 4, social studies 3, science 3 (laboratory 3) and foreign language 2. Math units should include geometry and algebra II.

2008-2009 Annual costs. Tuition/fees: $30,062. Per-credit charge: $1,233. Room/board: $8,496. Books/supplies: $1,000.

2007-2008 Financial aid. **Need-based:** 82% of total undergraduate aid awarded as scholarships/grants, 18% as loans/jobs. Need-based aid available for part-time students. Work-study available nights and weekends. **Non-need-based:** Scholarships awarded for academics, leadership, religious affiliation, state residency. **Additional information:** Deadline of November 1 to apply for Oxford College Scholars Program.

Application procedures. **Admission:** Priority date 1/15; no deadline. $50 fee, may be waived for applicants with need. Admission notification on a rolling basis beginning on or about 3/15. Must reply by May 1 or within 3 week(s) if notified thereafter. 11/1 deadline for academic scholars program. **Financial aid:** Priority date 2/1, closing date 3/1. FAFSA, CSS PROFILE required. Applicants notified by 4/1; must reply by 5/1 or within 2 week(s) of notification.

Academics. **Special study options:** Cooperative education, cross-registration, distance learning, double major, dual enrollment of high school students, independent study, internships, liberal arts/career combination, study abroad. **Credit/placement by examination:** AP, CLEP, IB, institutional tests. 16 credit hours maximum toward associate degree. **Support services:** Reduced course load, study skills assistance, tutoring, writing center.

Majors. **Liberal arts:** Arts/sciences.

Computing on campus. 80 workstations in dormitories, library, computer center, student center. Dormitories wired for high-speed internet access and linked to campus network. Commuter students can connect to campus network. Online course registration, online library, helpline, student web hosting, wireless network available.

Student life. **Freshman orientation:** Mandatory, $100 fee. Six-day program held prior to start of school year; includes registration. **Housing:** Guaranteed on-campus for all undergraduates. Coed dorms, single-sex dorms, special housing for disabled, wellness housing available. $75 nonrefundable deposit, deadline 5/1. **Activities:** Campus ministries, choral groups, dance, drama, film society, literary magazine, music ensembles, student government, student newspaper, volunteer club, fellowship club, outdoor club, College Republicans, Circle K, Jewish student union, Catholic student union, Muslim student association, Young Democrats, Hindu student council.

Athletics. NJCAA. **Intercollegiate:** Basketball M, soccer W, tennis. **Intramural:** Basketball, football (non-tackle), table tennis, volleyball. **Team name:** Eagles.

Student services. Alcohol/substance abuse counseling, chaplain/spiritual director, career counseling, financial aid counseling, health services, minority student services, personal counseling, placement for graduates. **Physically disabled:** Services for visually, speech, hearing impaired.

Contact. E-mail: oxadmission@emory.edu
Phone: (770) 784-8328 Toll-free number: (800) 723-8328
Fax: (770) 784-8359
Jennifer Taylor, Dean of Enrollment Services, Oxford College of Emory University, 100 Hamill Street, Oxford, GA 30054-1418

Savannah River College

Augusta, Georgia
www.savannahrivercollege.edu

- For-profit 2-year junior and technical college
- Small city
- Interview required

General. Regionally accredited; also accredited by ACICS. **Enrollment:** 268 degree-seeking undergraduates. **Degrees:** 35 associate awarded. **Calendar:** Quarter. **Full-time faculty:** 7 total; 43% have terminal degrees, 57% minority. **Part-time faculty:** 25 total; 20% have terminal degrees, 72% minority. **Class size:** 96% < 20, 4% 20-39.

Basis for selection. Interview very important. **Homeschooled:** Transcript of courses and grades, state high school equivalency certificate required.

2008-2009 Annual costs. Tuition/fees: $10,495. Books/supplies: $150.

2008-2009 Financial aid. All financial aid based on need. Need-based aid available for part-time students.

Application procedures. **Admission:** No deadline. $50 fee. **Financial aid:** No deadline. FAFSA, institutional form required.

Academics. **Special study options:** Double major, independent study, internships. **Credit/placement by examination:** CLEP. **Support services:** Learning center, reduced course load, study skills assistance, tutoring.

Majors. **Business:** Accounting, administrative services, business admin. **Health:** Insurance specialist, management/clinical assistant, office assistant. **Other:** Microsoft network engineer.

Most popular majors. Business/marketing 19%, computer/information sciences 8%, health sciences 74%.

Computing on campus. 133 workstations in library. Online library available.

Student life. **Freshman orientation:** Mandatory. **Activities:** Student newspaper.

Student services. **Transfer:** Pre-admission transcript evaluation for new students.

Contact. E-mail: info@savannahrivercollege.edu
Phone: (706) 738-5604 Fax: (706) 736-3599
Jeffrey Rainier, Director of Admissions, Savannah River College, 2528 Center West Parkway, Building A, Augusta, GA 30909

Savannah Technical College

Savannah, Georgia
www.savannahtech.edu **CB code: 3741**

- Public 2-year technical college
- Commuter campus in small city

General. Regionally accredited. Classes offered at satellite campuses in Liberty and Effingham Counties. **Enrollment:** 4,068 degree-seeking undergraduates; 512 non-degree-seeking students. **Degrees:** 157 associate awarded. **Location:** 250 miles from Atlanta. **Calendar:** Quarter, extensive summer session. **Full-time faculty:** 85 total; 40% minority, 53% women. **Part-time faculty:** 275 total; 52% minority, 62% women. **Class size:** 64% < 20, 36% 20-39.

Student profile. Among degree-seeking undergraduates, 991 enrolled as first-time, first-year students.

Part-time:	54%	**Asian American:**	3%
Out-of-state:	12%	**Hispanic American:**	4%
Women:	67%	**International:**	2%
African American:	51%	**25 or older:**	54%

Transfer out. **Colleges most students transferred to 2008:** Savannah State University, Oglethorpe Atlantic State University.

Basis for selection. Open admission, but selective for some programs. Competitive admissions for allied health programs. ACT or SAT may be accepted in lieu of COMPASS or ASSET for placement. **Learning Disabled:** Must meet with disability coordinator.

High school preparation. College-preparatory program recommended. 22 units recommended. Recommended units include English 4, mathematics 3, social studies 3, science 3, foreign language 1 and academic electives 3. 4 tech prep and 1 science recommended.

2008-2009 Annual costs. Tuition/fees: $1,539; $2,835 out-of-state. Per-credit charge: $36 in-state; $72 out-of-state. Books/supplies: $1,500.

2007-2008 Financial aid. **Need-based:** Need-based aid available for part-time students. **Non-need-based:** Scholarships awarded for academics, leadership, minority status, state residency.

Application procedures. **Admission:** No deadline. $15 fee. Application must be submitted on paper. Admission notification on a rolling basis. **Financial aid:** No deadline. FAFSA required. Applicants notified on a rolling basis.

Academics. **Special study options:** Distance learning, dual enrollment of high school students, weekend college. License preparation in dental hygiene, nursing, paramedic. **Credit/placement by examination:** AP, CLEP, institutional tests. **Support services:** GED preparation and test center, learning center, reduced course load, remedial instruction, study skills assistance, tutoring.

Majors. **Business:** Accounting technology, administrative services, marketing, office technology, operations, sales/distribution. **Computer sciences:** General, data processing, networking, programming. **Construction:** Electrician. **Education:** Early childhood. **Engineering technology:** Computer, drafting, electrical. **Health:** Dental assistant, EMT paramedic, licensed practical nurse, medical assistant, surgical technology. **Legal studies:** Paralegal. **Mechanic/repair:** Auto body, automotive, heating/ac/refrig, industrial. **Personal/culinary services:** Chef training, cosmetic. **Production:** Machine shop technology, welding. **Protective services:** Criminal justice.

Most popular majors. Business/marketing 43%, computer/information sciences 21%, education 19%, health sciences 6%, security/protective services 6%.

Computing on campus. 100 workstations in library, computer center. Online course registration, online library available.

Student life. **Freshman orientation:** Available. Preregistration for classes offered. **Activities:** Student government.

Student services. Career counseling, services for economically disadvantaged, student employment services, financial aid counseling, placement for graduates. **Physically disabled:** Services for visually, hearing impaired. **Transfer:** Re-entry adviser, pre-admission transcript evaluation for new students.

Contact. E-mail: webinfo@savannahtech.edu
Phone: (912) 443-5517 Toll-free number: (800) 769-6362
Fax: (912) 443-5705
Gail Eubanks, Vice President of Student Success, Savannah Technical College, 5717 White Bluff Road, Savannah, GA 31405-5521

South Georgia College
Douglas, Georgia
www.sgc.edu **CB code: 5619**

- Public 2-year community and junior college
- Commuter campus in large town

General. Founded in 1906. Regionally accredited. **Enrollment:** 1,860 degree-seeking undergraduates. **Degrees:** 191 associate awarded. **Location:** 200 miles from Atlanta; 120 miles from Jacksonville, Florida. **Calendar:** Semester, extensive summer session. **Full-time faculty:** 44 total. **Part-time faculty:** 41 total. **Class size:** 39% < 20, 55% 20-39, 6% 40-49, less than 1% 50-99. **Special facilities:** Mobile nursing clinic.

Transfer out. **Colleges most students transferred to 2008:** Valdosta State University, Georgia Southern University, University of Georgia.

Basis for selection. Open admission. Students who score below 400 SAT math (16 ACT math) or 430 SAT verbal (18 ACT English) required to take College Placement Exam in English, reading, and/or math. Interview required of nursing majors. **Homeschooled:** Statement describing homeschool structure and mission, transcript of courses and grades required.

High school preparation. 16 units recommended. Recommended units include English 4, mathematics 4, social studies 3, science 3 (laboratory 3) and foreign language 2.

2008-2009 Annual costs. Tuition/fees: $2,272; $7,774 out-of-state. Per-credit charge: $77 in-state; $306 out-of-state. Room/board: $7,350. Books/supplies: $660. Personal expenses: $825.

Financial aid. **Need-based:** Need-based aid available for part-time students. **Non-need-based:** Scholarships awarded for academics.

Application procedures. **Admission:** No deadline. $20 fee, may be waived for applicants with need. Admission notification on a rolling basis. **Financial aid:** Priority date 4/1; no closing date. FAFSA, institutional form required. Applicants notified on a rolling basis starting 7/6; must reply within 2 week(s) of notification.

Academics. Students may pursue associate in nursing through South Georgia College/Waycross College campus. **Special study options:** Cooperative education, distance learning, dual enrollment of high school students, independent study, study abroad, teacher certification program. Bachelor's degree programs available on campus. License preparation in nursing. **Credit/placement by examination:** AP, CLEP, IB, institutional tests. 30 credit hours maximum toward associate degree. **Support services:** Learning center, reduced course load, remedial instruction, tutoring.

Majors. **Biology:** General. **Business:** General, accounting, administrative services, banking/financial services, business admin, communications, finance, management information systems, managerial economics, marketing, office management, office technology, office/clerical, operations, statistics. **Communications:** General, journalism. **Computer sciences:** General, applications programming, programming. **Education:** General, business, health, physical. **Foreign languages:** General, French, German, Spanish. **Health:** Nursing (RN), predental, premedicine, prepharmacy. **History:** General. **Legal studies:** Prelaw. **Liberal arts:** Arts/sciences. **Math:** General. **Parks/recreation:** General, facilities management, health/fitness, sports admin. **Philosophy/religion:** Philosophy. **Physical sciences:** Chemistry, physics. **Protective services:** Criminal justice, law enforcement admin, police science. **Psychology:** General. **Social sciences:** General, criminology, economics, political science, sociology.

Most popular majors. Health sciences 26%, liberal arts 68%.

Computing on campus. 80 workstations in dormitories, library, computer center, student center. Dormitories wired for high-speed internet access. Online course registration, helpline available.

Student life. **Freshman orientation:** Mandatory. Preregistration for classes offered. **Housing:** Guaranteed on-campus for all undergraduates. Coed dorms available. $30 deposit. **Activities:** Campus ministries, dance, drama, international student organizations, literary magazine, student government, student newspaper, Baptist student union, Association of Student Nurses, Students for Multicultural Unity, Phi Beta Lambda.

Athletics. NJCAA. **Intercollegiate:** Baseball M, softball W, tennis W. **Intramural:** Basketball, softball, swimming, synchronized swimming, table tennis, tennis, volleyball. **Team name:** Tigers.

Student services. Student employment services, financial aid counseling, veterans' counselor. **Learning disabled:** Comprehensive services available. **Transfer:** Pre-admission transcript evaluation for new students. College fairs on campus for students transferring to 4-year colleges.

Contact. E-mail: admissions@sgc.edu
Phone: (912) 389-4510 Toll-free number: (800) 342-6364
Fax: (912) 389-4388
Wes Brown, Director of Enrollment Services, South Georgia College, 100 West College Park Drive, Douglas, GA 31533-5098

Southeastern Technical College
Vidalia, Georgia
www.southeasterntech.edu **CB code: 5652**

- Public 2-year technical college
- Large town

General. Regionally accredited. **Enrollment:** 1,003 degree-seeking undergraduates. **Degrees:** 32 associate awarded. **Calendar:** Quarter. **Full-time faculty:** 34 total. **Part-time faculty:** 34 total.

Student profile.

African American:	29%	**Hispanic American:**	4%

Basis for selection. Open admission.

High school preparation. College-preparatory program recommended. 22 units recommended. Recommended units include English 4, mathematics 3, social studies 3, science 3, foreign language 1 and academic electives 3.

2008-2009 Annual costs. Tuition/fees: $1,539; $2,835 out-of-state. Per-credit charge: $36 in-state; $62 out-of-state.

2007-2008 Financial aid. **Need-based:** Need-based aid available for part-time students. Work-study available nights and for part-time students. **Non-need-based:** Scholarships awarded for state residency.

Application procedures. **Admission:** $15 fee. **Financial aid:** No deadline. FAFSA, institutional form required. Applicants notified on a rolling basis starting 4/6.

Academics. **Special study options:** Distance learning, dual enrollment of high school students, weekend college. **Credit/placement by examination:** CLEP, institutional tests. **Support services:** GED preparation and test center, tutoring.

Majors. **Business:** Accounting, business admin, marketing. **Computer sciences:** Networking. **Construction:** Electrician. **Education:** Early childhood. **Health:** Clinical lab technology.

Most popular majors. Business/marketing 28%, computer/information sciences 28%, education 16%, health sciences 13%, security/protective services 9%, trade and industry 6%.

Computing on campus. Commuter students can connect to campus network. Online library, wireless network available.

Student life. **Freshman orientation:** Mandatory.

Athletics. **Intramural:** Bowling M, volleyball M.

Student services. **Physically disabled:** Services for visually, speech, hearing impaired.

Contact. E-mail: brhart@southeasterntech.edu
Phone: (912) 538-3121
Brad Hart, Director of Enrollment Services, Southeastern Technical College, 3001 East First Street, Vidalia, GA 30474

Southwest Georgia Technical College

Thomasville, Georgia
www.southwestgatech.edu **CB code: 3627**

- Public 2-year technical college
- Commuter campus in large town

General. Regionally accredited. **Enrollment:** 1,208 degree-seeking undergraduates; 307 non-degree-seeking students. **Degrees:** 107 associate awarded. **Location:** 35 miles from Tallahassee, Florida. **Calendar:** Quarter, extensive summer session. **Full-time faculty:** 62 total. **Partnerships:** Formal partnership with John Deere.

Student profile. Among degree-seeking undergraduates, 237 enrolled as first-time, first-year students.

Part-time:	58%	**African American:**	39%
Out-of-state:	3%	**Asian American:**	1%
Women:	72%	**Hispanic American:**	1%

Basis for selection. Open admission, but selective for some programs. Most health programs selective due to limited enrollment. Selection process may include required certifications, additional standardized testing, prerequisite courses and physical exam. ACT or SAT may be accepted in lieu of COMPASS or ASSET for placement. **Learning Disabled:** Students seeking accommodations should provide documentation of learning disability.

High school preparation. College-preparatory program recommended. 22 units recommended. Recommended units include English 4, mathematics 3, social studies 3, science 3, foreign language 1 and academic electives 3. 4 tech prep and 1 health science recommended.

2008-2009 Annual costs. Tuition/fees: $1,539; $2,835 out-of-state. Per-credit charge: $36 in-state; $72 out-of-state. Truck driving and flight technology are higher cost programs. Books/supplies: $990. Personal expenses: $4,400.

2007-2008 Financial aid. **Need-based:** Need-based aid available for part-time students. Work-study available nights. **Non-need-based:** Scholarships awarded for state residency.

Application procedures. **Admission:** No deadline. $20 fee. Admission notification on a rolling basis. **Financial aid:** No deadline. FAFSA, institutional form required. Applicants notified on a rolling basis starting 7/1.

Academics. **Special study options:** Cooperative education, distance learning, double major, dual enrollment of high school students, internships, liberal arts/career combination, weekend college. License preparation in nursing, paramedic, physical therapy, radiology, real estate. **Credit/placement by examination:** CLEP, institutional tests. **Support services:** GED preparation and test center, remedial instruction, tutoring.

Majors. **Agriculture:** Equipment technology, power machinery. **Business:** Accounting technology, administrative services, business admin, office/clerical, operations. **Computer sciences:** Data entry, data processing, networking. **Education:** Early childhood. **Health:** Clinical lab technology, medical assistant, medical radiologic technology/radiation therapy, nursing (RN), pharmacy assistant, radiologic technology/medical imaging, respiratory therapy technology, surgical technology. **Mechanic/repair:** Heavy equipment. **Protective services:** Criminal justice, police science.

Most popular majors. Business/marketing 20%, computer/information sciences 8%, education 7%, health sciences 51%, security/protective services 7%.

Computing on campus. 42 workstations in library. Online course registration, online library available.

Student life. **Freshman orientation:** Mandatory. Preregistration for classes offered. Held quarterly. **Activities:** Student government, National Vocational honor society, Phi Beta Lambda, SkillsUSA.

Student services. Adult student services, career counseling, services for economically disadvantaged, student employment services, financial aid counseling, personal counseling, placement for graduates. **Physically disabled:** Services for visually, hearing impaired. **Transfer:** Pre-admission transcript evaluation for new students.

Contact. E-mail: info@southwestgatech.edu
Phone: (229) 225-5060 Fax: (229) 227-2666
Deborah Gray, Registrar, Southwest Georgia Technical College, 15689 US Highway 19N, Thomasville, GA 31792

Valdosta Technical College

Valdosta, Georgia
www.valdostatech.edu

- Public 2-year technical college
- Small city

General. Regionally accredited. **Enrollment:** 2,391 degree-seeking undergraduates. **Calendar:** Quarter. **Full-time faculty:** 67 total. **Part-time faculty:** 60 total.

Academics. **Credit/placement by examination:** CLEP.

Majors. **Communications technology:** Graphic/printing. **Computer sciences:** General. **Education:** Early childhood. **Engineering technology:** Drafting. **Health:** Clinical lab technology, radiologic technology/medical imaging. **Protective services:** Firefighting.

Contact. E-mail: admissions@valdostatech.edu
Phone: (229) 333-2105
Charlotte Hesters, Director of Admissions, Valdosta Technical College, 4089 Val Tech Road, Valdosta, GA 31602

Waycross College

Waycross, Georgia
www.waycross.edu **CB code: 5889**

- Public 2-year community and liberal arts college
- Commuter campus in large town
- SAT or ACT required

General. Founded in 1976. Regionally accredited. **Enrollment:** 970 degree-seeking undergraduates. **Degrees:** 101 associate awarded. **Location:** 70 miles from Jacksonville, Florida. **Calendar:** Semester, limited summer session. **Full-time faculty:** 20 total. **Part-time faculty:** 27 total. **Special facilities:** Repository of materials about the Okefenokee Swamp.

Student profile.

Out-of-state:	10%	**25 or older:**	28%

Transfer out. **Colleges most students transferred to 2008:** Valdosta State University, Armstrong Atlantic University, Georgia Southern University, University of Georgia.

Basis for selection. 330 SAT verbal or 310 SAT math required. Open admissions for all students out of school for over 5 years with high school diploma or GED. Essay required of low-scoring SAT verbal or ACT English applicants and those who have not completed 4 years high school English. **Adult students:** SAT/ACT scores not required if out of high school 5 year(s) or more. COMPASS placement exams required.

High school preparation. 16 units required. Required units include English 4, mathematics 4, social studies 3, science 3 and foreign language 2.

2008-2009 Annual costs. Tuition/fees: $1,992; $7,494 out-of-state. Per-credit charge: $77 in-state; $306 out-of-state. Books/supplies: $500. Personal expenses: $900.

2007-2008 Financial aid. Need-based: Need-based aid available for part-time students. Work-study available nights and for part-time students. **Non-need-based:** Scholarships awarded for academics, alumni affiliation, leadership.

Application procedures. Admission: No deadline. $20 fee, may be waived for applicants with need. Admission notification on a rolling basis. **Financial aid:** Priority date 6/1; no closing date. FAFSA, institutional form required. Applicants notified on a rolling basis; must reply within 2 week(s) of notification.

Academics. Special study options: Dual enrollment of high school students, independent study, liberal arts/career combination, study abroad. Cooperative nursing programs (RN) with South Georgia College, Valdosta State College. Bachelor's degree programs available on campus. **Credit/placement by examination:** CLEP, institutional tests. 20 credit hours maximum toward associate degree. SAT Subject Tests used to replace courses students did not take in high school. **Support services:** Learning center, reduced course load, remedial instruction, study skills assistance, tutoring, writing center.

Majors. Biology: General. **Business:** Accounting, business admin. **Computer sciences:** General, programming. **Conservation:** Environmental science. **Education:** General, physical. **Family/consumer sciences:** Child care. **Health:** Clinical lab technology, dental hygiene, EMT paramedic, medical radiologic technology/radiation therapy, surgical technology. **History:** General. **Math:** General. **Mechanic/repair:** Automotive, electronics/electrical, heating/ac/refrig, industrial. **Parks/recreation:** Health/fitness. **Personal/culinary services:** Cosmetic. **Physical sciences:** Chemistry. **Psychology:** General. **Social sciences:** Political science, sociology.

Computing on campus. 100 workstations in library, computer center, student center. Online course registration available.

Student life. Freshman orientation: Mandatory. Preregistration for classes offered. **Activities:** Drama, literary magazine, student government, student newspaper, Baptist student union, multicultural student alliance, Circle-K.

Athletics. Intramural: Baseball M, basketball, football (non-tackle), softball. **Team name:** Swamp Fox.

Student services. Adult student services, alcohol/substance abuse counseling, career counseling, student employment services, financial aid counseling, minority student services, personal counseling, placement for graduates, veterans' counselor. **Physically disabled:** Services for visually, speech, hearing impaired. **Transfer:** Pre-admission transcript evaluation for new students. Transfer adviser, college fairs on campus for students transferring to 4-year colleges.

Contact. E-mail: admiss@waycross.edu
Phone: (912) 285-6133 Fax: (912) 285-6158
Robert Wingfield, Director of Admissions and Records, Waycross College, 2001 South Georgia Parkway, Waycross, GA 31503

West Central Technical College

Waco, Georgia
www.westcentraltech.edu

- Public 2-year technical college
- Commuter campus in rural community

General. Enrollment: 3,748 degree-seeking undergraduates; 335 non-degree-seeking students. **Degrees:** 195 associate awarded. **Calendar:** Quarter. **Full-time faculty:** 83 total. **Part-time faculty:** 227 total.

Student profile. Among degree-seeking undergraduates, 934 enrolled as first-time, first-year students.

Part-time:	68%	**Asian American:**	1%
Women:	74%	**Hispanic American:**	2%
African American:	26%		

Basis for selection. Open admission, but selective for some programs. Special requirements for health services programs. ACT or SAT may be accepted in lieu of COMPASS or ASSET for placement. **Homeschooled:** State high school equivalency certificate required.

High school preparation. College-preparatory program recommended. 22 units recommended. Recommended units include English 4, mathematics 3, social studies 3, science 3, foreign language 1 and academic electives 3. 4 tech prep and 1 health science recommended.

2008-2009 Annual costs. Tuition/fees: $1,539; $2,835 out-of-state. Per-credit charge: $36 in-state; $72 out-of-state. Truck driving and flight technology are higher cost programs.Tuition reciprocity with bordering states. Commercial truck driving program is $2,784. EMT programs are $45 per-credit-hour. Additional fees may apply. Books/supplies: $945. Personal expenses: $1,300.

Financial aid. Need-based: Need-based aid available for part-time students.

Application procedures. Admission: No deadline. $25 fee.

Academics. Special study options: Distance learning, dual enrollment of high school students. **Credit/placement by examination:** AP, CLEP. **Support services:** GED preparation and test center, remedial instruction, study skills assistance, tutoring.

Majors. Business: Accounting, business admin, marketing. **Education:** Early childhood. **Health:** Dental hygiene, radiologic technology/medical imaging. **Protective services:** Criminal justice.

Most popular majors. Business/marketing 24%, computer/information sciences 19%, health sciences 48%.

Computing on campus. Online course registration available.

Athletics. Intercollegiate: Basketball M, volleyball W. **Team name:** Golden Knights.

Student services. Career counseling, financial aid counseling, placement for graduates. **Physically disabled:** Services for visually, speech, hearing impaired.

Contact. Phone: (770) 537-5740 Fax: (770) 537-7995
Mary Aderhold, Admissions Director, West Central Technical College, 176 Murphy Campus Boulevard, Waco, GA 30182

West Georgia Technical College

LaGrange, Georgia
www.westgatech.edu **CB code: 3632**

- Public 2-year technical college
- Commuter campus in small city

General. Regionally accredited. **Enrollment:** 1,682 degree-seeking undergraduates; 124 non-degree-seeking students. **Degrees:** 83 associate awarded. **Location:** 60 miles from Atlanta. **Calendar:** Quarter, limited summer session. **Full-time faculty:** 46 total. **Part-time faculty:** 96 total. **Class size:** 80% < 20, 20% 20-39.

Student profile. Among degree-seeking undergraduates, 416 enrolled as first-time, first-year students.

Part-time:	57%	**Asian American:**	1%
Women:	59%	**Hispanic American:**	1%
African American:	36%	**25 or older:**	54.4%

Basis for selection. Open admission, but selective for some programs. Admission to radiology and nursing programs based on examination, interview and space availability. ACT or SAT may be accepted in lieu of COMPASS or ASSET for placement. **Homeschooled:** Transcript of courses and grades required. Must provide satisfactory documentation indicating the homeschool is approved. **Learning Disabled:** Disabilities must be documented with the on-site coordinator to receive consideration for accommodation.

High school preparation. College-preparatory program recommended. 22 units recommended. Recommended units include English 4, mathematics 3, social studies 3, science 3, foreign language 1 and academic electives 3. 4 tech prep and 1 health science recommended.

2008-2009 Annual costs. Tuition/fees: $1,539; $2,835 out-of-state. Per-credit charge: $36 in-state; $72 out-of-state. Tuition reciprocity with bordering states. Commercial truck driving program is $2,784. Basic welding and EMT programs are $45 per-credit-hour. Books/supplies: $1,283. Personal expenses: $1,300.

Financial aid. Need-based: Need-based aid available for part-time students. Work-study available nights and for part-time students. **Non-need-based:** Scholarships awarded for state residency.

Application procedures. Admission: No deadline. $15 fee. Admission notification on a rolling basis. **Financial aid:** No deadline. FAFSA, institutional form required. Applicants notified on a rolling basis; must reply within 1 week(s) of notification.

Academics. Tutorial program available. **Special study options:** Distance learning, dual enrollment of high school students, weekend college. License preparation in paramedic, radiology, real estate. **Credit/placement by examination:** AP, CLEP. 15 credit hours maximum toward associate degree. **Support services:** GED preparation and test center, learning center, study skills assistance, tutoring.

Majors. Business: Accounting, administrative services, business admin, executive assistant, management science. **Computer sciences:** General, data entry, networking, web page design. **Education:** Early childhood. **Health:** Medical records technology, pharmacy assistant. **Mechanic/repair:** General, electronics/electrical, industrial. **Protective services:** Criminal justice, firefighting.

Most popular majors. Business/marketing 27%, computer/information sciences 10%, education 12%, health sciences 23%, security/protective services 24%.

Computing on campus. 100 workstations in library, computer center. Online library available.

Student life. Freshman orientation: Mandatory. Preregistration for classes offered. **Activities:** Student government, TV station, Phi Beta Lambda.

Student services. Adult student services, career counseling, student employment services, financial aid counseling, on-campus daycare, placement for graduates, veterans' counselor, women's services. **Physically disabled:** Services for visually, hearing impaired.

Contact. E-mail: lbasham@westgatech.edu
Phone: (706) 845-4244 Fax: (706) 845-4340
Lori Basham, Director of Admission, West Georgia Technical College, One College Circle, LaGrange, GA 30240

Young Harris College

Young Harris, Georgia
www.yhc.edu **CB code: 5990**

- Private 2-year liberal arts college affiliated with United Methodist Church
- Residential campus in rural community
- SAT or ACT (ACT writing recommended) required

General. Founded in 1886. Regionally accredited. **Enrollment:** 649 degree-seeking undergraduates. **Degrees:** 129 associate awarded. **Location:** 120 miles from Atlanta. **Calendar:** Semester, limited summer session. **Full-time faculty:** 46 total; 54% have terminal degrees, 4% minority, 46% women. **Part-time faculty:** 12 total; 25% have terminal degrees, 33% women. **Class size:** 65% < 20, 34% 20-39, less than 1% 40-49. **Special facilities:** Planetarium, black box theater, observatory, climbing wall, cross country trail, PDGA certified disc golf course.

Student profile. Among degree-seeking undergraduates, 90% enrolled in a transfer program, 396 enrolled as first-time, first-year students.

Part-time:	4%	**25 or older:**	2%
Out-of-state:	5.5%	**Live on campus:**	83%
Women:	54%		

Transfer out. Colleges most students transferred to 2008: University of Georgia, Georgia College & State University, North Georgia College & State University, Kennesaw State University.

Basis for selection. Heavy emphasis on academic GPA and SAT/ACT scores. High school record, interview considered. Conditional admission possible. **Adult students:** SAT/ACT scores not required if out of high school 5 year(s) or more. **Homeschooled:** Transcript of courses and grades required. Possible GED requirement dependent upon SAT/ACT scores. **Learning Disabled:** Psycho-educational analysis required.

High school preparation. Recommended units include English 4, mathematics 4, social studies 3, science 3 and foreign language 2.

2008-2009 Annual costs. Tuition/fees: $16,630. Per-credit charge: $500. Room/board: $5,878. Books/supplies: $800. Personal expenses: $1,050.

2007-2008 Financial aid. Need-based: 252 full-time freshmen applied for aid; 187 were judged to have need; 187 of these received aid. Average need met was 78%. Average scholarship/grant was $9,841; average loan $2,783. 79% of total undergraduate aid awarded as scholarships/grants, 21% as loans/jobs. Need-based aid available for part-time students. Work-study available nights. **Non-need-based:** Awarded to 390 full-time undergraduates, including 206 freshmen. Scholarships awarded for academics, art, athletics, job skills, music/drama, state residency.

Application procedures. Admission: Priority date 1/1; no deadline. $30 fee, may be waived for applicants with need, free for online applicants. Admission notification on a rolling basis beginning on or about 9/1. Must reply by May 1 or within 4 week(s) if notified thereafter. **Financial aid:** Priority date 4/1; no closing date. FAFSA, institutional form required. Applicants notified on a rolling basis starting 3/1; must reply within 2 week(s) of notification.

Academics. Special study options: Dual enrollment of high school students, honors, study abroad. Bachelor's degree programs available on campus. **Credit/placement by examination:** AP, CLEP, IB, institutional tests. Student may exempt computer science 101 but will not receive credit. **Support services:** Pre-admission summer program, reduced course load, remedial instruction, study skills assistance, tutoring, writing center.

Majors. Biology: General. **Business:** General, hospitality admin. **Communications:** General. **Conservation:** Forestry. **Education:** General, art, music. **Engineering:** General. **Foreign languages:** General, French, Spanish. **Health:** Predental, premedicine, prenursing, prepharmacy, preveterinary. **History:** General. **Interdisciplinary:** Biological/physical sciences. **Legal studies:** Prelaw. **Liberal arts:** Arts/sciences. **Math:** General. **Parks/recreation:** Health/fitness. **Philosophy/religion:** Religion. **Physical sciences:** Astronomy, chemistry, physics. **Protective services:** Criminal justice. **Psychology:** General. **Social sciences:** General. **Visual/performing arts:** General, art, dramatic, studio arts.

Computing on campus. 37 workstations in dormitories, library, computer center. Dormitories wired for high-speed internet access and linked to campus network. Commuter students can connect to campus network. Online course registration, online library, helpline, wireless network available.

Student life. Freshman orientation: Mandatory. Preregistration for classes offered. Two-day,1-night program held during summer prior to fall enrollment. **Policies:** All single freshmen and sophomores under age 22 not living with family must reside in college dormitories. No alcohol allowed on campus. **Housing:** Guaranteed on-campus for all undergraduates. Coed dorms, single-sex dorms, wellness housing available. $200 fully refundable deposit. **Activities:** Jazz band, campus ministries, choral groups, dance, drama, literary magazine, music ensembles, musical theater, student government, student newspaper, Wesley Fellowship, College Republicans, Young Democrats, honorary service organizations.

Athletics. NJCAA. **Intercollegiate:** Baseball M, cross-country, golf, soccer, softball W, tennis W. **Intramural:** Basketball, football (non-tackle), softball, volleyball. **Team name:** Mountain Lions.

Student services. Alcohol/substance abuse counseling, chaplain/spiritual director, career counseling, financial aid counseling, health services, personal counseling, women's services. **Physically disabled:** Services for visually, speech, hearing impaired. **Learning disabled:** Comprehensive services available. **Transfer:** Pre-admission transcript evaluation for new students. Transfer center, transfer adviser for students transferring to 4-year colleges.

Contact. E-mail: admissions@yhc.edu
Phone: (706) 379-3111 Toll-free number: (800) 241-3754
Fax: (706) 379-3108
Clinton Hobbs, Vice President for Enrollment Management, Young Harris College, PO Box 116, Young Harris, GA 30582-0116

Hawaii

Hawaii Tokai International College

Honolulu, Hawaii
www.hawaiitokai.edu **CB code: 2588**

- Private 2-year junior and liberal arts college
- Residential campus in large city
- Application essay, interview required

General. Regionally accredited. **Enrollment:** 42 degree-seeking undergraduates; 53 non-degree-seeking students. **Degrees:** 39 associate awarded. **Calendar:** Quarter, limited summer session. **Full-time faculty:** 9 total; 33% have terminal degrees, 44% women. **Part-time faculty:** 15 total; 13% have terminal degrees, 60% minority, 47% women. **Class size:** 100% < 20.

Student profile. Among degree-seeking undergraduates, 100% enrolled in a transfer program, 12 enrolled as first-time, first-year students, 1 transferred in from other institutions.

Out-of-state:	5%	**Live on campus:**	67%
Women:	50%		

Transfer out. 89% of students enrolled in the transfer program go on to 4-year colleges. **Colleges most students transferred to 2008:** University of Hawaii at Manoa, Tokai University.

Basis for selection. Essay, academic GPA, recommendations, character, interview, and commitment to studies.

2008-2009 Annual costs. Tuition/fees: $9,450. Room/board: $6,375. Books/supplies: $800. Personal expenses: $1,200.

Financial aid. Non-need-based: Scholarships awarded for academics.

Application procedures. Admission: Closing date 8/2 (postmark date). $50 fee. Admission notification on a rolling basis. **Financial aid:** Institutional form required.

Academics. Special study options: ESL, study abroad. **Credit/placement by examination:** CLEP, institutional tests. **Support services:** Tutoring.

Majors. Liberal arts: Arts/sciences.

Computing on campus. 60 workstations in library, computer center. Dormitories wired for high-speed internet access and linked to campus network. Commuter students can connect to campus network. Online library, wireless network available.

Student life. Freshman orientation: Mandatory. Preregistration for classes offered. **Housing:** Guaranteed on-campus for all undergraduates. Coed dorms, wellness housing available. $25 nonrefundable deposit. **Activities:** Music ensembles, student government, student newspaper.

Athletics. Team name: T-Wave.

Student services. Career counseling, financial aid counseling, personal counseling. **Physically disabled:** Services for visually impaired. **Transfer:** Re-entry adviser, pre-admission transcript evaluation for new students. Transfer center, transfer adviser, college fairs on campus for students transferring to 4-year colleges.

Contact. E-mail: htic@tokai.edu
Phone: (808) 983-4154 Fax: (808) 983-4173
Noriko Ito, Director, Student Services, Hawaii Tokai International College, 2241 Kapiolani Boulevard, Honolulu, HI 96826

Heald College: Honolulu

Honolulu, Hawaii
www.heald.edu **CB code: 4324**

- For-profit 2-year technical and career college
- Commuter campus in very large city

General. Founded in 1863. Regionally accredited. **Enrollment:** 1,139 degree-seeking undergraduates. **Degrees:** 384 associate awarded. **Calendar:** Quarter. **Full-time faculty:** 25 total. **Part-time faculty:** 18 total.

Basis for selection. Open admission. COMPASS Test administered prior to application.

2008-2009 Annual costs. Tuition/fees: $11,550. Fees vary by program. Books/supplies: $1,500.

Financial aid. All financial aid based on need. Need-based aid available for part-time students. Work-study available nights, weekends and for part-time students.

Application procedures. Admission: No deadline. No application fee. Admission notification on a rolling basis. **Financial aid:** No deadline. FAFSA required.

Academics. Special study options: Internships. **Credit/placement by examination:** CLEP, institutional tests. **Support services:** Learning center, reduced course load, remedial instruction, study skills assistance, tutoring.

Majors. Business: Accounting, business admin, hospitality admin, tourism/travel. **Computer sciences:** General, vendor certification, web page design. **Engineering technology:** Electrical. **Health:** Dental assistant, medical assistant, medical records technology, medical secretary, office assistant. **Legal studies:** Legal secretary, paralegal. **Other:** Criminal justice administration, Software technologies.

Computing on campus. Online library, wireless network available.

Student life. Freshman orientation: Mandatory.

Student services. Career counseling, student employment services, financial aid counseling, placement for graduates. **Transfer:** Re-entry adviser, pre-admission transcript evaluation for new students. Transfer adviser for students transferring to 4-year colleges.

Contact. E-mail: evelyn_schemmel@heald.edu
Phone: (808) 955-1500 Toll-free number: (800) 940-0530
Fax: (808) 955-6964
Daniel Barnhart, Director of Admissions, Heald College: Honolulu, 1500 Kapiolani Boulevard, Honolulu, HI 96814-3715

Remington College: Honolulu

Honolulu, Hawaii
www.remingtoncollege.edu **CB code: 3507**

- For-profit 2-year branch campus college
- Commuter campus in very large city

General. Accredited by ACICS. **Calendar:** Quarter.

Annual costs/financial aid. Costs of entire programs leading to certificate, associate degree, and bachelor's degree range from $13,000 to $38,880; include books and supplies. Personal expenses: $1,764. Need-based financial aid available for full-time students.

Contact. Phone: (808) 942-1000
Campus President, 1111 Bishop Street, Suite 400, Honolulu, HI 96813-2811

TransPacific Hawaii College

Honolulu, Hawaii
www.transpacific.org **CB code: 4429**

- Private 2-year junior and liberal arts college
- Commuter campus in large city
- Application essay required

General. Regionally accredited. TransPacific serves as a transitional institution for students from Asia who have the desire to study in America but who lack the language ability and study skills. The college is in session 12 months per year and a student can become fluent in English and gain an Associate of Arts degree in 24 months. **Enrollment:** 176 degree-seeking undergraduates. **Degrees:** 120 associate awarded. **Location:** 6 miles from Honolulu. **Calendar:** Continuous. **Full-time faculty:** 11 total; 36% have terminal degrees, 64% women. **Part-time faculty:** 32 total; 28% have terminal degrees, 53% women. **Class size:** 100% < 20.

Transfer out. Colleges most students transferred to 2008: University of Hawaii, University of Washington, Alliant International University, Ritsumeikan Asia Pacific University, Marymount College.

Basis for selection. Secondary school record, essay important.

High school preparation. Recommended units include English 4, mathematics 4, social studies 2, history 2, science 2, computer science 1, visual/performing arts 1 and academic electives 5.

2008-2009 Annual costs. Tuition/fees: $16,300. Students are responsible for their board with a home stay family, about $750 per month. Books/supplies: $800.

Application procedures. **Admission:** Closing date 8/27 (postmark date). $50 fee. Admission notification on a rolling basis.

Academics. Academic program emphasizes crosscultural curriculum. **Special study options:** ESL, independent study, liberal arts/career combination. **Credit/placement by examination:** CLEP, institutional tests. **Support services:** Tutoring.

Majors. **Liberal arts:** Arts/sciences.

Computing on campus. 45 workstations in library, computer center. Repair service, wireless network available.

Student life. **Freshman orientation:** Mandatory. Held in Japan during the first week of March. **Housing:** Homestay for majority of students. **Activities:** Student government, student newspaper.

Student services. Career counseling, personal counseling. **Transfer:** Transfer center, transfer adviser, college fairs on campus for students transferring to 4-year colleges.

Contact. E-mail: akikotyler@transpacific.edu
Phone: (808) 377-5402 Fax: (808) 373-9735
Shungo Kawanishi, Vice President for Global Affairs, TransPacific Hawaii College, 5257 Kalanianaole Highway, Honolulu, HI 96821

University of Hawaii: Hawaii Community College

Hilo, Hawaii
www.hawcc.hawaii.edu **CB code: 1801**

- Public 2-year community college
- Small city

General. Founded in 1969. Regionally accredited. **Enrollment:** 2,378 degree-seeking undergraduates. **Degrees:** 262 associate awarded. **ROTC:** Naval. **Location:** 200 miles from Honolulu. **Calendar:** Semester, limited summer session. **Full-time faculty:** 100 total. **Part-time faculty:** 35 total.

Student profile.

25 or older:	32%	**Live on campus:**	35%

Basis for selection. Open admission.

2008-2009 Annual costs. Tuition/fees: $2,264; $8,054 out-of-state. Per-credit charge: $71 in-state; $264 out-of-state. Books/supplies: $672. Personal expenses: $953.

Financial aid. All financial aid based on need. Need-based aid available for part-time students. **Additional information:** Hawaii student incentive grants and tuition waivers (merit and need-based) available to Hawaii residents.

Application procedures. **Admission:** Closing date 7/30. No application fee in-state; $25 out-of-state. Admission notification on a rolling basis. **Financial aid:** Priority date 4/1; no closing date. FAFSA required. Applicants notified on a rolling basis starting 5/1; must reply within 2 week(s) of notification.

Academics. **Special study options:** Cooperative education, cross-registration, distance learning, double major, dual enrollment of high school students, ESL, honors, independent study. **Credit/placement by examination:** CLEP. 15 credit hours maximum toward associate degree. **Support services:** Learning center, pre-admission summer program, reduced course load, remedial instruction, tutoring.

Majors. **Agriculture:** General. **Business:** Accounting, administrative services, market research, marketing, operations. **Construction:** Carpentry, power transmission. **Education:** Early childhood. **Engineering technology:** Drafting, electrical. **Family/consumer sciences:** Food/nutrition. **Health:** Nursing (RN). **Liberal arts:** Arts/sciences. **Mechanic/repair:** Auto body, automotive, diesel, electronics/electrical. **Personal/culinary services:** Food service, restaurant/catering. **Protective services:** Criminal justice, law enforcement admin. **Other:** Architectural, engineering and CAD technologies.

Student life. **Freshman orientation:** Available. Preregistration for classes offered. **Housing:** Coed dorms, special housing for disabled, apartments, wellness housing available. **Activities:** Dance, drama, literary magazine, music ensembles, student government, student newspaper, TV station, Phi Theta Kappa honors society.

Athletics. **Team name:** Hawaii Hawks (i'eo).

Student services. Adult student services, career counseling, student employment services, financial aid counseling, health services, on-campus daycare, personal counseling, veterans' counselor. **Physically disabled:** Services for hearing impaired. **Transfer:** Transfer adviser, college fairs on campus for students transferring to 4-year colleges.

Contact. E-mail: hawccinf@hawaii.edu
Phone: (808) 974-7661 Fax: (808) 974-7692
David Loeding, Registrar, University of Hawaii: Hawaii Community College, 200 West Kawili Street, Hilo, HI 96720-4091

University of Hawaii: Honolulu Community College

Honolulu, Hawaii
honolulu.hawaii.edu **CB code: 4350**

- Public 2-year community and technical college
- Commuter campus in very large city

General. Founded in 1920. Regionally accredited. **Enrollment:** 3,300 degree-seeking undergraduates. **Degrees:** 460 associate awarded. **ROTC:** Army, Air Force. **Calendar:** Semester, limited summer session. **Full-time faculty:** 130 total. **Part-time faculty:** 60 total. **Class size:** 50% < 20, 50% 20-39.

Student profile. Among degree-seeking undergraduates, 1,522 transferred in from other institutions.

Out-of-state:	3%	**25 or older:**	36%

Transfer out. **Colleges most students transferred to 2008:** University of Hawaii at Manoa, University of Hawaii at Hilo, University of Hawaii West Oahu, Chaminade University, Hawaii Pacific University.

Basis for selection. Open admission, but selective for out-of-state students. Out-of-state and foreign applicants subject to non-resident quota. High school diploma required for cosmetology program.

2008-2009 Annual costs. Tuition/fees: $2,160; $7,950 out-of-state. Per-credit charge: $71 in-state; $264 out-of-state. Books/supplies: $773. Personal expenses: $1,166.

2007-2008 Financial aid. **Need-based:** Need-based aid available for part-time students. Work-study available for part-time students. **Non-need-based:** Scholarships awarded for academics, state residency. **Additional information:** Hawaii student incentive grants and tuition waivers (merit and need-based) available to Hawaii residents at participating institutions.

Application procedures. **Admission:** Priority date 7/1; no deadline. No application fee in-state; $25 out-of-state. Admission notification on a rolling basis beginning on or about 3/1. **Financial aid:** Priority date 4/1; no closing date. FAFSA required. Applicants notified on a rolling basis starting 7/1; must reply within 3 week(s) of notification.

Academics. **Special study options:** Cooperative education, cross-registration, distance learning, dual enrollment of high school students, ESL, independent study, internships, student-designed major. License preparation in aviation. **Credit/placement by examination:** AP, CLEP, institutional tests. 30 credit hours maximum toward associate degree. **Support services:** Learning center, remedial instruction, study skills assistance, tutoring.

Majors. **Business:** Fashion. **Communications technology:** Graphic/printing. **Computer sciences:** General, computer graphics, information systems. **Construction:** Carpentry, electrician. **Education:** Early childhood, technology/industrial arts, voc/tech. **Engineering:** Aerospace, architectural, computer, polymer. **Engineering technology:** Drafting, electrical, occupational safety. **Family/consumer sciences:** Child care, institutional food production. **Health:** Occupational health. **Liberal arts:** Arts/sciences. **Mechanic/repair:** General, aircraft, auto body, automotive, diesel, electronics/electrical, heating/ac/refrig, marine. **Personal/culinary services:** Cosmetic. **Protective services:** Criminal justice, fire safety technology, fire services admin, firefighting, law enforcement admin, police science. **Public administration:** Community org/advocacy, human services, social work. **Transportation:** Airline/commercial pilot, aviation management. **Visual/performing arts:** Commercial/advertising art, fashion design.

Most popular majors. Engineering/engineering technologies 37%, liberal arts 20%, public administration/social services 8%, security/protective services 11%, trade and industry 16%.

Computing on campus. 135 workstations in library, computer center, student center. Commuter students can connect to campus network. Online course registration, wireless network available.

Student life. **Freshman orientation:** Mandatory. **Housing:** Dorms and apartments available at University of Hawaii at Manoa campus. **Activities:** Literary magazine, student government, student newspaper, Pacific Islander association, Filipino club.

Student services. Career counseling, student employment services, financial aid counseling, health services, on-campus daycare, placement for graduates, veterans' counselor. **Physically disabled:** Services for visually, speech, hearing impaired. **Transfer:** Pre-admission transcript evaluation for new students. Transfer center, transfer adviser, college fairs on campus for students transferring to 4-year colleges.

Contact. E-mail: admissions@hcc.hawaii.edu
Phone: (808) 845-9129 Fax: (808) 847-9829
Funai Grace, Admissions Counselor, University of Hawaii: Honolulu Community College, 874 Dillingham Boulevard, Honolulu, HI 96817

University of Hawaii: Kapiolani Community College

Honolulu, Hawaii
www.kcc.hawaii.edu **CB code: 4377**

- Public 2-year community college
- Commuter campus in very large city

General. Founded in 1957. Regionally accredited. **Enrollment:** 4,909 degree-seeking undergraduates. **Degrees:** 649 associate awarded. **Calendar:** Semester, limited summer session. **Full-time faculty:** 245 total. **Part-time faculty:** 150 total. **Class size:** 55% < 20, 45% 20-39, less than 1% 40-49, less than 1% 50-99.

Student profile.

Out-of-state:	7%	**25 or older:**	41%

Transfer out. **Colleges most students transferred to 2008:** University of Hawaii at Manoa.

Basis for selection. Open admission, but selective for some programs. Special requirements for health science and nursing programs. High school diploma required for allied health and nursing programs and for students under age 18. Essay recommended. Interview required of allied health, legal assistant, and nursing programs.

2008-2009 Annual costs. Tuition/fees: $2,190; $7,980 out-of-state. Per-credit charge: $71 in-state; $264 out-of-state. Books/supplies: $725. Personal expenses: $1,143.

Financial aid. All financial aid based on need. Need-based aid available for part-time students. **Additional information:** Hawaii student incentive grants and tuition waivers (merit and need-based) available to Hawaii residents.

Application procedures. **Admission:** Closing date 7/17 (postmark date). $25 fee. Application must be submitted on paper. Admission notification on a rolling basis. Application deadline April 1 for allied health and legal assistant programs; February 1 for registered nursing program. **Financial aid:** Priority date 4/1; no closing date. FAFSA required. Applicants notified on a rolling basis; must reply within 2 week(s) of notification.

Academics. **Special study options:** Cross-registration, distance learning, double major, dual enrollment of high school students, ESL, exchange student, external degree, honors, independent study, internships, study abroad, teacher certification program, weekend college. Service learning. License preparation in nursing, paramedic. **Credit/placement by examination:** CLEP, institutional tests. **Support services:** Learning center, remedial instruction, tutoring.

Majors. **Business:** General, accounting, hospitality/recreation, office technology, sales/distribution. **Computer sciences:** Data processing. **Family/consumer sciences:** Institutional food production. **Health:** Clinical lab technology, dental assistant, dental hygiene, EMT paramedic, licensed practical nurse, medical assistant, medical radiologic technology/radiation therapy, nursing (RN), nursing assistant, occupational therapy assistant, physical therapy assistant, physician assistant, respiratory therapy technology, sonography. **Legal studies:** Legal secretary, paralegal. **Liberal arts:** Arts/sciences. **Personal/culinary services:** Culinary arts.

Most popular majors. Business/marketing 30%, computer/information sciences 6%, health sciences 21%, liberal arts 38%.

Computing on campus. 150 workstations in library, computer center, student center. Commuter students can connect to campus network. Online course registration, online library, student web hosting, wireless network available.

Student life. **Freshman orientation:** Mandatory. 15 two-hour sessions, any one of which may be attended by a new student. **Housing:** Coed dorms available. Housing available through University of Hawaii system. **Activities:** Choral groups, dance, drama, literary magazine, music ensembles, student government, student newspaper, international students club, marketing association, music club, Phi Theta Kappa, nursing association, Japanese, Chinese and Korean club, Catholic Ministry Association, pre-engineering club.

Student services. Career counseling, services for economically disadvantaged, student employment services, financial aid counseling, minority student services, on-campus daycare, personal counseling, placement for graduates, veterans' counselor. **Physically disabled:** Services for visually, speech, hearing impaired.

Contact. E-mail: kapinfo@hawaii.edu
Phone: (808) 734-9555 Fax: (808) 734-9896
Sharon Fowler, Coordinator of Enrollment Services, University of Hawaii: Kapiolani Community College, 4303 Diamond Head Road, Honolulu, HI 96816-4421

University of Hawaii: Kauai Community College

Lihue, Hawaii
www.kauai.hawaii.edu **CB code: 4378**

- Public 2-year community college
- Commuter campus in small city

General. Founded in 1928. Regionally accredited. **Enrollment:** 840 degree-seeking undergraduates. **Degrees:** 108 associate awarded. **Location:** 100 miles from Honolulu. **Calendar:** Semester, limited summer session. **Full-time faculty:** 70 total. **Part-time faculty:** 30 total. **Special facilities:** Botanical facilities.

Basis for selection. Open admission, but selective for out-of-state students. Special requirements for out-of-state residents in nursing, electrical installation and maintenance technology, facilities engineering technology, nurse's aide, electronics technology programs, and culinary arts.

2008-2009 Annual costs. Tuition/fees: $2,190; $7,980 out-of-state. Per-credit charge: $71 in-state; $264 out-of-state.

2008-2009 Financial aid. **Need-based:** Work-study available nights and for part-time students. **Additional information:** Hawaii student incentive grants and tuition waivers (merit and need-based) available to Hawaii residents.

Application procedures. **Admission:** Priority date 8/1; no deadline. Admission notification on a rolling basis beginning on or about 3/1. Institutional placement test. **Financial aid:** Priority date 4/1, closing date 5/1. FAFSA, institutional form required. Applicants notified on a rolling basis starting 5/1.

Academics. **Special study options:** Cooperative education, cross-registration, distance learning, ESL, internships. Bachelor's degree programs available on campus. **Credit/placement by examination:** AP, CLEP, institutional tests. **Support services:** Learning center, tutoring, writing center.

Majors. **Business:** Accounting, hospitality admin, office/clerical. **Construction:** Carpentry, electrician. **Education:** Early childhood. **Engineering technology:** Electrical. **Health:** Nursing (RN). **Liberal arts:** Arts/sciences. **Mechanic/repair:** Auto body, automotive. **Personal/culinary services:** Culinary arts.

Computing on campus. 150 workstations in computer center.

Student life. **Freshman orientation:** Available. **Activities:** Concert band, choral groups, international student organizations, music ensembles, student government, Hawaiian club, Pamantasan club, Hawaiian performing arts club, Japanese club, environmental club.

Athletics. **Intramural:** Basketball.

Student services. Adult student services, career counseling, student employment services, health services, on-campus daycare, personal counseling, placement for graduates, veterans' counselor. **Physically disabled:** Services for visually, speech, hearing impaired. **Transfer:** Transfer adviser, college fairs on campus for students transferring to 4-year colleges.

Contact. E-mail: arkauai@hawaii.edu
Phone: (808) 245-8225 Fax: (808) 245-8297
Leighton Oride, Admissions Officer and Registrar, University of Hawaii: Kauai Community College, 3-1901 Kaumualii Highway, Lihue, HI 96766-9500

University of Hawaii: Leeward Community College

Pearl City, Hawaii
www.lcc.hawaii.edu **CB code: 4410**

- Public 2-year community college
- Commuter campus in large town

General. Founded in 1968. Regionally accredited. **Enrollment:** 5,887 degree-seeking undergraduates. **Degrees:** 442 associate awarded. **ROTC:** Army, Air Force. **Location:** 10 miles from Honolulu. **Calendar:** Semester, limited summer session. **Full-time faculty:** 180 total. **Part-time faculty:** 80 total. **Special facilities:** Observatory.

Student profile.

Out-of-state:	10%	**25 or older:**	34%

Basis for selection. Open admission.

2008-2009 Annual costs. Tuition/fees: $2,155; $7,945 out-of-state. Per-credit charge: $71 in-state; $264 out-of-state. Books/supplies: $672. Personal expenses: $953.

Financial aid. Need-based: Need-based aid available for part-time students. **Additional information:** Leveraging Educational Assistance Partnership (LEAP) funds or tuition waivers available to students with financial need.

Application procedures. Admission: Closing date 7/15 (postmark date). No application fee in-state; $25 out-of-state. Admission notification on a rolling basis beginning on or about 12/1. **Financial aid:** Priority date 4/15; no closing date. FAFSA required. Applicants notified on a rolling basis starting 6/1; must reply within 2 week(s) of notification.

Academics. Special study options: Cross-registration, distance learning, dual enrollment of high school students, honors, independent study, internships, liberal arts/career combination, weekend college. **Credit/placement by examination:** CLEP, IB, institutional tests. 21 credit hours maximum toward associate degree. **Support services:** Learning center, pre-admission summer program, remedial instruction, study skills assistance, tutoring.

Majors. Business: Accounting, office/clerical. **Communications:** Broadcast journalism. **Computer sciences:** General. **Liberal arts:** Arts/sciences.

Computing on campus. 200 workstations in library, computer center. Commuter students can connect to campus network. Helpline available.

Student life. Activities: Bands, choral groups, dance, drama, film society, literary magazine, music ensembles, musical theater, student government, student newspaper, TV station, Filipino ethnic organization, club for physically handicapped, Campus Crusade for Christ, human services club.

Athletics. Intramural: Bowling, golf, soccer, tennis, volleyball.

Student services. Adult student services, career counseling, student employment services, health services, on-campus daycare, personal counseling, placement for graduates, veterans' counselor. **Physically disabled:** Services for visually, speech, hearing impaired. **Transfer:** Transfer adviser, college fairs on campus for students transferring to 4-year colleges.

Contact. E-mail: lccar@hawaii.edu
Phone: (808) 455-0217 Fax: (808) 454-8804
Warren Mau, Registrar, University of Hawaii: Leeward Community College, 96-045 Ala Ike, Pearl City, HI 96782

University of Hawaii: Maui Community College

Kahului, Hawaii
www.maui.hawaii.edu **CB code: 4510**

- Public 2-year community college
- Commuter campus in small city

General. Founded in 1931. Regionally accredited. Branch campuses on Molokai, Lanai and Hana. **Enrollment:** 2,659 degree-seeking undergraduates; 394 non-degree-seeking students. **Degrees:** 245 associate awarded. **Location:** 150 miles from Honolulu. **Calendar:** Semester, limited summer session. **Full-time faculty:** 116 total. **Part-time faculty:** 1 total.

Student profile. Among degree-seeking undergraduates, 746 enrolled as first-time, first-year students.

Part-time:	55%	**Women:**	65%
Out-of-state:	1%	**Live on campus:**	1%

Basis for selection. Open admission, but selective for some programs. Special requirements for nursing program. Interview required of nursing majors.

2008-2009 Annual costs. Tuition/fees: $2,252; $10,922 out-of-state. Per-credit charge: $71 in-state; $360 out-of-state. Room/board: $7,478. Books/supplies: $879.

2007-2008 Financial aid. Need-based: Need-based aid available for part-time students. Work-study available nights and for part-time students.

Application procedures. Admission: Priority date 7/31; no deadline. No application fee in-state; $25 out-of-state. Admission notification on a rolling basis. **Financial aid:** Priority date 4/1; no closing date. FAFSA, institutional form required. Applicants notified on a rolling basis starting 6/1; must reply within 4 week(s) of notification.

Academics. Special study options: Cooperative education, distance learning, double major, dual enrollment of high school students, ESL, independent study, liberal arts/career combination, weekend college. **Credit/placement by examination:** CLEP, institutional tests. 30 credit hours maximum toward associate degree. **Support services:** Learning center, pre-admission summer program, reduced course load, remedial instruction, tutoring.

Majors. Agriculture: General. **Business:** General, accounting, tourism/travel. **Construction:** Carpentry. **Education:** Early childhood. **Engineering technology:** Drafting. **Family/consumer sciences:** Apparel marketing, food/nutrition. **Liberal arts:** Arts/sciences. **Mechanic/repair:** Auto body, automotive. **Personal/culinary services:** Food service. **Public administration:** Human services.

Computing on campus. Dormitories wired for high-speed internet access and linked to campus network. Commuter students can connect to campus network. Online course registration, helpline available.

Student life. Freshman orientation: Available. **Housing:** Coed dorms available. $160 deposit, deadline 6/1. **Activities:** Student government, student newspaper, TV station.

Student services. Career counseling, student employment services, health services, on-campus daycare, personal counseling, veterans' counselor. **Physically disabled:** Services for visually, speech, hearing impaired. **Transfer:** Transfer adviser for students transferring to 4-year colleges.

Contact. Phone: (808) 984-3500 Toll-free number: (800) 479-6692
Fax: (808) 242-9618
Stephen Kameda, Admissions Officer/Registrar, University of Hawaii: Maui Community College, 310 West Kaahumanu Avenue, Kahului, HI 96732-1617

University of Hawaii: Windward Community College

Kaneohe, Hawaii
www.wcc.hawaii.edu **CB code: 4976**

- Public 2-year community college
- Commuter campus in small city

General. Founded in 1972. Regionally accredited. **Enrollment:** 1,824 degree-seeking undergraduates. **Degrees:** 130 associate awarded. **ROTC:** Army. **Location:** 10 miles from Honolulu. **Calendar:** Semester, limited summer session. **Full-time faculty:** 40 total. **Part-time faculty:** 32 total. **Special facilities:** Planetarium, greenhouse, observatory, NASA lab, biomedicinal garden.

Student profile. Among degree-seeking undergraduates, .77% enrolled in a transfer program, .01% enrolled in a vocational program.

Out-of-state:	9%	**25 or older:**	38%

Basis for selection. Open admission. **Adult students:** SAT/ACT scores not required.

2008-2009 Annual costs. Tuition/fees: $2,170; $7,960 out-of-state. Per-credit charge: $71 in-state; $264 out-of-state. Books/supplies: $987. Personal expenses: $1,730.

Financial aid. **Need-based:** Need-based aid available for part-time students. **Additional information:** Hawaii student incentive grants and tuition waivers (merit and need-based) available to Hawaii residents.

Application procedures. **Admission:** Priority date 8/1; no deadline. No application fee in-state; $25 out-of-state. Admission notification on a rolling basis. Out-of-state military dependents not required to pay application fee. **Financial aid:** Priority date 4/1; no closing date. FAFSA required. Applicants notified on a rolling basis starting 3/15; must reply within 2 week(s) of notification.

Academics. **Special study options:** Cooperative education, distance learning, double major, dual enrollment of high school students, independent study, internships, student-designed major. **Credit/placement by examination:** CLEP, institutional tests. **Support services:** Learning center, reduced course load, remedial instruction, study skills assistance, tutoring.

Majors. **Liberal arts:** Arts/sciences.

Computing on campus. 30 workstations in library, computer center, student center. Commuter students can connect to campus network. Online course registration, helpline, wireless network available.

Student life. **Freshman orientation:** Mandatory. Preregistration for classes offered. **Activities:** Choral groups, drama, student government, student newspaper.

Student services. Adult student services, career counseling, services for economically disadvantaged, student employment services, financial aid counseling, minority student services, personal counseling, placement for graduates, veterans' counselor. **Transfer:** Pre-admission transcript evaluation for new students. Transfer adviser, college fairs on campus for students transferring to 4-year colleges.

Contact. E-mail: wccinfo@hawaii.edu
Phone: (808) 235-7432 Fax: (808) 235-9148
Geri Imai, Registrar, University of Hawaii: Windward Community College, 45-720 Kea'ahala Road, Kaneohe, HI 96744

Idaho

College of Southern Idaho
Twin Falls, Idaho
www.csi.edu **CB code: 4114**

- Public 2-year community and junior college
- Commuter campus in large town

General. Founded in 1964. Regionally accredited. **Enrollment:** 4,960 degree-seeking undergraduates. **Degrees:** 667 associate awarded. **Location:** 130 miles from Boise. **Calendar:** Semester, limited summer session. **Full-time faculty:** 239 total. **Part-time faculty:** 261 total. **Special facilities:** Museum and planetarium including anthropology, archeology, fine arts collections.

Student profile.

Out-of-state:	5%	**Live on campus:**	5%
25 or older:	52%		

Transfer out. Colleges most students transferred to 2008: Boise State University, University of Idaho, Idaho State University, Utah State University, Albertsons College.

Basis for selection. Open admission, but selective for some programs. ACT recommended; letters of reference, letter of intent, and special tests required for applicants to registered nursing program. Interview required of registered nursing, technical majors.

2008-2009 Annual costs. Tuition/fees: $2,280; $6,360 out-of-state. Per-credit charge: $95 in-state; $265 out-of-state. Room/board: $4,700. Books/supplies: $990. Personal expenses: $1,900.

Financial aid. Need-based: Need-based aid available for part-time students. **Additional information:** Out-of-state tuition waivers based on GPA and activities.

Application procedures. Admission: No deadline. No application fee. Admission notification on a rolling basis. **Financial aid:** Priority date 3/1; no closing date. FAFSA required. Applicants notified on a rolling basis starting 4/30; must reply within 3 week(s) of notification.

Academics. Special study options: Distance learning, dual enrollment of high school students, ESL, honors. License preparation in real estate. **Credit/placement by examination:** AP, CLEP. 21 credit hours maximum toward associate degree. **Support services:** GED preparation and test center, learning center, reduced course load, remedial instruction, study skills assistance, tutoring, writing center.

Majors. Agriculture: Aquaculture, business, equestrian studies, horticultural science, range science. **Biology:** General. **Business:** General, accounting, hospitality/recreation, real estate, tourism promotion. **Communications:** General. **Computer sciences:** Computer graphics, computer science, LAN/WAN management. **Conservation:** General, forestry, water/wetlands/marine, wildlife. **Education:** Bilingual, early childhood, elementary, physical, secondary. **Engineering:** Civil, computer, electrical. **Engineering technology:** Computer systems, drafting. **Foreign languages:** General, sign language interpretation. **Health:** Dental hygiene, EMT paramedic, nursing (RN), pharmacy assistant, predental, premedicine, prepharmacy, preveterinary, respiratory therapy technology, veterinary technology/assistant. **History:** General. **Interdisciplinary:** Natural sciences. **Legal studies:** Prelaw. **Liberal arts:** Arts/sciences, library science. **Math:** General. **Mechanic/repair:** Auto body, automotive, diesel, heating/ac/refrig. **Parks/recreation:** Health/fitness. **Personal/culinary services:** Culinary arts. **Physical sciences:** Chemistry, geology, physics. **Production:** Welding, woodworking. **Protective services:** Fire safety technology, law enforcement admin. **Psychology:** General. **Public administration:** Human services. **Social sciences:** Anthropology, economics, geography, political science, sociology. **Visual/performing arts:** Art, commercial/advertising art, dramatic, photography.

Computing on campus. 350 workstations in dormitories, library, computer center, student center. Dormitories wired for high-speed internet access and linked to campus network. Commuter students can connect to campus network. Online course registration, online library, helpline, student web hosting, wireless network available.

Student life. Housing: Coed dorms, apartments, wellness housing available. $100 fully refundable deposit. **Activities:** Pep band, campus ministries, choral groups, drama, international student organizations, student government, student newspaper, Christian Fellowship, Latter-day Saints student association, Ambassadors, Latinos Unidos, Golden Eagle Native Americans, Chi Alpha, accent club.

Athletics. NJCAA. **Intercollegiate:** Baseball M, basketball, equestrian, rodeo, softball, volleyball W. **Intramural:** Basketball, bowling, football (non-tackle), golf, racquetball, soccer, softball, tennis, volleyball. **Team name:** Eagles.

Student services. Adult student services, alcohol/substance abuse counseling, career counseling, student employment services, financial aid counseling, health services, minority student services, on-campus daycare, personal counseling, veterans' counselor. **Physically disabled:** Services for visually, hearing impaired. **Transfer:** Re-entry adviser, pre-admission transcript evaluation for new students. College fairs on campus for students transferring to 4-year colleges.

Contact. Phone: (208) 732-6792 Fax: (208) 736-3014
Gail Schull, Director of Admissions, College of Southern Idaho, Box 1238, Twin Falls, ID 83303-1238

Two-Year Colleges

Eastern Idaho Technical College
Idaho Falls, Idaho
www.eitc.edu **CB code: 0975**

- Public 2-year technical college
- Commuter campus in small city

General. Founded in 1969. Regionally accredited. **Enrollment:** 651 degree-seeking undergraduates. **Degrees:** 71 associate awarded. **Location:** 280 miles from Boise, 230 miles from Salt Lake City. **Calendar:** Semester, limited summer session. **Full-time faculty:** 43 total; 58% women. **Part-time faculty:** 93 total; 56% women. **Class size:** 78% < 20, 21% 20-39, 2% 40-49.

Basis for selection. Open admission, but selective for some programs. Entrance exam, essay required for nursing. COMPASS required of all applicants. Students who score below acceptable level must take developmental classes before enrolling in degree program.

High school preparation. Recommended units include English 8, mathematics 6 and science 6.

2008-2009 Annual costs. Tuition/fees: $1,796; $6,238 out-of-state. Per-credit charge: $85 in-state; $170 out-of-state. Fees may vary according to the program of study. Books/supplies: $808. Personal expenses: $1,316.

Financial aid. Need-based: Need-based aid available for part-time students. Work-study available for part-time students. **Non-need-based:** Scholarships awarded for academics, job skills, state residency.

Application procedures. Admission: Closing date 8/20 (receipt date). $10 fee, may be waived for applicants with need. Application must be submitted on paper. Admission notification on a rolling basis. **Financial aid:** Priority date 6/1; no closing date. FAFSA, institutional form required. Applicants notified on a rolling basis starting 6/6; must reply within 4 week(s) of notification.

Academics. Special study options: Distance learning, ESL. License preparation in nursing, real estate. **Credit/placement by examination:** AP, CLEP. **Support services:** GED preparation and test center, learning center, pre-admission summer program, reduced course load, remedial instruction, study skills assistance, tutoring, writing center.

Majors. Business: Accounting, administrative services, marketing. **Computer sciences:** Networking, web page design. **Health:** Medical assistant, nursing (RN), surgical technology. **Legal studies:** Paralegal. **Mechanic/repair:** General, automotive, diesel. **Production:** Welding. **Protective services:** Firefighting.

Most popular majors. Business/marketing 24%, computer/information sciences 14%, engineering/engineering technologies 9%, health sciences 30%, legal studies 6%, trade and industry 18%.

Computing on campus. 209 workstations in library, computer center. Online library available.

Student life. Freshman orientation: Mandatory. Preregistration for classes offered. **Activities:** Student government.

Student services. Adult student services, alcohol/substance abuse counseling, career counseling, student employment services, financial aid counseling, personal counseling, placement for graduates, veterans' counselor, women's services. **Physically disabled:** Services for visually, speech, hearing impaired.

Contact. E-mail: jmeldrum@eitc.edu
Phone: (208) 524-3000 ext. 3337 Toll-free number: (800) 662-0261
Fax: (208) 525-7026
Jason Meldrum, Director of Admissions and Career Placement, Eastern Idaho Technical College, 1600 South 25th East, Idaho Falls, ID 83404-5788

North Idaho College

Coeur d'Alene, Idaho
www.nic.edu
CB member
CB code: 4539

- Public 2-year community college
- Commuter campus in large town

General. Founded in 1933. Regionally accredited. **Enrollment:** 3,958 degree-seeking undergraduates; 365 non-degree-seeking students. **Degrees:** 397 associate awarded. **ROTC:** Army. **Location:** 30 miles from Spokane, Washington. **Calendar:** Semester, limited summer session. **Full-time faculty:** 153 total; 8% have terminal degrees, 14% minority, 53% women. **Part-time faculty:** 154 total; 8% have terminal degrees, 7% minority, 53% women. **Partnerships:** Formal partnerships with local businesses.

Student profile. Among degree-seeking undergraduates, 1,047 enrolled as first-time, first-year students.

Part-time:	36%	**Asian American:**	2%
Women:	61%	**Hispanic American:**	3%
African American:	1%	**Native American:**	2%

Transfer out. **Colleges most students transferred to 2008:** University of Idaho, Lewis-Clark State College, Boise State University, Eastern Washington University, Spokane Community College.

Basis for selection. Open admission, but selective for some programs. RN, LPN and other allied health program applicants must submit 3 references and supplemental statement. Professional technical applicants should be interviewed by counselor. ACT, SAT, or COMPASS used for placement; scores must not be more than 2 years old. TOEFL scores used for placement of international students. Interview recommended for professional technical majors. **Homeschooled:** GED highly recommended. **Learning Disabled:** Contact Disability Support Services at time of application.

High school preparation. Recommended units include English 4, mathematics 3, social studies 2, science 3 (laboratory 1). Algebra, biology, 2 years chemistry with laboratory, or 1 year chemistry and 1 year physics, with cumulative 2.50 GPA required for registered nursing applicants. Physics, advanced algebra recommended for nursing applicants.

2008-2009 Annual costs. Tuition/fees: $2,246; $3,246 out-of-district; $7,798 out-of-state. Per-credit charge: $150 in-district; $213 out-of-district; $435 out-of-state. Room/board: $5,680. Books/supplies: $700. Personal expenses: $926.

2007-2008 Financial aid. **Need-based:** Need-based aid available for part-time students. Work-study available weekends and for part-time students. **Non-need-based:** Scholarships awarded for academics, art, athletics, leadership, minority status, music/drama, state residency.

Application procedures. **Admission:** No deadline. $25 fee, may be waived for applicants with need. Admission notification on a rolling basis beginning on or about 1/1. **Financial aid:** Priority date 3/15; no closing date. FAFSA required. Applicants notified on a rolling basis starting 4/1; must reply within 2 week(s) of notification.

Academics. **Special study options:** Distance learning, dual enrollment of high school students, independent study, internships. Lewis Clark State College and University of Idaho upper division and graduate classes on campus. Bachelor's degree programs available on campus. License preparation in nursing. **Credit/placement by examination:** CLEP, SAT, ACT, institutional tests. 24 credit hours maximum toward associate degree. **Support services:** GED preparation and test center, learning center, reduced course load, remedial instruction, study skills assistance, tutoring, writing center.

Majors. **Area/ethnic studies:** Native American. **Biology:** General, botany, zoology. **Business:** Administrative services, business admin. **Communications:** General, journalism, public relations. **Computer sciences:** General, applications programming, programming. **Conservation:** Fisheries, forestry, wildlife. **Construction:** Carpentry. **Education:** General, business, early childhood, elementary, secondary. **Engineering:** General, chemical, civil, electrical. **Engineering technology:** Drafting. **Foreign languages:** General. **Health:** Clinical lab assistant, health services, medical assistant, medical secretary, medical transcription, mental health services, nursing (RN), pharmacy assistant, physical therapy assistant, predental, premedicine, prepharmacy, preveterinary. **History:** General. **Legal studies:** Legal secretary, prelaw. **Liberal arts:** Arts/sciences. **Math:** General. **Mechanic/repair:** Auto body, automotive, diesel, heating/ac/refrig, industrial. **Parks/recreation:** Health/fitness. **Philosophy/religion:** Philosophy. **Physical sciences:** Astronomy, chemistry, geology, physics. **Protective services:** Criminal justice, police science. **Psychology:** General. **Public administration:** Human services. **Social sciences:** General, anthropology, political science, sociology. **Visual/performing arts:** Commercial/advertising art, music performance, music theory/composition, studio arts.

Most popular majors. Business/marketing 11%, engineering/engineering technologies 6%, health sciences 16%, liberal arts 41%.

Computing on campus. 150 workstations in dormitories, library, computer center, student center. Dormitories wired for high-speed internet access and linked to campus network. Commuter students can connect to campus network. Online course registration, helpline, repair service, wireless network available.

Student life. **Freshman orientation:** Available. **Housing:** Coed dorms available. $150 deposit, deadline 6/1. Apartment complex adjacent to campus available. **Activities:** Bands, campus ministries, choral groups, dance, drama, international student organizations, literary magazine, music ensembles, musical theater, student government, student newspaper, symphony orchestra, Students for Human Equality, creative writers club, nursing student association, veterans club.

Athletics. NJCAA. **Intercollegiate:** Basketball, cheerleading, soccer, softball W, volleyball W, wrestling M. **Intramural:** Basketball, bowling, football (non-tackle), golf, softball, table tennis, tennis, volleyball. **Team name:** Cardinals.

Student services. Adult student services, alcohol/substance abuse counseling, career counseling, services for economically disadvantaged, student employment services, financial aid counseling, health services, legal services, minority student services, on-campus daycare, personal counseling, placement for graduates, veterans' counselor, women's services. **Physically disabled:** Services for visually, speech, hearing impaired. **Transfer:** Transfer adviser, college fairs on campus for students transferring to 4-year colleges.

Contact. E-mail: admit@nic.edu
Phone: (208) 769-3311 Toll-free number: (877) 404-4536
Fax: (208) 769-3399
Maxine Gish, Director of Admissions, North Idaho College, 1000 West Garden Avenue, Coeur d'Alene, ID 83814-2199

Stevens-Henager College: Boise

Boise, Idaho
www.stevenshenager.edu/shc/campus/boise.cfm

- For-profit 2-year technical and career college
- Commuter campus in small city
- Application essay, interview required

General. Accredited by ACCSCT. **Enrollment:** 503 degree-seeking undergraduates. **Degrees:** 58 bachelor's, 150 associate awarded; master's offered. **Calendar:** Continuous, extensive summer session. **Full-time faculty:** 11 total; 18% have terminal degrees, 18% minority, 46% women. **Part-time faculty:** 32 total; 9% have terminal degrees, 6% minority, 28% women.

Student profile. Among degree-seeking undergraduates, 503 enrolled as first-time, first-year students, 39 transferred in from other institutions.

Out-of-state:	2%	**25 or older:**	55%
Women:	69%		

Transfer out. 30% of students enrolled in the transfer program go on to 4-year colleges.

Basis for selection. Open admission, but selective for some programs. All applicants must complete a personal interview and submit a personal statement. **Adult students:** SAT/ACT scores not required. **Homeschooled:** Transcript of courses and grades, state high school equivalency certificate, interview required.

High school preparation. 11 units required; 15 recommended. Required and recommended units include English 4, mathematics 2-3, social studies 1, history 2, science 2-3, foreign language 1 and computer science 1.

2009-2010 Annual costs. Tuition/fees (projected): $14,560. Tuition and fees can vary by program.

2007-2008 Financial aid. Need-based: 17% of total undergraduate aid awarded as scholarships/grants, 83% as loans/jobs.

Application procedures. Admission: No deadline. $75 fee. Application must be submitted on paper. Admission notification on a rolling basis.

Academics. Special study options: Accelerated study, distance learning, external degree, liberal arts/career combination, study abroad. Bachelor's degree programs available on campus. **Credit/placement by examination:** CLEP. **Support services:** Study skills assistance, tutoring, writing center.

Majors. Business: Accounting, business admin. **Health:** Office assistant. **Visual/performing arts:** Graphic design.

Computing on campus. 35 workstations in library, computer center, student center. Commuter students can connect to campus network. Online library, wireless network available.

Student life. Freshman orientation: Mandatory. **Activities:** Student newspaper.

Student services. Adult student services, career counseling, student employment services, financial aid counseling, placement for graduates. **Transfer:** Pre-admission transcript evaluation for new students.

Contact. E-mail: jaime.davis@stevenshenager.edu
Phone: (208) 283-5134 Fax: (208) 345-6999
David Breck, Director of Admissions, Stevens-Henager College: Boise, 1444 S Entertainment Avenue, Boise, ID 83709

Illinois

Black Hawk College
Moline, Illinois
www.bhc.edu **CB code: 1483**

- Public 2-year community college
- Commuter campus in large town

General. Founded in 1946. Regionally accredited. **Enrollment:** 4,263 degree-seeking undergraduates; 1,916 non-degree-seeking students. **Degrees:** 575 associate awarded. **Location:** 160 miles from Chicago, 60 miles from Iowa City. **Calendar:** Semester, limited summer session. **Full-time faculty:** 133 total; 16% have terminal degrees, 10% minority, 53% women. **Part-time faculty:** 194 total; 8% have terminal degrees, 10% minority, 54% women. **Class size:** 63% < 20, 36% 20-39, less than 1% 40-49, less than 1% 50-99. **Special facilities:** PBS television station.

Student profile. Among degree-seeking undergraduates, 53% enrolled in a transfer program, 47% enrolled in a vocational program, 5% already have a bachelor's degree or higher, 723 enrolled as first-time, first-year students, 225 transferred in from other institutions.

Part-time:	44%	**Asian American:**	1%
Out-of-state:	5%	**Hispanic American:**	9%
Women:	62%	**25 or older:**	39%
African American:	9%		

Transfer out. 75% of students enrolled in the transfer program go on to 4-year colleges. **Colleges most students transferred to 2008:** Western Illinois University, Illinois State University, St. Ambrose University, Northern Illinois University, University of Iowa.

Basis for selection. Open admission, but selective for some programs. Special requirements for health care-related programs, such as nursing and physical therapy assistant.

High school preparation. 15 units recommended. Recommended units include English 4, mathematics 3, social studies 3, science 3, foreign language 2 and visual/performing arts 2.

2008-2009 Annual costs. Tuition/fees: $2,535; $4,755 out-of-district; $8,325 out-of-state. Per-credit charge: $77 in-district; $151 out-of-district; $270 out-of-state. Agreement with 5 contiguous Iowa counties for special tuition rate of $111 per credit plus required fees. Online courses are $91 (tuition only) per credit hour in-state; $270, out-of-state. Books/supplies: $950. Personal expenses: $3,900.

2007-2008 Financial aid. **Need-based:** 530 full-time freshmen applied for aid; 328 were judged to have need; 293 of these received aid. Average need met was 64%. Average scholarship/grant was $2,137; average loan $1,445. 81% of total undergraduate aid awarded as scholarships/grants, 19% as loans/jobs. Need-based aid available for part-time students. Work-study available for part-time students. **Non-need-based:** Awarded to 412 full-time undergraduates, including 141 freshmen. Scholarships awarded for academics, art, athletics, leadership, music/drama, state residency. **Additional information:** 5/15 deadline for scholarships.

Application procedures. **Admission:** No deadline. No application fee. Admission notification on a rolling basis beginning on or about 3/1. **Financial aid:** Priority date 5/15; no closing date. FAFSA required. Applicants notified on a rolling basis starting 5/1.

Academics. **Special study options:** Accelerated study, cooperative education, cross-registration, distance learning, dual enrollment of high school students, ESL, independent study, internships, study abroad, weekend college. License preparation in nursing, physical therapy. **Credit/placement by examination:** AP, CLEP, ACT, institutional tests. 30 credit hours maximum toward associate degree. Most CLEP credit awarded to students pursuing associate degree in liberal studies. **Support services:** GED preparation, learning center, reduced course load, remedial instruction, study skills assistance, tutoring.

Majors. **Agriculture:** Animal husbandry, business, crop production, equestrian studies, horticulture, mechanization, production. **Business:** Accounting, accounting technology, administrative services, banking/financial services, business admin, human resources, international, office management, office technology, retailing, small business admin. **Communications technology:** Radio/tv. **Computer sciences:** Programming. **Construction:** Carpentry, electrician. **Education:** Early childhood, mathematics, special. **Engineering technology:** Environmental, manufacturing. **Foreign languages:** Sign language interpretation. **Health:** Electroencephalograph technology, EMT paramedic, medical radiologic technology/radiation therapy, medical records technology, nursing (RN), physical therapy assistant. **Interdisciplinary:** Biological/physical sciences. **Legal studies:** Legal secretary, paralegal. **Liberal arts:** Arts/sciences. **Mechanic/repair:** Auto body, automotive, diesel, heating/ac/refrig. **Personal/culinary services:** Restaurant/catering. **Protective services:** Fire services admin, police science. **Visual/performing arts:** Design, interior design.

Most popular majors. Agriculture 10%, health sciences 17%, interdisciplinary studies 12%, liberal arts 48%.

Computing on campus. 850 workstations in library, computer center. Commuter students can connect to campus network. Online course registration, wireless network available.

Student life. **Freshman orientation:** Mandatory. Preregistration for classes offered. **Activities:** Jazz band, choral groups, drama, international student organizations, music ensembles, student government, student newspaper, TV station, African-American student union, Alpha Beta Gamma, Association of Latin America, Brotherhood On Campus, College Democrats of America, College Republicans, Sisterhood On Campus, Social Action Connection, Clean Sphere, Habitat for Humanity.

Athletics. NJCAA. **Intercollegiate:** Baseball M, basketball, golf M, softball W, volleyball W. **Team name:** Braves.

Student services. Career counseling, services for economically disadvantaged, student employment services, financial aid counseling, minority student services, personal counseling, placement for graduates, women's services. **Physically disabled:** Services for visually, speech, hearing impaired. **Transfer:** Transfer center, transfer adviser, college fairs on campus for students transferring to 4-year colleges.

Contact. Phone: (309) 796-5300 Fax: (309) 796-5209
Richard Vallandingham, Dean of Student Support Services, Black Hawk College, 6600 34th Avenue, Moline, IL 61265-5899

Black Hawk College: East Campus
Galva, Illinois
www.bhc.edu **CB code: 0690**

- Public 2-year community college
- Commuter campus in small town

General. Founded in 1967. Regionally accredited. **Enrollment:** 800 degree-seeking undergraduates. **Degrees:** 575 associate awarded. **Location:** 45 miles from Peoria, 50 miles from Moline. **Calendar:** Semester, extensive summer session. **Full-time faculty:** 24 total. **Part-time faculty:** 40 total. **Special facilities:** Agricultural facilities for horse boarding.

Transfer out. **Colleges most students transferred to 2008:** Western Illinois University, Illinois State University, University of Illinois.

Basis for selection. Open admission, but selective for some programs. Special requirements for physical therapy assistant and nursing programs, limited enrollment in practical nursing and truck driving certificates. SAT or ACT may be used in lieu of placement exam. Interview required of nursing and physical therapy assistant majors.

2008-2009 Annual costs. Tuition/fees: $2,535; $4,755 out-of-district; $8,325 out-of-state. Per-credit charge: $77 in-state; $270 out-of-state. Agreement with 5 contiguous Iowa counties for special tuition rate of $111 per credit plus required fees. Online courses are $91 (tuition only) per credit hour in-state; $270, out-of-state. Books/supplies: $600.

Application procedures. **Admission:** No deadline. No application fee. Admission notification on a rolling basis. **Financial aid:** Priority date 5/15; no closing date. FAFSA required. Applicants notified on a rolling basis; must reply within 2 week(s) of notification.

Academics. **Special study options:** Cooperative education, cross-registration, distance learning, double major, dual enrollment of high school students, independent study, internships, study abroad. **Credit/placement by examination:** CLEP, institutional tests. 40 credit hours maximum toward associate degree. **Support services:** GED preparation and test center, learning center, pre-admission summer program, reduced course load, remedial instruction, tutoring.

Majors. Agriculture: Business, equestrian studies, horticulture. **Biology:** General. **Business:** General, accounting, administrative services, office technology. **Communications:** Journalism, public relations. **Computer sciences:** General, data processing, programming. **Education:** Elementary, secondary. **Health:** Predental, premedicine, prepharmacy. **History:** General. **Interdisciplinary:** Natural sciences. **Legal studies:** Paralegal, prelaw. **Liberal arts:** Arts/sciences. **Math:** General. **Mechanic/repair:** Automotive. **Physical sciences:** Chemistry, planetary. **Psychology:** General. **Social sciences:** Anthropology, economics, political science, sociology. **Visual/performing arts:** Art.

Computing on campus. 101 workstations in computer center.

Student life. Activities: Student government.

Athletics. NJCAA. **Intercollegiate:** Basketball. **Team name:** Warriors/Lady Warriors.

Student services. Career counseling, student employment services, personal counseling, placement for graduates, veterans' counselor. **Physically disabled:** Services for visually, speech, hearing impaired. **Transfer:** Transfer adviser, college fairs on campus for students transferring to 4-year colleges.

Contact. E-mail: riced@bhc.edu
Phone: (309) 854-1703 Fax: (309) 856-6005
Dede Rice, Assistant Registrar, Black Hawk College: East Campus, 26230 Black Hawk Road, Galva, IL 61434-9476

Carl Sandburg College

Galesburg, Illinois
www.sandburg.edu **CB code: 1982**

- Public 2-year community college
- Commuter campus in large town

General. Founded in 1966. Regionally accredited. Branch center in Carthage, extension center in Bushnell. **Enrollment:** 1,976 degree-seeking undergraduates; 639 non-degree-seeking students. **Degrees:** 245 associate awarded. **ROTC:** Army. **Location:** 198 miles from Chicago, 47 miles from Peoria. **Calendar:** Semester, limited summer session. **Full-time faculty:** 61 total; 8% have terminal degrees, 2% minority, 64% women. **Part-time faculty:** 126 total; 2% have terminal degrees, 5% minority, 60% women. **Class size:** 94% < 20, 6% 20-39, less than 1% 40-49, less than 1% 50-99. **Special facilities:** Greenhouse, 22-acre agriculture experience plot.

Student profile. Among degree-seeking undergraduates, 98% enrolled in a transfer program, 2% enrolled in a vocational program, 2% already have a bachelor's degree or higher, 237 enrolled as first-time, first-year students, 52 transferred in from other institutions.

Part-time:	42%	**Asian American:**	1%
Out-of-state:	3%	**Hispanic American:**	4%
Women:	67%	**25 or older:**	39%
African American:	5%		

Transfer out. 30% of students enrolled in the transfer program go on to 4-year colleges. **Colleges most students transferred to 2008:** Western Illinois University, Illinois State University.

Basis for selection. Open admission, but selective for some programs. Special requirements for allied health programs. Interview recommended for radiologic technology, mortuary science, and physical therapy assistant majors.

High school preparation. 15 units recommended. Recommended units include English 4, mathematics 3, social studies 2, science 2 (laboratory 2) and academic electives 2.

2008-2009 Annual costs. Tuition/fees: $3,810; $4,320 out-of-district; $6,360 out-of-state. Books/supplies: $710. Personal expenses: $880.

2007-2008 Financial aid. Need-based: 80 full-time freshmen applied for aid; 72 were judged to have need; 72 of these received aid. Average need met was 25%. Average scholarship/grant was $4,019; average loan $2,212. 84% of total undergraduate aid awarded as scholarships/grants, 16% as loans/jobs. Work-study available for part-time students. **Non-need-based:** Awarded to 193 full-time undergraduates, including 53 freshmen. Scholarships awarded for academics, art, athletics, music/drama.

Application procedures. Admission: No deadline. No application fee. Admission notification on a rolling basis. **Financial aid:** Priority date 5/1; no closing date. FAFSA, institutional form required. Applicants notified on a rolling basis starting 5/1; must reply by 8/25 or within 2 week(s) of notification.

Academics. Special study options: Cross-registration, dual enrollment of high school students, ESL, honors, independent study, internships, student-designed major, study abroad, teacher certification program. License preparation in dental hygiene, nursing, paramedic, radiology. **Credit/placement by examination:** AP, CLEP, institutional tests. 20 credit hours maximum toward associate degree. **Support services:** GED preparation and test center, learning center, remedial instruction, tutoring.

Majors. Agriculture: Business. **Business:** Accounting, administrative services, banking/financial services, business admin, operations. **Computer sciences:** General. **Engineering technology:** Drafting. **Family/consumer sciences:** Child care. **Health:** Nursing (RN). **Mechanic/repair:** Auto body. **Personal/culinary services:** Mortuary science. **Protective services:** Firefighting, law enforcement admin.

Most popular majors. Business/marketing 8%, health sciences 31%, interdisciplinary studies 17%, liberal arts 32%.

Computing on campus. 69 workstations in library, computer center. Commuter students can connect to campus network. Online library, helpline, wireless network available.

Student life. Activities: Bands, choral groups, drama, literary magazine, music ensembles, student government.

Athletics. NJCAA. **Intercollegiate:** Baseball M, basketball, softball W, volleyball W. **Team name:** Chargers.

Student services. Career counseling, services for economically disadvantaged, student employment services, on-campus daycare, personal counseling, placement for graduates, veterans' counselor. **Physically disabled:** Services for visually, hearing impaired. **Transfer:** Transfer adviser, college fairs on campus for students transferring to 4-year colleges.

Contact. Phone: (309) 344-2518 Fax: (309) 344-3526
Carol Kreider, Dean of Student Support Services, Carl Sandburg College, 2400 Tom L. Wilson Boulevard, Galesburg, IL 61401

City Colleges of Chicago: Harold Washington College

Chicago, Illinois
www.ccc.edu **CB code: 1089**

- Public 2-year community college
- Commuter campus in very large city

General. Founded in 1962. Regionally accredited. **Enrollment:** 7,748 degree-seeking undergraduates. **Degrees:** 281 associate awarded. **Calendar:** Semester, limited summer session. **Full-time faculty:** 111 total. **Part-time faculty:** 423 total. **Partnerships:** Formal partnerships with McDonalds, Dominicks, Chicago public schools.

Transfer out. Colleges most students transferred to 2008: Chicago State University, Northeastern Illinois University, University of Illinois-Chicago, DePaul University, Roosevelt University.

Basis for selection. Open admission, but selective for some programs. Special requirements for physicians assistant and police programs. All incoming freshmen required to take placement tests.

High school preparation. 20 units required. Required units include English 4, mathematics 4, social studies 4, science 3 and academic electives 3. 2 additional units in foreign language, art, music, computer science, or other electives required.

2008-2009 Annual costs. Tuition/fees: $2,510; $8,120 out-of-district; $9,557 out-of-state. Per-credit charge: $72 in-district; $259 out-of-district; $307 out-of-state. Books/supplies: $600. Personal expenses: $1,761.

Financial aid. All financial aid based on need. Need-based aid available for part-time students. Work-study available nights and for part-time students.

Application procedures. Admission: No deadline. No application fee. **Financial aid:** Priority date 5/1, closing date 6/30. FAFSA required. Applicants notified on a rolling basis starting 7/1; must reply within 2 week(s) of notification.

Academics. Special study options: Cooperative education, cross-registration, distance learning, double major, dual enrollment of high school

students, ESL, honors, independent study, internships, liberal arts/career combination. Courses by videocassette at Chicago public libraries; offer license preparation in taxi, limousine, foodservice and sanitation, and substance abuse counseling. **Credit/placement by examination:** AP, CLEP, institutional tests. **Support services:** GED preparation, learning center, reduced course load, remedial instruction, study skills assistance, tutoring.

Majors. Biology: General. **Business:** Accounting, administrative services, banking/financial services, business admin, hospitality admin, international, tourism/travel. **Communications:** Journalism. **Computer sciences:** General, data processing, information systems. **Education:** Early childhood, elementary, secondary, teacher assistance. **Engineering:** General. **Family/consumer sciences:** Family studies. **Foreign languages:** General, French, German, Japanese, Spanish. **Health:** Predental, premedicine, prepharmacy, substance abuse counseling. **Legal studies:** General, prelaw. **Liberal arts:** Arts/sciences. **Math:** General. **Philosophy/religion:** Philosophy. **Physical sciences:** Chemistry, physics. **Protective services:** Corrections, firefighting, law enforcement admin, police science. **Public administration:** Social work. **Social sciences:** General. **Visual/performing arts:** Art, commercial/advertising art, design, dramatic.

Most popular majors. Business/marketing 9%, education 7%, health sciences 6%, liberal arts 66%.

Computing on campus. 180 workstations in computer center. Online library available.

Student life. Freshman orientation: Mandatory. Preregistration for classes offered. One hour overview. **Activities:** Jazz band, choral groups, drama, literary magazine, music ensembles, student government, student newspaper, black student union, Organization of Latin American Students, Berean Bible club, Circle K.

Student services. Adult student services, career counseling, services for economically disadvantaged, student employment services, financial aid counseling, minority student services, personal counseling, placement for graduates, veterans' counselor. **Physically disabled:** Services for visually, speech, hearing impaired. **Learning disabled:** Comprehensive services available. **Transfer:** Transfer adviser, college fairs on campus for students transferring to 4-year colleges.

Contact. Phone: (312) 553-6071 Fax: (312) 553-6077
Robert Brown, Registrar, City Colleges of Chicago: Harold Washington College, 30 East Lake Street, Chicago, IL 60601

City Colleges of Chicago: Harry S. Truman College

Chicago, Illinois
www.ccc.edu **CB code: 1111**

- Public 2-year community college
- Commuter campus in very large city

General. Founded in 1956. Regionally accredited. **Enrollment:** 5,092 degree-seeking undergraduates. **Degrees:** 203 associate awarded. **Calendar:** Semester, limited summer session. **Full-time faculty:** 88 total. **Part-time faculty:** 467 total. **Special facilities:** Art gallery for Chicago artists, theater for performing arts. **Partnerships:** Formal partnerships with Chamber of Commerce and aldermanic representative for our ward.

Transfer out. Colleges most students transferred to 2008: University of Illinois, Loyola University of Chicago, Roosevelt University, Northeastern Illinois University.

Basis for selection. Open admission, but selective for some programs. Test scores, essay considered for nursing and certain allied health programs. Applicants without high school diploma must obtain GED prior to graduation. ACT required of nursing applicants.

2008-2009 Annual costs. Tuition/fees: $2,510; $8,120 out-of-district; $9,557 out-of-state. Per-credit charge: $72 in-district; $259 out-of-district; $307 out-of-state. Books/supplies: $800. Personal expenses: $1,530.

Financial aid. All financial aid based on need. Need-based aid available for part-time students. Work-study available nights and weekends.

Application procedures. Admission: No deadline. No application fee. Admission notification on a rolling basis. **Financial aid:** No deadline. FAFSA required. Applicants notified on a rolling basis starting 7/1; must reply within 3 week(s) of notification.

Academics. Special study options: Cooperative education, cross-registration, dual enrollment of high school students, honors, independent study, internships, liberal arts/career combination, weekend college. License preparation in nursing. **Credit/placement by examination:** AP, CLEP, institutional tests. 30 credit hours maximum toward associate degree. **Support services:** GED preparation and test center, learning center, reduced course load, remedial instruction, tutoring.

Majors. Business: Business admin. **Computer sciences:** General. **Health:** Nursing (RN).

Computing on campus. 86 workstations in library, computer center.

Student life. Freshman orientation: Available. **Activities:** Drama, student government, student newspaper, TV station, Latin American center, refugee center, Native American center.

Athletics. NJCAA.

Student services. Adult student services, career counseling, student employment services, health services, on-campus daycare, personal counseling, placement for graduates, veterans' counselor. **Transfer:** Transfer adviser for students transferring to 4-year colleges.

Contact. Phone: (773) 907-6814 Fax: (773) 907-4757
Mylinh Tran, Registrar, City Colleges of Chicago: Harry S. Truman College, 1145 West Wilson Avenue, Chicago, IL 60640

City Colleges of Chicago: Kennedy-King College

Chicago, Illinois
www.ccc.edu **CB code: 1910**

- Public 2-year community college
- Commuter campus in very large city

General. Founded in 1935. Regionally accredited. **Enrollment:** 4,581 degree-seeking undergraduates. **Degrees:** 124 associate awarded. **Calendar:** Semester, limited summer session. **Full-time faculty:** 65 total. **Part-time faculty:** 254 total. **Class size:** 19% < 20, 77% 20-39, 3% 40-49, less than 1% 50-99.

Student profile.

Out-of-state:	1%	**25 or older:**	65%

Transfer out. Colleges most students transferred to 2008: University of Illinois at Chicago, Chicago State University.

Basis for selection. Open admission. Applicants admitted without high school diploma must pass GED by end of first school year.

2008-2009 Annual costs. Tuition/fees: $2,510; $8,120 out-of-district; $9,557 out-of-state. Per-credit charge: $72 in-district; $259 out-of-district; $307 out-of-state. Lab fee of $30 for technical and vocational courses. Books/supplies: $1,000. Personal expenses: $2,000.

Financial aid. All financial aid based on need. Need-based aid available for part-time students.

Application procedures. Admission: No deadline. No application fee. **Financial aid:** Priority date 8/1; no closing date. FAFSA required. Applicants notified on a rolling basis starting 8/15; must reply within 2 week(s) of notification.

Academics. Special study options: Cooperative education, cross-registration, distance learning, dual enrollment of high school students, honors, independent study, internships, liberal arts/career combination, weekend college. License preparation in dental hygiene, nursing. **Credit/placement by examination:** AP, CLEP, institutional tests. 15 credit hours maximum toward associate degree. Interview recommended for placement and counseling. **Support services:** GED preparation, learning center, pre-admission summer program, reduced course load, remedial instruction, study skills assistance, tutoring, writing center.

Majors. Area/ethnic studies: African-American. **Business:** Accounting, administrative services, business admin. **Communications:** Broadcast journalism, journalism. **Communications technology:** Graphics, printing press operator. **Computer sciences:** General. **Education:** General, early childhood, elementary, middle, voc/tech. **Engineering technology:** Heat/ac/refrig. **Family/consumer sciences:** Child development. **Foreign languages:** General. **Health:** Dental hygiene, health services, nursing (RN), predental, premedicine, prepharmacy. **History:** General. **Legal studies:** Prelaw. **Liberal arts:** Arts/sciences. **Math:** General. **Mechanic/repair:** Automotive, heating/ac/refrig. **Physical sciences:** Chemistry, physics. **Psychology:** General. **Public administration:** Social work. **Social sciences:** General. **Visual/performing arts:** General, commercial/advertising art, dramatic, studio arts.

Computing on campus. 100 workstations in library, computer center.

Student life. Freshman orientation: Available. Preregistration for classes offered. **Activities:** Choral groups, drama, musical theater, radio station, student government, student newspaper, TV station, Phi Theta Kappa, Student Nursing Association, broadcasting club, math club, Future Teachers of Chicago.

Athletics. NJCAA. **Intercollegiate:** Basketball. **Intramural:** Basketball M, softball, swimming, volleyball. **Team name:** Statesman, Lady Statesman.

Student services. Adult student services, career counseling, student employment services, on-campus daycare, personal counseling, placement for graduates, veterans' counselor. **Physically disabled:** Services for visually, hearing impaired. **Transfer:** Re-entry adviser, pre-admission transcript evaluation for new students. Transfer center, transfer adviser, college fairs on campus for students transferring to 4-year colleges.

Contact. Phone: (773) 602-5273 Fax: (773) 602-5247
Marlene Sparrow-Oloko, Registrar, City Colleges of Chicago: Kennedy-King College, 6800 South Wentworth Avenue, Chicago, IL 60621

City Colleges of Chicago: Malcolm X College

Chicago, Illinois
www.malcolmx.ccc.edu **CB code: 1144**

- Public 2-year community and junior college
- Commuter campus in very large city

General. Founded in 1911. Regionally accredited. **Enrollment:** 3,534 degree-seeking undergraduates. **Degrees:** 252 associate awarded. **Location:** 3 miles from downtown. **Calendar:** Semester, limited summer session. **Full-time faculty:** 67 total. **Part-time faculty:** 293 total. **Class size:** 53% < 20, 47% 20-39. **Partnerships:** Formal partnerships with three middle and six high schools to provide TRIO Talent Search and Upward Bound programs.

Student profile.

Out-of-state:	1%	25 or older:	58%

Transfer out. Colleges most students transferred to 2008: University of Illinois at Chicago, Chicago State University, Northeastern Illinois University, Robert Morris College, National-Louis University.

Basis for selection. Open admission, but selective for some programs. Interview recommended for nursing and allied health applicants. Adults out of high school 5 years or more may be concurrently registered while obtaining GED.

2008-2009 Annual costs. Tuition/fees: $2,510; $8,120 out-of-district; $9,557 out-of-state. Per-credit charge: $72 in-district; $259 out-of-district; $307 out-of-state. Some courses require a $30 lab fee. Books/supplies: $800.

Financial aid. All financial aid based on need. Need-based aid available for part-time students. Work-study available nights, weekends and for part-time students.

Application procedures. Admission: No deadline. No application fee. Admission notification on a rolling basis. **Financial aid:** Priority date 7/1; no closing date. FAFSA, institutional form required. Applicants notified on a rolling basis starting 7/1; must reply within 2 week(s) of notification.

Academics. Special study options: Cooperative education, cross-registration, distance learning, dual enrollment of high school students, ESL, internships, liberal arts/career combination, weekend college. License preparation in nursing, paramedic, radiology. **Credit/placement by examination:** AP, CLEP, institutional tests. 30 credit hours maximum toward associate degree. **Support services:** GED preparation, learning center, pre-admission summer program, reduced course load, remedial instruction, study skills assistance, tutoring.

Majors. Agriculture: Food science. **Biology:** General. **Business:** General, accounting, administrative services, business admin, office technology. **Education:** Teacher assistance. **Family/consumer sciences:** Child care, institutional food production. **Health:** Clinical lab technology, dialysis technology, EMT paramedic, medical radiologic technology/radiation therapy, nursing (RN), respiratory therapy technology, surgical technology. **Liberal arts:** Arts/sciences. **Personal/culinary services:** Culinary arts, mortuary science.

Most popular majors. Biological/life sciences 9%, health sciences 63%, liberal arts 25%.

Computing on campus. 275 workstations in library, computer center. Online course registration, online library, repair service, wireless network available.

Student life. Freshman orientation: Available. Preregistration for classes offered. **Activities:** Dance, drama, literary magazine, student government, student newspaper.

Athletics. NJCAA. **Intercollegiate:** Basketball, cheerleading M, track and field. **Intramural:** Basketball, cheerleading W, table tennis, track and field, volleyball. **Team name:** Hawks.

Student services. Adult student services, career counseling, student employment services, financial aid counseling, minority student services, on-campus daycare, personal counseling, placement for graduates, veterans' counselor. **Physically disabled:** Services for visually, speech, hearing impaired. **Learning disabled:** Comprehensive services available. **Transfer:** Pre-admission transcript evaluation for new students. Transfer center, transfer adviser, college fairs on campus for students transferring to 4-year colleges.

Contact. Phone: (312) 850-7126 Fax: (312) 850-7092
Abdul-Rasheed Akbar, Registrar, City Colleges of Chicago: Malcolm X College, 1900 West Van Buren Street, Chicago, IL 60612

City Colleges of Chicago: Olive-Harvey College

Chicago, Illinois
www.ccc.edu **CB code: 1584**

- Public 2-year community college
- Commuter campus in very large city

General. Founded in 1970. Regionally accredited. **Enrollment:** 2,526 degree-seeking undergraduates. **Degrees:** 234 associate awarded. **Location:** 16 miles from downtown. **Calendar:** Semester, limited summer session. **Full-time faculty:** 55 total. **Part-time faculty:** 155 total. **Special facilities:** Child development, high technology centers.

Basis for selection. Open admission, but selective for some programs. Special requirements for nursing, electronics, respiratory care, and local area networking programs.

High school preparation. 15 units recommended. Recommended units include English 4, mathematics 3, social studies 3, science 3 and foreign language 2.

2008-2009 Annual costs. Tuition/fees: $2,510; $8,120 out-of-district; $9,557 out-of-state. Per-credit charge: $72 in-district; $259 out-of-district; $307 out-of-state. Books/supplies: $600.

Financial aid. Need-based: Need-based aid available for part-time students.

Application procedures. Admission: No deadline. No application fee. Admission notification on a rolling basis. **Financial aid:** Priority date 8/15; no closing date. FAFSA required. Applicants notified on a rolling basis; must reply within 3 week(s) of notification.

Academics. Special study options: Cooperative education, cross-registration, distance learning, dual enrollment of high school students, honors, independent study, internships, student-designed major, study abroad. **Credit/placement by examination:** AP, CLEP, institutional tests. 30 credit hours maximum toward associate degree. **Support services:** Learning center, reduced course load, remedial instruction, tutoring.

Majors. Area/ethnic studies: African-American. **Biology:** General. **Business:** General, accounting, administrative services, business admin, management information systems. **Computer sciences:** General, data processing, programming. **Education:** Art. **Engineering:** General, architectural, electrical. **Family/consumer sciences:** Child care, child development. **Foreign languages:** General. **Legal studies:** General. **Liberal arts:** Arts/sciences. **Math:** General. **Philosophy/religion:** Philosophy. **Physical sciences:** Chemistry, physics, planetary. **Social sciences:** General. **Visual/performing arts:** Drawing, painting, photography, studio arts.

Computing on campus. 517 workstations in library, computer center.

Student life. Activities: Student government, student newspaper, African-American and Latino student groups.

Athletics. NJCAA. **Intercollegiate:** Basketball M, volleyball W. **Intramural:** Basketball, volleyball.

Student services. Adult student services, career counseling, student employment services, on-campus daycare, placement for graduates, veterans' counselor. **Transfer:** Transfer center, transfer adviser, college fairs on campus for students transferring to 4-year colleges.

Contact. Phone: (773) 291-6384 Fax: (773) 291-6185
Valerie Davis, Registrar, City Colleges of Chicago: Olive-Harvey College, 10001 South Woodlawn Avenue, Chicago, IL 60628

City Colleges of Chicago: Richard J. Daley College

Chicago, Illinois
www.daley.ccc.edu/ **CB code: 1093**

- Public 2-year community college
- Commuter campus in very large city

General. Founded in 1960. Regionally accredited. **Enrollment:** 4,107 degree-seeking undergraduates. **Degrees:** 324 associate awarded. **Calendar:** Semester, limited summer session. **Full-time faculty:** 56 total. **Part-time faculty:** 308 total.

Basis for selection. Open admission, but selective for some programs. Special requirements for nursing program.

High school preparation. 15 units recommended. Recommended units include English 4, mathematics 3, social studies 3, science 3 and academic electives 2.

2008-2009 Annual costs. Tuition/fees: $2,510; $8,120 out-of-district; $9,557 out-of-state. Per-credit charge: $72 in-district; $259 out-of-district; $307 out-of-state. Books/supplies: $800. Personal expenses: $320.

Application procedures. **Admission:** No deadline. No application fee. Admission notification on a rolling basis. **Financial aid:** No deadline. FAFSA required. Applicants notified on a rolling basis.

Academics. Cross-registration with other City Colleges of Chicago. **Special study options:** Cooperative education, cross-registration, distance learning, dual enrollment of high school students, honors, independent study, internships, weekend college. **Credit/placement by examination:** AP, CLEP, institutional tests. 30 credit hours maximum toward associate degree. **Support services:** Learning center, reduced course load, remedial instruction, tutoring.

Majors. **Business:** General. **Liberal arts:** Arts/sciences. **Social sciences:** General.

Computing on campus. 250 workstations in library, computer center.

Student life. **Activities:** Student government, student newspaper, TV station.

Athletics. NJCAA.

Student services. Adult student services, career counseling, student employment services, on-campus daycare, personal counseling, placement for graduates, veterans' counselor. **Physically disabled:** Services for visually, speech, hearing impaired. **Transfer:** Transfer adviser, college fairs on campus for students transferring to 4-year colleges.

Contact. Phone: (773) 838-7606 Fax: (773) 838-7605
Milton Wright, Registrar, City Colleges of Chicago: Richard J. Daley College, 7500 South Pulaski Road, Chicago, IL 60652

City Colleges of Chicago: Wright College

Chicago, Illinois
www.ccc.edu **CB code: 1925**

- Public 2-year community college
- Commuter campus in very large city

General. Founded in 1934. Regionally accredited. **Enrollment:** 7,571 degree-seeking undergraduates. **Degrees:** 395 associate awarded. **Location:** 15 miles from downtown. **Calendar:** Semester, limited summer session. **Full-time faculty:** 107 total. **Part-time faculty:** 472 total. **Class size:** 100% 20-39.

Transfer out. **Colleges most students transferred to 2008:** Northeastern Illinois University, University of Illinois at Chicago, DePaul University.

Basis for selection. Open admission.

2008-2009 Annual costs. Tuition/fees: $2,510; $8,120 out-of-district; $9,557 out-of-state. Per-credit charge: $72 in-district; $259 out-of-district; $307 out-of-state. Books/supplies: $630. Personal expenses: $1,280.

Financial aid. **Need-based:** Need-based aid available for part-time students. Work-study available nights, weekends and for part-time students.

Application procedures. **Admission:** No deadline. No application fee. Admission notification on a rolling basis. **Financial aid:** Priority date 6/1; no closing date. FAFSA, institutional form required. Applicants notified on a rolling basis starting 7/15.

Academics. **Special study options:** Cross-registration, distance learning, dual enrollment of high school students, ESL, honors, independent study, internships, weekend college. License preparation in nursing, occupational therapy. **Credit/placement by examination:** AP, CLEP, IB, institutional tests. 10 credit hours maximum toward associate degree. **Support services:** GED preparation and test center, learning center, reduced course load, remedial instruction, tutoring.

Majors. **Business:** Accounting, administrative services, business admin, sales/distribution. **Computer sciences:** General, applications programming. **Engineering technology:** Mechanical drafting. **Health:** Licensed practical nurse, medical radiologic technology/radiation therapy, occupational therapy assistant, radiologic technology/medical imaging, sonography. **Interdisciplinary:** Gerontology. **Liberal arts:** Arts/sciences, library assistant. **Mechanic/repair:** Electronics/electrical. **Visual/performing arts:** Design.

Computing on campus. 534 workstations in computer center.

Student life. **Freshman orientation:** Available. Preregistration for classes offered. **Activities:** Concert band, choral groups, drama, film society, literary magazine, music ensembles, student government, student newspaper, symphony orchestra, Circle-K, service organization, honor society, various ethnic clubs.

Athletics. NJCAA. **Intercollegiate:** Basketball, wrestling M. **Team name:** Rams.

Student services. Adult student services, chaplain/spiritual director, career counseling, student employment services, financial aid counseling, health services, legal services, on-campus daycare, personal counseling, placement for graduates, veterans' counselor. **Physically disabled:** Services for visually, speech, hearing impaired. **Transfer:** Transfer center, transfer adviser, college fairs on campus for students transferring to 4-year colleges.

Contact. Phone: (773) 481-8259 Fax: (773) 481-8053
Linda Huertas, Registrar, City Colleges of Chicago: Wright College, 4300 North Narragansett Avenue, Chicago, IL 60634-4276

College of DuPage

Glen Ellyn, Illinois **CB member**
www.cod.edu **CB code: 1083**

- Public 2-year community college
- Commuter campus in large town

General. Founded in 1966. Regionally accredited. Continuing Education division offers courses at more than 50 off-campus locations. Selected courses available through the Internet. Adult fast-track program for highly motivated, self-disciplined students 24 years and older. **Enrollment:** 21,978 degree-seeking undergraduates; 3,690 non-degree-seeking students. **Degrees:** 1,556 associate awarded. **Location:** 25 miles from Chicago. **Calendar:** Semester, extensive summer session. **Full-time faculty:** 307 total; 28% have terminal degrees, 12% minority, 54% women. **Part-time faculty:** 1,149 total; 11% have terminal degrees, 12% minority, 58% women. **Class size:** 37% < 20, 60% 20-39, 2% 40-49, less than 1% 50-99, less than 1% >100. **Special facilities:** Older adult institute, prairie-marsh nature preserve, arts center, community recreation center.

Student profile. Among degree-seeking undergraduates, 2,959 enrolled as first-time, first-year students.

Part-time:	57%	**Asian American:**	11%
Women:	54%	**Hispanic American:**	10%
African American:	7%	**25 or older:**	53%

Transfer out. **Colleges most students transferred to 2008:** Northern Illinois University, Illinois State University, University of Illinois-Chicago, Elmhurst College, Benedictine University.

Basis for selection. Open admission, but selective for some programs. Special requirements for allied health programs.

2008-2009 Annual costs. Tuition/fees: $3,240; $8,880 out-of-district; $10,770 out-of-state. Per-credit charge: $88 in-district; $276 out-of-district; $339 out-of-state. Books/supplies: $1,370. Personal expenses: $1,435.

2007-2008 Financial aid. Need-based: 766 full-time freshmen applied for aid; 550 were judged to have need; 439 of these received aid. Average need met was 63%. Average scholarship/grant was $4,087; average loan $2,815. 52% of total undergraduate aid awarded as scholarships/grants, 48% as loans/jobs. Need-based aid available for part-time students. Work-study available nights, weekends and for part-time students. **Non-need-based:** Awarded to 338 full-time undergraduates, including 105 freshmen. Scholarships awarded for academics, art, leadership, minority status, music/drama, state residency.

Application procedures. Admission: No deadline. $20 fee, may be waived for applicants with need. Admission notification on a rolling basis. **Financial aid:** Priority date 4/30; no closing date. FAFSA required. Applicants notified on a rolling basis starting 6/1; must reply within 2 week(s) of notification.

Academics. Special study options: Accelerated study, cooperative education, cross-registration, distance learning, double major, dual enrollment of high school students, ESL, honors, independent study, internships, student-designed major, study abroad, weekend college. License preparation in dental hygiene, nursing, paramedic, real estate. **Credit/placement by examination:** AP, CLEP, institutional tests. 65 credit hours maximum toward associate degree. **Support services:** GED preparation and test center, learning center, pre-admission summer program, reduced course load, remedial instruction, study skills assistance, tutoring, writing center.

Majors. Agriculture: Horticulture. **Business:** Accounting, accounting technology, administrative services, business admin, fashion, office management, real estate, sales/distribution, tourism promotion. **Communications technology:** General, graphic/printing. **Computer sciences:** Applications programming. **Construction:** Maintenance. **Engineering:** General. **Engineering technology:** Drafting, electrical, plastics, robotics. **Family/consumer sciences:** Child care. **Health:** Dental hygiene, EMT paramedic, medical radiologic technology/radiation therapy, medical records technology, nursing (RN), occupational therapy assistant, physical therapy assistant, respiratory therapy technology, speech-language pathology assistant, substance abuse counseling, surgical technology. **Interdisciplinary:** Biological/physical sciences. **Legal studies:** Legal secretary. **Liberal arts:** Arts/sciences, library assistant. **Mechanic/repair:** Automotive, communications systems, electronics/electrical, heating/ac/refrig, industrial electronics. **Personal/culinary services:** Chef training, cosmetic, culinary arts, restaurant/catering. **Protective services:** Fire safety technology, police science. **Public administration:** Social work. **Visual/performing arts:** Art, commercial photography, design.

Most popular majors. Business/marketing 9%, health sciences 12%, interdisciplinary studies 7%, liberal arts 53%.

Computing on campus. 2,403 workstations in library, computer center. Commuter students can connect to campus network. Online course registration, online library, helpline, repair service available.

Student life. Freshman orientation: Available. Includes campus tour and general session. **Housing:** Housing available in cooperation with nearby private college. **Activities:** Bands, choral groups, dance, drama, international student organizations, literary magazine, music ensembles, Model UN, opera, radio station, student government, student newspaper, symphony orchestra, InterVarsity Christian Fellowship, Endowment for Future Generations, Brothers and Sisters in Christ, black student union, Latino ethnic awareness association, Japanese culture club, La Rencontre Francaise, Muslim student association.

Athletics. NJCAA. **Intercollegiate:** Baseball M, basketball, cross-country, diving, football (tackle) M, golf M, soccer, softball W, swimming, tennis, track and field, volleyball W. **Intramural:** Basketball, bowling, diving, football (non-tackle), golf, racquetball, soccer, softball, swimming, tennis, volleyball, weight lifting. **Team name:** Chaparrels.

Student services. Adult student services, career counseling, services for economically disadvantaged, student employment services, financial aid counseling, health services, minority student services, on-campus daycare, personal counseling, placement for graduates. **Physically disabled:** Services for visually, speech, hearing impaired. **Transfer:** Transfer center, transfer adviser, college fairs on campus for students transferring to 4-year colleges.

Contact. E-mail: admissions@cod.edu
Phone: (630) 942-2482 Fax: (630) 790-2686
Amy Hauenstein, Coordinator of Admission Services, College of DuPage, 425 Fawell Boulevard, Glen Ellyn, IL 60137-6599

College of Lake County

Grayslake, Illinois — **CB member**
www.clcillinois.edu — **CB code: 1983**

- Public 2-year community college
- Commuter campus in large town

General. Founded in 1967. Regionally accredited. **Enrollment:** 11,999 degree-seeking undergraduates; 4,360 non-degree-seeking students. **Degrees:** 998 associate awarded. **Location:** 40 miles from Chicago, 45 miles from Milwaukee. **Calendar:** Semester, extensive summer session. **Full-time faculty:** 182 total; 20% have terminal degrees, 21% minority, 52% women. **Part-time faculty:** 650 total; 9% have terminal degrees, 12% minority, 53% women. **Class size:** 49% < 20, 51% 20-39, less than 1% 50-99. **Special facilities:** CAD/CAM center, automated industrial center, performing arts center, child care center.

Student profile. Among degree-seeking undergraduates, 62% enrolled in a transfer program, 38% enrolled in a vocational program, 9% already have a bachelor's degree or higher, 1,955 enrolled as first-time, first-year students.

Part-time:	62%	**Asian American:**	6%
Out-of-state:	1%	**Hispanic American:**	18%
Women:	56%	**International:**	1%
African American:	8%	**25 or older:**	46%

Transfer out. Colleges most students transferred to 2008: Northern Illinois University, University of Wisconsin at Parkside, Northeastern Illinois University, Southern Illinois University, DePaul University.

Basis for selection. Open admission, but selective for some programs. Open admission for certificate and associate of applied science. College-preparatory high school program required for associate of arts and science. Selective admission for health career programs: academic record, class rank, test scores important; recommendations, interview considered. **Learning Disabled:** Accommodations provided when taking proficiency exams.

High school preparation. 15 units recommended. Recommended units include English 4, mathematics 3, social studies 3, (laboratory 3) and academic electives 2. 2 biology and 1 chemistry required for nursing program, mathematics for medical laboratory technician program, chemistry for radiology program. Recommended electives include foreign language, music, vocational education or art.

2009-2010 Annual costs. Tuition/fees: $2,850; $6,600 out-of-district; $8,730 out-of-state. Per-credit charge: $81 in-district; $206 out-of-district; $277 out-of-state. Books/supplies: $1,200. Personal expenses: $1,240.

Financial aid. Need-based: Need-based aid available for part-time students. Work-study available nights and for part-time students. **Non-need-based:** Scholarships awarded for academics, alumni affiliation, art, athletics, leadership, minority status, music/drama.

Application procedures. Admission: No deadline. No application fee. Admission notification on a rolling basis. Application deadlines vary for health career programs. **Financial aid:** Priority date 6/5; no closing date. FAFSA required. Applicants notified on a rolling basis starting 6/15; must reply within 2 week(s) of notification.

Academics. High school distribution requirement for associate degree applicants may be fulfilled at college. **Special study options:** Accelerated study, cooperative education, cross-registration, distance learning, dual enrollment of high school students, ESL, honors, independent study, internships, student-designed major, study abroad. License preparation in dental hygiene, nursing, paramedic, radiology, real estate. **Credit/placement by examination:** AP, CLEP, institutional tests. 30 credit hours maximum toward associate degree. **Support services:** GED preparation and test center, learning center, reduced course load, remedial instruction, study skills assistance, tutoring, writing center.

Majors. Agriculture: Landscaping, ornamental horticulture, turf management. **Business:** Accounting technology, administrative services, business admin, office technology. **Conservation:** Management/policy. **Construction:** Electrician. **Education:** Music. **Engineering:** General. **Engineering technology:** Civil, construction, electrical, mechanical. **Health:** Dental hygiene, medical radiologic technology/radiation therapy, nursing (RN), office admin, substance abuse counseling. **Interdisciplinary:** Biological/physical sciences. **Legal studies:** Paralegal. **Liberal arts:** Arts/sciences, library assistant. **Mechanic/repair:** Automotive, computer, heating/ac/refrig, industrial, industrial electronics. **Personal/culinary services:** Restaurant/catering. **Production:** Machine shop technology. **Protective services:** Fire safety technology, police science. **Public administration:** Social work. **Visual/performing arts:** Art.

Most popular majors. Biological/life sciences 10%, health sciences 18%, liberal arts 55%.

Computing on campus. 800 workstations in library, computer center. Online course registration, wireless network available.

Student life. Freshman orientation: Available. **Policies:** Alcohol-free campus, smoking allowed only outside the building. **Activities:** Bands, campus ministries, choral groups, dance, drama, literary magazine, music ensembles, musical theater, radio station, student government, student newspaper, 11 academic organizations, 6 ethnic organizations, 4 religious organizations, 6 health and fitness organizations.

Athletics. NJCAA. **Intercollegiate:** Baseball M, basketball, cross-country, golf, soccer, softball W, tennis, volleyball W. **Intramural:** Basketball, golf, soccer, table tennis, tennis, volleyball. **Team name:** Lancers.

Student services. Alcohol/substance abuse counseling, career counseling, services for economically disadvantaged, student employment services, financial aid counseling, health services, minority student services, on-campus daycare, personal counseling, placement for graduates, veterans' counselor, women's services. **Physically disabled:** Services for visually, speech, hearing impaired. **Transfer:** Re-entry adviser for new students. Transfer center, transfer adviser, college fairs on campus for students transferring to 4-year colleges.

Contact. E-mail: info@clcillinois.edu
Phone: (847) 543-2061 Fax: (847) 543-3061
Karen Hlavin, Director, College of Lake County, 19351 West Washington Street, Grayslake, IL 60030-1198

College of Office Technology

Chicago, Illinois
www.cot.edu **CB code: 3527**

- For-profit 2-year business college
- Commuter campus in very large city

General. Accredited by ACICS. **Enrollment:** 270 degree-seeking undergraduates. **Degrees:** 3 associate awarded. **Calendar:** Continuous, limited summer session. **Full-time faculty:** 16 total; 38% have terminal degrees, 88% minority, 25% women. **Part-time faculty:** 12 total; 92% minority, 33% women.

Basis for selection. Open admission.

2008-2009 Annual costs. Tuition/fees: $10,368. Personal expenses: $4,600.

Financial aid. All financial aid based on need. Need-based aid available for part-time students.

Application procedures. Admission: No deadline. $50 fee. Application must be submitted on paper. Admission notification on a rolling basis. **Financial aid:** No deadline. FAFSA required. Applicants notified on a rolling basis.

Academics. Credit/placement by examination: AP, CLEP. **Support services:** Tutoring.

Majors. Computer sciences: Data entry.

Computing on campus. 20 workstations in library.

Student life. Freshman orientation: Mandatory.

Contact. E-mail: info@cotedu.com
Phone: (773) 278-0042 Toll-free number: (800) 953-6161
Fax: (773) 278-0143
William Bolton, Director of Admissions, College of Office Technology, 1520 West Division Street, Chicago, IL 60622-3312

Cooking & Hospitality Institute of Chicago

Chicago, Illinois
www.chic.edu **CB code: 2564**

- For-profit 2-year culinary school
- Commuter campus in very large city
- Interview required

General. Regionally accredited. Affiliated with Le Cordon Bleu. **Enrollment:** 1,004 degree-seeking undergraduates. **Degrees:** 553 associate awarded. **Location:** Downtown. **Calendar:** Continuous, extensive summer session. **Full-time faculty:** 26 total; 15% minority, 35% women. **Part-time faculty:** 20 total; 15% minority, 55% women. **Special facilities:** Student-run restaurant.

Student profile. Among degree-seeking undergraduates, 154 enrolled as first-time, first-year students.

Out-of-state:	29%	**Asian American:**	2%
Women:	46%	**Hispanic American:**	13%
African American:	14%	**25 or older:**	46%

Basis for selection. Open admission. **Homeschooled:** Portfolio required. **Learning Disabled:** Documentation of learning disability and special accommodations needed must be provided.

2008-2009 Annual costs. Tuition for associate of applied science in Le Cordon Bleu Culinary Arts: $39,950; associate of applied science in Le Cordon Bleu Patisserie and Baking: $38,500; certificate in Le Cordon Bleu Culinary Arts: $12,200. Books/supplies: $3,400. Personal expenses: $5,006.

Financial aid. Need-based: Need-based aid available for part-time students. Work-study available nights and for part-time students.

Application procedures. Admission: No deadline. $100 fee. Admission notification on a rolling basis. **Financial aid:** No deadline. FAFSA, institutional form required. Applicants notified on a rolling basis.

Academics. All levels of developmental learning provided. **Special study options:** All programs contain an externship course. **Credit/placement by examination:** AP, CLEP. 12 credit hours maximum toward associate degree. **Support services:** Learning center, remedial instruction, tutoring.

Majors. Personal/culinary services: Baking, chef training.

Computing on campus. 70 workstations in library, computer center, student center. Commuter students can connect to campus network. Online library, wireless network available.

Student life. Freshman orientation: Mandatory. **Activities:** Student newspaper.

Student services. Career counseling, student employment services, financial aid counseling, placement for graduates, veterans' counselor.

Contact. E-mail: chic@chicnet.org
Phone: (312) 944-0882 Toll-free number: (877) 828-7772
Fax: (312) 944-8557
Robert Hiller, Senior Director of Admissions, Cooking & Hospitality Institute of Chicago, 361 West Chestnut, Chicago, IL 60610-3050

Danville Area Community College

Danville, Illinois
www.dacc.edu **CB code: 1160**

- Public 2-year community college
- Commuter campus in large town

General. Founded in 1946. Regionally accredited. **Enrollment:** 2,491 degree-seeking undergraduates; 231 non-degree-seeking students. **Degrees:** 269 associate awarded. **Location:** 150 miles from Chicago, 90 miles from Indianapolis. **Calendar:** Semester, limited summer session. **Full-time faculty:** 53 total; 74% have terminal degrees, 11% minority, 51% women. **Part-time faculty:** 82 total; 45% have terminal degrees, 8% minority, 60% women. **Class size:** 63% < 20, 35% 20-39, less than 1% 40-49, less than 1% 50-99.

Student profile. Among degree-seeking undergraduates, 67% enrolled in a transfer program, 33% enrolled in a vocational program, 464 enrolled as first-time, first-year students, 1,338 transferred in from other institutions.

Part-time:	55%	**Asian American:**	1%
Out-of-state:	1%	**Hispanic American:**	3%
Women:	62%	**25 or older:**	40%
African American:	12%		

Transfer out. Colleges most students transferred to 2008: Eastern Illinois University, Illinois State University, Southern Illinois University at Carbondale, University of Illinois at Urbana/Champaign.

Basis for selection. Open admission.

High school preparation. College-preparatory program recommended. 15 units recommended. Recommended units include English 4, mathematics 3, social studies 2, science 2 and academic electives 4.

2008-2009 Annual costs. Tuition/fees: $2,520; $4,800 out-of-district; $4,800 out-of-state. Per-credit charge: $74 in-district; $150 out-of-district; $150 out-of-state. Books/supplies: $700. Personal expenses: $1,575.

2007-2008 Financial aid. Need-based: Average need met was 67%. Average scholarship/grant was $1,620; average loan $2,625. 87% of total undergraduate aid awarded as scholarships/grants, 13% as loans/jobs. Need-based aid available for part-time students. Work-study available nights, weekends and for part-time students. **Non-need-based:** Scholarships awarded for academics, athletics, minority status.

Application procedures. Admission: No deadline. No application fee. Application must be submitted on paper. Admission notification on a rolling basis. **Financial aid:** Priority date 7/1; no closing date. FAFSA, institutional form required. Applicants notified on a rolling basis starting 4/1.

Academics. Special study options: Distance learning, double major, dual enrollment of high school students, ESL, independent study, internships, liberal arts/career combination. License preparation in nursing, real estate. **Credit/placement by examination:** AP, CLEP, IB, institutional tests. 45 credit hours maximum toward associate degree. **Support services:** GED preparation and test center, learning center, remedial instruction, study skills assistance, tutoring, writing center.

Majors. Agriculture: Business, floriculture, turf management. **Biology:** General. **Business:** Accounting technology, administrative services, management information systems, office technology, selling. **Communications:** General, advertising, journalism. **Computer sciences:** General, applications programming, networking, programming. **Education:** General. **Engineering:** General. **Engineering technology:** CAD/CADD, manufacturing. **Health:** Medical records technology, medical secretary, nursing (RN), radiologic technology/medical imaging. **History:** General. **Legal studies:** Prelaw. **Liberal arts:** Arts/sciences. **Math:** General. **Mechanic/repair:** General, automotive, electronics/electrical, industrial, industrial electronics. **Physical sciences:** Chemistry. **Protective services:** Law enforcement admin. **Psychology:** General. **Public administration:** Human services. **Social sciences:** Political science, sociology.

Most popular majors. Business/marketing 12%, computer/information sciences 7%, health sciences 17%, liberal arts 55%.

Computing on campus. 600 workstations in library, computer center, student center. Online course registration, helpline, repair service, wireless network available.

Student life. Freshman orientation: Available. Preregistration for classes offered. **Activities:** Choral groups, literary magazine, student government, symphony orchestra, Fellowship of Christian Athletes, Black student union, Hispanic student association, College Republicans, Minority Teacher Education Association, political affairs club, Powerhouse Collegian Ministry.

Athletics. NJCAA. **Intercollegiate:** Baseball M, basketball, cross-country, golf, soccer M, softball W, volleyball W. **Team name:** Jaguars.

Student services. Adult student services, career counseling, student employment services, financial aid counseling, on-campus daycare, personal counseling, placement for graduates, veterans' counselor. **Physically disabled:** Services for visually, speech, hearing impaired. **Transfer:** Preadmission transcript evaluation for new students. Transfer adviser, college fairs on campus for students transferring to 4-year colleges.

Contact. E-mail: stacy@dacc.edu
Phone: (217) 443-8800 Fax: (217) 443-8337
Stacy Ehmen, Director of Admissions and Records, Danville Area Community College, 2000 East Main Street, Danville, IL 61832

Elgin Community College

Elgin, Illinois
www.elgin.edu **CB code: 1203**

- Public 2-year community college
- Commuter campus in small city

General. Founded in 1949. Regionally accredited. **Enrollment:** 6,746 degree-seeking undergraduates; 3,075 non-degree-seeking students. **Degrees:** 768 associate awarded. **Location:** 35 miles from Chicago. **Calendar:** Semester, extensive summer session. **Full-time faculty:** 127 total; 22% have terminal degrees, 16% minority, 54% women. **Part-time faculty:** 372 total; 6% have terminal degrees, 14% minority, 54% women. **Special facilities:** Greenhouse, business conference center, visual and performing arts center, culinary arts program, student-run gourmet restaurant.

Student profile. Among degree-seeking undergraduates, 63% enrolled in a transfer program, 37% enrolled in a vocational program, 4% already have a bachelor's degree or higher, 1,234 enrolled as first-time, first-year students.

Part-time:	55%	**Asian American:**	8%
Women:	56%	**Hispanic American:**	19%
African American:	6%	**25 or older:**	41%

Transfer out. Colleges most students transferred to 2008: Northern Illinois University, Illinois State University, Southern Illinois University-Carbondale, University of Illinois, University of Illinois at Chicago.

Basis for selection. Open admission, but selective for some programs. Additional requirements for nursing and some health professions programs.

2008-2009 Annual costs. Tuition/fees: $2,740; $11,778 out-of-district; $14,184 out-of-state. Per-credit charge: $91 in-district; $392 out-of-district; $472 out-of-state. Books/supplies: $1,700. Personal expenses: $2,338.

Financial aid. Need-based: Need-based aid available for part-time students. Work-study available nights and weekends. **Non-need-based:** Scholarships awarded for academics, alumni affiliation, art, athletics, job skills, leadership, minority status, music/drama, religious affiliation, ROTC, state residency.

Application procedures. Admission: No deadline. No application fee. Admission notification on a rolling basis. **Financial aid:** Priority date 6/1; no closing date. FAFSA, institutional form required. Applicants notified on a rolling basis starting 4/6; must reply within 3 week(s) of notification.

Academics. Special study options: Accelerated study, cooperative education, distance learning, double major, dual enrollment of high school students, ESL, honors, independent study, internships, study abroad, weekend college. Dual admission with selected 4-year schools. Bachelor's degree programs available on campus. License preparation in aviation, dental hygiene, nursing, paramedic, physical therapy, radiology, real estate. **Credit/placement by examination:** AP, CLEP, institutional tests. 30 credit hours maximum toward associate degree. **Support services:** GED preparation and test center, learning center, reduced course load, remedial instruction, study skills assistance, tutoring, writing center.

Honors college/program. Top 20% of class, 3.5 GPA, or 25 ACT/1140 SAT required. Offers smaller class sizes and innovative learning experiences, including multidisciplinary approaches.

Majors. Business: Accounting, business admin, entrepreneurial studies, executive assistant, hotel/motel admin, marketing, retailing. **Computer sciences:** Computer graphics, data entry. **Education:** General, physical. **Engineering:** General. **Engineering technology:** CAD/CADD. **Health:** Clinical lab technology, nursing (RN), physical therapy assistant. **Interdisciplinary:** Biological/physical sciences. **Legal studies:** Legal secretary, paralegal. **Liberal arts:** Arts/sciences. **Math:** Applied. **Mechanic/repair:** Automotive, heating/ac/refrig, industrial. **Personal/culinary services:** Baking, chef training, restaurant/catering. **Production:** Machine tool. **Protective services:** Fire services admin, police science. **Public administration:** Social work. **Visual/performing arts:** Art, design, graphic design.

Computing on campus. 800 workstations in library, computer center, student center. Wireless network available.

Student life. Freshman orientation: Mandatory. **Activities:** Bands, choral groups, drama, literary magazine, music ensembles, musical theater, student government, student newspaper, symphony orchestra, Phi Theta Kappa, Alpha Beta Gamma, Latin American organization, United Students of All Cultures, black student association, single parents student group, Advocacy for Disabled and Abled Persons Together, Amnesty International, gay/lesbian/bi-sexual, Earth First.

Athletics. NJCAA. **Intercollegiate:** Baseball M, basketball, cross-country, golf M, soccer, softball W, tennis, volleyball W. **Team name:** Spartans.

Student services. Adult student services, career counseling, services for economically disadvantaged, student employment services, financial aid counseling, minority student services, on-campus daycare, personal counseling, placement for graduates, veterans' counselor. **Physically disabled:** Services for visually, speech, hearing impaired. **Transfer:** Transfer center, transfer adviser, college fairs on campus for students transferring to 4-year colleges.

Contact. E-mail: admissions@elgin.edu
Phone: (847) 214-7385 Fax: (847) 608-5458
Mary Perkins, Associate Dean of Enrollment Management, Elgin Community College, 1700 Spartan Drive, Elgin, IL 60123-7193

Fox College
Bedford Park, Illinois
www.foxcollege.edu **CB code: 2670**

- For-profit 2-year junior and technical college
- Commuter campus in very large city

General. Accredited by ACICS. Additional degree site in Tinley Park. **Enrollment:** 500 degree-seeking undergraduates. **Degrees:** 94 associate awarded. **Calendar:** Semester. **Full-time faculty:** 12 total. **Part-time faculty:** 10 total.

Basis for selection. Open admission, but selective for some programs. GED/High school academic record, writing sample, and interview considered for selective programs.

Application procedures. Admission: No deadline. $50 fee. **Financial aid:** No deadline.

Academics. Credit/placement by examination: CLEP.

Majors. Business: Accounting, administrative services. **Health:** Medical assistant, veterinary technology/assistant.

Student services. Career counseling, financial aid counseling, placement for graduates.

Contact. E-mail: admissions@foxcollege.edu
Phone: (708) 444-4500
Fox College, 6640 South Cicero Avenue, Bedford Park, IL 60638

Harper College
Palatine, Illinois
www.harpercollege.edu **CB code: 1932**

- Public 2-year community college
- Commuter campus in small city

General. Founded in 1965. Regionally accredited. Program for hearing-impaired offered. Bachelor completion program with Indiana University. **Enrollment:** 13,302 degree-seeking undergraduates; 1,948 non-degree-seeking students. **Degrees:** 1,231 associate awarded. **Location:** 30 miles from Chicago. **Calendar:** Semester, extensive summer session. **Full-time faculty:** 192 total; 92% have terminal degrees, 9% minority, 58% women. **Part-time faculty:** 606 total; 72% have terminal degrees, 5% minority, 50% women. **Class size:** 34% < 20, 50% 20-39, 12% 40-49, 3% 50-99, less than 1% >100. **Special facilities:** Observatory.

Student profile. Among degree-seeking undergraduates, 63% enrolled in a transfer program, 38% enrolled in a vocational program, 7% already have a bachelor's degree or higher, 2,699 enrolled as first-time, first-year students, 1,250 transferred in from other institutions.

Part-time:	50%	**Hispanic American:**	11%
Women:	55%	**International:**	1%
African American:	4%	**25 or older:**	36%
Asian American:	11%		

Transfer out. Colleges most students transferred to 2008: Northern Illinois University, University of Illinois-Urbana, University of Illinois-Chicago, Illinois State University, Roosevelt University.

Basis for selection. Open admission, but selective for some programs. Selective admission to cardiac technology, dental hygiene, emergency medical technician, certified nursing assistant, electrocardiograph technology, emergency medical service paramedic, and diagnostic medical sonography. Pre-nursing examinations for nursing applicants. Critical thinking test for legal technology applicants.

High school preparation. 17 units recommended. Recommended units include English 4, mathematics 4, social studies 2 and science 2.

2008-2009 Annual costs. Tuition/fees: $3,234; $10,194 out-of-district; $12,504 out-of-state. Per-credit charge: $90 in-district; $322 out-of-district; $399 out-of-state. In-district tuition rates available to employees of in-district companies who reside outside college district. Books/supplies: $1,000. Personal expenses: $1,800.

2007-2008 Financial aid. Need-based: Need-based aid available for part-time students. Work-study available nights and weekends. **Non-need-based:** Scholarships awarded for academics, art, leadership, minority status, music/drama, state residency.

Application procedures. Admission: No deadline. $25 fee, may be waived for applicants with need. Admission notification on a rolling basis. Priority given to applications to nursing program received by December 1. Priority given to applications received by February 1 for all other limited-enrollment programs. **Financial aid:** Priority date 3/1; no closing date. FAFSA, institutional form required. Applicants notified on a rolling basis starting 3/1; must reply within 2 week(s) of notification.

Academics. Cooperative career program with in-district high schools. Students begin specialized training in high school and continue in colleges. Team-taught interdisciplinary courses and courseloads offered each semester. **Special study options:** Accelerated study, cooperative education, distance learning, dual enrollment of high school students, ESL, honors, independent study, internships, study abroad, weekend college. Bachelor's degree programs available on campus. License preparation in dental hygiene, nursing, paramedic, radiology, real estate. **Credit/placement by examination:** AP, CLEP, institutional tests. 30 credit hours maximum toward associate degree. Maximum of 50% total hours in any degree program may be earned through credit by examination. **Support services:** GED preparation and test center, learning center, pre-admission summer program, reduced course load, remedial instruction, study skills assistance, tutoring, writing center.

Majors. Agriculture: Horticulture, turf management. **Business:** Accounting technology, banking/financial services, business admin, executive assistant, fashion, fashion modeling, hospitality admin, hospitality/recreation, international, sales/distribution, selling, small business admin. **Communications technology:** Graphic/printing. **Computer sciences:** General, applications programming, computer forensics, computer science, data processing, information systems, programming, systems analysis, web page design. **Construction:** Maintenance. **Education:** Teacher assistance. **Engineering:** General. **Engineering technology:** Architectural drafting, electrical. **Family/consumer sciences:** Fashion consultant, home furnishings. **Health:** Cardiovascular technology, dental hygiene, dietetic technician, EMT paramedic, medical secretary, nursing (RN), radiologic technology/medical imaging, sonography. **Legal studies:** Legal secretary, paralegal. **Liberal arts:** Arts/sciences. **Mechanic/repair:** Heating/ac/refrig. **Philosophy/religion:** Philosophy. **Physical sciences:** General. **Protective services:** Emergency management/homeland security, firefighting, police science. **Visual/performing arts:** Studio arts. **Other:** Nanoscience technology.

Most popular majors. Business/marketing 7%, health sciences 15%, liberal arts 63%.

Computing on campus. 1,698 workstations in library, computer center, student center. Online course registration, online library, wireless network available.

Student life. Freshman orientation: Mandatory. Preregistration for classes offered. Two-day program includes tour, assessment tests, academic advising. Optional for part-time students. **Activities:** Bands, campus ministries, choral groups, dance, drama, international student organizations, literary magazine, music ensembles, musical theater, radio station, student government, student newspaper, service organizations, professional organizations, student ambassadors.

Athletics. NJCAA. **Intercollegiate:** Baseball M, basketball, cross-country, football (tackle) M, soccer, softball W, track and field, volleyball W, wrestling M. **Intramural:** Baseball M, basketball M, football (non-tackle) M, racquetball, skiing, softball, table tennis, tennis, volleyball. **Team name:** Hawks.

Student services. Adult student services, career counseling, services for economically disadvantaged, student employment services, financial aid counseling, health services, legal services, minority student services, on-campus daycare, personal counseling, veterans' counselor, women's services. **Physically disabled:** Services for visually, speech, hearing impaired. **Transfer:** Transfer adviser, college fairs on campus for students transferring to 4-year colleges.

Contact. E-mail: admissions@harpercollege.edu
Phone: (847) 925-6707 Fax: (847) 925-6044
Robert Parzy, Director of Admissions Outreach, Harper College, 1200 West Algonquin Road, Palatine, IL 60067-7398

Heartland Community College
Normal, Illinois
www.heartland.edu **CB code: 1361**

- Public 2-year community college
- Commuter campus in small city

General. Regionally accredited. Green construction and technology employed in construction projects. **Enrollment:** 4,952 degree-seeking undergraduates; 31 non-degree-seeking students. **Degrees:** 502 associate awarded.

Calendar: Semester, extensive summer session. **Full-time faculty:** 84 total; 20% have terminal degrees, 10% minority, 56% women. **Part-time faculty:** 199 total; 10% have terminal degrees, 8% minority, 55% women. **Class size:** 54% < 20, 46% 20-39, less than 1% 40-49, less than 1% 50-99.

Student profile. Among degree-seeking undergraduates, 83% enrolled in a transfer program, 17% enrolled in a vocational program, 4% already have a bachelor's degree or higher, 1,140 enrolled as first-time, first-year students, 244 transferred in from other institutions.

Part-time:	54%	**Hispanic American:**	3%
Women:	54%	**International:**	2%
African American:	9%	**25 or older:**	31%
Asian American:	2%		

Transfer out. 90% of students enrolled in the transfer program go on to 4-year colleges. **Colleges most students transferred to 2008:** Illinois State University.

Basis for selection. Open admission, but selective for some programs. Nursing program requires 2.5 GPA; college-level skills attainment in reading, English, biology, and math. Placement testing required to determine readiness in reading, English, and math. Developmental courses may be required before proceeding to college-level courses.

High school preparation. Recommended units include English 4, mathematics 3, social studies 2, science 2 and foreign language 2. Social studies units should include history and government.

2009-2010 Annual costs. Tuition/fees: $2,850; $5,490 out-of-district; $8,130 out-of-state. Per-credit charge: $88 in-district; $176 out-of-district; $264 out-of-state. Books/supplies: $900. Personal expenses: $902.

2007-2008 Financial aid. Need-based: 96% of total undergraduate aid awarded as scholarships/grants, 4% as loans/jobs. Need-based aid available for part-time students. Work-study available nights, weekends and for part-time students. **Non-need-based:** Scholarships awarded for academics, alumni affiliation, athletics, job skills, leadership, minority status, state residency.

Application procedures. Admission: Priority date 6/1; no deadline. No application fee. Admission notification on a rolling basis. May defer admission up to one year. Early admission of high school students with recommendation of high school officials. **Financial aid:** Priority date 4/1; no closing date. FAFSA, institutional form required. Applicants notified on a rolling basis starting 5/15; must reply within 2 week(s) of notification.

Academics. Special study options: Distance learning, double major, dual enrollment of high school students, ESL, honors, independent study, internships, liberal arts/career combination, study abroad. License preparation in nursing, paramedic, radiology, real estate. **Credit/placement by examination:** AP, CLEP, institutional tests. 15 credit hours maximum toward associate degree. **Support services:** GED preparation and test center, learning center, remedial instruction, study skills assistance, tutoring, writing center.

Majors. Business: Insurance. **Computer sciences:** Data entry, information technology, networking. **Construction:** Electrician. **Education:** Mathematics, teacher assistance. **Engineering:** General. **Engineering technology:** CAD/CADD, electrical, manufacturing. **Health:** Nursing (RN), radiologic technology/medical imaging. **Interdisciplinary:** Biological/physical sciences. **Liberal arts:** Arts/sciences. **Mechanic/repair:** Industrial. **Production:** Welding. **Protective services:** Criminal justice. **Visual/performing arts:** Design.

Most popular majors. Interdisciplinary studies 12%, liberal arts 76%.

Computing on campus. 70 workstations in library, computer center. Commuter students can connect to campus network. Online course registration, online library, helpline, wireless network available.

Student life. Freshman orientation: Mandatory. Multiple half-day sessions for full-time students; reservations required. Online session required for part-time students. Program includes basic skills assessment, academic advising, and registration assistance. **Activities:** Campus ministries, international student organizations, student government, student newspaper, Phi Theta Kappa, Sigma Kappa Delta, Alpha Beta Gamma, Chi Gamma Iota, Rotoract, Toastmasters, culture club, environmental club, outdoor adventure club, Campus Crusade for Christ.

Athletics. NJCAA. **Intercollegiate:** Baseball M, soccer, softball W. **Intramural:** Basketball, softball, volleyball. **Team name:** Hawks.

Student services. Adult student services, alcohol/substance abuse counseling, career counseling, services for economically disadvantaged, student employment services, financial aid counseling, minority student services, on-campus daycare, personal counseling, placement for graduates, veterans' counselor. **Physically disabled:** Services for visually, speech, hearing impaired. **Transfer:** Pre-admission transcript evaluation for new students. Transfer adviser, college fairs on campus for students transferring to 4-year colleges.

Contact. E-mail: soar@heartland.edu
Phone: (309) 268-8000 Fax: (309) 268-7992
Kathleen Collins, Dean of Student Services, Heartland Community College, 1500 West Raab Road, Normal, IL 61761

Highland Community College
Freeport, Illinois
www.highland.edu **CB code: 1233**

- Public 2-year community college
- Commuter campus in large town

General. Founded in 1961. Regionally accredited. **Enrollment:** 1,876 degree-seeking undergraduates; 307 non-degree-seeking students. **Degrees:** 229 associate awarded. **Location:** 100 miles from Chicago, 38 miles from Rockford. **Calendar:** Semester, limited summer session. **Full-time faculty:** 46 total; 15% have terminal degrees, 2% minority, 33% women. **Part-time faculty:** 117 total; 2% have terminal degrees, 5% minority, 64% women. **Class size:** 71% < 20, 26% 20-39, 2% 40-49, less than 1% 50-99. **Special facilities:** Regional arboretum, YMCA on campus.

Student profile. Among degree-seeking undergraduates, 55% enrolled in a transfer program, 45% enrolled in a vocational program, 3% already have a bachelor's degree or higher, 410 enrolled as first-time, first-year students, 86 transferred in from other institutions.

Part-time:	44%	**Asian American:**	1%
Out-of-state:	3%	**Hispanic American:**	2%
Women:	63%	**25 or older:**	32%
African American:	10%		

Transfer out. Colleges most students transferred to 2008: Illinois State University, University of Wisconsin-Platteville, Northern Illinois University, Western Illinois University, Columbia College.

Basis for selection. Open admission, but selective for some programs. Special criteria for acceptance into nursing program: based on points accumulated by taking prerequisite courses; class rank, test scores considered. **Homeschooled:** Transcript of courses and grades required.

High school preparation. 15 units recommended. Recommended units include English 4, mathematics 3, social studies 2, science 2 (laboratory 2) and academic electives 4.

2008-2009 Annual costs. Tuition/fees: $2,490; $4,050 out-of-district; $4,050 out-of-state. Per-credit charge: $76 in-district; $128 out-of-district; $128 out-of-state. Books/supplies: $900. Personal expenses: $1,300.

2007-2008 Financial aid. Need-based: 74% of total undergraduate aid awarded as scholarships/grants, 26% as loans/jobs. Need-based aid available for part-time students. Work-study available nights and for part-time students. **Non-need-based:** Scholarships awarded for academics, athletics.

Application procedures. Admission: No deadline. No application fee. Admission notification on a rolling basis. **Financial aid:** No deadline. FAFSA, institutional form required. Applicants notified on a rolling basis starting 8/1; must reply within 2 week(s) of notification.

Academics. Special study options: Distance learning, dual enrollment of high school students, ESL, independent study, internships, student-designed major. Bachelor's degree programs available on campus. License preparation in nursing, real estate. **Credit/placement by examination:** AP, CLEP, institutional tests. 21 credit hours maximum toward associate degree. **Support services:** GED preparation, learning center, remedial instruction, study skills assistance, tutoring, writing center.

Majors. Agriculture: Business. **Business:** Accounting, administrative services, business admin. **Computer sciences:** Information technology. **Education:** Mathematics. **Engineering:** General. **Engineering technology:** Industrial. **Health:** Medical records technology, nursing (RN). **Interdisciplinary:** Biological/physical sciences. **Liberal arts:** Arts/sciences. **Mechanic/repair:** Auto body, automotive. **Visual/performing arts:** Art, graphic design.

Most popular majors. Health sciences 14%, interdisciplinary studies 27%, liberal arts 44%.

Computing on campus. 366 workstations in library, computer center, student center. Commuter students can connect to campus network. Online course registration, online library, helpline, repair service, wireless network available.

Student life. **Freshman orientation:** Available. **Activities:** Bands, choral groups, dance, drama, literary magazine, music ensembles, musical theater, student government, student newspaper, current issues club, environmental awareness, religious fellowship, international club, People of Color, pride club, student senate.

Athletics. NJCAA. **Intercollegiate:** Baseball M, basketball, golf M, softball W, volleyball W. **Intramural:** Basketball, volleyball. **Team name:** Cougars.

Student services. Adult student services, career counseling, services for economically disadvantaged, financial aid counseling, personal counseling, veterans' counselor. **Physically disabled:** Services for visually, speech, hearing impaired. **Transfer:** Pre-admission transcript evaluation for new students. Transfer center, transfer adviser, college fairs on campus for students transferring to 4-year colleges.

Contact. E-mail: karl.richards@highland.edu
Phone: (815) 235-6121 ext. 3414 Fax: (815) 235-6130
Karl Richards, Dean of Enrollment Services, Highland Community College, 2998 West Pearl City Road, Freeport, IL 61032-9341

Illinois Central College
East Peoria, Illinois
www.icc.edu **CB code: 1312**

- Public 2-year community college
- Commuter campus in large town

General. Founded in 1966. Regionally accredited. **Enrollment:** 9,457 degree-seeking undergraduates; 2,563 non-degree-seeking students. **Degrees:** 1,313 associate awarded. **Location:** 150 miles from Chicago, 5 miles from Peoria. **Calendar:** Semester, extensive summer session. **Full-time faculty:** 183 total. **Part-time faculty:** 650 total. **Partnerships:** Formal partnerships with Caterpillar Tractor Company and General Motors.

Student profile. Among degree-seeking undergraduates, 54% enrolled in a transfer program, 26% enrolled in a vocational program, 1,534 enrolled as first-time, first-year students.

Part-time:	53%	**African American:**	12%
Out-of-state:	1%	**Asian American:**	2%
Women:	59%	**Hispanic American:**	3%

Transfer out. 35% of students enrolled in the transfer program go on to 4-year colleges. **Colleges most students transferred to 2008:** Illinois State University, Bradley University, Western Illinois University, Southern Illinois University: Carbondale, University of Illinois: Urbana-Champaign.

Basis for selection. Open admission, but selective for some programs. Special requirements for health occupation programs and diesel mechanics. Some programs require ACT for admission and placement. Audition required of music majors.

High school preparation. 15 units recommended. Recommended units include English 4, mathematics 3, social studies 2 and science 2.

2008-2009 Annual costs. Tuition/fees: $2,460; $5,400 out-of-district; $5,400 out-of-state. Per-credit charge: $82 in-district; $180 out-of-district; $180 out-of-state. Books/supplies: $600. Personal expenses: $2,335.

Financial aid. **Non-need-based:** Scholarships awarded for athletics.

Application procedures. **Admission:** No deadline. No application fee. Admission notification on a rolling basis. **Financial aid:** Priority date 6/15; no closing date. FAFSA, institutional form required. Applicants notified on a rolling basis starting 6/1; must reply within 2 week(s) of notification.

Academics. Team-taught, multidisciplinary program available for transfers. **Special study options:** Distance learning, ESL, honors, independent study, internships, weekend college. Bachelor's degree programs available on campus. License preparation in dental hygiene, nursing, occupational therapy, paramedic, physical therapy, radiology, real estate. **Credit/placement by examination:** AP, CLEP, ACT, institutional tests. 30 credit hours maximum toward associate degree. **Support services:** GED preparation and test center, learning center, reduced course load, remedial instruction, study skills assistance, tutoring, writing center.

Majors. **Agriculture:** Business, horticulture. **Architecture:** Interior. **Business:** General, accounting, administrative services, banking/financial services, business admin, international, real estate. **Communications:** Broadcast journalism, journalism. **Computer sciences:** General, applications programming, programming. **Conservation:** General. **Education:** Elementary, physical, secondary, special. **Engineering:** General, agricultural, electrical. **Engineering technology:** Robotics. **Family/consumer sciences:** General, child care, food/nutrition. **Foreign languages:** General. **Health:** Clinical lab technology, dental hygiene, health care admin, medical radiologic technology/radiation therapy, medical records technology, occupational therapy assistant, physical therapy assistant, predental, premedicine, prepharmacy, preveterinary, respiratory therapy technology, surgical technology. **Legal studies:** Court reporting, paralegal, prelaw. **Liberal arts:** Arts/sciences, library assistant. **Math:** General. **Physical sciences:** Chemistry, geology, physics, planetary. **Protective services:** Criminal justice, fire safety technology. **Visual/performing arts:** Dance, dramatic, studio arts.

Computing on campus. 500 workstations in library, computer center.

Student life. **Freshman orientation:** Available. **Activities:** Bands, choral groups, dance, drama, international student organizations, music ensembles, student government, student newspaper, Tomorrow's Black Leaders, College Republicans, College Democrats, Inter-Varsity Christian Fellowship.

Athletics. NJCAA. **Intercollegiate:** Baseball M, basketball, cross-country, golf M, soccer, softball W, volleyball W. **Intramural:** Badminton, basketball, golf, table tennis, tennis, volleyball. **Team name:** Cougars.

Student services. Adult student services, career counseling, student employment services, health services, on-campus daycare, personal counseling, placement for graduates, veterans' counselor. **Physically disabled:** Services for visually, speech, hearing impaired. **Transfer:** Transfer center, transfer adviser, college fairs on campus for students transferring to 4-year colleges.

Contact. E-mail: enroll@icc.edu
Phone: (309) 694-5354 Fax: (309) 694-8461
Emily Peterson, Director of Enrollment Management, Illinois Central College, One College Drive, East Peoria, IL 61635-0001

Illinois Eastern Community Colleges: Frontier Community College
Fairfield, Illinois
www.iecc.edu/fcc **CB code: 1894**

- Public 2-year community college
- Commuter campus in small town

General. Founded in 1976. Regionally accredited. **Enrollment:** 1,529 degree-seeking undergraduates; 835 non-degree-seeking students. **Degrees:** 113 associate awarded. **Location:** 110 miles from St. Louis. **Calendar:** Semester, extensive summer session. **Full-time faculty:** 5 total. **Part-time faculty:** 230 total.

Student profile. Among degree-seeking undergraduates, 41% enrolled in a transfer program, 59% enrolled in a vocational program, 53 enrolled as first-time, first-year students.

Part-time:	81%	**Women:**	62%
Out-of-state:	1%	**25 or older:**	51%

Basis for selection. Open admission, but selective for some programs. Special requirements for nursing and radiography programs. Preference given to regional residents. Interview recommended for nursing and radiography technology.

High school preparation. Recommended units include English 3, mathematics 2 and science 1.

2008-2009 Annual costs. Tuition/fees: $1,910; $5,736 out-of-district; $7,140 out-of-state. Per-credit charge: $60 in-district; $188 out-of-district; $234 out-of-state. Students in qualifying Indiana districts pay per-credit-hour rate of $114. Books/supplies: $1,000. Personal expenses: $1,120.

Financial aid. **Need-based:** Need-based aid available for part-time students. **Non-need-based:** Scholarships awarded for academics, state residency.

Application procedures. **Admission:** No deadline. $10 fee. Admission notification on a rolling basis beginning on or about 8/1. **Financial aid:** No deadline. FAFSA, institutional form required. Applicants notified on a rolling basis starting 8/1; must reply within 2 week(s) of notification.

Academics. Students, with counselors' aid, design own academic programs through nontraditional alternatives to classroom study. **Special study options:** Distance learning, double major, dual enrollment of high school students, ESL, honors, independent study, student-designed major, study abroad, teacher certification program, weekend college. License preparation in nursing. **Credit/placement by examination:** AP, CLEP, institutional tests. 32 credit hours maximum toward associate degree. **Support services:** GED preparation, learning center, remedial instruction, study skills assistance, tutoring.

Majors. Business: Administrative services, office technology. **Computer sciences:** General. **Health:** Mental health services. **Liberal arts:** Arts/sciences.

Most popular majors. Business/marketing 8%, health sciences 9%, interdisciplinary studies 10%, liberal arts 54%.

Computing on campus. 40 workstations in library, computer center. Commuter students can connect to campus network.

Student life. Freshman orientation: Available. Preregistration for classes offered. Freshman orientation strongly recommended. **Activities:** Student government, student newspaper.

Student services. Adult student services, career counseling, services for economically disadvantaged, student employment services, financial aid counseling, minority student services, personal counseling, placement for graduates, veterans' counselor. **Physically disabled:** Services for visually, speech, hearing impaired. **Transfer:** Pre-admission transcript evaluation for new students. Transfer adviser, college fairs on campus for students transferring to 4-year colleges.

Contact. Phone: (618) 842-3711 Toll-free number: (877) 464-3687
Fax: (618) 842-6340
Mary Atkins, Director of Registration and Records, Illinois Eastern Community Colleges: Frontier Community College, 2 Frontier Drive, Fairfield, IL 62837-9801

Illinois Eastern Community Colleges: Lincoln Trail College

Robinson, Illinois
www.iecc.edu/ltc **CB code: 0758**

- Public 2-year community college
- Commuter campus in small town

General. Founded in 1969. Regionally accredited. **Enrollment:** 1,036 degree-seeking undergraduates; 340 non-degree-seeking students. **Degrees:** 193 associate awarded. **Location:** 200 miles from Indianapolis, 110 miles from St. Louis. **Calendar:** Semester, extensive summer session. **Full-time faculty:** 27 total. **Part-time faculty:** 61 total.

Student profile. Among degree-seeking undergraduates, 61% enrolled in a transfer program, 39% enrolled in a vocational program, 185 enrolled as first-time, first-year students.

Part-time:	53%	**Women:**	35%
Out-of-state:	1%	**25 or older:**	44%

Basis for selection. Open admission.

High school preparation. Recommended units include English 3, mathematics 2 and science 1.

2008-2009 Annual costs. Tuition/fees: $1,910; $5,736 out-of-district; $7,140 out-of-state. Per-credit charge: $60 in-district; $188 out-of-district; $234 out-of-state. Students in qualifying Indiana districts pay per-credit-hour rate of $114. Books/supplies: $1,000. Personal expenses: $1,120.

Financial aid. Need-based: Need-based aid available for part-time students. **Non-need-based:** Scholarships awarded for academics, athletics, state residency.

Application procedures. Admission: No deadline. $10 fee. Admission notification on a rolling basis beginning on or about 8/1. **Financial aid:** No deadline. FAFSA, institutional form required. Applicants notified on a rolling basis starting 8/1; must reply within 2 week(s) of notification.

Academics. Students (with counselors' aid) design academic programs through nontraditional alternatives to classroom study. **Special study options:** Distance learning, double major, dual enrollment of high school students, ESL, honors, independent study, internships, student-designed major, study abroad, weekend college. License preparation in nursing. **Credit/placement by examination:** AP, CLEP, institutional tests. 32 credit hours maximum toward associate degree. **Support services:** GED preparation, learning center, remedial instruction, study skills assistance, tutoring.

Majors. Agriculture: Horticulture. **Business:** Administrative services, banking/financial services, office technology. **Computer sciences:** General. **Education:** Music, teacher assistance. **Engineering technology:** Drafting. **Interdisciplinary:** Biological/physical sciences. **Liberal arts:** Arts/sciences. **Mechanic/repair:** Electronics/electrical, heating/ac/refrig.

Most popular majors. Engineering/engineering technologies 7%, health sciences 7%, liberal arts 70%.

Computing on campus. 91 workstations in library, computer center. Commuter students can connect to campus network.

Student life. Freshman orientation: Available. Preregistration for classes offered. **Activities:** Bands, choral groups, drama, music ensembles, musical theater, student government, student newspaper.

Athletics. NJCAA. **Intercollegiate:** Baseball M, basketball, softball W. **Intramural:** Basketball, softball. **Team name:** Statesmen.

Student services. Career counseling, services for economically disadvantaged, student employment services, financial aid counseling, minority student services, personal counseling, placement for graduates, veterans' counselor. **Physically disabled:** Services for visually, speech, hearing impaired. **Transfer:** Pre-admission transcript evaluation for new students. Transfer adviser, college fairs on campus for students transferring to 4-year colleges.

Contact. Phone: (618) 544-8657 Toll-free number: (866) 582-4322
Fax: (618) 544-3957
Becky Mikeworth, Director of Admissions, Illinois Eastern Community Colleges: Lincoln Trail College, 11220 State Highway 1, Robinson, IL 62454-5707

Illinois Eastern Community Colleges: Olney Central College

Olney, Illinois
www.iecc.edu/occ **CB code: 0827**

- Public 2-year community college
- Commuter campus in small town

General. Founded in 1962. Regionally accredited. **Enrollment:** 963 degree-seeking undergraduates; 523 non-degree-seeking students. **Degrees:** 303 associate awarded. **Location:** 200 miles from St. Louis. **Calendar:** Semester, extensive summer session. **Full-time faculty:** 47 total. **Part-time faculty:** 75 total.

Student profile. Among degree-seeking undergraduates, 60% enrolled in a transfer program, 40% enrolled in a vocational program, 146 enrolled as first-time, first-year students.

Part-time:	25%	**25 or older:**	40%
Women:	59%		

Basis for selection. Open admission, but selective for some programs. Special requirements for nursing, radiology programs. Preference given to Illinois Eastern Community College region residents. Interview recommended for nursing, radiology technology majors.

High school preparation. Recommended units include English 3, mathematics 2 and science 1.

2008-2009 Annual costs. Tuition/fees: $1,910; $5,736 out-of-district; $7,140 out-of-state. Per-credit charge: $60 in-district; $188 out-of-district; $234 out-of-state. Students in qualifying Indiana districts pay per-credit-hour rate of $114. Books/supplies: $1,000. Personal expenses: $1,120.

Financial aid. Need-based: Need-based aid available for part-time students. **Non-need-based:** Scholarships awarded for academics, athletics, state residency.

Application procedures. Admission: No deadline. $10 fee. Admission notification on a rolling basis beginning on or about 8/1. **Financial aid:** No deadline. FAFSA, institutional form required. Applicants notified on a rolling basis starting 8/1; must reply within 2 week(s) of notification.

Academics. Students design academic programs with aid of counselors through nontraditional alternatives to classroom study. **Special study options:** Distance learning, double major, dual enrollment of high school students, ESL, honors, independent study, internships, student-designed major, study abroad, weekend college. License preparation in nursing, radiology, real estate. **Credit/placement by examination:** AP, CLEP, institutional tests. 32 credit hours maximum toward associate degree. **Support services:** GED preparation, learning center, remedial instruction, study skills assistance, tutoring.

Majors. Business: Accounting, administrative services, office technology. **Education:** Music. **Health:** Medical radiologic technology/radiation therapy, medical secretary, nursing (RN). **Liberal arts:** Arts/sciences. **Mechanic/**

repair: Auto body, industrial. **Production:** Woodworking. **Protective services:** Police science.

Most popular majors. Health sciences 12%, liberal arts 70%, trade and industry 7%.

Computing on campus. 125 workstations in library, computer center. Commuter students can connect to campus network.

Student life. Freshman orientation: Available. Preregistration for classes offered. **Activities:** Bands, choral groups, drama, music ensembles, musical theater, student government, student newspaper.

Athletics. NJCAA. **Intercollegiate:** Baseball M, basketball, softball W. **Intramural:** Basketball, softball. **Team name:** Blue Knights.

Student services. Career counseling, services for economically disadvantaged, student employment services, financial aid counseling, minority student services, on-campus daycare, personal counseling, placement for graduates, veterans' counselor. **Physically disabled:** Services for visually, speech, hearing impaired. **Transfer:** Pre-admission transcript evaluation for new students. Transfer adviser, college fairs on campus for students transferring to 4-year colleges.

Contact. Phone: (618) 395-7777 Toll-free number: (866) 622-4322
Fax: (618) 392-5212
Chris Webber, Assistant Dean of Student Services, Illinois Eastern Community Colleges: Olney Central College, 305 North West Street, Olney, IL 62450

Illinois Eastern Community Colleges: Wabash Valley College

Mount Carmel, Illinois
www.iecc.edu/wvc — **CB code: 1936**

- Public 2-year community college
- Commuter campus in small town

General. Founded in 1960. Regionally accredited. **Enrollment:** 621 full-time, degree-seeking students. **Degrees:** 177 associate awarded. **Location:** 40 miles from Evansville, Indiana. **Calendar:** Semester, extensive summer session. **Full-time faculty:** 38 total. **Part-time faculty:** 130 total.

Student profile. Among full-time, degree-seeking students, 37% enrolled in a transfer program, 63% enrolled in a vocational program.

Out-of-state:	4%	**25 or older:**	56%

Basis for selection. Open admission.

High school preparation. Recommended units include English 3, mathematics 2 and science 1.

2008-2009 Annual costs. Tuition/fees: $1,910; $5,736 out-of-district; $7,140 out-of-state. Per-credit charge: $60 in-district; $188 out-of-district; $234 out-of-state. Students in qualifying Indiana districts pay per-credit-hour rate of $114. Books/supplies: $1,000. Personal expenses: $1,120.

Financial aid. Need-based: Need-based aid available for part-time students. **Non-need-based:** Scholarships awarded for academics, athletics, state residency.

Application procedures. Admission: No deadline. $10 fee. Admission notification on a rolling basis beginning on or about 8/1. **Financial aid:** No deadline. FAFSA, institutional form required. Applicants notified on a rolling basis starting 8/1; must reply within 2 week(s) of notification.

Academics. Students, with counselor's aid, design own academic programs through nontraditional alternatives to classroom study. **Special study options:** Distance learning, double major, dual enrollment of high school students, ESL, honors, independent study, internships, student-designed major, study abroad, weekend college. License preparation in nursing, real estate. **Credit/placement by examination:** AP, CLEP, institutional tests. 32 credit hours maximum toward associate degree. **Support services:** GED preparation, learning center, remedial instruction, study skills assistance, tutoring.

Majors. Agriculture: Business, horticulture, production. **Business:** Accounting technology, administrative services, office technology. **Communications:** Broadcast journalism. **Engineering technology:** Electrical, manufacturing. **Family/consumer sciences:** Child care. **Liberal arts:** Arts/sciences. **Mechanic/repair:** Diesel, industrial. **Production:** Machine shop technology. **Public administration:** Social work.

Most popular majors. Agriculture 6%, business/marketing 6%, interdisciplinary studies 22%, liberal arts 40%, trade and industry 9%.

Computing on campus. 100 workstations in library, computer center. Commuter students can connect to campus network.

Student life. Freshman orientation: Available. Preregistration for classes offered. **Activities:** Bands, choral groups, drama, music ensembles, musical theater, radio station, student government, student newspaper, TV station.

Athletics. NJCAA. **Intercollegiate:** Baseball M, basketball, softball W. **Intramural:** Basketball, softball. **Team name:** Warriors.

Student services. Career counseling, services for economically disadvantaged, student employment services, financial aid counseling, minority student services, on-campus daycare, personal counseling, placement for graduates, veterans' counselor. **Physically disabled:** Services for visually, speech, hearing impaired. **Transfer:** Pre-admission transcript evaluation for new students. Transfer adviser, college fairs on campus for students transferring to 4-year colleges.

Contact. Phone: (618) 262-8641 Toll-free number: (866) 982-4322
Fax: (618) 262-5347
Diana Spear, Assistant Dean for Student Services, Illinois Eastern Community Colleges: Wabash Valley College, 2200 College Drive, Mount Carmel, IL 62863-2657

Illinois Valley Community College

Oglesby, Illinois — **CB member**
www.ivcc.edu — **CB code: 1397**

- Public 2-year community college
- Commuter campus in small town

General. Founded in 1966. Regionally accredited. **Enrollment:** 2,940 degree-seeking undergraduates. **Degrees:** 414 associate awarded. **Location:** 60 miles from Peoria, 95 miles from Chicago. **Calendar:** Semester, extensive summer session. **Full-time faculty:** 81 total. **Part-time faculty:** 175 total. **Special facilities:** Federal and state nuclear regulatory commission document depositories.

Transfer out. Colleges most students transferred to 2008: Illinois State University, Northern Illinois University, Western Illinois University, University of Illinois/Urbana-Champaign, Eastern Illinois University.

Basis for selection. Open admission, but selective for some programs. Applicants to nursing programs must have 2.0 GPA for LPN, 2.5 GPA for RN and background in laboratory science; 2.0 GPA required for dental assisting. **Homeschooled:** Transcript of courses and grades required.

2008-2009 Annual costs. Tuition/fees: $2,168; $7,992 out-of-district; $9,092 out-of-state. Per-credit charge: $61 in-district; $243 out-of-district; $277 out-of-state. Books/supplies: $1,000. Personal expenses: $1,170.

2007-2008 Financial aid. Need-based: Need-based aid available for part-time students.

Application procedures. Admission: No deadline. No application fee. Admission notification on a rolling basis. **Financial aid:** Priority date 5/1; no closing date. FAFSA required. Applicants notified on a rolling basis starting 5/1.

Academics. Special study options: Cross-registration, distance learning, dual enrollment of high school students, honors, independent study, internships, study abroad. License preparation in nursing, real estate. **Credit/placement by examination:** AP, CLEP, institutional tests. 16 credit hours maximum toward associate degree. **Support services:** GED preparation and test center, learning center, pre-admission summer program, reduced course load, remedial instruction, study skills assistance, tutoring, writing center.

Majors. Agriculture: General. **Biology:** General. **Business:** Management science. **Communications:** General, journalism. **Computer sciences:** General, applications programming, information systems. **Education:** General. **Engineering:** General. **Engineering technology:** Drafting. **Family/consumer sciences:** Child care. **Foreign languages:** General. **Health:** Athletic training, nursing (RN). **History:** General. **Legal studies:** General. **Math:** General, applied. **Parks/recreation:** Health/fitness, sports admin. **Physical sciences:** Chemistry, geology, oceanography, physics, planetary. **Protective services:** Law enforcement admin, police science. **Psychology:** General. **Public administration:** Social work. **Social sciences:** General, political science, sociology. **Visual/performing arts:** General, art, art history/conservation, dramatic, music history, music performance, studio arts.

Computing on campus. 200 workstations in library, computer center. Online course registration, online library, helpline, wireless network available.

Student life. **Freshman orientation:** Available. Sessions held in spring and fall. **Activities:** Bands, choral groups, drama, literary magazine, music ensembles, musical theater, student government, student newspaper, Amnesty International, gay/straight alliance, People of the World End Racism (POWER), student nurses association, Young Republicans.

Athletics. NJCAA. **Intercollegiate:** Baseball M, basketball, golf M, softball W, tennis, volleyball W. **Intramural:** Basketball, softball, volleyball. **Team name:** Eagles.

Student services. Career counseling, student employment services, financial aid counseling, on-campus daycare, personal counseling, placement for graduates, veterans' counselor. **Physically disabled:** Services for visually, hearing impaired. **Transfer:** Transfer adviser for students transferring to 4-year colleges.

Contact. E-mail: tracy_morris@ivcc.edu
Phone: (815) 224-0439 Fax: (815) 224-6091
Tracy Morris, Director of Admissions and Records, Illinois Valley Community College, 815 North Orlando Smith Avenue, Oglesby, IL 61348-9693

John A. Logan College

Carterville, Illinois
www.jalc.edu **CB code: 1357**

- Public 2-year community college
- Commuter campus in small town

General. Founded in 1967. Regionally accredited. **Enrollment:** 2,306 degree-seeking undergraduates. **Degrees:** 542 associate awarded. **ROTC:** Army, Air Force. **Location:** 10 miles from Carbondale. **Calendar:** Semester, limited summer session. **Full-time faculty:** 100 total. **Part-time faculty:** 15 total. **Class size:** 53% < 20, 44% 20-39, less than 1% 40-49, less than 1% 50-99, less than 1% >100.

Student profile.

Out-of-state:	1%	**25 or older:**	21%

Transfer out. **Colleges most students transferred to 2008:** Southern Illinois University at Carbondale.

Basis for selection. Open admission, but selective for some programs. Admission to allied health programs competitive, unique criteria depending on program. ASSET and/or COMPASS accepted in place of SAT or ACT.

High school preparation. College preparatory program required of 2-year transfer degree applicants. Must have 15 high school course units: 4 English, 3 math, 3 laboratory science, 3 social science, 2 electives.

2008-2009 Annual costs. Tuition/fees: $2,130; $5,030 out-of-district; $6,984 out-of-state. Per-credit charge: $71 in-district; $168 out-of-district; $233 out-of-state. Books/supplies: $1,234. Personal expenses: $617.

Financial aid. All financial aid based on need. Need-based aid available for part-time students. Work-study available for part-time students.

Application procedures. **Admission:** No deadline. No application fee. Admission notification on a rolling basis. **Financial aid:** Priority date 5/1; no closing date. FAFSA, institutional form required. Applicants notified on a rolling basis starting 5/1.

Academics. **Special study options:** Distance learning, dual enrollment of high school students, liberal arts/career combination. Bachelor's degree programs available on campus. License preparation in dental hygiene, nursing, occupational therapy, paramedic, real estate. **Credit/placement by examination:** CLEP, institutional tests. 30 credit hours maximum toward associate degree. **Support services:** GED preparation and test center, study skills assistance, tutoring, writing center.

Majors. **Agriculture:** Business. **Biology:** General. **Business:** Accounting technology, business admin, executive assistant, office management. **Communications:** Journalism. **Computer sciences:** General. **Construction:** Carpentry. **Education:** Art, early childhood, elementary, history, mathematics, physical, secondary, social studies, special, teacher assistance. **Engineering:** General. **Engineering technology:** Drafting. **Health:** Clinical lab technology, dental hygiene, medical records technology, nursing (RN), occupational therapy assistant, prepharmacy, sonography. **Interdisciplinary:** Biological/physical sciences. **Liberal arts:** Arts/sciences. **Math:** General. **Mechanic/repair:** Auto body, automotive, electronics/electrical, industrial. **Personal/culinary services:** Cosmetic. **Physical sciences:** Chemistry, physics. **Production:** Machine shop technology, tool and die, welding. **Protective services:** Corrections, criminal justice. **Psychology:** General. **Public administration:** Social work. **Social sciences:** Economics, international relations, political science, sociology. **Visual/performing arts:** Art, dramatic.

Computing on campus. 651 workstations in library, computer center. Online course registration available.

Student life. **Freshman orientation:** Available. **Housing:** Housing at Southern Illinois University - Carbondale. **Activities:** Concert band, choral groups, drama, music ensembles, musical theater, student government, student newspaper.

Athletics. NJCAA. **Intercollegiate:** Baseball M, basketball, golf, softball W, volleyball W. **Team name:** Volunteers.

Student services. Adult student services, career counseling, student employment services, financial aid counseling, minority student services, on-campus daycare, placement for graduates, veterans' counselor. **Physically disabled:** Services for visually, hearing impaired. **Transfer:** Transfer center, college fairs on campus for students transferring to 4-year colleges.

Contact. E-mail: terrycrain@jalc.edu
Phone: (618) 985-3741 ext. 8298 Fax: (618) 985-4433
Terry Crain, Dean of Student Services, John A. Logan College, 700 Logan College Road, Carterville, IL 62918

John Wood Community College

Quincy, Illinois
www.jwcc.edu **CB code: 1374**

- Public 2-year community college
- Commuter campus in large town

General. Founded in 1974. Regionally accredited. Additional extension sites in Pittsfield and Mt. Sterling. **Enrollment:** 1,889 degree-seeking undergraduates; 514 non-degree-seeking students. **Degrees:** 328 associate awarded. **Location:** 140 miles from St. Louis, 100 miles from Springfield. **Calendar:** Semester, extensive summer session. **Full-time faculty:** 52 total; 6% minority, 62% women. **Part-time faculty:** 146 total; 6% minority, 40% women. **Class size:** 71% < 20, 29% 20-39, less than 1% 40-49. **Special facilities:** Truck driver training facility, greenhouse, agricultural center.

Student profile. Among degree-seeking undergraduates, 80% enrolled in a transfer program, 20% enrolled in a vocational program, 493 enrolled as first-time, first-year students, 173 transferred in from other institutions.

Part-time:	40%	**Asian American:**	2%
Out-of-state:	9%	**Hispanic American:**	1%
Women:	62%	**25 or older:**	38%
African American:	3%		

Transfer out. **Colleges most students transferred to 2008:** Western Illinois University, Eastern Illinois University, University of Illinois-Springfield, Quincy University.

Basis for selection. Open admission, but selective for some programs. Limited enrollment in certificate programs in dietary management, practical nursing, nurse assistant and in associate degree program in nursing and truck driver training.

High school preparation. Recommended units include English 4, mathematics 3, social studies 3 and science 4.

2008-2009 Annual costs. Tuition/fees: $3,120; $6,120 out-of-state. Per-credit charge: $96 in-state; $196 out-of-state. Books/supplies: $1,152. Personal expenses: $720.

Financial aid. **Need-based:** Need-based aid available for part-time students. Work-study available nights and weekends.

Application procedures. **Admission:** No deadline. No application fee. Admission notification on a rolling basis. **Financial aid:** No deadline. FAFSA required. Applicants notified on a rolling basis starting 3/1.

Academics. **Special study options:** Distance learning, dual enrollment of high school students, ESL, independent study, internships, liberal arts/career combination, student-designed major, study abroad. License preparation in nursing, paramedic, real estate. **Credit/placement by examination:** AP, CLEP, institutional tests. 30 credit hours maximum toward associate degree. **Support services:** GED preparation and test center, learning center, reduced course load, remedial instruction, study skills assistance, tutoring, writing center.

Majors. **Agriculture:** General, animal husbandry, animal sciences, business, horticulture. **Biology:** General. **Business:** General, accounting, accounting technology, administrative services, business admin, executive assistant, sales/distribution. **Communications:** General. **Computer sciences:** General, applications programming. **Construction:** Electrician. **Education:** General, early childhood. **Engineering:** General. **Engineering technology:** Mechanical drafting. **Family/consumer sciences:** Child care. **Foreign languages:** Spanish. **Health:** Clinical lab technology, EMT paramedic, medical radiologic technology/radiation therapy, medical secretary, nursing (RN). **History:** General. **Interdisciplinary:** Biological/physical sciences. **Legal studies:** Legal secretary, prelaw. **Liberal arts:** Arts/sciences. **Math:** General. **Mechanic/repair:** Industrial. **Parks/recreation:** Health/fitness. **Personal/culinary services:** Restaurant/catering. **Physical sciences:** General, physics. **Protective services:** Emergency management/homeland security, fire safety technology, police science. **Psychology:** General. **Social sciences:** Economics, sociology. **Visual/performing arts:** Art, graphic design.

Most popular majors. Health sciences 23%, interdisciplinary studies 39%, liberal arts 22%.

Computing on campus. 400 workstations in library, computer center. Online course registration, helpline available.

Student life. **Freshman orientation:** Mandatory. **Activities:** Jazz band, choral groups, drama, music ensembles, musical theater, student government, service organizations, honor society, Phi Theta Kappa.

Athletics. NJCAA. **Intercollegiate:** Baseball M, basketball, golf M, softball W, volleyball W. **Intramural:** Basketball M, bowling, volleyball. **Team name:** Trail Blazers.

Student services. Adult student services, career counseling, services for economically disadvantaged, student employment services, financial aid counseling, minority student services, veterans' counselor. **Physically disabled:** Services for visually, speech, hearing impaired. **Transfer:** Transfer adviser, college fairs on campus for students transferring to 4-year colleges.

Contact. E-mail: admissions@jwcc.edu
Phone: (217) 641-4338 Fax: (217) 224-4208
Kassie Daly, Director of Admissions, John Wood Community College, 1301 South 48th Street, Quincy, IL 62305-8736

Joliet Junior College
Joliet, Illinois
www.jjc.edu **CB code: 1346**

- Public 2-year community college
- Commuter campus in small city

General. Founded in 1901. Regionally accredited. **Enrollment:** 11,788 degree-seeking undergraduates. **Degrees:** 1,003 associate awarded. **Location:** 45 miles from Chicago. **Calendar:** Semester, extensive summer session. **Full-time faculty:** 209 total. **Part-time faculty:** 451 total. **Class size:** 48% < 20, 51% 20-39, less than 1% 40-49, less than 1% 50-99, less than 1% >100. **Special facilities:** Planetarium, nature trail, arboretum, working farm, fitness center.

Student profile.

Out-of-state:	1%	**25 or older:**	42%

Transfer out. **Colleges most students transferred to 2008:** Northern Illinois University, Illinois State University, University of St. Francis, Lewis University, Governors State University.

Basis for selection. Open admission, but selective for some programs and for out-of-state students. Preference given to cooperative programs and in-district applicants. Nursing applicants must have 20 ACT if in top third of high school class or 21 ACT if in top half of class. Interview recommended for some.

High school preparation. 15 units recommended. Recommended units include English 4, mathematics 3, social studies 3, science 3 and academic electives 2.

2008-2009 Annual costs. Tuition/fees: $2,640; $7,193 out-of-district; $8,042 out-of-state. Per-credit charge: $64 in-district; $216 out-of-district; $244 out-of-state. Additional course fees range from $3 to $90. Personal expenses: $1,500.

2007-2008 Financial aid. **Need-based:** 63% of total undergraduate aid awarded as scholarships/grants, 37% as loans/jobs. Need-based aid available for part-time students. Work-study available nights, weekends and for part-time students. **Non-need-based:** Scholarships awarded for academics.

Application procedures. **Admission:** No deadline. No application fee. Admission notification on a rolling basis. **Financial aid:** Closing date 5/1. FAFSA, institutional form required. Applicants notified on a rolling basis starting 5/15.

Academics. **Special study options:** Cooperative education, distance learning, dual enrollment of high school students, ESL, honors, independent study, internships, study abroad. License preparation in nursing, paramedic, radiology, real estate. **Credit/placement by examination:** AP, CLEP, institutional tests. 45 credit hours maximum toward associate degree. **Support services:** GED preparation, learning center, pre-admission summer program, reduced course load, remedial instruction, study skills assistance, tutoring, writing center.

Majors. **Agriculture:** General, greenhouse operations, horticulture, landscaping, nursery operations, ornamental horticulture, supplies, turf management. **Biology:** General. **Business:** Accounting, administrative services, business admin, fashion, office management, office technology, office/clerical. **Computer sciences:** General, information systems, programming. **Education:** Early childhood, elementary, secondary, special, teacher assistance. **Engineering:** Electrical. **Engineering technology:** Architectural, construction, drafting, electrical. **Family/consumer sciences:** Clothing/textiles. **Health:** Medical secretary, nursing (RN), veterinary technology/assistant. **History:** General. **Legal studies:** Legal secretary. **Liberal arts:** Arts/sciences. **Math:** General. **Mechanic/repair:** Auto body. **Personal/culinary services:** Culinary arts. **Physical sciences:** Chemistry. **Protective services:** Law enforcement admin. **Psychology:** General. **Social sciences:** Political science, sociology. **Visual/performing arts:** Art, interior design.

Most popular majors. Business/marketing 7%, health sciences 15%, liberal arts 49%.

Computing on campus. Helpline, repair service available.

Student life. **Freshman orientation:** Available. **Activities:** Bands, choral groups, drama, literary magazine, music ensembles, musical theater, student government, student newspaper, campus ministry, black student organization, Intervarsity Christian Fellowship, Latinos Unidos, Latter Day Saints association, unity club.

Athletics. NJCAA. **Intercollegiate:** Baseball M, basketball, cross-country, football (tackle) M, soccer, softball W, tennis, volleyball W. **Team name:** Wolves.

Student services. Career counseling, services for economically disadvantaged, student employment services, financial aid counseling, minority student services, on-campus daycare, personal counseling, placement for graduates, veterans' counselor, women's services. **Physically disabled:** Services for visually, speech, hearing impaired. **Transfer:** Transfer center, transfer adviser for students transferring to 4-year colleges.

Contact. E-mail: jkloberd@jjc.edu
Phone: (815) 729-9020 Fax: (815) 744-5507
Jennifer Kloberdanz, Director of Admissions and Recruitment, Joliet Junior College, 1215 Houbolt Road, Joliet, IL 60431-8938

Kankakee Community College
Kankakee, Illinois
www.kcc.edu **CB code: 1380**

- Public 2-year community college
- Commuter campus in large town

General. Founded in 1966. Regionally accredited. **Enrollment:** 2,906 degree-seeking undergraduates; 858 non-degree-seeking students. **Degrees:** 329 associate awarded. **ROTC:** Army. **Location:** 60 miles from Chicago. **Calendar:** Semester, extensive summer session. **Full-time faculty:** 60 total; 5% have terminal degrees, 10% minority, 52% women. **Part-time faculty:** 104 total; 4% have terminal degrees, 9% minority, 53% women.

Student profile. Among degree-seeking undergraduates, 34% enrolled in a transfer program, 66% enrolled in a vocational program, 2% already have a bachelor's degree or higher, 332 enrolled as first-time, first-year students.

Part-time:	54%	**African American:**	14%
Out-of-state:	5%	**Asian American:**	1%
Women:	68%	**Hispanic American:**	6%

Transfer out. **Colleges most students transferred to 2008:** Illinois State University, Governors State University, Olivet Nazarene University, University of Illinois, Eastern Illinois University.

Basis for selection. Open admission, but selective for some programs. Criteria for health career programs may include prerequisite coursework, high school record and test scores; separate application and COMPASS required. ASSET required of all students for placement. **Adult students:** COMPASS required.

High school preparation. College-preparatory program recommended. 15 units recommended. Recommended units include English 4, mathematics 3, social studies 2, science 2 (laboratory 1) and academic electives 4.

2009-2010 Annual costs. Tuition/fees (projected): $2,310; $5,160 out-of-district; $11,460 out-of-state. Per-credit charge: $77 in-district; $172 out-of-district; $382 out-of-state. Books/supplies: $950. Personal expenses: $1,400.

2007-2008 Financial aid. Need-based: 90% of total undergraduate aid awarded as scholarships/grants, 10% as loans/jobs. Need-based aid available for part-time students. **Non-need-based:** Scholarships awarded for athletics.

Application procedures. Admission: No deadline. No application fee. Application must be submitted online. Admission notification on a rolling basis. **Financial aid:** Priority date 6/1; no closing date. FAFSA required. Applicants notified on a rolling basis; must reply within 4 week(s) of notification.

Academics. Special study options: Cross-registration, distance learning, dual enrollment of high school students, ESL, honors, independent study, internships, study abroad, teacher certification program. License preparation in nursing, paramedic, physical therapy, radiology. **Credit/placement by examination:** AP, CLEP, institutional tests. 16 credit hours maximum toward associate degree. **Support services:** GED preparation and test center, learning center, pre-admission summer program, reduced course load, remedial instruction, study skills assistance, tutoring, writing center.

Majors. Biology: General. **Business:** Accounting, administrative services, business admin, construction management. **Communications technology:** Desktop publishing. **Computer sciences:** Information technology. **Education:** General, early childhood, elementary, mathematics, secondary, teacher assistance. **Engineering:** General. **Engineering technology:** Drafting, manufacturing. **Health:** Clinical lab technology, EMT paramedic, medical assistant, nursing (RN), physical therapy assistant, predental, premedicine, prepharmacy, preveterinary, radiologic technology/medical imaging, respiratory therapy technology. **Legal studies:** Paralegal. **Math:** General. **Mechanic/repair:** General, automotive, electronics/electrical, heating/ac/refrig, industrial electronics. **Production:** Welding. **Protective services:** Emergency management/homeland security, police science. **Psychology:** General. **Social sciences:** Political science. **Visual/performing arts:** General, art, studio arts.

Most popular majors. Business/marketing 8%, education 7%, health sciences 34%, liberal arts 7%, security/protective services 6%.

Computing on campus. 1,000 workstations in library, computer center, student center. Commuter students can connect to campus network. Online library, helpline, wireless network available.

Student life. Freshman orientation: Mandatory. Preregistration for classes offered. Two-hour orientation class held multiple dates and times at beginning of term. **Activities:** Radio station, student government.

Athletics. NJCAA. **Intercollegiate:** Baseball M, basketball, soccer M, softball W, volleyball W. **Intramural:** Basketball, golf. **Team name:** Cavaliers.

Student services. Adult student services, career counseling, student employment services, financial aid counseling, minority student services, on-campus daycare, placement for graduates, veterans' counselor. **Physically disabled:** Services for visually, speech, hearing impaired. **Transfer:** Pre-admission transcript evaluation for new students. Transfer center, transfer adviser, college fairs on campus for students transferring to 4-year colleges.

Contact. Phone: (815) 802-8520 Fax: (815) 802-8101
Michelle Driscoll, Assistant Dean of Student Services, Kankakee Community College, 100 College Drive, Kankakee, IL 60901-6505

Kaskaskia College

Centralia, Illinois
www.kaskaskia.edu **CB code: 1108**

- Public 2-year community college
- Commuter campus in large town

General. Founded in 1966. Regionally accredited. Child care center available. **Enrollment:** 1,824 full-time, degree-seeking students. **Degrees:** 516 associate awarded. **Location:** 60 miles from St. Louis. **Calendar:** Semester, limited summer session. **Full-time faculty:** 74 total; 7% have terminal degrees, 3% minority, 46% women. **Part-time faculty:** 160 total; 3% have terminal degrees, 8% minority, 61% women. **Partnerships:** Formal partnerships with local businesses, hospitals, factories/industries, and correctional institutions that participate in training, apprenticeship, and safety features.

Student profile. Among full-time, degree-seeking students, 62% enrolled in a transfer program, 38% enrolled in a vocational program, 4% already have a bachelor's degree or higher, 1,380 transferred in from other institutions.

Out-of-state:	1%	**Native American:**	1%
African American:	5%	**International:**	1%
Asian American:	1%	**25 or older:**	39%
Hispanic American:	1%		

Transfer out. Colleges most students transferred to 2008: Southern Illinois University at Carbondale, Southern Illinois University at Edwardsville, Eastern Illinois University.

Basis for selection. Open admission, but selective for some programs. Special requirements for health-related programs. ASSET test recommended for practical nursing, cosmetology, dental, radiologic technology, physical therapy assistant program applicants. Nelson-Denny Reading Test recommended and ASSET required for nursing assistant, diagnostic medical sonography, respiratory therapy applicants. Interview required of allied health majors. **Homeschooled:** COMPASS/ACT required.

High school preparation. 15 units recommended. Recommended units include English 4, mathematics 3, social studies 3, science 3, foreign language 2 and academic electives 2. Specific requirements for allied health.

2008-2009 Annual costs. Tuition/fees: $2,190; $4,140 out-of-district; $9,240 out-of-state. Per-credit charge: $65 in-district; $130 out-of-district; $300 out-of-state.

2008-2009 Financial aid. Need-based: Need-based aid available for part-time students. Work-study available for part-time students. **Non-need-based:** Scholarships awarded for academics, athletics, state residency.

Application procedures. Admission: No deadline. No application fee. Application must be submitted on paper. Admission notification on a rolling basis. Allied health programs have specific closing dates. **Financial aid:** Priority date 5/15; no closing date. FAFSA required. Applicants notified on a rolling basis starting 4/1; must reply within 2 week(s) of notification.

Academics. Learning communities available. **Special study options:** Accelerated study, cooperative education, distance learning, double major, dual enrollment of high school students, ESL, honors, independent study, internships, liberal arts/career combination, student-designed major, weekend college. License preparation in nursing, paramedic, physical therapy, radiology. **Credit/placement by examination:** CLEP, institutional tests. 30 credit hours maximum toward associate degree. **Support services:** GED preparation, learning center, reduced course load, remedial instruction, study skills assistance, tutoring.

Majors. Agriculture: General. **Business:** General, accounting, executive assistant, office technology. **Computer sciences:** Information systems, system admin. **Construction:** Carpentry. **Education:** Mathematics, teacher assistance. **Engineering technology:** Architectural drafting, electrical. **Health:** EMT paramedic, nursing (RN), physical therapy assistant, radiologic technology/medical imaging, respiratory therapy technology, veterinary technology/assistant. **Interdisciplinary:** Biological/physical sciences. **Liberal arts:** Arts/sciences. **Mechanic/repair:** Auto body, automotive, industrial. **Personal/culinary services:** Chef training. **Protective services:** Juvenile corrections, law enforcement admin.

Most popular majors. Business/marketing 7%, health sciences 31%, interdisciplinary studies 6%, liberal arts 43%.

Computing on campus. 187 workstations in library, computer center, student center. Commuter students can connect to campus network. Online library, helpline, repair service, wireless network available.

Student life. Freshman orientation: Available, $78 fee. Preregistration for classes offered. One-day session on campus held prior to semester; additional online session. **Activities:** Bands, choral groups, drama, film society, music ensembles, student government, student newspaper, Brothers and Sisters in Christ, Black Student Association.

Athletics. NJCAA. **Intercollegiate:** Baseball M, basketball, cheerleading, golf, softball W, volleyball W. **Team name:** Blue Devils.

Student services. Adult student services, career counseling, services for economically disadvantaged, student employment services, financial aid counseling, minority student services, on-campus daycare, personal counseling, placement for graduates, veterans' counselor. **Physically disabled:** Services for visually, speech, hearing impaired. **Transfer:** Pre-admission transcript

Two-Year Colleges

evaluation for new students. Transfer center, transfer adviser, college fairs on campus for students transferring to 4-year colleges.

Contact. Phone: (618) 545-3040 Fax: (618) 532-1135
Denise Derrick, Director of Admissions and Registration, Kaskaskia College, 27210 College Road, Centralia, IL 62801

Kishwaukee College

Malta, Illinois
www.kishwaukeecollege.edu **CB code: 0511**

- Public 2-year community college
- Commuter campus in rural community

General. Founded in 1967. Regionally accredited. **Enrollment:** 3,083 degree-seeking undergraduates. **Degrees:** 501 associate awarded. **ROTC:** Army. **Location:** 7 miles from DeKalb. **Calendar:** Semester, limited summer session. **Full-time faculty:** 83 total. **Part-time faculty:** 173 total.

Student profile.

Out-of-state:	1%	25 or older:	32%

Transfer out. Colleges most students transferred to 2008: Northern Illinois University.

Basis for selection. Open admission, but selective for some programs. Special requirements, including interview, for nursing, radiologic technology and therapeutic massage programs. Portfolio recommended for art majors. **Learning Disabled:** Students with learning disabilities should contact disabilities service office at least 30 days before enrollment to assist student with reasonable accommodations.

High school preparation. 15 units recommended. Recommended units include English 4, mathematics 3, social studies 3, science 3 and foreign language 2. High school diploma or equivalency required for nursing, radiologic technology, and therapeutic massage applicants.

2008-2009 Annual costs. Tuition/fees: $2,430; $7,410 out-of-district; $8,340 out-of-state. Per-credit charge: $71 in-district; $237 out-of-district; $268 out-of-state. Books/supplies: $1,000. Personal expenses: $1,000.

2007-2008 Financial aid. Need-based: Need-based aid available for part-time students. Work-study available nights, weekends and for part-time students. **Non-need-based:** Scholarships awarded for academics, athletics, leadership, music/drama, state residency.

Application procedures. Admission: No deadline. No application fee. Admission notification on a rolling basis. **Financial aid:** Priority date 5/1; no closing date. FAFSA, institutional form required. Applicants notified on a rolling basis starting 5/1; must reply within 2 week(s) of notification.

Academics. Cross-registration with Northern Illinois University and nearby community colleges. Distance Learning Consortium, member Illinois Virtual College (IVC). **Special study options:** Cross-registration, distance learning, double major, dual enrollment of high school students, ESL, independent study, internships, study abroad. License preparation in aviation, nursing, radiology, real estate. **Credit/placement by examination:** AP, CLEP, institutional tests. 48 credit hours maximum toward associate degree. Must complete 15 hours residency prior to posting proficiency credit. **Support services:** GED preparation and test center, learning center, pre-admission summer program, reduced course load, remedial instruction, study skills assistance, tutoring.

Majors. Agriculture: Agribusiness operations, animal breeding, business, greenhouse operations, horticultural science, horticulture, landscaping, nursery operations, ornamental horticulture, supplies. **Architecture:** Landscape. **Business:** General, accounting, human resources, management information systems, office management, office/clerical, operations. **Communications:** General, journalism. **Computer sciences:** Applications programming. **Education:** General, early childhood, elementary, physical, secondary, special. **Engineering:** General. **Engineering technology:** Drafting, electrical, manufacturing. **Family/consumer sciences:** General, child care. **Foreign languages:** General, French, Spanish. **Health:** Medical radiologic technology/radiation therapy, nursing (RN), predental, premedicine, prenursing, prepharmacy, preveterinary. **History:** General. **Interdisciplinary:** Biological/physical sciences. **Legal studies:** Prelaw. **Liberal arts:** Arts/sciences. **Math:** General. **Mechanic/repair:** Auto body, automotive, diesel. **Parks/recreation:** Health/fitness. **Physical sciences:** Astronomy, chemistry, physics. **Protective services:** Fire safety technology, firefighting, police science. **Psychology:** General. **Public administration:** Social work. **Social sciences:** General, criminology, economics, political science, sociology. **Visual/performing arts:** General, art, dramatic.

Most popular majors. Agriculture 7%, health sciences 10%, interdisciplinary studies 51%, liberal arts 29%.

Computing on campus. 376 workstations in library, computer center. Online library, helpline available.

Student life. Freshman orientation: Available. Preregistration for classes offered. Five sessions held during summer. **Activities:** Choral groups, drama, literary magazine, music ensembles, musical theater, student government, student newspaper, international student club, Nurses Christian Fellowship, Phi Theta Kappa, black student union, Vocational Industrial Clubs of America, Christian Fellowship, agriculture club, horticulture club, student nurses organization, student radiographers association.

Athletics. NJCAA. **Intercollegiate:** Baseball M, basketball, golf, soccer M, softball W, volleyball W. **Intramural:** Badminton, basketball, softball, volleyball. **Team name:** Kougars.

Student services. Adult student services, career counseling, services for economically disadvantaged, student employment services, financial aid counseling, health services, minority student services, on-campus daycare, personal counseling, placement for graduates, veterans' counselor, women's services. **Physically disabled:** Services for visually, speech, hearing impaired. **Learning disabled:** Comprehensive services available. **Transfer:** Re-entry adviser, pre-admission transcript evaluation for new students. Transfer center, transfer adviser, college fairs on campus for students transferring to 4-year colleges.

Contact. Phone: (815) 825-2086 ext. 218 Fax: (815) 825-2306
Jill Bier, Director of Admissions, Registration and Records, Kishwaukee College, 21193 Malta Road, Malta, IL 60150-9699

Lake Land College

Mattoon, Illinois
www.lakelandcollege.edu **CB code: 1424**

- Public 2-year community college
- Commuter campus in large town

General. Founded in 1966. Regionally accredited. **Enrollment:** 5,134 degree-seeking undergraduates. **Degrees:** 1,000 associate awarded. **Location:** 45 miles from Decatur, 45 miles from Champaign. **Calendar:** Semester, extensive summer session. **Full-time faculty:** 123 total; 72% have terminal degrees, 6% minority, 45% women. **Part-time faculty:** 329 total; 46% have terminal degrees, 3% minority, 55% women. **Class size:** 55% < 20, 45% 20-39.

Student profile. Among degree-seeking undergraduates, 50% enrolled in a transfer program, 50% enrolled in a vocational program, 10% already have a bachelor's degree or higher.

Out-of-state:	3%	25 or older:	46%

Transfer out. Colleges most students transferred to 2008: Eastern Illinois University, Southern Illinois University, University of Illinois.

Basis for selection. Open admission, but selective for some programs. Special requirements for dental hygiene, nursing, physical therapist assistant, John Deere agricultural technology, massage therapy, and cosmetology programs. ACT required of dental hygiene applicants for placement only. **Adult students:** Assessment battery test required.

High school preparation. Recommended units include English 4, mathematics 3, social studies 3, history 3, science 3 (laboratory 3), foreign language 2 and academic electives 2. Math and biology required for dental hygiene and nursing applicants.

2008-2009 Annual costs. Tuition/fees: $2,394; $5,087 out-of-district; $9,264 out-of-state. Per-credit charge: $64 in-district; $153 out-of-district; $293 out-of-state. Books/supplies: $318.

2007-2008 Financial aid. Need-based: 74% of total undergraduate aid awarded as scholarships/grants, 26% as loans/jobs. Need-based aid available for part-time students. Work-study available nights, weekends and for part-time students. **Non-need-based:** Scholarships awarded for academics, athletics.

Application procedures. Admission: No deadline. No application fee. Admission notification on a rolling basis. **Financial aid:** Priority date 5/1; no closing date. FAFSA required. Applicants notified on a rolling basis starting 6/1.

Academics. Special study options: Accelerated study, cooperative education, distance learning, dual enrollment of high school students, ESL, honors, independent study, internships, study abroad, weekend college. License preparation in dental hygiene, nursing, physical therapy. **Credit/placement by examination:** AP, CLEP, institutional tests. 32 credit hours maximum toward associate degree. **Support services:** GED preparation, learning center, reduced course load, remedial instruction, study skills assistance, tutoring.

Majors. **Agriculture:** General. **Business:** General, administrative services, human resources. **Communications:** Broadcast journalism, journalism. **Computer sciences:** LAN/WAN management, networking. **Conservation:** Wildlife. **Education:** General, biology, mathematics, social science. **Engineering:** General, civil. **Family/consumer sciences:** General, child care. **Health:** Dental hygiene, nursing (RN), physical therapy assistant, premedicine, prepharmacy, preveterinary. **Legal studies:** Legal secretary, prelaw. **Liberal arts:** Arts/sciences. **Math:** General. **Protective services:** Police science. **Psychology:** General. **Social sciences:** General, economics. **Visual/performing arts:** Studio arts.

Computing on campus. 500 workstations in library, computer center. Online course registration available.

Student life. **Freshman orientation:** Available. Preregistration for classes offered. Mandatory for degree-seeking students; approximately 4 hours in length. **Activities:** Choral groups, radio station, student government, student newspaper, Phi Theta Kappa.

Athletics. NJCAA. **Intercollegiate:** Baseball M, basketball, softball W, tennis, volleyball W. **Intramural:** Bowling, golf, softball, volleyball. **Team name:** Lakers.

Student services. Career counseling, student employment services, health services, on-campus daycare, personal counseling, placement for graduates, veterans' counselor. **Physically disabled:** Services for visually, speech, hearing impaired. **Transfer:** Transfer adviser, college fairs on campus for students transferring to 4-year colleges.

Contact. E-mail: admissions@lakeland.cc.il.us
Phone: (217) 234-5434 Fax: (217) 234-5390
Jon VanDyke, Dean of Admission Services, Lake Land College, 5001 Lake Land Boulevard, Mattoon, IL 61938-9366

Lewis and Clark Community College

Godfrey, Illinois — **CB member**
www.lc.edu — **CB code: 0623**

- Public 2-year community college
- Commuter campus in large town

General. Founded in 1970. Regionally accredited. **Enrollment:** 2,813 full-time, degree-seeking students. **Degrees:** 646 associate awarded. **ROTC:** Army. **Location:** 30 miles from St. Louis. **Calendar:** Semester, limited summer session. **Full-time faculty:** 96 total. **Part-time faculty:** 223 total.

Transfer out. **Colleges most students transferred to 2008:** Southern Illinois University: Edwardsville.

Basis for selection. Open admission, but selective for some programs. Special requirements for nursing and other allied health programs. Interview required for radio broadcasting, music majors. Audition required for music majors.

High school preparation. Recommended units include English 4, mathematics 3 and science 2.

2009-2010 Annual costs. Tuition/fees: $2,820; $7,620 out-of-district; $10,020 out-of-state. Per-credit charge: $80 in-district; $254 out-of-district; $334 out-of-state. Books/supplies: $435. Personal expenses: $1,100.

2008-2009 Financial aid. **Need-based:** Need-based aid available for part-time students.

Application procedures. **Admission:** No deadline. No application fee. Admission notification on a rolling basis. **Financial aid:** Priority date 6/1; no closing date. FAFSA required. Applicants notified on a rolling basis starting 8/1; must reply within 3 week(s) of notification.

Academics. **Special study options:** Cooperative education, cross-registration, distance learning, double major, dual enrollment of high school students, internships, liberal arts/career combination, student-designed major. Bachelor's degree programs available on campus. License preparation in dental hygiene, nursing, occupational therapy, paramedic, real estate. **Credit/placement by examination:** AP, CLEP, institutional tests. 32 credit hours maximum toward associate degree. **Support services:** GED preparation, learning center, remedial instruction, study skills assistance, tutoring, writing center.

Majors. **Business:** General, accounting, banking/financial services, business admin, office/clerical. **Communications:** Radio/tv. **Computer sciences:** General, computer graphics, computer science, data processing, information technology, LAN/WAN management, web page design, webmaster. **Education:** General, early childhood, teacher assistance. **Engineering technology:** Drafting. **Family/consumer sciences:** Child care. **Health:** Dental hygiene, nursing (RN), occupational therapy assistant, predental, premedicine, prenursing, prepharmacy. **Legal studies:** Legal secretary, prelaw. **Liberal arts:** Arts/sciences. **Mechanic/repair:** Automotive. **Protective services:** Criminal justice, firefighting. **Visual/performing arts:** Studio arts.

Computing on campus. 300 workstations in library, computer center. Online course registration, online library, wireless network available.

Student life. **Freshman orientation:** Mandatory. Preregistration for classes offered. **Activities:** Bands, choral groups, dance, drama, music ensembles, radio station, student government, student newspaper, TV station, veterans organization, Christian Campus Fellowship, disabled students organization, black student association, political action club.

Athletics. NJCAA. **Intercollegiate:** Baseball M, basketball, golf M, soccer, softball W, tennis, volleyball W. **Team name:** Trailblazers.

Student services. Adult student services, career counseling, student employment services, health services, on-campus daycare, personal counseling, placement for graduates, veterans' counselor. **Physically disabled:** Services for visually, hearing impaired. **Transfer:** Pre-admission transcript evaluation for new students. Transfer center, transfer adviser, college fairs on campus for students transferring to 4-year colleges.

Contact. E-mail: enroll@lc.edu
Phone: (618) 468-2222 Toll-free number: (800) 500-5222
Fax: (618) 468-2310
Peggy Hudson, Director Enrollment Center for Admissions Services, Lewis and Clark Community College, 5800 Godfrey Road, Godfrey, IL 62035-2466

Lincoln College

Lincoln, Illinois
www.lincolncollege.edu — **CB code: 1406**

- Private 2-year junior and liberal arts college
- Residential campus in large town
- SAT or ACT (ACT writing recommended) required

General. Founded in 1865. Regionally accredited. Liberal arts degree program offered only at main campus. Degree and vocational programs available at extension campus in Normal. **Enrollment:** 1,090 degree-seeking undergraduates. **Degrees:** 64 bachelor's, 222 associate awarded. **Location:** 185 miles from Chicago, 125 miles from St. Louis. **Calendar:** Semester, limited summer session. **Full-time faculty:** 33 total. **Part-time faculty:** 25 total. **Special facilities:** Abe Lincoln collections, museum of the presidents.

Student profile. Among degree-seeking undergraduates, 37 transferred in from other institutions.

Out-of-state:	9%	**Live on campus:**	90%

Transfer out. 85% of students enrolled in the transfer program go on to 4-year colleges. **Colleges most students transferred to 2008:** Illinois State University, Southern Illinois University, Eastern Illinois University, Northern Illinois University, Western Illinois University.

Basis for selection. Test scores and high school transcript are most important. Letters of recommendation and/or a personal statment or interview may be required. Normal campus requires 18 ACT score for resident students. Interview and a personal statment recommended for academically weak applicants. **Homeschooled:** Transcript of courses and grades, state high school equivalency certificate required. **Learning Disabled:** Office of Disability Services requires documentation of ADD/ADHD for consideration for special program. Students with other learning disabilities go through normal selection process.

High school preparation. College-preparatory program recommended. Recommended units include English 4, mathematics 3, social studies 2, history 2, science 3 (laboratory 1), foreign language 2 and computer science 2.

2008-2009 Annual costs. Tuition/fees: $20,000. Per-credit charge: $250. Room/board: $6,200. Books/supplies: $690. Personal expenses: $1,886.

2008-2009 Financial aid. **Need-based:** Average need met was 48%. Average scholarship/grant was $11,202; average loan $3,020. 67% of total undergraduate aid awarded as scholarships/grants, 33% as loans/jobs. Need-based aid available for part-time students. Work-study available nights and

Two-Year Colleges

weekends. **Non-need-based:** Scholarships awarded for academics, art, athletics, music/drama. **Additional information:** Auditions recommended for music, speech, theater, broadcasting, and dance scholarship candidates, portfolios recommended for art and technical theater scholarship candidates.

Application procedures. **Admission:** Closing date 8/18 (receipt date). $25 fee, may be waived for applicants with need. Admission notification on a rolling basis. Freshman enrollment limited. Application process closes early if maximum is reached. **Financial aid:** Priority date 6/1, closing date 7/1. FAFSA required. Applicants notified on a rolling basis starting 6/1; must reply within 3 week(s) of notification.

Academics. **Special study options:** Combined bachelor's/graduate degree, dual enrollment of high school students, honors, independent study, study abroad. Bachelor's degree programs available on campus. **Credit/placement by examination:** AP, CLEP, SAT, ACT, institutional tests. 15 credit hours maximum toward associate degree. **Support services:** Learning center, pre-admission summer program, reduced course load, study skills assistance, tutoring.

Majors. **Biology:** General. **Business:** General, accounting, business admin, tourism promotion, tourism/travel. **Communications:** General, journalism. **Computer sciences:** Computer science. **Conservation:** General, environmental studies. **Education:** General, art, elementary, multi-level teacher. **History:** General. **Liberal arts:** Arts/sciences. **Math:** General. **Parks/recreation:** Health/fitness. **Philosophy/religion:** Philosophy, religion. **Physical sciences:** Chemistry, physics. **Protective services:** Law enforcement admin, police science. **Psychology:** General. **Social sciences:** General, economics, geography, sociology. **Visual/performing arts:** General, art, art history/conservation, ceramics, dance, dramatic, drawing, jazz, music history, music performance, music theory/composition, painting, photography, piano/organ, sculpture, studio arts, theater design, voice/opera.

Computing on campus. 130 workstations in library, computer center, student center. Dormitories wired for high-speed internet access. Commuter students can connect to campus network. Helpline available.

Student life. **Freshman orientation:** Mandatory. Preregistration for classes offered. Orientation and class registration held in April, June, and July. **Housing:** Guaranteed on-campus for all undergraduates. Single-sex dorms available. $125 fully refundable deposit, deadline 8/1. **Activities:** Bands, choral groups, dance, drama, literary magazine, music ensembles, musical theater, radio station, student government, student newspaper, Black Student Union, Rotaract, Mosaic (Christian group).

Athletics. NJCAA. **Intercollegiate:** Baseball M, basketball, cross-country, diving, golf, soccer, softball W, swimming, track and field, volleyball W, wrestling M. **Intramural:** Baseball M, basketball, football (non-tackle), football (tackle), soccer, softball, table tennis, volleyball. **Team name:** Lynx.

Student services. Adult student services, career counseling, student employment services, health services, personal counseling, placement for graduates. **Learning disabled:** Comprehensive services available. **Transfer:** Pre-admission transcript evaluation for new students. Transfer center, transfer adviser, college fairs on campus for students transferring to 4-year colleges.

Contact. E-mail: admissions@lincolncollege.edu
Phone: (800) 569-0556 Fax: (217) 732-7715
Gretchen Bree, Director of Admission, Lincoln College, 300 Keokuk Street, Lincoln, IL 62656

Lincoln Land Community College

Springfield, Illinois
www.llcc.edu **CB code: 1428**

- Public 2-year community and junior college
- Commuter campus in small city

General. Founded in 1967. Regionally accredited. **Enrollment:** 4,937 degree-seeking undergraduates; 1,722 non-degree-seeking students. **Degrees:** 622 associate awarded. **ROTC:** Army, Naval, Air Force. **Location:** 180 miles from Chicago, 96 miles from St. Louis. **Calendar:** Semester, extensive summer session. **Full-time faculty:** 126 total; 92% have terminal degrees, 7% minority, 52% women. **Part-time faculty:** 248 total; 2% minority, 49% women. **Class size:** 60% < 20, 38% 20-39, less than 1% 40-49, 1% 50-99. **Special facilities:** Museum.

Student profile. Among degree-seeking undergraduates, 58% enrolled in a transfer program, 29% enrolled in a vocational program, 3% already have a bachelor's degree or higher, 817 enrolled as first-time, first-year students, 56 transferred in from other institutions.

Part-time:	53%	**Asian American:**	1%
Women:	59%	**Hispanic American:**	2%
African American:	9%	**25 or older:**	37%

Transfer out. 35% of students enrolled in the transfer program go on to 4-year colleges. **Colleges most students transferred to 2008:** University of Illinois: Springfield, Southern Illinois University: Carbondale, Eastern Illinois University, Western Illinois University, Illinois State University.

Basis for selection. Open admission, but selective for some programs. Nursing and allied health program applicants must rank in top half of high school class and have 20 ACT. Admissions assessment not required of students with 22 ACT or above.

High school preparation. Recommended units include English 4, mathematics 3, social studies 2, science 2 (laboratory 2) and academic electives 2.

2008-2009 Annual costs. Tuition/fees: $2,505; $4,710 out-of-district; $6,915 out-of-state. Per-credit charge: $74 in-district; $147 out-of-district; $221 out-of-state. Books/supplies: $840.

Financial aid. **Need-based:** Need-based aid available for part-time students. Work-study available nights. **Non-need-based:** Scholarships awarded for academics, athletics, minority status, state residency.

Application procedures. **Admission:** No deadline. No application fee. Application must be submitted on paper. Admission notification on a rolling basis. **Financial aid:** Priority date 5/1; no closing date. FAFSA, institutional form required. Applicants notified on a rolling basis starting 4/15; must reply within 2 week(s) of notification.

Academics. **Special study options:** Cooperative education, distance learning, double major, dual enrollment of high school students, ESL, honors, independent study, internships, liberal arts/career combination, study abroad, United Nations semester. License preparation in nursing, occupational therapy, paramedic, physical therapy, radiology, real estate. **Credit/placement by examination:** AP, CLEP, institutional tests. 30 credit hours maximum toward associate degree. **Support services:** GED preparation, learning center, reduced course load, remedial instruction, study skills assistance, tutoring, writing center.

Majors. **Agriculture:** Landscaping, production. **Business:** General, accounting, administrative services, hospitality admin, office technology. **Computer sciences:** Applications programming, networking, programming. **Construction:** Maintenance. **Education:** Teacher assistance. **Engineering:** General. **Engineering technology:** Architectural drafting, construction, electrical. **Health:** Nursing (RN), occupational therapy assistant, office assistant, radiologic technology/medical imaging. **Interdisciplinary:** Biological/physical sciences. **Legal studies:** Legal secretary. **Liberal arts:** Arts/sciences. **Mechanic/repair:** Aircraft, auto body, automotive, industrial electronics. **Protective services:** Firefighting, police science. **Transportation:** Aviation management. **Visual/performing arts:** Graphic design, studio arts.

Most popular majors. Health sciences 18%, interdisciplinary studies 22%, liberal arts 44%.

Computing on campus. 325 workstations in library, computer center, student center. Commuter students can connect to campus network. Online course registration, online library, helpline, wireless network available.

Student life. **Freshman orientation:** Available. Preregistration for classes offered. Half-day program offered at beginning of semester. **Activities:** Bands, choral groups, dance, drama, international student organizations, literary magazine, music ensembles, musical theater, student government, student newspaper.

Athletics. NJCAA. **Intercollegiate:** Baseball M, basketball, soccer M, softball W, volleyball W. **Team name:** Loggers.

Student services. Adult student services, career counseling, services for economically disadvantaged, student employment services, financial aid counseling, minority student services, on-campus daycare, personal counseling, placement for graduates, veterans' counselor. **Physically disabled:** Services for visually, speech, hearing impaired. **Learning disabled:** Comprehensive services available. **Transfer:** Pre-admission transcript evaluation for new students. Transfer adviser, college fairs on campus for students transferring to 4-year colleges.

Contact. E-mail: ron.gregoire@llcc.cc.il.us
Phone: (217) 786-2290 Toll-free number: (800) 727-4161
Fax: (217) 786-2492
Ron Gregoire, Director of Admissions and Records, Lincoln Land Community College, 5250 Shepherd Road, Springfield, IL 62794-9256

MacCormac College
Chicago, Illinois
www.maccormac.edu **CB code: 1520**

- Private 2-year junior college
- Commuter campus in very large city
- Interview required

General. Founded in 1904. Regionally accredited. **Enrollment:** 163 degree-seeking undergraduates. **Degrees:** 45 associate awarded. **Calendar:** Semester, extensive summer session. **Full-time faculty:** 5 total. **Part-time faculty:** 21 total.

Student profile.

Out-of-state:	1%	**25 or older:**	30%

Transfer out. Colleges most students transferred to 2008: Loyola University, DePaul University, Roosevelt University.

Basis for selection. Open admission, but selective for some programs. Minimum typing speed required for court reporting. ACT recommended.

High school preparation. 13 units required; 15 recommended. Required and recommended units include English 4, mathematics 2-3, social studies 3-4, history 1, science 2 (laboratory 1).

2008-2009 Annual costs. Tuition/fees: $10,060. Per-credit charge: $415. Books/supplies: $1,000.

2008-2009 Financial aid. Non-need-based: Scholarships awarded for academics, leadership.

Application procedures. Admission: No deadline. $20 fee, may be waived for applicants with need. Admission notification on a rolling basis. **Financial aid:** Closing date 8/15. FAFSA required. Must reply within 2 week(s) of notification.

Academics. Special study options: ESL, internships. **Credit/placement by examination:** CLEP, IB, institutional tests. 36 credit hours maximum toward associate degree. **Support services:** Learning center, study skills assistance, tutoring.

Majors. Business: General, accounting, administrative services, business admin, hospitality admin, international, international marketing, management information systems, marketing, office management, office technology, office/clerical, tourism promotion, tourism/travel. **Computer sciences:** General, computer science, information systems. **Health:** Medical transcription. **Legal studies:** Court reporting, legal secretary, paralegal.

Most popular majors. Business/marketing 80%, legal studies 15%.

Computing on campus. 118 workstations in library, computer center.

Student life. Freshman orientation: Mandatory. Preregistration for classes offered. **Activities:** Student government, student activities committee, Phi Theta Kappa.

Student services. Career counseling, student employment services, financial aid counseling, personal counseling, placement for graduates. **Transfer:** Transfer adviser for students transferring to 4-year colleges.

Contact. E-mail: admissions@maccormac.edu
Phone: (312) 922-1884 Fax: (312) 922-3196
David Grassi, Admissions Representative, MacCormac College, 29 East Madison Street, Chicago, IL 60602

McHenry County College
Crystal Lake, Illinois **CB member**
www.mchenry.edu **CB code: 1525**

- Public 2-year community college
- Commuter campus in large town

General. Founded in 1967. Regionally accredited. **Enrollment:** 5,374 degree-seeking undergraduates. **Degrees:** 440 associate awarded. **Location:** 50 miles from Chicago. **Calendar:** Semester, limited summer session. **Full-time faculty:** 92 total; 8% minority, 48% women. **Part-time faculty:** 185 total; 7% minority, 55% women. **Special facilities:** Planetarium, weather cam.

Transfer out. Colleges most students transferred to 2008: Northern Illinois University, Illinois State University, University of Illinois at Chicago, Southern Illinois University, Columbia College.

Basis for selection. Open admission, but selective for some programs. Selective admission to RN program.

High school preparation. 18 units recommended. Recommended units include English 4, mathematics 3, social studies 3, science 3 (laboratory 3) and academic electives 2. 2 units in foreign language, music, vocational education, or art recommended.

2008-2009 Annual costs. Tuition/fees: $2,594; $8,483 out-of-district; $9,619 out-of-state. Per-credit charge: $77 in-district; $273 out-of-district; $311 out-of-state. Books/supplies: $800. Personal expenses: $1,362.

2007-2008 Financial aid. Need-based: Need-based aid available for part-time students. Work-study available nights, weekends and for part-time students. **Non-need-based:** Scholarships awarded for academics, athletics, leadership, music/drama, state residency. **Additional information:** Students can apply throughout the award year for federal and state aid. Students with physical handicaps or learning disabilities may apply for special needs scholarship.

Application procedures. Admission: No deadline. $15 fee. Admission notification on a rolling basis. **Financial aid:** Priority date 6/1; no closing date. FAFSA, institutional form required. Applicants notified on a rolling basis starting 5/1.

Academics. Special study options: Accelerated study, cooperative education, distance learning, dual enrollment of high school students, ESL, honors, independent study, internships, liberal arts/career combination, study abroad. Cooperative programs (tech prep) with Education for Employment. License preparation in paramedic, real estate. **Credit/placement by examination:** AP, CLEP, institutional tests. 30 credit hours maximum toward associate degree. Local proficiency exams available for occupational course credit, DANTES exams accepted. **Support services:** GED preparation and test center, learning center, pre-admission summer program, reduced course load, remedial instruction, study skills assistance, tutoring, writing center.

Majors. Agriculture: Horticulture. **Business:** Accounting technology, administrative services, business admin, operations, real estate, selling. **Computer sciences:** Applications programming. **Construction:** Building inspection. **Engineering:** General. **Engineering technology:** Electrical, mechanical. **Health:** EMT paramedic. **Interdisciplinary:** Biological/physical sciences. **Liberal arts:** Arts/sciences. **Mechanic/repair:** Automotive. **Protective services:** Firefighting, police science. **Visual/performing arts:** Art.

Most popular majors. Business/marketing 6%, interdisciplinary studies 68%, liberal arts 12%.

Computing on campus. 153 workstations in library, computer center, student center. Commuter students can connect to campus network. Online course registration, online library available.

Student life. Freshman orientation: Available. Preregistration for classes offered. Admitted students from local high schools invited to participate in orientation and preregistration during April and May. **Activities:** Bands, choral groups, drama, literary magazine, music ensembles, student government, student newspaper, Latinos Unidos, Phi Theta Kappa, campus activities board, campus Christian fellowship, Club Concordia, Pride Alliance, black student alliance, Latter-day Saint student association, Special Needs Action Program.

Athletics. NJCAA. **Intercollegiate:** Baseball M, basketball, soccer M, softball W, tennis, volleyball W. **Intramural:** Basketball. **Team name:** Fighting Scots.

Student services. Adult student services, career counseling, student employment services, financial aid counseling, minority student services, on-campus daycare, personal counseling, placement for graduates, veterans' counselor. **Physically disabled:** Services for visually, speech, hearing impaired. **Transfer:** Pre-admission transcript evaluation for new students. Transfer center, transfer adviser, college fairs on campus for students transferring to 4-year colleges.

Contact. E-mail: admissions@mchenry.edu
Phone: (815) 455-8530 Toll-free number: (866) 743-6667
Fax: (815) 455-3766
Fran Duwaldt, Coordinator of Admissions, McHenry County College, 8900 U.S. Highway 14, Crystal Lake, IL 60012-2761

Moraine Valley Community College
Palos Hills, Illinois
www.morainevalley.edu **CB code: 1524**

- Public 2-year community college
- Commuter campus in large town

General. Founded in 1967. Regionally accredited. **Enrollment:** 11,133 degree-seeking undergraduates; 6,344 non-degree-seeking students. **Degrees:** 1,248 associate awarded. **Location:** 25 miles from Chicago. **Calendar:** Semester, extensive summer session. **Full-time faculty:** 180 total; 9% have terminal degrees, 57% women. **Part-time faculty:** 602 total; 7% have terminal degrees, 52% women. **Class size:** 37% < 20, 63% 20-39, less than 1% 40-49. **Special facilities:** Nature study area, center for contemporary technology, fine and performing arts center.

Student profile. Among degree-seeking undergraduates, 58% enrolled in a transfer program, 33% enrolled in a vocational program, 4% already have a bachelor's degree or higher, 1,722 enrolled as first-time, first-year students, 709 transferred in from other institutions.

Part-time:	46%	**Hispanic American:**	13%
Women:	57%	**International:**	2%
African American:	9%	**25 or older:**	29%
Asian American:	3%		

Transfer out. 88% of students enrolled in the transfer program go on to 4-year colleges. **Colleges most students transferred to 2008:** Governors State University, St. Xavier University, University of Illinois-Chicago, Illinois State University, Eastern Illinois University.

Basis for selection. Open admission, but selective for some programs. Some health science programs have special admission requirements and limited enrollment. Placement tests may be waived for students with specified ACT scores. COMPASS tests required of all full-time students. **Learning Disabled:** Students should register with Center for Disability Services before May 1.

High school preparation. College-preparatory program recommended. 15 units required. Required units include English 4, mathematics 2, social studies 2, science 2 (laboratory 2) and academic electives 5.

2009-2010 Annual costs. Tuition/fees (projected): $2,466; $6,816 out-of-district; $8,016 out-of-state. Per-credit charge: $82 in-district; $227 out-of-district; $267 out-of-state. Books/supplies: $1,920. Personal expenses: $1,673.

2007-2008 Financial aid. Need-based: 88% of total undergraduate aid awarded as scholarships/grants, 12% as loans/jobs. Need-based aid available for part-time students. Work-study available nights and for part-time students. **Non-need-based:** Scholarships awarded for academics, athletics, leadership.

Application procedures. Admission: No deadline. No application fee. Admission notification on a rolling basis. **Financial aid:** Priority date 5/1; no closing date. FAFSA, institutional form required. Applicants notified on a rolling basis starting 3/1; must reply within 4 week(s) of notification.

Academics. Special study options: Accelerated study, cooperative education, distance learning, double major, dual enrollment of high school students, ESL, honors, independent study, internships, liberal arts/career combination, study abroad, weekend college. License preparation in paramedic. **Credit/placement by examination:** AP, CLEP, ACT, institutional tests. **Support services:** GED preparation and test center, learning center, reduced course load, remedial instruction, study skills assistance, tutoring, writing center.

Majors. Business: General, administrative services, business admin, entrepreneurial studies, hospitality admin, human resources, management information systems, retailing, small business admin, tourism/travel. **Computer sciences:** LAN/WAN management, security, webmaster. **Education:** Mathematics, science, teacher assistance. **Engineering technology:** Instrumentation, mechanical. **Health:** Medical records technology, nursing (RN), radiologic technology/medical imaging, respiratory therapy assistant, respiratory therapy technology. **Interdisciplinary:** Biological/physical sciences. **Liberal arts:** Arts/sciences. **Mechanic/repair:** Automotive, heating/ac/refrig, industrial electronics. **Parks/recreation:** Facilities management. **Personal/culinary services:** Restaurant/catering. **Protective services:** Corrections, firefighting, juvenile corrections, police science. **Visual/performing arts:** General, graphic design. **Other:** Recreation therapy.

Most popular majors. Health sciences 12%, interdisciplinary studies 43%, liberal arts 30%.

Computing on campus. 1,263 workstations in library, computer center, student center. Online course registration, online library, helpline available.

Student life. Freshman orientation: Available. Students registering for 12 or more credit hours required to participate in orientation program prior to first registration. **Activities:** Bands, campus ministries, choral groups, dance, drama, international student organizations, literary magazine, music ensembles, musical theater, student government, student newspaper, community service volunteer program, forensics team, inter-club council, peers educating peers, student entertainment board, Muslim student association, Alliance for African-American students, Latin and Arab student groups.

Athletics. NJCAA. **Intercollegiate:** Baseball M, basketball, cross-country, golf M, soccer, softball W, tennis, volleyball W. **Intramural:** Badminton, basketball, volleyball W. **Team name:** Cyclones.

Student services. Adult student services, career counseling, services for economically disadvantaged, student employment services, financial aid counseling, minority student services, on-campus daycare, personal counseling, placement for graduates, women's services. **Physically disabled:** Services for visually, speech, hearing impaired. **Transfer:** Transfer center, transfer adviser, college fairs on campus for students transferring to 4-year colleges.

Contact. E-mail: admissions@morainevalley.edu
Phone: (708) 974-2110 Fax: (708) 974-0974
Wendy Manser, Dean of Enrollment Services, Moraine Valley Community College, 9000 West College Parkway, Palos Hills, IL 60465-0937

Morrison Institute of Technology

Morrison, Illinois
www.morrison.tec.il.us **CB code: 1269**

- Private 2-year junior and technical college
- Residential campus in small town

General. Founded in 1973. Accredited by Technology Accreditation Commission of Accreditation Board of Engineering and Technology. **Enrollment:** 132 degree-seeking undergraduates. **Degrees:** 55 associate awarded. **Location:** 100 miles from Chicago, 50 miles from Davenport, Iowa. **Calendar:** Semester, limited summer session. **Full-time faculty:** 10 total. **Part-time faculty:** 1 total. **Class size:** 46% < 20, 54% 20-39. **Special facilities:** 4 computer-aided design (CAD) laboratories.

Student profile.

Out-of-state:	6%	**Live on campus:**	70%
25 or older:	10%		

Transfer out. Colleges most students transferred to 2008: Bradley University, University of Wisconsin at Platteville.

Basis for selection. Open admission. Interview recommended.

High school preparation. Recommended units include mathematics 2 and science 1. Algebra, geometry and drafting recommended.

2008-2009 Annual costs. Tuition/fees: $13,360. Per-credit charge: $545. Room only: $2,700. Books/supplies: $850. Personal expenses: $900.

2007-2008 Financial aid. Need-based: Need-based aid available for part-time students. Work-study available nights and weekends. **Non-need-based:** Scholarships awarded for academics.

Application procedures. Admission: Priority date 8/1; no deadline. $30 fee. Admission notification on a rolling basis. **Financial aid:** No deadline. FAFSA, institutional form required. Applicants notified on a rolling basis; must reply within 2 week(s) of notification.

Academics. Special study options: Double major. **Credit/placement by examination:** AP, CLEP, IB, institutional tests. 25 credit hours maximum toward associate degree. SOC approved guidelines. **Support services:** Reduced course load, tutoring.

Majors. Architecture: Technology. **Computer sciences:** LAN/WAN management. **Engineering technology:** Architectural, CAD/CADD, civil, construction, manufacturing, surveying.

Computing on campus. 80 workstations in library, computer center. Dormitories wired for high-speed internet access and linked to campus network. Wireless network available.

Student life. Freshman orientation: Mandatory. Preregistration for classes offered. Five 1-hour presentations during first 5 weeks of semester. **Housing:** Guaranteed on-campus for all undergraduates. Coed dorms, special housing for disabled, wellness housing available. $100 deposit. **Activities:** Student government, student newspaper, professional societies, student chapters.

Athletics. Intramural: Basketball M, bowling, volleyball.

Student services. Career counseling, student employment services, personal counseling, placement for graduates. **Transfer:** Transfer adviser, college fairs on campus for students transferring to 4-year colleges.

Contact. E-mail: admissions@morrison.tec.il.us
Phone: (815) 772-7218 ext. 11 Fax: (815) 772-7548
Jodie Eaker, Director of Admissions, Morrison Institute of Technology, 701 Portland Avenue, Morrison, IL 61270-2959

Morton College
Cicero, Illinois
www.morton.edu **CB code: 1489**

- Public 2-year community college
- Commuter campus in small city

General. Founded in 1924. Regionally accredited. **Enrollment:** 2,271 degree-seeking undergraduates; 2,688 non-degree-seeking students. **Degrees:** 332 associate awarded. **Location:** 6 miles from Chicago Loop. **Calendar:** Semester, limited summer session. **Full-time faculty:** 55 total; 13% have terminal degrees, 13% minority, 54% women. **Part-time faculty:** 168 total; 10% have terminal degrees, 25% minority, 52% women. **Special facilities:** Planetarium, museum.

Student profile. Among degree-seeking undergraduates, 50% enrolled in a transfer program, 45% enrolled in a vocational program, 436 enrolled as first-time, first-year students.

Part-time:	58%	**Hispanic American:**	73%
Women:	55%	**International:**	3%
African American:	5%	**25 or older:**	26%
Asian American:	2%		

Basis for selection. Open admission, but selective for some programs and for out-of-state students. Nursing and physical therapist assistant programs have limited space. Preference given to in-district applicants using class rank, mathematics and science course prerequisites, and placement tests as guides.

High school preparation. 15 units recommended. Recommended units include English 4, mathematics 3, social studies 3, science 3 and foreign language 2.

2008-2009 Annual costs. Tuition/fees: $2,580; $6,676 out-of-district; $8,724 out-of-state. Per-credit charge: $64 in-district; $192 out-of-district; $256 out-of-state.

2007-2008 Financial aid. Need-based: Need-based aid available for part-time students. Work-study available nights, weekends and for part-time students.

Application procedures. Admission: No deadline. $10 fee. Admission notification on a rolling basis. **Financial aid:** Priority date 6/1; no closing date. FAFSA, institutional form required. Applicants notified on a rolling basis starting 8/3.

Academics. Special study options: Distance learning, double major, dual enrollment of high school students, ESL, internships, weekend college. License preparation in nursing, physical therapy. **Credit/placement by examination:** AP, CLEP, IB, institutional tests. 30 credit hours maximum toward associate degree. **Support services:** GED preparation, learning center, pre-admission summer program, remedial instruction, tutoring, writing center.

Majors. Business: Accounting, administrative services, business admin. **Computer sciences:** Information technology. **Engineering technology:** CAD/CADD. **Health:** Nursing (RN), physical therapy assistant. **Interdisciplinary:** Biological/physical sciences. **Liberal arts:** Arts/sciences. **Mechanic/repair:** Automotive, heating/ac/refrig. **Protective services:** Police science. **Visual/performing arts:** Studio arts.

Most popular majors. Business/marketing 7%, health sciences 22%, interdisciplinary studies 9%, liberal arts 48%, security/protective services 7%.

Computing on campus. 314 workstations in library, computer center, student center. Wireless network available.

Student life. Freshman orientation: Available. Preregistration for classes offered. **Activities:** Jazz band, choral groups, dance, drama, music ensembles, musical theater, student government, student newspaper, art club, nursing students association, Phi Theta Kappa, HALO, College Bowl, film club, Yes We Can!-Si Se Puede!, open options, student success club, automotive club.

Athletics. NJCAA. **Intercollegiate:** Baseball M, basketball, cross-country, soccer M, softball W, volleyball W. **Team name:** Panthers.

Student services. Career counseling, services for economically disadvantaged, student employment services, financial aid counseling, on-campus daycare, personal counseling, placement for graduates. **Physically disabled:** Services for visually, speech, hearing impaired. **Transfer:** Pre-admission transcript evaluation for new students. Transfer center, transfer adviser, college fairs on campus for students transferring to 4-year colleges.

Contact. E-mail: enroll@morton.edu
Phone: (708) 656-8000 ext. 346 Fax: (708) 656-9592
Lizette Urbina, Associate Dean Student Development & Records, Morton College, 3801 South Central Avenue, Cicero, IL 60804-4398

Northwestern Business College
Chicago, Illinois
www.northwesternbc.edu **CB code: 2433**

- For-profit 2-year technical college
- Commuter campus in very large city

General. Founded in 1902. Regionally accredited. Additional campuses in Bridgeview and Naperville. **Enrollment:** 1,372 degree-seeking undergraduates; 434 non-degree-seeking students. **Degrees:** 403 associate awarded. **Calendar:** Quarter, extensive summer session. **Full-time faculty:** 41 total; 27% minority. **Part-time faculty:** 100 total; 44% minority. **Class size:** 78% < 20, 22% 20-39, less than 1% 40-49. **Special facilities:** Health sciences laboratories.

Student profile. Among degree-seeking undergraduates, 679 enrolled as first-time, first-year students.

Part-time:	55%	**Asian American:**	2%
Women:	78%	**Hispanic American:**	34%
African American:	40%	**25 or older:**	31%

Basis for selection. Students must have a 15 ACT, 550 SAT (exclusive of Writing) or pass admissions test administered on campus. COMPASS or ASSET used for placement.

2008-2009 Annual costs. Tuition/fees: $17,890. Per-credit charge: $390. Tuition may be higher for some classes. Books/supplies: $1,250. Personal expenses: $1,000.

2008-2009 Financial aid. Need-based: Need-based aid available for part-time students. Work-study available nights and for part-time students. **Non-need-based:** Scholarships awarded for academics. **Additional information:** State grant programs for Illinois residents and alternative loans offered.

Application procedures. Admission: No deadline. $25 fee. Admission notification on a rolling basis. **Financial aid:** Priority date 6/30; no closing date. FAFSA, institutional form required. Applicants notified on a rolling basis starting 8/15; must reply within 4 week(s) of notification.

Academics. Students wishing to graduate early may attend summer quarter. **Special study options:** Double major, internships. License preparation in real estate. **Credit/placement by examination:** AP, CLEP, IB, institutional tests. 50 credit hours maximum toward associate degree. Maximum credit awarded by examination is 25% of major, 50% of program. **Support services:** Learning center, reduced course load, remedial instruction, study skills assistance, tutoring.

Majors. Business: Accounting, administrative services, business admin, entrepreneurial studies, hospitality admin, tourism/travel. **Computer sciences:** General, applications programming, programming. **Health:** Medical assistant, medical records technology, medical secretary. **Legal studies:** Paralegal.

Most popular majors. Business/marketing 29%, health sciences 9%, legal studies 7%.

Computing on campus. 413 workstations in library, computer center.

Student life. Freshman orientation: Mandatory. Preregistration for classes offered. Three-hour program offered day and evening. **Activities:** Honor society, clubs related to majors, Junior Achievement.

Student services. Alcohol/substance abuse counseling, career counseling, student employment services, financial aid counseling, personal counseling, placement for graduates. **Physically disabled:** Services for visually, speech, hearing impaired. **Transfer:** Pre-admission transcript evaluation for new students. Transfer center, transfer adviser, college fairs on campus for students transferring to 4-year colleges.

Contact. Phone: (773) 481-3730 Toll-free number: (800) 396-5613
Fax: (773) 481-3738
Mark Sliz, Director of Admissions, Northwestern Business College, 4839 North Milwaukee Avenue, Chicago, IL 60630

Oakton Community College
Des Plaines, Illinois
www.oakton.edu **CB code: 1573**

- Public 2-year community college
- Commuter campus in small city

General. Founded in 1969. Regionally accredited. **Enrollment:** 5,529 degree-seeking undergraduates. **Degrees:** 410 associate awarded. **Location:** 15 miles from Chicago. **Calendar:** Semester, limited summer session. **Full-time faculty:** 160 total. **Part-time faculty:** 520 total. **Special facilities:** Wildlife preserve, visual arts center.

Student profile.

Out-of-state:	7%	25 or older:	45%

Transfer out. Colleges most students transferred to 2008: University of Illinois-Chicago, Northeastern Illinois University, DePaul University, Loyola University-Chicago.

Basis for selection. Open admission, but selective for some programs. Special requirements for health career programs and international students. Interview required of non-nursing health career majors. **Learning Disabled:** After applying for admission, students provide documentation of disability and arrange meetings for testing and registration.

2008-2009 Annual costs. Tuition/fees: $2,678; $8,002 out-of-district; $9,677 out-of-state. Per-credit charge: $84 in-district; $261 out-of-district; $317 out-of-state. Books/supplies: $800. Personal expenses: $1,000.

2007-2008 Financial aid. Need-based: 93% of total undergraduate aid awarded as scholarships/grants, 7% as loans/jobs. Need-based aid available for part-time students. Work-study available nights, weekends and for part-time students. **Non-need-based:** Scholarships awarded for academics, art, athletics, leadership, minority status, music/drama, state residency.

Application procedures. Admission: No deadline. $25 fee. Admission notification on a rolling basis. **Financial aid:** Priority date 3/1; no closing date. FAFSA, institutional form required. Applicants notified on a rolling basis starting 3/1; must reply within 2 week(s) of notification.

Academics. Special study options: Accelerated study, distance learning, dual enrollment of high school students, exchange student, honors, independent study, internships, study abroad, teacher certification program, weekend college. License preparation in nursing, real estate. **Credit/placement by examination:** AP, CLEP, SAT, ACT, institutional tests. 30 credit hours maximum toward associate degree. **Support services:** GED preparation, learning center, remedial instruction, study skills assistance, tutoring, writing center.

Majors. Business: Accounting, business admin, international, office management, real estate. **Computer sciences:** General, data processing. **Construction:** Maintenance. **Education:** Early childhood. **Engineering:** General. **Engineering technology:** Architectural, construction, drafting, electrical, electrical drafting, robotics. **Health:** Clinical lab assistant, medical records technology, nursing (RN), physical therapy assistant. **Liberal arts:** Arts/sciences. **Mechanic/repair:** Automotive. **Production:** Machine shop technology. **Protective services:** Firefighting, police science. **Visual/performing arts:** Commercial/advertising art.

Computing on campus. 800 workstations in library, computer center, student center. Commuter students can connect to campus network. Online course registration, online library, helpline, wireless network available.

Student life. Freshman orientation: Available. Preregistration for classes offered. **Activities:** Jazz band, choral groups, drama, literary magazine, music ensembles, student government, student newspaper, Christian student association, Indian student association, political science forum, black student union, Hillel, Japanese club, desktop publishing club.

Athletics. NJCAA. **Intercollegiate:** Baseball M, basketball, cross-country, golf M, soccer, softball W, tennis, track and field, volleyball W. **Intramural:** Basketball, volleyball. **Team name:** Raiders.

Student services. Adult student services, alcohol/substance abuse counseling, career counseling, student employment services, financial aid counseling, health services, minority student services, on-campus daycare, personal counseling, placement for graduates, veterans' counselor. **Transfer:** Transfer center, transfer adviser, college fairs on campus for students transferring to 4-year colleges.

Contact. E-mail: admiss@oakton.edu
Phone: (847) 635-1629 Fax: (847) 635-1890
Michele Brown, Director of Admission and Enrollment Management,
Oakton Community College, 1600 East Golf Road, Des Plaines, IL 60016

Parkland College
Champaign, Illinois
www.parkland.edu **CB code: 1619**

- Public 2-year community college
- Commuter campus in small city
- Interview required

General. Founded in 1966. Regionally accredited. Students have access to resources at University of Illinois and within certain guidelines may enroll in University of Illinois classes. **Enrollment:** 6,501 degree-seeking undergraduates. **Degrees:** 903 associate awarded. **ROTC:** Army, Naval, Air Force. **Location:** 150 miles from Chicago, 120 miles from Indianapolis. **Calendar:** Semester, extensive summer session. **Full-time faculty:** 169 total; 16% have terminal degrees, 12% minority, 49% women. **Part-time faculty:** 350 total; 9% have terminal degrees, 8% minority, 55% women. **Class size:** 64% < 20, 34% 20-39, less than 1% 40-49, less than 1% 50-99, less than 1% >100. **Special facilities:** Planetarium, nature preserve, agricultural technology applications center, land laboratory. **Partnerships:** Formal partnerships with local businesses including CISCO Systems, Case Corporation, Microsoft, Ford ASSET, LINUX Professional Institute.

Student profile.

Out-of-state:	65%	25 or older:	33%

Transfer out. Colleges most students transferred to 2008: University of Illinois at Urbana-Champaign.

Basis for selection. Open admission, but selective for some programs. Limited admissions to health professions and trade union programs. ACT required for health programs. **Homeschooled:** Recommended that students meet with admissions adviser. **Learning Disabled:** Students with learning disabilities encouraged to contact learning disabilities specialist prior to enrolling.

High school preparation. 15 units required. Required units include English 4, mathematics 3, social studies 2, science 2, foreign language 2 and academic electives 2.

2008-2009 Annual costs. Tuition/fees: $2,610; $6,900 out-of-district; $10,740 out-of-state. Per-credit charge: $87 in-district; $230 out-of-district; $358 out-of-state. For Internet classes, in-district students pay $87, all others pay $127 per credit hour. Books/supplies: $1,200. Personal expenses: $1,500.

2007-2008 Financial aid. Need-based: Work-study available nights. **Non-need-based:** Scholarships awarded for academics, art, athletics, leadership, minority status, music/drama, state residency.

Application procedures. Admission: No deadline. No application fee. Admission notification on a rolling basis. **Financial aid:** Priority date 3/1; no closing date. FAFSA, institutional form required. Applicants notified on a rolling basis starting 6/1; must reply within 2 week(s) of notification.

Academics. Special study options: Accelerated study, cross-registration, distance learning, double major, dual enrollment of high school students, ESL, honors, independent study, internships, student-designed major, study abroad. Bachelor's degree programs available on campus. License preparation in dental hygiene, nursing, paramedic. **Credit/placement by examination:** AP, CLEP, SAT, ACT, institutional tests. 25 credit hours maximum toward associate degree. Institutionally-prepared proficiency exams are available. **Support services:** GED preparation and test center, learning center, reduced course load, remedial instruction, study skills assistance, tutoring, writing center.

Majors. Agriculture: General, animal husbandry, business, landscaping, mechanization. **Business:** General, accounting technology, business admin, executive assistant, hotel/motel admin, marketing, selling. **Communications:** Radio/tv. **Communications technology:** Radio/tv. **Computer sciences:** Applications programming, networking. **Construction:** General, electrician. **Education:** Art, music. **Engineering:** General. **Engineering technology:** Computer systems, industrial, surveying. **Health:** Dental hygiene, nursing (RN), occupational therapy assistant, radiologic technology/medical imaging, respiratory therapy technology, surgical technology, veterinary technology/assistant. **Interdisciplinary:** Biological/physical sciences. **Liberal arts:** Arts/sciences. **Mechanic/repair:** Auto body, automotive, diesel. **Personal/culinary services:** Restaurant/catering. **Protective services:** Fire safety technology, police science. **Public administration:** Social work. **Visual/performing arts:** Art, commercial/advertising art.

Most popular majors. Business/marketing 14%, education 7%, health sciences 18%, interdisciplinary studies 20%, liberal arts 14%.

Computing on campus. 1,425 workstations in library, computer center. Online course registration available.

Student life. **Freshman orientation:** Mandatory. Preregistration for classes offered. Held at beginning of semester. **Policies:** Students may take part in activities at University of Illinois. **Housing:** Housing available at University of Illinois facilities. **Activities:** Bands, choral groups, dance, drama, international student organizations, literary magazine, music ensembles, musical theater, radio station, student government, student newspaper, TV station, black student association, Phi Theta Kappa, student nurses association, veterinary technology association, Christian Fellowship, Colours, dental assisting association, dental hygienists association.

Athletics. NJCAA. **Intercollegiate:** Baseball M, basketball, golf M, soccer, softball W, volleyball W. **Intramural:** Basketball, bowling, softball, tennis, volleyball. **Team name:** Cobras.

Student services. Adult student services, career counseling, services for economically disadvantaged, student employment services, financial aid counseling, minority student services, on-campus daycare, personal counseling, placement for graduates, veterans' counselor, women's services. **Physically disabled:** Services for visually, speech, hearing impaired. **Learning disabled:** Comprehensive services available. **Transfer:** Transfer center, transfer adviser, college fairs on campus for students transferring to 4-year colleges.

Contact. E-mail: mhenry@parkland.edu
Phone: (217) 351-2208 Toll-free number: (800) 346-8089
Fax: (217) 353-2640
Micheal Henry, Director of Admissions and Records, Parkland College, 2400 West Bradley Avenue, Champaign, IL 61821-1899

Prairie State College

Chicago Heights, Illinois
www.prairiestate.edu **CB code: 1077**

- Public 2-year community college
- Commuter campus in large town

General. Founded in 1957. Regionally accredited. **Enrollment:** 4,709 degree-seeking undergraduates. **Degrees:** 329 associate awarded. **Location:** 30 miles from Chicago. **Calendar:** Semester, limited summer session. **Full-time faculty:** 85 total. **Part-time faculty:** 200 total.

Transfer out. **Colleges most students transferred to 2008:** Governors State University, University of Illinois - Chicago.

Basis for selection. Open admission, but selective for some programs. Admission to nursing and dental hygiene programs based on GPA in required courses and test scores.

High school preparation. One unit each of chemistry and algebra required for nursing and dental programs, plus 1 unit biology for nursing.

2008-2009 Annual costs. Tuition/fees: $2,620; $7,340 out-of-district; $9,980 out-of-state. Per-credit charge: $87 in-district; $244 out-of-district; $332 out-of-state. Books/supplies: $750. Personal expenses: $1,700.

Financial aid. **Need-based:** Need-based aid available for part-time students. Work-study available nights, weekends and for part-time students.

Application procedures. **Admission:** No deadline. $10 fee, may be waived for applicants with need. Admission notification on a rolling basis. **Financial aid:** Priority date 7/1; no closing date. FAFSA, institutional form required. Applicants notified on a rolling basis; must reply within 2 week(s) of notification.

Academics. Students completing an Associate in Arts or Science degree are guaranteed their classes will transfer to other Illinois colleges. **Special study options:** Cross-registration, distance learning, dual enrollment of high school students, ESL, honors, independent study, internships, study abroad, weekend college. License preparation in dental hygiene, nursing. **Credit/placement by examination:** CLEP, institutional tests. 45 credit hours maximum toward associate degree. **Support services:** GED preparation and test center, learning center, pre-admission summer program, reduced course load, remedial instruction, study skills assistance, tutoring.

Majors. **Business:** Administrative services, operations. **Computer sciences:** Applications programming, programming. **Construction:** Electrician. **Engineering technology:** Electrical. **Family/consumer sciences:** Child care. **Health:** Dental hygiene, mental health services, nursing (RN), substance abuse counseling. **Interdisciplinary:** Biological/physical sciences. **Liberal arts:** Arts/sciences. **Mechanic/repair:** Automotive. **Protective services:** Fire safety technology, police science. **Visual/performing arts:** Commercial photography, design, interior design, photography.

Most popular majors. Business/marketing 12%, education 12%, health sciences 27%, liberal arts 17%, psychology 8%.

Computing on campus. 248 workstations in library, computer center, student center. Helpline available.

Student life. **Freshman orientation:** Available. **Activities:** Jazz band, choral groups, dance, drama, musical theater, student government, student newspaper, symphony orchestra, All Latin Alliance, Black Student Union.

Athletics. **Intercollegiate:** Baseball M, basketball M, golf M, soccer M. **Team name:** Pioneers.

Student services. Student employment services, financial aid counseling, minority student services, on-campus daycare, personal counseling, placement for graduates. **Physically disabled:** Services for visually, speech, hearing impaired. **Transfer:** Transfer center, transfer adviser, college fairs on campus for students transferring to 4-year colleges.

Contact. Phone: (708) 709-3516
Marietta Turner, Coordinator of Admissions and Records, Prairie State College, 202 South Halsted Street, Chicago Heights, IL 60411

Rasmussen College: Aurora

Aurora, Illinois
www.rasmussen.edu

- For-profit 2-year technical college
- Small city

General. Regionally accredited. **Enrollment:** 72 degree-seeking undergraduates. **Calendar:** Quarter. **Part-time faculty:** 6 total.

Basis for selection. Open admission, but selective for some programs.

2009-2010 Annual costs. Regular courses: $350/credit; networking courses: $395/credit; multimedia and web programming courses: $430/credit.

Application procedures. **Admission:** $60 fee.

Academics. **Credit/placement by examination:** CLEP.

Majors. **Business:** Accounting, business admin. **Computer sciences:** Information technology, web page design. **Health:** Health services, massage therapy, medical transcription, pharmacy assistant. **Protective services:** Law enforcement admin.

Contact. Phone: (630) 888-3500
Tony Perez, Director of Admissions, Rasmussen College: Aurora, 2363 Sequoia Drive, Suite 131, Aurora, IL 60506

Rasmussen College: Rockford

Rockford, Illinois
www.rasmussen.edu

- For-profit 2-year technical college
- Small city

General. Regionally accredited. **Enrollment:** 632 degree-seeking undergraduates. **Degrees:** 6 associate awarded. **Calendar:** Quarter. **Full-time faculty:** 5 total. **Part-time faculty:** 28 total.

Basis for selection. Open admission, but selective for some programs.

2009-2010 Annual costs. Regular courses: $350/credit; networking courses: $395/credit; multimedia and web programming courses: $430/credit.

Application procedures. **Admission:** $60 fee.

Academics. **Credit/placement by examination:** CLEP.

Majors. **Business:** Accounting, business admin. **Computer sciences:** Information technology, webmaster. **Health:** Massage therapy, medical records technology, medical transcription, pharmacy assistant. **Protective services:** Law enforcement admin.

Contact. Phone: (815) 316-4800
Michael Plocinski, Director of Admissions, Rasmussen College: Rockford, 6000 East State Street, Fourth Floor, Rockford, IL 61108-2513

Two-Year Colleges

Rend Lake College
Ina, Illinois
www.rlc.edu **CB code: 1673**

- Public 2-year community college
- Commuter campus in rural community

General. Founded in 1955. Regionally accredited. Satellite campuses located in Mt. Vernon and Pinckneyville. **Enrollment:** 4,821 degree-seeking undergraduates. **Degrees:** 628 associate awarded. **Location:** 45 miles from Carbondale, 85 miles from St. Louis. **Calendar:** Semester, limited summer session. **Full-time faculty:** 64 total. **Part-time faculty:** 123 total. **Class size:** 68% < 20, 29% 20-39, 2% 40-49, less than 1% 50-99. **Partnerships:** Formal partnerships to provide technical training for employees of General Tire (Mt. Vernon) and Matsushita Universal; mandated federal training provided to Department of Natural Resources-Mines and Minerals; authorized training provided for Cisco curriculum.

Student profile.

Out-of-state:	1%	**Live on campus:**	1%
25 or older:	70%		

Transfer out. Colleges most students transferred to 2008: Southern Illinois University-Carbondale, Southern Illinois University-Edwardsville, Eastern Illinois University, Southeast Missouri State University, Murray State University.

Basis for selection. Open admission, but selective for some programs. Special requirements for allied health programs. SAT, ACT, ASSET, or COMPASS scores required for degree-seeking students for placement.

High school preparation. 15 units recommended. Recommended units include English 4, mathematics 3, social studies 3, science 3 (laboratory 3) and academic electives 2. Social studies units should include history and government. Electives may include foreign language, vocational education, music, or art. Lowest level math accepted is algebra 1.

2008-2009 Annual costs. Tuition/fees: $2,220; $3,375 out-of-district; $4,500 out-of-state. Per-credit charge: $74 in-district; $113 out-of-district; $150 out-of-state. Books/supplies: $900. Personal expenses: $1,636.

2007-2008 Financial aid. Need-based: 73% of total undergraduate aid awarded as scholarships/grants, 27% as loans/jobs. Need-based aid available for part-time students. **Non-need-based:** Scholarships awarded for academics, art, athletics, leadership, music/drama, state residency.

Application procedures. Admission: No deadline. No application fee. Admission notification on a rolling basis. **Financial aid:** No deadline. FAFSA required. Applicants notified on a rolling basis starting 3/15; must reply within 4 week(s) of notification.

Academics. Special study options: Cooperative education, distance learning, dual enrollment of high school students, ESL, honors, independent study, internships, study abroad. Bachelor's degree programs available on campus. License preparation in nursing, occupational therapy, paramedic, real estate. **Credit/placement by examination:** AP, CLEP, institutional tests. 16 credit hours maximum toward associate degree. Credits awarded for CLEP, proficiency exams and AP scores. **Support services:** GED preparation, learning center, remedial instruction, study skills assistance, tutoring.

Majors. Agriculture: Business, horticulture, mechanization, production. **Architecture:** Technology. **Business:** Administrative services, business admin. **Computer sciences:** Applications programming, LAN/WAN management. **Engineering:** General. **Engineering technology:** Manufacturing, surveying. **Family/consumer sciences:** Child development. **Health:** Clinical lab technology, EMT paramedic, medical records technology, nursing (RN), occupational therapy assistant. **Interdisciplinary:** Biological/physical sciences. **Liberal arts:** Arts/sciences. **Mechanic/repair:** Automotive, diesel, heavy equipment, industrial. **Personal/culinary services:** Chef training. **Protective services:** Corrections, fire services admin, police science. **Visual/performing arts:** Art, commercial/advertising art.

Computing on campus. 496 workstations in library, computer center. Commuter students can connect to campus network. Online library, wireless network available.

Student life. Freshman orientation: Mandatory. **Activities:** Bands, choral groups, dance, drama, music ensembles, musical theater, student government, student newspaper, symphony orchestra, culinary arts club, Active College Christians, practical nursing club, automotive club, horticulture club, art league, criminal justice club.

Athletics. NJCAA. **Intercollegiate:** Baseball M, basketball, cheerleading M, cross-country, golf, softball W, tennis W, track and field, volleyball W, wrestling M. **Team name:** Warriors.

Student services. Adult student services, career counseling, services for economically disadvantaged, student employment services, financial aid counseling, on-campus daycare, personal counseling, placement for graduates, veterans' counselor. **Physically disabled:** Services for visually, speech, hearing impaired. **Transfer:** Pre-admission transcript evaluation for new students. Transfer adviser, college fairs on campus for students transferring to 4-year colleges.

Contact. E-mail: admiss@rlc.edu
Phone: (618) 437-5321 ext. 1230 Fax: (618) 437-5677
Vickie Schulte, Director of Student Records, Rend Lake College, 468 North Ken Gray Parkway, Ina, IL 62846

Richland Community College
Decatur, Illinois **CB member**
www.richland.edu **CB code: 0738**

- Public 2-year community college
- Commuter campus in small city

General. Founded in 1971. Regionally accredited. **Enrollment:** 2,131 degree-seeking undergraduates; 1,153 non-degree-seeking students. **Degrees:** 280 associate awarded. **Location:** 180 miles from Chicago, 120 miles from St. Louis. **Calendar:** Semester, limited summer session. **Full-time faculty:** 92 total. **Part-time faculty:** 147 total. **Class size:** 76% < 20, 24% 20-39, less than 1% 40-49. **Special facilities:** Human patient simulator for allied health students.

Student profile. Among degree-seeking undergraduates, 54% enrolled in a transfer program, 46% enrolled in a vocational program, 1% already have a bachelor's degree or higher, 369 enrolled as first-time, first-year students.

Part-time:	60%	**Asian American:**	1%
Women:	55%	**Hispanic American:**	2%
African American:	18%	**25 or older:**	50%

Transfer out. Colleges most students transferred to 2008: Illinois State University, Millikin University, Southern Illinois University-Carbondale, Eastern Illinois University, University of Illinois-Springfield.

Basis for selection. Open admission, but selective for some programs. Separate admission process for allied health programs.

High school preparation. Required units include English 4, mathematics 3, social studies 3, science 3 and foreign language 2.

2008-2009 Annual costs. Tuition/fees: $2,230; $11,304 out-of-district; $14,768 out-of-state. Per-credit charge: $70 in-district; $372 out-of-district; $487 out-of-state. Books/supplies: $1,000.

2007-2008 Financial aid. Need-based: 152 full-time freshmen applied for aid; 85 were judged to have need; 73 of these received aid. Average need met was 48%. Average scholarship/grant was $3,578; average loan $2,687. 83% of total undergraduate aid awarded as scholarships/grants, 17% as loans/jobs. Need-based aid available for part-time students. Work-study available nights and for part-time students. **Non-need-based:** Awarded to 100 full-time undergraduates, including 32 freshmen. Scholarships awarded for academics.

Application procedures. Admission: No deadline. No application fee. Admission notification on a rolling basis. **Financial aid:** Closing date 6/30. FAFSA required. Applicants notified on a rolling basis starting 3/20.

Academics. Special study options: Distance learning, dual enrollment of high school students, ESL, honors, independent study, internships, liberal arts/career combination, teacher certification program. License preparation in nursing, paramedic, radiology. **Credit/placement by examination:** AP, CLEP, institutional tests. **Support services:** GED preparation, learning center, reduced course load, remedial instruction, study skills assistance, tutoring, writing center.

Majors. Agriculture: Business, horticultural science, horticulture. **Biology:** General. **Business:** General, accounting, hospitality admin, management information systems. **Communications:** Journalism. **Computer sciences:** General, computer graphics, computer science, data entry, programming. **Construction:** Electrician. **Education:** General. **Engineering:** General. **Engineering technology:** Drafting. **Foreign languages:** French, German, Spanish. **Health:** EMT paramedic, nursing (RN), radiologic technology/medical imaging, surgical technology. **History:** General. **Legal studies:** Prelaw. **Liberal arts:** Arts/sciences. **Math:** General. **Mechanic/repair:** General, automotive, electronics/electrical, heating/ac/refrig, industrial. **Philosophy/**

religion: Philosophy. **Physical sciences:** Planetary. **Protective services:** Criminal justice, firefighting, police science. **Psychology:** General. **Social sciences:** General, anthropology, archaeology, economics, geography, political science, sociology. **Visual/performing arts:** General, art, art history/conservation, ceramics, drawing, painting, sculpture.

Most popular majors. Health sciences 26%, interdisciplinary studies 24%, liberal arts 27%.

Computing on campus. 245 workstations in library, computer center. Commuter students can connect to campus network. Online course registration, online library, helpline available.

Student life. Freshman orientation: Mandatory. Preregistration for classes offered. 2 hours, includes registering for courses, variety of times available. **Activities:** Drama, student government, student newspaper.

Athletics. Team name: Knights.

Student services. Adult student services, career counseling, services for economically disadvantaged, student employment services, financial aid counseling, minority student services, on-campus daycare, personal counseling, placement for graduates, veterans' counselor, women's services. **Physically disabled:** Services for visually, speech, hearing impaired. **Transfer:** Pre-admission transcript evaluation for new students. Transfer center, transfer adviser, college fairs on campus for students transferring to 4-year colleges.

Contact. Phone: (217) 875-7200 ext. 257 Fax: (217) 875-7783
JoAnn Wirey, Registrar, Richland Community College, One College Park, Decatur, IL 62521

Rock Valley College

Rockford, Illinois — **CB member**
www.rockvalleycollege.edu — **CB code: 1674**

- Public 2-year community college
- Commuter campus in small city

General. Founded in 1964. Regionally accredited. **Enrollment:** 5,871 degree-seeking undergraduates. **Degrees:** 560 associate awarded. **Location:** 85 miles from Chicago. **Calendar:** Semester, limited summer session. **Full-time faculty:** 149 total. **Part-time faculty:** 161 total. **Special facilities:** Outdoor theater. **Partnerships:** Formal partnership with CISCO.

Transfer out. Colleges most students transferred to 2008: Northern Illinois University, Illinois State University, Western Illinois University.

Basis for selection. Open admission, but selective for some programs. Special requirements for nursing and respiratory therapy programs. Test scores used for nursing students only. Interview required of respiratory therapy, nursing, aviation maintenance majors. Audition required of music majors.

High school preparation. Recommended units include English 4, mathematics 3, social studies 2 and science 2. One chemistry required for nursing applicants, 1 chemistry and 1 algebra for respiratory therapy applicants.

2008-2009 Annual costs. Tuition/fees: $2,220; $8,670 out-of-district; $13,560 out-of-state. Per-credit charge: $66 in-district; $281 out-of-district; $444 out-of-state. Costs vary by program. Books/supplies: $1,000.

2007-2008 Financial aid. Need-based: 70% of total undergraduate aid awarded as scholarships/grants, 30% as loans/jobs. Need-based aid available for part-time students. Work-study available nights and for part-time students. **Non-need-based:** Scholarships awarded for academics, ROTC.

Application procedures. Admission: No deadline. No application fee. Application must be submitted on paper. Admission notification on a rolling basis. **Financial aid:** Closing date 5/1. FAFSA required. Applicants notified on a rolling basis starting 4/1; must reply within 2 week(s) of notification.

Academics. Special study options: Cooperative education, dual enrollment of high school students, ESL, external degree, independent study, internships, liberal arts/career combination, student-designed major, study abroad. License preparation in aviation, dental hygiene, nursing. **Credit/placement by examination:** AP, CLEP, institutional tests. 39 credit hours maximum toward associate degree. **Support services:** GED preparation, learning center, reduced course load, remedial instruction, study skills assistance, tutoring, writing center.

Majors. Business: General, accounting, administrative services, business admin, logistics, marketing. **Computer sciences:** General. **Engineering technology:** Construction, electrical, manufacturing. **Family/consumer sciences:** Child care. **Health:** Medical records technology, nursing (RN), respiratory therapy technology. **Legal studies:** Paralegal. **Liberal arts:** Arts/sciences. **Mechanic/repair:** Aircraft, automotive. **Protective services:** Firefighting, law enforcement admin. **Public administration:** Human services.

Computing on campus. 130 workstations in library, computer center, student center. Commuter students can connect to campus network. Online course registration, online library, helpline, wireless network available.

Student life. Freshman orientation: Available. Preregistration for classes offered. **Activities:** Bands, choral groups, dance, drama, literary magazine, music ensembles, musical theater, student government, student newspaper, 21 student interest groups.

Athletics. NJCAA. **Intercollegiate:** Baseball M, basketball, football (tackle) M, golf M, soccer, softball W, squash W, tennis, volleyball W. **Intramural:** Basketball M, skiing. **Team name:** Eagles.

Student services. Adult student services, career counseling, student employment services, financial aid counseling, personal counseling, placement for graduates, veterans' counselor. **Physically disabled:** Services for visually, speech, hearing impaired. **Transfer:** Transfer adviser, college fairs on campus for students transferring to 4-year colleges.

Contact. Phone: (815) 921-4250 Fax: (815) 921-4269
Lynn Perkins, Admissions Director, Rock Valley College, 3301 North Mulford Road, Rockford, IL 61114-5699

Rockford Business College

Rockford, Illinois
www.rockfordcareercollege.edu — **CB code: 2459**

- For-profit 2-year career college
- Commuter campus in small city
- Interview required

General. Founded in 1862. Accredited by ACICS. **Enrollment:** 560 degree-seeking undergraduates. **Degrees:** 100 associate awarded. **Location:** 90 miles from Chicago, 75 miles from Madison, Wisconsin. **Calendar:** Quarter, extensive summer session. **Full-time faculty:** 10 total; 40% have terminal degrees, 10% minority, 60% women. **Part-time faculty:** 50 total; 30% have terminal degrees, 20% minority, 70% women. **Class size:** 88% < 20, 11% 20-39, 1% 40-49.

Basis for selection. Open admission. **Homeschooled:** State high school equivalency certificate required.

2009-2010 Annual costs. Tuition/fees (projected): $7,350. Per-credit charge: $200. Books/supplies: $800. Personal expenses: $2,880.

Financial aid. All financial aid based on need. Need-based aid available for part-time students. Work-study available nights.

Application procedures. Admission: No deadline. $150 fee. Application must be submitted on paper. Admission notification on a rolling basis. **Financial aid:** No deadline. FAFSA required. Applicants notified on a rolling basis.

Academics. Special study options: Independent study, internships. **Credit/placement by examination:** CLEP, IB, institutional tests. 50 credit hours maximum toward associate degree. **Support services:** Study skills assistance, tutoring.

Majors. Business: General, accounting, business admin, marketing, office/clerical. **Computer sciences:** General, data processing, information systems. **Health:** Massage therapy, medical assistant, medical secretary, pharmacy assistant, veterinary technology/assistant. **Legal studies:** Legal secretary, paralegal.

Most popular majors. Business/marketing 11%, health sciences 36%.

Computing on campus. 75 workstations in library, computer center.

Student life. Freshman orientation: Mandatory. Preregistration for classes offered.

Student services. Career counseling, student employment services, financial aid counseling, placement for graduates. **Transfer:** Pre-admission transcript evaluation for new students.

Contact. E-mail: info@rockfordcareercollege.edu
Phone: (815) 965-8616 Toll-free number: (866) 722-4632
Fax: (815) 965-0360
David Julius, Director of Enrollment Services, Rockford Business College, 1130 South Alpine Road, Rockford, IL 61108

Sauk Valley Community College

Dixon, Illinois
www.svcc.edu **CB code: 1780**

- Public 2-year community college
- Commuter campus in large town

General. Founded in 1965. Regionally accredited. **Enrollment:** 1,905 degree-seeking undergraduates. **Degrees:** 249 associate awarded. **Location:** 110 miles from Chicago. **Calendar:** Semester, limited summer session. **Full-time faculty:** 43 total. **Part-time faculty:** 99 total. **Class size:** 63% < 20, 33% 20-39, 3% 40-49, less than 1% 50-99. **Special facilities:** Observatory, prairie plots.

Student profile.

25 or older:	38%	**Live on campus:**	1%

Transfer out. Colleges most students transferred to 2008: Northern Illinois University, Illinois State University, Western Illinois University, University of Illinois, Southern Illinois University.

Basis for selection. Open admission, but selective for some programs. Special requirements for allied health programs: academic record, state residency important; class rank, test scores considered. Placement exam required of all students who plan to enroll in English or math courses. **Homeschooled:** Transcript of courses and grades required.

High school preparation. 15 units recommended. Recommended units include English 4, mathematics 3, social studies 2, science 2 (laboratory 2) and academic electives 4. Special course requirements for allied health programs.

2008-2009 Annual costs. Tuition/fees: $2,550; $7,500 out-of-district; $8,460 out-of-state. Per-credit charge: $85 in-district; $250 out-of-district; $282 out-of-state. Room only: $4,131. Books/supplies: $500.

2007-2008 Financial aid. Need-based: 73% of total undergraduate aid awarded as scholarships/grants, 27% as loans/jobs. Need-based aid available for part-time students. Work-study available nights, weekends and for part-time students. **Non-need-based:** Scholarships awarded for academics, art, athletics, leadership, minority status, ROTC, state residency.

Application procedures. Admission: No deadline. No application fee. Admission notification on a rolling basis. **Financial aid:** Priority date 3/1; no closing date. FAFSA, institutional form required. Applicants notified on a rolling basis starting 5/1; must reply within 4 week(s) of notification.

Academics. Special study options: Cooperative education, distance learning, dual enrollment of high school students, ESL, honors, independent study, internships. License preparation in nursing, paramedic, radiology, real estate. **Credit/placement by examination:** AP, CLEP, institutional tests. 30 credit hours maximum toward associate degree. Both CLEP and DANTES exams are used. **Support services:** GED preparation and test center, learning center, remedial instruction, study skills assistance, tutoring, writing center.

Majors. Biology: General. **Business:** General, accounting, administrative services, business admin, management information systems, marketing, office management, office technology, office/clerical. **Communications:** General, journalism, public relations. **Computer sciences:** General, applications programming, data processing, programming. **Education:** General, art, bilingual, biology, chemistry, elementary, English, family/consumer sciences, French, German, gifted/talented, health, history, mathematics, middle, multi-level teacher, music, physical, physically handicapped, physics, sales/marketing, science, secondary, social science, social studies, Spanish, special, speech, technology/industrial arts, voc/tech. **Engineering:** General, civil, electrical, physics. **Engineering technology:** Drafting, manufacturing, solar energy. **Family/consumer sciences:** Child care. **Foreign languages:** General, French, German, Spanish. **Health:** Athletic training, medical radiologic technology/radiation therapy, medical secretary, nursing (RN), predental, premedicine, prenursing, prepharmacy, preveterinary. **History:** General. **Interdisciplinary:** Math/computer science. **Legal studies:** Legal secretary, prelaw. **Liberal arts:** Arts/sciences. **Math:** General. **Mechanic/repair:** Diesel, heating/ac/refrig. **Parks/recreation:** Exercise sciences, sports admin. **Philosophy/religion:** Philosophy. **Physical sciences:** Chemistry, physics. **Protective services:** Criminal justice, law enforcement admin, police science. **Psychology:** General. **Public administration:** Human services, social work. **Social sciences:** General, economics, political science, sociology. **Visual/performing arts:** Art, art history/conservation, commercial/advertising art, dramatic, fashion design, music performance, studio arts, voice/opera.

Most popular majors. Business/marketing 17%, health sciences 19%, interdisciplinary studies 28%, liberal arts 25%.

Computing on campus. 120 workstations in library, computer center, student center. Dormitories wired for high-speed internet access. Online library, helpline, wireless network available.

Student life. Freshman orientation: Mandatory, $82 fee. Preregistration for classes offered. 15 hours held throughout first semester or prior to start of semester. **Housing:** Apartments available. **Activities:** Bands, choral groups, drama, music ensembles, musical theater, student government, student newspaper, symphony orchestra, Association of Latin American Students, Campus Crusade for Christ, Phi Theta Kappa.

Athletics. NJCAA. **Intercollegiate:** Baseball M, basketball, cheerleading M, cross-country, golf M, softball W, tennis, volleyball W. **Team name:** Skyhawks.

Student services. Adult student services, career counseling, services for economically disadvantaged, student employment services, financial aid counseling, minority student services, on-campus daycare, personal counseling, placement for graduates, veterans' counselor. **Physically disabled:** Services for visually, speech, hearing impaired. **Transfer:** Pre-admission transcript evaluation for new students. Transfer center, transfer adviser, college fairs on campus for students transferring to 4-year colleges.

Contact. Phone: (815) 288-5511 ext. 343 Fax: (815) 288-3190
Pamela Medema, Registrar, Sauk Valley Community College, 173 Illinois Route 2, Dixon, IL 61021-9110

Shawnee Community College

Ullin, Illinois
www.shawneecc.edu **CB code: 0882**

- Public 2-year community college
- Commuter campus in rural community

General. Founded in 1967. Regionally accredited. Extension centers in Anna, Cairo, and Metropolis. **Enrollment:** 1,954 degree-seeking undergraduates. **Degrees:** 241 associate awarded. **ROTC:** Army, Naval, Air Force. **Location:** 40 miles from Paducah, Kentucky. **Calendar:** Semester, extensive summer session. **Full-time faculty:** 42 total. **Part-time faculty:** 170 total.

Basis for selection. Open admission, but selective for some programs. Applicants for allied health programs selected on basis of entrance examination score. ACT recommended for placement and counseling. Interview recommended for art, music, speech majors. Audition recommended for speech and music majors. Portfolio recommended for art majors.

High school preparation. 15 units recommended. Recommended units include English 4, mathematics 3, social studies 3, science 3 and foreign language 2. 2 units recommended in foreign language, music, or art. Transfer program applicants must have state mandated high school course requirements or demonstrate proficiency through placement tests.

2008-2009 Annual costs. Tuition/fees: $2,160; $3,240 out-of-state. Per-credit charge: $66 in-state; $102 out-of-state. Books/supplies: $500. Personal expenses: $680.

Financial aid. All financial aid based on need. Need-based aid available for part-time students.

Application procedures. Admission: No deadline. No application fee. Admission notification on a rolling basis beginning on or about 1/15. **Financial aid:** Priority date 9/1; no closing date. FAFSA required. Applicants notified on a rolling basis; must reply within 2 week(s) of notification.

Academics. Special study options: Cooperative education, distance learning, dual enrollment of high school students, honors, independent study, internships, liberal arts/career combination. License preparation in nursing, occupational therapy, paramedic, real estate. **Credit/placement by examination:** AP, CLEP, institutional tests. 15 credit hours maximum toward associate degree. **Support services:** GED preparation and test center, learning center, pre-admission summer program, remedial instruction, study skills assistance, tutoring, writing center.

Majors. Agriculture: Business, horticulture. **Business:** General, accounting, management science. **Conservation:** Forestry, wildlife. **Engineering technology:** Drafting, electrical. **Family/consumer sciences:** Family/community services, food/nutrition. **Health:** Medical records technology, medical secretary. **Interdisciplinary:** Biological/physical sciences. **Legal studies:** Legal secretary. **Liberal arts:** Arts/sciences.

Computing on campus. 120 workstations in library, computer center, student center. Online course registration, online library, helpline, wireless network available.

Student life. **Freshman orientation:** Mandatory. Preregistration for classes offered. **Activities:** Concert band, choral groups, dance, drama, music ensembles, musical theater, student government, student newspaper.

Athletics. NJCAA. **Intercollegiate:** Baseball M, basketball, softball W, volleyball W. **Intramural:** Baseball M, basketball, football (non-tackle), table tennis, volleyball. **Team name:** Saints.

Student services. Career counseling, services for economically disadvantaged, student employment services, financial aid counseling, on-campus daycare, personal counseling, placement for graduates, veterans' counselor. **Physically disabled:** Services for visually, speech, hearing impaired. **Transfer:** Pre-admission transcript evaluation for new students. Transfer center, transfer adviser, college fairs on campus for students transferring to 4-year colleges.

Contact. E-mail: admissions@shawneecc.edu
Phone: (618) 634-3200 ext. 3247 Fax: (618) 634-3346
Dee Blakely, Director of Admissions and Counseling, Shawnee Community College, 8364 Shawnee College Road, Ullin, IL 62992

South Suburban College of Cook County

South Holland, Illinois
www.southsuburbancollege.edu **CB code: 1806**

- Public 2-year community college
- Commuter campus in large town

General. Founded in 1927. Regionally accredited. **Enrollment:** 4,983 degree-seeking undergraduates. **Degrees:** 381 associate awarded. **Location:** 20 miles from the Chicago Loop. **Calendar:** Semester, limited summer session. **Full-time faculty:** 120 total. **Part-time faculty:** 217 total.

Student profile.

Out-of-state:	5%	**25 or older:**	48%

Transfer out. **Colleges most students transferred to 2008:** Governors State University, University of Illinois-Chicago, Purdue University-Calumet, Chicago State University.

Basis for selection. Open admission, but selective for some programs. Separate requirements for health career programs. Audition recommended for music majors. **Learning Disabled:** Students need to self-declare with counseling center. Accommodations provided as needed.

High school preparation. 15 units required. Required units include English 4, mathematics 3, social studies 2, science 2 (laboratory 1) and academic electives 4.

2009-2010 Annual costs. Tuition/fees (projected): $3,112; $8,452 out-of-district; $10,102 out-of-state. Per-credit charge: $90 in-district; $268 out-of-district; $323 out-of-state. Some students may qualify for a tuition rate of $105 per credit hour for special programs in other in-state community college districts, in Lake County Illinois and in Chicago. Books/supplies: $600.

2007-2008 Financial aid. **Need-based:** 98% of total undergraduate aid awarded as scholarships/grants, 2% as loans/jobs. Need-based aid available for part-time students. Work-study available nights and for part-time students. **Non-need-based:** Scholarships awarded for academics, art, athletics, music/drama, state residency.

Application procedures. **Admission:** No deadline. No application fee. Application must be submitted on paper. Admission notification on a rolling basis. **Financial aid:** No deadline. FAFSA required. Applicants notified on a rolling basis.

Academics. **Special study options:** Distance learning, double major, dual enrollment of high school students, ESL, honors, internships, liberal arts/career combination, study abroad. License preparation in nursing, occupational therapy, paramedic, radiology, real estate. **Credit/placement by examination:** AP, CLEP, institutional tests. 15 credit hours maximum toward associate degree. ECEP (institutional evaluation/award process), DANTES accepted. **Support services:** GED preparation and test center, learning center, reduced course load, remedial instruction, study skills assistance, tutoring.

Majors. **Biology:** General, biomedical sciences. **Business:** General, accounting, administrative services, fashion, finance, marketing, office management. **Computer sciences:** General. **Construction:** Maintenance. **Education:** General, early childhood, special, teacher assistance. **Engineering:** General, science. **Engineering technology:** Construction, drafting, electrical. **Foreign languages:** Spanish. **Health:** Medical radiologic technology/radiation therapy, nursing (RN), occupational therapy assistant, pharmacy assistant. **History:** General. **Legal studies:** Court reporting, paralegal. **Liberal arts:** Arts/sciences. **Math:** General. **Parks/recreation:** Health/fitness, sports admin. **Philosophy/religion:** Philosophy. **Physical sciences:** Astronomy, chemistry, geology, physics. **Protective services:** Criminal justice. **Psychology:** General. **Public administration:** Human services. **Social sciences:** Anthropology, economics, geography, political science, sociology. **Visual/performing arts:** Dramatic, studio arts.

Computing on campus. 1,500 workstations in library, computer center, student center. Online course registration, online library available.

Student life. **Freshman orientation:** Mandatory. Preregistration for classes offered. Continuous orientation program; specialized high school student success program in summer. **Activities:** Bands, choral groups, drama, literary magazine, music ensembles, student government, TV station, business professionals, veterans organization, paralegal association, occupational therapy organization, human service club, Creative Dimensions, nursing club.

Athletics. NJCAA. **Intercollegiate:** Baseball M, basketball, soccer M, softball W, volleyball W. **Intramural:** Baseball M, basketball, softball, volleyball. **Team name:** Bulldogs.

Student services. Career counseling, student employment services, financial aid counseling, on-campus daycare, personal counseling, veterans' counselor. **Physically disabled:** Services for visually, speech, hearing impaired. **Learning disabled:** Comprehensive services available. **Transfer:** Transfer center, transfer adviser, college fairs on campus for students transferring to 4-year colleges.

Contact. E-mail: admissions@southsuburbancollege.edu
Phone: (708) 596-2000 ext. 2329 Fax: (708) 225-5806
Robin Rihacek, Director of Admissions, Registration and Records, South Suburban College of Cook County, 15800 South State Street, South Holland, IL 60473

Southeastern Illinois College

Harrisburg, Illinois
www.sic.edu **CB code: 1777**

- Public 2-year community college
- Commuter campus in small town

General. Founded in 1960. Regionally accredited. **Enrollment:** 848 full-time, degree-seeking students. **Degrees:** 239 associate awarded. **Location:** 45 miles from Carbondale; 65 miles from Evansville, Indiana. **Calendar:** Semester, extensive summer session. **Full-time faculty:** 66 total; 9% have terminal degrees, 3% minority, 33% women. **Part-time faculty:** 241 total; 5% have terminal degrees, 3% minority, 56% women. **Special facilities:** Game preserve management facility, archery range, fire science center. **Partnerships:** Formal partnership with Cummins Corporation for diesel technology.

Student profile. Among full-time, degree-seeking students, 35% enrolled in a transfer program, 57% enrolled in a vocational program, 3% already have a bachelor's degree or higher.

Transfer out. **Colleges most students transferred to 2008:** Southern Illinois University at Carbondale.

Basis for selection. Open admission, but selective for some programs. Special requirements for nursing, medical records, health information technology, surgical nurse, occupational therapy assistant, and conservation game management programs. Admission to health programs based on test scores. Psychological Services Bureau-Health Occupations Examination required for medical laboratory technician, ASSET for health information systems. NET test required for associate degree and practical nursing programs. **Homeschooled:** Transcript of courses and grades required.

High school preparation. 15 units recommended. Recommended units include English 4, mathematics 3, social studies 3, science 3 and academic electives 2.

2008-2009 Annual costs. Tuition/fees: $2,220; $3,300 out-of-district; $3,660 out-of-state. Per-credit charge: $72 in-district; $108 out-of-district; $120 out-of-state. Books/supplies: $450. Personal expenses: $1,357.

2007-2008 Financial aid. **Need-based:** Need-based aid available for part-time students. Work-study available for part-time students. **Non-need-based:** Scholarships awarded for academics, alumni affiliation, art, athletics, music/drama.

Application procedures. **Admission:** No deadline. No application fee. Admission notification on a rolling basis beginning on or about 5/1. **Financial aid:** No deadline. FAFSA required. Applicants notified on a rolling basis starting 4/15; must reply within 2 week(s) of notification.

Academics. **Special study options:** Cross-registration, distance learning, double major, dual enrollment of high school students, independent study, internships, student-designed major. Bachelor's degree programs available on campus. License preparation in nursing, paramedic, real estate. **Credit/placement by examination:** AP, CLEP, institutional tests. 29 credit hours maximum toward associate degree. **Support services:** GED preparation and test center, learning center, pre-admission summer program, reduced course load, remedial instruction, tutoring.

Majors. **Business:** Administrative services, business admin, office technology. **Computer sciences:** Information systems, LAN/WAN management. **Conservation:** Wildlife. **Education:** General. **Family/consumer sciences:** Child care. **Health:** Clinical lab technology, medical records technology, nursing (RN), occupational therapy assistant, office assistant. **Interdisciplinary:** Behavioral sciences, math/computer science, natural sciences. **Legal studies:** Prelaw. **Liberal arts:** Arts/sciences. **Math:** General. **Mechanic/repair:** Diesel. **Protective services:** Police science. **Public administration:** Human services.

Computing on campus. 75 workstations in library, computer center. Wireless network available.

Student life. **Freshman orientation:** Available. Preregistration for classes offered. Individual orientation/advisement/registration appointments held for degree-seeking students. **Activities:** Bands, choral groups, drama, music ensembles, musical theater, student government, student newspaper, art club, math and science club, BASIC, Students in Free Enterprise, Phi Theta Kappa, Phi Beta Lambda, Theta Sigma Phi, Student Association of Family and Consumer Sciences, forensics club.

Athletics. NJCAA. **Intercollegiate:** Baseball M, basketball, cheerleading M, softball W. **Intramural:** Basketball, cheerleading W. **Team name:** Falcons.

Student services. Career counseling, student employment services, financial aid counseling, on-campus daycare, personal counseling, placement for graduates, veterans' counselor. **Physically disabled:** Services for visually, hearing impaired. **Transfer:** Transfer adviser, college fairs on campus for students transferring to 4-year colleges.

Contact. E-mail: admissions@sic.edu
Phone: (618) 252-5400 ext. 2441 Toll-free number: (866) 338-2742
Fax: (618) 252-3062
Kelly Boyd, Director of Enrollment Services, Southeastern Illinois College, 3575 College Road, Harrisburg, IL 62946

Southwestern Illinois College

Belleville, Illinois
www.swic.edu **CB code: 1057**

- Public 2-year community college
- Commuter campus in small city

General. Founded in 1946. Regionally accredited. **Location:** 20 miles from St. Louis. **Calendar:** Semester.

Annual costs/financial aid. Tuition/fees (2008-2009): $2,250; $5,790 out-of-district; $8,790 out-of-state. Required fees vary by course taken. Those age 60 and over receive a $5 per-credit-hour tuition reduction. Books/supplies: $500. Personal expenses: $1,320. Need-based financial aid available to full-time and part-time students.

Contact. Phone: (618) 235-2700 ext. 5526
Director of Admissions, 2500 Carlyle Avenue, Belleville, IL 62221-5899

Spoon River College

Canton, Illinois
www.src.edu **CB code: 1154**

- Public 2-year community college
- Commuter campus in large town

General. Founded in 1959. Regionally accredited. **Enrollment:** 1,616 degree-seeking undergraduates. **Degrees:** 233 associate awarded. **ROTC:** Army. **Location:** 35 miles from Peoria. **Calendar:** Semester, limited summer session. **Full-time faculty:** 36 total; 11% have terminal degrees, 6% minority, 56% women. **Part-time faculty:** 77 total; 46% women. **Special facilities:** Natural arboretum, walking trail, agricultural test plots.

Transfer out. **Colleges most students transferred to 2008:** Western Illinois University.

Basis for selection. Open admission, but selective for some programs. Special requirements for nursing program. All students must take COMPASS exam for placement; if score indicates, student must be remediated before taking college-level courses. College-preparatory program recommended for transfer degree programs. Vocational students not required to have specific high school courses.

High school preparation. 15 units recommended. Recommended units include English 4, mathematics 3, social studies 3, science 3 (laboratory 3) and academic electives 2.

2008-2009 Annual costs. Tuition/fees: $2,640; $6,030 out-of-district; $7,110 out-of-state. Per-credit charge: $78 in-district; $191 out-of-district; $227 out-of-state. Books/supplies: $600.

2007-2008 Financial aid. **Need-based:** Need-based aid available for part-time students. Work-study available nights and for part-time students. **Non-need-based:** Scholarships awarded for academics, athletics.

Application procedures. **Admission:** No deadline. No application fee. Admission notification on a rolling basis. **Financial aid:** Closing date 7/2. FAFSA required. Applicants notified on a rolling basis starting 3/15.

Academics. **Special study options:** Distance learning, dual enrollment of high school students, ESL, honors, internships. License preparation in nursing. **Credit/placement by examination:** AP, CLEP, IB, institutional tests. 32 credit hours maximum toward associate degree. Maximum 50% of credit hours toward degree may be awarded through CLEP. **Support services:** GED preparation, learning center, reduced course load, remedial instruction, study skills assistance, tutoring, writing center.

Majors. **Agriculture:** Business, equipment technology. **Business:** General, administrative services, managerial economics. **Computer sciences:** Information technology, web page design. **Conservation:** Management/policy. **Education:** Adult/continuing, early childhood, ESL. **Health:** Health care admin. **History:** General. **Interdisciplinary:** Biological/physical sciences. **Legal studies:** Prelaw. **Mechanic/repair:** Automotive. **Protective services:** Law enforcement admin. **Visual/performing arts:** Art.

Computing on campus. 100 workstations in library, computer center, student center. Online course registration, online library, helpline available.

Student life. **Freshman orientation:** Available. Offered prior to fall semester. **Activities:** Drama, literary magazine, student government, agriculture fraternity, honors fraternity, peer ambassador program, diesel fraternity, Fellowship of Christian Athletes.

Athletics. NJCAA. **Intercollegiate:** Baseball M, basketball, softball W. **Team name:** Mudcats.

Student services. Adult student services, career counseling, student employment services, financial aid counseling, on-campus daycare, personal counseling, placement for graduates, veterans' counselor. **Physically disabled:** Services for visually, speech, hearing impaired. **Transfer:** Pre-admission transcript evaluation for new students. Transfer adviser, college fairs on campus for students transferring to 4-year colleges.

Contact. E-mail: admissions@src.edu
Phone: (309) 649-7020 Toll-free number: (800) 334-7337
Fax: (309) 649-6393
Melissa Wilkinson, Director of Admissions and Records, Spoon River College, 23235 North County Road 22, Canton, IL 61520

Springfield College in Illinois

Springfield, Illinois
www.sci.edu **CB code: 1734**

- Private 2-year junior and liberal arts college affiliated with Roman Catholic Church
- Commuter campus in small city
- SAT or ACT (ACT writing optional) required

General. Founded in 1929. Regionally accredited. **Enrollment:** 522 degree-seeking undergraduates. **Degrees:** 143 associate awarded. **Location:** 200 miles from Chicago, 100 miles from St. Louis. **Calendar:** 4-1-4, limited summer session. **Full-time faculty:** 25 total. **Part-time faculty:** 51 total.

Transfer out. **Colleges most students transferred to 2008:** Southern Illinois University-Edwardsville, University of Illinois-Springfield, Illinois State University, Eastern Illinois University, Southern Illinois University-Carbondale.

Basis for selection. High school course work, test scores, GPA, class rank required criteria. Interview may be recommended for academically weak applicants. Portfolio recommended for art majors. **Adult students:** SAT/ACT scores not required if applicant over 24. **Homeschooled:** Transcript of courses and grades, state high school equivalency certificate required. GED required to qualify for federal and state financial aid. **Learning Disabled:** Admission requirements for students with learning disabilities handled on case by case basis.

High school preparation. Recommended units include English 4, mathematics 3, social studies 2, science 2 and academic electives 2. Mathematics and physical science recommended for all applicants, foreign language for some.

2008-2009 Annual costs. Tuition/fees: $8,300. 15 meals per week provded. Room/board: $6,900. Books/supplies: $850. Personal expenses: $1,210.

Financial aid. Need-based: Need-based aid available for part-time students. Work-study available nights, weekends and for part-time students. **Non-need-based:** Scholarships awarded for academics, art, athletics, leadership, religious affiliation.

Application procedures. Admission: No deadline. $20 fee, may be waived for applicants with need. Admission notification on a rolling basis. **Financial aid:** Priority date 3/1; no closing date. FAFSA, institutional form required. Applicants notified on a rolling basis starting 3/15; must reply within 2 week(s) of notification.

Academics. Special study options: Cross-registration, double major, dual enrollment of high school students, honors, independent study, internships, study abroad. **Credit/placement by examination:** AP, CLEP, ACT, institutional tests. 30 credit hours maximum toward associate degree. **Support services:** Learning center, reduced course load, remedial instruction, study skills assistance, tutoring.

Majors. Business: General, business admin. **Education:** Elementary, secondary. **Health:** Clinical lab science, predental, premedicine, prenursing, prepharmacy, preveterinary. **Legal studies:** Prelaw. **Liberal arts:** Arts/sciences. **Math:** General. **Philosophy/religion:** Religion. **Public administration:** Social work. **Transportation:** Aviation. **Visual/performing arts:** Art.

Computing on campus. 45 workstations in library, computer center. Wireless network available.

Student life. Freshman orientation: Mandatory. Preregistration for classes offered. Held Friday before classes begin. **Policies:** Alcohol and other drugs prohibited. **Housing:** Single-sex dorms, wellness housing available. $300 nonrefundable deposit. **Activities:** Campus ministries, international student organizations, literary magazine, student government, student newspaper, Student Ambassadors, Phi Theta Kappa, arts and cultural events club, Alpha Sigma Lambda.

Athletics. NJCAA. **Intercollegiate:** Baseball M, golf M, soccer, softball W, volleyball W. **Team name:** Bulldogs.

Student services. Alcohol/substance abuse counseling, chaplain/spiritual director, career counseling, financial aid counseling, personal counseling, veterans' counselor. **Transfer:** Pre-admission transcript evaluation for new students. Transfer adviser for students transferring to 4-year colleges.

Contact. E-mail: admissions@sci.edu
Phone: (217) 525-1420 ext. 287 Toll-free number: (800) 635-7289
Fax: (217) 525-1497
Susan Boehler, Director of Enrollment Services, Springfield College in Illinois, 1500 North Fifth Street, Springfield, IL 62702-2694

Taylor Business Institute

Chicago, Illinois
www.tbiil.edu **CB code: 2488**

- For-profit 2-year business college
- Very large city

General. Accredited by ACICS. **Enrollment:** 185 degree-seeking undergraduates. **Degrees:** 58 associate awarded. **Calendar:** Continuous. **Full-time faculty:** 29 total. **Part-time faculty:** 15 total.

Basis for selection. Open admission. CPAT required for placement and assessment after admission.

Financial aid. Need-based: Work-study available nights.

Application procedures. Admission: No deadline. $25 fee, may be waived for applicants with need. **Financial aid:** FAFSA, institutional form required.

Academics. Credit/placement by examination: CLEP.

Majors. Business: Accounting.

Student life. Freshman orientation: Available.

Student services. Alcohol/substance abuse counseling, career counseling, services for economically disadvantaged, student employment services, financial aid counseling, minority student services, personal counseling, placement for graduates, veterans' counselor, women's services.

Contact. Phone: (312) 658-5100
Ken Hatcher, Director of Admissions, Taylor Business Institute, 318 West Adams Street, 5th Floor, Chicago, IL 60606

Triton College

River Grove, Illinois **CB member**
www.triton.edu **CB code: 1821**

- Public 2-year community and junior college
- Commuter campus in large town

General. Founded in 1964. Regionally accredited. **Enrollment:** 9,610 degree-seeking undergraduates; 5,937 non-degree-seeking students. **Degrees:** 825 associate awarded. **Location:** 5 miles from Chicago. **Calendar:** Semester, extensive summer session. **Full-time faculty:** 121 total; 21% have terminal degrees, 22% minority, 55% women. **Part-time faculty:** 567 total; 18% have terminal degrees, 20% minority, 45% women. **Class size:** 46% < 20, 53% 20-39, less than 1% 40-49. **Special facilities:** Earth and space center with planetarium, and theater, performing arts center, botanical gardens, educational technology resource center, culinary arts operated dinning facility. **Partnerships:** Formal partnerships with Toyota, General Motors, Disney Corporation, over 24 hospitals and health care providers in Chicago area.

Student profile. Among degree-seeking undergraduates, 66% enrolled in a transfer program, 34% enrolled in a vocational program, 2% already have a bachelor's degree or higher, 2,321 enrolled as first-time, first-year students, 507 transferred in from other institutions.

Part-time:	60%	**Asian American:**	5%
Out-of-state:	1%	**Hispanic American:**	23%
Women:	56%	**25 or older:**	52%
African American:	22%		

Transfer out. 44% of students enrolled in the transfer program go on to 4-year colleges. **Colleges most students transferred to 2008:** Northern Illinois University, Northeastern Illinois University, University of Illinois at Chicago, DePaul University, Eastern Illinois University.

Basis for selection. Open admission, but selective for some programs. Special requirements for most health programs and two manufacturer-related automotive programs. Applicants to allied health program must attend information session. **Learning Disabled:** Students must self-identify.

High school preparation. 15 units recommended. Recommended units include English 4, mathematics 3, social studies 3, science 3 and academic electives 2. Biology, chemistry, or algebra required for most allied health programs. 15 specified units required for university transfer programs.

2008-2009 Annual costs. Tuition/fees: $2,170; $5,740 out-of-district; $7,150 out-of-state. Per-credit charge: $64 in-district; $183 out-of-district; $230 out-of-state. Books/supplies: $1,120. Personal expenses: $1,405.

2007-2008 Financial aid. Need-based: 634 full-time freshmen applied for aid; 428 were judged to have need; 428 of these received aid. Average scholarship/grant was $4,050; average loan $2,592. 86% of total undergraduate aid awarded as scholarships/grants, 14% as loans/jobs. Need-based aid available for part-time students. Work-study available nights, weekends and for part-time students. **Non-need-based:** Awarded to 366 full-time undergraduates, including 111 freshmen. Scholarships awarded for academics, athletics, leadership.

Application procedures. Admission: No deadline. No application fee. Admission notification on a rolling basis. **Financial aid:** Priority date 4/15; no closing date. FAFSA, institutional form required. Applicants notified on a rolling basis starting 4/1; must reply within 2 week(s) of notification.

Academics. Special study options: Accelerated study, cooperative education, cross-registration, distance learning, dual enrollment of high school students, ESL, exchange student, honors, independent study, internships, liberal arts/career combination, teacher certification program, weekend college. Bachelor's degree programs available on campus. License preparation in nursing, paramedic, radiology, real estate. **Credit/placement by examination:** AP, CLEP, institutional tests. 30 credit hours maximum toward associate degree. **Support services:** GED preparation, learning center, reduced course load, remedial instruction, study skills assistance, tutoring.

Honors college/program. 25 ACT and/or 3.35 GPA required; about 25 admitted each year.

Majors. Agriculture: Greenhouse operations, horticulture, landscaping, ornamental horticulture. **Architecture:** Interior. **Area/ethnic studies:** Women's. **Biology:** General. **Business:** Accounting, business admin, construction management, executive assistant, financial planning, hospitality admin, hotel/motel admin, human resources, international, management information systems, marketing, restaurant/food services, sales/distribution, selling. **Communications:** Digital media. **Computer sciences:** Information systems, networking. **Education:** General, early childhood, mathematics, science. **Engineering:** General. **Engineering technology:** Architectural drafting, construction, drafting, electrical, mechanical, surveying. **Foreign languages:** General, French, Italian, Spanish. **Health:** EMT paramedic, medical radiologic technology/radiation therapy, nuclear medical technology, nursing (RN), ophthalmic technology, predental, premedicine, prenursing, prepharmacy, preveterinary, radiologic technology/medical imaging, respiratory therapy technology, sonography, substance abuse counseling. **History:** General. **Interdisciplinary:** Biological/physical sciences, intercultural. **Legal studies:** Prelaw. **Liberal arts:** Arts/sciences. **Math:** General. **Mechanic/repair:** Automotive, avionics, heating/ac/refrig, industrial. **Personal/culinary services:** Chef training, culinary arts. **Philosophy/religion:** Philosophy. **Physical sciences:** Chemistry, geology, physics. **Production:** Welding. **Protective services:** Firefighting, law enforcement admin, police science. **Psychology:** General. **Public administration:** Community org/advocacy, social work. **Social sciences:** Anthropology, econometrics, economics, geography, political science, sociology. **Visual/performing arts:** Art, commercial/advertising art, design, dramatic, interior design, studio arts.

Most popular majors. Health sciences 39%, interdisciplinary studies 13%, liberal arts 28%, trade and industry 7%.

Computing on campus. 946 workstations in library, computer center. Commuter students can connect to campus network. Online course registration, online library, helpline, wireless network available.

Student life. Freshman orientation: Available. Sessions held throughout summer months. **Activities:** Jazz band, choral groups, dance, drama, music ensembles, musical theater, radio station, student government, student newspaper, over 30 clubs and organizations available.

Athletics. NJCAA. **Intercollegiate:** Baseball M, basketball, soccer, softball W, volleyball W, wrestling M. **Team name:** Trojans.

Student services. Career counseling, services for economically disadvantaged, student employment services, financial aid counseling, health services, minority student services, on-campus daycare, personal counseling, placement for graduates, veterans' counselor. **Physically disabled:** Services for visually, speech, hearing impaired. **Transfer:** Pre-admission transcript evaluation for new students. Transfer center, transfer adviser, college fairs on campus for students transferring to 4-year colleges.

Contact. E-mail: triton@triton.edu
Phone: (708) 456-0300 ext. 3130 Fax: (708) 583-3162
Mary-Rita Moore, Dean, Enrollment Services, Triton College, 2000 North Fifth Avenue, River Grove, IL 60171

Vatterott College: Quincy

Quincy, Illinois
www.vatterott-college.edu

- For-profit 2-year technical college
- Commuter campus in small city

General. Accredited by ACCSCT. **Enrollment:** 259 degree-seeking undergraduates. **Degrees:** 23 associate awarded. **Calendar:** Continuous. **Full-time faculty:** 15 total. **Part-time faculty:** 30 total.

Student profile. Among degree-seeking undergraduates, 100% enrolled in a vocational program.

Basis for selection. Open admission.

2008-2009 Annual costs. Program cost ranges: $15,750 to $18,600 for certificate/diploma. Books and tools: $1850-$3700.

Application procedures. Admission: No deadline. No application fee.

Academics. Credit/placement by examination: CLEP.

Majors. Computer sciences: Computer science. **Engineering technology:** CAD/CADD. **Health:** Medical assistant. **Mechanic/repair:** Heating/ac/refrig.

Contact. Phone: (217) 224-0600 Toll-free number: (800) 438-5621
Fax: (217) 223-6771
Kim Otte, Director of Admissions, Vatterott College: Quincy, 3609 North Marx Drive, Quincy, IL 62305

Waubonsee Community College

Sugar Grove, Illinois
www.waubonsee.edu **CB code: 1938**

- Public 2-year community college
- Commuter campus in small town

General. Founded in 1966. Regionally accredited. Public, comprehensive community college organized in 1966. **Enrollment:** 6,813 degree-seeking undergraduates; 2,494 non-degree-seeking students. **Degrees:** 635 associate awarded. **ROTC:** Army. **Location:** 9 miles from Aurora. **Calendar:** 4-4-1 semester system. Extensive summer session. **Full-time faculty:** 105 total; 15% have terminal degrees, 10% minority, 58% women. **Part-time faculty:** 621 total; 7% have terminal degrees, 13% minority, 60% women. **Special facilities:** Observatory, nature trail. **Partnerships:** Formal partnership with Valley Education for Employment System.

Student profile. Among degree-seeking undergraduates, 48% enrolled in a transfer program, 52% enrolled in a vocational program, 1,529 enrolled as first-time, first-year students.

Part-time:	52%	**Asian American:**	3%
Women:	57%	**Hispanic American:**	19%
African American:	7%	**25 or older:**	33%

Transfer out. 72% of students enrolled in the transfer program go on to 4-year colleges. **Colleges most students transferred to 2008:** Northern Illinois University, Illinois State University, Aurora University-Illinois, University of Illinois at Urbana-Champaign, University of Illinois at Chicago.

Basis for selection. Open admission, but selective for some programs. Admission to limited enrollment programs based on specific assessment testing and/or successful completion of prerequisite coursework.

High school preparation. College-preparatory program recommended. 15 units recommended. Recommended units include English 4, mathematics 3, social studies 3, science 3 and academic electives 2.

2009-2010 Annual costs. Tuition/fees (projected): $2,460; $8,027 out-of-district; $8,838 out-of-state. Per-credit charge: $79 in-district; $265 out-of-district; $292 out-of-state. Books/supplies: $1,156. Personal expenses: $1,306.

2007-2008 Financial aid. Need-based: 74% of total undergraduate aid awarded as scholarships/grants, 26% as loans/jobs. Need-based aid available for part-time students. Work-study available nights and for part-time students. **Non-need-based:** Scholarships awarded for academics, art, athletics, leadership, minority status, music/drama.

Application procedures. Admission: No deadline. No application fee. Application must be submitted on paper. Admission notification on a rolling basis. **Financial aid:** Closing date 12/1. FAFSA required. Applicants notified on a rolling basis.

Academics. Review classes offered for various levels of math, English, and reading. **Special study options:** Accelerated study, distance learning, dual enrollment of high school students, ESL, honors, independent study, internships, liberal arts/career combination, study abroad, weekend college. License preparation in nursing, real estate. **Credit/placement by examination:** AP, CLEP, institutional tests. 30 credit hours maximum toward associate degree. Student must be enrolled before scores can be recorded on transcript. Recording fee may apply. **Support services:** GED preparation and test center, learning center, reduced course load, remedial instruction, study skills assistance, tutoring, writing center.

Majors. Business: Accounting technology, administrative services, business admin, construction management, executive assistant, human resources, logistics, office technology, retailing, small business admin. **Communications technology:** Radio/tv. **Computer sciences:** LAN/WAN management, programming, web page design. **Construction:** Electrician. **Education:** Art, mathematics, multi-level teacher, music, teacher assistance. **Engineering:** General. **Engineering technology:** CAD/CADD, electrical. **Foreign languages:** Sign language interpretation, translation. **Health:**

Massage therapy, nursing (RN). **Interdisciplinary:** Biological/physical sciences. **Liberal arts:** Arts/sciences. **Mechanic/repair:** Auto body, automotive, heating/ac/refrig, industrial. **Protective services:** Police science. **Public administration:** Social work. **Visual/performing arts:** Graphic design, studio arts.

Most popular majors. Health sciences 16%, interdisciplinary studies 47%, liberal arts 24%.

Computing on campus. 140 workstations in library, computer center, student center. Commuter students can connect to campus network. Online course registration, helpline, wireless network available.

Student life. Freshman orientation: Available. Optional 1-day program offered before semester begins. **Activities:** Bands, choral groups, dance, drama, literary magazine, music ensembles, musical theater, opera, student government, student newspaper, Latino Unidos, Christian fellowship, Amnesty International, African cultural alliance, model Illinois government, Students for a Diverse Society.

Athletics. NJCAA. **Intercollegiate:** Baseball M, basketball, cross-country, golf M, soccer, softball W, tennis, volleyball W, wrestling M. **Intramural:** Basketball, bowling, table tennis. **Team name:** Chiefs.

Student services. Career counseling, services for economically disadvantaged, student employment services, financial aid counseling, minority student services, on-campus daycare, personal counseling, placement for graduates, veterans' counselor. **Physically disabled:** Services for visually, speech, hearing impaired. **Transfer:** Transfer adviser, college fairs on campus for students transferring to 4-year colleges.

Contact. E-mail: recruitment@waubonsee.edu
Phone: (630) 466-7900 ext. 2370 Fax: (630) 466-4964
Joy Baish, Admissions Manager, Waubonsee Community College, Route 47 at Waubonsee Drive, Sugar Grove, IL 60554-9454

Indiana

Ancilla College

Donaldson, Indiana
www.ancilla.edu **CB code: 1015**

- Private 2-year community and liberal arts college affiliated with Roman Catholic Church
- Commuter campus in rural community

General. Founded in 1937. Regionally accredited. **Enrollment:** 495 degree-seeking undergraduates. **Degrees:** 90 associate awarded. **Location:** 30 miles from South Bend, 7 miles from Plymouth. **Calendar:** Semester, limited summer session. **Full-time faculty:** 25 total; 68% have terminal degrees, 52% women. **Part-time faculty:** 33 total; 82% have terminal degrees, 67% women. **Class size:** 67% < 20, 33% 20-39.

Student profile. Among degree-seeking undergraduates, 60 transferred in from other institutions.

Out-of-state:	1%	**25 or older:**	36%

Transfer out. Colleges most students transferred to 2008: Indiana University South Bend, Purdue North Central, Bethel College.

Basis for selection. Open admission, but selective for some programs. Special requirements for nursing program. **Adult students:** SAT/ACT scores not required if out of high school 3 year(s) or more. **Homeschooled:** Transcript of courses and grades required.

High school preparation. 21 units recommended. Recommended units include English 4, mathematics 4, social studies 2, history 3, science 3 (laboratory 3) and foreign language 2.

2008-2009 Annual costs. Tuition/fees: $12,080. Per-credit charge: $395. Books/supplies: $1,250. Personal expenses: $680.

2008-2009 Financial aid. Need-based: Need-based aid available for part-time students. Work-study available for part-time students. **Non-need-based:** Scholarships awarded for academics, athletics, job skills, leadership.

Application procedures. Admission: No deadline. No application fee. Admission notification on a rolling basis. **Financial aid:** Closing date 3/1. FAFSA, institutional form required. Applicants notified on a rolling basis starting 3/1; must reply within 2 week(s) of notification.

Academics. Special study options: Double major, dual enrollment of high school students, independent study, liberal arts/career combination. License preparation in real estate. **Credit/placement by examination:** CLEP, institutional tests. 12 credit hours maximum toward associate degree. **Support services:** Learning center, reduced course load, remedial instruction, study skills assistance, tutoring, writing center.

Majors. Biology: General. **Business:** Business admin. **Education:** Early childhood, elementary, secondary. **Health:** Nursing (RN), prenursing. **History:** General. **Interdisciplinary:** Behavioral sciences. **Liberal arts:** Arts/sciences. **Physical sciences:** Chemistry. **Protective services:** Criminal justice.

Computing on campus. 53 workstations in library, computer center. Online library available.

Student life. Freshman orientation: Mandatory. Preregistration for classes offered. **Activities:** Campus ministries, literary magazine, student government, student newspaper, Student Ambassadors, Phi Theta Kappa.

Athletics. NJCAA. **Intercollegiate:** Baseball M, basketball, cheerleading, golf, soccer M, softball W, volleyball W. **Team name:** Chargers.

Student services. Chaplain/spiritual director, career counseling, student employment services, financial aid counseling, personal counseling. **Transfer:** Transfer adviser for students transferring to 4-year colleges.

Contact. E-mail: admissions@ancilla.edu
Phone: (574) 936-8898 ext. 330 Toll-free number: (866) 262-4552
Fax: (574) 935-1773
Erin Alonzo, Director of Admissions, Ancilla College, 9001 Union Road, Donaldson, IN 46513

Aviation Institute of Maintenance: Indianapolis

Indianapolis, Indiana
www.aviationmaintenance.edu **CB code: 3192**

- For-profit 2-year technical college
- Commuter campus in very large city
- Interview required

General. Accredited by ACCSCT. Fast track program for airframe and powerplant training. **Enrollment:** 157 degree-seeking undergraduates. **Degrees:** 50 associate awarded. **Location:** 10 miles from downtown. **Calendar:** Continuous, extensive summer session. **Full-time faculty:** 16 total. **Part-time faculty:** 1 total. **Special facilities:** Aircraft, engines, and aircraft hangar on site.

Basis for selection. Open admission, but selective for some programs. Academy entrance exam, high school diploma or GED, interview with admissions representatives, college tour, English comprehension at eighth-grade level, physical ability very important.

2008-2009 Annual costs. Tuition: $240 per credit hour.

Application procedures. Admission: No deadline. $25 fee. Admission notification on a rolling basis. **Financial aid:** FAFSA required.

Academics. Special study options: FAA certified license in airframe, FAA certified license in power plant. License preparation in aviation. **Credit/placement by examination:** CLEP, institutional tests. 50% of credits toward degree must be earned in residence.

Majors. Mechanic/repair: Aircraft. **Transportation:** Aviation.

Student life. Freshman orientation: Mandatory. Held prior to start of program for 2-3 days. Students obtain mandatory uniforms. **Policies:** Airlines mandate random mandatory drug testing. Criminal background check conducted.

Student services. Student employment services, placement for graduates. **Transfer:** Pre-admission transcript evaluation for new students.

Contact. E-mail: directorami@tidetech.com
Phone: (317) 243-4519 Toll-free number: (888) 349-5387
Fax: (317) 243-4569
Andy Duncan, Managing Director, Aviation Institute of Maintenance: Indianapolis, 7251 West McCarty Street, Indianapolis, IN 46241-1445

Brown Mackie College: Fort Wayne

Fort Wayne, Indiana
www.brownmackie.com **CB code: 3379**

- For-profit 2-year branch campus and business college
- Large city

General. Accredited by ACICS. **Enrollment:** 1,300 full-time, degree-seeking students. **Degrees:** 155 associate awarded. **Calendar:** Quarter. **Full-time faculty:** 35 total. **Part-time faculty:** 80 total.

Basis for selection. Open admission.

2008-2009 Annual costs. Nursing program tuition $295 per credit hour. Occupational therapy courses $350 per credit hour; general education courses for occupational therapy $235 per credit hour. $20 per-credit-hour charge for all courses. All other programs $235 per credit hour. Books/supplies: $1,100.

Application procedures. Admission: No deadline. $20 fee.

Academics. Credit/placement by examination: CLEP.

Majors. Business: Accounting, business admin. **Computer sciences:** General. **Health:** Medical assistant, occupational therapy assistant. **Legal studies:** Paralegal.

Contact. E-mail: ktaboh@brownmackie.edu
Phone: (260) 484-4400 Toll-free number: (866) 433-2289
Fax: (260) 484-2678
Phil Hooks, Director of Admissions, Brown Mackie College: Fort Wayne, 3000 Coliseum Boulevard, Suite 100, Fort Wayne, IN 46805

Brown Mackie College: Merrillville
Merrillville, Indiana
www.brownmackie.edu **CB code: 7115**

- For-profit 2-year business college
- Small city

General. Accredited by ACICS. **Calendar:** Continuous.

Annual costs/financial aid. Nursing program tuition $295 per credit hour. Occupational therapy courses $350 per credit hour; general education courses for occupational therapy $235 per credit hour. Fees are $15 per credit hour for all programs except nursing which is $20. Books/supplies: $720. Personal expenses: $845.

Contact. Phone: (219) 769-3321
Director of Admissions, 1000 East 80th Place, Suite 101N, Merrillville, IN 46410

Brown Mackie College: Michigan City
Michigan City, Indiana
www.cbcaec.com **CB code: 3345**

- For-profit 2-year branch campus college
- Large town

General. Accredited by ACICS. **Calendar:** Continuous.

Annual costs/financial aid. Per-credit-hour charge (tuition only) is $235; required fees are $15 per credit hour. Books/supplies: $630. Personal expenses: $2,664.

Contact. Phone: (219) 877-3100
Director of Admissions, 325 East US Highway 20, Michigan City, IN 46360-7362

Brown Mackie College: South Bend
South Bend, Indiana
www.brownmackie.edu **CB code: 3140**

- For-profit 2-year community and technical college
- Commuter campus in small city
- Application essay, interview required

General. Founded in 1882. Accredited by ACICS. **Enrollment:** 905 degree-seeking undergraduates. **Degrees:** 135 associate awarded. **Location:** 90 miles from Chicago, 150 miles from Indianapolis. **Calendar:** Quarter, extensive summer session. **Full-time faculty:** 26 total. **Part-time faculty:** 29 total. **Class size:** 81% < 20, 19% 20-39.

Student profile.

Out-of-state:	7%	**25 or older:**	45%

Basis for selection. Open admission.

2008-2009 Annual costs. Nursing program tuition $295 per credit hour. Occupational therapy courses $350 per credit hour; general education courses for occupational therapy $235 per credit hour. Fees are $15 per credit hour for all programs except nursing which is $20. Books/supplies: $1,200.

2008-2009 Financial aid. All financial aid based on need. 30% of total undergraduate aid awarded as scholarships/grants, 70% as loans/jobs. Need-based aid available for part-time students.

Application procedures. Admission: No deadline. No application fee. Must reply by May 1 or within 1 week(s) if notified thereafter. **Financial aid:** No deadline. FAFSA required. Applicants notified on a rolling basis; must reply within 1 week(s) of notification.

Academics. Four-day academic week. Optional Friday tutorial sessions available. **Special study options:** Accelerated study, double major, independent study, internships. **Credit/placement by examination:** CLEP. 28 credit hours maximum toward associate degree. **Support services:** Remedial instruction, study skills assistance, tutoring.

Majors. Business: Accounting, administrative services. **Computer sciences:** General. **Health:** Medical assistant, medical transcription, occupational therapy assistant, physical therapy assistant. **Legal studies:** Legal secretary.

Most popular majors. Business/marketing 39%, health sciences 61%.

Computing on campus. 60 workstations in computer center.

Student life. Freshman orientation: Mandatory. Preregistration for classes offered. Two-hour sessions held Thursday before class starts. **Housing:** Students are referred to local apartment complexes.

Student services. Career counseling, student employment services, personal counseling, placement for graduates, veterans' counselor. **Transfer:** Transfer adviser for students transferring to 4-year colleges.

Contact. E-mail: bmcsbadm@brownmackie.edu
Phone: (574) 237-0774 Toll-free number: (800) 743-2447
Amy Wolf, Director of Admissions, Brown Mackie College: South Bend, 1030 East Jefferson Boulevard, South Bend, IN 46617

College of Court Reporting
Hobart, Indiana
www.ccr.edu **CB code: 3532**

- For-profit 2-year business and technical college
- Small city

General. Accredited by ACICS. **Enrollment:** 230 degree-seeking undergraduates. **Degrees:** 18 associate awarded. **Calendar:** Semester. **Part-time faculty:** 20 total.

Basis for selection. Open admission.

2008-2009 Annual costs. Tuition/fees: $7,080. Per-credit charge: $295. Books/supplies: $1,500.

Application procedures. Admission: Closing date 9/30. $50 fee.

Academics. Credit/placement by examination: CLEP.

Majors. Business: Office technology. **Health:** Medical transcription. **Legal studies:** Court reporting.

Contact. E-mail: information@ccr.edu
Phone: (219) 942-1459 Fax: (219) 942-1631
Nicky Rodriguez, Director of Admissions, College of Court Reporting, 111 West 10th Street, Suite 111, Hobart, IN 46342

Indiana Business College: Anderson
Anderson, Indiana
www.ibcschools.edu **CB code: 3364**

- For-profit 2-year business and health science college
- Commuter campus in small city
- Interview required

General. Accredited by ACICS. **Enrollment:** 174 degree-seeking undergraduates. **Degrees:** 60 associate awarded. **Location:** 45 miles from Indianapolis. **Calendar:** Quarter, extensive summer session. **Full-time faculty:** 5 total. **Part-time faculty:** 11 total.

Basis for selection. Interview and Wonderlic evaluation are main admission criteria.

2008-2009 Annual costs. Tuition and fees vary by program.

Financial aid. Need-based: Need-based aid available for part-time students. **Additional information:** Work-study programs available.

Application procedures. Admission: No deadline. $50 fee. Admission notification on a rolling basis. **Financial aid:** FAFSA required. Applicants notified on a rolling basis.

Academics. Special study options: Distance learning, dual enrollment of high school students, internships. Bachelor's degree programs available on campus. **Credit/placement by examination:** CLEP, institutional tests. Free test-out program is available to high school seniors. Test-outs are available to all other students for a $30 fee.

Majors. Business: Accounting, accounting/finance, administrative services, banking/financial services, business admin, human resources, marketing. **Health:** Insurance coding, insurance specialist, medical assistant, medical records technology. **Protective services:** Law enforcement admin.

Student life. Housing: Apartments available. **Activities:** Student government.

Student services. Career counseling, student employment services, financial aid counseling, placement for graduates.

Contact. E-mail: anderson@ibcschools.edu
Phone: (765) 644-7514 Toll-free number: (800) 422-4723
Fax: (765) 644-5724
Matt Stein, Associate Director of Admissions, Indiana Business College: Anderson, 140 East 53rd Street, Anderson, IN 46013

Indiana Business College: Columbus
Columbus, Indiana
www.ibcschools.edu **CB code: 3349**

- For-profit 2-year business and health science college
- Commuter campus in large town
- Interview required

General. Accredited by ACICS. **Enrollment:** 207 degree-seeking undergraduates. **Degrees:** 90 associate awarded. **Location:** 50 miles from Indianapolis. **Calendar:** Quarter, extensive summer session. **Full-time faculty:** 5 total. **Part-time faculty:** 4 total.

Basis for selection. Interview and Wonderlic evaluation are main admission criteria.

2008-2009 Annual costs. Tuition and fees vary by program.

Financial aid. Need-based: Need-based aid available for part-time students. **Additional information:** Work-study programs available.

Application procedures. Admission: No deadline. $50 fee. Admission notification on a rolling basis. **Financial aid:** FAFSA required. Applicants notified on a rolling basis.

Academics. Special study options: Distance learning, dual enrollment of high school students, internships. **Credit/placement by examination:** CLEP, institutional tests. Free test-out program available to high school seniors. Test-outs available to other students for $30 fee.

Majors. Business: Accounting, accounting/finance, administrative services, banking/financial services, business admin, marketing. **Health:** Insurance coding, insurance specialist, medical assistant, medical records technology.

Student services. Career counseling, student employment services, financial aid counseling, placement for graduates.

Contact. E-mail: columbus@ibcschools.edu
Phone: (812) 379-9000 Toll-free number: (800) 422-4723
Fax: (812) 375-0414
Gina Pate, Director of Admissions, Indiana Business College: Columbus, 2222 Poshard Drive, Columbus, IN 47203

Indiana Business College: Elkhart
Elkhart, Indiana
www.ibcschools.edu

- For-profit 2-year business and health science college
- Small city

General. Regionally accredited. **Enrollment:** 220 degree-seeking undergraduates. **Calendar:** Quarter.

Basis for selection. Open admission.

2008-2009 Annual costs. Tuition and fees vary by program.

Application procedures. Admission: No deadline. No application fee.

Academics. Credit/placement by examination: CLEP.

Majors. Business: Accounting, accounting/finance, business admin, human resources, marketing. **Health:** Insurance coding, medical assistant. **Protective services:** Law enforcement admin.

Contact. Phone: (574) 522-0397
Indiana Business College: Elkhart, 56075 Parkway Ave., Elkhart, IN 46516

Indiana Business College: Evansville
Evansville, Indiana
www.ibcschools.edu **CB code: 3346**

- For-profit 2-year business and health science college
- Commuter campus in small city
- Interview required

General. Accredited by ACICS. **Enrollment:** 226 degree-seeking undergraduates. **Degrees:** 83 associate awarded. **Calendar:** Quarter, extensive summer session. **Full-time faculty:** 8 total. **Part-time faculty:** 8 total.

Basis for selection. Interview and Wonderlic evaluation are main admission criteria.

2008-2009 Annual costs. Tuition and fees vary by program.

Financial aid. Need-based: Need-based aid available for part-time students. **Additional information:** Work-study programs available.

Application procedures. Admission: No deadline. $50 fee. Admission notification on a rolling basis. **Financial aid:** FAFSA required. Applicants notified on a rolling basis.

Academics. Special study options: Distance learning, dual enrollment of high school students, internships. Bachelor's degree programs available on campus. **Credit/placement by examination:** CLEP, institutional tests. Free test-out program available to high school seniors. Test-outs available to all other students for $30 fee.

Majors. Business: Accounting, accounting/finance, administrative services, banking/financial services, business admin, marketing. **Computer sciences:** Information technology. **Health:** Insurance coding, medical assistant, medical records technology. **Protective services:** Law enforcement admin. **Other:** Help desk administration.

Student services. Career counseling, student employment services, financial aid counseling, placement for graduates.

Contact. Phone: (812) 476-6000 Toll-free number: (800) 422-4723
Fax: (812) 471-8576
Starlet Gupton, Director of Admissions, Indiana Business College: Evansville, 4601 Theater Drive, Evansville, IN 47715

Indiana Business College: Fort Wayne
Fort Wayne, Indiana
www.ibcschools.edu **CB code: 3867**

- For-profit 2-year business and health science college
- Commuter campus in large city
- Interview required

General. Accredited by ACICS. **Enrollment:** 492 degree-seeking undergraduates. **Degrees:** 126 associate awarded. **Calendar:** Quarter, extensive summer session. **Full-time faculty:** 6 total. **Part-time faculty:** 14 total.

Basis for selection. Interview and Wonderlic evaluation are main admission criteria.

2008-2009 Annual costs. Tuition and fees vary by program.

Financial aid. Need-based: Need-based aid available for part-time students. **Additional information:** Work-study programs available.

Application procedures. Admission: No deadline. $50 fee. Admission notification on a rolling basis. **Financial aid:** FAFSA required.

Academics. Special study options: Distance learning, dual enrollment of high school students, internships. Bachelor's degree programs available on campus. **Credit/placement by examination:** CLEP, institutional tests. Free test-out program is available to high school seniors. Test-outs are available to all other students for a $30 fee.

Majors. Business: Accounting, accounting/finance, administrative services, banking/financial services, business admin, marketing. **Computer sciences:** Information technology. **Health:** Insurance specialist, medical assistant, medical records technology, surgical technology. **Protective services:** Law enforcement admin. **Other:** Help desk administration.

Student services. Career counseling, student employment services, financial aid counseling, placement for graduates.

Contact. E-mail: fortwayne@ibcschools.edu
Phone: (260) 471-7667 Toll-free number: (800) 422-4723
Fax: (260) 471-6918
Janet Herman, Executive Director, Indiana Business College: Fort Wayne, 6413 North Clinton Street, Fort Wayne, IN 46825

Indiana Business College: Indianapolis
Indianapolis, Indiana
www.ibcschools.edu **CB code: 2317**

- For-profit 2-year business and health science college
- Commuter campus in very large city

General. Founded in 1902. Accredited by ACICS. **Enrollment:** 1,889 degree-seeking undergraduates. **Degrees:** 240 associate awarded. **Calendar:** Quarter, extensive summer session. **Full-time faculty:** 30 total. **Part-time faculty:** 10 total.

Basis for selection. Interview and Wonderlic evaluation are main admission criteria.

2008-2009 Annual costs. Tuition and fees vary by program.

Financial aid. Need-based: Need-based aid available for part-time students. **Additional information:** Work-study programs available.

Application procedures. Admission: No deadline. $50 fee. Admission notification on a rolling basis. **Financial aid:** FAFSA required. Applicants notified on a rolling basis.

Academics. Special study options: Distance learning, dual enrollment of high school students, internships. Bachelor's degree programs available on campus. **Credit/placement by examination:** CLEP, institutional tests. Free test-out program available to high school seniors. Test-outs available to all other students for $30 fee per exam.

Majors. Business: Accounting, accounting/finance, administrative services, banking/financial services, business admin, fashion, human resources, marketing. **Computer sciences:** Information technology, networking. **Engineering technology:** Computer systems. **Health:** Medical assistant. **Personal/culinary services:** Baking, culinary arts. **Protective services:** Law enforcement admin. **Other:** Cisco network associate, Help desk administration.

Student life. Activities: Student government.

Student services. Career counseling, student employment services, financial aid counseling, placement for graduates.

Contact. E-mail: indianapolis@ibcschools.edu
Phone: (317) 264-5656 Toll-free number: (800) 422-4723
Fax: (317) 264-5650
Ted Lukomski, Director of Admissions, Indiana Business College: Indianapolis, 550 East Washington Street, Indianapolis, IN 46204

Indiana Business College: Indianapolis Northwest
Indianapolis, Indiana
www.ibcschools.edu

- For-profit 2-year business and health science college
- Very large city

General. Accredited by ACICS. **Enrollment:** 247 degree-seeking undergraduates. **Degrees:** 12 associate awarded. **Calendar:** Quarter. **Full-time faculty:** 8 total. **Part-time faculty:** 5 total.

Basis for selection. Interview and Wonderlic evaluation are main admission criteria.

2008-2009 Annual costs. Tuition and fees vary by program.

Application procedures. Admission: No deadline. $50 fee. Admission notification on a rolling basis. **Financial aid:** FAFSA required.

Academics. Special study options: Distance learning, dual enrollment of high school students, internships. **Credit/placement by examination:** CLEP, institutional tests.

Majors. Business: Accounting, administrative services, banking/financial services, business admin, marketing. **Health:** Insurance coding, insurance specialist, medical assistant, medical records technology, surgical technology, veterinary technology/assistant.

Contact. E-mail: northwest@ibcschools.edu
Phone: (317) 873-6500 Toll-free number: (800) IBC-GRAD
Mark Jones, Director of Admissions, Indiana Business College: Indianapolis Northwest, 6300 Technology Center Drive, Indianapolis, IN 46278

Indiana Business College: Lafayette
Lafayette, Indiana
www.ibcschools.edu **CB code: 3353**

- For-profit 2-year business and health science college
- Commuter campus in small city
- Interview required

General. Accredited by ACICS. **Enrollment:** 272 degree-seeking undergraduates. **Degrees:** 70 associate awarded. **Location:** 60 miles from Indianapolis. **Calendar:** Quarter, extensive summer session. **Full-time faculty:** 7 total. **Part-time faculty:** 6 total.

Basis for selection. Interview and Wonderlic evaluation are main admission criteria.

2008-2009 Annual costs. Tuition and fees vary by program.

Financial aid. Need-based: Need-based aid available for part-time students. **Additional information:** Work-study programs available.

Application procedures. Admission: No deadline. $50 fee. Admission notification on a rolling basis. **Financial aid:** FAFSA required. Applicants notified on a rolling basis.

Academics. Special study options: Distance learning, dual enrollment of high school students, internships. **Credit/placement by examination:** CLEP, institutional tests. Free test-out program available to high school seniors. Test-outs available to all other students for a $30 fee.

Majors. Business: Accounting, accounting/finance, administrative services, banking/financial services, business admin, human resources, marketing. **Health:** Insurance coding, insurance specialist, medical assistant, medical records technology.

Student services. Career counseling, student employment services, financial aid counseling, placement for graduates.

Contact. E-mail: lafayette@ibcschools.edu
Phone: (765) 447-9550 Toll-free number: (800) 422-4723
Fax: (765) 447-0868
Stacy Golleher, Director of Admissions, Indiana Business College: Lafayette, 4705 Meijer Court, Lafayette, IN 47905

Indiana Business College: Marion
Marion, Indiana
www.ibcschools.edu **CB code: 3360**

- For-profit 2-year business and health science college
- Commuter campus in large town
- Interview required

General. Accredited by ACICS. **Enrollment:** 114 degree-seeking undergraduates. **Degrees:** 30 associate awarded. **Location:** 70 miles from Indianapolis. **Calendar:** Quarter, extensive summer session. **Full-time faculty:** 3 total. **Part-time faculty:** 8 total.

Basis for selection. Interview and Wonderlic evaluation are main admission criteria.

2008-2009 Annual costs. Tuition and fees vary by program.

Financial aid. Need-based: Need-based aid available for part-time students. **Additional information:** Work-study programs available.

Application procedures. Admission: No deadline. $50 fee. Admission notification on a rolling basis. **Financial aid:** FAFSA required. Applicants notified on a rolling basis.

Academics. Special study options: Distance learning, dual enrollment of high school students, internships. **Credit/placement by examination:** CLEP, institutional tests. Free test-out program available to high school seniors. Test-outs are available to all other students for a $30 fee per exam.

Majors. **Business:** Accounting, accounting/finance, administrative services, banking/financial services, business admin, marketing. **Health:** Insurance coding, medical assistant. **Protective services:** Law enforcement admin.

Student services. Career counseling, student employment services, financial aid counseling, placement for graduates.

Contact. E-mail: marion@ibcschools.edu
Phone: (765) 662-7497 Toll-free number: (800) 422-4723
Fax: (765) 651-9421
Richard Herman, Executive Director, Indiana Business College: Marion, 830 North Miller Avenue, Marion, IN 46952

Indiana Business College: Medical

Indianapolis, Indiana
www.ibcschools.edu **CB code: 3370**

- For-profit 2-year health science college
- Commuter campus in very large city
- Interview required

General. Accredited by ACICS. **Enrollment:** 458 degree-seeking undergraduates. **Degrees:** 196 associate awarded. **Calendar:** Quarter, extensive summer session. **Full-time faculty:** 20 total. **Part-time faculty:** 10 total.

Basis for selection. Interview and Wonderlic evaluation are main admission criteria.

2008-2009 Annual costs. Tuition and fees vary by program.

Financial aid. **Need-based:** Need-based aid available for part-time students. **Additional information:** Work-study programs available.

Application procedures. **Admission:** No deadline. $50 fee. Admission notification on a rolling basis. **Financial aid:** FAFSA required. Applicants notified on a rolling basis.

Academics. **Special study options:** Distance learning, dual enrollment of high school students, internships. **Credit/placement by examination:** CLEP, institutional tests. Free test-out program available to high school seniors. Test-outs available to all other students for $30 fee per exam. **Support services:** Reduced course load, study skills assistance, tutoring.

Majors. **Business:** Insurance. **Health:** Clinical lab science, insurance coding, insurance specialist, massage therapy, medical assistant, medical records technology, nursing (RN), surgical technology. **Other:** Property and casualty claims.

Student life. **Freshman orientation:** Available. One-hour orientation held quarterly on first day of classes.

Student services. Career counseling, student employment services, financial aid counseling, placement for graduates.

Contact. E-mail: medical@ibcschools.edu
Phone: (317) 375-8000 Toll-free number: (800) 422-4723
Fax: (317) 351-1871
Alan Bacon, Director of Admissions, Indiana Business College: Medical, 8150 Brookville Road, Indianapolis, IN 46239

Indiana Business College: Muncie

Muncie, Indiana
www.ibcschools.edu **CB code: 3347**

- For-profit 2-year business and health science college
- Commuter campus in small city
- Interview required

General. Accredited by ACICS. **Enrollment:** 201 degree-seeking undergraduates. **Degrees:** 99 associate awarded. **Calendar:** Quarter, extensive summer session. **Full-time faculty:** 4 total. **Part-time faculty:** 13 total.

Basis for selection. Interview and Wonderlic evaluation are main admission criteria.

2008-2009 Annual costs. Tuition and fees vary by program.

Financial aid. **Need-based:** Need-based aid available for part-time students. **Additional information:** Work-study programs available.

Application procedures. **Admission:** No deadline. $50 fee. Admission notification on a rolling basis. **Financial aid:** FAFSA required. Applicants notified on a rolling basis.

Academics. **Special study options:** Distance learning, dual enrollment of high school students, internships. Bachelor's degree programs available on campus. **Credit/placement by examination:** CLEP, institutional tests. Free test-out program available to high school seniors. Test-outs available to all other students for a $30 fee per exam. **Support services:** Study skills assistance, tutoring.

Majors. **Business:** Accounting, accounting/finance, administrative services, banking/financial services, business admin, human resources, marketing. **Computer sciences:** Information technology. **Engineering technology:** Computer systems. **Health:** Health care admin, insurance coding, medical assistant. **Protective services:** Law enforcement admin. **Other:** Help desk administration.

Student life. **Freshman orientation:** Mandatory.

Student services. Career counseling, student employment services, financial aid counseling, placement for graduates.

Contact. E-mail: muncie@ibcschools.edu
Phone: (765) 288-8681 Toll-free number: (800) 422-4723
Fax: (765) 288-8797
Jeremy Linder, Associate Director of Admissions, Indiana Business College: Muncie, 411 West Riggin Road, Muncie, IN 47303

Indiana Business College: Terre Haute

Terre Haute, Indiana
www.ibcschools.edu **CB code: 3348**

- For-profit 2-year business and health science college
- Commuter campus in small city
- Interview required

General. Accredited by ACICS. **Enrollment:** 257 degree-seeking undergraduates. **Degrees:** 76 associate awarded. **Calendar:** Quarter, extensive summer session. **Full-time faculty:** 4 total. **Part-time faculty:** 7 total.

Basis for selection. Interview, Wonderlic evaluation, and recommendation are main admission criteria.

2008-2009 Annual costs. Tuition and fees vary by program.

Financial aid. **Need-based:** Need-based aid available for part-time students. **Additional information:** Work-study programs available.

Application procedures. **Admission:** No deadline. $50 fee. Admission notification on a rolling basis. **Financial aid:** FAFSA required. Applicants notified on a rolling basis.

Academics. **Special study options:** Cooperative education, distance learning, dual enrollment of high school students, internships. Bachelor's degree programs available on campus. **Credit/placement by examination:** CLEP, institutional tests. Free test-out program available to high school seniors. Test-outs are available to all other students for a fee of $30 per test. **Support services:** Study skills assistance, tutoring.

Majors. **Business:** Accounting, accounting/finance, administrative services, banking/financial services, business admin, human resources, marketing. **Computer sciences:** Information technology, system admin. **Health:** Insurance coding, medical assistant, medical records technology.

Student services. Career counseling, student employment services, financial aid counseling, placement for graduates.

Contact. E-mail: terrehaute@ibcschools.edu
Phone: (812) 877-2100 Toll-free number: (800) 422-4723
Fax: (812) 877-4440
Sarah Stultz, Regional Director, Indiana Business College: Terre Haute, 1378 South State Road 46, Terre Haute, IN 47803

International Business College: Indianapolis

Indianapolis, Indiana
www.intlbusinesscollege.com **CB code: 3374**

- For-profit 2-year business college
- Commuter campus in very large city

General. Accredited by ACICS. **Calendar:** Continuous.

Annual costs/financial aid. Tuition/fees (2008-2009): $12,960. Room: $6,320. Books/supplies: $1,400.

Contact. Phone: (317) 841-6400
7205 Shadeland Station, Indianapolis, IN 46256

ITT Technical Institute: Newburgh
Newburgh, Indiana

- For-profit 2-year business and technical college
- Small town

General. Accredited by ACICS. **Calendar:** Quarter.

Contact. 10999 Stahl Road, Newburgh, IN 47630

Ivy Tech Community College: Bloomington
Bloomington, Indiana
www.ivytech.edu **CB code: 1455**

- Public 2-year community college
- Commuter campus in small city

General. Enrollment: 5,136 degree-seeking undergraduates; 487 non-degree-seeking students. **Degrees:** 339 associate awarded. **Calendar:** Semester, extensive summer session. **Full-time faculty:** 62 total. **Part-time faculty:** 277 total.

Student profile. Among degree-seeking undergraduates, 70% enrolled in a transfer program, 30% enrolled in a vocational program, 1,283 enrolled as first-time, first-year students, 174 transferred in from other institutions.

Part-time:	48%	**Asian American:**	1%
Out-of-state:	1%	**Hispanic American:**	1%
Women:	59%	**25 or older:**	38%
African American:	4%		

Transfer out. Colleges most students transferred to 2008: Indiana University-Bloomington.

Basis for selection. Open admission, but selective for some programs. Special requirements for human services and health technology programs based on test scores and prior academic work.

2008-2009 Annual costs. Tuition/fees: $2,930; $5,879 out-of-state. Per-credit charge: $95 in-state; $193 out-of-state. Out-of-state distance education tuition: $124 per credit hour ($3,731 for academic year).

2007-2008 Financial aid. Need-based: Need-based aid available for part-time students. Work-study available nights and for part-time students.

Application procedures. Admission: No deadline. No application fee. Admission notification on a rolling basis. Application closing date for international students at least 60 days prior to start of semester. **Financial aid:** Priority date 3/1; no closing date. FAFSA required. Applicants notified on a rolling basis starting 7/1.

Academics. Special study options: Distance learning, dual enrollment of high school students, internships, liberal arts/career combination, teacher certification program, weekend college. License preparation in nursing. **Credit/placement by examination:** AP, CLEP, institutional tests. 45 credit hours maximum toward associate degree. 15 credits must be earned in residence. **Support services:** Learning center, reduced course load, remedial instruction, tutoring.

Majors. Biology: Biotechnology. **Business:** Accounting technology, business admin, executive assistant, hospitality admin. **Computer sciences:** General, information technology. **Construction:** Electrician, maintenance, plumbing. **Education:** General, early childhood. **Engineering technology:** Drafting, electrical. **Health:** EMT paramedic, medical radiologic technology/radiation therapy, medical records technology, mental health services, nursing (RN), respiratory therapy technology. **Legal studies:** Paralegal. **Liberal arts:** Arts/sciences, library assistant. **Mechanic/repair:** General, heating/ac/refrig. **Parks/recreation:** Exercise sciences. **Production:** Cabinetmaking/millwright, machine tool, sheet metal, tool and die. **Protective services:** Criminal justice. **Other:** Manufacturing and industrial technology, Mold and die, Stationary power plant operator.

Most popular majors. Business/marketing 32%, computer/information sciences 7%, engineering/engineering technologies 12%, health sciences 22%, liberal arts 10%.

Computing on campus. 884 workstations in library, computer center. Online course registration, online library, helpline, repair service, student web hosting available.

Student life. Freshman orientation: Available. **Activities:** Student government, Phi Theta Kappa, College Democrats, student leadership academy, Christian Challenge, computer club, cultural awareness.

Student services. Adult student services, career counseling, student employment services, financial aid counseling, minority student services, placement for graduates, veterans' counselor. **Physically disabled:** Services for visually, speech, hearing impaired. **Transfer:** Transfer center, transfer adviser, college fairs on campus for students transferring to 4-year colleges.

Contact. E-mail: lhandy1@ivytech.edu
Phone: (812) 330-6023 Toll-free number: (800) 447-0700 ext. 6350
Fax: (812) 330-106
Lori Handy, Director of Enrollment Services, Ivy Tech Community College: Bloomington, 200 Daniels Way, Bloomington, IN 47404-1511

Ivy Tech Community College: Central Indiana
Indianapolis, Indiana
www.ivytech.edu **CB code: 1311**

- Public 2-year community college
- Commuter campus in very large city

General. Founded in 1966. Regionally accredited. Branch location at Lawrence. **Enrollment:** 15,795 degree-seeking undergraduates; 1,913 non-degree-seeking students. **Degrees:** 897 associate awarded. **Location:** 2 miles from downtown. **Calendar:** Semester, extensive summer session. **Full-time faculty:** 153 total. **Part-time faculty:** 440 total.

Student profile. Among degree-seeking undergraduates, 59% enrolled in a transfer program, 41% enrolled in a vocational program, 3,707 enrolled as first-time, first-year students, 610 transferred in from other institutions.

Part-time:	67%	**Asian American:**	2%
Women:	58%	**Hispanic American:**	3%
African American:	26%	**25 or older:**	46%

Transfer out. Colleges most students transferred to 2008: Indiana University-Purdue University Indianapolis, Vincennes University, Indiana University-Bloomington, Purdue University-West Lafayette, Ball State University.

Basis for selection. Open admission, but selective for some programs. Special requirements for human services and health technology programs based on test scores and prior academic work.

2008-2009 Annual costs. Tuition/fees: $2,930; $5,879 out-of-state. Per-credit charge: $95 in-state; $193 out-of-state. Out-of-state distance education tuition: $124 per credit hour ($3,731 for academic year).

2007-2008 Financial aid. Need-based: Need-based aid available for part-time students. Work-study available nights and for part-time students.

Application procedures. Admission: No deadline. No application fee. Admission notification on a rolling basis. Application closing date for undergraduate international students at least 60 days prior to start of semester. **Financial aid:** Priority date 3/1; no closing date. FAFSA required. Applicants notified on a rolling basis starting 7/1.

Academics. Special study options: Cooperative education, distance learning, dual enrollment of high school students, ESL, internships, liberal arts/career combination, teacher certification program, weekend college. License preparation in nursing, radiology. **Credit/placement by examination:** AP, CLEP, institutional tests. 45 credit hours maximum toward associate degree. 15 credits must be earned in residence. **Support services:** GED preparation and test center, learning center, reduced course load, remedial instruction, tutoring.

Majors. Biology: Biotechnology. **Business:** Accounting technology, business admin, executive assistant, hospitality admin, logistics. **Computer sciences:** General, information technology. **Construction:** Carpentry, electrician, glazier, maintenance, masonry, painting, pipefitting, plumbing. **Education:** General, early childhood. **Engineering technology:** Electrical, industrial, occupational safety, telecommunications. **Health:** EMT paramedic, medical assistant, medical radiologic technology/radiation therapy, medical records technology, mental health services, nursing (RN), respiratory therapy technology, surgical technology. **Legal studies:** Paralegal. **Liberal arts:** Arts/sciences, library assistant. **Mechanic/repair:** General, automotive, electronics/electrical, heating/ac/refrig, industrial electronics. **Personal/culinary services:**

Mortuary science. **Production:** Cabinetmaking/millwright, ironworking, machine shop technology, machine tool, sheet metal, tool and die. **Protective services:** Criminal justice, emergency management/homeland security. **Visual/performing arts:** Design. **Other:** Floorlayers, Stationary power plant operator.

Most popular majors. Business/marketing 21%, computer/information sciences 7%, engineering/engineering technologies 7%, health sciences 28%, trade and industry 19%.

Computing on campus. 1,599 workstations in library, computer center. Online course registration, online library, helpline, repair service, student web hosting, wireless network available.

Student life. **Freshman orientation:** Available. **Activities:** Student government, Phi Theta Kappa, accounting association, human service club, radiology technology club, student leadership academy, black student union, Veterans Association.

Student services. Adult student services, career counseling, student employment services, financial aid counseling, minority student services, placement for graduates, veterans' counselor. **Physically disabled:** Services for visually, speech, hearing impaired. **Transfer:** Transfer center, transfer adviser, college fairs on campus for students transferring to 4-year colleges.

Contact. E-mail: tfunk@ivytech.edu
Phone: (317) 921-4882 Toll-free number: (800) 732-1470
Fax: (317) 921-4753
Tracy Funk, Director of Admissions, Ivy Tech Community College: Central Indiana, 50 West Fall Creek Parkway North Drive, Indianapolis, IN 46208-5752

Ivy Tech Community College: Columbus

Columbus, Indiana
www.ivytech.edu **CB code: 1286**

- Public 2-year community college
- Commuter campus in large town

General. Founded in 1963. Regionally accredited. **Enrollment:** 3,174 degree-seeking undergraduates; 247 non-degree-seeking students. **Degrees:** 282 associate awarded. **Location:** 40 miles from Indianapolis. **Calendar:** Semester, extensive summer session. **Full-time faculty:** 45 total. **Part-time faculty:** 205 total. **Special facilities:** Visual communications gallery.

Student profile. Among degree-seeking undergraduates, 52% enrolled in a transfer program, 48% enrolled in a vocational program, 620 enrolled as first-time, first-year students, 110 transferred in from other institutions.

Part-time:	60%	**Asian American:**	1%
Out-of-state:	1%	**Hispanic American:**	2%
Women:	72%	**25 or older:**	52%
African American:	2%		

Transfer out. **Colleges most students transferred to 2008:** Indiana University-Purdue University Indianapolis, Indiana University-Bloomington, Purdue University, Vincennes University, Indiana State University.

Basis for selection. Open admission, but selective for some programs. Special requirements for human services and health technology programs based on test scores and prior academic work.

2008-2009 Annual costs. Tuition/fees: $2,930; $5,879 out-of-state. Per-credit charge: $95 in-state; $193 out-of-state. Out-of-state distance education tuition: $124 per credit hour ($3,731 for academic year).

2007-2008 Financial aid. **Need-based:** Need-based aid available for part-time students. Work-study available nights and for part-time students.

Application procedures. **Admission:** No deadline. No application fee. Admission notification on a rolling basis. Application closing date for international students at least 60 days prior to start of semester. **Financial aid:** Priority date 3/1; no closing date. FAFSA required. Applicants notified on a rolling basis starting 7/1.

Academics. **Special study options:** Distance learning, dual enrollment of high school students, internships, liberal arts/career combination, teacher certification program, weekend college. License preparation in dental hygiene, nursing, paramedic, radiology. **Credit/placement by examination:** AP, CLEP, institutional tests. 45 credit hours maximum toward associate degree. 15 credits must be earned in residence. **Support services:** Learning center, reduced course load, remedial instruction, tutoring.

Majors. **Agriculture:** General. **Business:** Accounting technology, business admin, executive assistant. **Computer sciences:** General, information technology. **Construction:** Maintenance, masonry. **Education:** General, early childhood. **Engineering technology:** Drafting, electrical. **Health:** EMT paramedic, medical assistant, medical radiologic technology/radiation therapy, mental health services, nursing (RN), ophthalmic technology, surgical technology. **Legal studies:** Paralegal. **Liberal arts:** Arts/sciences, library assistant. **Mechanic/repair:** Automotive, heating/ac/refrig. **Production:** Machine tool, tool and die. **Protective services:** Criminal justice. **Visual/performing arts:** Design, interior design. **Other:** Industrial millwright, Industrial plumber, Manufacturing and industrial technology, Stationary power plant operator.

Most popular majors. Business/marketing 9%, health sciences 73%.

Computing on campus. 524 workstations in library, computer center. Online course registration, online library, helpline, repair service, student web hosting available.

Student life. **Freshman orientation:** Available. **Activities:** Student government, student newspaper, Phi Theta Kappa, student leadership academy.

Student services. Adult student services, career counseling, student employment services, financial aid counseling, minority student services, placement for graduates, veterans' counselor. **Physically disabled:** Services for visually, speech, hearing impaired. **Transfer:** Transfer adviser, college fairs on campus for students transferring to 4-year colleges.

Contact. E-mail: nbagadio@ivytech.edu
Phone: (812) 374-5129 Toll-free number: (800) 922-4838
Fax: (812) 372-0311
Neil Bagadiong, Director of Admissions/Assistant Director of Student Affairs, Ivy Tech Community College: Columbus, 4475 Central Avenue, Columbus, IN 47203-1868

Ivy Tech Community College: East Central

Muncie, Indiana
www.ivytech.edu **CB code: 1279**

- Public 2-year community college
- Commuter campus in small city

General. Founded in 1968. Regionally accredited. Campuses also at Anderson and Marion. **Enrollment:** 6,702 degree-seeking undergraduates; 500 non-degree-seeking students. **Degrees:** 446 associate awarded. **Location:** 50 miles from Indianapolis. **Calendar:** Semester, extensive summer session. **Full-time faculty:** 96 total. **Part-time faculty:** 366 total.

Student profile. Among degree-seeking undergraduates, 60% enrolled in a transfer program, 40% enrolled in a vocational program, 1,455 enrolled as first-time, first-year students, 253 transferred in from other institutions.

Part-time:	52%	**Hispanic American:**	1%
Women:	67%	**25 or older:**	48%
African American:	8%		

Transfer out. **Colleges most students transferred to 2008:** Ball State University, Purdue University-West Lafayette, Indiana University-Kokomo.

Basis for selection. Open admission, but selective for some programs. Special requirements for human services and health technology programs based on test scores and prior academic work. **Adult students:** SAT/ACT scores not required.

2008-2009 Annual costs. Tuition/fees: $2,930; $5,879 out-of-state. Per-credit charge: $95 in-state; $193 out-of-state. Out-of-state distance education tuition: $124 per credit hour ($3,731 for academic year).

2007-2008 Financial aid. **Need-based:** Need-based aid available for part-time students. Work-study available nights and for part-time students. **Additional information:** Higher Education Aid (HEA), Child of Disabled/Deceased Veterans (CDV), Ivy Tech Scholarships (IVTC) and grants, vocational rehabilitation and veteran's assistance available. None require repayment.

Application procedures. **Admission:** No deadline. No application fee. Admission notification on a rolling basis. Application closing date for international students at least 60 days prior to start of semester. **Financial aid:** Priority date 3/1; no closing date. FAFSA required. Applicants notified on a rolling basis starting 7/1.

Academics. **Special study options:** Distance learning, dual enrollment of high school students, internships, liberal arts/career combination, teacher certification program, weekend college. License preparation in dental hygiene, nursing, physical therapy, radiology. **Credit/placement by examination:** AP, CLEP, institutional tests. 45 credit hours maximum toward associate degree. 15 credits must be earned in residence. **Support services:** GED preparation and test center, learning center, reduced course load, remedial instruction, tutoring.

Majors. Agriculture: General. **Business:** Accounting technology, business admin, executive assistant, hospitality admin. **Computer sciences:** General, information technology. **Construction:** Carpentry, electrician, maintenance, masonry, painting, pipefitting. **Education:** General, early childhood. **Engineering technology:** Drafting, electrical, occupational safety. **Health:** Medical assistant, medical radiologic technology/radiation therapy, mental health services, nursing (RN), physical therapy assistant, respiratory therapy technology, surgical technology. **Legal studies:** Paralegal. **Liberal arts:** Arts/sciences, library assistant. **Mechanic/repair:** Automotive, heating/ac/refrig. **Production:** Machine tool, tool and die. **Protective services:** Criminal justice. **Other:** Industrial millwright, Industrial plumber/pipefitter, Manufacturing and industrial technology, Stationary power plant operator.

Most popular majors. Business/marketing 21%, engineering/engineering technologies 8%, health sciences 50%.

Computing on campus. 1,481 workstations in library, computer center. Online course registration, online library, helpline, repair service, student web hosting available.

Student life. Freshman orientation: Available. **Activities:** Student government, Phi Theta Kappa, Skills USA-VICA, early childhood education club, human services club, student leadership academy.

Student services. Adult student services, career counseling, student employment services, financial aid counseling, minority student services, placement for graduates, veterans' counselor. **Physically disabled:** Services for visually, speech, hearing impaired. **Transfer:** Transfer center, transfer adviser, college fairs on campus for students transferring to 4-year colleges.

Contact. E-mail: csharp@ivytech.edu
Phone: (765) 289-2291 ext. 1479 Toll-free number: (800) 589-8324
Fax: (765) 289-2292 ext. 502
Corey Sharp, Director of Enrollment Management, Ivy Tech Community College: East Central, 4301 South Cowan Road, Muncie, IN 47302-9448

Ivy Tech Community College: Kokomo

Kokomo, Indiana
www.ivytech.edu **CB code: 1329**

- Public 2-year community college
- Commuter campus in large town

General. Founded in 1968. Regionally accredited. Campus also at Logansport. Branch location at Wabash. **Enrollment:** 3,905 degree-seeking undergraduates; 291 non-degree-seeking students. **Degrees:** 212 associate awarded. **Location:** 50 miles from Indianapolis. **Calendar:** Semester, extensive summer session. **Full-time faculty:** 67 total. **Part-time faculty:** 196 total.

Student profile. Among degree-seeking undergraduates, 52% enrolled in a transfer program, 48% enrolled in a vocational program, 702 enrolled as first-time, first-year students, 142 transferred in from other institutions.

Part-time:	63%	**Hispanic American:**	2%
Women:	69%	**Native American:**	1%
African American:	6%	**25 or older:**	58%

Transfer out. Colleges most students transferred to 2008: Indiana University-Kokomo, Purdue University-West Lafayette, Ball State University.

Basis for selection. Open admission, but selective for some programs. Special requirements for human services and health technology programs based on test scores and prior academic work.

2008-2009 Annual costs. Tuition/fees: $2,930; $5,879 out-of-state. Per-credit charge: $95 in-state; $193 out-of-state. Out-of-state distance education tuition: $124 per credit hour ($3,731 for academic year).

2007-2008 Financial aid. Need-based: Need-based aid available for part-time students. Work-study available nights and for part-time students.

Application procedures. Admission: No deadline. No application fee. Admission notification on a rolling basis. Application closing date for international students at least 60 days prior to start of semester. **Financial aid:** Priority date 3/1; no closing date. FAFSA required. Applicants notified on a rolling basis starting 7/1.

Academics. Special study options: Distance learning, dual enrollment of high school students, independent study, internships, liberal arts/career combination, teacher certification program, weekend college. License preparation in nursing, paramedic, physical therapy. **Credit/placement by examination:** AP, CLEP, institutional tests. 45 credit hours maximum toward associate degree. 15 credits must be earned in residence. **Support services:** Learning center, reduced course load, remedial instruction, tutoring.

Majors. Agriculture: General. **Business:** Accounting technology, business admin, executive assistant. **Communications:** General. **Computer sciences:** General, information technology. **Construction:** Electrician, maintenance, site management. **Education:** General, early childhood. **Engineering technology:** Drafting, occupational safety. **Health:** EMT paramedic, medical assistant, mental health services, nursing (RN), surgical technology. **Legal studies:** Paralegal. **Liberal arts:** Arts/sciences, library assistant. **Mechanic/repair:** Automotive, heating/ac/refrig. **Production:** Machine tool, tool and die. **Protective services:** Criminal justice. **Visual/performing arts:** Design. **Other:** Industrial millwright, Industrial plumber/pipefitter, Manufacturing and industrial technology, Stationary power plant operator.

Most popular majors. Business/marketing 14%, computer/information sciences 7%, engineering/engineering technologies 10%, health sciences 35%, security/protective services 7%, trade and industry 16%.

Computing on campus. 699 workstations in library, computer center. Online course registration, online library, helpline, repair service, student web hosting available.

Student life. Freshman orientation: Available. **Activities:** Student government, Phi Theta Kappa, student leadership academy, business administration student organization, professional and trade organization.

Student services. Adult student services, career counseling, student employment services, financial aid counseling, minority student services, placement for graduates, veterans' counselor. **Physically disabled:** Services for visually, speech, hearing impaired. **Transfer:** Transfer adviser, college fairs on campus for students transferring to 4-year colleges.

Contact. E-mail: sdillman@ivytech.edu
Phone: (765) 459-0561 ext. 318 Toll-free number: (800) 459-0561
Fax: (765) 454-5111
Suzanne Dillman, Director of Admissions, Ivy Tech Community College: Kokomo, 1815 East Morgan Street, Kokomo, IN 46903-1373

Ivy Tech Community College: Lafayette

Lafayette, Indiana
www.ivytech.edu **CB code: 1282**

- Public 2-year community college
- Commuter campus in large town

General. Founded in 1968. Regionally accredited. **Enrollment:** 5,563 degree-seeking undergraduates; 1,370 non-degree-seeking students. **Degrees:** 369 associate awarded. **Location:** 60 miles from Indianapolis. **Calendar:** Semester, extensive summer session. **Full-time faculty:** 84 total. **Part-time faculty:** 256 total. **Special facilities:** Multimedia laboratory.

Student profile. Among degree-seeking undergraduates, 47% enrolled in a transfer program, 53% enrolled in a vocational program, 1,180 enrolled as first-time, first-year students, 201 transferred in from other institutions.

Part-time:	49%	**Asian American:**	1%
Out-of-state:	1%	**Hispanic American:**	4%
Women:	57%	**Native American:**	1%
African American:	4%	**25 or older:**	38%

Transfer out. Colleges most students transferred to 2008: Purdue University-West Lafayette, Indiana University-Purdue University Indianapolis.

Basis for selection. Open admission, but selective for some programs. Special requirements for human services and health technology programs based on test scores and prior academic work. **Adult students:** SAT/ACT scores not required.

2008-2009 Annual costs. Tuition/fees: $2,930; $5,879 out-of-state. Per-credit charge: $95 in-state; $193 out-of-state. Out-of-state distance education tuition: $124 per credit hour ($3,731 for academic year).

2007-2008 Financial aid. Need-based: Need-based aid available for part-time students. Work-study available nights and for part-time students.

Application procedures. Admission: No deadline. No application fee. Admission notification on a rolling basis. Application closing date for international students at least 60 days prior to start of semester. **Financial aid:**

Priority date 3/1; no closing date. FAFSA required. Applicants notified on a rolling basis starting 7/1.

Academics. **Special study options:** Distance learning, dual enrollment of high school students, internships, liberal arts/career combination, teacher certification program, weekend college. License preparation in dental hygiene, nursing. **Credit/placement by examination:** AP, CLEP, institutional tests. 45 credit hours maximum toward associate degree. 15 credits must be earned in residence. **Support services:** Learning center, reduced course load, remedial instruction, tutoring.

Majors. **Agriculture:** General. **Biology:** Biotechnology. **Business:** Accounting technology, business admin, executive assistant. **Computer sciences:** General, information technology. **Construction:** Carpentry, electrician, lineworker, maintenance, masonry, painting. **Education:** General, early childhood. **Engineering technology:** Drafting, electrical. **Health:** Medical assistant, medical records technology, mental health services, nursing (RN), respiratory therapy technology, surgical technology. **Legal studies:** Paralegal. **Liberal arts:** Arts/sciences, library assistant. **Mechanic/repair:** Automotive, heating/ac/refrig. **Production:** Cabinetmaking/millwright, ironworking, machine tool, sheet metal, tool and die. **Protective services:** Criminal justice. **Other:** Industrial millwright, Industrial plumber, Manufacturing and industrial technology, Stationary power plant operator.

Most popular majors. Business/marketing 21%, computer/information sciences 6%, engineering/engineering technologies 9%, health sciences 31%, liberal arts 9%, security/protective services 7%, trade and industry 9%.

Computing on campus. 1,313 workstations in library, computer center. Online course registration, online library, helpline, repair service, student web hosting available.

Student life. **Freshman orientation:** Available. **Activities:** Student government, Phi Theta Kappa, American Chemical Society, Dental Assistant Society, Respiratory Care Society, student leadership academy, culture club.

Student services. Adult student services, career counseling, student employment services, financial aid counseling, minority student services, placement for graduates, veterans' counselor. **Physically disabled:** Services for visually, speech, hearing impaired. **Transfer:** Transfer center, transfer adviser for students transferring to 4-year colleges.

Contact. E-mail: jdoppelf@ivytech.edu
Phone: (765) 269-5200 Toll-free number: (800) 669-4882 ext. 5200
Fax: (765) 772-9293
Ivan Hernadez, Director of Admissions, Ivy Tech Community College: Lafayette, 3101 South Creasy Lane, Lafayette, IN 47905-6299

Ivy Tech Community College: North Central

South Bend, Indiana
www.ivytech.edu **CB code: 1280**

- Public 2-year community college
- Commuter campus in small city

General. Founded in 1968. Regionally accredited. Campuses also at Warsaw and Elkhart. **Enrollment:** 6,090 degree-seeking undergraduates; 669 non-degree-seeking students. **Degrees:** 300 associate awarded. **Location:** 100 miles from Chicago. **Calendar:** Semester, extensive summer session. **Full-time faculty:** 82 total. **Part-time faculty:** 232 total.

Student profile. Among degree-seeking undergraduates, 32% enrolled in a transfer program, 68% enrolled in a vocational program, 1,163 enrolled as first-time, first-year students, 637 transferred in from other institutions.

Part-time:	69%	**Asian American:**	1%
Women:	60%	**Hispanic American:**	6%
African American:	16%	**25 or older:**	56%

Transfer out. **Colleges most students transferred to 2008:** Indiana University-South Bend, Indiana University-Purdue University Fort Wayne, Purdue University-West Lafayette, Purdue University-North Central.

Basis for selection. Open admission, but selective for some programs. Special requirements for human services and health technology programs based on test scores and prior academic work. Comparative Guidance and Placement Program required for admission of allied health applicants. Interview required of allied health majors. Portfolio recommended for photographic technology and graphic arts technology majors.

High school preparation. Medical laboratory assistant program requires 1 chemistry and 1 algebra.

2008-2009 Annual costs. Tuition/fees: $2,930; $5,879 out-of-state. Per-credit charge: $95 in-state; $193 out-of-state. Out-of-state distance education tuition: $124 per credit hour ($3,731 for academic year).

2007-2008 Financial aid. **Need-based:** Need-based aid available for part-time students. Work-study available nights and for part-time students.

Application procedures. **Admission:** No deadline. No application fee. Admission notification on a rolling basis. **Financial aid:** Priority date 3/1; no closing date. FAFSA required. Applicants notified on a rolling basis starting 7/1.

Academics. Industrial training division offers customized courses and seminars to companies and corporations in surrounding community. **Special study options:** Distance learning, dual enrollment of high school students, ESL, internships, liberal arts/career combination, teacher certification program, weekend college. License preparation in nursing. **Credit/placement by examination:** AP, CLEP, institutional tests. 45 credit hours maximum toward associate degree. 15 credits must be earned in residence. **Support services:** Learning center, reduced course load, remedial instruction, tutoring.

Majors. **Agriculture:** General. **Biology:** Biotechnology. **Business:** Accounting technology, business admin, executive assistant, hospitality admin. **Computer sciences:** General, information technology. **Construction:** Carpentry, electrician, maintenance, masonry, painting, pipefitting, plumbing, roofing. **Education:** General, early childhood. **Engineering technology:** Drafting, electrical, occupational safety, telecommunications. **Health:** Clinical lab technology, EMT paramedic, medical assistant, medical radiologic technology/radiation therapy, mental health services, nursing (RN), respiratory therapy technology. **Legal studies:** Paralegal. **Liberal arts:** Arts/sciences, library assistant. **Mechanic/repair:** Automotive, heating/ac/refrig. **Production:** Cabinetmaking/millwright, ironworking, machine tool, sheet metal, tool and die. **Protective services:** Criminal justice. **Visual/performing arts:** Design, interior design. **Other:** Floorlayer, Industrial millwright, Manufacturing and Industrial Technology, Stationary power plant operator.

Most popular majors. Business/marketing 18%, engineering/engineering technologies 6%, health sciences 38%, trade and industry 18%, visual/performing arts 7%.

Computing on campus. 1,178 workstations in library, computer center. Online course registration, online library, helpline, repair service, student web hosting available.

Student life. **Freshman orientation:** Available. **Activities:** Student government, Phi Theta Kappa, student leadership academy, student ad club.

Student services. Adult student services, career counseling, student employment services, financial aid counseling, minority student services, placement for graduates, veterans' counselor. **Physically disabled:** Services for visually, speech, hearing impaired. **Transfer:** Transfer adviser, college fairs on campus for students transferring to 4-year colleges.

Contact. E-mail: jaustin@ivytech.edu
Phone: (574) 289-7001 Toll-free number: (888) 489-5463
Fax: (574) 236-7177
Pam Decker, Director of Admissions, Ivy Tech Community College: North Central, 220 Dean Johnson Boulevard, South Bend, IN 46601-3415

Ivy Tech Community College: Northeast

Fort Wayne, Indiana
www.ivytech.edu **CB code: 1278**

- Public 2-year community college
- Commuter campus in small city

General. Founded in 1963. Regionally accredited. **Enrollment:** 7,458 degree-seeking undergraduates; 1,031 non-degree-seeking students. **Degrees:** 514 associate awarded. **Location:** 120 miles from Indianapolis. **Calendar:** Semester, extensive summer session. **Full-time faculty:** 107 total. **Part-time faculty:** 316 total.

Student profile. Among degree-seeking undergraduates, 45% enrolled in a transfer program, 55% enrolled in a vocational program, 1,579 enrolled as first-time, first-year students, 346 transferred in from other institutions.

Part-time:	60%	**Asian American:**	1%
Out-of-state:	2%	**Hispanic American:**	4%
Women:	63%	**25 or older:**	49%
African American:	15%		

Transfer out. **Colleges most students transferred to 2008:** Indiana University, Purdue University-Ft. Wayne, Ball State University.

Basis for selection. Open admission, but selective for some programs. Special requirements for human services and health technology programs based on test scores and prior academic work.

2008-2009 Annual costs. Tuition/fees: $2,930; $5,879 out-of-state. Per-credit charge: $95 in-state; $193 out-of-state. Out-of-state distance education tuition: $124 per credit hour ($3,731 for academic year).

2007-2008 Financial aid. Need-based: Need-based aid available for part-time students. Work-study available nights and for part-time students.

Application procedures. Admission: No deadline. No application fee. Admission notification on a rolling basis. Application closing dates for international students at least 60 days prior to start of semester. **Financial aid:** Priority date 3/1; no closing date. FAFSA required. Applicants notified on a rolling basis starting 7/1.

Academics. Special study options: Distance learning, dual enrollment of high school students, ESL, internships, liberal arts/career combination, teacher certification program, weekend college. License preparation in nursing. **Credit/placement by examination:** AP, CLEP, institutional tests. 45 credit hours maximum toward associate degree. 15 credits must be completed in residence. **Support services:** GED preparation and test center, learning center, reduced course load, remedial instruction, tutoring.

Majors. Business: Accounting technology, business admin, executive assistant, hospitality admin. **Computer sciences:** General, information technology. **Construction:** Electrician, maintenance, masonry, painting, pipefitting, site management. **Education:** General, early childhood. **Engineering technology:** Drafting, occupational safety, telecommunications. **Health:** EMT paramedic, massage therapy, medical assistant, mental health services, nursing (RN), respiratory therapy technology. **Legal studies:** Paralegal. **Liberal arts:** Arts/sciences, library assistant. **Mechanic/repair:** Automotive, heating/ac/refrig. **Production:** Ironworking, machine tool, sheet metal, tool and die. **Protective services:** Criminal justice. **Other:** Construction technology, Industrial millwright, Manufacturing and industrial technology, Stationary power plant operator.

Most popular majors. Business/marketing 29%, engineering/engineering technologies 11%, health sciences 32%, trade and industry 12%.

Computing on campus. 1,511 workstations in library, computer center. Online course registration, online library, helpline, repair service, student web hosting available.

Student life. Freshman orientation: Available. **Activities:** Student government, student newspaper, Phi Theta Kappa, multi-cultural organization, Society of Manufacturing Engineers, student leadership academy, Association of Construction Technology Students.

Student services. Adult student services, career counseling, student employment services, financial aid counseling, minority student services, placement for graduates, veterans' counselor. **Physically disabled:** Services for visually, speech, hearing impaired. **Transfer:** Transfer center, transfer adviser, college fairs on campus for students transferring to 4-year colleges.

Contact. E-mail: sscheer@ivytech.edu
Phone: (260) 480-4221 Toll-free number: (800) 859-4882 ext. 4268
Fax: (260) 480-2053
Steve Scheer, Director of Admissions, Ivy Tech Community College: Northeast, 3800 North Anthony Boulevard, Fort Wayne, IN 46805-1489

Ivy Tech Community College: Northwest

Gary, Indiana
www.ivytech.edu **CB code: 1281**

- Public 2-year community college
- Commuter campus in small city

General. Founded in 1968. Regionally accredited. Campuses also at East Chicago, Valparaiso, and Michigan City. **Enrollment:** 5,701 degree-seeking undergraduates; 673 non-degree-seeking students. **Degrees:** 417 associate awarded. **Location:** 30 miles from Chicago. **Calendar:** Semester, extensive summer session. **Full-time faculty:** 94 total. **Part-time faculty:** 245 total.

Student profile. Among degree-seeking undergraduates, 49% enrolled in a transfer program, 51% enrolled in a vocational program, 1,205 enrolled as first-time, first-year students.

Part-time:	61%	**Asian American:**	1%
Women:	67%	**Hispanic American:**	10%
African American:	26%	**25 or older:**	55%

Transfer out. Colleges most students transferred to 2008: Purdue University- Calumet, Indiana University-Northwest, Purdue University-North Central.

Basis for selection. Open admission, but selective for some programs. Special requirements for human services and health technology programs based on test scores and prior academic work.

2008-2009 Annual costs. Tuition/fees: $2,930; $5,879 out-of-state. Per-credit charge: $95 in-state; $193 out-of-state. Out-of-state distance education tuition: $124 per credit hour ($3,731 for academic year).

2007-2008 Financial aid. Need-based: Need-based aid available for part-time students. Work-study available nights and for part-time students.

Application procedures. Admission: No deadline. No application fee. Admission notification on a rolling basis. Application closing date for international students at least 60 days prior to start of semester. **Financial aid:** Priority date 3/1; no closing date. FAFSA required. Applicants notified on a rolling basis starting 7/1.

Academics. Special study options: Distance learning, dual enrollment of high school students, internships, liberal arts/career combination, teacher certification program, weekend college. License preparation in nursing, physical therapy, real estate. **Credit/placement by examination:** AP, CLEP, institutional tests. 45 credit hours maximum toward associate degree. 15 credits must be earned in residence. **Support services:** Learning center, reduced course load, remedial instruction, tutoring.

Majors. Business: Accounting technology, administrative services, business admin, executive assistant, hospitality admin. **Computer sciences:** General, information technology. **Construction:** Carpentry, electrician, maintenance, masonry, painting, pipefitting, site management. **Education:** General, early childhood. **Engineering:** General. **Engineering technology:** Drafting, electrical, occupational safety, telecommunications. **Health:** EMT paramedic, medical assistant, medical radiologic technology/radiation therapy, mental health services, nursing (RN), physical therapy assistant, respiratory therapy technology, surgical technology. **Legal studies:** Paralegal. **Liberal arts:** Arts/sciences, library assistant. **Mechanic/repair:** General, automotive, heating/ac/refrig. **Personal/culinary services:** Mortuary science. **Production:** Cabinetmaking/millwright, ironworking, machine tool, sheet metal, tool and die. **Protective services:** Criminal justice. **Other:** Floorlayers, Manufacturing and industrial technology, Stationary power plant operator.

Most popular majors. Business/marketing 25%, computer/information sciences 8%, health sciences 35%, trade and industry 14%.

Computing on campus. 419 workstations in library, computer center. Online course registration, online library, helpline, repair service, student web hosting available.

Student life. Freshman orientation: Available. **Activities:** Student government, Phi Theta Kappa,computer club, business club, culinary arts club, medical assistants, mortuary science club, student leadership academy, early childhood development club, nursing club.

Student services. Adult student services, career counseling, student employment services, financial aid counseling, minority student services, placement for graduates, veterans' counselor. **Physically disabled:** Services for visually, speech, hearing impaired. **Transfer:** Transfer adviser, college fairs on campus for students transferring to 4-year colleges.

Contact. E-mail: tlewis@ivytech.edu
Phone: (219) 981-1111 ext. 2273 Toll-free number: (888) 489-5463
Fax: (219) 981-4415
Twilla Lewis, Associate Dean of Student Affairs, Ivy Tech Community College: Northwest, 1440 East 35th Avenue, Gary, IN 46409-1499

Ivy Tech Community College: Richmond

Richmond, Indiana
www.ivytech.edu **CB code: 1283**

- Public 2-year community college
- Commuter campus in large town

General. Founded in 1968. Regionally accredited. Branch location at Connersville. **Enrollment:** 2,457 degree-seeking undergraduates; 336 non-degree-seeking students. **Degrees:** 179 associate awarded. **Location:** 70 miles from Indianapolis; 45 miles from Dayton, Ohio. **Calendar:** Semester, extensive summer session. **Full-time faculty:** 37 total. **Part-time faculty:** 142 total. **Special facilities:** Student-operated restaurant.

Two-Year Colleges

Student profile. Among degree-seeking undergraduates, 26% enrolled in a transfer program, 74% enrolled in a vocational program, 400 enrolled as first-time, first-year students, 75 transferred in from other institutions.

Part-time:	64%	**African American:**	4%
Out-of-state:	2%	**25 or older:**	62%
Women:	72%		

Transfer out. Colleges most students transferred to 2008: Indiana University East, Purdue University-West Lafayette.

Basis for selection. Open admission, but selective for some programs. Special requirements for human services and health technology programs based on test scores and prior academic work.

2008-2009 Annual costs. Tuition/fees: $2,930; $5,879 out-of-state. Per-credit charge: $95 in-state; $193 out-of-state. Out-of-state distance education tuition: $124 per credit hour ($3,731 for academic year).

2007-2008 Financial aid. Need-based: Need-based aid available for part-time students. Work-study available nights and for part-time students.

Application procedures. Admission: No deadline. No application fee. Admission notification on a rolling basis. Application closing date for international students at least 60 days prior to start of semester. **Financial aid:** Priority date 3/1; no closing date. FAFSA required. Applicants notified on a rolling basis starting 7/1.

Academics. Special study options: Distance learning, dual enrollment of high school students, independent study, internships, liberal arts/career combination, teacher certification program, weekend college. License preparation in nursing. **Credit/placement by examination:** AP, CLEP, institutional tests. 45 credit hours maximum toward associate degree. 15 credits must be earned in residence. **Support services:** Learning center, reduced course load, remedial instruction, tutoring.

Majors. Agriculture: General. **Business:** Accounting technology, business admin, executive assistant. **Computer sciences:** General, information technology. **Construction:** Electrician, maintenance, plumbing. **Education:** General, early childhood. **Engineering technology:** Drafting, electrical, industrial. **Health:** EMT paramedic, medical assistant, medical radiologic technology/radiation therapy, mental health services, nursing (RN), respiratory therapy technology. **Legal studies:** Paralegal. **Liberal arts:** Arts/sciences, library assistant. **Mechanic/repair:** General, automotive, heating/ac/refrig. **Production:** Machine tool, sheet metal, tool and die. **Protective services:** Criminal justice. **Other:** Stationary power plant operator.

Most popular majors. Business/marketing 24%, computer/information sciences 8%, health sciences 41%, liberal arts 8%, trade and industry 6%.

Computing on campus. 857 workstations in library, computer center. Online course registration, online library, helpline, repair service, student web hosting available.

Student life. Freshman orientation: Available. **Activities:** Student government, Phi Theta Kappa, Business Professionals of America, student computer association, Student Chapter of the Institute of Management Accounts, Refrigeration service engineers society, student leadership academy, multicultural student organization.

Student services. Adult student services, career counseling, student employment services, financial aid counseling, minority student services, placement for graduates, veterans' counselor. **Physically disabled:** Services for visually, speech, hearing impaired. **Transfer:** Transfer adviser for students transferring to 4-year colleges.

Contact. E-mail: jplaster@ivytech.edu
Phone: (765) 966-2656 ext. 1212 Toll-free number: (800) 659-4562
Fax: (765) 962-8741
Jeff Plasterer, Director of Admissions, Ivy Tech Community College: Richmond, 2357 Chester Boulevard, Richmond, IN 47374-1298

Ivy Tech Community College: South Central

Sellersburg, Indiana
www.ivytech.edu **CB code: 1273**

- Public 2-year community college
- Commuter campus in small town

General. Founded in 1968. Regionally accredited. **Enrollment:** 3,826 degree-seeking undergraduates; 520 non-degree-seeking students. **Degrees:** 359 associate awarded. **Location:** 10 miles from Louisville, Kentucky. **Calendar:** Semester, extensive summer session. **Full-time faculty:** 55 total. **Part-time faculty:** 141 total.

Student profile. Among degree-seeking undergraduates, 36% enrolled in a transfer program, 64% enrolled in a vocational program, 883 enrolled as first-time, first-year students, 163 transferred in from other institutions.

Part-time:	64%	**African American:**	5%
Out-of-state:	6%	**Hispanic American:**	1%
Women:	53%	**25 or older:**	55%

Transfer out. Colleges most students transferred to 2008: Indiana University Southeast.

Basis for selection. Open admission, but selective for some programs. Special requirements for human services and health technology programs based on test scores and prior academic work. **Adult students:** SAT/ACT scores not required.

2008-2009 Annual costs. Tuition/fees: $2,930; $5,879 out-of-state. Per-credit charge: $95 in-state; $193 out-of-state. Out-of-state distance education tuition: $124 per credit hour ($3,731 for academic year).

2007-2008 Financial aid. Need-based: Need-based aid available for part-time students. Work-study available nights and for part-time students.

Application procedures. Admission: No deadline. No application fee. Admission notification on a rolling basis. Application closing date for international students at least 60 days prior to start of semester. **Financial aid:** Priority date 3/1; no closing date. FAFSA required. Applicants notified on a rolling basis starting 7/1.

Academics. Special study options: Cooperative education, distance learning, dual enrollment of high school students, internships, liberal arts/career combination, teacher certification program, weekend college. License preparation in nursing, real estate. **Credit/placement by examination:** AP, CLEP, institutional tests. 45 credit hours maximum toward associate degree. 15 credits must be earned in residence. **Support services:** GED preparation and test center, learning center, reduced course load, remedial instruction, tutoring.

Majors. Business: Accounting technology, business admin, executive assistant. **Computer sciences:** General, information technology. **Construction:** Electrician, maintenance, masonry, pipefitting. **Education:** General, early childhood. **Engineering technology:** Drafting, electrical, telecommunications. **Health:** Clinical lab technology, medical assistant, medical radiologic technology/radiation therapy, mental health services, nursing (RN), respiratory therapy technology. **Legal studies:** Paralegal. **Liberal arts:** Arts/sciences, library assistant. **Mechanic/repair:** Automotive, heating/ac/refrig. **Production:** Cabinetmaking/millwright, machine tool, sheet metal, tool and die. **Protective services:** Criminal justice. **Visual/performing arts:** Design. **Other:** Floorlayers, Industrial millwright, Industrial sheet metal, Manufacturing and industrial technology.

Most popular majors. Business/marketing 20%, computer/information sciences 6%, engineering/engineering technologies 15%, health sciences 39%, trade and industry 6%.

Computing on campus. 505 workstations in library, computer center. Online course registration, online library, helpline, repair service, student web hosting available.

Student life. Freshman orientation: Mandatory. **Activities:** Student government, student newspaper, Phi Theta Kappa, art club, Christian Student Fellowship, C.A.R.E. club, ASN club, Business Professionals of America, human services club, computer information club, student leadership academy.

Student services. Career counseling, student employment services, financial aid counseling, minority student services, placement for graduates, veterans' counselor. **Transfer:** Transfer center, transfer adviser, college fairs on campus for students transferring to 4-year colleges.

Contact. E-mail: pfawcett@ivytech.edu
Phone: (812) 246-3301 ext. 4136 Toll-free number: (800) 321-9021
Fax: (812) 246-9905
Pat Fawcett, Director of Enrollment Services, Ivy Tech Community College: South Central, 8204 Highway 311, Sellersburg, IN 47172-1897

Ivy Tech Community College: Southeast

Madison, Indiana
www.ivytech.edu **CB code: 1334**

- Public 2-year community college
- Commuter campus in large town

General. Founded in 1968. Regionally accredited. Branch in Lawrenceburg. **Enrollment:** 2,056 degree-seeking undergraduates; 323 non-degree-seeking students. **Degrees:** 177 associate awarded. **Location:** 46 miles from Columbus, Ohio; 88 miles from Indianapolis. **Calendar:** Semester, extensive summer session. **Full-time faculty:** 39 total. **Part-time faculty:** 122 total. **Special facilities:** Gaming training center in Aurora, Indiana.

Student profile. Among degree-seeking undergraduates, 51% enrolled in a transfer program, 49% enrolled in a vocational program, 414 enrolled as first-time, first-year students, 75 transferred in from other institutions.

Part-time:	55%	**African American:**	1%
Out-of-state:	1%	**Hispanic American:**	1%
Women:	74%	**25 or older:**	47%

Transfer out. Colleges most students transferred to 2008: Indiana University-Southeast.

Basis for selection. Open admission, but selective for some programs. Special requirements for human services and health technology programs based on test scores and prior academic work.

2008-2009 Annual costs. Tuition/fees: $2,930; $5,879 out-of-state. Per-credit charge: $95 in-state; $193 out-of-state. Out-of-state distance education tuition: $124 per credit hour ($3,731 for academic year).

2007-2008 Financial aid. Need-based: Need-based aid available for part-time students. Work-study available nights and for part-time students.

Application procedures. Admission: No deadline. No application fee. Admission notification on a rolling basis. Application closing date for international students at least 60 days prior to start of semester. **Financial aid:** Priority date 3/1; no closing date. FAFSA required. Applicants notified on a rolling basis starting 7/1.

Academics. Special study options: Distance learning, dual enrollment of high school students, internships, liberal arts/career combination, teacher certification program, weekend college. License preparation in nursing. **Credit/placement by examination:** AP, CLEP, institutional tests. 45 credit hours maximum toward associate degree. 15 credit hours must be earned in residence. **Support services:** Learning center, reduced course load, remedial instruction, tutoring.

Majors. Business: Accounting technology, business admin, executive assistant. **Computer sciences:** General, information technology. **Education:** General, early childhood. **Engineering technology:** Drafting, electrical. **Health:** Medical assistant, mental health services, nursing (RN). **Legal studies:** Paralegal. **Liberal arts:** Arts/sciences, library assistant. **Protective services:** Criminal justice. **Other:** Manufacturing and industrial technology.

Most popular majors. Business/marketing 27%, health sciences 57%.

Computing on campus. 710 workstations in library, computer center. Online course registration, online library, helpline, repair service, student web hosting available.

Student life. Freshman orientation: Available. **Activities:** Student government, Phi Theta Kappa, student leadership academy, computer club, fitness club.

Student services. Career counseling, student employment services, financial aid counseling, minority student services, placement for graduates, veterans' counselor. **Physically disabled:** Services for visually, speech, hearing impaired. **Transfer:** Transfer adviser, college fairs on campus for students transferring to 4-year colleges.

Contact. E-mail: chutcher@ivytech.edu
Phone: (812) 265-2580 ext. 4142 Toll-free number: (800) 403-2190
Fax: (812) 265-4028
Cindy Hutcherson, Assistant Director of Admission/Career Services, Ivy Tech Community College: Southeast, 590 Ivy Tech Drive, Madison, IN 47250-1881

Ivy Tech Community College: Southwest

Evansville, Indiana
www.ivytech.edu **CB code: 1277**

- Public 2-year community college
- Commuter campus in small city

General. Founded in 1968. Regionally accredited. Branch location at Tell City. **Enrollment:** 4,783 degree-seeking undergraduates; 812 non-degree-seeking students. **Degrees:** 400 associate awarded. **Location:** 180 miles from Indianapolis; 112 miles from Louisville, Kentucky. **Calendar:** Semester, extensive summer session. **Full-time faculty:** 77 total. **Part-time faculty:** 215 total. **Special facilities:** Plastics lab, computer integrated manufacturing lab.

Student profile. Among degree-seeking undergraduates, 36% enrolled in a transfer program, 64% enrolled in a vocational program, 806 enrolled as first-time, first-year students, 252 transferred in from other institutions.

Part-time:	59%	**African American:**	8%
Out-of-state:	2%	**Hispanic American:**	1%
Women:	57%	**25 or older:**	50%

Transfer out. Colleges most students transferred to 2008: University of Southern Indiana, Vincennes University, Indiana State University.

Basis for selection. Open admission, but selective for some programs. Special requirements for human services and health technology programs based on test scores and prior academic work.

2008-2009 Annual costs. Tuition/fees: $2,930; $5,879 out-of-state. Per-credit charge: $95 in-state; $193 out-of-state. Out-of-state distance education tuition: $124 per credit hour ($3,731 for academic year).

2007-2008 Financial aid. Need-based: Need-based aid available for part-time students. Work-study available nights and for part-time students.

Application procedures. Admission: No deadline. No application fee. Admission notification on a rolling basis. Application closing date for international students at least 60 days prior to start of semester. **Financial aid:** Priority date 3/1; no closing date. FAFSA required. Applicants notified on a rolling basis starting 7/1.

Academics. Special study options: Cooperative education, distance learning, dual enrollment of high school students, independent study, internships, liberal arts/career combination, teacher certification program, weekend college. License preparation in nursing, paramedic. **Credit/placement by examination:** AP, CLEP, institutional tests. 45 credit hours maximum toward associate degree. 15 credit hours must be earned in residence. **Support services:** Learning center, reduced course load, remedial instruction, tutoring.

Majors. Agriculture: General. **Biology:** Biotechnology. **Business:** Accounting technology, business admin, executive assistant, hospitality admin. **Computer sciences:** General, information technology. **Construction:** Carpentry, electrician, maintenance, masonry, painting, pipefitting, site management. **Education:** General, early childhood. **Engineering:** General. **Engineering technology:** Drafting, electrical, occupational safety, telecommunications. **Health:** EMT paramedic, medical assistant, mental health services, nursing (RN), surgical technology. **Legal studies:** Paralegal. **Liberal arts:** Arts/sciences, library assistant. **Mechanic/repair:** Automotive, heating/ac/refrig. **Production:** Boilermaking, cabinetmaking/millwright, ironworking, machine tool, sheet metal, tool and die. **Protective services:** Criminal justice. **Transportation:** Heavy/earthmoving equipment. **Visual/performing arts:** Design, interior design. **Other:** Heat frost and asbestos, Industrial millwight, Manufacturing and industrial technology, Stationary power plant operator.

Most popular majors. Business/marketing 25%, computer/information sciences 6%, engineering/engineering technologies 11%, health sciences 20%, trade and industry 17%, visual/performing arts 10%.

Computing on campus. 1,021 workstations in library, computer center. Online course registration, online library, helpline, repair service, student web hosting available.

Student life. Freshman orientation: Available. **Housing:** Housing available at University of Southern Indiana. **Activities:** Student government, Phi Theta Kappa, American Institute of Architectural Students, National Association of Industrial Technicians, International Association Of Administrative Professionals, human services club, student leadership academy, art and design club.

Student services. Adult student services, career counseling, student employment services, financial aid counseling, minority student services, placement for graduates, veterans' counselor. **Physically disabled:** Services for visually, speech, hearing impaired. **Transfer:** Transfer adviser, college fairs on campus for students transferring to 4-year colleges.

Contact. E-mail: ajohnson@ivytech.edu
Phone: (812) 429-1430 Toll-free number: (888) 489-5463
Fax: (812) 429-9878
Denise Johnson-Kincaid, Director of Admissions, Ivy Tech Community College: Southwest, 3501 First Avenue, Evansville, IN 47710-3398

Ivy Tech Community College: Wabash Valley

Terre Haute, Indiana
www.ivytech.edu **CB code: 1284**

- Public 2-year community college
- Commuter campus in small city

General. Founded in 1966. Regionally accredited. Branch location at Greencastle. **Enrollment:** 5,084 degree-seeking undergraduates; 767 non-degree-seeking students. **Degrees:** 486 associate awarded. **Location:** 80 miles from Indianapolis. **Calendar:** Semester, extensive summer session. **Full-time faculty:** 88 total. **Part-time faculty:** 199 total. **Special facilities:** Plastics productivity center.

Student profile. Among degree-seeking undergraduates, 45% enrolled in a transfer program, 55% enrolled in a vocational program, 857 enrolled as first-time, first-year students, 215 transferred in from other institutions.

Part-time:	55%	**Hispanic American:**	1%
Out-of-state:	4%	**Native American:**	1%
Women:	60%	**25 or older:**	50%
African American:	4%		

Transfer out. Colleges most students transferred to 2008: Indiana State University, Vincennes University, Purdue University-West Lafayette.

Basis for selection. Open admission, but selective for some programs. Special requirements for human services and health technology programs based on test scores and prior academic work.

2008-2009 Annual costs. Tuition/fees: $2,930; $5,879 out-of-state. Per-credit charge: $95 in-state; $193 out-of-state. Out-of-state distance education tuition: $124 per credit hour ($3,731 for academic year).

2007-2008 Financial aid. Need-based: Need-based aid available for part-time students. Work-study available nights and for part-time students.

Application procedures. Admission: No deadline. No application fee. Admission notification on a rolling basis. Application closing date for international students is at least 60 days prior to start of semester. **Financial aid:** Priority date 3/1; no closing date. FAFSA required. Applicants notified on a rolling basis starting 7/1.

Academics. Special study options: Distance learning, dual enrollment of high school students, internships, liberal arts/career combination, teacher certification program, weekend college. License preparation in aviation, nursing, paramedic, radiology. **Credit/placement by examination:** AP, CLEP, institutional tests. 45 credit hours maximum toward associate degree. 15 credits must be earned in residence. **Support services:** Learning center, reduced course load, remedial instruction, tutoring.

Majors. Agriculture: General. **Biology:** Biotechnology. **Business:** Accounting technology, business admin, executive assistant. **Computer sciences:** General, information technology. **Construction:** Carpentry, electrician, maintenance, masonry, painting, pipefitting. **Education:** General, early childhood. **Engineering technology:** Drafting, electrical, occupational safety. **Health:** Clinical lab technology, EMT paramedic, medical assistant, medical radiologic technology/radiation therapy, mental health services, nursing (RN), respiratory therapy technology, surgical technology. **Legal studies:** Paralegal. **Liberal arts:** Arts/sciences, library assistant. **Mechanic/repair:** Automotive, heating/ac/refrig. **Production:** Ironworking, machine tool, sheet metal, tool and die. **Protective services:** Criminal justice. **Transportation:** Heavy/earthmoving equipment. **Visual/performing arts:** Design. **Other:** Industrial millwright, Industrial plumber/pipefitter, Manufacturing and industrial technology, Stationary power plant operator.

Most popular majors. Business/marketing 16%, health sciences 41%, trade and industry 16%.

Computing on campus. 1,589 workstations in library, computer center. Online course registration, online library, helpline, repair service, student web hosting, wireless network available.

Student life. Freshman orientation: Available. **Activities:** Student government, Phi Theta Kappa, student leadership academy, practical nurses class organization.

Student services. Adult student services, career counseling, student employment services, financial aid counseling, minority student services, on-campus daycare, placement for graduates, veterans' counselor. **Physically disabled:** Services for visually, speech, hearing impaired. **Transfer:** Transfer center, transfer adviser, college fairs on campus for students transferring to 4-year colleges.

Contact. E-mail: mfisher@ivytech.edu
Phone: (812) 298-2300 Toll-free number: (800) 377-4882
Fax: (812) 299-5723
Michael Fisher, Director of Admissions, Ivy Tech Community College: Wabash Valley, 8000 South Education Drive, Terre Haute, IN 47802-4898

Kaplan College: Hammond

Hammond, Indiana
www.kaplan.com **CB code: 2461**

- For-profit 2-year business and technical college
- Commuter campus in small city

General. Founded in 1969. Accredited by ACICS. **Location:** 30 miles from Chicago, 15 miles from Merrillville. **Calendar:** Quarter.

Annual costs/financial aid. Tuition/fees (2008-2009): $10,200.

Contact. Phone: (219) 844-0100
Admissions Director, 7833 Indianapolis Boulevard, Hammond, IN 46324

Kaplan College: Indianapolis

Indianapolis, Indiana
www.kcindy.com **CB code: 7700**

- For-profit 2-year business and health science college
- Commuter campus in very large city

General. Accredited by ACCSCT. **Calendar:** Continuous.

Annual costs/financial aid. Books/supplies: $500. Personal expenses: $1,472. Need-based financial aid available for full-time students.

Contact. Phone: (317) 299-6001
Director of Admissions, 7302 Woodland Drive, Indianapolis, IN 46278-1736

Kaplan College: Merrillville

Merrillville, Indiana
www.sawyercollege.edu **CB code: 3381**

- For-profit 2-year technical college
- Commuter campus in large town
- Interview required

General. Accredited by ACICS. **Enrollment:** 390 degree-seeking undergraduates. **Degrees:** 80 associate awarded. **Location:** 35 miles from Chicago. **Calendar:** Quarter. **Full-time faculty:** 12 total.

Basis for selection. Open admission. **Homeschooled:** State high school equivalency certificate required.

2008-2009 Annual costs. Tuition/fees: $12,316. Books/supplies: $1,324.

Financial aid. Need-based: Need-based aid available for part-time students.

Application procedures. Admission: No deadline. $20 fee. Admission notification on a rolling basis. **Financial aid:** No deadline. FAFSA required. Applicants notified on a rolling basis.

Academics. Special study options: Liberal arts/career combination. **Credit/placement by examination:** CLEP. 50 credit hours maximum toward associate degree. **Support services:** Reduced course load, study skills assistance, tutoring.

Majors. Health: Massage therapy, medical assistant, office admin. **Other:** Computer business specialist.

Computing on campus. 72 workstations in library, computer center. Online library available.

Student life. Freshman orientation: Mandatory. Preregistration for classes offered.

Student services. Adult student services, career counseling, student employment services, financial aid counseling, placement for graduates. **Transfer:** Pre-admission transcript evaluation for new students.

Contact. Phone: (219) 736-0436 Toll-free number: (800) 964-0218
Fax: (219) 942-3762
Sonya Vance-Brown, Director of Admissions, Kaplan College: Merrillville, 3803 East Lincoln Highway, Merrillville, IN 46410

Lincoln College of Technology: Indianapolis

Indianapolis, Indiana
www.lincolntech.com **CB code: 3058**

- For-profit 2-year technical college
- Very large city

General. Accredited by ACCSCT. **Calendar:** Continuous.

Annual costs/financial aid. Cost for entire AAS diesel & truck service management program $28,385. Other program costs vary. Books/supplies: $1,815.

Contact. Phone: (317) 632-5553
7225 Winton Drive, Building 128, Indianapolis, IN 46268

Mid-America College of Funeral Service

Jeffersonville, Indiana
www.mid-america.edu **CB code: 0644**

- Private 2-year school of mortuary science
- Commuter campus in large town

General. Founded in 1905. **Enrollment:** 48 degree-seeking undergraduates. **Degrees:** 33 associate awarded. **Location:** 5 miles from Louisville, Kentucky. **Calendar:** Quarter. **Full-time faculty:** 8 total.

Basis for selection. Open admission. **Homeschooled:** Transcript of courses and grades required.

2008-2009 Annual costs. Tuition/fees: $9,000. Cost of AAS degree program (including tuition, books, fees) $22,400. Personal expenses: $2,520.

Application procedures. Admission: No deadline. $50 fee. Admission notification on a rolling basis. **Financial aid:** No deadline. FAFSA required. Applicants notified on a rolling basis.

Academics. Credit/placement by examination: CLEP.

Majors. Personal/culinary services: Mortuary science.

Computing on campus. 15 workstations in library, computer center.

Student life. Activities: Student government.

Student services. Student employment services, personal counseling, placement for graduates. **Transfer:** Pre-admission transcript evaluation for new students.

Contact. E-mail: macfs@mindspring.com
Phone: (812) 288-8878 Fax: (812) 288-5942
Cathy Denison, Director of Admissions, Mid-America College of Funeral Service, 3111 Hamburg Pike, Jeffersonville, IN 47130

National College: Indianapolis

Indianapolis, Indiana

- For-profit 2-year branch campus college
- Very large city

General. Regionally accredited; also accredited by ACICS. **Enrollment:** 314 degree-seeking undergraduates. **Degrees:** 28 associate awarded. **Calendar:** Quarter. **Full-time faculty:** 5 total. **Part-time faculty:** 33 total.

Basis for selection. Open admission.

2008-2009 Annual costs. Tuition/fees: $9,585. Per-credit charge: $212.

Application procedures. Admission: No deadline. $30 fee.

Academics. Credit/placement by examination: CLEP.

Majors. Business: Accounting/business management, administrative services, business admin. **Engineering technology:** Computer systems. **Health:** Medical assistant, medical records technology, pharmacy assistant, surgical technology.

Contact. Phone: (317) 578-7353
Larry Steele, Vice President of Admissions, National College: Indianapolis, 6060 Castleway Drive West, Indianapolis, IN 46250

Vincennes University

Vincennes, Indiana **CB member**
www.vinu.edu **CB code: 1877**

- Public 2-year junior college
- Residential campus in large town

General. Founded in 1801. Regionally accredited. Additional campus in Jasper, Aviation Technology Center at Indianapolis International Airport, ASL program at Indiana School for the Deaf. **Enrollment:** 8,848 degree-seeking undergraduates; 2,741 non-degree-seeking students. **Degrees:** 26 bachelor's, 1,178 associate awarded. **ROTC:** Army, Air Force. **Location:** 120 miles from Indianapolis, 55 miles from Evansville. **Calendar:** Semester, extensive summer session. **Full-time faculty:** 320 total. **Part-time faculty:** 120 total. **Special facilities:** Two college-owned airports, performing arts center, center for applied technology.

Student profile. Among degree-seeking undergraduates, 22% enrolled in a transfer program, 55% enrolled in a vocational program, 3,248 enrolled as first-time, first-year students, 219 transferred in from other institutions.

Part-time:	42%	**Hispanic American:**	2%
Out-of-state:	36%	**International:**	1%
Women:	40%	**25 or older:**	36%
African American:	9%	**Live on campus:**	36%
Asian American:	1%		

Transfer out. Colleges most students transferred to 2008: Indiana University, Indiana State University, Purdue University, University of Southern Indiana, Ball State University.

Basis for selection. Open admission, but selective for some programs. Admission to health occupation programs based primarily on high school transcripts, test scores, school and community activities, special talents/skills. SAT or ACT (SAT preferred) required for health occupation programs. Audition required of music majors. Portfolio recommended for fine arts, commercial art, design majors. **Homeschooled:** Statement describing homeschool structure and mission, transcript of courses and grades required. **Learning Disabled:** Students needing special accommodations required to submit psychometric testing indicating diagnosis of specific disability, along with list of any special services required.

High school preparation. College-preparatory program recommended. Recommended units include English 4, mathematics 3, social studies 2, history 2, science 3 (laboratory 2) and foreign language 2.

2008-2009 Annual costs. Tuition/fees: $4,398; $10,126 out-of-state. Per-credit charge: $134 in-state; $325 out-of-state. Students from Crawford, Richland, Lawrence and Wabash counties in Illinois pay tuition of $209 per credit hour (including capital improvement and technology fees, not including student activity fee). Room/board: $7,036. Books/supplies: $980. Personal expenses: $900.

Financial aid. Need-based: Need-based aid available for part-time students. Work-study available nights, weekends and for part-time students. **Non-need-based:** Scholarships awarded for academics, art, athletics, leadership, music/drama, state residency.

Application procedures. Admission: No deadline. $20 fee, may be waived for applicants with need. Admission notification on a rolling basis. **Financial aid:** Priority date 3/1, closing date 5/1. FAFSA required. Applicants notified on a rolling basis starting 5/1; must reply by 8/24.

Academics. Free tutoring provided in most subjects. **Special study options:** Accelerated study, distance learning, dual enrollment of high school students, ESL, external degree, honors, independent study, internships, student-designed major, weekend college. Bachelor's degree programs available on campus. License preparation in aviation, dental hygiene, nursing, paramedic, physical therapy, real estate. **Credit/placement by examination:** AP, CLEP, IB, institutional tests. **Support services:** Learning center, pre-admission summer program, reduced course load, remedial instruction, study skills assistance, tutoring, writing center.

Honors college/program. 1100 SAT (exclusive of Writing), 25 ACT, leadership qualities, writing sample, 3 references. 20 students admitted for fall.

Majors. Agriculture: General, business, food processing, food science, horticulture. **Biology:** General, biochemistry, biotechnology. **Business:** General, accounting technology, administrative services, business admin, fashion, hospitality admin, hotel/motel admin, logistics. **Communications:** Journalism, photojournalism, public relations. **Communications technology:** Graphic/printing, radio/tv, recording arts. **Computer sciences:** General, computer science, networking, programming, webmaster. **Conservation:** General. **Construction:** General. **Education:** Art, business, chemistry, early childhood, elementary, English, family/consumer sciences, health, mathematics, music, physical, secondary, special, speech, teacher assistance, technology/industrial arts. **Engineering:** Agricultural, biomedical, chemical, civil, electrical, mechanical, surveying. **Engineering technology:** General, architectural drafting, electrical, manufacturing, mechanical drafting, mining, surveying. **Family/consumer sciences:** General, child care. **Foreign languages:** General, American Sign Language. **Health:** Art therapy, dietetics, EMT paramedic, environmental health, health care admin, massage therapy, medical radiologic technology/radiation therapy, medical records technology, nuclear medical technology, nursing (RN), pharmacy assistant, physical therapy assistant, predental, premedicine, prepharmacy, preveterinary, surgical technology. **History:** General. **Interdisciplinary:** Behavioral sciences, biological/physical sciences. **Legal studies:** Paralegal. **Liberal arts:** Arts/sciences. **Math:** General. **Mechanic/repair:** Auto body, automotive, diesel. **Parks/recreation:** Health/fitness, sports admin. **Personal/culinary services:** Chef training, cosmetic, mortuary science, restaurant/catering. **Philosophy/religion:** Philosophy. **Physical sciences:** Chemistry, geology, physics. **Production:** Tool and die. **Protective services:** Firefighting, police science, security management, security services. **Psychology:** General. **Public administration:** General, social work. **Social sciences:** General, anthropology, economics, geography, political science, sociology. **Transportation:** Airline/commercial pilot. **Visual/performing arts:** Art, commercial/advertising art, dramatic, music performance, theater design. **Other:** Assistive Technology, Computer/ Software Support Specialist, Construction Technology/Building Materials Marketing Option, Drafting and design/CAD, General Science/ Earth Sciences Concentration, Liberal Arts/Pre-Law Concentration, Multimedia Communications.

Computing on campus. 350 workstations in dormitories, library, computer center, student center. Dormitories wired for high-speed internet access and linked to campus network. Commuter students can connect to campus network. Online library, student web hosting, wireless network available.

Student life. Freshman orientation: Mandatory. Preregistration for classes offered. Held the weekend prior to first day of classes; includes study skills, social activities, parent orientation. **Housing:** Guaranteed on-campus for freshmen. Coed dorms, single-sex dorms, special housing for disabled, fraternity/sorority housing, wellness housing available. $150 partly refundable deposit. **Activities:** Bands, campus ministries, choral groups, dance, drama, international student organizations, literary magazine, music ensembles, musical theater, radio station, student government, student newspaper, TV station, Latter Day Saints, student government association, black male initiative, College Republicans, Christian Campus Fellowship, Democrat club, Women of Essence and Gospel Choir, Embracing Latino Heritage, Pride.

Athletics. NJCAA. **Intercollegiate:** Baseball M, basketball, bowling, cheerleading, cross-country, diving, golf M, tennis M, track and field, volleyball W. **Intramural:** Baseball M, basketball, bowling, cross-country, golf, gymnastics, handball, racquetball, skiing, softball, swimming, table tennis, tennis, track and field, volleyball, wrestling M. **Team name:** Trailblazers.

Student services. Adult student services, alcohol/substance abuse counseling, chaplain/spiritual director, career counseling, student employment services, financial aid counseling, health services, minority student services, on-campus daycare, personal counseling, placement for graduates, veterans' counselor. **Physically disabled:** Services for visually, hearing impaired. **Learning disabled:** Comprehensive services available. **Transfer:** Pre-admission transcript evaluation for new students. Transfer adviser for students transferring to 4-year colleges.

Contact. E-mail: vuadmit@vinu.edu
Phone: (812) 888-4313 Toll-free number: (800) 742-9198
Fax: (812) 888-5707
Christian Blome, Director of Admissions, Vincennes University, 1002 North First Street, Vincennes, IN 47591

Iowa

AIB College of Business
Des Moines, Iowa
www.aib.edu **CB code: 7302**

- Private 2-year business college
- Residential campus in large city

General. Founded in 1921. Regionally accredited. **Enrollment:** 975 degree-seeking undergraduates; 10 non-degree-seeking students. **Degrees:** 26 bachelor's, 239 associate awarded. **Location:** 2 miles from downtown. **Calendar:** Quarter, extensive summer session. **Full-time faculty:** 26 total; 12% have terminal degrees, 69% women. **Part-time faculty:** 49 total; 20% have terminal degrees, 51% women. **Class size:** 86% < 20, 14% 20-39. **Special facilities:** Dictation tape library, video collection, CISCO and Microsoft labs, voice captioning laptops.

Student profile. Among degree-seeking undergraduates, 1% already have a bachelor's degree or higher, 134 enrolled as first-time, first-year students.

Part-time:	42%	**Hispanic American:**	2%
Out-of-state:	5%	**Native American:**	1%
Women:	72%	**25 or older:**	21%
African American:	2%	**Live on campus:**	42%
Asian American:	2%		

Transfer out. Colleges most students transferred to 2008: Graceland College, Simpson College, Upper Iowa University.

Basis for selection. High school record important, test scores considered. SAT or ACT recommended. Institution's own test administered for students without ACT or for students with less than 18 ACT. **Adult students:** SAT/ACT scores not required if applicant over 24 or out of high school 5 years or more. **Homeschooled:** Transcript of courses and grades required.

2008-2009 Annual costs. Tuition/fees: $12,120. Per-credit charge: $220. Room only: $3,150. Books/supplies: $996. Personal expenses: $1,170.

2007-2008 Financial aid. Need-based: Need-based aid available for part-time students. Work-study available nights, weekends and for part-time students. **Non-need-based:** Scholarships awarded for academics, alumni affiliation, leadership.

Application procedures. Admission: Closing date 8/1 (receipt date). $25 fee, may be waived for applicants with need. Admission notification on a rolling basis beginning on or about 9/15. **Financial aid:** Priority date 4/1; no closing date. FAFSA, institutional form required. Applicants notified on a rolling basis starting 3/1; must reply within 2 week(s) of notification.

Academics. Real-time reporting program approved by National Court Reporters Association. Online bachelor's program available. **Special study options:** Cross-registration, distance learning, double major, dual enrollment of high school students, internships, liberal arts/career combination. Bachelor's degree programs available on campus. **Credit/placement by examination:** AP, CLEP, SAT, ACT, institutional tests. **Support services:** Reduced course load, remedial instruction, study skills assistance, tutoring.

Majors. Business: General, accounting, accounting/business management, accounting/finance, administrative services, business admin, marketing, office management, selling, tourism/travel. **Computer sciences:** Information technology. **Legal studies:** Court reporting. **Other:** Communications design/management.

Most popular majors. Business/marketing 19%, history 30%.

Computing on campus. 404 workstations in dormitories, library, student center. Dormitories wired for high-speed internet access and linked to campus network. Commuter students can connect to campus network. Online library, helpline, wireless network available.

Student life. Freshman orientation: Available. Five 1-day sessions held in late August for students and families. **Housing:** Coed dorms, special housing for disabled, apartments, fraternity/sorority housing available. $200 fully refundable deposit, deadline 5/1. Housing available for single-parents, married students, families. **Activities:** Campus ministries, student government.

Athletics. NJCAA. **Intercollegiate:** Basketball W, cheerleading, golf. **Intramural:** Badminton, basketball, bowling, football (non-tackle), golf, softball, table tennis, tennis, volleyball. **Team name:** Eagles.

Student services. Adult student services, alcohol/substance abuse counseling, career counseling, student employment services, financial aid counseling, health services, personal counseling, placement for graduates. **Physically disabled:** Services for visually, speech, hearing impaired. **Transfer:** Pre-admission transcript evaluation for new students. Transfer adviser for students transferring to 4-year colleges.

Contact. E-mail: admissions@aib.edu
Phone: (515) 246-5358 Toll-free number: (800) 444-1921
Fax: (515) 244-6773
Shirlee Krouch, Vice President of Enrollment, AIB College of Business, 2500 Fleur Drive, Des Moines, IA 50321-1799

Clinton Community College
Clinton, Iowa
www.eicc.edu **CB code: 6100**

- Public 2-year community college
- Commuter campus in large town

General. Founded in 1946. Regionally accredited. **Enrollment:** 990 degree-seeking undergraduates; 250 non-degree-seeking students. **Degrees:** 141 associate awarded. **Location:** 40 miles from Davenport. **Calendar:** Semester, limited summer session. **Full-time faculty:** 32 total; 6% minority, 44% women. **Part-time faculty:** 100 total; 2% minority, 58% women. **Class size:** 90% < 20, 9% 20-39, less than 1% 40-49.

Student profile. Among degree-seeking undergraduates, 73% enrolled in a transfer program, 27% enrolled in a vocational program, 1% already have a bachelor's degree or higher, 253 enrolled as first-time, first-year students, 11 transferred in from other institutions.

Part-time:	50%	**Hispanic American:**	2%
Out-of-state:	12%	**Native American:**	1%
Women:	67%	**International:**	1%
African American:	5%	**25 or older:**	35%

Transfer out. Colleges most students transferred to 2008: Ashford University, University of Iowa, Iowa State University, University of Northern Iowa, St. Ambrose University.

Basis for selection. Open admission, but selective for some programs. Special requirements for nursing program. Interview recommended.

2008-2009 Annual costs. Tuition/fees: $3,210; $4,815 out-of-state. Per-credit charge: $107 in-state; $161 out-of-state. Books/supplies: $1,140. Personal expenses: $1,090.

Application procedures. Admission: No deadline. No application fee. Admission notification on a rolling basis beginning on or about 9/1. **Financial aid:** Priority date 4/20; no closing date. FAFSA, institutional form required. Applicants notified on a rolling basis starting 5/15; must reply within 2 week(s) of notification.

Academics. Special study options: Accelerated study, cooperative education, cross-registration, distance learning, double major, dual enrollment of high school students, ESL, honors, independent study, study abroad, weekend college. License preparation in nursing, paramedic, real estate. **Credit/placement by examination:** AP, CLEP, institutional tests. 30 credit hours maximum toward associate degree. **Support services:** GED preparation and test center, learning center, reduced course load, remedial instruction, study skills assistance, tutoring.

Majors. Agriculture: Equine science. **Business:** Administrative services, business admin. **Communications technology:** Graphic/printing, graphics. **Computer sciences:** Applications programming. **Engineering technology:** Architectural drafting, drafting, electrical, environmental, manufacturing, occupational safety. **Health:** Dental hygiene, electroencephalograph technology, EMT paramedic, nuclear medical technology, nursing (RN), physical therapy assistant, radiologic technology/medical imaging, sonography. **Liberal arts:** Arts/sciences. **Personal/culinary services:** Restaurant/catering. **Protective services:** Firefighting, police science.

Most popular majors. Health sciences 11%, liberal arts 77%.

Computing on campus. 55 workstations in library, computer center. Commuter students can connect to campus network. Online course registration, helpline, wireless network available.

Student life. Freshman orientation: Available. Preregistration for classes offered. **Activities:** Drama, literary magazine, student government, student newspaper, Phi Beta Lambda, Phi Theta Kappa, student senate, peer ambassadors, drama/fine arts club, S.N.A.P., drafting club, nursing club, graphic arts/printer club, Leadership Connection.

Athletics. NJCAA. **Intercollegiate:** Basketball M, volleyball W. **Intramural:** Basketball, bowling, softball, table tennis, tennis, volleyball. **Team name:** Cougars.

Student services. Career counseling, student employment services, financial aid counseling, personal counseling, placement for graduates, veterans' counselor. **Physically disabled:** Services for visually, speech, hearing impaired. **Transfer:** Transfer adviser, college fairs on campus for students transferring to 4-year colleges.

Contact. E-mail: scarmody@eicc.edu
Phone: (888) 336-390 Toll-free number: (888) 336-3907
Fax: (563) 244-7107
Susan Carmody, Admissions Officer, Clinton Community College, 1000 Lincoln Boulevard, Clinton, IA 52732

Des Moines Area Community College

Ankeny, Iowa — **CB member**
www.dmacc.edu — **CB code: 6177**

- Public 2-year community college
- Commuter campus in large town

General. Founded in 1966. Regionally accredited. Multilocation institution with campuses at Boone, Des Moines, West Des Moines, Carroll, and Newton. Ankeny campus is primary location and administrative center. **Enrollment:** 13,443 degree-seeking undergraduates; 5,252 non-degree-seeking students. **Degrees:** 1,554 associate awarded. **Location:** 15 miles from downtown Des Moines, 25 miles from Ames. **Calendar:** Semester, extensive summer session. **Full-time faculty:** 330 total; 5% minority, 47% women. **Part-time faculty:** 5 total; 60% women. **Special facilities:** Wireless computer technology campus, career academies.

Student profile. Among degree-seeking undergraduates, 19% enrolled in a transfer program, 23% enrolled in a vocational program, 2% already have a bachelor's degree or higher, 3,199 enrolled as first-time, first-year students.

Part-time:	46%	**Hispanic American:**	4%
Women:	57%	**Native American:**	1%
African American:	7%	**International:**	1%
Asian American:	3%	**25 or older:**	24%

Transfer out. Colleges most students transferred to 2008: Iowa State University, Grand View College, University of Northern Iowa.

Basis for selection. Open admission, but selective for some programs. Special requirements for dental hygiene, commercial art, nursing, CAP programs. Interview required of dental hygiene, commercial art majors. Portfolio required of commercial art majors.

High school preparation. Recommended units include English 4, mathematics 3 and science 3.

2008-2009 Annual costs. Tuition/fees: $3,210; $6,420 out-of-state. Per-credit charge: $107 in-state; $214 out-of-state. Books/supplies: $1,000. Personal expenses: $1,646.

2007-2008 Financial aid. Need-based: 29% of total undergraduate aid awarded as scholarships/grants, 71% as loans/jobs. Need-based aid available for part-time students. Work-study available nights, weekends and for part-time students. **Non-need-based:** Scholarships awarded for academics, athletics, state residency.

Application procedures. Admission: No deadline. No application fee. Admission notification on a rolling basis. **Financial aid:** Priority date 4/1; no closing date. FAFSA required. Applicants notified on a rolling basis starting 4/1; must reply within 2 week(s) of notification.

Academics. Special study options: Cooperative education, cross-registration, distance learning, dual enrollment of high school students, ESL, honors, independent study, internships, liberal arts/career combination, study abroad, weekend college. Bachelor's degree programs available on campus. License preparation in dental hygiene, nursing, paramedic, real estate. **Credit/placement by examination:** AP, CLEP, institutional tests. 28 credit hours maximum toward associate degree. **Support services:** GED preparation and test center, learning center, pre-admission summer program, reduced course load, remedial instruction, study skills assistance, tutoring, writing center.

Majors. Agriculture: Horticulture, supplies. **Biology:** Biotechnology. **Business:** Accounting, accounting technology, apparel, business admin, hospitality admin, marketing, office management, sales/distribution. **Communications technology:** Desktop publishing. **Computer sciences:** Applications programming, information technology, networking. **Construction:** Carpentry. **Engineering:** Surveying. **Engineering technology:** Architectural drafting, civil, electrical, mechanical drafting. **Foreign languages:** Translation. **Health:** Clinical lab technology, dental hygiene, health care admin, medical secretary, nursing (RN), respiratory therapy technology, veterinary technology/assistant. **Legal studies:** Paralegal. **Liberal arts:** Arts/sciences. **Mechanic/repair:** Auto body, automotive, communications systems, diesel, heating/ac/refrig, industrial, industrial electronics. **Parks/recreation:** Sports admin. **Personal/culinary services:** Chef training. **Production:** Machine tool, tool and die, welding. **Protective services:** Fire safety technology, police science. **Public administration:** Community org/advocacy. **Visual/performing arts:** Commercial/advertising art.

Most popular majors. Business/marketing 14%, health sciences 12%, liberal arts 47%, trade and industry 8%.

Computing on campus. 200 workstations in library, computer center. Commuter students can connect to campus network. Online course registration, online library, helpline, wireless network available.

Student life. Freshman orientation: Available. Preregistration for classes offered. Half-day program offered. **Policies:** Student Action Board responsible for many on-campus professional and social activities. **Activities:** Choral groups, drama, literary magazine, student government, student newspaper.

Athletics. NJCAA. **Intercollegiate:** Baseball M, basketball, volleyball W. **Intramural:** Badminton, basketball, bowling, football (non-tackle), golf, softball, table tennis, tennis, volleyball. **Team name:** Bears (Boone campus only).

Student services. Adult student services, career counseling, student employment services, financial aid counseling, health services, on-campus daycare, personal counseling, placement for graduates, veterans' counselor. **Physically disabled:** Services for visually, speech, hearing impaired. **Transfer:** Transfer adviser, college fairs on campus for students transferring to 4-year colleges.

Contact. E-mail: admissions@dmacc.edu
Phone: (515) 964-6241 Toll-free number: (800) 362-2127 ext. 6241
Fax: (515) 964-6391
Michael Lentsch, Director of Enrollment Management, Des Moines Area Community College, 2006 South Ankeny Boulevard, Ankeny, IA 50023-3993

Ellsworth Community College

Iowa Falls, Iowa
www.iavalley.cc.ia.us/ecc — **CB code: 5528**

- Public 2-year community college
- Residential campus in small town

General. Founded in 1890. Regionally accredited. **Enrollment:** 1,106 degree-seeking undergraduates. **Degrees:** 163 associate awarded. **Location:** 70 miles from Des Moines. **Calendar:** Semester, limited summer session. **Full-time faculty:** 38 total. **Part-time faculty:** 46 total. **Special facilities:** 80-acre wildlife area.

Transfer out. Colleges most students transferred to 2008: University of Northern Iowa, Buena Vista University, Iowa State University, Wartburg College, University of Iowa.

Basis for selection. Open admission, but selective for some programs. Special requirements for some nursing programs.

2008-2009 Annual costs. Tuition/fees: $4,290; $5,190 out-of-state. Per-credit charge: $119 in-state; $149 out-of-state. Room/board: $4,852. Books/supplies: $700. Personal expenses: $1,400.

2007-2008 Financial aid. Need-based: Need-based aid available for part-time students. Work-study available nights, weekends and for part-time students. **Non-need-based:** Scholarships awarded for academics, art, athletics, leadership, minority status, music/drama.

Application procedures. Admission: No deadline. No application fee. Admission notification on a rolling basis. COMPASS required of applicants without SAT or ACT. **Financial aid:** Priority date 4/1; no closing date. FAFSA, institutional form required. Applicants notified on a rolling basis starting 2/15; must reply within 4 week(s) of notification.

Academics. **Special study options:** Cooperative education, cross-registration, distance learning, double major, dual enrollment of high school students, ESL, honors, independent study, internships, liberal arts/career combination. Bachelor's degree programs available on campus. License preparation in nursing. **Credit/placement by examination:** AP, CLEP, institutional tests. 24 credit hours maximum toward associate degree. **Support services:** GED preparation and test center, learning center, remedial instruction, study skills assistance, tutoring, writing center.

Majors. **Agriculture:** Business, equestrian studies, farm/ranch. **Biology:** General, biotechnology. **Business:** General, accounting, administrative services, fashion, insurance, office technology, office/clerical. **Communications:** General. **Computer sciences:** General, computer graphics, computer science, data processing, information systems, LAN/WAN management, programming. **Conservation:** General, wildlife. **Construction:** Carpentry. **Education:** General, agricultural, biology, business, chemistry, elementary, family/consumer sciences, history, mathematics, middle, multi-level teacher, physical, physics, science, secondary, social science, social studies, teacher assistance. **Engineering:** General. **Family/consumer sciences:** General, clothing/textiles, family/community services. **Health:** Athletic training, medical secretary, nursing (RN), predental, premedicine, prepharmacy, preveterinary. **History:** General. **Interdisciplinary:** Behavioral sciences, natural sciences. **Legal studies:** Legal secretary, prelaw. **Liberal arts:** Arts/sciences. **Math:** General. **Parks/recreation:** Health/fitness. **Physical sciences:** Chemistry, physics. **Protective services:** Criminal justice, law enforcement admin. **Psychology:** General. **Public administration:** Human services, social work. **Science technology:** Biological. **Social sciences:** General, criminology, sociology. **Visual/performing arts:** Art, commercial/advertising art, dramatic, studio arts.

Most popular majors. Business/marketing 10%, health sciences 10%, liberal arts 59%.

Computing on campus. 100 workstations in dormitories, library, computer center, student center. Dormitories wired for high-speed internet access and linked to campus network. Commuter students can connect to campus network. Online library, repair service, wireless network available.

Student life. **Freshman orientation:** Mandatory. Preregistration for classes offered. Various dates to chose from for orientation, advising, and preregistration. **Housing:** Guaranteed on-campus for freshmen. Single-sex dorms available. $200 deposit. **Activities:** Bands, choral groups, dance, drama, international student organizations, literary magazine, music ensembles, musical theater, student government, student newspaper, Young Democrats, Young Republicans, minority student organization, human services club, agricultural science club, criminal justice club.

Athletics. NJCAA. **Intercollegiate:** Baseball M, basketball, cross-country, football (tackle) M, golf, softball W, volleyball W, wrestling M. **Intramural:** Badminton, basketball, bowling, football (non-tackle), handball, racquetball, swimming, tennis, volleyball. **Team name:** Panthers.

Student services. Adult student services, alcohol/substance abuse counseling, career counseling, services for economically disadvantaged, student employment services, financial aid counseling, health services, personal counseling, placement for graduates, veterans' counselor. **Transfer:** Pre-admission transcript evaluation for new students. Transfer adviser, college fairs on campus for students transferring to 4-year colleges.

Contact. Phone: (641) 648-4611 ext. 431 Toll-free number: (800) 322-9253 Fax: (641) 648-3128
Annie Kalous, Director of Admissions, Ellsworth Community College, 1100 College Avenue, Iowa Falls, IA 50126

Hawkeye Community College
Waterloo, Iowa
www.hawkeyecollege.edu **CB code: 6288**

- Public 2-year community and technical college
- Commuter campus in small city

General. Founded in 1966. Regionally accredited. **Enrollment:** 4,086 degree-seeking undergraduates; 1,677 non-degree-seeking students. **Degrees:** 824 associate awarded. **ROTC:** Army, Naval, Air Force. **Location:** 120 miles from Des Moines; 90 miles from Cedar Rapids. **Calendar:** Semester, limited summer session. **Full-time faculty:** 125 total; 10% have terminal degrees, 4% minority. **Part-time faculty:** 162 total; 2% have terminal degrees, 5% minority.

Student profile. Among degree-seeking undergraduates, 1,286 enrolled as first-time, first-year students.

Part-time:	24%	**Asian American:**	1%
Out-of-state:	1%	**Hispanic American:**	2%
Women:	53%	**Native American:**	1%
African American:	7%	**25 or older:**	20%

Transfer out. **Colleges most students transferred to 2008:** University of Northern Iowa, University of Iowa, Iowa State University.

Basis for selection. Open admission, but selective for some programs. Selective admission to health, engineering and information systems programs. ACT required for admission to medical laboratory technician and dental hygiene programs. Specific placement scores may be required in reading, writing and math for selective programs. **Homeschooled:** Transcript of courses and grades required.

High school preparation. 1 year biology for nursing and medical laboratory technicians. 1 year chemistry for respiratory care and nursing. 2 semesters studio art and 1 computer course for graphic communications.

2008-2009 Annual costs. Tuition/fees: $4,050; $5,910 out-of-state. Per-credit charge: $124 in-state; $186 out-of-state. Books/supplies: $840. Personal expenses: $3,720.

2008-2009 Financial aid. **Need-based:** Work-study available nights, weekends and for part-time students. **Non-need-based:** Scholarships awarded for academics, state residency.

Application procedures. **Admission:** No deadline. No application fee. Admission notification on a rolling basis. Accepted students asked to pay first-semester tuition in August to confirm fall enrollment or enter into a tuition payment plan. **Financial aid:** Priority date 7/1; no closing date. FAFSA required. Applicants notified on a rolling basis starting 5/1; must reply within 2 week(s) of notification.

Academics. **Special study options:** Cooperative education, distance learning, dual enrollment of high school students, external degree, honors, independent study, internships, liberal arts/career combination, study abroad, weekend college. License preparation in dental hygiene, nursing. **Credit/placement by examination:** AP, CLEP, institutional tests. 30 credit hours maximum toward associate degree. **Support services:** GED preparation and test center, learning center, reduced course load, remedial instruction, study skills assistance, tutoring.

Majors. **Agriculture:** Animal husbandry, horticulture, power machinery, supplies. **Business:** Accounting, executive assistant, sales/distribution. **Communications technology:** Graphics. **Computer sciences:** General, networking, web page design. **Conservation:** Management/policy. **Engineering technology:** Architectural drafting, civil, electrical, manufacturing. **Health:** Clinical lab technology, dental hygiene, medical secretary, nursing (RN), respiratory therapy technology. **Liberal arts:** Arts/sciences. **Mechanic/repair:** Auto body, automotive, diesel. **Production:** Machine tool, tool and die. **Protective services:** Police science. **Visual/performing arts:** Commercial photography, interior design.

Most popular majors. Engineering/engineering technologies 6%, health sciences 16%, liberal arts 44%, trade and industry 8%.

Computing on campus. 300 workstations in library, computer center. Commuter students can connect to campus network. Online course registration available.

Student life. **Freshman orientation:** Available. Preregistration for classes offered. Held week before classes begin. **Activities:** Student government.

Athletics. **Intramural:** Basketball, bowling, football (non-tackle), soccer, softball, volleyball.

Student services. Career counseling, student employment services, financial aid counseling, on-campus daycare, personal counseling, placement for graduates, veterans' counselor. **Physically disabled:** Services for visually, hearing impaired. **Transfer:** Pre-admission transcript evaluation for new students. Transfer center, transfer adviser, college fairs on campus for students transferring to 4-year colleges.

Contact. E-mail: admission@hawkeyecollege.edu
Phone: (319) 296-4000 Toll-free number: (800) 670-4769 ext. 4000
Fax: (319) 296-4490
David Ball, Director of Admissions & Recruiting, Hawkeye Community College, Box 8015, Waterloo, IA 50704-8015

Two-Year Colleges

Indian Hills Community College
Ottumwa, Iowa
www.indianhills.edu **CB code: 6312**

- Public 2-year community and technical college
- Commuter campus in large town

General. Founded in 1966. Regionally accredited. **Enrollment:** 2,863 degree-seeking undergraduates; 1,366 non-degree-seeking students. **Degrees:** 828 associate awarded. **Location:** 90 miles from Des Moines. **Calendar:** Quarter, extensive summer session. **Full-time faculty:** 108 total; 7% have terminal degrees, less than 1% minority, 44% women. **Part-time faculty:** 122 total; 7% have terminal degrees, 2% minority, 56% women. **Class size:** 68% < 20, 26% 20-39, 4% 40-49, 3% 50-99, less than 1% >100. **Special facilities:** Wildlife sanctuary, outdoor stage, grotto.

Student profile. Among degree-seeking undergraduates, 56% enrolled in a transfer program, 41% enrolled in a vocational program, 2% already have a bachelor's degree or higher, 1,012 enrolled as first-time, first-year students, 177 transferred in from other institutions.

Part-time:	21%	**Hispanic American:**	3%
Out-of-state:	7%	**Native American:**	1%
Women:	57%	**International:**	1%
African American:	1%	**25 or older:**	28%
Asian American:	1%	**Live on campus:**	15%

Transfer out. Colleges most students transferred to 2008: Buena Vista, University of Northern Iowa, William Penn University, University of Iowa, Iowa State University.

Basis for selection. Open admission, but selective for some programs. GPA, any prior college credit, test scores considered for limited enrollment programs. ACT required for technology programs and for counseling. College Qualification Test required for some health occupation program applicants. **Homeschooled:** Transcript of courses and grades required.

High school preparation. Recommended units include English 2, mathematics 2, science 2 (laboratory 2).

2008-2009 Annual costs. Tuition/fees: $3,540; $5,310 out-of-state. Per-credit charge: $118 in-state; $177 out-of-state. Room/board: $5,175. Books/supplies: $675. Personal expenses: $750.

2007-2008 Financial aid. Need-based: Need-based aid available for part-time students. Work-study available nights, weekends and for part-time students. **Non-need-based:** Scholarships awarded for academics, athletics, state residency.

Application procedures. Admission: Priority date 7/1; no deadline. No application fee. Admission notification on a rolling basis. **Financial aid:** Priority date 4/1; no closing date. FAFSA, institutional form required. Applicants notified on a rolling basis starting 6/1; must reply within 2 week(s) of notification.

Academics. Special study options: Cooperative education, distance learning, dual enrollment of high school students, ESL, honors, independent study, internships, liberal arts/career combination. Bachelor's degree programs available on campus. License preparation in aviation, nursing, paramedic, physical therapy, radiology, real estate. **Credit/placement by examination:** AP, CLEP, institutional tests. 16 credit hours maximum toward associate degree. **Support services:** GED preparation and test center, learning center, pre-admission summer program, reduced course load, remedial instruction, study skills assistance, tutoring, writing center.

Majors. Agriculture: Production. **Business:** Business admin. **Computer sciences:** Applications programming, networking, security. **Construction:** General. **Engineering:** Agricultural. **Engineering technology:** Electrical, laser/optical, mechanical drafting, robotics. **Health:** Clinical lab technology, EMT paramedic, medical records technology, nursing (RN), physical therapy assistant, radiologic technology/medical imaging. **Liberal arts:** Arts/sciences. **Mechanic/repair:** Auto body, automotive, avionics, diesel. **Personal/culinary services:** Chef training. **Production:** Machine tool. **Protective services:** Police science. **Science technology:** Biological. **Transportation:** Airline/commercial pilot.

Most popular majors. Computer/information sciences 8%, health sciences 27%, liberal arts 44%, trade and industry 11%.

Computing on campus. 742 workstations in dormitories, library, computer center, student center. Commuter students can connect to campus network. Online course registration, online library, helpline, wireless network available.

Student life. Freshman orientation: Available. **Housing:** Coed dorms, single-sex dorms available. $200 fully refundable deposit. **Activities:** Jazz band, campus ministries, choral groups, dance, drama, music ensembles, musical theater, student government, student newspaper.

Athletics. NJCAA. **Intercollegiate:** Baseball M, basketball M, golf M, softball W, volleyball W. **Intramural:** Basketball, bowling, fencing, racquetball, softball, tennis, volleyball. **Team name:** Warriors.

Student services. Adult student services, career counseling, services for economically disadvantaged, student employment services, financial aid counseling, health services, on-campus daycare, personal counseling, placement for graduates, veterans' counselor. **Physically disabled:** Services for visually, hearing impaired. **Transfer:** Transfer adviser, college fairs on campus for students transferring to 4-year colleges.

Contact. E-mail: enrollment_services@ihcc.cc
Phone: (641) 683-5153 Toll-free number: (800) 726-2585 ext. 5153
Fax: (641) 683-5184
Jane Sapp, Admissions Officer, Indian Hills Community College, 623 Indian Hills Drive, Building 12, Ottumwa, IA 52501

Iowa Central Community College
Fort Dodge, Iowa
www.iowacentral.edu **CB code: 6217**

- Public 2-year community college
- Commuter campus in large town

General. Founded in 1966. Regionally accredited. Courses available at 2 branch campuses: Webster City and Storm Lake. **Enrollment:** 5,731 degree-seeking undergraduates. **Degrees:** 663 associate awarded. **Location:** 90 miles from Des Moines. **Calendar:** Semester, limited summer session. **Full-time faculty:** 77 total. **Part-time faculty:** 351 total. **Special facilities:** Broadcasting suite.

Student profile. Among degree-seeking undergraduates, 66% enrolled in a transfer program, 33% enrolled in a vocational program, 8% already have a bachelor's degree or higher.

Out-of-state:	5%	**Live on campus:**	25%

Transfer out. Colleges most students transferred to 2008: Buena Vista University, Iowa State University, University of Northern Iowa.

Basis for selection. Open admission, but selective for some programs.

2008-2009 Annual costs. Tuition/fees: $3,600; $5,235 out-of-state. Per-credit charge: $109 in-state; $164 out-of-state. Room/board: $4,850. Books/supplies: $850. Personal expenses: $1,550.

Financial aid. Need-based: Need-based aid available for part-time students. Work-study available nights, weekends and for part-time students. **Non-need-based:** Scholarships awarded for academics, art, athletics, leadership, music/drama.

Application procedures. Admission: No deadline. No application fee. Admission notification on a rolling basis. **Financial aid:** Priority date 3/8; no closing date. FAFSA required. Applicants notified on a rolling basis starting 4/15; must reply within 2 week(s) of notification.

Academics. Special study options: Accelerated study, cooperative education, cross-registration, distance learning, dual enrollment of high school students, external degree, independent study, internships, study abroad. 2 Plus 2 Agreements with Iowa State University and the University of Iowa, University of Iowa College of Nursing RN-BSN program. Bachelor's degree programs available on campus. License preparation in aviation, dental hygiene, nursing, paramedic, radiology. **Credit/placement by examination:** AP, CLEP. 30 credit hours maximum toward associate degree. ACT may be submitted for placement in lieu of COMPASS or ASSET. **Support services:** GED preparation and test center, learning center, pre-admission summer program, reduced course load, remedial instruction, study skills assistance, tutoring.

Majors. Agriculture: Agribusiness operations, turf management. **Business:** Accounting, administrative services, business admin, logistics, operations. **Communications technology:** General, desktop publishing, radio/tv. **Computer sciences:** Web page design, webmaster. **Construction:** General. **Engineering technology:** Electrical, energy systems, manufacturing. **Health:** Clinical lab technology, EMT paramedic, medical assistant, medical radiologic technology/radiation therapy, nursing (RN), occupational therapy assistant, physical therapy assistant, premedicine, prepharmacy, preveterinary, radiologic technology/medical imaging. **Legal studies:** Prelaw. **Liberal arts:** Arts/sciences. **Mechanic/repair:** Auto body, automotive, diesel, industrial electronics. **Personal/culinary services:** Cosmetic, culinary arts. **Production:** Machine tool. **Protective services:** Firefighting, police science. **Public administration:** Social work. **Science technology:** Chemical. **Transportation:** Aviation. **Other:** Industrial business.

Computing on campus. 500 workstations in library, computer center, student center. Dormitories wired for high-speed internet access and linked to campus network. Commuter students can connect to campus network. Online course registration, helpline available.

Student life. **Freshman orientation:** Mandatory. Preregistration for classes offered. **Housing:** Coed dorms, single-sex dorms, special housing for disabled, apartments available. $100 nonrefundable deposit. **Activities:** Bands, choral groups, dance, drama, music ensembles, musical theater, radio station, student government, student newspaper, symphony orchestra.

Athletics. NJCAA. **Intercollegiate:** Baseball M, basketball, cross-country, football (tackle) M, golf, rodeo, soccer, softball W, swimming, track and field, volleyball W, wrestling M. **Intramural:** Basketball, bowling, golf, volleyball. **Team name:** Tritons.

Student services. Career counseling, services for economically disadvantaged, student employment services, financial aid counseling, health services, minority student services, personal counseling, placement for graduates, veterans' counselor. **Physically disabled:** Services for visually, speech, hearing impaired. **Transfer:** Pre-admission transcript evaluation for new students. Transfer adviser, college fairs on campus for students transferring to 4-year colleges.

Contact. Phone: (515) 576-7201 ext. 1008 Toll-free number: (800) 362-2793 ext. 1008 Fax: (515) 576-7724
Samantha McClain, Director of Admissions, Iowa Central Community College, One Triton Circle, Fort Dodge, IA 50501

Iowa Lakes Community College

Estherville, Iowa
www.iowalakes.edu **CB code: 6196**

- Public 2-year community college
- Commuter campus in small town

General. Founded in 1967. Regionally accredited. 3 campuses with dormitories and food service operating in Emmetsburg, Estherville and Spencer. Classes also offered at campuses located in Algona and Spirit Lake. **Enrollment:** 1,973 degree-seeking undergraduates; 964 non-degree-seeking students. **Degrees:** 440 associate awarded. **Location:** 100 miles from Mason City; 100 miles from Sioux Falls, South Dakota. **Calendar:** Semester, limited summer session. **Full-time faculty:** 97 total; 46% women. **Part-time faculty:** 115 total; less than 1% minority, 70% women. **Special facilities:** 360-acre farm, print collection, wind turbine.

Student profile. Among degree-seeking undergraduates, 38% enrolled in a transfer program, 62% enrolled in a vocational program, 1% already have a bachelor's degree or higher, 736 enrolled as first-time, first-year students, 327 transferred in from other institutions.

Part-time:	21%	**25 or older:**	28%
Out-of-state:	11%	**Live on campus:**	17%
Women:	54%		

Transfer out. 11% of students enrolled in the transfer program go on to 4-year colleges. **Colleges most students transferred to 2008:** University of Northern Iowa, Iowa State University, University of Iowa, Minnesota State University-Mankato, Buena Vista University.

Basis for selection. Open admission, but selective for some programs. Special requirements for nursing, aviation/airport management, wind turbine technology, and computer-aided drafting and design programs. ACT required for nursing students. Interview required of career programs. Audition recommended for music majors. Portfolio recommended for advertising design majors.

2008-2009 Annual costs. Tuition/fees: $4,121; $4,181 out-of-state. Per-credit charge: $120 in-state; $122 out-of-state. Room/board: $4,600. Books/supplies: $600. Personal expenses: $500.

2008-2009 Financial aid. All financial aid based on need. Need-based aid available for part-time students.

Application procedures. **Admission:** No deadline. No application fee. Admission notification on a rolling basis. **Financial aid:** Priority date 4/22; no closing date. FAFSA, institutional form required. Applicants notified on a rolling basis starting 4/15.

Academics. **Special study options:** Cooperative education, cross-registration, distance learning, dual enrollment of high school students, ESL, honors, internships, liberal arts/career combination, weekend college. Evening college. License preparation in aviation, nursing, paramedic, real estate. **Credit/placement by examination:** CLEP, institutional tests. 30 credit hours maximum toward associate degree. **Support services:** GED preparation and test center, learning center, reduced course load, remedial instruction, study skills assistance, tutoring.

Majors. **Agriculture:** Landscaping, power machinery, production, supplies. **Business:** Accounting, business admin, hotel/motel admin, office management, restaurant/food services, sales/distribution, tourism promotion. **Communications:** Broadcast journalism, journalism. **Computer sciences:** Applications programming, networking. **Conservation:** Environmental studies. **Engineering:** Agricultural. **Engineering technology:** Drafting, energy systems, environmental, mechanical drafting. **Health:** EMT paramedic, health care admin, nursing (RN). **Legal studies:** Paralegal. **Liberal arts:** Arts/sciences. **Parks/recreation:** Facilities management. **Protective services:** Police science. **Social sciences:** Cartography. **Transportation:** Aviation. **Visual/performing arts:** Commercial/advertising art, photography. **Other:** Rehabilitation and therapeutic services.

Most popular majors. Agriculture 6%, business/marketing 10%, health sciences 19%, liberal arts 41%, trade and industry 7%.

Computing on campus. 800 workstations in library, computer center, student center. Dormitories wired for high-speed internet access. Online course registration, online library, helpline, repair service, wireless network available.

Student life. **Freshman orientation:** Mandatory. Preregistration for classes offered. **Housing:** Coed dorms, special housing for disabled, apartments available. **Activities:** Bands, choral groups, drama, international student organizations, literary magazine, music ensembles, musical theater, radio station, student government, student newspaper, TV station.

Athletics. NJCAA. **Intercollegiate:** Baseball M, basketball, cross-country, golf, soccer, softball W, track and field, volleyball W, wrestling M. **Intramural:** Basketball, bowling, racquetball, skiing, softball, table tennis, volleyball. **Team name:** Lakers.

Student services. Adult student services, alcohol/substance abuse counseling, career counseling, services for economically disadvantaged, financial aid counseling, personal counseling, placement for graduates, veterans' counselor, women's services. **Transfer:** Pre-admission transcript evaluation for new students. Transfer adviser, college fairs on campus for students transferring to 4-year colleges.

Contact. E-mail: info@iowalakes.edu
Phone: (712) 362-7946 Toll-free number: (800) 521-5054
Julie Carlson, Dean, Enrollment Management, Iowa Lakes Community College, 300 South 18th Street, Estherville, IA 51334-2725

Iowa Western Community College

Council Bluffs, Iowa
www.iwcc.edu **CB code: 6302**

- Public 2-year community and technical college
- Commuter campus in small city

General. Founded in 1966. Regionally accredited. Branch campus at Clarinda offers liberal arts and vocational programs in practical nursing, secretarial, mechanical technology, and electromechanical technology. Centers in Harlan and Atlantic offer evening programs in liberal arts and business administration. Practical nursing offered at Harlan. **Enrollment:** 3,897 degree-seeking undergraduates. **Degrees:** 615 associate awarded. **ROTC:** Army, Air Force. **Location:** 10 miles from Omaha. **Calendar:** Semester, extensive summer session. **Full-time faculty:** 136 total. **Part-time faculty:** 173 total.

Student profile.

Out-of-state:	10%	**Live on campus:**	21%

Transfer out. **Colleges most students transferred to 2008:** University of Iowa, Iowa State University, Northwest Missouri State University, University of Nebraska at Omaha, Buena Vista University.

Basis for selection. Open admission, but selective for some programs. Selective admission to nursing, dental hygiene, music, automotive technology and veterinary technology. Academic enrichment courses available to help gain proficiency needed for admission to specific programs. COMPASS or ACT/SAT required for placement. Interview required of vocational-technical applicants.

High school preparation. Specific subject requirements for some career programs.

2008-2009 Annual costs. Tuition/fees: $3,660; $5,325 out-of-state. Per-credit charge: $111 in-state; $167 out-of-state. Room/board: $5,910. Books/supplies: $800. Personal expenses: $1,440.

2007-2008 Financial aid. Need-based: 83% of total undergraduate aid awarded as scholarships/grants, 17% as loans/jobs. Need-based aid available for part-time students. **Non-need-based:** Scholarships awarded for athletics, music/drama.

Application procedures. Admission: No deadline. No application fee. Admission notification on a rolling basis. Applicants for limited-enrollment programs considered on first applied, first accepted basis. **Financial aid:** Priority date 7/1; no closing date. FAFSA required. Applicants notified on a rolling basis starting 3/1; must reply within 3 week(s) of notification.

Academics. Special study options: Cooperative education, distance learning, dual enrollment of high school students, ESL, independent study, internships, student-designed major. License preparation in aviation, dental hygiene, nursing, paramedic. **Credit/placement by examination:** CLEP, institutional tests. 40 credit hours maximum toward associate degree. **Support services:** GED preparation and test center, learning center, reduced course load, remedial instruction, study skills assistance, tutoring, writing center.

Majors. Agriculture: General, agribusiness operations, business. **Biology:** General. **Business:** Administrative services, sales/distribution. **Communications technology:** Graphic/printing. **Computer sciences:** Programming. **Education:** General. **Engineering technology:** Architectural, civil, electrical. **Family/consumer sciences:** Child care, institutional food production. **Foreign languages:** Sign language interpretation. **Health:** Dental hygiene, medical secretary, nursing (RN), substance abuse counseling. **Legal studies:** Legal secretary, paralegal. **Liberal arts:** Arts/sciences. **Math:** General. **Mechanic/repair:** General, aircraft. **Personal/culinary services:** Culinary arts. **Protective services:** Firefighting, forensics. **Psychology:** General. **Public administration:** Human services, social work.

Computing on campus. 250 workstations in dormitories, library, computer center, student center. Dormitories wired for high-speed internet access.

Student life. Freshman orientation: Mandatory. Preregistration for classes offered. **Housing:** Coed dorms, apartments available. **Activities:** Bands, choral groups, dance, drama, literary magazine, musical theater, radio station, student government, student newspaper, TV station, Christian Fellowship, special interest clubs, Phi Theta Kappa.

Athletics. NJCAA. **Intercollegiate:** Baseball M, basketball, softball W, volleyball W. **Intramural:** Basketball, bowling, football (non-tackle), softball, tennis, volleyball. **Team name:** Reivers.

Student services. Career counseling, services for economically disadvantaged, student employment services, financial aid counseling, health services, on-campus daycare, placement for graduates, veterans' counselor. **Physically disabled:** Services for visually, speech, hearing impaired. **Transfer:** Pre-admission transcript evaluation for new students. Transfer center, transfer adviser, college fairs on campus for students transferring to 4-year colleges.

Contact. E-mail: admissions@iwcc.edu
Phone: (712) 325-3277 Toll-free number: (800) 432-5852
Fax: (712) 325-3720
Chris LaFerla, Director of Admissions, Iowa Western Community College, 2700 College Road, Council Bluffs, IA 51502-3004

Kaplan University: Cedar Rapids

Cedar Rapids, Iowa
www.kucampus.edu **CB code: 3384**

- For-profit 2-year liberal arts college
- Commuter campus in small city
- Application essay, interview required

General. Regionally accredited. **Enrollment:** 572 degree-seeking undergraduates. **Degrees:** 62 bachelor's, 110 associate awarded. **Calendar:** Differs by program, extensive summer session. **Full-time faculty:** 15 total; 7% have terminal degrees, 7% minority, 67% women. **Part-time faculty:** 29 total; 10% have terminal degrees, 3% minority, 62% women. **Class size:** 49% < 20, 51% 20-39.

Student profile. Among degree-seeking undergraduates, 201 enrolled as first-time, first-year students.

Part-time:	34%	**25 or older:**	62%
Women:	80%		

Basis for selection. Open admission, but selective for some programs. All students must take WonderLic test on campus during initial interview. **Homeschooled:** State high school equivalency certificate required.

2008-2009 Annual costs. Tuition/fees: $14,075. Per-credit charge: $390. Cost is for 3 terms of 12 hours each. Tuition includes books and supplies; may vary by program.

2007-2008 Financial aid. Need-based: Need-based aid available for part-time students. Work-study available nights and weekends. **Non-need-based:** Scholarships awarded for academics.

Application procedures. Admission: No deadline. No application fee. Application must be submitted on paper. Admission notification on a rolling basis. **Financial aid:** Priority date 6/30; no closing date. FAFSA, institutional form required. Applicants notified on a rolling basis.

Academics. Special study options: Accelerated study, distance learning, honors, independent study, internships. Bachelor's degree programs available on campus. License preparation in nursing. **Credit/placement by examination:** AP, CLEP, institutional tests. Combined credit by examination and for life/work experiences shall not exceed 25% of program requirements. **Support services:** Learning center, remedial instruction, tutoring.

Majors. Business: Accounting, business admin. **Computer sciences:** Information technology. **Health:** Medical assistant. **Protective services:** Criminal justice.

Most popular majors. Business/marketing 19%, computer/information sciences 14%, health sciences 34%, security/protective services 19%.

Computing on campus. 207 workstations in library. Commuter students can connect to campus network. Online library available.

Student life. Freshman orientation: Mandatory.

Student services. Adult student services, career counseling, student employment services, financial aid counseling, placement for graduates. **Physically disabled:** Services for visually, hearing impaired. **Transfer:** Re-entry adviser for new students.

Contact. E-mail: nidonahue@hamiltonia.edu
Phone: (319) 363-0481 Toll-free number: (800) 728-0481
Fax: (319) 363-3812
Niki Donahue, Director of Admissions, Kaplan University: Cedar Rapids, 3165 Edgewood Parkway, SW, Cedar Rapids, IA 52404

Kirkwood Community College

Cedar Rapids, Iowa
www.kirkwood.edu **CB code: 6027**

- Public 2-year community college
- Commuter campus in small city

General. Founded in 1966. Regionally accredited. Off-campus sites in Iowa City, Vinton, Tipton, Williamsburg, Monticello, Washington, Belle Plaine, Marion, Cedar Rapids. **Enrollment:** 12,563 degree-seeking undergraduates; 2,678 non-degree-seeking students. **Degrees:** 1,920 associate awarded. **Location:** 128 miles from Des Moines. **Calendar:** Semester, extensive summer session. **Full-time faculty:** 281 total. **Part-time faculty:** 550 total. **Special facilities:** Telecommunications center, raptor center, equestrian center. **Partnerships:** Formal partnerships with CISCO LAN Management.

Student profile. Among degree-seeking undergraduates, 3,420 enrolled as first-time, first-year students.

Part-time:	36%	**Hispanic American:**	2%
Out-of-state:	2%	**Native American:**	1%
Women:	54%	**International:**	1%
African American:	5%	**25 or older:**	27%
Asian American:	2%		

Transfer out. Colleges most students transferred to 2008: University of Iowa, University of Northern Iowa, Iowa State University, Mount Mercy College, Coe College.

Basis for selection. Open admission, but selective for some programs. Some health science programs require minimum scores on COMPASS exam for admission to program. Interview required of vocational-technical, career option applicants.

2008-2009 Annual costs. Tuition/fees: $3,210; $3,960 out-of-state. Per-credit charge: $107 in-state; $132 out-of-state. Books/supplies: $1,410.

Financial aid. Need-based: Need-based aid available for part-time students. Work-study available nights, weekends and for part-time students. **Non-need-based:** Scholarships awarded for art, athletics, leadership, music/drama.

Application procedures. Admission: Priority date 3/15; no deadline. No application fee. Admission notification on a rolling basis. **Financial aid:** Priority date 7/1; no closing date. FAFSA required. Applicants notified on a rolling basis starting 4/1.

Academics. Special study options: Accelerated study, cooperative education, cross-registration, distance learning, dual enrollment of high school students, ESL, exchange student, external degree, honors, independent study, internships, liberal arts/career combination, student-designed major, study abroad, weekend college. License preparation in dental hygiene, nursing, paramedic, physical therapy, real estate. **Credit/placement by examination:** CLEP, IB, institutional tests. 21 credit hours maximum toward associate degree. **Support services:** GED preparation and test center, learning center, pre-admission summer program, reduced course load, remedial instruction, study skills assistance, tutoring, writing center.

Majors. Agriculture: Equestrian studies, nursery operations, supplies, turf management. **Biology:** Biotechnology. **Business:** Accounting, administrative services, business admin, fashion, finance, office technology, sales/distribution. **Communications technology:** General, graphic/printing. **Computer sciences:** Applications programming. **Conservation:** General. **Construction:** Maintenance, power transmission. **Engineering:** General. **Engineering technology:** Drafting, electrical, surveying. **Family/consumer sciences:** Child care, institutional food production. **Foreign languages:** Sign language interpretation. **Health:** Dental assistant, dental hygiene, dental lab technology, electroencephalograph technology, EMT ambulance attendant, EMT paramedic, medical assistant, medical records technology, medical secretary, nursing (RN), occupational therapy assistant, physical therapy assistant, respiratory therapy technology, surgical technology, veterinary technology/assistant. **Legal studies:** Legal secretary, paralegal. **Liberal arts:** Arts/sciences. **Mechanic/repair:** Automotive, diesel, electronics/electrical. **Personal/culinary services:** Culinary arts. **Protective services:** Fire services admin, firefighting, police science. **Public administration:** Community org/advocacy.

Computing on campus. 1,000 workstations in library, computer center, student center. Commuter students can connect to campus network. Online course registration, online library, helpline, wireless network available.

Student life. Freshman orientation: Available. Preregistration for classes offered. Various group sessions held throughout the year. Additional 2-day session held week before fall classes start. **Activities:** Bands, campus ministries, choral groups, drama, film society, literary magazine, music ensembles, musical theater, radio station, student government, student newspaper, symphony orchestra, TV station, over 50 organizations.

Athletics. NJCAA. **Intercollegiate:** Baseball M, basketball, golf M, softball W, volleyball W. **Intramural:** Basketball, cheerleading, handball, racquetball, soccer, volleyball. **Team name:** Eagles.

Student services. Adult student services, alcohol/substance abuse counseling, career counseling, services for economically disadvantaged, student employment services, financial aid counseling, health services, minority student services, on-campus daycare, personal counseling, placement for graduates, veterans' counselor. **Physically disabled:** Services for visually, speech, hearing impaired. **Learning disabled:** Comprehensive services available. **Transfer:** Pre-admission transcript evaluation for new students. Transfer center, transfer adviser, college fairs on campus for students transferring to 4-year colleges.

Contact. E-mail: info@kirkwood.edu
Phone: (319) 398-5517 Toll-free number: (800) 332-2055 ext. 5517
Fax: (319) 398-1244
Doug Bannon, Director of Admissions Services, Kirkwood Community College, 6301 Kirkwood Boulevard SW, Cedar Rapids, IA 52406

Marshalltown Community College

Marshalltown, Iowa
www.iavalley.edu/mcc/ **CB code: 6394**

- Public 2-year community college
- Residential campus in large town

General. Founded in 1927. Regionally accredited. **Enrollment:** 1,877 degree-seeking undergraduates. **Degrees:** 212 associate awarded. **Location:** 50 miles from Des Moines. **Calendar:** Semester, limited summer session. **Full-time faculty:** 48 total. **Part-time faculty:** 87 total. **Special facilities:** Prairie, challenge course.

Transfer out. Colleges most students transferred to 2008: Iowa State University, University of Northern Iowa, University of Iowa.

Basis for selection. Open admission, but selective for some programs. Special requirements for health career programs. Interview recommended for health careers majors.

2008-2009 Annual costs. Tuition/fees: $4,290; $5,190 out-of-state. Per-credit charge: $119 in-state; $149 out-of-state. Room only: $3,750. Books/supplies: $425.

Application procedures. Admission: No deadline. No application fee. Admission notification on a rolling basis. **Financial aid:** Priority date 3/1; no closing date. Institutional form required. Applicants notified on a rolling basis starting 6/1; must reply within 2 week(s) of notification.

Academics. Special study options: Accelerated study, cooperative education, cross-registration, distance learning, dual enrollment of high school students, ESL, honors, independent study, internships, liberal arts/career combination, study abroad. Bachelor's degree programs available on campus. License preparation in nursing, real estate. **Credit/placement by examination:** AP, CLEP, institutional tests. 30 credit hours maximum toward associate degree. **Support services:** GED preparation and test center, learning center, reduced course load, remedial instruction, study skills assistance, tutoring, writing center.

Majors. Agriculture: Business. **Biology:** General, botany. **Business:** General, accounting, administrative services, business admin. **Communications:** Journalism. **Communications technology:** General. **Computer sciences:** General, networking, systems analysis. **Conservation:** Forestry. **Education:** General, elementary, physical, secondary. **Engineering:** General. **Engineering technology:** Drafting. **Family/consumer sciences:** General, child care. **Foreign languages:** Spanish. **Health:** Health services, nursing (RN), predental, premedicine, prenursing, prepharmacy, preveterinary, surgical technology. **Legal studies:** Prelaw. **Liberal arts:** Arts/sciences. **Math:** General. **Mechanic/repair:** Heating/ac/refrig, industrial. **Personal/culinary services:** Embalming, mortuary science. **Protective services:** Law enforcement admin, police science. **Psychology:** General. **Public administration:** Community org/advocacy. **Social sciences:** General. **Visual/performing arts:** General, studio arts.

Most popular majors. Computer/information sciences 7%, education 8%, health sciences 10%, liberal arts 65%.

Computing on campus. 250 workstations in dormitories, library, computer center. Commuter students can connect to campus network. Online library, helpline available.

Student life. Freshman orientation: Available. Preregistration for classes offered. **Housing:** Special housing for disabled, apartments available. $300 deposit. **Activities:** Concert band, choral groups, drama, international student organizations, radio station, student government, student newspaper, TV station.

Athletics. NJCAA. **Intercollegiate:** Baseball M, basketball, golf, soccer M, softball W. **Intramural:** Basketball, racquetball. **Team name:** Tigers.

Student services. Adult student services, career counseling, services for economically disadvantaged, student employment services, financial aid counseling, health services, on-campus daycare, personal counseling, placement for graduates, veterans' counselor. **Physically disabled:** Services for visually, speech, hearing impaired. **Learning disabled:** Comprehensive services available. **Transfer:** College fairs on campus for students transferring to 4-year colleges.

Contact. Phone: (641) 752-7106 ext. 216 Fax: (641) 752-8149
Deana Inman, Director of Admissions, Marshalltown Community College, 3700 South Center Street, Marshalltown, IA 50158

Muscatine Community College

Muscatine, Iowa
www.eicc.edu **CB code: 6422**

- Public 2-year community college
- Commuter campus in large town

General. Founded in 1929. Regionally accredited. **Enrollment:** 1,306 degree-seeking undergraduates; 318 non-degree-seeking students. **Degrees:** 155 associate awarded. **Location:** 30 miles from Davenport. **Calendar:** Semester, extensive summer session. **Full-time faculty:** 32 total; 9% minority, 53% women. **Part-time faculty:** 101 total; 8% minority, 57% women. **Class size:** 28% < 20, 4% 20-39, 68% 40-49.

Student profile. Among degree-seeking undergraduates, 76% enrolled in a transfer program, 24% enrolled in a vocational program, 2% already have a bachelor's degree or higher, 311 enrolled as first-time, first-year students, 23 transferred in from other institutions.

Part-time:	59%	**Hispanic American:**	14%
Out-of-state:	5%	**Native American:**	1%
Women:	55%	**International:**	1%
African American:	2%	**25 or older:**	26%
Asian American:	1%	**Live on campus:**	5%

Basis for selection. Open admission, but selective for some programs. Special requirements for nursing program.

2008-2009 Annual costs. Tuition/fees: $3,210; $4,815 out-of-state. Per-credit charge: $107 in-state; $161 out-of-state. Online course tuition: $138 per credit hour. Room only: $3,600. Books/supplies: $900.

Application procedures. Admission: No deadline. No application fee. Admission notification on a rolling basis beginning on or about 9/1. **Financial aid:** Priority date 4/20; no closing date. FAFSA required. Applicants notified on a rolling basis starting 5/15; must reply within 2 week(s) of notification.

Academics. Special study options: Accelerated study, cooperative education, cross-registration, distance learning, double major, dual enrollment of high school students, ESL, honors, independent study, internships, study abroad. Bachelor's degree programs available on campus. License preparation in nursing, real estate. **Credit/placement by examination:** AP, CLEP, institutional tests. 30 credit hours maximum toward associate degree. **Support services:** Learning center, reduced course load, remedial instruction, tutoring.

Majors. Agriculture: Horticulture, production, supplies. **Business:** Accounting, administrative services, business admin, logistics. **Computer sciences:** Applications programming. **Conservation:** General. **Construction:** Electrician. **Engineering technology:** Environmental, manufacturing. **Health:** Dental hygiene, electroencephalograph technology, EMT paramedic, nuclear medical technology, physical therapy assistant, radiologic technology/medical imaging, respiratory therapy technology, sonography, veterinary technology/assistant. **Liberal arts:** Arts/sciences. **Mechanic/repair:** Industrial. **Personal/culinary services:** Restaurant/catering. **Protective services:** Firefighting, police science.

Most popular majors. Agriculture 11%, liberal arts 82%.

Computing on campus. 60 workstations in library, computer center. Dormitories wired for high-speed internet access and linked to campus network. Commuter students can connect to campus network. Online course registration, online library, helpline available.

Student life. Freshman orientation: Available. Preregistration for classes offered. **Housing:** Apartments, cooperative housing available. **Activities:** Choral groups, drama, film society, music ensembles, student government, student newspaper, TV station, agriculture technology club, All Kinds of People, College Democrats, College Republicans, Delta Epsilon Chi, Business Professionals of America, horticulture club, Phi Theta Kappa.

Athletics. NJCAA. **Intercollegiate:** Baseball M, softball W. **Intramural:** Bowling, football (non-tackle), golf, skiing, soccer, table tennis. **Team name:** Cardinals.

Student services. Adult student services, career counseling, student employment services, financial aid counseling, on-campus daycare, placement for graduates. **Physically disabled:** Services for visually, speech, hearing impaired. **Transfer:** Transfer adviser, college fairs on campus for students transferring to 4-year colleges.

Contact. Phone: (563) 288-6000 Toll-free number: (888) 336-3907
Fax: (563) 264-8341
Gary Mohr, Executive Director of External Affairs, Muscatine Community College, 152 Colorado Street, Muscatine, IA 52761-5396

North Iowa Area Community College

Mason City, Iowa
www.niacc.edu **CB code: 6400**

- Public 2-year community college
- Commuter campus in large town

General. Founded in 1918. Regionally accredited. **Enrollment:** 3,335 degree-seeking undergraduates; 150 non-degree-seeking students. **Degrees:** 484 associate awarded. **Location:** 120 miles from Des Moines, 120 miles from Minneapolis-St. Paul. **Calendar:** Semester, limited summer session. **Full-time faculty:** 85 total; 9% have terminal degrees, 1% minority, 35% women. **Part-time faculty:** 69 total; 12% have terminal degrees, 49% women. **Special facilities:** Manufacturing technology center, entrepreneurial center, community auditorium, business incubator.

Student profile. Among degree-seeking undergraduates, 839 enrolled as first-time, first-year students.

Part-time:	45%	**25 or older:**	5%
Out-of-state:	6%	**Live on campus:**	7%
Women:	52%		

Transfer out. Colleges most students transferred to 2008: University of Northern Iowa, Iowa State University, University of Iowa.

Basis for selection. Open admission, but selective for some programs. Special admission requirements for nursing and physical therapy assistants.

2008-2009 Annual costs. Tuition/fees: $3,487; $5,041 out-of-state. Per-credit charge: $103 in-state; $155 out-of-state. Room/board: $4,536. Books/supplies: $817. Personal expenses: $1,652.

2007-2008 Financial aid. Need-based: 705 full-time freshmen applied for aid; 585 were judged to have need; 562 of these received aid. Average need met was 68%. Average scholarship/grant was $3,794; average loan $4,391. 51% of total undergraduate aid awarded as scholarships/grants, 49% as loans/jobs. Need-based aid available for part-time students. Work-study available nights and for part-time students. **Non-need-based:** Scholarships awarded for academics, alumni affiliation, art, athletics, leadership, music/drama.

Application procedures. Admission: No deadline. No application fee. Admission notification on a rolling basis. **Financial aid:** Priority date 3/1; no closing date. FAFSA, institutional form required. Applicants notified on a rolling basis starting 4/1; must reply within 2 week(s) of notification.

Academics. Special study options: Cooperative education, distance learning, dual enrollment of high school students, honors, independent study, internships, liberal arts/career combination, study abroad. Bachelor's degree programs available on campus. License preparation in real estate. **Credit/placement by examination:** AP, CLEP, institutional tests. 30 credit hours maximum toward associate degree. **Support services:** GED preparation and test center, learning center, remedial instruction, study skills assistance, tutoring, writing center.

Majors. Agriculture: General, agribusiness operations, business, farm/ranch, production, supplies. **Business:** Accounting, administrative services, business admin, entrepreneurial studies, hospitality admin. **Computer sciences:** System admin. **Education:** General, early childhood, physical, secondary. **Engineering technology:** Electrical. **Family/consumer sciences:** General. **Health:** Clinical lab technology, EMT paramedic, nursing (RN), physical therapy assistant. **Liberal arts:** Arts/sciences. **Mechanic/repair:** Automotive, heating/ac/refrig, industrial electronics. **Parks/recreation:** Sports admin. **Personal/culinary services:** Mortuary science. **Production:** Machine tool, tool and die. **Protective services:** Fire services admin, police science. **Social sciences:** General, criminology, geography, political science, sociology.

Most popular majors. Business/marketing 10%, health sciences 12%, liberal arts 60%.

Computing on campus. 350 workstations in dormitories, library, computer center. Dormitories wired for high-speed internet access and linked to campus network. Commuter students can connect to campus network. Online library, wireless network available.

Student life. Freshman orientation: Mandatory. Online program. **Housing:** Coed dorms, apartments, wellness housing available. $50 partly refundable deposit. **Activities:** Bands, choral groups, dance, drama, music ensembles, student government, student newspaper, symphony orchestra, OK House, multicultural student union.

Athletics. NJCAA. **Intercollegiate:** Baseball M, basketball, cross-country, football (tackle) M, golf, soccer M, softball W, track and field, volleyball W, wrestling M. **Intramural:** Basketball, football (non-tackle), softball, volleyball. **Team name:** Trojans.

Student services. Adult student services, alcohol/substance abuse counseling, career counseling, student employment services, financial aid counseling, health services, personal counseling, placement for graduates, veterans' counselor. **Physically disabled:** Services for visually, speech, hearing impaired. **Transfer:** Transfer adviser, college fairs on campus for students transferring to 4-year colleges.

Contact. E-mail: request@niacc.cc.ia.us
Phone: (641) 422-4245 Toll-free number: (888) 466-4222 ext. 4245
Fax: (641) 422-4385
Rachel McGuire, Director of Admissions, North Iowa Area Community College, 500 College Drive, Mason City, IA 50401

Northeast Iowa Community College

Calmar, Iowa — **CB member**
www.nicc.edu — **CB code: 6751**

- Public 2-year community college
- Commuter campus in rural community

General. Founded in 1966. Regionally accredited. Branch campus at Peosta, 10 miles from Dubuque. **Enrollment:** 3,200 degree-seeking undergraduates. **Degrees:** 335 associate awarded. **Location:** 60 miles from Waterloo. **Calendar:** Semester, extensive summer session. **Full-time faculty:** 121 total; 62% women. **Part-time faculty:** 204 total; 72% women.

Student profile. Among degree-seeking undergraduates, 721 transferred in from other institutions.

Out-of-state:	9%	**25 or older:**	23%

Transfer out. Colleges most students transferred to 2008: University of Northern Iowa-Cedar Fall, Loras College, Clarke College, University of Dubuque.

Basis for selection. Open admission, but selective for some programs. Health students required to meet program specific admission criteria. All degree-seeking students required to submit placement test scores.

2008-2009 Annual costs. Tuition/fees: $4,050. Per-credit charge: $122. Books/supplies: $1,300. Personal expenses: $1,652.

Financial aid. Need-based: Need-based aid available for part-time students. Work-study available nights and for part-time students. **Non-need-based:** Scholarships awarded for academics, leadership.

Application procedures. Admission: No deadline. No application fee. Admission notification on a rolling basis. **Financial aid:** Priority date 7/1; no closing date. FAFSA required. Applicants notified on a rolling basis starting 5/1.

Academics. Dental assisting certification exam given on-campus. **Special study options:** Cooperative education, distance learning, double major, dual enrollment of high school students, ESL, honors, independent study, internships, student-designed major, study abroad. **Credit/placement by examination:** AP, CLEP. **Support services:** GED preparation and test center, learning center, reduced course load, remedial instruction, study skills assistance, tutoring, writing center.

Majors. Agriculture: Agribusiness operations, crop production, dairy husbandry, horticultural science, power machinery, production, products processing, supplies. **Business:** Accounting, administrative services, business admin, office technology, sales/distribution. **Computer sciences:** Applications programming. **Construction:** General, carpentry, electrician, plumbing. **Engineering technology:** Electrical. **Health:** Clinical lab technology, EMT paramedic, massage therapy, medical records technology, nursing (RN), radiologic technology/medical imaging, respiratory therapy technology. **Liberal arts:** Arts/sciences. **Mechanic/repair:** Automotive. **Personal/culinary services:** Cosmetic. **Public administration:** Community org/advocacy, social work. **Other:** Gas utility construction and service.

Most popular majors. Agriculture 9%, business/marketing 13%, health sciences 33%, liberal arts 35%.

Computing on campus. 800 workstations in library, computer center. Helpline, repair service, wireless network available.

Student life. Freshman orientation: Available. One-day program with different interest sessions available. **Activities:** Student government, student newspaper.

Athletics. Intramural: Basketball, bowling, golf, skiing, softball, volleyball. **Team name:** Cougars.

Student services. Adult student services, alcohol/substance abuse counseling, career counseling, services for economically disadvantaged, student employment services, financial aid counseling, health services, on-campus daycare, personal counseling, placement for graduates, veterans' counselor, women's services. **Physically disabled:** Services for visually, speech, hearing impaired. **Transfer:** Pre-admission transcript evaluation for new students. Transfer adviser, college fairs on campus for students transferring to 4-year colleges.

Contact. Phone: (563) 562-3263 ext. 234 Toll-free number: (800) 778-2256 ext. 234 Fax: (563) 562-4369
Kristi Strief, Admissions Manager, Northeast Iowa Community College, Box 400, Calmar, IA 52132

Northwest Iowa Community College

Sheldon, Iowa
www.nwicc.edu — **CB code: 1359**

- Public 2-year community college
- Commuter campus in small town

General. Founded in 1966. Regionally accredited. **Enrollment:** 1,256 degree-seeking undergraduates. **Degrees:** 174 associate awarded. **Location:** 60 miles from Sioux City; 65 miles from Sioux Falls, South Dakota. **Calendar:** Semester, extensive summer session. **Full-time faculty:** 41 total; 42% women. **Part-time faculty:** 89 total; 7% have terminal degrees, 1% minority, 53% women. **Class size:** 89% < 20, 11% 20-39, less than 1% 40-49. **Special facilities:** Natural prairie preserve.

Student profile.

Out-of-state:	5%	**Live on campus:**	3%
25 or older:	17%		

Basis for selection. Open admission, but selective for some programs. 2.0 GPA and 2 science required for LPN program. Algebra required for some technical programs. Minimum COMPASS scores for ADN and Powerline programs.

2008-2009 Annual costs. Tuition/fees: $4,110; $5,160 out-of-state. Per-credit charge: $113 in-state; $148 out-of-state. Room/board: $3,550. Books/supplies: $716. Personal expenses: $854.

Financial aid. Need-based: Need-based aid available for part-time students.

Application procedures. Admission: No deadline. $10 fee. Admission notification on a rolling basis. **Financial aid:** Priority date 4/1; no closing date. FAFSA, institutional form required. Applicants notified on a rolling basis starting 5/1.

Academics. Special study options: Cooperative education, distance learning, dual enrollment of high school students, ESL, independent study, liberal arts/career combination. Bachelor's degree programs available on campus. License preparation in nursing, paramedic, radiology. **Credit/placement by examination:** AP, CLEP, institutional tests. 30 credit hours maximum toward associate degree. **Support services:** GED preparation and test center, learning center, pre-admission summer program, reduced course load, remedial instruction, study skills assistance, tutoring.

Majors. Business: Accounting, business admin. **Computer sciences:** Networking, system admin. **Construction:** Carpentry, lineworker. **Engineering technology:** Electrical, manufacturing. **Health:** EMT paramedic, medical records technology, nursing (RN), radiologic technology/medical imaging. **Liberal arts:** Arts/sciences. **Mechanic/repair:** Auto body, automotive, diesel, industrial electronics. **Production:** Tool and die.

Computing on campus. 362 workstations in library, computer center, student center. Commuter students can connect to campus network. Online course registration, online library, helpline, wireless network available.

Student life. Freshman orientation: Available. Preregistration for classes offered. **Policies:** Student housing is non-smoking; no alcohol allowed. **Housing:** Apartments available. $190 partly refundable deposit. **Activities:** Student government, student newspaper, Campus Crusade for Christ.

Athletics. Intramural: Basketball, bowling, football (non-tackle).

Student services. Career counseling, student employment services, financial aid counseling, minority student services, personal counseling, placement for graduates, veterans' counselor. **Physically disabled:** Services for visually, speech, hearing impaired. **Transfer:** Pre-admission transcript evaluation for new students. Transfer adviser, college fairs on campus for students transferring to 4-year colleges.

Contact. E-mail: lstory@nwicc.edu
Phone: (712) 324-5061 Toll-free number: (800) 352-4907
Fax: (712) 324-4136
Lisa Story, Director of Admissions, Northwest Iowa Community College, 603 West Park Street, Sheldon, IA 51201

St. Luke's College
Sioux City, Iowa
www.stlukescollege.edu **CB code: 3625**

- Private 2-year health science college affiliated with Lutheran and Methodist churches
- Commuter campus in small city
- ACT (writing optional), application essay, interview required

General. Regionally accredited. Offers hospital-based health care provider programs. **Enrollment:** 149 degree-seeking undergraduates. **Degrees:** 70 associate awarded. **Location:** 90 miles from Omaha. **Calendar:** Semester, limited summer session. **Full-time faculty:** 17 total; 88% women. **Part-time faculty:** 9 total; 56% women. **Class size:** 77% < 20, 23% 20-39.

Student profile. Among degree-seeking undergraduates, 22% enrolled in a transfer program, 4% already have a bachelor's degree or higher, 4 enrolled as first-time, first-year students, 18 transferred in from other institutions.

Part-time:	31%	**Hispanic American:**	3%
Women:	84%	**Native American:**	1%
African American:	1%	**25 or older:**	26%
Asian American:	3%		

Transfer out. 71% of students enrolled in the transfer program go on to 4-year colleges. **Colleges most students transferred to 2008:** Morningside College, Briar Cliff College, Western Iowa Tech Community College, Dordt College.

Basis for selection. Professional programs require 2.5 GPA or GED and 19 ACT. Pre-professional programs require only one of these criteria. **Homeschooled:** Transcript of courses and grades required. **Learning Disabled:** Job shadowing recommended.

High school preparation. 8 units recommended. Recommended units include English 4, mathematics 2 and science 2. Electives recommended include psychology, computer operations, typing or keyboarding.

2009-2010 Annual costs. Tuition/fees: $14,270. Per-credit charge: $390. Summer general fee: $125. Books/supplies: $1,250. Personal expenses: $1,245.

2008-2009 Financial aid. Need-based: 28% of total undergraduate aid awarded as scholarships/grants, 72% as loans/jobs. Need-based aid available for part-time students. Work-study available nights, weekends and for part-time students. **Non-need-based:** Scholarships awarded for academics, job skills, leadership.

Application procedures. Admission: Closing date 8/1 (receipt date). $100 fee, may be waived for applicants with need. Admission notification on a rolling basis. Must reply within 2 weeks of acceptance. **Financial aid:** Priority date 3/1; no closing date. FAFSA required. Applicants notified on a rolling basis starting 4/1; must reply within 2 week(s) of notification.

Academics. Students can attend any bachelor's nursing program in Iowa after graduating with associate degree in nursing. Local college offers students access to learning and writing center. **Special study options:** Combined bachelor's/graduate degree, internships. License preparation in nursing, radiology. **Credit/placement by examination:** AP, CLEP. 22 credit hours maximum toward associate degree. **Support services:** Learning center, reduced course load, study skills assistance, tutoring.

Majors. Health: Medical radiologic technology/radiation therapy, nursing (RN), respiratory therapy technology.

Computing on campus. 18 workstations in library, computer center, student center. Online library, helpline, wireless network available.

Student life. Freshman orientation: Mandatory, $20 fee. Preregistration for classes offered. Held week prior to classes. **Policies:** Alcohol- and drug-free campus. **Activities:** Community service organization.

Student services. Alcohol/substance abuse counseling, chaplain/spiritual director, student employment services, financial aid counseling, health services, on-campus daycare, personal counseling. **Transfer:** Pre-admission transcript evaluation for new students.

Contact. E-mail: mccartsj@stlukes.org
Phone: (712) 279-3158 Toll-free number: (800) 352-4660 ext. 3158
Fax: (712) 233-8017
Sherry McCarthy, Enrollment Coordinator, St. Luke's College, 2720 Stone Park Boulevard, Sioux City, IA 51104

Scott Community College
Bettendorf, Iowa
www.eicc.edu **CB code: 0282**

- Public 2-year community college
- Commuter campus in small city

General. Founded in 1966. Regionally accredited. **Enrollment:** 3,520 degree-seeking undergraduates; 591 non-degree-seeking students. **Degrees:** 537 associate awarded. **Location:** 3 miles from Davenport. **Calendar:** Semester, extensive summer session. **Full-time faculty:** 80 total; 6% minority, 52% women. **Part-time faculty:** 252 total; 8% minority, 58% women. **Class size:** 80% < 20, 20% 20-39, less than 1% 40-49, less than 1% 50-99.

Student profile. Among degree-seeking undergraduates, 56% enrolled in a transfer program, 44% enrolled in a vocational program, 3% already have a bachelor's degree or higher, 903 enrolled as first-time, first-year students, 96 transferred in from other institutions.

Part-time:	49%	**Hispanic American:**	5%
Out-of-state:	11%	**Native American:**	1%
Women:	63%	**International:**	1%
African American:	10%	**25 or older:**	40%
Asian American:	2%		

Transfer out. Colleges most students transferred to 2008: University of Iowa, Iowa State University, University of Northern Iowa, St. Ambrose University, Western Illinois University.

Basis for selection. Open admission, but selective for some programs. Admission to some programs, particularly health occupations, based on academic achievement and previous courses. Interview required for radiologic technology and medical laboratory technician; recommended for nursing, electroneuro diagnostic technology and pharmacy technician.

2008-2009 Annual costs. Tuition/fees: $3,210; $4,815 out-of-state. Per-credit charge: $107 in-state; $161 out-of-state. Books/supplies: $1,140. Personal expenses: $1,090.

Application procedures. Admission: No deadline. No application fee. Admission notification on a rolling basis beginning on or about 9/1. **Financial aid:** Priority date 4/20; no closing date. FAFSA required. Applicants notified on a rolling basis starting 5/15; must reply within 2 week(s) of notification.

Academics. Special study options: Accelerated study, cooperative education, cross-registration, distance learning, double major, dual enrollment of high school students, ESL, honors, independent study, internships, liberal arts/career combination, study abroad, weekend college. License preparation in nursing, real estate. **Credit/placement by examination:** AP, CLEP, institutional tests. 30 credit hours maximum toward associate degree. **Support services:** GED preparation and test center, learning center, reduced course load, remedial instruction, tutoring.

Majors. Agriculture: Equine science. **Business:** Accounting, administrative services, hospitality admin, logistics. **Communications technology:** General. **Computer sciences:** Applications programming. **Engineering technology:** Environmental, mechanical drafting. **Foreign languages:** Sign language interpretation. **Health:** Dental hygiene, electroencephalograph technology, EMT paramedic, medical records technology, nuclear medical technology, nursing (RN), physical therapy assistant, radiologic technology/medical imaging, respiratory therapy technology, sonography. **Liberal arts:** Arts/sciences. **Mechanic/repair:** Auto body, automotive, diesel, heating/ac/refrig. **Personal/culinary services:** Chef training, culinary arts, restaurant/catering. **Production:** Machine tool, welding. **Protective services:** Police science. **Visual/performing arts:** Interior design.

Most popular majors. Business/marketing 8%, health sciences 18%, liberal arts 58%, trade and industry 6%.

Computing on campus. 125 workstations in library, computer center, student center. Commuter students can connect to campus network. Online course registration, helpline, wireless network available.

Student life. Freshman orientation: Available. Preregistration for classes offered. **Activities:** Campus ministries, international student organizations, literary magazine, student government, student newspaper, auto collision repair club, volunteer club, Phi Theta Kappa, nursing club, RadTech club, environmental club, dental assisting club.

Athletics. Intercollegiate: Golf, soccer. **Team name:** Eagles.

Student services. Career counseling, student employment services, financial aid counseling, on-campus daycare, personal counseling, placement for graduates, veterans' counselor. **Physically disabled:** Services for visually, speech, hearing impaired. **Transfer:** Transfer adviser, college fairs on campus for students transferring to 4-year colleges.

Contact. Phone: (563) 441-4004 Toll-free number: (888) 336-3907
Fax: (563) 441-4101
Gary Mohr, Admissions Officer, Scott Community College, 500 Belmont Road, Bettendorf, IA 52722-6804

Southeastern Community College: North Campus

West Burlington, Iowa
www.scciowa.edu **CB code: 6048**

- Public 2-year community and junior college
- Commuter campus in large town

General. Founded in 1966. Regionally accredited. Campuses in West Burlington, Keokuk, Mt. Pleasant, and Ft. Madison. **Enrollment:** 2,363 degree-seeking undergraduates; 1,049 non-degree-seeking students. **Degrees:** 472 associate awarded. **Location:** 200 miles from Des Moines, 300 miles from Chicago. **Calendar:** Semester, limited summer session. **Full-time faculty:** 55 total; 14% have terminal degrees, 6% minority, 47% women. **Part-time faculty:** 120 total; 2% have terminal degrees, 4% minority, 65% women. **Class size:** 68% < 20, 30% 20-39, 2% 40-49, less than 1% 50-99. **Special facilities:** Greenhouse, college operated farm.

Student profile. Among degree-seeking undergraduates, 386 enrolled as first-time, first-year students.

Part-time:	37%	**Hispanic American:**	3%
Out-of-state:	14%	**Native American:**	1%
Women:	64%	**International:**	1%
African American:	4%	**25 or older:**	33%
Asian American:	1%	**Live on campus:**	2%

Transfer out. Colleges most students transferred to 2008: University of Iowa, Western Illinois University, Iowa State University, University of Northern Iowa, Iowa Wesleyan College.

Basis for selection. Open admission, but selective for some programs. Special requirements for nursing, electronic technology, medical assistant, medical coding and billing, medical transcription, chemical dependency counselor, EMT- Paramedic, and respiratory care.

2008-2009 Annual costs. Tuition/fees: $3,450; $3,600 out-of-state. Per-credit charge: $115 in-state; $120 out-of-state. Books/supplies: $936. Personal expenses: $1,654.

2007-2008 Financial aid. Need-based: 261 full-time freshmen applied for aid; 210 were judged to have need; 201 of these received aid. Average scholarship/grant was $1,434; average loan $2,722. 50% of total undergraduate aid awarded as scholarships/grants, 50% as loans/jobs. Need-based aid available for part-time students. **Non-need-based:** Awarded to 369 full-time undergraduates, including 92 freshmen. Scholarships awarded for academics, art, athletics, minority status.

Application procedures. Admission: No deadline. No application fee. Admission notification on a rolling basis. **Financial aid:** Priority date 7/1; no closing date. FAFSA required. Applicants notified on a rolling basis starting 3/1; must reply within 4 week(s) of notification.

Academics. Special study options: Cooperative education, cross-registration, distance learning, dual enrollment of high school students, ESL, independent study, internships, weekend college. Bachelor's degree programs available on campus. License preparation in dental hygiene, nursing, occupational therapy, paramedic, physical therapy, radiology, real estate. **Credit/placement by examination:** AP, CLEP, ACT, institutional tests. 30 credit hours maximum toward associate degree. **Support services:** GED preparation and test center, learning center, pre-admission summer program, reduced course load, remedial instruction, study skills assistance, tutoring.

Majors. Agriculture: General, business, supplies. **Business:** General, accounting, administrative services, business admin, construction management, executive assistant, office management, office technology, office/clerical, receptionist. **Communications:** Digital media, journalism. **Communications technology:** Desktop publishing, graphics. **Computer sciences:** Computer graphics, data processing, networking, programming, web page design. **Construction:** Carpentry, maintenance. **Engineering:** Electrical, mechanics. **Engineering technology:** Construction, drafting, electrical, robotics. **Family/consumer sciences:** Child care. **Health:** EMT paramedic, medical assistant, medical radiologic technology/radiation therapy, nursing (RN), substance abuse counseling. **Legal studies:** Legal secretary. **Liberal arts:** Arts/sciences. **Mechanic/repair:** General. **Production:** General, machine tool, tool and die. **Protective services:** Law enforcement admin. **Public administration:** Human services.

Most popular majors. Business/marketing 11%, health sciences 16%, liberal arts 54%.

Computing on campus. 100 workstations in library, computer center. Dormitories wired for high-speed internet access. Helpline, wireless network available.

Student life. Freshman orientation: Mandatory. Preregistration for classes offered. Two-hour session offered both day and evening before term begins. **Housing:** Coed dorms, single-sex dorms, special housing for disabled, apartments available. $300 partly refundable deposit. **Activities:** Campus ministries, choral groups, drama, international student organizations, literary magazine, music ensembles, musical theater, student government, student newspaper, symphony orchestra, Campus Crusade for Christ, multicultural club.

Athletics. NJCAA. **Intercollegiate:** Baseball M, basketball, golf, softball W, volleyball W. **Intramural:** Basketball, bowling, cheerleading, football (non-tackle), softball, volleyball. **Team name:** Black Hawks.

Student services. Career counseling, services for economically disadvantaged, student employment services, financial aid counseling, minority student services, on-campus daycare, personal counseling, placement for graduates, veterans' counselor. **Physically disabled:** Services for visually, speech, hearing impaired. **Learning disabled:** Comprehensive services available. **Transfer:** Pre-admission transcript evaluation for new students. Transfer adviser, college fairs on campus for students transferring to 4-year colleges.

Contact. E-mail: admoff@scciowa.edu
Phone: (319) 752-2731 ext. 5012 Toll-free number: (866) 722-4692 ext. 5012 Fax: (319) 758-6725
Dana Chrisman, Senior Enrollment Officer, Southeastern Community College: North Campus, 1500 West Agency Road, West Burlington, IA 52655-0605

Southeastern Community College: South Campus

Keokuk, Iowa
www.scciowa.edu **CB code: 6340**

- Public 2-year community college
- Commuter campus in large town

General. Founded in 1966. Regionally accredited. **Location:** 45 miles from Burlington; 45 miles from Quincy, Illinois. **Calendar:** Semester.

Annual costs/financial aid. Tuition/fees (2008-2009): $3,450; $3,600 out-of-state. Books/supplies: $600. Need-based financial aid available to full-time and part-time students.

Contact. Phone: (319) 524-3221 ext. 8416
Senior Enrollment Officer, Box 6007, Keokuk, IA 52632-6007

Southwestern Community College

Creston, Iowa
www.swcciowa.edu **CB code: 6122**

- Public 2-year community college
- Commuter campus in small town

General. Founded in 1966. Regionally accredited. **Enrollment:** 908 degree-seeking undergraduates; 560 non-degree-seeking students. **Degrees:** 215 associate awarded. **Location:** 75 miles from Des Moines; 110 miles from Omaha, Nebraska. **Calendar:** Semester, limited summer session. **Full-time faculty:** 48 total; 4% have terminal degrees, 48% women. **Part-time faculty:** 71 total; 8% have terminal degrees, 1% minority, 51% women. **Class size:** 79% < 20, 18% 20-39, 2% 40-49, 1% 50-99. **Special facilities:** Recording studio.

Student profile. Among degree-seeking undergraduates, 188 enrolled as first-time, first-year students.

Part-time:	24%	**25 or older:**	38%
Out-of-state:	4%	**Live on campus:**	5%
Women:	66%		

Two-Year Colleges

Transfer out. Colleges most students transferred to 2008: Northwest Missouri State University, Buena Vista University, Iowa State University, Graceland College, University of Northern Iowa.

Basis for selection. Open admission, but selective for some programs. Special requirements for nursing. LPN criteria includes date nursing application is received and date COMPASS test scores are achieved. ADN requirements contingent on application, COMPASS test scores, and a ranking selection process. **Adult students:** Students must take COMPASS test for placement.

High school preparation. One chemistry required for health programs.

2008-2009 Annual costs. Tuition/fees: $3,920; $4,934 out-of-state. Per-credit charge: $111 in-state; $143 out-of-state. Room/board: $4,700. Books/supplies: $600. Personal expenses: $1,500.

2007-2008 Financial aid. Need-based: Need-based aid available for part-time students. Work-study available nights, weekends and for part-time students. **Non-need-based:** Scholarships awarded for academics, athletics, leadership, music/drama, state residency.

Application procedures. Admission: Priority date 8/1; no deadline. No application fee. Admission notification on a rolling basis. **Financial aid:** Priority date 7/1; no closing date. FAFSA required. Applicants notified on a rolling basis starting 6/1; must reply within 2 week(s) of notification.

Academics. Special study options: Cooperative education, distance learning, double major, dual enrollment of high school students, independent study, internships, liberal arts/career combination. License preparation in nursing. **Credit/placement by examination:** AP, CLEP. 30 credit hours maximum toward associate degree. Arts and science students without 19 ACT required to take ASSET exam. **Support services:** GED preparation and test center, learning center, reduced course load, remedial instruction, study skills assistance, tutoring.

Majors. Agriculture: Business, production. **Business:** General, accounting, administrative services, marketing. **Computer sciences:** Applications programming, information systems, webmaster. **Construction:** Carpentry. **Education:** General. **Engineering technology:** Drafting, electrical. **Health:** Medical transcription, nursing (RN). **Liberal arts:** Arts/sciences. **Mechanic/repair:** Auto body, electronics/electrical. **Visual/performing arts:** Music performance.

Most popular majors. Business/marketing 10%, computer/information sciences 6%, health sciences 20%, liberal arts 43%, trade and industry 12%.

Computing on campus. 140 workstations in dormitories, library, computer center, student center. Dormitories wired for high-speed internet access and linked to campus network. Helpline, repair service, wireless network available.

Student life. Freshman orientation: Mandatory. Preregistration for classes offered. **Housing:** Coed dorms, single-sex dorms, wellness housing available. $100 deposit. **Activities:** Bands, choral groups, music ensembles, student government, student newspaper.

Athletics. NJCAA. **Intercollegiate:** Baseball M, basketball, cross-country, golf M, softball W, volleyball W. **Intramural:** Basketball, table tennis, tennis, volleyball. **Team name:** Spartans.

Student services. Adult student services, career counseling, services for economically disadvantaged, student employment services, health services, legal services, personal counseling, placement for graduates, veterans' counselor. **Physically disabled:** Services for visually, speech, hearing impaired. **Transfer:** Pre-admission transcript evaluation for new students. Transfer adviser, college fairs on campus for students transferring to 4-year colleges.

Contact. Phone: (641) 782-7081 ext. 421 Toll-free number: (800) 247-4023 Fax: (641) 782-3312
Lisa Carstens, Director of Admissions, Southwestern Community College, 1501 West Townline Street, Creston, IA 50801

Vatterott College

Des Moines, Iowa
www.vatterott-college.edu **CB code: 2909**

- For-profit 2-year health science and technical college
- Commuter campus in large city
- Interview required

General. Accredited by ACCSCT. **Enrollment:** 238 degree-seeking undergraduates. **Degrees:** 74 associate awarded. **Calendar:** Continuous, extensive summer session. **Full-time faculty:** 13 total. **Part-time faculty:** 18 total.

Basis for selection. Open admission.

2008-2009 Annual costs. Program cost ranges: $14,300 to $22,000 (certificate/diploma); $21,450 to $31,050 (associate degree).

Financial aid. All financial aid based on need.

Application procedures. Admission: No deadline. No application fee. Admission notification on a rolling basis. School tour, interview with admissions representative, financial clearance, completion of placement evaluation, application, and enrollment forms required. **Financial aid:** No deadline. FAFSA required. Applicants notified on a rolling basis.

Academics. Credit/placement by examination: CLEP, institutional tests. 24 credit hours maximum toward associate degree. Credits may be counted toward diploma if student passes and is awarded credit for previous training.

Majors. Computer sciences: Networking, programming. **Engineering technology:** Drafting.

Computing on campus. 125 workstations in library, computer center.

Student life. Freshman orientation: Mandatory.

Student services. Financial aid counseling, placement for graduates. **Transfer:** Pre-admission transcript evaluation for new students.

Contact. E-mail: desmoines@vatterott-college.edu
Phone: (515) 309-9000 Toll-free number: (800) 353-7264
Fax: (515) 309-0366
Darin Boots, Director of Admissions, Vatterott College, 6100 Thornton, Suite 290, Des Moines, IA 50321

Western Iowa Tech Community College

Sioux City, Iowa **CB member**
www.witcc.com **CB code: 6950**

- Public 2-year community college
- Commuter campus in small city

General. Founded in 1966. Regionally accredited. **Enrollment:** 2,426 degree-seeking undergraduates; 2,999 non-degree-seeking students. **Degrees:** 436 associate awarded. **Location:** 200 miles from Des Moines; 90 miles from Omaha, Nebraska. **Calendar:** Semester, extensive summer session. **Full-time faculty:** 81 total; 6% minority, 54% women. **Part-time faculty:** 241 total; 27% minority, 59% women. **Class size:** 81% < 20, 17% 20-39, 1% 40-49, less than 1% 50-99, less than 1% >100.

Student profile. Among degree-seeking undergraduates, 372 enrolled as first-time, first-year students.

Part-time:	36%	**Hispanic American:**	7%
Out-of-state:	10%	**Native American:**	2%
Women:	63%	**25 or older:**	28%
African American:	3%	**Live on campus:**	3%
Asian American:	2%		

Transfer out. Colleges most students transferred to 2008: Iowa State University, Briar Cliff College, Morningside College, University of Northern Iowa, Bellevue University.

Basis for selection. Open admission, but selective for some programs. Special requirements for nursing, surgical technician, dental assistant, physical therapy assistant, childcare supervision and management, emergency medical technician, police science, and business. Computerized placement test (CPT or ACT) required of all diploma and degree-seeking students and of all students taking English composition and math courses.

High school preparation. Recommended units include English 4, mathematics 2, social studies 2, history 2, science 2 and foreign language 1.

2008-2009 Annual costs. Tuition/fees: $3,735; $4,455 out-of-state. Per-credit charge: $109 in-state; $133 out-of-state. Room/board: $4,887. Books/supplies: $900. Personal expenses: $1,170.

2007-2008 Financial aid. Need-based: Need-based aid available for part-time students. Work-study available nights, weekends and for part-time students. **Non-need-based:** Scholarships awarded for academics, leadership, music/drama.

Application procedures. Admission: No deadline. No application fee. Admission notification on a rolling basis. **Financial aid:** No deadline. FAFSA required. Applicants notified on a rolling basis starting 4/1.

Academics. Special study options: Accelerated study, distance learning, double major, dual enrollment of high school students, ESL, honors, independent study, internships. License preparation in paramedic. **Credit/placement by examination:** AP, CLEP, institutional tests. **Support services:** GED preparation and test center, learning center, pre-admission summer program, reduced course load, remedial instruction, study skills assistance, tutoring.

Majors. Agriculture: Supplies, turf management. **Biology:** Biotechnology. **Business:** Accounting, administrative services, business admin, finance, human resources, office technology, sales/distribution. **Communications technology:** Desktop publishing. **Computer sciences:** Web page design. **Engineering technology:** Architectural, mechanical drafting, telecommunications. **Health:** Clinical lab technology, dental hygiene, EMT paramedic, medical secretary, nursing (RN), office admin, physical therapy assistant, surgical technology. **Legal studies:** Legal secretary. **Liberal arts:** Arts/sciences. **Mechanic/repair:** Auto body, automotive, industrial, musical instruments. **Protective services:** Firefighting, juvenile corrections, police science. **Visual/performing arts:** Interior design. **Other:** Cyber crime investigation, Multi/interdisciplinary technical study.

Most popular majors. Business/marketing 14%, engineering/engineering technologies 7%, health sciences 25%, liberal arts 30%, security/protective services 7%.

Computing on campus. 1,700 workstations in dormitories, library, computer center, student center. Dormitories wired for high-speed internet access and linked to campus network. Commuter students can connect to campus network. Online course registration, online library, helpline, wireless network available.

Student life. Freshman orientation: Available. Preregistration for classes offered. **Housing:** Apartments available. $100 deposit. **Activities:** Choral groups, drama, music ensembles, student government, celebrations, multicultural group, sociology club.

Athletics. Intramural: Golf, volleyball.

Student services. Adult student services, career counseling, services for economically disadvantaged, student employment services, health services, personal counseling, placement for graduates. **Physically disabled:** Services for visually, speech, hearing impaired. **Transfer:** Transfer center, transfer adviser, college fairs on campus for students transferring to 4-year colleges.

Contact. Phone: (712) 274-6403 Toll-free number: (800) 352-4649 ext. 6403 Fax: (712) 274-6441
Lora VanderZwaag, Director of Admissions, Western Iowa Tech Community College, Box 5199, Sioux City, IA 51102-5199

Kansas

Allen County Community College
Iola, Kansas
www.allencc.edu **CB code: 6305**

- Public 2-year community college
- Commuter campus in small town

General. Founded in 1923. Regionally accredited. Two campuses available to serve students in rural or metropolitan area. **Enrollment:** 2,821 degree-seeking undergraduates. **Degrees:** 277 associate awarded. **Location:** 100 miles from Kansas City. **Calendar:** Semester, limited summer session. **Full-time faculty:** 36 total. **Part-time faculty:** 145 total. **Special facilities:** College-operated farm.

Student profile.

Out-of-state:	3%	**Live on campus:**	20%
25 or older:	31%		

Transfer out. Colleges most students transferred to 2008: Pittsburg State University, Kansas State University, Emporia State University, University of Kansas, Washburn University.

Basis for selection. Open admission. TOEFL score of 520 or higher required for admission of non-English-speaking students. Placement test required. **Homeschooled:** Transcript of courses and grades required. Placement test required (ACT, COMPASS or ASSET). **Learning Disabled:** Copies of a high school IEP are helpful, but not required.

2008-2009 Annual costs. Tuition/fees: $1,710; $1,800 out-of-district; $1,800 out-of-state. Per-credit charge: $41 in-district; $44 out-of-district; $44 out-of-state. Room/board: $4,100. Books/supplies: $300. Personal expenses: $1,620.

2007-2008 Financial aid. Need-based: 53% of total undergraduate aid awarded as scholarships/grants, 47% as loans/jobs. Need-based aid available for part-time students. Work-study available nights and weekends. **Non-need-based:** Scholarships awarded for academics, art, athletics, music/drama, state residency. **Additional information:** Scholarships for livestock judging, cheerleading, choir, dance, drama, art, academic challenge, and student ambassadors.

Application procedures. Admission: No deadline. No application fee. Admission notification on a rolling basis. **Financial aid:** Closing date 6/1. FAFSA required. Applicants notified on a rolling basis starting 6/1; must reply within 2 week(s) of notification.

Academics. Special study options: Cooperative education, distance learning, double major, dual enrollment of high school students, independent study, internships, liberal arts/career combination, student-designed major, weekend college. Bachelor's degree programs available on campus. **Credit/placement by examination:** AP, CLEP, institutional tests. 12 credit hours maximum toward associate degree. **Support services:** GED preparation and test center, learning center, reduced course load, remedial instruction, study skills assistance, tutoring, writing center.

Majors. Agriculture: Farm/ranch. **Biology:** General. **Business:** Accounting, administrative services, business admin, office management, sales/distribution. **Computer sciences:** General, computer science. **Education:** Mathematics, music, secondary. **Engineering:** Electrical. **Engineering technology:** Drafting. **Health:** EMT paramedic, nursing assistant. **History:** General. **Liberal arts:** Library science. **Math:** General. **Mechanic/repair:** Electronics/electrical. **Physical sciences:** Chemistry, physics. **Production:** Woodworking. **Protective services:** Police science. **Social sciences:** Economics, geography, sociology. **Visual/performing arts:** Art, ceramics, crafts, drawing, painting, studio arts, voice/opera.

Most popular majors. Business/marketing 28%, communications/journalism 16%, education 12%, health sciences 12%, liberal arts 13%.

Computing on campus. 100 workstations in dormitories, library, computer center, student center. Dormitories wired for high-speed internet access. Online library, repair service, wireless network available.

Student life. Freshman orientation: Mandatory. Preregistration for classes offered. **Housing:** Coed dorms, apartments available. $125 fully refundable deposit, deadline 7/7. **Activities:** Bands, choral groups, dance, drama, music ensembles, musical theater, student government, Aggie Club, biology club, Phi Theta Kappa.

Athletics. NJCAA. **Intercollegiate:** Baseball M, basketball, cheerleading, cross-country, golf, soccer, softball W, track and field, volleyball W. **Intramural:** Basketball, football (non-tackle), softball, table tennis, tennis, volleyball. **Team name:** Red Devils.

Student services. Adult student services, alcohol/substance abuse counseling, career counseling, services for economically disadvantaged, student employment services, financial aid counseling, minority student services, personal counseling, placement for graduates, veterans' counselor, women's services. **Physically disabled:** Services for visually, hearing impaired. **Transfer:** Pre-admission transcript evaluation for new students. Transfer adviser, college fairs on campus for students transferring to 4-year colleges.

Contact. E-mail: weber@allencc.edu
Phone: (620) 365-5116 ext. 268 Fax: (620) 365-3284
Rebecca Bilderback, Admissions Director, Allen County Community College, 1801 North Cottonwood, Iola, KS 66749

Barton County Community College
Great Bend, Kansas
www.bartonccc.edu **CB code: 0784**

- Public 2-year community college
- Commuter campus in large town

General. Founded in 1965. Regionally accredited. **Enrollment:** 3,060 degree-seeking undergraduates. **Degrees:** 440 associate awarded. **Location:** 125 miles from Wichita. **Calendar:** Semester, limited summer session. **Full-time faculty:** 72 total; 7% have terminal degrees, 4% minority, 42% women. **Part-time faculty:** 110 total; 2% have terminal degrees, 6% minority, 57% women. **Class size:** 79% < 20, 20% 20-39, 1% 40-49, less than 1% 50-99. **Special facilities:** Natatorium, planetarium.

Student profile.

Out-of-state:	5%	**Live on campus:**	8%
25 or older:	46%		

Transfer out. Colleges most students transferred to 2008: Fort Hays State University, Kansas State University, University of Kansas, Wichita State University, Emporia State University.

Basis for selection. Open admission, but selective for some programs. Special requirements for medical laboratory technician, nursing, and mobile intensive care technician programs. ACT, SAT, ASSET or ACCUPLACER required for placement in math or English courses. Interview required of nursing majors.

2008-2009 Annual costs. Tuition/fees: $2,130; $2,700 out-of-state. Per-credit charge: $49 in-state; $68 out-of-state. Room/board: $4,342. Books/supplies: $830. Personal expenses: $3,042.

2007-2008 Financial aid. Need-based: Need-based aid available for part-time students. **Non-need-based:** Scholarships awarded for academics, athletics.

Application procedures. Admission: No deadline. No application fee. Application must be submitted on paper. Admission notification on a rolling basis. **Financial aid:** Priority date 3/1; no closing date. FAFSA required. Applicants notified on a rolling basis starting 6/1; must reply within 4 week(s) of notification.

Academics. Special study options: Accelerated study, cooperative education, distance learning, dual enrollment of high school students, ESL, honors, independent study, internships. License preparation in nursing, paramedic, real estate. **Credit/placement by examination:** AP, CLEP, IB, institutional tests. ACT, SAT, ASSET, or ACCUPLACER is required for enrollment in Math or English coursework. **Support services:** GED preparation and test center, learning center, remedial instruction, tutoring.

Majors. Agriculture: General, production. **Biology:** General, wildlife. **Business:** General, accounting, accounting technology, administrative services, human resources, operations. **Communications:** General, journalism. **Computer sciences:** Computer science, data processing, information systems. **Conservation:** Forestry. **Education:** General. **Engineering:** General. **Engineering technology:** Computer systems, hazardous materials. **Family/consumer sciences:** Child care. **Foreign languages:** General. **Health:** Athletic training, clinical lab science, clinical lab technology, dietician assistant, EMT paramedic, health services, medical assistant, medical records admin, nursing (RN), predental, premedicine, prenursing, prepharmacy, preveterinary. **History:** General. **Legal studies:** Prelaw. **Liberal arts:** Arts/sciences. **Math:** General. **Mechanic/repair:** Automotive. **Military:** General. **Parks/recreation:** Exercise sciences, health/fitness, sports admin. **Personal/culinary services:** Mortuary science. **Philosophy/religion:** Philosophy. **Physical sciences:** General, chemistry, physics. **Protective services:** Firefighting, police science, security management. **Psychology:** General. **Public administration:** General, social work. **Social sciences:** Anthropology, economics, political science, sociology. **Visual/performing arts:** Art, dance, dramatic, graphic design.

Most popular majors. Business/marketing 11%, health sciences 16%, liberal arts 51%.

Computing on campus. 350 workstations in dormitories, library, computer center, student center. Dormitories wired for high-speed internet access and linked to campus network. Commuter students can connect to campus network. Online course registration, online library, helpline available.

Student life. Freshman orientation: Mandatory. Preregistration for classes offered. **Housing:** Guaranteed on-campus for freshmen. Coed dorms, wellness housing available. $100 fully refundable deposit. **Activities:** Bands, choral groups, dance, drama, literary magazine, music ensembles, musical theater, student government, student newspaper, Newman Club, Fellowship of Christian Athletes, Campus Christian Fellowship, Student Ambassadors.

Athletics. NJCAA. **Intercollegiate:** Baseball M, basketball, cheerleading, cross-country, golf, soccer, softball W, tennis, track and field, volleyball W. **Intramural:** Baseball M, basketball, football (non-tackle), softball, table tennis, tennis, volleyball. **Team name:** Cougars.

Student services. Adult student services, alcohol/substance abuse counseling, career counseling, services for economically disadvantaged, student employment services, financial aid counseling, health services, on-campus daycare, personal counseling, placement for graduates, veterans' counselor. **Physically disabled:** Services for hearing impaired. **Transfer:** Pre-admission transcript evaluation for new students. Transfer adviser, college fairs on campus for students transferring to 4-year colleges.

Contact. E-mail: admissions@bartonccc.edu
Phone: (620) 792-2701 ext. 286 Toll-free number: (800) 722-6842
Fax: (620) 786-1160
Todd Moore, Director of Marketing, Barton County Community College, 245 North East 30th Road, Great Bend, KS 67530-9283

Brown Mackie College: Salina

Salina, Kansas
www.brownmackie.edu/Salina/ **CB code: 3366**

- For-profit 2-year junior college
- Commuter campus in large town

General. Regionally accredited. Branch campus in Kansas City. **Enrollment:** 447 degree-seeking undergraduates. **Degrees:** 77 associate awarded. **Location:** 90 miles from Wichita, 108 miles from Topeka. **Calendar:** Quarter, extensive summer session. **Full-time faculty:** 17 total. **Part-time faculty:** 19 total.

Student profile. Among degree-seeking undergraduates, 94 enrolled as first-time, first-year students.

Transfer out. Colleges most students transferred to 2008: Kansas Wesleyan University, Kansas State University.

Basis for selection. Open admission. **Homeschooled:** Transcript of courses and grades required. Home-school must be registered by state department of education.

2008-2009 Annual costs. Tuition/fees: $8,028. Computer networking program $300 per-credit-hour; required fees: $25 per-credit-hour. Nursing program $260 per-credit-hour; required fees: $20 per-credit-hour. Books/supplies: $1,440. Personal expenses: $1,520.

Application procedures. Admission: No deadline. No application fee. Application must be submitted on paper. Admission notification on a rolling basis. **Financial aid:** No deadline. Applicants notified on a rolling basis.

Academics. Special study options: Internships, weekend college. License preparation in nursing. **Credit/placement by examination:** CLEP, institutional tests. **Support services:** Remedial instruction, study skills assistance, tutoring.

Majors. Business: Accounting, business admin, selling. **Computer sciences:** Information technology, networking. **Engineering technology:** CAD/CADD. **Health:** Office admin. **Legal studies:** Paralegal. **Protective services:** Law enforcement admin.

Computing on campus. 134 workstations in library, computer center.

Student life. Freshman orientation: Mandatory. Part-day program held prior to start of classes. **Activities:** Student government, student newspaper.

Athletics. NJCAA. **Intercollegiate:** Baseball M, basketball, softball W. **Intramural:** Softball. **Team name:** Lions.

Student services. Career counseling, student employment services, placement for graduates.

Contact. E-mail: dheath@brownmackie.edu
Phone: (785) 825-5422 Toll-free number: (800) 365-0433
Fax: (785) 827-7623
Diann Heath, Director of Admissions, Brown Mackie College: Salina, 2106 South Ninth Street, Salina, KS 67401

Butler County Community College

El Dorado, Kansas
www.butlercc.edu **CB code: 6191**

- Public 2-year community college
- Commuter campus in large town

General. Founded in 1927. Regionally accredited. **Location:** 25 miles from Wichita. **Calendar:** Semester.

Annual costs/financial aid. Tuition/fees (2008-2009): $1,890; $2,220 out-of-district; $3,630 out-of-state. Room/board: $4,765. Books/supplies: $1,000. Personal expenses: $1,350. Need-based financial aid available to full-time and part-time students.

Contact. Phone: (316) 322-3255
Director of Enrollment Management, 901 South Haverhill Road, El Dorado, KS 67042-3280

Cloud County Community College

Concordia, Kansas
www.cloud.edu **CB code: 6137**

- Public 2-year community college
- Commuter campus in small town

General. Founded in 1965. Regionally accredited. **Enrollment:** 800 degree-seeking undergraduates; 1,326 non-degree-seeking students. **Degrees:** 206 associate awarded. **Location:** 200 miles from Kansas City, 140 miles from Topeka. **Calendar:** Semester, limited summer session. **Full-time faculty:** 42 total. **Part-time faculty:** 198 total. **Class size:** 88% < 20, 12% 20-39, less than 1% 40-49. **Special facilities:** Theater, observatory, children's center, human cadaver lab. **Partnerships:** Formal partnerships with Tallgrass TechPrep Consortium.

Student profile. Among degree-seeking undergraduates, 245 enrolled as first-time, first-year students.

Part-time:	32%	**Hispanic American:**	6%
Out-of-state:	5%	**Native American:**	1%
Women:	60%	**International:**	1%
African American:	11%	**25 or older:**	35%
Asian American:	1%	**Live on campus:**	4%

Transfer out. Colleges most students transferred to 2008: Kansas State University, Fort Hays State University, Wichita State University, Kansas Wesleyan University, Kansas University.

Basis for selection. Open admission.

High school preparation. 18 units recommended. Recommended units include English 4, mathematics 3, social studies 2 and science 4.

2008-2009 Annual costs. Tuition/fees: $2,438; $2,438 out-of-state. Per-credit charge: $61. Room/board: $4,540. Books/supplies: $700. Personal expenses: $1,650.

Financial aid. Need-based: Need-based aid available for part-time students. Work-study available nights, weekends and for part-time students.

Application procedures. Admission: No deadline. No application fee. Admission notification on a rolling basis. **Financial aid:** Priority date 4/1;

no closing date. FAFSA required. Applicants notified on a rolling basis starting 5/1; must reply within 4 week(s) of notification.

Academics. **Special study options:** Cooperative education, distance learning, dual enrollment of high school students, ESL, independent study, internships, teacher certification program. License preparation in nursing. **Credit/placement by examination:** AP, CLEP, institutional tests. 30 credit hours maximum toward associate degree. **Support services:** GED preparation and test center, learning center, remedial instruction, study skills assistance, tutoring, writing center.

Majors. **Agriculture:** Production, supplies. **Business:** Administrative services, business admin, office technology, tourism promotion. **Communications:** Journalism. **Communications technology:** Radio/tv. **Computer sciences:** LAN/WAN management, web page design. **Education:** Teacher assistance. **Family/consumer sciences:** Child care. **Health:** Nursing (RN). **Legal studies:** Paralegal. **Liberal arts:** Arts/sciences. **Protective services:** Police science. **Visual/performing arts:** Graphic design.

Most popular majors. Health sciences 14%, liberal arts 75%.

Computing on campus. 100 workstations in dormitories, library, computer center. Dormitories wired for high-speed internet access and linked to campus network. Online library, wireless network available.

Student life. **Freshman orientation:** Mandatory. Preregistration for classes offered. Held one day prior to registration each Fall semester, from 9am to 3pm. Offers a variety of activities to acquaint students with services available both at the college and in the community. **Housing:** Special housing for disabled, apartments available. $100 deposit. **Activities:** Bands, choral groups, dance, drama, music ensembles, radio station, student government, student newspaper, Fellowship of Christian Athletes.

Athletics. NJCAA. **Intercollegiate:** Baseball M, basketball, cross-country, soccer, softball W, track and field, volleyball W. **Intramural:** Basketball, football (non-tackle), soccer, softball, volleyball. **Team name:** Thunderbirds.

Student services. Alcohol/substance abuse counseling, career counseling, services for economically disadvantaged, student employment services, financial aid counseling, health services, on-campus daycare, personal counseling, placement for graduates, veterans' counselor. **Physically disabled:** Services for visually, speech, hearing impaired. **Transfer:** Pre-admission transcript evaluation for new students.

Contact. E-mail: admit@cloud.edu
Phone: (785) 243-1435 ext. 212 Toll-free number: (800) 729-5101 ext. 212
Fax: (785) 243-9380
Kim Reynolds, Director of Admissions, Cloud County Community College, 2221 Campus Drive, Concordia, KS 66901-1002

Coffeyville Community College

Coffeyville, Kansas
www.coffeyville.edu
CB code: 6102

- Public 2-year community and technical college
- Commuter campus in large town

General. Founded in 1923. Regionally accredited. **Enrollment:** 1,500 degree-seeking undergraduates. **Degrees:** 217 associate awarded. **Location:** 75 miles from Tulsa, Oklahoma, 137 miles from Wichita. **Calendar:** Semester, limited summer session. **Full-time faculty:** 50 total. **Part-time faculty:** 25 total. **Class size:** 64% < 20, 33% 20-39, less than 1% 40-49, 3% 50-99. **Special facilities:** Greenhouse, commercial television station. **Partnerships:** Formal partnership with Wal-Mart.

Student profile. Among degree-seeking undergraduates, 70% enrolled in a transfer program, 13% enrolled in a vocational program, 663 enrolled as first-time, first-year students, 45 transferred in from other institutions.

Part-time:	25%	**Women:**	47%
Out-of-state:	15%	**Live on campus:**	31%

Transfer out. 70% of students enrolled in the transfer program go on to 4-year colleges. **Colleges most students transferred to 2008:** Pittsburg State University, Kansas State University, University of Kansas.

Basis for selection. Open admission. **Homeschooled:** ACT or placement test required for placement. **Learning Disabled:** Require IEP.

High school preparation. 20 units recommended. Recommended units include English 4, mathematics 4, social studies 3, history 2, science 3 (laboratory 2), foreign language 1, computer science 1 and visual/performing arts 1.

2008-2009 Annual costs. Tuition/fees: $1,840; $3,240 out-of-state. Per-credit charge: $27 in-state; $67 out-of-state. Oklahoma border county resident tuition: $35 per-credit-hour. Room/board: $4,796. Books/supplies: $700. Personal expenses: $1,200.

2007-2008 Financial aid. **Need-based:** Need-based aid available for part-time students. Work-study available nights, weekends and for part-time students. **Non-need-based:** Scholarships awarded for academics, alumni affiliation, art, athletics, leadership, music/drama, state residency.

Application procedures. **Admission:** No deadline. No application fee. Admission notification on a rolling basis. **Financial aid:** Priority date 8/1; no closing date. FAFSA required. Applicants notified on a rolling basis starting 6/20.

Academics. **Special study options:** Distance learning, double major, dual enrollment of high school students, ESL, honors, independent study, internships, liberal arts/career combination, student-designed major. License preparation in paramedic. **Credit/placement by examination:** AP, CLEP, institutional tests. **Support services:** GED preparation, learning center, reduced course load, remedial instruction, study skills assistance, tutoring.

Honors college/program. Application for Presidential Scholarship, minimum ACT score of 24, minimum 3.5 high school GPA, essay required. Top 12-15 applicants accepted each fall.

Majors. **Agriculture:** General, business, horticulture, supplies. **Biology:** General. **Business:** General, accounting, administrative services, business admin, entrepreneurial studies, management information systems, office management, office/clerical, retailing. **Communications:** General, broadcast journalism, journalism. **Communications technology:** General. **Computer sciences:** General, networking. **Education:** General, early childhood, elementary, multi-level teacher, physical, secondary, speech. **Engineering:** General. **Family/consumer sciences:** General, institutional food production. **Foreign languages:** General, Spanish. **Health:** Athletic training, EMT paramedic, predental, premedicine, prenursing, prepharmacy, preveterinary. **History:** General. **Legal studies:** Prelaw. **Liberal arts:** Arts/sciences. **Math:** General. **Parks/recreation:** Health/fitness. **Physical sciences:** Chemistry, physics. **Psychology:** General. **Public administration:** Social work. **Social sciences:** General, economics, political science, sociology. **Visual/performing arts:** General, art, dramatic, studio arts.

Computing on campus. 100 workstations in dormitories, library, computer center, student center. Dormitories wired for high-speed internet access. Online course registration, wireless network available.

Student life. **Freshman orientation:** Mandatory. Preregistration for classes offered. **Housing:** Single-sex dorms, apartments available. $100 partly refundable deposit. **Activities:** Bands, choral groups, dance, drama, film society, international student organizations, music ensembles, musical theater, student government, TV station, Phi Theta Kappa, agriculture club.

Athletics. NJCAA. **Intercollegiate:** Baseball M, basketball, cheerleading, cross-country, football (tackle) M, golf, rodeo, soccer, softball W, track and field, volleyball W. **Intramural:** Basketball, bowling, golf, table tennis, volleyball. **Team name:** Red Ravens.

Student services. Adult student services, career counseling, student employment services, financial aid counseling, health services, personal counseling, veterans' counselor. **Physically disabled:** Services for visually, speech, hearing impaired. **Learning disabled:** Comprehensive services available. **Transfer:** Transfer adviser, college fairs on campus for students transferring to 4-year colleges.

Contact. E-mail: admissions@coffeyville.edu
Phone: (620) 252-7047 Toll-free number: (877) 517-2836
Fax: (620) 252-7399
Kelli Bauer, Admissions Coordinator, Coffeyville Community College, 400 West 11th Street, Coffeyville, KS 67337-5064

Colby Community College

Colby, Kansas
www.colbycc.edu
CB code: 6129

- Public 2-year community college
- Commuter campus in small town
- Interview required

General. Founded in 1964. Regionally accredited. **Enrollment:** 577 degree-seeking undergraduates; 928 non-degree-seeking students. **Degrees:** 265 associate awarded. **Location:** 100 miles from Hays, 200 miles from Denver. **Calendar:** Semester, limited summer session. **Full-time faculty:** 58 total; 17% have terminal degrees, 3% minority, 64% women. **Part-time faculty:** 95 total; 61% women. **Class size:** 72% < 20, 26% 20-39, less than 1%

40-49, less than 1% 50-99. **Special facilities:** 64-acre farm, cultural arts center, fitness laboratory.

Student profile. Among degree-seeking undergraduates, 48% enrolled in a transfer program, 52% enrolled in a vocational program, 205 enrolled as first-time, first-year students, 61 transferred in from other institutions.

Part-time:	11%	**Hispanic American:**	3%
Out-of-state:	30%	**Native American:**	1%
Women:	63%	**International:**	2%
African American:	3%	**25 or older:**	12%
Asian American:	2%	**Live on campus:**	30%

Transfer out. Colleges most students transferred to 2008: Fort Hays State University, Kansas State University, University of Kansas.

Basis for selection. Open admission, but selective for some programs. Interview required for physical therapist assistant, veterinary technology, dental hygiene, and nursing programs. Audition recommended for music majors. Portfolios recommended for art majors. **Adult students:** COMPASS required if 2 or more years since ACT/SAT was taken. **Home-schooled:** Transcript of courses and grades, state high school equivalency certificate required.

High school preparation. College-preparatory program recommended.

2008-2009 Annual costs. Tuition/fees: $2,430; $3,600 out-of-state. Per-credit charge: $48 in-state; $87 out-of-state. Nebraska and Colorado border county residents pay $58 per credit hour for tuition, and additional $33 per credit hour for required fees. Room/board: $3,900. Books/supplies: $888. Personal expenses: $850.

2007-2008 Financial aid. Need-based: 163 full-time freshmen applied for aid; 132 were judged to have need; 129 of these received aid. Average need met was 77%. Average scholarship/grant was $4,405; average loan $1,583. 57% of total undergraduate aid awarded as scholarships/grants, 43% as loans/jobs. Need-based aid available for part-time students. Work-study available nights, weekends and for part-time students. **Non-need-based:** Awarded to 167 full-time undergraduates, including 85 freshmen. Scholarships awarded for academics, athletics, music/drama.

Application procedures. Admission: No deadline. No application fee. Admission notification on a rolling basis. **Financial aid:** Priority date 6/1; no closing date. FAFSA required. Applicants notified on a rolling basis starting 5/1.

Academics. Special study options: Cooperative education, distance learning, dual enrollment of high school students, honors, independent study, internships, liberal arts/career combination. License preparation in nursing. **Credit/placement by examination:** AP, CLEP, institutional tests. 30 credit hours maximum toward associate degree. **Support services:** GED preparation and test center, learning center, pre-admission summer program, reduced course load, remedial instruction, study skills assistance, tutoring, writing center.

Majors. Agriculture: Agribusiness operations, agronomy, equestrian studies, equine science, farm/ranch. **Biology:** General. **Business:** Administrative services, business admin. **Communications:** Broadcast journalism, journalism. **Conservation:** Forestry, wildlife. **Education:** General, agricultural, art, biology, business, chemistry, elementary, family/consumer sciences, mathematics, music, physical, science, secondary. **Engineering:** General. **Family/consumer sciences:** General, child care. **Health:** Dental hygiene, medical secretary, nursing (RN), physical therapy assistant, premedicine, prenursing, prepharmacy, preveterinary, veterinary technology/assistant. **History:** General. **Legal studies:** Prelaw. **Liberal arts:** Arts/sciences. **Math:** General. **Physical sciences:** Chemistry. **Psychology:** General. **Public administration:** Social work. **Social sciences:** Sociology. **Visual/performing arts:** General, dramatic.

Most popular majors. Agriculture 10%, business/marketing 11%, health sciences 28%, liberal arts 46%.

Computing on campus. 100 workstations in dormitories, library, computer center, student center. Dormitories wired for high-speed internet access. Online course registration, online library, helpline, wireless network available.

Student life. Freshman orientation: Mandatory, $15 fee. Preregistration for classes offered. **Housing:** Coed dorms, single-sex dorms, special housing for disabled, wellness housing available. $100 fully refundable deposit. **Activities:** Bands, choral groups, drama, literary magazine, music ensembles, musical theater, radio station, student government, student newspaper, TV station.

Athletics. NJCAA. **Intercollegiate:** Baseball M, basketball, cross-country, equestrian, golf, rodeo, softball W, track and field, volleyball W, wrestling M. **Intramural:** Basketball, softball, volleyball. **Team name:** Trojans.

Student services. Adult student services, alcohol/substance abuse counseling, career counseling, services for economically disadvantaged, student employment services, financial aid counseling, health services, personal counseling, placement for graduates, veterans' counselor. **Physically disabled:** Services for visually, speech, hearing impaired. **Transfer:** Pre-admission transcript evaluation for new students. Transfer adviser, college fairs on campus for students transferring to 4-year colleges.

Contact. E-mail: admissions@colbycc.edu
Phone: (785) 460-4690 Toll-free number: (888) 634-9350
Fax: (785) 460-4691
Nikol Nolan, Director of Admissions, Colby Community College, 1255 South Range Avenue, Colby, KS 67701

Cowley County Community College
Arkansas City, Kansas
www.cowley.edu **CB code: 6008**

- Public 2-year community and technical college
- Commuter campus in large town

General. Founded in 1922. Regionally accredited. **Enrollment:** 3,372 degree-seeking undergraduates; 257 non-degree-seeking students. **Degrees:** 561 associate awarded. **Location:** 50 miles from Wichita. **Calendar:** Semester, limited summer session. **Full-time faculty:** 41 total; 56% women. **Part-time faculty:** 179 total; 1% minority, 59% women. **Class size:** 69% < 20, 30% 20-39, less than 1% 50-99, less than 1% >100.

Student profile. Among degree-seeking undergraduates, 79% enrolled in a transfer program, 21% enrolled in a vocational program, 3% already have a bachelor's degree or higher, 527 enrolled as first-time, first-year students.

Part-time:	55%	**Hispanic American:**	4%
Out-of-state:	6%	**Native American:**	1%
Women:	61%	**25 or older:**	33%
African American:	8%	**Live on campus:**	10%
Asian American:	4%		

Basis for selection. Open admission, but selective for some programs. Special requirements for mobile intensive care training program. **Home-schooled:** Transcript of courses and grades required.

2008-2009 Annual costs. Tuition/fees: $2,040; $2,190 out-of-district; $3,750 out-of-state. Per-credit charge: $45 in-district; $50 out-of-district; $102 out-of-state. Oklahoma border county resident tuition: $50 per-credit-hour. Room/board: $4,200. Books/supplies: $600. Personal expenses: $900.

2008-2009 Financial aid. Need-based: Average scholarship/grant was $3,796; average loan $3,242. 53% of total undergraduate aid awarded as scholarships/grants, 47% as loans/jobs. Need-based aid available for part-time students. **Non-need-based:** Scholarships awarded for academics, alumni affiliation, art, athletics, leadership, music/drama, state residency.

Application procedures. Admission: No deadline. No application fee. Admission notification on a rolling basis. **Financial aid:** Priority date 4/15; no closing date. FAFSA required. Applicants notified on a rolling basis starting 1/15; must reply within 2 week(s) of notification.

Academics. Special study options: Cooperative education, distance learning, double major, dual enrollment of high school students, independent study, internships, teacher certification program. Area vocational-technical school programs available. **Credit/placement by examination:** AP, CLEP. 15 credit hours maximum toward associate degree. Students with ACT scores of 21 on verbal and math not required to take placement test. **Support services:** GED preparation and test center, learning center, reduced course load, remedial instruction, study skills assistance, tutoring.

Majors. Agriculture: Farm/ranch. **Business:** General, administrative services, business admin, entrepreneurial studies, office/clerical, organizational behavior. **Communications:** General, journalism. **Computer sciences:** Networking. **Education:** General. **Engineering:** General. **Family/consumer sciences:** Child care. **Foreign languages:** General, sign language interpretation. **Health:** EMT paramedic, nursing assistant. **Liberal arts:** Arts/sciences. **Math:** General. **Mechanic/repair:** Aircraft, automotive, avionics. **Personal/culinary services:** Cosmetic. **Philosophy/religion:** Philosophy, religion. **Physical sciences:** General, chemistry. **Production:** Machine shop technology, welding. **Protective services:** Corrections, law enforcement admin, police science. **Science technology:** Radiologic. **Social sciences:** General. **Visual/performing arts:** General, art, commercial/advertising art, music.

Most popular majors. Liberal arts 86%.

Computing on campus. 130 workstations in dormitories, library, computer center, student center. Dormitories wired for high-speed internet access and linked to campus network. Commuter students can connect to campus network.

Student life. **Freshman orientation:** Available. Preregistration for classes offered. **Housing:** Single-sex dorms, wellness housing available. $100 nonrefundable deposit. **Activities:** Bands, choral groups, drama, music ensembles, student government, student newspaper, Academic Civic Engagement through Service, Campus Christian Fellowship, Black Student Union, Young Democrats, College Republicans.

Athletics. NJCAA. **Intercollegiate:** Baseball M, basketball, cheerleading, cross-country, softball W, tennis, track and field, volleyball W. **Intramural:** Basketball, football (non-tackle), softball, volleyball. **Team name:** Tigers.

Student services. Career counseling, student employment services, health services, personal counseling, placement for graduates, veterans' counselor.

Contact. Phone: (620) 442-0430 Toll-free number: (800) 593-2222
Fax: (620) 441-5350
Shayla McDonald, Director of Admissions, Cowley County Community College, PO Box 1147, Arkansas City, KS 67005-1147

Dodge City Community College
Dodge City, Kansas
www.dc3.edu **CB code: 6166**

- Public 2-year community and technical college
- Commuter campus in large town

General. Founded in 1935. Regionally accredited. **Enrollment:** 1,554 degree-seeking undergraduates. **Degrees:** 124 associate awarded. **Location:** 150 miles from Wichita. **Calendar:** Semester, limited summer session. **Full-time faculty:** 60 total. **Part-time faculty:** 110 total. **Class size:** 25% < 20, 75% 20-39. **Special facilities:** Federal depository of books and documents, horse barn, rodeo practice arena, astronomy center.

Student profile.

Out-of-state:	5%	**Live on campus:**	33%
25 or older:	45%		

Transfer out. **Colleges most students transferred to 2008:** Kansas State University, Fort Hays State University, University of Kansas, Pittsburg State University, Wichita State University.

Basis for selection. Open admission, but selective for some programs. Special requirements for nursing program. Students without GED or high school diploma must take test to demonstrate ability to benefit. ASSET used as placement test. Michigan test given to ESL students. Interview recommended for nursing majors. Audition recommended for music majors. Portfolio recommended for art majors.

High school preparation. Recommended units include English 4, mathematics 3, social studies 3 and science 3.

2008-2009 Annual costs. Tuition/fees: $1,950; $2,700 out-of-state. Per-credit charge: $35 in-district; $35 out-of-district; $45 out-of-state. Room/board: $4,370. Books/supplies: $600. Personal expenses: $1,000.

2007-2008 Financial aid. **Need-based:** Need-based aid available for part-time students. Work-study available nights, weekends and for part-time students. **Non-need-based:** Scholarships awarded for academics, athletics, music/drama, state residency.

Application procedures. **Admission:** No deadline. No application fee. Admission notification on a rolling basis. **Financial aid:** Priority date 3/15; no closing date. FAFSA, institutional form required. Applicants notified on a rolling basis; must reply within 2 week(s) of notification.

Academics. **Special study options:** Cross-registration, distance learning, double major, dual enrollment of high school students, ESL, independent study, internships. Bachelor's degree programs available on campus. License preparation in nursing, paramedic. **Credit/placement by examination:** CLEP. 30 credit hours maximum toward associate degree. **Support services:** GED preparation and test center, learning center, reduced course load, remedial instruction, tutoring, writing center.

Majors. **Agriculture:** Agribusiness operations, business, equestrian studies, farm/ranch, horticulture. **Biology:** General. **Business:** General, accounting, banking/financial services, management information systems, office management. **Communications:** Broadcast journalism, journalism. **Computer sciences:** General, computer science, data processing. **Education:** General, elementary, secondary. **Engineering:** General. **Family/consumer sciences:** Child care. **Health:** Athletic training, licensed practical nurse, medical records technology, nursing (RN), nursing assistant, premedicine, prepharmacy, preveterinary, substance abuse counseling. **Legal studies:** Legal secretary, prelaw. **Math:** General. **Mechanic/repair:** Electronics/electrical. **Parks/recreation:** Health/fitness. **Physical sciences:** Chemistry. **Protective services:** Firefighting. **Social sciences:** General, economics, sociology. **Visual/performing arts:** Art.

Computing on campus. 125 workstations in dormitories, library, computer center, student center. Dormitories wired for high-speed internet access.

Student life. **Freshman orientation:** Mandatory. Held 2 days before classes begins. **Housing:** Guaranteed on-campus for freshmen. Single-sex dorms, wellness housing available. **Activities:** Bands, choral groups, dance, drama, music ensembles, radio station, student government, student newspaper, TV station, Black student union, Fellowship of Christian Athletes, Hispanic American leadership organization, Newman club.

Athletics. NJCAA. **Intercollegiate:** Baseball M, basketball, cross-country, football (tackle) M, golf, softball W, track and field, volleyball W. **Intramural:** Basketball, handball, racquetball, softball W. **Team name:** Conquistadors.

Student services. Adult student services, career counseling, student employment services, veterans' counselor. **Physically disabled:** Services for visually, speech, hearing impaired. **Transfer:** Transfer adviser, college fairs on campus for students transferring to 4-year colleges.

Contact. Phone: (620) 227-9217 Toll-free number: (800) 367-3222
Fax: (620) 227-9277
Tammy Tabor, Director of Admissions, Dodge City Community College, 2501 North 14th Avenue, Dodge City, KS 67801-2399

Donnelly College
Kansas City, Kansas
www.donnelly.edu **CB code: 6167**

- Private 2-year junior and liberal arts college affiliated with Roman Catholic Church
- Commuter campus in large city

General. Founded in 1949. Regionally accredited. **Enrollment:** 631 degree-seeking undergraduates; 3 non-degree-seeking students. **Degrees:** 5 bachelor's, 42 associate awarded. **Location:** 5 miles from downtown. **Calendar:** Semester, limited summer session. **Full-time faculty:** 13 total; 15% have terminal degrees, 8% minority, 54% women. **Part-time faculty:** 28 total; 4% have terminal degrees, 29% minority, 54% women. **Class size:** 69% < 20, 31% 20-39.

Student profile. Among degree-seeking undergraduates, 90% enrolled in a transfer program, 106 enrolled as first-time, first-year students, 60 transferred in from other institutions.

Part-time:	53%	**Hispanic American:**	31%
Out-of-state:	11%	**Native American:**	1%
Women:	70%	**International:**	8%
African American:	45%	**25 or older:**	52%
Asian American:	5%	**Live on campus:**	3%

Transfer out. 31% of students enrolled in the transfer program go on to 4-year colleges. **Colleges most students transferred to 2008:** University of Kansas, University of Missouri-Kansas City, Kansas City Kansas Community College, Kansas State, Johnson County Community College.

Basis for selection. Open admission. Michigan Proficiency Test required of foreign applicants. **Homeschooled:** Must take the Ability to Benefit test or have a GED.

2008-2009 Annual costs. Tuition/fees: $5,040. Per-credit charge: $180. Books/supplies: $830. Personal expenses: $1,860.

2008-2009 Financial aid. **Need-based:** 39 full-time freshmen applied for aid; 39 were judged to have need; 39 of these received aid. Average need met was 99%. Average scholarship/grant was $2,057; average loan $1,290. 77% of total undergraduate aid awarded as scholarships/grants, 23% as loans/jobs. Need-based aid available for part-time students. Work-study available for part-time students. **Non-need-based:** Awarded to 4 full-time undergraduates, including 2 freshmen. Scholarships awarded for academics, religious affiliation.

Application procedures. **Admission:** No deadline. No application fee. Admission notification on a rolling basis. **Financial aid:** Priority date 4/1;

no closing date. FAFSA, institutional form required. Applicants notified on a rolling basis starting 7/1.

Academics. Special study options: Distance learning, dual enrollment of high school students, ESL, liberal arts/career combination, weekend college. Bachelor's degree programs available on campus. **Credit/placement by examination:** CLEP, institutional tests. 20 credit hours maximum toward associate degree. **Support services:** GED preparation, learning center, reduced course load, remedial instruction, study skills assistance, tutoring.

Majors. Biology: General. **Business:** General, accounting, office/clerical. **Computer sciences:** Data processing, programming. **Education:** Elementary. **Engineering:** General. **Health:** Prenursing. **Math:** General. **Physical sciences:** General. **Psychology:** General. **Social sciences:** General.

Most popular majors. Business/marketing 26%, education 28%, liberal arts 28%.

Computing on campus. 75 workstations in library, computer center. Online library available.

Student life. Freshman orientation: Mandatory. Preregistration for classes offered. **Housing:** Coed dorms available. $100 nonrefundable deposit, deadline 8/1. **Activities:** Campus ministries, Orginazation of Student Leadership.

Student services. Career counseling, services for economically disadvantaged, student employment services, financial aid counseling, personal counseling, placement for graduates, veterans' counselor. **Physically disabled:** Services for visually, speech, hearing impaired. **Transfer:** Transfer adviser, college fairs on campus for students transferring to 4-year colleges.

Contact. E-mail: sanders@donnelly.edu
Phone: (913) 621-8713 Fax: (913) 621-8719
Frances Sanders, Dean of Enrollment Services, Donnelly College, 608 North 18th Street, Kansas City, KS 66102-4210

Fort Scott Community College

Fort Scott, Kansas
www.fortscott.edu **CB code: 6219**

- Public 2-year community college
- Commuter campus in small town

General. Founded in 1919. Regionally accredited. **Enrollment:** 1,587 degree-seeking undergraduates. **Degrees:** 233 associate awarded. **Location:** 25 miles from Pittsburg. **Calendar:** Semester, limited summer session. **Full-time faculty:** 60 total. **Part-time faculty:** 75 total. **Special facilities:** Indoor and outdoor rodeo training facilities.

Student profile.

Out-of-state:	14%	**Live on campus:**	14%

Basis for selection. Open admission.

2008-2009 Annual costs. Tuition/fees: $2,100; $3,780 out-of-state. Per-credit charge: $40 in-state; $96 out-of-state. Students from bordering states of Oklahoma, Nebraska, Arkansas, Missouri, and Colorado pay $2,940 annual full-time tuition or $98 per credit hour. Room/board: $4,320. Books/supplies: $550. Personal expenses: $1,020.

Application procedures. Admission: No deadline. No application fee. Admission notification on a rolling basis. **Financial aid:** No deadline. Applicants notified on a rolling basis starting 10/1.

Academics. Special study options: Cooperative education, distance learning, dual enrollment of high school students, ESL, independent study, internships, study abroad, teacher certification program, weekend college. **Credit/placement by examination:** AP, CLEP. 18 credit hours maximum toward associate degree. **Support services:** Learning center, pre-admission summer program, remedial instruction, tutoring.

Majors. Agriculture: Animal sciences, business. **Business:** General, administrative services, business admin, management information systems. **Communications:** General, public relations. **Communications technology:** Graphic/printing. **Computer sciences:** General. **Conservation:** General. **Education:** General. **Health:** Licensed practical nurse. **History:** General. **Liberal arts:** Arts/sciences. **Physical sciences:** Chemistry, physics. **Protective services:** Law enforcement admin. **Psychology:** General. **Social sciences:** General, criminology.

Student life. Freshman orientation: Available. Preregistration for classes offered. **Housing:** Coed dorms available. **Activities:** Bands, choral groups, dance, drama, literary magazine, music ensembles, musical theater, student government, student newspaper, symphony orchestra, Christians on Campus.

Athletics. NJCAA. **Intercollegiate:** Baseball M, basketball, cheerleading M, cross-country, football (tackle) M, rodeo, softball W, volleyball W. **Intramural:** Basketball, bowling, racquetball. **Team name:** Greyhounds.

Student services. Adult student services, services for economically disadvantaged, student employment services, financial aid counseling. **Transfer:** Transfer adviser, college fairs on campus for students transferring to 4-year colleges.

Contact. Phone: (620) 223-2700 ext. 353 Fax: (620) 223-6530
Mert Barrows, Director of Admissions, Fort Scott Community College, 2108 South Horton Street, Fort Scott, KS 66701

Garden City Community College

Garden City, Kansas
www.gcccks.edu **CB code: 6246**

- Public 2-year community college
- Commuter campus in large town

General. Founded in 1919. Regionally accredited. **Enrollment:** 1,984 undergraduates. **Degrees:** 205 associate awarded. **Location:** 200 miles from Wichita. **Calendar:** Semester, limited summer session. **Full-time faculty:** 67 total; 46% women. **Part-time faculty:** 72 total; 39% women. **Class size:** 80% < 20, 19% 20-39, less than 1% 40-49, less than 1% 50-99, less than 1% >100. **Special facilities:** Cadaver lab, fire arms training system, fire training tower. **Partnerships:** Formal partnerships with John Deere Company and dealers (John Deere Agricultural technical program,) Centers of excellence in automotive, cosmetology and broadcasting offered in cooperation with area high schools, and Ford Motor Company.

Student profile.

Out-of-state:	7%	**Live on campus:**	15%
25 or older:	40%		

Basis for selection. Open admission, but selective for some programs. Additional requirements and/or an additional application is required for Nursing, Automotive Technology, Industrial Maintenance Technology, Emergency Medical Services Technology, Information Technology, and John Deere Agricultural Technology programs. Michigan English Placement Test required. Audition recommended for music majors. Portfolio recommended for art and photography majors.

High school preparation. College-preparatory program recommended. Recommended units include English 4, mathematics 2, social studies 2 and science 2.

2008-2009 Annual costs. Tuition/fees: $1,860; $2,580 out-of-state. Per-credit charge: $41 in-state; $65 out-of-state. Room/board: $4,350. Books/supplies: $790. Personal expenses: $1,585.

2007-2008 Financial aid. Need-based: 73% of total undergraduate aid awarded as scholarships/grants, 27% as loans/jobs. Need-based aid available for part-time students. Work-study available nights, weekends and for part-time students. **Non-need-based:** Scholarships awarded for academics, art, athletics, job skills, leadership, minority status, music/drama, state residency.

Application procedures. Admission: No deadline. No application fee. Application must be submitted on paper. Admission notification on a rolling basis. **Financial aid:** Priority date 3/1; no closing date. FAFSA, institutional form required. Applicants notified on a rolling basis starting 4/15; must reply within 2 week(s) of notification.

Academics. Special study options: Cooperative education, cross-registration, distance learning, dual enrollment of high school students, ESL, internships, liberal arts/career combination, student-designed major. Bachelor's degree programs available on campus. License preparation in nursing, paramedic, radiology. **Credit/placement by examination:** AP, CLEP, IB, institutional tests. 30 credit hours maximum toward associate degree. **Support services:** GED preparation and test center, learning center, remedial instruction, study skills assistance, tutoring.

Majors. Agriculture: General, agronomy, animal sciences, business, economics, farm/ranch. **Biology:** General. **Business:** General. **Communications:** General, journalism. **Computer sciences:** General, computer science, networking. **Conservation:** Forestry, management/policy, wildlife. **Education:** General, art, business, chemistry, early childhood, elementary, health, history, mathematics, middle, music, physical, physics, reading, science, secondary, social science, social studies. **Engineering:** General, science. **Engineering technology:** Drafting. **Family/consumer sciences:** General, child care. **Health:** Athletic training, nursing (RN). **Interdisciplinary:** Behavioral sciences, natural sciences. **Legal studies:** Prelaw. **Liberal arts:** Arts/sciences. **Math:** General. **Parks/recreation:** Health/fitness. **Physical sciences:** General, chemistry. **Protective services:** Firefighting, law enforcement admin, police science. **Psychology:** General. **Social sciences:** General. **Visual/performing arts:** General, art, dramatic.

Most popular majors. Agriculture 6%, biological/life sciences 8%, business/marketing 14%, education 15%, health sciences 12%, liberal arts 16%.

Computing on campus. 300 workstations in dormitories, library, computer center, student center. Dormitories wired for high-speed internet access and linked to campus network.

Student life. Freshman orientation: Available. Held prior to start of classes. **Housing:** Coed dorms, apartments, wellness housing available. $300 deposit, deadline 8/1. **Activities:** Bands, choral groups, dance, drama, literary magazine, music ensembles, musical theater, student government, student newspaper, Newman Club, Hispanic American Leadership Organization, Black Student Union.

Athletics. NJCAA. **Intercollegiate:** Baseball M, basketball, cheerleading, cross-country, football (tackle) M, rodeo, soccer, softball W, track and field, volleyball W. **Intramural:** Archery, basketball, bowling, racquetball, rifle, softball, swimming, table tennis, tennis, track and field, volleyball. **Team name:** Broncbusters.

Student services. Career counseling, services for economically disadvantaged, student employment services, financial aid counseling, health services, on-campus daycare, personal counseling, veterans' counselor. **Physically disabled:** Services for visually, speech, hearing impaired. **Transfer:** Transfer adviser, college fairs on campus for students transferring to 4-year colleges.

Contact. E-mail: nikki.geier@gcccks.edu
Phone: (620) 276-9608 Toll-free number: (800) 658-1696
Fax: (620) 276-9650
Nikki Geier, Director of Admissions, Garden City Community College, 801 Campus Drive, Garden City, KS 67846-6333

Hesston College

Hesston, Kansas
www.hesston.edu **CB code: 6274**

- Private 2-year junior college affiliated with Mennonite Church
- Residential campus in small town

General. Founded in 1909. Regionally accredited. **Enrollment:** 419 degree-seeking undergraduates; 6 non-degree-seeking students. **Degrees:** 163 associate awarded. **Location:** 35 miles from Wichita. **Calendar:** Semester, limited summer session. **Full-time faculty:** 24 total; 4% have terminal degrees, 50% women. **Part-time faculty:** 19 total; 10% have terminal degrees, 5% minority, 53% women. **Class size:** 63% < 20, 33% 20-39, 4% 40-49. **Special facilities:** Arboretum, retreat center. **Partnerships:** Formal partnerships with schools in the Mennonite Secondary Education Council.

Student profile. Among degree-seeking undergraduates, 60% enrolled in a transfer program, 40% enrolled in a vocational program, 1% already have a bachelor's degree or higher, 176 enrolled as first-time, first-year students, 39 transferred in from other institutions.

Part-time:	11%	**Hispanic American:**	4%
Out-of-state:	57%	**International:**	10%
Women:	55%	**25 or older:**	14%
African American:	5%	**Live on campus:**	71%

Transfer out. 70% of students enrolled in the transfer program go on to 4-year colleges. **Colleges most students transferred to 2008:** Eastern Mennonite College, Goshen College, Wichita State University, Bethel College.

Basis for selection. Open admission, but selective for some programs. Special requirements for nursing and pastoral ministries programs. A supplementary application is required for admission to the nursing and pastoral ministries programs. ASSET required for placement if ACT/SAT scores not submitted. **Homeschooled:** Must provide ACT, SAT, ASSET, or COMPASS scores.

High school preparation. Recommended units include English 4, mathematics 3, social studies 3 and science 3.

2008-2009 Annual costs. Tuition/fees: $18,776. Room/board: $6,220. Books/supplies: $1,500. Personal expenses: $1,500.

2007-2008 Financial aid. Need-based: 165 full-time freshmen applied for aid; 149 were judged to have need; 149 of these received aid. Average need met was 80%. Average scholarship/grant was $10,237; average loan $3,750. 63% of total undergraduate aid awarded as scholarships/grants, 37% as loans/jobs. Need-based aid available for part-time students. Work-study available nights, weekends and for part-time students. **Non-need-based:** Awarded to 200 full-time undergraduates, including 107 freshmen. Scholarships awarded for academics, alumni affiliation, art, athletics, job skills, music/drama.

Application procedures. Admission: Priority date 5/1; no deadline. $15 fee. Admission notification on a rolling basis. **Financial aid:** Priority date 4/1; no closing date. FAFSA required. Applicants notified on a rolling basis starting 2/1; must reply within 4 week(s) of notification.

Academics. Special study options: Cooperative education, ESL, independent study, internships, liberal arts/career combination. License preparation in aviation, nursing. **Credit/placement by examination:** AP, CLEP, IB, institutional tests. 12 credit hours maximum toward associate degree. **Support services:** Learning center, reduced course load, remedial instruction, study skills assistance, tutoring, writing center.

Majors. Business: General. **Computer sciences:** General. **Education:** Early childhood. **Health:** Nursing (RN). **Liberal arts:** Arts/sciences. **Theology:** Theology. **Transportation:** Aviation.

Most popular majors. Health sciences 45%, theological studies 7%, trade and industry 16%.

Computing on campus. 78 workstations in library, computer center, student center. Dormitories wired for high-speed internet access and linked to campus network. Wireless network available.

Student life. Freshman orientation: Mandatory. Preregistration for classes offered. Held one-day prior to the beginning of classes. All new first-time students are required to enroll during the first semester in either College Orientation/Success or College Learning Strategies. **Policies:** Use of alcohol, drugs, smoking and possession of firearms/fireworks prohibited. Decency in dress and appearance is expected. Chapel attendance is required. Religious observance required. **Housing:** Guaranteed on-campus for all undergraduates. Single-sex dorms, wellness housing available. $50 deposit. **Activities:** Pep band, choral groups, drama, music ensembles, musical theater, student newspaper, peace and service club, prison ministries, International Christian Fellowship, Students for Responsible Citizenship.

Athletics. NJCAA. **Intercollegiate:** Baseball M, basketball, soccer, softball W, tennis, volleyball W. **Intramural:** Basketball, soccer, volleyball. **Team name:** Larks.

Student services. Alcohol/substance abuse counseling, chaplain/spiritual director, career counseling, financial aid counseling, minority student services, personal counseling, veterans' counselor. **Physically disabled:** Services for hearing impaired. **Learning disabled:** Comprehensive services available. **Transfer:** Pre-admission transcript evaluation for new students. Transfer adviser, college fairs on campus for students transferring to 4-year colleges.

Contact. E-mail: admissions@hesston.edu
Phone: (620) 327-8222 Toll-free number: (800) 995-2757
Fax: (620) 327-8300
Joel Kauffman, Director of Admissions, Hesston College, Box 3000, Hesston, KS 67062-2093

Highland Community College

Highland, Kansas
www.highlandcc.edu **CB code: 6276**

- Public 2-year community college
- Residential campus in rural community

General. Founded in 1857. Regionally accredited. **Enrollment:** 1,689 degree-seeking undergraduates. **Degrees:** 196 associate awarded. **Location:** 26 miles from St. Joseph, Missouri. **Calendar:** Semester, limited summer session. **Full-time faculty:** 38 total; 5% have terminal degrees, 3% minority, 50% women. **Part-time faculty:** 192 total; 5% have terminal degrees, 4% minority, 55% women. **Class size:** 75% < 20, 24% 20-39, less than 1% 40-49, less than 1% 50-99. **Special facilities:** Photography studio, sports medicine/athletic trainer facilities, learning skills center, communication technology complex, wellness center.

Student profile. Among degree-seeking undergraduates, 90% enrolled in a transfer program, 9% enrolled in a vocational program.

Out-of-state:	7%	**Native American:**	3%
African American:	7%	**25 or older:**	29%
Asian American:	1%	**Live on campus:**	19%
Hispanic American:	3%		

Transfer out. 80% of students enrolled in the transfer program go on to 4-year colleges. **Colleges most students transferred to 2008:** Kansas State University, Emporia State University, University of Kansas, Washburn University, Missouri Western State College.

Basis for selection. Open admission, but selective for out-of-state students. Out-of-state applicants must be in top two-thirds of graduating class or have 14 ACT or 660 SAT (exclusive of Writing). Placement tests determine program eligibility. **Adult students:** Full Compass Placement. **Homeschooled:** Transcript of courses and grades required. **Learning Disabled:** Students are asked to self-identify if they have an IEP or other verified disability. There are no special requirements or procedures.

High school preparation. College-preparatory program required. 11 units recommended. Recommended units include English 3, mathematics 2, social studies 2 and science 4.

2008-2009 Annual costs. Tuition/fees: $1,980; $2,370 out-of-district; $3,900 out-of-state. Per-credit charge: $39 in-district; $52 out-of-district; $103 out-of-state. Out-of-state within 150 miles: $65 per-credit-hour. Room/board: $4,690. Books/supplies: $400. Personal expenses: $915.

2007-2008 Financial aid. Need-based: 58% of total undergraduate aid awarded as scholarships/grants, 42% as loans/jobs. Need-based aid available for part-time students. Work-study available nights, weekends and for part-time students. **Non-need-based:** Scholarships awarded for academics, alumni affiliation, art, athletics, job skills, leadership, music/drama. **Additional information:** Auditions and portfolios important for certain scholarship candidates.

Application procedures. Admission: Priority date 7/1; no deadline. No application fee. Admission notification on a rolling basis beginning on or about 4/1. Application deadline for out-of-state applicants August 1, must reply within 2 weeks. SAT or ACT recommended, ACT preferred. Score report by August 1. **Financial aid:** Priority date 4/1; no closing date. FAFSA, institutional form required. Applicants notified on a rolling basis starting 4/15; must reply within 14 week(s) of notification.

Academics. Special study options: Cooperative education, distance learning, double major, dual enrollment of high school students, independent study, student-designed major. 5 non-credit classes given through website. License preparation in nursing. **Credit/placement by examination:** AP, CLEP, institutional tests. 15 credit hours maximum toward associate degree. **Support services:** GED preparation and test center, learning center, preadmission summer program, reduced course load, remedial instruction, study skills assistance, tutoring.

Majors. Agriculture: General, business, economics. **Biology:** General. **Business:** General, accounting, business admin, marketing. **Construction:** General, electrician. **Education:** General, early childhood, elementary, secondary. **Health:** Health services, licensed practical nurse, medical records technology, nursing assistant. **History:** General. **Math:** General. **Mechanic/repair:** Auto body, automotive, diesel, heating/ac/refrig. **Parks/recreation:** Health/fitness. **Physical sciences:** General. **Protective services:** Law enforcement admin, security services. **Psychology:** General. **Visual/performing arts:** Commercial photography, dramatic, music performance, photography, studio arts. **Other:** Computer technology, Industrial welding.

Most popular majors. Business/marketing 13%, education 13%, health sciences 18%, security/protective services 6%.

Computing on campus. 96 workstations in library, computer center. Dormitories linked to campus network. Commuter students can connect to campus network. Online course registration available.

Student life. Freshman orientation: Mandatory. Preregistration for classes offered. **Housing:** Coed dorms, single-sex dorms, apartments, wellness housing available. $150 fully refundable deposit. **Activities:** Bands, choral groups, dance, drama, music ensembles, musical theater, student government, student newspaper, campus Christian fellowship, Christian athletes association.

Athletics. NJCAA. **Intercollegiate:** Baseball M, basketball, cheerleading, cross-country, football (tackle) M, softball W, track and field, volleyball W. **Intramural:** Badminton, basketball, football (non-tackle), softball, table tennis, tennis, volleyball. **Team name:** Scotties.

Student services. Adult student services, career counseling, student employment services, financial aid counseling, personal counseling, placement for graduates, veterans' counselor. **Physically disabled:** Services for visually, speech, hearing impaired. **Transfer:** Transfer adviser, college fairs on campus for students transferring to 4-year colleges.

Contact. E-mail: mscott@highlandcc.edu
Phone: (785) 442-6020 Fax: (785) 442-6106
Cheryl Rasmussen, Vice President for Student Services, Highland Community College, 606 West Main Street, Highland, KS 66035-0068

Hutchinson Community College

Hutchinson, Kansas
www.hutchcc.edu **CB code: 6281**

- Public 2-year community college
- Commuter campus in large town

General. Founded in 1928. Regionally accredited. Additional centers in Newton, McPherson. **Enrollment:** 3,475 degree-seeking undergraduates; 1,378 non-degree-seeking students. **Degrees:** 632 associate awarded. **Location:** 45 miles from Wichita, 200 miles from Kansas City. **Calendar:** Semester, limited summer session. **Full-time faculty:** 116 total; 14% have terminal degrees, 3% minority, 45% women. **Part-time faculty:** 216 total; 3% have terminal degrees, 1% minority, 51% women. **Class size:** 83% < 20, 16% 20-39, less than 1% 40-49, less than 1% 50-99. **Special facilities:** Cosmosphere space center, Kansas state fair, underground salt mine museum.

Student profile. Among degree-seeking undergraduates, 51% enrolled in a transfer program, 49% enrolled in a vocational program, 4% already have a bachelor's degree or higher, 1,065 enrolled as first-time, first-year students, 460 transferred in from other institutions.

Part-time:	39%	**Hispanic American:**	5%
Out-of-state:	7%	**Native American:**	1%
Women:	56%	**International:**	1%
African American:	6%	**25 or older:**	35%
Asian American:	1%	**Live on campus:**	11%

Transfer out. 70% of students enrolled in the transfer program go on to 4-year colleges. **Colleges most students transferred to 2008:** Kansas State University, University of Kansas, Wichita State University, Emporia State University, Fort Hays State University.

Basis for selection. Open admission, but selective for some programs. Special requirements for nursing, radiology, emergency medical sciences paramedic, health information technology, licensed practical nursing, and surgical technology. C-NET exam required for nursing program applicants. Interview required for nursing, radiology, paramedic, health information technology, and surgical technology programs. **Homeschooled:** Provide home school/high school diploma or GED.

2008-2009 Annual costs. Tuition/fees: $2,130; $3,150 out-of-state. Per-credit charge: $55 in-state; $89 out-of-state. Room/board: $4,724. Books/supplies: $1,100. Personal expenses: $1,100.

Financial aid. Need-based: Need-based aid available for part-time students. **Non-need-based:** Scholarships awarded for academics, athletics, minority status, state residency.

Application procedures. Admission: No deadline. No application fee. Admission notification on a rolling basis. Priority application dates: 1/15 practical nursing, 1/15 nursing, 5/24 radiology, 6/1 health information. **Financial aid:** Priority date 2/1; no closing date. FAFSA, institutional form required. Applicants notified on a rolling basis starting 4/1; must reply within 2 week(s) of notification.

Academics. Special study options: Cooperative education, distance learning, double major, dual enrollment of high school students, ESL, honors, independent study, internships, weekend college. Bachelor's degree programs available on campus. **Credit/placement by examination:** AP, CLEP, institutional tests. 16 credit hours maximum toward associate degree. **Support services:** GED preparation and test center, learning center, remedial instruction, study skills assistance, tutoring, writing center.

Majors. Agriculture: General, farm/ranch, power machinery. **Biology:** General, biotechnology. **Business:** General, administrative services, personal/financial services, retailing. **Communications:** General. **Communications technology:** General. **Computer sciences:** General, networking, systems analysis. **Construction:** Carpentry. **Education:** General. **Engineering:** General. **Engineering technology:** Drafting, manufacturing. **Family/consumer sciences:** General, child care. **Foreign languages:** General. **Health:** EMT paramedic, medical radiologic technology/radiation therapy, medical records technology, nursing (RN), physical therapy assistant. **Legal studies:** Paralegal. **Liberal arts:** Arts/sciences. **Math:** General. **Mechanic/repair:** Auto body, automotive, electronics/electrical. **Physical sciences:** General. **Production:** Machine tool, welding. **Protective services:** Fire safety technology, police science. **Psychology:** General. **Social sciences:** General. **Visual/performing arts:** General.

Most popular majors. Agriculture 6%, business/marketing 16%, health sciences 22%, liberal arts 20%, security/protective services 11%.

Computing on campus. 600 workstations in dormitories, library, computer center, student center. Dormitories wired for high-speed internet access. Helpline, wireless network available.

Student life. **Freshman orientation:** Available. Preregistration for classes offered. **Housing:** Single-sex dorms available. $100 deposit, deadline 7/15. **Activities:** Bands, choral groups, dance, drama, literary magazine, music ensembles, student government, student newspaper, symphony orchestra, Black Cultural Society, Hispanic American leadership organization, Hutchinson Christian Fellowship, Campus Crusade for Christ, Right to Life.

Athletics. NJCAA. **Intercollegiate:** Baseball M, basketball, cross-country, football (tackle) M, golf M, soccer W, softball W, tennis, track and field, volleyball W. **Intramural:** Badminton, basketball, bowling, racquetball, soccer, softball, table tennis, tennis, track and field, volleyball. **Team name:** Blue Dragons.

Student services. Adult student services, career counseling, student employment services, financial aid counseling, health services, on-campus daycare, personal counseling, placement for graduates, veterans' counselor. **Physically disabled:** Services for visually, speech, hearing impaired. **Transfer:** Pre-admission transcript evaluation for new students. Transfer adviser, college fairs on campus for students transferring to 4-year colleges.

Contact. E-mail: info@hutchcc.edu
Phone: (620) 665-3536 Toll-free number: (800) 289-3501
Fax: (620) 665-3301
Corbin Strobel, Director of Admissions, Hutchinson Community College, 1300 North Plum, Hutchinson, KS 67501

Independence Community College

Independence, Kansas
www.indycc.edu **CB code: 6304**

- Public 2-year community and junior college
- Commuter campus in large town

General. Founded in 1925. Regionally accredited. **Enrollment:** 622 degree-seeking undergraduates. **Degrees:** 75 associate awarded. **Location:** 110 miles from Tulsa, Oklahoma. **Calendar:** Semester, extensive summer session. **Full-time faculty:** 31 total. **Part-time faculty:** 105 total. **Special facilities:** Collection of original manuscripts, press clippings, personal books and recordings of playwright William Inge.

Student profile.

Out-of-state:	9%	**Live on campus:**	10%
25 or older:	53%		

Transfer out. **Colleges most students transferred to 2008:** Pittsburg State University, Emporia State University, Wichita State University, Kansas State University, University of Kansas.

Basis for selection. Open admission.

High school preparation. 17 units recommended. Recommended units include English 4, mathematics 4, social studies 2, history 2, science 2 (laboratory 1) and foreign language 2.

2008-2009 Annual costs. Tuition/fees: $1,575; $1,650 out-of-district; $2,850 out-of-state. Per-credit charge: $25 in-district; $28 out-of-district; $68 out-of-state. Room/board: $4,400. Books/supplies: $500.

Financial aid. **Need-based:** Need-based aid available for part-time students. **Non-need-based:** Scholarships awarded for academics, athletics.

Application procedures. **Admission:** No deadline. No application fee. Admission notification on a rolling basis beginning on or about 5/1. **Financial aid:** Priority date 4/1; no closing date. FAFSA required. Applicants notified on a rolling basis.

Academics. **Special study options:** Distance learning, double major, dual enrollment of high school students, ESL, independent study, internships. Bachelor's degree programs available on campus. **Credit/placement by examination:** CLEP, institutional tests. **Support services:** GED preparation and test center, learning center, reduced course load, remedial instruction, study skills assistance, tutoring, writing center.

Majors. **Agriculture:** Business. **Biology:** General, botany, zoology. **Business:** General, accounting, administrative services, business admin, office technology, office/clerical. **Communications:** General, advertising, broadcast journalism, journalism. **Computer sciences:** General, data processing, information systems, programming, systems analysis. **Education:** General, art, biology, chemistry, computer, early childhood, elementary, English, health, history, mathematics, middle, music, physical, sales/marketing, school counseling, science, social science, social studies, technology/industrial arts, voc/tech. **Engineering:** General, architectural, chemical, civil. **Engineering technology:** Architectural, civil, drafting. **Family/consumer sciences:** Child care. **Foreign languages:** General, French, Spanish. **Health:** EMT paramedic, medical secretary, nursing assistant. **History:** General. **Legal studies:** Legal secretary, paralegal, prelaw. **Liberal arts:** Arts/sciences. **Math:** General, applied, statistics. **Physical sciences:** Chemistry. **Psychology:** General. **Public administration:** Human services, social work. **Social sciences:** General, economics, political science, sociology. **Visual/performing arts:** Art, dramatic, studio arts.

Most popular majors. Business/marketing 30%, education 10%, liberal arts 52%.

Computing on campus. 130 workstations in library, computer center, student center. Online course registration available.

Student life. **Freshman orientation:** Mandatory, $15 fee. **Housing:** Coed dorms available. $50 deposit. **Activities:** Bands, choral groups, drama, music ensembles, musical theater, radio station, student government, student newspaper.

Athletics. NJCAA. **Intercollegiate:** Baseball M, basketball, football (tackle) M, softball W, tennis, track and field, volleyball W. **Intramural:** Basketball. **Team name:** Pirates.

Student services. Adult student services, career counseling, student employment services, financial aid counseling, personal counseling, placement for graduates, veterans' counselor. **Transfer:** Pre-admission transcript evaluation for new students. Transfer adviser, college fairs on campus for students transferring to 4-year colleges.

Contact. E-mail: admissions@indycc.edu
Phone: (620) 331-4100 Toll-free number: (800) 842-6063 ext. 5400
Fax: (620) 331-0946
Sheila Smither, Director of Admissions, Independence Community College, 1057 West College Avenue, Independence, KS 67301

Johnson County Community College

Overland Park, Kansas
www.jccc.edu **CB code: 6325**

- Public 2-year community college
- Commuter campus in very large city

General. Founded in 1967. Regionally accredited. **Enrollment:** 19,056 undergraduates. **Degrees:** 1,162 associate awarded. **Location:** 20 miles from downtown Kansas City. **Calendar:** Semester, extensive summer session. **Full-time faculty:** 230 total. **Part-time faculty:** 500 total. **Special facilities:** National academy of railroad sciences.

Student profile.

Out-of-state:	6%	**25 or older:**	37%

Transfer out. **Colleges most students transferred to 2008:** Kansas University, Kansas State University.

Basis for selection. Open admission, but selective for some programs. Special requirements for some allied health programs. ACT required for admission for nursing and dental hygiene applicants. Test scores cannot be older than two years. SAT critial reading not accepted. Interview required for nursing, dental hygiene, emergency medical intensive care technician, respiratory therapy, and paralegal programs. Portfolio required of art majors. **Adult students:** SAT/ACT scores not required. **Homeschooled:** Transcript of courses and grades required. **Learning Disabled:** Access services office assists students with documented disabilities.

2008-2009 Annual costs. Tuition/fees: $1,950; $2,400 out-of-district; $4,470 out-of-state. Per-credit charge: $65 in-district; $80 out-of-district; $149 out-of-state. Books/supplies: $1,000. Personal expenses: $1,500.

2008-2009 Financial aid. **Need-based:** Need-based aid available for part-time students. **Non-need-based:** Scholarships awarded for academics.

Application procedures. Admission: No deadline. No application fee. Admission notification on a rolling basis. **Financial aid:** Priority date 4/1; no closing date. FAFSA required. Applicants notified on a rolling basis starting 4/15; must reply within 2 week(s) of notification.

Academics. Wide variety of telecourses and courses offered by special arrangement. **Special study options:** Cooperative education, cross-registration, distance learning, double major, dual enrollment of high school students, ESL, exchange student, honors, independent study, internships, study abroad, weekend college. **Credit/placement by examination:** AP, CLEP, institutional tests. 30 credit hours maximum toward associate degree. **Support services:** GED preparation and test center, learning center, reduced course load, remedial instruction, tutoring, writing center.

Majors. Business: Accounting, administrative services, business admin, sales/distribution. **Computer sciences:** Applications programming, networking. **Construction:** Power transmission. **Engineering technology:** Civil, drafting, electrical. **Family/consumer sciences:** Child care, institutional food production. **Foreign languages:** Sign language interpretation. **Health:** Dental hygiene, EMT paramedic, medical radiologic technology/radiation therapy, medical records technology, nursing (RN), occupational therapy assistant, physical therapy assistant, respiratory therapy technology, surgical technology, veterinary technology/assistant. **Legal studies:** Paralegal. **Liberal arts:** Arts/sciences. **Mechanic/repair:** Automotive, electronics/electrical. **Protective services:** Firefighting, police science. **Visual/performing arts:** Commercial/advertising art.

Most popular majors. Business/marketing 7%, family/consumer sciences 8%, health sciences 12%, liberal arts 60%.

Computing on campus. 800 workstations in library, computer center, student center. Online course registration, online library, helpline, wireless network available.

Student life. Freshman orientation: Available. **Activities:** Bands, choral groups, drama, student government, student newspaper.

Athletics. NJCAA. **Intercollegiate:** Baseball M, basketball, cross-country, golf M, soccer M, softball W, tennis, track and field, volleyball W. **Intramural:** Basketball M, bowling, handball, racquetball, softball M, table tennis M, tennis M, volleyball M. **Team name:** Cavaliers.

Student services. Adult student services, career counseling, student employment services, on-campus daycare, personal counseling, placement for graduates, veterans' counselor. **Physically disabled:** Services for visually, hearing impaired. **Transfer:** Transfer adviser, college fairs on campus for students transferring to 4-year colleges.

Contact. E-mail: jcccadmissions@jccc.edu
Phone: (913) 469-3803 Toll-free number: (866) 896-5893
Fax: (913) 469-2524
Pete Belk, Director of Admission, Johnson County Community College, 12345 College Boulevard, Overland Park, KS 66210-1299

Kansas City Kansas Community College

Kansas City, Kansas — **CB member**
www.kckcc.edu — **CB code: 6333**

- Public 2-year community and junior college
- Commuter campus in very large city

General. Founded in 1923. Regionally accredited. **Enrollment:** 4,364 degree-seeking undergraduates; 1,456 non-degree-seeking students. **Degrees:** 506 associate awarded. **Calendar:** Semester, extensive summer session. **Full-time faculty:** 119 total; 25% have terminal degrees, 20% minority, 54% women. **Part-time faculty:** 308 total. **Class size:** 76% < 20, 23% 20-39, less than 1% 40-49, less than 1% 50-99. **Partnerships:** Formal partnerships with National Retail Federation Foundation (Industry Standard Certification Affiliation); American Hotel and Lodging Educational Institute (Industry Standard Certification Affiliation); General Motors - Fairfax (Skill Center).

Student profile. Among degree-seeking undergraduates, 80% enrolled in a transfer program, 29% enrolled in a vocational program, 11% already have a bachelor's degree or higher, 821 enrolled as first-time, first-year students, 381 transferred in from other institutions.

Part-time:	58%	**Hispanic American:**	7%
Out-of-state:	5%	**Native American:**	1%
Women:	66%	**International:**	3%
African American:	26%	**25 or older:**	49%
Asian American:	2%		

Basis for selection. Open admission, but selective for some programs. Special requirements for nursing program. **Homeschooled:** Interview required. Admission based on ACT, SAT, or GED scores and interview.

High school preparation. 21 units recommended. Recommended units include English 4, mathematics 4, social studies 4, history 4, science 3 and foreign language 2.

2008-2009 Annual costs. Tuition/fees: $1,770; $4,710 out-of-state. Per-credit charge: $49 in-state; $147 out-of-state. Fees vary by program. Books/supplies: $920. Personal expenses: $2,250.

2007-2008 Financial aid. Need-based: 43% of total undergraduate aid awarded as scholarships/grants, 57% as loans/jobs. Need-based aid available for part-time students. Work-study available nights, weekends and for part-time students. **Non-need-based:** Scholarships awarded for academics, art, athletics, music/drama.

Application procedures. Admission: No deadline. No application fee. Admission notification on a rolling basis. **Financial aid:** Priority date 4/15; no closing date. FAFSA required. Applicants notified on a rolling basis starting 5/1; must reply within 4 week(s) of notification.

Academics. Extensive online classes. **Special study options:** Cooperative education, distance learning, dual enrollment of high school students, ESL, external degree, honors, internships, liberal arts/career combination, weekend college. **Credit/placement by examination:** AP, CLEP, IB, institutional tests. 15 credit hours maximum toward associate degree. **Support services:** GED preparation and test center, learning center, reduced course load, remedial instruction, study skills assistance, tutoring, writing center.

Majors. Business: Accounting/business management, administrative services, business admin, marketing. **Communications technology:** Desktop publishing, recording arts. **Computer sciences:** Networking. **Engineering technology:** CAD/CADD, computer, hazardous materials, software. **Family/consumer sciences:** Child care. **Health:** EMT paramedic, nursing (RN), physical therapy assistant, respiratory therapy assistant, respiratory therapy technology, substance abuse counseling. **Legal studies:** Paralegal. **Liberal arts:** Arts/sciences. **Personal/culinary services:** Mortuary science. **Protective services:** Corrections, firefighting, police science. **Other:** Victim/Survivor services.

Most popular majors. Business/marketing 6%, health sciences 28%, liberal arts 46%, personal/culinary services 7%.

Computing on campus. 900 workstations in library, computer center. Commuter students can connect to campus network. Online course registration, online library, helpline, wireless network available.

Student life. Freshman orientation: Mandatory, $59 fee. Preregistration for classes offered. One credit hour course taken in first semester. **Activities:** Bands, choral groups, drama, international student organizations, music ensembles, musical theater, student government, student newspaper, TV station, African American Student Union, International Student Organization, Campus Forum, Christian Student Union, Phi Theta Kappa, Student Senate, Out Questioning & Straight Diversity Club, Student Organization of Latinos, Economics Club, Students in Free Enterprise.

Athletics. NJCAA. **Intercollegiate:** Baseball M, basketball, cross-country, golf M, soccer M, softball W, track and field, volleyball W. **Team name:** Blue Devils.

Student services. Adult student services, alcohol/substance abuse counseling, career counseling, services for economically disadvantaged, student employment services, financial aid counseling, health services, on-campus daycare, personal counseling, veterans' counselor, women's services. **Physically disabled:** Services for visually, speech, hearing impaired. **Learning disabled:** Comprehensive services available. **Transfer:** Transfer adviser, college fairs on campus for students transferring to 4-year colleges.

Contact. E-mail: admiss@kckcc.edu
Phone: (913) 288-7600 Fax: (913) 288-7648
Denise McDowell, Dean of Enrollment Management and Registrar, Kansas City Kansas Community College, 7250 State Avenue, Kansas City, KS 66112

Labette Community College

Parsons, Kansas
www.labette.edu — **CB code: 6576**

- Public 2-year community college
- Commuter campus in large town

General. Founded in 1923. Regionally accredited. **Enrollment:** 934 degree-seeking undergraduates. **Degrees:** 212 associate awarded. **Location:** 130

miles from Kansas City, 50 miles from Tulsa, Oklahoma. **Calendar:** Semester, extensive summer session. **Full-time faculty:** 30 total; 23% have terminal degrees, 10% minority, 50% women. **Part-time faculty:** 97 total; 3% have terminal degrees, 65% women. **Class size:** 78% < 20, 22% 20-39, less than 1% 40-49. **Special facilities:** Recording technology program equipment and health science equipment. **Partnerships:** Formal partnerships with local businesses.

Student profile.

Out-of-state:	5%	**Live on campus:**	3%
25 or older:	41%		

Transfer out. **Colleges most students transferred to 2008:** Pittsburg State, Emporia State, Wichita State, Kansas University, Kansas State University.

Basis for selection. Open admission, but selective for some programs. Special requirements for health and commercial music programs. ACT, school and College Ability Tests required of nursing applicants. COMPASS also used to measure language proficiency. Interview required for nursing, radiology, respiratory therapy programs, and commercial music programs. **Homeschooled:** Transcript of courses and grades required. GED and ACT scores may be considered. Placement testing available. **Learning Disabled:** Student must notify campus ADA coordinator at least 30 days prior to first day of classes (earlier in special circumstances).

2008-2009 Annual costs. Tuition/fees: $2,130; $2,880 out-of-state. Per-credit charge: $42 in-state; $67 out-of-state. Residents of neighboring states (AR, MO, OK) pay per-credit-hour tuition rate of $63. Books/supplies: $550. Personal expenses: $2,000.

Financial aid. **Need-based:** Need-based aid available for part-time students. Work-study available nights. **Non-need-based:** Scholarships awarded for academics, leadership.

Application procedures. **Admission:** No deadline. No application fee. Admission notification on a rolling basis. **Financial aid:** No deadline. FAFSA required. Applicants notified on a rolling basis starting 4/4; must reply within 2 week(s) of notification.

Academics. Extensive PLATO learning system available. Four-year bachelor's program with Emporia State University, Washburn University. **Special study options:** Distance learning, dual enrollment of high school students, liberal arts/career combination. License preparation in nursing, radiology. **Credit/placement by examination:** AP, CLEP, institutional tests. 12 credit hours maximum toward associate degree. **Support services:** GED preparation and test center, learning center, remedial instruction, study skills assistance, tutoring, writing center.

Majors. **Biology:** General. **Business:** Accounting, business admin, office/clerical. **Communications:** Journalism. **Computer sciences:** General, data processing, LAN/WAN management, networking, programming. **Education:** General, business, early childhood, elementary, music, secondary. **Health:** Medical secretary, nursing (RN), radiologic technology/medical imaging, respiratory therapy technology. **History:** General. **Legal studies:** Legal secretary, prelaw. **Liberal arts:** Arts/sciences. **Protective services:** Corrections, firefighting, law enforcement admin. **Psychology:** General. **Social sciences:** General, political science. **Visual/performing arts:** Commercial/advertising art, music management, studio arts.

Most popular majors. Business/marketing 11%, education 15%, health sciences 53%.

Computing on campus. 150 workstations in library, computer center, student center. Commuter students can connect to campus network. Online library, helpline, student web hosting, wireless network available.

Student life. **Freshman orientation:** Mandatory. **Activities:** Bands, choral groups, dance, drama, music ensembles, student government, Christian Club, Phi Beta Lambda, Phi Theta Kappa.

Athletics. NJCAA. **Intercollegiate:** Baseball M, basketball, cheerleading, softball W, tennis W, volleyball W, wrestling M. **Team name:** Cardinals.

Student services. Adult student services, career counseling, services for economically disadvantaged, student employment services, financial aid counseling, personal counseling, placement for graduates, veterans' counselor. **Physically disabled:** Services for visually, speech, hearing impaired. **Transfer:** Transfer adviser, college fairs on campus for students transferring to 4-year colleges.

Contact. Phone: (620) 421-6700 Toll-free number: (888) 522-3883
Fax: (620) 421-0180
Tammy Fuentez, Director of Admissions, Labette Community College, 200 South 14th Street, Parsons, KS 67357

Manhattan Area Technical College
Manhattan, Kansas
www.matc.net

- Public 2-year technical college
- Commuter campus in large town

General. **Location:** 125 miles from Kansas City. **Calendar:** Semester.

Annual costs/financial aid. Tuition/fees (2008-2009): $2,400. Need-based financial aid available to full-time and part-time students.

Contact. Phone: (785) 587-2800 ext. 104
Director of Admissions, 3136 Dickens Avenue, Manhattan, KS 66503-2499

Neosho County Community College
Chanute, Kansas
www.neosho.edu **CB code: 6093**

- Public 2-year community college
- Commuter campus in small town

General. Founded in 1936. Regionally accredited. **Enrollment:** 2,025 undergraduates. **Degrees:** 192 associate awarded. **Location:** 110 miles from Kansas City, Missouri, 100 miles from Wichita. **Calendar:** Semester, limited summer session. **Full-time faculty:** 50 total. **Part-time faculty:** 130 total. **Class size:** 83% < 20, 15% 20-39, 2% 40-49.

Student profile.

Out-of-state:	14%	**Live on campus:**	28%

Transfer out. **Colleges most students transferred to 2008:** Pittsburg State University, Emporia State University, Kansas State University, University of Kansas, Wichita State University.

Basis for selection. Open admission, but selective for some programs. Special requirements for nursing program, nursing entrance test (NET) required. Students not submitting ACT scores take college-administered placement exam. **Homeschooled:** Must take GED.

2008-2009 Annual costs. Tuition/fees: $2,010; $2,310 out-of-district; $3,030 out-of-state. Per-credit charge: $44. Room/board: $4,400. Books/supplies: $430. Personal expenses: $800.

2007-2008 Financial aid. **Need-based:** Need-based aid available for part-time students. Work-study available nights, weekends and for part-time students. **Non-need-based:** Scholarships awarded for academics, art, athletics, leadership, music/drama, state residency.

Application procedures. **Admission:** Priority date 8/15; no deadline. No application fee. Admission notification on a rolling basis. **Financial aid:** Priority date 4/1; no closing date. FAFSA required. Applicants notified on a rolling basis; must reply within 6 week(s) of notification.

Academics. **Special study options:** Cooperative education, distance learning, dual enrollment of high school students, ESL, honors, independent study, liberal arts/career combination, weekend college. License preparation in nursing, real estate. **Credit/placement by examination:** CLEP, institutional tests. 15 credit hours maximum toward associate degree. **Support services:** GED preparation and test center, learning center, reduced course load, remedial instruction, study skills assistance, tutoring, writing center.

Majors. **Biology:** General. **Business:** Accounting, administrative services, banking/financial services, business admin, office management. **Communications:** General. **Computer sciences:** General. **Education:** General, secondary. **Engineering technology:** Computer systems, drafting, industrial. **Family/consumer sciences:** General. **Foreign languages:** General. **Health:** Athletic training, health care admin, licensed practical nurse, nursing (RN). **Interdisciplinary:** Natural sciences. **Liberal arts:** Arts/sciences. **Math:** General. **Parks/recreation:** Exercise sciences. **Physical sciences:** Chemistry. **Psychology:** General. **Public administration:** Social work. **Social sciences:** General. **Visual/performing arts:** Art, dramatic, studio arts.

Most popular majors. Business/marketing 15%, health sciences 49%, liberal arts 24%.

Computing on campus. 120 workstations in dormitories, library, computer center, student center. Dormitories wired for high-speed internet access. Online library, helpline, wireless network available.

Student life. Freshman orientation: Mandatory. Preregistration for classes offered. **Housing:** Guaranteed on-campus for freshmen. Coed dorms available. $100 nonrefundable deposit. Home stays with host families for international students. **Activities:** Choral groups, dance, drama, music ensembles, musical theater, student government.

Athletics. NJCAA. **Intercollegiate:** Baseball M, basketball, cheerleading, cross-country, soccer, softball W, track and field, volleyball W, wrestling M. **Team name:** Panthers.

Student services. Adult student services, career counseling, student employment services, financial aid counseling, personal counseling, placement for graduates, veterans' counselor. **Physically disabled:** Services for visually, speech, hearing impaired. **Transfer:** Pre-admission transcript evaluation for new students. Transfer center, transfer adviser, college fairs on campus for students transferring to 4-year colleges.

Contact. E-mail: amkiefer@neosho.edu
Phone: (620) 431-2820 ext. 233 Toll-free number: (800) 729-6222
Fax: (316) 431-6056
Eric Tincher, Dean of Student Development, Neosho County Community College, 800 West 14th Street, Chanute, KS 66720

North Central Kansas Technical College

Beloit, Kansas
www.ncktc.edu **CB code: 2616**

- Public 2-year technical college
- Small town

General. Regionally accredited. Multicampus institution. **Enrollment:** 355 degree-seeking undergraduates. **Degrees:** 198 associate awarded. **Location:** 107 miles from Hays, 175 miles from Topeka. **Calendar:** Semester. **Full-time faculty:** 43 total. **Part-time faculty:** 7 total.

Student profile. Among degree-seeking undergraduates, 100% enrolled in a vocational program.

Basis for selection. Open admission. **Learning Disabled:** Students must present written documentation from certified professional identifying disability with recommendations for accommodations.

2008-2009 Annual costs. Tuition/fees: $3,497. Room/board: $4,150. Books/supplies: $800.

2008-2009 Financial aid. All financial aid based on need. Need-based aid available for part-time students. Work-study available nights and for part-time students.

Application procedures. Admission: No deadline. $50 fee. Admission notification on a rolling basis. **Financial aid:** No deadline. FAFSA required.

Academics. Credit/placement by examination: CLEP. **Support services:** Learning center, remedial instruction, tutoring.

Majors. Agriculture: Equipment technology. **Engineering technology:** Electrical. **Health:** Nursing (RN). **Mechanic/repair:** Automotive, diesel, electronics/electrical.

Computing on campus. 50 workstations in library, computer center. Dormitories wired for high-speed internet access. Repair service available.

Student life. Freshman orientation: Available. Preregistration for classes offered. **Housing:** Coed dorms available. **Activities:** Student government.

Athletics. Intramural: Basketball M, football (non-tackle) M, volleyball, wrestling M.

Student services. Career counseling, financial aid counseling, placement for graduates.

Contact. E-mail: dhughes@ncktc.edu
Phone: (800) 658-4655 Toll-free number: (800) 658-4655
Fax: (785) 738-2903
David Hughes, Admissions Director, North Central Kansas Technical College, P.O. Box 507, Beloit, KS 67420

Pratt Community College

Pratt, Kansas
www.prattcc.edu **CB code: 6581**

- Public 2-year community and technical college
- Commuter campus in small town

General. Founded in 1938. Regionally accredited. **Enrollment:** 705 degree-seeking undergraduates; 917 non-degree-seeking students. **Degrees:** 190 associate awarded. **Location:** 70 miles from Wichita. **Calendar:** Semester, limited summer session. **Full-time faculty:** 49 total; 4% have terminal degrees, 2% minority, 61% women. **Part-time faculty:** 124 total; 8% have terminal degrees, 8% minority, 52% women. **Class size:** 64% < 20, 33% 20-39, 2% 40-49, less than 1% 50-99. **Special facilities:** Indoor and outdoor rodeo facilities, electrical powerlineman training facility.

Student profile. Among degree-seeking undergraduates, 60% enrolled in a transfer program, 40% enrolled in a vocational program, 277 enrolled as first-time, first-year students.

Part-time:	13%	**Native American:**	1%
Out-of-state:	11%	**International:**	3%
Women:	49%	**25 or older:**	20%
African American:	4%	**Live on campus:**	40%
Hispanic American:	6%		

Transfer out. Colleges most students transferred to 2008: Fort Hays State University, Emporia State University, Kansas State University.

Basis for selection. Open admission, but selective for some programs. Special requirements for nursing, agriculture power technology, and electrical power distribution programs. ACT scores used for course placement; if not, ASSET administered. Interview required of nursing majors. Audition required of music and drama majors. Portfolio recommended for art majors. **Homeschooled:** Transcript of courses and grades required. **Learning Disabled:** IEP's must be submitted to admissions before initial enrollment and request of services.

2008-2009 Annual costs. Tuition/fees: $2,220; $2,280 out-of-state. Per-credit charge: $45 in-state; $47 out-of-state. Out-of-district Kansas residents have additional fee of $100; out-of-state $200, and international students $300 for the year. Technology fee of $150 per semester applicable for auto, ag power, and electrical power areas. Room/board: $4,576. Books/supplies: $800. Personal expenses: $1,000.

2008-2009 Financial aid. Need-based: 69% of total undergraduate aid awarded as scholarships/grants, 31% as loans/jobs. Need-based aid available for part-time students. Work-study available for part-time students. **Non-need-based:** Scholarships awarded for academics, art, athletics, leadership, minority status, music/drama, state residency.

Application procedures. Admission: No deadline. No application fee. Admission notification on a rolling basis beginning on or about 1/1. **Financial aid:** Priority date 5/1, closing date 8/1. FAFSA, institutional form required. Applicants notified on a rolling basis starting 2/1; must reply within 2 week(s) of notification.

Academics. Special study options: Distance learning, dual enrollment of high school students, honors, independent study, internships, liberal arts/career combination, weekend college. Bachelor's degree programs available on campus. License preparation in nursing. **Credit/placement by examination:** CLEP, IB, institutional tests. 15 credit hours maximum toward associate degree. **Support services:** GED preparation, learning center, remedial instruction, tutoring.

Majors. Agriculture: General, animal sciences, business, farm/ranch, range science. **Biology:** General, botany. **Business:** Accounting, business admin, entrepreneurial studies, office management, office technology, office/clerical. **Communications:** General, journalism. **Computer sciences:** General. **Conservation:** Wildlife. **Education:** General, early childhood, elementary, secondary. **Engineering:** General. **Health:** Licensed practical nurse, medical secretary, nursing (RN), predental, premedicine, prepharmacy, preveterinary. **History:** General. **Interdisciplinary:** Biological/physical sciences. **Legal studies:** Legal secretary, prelaw. **Liberal arts:** Arts/sciences. **Math:** General. **Mechanic/repair:** Automotive. **Physical sciences:** Chemistry, inorganic chemistry, physics. **Psychology:** General. **Social sciences:** General, political science, sociology. **Visual/performing arts:** General, ceramics, commercial/advertising art, dramatic, drawing, painting, studio arts.

Most popular majors. Agriculture 9%, business/marketing 6%, education 7%, health sciences 39%, trade and industry 18%.

Computing on campus. 125 workstations in dormitories, library, computer center. Dormitories wired for high-speed internet access and linked to campus network. Commuter students can connect to campus network. Online course registration, online library, helpline, wireless network available.

Student life. Freshman orientation: Available. Preregistration for classes offered. Held preceding each fall and spring semester. One to 2 days before classes begin. **Policies:** 2 MMR (Measle, Mumps, Rubella) inoculations and Meningitis inoculations required for dorm students. **Housing:** Coed dorms, single-sex dorms, wellness housing available. $200 deposit. **Activities:** Bands, choral groups, dance, drama, international student organizations, literary magazine, music ensembles, musical theater, student government, student newspaper, Christian Challenge, Student Senate, Student Ambassadors, Rotaract.

Athletics. NJCAA. **Intercollegiate:** Baseball M, basketball, cheerleading, cross-country, golf, rodeo, softball W, track and field, volleyball W, wrestling M. **Intramural:** Basketball, football (non-tackle), rodeo, softball, table tennis, volleyball. **Team name:** Beavers.

Student services. Adult student services, career counseling, student employment services, financial aid counseling, health services, on-campus daycare, personal counseling, placement for graduates, veterans' counselor. **Physically disabled:** Services for visually, speech, hearing impaired. **Transfer:** College fairs on campus for students transferring to 4-year colleges.

Contact. E-mail: lynnp@prattcc.edu
Phone: (620) 672-5641 ext. 217 Toll-free number: (800) 794-3091 ext. 217
Fax: (620) 672-5288
Lynn Perez, Director of Admissions, Pratt Community College, 348 Northeast State Road 61, Pratt, KS 67124-8317

Seward County Community College

Liberal, Kansas
www.sccc.edu **CB code: 0286**

- Public 2-year community college
- Commuter campus in large town

General. Founded in 1967. Regionally accredited. Off-campus classes offered in 7 locations, adult learning center with ESL classes, interactive television classrooms to off-site locations, adult basic education classes, GED testing available. **Enrollment:** 1,687 degree-seeking undergraduates. **Degrees:** 203 associate awarded. **Location:** 210 miles from Wichita, 150 miles from Amarillo, Texas. **Calendar:** Semester, limited summer session. **Full-time faculty:** 65 total. **Part-time faculty:** 73 total. **Class size:** 83% < 20, 16% 20-39, less than 1% 40-49, less than 1% 50-99. **Special facilities:** Wellness center.

Student profile.

Out-of-state:	19%	**Live on campus:**	15%
25 or older:	34%		

Transfer out. Colleges most students transferred to 2008: Kansas State University, Texas Christian University, University of Texas-Arlington, University of Central Oklahoma, Fort Hays State University.

Basis for selection. Open admission, but selective for some programs.

High school preparation. 20 units recommended. Recommended units include English 4, mathematics 3, social studies 2, science 2 and foreign language 1.

2008-2009 Annual costs. Tuition/fees: $1,860; $2,550 out-of-state. Per-credit charge: $40 in-state; $63 out-of-state. Residents of neighboring counties in OK, TX and CO pay per-credit-hour rate of $50. Room/board: $4,100. Books/supplies: $700. Personal expenses: $1,000.

2007-2008 Financial aid. Need-based: Need-based aid available for part-time students. **Non-need-based:** Scholarships awarded for academics, athletics.

Application procedures. Admission: Priority date 4/1; no deadline. No application fee. Admission notification on a rolling basis. **Financial aid:** Priority date 4/1; no closing date. FAFSA, institutional form required. Applicants notified on a rolling basis starting 6/15; must reply within 4 week(s) of notification.

Academics. Special study options: Cooperative education, cross-registration, distance learning, double major, dual enrollment of high school students, ESL, external degree, honors, independent study, internships, liberal arts/career combination. Bachelor's degree programs available on campus. License preparation in nursing, paramedic. **Credit/placement by examination:** AP, CLEP, institutional tests. 24 credit hours maximum toward associate degree. **Support services:** GED preparation and test center, learning center, remedial instruction, study skills assistance, tutoring, writing center.

Majors. Agriculture: General, animal sciences, business, economics, farm/ranch. **Biology:** General. **Business:** General, accounting, administrative services, business admin, fashion, finance, hospitality admin, office management, office technology, office/clerical, sales/distribution. **Communications:** General, journalism. **Computer sciences:** General, applications programming, computer graphics, computer science, data entry, data processing, information technology, programming. **Conservation:** Forestry, wildlife. **Education:** General, teacher assistance. **Engineering:** General. **Health:** Athletic training, clinical lab assistant, clinical lab technology, dental hygiene, medical secretary, nursing (RN), predental, premedicine, prenursing, prepharmacy, preveterinary, respiratory therapy technology. **History:** General. **Interdisciplinary:** Biological/physical sciences, math/computer science, natural sciences. **Legal studies:** Legal secretary, prelaw. **Liberal arts:** Arts/sciences, library assistant. **Math:** General. **Military:** General. **Parks/recreation:** General, exercise sciences, health/fitness. **Personal/culinary services:** Cosmetology. **Philosophy/religion:** Religion. **Physical sciences:** Chemistry, physics. **Protective services:** Law enforcement admin, police science. **Psychology:** General. **Public administration:** Social work. **Social sciences:** General, economics, sociology. **Visual/performing arts:** General, art, ceramics, dramatic, music performance, painting, studio arts, voice/opera.

Computing on campus. 450 workstations in dormitories, library, computer center, student center. Dormitories wired for high-speed internet access. Commuter students can connect to campus network. Online course registration, online library, wireless network available.

Student life. Freshman orientation: Mandatory. Preregistration for classes offered. **Housing:** Coed dorms available. $100 deposit, deadline 6/30. **Activities:** Bands, choral groups, drama, film society, literary magazine, music ensembles, musical theater, student government, student newspaper, symphony orchestra, TV station.

Athletics. NJCAA. **Intercollegiate:** Baseball M, basketball, softball W, tennis, volleyball W. **Intramural:** Basketball, bowling, football (non-tackle), golf, soccer, swimming, table tennis, volleyball. **Team name:** Saints.

Student services. Adult student services, career counseling, student employment services, financial aid counseling, personal counseling, veterans' counselor. **Learning disabled:** Comprehensive services available. **Transfer:** Transfer adviser, college fairs on campus for students transferring to 4-year colleges.

Contact. E-mail: desiree.maxwell@sccc.edu
Phone: (620) 417-1102 Toll-free number: (800) 373-9951 ext. 1102
Fax: (620) 417-1079
JR Doney, Director of Marketing and Admissions, Seward County Community College, 1801 North Kansas Avenue, Liberal, KS 67905-1137

Kentucky

Ashland Community and Technical College
Ashland, Kentucky
www.ashland.kctcs.edu **CB code: 0703**

- Public 2-year community college
- Commuter campus in large town

General. Founded in 1957. Regionally accredited. Off-campus classes in surrounding counties. **Enrollment:** 2,425 degree-seeking undergraduates. **Degrees:** 281 associate awarded. **Location:** 120 miles from Lexington; 15 miles from Huntington, West Virginia. **Calendar:** Semester, limited summer session. **Full-time faculty:** 95 total. **Part-time faculty:** 120 total. **Special facilities:** 3 open computer labs, learning assistance center, early intervention program for students at risk.

Student profile.

Out-of-state:	26%	25 or older:	43%

Transfer out. Colleges most students transferred to 2008: Morehead State University, Marshall University, Shawnee State University.

Basis for selection. Open admission, but selective for some programs. Admission to nursing program based on test scores and academic record. Interview recommended.

High school preparation. 11 units recommended. Recommended units include English 4, mathematics 3, social studies 2, science 2 (laboratory 2).

2008-2009 Annual costs. Tuition/fees: $3,630; $11,700 out-of-state. Per-credit charge: $121 in-state; $390 out-of-state. Tuition reduction program available for qualified residents of contiguous states. Books/supplies: $750. Personal expenses: $800.

Financial aid. Non-need-based: Scholarships awarded for academics, job skills, leadership, minority status, music/drama. **Additional information:** In-state 100% disabled or deceased veterans' children receive tuition waiver from state.

Application procedures. Admission: No deadline. No application fee. Admission notification on a rolling basis. Nursing applications due by March 1. **Financial aid:** Priority date 3/15; no closing date. FAFSA, institutional form required. Applicants notified on a rolling basis starting 5/1; must reply within 3 week(s) of notification.

Academics. Special study options: Cooperative education, cross-registration, distance learning, dual enrollment of high school students, honors, internships, liberal arts/career combination, weekend college. **Credit/placement by examination:** AP, CLEP, institutional tests. 40 credit hours maximum toward associate degree. **Support services:** GED test center, learning center, pre-admission summer program, reduced course load, remedial instruction, study skills assistance, tutoring.

Honors college/program. Participants have option of taking selected honors courses.

Majors. Business: Accounting, banking/financial services, business admin, management information systems, office/clerical, real estate. **Computer sciences:** Information systems, vendor certification. **Health:** Medical secretary, nursing (RN), physical therapy assistant, respiratory therapy technology. **Legal studies:** Legal secretary. **Liberal arts:** Arts/sciences. **Protective services:** Police science.

Most popular majors. Biological/life sciences 14%, business/marketing 16%, health sciences 49%, liberal arts 16%.

Computing on campus. 138 workstations in library, computer center. Commuter students can connect to campus network. Online course registration, helpline available.

Student life. Freshman orientation: Mandatory. Preregistration for classes offered. **Activities:** Choral groups, drama, literary magazine, music ensembles, musical theater, student government, student newspaper, Baptist student union/students for Christ, Circle K, drama club, multicultural student affairs, Phi Theta Kappa, students in free enterprise.

Athletics. Intramural: Basketball, bowling, fencing, softball, table tennis, tennis, volleyball.

Student services. Adult student services, career counseling, student employment services, financial aid counseling, health services, minority student services, on-campus daycare, personal counseling, placement for graduates, veterans' counselor. **Physically disabled:** Services for visually, speech, hearing impaired. **Transfer:** Re-entry adviser for new students. Transfer center, transfer adviser for students transferring to 4-year colleges.

Contact. E-mail: willie.mccullough@kctcs.net
Phone: (606) 326-2000 Toll-free number: (800) 370-7191
Fax: (606) 325-8124
Willie McCullough, Dean for Student Affairs, Ashland Community and Technical College, 1400 College Drive, Ashland, KY 41101-3683

Big Sandy Community and Technical College
Prestonsburg, Kentucky
www.bigsandy.kctcs.edu **CB code: 0869**

- Public 2-year community and technical college
- Commuter campus in small town

General. Founded in 1964. Regionally accredited. Four campuses located at Hager Hill, Paintsville, Pikeville, and Prestonsburg. **Enrollment:** 1,880 full-time, degree-seeking students. **Degrees:** 255 associate awarded. **Location:** 120 miles from Lexington. **Calendar:** Semester, limited summer session. **Special facilities:** East Kentucky Science Center, planetarium, nature trail.

Student profile.

Out-of-state:	1%	25 or older:	36%

Basis for selection. Open admission, but selective for some programs. Nursing and dental hygiene programs require minimum ACT score of 20 for admission. All others required to submit COMPASS or ASSET scores for placement, but ACT or SAT will be considered if submitted.

2008-2009 Annual costs. Tuition/fees: $3,630; $11,700 out-of-state. Per-credit charge: $121 in-state; $390 out-of-state. Tuition reduction program available for qualified residents of contiguous states. Books/supplies: $450. Personal expenses: $3,000.

2008-2009 Financial aid. Need-based: Need-based aid available for part-time students. **Non-need-based:** Scholarships awarded for academics.

Application procedures. Admission: No deadline. No application fee. Application must be submitted on paper. Admission notification on a rolling basis. Must have completed junior year of high school prior to enrolling full-time; may audit courses if junior or sophomore, except English 101/102. **Financial aid:** Priority date 4/1; no closing date. FAFSA required. Applicants notified on a rolling basis; must reply within 2 week(s) of notification.

Academics. Special study options: Cooperative education, distance learning, dual enrollment of high school students, independent study, internships, liberal arts/career combination, weekend college. Bachelor's degree programs available on campus. **Credit/placement by examination:** AP, CLEP, institutional tests. 36 credit hours maximum toward associate degree. **Support services:** GED preparation and test center, learning center, remedial instruction, study skills assistance, tutoring, writing center.

Majors. Business: Accounting, administrative services, management information systems, management science, real estate. **Computer sciences:** Information technology, networking, programming, webmaster. **Health:** Dental hygiene, nursing (RN). **Liberal arts:** Arts/sciences. **Mechanic/repair:** Automotive, heating/ac/refrig. **Protective services:** Police science. **Public administration:** Human services.

Computing on campus. 575 workstations in library, computer center, student center. Online course registration, online library, wireless network available.

Student life. Freshman orientation: Available. Preregistration for classes offered. **Activities:** Choral groups, drama, literary magazine, student government, Baptist Student Union, Phi Theta Kappa, Phi Beta Lambda, Kentucky Association of Nursing Students, CARE, law enforcement club.

Student services. Career counseling, services for economically disadvantaged, financial aid counseling, personal counseling, veterans' counselor. **Physically disabled:** Services for visually, speech, hearing impaired. **Transfer:** Pre-admission transcript evaluation for new students. Transfer center, transfer adviser, college fairs on campus for students transferring to 4-year colleges.

Contact. E-mail: jimmy.wright@kctcs.edu
Phone: (606) 886-3863 ext. 67366 Toll-free number: (888) 641-4132 ext. 67366 Fax: (606) 886-6943
Jimmy Wright, Associate Dean of Students, Big Sandy Community and Technical College, One Bert T. Combs Drive, Prestonsburg, KY 41653

Bluegrass Community and Technical College

Lexington, Kentucky **CB member**
www.bluegrass.kctcs.edu **CB code: 0645**

- Public 2-year community and technical college
- Commuter campus in large city

General. Founded in 1965. Regionally accredited. **Location:** 90 miles from Cincinnati, 75 miles from Louisville. **Calendar:** Semester.

Annual costs/financial aid. Tuition/fees (2008-2009): $3,630; $11,700 out-of-state. Tuition reduction program available for qualified residents of contiguous states. Room/board: $5,816. Books/supplies: $800. Personal expenses: $800. Need-based financial aid available to full-time and part-time students.

Contact. Phone: (859) 246-6210
Director of Admissions, 200 Oswald Building, Cooper Drive, Lexington, KY 40506-0235

Brown Mackie College: Hopkinsville

Hopkinsville, Kentucky
www.brownmackie.edu **CB code: 5375**

- For-profit 2-year business and junior college
- Large town

General. Accredited by ACICS. **Calendar:** Quarter.

Annual costs/financial aid. Tuition/fees (2008-2009): $10,275. Occupational Therapy Assistant program $300 per-credit-hour, COA $12,615. Need-based financial aid available for full-time students.

Contact. Phone: (270) 886-1302
4001 Fort Campbell Boulevard, Hopkinsville, KY 42240

Brown Mackie College: Louisville

Louisville, Kentucky
www.brownmackie.edu **CB code: 0305**

- For-profit 2-year technical college
- Commuter campus in large city

General. Founded in 1972. Accredited by ACICS. **Calendar:** Quarter.

Annual costs/financial aid. Tuition/fees (2008-2009): $10,035. Personal expenses: $896.

Contact. Phone: (502) 968-7191
Admissions Director, 3605 Fern Valley Road, Louisville, KY 40219

Brown Mackie College: North Kentucky

Fort Mitchell, Kentucky
www.brownmackie.edu **CB code: 3419**

- For-profit 2-year business and health science college
- Small town

General. Accredited by ACICS. **Enrollment:** 500 degree-seeking undergraduates. **Degrees:** 200 associate awarded. **Location:** 8 miles from Cincinnati. **Calendar:** Continuous. **Full-time faculty:** 15 total; 27% have terminal degrees, 67% women. **Part-time faculty:** 24 total; 46% women.

Basis for selection. Open admission.

2008-2009 Annual costs. Tuition/fees: $9,000. Per-credit charge: $235. Books/supplies: $1,380.

Application procedures. Admission: No deadline. No application fee. Admission notification on a rolling basis.

Academics. Special study options: License preparation in nursing, occupational therapy. **Credit/placement by examination:** CLEP. **Support services:** Remedial instruction, tutoring.

Majors. Business: Accounting technology, business admin. **Computer sciences:** General. **Health:** Health services.

Computing on campus. 16 workstations in library.

Student life. Freshman orientation: Mandatory.

Contact. Phone: (859) 341-5627 Toll-free number: (800) 888-1445 Fax: (859) 341-6483
Greg Hitt, Director of Admissions, Brown Mackie College: North Kentucky, 309 Buttermilk Pike, Fort Mitchell, KY 41017

Daymar College: Louisville

Louisville, Kentucky
www.daymarcollege.edu **CB code: 3407**

- For-profit 2-year business college
- Large city

General. Accredited by ACICS. **Calendar:** Quarter.

Annual costs/financial aid. Tuition/fees (2008-2009): $12,000. Books/supplies: $2,000.

Contact. Phone: (502) 495-1040
Director of Admissions, 4112 Fern Valley Road, Louisville, KY 40219-1973

Daymar College: Owensboro

Owensboro, Kentucky
www.daymarcollege.edu **CB code: 0772**

- For-profit 2-year business and junior college
- Commuter campus in small city
- Interview required

General. Founded in 1963. Accredited by ACICS. Provides hands-on training with practical theory. In Medical Assisting - Clinical Track, students have 3 classes at Owensboro Medical Health System. **Enrollment:** 300 degree-seeking undergraduates. **Degrees:** 73 associate awarded. **Location:** 120 miles from Louisville, 35 miles from Evansville, Indiana. **Calendar:** Quarter, extensive summer session. **Full-time faculty:** 15 total. **Part-time faculty:** 25 total.

Basis for selection. Open admission. Must have high school diploma or GED, admissions interview. SAT, ACT, or Wonderlic Scholastic Level Exam required for placement. **Homeschooled:** Interview required. **Learning Disabled:** Copy of IEP from high school required.

High school preparation. Recommended units include English 3, mathematics 1, social studies 1 and science 1. One human relations also recommended.

2008-2009 Annual costs. Tuition/fees: $12,000. Books/supplies: $2,000.

Financial aid. All financial aid based on need. Need-based aid available for part-time students. Work-study available for part-time students.

Application procedures. Admission: No deadline. No application fee. Admission notification on a rolling basis. **Financial aid:** No deadline. FAFSA required. Applicants notified on a rolling basis.

Academics. Special study options: Cooperative education, distance learning, double major, dual enrollment of high school students, honors, independent study, internships. **Credit/placement by examination:** AP, CLEP, institutional tests. 12 credit hours maximum toward associate degree. **Support services:** GED preparation, remedial instruction, tutoring.

Majors. Business: Administrative services, business admin, office management, office technology, office/clerical, operations. **Computer sciences:** General, data processing, information systems, networking, systems analysis. **Health:** Medical assistant, medical secretary, pharmacy assistant. **Legal studies:** Legal secretary, paralegal.

Most popular majors. Business/marketing 14%, computer/information sciences 36%, health sciences 32%, legal studies 19%.

Computing on campus. 115 workstations in library, computer center.

Student life. Freshman orientation: Mandatory. **Activities:** Student newspaper.

Student services. Alcohol/substance abuse counseling, career counseling, student employment services, financial aid counseling, personal counseling, placement for graduates. **Physically disabled:** Services for visually, hearing impaired. **Transfer:** Re-entry adviser, pre-admission transcript evaluation for new students. Transfer adviser for students transferring to 4-year colleges.

Contact. E-mail: eandryszak@daymarcollege.edu
Phone: (270) 926-4040 Toll-free number: (800) 960-4090
Fax: (270) 685-4090
Erik Andryszak, Director of Admissions, Daymar College: Owensboro, 3361 Buckland Square, Owensboro, KY 42301

Daymar College: Paducah

Paducah, Kentucky
www.daymarcollege.edu **CB code: 0669**

- For-profit 2-year technical college
- Commuter campus in small city
- Interview required

General. Founded in 1964. Accredited by ACICS. Associate program completes 3 academic years in 2 calendar years. **Enrollment:** 350 degree-seeking undergraduates. **Degrees:** 40 associate awarded. **Location:** 150 miles from Nashville, Tennessee and St. Louis. **Calendar:** Quarter, extensive summer session. **Full-time faculty:** 8 total. **Part-time faculty:** 30 total.

Basis for selection. Open admission.

2008-2009 Annual costs. Tuition/fees: $12,000. Books/supplies: $2,000.

Application procedures. Admission: No deadline. No application fee. Admission notification on a rolling basis. **Financial aid:** No deadline. FAFSA, CSS PROFILE required. Applicants notified on a rolling basis; must reply within 3 week(s) of notification.

Academics. Special study options: Distance learning, internships. **Credit/placement by examination:** CLEP. **Support services:** Learning center, tutoring.

Majors. Engineering: Electrical. **Engineering technology:** Electrical. **Health:** Insurance coding, insurance specialist, pharmacy assistant. **Math:** Applied.

Computing on campus. 50 workstations in library, computer center. Commuter students can connect to campus network. Online library, helpline, wireless network available.

Student life. Freshman orientation: Mandatory. Preregistration for classes offered.

Student services. Alcohol/substance abuse counseling, career counseling, student employment services, financial aid counseling, personal counseling, placement for graduates, veterans' counselor. **Transfer:** Pre-admission transcript evaluation for new students.

Contact. Phone: (270) 444-9676 Toll-free number: (800) 995-4438
Fax: (270) 441-7202
Shannon Jones, Director of Admission, Daymar College: Paducah, 509 South 30th Street, Paducah, KY 42001

Draughons Junior College

Bowling Green, Kentucky
www.draughons.edu **CB code: 3399**

- For-profit 2-year branch campus and junior college
- Commuter campus in large town

General. Accredited by ACICS. **Location:** 120 miles from Louisville, 60 miles from Nashville, Tennessee. **Calendar:** Quarter.

Annual costs/financial aid. Tuition/fees (2008-2009): $9,675. Books/supplies: $2,030. Need-based financial aid available to full-time and part-time students.

Contact. Phone: (270) 843-6750
Admissions, 2421 Fitzgerald Industrial Drive, Bowling Green, KY 42101

Elizabethtown Community and Technical College

Elizabethtown, Kentucky
www.elizabethtown.kctcs.edu **CB code: 1211**

- Public 2-year community and technical college
- Commuter campus in large town

General. Founded in 1964. Regionally accredited. Off-campus locations at Fort Knox, Bardstown, Leitchfield, Hardinsburg, and Brandenburg. **Enrollment:** 2,481 full-time, degree-seeking students. **Degrees:** 447 associate awarded. **ROTC:** Army. **Location:** 40 miles southwest from Louisville. **Calendar:** Semester, limited summer session. **Special facilities:** Regional Home for the Arts center.

Student profile.

Out-of-state:	1%	**25 or older:**	52%

Transfer out. Colleges most students transferred to 2008: Western Kentucky University, University of Louisville, University of Kentucky.

Basis for selection. Open admission, but selective for some programs. All nursing, radiography and dental hygiene programs have criteria specific to each. Enrolled freshmen must take ACT or ACT/Career Planning Profile or ASSET by start of second semester. **Learning Disabled:** An ADA counselor is on campus to assist those with special needs or disabilities.

High school preparation. College-preparatory program recommended.

2008-2009 Annual costs. Tuition/fees: $3,630; $11,700 out-of-state. Per-credit charge: $121 in-state; $390 out-of-state. Tuition reduction program available for qualified residents of contiguous states. Books/supplies: $400.

Financial aid. All financial aid based on need. Need-based aid available for part-time students. Work-study available nights, weekends and for part-time students.

Application procedures. Admission: No deadline. No application fee. Admission notification on a rolling basis. Early admission available for specially qualified high school students on part-time basis. **Financial aid:** Priority date 4/1; no closing date. FAFSA required. Applicants notified on a rolling basis starting 6/1; must reply within 2 week(s) of notification.

Academics. Special study options: Cooperative education, distance learning, dual enrollment of high school students, honors, internships, liberal arts/career combination, teacher certification program, weekend college. Bachelor's degree programs available on campus. License preparation in dental hygiene, nursing, radiology, real estate. **Credit/placement by examination:** AP, CLEP, institutional tests. 6 credit hours maximum toward associate degree. **Support services:** GED test center, learning center, remedial instruction, study skills assistance, tutoring, writing center.

Majors. Business: Business admin, executive assistant, real estate. **Computer sciences:** General. **Construction:** Electrician. **Education:** Early childhood, teacher assistance. **Engineering technology:** General, quality control. **Health:** Dental hygiene, medical radiologic technology/radiation therapy, medical secretary, nursing (RN). **Liberal arts:** Arts/sciences. **Mechanic/repair:** Appliance, automotive, diesel, locksmithing. **Production:** Machine shop technology, welding. **Protective services:** Firefighting, law enforcement admin. **Public administration:** Human services, social work.

Computing on campus. 87 workstations in library, computer center, student center. Online library, helpline, wireless network available.

Student life. Freshman orientation: Available. Preregistration for classes offered. Online orientation or on-campus orientation available. **Activities:** Choral groups, drama, literary magazine, student government, student newspaper, Baptist Campus Ministry, Association of Nursing Students, Phi Theta Kappa, Phi Beta Lambda, Gay Straight Alliance, Students in Free Enterprise, Skills USA, Phoenix Club.

Student services. Adult student services, career counseling, services for economically disadvantaged, financial aid counseling, personal counseling, placement for graduates, veterans' counselor, women's services. **Physically disabled:** Services for visually, speech, hearing impaired. **Transfer:** Transfer adviser, college fairs on campus for students transferring to 4-year colleges.

Contact. E-mail: Elizabethtown-Admissions@kctcs.edu
Phone: (270) 769-1632 Toll-free number: (877) 246-2322
Fax: (270) 769-1618
Bryan Smith, Counselor, Elizabethtown Community and Technical College, 600 College Street Road, Elizabethtown, KY 42701

Gateway Community and Technical College
Covington, Kentucky
www.gateway.kctcs.edu

- Public 2-year community and technical college
- Large city

General. Candidate for regional accreditation. **Calendar:** Semester.

Annual costs/financial aid. Tuition/fees: $3,750; $12,750 out-of-state.

Contact. Phone: (859) 441-4500
Assistant Director of Admissions, 1025 Amsterdam Road, Covington, KY 41011

Hazard Community and Technical College
Hazard, Kentucky
www.hazard.kctcs.edu **CB code: 0815**

- Public 2-year community and technical college
- Commuter campus in small town

General. Founded in 1968. Regionally accredited. **Enrollment:** 2,065 degree-seeking undergraduates. **Degrees:** 245 associate awarded. **Location:** 100 miles from Lexington. **Calendar:** Semester, limited summer session. **Full-time faculty:** 88 total. **Part-time faculty:** 56 total.

Transfer out. Colleges most students transferred to 2008: Morehead State University, Eastern Kentucky University, University of Kentucky, Lindsey Wilson College.

Basis for selection. Open admission, but selective for some programs. Out-of-state applicants must rank in top half of high school class or have 3.0 GPA.

High school preparation. 11 units recommended. Recommended units include English 4, mathematics 3, social studies 1, history 1 and science 2.

2008-2009 Annual costs. Tuition/fees: $3,630; $11,700 out-of-state. Per-credit charge: $121 in-state; $390 out-of-state. Tuition reduction program available for qualified residents of contiguous states. Books/supplies: $800. Personal expenses: $800.

2008-2009 Financial aid. All financial aid based on need. Need-based aid available for part-time students.

Application procedures. Admission: Priority date 8/1; no deadline. No application fee. Admission notification on a rolling basis beginning on or about 6/15. **Financial aid:** Priority date 4/1; no closing date. FAFSA required. Applicants notified on a rolling basis starting 6/15; must reply within 2 week(s) of notification.

Academics. Special study options: Cooperative education, distance learning, dual enrollment of high school students, honors, independent study, internships, liberal arts/career combination. 2+2 bachelor's degree programs in business administration, elementary education and University Studies with Morehead State University; 2+2 bachelor's degree program in criminal justice, Individualized Studies, nursing and social work with Eastern Kentucky University; 2+2 bachelor's degree in Arts/Human Services and Counseling with Lindsey Wilson and a Master of Education in Mental Health Counseling with Lindsey Wilson. Bachelor's degree programs available on campus. **Credit/placement by examination:** CLEP, institutional tests. **Support services:** GED test center, learning center, remedial instruction, study skills assistance, tutoring, writing center.

Majors. Business: Marketing. **Computer sciences:** General. **Education:** Early childhood. **Health:** Medical radiologic technology/radiation therapy, nursing (RN), physical therapy assistant. **Liberal arts:** Arts/sciences. **Mechanic/repair:** Automotive. **Public administration:** Human services.

Computing on campus. 494 workstations in library, computer center, student center.

Student life. Freshman orientation: Available. **Activities:** Student government.

Student services. Physically disabled: Services for visually, speech, hearing impaired. **Transfer:** Pre-admission transcript evaluation for new students. College fairs on campus for students transferring to 4-year colleges.

Contact. E-mail: angie.bedwell@kctcs.edu
Phone: (606) 436-5721 ext. 73525 Toll-free number: (800) 246-7521 ext. 73525 Fax: (606) 666-4312
Scott Gross, Director of Admissions, Hazard Community and Technical College, One Community College Drive, Hazard, KY 41701

Henderson Community College
Henderson, Kentucky
www.hencc.kctcs.edu **CB code: 1307**

- Public 2-year community college
- Commuter campus in large town

General. Founded in 1960. Regionally accredited. **Enrollment:** 1,250 degree-seeking undergraduates. **Degrees:** 176 associate awarded. **Location:** 10 miles from Evansville, Indiana. **Calendar:** Semester, limited summer session. **Full-time faculty:** 39 total. **Part-time faculty:** 52 total. **Special facilities:** Fine arts center hosting variety of social and cultural activities in visual and performing arts.

Transfer out. Colleges most students transferred to 2008: Western Kentucky University, Murray State University, University of Kentucky, University of Southern Indiana, Wesley University.

Basis for selection. Open admission, but selective for some programs. Dental hygiene, nursing and clinical lab technician programs selective; test scores and high school GPA important admissions criteria. Interview required for nursing program.

2008-2009 Annual costs. Tuition/fees: $3,630; $11,700 out-of-state. Per-credit charge: $121 in-state; $390 out-of-state. Tuition reduction program available for qualified residents of contiguous states. Books/supplies: $500.

Application procedures. Admission: No application fee. Admission notification on a rolling basis beginning on or about 3/1. **Financial aid:** Priority date 4/1; no closing date. FAFSA required. Applicants notified on a rolling basis starting 5/1.

Academics. Special study options: Cooperative education, cross-registration, distance learning, double major, dual enrollment of high school students, honors, independent study, liberal arts/career combination, weekend college. License preparation in dental hygiene, nursing. **Credit/placement by examination:** AP, CLEP. **Support services:** GED preparation and test center, learning center, pre-admission summer program, reduced course load, remedial instruction, study skills assistance, tutoring, writing center.

Majors. Agriculture: Business technology. **Business:** Administrative services, business admin, management information systems. **Communications:** General. **Computer sciences:** Data processing. **Education:** Early childhood. **Engineering technology:** Electrical. **Health:** Clinical lab technology. **Liberal arts:** Arts/sciences. **Public administration:** Community org/advocacy, social work.

Computing on campus. 99 workstations in library, computer center, student center. Commuter students can connect to campus network. Online course registration, online library, repair service available.

Student life. Freshman orientation: Available. Preregistration for classes offered. **Activities:** Choral groups, literary magazine, student government, student newspaper, Baptist Student Union.

Student services. Career counseling, financial aid counseling, minority student services, personal counseling, placement for graduates, veterans' counselor. **Transfer:** Re-entry adviser, pre-admission transcript evaluation for new students. Transfer center, transfer adviser, college fairs on campus for students transferring to 4-year colleges.

Contact. Phone: (270) 830-5256
Patty Mitchell, Director of Admissions, Henderson Community College, 2660 South Green Street, Henderson, KY 42420

Hopkinsville Community College
Hopkinsville, Kentucky
www.hopkinsville.kctcs.edu **CB code: 1274**

- Public 2-year community college
- Commuter campus in small city

General. Founded in 1965. Regionally accredited. **Enrollment:** 2,430 degree-seeking undergraduates; 325 non-degree-seeking students. **Degrees:** 304 associate awarded. **Location:** 70 miles from Nashville, Tennessee, 25 miles from Clarksville, Tennessee. **Calendar:** Semester, limited summer session.

Full-time faculty: 67 total; 12% have terminal degrees, 10% minority, 49% women. **Part-time faculty:** 95 total. **Class size:** 53% < 20, 43% 20-39, 3% 40-49, less than 1% 50-99.

Student profile. Among degree-seeking undergraduates, 38% enrolled in a transfer program, 51% enrolled in a vocational program, 453 enrolled as first-time, first-year students, 176 transferred in from other institutions.

Part-time:	60%	**Women:**	73%
Out-of-state:	34%		

Transfer out. 19% of students enrolled in the transfer program go on to 4-year colleges. **Colleges most students transferred to 2008:** Murray State University, Austin Peay State University, Western Kentucky University.

Basis for selection. Open admission. ACT scores below 19 require COMPASS for placement.

2008-2009 Annual costs. Tuition/fees: $3,630; $11,700 out-of-state. Per-credit charge: $121 in-state; $390 out-of-state. Tuition reduction program available for qualified residents of contiguous states. Books/supplies: $1,000. Personal expenses: $2,820.

Financial aid. Need-based: Need-based aid available for part-time students. Work-study available nights. **Non-need-based:** Scholarships awarded for academics, leadership, minority status, state residency. **Additional information:** ACT required for academic scholarships.

Application procedures. Admission: No deadline. No application fee. Admission notification on a rolling basis. **Financial aid:** No deadline. FAFSA required. Applicants notified on a rolling basis starting 7/1.

Academics. Special study options: Cooperative education, distance learning, dual enrollment of high school students, independent study, internships. License preparation in nursing. **Credit/placement by examination:** AP, CLEP. **Support services:** GED preparation and test center, learning center, remedial instruction, study skills assistance, tutoring, writing center.

Majors. Agriculture: Production. **Business:** Business admin, executive assistant. **Computer sciences:** General. **Education:** Teacher assistance. **Engineering technology:** General, electromechanical. **Health:** Nursing (RN). **Liberal arts:** Arts/sciences. **Protective services:** Law enforcement admin, police science. **Public administration:** Social work. **Other:** Gen occupational technical stu.

Most popular majors. Business/marketing 9%, education 8%, health sciences 9%, liberal arts 57%.

Computing on campus. Commuter students can connect to campus network. Online course registration, online library, helpline, wireless network available.

Student life. Freshman orientation: Available. Preregistration for classes offered. On-campus orientations held prior to semester; web-based orientation available through a series of video clips. **Activities:** Campus ministries, literary magazine, student government, student newspaper, TV station, Baptist Campus Ministry, Religion & Philosophy, College Democrats, College Republicans, Minority Student Union.

Athletics. Intramural: Football (tackle) M.

Student services. Career counseling, student employment services, financial aid counseling, minority student services, placement for graduates, veterans' counselor. **Physically disabled:** Services for visually, speech, hearing impaired. **Transfer:** Transfer adviser, college fairs on campus for students transferring to 4-year colleges.

Contact. E-mail: jlevel0001@kctcs.edu
Phone: (270) 707-3810 Fax: (270) 886-0237
Ruth Ann Rettie, Registrar, Hopkinsville Community College, PO Box 2100, Hopkinsville, KY 42241-2100

Jefferson Community and Technical College

Louisville, Kentucky
www.jefferson.kctcs.edu **CB code: 1328**

- Public 2-year community and technical college
- Commuter campus in large city
- Interview required

General. Founded in 1968. Regionally accredited. 3 other campuses: southwestern Jefferson County, Shelby County and Carrollton. Courses also offered off-campus and online. **Enrollment:** 11,230 degree-seeking undergraduates. **Degrees:** 869 associate awarded. **ROTC:** Army. **Location:** Downtown. **Calendar:** Semester, extensive summer session. **Full-time faculty:** 330 total. **Part-time faculty:** 310 total. **Class size:** 54% < 20, 40% 20-39, 2% 40-49, 2% 50-99, less than 1% >100. **Special facilities:** Classes taught at local zoo, local pottery, local truck manufacturing plant, multimedia allied health lab, machine shop lab. **Partnerships:** Formal partnerships with United Parcel Service, Ford Motor Company, Norton Hospital, Jewish Hospital, St. Mary's Health Care System and local area technology centers.

Student profile.

Out-of-state:	4%	**25 or older:**	45%

Transfer out. Colleges most students transferred to 2008: University of Louisville, Spalding University, University of Kentucky, Bellarmine University.

Basis for selection. Open admission, but selective for some programs. Special requirements for nursing and other allied health programs. Entering freshmen required to take ACT for placement before start of second semester. Interview required for allied health programs: nursing, respiratory therapy, radiology, nuclear medicine, health information technology, occupational therapy, physical therapy, surgical technology, and practical nursing.

2008-2009 Annual costs. Tuition/fees: $3,630; $11,700 out-of-state. Per-credit charge: $121 in-state; $390 out-of-state. Tuition reduction program available for qualified residents of contiguous states. Books/supplies: $800. Personal expenses: $848.

Financial aid. Need-based: Need-based aid available for part-time students. Work-study available for part-time students. **Non-need-based:** Scholarships awarded for academics, art, minority status.

Application procedures. Admission: No deadline. No application fee. Admission notification on a rolling basis. **Financial aid:** Priority date 3/15; no closing date. FAFSA, institutional form required. Applicants notified on a rolling basis starting 6/15; must reply within 3 week(s) of notification.

Academics. Special study options: Cooperative education, cross-registration, distance learning, dual enrollment of high school students, ESL, honors, independent study, internships, teacher certification program, weekend college. License preparation in aviation, nursing, occupational therapy, physical therapy, radiology, real estate. **Credit/placement by examination:** AP, CLEP, IB, institutional tests. STEP test, challenge exams available. **Support services:** GED preparation and test center, learning center, reduced course load, remedial instruction, study skills assistance, tutoring, writing center.

Majors. Agriculture: Horticulture. **Business:** Accounting technology, business admin, executive assistant, real estate. **Communications technology:** General. **Computer sciences:** General, data processing. **Education:** Teacher assistance. **Engineering technology:** General, electromechanical. **Health:** Electrocardiograph technology, medical records technology, nuclear medical technology, nursing (RN), occupational therapy assistant, physical therapy assistant, respiratory therapy technology, sonography. **Liberal arts:** Arts/sciences. **Mechanic/repair:** Automotive. **Personal/culinary services:** Chef training. **Production:** Welding. **Protective services:** Firefighting. **Public administration:** Social work. **Science technology:** Chemical.

Most popular majors. Health sciences 30%, interdisciplinary studies 7%, liberal arts 43%.

Computing on campus. 1,500 workstations in library, computer center, student center. Commuter students can connect to campus network. Online course registration, online library, helpline available.

Student life. Freshman orientation: Mandatory. Preregistration for classes offered. **Activities:** Drama, literary magazine, student government, student newspaper, black student union, Baptist student union, Earth-ecology club, Aspire, international student club, WOW.

Student services. Adult student services, career counseling, services for economically disadvantaged, student employment services, financial aid counseling, health services, minority student services, on-campus daycare, personal counseling, placement for graduates, veterans' counselor, women's services. **Physically disabled:** Services for visually, speech, hearing impaired. **Transfer:** Re-entry adviser, pre-admission transcript evaluation for new students. Transfer adviser, college fairs on campus for students transferring to 4-year colleges.

Contact. Phone: (502) 213-5333
Denise Gray-Lackey, Dean of Student Affairs, Jefferson Community and Technical College, 109 East Broadway, Louisville, KY 40202

Louisville Technical Institute
Louisville, Kentucky
www.louisvilletech.edu **CB code: 1501**

- For-profit 2-year visual arts, technical and career college
- Commuter campus in very large city
- Interview required

General. Founded in 1961. Accredited by ACICS. **Enrollment:** 575 degree-seeking undergraduates; 6 non-degree-seeking students. **Degrees:** 5 bachelor's, 158 associate awarded. **Location:** 7 miles from downtown. **Calendar:** Quarter, extensive summer session. **Full-time faculty:** 30 total; 3% minority, 37% women. **Part-time faculty:** 38 total; 5% have terminal degrees, 8% minority, 45% women. **Class size:** 97% < 20, 3% 20-39. **Special facilities:** Laboratories for computer-aided graphics, computer-aided drafting, electronics, computer networking, computer security and forensics and robotics.

Student profile. Among degree-seeking undergraduates, 100% enrolled in a vocational program, 2% already have a bachelor's degree or higher, 167 enrolled as first-time, first-year students, 88 transferred in from other institutions.

Part-time:	46%	**Asian American:**	2%
Out-of-state:	11%	**Hispanic American:**	1%
Women:	41%	**Live on campus:**	2%
African American:	15%		

Transfer out. 5% of students enrolled in the transfer program go on to 4-year colleges. **Colleges most students transferred to 2008:** Sullivan University.

Basis for selection. Entrance test (CPAt) scores, previous school record and the interview process with an admissions representative are the most important factors in admissions decisions. Equivalent scores from the ACT or SAT can be accepted in place of a CPAt score. **Homeschooled:** Statement describing homeschool structure and mission, transcript of courses and grades, state high school equivalency certificate required. **Learning Disabled:** Students seeking special accommodations must provide in advance documentation from professional analysis indicating the level of disability and types of recommended accommodations.

High school preparation. Recommended units include English 4, mathematics 4, social studies 2, science 3, computer science 1 and visual/performing arts 1.

2008-2009 Annual costs. Tuition and fees vary depending upon the career/academic program in which a student enrolls. Books/supplies: $1,500. Personal expenses: $2,400.

2007-2008 Financial aid. Need-based: 25% of total undergraduate aid awarded as scholarships/grants, 75% as loans/jobs. Need-based aid available for part-time students. Work-study available nights. **Non-need-based:** Scholarships awarded for academics, art, job skills.

Application procedures. Admission: No deadline. $100 fee, may be waived for applicants with need. Application must be submitted on paper. Admission notification on a rolling basis. **Financial aid:** No deadline. FAFSA required. Applicants notified on a rolling basis; must reply within 2 week(s) of notification.

Academics. Special study options: Accelerated study, cooperative education, double major, internships. Bachelor's degree programs available on campus. **Credit/placement by examination:** AP, CLEP, institutional tests. 51 credit hours maximum toward associate degree, 99 toward bachelor's. **Support services:** Learning center, reduced course load, remedial instruction, study skills assistance, tutoring.

Majors. Architecture: Interior. **Communications technology:** Animation/special effects, desktop publishing, graphics. **Computer sciences:** Computer graphics, information systems, information technology, LAN/WAN management, security, system admin, vendor certification, web page design. **Engineering:** Architectural. **Engineering technology:** Architectural, architectural drafting, CAD/CADD, computer, computer hardware, drafting, electrical, mechanical drafting, robotics. **Mechanic/repair:** Computer. **Visual/performing arts:** Commercial/advertising art, graphic design, illustration, interior design.

Most popular majors. Computer/information sciences 30%, engineering/engineering technologies 47%, visual/performing arts 23%.

Computing on campus. 250 workstations in library, computer center. Commuter students can connect to campus network. Online library, helpline, repair service, wireless network available.

Student life. Freshman orientation: Mandatory. Preregistration for classes offered. A three-hour orientation program including basic policy information, breakout sessions by academic program, a learning style survey and a Q - A session is conducted at the start of each quarter for day and evening students. **Housing:** Apartments, wellness housing available. $95 nonrefundable deposit. **Activities:** Student chapters of SkillsUSA, American Design Drafting Association (ADDA), American Society of Interior Designers (ASID), International Interior Design Association (IIDA) and the Louisville Ad Federation, Greener Living Club.

Student services. Adult student services, career counseling, student employment services, financial aid counseling, placement for graduates, veterans' counselor. **Transfer:** Re-entry adviser, pre-admission transcript evaluation for new students.

Contact. E-mail: kripperdan@louisvilletech.edu
Phone: (502) 456-6509 Toll-free number: (800) 844-6528
Fax: (502) 456-2341
Kevin Ripperdan, Director of Admissions, Louisville Technical Institute, 3901 Atkinson Square Drive, Louisville, KY 40218-4524

Madisonville Community College
Madisonville, Kentucky
www.madisonville.kctcs.edu **CB code: 1606**

- Public 2-year community college
- Commuter campus in large town

General. Founded in 1968. Regionally accredited. Campuses include: North Campus, Health Campus, Technology Campus and Muhlenberg County Campus. Classes also offered at area high schools and other off-campus locations, including KET telecourses and online. **Enrollment:** 4,000 degree-seeking undergraduates. **Degrees:** 410 associate awarded. **Location:** 50 miles from Evansville, Indiana. **Calendar:** Semester, extensive summer session. **Full-time faculty:** 100 total. **Part-time faculty:** 75 total. **Special facilities:** Glema Mahr center for the arts.

Student profile.

Out-of-state:	1%	**25 or older:**	50%

Transfer out. Colleges most students transferred to 2008: Murray State University, Western Kentucky University, University of Kentucky.

Basis for selection. Open admission. ACT or CAPS scores required for placement/counseling. Special requirements for health programs (nursing, physical therapy assistant, radiography, resipiratory, biomedical, occupational therapy assistant, clinical lab technology). Interview recommended for nursing and physical therapy assistant applicants. **Adult students:** ACT or COMPASS test scores required of all students; scores must be less than 5 years old to be considered. **Homeschooled:** Encouraged to apply for early admissions status prior to completion of high school credential. **Learning Disabled:** Disability resources provided for qualified students.

High school preparation. 14 units recommended. Recommended units include English 4, mathematics 3, social studies 2, history 2, science 2 (laboratory 1).

2008-2009 Annual costs. Tuition/fees: $3,630; $11,700 out-of-state. Per-credit charge: $121 in-state; $390 out-of-state. Tuition reduction program available for qualified residents of contiguous states. Books/supplies: $500. Personal expenses: $1,000.

2007-2008 Financial aid. Need-based: Need-based aid available for part-time students. Work-study available nights, weekends and for part-time students. **Non-need-based:** Scholarships awarded for minority status.

Application procedures. Admission: Closing date 8/1 (receipt date). No application fee. Admission notification on a rolling basis. **Financial aid:** Priority date 3/15; no closing date. FAFSA, institutional form required. Applicants notified on a rolling basis; must reply within 3 week(s) of notification.

Academics. Adult and continuing education programs available both on and off-campus. Tech prep and school-to-work programs available. **Special study options:** Cooperative education, distance learning, double major, dual enrollment of high school students, honors, independent study, internships, liberal arts/career combination, weekend college. Bachelor's degree programs available on campus. License preparation in nursing, occupational therapy, physical therapy, radiology, real estate. **Credit/placement by examination:** AP, CLEP, institutional tests. **Support services:** GED preparation and test center, learning center, remedial instruction, study skills assistance, tutoring, writing center.

Majors. Agriculture: Production. **Business:** Accounting, administrative services, business admin, finance, management information systems, real estate, sales/distribution. **Computer sciences:** General. **Construction:** Electrician. **Education:** General, early childhood. **Engineering technology:** General, drafting, electromechanical. **Health:** Clinical lab science, clinical lab technology, medical radiologic technology/radiation therapy, medical secretary, nursing (RN), occupational therapy assistant, physical therapy assistant, respiratory therapy technology. **Liberal arts:** Arts/sciences. **Production:** Machine shop technology. **Protective services:** Law enforcement admin.

Most popular majors. Business/marketing 14%, health sciences 39%, liberal arts 36%.

Computing on campus. 200 workstations in library, computer center, student center. Commuter students can connect to campus network. Online course registration, online library, helpline, wireless network available.

Student life. **Freshman orientation:** Mandatory. Preregistration for classes offered. **Activities:** Choral groups, drama, literary magazine, musical theater, student government, student newspaper, multicultural student organization, Lions Club, Student Ambassadors, Socratic Society, Phi Theta Kappa, Baptist Student Union.

Athletics. **Intramural:** Basketball.

Student services. Adult student services, career counseling, services for economically disadvantaged, student employment services, financial aid counseling, health services, minority student services, placement for graduates, veterans' counselor. **Physically disabled:** Services for visually, speech, hearing impaired. **Transfer:** Pre-admission transcript evaluation for new students. Transfer adviser, college fairs on campus for students transferring to 4-year colleges.

Contact. E-mail: aimee.bullock@kctcs.edu
Phone: (270) 821-2250 Toll-free number: (866) 227-4812
Fax: (270) 825-8553
Aimee Bullock, Director of Enrollment Management, Madisonville Community College, 2000 College Drive, Madisonville, KY 42431

Maysville Community and Technical College

Maysville, Kentucky
www.maysville.kctcs.edu **CB code: 0693**

- Public 2-year community and technical college
- Commuter campus in small town

General. Founded in 1968. Regionally accredited. Access to University of Kentucky library through automated system (KYVU). **Enrollment:** 2,086 degree-seeking undergraduates. **Degrees:** 184 associate awarded. **Location:** 60 miles from Lexington, 60 miles from Cincinnati. **Calendar:** Semester, limited summer session. **Full-time faculty:** 93 total. **Part-time faculty:** 87 total. **Class size:** 78% < 20, 22% 20-39, less than 1% 50-99.

Student profile.

Out-of-state:	8%	**25 or older:**	54%

Basis for selection. Open admission, but selective for some programs. High school diploma required and ACT scores considered for nursing program. ACT or COMPASS may be required for placement in degree-seeking programs. Interview required of nursing majors.

High school preparation. Recommended units include English 4, mathematics 3, social studies 2, science 2 and foreign language 2.

2008-2009 Annual costs. Tuition/fees: $3,630; $11,700 out-of-state. Per-credit charge: $121 in-state; $390 out-of-state. Tuition reduction program available for qualified residents of contiguous states. Books/supplies: $2,000. Personal expenses: $1,400.

2007-2008 Financial aid. **Need-based:** 57% of total undergraduate aid awarded as scholarships/grants, 43% as loans/jobs. Need-based aid available for part-time students. Work-study available nights. **Non-need-based:** Scholarships awarded for academics.

Application procedures. **Admission:** No deadline. $5 fee. Admission notification on a rolling basis. March 1 priority date for nursing applicants. **Financial aid:** Priority date 4/1; no closing date. FAFSA, institutional form required. Applicants notified on a rolling basis starting 3/1; must reply within 3 week(s) of notification.

Academics. **Special study options:** Cooperative education, distance learning, double major, dual enrollment of high school students, honors, independent study, internships, teacher certification program. Bachelor's degree programs available on campus. License preparation in nursing, real estate. **Credit/placement by examination:** AP, CLEP, institutional tests. **Support services:** GED preparation and test center, learning center, reduced course load, remedial instruction, study skills assistance, tutoring.

Majors. **Agriculture:** Horticultural science. **Business:** General, accounting, business admin, e-commerce, executive assistant, office management. **Computer sciences:** General, computer science, data processing, database management, information systems, programming, security, system admin, web page design. **Conservation:** Environmental studies. **Construction:** Carpentry. **Education:** Early childhood. **Engineering:** Industrial, manufacturing. **Engineering technology:** Electrical, electromechanical, energy systems, industrial, manufacturing. **Health:** Licensed practical nurse, medical secretary, nursing (RN), surgical technology. **Liberal arts:** Arts/sciences. **Mechanic/repair:** General, automotive, diesel, industrial.

Computing on campus. 375 workstations in library, computer center. Commuter students can connect to campus network.

Student life. **Freshman orientation:** Mandatory. Preregistration for classes offered. **Activities:** Drama, student government, Phi Theta Kappa, student education association, society of manufacturing student engineers, association of nursing students.

Athletics. **Intramural:** Badminton, volleyball.

Student services. Adult student services, alcohol/substance abuse counseling, career counseling, services for economically disadvantaged, student employment services, financial aid counseling, personal counseling, placement for graduates, veterans' counselor. **Physically disabled:** Services for hearing impaired. **Transfer:** Transfer adviser, college fairs on campus for students transferring to 4-year colleges.

Contact. E-mail: patee.massie@kctcs.edu
Phone: (606) 759-5818 ext. 66186 Fax: (606) 759-5818
Patricia Massie, Registrar/Admissions Officer, Maysville Community and Technical College, 1755 US HIghway 68, Maysville, KY 41056

National College: Danville

Danville, Kentucky
www.ncbt.edu **CB code: 3413**

- For-profit 2-year business college
- Commuter campus in large town

General. Accredited by ACICS. **Enrollment:** 295 degree-seeking undergraduates. **Degrees:** 56 associate awarded. **Calendar:** Quarter, extensive summer session. **Full-time faculty:** 1 total. **Part-time faculty:** 24 total.

Basis for selection. Open admission. Interviews highly recommended.

2008-2009 Annual costs. Tuition/fees: $9,585. Per-credit charge: $212. Books/supplies: $1,500.

Financial aid. All financial aid based on need. Need-based aid available for part-time students.

Application procedures. **Admission:** No deadline. $30 fee, may be waived for applicants with need. Admission notification on a rolling basis. **Financial aid:** No deadline. FAFSA required. Applicants notified on a rolling basis.

Academics. **Special study options:** Double major, internships, liberal arts/career combination. **Credit/placement by examination:** CLEP, institutional tests. **Support services:** Learning center, remedial instruction, tutoring.

Majors. **Business:** Accounting, administrative services, business admin. **Computer sciences:** Computer science. **Health:** Medical assistant, medical secretary, physician assistant.

Computing on campus. 35 workstations in library, computer center.

Student life. **Freshman orientation:** Mandatory. Preregistration for classes offered. **Activities:** Student government.

Student services. Career counseling, student employment services, financial aid counseling, personal counseling, placement for graduates, veterans' counselor.

Contact. E-mail: market@educorp.edu
Phone: (859) 236-6991 Toll-free number: (800) 664-1886
Fax: (859) 236-1063
Larry Steele, Vice President of Admissions, National College: Danville, PO Box 6400, Roanoke, VA 24017

National College: Florence
Florence, Kentucky
www.ncbt.edu **CB code: 3408**

- For-profit 2-year business college
- Commuter campus in large town

General. Accredited by ACICS. **Enrollment:** 137 degree-seeking undergraduates. **Degrees:** 56 associate awarded. **Calendar:** Quarter, limited summer session. **Full-time faculty:** 4 total. **Part-time faculty:** 28 total.

Basis for selection. Open admission. Interview highly recommended.

2008-2009 Annual costs. Tuition/fees: $9,585. Per-credit charge: $212. Books/supplies: $1,500.

Financial aid. All financial aid based on need. Need-based aid available for part-time students.

Application procedures. Admission: No deadline. $30 fee. Admission notification on a rolling basis. **Financial aid:** No deadline. FAFSA required. Applicants notified on a rolling basis.

Academics. Special study options: Double major, internships. **Credit/placement by examination:** CLEP, institutional tests. **Support services:** Learning center, remedial instruction, tutoring.

Majors. Business: Accounting, administrative services, business admin. **Computer sciences:** Computer science. **Health:** Medical assistant, medical secretary.

Computing on campus. 35 workstations in library, computer center.

Student life. Freshman orientation: Mandatory. Preregistration for classes offered. **Activities:** Student government.

Student services. Career counseling, student employment services, financial aid counseling, personal counseling, placement for graduates, veterans' counselor.

Contact. E-mail: market@educorp.edu
Phone: (606) 525-6510 Fax: (606) 525-8961
Larry Steele, Vice President of Admissions, National College: Florence, PO Box 6400, Roanoke, VA 24017

National College: Lexington
Lexington, Kentucky
www.ncbt.edu **CB code: 0987**

- For-profit 2-year business and junior college
- Commuter campus in small city

General. Founded in 1941. Accredited by ACICS. **Enrollment:** 548 degree-seeking undergraduates. **Degrees:** 87 associate awarded. **Location:** 100 miles from Cincinnati. **Calendar:** Quarter, limited summer session. **Full-time faculty:** 5 total. **Part-time faculty:** 46 total.

Basis for selection. Open admission. Interview recommended.

2008-2009 Annual costs. Tuition/fees: $9,585. Per-credit charge: $212. Books/supplies: $1,500.

Financial aid. All financial aid based on need. Need-based aid available for part-time students.

Application procedures. Admission: No deadline. $30 fee, may be waived for applicants with need. Admission notification on a rolling basis. **Financial aid:** No deadline. FAFSA required. Applicants notified on a rolling basis.

Academics. Special study options: Double major, internships. **Credit/placement by examination:** CLEP, institutional tests. **Support services:** Learning center, remedial instruction, tutoring.

Majors. Business: Accounting, administrative services, business admin, office management, office/clerical. **Computer sciences:** Computer science. **Health:** Medical assistant, medical secretary, physician assistant. **Legal studies:** Legal secretary.

Computing on campus. 35 workstations in library, computer center.

Student life. Freshman orientation: Mandatory. Preregistration for classes offered. **Activities:** Student government.

Student services. Career counseling, student employment services, personal counseling, placement for graduates, veterans' counselor.

Contact. E-mail: market@educorp.edu
Phone: (859) 253-0621 Toll-free number: (800) 664-1886
Fax: (859) 233-3054
Larry Steele, Vice President of Admissions, National College: Lexington, PO Box 6400, Roanoke, VA 24017

National College: Louisville
Louisville, Kentucky
www.ncbt.edu **CB code: 3415**

- For-profit 2-year business college
- Commuter campus in large city

General. Accredited by ACICS. **Enrollment:** 767 degree-seeking undergraduates. **Degrees:** 140 associate awarded. **Calendar:** Quarter, limited summer session. **Full-time faculty:** 4 total. **Part-time faculty:** 49 total.

Basis for selection. Open admission. Interviews highly recommended.

2008-2009 Annual costs. Tuition/fees: $9,585. Per-credit charge: $212. Books/supplies: $1,500.

Financial aid. All financial aid based on need. Need-based aid available for part-time students.

Application procedures. Admission: No deadline. $30 fee, may be waived for applicants with need. Admission notification on a rolling basis. **Financial aid:** No deadline. FAFSA required. Applicants notified on a rolling basis.

Academics. Special study options: Internships. **Credit/placement by examination:** CLEP, institutional tests. **Support services:** Learning center, remedial instruction, tutoring.

Majors. Business: Accounting, administrative services, business admin. **Computer sciences:** Computer science. **Health:** Medical assistant, medical secretary. **Legal studies:** Legal secretary.

Computing on campus. 35 workstations in library, computer center.

Student life. Freshman orientation: Mandatory. Preregistration for classes offered. **Activities:** Student government.

Student services. Career counseling, student employment services, personal counseling, placement for graduates, veterans' counselor.

Contact. E-mail: market@educorp.edu
Phone: (502) 447-7634 Toll-free number: (800) 664-1886
Fax: (502) 447-7665
Larry Steele, Vice President of Admissions, National College: Louisville, PO Box 6400, Roanoke, VA 24017

National College: Pikeville
Pikeville, Kentucky
www.ncbt.edu **CB code: 3412**

- For-profit 2-year business college
- Commuter campus in large town

General. Accredited by ACICS. **Enrollment:** 191 degree-seeking undergraduates. **Degrees:** 27 associate awarded. **Calendar:** Quarter, extensive summer session. **Full-time faculty:** 2 total. **Part-time faculty:** 15 total.

Basis for selection. Open admission. Interviews highly recommended.

2008-2009 Annual costs. Tuition/fees: $9,585. Per-credit charge: $212. Books/supplies: $1,500.

Financial aid. All financial aid based on need. Need-based aid available for part-time students.

Application procedures. Admission: No deadline. $30 fee, may be waived for applicants with need. Admission notification on a rolling basis. **Financial aid:** No deadline. FAFSA required.

Academics. Special study options: Double major, internships. **Credit/placement by examination:** CLEP, institutional tests. **Support services:** Learning center, remedial instruction, tutoring.

Majors. Business: Accounting, administrative services, business admin. **Health:** Medical assistant, medical secretary. **Legal studies:** Legal secretary.

Computing on campus. 35 workstations in library, computer center.

Student life. Freshman orientation: Mandatory. Preregistration for classes offered. **Activities:** Student government.

Student services. Career counseling, student employment services, financial aid counseling, personal counseling, placement for graduates, veterans' counselor.

Contact. E-mail: market@educorp.edu
Phone: (606) 432-5477 Toll-free number: (800) 664-1886
Fax: (606) 437-4952
Larry Steele, Vice President of Admissions, National College: Pikeville, PO Box 6400, Roanoke, VA 24017

National College: Richmond

Richmond, Kentucky
www.ncbt.edu **CB code: 3414**

- For-profit 2-year business college
- Commuter campus in large town

General. Accredited by ACICS. **Enrollment:** 306 degree-seeking undergraduates. **Degrees:** 60 associate awarded. **Calendar:** Quarter, limited summer session. **Full-time faculty:** 1 total. **Part-time faculty:** 33 total.

Basis for selection. Open admission. Interviews highly recommended.

2008-2009 Annual costs. Tuition/fees: $9,585. Per-credit charge: $212. Books/supplies: $1,500.

Financial aid. All financial aid based on need. Need-based aid available for part-time students.

Application procedures. Admission: No deadline. $30 fee, may be waived for applicants with need. Admission notification on a rolling basis. **Financial aid:** No deadline. FAFSA required. Applicants notified on a rolling basis.

Academics. Special study options: Double major, internships. **Credit/placement by examination:** CLEP, institutional tests. **Support services:** Learning center, remedial instruction, tutoring.

Majors. Business: Accounting, administrative services, business admin. **Computer sciences:** Computer science. **Health:** Medical assistant, medical secretary.

Computing on campus. 35 workstations in library, computer center.

Student life. Freshman orientation: Mandatory. Preregistration for classes offered. **Activities:** Student government.

Student services. Career counseling, student employment services, financial aid counseling, personal counseling, placement for graduates, veterans' counselor.

Contact. E-mail: market@educorp.edu
Phone: (859) 623-8956 Toll-free number: (800) 664-1886
Fax: (859) 624-5544
Larry Steele, Vice President of Admissions, National College: Richmond, PO Box 6400, Roanoke, VA 24017

Owensboro Community and Technical College

Owensboro, Kentucky
www.octc.kctcs.edu **CB code: 0613**

- Public 2-year community and technical college
- Commuter campus in small city

General. Founded in 1986. Regionally accredited. **Enrollment:** 2,986 degree-seeking undergraduates; 2,599 non-degree-seeking students. **Degrees:** 413 associate awarded. **Location:** 120 miles from Louisville; 40 miles from Evansville, Indiana. **Calendar:** Semester, extensive summer session. **Full-time faculty:** 100 total; 13% have terminal degrees, 5% minority, 54% women. **Part-time faculty:** 115 total. **Class size:** 60% < 20, 39% 20-39, 2% 40-49. **Special facilities:** Outdoor classroom/nature area, early Head-start program.

Student profile. Among degree-seeking undergraduates, 43% enrolled in a transfer program, 57% enrolled in a vocational program, 692 enrolled as first-time, first-year students.

Part-time:	42%	**African American:**	4%
Out-of-state:	3%	**Hispanic American:**	1%
Women:	65%	**25 or older:**	32%

Transfer out. Colleges most students transferred to 2008: Western Kentucky University, Kentucky Wesleyan College, Brescia University, University of Southern Indiana, University of Kentucky.

Basis for selection. Open admission, but selective for some programs. ACT scores required for nursing, radiography, diagnostic medical sonography, surgical technology, and early childhood education programs. **Home-schooled:** Documentation of courses required.

High school preparation. 11 units recommended. Recommended units include English 4, mathematics 3, social studies 1, history 2, science 3 (laboratory 1).

2008-2009 Annual costs. Tuition/fees: $3,630; $11,700 out-of-state. Per-credit charge: $121 in-state; $390 out-of-state. Tuition reduction program available for qualified residents of contiguous states. Books/supplies: $950. Personal expenses: $1,040.

2007-2008 Financial aid. Need-based: Need-based aid available for part-time students. Work-study available for part-time students. **Non-need-based:** Scholarships awarded for academics, state residency.

Application procedures. Admission: Priority date 4/1; deadline 8/15 (receipt date). No application fee. Admission notification on a rolling basis beginning on or about 3/1. **Financial aid:** Priority date 3/16; no closing date. FAFSA required. Applicants notified by 6/1; must reply within 2 week(s) of notification.

Academics. Special study options: Cooperative education, distance learning, double major, dual enrollment of high school students, independent study, study abroad. License preparation in nursing, paramedic, radiology, real estate. **Credit/placement by examination:** AP, CLEP, IB, institutional tests. **Support services:** Learning center, remedial instruction, study skills assistance, tutoring.

Majors. Agriculture: Business. **Biology:** Biotechnology. **Business:** General, accounting, administrative services, business admin, management information systems, office/clerical. **Computer sciences:** Information systems. **Construction:** Carpentry, electrician. **Education:** General, early childhood. **Engineering technology:** Architectural drafting, CAD/CADD, electrical. **Health:** Medical radiologic technology/radiation therapy, medical secretary, medical transcription, nursing (RN), office assistant, sonography. **Liberal arts:** Arts/sciences. **Personal/culinary services:** Chef training. **Production:** Machine tool, welding. **Protective services:** Police science. **Public administration:** Social work.

Most popular majors. Business/marketing 8%, health sciences 17%, interdisciplinary studies 14%, liberal arts 45%.

Computing on campus. 120 workstations in library, computer center, student center. Online course registration, online library, helpline, wireless network available.

Student life. Freshman orientation: Mandatory. Preregistration for classes offered. Half-day session conducted a month before classes begin. **Activities:** Choral groups, drama, literary magazine, radio station, student government, student newspaper, TV station.

Athletics. Intramural: Basketball, softball.

Student services. Career counseling, services for economically disadvantaged, student employment services, financial aid counseling, on-campus daycare, personal counseling, placement for graduates, veterans' counselor. **Physically disabled:** Services for visually, speech, hearing impaired. **Transfer:** Pre-admission transcript evaluation for new students. Transfer adviser, college fairs on campus for students transferring to 4-year colleges.

Contact. E-mail: octc.info@kctcs.edu
Phone: (270) 686-4527 Toll-free number: (866) 755-6282
Fax: (270) 686-4648
Kevin Beardmore, Vice President of Student Affairs, Owensboro Community and Technical College, 4800 New Hartford Road, Owensboro, KY 42303-1899

Somerset Community College

Somerset, Kentucky
www.somerset.kctcs.edu **CB code: 1779**

- Public 2-year community and technical college
- Commuter campus in large town

General. Founded in 1965. Regionally accredited. One of 15 community colleges and 12 technical colleges consolidated under one administration. **Enrollment:** 4,860 degree-seeking undergraduates. **Degrees:** 550 associate awarded. **Location:** 70 miles from Lexington. **Calendar:** Semester, limited summer session. **Full-time faculty:** 148 total. **Part-time faculty:** 160 total. **Class size:** 66% < 20, 32% 20-39, less than 1% 40-49, less than 1% 50-99.

Student profile.

Out-of-state:	1%	**25 or older:**	47%

Transfer out. Colleges most students transferred to 2008: Morehead State University, University of Kentucky, Western Kentucky University, Eastern Kentucky University.

Basis for selection. Open admission, but selective for some programs. Test scores, letters of recommendation, and interview required for limited enrollment programs in allied health. ACT required in admissions process but not ordinarily used as selective criterion.

High school preparation. 20 units recommended. Recommended units include English 4, mathematics 3, social studies 2, science 2 and academic electives 9.

2008-2009 Annual costs. Tuition/fees: $3,630; $11,700 out-of-state. Per-credit charge: $121 in-state; $390 out-of-state. Tuition reduction program available for qualified residents of contiguous states. Books/supplies: $500. Personal expenses: $800.

2007-2008 Financial aid. All financial aid based on need. 79% of total undergraduate aid awarded as scholarships/grants, 21% as loans/jobs. Need-based aid available for part-time students. Work-study available for part-time students.

Application procedures. Admission: No deadline. No application fee. Application must be submitted on paper. Admission notification on a rolling basis. Admitted students in nursing, clinical laboratory techniques, and physical therapy assisting must reply within 10 days. **Financial aid:** Priority date 3/1; no closing date. FAFSA required. Applicants notified on a rolling basis starting 5/1; must reply within 2 week(s) of notification.

Academics. Special study options: Cooperative education, distance learning, dual enrollment of high school students, ESL, external degree, independent study, internships, liberal arts/career combination. Bachelor's degree programs available on campus. License preparation in aviation, dental hygiene, nursing, physical therapy, radiology, real estate. **Credit/placement by examination:** AP, CLEP. 12 credit hours maximum toward associate degree. **Support services:** GED preparation and test center, learning center, reduced course load, remedial instruction, study skills assistance, tutoring, writing center.

Majors. Business: Business admin, executive assistant. **Communications technology:** Graphics, printing management. **Computer sciences:** General. **Construction:** Carpentry, electrician, masonry, pipefitting, plumbing. **Education:** General, teacher assistance. **Family/consumer sciences:** Child care. **Health:** Clinical lab assistant, clinical lab technology, licensed practical nurse, medical assistant, medical secretary, nursing (RN), physical therapy assistant. **Liberal arts:** Arts/sciences. **Mechanic/repair:** Aircraft powerplant, auto body, automotive, diesel, industrial, industrial electronics. **Personal/culinary services:** Cosmetology. **Production:** Machine shop technology, welding. **Protective services:** Law enforcement admin, police science.

Computing on campus. 947 workstations in library, computer center, student center. Commuter students can connect to campus network. Online course registration, online library, repair service available.

Student life. Freshman orientation: Mandatory. Preregistration for classes offered. **Activities:** Choral groups, drama, film society, music ensembles, student government, student newspaper, Baptist Student Union, student government association, Students for Free Enterprise, Phi Beta Lambda, Phi Theta Kappa, criminal justice student organization.

Athletics. Intramural: Basketball, football (non-tackle), racquetball, softball, volleyball. **Team name:** Cougars.

Student services. Adult student services, career counseling, services for economically disadvantaged, student employment services, financial aid counseling, minority student services, personal counseling, placement for graduates, veterans' counselor. **Physically disabled:** Services for visually, speech, hearing impaired. **Transfer:** Pre-admission transcript evaluation for new students. Transfer adviser, college fairs on campus for students transferring to 4-year colleges.

Contact. E-mail: tracy.casada@kctcs.edu
Phone: (606) 451-6630 Toll-free number: (877) 629-9722
Fax: (606) 679-4369
Tracy Casada, Dean of Student Affairs, Somerset Community College, 808 Monticello Street, Somerset, KY 42501

Southeast Kentucky Community and Technical College

Cumberland, Kentucky
www.secc.kctcs.edu **CB code: 1770**

- Public 2-year community and technical college
- Commuter campus in small town

General. Founded in 1960. Regionally accredited. Branch campuses at Harlan, Middlesboro, Pineville and Whitesburg. **Enrollment:** 2,104 degree-seeking undergraduates; 3,416 non-degree-seeking students. **Degrees:** 415 associate awarded. **Location:** 150 miles from Lexington. **Calendar:** Semester, limited summer session. **Full-time faculty:** 114 total; 10% minority, 46% women. **Part-time faculty:** 66 total; 4% minority, 50% women. **Class size:** 32% < 20, 53% 20-39, 10% 40-49, 4% 50-99. **Special facilities:** Appalachian archives.

Student profile. Among degree-seeking undergraduates, 35% enrolled in a transfer program, 65% enrolled in a vocational program, 777 enrolled as first-time, first-year students, 81 transferred in from other institutions.

Part-time:	39%	**Women:**	61%
Out-of-state:	4%	**25 or older:**	40%

Transfer out. 25% of students enrolled in the transfer program go on to 4-year colleges. **Colleges most students transferred to 2008:** Lincoln Memorial University, University of Louisville, Eastern Kentucky University.

Basis for selection. Open admission, but selective for some programs. ACT required for nursing, radiography, respiratory care and physical therapy programs. **Homeschooled:** Transcript of courses and grades required.

High school preparation. 12 units recommended. Recommended units include English 4, mathematics 3, history 2, science 2 (laboratory 1).

2008-2009 Annual costs. Tuition/fees: $3,630; $11,844 out-of-state. Per-credit charge: $121 in-state; $390 out-of-state. Tuition reduction program available for qualified residents of contiguous states. Books/supplies: $450. Personal expenses: $1,100.

2008-2009 Financial aid. All financial aid based on need. Need-based aid available for part-time students. Work-study available for part-time students. **Additional information:** March 15 deadline for state financial aid.

Application procedures. Admission: No deadline. No application fee. Admission notification on a rolling basis. **Financial aid:** Priority date 3/15; no closing date. FAFSA required. Applicants notified by 6/15; must reply within 2 week(s) of notification.

Academics. Special study options: Cross-registration, distance learning, dual enrollment of high school students, internships, liberal arts/career combination. License preparation in nursing. **Credit/placement by examination:** AP, CLEP, institutional tests. 30 credit hours maximum toward associate degree. **Support services:** GED preparation and test center, learning center, pre-admission summer program, reduced course load, remedial instruction, study skills assistance, tutoring, writing center.

Majors. Business: Administrative services, banking/financial services, business admin, finance, management information systems. **Computer sciences:** General, data processing. **Engineering technology:** Computer. **Health:** Clinical lab assistant, medical radiologic technology/radiation therapy, nursing (RN), physical therapy assistant, respiratory therapy technology. **Liberal arts:** Arts/sciences. **Protective services:** Police science.

Most popular majors. Business/marketing 15%, education 10%, health sciences 20%, liberal arts 52%.

Computing on campus. 46 workstations in library, computer center. Commuter students can connect to campus network. Online course registration, wireless network available.

Student life. Freshman orientation: Mandatory. **Activities:** Choral groups, dance, drama, student government, student newspaper, Christian student union, black student union, Professional Business Leaders, wilderness club, nursing club.

Athletics. **Intramural:** Basketball, golf, table tennis, volleyball.

Student services. Adult student services, career counseling, financial aid counseling, personal counseling, placement for graduates, veterans' counselor. **Physically disabled:** Services for visually impaired. **Transfer:** Transfer adviser, college fairs on campus for students transferring to 4-year colleges.

Contact. E-mail: cookie.baker@kctcs.edu
Phone: (606) 589-2145 Toll-free number: (888) 274-7332
Fax: (606) 589-5423
Veria Baldwin, Director of Admissions, Southeast Kentucky Community and Technical College, 700 College Road, Cumberland, KY 40823

Southwestern College: Florence

Florence, Kentucky
www.swcollege.net **CB code: 2482**

- For-profit 2-year health science and career college
- Residential campus in small city
- Interview required

General. Accredited by ACICS. **Enrollment:** 315 undergraduates. **Degrees:** 6 associate awarded. **Location:** 5 miles from Cincinnati. **Calendar:** Quarter, extensive summer session. **Full-time faculty:** 10 total; 50% have terminal degrees, 20% minority, 60% women. **Part-time faculty:** 10 total; 50% have terminal degrees, 40% women.

Student profile. 10% enrolled in a transfer program, 90% enrolled in a vocational program, 2% already have a bachelor's degree or higher.

Out-of-state:	3%	**Asian American:**	1%
African American:	5%	**Hispanic American:**	1%

Transfer out. **Colleges most students transferred to 2008:** Brown Mackie, Beckfield, Northern Kentucky University, Gateway Technical Community College.

Basis for selection. Open admission. **Homeschooled:** State high school equivalency certificate required.

High school preparation. College-preparatory program required.

2008-2009 Annual costs. Tuition/fees: $10,825.

2007-2008 Financial aid. All financial aid based on need. 300 full-time freshmen applied for aid; 280 were judged to have need; 280 of these received aid. Average need met was 100%. Average scholarship/grant was $400. 25% of total undergraduate aid awarded as scholarships/grants, 75% as loans/jobs. Need-based aid available for part-time students.

Application procedures. **Admission:** No deadline. $20 fee. Application must be submitted on paper. Admission notification on a rolling basis. **Financial aid:** No deadline. FAFSA required. Applicants notified on a rolling basis.

Academics. **Special study options:** Independent study, liberal arts/career combination. **Credit/placement by examination:** CLEP. **Support services:** GED preparation, study skills assistance, tutoring.

Majors. **Business:** Business admin. **Computer sciences:** General. **Health:** Medical assistant. **Protective services:** Law enforcement admin.

Computing on campus. 50 workstations in library, computer center. Online library available.

Student life. **Freshman orientation:** Mandatory. Preregistration for classes offered. Held on campus before each quarter in mornings and evenings. **Activities:** Student government, student newspaper.

Student services. Career counseling, services for economically disadvantaged, student employment services, financial aid counseling, placement for graduates. **Transfer:** Pre-admission transcript evaluation for new students.

Contact. E-mail: cbaird@swcollege.net
Phone: (859) 282-9999 Fax: (859) 282-7940
Cathy Baird, Director of Admissions, Southwestern College: Florence, 8095 Connector Drive, Florence, KY 41042

Spencerian College

Louisville, Kentucky
www.spencerian.edu **CB code: 3422**

- For-profit 2-year health science and nursing college
- Commuter campus in large city

General. Accredited by ACICS. **Enrollment:** 1,202 degree-seeking undergraduates. **Degrees:** 128 associate awarded. **Location:** 10 miles from downtown. **Calendar:** Quarter, extensive summer session. **Full-time faculty:** 45 total; 2% have terminal degrees, 84% women. **Part-time faculty:** 54 total; 7% have terminal degrees, 63% women. **Special facilities:** Radiology labs, surgical technology lab, mock operating room, massage therapy lab.

Student profile. Among degree-seeking undergraduates, 100% enrolled in a vocational program, 380 enrolled as first-time, first-year students.

Basis for selection. Open admission, but selective for some programs. Requirements vary by program. Interview may be required for selective admission programs such as nursing, medical laboratory technology, invasive cardiovascular technology, and surgical technology programs. **Homeschooled:** Transcript of courses and grades required.

2008-2009 Annual costs. Tuition/fees: $14,620. Room only: $4,680.

Application procedures. **Admission:** No deadline. $100 fee. Admission notification on a rolling basis.

Academics. Fridays set aside for catch-up and make-up work for all students whose programs do not require Friday classes or clinicals. **Special study options:** Distance learning, independent study, internships. **Credit/placement by examination:** CLEP, institutional tests. **Support services:** Learning center, tutoring.

Majors. **Business:** Accounting, business admin. **Health:** Cardiovascular technology, clinical lab technology, insurance specialist, medical radiologic technology/radiation therapy, nursing (RN), office admin, surgical technology.

Most popular majors. Health sciences 95%.

Computing on campus. 86 workstations in library, computer center. Commuter students can connect to campus network.

Student life. **Freshman orientation:** Mandatory. One day and one evening session held week before classes begin. **Housing:** Apartments available. $95 deposit.

Student services. Career counseling, financial aid counseling, placement for graduates. **Transfer:** Re-entry adviser, pre-admission transcript evaluation for new students.

Contact. Phone: (502) 447-1000 Toll-free number: (800) 264-1799
Fax: (502) 447-4574
Kathleen Belanger, Director of Admissions, Spencerian College, 4627 Dixie Highway, Louisville, KY 40216

Spencerian College: Lexington

Lexington, Kentucky
www.spencerian.edu **CB code: 3424**

- For-profit 2-year branch campus and technical college
- Commuter campus in small city
- Interview required

General. Accredited by ACICS. **Enrollment:** 601 degree-seeking undergraduates; 3 non-degree-seeking students. **Degrees:** 89 associate awarded. **Location:** 72 miles from Louisville. **Calendar:** Quarter, limited summer session. **Full-time faculty:** 30 total; 3% have terminal degrees, 7% minority, 53% women. **Part-time faculty:** 25 total; 16% minority, 48% women. **Class size:** 93% < 20, 7% 20-39.

Student profile. Among degree-seeking undergraduates, 45% enrolled in a vocational program, 10% already have a bachelor's degree or higher, 133 enrolled as first-time, first-year students.

Part-time:	41%	**African American:**	13%
Women:	55%	**Hispanic American:**	1%

Transfer out. 1% of students enrolled in the transfer program go on to 4-year colleges. **Colleges most students transferred to 2008:** Lexington Community College, University of Kentucky, Eastern Kentucky University, KCTCS.

Basis for selection. Open admission, but selective for some programs. Passing score on CPAt or HOBET (for certain medical programs) or at least 16 on ACT.required for selective programs. **Homeschooled:** Transcript of courses and grades, state high school equivalency certificate required.

2008-2009 Annual costs. Tuition/fees: $2,775. Cost of programs ranges from $9,000 to $41,000; program-specific fees are additional. Cost of housing is $520 per month. Per-credit-hour charge ranges from $235 to $380 depending on program. Books/supplies: $1,200. Personal expenses: $450.

2008-2009 Financial aid. All financial aid based on need. 41% of total undergraduate aid awarded as scholarships/grants, 59% as loans/jobs. Need-based aid available for part-time students.

Application procedures. Admission: No deadline. $100 fee. Admission notification on a rolling basis. **Financial aid:** No deadline. FAFSA, institutional form required. Applicants notified on a rolling basis starting 1/1.

Academics. Special study options: Cooperative education, double major, independent study, weekend college. License preparation in radiology. **Credit/placement by examination:** CLEP, IB. 23 credit hours maximum toward associate degree. **Support services:** Reduced course load, study skills assistance, tutoring.

Majors. Computer sciences: Computer graphics. **Engineering:** Electrical. **Engineering technology:** Computer, computer systems, drafting, electrical. **Health:** Health services. **Mechanic/repair:** Electronics/electrical. **Visual/performing arts:** Commercial/advertising art.

Most popular majors. Architecture 11%, computer/information sciences 30%, engineering/engineering technologies 17%, health sciences 19%.

Computing on campus. PC or laptop required. 170 workstations in library, computer center. Commuter students can connect to campus network. Online library, helpline, wireless network available.

Student life. Freshman orientation: Mandatory. Preregistration for classes offered. 4-hour session held at the beginning of each quarter. **Policies:** Students must be under the age of 21 to live in dorm. **Housing:** Guaranteed on-campus for freshmen. Coed dorms, special housing for disabled, apartments available. $95 nonrefundable deposit. **Activities:** Student newspaper, Healing Hands student organization, Skeleton Crew (Radiography), CADD Student Organization, Allied Health Student Organization.

Athletics. Intramural: Football (non-tackle), softball, volleyball.

Student services. Adult student services, career counseling, student employment services, financial aid counseling, personal counseling, placement for graduates, veterans' counselor. **Physically disabled:** Services for visually, speech, hearing impaired. **Transfer:** Pre-admission transcript evaluation for new students.

Contact. Phone: (859) 223-9608 ext. 5460 Toll-free number: (800) 456-3253 ext. 5460 Fax: (859) 224-7744
David Profita, Director of Admissions, Spencerian College: Lexington, 1575 Winchester Road, Lexington, KY 40505

West Kentucky Community and Technical College

Paducah, Kentucky
www.westkentucky.kctcs.edu **CB code: 1620**

- Public 2-year community and technical college
- Commuter campus in large town

General. Founded in 1932. Regionally accredited. **Enrollment:** 3,514 degree-seeking undergraduates. **Degrees:** 523 associate awarded. **Location:** 140 miles from Nashville, Tennessee. **Calendar:** Semester, limited summer session. **Full-time faculty:** 341 total. **Part-time faculty:** 208 total.

Student profile.

Out-of-state:	4%	**25 or older:**	39%

Basis for selection. Open admission, but selective for some programs. ACT score of 19 required for nursing and physical therapist assistant applicants. CPP placement test required for non-traditional students. ACT required for some applicants and must be received by August 25. Interview required of nursing applicants.

High school preparation. 20 units recommended. Recommended units include English 4, mathematics 3, social studies 2 and science 2.

2008-2009 Annual costs. Tuition/fees: $3,630; $11,700 out-of-state. Per-credit charge: $121 in-state; $390 out-of-state. Tuition reduction program available for qualified residents of contiguous states. Books/supplies: $400. Personal expenses: $425.

Financial aid. Need-based: Need-based aid available for part-time students.

Application procedures. Admission: No deadline. No application fee. Admission notification on a rolling basis beginning on or about 4/1. **Financial aid:** Priority date 4/1; no closing date. FAFSA required. Applicants notified on a rolling basis starting 7/15; must reply within 4 week(s) of notification.

Academics. Special study options: Cooperative education, distance learning, dual enrollment of high school students, ESL, honors, weekend college. License preparation in real estate. **Credit/placement by examination:** CLEP. **Support services:** GED preparation and test center, learning center, reduced course load, remedial instruction, tutoring.

Majors. Business: Accounting, administrative services, banking/financial services, business admin, management information systems, office technology, real estate. **Communications:** General. **Computer sciences:** General, applications programming. **Construction:** Electrician. **Health:** Clinical lab technology, medical radiologic technology/radiation therapy, nursing (RN), physical therapy assistant, physics/radiologic health, respiratory therapy technology, sonography. **Legal studies:** Court reporting. **Liberal arts:** Arts/sciences. **Mechanic/repair:** Industrial. **Personal/culinary services:** Culinary arts.

Computing on campus. 70 workstations in library, computer center.

Student life. Freshman orientation: Mandatory. **Activities:** Choral groups, drama, musical theater, radio station, student government, student newspaper, TV station.

Athletics. Intramural: Basketball M, golf, volleyball.

Student services. Adult student services, career counseling, student employment services, personal counseling, placement for graduates, veterans' counselor. **Physically disabled:** Services for visually, speech, hearing impaired. **Transfer:** Transfer adviser for students transferring to 4-year colleges.

Contact. Phone: (270) 534-3264 Fax: (270) 534-6304
Maria Rosa, Director of Admissions, West Kentucky Community and Technical College, 4810 Alben Barkley Drive/ Box 7380, Paducah, KY 42002-7380

Louisiana

Baton Rouge Community College
Baton Rouge, Louisiana
www.mybrcc.edu **CB code: 6023**

- Public 2-year community college
- Commuter campus in large city

General. Regionally accredited. **Enrollment:** 6,929 degree-seeking undergraduates; 679 non-degree-seeking students. **Degrees:** 310 associate awarded. **Calendar:** Semester, extensive summer session. **Full-time faculty:** 136 total; 60% minority, 65% women. **Part-time faculty:** 152 total; 53% minority, 59% women. **Class size:** 15% < 20, 75% 20-39, 10% 40-49, less than 1% 50-99. **Special facilities:** Health and wellness facility, rock climbing wall.

Student profile. Among degree-seeking undergraduates, 12% enrolled in a vocational program, 1,473 enrolled as first-time, first-year students, 793 transferred in from other institutions.

Part-time:	43%	**Women:**	59%
Out-of-state:	1%	**25 or older:**	28%

Transfer out. Colleges most students transferred to 2008: Louisiana State University, Southern University, Southeastern University.

Basis for selection. Open admission, but selective for some programs. **Homeschooled:** GED or documentation from state verifying completion of SBESE-approved home study program required.

2008-2009 Annual costs. Tuition/fees: $1,846; $4,794 out-of-state. Books/supplies: $1,200. Personal expenses: $1,692.

2007-2008 Financial aid. Need-based: 99% of total undergraduate aid awarded as scholarships/grants, 1% as loans/jobs. Need-based aid available for part-time students. Work-study available weekends and for part-time students. **Non-need-based:** Scholarships awarded for academics, athletics.

Application procedures. Admission: No deadline. $7 fee. Admission notification on a rolling basis. **Financial aid:** Priority date 4/15; no closing date. FAFSA, institutional form required. Applicants notified on a rolling basis.

Academics. Special study options: Cross-registration, distance learning, double major, dual enrollment of high school students, honors, teacher certification program, weekend college. License preparation in nursing. **Credit/placement by examination:** CLEP, institutional tests. **Support services:** Learning center, remedial instruction, study skills assistance, tutoring, writing center.

Majors. Business: General, office technology. **Computer sciences:** General. **Education:** General. **Engineering technology:** Industrial. **Health:** Nursing (RN). **Liberal arts:** Arts/sciences. **Protective services:** Police science. **Visual/performing arts:** Cinematography.

Most popular majors. Education 19%, liberal arts 56%.

Computing on campus. 175 workstations in library, computer center, student center. Online course registration, online library, helpline, wireless network available.

Student life. Freshman orientation: Mandatory. Preregistration for classes offered. **Policies:** All student club members must maintain 2.0 GPA to be active in campus clubs. All student government association officers must maintain 2.5 GPA to remain in office. **Activities:** Jazz band, dance, drama, international student organizations, literary magazine, music ensembles, student government, student newspaper, Christian student association, future educators club, center for peace, peer advisors and leaders, poetry club, self-esteem club, twenty-five plus society, student government association.

Athletics. NJCAA. **Intercollegiate:** Baseball M, softball W. **Intramural:** Football (non-tackle) M, soccer. **Team name:** Bears.

Student services. Alcohol/substance abuse counseling, career counseling, financial aid counseling, personal counseling, veterans' counselor. **Physically disabled:** Services for visually, speech, hearing impaired. **Learning disabled:** Comprehensive services available.

Contact. E-mail: clayn@mybrcc.edu
Phone: (225) 216-8700
Nancy Clay, Executive Director of Enrollment Services, Baton Rouge Community College, 201 Community College Drive, Baton Rouge, LA 70806

Baton Rouge School of Computers
Baton Rouge, Louisiana
www.brsc.net **CB code: 3197**

- For-profit 2-year technical college
- Small city

General. Accredited by ACCSCT. **Enrollment:** 85 degree-seeking undergraduates. **Degrees:** 29 associate awarded. **Calendar:** Continuous. **Full-time faculty:** 17 total. **Part-time faculty:** 2 total.

Basis for selection. Open admission.

2008-2009 Annual costs. $11,500 tuition for diploma program, $25,000 for associate degree; $150 registration fee. Additional charge for textbooks. Books/supplies: $500. Personal expenses: $2,400.

Application procedures. Admission: No deadline. $25 fee, may be waived for applicants with need.

Academics. Credit/placement by examination: CLEP.

Majors. Business: General. **Computer sciences:** General. **Mechanic/repair:** General.

Student life. Freshman orientation: Mandatory.

Contact. Phone: (225) 923-2525 Fax: (225) 923-2979
Brenda Boss, Director of Admissions, Baton Rouge School of Computers, 10425 Plaza Americana, Baton Rouge, LA 70816

Blue Cliff College: Houma
Houma, Louisiana
www.bluecliffcollege.com

- For-profit 2-year technical college
- Commuter campus in large town

General. Accredited by ACCSCT. **Enrollment:** 170 degree-seeking undergraduates. **Degrees:** 34 associate awarded. **Calendar:** Quarter. **Full-time faculty:** 6 total. **Part-time faculty:** 8 total.

Basis for selection. Open admission.

2008-2009 Annual costs. Associate degree program in medical assisting or massage therapy, $21,140; diploma program in medical assisting, $11,825, plus $500 in fees; massage therapy diploma program, $11,395, plus $500 in fees.

Application procedures. Admission: No deadline. $25 fee. Admission notification on a rolling basis.

Academics. Credit/placement by examination: CLEP.

Majors. Health: Medical assistant. **Protective services:** Criminal justice.

Student services. Transfer: Pre-admission transcript evaluation for new students.

Contact. Phone: (985) 601-4000 Toll-free number: (800) 511-2609
Joe Rogalski, Director of Admissions, Blue Cliff College: Houma, 803 Barrow Street, Houma, LA 70360

Blue Cliff College: Lafayette
Lafayette, Louisiana
www.bluecliffcollege.com

- For-profit 2-year health science and technical college
- Commuter campus in small city
- Application essay, interview required

General. Accredited by ACCSCT. **Enrollment:** 115 degree-seeking undergraduates. **Location:** 60 miles from Baton Rouge. **Calendar:** Quarter, extensive summer session. **Full-time faculty:** 3 total. **Part-time faculty:** 7 total. **Special facilities:** Massage therapy clinics.

Basis for selection. Open admission. Wonderlic test given as skills assessment before enrollment. **Homeschooled:** State high school equivalency certificate required.

High school preparation. 25 units recommended. Recommended units include English 4, mathematics 3, history 3, science 4, foreign language 1 and academic electives 10.

2008-2009 Annual costs. Associate degree program in medical assisting or massage therapy, $21,140; diploma program in medical assisting, $11,825, plus $500 in fees; massage therapy diploma program, $11,395, plus $500 in fees.

Application procedures. Admission: $25 fee. Application must be submitted on paper.

Academics. Credit/placement by examination: CLEP.

Majors. Health: Massage therapy. **Protective services:** Criminal justice.

Athletics. Team name: Humming Birds.

Contact. E-mail: hildaj@bluecliffcollege.com
Phone: (337) 269-0620 ext. 3209 Toll-free number: (877) 269-0615 ext. 3204 Fax: (337) 269-0688
Kathy Johnson, Admissions Director, Blue Cliff College: Lafayette, 100 Asma Boulevard, Suite 350, Lafayette, LA 70508

Blue Cliff College: Metairie

Metairie, Louisiana
www.bluecliffcollege.com

- For-profit 2-year technical college
- Commuter campus in large town

General. Accredited by ACCSCT. **Enrollment:** 132 full-time, degree-seeking students. **Degrees:** 10 associate awarded. **Calendar:** Quarter. **Full-time faculty:** 4 total. **Part-time faculty:** 8 total.

Student profile. Among full-time, degree-seeking students, 3 transferred in from other institutions.

Basis for selection. Open admission. Wonderlic test given as skills assessment before enrollment.

2008-2009 Annual costs. Associate degree program in medical assisting or massage therapy, $21,140; diploma program in medical assisting, $11,825, plus $500 in fees; massage therapy diploma program, $11,395, plus $500 in fees.

Application procedures. Admission: No deadline. $25 fee.

Academics. Credit/placement by examination: CLEP.

Majors. Health: Massage therapy.

Student services. Transfer: Pre-admission transcript evaluation for new students.

Contact. E-mail: lisaf@bluecliffcollege.com
Phone: (504) 456-3141 Toll-free number: (800) 517-8176
Fax: (504) 456-7849
Lisa Francis, Admissions Officer, Blue Cliff College: Metairie, 3200 Cleary Avenue, Metairie, LA 70002

Blue Cliff College: Shreveport

Shreveport, Louisiana
www.bluecliffcollege.com

- For-profit 2-year technical college
- Commuter campus in small city

General. Accredited by ACCSCT. **Enrollment:** 170 full-time, degree-seeking students. **Degrees:** 5 associate awarded. **Calendar:** Quarter. **Full-time faculty:** 4 total. **Part-time faculty:** 8 total.

Basis for selection. Open admission.

2008-2009 Annual costs. Associate degree program in medical assisting or massage therapy, $21,140; diploma program in medical assisting, $11,825, plus $500 in fees; massage therapy diploma program, $11,395, plus $500 in fees.

Application procedures. Admission: No deadline. $25 fee. Admission notification on a rolling basis.

Academics. Credit/placement by examination: CLEP.

Majors. Health: Massage therapy, medical assistant.

Contact. Phone: (318) 425-7941
Admissions Representative, Blue Cliff College: Shreveport, 8731 Park Plaza Drive, Shreveport, LA 71105-5682

Bossier Parish Community College

Bossier City, Louisiana
www.bpcc.edu **CB code: 0787**

- Public 2-year community college
- Commuter campus in small city

General. Founded in 1966. Regionally accredited. **Enrollment:** 3,828 degree-seeking undergraduates; 837 non-degree-seeking students. **Degrees:** 363 associate awarded. **Location:** 6 miles from downtown Shreveport. **Calendar:** Semester, limited summer session. **Full-time faculty:** 110 total; 8% have terminal degrees, 10% minority, 64% women. **Part-time faculty:** 176 total; 2% have terminal degrees, 12% minority, 54% women. **Class size:** 47% < 20, 52% 20-39, less than 1% 40-49, less than 1% 50-99. **Partnerships:** Formal partnerships with General Motors, Libby Glass.

Student profile. Among degree-seeking undergraduates, 90% enrolled in a transfer program, 7% enrolled in a vocational program, 918 enrolled as first-time, first-year students, 265 transferred in from other institutions.

Part-time:	35%	**Asian American:**	1%
Out-of-state:	3%	**Hispanic American:**	2%
Women:	66%	**25 or older:**	37%
African American:	26%		

Transfer out. 18% of students enrolled in the transfer program go on to 4-year colleges. **Colleges most students transferred to 2008:** Louisiana State University in Shreveport, Northwestern State University of Louisiana, Louisiana Tech University, Southern Arkansas University, Grambling State University.

Basis for selection. Open admission, but selective for out-of-state students. **Homeschooled:** Students generally expected to complete requirements for GED.

2008-2009 Annual costs. Tuition/fees: $1,760; $3,900 out-of-state. Books/supplies: $1,200. Personal expenses: $1,692.

2007-2008 Financial aid. Need-based: 655 full-time freshmen applied for aid; 530 were judged to have need; 491 of these received aid. Average need met was 74%. Average scholarship/grant was $5,730; average loan $4,377. 43% of total undergraduate aid awarded as scholarships/grants, 57% as loans/jobs. Need-based aid available for part-time students. Work-study available nights and for part-time students. **Non-need-based:** Awarded to 392 full-time undergraduates, including 331 freshmen. Scholarships awarded for academics, alumni affiliation, athletics, minority status, music/drama.

Application procedures. Admission: Closing date 8/8 (receipt date). $15 fee. Application must be submitted on paper. Admission notification on a rolling basis. **Financial aid:** Closing date 7/1. FAFSA required. Applicants notified on a rolling basis.

Academics. Special study options: Accelerated study, distance learning, double major, dual enrollment of high school students, honors, internships, teacher certification program. **Credit/placement by examination:** AP, CLEP, institutional tests. 30 credit hours maximum toward associate degree. **Support services:** GED preparation, learning center, remedial instruction, study skills assistance, tutoring, writing center.

Majors. Business: General. **Communications technology:** Recording arts. **Computer sciences:** Information systems, web page design. **Engineering technology:** CAD/CADD, industrial. **Health:** EMT paramedic, medical assistant, pharmacy assistant, physical therapy assistant, respiratory therapy technology. **Liberal arts:** Arts/sciences. **Mechanic/repair:** Industrial. **Protective services:** Criminal justice. **Visual/performing arts:** Dramatic.

Most popular majors. Business/marketing 16%, communications/journalism 10%, computer/information sciences 6%, health sciences 18%, liberal arts 38%, security/protective services 8%.

Computing on campus. 120 workstations in library. Online course registration, online library, wireless network available.

Student life. **Freshman orientation:** Available. Preregistration for classes offered. **Activities:** Bands, campus ministries, choral groups, dance, drama, international student organizations, literary magazine, music ensembles, musical theater, radio station, student government, student newspaper, TV station, College Republicans, gospel choir, ADAPTS, Maroon Jackets, NAACP, FCA, SGA.

Athletics. NJCAA. **Intercollegiate:** Baseball M, basketball M, cheerleading, softball W. **Team name:** Cavaliers.

Student services. Career counseling, services for economically disadvantaged, student employment services, financial aid counseling, minority student services, personal counseling, veterans' counselor. **Physically disabled:** Services for visually, speech, hearing impaired. **Transfer:** Pre-admission transcript evaluation for new students. College fairs on campus for students transferring to 4-year colleges.

Contact. E-mail: admissions@bpcc.edu
Phone: (318) 678-6004 Fax: (318) 678-6390
Patty Stewart, Admissions Officer, Bossier Parish Community College, 6220 East Texas Street, Bossier City, LA 71111-6922

Camelot College
Baton Rouge, Louisiana
www.camelotcollege.com **CB code: 3427**

- For-profit 2-year health science and technical college
- Small city

General. Accredited by ACICS. **Enrollment:** 280 degree-seeking undergraduates. **Calendar:** Continuous.

Basis for selection. Open admission.

2008-2009 Annual costs. Annual tuition $9,340 for computer data processing and medical assistant programs, $10,900 for paralegal and cosmetology programs, $8,141 for cosmetology instructor's training program.

Application procedures. **Admission:** No deadline. $10 fee, may be waived for applicants with need. Admission notification on a rolling basis.

Academics. **Credit/placement by examination:** CLEP.

Majors. **Computer sciences:** General.

Contact. E-mail: home@camelotcollege.com
Phone: (225) 928-3005 Toll-free number: (800) 470-3320
Fax: (225) 927-3794
Mark Haywood, Admissions Representative, Camelot College, 2618 Wooddale Boulevard, Suite A, Baton Rouge, LA 70805

Delgado Community College
New Orleans, Louisiana **CB member**
www.dcc.edu **CB code: 6176**

- Public 2-year community college
- Commuter campus in very large city

General. Founded in 1921. Regionally accredited. **Enrollment:** 13,015 degree-seeking undergraduates; 1,435 non-degree-seeking students. **Degrees:** 824 associate awarded. **ROTC:** Army, Air Force. **Calendar:** Semester, extensive summer session. **Full-time faculty:** 425 total; 6% have terminal degrees, 24% minority, 65% women. **Part-time faculty:** 353 total; 38% minority, 50% women. **Class size:** 48% < 20, 49% 20-39, 2% 40-49, less than 1% 50-99. **Special facilities:** Ship simulator, fine arts gallery.

Student profile. Among degree-seeking undergraduates, 13% enrolled in a transfer program, 87% enrolled in a vocational program, 2,307 enrolled as first-time, first-year students.

Part-time:	54%	**Hispanic American:**	6%
Out-of-state:	3%	**Native American:**	1%
Women:	69%	**International:**	1%
African American:	37%	**25 or older:**	44%
Asian American:	3%		

Transfer out. **Colleges most students transferred to 2008:** University of New Orleans, Southern University at New Orleans, Louisiana State University, Nicholls State University, Southeastern Louisiana University.

Basis for selection. Open admission, but selective for some programs. **Adult students:** SAT/ACT scores not required if applicant over 25. Adult students without high school diploma or GED required to pass Ability to Benefit Exam. **Homeschooled:** Applicants who have not completed state or regionally approved program required to have GED or successfully pass Ability to Benefit Exam.

2008-2009 Annual costs. Tuition/fees: $1,928; $4,908 out-of-state. Books/supplies: $1,200. Personal expenses: $4,645.

Financial aid. **Need-based:** Need-based aid available for part-time students. Work-study available nights, weekends and for part-time students. **Non-need-based:** Scholarships awarded for academics, athletics, leadership, music/drama, state residency.

Application procedures. **Admission:** No deadline. $25 fee. Admission notification on a rolling basis. **Financial aid:** Priority date 5/1, closing date 7/15. FAFSA, institutional form required. Applicants notified on a rolling basis starting 4/1; must reply within 2 week(s) of notification.

Academics. **Special study options:** Cooperative education, cross-registration, distance learning, double major, dual enrollment of high school students, ESL, honors, independent study, internships, liberal arts/career combination, student-designed major, weekend college. License preparation in nursing, paramedic, physical therapy, real estate. **Credit/placement by examination:** AP, CLEP, institutional tests. 24 credit hours maximum toward associate degree. **Support services:** Learning center, pre-admission summer program, remedial instruction, tutoring.

Majors. **Agriculture:** Horticulture. **Architecture:** Interior. **Business:** Accounting, administrative services, business admin, hospitality admin. **Computer sciences:** Data processing. **Construction:** Maintenance. **Education:** Early childhood. **Engineering technology:** Architectural, biomedical, civil, electrical, occupational safety. **Family/consumer sciences:** Institutional food production. **Foreign languages:** Sign language interpretation. **Health:** Clinical lab technology, dental hygiene, dental lab technology, EMT paramedic, medical radiologic technology/radiation therapy, medical records technology, nursing (RN), occupational therapy assistant, physical therapy assistant, respiratory therapy technology. **Interdisciplinary:** Biological/physical sciences. **Liberal arts:** Arts/sciences. **Mechanic/repair:** Automotive, computer, electronics/electrical. **Personal/culinary services:** Mortuary science. **Production:** Machine shop technology. **Protective services:** Fire safety technology, police science. **Visual/performing arts:** Art, commercial/advertising art, design.

Most popular majors. Business/marketing 17%, health sciences 44%, liberal arts 10%, security/protective services 6%.

Computing on campus. 555 workstations in library, computer center, student center. Online library, wireless network available.

Student life. **Freshman orientation:** Available. Preregistration for classes offered. **Activities:** Concert band, choral groups, dance, drama, film society, music ensembles, musical theater, student government, student newspaper, TV station, religious organizations available.

Athletics. NJCAA. **Intercollegiate:** Baseball M, basketball M, cheerleading. **Intramural:** Archery, badminton, baseball M, basketball, golf, soccer, softball, swimming, table tennis, tennis, volleyball. **Team name:** Dolphins.

Student services. Adult student services, career counseling, services for economically disadvantaged, student employment services, financial aid counseling, health services, on-campus daycare, personal counseling, placement for graduates, veterans' counselor. **Physically disabled:** Services for visually, speech, hearing impaired. **Transfer:** Re-entry adviser for new students. Transfer center, transfer adviser, college fairs on campus for students transferring to 4-year colleges.

Contact. E-mail: gboutte@dcc.edu
Phone: (504) 671-5099 Fax: (504) 483-1895
Gwen Boutte, Director of Admissions & Enrollment Services, Delgado Community College, 615 City Park Avenue, New Orleans, LA 70119

Delta College of Arts & Technology
Baton Rouge, Louisiana
www.deltacollege.com **CB code: 3131**

- For-profit 2-year visual arts and technical college
- Large city

General. Accredited by ACCSCT. **Enrollment:** 140 degree-seeking undergraduates. **Degrees:** 10 associate awarded. **Calendar:** Continuous. **Full-time faculty:** 22 total. **Part-time faculty:** 13 total.

Basis for selection. Open admission.

2008-2009 Annual costs. Tuition for full programs ranges from $8,250 to $19,500 and includes books and supplies. Registration fee $100. Books/supplies: $775. Personal expenses: $250.

Application procedures. Admission: No deadline. $100 fee. Admission notification on a rolling basis. **Financial aid:** No deadline.

Academics. Credit/placement by examination: CLEP.

Majors. Health: Licensed practical nurse. **Visual/performing arts:** General.

Contact. E-mail: admissions@deltacollege.com
Phone: (225) 928-7770 Fax: (225) 927-9096
David Clark, General Manager, Delta College of Arts & Technology, 7380 Exchange Place, Baton Rouge, LA 70806

Delta School of Business & Technology
Lake Charles, Louisiana
www.deltatech.edu **CB code: 2252**

- For-profit 2-year business and technical college
- Small city

General. Founded in 1970. Accredited by ACICS. **Enrollment:** 360 degree-seeking undergraduates. **Degrees:** 124 associate awarded. **Location:** 128 miles from Baton Rouge. **Calendar:** Continuous. **Full-time faculty:** 22 total. **Part-time faculty:** 13 total.

Student profile.

Out-of-state:	10%	**25 or older:**	40%

Basis for selection. Open admission.

2008-2009 Annual costs. Cost of associate degree program $9,590 per year, plus books and fees of approximately $2,540; IT program slightly higher at $10,260 per year, plus books and fees of approximately $2,790. One-year diploma programs also available at similar cost. Books/supplies: $800.

Application procedures. Admission: No deadline. No application fee. Admission notification on a rolling basis.

Academics. Special study options: Accelerated study, distance learning, double major, honors, internships. **Credit/placement by examination:** CLEP. **Support services:** Reduced course load, tutoring.

Majors. Business: Accounting, business admin. **Engineering technology:** Drafting. **Health:** Medical assistant. **Mechanic/repair:** Electronics/electrical.

Computing on campus. 30 workstations in computer center.

Student services. Career counseling, student employment services, placement for graduates.

Contact. E-mail: barbara@deltatech.edu
Phone: (337) 439-5765 Toll-free number: (800) 259-5627
Fax: (337) 436-5151
Barbara Holt, Director of Admissions, Delta School of Business & Technology, 517 Broad Street, Lake Charles, LA 70601

Gretna Career College
Gretna, Louisiana
www.gretnacareercollege.edu

- For-profit 2-year technical college
- Commuter campus in large town

General. Accredited by ACCSCT. **Enrollment:** 55 degree-seeking undergraduates. **Degrees:** 3 associate awarded. **Calendar:** Semester. **Full-time faculty:** 35 total.

Basis for selection. Open admission.

2008-2009 Annual costs. Tuition varies by program and ranges from $7,340-$12,875 for certificate and diploma programs; $23,700-$24,200 for associate degree programs. Costs include books and supplies.

Application procedures. Admission: No deadline. $50 fee. Admission notification on a rolling basis.

Academics. Credit/placement by examination: CLEP.

Majors. Health: Nursing assistant, office assistant. **Mechanic/repair:** Auto body.

Contact. E-mail: admissions@gretnacareercollege.edu
Phone: (504) 366-5409 ext. 23
Ana Heimes, Director of Admissions, Gretna Career College, 1415 Whitney Avenue, Gretna, LA 70053

ITI Technical College
Baton Rouge, Louisiana
www.iticollege.edu

- For-profit 2-year technical college
- Commuter campus in large city
- Interview required

General. Accredited by ACCSCT. **Enrollment:** 370 degree-seeking undergraduates; 75 non-degree-seeking students. **Degrees:** 131 associate awarded. **Calendar:** Differs by program. **Full-time faculty:** 20 total; 25% minority, 20% women. **Part-time faculty:** 30 total; 13% minority, 10% women.

Student profile. Among degree-seeking undergraduates, 100% enrolled in a vocational program, 163 enrolled as first-time, first-year students.

Out-of-state:	1%	**25 or older:**	47%
Women:	19%		

Basis for selection. Open admission. Applicant completes application, must interview and tour campus, complete entrance evaluation, settle funding, sign enrollment agreement. **Homeschooled:** Students must have acceptable certificate or diploma at time of enrollment. **Learning Disabled:** Students must meet with school director regarding special needs and referral for assistance.

2008-2009 Annual costs. Full-time tuition varies by program from $12,000 to $24,100.

Financial aid. All financial aid based on need. Need-based aid available for part-time students.

Application procedures. Admission: No deadline. No application fee. Admission notification on a rolling basis. **Financial aid:** No deadline. FAFSA required.

Academics. Credit/placement by examination: CLEP. **Support services:** Study skills assistance, tutoring.

Majors. Business: Administrative services, business admin, executive assistant, office management, office technology. **Communications technology:** General. **Computer sciences:** Data processing, information systems. **Engineering technology:** Drafting, electrical, instrumentation. **Health:** Insurance coding, insurance specialist, medical records admin, medical records technology, medical secretary, medical transcription, office admin, office assistant, office computer specialist, receptionist.

Computing on campus. 5 workstations in library.

Student life. Freshman orientation: Mandatory.

Student services. Career counseling, financial aid counseling, placement for graduates.

Contact. E-mail: admissions@iticollege.edu
Phone: (225) 752-4233 Toll-free number: (800) 467-4484
Fax: (225) 756-0903
Joe Martin, Director of Admissions, ITI Technical College, 13944 Airline Highway, Baton Rouge, LA 70817

Louisiana State University at Eunice
Eunice, Louisiana
www.lsue.edu **CB code: 6386**

- Public 2-year branch campus and community college
- Commuter campus in large town

General. Founded in 1964. Regionally accredited. **Enrollment:** 3,031 degree-seeking undergraduates. **Degrees:** 223 associate awarded. **Location:** 40 miles from Lafayette, 90 miles from Baton Rouge. **Calendar:** Semester, limited summer session. **Full-time faculty:** 81 total. **Part-time faculty:** 85 total.

Student profile.

Out-of-state:	1%	**25 or older:**	37%

Transfer out. Colleges most students transferred to 2008: Louisiana State University-Baton Rouge, University of Louisiana at Lafayette, McNeese State University, Southern University.

Basis for selection. Open admission, but selective for some programs. Test scores, school achievement record, interview considered for admission to nursing and respiratory care programs. **Homeschooled:** Transcript of courses and grades required. Applicants must be from nationally recognized program from accredited agency and have GED or ACT score equal to or greater than current state average.

2008-2009 Annual costs. Tuition/fees: $2,355; $5,445 out-of-state. Per-credit charge: $110. Books/supplies: $1,000.

2008-2009 Financial aid. Need-based: Need-based aid available for part-time students.

Application procedures. Admission: Closing date 8/1. $25 fee. Admission notification on a rolling basis. **Financial aid:** Priority date 6/1; no closing date. FAFSA, institutional form required. Applicants notified on a rolling basis starting 4/1; must reply within 2 week(s) of notification.

Academics. Special study options: Distance learning, dual enrollment of high school students, honors, independent study, liberal arts/career combination. Bachelor's degree programs available on campus. License preparation in nursing, physical therapy. **Credit/placement by examination:** AP, CLEP, institutional tests. 30 credit hours maximum toward associate degree. **Support services:** Learning center, remedial instruction, study skills assistance, tutoring.

Majors. Business: General, administrative services. **Computer sciences:** General. **Education:** Early childhood. **Health:** Licensed practical nurse, medical radiologic technology/radiation therapy, respiratory therapy technology. **Interdisciplinary:** Natural sciences. **Legal studies:** Paralegal. **Liberal arts:** Arts/sciences. **Protective services:** Criminal justice, fire safety technology.

Computing on campus. 150 workstations in library, computer center. Commuter students can connect to campus network. Online course registration, helpline available.

Student life. Freshman orientation: Available. Preregistration for classes offered. **Activities:** Drama, student government, student newspaper, Circle-K, Baptist collegiate ministry, Newman Club, Rotoract, African American student alliance, Students in Free Enterprise, Catholic student center.

Athletics. NJCAA. **Intercollegiate:** Baseball M, basketball W. **Intramural:** Baseball M, basketball, football (non-tackle) M, softball W, tennis W, volleyball. **Team name:** Bengals.

Student services. Adult student services, chaplain/spiritual director, career counseling, financial aid counseling, health services, personal counseling, placement for graduates, veterans' counselor. **Physically disabled:** Services for visually, hearing impaired. **Transfer:** Transfer adviser, college fairs on campus for students transferring to 4-year colleges.

Contact. E-mail: rryder@lsue.edu
Phone: (337) 550-1305 Toll-free number: (888) 367-5783
Fax: (337) 550-1306
Ronald Ryder, Admissions Director, Louisiana State University at Eunice, Box 1129, Eunice, LA 70535

Nunez Community College

Chalmette, Louisiana
www.nunez.edu **CB code: 0295**

- Public 2-year community and technical college
- Commuter campus in large town

General. Founded in 1992. Regionally accredited. **Enrollment:** 1,046 degree-seeking undergraduates; 618 non-degree-seeking students. **Degrees:** 100 associate awarded. **Location:** 11 miles from New Orleans. **Calendar:** Semester, limited summer session. **Full-time faculty:** 39 total; 15% have terminal degrees, 15% minority, 59% women. **Part-time faculty:** 27 total; 15% have terminal degrees, 11% minority, 37% women. **Class size:** 60% < 20, 35% 20-39, 4% 40-49, 2% 50-99.

Student profile. Among degree-seeking undergraduates, 26% enrolled in a transfer program, 74% enrolled in a vocational program, 115 enrolled as first-time, first-year students, 164 transferred in from other institutions.

Part-time:	40%	**Hispanic American:**	3%
Women:	64%	**Native American:**	2%
African American:	35%	**25 or older:**	30%
Asian American:	2%		

Transfer out. Colleges most students transferred to 2008: University of New Orleans, Southern University of New Orleans, Louisiana State University-Baton Rouge, Our Lady of Holy Cross College, Loyola University of New Orleans.

Basis for selection. Open admission, but selective for some programs. Additional requirements for Practical Nursing, Emergency Medical Technician and Associate of Science in Teaching (Grades 1-5).

High school preparation. 12 units recommended. Recommended units include English 4, mathematics 4, social studies 1, history 1, science 2 (laboratory 1).

2008-2009 Annual costs. Tuition/fees: $1,858; $4,378 out-of-state. Books/supplies: $1,700.

2007-2008 Financial aid. Need-based: 89% of total undergraduate aid awarded as scholarships/grants, 11% as loans/jobs. Need-based aid available for part-time students. Work-study available nights and for part-time students. **Additional information:** Pell Grants, Stafford Loans, campus work-study, and tuition waiver scholarships available. Louisiana National Guard tuition exemption, teacher tuition exemption, dependents of injured fire-police tuition waivers.

Application procedures. Admission: Priority date 8/1; no deadline. $10 fee. Application must be submitted on paper. Admission notification on a rolling basis. **Financial aid:** Priority date 6/1, closing date 8/1. FAFSA required. Applicants notified by 9/1; must reply by 10/15.

Academics. Special study options: Cooperative education, cross-registration, distance learning, double major, dual enrollment of high school students, honors, independent study, internships, student-designed major, weekend college. License preparation in nursing, paramedic. **Credit/placement by examination:** AP, CLEP, institutional tests. 24 credit hours maximum toward associate degree. **Support services:** Learning center, reduced course load, remedial instruction, tutoring.

Majors. Business: General. **Computer sciences:** Computer science, information systems. **Education:** General. **Engineering technology:** Industrial. **Health:** Office admin. **Legal studies:** Paralegal. **Mechanic/repair:** Heating/ac/refrig. **Personal/culinary services:** Chef training. **Other:** General science.

Most popular majors. Business/marketing 24%, education 14%, health sciences 13%, legal studies 6%, liberal arts 33%.

Computing on campus. 75 workstations in library, computer center, student center. Online library, helpline available.

Student life. Freshman orientation: Mandatory. Preregistration for classes offered. Two-hour orientation offered during registration period. **Activities:** Concert band, drama, student government, student newspaper.

Athletics. Team name: Pelicans.

Student services. Career counseling, financial aid counseling, personal counseling, placement for graduates, veterans' counselor. **Physically disabled:** Services for visually, hearing impaired. **Transfer:** Transfer adviser, college fairs on campus for students transferring to 4-year colleges.

Contact. E-mail: bmaillet@nunez.edu
Phone: (504) 278-7467 Fax: (504) 278-7487
Becky Maillet, Director of Admissions and Registration, Nunez Community College, 3710 Paris Road, Chalmette, LA 70043

Remington College: Baton Rouge

Baton Rouge, Louisiana
www.remingtoncollege.edu/batonrouge **CB code: 3428**

- For-profit 2-year technical college
- Commuter campus in large city
- Interview required

General. Accredited by ACICS. **Enrollment:** 525 degree-seeking undergraduates. **Degrees:** 76 associate awarded. **Calendar:** Quarter. **Full-time faculty:** 12 total. **Part-time faculty:** 8 total.

Basis for selection. Open admission, but selective for some programs.

2008-2009 Annual costs. Costs of entire programs leading to certificate, associate degree, bachelor's degree range from $13,000 to $38,880; includes books and supplies.

Financial aid. All financial aid based on need. Work-study available nights.

Application procedures. Admission: No deadline. $50 fee. Admission notification on a rolling basis. **Financial aid:** No deadline. FAFSA required. Applicants notified on a rolling basis; must reply within 1 week(s) of notification.

Academics. Special study options: Liberal arts/career combination. **Credit/placement by examination:** CLEP. **Support services:** Tutoring.

Majors. Computer sciences: General, information systems, LAN/WAN management.

Computing on campus. PC or laptop required.

Student life. Freshman orientation: Mandatory. **Activities:** Student government.

Student services. Financial aid counseling, placement for graduates.

Contact. Phone: (225) 922-3990 Fax: (225) 922-6569
AcQueena Fuller, Director of Admissions, Remington College: Baton Rouge, 10551 Coursey Boulevard, Baton Rouge, LA 70816

Remington College: Lafayette

Lafayette, Louisiana
www.remingtoncollege.edu **CB code: 7117**

- For-profit 2-year junior college
- Commuter campus in small city
- Interview required

General. Founded in 1940. Accredited by ACICS. **Enrollment:** 207 degree-seeking undergraduates. **Degrees:** 174 associate awarded. **Location:** 50 miles from Baton Rouge. **Calendar:** Quarter, extensive summer session. **Full-time faculty:** 12 total; 8% have terminal degrees, 17% minority. **Part-time faculty:** 17 total; 24% minority.

Student profile. Among degree-seeking undergraduates, 30 enrolled as first-time, first-year students.

African American:	56%	**25 or older:**	40%
Hispanic American:	1%		

Transfer out. 5% of students enrolled in the transfer program go on to 4-year colleges.

Basis for selection. Open admission, but selective for some programs. **Homeschooled:** State high school equivalency certificate required.

2008-2009 Annual costs. Costs of entire programs leading to certificate, associate degree, bachelor's degree range from $14,000 to $39,900; includes books and supplies.

2007-2008 Financial aid. All financial aid based on need. Work-study available nights.

Application procedures. Admission: No deadline. $50 fee. Application must be submitted on paper. Admission notification on a rolling basis. **Financial aid:** No deadline. FAFSA, institutional form required.

Academics. Laptop computer provided to each student. **Special study options:** Accelerated study, independent study, liberal arts/career combination. **Credit/placement by examination:** CLEP. **Support services:** GED preparation, tutoring.

Majors. Business: Business admin. **Computer sciences:** General. **Protective services:** Law enforcement admin.

Computing on campus. 110 workstations in library, computer center. Online library, helpline, repair service available.

Student life. Freshman orientation: Mandatory. Preregistration for classes offered. **Activities:** National Vocational Technical Society (associate degree honors society), Nightingale Medical Honor Society (diploma honors society).

Student services. Student employment services, financial aid counseling, placement for graduates. **Transfer:** Pre-admission transcript evaluation for new students.

Contact. Phone: (337) 981-4010 Fax: (337) 983-7130
Lee Williams, Director of Admissions, Remington College: Lafayette, 303 Rue Louis XIV, Lafayette, LA 70508

Remington College: Shreveport

Shreveport, Louisiana
www.remingtoncollege.edu

- Private 2-year technical college
- Small city

General. Regionally accredited; also accredited by ACCSCT. **Enrollment:** 100 degree-seeking undergraduates. **Calendar:** Continuous. **Full-time faculty:** 16 total. **Part-time faculty:** 14 total.

Basis for selection. Open admission.

Academics. Credit/placement by examination: CLEP.

Majors. Business: Business admin. **Protective services:** Law enforcement admin.

Contact. Remington College: Shreveport, 2106 Bert Kouns Industrial Loop, Shreveport, LA 71118

River Parishes Community College

Sorrento, Louisiana
www.rpcc.edu

- Public 2-year community college
- Commuter campus in rural community

General. Regionally accredited. **Enrollment:** 450 full-time, degree-seeking students. **Degrees:** 53 associate awarded. **Location:** 20 miles from Baton Rouge, 40 miles from New Orleans. **Calendar:** Semester, limited summer session. **Full-time faculty:** 17 total. **Part-time faculty:** 35 total.

Student profile.

Out-of-state:	1%	**25 or older:**	27%

Basis for selection. Open admission. **Homeschooled:** Transcript of courses and grades required.

2008-2009 Annual costs. Tuition/fees: $2,256; $4,684 out-of-state. Per-credit charge: $70. Books/supplies: $1,200. Personal expenses: $1,726.

Application procedures. Admission: No deadline. $10 fee. Admission notification on a rolling basis. **Financial aid:** Priority date 4/15; no closing date. FAFSA required. Applicants notified on a rolling basis starting 3/1.

Academics. Credit/placement by examination: CLEP, SAT, ACT.

Majors. Liberal arts: Arts/sciences.

Computing on campus. Online library, wireless network available.

Contact. Phone: (225) 675-8270 Fax: (225) 675-5478
Jennifer Kleinpeter, Admissions Director, River Parishes Community College, PO Box 310, Sorrento, LA 70778

South Louisiana Community College

Lafayette, Louisiana
www.southlouisiana.edu **CB code: 4521**

- Public 2-year community college
- Commuter campus in small city

General. Regionally accredited. **Enrollment:** 1,711 degree-seeking undergraduates; 1,820 non-degree-seeking students. **Degrees:** 100 associate awarded. **Calendar:** Semester, extensive summer session. **Full-time faculty:** 36 total; 17% have terminal degrees, 22% minority, 44% women. **Part-time faculty:** 111 total; 15% minority, 60% women. **Class size:** 46% < 20, 53% 20-39, less than 1% 40-49, less than 1% 50-99.

Student profile. Among degree-seeking undergraduates, 19% enrolled in a transfer program, 447 enrolled as first-time, first-year students.

Part-time:	45%	**Asian American:**	2%
Women:	55%	**Hispanic American:**	1%
African American:	29%	**Native American:**	1%

Basis for selection. Open admission, but selective for some programs.

High school preparation. College-preparatory program recommended. 17.5 units recommended. Recommended units include English 4, mathematics 4, social studies 1, history 2, science 3, foreign language 2, computer science .5 and visual/performing arts 1.

2008-2009 Annual costs. Tuition/fees: $1,862; $4,022 out-of-state.

Financial aid. Need-based: Need-based aid available for part-time students.

Application procedures. Admission: Priority date 7/1; no deadline. $5 fee. Application must be submitted on paper. **Financial aid:** Priority date 7/1; no closing date. FAFSA, institutional form required.

Academics. Special study options: Cross-registration, distance learning, dual enrollment of high school students. **Credit/placement by examination:** CLEP, ACT, institutional tests. **Support services:** Learning center, remedial instruction, study skills assistance, tutoring, writing center.

Majors. Business: General. **Education:** Kindergarten/preschool. **Engineering technology:** Industrial. **Health:** EMT paramedic. **Liberal arts:** Arts/sciences. **Protective services:** Criminal justice.

Most popular majors. Business/marketing 18%, education 16%, engineering/engineering technologies 13%, health sciences 20%, liberal arts 26%, security/protective services 6%.

Computing on campus. 50 workstations in library, student center. Online library, helpline, wireless network available.

Student life. Freshman orientation: Mandatory. **Activities:** Literary magazine, student government.

Student services. Career counseling, financial aid counseling, personal counseling. **Physically disabled:** Services for visually, speech, hearing impaired.

Contact. E-mail: admissions@southlouisiana.edu
Phone: (337) 521-8923 Fax: (337) 262-2101
Arthur Gillis, Director of Admissions, South Louisiana Community College, 320 Devalcourt, Lafayette, LA 70506-4124

Southern University at Shreveport

Shreveport, Louisiana
www.susla.edu **CB code: 0322**

- Public 2-year community college
- Commuter campus in small city

General. Founded in 1964. Regionally accredited. **Enrollment:** 2,340 degree-seeking undergraduates. **Degrees:** 252 associate awarded. **Calendar:** Semester, limited summer session. **Full-time faculty:** 81 total; 100% have terminal degrees, 69% women. **Part-time faculty:** 81 total; 100% have terminal degrees, 63% women.

Basis for selection. Open admission.

High school preparation. 15 units recommended. Recommended units include English 3, mathematics 2, social studies 2 and science 5.

2008-2009 Annual costs. Tuition/fees: $2,318; $3,448 out-of-state. Books/supplies: $600. Personal expenses: $1,420.

Application procedures. Admission: No deadline. $5 fee ($15 out-of-state). Admission notification on a rolling basis. **Financial aid:** No deadline. FAFSA required. Applicants notified on a rolling basis.

Academics. Special study options: Cross-registration, internships. License preparation in dental hygiene, nursing, radiology. **Credit/placement by examination:** CLEP, institutional tests. 3 credit hours maximum toward associate degree. **Support services:** GED preparation, remedial instruction, study skills assistance, tutoring, writing center.

Majors. Biology: General. **Business:** Accounting, banking/financial services, business admin. **Computer sciences:** General, applications programming, computer science. **Education:** Early childhood. **Engineering technology:** Electrical. **Health:** Clinical lab technology, dental hygiene, health services, medical radiologic technology/radiation therapy, medical records technology, respiratory therapy technology, surgical technology. **Liberal arts:** Arts/sciences. **Physical sciences:** Chemistry. **Protective services:** Law enforcement admin. **Public administration:** Human services. **Social sciences:** General, sociology. **Transportation:** Aviation management.

Most popular majors. Business/marketing 20%, education 9%, health sciences 41%, liberal arts 15%.

Computing on campus. 50 workstations in library, computer center. Commuter students can connect to campus network. Online course registration, online library available.

Student life. Freshman orientation: Mandatory. Preregistration for classes offered. **Activities:** Choral groups, dance, student government, student newspaper, Baptist student union, Afro-American society.

Athletics. NJCAA. **Intercollegiate:** Basketball. **Team name:** Jaguars.

Student services. Health services, personal counseling, placement for graduates, veterans' counselor.

Contact. Phone: (318) 674-3342 Fax: (318) 674-3489
Associate Vice Chancellor Enrollment Management, Southern University at Shreveport, 3050 Martin Luther King, Jr. Drive, Shreveport, LA 71107

Maine

Andover College
South Portland, Maine
www.andovercollege.edu CB code: 0688

- For-profit 2-year business and junior college
- Commuter campus in small city
- Interview required

General. Founded in 1966. Regionally accredited. **Enrollment:** 900 degree-seeking undergraduates. **Degrees:** 454 associate awarded. **Location:** 115 miles from Boston. **Calendar:** Six 8-week terms. Extensive summer session. **Full-time faculty:** 17 total. **Part-time faculty:** 80 total. **Class size:** 98% < 20, 2% 20-39.

Student profile.

Out-of-state:	4%	**25 or older:**	90%

Transfer out. Colleges most students transferred to 2008: University of Southern Maine.

Basis for selection. Open admission. **Homeschooled:** Transcript of courses and grades required.

2008-2009 Annual costs. Tuition/fees: $9,150. Per-credit charge: $284. Books/supplies: $1,250.

2007-2008 Financial aid. All financial aid based on need. **Additional information:** Work-study positions available.

Application procedures. Admission: No deadline. $20 fee, may be waived for applicants with need. Application must be submitted on paper. Admission notification on a rolling basis. **Financial aid:** No deadline. FAFSA required. Applicants notified on a rolling basis.

Academics. Special study options: Accelerated study, cooperative education, double major, dual enrollment of high school students, independent study, internships, liberal arts/career combination, teacher certification program. **Credit/placement by examination:** AP, CLEP, institutional tests. 12 credit hours maximum toward associate degree. **Support services:** Learning center, reduced course load, remedial instruction, study skills assistance, tutoring, writing center.

Majors. Business: Accounting, administrative services, business admin, hospitality admin, hospitality/recreation, office management, office technology, office/clerical, tourism promotion, tourism/travel. **Computer sciences:** General, computer science, data processing, programming. **Education:** Early childhood. **Family/consumer sciences:** Child care. **Health:** Medical assistant, medical records admin, medical records technology, medical secretary, medical transcription. **Legal studies:** Legal secretary, paralegal. **Protective services:** Criminal justice, law enforcement admin, police science.

Most popular majors. Business/marketing 21%, computer/information sciences 9%, health sciences 17%, legal studies 12%.

Computing on campus. 90 workstations in library, computer center, student center. Helpline available.

Student life. Freshman orientation: Mandatory. Preregistration for classes offered. **Activities:** Student newspaper, Phi Beta Lambda, C.O.P.S. (criminal justice), APPEAL paralegal professionals, college student advisors.

Student services. Adult student services, career counseling, student employment services, financial aid counseling, personal counseling, placement for graduates. **Physically disabled:** Services for hearing impaired.

Contact. E-mail: enroll@andovercollege.edu
Phone: (207) 774-6126 Toll-free number: (800) 639-3110
Fax: (207) 774-1715
Wendy Burbank, Director of Admissions, Andover College, 265 Western Avenue, South Portland, ME 04106

Beal College
Bangor, Maine
www.bealcollege.edu CB code: 3114

- For-profit 2-year junior and career college
- Commuter campus in large town

General. Founded in 1891. Accredited by ACICS. **Enrollment:** 399 degree-seeking undergraduates; 12 non-degree-seeking students. **Degrees:** 117 associate awarded. **Location:** 250 miles from Boston. **Calendar:** Six 8-week modules per year. Extensive summer session. **Full-time faculty:** 8 total. **Part-time faculty:** 9 total. **Class size:** 59% < 20, 41% 20-39.

Student profile. Among degree-seeking undergraduates, 5% already have a bachelor's degree or higher, 57 enrolled as first-time, first-year students.

Part-time:	32%	**Hispanic American:**	1%
Women:	80%	**Native American:**	1%
African American:	1%	**25 or older:**	54%

Basis for selection. Open admission. Interview recommended. **Homeschooled:** Students who earned high school diploma through home school education must provide passing GED scores.

High school preparation. Recommended units include English 4, mathematics 4 and science 1.

2008-2009 Annual costs. Tuition/fees: $6,505. Per-credit charge: $175. Books/supplies: $1,000. Personal expenses: $700.

Application procedures. Admission: No deadline. $25 fee, may be waived for applicants with need. Admission notification on a rolling basis. **Financial aid:** No deadline. FAFSA, institutional form required. Applicants notified on a rolling basis starting 6/15; must reply within 2 week(s) of notification.

Academics. Students in medical assisting program must complete 160-hour practicum. **Special study options:** Accelerated study, double major, independent study. Externships. **Credit/placement by examination:** CLEP, institutional tests. 30 credit hours maximum toward associate degree. **Support services:** Reduced course load, remedial instruction, tutoring.

Majors. Business: Accounting, administrative services, business admin, office management, sales/distribution, tourism promotion. **Education:** Early childhood. **Family/consumer sciences:** Family/community services. **Health:** Medical assistant, medical secretary. **Legal studies:** Legal secretary, paralegal. **Protective services:** Police science.

Computing on campus. 45 workstations in library, computer center. Wireless network available.

Student life. Freshman orientation: Available. **Activities:** Student newspaper.

Student services. Adult student services, career counseling, student employment services, placement for graduates, veterans' counselor. **Transfer:** Pre-admission transcript evaluation for new students.

Contact. E-mail: admissions@bealcollege.edu
Phone: (207) 947-4591 Fax: (207) 947-0208
Erin Morgan, Admissions Director, Beal College, 99 Farm Road, Bangor, ME 04401

Central Maine Community College
Auburn, Maine CB member
www.cmcc.edu CB code: 3309

- Public 2-year community and technical college
- Commuter campus in small city

General. Founded in 1964. Regionally accredited. **Enrollment:** 2,018 degree-seeking undergraduates; 482 non-degree-seeking students. **Degrees:** 261 associate awarded. **Location:** One mile from downtown. **Calendar:** Semester, limited summer session. **Full-time faculty:** 55 total. **Part-time faculty:** 146 total. **Partnerships:** Formal partnership with Verizon Telecommunications Technology program.

Student profile. Among degree-seeking undergraduates, 739 enrolled as first-time, first-year students, 140 transferred in from other institutions.

Part-time:	43%	**25 or older:**	32%
Out-of-state:	2%	**Live on campus:**	13%
Women:	55%		

Transfer out. **Colleges most students transferred to 2008:** University of Maine System.

Basis for selection. Open admission, but selective for some programs. Special requirements for nursing and radiologic technology. Many other academic programs have specific academic prerequisites but are not selective in terms of admission to the program. SAT scores or institutional placement test required for all applicants. **Homeschooled:** Transcript of courses and grades required. A copy of the state department of education correspondence granting approval of homeschooling program and the most recent teacher certification recognizing student's grade level and/or appropriate test results required. **Learning Disabled:** Applicants with documented disabilities should contact the college's disability coordinator.

High school preparation. Recommended units include English 4, mathematics 2, social studies 1, history 1 and science 2.

2008-2009 Annual costs. Tuition/fees: $3,192; $5,652 out-of-state. Per-credit charge: $82 in-state; $164 out-of-state. Additional lab and technology fees may apply to specific programs and courses. Room/board: $6,820. Books/supplies: $1,200. Personal expenses: $1,300.

2008-2009 Financial aid. All financial aid based on need. Need-based aid available for part-time students. Work-study available nights, weekends and for part-time students. **Additional information:** Tuition and/or fee waivers may be available to orphans, Native Americans, fire fighters, police, disabled veterans, dependents or survivors of veterans killed in line of duty.

Application procedures. **Admission:** No deadline. $20 fee, may be waived for applicants with need. Admission notification on a rolling basis beginning on or about 10/1. **Financial aid:** Priority date 5/8; no closing date. FAFSA, institutional form required. Applicants notified on a rolling basis starting 3/15; must reply within 2 week(s) of notification.

Academics. **Special study options:** Distance learning, ESL, independent study, internships, liberal arts/career combination. License preparation in nursing, radiology, real estate. **Credit/placement by examination:** AP, CLEP, IB, institutional tests. Up to 75% of credits may meet curriculum requirements; 25% of credits must be completed in residence. **Support services:** Learning center, reduced course load, remedial instruction, study skills assistance, tutoring, writing center.

Majors. **Business:** Accounting, business admin, hospitality admin, office technology. **Communications technology:** Graphic/printing. **Computer sciences:** Data entry, LAN/WAN management. **Construction:** Maintenance. **Education:** Early childhood, teacher assistance. **Engineering technology:** Civil. **Health:** Medical assistant, medical radiologic technology/radiation therapy, nursing (RN). **Liberal arts:** Arts/sciences. **Mechanic/repair:** Automotive, electronics/electrical. **Production:** Machine tool. **Protective services:** Law enforcement admin.

Most popular majors. Business/marketing 24%, engineering/engineering technologies 9%, family/consumer sciences 6%, health sciences 23%, liberal arts 11%, trade and industry 22%.

Computing on campus. 400 workstations in library, computer center. Dormitories wired for high-speed internet access and linked to campus network. Commuter students can connect to campus network. Online library, helpline, wireless network available.

Student life. **Freshman orientation:** Available. Preregistration for classes offered. **Policies:** Student code of conduct observed. **Housing:** Single-sex dorms, apartments available. $50 nonrefundable deposit. **Activities:** Drama, literary magazine, student government.

Athletics. USCAA. **Intercollegiate:** Baseball M, basketball. **Intramural:** Basketball, skiing. **Team name:** Mustangs.

Student services. Career counseling, services for economically disadvantaged, student employment services, financial aid counseling, personal counseling, placement for graduates, women's services. **Physically disabled:** Services for visually, speech, hearing impaired. **Transfer:** Transfer adviser, college fairs on campus for students transferring to 4-year colleges.

Contact. E-mail: enroll@cmcc.edu
Phone: (207) 755-5273 Toll-free number: (800) 891-2002 ext. 273
Fax: (207) 755-5493
Betsy Libby, Director of Admissions, Central Maine Community College, 1250 Turner Street, Auburn, ME 04210

Central Maine Medical Center College of Nursing and Health Professions

Lewiston, Maine **CB member**
www.cmmcson.edu **CB code: 3302**

- Private 2-year nursing college
- Commuter campus in large town
- SAT, application essay required

General. Founded in 1891. Regionally accredited. **Enrollment:** 122 degree-seeking undergraduates; 24 non-degree-seeking students. **Degrees:** 38 associate awarded. **Location:** 35 miles from Portland. **Calendar:** Semester, limited summer session. **Full-time faculty:** 13 total; 8% have terminal degrees, 85% women. **Part-time faculty:** 6 total; 100% women.

Student profile.

Part-time:	79%	**Asian American:**	1%
Out-of-state:	3%	**Hispanic American:**	2%
Women:	87%	**25 or older:**	74%
African American:	2%	**Live on campus:**	4%

Basis for selection. Test scores required. Essay, academic ability very important. SAT may be waived if applicant has completed 12 academic college credits with minimum grade of 2.0. **Homeschooled:** High school diploma or GED required.

High school preparation. College-preparatory program recommended. Required units include science 1. Biology course required.

2009-2010 Annual costs. Tuition/fees (projected): $7,638. Per-credit charge: $182. Room only: $1,500. Books/supplies: $2,152. Personal expenses: $2,580.

2007-2008 Financial aid. All financial aid based on need. 22 full-time freshmen applied for aid; 21 were judged to have need; 21 of these received aid. Average need met was 28%. Average scholarship/grant was $6,800; average loan $4,000. 32% of total undergraduate aid awarded as scholarships/grants, 68% as loans/jobs. Need-based aid available for part-time students.

Application procedures. **Admission:** Closing date 2/15 (receipt date). $40 fee, may be waived for applicants with need. Admission notification 3/15. Must reply by 5/1. **Financial aid:** Priority date 5/1, closing date 7/1. FAFSA, institutional form required. Applicants notified on a rolling basis starting 4/1; must reply within 2 week(s) of notification.

Academics. **Special study options:** Distance learning, internships. License preparation in nursing. **Credit/placement by examination:** AP, CLEP. 15 credit hours maximum toward associate degree. **Support services:** Learning center, remedial instruction, study skills assistance.

Majors. **Health:** Nursing (RN).

Computing on campus. PC or laptop required. 12 workstations in computer center. Wireless network available.

Student life. **Freshman orientation:** Mandatory. Preregistration for classes offered. **Policies:** Entire campus is smoke-free; zero tolerance for alcohol, drugs, weapons. **Housing:** Coed dorms, wellness housing available. $50 nonrefundable deposit, deadline 8/15. Single rooms available at extra cost. **Activities:** Student government.

Student services. Financial aid counseling, health services, personal counseling, veterans' counselor. **Transfer:** Pre-admission transcript evaluation for new students. College fairs on campus for students transferring to 4-year colleges.

Contact. E-mail: jenisod@cmhc.org
Phone: (207) 795-2843 Fax: (207) 795-2849
Peter Miller, Admissions Committee Chairperson, Central Maine Medical Center College of Nursing and Health Professions, 70 Middle Street, Lewiston, ME 04240

Eastern Maine Community College

Bangor, Maine **CB member**
www.emcc.edu **CB code: 3372**

- Public 2-year community and technical college
- Commuter campus in large town
- Application essay required

General. Founded in 1966. Regionally accredited. **Enrollment:** 1,607 degree-seeking undergraduates. **Degrees:** 237 associate awarded. **Location:** 250

Two-Year Colleges

miles from Boston, 130 miles from Portland. **Calendar:** Semester, limited summer session. **Full-time faculty:** 54 total. **Part-time faculty:** 106 total.

Transfer out. Colleges most students transferred to 2008: University of Maine-Orono, Husson College.

Basis for selection. Open admission, but selective for some programs. School record, recommendations, and essays most important. Entrance requirements vary by program. SAT required for engineering technologies, registered nursing, and medical radiography applicants; score report preferred by April 30. Interview recommended for some majors.

High school preparation. Recommended units include English 4, mathematics 3 and science 2. Academic requirements vary by program.

2008-2009 Annual costs. Tuition/fees: $3,255; $5,715 out-of-state. Per-credit charge: $82 in-state; $164 out-of-state. Additional lab and technology fees may apply to specific programs and courses. Room/board: $6,360. Books/supplies: $800. Personal expenses: $1,500.

2007-2008 Financial aid. All financial aid based on need. Need-based aid available for part-time students. Work-study available nights, weekends and for part-time students.

Application procedures. Admission: No deadline. $20 fee, may be waived for applicants with need. Admission notification on a rolling basis. Must reply by May 1 or within 4 week(s) if notified thereafter. Deposit refundable up to 60 days before program begins. **Financial aid:** Priority date 5/1; no closing date. FAFSA, institutional form required. Applicants notified on a rolling basis starting 5/1; must reply within 3 week(s) of notification.

Academics. Special study options: External degree, internships, student-designed major. **Credit/placement by examination:** CLEP, institutional tests. Maximum of 40% of required credit total in student's field of study may be obtained through credit by examination. **Support services:** Learning center, reduced course load, remedial instruction, study skills assistance, tutoring.

Majors. Agriculture: Food science. **Business:** General, administrative services, banking/financial services, business admin, office management. **Construction:** Carpentry, pipefitting, power transmission. **Education:** Early childhood. **Engineering technology:** Construction, electrical. **Health:** Medical radiologic technology/radiation therapy, nursing (RN), preop/surgical nursing. **Liberal arts:** Arts/sciences. **Mechanic/repair:** Automotive, heating/ac/refrig. **Personal/culinary services:** Culinary arts. **Production:** Machine tool, welding. **Protective services:** Firefighting.

Most popular majors. Business/marketing 36%, computer/information sciences 17%, health sciences 22%, interdisciplinary studies 11%, personal/culinary services 14%.

Computing on campus. 75 workstations in dormitories, library, computer center. Commuter students can connect to campus network. Helpline, wireless network available.

Student life. Freshman orientation: Mandatory. Preregistration for classes offered. **Housing:** Guaranteed on-campus for all undergraduates. Coed dorms available. $50 nonrefundable deposit, deadline 7/1. **Activities:** Student government, student newspaper.

Athletics. Intercollegiate: Basketball M, golf, soccer. **Intramural:** Badminton, basketball, bowling, ice hockey M, skiing, softball, table tennis, volleyball. **Team name:** Golden Eagles.

Student services. Adult student services, career counseling, student employment services, personal counseling, placement for graduates, veterans' counselor.

Contact. E-mail: admissions@emcc.edu
Phone: (207) 974-4680 Toll-free number: (800) 286-9357
Fax: (207) 974-4683
Elizabeth Russell, Director of Admissions, Eastern Maine Community College, 354 Hogan Road, Bangor, ME 04401

Kennebec Valley Community College

Fairfield, Maine
www.kvcc.me.edu **CB code: 3475**

- Public 2-year community and technical college
- Commuter campus in small town

General. Founded in 1969. Regionally accredited. **Enrollment:** 1,495 degree-seeking undergraduates; 709 non-degree-seeking students. **Degrees:** 253 associate awarded. **Location:** 24 miles from Augusta, 75 miles from Portland. **Calendar:** Semester, limited summer session. **Full-time faculty:** 40 total; 5% have terminal degrees, 5% minority, 65% women. **Part-time faculty:** 117 total; 5% have terminal degrees, 2% minority, 51% women. **Class size:** 70% < 20, 30% 20-39, less than 1% 40-49.

Student profile. Among degree-seeking undergraduates, 329 enrolled as first-time, first-year students.

Part-time:	60%	**Hispanic American:**	1%
Women:	62%	**Native American:**	1%
Asian American:	1%		

Basis for selection. Open admission, but selective for some programs. Special requirements for nursing and allied health programs.

2008-2009 Annual costs. Tuition/fees: $3,012; $5,472 out-of-state. Per-credit charge: $82 in-state; $164 out-of-state. Additional lab and technology fees apply to specific programs and courses. Books/supplies: $737.

2007-2008 Financial aid. Need-based: 154 full-time freshmen applied for aid; 128 were judged to have need; 104 of these received aid. Average need met was 41%. Average scholarship/grant was $3,880; average loan $2,458. 64% of total undergraduate aid awarded as scholarships/grants, 36% as loans/jobs. Need-based aid available for part-time students. **Non-need-based:** Awarded to 42 full-time undergraduates, including 19 freshmen.

Application procedures. Admission: No deadline. $20 fee. Admission notification on a rolling basis. Only allied health programs have application deadline. **Financial aid:** Priority date 4/1; no closing date. FAFSA, institutional form required. Applicants notified on a rolling basis starting 5/1.

Academics. Special study options: Cooperative education, cross-registration, distance learning, dual enrollment of high school students, internships, liberal arts/career combination. License preparation in nursing, occupational therapy, paramedic, physical therapy, radiology. **Credit/placement by examination:** AP, CLEP. **Support services:** Learning center, remedial instruction, study skills assistance, tutoring.

Majors. Business: Accounting technology, management information systems, marketing. **Conservation:** Forest technology. **Construction:** Electrician. **Education:** Teacher assistance. **Engineering technology:** Electrical. **Family/consumer sciences:** Child development. **Health:** EMT paramedic, medical assistant, medical records technology, nursing (RN), occupational therapy assistant, physical therapy assistant, radiologic technology/medical imaging, respiratory therapy technology. **Production:** Machine tool. **Science technology:** Biological.

Most popular majors. Business/marketing 12%, education 8%, family/consumer sciences 7%, health sciences 47%, liberal arts 12%, trade and industry 9%.

Computing on campus. 400 workstations in library, computer center. Commuter students can connect to campus network. Online library, helpline, wireless network available.

Student life. Freshman orientation: Available. **Activities:** Choral groups, student government, student newspaper.

Athletics. Intercollegiate: Basketball. **Intramural:** Basketball, volleyball. **Team name:** Lynx.

Student services. Career counseling, student employment services, on-campus daycare, personal counseling, placement for graduates. **Transfer:** Transfer adviser, college fairs on campus for students transferring to 4-year colleges.

Contact. E-mail: jbourgoin@kvcc.me.edu
Phone: (207) 453-5131 Toll-free number: (800) 528-5882
Fax: (207) 453-5011
Jim Bourgoin, Director of Admissions, Kennebec Valley Community College, 92 Western Avenue, Fairfield, ME 04937-1367

Northern Maine Community College

Presque Isle, Maine
www.nmcc.edu **CB code: 3631**

- Public 2-year technical college
- Commuter campus in small town
- Application essay, interview required

General. Founded in 1961. Regionally accredited. **Enrollment:** 840 degree-seeking undergraduates. **Degrees:** 102 associate awarded. **Location:** 165 miles from Bangor. **Calendar:** Semester, limited summer session. **Full-time faculty:** 45 total. **Part-time faculty:** 35 total.

Basis for selection. School achievement record and test scores important.

High school preparation. Required units include English 4 and mathematics 2.

2008-2009 Annual costs. Tuition/fees: $3,121; $5,581 out-of-state. Per-credit charge: $82 in-state; $164 out-of-state. Additional lab and technology fees may apply to specific programs and courses. Room/board: $5,500. Books/supplies: $1,200. Personal expenses: $1,200.

Financial aid. **Need-based:** Need-based aid available for part-time students.

Application procedures. **Admission:** No deadline. $20 fee, may be waived for applicants with need. Admission notification on a rolling basis. **Financial aid:** Priority date 5/1; no closing date. FAFSA, institutional form required. Applicants notified on a rolling basis starting 4/15; must reply within 2 week(s) of notification.

Academics. **Special study options:** Cross-registration, double major, internships, liberal arts/career combination. **Credit/placement by examination:** CLEP. 15 credit hours maximum toward associate degree. **Support services:** Learning center, pre-admission summer program, reduced course load, remedial instruction, tutoring.

Majors. **Agriculture:** Business. **Business:** Accounting, administrative services, business admin, management information systems, office management, office technology, operations. **Computer sciences:** Applications programming, data processing, programming. **Construction:** Carpentry, electrician, pipefitting, power transmission. **Education:** Early childhood. **Engineering technology:** Drafting, electrical. **Health:** Medical secretary, nursing (RN). **Legal studies:** Legal secretary. **Mechanic/repair:** Auto body, automotive, diesel, electronics/electrical, heating/ac/refrig, industrial. **Production:** Woodworking.

Computing on campus. Commuter students can connect to campus network.

Student life. **Freshman orientation:** Mandatory, $30 fee. Preregistration for classes offered. Held both in fall and spring semester. **Housing:** Coed dorms, apartments available. $25 deposit. **Activities:** Student government, student newspaper.

Athletics. **Intercollegiate:** Basketball M, golf, ice hockey, soccer. **Intramural:** Archery, badminton, baseball M, basketball M, racquetball, softball, table tennis, tennis, volleyball.

Student services. Adult student services, alcohol/substance abuse counseling, career counseling, student employment services, financial aid counseling, health services, personal counseling, placement for graduates, veterans' counselor. **Transfer:** Transfer adviser for students transferring to 4-year colleges.

Contact. E-mail: nbcasava@nmcc.edu
Phone: (207) 768-2700 Fax: (207) 768-2831
William Casavant, Director of Admissions, Northern Maine Community College, 33 Edgemont Drive, Presque Isle, ME 04769

Southern Maine Community College

South Portland, Maine — **CB member**
www.smccme.edu — **CB code: 3535**

- Public 2-year community and technical college
- Commuter campus in large town

General. Founded in 1946. Regionally accredited. **Enrollment:** 5,235 degree-seeking undergraduates; 438 non-degree-seeking students. **Degrees:** 556 associate awarded. **Location:** 3 miles from Portland, 120 miles from Boston. **Calendar:** Semester, limited summer session. **Full-time faculty:** 90 total. **Part-time faculty:** 170 total.

Student profile.

Part-time:	48%	**Women:**	51%

Basis for selection. Open admission, but selective for some programs. Special requirements for allied health science programs. Must have prerequisites completed prior to being accepted into the programs.

High school preparation. Recommended units include English 4, mathematics 3, science 1 (laboratory 1). Academic subject requirements vary by program.

2008-2009 Annual costs. Tuition/fees: $3,167; $5,627 out-of-state. Per-credit charge: $82 in-state; $164 out-of-state. Additional lab and technology fees may apply to specific programs and courses. Room/board: $7,746.

Financial aid. All financial aid based on need. Need-based aid available for part-time students. Work-study available nights, weekends and for part-time students.

Application procedures. **Admission:** Priority date 7/15; no deadline. $20 fee, may be waived for applicants with need. Admission notification on a rolling basis. Must reply by May 1 or within 4 week(s) if notified thereafter. **Financial aid:** Priority date 3/30; no closing date. FAFSA required. Applicants notified on a rolling basis; must reply by 5/1 or within 2 week(s) of notification.

Academics. **Special study options:** Cross-registration, distance learning, double major, dual enrollment of high school students, honors, independent study, internships, liberal arts/career combination. License preparation in nursing, paramedic, radiology. **Credit/placement by examination:** AP, CLEP, institutional tests. **Support services:** Learning center, reduced course load, remedial instruction, study skills assistance, tutoring.

Majors. **Agriculture:** Horticulture. **Biology:** Biotechnology, marine. **Business:** Business admin, hotel/motel admin. **Communications:** Digital media. **Construction:** General. **Education:** Early childhood. **Engineering technology:** Architectural drafting, computer, electrical. **Health:** Cardiovascular technology, dietetic technician, EMT paramedic, medical assistant, medical radiologic technology/radiation therapy, nursing (RN), radiologic technology/medical imaging, respiratory therapy technology, surgical technology. **Mechanic/repair:** Automotive, heating/ac/refrig. **Personal/culinary services:** Chef training. **Production:** Machine tool. **Protective services:** Firefighting, police science.

Computing on campus. 300 workstations in library, computer center, student center. Dormitories wired for high-speed internet access and linked to campus network. Commuter students can connect to campus network. Online course registration, online library, helpline, wireless network available.

Student life. **Freshman orientation:** Available, $70 fee. Preregistration for classes offered. **Housing:** Coed dorms available. $50 nonrefundable deposit. **Activities:** Choral groups, international student organizations, literary magazine, student government, student newspaper.

Athletics. USCAA. **Intercollegiate:** Baseball M, basketball, golf, soccer, softball W. **Intramural:** Basketball, ice hockey M, soccer, volleyball. **Team name:** Seawolves.

Student services. Career counseling, student employment services, financial aid counseling, on-campus daycare, personal counseling, placement for graduates, veterans' counselor. **Physically disabled:** Services for visually, speech, hearing impaired. **Transfer:** Pre-admission transcript evaluation for new students. Transfer adviser, college fairs on campus for students transferring to 4-year colleges.

Contact. E-mail: enrollmentservices@smccme.edu
Phone: (207) 741-5155 Toll-free number: (877) 282-2182
Fax: (207) 741-5760
Staci Grasky, Associate Dean for Information and Enrollment Services / Registrar, Southern Maine Community College, 2 Fort Road, South Portland, ME 04106

Washington County Community College

Calais, Maine
www.wccc.me.edu — **CB code: 3961**

- Public 2-year community and technical college
- Commuter campus in small town

General. Founded in 1969. Regionally accredited. **Enrollment:** 380 degree-seeking undergraduates. **Degrees:** 55 associate awarded. **Location:** 98 miles from Bangor, 75 miles from St. John, Canada. **Calendar:** Semester, limited summer session. **Full-time faculty:** 21 total. **Part-time faculty:** 20 total.

Student profile. Among degree-seeking undergraduates, 20% enrolled in a transfer program, 80% enrolled in a vocational program, 2% already have a bachelor's degree or higher.

Out-of-state:	5%	**Live on campus:**	25%
25 or older:	34%		

Transfer out. 50% of students enrolled in the transfer program go on to 4-year colleges. **Colleges most students transferred to 2008:** University of Maine at Machias, University of Maine at Augusta, Husson College.

Two-Year Colleges

Basis for selection. Open admission, but selective for some programs. Algebra I required or placement in the equivalent of MAT106 on ACCUPLACER exam for residential and commercial electricity program. **Homeschooled:** Applicants required to take GED exam or equivalent.

High school preparation. 20 units recommended. Recommended units include English 4, mathematics 2, social studies 1, history 2 and science 2. Program-specific requirements apply in some areas.

2008-2009 Annual costs. Tuition/fees: $3,062; $5,522 out-of-state. Per-credit charge: $82 in-state; $164 out-of-state. Additional lab and technology fees may apply to specific programs and courses. Room only: $2,730. Books/supplies: $1,000. Personal expenses: $1,669.

Financial aid. Need-based: Need-based aid available for part-time students. Work-study available for part-time students. **Non-need-based:** Scholarships awarded for academics.

Application procedures. Admission: Closing date 8/14. $20 fee, may be waived for applicants with need. Admission notification on a rolling basis. **Financial aid:** Priority date 5/1; no closing date. FAFSA, institutional form required. Applicants notified on a rolling basis starting 6/1; must reply within 2 week(s) of notification.

Academics. Special study options: Cooperative education, distance learning, double major, dual enrollment of high school students, independent study, liberal arts/career combination. Offer license preparation program in heating and plumbing. **Credit/placement by examination:** CLEP, IB. **Support services:** GED preparation and test center, learning center, reduced course load, remedial instruction, study skills assistance, tutoring, writing center.

Majors. Business: Business admin, office management, small business admin. **Education:** Early childhood. **Family/consumer sciences:** Food/nutrition, institutional food production. **Liberal arts:** Arts/sciences. **Mechanic/repair:** General. **Other:** Adventure Recreation & Tourism.

Most popular majors. Business/marketing 19%, computer/information sciences 33%, liberal arts 13%, trade and industry 35%.

Computing on campus. 117 workstations in dormitories, library, computer center, student center. Dormitories linked to campus network. Helpline, wireless network available.

Student life. Freshman orientation: Mandatory. Preregistration for classes offered. **Housing:** Guaranteed on-campus for all undergraduates. Special housing for disabled, apartments available. $150 deposit. **Activities:** Student government, Gender Equity, Native American club.

Athletics. Intramural: Baseball M, basketball, cross-country, golf, skiing, volleyball. **Team name:** Polar Bears.

Student services. Adult student services, career counseling, student employment services, on-campus daycare, personal counseling, placement for graduates, veterans' counselor. **Physically disabled:** Services for visually, speech, hearing impaired. **Transfer:** Pre-admission transcript evaluation for new students. College fairs on campus for students transferring to 4-year colleges.

Contact. E-mail: admissions@wccc.me.edu
Phone: (207) 454-1000 Toll-free number: (800) 210-6932
Fax: (207) 454-1092
Kent Lyons, Admissions Counselor, Washington County Community College, One College Drive, Calais, ME 04619

York County Community College

Wells, Maine — **CB member**
www.yccc.edu — **CB code: 3990**

- Public 2-year community and technical college
- Commuter campus in small town

General. Regionally accredited. **Enrollment:** 850 degree-seeking undergraduates; 269 non-degree-seeking students. **Degrees:** 94 associate awarded. **Location:** 30 miles from Portland. **Calendar:** Semester, extensive summer session. **Full-time faculty:** 13 total; 31% have terminal degrees, 38% women. **Part-time faculty:** 70 total; 13% have terminal degrees, 59% women. **Class size:** 65% < 20, 35% 20-39.

Student profile. Among degree-seeking undergraduates, 273 enrolled as first-time, first-year students.

Part-time:	55%	**Women:**	63%
Out-of-state:	3%	**25 or older:**	33%

Transfer out. Colleges most students transferred to 2008: University of Southern Maine, University of New England, University of New Hampshire.

Basis for selection. Open admission. **Homeschooled:** Transcript of courses and grades, state high school equivalency certificate required.

2008-2009 Annual costs. Tuition/fees: $3,042; $5,502 out-of-state. Per-credit charge: $82 in-state; $164 out-of-state. Additional lab and technology fees may apply to specific programs and courses. Books/supplies: $1,000. Personal expenses: $1,000.

2007-2008 Financial aid. Need-based: Need-based aid available for part-time students. Work-study available nights, weekends and for part-time students. **Non-need-based:** Scholarships awarded for academics, art, leadership.

Application procedures. Admission: No deadline. $20 fee, may be waived for applicants with need, free for online applicants. **Financial aid:** Priority date 5/1; no closing date. FAFSA required. Applicants notified by 3/1; must reply within 2 week(s) of notification.

Academics. Special study options: Distance learning, dual enrollment of high school students, honors, liberal arts/career combination. License preparation in nursing, real estate. **Credit/placement by examination:** CLEP, institutional tests. 45 credit hours maximum toward associate degree. **Support services:** Learning center, remedial instruction, study skills assistance, tutoring, writing center.

Majors. Business: Accounting, business admin, management information systems. **Engineering technology:** CAD/CADD. **Family/consumer sciences:** General. **Personal/culinary services:** Culinary arts. **Protective services:** Law enforcement admin. **Visual/performing arts:** Design. **Other:** Career studies, Trade technical occupations.

Most popular majors. Architecture 8%, business/marketing 20%, computer/information sciences 10%, education 8%, liberal arts 39%.

Computing on campus. 160 workstations in library, computer center, student center. Wireless network available.

Student life. Freshman orientation: Available. Preregistration for classes offered. **Activities:** Dance, literary magazine, student government, student newspaper.

Student services. Career counseling, services for economically disadvantaged, student employment services, financial aid counseling, veterans' counselor. **Transfer:** Transfer adviser, college fairs on campus for students transferring to 4-year colleges.

Contact. E-mail: admissions@yccc.edu
Phone: (207) 646-9282 ext. 304
Fred Quistgard, Director of Admissions, York County Community College, 112 College Drive, Wells, ME 04090

Maryland

Allegany College of Maryland
Cumberland, Maryland
www.allegany.edu **CB code: 5028**

- Public 2-year community college
- Commuter campus in large town

General. Founded in 1961. Regionally accredited. **Enrollment:** 2,994 degree-seeking undergraduates; 951 non-degree-seeking students. **Degrees:** 500 associate awarded. **ROTC:** Army. **Location:** 150 miles from Baltimore, 150 miles from Washington, DC. **Calendar:** Semester, limited summer session. **Full-time faculty:** 111 total; 15% have terminal degrees, 57% women. **Part-time faculty:** 151 total; 4% have terminal degrees, 75% women. **Class size:** 77% < 20, 22% 20-39, 1% 40-49, less than 1% >100. **Special facilities:** Greenhouse, arboretum, wetlands, Appalachian Room, labyrinth and serenity garden.

Student profile. Among degree-seeking undergraduates, 21% enrolled in a transfer program, 79% enrolled in a vocational program, 2% already have a bachelor's degree or higher, 887 enrolled as first-time, first-year students, 236 transferred in from other institutions.

Part-time:	31%	**Asian American:**	1%
Out-of-state:	54%	**Hispanic American:**	1%
Women:	68%	**25 or older:**	32%
African American:	10%	**Live on campus:**	7%

Transfer out. 70% of students enrolled in the transfer program go on to 4-year colleges. **Colleges most students transferred to 2008:** Frostburg State University, Shippensburg University, University of Pittsburgh at Johnstown.

Basis for selection. Open admission, but selective for some programs. Admission to allied health programs based on high school records, test scores.

2009-2010 Annual costs. Tuition/fees (projected): $3,336; $5,632 out-of-district; $6,472 out-of-state. Per-credit charge: $99 in-district; $182 out-of-district; $213 out-of-state. Books/supplies: $1,000. Personal expenses: $1,200.

2007-2008 Financial aid. Need-based: 66% of total undergraduate aid awarded as scholarships/grants, 34% as loans/jobs. Need-based aid available for part-time students. Work-study available nights and for part-time students. **Non-need-based:** Scholarships awarded for academics, athletics, leadership, state residency.

Application procedures. Admission: No deadline. No application fee. Admission notification on a rolling basis. High school and/or college transcript and placement tests in English, reading, and mathematics required. **Financial aid:** Priority date 3/1; no closing date. FAFSA, institutional form required. Applicants notified on a rolling basis starting 4/15; must reply within 2 week(s) of notification.

Academics. Special study options: Accelerated study, distance learning, double major, dual enrollment of high school students, ESL, honors, independent study, internships, liberal arts/career combination. Bachelor's degree programs available on campus. License preparation in dental hygiene, nursing, occupational therapy, physical therapy, radiology, real estate. **Credit/placement by examination:** AP, CLEP, institutional tests. 30 credit hours maximum toward associate degree. **Support services:** Learning center, reduced course load, remedial instruction, study skills assistance, tutoring.

Majors. Biology: General. **Business:** General, accounting, accounting technology, administrative services, business admin, hospitality admin, hospitality/recreation, management information systems, managerial economics, marketing. **Communications:** General. **Communications technology:** General. **Computer sciences:** General, computer science, information systems. **Conservation:** Forest management. **Education:** Early childhood, elementary, health, physical, secondary. **Engineering:** General. **Foreign languages:** Spanish. **Health:** Clinical lab technology, dental hygiene, health services, massage therapy, medical assistant, medical radiologic technology/radiation therapy, medical secretary, medical transcription, mental health services, nursing (RN), occupational therapy assistant, physical therapy assistant, prepharmacy, respiratory therapy technology. **History:** General. **Liberal arts:** Arts/sciences. **Math:** General. **Mechanic/repair:** Automotive. **Parks/recreation:** Facilities management. **Personal/culinary services:** General, chef training. **Physical sciences:** Chemistry, physics. **Protective services:** Police science. **Psychology:** General. **Public administration:** Social work. **Social sciences:** General, economics, political science, sociology. **Visual/performing arts:** Art. **Other:** Nanotechnology.

Most popular majors. Business/marketing 14%, health sciences 45%, liberal arts 23%.

Computing on campus. 450 workstations in library, computer center. Online course registration, online library, student web hosting, wireless network available.

Student life. Freshman orientation: Available, $4 fee. Preregistration for classes offered. **Housing:** Apartments, wellness housing available. $300 partly refundable deposit, deadline 8/26. **Activities:** Choral groups, dance, literary magazine, student government, forestry club, Older and Wiser Club, Phi Theta Kappa-Honors Society, Christian Fellowship, chess club, respiratory therapy club, dental hygiene club, medical laboratory technology club.

Athletics. NJCAA. **Intercollegiate:** Baseball M, basketball, soccer M, softball W, volleyball W. **Team name:** Trojans.

Student services. Career counseling, student employment services, financial aid counseling, on-campus daycare, personal counseling, placement for graduates, veterans' counselor, women's services. **Physically disabled:** Services for visually, speech, hearing impaired. **Transfer:** Pre-admission transcript evaluation for new students. Transfer adviser, college fairs on campus for students transferring to 4-year colleges.

Contact. E-mail: cnolan@allegany.edu
Phone: (301) 784-5199 Fax: (301) 784-5027
Cathy Nolan, Director of Admissions and Registration, Allegany College of Maryland, 12401 Willowbrook Road, SE, Cumberland, MD 21502

Anne Arundel Community College
Arnold, Maryland **CB member**
www.aacc.edu **CB code: 5019**

- Public 2-year community college
- Commuter campus in large town

General. Founded in 1964. Regionally accredited. 3 off-campus academic/student services centers: Fort Meade Army Education Center, Glen Burnie Town Center and Arundel Mills. **Enrollment:** 12,492 degree-seeking undergraduates. **Degrees:** 1,247 associate awarded. **Location:** 20 miles from Baltimore, 8 miles from Annapolis. **Calendar:** Semester, limited summer session. **Full-time faculty:** 263 total. **Part-time faculty:** 718 total. **Special facilities:** Off-campus workforce center at Baltimore-Washington International airport, environmental center, astronomy laboratory, center for performing arts, fine arts academic center, allied health/public services center, technology center, architectural, engineering, computer science and cybercrime labs, hospitality, culinary arts and tourism institute, entrepreneurial studies institute.

Transfer out. Colleges most students transferred to 2008: University of Maryland-Baltimore County, Towson University, University of Maryland-College Park, Salisbury University, University of Maryland University College.

Basis for selection. Open admission, but selective for some programs. Special requirements for certain allied health programs. International students must provide certification of finances. Interview recommended for applicants to nursing, human services, radiologic technology, physician's assistant programs.

2008-2009 Annual costs. Tuition/fees: $2,860; $5,230 out-of-district; $9,040 out-of-state. Per-credit charge: $86 in-district; $165 out-of-district; $292 out-of-state. Books/supplies: $900. Personal expenses: $1,300.

2007-2008 Financial aid. Need-based: 42% of total undergraduate aid awarded as scholarships/grants, 58% as loans/jobs. Need-based aid available for part-time students. Work-study available nights, weekends and for part-time students.

Application procedures. Admission: No deadline. No application fee. Admission notification on a rolling basis. **Financial aid:** Priority date 5/15; no closing date. FAFSA, institutional form required. Applicants notified on a rolling basis starting 7/1; must reply within 2 week(s) of notification.

Academics. Special study options: Cooperative education, distance learning, double major, dual enrollment of high school students, ESL, honors, independent study, internships, liberal arts/career combination, student-designed major, weekend college. Bachelor's degree programs available on campus. License preparation in nursing, paramedic, radiology, real estate. **Credit/placement by examination:** AP, CLEP, institutional tests. 15 credit hours maximum toward associate degree. **Support services:** GED preparation, learning center, reduced course load, remedial instruction, study skills assistance, tutoring, writing center.

Majors. Business: General, accounting. **Computer sciences:** General. **Education:** General, elementary, secondary. **Engineering:** General. **Engineering technology:** Drafting, electrical. **Family/consumer sciences:** Child care. **Health:** Dental assistant, EMT paramedic, health services, medical assistant, medical radiologic technology/radiation therapy, nursing (RN), pharmacy assistant, physical therapy assistant. **Legal studies:** Paralegal. **Liberal arts:** Arts/sciences. **Math:** General. **Mechanic/repair:** Electronics/electrical. **Parks/recreation:** Health/fitness. **Personal/culinary services:** Baking, chef training, culinary arts, restaurant/catering. **Protective services:** Forensics, law enforcement admin. **Public administration:** Human services. **Visual/performing arts:** Commercial/advertising art, interior design.

Most popular majors. Business/marketing 16%, health sciences 13%, liberal arts 56%.

Computing on campus. Commuter students can connect to campus network. Online library, helpline, wireless network available.

Student life. Freshman orientation: Mandatory. One day orientation program required for all first-time, full-time students. **Activities:** Bands, campus ministries, choral groups, dance, drama, international student organizations, literary magazine, music ensembles, musical theater, opera, student government, student newspaper, symphony orchestra, Black student union, Lambda Pioneers, Fellowship of Christian Athletes.

Athletics. NJCAA. **Intercollegiate:** Baseball M, basketball, golf M, lacrosse, soccer, softball W, volleyball W. **Intramural:** Basketball, softball, swimming, table tennis, tennis, volleyball, weight lifting. **Team name:** Pioneers.

Student services. Adult student services, alcohol/substance abuse counseling, career counseling, student employment services, financial aid counseling, health services, minority student services, on-campus daycare, personal counseling, placement for graduates, veterans' counselor. **Physically disabled:** Services for visually, speech, hearing impaired. **Transfer:** Transfer center, transfer adviser, college fairs on campus for students transferring to 4-year colleges.

Contact. E-mail: admissions@aacc.edu
Phone: (410) 777-2246 Fax: (410) 777-4246
Thomas McGinn, Director of Enrollment Development and Admissions, Anne Arundel Community College, 101 College Parkway, Arnold, MD 21012-1895

Baltimore City Community College

Baltimore, Maryland
www.bccc.edu **CB code: 5051**

- Public 2-year community college
- Commuter campus in very large city

General. Founded in 1947. Regionally accredited. Sites throughout Baltimore. **Enrollment:** 6,818 degree-seeking undergraduates. **Degrees:** 419 associate awarded. **Location:** 50 miles from Washington, DC, 75 miles from Philadelphia. **Calendar:** Semester, extensive summer session. **Full-time faculty:** 133 total. **Part-time faculty:** 246 total. **Special facilities:** Greenhouse, planetarium.

Student profile.

Out-of-state:	1%	**25 or older:**	58%

Transfer out. Colleges most students transferred to 2008: Coppin State University, Morgan State University, University of Baltimore, Towson University, University of Maryland Baltimore County.

Basis for selection. Open admission, but selective for some programs. Special requirements for nursing and allied health. SAT and ACT scores may be used in place of reading, math, and English proficiency tests required of all first-time students. Interview recommended for applicants to allied health, paralegal, emergency medical services programs. Portfolio recommended for art, fashion design majors.

2008-2009 Annual costs. Tuition/fees: $3,062; $6,722 out-of-state. Books/supplies: $700.

Financial aid. All financial aid based on need. Need-based aid available for part-time students. Work-study available nights, weekends and for part-time students.

Application procedures. Admission: No deadline. $10 fee, may be waived for applicants with need. Admission notification on a rolling basis. **Financial aid:** Priority date 6/1; no closing date. FAFSA, institutional form required. Applicants notified on a rolling basis starting 7/1; must reply within 2 week(s) of notification.

Academics. Adults without diploma or GED become eligible for degree programs after successfully completing 15 college-level credits. **Special study options:** Cooperative education, distance learning, double major, dual enrollment of high school students, ESL, honors, independent study, internships, liberal arts/career combination, study abroad, teacher certification program, weekend college. License preparation in dental hygiene, nursing, paramedic, physical therapy, real estate. **Credit/placement by examination:** CLEP, IB, institutional tests. 15 credit hours maximum toward associate degree. **Support services:** GED preparation, learning center, preadmission summer program, reduced course load, remedial instruction, study skills assistance, tutoring, writing center.

Majors. Biology: Biotechnology. **Business:** General, accounting, administrative services, business admin, fashion, hospitality admin, management information systems, marketing, office management, office technology. **Computer sciences:** General, computer graphics, computer science, information systems, systems analysis. **Education:** General, early childhood, multilevel teacher. **Engineering:** General. **Engineering technology:** Drafting, electrical. **Family/consumer sciences:** Clothing/textiles. **Health:** Dental hygiene, EMT paramedic, health care admin, health services, licensed practical nurse, medical records admin, medical records technology, medical secretary, nursing (RN), physical therapy assistant, respiratory therapy technology. **Interdisciplinary:** Biological/physical sciences. **Legal studies:** Legal secretary, paralegal. **Liberal arts:** Arts/sciences. **Protective services:** Corrections, law enforcement admin, police science. **Public administration:** Social work. **Visual/performing arts:** Art, fashion design.

Most popular majors. Business/marketing 14%, computer/information sciences 7%, health sciences 30%, liberal arts 26%, security/protective services 9%.

Computing on campus. 200 workstations in library, computer center, student center. Online library available.

Student life. Freshman orientation: Mandatory. Preregistration for classes offered. **Activities:** Choral groups, drama, international student organizations, musical theater, radio station, student government, student newspaper, fashion club, human services club, media club, civic organizations, computer club.

Athletics. NJCAA. **Intercollegiate:** Baseball M, basketball, volleyball W. **Team name:** Panthers.

Student services. Career counseling, student employment services, financial aid counseling, health services, on-campus daycare, personal counseling, placement for graduates, veterans' counselor. **Physically disabled:** Services for visually, speech, hearing impaired. **Learning disabled:** Comprehensive services available. **Transfer:** Pre-admission transcript evaluation for new students. Transfer adviser, college fairs on campus for students transferring to 4-year colleges.

Contact. E-mail: admissions@bccc.edu
Phone: (410) 462-8300 Toll-free number: (888) 203-1261
Fax: (410) 462-8345
Deneen Dangerfield, Director of Admissions, Baltimore City Community College, 2901 Liberty Heights Avenue, Baltimore, MD 21215-7893

Carroll Community College

Westminster, Maryland
www.carrollcc.edu **CB code: 5797**

- Public 2-year community college
- Commuter campus in large town

General. Founded in 1993. Regionally accredited. **Enrollment:** 3,460 degree-seeking undergraduates. **Degrees:** 371 associate awarded. **Location:** 30 miles from Baltimore. **Calendar:** Semester, extensive summer session. **Full-time faculty:** 68 total; 15% have terminal degrees, 3% minority, 62% women. **Part-time faculty:** 190 total; 6% minority, 61% women. **Class size:** 45% < 20, 55% 20-39. **Special facilities:** Theater, amphitheatre, art gallery.

Student profile. Among degree-seeking undergraduates, 820 enrolled as first-time, first-year students, 289 transferred in from other institutions.

Part-time:	53%	**Asian American:**	1%
Out-of-state:	3%	**Hispanic American:**	2%
Women:	63%	**25 or older:**	28%
African American:	3%		

Two-Year Colleges

Transfer out. **Colleges most students transferred to 2008:** Towson University, McDaniel College, University of Maryland Baltimore County, Salisbury University, University of Baltimore.

Basis for selection. Open admission, but selective for some programs.

2008-2009 Annual costs. Tuition/fees: $3,407; $4,925 out-of-district; $6,926 out-of-state. Per-credit charge: $114 in-district; $164 out-of-district; $231 out-of-state. Books/supplies: $1,200. Personal expenses: $1,000.

2007-2008 Financial aid. **Need-based:** 98% of total undergraduate aid awarded as scholarships/grants, 2% as loans/jobs. Need-based aid available for part-time students. Work-study available nights, weekends and for part-time students. **Non-need-based:** Scholarships awarded for academics, art, job skills, leadership, state residency.

Application procedures. **Admission:** No deadline. No application fee. Application must be submitted on paper. Admission notification on a rolling basis. **Financial aid:** Priority date 3/1; no closing date. FAFSA required. Applicants notified by 6/1; must reply within 2 week(s) of notification.

Academics. **Special study options:** Distance learning, dual enrollment of high school students, ESL, honors, independent study, internships, liberal arts/career combination, weekend college. **Credit/placement by examination:** AP, CLEP, institutional tests. 30 credit hours maximum toward associate degree. **Support services:** GED preparation, learning center, remedial instruction, study skills assistance, tutoring, writing center.

Majors. **Business:** General, accounting technology, administrative services, international, management information systems. **Computer sciences:** Computer graphics. **Education:** General, chemistry, early childhood, elementary, mathematics, Spanish. **Engineering technology:** Architectural drafting. **Family/consumer sciences:** Child care. **Health:** Dental hygiene, EMT ambulance attendant, nuclear medical technology, nursing (RN), physical therapy assistant, prenursing, radiologic technology/medical imaging, respiratory therapy technology, sonography, surgical technology. **Legal studies:** General. **Liberal arts:** Arts/sciences. **Parks/recreation:** Exercise sciences. **Protective services:** Forensics, police science. **Psychology:** General. **Visual/performing arts:** Art, commercial/advertising art, theater design.

Most popular majors. Business/marketing 13%, education 6%, health sciences 21%, liberal arts 57%.

Computing on campus. 684 workstations in library, computer center, student center. Commuter students can connect to campus network. Online library, helpline, wireless network available.

Student life. **Freshman orientation:** Available. Preregistration for classes offered. One-day program in late August. **Activities:** Jazz band, choral groups, drama, film society, literary magazine, music ensembles, musical theater, student government, symphony orchestra, Alliance, Christian club, Leadership Challenge, juggling club, campus activities board, outdoor club, Green Team, game design.

Student services. Career counseling, student employment services, financial aid counseling, on-campus daycare, personal counseling. **Physically disabled:** Services for visually, speech, hearing impaired. **Transfer:** Reentry adviser, pre-admission transcript evaluation for new students. Transfer center, transfer adviser, college fairs on campus for students transferring to 4-year colleges.

Contact. E-mail: cedwards@carrollcc.edu
Phone: (410) 386-8430 Toll-free number: (888) 221-9748
Fax: (410) 386-8446
Candace Edwards, Coordinator of Admissions, Carroll Community College, 1601 Washington Road, Westminster, MD 21157

Cecil College

North East, Maryland
www.cecil.edu **CB code: 5091**

- Public 2-year community college
- Commuter campus in large town

General. Founded in 1968. Regionally accredited. **Enrollment:** 2,086 degree-seeking undergraduates; 190 non-degree-seeking students. **Degrees:** 178 associate awarded. **Location:** 50 miles from Baltimore, 50 miles from Philadelphia. **Calendar:** Semester, limited summer session. **Full-time faculty:** 45 total; 20% have terminal degrees, 9% minority, 69% women. **Part-time faculty:** 146 total; 1% have terminal degrees, 6% minority, 58% women. **Class size:** 79% < 20, 19% 20-39, 1% 40-49, less than 1% 50-99, less than 1% >100.

Student profile. Among degree-seeking undergraduates, 49% enrolled in a transfer program, 51% enrolled in a vocational program, 594 enrolled as first-time, first-year students, 9 transferred in from other institutions.

Part-time:	62%	**Asian American:**	1%
Out-of-state:	10%	**Hispanic American:**	2%
Women:	64%	**25 or older:**	32%
African American:	7%		

Basis for selection. Open admission, but selective for some programs. Admission to nursing programs based on high school record, test scores, required interview. All students must take Cecil College placement tests.

High school preparation. College-preparatory program recommended.

2008-2009 Annual costs. Tuition/fees: $2,912; $5,612 out-of-district; $6,962 out-of-state. Per-credit charge: $85 in-district; $175 out-of-district; $220 out-of-state. Books/supplies: $935. Personal expenses: $2,000.

2007-2008 Financial aid. **Need-based:** 45% of total undergraduate aid awarded as scholarships/grants, 55% as loans/jobs. Work-study available nights, weekends and for part-time students. **Non-need-based:** Scholarships awarded for academics, alumni affiliation, athletics, job skills, state residency.

Application procedures. **Admission:** No deadline. No application fee. Admission notification on a rolling basis. Application deadline for nursing program March 1. **Financial aid:** Priority date 8/1; no closing date. FAFSA required. Applicants notified on a rolling basis; must reply within 2 week(s) of notification.

Academics. **Special study options:** Accelerated study, cooperative education, distance learning, double major, dual enrollment of high school students, ESL, honors, independent study, internships, teacher certification program, weekend college. Bachelor's degree programs available on campus. License preparation in aviation, nursing. **Credit/placement by examination:** AP, CLEP, institutional tests. 45 credit hours maximum toward associate degree. **Support services:** Learning center, reduced course load, remedial instruction, tutoring, writing center.

Majors. **Agriculture:** Equine science. **Biology:** General. **Business:** General, accounting, administrative services, business admin, communications, financial planning, management information systems, marketing, office management, transportation. **Computer sciences:** General, applications programming, programming, web page design. **Education:** General, early childhood, elementary, secondary. **Engineering technology:** CAD/CADD, electrical, heat/ac/refrig. **Health:** EMT paramedic, nursing (RN). **Liberal arts:** Arts/sciences. **Math:** General. **Physical sciences:** Chemistry, physics. **Protective services:** Firefighting, police science. **Transportation:** General, air traffic control, aviation. **Visual/performing arts:** Commercial photography, design, drawing, photography, studio arts.

Most popular majors. Business/marketing 17%, health sciences 32%, liberal arts 34%, visual/performing arts 7%.

Computing on campus. 97 workstations in library, computer center, student center. Commuter students can connect to campus network. Online course registration, online library available.

Student life. **Freshman orientation:** Available. Preregistration for classes offered. **Activities:** Dance, drama, musical theater, student government, student newspaper.

Athletics. NJCAA. **Intercollegiate:** Baseball M, basketball, cheerleading M, golf M, soccer, softball W, tennis, volleyball W. **Team name:** Seahawks.

Student services. Adult student services, alcohol/substance abuse counseling, career counseling, student employment services, financial aid counseling, legal services, minority student services, personal counseling, placement for graduates, veterans' counselor. **Transfer:** Transfer adviser, college fairs on campus for students transferring to 4-year colleges.

Contact. E-mail: dlane@cecil.edu
Phone: (410) 287-6060 Fax: (410) 287-1026
Diane Lane, Vice President of Student Services, Cecil College, One Seahawk Drive, North East, MD 21901

Chesapeake College

Wye Mills, Maryland
www.chesapeake.edu **CB code: 5143**

- Public 2-year community college
- Commuter campus in rural community

General. Founded in 1965. Regionally accredited. **Enrollment:** 2,038 degree-seeking undergraduates. **Degrees:** 196 associate awarded. **Location:** 50 miles from Washington, DC, 50 miles from Baltimore. **Calendar:** Semester, limited summer session. **Full-time faculty:** 56 total. **Part-time faculty:** 77 total. **Special facilities:** Performing arts center.

Student profile.

Out-of-state:	1%	**25 or older:**	47%

Transfer out. Colleges most students transferred to 2008: Salisbury State College, Towson University, Frostburg State College, University of Maryland.

Basis for selection. Open admission, but selective for some programs. Admission to radiological technology, surgical technology, physical therapist assistant and nursing programs based on specific high school courses, cumulative grade point averages, and/or test scores.

2008-2009 Annual costs. Tuition/fees: $3,304; $5,374 out-of-district; $7,684 out-of-state. Per-credit charge: $91 in-district; $159 out-of-district; $236 out-of-state. Books/supplies: $1,400. Personal expenses: $1,000.

Financial aid. Need-based: Need-based aid available for part-time students. **Non-need-based:** Scholarships awarded for academics, art, athletics, state residency.

Application procedures. Admission: No deadline. No application fee. Admission notification on a rolling basis. Early application advised for radiologic technology and nursing programs. **Financial aid:** Priority date 5/1; no closing date. FAFSA, institutional form required. Applicants notified on a rolling basis starting 5/1; must reply within 2 week(s) of notification.

Academics. Special study options: Cooperative education, cross-registration, distance learning, dual enrollment of high school students, ESL, honors, independent study, internships, student-designed major, teacher certification program, weekend college. License preparation in nursing, paramedic, physical therapy. **Credit/placement by examination:** CLEP, institutional tests. 32 credit hours maximum toward associate degree. **Support services:** Learning center, reduced course load, remedial instruction, study skills assistance, tutoring, writing center.

Majors. Business: General, accounting, administrative services, management information systems, tourism promotion. **Computer sciences:** General. **Education:** General, elementary, secondary. **Engineering technology:** Drafting, manufacturing. **Family/consumer sciences:** Child care. **Health:** Medical radiologic technology/radiation therapy, medical records technology, mental health services, nursing (RN), physical therapy assistant. **Legal studies:** Paralegal. **Liberal arts:** Arts/sciences. **Mechanic/repair:** Aircraft. **Protective services:** Criminal justice, police science. **Psychology:** General. **Social sciences:** General.

Computing on campus. Commuter students can connect to campus network. Helpline available.

Student life. Freshman orientation: Available. Preregistration for classes offered. **Activities:** Choral groups, drama, student government, TV station, action teams, peer associates, African American student union, Phi Theta Kappa honor society, Best Buddies.

Athletics. NJCAA. **Intercollegiate:** Baseball M, basketball, soccer, softball W. **Intramural:** Basketball, soccer. **Team name:** Skipjacks.

Student services. Adult student services, career counseling, student employment services, financial aid counseling, minority student services, on-campus daycare, personal counseling, placement for graduates, veterans' counselor. **Physically disabled:** Services for visually, speech, hearing impaired. **Transfer:** Transfer adviser, college fairs on campus for students transferring to 4-year colleges.

Contact. E-mail: kpetrichenko@chesapeake.edu
Phone: (410) 822-5400 ext. 287 Fax: (410) 827-5878
Kathy Petrichenko, Dean of Recruitment, Chesapeake College, Box 8, Wye Mills, MD 21679-0008

College of Southern Maryland

La Plata, Maryland
www.csmd.edu **CB code: 5144**

- Public 2-year community college
- Commuter campus in large town

General. Founded in 1958. Regionally accredited. Additional campuses located in Charles County, Calvert County, and St. Mary's County. **Enrollment:** 6,687 degree-seeking undergraduates; 1,553 non-degree-seeking students. **Degrees:** 683 associate awarded. **Location:** 30 miles from Washington, DC. **Calendar:** Semester, limited summer session. **Full-time faculty:** 119 total; 25% have terminal degrees, 14% minority, 53% women. **Part-time faculty:** 496 total; 6% have terminal degrees, 18% minority, 43% women. **Class size:** 38% < 20, 61% 20-39, less than 1% 40-49, less than 1% 50-99.

Student profile. Among degree-seeking undergraduates, 56% enrolled in a transfer program, 44% enrolled in a vocational program, 1,549 enrolled as first-time, first-year students, 243 transferred in from other institutions.

Part-time:	60%	**Hispanic American:**	3%
Women:	66%	**Native American:**	1%
African American:	22%	**25 or older:**	36%
Asian American:	4%		

Transfer out. Colleges most students transferred to 2008: University of Maryland: University College, University of Maryland: College Park, Towson University, Salisbury University, St. Mary's College of Maryland.

Basis for selection. Open admission, but selective for some programs. Specific requirements for clinical nursing courses include high school diploma or GED, special testing (ACT), minimum 2.0 GPA in high school. Must have graduated from high school, earned high school equivalency or have met the criteria of one of the college's special admissions programs. Students must take the college skills assessment test unless they have taken the SAT, scored 550 in English and math or the ACT, scored 21 or higher. Interview required of early admission and nursing applicants. **Adult students:** SAT/ACT scores not required.

2008-2009 Annual costs. Tuition/fees: $3,528; $7,956 out-of-state. Per-credit charge: $98 in-district; $171 out-of-district; $221 out-of-state. Out-of-district fees are an additional $420; out-of-state fees are an additional $690. The required fees figure is based on in-county rates. Books/supplies: $1,400. Personal expenses: $1,555.

2007-2008 Financial aid. Need-based: 83% of total undergraduate aid awarded as scholarships/grants, 17% as loans/jobs. Need-based aid available for part-time students. Work-study available nights, weekends and for part-time students. **Non-need-based:** Scholarships awarded for academics, athletics, state residency.

Application procedures. Admission: No deadline. No application fee. Admission notification on a rolling basis. **Financial aid:** Priority date 3/1; no closing date. FAFSA required. Applicants notified on a rolling basis starting 5/15; must reply within 2 week(s) of notification.

Academics. Special study options: Accelerated study, cooperative education, distance learning, dual enrollment of high school students, honors, independent study, liberal arts/career combination, weekend college. Bachelor's degree programs available on campus. License preparation in nursing, paramedic, physical therapy, radiology. **Credit/placement by examination:** AP, CLEP, institutional tests. 30 credit hours maximum toward associate degree. **Support services:** Learning center, reduced course load, remedial instruction, study skills assistance, tutoring.

Majors. Business: General, accounting technology, business admin. **Computer sciences:** General, information technology, programming. **Construction:** Lineworker. **Education:** General, elementary. **Engineering:** General. **Engineering technology:** Electrical, environmental. **Family/consumer sciences:** Child care. **Health:** Clinical lab technology, EMT paramedic, licensed practical nurse, massage therapy, nursing (RN), physical therapy assistant. **Legal studies:** Paralegal. **Liberal arts:** Arts/sciences. **Parks/recreation:** Health/fitness. **Protective services:** Firefighting, law enforcement admin. **Other:** Mental and Social Health Services and Allied Professions.

Most popular majors. Business/marketing 25%, computer/information sciences 7%, engineering/engineering technologies 13%, health sciences 15%, liberal arts 39%.

Computing on campus. 1,037 workstations in library, computer center. Commuter students can connect to campus network. Online course registration, helpline available.

Student life. Freshman orientation: Available. Preregistration for classes offered. **Activities:** Jazz band, choral groups, drama, literary magazine, music ensembles, musical theater, student government, student newspaper, BACCHUS Peer Education Network, Black Student Union, Campus Crusade for Christ, El Circulo Cultural Hispanico, Future Teachers Club, The Hawkeye, nursing student association, Phi Theta Kappa, student activities committee, Women on Campus.

Athletics. NJCAA. **Intercollegiate:** Baseball M, basketball, golf, soccer, softball W, tennis, volleyball W. **Team name:** Hawks.

Student services. Adult student services, career counseling, student employment services, financial aid counseling, personal counseling, placement for graduates, veterans' counselor. **Physically disabled:** Services for visually, speech, hearing impaired. **Transfer:** Re-entry adviser for new students. Transfer adviser, college fairs on campus for students transferring to 4-year colleges.

Contact. E-mail: info@csmd.edu
Phone: (301) 934-7765 Toll-free number: (800) 933-9177 ext. 7765
Fax: (301) 934-7698
Bertha Clay, Director of Admissions, College of Southern Maryland, College of Southern Maryland-AOD, La Plata, MD 20646-0910

Community College of Baltimore County

Baltimore, Maryland **CB member**
www.ccbcmd.edu **CB code: 5137**

- Public 2-year community college
- Commuter campus in very large city

General. Founded in 1956. Regionally accredited. 3 campuses-Catonsville, Dundalk and Essex; 2 extension centers in Owings Mills and Hunt Valley. **Enrollment:** 17,105 degree-seeking undergraduates; 3,568 non-degree-seeking students. **Degrees:** 1,654 associate awarded. **Location:** 8 miles from Baltimore. **Calendar:** Semester, limited summer session. **Full-time faculty:** 384 total; 23% have terminal degrees, 17% minority, 57% women. **Part-time faculty:** 723 total; 2% have terminal degrees, 21% minority, 57% women. **Special facilities:** Planetarium, occupational training center, performing arts theater, computer integrated manufacturing center. **Partnerships:** Formal partnership with the Baltimore County Public Schools for the Early Assessment and Intervention Project.

Student profile. Among degree-seeking undergraduates, 3,248 enrolled as first-time, first-year students.

Part-time:	62%	**Hispanic American:**	3%
Women:	63%	**International:**	2%
African American:	33%	**25 or older:**	42%
Asian American:	4%		

Transfer out. Colleges most students transferred to 2008: University of Baltimore, University of Maryland Baltimore County, Towson University, Morgan State University.

Basis for selection. Open admission, but selective for some programs. Additional requirements for School of Health Professions. In-house placement tests required of applicants not presenting SAT or ACT scores. Score reports preferred by July 1. Interview recommended for applicants under age 16 and early admission applicants.

High school preparation. 21 units recommended. Recommended units include English 4, mathematics 3, social studies 4, science 3, foreign language 2 and academic electives 6.

2008-2009 Annual costs. Tuition/fees: $3,080; $5,600 out-of-district; $8,210 out-of-state. Per-credit charge: $90 in-district; $174 out-of-district; $261 out-of-state. Books/supplies: $1,200. Personal expenses: $1,400.

2007-2008 Financial aid. Need-based: Need-based aid available for part-time students. Work-study available nights, weekends and for part-time students. **Non-need-based:** Scholarships awarded for academics, athletics, state residency. **Additional information:** On-campus employment typically available.

Application procedures. Admission: No deadline. $15 fee, may be waived for applicants with need, free for online applicants. Admission notification on a rolling basis. **Financial aid:** Closing date 3/1. FAFSA required. Applicants notified on a rolling basis starting 5/1; must reply within 2 week(s) of notification.

Academics. Special study options: Cooperative education, cross-registration, distance learning, dual enrollment of high school students, ESL, honors, independent study, internships, liberal arts/career combination, study abroad, teacher certification program. Weekend Courses available. License preparation in aviation, dental hygiene, nursing. **Credit/placement by examination:** AP, CLEP, institutional tests. 30 credit hours maximum toward associate degree. **Support services:** GED preparation, learning center, reduced course load, remedial instruction, tutoring.

Majors. Agriculture: Horticulture, plant sciences. **Business:** General, accounting technology, administrative services, business admin, construction management, hotel/motel admin, labor relations, management information systems, real estate. **Communications technology:** Graphic/printing, radio/tv. **Computer sciences:** General, computer graphics. **Construction:** Site management. **Education:** General, chemistry, early childhood, elementary, mathematics, physics, Spanish, special. **Engineering:** General. **Engineering technology:** Architectural drafting, civil, computer systems, drafting, electrical, environmental, hydraulics, industrial, mechanical, occupational safety, quality control. **Family/consumer sciences:** Child care. **Foreign languages:** Sign language interpretation. **Health:** Clinical lab technology, dental hygiene, EMT paramedic, medical assistant, medical informatics, medical radiologic technology/radiation therapy, medical records technology, medical secretary, mental health services, nursing (RN), respiratory therapy technology, substance abuse counseling, veterinary technology/assistant. **Interdisciplinary:** Biological/physical sciences. **Legal studies:** Paralegal. **Liberal arts:** Arts/sciences. **Mechanic/repair:** Auto body, automotive, diesel, heating/ac/refrig. **Parks/recreation:** General. **Personal/culinary services:** Mortuary science. **Protective services:** Police science. **Social sciences:** Geography. **Transportation:** Aviation. **Visual/performing arts:** General, commercial photography, commercial/advertising art. **Other:** Biotechnology, Engineering technology, Industrial maintenance technician, Marketing management, Occupational therapy assistant.

Computing on campus. Online course registration, online library available.

Student life. Freshman orientation: Available. Preregistration for classes offered. One-day program. **Activities:** Choral groups, dance, drama, international student organizations, literary magazine, music ensembles, musical theater, radio station, student government, student newspaper, TV station, black student union, Adventure Society, Christian fellowship.

Athletics. NJCAA. **Intercollegiate:** Baseball M, basketball, lacrosse, soccer, softball W, volleyball W.

Student services. Career counseling, services for economically disadvantaged, student employment services, financial aid counseling, minority student services, on-campus daycare, personal counseling, placement for graduates, veterans' counselor. **Physically disabled:** Services for visually, speech, hearing impaired. **Transfer:** Pre-admission transcript evaluation for new students. Transfer adviser, college fairs on campus for students transferring to 4-year colleges.

Contact. E-mail: catonsvilleadmissions@ccbcmd.edu
Phone: (443) 840-4392 Fax: (443) 840-5046
Diane Drake, Director of Admissions, Community College of Baltimore County, 800 South Rolling Road, Baltimore, MD 21228

Frederick Community College

Frederick, Maryland **CB member**
www.frederick.edu **CB code: 5230**

- Public 2-year community college
- Commuter campus in small city

General. Founded in 1957. Regionally accredited. **Enrollment:** 5,172 degree-seeking undergraduates; 576 non-degree-seeking students. **Degrees:** 577 associate awarded. **Location:** 40 miles from Washington, DC, 40 miles from Baltimore. **Calendar:** Semester, extensive summer session. **Full-time faculty:** 88 total. **Part-time faculty:** 350 total. **Special facilities:** Culinary arts institute, advanced workforce training center.

Student profile. Among degree-seeking undergraduates, 81% enrolled in a transfer program, 8% enrolled in a vocational program, 1,331 enrolled as first-time, first-year students.

Part-time:	59%	**Women:**	57%
Out-of-state:	1%	**25 or older:**	50%

Transfer out. Colleges most students transferred to 2008: Hood College, Mount St. Mary's University, Towson University, University of Maryland: College Park, Frostburg University.

Basis for selection. Open admission, but selective for some programs. All nursing programs, respiratory therapy, and surgical technology have special requirements. Students must show successful completion of appropriate general education requirements. Score of 550 or higher on either SAT math or verbal will exempt student from appropriate assessment. Interview required of nursing, respiratory therapy applicants. **Homeschooled:** Transcript of courses and grades required. **Learning Disabled:** Meet with Office of Services for Students with Disabilities staff prior to testing/registration.

2008-2009 Annual costs. Tuition/fees: $3,128; $6,368 out-of-district; $8,528 out-of-state. Per-credit charge: $92 in-district; $200 out-of-district; $272 out-of-state. Books/supplies: $1,200. Personal expenses: $1,000.

2007-2008 Financial aid. Need-based: 82% of total undergraduate aid awarded as scholarships/grants, 18% as loans/jobs. Need-based aid available for part-time students. Work-study available for part-time students. **Non-need-based:** Scholarships awarded for academics, athletics, state residency.

Application procedures. **Admission:** No deadline. No application fee. Admission notification on a rolling basis beginning on or about 1/1. Application deadline for nursing applicants December 15, surgical technology and emergency medical services applicants February 1. **Financial aid:** Priority date 6/1; no closing date. FAFSA, institutional form required. Applicants notified on a rolling basis starting 5/15; must reply within 2 week(s) of notification.

Academics. **Special study options:** Cooperative education, distance learning, dual enrollment of high school students, ESL, honors, independent study, internships, liberal arts/career combination, study abroad, teacher certification program, weekend college. License preparation in nursing, real estate. **Credit/placement by examination:** AP, CLEP, institutional tests. 30 credit hours maximum toward associate degree. **Support services:** Learning center, pre-admission summer program, reduced course load, remedial instruction, study skills assistance, tutoring, writing center.

Majors. **Biology:** General. **Business:** Accounting, banking/financial services, business admin, hospitality admin, international. **Communications:** General. **Communications technology:** General. **Computer sciences:** General, applications programming, computer science, information systems, information technology, system admin, systems analysis. **Construction:** General. **Education:** General, early childhood, multi-level teacher, physical, Spanish. **Engineering:** General. **Engineering technology:** Biomedical, CAD/CADD, computer, computer hardware, computer systems, software. **Family/consumer sciences:** Child care. **Health:** Nuclear medical technology, nursing (RN), prenursing, prepharmacy, respiratory therapy technology, surgical technology. **History:** General. **Legal studies:** Legal secretary, paralegal. **Liberal arts:** Arts/sciences. **Math:** General. **Personal/culinary services:** Culinary arts. **Philosophy/religion:** Philosophy. **Physical sciences:** Chemistry. **Protective services:** Criminal justice, emergency management/homeland security, fire services admin, police science. **Psychology:** General. **Public administration:** Human services. **Science technology:** Biological. **Social sciences:** Economics, political science, sociology. **Visual/performing arts:** Art, dramatic.

Computing on campus. 150 workstations in library, computer center. Commuter students can connect to campus network. Online course registration, online library, wireless network available.

Student life. **Freshman orientation:** Mandatory. Preregistration for classes offered. Held throughout summer; include advisement and pre-registration. **Activities:** Jazz band, choral groups, dance, drama, film society, literary magazine, music ensembles, student government, student newspaper, multicultural student union, Christian students club, chess club, community service club, environmental awareness club, honors student association, international students club, gay/lesbian/bisexual group, nursing club, young Democrats and Republicans.

Athletics. NJCAA. **Intercollegiate:** Baseball M, basketball, golf, soccer, softball W, volleyball W. **Team name:** Cougars.

Student services. Adult student services, alcohol/substance abuse counseling, career counseling, student employment services, financial aid counseling, minority student services, on-campus daycare, personal counseling, placement for graduates, veterans' counselor, women's services. **Physically disabled:** Services for visually, speech, hearing impaired. **Transfer:** Transfer center, transfer adviser, college fairs on campus for students transferring to 4-year colleges.

Contact. E-mail: kfrawley@frederick.edu
Phone: (301) 846-2431 Fax: (301) 624-2799
Kathy Frawley, Associate Vice President/Registrar, Frederick Community College, 7932 Opossumtown Pike, Frederick, MD 21702

Garrett College
McHenry, Maryland
www.garrettcollege.edu **CB code: 5279**

- Public 2-year community college
- Commuter campus in rural community

General. Founded in 1971. Regionally accredited. **Enrollment:** 656 degree-seeking undergraduates. **Degrees:** 96 associate awarded. **Location:** 45 miles from Cumberland, 40 miles from Morgantown, West Virginia. **Calendar:** Semester, limited summer session. **Full-time faculty:** 17 total; 29% have terminal degrees, 6% minority, 29% women. **Part-time faculty:** 76 total; 5% have terminal degrees.

Student profile. Among degree-seeking undergraduates, 46 transferred in from other institutions.

Out-of-state:	19%	**Live on campus:**	10%
25 or older:	21%		

Transfer out. **Colleges most students transferred to 2008:** Frostburg State University.

Basis for selection. Open admission. Applicants without high school diploma must earn diploma or GED before completing 20 credit hours when enrolling in certificate program, and complete 30 credit hours when enrolling in degree program. **Adult students:** SAT/ACT scores not required. **Homeschooled:** Transcript of courses and grades required.

High school preparation. College-preparatory program recommended.

2008-2009 Annual costs. Tuition/fees: $2,970; $6,510 out-of-district; $7,590 out-of-state. Per-credit charge: $78 in-district; $196 out-of-district; $232 out-of-state. Room/board: $4,300. Books/supplies: $2,000. Personal expenses: $3,000.

Financial aid. **Need-based:** Need-based aid available for part-time students. **Non-need-based:** Scholarships awarded for academics, athletics, leadership. **Additional information:** Many local scholarships both merit and need based.

Application procedures. **Admission:** No deadline. No application fee. Admission notification on a rolling basis. **Financial aid:** Closing date 3/1. FAFSA required. Applicants notified on a rolling basis starting 5/15; must reply within 2 week(s) of notification.

Academics. **Special study options:** Distance learning, double major, dual enrollment of high school students, honors, independent study. **Credit/placement by examination:** AP, CLEP, institutional tests. 30 credit hours maximum toward associate degree. **Support services:** GED preparation and test center, learning center, pre-admission summer program, reduced course load, remedial instruction, tutoring, writing center.

Majors. **Agriculture:** Business. **Business:** General, business admin, office technology. **Computer sciences:** Information systems. **Conservation:** General, fisheries, wildlife. **Education:** General, elementary, physical, secondary. **Interdisciplinary:** Behavioral sciences. **Liberal arts:** Arts/sciences. **Math:** General. **Parks/recreation:** General. **Protective services:** Police science. **Psychology:** General. **Visual/performing arts:** General.

Most popular majors. Business/marketing 17%, education 12%, liberal arts 51%, natural resources/environmental science 12%.

Computing on campus. 80 workstations in library, computer center. Dormitories wired for high-speed internet access. Online library, helpline, wireless network available.

Student life. **Freshman orientation:** Available. Preregistration for classes offered. **Housing:** Coed dorms, wellness housing available. $200 nonrefundable deposit. **Activities:** Concert band, drama, international student organizations, student government, student newspaper, art club, adventure sports club, math club, wildlife club, women's athletic club, world view international club.

Athletics. NJCAA. **Intercollegiate:** Baseball M, basketball, golf M, softball W, volleyball W. **Intramural:** Softball W, volleyball W. **Team name:** Lakers.

Student services. Career counseling, student employment services, financial aid counseling. **Physically disabled:** Services for visually, speech, hearing impaired. **Transfer:** Transfer adviser, college fairs on campus for students transferring to 4-year colleges.

Contact. E-mail: admissions@garrettcollege.edu
Phone: (301) 387-3044 Toll-free number: (866) 554-2773
Fax: (301) 387-3038
Rachell Davis, Coordinator of Enrollment Management, Garrett College, 687 Mosser Road, McHenry, MD 21541

Hagerstown Community College
Hagerstown, Maryland
www.hagerstowncc.edu **CB code: 5290**

- Public 2-year community college
- Commuter campus in small city

General. Founded in 1946. Regionally accredited. **Enrollment:** 1,260 full-time, degree-seeking students. **Degrees:** 361 associate awarded. **Location:**

70 miles from Baltimore. **Calendar:** Semester, extensive summer session. **Full-time faculty:** 71 total. **Part-time faculty:** 168 total. **Special facilities:** Technology center, distance learning classrooms, amphitheater, biotechnology/wet labs.

Student profile.

Out-of-state:	23%	**25 or older:**	34%

Transfer out. Colleges most students transferred to 2008: Frostburg State University, Towson State University, Shepherd University, Shippensburg University, University of Maryland.

Basis for selection. Open admission, but selective for some programs. Admission to nursing and radiography programs based on 2.0 GPA, ACT composite score of 21, 1 laboratory chemistry and algebra. SAT/ACT (ACT preferred) and interview required for nursing and radiography program.

High school preparation. 16 units recommended. Recommended units include English 4, mathematics 3, social studies 1, history 1, science 3 (laboratory 2) and academic electives 2. One chemistry, 1 biology, 2 algebra required of nursing applicants; 1 physics, 1 chemistry, 2 algebra required of radiologic technologies applicants.

2008-2009 Annual costs. Tuition/fees: $3,210; $4,860 out-of-district; $6,270 out-of-state. Per-credit charge: $96 in-district; $151 out-of-district; $198 out-of-state. Books/supplies: $1,200. Personal expenses: $400.

2007-2008 Financial aid. All financial aid based on need. Need-based aid available for part-time students. Work-study available nights, weekends and for part-time students.

Application procedures. Admission: No deadline. No application fee. Admission notification on a rolling basis. **Financial aid:** Priority date 3/1; no closing date. FAFSA required. Applicants notified on a rolling basis starting 5/1.

Academics. Special study options: Accelerated study, cooperative education, cross-registration, distance learning, double major, dual enrollment of high school students, ESL, honors, independent study, internships, liberal arts/career combination. License preparation in nursing, paramedic, radiology, real estate. **Credit/placement by examination:** AP, CLEP, institutional tests. 30 credit hours maximum toward associate degree. **Support services:** GED preparation and test center, learning center, pre-admission summer program, reduced course load, remedial instruction, study skills assistance, tutoring.

Majors. Business: General, accounting technology, banking/financial services, business admin, management information systems, transportation. **Communications technology:** Animation/special effects. **Computer sciences:** General, web page design. **Education:** General, early childhood, elementary. **Engineering:** General. **Engineering technology:** Electromechanical, industrial, mechanical. **Family/consumer sciences:** Child care. **Health:** EMT paramedic, medical radiologic technology/radiation therapy, medical secretary, mental health services, nursing (RN). **Liberal arts:** Arts/sciences. **Protective services:** Police science. **Science technology:** Biological. **Visual/performing arts:** Commercial/advertising art.

Most popular majors. Business/marketing 18%, education 8%, health sciences 21%, liberal arts 43%.

Computing on campus. 500 workstations in library, computer center, student center. Commuter students can connect to campus network. Online course registration, online library, helpline, repair service available.

Student life. Freshman orientation: Available. **Activities:** Jazz band, choral groups, drama, international student organizations, literary magazine, musical theater, student government, student newspaper, Intervarsity Christian Fellowship.

Athletics. NJCAA. **Intercollegiate:** Baseball M, basketball, cheerleading, cross-country, golf, soccer, softball W, tennis, track and field, volleyball W. **Team name:** Hawks.

Student services. Adult student services, career counseling, services for economically disadvantaged, student employment services, financial aid counseling, health services, on-campus daycare, personal counseling, placement for graduates, veterans' counselor. **Physically disabled:** Services for visually, speech, hearing impaired. **Transfer:** Pre-admission transcript evaluation for new students. Transfer adviser, college fairs on campus for students transferring to 4-year colleges.

Contact. E-mail: admissions@hagerstowncc.edu
Phone: (301) 790-2800 ext. 238 Fax: (301) 791-9165
Jennifer Fisher, Director of Admissions, Records and Registration, Hagerstown Community College, 11400 Robinwood Drive, Hagerstown, MD 21742

Harford Community College

Bel Air, Maryland
www.harford.edu **CB code: 5303**

- Public 2-year community college
- Commuter campus in small city

General. Founded in 1957. Regionally accredited. **Enrollment:** 4,936 degree-seeking undergraduates; 1,278 non-degree-seeking students. **Degrees:** 535 associate awarded. **Location:** 25 miles from Baltimore. **Calendar:** Semester, limited summer session. **Full-time faculty:** 100 total; 7% minority, 52% women. **Part-time faculty:** 248 total; 7% minority, 56% women. **Special facilities:** Observatory, art galleries, theater.

Student profile. Among degree-seeking undergraduates, 1,202 enrolled as first-time, first-year students, 429 transferred in from other institutions.

Part-time:	51%	**Hispanic American:**	3%
Out-of-state:	1%	**Native American:**	1%
Women:	61%	**International:**	1%
African American:	14%	**25 or older:**	47%
Asian American:	3%		

Transfer out. Colleges most students transferred to 2008: Towson University, University of Maryland at College Park, University of Baltimore, Salisbury University, University of Maryland Baltimore County.

Basis for selection. Open admission, but selective for some programs. Some restrictions apply for applicants under 16 years old and international students. Nursing program has specific selection criteria. Students with a SAT score of 550 or higher in the critical reading portion or the math section will be exempt from the corresponding Accuplacer section of the assessment. Students not meeting basic requirements must complete transitional courses. **Adult students:** SAT/ACT scores not required.

High school preparation. 12 units recommended. Recommended units include English 4, mathematics 3, social studies 2 and science 3. Several degree programs require additional preparation.

2008-2009 Annual costs. Tuition/fees: $2,607; $5,077 out-of-district; $7,347 out-of-state. Per-credit charge: $79 in-district; $158 out-of-district; $237 out-of-state. Required fees based on $79 per credit in-county fee. Books/supplies: $1,300. Personal expenses: $1,000.

2007-2008 Financial aid. Need-based: Work-study available for part-time students.

Application procedures. Admission: No deadline. No application fee. Admission notification on a rolling basis. Application deadline for nursing June 1. Notification within 30 days. **Financial aid:** Priority date 3/15; no closing date. FAFSA, institutional form required. Applicants notified on a rolling basis starting 4/1; must reply within 2 week(s) of notification.

Academics. Special study options: Cooperative education, distance learning, double major, dual enrollment of high school students, independent study, internships, liberal arts/career combination, weekend college. License preparation in nursing. **Credit/placement by examination:** AP, CLEP, IB, institutional tests. 30 credit hours maximum toward associate degree. **Support services:** GED preparation and test center, learning center, reduced course load, remedial instruction, study skills assistance, tutoring, writing center.

Majors. Agriculture: Business, equestrian studies, horticulture, landscaping, turf management. **Biology:** General. **Business:** General, accounting technology, business admin, management information systems. **Communications:** Media studies. **Computer sciences:** General, computer science, security. **Conservation:** Environmental science, environmental studies. **Education:** General, chemistry, early childhood, elementary, mathematics, physics, secondary. **Engineering:** General. **Engineering technology:** General, CAD/CADD. **Health:** Electroencephalograph technology, massage therapy, medical assistant, nursing (RN). **History:** General. **Interdisciplinary:** Historic preservation. **Legal studies:** General. **Math:** General. **Philosophy/religion:** Philosophy. **Physical sciences:** Chemistry, physics. **Protective services:** Police science. **Psychology:** General. **Public administration:** Social work. **Social sciences:** Anthropology, international relations, political science, sociology. **Visual/performing arts:** General, commercial photography, design, interior design, studio arts, theater design. **Other:** Histotechnology.

Most popular majors. Business/marketing 19%, health sciences 16%, liberal arts 40%, personal/culinary services 9%.

Computing on campus. 750 workstations in library, computer center, student center. Commuter students can connect to campus network. Online course registration, online library, helpline, student web hosting, wireless network available.

Student life. **Freshman orientation:** Available. Preregistration for classes offered. **Activities:** Bands, choral groups, dance, drama, film society, literary magazine, music ensembles, musical theater, radio station, student government, student newspaper, TV station, Black student union, multinational Hispanic student association, political awareness association, Phi Theta Kappa, Campus Christian Life club, College Democrats, College Republicans, multicultural student association.

Athletics. NJCAA. **Intercollegiate:** Baseball M, basketball, golf M, lacrosse, soccer, softball W, tennis, volleyball W. **Intramural:** Badminton, basketball, football (non-tackle), soccer, softball, tennis, volleyball. **Team name:** Fighting Owls.

Student services. Career counseling, student employment services, financial aid counseling, on-campus daycare, personal counseling, placement for graduates, veterans' counselor. **Physically disabled:** Services for visually, speech, hearing impaired. **Transfer:** Pre-admission transcript evaluation for new students. Transfer adviser, college fairs on campus for students transferring to 4-year colleges.

Contact. E-mail: sendinfo@harford.edu
Phone: (410) 836-4107 Fax: (410) 836-4169
Brian Hammond, Coordinator of Admissions, Harford Community College, 401 Thomas Run Road, Bel Air, MD 21015

Howard Community College

Columbia, Maryland
www.howardcc.edu **CB code: 5308**

- Public 2-year community college
- Commuter campus in small city

General. Founded in 1966. Regionally accredited. **Enrollment:** 7,143 degree-seeking undergraduates; 762 non-degree-seeking students. **Degrees:** 635 associate awarded. **Location:** 20 miles from Baltimore, 30 miles from Washington, DC. **Calendar:** Semester, extensive summer session. **Full-time faculty:** 148 total; 27% have terminal degrees, 21% minority, 63% women. **Part-time faculty:** 523 total; 12% have terminal degrees, 27% minority, 62% women. **Class size:** 52% < 20, 45% 20-39, 2% 40-49, 2% 50-99. **Special facilities:** Practice rooms, recital hall, black box theater, art and dance studios, child care facility, conference center, Center for Entrepreneurial and Business Excellence, wellness center, mediation and conflict resolution center, World Languages Institute. **Partnerships:** Formal partnerships with Novell Education Academic Partner, Microsoft Authorized Academic Training Program, Sylvan/Prometric Authorized Testing/Academic Center, Comp Tia Authorized Education Partner, and Regional Cisco Networking Academy.

Student profile. Among degree-seeking undergraduates, 70% enrolled in a transfer program, 30% enrolled in a vocational program, 15% already have a bachelor's degree or higher, 1,651 enrolled as first-time, first-year students.

Part-time:	59%	**Hispanic American:**	5%
Women:	57%	**Native American:**	1%
African American:	23%	**International:**	6%
Asian American:	10%	**25 or older:**	37%

Transfer out. 70% of students enrolled in the transfer program go on to 4-year colleges. **Colleges most students transferred to 2008:** University of Maryland-College Park, University of Maryland-Baltimore County, Towson University, Salisbury University.

Basis for selection. Open admission, but selective for some programs. Special requirements for clinical nursing, radiologic technology, emergency medical services, cardiovascular technology applicants. Selective admission to James W. Rouse Scholars and Silas Craft Collegians programs. SAT or ACT required for admission to James W. Rouse Scholars Program. Mandatory assessment policy. Most students must complete placement testing before completing 12 credits. Placement test exemptions allowed based on SAT/ACT scores. Interview and portfolio recommended for some selective admissions programs. **Adult students:** SAT/ACT scores not required.

High school preparation. College-preparatory program recommended. Recommended units include English 4, mathematics 4, social studies 4, history 3, science 3 (laboratory 2) and foreign language 3. Computer related course involving skills such as word-processing, databases and spreadsheets, as well as the Internet.

2008-2009 Annual costs. Tuition/fees: $3,993; $6,483 out-of-district; $8,193 out-of-state. Books/supplies: $1,200. Personal expenses: $1,000.

2007-2008 Financial aid. **Need-based:** 73% of total undergraduate aid awarded as scholarships/grants, 27% as loans/jobs. Need-based aid available for part-time students. Work-study available nights, weekends and for part-time students.

Application procedures. **Admission:** No deadline. $25 fee, may be waived for applicants with need. Admission notification on a rolling basis. Specific deadlines apply for applications to James W. Rouse Scholars program and clinical nursing program. **Financial aid:** Priority date 3/1; no closing date. FAFSA required. Applicants notified on a rolling basis starting 5/1.

Academics. Pre-admission summer program for disabled students only. **Special study options:** Accelerated study, cooperative education, distance learning, dual enrollment of high school students, ESL, external degree, honors, independent study, internships, liberal arts/career combination, study abroad, teacher certification program, weekend college. License preparation in nursing, paramedic, radiology. **Credit/placement by examination:** AP, CLEP, IB, institutional tests. 30 credit hours maximum toward associate degree. **Support services:** GED preparation, learning center, pre-admission summer program, reduced course load, remedial instruction, study skills assistance, tutoring, writing center.

Majors. **Agriculture:** Horticultural science. **Area/ethnic studies:** American, women's. **Biology:** Biomedical sciences. **Business:** Business admin, financial planning, hospitality admin, management information systems, office management, retailing, sales/distribution. **Communications:** Digital media. **Communications technology:** Desktop publishing. **Computer sciences:** Computer graphics, computer science, information technology, networking, security. **Conservation:** General. **Education:** Early childhood, elementary, secondary. **Engineering:** General. **Engineering technology:** Biomedical, CAD/CADD, electrical, laser/optical, telecommunications. **Family/consumer sciences:** Child development. **Health:** Athletic training, cardiovascular technology, clinical lab technology, EMT paramedic, health services admin, licensed practical nurse, massage therapy, music therapy, nursing (RN), physical therapy assistant, predental, premedicine, prepharmacy, preveterinary, radiologic technology/medical imaging, respiratory therapy assistant, substance abuse counseling, surgical technology. **History:** General. **Interdisciplinary:** Global studies, intercultural. **Legal studies:** Legal secretary. **Liberal arts:** Arts/sciences. **Math:** General. **Mechanic/repair:** Electronics/electrical. **Parks/recreation:** Exercise sciences, health/fitness. **Philosophy/religion:** Philosophy. **Physical sciences:** General. **Protective services:** Criminal justice. **Psychology:** General. **Social sciences:** General, anthropology, criminology, international economics. **Visual/performing arts:** Art, cinematography, commercial/advertising art, dance, design, dramatic, photography, studio arts, theater design.

Most popular majors. Business/marketing 12%, education 6%, health sciences 24%, liberal arts 52%.

Computing on campus. 135 workstations in library, computer center, student center. Commuter students can connect to campus network. Online course registration, online library, helpline, repair service, student web hosting, wireless network available.

Student life. **Freshman orientation:** Available. Preregistration for classes offered. 3-4 hour day or evening program the week before start of fall and spring semesters. **Policies:** Drug- and alcohol-free campus, code of conduct, academic honesty. **Activities:** Jazz band, choral groups, dance, drama, literary magazine, music ensembles, musical theater, student government, student newspaper, TV station, Christian fellowship, Muslim student association, Jewish student union, Desi club, peace/human rights clubs, environmental club, nursing club, ASL/deaf club, leadership club, hospitality club.

Athletics. NJCAA. **Intercollegiate:** Basketball, cross-country, lacrosse, soccer, track and field, volleyball W. **Team name:** Dragons.

Student services. Adult student services, career counseling, services for economically disadvantaged, student employment services, financial aid counseling, on-campus daycare, personal counseling, placement for graduates, veterans' counselor, women's services. **Physically disabled:** Services for visually, speech, hearing impaired. **Learning disabled:** Comprehensive services available. **Transfer:** Pre-admission transcript evaluation for new students. Transfer center, transfer adviser, college fairs on campus for students transferring to 4-year colleges.

Contact. E-mail: adm-adv@howardcc.edu
Phone: (410) 772-4856 Fax: (410) 772-4589
Christy Thomson, Assistant Director of Admissions, Howard Community College, 10901 Little Patuxent Parkway, Columbia, MD 21044-3197

Kaplan College: Hagerstown

Hagerstown, Maryland
www.KC-Hagerstown.com **CB code: 0804**

- For-profit 2-year business and junior college
- Commuter campus in large town
- Interview required

General. Founded in 1938. Accredited by ACICS. **Enrollment:** 611 degree-seeking undergraduates. **Degrees:** 129 associate awarded. **Location:** 70 miles from Baltimore, 70 miles from Washington, DC. **Calendar:** Quarter, limited summer session. **Full-time faculty:** 55 total. **Part-time faculty:** 25 total. **Special facilities:** Firearms training simulator, forensic recovery and evidence detection lab.

Student profile.

Out-of-state:	60%	**Live on campus:**	3%
25 or older:	55%		

Basis for selection. Open admission, but selective for some programs.

2008-2009 Annual costs. Books/supplies: $875. Personal expenses: $960.

2007-2008 Financial aid. Need-based: Need-based aid available for part-time students.

Application procedures. Admission: No deadline. $20 fee. Admission notification on a rolling basis. **Financial aid:** No deadline. FAFSA, institutional form required. Applicants notified on a rolling basis starting 6/1; must reply within 2 week(s) of notification.

Academics. College includes allied health, legal, business, criminal justice, computer forensics and information technology divisions. Several bachelor's programs offered in online courses. **Special study options:** Distance learning, double major, internships. **Credit/placement by examination:** AP, CLEP, institutional tests. 15 credit hours maximum toward associate degree. **Support services:** Reduced course load, remedial instruction, tutoring.

Majors. Business: Accounting, administrative services, business admin, office technology. **Computer sciences:** Computer graphics, data processing, LAN/WAN management, system admin, webmaster. **Health:** Medical assistant, medical records technology, medical secretary, medical transcription. **Legal studies:** Paralegal. **Protective services:** Criminal justice, forensics, law enforcement admin.

Most popular majors. Business/marketing 22%, computer/information sciences 28%, health sciences 39%, legal studies 11%.

Computing on campus. 85 workstations in library, computer center.

Student life. Freshman orientation: Mandatory. **Housing:** Coed dorms available. $150 deposit. **Activities:** Student government.

Student services. Career counseling, student employment services, financial aid counseling, personal counseling, placement for graduates.

Contact. E-mail: info@kc-hagerstown.edu
Phone: (301) 739-2670 Toll-free number: (800) 422-2670
Fax: (301) 791-7661
Jon Filkins, Director of Admissions, Kaplan College: Hagerstown, 18618 Crestwood Drive, Hagerstown, MD 21742

Montgomery College

Rockville, Maryland — **CB member**
www.montgomerycollege.edu — **CB code: 5440**

- Public 2-year community college
- Commuter campus in very large city

General. Founded in 1946. Regionally accredited. Additional campuses in Takoma Park/Silver Spring and Germantown. **Enrollment:** 18,004 degree-seeking undergraduates; 6,448 non-degree-seeking students. **Degrees:** 1,736 associate awarded. **Location:** 5 miles from Washington, DC. **Calendar:** Semester, extensive summer session. **Full-time faculty:** 517 total; 34% have terminal degrees, 29% minority, 56% women. **Part-time faculty:** 763 total; 25% have terminal degrees, 30% minority, 56% women. **Class size:** 36% < 20, 62% 20-39, less than 1% 40-49, 2% 50-99. **Special facilities:** Performing arts center, child care center, planetarium.

Student profile. Among degree-seeking undergraduates, 55% enrolled in a transfer program, 18% enrolled in a vocational program, 4% already have a bachelor's degree or higher, 4,965 enrolled as first-time, first-year students, 988 transferred in from other institutions.

Part-time:	59%	**Women:**	52%
Out-of-state:	4%	**25 or older:**	36%

Transfer out. 60% of students enrolled in the transfer program go on to 4-year colleges. **Colleges most students transferred to 2008:** University of Maryland: College Park, University of Maryland: Baltimore County, Towson State University, University of Maryland: University College, Salisbury University.

Basis for selection. Open admission, but selective for some programs. Admission to allied medical health programs considers standardized test scores, secondary school record, geographical residence, and state residence. Montgomery County residents get first priority; GPA rank within residency category is important. Audition required for music majors and School of Art & Design admissions process requires a portfolio review/interview.

High school preparation. College-preparatory program recommended. Recommended units include English 4, mathematics 3 and science 2.

2008-2009 Annual costs. Tuition/fees: $3,984; $7,728 out-of-district; $10,320 out-of-state. Books/supplies: $1,200. Personal expenses: $1,380.

2007-2008 Financial aid. Need-based: 78% of total undergraduate aid awarded as scholarships/grants, 22% as loans/jobs. Need-based aid available for part-time students. Work-study available nights, weekends and for part-time students. **Non-need-based:** Scholarships awarded for academics, alumni affiliation, art, music/drama, state residency.

Application procedures. Admission: No deadline. $25 fee, may be waived for applicants with need. Admission notification on a rolling basis. **Financial aid:** Priority date 5/15; no closing date. FAFSA, institutional form required. Applicants notified on a rolling basis starting 5/30.

Academics. Special study options: Accelerated study, cooperative education, distance learning, double major, dual enrollment of high school students, ESL, honors, independent study, internships, student-designed major, study abroad, teacher certification program, weekend college. License preparation in nursing, physical therapy, radiology, real estate. **Credit/placement by examination:** AP, CLEP, institutional tests. 45 credit hours maximum toward associate degree. **Support services:** GED preparation and test center, learning center, pre-admission summer program, remedial instruction, study skills assistance, tutoring, writing center.

Majors. Agriculture: General. **Architecture:** Technology. **Biology:** Biochemistry. **Business:** General, accounting technology, business admin, construction management, hospitality admin, hotel/motel admin, international, management information systems. **Communications:** Advertising, broadcast journalism. **Communications technology:** Desktop publishing, graphic/printing, graphics. **Computer sciences:** General, computer graphics, computer science, information systems, programming. **Education:** General, early childhood, science. **Engineering:** General, civil. **Engineering technology:** Architectural, biomedical, civil, drafting, electrical. **Family/consumer sciences:** Child care, institutional food production. **Foreign languages:** American Sign Language. **Health:** Medical radiologic technology/radiation therapy, medical records technology, nursing (RN), physical therapy assistant, predental, premedicine, prepharmacy, sonography, surgical technology. **Interdisciplinary:** Biological/physical sciences. **Legal studies:** Paralegal. **Liberal arts:** Arts/sciences. **Math:** General. **Mechanic/repair:** Automotive. **Parks/recreation:** Exercise sciences. **Personal/culinary services:** Food service. **Physical sciences:** Physics. **Protective services:** Firefighting, law enforcement admin. **Science technology:** Biological. **Visual/performing arts:** General, art history/conservation, commercial photography, commercial/advertising art, dance, interior design, photography, studio arts, theater design. **Other:** Applied geography.

Most popular majors. Business/marketing 18%, engineering/engineering technologies 6%, health sciences 11%, liberal arts 52%.

Computing on campus. 400 workstations in library, computer center. Commuter students can connect to campus network. Online course registration, online library, helpline, wireless network available.

Student life. Freshman orientation: Available. Preregistration for classes offered. **Activities:** Concert band, choral groups, dance, drama, international student organizations, music ensembles, musical theater, radio station, student government, student newspaper, TV station, Jewish student association, progressive student alliance, Christian fellowship, lesbian student alliance, Students Against Driving Drunk, African-American student organization, Hispanic student organization, Asian student organization.

Athletics. NJCAA. **Intercollegiate:** Baseball M, basketball, cross-country, field hockey W, golf M, lacrosse M, soccer, softball W, tennis, track and field, volleyball W, wrestling M. **Intramural:** Basketball.

Student services. Adult student services, career counseling, services for economically disadvantaged, student employment services, financial aid counseling, minority student services, on-campus daycare, personal counseling, placement for graduates, veterans' counselor. **Physically disabled:** Services for visually, speech, hearing impaired. **Learning disabled:** Comprehensive services available. **Transfer:** Re-entry adviser, pre-admission transcript evaluation for new students. Transfer center, transfer adviser, college fairs on campus for students transferring to 4-year colleges.

Contact. Phone: (240) 567-5034 Fax: (240) 567-5037
Sherman Helberg, Director of Enrollment Management, Montgomery College, 51 Mannakee Street, Rockville, MD 20850

Prince George's Community College

Largo, Maryland
www.pgcc.edu
CB member
CB code: 5545

- Public 2-year community college
- Commuter campus in very large city

General. Founded in 1958. Regionally accredited. Extension center at Andrews Air Force Base serves both military and civilian personnel. **Enrollment:** 10,752 degree-seeking undergraduates. **Degrees:** 734 associate awarded. **ROTC:** Army, Air Force. **Location:** 10 miles from Washington, DC. **Calendar:** Semester, limited summer session. **Full-time faculty:** 244 total. **Part-time faculty:** 457 total. **Class size:** 64% < 20, 35% 20-39, less than 1% 40-49, less than 1% 50-99. **Special facilities:** Natatorium, art gallery.

Student profile.

Out-of-state:	4%	**25 or older:**	47%

Transfer out. Colleges most students transferred to 2008: University of Maryland-College Park, Bowie State University, University of Maryland-University College, Morgan State University.

Basis for selection. Open admission, but selective for some programs. Special requirements for health technology programs and for international students. Health technology program requires high school diploma or GED. For some scholarship awards or honors program consideration, SAT combined score of 1050 or above (exclusive of writing) required. SAT or ACT scores may be used in place of college's placement tests.

High school preparation. Recommended units include English 4, mathematics 4, social studies 3, history 3, science 3 (laboratory 2) and academic electives 4. One computer literacy recommended.

2008-2009 Annual costs. Tuition/fees: $3,920; $6,050 out-of-district; $8,690 out-of-state. Per-credit charge: $96 in-district; $167 out-of-district; $255 out-of-state. Instructional services fees range from $27 to $37 per credit depending on course. Books/supplies: $723.

2007-2008 Financial aid. All financial aid based on need. 77% of total undergraduate aid awarded as scholarships/grants, 23% as loans/jobs. Need-based aid available for part-time students. Work-study available for part-time students.

Application procedures. Admission: No deadline. $25 fee. Admission notification on a rolling basis. **Financial aid:** Priority date 6/1; no closing date. FAFSA, institutional form required. Applicants notified on a rolling basis starting 6/1; must reply within 2 week(s) of notification.

Academics. Special study options: Cooperative education, distance learning, double major, dual enrollment of high school students, ESL, honors, independent study, liberal arts/career combination, teacher certification program, weekend college. License preparation in nursing, paramedic, real estate. **Credit/placement by examination:** AP, CLEP, institutional tests. 30 credit hours maximum toward associate degree. **Support services:** GED preparation, learning center, reduced course load, remedial instruction, study skills assistance, tutoring, writing center.

Majors. Area/ethnic studies: African-American, American, women's. **Biology:** General. **Business:** Accounting, administrative services, business admin, marketing, office management, office technology. **Computer sciences:** General, computer science, information systems, programming, systems analysis. **Education:** Business, early childhood, elementary, health, mathematics, physical, science, secondary. **Engineering:** General, aerospace. **Engineering technology:** Drafting, electrical. **Family/consumer sciences:** Child care. **Health:** EMT paramedic, medical radiologic technology/radiation therapy, medical records admin, medical records technology, medical secretary, nuclear medical technology, nursing (RN), premedicine, prepharmacy, respiratory therapy technology. **Legal studies:** Legal secretary, paralegal. **Liberal arts:** Arts/sciences. **Physical sciences:** Chemistry. **Protective services:** Criminal justice, forensics. **Psychology:** General. **Visual/performing arts:** Commercial/advertising art, studio arts.

Computing on campus. 950 workstations in library, computer center, student center. Commuter students can connect to campus network. Helpline, repair service available.

Student life. Freshman orientation: Available. Preregistration for classes offered. **Activities:** Choral groups, drama, film society, international student organizations, literary magazine, music ensembles, musical theater, opera, student government, student newspaper, TV station, Union of Black Scholars, Active Seniors (for senior citizens), student program board, Spanish club, French club, Caribbean students club, Muslim society, women's Bible study.

Athletics. NJCAA. **Intercollegiate:** Baseball M, basketball, bowling, golf, soccer, softball W, tennis M, volleyball W. **Intramural:** Basketball, bowling, golf, racquetball, soccer, table tennis, volleyball. **Team name:** Owls.

Student services. Adult student services, career counseling, services for economically disadvantaged, student employment services, financial aid counseling, health services, minority student services, on-campus daycare, personal counseling, placement for graduates, veterans' counselor. **Physically disabled:** Services for visually, speech, hearing impaired. **Learning disabled:** Comprehensive services available. **Transfer:** Re-entry adviser for new students. Transfer center, transfer adviser, college fairs on campus for students transferring to 4-year colleges.

Contact. E-mail: enrollmentservices@pgcc.edu
Phone: (301) 322-0801 Fax: (301) 322-0119
Vera Bagley, Director of Admissions and Records, Prince George's Community College, 301 Largo Road, Largo, MD 20774

TESST College of Technology: Baltimore

Baltimore, Maryland
www.tesst.com/tesstPortal

- For-profit 2-year technical college
- Very large city

General. Regionally accredited; also accredited by ACCSCT. **Enrollment:** 900 degree-seeking undergraduates. **Degrees:** 27 associate awarded. **Calendar:** Semester. **Full-time faculty:** 32 total. **Part-time faculty:** 22 total.

Basis for selection. Open admission, but selective for some programs. Institutional evaluation test may be accepted in lieu of SAT/ACT.

2008-2009 Annual costs. Cost for complete program is $13,300-$31,200, depending on field of study.

Application procedures. Admission: No deadline. $20 fee. Admission notification on a rolling basis. **Financial aid:** No deadline.

Academics. Credit/placement by examination: AP, CLEP.

Majors. Computer sciences: Information systems. **Engineering technology:** Electrical, telecommunications.

Contact. Phone: (410) 644-6400 Fax: (410) 644-6481
William Scott, Director of Admissions, TESST College of Technology: Baltimore, 1520 South Caton Avenue, Baltimore, MD 21227-1063

TESST College of Technology: Beltsville

Beltsville, Maryland
www.tesst.com

- For-profit 2-year technical college
- Large town

General. Accredited by ACCSCT. **Enrollment:** 615 degree-seeking undergraduates. **Degrees:** 76 associate awarded. **Calendar:** Semester. **Full-time faculty:** 10 total.

Basis for selection. Open admission.

2008-2009 Annual costs. Cost for complete program is $13,300-$31,200 depending on field of study.

Academics. Credit/placement by examination: CLEP.

Majors. Computer sciences: Data entry, information systems.

Contact. E-mail: dedmonds@tesst.com
Phone: (301) 937-8448 Toll-free number: (800) 488-3778
Sandra Ugol, President, TESST College of Technology: Beltsville, 4600 Powder Mill Road, Beltsville, MD 20705

TESST College of Technology: Towson

Towson, Maryland
www.tesst.com

- For-profit 2-year technical college
- Small city

General. Accredited by ACCSCT. **Location:** 15 miles from Baltimore. **Calendar:** Semester.

Contact. Phone: (410) 296-5350
Director of Admissions, 803 Glen Eagles Court, Towson, MD 21286

Wor-Wic Community College
Salisbury, Maryland
www.worwic.edu **CB code: 1613**

- Public 2-year community college
- Commuter campus in large town

General. Founded in 1975. Regionally accredited. **Enrollment:** 3,278 degree-seeking undergraduates; 394 non-degree-seeking students. **Degrees:** 246 associate awarded. **Location:** 110 miles from Baltimore, 120 miles from Washington, DC. **Calendar:** Semester, limited summer session. **Full-time faculty:** 67 total; 27% have terminal degrees, 9% minority, 58% women. **Part-time faculty:** 105 total; 8% have terminal degrees, 10% minority, 69% women. **Class size:** 44% < 20, 47% 20-39, 6% 40-49, 3% 50-99. **Partnerships:** Formal partnership with local medical center to provide financial and clinical support to the college's health programs.

Student profile. Among degree-seeking undergraduates, 42% enrolled in a transfer program, 58% enrolled in a vocational program, 808 enrolled as first-time, first-year students, 307 transferred in from other institutions.

Part-time:	64%	**Asian American:**	1%
Out-of-state:	2%	**Hispanic American:**	1%
Women:	66%	**Native American:**	1%
African American:	25%	**25 or older:**	41%

Transfer out. 81% of students enrolled in the transfer program go on to 4-year colleges. **Colleges most students transferred to 2008:** Salisbury University, University of Maryland Eastern Shore.

Basis for selection. Open admission, but selective for some programs. Special requirements for emergency medical services, nursing and radiologic technology programs.

High school preparation. College-preparatory program recommended. Recommended units include English 4 and mathematics 2.

2009-2010 Annual costs. Tuition/fees (projected): $2,594; $6,104 out-of-district; $7,094 out-of-state. Per-credit charge: $80 in-district; $197 out-of-district; $230 out-of-state. Books/supplies: $1,400. Personal expenses: $1,000.

2008-2009 Financial aid. Need-based: Need-based aid available for part-time students. Work-study available nights, weekends and for part-time students. **Non-need-based:** Scholarships awarded for academics, state residency.

Application procedures. Admission: No deadline. No application fee. Application must be submitted on paper. Admission notification on a rolling basis. **Financial aid:** Priority date 6/1; no closing date. FAFSA, institutional form required. Applicants notified on a rolling basis starting 4/1.

Academics. Special study options: Distance learning, double major, dual enrollment of high school students, ESL, honors, internships. License preparation in nursing, paramedic, radiology. **Credit/placement by examination:** AP, CLEP, institutional tests. 30 credit hours maximum toward associate degree. **Support services:** Learning center, reduced course load, remedial instruction, tutoring, writing center.

Majors. Business: General, accounting technology, administrative services, business admin, hospitality admin. **Computer sciences:** General, systems analysis. **Education:** General, early childhood, elementary. **Engineering technology:** Drafting, electrical. **Family/consumer sciences:** Child care. **Health:** EMT paramedic, medical radiologic technology/radiation therapy, nursing (RN), substance abuse counseling. **Interdisciplinary:** Biological/physical sciences. **Protective services:** Police science.

Most popular majors. Business/marketing 18%, computer/information sciences 6%, health sciences 28%, liberal arts 31%.

Computing on campus. 613 workstations in library, computer center, student center. Commuter students can connect to campus network. Online library available.

Student life. Freshman orientation: Available. Preregistration for classes offered. **Activities:** Choral groups, drama, literary magazine, student government, student newspaper.

Student services. Career counseling, student employment services, financial aid counseling, on-campus daycare, personal counseling, placement for graduates, veterans' counselor. **Physically disabled:** Services for visually, speech, hearing impaired. **Transfer:** College fairs on campus for students transferring to 4-year colleges.

Contact. E-mail: admissions@worwic.edu
Phone: (410) 334-2895 Fax: (410) 334-2954
Richard Webster, Director of Admissions, Wor-Wic Community College, 32000 Campus Drive, Salisbury, MD 21804

Massachusetts

Bay State College

Boston, Massachusetts
www.baystate.edu
CB code: 3120

- Private 2-year junior college
- Commuter campus in very large city
- Application essay, interview required

General. Founded in 1946. Regionally accredited. **Enrollment:** 810 degree-seeking undergraduates. **Degrees:** 35 bachelor's, 132 associate awarded. **Calendar:** Semester, limited summer session. **Full-time faculty:** 17 total. **Part-time faculty:** 73 total.

Student profile.

25 or older:	12%	**Live on campus:**	30%

Basis for selection. Special consideration to students with lower than 2.0 GPA; interview and 2 recommendations from guidance counselors. Writing sample and second interview may be requested.

High school preparation. Recommended units include English 4, mathematics 2, social studies 1, history 1, science 2 (laboratory 1).

2008-2009 Annual costs. Tuition/fees: $19,350. Per-credit charge: $788. Program specific fees for allied health, $475 and fashion design, $300. Room/board: $11,130. Books/supplies: $1,000. Personal expenses: $1,800.

2007-2008 Financial aid. Need-based: 28% of total undergraduate aid awarded as scholarships/grants, 72% as loans/jobs. Need-based aid available for part-time students. Work-study available nights, weekends and for part-time students.

Application procedures. Admission: No deadline. $40 fee, may be waived for applicants with need. Admission notification on a rolling basis. **Financial aid:** Priority date 3/15; no closing date. FAFSA, institutional form required. Applicants notified on a rolling basis starting 3/15; must reply within 3 week(s) of notification.

Academics. Special study options: Cooperative education, ESL, honors, independent study, internships. Bachelor's degree programs available on campus. License preparation in occupational therapy, physical therapy. **Credit/placement by examination:** CLEP, IB, institutional tests. 9 credit hours maximum toward associate degree. **Support services:** Learning center, reduced course load, study skills assistance, tutoring.

Majors. Business: Accounting, administrative services, business admin, fashion, hospitality/recreation, marketing, office management, sales/distribution, tourism promotion. **Computer sciences:** General. **Education:** Early childhood. **Health:** Medical assistant, medical secretary, occupational therapy assistant, physical therapy assistant. **Legal studies:** Legal secretary, paralegal. **Protective services:** Law enforcement admin. **Visual/performing arts:** Fashion design. **Other:** Entertainment management.

Most popular majors. Business/marketing 73%, health sciences 27%.

Computing on campus. 62 workstations in computer center, student center.

Student life. Freshman orientation: Mandatory. Preregistration for classes offered. **Housing:** Coed dorms, single-sex dorms available. $200 deposit, deadline 3/1. **Activities:** Literary magazine, clubs associated with majors, student activities club, international club, community service.

Student services. Adult student services, career counseling, student employment services, financial aid counseling, health services, personal counseling, placement for graduates, veterans' counselor. **Transfer:** Pre-admission transcript evaluation for new students. Transfer adviser, college fairs on campus for students transferring to 4-year colleges.

Contact. E-mail: admissions@baystate.edu
Phone: (617) 217-9155 Toll-free number: (800) 815-3276
Fax: (617) 536-1735
Kim Olds, Director of Admissions, Bay State College, 122 Commonwealth Avenue, Boston, MA 02116

Benjamin Franklin Institute of Technology

Boston, Massachusetts
www.bfit.edu
CB member
CB code: 3394

- Private 2-year technical college
- Commuter campus in very large city

General. Founded in 1908. Regionally accredited. Founded under provisions of the will of Benjamin Franklin and managed by Franklin Foundation. **Enrollment:** 529 degree-seeking undergraduates. **Degrees:** 5 bachelor's, 85 associate awarded. **Calendar:** Semester, limited summer session. **Full-time faculty:** 31 total. **Part-time faculty:** 35 total. **Special facilities:** Extensive labs for automotive, architecture, computer, electronic, electrical, opticianry, pharmacy, and mechanized engineering technologies.

Student profile.

Out-of-state:	5%	**25 or older:**	13%

Transfer out. Colleges most students transferred to 2008: Northeastern University, University of Massachusetts at Lowell, Worcester Polytech, Wentworth Institute.

Basis for selection. School achievement record, particularly in math and science, most important. SAT or ACT recommended. Interview and essay recommended.

High school preparation. 8 units required. Required and recommended units include English 4, mathematics 3-5 and science 1-3. Level of math and science required varies by program.

2008-2009 Annual costs. Tuition/fees: $13,350. Per-credit charge: $556. Cost shown is for certificate program. Books/supplies: $600.

2007-2008 Financial aid. Need-based: Need-based aid available for part-time students. **Non-need-based:** Scholarships awarded for academics.

Application procedures. Admission: Priority date 5/1; no deadline. $25 fee, may be waived for applicants with need. Admission notification on a rolling basis. **Financial aid:** Priority date 4/1; no closing date. FAFSA required. Applicants notified on a rolling basis starting 3/1; must reply within 4 week(s) of notification.

Academics. Special study options: ESL, liberal arts/career combination. Bachelor's degree programs available on campus. **Credit/placement by examination:** CLEP, IB, institutional tests. **Support services:** Learning center, pre-admission summer program, reduced course load, remedial instruction, study skills assistance, tutoring.

Majors. Architecture: Technology. **Biology:** Biomedical sciences. **Computer sciences:** General, programming. **Construction:** Electrician. **Engineering technology:** Architectural, automotive, biomedical, computer, computer hardware, computer systems, electrical, mechanical, mechanical drafting. **Mechanic/repair:** General, automotive.

Computing on campus. 120 workstations in library, computer center. Wireless network available.

Student life. Freshman orientation: Mandatory. Preregistration for classes offered. Half-day program held in August. **Housing:** Student housing available at Boston University. **Activities:** Student government, student newspaper.

Athletics. NJCAA. **Intercollegiate:** Soccer M. **Intramural:** Basketball M. **Team name:** Shockers.

Student services. Career counseling, student employment services, financial aid counseling, personal counseling, placement for graduates, veterans' counselor. **Transfer:** Pre-admission transcript evaluation for new students. Transfer adviser, college fairs on campus for students transferring to 4-year colleges.

Contact. E-mail: admissions@bfit.edu
Phone: (617) 423-4630 ext. 121 Fax: (617) 482-3706
Andrea Dawes, Director of Admissions, Benjamin Franklin Institute of Technology, 41 Berkeley Street, Boston, MA 02116

Berkshire Community College

Pittsfield, Massachusetts
www.berkshirecc.edu
CB member
CB code: 3102

- Public 2-year community college
- Commuter campus in large town

General. Founded in 1960. Regionally accredited. Elderhostel program site, children's circus. **Enrollment:** 1,841 degree-seeking undergraduates; 434 non-degree-seeking students. **Degrees:** 235 associate awarded. **Location:** 40 miles from Albany, New York. **Calendar:** Semester, limited summer session. **Full-time faculty:** 53 total; 72% have terminal degrees, 68% women. **Part-time faculty:** 122 total; 50% have terminal degrees, less than 1% minority, 44% women. **Class size:** 16% < 20, 84% 20-39. **Special facilities:** Global positioning laboratory, nature trail, computer animation, graphics laboratory. **Partnerships:** Formal partnerships with Plastics Network, Applied Technology Council, Berkshire Works, Tech-Prep programs, service learning programs.

Student profile. Among degree-seeking undergraduates, 39% enrolled in a transfer program, 61% enrolled in a vocational program, 497 enrolled as first-time, first-year students.

Part-time:	47%	**Asian American:**	2%
Out-of-state:	3%	**Hispanic American:**	4%
Women:	62%	**International:**	2%
African American:	6%	**25 or older:**	36%

Transfer out. 48% of students enrolled in the transfer program go on to 4-year colleges. **Colleges most students transferred to 2008:** University of Massachusetts-Amherst, Massachusetts College of Liberal Arts, Westfield State College, SUNY, Sage Colleges.

Basis for selection. Open admission, but selective for some programs. Special requirements for nursing and allied health programs. Fall-only admission to nursing and allied health programs.

High school preparation. 1 chemistry, 1 biology, 1 algebra, demonstrated college level English skills required for nursing and health program applicants.

2008-2009 Annual costs. Tuition/fees: $3,930; $11,550 out-of-state. Per-credit charge: $26 in-state; $280 out-of-state. Books/supplies: $810. Personal expenses: $2,316.

2007-2008 Financial aid. Need-based: 68% of total undergraduate aid awarded as scholarships/grants, 32% as loans/jobs. Need-based aid available for part-time students. Work-study available nights, weekends and for part-time students. **Non-need-based:** Scholarships awarded for academics, job skills, leadership, state residency. **Additional information:** Tuition waivers available to Massachusetts residents who fall into one of the following categories: Department of Social Services adopted or foster children, Massachusetts Rehabilitation Commission clients, high-scoring MCAS students, National Guard members, Native Americans, state employees and their dependents, veterans.

Application procedures. Admission: No deadline. $10 fee ($35 out-of-state), may be waived for applicants with need. Application must be submitted on paper. Admission notification on a rolling basis. **Financial aid:** Priority date 5/1; no closing date. FAFSA required. Applicants notified on a rolling basis starting 5/10; must reply within 2 week(s) of notification.

Academics. Special study options: Cooperative education, cross-registration, distance learning, double major, dual enrollment of high school students, ESL, honors, independent study, internships, liberal arts/career combination, student-designed major, study abroad. License preparation in nursing, occupational therapy, physical therapy. **Credit/placement by examination:** AP, CLEP, IB, institutional tests. 30 credit hours maximum toward associate degree. **Support services:** GED test center, learning center, pre-admission summer program, reduced course load, remedial instruction, study skills assistance, tutoring, writing center.

Majors. Business: General, business admin, hospitality admin, office technology. **Computer sciences:** General. **Conservation:** Environmental science. **Engineering:** General. **Engineering technology:** Electrical. **Health:** Health services, nursing (RN), physical therapy assistant, respiratory therapy technology. **Liberal arts:** Arts/sciences. **Protective services:** Criminal justice, firefighting. **Public administration:** Community org/advocacy. **Visual/performing arts:** General.

Most popular majors. Business/marketing 19%, health sciences 22%, liberal arts 34%, security/protective services 6%, visual/performing arts 7%.

Computing on campus. 376 workstations in library, computer center, student center. Online library, helpline, wireless network available.

Student life. Freshman orientation: Mandatory. Preregistration for classes offered. Variety of options, including 1-day orientation/registration and 2-week summer transition program. **Policies:** Alcohol-free campus. **Activities:** Bands, choral groups, dance, drama, literary magazine, music ensembles, musical theater, student government, TV station, Phi Theta Kappa honor society.

Student services. Adult student services, alcohol/substance abuse counseling, career counseling, services for economically disadvantaged, student employment services, financial aid counseling, minority student services, on-campus daycare, personal counseling, placement for graduates, veterans' counselor, women's services. **Physically disabled:** Services for visually, speech, hearing impaired. **Learning disabled:** Comprehensive services available. **Transfer:** Re-entry adviser, pre-admission transcript evaluation for new students. Transfer adviser, college fairs on campus for students transferring to 4-year colleges.

Contact. E-mail: admissions@berkshirecc.edu
Phone: (413) 236-1630 Toll-free number: (800) 816-1233 ext. 1630
Fax: (413) 496-9511
Michael Bullock, Dean of Student Affairs and Enrollment Services, Berkshire Community College, 1350 West Street, Pittsfield, MA 01201-5786

Bristol Community College

Fall River, Massachusetts — **CB member**
www.bristolcc.edu — **CB code: 3110**

- Public 2-year community college
- Commuter campus in small city

General. Founded in 1965. Regionally accredited. **Enrollment:** 6,598 degree-seeking undergraduates; 1,502 non-degree-seeking students. **Degrees:** 728 associate awarded. **Location:** 48 miles from Boston; 17 miles from Providence, Rhode Island. **Calendar:** Semester, extensive summer session. **Full-time faculty:** 100 total. **Part-time faculty:** 330 total. **Special facilities:** Planetarium, greenhouse, robotics laboratory, aquaculture laboratory. **Partnerships:** Formal partnerships with local businesses and non-profit organizations.

Student profile. Among degree-seeking undergraduates, 1,820 enrolled as first-time, first-year students.

Part-time:	47%	**Women:**	61%
Out-of-state:	15%	**25 or older:**	49%

Basis for selection. Open admission, but selective for some programs. Special requirements for health science and culinary arts programs. SAT scores required for allied health programs. **Homeschooled:** Letter of approval from student's school district that authenticates homeschool education required.

High school preparation. Health science programs require certain grades on specified courses.

2008-2009 Annual costs. Tuition/fees: $3,840; $10,020 out-of-state. Per-credit charge: $24 in-state; $230 out-of-state. Books/supplies: $1,000. Personal expenses: $4,840.

2007-2008 Financial aid. Need-based: Need-based aid available for part-time students. Work-study available nights, weekends and for part-time students. **Non-need-based:** Scholarships awarded for academics, art, leadership, minority status, music/drama.

Application procedures. Admission: No deadline. $10 fee ($35 out-of-state), may be waived for applicants with need, free for online applicants. Admission notification on a rolling basis beginning on or about 12/1. Must reply by May 1 or within 2 week(s) if notified thereafter. **Financial aid:** Priority date 5/1; no closing date. FAFSA, institutional form required. Applicants notified on a rolling basis starting 5/1; must reply within 2 week(s) of notification.

Academics. Students must complete general education requirement core curriculum prior to graduation. **Special study options:** Cooperative education, cross-registration, distance learning, dual enrollment of high school students, ESL, honors, independent study, internships, student-designed major, weekend college. **Credit/placement by examination:** CLEP, institutional tests. 30 credit hours maximum toward associate degree. **Support services:** GED preparation and test center, learning center, pre-admission summer program, reduced course load, remedial instruction, tutoring, writing center.

Majors. Business: Accounting, banking/financial services, business admin. **Communications:** General. **Computer sciences:** General, computer science, data processing, information systems, programming. **Education:** Early childhood, elementary, kindergarten/preschool. **Engineering:** General, environmental, manufacturing, mechanical, science, structural. **Engineering technology:** Environmental, water quality. **Family/consumer sciences:** Child care. **Foreign languages:** American Sign Language. **Health:** Clinical lab technology, dental hygiene, medical records technology, medical secretary, nursing (RN), occupational therapy assistant. **Legal studies:** Paralegal. **Liberal arts:** Arts/sciences. **Protective services:** Criminal justice, firefighting. **Visual/performing arts:** Art, dramatic.

Most popular majors. Business/marketing 23%, education 8%, health sciences 12%, liberal arts 31%, security/protective services 9%.

Computing on campus. Dormitories linked to campus network. Commuter students can connect to campus network. Online course registration, online library, helpline available.

Student life. **Freshman orientation:** Available. Preregistration for classes offered. **Activities:** Campus ministries, choral groups, dance, drama, international student organizations, radio station, student government, student newspaper, TV station, Catholic student association, Christian Fellowship, water watch, international club, Portuguese club, Latino club, Cambodian association, human services club, coalition for social justice.

Athletics. NJCAA. **Intercollegiate:** Basketball, soccer. **Team name:** Bristol Bee's.

Student services. Adult student services, alcohol/substance abuse counseling, chaplain/spiritual director, career counseling, student employment services, financial aid counseling, health services, minority student services, on-campus daycare, personal counseling, placement for graduates, veterans' counselor. **Physically disabled:** Services for visually, speech, hearing impaired. **Learning disabled:** Comprehensive services available. **Transfer:** Transfer adviser, college fairs on campus for students transferring to 4-year colleges.

Contact. E-mail: admissions@bristolcc.edu
Phone: (508) 678-2811 ext. 2516 Toll-free number: (800) 462-0035
Fax: (508) 730-3265
Rodney Clark, Dean of Admissions, Bristol Community College, 777 Elsbree Street, Fall River, MA 02720-7395

Bunker Hill Community College

Boston, Massachusetts — **CB member**
www.bhcc.mass.edu — **CB code: 3123**

- Public 2-year community college
- Commuter campus in very large city

General. Founded in 1973. Regionally accredited. **Enrollment:** 7,313 degree-seeking undergraduates; 2,184 non-degree-seeking students. **Degrees:** 621 associate awarded. **Location:** 5 miles from downtown. **Calendar:** Semester, extensive summer session. **Full-time faculty:** 130 total. **Part-time faculty:** 413 total. **Class size:** 38% < 20, 62% 20-39, less than 1% 40-49, less than 1% 50-99.

Student profile. Among degree-seeking undergraduates, 58% enrolled in a transfer program, 42% enrolled in a vocational program, 1,590 enrolled as first-time, first-year students.

Part-time:	60%	**Hispanic American:**	16%
Women:	59%	**International:**	9%
African American:	25%	**25 or older:**	49%
Asian American:	13%		

Transfer out. **Colleges most students transferred to 2008:** University of Massachusetts Boston, Salem State College, Northeastern University, Bentley College, Suffolk University.

Basis for selection. Open admission, but selective for some programs. Special requirements for nursing, medical radiography, surgical technology, ultrasound, overhead electrical line worker programs. **Homeschooled:** Must submit evidence that program was approved by school district's superintendent or school committee. If under the age of 16, a letter from school district's superintendent or school committe required as well.

2008-2009 Annual costs. Tuition/fees: $3,480; $9,660 out-of-state. Per-credit charge: $24 in-state; $230 out-of-state. New England Regional Tuition: $112 per-credit-hour. Books/supplies: $1,200. Personal expenses: $1,600.

2007-2008 Financial aid. **Need-based:** 89% of total undergraduate aid awarded as scholarships/grants, 11% as loans/jobs. Need-based aid available for part-time students. Work-study available for part-time students. **Non-need-based:** Scholarships awarded for academics.

Application procedures. **Admission:** Priority date 5/1; deadline 9/2. $10 fee ($35 out-of-state), may be waived for applicants with need. Application must be submitted on paper. Admission notification on a rolling basis. Must reply by May 1 or within 2 week(s) if notified thereafter. **Financial aid:** Priority date 4/15; no closing date. FAFSA required. Applicants notified on a rolling basis starting 6/1; must reply within 2 week(s) of notification.

Academics. Some courses taught off-campus in the community. **Special study options:** Cross-registration, distance learning, double major, dual enrollment of high school students, ESL, external degree, honors, independent study, internships, liberal arts/career combination, study abroad, weekend college. License preparation in nursing, paramedic, radiology, real estate. **Credit/placement by examination:** AP, CLEP, institutional tests. 45 credit hours maximum toward associate degree. **Support services:** GED preparation, learning center, pre-admission summer program, reduced course load, remedial instruction, study skills assistance, tutoring, writing center.

Majors. **Biology:** General. **Business:** Accounting, business admin, finance, hospitality admin, international, office/clerical, operations, tourism/travel. **Communications:** General. **Computer sciences:** Applications programming, computer science, data entry, networking, system admin, web page design, word processing. **Education:** General. **Engineering:** General, biomedical. **Foreign languages:** General. **Health:** Cardiovascular technology, medical radiologic technology/radiation therapy, medical secretary, nuclear medical technology, nursing (RN), respiratory therapy technology, sonography. **History:** General. **Math:** General. **Physical sciences:** Chemistry, physics. **Protective services:** Corrections, law enforcement admin, security management. **Psychology:** General. **Public administration:** Human services. **Social sciences:** Sociology. **Visual/performing arts:** Art, design, dramatic.

Most popular majors. Business/marketing 29%, health sciences 28%, liberal arts 10%.

Computing on campus. 668 workstations in library, computer center. Commuter students can connect to campus network. Online course registration, online library, helpline, wireless network available.

Student life. **Freshman orientation:** Available. Preregistration for classes offered. **Activities:** Jazz band, choral groups, dance, drama, film society, international student organizations, literary magazine, music ensembles, radio station, student government, African American cultural society, African student club, Alpha Kappa Mu honor society, Amnesty International, Arab students association, Asian students association, Brazilian cultural club, criminal justice society, gay/lesbian/bisexual/transgender student union, multicultural club.

Athletics. NJCAA. **Intercollegiate:** Baseball M, basketball, golf, soccer, softball W. **Intramural:** Basketball, table tennis, tennis. **Team name:** Bulldogs.

Student services. Adult student services, career counseling, services for economically disadvantaged, student employment services, financial aid counseling, health services, on-campus daycare, personal counseling, placement for graduates, veterans' counselor. **Physically disabled:** Services for visually, speech, hearing impaired. **Transfer:** Re-entry adviser, pre-admission transcript evaluation for new students. Transfer center, transfer adviser, college fairs on campus for students transferring to 4-year colleges.

Contact. E-mail: admissions@bhcc.mass.edu
Phone: (617) 228-2422 Fax: (617) 228-2082
Debra Boyer, Registrar/Director of Enrollment Services, Bunker Hill Community College, 250 New Rutherford Avenue, Boston, MA 02129-2925

Cape Cod Community College

West Barnstable, Massachusetts — **CB member**
www.capecod.edu — **CB code: 3289**

- Public 2-year community college
- Commuter campus in small town

General. Founded in 1961. Regionally accredited. **Enrollment:** 3,432 degree-seeking undergraduates. **Degrees:** 429 associate awarded. **Location:** 79 miles from Boston; 80 miles from Providence, Rhode Island. **Calendar:** Semester, limited summer session. **Full-time faculty:** 64 total. **Part-time faculty:** 257 total. **Special facilities:** Source collection for Cape Cod history, marshland nature preserve, maritime studies collection, art gallery. **Partnerships:** Formal partnerships with Tech Prep, School-to-Career, Cape Cod Technology Council Apprenticeship Program.

Transfer out. **Colleges most students transferred to 2008:** Bridgewater State College, University of Massachusetts (Amherst, Boston, Dartmouth), Suffolk University.

Basis for selection. Open admission, but selective for some programs. Special requirements for dental hygiene and nursing programs; priority given to Massachusetts residents. Interview recommended for dental hygiene and nursing programs. **Homeschooled:** Ability To Benefit required.

High school preparation. Chemistry with lab and algebra required for dental hygiene and nursing programs. Nursing also requires biology with anatomy and physiology unit labs.

2008-2009 Annual costs. Tuition/fees: $4,080; $10,260 out-of-state. Per-credit charge: $24 in-state; $230 out-of-state. Books/supplies: $1,000. Personal expenses: $1,336.

2008-2009 Financial aid. Need-based: Need-based aid available for part-time students. Work-study available for part-time students. **Non-need-based:** Scholarships awarded for academics, art, job skills, leadership, music/drama, state residency.

Application procedures. Admission: Priority date 8/10; no deadline. No application fee. Application must be submitted on paper. Admission notification on a rolling basis. Must reply by May 1 or within 4 week(s) if notified thereafter. January 5 application priority date for nursing, February 1 for dental hygiene. **Financial aid:** Priority date 5/1; no closing date. FAFSA required. Applicants notified on a rolling basis starting 5/1.

Academics. Special study options: Accelerated study, cooperative education, cross-registration, distance learning, dual enrollment of high school students, ESL, honors, independent study, internships, study abroad. Bachelor's degree programs available on campus. License preparation in dental hygiene, nursing, paramedic, real estate. **Credit/placement by examination:** AP, CLEP, institutional tests. 30 credit hours maximum toward associate degree. **Support services:** GED preparation and test center, learning center, reduced course load, remedial instruction, study skills assistance, tutoring, writing center.

Majors. Business: Accounting, accounting/business management, administrative services, business admin, executive assistant, hotel/motel admin, management science, marketing, office management, office/clerical. **Communications:** General, journalism, media studies, public relations. **Computer sciences:** General, applications programming, computer science, information systems, information technology, LAN/WAN management, networking, web page design, webmaster. **Conservation:** General, environmental science, environmental studies. **Education:** General, early childhood, kindergarten/preschool. **Engineering:** General. **Foreign languages:** General. **Health:** Dental hygiene, EMT paramedic, medical secretary, nursing (RN), predental, prenursing. **History:** General. **Interdisciplinary:** Behavioral sciences, global studies, natural sciences. **Legal studies:** Legal secretary. **Liberal arts:** Arts/sciences. **Math:** General. **Philosophy/religion:** Philosophy. **Physical sciences:** General. **Protective services:** Criminal justice, fire safety technology, firefighting, law enforcement admin. **Psychology:** General. **Public administration:** Human services. **Social sciences:** General, sociology. **Visual/performing arts:** General, commercial/advertising art, dance, dramatic, graphic design.

Computing on campus. 240 workstations in library, computer center, student center. Commuter students can connect to campus network. Helpline, wireless network available.

Student life. Freshman orientation: Mandatory. Preregistration for classes offered. Half-day program includes meeting with assigned adviser. **Activities:** Choral groups, dance, drama, literary magazine, music ensembles, musical theater, radio station, student government, student newspaper, TV station, Phi Theta Kappa honor society, service learning, unity club, academic support club, gay-bi-lesbian club, recycling club, rotary club.

Athletics. Intramural: Badminton, basketball, racquetball, table tennis, tennis, volleyball. **Team name:** Helmsmen.

Student services. Adult student services, alcohol/substance abuse counseling, career counseling, services for economically disadvantaged, student employment services, financial aid counseling, health services, minority student services, on-campus daycare, personal counseling, placement for graduates, veterans' counselor, women's services. **Physically disabled:** Services for visually, speech, hearing impaired. **Transfer:** Re-entry adviser, preadmission transcript evaluation for new students. Transfer adviser, college fairs on campus for students transferring to 4-year colleges.

Contact. E-mail: admiss@capecod.edu
Phone: (508) 362-2131 ext. 4311 Toll-free
number: (877) 846-3672 ext. 4311 Fax: (508) 375-4089
Susan Kline-Symington, Director of Admissions, Cape Cod Community College, 2240 Iyannough Road, West Barnstable, MA 02668-1599

Caritas Laboure College
Boston, Massachusetts
www.laboure.edu — **CB code: 3287**

- Private 2-year health science and junior college affiliated with Roman Catholic Church
- Commuter campus in very large city
- Interview required

General. Founded in 1971. Regionally accredited. Affiliated with more than 100 health care agencies in Greater Boston area. **Enrollment:** 535 degree-seeking undergraduates. **Degrees:** 104 associate awarded. **Location:** 5 miles from downtown. **Calendar:** Semester, limited summer session. **Full-time faculty:** 34 total. **Part-time faculty:** 33 total. **Class size:** 87% < 20, 13% 20-39.

Student profile.

Out-of-state:	1%	**25 or older:**	70%

Basis for selection. School achievement record, recommendations, interview important, work experience considered.

High school preparation. 10 units required; 16 recommended. Required and recommended units include English 4, mathematics 3, science 1-2 (laboratory 1).

2008-2009 Annual costs. Per-credit charge: $585. Cost of 4-term year is $21,878, inclusive of fees. Professional study courses are $645 per credit. General Education courses are $585 per credit. Books/supplies: $400.

2008-2009 Financial aid. Need-based: Need-based aid available for part-time students. Work-study available nights and for part-time students. **Non-need-based:** Scholarships awarded for academics, alumni affiliation, leadership, religious affiliation.

Application procedures. Admission: No deadline. $25 fee, may be waived for applicants with need. Admission notification on a rolling basis. **Financial aid:** Priority date 4/1; no closing date. FAFSA, institutional form required. Applicants notified on a rolling basis starting 5/15; must reply within 2 week(s) of notification.

Academics. Special study options: Accelerated study, independent study, liberal arts/career combination. Bachelor's degree programs available on campus. License preparation in nursing. **Credit/placement by examination:** CLEP, institutional tests. 23 credit hours maximum toward associate degree. **Support services:** Learning center, pre-admission summer program, reduced course load, remedial instruction, tutoring.

Majors. Health: Clinical lab science, dietetics, medical radiologic technology/radiation therapy, medical records technology, nuclear medical technology, nursing (RN), radiologic technology/medical imaging.

Most popular majors. Family/consumer sciences 8%, health sciences 92%.

Computing on campus. 20 workstations in library, computer center.

Student life. Freshman orientation: Available, $100 fee. Preregistration for classes offered. One-day information session and tour prior to fall term. **Activities:** Student government.

Student services. Chaplain/spiritual director, career counseling, financial aid counseling, personal counseling.

Contact. E-mail: admit@laboure.edu
Phone: (617) 296-8300 ext. 4016 Fax: (617) 296-7947
Gina Morrissette, Director of Admissions, Caritas Laboure College, 2120 Dorchester Avenue, Boston, MA 02124-5698

Dean College
Franklin, Massachusetts — **CB member**
www.dean.edu — **CB code: 3352**

- Private 2-year junior and liberal arts college
- Residential campus in large town
- SAT or ACT (ACT writing optional), application essay required

General. Founded in 1865. Regionally accredited. **Enrollment:** 1,147 degree-seeking undergraduates; 194 non-degree-seeking students. **Degrees:** 19 bachelor's, 230 associate awarded. **Location:** 30 miles from Boston; 30 miles from Providence, Rhode Island. **Calendar:** Semester, limited summer session. **Full-time faculty:** 35 total; 43% have terminal degrees, 6% minority, 54% women. **Part-time faculty:** 68 total; 16% have terminal degrees, 4% minority, 66% women. **Class size:** 63% < 20, 36% 20-39, less than 1% 40-49. **Special facilities:** Telecommunications center, childcare center, radio station. **Partnerships:** Formal partnerships with Putnam Investments (students may earn associate degree while working).

Student profile. Among degree-seeking undergraduates, 575 enrolled as first-time, first-year students, 55 transferred in from other institutions.

Part-time:	10%	**Women:**	49%
Out-of-state:	42%	**Live on campus:**	87%

Transfer out. 99% of students enrolled in the transfer program go on to 4-year colleges. **Colleges most students transferred to 2008:** Suffolk University, Northeastern University, University of Massachusetts Amherst, Emerson, Bridgewater State.

Basis for selection. School achievement record, recommendations most important. Interview recommended. **Learning Disabled:** Arch program applicants must submit appropriate materials that identify and describe the student's learning abilities and any issues relevant to successful completion of a college program.

High school preparation. College-preparatory program recommended. 8 units required; 14 recommended. Required and recommended units include English 3-4, mathematics 1-2, social studies 1-2, history 1-2, science 1-2 (laboratory 1), foreign language 1 and academic electives 1.

2009-2010 Annual costs. Tuition/fees (projected): $28,020. Room/board: $11,964. Books/supplies: $1,000. Personal expenses: $200.

2007-2008 Financial aid. Need-based: 396 full-time freshmen applied for aid; 353 were judged to have need; 353 of these received aid. Average need met was 93%. Average scholarship/grant was $12,769; average loan $3,535. 78% of total undergraduate aid awarded as scholarships/grants, 22% as loans/jobs. Need-based aid available for part-time students. Work-study available nights, weekends and for part-time students. **Non-need-based:** Awarded to 601 full-time undergraduates, including 322 freshmen. Scholarships awarded for academics, athletics, leadership, music/drama, state residency.

Application procedures. Admission: No deadline. $35 fee, may be waived for applicants with need. Admission notification on a rolling basis beginning on or about 12/1. Must reply by May 1 or within 2 week(s) if notified thereafter. **Financial aid:** Priority date 3/15; no closing date. FAFSA required. Applicants notified on a rolling basis starting 3/6; must reply by 5/1 or within 2 week(s) of notification.

Academics. Special study options: ESL, honors, independent study, student-designed major. Bachelor's degree programs available on campus. **Credit/placement by examination:** AP, CLEP, IB, SAT. **Support services:** Learning center, reduced course load, remedial instruction, study skills assistance, tutoring, writing center.

Majors. Business: General, business admin. **Communications:** General. **Computer sciences:** General. **Education:** Early childhood, physical. **Health:** Athletic training, health services. **History:** General. **Liberal arts:** Arts/sciences. **Math:** General. **Parks/recreation:** Health/fitness, sports admin. **Physical sciences:** General. **Protective services:** Criminal justice, law enforcement admin. **Psychology:** General. **Visual/performing arts:** Dance, dramatic.

Most popular majors. Business/marketing 25%, communications/journalism 7%, education 6%, health sciences 11%, liberal arts 34%, visual/performing arts 10%.

Computing on campus. PC or laptop required. Wireless network available.

Student life. Freshman orientation: Mandatory, $200 fee. Preregistration for classes offered. **Housing:** Guaranteed on-campus for all undergraduates. Coed dorms, single-sex dorms, wellness housing available. $400 deposit, deadline 5/1. Off-campus condos. **Activities:** Jazz band, choral groups, dance, drama, international student organizations, literary magazine, music ensembles, musical theater, radio station, student government, TV station, Hillel, Christian Fellowship.

Athletics. NJCAA. **Intercollegiate:** Baseball M, basketball, football (tackle) M, golf M, lacrosse, soccer, softball W. **Intramural:** Basketball, soccer, softball W. **Team name:** Bulldogs.

Student services. Adult student services, alcohol/substance abuse counseling, career counseling, financial aid counseling, health services, personal counseling. **Physically disabled:** Services for visually, speech, hearing impaired. **Learning disabled:** Comprehensive services available. **Transfer:** Transfer center, transfer adviser, college fairs on campus for students transferring to 4-year colleges.

Contact. E-mail: admission@dean.edu
Phone: (508) 541-1508 Toll-free number: (877) 879-3326
Fax: (508) 541-8726
Jay Leiendecker, Vice President of Enrollment Services, Dean College, 99 Main Street, Franklin, MA 02038-1994

Fisher College

Boston, Massachusetts
www.fisher.edu **CB code: 3391**

- Private 2-year liberal arts college
- Residential campus in very large city

General. Founded in 1903. Regionally accredited. Branch campuses in Boston, North Attleboro and New Bedford. **Enrollment:** 1,230 degree-seeking undergraduates. **Degrees:** 69 bachelor's, 176 associate awarded. **Location:** Downtown. **Calendar:** Semester, limited summer session. **Full-time faculty:** 21 total; 33% have terminal degrees, 5% minority, 67% women. **Part-time faculty:** 24 total; 12% minority, 50% women. **Class size:** 53% < 20, 47% 20-39. **Partnerships:** Formal agreements with TechPrep programs in Massachusetts.

Student profile. Among degree-seeking undergraduates, 333 enrolled as first-time, first-year students.

Part-time:	30%	**25 or older:**	4%
Out-of-state:	29%	**Live on campus:**	51%
Women:	71%		

Transfer out. 30% of students enrolled in the transfer program go on to 4-year colleges.

Basis for selection. High school GPA, test scores, personal essays and recommendation letters reviewed. Essay recommended. **Homeschooled:** Statement describing homeschool structure and mission required. **Learning Disabled:** Accommodation review available upon request. Students requesting review should submit latest IEP as well as current psychoeducational testing.

High school preparation. Recommended units include English 4, mathematics 3, social studies 3 and science 2.

2008-2009 Annual costs. Tuition/fees: $23,225. Room/board: $12,250. Books/supplies: $1,200. Personal expenses: $1,200.

2008-2009 Financial aid. Need-based: Need-based aid available for part-time students. Work-study available nights, weekends and for part-time students. **Non-need-based:** Scholarships awarded for academics, alumni affiliation, state residency.

Application procedures. Admission: No deadline. $50 fee, may be waived for applicants with need, free for online applicants. Admission notification on a rolling basis. **Financial aid:** Priority date 3/1; no closing date. FAFSA required. Applicants notified on a rolling basis starting 3/1; must reply within 2 week(s) of notification.

Academics. Special study options: Cross-registration, distance learning, double major, ESL, honors, internships, liberal arts/career combination. Bachelor's degree programs available on campus. **Credit/placement by examination:** AP, CLEP, IB, institutional tests. 30 credit hours maximum toward associate degree, 75 toward bachelor's. Institution follows ACE guide for credit by examination. **Support services:** Learning center, reduced course load, remedial instruction, study skills assistance, tutoring, writing center.

Majors. Business: Business admin, fashion, hospitality admin, tourism/travel. **Education:** Early childhood. **Family/consumer sciences:** Clothing/textiles. **Liberal arts:** Arts/sciences. **Psychology:** General.

Most popular majors. Business/marketing 47%, education 9%, liberal arts 25%, visual/performing arts 7%.

Computing on campus. 60 workstations in dormitories, library, computer center, student center. Dormitories wired for high-speed internet access and linked to campus network. Online course registration, helpline, repair service available.

Student life. Freshman orientation: Mandatory. Preregistration for classes offered. Several 1-day preregistration days scheduled throughout summer with full 2-day orientation program prior to start of classes. **Housing:** Coed dorms, single-sex dorms available. $500 fully refundable deposit. **Activities:** Drama, film society, literary magazine, student government.

Athletics. NAIA. **Intercollegiate:** Baseball M, basketball, softball W. **Team name:** Falcons.

Student services. Adult student services, alcohol/substance abuse counseling, career counseling, student employment services, financial aid counseling, health services, personal counseling, placement for graduates, veterans' counselor. **Transfer:** Re-entry adviser, pre-admission transcript evaluation for new students. Transfer adviser, college fairs on campus for students transferring to 4-year colleges.

Contact. E-mail: admissions@fisher.edu
Phone: (617) 236-8818 Toll-free number: (866) 266-6007
Fax: (617) 236-5473
Robert Melaragni, Dean of Admissions, Fisher College, 118 Beacon Street, Boston, MA 02116

Greenfield Community College

Greenfield, Massachusetts **CB member**
www.gcc.mass.edu **CB code: 3420**

- Public 2-year community college
- Commuter campus in large town

General. Founded in 1962. Regionally accredited. Students may enroll in credit courses taught at Smith College, Veterans Hospital (Northampton), Massachusetts College of Art, Massachusetts College of Liberal Arts. **Enrollment:** 1,969 degree-seeking undergraduates; 348 non-degree-seeking students. **Degrees:** 280 associate awarded. **Location:** 40 miles from Springfield. **Calendar:** Semester, limited summer session. **Full-time faculty:** 54 total; 54% women. **Part-time faculty:** 133 total. **Class size:** 62% < 20, 37% 20-39, less than 1% 40-49, less than 1% 50-99.

Student profile. Among degree-seeking undergraduates, 325 enrolled as first-time, first-year students, 156 transferred in from other institutions.

Part-time:	58%	**Asian American:**	3%
Out-of-state:	44%	**Hispanic American:**	2%
Women:	62%	**Native American:**	1%
African American:	4%	**25 or older:**	45%

Transfer out. Colleges most students transferred to 2008: University of Massachusetts: Amherst, Westfield State College, Massachusetts College of Liberal Arts, Smith College, Elms College.

Basis for selection. Open admission, but selective for some programs. Special entrance requirements for occupational technology, nursing, paramedic, massage therapy, outdoor leadership programs.

High school preparation. Students from public high schools in the Commonwealth must be MCAS graduates, or demonstrate an ability to benefit.

2008-2009 Annual costs. Tuition/fees: $4,637; $12,287 out-of-state. Per-credit charge: $26 in-state; $281 out-of-state. Books/supplies: $850. Personal expenses: $1,560.

Financial aid. All financial aid based on need. Need-based aid available for part-time students. Work-study available nights, weekends and for part-time students.

Application procedures. Admission: No deadline. $10 fee ($35 out-of-state), may be waived for applicants with need. Admission notification on a rolling basis. Limited space available in nursing and outdoor leadership programs. Application priority date 2/1. **Financial aid:** Priority date 4/15; no closing date. FAFSA, institutional form required. Applicants notified on a rolling basis starting 5/1; must reply within 2 week(s) of notification.

Academics. Special study options: Cooperative education, cross-registration, distance learning, double major, dual enrollment of high school students, ESL, independent study, internships, liberal arts/career combination. License preparation in nursing, paramedic, real estate. **Credit/placement by examination:** AP, CLEP, institutional tests. 15 credit hours maximum toward associate degree. **Support services:** GED test center, learning center, reduced course load, remedial instruction, study skills assistance, tutoring.

Majors. Business: General, accounting, administrative services, business admin. **Computer sciences:** General. **Conservation:** General, environmental science. **Education:** Early childhood. **Engineering:** Science. **Health:** Nursing (RN), occupational therapy assistant. **Liberal arts:** Arts/sciences. **Personal/culinary services:** Cosmetic. **Protective services:** Police science. **Visual/performing arts:** Commercial/advertising art. **Other:** Renewable energy/efficiency.

Most popular majors. Business/marketing 12%, health sciences 12%, liberal arts 49%, security/protective services 8%, visual/performing arts 9%.

Computing on campus. 212 workstations in library, computer center. Commuter students can connect to campus network. Online library, helpline, wireless network available.

Student life. Freshman orientation: Available. Preregistration for classes offered. **Activities:** Jazz band, choral groups, dance, drama, music ensembles, student government.

Student services. Adult student services, career counseling, services for economically disadvantaged, student employment services, financial aid counseling, health services, personal counseling, placement for graduates, veterans' counselor, women's services. **Physically disabled:** Services for visually, speech, hearing impaired. **Transfer:** Re-entry adviser, pre-admission transcript evaluation for new students. Transfer adviser, college fairs on campus for students transferring to 4-year colleges.

Contact. E-mail: admissions@gcc.mass.edu
Phone: (413) 775-1809 Fax: (413) 773-5129
Herbert Hentz, Director of Admissions, Greenfield Community College, One College Drive, Greenfield, MA 01301

Holyoke Community College

Holyoke, Massachusetts **CB member**
www.hcc.edu **CB code: 3437**

- Public 2-year community college
- Commuter campus in large town

General. Founded in 1946. Regionally accredited. **Enrollment:** 6,131 degree-seeking undergraduates; 461 non-degree-seeking students. **Degrees:** 777 associate awarded. **ROTC:** Army, Air Force. **Location:** 8 miles from Springfield. **Calendar:** Semester, extensive summer session. **Full-time faculty:** 130 total; 11% minority, 62% women. **Part-time faculty:** 334 total; 10% minority, 52% women. **Class size:** 43% < 20, 56% 20-39, less than 1% 40-49.

Student profile. Among degree-seeking undergraduates, 1,698 enrolled as first-time, first-year students.

Part-time:	44%	**Asian American:**	2%
Out-of-state:	1%	**Hispanic American:**	16%
Women:	62%	**International:**	1%
African American:	6%	**25 or older:**	30%

Transfer out. Colleges most students transferred to 2008: University of Massachusetts-Amherst, Western New England College, American International College, Westfield State College, Elms College.

Basis for selection. Open admission, but selective for some programs. Special requirements for nursing, radiography, animal sciences, practical nursing programs. Audition required of music majors. Portfolio required of fine arts majors.

2008-2009 Annual costs. Tuition/fees: $3,558; $9,738 out-of-state. Per-credit charge: $24 in-state; $230 out-of-state. Books/supplies: $1,000. Personal expenses: $3,500.

2007-2008 Financial aid. Need-based: 76% of total undergraduate aid awarded as scholarships/grants, 24% as loans/jobs. Need-based aid available for part-time students. Work-study available nights and for part-time students. **Non-need-based:** Scholarships awarded for academics, art, leadership, music/drama.

Application procedures. Admission: No deadline. No application fee. Admission notification on a rolling basis. **Financial aid:** Priority date 5/1; no closing date. FAFSA required. Applicants notified on a rolling basis starting 5/1; must reply within 2 week(s) of notification.

Academics. Special study options: Cooperative education, cross-registration, distance learning, double major, dual enrollment of high school students, ESL, honors, independent study, internships, liberal arts/career combination, student-designed major, study abroad, teacher certification program, weekend college. License preparation in nursing. **Credit/placement by examination:** AP, CLEP, institutional tests. 30 credit hours maximum toward associate degree. **Support services:** GED preparation and test center, learning center, reduced course load, remedial instruction, study skills assistance, tutoring, writing center.

Majors. Business: Accounting technology, administrative services, business admin, hospitality admin, human resources, restaurant/food services, retailing. **Computer sciences:** Applications programming. **Engineering:** General. **Engineering technology:** Environmental. **Family/consumer sciences:** Child care. **Health:** Medical radiologic technology/radiation therapy, nursing (RN), optician, veterinary technology/assistant. **Liberal arts:** Arts/sciences. **Parks/recreation:** Health/fitness, sports admin. **Protective services:** Criminal justice. **Public administration:** Social work. **Social sciences:** Geography. **Visual/performing arts:** Art.

Most popular majors. Business/marketing 21%, family/consumer sciences 6%, health sciences 11%, liberal arts 44%, security/protective services 6%.

Computing on campus. 67 workstations in computer center. Commuter students can connect to campus network. Online course registration, online library, helpline, wireless network available.

Student life. Freshman orientation: Mandatory. Preregistration for classes offered. **Activities:** Jazz band, choral groups, drama, literary magazine, music ensembles, musical theater, radio station, student government, student newspaper, symphony orchestra, more than 30 clubs and organizations.

Athletics. NJCAA. **Intercollegiate:** Baseball M, basketball, cross-country, golf, soccer, softball W, volleyball W. **Intramural:** Basketball, soccer, softball, volleyball. **Team name:** Cougars.

Student services. Adult student services, alcohol/substance abuse counseling, chaplain/spiritual director, career counseling, services for economically disadvantaged, student employment services, financial aid counseling, health services, minority student services, on-campus daycare, personal counseling, placement for graduates, veterans' counselor, women's services. **Physically disabled:** Services for visually, speech, hearing impaired. **Transfer:** Transfer adviser, college fairs on campus for students transferring to 4-year colleges.

Contact. E-mail: admissions@hcc.mass.edu
Phone: (413) 552-2001 Fax: (413) 552-2045
Marcia Rosbury-Henne, Director of Admissions and Transfer Affairs, Holyoke Community College, 303 Homestead Avenue, Holyoke, MA 01040

ITT Technical Institute: Norwood

Norwood, Massachusetts
www.itt-tech.edu **CB code: 2699**

- For-profit 2-year technical college
- Commuter campus in small city

General. Accredited by ACICS. **Calendar:** Quarter.

Contact. Phone: (781) 278-7200
Director of Recruitment, 333 Providence Highway, Norwood, MA 02062

ITT Technical Institute: Woburn

Woburn, Massachusetts
www.itt-tech.edu

- For-profit 2-year technical college
- Small city

General. Accredited by ACICS. **Calendar:** Quarter.

Contact. Phone: (781) 937-8324
Director of Recruitment, 10 Forbes Road, Woburn, MA 01801

Marian Court College

Swampscott, Massachusetts **CB member**
www.mariancourt.edu **CB code: 9100**

- Private 2-year junior college affiliated with Roman Catholic Church
- Commuter campus in large town
- Application essay, interview required

General. Founded in 1964. Regionally accredited. Evening division on quarter system. **Enrollment:** 216 full-time, degree-seeking students. **Degrees:** 63 associate awarded. **Location:** 5 miles from Lynn, 20 miles from Boston. **Calendar:** Semester, limited summer session. **Full-time faculty:** 7 total. **Part-time faculty:** 20 total.

Basis for selection. High school grades, recommendations, interview important. Institutional English and math tests used for placement.

2008-2009 Annual costs. Tuition/fees: $13,956. Evening program: $675 for 3 credit course. Books/supplies: $600. Personal expenses: $1,957.

2007-2008 Financial aid. Need-based: Need-based aid available for part-time students. **Non-need-based:** Scholarships awarded for academics.

Application procedures. Admission: Priority date 5/1; no deadline. No application fee. Admission notification on a rolling basis. Must reply by May 1 or within 2 week(s) if notified thereafter. **Financial aid:** Priority date 4/1; no closing date. FAFSA, institutional form required. Applicants notified on a rolling basis starting 4/15.

Academics. Freshman seminar required of all freshmen. Special adult learner freshman seminars available. Writing lab available evenings for extra assistance. **Special study options:** Cross-registration, double major, honors, independent study, internships, weekend college. Member Northeast Consortium of Colleges and Universities in Massachusetts. **Credit/placement by examination:** CLEP, institutional tests. 15 credit hours maximum toward associate degree. **Support services:** Reduced course load, tutoring.

Majors. Business: Accounting, administrative services, business admin, hospitality admin, human resources, management information systems, marketing, tourism/travel. **Computer sciences:** Data entry, web page design. **Health:** Medical secretary, medical transcription. **Legal studies:** Legal secretary, paralegal. **Liberal arts:** Arts/sciences. **Protective services:** Law enforcement admin, security services.

Computing on campus. 53 workstations in library, computer center, student center.

Student life. Activities: Literary magazine, student government, Mercy Outreach, travel club, student life organization.

Student services. Adult student services, career counseling, student employment services, health services, personal counseling, placement for graduates. **Transfer:** Transfer adviser, college fairs on campus for students transferring to 4-year colleges.

Contact. E-mail: info@mariancourt.edu
Phone: (781) 595-6768 Fax: (781) 595-3560
Bryan Boppert, Associate Director of Admissions, Marian Court College, 35 Little's Point Road, Swampscott, MA 01907-2896

Massachusetts Bay Community College

Wellesley Hills, Massachusetts **CB member**
www.massbay.edu **CB code: 3294**

- Public 2-year community college
- Commuter campus in large town

General. Founded in 1961. Regionally accredited. **Enrollment:** 4,577 degree-seeking undergraduates; 541 non-degree-seeking students. **Degrees:** 442 associate awarded. **Location:** 13 miles from Boston. **Calendar:** Semester, extensive summer session. **Full-time faculty:** 74 total; 23% minority, 62% women. **Part-time faculty:** 250 total; 49% women. **Class size:** 42% < 20, 57% 20-39, less than 1% 40-49, less than 1% 50-99. **Special facilities:** Advanced technology center (technology and health science laboratories). **Partnerships:** Formal partnerships with Toyota, Chrysler, General Motors, EMC2.

Student profile. Among degree-seeking undergraduates, 79% enrolled in a vocational program, 6% already have a bachelor's degree or higher, 1,275 enrolled as first-time, first-year students, 187 transferred in from other institutions.

Part-time:	57%	**Asian American:**	4%
Out-of-state:	1%	**Hispanic American:**	10%
Women:	59%	**International:**	3%
African American:	15%	**25 or older:**	41%

Transfer out. Colleges most students transferred to 2008: Framingham State College, University of Massachusetts-Boston, Northeastern University, Bentley College.

Basis for selection. Open admission, but selective for some programs. Special requirements for nursing, radiologic technology, paramedic, respiratory therapy programs.

High school preparation. Some programs require special academic preparation.

2008-2009 Annual costs. Tuition/fees: $4,530; $10,710 out-of-state. Per-credit charge: $24 in-state; $230 out-of-state. NEBHE tuition rate is 150% of in-state cost and fees are approximately the same. Books/supplies: $982. Personal expenses: $3,638.

2007-2008 Financial aid. Need-based: Need-based aid available for part-time students.

Application procedures. Admission: No deadline. $20 fee, may be waived for applicants with need. Admission notification on a rolling basis. **Financial aid:** Priority date 8/30; no closing date. FAFSA, institutional form required. Applicants notified on a rolling basis starting 4/1.

Academics. Special study options: Cooperative education, distance learning, dual enrollment of high school students, honors, internships, liberal arts/career combination, study abroad. License preparation in nursing, paramedic, physical therapy, radiology. **Credit/placement by examination:** AP, CLEP, IB, institutional tests. 30 credit hours maximum toward associate degree. **Support services:** Learning center, reduced course load, remedial instruction, study skills assistance, tutoring, writing center.

Majors. Biology: Marine. **Business:** General, accounting, business admin, hospitality admin. **Communications:** General. **Computer sciences:** General, computer science, information systems. **Engineering technology:** Automotive, computer, electrical, laser/optical. **Family/consumer sciences:** Child care. **Health:** Medical informatics, medical radiologic technology/radiation therapy, nursing (RN), physical therapy assistant, respiratory therapy technology. **Legal studies:** Paralegal. **Liberal arts:** Arts/sciences. **Protective services:** Forensics, law enforcement admin. **Public administration:** Human services. **Science technology:** Biological, chemical. **Social sciences:** General.

Most popular majors. Business/marketing 15%, engineering/engineering technologies 8%, health sciences 38%, liberal arts 22%, security/protective services 7%.

Computing on campus. 550 workstations in library, computer center, student center. Commuter students can connect to campus network. Wireless network available.

Student life. Freshman orientation: Available. **Activities:** Drama, student government, student newspaper, volunteer service corps, Christian Fellowship, Hillel, New World club, Latino club, sexual orientation support group.

Athletics. NJCAA. **Intercollegiate:** Baseball M, basketball, cheerleading M, golf, soccer, softball W. **Intramural:** Ice hockey M. **Team name:** Buccaneers.

Student services. Adult student services, career counseling, student employment services, financial aid counseling, health services, minority student services, personal counseling, placement for graduates, veterans' counselor. **Physically disabled:** Services for visually, speech, hearing impaired. **Transfer:** Pre-admission transcript evaluation for new students. Transfer adviser, college fairs on campus for students transferring to 4-year colleges.

Contact. E-mail: info@massbay.edu
Phone: (781) 239-2500 Fax: (781) 239-1047
Donna Raposa, Director for Admissions, Massachusetts Bay Community College, 50 Oakland Street, Wellesley Hills, MA 02481

Massasoit Community College

Brockton, Massachusetts — **CB member**
www.massasoit.mass.edu — **CB code: 3549**

- Public 2-year community college
- Commuter campus in small city

General. Founded in 1966. Regionally accredited. Second campus located in Canton, 10 miles from Boston. **Enrollment:** 5,377 degree-seeking undergraduates; 2,017 non-degree-seeking students. **Degrees:** 722 associate awarded. **Location:** 25 miles from Boston. **Calendar:** Semester, extensive summer session. **Full-time faculty:** 100 total; 49% women. **Part-time faculty:** 382 total; 53% women. **Special facilities:** Theater, conference center.

Student profile. Among degree-seeking undergraduates, 1,706 enrolled as first-time, first-year students, 462 transferred in from other institutions.

Part-time:	44%	**Asian American:**	2%
Out-of-state:	1%	**Hispanic American:**	3%
Women:	57%	**25 or older:**	39%
African American:	19%		

Transfer out. Colleges most students transferred to 2008: Bridgewater State College, University of Massachusetts Boston, University of Massachusetts Amherst, Stonehill College, Northeastern University.

Basis for selection. Open admission, but selective for some programs. Special requirements for allied health programs. Interview recommended for allied health applicants.

2008-2009 Annual costs. Tuition/fees: $3,510; $9,690 out-of-state. Per-credit charge: $24 in-state; $230 out-of-state. Books/supplies: $800. Personal expenses: $1,800.

Financial aid. All financial aid based on need.

Application procedures. Admission: No deadline. No application fee. Application must be submitted on paper. Admission notification on a rolling basis. Application priority date of 2/1 for nursing and radiology programs. **Financial aid:** Priority date 4/15; no closing date. FAFSA required. Applicants notified on a rolling basis starting 6/1.

Academics. Special study options: Accelerated study, cooperative education, cross-registration, distance learning, dual enrollment of high school students, ESL, honors, independent study, internships, liberal arts/career combination, weekend college. License preparation in dental hygiene, nursing, radiology, real estate. **Credit/placement by examination:** CLEP, institutional tests. 30 credit hours maximum toward associate degree. **Support services:** GED preparation and test center, learning center, pre-admission summer program, reduced course load, remedial instruction, study skills assistance, tutoring, writing center.

Majors. Business: Accounting, administrative services, business admin, hospitality admin, management information systems, marketing, office management, operations, tourism/travel. **Communications:** Media studies. **Computer sciences:** General, programming. **Education:** Teacher assistance. **Engineering technology:** Architectural, electrical, heat/ac/refrig, telecommunications. **Family/consumer sciences:** Child care. **Health:** Medical radiologic technology/radiation therapy, nursing (RN), respiratory therapy technology. **Legal studies:** Legal secretary, paralegal. **Liberal arts:** Arts/sciences. **Mechanic/repair:** Diesel. **Personal/culinary services:** Chef training. **Protective services:** Firefighting, police science. **Public administration:** Human services. **Visual/performing arts:** Commercial/advertising art, dramatic, studio arts.

Most popular majors. Business/marketing 20%, health sciences 19%, liberal arts 27%, security/protective services 11%.

Computing on campus. 280 workstations in library, computer center, student center. Commuter students can connect to campus network. Helpline, repair service, student web hosting, wireless network available.

Student life. Freshman orientation: Available. Preregistration for classes offered. **Activities:** Jazz band, choral groups, dance, drama, literary magazine, music ensembles, musical theater, opera, radio station, student government, student newspaper, TV station, Phi Theta Kappa, art and museum association, Helping Hands, International Touch, senior center, women's resource center, Top of the Rainbow.

Athletics. NJCAA. **Intercollegiate:** Baseball M, basketball, soccer, softball W. **Intramural:** Swimming, weight lifting. **Team name:** Warriors.

Student services. Adult student services, alcohol/substance abuse counseling, career counseling, services for economically disadvantaged, student employment services, financial aid counseling, health services, minority student services, on-campus daycare, personal counseling, placement for graduates, veterans' counselor, women's services. **Physically disabled:** Services for visually, speech, hearing impaired. **Transfer:** Transfer adviser, college fairs on campus for students transferring to 4-year colleges.

Contact. E-mail: admoffice@massasoit.mass.edu
Phone: (508) 588-9100 ext. 1411 Fax: (508) 427-1255
Michelle Hughes, Director of Admissions, Massasoit Community College, One Massasoit Boulevard, Brockton, MA 02302-3996

Middlesex Community College

Bedford, Massachusetts — **CB member**
www.middlesex.mass.edu — **CB code: 3554**

- Public 2-year community college
- Commuter campus in small city

General. Founded in 1969. Regionally accredited. Second main campus located in Lowell. **Enrollment:** 7,569 degree-seeking undergraduates. **Degrees:** 835 associate awarded. **ROTC:** Air Force. **Location:** 16 miles from Boston. **Calendar:** Semester, limited summer session. **Full-time faculty:** 130 total. **Part-time faculty:** 415 total. **Special facilities:** Dental clinic, law center. **Partnerships:** Formal partnerships with business and industry links.

Student profile.

Out-of-state:	1%	**25 or older:**	49%

Basis for selection. Open admission, but selective for some programs. Admission to some health programs based on prerequisite courses in math and science and placement test scores. Some health, counseling, business honors and biotechnology programs require essays, letters of reference and interview.

High school preparation. For some health programs, 1 unit each of biology and chemistry required in addition to 2 units of math at Algebra I level and above.

2008-2009 Annual costs. Tuition/fees: $4,010; $10,190 out-of-state. Per-credit charge: $132 in-state; $338 out-of-state. New England resident tuition $144 per credit hour. Books/supplies: $900. Personal expenses: $600.

2007-2008 Financial aid. All financial aid based on need. Need-based aid available for part-time students. Work-study available nights, weekends and for part-time students. **Additional information:** Application priority date 5/1 for Massachusetts state funds.

Application procedures. Admission: No deadline. No application fee. Admission notification on a rolling basis. Closing date February 1 for dental hygiene, April 1 for diagnostic medical sonography. Applications received later considered on space-available basis. Applicants must reply within 2 weeks of acceptance. **Financial aid:** Priority date 5/1; no closing date. FAFSA, institutional form required. Applicants notified on a rolling basis starting 6/1; must reply within 2 week(s) of notification.

Academics. Special study options: Accelerated study, cooperative education, cross-registration, distance learning, dual enrollment of high school students, ESL, exchange student, honors, independent study, internships, liberal arts/career combination, study abroad, weekend college. **Credit/placement by examination:** AP, CLEP, institutional tests. 45 credit hours maximum toward associate degree. **Support services:** GED preparation, learning center, pre-admission summer program, reduced course load, remedial instruction, study skills assistance, tutoring, writing center.

Majors. Biology: Biotechnology. **Business:** Accounting, administrative services, business admin, fashion, hospitality admin, office management, office technology, sales/distribution. **Communications:** General. **Communications technology:** Desktop publishing. **Computer sciences:** Computer science, networking. **Education:** Early childhood. **Engineering:** Science. **Engineering technology:** Drafting. **Health:** Clinical lab technology, dental assistant, dental hygiene, dental lab technology, health services, medical assistant, medical radiologic technology/radiation therapy, nursing (RN), sonography. **Legal studies:** Paralegal. **Liberal arts:** Arts/sciences. **Mechanic/repair:** Aircraft, automotive. **Protective services:** Fire safety technology, law enforcement admin. **Science technology:** Biological. **Visual/performing arts:** General, commercial/advertising art, dramatic, studio arts.

Most popular majors. Business/marketing 24%, health sciences 19%, liberal arts 32%, security/protective services 10%, trade and industry 10%.

Computing on campus. 350 workstations in library, computer center. Helpline available.

Student life. Freshman orientation: Available. **Housing:** Dorm rooms contractable on space-available basis at University of Massachusetts-Lowell. **Activities:** Drama, student government, student newspaper, international club, student activities, mental health club, early childhood education club, art club, MassPIRG.

Athletics. Intramural: Table tennis, volleyball.

Student services. Adult student services, career counseling, student employment services, health services, on-campus daycare, personal counseling, placement for graduates, veterans' counselor. **Physically disabled:** Services for visually, speech, hearing impaired. **Transfer:** Pre-admission transcript evaluation for new students. Transfer adviser, college fairs on campus for students transferring to 4-year colleges.

Contact. E-mail: admissions@middlesex.mass.edu
Phone: (978) 656-3207 Toll-free number: (800) 818-3434
Fax: (978) 656-3322
Marilynn Gallagan, Dean of Admissions, Middlesex Community College, 33 Kearney Square, Lowell, MA 01852-1987

Mount Wachusett Community College

Gardner, Massachusetts — **CB member**
www.mwcc.edu — **CB code: 3545**

- Public 2-year community college
- Commuter campus in large town

General. Founded in 1963. Regionally accredited. **Enrollment:** 3,907 degree-seeking undergraduates; 478 non-degree-seeking students. **Degrees:** 446 associate awarded. **Location:** 59 miles from Boston. **Calendar:** Semester, extensive summer session. **Full-time faculty:** 77 total; 4% minority, 66% women. **Part-time faculty:** 135 total; 3% minority, 53% women. **Class size:** 66% < 20, 33% 20-39, less than 1% 40-49, less than 1% 50-99. **Special facilities:** On-site child-care facility, theater, fitness and wellness center, pool. **Partnerships:** Formal partnership with Tech Prep (high school articulation programs), Nypro, Adams and Associates.

Student profile. Among degree-seeking undergraduates, 1,063 enrolled as first-time, first-year students, 297 transferred in from other institutions.

Part-time:	53%	**Asian American:**	3%
Out-of-state:	5%	**Hispanic American:**	11%
Women:	66%	**International:**	1%
African American:	6%	**25 or older:**	59%

Transfer out. Colleges most students transferred to 2008: Fitchburg State College, University of Massachusetts Amherst, Worcester State College, University of Massachusetts Lowell.

Basis for selection. Open admission, but selective for some programs. Special requirements for all health science programs with emphasis on college level academic coursework, life science or other science programs, other academic preparation and work experience. Interview required for early admission of high school students. Portfolio recommended for art programs. **Homeschooled:** Statement describing homeschool structure and mission, transcript of courses and grades, interview required. Applicants must submit copies of curriculum approvals from local secondary school district. **Learning Disabled:** Students advised to meet with coordinator of disabilities services during admissions process.

High school preparation. College-preparatory program recommended. 16 units recommended. Recommended units include English 4, mathematics 3, social studies 1, history 1, science 2 (laboratory 2), foreign language 2 and academic electives 3.

2008-2009 Annual costs. Tuition/fees: $4,530; $10,680 out-of-state. Per-credit charge: $25 in-state; $230 out-of-state. New England resident tuition is $1,125. Books/supplies: $1,000. Personal expenses: $1,700.

2007-2008 Financial aid. All financial aid based on need. 500 full-time freshmen applied for aid; 345 were judged to have need; 320 of these received aid. Average need met was 91%. Average scholarship/grant was $3,764; average loan $886. 69% of total undergraduate aid awarded as scholarships/grants, 31% as loans/jobs. Need-based aid available for part-time students. Work-study available nights and for part-time students.

Application procedures. Admission: Priority date 4/1; no deadline. $10 fee, may be waived for applicants with need, free for online applicants. Admission notification on a rolling basis beginning on or about 12/1. Nursing, Dental Hygiene must apply by February 1. Clinical Laboratory Science, Physical Therapy Assistant, and Massage Therapy must apply by March 1. **Financial aid:** Priority date 4/15; no closing date. FAFSA, institutional form required. Applicants notified on a rolling basis starting 5/1.

Academics. Special study options: Accelerated study, cooperative education, cross-registration, distance learning, double major, dual enrollment of high school students, ESL, honors, independent study, internships, liberal arts/career combination, study abroad, weekend college. License preparation in dental hygiene, nursing, physical therapy. **Credit/placement by examination:** AP, CLEP, IB, institutional tests. 30 credit hours maximum toward associate degree. **Support services:** GED preparation and test center, learning center, pre-admission summer program, reduced course load, remedial instruction, study skills assistance, tutoring, writing center.

Majors. Biology: Biotechnology. **Business:** Business admin, executive assistant. **Communications technology:** Radio/tv. **Computer sciences:** General, computer graphics, web page design. **Conservation:** Environmental studies. **Engineering technology:** Computer, plastics. **Family/consumer sciences:** Child care, child development. **Health:** Clinical lab technology, dental hygiene, medical assistant, mental health services, nursing (RN), physical therapy assistant. **Legal studies:** Paralegal. **Liberal arts:** Arts/sciences. **Mechanic/repair:** Automotive. **Protective services:** Corrections, criminal justice, fire safety technology, law enforcement admin. **Public administration:** Human services. **Visual/performing arts:** Art.

Most popular majors. Business/marketing 16%, computer/information sciences 7%, health sciences 29%, liberal arts 23%, public administration/social services 7%.

Computing on campus. 415 workstations in library, computer center. Commuter students can connect to campus network. Online course registration, online library, helpline, wireless network available.

Student life. Freshman orientation: Available. Preregistration for classes offered. One-day session held week before start of classes. **Housing:** Limited housing available on campus of Fitchburg State College. **Activities:** Drama, literary magazine, musical theater, student government, student newspaper, art club, nursing clubs, student government association, pride club, dental hygiene club, green society, Campus Crusade for Christ, campus activities team for students, MassPIRG, ALANA club.

Athletics. Intramural: Badminton, basketball, football (tackle), softball, table tennis, volleyball, water polo. **Team name:** Mountain Lions.

Student services. Adult student services, alcohol/substance abuse counseling, chaplain/spiritual director, career counseling, services for economically disadvantaged, student employment services, financial aid counseling, health services, minority student services, on-campus daycare, personal counseling, placement for graduates, veterans' counselor, women's services. **Physically disabled:** Services for visually, speech, hearing impaired. **Learning disabled:** Comprehensive services available. **Transfer:** Pre-admission transcript evaluation for new students. Transfer adviser, college fairs on campus for students transferring to 4-year colleges.

Contact. E-mail: admissions@mwcc.mass.edu
Phone: (978) 630-9554 Fax: (978) 630-9554
John Walsh, Director of Admissions, Mount Wachusett Community College, 444 Green Street, Gardner, MA 01440-1000

New England College of Finance

Boston, Massachusetts
www.finance.edu **CB code: 3376**

- For-profit 2-year business college
- Very large city
- Interview required

General. Founded in 1909. Regionally accredited. **Enrollment:** 657 degree-seeking undergraduates. **Degrees:** 49 associate awarded; master's offered. **Calendar:** Continuous, limited summer session. **Part-time faculty:** 180 total. **Partnerships:** Formal partnerships with several financial services companies.

Basis for selection. Open admission, but selective for some programs. Academic background, professional recommendation, demonstrated commitment to program and banking, and interview considered.

2008-2009 Annual costs. Cost of 3 credit course is $925 for employees of member companies; cost for non-members is $1100.

Financial aid. Additional information: No college-administered financial aid. 90% of students receive tuition reimbursement from employer.

Application procedures. Admission: No deadline. $50 fee. Admission notification on a rolling basis. **Financial aid:** No deadline.

Academics. Special study options: Accelerated study, distance learning, dual enrollment of high school students, independent study. **Credit/placement by examination:** CLEP. 9 credit hours maximum toward associate degree. **Support services:** Remedial instruction, tutoring.

Majors. Business: General, banking/financial services, business admin.

Computing on campus. 24 workstations in computer center.

Student life. Activities: Literary magazine.

Student services. Career counseling, personal counseling. **Transfer:** Pre-admission transcript evaluation for new students. Transfer adviser for students transferring to 4-year colleges.

Contact. E-mail: admissions@finance.edu
Phone: (617) 951-2350 Fax: (617) 951-2533
Mina Goldman, Vice President of Admissions, New England College of Finance, 10 High Street, Suite 204, Boston, MA 02110

North Shore Community College

Danvers, Massachusetts **CB member**
www.northshore.edu **CB code: 3651**

- Public 2-year community college
- Commuter campus in small city

General. Founded in 1965. Regionally accredited. Additional campus in Lynn, corporate training center in Beverly. **Enrollment:** 6,331 degree-seeking undergraduates; 892 non-degree-seeking students. **Degrees:** 658 associate awarded. **Location:** 25 miles from Boston. **Calendar:** Semester, limited summer session. **Full-time faculty:** 135 total; 90% have terminal degrees, 12% minority, 66% women. **Part-time faculty:** 361 total; 11% have terminal degrees, 6% minority, 54% women. **Class size:** 49% < 20, 51% 20-39, less than 1% 40-49, less than 1% 50-99. **Special facilities:** Agricultural facility for horticulture, animal science, culinary arts. **Partnerships:** Formal partnership with Verizon, area high schools for Tech Prep, consortium providing distance learning opportunities.

Student profile. Among degree-seeking undergraduates, 35% enrolled in a transfer program, 54% enrolled in a vocational program, 1,523 enrolled as first-time, first-year students, 654 transferred in from other institutions.

Part-time:	52%	**Asian American:**	4%
Women:	60%	**Hispanic American:**	15%
African American:	8%	**25 or older:**	40%

Transfer out. 80% of students enrolled in the transfer program go on to 4-year colleges. **Colleges most students transferred to 2008:** Salem State College, University of Massachusetts-Boston, University of Massachusetts-Lowell, Suffolk University, Northeastern University, Lesley College.

Basis for selection. Open admission, but selective for some programs. School achievement record considered for health, engineering, computer science programs; some prerequisite course requirements exist. Pre-Nursing Assessment Test required for pre-nursing program; Nurse Entrance Exam required for LPN program. Essay and/or interview may be required in some programs, including health and human services. **Homeschooled:** Home program must be affiliated with accredited agency or local school system. **Learning Disabled:** Students must identify disability, individual test administration available.

High school preparation. One algebra, 1 biology, and 1 chemistry required for some health programs and for biotechnology. Trigonometry, physics, chemistry required for engineering. Trigonometry, computer literacy required for computer science.

2008-2009 Annual costs. Tuition/fees: $3,750; $10,710 out-of-state. Per-credit charge: $25 in-state; $257 out-of-state. New England regional tuition: $138 per credit hour. Books/supplies: $800. Personal expenses: $1,300.

2007-2008 Financial aid. All financial aid based on need. 84% of total undergraduate aid awarded as scholarships/grants, 16% as loans/jobs. Need-based aid available for part-time students. Work-study available for part-time students.

Application procedures. Admission: No deadline. No application fee. Admission notification on a rolling basis. **Financial aid:** Priority date 5/1; no closing date. FAFSA required. Applicants notified on a rolling basis starting 6/1; must reply within 2 week(s) of notification.

Academics. Participation in state dual enrollment program which allows high school juniors and seniors to take credit courses contingent upon approval of high school principal. Tuition and fees paid by state. **Special study options:** Accelerated study, cross-registration, distance learning, double major, dual enrollment of high school students, ESL, honors, independent study, internships, student-designed major, study abroad, weekend college. License preparation in aviation, nursing, occupational therapy, physical therapy, radiology, real estate. **Credit/placement by examination:** AP, CLEP, institutional tests. 45 credit hours maximum toward associate degree. DANTES, Excelsior, CLEP tests accepted. CLEP tests in Freshman Composition and Analyzing and Interpreting Literature must be accompanied by essay; lab credit not awarded for Biology and Chemistry tests. **Support services:** GED preparation and test center, learning center, remedial instruction, study skills assistance, tutoring, writing center.

Majors. Agriculture: Floriculture, horticulture. **Business:** Accounting technology, business admin, executive assistant, hospitality admin, hotel/motel admin, marketing. **Computer sciences:** General, computer science, programming. **Education:** Early childhood, elementary, kindergarten/preschool, teacher assistance. **Engineering:** General. **Engineering technology:** Telecommunications. **Family/consumer sciences:** Aging. **Health:** Dietetic technician, medical secretary, mental health services, nursing (RN), occupational therapy assistant, physical therapy assistant, radiologic technology/medical imaging, respiratory therapy technology, substance abuse counseling, veterinary technology/assistant. **Legal studies:** Legal secretary, paralegal. **Liberal arts:** Arts/sciences. **Personal/culinary services:** Chef training. **Protective services:** Criminal justice, fire safety technology. **Science technology:** Biological. **Transportation:** Airline/commercial pilot, aviation management. **Visual/performing arts:** Graphic design.

Most popular majors. Business/marketing 11%, family/consumer sciences 7%, health sciences 29%, liberal arts 30%, security/protective services 17%.

Computing on campus. 300 workstations in library, computer center, student center. Commuter students can connect to campus network. Online course registration, online library, helpline available.

Student life. Freshman orientation: Available. Preregistration for classes offered. All day event includes placement testing, adviser assistance. **Activities:** Drama, Model UN, student government, student newspaper, students against drug abuse, early childhood club, marketing club, engineering club, women in transition club, multicultural society, poets and writers club, gerontology club, occupational therapy assistant club.

Athletics. Team name: Seahawks.

Student services. Adult student services, career counseling, services for economically disadvantaged, student employment services, financial aid counseling, health services, on-campus daycare, personal counseling, placement for graduates, veterans' counselor, women's services. **Physically disabled:** Services for visually, speech, hearing impaired. **Learning disabled:** Comprehensive services available. **Transfer:** Pre-admission transcript evaluation for new students. Transfer adviser, college fairs on campus for students transferring to 4-year colleges.

Contact. E-mail: info@northshore.edu
Phone: (978) 762-4188 Fax: (978) 762-4015
Jennifer Kirk, Director of Recruitment, North Shore Community College, One Ferncroft Road, Danvers, MA 01923-0840

Northern Essex Community College

Haverhill, Massachusetts **CB member**
www.necc.mass.edu **CB code: 3674**

- Public 2-year community and junior college
- Commuter campus in small city

General. Founded in 1960. Regionally accredited. Additional campus in Lawrence. **Enrollment:** 6,146 degree-seeking undergraduates; 874 non-degree-seeking students. **Degrees:** 605 associate awarded. **Location:** 40 miles from Boston. **Calendar:** Semester, extensive summer session. **Full-time faculty:** 99 total; 11% minority, 62% women. **Part-time faculty:** 388 total; 6% minority, 58% women. **Class size:** 38% < 20, 62% 20-39.

Student profile. Among degree-seeking undergraduates, 40% enrolled in a transfer program, 60% enrolled in a vocational program, 1,537 enrolled as first-time, first-year students, 391 transferred in from other institutions.

Part-time:	59%	**Women:**	63%
Out-of-state:	18%		

Basis for selection. Open admission, but selective for some programs. Special requirements for technology studies (engineering, computer, computer maintenance, electronics) and health and human services. Interview required of health and human services majors.

High school preparation. Health and technologies programs have specific math and/or science requirements.

2008-2009 Annual costs. Tuition/fees: $3,510; $10,740 out-of-state. Per-credit charge: $25 in-state; $266 out-of-state. New England residents pay $134 per credit hour. Books/supplies: $800. Personal expenses: $850.

Financial aid. Need-based: Need-based aid available for part-time students. **Non-need-based:** Scholarships awarded for academics.

Application procedures. Admission: Priority date 2/1; no deadline. $25 fee. Admission notification on a rolling basis. Entrance examination required for schools of practical/vocational nursing. **Financial aid:** Priority date 5/1; no closing date. FAFSA required. Applicants notified on a rolling basis starting 3/1; must reply within 2 week(s) of notification.

Academics. Special study options: Accelerated study, cooperative education, cross-registration, distance learning, double major, dual enrollment of high school students, ESL, exchange student, honors, internships, liberal arts/career combination, study abroad, weekend college. License preparation in dental hygiene, nursing, paramedic, radiology, real estate. **Credit/placement by examination:** AP, CLEP, institutional tests. 36 credit hours maximum toward associate degree. **Support services:** GED preparation and test center, learning center, pre-admission summer program, reduced course load, remedial instruction, study skills assistance, tutoring, writing center.

Majors. Business: General, accounting, administrative services, business admin, finance, international, logistics, marketing, office management, office technology, tourism promotion, tourism/travel. **Communications:** Broadcast journalism, journalism. **Communications technology:** General. **Computer sciences:** General, computer graphics, computer science, information systems, programming. **Education:** Business, early childhood. **Engineering:** Science. **Engineering technology:** Biomedical, electrical. **Family/consumer sciences:** Child care. **Foreign languages:** Sign language interpretation. **Health:** EMT paramedic, medical records admin, medical secretary, mental health services, nursing (RN), respiratory therapy technology, substance abuse counseling. **Legal studies:** Paralegal. **Liberal arts:** Arts/sciences. **Parks/recreation:** Sports admin. **Protective services:** Criminal justice. **Public administration:** Social work. **Visual/performing arts:** Commercial/advertising art, design. **Other:** Polysomnography/sleep technology.

Computing on campus. 400 workstations in library, computer center, student center. Commuter students can connect to campus network. Online course registration, online library, helpline, wireless network available.

Student life. Freshman orientation: Mandatory. Preregistration for classes offered. **Activities:** Choral groups, dance, drama, literary magazine, student government, student newspaper, American Sign Language club, Hispanic cultural club, women's resource network, social club (students with disabilities), Bible club.

Athletics. NJCAA. **Intercollegiate:** Baseball M, basketball, golf, soccer M, softball W. **Intramural:** Basketball, cross-country, golf, skiing, softball, table tennis, volleyball. **Team name:** Scarlet Knights.

Student services. Adult student services, career counseling, services for economically disadvantaged, student employment services, financial aid counseling, health services, on-campus daycare, personal counseling, placement for graduates, veterans' counselor, women's services. **Physically disabled:** Services for visually, speech, hearing impaired. **Learning disabled:** Comprehensive services available. **Transfer:** Transfer adviser, college fairs on campus for students transferring to 4-year colleges.

Contact. E-mail: admissions@necc.mass.edu
Phone: (978) 556-3600
Nora Sheridan, Director of Admissions, Northern Essex Community College, 100 Elliott Street, Haverhill, MA 01830-2399

Quincy College

Quincy, Massachusetts **CB member**
www.quincycollege.edu **CB code: 3713**

- Public 2-year community college
- Commuter campus in small city

General. Founded in 1956. Regionally accredited. Branch campus in Plymouth. **Enrollment:** 3,823 degree-seeking undergraduates. **Degrees:** 426 associate awarded. **Location:** 10 miles from downtown Boston. **Calendar:** Semester, extensive summer session. **Full-time faculty:** 34 total. **Part-time faculty:** 270 total.

Student profile.

Out-of-state:	1%	**25 or older:**	51%

Basis for selection. Open admission, but selective for some programs. Admission to health career programs based on test scores and high school record.

High school preparation. College-preparatory program with biology and chemistry required for registered nursing program.

2008-2009 Annual costs. Tuition/fees: $4,950. Per-credit charge: $165. Books/supplies: $500. Personal expenses: $400.

Application procedures. Admission: No deadline. $30 fee, may be waived for applicants with need. Admission notification on a rolling basis. **Financial aid:** FAFSA required. Applicants notified on a rolling basis starting 5/1; must reply within 2 week(s) of notification.

Academics. Special study options: Accelerated study, dual enrollment of high school students, independent study, internships. **Credit/placement by examination:** CLEP, institutional tests. 30 credit hours maximum toward associate degree. **Support services:** Learning center, pre-admission summer program, reduced course load, remedial instruction, tutoring.

Majors. Business: General, office technology, tourism/travel. **Computer sciences:** Computer science. **Conservation:** General. **Education:** Early childhood. **Health:** Nursing (RN). **Legal studies:** Paralegal. **Liberal arts:** Arts/sciences. **Protective services:** Criminal justice.

Computing on campus. 60 workstations in library, computer center. Wireless network available.

Student life. Freshman orientation: Available. **Activities:** Drama.

Student services. Adult student services, alcohol/substance abuse counseling, career counseling, student employment services, financial aid counseling, minority student services. **Transfer:** College fairs on campus for students transferring to 4-year colleges.

Contact. E-mail: admissions@quincycollege.edu
Phone: (617) 984-1700 Toll-free number: (800) 698-1700
Fax: (617) 984-1669
Lisa Stack, Director of Admissions, Quincy College, 24 Saville Avenue, Quincy, MA 02169

Quinsigamond Community College

Worcester, Massachusetts **CB member**
www.qcc.edu **CB code: 3714**

- Public 2-year community college
- Commuter campus in small city

General. Founded in 1963. Regionally accredited. **Enrollment:** 5,923 degree-seeking undergraduates; 1,302 non-degree-seeking students. **Degrees:** 600 associate awarded. **ROTC:** Army, Air Force. **Location:** 45 miles from Boston. **Calendar:** Semester, extensive summer session. **Full-time faculty:** 118 total. **Part-time faculty:** 378 total. **Class size:** 64% < 20, 35% 20-39, less than 1% 40-49. **Special facilities:** Dental hygiene clinic, athletic center, child care center. **Partnerships:** Formal partnerships with Intel Corporation, Verizon, National Grid.

Student profile. Among degree-seeking undergraduates, 75% enrolled in a transfer program, 58% enrolled in a vocational program, 2% already have a bachelor's degree or higher, 1,670 enrolled as first-time, first-year students, 921 transferred in from other institutions.

Part-time:	47%	**Asian American:**	4%
Out-of-state:	2%	**Hispanic American:**	12%
Women:	57%	**Native American:**	1%
African American:	10%	**25 or older:**	35%

Transfer out. 44% of students enrolled in the transfer program go on to 4-year colleges. **Colleges most students transferred to 2008:** Worcester State College, University of Massachusetts-Amherst, Assumption College, Anna Maria College, Framingham State College.

Basis for selection. Open admission, but selective for some programs. Special requirements for health programs.

High school preparation. Recommended units include English 4, mathematics 3, social studies 2, history 1, science 3 (laboratory 2), foreign language 2 and computer science 1. English, college math, and laboratory sciences required for health programs. English and math required for business, technology, and early childhood education.

2008-2009 Annual costs. Tuition/fees: $3,960; $10,140 out-of-state. Per-credit charge: $24 in-state; $230 out-of-state. Books/supplies: $900. Personal expenses: $1,362.

2007-2008 Financial aid. Need-based: Need-based aid available for part-time students. Work-study available nights, weekends and for part-time students. **Non-need-based:** Scholarships awarded for academics, leadership, minority status.

Application procedures. Admission: No deadline. $20 fee ($50 out-of-state), may be waived for applicants with need. Admission notification on a rolling basis beginning on or about 10/1. Must reply by May 1 or within 2 week(s) if notified thereafter. **Financial aid:** Priority date 4/1; no closing date. FAFSA required. Applicants notified on a rolling basis starting 4/1.

Academics. Specialized academic support to those with disabilities. **Special study options:** Accelerated study, cooperative education, cross-registration, distance learning, double major, dual enrollment of high school students, ESL, honors, independent study, internships, liberal arts/career combination, weekend college. Member 13-school Worcester consortium. License preparation in dental hygiene, nursing, occupational therapy, paramedic, radiology. **Credit/placement by examination:** AP, CLEP, IB, institutional tests. **Support services:** GED preparation and test center, learning center, reduced course load, remedial instruction, study skills assistance, tutoring, writing center.

Majors. Biology: Biotechnology. **Business:** Administrative services, business admin, hotel/motel admin, office/clerical, restaurant/food services. **Communications technology:** Graphics. **Computer sciences:** General, applications programming, computer forensics, programming. **Education:** Early childhood. **Engineering:** General, computer, computer hardware, electrical, manufacturing. **Engineering technology:** Computer, electrical, electromechanical, manufacturing, telecommunications. **Family/consumer sciences:** Institutional food production. **Health:** Dental hygiene, EMT paramedic, medical assistant, medical radiologic technology/radiation therapy, medical secretary, nursing (RN), occupational therapy assistant, office assistant, respiratory therapy technology. **Liberal arts:** Arts/sciences. **Mechanic/repair:** Automotive, electronics/electrical. **Personal/culinary services:** Food service, restaurant/catering. **Protective services:** Firefighting, forensics, law enforcement admin. **Public administration:** Human services.

Most popular majors. Business/marketing 14%, health sciences 16%, liberal arts 21%, security/protective services 6%.

Computing on campus. 400 workstations in library, computer center. Helpline, wireless network available.

Student life. Freshman orientation: Available. Preregistration for classes offered. Half-day program; some academic majors hold specialized orientation programs. **Activities:** Campus ministries, choral groups, drama, literary magazine, student government, student newspaper, multicultural club, several occupational groups, academic clubs.

Athletics. NJCAA. **Intercollegiate:** Baseball M, basketball, softball W. **Intramural:** Basketball, football (non-tackle), soccer, volleyball. **Team name:** Chiefs.

Student services. Chaplain/spiritual director, career counseling, student employment services, financial aid counseling, minority student services, on-campus daycare, personal counseling, placement for graduates, veterans' counselor. **Physically disabled:** Services for visually, speech, hearing impaired. **Learning disabled:** Comprehensive services available. **Transfer:** Transfer adviser, college fairs on campus for students transferring to 4-year colleges.

Contact. E-mail: admissions@qcc.mass.edu
Phone: (508) 854-4262 Fax: (508) 854-7525
James Fowler, Director of Admissions, Quinsigamond Community College, 670 West Boylston Street, Worcester, MA 01606

Roxbury Community College

Roxbury Crossing, Massachusetts **CB member**
www.rcc.mass.edu **CB code: 3740**

- Public 2-year community college
- Commuter campus in very large city

General. Founded in 1973. Regionally accredited. **Enrollment:** 2,154 degree-seeking undergraduates; 328 non-degree-seeking students. **Degrees:** 171 associate awarded. **ROTC:** Army. **Calendar:** Semester, extensive summer session. **Full-time faculty:** 50 total; 52% minority, 56% women. **Part-time faculty:** 106 total; 42% women. **Class size:** 73% < 20, 27% 20-39. **Special facilities:** Indoor track and field facilities. **Partnerships:** Formal partnerships with local employers.

Student profile. Among degree-seeking undergraduates, 49% enrolled in a transfer program, 51% enrolled in a vocational program, 539 enrolled as first-time, first-year students, 105 transferred in from other institutions.

Part-time:	61%	**Hispanic American:**	14%
Women:	69%	**International:**	1%
African American:	53%	**25 or older:**	61%
Asian American:	1%		

Basis for selection. Open admission, but selective for some programs. Specific admissions criteria for Nursing and Radiologic Technology programs.

High school preparation. College-preparatory program required.

2008-2009 Annual costs. Tuition/fees: $3,660; $11,310 out-of-state. Per-credit charge: $26 in-state; $281 out-of-state. New England Regional per-credit-hour charge $105. Books/supplies: $800. Personal expenses: $1,800.

Financial aid. All financial aid based on need. Need-based aid available for part-time students.

Application procedures. Admission: No deadline. $10 fee ($35 out-of-state), may be waived for applicants with need. Admission notification on a rolling basis. **Financial aid:** Priority date 5/1; no closing date. FAFSA, institutional form required. Applicants notified on a rolling basis starting 6/15; must reply within 2 week(s) of notification.

Academics. Special study options: Cross-registration, double major, dual enrollment of high school students, ESL, honors, independent study, internships, liberal arts/career combination. License preparation in nursing. **Credit/placement by examination:** CLEP, institutional tests. **Support services:** GED preparation and test center, learning center, remedial instruction, tutoring.

Majors. Architecture: Technology. **Biology:** General. **Business:** Accounting, administrative services, business admin, hospitality/recreation, management information systems, office management, office technology. **Communications technology:** Radio/tv. **Computer sciences:** General, applications programming. **Conservation:** General. **Education:** Early childhood. **Engineering technology:** CAD/CADD, drafting. **Family/consumer sciences:** Child care. **Foreign languages:** French. **Health:** Medical secretary, nursing (RN), prenursing. **Legal studies:** Legal secretary, paralegal. **Liberal arts:** Arts/sciences, humanities. **Math:** General. **Physical sciences:** General. **Protective services:** Law enforcement admin. **Social sciences:** General. **Visual/performing arts:** General.

Most popular majors. Business/marketing 27%, health sciences 27%, liberal arts 29%, security/protective services 11%.

Computing on campus. 52 workstations in library, computer center.

Student life. Freshman orientation: Available. Preregistration for classes offered. **Activities:** Choral groups, dance, drama, student government, student newspaper, Union Estudiantil Latina, international student association, Christian ministry.

Athletics. NJCAA. **Intercollegiate:** Basketball, soccer M.

Student services. Career counseling, student employment services, financial aid counseling, health services, on-campus daycare, personal counseling, placement for graduates. **Transfer:** Transfer adviser, college fairs on campus for students transferring to 4-year colleges.

Contact. Phone: (617) 541-5310 Fax: (617) 541-5316
Walter Clark, Director of Admissions, Roxbury Community College, 1234 Columbus Avenue, Roxbury Crossing, MA 02120-3400

Springfield Technical Community College

Springfield, Massachusetts **CB member**
www.stcc.edu **CB code: 3791**

- Public 2-year community and technical college
- Commuter campus in small city

General. Founded in 1967. Regionally accredited. **Enrollment:** 5,330 degree-seeking undergraduates; 1,001 non-degree-seeking students. **Degrees:** 702 associate awarded. **Location:** 90 miles from Boston; 30 miles from Hartford, Connecticut. **Calendar:** Semester, limited summer session. **Full-time faculty:** 157 total. **Part-time faculty:** 236 total. **Special facilities:** Springfield Armory Museum (national historic site). **Partnerships:** Formal partnerships with Verizon, Microsoft, Novell, A+, Cisco, Ford Asset, IBM.

Student profile. Among degree-seeking undergraduates, 1,411 enrolled as first-time, first-year students.

Part-time:	51%	**Hispanic American:**	19%
Out-of-state:	4%	**Native American:**	1%
Women:	57%	**International:**	1%
African American:	16%	**25 or older:**	43%
Asian American:	2%		

Transfer out. Colleges most students transferred to 2008: University of Massachusetts-Amherst, Westfield State College, Elms College, American International College, Springfield College.

Basis for selection. Open admission, but selective for some programs. Special requirements for certain health, engineering and science programs. SAT required for selective health and engineering programs. **Home-schooled:** Statement describing homeschool structure and mission required.

High school preparation. Math, chemistry, biology and/or physics required for many competitive programs.

2008-2009 Annual costs. Tuition/fees: $3,696; $10,206 out-of-state. Per-credit charge: $25 in-state; $242 out-of-state. New England reciprocal rate $237 per credit hour, including fees. Books/supplies: $1,000. Personal expenses: $1,836.

2007-2008 Financial aid. All financial aid based on need. 77% of total undergraduate aid awarded as scholarships/grants, 23% as loans/jobs. Need-based aid available for part-time students. Work-study available for part-time students.

Application procedures. Admission: No deadline. $10 fee ($35 out-of-state), may be waived for applicants with need. Admission notification on a rolling basis beginning on or about 3/1. Applicants must reply within 3 weeks of notification of admission. **Financial aid:** Priority date 5/1; no closing date. FAFSA, institutional form required. Applicants notified on a rolling basis starting 7/1.

Academics. Special study options: Cooperative education, cross-registration, distance learning, dual enrollment of high school students, ESL, honors, independent study, internships, liberal arts/career combination. License preparation in nursing, radiology. **Credit/placement by examination:** AP, CLEP, institutional tests. 45 credit hours maximum toward associate degree. **Support services:** GED preparation and test center, learning center, reduced course load, remedial instruction, study skills assistance, tutoring, writing center.

Majors. Agriculture: Landscaping. **Biology:** General, biotechnology. **Business:** General, accounting, business admin, executive assistant, finance, marketing, small business admin. **Communications technology:** Animation/special effects, radio/tv. **Computer sciences:** Applications programming, computer science, data processing, security, system admin, web page design. **Education:** Early childhood, elementary. **Engineering:** General. **Engineering technology:** Automotive, civil, computer, electrical, electromechanical, heat/ac/refrig, laser/optical, mechanical, telecommunications. **Health:** Clinical lab technology, dental hygiene, insurance coding, massage therapy, medical assistant, medical secretary, nuclear medical technology, nursing (RN), occupational therapy assistant, physical therapy assistant, premedicine, radiologic technology/medical imaging, respiratory therapy technology, sonography, surgical technology. **Liberal arts:** Arts/sciences. **Math:** General. **Parks/recreation:** Sports admin. **Physical sciences:** Chemistry, physics. **Protective services:** Fire safety technology, police science. **Visual/performing arts:** Commercial photography, commercial/advertising art, studio arts.

Most popular majors. Business/marketing 14%, engineering/engineering technologies 14%, health sciences 31%, liberal arts 18%, security/protective services 7%.

Computing on campus. 1,420 workstations in library, student center. Commuter students can connect to campus network. Online course registration, online library, helpline, student web hosting, wireless network available.

Student life. Freshman orientation: Available. Half-day session held 3 weeks before start of classes. **Policies:** No alcohol permitted. **Activities:** Drama, student government, student newspaper, TV station, business club, gay/lesbian/bisexual alliance, Christian Fellowship, Phi Theta Kappa, Campus Civitan, computer club, gallery players, engineering club, criminal justice club, massage therapy club.

Athletics. NJCAA. **Intercollegiate:** Basketball, golf, soccer, tennis, wrestling M. **Team name:** Rams.

Student services. Adult student services, alcohol/substance abuse counseling, career counseling, services for economically disadvantaged, student employment services, financial aid counseling, health services, on-campus daycare, personal counseling, placement for graduates, veterans' counselor, women's services. **Physically disabled:** Services for visually, speech, hearing impaired. **Learning disabled:** Comprehensive services available. **Transfer:** Pre-admission transcript evaluation for new students. Transfer center, transfer adviser, college fairs on campus for students transferring to 4-year colleges.

Contact. E-mail: admissions@stcc.edu
Phone: (413) 755-4202
Louisa Davis-Freeman, Dean of Admissions, Springfield Technical Community College, One Armory Square, Springfield, MA 01102-9000

Urban College of Boston

Boston, Massachusetts
www.urbancollege.edu **CB code: 3630**

- Private 2-year community college
- Commuter campus in very large city

General. Regionally accredited. **Enrollment:** 3 full-time, degree-seeking students. **Degrees:** 89 associate awarded. **Calendar:** Semester, limited summer session. **Full-time faculty:** 3 total. **Part-time faculty:** 42 total. **Class size:** 57% < 20, 43% 20-39.

Transfer out. Colleges most students transferred to 2008: Lesley College, Springfield College, Cambridge College.

Basis for selection. Open admission.

2008-2009 Annual costs. Tuition/fees: $4,700. Per-credit charge: $155. Books/supplies: $1,000. Personal expenses: $2,860.

2007-2008 Financial aid. All financial aid based on need. Need-based aid available for part-time students.

Application procedures. Admission: No deadline. $10 fee, may be waived for applicants with need. Admission notification on a rolling basis. **Financial aid:** No deadline. FAFSA required. Applicants notified on a rolling basis starting 4/15.

Academics. Special study options: Independent study, internships. **Credit/placement by examination:** AP, CLEP, IB. **Support services:** Learning center, study skills assistance, tutoring.

Majors. Education: Early childhood. **Liberal arts:** Arts/sciences. **Public administration:** Human services.

Computing on campus. 2 workstations in library, computer center.

Student life. Freshman orientation: Available. Preregistration for classes offered. **Policies:** Drug and alcohol use prohibited.

Student services. Career counseling, services for economically disadvantaged, financial aid counseling, minority student services, personal counseling, placement for graduates. **Transfer:** Transfer adviser for students transferring to 4-year colleges.

Contact. Phone: (617) 348-6359 Fax: (617) 423-4758
Henry Johnson, Dean of Enrollment Services, Urban College of Boston, 178 Tremont Street, Seventh Floor, Boston, MA 02111

Two-Year Colleges

Michigan

Alpena Community College
Alpena, Michigan
www.alpenacc.edu **CB code: 1011**

- Public 2-year community college
- Commuter campus in large town

General. Founded in 1952. Regionally accredited. **Enrollment:** 2,047 degree-seeking undergraduates. **Degrees:** 280 associate awarded. **Location:** 240 miles from Detroit. **Calendar:** Semester, limited summer session. **Full-time faculty:** 50 total. **Part-time faculty:** 85 total. **Special facilities:** Museum, planetarium.

Student profile.

Out-of-state:	1%	**Live on campus:**	3%
25 or older:	48%		

Transfer out. Colleges most students transferred to 2008: Lake Superior State University, Central Michigan University, Michigan State University, Ferris State University, Saginaw Valley State University.

Basis for selection. Open admission, but selective for some programs. Special requirements for practical nursing, registered nursing, and utility technician programs. ACT may be used for scholarship consideration or as basis for corroboration of institutional placement exam results. Placement test requirement waived for applicants with ACT composite score of 20 or higher.

High school preparation. High school diploma or equivalent required for nursing applicants.

2008-2009 Annual costs. Tuition/fees: $3,040; $4,300 out-of-district; $5,560 out-of-state. Per-credit charge: $84 in-district; $126 out-of-district; $168 out-of-state. Books/supplies: $500. Personal expenses: $600.

2008-2009 Financial aid. Need-based: 97% of total undergraduate aid awarded as scholarships/grants, 3% as loans/jobs. Need-based aid available for part-time students. Work-study available for part-time students. **Non-need-based:** Scholarships awarded for academics, art, athletics, job skills, leadership, music/drama.

Application procedures. Admission: Priority date 6/15; no deadline. No application fee. Admission notification on a rolling basis beginning on or about 2/15. **Financial aid:** Priority date 8/1; no closing date. FAFSA required. Applicants notified on a rolling basis starting 5/15; must reply within 3 week(s) of notification.

Academics. Special study options: Distance learning, double major, dual enrollment of high school students, internships, liberal arts/career combination. Bachelor's degree programs available on campus. License preparation in nursing. **Credit/placement by examination:** AP, CLEP, institutional tests. 30 credit hours maximum toward associate degree. **Support services:** Learning center, reduced course load, remedial instruction, study skills assistance, tutoring, writing center.

Majors. Business: Accounting, business admin, management information systems. **Communications technology:** Graphic/printing. **Computer sciences:** General, information systems, LAN/WAN management, networking. **Education:** General. **Engineering:** General. **Engineering technology:** Construction, drafting, manufacturing. **Health:** Medical assistant, nursing (RN). **Liberal arts:** Arts/sciences. **Mechanic/repair:** Automotive. **Protective services:** Corrections, law enforcement admin.

Computing on campus. 75 workstations in library, computer center. Commuter students can connect to campus network. Online library available.

Student life. Freshman orientation: Available. Preregistration for classes offered. One-day program during week prior to start of each semester. **Housing:** Apartments available. $300 deposit, deadline 8/1. **Activities:** Jazz band, dance, drama, musical theater, student government, student newspaper.

Athletics. NJCAA. **Intercollegiate:** Basketball, golf M, softball W, volleyball W. **Intramural:** Basketball, bowling, softball, volleyball. **Team name:** Lumberjacks.

Student services. Adult student services, alcohol/substance abuse counseling, career counseling, student employment services, financial aid counseling, personal counseling, placement for graduates, veterans' counselor, women's services. **Transfer:** Pre-admission transcript evaluation for new students. Transfer adviser, college fairs on campus for students transferring to 4-year colleges.

Contact. E-mail: kollienm@alpenacc.edu
Phone: (989) 358-7339 Toll-free number: (888) 468-6222
Fax: (989) 358-7540
Michael Kollien, Director of Admissions, Alpena Community College, 665 Johnson Street, Alpena, MI 49707

Bay de Noc Community College
Escanaba, Michigan
www.baycollege.edu **CB code: 1049**

- Public 2-year community college
- Commuter campus in large town

General. Founded in 1962. Regionally accredited. **Enrollment:** 2,170 degree-seeking undergraduates; 244 non-degree-seeking students. **Degrees:** 280 associate awarded. **Location:** 110 miles from Green Bay, Wisconsin. **Calendar:** Semester, limited summer session. **Full-time faculty:** 47 total. **Part-time faculty:** 106 total. **Class size:** 65% < 20, 34% 20-39, less than 1% 40-49. **Special facilities:** Reading, writing, math and computer-assisted instructional laboratories, center for performing arts, art gallery.

Student profile. Among degree-seeking undergraduates, 38% enrolled in a transfer program, 52% enrolled in a vocational program, 623 enrolled as first-time, first-year students.

Part-time:	36%	**25 or older:**	33%
Out-of-state:	5%	**Live on campus:**	2%
Women:	60%		

Transfer out. 48% of students enrolled in the transfer program go on to 4-year colleges. **Colleges most students transferred to 2008:** Northern Michigan University, Lake Superior State University, Michigan Technological University.

Basis for selection. Open admission, but selective for some programs. Special requirements for nursing program.

High school preparation. College-preparatory program recommended.

2008-2009 Annual costs. Tuition/fees: $2,565; $4,035 out-of-district; $5,055 out-of-state. Per-credit charge: $77 in-district; $126 out-of-district; $160 out-of-state. Tuition and instructional fees based on contact hours. Room/board: $2,600. Books/supplies: $1,072. Personal expenses: $500.

2008-2009 Financial aid. Need-based: Need-based aid available for part-time students. Work-study available nights, weekends and for part-time students. **Non-need-based:** Scholarships awarded for academics.

Application procedures. Admission: Closing date 8/15 (receipt date). $25 fee. Admission notification on a rolling basis. **Financial aid:** Priority date 4/1; no closing date. FAFSA required. Applicants notified on a rolling basis starting 2/1; must reply within 2 week(s) of notification.

Academics. Special study options: Cooperative education, distance learning, dual enrollment of high school students, internships, liberal arts/career combination, weekend college. Bachelor's degree programs available on campus. License preparation in nursing. **Credit/placement by examination:** AP, CLEP, institutional tests. 40 credit hours maximum toward associate degree. **Support services:** Pre-admission summer program, reduced course load, remedial instruction, study skills assistance, tutoring, writing center.

Majors. Architecture: Landscape. **Business:** Accounting, administrative services, business admin, sales/distribution. **Computer sciences:** Data processing. **Conservation:** Wood science. **Engineering technology:** Drafting, electrical, water quality. **Family/consumer sciences:** Child care. **Health:** Nursing (RN). **Legal studies:** Prelaw. **Liberal arts:** Arts/sciences. **Mechanic/repair:** General, automotive. **Physical sciences:** Astronomy.

Most popular majors. Business/marketing 22%, engineering/engineering technologies 8%, health sciences 24%, liberal arts 32%, security/protective services 7%.

Computing on campus. 535 workstations in library, computer center. Dormitories wired for high-speed internet access and linked to campus network. Commuter students can connect to campus network. Online course registration, online library, helpline, wireless network available.

Student life. **Freshman orientation:** Available. Students meet with counselors, financial aid officers, student services representatives to determine course of study and expenses. **Housing:** Apartments available. $150 partly refundable deposit, deadline 8/15. **Activities:** Campus ministries, choral groups, drama, literary magazine, Model UN, student government, student newspaper, student volunteer association, nurses association, student activities board, history club, water tech club, art club.

Athletics. **Intramural:** Basketball, bowling, golf, skiing, softball, swimming, table tennis, volleyball.

Student services. Adult student services, career counseling, student employment services, financial aid counseling, on-campus daycare, personal counseling, veterans' counselor. **Physically disabled:** Services for visually, hearing impaired. **Transfer:** Transfer adviser, college fairs on campus for students transferring to 4-year colleges.

Contact. E-mail: carterc@baycollege.edu
Phone: (906) 786-5802 ext. 1276 Toll-free number: (800) 221-2001 ext. 1276 Fax: (906) 786-8515
Cynthia Carter, Director of Admissions, Bay de Noc Community College, 2001 North Lincoln Road, Escanaba, MI 49829-2511

Bay Mills Community College

Brimley, Michigan
www.bmcc.edu **CB code: 2101**

- Public 2-year community college
- Commuter campus in rural community

General. Regionally accredited. **Enrollment:** 210 full-time, degree-seeking students. **Degrees:** 34 associate awarded. **Location:** 20 miles from Sault Ste. Marie. **Calendar:** Semester. **Full-time faculty:** 10 total; 40% women. **Part-time faculty:** 20 total; 70% women.

Transfer out. **Colleges most students transferred to 2008:** Lake Superior State University.

Basis for selection. Open admission. **Homeschooled:** Transcript of courses and grades required.

2008-2009 Annual costs. Tuition/fees: $2,910. Per-credit charge: $85. Books/supplies: $200.

Financial aid. **Need-based:** Work-study available nights and for part-time students.

Application procedures. **Admission:** Closing date 9/4 (receipt date). No application fee. Admission notification on a rolling basis. **Financial aid:** Priority date 6/30; no closing date. FAFSA required.

Academics. **Special study options:** Cooperative education, distance learning, double major, dual enrollment of high school students, independent study, internships. License preparation in paramedic. **Credit/placement by examination:** AP, CLEP, institutional tests. **Support services:** GED preparation and test center, learning center, remedial instruction, study skills assistance, tutoring.

Majors. **Area/ethnic studies:** Native American. **Business:** Business admin. **Computer sciences:** General, computer science. **Construction:** General. **Education:** Early childhood. **Parks/recreation:** Health/fitness.

Computing on campus. 30 workstations in library, computer center. Online library, repair service, wireless network available.

Student life. **Freshman orientation:** Mandatory. Preregistration for classes offered. **Activities:** Student government.

Student services. Career counseling, financial aid counseling. **Transfer:** Pre-admission transcript evaluation for new students. College fairs on campus for students transferring to 4-year colleges.

Contact. E-mail: elehre@bmcc.edu
Phone: (906) 248-3354 ext. 8422 Toll-free number: (800) 844-2622
Fax: (906) 248-3351
Elaine Lehre, Admissions Officer, Bay Mills Community College, 12214 West Lakeshore Drive, Brimley, MI 49715

Delta College

University Center, Michigan
www.delta.edu **CB code: 1816**

- Public 2-year community and junior college
- Commuter campus in small city

General. Founded in 1957. Regionally accredited. **Location:** 10 miles from Saginaw, 12 miles from Midland. **Calendar:** Semester.

Annual costs/financial aid. Tuition/fees (2008-2009): $2,922; $4,122 out-of-district; $5,712 out-of-state. Books/supplies: $1,380. Personal expenses: $855. Need-based financial aid available to full-time and part-time students.

Contact. Phone: (989) 686-9093
Director of Enrollment Services, 1961 Delta Road, University Center, MI 48710

Glen Oaks Community College

Centreville, Michigan **CB member**
www.glenoaks.edu **CB code: 1261**

- Public 2-year community college
- Commuter campus in rural community

General. Founded in 1965. Regionally accredited. **Enrollment:** 1,700 degree-seeking undergraduates. **Degrees:** 204 associate awarded. **Location:** 35 miles from Kalamazoo. **Calendar:** Semester, limited summer session. **Full-time faculty:** 27 total. **Part-time faculty:** 80 total. **Special facilities:** Fitness center, nature trails and habitat.

Student profile. Among degree-seeking undergraduates, 42% enrolled in a transfer program, 58% enrolled in a vocational program, 12% already have a bachelor's degree or higher.

Out-of-state:	18%	**25 or older:**	82%

Transfer out. **Colleges most students transferred to 2008:** Western Michigan University, Grand Valley State University, Kalamazoo Valley Community College, Kellogg Community College, Michigan State University.

Basis for selection. Open admission, but selective for some programs. Admission to nursing program based on pre-admission test, high school grades, and health form. ACCUPLACER test requested for certain programs. ACT or SAT may be considered in lieu of ACCUPLACER.

2008-2009 Annual costs. Tuition/fees: $2,990. Per-credit charge: $72. In-county residents pay $72 per contact hour. Students from service area counties (Branch and Cass counties in Michigan and LaGrange, Elkheart, Steuben counties in Indiana) pay $108 per contact hour. All others pay $144 per contact hour. Books/supplies: $500. Personal expenses: $775.

Financial aid. **Need-based:** Need-based aid available for part-time students. Work-study available nights and for part-time students. **Non-need-based:** Scholarships awarded for academics, art, athletics, leadership, minority status, music/drama.

Application procedures. **Admission:** No deadline. No application fee. Admission notification on a rolling basis. **Financial aid:** No deadline. FAFSA, institutional form required. Applicants notified on a rolling basis.

Academics. **Special study options:** Accelerated study, distance learning, double major, dual enrollment of high school students, independent study, internships, liberal arts/career combination. Bachelor's degree programs available on campus. License preparation in paramedic. **Credit/placement by examination:** AP, CLEP, institutional tests. 47 credit hours maximum toward associate degree. **Support services:** Learning center, remedial instruction, study skills assistance, tutoring.

Majors. **Business:** General. **Education:** Early childhood. **Engineering:** Science. **Family/consumer sciences:** Child care. **Health:** Nursing (RN). **Liberal arts:** Arts/sciences.

Most popular majors. Business/marketing 32%, engineering/engineering technologies 7%, health sciences 16%, liberal arts 41%.

Computing on campus. 85 workstations in library, computer center. Online library, wireless network available.

Student life. **Freshman orientation:** Available. Preregistration for classes offered. **Activities:** Choral groups, music ensembles, student government, academic honorary society, Phi Theta Kappa.

Athletics. NJCAA. **Intercollegiate:** Baseball M, basketball, cross-country, golf, softball W. **Intramural:** Table tennis. **Team name:** Vikings.

Student services. Career counseling, services for economically disadvantaged, student employment services, financial aid counseling, on-campus daycare, personal counseling, women's services. **Physically disabled:** Services for visually, speech, hearing impaired. **Transfer:** Transfer adviser, college fairs on campus for students transferring to 4-year colleges.

Contact. E-mail: jzimmerman@glenoaks.edu
Phone: (269) 467-9945 ext. 320 Toll-free number: (888) 994-7818 ext. 320
Fax: (269) 467-9068
Jean Zimmerman, Director of Admissions, Glen Oaks Community College, 62249 Shimmel Road, Centreville, MI 49032-9719

Gogebic Community College
Ironwood, Michigan
www.gogebic.edu **CB code: 1250**

- Public 2-year community college
- Commuter campus in small town

General. Founded in 1932. Regionally accredited. **Enrollment:** 904 degree-seeking undergraduates. **Degrees:** 139 associate awarded. **Location:** 100 miles from Duluth, Minnesota, 150 miles from Marquette. **Calendar:** Semester, limited summer session. **Full-time faculty:** 33 total. **Part-time faculty:** 40 total. **Class size:** 72% < 20, 27% 20-39, less than 1% 40-49, less than 1% 50-99. **Special facilities:** Arboretum, ski hill, terrain park, tubing park, cross-country ski trails.

Student profile. Among degree-seeking undergraduates, 38% enrolled in a transfer program, 54% enrolled in a vocational program.

Transfer out. Colleges most students transferred to 2008: Northern Michigan University, University of Wisconsin-Superior, Northland College, Michigan Technological University.

Basis for selection. Open admission, but selective for some programs. Students applying to nursing programs required to show competency in biology and chemistry. Admission based on assessment test scores and academic achievement. Interview recommended. **Homeschooled:** Interview required.

High school preparation. Nursing applicants must have background in chemistry, math, and biology.

2008-2009 Annual costs. Tuition/fees: $3,028; $3,679 out-of-district; $4,485 out-of-state. Per-credit charge: $81 in-district; $102 out-of-district; $128 out-of-state. Room only: $3,680. Books/supplies: $950. Personal expenses: $700.

Financial aid. Need-based: Need-based aid available for part-time students. Work-study available nights, weekends and for part-time students. **Non-need-based:** Scholarships awarded for academics, art, athletics, job skills, leadership, music/drama, state residency.

Application procedures. Admission: No deadline. $10 fee, may be waived for applicants with need. Admission notification on a rolling basis. **Financial aid:** Priority date 5/1; no closing date. FAFSA required. Applicants notified on a rolling basis starting 3/15; must reply within 2 week(s) of notification.

Academics. Special study options: Cooperative education, distance learning, double major, dual enrollment of high school students, honors, independent study, internships, student-designed major. License preparation in nursing, paramedic. **Credit/placement by examination:** AP, CLEP, institutional tests. 12 credit hours maximum toward associate degree. AP exam scores not listed in policy evaluated on individual basis. **Support services:** GED test center, learning center, reduced course load, remedial instruction, study skills assistance, tutoring.

Majors. Biology: General. **Business:** General, accounting, administrative services, business admin, entrepreneurial studies, office management, office technology. **Communications technology:** Graphics. **Computer sciences:** General, data processing, programming. **Conservation:** General, forestry. **Construction:** General, carpentry. **Education:** General, early childhood, elementary, secondary, special, teacher assistance. **Engineering:** General. **Engineering technology:** Automotive, CAD/CADD, construction. **Health:** Clinical lab science, EMT paramedic, nursing (RN), predental, premedicine, prenursing, prepharmacy, preveterinary. **History:** General. **Legal studies:** Prelaw. **Liberal arts:** Arts/sciences. **Math:** General. **Mechanic/repair:** Automotive. **Parks/recreation:** Facilities management. **Personal/culinary services:** Mortuary science. **Physical sciences:** General, chemistry, physics. **Protective services:** Law enforcement admin. **Psychology:** General. **Public administration:** Social work. **Social sciences:** General. **Visual/performing arts:** Art, commercial/advertising art.

Computing on campus. 240 workstations in dormitories, library, computer center. Dormitories wired for high-speed internet access and linked to campus network. Commuter students can connect to campus network. Online library, wireless network available.

Student life. Freshman orientation: Mandatory. Preregistration for classes offered. Early orientation held in April for accepted students who have completed assessment. Other orientation programs in August and June. **Housing:** Guaranteed on-campus for freshmen. Coed dorms available. **Activities:** Concert band, drama, music ensembles, student government, student newspaper, student senate, student nurses association.

Athletics. NJCAA. **Intercollegiate:** Basketball. **Intramural:** Basketball, bowling, cheerleading, football (non-tackle) M, golf, skiing, soccer, softball, tennis, volleyball. **Team name:** Samsons.

Student services. Alcohol/substance abuse counseling, career counseling, services for economically disadvantaged, student employment services, financial aid counseling, personal counseling, placement for graduates, veterans' counselor. **Physically disabled:** Services for visually, hearing impaired. **Transfer:** Re-entry adviser for new students. Transfer adviser, college fairs on campus for students transferring to 4-year colleges.

Contact. E-mail: debbiej@gogebic.edu
Phone: (906) 932-4231 ext. 207 Toll-free number: (800) 682-5910 ext. 207
Fax: (906) 932-2339
Jeanne Graham, Director of Admissions and Public Information, Gogebic Community College, E4946 Jackson Road, Ironwood, MI 49938

Grand Rapids Community College
Grand Rapids, Michigan **CB member**
www.grcc.edu **CB code: 1254**

- Public 2-year community college
- Commuter campus in small city

General. Founded in 1914. Regionally accredited. Evening courses offered at 9 off-campus sites in Western Michigan. **Enrollment:** 14,392 degree-seeking undergraduates; 1,011 non-degree-seeking students. **Degrees:** 1,534 associate awarded. **Location:** 70 miles from Lansing, 180 miles from Chicago. **Calendar:** Semester, extensive summer session. **Full-time faculty:** 266 total; 10% have terminal degrees, 15% minority, 51% women. **Part-time faculty:** 488 total; 6% have terminal degrees, 8% minority, 49% women. **Class size:** 19% < 20, 81% 20-39, less than 1% 40-49, less than 1% 50-99.

Student profile. Among degree-seeking undergraduates, 41% enrolled in a transfer program, 46% enrolled in a vocational program, 3,542 enrolled as first-time, first-year students, 693 transferred in from other institutions.

Part-time:	54%	**Asian American:**	3%
Out-of-state:	1%	**Hispanic American:**	7%
Women:	52%	**Native American:**	1%
African American:	11%	**25 or older:**	30%

Transfer out. Colleges most students transferred to 2008: Grand Valley State University, Ferris State University, Western Michigan University, Michigan State University, Aquinas College.

Basis for selection. Open admission, but selective for some programs. Occupational health program applicants must be high school graduates, have GPAs and completed specific classes with a 2.0 grade or better. **Homeschooled:** Assessment exam required.

High school preparation. Recommended units include English 4, mathematics 3, social studies 2 and science 3.

2008-2009 Annual costs. Tuition/fees: $2,555; $5,250 out-of-district; $7,670 out-of-state. Per-credit charge: $83 in-district; $173 out-of-district; $253 out-of-state. Books/supplies: $1,524. Personal expenses: $575.

2008-2009 Financial aid. Need-based: Need-based aid available for part-time students. Work-study available nights, weekends and for part-time students. **Non-need-based:** Scholarships awarded for academics, alumni affiliation, art, athletics, leadership, minority status, music/drama, state residency. **Additional information:** Tuition reimbursement and/or child-care services for single parents and displaced homemakers who meet Perkins guidelines.

Application procedures. Admission: Closing date 8/30 (receipt date). $20 fee, may be waived for applicants with need. Admission notification on a rolling basis. **Financial aid:** Priority date 4/1; no closing date. FAFSA required. Applicants notified on a rolling basis starting 5/1; must reply within 3 week(s) of notification.

Academics. Liberal arts and pre-professional curricula along with extensive work-force training and technical seminars offered. **Special study options:** Cooperative education, distance learning, dual enrollment of high school students, ESL, independent study, internships, study abroad, weekend college. License preparation in dental hygiene, nursing, occupational therapy, radiology. **Credit/placement by examination:** AP, CLEP, institutional tests. 30 credit hours maximum toward associate degree. **Support**

services: GED test center, learning center, reduced course load, remedial instruction, study skills assistance, tutoring, writing center.

Majors. Agriculture: Landscaping. **Architecture:** Technology. **Biology:** General. **Business:** General, accounting technology, business admin, executive assistant, fashion, sales/distribution. **Communications:** Journalism. **Computer sciences:** General, LAN/WAN management, networking, programming, web page design, webmaster. **Conservation:** Fisheries, forestry, management/policy, wildlife. **Education:** Art, business, chemistry, elementary, English, mathematics, multi-level teacher, music, physical, science, teacher assistance, technology/industrial arts. **Engineering:** General. **Engineering technology:** General, architectural drafting, automotive, electrical, heat/ac/refrig, mechanical drafting, plastics, quality control, water quality. **Family/consumer sciences:** Aging, child care, child development. **Foreign languages:** General. **Health:** Clinical lab science, dental assistant, dental hygiene, licensed practical nurse, medical radiologic technology/radiation therapy, nursing (RN), occupational therapy assistant, predental, premedicine, prepharmacy, preveterinary, surgical technology. **Legal studies:** Prelaw. **Liberal arts:** Arts/sciences, library science. **Math:** General. **Mechanic/repair:** Electronics/electrical, heating/ac/refrig. **Personal/culinary services:** Chef training, mortuary science, restaurant/catering. **Physical sciences:** Chemistry, geology, oceanography, physics. **Production:** General, machine shop technology, welding. **Protective services:** Corrections, firefighting, law enforcement admin, police science. **Psychology:** General. **Public administration:** Social work. **Science technology:** Chemical. **Social sciences:** Economics, political science, sociology. **Visual/performing arts:** Art, commercial/advertising art, dramatic, interior design, music management, music performance, photography, piano/organ, studio arts, voice/opera. **Other:** Music recording technology, Pre-optometry.

Most popular majors. Business/marketing 15%, education 6%, engineering/engineering technologies 8%, health sciences 11%, liberal arts 31%, security/protective services 6%.

Computing on campus. 1,254 workstations in library, computer center. Commuter students can connect to campus network. Online course registration, online library, helpline, wireless network available.

Student life. Freshman orientation: Available. Preregistration for classes offered. Provides campus tours and general information about the college. **Policies:** No smoking on campus. **Activities:** Bands, choral groups, dance, drama, film society, international student organizations, literary magazine, music ensembles, musical theater, student government, student newspaper, symphony orchestra, TV station, Black student organization, Hispanic student organization, Native American student organization, Vietnamese student organization, Christian Fellowship, content area student organizations, service learning.

Athletics. NJCAA. **Intercollegiate:** Baseball M, basketball, cross-country, diving, football (tackle) M, golf M, softball W, swimming, tennis, track and field, volleyball W, wrestling M. **Intramural:** Basketball, racquetball, skiing, soccer M, swimming. **Team name:** Raiders.

Student services. Adult student services, career counseling, student employment services, financial aid counseling, on-campus daycare, personal counseling, placement for graduates. **Physically disabled:** Services for visually, speech, hearing impaired. **Transfer:** Pre-admission transcript evaluation for new students. Transfer adviser, college fairs on campus for students transferring to 4-year colleges.

Contact. E-mail: enroll@grcc.edu
Phone: (616) 234-7623 Fax: (616) 234-4107
Diane Patrick, Director of Admissions, Grand Rapids Community College, 143 Bostwick Avenue NE, Grand Rapids, MI 49503-3295

Henry Ford Community College

Dearborn, Michigan
www.hfcc.edu **CB code: 1293**

- Public 2-year community college
- Commuter campus in small city

General. Founded in 1938. Regionally accredited. **Enrollment:** 14,282 degree-seeking undergraduates; 1,289 non-degree-seeking students. **Degrees:** 1,128 associate awarded. **Location:** 8 miles from Detroit. **Calendar:** Semester, extensive summer session. **Full-time faculty:** 201 total. **Part-time faculty:** 551 total.

Student profile. Among degree-seeking undergraduates, 3,002 enrolled as first-time, first-year students.

Part-time:	59%	**Women:**	58%
Out-of-state:	2%	**25 or older:**	47%

Transfer out. Colleges most students transferred to 2008: The University of Michigan-Dearborn, Wayne State University, Eastern Michigan University, Michigan State University.

Basis for selection. Open admission, but selective for some programs. Special requirements for specific allied health programs.

High school preparation. For allied health programs: 1 year high school biology, chemistry, and algebra.

2008-2009 Annual costs. Tuition/fees: $2,412; $4,062 out-of-district; $4,212 out-of-state. Per-credit charge: $65 in-district; $120 out-of-district; $125 out-of-state. Books/supplies: $500. Personal expenses: $585.

Financial aid. Need-based: Work-study available nights, weekends and for part-time students.

Application procedures. Admission: No deadline. $30 fee, may be waived for applicants with need. Admission notification on a rolling basis. **Financial aid:** Priority date 4/1; no closing date. FAFSA required. Applicants notified on a rolling basis starting 3/1.

Academics. Special study options: Accelerated study, cooperative education, distance learning, double major, dual enrollment of high school students, ESL, honors, independent study. License preparation in nursing, paramedic, physical therapy, radiology. **Credit/placement by examination:** CLEP. 20 credit hours maximum toward associate degree. **Support services:** Learning center, pre-admission summer program, reduced course load, remedial instruction, study skills assistance, tutoring, writing center.

Majors. Architecture: Technology. **Business:** General, accounting, business admin, executive assistant, hospitality admin, management science, office/clerical, real estate. **Communications:** Broadcast journalism. **Communications technology:** Animation/special effects. **Computer sciences:** General, security. **Conservation:** Environmental studies. **Construction:** General. **Education:** Early childhood, elementary, secondary, special. **Engineering:** General. **Engineering technology:** CAD/CADD, drafting, electrical, energy systems, manufacturing. **Family/consumer sciences:** Child development. **Health:** EMT paramedic, licensed practical nurse, management/clinical assistant, medical records technology, nursing (RN), office admin, physical therapy assistant, prepharmacy, radiologic technology/medical imaging, respiratory therapy technology, surgical technology. **Legal studies:** Legal secretary, paralegal. **Liberal arts:** Arts/sciences. **Mechanic/repair:** Automotive, industrial. **Parks/recreation:** Exercise sciences. **Personal/culinary services:** Chef training, restaurant/catering. **Philosophy/religion:** Religion. **Physical sciences:** Chemistry. **Protective services:** Firefighting, law enforcement admin, security management. **Transportation:** General. **Visual/performing arts:** Art, commercial/advertising art, dramatic, interior design, studio arts.

Computing on campus. Commuter students can connect to campus network. Online course registration, online library, helpline, wireless network available.

Student life. Freshman orientation: Available. Preregistration for classes offered. **Activities:** Bands, choral groups, drama, film society, literary magazine, music ensembles, radio station, student government, student newspaper, Muslim student association, African American association, community service club, Campus Crusade for Christ, international relations organization, Students for a Democratic Society, Crazy Antics club, Yemen student association, multicultural club, diversity club.

Athletics. NJCAA. **Intercollegiate:** Baseball M, basketball, golf, softball W, volleyball W. **Intramural:** Basketball, bowling, golf, table tennis, tennis, track and field, volleyball. **Team name:** Hawks.

Student services. Adult student services, career counseling, services for economically disadvantaged, student employment services, financial aid counseling, on-campus daycare, personal counseling, placement for graduates, veterans' counselor. **Physically disabled:** Services for visually, hearing impaired. **Transfer:** Re-entry adviser, pre-admission transcript evaluation for new students. Transfer center, transfer adviser, college fairs on campus for students transferring to 4-year colleges.

Contact. Phone: (313) 845-9613 Toll-free number: (800) 585-4322
Fax: (313) 845-9891
Douglas Freed, Director of Enrollment Management, Henry Ford Community College, 5101 Evergreen Road, Dearborn, MI 48128

ITT Technical Institute: Canton

Canton, Michigan

- For-profit 2-year business and technical college
- Commuter campus in small city

General. Accredited by ACICS. **Calendar:** Quarter.

Contact. 1905 South Haggerty Road, Canton, MI 48188

ITT Technical Institute: Grand Rapids

Grand Rapids, Michigan
www.itt-tech.edu
CB code: 2705

- For-profit 2-year technical college
- Commuter campus in small city

General. Accredited by ACICS. **Calendar:** Quarter.

Contact. Phone: (616) 956-1060
Director of Recruitment, 4020 Sparks Drive Southeast, Grand Rapids, MI 49546

ITT Technical Institute: Troy

Troy, Michigan
www.itt-tech.edu
CB code: 2784

- For-profit 2-year technical college
- Commuter campus in small city

General. Accredited by ACICS. **Calendar:** Quarter.

Contact. Phone: (248) 524-1800
Director of Recruitment, 1522 East Big Beaver Road, Troy, MI 48083-1905

Jackson Community College

Jackson, Michigan
www.jccmi.edu
CB member
CB code: 1340

- Public 2-year community college
- Commuter campus in small city

General. Founded in 1928. Regionally accredited. Off-campus locations in Hillsdale County and Lenawee County. **Enrollment:** 6,200 degree-seeking undergraduates. **Degrees:** 550 associate awarded. **Location:** 6 miles from downtown. **Calendar:** Semester, limited summer session. **Full-time faculty:** 90 total. **Part-time faculty:** 302 total. **Class size:** 65% < 20, 34% 20-39, 1% 40-49. **Partnerships:** Formal partnership with Foote Health University to provide education and training for employees.

Transfer out. Colleges most students transferred to 2008: Michigan State University, Spring Arbor University, Eastern Michigan University, Siena Heights University, Western Michigan University.

Basis for selection. Open admission, but selective for some programs. Special requirements for allied health programs and nursing program. ACT scores used for placement if submitted. Students not submitting ACT scores are required to take college-administered placement tests. Second admit programs require interviews and specific academic prerequisites.

2008-2009 Annual costs. Tuition/fees: $3,240; $4,305 out-of-district; $5,865 out-of-state. Per-credit charge: $87 in-district; $122 out-of-district; $174 out-of-state. Books/supplies: $672. Personal expenses: $720.

2008-2009 Financial aid. Need-based: Need-based aid available for part-time students. Work-study available nights, weekends and for part-time students. **Non-need-based:** Scholarships awarded for academics, art, leadership, music/drama, state residency.

Application procedures. Admission: No deadline. No application fee. Admission notification on a rolling basis. **Financial aid:** Priority date 6/15; no closing date. FAFSA, institutional form required. Applicants notified on a rolling basis starting 3/1.

Academics. Extensive on-line offerings. Students may also complete bachelor's degrees on-campus from partner universities. **Special study options:** Distance learning, dual enrollment of high school students, ESL, independent study, internships, liberal arts/career combination. Bachelor's degree programs available on campus. License preparation in aviation, nursing, paramedic, radiology. **Credit/placement by examination:** AP, CLEP, IB, institutional tests. 30 credit hours maximum toward associate degree. **Support services:** GED preparation and test center, learning center, preadmission summer program, remedial instruction, study skills assistance, tutoring, writing center.

Majors. Business: General, accounting, business admin, finance. **Computer sciences:** Applications programming, computer graphics, data processing, programming, web page design. **Construction:** Electrician. **Education:** Early childhood. **Engineering technology:** Electrical, heat/ac/refrig. **Health:** EMT paramedic, medical assistant, medical transcription, nursing (RN), radiologic technology/medical imaging, sonography. **Liberal arts:** Arts/sciences. **Mechanic/repair:** Automotive, electronics/electrical, heating/ac/refrig. **Protective services:** Criminal justice. **Visual/performing arts:** Graphic design.

Most popular majors. Business/marketing 12%, health sciences 28%, liberal arts 39%, trade and industry 9%.

Computing on campus. 356 workstations in library, computer center, student center. Online course registration, helpline available.

Student life. Freshman orientation: Available. 2- to 3-hour program prior to each semester. **Activities:** Bands, choral groups, dance, drama, music ensembles, musical theater, student government, student newspaper.

Athletics. Intramural: Basketball M, football (non-tackle) M, soccer M. **Team name:** Golden Jets.

Student services. Adult student services, career counseling, services for economically disadvantaged, financial aid counseling, minority student services, on-campus daycare. **Physically disabled:** Services for visually, speech, hearing impaired. **Transfer:** Pre-admission transcript evaluation for new students. Transfer center, transfer adviser, college fairs on campus for students transferring to 4-year colleges.

Contact. E-mail: admissions@jccmi.edu
Phone: (517) 796-8425 Toll-free number: (888) 522-7344
Fax: (517) 796-8631
Julie Hand, Enrollment Services Team Leader, Jackson Community College, 2111 Emmons Road, Jackson, MI 49201-8399

Kalamazoo Valley Community College

Kalamazoo, Michigan
www.kvcc.edu
CB code: 1378

- Public 2-year community college
- Commuter campus in small city

General. Founded in 1966. Regionally accredited. Additional campus downtown. **Enrollment:** 10,173 degree-seeking undergraduates. **Degrees:** 784 associate awarded. **Location:** 130 miles from Detroit, 150 miles from Chicago. **Calendar:** Semester, limited summer session. **Full-time faculty:** 135 total. **Part-time faculty:** 385 total. **Class size:** 30% < 20, 59% 20-39, 10% 40-49, less than 1% 50-99.

Student profile.

Out-of-state:	1%	**25 or older:**	50%

Transfer out. Colleges most students transferred to 2008: Western Michigan University.

Basis for selection. Open admission.

2008-2009 Annual costs. Tuition/fees: $2,040; $3,240 out-of-district; $4,350 out-of-state. Per-credit charge: $68 in-district; $108 out-of-district; $145 out-of-state. Books/supplies: $1,350. Personal expenses: $1,282.

Financial aid. Need-based: Need-based aid available for part-time students. Work-study available nights, weekends and for part-time students. **Non-need-based:** Scholarships awarded for academics, athletics.

Application procedures. Admission: No deadline. No application fee. Admission notification on a rolling basis. **Financial aid:** Priority date 6/1; no closing date. FAFSA, institutional form required. Applicants notified on a rolling basis starting 5/1; must reply within 2 week(s) of notification.

Academics. Special study options: Cooperative education, cross-registration, distance learning, dual enrollment of high school students, ESL, honors, independent study, internships, liberal arts/career combination, weekend college. License preparation in dental hygiene, nursing. **Credit/placement by examination:** CLEP, institutional tests. 32 credit hours maximum toward associate degree. Michigan Language Assessment Battery may be used for placement. **Support services:** Learning center, reduced course load, remedial instruction, tutoring, writing center.

Majors. Business: Accounting, administrative services, business admin, management information systems. **Communications technology:** General. **Computer sciences:** Computer graphics, data processing, programming. **Education:** General. **Engineering:** General. **Engineering technology:** Drafting, electrical. **Family/consumer sciences:** Family studies. **Health:** Dental hygiene, licensed practical nurse, medical assistant, medical secretary, nursing (RN), respiratory therapy technology. **Legal studies:** Legal secretary.

Liberal arts: Arts/sciences. **Mechanic/repair:** Automotive. **Physical sciences:** General. **Protective services:** Firefighting, law enforcement admin, police science. **Visual/performing arts:** Commercial/advertising art.

Most popular majors. Business/marketing 11%, education 11%, engineering/engineering technologies 7%, health sciences 12%, liberal arts 43%.

Computing on campus. 1,000 workstations in library, computer center, student center. Online course registration, wireless network available.

Student life. Freshman orientation: Available. **Activities:** Choral groups, dance, Fellowship of Christian Athletes, international student club, Student American Dental Hygiene Association, data processing association, African American association, Latino student association, Native American association, deaf student association.

Athletics. NJCAA. **Intercollegiate:** Baseball M, basketball, golf M, softball W, tennis, volleyball W. **Intramural:** Basketball M, tennis W, volleyball W. **Team name:** Cougars.

Student services. Career counseling, services for economically disadvantaged, student employment services, financial aid counseling, minority student services, on-campus daycare, personal counseling, placement for graduates, women's services. **Physically disabled:** Services for visually, speech, hearing impaired. **Transfer:** Transfer adviser, college fairs on campus for students transferring to 4-year colleges.

Contact. E-mail: admissions@kvcc.edu
Phone: (269) 488-4400 Fax: (269) 488-4161
Michael McCall, Director of Admissions, Registration and Records, Kalamazoo Valley Community College, 6767 West O Avenue, Kalamazoo, MI 49003-4070

Kellogg Community College
Battle Creek, Michigan
www.kellogg.edu **CB code: 1375**

- Public 2-year community college
- Commuter campus in small city

General. Founded in 1956. Regionally accredited. Academic centers in Coldwater, Hastings and Albion. Regional manufacturing technical center with open entry/open exit programs in 7 different technical areas. **Enrollment:** 4,535 degree-seeking undergraduates; 1,040 non-degree-seeking students. **Degrees:** 740 associate awarded. **Location:** 20 miles from Kalamazoo, 80 miles from Grand Rapids. **Calendar:** Semester, limited summer session. **Full-time faculty:** 90 total. **Part-time faculty:** 290 total.

Student profile. Among degree-seeking undergraduates, 862 enrolled as first-time, first-year students.

Part-time:	62%	**Hispanic American:**	2%
Women:	68%	**Native American:**	1%
African American:	8%	**25 or older:**	47%
Asian American:	1%		

Transfer out. Colleges most students transferred to 2008: Western Michigan University, Michigan State University, Ferris State University, Grand Valley State University, Central Michigan University.

Basis for selection. Open admission, but selective for some programs. Allied health and nursing program applicants must supply high school record, previous college transcripts, ACT/SAT test scores, and meet specific academic criteria.

High school preparation. College-preparatory program recommended. Recommended units include English 4, mathematics 4, social studies 1, history 3, science 4 (laboratory 1), foreign language 1 and academic electives 6.

2008-2009 Annual costs. Tuition/fees: $2,325; $3,638 out-of-district; $5,123 out-of-state. Books/supplies: $1,300. Personal expenses: $5,782.

2008-2009 Financial aid. Need-based: Need-based aid available for part-time students. Work-study available nights and for part-time students. **Non-need-based:** Scholarships awarded for academics, alumni affiliation, athletics.

Application procedures. Admission: Priority date 8/1; no deadline. No application fee. Admission notification on a rolling basis. **Financial aid:** Priority date 4/1; no closing date. FAFSA, institutional form required. Applicants notified on a rolling basis starting 4/1.

Academics. Special study options: Accelerated study, cooperative education, distance learning, double major, dual enrollment of high school students, honors, independent study, internships, liberal arts/career combination, weekend college. Bachelor's degree programs available on campus. License preparation in dental hygiene, nursing, paramedic, physical therapy, radiology. **Credit/placement by examination:** AP, CLEP, IB, institutional tests. Must be 2.0 or above for credit. **Support services:** Learning center, reduced course load, remedial instruction, study skills assistance, tutoring, writing center.

Majors. Business: Accounting, administrative services, business admin. **Communications technology:** General. **Computer sciences:** Programming. **Construction:** Electrician, pipefitting. **Engineering technology:** Drafting, electrical. **Family/consumer sciences:** Child care. **Health:** Clinical lab technology, dental hygiene, EMT paramedic, health services, medical radiologic technology/radiation therapy, medical secretary, nursing (RN), physical therapy assistant. **Legal studies:** Legal secretary, paralegal. **Liberal arts:** Arts/sciences. **Mechanic/repair:** Heating/ac/refrig, industrial. **Protective services:** Corrections, fire safety technology, police science. **Public administration:** Social work. **Visual/performing arts:** Commercial/advertising art.

Most popular majors. Business/marketing 12%, health sciences 27%, liberal arts 47%.

Computing on campus. 1,000 workstations in library, computer center. Commuter students can connect to campus network. Online course registration, online library, helpline, wireless network available.

Student life. Freshman orientation: Available. **Activities:** Bands, campus ministries, choral groups, drama, international student organizations, literary magazine, music ensembles, student newspaper, African American cultural enhancement association, human services club, Phi Theta Kappa, literary/photography magazine, art league, crude arts club, tech club.

Athletics. NJCAA. **Intercollegiate:** Baseball M, basketball, soccer M, softball W, volleyball W. **Team name:** Bruins.

Student services. Student employment services, financial aid counseling, personal counseling, placement for graduates, veterans' counselor. **Physically disabled:** Services for visually, speech, hearing impaired. **Transfer:** Pre-admission transcript evaluation for new students. Transfer adviser, college fairs on campus for students transferring to 4-year colleges.

Contact. E-mail: admissions@kellogg.edu
Phone: (269) 365-4153 Fax: (269) 966-4089
Denise Newman, Director of Enrollment Services, Kellogg Community College, 450 North Avenue, Battle Creek, MI 49017-3397

Kirtland Community College
Roscommon, Michigan
www.kirtland.edu **CB code: 1382**

- Public 2-year community college
- Commuter campus in rural community

General. Founded in 1966. Regionally accredited. Additional campuses in Roscommon and Gaylord. **Enrollment:** 1,475 degree-seeking undergraduates; 182 non-degree-seeking students. **Degrees:** 153 associate awarded. **Location:** 192 miles from Detroit, 150 miles from Grand Rapids. **Calendar:** Semester, extensive summer session. **Full-time faculty:** 35 total; 11% have terminal degrees, 6% minority, 46% women. **Part-time faculty:** 104 total; 3% minority, 58% women. **Class size:** 87% < 20, 13% 20-39. **Special facilities:** Fitness and nature trail, firing range, Michigan Technical Education Center.

Student profile. Among degree-seeking undergraduates, 17% enrolled in a transfer program, 66% enrolled in a vocational program, 259 enrolled as first-time, first-year students, 85 transferred in from other institutions.

Part-time:	55%	**Hispanic American:**	1%
Women:	63%	**Native American:**	2%
African American:	1%	**25 or older:**	43%
Asian American:	1%		

Transfer out. Colleges most students transferred to 2008: Central Michigan University, Saginaw Valley State University, Mid-Michigan Community College, North Central Michigan College, Delta College.

Basis for selection. Open admission, but selective for some programs. Special requirements for nursing (levels I and II), pre-corrections, criminal justice administration, criminal justice pre-services, cardiovascular sonography and corrections administration programs. **Homeschooled:** Transcript or record of courses and grades requested.

Two-Year Colleges

High school preparation. 10 units recommended. Recommended units include English 4, mathematics 2, social studies 2 and science 2.

2008-2009 Annual costs. Tuition/fees: $2,865; $4,800 out-of-district; $5,805 out-of-state. Per-credit charge: $78 in-district; $142 out-of-district; $176 out-of-state. Books/supplies: $900. Personal expenses: $540.

2008-2009 Financial aid. Need-based: Average need met was 33%. Average scholarship/grant was $2,527; average loan $1,180. 62% of total undergraduate aid awarded as scholarships/grants, 38% as loans/jobs. Need-based aid available for part-time students. Work-study available nights, weekends and for part-time students. **Non-need-based:** Scholarships awarded for academics, athletics, minority status. **Additional information:** Federal, state, and institutional work-study programs available.

Application procedures. Admission: No deadline. No application fee. Admission notification on a rolling basis. **Financial aid:** Priority date 5/1; no closing date. FAFSA required. Applicants notified on a rolling basis.

Academics. Special study options: Accelerated study, cooperative education, distance learning, dual enrollment of high school students, ESL, honors, independent study, internships. License preparation in nursing. **Credit/placement by examination:** AP, CLEP, institutional tests. 45 credit hours maximum toward associate degree. **Support services:** Learning center, reduced course load, remedial instruction, tutoring, writing center.

Majors. Business: Administrative services, business admin, management information systems. **Computer sciences:** Systems analysis, webmaster, word processing. **Construction:** Carpentry. **Education:** Multi-level teacher, teacher assistance. **Engineering:** Computer. **Engineering technology:** Drafting, electrical, industrial, manufacturing. **Health:** Cardiovascular technology, EMT paramedic, massage therapy, medical assistant, medical secretary, medical transcription, nursing (RN), predental, premedicine, prepharmacy, preveterinary. **Legal studies:** Legal secretary. **Liberal arts:** Arts/sciences, humanities. **Mechanic/repair:** Automotive, heating/ac/refrig, industrial, small engine. **Personal/culinary services:** Aesthetician, cosmetic, cosmetology, manicurist, salon management. **Production:** Machine tool, welding. **Protective services:** Correctional facilities, corrections, law enforcement admin, police science. **Visual/performing arts:** Graphic design.

Most popular majors. Business/marketing 13%, computer/information sciences 7%, health sciences 35%, liberal arts 17%, security/protective services 15%, trade and industry 7%.

Computing on campus. 180 workstations in library, computer center, student center. Commuter students can connect to campus network. Online course registration, online library, helpline, wireless network available.

Student life. Freshman orientation: Available. Preregistration for classes offered. Held in August for students and parents. **Activities:** Choral groups, drama, literary magazine, student government, student newspaper, student senate, Phi Theta Kappa, Christian Fellowship, student activities committee, student medieval club, criminal justice club.

Athletics. NJCAA. **Intercollegiate:** Basketball, cross-country, golf. **Team name:** Firebirds.

Student services. Adult student services, career counseling, services for economically disadvantaged, student employment services, financial aid counseling, on-campus daycare, personal counseling, placement for graduates, veterans' counselor. **Physically disabled:** Services for visually, speech, hearing impaired. **Transfer:** Transfer adviser, college fairs on campus for students transferring to 4-year colleges.

Contact. E-mail: admissions@kirtland.edu
Phone: (989) 275-5121 ext. 284 Fax: (989) 275-6727
Susie Allen, Coordinator of Admissions, Kirtland Community College, 10775 North Saint Helen Road, Roscommon, MI 48653

Lake Michigan College

Benton Harbor, Michigan
www.lakemichigancollege.edu **CB code: 1137**

- Public 2-year community and junior college
- Residential campus in large town

General. Founded in 1946. Regionally accredited. Additional campuses located in South Haven and Bertrand Crossing. Michigan Technical Education Center (M-TEC) located in Benton Harbor. **Enrollment:** 3,844 degree-seeking undergraduates; 103 non-degree-seeking students. **Degrees:** 305 associate awarded. **Location:** 80 miles from Grand Rapids, 40 miles from South Bend, Indiana. **Calendar:** Semester, limited summer session. **Full-time faculty:** 57 total; 33% have terminal degrees, 49% women. **Part-time faculty:** 221 total; 8% have terminal degrees, 52% women. **Class size:** 76% <20, 22% 20-39, less than 1% 40-49, less than 1% 50-99, less than 1% >100. **Special facilities:** Video production facility, nature area.

Student profile. Among degree-seeking undergraduates, 48% enrolled in a transfer program, 52% enrolled in a vocational program, 4% already have a bachelor's degree or higher, 744 enrolled as first-time, first-year students, 125 transferred in from other institutions.

Part-time:	67%	**Asian American:**	2%
Out-of-state:	1%	**Hispanic American:**	4%
Women:	60%	**Native American:**	1%
African American:	17%	**25 or older:**	16%

Transfer out. Colleges most students transferred to 2008: Western Michigan University, Sienna Heights University, Grand Valley State University, Michigan State University, Ferris State University.

Basis for selection. Open admission, but selective for some programs. Admission to health sciences programs based on 2.5 high school GPA in academic subjects. Interview required for dental assistant, radiologic technology, nursing majors. **Homeschooled:** State high school equivalency certificate required.

2008-2009 Annual costs. Tuition/fees: $3,105; $4,170 out-of-district; $5,190 out-of-state. Per-credit charge: $73 in-district; $108 out-of-district; $142 out-of-state. Books/supplies: $1,120. Personal expenses: $1,400.

2007-2008 Financial aid. Need-based: 96% of total undergraduate aid awarded as scholarships/grants, 4% as loans/jobs.

Application procedures. Admission: No deadline. No application fee. Admission notification on a rolling basis. **Financial aid:** Priority date 3/1; no closing date. FAFSA required. Applicants notified on a rolling basis; must reply within 2 week(s) of notification.

Academics. Special study options: Cooperative education, cross-registration, distance learning, double major, dual enrollment of high school students, ESL, honors, independent study, internships, liberal arts/career combination, teacher certification program, weekend college. Bachelor's degree programs available on campus. License preparation in nursing, paramedic, radiology. **Credit/placement by examination:** AP, CLEP, institutional tests. 30 credit hours maximum toward associate degree. **Support services:** GED test center, learning center, remedial instruction, tutoring.

Majors. Biology: General. **Business:** Accounting, administrative services, business admin, hospitality admin, marketing, tourism/travel. **Computer sciences:** Information technology, networking, programming. **Conservation:** Environmental science. **Education:** Early childhood, elementary, secondary. **Engineering:** General. **Engineering technology:** CAD/CADD, electrical, energy systems. **Foreign languages:** General. **Health:** Dental assistant, EMT paramedic, medical radiologic technology/radiation therapy, medical secretary, nursing (RN), office assistant, predental, premedicine, prenursing, prepharmacy, preveterinary, radiologic technology/medical imaging, sonography. **History:** General. **Legal studies:** Legal secretary. **Liberal arts:** Arts/sciences, humanities. **Math:** General. **Parks/recreation:** Health/fitness. **Philosophy/religion:** Philosophy. **Physical sciences:** General, chemistry, geology, physics. **Production:** Machine tool. **Protective services:** Corrections, firefighting, police science. **Psychology:** General. **Science technology:** Nuclear power. **Social sciences:** Geography, political science, sociology. **Visual/performing arts:** Art, dramatic, graphic design, music performance.

Most popular majors. Business/marketing 17%, health sciences 27%, interdisciplinary studies 9%, liberal arts 30%, trade and industry 6%.

Computing on campus. 100 workstations in library, computer center. Commuter students can connect to campus network. Online course registration, helpline, wireless network available.

Student life. Freshman orientation: Mandatory. **Activities:** Bands, choral groups, drama, music ensembles, student government, student newspaper.

Athletics. NJCAA. **Intercollegiate:** Baseball M, basketball, golf M, softball W, volleyball W. **Intramural:** Badminton, baseball M, basketball, bowling, softball, table tennis, tennis, volleyball. **Team name:** Indians.

Student services. Adult student services, career counseling, student employment services, health services, on-campus daycare, personal counseling, placement for graduates, veterans' counselor. **Physically disabled:** Services for visually, hearing impaired. **Transfer:** Re-entry adviser, pre-admission transcript evaluation for new students. College fairs on campus for students transferring to 4-year colleges.

Contact. E-mail: admissions@lakemichigancollege.edu
Phone: (269) 927-8107 Toll-free number: (800) 252-1562
Fax: (269) 927-6875
Cindy Reuss, Lead Admissions Representative, Lake Michigan College, 2755 East Napier Avenue, Benton Harbor, MI 49022-1899

Lansing Community College

Lansing, Michigan — **CB member**
www.lansing.cc.mi.us — **CB code: 1414**

- Public 2-year community college
- Commuter campus in small city

General. Founded in 1957. Regionally accredited. **Enrollment:** 14,523 degree-seeking undergraduates; 4,922 non-degree-seeking students. **Degrees:** 1,364 associate awarded. **ROTC:** Army, Air Force. **Location:** 90 miles from Detroit. **Calendar:** Semester, extensive summer session. **Full-time faculty:** 250 total; 15% minority, 53% women. **Part-time faculty:** 1,670 total; 12% minority, 54% women. **Class size:** 48% < 20, 51% 20-39, less than 1% 40-49, less than 1% 50-99, less than 1% >100. **Special facilities:** Planetarium, observatory, science concepts laboratory, computer-integrated manufacturing institute, in-depth photography institute, truck driver training range, technical library.

Student profile. Among degree-seeking undergraduates, 30% enrolled in a transfer program, 30% enrolled in a vocational program, 3,258 enrolled as first-time, first-year students.

Part-time:	64%	**Hispanic American:**	4%
Women:	54%	**Native American:**	1%
African American:	9%	**International:**	3%
Asian American:	2%	**25 or older:**	38%

Transfer out. Colleges most students transferred to 2008: Michigan State University, Central Michigan University.

Basis for selection. Open admission, but selective for some programs. Special requirements for health, aviation, music, police academy programs, fire academy. MELAB required of foreign students. TOEFL also accepted. Interview required of health program applicants and international applicants. Audition recommended for music, dance, theater majors. Portfolio recommended for art majors.

2008-2009 Annual costs. Tuition/fees: $2,240; $4,070 out-of-district; $6,080 out-of-state. Per-credit charge: $73 in-district; $134 out-of-district; $201 out-of-state. There is a $10 online course fee applied to all online courses, and separate course fees may be assessed for courses required special supplies, equipment, or travel. A $5 per billable hour facility fee is charged to students on all credit classes. Books/supplies: $693. Personal expenses: $1,071.

2007-2008 Financial aid. Need-based: Need-based aid available for part-time students. Work-study available nights, weekends and for part-time students. **Non-need-based:** Scholarships awarded for academics, athletics.

Application procedures. Admission: No deadline. No application fee. Admission notification on a rolling basis. SAT or ACT recommended for assessment waivers and counseling. **Financial aid:** Priority date 7/5; no closing date. FAFSA required. Applicants notified on a rolling basis starting 4/3.

Academics. Several 4-year degree course studies available, students complete 3 years at LCC and 4th year at a 4-year degree institution. **Special study options:** Accelerated study, cooperative education, cross-registration, distance learning, double major, dual enrollment of high school students, exchange student, honors, independent study, internships, study abroad, teacher certification program, weekend college. External bachelor's degree with Northwood Institute, 3+1 degree program, 2+2 degree program. Bachelor's degree programs available on campus. License preparation in aviation, dental hygiene, nursing, paramedic, real estate. **Credit/placement by examination:** AP, CLEP, IB, institutional tests. 40 credit hours maximum toward associate degree. **Support services:** Learning center, pre-admission summer program, reduced course load, remedial instruction, study skills assistance, tutoring, writing center.

Majors. Architecture: Interior, landscape. **Area/ethnic studies:** African. **Biology:** General. **Business:** General, accounting, administrative services, business admin, fashion, hospitality/recreation, human resources, insurance, international, management information systems, marketing, office management, office technology, real estate, sales/distribution, tourism promotion, tourism/travel. **Communications:** General, advertising, broadcast journalism, journalism. **Communications technology:** General, graphic/printing. **Computer sciences:** General, applications programming, data processing, networking, programming, systems analysis, vendor certification. **Conservation:** General. **Construction:** Carpentry, maintenance, masonry, pipefitting, power transmission. **Education:** General, art, elementary, mathematics, music, physical, science, secondary, special, speech, trade/industrial. **Engineering:** General. **Engineering technology:** Civil, drafting, electrical, environmental, hydraulics. **Family/consumer sciences:** General, child care, institutional food production. **Foreign languages:** General, French, German, sign language interpretation, Spanish. **Health:** Clinical lab science, dental hygiene, EMT paramedic, health care admin, licensed practical nurse, medical assistant, medical radiologic technology/radiation therapy, medical secretary, nuclear medical technology, physician assistant, predental, respiratory therapy technology, sonography, surgical technology. **History:** General. **Interdisciplinary:** Biological/physical sciences, gerontology. **Legal studies:** Court reporting, legal secretary, paralegal, prelaw. **Liberal arts:** Arts/sciences. **Math:** General, applied. **Mechanic/repair:** General, aircraft, avionics, electronics/electrical, heating/ac/refrig, industrial. **Parks/recreation:** Facilities management. **Personal/culinary services:** Cosmetic, culinary arts. **Philosophy/religion:** Philosophy, religion. **Physical sciences:** Chemistry. **Protective services:** Criminal justice, firefighting, law enforcement admin, police science. **Psychology:** General. **Public administration:** Social work. **Social sciences:** General, anthropology, geography, political science, sociology. **Transportation:** Aviation. **Visual/performing arts:** General, art, cinematography, commercial/advertising art, dance, dramatic, drawing, music performance, music theory/composition, painting, photography.

Most popular majors. Business/marketing 13%, health sciences 40%, visual/performing arts 7%.

Computing on campus. 200 workstations in library, computer center. Commuter students can connect to campus network. Online course registration, helpline, wireless network available.

Student life. Freshman orientation: Available. Preregistration for classes offered. Occurs first 5 days of open registration. **Activities:** Bands, choral groups, dance, drama, film society, music ensembles, musical theater, radio station, student government, student newspaper, symphony orchestra, TV station, Newman club, black student delegates, Hispanic club, Campus Disciples, Baptist student union, international club, Maranatha Christian Fellowship, student adviser club, substance abuse association.

Athletics. NJCAA. **Intercollegiate:** Basketball, cross-country, golf, track and field, volleyball W. **Intramural:** Basketball, bowling, boxing M. **Team name:** Stars.

Student services. Adult student services, career counseling, services for economically disadvantaged, student employment services, financial aid counseling, minority student services, personal counseling, placement for graduates, veterans' counselor, women's services. **Physically disabled:** Services for visually, speech, hearing impaired. **Transfer:** Transfer adviser, college fairs on campus for students transferring to 4-year colleges.

Contact. Phone: (517) 483-1200 Toll-free number: (800) 644-4522
Fax: (517) 483-9668
Director of Admissions, Lansing Community College, 422 North Washington Square, Lansing, MI 48901

Macomb Community College

Warren, Michigan — **CB member**
www.macomb.edu — **CB code: 1722**

- Public 2-year community college
- Commuter campus in small city

General. Founded in 1954. Regionally accredited. **Enrollment:** 12,901 degree-seeking undergraduates; 10,084 non-degree-seeking students. **Degrees:** 2,233 associate awarded. **Location:** 20 miles from Detroit. **Calendar:** Semester, extensive summer session. **Full-time faculty:** 229 total; 14% have terminal degrees, 4% minority, 44% women. **Part-time faculty:** 803 total; 9% have terminal degrees, 5% minority, 42% women. **Special facilities:** Nature preserves, center for performing arts.

Student profile. Among degree-seeking undergraduates, 1,252 enrolled as first-time, first-year students.

Part-time:	62%	**Hispanic American:**	1%
Women:	51%	**Native American:**	1%
African American:	7%	**International:**	2%
Asian American:	3%	**25 or older:**	39%

Transfer out. Colleges most students transferred to 2008: Central Michigan University, Oakland University, Walsh College, Wayne State University, Michigan State University.

Basis for selection. Open admission, but selective for some programs. Special requirements for nursing, physical therapy assistant, occupational therapy assistant, respiratory therapy assistant, veterinarian technician programs; combination of GPA and test scores considered.

2008-2009 Annual costs. Tuition/fees: $2,200; $3,340 out-of-district; $4,330 out-of-state. Per-credit charge: $72 in-district; $110 out-of-district; $142 out-of-state. Books/supplies: $578. Personal expenses: $791.

2007-2008 Financial aid. Need-based: Need-based aid available for part-time students. Work-study available nights, weekends and for part-time students. **Non-need-based:** Scholarships awarded for academics, athletics, leadership, music/drama, state residency.

Application procedures. Admission: No deadline. No application fee. Admission notification on a rolling basis. January 31 closing date for nursing and physical therapy assistant programs. **Financial aid:** Priority date 4/15; no closing date. FAFSA, institutional form required. Applicants notified on a rolling basis starting 5/15; must reply within 2 week(s) of notification.

Academics. Courses toward bachelor's degrees offered on campus by University of Detroit, Walsh College of Accountancy and Business Administration, Wayne State University, Central Michigan University, Oakland University, University of Detroit Mercy, Davenport University, Rochester College. On-line degree program with Franklin University. **Special study options:** Cooperative education, cross-registration, distance learning, dual enrollment of high school students, ESL, independent study, internships, liberal arts/career combination, study abroad, weekend college. **Credit/placement by examination:** AP, CLEP, institutional tests. 47 credit hours maximum toward associate degree. **Support services:** Learning center, reduced course load, remedial instruction, tutoring.

Majors. Biology: General. **Business:** General, accounting, administrative services, business admin, marketing, office technology, operations. **Communications:** General, broadcast journalism, public relations. **Communications technology:** Graphic/printing. **Computer sciences:** General, data entry, networking, programming, web page design. **Engineering technology:** Civil, construction, drafting, electrical, manufacturing, surveying. **Family/consumer sciences:** Child care. **Health:** EMT paramedic, health services, medical assistant, medical secretary, nursing (RN), occupational therapy assistant, physical therapy assistant, respiratory therapy technology, surgical technology, veterinary technology/assistant. **Legal studies:** Paralegal. **Liberal arts:** Arts/sciences. **Math:** General. **Mechanic/repair:** Automotive, electronics/electrical, heating/ac/refrig. **Personal/culinary services:** Culinary arts. **Physical sciences:** Chemistry. **Protective services:** Fire safety technology, firefighting, forensics, police science. **Visual/performing arts:** Commercial/advertising art.

Most popular majors. Business/marketing 12%, engineering/engineering technologies 6%, health sciences 13%, liberal arts 51%.

Computing on campus. 1,800 workstations in library, computer center. Commuter students can connect to campus network.

Student life. Freshman orientation: Available. Occurs beginning of semester. **Activities:** Bands, choral groups, dance, drama, music ensembles, musical theater, symphony orchestra, student activities board, College Republicans, service learning and volunteerism, Newman Club, Campus Crusade for Christ, Young Democrats, African American alliance, international culture club, Phi Theta Kappa.

Athletics. NJCAA. **Intercollegiate:** Baseball M, basketball, cross-country, soccer M, softball W, volleyball W.

Student services. Chaplain/spiritual director, career counseling, student employment services, financial aid counseling, health services, personal counseling, placement for graduates. **Physically disabled:** Services for visually, speech, hearing impaired. **Transfer:** Transfer adviser, college fairs on campus for students transferring to 4-year colleges.

Contact. Phone: (586) 445-7999 Toll-free number: (866) 622-6621
Fax: (586) 445-7157
Ronald Hughes, Director of Enrollment Services, Macomb Community College, 14500 East Twelve Mile Road, Warren, MI 48088-3896

Mid Michigan Community College

Harrison, Michigan
www.midmich.edu **CB code: 1523**

- Public 2-year community college
- Commuter campus in small town

General. Founded in 1965. Regionally accredited. **Location:** 30 miles from Mount Pleasant, 100 miles from Lansing. **Calendar:** Semester.

Annual costs/financial aid. Tuition/fees (2008-2009): $2,415; $4,020 out-of-district; $7,890 out-of-state. Books/supplies: $1,118. Personal expenses: $1,600. Need-based financial aid available to full-time and part-time students.

Contact. Phone: (989) 386-6661
Director of Admissions and Registration, 1375 South Clare Avenue, Harrison, MI 48625

Monroe County Community College

Monroe, Michigan
www.monroeccc.edu **CB code: 1514**

- Public 2-year community college
- Commuter campus in large town

General. Founded in 1964. Regionally accredited. Off-campus site at Whitman Center. **Enrollment:** 4,514 undergraduates. **Degrees:** 465 associate awarded. **Location:** 45 miles from Detroit, 20 miles from Toledo, Ohio. **Calendar:** Semester, limited summer session. **Full-time faculty:** 62 total. **Part-time faculty:** 125 total.

Student profile. 53% enrolled in a transfer program, 47% enrolled in a vocational program.

Out-of-state:	3%	**25 or older:**	40%

Transfer out. Colleges most students transferred to 2008: Eastern Michigan University, University of Toledo, Siena Heights University, Western Michigan University, University of Michigan.

Basis for selection. Open admission, but selective for some programs. Selective admission for nursing, respiratory therapy, medical assistance and culinary skills program. ACT required for nursing and respiratory therapy applicants. Test scores required by March 31. Interview required of respiratory therapy and culinary program applicants.

High school preparation. Recommended units include English 4, mathematics 3, social studies 3, history 1 and science 3. Nursing and respiratory therapy applicants must have 1 unit chemistry and 1 biology. Strong science background highly recommended.

2008-2009 Annual costs. Tuition/fees: $2,240; $3,680 out-of-district; $4,070 out-of-state. Per-credit charge: $73 in-district; $121 out-of-district; $134 out-of-state. Books/supplies: $1,000. Personal expenses: $560.

Financial aid. Need-based: Need-based aid available for part-time students. Work-study available nights, weekends and for part-time students. **Non-need-based:** Scholarships awarded for academics, alumni affiliation, art, leadership, music/drama, state residency.

Application procedures. Admission: Priority date 5/1; no deadline. No application fee. Admission notification on a rolling basis. Closing date for nursing and respiratory therapy applications: 5/10. **Financial aid:** Priority date 4/1; no closing date. FAFSA, institutional form required. Applicants notified on a rolling basis starting 4/1; must reply within 2 week(s) of notification.

Academics. Special study options: Accelerated study, cooperative education, dual enrollment of high school students, independent study. Bachelor's degree programs available on campus. License preparation in nursing, paramedic, real estate. **Credit/placement by examination:** AP, CLEP, institutional tests. 30 credit hours maximum toward associate degree. **Support services:** Learning center, reduced course load, remedial instruction, tutoring, writing center.

Majors. Business: Accounting, administrative services, banking/financial services, business admin, office technology, office/clerical. **Computer sciences:** General, applications programming, programming. **Education:** Early childhood. **Engineering:** Electrical. **Engineering technology:** Architectural, drafting, electrical, manufacturing. **Family/consumer sciences:** Child care. **Health:** Medical secretary, nursing (RN), respiratory therapy technology. **Legal studies:** Legal secretary. **Liberal arts:** Arts/sciences. **Personal/culinary services:** Culinary arts. **Visual/performing arts:** Studio arts.

Computing on campus. 150 workstations in library, computer center, student center. Helpline, wireless network available.

Student life. Freshman orientation: Available. **Activities:** Concert band, choral groups, drama, international student organizations, radio station, student government, student newspaper, symphony orchestra, respiratory therapy club, nursing club, Society of Automotive Engineers, campus Bible study.

Athletics. Team name: Huskies.

Student services. Career counseling, student employment services, on-campus daycare, personal counseling, placement for graduates. **Physically disabled:** Services for visually, speech, hearing impaired. **Transfer:** Transfer adviser, college fairs on campus for students transferring to 4-year colleges.

Contact. E-mail: mhall@monroeccc.edu
Phone: (734) 384-4104 Toll-free number: (877) 937-6222
Fax: (734) 242-9711
Mark Hall, Director of Admissions and Guidance Services, Monroe County Community College, 1555 South Raisinville Road, Monroe, MI 48161-9746

Montcalm Community College

Sidney, Michigan
www.montcalm.edu **CB code: 1522**

- Public 2-year community and liberal arts college
- Commuter campus in rural community

General. Founded in 1965. Regionally accredited. Off-campus centers in Ionia, Howard City, Greenville and Alma. **Enrollment:** 1,937 degree-seeking undergraduates; 353 non-degree-seeking students. **Degrees:** 334 associate awarded. **Location:** 50 miles from Grand Rapids, 65 miles from Lansing. **Calendar:** Semester, limited summer session. **Full-time faculty:** 34 total. **Part-time faculty:** 145 total. **Class size:** 55% < 20, 44% 20-39, less than 1% 40-49, less than 1% >100. **Special facilities:** Marked nature preserves and trails, barn theatre.

Student profile. Among degree-seeking undergraduates, 286 enrolled as first-time, first-year students.

Part-time:	57%	**Hispanic American:**	1%
Women:	70%	**Native American:**	1%

Transfer out. Colleges most students transferred to 2008: Central Michigan University, Ferris State University, Grand Valley State University, Davenport University.

Basis for selection. Open admission, but selective for some programs. Applicants to nursing program must score at least a COMPASS pre-algebra of 44 and reading of 80.

2008-2009 Annual costs. Tuition/fees: $2,385; $4,005 out-of-district; $5,295 out-of-state. Per-credit charge: $74 in-district; $128 out-of-district; $171 out-of-state. Books/supplies: $901. Personal expenses: $1,072.

Financial aid. Need-based: Need-based aid available for part-time students. Work-study available for part-time students. **Non-need-based:** Scholarships awarded for academics, state residency.

Application procedures. Admission: No deadline. No application fee. Admission notification on a rolling basis. **Financial aid:** Priority date 2/15; no closing date. FAFSA, institutional form required. Applicants notified on a rolling basis starting 6/15; must reply within 2 week(s) of notification.

Academics. Special study options: Cooperative education, distance learning, dual enrollment of high school students, independent study, internships, liberal arts/career combination. License preparation in nursing, paramedic. **Credit/placement by examination:** AP, CLEP, institutional tests. **Support services:** GED test center, learning center, reduced course load, remedial instruction, study skills assistance, tutoring.

Majors. Business: Accounting, administrative services, business admin, construction management, entrepreneurial studies, executive assistant, information resources management, management information systems, office technology. **Computer sciences:** General, data processing. **Education:** Teacher assistance. **Engineering technology:** Automotive, drafting, electrical, industrial, manufacturing, surveying. **Family/consumer sciences:** Child care. **Health:** Medical secretary, nursing (RN). **Liberal arts:** Arts/sciences. **Mechanic/repair:** Computer, electronics/electrical. **Personal/culinary services:** Cosmetic. **Protective services:** Criminal justice.

Most popular majors. Business/marketing 22%, education 6%, health sciences 31%, liberal arts 23%, security/protective services 6%, trade and industry 6%.

Computing on campus. 450 workstations in library, computer center. Helpline available.

Student life. Freshman orientation: Mandatory. **Activities:** Jazz band, choral groups, drama, music ensembles, musical theater, student newspaper, Phi Theta Kappa, future business professionals club, Native American club, nursing club, judo club.

Athletics. Intramural: Volleyball.

Student services. Career counseling, student employment services, financial aid counseling, placement for graduates. **Physically disabled:** Services for visually, speech, hearing impaired. **Transfer:** Pre-admission transcript evaluation for new students. Transfer adviser, college fairs on campus for students transferring to 4-year colleges.

Contact. E-mail: admissions@montcalm.edu
Phone: (989) 328-1250 Toll-free number: (877) 328-2111
Fax: (989) 328-2950
Debra Alexander, Director of Admissions, Montcalm Community College, 2800 College Drive, Sidney, MI 48885

Mott Community College

Flint, Michigan **CB member**
www.mcc.edu **CB code: 1225**

- Public 2-year community college
- Commuter campus in large city

General. Founded in 1923. Regionally accredited. Branch campuses located in Fenton, Lapeer, Livingston, and Clio. **Enrollment:** 7,567 degree-seeking undergraduates; 3,246 non-degree-seeking students. **Degrees:** 1,114 associate awarded. **Location:** 65 miles from Detroit. **Calendar:** Semester, extensive summer session. **Full-time faculty:** 153 total; 20% have terminal degrees, 17% minority, 60% women. **Part-time faculty:** 348 total; 6% have terminal degrees, 16% minority, 59% women. **Special facilities:** Geology museum, regional technology center, dental clinic, visual arts and design center, greenhouse, student-operated cosmetology/nail technology salon, hospital wing replica, SimMan room, esthetician labs.

Student profile. Among degree-seeking undergraduates, 12% enrolled in a transfer program, 75% enrolled in a vocational program, 20% already have a bachelor's degree or higher, 795 enrolled as first-time, first-year students, 369 transferred in from other institutions.

Part-time:	60%	**Hispanic American:**	2%
Women:	63%	**Native American:**	1%
African American:	19%	**International:**	1%
Asian American:	1%	**25 or older:**	48%

Transfer out. Colleges most students transferred to 2008: University of Michigan: Flint, Ferris State University, Central Michigan University, Saginaw Valley State University, Eastern Michigan University.

Basis for selection. Open admission, but selective for some programs. Special requirements for nursing and allied health programs. Audition recommended for music majors. **Learning Disabled:** Students must request assistance, provide documentation of disabilities, and register with Disability Services before classes begin.

2008-2009 Annual costs. Tuition/fees: $2,801; $4,064 out-of-district; $5,336 out-of-state. Per-credit charge: $85 in-district; $127 out-of-district; $169 out-of-state. Books/supplies: $983. Personal expenses: $934.

2008-2009 Financial aid. Need-based: 61% of total undergraduate aid awarded as scholarships/grants, 39% as loans/jobs. Need-based aid available for part-time students. Work-study available nights and for part-time students. **Non-need-based:** Scholarships awarded for academics, alumni affiliation, art, athletics, leadership, minority status, music/drama, state residency.

Application procedures. Admission: No deadline. No application fee. Admission notification on a rolling basis. **Financial aid:** No deadline. FAFSA required. Applicants notified on a rolling basis starting 5/1.

Academics. Distance learning and open entry/open exit modular courses being expanded in Regional Technology Center. **Special study options:** Cooperative education, distance learning, double major, dual enrollment of high school students, ESL, honors, independent study, internships, liberal arts/career combination. License preparation in dental hygiene, nursing, occupational therapy, physical therapy. **Credit/placement by examination:** AP, CLEP, institutional tests. 16 credit hours maximum toward associate degree. **Support services:** Learning center, remedial instruction, study skills assistance, tutoring, writing center.

Majors. Business: General, accounting technology, administrative services, business admin, entrepreneurial studies, executive assistant, international, management information systems, marketing, office management, office technology. **Communications technology:** General. **Computer sciences:** Networking. **Education:** Early childhood, teacher assistance. **Engineering technology:** Architectural, drafting, electrical, heat/ac/refrig, manufacturing, mechanical, mechanical drafting, quality control, surveying. **Family/consumer sciences:** Institutional food production. **Foreign languages:** Sign language interpretation. **Health:** Community health services, dental assistant, dental hygiene, EMT paramedic, histologic assistant, medical radiologic technology/radiation therapy, nursing (RN), occupational therapy assistant, physical therapy assistant, respiratory therapy technology. **Liberal arts:** Arts/sciences. **Mechanic/repair:** Auto body, automotive. **Personal/culinary services:** Baking, chef training, salon management. **Protective services:** Fire safety technology, police science. **Visual/performing arts:** Art, graphic design, photography. **Other:** Applied technology, Industrial technology.

Most popular majors. Biological/life sciences 13%, business/marketing 7%, engineering/engineering technologies 6%, health sciences 25%, liberal arts 29%, security/protective services 8%.

Computing on campus. 1,290 workstations in library, computer center, student center. Commuter students can connect to campus network. Online course registration, wireless network available.

Student life. Freshman orientation: Mandatory. Three-hour sessions. **Activities:** Bands, choral groups, music ensembles, student government, student newspaper, criminal justice club, connoisseur club, environmental club, Phi Theta Kappa, student nurses association, dental hygiene club, gardening association, social work club, ballroomers/steppers, travel club.

Athletics. NJCAA. **Intercollegiate:** Baseball M, basketball, cross-country, golf M, softball W, volleyball W. **Team name:** Bears.

Student services. Career counseling, services for economically disadvantaged, student employment services, financial aid counseling, health services, on-campus daycare, personal counseling, placement for graduates. **Physically disabled:** Services for visually, speech, hearing impaired. **Transfer:** Pre-admission transcript evaluation for new students. Transfer adviser, college fairs on campus for students transferring to 4-year colleges.

Contact. E-mail: inquiry@mcc.edu
Phone: (810) 762-0315 Toll-free number: (800) 852-8614
Fax: (810) 232-9442
Delores Deen, Executive Dean, Student Services, Mott Community College, 1401 East Court Street, Flint, MI 48503-2089

Muskegon Community College

Muskegon, Michigan
www.muskegoncc.edu **CB code: 1495**

- Public 2-year community college
- Commuter campus in small city

General. Founded in 1926. Regionally accredited. Bachelor's and graduate programs offered on-campus with participating 4-year institutions. **Enrollment:** 4,715 degree-seeking undergraduates. **Degrees:** 296 associate awarded. **Location:** 45 miles from Grand Rapids. **Calendar:** Semester, limited summer session. **Full-time faculty:** 97 total. **Part-time faculty:** 178 total. **Special facilities:** Planetarium, nature preserve, herbal garden, observatory.

Basis for selection. Open admission, but selective for some programs. Nursing applicants must have math (level 35) and basic college chemistry. High school diploma, GED, 10th-grade reading level on Nelson Denny, or 22 ACT required for select programs and courses. High school diploma, GED or completion of 15 credits with at least a C average required for degree-seeking candidates. **Homeschooled:** Transcript of courses and grades required.

2008-2009 Annual costs. Tuition/fees: $2,350; $3,685 out-of-district; $4,900 out-of-state. Per-credit charge: $69 in-district; $114 out-of-district; $154 out-of-state. Students also assessed contact hour fees, which vary according to residency status, and course fees, which vary. Books/supplies: $1,000. Personal expenses: $800.

Financial aid. Need-based: Work-study available nights, weekends and for part-time students.

Application procedures. Admission: Priority date 5/1; no deadline. No application fee. Admission notification on a rolling basis. **Financial aid:** Priority date 5/1; no closing date. FAFSA, institutional form required. Applicants notified on a rolling basis starting 6/1; must reply within 2 week(s) of notification.

Academics. Special study options: Cooperative education, cross-registration, distance learning, double major, dual enrollment of high school students, honors, independent study, internships. License preparation in nursing, real estate. **Credit/placement by examination:** AP, CLEP, institutional tests. 30 credit hours maximum toward associate degree. **Support services:** Learning center, remedial instruction, tutoring, writing center.

Majors. Business: Accounting, administrative services, international, marketing. **Communications technology:** Graphic/printing. **Computer sciences:** General, data processing. **Engineering technology:** Drafting, electrical. **Health:** Licensed practical nurse, medical secretary, nursing (RN), respiratory therapy technology. **Legal studies:** Legal secretary. **Mechanic/repair:** General. **Protective services:** Law enforcement admin. **Visual/performing arts:** Commercial/advertising art.

Computing on campus. Wireless network available.

Student life. Freshman orientation: Available. **Activities:** Bands, choral groups, dance, drama, music ensembles, musical theater, student government, student newspaper, TV station, interdenominational religious group, black student alliance, Students Again Gaining Enlightenment.

Athletics. NJCAA. **Intercollegiate:** Baseball M, basketball, golf, softball W, tennis W, volleyball W, wrestling M. **Intramural:** Baseball M, basketball, bowling, golf, softball W, table tennis. **Team name:** Jayhawks.

Student services. Career counseling, student employment services, health services, personal counseling, placement for graduates, veterans' counselor. **Physically disabled:** Services for visually, speech, hearing impaired. **Transfer:** College fairs on campus for students transferring to 4-year colleges.

Contact. E-mail: darlene.peklar@muskegoncc.edu
Phone: (231) 777-0366 Toll-free number: (866) 711-4622
Fax: (231) 777-0443
Jean Roberts, Director of Records and Registration, Muskegon Community College, 221 South Quarterline Road, Muskegon, MI 49442

North Central Michigan College

Petoskey, Michigan
www.ncmich.edu **CB code: 1569**

- Public 2-year community college
- Commuter campus in small town

General. Founded in 1958. Regionally accredited. **Enrollment:** 2,240 degree-seeking undergraduates. **Degrees:** 230 associate awarded. **Location:** 40 miles from Mackinaw City, 60 miles from Traverse City. **Calendar:** Semester, limited summer session. **Full-time faculty:** 35 total. **Part-time faculty:** 140 total. **Class size:** 100% 20-39. **Special facilities:** Nature preserve.

Student profile.

Out-of-state:	5%	**Live on campus:**	5%
25 or older:	57%		

Transfer out. Colleges most students transferred to 2008: Lake Superior State University, Grand Valley State University, Central Michigan University, Northern Michigan University, Ferris State University.

Basis for selection. Open admission, but selective for some programs. Special requirements for nursing program. All degree-seeking students must provide ACT, SAT or COMPASS scores for mandatory placement.

High school preparation. Recommended units include English 3, mathematics 3 and science 3. Chemistry recommended for nursing applicants.

2008-2009 Annual costs. Tuition/fees: $2,340; $3,681 out-of-district; $4,674 out-of-state. Per-credit charge: $70 in-district; $114 out-of-district; $147 out-of-state. Room/board: $4,432. Books/supplies: $1,050. Personal expenses: $650.

Financial aid. Need-based: Need-based aid available for part-time students. Work-study available nights, weekends and for part-time students.

Application procedures. Admission: No deadline. No application fee. Application must be submitted online. Admission notification on a rolling basis. **Financial aid:** Closing date 4/1. FAFSA, institutional form required. Applicants notified on a rolling basis starting 4/30.

Academics. Special study options: Cooperative education, cross-registration, distance learning, dual enrollment of high school students, independent study, internships. Bachelor's degree programs available on campus. **Credit/placement by examination:** AP, CLEP, IB. 15 credit hours maximum toward associate degree. **Support services:** Learning center, remedial instruction, tutoring.

Majors. Business: General, accounting, administrative services, business admin, office/clerical. **Computer sciences:** General. **Education:** Early childhood. **Health:** EMT paramedic, nursing (RN). **Legal studies:** Paralegal. **Liberal arts:** Arts/sciences.

Most popular majors. Health sciences 21%, liberal arts 71%.

Computing on campus. 133 workstations in dormitories, library, computer center, student center. Dormitories wired for high-speed internet access and linked to campus network. Commuter students can connect to campus network. Online course registration, wireless network available.

Student life. Freshman orientation: Available. Preregistration for classes offered. Held in summer before classes begin. **Housing:** Coed dorms available. $50 deposit. **Activities:** Student government, student newspaper, nursing student association, Phi Theta Kappa, Campus Crusade.

Athletics. Intramural: Basketball, volleyball.

Student services. Career counseling, services for economically disadvantaged, financial aid counseling, personal counseling, veterans' counselor, women's services. **Physically disabled:** Services for visually, speech, hearing impaired. **Learning disabled:** Comprehensive services available. **Transfer:** Transfer adviser, college fairs on campus for students transferring to 4-year colleges.

Contact. E-mail: advisor@ncmich.edu
Phone: (231) 348-6600 Toll-free number: (888) 298-6605
Fax: (231) 348-6672
Julieanne Tobin, Director Enrollment Management, North Central Michigan College, 1515 Howard Street, Petoskey, MI 49770

Northwestern Michigan College

Traverse City, Michigan
www.nmc.edu **CB code: 1564**

- Public 2-year community and maritime college
- Commuter campus in large town

General. Founded in 1951. Regionally accredited. **Enrollment:** 4,095 degree-seeking undergraduates; 460 non-degree-seeking students. **Degrees:** 530 associate awarded. **Location:** 180 miles from Lansing, 265 miles from Detroit. **Calendar:** Semester, extensive summer session. **Full-time faculty:** 90 total. **Part-time faculty:** 120 total. **Class size:** 100% 20-39. **Special facilities:** Great Lakes Maritime Academy, pilot training center, observatory, culinary arts, restaurant, museum, water studies institute.

Student profile. Among degree-seeking undergraduates, 47% enrolled in a transfer program, 53% enrolled in a vocational program, 923 enrolled as first-time, first-year students.

Part-time:	50%	**Hispanic American:**	2%
Out-of-state:	5%	**Native American:**	2%
Women:	57%	**25 or older:**	64%
African American:	1%	**Live on campus:**	3%
Asian American:	1%		

Transfer out. Colleges most students transferred to 2008: Michigan State University, Grand Valley State University, Ferris State University, Central Michigan University.

Basis for selection. Open admission, but selective for some programs. Admission for maritime, nursing, dental assistant and aviation programs based on school GPA, recommendation and test scores. ACT or SAT required for maritime program. **Adult students:** SAT/ACT scores not required. **Homeschooled:** Transcript of courses and grades required. **Learning Disabled:** COMPASS testing to show ability to benefit.

2008-2009 Annual costs. Tuition/fees: $2,868; $4,936 out-of-district; $6,164 out-of-state. Per-credit charge: $77 in-district; $142 out-of-district; $180 out-of-state. Room/board: $7,853. Books/supplies: $690. Personal expenses: $690.

2007-2008 Financial aid. Need-based: Need-based aid available for part-time students. Work-study available nights, weekends and for part-time students. **Non-need-based:** Scholarships awarded for academics, art, job skills, leadership, minority status, music/drama, ROTC, state residency.

Application procedures. Admission: No deadline. $20 fee, may be waived for applicants with need. Admission notification on a rolling basis. **Financial aid:** Priority date 4/1; no closing date. FAFSA required. Applicants notified on a rolling basis starting 5/1; must reply within 2 week(s) of notification.

Academics. Great Lakes Maritime Academy (4-year deck officer and marine engineer training program) for service in shipping industry on campus. 9 months spent aboard commercial vessels. Bachelor's degree awarded to maritime academy graduates in conjunction with Ferris State University. **Special study options:** Cooperative education, distance learning, dual enrollment of high school students, ESL, honors, independent study, internships, liberal arts/career combination, study abroad. Study broad includes two summer programs - Germany for the Business Division and Russia for the pre-engineering students. Bachelor's degree programs available on campus. **Credit/placement by examination:** AP, CLEP, institutional tests. 32 credit hours maximum toward associate degree. **Support services:** Learning center, pre-admission summer program, reduced course load, remedial instruction, study skills assistance, tutoring, writing center.

Majors. Agriculture: Crop production, landscaping, nursery operations, turf management. **Biology:** General. **Business:** General, accounting, accounting technology, business admin, management information systems, office technology. **Communications:** General. **Computer sciences:** Information systems. **Education:** General. **Engineering:** General. **Engineering technology:** Drafting, electrical. **Health:** Dental assistant, medical assistant, nursing (RN). **Liberal arts:** Arts/sciences. **Math:** General. **Mechanic/repair:** Automotive, electronics/electrical. **Personal/culinary services:** Chef training, culinary arts. **Physical sciences:** General. **Protective services:** Law enforcement admin, police science. **Social sciences:** General. **Transportation:** Airline/commercial pilot, aviation, maritime/Merchant Marine. **Visual/performing arts:** Art, commercial/advertising art, dramatic, piano/organ, studio arts, voice/opera.

Most popular majors. Health sciences 19%, liberal arts 52%.

Computing on campus. 625 workstations in dormitories, library, computer center, student center. Dormitories wired for high-speed internet access and linked to campus network. Commuter students can connect to campus network. Online course registration, online library, helpline, wireless network available.

Student life. Freshman orientation: Mandatory. Multiple one-day sessions prior to the start of each semester. **Housing:** Guaranteed on-campus for freshmen. Coed dorms, special housing for disabled, apartments available. $500 fully refundable deposit. **Activities:** Bands, choral groups, dance, drama, international student organizations, literary magazine, music ensembles, musical theater, radio station, student government, student newspaper, symphony orchestra, residence hall council, propeller club, Phi Theta Kappa, engineer club, botany club, law enforcement club, diverse student body group, Native American student group.

Student services. Adult student services, career counseling, student employment services, health services, minority student services, personal counseling, placement for graduates, veterans' counselor. **Physically disabled:** Services for visually, speech, hearing impaired. **Transfer:** Re-entry adviser, pre-admission transcript evaluation for new students. Transfer adviser, college fairs on campus for students transferring to 4-year colleges.

Contact. E-mail: jbensley@nmc.edu
Phone: (231) 995-1054 Toll-free number: (800) 748-0566
Fax: (231) 995-1339
James Bensley, Director of Admissions, Northwestern Michigan College, 1701 East Front Street, Traverse City, MI 49686

Oakland Community College

Bloomfield Hills, Michigan **CB member**
www.oaklandcc.edu **CB code: 1607**

- Public 2-year community college
- Commuter campus in very large city

General. Founded in 1964. Regionally accredited. Multicampus institution with locations in Auburn Hills, Farmington Hills, Southfield, Royal Oak, and Waterford. CREST (Combined Regional Emergency Services Training Center) located in Auburn Hills. **Enrollment:** 14,116 degree-seeking undergraduates; 10,841 non-degree-seeking students. **Degrees:** 1,956 associate awarded. **Location:** 30 miles from Detroit. **Calendar:** Semester, limited summer session. **Full-time faculty:** 241 total; 8% minority, 51% women. **Part-time faculty:** 741 total; 10% minority, 51% women. **Class size:** 23% < 20, 77% 20-39, less than 1% 40-49.

Student profile. Among degree-seeking undergraduates, 25% enrolled in a transfer program, 72% enrolled in a vocational program, 1% already have a bachelor's degree or higher, 2,006 enrolled as first-time, first-year students.

Part-time:	67%	**Hispanic American:**	2%
Women:	61%	**Native American:**	1%
African American:	18%	**International:**	7%
Asian American:	2%	**25 or older:**	49%

Transfer out. 24% of students enrolled in the transfer program go on to 4-year colleges. **Colleges most students transferred to 2008:** Oakland University, Wayne State University, Walsh College, Eastern Michigan University, University of Michigan-Dearborn.

Basis for selection. Open admission. Interview recommended. **Homeschooled:** English and math placement testing mandatory.

2008-2009 Annual costs. Tuition/fees: $1,873; $3,121 out-of-district; $4,351 out-of-state. Per-credit charge: $60 in-district; $102 out-of-district; $143 out-of-state. Books/supplies: $960. Personal expenses: $700.

2008-2009 Financial aid. **Need-based:** Need-based aid available for part-time students. Work-study available for part-time students. **Non-need-based:** Scholarships awarded for academics, athletics.

Application procedures. **Admission:** No deadline. No application fee. Admission notification on a rolling basis. **Financial aid:** Priority date 4/15; no closing date. FAFSA required. Applicants notified on a rolling basis starting 4/15.

Academics. **Special study options:** Cooperative education, distance learning, dual enrollment of high school students, ESL, internships, study abroad. Saturday classes offered. License preparation in dental hygiene, nursing, occupational therapy, paramedic, physical therapy, radiology. **Credit/placement by examination:** AP, CLEP, institutional tests. Last 15 credit hours toward degree program must be satisfied with institution's coursework, not credit by exam. **Support services:** Learning center, reduced course load, remedial instruction, study skills assistance, tutoring, writing center.

Majors. **Agriculture:** Landscaping. **Business:** Accounting technology, accounting/business management, business admin, construction management, entrepreneurial studies, hotel/motel admin, international, office management, office technology, restaurant/food services. **Communications technology:** Photo/film/video, radio/tv. **Computer sciences:** General, data processing, information technology, programming, security, systems analysis. **Construction:** Carpentry, electrician, pipefitting. **Engineering:** General. **Engineering technology:** Architectural, computer hardware, computer systems, drafting, electrical, electromechanical, heat/ac/refrig, industrial, manufacturing, mechanical drafting, robotics. **Family/consumer sciences:** Child care. **Foreign languages:** Sign language interpretation. **Health:** Community health services, dental hygiene, EMT paramedic, health care admin, histologic technology, massage therapy, medical assistant, medical radiologic technology/radiation therapy, medical transcription, nuclear medical technology, nursing (RN), occupational therapy assistant, pharmacy assistant, physical therapy assistant, respiratory therapy technology, sonography, surgical technology, veterinary technology/assistant. **Legal studies:** Court reporting, paralegal. **Liberal arts:** Arts/sciences, library assistant. **Mechanic/repair:** General, automotive, medium/heavy vehicle. **Parks/recreation:** Exercise sciences. **Personal/culinary services:** Chef training, cosmetic, salon management. **Production:** Machine tool, sheet metal, tool and die, welding. **Protective services:** Corrections, criminalistics, firefighting, law enforcement admin, police science. **Visual/performing arts:** Art, ceramics, dramatic, graphic design, interior design, music performance, music theory/composition, photography, voice/opera. **Other:** Milwright, Polysomnographic technology, Science.

Most popular majors. Business/marketing 14%, health sciences 19%, liberal arts 46%.

Computing on campus. 2,501 workstations in library, computer center, student center. Commuter students can connect to campus network. Online course registration, online library, helpline, wireless network available.

Student life. **Freshman orientation:** Available. Held in the first two weeks of class. **Activities:** Bands, choral groups, dance, drama, film society, international student organizations, literary magazine, music ensembles, student government, symphony orchestra, PTK, film society, Writers Block, student mentor program, dance team, Rhythm of the Cultures, anime club, Gamers Guild, psychology club.

Athletics. NJCAA. **Intercollegiate:** Basketball, cross-country, golf M, softball W, tennis W, volleyball W. **Intramural:** Cross-country, racquetball. **Team name:** Raiders.

Student services. Career counseling, services for economically disadvantaged, student employment services, financial aid counseling, on-campus daycare, personal counseling, placement for graduates, veterans' counselor, women's services. **Physically disabled:** Services for visually, speech, hearing impaired. **Transfer:** Pre-admission transcript evaluation for new students. Transfer center, transfer adviser, college fairs on campus for students transferring to 4-year colleges.

Contact. Phone: (248) 341-2200 Fax: (248) 341-2099
Maurice McCall, Director of Enrollment Services/Registrar, Oakland Community College, 2480 Opdyke Road, Bloomfield Hills, MI 48304-2266

Saginaw Chippewa Tribal College

Mount Pleasant, Michigan
www.sagchip.org/tribalcollege

- Public 2-year community college
- Large town

General. **Enrollment:** 109 degree-seeking undergraduates. **Degrees:** 12 associate awarded. **Calendar:** Semester, limited summer session. **Full-time faculty:** 4 total. **Part-time faculty:** 11 total.

Basis for selection. Open admission.

2008-2009 Annual costs. Tuition/fees: $1,950. Per-credit charge: $60.

Application procedures. **Admission:** No deadline. $25 fee. Admission notification on a rolling basis. **Financial aid:** No deadline.

Academics. **Special study options:** Dual enrollment of high school students. **Credit/placement by examination:** CLEP.

Majors. **Area/ethnic studies:** Native American. **Business:** Business admin.

Contact. Phone: (989) 775-4123
Tracy Reed, Director of Admissions, Saginaw Chippewa Tribal College, 2274 Enterprise Drive, Mount Pleasant, MI 48858

St. Clair County Community College

Port Huron, Michigan
www.sc4.edu **CB code: 1628**

- Public 2-year community college
- Commuter campus in large town

General. Founded in 1923. Regionally accredited. **Enrollment:** 4,000 degree-seeking undergraduates. **Degrees:** 520 associate awarded. **Location:** 55 miles from Detroit. **Calendar:** Semester, limited summer session. **Full-time faculty:** 90 total. **Part-time faculty:** 180 total. **Special facilities:** Fine arts facility, natural history museum.

Student profile.

Out-of-state:	2%	**25 or older:**	44%

Basis for selection. Open admission.

2008-2009 Annual costs. Tuition/fees: $3,087; $5,442 out-of-district; $7,692 out-of-state. Per-credit charge: $87 in-district; $165 out-of-district; $240 out-of-state. Residents of Lambton County, Canada pay in-state, out-of-district rate for tuition. Lambton County residents pay in-district tuition rate if enrolled in program of study not offered at Lambton College. Books/supplies: $850. Personal expenses: $439.

Application procedures. **Admission:** Closing date 9/1. No application fee. Admission notification on a rolling basis. **Financial aid:** Priority date 6/1; no closing date. FAFSA required. Applicants notified on a rolling basis starting 5/15; must reply within 2 week(s) of notification.

Academics. **Special study options:** Accelerated study, cooperative education, distance learning, double major, dual enrollment of high school students, honors, internships, weekend college. Bachelor's degree programs available on campus. License preparation in nursing. **Credit/placement by examination:** AP, CLEP, institutional tests. 45 credit hours maximum toward associate degree. **Support services:** GED preparation and test center, learning center, reduced course load, remedial instruction, study skills assistance, tutoring.

Majors. **Agriculture:** Horticultural science, supplies. **Business:** General, accounting, administrative services, business admin, office technology, office/clerical. **Communications:** Broadcast journalism, journalism. **Computer sciences:** Data processing. **Education:** General. **Engineering:** General. **Engineering technology:** Architectural drafting, drafting, electrical, manufacturing. **Family/consumer sciences:** Child care. **Health:** Medical secretary, nursing (RN). **Legal studies:** Legal secretary. **Liberal arts:** Arts/sciences. **Production:** Machine tool, welding. **Protective services:** Law enforcement admin. **Visual/performing arts:** Commercial/advertising art, studio arts. **Other:** Industrial automation.

Computing on campus. 229 workstations in library, computer center, student center.

Student life. **Freshman orientation:** Mandatory. Online orientation for all new students. On-campus orientation option available, but limited in dates and times. **Activities:** Concert band, choral groups, drama, music ensembles, radio station, student government, student newspaper, symphony orchestra, TV station, global awareness club.

Athletics. NJCAA. **Intercollegiate:** Baseball M, basketball, golf, softball W, volleyball W. **Intramural:** Volleyball M. **Team name:** Skippers.

Student services. Career counseling, student employment services, financial aid counseling, on-campus daycare, personal counseling, placement for graduates, veterans' counselor. **Physically disabled:** Services for visually, speech, hearing impaired. **Transfer:** Transfer adviser, college fairs on campus for students transferring to 4-year colleges.

Contact. E-mail: enrollment@sc4.edu
Phone: (810) 989-5500 Fax: (810) 984-4730
Pete Lacey, Registrar, St. Clair County Community College, 323 Erie Street, Port Huron, MI 48061-5015

Schoolcraft College

Livonia, Michigan — **CB member**
www.schoolcraft.edu — **CB code: 1764**

- Public 2-year community college
- Commuter campus in small city

General. Founded in 1961. Regionally accredited. **Enrollment:** 9,760 degree-seeking undergraduates; 2,800 non-degree-seeking students. **Degrees:** 1,025 associate awarded. **Location:** 20 miles from Ann Arbor. **Calendar:** Semester, limited summer session. **Full-time faculty:** 95 total. **Part-time faculty:** 390 total.

Student profile. Among degree-seeking undergraduates, 33% enrolled in a transfer program, 67% enrolled in a vocational program, 2,014 enrolled as first-time, first-year students.

Part-time:	57%	**25 or older:**	36%
Women:	56%		

Transfer out. Colleges most students transferred to 2008: Henry Ford Community College, Oakland Community College, Eastern Michigan University, Michigan State University, Wayne State University.

Basis for selection. Open admission, but selective for some programs. International students advised to start application process 3 months prior to start date of semester. **Homeschooled:** Interview required.

2008-2009 Annual costs. Tuition/fees: $2,380; $3,400 out-of-district; $4,990 out-of-state.

Financial aid. Need-based: Need-based aid available for part-time students. Work-study available nights, weekends and for part-time students. **Non-need-based:** Scholarships awarded for academics, athletics, leadership, music/drama, state residency.

Application procedures. Admission: No deadline. No application fee. Admission notification on a rolling basis. **Financial aid:** No deadline. FAFSA required. Applicants notified on a rolling basis starting 6/1.

Academics. Special study options: Accelerated study, cooperative education, distance learning, double major, dual enrollment of high school students, ESL, external degree, honors, liberal arts/career combination, weekend college. **Credit/placement by examination:** AP, CLEP, institutional tests. 30 credit hours maximum toward associate degree. **Support services:** GED preparation and test center, learning center, remedial instruction, tutoring.

Honors college/program. Minimum 3.5 GPA, 25 ACT or 1100 SAT (exclusive of Writing), writing sample, personal interview and 2 letters of recommendation required.

Majors. Business: General, accounting technology, administrative services, business admin, entrepreneurial studies, executive assistant, marketing, office technology, small business admin. **Communications technology:** Radio/tv, recording arts. **Computer sciences:** General, applications programming, computer graphics, programming, web page design. **Education:** General. **Engineering:** General. **Engineering technology:** Biomedical, drafting, electrical, environmental, manufacturing, metallurgical, quality control. **Family/consumer sciences:** Child care, child development. **Health:** EMT paramedic, health services, licensed practical nurse, massage therapy, medical records technology, nursing (RN), occupational therapy assistant. **Personal/culinary services:** Chef training. **Protective services:** Corrections, firefighting, police science, security services. **Transportation:** Aviation management.

Most popular majors. Business/marketing 18%, education 10%, health sciences 16%, liberal arts 28%, security/protective services 10%.

Computing on campus. 930 workstations in library, computer center.

Student life. Freshman orientation: Mandatory. **Activities:** Concert band, choral groups, drama, literary magazine, music ensembles, musical theater, student newspaper, music club, beekeepers club, international students club, quilting club, student activities board, Phi Theta Kappa, honors society, gourmet club, occupational therapy club.

Athletics. NJCAA. **Intercollegiate:** Basketball, bowling, cross-country W, golf, soccer, volleyball W. **Team name:** Ocelots.

Student services. Adult student services, career counseling, services for economically disadvantaged, student employment services, financial aid counseling, health services, legal services, on-campus daycare, personal counseling, placement for graduates, veterans' counselor, women's services. **Physically disabled:** Services for visually, speech, hearing impaired. **Transfer:** College fairs on campus for students transferring to 4-year colleges.

Contact. E-mail: admissions@schoolcraft.edu
Phone: (734) 462-4426 Fax: (734) 462-4553
Nicole Wilson-Fennell, Director of Enrollment Management, Schoolcraft College, 18600 Haggerty Road, Livonia, MI 48152-2696

Southwestern Michigan College

Dowagiac, Michigan
www.swmich.edu — **CB code: 1783**

- Public 2-year community college
- Commuter campus in small town

General. Founded in 1964. Regionally accredited. Two traditional semesters (fall and winter) and one optional spring term. Bachelor's degree programs offered in agreement with 4-year colleges and universities including Bethel College and Ferris State University. **Enrollment:** 2,163 degree-seeking undergraduates; 434 non-degree-seeking students. **Degrees:** 227 associate awarded. **Location:** 30 miles from South Bend, Indiana. **Calendar:** Semester, extensive summer session. **Full-time faculty:** 52 total; 21% have terminal degrees, 8% minority, 44% women. **Part-time faculty:** 91 total; 12% have terminal degrees, 11% minority, 56% women. **Special facilities:** Museum, wooded trails.

Student profile. Among degree-seeking undergraduates, 51% enrolled in a transfer program, 49% enrolled in a vocational program, 567 enrolled as first-time, first-year students, 189 transferred in from other institutions.

Part-time:	48%	**Asian American:**	1%
Out-of-state:	6%	**Hispanic American:**	4%
Women:	65%	**International:**	3%
African American:	9%	**25 or older:**	41%

Transfer out. Colleges most students transferred to 2008: Western Michigan University, Ferris State University, Bethel College, Indiana University of South Bend, Grand Valley State University.

Basis for selection. Open admission, but selective for some programs. Assessment tests in reading, writing, and math administered prior to registration for classes. Students may be exempted based upon ACT/SAT scores. Special requirements for nursing programs. Interview required for nursing applicants.

2008-2009 Annual costs. Tuition/fees: $3,165; $3,848 out-of-district; $4,103 out-of-state. Per-credit charge: $83 in-district; $105 out-of-district; $114 out-of-state. Books/supplies: $1,200. Personal expenses: $1,080.

2007-2008 Financial aid. Need-based: Need-based aid available for part-time students. Work-study available nights, weekends and for part-time students. **Non-need-based:** Scholarships awarded for academics, art, leadership, music/drama.

Application procedures. Admission: No deadline. No application fee. Admission notification on a rolling basis. **Financial aid:** Priority date 7/1; no closing date. FAFSA, institutional form required. Applicants notified on a rolling basis starting 4/1; must reply within 2 week(s) of notification.

Academics. Special study options: Accelerated study, cooperative education, distance learning, double major, dual enrollment of high school students, ESL, independent study, internships, weekend college. Bachelor's degree programs available on campus. License preparation in nursing, paramedic. **Credit/placement by examination:** AP, CLEP, institutional tests. 13 credit hours maximum toward associate degree. Credit for specific courses may be earned through ACE (Achieved Credit by Examination) testing. **Support services:** Learning center, reduced course load, remedial instruction, study skills assistance, tutoring, writing center.

Majors. Business: Accounting technology, business admin, executive assistant. **Communications technology:** Graphic/printing. **Computer sciences:** General. **Education:** Early childhood, teacher assistance. **Engineering technology:** Drafting, electrical. **Health:** EMT paramedic, medical assistant, medical records technology, nursing (RN). **Liberal arts:** Arts/sciences. **Mechanic/repair:** Automotive, industrial. **Production:** Machine tool, tool and die. **Protective services:** Firefighting. **Public administration:** Social work. **Other:** Occupational technology.

Most popular majors. Health sciences 23%, liberal arts 60%.

Computing on campus. 82 workstations in library, computer center, student center. Commuter students can connect to campus network. Online course registration, online library, helpline, wireless network available.

Student life. Freshman orientation: Available. Preregistration for classes offered. Several half-day sessions available. **Housing:** Coed dorms available. $275 nonrefundable deposit, deadline 6/1. **Activities:** Bands, choral groups, dance, drama, international student organizations, music ensembles, musical theater, student newspaper, Phi Theta Kappa, Business Professionals of America, Christian Bible study, dance club, Green club, music club, Alpha Kappa Omega, library club.

Athletics. Intramural: Basketball, football (non-tackle), golf, soccer, softball.

Student services. Career counseling, student employment services, financial aid counseling. **Physically disabled:** Services for visually, speech, hearing impaired. **Transfer:** Transfer adviser, college fairs on campus for students transferring to 4-year colleges.

Contact. E-mail: enrollment@swmich.edu
Phone: (269) 782-1413 Toll-free number: (800) 456-8675 ext. 1413
Fax: (269) 782-1371
Margaret Hay, Dean of Academic Support, Southwestern Michigan College, 58900 Cherry Grove Road, Dowagiac, MI 49047-9793

Washtenaw Community College

Ann Arbor, Michigan
www.wccnet.edu
CB member
CB code: 1935

- Public 2-year community college
- Commuter campus in small city

General. Founded in 1965. Regionally accredited. Classes taught in Brighton, Saline, Chelsea, Ypsilanti and Hartland. **Enrollment:** 10,339 degree-seeking undergraduates. **Degrees:** 1,107 associate awarded. **ROTC:** Army. **Location:** 40 miles from Detroit. **Calendar:** Trimester, extensive summer session. **Full-time faculty:** 181 total. **Part-time faculty:** 539 total.

Basis for selection. Open admission, but selective for some programs. Special requirements for health service technologies programs and some computer technology programs.

High school preparation. 15 units recommended. Recommended units include English 4, mathematics 4, social studies 2, science 4 and foreign language 1. Biology, chemistry, and algebra required for health programs. Trigonometry and drafting required for technical programs.

2008-2009 Annual costs. Tuition/fees: $2,310; $3,840 out-of-district; $5,130 out-of-state. Per-credit charge: $70 in-district; $120 out-of-district; $164 out-of-state. Books/supplies: $600. Personal expenses: $2,000.

Financial aid. Non-need-based: Scholarships awarded for academics.

Application procedures. Admission: Priority date 8/12; no deadline. No application fee. Admission notification on a rolling basis beginning on or about 2/20. **Financial aid:** Priority date 6/1, closing date 7/1. FAFSA, institutional form required. Applicants notified on a rolling basis.

Academics. Special study options: Cooperative education, cross-registration, distance learning, dual enrollment of high school students, ESL, honors, independent study, internships, liberal arts/career combination, weekend college. Bachelor's degree programs available on campus. **Credit/placement by examination:** AP, CLEP, institutional tests. 45 credit hours maximum toward associate degree. **Support services:** GED preparation and test center, learning center, remedial instruction, study skills assistance, tutoring, writing center.

Majors. Architecture: Technology. **Business:** Accounting, administrative services, business admin. **Communications technology:** Graphic/printing. **Computer sciences:** General, applications programming, computer graphics, computer science, data processing, information systems, LAN/WAN management, networking, programming, security, web page design. **Construction:** Maintenance. **Education:** Early childhood, elementary, secondary. **Engineering:** General, mechanics, science. **Engineering technology:** Construction, drafting, electrical. **Health:** Medical radiologic technology/radiation therapy, medical records admin, nursing (RN), premedicine, respiratory therapy technology, substance abuse counseling. **Liberal arts:** Arts/sciences. **Mechanic/repair:** Auto body, automotive, electronics/electrical, heating/ac/refrig. **Personal/culinary services:** Culinary arts. **Protective services:** Corrections, law enforcement admin, police science. **Social sciences:** General. **Visual/performing arts:** Commercial photography, photography.

Computing on campus. 211 workstations in library, computer center, student center. Commuter students can connect to campus network. Online course registration, online library, helpline, repair service, student web hosting available.

Student life. Freshman orientation: Mandatory. **Activities:** Jazz band, choral groups, dance, drama, literary magazine, musical theater, student government, student newspaper, African-American student association, Christian Challenge Student Advisory Council, international student association, Phi Theta Kappa, student assembly.

Student services. Adult student services, alcohol/substance abuse counseling, career counseling, services for economically disadvantaged, student employment services, financial aid counseling, minority student services, on-campus daycare, personal counseling, placement for graduates, veterans' counselor, women's services. **Physically disabled:** Services for visually, speech, hearing impaired. **Transfer:** Pre-admission transcript evaluation for new students. Transfer center, transfer adviser, college fairs on campus for students transferring to 4-year colleges.

Contact. E-mail: studrec@wccnet.org
Phone: (734) 973-3543 Fax: (734) 677-5414
Larry Aeilts, Director of Admissions, Washtenaw Community College, 4800 East Huron River Drive, Ann Arbor, MI 48106-1610

Wayne County Community College

Detroit, Michigan
www.wcccd.edu
CB code: 1937

- Public 2-year community and liberal arts college
- Commuter campus in very large city

General. Founded in 1967. Regionally accredited. Five campuses and extension site. **Enrollment:** 19,686 degree-seeking undergraduates; 1,854 non-degree-seeking students. **Degrees:** 1,100 associate awarded. **Calendar:** Semester, extensive summer session. **Full-time faculty:** 97 total. **Part-time faculty:** 974 total. **Class size:** 36% < 20, 52% 20-39, 10% 40-49, 2% 50-99. **Partnerships:** Formal partnerships with corporations and high schools.

Student profile. Among degree-seeking undergraduates, 4,117 enrolled as first-time, first-year students.

Part-time:	76%	**Asian American:**	1%
Women:	69%	**Hispanic American:**	2%
African American:	63%	**25 or older:**	58%

Transfer out. Colleges most students transferred to 2008: Wayne State University.

Basis for selection. Open admission. Select carrer programs require interviews and pre-requisite classes. **Adult students:** COMPASS placement exam required. **Homeschooled:** Transcript of courses and grades, state high school equivalency certificate required. **Learning Disabled:** Students with learning disabilities must register with the campus Learning Center Coordinatior and provide appropriate documentation.

2008-2009 Annual costs. Tuition/fees: $2,020; $2,990 out-of-district; $3,890 out-of-state. Per-credit charge: $58 in-district; $90 out-of-district; $120 out-of-state. Books/supplies: $850.

2007-2008 Financial aid. Need-based: 60% of total undergraduate aid awarded as scholarships/grants, 40% as loans/jobs. Need-based aid available for part-time students. Work-study available nights, weekends and for part-time students. **Additional information:** High school diploma, GED, or passing grade on ABT required for financial aid.

Application procedures. Admission: Closing date 9/2 (receipt date). $10 fee, may be waived for applicants with need. Admission notification on a rolling basis. **Financial aid:** Priority date 5/1; no closing date. FAFSA required. Applicants notified on a rolling basis starting 5/1.

Academics. Special study options: Accelerated study, distance learning, double major, dual enrollment of high school students, honors, independent study, internships, liberal arts/career combination, study abroad, weekend college. License preparation in dental hygiene, nursing, occupational therapy, paramedic, real estate. **Credit/placement by examination:** AP, CLEP, institutional tests. 45 credit hours maximum toward associate degree. Recommendation of CAO or program chair. **Support services:** GED preparation, learning center, remedial instruction, study skills assistance, tutoring.

Majors. Business: Accounting technology, business admin, labor relations. **Computer sciences:** General, programming. **Education:** General, elementary, secondary. **Engineering:** General. **Engineering technology:** Computer, electrical, electromechanical, telecommunications. **Family/consumer sciences:** Aging, child care, institutional food production. **Health:** Dental hygiene, EMT paramedic, mental health services, nursing (RN), occupational therapy assistant, pharmacy assistant, substance abuse counseling, surgical technology, veterinary technology/assistant. **Legal studies:** Paralegal.

Liberal arts: Arts/sciences. **Mechanic/repair:** Aircraft, aircraft powerplant, automotive, diesel, heating/ac/refrig. **Philosophy/religion:** Islamic, religion. **Production:** Machine tool, tool and die, welding. **Protective services:** Corrections, fire safety technology, law enforcement admin. **Public administration:** Social work. **Social sciences:** General.

Most popular majors. Business/marketing 7%, health sciences 7%, liberal arts 60%.

Computing on campus. Commuter students can connect to campus network. Online course registration, online library, helpline, repair service, wireless network available.

Student life. **Freshman orientation:** Available. Includes assessment testing. **Policies:** Students must follow the student code of conduct. **Activities:** Dance, drama, student government.

Athletics. NJCAA. **Intramural:** Basketball, cross-country M, golf M, volleyball W. **Team name:** Wild Cats.

Student services. Adult student services, career counseling, services for economically disadvantaged, student employment services, financial aid counseling, on-campus daycare, personal counseling, placement for graduates, veterans' counselor, women's services. **Physically disabled:** Services for visually, speech, hearing impaired. **Learning disabled:** Comprehensive services available. **Transfer:** Re-entry adviser, pre-admission transcript evaluation for new students. Transfer adviser, college fairs on campus for students transferring to 4-year colleges.

Contact. Phone: (313) 496-2600 Fax: (313) 962-1643
Adrian Phillips, Associate Vice Chancellor Student Services, Wayne County Community College, 801 West Fort Street, Detroit, MI 48226

West Shore Community College

Scottville, Michigan
www.westshore.edu **CB code: 1941**

- Public 2-year community college
- Commuter campus in rural community

General. Founded in 1967. Regionally accredited. **Enrollment:** 515 full-time, degree-seeking students. **Degrees:** 156 associate awarded. **Location:** 54 miles from Muskegon. **Calendar:** Semester, limited summer session. **Full-time faculty:** 26 total. **Part-time faculty:** 69 total.

Transfer out. **Colleges most students transferred to 2008:** Grand Valley State University, Ferris State University, Davenport College, Central Michigan University.

Basis for selection. Open admission, but selective for some programs. Applicants to nursing programs must complete prerequisite course work with minimum 2.0 GPA.

2008-2009 Annual costs. Tuition/fees: $2,340; $3,780 out-of-district; $4,980 out-of-state. Per-credit charge: $72 in-district; $120 out-of-district; $160 out-of-state. Books/supplies: $700. Personal expenses: $650.

2008-2009 Financial aid. **Need-based:** Need-based aid available for part-time students. Work-study available nights, weekends and for part-time students.

Application procedures. **Admission:** No deadline. $15 fee. Admission notification on a rolling basis. Applicants for associate degree in nursing must apply by January 1, practical nursing applicants by June 1. **Financial aid:** Priority date 3/15; no closing date. FAFSA required. Applicants notified on a rolling basis starting 5/15; must reply within 2 week(s) of notification.

Academics. **Special study options:** Distance learning, dual enrollment of high school students, independent study, internships. Bachelor's degree programs available on campus. License preparation in nursing. **Credit/placement by examination:** AP, CLEP, institutional tests. 10 credit hours maximum toward associate degree. **Support services:** GED test center, learning center, reduced course load, remedial instruction, study skills assistance, tutoring.

Majors. **Business:** General, accounting, administrative services, management information systems, marketing, office technology, office/clerical. **Computer sciences:** Data processing. **Education:** General. **Engineering technology:** CAD/CADD, electrical. **Health:** EMT paramedic, nursing (RN), nursing assistant, prepharmacy. **Legal studies:** Prelaw. **Liberal arts:** Arts/sciences. **Math:** General. **Production:** Welding. **Protective services:** Law enforcement admin.

Computing on campus. 300 workstations in library, computer center, student center. Commuter students can connect to campus network. Helpline available.

Student life. **Freshman orientation:** Mandatory. Preregistration for classes offered. Each student meets one-on-one with academic counselor during registration period before classes begin. **Activities:** Choral groups, drama, music ensembles, musical theater, student government, student newspaper, Phi Theta Kappa honor society, law enforcement club, art club, science club, additional special interest clubs.

Athletics. **Intramural:** Basketball, racquetball, softball, volleyball.

Student services. Career counseling, student employment services, personal counseling, placement for graduates, veterans' counselor. **Physically disabled:** Services for visually, speech, hearing impaired. **Transfer:** Pre-admission transcript evaluation for new students. Transfer adviser, college fairs on campus for students transferring to 4-year colleges.

Contact. E-mail: admissions@westshore.edu
Phone: (231) 845-6211 ext. 3117 Fax: (231) 845-3944
Tom Bell, Director of Admissions, West Shore Community College, 3000 North Stiles Road, Scottville, MI 49454-0277

Minnesota

Academy College

Bloomington, Minnesota
www.academycollege.edu **CB code: 3311**

- For-profit 2-year junior and career college
- Large city
- Interview required

General. Accredited by ACICS. **Enrollment:** 168 degree-seeking undergraduates. **Degrees:** 17 bachelor's, 19 associate awarded. **Calendar:** Quarter, extensive summer session. **Full-time faculty:** 5 total. **Part-time faculty:** 50 total. **Class size:** 100% < 20.

Student profile.

Out-of-state:	27%	**25 or older:**	65%

Basis for selection. Open admission.

2008-2009 Annual costs. Tuition ranges from $335 to $399 per credit hour depending on program. Books/supplies: $700. Personal expenses: $2,200.

2007-2008 Financial aid. Need-based: Need-based aid available for part-time students. Work-study available nights, weekends and for part-time students.

Application procedures. Admission: No deadline. $30 fee. Application must be submitted on paper. Admission notification on a rolling basis. **Financial aid:** No deadline. FAFSA, institutional form required. Applicants notified on a rolling basis.

Academics. Special study options: Distance learning, internships. License preparation in aviation. **Credit/placement by examination:** AP, CLEP. **Support services:** Learning center, reduced course load, study skills assistance, tutoring.

Majors. Business: Accounting, business admin, finance, sales/distribution, training/development. **Communications technology:** General, animation/special effects. **Computer sciences:** General, computer graphics, programming, system admin, web page design. **Transportation:** Airline/commercial pilot, aviation, aviation management. **Visual/performing arts:** General, commercial/advertising art.

Computing on campus. 100 workstations in library, computer center. Online library, wireless network available.

Student life. Freshman orientation: Mandatory.

Student services. Placement for graduates. **Transfer:** Pre-admission transcript evaluation for new students.

Contact. E-mail: admissions@academycollege.edu
Phone: (952) 851-0066 Toll-free number: (800) 292-9149
Fax: (952) 851-0094
Tracey Schantz, Campus Director, Academy College, 1101 East 78th Street, Bloomington, MN 55420

Alexandria Technical College

Alexandria, Minnesota
www.alextech.edu **CB code: 0771**

- Public 2-year technical college
- Commuter campus in large town
- Interview required

General. Founded in 1961. Regionally accredited. **Enrollment:** 1,685 degree-seeking undergraduates. **Degrees:** 482 associate awarded. **Location:** 135 miles from Minneapolis-St. Paul. **Calendar:** Semester, limited summer session. **Full-time faculty:** 70 total; 39% women. **Part-time faculty:** 27 total; 48% women.

Student profile.

Out-of-state:	4%	**25 or older:**	25%

Basis for selection. Open admission, but selective for some programs. School achievement record, test scores, and interview considered for course placement. Minnesota Multiphasic Personality Inventory required. ACT recommended and physical agility test required for law enforcement applicants. NET test for practical nursing examination required for practical nursing applicants. Mechanical reasoning tests required for marine and small engine mechanics and diesel mechanics applicants. Applicants considered in order of applications received. Portfolio required for communications art and design students.

2008-2009 Annual costs. Tuition/fees: $4,506; $4,506 out-of-state. Per-credit charge: $135 in-state; $135 out-of-state. In-state and out-of-state tuition rates are the same. Books/supplies: $1,200.

Financial aid. All financial aid based on need. Need-based aid available for part-time students. Work-study available for part-time students.

Application procedures. Admission: Priority date 8/1; no deadline. $20 fee. Admission notification on a rolling basis. **Financial aid:** Priority date 5/1; no closing date. FAFSA, institutional form required. Applicants notified on a rolling basis starting 6/30; must reply within 2 week(s) of notification.

Academics. Special study options: Distance learning, double major, independent study, internships, liberal arts/career combination, student-designed major. Bachelor's degree programs available on campus. License preparation in nursing, real estate. **Credit/placement by examination:** AP, CLEP, institutional tests. No separate limits on CLEP and credit by exam. **Support services:** Reduced course load, remedial instruction, study skills assistance, tutoring, writing center.

Majors. Business: Accounting, banking/financial services, business admin, fashion, hospitality admin, marketing, office management, operations. **Computer sciences:** General, networking, programming, web page design. **Engineering technology:** Hydraulics, industrial, manufacturing, mechanical drafting. **Family/consumer sciences:** Child care. **Health:** Clinical lab technology, medical secretary, nursing (RN). **Legal studies:** Legal secretary, paralegal. **Mechanic/repair:** Diesel. **Parks/recreation:** Health/fitness. **Production:** Machine tool. **Protective services:** Police science. **Public administration:** Human services. **Visual/performing arts:** Commercial/advertising art, interior design.

Most popular majors. Business/marketing 24%, computer/information sciences 9%, health sciences 13%, security/protective services 22%, trade and industry 6%, visual/performing arts 12%.

Computing on campus. 1,100 workstations in library, computer center. Online course registration, online library, helpline, repair service, wireless network available.

Student life. Freshman orientation: Available. Preregistration for classes offered. **Activities:** Campus ministries, student government, Phi Theta Kappa, Business Professionals of America, Delta Epsilon Chi, Skills USA, student senate.

Athletics. Intramural: Basketball, softball, volleyball.

Student services. Alcohol/substance abuse counseling, chaplain/spiritual director, career counseling, services for economically disadvantaged, student employment services, financial aid counseling, health services, minority student services, personal counseling, placement for graduates, veterans' counselor. **Physically disabled:** Services for visually, speech, hearing impaired. **Transfer:** Pre-admission transcript evaluation for new students. Transfer adviser, college fairs on campus for students transferring to 4-year colleges.

Contact. E-mail: admissionsrep@alextech.edu
Phone: (320) 762-4520 Toll-free number: (888) 234-1222
Fax: (320) 762-4603
Doug Tatge, Dean of Student Affairs, Alexandria Technical College, 1601 Jefferson Street, Alexandria, MN 56308-3799

Anoka Technical College

Anoka, Minnesota
www.anokatech.edu **CB code: 6084**

- Public 2-year technical college
- Commuter campus in large town

General. Regionally accredited. **Enrollment:** 2,230 degree-seeking undergraduates. **Degrees:** 164 associate awarded. **Location:** 25 miles from

Minneapolis-St. Paul. **Calendar:** Semester, limited summer session. **Full-time faculty:** 75 total. **Part-time faculty:** 30 total.

Basis for selection. Open admission. All new students are required to take the computer-based Accuplacer entrance examination to determine their skill level in mathematics, reading and writing. **Adult students:** SAT/ACT scores not required.

2008-2009 Annual costs. Tuition/fees: $4,669; $4,669 out-of-state. Per-credit charge: $142 in-state; $142 out-of-state. In-state and out-of-state tuition rates are the same.

Financial aid. All financial aid based on need. Need-based aid available for part-time students. Work-study available nights.

Application procedures. Admission: Closing date 8/15 (postmark date). $20 fee, may be waived for applicants with need. Admission notification on a rolling basis. **Financial aid:** No deadline. FAFSA, institutional form required. Applicants notified on a rolling basis starting 5/1.

Academics. Special study options: Distance learning, internships, liberal arts/career combination. License preparation in nursing, occupational therapy, paramedic. **Credit/placement by examination:** CLEP, institutional tests. 72 credit hours maximum toward associate degree. **Support services:** GED preparation and test center, learning center, reduced course load, remedial instruction, study skills assistance, tutoring, writing center.

Majors. Agriculture: Horticulture, landscaping, nursery operations, turf management. **Computer sciences:** Information systems. **Engineering technology:** Drafting, electrical. **Family/consumer sciences:** Child care. **Health:** Licensed practical nurse, medical secretary, occupational therapy assistant, physical therapy assistant. **Mechanic/repair:** Automotive. **Parks/recreation:** Facilities management. **Transportation:** Air traffic control, aviation, aviation management.

Computing on campus. 250 workstations in library, computer center, student center. Online library available.

Student life. Freshman orientation: Mandatory. **Activities:** Student government.

Student services. Career counseling, student employment services, health services, on-campus daycare, personal counseling, placement for graduates, veterans' counselor. **Physically disabled:** Services for visually, speech, hearing impaired.

Contact. E-mail: admissions@anokatech.edu
Phone: (763) 576-4850 Fax: (763) 576-4756
Leo Christenson, Dean of Academic Resources, Anoka Technical College, 1355 West Highway 10, Anoka, MN 55303

Anoka-Ramsey Community College

Coon Rapids, Minnesota
www.anokaramsey.edu **CB code: 6024**

- Public 2-year community college
- Commuter campus in small city

General. Founded in 1965. Regionally accredited. Extension sites at Elk River and Fridley. **Enrollment:** 6,586 degree-seeking undergraduates. **Degrees:** 803 associate awarded. **ROTC:** Army, Naval, Air Force. **Location:** 20 miles from Minneapolis-St. Paul. **Calendar:** Semester, limited summer session. **Full-time faculty:** 115 total. **Part-time faculty:** 174 total. **Special facilities:** Glass-blowing studio, native prairie ground.

Transfer out. Colleges most students transferred to 2008: University of Minnesota-Twin Cities, St. Cloud State University.

Basis for selection. Open admission, but selective for some programs. Special requirements for nursing, biomedical technology, computer networking, and telecommunications programs. National League of Nursing Pre-admissions Test required for nursing applicants.

High school preparation. One year laboratory chemistry and 1 year laboratory biology required for nursing applicants out of high school less than 5 years.

2008-2009 Annual costs. Tuition/fees: $4,100; $4,100 out-of-state. Per-credit charge: $120 in-state; $120 out-of-state. In-state and out-of-state tuition rates are the same. Books/supplies: $600. Personal expenses: $600.

Financial aid. All financial aid based on need. Work-study available nights, weekends and for part-time students.

Application procedures. Admission: No deadline. $20 fee, may be waived for applicants with need. Admission notification on a rolling basis. **Financial aid:** Priority date 4/1; no closing date. FAFSA, institutional form required. Applicants notified on a rolling basis; must reply within 2 week(s) of notification.

Academics. Special study options: Cross-registration, distance learning, dual enrollment of high school students, independent study, internships, study abroad, weekend college. Joint admission with Colleges of Science and Engineering at Duluth and Mankato State University, University of Minnesota, St. Cloud State University, and University of Minnesota-Twin Cities in agriculture, natural resources, human ecology, and liberal arts. **Credit/placement by examination:** AP, CLEP, institutional tests. 30 credit hours maximum toward associate degree. **Support services:** Learning center, reduced course load, remedial instruction, study skills assistance, tutoring, writing center.

Majors. Agriculture: Landscaping, nursery operations, turf management. **Business:** Accounting, administrative services, business admin, marketing. **Computer sciences:** Information systems. **Conservation:** Environmental science. **Engineering:** General. **Engineering technology:** Architectural, electrical. **Family/consumer sciences:** Child care. **Health:** Medical secretary, nursing (RN), occupational therapy assistant, optician, physical therapy assistant. **Legal studies:** Legal secretary. **Liberal arts:** Arts/sciences. **Mechanic/repair:** Automotive. **Parks/recreation:** General.

Most popular majors. Business/marketing 11%, health sciences 27%, liberal arts 56%.

Computing on campus. 300 workstations in library, computer center.

Student life. Freshman orientation: Mandatory. **Activities:** Bands, choral groups, drama, international student organizations, literary magazine, music ensembles, musical theater, student government, student newspaper, symphony orchestra, Phi Theta Kappa, humanities club, Intervarsity Christian Fellowship.

Athletics. NJCAA. **Intercollegiate:** Baseball M, basketball, volleyball W. **Intramural:** Archery M, baseball M, basketball, bowling, golf, ice hockey, soccer, softball, volleyball.

Student services. Adult student services, career counseling, student employment services, personal counseling, veterans' counselor. **Physically disabled:** Services for visually, speech, hearing impaired. **Transfer:** Transfer adviser, college fairs on campus for students transferring to 4-year colleges.

Contact. Phone: (763) 422-3333 Fax: (763) 422-3636
Anoka-Ramsey Community College, 11200 Mississippi Boulevard NW, Coon Rapids, MN 55433

Central Lakes College

Brainerd, Minnesota
www.clcmn.edu **CB code: 6045**

- Public 2-year community and technical college
- Commuter campus in large town

General. Founded in 1938. Regionally accredited. Access to 1.5 million book titles through participation in online catalog system with 28 other libraries. **Enrollment:** 3,087 degree-seeking undergraduates. **Degrees:** 423 associate awarded. **Location:** 125 miles from Minneapolis-St. Paul. **Calendar:** Semester, limited summer session. **Full-time faculty:** 101 total. **Part-time faculty:** 67 total. **Class size:** 54% < 20, 51% 20-39, 2% 40-49. **Special facilities:** Conservatory, American Indian studies center.

Student profile. Among degree-seeking undergraduates, 220 transferred in from other institutions.

Basis for selection. Open admission, but selective for some programs. Applicants to mobility nursing program must have graduate license in practical nursing (LPN). Practical nurse program grades and college grades considered. Instructor and employer references, practical to registered nursing mobility profile, and mathematics test scores also considered.

2008-2009 Annual costs. Tuition/fees: $4,540. Per-credit charge: $133. In-state and out-of-state tuition rates same. Books/supplies: $800. Personal expenses: $1,500.

2007-2008 Financial aid. Need-based: 44% of total undergraduate aid awarded as scholarships/grants, 56% as loans/jobs. Need-based aid available for part-time students. Work-study available for part-time students.

Application procedures. Admission: No deadline. $20 fee. Admission notification on a rolling basis. **Financial aid:** Priority date 6/1; no closing

Two-Year Colleges

date. FAFSA, institutional form required. Applicants notified on a rolling basis starting 6/10; must reply within 2 week(s) of notification.

Academics. Special study options: Combined bachelor's/graduate degree, distance learning, dual enrollment of high school students, independent study, internships, liberal arts/career combination. 2+2 management program with College of St. Scholastica, 2+2 programs with Southwest State in organizational management and teacher education, 2+2 natural resources with University of Minnesota: Crookston. Bachelor's degree programs available on campus. License preparation in nursing. **Credit/placement by examination:** AP, CLEP, IB, institutional tests. **Support services:** Learning center, remedial instruction, study skills assistance, tutoring.

Majors. Agriculture: Horticulture. **Business:** Accounting, administrative services, business admin, tourism/travel. **Communications technology:** Photo/film/video. **Computer sciences:** Data processing, networking, programming. **Conservation:** General. **Education:** Teacher assistance. **Engineering:** General. **Engineering technology:** Computer systems, robotics. **Family/consumer sciences:** Child care. **Health:** Medical secretary, nursing (RN). **Liberal arts:** Arts/sciences. **Mechanic/repair:** Automotive, heavy equipment, industrial electronics, marine. **Production:** Welding. **Protective services:** Criminal justice, criminalistics, police science. **Visual/performing arts:** Commercial/advertising art.

Most popular majors. Business/marketing 8%, health sciences 11%, liberal arts 57%.

Computing on campus. 150 workstations in library, computer center. Commuter students can connect to campus network. Online course registration, online library, repair service, wireless network available.

Student life. Freshman orientation: Mandatory. Online orientation required. Orientations also held in-person throughout spring and summer. **Activities:** Bands, choral groups, drama, international student organizations, music ensembles, musical theater, student government, student newspaper, Anishinabe Student Association, campus ambassadors, law enforcement club, mentoring, theater club, Phi Theta Kappa, Spanish club, minority student forum.

Athletics. NJCAA. **Intercollegiate:** Baseball M, basketball, football (tackle) M, golf, softball W, volleyball W. **Intramural:** Baseball M, basketball, bowling, golf, softball, volleyball. **Team name:** Raiders.

Student services. Adult student services, career counseling, services for economically disadvantaged, financial aid counseling, health services, minority student services, on-campus daycare, personal counseling, placement for graduates, veterans' counselor, women's services. **Physically disabled:** Services for visually, speech, hearing impaired. **Transfer:** Pre-admission transcript evaluation for new students. Transfer adviser, college fairs on campus for students transferring to 4-year colleges.

Contact. E-mail: rtretter@clcmn.edu
Phone: (218) 855-8037 Toll-free number: (800) 933-0346
Fax: (218) 855-8230
Charlotte Daniels, Director of Admissions, Central Lakes College, 501 West College Drive, Brainerd, MN 56401

Century Community and Technical College

White Bear Lake, Minnesota
www.century.edu **CB code: 6388**

- Public 2-year community and technical college
- Commuter campus in large town

General. Founded in 1967. Regionally accredited. **Enrollment:** 8,548 degree-seeking undergraduates; 728 non-degree-seeking students. **Degrees:** 888 associate awarded. **ROTC:** Air Force. **Location:** 16 miles from Minneapolis-St. Paul. **Calendar:** Semester, limited summer session. **Full-time faculty:** 180 total; 19% have terminal degrees, 8% minority, 53% women. **Part-time faculty:** 164 total; 7% minority, 48% women. **Class size:** 30% < 20, 60% 20-39, 7% 40-49, 3% 50-99. **Special facilities:** 92-acre nature area, walking trail.

Student profile. Among degree-seeking undergraduates, 28% enrolled in a transfer program, 72% enrolled in a vocational program, 3% already have a bachelor's degree or higher, 1,637 enrolled as first-time, first-year students, 998 transferred in from other institutions.

Part-time:	52%	**Hispanic American:**	2%
Out-of-state:	6%	**Native American:**	1%
Women:	57%	**International:**	1%
African American:	10%	**25 or older:**	36%
Asian American:	14%		

Transfer out. Colleges most students transferred to 2008: Metropolitan State University, University of Minnesota, University of Wisconsin-River Falls, St. Cloud State University, University of Wisconsin-Stout.

Basis for selection. Open admission, but selective for some programs. Special requirements for nursing, radiology, orthotics, prosthetics, paramedic, dental assist and dental hygiene programs. LOEP used to determine English proficiency. **Learning Disabled:** Documentation of disability must be provided within the first semester of service.

2008-2009 Annual costs. Tuition/fees: $4,565; $4,565 out-of-state. Per-credit charge: $135 in-state; $135 out-of-state. In-state and out-of-state tuition rates are the same. Books/supplies: $1,000.

2007-2008 Financial aid. All financial aid based on need. 35% of total undergraduate aid awarded as scholarships/grants, 65% as loans/jobs. Need-based aid available for part-time students. Work-study available for part-time students. **Additional information:** Minnesota resident out of high school or not enrolled in college for 7 years without bachelor's or other higher degree offered cost of tuition and books for 1 course in 1 semester up to maximum of 5 credits.

Application procedures. Admission: No deadline. $20 fee, may be waived for applicants with need. Admission notification on a rolling basis. **Financial aid:** No deadline. FAFSA required. Applicants notified on a rolling basis starting 5/15.

Academics. Special study options: Dual enrollment of high school students, ESL, honors, internships, liberal arts/career combination. License preparation in dental hygiene, nursing, paramedic, radiology. **Credit/placement by examination:** AP, CLEP, IB. **Support services:** Learning center, remedial instruction, study skills assistance, tutoring, writing center.

Majors. Agriculture: Greenhouse operations, horticultural science, landscaping. **Business:** Accounting, administrative services, business admin, marketing. **Communications:** Digital media. **Computer sciences:** General, computer science, networking, security. **Construction:** Maintenance. **Education:** Multi-level teacher, teacher assistance. **Engineering:** General. **Engineering technology:** CAD/CADD, computer systems. **Foreign languages:** Translation. **Health:** Dental assistant, dental hygiene, EMT paramedic, medical secretary, nursing (RN), orthotics/prosthetics, radiologic technology/medical imaging, substance abuse counseling. **Interdisciplinary:** Global studies. **Liberal arts:** Arts/sciences. **Mechanic/repair:** Auto body, automotive, heating/ac/refrig. **Parks/recreation:** Sports admin. **Personal/culinary services:** Cosmetic. **Protective services:** Criminal justice, criminalistics, police science, security services. **Public administration:** Human services. **Visual/performing arts:** Interior design.

Most popular majors. Health sciences 32%, liberal arts 41%, security/protective services 7%.

Computing on campus. 1,450 workstations in library, computer center. Commuter students can connect to campus network. Online course registration, wireless network available.

Student life. Freshman orientation: Mandatory. Preregistration for classes offered. 4-hour session preceding semester start. Online orientation also available. **Activities:** Bands, choral groups, drama, literary magazine, music ensembles, student government, student newspaper, symphony orchestra, Alpha & Omega, Asian student association, Black student association, Democrats club, drama club, intercultural club, Phi Theta Kappa, Republicans club, Student Ambassadors, Creative Arts Alliance.

Athletics. NJCAA. **Intercollegiate:** Golf. **Intramural:** Badminton, basketball, golf, softball, volleyball.

Student services. Career counseling, student employment services, financial aid counseling, health services, minority student services, on-campus daycare, personal counseling. **Physically disabled:** Services for visually, speech, hearing impaired. **Transfer:** Transfer adviser, college fairs on campus for students transferring to 4-year colleges.

Contact. E-mail: admissions@century.edu
Phone: (651) 779-1700 Toll-free number: (800) 228-1978
Fax: (651) 779-1796
Christine Paulos, Director of Admissions, Century Community and Technical College, 3300 Century Avenue North, White Bear Lake, MN 55110

Dakota County Technical College

Rosemount, Minnesota
www.dctc.edu **CB code: 7149**

- Public 2-year technical college
- Commuter campus in large town

General. Regionally accredited. **Enrollment:** 2,393 degree-seeking undergraduates; 355 non-degree-seeking students. **Degrees:** 294 associate awarded. **Location:** 20 miles from Minneapolis-St. Paul. **Calendar:** Semester, limited summer session. **Full-time faculty:** 80 total; 4% minority, 42% women. **Part-time faculty:** 100 total; 9% minority, 47% women. **Class size:** 58% < 20, 41% 20-39, less than 1% 40-49. **Special facilities:** Greenhouse, truck driving rodeo, skid pad. **Partnerships:** Formal partnership with General Motors for Automotive Service Education Program/Body Service Education Program.

Student profile. Among degree-seeking undergraduates, 100% enrolled in a vocational program, 917 enrolled as first-time, first-year students, 570 transferred in from other institutions.

Part-time:	38%	**Hispanic American:**	3%
Women:	50%	**Native American:**	1%
African American:	8%	**International:**	1%
Asian American:	4%	**25 or older:**	53%

Basis for selection. Open admission, but selective for some programs. Minimum test scores required for certain programs. TOEFL required for international students. Admissions visit including meeting with the program instructor(s) required. **Homeschooled:** Transcript of courses and grades required.

High school preparation. College-preparatory program recommended.

2008-2009 Annual costs. Tuition/fees: $4,909; $9,239 out-of-state. Per-credit charge: $144 in-state; $289 out-of-state. Books/supplies: $1,625. Personal expenses: $2,250.

Financial aid. Need-based: Need-based aid available for part-time students. Work-study available nights, weekends and for part-time students. **Non-need-based:** Scholarships awarded for academics, leadership.

Application procedures. Admission: No deadline. $20 fee, may be waived for applicants with need. Admission notification on a rolling basis. **Financial aid:** No deadline. FAFSA required. Applicants notified on a rolling basis starting 3/15.

Academics. Special study options: Accelerated study, cooperative education, cross-registration, distance learning, double major, ESL, independent study, internships, liberal arts/career combination. Bachelor's degree programs available on campus. License preparation in nursing, real estate. **Credit/placement by examination:** AP, CLEP, institutional tests. **Support services:** Learning center, pre-admission summer program, remedial instruction, study skills assistance, tutoring, writing center.

Majors. Agriculture: Landscaping. **Business:** Accounting, business admin, executive assistant, management information systems, marketing, real estate, sales/distribution, tourism/travel, travel services. **Communications:** Digital media. **Computer sciences:** Database management, networking, programming. **Construction:** Electrician, lineworker, masonry. **Engineering technology:** Architectural drafting, biomedical, manufacturing. **Health:** Dental assistant, medical assistant, medical secretary. **Legal studies:** Legal secretary. **Mechanic/repair:** Auto body, automotive, heavy equipment, medium/heavy vehicle. **Parks/recreation:** Exercise sciences. **Transportation:** Aviation management. **Visual/performing arts:** Commercial/advertising art, graphic design, interior design, photography.

Most popular majors. Business/marketing 24%, engineering/engineering technologies 12%, health sciences 8%, parks/recreation 7%, trade and industry 17%, visual/performing arts 23%.

Computing on campus. 200 workstations in library, computer center, student center. Online course registration, online library, helpline, wireless network available.

Student life. Freshman orientation: Mandatory. Preregistration for classes offered. Sessions available 2-3 months prior to semester. **Activities:** International student organizations, student government, student newspaper, multicultural club, veterans center.

Athletics. NJCAA. **Intercollegiate:** Baseball M, soccer, softball W. **Intramural:** Basketball. **Team name:** Blue Knights.

Student services. Career counseling, services for economically disadvantaged, student employment services, financial aid counseling, health services, minority student services, personal counseling, placement for graduates, veterans' counselor. **Physically disabled:** Services for visually, speech, hearing impaired. **Learning disabled:** Comprehensive services available. **Transfer:** Re-entry adviser, pre-admission transcript evaluation for new students. Transfer adviser, college fairs on campus for students transferring to 4-year colleges.

Contact. E-mail: admissions@dctc.edu
Phone: (651) 423-8301 Toll-free number: (877) 937-3282
Fax: (651) 423-8775
Patrick Lair, Admissions Director, Dakota County Technical College, 1300 145th Street East, Rosemount, MN 55068

Duluth Business University

Duluth, Minnesota
www.dbumn.edu **CB code: 3312**

- For-profit 2-year business college
- Small city
- Interview required

General. Accredited by ACICS. **Enrollment:** 309 degree-seeking undergraduates. **Degrees:** 32 associate awarded. **Location:** 150 miles from Minneapolis-St. Paul. **Calendar:** Quarter, extensive summer session. **Full-time faculty:** 13 total. **Part-time faculty:** 19 total. **Class size:** 96% < 20, 4% 20-39.

Student profile. Among degree-seeking undergraduates, 104 enrolled as first-time, first-year students.

Part-time:	29%	**Women:**	84%

Basis for selection. High school diploma or GED and interview required.

2008-2009 Annual costs. Tuition/fees: $13,995. Per-credit charge: $310. Vet tech and Graphics programs $330/credit hour. Books/supplies: $1,462.

Application procedures. Admission: No deadline. $35 fee. Application must be submitted on paper. Admission notification on a rolling basis.

Academics. Special study options: Distance learning, internships. **Credit/placement by examination:** AP, CLEP. **Support services:** Remedial instruction, tutoring.

Majors. Business: Business admin. **Legal studies:** Paralegal.

Most popular majors. Business/marketing 12%, health sciences 88%.

Computing on campus. Helpline, repair service, wireless network available.

Student life. Freshman orientation: Mandatory. Preregistration for classes offered.

Student services. Career counseling. **Transfer:** Re-entry adviser, pre-admission transcript evaluation for new students.

Contact. E-mail: info@dbumn.edu
Phone: (218) 722-4000 Toll-free number: (800) 777-8406
Fax: (218) 628-2127
David Cook, Educational Recruitment Manager, Duluth Business University, 4727 Mike Colalillo Drive, Duluth, MN 55807

Dunwoody College of Technology

Minneapolis, Minnesota
www.dunwoody.edu **CB code: 2265**

- Private 2-year technical college
- Commuter campus in very large city
- Application essay, interview required

General. Founded in 1914. Regionally accredited. **Enrollment:** 1,571 degree-seeking undergraduates. **Degrees:** 8 bachelor's, 371 associate awarded. **Calendar:** Quarter, limited summer session. **Full-time faculty:** 87 total; 6% have terminal degrees, 12% minority, 20% women. **Part-time faculty:** 43 total; 2% have terminal degrees, 14% minority, 21% women. **Class size:** 76% < 20, 23% 20-39, less than 1% 50-99.

Student profile.

Out-of-state:	2%	**25 or older:**	30%

Transfer out. Colleges most students transferred to 2008: Minneapolis Community and Technical College, Normandale Community College, University of Minnesota-Twin Cities, Inver Hills Community College, Century College.

Basis for selection. Institutional entrance test required. Rank in upper-half of high school class preferred. Essay or personal statement required at time of admissions testing. **Homeschooled:** Transcript of courses and grades required. **Learning Disabled:** Students must submit official documentation.

High school preparation. 8 units required; 20 recommended. Required and recommended units include English 3-4, mathematics 3-4, social studies 2, history 2, science 1-2 (laboratory 1-2) and academic electives 4.

2008-2009 Annual costs. Tuition/fees: $13,931. Per-credit charge: $183. Books/supplies: $915. Personal expenses: $1,035.

2007-2008 Financial aid. Need-based: Need-based aid available for part-time students. **Non-need-based:** Scholarships awarded for academics.

Application procedures. Admission: No deadline. $50 fee, may be waived for applicants with need. Admission notification on a rolling basis. Applicants to architecture, computer and electrical programs should apply at least 6 months prior to beginning of quarter. **Financial aid:** Priority date 6/1; no closing date. FAFSA required. Applicants notified on a rolling basis starting 2/1; must reply within 4 week(s) of notification.

Academics. Special study options: Distance learning, double major, ESL, independent study, internships. Bachelor's degree programs available on campus. **Credit/placement by examination:** CLEP, IB, institutional tests. **Support services:** Learning center, pre-admission summer program, reduced course load, remedial instruction, study skills assistance, tutoring, writing center.

Majors. Agriculture: Food processing. **Communications technology:** Desktop publishing, printing press operator. **Computer sciences:** Applications programming, networking. **Construction:** Electrician, site management. **Engineering:** Manufacturing. **Engineering technology:** Architectural drafting, electrical, electrical drafting, electromechanical, heat/ac/refrig, robotics, surveying. **Mechanic/repair:** Auto body, automotive, heating/ac/refrig. **Production:** Machine tool. **Visual/performing arts:** Graphic design, interior design.

Most popular majors. Computer/information sciences 8%, engineering/engineering technologies 28%, trade and industry 61%.

Computing on campus. PC or laptop required. 1,900 workstations in library, computer center. Commuter students can connect to campus network. Helpline, repair service, wireless network available.

Student life. Freshman orientation: Mandatory. One-day program, offered multiple times. **Activities:** Student government.

Student services. Career counseling, student employment services, financial aid counseling, minority student services, personal counseling, placement for graduates, veterans' counselor, women's services. **Transfer:** Reentry adviser, pre-admission transcript evaluation for new students. Transfer adviser for students transferring to 4-year colleges.

Contact. E-mail: info@dunwoody.edu
Phone: (612) 374-5800 Toll-free number: (800) 292-4625
Fax: (612) 677-3131
Shaun Manning, Director of Admissions, Dunwoody College of Technology, 818 Dunwoody Boulevard, Minneapolis, MN 55403-1192

Fond du Lac Tribal and Community College

Cloquet, Minnesota
www.fdltcc.edu **CB code: 7119**

- Public 2-year community college
- Commuter campus in large town

General. Founded in 1987. Regionally accredited. Combined state community college and tribal college. **Enrollment:** 767 full-time, degree-seeking students. **Degrees:** 194 associate awarded. **Location:** 16 miles from Duluth. **Calendar:** Semester, limited summer session. **Full-time faculty:** 36 total. **Part-time faculty:** 30 total. **Special facilities:** 21,000 acre environmental study area.

Student profile.

Out-of-state:	5%	**Live on campus:**	8%
25 or older:	34%		

Basis for selection. Open admission. ASSET required. ACT or SAT may be substituted for ASSET.

High school preparation. Recommended units include English 4, mathematics 3 and foreign language 4.

2008-2009 Annual costs. Tuition/fees: $4,440; $8,428 out-of-state. Per-credit charge: $133 in-state; $266 out-of-state. Books/supplies: $876. Personal expenses: $1,050.

Financial aid. Need-based: Need-based aid available for part-time students. **Non-need-based:** Scholarships awarded for academics.

Application procedures. Admission: No deadline. $20 fee, may be waived for applicants with need. Admission notification on a rolling basis. **Financial aid:** Priority date 3/15; no closing date. FAFSA, institutional form required. Applicants notified on a rolling basis starting 4/15.

Academics. Special study options: Cooperative education, distance learning, dual enrollment of high school students, liberal arts/career combination, weekend college. Bachelor's degree programs available on campus. License preparation in nursing. **Credit/placement by examination:** CLEP, IB, institutional tests. 24 credit hours maximum toward associate degree. **Support services:** Learning center, remedial instruction, study skills assistance, tutoring.

Majors. Business: Administrative services, finance. **Computer sciences:** Information technology, security. **Conservation:** Environmental science. **Construction:** Power transmission. **Family/consumer sciences:** Food/nutrition. **Health:** Clinical nutrition, licensed practical nurse, nursing (RN), prenursing. **Liberal arts:** Arts/sciences. **Protective services:** Corrections, forensics, law enforcement admin, police science. **Public administration:** Human services. **Social sciences:** Cartography.

Computing on campus. 100 workstations in dormitories, library, computer center, student center. Dormitories linked to campus network.

Student life. Freshman orientation: Mandatory. **Housing:** Coed dorms, special housing for disabled, apartments available. $150 deposit, deadline 6/15. **Activities:** Choral groups, drama, student government, student newspaper, Phi Theta Kappa Honor Society, law enforcement club, human services club, science club, volunteer information program, Anishinaabe Congress, math club, veterans club, American Indian Business Leaders.

Athletics. Intramural: Bowling, softball, volleyball.

Student services. Adult student services, career counseling, student employment services, financial aid counseling, health services, minority student services, on-campus daycare, personal counseling, placement for graduates, veterans' counselor. **Physically disabled:** Services for visually, speech, hearing impaired. **Transfer:** Pre-admission transcript evaluation for new students. Transfer adviser, college fairs on campus for students transferring to 4-year colleges.

Contact. E-mail: admissions@fdltcc.edu
Phone: (218) 879-0808 Toll-free number: (800) 657-3712
Fax: (218) 879-0814
Kathy Jubie, Admissions Representative, Fond du Lac Tribal and Community College, 2101 14th Street, Cloquet, MN 55720

Hennepin Technical College

Brooklyn Park, Minnesota
www.hennepintech.edu **CB code: 6290**

- Public 2-year technical college
- Commuter campus in small city

General. Regionally accredited. **Enrollment:** 4,369 full-time, degree-seeking students. **Degrees:** 506 associate awarded. **Location:** 10 miles from Minneapolis-St. Paul. **Calendar:** Semester, limited summer session. **Full-time faculty:** 685 total. **Part-time faculty:** 548 total.

Student profile. Among full-time, degree-seeking students, 100% enrolled in a vocational program.

Out-of-state:	2%	**25 or older:**	64%

Basis for selection. Open admission, but selective for some programs. Special requirements for nursing and dental program. Accuplacer for placement only.

2008-2009 Annual costs. Tuition/fees: $4,271; $4,271 out-of-state. Per-credit charge: $133 in-state; $133 out-of-state. Books/supplies: $1,000.

Financial aid. All financial aid based on need.

Application procedures. Admission: No deadline. $20 fee, may be waived for applicants with need. Admission notification on a rolling basis. **Financial aid:** No deadline. FAFSA, institutional form required. Applicants notified on a rolling basis starting 3/1.

Academics. **Special study options:** Cross-registration, ESL, honors, independent study, internships, student-designed major. Bachelor's degree programs available on campus. License preparation in nursing, paramedic. **Credit/placement by examination:** AP, CLEP. **Support services:** Learning center, pre-admission summer program, reduced course load, remedial instruction, study skills assistance, tutoring.

Majors. **Agriculture:** Floriculture, landscaping, nursery operations. **Business:** Accounting, accounting technology, office technology, office/clerical. **Communications:** Advertising, digital media, publishing. **Communications technology:** General, desktop publishing, graphic/printing, graphics, photo/film/video, printing press operator, recording arts. **Computer sciences:** General, applications programming, computer graphics, data processing, information systems, programming, security, systems analysis, web page design. **Construction:** Carpentry, electrician, maintenance. **Engineering technology:** Architectural drafting, automotive, construction, drafting, electrical, heat/ac/refrig, hydraulics, industrial, manufacturing, mechanical, plastics. **Family/consumer sciences:** Child development. **Health:** Dental assistant, EMT paramedic, licensed practical nurse, medical secretary, office admin, ward clerk. **Mechanic/repair:** General, auto body, automotive, diesel, electronics/electrical, heating/ac/refrig, industrial, marine, medium/heavy vehicle, motorcycle, small engine. **Personal/culinary services:** Chef training, culinary arts, food prep, restaurant/catering. **Production:** Ironworking, machine shop technology, machine tool, sheet metal, tool and die, welding, woodworking.

Computing on campus. 75 workstations in library, computer center, student center. Online course registration, online library available.

Student life. **Freshman orientation:** Mandatory. Preregistration for classes offered. A week before school starts. **Activities:** Student government.

Student services. Career counseling, student employment services, financial aid counseling, personal counseling, placement for graduates, veterans' counselor. **Physically disabled:** Services for visually, speech, hearing impaired. **Transfer:** Pre-admission transcript evaluation for new students. Transfer adviser for students transferring to 4-year colleges.

Contact. E-mail: info@hennepintech.edu
Phone: (763) 488-2500 Toll-free number: (800) 345-4655
Fax: (763) 488-2944
Joy Bodin, Director of Admissions, Hennepin Technical College, 9000 Brooklyn Boulevard, Brooklyn Park, MN 55455

Hibbing Community College
Hibbing, Minnesota
www.hibbing.edu **CB code: 6275**

- Public 2-year community and technical college
- Commuter campus in large town

General. Founded in 1916. Regionally accredited. **Enrollment:** 1,502 degree-seeking undergraduates. **Degrees:** 222 associate awarded. **Location:** 75 miles from Duluth. **Calendar:** Semester, limited summer session. **Full-time faculty:** 63 total. **Part-time faculty:** 45 total. **Special facilities:** Space planetarium.

Student profile.

Out-of-state:	13%	**Live on campus:**	7%
25 or older:	40%		

Transfer out. **Colleges most students transferred to 2008:** Bemidji State University, University of Minnesota: Duluth, College of St. Scholastica, University of Wisconsin-Superior.

Basis for selection. Open admission, but selective for some programs. Academic placement test required. Special requirements for nursing, dental assistant and law enforcement programs. **Homeschooled:** Transcript of courses and grades required.

2008-2009 Annual costs. Tuition/fees: $4,481; $5,468 out-of-state. Per-credit charge: $132 in-state; $164 out-of-state. Online students pay an additional $25 per-credit-hour charge. Books/supplies: $825.

Application procedures. **Admission:** Priority date 4/15; no deadline. $20 fee, may be waived for applicants with need. Admission notification on a rolling basis. **Financial aid:** Priority date 7/1; no closing date. Institutional form required. Applicants notified on a rolling basis starting 6/30; must reply within 2 week(s) of notification.

Academics. **Special study options:** Cooperative education, cross-registration, distance learning, dual enrollment of high school students, honors, independent study, internships, liberal arts/career combination, study abroad. Bachelor's degree programs available on campus. License preparation in aviation, nursing. **Credit/placement by examination:** CLEP, institutional tests. 12 credit hours maximum toward associate degree. **Support services:** Learning center, pre-admission summer program, reduced course load, remedial instruction, study skills assistance, tutoring.

Majors. **Business:** Administrative services, business admin, office/clerical. **Computer sciences:** General, security, web page design. **Health:** Clinical lab technology, dental assistant, medical secretary, nursing (RN). **Legal studies:** Legal secretary. **Liberal arts:** Arts/sciences. **Personal/culinary services:** Culinary arts. **Protective services:** Police science. **Other:** Professional helicopter training.

Computing on campus. 100 workstations in dormitories, library, computer center. Commuter students can connect to campus network. Online course registration, online library available.

Student life. **Freshman orientation:** Available. Preregistration for classes offered. Registration orientation held throughout the summer; all-student orientation held day before classes begin. **Housing:** Coed dorms available. $250 fully refundable deposit. On-campus apartments are available to students. **Activities:** Bands, choral groups, drama, music ensembles, musical theater, student government, student newspaper, Phi Theta Kappa.

Athletics. NJCAA. **Intercollegiate:** Baseball M, basketball, golf, softball W, volleyball W. **Intramural:** Badminton, baseball M, basketball, bowling, skiing, volleyball. **Team name:** Cardinals.

Student services. Adult student services, career counseling, services for economically disadvantaged, student employment services, financial aid counseling, minority student services, personal counseling, placement for graduates, veterans' counselor. **Physically disabled:** Services for visually, speech, hearing impaired. **Transfer:** Pre-admission transcript evaluation for new students. Transfer adviser, college fairs on campus for students transferring to 4-year colleges.

Contact. E-mail: admissions@hibbing.edu
Phone: (218) 262-7207 Toll-free number: (800) 224-4422
Fax: (218) 263-2992
Sarah Merhar, Admissions Representative, Hibbing Community College, 1515 East 25th Street, Hibbing, MN 55746

High-Tech Institute
St. Louis Park, Minnesota
www.hightechschools.com **CB code: 3042**

- For-profit 2-year technical college
- Small city

General. Accredited by ACCSCT. **Calendar:** Continuous.

Annual costs/financial aid. Costs for diploma programs range from $12,150 to $25,850. Fees, books, uniforms and tools included.

Contact. Phone: (952) 417-2200
5100 Gamble Drive, St. Louis Park, MN 55416

Inver Hills Community College
Inver Grove Heights, Minnesota **CB member**
www.inverhills.edu **CB code: 6300**

- Public 2-year community college
- Commuter campus in large town

General. Founded in 1967. Regionally accredited. **Enrollment:** 4,469 degree-seeking undergraduates; 1,348 non-degree-seeking students. **Degrees:** 584 associate awarded. **ROTC:** Air Force. **Location:** 6 miles from Minneapolis-St. Paul. **Calendar:** Semester, limited summer session. **Full-time faculty:** 91 total; 6% minority, 57% women. **Part-time faculty:** 141 total; 4% minority, 47% women.

Student profile. Among degree-seeking undergraduates, 715 enrolled as first-time, first-year students.

Part-time:	58%	**Women:**	60%
Out-of-state:	2%	**25 or older:**	38%

Transfer out. **Colleges most students transferred to 2008:** University of Minnesota, Metro State University, St. Thomas/St. Catherine's University, University of Wisconsin-River Falls, Minnesota State University-Mankato.

Basis for selection. Open admission, but selective for some programs. Special requirements for nursing and emergency health service programs,

Two-Year Colleges

Computer and Networking Technology and international students. **Adult students:** SAT/ACT scores not required. **Homeschooled:** Transcript of courses and grades, state high school equivalency certificate required.

2008-2009 Annual costs. Tuition/fees: $4,655; $4,655 out-of-state. Per-credit charge: $140 in-state; $140 out-of-state. In-state and out-of-state tuition rates are the same.

2008-2009 Financial aid. All financial aid based on need. Need-based aid available for part-time students. Work-study available nights, weekends and for part-time students.

Application procedures. Admission: Priority date 8/1; no deadline. $20 fee, may be waived for applicants with need. Admission notification on a rolling basis. **Financial aid:** No deadline. FAFSA required. Applicants notified on a rolling basis starting 6/1.

Academics. Special study options: Accelerated study, distance learning, dual enrollment of high school students, honors, independent study, internships, liberal arts/career combination, student-designed major, study abroad, weekend college. License preparation in aviation, nursing, paramedic. **Credit/placement by examination:** AP, CLEP, IB, institutional tests. 30 credit hours maximum toward associate degree. **Support services:** GED test center, learning center, pre-admission summer program, reduced course load, remedial instruction, study skills assistance, tutoring, writing center.

Majors. Business: Accounting, business admin, construction management. **Computer sciences:** Computer science, networking, programming. **Construction:** Building inspection. **Health:** EMT paramedic, nursing (RN). **Legal studies:** Legal secretary, paralegal. **Liberal arts:** Arts/sciences. **Parks/recreation:** Health/fitness. **Protective services:** Law enforcement admin, police science. **Public administration:** Social work. **Transportation:** Air traffic control, airline/commercial pilot, aviation management.

Most popular majors. Business/marketing 10%, health sciences 27%, legal studies 13%, liberal arts 28%, security/protective services 11%.

Computing on campus. 141 workstations in library, computer center, student center. Commuter students can connect to campus network. Online course registration, online library, helpline, repair service, wireless network available.

Student life. Freshman orientation: Mandatory. Preregistration for classes offered. Three-hour session before start of semester. Online orientation is also available. **Activities:** Concert band, choral groups, dance, drama, international student organizations, literary magazine, music ensembles, musical theater, student government, French club, German club, Spanish club, student senate, Christian Fellowship, international club, Black student union, Progressive Student Alliance, Gay-Straight Alliance, Somali club.

Athletics. Intramural: Badminton, baseball, basketball, bowling, football (non-tackle), golf, ice hockey, lacrosse, skiing, soccer, softball, table tennis, volleyball.

Student services. Adult student services, alcohol/substance abuse counseling, career counseling, services for economically disadvantaged, student employment services, financial aid counseling, health services, minority student services, on-campus daycare, personal counseling, placement for graduates, veterans' counselor. **Physically disabled:** Services for visually, speech, hearing impaired. **Transfer:** Pre-admission transcript evaluation for new students. Transfer adviser, college fairs on campus for students transferring to 4-year colleges.

Contact. E-mail: iseekinfo@inverhills.edu
Phone: (651) 450-8503 Fax: (651) 450-8677
Landon Pirius, Dean of Students, Inver Hills Community College, 2500 80th Street East, Inver Grove Heights, MN 55076-3224

Itasca Community College

Grand Rapids, Minnesota
www.itascacc.edu **CB code: 6309**

- Public 2-year junior and liberal arts college
- Commuter campus in large town

General. Founded in 1922. Regionally accredited. **Enrollment:** 966 degree-seeking undergraduates; 110 non-degree-seeking students. **Degrees:** 227 associate awarded. **Location:** 80 miles from Duluth, 180 miles from Minneapolis-St. Paul. **Calendar:** Semester, limited summer session. **Full-time faculty:** 42 total; 2% have terminal degrees, 5% minority. **Part-time faculty:** 28 total; 7% have terminal degrees, 4% minority. **Special facilities:** Educational wetland habitat, University of Minnesota agricultural station, U.S. Forest Service share campus, 500 acres experimental forest. **Partnerships:** Formal partnerships with local businesses for training, partnership council with area high schools.

Student profile. Among degree-seeking undergraduates, 301 enrolled as first-time, first-year students, 556 transferred in from other institutions.

Part-time:	22%	**25 or older:**	24%
Out-of-state:	7%	**Live on campus:**	14%
Women:	47%		

Transfer out. Colleges most students transferred to 2008: Bemidji State University, College of St. Scholastica, University of Minnesota: Duluth, St. Cloud State University, University of North Dakota.

Basis for selection. Open admission. College-level reading and English testing required for class act teacher education program.

High school preparation. 12 units recommended. Recommended units include English 4, mathematics 2, social studies 2, science 2 and foreign language 2. Computer skills recommended.

2008-2009 Annual costs. Tuition/fees: $4,489; $5,476 out-of-state. Per-credit charge: $132 in-state; $164 out-of-state. Books/supplies: $1,000. Personal expenses: $1,387.

2007-2008 Financial aid. Need-based: 60% of total undergraduate aid awarded as scholarships/grants, 40% as loans/jobs. Need-based aid available for part-time students. Work-study available nights, weekends and for part-time students. **Non-need-based:** Scholarships awarded for academics, leadership, music/drama, state residency.

Application procedures. Admission: Priority date 8/1; deadline 8/29 (postmark date). $20 fee, may be waived for applicants with need. Admission notification on a rolling basis. **Financial aid:** Priority date 5/1; no closing date. FAFSA required. Applicants notified on a rolling basis starting 4/1.

Academics. Special study options: Cooperative education, dual enrollment of high school students, independent study, internships, liberal arts/career combination, study abroad. License preparation in nursing, real estate. **Credit/placement by examination:** AP, CLEP, IB, institutional tests. 10 credit hours maximum toward associate degree. **Support services:** GED test center, learning center, pre-admission summer program, reduced course load, remedial instruction, study skills assistance, tutoring.

Majors. Area/ethnic studies: Native American. **Business:** Accounting, business admin. **Communications:** Media studies. **Conservation:** General, forestry. **Education:** General, early childhood. **Engineering:** General. **Engineering technology:** General. **Health:** Prenursing. **Liberal arts:** Arts/sciences. **Psychology:** General. **Public administration:** Human services, social work. **Social sciences:** Geography. **Other:** Pulp and paper technician, Wildland firefighting.

Computing on campus. 275 workstations in dormitories, library, computer center, student center. Dormitories wired for high-speed internet access and linked to campus network. Commuter students can connect to campus network. Online course registration, online library, wireless network available.

Student life. Freshman orientation: Available. Preregistration for classes offered. Orientation held before classes begin. **Housing:** Coed dorms available. $200 nonrefundable deposit, deadline 6/30. **Activities:** Literary magazine, student government, Circle-K, business club, Student Ambassadors, Panarama, Global Ed, engineering club, psychology club, STARS.

Athletics. NJCAA. **Intercollegiate:** Baseball M, basketball, football (tackle) M, softball W, volleyball W, wrestling M. **Intramural:** Basketball M, bowling, football (non-tackle), softball, table tennis, volleyball. **Team name:** Vikings.

Student services. Adult student services, career counseling, student employment services, financial aid counseling, minority student services, personal counseling. **Physically disabled:** Services for visually, speech, hearing impaired. **Learning disabled:** Comprehensive services available. **Transfer:** Transfer adviser for students transferring to 4-year colleges.

Contact. E-mail: info@itascacc.edu
Phone: (218) 322-2330 Toll-free number: (800) 996-6422
Fax: (218) 322-2332
Candace Perry, Director of Enrollment Services, Itasca Community College, 1851 Highway 169 East, Grand Rapids, MN 55744

ITT Technical Institute: Eden Prairie

Eden Prairie, Minnesota
www.itt-tech.edu/campus/school.cfm?lloc_num=27

- For-profit 2-year technical college
- Small city

General. Accredited by ACICS. **Calendar:** Quarter.

Contact. Phone: (952) 914-5300
8911 Columbine Road, Eden Prairie, MN 55347

Lake Superior College

Duluth, Minnesota
www.lsc.edu **CB code: 6352**

- Public 2-year community and technical college
- Commuter campus in small city

General. Regionally accredited. **Enrollment:** 3,516 degree-seeking undergraduates; 596 non-degree-seeking students. **Degrees:** 574 associate awarded. **ROTC:** Army, Naval. **Location:** 150 miles from Minneapolis-St. Paul. **Calendar:** Semester, limited summer session. **Full-time faculty:** 97 total; 3% minority, 54% women. **Part-time faculty:** 172 total; 5% minority, 48% women. **Class size:** 51% < 20, 48% 20-39, less than 1% 40-49, less than 1% 50-99. **Special facilities:** Emergency response training center, professional pilot programs.

Student profile. Among degree-seeking undergraduates, 44% enrolled in a transfer program, 56% enrolled in a vocational program, 759 enrolled as first-time, first-year students, 427 transferred in from other institutions.

Part-time:	37%	**Asian American:**	2%
Out-of-state:	11%	**Hispanic American:**	1%
Women:	58%	**Native American:**	2%
African American:	2%	**25 or older:**	34%

Transfer out. Colleges most students transferred to 2008: University of Minnesota-Duluth, University of Minnesota-Twin Cities.

Basis for selection. Open admission, but selective for some programs. Special requirements for radiology and dental hygiene with minimum 2.6 GPA and nursing with a minimum 2.8 GPA. The Academic Skills Assessment Program Computerized Placement Test required for all students unless transcript shows completion of college level math and English composition.

High school preparation. College-preparatory program recommended.

2008-2009 Annual costs. Tuition/fees: $4,261; $7,921 out-of-state. Per-credit charge: $122 in-state; $244 out-of-state. Books/supplies: $1,500. Personal expenses: $3,475.

2007-2008 Financial aid. Need-based: Average scholarship/grant was $1,110; average loan $1,906. 32% of total undergraduate aid awarded as scholarships/grants, 68% as loans/jobs. Need-based aid available for part-time students. Work-study available nights, weekends and for part-time students. **Non-need-based:** Scholarships awarded for academics, leadership.

Application procedures. Admission: Closing date 8/18 (postmark date). $20 fee, may be waived for applicants with need. Admission notification on a rolling basis. **Financial aid:** Priority date 5/1; no closing date. FAFSA required. Applicants notified on a rolling basis starting 5/1.

Academics. Special study options: Accelerated study, cooperative education, distance learning, double major, dual enrollment of high school students, ESL, honors, independent study, internships, liberal arts/career combination, study abroad. License preparation in aviation, dental hygiene, nursing, paramedic, physical therapy, radiology, real estate. **Credit/placement by examination:** AP, CLEP, institutional tests. 30 credit hours maximum toward associate degree. **Support services:** Learning center, reduced course load, remedial instruction, study skills assistance, tutoring, writing center.

Majors. Business: Accounting, administrative services, business admin, management information systems, marketing, selling. **Computer sciences:** General, database management, networking, programming. **Construction:** Carpentry, electrician. **Engineering technology:** Architectural drafting, CAD/CADD, civil, computer hardware, computer systems, electrical, mechanical drafting, telecommunications. **Health:** Clinical lab technology, dental hygiene, medical secretary, nursing (RN), occupational therapy assistant, physical therapy assistant, physician assistant, radiologic technology/medical imaging, respiratory therapy technology, sonography, surgical technology. **Legal studies:** Legal secretary, paralegal. **Liberal arts:** Arts/sciences. **Mechanic/repair:** Aircraft, automotive. **Production:** Machine tool, welding. **Protective services:** Fire safety technology. **Transportation:** Airline/commercial pilot, aviation management. **Visual/performing arts:** Studio arts.

Most popular majors. Business/marketing 7%, health sciences 35%, liberal arts 40%.

Computing on campus. 514 workstations in library, computer center, student center. Commuter students can connect to campus network. Online course registration, online library, helpline, repair service, student web hosting, wireless network available.

Student life. Freshman orientation: Available. Preregistration for classes offered. Half day each semester prior to start of term. **Policies:** Policy describes the student role in the allocation of student activity fees. Students are involved in decision making policies through shared governance. **Activities:** Choral groups, drama, student government, student newspaper, Intervarsity Christian Fellowship, Phi Theta Kappa, Teachers of Tomorrow, United Multicultural Group, art club, skills, nursing, dental hygiene club, radiology club.

Athletics. Intramural: Baseball, basketball, bowling, ice hockey, skiing, softball, volleyball. **Team name:** Huskies.

Student services. Adult student services, alcohol/substance abuse counseling, career counseling, services for economically disadvantaged, student employment services, financial aid counseling, minority student services, on-campus daycare, personal counseling, placement for graduates, veterans' counselor, women's services. **Physically disabled:** Services for visually, speech, hearing impaired. **Transfer:** Pre-admission transcript evaluation for new students. Transfer center, transfer adviser, college fairs on campus for students transferring to 4-year colleges.

Contact. E-mail: enroll@lsc.edu
Phone: (218) 733-7601 Toll-free number: (800) 432-2884
Fax: (218) 733-5945
Melissa Leno, Director of Admissions, Lake Superior College, 2101 Trinity Road, Duluth, MN 55811

Lakeland Academy Division of Herzing College

Crystal, Minnesota
www.herzing.edu **CB code: 3051**

- For-profit 2-year health science college
- Large city

General. Regionally accredited. **Enrollment:** 232 degree-seeking undergraduates. **Degrees:** 1 bachelor's, 81 associate awarded. **Calendar:** Continuous. **Full-time faculty:** 30 total. **Part-time faculty:** 27 total.

Basis for selection. Open admission, but selective for some programs. Qualifications for dental hygiene program include completion of dental hygiene application along with supporting documentation as requested.

2008-2009 Annual costs. Cost of full programs ranges from $11,272 to $48,407, including fees and books.

Application procedures. Admission: No deadline. No application fee. Admission notification on a rolling basis. **Financial aid:** Priority date 3/1; no closing date. FAFSA required.

Academics. Special study options: Bachelor's degree programs available on campus. **Credit/placement by examination:** CLEP.

Majors. Business: General.

Contact. E-mail: info@mpls.herzing.edu
Phone: (763) 535-3000
Shelly Larson, Director of Admissions, Lakeland Academy Division of Herzing College, 5700 West Broadway, Crystal, MN 55428

Le Cordon Bleu College of Culinary Arts

Mendota Heights, Minnesota
www.twincitiesculinary.com

- For-profit 2-year culinary school and career college
- Commuter campus in very large city
- Interview required

General. Accredited by ACCSCT. **Enrollment:** 558 full-time, degree-seeking students. **Degrees:** 366 associate awarded. **Location:** 12 miles from Minneapolis-St. Paul. **Calendar:** Quarter, extensive summer session. **Full-time faculty:** 40 total. **Part-time faculty:** 10 total.

Basis for selection. Open admission. **Homeschooled:** Transcript of courses and grades required. **Learning Disabled:** Current IEP.

High school preparation. Recommended units include English 3, mathematics 2, social studies 1, history 1 and science 1.

2008-2009 Annual costs. Program tuition and fees: $42,500 (culinary), $34,400 (patisserie).

Financial aid. Non-need-based: Scholarships awarded for academics, job skills, leadership.

Application procedures. Admission: No deadline. $50 fee, may be waived for applicants with need. Admission notification on a rolling basis.

Academics. Special study options: Internships. **Credit/placement by examination:** CLEP. **Support services:** Remedial instruction, study skills assistance, tutoring.

Majors. Personal/culinary services: General, baking.

Computing on campus. 40 workstations in library, computer center. Online library, wireless network available.

Student life. Freshman orientation: Mandatory. Several options for orientation including the Saturday prior to beginning classes. **Activities:** Student newspaper.

Student services. Adult student services, alcohol/substance abuse counseling, career counseling, student employment services, financial aid counseling, legal services, personal counseling, placement for graduates. **Transfer:** Pre-admission transcript evaluation for new students.

Contact. E-mail: info@twincitiesculinary.com
Phone: (651) 675-4700 Toll-free number: (800) 931-6855
Fax: (651) 452-5282
Angela Caputo, Associate Director of Admissions, Le Cordon Bleu College of Culinary Arts, 1315 Mendota Heights Road, Mendota Heights, MN 55120

Leech Lake Tribal College

Cass Lake, Minnesota
www.lltc.edu **CB code: 3931**

- Public 2-year Tribal college grounded in Anishinaabe knowledge and culture
- Commuter campus in small town

General. Regionally accredited. Chartered by the Leech Lake Band of Ojibwe. Grounded in Anishinaabe knowledge and culture. **Enrollment:** 216 degree-seeking undergraduates. **Degrees:** 14 associate awarded. **Location:** 15 miles from Bemidji. **Calendar:** Semester, limited summer session. **Full-time faculty:** 13 total. **Part-time faculty:** 8 total. **Class size:** 100% < 20.

Basis for selection. Open admission. **Homeschooled:** Documentation of high school classes required.

2008-2009 Annual costs. Tuition/fees: $3,980. Per-credit charge: $125. Books/supplies: $600.

Financial aid. All financial aid based on need. Need-based aid available for part-time students.

Application procedures. Admission: $15 fee. Application must be submitted on paper. Admission notification on a rolling basis. **Financial aid:** Closing date 6/30. FAFSA required.

Academics. Special study options: Cooperative education, double major, independent study, internships, liberal arts/career combination, teacher certification program. **Credit/placement by examination:** CLEP, institutional tests. **Support services:** Reduced course load, remedial instruction, study skills assistance, tutoring.

Majors. Area/ethnic studies: Native American. **Business:** Business admin. **Education:** Early childhood. **Health:** Clinical nutrition. **Liberal arts:** Arts/sciences. **Protective services:** Police science.

Computing on campus. 31 workstations in library, computer center, student center.

Student life. Freshman orientation: Available. Preregistration for classes offered. **Activities:** Choral groups, student government.

Student services. Adult student services, financial aid counseling, personal counseling. **Transfer:** Transfer adviser for students transferring to 4-year colleges.

Contact. E-mail: registrar@lltc.edu
Phone: (218) 335-4222 Fax: (218) 335-4217
Veronica Veaux, Registrar, Leech Lake Tribal College, PO Box 180, Cass Lake, MN 56633

Mesabi Range Community and Technical College

Virginia, Minnesota
www.mr.mnscu.edu **CB code: 6432**

- Public 2-year community and technical college
- Commuter campus in large town

General. Founded in 1918. Regionally accredited. Career/technical programs offered at Eveleth campus. **Enrollment:** 913 full-time, degree-seeking students. **Degrees:** 185 associate awarded. **Location:** 60 miles from Duluth. **Calendar:** Semester, limited summer session. **Full-time faculty:** 47 total; 15% minority. **Part-time faculty:** 42 total.

Student profile.

Out-of-state:	9%	**Live on campus:**	8%
25 or older:	26%		

Transfer out. Colleges most students transferred to 2008: University of Minnesota-Duluth, Bemidji State University, St. Cloud State University, Mankato State University, University of Minnesota-Minneapolis.

Basis for selection. Open admission.

2008-2009 Annual costs. Tuition/fees: $4,481; $5,468 out-of-state. Per-credit charge: $132 in-state; $164 out-of-state. Books/supplies: $1,000. Personal expenses: $1,000.

2008-2009 Financial aid. Need-based: Need-based aid available for part-time students. Work-study available nights, weekends and for part-time students. **Non-need-based:** Scholarships awarded for state residency.

Application procedures. Admission: No deadline. $20 fee, may be waived for applicants with need. Admission notification on a rolling basis beginning on or about 1/1. **Financial aid:** Priority date 4/22; no closing date. FAFSA, institutional form required. Applicants notified on a rolling basis starting 5/1; must reply within 2 week(s) of notification.

Academics. Special study options: Dual enrollment of high school students, independent study, internships, liberal arts/career combination, study abroad. Bachelor's degree programs available on campus. License preparation in nursing, paramedic. **Credit/placement by examination:** CLEP, institutional tests. **Support services:** Learning center, reduced course load, remedial instruction, study skills assistance, tutoring.

Majors. Biology: General. **Business:** General, administrative services, marketing, office technology. **Communications technology:** Graphic/printing. **Computer sciences:** General, programming, systems analysis. **Construction:** Carpentry. **Education:** General, teacher assistance. **Engineering:** Computer. **Engineering technology:** Robotics. **Health:** Substance abuse counseling. **Liberal arts:** Arts/sciences. **Mechanic/repair:** General, automotive, industrial electronics. **Parks/recreation:** Exercise sciences. **Public administration:** Human services.

Computing on campus. Dormitories linked to campus network. Online course registration available.

Student life. Freshman orientation: Mandatory. **Housing:** Apartments available. $300 deposit, deadline 9/1. **Activities:** Bands, choral groups, dance, drama, literary magazine, music ensembles, musical theater, student government, student newspaper, symphony orchestra.

Athletics. NJCAA. **Intercollegiate:** Baseball M, basketball, football (tackle) M, softball W, volleyball W. **Intramural:** Badminton, basketball, bowling, field hockey W, ice hockey, racquetball, softball, table tennis, volleyball. **Team name:** Norseman.

Student services. Career counseling, student employment services, minority student services, on-campus daycare, personal counseling, placement for graduates. **Physically disabled:** Services for visually, hearing impaired. **Transfer:** Pre-admission transcript evaluation for new students.

Contact. E-mail: s.twaddle@mr.mnscu.edu
Phone: (218) 749-0315 Fax: (218) 749-0318
Brenda Kochevar, Director of Enrollment Services, Mesabi Range Community and Technical College, 1001 Chestnut Street West, Virginia, MN 55792-3448

Minneapolis Business College

Roseville, Minnesota
www.mplsbusinesscollege.com **CB code: 7126**

- For-profit 2-year business and technical college
- Very large city

General. Founded in 1874. Accredited by ACICS. **Location:** 10 miles from Minneapolis-St. Paul. **Calendar:** Semester.

Annual costs/financial aid. Tuition/fees (2008-2009): $13,400. Fees for books and supplies vary from $40 to $1,320 per academic year depending on program. Lab fee for medical assistant program $1,160. Room: $6,640.

Contact. Phone: (651) 636-7406
Admissions Supervisor, 1711 West County Road B, Roseville, MN 55113

Minneapolis Community and Technical College

Minneapolis, Minnesota
www.minneapolis.edu **CB code: 6434**

- Public 2-year community and technical college
- Commuter campus in large city

General. Founded in 1965. Regionally accredited. **Enrollment:** 9,539 degree-seeking undergraduates. **Degrees:** 648 associate awarded. **Location:** Downtown. **Calendar:** Semester, limited summer session. **Class size:** 48% < 20, 44% 20-39, 5% 40-49, 3% 50-99.

Student profile.

African American:	29%	**Native American:**	2%
Asian American:	7%	**International:**	2%
Hispanic American:	5%		

Transfer out. Colleges most students transferred to 2008: University of Minnesota, Metro State University.

Basis for selection. Open admission, but selective for some programs. The following programs have additional requirements for admission: air traffic control, cinema division (cinematography, directing and producing, editing and post production and screenwriting), dental assistant, nursing, professional peace officers program.

2008-2009 Annual costs. Tuition/fees: $4,532; $4,532 out-of-state. Per-credit charge: $138. In-state and out-of-state tuition rates are the same.

2007-2008 Financial aid. All financial aid based on need. Need-based aid available for part-time students. Work-study available nights, weekends and for part-time students.

Application procedures. Admission: No deadline. $20 fee, may be waived for applicants with need. Admission notification on a rolling basis. **Financial aid:** Priority date 6/1; no closing date. FAFSA required. Applicants notified on a rolling basis starting 7/15; must reply within 2 week(s) of notification.

Academics. Special study options: Accelerated study, cross-registration, distance learning, dual enrollment of high school students, ESL, honors, independent study, internships, liberal arts/career combination, weekend college. Bachelor's degree programs available on campus. **Credit/placement by examination:** AP, CLEP, IB, institutional tests. **Support services:** Learning center, remedial instruction, tutoring.

Majors. Biology: General, biotechnology. **Business:** Accounting, administrative services, business admin, office technology. **Communications:** Digital media. **Communications technology:** Photo/film/video, recording arts. **Computer sciences:** Networking, programming, security, web page design. **Education:** General. **Family/consumer sciences:** Child care. **Health:** Electroencephalograph technology, nursing (RN), substance abuse counseling. **Liberal arts:** Arts/sciences, library assistant. **Math:** General. **Mechanic/repair:** Aircraft, aircraft powerplant, heating/ac/refrig, watch/jewelry. **Parks/recreation:** General. **Personal/culinary services:** Chef training. **Physical sciences:** Chemistry. **Production:** Cabinetmaking/millwright. **Protective services:** Criminal justice, police science. **Public administration:** General, human services. **Transportation:** Air traffic control. **Visual/performing arts:** Cinematography, commercial photography, design, play/screenwriting, studio arts. **Other:** Polysomnography technology, Women's studies.

Computing on campus. 278 workstations in library, computer center. Online course registration, online library, wireless network available.

Student life. Freshman orientation: Mandatory. Preregistration for classes offered. **Activities:** Jazz band, choral groups, drama, literary magazine, music ensembles, student government, student newspaper, International Student Association, Phi Theta Kappa Honor Society, Vocational Industrial Clubs of America, Association of Black Collegiates, Student Nurses Association, Business Professionals of America, Chess Club, Education Club, United Nations of Indian Tribes for Education, Out Campus Alliance.

Athletics. NJCAA. **Intercollegiate:** Basketball, golf. **Team name:** Mavericks.

Student services. Adult student services, career counseling, services for economically disadvantaged, student employment services, financial aid counseling, minority student services, personal counseling, placement for graduates, veterans' counselor. **Physically disabled:** Services for visually, speech, hearing impaired. **Learning disabled:** Comprehensive services available. **Transfer:** Transfer adviser, college fairs on campus for students transferring to 4-year colleges.

Contact. E-mail: admissions.office@minneapolis.edu
Phone: (612) 659-6200 Toll-free number: (800) 247-0911
Fax: (612) 659-6210
Kerri Carlson, Director of Admissions, Minneapolis Community and Technical College, 1501 Hennepin Avenue, Minneapolis, MN 55403-1779

Minneapolis Drafting School Division of Herzing College

Minneapolis, Minnesota
www.herzing.edu

- For-profit 2-year technical college
- Large city

General. Regionally accredited. **Enrollment:** 285 degree-seeking undergraduates. **Degrees:** 1 bachelor's, 81 associate awarded. **Calendar:** Semester. **Full-time faculty:** 15 total. **Part-time faculty:** 25 total.

Basis for selection. Open admission, but selective for some programs. Admissions decisions based on applicant's interest, professional attitude, and performance on standardized tests. Applicants who don't submit SAT or ACT scores must complete an entrance examination for admission.

2008-2009 Annual costs. Tuition/fees: $12,022. Per-credit charge: $400. Cost varies; tuition figures shown weighted average of all programs.

Application procedures. Admission: No deadline. No application fee. Admission notification on a rolling basis. **Financial aid:** No deadline.

Academics. Credit/placement by examination: CLEP.

Majors. Computer sciences: System admin. **Engineering technology:** Drafting, mechanical drafting.

Contact. E-mail: info@mpls.herzing.edu
Phone: (763) 535-3000
Shelly Larson, Director of Admissions, Minneapolis Drafting School Division of Herzing College, 5700 West Broadway, Minneapolis, MN 55428

Minnesota School of Business: Brooklyn Center

Brooklyn Center, Minnesota
www.msbcollege.edu **CB code: 3314**

- For-profit 2-year business college
- Large town
- SAT or ACT (ACT writing optional), interview required

General. Accredited by ACICS. **Enrollment:** 347 full-time, degree-seeking students. **Degrees:** 79 associate awarded. **Calendar:** Continuous. **Full-time faculty:** 8 total. **Part-time faculty:** 30 total.

Basis for selection. Personal interview and assessment examination most important. Applicants must submit ACT scores of 17 or above, SAT equivalent, or take an entrance exam.

2008-2009 Annual costs. Tuition/fees: $18,770. Per-credit charge: $390. Books/supplies: $1,800.

2008-2009 Financial aid. All financial aid based on need. Need-based aid available for part-time students.

Application procedures. Admission: No deadline. $50 fee. Admission notification on a rolling basis. **Financial aid:** FAFSA required.

Academics. Special study options: Bachelor's degree programs available on campus. **Credit/placement by examination:** CLEP.

Majors. Business: Business admin. **Legal studies:** General. **Visual/performing arts:** General.

Contact. Phone: (763) 566-7777
Jennifer Sekula, Director of Admissions, Minnesota School of Business: Brooklyn Center, 5910 Shingle Creek Parkway, Brooklyn Center, MN 55430

Minnesota State College - Southeast Technical

Winona, Minnesota
www.southeastmn.edu **CB code: 7123**

- Public 2-year technical college
- Commuter campus in large town

General. Founded in 1949. Regionally accredited. **Enrollment:** 1,874 degree-seeking undergraduates; 172 non-degree-seeking students. **Degrees:** 173 associate awarded. **Location:** 55 miles from Rochester, 32 miles from La Crosse, Wisconsin. **Calendar:** Semester, limited summer session. **Full-time faculty:** 51 total; 2% minority, 39% women. **Part-time faculty:** 66 total; 3% minority, 59% women. **Class size:** 67% < 20, 29% 20-39, 3% 40-49, less than 1% 50-99. **Partnerships:** Formal partnerships with School-to-Work and Tech Prep programs.

Student profile. Among degree-seeking undergraduates, 8% enrolled in a transfer program, 92% enrolled in a vocational program, 627 enrolled as first-time, first-year students, 287 transferred in from other institutions.

Part-time:	40%	**Asian American:**	2%
Out-of-state:	28%	**Hispanic American:**	1%
Women:	61%	**Native American:**	1%
African American:	6%	**25 or older:**	43%

Basis for selection. Open admission, but selective for some programs. Practical Nursing requires several academic standards be met before admission to program. Truck Driver Training requires Department of Transportation (DOT) medical certificate and Commercial Drivers License (CDL) learner's permit . **Homeschooled:** Transcript of courses and grades required. **Learning Disabled:** Disability documentation required to receive accommodations.

High school preparation. College-preparatory program recommended. 7 units recommended. Recommended units include English 4, mathematics 2 and science 1.

2008-2009 Annual costs. Tuition/fees: $4,584; $8,812 out-of-state. Per-credit charge: $141 in-state; $282 out-of-state. Books/supplies: $900. Personal expenses: $3,654.

2007-2008 Financial aid. Need-based: Need-based aid available for part-time students. Work-study available for part-time students. **Non-need-based:** Scholarships awarded for academics, leadership.

Application procedures. Admission: No deadline. $20 fee, may be waived for applicants with need. Admission notification on a rolling basis. **Financial aid:** Priority date 5/15, closing date 6/30. FAFSA, institutional form required. Applicants notified on a rolling basis; must reply within 3 week(s) of notification.

Academics. Special study options: Accelerated study, distance learning, double major, dual enrollment of high school students, internships, liberal arts/career combination. License preparation in nursing. **Credit/placement by examination:** AP, CLEP, IB, institutional tests. **Support services:** Learning center, reduced course load, remedial instruction, tutoring.

Majors. Business: Accounting, accounting technology, administrative services, business admin, retailing, sales/distribution, selling. **Computer sciences:** Networking, programming, web page design. **Construction:** Carpentry. **Engineering technology:** Computer systems, drafting, electrical, electromechanical. **Family/consumer sciences:** Child care. **Health:** Massage therapy, medical secretary, nursing (RN). **Legal studies:** Legal secretary. **Mechanic/repair:** Auto body, heating/ac/refrig, industrial. **Personal/culinary services:** Cosmetic.

Most popular majors. Business/marketing 25%, computer/information sciences 8%, engineering/engineering technologies 8%, health sciences 48%, trade and industry 8%.

Computing on campus. 75 workstations in library. Online course registration, online library, wireless network available.

Student life. Freshman orientation: Mandatory. **Housing:** Cooperative housing available. For Red Wing campus students: Privately-owned dormitory near college available. For Winona campus students: Winona State University dormitory near college available by cooperative arrangement. **Activities:** Student government, student newspaper, Student Senate, Business Professionals of America (BPA), Skills USA, Delta Epsilon Chi (DEX), Guild of American Luthiers, Association of Stringed Instrument Artisans, Violin Society of America, Musical Instrument Technicians Association (MITA), National Association of Professional Band Instrument Repair Technicians (NAPBIRT), Data Processing Management Association.

Student services. Adult student services, alcohol/substance abuse counseling, career counseling, student employment services, financial aid counseling, health services, minority student services, personal counseling, placement for graduates, veterans' counselor. **Physically disabled:** Services for visually, speech, hearing impaired. **Transfer:** Pre-admission transcript evaluation for new students.

Contact. E-mail: enrollmentservices@southeastmn.edu
Phone: (507) 453-2700 Toll-free number: (877) 853-8324
Fax: (507) 453-2715
Al DuCett, Director of Admissions, Minnesota State College - Southeast Technical, 1250 Homer Road, Winona, MN 55987-0409

Minnesota State Community and Technical College

Fergus Falls, Minnesota
www.minnesota.edu **CB code: 2110**

- Public 2-year community and technical college
- Commuter campus in large town

General. Founded in 1960. Regionally accredited. Campuses in Detroit Lakes, Fergus Falls, Moorhead, and Wadena. **Enrollment:** 3,228 full-time, degree-seeking students. **Degrees:** 786 associate awarded. **Location:** 180 miles from Minneapolis-St. Paul, 60 miles from Fargo, North Dakota. **Calendar:** Semester, limited summer session. **Full-time faculty:** 173 total. **Part-time faculty:** 125 total. **Partnerships:** Formal partnerships with local high schools; juniors and seniors can enroll in specially designed courses for college credit at their high school.

Student profile. Among full-time, degree-seeking students, 550 transferred in from other institutions.

Out-of-state:	10%	**Live on campus:**	10%
25 or older:	31%		

Transfer out. Colleges most students transferred to 2008: Minnesota State University: Moorhead, St. Cloud State University, Bemidji State University, Minnesota State University: Mankato, University of Minnesota: Twin Cities.

Basis for selection. Open admission. **Homeschooled:** Statement describing homeschool structure and mission, transcript of courses and grades required. **Learning Disabled:** Special accommodations available for students during placement assessment tests.

2008-2009 Annual costs. Tuition/fees: $4,876; $4,876 out-of-state. Per-credit charge: $141 in-state; $141 out-of-state. Room only: $2,450.

Financial aid. Need-based: Need-based aid available for part-time students. Work-study available nights and weekends. **Non-need-based:** Scholarships awarded for academics, art, leadership, minority status, music/drama, state residency.

Application procedures. Admission: No deadline. $20 fee. Admission notification on a rolling basis. **Financial aid:** Priority date 6/1; no closing date. FAFSA, institutional form required. Applicants notified on a rolling basis starting 7/1.

Academics. Special study options: Distance learning, dual enrollment of high school students, ESL, honors, internships, liberal arts/career combination, study abroad, weekend college. Bachelor's degree programs available on campus. License preparation in dental hygiene, nursing. **Credit/placement by examination:** AP, CLEP, IB, institutional tests. **Support services:** Learning center, reduced course load, remedial instruction, study skills assistance, tutoring, writing center.

Majors. Biology: General. **Business:** Accounting, administrative services, banking/financial services, business admin, fashion, human resources, office technology, sales/distribution, selling. **Computer sciences:** Networking, programming, security, web page design. **Construction:** Carpentry, site management. **Education:** Teacher assistance. **Engineering technology:** Architectural drafting, computer, computer systems, electrical, manufacturing, mechanical drafting, telecommunications. **Health:** Clinical lab technology, dental hygiene, licensed practical nurse, medical records technology, medical secretary, nursing (RN), pharmacy assistant, radiologic technology/medical imaging. **Legal studies:** Legal secretary, paralegal. **Liberal arts:** Arts/sciences. **Mechanic/repair:** Auto body, automotive, diesel, industrial, marine. **Protective services:** Criminal justice. **Visual/performing arts:** Graphic design.

Most popular majors. Business/marketing 16%, health sciences 44%, liberal arts 20%.

Computing on campus. 200 workstations in library, computer center, student center. Dormitories wired for high-speed internet access and linked to campus network. Online course registration, online library, helpline, wireless network available.

Student life. **Freshman orientation:** Mandatory. Preregistration for classes offered. 5-8 hour session held in summer. **Housing:** Apartments available. Privately owned dormitories within walking distance of the college. **Activities:** Bands, choral groups, drama, music ensembles, musical theater, student government, student newspaper, cactus (campus diversity organization).

Athletics. NJCAA. **Intercollegiate:** Baseball M, basketball, football (tackle) M, golf, softball W, volleyball W. **Intramural:** Basketball, bowling, football (non-tackle), football (tackle) M, golf, soccer, softball, volleyball. **Team name:** Spartans.

Student services. Adult student services, alcohol/substance abuse counseling, career counseling, student employment services, financial aid counseling, minority student services, personal counseling, placement for graduates, veterans' counselor, women's services. **Physically disabled:** Services for visually, speech, hearing impaired. **Transfer:** Pre-admission transcript evaluation for new students. Transfer adviser, college fairs on campus for students transferring to 4-year colleges.

Contact. E-mail: enroll@minnesota.edu
Phone: (218) 736-1525 Toll-free number: (877) 450-3322
Fax: (218) 736-1510
Carrie Brimhall, Director of Enrollment Management, Minnesota State Community and Technical College, 1414 College Way, Fergus Falls, MN 56537-1000

Minnesota West Community and Technical College

Pipestone, Minnesota
www.mnwest.edu **CB code: 6945**

- Public 2-year community and technical college
- Commuter campus in large town

General. Founded in 1936. Regionally accredited. In addition to the administrative campus at Granite Falls, there are campuses at Canby, Jackson, Pipestone, and Worthington and three learning sites in Fairmont, Luverne and Marshall, Minnesota. **Enrollment:** 2,630 degree-seeking undergraduates. **Degrees:** 328 associate awarded. **Location:** 200 miles from Minneapolis-St. Paul, 60 miles from Sioux Falls, South Dakota. **Calendar:** Semester, limited summer session. **Full-time faculty:** 86 total. **Part-time faculty:** 136 total.

Basis for selection. Open admission. PSB-Aptitude for Practical Nursing Examination required of nursing applicants. Test scores not required for continuing education students. Interview recommended. **Homeschooled:** Transcript of courses and grades required.

2008-2009 Annual costs. Tuition/fees: $4,807; $4,807 out-of-state. Per-credit charge: $144. In-state and out-of-state tuition rates are the same. Books/supplies: $600.

2008-2009 Financial aid. **Need-based:** 48% of total undergraduate aid awarded as scholarships/grants, 52% as loans/jobs. Need-based aid available for part-time students. Work-study available nights, weekends and for part-time students.

Application procedures. **Admission:** No deadline. $20 fee, may be waived for applicants with need. Admission notification on a rolling basis. Priority deadline for practical nursing applicants 02/15. **Financial aid:** Priority date 6/9; no closing date. FAFSA required. Applicants notified on a rolling basis starting 4/9; must reply within 2 week(s) of notification.

Academics. **Special study options:** Cooperative education, cross-registration, distance learning, double major, dual enrollment of high school students, independent study, internships, liberal arts/career combination, student-designed major, study abroad. License preparation in nursing, radiology. **Credit/placement by examination:** AP, CLEP, IB, institutional tests. 60 credit hours maximum toward associate degree. **Support services:** Learning center, pre-admission summer program, reduced course load, remedial instruction, study skills assistance, tutoring.

Majors. **Agriculture:** General, agronomy, business, equipment technology, farm/ranch, plant sciences, production. **Biology:** General. **Business:** General, accounting, accounting/business management, accounting/finance, administrative services, business admin, executive assistant, office management. **Communications:** General, media studies. **Computer sciences:** General. **Construction:** General, electrician, lineworker, plumbing, power transmission. **Education:** General, business, elementary, physical, secondary, special. **Engineering:** General. **Engineering technology:** Computer, heat/ac/refrig, manufacturing, robotics. **Family/consumer sciences:** Child care. **Health:** Clinical lab technology, dental assistant, health services, medical assistant, medical secretary, nursing (RN), predental, premedicine, prenursing, prepharmacy, preveterinary, radiologic technology/medical imaging. **History:** General. **Legal studies:** General. **Liberal arts:** Arts/sciences. **Math:** General. **Mechanic/repair:** Auto body, automotive, diesel, heating/ac/refrig. **Philosophy/religion:** Philosophy. **Physical sciences:** Chemistry, physics. **Production:** Machine tool. **Protective services:** Corrections, law enforcement admin, police science. **Psychology:** General. **Public administration:** Human services. **Social sciences:** Economics, geography, political science, sociology. **Visual/performing arts:** General, art. **Other:** Heating/ventilating/air conditioning.

Most popular majors. Business/marketing 18%, engineering/engineering technologies 8%, health sciences 29%, liberal arts 30%.

Computing on campus. Online course registration, online library, helpline, wireless network available.

Student life. **Freshman orientation:** Mandatory. **Housing:** Subsidized apartments adjacent to campus. **Activities:** Jazz band, choral groups, drama, music ensembles, musical theater, radio station, student government, student newspaper, TV station, non-traditional student club, student senate, Phi Beta Kappa.

Athletics. NJCAA. **Intercollegiate:** Basketball, cheerleading, football (tackle) M, golf, softball W, volleyball W, wrestling M. **Intramural:** Basketball, bowling, golf, skiing, softball, tennis. **Team name:** Blue Jays.

Student services. Adult student services, career counseling, student employment services, financial aid counseling, minority student services, personal counseling, veterans' counselor. **Physically disabled:** Services for visually, speech, hearing impaired. **Transfer:** Pre-admission transcript evaluation for new students. Transfer adviser, college fairs on campus for students transferring to 4-year colleges.

Contact. E-mail: barbara.reinders@mnwest.edu
Phone: (800) 658-2330 Toll-free number: (800) 658-2330
Fax: (507) 825-4656
Barbara Reinders, Admissions Coordinator, Minnesota West Community and Technical College, 1314 North Hiawatha Avenue, Pipestone, MN 56164

Normandale Community College

Bloomington, Minnesota **CB member**
www.normandale.edu **CB code: 6501**

- Public 2-year community college
- Commuter campus in very large city

General. Founded in 1968. Regionally accredited. **Enrollment:** 9,482 degree-seeking undergraduates. **Degrees:** 814 associate awarded. **ROTC:** Army, Naval, Air Force. **Location:** 12 miles from Minneapolis-St. Paul. **Calendar:** Semester, extensive summer session. **Full-time faculty:** 192 total. **Part-time faculty:** 150 total. **Class size:** 31% < 20, 52% 20-39, 15% 40-49, 2% 50-99. **Special facilities:** Japanese garden, marshland area, career and academic planning center.

Student profile.

Out-of-state:	1%	**25 or older:**	33%

Transfer out. **Colleges most students transferred to 2008:** University of Minnesota, University of St. Thomas, Minnesota State University: Mankato, St. Cloud State University, Metropolitan State University.

Basis for selection. Open admission, but selective for some programs. Admission to health-related programs (dental hygiene, nursing, dietetic technology, radiologic technology) based on high school GPA and completion of specific course requirements. In-house placement tests in English, mathematics, reading administered before registration. **Adult students:** SAT/ACT scores not required.

2008-2009 Annual costs. Tuition/fees: $4,607; $4,607 out-of-state. Per-credit charge: $137 in-state; $137 out-of-state. In-state and out-of-state tuition rates are the same. Books/supplies: $1,130. Personal expenses: $2,700.

2007-2008 Financial aid. **Need-based:** 56% of total undergraduate aid awarded as scholarships/grants, 44% as loans/jobs. Need-based aid available for part-time students. Work-study available nights, weekends and for part-time students. **Non-need-based:** Scholarships awarded for academics, leadership, music/drama, state residency.

Application procedures. **Admission:** No deadline. $20 fee, may be waived for applicants with need. Admission notification on a rolling basis. **Financial aid:** Priority date 4/1; no closing date. FAFSA required. Applicants notified on a rolling basis starting 4/15.

Academics. **Special study options:** Accelerated study, cooperative education, distance learning, double major, dual enrollment of high school students, ESL, honors, independent study, internships, liberal arts/career combination, study abroad, teacher certification program, weekend college. Bachelor's degree programs available on campus. License preparation in dental hygiene, nursing, radiology. **Credit/placement by examination:** AP, CLEP, IB, institutional tests. No limit to the number of credits that can be applied toward a student's degree, provided the student meets the college's credits-in-residence requirement. **Support services:** Learning center, reduced course load, remedial instruction, study skills assistance, tutoring, writing center.

Majors. **Business:** Accounting, business admin, hospitality admin, marketing. **Computer sciences:** General, computer science. **Education:** General, elementary, special. **Engineering:** General. **Engineering technology:** Biomedical, computer systems, manufacturing. **Health:** Dental hygiene, dietetics, nursing (RN), radiologic technology/medical imaging. **Liberal arts:** Arts/sciences. **Protective services:** Criminal justice, police science. **Visual/performing arts:** Dramatic, studio arts.

Most popular majors. Health sciences 15%, liberal arts 69%, security/protective services 6%.

Computing on campus. 575 workstations in library, computer center, student center. Commuter students can connect to campus network. Online course registration, online library, helpline, repair service, wireless network available.

Student life. **Freshman orientation:** Mandatory, $25 fee. **Activities:** Bands, choral groups, drama, literary magazine, music ensembles, musical theater, student government, student newspaper, Christian Fellowship club, Black student alliance, ASIA, single parents, wellness support group, Phi Theta Kappa, Somali student association, Ethiopian student association, Club Latino.

Athletics. **Intramural:** Archery, baseball, basketball, bowling, boxing, cross-country, fencing, field hockey, football (non-tackle), golf, handball, ice hockey, judo, racquetball, skiing, soccer, softball, table tennis, tennis, volleyball, weight lifting. **Team name:** Lions.

Student services. Adult student services, career counseling, services for economically disadvantaged, student employment services, financial aid counseling, on-campus daycare, personal counseling, placement for graduates, veterans' counselor. **Physically disabled:** Services for visually, speech, hearing impaired. **Transfer:** Pre-admission transcript evaluation for new students. Transfer adviser, college fairs on campus for students transferring to 4-year colleges.

Contact. E-mail: admissions@normandale.edu
Phone: (952) 487-8201 Toll-free number: (866) 880-8740
Fax: (952) 487-8230
Matt Crawford, Director of Admissions, Normandale Community College, 9700 France Avenue South, Bloomington, MN 55431

North Hennepin Community College

Brooklyn Park, Minnesota
www.nhcc.edu **CB code: 6498**

- Public 2-year community college
- Commuter campus in small city

General. Founded in 1966. Regionally accredited. **Enrollment:** 6,389 degree-seeking undergraduates; 527 non-degree-seeking students. **Degrees:** 708 associate awarded. **ROTC:** Army, Naval, Air Force. **Location:** 12 miles from downtown. **Calendar:** Semester, limited summer session. **Full-time faculty:** 104 total; 9% minority, 65% women. **Part-time faculty:** 145 total; 8% minority, 48% women. **Class size:** 33% < 20, 51% 20-39, 7% 40-49, 8% 50-99, less than 1% >100.

Student profile. Among degree-seeking undergraduates, 1% already have a bachelor's degree or higher, 1,401 enrolled as first-time, first-year students.

Part-time:	60%	**Hispanic American:**	2%
Women:	58%	**Native American:**	1%
African American:	16%	**International:**	1%
Asian American:	10%	**25 or older:**	52%

Transfer out. 48% of students enrolled in the transfer program go on to 4-year colleges.

Basis for selection. Open admission, but selective for some programs. Competitive admission for medical programs: nursing, medical lab technician, histo technician, graphic design. Must show proof of immunization to be enrolled in classes. Assessment test or approved waiver required for registration. **Homeschooled:** State high school equivalency certificate required.

High school preparation. 1 unit chemistry and algebra are required for nursing program.

2008-2009 Annual costs. Tuition/fees: $4,623; $4,623 out-of-state. Per-credit charge: $140 in-state; $140 out-of-state. In-state and out-of-state tuition rates are the same. Books/supplies: $1,000. Personal expenses: $3,586.

2007-2008 Financial aid. **Need-based:** 43% of total undergraduate aid awarded as scholarships/grants, 57% as loans/jobs. Need-based aid available for part-time students. Work-study available nights, weekends and for part-time students. **Non-need-based:** Scholarships awarded for academics, art, leadership. **Additional information:** Computerized financial aid application.

Application procedures. **Admission:** No deadline. $20 fee. Admission notification on a rolling basis. **Financial aid:** Priority date 4/15; no closing date. FAFSA required. Applicants notified on a rolling basis starting 6/1.

Academics. **Special study options:** Cross-registration, distance learning, double major, dual enrollment of high school students, ESL, honors, independent study, internships, student-designed major, study abroad, weekend college. Bachelor's degree programs available on campus. License preparation in nursing. **Credit/placement by examination:** AP, CLEP, IB, institutional tests. 30 credit hours maximum toward associate degree. **Support services:** GED test center, learning center, reduced course load, remedial instruction, study skills assistance, tutoring, writing center.

Majors. **Biology:** General. **Business:** Accounting, accounting technology, business admin, finance, management information systems, marketing, small business admin. **Computer sciences:** Computer science. **Construction:** Building inspection, site management. **Engineering:** General. **Health:** Cardiovascular technology, clinical lab technology, histologic assistant, nursing (RN), radiologic technology/medical imaging. **Legal studies:** Paralegal. **Liberal arts:** Arts/sciences. **Physical sciences:** Chemistry. **Protective services:** Criminal justice, police science. **Visual/performing arts:** Graphic design, studio arts.

Most popular majors. Business/marketing 16%, health sciences 18%, liberal arts 48%, security/protective services 8%.

Computing on campus. 700 workstations in library, computer center, student center. Online course registration, online library, helpline, wireless network available.

Student life. **Freshman orientation:** Mandatory. Preregistration for classes offered. 2 to 3 hour session held prior to the start of each term for all new students. **Activities:** Choral groups, drama, literary magazine, musical theater, student government, student newspaper.

Athletics. **Intramural:** Basketball, bowling, soccer, softball, tennis, volleyball.

Student services. Career counseling, student employment services, financial aid counseling, on-campus daycare, personal counseling, placement for graduates. **Physically disabled:** Services for visually, speech, hearing impaired. **Learning disabled:** Comprehensive services available. **Transfer:** Pre-admission transcript evaluation for new students. Transfer adviser, college fairs on campus for students transferring to 4-year colleges.

Contact. E-mail: admissions@nhcc.edu
Phone: (763) 424-0719 Toll-free number: (800) 818-0395
Fax: (763) 493-0563
Lori Kirkeby, Registrar, North Hennepin Community College, 7411 85th Avenue North, Brooklyn Park, MN 55445

Northland Community & Technical College

Thief River Falls, Minnesota
www.northlandcollege.edu **CB code: 6500**

- Public 2-year community and technical college
- Commuter campus in small town

General. Founded in 1965. Regionally accredited. Campuses in East Grand Forks and Thief River Falls. **Enrollment:** 1,752 full-time, degree-seeking students. **Degrees:** 564 associate awarded. **Location:** 55 miles from Grand Forks, North Dakota. **Calendar:** Semester, limited summer session. **Full-time faculty:** 128 total. **Part-time faculty:** 106 total. **Class size:** 50% < 20, 48% 20-39, 2% 40-49, less than 1% 50-99, less than 1% >100.

Transfer out. Colleges most students transferred to 2008: University of North Dakota, North Dakota State University, Bemidji State University, University of Minnesota: Crookston, Moorhead State University, St. Cloud State University.

Basis for selection. Open admission. Students are required to go through the ACCUPLACER assessment program to determine level of mathematics, reading and English skills. **Homeschooled:** Transcript of courses and grades required.

2008-2009 Annual costs. Tuition/fees: $4,926. Per-credit charge: $147. In-state and out-of-state tuition rates are the same. Books/supplies: $600. Personal expenses: $1,350.

2007-2008 Financial aid. Need-based: 34% of total undergraduate aid awarded as scholarships/grants, 66% as loans/jobs. Need-based aid available for part-time students. Work-study available nights and for part-time students. **Non-need-based:** Scholarships awarded for academics.

Application procedures. Admission: No deadline. $20 fee. Admission notification on a rolling basis. **Financial aid:** Priority date 5/1; no closing date. FAFSA required. Applicants notified on a rolling basis starting 5/15.

Academics. Special study options: Distance learning, double major, dual enrollment of high school students, external degree, internships, liberal arts/career combination. License preparation in aviation, nursing, occupational therapy, paramedic, physical therapy, radiology. **Credit/placement by examination:** AP, CLEP, institutional tests. 44 credit hours maximum toward associate degree. **Support services:** GED test center, learning center, reduced course load, remedial instruction, study skills assistance, tutoring, writing center.

Majors. Agriculture: Business, economics, farm/ranch. **Architecture:** Technology. **Biology:** General. **Business:** Accounting, administrative services, management information systems, marketing, sales/distribution. **Communications:** General, broadcast journalism, journalism, media studies, radio/tv. **Computer sciences:** Networking. **Conservation:** Environmental science, management/policy. **Construction:** General. **Education:** General, early childhood. **Engineering:** General, electrical. **Engineering technology:** Drafting. **Foreign languages:** General. **Health:** Athletic training, cardiovascular technology, clinical lab science, clinical lab technology, EMT ambulance attendant, EMT paramedic, health services, insurance coding, medical assistant, medical secretary, medical transcription, nursing (RN), occupational therapy assistant, office assistant, pharmacy assistant, physical therapy assistant, radiologic technology/medical imaging, respiratory therapy assistant, respiratory therapy technology, surgical technology. **Interdisciplinary:** Math/computer science. **Legal studies:** Prelaw. **Liberal arts:** Arts/sciences. **Math:** General. **Mechanic/repair:** Aircraft, auto body, automotive, avionics, electronics/electrical. **Parks/recreation:** General. **Production:** Welding. **Protective services:** Corrections, criminal justice, law enforcement admin, police science. **Psychology:** General. **Public administration:** Human services. **Social sciences:** General. **Visual/performing arts:** General, art, studio arts.

Computing on campus. 356 workstations in library, computer center, student center. Online course registration, online library, helpline, repair service, wireless network available.

Student life. Freshman orientation: Mandatory. **Activities:** Bands, choral groups, dance, drama, music ensembles, musical theater, radio station, student government, student newspaper, Phi Theta Kappa honor society, multicultural club, SOS club, diversity committee.

Athletics. NJCAA. **Intercollegiate:** Baseball M, basketball, football (tackle) M, softball W, volleyball W. **Intramural:** Basketball, bowling, golf, soccer, softball, tennis, volleyball. **Team name:** Pioneers.

Student services. Adult student services, career counseling, services for economically disadvantaged, student employment services, financial aid counseling, minority student services, on-campus daycare, personal counseling, placement for graduates, veterans' counselor, women's services. **Physically disabled:** Services for visually, speech, hearing impaired. **Transfer:** Reentry adviser, pre-admission transcript evaluation for new students. Transfer adviser, college fairs on campus for students transferring to 4-year colleges.

Contact. E-mail: admissions@northlandcollege.edu
Phone: (218) 773-3441 Toll-free number: (800) 959-6282
Fax: (218) 681-0774
Eugene Klinke, Enrollment Management Coordinator, Northland Community & Technical College, 1101 Highway One East, Thief River Falls, MN 56701

Northwest Technical College

Bemidji, Minnesota
www.ntcmn.edu **CB code: 3626**

- Public 2-year technical college
- Commuter campus in large town

General. Regionally accredited. Northwest Technical College is affiliated with Bemidji State University. **Enrollment:** 892 degree-seeking undergraduates; 481 non-degree-seeking students. **Degrees:** 114 associate awarded. **Location:** 229 miles from Minneapolis-St. Paul, 152 miles from Duluth. **Calendar:** Semester, limited summer session. **Full-time faculty:** 32 total; 3% minority, 69% women. **Part-time faculty:** 37 total; 54% women. **Class size:** 71% < 20, 27% 20-39, 2% 40-49, less than 1% 50-99. **Special facilities:** American Indian resource center, lake, 3D hologram technology.

Student profile. Among degree-seeking undergraduates, 100% enrolled in a vocational program, 4% already have a bachelor's degree or higher, 186 enrolled as first-time, first-year students, 111 transferred in from other institutions.

Part-time:	45%	**Hispanic American:**	1%
Out-of-state:	5%	**Native American:**	12%
Women:	67%	**25 or older:**	44%
African American:	1%	**Live on campus:**	5%
Asian American:	1%		

Transfer out. Colleges most students transferred to 2008: Bemidji State University, Northland Community and Technical College, Minnesota State Community and Technical College.

Basis for selection. Open admission. **Learning Disabled:** Procedure: Learners with learning disabilities are encouraged to have an IEP on file with the Learning Services Coordinator and meet with her prior to the start of the semester to develop a Personal Education Plan.

2008-2009 Annual costs. Tuition/fees: $4,766; $4,766 out-of-state. Per-credit charge: $149 in-state; $149 out-of-state. Books/supplies: $1,200.

2008-2009 Financial aid. All financial aid based on need. 56% of total undergraduate aid awarded as scholarships/grants, 44% as loans/jobs. Need-based aid available for part-time students. Work-study available nights and for part-time students.

Application procedures. Admission: No deadline. $20 fee, may be waived for applicants with need. Admission notification on a rolling basis. High school learners can attend the college under the Post-Secondary Enrollment Options program. **Financial aid:** Priority date 7/1; no closing date. FAFSA, institutional form required. Applicants notified on a rolling basis.

Academics. NTC learners can take General Education courses from Bemidji State University and/or online from a regional consortium of colleges in fulfillment of general education requirements of degrees at NTC. **Special study options:** Cross-registration, distance learning, double major, dual enrollment of high school students, ESL, independent study, internships, student-designed major. Study abroad options are available through our partnership with Bemidji State University. License preparation in nursing. **Credit/placement by examination:** AP, CLEP, IB, institutional tests. **Support services:** Learning center, reduced course load, remedial instruction, study skills assistance, tutoring.

Majors. Agriculture: Landscaping. **Business:** Accounting, administrative services, business admin, sales/distribution. **Engineering technology:** Industrial, manufacturing. **Family/consumer sciences:** Child care. **Health:** Licensed practical nurse, massage therapy, medical secretary, nursing (RN). **Mechanic/repair:** Automotive, engine machinist.

Most popular majors. Business/marketing 17%, health sciences 76%.

Computing on campus. PC or laptop required. 140 workstations in dormitories, library, computer center, student center. Dormitories wired for high-speed internet access. Commuter students can connect to campus network. Online course registration, online library, helpline, repair service, wireless network available.

Student life. **Freshman orientation:** Mandatory. Preregistration for classes offered. **Housing:** Coed dorms, apartments, wellness housing available. $150 partly refundable deposit. NTC learners may reside in Bemidji State University residence halls. **Activities:** Student government, Phi Theta Kappa, Skills USA.

Student services. Adult student services, chaplain/spiritual director, career counseling, services for economically disadvantaged, student employment services, financial aid counseling, health services, minority student services, personal counseling, placement for graduates, veterans' counselor. **Physically disabled:** Services for visually, speech, hearing impaired. **Learning disabled:** Comprehensive services available. **Transfer:** Re-entry adviser, pre-admission transcript evaluation for new students. Transfer adviser, college fairs on campus for students transferring to 4-year colleges.

Contact. E-mail: richard.lehmann@ntcmn.edu
Phone: (218) 333-6647 Toll-free number: (800) 942-8324
Fax: (218) 333-6697
Richard Lehmann, Admissions Specialist, Northwest Technical College, 905 Grant Avenue Southeast, Bemidji, MN 56601-4907

Northwest Technical Institute

Eagan, Minnesota
www.nti.edu **CB code: 1388**

- For-profit 2-year technical college
- Commuter campus in small city
- Application essay, interview required

General. Founded in 1957. Accredited by ACCSCT. **Enrollment:** 133 degree-seeking undergraduates. **Degrees:** 56 associate awarded. **Location:** 10 miles from Minneapolis-St. Paul. **Calendar:** Semester, extensive summer session. **Full-time faculty:** 12 total; 17% have terminal degrees, 50% women. **Part-time faculty:** 2 total; 50% women. **Class size:** 100% < 20.

Student profile. Among degree-seeking undergraduates, 100% enrolled in a vocational program, 1% already have a bachelor's degree or higher, 90 enrolled as first-time, first-year students.

Women:	18%	25 or older:	19%

Transfer out. 15% of students enrolled in the transfer program go on to 4-year colleges.

Basis for selection. Open admission.

High school preparation. Recommended units include English 2, mathematics 3 and science 2.

2008-2009 Annual costs. Tuition/fees: $14,845. Per-credit charge: $463. Books/supplies: $650. Personal expenses: $3,192.

Financial aid. **Need-based:** Need-based aid available for part-time students.

Application procedures. **Admission:** No deadline. $25 fee. Admission notification on a rolling basis. **Financial aid:** No deadline. FAFSA, institutional form required. Applicants notified on a rolling basis; must reply within 2 week(s) of notification.

Academics. **Special study options:** Honors, liberal arts/career combination. **Credit/placement by examination:** AP, CLEP. **Support services:** Tutoring.

Majors. **Architecture:** Technology. **Engineering:** General, mechanical. **Engineering technology:** General, architectural, architectural drafting, drafting, mechanical, mechanical drafting.

Computing on campus. 120 workstations in student center.

Student life. **Freshman orientation:** Mandatory.

Student services. Career counseling, student employment services, placement for graduates. **Transfer:** Re-entry adviser, pre-admission transcript evaluation for new students.

Contact. E-mail: info@nti.edu
Phone: (952) 944-0080 Toll-free number: (800) 443-4223
Fax: (952) 944-9274
Keith Fossen, President, Northwest Technical Institute, 950 Blue Gentian Road, Eagan, MN 55121

Pine Technical College

Pine City, Minnesota
www.pinetech.edu **CB code: 7118**

- Public 2-year technical college
- Commuter campus in small town

General. Regionally accredited. **Enrollment:** 548 degree-seeking undergraduates. **Degrees:** 22 associate awarded. **Location:** 60 miles from Minneapolis-St. Paul. **Calendar:** Semester, limited summer session. **Full-time faculty:** 18 total. **Part-time faculty:** 21 total. **Class size:** 77% < 20, 18% 20-39, 2% 40-49, 2% 50-99.

Student profile.

Out-of-state:	11%	25 or older:	35%

Transfer out. **Colleges most students transferred to 2008:** St. Cloud Technical College, Anoka-Ramsey Community College, Lake Superior Community College, Mesabi Community College, North Hennepin College.

Basis for selection. Open admission, but selective for some programs. Additional requirements for some majors. Criminal history check. **Home-schooled:** State high school equivalency certificate required.

2008-2009 Annual costs. Tuition/fees: $4,341; $8,196 out-of-state. Per-credit charge: $129 in-state; $257 out-of-state. Books/supplies: $800. Personal expenses: $600.

Financial aid. **Need-based:** Need-based aid available for part-time students. Work-study available for part-time students. **Non-need-based:** Scholarships awarded for academics, state residency.

Application procedures. **Admission:** No deadline. $20 fee, may be waived for applicants with need. Admission notification on a rolling basis. **Financial aid:** Priority date 5/5; no closing date. FAFSA, institutional form required. Applicants notified on a rolling basis starting 6/5.

Academics. **Special study options:** Cross-registration, distance learning, double major, dual enrollment of high school students, honors, independent study, internships, liberal arts/career combination. License preparation in nursing. **Credit/placement by examination:** AP, CLEP, institutional tests. 35 credit hours maximum toward associate degree. **Support services:** Learning center, reduced course load, remedial instruction, study skills assistance, tutoring.

Majors. **Biology:** Biotechnology. **Business:** Accounting, business admin. **Computer sciences:** Data processing, information systems, programming. **Engineering technology:** Manufacturing. **Family/consumer sciences:** Child care. **Health:** Insurance coding. **Mechanic/repair:** Automotive, gunsmithing. **Production:** Machine tool. **Public administration:** Human services.

Most popular majors. Business/marketing 62%, family/consumer sciences 31%.

Computing on campus. 100 workstations in library, computer center. Commuter students can connect to campus network. Online course registration, online library, helpline, wireless network available.

Student life. **Freshman orientation:** Mandatory. **Activities:** Student government.

Athletics. **Intercollegiate:** Rifle. **Intramural:** Rifle, tennis.

Student services. Career counseling, services for economically disadvantaged, student employment services, financial aid counseling, on-campus daycare, personal counseling, placement for graduates. **Physically disabled:** Services for visually, hearing impaired. **Transfer:** Pre-admission transcript evaluation for new students. Transfer adviser, college fairs on campus for students transferring to 4-year colleges.

Contact. E-mail: information@pinetech.edu
Phone: (320) 629-5100 Toll-free number: (800) 521-7463
Fax: (320) 629-5101
James Stumne, Admissions Director, Pine Technical College, 900 Fourth Street, SE, Pine City, MN 55063

Rainy River Community College

International Falls, Minnesota
www.rrcc.mnscu.edu **CB code: 1637**

- Public 2-year community and technical college
- Commuter campus in small town

General. Founded in 1967. Regionally accredited. **Enrollment:** 343 degree-seeking undergraduates. **Degrees:** 47 associate awarded. **Location:** 300 miles from Minneapolis-St. Paul, 150 miles from Duluth. **Calendar:** Semester, limited summer session. **Full-time faculty:** 11 total. **Part-time faculty:** 14 total.

Student profile. Among degree-seeking undergraduates, 343 enrolled as first-time, first-year students.

Transfer out. Colleges most students transferred to 2008: St. Cloud State University, Bemidji State University, University of Minnesota-Duluth.

Basis for selection. Open admission.

2008-2009 Annual costs. Tuition/fees: $4,517; $5,504 out-of-state. Per-credit charge: $132 in-state; $164 out-of-state. Books/supplies: $600. Personal expenses: $900.

2008-2009 Financial aid. Need-based: Need-based aid available for part-time students. Work-study available nights, weekends and for part-time students. **Non-need-based:** Scholarships awarded for academics, alumni affiliation, minority status, state residency. **Additional information:** Many scholarship and employment opportunities for applicants showing little or no need.

Application procedures. Admission: No deadline. $20 fee. Admission notification on a rolling basis. **Financial aid:** Priority date 6/1; no closing date. FAFSA, institutional form required. Applicants notified on a rolling basis starting 5/1; must reply within 3 week(s) of notification.

Academics. Special study options: Distance learning, dual enrollment of high school students, honors, independent study, internships, liberal arts/career combination. License preparation in aviation, nursing. **Credit/placement by examination:** AP, CLEP, IB, institutional tests. **Support services:** Learning center, pre-admission summer program, reduced course load, remedial instruction, study skills assistance, tutoring, writing center.

Majors. Area/ethnic studies: Native American. **Education:** Science. **Liberal arts:** Arts/sciences. **Math:** General. **Mechanic/repair:** Industrial.

Computing on campus. 100 workstations in dormitories, library, computer center. Online course registration available.

Student life. Freshman orientation: Mandatory. **Housing:** Special housing for disabled, apartments available. $200 deposit. Student apartments equipped with computers. **Activities:** Choral groups, drama, literary magazine, music ensembles, musical theater, student government, Black Student Association club, Native Student club, environment club.

Athletics. NJCAA. **Intercollegiate:** Basketball, football (tackle) M, softball W, volleyball W. **Intramural:** Archery, badminton, bowling, cheerleading, cross-country, golf, ice hockey W, racquetball, skiing, softball, table tennis, tennis, volleyball. **Team name:** Voyageurs.

Student services. Adult student services, career counseling, services for economically disadvantaged, student employment services, financial aid counseling, minority student services, personal counseling, placement for graduates, veterans' counselor. **Physically disabled:** Services for visually, speech, hearing impaired. **Transfer:** Re-entry adviser, pre-admission transcript evaluation for new students. Transfer adviser, college fairs on campus for students transferring to 4-year colleges.

Contact. E-mail: admissions@rrcc.mnscu.edu
Phone: (218) 285-2207 Toll-free number: (800) 456-3996
Fax: (218) 285-2239
Berta Hagen, Registrar, Rainy River Community College, 1501 Highway 71, International Falls, MN 56649

Rasmussen College: Brooklyn Park

Brooklyn Park, Minnesota
www.rasmussen.edu

- For-profit 2-year career college
- Commuter campus in small city

General. Regionally accredited. **Enrollment:** 913 degree-seeking undergraduates. **Degrees:** 125 associate awarded. **Location:** 10 miles from Minneapolis-St. Paul. **Calendar:** Quarter, extensive summer session. **Full-time faculty:** 11 total. **Part-time faculty:** 40 total.

Basis for selection. Open admission, but selective for some programs. Programs in allied health, justice studies, and education require students to complete a background check. **Adult students:** SAT/ACT scores not required.

Financial aid. Need-based: Need-based aid available for part-time students.

Application procedures. Admission: No deadline. $60 fee. Admission notification on a rolling basis. **Financial aid:** No deadline. FAFSA, institutional form required. Applicants notified on a rolling basis.

Academics. Special study options: Distance learning, double major, honors, independent study, internships. **Credit/placement by examination:** AP, CLEP, institutional tests. 45 credit hours maximum toward associate degree, 90 toward bachelor's. Credit limited to specific programs and to courses for which examinations are available. 50% of a student's program credits must be completed through coursework at Rasmussen College. **Support services:** Learning center, remedial instruction, study skills assistance, tutoring, writing center.

Majors. Business: Accounting, administrative services, business admin. **Computer sciences:** Web page design. **Family/consumer sciences:** Child care. **Health:** Clinical lab assistant, licensed practical nurse, massage therapy, medical assistant, medical records technology, medical secretary, medical transcription, pharmacy assistant, surgical technology. **Legal studies:** Paralegal. **Other:** Criminal justice, Information systems management.

Computing on campus. 100 workstations in library, computer center, student center. Online course registration, online library, helpline, wireless network available.

Student life. Freshman orientation: Mandatory.

Student services. Adult student services, career counseling, services for economically disadvantaged, student employment services, financial aid counseling, placement for graduates.

Contact. E-mail: lori.kaiser@rasmussen.edu
Phone: (763) 493-4500 Toll-free number: (877) 495-4500
Lori Kaiser, Director of Admissions, Rasmussen College: Brooklyn Park, 8301 93rd Avenue North, Brooklyn Park, MN 55445

Rasmussen College: Eagan

Eagan, Minnesota
www.rasmussen.edu **CB code: 2449**

- For-profit 2-year career college
- Commuter campus in small city

General. Regionally accredited. **Enrollment:** 719 degree-seeking undergraduates. **Degrees:** 1 bachelor's, 83 associate awarded. **Location:** 12 miles from Minneapolis-St. Paul. **Calendar:** Quarter, extensive summer session. **Full-time faculty:** 11 total. **Part-time faculty:** 20 total.

Basis for selection. Open admission, but selective for some programs. The Practical Nursing AAS program has selective admissions requirements, including entrance examinations, background checks, and health screenings. Some additional programs in allied health, justice studies, and education require students to complete a background check. **Adult students:** SAT/ACT scores not required.

2007-2008 Financial aid. Need-based: Need-based aid available for part-time students.

Application procedures. Admission: No deadline. $60 fee. Admission notification on a rolling basis. **Financial aid:** No deadline. FAFSA, institutional form required. Applicants notified on a rolling basis.

Academics. Special study options: Distance learning, double major, honors, independent study, internships. **Credit/placement by examination:** AP, CLEP, institutional tests. 45 credit hours maximum toward associate degree, 90 toward bachelor's. Credit limited to specific programs and to courses for which examinations are available. 50% of the student's program credits must be completed through coursework at Rasmussen College. **Support services:** Learning center, remedial instruction, study skills assistance, tutoring, writing center.

Majors. Business: Accounting, administrative services, business admin. **Computer sciences:** Web page design. **Family/consumer sciences:** Child care. **Health:** Licensed practical nurse, massage therapy, medical assistant, medical records technology, medical secretary, medical transcription, pharmacy assistant. **Legal studies:** Paralegal. **Other:** Criminal justice, Information systems management.

Computing on campus. 100 workstations in library, computer center, student center. Online course registration, online library, helpline, wireless network available.

Student life. Freshman orientation: Mandatory.

Student services. Adult student services, career counseling, services for economically disadvantaged, student employment services, financial aid counseling, placement for graduates.

Contact. E-mail: jon.peterson@rasmussen.edu
Phone: (651) 687-9000 Toll-free number: (800) 852-6367
Fax: (651) 687-0507
Jon Peterson, Director of Admissions, Rasmussen College: Eagan, 3500 Federal Drive, Eagan, MN 55122

Rasmussen College: Eden Prairie

Eden Prairie, Minnesota
www.rasmussen.edu **CB code: 2448**

- For-profit 2-year career college
- Commuter campus in small city

General. Regionally accredited. **Enrollment:** 1,037 degree-seeking undergraduates. **Degrees:** 1 bachelor's, 133 associate awarded. **Location:** 10 miles from Minneapolis-St. Paul. **Calendar:** Quarter, extensive summer session. **Full-time faculty:** 10 total. **Part-time faculty:** 147 total.

Basis for selection. Open admission, but selective for some programs. Programs in allied health, justice studies, and education require students to complete a background check. **Adult students:** SAT/ACT scores not required.

Financial aid. Need-based: Need-based aid available for part-time students.

Application procedures. Admission: No deadline. $60 fee. Admission notification on a rolling basis. **Financial aid:** No deadline. FAFSA, institutional form required. Applicants notified on a rolling basis.

Academics. Special study options: Distance learning, double major, honors, independent study, internships. **Credit/placement by examination:** AP, CLEP. 45 credit hours maximum toward associate degree, 90 toward bachelor's. Credit limited to specific programs and to courses for which examinations are available. 50% of the student's program credits must be completed through coursework at Rasmussen College. **Support services:** Learning center, remedial instruction, study skills assistance, tutoring, writing center.

Majors. Business: Accounting, administrative services, business admin. **Computer sciences:** Web page design. **Family/consumer sciences:** Child care. **Health:** Massage therapy, medical assistant, medical records technology, medical secretary, medical transcription, pharmacy assistant. **Legal studies:** Paralegal. **Other:** Information systems management.

Computing on campus. 100 workstations in library, computer center, student center. Online course registration, online library, helpline, wireless network available.

Student life. Freshman orientation: Mandatory.

Student services. Adult student services, career counseling, services for economically disadvantaged, student employment services, financial aid counseling, placement for graduates.

Contact. E-mail: jeff.lust@rasmussen.edu
Phone: (952) 545-2000 Toll-free number: (800) 852-0929
Jeff Lust, Director of Admissions, Rasmussen College: Eden Prairie, 7905 Golden Triangle Drive, Suite 100, Eden Prairie, MN 55344

Rasmussen College: Mankato

Mankato, Minnesota
www.rasmussen.edu **CB code: 2453**

- For-profit 2-year career college
- Commuter campus in large town

General. Founded in 1983. Regionally accredited. **Enrollment:** 666 degree-seeking undergraduates. **Degrees:** 1 bachelor's, 141 associate awarded. **Location:** 60 miles from Minneapolis-St. Paul. **Calendar:** Quarter, extensive summer session. **Full-time faculty:** 14 total. **Part-time faculty:** 19 total.

Basis for selection. Open admission, but selective for some programs. The Medical Laboratory Technician and Practical Nursing AAS programs have selective admissions requirements, including entrance examinations, background checks, and health screenings. Some additional programs in allied health, justice studies, and education require students to complete a background check. **Adult students:** SAT/ACT scores not required.

Financial aid. Need-based: Need-based aid available for part-time students.

Application procedures. Admission: No deadline. $60 fee. Admission notification on a rolling basis. **Financial aid:** No deadline. FAFSA, institutional form required. Applicants notified on a rolling basis.

Academics. Special study options: Distance learning, double major, honors, independent study, internships. **Credit/placement by examination:** AP, CLEP, IB, institutional tests. 45 credit hours maximum toward associate degree, 90 toward bachelor's. Credit limited to specific programs and to courses for which examinations are available. 50% of the student's program must be completed through coursework at Rasmussen College. **Support services:** Learning center, remedial instruction, study skills assistance, tutoring, writing center.

Majors. Business: Accounting, administrative services, business admin. **Family/consumer sciences:** Child care. **Health:** Clinical lab technology, licensed practical nurse, massage therapy, medical assistant, medical records technology, medical secretary, medical transcription, pharmacy assistant. **Legal studies:** Paralegal. **Other:** Criminal justice, Information systems management.

Computing on campus. 100 workstations in library, computer center, student center. Online course registration, online library, helpline available.

Student life. Freshman orientation: Mandatory.

Student services. Adult student services, career counseling, services for economically disadvantaged, student employment services, financial aid counseling, placement for graduates.

Contact. E-mail: kathy.clifford@rasmussen.edu
Phone: (507) 625-6556 Fax: (507) 625-6557
Kathy Clifford, Director of Admissions, Rasmussen College: Mankato, 130 Saint Andrews Drive, Mankato, MN 56001

Rasmussen College: St. Cloud

St. Cloud, Minnesota
www.rasmussen.edu **CB code: 3315**

- For-profit 2-year community and career college
- Commuter campus in small city

General. Regionally accredited. **Enrollment:** 904 degree-seeking undergraduates. **Degrees:** 153 associate awarded. **Location:** 60 miles from Minneapolis-St. Paul. **Calendar:** Quarter, extensive summer session. **Full-time faculty:** 15 total. **Part-time faculty:** 9 total.

Basis for selection. Open admission, but selective for some programs. The Medical Laboratory Technician, Surgical Technologist, and Practical Nursing AAS programs have selective admissions requirements, including entrance examinations, background checks, and health screenings. Some additional programs in allied health, justice studies, and education require students to complete a background check. **Adult students:** SAT/ACT scores not required.

2008-2009 Financial aid. Need-based: Need-based aid available for part-time students.

Application procedures. Admission: No deadline. $60 fee. Admission notification on a rolling basis. **Financial aid:** No deadline. FAFSA, institutional form required. Applicants notified on a rolling basis.

Academics. Special study options: Distance learning, double major, honors, independent study, internships. **Credit/placement by examination:** AP, CLEP, institutional tests. 45 credit hours maximum toward associate degree, 90 toward bachelor's. Credit limited to specific programs and to courses for which examinations are available. 50% of a student's program credits must be completed through coursework at Rasmussen College. **Support services:** Learning center, remedial instruction, study skills assistance, tutoring, writing center.

Majors. Business: Accounting, administrative services, business admin. **Computer sciences:** Web page design. **Family/consumer sciences:** Child care. **Health:** Clinical lab technology, licensed practical nurse, massage therapy, medical assistant, medical records technology, medical secretary, medical transcription, pharmacy assistant, surgical technology. **Legal studies:** Paralegal. **Other:** Criminal justice, Information systems management.

Computing on campus. 100 workstations in library, computer center, student center. Online course registration, online library, helpline, wireless network available.

Student life. Freshman orientation: Mandatory.

Student services. Adult student services, career counseling, services for economically disadvantaged, student employment services, financial aid counseling, placement for graduates.

Contact. E-mail: andrea.peters@rasmussen.edu
Phone: (320) 251-5600 Toll-free number: (800) 852-0460
Fax: (320) 251-3702
Andrea Peters, Director of Admissions, Rasmussen College: St. Cloud, 226 Park Avenue South, St. Cloud, MN 56301-3713

Ridgewater College
Willmar, Minnesota
www.ridgewater.edu **CB code: 6949**

- Public 2-year community and technical college
- Commuter campus in large town

General. Founded in 1961. Regionally accredited. Two campuses: Willmar and Hutchinson. **Enrollment:** 3,676 degree-seeking undergraduates. **Degrees:** 528 associate awarded. **Location:** 100 miles from Minneapolis-St. Paul. **Calendar:** Semester, limited summer session. **Special facilities:** Natural wooded prairie and wetlands areas for biological study, nursing simulation centers.

Student profile. Among degree-seeking undergraduates, 51% enrolled in a transfer program, 49% enrolled in a vocational program, 891 enrolled as first-time, first-year students.

Basis for selection. Open admission, but selective for some programs. Special requirements for practical nursing, registered nursing, radiologic technology, chemical dependency counseling, veterinary technology, and post-secondary programs. An interview is recommended for the law enforcement, nursing, radiologic technology, and veterinary technology programs.

High school preparation. Chemistry and mathematics are recommended for mathematics, science, and health science majors.

2008-2009 Annual costs. Tuition/fees: $4,606; $4,606 out-of-state. Per-credit charge: $136 in-state; $136 out-of-state. In-state and out-of-state tuition rates are the same. Books/supplies: $800. Personal expenses: $1,660.

2008-2009 Financial aid. Need-based: 33% of total undergraduate aid awarded as scholarships/grants, 67% as loans/jobs. Need-based aid available for part-time students. Work-study available nights, weekends and for part-time students. **Additional information:** Special funds are available for adult transfer students returning or continuing education after a 7-year absence from academic training. ALLISS grants provide reimbursement for one class, up to five credits for one semester.

Application procedures. Admission: Priority date 8/1; no deadline. $20 fee. Application must be submitted on paper. Admission notification on a rolling basis. **Financial aid:** No deadline. FAFSA, institutional form required. Applicants notified on a rolling basis.

Academics. Four-year baccalaureate degrees including business administration, early childhood education and criminal justice are taught by state universities and are available on campus. **Special study options:** Cooperative education, distance learning, dual enrollment of high school students, internships, liberal arts/career combination, student-designed major, study abroad. Bachelor's degree programs available on campus. License preparation in nursing, paramedic, real estate. **Credit/placement by examination:** AP, CLEP, institutional tests. 20 credit hours maximum toward associate degree. **Support services:** GED test center, learning center, pre-admission summer program, reduced course load, remedial instruction, study skills assistance, tutoring.

Majors. Agriculture: General, agribusiness operations, agronomy, business, dairy, economics, farm/ranch, production. **Biology:** General, conservation. **Business:** General, accounting, management information systems, marketing, retailing, sales/distribution. **Communications:** General, journalism, media studies, publishing. **Communications technology:** Desktop publishing. **Computer sciences:** General, computer science, networking, web page design, webmaster. **Construction:** Carpentry, electrician. **Education:** General, adult/continuing, art, business, elementary, health, instructional media, mathematics, middle, multi-level teacher, music, physical, science, secondary, special, teacher assistance, voc/tech. **Engineering technology:** General, CAD/CADD, drafting, electrical, instrumentation, metallurgical. **Family/consumer sciences:** Family studies. **Health:** Athletic training, health care admin, medical assistant, medical radiologic technology/radiation therapy, medical records technology, medical secretary, nursing (RN), substance abuse counseling, veterinary technology/assistant. **History:** General. **Interdisciplinary:** Math/computer science. **Legal studies:** Legal secretary, prelaw. **Liberal arts:** Arts/sciences. **Math:** General. **Mechanic/repair:** Auto body, automotive. **Parks/recreation:** General, health/fitness. **Personal/culinary services:** Cosmetic. **Physical sciences:** Chemistry, geology. **Production:** Machine tool, tool and die, welding. **Protective services:** Criminal justice, police science. **Psychology:** General. **Public administration:** Social work. **Social sciences:** General, criminology, economics, political science, sociology, urban studies. **Visual/performing arts:** Art, commercial photography, photography, studio arts. **Other:** Activity director, Nondestructive testing technology.

Computing on campus. 1,000 workstations in library, computer center. Commuter students can connect to campus network. Online course registration, helpline, repair service, wireless network available.

Student life. Freshman orientation: Mandatory. **Housing:** Apartment buildings are adjacent to campus. **Activities:** Choral groups, drama, music ensembles, musical theater, student government, student newspaper, CIA, multicultural club, Phi Theta Kappa, PRISM (GLBTQ organization), Ridgewater Democrats, Ridgewater Republicans.

Athletics. NJCAA. **Intercollegiate:** Baseball M, basketball, football (tackle) M, golf, softball W, volleyball W, wrestling M. **Intramural:** Basketball, football (non-tackle) M, skiing, softball, volleyball, weight lifting. **Team name:** Warriors.

Student services. Adult student services, alcohol/substance abuse counseling, career counseling, services for economically disadvantaged, student employment services, financial aid counseling, health services, minority student services, personal counseling, placement for graduates, veterans' counselor. **Physically disabled:** Services for visually, speech, hearing impaired. **Transfer:** Transfer adviser, college fairs on campus for students transferring to 4-year colleges.

Contact. E-mail: info@ridgewater.edu
Phone: (320) 222-5976 Toll-free number: (800) 722-1151
Fax: (320) 222-5216
Sally Kerfeld, Director of Admissions, Ridgewater College, 2101 15th Avenue Northwest, Willmar, MN 56201

Riverland Community College
Austin, Minnesota
www.riverland.edu **CB code: 6017**

- Public 2-year community and technical college
- Commuter campus in large town

General. Founded in 1996. Regionally accredited. **Enrollment:** 3,279 degree-seeking undergraduates. **Degrees:** 356 associate awarded. **Location:** 90 miles from Minneapolis-St. Paul. **Calendar:** Semester, limited summer session. **Full-time faculty:** 97 total; 7% have terminal degrees, 3% minority, 41% women. **Part-time faculty:** 77 total; 10% have terminal degrees, 1% minority, 46% women. **Class size:** 68% < 20, 29% 20-39, 2% 40-49, less than 1% 50-99.

Student profile. Among degree-seeking undergraduates, 45% enrolled in a transfer program, 55% enrolled in a vocational program, 3% already have a bachelor's degree or higher, 1,596 enrolled as first-time, first-year students.

Part-time:	59%	**25 or older:**	46%
Out-of-state:	2%	**Live on campus:**	3%
Women:	54%		

Transfer out. Colleges most students transferred to 2008: Mankato State University, Winona State University, Southwest Minnesota State University.

Basis for selection. Open admission, but selective for some programs. Special requirements for human services, nursing, corrections, radiography, and construction electrician. **Homeschooled:** Transcript of courses and grades required.

High school preparation. Chemistry required of nursing applicants.

2008-2009 Annual costs. Tuition/fees: $4,701; $4,701 out-of-state. Per-credit charge: $138. In-state and out-of-state tuition rates are the same. Room/board: $2,640. Books/supplies: $800. Personal expenses: $3,990.

2007-2008 Financial aid. Need-based: Average scholarship/grant was $2,633; average loan $3,248. 37% of total undergraduate aid awarded as scholarships/grants, 63% as loans/jobs. Need-based aid available for part-time students. Work-study available for part-time students. **Non-need-based:** Scholarships awarded for alumni affiliation, art, job skills, leadership, music/drama, state residency. **Additional information:** One class tuition-free for Minnesota residents over 25 who have not attended college for at least 7 years.

Application procedures. Admission: Closing date 8/31. $20 fee, may be waived for applicants with need. Admission notification on a rolling basis. **Financial aid:** Priority date 5/15; no closing date. FAFSA required. Applicants notified on a rolling basis; must reply within 5 week(s) of notification.

Academics. Special study options: Cross-registration, distance learning, double major, dual enrollment of high school students, ESL, internships, liberal arts/career combination, study abroad, weekend college. Bachelor's degree programs available on campus. License preparation in nursing, radiology, real estate. **Credit/placement by examination:** AP, CLEP, institutional tests. 20 credit hours maximum toward associate degree. **Support services:** Learning center, reduced course load, remedial instruction, study skills assistance, tutoring, writing center.

Majors. Business: Accounting, administrative services, management science. **Computer sciences:** General, LAN/WAN management. **Engineering:** Software. **Health:** Medical radiologic technology/radiation therapy, medical secretary, nursing (RN). **Legal studies:** Legal secretary. **Liberal arts:** Arts/sciences. **Mechanic/repair:** Automotive. **Protective services:** Police science. **Public administration:** Human services.

Most popular majors. Business/marketing 6%, health sciences 26%, liberal arts 53%, security/protective services 7%.

Computing on campus. 250 workstations in library, computer center, student center. Online course registration, helpline, wireless network available.

Student life. Freshman orientation: Mandatory. **Housing:** Coed dorms, wellness housing available. $350 partly refundable deposit, deadline 9/1. College foundation-owned student housing. **Activities:** Concert band, choral groups, drama, music ensembles, musical theater, student government, student newspaper, diversity club, DEEDS (Human Service) club, Criminal Justice Society, RIOT (Christian Fellowship) club, Amnesty International.

Athletics. NJCAA. **Intercollegiate:** Baseball M, basketball, golf, softball W, volleyball W. **Intramural:** Basketball, football (tackle) M, weight lifting. **Team name:** Blue Devils.

Student services. Career counseling, services for economically disadvantaged, student employment services, financial aid counseling, minority student services, on-campus daycare, personal counseling, placement for graduates, veterans' counselor, women's services. **Physically disabled:** Services for visually, speech, hearing impaired. **Transfer:** Transfer adviser, college fairs on campus for students transferring to 4-year colleges.

Contact. E-mail: admissions@riverland.edu
Phone: (507) 433-0517 Toll-free number: (800) 247-5039
Fax: (507) 433-0515
Dani Heiny, Admissions, Riverland Community College, 1900 Eighth Avenue, NW, Austin, MN 55912-1407

Rochester Community and Technical College

Rochester, Minnesota
www.roch.edu **CB code: 6610**

- Public 2-year community and technical college
- Commuter campus in small city

General. Founded in 1915. Regionally accredited. 2 + 2 and other career pathways spanning certificate to Master's degree programs through a partnership with Winona State University. **Enrollment:** 3,239 full-time, degree-seeking students. **Degrees:** 833 associate awarded. **Location:** 80 miles from Minneapolis-St. Paul. **Calendar:** Semester, limited summer session. **Full-time faculty:** 147 total; 55% have terminal degrees, 8% minority, 60% women. **Part-time faculty:** 156 total; 3% minority, 55% women. **Class size:** 28% < 20, 68% 20-39, 3% 40-49, less than 1% 50-99. **Special facilities:** Observatory, dental clinic, horticulture technology facility, regional sports center.

Student profile.

Out-of-state:	5%	**25 or older:**	40%

Transfer out. 32% of students enrolled in the transfer program go on to 4-year colleges. **Colleges most students transferred to 2008:** Winona State University, Minnesota State College: Mankato, University of Minnesota.

Basis for selection. Open admission, but selective for some programs. Admission to allied health and technology programs based on course work, class rank, institutional placement test scores. **Adult students:** SAT/ACT scores not required.

High school preparation. Biology, chemistry, algebra and/or English required for some programs.

2008-2009 Annual costs. Tuition/fees: $4,820; $4,820 out-of-state. Per-credit charge: $138 in-state; $138 out-of-state. Books/supplies: $1,000. Personal expenses: $3,475.

Financial aid. Need-based: Need-based aid available for part-time students. Work-study available nights, weekends and for part-time students.

Application procedures. Admission: Priority date 6/1; deadline 8/10 (postmark date). $20 fee, may be waived for applicants with need. Admission notification on a rolling basis. **Financial aid:** Priority date 4/15; no closing date. FAFSA required. Applicants notified on a rolling basis.

Academics. Special study options: Combined bachelor's/graduate degree, distance learning, dual enrollment of high school students, honors, independent study, internships, study abroad. Bachelor's degree programs available on campus. License preparation in dental hygiene, nursing, paramedic. **Credit/placement by examination:** AP, CLEP, institutional tests. 16 credit hours maximum toward associate degree. **Support services:** Learning center, reduced course load, remedial instruction, study skills assistance, tutoring, writing center.

Majors. Agriculture: Equine science, greenhouse operations, horticultural science, turf management. **Biology:** Biomedical sciences. **Business:** Accounting, administrative services, business admin, retailing, special products marketing. **Communications:** Digital media, media studies. **Computer sciences:** General, computer science, web page design. **Conservation:** Environmental science. **Education:** Music, teacher assistance. **Engineering:** General. **Engineering technology:** CAD/CADD, computer systems, mechanical. **Family/consumer sciences:** Child care. **Health:** Cardiovascular technology, dental assistant, dental hygiene, electroencephalograph technology, EMT paramedic, health services, medical records technology, medical secretary, mental health services, nursing (RN), radiologic technology/medical imaging, surgical technology, veterinary technology/assistant. **Interdisciplinary:** Natural sciences. **Liberal arts:** Arts/sciences. **Parks/recreation:** Sports admin. **Protective services:** Criminal justice, police science. **Visual/performing arts:** Graphic design, music management, music theory/composition. **Other:** Professional studies.

Most popular majors. Business/marketing 8%, health sciences 32%, liberal arts 43%, security/protective services 7%.

Computing on campus. 390 workstations in library, computer center. Commuter students can connect to campus network. Online course registration, online library, helpline available.

Student life. Freshman orientation: Available. Preregistration for classes offered. **Housing:** Non-college-affiliated student-only housing available near campus. **Activities:** Bands, choral groups, dance, drama, international student organizations, music ensembles, musical theater, radio station, student government, student newspaper, student senate, ECHO (student newspaper), Asian student association, African student organization, Muslim student association, environmentalism club, Armed Forces and Veterans club, Circle of Friends-GLBTQA, international student association, law enforcement club.

Athletics. NJCAA. **Intercollegiate:** Baseball M, basketball, football (tackle) M, golf, soccer W, softball W, volleyball W, wrestling M. **Intramural:** Badminton, basketball, football (non-tackle), golf, soccer, softball, volleyball. **Team name:** Yellowjackets.

Student services. Alcohol/substance abuse counseling, career counseling, services for economically disadvantaged, financial aid counseling, health services, minority student services, on-campus daycare, personal counseling, veterans' counselor. **Physically disabled:** Services for visually, speech, hearing impaired. **Transfer:** Pre-admission transcript evaluation for new students. Transfer adviser, college fairs on campus for students transferring to 4-year colleges.

Contact. Phone: (507) 285-7265 Fax: (507) 280-3529
Holly Bigelow, Registrar, Rochester Community and Technical College, 851 30th Avenue SE, Rochester, MN 55904-4999

St. Cloud Technical College

St. Cloud, Minnesota
www.sctc.edu **CB code: 1986**

- Public 2-year technical college
- Commuter campus in small city

General. Founded in 1948. Regionally accredited. **Enrollment:** 3,451 degree-seeking undergraduates; 479 non-degree-seeking students. **Degrees:** 397 associate awarded. **Location:** 65 miles from Minneapolis-St. Paul. **Calendar:** Semester, limited summer session. **Full-time faculty:** 115 total. **Part-time faculty:** 83 total.

Student profile. Among degree-seeking undergraduates, 17% enrolled in a transfer program, 83% enrolled in a vocational program, 936 enrolled as first-time, first-year students.

Part-time:	30%	**Asian American:**	1%
Out-of-state:	2%	**Hispanic American:**	1%
Women:	51%	**Native American:**	1%
African American:	3%	**25 or older:**	24%

Transfer out. **Colleges most students transferred to 2008:** St. Cloud State University, Bemidji State University, University of Minnesota.

Basis for selection. Open admission, but selective for some programs. Paramedicine applicants must complete EMT basic and emergency cardiac care courses prior to acceptance. Echocardiography, sonography, cardiovascular technician, practical nursing, dental assisting, and dental hygiene all require pre-requisite courses to be completed prior to admission to the major. Programs such as echocardiography, sonography and cardiovascular technician require that students are interviewed as part of the acceptance process. **Homeschooled:** Proof of high school graduation required. **Learning Disabled:** Students with developmental disabilities may take the course placement test with accommodations.

High school preparation. Recommended units include English 2, mathematics 2, science 1 (laboratory 1). Mathematics and science classes recommended for technical programs; algebra required for civil engineering; dental hygiene applicants must have all science and nutrition coursework completed; anatomy and physiology, college algebra, and physics required for echocardiography, sonography, and cardiovascular technology.

2008-2009 Annual costs. Tuition/fees: $4,614; $4,614 out-of-state. Per-credit charge: $137. In-state and out-of-state tuition rates are the same. Books/supplies: $950. Personal expenses: $1,000.

2007-2008 Financial aid. **Need-based:** 56% of total undergraduate aid awarded as scholarships/grants, 44% as loans/jobs. Need-based aid available for part-time students. Work-study available nights, weekends and for part-time students. **Non-need-based:** Scholarships awarded for academics, leadership, state residency.

Application procedures. **Admission:** Closing date 8/7 (postmark date). $20 fee. Application must be submitted on paper. Admission notification on a rolling basis beginning on or about 10/7. **Financial aid:** No deadline. FAFSA, institutional form required. Applicants notified on a rolling basis starting 6/1.

Academics. **Special study options:** Accelerated study, cooperative education, cross-registration, distance learning, double major, dual enrollment of high school students, independent study, internships. Bachelor's degree programs available on campus. License preparation in dental hygiene, nursing, paramedic, real estate. **Credit/placement by examination:** AP, CLEP, institutional tests. **Support services:** Learning center, pre-admission summer program, reduced course load, remedial instruction, study skills assistance, tutoring, writing center.

Majors. **Business:** Accounting, banking/financial services, business admin, executive assistant, sales/distribution. **Communications:** Advertising. **Computer sciences:** Networking, programming. **Construction:** Carpentry, electrician, plumbing. **Education:** Teacher assistance. **Engineering technology:** Architectural drafting, CAD/CADD, civil, electrical, instrumentation, mechanical drafting, water quality. **Family/consumer sciences:** Child care. **Health:** Cardiovascular technology, dental assistant, dental hygiene, EMT paramedic, licensed practical nurse, medical records technology, sonography, surgical technology. **Legal studies:** Legal secretary. **Mechanic/repair:** Auto body, automotive, heating/ac/refrig, medium/heavy vehicle. **Production:** Machine tool.

Most popular majors. Business/marketing 22%, communications/journalism 7%, computer/information sciences 6%, engineering/engineering technologies 14%, health sciences 42%, trade and industry 6%.

Computing on campus. PC or laptop required. 468 workstations in library, computer center, student center. Commuter students can connect to campus network. Online course registration, helpline, repair service, wireless network available.

Student life. **Freshman orientation:** Mandatory. **Housing:** Privately-owned dormitory next to campus. Housing also available at St. Cloud State University. **Activities:** Student government, student newspaper, TV station, Campus Crusade for Christ, Newman Center, Delta Kappa Phi.

Athletics. NJCAA. **Intercollegiate:** Baseball M, basketball, softball W, volleyball W. **Intramural:** Basketball, football (non-tackle), football (tackle), golf, ice hockey, racquetball, soccer, softball, tennis, track and field, volleyball. **Team name:** Cyclones.

Student services. Adult student services, career counseling, student employment services, financial aid counseling, on-campus daycare, personal counseling, placement for graduates, veterans' counselor. **Physically disabled:** Services for visually, speech, hearing impaired. **Transfer:** Pre-admission transcript evaluation for new students. Transfer adviser for students transferring to 4-year colleges.

Contact. E-mail: enroll@sctc.edu
Phone: (320) 308-5089 Toll-free number: (800) 222-1009 ext. 5089
Fax: (320) 308-5981
Jodi Elness, Director of Enrollment Management, St. Cloud Technical College, 1540 Northway Drive, St. Cloud, MN 56303

St. Paul College

Saint Paul, Minnesota
www.saintpaul.edu **CB code: 0534**

Two-Year Colleges

- Public 2-year community and technical college
- Commuter campus in large city

General. Founded in 1919. Regionally accredited. **Enrollment:** 5,387 degree-seeking undergraduates. **Degrees:** 283 associate awarded. **Calendar:** Semester, limited summer session. **Full-time faculty:** 115 total; 8% have terminal degrees, 11% minority. **Part-time faculty:** 140 total; 6% minority. **Class size:** 57% < 20, 41% 20-39, 2% 40-49.

Student profile. Among degree-seeking undergraduates, 27% enrolled in a transfer program, 76% enrolled in a vocational program, 978 enrolled as first-time, first-year students, 586 transferred in from other institutions.

Part-time:	62%	**Women:**	51%
Out-of-state:	1%	**25 or older:**	56%

Transfer out. **Colleges most students transferred to 2008:** Metropoltian State University, Century Community and Technical College, Inver Hills Community College.

Basis for selection. Open admission, but selective for some programs. ACT considered for placement if submitted; scores must be received by July 1. Interview recommended for selected programs. **Homeschooled:** Transcript of courses and grades required.

High school preparation. College-preparatory program recommended. Recommended units include English 3, mathematics 2, social studies 3 and history 3.

2008-2009 Annual costs. Tuition/fees: $4,399; $4,399 out-of-state. Per-credit charge: $136 in-state; $136 out-of-state. In-state and out-of-state tuition rates are the same. Books/supplies: $800. Personal expenses: $1,640.

2008-2009 Financial aid. **Need-based:** Average scholarship/grant was $2,633. 46% of total undergraduate aid awarded as scholarships/grants, 54% as loans/jobs. Need-based aid available for part-time students. Work-study available nights and for part-time students. **Non-need-based:** Scholarships awarded for leadership.

Application procedures. **Admission:** Priority date 7/1; no deadline. $20 fee. Application must be submitted online. Admission notification on a rolling basis. **Financial aid:** No deadline. FAFSA required. Applicants notified on a rolling basis starting 6/1.

Academics. **Special study options:** Combined bachelor's/graduate degree, distance learning, dual enrollment of high school students, ESL, honors, internships. License preparation in nursing. **Credit/placement by examination:** AP, CLEP, IB, institutional tests. **Support services:** Learning center, reduced course load, remedial instruction, study skills assistance, tutoring.

Majors. **Business:** General, accounting, administrative services, entrepreneurial studies, hospitality admin, human resources, international marketing, logistics, management information systems, office management. **Communications technology:** Animation/special effects. **Computer sciences:** Applications programming, computer graphics, computer science, networking, programming. **Construction:** Site management. **Engineering technology:** Biomedical, electrical, manufacturing, surveying. **Family/consumer sciences:** Child care. **Foreign languages:** Sign language interpretation. **Health:** Athletic training, clinical lab technology, licensed practical nurse, massage therapy, medical records technology, office assistant, respiratory therapy technology. **Liberal arts:** Arts/sciences. **Mechanic/repair:** Auto body, automotive, industrial. **Personal/culinary services:** Aesthetician, chef training, cosmetic. **Science technology:** Chemical.

Most popular majors. Business/marketing 18%, engineering/engineering technologies 8%, family/consumer sciences 6%, foreign language 10%, health sciences 18%, liberal arts 17%, personal/culinary services 8%.

Computing on campus. 1,000 workstations in library, computer center. Commuter students can connect to campus network. Online course registration, online library, helpline, repair service, wireless network available.

Student life. **Freshman orientation:** Available. Preregistration for classes offered. **Activities:** Student government, Business Professionals of America, Vocational-Industrial Clubs of America, Student Senate, African Heritage student association, Hispanic student association, Asian student association.

Student services. Adult student services, alcohol/substance abuse counseling, career counseling, student employment services, financial aid counseling, on-campus daycare, personal counseling, placement for graduates, veterans' counselor. **Physically disabled:** Services for visually, speech, hearing impaired. **Learning disabled:** Comprehensive services available. **Transfer:** Pre-admission transcript evaluation for new students. Transfer center, transfer adviser, college fairs on campus for students transferring to 4-year colleges.

Contact. E-mail: admissions@saintpaul.edu
Phone: (651) 846-1555 Toll-free number: (800) 227-6029
Fax: (651) 846-1468
Sarah Carrico, Director of Office of Enrollment Services, St. Paul College, 235 Marshall Avenue, Saint Paul, MN 55102-1800

South Central College
North Mankato, Minnesota
www.southcentral.edu **CB code: 7124**

- Public 2-year community and technical college
- Commuter campus in large town

General. Founded in 1946. Regionally accredited. Campuses in North Mankato and Faribault, MN. **Enrollment:** 3,424 degree-seeking undergraduates. **Degrees:** 326 associate awarded. **Location:** 80 miles from Minneapolis-St. Paul. **Calendar:** Semester, limited summer session. **Full-time faculty:** 123 total. **Part-time faculty:** 53 total.

Basis for selection. Open admission. **Homeschooled:** State high school equivalency certificate required.

2008-2009 Annual costs. Tuition/fees: $4,515. Per-credit charge: $135. Books/supplies: $650.

2007-2008 Financial aid. **Need-based:** Need-based aid available for part-time students. Work-study available nights and for part-time students.

Application procedures. **Admission:** $20 fee. Application must be submitted on paper. Admission notification on a rolling basis. **Financial aid:** Priority date 5/1; no closing date. FAFSA, institutional form required. Applicants notified on a rolling basis starting 6/1.

Academics. **Special study options:** Distance learning, dual enrollment of high school students, honors, independent study, internships, liberal arts/career combination. License preparation in nursing, paramedic. **Credit/placement by examination:** AP, CLEP, IB, institutional tests. **Support services:** GED preparation and test center, learning center, reduced course load, remedial instruction, study skills assistance, tutoring, writing center.

Majors. **Agriculture:** General, animal sciences, equipment technology, production. **Business:** Accounting, accounting technology, administrative services, business admin, marketing, restaurant/food services. **Communications technology:** Graphic/printing. **Computer sciences:** Data processing, information technology, LAN/WAN management. **Construction:** General, site management. **Engineering technology:** Civil, drafting, heat/ac/refrig, occupational safety. **Family/consumer sciences:** Child development. **Health:** Clinical lab technology, dental assistant, EMT paramedic, licensed practical nurse, nursing (RN). **Legal studies:** Legal secretary. **Liberal arts:** Arts/sciences. **Mechanic/repair:** Auto body, automotive, heating/ac/refrig. **Personal/culinary services:** Culinary arts, restaurant/catering. **Production:** Cabinetmaking/millwright, machine tool. **Public administration:** Human services. **Visual/performing arts:** Commercial/advertising art, graphic design. **Other:** Mechatronics.

Computing on campus. 725 workstations in library, computer center, student center. Commuter students can connect to campus network. Online course registration, online library, helpline, wireless network available.

Student life. **Freshman orientation:** Mandatory. **Activities:** Music ensembles, student government, student newspaper.

Student services. Alcohol/substance abuse counseling, career counseling, student employment services, financial aid counseling, on-campus daycare, personal counseling, placement for graduates, veterans' counselor. **Physically disabled:** Services for visually, speech, hearing impaired. **Transfer:** Pre-admission transcript evaluation for new students.

Contact. E-mail: admissions@southcentral.edu
Phone: (507) 389-7451 Toll-free number: (800) 722-9359
Fax: (507) 388-9951
Bev Herda, Admissions Director, South Central College, 1920 Lee Boulevard, North Mankato, MN 56003

Vermilion Community College
Ely, Minnesota
www.vcc.edu **CB code: 6194**

- Public 2-year community and technical college
- Residential campus in small town

General. Founded in 1922. Regionally accredited. **Enrollment:** 610 degree-seeking undergraduates. **Degrees:** 113 associate awarded. **Location:** 100 miles from Duluth. **Calendar:** Semester, limited summer session. **Full-time faculty:** 22 total; 4% minority, 32% women. **Part-time faculty:** 18 total; 6% minority, 39% women. **Special facilities:** 40-acre outdoor learning center near Boundary Waters Canoe Area.

Student profile.

Out-of-state:	5%	**Live on campus:**	40%
25 or older:	18%		

Basis for selection. Open admission. Interview required for law enforcement, natural resources, parks and recreation students.

2008-2009 Annual costs. Tuition/fees: $4,511; $5,498 out-of-state. Per-credit charge: $132 in-state; $164 out-of-state. Various reciprocity agreements with some neighboring states provide tuition reduction to out-of-state students. Room/board: $4,780. Books/supplies: $600. Personal expenses: $1,500.

Financial aid. **Need-based:** Need-based aid available for part-time students. Work-study available nights and weekends.

Application procedures. **Admission:** No deadline. $20 fee, may be waived for applicants with need. Admission notification on a rolling basis beginning on or about 1/1. **Financial aid:** No deadline. FAFSA, institutional form required. Applicants notified on a rolling basis starting 4/1.

Academics. **Special study options:** Cooperative education, cross-registration, dual enrollment of high school students, honors, independent study, internships, liberal arts/career combination. **Credit/placement by examination:** CLEP. **Support services:** Learning center, pre-admission summer program, reduced course load, remedial instruction, tutoring.

Majors. **Biology:** General. **Business:** General, accounting, business admin. **Communications:** General, journalism. **Conservation:** General, environmental studies, fisheries, forest resources, forestry, management/policy, wildlife. **Education:** General, art, biology, business, chemistry, computer, elementary, geography, health, history, kindergarten/preschool, mathematics, middle, physics, science, secondary, social studies. **Engineering:** Civil. **Family/consumer sciences:** General. **Health:** Environmental health, predental, premedicine, preveterinary. **History:** General. **Legal studies:** Prelaw. **Parks/recreation:** General, facilities management. **Physical sciences:** General, astronomy, chemistry, geology, physics. **Protective services:** Criminal justice, law enforcement admin, police science. **Psychology:** General. **Social sciences:** General, criminology, geography, political science. **Transportation:** Aviation, aviation management. **Visual/performing arts:** Dramatic.

Computing on campus. Dormitories linked to campus network.

Student life. **Freshman orientation:** Mandatory. 6 different programs from April through start of classes. **Housing:** Coed dorms available. **Activities:** Choral groups, drama, musical theater, student government, student newspaper.

Athletics. NJCAA. **Intercollegiate:** Baseball M, basketball, football (tackle) M, softball W, volleyball W. **Intramural:** Basketball, bowling, softball, tennis, volleyball. **Team name:** Ironmen, Ironwomen.

Student services. Career counseling, student employment services, personal counseling, placement for graduates, veterans' counselor. **Physically disabled:** Services for visually, speech, hearing impaired. **Transfer:** Transfer adviser, college fairs on campus for students transferring to 4-year colleges.

Contact. E-mail: admissions@vcc.edu
Phone: (218) 235-2191 Toll-free number: (800) 657-3608
Fax: (218) 235-2173
Jeff Nelson, Director of Enrollment Services, Vermilion Community College, 1900 East Camp Street, Ely, MN 55731-9989

White Earth Tribal and Community College
Mahnomen, Minnesota
www.wetcc.org

- Private 2-year community college
- Rural community

General. Location: 70 miles east of Fargo/Moorhead and 65 miles west of Bemidji, MN. **Calendar:** Semester.

Annual costs/financial aid. Tuition/fees (2008-2009): $3,050. Books/supplies: $850. Personal expenses: $1,350.

Contact. Phone: (218) 936-5731
Registrar, 202 South Main Street, Mahnomen, MN 56557

Mississippi

Antonelli College: Hattiesburg

Hattiesburg, Mississippi
www.antonellicollege.edu **CB code: 3195**

- For-profit 2-year branch campus and technical college
- Large town
- Interview required

General. Accredited by ACCSCT. **Enrollment:** 400 degree-seeking undergraduates. **Degrees:** 110 associate awarded. **Location:** 90 miles from Jacksonville. **Calendar:** Continuous. **Full-time faculty:** 18 total. **Part-time faculty:** 10 total.

Basis for selection. Open admission. **Homeschooled:** State high school equivalency certificate required.

2008-2009 Annual costs. Tuition/fees: $12,120. Books/supplies: $1,200.

Application procedures. Admission: No deadline. $75 fee, may be waived for applicants with need. Application must be submitted on paper. Admission notification on a rolling basis beginning on or about 8/17.

Academics. Special study options: Dual enrollment of high school students, internships. **Credit/placement by examination:** CLEP. **Support services:** GED preparation.

Majors. Computer sciences: General.

Contact. E-mail: karen.gautreau@antonellicollege.edu
Phone: (601) 583-4100 Fax: (601) 583-0839
Jarita Large, Director of Admissions, Antonelli College: Hattiesburg, 1500 North 31st Avenue, Hattiesburg, MS 39401

Antonelli College: Jackson

Jackson, Mississippi
www.antonellicollege.edu **CB code: 3193**

- For-profit 2-year technical college
- Commuter campus in small city

General. Accredited by ACCSCT. **Enrollment:** 287 degree-seeking undergraduates. **Degrees:** 99 associate awarded. **Calendar:** Quarter. **Full-time faculty:** 18 total. **Part-time faculty:** 20 total.

Basis for selection. Open admission.

2008-2009 Annual costs. Tuition/fees: $12,120. Books/supplies: $1,200.

Application procedures. Admission: No deadline. $75 fee. **Financial aid:** No deadline.

Academics. Credit/placement by examination: CLEP, institutional tests. 14 credit hours maximum toward associate degree. **Support services:** Study skills assistance, tutoring.

Majors. Business: Accounting, office technology. **Computer sciences:** Computer graphics, data entry, networking, security, web page design, webmaster. **Health:** Insurance coding, massage therapy, medical assistant, medical transcription. **Legal studies:** General. **Visual/performing arts:** Graphic design, interior design.

Computing on campus. 100 workstations in library, computer center. Wireless network available.

Student life. Freshman orientation: Mandatory. Preregistration for classes offered. Held 2 days prior to start of class. **Activities:** Student newspaper.

Student services. Student employment services, financial aid counseling, placement for graduates.

Contact. Phone: (601) 362-9991
Adam Grosch, Admissions Director, Antonelli College: Jackson, 2323 Lakeland Drive, Jackson, MS 39232

Blue Cliff College: Gulfport

Gulfport, Mississippi
www.bluecliffcollege.com

- For-profit 2-year technical college
- Small city
- Interview required

General. Accredited by ACCSCT. Medical assisting program graduates eligible to sit for the AMA exam. Massage therapy program graduates eligible for provisional license for up to six months until they take national boards. Fees for these exams included in tuition. **Enrollment:** 142 degree-seeking undergraduates. **Degrees:** 1 associate awarded. **Calendar:** Quarter, extensive summer session. **Full-time faculty:** 10 total. **Part-time faculty:** 6 total.

Basis for selection. Open admission. WONDERLIC test required. **Homeschooled:** Transcript of courses and grades required.

2008-2009 Financial aid. All financial aid based on need. Need-based aid available for part-time students.

Application procedures. Admission: No deadline. $100 fee. Application must be submitted on paper. **Financial aid:** FAFSA required.

Academics. Credit/placement by examination: CLEP. **Support services:** Tutoring.

Majors. Health: Massage therapy, office assistant.

Computing on campus. 20 workstations in library, computer center, student center. Commuter students can connect to campus network. Online library, helpline, wireless network available.

Student life. Freshman orientation: Mandatory.

Student services. Career counseling, student employment services, financial aid counseling.

Contact. Phone: (288) 896-9727 Fax: (228) 896-8659
Blue Cliff College: Gulfport, 12251 Bernard Parkway, Gulfport, MS 39503

Coahoma Community College

Clarksdale, Mississippi
www.coahomacc.edu **CB code: 1126**

- Public 2-year community college
- Commuter campus in large town

General. Founded in 1949. Regionally accredited. **Enrollment:** 2,215 degree-seeking undergraduates. **Degrees:** 199 associate awarded. **Location:** 65 miles from Memphis, Tennessee. **Calendar:** Semester, limited summer session. **Full-time faculty:** 53 total. **Part-time faculty:** 68 total.

Transfer out. Colleges most students transferred to 2008: Alcorn State University, Delta State University, Jackson State University, Mississippi Valley State University, University of Mississippi.

Basis for selection. Open admission, but selective for some programs. High school record most important for admission to degree programs. Open admissions to vocational programs. Limited admission to associate degree nursing, licensed practical nursing, and respiratory therapy. ACT/SAT required for nursing. Interview required for nursing students; audition required for music students. **Homeschooled:** Transcript of courses and grades, letter of recommendation (nonparent) required.

High school preparation. College-preparatory program required. Recommended units include English 4, mathematics 3, social studies 2, science 3 (laboratory 3) and foreign language 1.

2008-2009 Annual costs. Tuition/fees: $1,800; $4,700 out-of-state. Per-credit charge: $90. Room/board: $3,514. Books/supplies: $800. Personal expenses: $700.

2008-2009 Financial aid. All financial aid based on need. Need-based aid available for part-time students.

Application procedures. Admission: No deadline. No application fee. Admission notification on a rolling basis. **Financial aid:** Priority date 4/1; no closing date. FAFSA, institutional form required. Applicants notified on a rolling basis starting 7/1.

Academics. **Special study options:** Distance learning, dual enrollment of high school students. License preparation in nursing. **Credit/placement by examination:** CLEP. **Support services:** GED preparation and test center, reduced course load, remedial instruction, tutoring, writing center.

Majors. **Biology:** General. **Business:** General, accounting, hotel/motel admin, office technology. **Communications:** Broadcast journalism, journalism. **Computer sciences:** General, computer science. **Education:** General, art, business, early childhood, elementary, health, mathematics, music, physical, science, social science. **Engineering technology:** Electrical. **Family/consumer sciences:** Child care. **Health:** Clinical lab science, medical records admin, nursing (RN), predental, premedicine, prenursing, prepharmacy, preveterinary, respiratory therapy technology. **Legal studies:** Prelaw. **Math:** General. **Mechanic/repair:** Industrial. **Parks/recreation:** Sports admin. **Physical sciences:** Chemistry. **Protective services:** Criminal justice. **Public administration:** Social work. **Social sciences:** General. **Visual/performing arts:** General.

Most popular majors. Business/marketing 16%, education 41%, health sciences 15%, public administration/social services 11%.

Computing on campus. Dormitories wired for high-speed internet access and linked to campus network. Online course registration, online library, helpline, wireless network available.

Student life. **Freshman orientation:** Mandatory. Preregistration for classes offered. Semester-long course offered each semester. **Housing:** Single-sex dorms, special housing for disabled, wellness housing available. $100 deposit, deadline 8/1. **Activities:** Bands, choral groups, music ensembles, student government, student newspaper, Baptist student union, Wesley Foundation, Black literary society.

Athletics. NJCAA. **Intercollegiate:** Baseball M, basketball, football (tackle) M, softball W. **Intramural:** Badminton, basketball, bowling, cheerleading W, football (non-tackle) M, football (tackle) M, softball, table tennis, volleyball. **Team name:** Tigers.

Student services. Career counseling, services for economically disadvantaged, financial aid counseling, health services, personal counseling. **Physically disabled:** Services for visually, speech, hearing impaired. **Transfer:** Pre-admission transcript evaluation for new students. Transfer adviser, college fairs on campus for students transferring to 4-year colleges.

Contact. E-mail: wholmes@coahomacc.edu
Phone: (662) 621-4205 Toll-free number: (800) 844-1222
Fax: (800) 844-1222
Wanda Holmes, Director of Admissions, Coahoma Community College, 3240 Friars Point Road, Clarksdale, MS 38614-9799

Copiah-Lincoln Community College

Wesson, Mississippi
www.colin.edu **CB code: 1142**

- Public 2-year community college
- Commuter campus in small town

General. Founded in 1928. Regionally accredited. Branch campuses in Natchez and Simpson County. **Enrollment:** 3,351 degree-seeking undergraduates. **Degrees:** 434 associate awarded. **Location:** 45 miles from Jackson. **Calendar:** Semester, limited summer session. **Full-time faculty:** 113 total. **Part-time faculty:** 79 total. **Special facilities:** Walking trail, golf course. **Partnerships:** Formal partnerships with over 300 local business and industry, health occupation affiliates, government agencies, and public service groups.

Student profile.

Out-of-state:	2%	**Live on campus:**	35%
25 or older:	30%		

Transfer out. **Colleges most students transferred to 2008:** University of Southern Mississippi, Alcorn State University, University of Mississippi, Mississippi State University, Jackson State University.

Basis for selection. Open admission, but selective for some programs. ACT required for certain technology and health occupation professions programs. **Homeschooled:** Transcript of courses and grades required. ACT required.

2008-2009 Annual costs. Tuition/fees: $1,800; $3,600 out-of-state. Per-credit charge: $105 in-state; $180 out-of-state. Housing deposit: $100.00, parking fee: $20.00. Room/board: $2,525. Books/supplies: $800.

2007-2008 Financial aid. **Need-based:** 67% of total undergraduate aid awarded as scholarships/grants, 33% as loans/jobs. Need-based aid available for part-time students. Work-study available nights, weekends and for part-time students. **Non-need-based:** Scholarships awarded for academics, art, athletics, job skills, leadership, music/drama, state residency.

Application procedures. **Admission:** No deadline. No application fee. Admission notification on a rolling basis. **Financial aid:** Priority date 4/1; no closing date. FAFSA required. Applicants notified on a rolling basis starting 4/1; must reply within 2 week(s) of notification.

Academics. **Special study options:** Distance learning, dual enrollment of high school students, honors. License preparation in nursing, paramedic, radiology. **Credit/placement by examination:** AP, CLEP, institutional tests. 12 credit hours maximum toward associate degree. **Support services:** GED preparation and test center, learning center, remedial instruction, study skills assistance, tutoring.

Majors. **Business:** Accounting, administrative services, business admin, hospitality admin, office technology. **Computer sciences:** Data processing, networking. **Conservation:** Wood science. **Engineering technology:** Drafting, electrical. **Health:** Clinical lab science, clinical lab technology, medical radiologic technology/radiation therapy, nursing (RN), respiratory therapy technology. **Liberal arts:** Arts/sciences. **Mechanic/repair:** Automotive, diesel, electronics/electrical. **Personal/culinary services:** Food service. **Production:** Machine tool. **Other:** Oil/Gas technology.

Computing on campus. 1,225 workstations in library, computer center. Dormitories linked to campus network. Online course registration, online library, helpline, student web hosting, wireless network available.

Student life. **Freshman orientation:** Mandatory. Preregistration for classes offered. **Housing:** Guaranteed on-campus for all undergraduates. Single-sex dorms, special housing for disabled, apartments, wellness housing available. $50 deposit. **Activities:** Bands, campus ministries, choral groups, literary magazine, music ensembles, radio station, student government, student newspaper, Baptist student union, Wesley Foundation, student Christian association, African-American studies club,Co-Lin College Republicans.

Athletics. NJCAA. **Intercollegiate:** Baseball M, basketball, cheerleading W, football (tackle) M, golf, soccer, softball W, tennis, track and field M. **Intramural:** Basketball, softball M, volleyball. **Team name:** Wolves.

Student services. Career counseling, services for economically disadvantaged, financial aid counseling, health services, on-campus daycare, personal counseling, veterans' counselor. **Physically disabled:** Services for visually, speech, hearing impaired. **Transfer:** Pre-admission transcript evaluation for new students. College fairs on campus for students transferring to 4-year colleges.

Contact. E-mail: phil.broome@colin.edu
Phone: (601) 643-8307 Fax: (601) 643-8225
Phil Broome, Dean of Administrative Services, Copiah-Lincoln Community College, Box 649, Wesson, MS 39191

East Central Community College

Decatur, Mississippi
www.eccc.edu **CB code: 1196**

- Public 2-year community college
- Commuter campus in rural community

General. Founded in 1928. Regionally accredited. **Enrollment:** 2,395 degree-seeking undergraduates. **Degrees:** 378 associate awarded. **Location:** 30 miles from Meridian, 85 miles from Jackson. **Calendar:** Semester, limited summer session. **Full-time faculty:** 69 total. **Part-time faculty:** 76 total.

Student profile.

Out-of-state:	2%	**Live on campus:**	30%
25 or older:	32%		

Basis for selection. Open admission, but selective for some programs. All applicants must submit ACT. No minimum score required. Special requirements for nursing program.

2008-2009 Annual costs. Tuition/fees: $1,520; $3,620 out-of-state. Per-credit charge: $75 in-state; $162 out-of-state. Room/board: $2,930. Books/supplies: $800. Personal expenses: $900.

2007-2008 Financial aid. **Need-based:** 72% of total undergraduate aid awarded as scholarships/grants, 28% as loans/jobs. **Non-need-based:** Scholarships awarded for academics, athletics, state residency.

Application procedures. **Admission:** No deadline. No application fee. **Financial aid:** No deadline. FAFSA, institutional form required. Applicants notified on a rolling basis starting 7/31; must reply within 2 week(s) of notification.

Academics. **Special study options:** Distance learning, dual enrollment of high school students, honors. **Credit/placement by examination:** CLEP, institutional tests. 6 credit hours maximum toward associate degree. **Support services:** GED preparation and test center, remedial instruction, study skills assistance, tutoring.

Majors. **Biology:** General. **Business:** General. **Computer sciences:** General, applications programming, data processing, programming. **Education:** General. **Engineering:** General. **Engineering technology:** Drafting, electrical. **Health:** Predental, premedicine, prepharmacy, preveterinary. **Interdisciplinary:** Gerontology. **Liberal arts:** Arts/sciences. **Math:** General. **Physical sciences:** Chemistry. **Psychology:** General. **Visual/performing arts:** Studio arts.

Student life. **Housing:** Guaranteed on-campus for freshmen. Single-sex dorms, apartments available. **Activities:** Bands, choral groups, drama, student government, student newspaper.

Athletics. NJCAA. **Intercollegiate:** Baseball M, basketball, football (tackle) M, golf, soccer, softball W, tennis. **Intramural:** Basketball, softball, table tennis. **Team name:** Warriors.

Student services. Career counseling, health services, on-campus daycare, personal counseling, veterans' counselor. **Transfer:** College fairs on campus for students transferring to 4-year colleges.

Contact. Phone: (601) 635-2111 ext. 392 Toll-free number: (877) 462-3222 Fax: (601) 635-4060
Donna Luke, Director of Admissions, East Central Community College, Box 129, Decatur, MS 39327

East Mississippi Community College

Scooba, Mississippi
www.eastms.edu **CB code: 1197**

- Public 2-year community college
- Residential campus in rural community

General. Founded in 1927. Regionally accredited. **Enrollment:** 4,184 degree-seeking undergraduates. **Degrees:** 1,565 associate awarded. **ROTC:** Naval. **Location:** 37 miles from Meridian. **Calendar:** Semester, limited summer session. **Full-time faculty:** 103 total. **Part-time faculty:** 108 total.

Student profile. Among degree-seeking undergraduates, 81% enrolled in a transfer program, 19% enrolled in a vocational program, 1,237 enrolled as first-time, first-year students, 471 transferred in from other institutions.

Part-time:	33%	**African American:**	54%
Women:	62%	**Hispanic American:**	1%

Basis for selection. Open admission, but selective for some programs. Special requirements for practical nursing, cosmetology, and funeral service technology. **Adult students:** SAT/ACT scores not required if applicant over 21.

2008-2009 Annual costs. Tuition/fees: $1,820; $3,570 out-of-state. $50 health fee for on-campus residents. Room/board: $3,000. Books/supplies: $900. Personal expenses: $2,200.

Financial aid. **Need-based:** Need-based aid available for part-time students. **Non-need-based:** Scholarships awarded for academics, art, athletics, leadership, music/drama, state residency.

Application procedures. **Admission:** No deadline. No application fee. Admission notification on a rolling basis. **Financial aid:** Priority date 4/1; no closing date. FAFSA, institutional form required. Applicants notified on a rolling basis starting 4/1; must reply within 2 week(s) of notification.

Academics. **Special study options:** Distance learning, dual enrollment of high school students, honors. License preparation in nursing. **Credit/placement by examination:** CLEP, institutional tests. **Support services:** GED preparation and test center, learning center, reduced course load, remedial instruction, tutoring.

Majors. **Business:** Banking/financial services. **Computer sciences:** General, programming. **Engineering technology:** Drafting.

Most popular majors. Business/marketing 17%, education 12%, health sciences 24%, liberal arts 21%, personal/culinary services 6%.

Computing on campus. 30 workstations in library, computer center. Dormitories wired for high-speed internet access. Online library, helpline available.

Student life. **Freshman orientation:** Mandatory. Preregistration for classes offered. **Housing:** Single-sex dorms available. $50 deposit. **Activities:** Marching band, choral groups, drama, literary magazine, music ensembles, student government, student newspaper, Gospel Choir, Interdenominational Christian Fellowship Group, Fellowship of Christian Athletes.

Athletics. NJCAA. **Intercollegiate:** Baseball M, basketball, football (tackle) M, golf, soccer M, softball W. **Team name:** Lions.

Student services. Adult student services, career counseling, services for economically disadvantaged, financial aid counseling, health services, personal counseling, placement for graduates. **Transfer:** Pre-admission transcript evaluation for new students. Transfer adviser, college fairs on campus for students transferring to 4-year colleges.

Contact. Phone: (662) 476-5040 Fax: (662) 476-5038
Karen Briggs, Director of Admissions, East Mississippi Community College, Admissions Office, Scooba, MS 39358

Hinds Community College

Raymond, Mississippi
www.hindscc.edu **CB code: 1296**

- Public 2-year branch campus and community college
- Commuter campus in small town

General. Founded in 1917. Regionally accredited. 6 off-campus credit bearing locations: Raymond, Utica, Rankin, Academic/Technical Center, Nursing/Allied Health Center, Vicksburg Warren County Center. **Enrollment:** 10,015 degree-seeking undergraduates. **Degrees:** 1,149 associate awarded. **ROTC:** Army. **Location:** 10 miles from Jackson. **Calendar:** Semester, extensive summer session. **Full-time faculty:** 390 total. **Part-time faculty:** 530 total. **Class size:** 45% < 20, 48% 20-39, 5% 40-49, less than 1% 50-99, less than 1% >100.

Student profile.

Out-of-state:	1%	**Live on campus:**	16%
25 or older:	43%		

Transfer out. **Colleges most students transferred to 2008:** Mississippi State University, University of Southern Mississippi, Jackson State, University of Mississippi, Mississippi College.

Basis for selection. Open admission, but selective for some programs. Special requirements for allied health, data processing programs. ACT not required for placement in vocational programs. 19 high school units, ACT composite score of 18 may be substituted for diploma. Interview required for allied health, vocational majors.

High school preparation. 19 units recommended. Recommended units include English 4, mathematics 2, social studies 2 and science 2.

2008-2009 Annual costs. Tuition/fees: $1,740; $3,946 out-of-state. Per-credit charge: $85 in-state; $170 out-of-state. Room/board: $2,920. Books/supplies: $420. Personal expenses: $1,500.

2007-2008 Financial aid. **Need-based:** Need-based aid available for part-time students. **Non-need-based:** Scholarships awarded for academics, art, athletics, job skills, leadership, minority status, music/drama, state residency.

Application procedures. **Admission:** No deadline. No application fee. Admission notification on a rolling basis beginning on or about 3/1. **Financial aid:** Priority date 4/1; no closing date. FAFSA required. Applicants notified on a rolling basis starting 5/15; must reply within 2 week(s) of notification.

Academics. **Special study options:** Accelerated study, cooperative education, distance learning, double major, dual enrollment of high school students, honors, independent study, internships, liberal arts/career combination, study abroad. License preparation in nursing. **Credit/placement by examination:** CLEP, institutional tests. 18 credit hours maximum toward associate degree. **Support services:** GED preparation and test center, learning center, remedial instruction, tutoring.

Majors. **Agriculture:** General, agribusiness operations, animal breeding, food science, landscaping. **Biology:** General. **Business:** Administrative services, fashion, finance, management information systems, office management, operations, sales/distribution, tourism promotion. **Communications:**

Journalism. **Communications technology:** General, graphic/printing. **Computer sciences:** General, data processing. **Education:** Business, elementary, physical, secondary, trade/industrial. **Engineering:** General. **Engineering technology:** Civil, drafting, electrical. **Family/consumer sciences:** General, child care, institutional food production. **Foreign languages:** Sign language interpretation. **Health:** Clinical lab assistant, clinical lab technology, dental assistant, EMT paramedic, licensed practical nurse, medical records technology, nursing assistant, respiratory therapy technology, surgical technology, veterinary technology/assistant. **History:** General. **Legal studies:** Legal secretary, paralegal, prelaw. **Liberal arts:** Arts/sciences. **Math:** General. **Mechanic/repair:** Electronics/electrical. **Personal/culinary services:** Culinary arts. **Physical sciences:** Chemistry, geology, physics. **Protective services:** Criminal justice, fire safety technology. **Psychology:** General. **Social sciences:** Political science, sociology. **Visual/performing arts:** Art, commercial/advertising art, dramatic.

Most popular majors. Business/marketing 12%, health sciences 28%, liberal arts 45%.

Computing on campus. 55 workstations in library, computer center. Online course registration, helpline, repair service available.

Student life. **Freshman orientation:** Available, $65 fee. Preregistration for classes offered. **Housing:** Single-sex dorms available. $50 deposit. **Activities:** Bands, choral groups, dance, drama, music ensembles, musical theater, student government, student newspaper, Baptist Student Union, Afro-American Cultural Society, Catholic Student Organization, College Independents, College Republicans, Fellowship of Christian Athletes, Class/Leadership/Authority and Womanhood, Campus Christian Fellowship.

Athletics. NJCAA. **Intercollegiate:** Baseball M, basketball, football (tackle) M, golf M, soccer M, softball W, tennis, track and field M. **Intramural:** Basketball, football (tackle) M, softball M, volleyball. **Team name:** Eagles.

Student services. Career counseling, student employment services, personal counseling, placement for graduates. **Physically disabled:** Services for visually, hearing impaired. **Transfer:** Transfer adviser, college fairs on campus for students transferring to 4-year colleges.

Contact. E-mail: records@hindscc.edu
Phone: (601) 857-3212 Toll-free number: (800) 446-3722
Fax: (601) 857-3539
Ginger Turner, Director of Admissions and Records, Hinds Community College, 505 East Main Street, Raymond, MS 39154-1100

Holmes Community College

Goodman, Mississippi
www.holmescc.edu **CB code: 1299**

- Public 2-year community college
- Residential campus in rural community

General. Founded in 1925. Regionally accredited. Additional campus in Ridgeland and center in Grenada. **Enrollment:** 4,898 degree-seeking undergraduates. **Degrees:** 541 associate awarded. **Location:** 10 miles from Jackson. **Calendar:** Semester, extensive summer session. **Full-time faculty:** 128 total. **Part-time faculty:** 80 total. **Special facilities:** Observatory.

Student profile.

Out-of-state:	5%	**Live on campus:**	25%
25 or older:	33%		

Transfer out. **Colleges most students transferred to 2008:** Mississippi State University, University of Mississippi, Delta State University, University of Southern Mississippi.

Basis for selection. Open admission, but selective for some programs. Official high school transcripts must show the date of graduation and be signed by the principal. Applicants for the nursing program are required to have an ACT composite score of 18 or higher, with a score of 17 or higher in math and an 18 or higher in reading. ACT is preferred for placement; however, other tests are available and accepted. **Adult students:** SAT/ACT scores not required if applicant over 21.

High school preparation. College-preparatory program recommended. 20 units required. Required units include English 4, mathematics 3, social studies 2, science 2 and academic electives 9.

2008-2009 Annual costs. Tuition/fees: $1,630; $3,580 out-of-state. Per-credit charge: $75. Room/board: $1,980. Books/supplies: $600. Personal expenses: $1,600.

Financial aid. **Non-need-based:** Scholarships awarded for academics, athletics.

Application procedures. **Admission:** Closing date 8/21. No application fee. Admission notification on a rolling basis. **Financial aid:** Priority date 6/1; no closing date. FAFSA, institutional form required. Applicants notified on a rolling basis.

Academics. **Special study options:** Cooperative education, distance learning, dual enrollment of high school students, honors, internships, liberal arts/career combination, weekend college. License preparation in nursing, paramedic. **Credit/placement by examination:** AP, CLEP, SAT, ACT, institutional tests. **Support services:** GED test center, learning center, reduced course load, remedial instruction, study skills assistance, tutoring.

Majors. **Business:** Administrative services, business admin, fashion. **Computer sciences:** General, computer science, programming. **Conservation:** Forestry. **Education:** Elementary, secondary. **Engineering:** General, architectural, electrical. **Engineering technology:** Drafting. **Health:** Predental, premedicine, prepharmacy, preveterinary. **Liberal arts:** Arts/sciences. **Math:** General. **Mechanic/repair:** Heating/ac/refrig.

Computing on campus. 400 workstations in library, computer center. Dormitories wired for high-speed internet access. Commuter students can connect to campus network. Online course registration, helpline, repair service available.

Student life. **Freshman orientation:** Available. **Housing:** Single-sex dorms available. **Activities:** Bands, choral groups, dance, drama, literary magazine, music ensembles, musical theater, student government, student newspaper, Baptist Student Union, Wesley Foundation, College Republican Club, Fellowship of Christian Athletes.

Athletics. NJCAA. **Intercollegiate:** Baseball M, basketball, football (tackle) M, golf M, soccer, softball W, tennis, track and field. **Intramural:** Basketball, football (tackle) M, soccer M, softball, track and field M, volleyball. **Team name:** Bulldogs.

Student services. Adult student services, career counseling, personal counseling, veterans' counselor. **Physically disabled:** Services for visually, speech, hearing impaired. **Transfer:** Pre-admission transcript evaluation for new students. Transfer adviser, college fairs on campus for students transferring to 4-year colleges.

Contact. E-mail: progers@holmescc.edu
Phone: (662) 472-9073 Toll-free number: (800) 465-6374
Fax: (662) 472-9152
Don Burnham, Director of Admissions and Records, Holmes Community College, Box 398, Goodman, MS 39079

Itawamba Community College

Fulton, Mississippi
www.iccms.edu **CB code: 1326**

- Public 2-year community and technical college
- Commuter campus in small town

General. Founded in 1948. Regionally accredited. Additional campuses in Fulton, Tupelo, as well as online instruction. **Enrollment:** 6,627 degree-seeking undergraduates. **Degrees:** 577 associate awarded. **Location:** 115 miles from Memphis, Tennessee, 135 miles from Birmingham, Alabama. **Calendar:** Semester, limited summer session. **Full-time faculty:** 153 total. **Part-time faculty:** 146 total. **Class size:** 51% < 20, 43% 20-39, 5% 40-49, 1% 50-99.

Transfer out. **Colleges most students transferred to 2008:** Mississippi State University, University of Mississippi.

Basis for selection. Open admission, but selective for some programs. Special requirements for health science programs, including minimum test scores on ACT or other discipline-specific tests and grade of at least 2.0 in program prerequisite courses. **Homeschooled:** Must complete GED or appeal to Admissions and Guidance Committee. **Learning Disabled:** Developmental courses recommended. Assistance provided by special needs counselor.

2008-2009 Annual costs. Tuition/fees: $1,630; $3,380 out-of-state. Per-credit charge: $85. Room/board: $2,700. Books/supplies: $900. Personal expenses: $180.

2007-2008 Financial aid. **Need-based:** 49% of total undergraduate aid awarded as scholarships/grants, 51% as loans/jobs. Need-based aid available for part-time students. Work-study available for part-time students. **Non-need-based:** Scholarships awarded for academics, art, athletics, leadership, music/drama, state residency.

Application procedures. **Admission:** No deadline. No application fee. Admission notification on a rolling basis. **Financial aid:** Priority date 4/30;

no closing date. FAFSA, institutional form required. Applicants notified on a rolling basis starting 4/15.

Academics. **Special study options:** Accelerated study, cooperative education, distance learning, double major, dual enrollment of high school students, ESL, honors, independent study, internships. License preparation in nursing, paramedic, physical therapy, radiology, real estate. **Credit/placement by examination:** CLEP, institutional tests. 15 credit hours maximum toward associate degree. **Support services:** GED preparation and test center, learning center, reduced course load, remedial instruction, study skills assistance, tutoring, writing center.

Majors. **Agriculture:** Business. **Business:** General, accounting, administrative services, management information systems, office/clerical. **Communications:** Broadcast journalism, journalism, public relations. **Computer sciences:** General, computer science, data processing, programming. **Conservation:** Forestry. **Construction:** Electrician. **Education:** Art, biology, business, chemistry, elementary, French, health, history, mathematics, music, physical, physics, science, secondary, social studies, Spanish, special, speech. **Engineering:** General, electrical. **Engineering technology:** Electrical. **Family/consumer sciences:** General, child care. **Foreign languages:** French, sign language interpretation, Spanish. **Health:** EMT paramedic, medical radiologic technology/radiation therapy, medical records admin, medical records technology, nursing (RN), occupational health, physical therapy assistant, predental, premedicine, prepharmacy, preveterinary, respiratory therapy technology, sonography, surgical technology. **History:** General. **Legal studies:** Paralegal, prelaw. **Liberal arts:** Arts/sciences, library science. **Math:** General. **Mechanic/repair:** Automotive, diesel, electronics/electrical. **Philosophy/religion:** Philosophy. **Physical sciences:** Chemistry, geology, physics. **Production:** Tool and die. **Protective services:** Criminal justice. **Psychology:** General. **Public administration:** Social work. **Social sciences:** Economics, sociology. **Visual/performing arts:** Art.

Most popular majors. Business/marketing 11%, family/consumer sciences 6%, health sciences 36%, liberal arts 42%.

Computing on campus. 600 workstations in dormitories, library, computer center. Dormitories wired for high-speed internet access and linked to campus network. Commuter students can connect to campus network. Online course registration, online library, helpline, wireless network available.

Student life. **Freshman orientation:** Available. Preregistration for classes offered. **Housing:** Single-sex dorms, wellness housing available. $50 deposit. **Activities:** Bands, choral groups, dance, drama, literary magazine, music ensembles, musical theater, student government, student newspaper.

Athletics. NJCAA. **Intercollegiate:** Baseball M, basketball, cheerleading, football (tackle) M, golf M, soccer M, softball W. **Intramural:** Basketball. **Team name:** Indians.

Student services. Alcohol/substance abuse counseling, chaplain/spiritual director, career counseling, services for economically disadvantaged, student employment services, financial aid counseling, minority student services, on-campus daycare, placement for graduates, veterans' counselor, women's services. **Physically disabled:** Services for visually, hearing impaired. **Transfer:** Transfer adviser, college fairs on campus for students transferring to 4-year colleges.

Contact. E-mail: hgjefcoat@iccms.edu
Phone: (662) 862-8031 Fax: (662) 862-8036
Gregg Jefcoat, Director of Admissions, Itawamba Community College, 602 West Hill Street, Fulton, MS 38843-1099

Jones County Junior College

Ellisville, Mississippi
www.jcjc.cc.ms.us **CB code: 1347**

- Public 2-year junior college
- Commuter campus in small town

General. Founded in 1927. Regionally accredited. **Location:** 7 miles from Laurel, 20 miles from Hattiesburg. **Calendar:** Semester.

Annual costs/financial aid. Tuition/fees (2008-2009): $1,920; $3,920 out-of-state. Room/board: $2,972. Books/supplies: $600. Personal expenses: $1,299. Need-based financial aid available to full-time and part-time students.

Contact. Phone: (601) 477-4025
Director of Admissions & Records, 900 South Court Street, Ellisville, MS 39437

Meridian Community College

Meridian, Mississippi **CB member**
www.meridiancc.edu **CB code: 1461**

- Public 2-year community college
- Commuter campus in large town

General. Founded in 1937. Regionally accredited. **Enrollment:** 3,614 degree-seeking undergraduates. **Degrees:** 478 associate awarded. **Location:** 90 miles from Jackson, 90 miles from Tuscaloosa, Alabama. **Calendar:** Semester, extensive summer session. **Full-time faculty:** 298 total. **Part-time faculty:** 55 total.

Student profile.

Out-of-state:	4%	**Live on campus:**	7%
25 or older:	50%		

Basis for selection. Open admission, but selective for some programs. Test scores, recommendations considered for health education applicants. Interview recommended for broadcast technology, data processing, graphic communication technology, and health programs majors.

High school preparation. Recommended units include English 4, mathematics 3, social studies 3, science 3 and academic electives 2. .5 unit computer applications recommended.

2008-2009 Annual costs. Tuition/fees: $1,660; $2,950 out-of-state. Per-credit charge: $80 in-state; $137 out-of-state. Room/board: $3,350. Books/supplies: $1,400. Personal expenses: $1,400.

Financial aid. **Need-based:** Need-based aid available for part-time students. **Non-need-based:** Scholarships awarded for academics, art, athletics, leadership, music/drama, state residency.

Application procedures. **Admission:** No application fee. Admission notification on a rolling basis. **Financial aid:** Priority date 6/1; no closing date. FAFSA, institutional form required. Applicants notified on a rolling basis starting 5/15; must reply within 2 week(s) of notification.

Academics. **Special study options:** Accelerated study, cooperative education, distance learning, dual enrollment of high school students, independent study, internships, weekend college. License preparation in dental hygiene, nursing, occupational therapy, paramedic, physical therapy, radiology, real estate. **Credit/placement by examination:** CLEP. 45 credit hours maximum toward associate degree. **Support services:** GED preparation and test center, learning center, remedial instruction, study skills assistance, tutoring.

Majors. **Agriculture:** Horticulture. **Business:** Administrative services, management information systems. **Communications:** General, broadcast journalism. **Communications technology:** General. **Computer sciences:** General, computer graphics, programming. **Engineering technology:** Drafting. **Family/consumer sciences:** Child care. **Health:** Clinical lab technology, dental hygiene, licensed practical nurse, medical radiologic technology/radiation therapy, medical records technology, medical secretary, physical therapy assistant, respiratory therapy technology. **Legal studies:** Prelaw. **Mechanic/repair:** Electronics/electrical. **Protective services:** Firefighting.

Computing on campus. 85 workstations in library, computer center. Dormitories wired for high-speed internet access and linked to campus network. Commuter students can connect to campus network. Online course registration, online library, helpline, repair service available.

Student life. **Freshman orientation:** Mandatory. Orientation sessions specific to certain programs. **Housing:** Coed dorms, single-sex dorms, apartments, wellness housing available. $100 fully refundable deposit. **Activities:** Bands, campus ministries, choral groups, drama, international student organizations, literary magazine, music ensembles, musical theater, radio station, student government, student newspaper, TV station, Baptist Student Union, T.J. Harris Organization, Wesley Foundation, Fellowship of Christian Athletes, Phi Theta Kappa, multicultural student association.

Athletics. NJCAA. **Intercollegiate:** Baseball M, basketball, golf M, soccer M, softball W, tennis. **Intramural:** Basketball, bowling, softball W, swimming, tennis, volleyball. **Team name:** Eagles.

Student services. Career counseling, student employment services, personal counseling, placement for graduates, veterans' counselor. **Physically disabled:** Services for visually, speech, hearing impaired. **Transfer:** Pre-admission transcript evaluation for new students. Transfer adviser, college fairs on campus for students transferring to 4-year colleges.

Contact. E-mail: apayne@meridiancc.edu
Phone: (601) 484-8895 Toll-free number: (800) 622-8431
Fax: (601) 484-8838
Angela Payne, Director of Admissions, Meridian Community College, 910 Highway 19 North, Meridian, MS 39307-5890

Mississippi Delta Community College

Moorhead, Mississippi
www.msdelta.edu **CB code: 1742**

- Public 2-year community college
- Commuter campus in rural community

General. Founded in 1926. Regionally accredited. **Enrollment:** 3,154 degree-seeking undergraduates. **Degrees:** 303 associate awarded. **Location:** 20 miles from Greenwood. **Calendar:** Semester, limited summer session. **Full-time faculty:** 120 total. **Part-time faculty:** 94 total.

Student profile.

Out-of-state:	3%	**Live on campus:**	25%

Transfer out. Colleges most students transferred to 2008: Delta State University, Mississippi State University, University of Mississippi, University of Southern Mississippi.

Basis for selection. Open admission, but selective for some programs. Test scores most important. Open admission to vocational programs. Limited admission to health occupations and computer technology curriculum.

High school preparation. 19 units recommended. Recommended units include English 3, mathematics 3, social studies 3, science 3, foreign language 3 and academic electives 4. 12 of the recommended units may be distributed in any combination in mathematics, science, foreign language, social studies, and history.

2008-2009 Annual costs. Tuition/fees: $1,920; $3,528 out-of-state. Room/board: $4,390. Books/supplies: $450. Personal expenses: $400.

Financial aid. Non-need-based: Scholarships awarded for academics, athletics, state residency.

Application procedures. Admission: Priority date 7/1; no deadline. No application fee. Admission notification on a rolling basis beginning on or about 5/30. **Financial aid:** Priority date 8/1; no closing date. FAFSA, institutional form required. Applicants notified on a rolling basis; must reply within 2 week(s) of notification.

Academics. Special study options: Distance learning. License preparation in nursing. **Credit/placement by examination:** CLEP. 15 credit hours maximum toward associate degree. **Support services:** GED preparation and test center, reduced course load, remedial instruction.

Majors. Agriculture: Business, economics, farm/ranch, horticulture. **Area/ethnic studies:** American. **Biology:** General. **Business:** Accounting, administrative services. **Communications:** General, advertising. **Computer sciences:** Programming. **Conservation:** Forestry. **Construction:** Maintenance. **Education:** General, art, business, elementary, health, physical, secondary, special, speech. **Engineering:** General. **Engineering technology:** Architectural, electrical. **Family/consumer sciences:** General. **Health:** Clinical lab technology, dental hygiene, EMT paramedic, medical radiologic technology/radiation therapy, medical records admin, predental, prepharmacy, preveterinary. **History:** General. **Legal studies:** Prelaw. **Liberal arts:** Arts/sciences. **Mechanic/repair:** Heating/ac/refrig. **Protective services:** Law enforcement admin. **Psychology:** General. **Public administration:** Social work. **Social sciences:** General, sociology. **Visual/performing arts:** Studio arts.

Student life. Freshman orientation: Available. **Housing:** Single-sex dorms available. **Activities:** Bands, choral groups, dance, drama, student government, student newspaper, Baptist Student Union, Wesley Foundation, Vocational Industrial Clubs of America.

Athletics. NJCAA. **Intercollegiate:** Baseball M, basketball, football (tackle) M, golf M, soccer M, softball W, tennis, track and field M. **Intramural:** Basketball, softball, tennis, track and field, volleyball.

Student services. Career counseling, student employment services, personal counseling, placement for graduates, veterans' counselor. **Transfer:** Transfer adviser for students transferring to 4-year colleges.

Contact. E-mail: admissions@msdelta.edu
Phone: (662) 246-6306 Fax: (662) 246-6321
Joe Ray, Chief Admissions Officer, Mississippi Delta Community College, Box 668, Moorhead, MS 38761

Mississippi Gulf Coast Community College

Perkinston, Mississippi
www.mgccc.edu **CB code: 1353**

- Public 2-year community college
- Commuter campus in large city

General. Founded in 1965. Regionally accredited. Instruction is available at our 3 campuses and 4 centers. **Enrollment:** 9,073 degree-seeking undergraduates; 101 non-degree-seeking students. **Degrees:** 255 associate awarded. **Location:** 30 miles from Biloxi, 90 miles from New Orleans. **Calendar:** Semester, limited summer session. **Full-time faculty:** 342 total. **Part-time faculty:** 205 total.

Student profile. Among degree-seeking undergraduates, 2,034 enrolled as first-time, first-year students.

Part-time:	36%	**25 or older:**	35%
Out-of-state:	3%	**Live on campus:**	8%
Women:	61%		

Transfer out. Colleges most students transferred to 2008: University of Southern MS; Mississippi State University; University of South Alabama.

Basis for selection. Open admission, but selective for some programs. Special requirements for health occupations programs.

High school preparation. 19 units recommended. Recommended units include English 3, mathematics 3 and science 3.

2009-2010 Annual costs. Tuition/fees (projected): $1,852; $3,698 out-of-state. Per-credit charge: $80 in-state; $157 out-of-state. $25 rental fee required per book. Books/supplies: $520. Personal expenses: $5,268.

2007-2008 Financial aid. All financial aid based on need.

Application procedures. Admission: No deadline. No application fee. **Financial aid:** Priority date 6/1; no closing date. Institutional form required. Applicants notified on a rolling basis starting 7/1.

Academics. Special study options: Accelerated study, cooperative education, distance learning, dual enrollment of high school students, honors, weekend college. License preparation in nursing, paramedic, radiology. **Credit/placement by examination:** CLEP. 32 credit hours maximum toward associate degree. **Support services:** GED preparation and test center, learning center, reduced course load, remedial instruction, study skills assistance, tutoring.

Majors. Agriculture: General, food science, landscaping, ornamental horticulture, turf management. **Biology:** General, biotechnology. **Business:** General, accounting, administrative services, banking/financial services, business admin, fashion, management information systems, marketing, office technology. **Communications:** General. **Computer sciences:** General. **Conservation:** Fisheries, forestry. **Construction:** Lineworker, pipefitting, power transmission. **Education:** General, art, business, elementary, mathematics, multi-level teacher, science, secondary, trade/industrial. **Engineering:** General. **Engineering technology:** CAD/CADD, drafting. **Health:** Clinical lab science, clinical lab technology, EMT paramedic, medical radiologic technology/radiation therapy, medical records admin, medical secretary, nursing (RN), optician, orthotics/prosthetics, prepharmacy, respiratory therapy technology, veterinary technology/assistant. **Legal studies:** Court reporting, paralegal, prelaw. **Liberal arts:** Arts/sciences. **Math:** General. **Mechanic/repair:** Electronics/electrical. **Personal/culinary services:** Cosmetic, funeral direction. **Protective services:** Criminal justice, fire safety technology. **Psychology:** General. **Public administration:** Social work. **Visual/performing arts:** Art, commercial/advertising art, interior design, sculpture.

Most popular majors. Business/marketing 20%, education 12%, engineering/engineering technologies 9%, health sciences 23%, liberal arts 22%.

Computing on campus. 375 workstations in library, computer center, student center. Dormitories wired for high-speed internet access and linked to campus network. Commuter students can connect to campus network. Online course registration, wireless network available.

Student life. Freshman orientation: Mandatory. Preregistration for classes offered. **Housing:** Single-sex dorms, special housing for disabled available. $50 nonrefundable deposit. **Activities:** Bands, campus ministries, choral groups, dance, drama, music ensembles, musical theater, student government, student newspaper, Baptist student union, Wesley Foundation, Newman Club, A.D.U.L.T.

Athletics. NJCAA. **Intercollegiate:** Baseball M, basketball, cheerleading, football (tackle) M, golf M, softball, tennis. **Intramural:** Baseball, basketball, football (tackle), softball, tennis. **Team name:** Bulldogs.

Student services. Adult student services, career counseling, student employment services, financial aid counseling, health services, on-campus daycare, personal counseling, placement for graduates, veterans' counselor. **Physically disabled:** Services for visually, hearing impaired. **Transfer:** Transfer adviser, college fairs on campus for students transferring to 4-year colleges.

Contact. E-mail: nichol.armstrong@mgccc.edu
Phone: (601) 928-6333 Toll-free number: (866) 735-1122
Fax: (601) 928-6345
Nichol Armstrong, Director of Admissions, Mississippi Gulf Coast Community College, PO Box 548, Perkinston, MS 39573

Northeast Mississippi Community College
Booneville, Mississippi
www.nemcc.edu **CB code: 1557**

- Public 2-year community college
- Commuter campus in small town

General. Founded in 1948. Regionally accredited. **Enrollment:** 3,297 degree-seeking undergraduates. **Degrees:** 397 associate awarded. **Location:** 30 miles from Tupelo, 110 miles from Memphis, Tennessee. **Calendar:** Semester, extensive summer session. **Full-time faculty:** 126 total. **Part-time faculty:** 27 total.

Basis for selection. Open admission, but selective for some programs. Admission to nursing, dental hygiene, and medical laboratory, medical assistance, practical nursing, radiologic technology, and respiratory technician programs based on test scores. Interview required for dental hygiene, medical laboratory technology, and nursing students. **Adult students:** SAT/ACT scores not required if applicant over 21.

High school preparation. 18 units recommended. Recommended units include English 4, mathematics 2, social studies 2 and science 2.

2008-2009 Annual costs. Tuition/fees: $1,920; $3,850 out-of-state. Per-credit charge: $105 in-state; $212 out-of-state. Room/board: $2,984. Books/supplies: $840. Personal expenses: $1,989.

2008-2009 Financial aid. Need-based: 73% of total undergraduate aid awarded as scholarships/grants, 27% as loans/jobs.

Application procedures. Admission: No deadline. No application fee. Application must be submitted on paper. Admission notification on a rolling basis. **Financial aid:** Priority date 4/1, closing date 6/30. FAFSA, institutional form required. Applicants notified on a rolling basis.

Academics. Special study options: Distance learning, dual enrollment of high school students, study abroad. **Credit/placement by examination:** AP, CLEP, institutional tests. 18 credit hours maximum toward associate degree. **Support services:** GED preparation and test center, learning center, pre-admission summer program, reduced course load, remedial instruction, tutoring.

Majors. Health: Clinical lab assistant, licensed practical nurse, medical assistant, medical radiologic technology/radiation therapy, pharmacy assistant, respiratory therapy technology.

Computing on campus. Dormitories wired for high-speed internet access and linked to campus network. Commuter students can connect to campus network. Online library, wireless network available.

Student life. Freshman orientation: Available, $25 fee. Preregistration for classes offered. Two one-day orientation/registration sessions are planned for entering freshman and transfer students. New and transfer students will attend Orientation/Registration one of the dates according to their college major. Attendance is highly encouraged. **Housing:** Single-sex dorms available. $100 fully refundable deposit. **Activities:** Bands, choral groups, dance, drama, film society, music ensembles, musical theater, radio station, student government, student newspaper.

Athletics. NJCAA. **Intercollegiate:** Baseball M, basketball, football (tackle) M, golf M, softball W, tennis. **Intramural:** Basketball, softball, table tennis, volleyball. **Team name:** Tigers.

Student services. Adult student services, career counseling, student employment services, health services, on-campus daycare, personal counseling, placement for graduates. **Physically disabled:** Services for visually, speech, hearing impaired. **Transfer:** Transfer adviser for students transferring to 4-year colleges.

Contact. E-mail: admitme@nemcc.edu
Phone: (662) 720-7290 Toll-free number: (800) 555-2154
Fax: (662) 728-1165
Robert Gibson, Director of Enrollment Services/Registrar, Northeast Mississippi Community College, 101 Cunningham Boulevard, Booneville, MS 38829

Northwest Mississippi Community College
Senatobia, Mississippi
www.northwestms.edu **CB code: 1562**

- Public 2-year community college
- Commuter campus in small town

General. Founded in 1927. Regionally accredited. **Enrollment:** 7,118 degree-seeking undergraduates. **Degrees:** 186 associate awarded. **ROTC:** Air Force. **Location:** 30 miles from Memphis, Tennessee. **Calendar:** Semester, extensive summer session. **Full-time faculty:** 200 total. **Part-time faculty:** 172 total. **Class size:** 45% < 20, 49% 20-39, 6% 40-49, less than 1% 50-99.

Student profile. Among degree-seeking undergraduates, 2,739 enrolled as first-time, first-year students.

Part-time:	24%	**Women:**	64%
Out-of-state:	10%	**Live on campus:**	14%

Transfer out. Colleges most students transferred to 2008: University of Mississippi.

Basis for selection. Open admission, but selective for some programs. Special requirements for some technical programs.

High school preparation. 17 units recommended. Recommended units include English 4, mathematics 3, social studies 4 and science 2.

2008-2009 Annual costs. Tuition/fees: $1,700; $3,700 out-of-state. Per-credit charge: $80 in-state; $125 out-of-state. Lab fees range from $15 to $25 per course. Room/board: $2,700. Books/supplies: $600. Personal expenses: $375.

Application procedures. Admission: No deadline. No application fee. Admission notification on a rolling basis beginning on or about 7/1. **Financial aid:** Priority date 4/1; no closing date. FAFSA required. Applicants notified by 8/16.

Academics. Special study options: Accelerated study, distance learning, dual enrollment of high school students. Bachelor's degree programs available on campus. License preparation in aviation, nursing, paramedic, real estate. **Credit/placement by examination:** CLEP, institutional tests. **Support services:** GED preparation and test center, reduced course load, remedial instruction, tutoring.

Majors. Agriculture: Agribusiness operations, animal sciences, dairy, economics, food science, horticulture, plant sciences, poultry. **Business:** Accounting, business admin, fashion, hospitality/recreation, management information systems, office technology. **Communications:** Broadcast journalism, journalism, public relations. **Communications technology:** General, graphic/printing. **Computer sciences:** General, applications programming, data processing, networking, programming. **Education:** General, art, business, elementary, family/consumer sciences, mathematics, music, physical, sales/marketing, science, secondary, social science, social studies, special. **Engineering technology:** Civil, drafting, electrical. **Health:** Medical secretary, respiratory therapy technology. **Legal studies:** Court reporting, legal secretary, paralegal. **Liberal arts:** Arts/sciences. **Mechanic/repair:** Heating/ac/refrig. **Visual/performing arts:** Commercial/advertising art.

Most popular majors. Business/marketing 31%, computer/information sciences 23%, education 15%, health sciences 31%.

Student life. Freshman orientation: Available. **Housing:** Single-sex dorms, apartments available. **Activities:** Bands, choral groups, drama, music ensembles, musical theater, student government, student newspaper.

Athletics. NJCAA. **Intercollegiate:** Baseball M, basketball, cheerleading, football (tackle) M, golf, rodeo, soccer, softball W, tennis, track and field M. **Intramural:** Archery, badminton. **Team name:** Rangers.

Student services. Career counseling, health services, personal counseling, veterans' counselor. **Physically disabled:** Services for visually, speech, hearing impaired.

Contact. E-mail: jlsimpson@northwestms.edu
Phone: (601) 562-3200 ext. 3219 Fax: (662) 562-3221
Larry Simpson, Registrar, Northwest Mississippi Community College, 4975 Highway 51 North, Senatobia, MS 38668

Pearl River Community College
Poplarville, Mississippi
www.prcc.edu **CB code: 1622**

- Public 2-year community college
- Commuter campus in small town

General. Founded in 1921. Regionally accredited. **Enrollment:** 3,790 degree-seeking undergraduates. **Degrees:** 485 associate awarded. **Location:** 35 miles from Hattiesburg, 70 miles from New Orleans. **Calendar:** Semester, limited summer session. **Full-time faculty:** 135 total. **Part-time faculty:** 50 total.

Student profile.

Out-of-state:	9%	**Live on campus:**	25%
25 or older:	23%		

Basis for selection. Open admission, but selective for some programs. Special requirements for health occupation programs. Interview recommended for nursing majors.

2008-2009 Annual costs. Tuition/fees: $1,806; $5,511 out-of-state. Per-credit charge: $90 in-state; $244 out-of-state. Room/board: $3,400. Books/supplies: $500.

2007-2008 Financial aid. Need-based: Need-based aid available for part-time students. **Non-need-based:** Scholarships awarded for academics, alumni affiliation, athletics, leadership, music/drama, state residency.

Application procedures. Admission: No deadline. No application fee. Admission notification on a rolling basis. **Financial aid:** Priority date 4/17; no closing date. FAFSA, institutional form required. Applicants notified on a rolling basis.

Academics. Special study options: Cooperative education, dual enrollment of high school students. License preparation in dental hygiene, nursing, occupational therapy, physical therapy, radiology. **Credit/placement by examination:** AP, CLEP, ACT. 30 credit hours maximum toward associate degree. **Support services:** GED preparation and test center, learning center, reduced course load, remedial instruction, tutoring.

Majors. Business: Business admin, management information systems, office technology. **Computer sciences:** Applications programming, data processing. **Construction:** Carpentry, masonry, power transmission. **Education:** Multi-level teacher. **Engineering technology:** Drafting, electrical. **Health:** Licensed practical nurse, medical secretary, respiratory therapy technology. **Legal studies:** Legal secretary. **Liberal arts:** Arts/sciences. **Mechanic/repair:** Auto body, heating/ac/refrig.

Computing on campus. 150 workstations in library, computer center. Dormitories wired for high-speed internet access and linked to campus network. Commuter students can connect to campus network. Online course registration, helpline, wireless network available.

Student life. Freshman orientation: Available, $25 fee. Preregistration for classes offered. **Housing:** Single-sex dorms, special housing for disabled available. $50 deposit. **Activities:** Bands, choral groups, drama, music ensembles, student government, student newspaper, Black Student Union, Wesley and Newman Clubs, Phi Theta Kappa, Afro-American Club, Baptist Student Union.

Athletics. NJCAA. **Intercollegiate:** Baseball M, basketball, football (tackle) M, golf M, softball W, tennis. **Intramural:** Badminton, basketball, softball, table tennis, tennis, volleyball. **Team name:** Wildcats.

Student services. Career counseling, student employment services, health services, personal counseling, placement for graduates, veterans' counselor.

Contact. E-mail: dford@prcc.edu
Phone: (601) 403-1214 Fax: (601) 403-1339
Dow Ford, Director of Admissions, Pearl River Community College, 101 Highway 11 North, Poplarville, MS 39470

Southwest Mississippi Community College
Summit, Mississippi
www.smcc.edu **CB code: 1729**

- Public 2-year community college
- Commuter campus in rural community

General. Founded in 1918. Regionally accredited. **Enrollment:** 1,638 degree-seeking undergraduates; 419 non-degree-seeking students. **Degrees:** 256 associate awarded. **Location:** 76 miles from Jackson, 100 miles from New Orleans. **Calendar:** Semester, limited summer session. **Full-time faculty:** 84 total. **Part-time faculty:** 16 total. **Class size:** 67% < 20, 26% 20-39, 4% 40-49, 2% 50-99, less than 1% >100. **Special facilities:** Observatory.

Student profile. Among degree-seeking undergraduates, 598 enrolled as first-time, first-year students, 130 transferred in from other institutions.

Part-time:	8%	**African American:**	45%
Out-of-state:	10%	**25 or older:**	28%
Women:	60%	**Live on campus:**	20%

Transfer out. Colleges most students transferred to 2008: The Univeristy of Southern Mississippi, Southeastern Louisiana University, Mississippi State University, The University of Mississippi, Jackson State University.

Basis for selection. Open admission, but selective for some programs. Some career-technical programs have additional requirements for admission, such as minimum ACT scores and/or sufficient grades in pre-requisite courses. For ability to benefit from career programs, high school graduation or GED preferred. **Homeschooled:** Transcript of courses and grades required. ACT scores highly recommended.

High school preparation. College-preparatory program recommended.

2008-2009 Annual costs. Tuition/fees: $1,800; $4,500 out-of-state. Per-credit charge: $75 in-state; $190 out-of-state. Room/board: $2,530. Books/supplies: $600. Personal expenses: $2,840.

2008-2009 Financial aid. Need-based: 99% of total undergraduate aid awarded as scholarships/grants, 1% as loans/jobs. Need-based aid available for part-time students.

Application procedures. Admission: Priority date 8/1; no deadline. No application fee. Application must be submitted on paper. Admission notification on a rolling basis. **Financial aid:** No deadline. Applicants notified on a rolling basis.

Academics. Special study options: Distance learning, dual enrollment of high school students. License preparation in nursing. **Credit/placement by examination:** AP, CLEP. 12 credit hours maximum toward associate degree. **Support services:** GED preparation and test center, learning center, reduced course load, remedial instruction, tutoring.

Majors. Business: Marketing, office/clerical. **Computer sciences:** Data processing. **Construction:** Well drilling. **Engineering technology:** Petroleum. **Health:** Insurance specialist, massage therapy, medical records admin, medical records technology, nursing (RN). **Liberal arts:** Arts/sciences. **Mechanic/repair:** Automotive, diesel.

Most popular majors. Business/marketing 6%, health sciences 36%, liberal arts 42%.

Computing on campus. 150 workstations in library, computer center. Dormitories wired for high-speed internet access. Online course registration, wireless network available.

Student life. Freshman orientation: Mandatory. Preregistration for classes offered. 4-hour sessions offered during summer and week before class begins. **Housing:** Single-sex dorms available. $60 partly refundable deposit, deadline 8/1. **Activities:** Bands, campus ministries, choral groups, dance, music ensembles, student government, student newspaper, Baptist student union, Wesley Foundation.

Athletics. NJCAA. **Intercollegiate:** Baseball M, basketball, football (tackle) M, soccer, softball W, tennis, track and field. **Intramural:** Basketball, tennis, volleyball. **Team name:** Bears.

Student services. Career counseling, health services, personal counseling, placement for graduates, veterans' counselor. **Physically disabled:** Services for visually, speech, hearing impaired. **Transfer:** Transfer adviser, college fairs on campus for students transferring to 4-year colleges.

Contact. E-mail: mattc@smcc.edu
Phone: (601) 276-2001 Fax: (601) 276-3888
Matthew Calhoun, Vice President of Admissions, Southwest Mississippi Community College, 1156 College Drive, Summit, MS 39666

Virginia College
Jackson, Mississippi
www.vc.edu

- For-profit 2-year community college
- Small city

General. Accredited by ACICS. **Enrollment:** 870 degree-seeking undergraduates. **Degrees:** 91 associate awarded. **Calendar:** Quarter.

Basis for selection. Passing score on CPAT exam required.

2008-2009 Annual costs. Per-credit-hour charge ranges from $207-$321 depending on program and includes fees and books.

Application procedures. Admission: No deadline.

Academics. Credit/placement by examination: CLEP.

Majors. Business: Business admin. **Health:** Office assistant.

Contact. E-mail: mtlittle@vc.edu
Phone: (601) 977-0960 Fax: (601) 977-2719
Madeline Little, Director, Virginia College, 4795 Interstate 55 North, Jackson, MS 39206

Virginia College Gulf Coast

Biloxi, Mississippi
www.vc.edu/gulfcoast/index.cfm

- For-profit 2-year business and health science college
- Small city

General. Accredited by ACICS. **Enrollment:** 381 degree-seeking undergraduates. **Degrees:** 56 associate awarded. **Calendar:** Quarter. **Full-time faculty:** 5 total. **Part-time faculty:** 45 total.

2008-2009 Annual costs. Per-credit-hour charge ranges from $294-$312, depending on program, and includes fees and books.

Application procedures. Admission: No deadline.

Academics. Credit/placement by examination: CLEP.

Majors. Business: Accounting, human resources, office management, resort management. **Health:** Insurance coding, surgical technology. **Legal studies:** Paralegal. **Protective services:** Criminal justice, police science.

Contact. Phone: (228) 392-2994
Virginia College Gulf Coast, 920 Cedar Lake Road, BIloxi, MS 39532

Missouri

Aviation Institute of Maintenance: Kansas City
Kansas City, Missouri
www.aviationmaintenance.edu

- For-profit 2-year technical college
- Large city

General. Accredited by ACCSCT. **Enrollment:** 97 degree-seeking undergraduates. **Degrees:** 10 associate awarded. **Calendar:** Continuous. **Full-time faculty:** 10 total.

Basis for selection. Open admission.

2008-2009 Annual costs. Tuition/fees: $10,800.

Application procedures. Admission: $25 fee.

Academics. Credit/placement by examination: CLEP.

Majors. Mechanic/repair: Aircraft.

Contact. E-mail: admdiramk@aviationmaintenance.edu
Phone: (816) 753-9920 Fax: (816) 753-9941
Aviation Institute of Maintenance: Kansas City, 4100 Raytown Road, Kansas City, MO 64129-3634

Bolivar Technical College
Bolivar, Missouri
www.bolivarcollege.org

- Private 2-year branch campus and technical college
- Commuter campus in small town
- Application essay required

General. Accredited by ACICS. Home campus in Houston Missouri. Consortium agreement with Drury University. **Enrollment:** 163 degree-seeking undergraduates. **Degrees:** 22 associate awarded. **Location:** 120 miles from Kansas City. **Calendar:** Semester. **Full-time faculty:** 5 total; 100% have terminal degrees, 80% women. **Part-time faculty:** 11 total; 100% have terminal degrees, 64% women.

Student profile. Among degree-seeking undergraduates, 10% enrolled in a transfer program, 9% enrolled in a vocational program, 1% already have a bachelor's degree or higher, 135 enrolled as first-time, first-year students, 10 transferred in from other institutions.

Women:	98%	**25 or older:**	95%

Transfer out. Colleges most students transferred to 2008: Missouri State University, Ozarks Technical Community College.

Basis for selection. Open admission, but selective for some programs. Admission based on composite score of 75% or higher on institutional entrance exams; requires a minimum passing score on each section of the exam. CPAt exam administered to all admitted students; additional testing for nursing students. **Homeschooled:** Transcript of courses and grades required. Act score of 18 or higher required. **Learning Disabled:** High school IEP from the junior or senior year allowed; adult diagnosis of special needs required if out of high school 2 or more years.

2008-2009 Annual costs. Tuition/fees: $11,940. Per-credit charge: $335. Tuition varies by program. Books/supplies: $2,000. Personal expenses: $13,688.

2007-2008 Financial aid. Need-based: 65% of total undergraduate aid awarded as scholarships/grants, 35% as loans/jobs.

Application procedures. Admission: No deadline. $45 fee. **Financial aid:** Priority date 4/1; no closing date.

Academics. Special study options: Internships. License preparation in nursing, paramedic. **Credit/placement by examination:** CLEP, institutional tests. **Support services:** Remedial instruction, study skills assistance, tutoring.

Majors. Business: Accounting. **Health:** EMT paramedic, medical secretary, nursing (RN).

Computing on campus. 40 workstations in library, computer center. Commuter students can connect to campus network. Online course registration, online library available.

Student life. Freshman orientation: Mandatory. Preregistration for classes offered. **Activities:** Student newspaper.

Student services. Financial aid counseling. **Transfer:** Pre-admission transcript evaluation for new students.

Contact. E-mail: info@bolivarcollege.org
Phone: (417) 777-5062 Toll-free number: (800) 440-6135
Fax: (417) 777-8908
Charlotte Gray, Admissions Director, Bolivar Technical College, PO Box 592, Bolivar, MO 65613

Colorado Technical University: North Kansas City
North Kansas City, Missouri
www.ctukansascity.com **CB code: 3322**

- For-profit 2-year health science and technical college
- Rural community

General. Calendar: Continuous.

Annual costs/financial aid. Associate programs: $15,500-$34,170; bachelor's programs: $23,760-48,600, inclusive of books and fees. Books/supplies: $1,620.

Contact. Phone: (816) 472-7400
Admissions Director, 520 East 19th Avenue, North Kansas City, MO 64116

Concorde Career College: Kansas City
Kansas City, Missouri
www.concorde.edu/kansas **CB code: 3126**

- For-profit 2-year business and health science college
- Large city

General. Accredited by ACCSCT. **Enrollment:** 632 degree-seeking undergraduates. **Degrees:** 34 associate awarded. **Calendar:** Continuous. **Full-time faculty:** 20 total. **Part-time faculty:** 11 total.

Basis for selection. Open admission, but selective for some programs.

2008-2009 Annual costs. Associate degree in respiratory therapy, $25,000; certificates range from $12,600 to $13,000; practical nursing, $23,566, practical nursing weekend program, $24,837; associate degree in nursing $35,000. All prices are inclusive of books, uniforms, and fees. Books/supplies: $348.

Application procedures. Admission: $100 fee.

Academics. Credit/placement by examination: CLEP.

Majors. Business: Business admin. **Health:** Licensed practical nurse, respiratory therapy assistant.

Contact. E-mail: dcrow@concorde.edu
Phone: (816) 531-5223 Toll-free number: (800) 464-1212
Fax: (816) 756-3231
Deborah Crow, Campus Director, Concorde Career College: Kansas City, 3239 Broadway, Kansas City, MO 64111

Cottey College
Nevada, Missouri **CB member**
www.cottey.edu **CB code: 6120**

- Private 2-year junior and liberal arts college for women
- Residential campus in small town
- SAT or ACT (ACT writing optional) required

General. Founded in 1884. Regionally accredited. Sponsored and supported by P.E.O. Sisterhood, nonsectarian philanthropic educational organization. College owned and supported by women for women. **Enrollment:**

330 degree-seeking undergraduates. **Degrees:** 91 associate awarded. **Location:** 100 miles from Kansas City, 60 miles from Joplin. **Calendar:** Semester. **Full-time faculty:** 36 total. **Part-time faculty:** 4 total. **Special facilities:** 33-acre wooded area with lodge for outings and nature laboratory, women's leadership center.

Student profile.

Out-of-state:	90%	**Live on campus:**	99%

Transfer out. **Colleges most students transferred to 2008:** Smith College, Hood College, Truman State University, Boston University, Mount Holyoke College.

Basis for selection. High school course of study most important; rank in top half of graduating class, test scores, essay also important. Recommendations and interviews considered when other criteria not met. Interview recommended for all students. Audition recommended for music students; portfolio recommended for art students. Essay requested sometimes. **Homeschooled:** Statement describing homeschool structure and mission, transcript of courses and grades required. Students should take GED examination.

High school preparation. 18 units required. Required units include English 4, mathematics 3, social studies 2, science 2 (laboratory 2) and foreign language 2. Mathematics should include algebra I, algebra II, geometry.

2008-2009 Annual costs. Tuition/fees: $13,960. Room/board: $5,400. Books/supplies: $800. Personal expenses: $900.

2008-2009 Financial aid. **Need-based:** Need-based aid available for part-time students. Work-study available nights and weekends. **Non-need-based:** Scholarships awarded for academics, alumni affiliation, art, athletics, leadership, music/drama.

Application procedures. **Admission:** Priority date 5/1; no deadline. $20 fee, may be waived for applicants with need, free for online applicants. Admission notification on a rolling basis. Must reply by May 1 or within 2 week(s) if notified thereafter. Tuition deposit of $100 required to reserve spot in class and in student housing. **Financial aid:** Priority date 3/1; no closing date. FAFSA required. Applicants notified on a rolling basis starting 3/15; must reply by 5/1 or within 4 week(s) of notification.

Academics. **Special study options:** Cross-registration, dual enrollment of high school students, independent study, internships. **Credit/placement by examination:** AP, CLEP, IB, institutional tests. **Support services:** Study skills assistance, tutoring, writing center.

Majors. **Liberal arts:** Arts/sciences.

Computing on campus. 62 workstations in dormitories, library, computer center. Commuter students can connect to campus network. Wireless network available.

Student life. **Freshman orientation:** Mandatory. Held in late August, 5 days prior to the first day of class. **Housing:** Guaranteed on-campus for all undergraduates. Wellness housing available. **Activities:** Jazz band, choral groups, dance, drama, literary magazine, music ensembles, student government, student newspaper, 35 campus service and social organizations available.

Athletics. NJCAA. **Intercollegiate:** Basketball W, volleyball W. **Intramural:** Badminton W, basketball W, cheerleading W, golf W, soccer W, softball W, swimming W, synchronized swimming W, table tennis W, tennis W, volleyball W. **Team name:** Comets.

Student services. Chaplain/spiritual director, career counseling, student employment services, financial aid counseling, health services, personal counseling. **Transfer:** Pre-admission transcript evaluation for new students. Transfer center, transfer adviser, college fairs on campus for students transferring to 4-year colleges.

Contact. E-mail: enrollmgt@cottey.edu
Phone: (417) 667-8181 Toll-free number: (888) 526-8839
Fax: (417) 667-1025
Judi Steege, Director of Admission, Cottey College, 1000 West Austin Boulevard, Nevada, MO 64772

Crowder College
Neosho, Missouri
www.crowder.edu **CB code: 6138**

- Public 2-year community and liberal arts college
- Commuter campus in small town

General. Founded in 1963. Regionally accredited. Internationally recognized water resource school and active/passive solar program. **Enrollment:** 2,816 degree-seeking undergraduates; 715 non-degree-seeking students. **Degrees:** 369 associate awarded. **Location:** 70 miles from Springfield, 28 miles from Joplin. **Calendar:** Semester, limited summer session. **Full-time faculty:** 71 total. **Part-time faculty:** 185 total.

Student profile. Among degree-seeking undergraduates, 666 enrolled as first-time, first-year students.

Part-time:	44%	**Live on campus:**	10%
Women:	66%		

Transfer out. **Colleges most students transferred to 2008:** Missouri Southern State College, Pittsburg State University, Southwest Missouri State University.

Basis for selection. Open admission, but selective for some programs. For nursing program: interview, 2.75 GPA and minimum 19 ACT score required. **Homeschooled:** Must pass GED.

High school preparation. Recommended units include English 4, mathematics 3 and science 3.

2008-2009 Annual costs. Tuition/fees: $2,400; $3,210 out-of-district; $4,050 out-of-state. Per-credit charge: $68 in-district; $95 out-of-district; $123 out-of-state. Room/board: $3,870. Books/supplies: $800.

2007-2008 Financial aid. All financial aid based on need. Need-based aid available for part-time students. Work-study available nights, weekends and for part-time students.

Application procedures. **Admission:** No deadline. $25 fee, may be waived for applicants with need. Admission notification on a rolling basis. **Financial aid:** Priority date 7/1; no closing date. FAFSA, institutional form required. Applicants notified on a rolling basis starting 5/15.

Academics. **Special study options:** Distance learning, dual enrollment of high school students, ESL, honors, independent study, internships, liberal arts/career combination, study abroad, weekend college. License preparation in nursing. **Credit/placement by examination:** AP, CLEP, institutional tests. 15 credit hours maximum toward associate degree. **Support services:** GED preparation and test center, learning center, reduced course load, remedial instruction, study skills assistance, tutoring.

Majors. **Agriculture:** Agribusiness operations, farm/ranch, poultry, production. **Biology:** General. **Business:** General, administrative services, office/clerical. **Communications:** Journalism, public relations. **Computer sciences:** General, system admin. **Education:** Elementary, physical, secondary. **Engineering:** General. **Engineering technology:** Electrical, solar energy. **Foreign languages:** Spanish. **Health:** Environmental health, nursing (RN), office assistant. **History:** General. **Interdisciplinary:** Math/computer science. **Liberal arts:** Arts/sciences. **Math:** General. **Mechanic/repair:** Automotive, diesel, industrial electronics. **Physical sciences:** General, chemistry, physics. **Psychology:** General. **Social sciences:** General. **Visual/performing arts:** Art, theater arts management.

Most popular majors. Business/marketing 12%, health sciences 19%, liberal arts 46%.

Computing on campus. 1,000 workstations in dormitories, library, computer center. Dormitories wired for high-speed internet access. Online library, helpline, wireless network available.

Student life. **Freshman orientation:** Mandatory. Preregistration for classes offered. **Housing:** Guaranteed on-campus for all undergraduates. Single-sex dorms, wellness housing available. $150 deposit. **Activities:** Bands, choral groups, dance, drama, literary magazine, music ensembles, musical theater, student government, student newspaper, Aggies (agricultural club), art club, Baptist student union, Students in Free Enterprise, Student-Missouri State Teacher's Association, Phi Theta Kappa, Latino union, Habitat for Humanity.

Athletics. NJCAA. **Intercollegiate:** Baseball M, basketball W, soccer M, softball W. **Team name:** Roughriders.

Student services. Career counseling, student employment services, financial aid counseling, personal counseling, placement for graduates. **Transfer:** Transfer adviser, college fairs on campus for students transferring to 4-year colleges.

Contact. E-mail: admissions@crowder.edu
Phone: (417) 455-5718 Toll-free number: (866) 238-7788
Fax: (417) 455-2439
Jim Riggs, Director of Admission, Crowder College, 601 LaClede Avenue, Neosho, MO 64850

East Central College

Union, Missouri CB member
www.eastcentral.edu CB code: 0845

- Public 2-year community college
- Commuter campus in small town

General. Founded in 1968. Regionally accredited. **Enrollment:** 2,396 degree-seeking undergraduates; 1,195 non-degree-seeking students. **Degrees:** 300 associate awarded. **Location:** 45 miles from St. Louis. **Calendar:** Semester, limited summer session. **Full-time faculty:** 68 total; 25% have terminal degrees, 6% minority, 56% women. **Part-time faculty:** 146 total; 6% have terminal degrees, 3% minority, 53% women. **Special facilities:** Learning and assessment center, observatory, natural prairie.

Student profile. Among degree-seeking undergraduates, 690 enrolled as first-time, first-year students.

Part-time:	37%	**Asian American:**	1%
Women:	64%	**Hispanic American:**	1%
African American:	2%	**25 or older:**	28%

Basis for selection. Open admission, but selective for some programs. Special requirements for nursing program and AAT. ASSET required for placement for degree seeking students but not required for all certificate programs. **Homeschooled:** 21 ACT required without GED.

2008-2009 Annual costs. Tuition/fees: $2,130; $2,910 out-of-district; $4,230 out-of-state. Per-credit charge: $61 in-district; $87 out-of-district; $131 out-of-state.

2007-2008 Financial aid. Need-based: Need-based aid available for part-time students. **Non-need-based:** Scholarships awarded for academics, alumni affiliation, art, athletics, music/drama, state residency.

Application procedures. Admission: No deadline. No application fee. Application must be submitted on paper. Admission notification on a rolling basis. **Financial aid:** Priority date 3/1; no closing date. FAFSA required. Applicants notified on a rolling basis starting 3/15.

Academics. Special study options: Distance learning, dual enrollment of high school students, ESL, honors, independent study, internships, liberal arts/career combination. Central Methodist University classes offered on campus and may count toward 4-year degree. Bachelor's degree programs available on campus. License preparation in nursing, paramedic, radiology. **Credit/placement by examination:** AP, CLEP, institutional tests. **Support services:** GED preparation and test center, learning center, reduced course load, remedial instruction, study skills assistance, tutoring, writing center.

Majors. Business: Accounting technology, administrative services, business admin. **Computer sciences:** Networking. **Construction:** General. **Education:** General, teacher assistance. **Engineering:** General. **Engineering technology:** Drafting, manufacturing. **Family/consumer sciences:** Child care. **Health:** EMT paramedic, medical radiologic technology/radiation therapy, medical secretary, nursing (RN), respiratory therapy technology. **Legal studies:** Legal secretary. **Mechanic/repair:** Automotive, heating/ac/refrig. **Personal/culinary services:** Chef training. **Production:** Machine tool, welding. **Protective services:** Firefighting, police science. **Science technology:** Biological. **Visual/performing arts:** Commercial/advertising art. **Other:** Apprenticeship training - communication trades, Apprenticeship training - construction trades, Industrial engineering technology, Occupational education.

Most popular majors. Business/marketing 12%, education 9%, health sciences 18%, liberal arts 48%.

Computing on campus. 315 workstations in library, computer center, student center. Online course registration, online library, wireless network available.

Student life. Freshman orientation: Mandatory. Preregistration for classes offered. Held prior to start of classes, includes tours, seminars, adviser activities, social activities. **Activities:** Jazz band, choral groups, drama, music ensembles, musical theater, student government, student newspaper, TV station, Phi Theta Kappa honor society, variety of religious and social clubs.

Athletics. NJCAA. **Intercollegiate:** Soccer M, softball W, volleyball W. **Team name:** Falcons.

Student services. Adult student services, career counseling, student employment services, financial aid counseling, personal counseling, placement for graduates, veterans' counselor. **Physically disabled:** Services for visually, hearing impaired. **Transfer:** Pre-admission transcript evaluation for new students. Transfer adviser, college fairs on campus for students transferring to 4-year colleges.

Contact. E-mail: wiedaks@eastcentral.edu
Phone: (636) 583-5195 ext. 2221 Fax: (636) 583-1897
Karen Wieda, Registrar, East Central College, 1964 Prairie Dell Road, Union, MO 63084-0529

High-Tech Institute

Kansas City, Missouri
www.hightechinstitute.edu

- For-profit 2-year technical college
- Very large city

General. Accredited by ACCSCT. **Enrollment:** 250 degree-seeking undergraduates. **Degrees:** 139 associate awarded. **Calendar:** Continuous. **Full-time faculty:** 10 total. **Part-time faculty:** 5 total.

Basis for selection. Open admission.

Academics. Credit/placement by examination: CLEP.

Majors. Health: Dental assistant, insurance coding, surgical technology.

Student life. Activities: Alpha Beta Kappa, student organization.

Contact. Phone: (816) 444-4300
Director of Admissions, High-Tech Institute, 9001 State Line Road, Kansas City, MO 64114

ITT Technical Institute: Kansas City

Kansas City, Missouri

- For-profit 2-year business and technical college
- Large city

General. Accredited by ACICS. **Calendar:** Quarter.

Contact. 9150 East 41st Terrace, Kansas City, MO 64133

Jefferson College

Hillsboro, Missouri
www.jeffco.edu CB code: 6320

- Public 2-year community and technical college
- Commuter campus in rural community

General. Founded in 1963. Regionally accredited. College also serves as area vocational school, continuing education program, adult basic education center and business and technology training center. **Enrollment:** 4,609 degree-seeking undergraduates; 536 non-degree-seeking students. **Degrees:** 576 associate awarded. **Location:** 30 miles from St. Louis. **Calendar:** Semester, limited summer session. **Full-time faculty:** 94 total; 13% have terminal degrees, 3% minority, 52% women. **Part-time faculty:** 193 total; 8% have terminal degrees, 7% minority, 46% women. **Class size:** 48% < 20, 48% 20-39, 2% 40-49, 2% 50-99, less than 1% >100. **Special facilities:** Outdoor theater, facility for computer-related technologies, graphic design lab, veterinary technology clinic, law enforcement academy.

Student profile. Among degree-seeking undergraduates, 55% enrolled in a transfer program, 45% enrolled in a vocational program, 1% already have a bachelor's degree or higher, 1,198 enrolled as first-time, first-year students.

Part-time:	45%	**25 or older:**	33%
Out-of-state:	2%	**Live on campus:**	4%
Women:	61%		

Transfer out. Colleges most students transferred to 2008: University of Missouri: St. Louis, Missouri Baptist University, Southeast Missouri State University.

Basis for selection. Open admission, but selective for some programs. Special requirements for nursing, veterinary technology programs, and law enforcement academy. Interview required for health services technologies students. **Homeschooled:** Transcript of courses and grades required. Minimum placement test scores if high school transcript is not from an approved accrediting body. **Learning Disabled:** Suggested that students with disabilities meet with the campus Disability Support Services Coordinator prior to enrollment.

High school preparation. Elementary algebra required for electronics; chemistry required for nursing and veterinary technology.

2008-2009 Annual costs. Tuition/fees: $2,550; $3,840 out-of-district; $5,100 out-of-state. Per-credit charge: $85 in-district; $128 out-of-district; $170 out-of-state. Room only: $3,400. Books/supplies: $1,000. Personal expenses: $1,000.

2007-2008 Financial aid. **Need-based:** 819 full-time freshmen applied for aid; 529 were judged to have need; 505 of these received aid. Average need met was 51%. Average scholarship/grant was $1,806; average loan $2,454. 58% of total undergraduate aid awarded as scholarships/grants, 42% as loans/jobs. Need-based aid available for part-time students. Work-study available nights and for part-time students. **Non-need-based:** Awarded to 1,127 full-time undergraduates, including 488 freshmen. Scholarships awarded for academics, art, athletics, leadership, music/drama, state residency.

Application procedures. **Admission:** Priority date 5/3; no deadline. $20 fee, may be waived for applicants with need. Admission notification on a rolling basis. **Financial aid:** Priority date 4/1; no closing date. FAFSA required. Applicants notified on a rolling basis starting 4/15.

Academics. Advising and Retention Center available. **Special study options:** Distance learning, double major, dual enrollment of high school students, ESL, honors, independent study, internships, liberal arts/career combination, study abroad. Cooperative agreement with 2 neighboring community colleges. License preparation in nursing, paramedic. **Credit/placement by examination:** AP, CLEP, IB, institutional tests. 30 credit hours maximum toward associate degree. **Support services:** GED preparation and test center, learning center, reduced course load, remedial instruction, study skills assistance, tutoring, writing center.

Majors. **Business:** General, administrative services, office/clerical. **Computer sciences:** General, security. **Education:** Early childhood, secondary. **Engineering:** General. **Engineering technology:** Architectural drafting, drafting, electrical. **Health:** EMT paramedic, medical secretary, nursing (RN), veterinary technology/assistant. **Liberal arts:** Arts/sciences. **Mechanic/repair:** Automotive, heating/ac/refrig, industrial. **Personal/culinary services:** Chef training, culinary arts, food prep, food service, restaurant/catering. **Production:** Machine tool, welding. **Protective services:** Fire safety technology, law enforcement admin, police science. **Science technology:** Biological.

Most popular majors. Business/marketing 7%, engineering/engineering technologies 6%, health sciences 13%, liberal arts 62%.

Computing on campus. 250 workstations in dormitories, library, computer center, student center. Dormitories wired for high-speed internet access and linked to campus network. Commuter students can connect to campus network. Online course registration, online library, helpline, wireless network available.

Student life. **Freshman orientation:** Mandatory, $85 fee. Preregistration for classes offered. One-credit hour first-year experience course. **Housing:** Apartments, wellness housing available. $200 fully refundable deposit. **Activities:** Bands, choral groups, drama, literary magazine, music ensembles, musical theater, student government, student newspaper, TV station, Phi Theta Kappa, College Ambassadors, Habitat for Humanity, academic clubs, cultural club, Missouri Student National Educational Association.

Athletics. NJCAA. **Intercollegiate:** Baseball M, basketball W, soccer M, softball W, volleyball W. **Team name:** Vikings.

Student services. Adult student services, alcohol/substance abuse counseling, career counseling, services for economically disadvantaged, student employment services, financial aid counseling, on-campus daycare, personal counseling, placement for graduates, veterans' counselor. **Physically disabled:** Services for visually, speech, hearing impaired. **Learning disabled:** Comprehensive services available. **Transfer:** Transfer adviser, college fairs on campus for students transferring to 4-year colleges.

Contact. E-mail: admissions@jeffco.edu
Phone: (636) 797-3000 ext. 217 Fax: (636) 789-5103
Julie Fraser, Director of Admissions and Financial Aid, Jefferson College, 1000 Viking Drive, Hillsboro, MO 63050-2441

L'Ecole Culinaire
St. Louis, Missouri
www.lecoleculinaire.com

- For-profit 2-year culinary school
- Large city

General. Accredited by ACCSCT. **Calendar:** Quarter.

Annual costs/financial aid. Program costs: $25,000 (certificate/diploma); $36,100 (associate degree).

Contact. 9811 South Outer Forty Drive, St. Louis, MO 63124

Linn State Technical College
Linn, Missouri
www.linnstate.edu

- Public 2-year technical college
- Residential campus in small town

General. **Enrollment:** 945 degree-seeking undergraduates; 28 non-degree-seeking students. **Degrees:** 256 associate awarded. **Location:** 30 from Jefferson City. **Calendar:** Semester, limited summer session. **Full-time faculty:** 82 total; 26% have terminal degrees, 1% minority, 27% women. **Part-time faculty:** 5 total; 20% have terminal degrees, 20% women. **Special facilities:** 3,200 feet hard surface runway, hangers, and fixed base operations.

Student profile. Among degree-seeking undergraduates, 463 enrolled as first-time, first-year students.

Part-time:	9%	**Women:**	9%

Basis for selection. Open admission, but selective for some programs.

2008-2009 Annual costs. Tuition/fees: $5,370; $9,750 out-of-state. Per-credit charge: $146 in-state; $292 out-of-state. Room/board: $4,920. Books/supplies: $910. Personal expenses: $1,200.

2007-2008 Financial aid. **Need-based:** 59% of total undergraduate aid awarded as scholarships/grants, 41% as loans/jobs.

Application procedures. **Admission:** No application fee. **Financial aid:** Priority date 3/1; no closing date.

Academics. **Credit/placement by examination:** CLEP.

Majors. **Computer sciences:** Networking, programming, systems analysis. **Construction:** Electrician, lineworker, maintenance. **Engineering technology:** Civil, drafting, electrical, manufacturing. **Health:** Physical therapy assistant. **Mechanic/repair:** Aircraft, aircraft powerplant, auto body, automotive, electronics/electrical, heating/ac/refrig, heavy equipment, medium/heavy vehicle, motorcycle. **Production:** Machine tool. **Science technology:** Nuclear power.

Most popular majors. Computer/information sciences 14%, engineering/engineering technologies 15%, science technologies 6%, trade and industry 58%.

Athletics. **Team name:** Eagle.

Contact. E-mail: admissions@linnstate.edu
Phone: (573) 897-5196 Toll-free number: (800) 743-8324
Fax: (573) 897-5026
Director of Admissions, Linn State Technical College, One Technology Drive, Linn, MO 65051

Metro Business College
Cape Girardeau, Missouri
www.metrobusinesscollege.edu **CB code: 3316**

- For-profit 2-year business and career college
- Commuter campus in large town
- Interview required

General. Accredited by ACICS. Parent campus in Cape Girardeau. **Enrollment:** 125 degree-seeking undergraduates. **Degrees:** 142 associate awarded. **Location:** 125 miles from St. Louis. **Calendar:** Continuous. **Full-time faculty:** 12 total. **Part-time faculty:** 5 total.

Basis for selection. Open admission, but selective for some programs. Open Admission Policy. **Homeschooled:** State high school equivalency certificate required.

2008-2009 Annual costs. Tuition/fees: $9,110.

Application procedures. **Admission:** No deadline. $25 fee.

Academics. **Credit/placement by examination:** CLEP. **Support services:** Study skills assistance, tutoring.

Majors. **Business:** Business admin.

Computing on campus. Online library available.

Student life. **Freshman orientation:** Mandatory.

Student services. Adult student services, alcohol/substance abuse counseling, career counseling, services for economically disadvantaged, student employment services, financial aid counseling, minority student services, personal counseling, placement for graduates, veterans' counselor. **Physically disabled:** Services for visually impaired.

Contact. E-mail: randy@metrobusinesscollege.edu
Phone: (573) 334-9181 Toll-free number: (800) 467-0785
Fax: (573) 334-0617
Denise Acey, Director of Admissions, Metro Business College, 1732 North Kingshighway, Cape Girardeau, MO 36701

Metro Business College: Jefferson City

Jefferson City, Missouri
www.metrobusinesscollege.edu **CB code: 3318**

- For-profit 2-year business and health science college
- Commuter campus in large town
- Interview required

General. Accredited by ACICS. **Enrollment:** 178 degree-seeking undergraduates. **Degrees:** 42 associate awarded. **Location:** 35 miles from Columbia. **Calendar:** Quarter, extensive summer session. **Full-time faculty:** 7 total; 29% have terminal degrees, 57% women. **Part-time faculty:** 12 total; 17% have terminal degrees, 8% minority, 50% women. **Class size:** 100% 40-49.

Student profile. Among degree-seeking undergraduates, 100% enrolled in a vocational program, 1% already have a bachelor's degree or higher, 56 enrolled as first-time, first-year students.

Part-time:	8%	**Hispanic American:**	3%
Women:	77%	**25 or older:**	54%
African American:	20%		

Transfer out. 2% of students enrolled in the transfer program go on to 4-year colleges.

Basis for selection. Open admission, but selective for some programs. Students must take entrance exam. Required scores vary by program.

2008-2009 Annual costs. Tuition/fees: $9,110.

Financial aid. **Need-based:** Need-based aid available for part-time students.

Application procedures. **Admission:** No deadline. $25 fee. Application must be submitted on paper. Admission notification on a rolling basis. **Financial aid:** No deadline. FAFSA, institutional form required. Applicants notified on a rolling basis.

Academics. **Credit/placement by examination:** CLEP. **Support services:** Reduced course load, remedial instruction, study skills assistance, tutoring.

Majors. **Business:** Business admin. **Health:** Office assistant.

Most popular majors. Computer/information sciences 57%, health sciences 43%.

Computing on campus. 7 workstations in library. Online library, repair service available.

Student life. **Freshman orientation:** Mandatory. **Activities:** Student government.

Student services. Adult student services, alcohol/substance abuse counseling, services for economically disadvantaged, student employment services, financial aid counseling, personal counseling, placement for graduates. **Transfer:** Pre-admission transcript evaluation for new students.

Contact. E-mail: infojeff@metrobusinesscollege.edu
Phone: (573) 635-6600 Toll-free number: (888) 436-3876
Fax: (573) 635-6999
Tanita Jeffries, Admissions Representative, Metro Business College: Jefferson City, 1407 Southwest Boulevard, Jefferson City, MO 65109

Metro Business College: Rolla

Rolla, Missouri
www.metrobusinesscollege.edu **CB code: 3317**

- For-profit 2-year business college
- Large town

General. Accredited by ACICS. **Calendar:** Continuous.

Annual costs/financial aid. Tuition/fees (2008-2009): $9,110.

Contact. Phone: (573) 364-8464
Director, 1202 East Highway 72, Rolla, MO 65401

Metropolitan Community College: Blue River

Independence, Missouri
www.mcckc.edu **CB code: 6060**

- Public 2-year community college
- Commuter campus in small city

General. Regionally accredited. **Enrollment:** 2,183 degree-seeking undergraduates; 877 non-degree-seeking students. **Degrees:** 247 associate awarded. **Location:** 25 miles from Kansas City. **Calendar:** Semester, limited summer session. **Full-time faculty:** 40 total; 25% have terminal degrees, 8% minority, 55% women. **Part-time faculty:** 321 total; 1% have terminal degrees, 8% minority, 40% women. **Class size:** 30% < 20, 69% 20-39, less than 1% 40-49, less than 1% 50-99.

Student profile. Among degree-seeking undergraduates, 1% already have a bachelor's degree or higher, 660 enrolled as first-time, first-year students, 41 transferred in from other institutions.

Part-time:	49%	**Hispanic American:**	4%
Women:	61%	**25 or older:**	1%
African American:	4%		

Basis for selection. Open admission. **Homeschooled:** Statement describing homeschool structure and mission, transcript of courses and grades, interview required. Provide proof of graduation requirements. Applicants under age 16 must meet with Dean of Student Services and bring student portfolio.

High school preparation. 16 units recommended. Recommended units include English 4, mathematics 3, social studies 3, science 3 and foreign language 2. 1 visual/performing arts recommended.

2008-2009 Annual costs. Tuition/fees: $2,460; $4,380 out-of-district; $5,850 out-of-state. Per-credit charge: $77 in-district; $141 out-of-district; $190 out-of-state. Books/supplies: $1,000. Personal expenses: $3,279.

2007-2008 Financial aid. **Need-based:** Average scholarship/grant was $1,712; average loan $1,516. 73% of total undergraduate aid awarded as scholarships/grants, 27% as loans/jobs. Need-based aid available for part-time students. Work-study available nights and for part-time students. **Non-need-based:** Scholarships awarded for academics, athletics, leadership.

Application procedures. **Admission:** No deadline. No application fee. Admission notification on a rolling basis. **Financial aid:** Priority date 5/30, closing date 8/20. FAFSA, institutional form required. Applicants notified on a rolling basis starting 4/8.

Academics. **Special study options:** Accelerated study, cooperative education, cross-registration, distance learning, dual enrollment of high school students, honors, independent study, internships, weekend college. **Credit/placement by examination:** AP, CLEP, institutional tests. 30 credit hours maximum toward associate degree. **Support services:** GED test center, learning center, remedial instruction, tutoring.

Majors. **Business:** General, business admin. **Computer sciences:** Computer science. **Education:** General. **Engineering:** General. **Engineering technology:** Software. **Liberal arts:** Arts/sciences. **Protective services:** Firefighting, law enforcement admin, police science.

Most popular majors. Business/marketing 8%, liberal arts 85%.

Computing on campus. 350 workstations in library, computer center. Commuter students can connect to campus network. Online course registration, online library, helpline available.

Student life. **Freshman orientation:** Available. Preregistration for classes offered. **Activities:** Choral groups, student government, student newspaper.

Athletics. **Intercollegiate:** Soccer. **Team name:** Trail Blazers.

Student services. Adult student services, career counseling, student employment services, personal counseling, placement for graduates, veterans' counselor. **Physically disabled:** Services for visually, speech, hearing impaired. **Transfer:** Transfer adviser for students transferring to 4-year colleges.

Contact. Phone: (816) 220-6577
Basil Lister, Registrar, Metropolitan Community College: Blue River, 3200 Broadway, Kansas City, MO 64111-2429

Metropolitan Community College: Longview

Lee's Summit, Missouri
www.mcckc.edu **CB code: 6359**

- Public 2-year community college
- Commuter campus in small city

General. Founded in 1968. Regionally accredited. **Enrollment:** 4,449 degree-seeking undergraduates; 1,399 non-degree-seeking students. **Degrees:** 479 associate awarded. **Location:** 10 miles from Kansas City. **Calendar:** Semester, extensive summer session. **Full-time faculty:** 88 total; 17% have terminal degrees, 9% minority, 48% women. **Part-time faculty:** 329 total; 4% have terminal degrees, 8% minority, 58% women. **Class size:** 41% < 20, 57% 20-39, less than 1% 40-49, less than 1% 50-99.

Student profile. Among degree-seeking undergraduates, 82% enrolled in a transfer program, 18% enrolled in a vocational program, 2% already have a bachelor's degree or higher, 1,409 enrolled as first-time, first-year students, 81 transferred in from other institutions.

Part-time:	46%	**Asian American:**	1%
Out-of-state:	1%	**Hispanic American:**	3%
Women:	58%	**Native American:**	1%
African American:	14%	**25 or older:**	25%

Basis for selection. Open admission. **Homeschooled:** Statement describing homeschool structure and mission, transcript of courses and grades, interview required. Provide proof of graduation requirements. Applicants under the age of 16 must meet with Dean of Student Services and bring student portfolio.

High school preparation. 16 units recommended. Recommended units include English 4, mathematics 3, social studies 3, science 3 and foreign language 2. 1 unit in visual/performing arts recommended.

2008-2009 Annual costs. Tuition/fees: $2,460; $4,380 out-of-district; $5,850 out-of-state. Per-credit charge: $77 in-district; $141 out-of-district; $190 out-of-state. Books/supplies: $1,000. Personal expenses: $3,279.

2007-2008 Financial aid. Need-based: Average scholarship/grant was $1,668; average loan $1,443. 73% of total undergraduate aid awarded as scholarships/grants, 27% as loans/jobs. Work-study available nights and for part-time students. **Non-need-based:** Scholarships awarded for academics, athletics, leadership.

Application procedures. Admission: No deadline. No application fee. Admission notification on a rolling basis. **Financial aid:** Priority date 5/30, closing date 8/20. FAFSA, institutional form required. Applicants notified on a rolling basis starting 4/8.

Academics. Special study options: Accelerated study, cooperative education, cross-registration, distance learning, dual enrollment of high school students, honors, independent study, internships, weekend college. **Credit/placement by examination:** AP, CLEP, institutional tests. 30 credit hours maximum toward associate degree. **Support services:** GED test center, learning center, remedial instruction, tutoring.

Majors. Agriculture: Turf management. **Business:** General, accounting, administrative services, business admin, office management, office technology, sales/distribution. **Computer sciences:** General, applications programming. **Education:** General. **Engineering:** General. **Engineering technology:** Surveying. **Liberal arts:** Arts/sciences. **Mechanic/repair:** Auto body, automotive. **Protective services:** Corrections, criminal justice.

Most popular majors. Business/marketing 7%, engineering/engineering technologies 9%, liberal arts 81%.

Computing on campus. 627 workstations in library, computer center. Commuter students can connect to campus network. Online course registration, helpline available.

Student life. Freshman orientation: Available. Preregistration for classes offered. **Activities:** Choral groups, drama, literary magazine, student government, student newspaper.

Athletics. NJCAA. **Intercollegiate:** Baseball M, volleyball W. **Intramural:** Basketball, swimming, volleyball. **Team name:** Lakers.

Student services. Adult student services, career counseling, student employment services, on-campus daycare, personal counseling, placement for graduates, veterans' counselor. **Physically disabled:** Services for visually, hearing impaired. **Transfer:** Transfer adviser for students transferring to 4-year colleges.

Contact. Phone: (816) 672-2000 Fax: (816) 672-2025
Kathy Hale, Registrar, Metropolitan Community College: Longview, 500 Longview Road, Lee's Summit, MO 64081-2105

Metropolitan Community College: Maple Woods

Kansas City, Missouri
www.mcckc.edu **CB code: 6436**

- Public 2-year community college
- Commuter campus in large city

General. Founded in 1968. Regionally accredited. **Enrollment:** 3,142 degree-seeking undergraduates; 1,407 non-degree-seeking students. **Degrees:** 351 associate awarded. **Location:** 15 miles from downtown. **Calendar:** Semester, limited summer session. **Full-time faculty:** 55 total; 20% have terminal degrees, 13% minority, 56% women. **Part-time faculty:** 302 total; 3% have terminal degrees, 5% minority, 55% women. **Class size:** 40% < 20, 60% 20-39, less than 1% 40-49, less than 1% 50-99.

Student profile. Among degree-seeking undergraduates, 84% enrolled in a transfer program, 16% enrolled in a vocational program, 2% already have a bachelor's degree or higher, 930 enrolled as first-time, first-year students, 65 transferred in from other institutions.

Part-time:	47%	**Asian American:**	2%
Women:	57%	**Hispanic American:**	5%
African American:	4%	**25 or older:**	31%

Basis for selection. Open admission, but selective for some programs. Special requirements for animal health technology program. **Homeschooled:** Provide proof of high school graduation. If under 16 years old must meet with Dean of Student Services and bring student portfolio.

High school preparation. 16 units recommended. Recommended units include English 4, mathematics 3, social studies 3, science 3 and foreign language 2. 1 unit in visual/performing arts recommended.

2008-2009 Annual costs. Tuition/fees: $2,460; $4,380 out-of-district; $5,850 out-of-state. Per-credit charge: $77 in-district; $141 out-of-district; $190 out-of-state. Books/supplies: $1,000. Personal expenses: $3,279.

2007-2008 Financial aid. Need-based: Average scholarship/grant was $2,433; average loan $1,541. 79% of total undergraduate aid awarded as scholarships/grants, 21% as loans/jobs. Need-based aid available for part-time students. Work-study available nights and for part-time students. **Non-need-based:** Scholarships awarded for academics, athletics, leadership.

Application procedures. Admission: No deadline. No application fee. Admission notification on a rolling basis. Separate application required for animal health technology; deadline March 1. **Financial aid:** Priority date 5/30; no closing date. FAFSA, institutional form required. Applicants notified on a rolling basis.

Academics. Special study options: Cross-registration, distance learning, dual enrollment of high school students, exchange student, honors, internships. **Credit/placement by examination:** AP, CLEP, institutional tests. 30 credit hours maximum toward associate degree. **Support services:** GED test center, learning center, reduced course load, remedial instruction, tutoring.

Majors. Business: General, administrative services, business admin, office technology, sales/distribution. **Computer sciences:** General, applications programming. **Education:** General. **Engineering:** General. **Foreign languages:** Sign language interpretation. **Health:** Nursing (RN), veterinary technology/assistant. **Liberal arts:** Arts/sciences. **Physical sciences:** General. **Protective services:** Criminal justice, law enforcement admin.

Most popular majors. Business/marketing 6%, health sciences 7%, liberal arts 83%.

Computing on campus. 370 workstations in computer center. Commuter students can connect to campus network. Online course registration, online library, helpline available.

Student life. Freshman orientation: Available. Preregistration for classes offered. **Activities:** Choral groups, student government, student newspaper.

Athletics. NJCAA. **Intercollegiate:** Baseball M, softball W. **Intramural:** Softball, volleyball W. **Team name:** Centaurs.

Student services. Adult student services, career counseling, student employment services, personal counseling, placement for graduates, veterans' counselor. **Physically disabled:** Services for visually, speech, hearing impaired. **Transfer:** Transfer adviser, college fairs on campus for students transferring to 4-year colleges.

Contact. Phone: (816) 437-3100 Fax: (816) 437-3049
Dawn Hatterman, Registrar, Metropolitan Community College: Maple Woods, 2601 NE Barry Road, Kansas City, MO 64156-1299

Metropolitan Community College: Penn Valley

Kansas City, Missouri
www.mcckc.edu **CB code: 6324**

- Public 2-year community college
- Commuter campus in large city

General. Regionally accredited. **Enrollment:** 3,540 degree-seeking undergraduates; 800 non-degree-seeking students. **Degrees:** 389 associate awarded. **Location:** 2 miles from downtown. **Calendar:** Semester, extensive summer session. **Full-time faculty:** 105 total; 19% have terminal degrees, 25% minority, 66% women. **Part-time faculty:** 320 total; less than 1% have terminal degrees, 32% minority, 64% women. **Class size:** 56% < 20, 41% 20-39, 1% 40-49, 2% 50-99.

Student profile. Among degree-seeking undergraduates, 68% enrolled in a transfer program, 32% enrolled in a vocational program, 4% already have a bachelor's degree or higher, 757 enrolled as first-time, first-year students, 66 transferred in from other institutions.

Part-time:	63%	**Asian American:**	4%
Out-of-state:	3%	**Hispanic American:**	7%
Women:	72%	**25 or older:**	52%
African American:	34%		

Basis for selection. Open admission, but selective for some programs. Special requirements for allied health programs. ACT or ASSET required for placement and counseling. **Homeschooled:** Statement describing homeschool structure and mission, transcript of courses and grades, interview required. Students under 16 must bring portfolio to Dean of Student Services.

High school preparation. 16 units recommended. Recommended units include English 4, mathematics 3, social studies 3, science 3 and foreign language 2. One unit visual/performing arts recommended.

2008-2009 Annual costs. Tuition/fees: $2,460; $4,380 out-of-district; $5,850 out-of-state. Per-credit charge: $77 in-district; $141 out-of-district; $190 out-of-state. Books/supplies: $1,000. Personal expenses: $3,279.

2007-2008 Financial aid. Need-based: Average scholarship/grant was $1,880; average loan $1,320. 74% of total undergraduate aid awarded as scholarships/grants, 26% as loans/jobs. Work-study available nights and for part-time students. **Non-need-based:** Scholarships awarded for academics, athletics, leadership.

Application procedures. Admission: No deadline. No application fee. Admission notification on a rolling basis. **Financial aid:** Priority date 5/30; no closing date. FAFSA, institutional form required. Applicants notified on a rolling basis starting 4/8.

Academics. Special study options: Cross-registration, distance learning, dual enrollment of high school students, ESL, honors, internships, liberal arts/career combination, weekend college. Cooperative programs in allied health with Johnson County Community College. License preparation in dental hygiene, nursing, occupational therapy, paramedic, physical therapy, radiology. **Credit/placement by examination:** AP, CLEP, institutional tests. 30 credit hours maximum toward associate degree. **Support services:** GED test center, learning center, reduced course load, remedial instruction, tutoring.

Majors. Business: General, accounting, administrative services, business admin, fashion, office management, office technology, sales/distribution. **Computer sciences:** General. **Education:** General. **Engineering:** General. **Family/consumer sciences:** Child care. **Health:** Dental assistant, EMT paramedic, medical radiologic technology/radiation therapy, mental health services, nursing (RN), occupational therapy assistant, physical therapy assistant, respiratory therapy technology. **Legal studies:** Paralegal. **Liberal arts:** Arts/sciences. **Mechanic/repair:** Heating/ac/refrig. **Protective services:** Corrections, criminal justice, law enforcement admin. **Visual/performing arts:** Commercial/advertising art, fashion design, graphic design, music.

Most popular majors. Family/consumer sciences 9%, health sciences 43%, liberal arts 32%, visual/performing arts 12%.

Computing on campus. 1,095 workstations in library, computer center.

Student life. Freshman orientation: Available. **Activities:** Jazz band, drama, music ensembles, opera, student government, student newspaper, Black student association, Los Americanos.

Athletics. NJCAA. **Intercollegiate:** Basketball M, golf M. **Team name:** Scouts.

Student services. Career counseling, student employment services, on-campus daycare, personal counseling, placement for graduates, veterans' counselor. **Physically disabled:** Services for visually, speech, hearing impaired.

Contact. Phone: (816) 759-4100 Fax: (816) 759-4161
Carroll O'Neal, Registrar, Metropolitan Community College: Penn Valley, 3201 Southwest Trafficway, Kansas City, MO 64111-2429

Mineral Area College

Park Hills, Missouri
www.mineralarea.edu **CB code: 6323**

- Public 2-year community college
- Commuter campus in small town

General. Founded in 1922. Regionally accredited. **Enrollment:** 2,989 degree-seeking undergraduates. **Degrees:** 465 associate awarded. **Location:** 60 miles from St. Louis. **Calendar:** Semester, limited summer session. **Full-time faculty:** 55 total. **Part-time faculty:** 195 total. **Class size:** 49% < 20, 51% 20-39.

Student profile.

Out-of-state:	1%	**Live on campus:**	4%
25 or older:	34%		

Transfer out. Colleges most students transferred to 2008: Central Methodist College at Park Hills, Southeast Missouri State University, Southwest Missouri State University, University of Missouri - St. Louis, University of Missouri - Columbia.

Basis for selection. Open admission, but selective for some programs. Interview required for health majors and law enforcement academy. **Homeschooled:** Must submit documentation as required by Missouri State Statute 167.031.

2008-2009 Annual costs. Tuition/fees: $2,490; $3,240 out-of-district; $3,960 out-of-state. Per-credit charge: $83 in-district; $108 out-of-district; $132 out-of-state. Room/board: $2,925. Books/supplies: $1,400.

2007-2008 Financial aid. Need-based: Need-based aid available for part-time students. Work-study available for part-time students. **Non-need-based:** Scholarships awarded for academics, alumni affiliation, art, athletics, leadership, music/drama, state residency.

Application procedures. Admission: Priority date 8/1; no deadline. $15 fee. Admission notification on a rolling basis beginning on or about 2/15. **Financial aid:** Priority date 4/1; no closing date. FAFSA required. Applicants notified on a rolling basis starting 2/15; must reply within 4 week(s) of notification.

Academics. Special study options: Cross-registration, distance learning, dual enrollment of high school students, honors, independent study, internships, liberal arts/career combination, study abroad. Bachelor's degree programs available on campus. License preparation in nursing. **Credit/placement by examination:** AP, CLEP, institutional tests. 30 credit hours maximum toward associate degree. Credit held in escrow for 1 semester. **Support services:** GED test center, learning center, pre-admission summer program, reduced course load, remedial instruction, study skills assistance, tutoring, writing center.

Majors. Agriculture: Horticulture, production. **Business:** General, accounting, administrative services, banking/financial services, business admin. **Communications technology:** Graphic/printing. **Computer sciences:** Networking, programming. **Education:** Voc/tech. **Engineering technology:** CAD/CADD, civil, construction, electrical, manufacturing, occupational safety. **Family/consumer sciences:** Child development. **Health:** Clinical lab technology, health services, nursing (RN), respiratory therapy technology. **Liberal arts:** Arts/sciences. **Mechanic/repair:** Auto body, automotive, heating/ac/refrig, industrial. **Production:** General, machine tool, welding. **Protective services:** Firefighting, police science. **Social sciences:** General.

Computing on campus. Dormitories wired for high-speed internet access. Online course registration, helpline available.

Student life. **Freshman orientation:** Mandatory. Preregistration for classes offered. One-day program for students and parents. **Housing:** Coed dorms, wellness housing available. $200 deposit. Privatized housing available. **Activities:** Bands, choral groups, drama, music ensembles, musical theater, student government, Young Democrats, Young Republicans, Baptist Youth.

Athletics. NJCAA. **Intercollegiate:** Baseball M, basketball, volleyball W. **Team name:** Cardinals.

Student services. Adult student services, career counseling, student employment services, financial aid counseling, personal counseling, placement for graduates, veterans' counselor. **Physically disabled:** Services for visually, speech, hearing impaired. **Transfer:** Pre-admission transcript evaluation for new students. Transfer adviser, college fairs on campus for students transferring to 4-year colleges.

Contact. E-mail: admissions@mineralarea.edu
Phone: (573) 518-2206 Fax: (573) 518-2166
Julie Sheets, Admissions Officer, Mineral Area College, PO Box 1000, Park Hills, MO 63601-1000

Missouri College
St. Louis, Missouri
www.missouricollege.com **CB code: 3074**

- For-profit 2-year technical college
- Commuter campus in large city
- Interview required

General. Accredited by ACCSCT. **Enrollment:** 508 degree-seeking undergraduates. **Degrees:** 24 associate awarded. **Calendar:** Continuous. **Full-time faculty:** 14 total. **Part-time faculty:** 20 total. **Class size:** 59% < 20, 41% 20-39.

Basis for selection. Open admission. All applicants required to take personnel test.

2008-2009 Annual costs. Tuition/fees: $10,650. Diploma programs are $345 per semester credit hour, degree programs are $365 per semester credit hour.

Financial aid. **Need-based:** Need-based aid available for part-time students. Work-study available nights.

Application procedures. **Admission:** No deadline. $35 fee. Admission notification on a rolling basis. **Financial aid:** No deadline. FAFSA required.

Academics. **Special study options:** Distance learning. Bachelor's degree programs available on campus. **Credit/placement by examination:** CLEP.

Majors. **Business:** Business admin. **Health:** Dental assistant, dietician assistant, massage therapy, medical assistant.

Most popular majors. Business/marketing 20%, health sciences 80%.

Student life. **Freshman orientation:** Mandatory.

Student services. Career counseling, financial aid counseling, personal counseling, placement for graduates. **Physically disabled:** Services for visually impaired.

Contact. E-mail: kjefferson@missouricollege.com
Phone: (314) 821-7700 Toll-free number: (800) 216-6732
Karl Jefferson, Director of Admissions, Missouri College, 10121 Manchester Road, St. Louis, MO 63122-1583

Missouri State University: West Plains
West Plains, Missouri
www.wp.missouristate.edu **CB code: 6662**

- Public 2-year branch campus college
- Commuter campus in large town

General. Regionally accredited. **Enrollment:** 1,458 degree-seeking undergraduates; 376 non-degree-seeking students. **Degrees:** 248 associate awarded. **Location:** 110 miles from Springfield. **Calendar:** Semester, limited summer session. **Full-time faculty:** 33 total; 24% have terminal degrees, 6% minority, 48% women. **Part-time faculty:** 77 total; 13% have terminal degrees, 60% women. **Class size:** 43% < 20, 57% 20-39, less than 1% 40-49.

Student profile. Among degree-seeking undergraduates, 74% enrolled in a transfer program, 26% enrolled in a vocational program, 1% already have a bachelor's degree or higher, 443 enrolled as first-time, first-year students, 87 transferred in from other institutions.

Part-time:	27%	**Women:**	62%
Out-of-state:	7%	**Live on campus:**	4%

Transfer out. 40% of students enrolled in the transfer program go on to 4-year colleges. **Colleges most students transferred to 2008:** Missouri State University: Springfield.

Basis for selection. Open admission, but selective for some programs. Nursing and respiratory therapy programs require separate application and applicants are considered competitively. **Homeschooled:** Transcript of courses and grades required. Must submit ACT score (minimum 18) or official GED transcript.

2008-2009 Annual costs. Tuition/fees: $3,304; $6,364 out-of-state. Per-credit charge: $102 in-state; $204 out-of-state. Room/board: $4,730. Books/supplies: $950. Personal expenses: $2,800.

2007-2008 Financial aid. **Need-based:** 89% of total undergraduate aid awarded as scholarships/grants, 11% as loans/jobs. Need-based aid available for part-time students. Work-study available nights, weekends and for part-time students. **Non-need-based:** Scholarships awarded for academics, athletics, state residency.

Application procedures. **Admission:** Closing date 8/21 (receipt date). $15 fee, may be waived for applicants with need. Admission notification on a rolling basis. **Financial aid:** Priority date 3/31; no closing date. FAFSA, institutional form required. Applicants notified on a rolling basis; must reply by 4/15.

Academics. **Special study options:** Distance learning, dual enrollment of high school students, honors, independent study, internships, liberal arts/career combination, student-designed major, study abroad. Bachelor's degree programs available on campus. License preparation in nursing. **Credit/placement by examination:** AP, CLEP, IB, institutional tests. 15 credit hours maximum toward associate degree. **Support services:** GED test center, learning center, remedial instruction, study skills assistance, tutoring, writing center.

Majors. **Agriculture:** Business, food science, horticultural science. **Business:** General, entrepreneurial studies. **Communications technology:** Animation/special effects. **Computer sciences:** General. **Engineering technology:** Manufacturing. **Family/consumer sciences:** Child care. **Health:** Nursing (RN), respiratory therapy technology. **Liberal arts:** Arts/sciences. **Protective services:** Police science.

Most popular majors. Health sciences 20%, liberal arts 73%.

Computing on campus. 104 workstations in dormitories, library, computer center, student center. Dormitories wired for high-speed internet access and linked to campus network. Commuter students can connect to campus network. Online course registration, online library, helpline, repair service, wireless network available.

Student life. **Freshman orientation:** Mandatory. Preregistration for classes offered. Half-day sessions held throughout summer. **Housing:** Coed dorms, special housing for disabled, wellness housing available. $100 fully refundable deposit. **Activities:** Campus ministries, choral groups, drama, student government, Campus Crusade for Christ, Christian Campus House, Young Democrats, Young Republicans.

Athletics. NJCAA. **Intercollegiate:** Basketball M, cheerleading, volleyball W. **Team name:** Grizzlies.

Student services. Career counseling, student employment services, financial aid counseling, health services, legal services, minority student services, personal counseling, placement for graduates, veterans' counselor. **Physically disabled:** Services for visually, hearing impaired. **Transfer:** Transfer adviser, college fairs on campus for students transferring to 4-year colleges.

Contact. E-mail: wpadmissions@missouristate.edu
Phone: (417) 255-7955 Toll-free number: (888) 466-7897
Fax: (417) 255-7959
Melissa Jett, Coordinator of Admissions, Missouri State University: West Plains, 128 Garfield Avenue, West Plains, MO 65775-2715

Moberly Area Community College
Moberly, Missouri
www.macc.edu **CB code: 6414**

- Public 2-year community college
- Commuter campus in large town

General. Founded in 1927. Regionally accredited. **Enrollment:** 3,126 degree-seeking undergraduates; 845 non-degree-seeking students. **Degrees:** 424 associate awarded. **Location:** 35 miles from Columbia. **Calendar:** Semester, extensive summer session. **Full-time faculty:** 62 total; 79% have terminal degrees, 2% minority, 60% women. **Part-time faculty:** 215 total; 76% have terminal degrees, 9% minority, 54% women. **Special facilities:** Multimedia/instructional television center, graphic arts/fine arts gallery, alumni museum.

Student profile. Among degree-seeking undergraduates, 77% enrolled in a transfer program, 23% enrolled in a vocational program, 937 enrolled as first-time, first-year students, 209 transferred in from other institutions.

Part-time:	37%	**Asian American:**	1%
Out-of-state:	2%	**Hispanic American:**	1%
Women:	60%	**25 or older:**	24%
African American:	10%	**Live on campus:**	2%

Transfer out. 75% of students enrolled in the transfer program go on to 4-year colleges. **Colleges most students transferred to 2008:** Central Methodist University, Columbia College, University of Missouri.

Basis for selection. Open admission, but selective for some programs. Special requirements for allied health and law enforcement programs. ACT scores required for admission to nursing programs. Degree-seeking students, or those taking 14 or more credits, must have ACT or ASSET score for placement purposes; tests also required for students enrolling in English or math courses. **Homeschooled:** Transcript of courses and grades, state high school equivalency certificate required. Applicants must provide transcript outlining educational process or take GED.

2008-2009 Annual costs. Tuition/fees: $2,280; $3,150 out-of-district; $4,560 out-of-state. Per-credit charge: $65 in-district; $94 out-of-district; $141 out-of-state. Meal plan covers 14 meals per week. Room only: $3,200. Books/supplies: $800. Personal expenses: $1,500.

2008-2009 Financial aid. Need-based: 73% of total undergraduate aid awarded as scholarships/grants, 27% as loans/jobs. Need-based aid available for part-time students. Work-study available nights, weekends and for part-time students. **Non-need-based:** Scholarships awarded for academics, alumni affiliation, art, athletics, leadership, music/drama.

Application procedures. Admission: No deadline. No application fee. Admission notification on a rolling basis. **Financial aid:** Priority date 4/1; no closing date. FAFSA required. Applicants notified on a rolling basis starting 4/1; must reply by 7/15 or within 2 week(s) of notification.

Academics. Special study options: Cooperative education, distance learning, dual enrollment of high school students, honors, internships, study abroad, teacher certification program. License preparation in nursing, paramedic. **Credit/placement by examination:** AP, CLEP, IB, institutional tests. 30 credit hours maximum toward associate degree. **Support services:** GED preparation and test center, learning center, remedial instruction, study skills assistance, tutoring.

Majors. Business: Accounting technology, marketing, office/clerical. **Communications:** Journalism. **Communications technology:** Graphic/printing. **Computer sciences:** Programming. **Education:** Voc/tech. **Engineering:** General. **Engineering technology:** Biomedical, drafting, electrical, manufacturing. **Family/consumer sciences:** Child care. **Health:** Nursing (RN). **Liberal arts:** Arts/sciences. **Production:** Welding.

Most popular majors. Business/marketing 6%, liberal arts 74%.

Computing on campus. 750 workstations in dormitories, library, computer center. Dormitories wired for high-speed internet access. Commuter students can connect to campus network. Online library, helpline, repair service, wireless network available.

Student life. Freshman orientation: Available. Preregistration for classes offered. Half-day program held during late summer. **Housing:** Single-sex dorms, wellness housing available. $150 partly refundable deposit, deadline 8/20. Limited housing available. **Activities:** Choral groups, drama, literary magazine, student government, student newspaper, Phi Theta Kappa, Association for the Education of Young Children, Brothers OX, service organizations, multicultural club.

Athletics. NJCAA. **Intercollegiate:** Basketball, cheerleading. **Intramural:** Basketball, volleyball. **Team name:** Greyhounds.

Student services. Adult student services, career counseling, services for economically disadvantaged, student employment services, financial aid counseling, placement for graduates. **Physically disabled:** Services for visually, speech, hearing impaired. **Transfer:** Pre-admission transcript evaluation for new students. Transfer adviser, college fairs on campus for students transferring to 4-year colleges.

Contact. E-mail: info@macc.edu
Phone: (660) 263-4110 ext. 270 Toll-free number: (800) 622-2070 ext. 270
Fax: (660) 263-2406
James Grant, Dean of Student Services, Moberly Area Community College, 101 College Avenue, Moberly, MO 65270-1304

North Central Missouri College

Trenton, Missouri
www.ncmissouri.edu **CB code: 6830**

- Public 2-year community college
- Commuter campus in small town

General. Founded in 1925. Regionally accredited. Evening classes offered at outreach sites in many area communities. **Enrollment:** 1,049 degree-seeking undergraduates; 471 non-degree-seeking students. **Degrees:** 243 associate awarded. **Location:** 90 miles from Kansas City. **Calendar:** Semester, limited summer session. **Full-time faculty:** 29 total. **Part-time faculty:** 75 total. **Special facilities:** Academic reinforcement center.

Student profile. Among degree-seeking undergraduates, 342 enrolled as first-time, first-year students.

Part-time:	23%	**Hispanic American:**	1%
Out-of-state:	2%	**25 or older:**	28%
Women:	75%	**Live on campus:**	8%
African American:	1%		

Transfer out. Colleges most students transferred to 2008: Missouri Western State College, Northwest Missouri State University, Southwest Missouri State University, Central Missouri State University.

Basis for selection. Open admission, but selective for some programs. Special requirements for associate and certificate programs in nursing. Interview required for nursing students.

2008-2009 Annual costs. Tuition/fees: $2,550; $3,510 out-of-district; $4,650 out-of-state. Per-credit charge: $65 in-district; $97 out-of-district; $135 out-of-state. Room/board: $4,924. Books/supplies: $800. Personal expenses: $1,029.

2007-2008 Financial aid. Need-based: Need-based aid available for part-time students. **Non-need-based:** Scholarships awarded for academics, athletics, minority status, music/drama.

Application procedures. Admission: No deadline. $15 fee. Application must be submitted on paper. Admission notification on a rolling basis beginning on or about 2/1. **Financial aid:** Priority date 3/15; no closing date. FAFSA, institutional form required. Applicants notified on a rolling basis starting 3/15.

Academics. Special study options: Cooperative education, distance learning, double major, dual enrollment of high school students, internships, liberal arts/career combination. Bachelor's degree programs available on campus. License preparation in nursing, paramedic. **Credit/placement by examination:** AP, CLEP, institutional tests. 30 credit hours maximum toward associate degree. **Support services:** GED preparation and test center, learning center, reduced course load, remedial instruction, study skills assistance, tutoring.

Majors. Agriculture: Agribusiness operations, farm/ranch. **Business:** Accounting, business admin, office technology, office/clerical. **Computer sciences:** General. **Construction:** Maintenance. **Education:** General. **Health:** Nursing (RN), office assistant. **Liberal arts:** Arts/sciences. **Mechanic/repair:** General, auto body, electronics/electrical. **Protective services:** Criminal justice. **Public administration:** Human services.

Most popular majors. Business/marketing 10%, health sciences 22%, liberal arts 54%.

Computing on campus. 163 workstations in dormitories, library, computer center, student center. Dormitories wired for high-speed internet access. Helpline available.

Student life. Freshman orientation: Available. **Housing:** Single-sex dorms, wellness housing available. $100 partly refundable deposit. **Activities:** Drama, student government, Baptist Student Union.

Athletics. NJCAA. **Intercollegiate:** Baseball M, basketball, softball W. **Intramural:** Volleyball. **Team name:** Pirates.

Student services. Alcohol/substance abuse counseling, career counseling, student employment services, financial aid counseling, personal counseling, placement for graduates. **Physically disabled:** Services for visually, speech, hearing impaired. **Transfer:** Transfer adviser, college fairs on campus for students transferring to 4-year colleges.

Contact. E-mail: admissions@mail.ncmissouri.edu
Phone: (660) 359-3948 ext. 401 Toll-free number: (800) 880-6180 ext. 401
Fax: (660) 359-2211
Karla McCollum, Admission Director, North Central Missouri College, 1301 Main Street, Trenton, MO 64683

Ozarks Technical Community College

Springfield, Missouri
www.otc.edu **CB code: 2583**

- Public 2-year community and technical college
- Commuter campus in small city

General. Regionally accredited. **Enrollment:** 9,475 degree-seeking undergraduates. **Degrees:** 846 associate awarded. **Location:** 160 miles from Kansas City, 250 miles from St. Louis. **Calendar:** Semester, extensive summer session. **Full-time faculty:** 160 total. **Part-time faculty:** 400 total.

Student profile.

Out-of-state:	1%	25 or older:	29%

Transfer out. Colleges most students transferred to 2008: Drury University, Evangel University, Southwest Missouri State University.

Basis for selection. Open admission, but selective for some programs. Special requirements for some allied health programs.

2008-2009 Annual costs. Tuition/fees: $2,940; $3,870 out-of-district; $4,905 out-of-state. Per-credit charge: $81 in-district; $112 out-of-district; $147 out-of-state. Books/supplies: $600. Personal expenses: $1,100.

2007-2008 Financial aid. All financial aid based on need. 58% of total undergraduate aid awarded as scholarships/grants, 42% as loans/jobs. Need-based aid available for part-time students. Work-study available for part-time students.

Application procedures. Admission: No deadline. No application fee. Admission notification on a rolling basis. **Financial aid:** Closing date 3/31. FAFSA, institutional form required. Applicants notified on a rolling basis starting 5/16.

Academics. Special study options: Cooperative education, distance learning, dual enrollment of high school students, ESL, independent study, internships. License preparation in dental hygiene, nursing, paramedic. **Credit/placement by examination:** CLEP, IB, institutional tests. **Support services:** GED preparation and test center, learning center, reduced course load, remedial instruction, study skills assistance, tutoring, writing center.

Majors. Agriculture: Turf management. **Business:** Accounting, business admin, hospitality admin, hotel/motel admin, office technology. **Communications:** Digital media. **Communications technology:** Graphic/printing. **Computer sciences:** Information technology, LAN/WAN management, web page design. **Engineering:** Electrical. **Engineering technology:** CAD/CADD, construction, electrical, industrial. **Family/consumer sciences:** Child development. **Health:** Dental hygiene, EMT paramedic, licensed practical nurse, medical records technology, occupational therapy assistant, physical therapy assistant, respiratory therapy technology. **Liberal arts:** Arts/sciences. **Mechanic/repair:** Auto body, automotive, diesel, heating/ac/refrig, industrial. **Personal/culinary services:** Culinary arts. **Production:** Machine tool, welding. **Protective services:** Fire safety technology. **Visual/performing arts:** Graphic design.

Most popular majors. Business/marketing 19%, computer/information sciences 6%, health sciences 7%, liberal arts 50%, trade and industry 8%.

Computing on campus. 250 workstations in library, computer center. Commuter students can connect to campus network. Online course registration, online library, helpline, wireless network available.

Student life. Freshman orientation: Available. Preregistration for classes offered. **Activities:** Student government, student newspaper, Phi Theta Kappa, National Honor Society, Women in Construction, nursing students groups, Phi Beta Lambda, national business organizations, electronics club, Society of Manufacturing Engineers.

Athletics. Team name: Eagles.

Student services. Career counseling, student employment services, financial aid counseling, on-campus daycare, personal counseling, placement for graduates. **Physically disabled:** Services for visually, speech, hearing impaired. **Transfer:** Transfer adviser, college fairs on campus for students transferring to 4-year colleges.

Contact. Phone: (417) 447-6900 Fax: (417) 447-6906
Joan Barrett, Director of Admissions, Ozarks Technical Community College, 1001 East Chestnut Expressway, Springfield, MO 65802

Patricia Stevens College

St. Louis, Missouri
www.patriciastevenscollege.edu **CB code: 3319**

- For-profit 2-year junior and liberal arts college
- Commuter campus in very large city
- Application essay, interview required

General. Accredited by ACICS. **Enrollment:** 105 degree-seeking undergraduates. **Degrees:** 62 associate awarded. **Location:** Downtown. **Calendar:** Quarter, extensive summer session. **Full-time faculty:** 5 total. **Part-time faculty:** 18 total. **Class size:** 95% < 20, 5% 20-39.

Student profile.

Out-of-state:	26%	25 or older:	39%

Transfer out. Colleges most students transferred to 2008: Fontbonne University, Lindenwood University, Maryville University, University of Phoenix, Webster University.

Basis for selection. Open admission, but selective for some programs. Every applicant is interviewed by the admissions staff. High school and other college transcripts are analyzed, as are attendance records and college entrance examinations such as SAT and ACT. Other achievements in the community and workplace considered. SAT or ACT scores are only required of students enrolling in a bachelor's degree program with less than 90 quarter hours in transfer credits. SAT or ACT scores are not required for students enrolling in an AAS program. **Homeschooled:** Statement describing homeschool structure and mission, transcript of courses and grades, interview required.

2008-2009 Annual costs. Tuition/fees: $9,450. Per-credit charge: $210. Use of textbooks included in tuition.

Financial aid. All financial aid based on need. Need-based aid available for part-time students.

Application procedures. Admission: No deadline. $15 fee. Application must be submitted on paper. Admission notification on a rolling basis. **Financial aid:** No deadline. FAFSA required. Applicants notified on a rolling basis.

Academics. Special study options: Accelerated study, double major, internships. **Credit/placement by examination:** AP, CLEP. **Support services:** Reduced course load, study skills assistance, tutoring.

Majors. Business: Business admin, fashion, hospitality admin, retailing, tourism/travel, travel services. **Legal studies:** Paralegal. **Visual/performing arts:** Interior design.

Most popular majors. Business/marketing 26%, health sciences 7%, legal studies 24%.

Computing on campus. 42 workstations in library, computer center. Wireless network available.

Student life. Freshman orientation: Mandatory. Preregistration for classes offered. Held each quarter before start of classes. **Policies:** Dress code and attendance policies enforced.

Student services. Adult student services, alcohol/substance abuse counseling, career counseling, student employment services, financial aid counseling, placement for graduates. **Transfer:** Pre-admission transcript evaluation for new students. Transfer adviser, college fairs on campus for students transferring to 4-year colleges.

Contact. E-mail: admissions@patriciastevenscollege.edu
Phone: (314) 421-0949 ext. 12 Toll-free number: (800) 871-0949 ext. 12
Fax: (314) 421-0304
John Willmon, Director of Admissions, Patricia Stevens College, 330 North Fourth Street, Suite 306, St. Louis, MO 63102

Pinnacle Career Institute: Kansas City

Kansas City, Missouri
www.pcitraining.edu **CB code: 2271**

- For-profit 2-year technical and career college
- Commuter campus in large city
- Interview required

General. Accredited by ACCSCT. **Enrollment:** 629 degree-seeking undergraduates. **Degrees:** 24 associate awarded. **Calendar:** Quarter, limited summer session. **Full-time faculty:** 10 total; 40% minority, 40% women. **Part-time faculty:** 11 total; 18% have terminal degrees, 64% minority, 54% women. **Class size:** 100% >100.

Student profile. Among degree-seeking undergraduates, 100% enrolled in a vocational program, 1% already have a bachelor's degree or higher, 15 enrolled as first-time, first-year students.

Basis for selection. Open admission. **Homeschooled:** Transcript of courses and grades, state high school equivalency certificate, interview required.

2008-2009 Annual costs. Tuition/fees: $11,232. Books/supplies: $1,500.

Application procedures. Admission: No deadline. $50 fee. Application must be submitted online. Admission notification on a rolling basis. **Financial aid:** No deadline.

Academics. Special study options: Distance learning. **Credit/placement by examination:** CLEP. **Support services:** Study skills assistance, tutoring.

Majors. Business: Executive assistant. **Engineering technology:** Electrical. **Health:** Medical assistant.

Most popular majors. Business/marketing 8%, engineering/engineering technologies 46%, health sciences 46%.

Computing on campus. 30 workstations in computer center. Online library, helpline, wireless network available.

Student life. Freshman orientation: Mandatory.

Student services. Career counseling, services for economically disadvantaged, student employment services, financial aid counseling, placement for graduates, veterans' counselor. **Transfer:** Pre-admission transcript evaluation for new students.

Contact. E-mail: bricks@pcitraining.edu
Phone: (816) 331-5700 Toll-free number: (800) 676-7912
Fax: (816) 331-2026
Allison Johnson, Director of Admissions, Pinnacle Career Institute: Kansas City, 1001 East 101st Terrace, Suite 325, Kansas City, MO 64131-3367

Ranken Technical College
St. Louis, Missouri
www.ranken.edu **CB code: 7028**

- Private 2-year technical college
- Commuter campus in very large city
- Interview required

General. Founded in 1907. Regionally accredited. **Enrollment:** 1,626 degree-seeking undergraduates. **Degrees:** 30 bachelor's, 339 associate awarded. **Location:** 3 miles from downtown. **Calendar:** Semester, limited summer session. **Full-time faculty:** 58 total; 2% have terminal degrees, 10% minority, 9% women. **Part-time faculty:** 49 total; 4% have terminal degrees, 14% women. **Partnerships:** Formal partnership with the GM-ASEP program.

Student profile. Among degree-seeking undergraduates, 100% enrolled in a vocational program, 1% already have a bachelor's degree or higher, 633 enrolled as first-time, first-year students.

Part-time:	35%	**Asian American:**	1%
Out-of-state:	43%	**Hispanic American:**	1%
Women:	4%	**Live on campus:**	3%
African American:	16%		

Basis for selection. Open admission. Institutional placement test and counseling session required. **Homeschooled:** State high school equivalency certificate required. **Learning Disabled:** Special accommodations available with appropriate documentation.

2009-2010 Annual costs. Tuition/fees: $12,498. Per-credit charge: $515. Book and tool costs vary by program. Books/supplies: $1,700. Personal expenses: $1,774.

2007-2008 Financial aid. Need-based: 18% of total undergraduate aid awarded as scholarships/grants, 82% as loans/jobs. Need-based aid available for part-time students. Work-study available nights.

Application procedures. Admission: No deadline. $25 fee, may be waived for applicants with need, free for online applicants. Admission notification on a rolling basis. Interview and tour recommended for new applicants. **Financial aid:** No deadline. FAFSA required. Applicants notified on a rolling basis starting 4/1.

Academics. Special study options: Cooperative education, distance learning, double major, dual enrollment of high school students, independent study, internships, study abroad. Bachelor's degree programs available on campus. **Credit/placement by examination:** AP, CLEP, IB, institutional tests. **Support services:** Learning center, pre-admission summer program, reduced course load, remedial instruction, study skills assistance, tutoring, writing center.

Majors. Architecture: Environmental design. **Communications technology:** General. **Computer sciences:** General, LAN/WAN management, webmaster. **Construction:** Carpentry. **Engineering technology:** Electrical. **Mechanic/repair:** Auto body, automotive, electronics/electrical, heating/ac/refrig, industrial. **Production:** Machine shop technology.

Computing on campus. 60 workstations in dormitories, library, computer center, student center. Dormitories wired for high-speed internet access and linked to campus network. Commuter students can connect to campus network. Online library, repair service, wireless network available.

Student life. Freshman orientation: Mandatory. Preregistration for classes offered. Four hour session held the week before classes begin. **Housing:** Guaranteed on-campus for all undergraduates. Coed dorms, special housing for disabled available. $150 partly refundable deposit, deadline 7/1. **Activities:** Student government, student newspaper, women's support program, Phi Theta Kappa.

Student services. Adult student services, alcohol/substance abuse counseling, career counseling, services for economically disadvantaged, student employment services, financial aid counseling, minority student services, personal counseling, placement for graduates, veterans' counselor, women's services. **Physically disabled:** Services for visually, speech, hearing impaired. **Transfer:** Pre-admission transcript evaluation for new students. Transfer adviser, college fairs on campus for students transferring to 4-year colleges.

Contact. E-mail: admissions@ranken.edu
Phone: (314) 286-4809 Toll-free number: (866) 472-6536
Fax: (314) 371-0241
Michael Hawley, Director of Admissions, Ranken Technical College, 4431 Finney Avenue, St. Louis, MO 63113

St. Charles Community College
Cottleville, Missouri
www.stchas.edu **CB code: 0168**

- Public 2-year community college
- Commuter campus in small city

General. Founded in 1986. Regionally accredited. **Enrollment:** 6,393 degree-seeking undergraduates; 1,021 non-degree-seeking students. **Degrees:** 633 associate awarded. **Location:** 35 miles from St. Louis. **Calendar:** Semester, limited summer session. **Full-time faculty:** 94 total; 26% have terminal degrees, 4% minority, 60% women. **Part-time faculty:** 323 total; 12% have terminal degrees, 4% minority, 59% women.

Student profile. Among degree-seeking undergraduates, 85% enrolled in a transfer program, 15% enrolled in a vocational program, 1,774 enrolled as first-time, first-year students.

Part-time:	45%	**Hispanic American:**	2%
Women:	59%	**International:**	1%
African American:	4%	**25 or older:**	28%
Asian American:	2%		

Transfer out. 58% of students enrolled in the transfer program go on to 4-year colleges. **Colleges most students transferred to 2008:** University of Missouri: St. Louis, Lindenwood University, University of Missouri: Columbia, Southwest Missouri State University, Maryville University.

Basis for selection. Open admission, but selective for some programs. Special requirements for nursing and allied health programs, including ACT. Limited enrollment for nursing program with preference given to in-state applicants. Must submit ACT scores by August 20th for allied health and nursing programs. **Homeschooled:** Transcript of courses and grades required.

High school preparation. 16 units recommended. Recommended units include English 4, mathematics 3, social studies 3, science 2, foreign language 2 and academic electives 1. One visual or performing arts recommended.

2009-2010 Annual costs. Tuition/fees: $2,400; $3,540 out-of-district; $5,250 out-of-state. Per-credit charge: $80 in-district; $118 out-of-district; $175 out-of-state. Books/supplies: $1,020. Personal expenses: $1,800.

2007-2008 Financial aid. Need-based: 59% of total undergraduate aid awarded as scholarships/grants, 41% as loans/jobs. Need-based aid available for part-time students. Work-study available for part-time students. **Non-need-based:** Scholarships awarded for academics, art, athletics, leadership, music/drama.

Application procedures. Admission: No deadline. No application fee. Application must be submitted on paper. Admission notification on a rolling basis. **Financial aid:** Priority date 7/1; no closing date. FAFSA, institutional form required. Applicants notified on a rolling basis starting 3/1.

Academics. Special study options: Distance learning, double major, dual enrollment of high school students, ESL, independent study, internships, liberal arts/career combination, study abroad, teacher certification program. License preparation in nursing, occupational therapy, real estate. **Credit/placement by examination:** AP, CLEP, IB, ACT, institutional tests. 49 credit hours maximum toward associate degree. **Support services:** GED preparation and test center, learning center, pre-admission summer program, remedial instruction, study skills assistance, tutoring, writing center.

Majors. Biology: General. **Business:** Accounting technology, marketing, office management. **Computer sciences:** Programming. **Education:** General, teacher assistance. **Engineering:** General, civil, mechanical. **Engineering technology:** Drafting, industrial. **Family/consumer sciences:** Child care. **Foreign languages:** General, French, Spanish. **Health:** EMT paramedic, massage therapy, medical records technology, nursing (RN), occupational therapy assistant. **History:** General. **Liberal arts:** Arts/sciences. **Math:** General. **Philosophy/religion:** Philosophy. **Physical sciences:** Chemistry. **Production:** General. **Protective services:** Firefighting, police science. **Psychology:** General. **Public administration:** Human services, social work. **Social sciences:** Economics, political science, sociology. **Visual/performing arts:** Commercial/advertising art, dramatic, music history. **Other:** Human services, Teacher education.

Most popular majors. Health sciences 15%, liberal arts 74%.

Computing on campus. 169 workstations in library, computer center, student center. Online library, helpline, wireless network available.

Student life. Freshman orientation: Available. **Activities:** Bands, choral groups, drama, international student organizations, literary magazine, music ensembles, student government, student newspaper, Campus Crusade for Christ, Global Student Network, Human Services Student organization, Phi Theta Kappa, Straights and Gays for Equality, SCC Outdoors Crew, Social Science Society, Student Nurse Organization.

Athletics. NJCAA. **Intercollegiate:** Baseball M, soccer, softball W. **Team name:** Cougars.

Student services. Adult student services, career counseling, student employment services, financial aid counseling, on-campus daycare, personal counseling, placement for graduates, veterans' counselor. **Physically disabled:** Services for visually, speech, hearing impaired. **Transfer:** Preadmission transcript evaluation for new students. Transfer adviser, college fairs on campus for students transferring to 4-year colleges.

Contact. E-mail: adm-reg@stchas.edu
Phone: (636) 922-8237 Fax: (636) 922-8236
Kathy Brockgreitens-Gober, Dean of Enrollment Services, St. Charles Community College, 4601 Mid Rivers Mall Drive, Cottleville, MO 63376

St. Louis Community College

Saint Louis, Missouri — **CB member**
www.stlcc.edu — **CB code: 6226**

- Public 2-year community and junior college
- Commuter campus in large city

General. Founded in 1962. Regionally accredited. Four campus locations: Forest Park (St. Louis), Florissant Valley (Ferguson), Meramec (Kirkwood), and Wildwood (Wildwood). **Enrollment:** 6,578 degree-seeking undergraduates. **Degrees:** 547 associate awarded. **Calendar:** Semester, extensive summer session. **Full-time faculty:** 132 total. **Part-time faculty:** 535 total.

Student profile.

Out-of-state:	4%	25 or older:	52%

Transfer out. Colleges most students transferred to 2008: St. Louis University, Washington University, University of Missouri: St. Louis, University of Missouri: Columbia, Webster University.

Basis for selection. Open admission.

2008-2009 Annual costs. Tuition/fees: $2,490; $3,690 out-of-district; $4,740 out-of-state. Per-credit charge: $83 in-district; $123 out-of-district; $158 out-of-state. Books/supplies: $800. Personal expenses: $2,100.

Financial aid. Need-based: Need-based aid available for part-time students. Work-study available for part-time students. **Non-need-based:** Scholarships awarded for academics, art, athletics, leadership, music/drama.

Application procedures. Admission: No deadline. No application fee. Admission notification on a rolling basis beginning on or about 4/1. **Financial aid:** Priority date 4/15; no closing date. FAFSA required. Applicants notified on a rolling basis starting 4/1.

Academics. Special study options: Cross-registration, distance learning, double major, dual enrollment of high school students, ESL, honors, independent study, liberal arts/career combination, study abroad, weekend college. License preparation in dental hygiene, nursing, paramedic, radiology, real estate. **Credit/placement by examination:** AP, CLEP, institutional tests. 30 credit hours maximum toward associate degree. **Support services:** GED preparation and test center, learning center, remedial instruction, study skills assistance, tutoring, writing center.

Majors. Biology: General. **Business:** General, accounting, administrative services, banking/financial services, international, organizational behavior, tourism/travel. **Communications:** General. **Communications technology:** Graphic/printing. **Computer sciences:** General, data processing, programming, systems analysis. **Construction:** Carpentry, electrician, maintenance, pipefitting. **Education:** Teacher assistance. **Engineering:** General. **Engineering technology:** Drafting, electrical. **Family/consumer sciences:** Child care, food/nutrition, institutional food production. **Health:** Clinical lab science, dental assistant, dental hygiene, EMT paramedic, medical radiologic technology/radiation therapy, respiratory therapy technology, sonography, surgical technology. **Liberal arts:** Arts/sciences. **Math:** General. **Mechanic/repair:** Automotive. **Personal/culinary services:** Culinary arts, mortuary science. **Physical sciences:** Chemistry, physics. **Protective services:** Fire safety technology. **Psychology:** General. **Social sciences:** General. **Visual/performing arts:** Photography, studio arts.

Most popular majors. Business/marketing 7%, computer/information sciences 9%, health sciences 20%, liberal arts 34%, personal/culinary services 12%.

Computing on campus. Commuter students can connect to campus network. Online course registration, online library available.

Student life. Freshman orientation: Available. Preregistration for classes offered. **Activities:** Choral groups, drama, literary magazine, musical theater, student government, student newspaper, TV station.

Athletics. NJCAA. **Intercollegiate:** Baseball M, basketball, soccer M, softball W. **Team name:** Highlanders.

Student services. Career counseling, services for economically disadvantaged, student employment services, financial aid counseling, health services, on-campus daycare, personal counseling, placement for graduates, veterans' counselor. **Physically disabled:** Services for visually, speech, hearing impaired. **Transfer:** Transfer adviser, college fairs on campus for students transferring to 4-year colleges.

Contact. E-mail: gmarshall@stlcc.edu
Phone: (314) 644-9127 Fax: (314) 644-9375
Glenn Marshall, Manager, Admissions/Registration, St. Louis Community College, 300 South Broadway, St. Louis, MO 63102-2800

St. Louis Community College at Florissant Valley

St. Louis, Missouri
www.stlcc.edu — **CB code: 6225**

- Public 2-year branch campus and community college
- Commuter campus in large city

General. Founded in 1962. Regionally accredited. **Enrollment:** 5,761 degree-seeking undergraduates. **Degrees:** 490 associate awarded. **ROTC:** Army.

Location: 17 miles from downtown. **Calendar:** Semester, extensive summer session. **Full-time faculty:** 140 total. **Part-time faculty:** 250 total. **Special facilities:** Observatory, child development center.

Student profile.

Out-of-state:	2%	**25 or older:**	48%

Basis for selection. Open admission, but selective for some programs. Nursing program applicants required to pass institutional test.

2008-2009 Annual costs. Tuition/fees: $2,490; $3,690 out-of-district; $4,740 out-of-state. Per-credit charge: $83 in-district; $123 out-of-district; $158 out-of-state. Books/supplies: $1,000. Personal expenses: $2,100.

Application procedures. Admission: No deadline. No application fee. Admission notification on a rolling basis. **Financial aid:** Priority date 8/1; no closing date. FAFSA required. Applicants notified on a rolling basis starting 5/1.

Academics. Special study options: Cooperative education, cross-registration, distance learning, dual enrollment of high school students, ESL, exchange student, honors, independent study, internships, study abroad, teacher certification program, weekend college. Bachelor's degree programs available on campus. **Credit/placement by examination:** CLEP, institutional tests. 49 credit hours maximum toward associate degree. **Support services:** Learning center, remedial instruction, tutoring.

Majors. Biology: General. **Business:** Administrative services, banking/financial services, business admin, fashion, management information systems, office technology. **Communications:** General, advertising, broadcast journalism, journalism, public relations. **Communications technology:** Graphic/printing. **Computer sciences:** General, applications programming, data processing, programming, systems analysis. **Education:** Early childhood, teacher assistance. **Engineering:** General. **Engineering technology:** Civil, computer hardware, drafting, electrical, manufacturing, mechanical. **Family/consumer sciences:** Child care. **Foreign languages:** Sign language interpretation. **Health:** Predental, premedicine, prepharmacy. **Liberal arts:** Arts/sciences. **Math:** General. **Personal/culinary services:** Culinary arts. **Physical sciences:** Chemistry, physics. **Protective services:** Fire safety technology, police science. **Psychology:** General. **Social sciences:** General. **Visual/performing arts:** General, commercial/advertising art, dramatic, studio arts.

Student life. Activities: Concert band, drama, musical theater, radio station, student government, student newspaper, TV station, Black student association.

Athletics. NJCAA. **Intercollegiate:** Baseball M, basketball, cross-country, soccer, softball W, track and field, volleyball W.

Student services. Career counseling, student employment services, health services, on-campus daycare, personal counseling, placement for graduates. **Physically disabled:** Services for visually, speech, hearing impaired. **Transfer:** Transfer adviser, college fairs on campus for students transferring to 4-year colleges.

Contact. Phone: (314) 513-4244 Fax: (314) 513-4724
Brenda Davenport, Manager of Admissions/Registration, St. Louis Community College at Florissant Valley, 3400 Pershall Road, St. Louis, MO 63135

St. Louis Community College at Meramec
St. Louis, Missouri
www.stlcc.edu **CB code: 6430**

- Public 2-year community college
- Commuter campus in large city

General. Founded in 1963. Regionally accredited. Two off-campus sites at South County Education Center and West County Education Center. **Enrollment:** 24,567 undergraduates. **Degrees:** 970 associate awarded. **ROTC:** Army, Air Force. **Location:** 15 miles from St. Louis. **Calendar:** Semester, extensive summer session. **Full-time faculty:** 190 total. **Part-time faculty:** 500 total. **Special facilities:** Center for advanced imaging.

Student profile.

Out-of-state:	1%	**25 or older:**	66%

Basis for selection. Open admission, but selective for some programs. Nursing, occupational therapy assistant, physical therapist assistant, paramedic technology programs have specific admission requirements. SAT or ACT score used to waive Accuplacer Test. Interview required for some health programs. **Homeschooled:** Transcript of courses and grades, interview required.

High school preparation. 22 units recommended. Recommended units include English 4, mathematics 2, social studies 3 and science 2.

2008-2009 Annual costs. Tuition/fees: $2,490; $3,690 out-of-district; $4,740 out-of-state. Per-credit charge: $83 in-district; $123 out-of-district; $158 out-of-state. Books/supplies: $800. Personal expenses: $2,100.

Financial aid. Need-based: Need-based aid available for part-time students.

Application procedures. Admission: Priority date 8/1; no deadline. No application fee. Admission notification on a rolling basis beginning on or about 3/1. **Financial aid:** Closing date 6/30. FAFSA, institutional form required. Applicants notified on a rolling basis starting 2/1.

Academics. Special study options: Accelerated study, cross-registration, distance learning, dual enrollment of high school students, ESL, honors, independent study, internships, study abroad. **Credit/placement by examination:** AP, CLEP, institutional tests. 49 credit hours maximum toward associate degree. **Support services:** GED preparation, learning center, pre-admission summer program, reduced course load, remedial instruction, tutoring, writing center.

Majors. Agriculture: Horticultural science, ornamental horticulture. **Architecture:** Interior. **Business:** General, accounting, administrative services, banking/financial services, management information systems, office technology, office/clerical, real estate. **Communications:** General. **Computer sciences:** General, applications programming, data processing. **Education:** General, elementary, secondary. **Engineering:** General. **Engineering technology:** Architectural, electrical. **Health:** EMT paramedic, occupational therapy assistant, physical therapy assistant. **Interdisciplinary:** Biological/physical sciences. **Legal studies:** Court reporting, legal secretary, paralegal. **Liberal arts:** Arts/sciences. **Math:** General. **Protective services:** Criminal justice, police science. **Public administration:** Social work. **Social sciences:** General. **Transportation:** Air traffic control. **Visual/performing arts:** Commercial/advertising art, photography, studio arts.

Computing on campus. 420 workstations in library, computer center.

Student life. Freshman orientation: Mandatory. Preregistration for classes offered. **Activities:** Bands, choral groups, drama, literary magazine, music ensembles, musical theater, student government, student newspaper, symphony orchestra, Phi Theta Kappa, international club, Intervarsity Christian Fellowship, horticulture club, bridge club, engineering club, photo club, scuba club, Student Ambassadors.

Athletics. NJCAA. **Intercollegiate:** Baseball M, basketball M, soccer, softball W, volleyball W, wrestling M. **Intramural:** Basketball, volleyball. **Team name:** Magic.

Student services. Career counseling, student employment services, financial aid counseling, health services, on-campus daycare, personal counseling, placement for graduates, veterans' counselor. **Physically disabled:** Services for visually, speech, hearing impaired. **Learning disabled:** Comprehensive services available. **Transfer:** Transfer adviser, college fairs on campus for students transferring to 4-year colleges.

Contact. Phone: (314) 984-7601 Fax: (314) 984-7051
Mike Cundiff, Director of Admissions, St. Louis Community College at Meramec, 11333 Big Bend Boulevard, Kirkwood, MO 63122-5799

Sanford-Brown College
Fenton, Missouri
www.sbcfenton.com **CB code: 3320**

- For-profit 2-year business and health science college
- Commuter campus in small town

General. Accredited by ACICS. **Calendar:** Continuous.

Annual costs/financial aid. Books/supplies: $1,714. Need-based financial aid available to full-time and part-time students.

Contact. Phone: (636) 349-4900
Dean, 1345 Smizer Mill Road, Fenton, MO 63026-1583

Sanford-Brown College: Hazelwood
Hazelwood, Missouri
www.sanford-brown.edu **CB code: 3321**

- For-profit 2-year technical and career college
- Large city

General. Accredited by ACICS. Hands on training. **Enrollment:** 656 degree-seeking undergraduates. **Degrees:** 215 associate awarded. **Calendar:** Quarter. **Full-time faculty:** 12 total. **Part-time faculty:** 42 total.

Basis for selection. Open admission.

2008-2009 Annual costs. Books/supplies: $909.

Application procedures. Admission: No deadline. $25 fee. **Financial aid:** No deadline.

Academics. Credit/placement by examination: CLEP.

Majors. Business: Accounting/business management, office technology. **Computer sciences:** General. **Health:** Health services. **Legal studies:** General.

Contact. Phone: (314) 687-2900 Fax: (314) 731-0550
Phyllis Forney, Director of Admissions, Sanford-Brown College: Hazelwood, 75 Village Square, Hazelwood, MO 63042

Sanford-Brown College: St. Peters

St. Peters, Missouri
www.sbcstpeters.com **CB code: 3323**

- For-profit 2-year career college
- Commuter campus in small city

General. Accredited by ACICS. **Enrollment:** 595 degree-seeking undergraduates. **Degrees:** 184 associate awarded. **Location:** 40 miles from St. Louis. **Calendar:** Continuous, extensive summer session. **Full-time faculty:** 19 total. **Part-time faculty:** 32 total.

Basis for selection. Open admission, but selective for some programs. Tests required for nursing programs.

Application procedures. Admission: No deadline. $25 fee.

Academics. Special study options: Bachelor's degree programs available on campus. **Credit/placement by examination:** CLEP. **Support services:** Learning center, study skills assistance, tutoring.

Majors. Business: Business admin. **Computer sciences:** Web page design. **Health:** Massage therapy, medical records technology, nursing (RN). **Legal studies:** Paralegal. **Protective services:** Corrections.

Computing on campus. Commuter students can connect to campus network. Online course registration, online library available.

Student life. Activities: Student newspaper.

Student services. Alcohol/substance abuse counseling, career counseling, student employment services, financial aid counseling, placement for graduates, veterans' counselor. **Physically disabled:** Services for visually, speech, hearing impaired.

Contact. E-mail: dgoodwin@sbc-stpeters.com
Phone: (636) 696-2300 Toll-free number: (888) 793-2433
Doug Goodwin, Director of Admissions, Sanford-Brown College: St. Peters, 100 Richmond Center Boulevard, St. Peters, MO 63376

Southeast Missouri Hospital College of Nursing and Health Sciences

Cape Girardeau, Missouri
www.sehosp.org **CB code: 4459**

- Private 2-year health science and nursing college
- Large town

General. Enrollment: 210 degree-seeking undergraduates. **Degrees:** 80 associate awarded. **Calendar:** Semester. **Full-time faculty:** 35 total.

Basis for selection. Open admission, but selective for some programs. Selective admission to associate degree program in nursing and some allied health programs.

High school preparation. College-preparatory program recommended.

2008-2009 Annual costs. Tuition/fees: $10,764. Books/supplies: $500.

Application procedures. Admission: No deadline. $40 fee. Admission notification on a rolling basis.

Academics. Special study options: License preparation in nursing, radiology. **Credit/placement by examination:** AP, CLEP.

Majors. Health: Nursing (RN), radiologic technology/medical imaging.

Contact. E-mail: dpugh@sehosp.org
Phone: (573) 334-6825 ext. 23 Fax: (573) 339-7805
Don Pugh, Registrar/Enrollment Counselor, Southeast Missouri Hospital College of Nursing and Health Sciences, 2001 William Street, Second Floor, Cape Girardeau, MO 63703

State Fair Community College

Sedalia, Missouri
www.sfccmo.edu **CB code: 6709**

- Public 2-year community college
- Commuter campus in large town

General. Founded in 1966. Regionally accredited. **Enrollment:** 2,941 degree-seeking undergraduates. **Degrees:** 488 associate awarded. **ROTC:** Army. **Location:** 78 miles from Kansas City. **Calendar:** Semester, limited summer session. **Full-time faculty:** 65 total; 100% have terminal degrees, 2% minority, 55% women. **Part-time faculty:** 185 total; 100% have terminal degrees, 5% minority, 60% women.

Student profile.

Out-of-state:	2%	**Live on campus:**	4%
25 or older:	38%		

Transfer out. Colleges most students transferred to 2008: University of Central Missouri, Missouri State University.

Basis for selection. Open admission, but selective for some programs. Special requirements for some health programs. ACT, ASSET, or COMPASS score current within the last five years required of full-time students and all degree-seeking students. Mechanical knowledge test required for auto mechanics program. Interview required for radiologic technology program applicants. **Learning Disabled:** Students are encouraged to establish documentation at least two weeks prior to the first day of each semester in order to receive accommodations.

2008-2009 Annual costs. Tuition/fees: $2,460; $3,300 out-of-district; $4,980 out-of-state. Per-credit charge: $68 in-district; $96 out-of-district; $152 out-of-state. Books/supplies: $1,100. Personal expenses: $1,400.

2007-2008 Financial aid. All financial aid based on need. Need-based aid available for part-time students. Work-study available nights and weekends.

Application procedures. Admission: No deadline. $25 fee, may be waived for applicants with need. Admission notification on a rolling basis. **Financial aid:** Priority date 7/1; no closing date. FAFSA required. Applicants notified on a rolling basis starting 7/15; must reply within 3 week(s) of notification.

Academics. Special study options: Cooperative education, cross-registration, distance learning, dual enrollment of high school students, ESL, internships, study abroad. License preparation in dental hygiene, nursing, paramedic, radiology, real estate. **Credit/placement by examination:** AP, CLEP, institutional tests. 30 credit hours maximum toward associate degree. Students may earn a maximum of 30 hours in combination from credit by exam or nontraditional credit toward an AA or AAS degree. **Support services:** GED preparation, learning center, reduced course load, remedial instruction, study skills assistance, tutoring, writing center.

Majors. Agriculture: Business, horticulture. **Business:** Accounting, administrative services, business admin, management information systems, special products marketing. **Computer sciences:** Applications programming, networking, programming, web page design. **Construction:** Site management. **Education:** Voc/tech. **Engineering technology:** CAD/CADD. **Family/consumer sciences:** Child care. **Health:** Dental hygiene, insurance coding, medical secretary, medical transcription, nursing (RN), office admin, radiologic technology/medical imaging. **Interdisciplinary:** Accounting/computer science. **Liberal arts:** Arts/sciences. **Mechanic/repair:** Automotive, electronics/electrical, industrial, industrial electronics, marine. **Production:** Machine tool. **Protective services:** Firefighting, police science.

Most popular majors. Business/marketing 9%, health sciences 19%, liberal arts 52%.

Computing on campus. 360 workstations in dormitories, library, computer center, student center. Dormitories wired for high-speed internet access and linked to campus network. Commuter students can connect to campus network. Online course registration, online library, helpline, wireless network available.

Student life. Freshman orientation: Available. Preregistration for classes offered. **Housing:** Coed dorms, wellness housing available. $100 nonrefundable deposit, deadline 7/15. **Activities:** Jazz band, choral groups, dance, drama, music ensembles, student government.

Athletics. NJCAA. **Intercollegiate:** Basketball, volleyball W. **Intramural:** Bowling, softball, volleyball. **Team name:** Roadrunners.

Student services. Career counseling, services for economically disadvantaged, student employment services, financial aid counseling, minority student services, personal counseling, placement for graduates, veterans' counselor. **Physically disabled:** Services for visually, speech, hearing impaired. **Transfer:** Pre-admission transcript evaluation for new students. Transfer adviser, college fairs on campus for students transferring to 4-year colleges.

Contact. E-mail: mcarter@sfccmo.edu
Phone: (660) 530-5833 Toll-free number: (877) 311-7322
Fax: (660) 596-7472
Mark Carter, Director of Admissions, State Fair Community College, 3201 West 16th Street, Sedalia, MO 65301-2199

Texas County Technical Institute
Houston, Missouri
www.texascountytech.edu

- Private 2-year nursing and technical college
- Small town

General. Accredited by ACICS. **Enrollment:** 150 degree-seeking undergraduates. **Degrees:** 25 associate awarded. **Calendar:** Semester. **Full-time faculty:** 10 total; 100% have terminal degrees, 80% women. **Part-time faculty:** 20 total; 10% have terminal degrees, 90% women.

2008-2009 Annual costs. Tuition/fees: $11,785. Tuition varies by program, $150 to $386 per credit hour. Books/supplies: $1,000. Personal expenses: $1,083.

Application procedures. Admission: No deadline. $45 fee.

Academics. Special study options: License preparation in nursing, paramedic. **Credit/placement by examination:** CLEP.

Majors. Business: Accounting, administrative services. **Computer sciences:** Data processing. **Health:** EMT paramedic, health services, medical secretary, nursing (RN).

Contact. E-mail: info@texascountytech.edu
Phone: (417) 967-5466 Toll-free number: (800) 835-1130
Fax: (417) 967-4604
Clarice Casebeer, Director of Admissions, Texas County Technical Institute, 6915 South Highway 63, Houston, MO 65483

Three Rivers Community College
Poplar Bluff, Missouri
www.trcc.edu **CB code: 6836**

- Public 2-year community college
- Commuter campus in large town

General. Founded in 1966. Regionally accredited. Selected courses offered at area high schools, vocational schools and other off-campus facilities. **Enrollment:** 2,481 degree-seeking undergraduates; 633 non-degree-seeking students. **Degrees:** 379 associate awarded. **Location:** 160 miles from St. Louis. **Calendar:** Semester, limited summer session. **Full-time faculty:** 66 total; 4% minority, 64% women. **Part-time faculty:** 103 total; 53% women.

Student profile. Among degree-seeking undergraduates, 75% enrolled in a transfer program, 25% enrolled in a vocational program, 633 enrolled as first-time, first-year students.

Part-time:	34%	**Hispanic American:**	2%
Out-of-state:	1%	**25 or older:**	39%
Women:	68%	**Live on campus:**	6%
African American:	10%		

Transfer out. Colleges most students transferred to 2008: Southeast Missouri State University, Arkansas State University, Southwest Missouri State University.

Basis for selection. Open admission, but selective for some programs. Special requirements for allied health programs and nursing. **Homeschooled:** Statement describing homeschool structure and mission required.

2009-2010 Annual costs. Tuition/fees: $2,505; $3,765 out-of-district; $4,605 out-of-state. Per-credit charge: $70 in-district; $112 out-of-district; $140 out-of-state. Book rental $20 per book. Lab fees vary per course. Room only: $3,114. Books/supplies: $450. Personal expenses: $1,249.

2007-2008 Financial aid. Need-based: 71% of total undergraduate aid awarded as scholarships/grants, 29% as loans/jobs. Need-based aid available for part-time students. Work-study available for part-time students. **Non-need-based:** Scholarships awarded for academics, athletics, state residency.

Application procedures. Admission: No deadline. $20 fee. Application must be submitted on paper. Admission notification on a rolling basis. **Financial aid:** Priority date 5/1; no closing date. FAFSA, institutional form required. Applicants notified on a rolling basis starting 6/1; must reply within 2 week(s) of notification.

Academics. Special study options: Accelerated study, distance learning, dual enrollment of high school students, independent study, internships, liberal arts/career combination. Bachelor's degree programs available on campus. License preparation in nursing, paramedic. **Credit/placement by examination:** AP, CLEP. 30 credit hours maximum toward associate degree. **Support services:** GED test center, learning center, remedial instruction, study skills assistance, tutoring, writing center.

Majors. Agriculture: Business. **Biology:** General. **Business:** Accounting, administrative services, entrepreneurial studies, management information systems, marketing. **Education:** General. **Engineering technology:** Civil, drafting. **Foreign languages:** General. **Health:** Clinical lab technology, nursing (RN), premedicine, prepharmacy, preveterinary. **History:** General. **Legal studies:** Prelaw. **Liberal arts:** Arts/sciences, library science. **Math:** General. **Parks/recreation:** Health/fitness. **Philosophy/religion:** Philosophy. **Physical sciences:** Chemistry. **Protective services:** Police science. **Psychology:** General. **Social sciences:** Economics, geography, political science, sociology. **Visual/performing arts:** Studio arts.

Most popular majors. Business/marketing 10%, health sciences 19%, liberal arts 48%, trade and industry 7%.

Computing on campus. 100 workstations in dormitories, library, computer center, student center. Dormitories wired for high-speed internet access.

Student life. Freshman orientation: Available. Preregistration for classes offered. Mini orientation activities are held for incoming freshmen during the registration process. Orientation for new students is offered at the beginning of each semester for students, family and friends. **Housing:** Apartments, wellness housing available. $200 partly refundable deposit. **Activities:** Concert band, choral groups, drama, music ensembles, student government, Student Senate, Phi Theta Kappa, Marketing Management Association,.

Athletics. NJCAA. **Intercollegiate:** Baseball M, basketball, softball W. **Intramural:** Baseball M, basketball, volleyball W. **Team name:** Raiders.

Student services. Career counseling, student employment services, on-campus daycare, placement for graduates, veterans' counselor. **Transfer:** Transfer adviser, college fairs on campus for students transferring to 4-year colleges.

Contact. E-mail: mfields@trcc.edu
Phone: (573) 840-9605 Toll-free number: (877) 879-8722 ext. 605
Fax: (573) 840-9058
Marcia Fields, Director of Admissions, Three Rivers Community College, 2080 Three Rivers Boulevard, Poplar Bluff, MO 63901-1308

Vatterott College
Berkeley, Missouri
www.vatterott-college.edu **CB code: 2507**

- For-profit 2-year technical college
- Large city

General. Accredited by ACCSCT. **Location:** 20 miles from St. Louis, 310 miles from Chicago. **Calendar:** Continuous.

Annual costs/financial aid. Program cost ranges: $14,350 to $22,000 (certificate/diploma); $32,050 to $33,850 (associate degree); $66,000 (bachelor's degree).

Contact. Phone: (314) 264-1040
Director of Admissions, 8580 Evans Avenue, Berkeley, MO 63134

Vatterott College: Joplin
Joplin, Missouri
www.vatterott-college.com

- For-profit 2-year technical college
- Large town

General. Accredited by ACCSCT. **Enrollment:** 286 degree-seeking undergraduates. **Degrees:** 36 associate awarded. **Calendar:** Continuous.

2008-2009 Annual costs. Program cost ranges: $9,550 to $20,800 (certificate/diploma); $30,250 to $32,050 (associate degree).

Academics. Credit/placement by examination: CLEP.

Majors. Computer sciences: General. **Engineering technology:** CAD/CADD. **Health:** Medical assistant, pharmacy assistant.

Contact. Phone: (417) 781-5633
Vatterott College: Joplin, 809 Illinois Avenue, Joplin, MO 64801

Vatterott College: Kansas City
Kansas City, Missouri
www.vatterott-college.edu **CB code: 2893**

- For-profit 2-year technical college
- Large city

General. Accredited by ACCSCT. **Enrollment:** 560 degree-seeking undergraduates. **Degrees:** 94 associate awarded. **Calendar:** Continuous. **Full-time faculty:** 18 total. **Part-time faculty:** 1 total.

2008-2009 Annual costs. Program cost ranges: $20,800 to $22,000 (certificate/diploma); $32,050 to $33,850 (associate degree).

Academics. Credit/placement by examination: CLEP.

Majors. Business: Business admin. **Computer sciences:** General, information systems. **Engineering technology:** Drafting. **Mechanic/repair:** Electronics/electrical, heating/ac/refrig.

Contact. E-mail: kc@vatterott-college.edu
Phone: (816) 861-1000 Toll-free number: (800) 466-3997
Fax: (816) 861-1400
David Payne, Director of Admissions, Vatterott College: Kansas City, 8955 East 38th Terrace, Kansas City, MO 64129

Vatterott College: O'Fallon
O'Fallon, Missouri
www.vatterott-college.edu

- For-profit 2-year branch campus and technical college
- Small city

General. Accredited by ACCSCT. **Enrollment:** 275 degree-seeking undergraduates. **Degrees:** 75 associate awarded. **Location:** 30 miles from St. Louis. **Calendar:** Continuous. **Full-time faculty:** 15 total. **Part-time faculty:** 8 total.

Student profile. Among degree-seeking undergraduates, 100% enrolled in a vocational program.

Basis for selection. Open admission.

2008-2009 Annual costs. Program cost ranges: $14,350 to $22,000 (certificate/diploma); $32,050 to $33,850 (associate degree).

Academics. Credit/placement by examination: CLEP.

Majors. Computer sciences: Networking. **Engineering technology:** Electromechanical, heat/ac/refrig. **Health:** Medical assistant.

Contact. E-mail: ofallon@vatterott-college.edu
Phone: (636) 978-7488 Toll-free number: (888) 766-3601
Fax: (636) 978-5121
Gertrude Bogan-Jones, Director of Admissions, Vatterott College: O'Fallon, 927 East Terra Lane, O'Fallon, MO 63366

Vatterott College: St. Joseph
St. Joseph, Missouri
www.vatterott-college.edu **CB code: 2896**

- For-profit 2-year branch campus and technical college
- Commuter campus in small city

General. Accredited by ACCSCT. **Enrollment:** 215 degree-seeking undergraduates. **Degrees:** 35 associate awarded. **Location:** 50 miles from Kansas City. **Calendar:** Quarter, extensive summer session. **Full-time faculty:** 14 total. **Part-time faculty:** 8 total.

Basis for selection. Open admission.

2008-2009 Annual costs. Program cost ranges: $10,800 to $21,000 (certificate/diploma); $24,500 to $30,600 (associate degree). Personal expenses: $1,288.

Financial aid. Need-based: Need-based aid available for part-time students.

Application procedures. Admission: No deadline. No application fee. **Financial aid:** No deadline. FAFSA required.

Academics. Credit/placement by examination: CLEP, institutional tests. 36 credit hours maximum toward associate degree. **Support services:** Tutoring.

Majors. Computer sciences: General. **Health:** Medical secretary.

Student life. Freshman orientation: Mandatory. Preregistration for classes offered. Held first day of classes. Students are briefed on policies and procedures and are introduced to the directors, career services, instructors and financial aid paperwork.

Student services. Career counseling, student employment services, financial aid counseling, placement for graduates, veterans' counselor.

Contact. E-mail: jaymi.evans@vatterott-college.edu
Phone: (816) 364-5399 Toll-free number: (800) 282-5327
Fax: (816) 364-1593
Jaymi Evans, Director of Admissions, Vatterott College: St. Joseph, 3131 Frederick Avenue, St. Joseph, MO 64506

Vatterott College: Springfield
Springfield, Missouri
www.vatterott-college.edu **CB code: 2895**

- For-profit 2-year branch campus and technical college
- Commuter campus in small city
- Application essay, interview required

General. Accredited by ACCSCT. **Enrollment:** 253 degree-seeking undergraduates. **Degrees:** 26 associate awarded. **Calendar:** Quarter. **Full-time faculty:** 30 total. **Part-time faculty:** 10 total.

Student profile. Among degree-seeking undergraduates, 244 enrolled as first-time, first-year students.

Basis for selection. Open admission, but selective for some programs. **Adult students:** SAT/ACT scores not required. **Homeschooled:** Transcript of courses and grades, state high school equivalency certificate required.

2008-2009 Annual costs. Program cost ranges: $14,300 to $20,800 (certificate/diploma); $30,250 to $32,050 (associate degree). Books/supplies: $2,388. Personal expenses: $2,289.

Financial aid. All financial aid based on need.

Application procedures. Admission: No deadline. No application fee. Application must be submitted on paper. Admission notification on a rolling basis. **Financial aid:** No deadline. FAFSA required.

Academics. Credit/placement by examination: CLEP, institutional tests. 36 credit hours maximum toward associate degree. **Support services:** Tutoring.

Majors. **Engineering technology:** CAD/CADD. **Health:** Medical assistant, pharmacy assistant. **Legal studies:** Paralegal.

Computing on campus. 2 workstations in library, computer center.

Student life. **Freshman orientation:** Mandatory. Preregistration for classes offered. Held the week before class term is scheduled to start.

Student services. Adult student services, student employment services, financial aid counseling, placement for graduates, veterans' counselor.

Contact. E-mail: springfield@vatterott-college.edu
Phone: (417) 831-8116 Toll-free number: (800) 766-5829
Fax: (417) 831-5099
Scott Lester, Director of Admissions, Vatterott College: Springfield, 3850 South Campbell, Springfield, MO 65807

Vatterott College: Sunset Hills

Sunset Hills, Missouri
www.vatterott-college.com **CB code: 2898**

- For-profit 2-year branch campus and technical college
- Very large city

General. Accredited by ACCSCT. **Enrollment:** 630 degree-seeking undergraduates. **Degrees:** 3 associate awarded. **Calendar:** Continuous. **Full-time faculty:** 25 total. **Part-time faculty:** 5 total.

Basis for selection. Open admission, but selective for some programs.

2008-2009 Annual costs. Program cost ranges: $14,350 to $22,000 (certificate/diploma); $26,650 to $33,850 (associate degree); $66,000 (bachelor's degree).

Application procedures. **Admission:** No deadline. No application fee. **Financial aid:** No deadline.

Academics. **Special study options:** Bachelor's degree programs available on campus. **Credit/placement by examination:** CLEP.

Majors. **Computer sciences:** General, networking. **Engineering technology:** Drafting. **Mechanic/repair:** Electronics/electrical, heating/ac/refrig.

Contact. E-mail: lisad@vatterott-college.com
Phone: (314) 843-4200
Director, Vatterott College: Sunset Hills, 12970 Maurer Industrial Drive, Sunset Hills, MO 63127

Wentworth Military Junior College

Lexington, Missouri
http://wma.edu/college **CB code: 6934**

- Private 2-year junior and military college
- Commuter campus in small town
- Interview required

General. Founded in 1880. Regionally accredited. Adult evening program open to both men and women. **Enrollment:** 927 degree-seeking undergraduates. **Degrees:** 64 associate awarded. **ROTC:** Army. **Location:** 40 miles from Kansas City. **Calendar:** Semester, extensive summer session. **Full-time faculty:** 10 total. **Part-time faculty:** 40 total. **Class size:** 100% < 20. **Special facilities:** Nature trail, military history library, indoor rifle range, athletic facilities.

Student profile.

Out-of-state:	55%	**Live on campus:**	23%
25 or older:	30%		

Transfer out. **Colleges most students transferred to 2008:** Central Missouri State University, Texas A&M University, Kansas University, Kansas State University, University of Missouri.

Basis for selection. Open admission, but selective for some programs. Admittees to senior ROTC programs must meet ROTC admission criteria. ACT/SAT required of applicants to ROTC commissioning program for admission, placement, counseling. Score report by August 1. **Homeschooled:** Transcript of courses and grades, letter of recommendation (nonparent) required.

High school preparation. 24 units recommended. Recommended units include English 4, mathematics 3, social studies 3, science 2 (laboratory 2), foreign language 2 and academic electives 8.

2008-2009 Annual costs. Tuition/fees: $16,430. Uniform: $2,150 for men and women. Room/board: $5,480. Books/supplies: $450. Personal expenses: $3,430.

Financial aid. All financial aid based on need.

Application procedures. **Admission:** No deadline. $100 fee. Admission notification on a rolling basis. **Financial aid:** Priority date 4/30, closing date 6/30. FAFSA required. Applicants notified on a rolling basis.

Academics. Service academy preparatory program. **Special study options:** Accelerated study, combined bachelor's/graduate degree, distance learning, dual enrollment of high school students, ESL, independent study, liberal arts/career combination, teacher certification program. License preparation in aviation, nursing. **Credit/placement by examination:** CLEP, institutional tests. 30 credit hours maximum toward associate degree. **Support services:** Tutoring.

Majors. **Liberal arts:** Arts/sciences.

Computing on campus. 50 workstations in library, computer center. Dormitories wired for high-speed internet access and linked to campus network. Commuter students can connect to campus network. Helpline, wireless network available.

Student life. **Policies:** Religious observance required. **Housing:** Single-sex dorms available. $1,500 deposit, deadline 6/30. **Activities:** Bands, choral groups, dance, drama, music ensembles, student government, student newspaper.

Athletics. NJCAA. **Intercollegiate:** Cross-country, rifle M, track and field, wrestling M. **Intramural:** Baseball M, basketball M, cheerleading W, football (non-tackle) M, golf, racquetball, rifle, soccer, swimming, tennis, volleyball, weight lifting M. **Team name:** Red Dragons.

Student services. Career counseling, financial aid counseling, health services, personal counseling. **Transfer:** Transfer adviser, college fairs on campus for students transferring to 4-year colleges.

Contact. E-mail: admissions@wma.edu
Phone: (660) 259-2221 Toll-free number: (800) 962-7682
Fax: (660) 259-2677
William Nodle, Admissions Director, Wentworth Military Junior College, 1880 Washington Avenue, Lexington, MO 64067-1799

Two-Year Colleges

Montana

Blackfeet Community College
Browning, Montana
www.bfcc.org **CB code: 0379**

- Public 2-year community college
- Commuter campus in small town

General. Founded in 1976. Regionally accredited. **Location:** 126 miles from Great Falls. **Calendar:** Semester.

Annual costs/financial aid. Tuition/fees (2008-2009): $2,190; $2,190 out-of-state. Books/supplies: $750. Need-based financial aid available to full-time and part-time students.

Contact. Phone: (406) 338-5421 ext. 243
Registrar/Admissions Officer, Highway 2 & 89, Browning, MT 59417

Chief Dull Knife College
Lame Deer, Montana
www.cdkc.edu **CB code: 5938**

- Public 2-year junior college
- Commuter campus in rural community

General. Regionally accredited. **Enrollment:** 119 full-time, degree-seeking students. **Degrees:** 20 associate awarded. **Location:** 110 miles from Billings. **Calendar:** Semester, limited summer session. **Full-time faculty:** 13 total. **Part-time faculty:** 31 total.

Basis for selection. Open admission.

2008-2009 Annual costs. Tuition/fees: $2,260. Per-credit charge: $70. Books/supplies: $850. Personal expenses: $800.

2008-2009 Financial aid. Need-based: Need-based aid available for part-time students. Work-study available nights and for part-time students.

Application procedures. Admission: No deadline. No application fee. Application must be submitted on paper. Admission notification on a rolling basis. **Financial aid:** Priority date 3/1; no closing date. FAFSA, institutional form required. Applicants notified on a rolling basis; must reply within 2 week(s) of notification.

Academics. Special study options: Cooperative education, double major, internships. Bachelor's degree programs available on campus. **Credit/placement by examination:** CLEP, institutional tests. 9 credit hours maximum toward associate degree. **Support services:** GED preparation and test center, learning center, remedial instruction, tutoring.

Computing on campus. 25 workstations in library, computer center. Online library available.

Student life. Freshman orientation: Mandatory. Preregistration for classes offered. **Activities:** Student government, student newspaper.

Athletics. Intramural: Basketball.

Student services. Career counseling, financial aid counseling, on-campus daycare, personal counseling, veterans' counselor. **Transfer:** Transfer adviser for students transferring to 4-year colleges.

Contact. E-mail: zspang@cdkc.edu
Phone: (406) 477-6215 Fax: (406) 477-6219
Zane Spang, Dean of Student Affairs, Chief Dull Knife College, Box 98, Lame Deer, MT 59043

Dawson Community College
Glendive, Montana
www.dawson.edu **CB code: 4280**

- Public 2-year community college
- Commuter campus in small town

General. Founded in 1940. Regionally accredited. **Enrollment:** 335 degree-seeking undergraduates; 79 non-degree-seeking students. **Degrees:** 72 associate awarded. **Location:** 220 miles from Billings, 100 miles from Dickinson, North Dakota. **Calendar:** Semester, limited summer session. **Full-time faculty:** 32 total. **Part-time faculty:** 25 total.

Student profile. Among degree-seeking undergraduates, 129 enrolled as first-time, first-year students.

Part-time:	13%	**Women:**	51%
Out-of-state:	15%	**Live on campus:**	48%

Transfer out. Colleges most students transferred to 2008: Dickinson State University, Montana State University-Bozeman, Montana State University-Billings, University of Montana.

Basis for selection. Open admission.

2008-2009 Annual costs. Tuition/fees: $2,736; $3,843 out-of-district; $8,499 out-of-state. Per-credit charge: $52 in-district; $89 out-of-district; $244 out-of-state. Mandatory $600-per-semester a la carte meal plan for on-campus residents. Full-time tuition for Western Undergraduate Exchange students: $3,211 ($134 per credit hour). Room only: $2,100. Books/supplies: $900. Personal expenses: $1,048.

2007-2008 Financial aid. Need-based: 56% of total undergraduate aid awarded as scholarships/grants, 44% as loans/jobs. Work-study available nights, weekends and for part-time students. **Non-need-based:** Scholarships awarded for academics, art, athletics, music/drama.

Application procedures. Admission: No deadline. $30 fee. Admission notification on a rolling basis. **Financial aid:** Priority date 3/1; no closing date. FAFSA required. Applicants notified on a rolling basis starting 5/15; must reply within 2 week(s) of notification.

Academics. Special study options: Distance learning, double major, dual enrollment of high school students, independent study, internships. **Credit/placement by examination:** CLEP, institutional tests. 15 credit hours maximum toward associate degree. **Support services:** GED preparation and test center, learning center, reduced course load, remedial instruction, study skills assistance, tutoring.

Majors. Agriculture: Business, equestrian studies, farm/ranch, power machinery. **Business:** General, administrative services. **Computer sciences:** General, vendor certification. **Education:** Early childhood. **Health:** Medical transcription, substance abuse counseling. **Liberal arts:** Arts/sciences. **Mechanic/repair:** Automotive. **Protective services:** Police science.

Computing on campus. 70 workstations in dormitories, library, computer center. Dormitories wired for high-speed internet access and linked to campus network. Wireless network available.

Student life. Freshman orientation: Mandatory. Preregistration for classes offered. Held during June and July. **Housing:** Coed dorms available. $150 deposit. Student dormitories include kitchen facilities. **Activities:** Bands, choral groups, drama, music ensembles, musical theater, student government, human services club, law enforcement club, Intervarsity Christian Fellowship.

Athletics. NJCAA. **Intercollegiate:** Baseball M, basketball, rodeo, softball W. **Intramural:** Basketball, bowling, golf, racquetball, softball, table tennis, tennis, volleyball. **Team name:** Buccaneers.

Student services. Adult student services, career counseling, student employment services, placement for graduates, veterans' counselor. **Physically disabled:** Services for visually, speech, hearing impaired. **Transfer:** Pre-admission transcript evaluation for new students. College fairs on campus for students transferring to 4-year colleges.

Contact. E-mail: myers@dawson.edu
Phone: (406) 377-3396 ext. 410 Toll-free number: (800) 821-8320 ext. 410
Fax: (406) 377-8132
Jolene Myers, Director of Admissions, Dawson Community College, 300 College Drive, Glendive, MT 59330

Flathead Valley Community College
Kalispell, Montana
www.fvcc.edu **CB code: 4317**

- Public 2-year community college
- Commuter campus in large town

General. Founded in 1967. Regionally accredited. **Enrollment:** 1,395 degree-seeking undergraduates; 504 non-degree-seeking students. **Degrees:** 181 associate awarded. **Location:** 250 miles from Spokane, Washington. **Calendar:** Semester, limited summer session. **Full-time faculty:** 42 total. **Part-time faculty:** 100 total. **Class size:** 86% < 20, 14% 20-39. **Partnerships:** Formal partnerships with Tech Prep and Running Start programs with area high schools.

Student profile. Among degree-seeking undergraduates, 293 enrolled as first-time, first-year students.

Part-time:	36%	**Women:**	61%
Out-of-state:	3%		

Transfer out. Colleges most students transferred to 2008: University of Montana, Montana State University - Bozeman.

Basis for selection. Open admission, but selective for some programs. Radiological technology program requires anatomy and physiology I and II, English composition, intermediate algebra, and medical terminology with a grade of C or better. Practical nursing program requires 8 prerequisite courses with GPA of 3.0. ASSET and COMPASS used for placement purposes. **Homeschooled:** Applicants must have GED or COMPASS test scores.

2008-2009 Annual costs. Tuition/fees: $3,472; $4,844 out-of-district; $10,612 out-of-state. Per-credit charge: $124 in-district; $173 out-of-district; $379 out-of-state. Books/supplies: $1,000. Personal expenses: $2,240.

2008-2009 Financial aid. Need-based: 62% of total undergraduate aid awarded as scholarships/grants, 38% as loans/jobs. Need-based aid available for part-time students. Work-study available for part-time students. **Non-need-based:** Scholarships awarded for academics, athletics.

Application procedures. Admission: No deadline. $15 fee. Application must be submitted on paper. Admission notification on a rolling basis. **Financial aid:** Priority date 3/1; no closing date. FAFSA required. Applicants notified by 4/15; must reply within 2 week(s) of notification.

Academics. Special study options: Distance learning, dual enrollment of high school students, independent study, internships, liberal arts/career combination, study abroad. Bachelor's degree programs available on campus. **Credit/placement by examination:** AP, CLEP, IB, institutional tests. 12 AP credits allowed toward associate degree. **Support services:** GED preparation and test center, learning center, reduced course load, remedial instruction, study skills assistance, tutoring, writing center.

Majors. Business: General, accounting, management information systems, marketing, office technology. **Conservation:** Management/policy. **Construction:** General. **Engineering:** General. **Engineering technology:** Surveying. **Health:** Health care admin, health services, medical assistant, medical records technology, medical secretary, medical transcription, office admin, office assistant, office computer specialist, receptionist, substance abuse counseling. **Legal studies:** Legal secretary. **Liberal arts:** Arts/sciences, humanities. **Mechanic/repair:** Watch/jewelry. **Protective services:** Law enforcement admin. **Public administration:** Human services.

Most popular majors. Business/marketing 6%, health sciences 8%, liberal arts 73%.

Computing on campus. 175 workstations in library, computer center. Commuter students can connect to campus network. Online course registration, helpline, wireless network available.

Student life. Freshman orientation: Available. Preregistration for classes offered. 4 half-day summer advising and registration programs. **Activities:** Drama, student government, student newspaper, Phi Theta Kappa, veterans organization, forestry club, campus ministry group, Bitta club (Native American), human service club, international student association.

Athletics. NJCAA. **Intercollegiate:** Cross-country, soccer M. **Intramural:** Badminton, basketball, football (tackle), golf, skiing, softball, table tennis, tennis, volleyball. **Team name:** Eagles.

Student services. Adult student services, career counseling, services for economically disadvantaged, student employment services, financial aid counseling, health services, personal counseling, placement for graduates, veterans' counselor. **Physically disabled:** Services for visually, hearing impaired. **Transfer:** Pre-admission transcript evaluation for new students. Transfer adviser for students transferring to 4-year colleges.

Contact. E-mail: mstoltz@fvcc.edu
Phone: (406) 756-3846 Toll-free number: (800) 313-3822
Fax: (406) 756-3965
Marlene Stoltz, Registrar/Admissions and Records Coordinator, Flathead Valley Community College, 777 Grandview Drive, Kalispell, MT 59901

Fort Belknap College

Harlem, Montana
www.fbcc.edu **CB code: 5971**

- Public 2-year community college
- Commuter campus in rural community

General. Regionally accredited. **Enrollment:** 145 degree-seeking undergraduates. **Degrees:** 20 associate awarded. **Location:** On Fort Belknap Reservation. **Calendar:** Semester. **Full-time faculty:** 13 total. **Part-time faculty:** 2 total. **Special facilities:** Native American cultural center.

Transfer out. Colleges most students transferred to 2008: University of Missoula.

Basis for selection. Open admission. Compass Placement Test required. **Homeschooled:** Transcript of courses and grades, state high school equivalency certificate required.

2008-2009 Annual costs. Tuition/fees: $2,410. Per-credit charge: $70. Books/supplies: $910. Personal expenses: $960.

Application procedures. Admission: No deadline. $10 fee. Admission notification on a rolling basis. **Financial aid:** No deadline. Applicants notified on a rolling basis.

Academics. Special study options: Dual enrollment of high school students. **Credit/placement by examination:** CLEP. **Support services:** GED preparation, learning center, tutoring.

Majors. Area/ethnic studies: Native American. **Business:** General. **Computer sciences:** Data processing. **Conservation:** Management/policy. **Education:** Elementary. **Health:** Substance abuse counseling. **Liberal arts:** Arts/sciences. **Public administration:** Human services.

Most popular majors. Biological/life sciences 21%, business/marketing 7%, computer/information sciences 29%, education 7%, liberal arts 7%, natural resources/environmental science 21%, psychology 7%.

Student life. Freshman orientation: Mandatory. **Activities:** Student government.

Student services. Career counseling, financial aid counseling.

Contact. Phone: (406) 353-2607 Fax: (406) 353-2898
Dixie Brockie, Registrar/Admissions Officer, Fort Belknap College, Box 159, Harlem, MT 59526-0159

Fort Peck Community College

Poplar, Montana
www.fpcc.edu **CB code: 5972**

- Public 2-year community college
- Commuter campus in small town

General. Regionally accredited. Tribally controlled college. **Enrollment:** 371 degree-seeking undergraduates. **Degrees:** 39 associate awarded. **Location:** 70 miles from Williston, North Dakota; 300 miles from Billings. **Calendar:** Semester, limited summer session. **Full-time faculty:** 25 total. **Part-time faculty:** 15 total. **Special facilities:** Individual student science lab stations.

Transfer out. Colleges most students transferred to 2008: Rocky Mountain College.

Basis for selection. Open admission. Interview recommended.

2008-2009 Annual costs. Tuition/fees: $1,940. Per-credit charge: $60. Books/supplies: $500. Personal expenses: $2,000.

Financial aid. Need-based: Need-based aid available for part-time students. Work-study available nights and for part-time students.

Application procedures. Admission: Closing date 9/16. $15 fee, may be waived for applicants with need. Admission notification on a rolling basis. **Financial aid:** No deadline. FAFSA, institutional form required. Applicants notified on a rolling basis; must reply within 2 week(s) of notification.

Academics. Special study options: Distance learning, double major, dual enrollment of high school students, independent study, internships, teacher certification program. **Credit/placement by examination:** CLEP. **Support services:** GED preparation and test center, learning center, remedial instruction, study skills assistance, tutoring.

Two-Year Colleges

Majors. **Area/ethnic studies:** Native American. **Biology:** Biomedical sciences. **Business:** General, administrative services, business admin. **Computer sciences:** Computer graphics, data processing. **Conservation:** General, management/policy. **Education:** General, science. **Health:** Substance abuse counseling. **Mechanic/repair:** Automotive. **Public administration:** Human services. **Visual/performing arts:** Studio arts.

Computing on campus. 65 workstations in library, computer center.

Student life. **Freshman orientation:** Available. **Activities:** Student government, student newspaper, American Indian Business Leaders.

Student services. Adult student services, career counseling, student employment services, on-campus daycare, personal counseling, placement for graduates, veterans' counselor. **Transfer:** Pre-admission transcript evaluation for new students. Transfer adviser, college fairs on campus for students transferring to 4-year colleges.

Contact. Phone: (406) 768-5553 Fax: (406) 768-5552
Leigh Melbourne, Director of Admissions, Fort Peck Community College, Box 398 605 Indian, Poplar, MT 59255-0398

Helena College of Technology of the University of Montana

Helena, Montana
www.umhelena.edu **CB code: 2022**

- Public 2-year community and technical college
- Commuter campus in large town

General. Founded in 1939. Regionally accredited. **Enrollment:** 908 degree-seeking undergraduates. **Degrees:** 117 associate awarded. **Location:** 90 miles from Great Falls. **Calendar:** Semester, limited summer session. **Full-time faculty:** 34 total. **Part-time faculty:** 56 total.

Student profile. Among degree-seeking undergraduates, 37% enrolled in a transfer program, 38% enrolled in a vocational program, 1% already have a bachelor's degree or higher, 251 enrolled as first-time, first-year students, 91 transferred in from other institutions.

Basis for selection. Open admission. Interview recommended.

High school preparation. Recommended units include English 3 and mathematics 3.

2008-2009 Annual costs. Tuition/fees: $3,025; $8,589 out-of-state. Books/supplies: $600. Personal expenses: $710.

2007-2008 Financial aid. **Need-based:** Need-based aid available for part-time students.

Application procedures. **Admission:** No deadline. $30 fee. Admission notification on a rolling basis beginning on or about 2/15. **Financial aid:** Priority date 3/1; no closing date. FAFSA, institutional form required. Applicants notified on a rolling basis starting 5/1.

Academics. **Special study options:** Dual enrollment of high school students, independent study, internships. License preparation in nursing. **Credit/placement by examination:** AP, CLEP. **Support services:** Learning center, pre-admission summer program, remedial instruction, study skills assistance, tutoring, writing center.

Majors. **Business:** Accounting, administrative services, office technology. **Computer sciences:** Programming. **Construction:** Carpentry. **Health:** Medical secretary. **Legal studies:** Legal secretary, paralegal. **Liberal arts:** Arts/sciences. **Mechanic/repair:** Aircraft, automotive, diesel, electronics/electrical. **Protective services:** Firefighting.

Computing on campus. 160 workstations in library, computer center. Commuter students can connect to campus network. Online course registration, online library, helpline, wireless network available.

Student life. **Freshman orientation:** Mandatory. Preregistration for classes offered. **Activities:** Student government, student newspaper.

Athletics. **Intramural:** Basketball, volleyball.

Student services. Adult student services, career counseling, student employment services, personal counseling, placement for graduates, veterans' counselor. **Physically disabled:** Services for visually, speech, hearing impaired. **Transfer:** Transfer adviser for students transferring to 4-year colleges.

Contact. E-mail: admissions@umh.umt.edu
Phone: (406) 444-6800 Toll-free number: (800) 241-4882
Fax: (406) 444-6892
Michael Brown, Executive Director of Enrollment Services, Helena College of Technology of the University of Montana, 1115 North Roberts Street, Helena, MT 59601-3098

Little Big Horn College

Crow Agency, Montana
www.lbhc.cc.mt.us **CB code: 0536**

- Private 2-year community college
- Commuter campus in rural community

General. Founded in 1980. Regionally accredited. Provides education for Crow Indian community. Crow lifeways, economic environment, history, language, and culture emphasized with standard curriculum. **Enrollment:** 265 degree-seeking undergraduates. **Degrees:** 47 associate awarded. **Location:** 60 miles from Billings. **Calendar:** Quarter. **Full-time faculty:** 15 total. **Part-time faculty:** 10 total.

Basis for selection. Open admission.

2008-2009 Annual costs. Tuition/fees: $2,760. Per-credit charge: $75. Books/supplies: $600. Personal expenses: $600.

2008-2009 Financial aid. **Need-based:** Need-based aid available for part-time students.

Application procedures. **Admission:** No deadline. No application fee. Admission notification on a rolling basis. **Financial aid:** No deadline. Applicants notified on a rolling basis.

Academics. Bilingual methodologies approach in some course work. **Special study options:** Distance learning, exchange student, internships. **Credit/placement by examination:** CLEP, institutional tests. **Support services:** Remedial instruction, tutoring.

Majors. **Area/ethnic studies:** Native American. **Biology:** General. **Business:** General, business admin, management information systems. **Computer sciences:** Data processing, information systems. **Family/consumer sciences:** General, child care. **Health:** Substance abuse counseling. **Liberal arts:** Arts/sciences. **Math:** General. **Psychology:** General. **Social sciences:** General.

Most popular majors. Business/marketing 10%, liberal arts 90%.

Student life. **Policies:** Native religious ceremonies offered. **Activities:** Student government.

Athletics. **Intercollegiate:** Basketball.

Student services. Career counseling, student employment services, personal counseling. **Transfer:** Transfer adviser, college fairs on campus for students transferring to 4-year colleges.

Contact. Phone: (406) 638-3116 Fax: (406) 638-3169
Tina Pretty On Top, Admissions Officer, Little Big Horn College, Box 370, Crow Agency, MT 59022

Miles Community College

Miles City, Montana
www.milescc.edu/ **CB code: 4081**

- Public 2-year community college
- Commuter campus in small town

General. Founded in 1939. Regionally accredited. **Enrollment:** 450 degree-seeking undergraduates; 23 non-degree-seeking students. **Degrees:** 107 associate awarded. **Location:** 150 miles from Billings. **Calendar:** Semester, limited summer session. **Full-time faculty:** 20 total. **Part-time faculty:** 31 total.

Student profile. Among degree-seeking undergraduates, 141 enrolled as first-time, first-year students, 23 transferred in from other institutions.

Part-time:	22%	**25 or older:**	45%
Out-of-state:	1%	**Live on campus:**	25%
Women:	63%		

Transfer out. Colleges most students transferred to 2008: Montana State University-Billings, Montana State University-Bozeman, Dickinson State University, University of Montana, South Dakota State University.

Basis for selection. Open admission, but selective for some programs. Special requirements for nursing program: National League for Nursing Pre-Admission Examination required, Certified Nurse's Aide required. COMPASS required for all students. **Homeschooled:** Minimum COMPASS scores: Writing, 32; Reading, 62; Pre-Algebra/Number Skills, 25; may be used in lieu of high school diploma or GED.

2008-2009 Annual costs. Tuition/fees: $3,420; $4,290 out-of-district; $7,080 out-of-state. Per-credit charge: $71 in-district; $100 out-of-district; $193 out-of-state. Room/board: $4,250. Books/supplies: $800. Personal expenses: $630.

Financial aid. Need-based: Need-based aid available for part-time students. Work-study available nights, weekends and for part-time students. **Non-need-based:** Scholarships awarded for academics, athletics, leadership.

Application procedures. Admission: No deadline. $30 fee. Admission notification on a rolling basis. **Financial aid:** Priority date 3/1; no closing date. FAFSA required. Applicants notified on a rolling basis starting 4/15; must reply within 4 week(s) of notification.

Academics. Special study options: Cooperative education, cross-registration, distance learning, dual enrollment of high school students, ESL, independent study, internships. License preparation in nursing. **Credit/placement by examination:** AP, CLEP, IB, institutional tests. 15 credit hours maximum toward associate degree. **Support services:** GED preparation and test center, learning center, pre-admission summer program, reduced course load, remedial instruction, study skills assistance, tutoring, writing center.

Majors. Agriculture: Business. **Biology:** General. **Business:** Administrative services, business admin, office management, office/clerical. **Communications:** Journalism. **Computer sciences:** General, computer graphics, data processing. **Conservation:** General, forestry, wildlife. **Construction:** Carpentry, maintenance, power transmission. **Education:** General. **Engineering:** General. **Family/consumer sciences:** General. **Foreign languages:** General. **Health:** Medical secretary, nursing (RN), prenursing. **Liberal arts:** Arts/sciences. **Math:** General. **Parks/recreation:** Health/fitness. **Physical sciences:** General. **Psychology:** General. **Public administration:** General, human services, social work. **Social sciences:** General, economics, political science. **Visual/performing arts:** Art, crafts, dramatic, photography.

Computing on campus. 90 workstations in library, computer center. Dormitories wired for high-speed internet access. Commuter students can connect to campus network. Online course registration available.

Student life. Freshman orientation: Mandatory. Preregistration for classes offered. **Housing:** Coed dorms available. $200 deposit. **Activities:** Campus ministries, choral groups, dance, drama, international student organizations, student government, Phi Theta Kappa, rodeo club, student senate, student ambassadors.

Athletics. NJCAA. **Intercollegiate:** Baseball M, basketball, cheerleading M, golf, rodeo, volleyball W. **Intramural:** Basketball, bowling, fencing, golf, handball, ice hockey, racquetball, soccer, tennis, volleyball, weight lifting. **Team name:** Pioneers.

Student services. Adult student services, career counseling, student employment services, financial aid counseling, personal counseling, placement for graduates, veterans' counselor. **Transfer:** Pre-admission transcript evaluation for new students. College fairs on campus for students transferring to 4-year colleges.

Contact. E-mail: bluntl@milescc.edu
Phone: (406) 874-6217 Toll-free number: (800) 541-9281
Fax: (406) 874-6283
Darren Pitcher, Dean of Student Services, Miles Community College, 2715 Dickinson Street, Miles City, MT 59301

Montana State University College of Technology: Great Falls

Great Falls, Montana
www.msugf.edu **CB code: 4482**

- Public 2-year community and technical college
- Commuter campus in small city

General. Founded in 1969. Regionally accredited. **Enrollment:** 1,466 degree-seeking undergraduates. **Degrees:** 171 associate awarded. **Location:** 200 miles from Billings, 150 miles from Missoula. **Calendar:** Semester, limited summer session. **Full-time faculty:** 51 total; 12% have terminal degrees, 4% minority, 53% women. **Part-time faculty:** 86 total; 5% minority, 62% women. **Class size:** 66% < 20, 34% 20-39.

Student profile.

Out-of-state:	9%	**25 or older:**	36%

Basis for selection. Open admission, but selective for some programs. Special requirements for dental hygiene, radiologic technology, practical nursing, dental assistant, surgical technology, and physical therapist assistant programs. **Adult students:** COMPASS test used to determine placement in courses. All placement tests must have been taken within the past three years. **Homeschooled:** Transcript of courses and grades, letter of recommendation (nonparent) required. Notarized copy of the homeschool curriculum, 2 letters of recommendation from non-family members, parental approval form if under 18 required.

2008-2009 Annual costs. Tuition/fees: $2,999; $9,151 out-of-state. Books/supplies: $1,200. Personal expenses: $2,072.

2007-2008 Financial aid. Need-based: 139 full-time freshmen applied for aid; 119 were judged to have need; 115 of these received aid. Average need met was 61%. Average scholarship/grant was $3,897; average loan $2,621. 48% of total undergraduate aid awarded as scholarships/grants, 52% as loans/jobs. Need-based aid available for part-time students. Work-study available nights, weekends and for part-time students. **Non-need-based:** Awarded to 7 full-time undergraduates, including 1 freshmen.

Application procedures. Admission: No deadline. $30 fee. Application must be submitted on paper. Admission notification on a rolling basis. **Financial aid:** Priority date 3/1; no closing date. FAFSA, institutional form required. Applicants notified on a rolling basis starting 4/1; must reply within 3 week(s) of notification.

Academics. Special study options: Combined bachelor's/graduate degree, cooperative education, distance learning, double major, dual enrollment of high school students, independent study, internships, liberal arts/career combination. License preparation in aviation, dental hygiene, nursing, paramedic, physical therapy, radiology. **Credit/placement by examination:** AP, CLEP, SAT, ACT, institutional tests. 25 credit hours maximum toward associate degree. **Support services:** Learning center, remedial instruction, study skills assistance, tutoring.

Majors. Business: Accounting, accounting technology, business admin. **Computer sciences:** General, networking. **Engineering technology:** Drafting. **Health:** Dental hygiene, EMT ambulance attendant, EMT paramedic, insurance specialist, licensed practical nurse, medical assistant, medical transcription, physical therapy assistant, radiologic technology/medical imaging, respiratory therapy assistant. **Mechanic/repair:** Auto body. **Protective services:** Firefighting. **Transportation:** Aviation. **Visual/performing arts:** Interior design.

Most popular majors. Business/marketing 11%, computer/information sciences 8%, education 12%, health sciences 37%, liberal arts 19%, visual/performing arts 7%.

Computing on campus. 202 workstations in library, computer center. Commuter students can connect to campus network. Online course registration, online library, helpline, wireless network available.

Student life. Freshman orientation: Mandatory, $10 fee. Two-hour session in May; day session held week prior to the beginning of fall semester. **Activities:** Drama, literary magazine, student government, student newspaper, Phi Theta Kappa, drama club, literary guild, health occupations student association, Native American student council, interior design students, Chi Alpha, nursing students, dental hygiene students, auto body students.

Student services. Career counseling, student employment services, financial aid counseling, placement for graduates. **Physically disabled:** Services for visually, hearing impaired. **Transfer:** Transfer adviser, college fairs on campus for students transferring to 4-year colleges.

Contact. E-mail: information@msugf.edu
Phone: (406) 771-4420 Toll-free number: (800) 446-2698
Fax: (406) 771-4329
Dena Wagner-Fossen, Registrar, Montana State University College of Technology: Great Falls, 2100 16th Avenue South, Great Falls, MT 59405

Stone Child College

Box Elder, Montana
www.stonechild.edu **CB code: 7044**

- Public 2-year community and junior college
- Commuter campus in rural community

General. Founded in 1984. Regionally accredited. Tribally-controlled college located on the Rocky Boys Indian Reservation. **Enrollment:** 213 degree-seeking undergraduates. **Degrees:** 34 associate awarded. **Location:** 26 miles from Havre, 100 miles from Great Falls. **Calendar:** Semester, limited summer session. **Full-time faculty:** 10 total. **Part-time faculty:** 29 total.

Student profile.

Out-of-state:	2%	25 or older:	56%

Transfer out. Colleges most students transferred to 2008: Montana State University-Northern, Montana State University-Billings, University of Montana, University of Great Falls.

Basis for selection. Open admission.

High school preparation. 22 units recommended. Recommended units include English 4, mathematics 3, social studies 3, history 4, science 3, foreign language 1 and academic electives 4.

2008-2009 Annual costs. Tuition/fees: $2,350. Per-credit charge: $60. Students not members of Federally-recognized Native American tribe pay additional $420 in fees/year. Books/supplies: $800. Personal expenses: $1,520.

Financial aid. Need-based: Need-based aid available for part-time students. Work-study available for part-time students. **Non-need-based:** Scholarships awarded for academics. **Additional information:** Scholarships available to high school and GED graduates who apply for college admission during the first term after graduation.

Application procedures. Admission: No deadline. $10 fee. Admission notification on a rolling basis. **Financial aid:** Priority date 3/1, closing date 6/30. FAFSA, institutional form required. Applicants notified on a rolling basis.

Academics. Special study options: Cooperative education, distance learning, double major, dual enrollment of high school students, independent study, liberal arts/career combination. Hosts distance learning programs from 4-year institutions, bachelors available in computer science, counseling, psychology, criminal justice, health care administration, human services management, marketing, paralegal studies, sociology, theology and religion. **Credit/placement by examination:** CLEP, institutional tests. 12 credit hours maximum toward associate degree. **Support services:** GED preparation, learning center, remedial instruction, tutoring.

Majors. Area/ethnic studies: Native American. **Business:** General, management information systems, office/clerical. **Computer sciences:** Data processing, information systems. **Education:** Elementary. **Health:** Substance abuse counseling. **Interdisciplinary:** Biological/physical sciences. **Liberal arts:** Arts/sciences. **Public administration:** Human services.

Computing on campus. 64 workstations in library, computer center, student center.

Student life. Freshman orientation: Mandatory. **Activities:** Student government, student newspaper.

Athletics. Intercollegiate: Basketball. **Intramural:** Basketball. **Team name:** Bear Paws.

Student services. Career counseling, on-campus daycare, personal counseling. **Transfer:** Transfer adviser, college fairs on campus for students transferring to 4-year colleges.

Contact. E-mail: tedewhitford@hotmail.com
Phone: (406) 395-4313 ext. 222 Fax: (406) 395-4836
Theodore Whitford, Director of Admissions, Stone Child College, RR1 Box 1082, Box Elder, MT 59521-9796

Nebraska

Central Community College

Grand Island, Nebraska
www.cccneb.edu **CB code: 6136**

- Public 2-year community and technical college
- Commuter campus in large town

General. Founded in 1966. Regionally accredited. Multilocation institution with campuses at Columbus, Grand Island, and Hastings. Centers located in Holdrege, Kearney, and Lexington. Multiple starting dates for most programs and courses. **Enrollment:** 4,091 degree-seeking undergraduates; 2,794 non-degree-seeking students. **Degrees:** 534 associate awarded. **Location:** 100 miles from Lincoln. **Calendar:** Semester, extensive summer session. **Full-time faculty:** 152 total; 27% have terminal degrees, 3% minority, 50% women. **Part-time faculty:** 112 total; 29% have terminal degrees, 3% minority, 54% women.

Student profile. Among degree-seeking undergraduates, 45% enrolled in a transfer program, 54% enrolled in a vocational program, 945 enrolled as first-time, first-year students.

Part-time:	46%	**Asian American:**	1%
Out-of-state:	1%	**Hispanic American:**	9%
Women:	64%	**25 or older:**	41%
African American:	1%	**Live on campus:**	20%

Transfer out. Colleges most students transferred to 2008: University of Nebraska-Kearney, University of Nebraska-Lincoln, University of Nebraska-Omaha, Bellevue University.

Basis for selection. Open admission, but selective for some programs and for out-of-state students. Special requirements for dental assisting, medical assisting, medical laboratory technician, health information management services, truck driving programs. ACT or Dental Hygiene Aptitude Test required for dental hygiene program. ACT or ASSET required for nursing programs. Interview recommended for health information management services.

2008-2009 Annual costs. Tuition/fees: $2,190; $3,045 out-of-state. Per-credit charge: $73 in-state; $106 out-of-state. Room/board: $4,080. Books/supplies: $1,000. Personal expenses: $1,380.

Financial aid. Need-based: Need-based aid available for part-time students. Work-study available nights and for part-time students. **Non-need-based:** Scholarships awarded for academics, art, athletics, job skills, leadership, music/drama.

Application procedures. Admission: No deadline. No application fee. Admission notification on a rolling basis. Score report for dental hygiene applicants due 09/01. Application deadlines: January 15 for dental hygiene, February 15 for associate degree nursing and practical nursing. **Financial aid:** Priority date 6/1; no closing date. FAFSA, institutional form required. Applicants notified on a rolling basis starting 3/1; must reply within 1 week(s) of notification.

Academics. Open entry/open exit, self-paced, flexible scheduling for most programs. **Special study options:** Accelerated study, cooperative education, distance learning, double major, dual enrollment of high school students, ESL, honors, independent study, internships, weekend college. License preparation in dental hygiene, nursing, real estate. **Credit/placement by examination:** AP, CLEP, institutional tests. 48 credit hours maximum toward associate degree. **Support services:** GED preparation and test center, learning center, reduced course load, remedial instruction, study skills assistance, tutoring.

Majors. Agriculture: Business, horticulture. **Business:** Administrative services, business admin, vehicle parts marketing. **Communications:** Digital media. **Computer sciences:** General. **Construction:** Electrician. **Engineering technology:** Drafting, electrical, quality control. **Family/consumer sciences:** General, child care. **Health:** Clinical lab technology, dental assistant, dental hygiene, licensed practical nurse, medical assistant, medical records technology, nursing (RN). **Legal studies:** Paralegal. **Liberal arts:** Arts/sciences. **Mechanic/repair:** Auto body, automotive, diesel, heating/ac/refrig, industrial. **Personal/culinary services:** Restaurant/catering. **Production:** General, machine tool, welding. **Protective services:** Criminal justice. **Visual/performing arts:** Commercial/advertising art.

Most popular majors. Business/marketing 16%, engineering/engineering technologies 8%, family/consumer sciences 6%, health sciences 24%, liberal arts 18%, trade and industry 13%.

Computing on campus. Dormitories linked to campus network. Commuter students can connect to campus network. Online course registration, online library, helpline available.

Student life. Freshman orientation: Available. Preregistration for classes offered. **Housing:** Coed dorms, single-sex dorms, apartments, wellness housing available. $150 partly refundable deposit. **Activities:** Jazz band, choral groups, dance, drama, music ensembles, musical theater, radio station, student government, student newspaper.

Athletics. NJCAA. **Intercollegiate:** Basketball M, golf M, softball W, volleyball W. **Intramural:** Basketball, bowling, table tennis, volleyball, weight lifting.

Student services. Adult student services, career counseling, services for economically disadvantaged, student employment services, financial aid counseling, health services, minority student services, on-campus daycare, personal counseling, placement for graduates, veterans' counselor, women's services. **Physically disabled:** Services for visually, speech, hearing impaired. **Transfer:** Pre-admission transcript evaluation for new students. Transfer adviser, college fairs on campus for students transferring to 4-year colleges.

Contact. E-mail: lkohout@cccneb.edu
Phone: (308) 398-7406 Toll-free number: (877) 222-0780
Fax: (308) 398-7398
Liz Kohout, Admissions Director, Central Community College, 3134 West Highway 34, Grand Island, NE 68802-4903

Kaplan University: Lincoln

Lincoln, Nebraska
www.kucampus.edu **CB code: 3385**

- For-profit 2-year branch campus college
- Commuter campus in small city

General. Founded in 1884. **Enrollment:** 496 degree-seeking undergraduates. **Degrees:** 19 bachelor's, 136 associate awarded. **Calendar:** Continuous, extensive summer session. **Full-time faculty:** 25 total. **Part-time faculty:** 40 total. **Class size:** 83% < 20, 17% 20-39.

Student profile.

Out-of-state:	2%	**25 or older:**	54%

Transfer out. Colleges most students transferred to 2008: Southeast Community College.

Basis for selection. Open admission, but selective for some programs. CPAT required of all applicants. Students must pass entrance exam.

2008-2009 Annual costs. Tuition/fees: $14,070. Cost is for 3 terms of 12 hours each. Tuition includes books and supplies; may vary by program.

2007-2008 Financial aid. All financial aid based on need. Need-based aid available for part-time students. Work-study available nights, weekends and for part-time students.

Application procedures. Admission: No deadline. $25 fee. Admission notification on a rolling basis. **Financial aid:** No deadline. FAFSA, institutional form required. Applicants notified on a rolling basis starting 2/1.

Academics. Special study options: Internships. Bachelor's degree programs available on campus. License preparation in nursing. **Credit/placement by examination:** CLEP. **Support services:** Learning center, study skills assistance, tutoring.

Majors. Business: Accounting, administrative services, business admin. **Computer sciences:** Information technology. **Health:** Medical assistant. **Legal studies:** Paralegal. **Protective services:** Criminal justice. **Other:** Multi-interdisciplinary studies.

Most popular majors. Business/marketing 20%, computer/information sciences 11%, health sciences 31%, legal studies 9%, security/protective services 23%.

Computing on campus. 70 workstations in library, computer center.

Student life. Freshman orientation: Mandatory. Orientation held on first day of classes for all new students. **Housing:** $150 deposit. **Activities:** Tour and travel club, medical club, association of information technology professionals, business club, legal assisting club.

Athletics. NJCAA. **Team name:** Aliens.

Student services. Career counseling, student employment services, financial aid counseling, placement for graduates, veterans' counselor. **Physically disabled:** Services for visually, hearing impaired. **Transfer:** Pre-admission transcript evaluation for new students.

Contact. E-mail: jmathers@kaplan.edu
Phone: (402) 474-5315 Toll-free number: (800) 742-7738
Fax: (402) 474-0896
Kelly Frette, Director of Admissions, Kaplan University: Lincoln, 1821 K Street, Lincoln, NE 68508

Kaplan University: Omaha

Omaha, Nebraska
www.khenet.kaplan.edu **CB code: 3326**

- For-profit 2-year career college
- Commuter campus in large city
- Interview required

General. **Enrollment:** 696 degree-seeking undergraduates. **Degrees:** 8 bachelor's, 92 associate awarded. **Calendar:** Quarter, extensive summer session. **Full-time faculty:** 26 total; 8% minority. **Part-time faculty:** 35 total; 11% minority. **Class size:** 54% < 20, 46% 20-39.

Student profile. Among degree-seeking undergraduates, 404 enrolled as first-time, first-year students.

Part-time:	27%	**Women:**	86%
Out-of-state:	96%	**25 or older:**	60%

Basis for selection. Open admission.

2008-2009 Annual costs. Tuition/fees: $14,050. Books/supplies: $100. Personal expenses: $378.

Financial aid. All financial aid based on need. Need-based aid available for part-time students.

Application procedures. **Admission:** No deadline. $20 fee. Application must be submitted on paper. Admission notification on a rolling basis. **Financial aid:** No deadline. FAFSA, institutional form required. Applicants notified on a rolling basis.

Academics. **Special study options:** Accelerated study, double major, internships. License preparation in nursing. **Credit/placement by examination:** CLEP, institutional tests. 32 credit hours maximum toward associate degree. **Support services:** Learning center, reduced course load, study skills assistance, tutoring, writing center.

Majors. **Business:** Accounting, business admin. **Computer sciences:** Data processing. **Health:** Medical assistant. **Legal studies:** Paralegal. **Protective services:** Criminal justice.

Most popular majors. Business/marketing 17%, health sciences 41%, interdisciplinary studies 7%, legal studies 17%, security/protective services 14%.

Computing on campus. Commuter students can connect to campus network. Online library available.

Student life. **Freshman orientation:** Mandatory.

Student services. Adult student services, career counseling, services for economically disadvantaged, student employment services, financial aid counseling, placement for graduates. **Physically disabled:** Services for visually, speech, hearing impaired. **Transfer:** Pre-admission transcript evaluation for new students.

Contact. E-mail: mbaum@kaplan.edu
Phone: (402) 431-6100 Toll-free number: (800) 642-1456
Fax: (402) 573-6482
Mike Baum, Director of Admissions, Kaplan University: Omaha, 5425 North 103rd. Street, Omaha, NE 68134

Little Priest Tribal College

Winnebago, Nebraska
www.lptc.bia.edu **CB code: 3616**

- Private 2-year community college
- Commuter campus in rural community

General. Regionally accredited. **Enrollment:** 112 degree-seeking undergraduates. **Degrees:** 5 associate awarded. **Location:** 30 miles from Sioux City, Iowa. **Calendar:** Semester, limited summer session. **Full-time faculty:** 5 total. **Part-time faculty:** 10 total. **Class size:** 82% < 20, 18% 20-39.

Transfer out. **Colleges most students transferred to 2008:** Wayne State College, Haskell Indian Nations University.

Basis for selection. Open admission.

High school preparation. 11 units recommended. Recommended units include English 3, mathematics 3, social studies 3 and science 2.

2008-2009 Annual costs. Tuition/fees: $2,985. Per-credit charge: $80. Books/supplies: $700.

Financial aid. **Need-based:** Need-based aid available for part-time students. Work-study available for part-time students.

Application procedures. **Admission:** No deadline. $10 fee. **Financial aid:** No deadline. FAFSA, institutional form required.

Academics. **Special study options:** Dual enrollment of high school students, independent study, liberal arts/career combination. **Credit/placement by examination:** CLEP. **Support services:** GED preparation and test center, learning center, reduced course load, remedial instruction, study skills assistance, tutoring.

Majors. **Area/ethnic studies:** Native American. **Business:** General. **Computer sciences:** General. **Conservation:** General. **Education:** General. **Health:** Health services, substance abuse counseling. **Liberal arts:** Arts/sciences. **Math:** General.

Most popular majors. Area/ethnic studies 20%, business/marketing 20%, health sciences 20%, liberal arts 40%.

Computing on campus. 20 workstations in library, computer center, student center.

Student life. **Freshman orientation:** Available. Preregistration for classes offered. **Activities:** Student government, student newspaper.

Student services. Adult student services, financial aid counseling, personal counseling. **Transfer:** Pre-admission transcript evaluation for new students. College fairs on campus for students transferring to 4-year colleges.

Contact. Phone: (402) 878-2380 ext. 160 Fax: (402) 878-2355
Darla LaPointe, Dean of Admissions, Little Priest Tribal College, PO Box 270, Winnebago, NE 68071

Metropolitan Community College

Omaha, Nebraska **CB member**
www.mccneb.edu **CB code: 5755**

- Public 2-year community and technical college
- Commuter campus in large city

General. Founded in 1974. Regionally accredited. Additional locations: Fort Omaha, Elkhorn Valley, South Omaha, Applied Technology Center, Fremont Area Center, Sarpy Center in La Vista. **Enrollment:** 6,609 degree-seeking undergraduates; 8,446 non-degree-seeking students. **Degrees:** 1,003 associate awarded. **Location:** 50 miles from Lincoln. **Calendar:** Quarter, extensive summer session. **Full-time faculty:** 212 total; 13% minority, 49% women. **Part-time faculty:** 723 total; 10% minority, 50% women. **Class size:** 66% < 20, 33% 20-39, less than 1% 40-49, less than 1% 50-99. **Special facilities:** CAD/CAM and electronic graphics facilities.

Student profile. Among degree-seeking undergraduates, 25% enrolled in a transfer program, 52% enrolled in a vocational program, 1,443 enrolled as first-time, first-year students.

Part-time:	57%	**Hispanic American:**	6%
Out-of-state:	3%	**Native American:**	1%
Women:	58%	**25 or older:**	43%
African American:	15%	**Live on campus:**	1%
Asian American:	4%		

Transfer out. **Colleges most students transferred to 2008:** University of Nebraska-Omaha, Bellevue University.

Basis for selection. Open admission, but selective for some programs. Admission to nursing and allied health programs based on test scores and references. Assessment testing and standardized RN entrance examination required for nursing associate degree programs. Human services programs require a "C" and approval from Human Services Faculty Review Committee. Certain programs may require preparatory work before attending classes. Interview required for nursing and allied health programs.

High school preparation. High school diploma or GED required of nursing and allied health applicants.

2008-2009 Annual costs. Tuition/fees: $2,160; $3,128 out-of-state. Per-credit charge: $43 in-state; $65 out-of-state. Room/board: $3,555. Books/supplies: $1,800.

2008-2009 Financial aid. Need-based: Need-based aid available for part-time students. **Non-need-based:** Scholarships awarded for academics.

Application procedures. Admission: No deadline. No application fee. Admission notification on a rolling basis. **Financial aid:** Priority date 3/15; no closing date. FAFSA, institutional form required. Applicants notified on a rolling basis starting 4/15.

Academics. Individualized, self-paced instruction. Degree through telecourses available. **Special study options:** Cooperative education, distance learning, double major, dual enrollment of high school students, ESL, honors, independent study, internships, weekend college. License preparation in nursing. **Credit/placement by examination:** AP, CLEP, institutional tests. 81 credit hours maximum toward associate degree. **Support services:** GED preparation and test center, learning center, remedial instruction, tutoring, writing center.

Majors. Agriculture: Horticulture, nursery operations. **Architecture:** Interior. **Business:** General, accounting, administrative services, business admin, management information systems. **Communications technology:** Graphic/printing. **Computer sciences:** General, networking. **Construction:** Maintenance, power transmission. **Engineering technology:** Architectural drafting, civil, drafting, electrical, software. **Family/consumer sciences:** Child care, institutional food production. **Foreign languages:** Sign language interpretation. **Health:** Nursing (RN), respiratory therapy technology. **Legal studies:** Paralegal. **Liberal arts:** Arts/sciences. **Mechanic/repair:** Auto body, automotive, heating/ac/refrig, industrial. **Personal/culinary services:** Culinary arts. **Protective services:** Fire services admin, police science. **Public administration:** Social work. **Visual/performing arts:** Commercial photography, commercial/advertising art, studio arts, theater arts management.

Most popular majors. Business/marketing 18%, health sciences 11%, liberal arts 30%, security/protective services 6%, trade and industry 10%, visual/performing arts 9%.

Computing on campus. 1,550 workstations in library, computer center. Commuter students can connect to campus network. Online course registration, helpline available.

Student life. Freshman orientation: Available. Preregistration for classes offered. **Housing:** Coed dorms, single-sex dorms, wellness housing available. **Activities:** Phi Theta Kappa scholastic honor society.

Student services. Adult student services, career counseling, services for economically disadvantaged, student employment services, financial aid counseling, minority student services, personal counseling, placement for graduates, veterans' counselor, women's services. **Physically disabled:** Services for visually, speech, hearing impaired. **Transfer:** Transfer adviser for students transferring to 4-year colleges.

Contact. E-mail: plewisrodriguez@mccneb.edu
Phone: (402) 457-2422 Toll-free number: (800) 228-9553
Fax: (402) 457-2616
Pam Lewis-Rodriguez, Assistant Dean of Enrollment Services,
Metropolitan Community College, Box 3777, Omaha, NE 68103-0777

Mid-Plains Community College Area

North Platte, Nebraska
www.mpcc.edu **CB code: 6497**

- Public 2-year community and technical college
- Commuter campus in large town

General. Founded in 1964. Regionally accredited. Two major sites, North Platte and McCook; extended campus sites in Broken Bow, Imperial, Ogallala, and Valentine. **Enrollment:** 1,252 degree-seeking undergraduates; 1,456 non-degree-seeking students. **Degrees:** 244 associate awarded. **Location:** 230 miles from Lincoln, 270 miles from Denver. **Calendar:** Semester, limited summer session. **Full-time faculty:** 65 total; 6% have terminal degrees, 52% women. **Part-time faculty:** 238 total. **Partnerships:** Formal partnership with Union Pacific Railroad for apprenticeships, technical training, continuing education.

Student profile. Among degree-seeking undergraduates, 40% enrolled in a transfer program, 60% enrolled in a vocational program, 2% already have a bachelor's degree or higher, 302 enrolled as first-time, first-year students, 15 transferred in from other institutions.

Part-time:	29%	**Hispanic American:**	4%
Out-of-state:	5%	**Native American:**	1%
Women:	62%	**25 or older:**	65%
African American:	4%	**Live on campus:**	5%

Transfer out. Colleges most students transferred to 2008: University of Nebraska at Lincoln, University of Nebraska at Kearney, Chadron State College.

Basis for selection. Open admission, but selective for some programs. Special requirements, including interview, for nursing and laboratory technology programs. Psychological Corporation Pre-Nursing Examination required of applicants to nursing program. Minimum ACT score of 17 required for licensed practical nursing and 21 for associate degree nursing. Minimum ASSET score of 40 in all areas required for medical laboratory technology program. **Adult students:** SAT/ACT scores not required. **Home-schooled:** State high school equivalency certificate required. **Learning Disabled:** Student should have physician's documentation of learning disability.

High school preparation. College-preparatory program recommended. Recommended units include English 4, mathematics 4, social studies 1, history 1, science 2, foreign language 1, computer science 1 and visual/performing arts 1.

2008-2009 Annual costs. Tuition/fees: $2,370; $2,970 out-of-state. Per-credit charge: $65 in-state; $85 out-of-state. Room/board: $4,700. Books/supplies: $1,000. Personal expenses: $750.

2007-2008 Financial aid. Need-based: 60% of total undergraduate aid awarded as scholarships/grants, 40% as loans/jobs. Need-based aid available for part-time students. Work-study available nights. **Non-need-based:** Scholarships awarded for academics, art, athletics, music/drama.

Application procedures. Admission: No deadline. No application fee. Admission notification on a rolling basis. **Financial aid:** Priority date 5/1; no closing date. FAFSA, institutional form required. Applicants notified on a rolling basis starting 5/1; must reply within 3 week(s) of notification.

Academics. Special study options: Cooperative education, distance learning, dual enrollment of high school students, exchange student, honors, independent study, internships, liberal arts/career combination. Bachelor's degree programs available on campus. License preparation in dental hygiene, nursing, paramedic, real estate. **Credit/placement by examination:** AP, CLEP. 20 credit hours maximum toward associate degree. **Support services:** GED preparation and test center, remedial instruction, study skills assistance, tutoring.

Majors. Business: Business admin, office management. **Computer sciences:** Information technology. **Construction:** Electrician, maintenance. **Engineering technology:** Electrical. **Family/consumer sciences:** Child care. **Health:** Clinical lab technology, dental assistant, nursing (RN). **Liberal arts:** Arts/sciences, library assistant. **Mechanic/repair:** General, auto body, automotive, diesel, electronics/electrical, heating/ac/refrig. **Production:** Welding. **Protective services:** Firefighting, police science. **Visual/performing arts:** Graphic design. **Other:** Electro-mechanical technology.

Most popular majors. Business/marketing 14%, health sciences 14%, liberal arts 58%, trade and industry 12%.

Computing on campus. 100 workstations in dormitories, library, computer center, student center. Dormitories wired for high-speed internet access. Commuter students can connect to campus network. Online library, wireless network available.

Student life. Freshman orientation: Available. Preregistration for classes offered. **Policies:** Drugs, alcohol, tobacco strictly prohibited. **Housing:** Coed dorms, single-sex dorms, special housing for disabled, apartments available. $200 deposit, deadline 8/15. **Activities:** Bands, choral groups, drama, music ensembles, student government, student newspaper.

Athletics. NJCAA. **Intercollegiate:** Baseball M, basketball, golf M, softball W, volleyball W. **Intramural:** Basketball, volleyball.

Student services. Career counseling, services for economically disadvantaged, student employment services, financial aid counseling, on-campus daycare, placement for graduates. **Transfer:** Transfer adviser for students transferring to 4-year colleges.

Contact. E-mail: rippenk@mpcc.edu
Phone: (308) 535-3609 Toll-free number: (800) 658-4308 ext. 3609
Fax: (308) 534-5767
Kelly Rippen, Area Admissions Coordinator, Mid-Plains Community College Area, 1101 Halligan Drive, North Platte, NE 69101

Myotherapy Institute
Lincoln, Nebraska
www.myotherapy.edu

- For-profit 2-year health science and community college
- Small city

General. Accredited by ACCSCT. **Calendar:** Continuous.

Annual costs/financial aid. Diploma program $10,500. Associate program $12,000.

Contact. Phone: (402) 421-7410
Director, 6020 South 58th Street, Lincoln, NE 68516

Nebraska College of Technical Agriculture
Curtis, Nebraska
www.ncta.unl.edu **CB code: 1305**

- Public 2-year agricultural college
- Residential campus in rural community

General. Founded in 1965. Regionally accredited. **Enrollment:** 250 full-time, degree-seeking students. **Degrees:** 64 associate awarded. **Location:** 40 miles from North Platte, 40 miles from McCook. **Calendar:** Semester, extensive summer session. **Full-time faculty:** 15 total; 27% have terminal degrees, 47% women. **Part-time faculty:** 10 total; 30% women. **Special facilities:** Farm, community golf course, land lab, cattle working facilities, indoor arena, horticulture greenhouse, vet tech surgery and lab facilities.

Student profile.

Out-of-state:	22%	**Live on campus:**	29%
25 or older:	5%		

Basis for selection. Open admission. Students are required to take the ACT test in order to be considered for scholarships but the ACT is not required to be admitted. **Homeschooled:** State high school equivalency certificate, interview required.

High school preparation. College-preparatory program recommended. 14 units recommended. Recommended units include English 4, mathematics 3, social studies 3, science 3 (laboratory 1).

2008-2009 Annual costs. Tuition/fees: $3,369; $6,256 out-of-state. Per-credit charge: $97 in-state; $193 out-of-state. Room/board: $4,309. Books/supplies: $1,000. Personal expenses: $1,375.

2007-2008 Financial aid. All financial aid based on need. 51% of total undergraduate aid awarded as scholarships/grants, 49% as loans/jobs. Need-based aid available for part-time students.

Application procedures. Admission: Closing date 8/15. $25 fee. Admission notification on a rolling basis. **Financial aid:** Priority date 4/1; no closing date. FAFSA required. Applicants notified on a rolling basis starting 5/1; must reply within 2 week(s) of notification.

Academics. Special study options: Cooperative education, distance learning, double major, dual enrollment of high school students, ESL, internships. Bachelor's degree programs available on campus. **Credit/placement by examination:** AP, CLEP, institutional tests. **Support services:** Reduced course load, remedial instruction, study skills assistance, tutoring.

Majors. Agriculture: General, agribusiness operations, animal health, business, equestrian studies, greenhouse operations, horticultural science, horticulture, landscaping, nursery operations, ornamental horticulture, turf management. **Conservation:** Management/policy. **Health:** Veterinary technology/assistant.

Computing on campus. 75 workstations in dormitories, library, computer center. Dormitories wired for high-speed internet access and linked to campus network. Online course registration, online library, repair service, wireless network available.

Student life. Freshman orientation: Mandatory. Preregistration for classes offered. 2-day program. **Housing:** Guaranteed on-campus for freshmen. Single-sex dorms, wellness housing available. $200 partly refundable deposit, deadline 8/15. **Activities:** Dance, drama, student government, student newspaper.

Athletics. Intercollegiate: Basketball, equestrian, golf, rodeo, volleyball. **Intramural:** Basketball, football (non-tackle), softball, volleyball. **Team name:** Aggies.

Student services. Alcohol/substance abuse counseling, chaplain/spiritual director, career counseling, student employment services, financial aid counseling, health services, personal counseling, placement for graduates, veterans' counselor. **Transfer:** Pre-admission transcript evaluation for new students. Transfer adviser, college fairs on campus for students transferring to 4-year colleges.

Contact. E-mail: lcooper5@unlnotes.unl.edu
Phone: (308) 367-4124 Toll-free number: (800) 328-7847
Fax: (308) 367-5209
Kevin Mills, Assistant Dean of Student Services, Nebraska College of Technical Agriculture, 404 East 7th Street, Curtis, NE 69025-0069

Nebraska Indian Community College
Macy, Nebraska
www.thenicc.edu **CB code: 1431**

- Public 2-year community college
- Commuter campus in rural community

General. Founded in 1979. Regionally accredited. Tribal college. **Enrollment:** 94 degree-seeking undergraduates. **Degrees:** 3 associate awarded. **Location:** 70 miles from Omaha, 30 miles from Sioux City, Iowa. **Calendar:** Semester, limited summer session. **Full-time faculty:** 7 total. **Part-time faculty:** 6 total. **Class size:** 100% < 20.

Student profile.

Out-of-state:	23%	**25 or older:**	69%

Basis for selection. Open admission.

High school preparation. Strong background in English, mathematics, and science recommended.

2008-2009 Annual costs. Tuition/fees: $3,200. Per-credit charge: $80. Books/supplies: $800. Personal expenses: $700.

Financial aid. All financial aid based on need. Need-based aid available for part-time students. Work-study available for part-time students.

Application procedures. Admission: No deadline. $50 fee, may be waived for applicants with need. Admission notification on a rolling basis. **Financial aid:** Priority date 7/15; no closing date. FAFSA, institutional form required. Applicants notified on a rolling basis starting 8/30; must reply within 2 week(s) of notification.

Academics. Special study options: Double major, dual enrollment of high school students, independent study, internships. **Credit/placement by examination:** CLEP, institutional tests. 15 credit hours maximum toward associate degree. **Support services:** Remedial instruction, study skills assistance, tutoring.

Majors. Area/ethnic studies: Native American. **Business:** Business admin. **Computer sciences:** General, data entry. **Conservation:** General. **Construction:** Carpentry. **Education:** Early childhood. **Liberal arts:** Arts/sciences. **Protective services:** Police science. **Public administration:** Social work.

Most popular majors. Business/marketing 33%, liberal arts 66%.

Computing on campus. 40 workstations in library, computer center.

Student life. Freshman orientation: Available. Preregistration for classes offered. **Activities:** Student government, student newspaper.

Student services. Adult student services, career counseling, financial aid counseling. **Transfer:** Pre-admission transcript evaluation for new students. Transfer adviser, college fairs on campus for students transferring to 4-year colleges.

Contact. E-mail: vwebster@thenicc.edu
Phone: (402) 837-5078 ext. 2581
Veda Webster, Dean of Student Services, Nebraska Indian Community College, PO Box 428, Macy, NE 68039

Northeast Community College
Norfolk, Nebraska
www.northeast.edu **CB code: 6473**

- Public 2-year community college
- Commuter campus in large town

General. Founded in 1973. Regionally accredited. **Enrollment:** 2,528 degree-seeking undergraduates; 2,612 non-degree-seeking students. **Degrees:** 633 associate awarded. **Location:** 110 miles from Omaha. **Calendar:** Semester, limited summer session. **Full-time faculty:** 106 total; 4% have terminal degrees, less than 1% minority, 38% women. **Part-time faculty:** 286 total; 4% have terminal degrees, less than 1% minority, 57% women. **Class size:** 78% < 20, 22% 20-39, less than 1% 40-49, less than 1% >100. **Special facilities:** College farm.

Student profile. Among degree-seeking undergraduates, 27% enrolled in a transfer program, 73% enrolled in a vocational program, 791 enrolled as first-time, first-year students.

Part-time:	22%	**Hispanic American:**	5%
Out-of-state:	6%	**Native American:**	1%
Women:	53%	**25 or older:**	12%
African American:	1%	**Live on campus:**	18%
Asian American:	1%		

Transfer out. Colleges most students transferred to 2008: Wayne State College, University of Nebraska-Lincoln, University of Nebraska-Omaha, University of Nebraska-Kearney, University of South Dakota.

Basis for selection. Open admission, but selective for some programs. Special requirements for nursing programs, physical therapy assistant program, and veterinary technician program. ACT or ASSET scores required for placement for students enrolling in 6 or more credit hours.

2009-2010 Annual costs. Tuition/fees: $2,430; $2,933 out-of-state. Per-credit charge: $67 in-state; $84 out-of-state. Room/board: $4,656. Books/supplies: $1,000. Personal expenses: $900.

2007-2008 Financial aid. Need-based: Need-based aid available for part-time students. Work-study available nights, weekends and for part-time students. **Non-need-based:** Scholarships awarded for academics, athletics, music/drama.

Application procedures. Admission: No deadline. No application fee. Admission notification on a rolling basis. **Financial aid:** No deadline. FAFSA, institutional form required. Applicants notified on a rolling basis; must reply within 2 week(s) of notification.

Academics. Off-campus credit classes available. Lifelong Learning Center offers students opportunity to earn advanced degrees on NECC campus. **Special study options:** Accelerated study, cooperative education, cross-registration, distance learning, dual enrollment of high school students, ESL, independent study, internships, liberal arts/career combination. License preparation in nursing, paramedic, real estate. **Credit/placement by examination:** AP, CLEP, institutional tests. **Support services:** GED preparation and test center, learning center, reduced course load, remedial instruction, study skills assistance, tutoring, writing center.

Majors. Agriculture: General, agribusiness operations, agronomy, animal sciences, business, equipment technology, farm/ranch, horticultural science, horticulture, livestock, mechanization, production. **Biology:** General. **Business:** Accounting, administrative services, banking/financial services, business admin, entrepreneurial studies, international, marketing, merchandising, office/clerical, real estate. **Communications:** Journalism. **Communications technology:** Radio/tv, recording arts. **Computer sciences:** General, computer science, computer support specialist, programming. **Construction:** Electrician, lineworker. **Education:** Early childhood, elementary, music, secondary. **Engineering:** General. **Engineering technology:** Architectural drafting, electrical, electromechanical, energy systems, heat/ac/refrig. **Health:** Dietetics, EMT paramedic, medical radiologic technology/radiation therapy, medical records technology, medical secretary, nursing (RN), physical therapy assistant, predental, premedicine, prenursing, prepharmacy, preveterinary, surgical technology, veterinary technology/assistant. **Legal studies:** Legal secretary, paralegal, prelaw. **Liberal arts:** Arts/sciences, library assistant. **Math:** General. **Mechanic/repair:** Auto body, automotive, diesel, heating/ac/refrig, medium/heavy vehicle. **Parks/recreation:** Health/fitness. **Personal/culinary services:** Chef training. **Physical sciences:** Chemistry, physics. **Protective services:** Corrections. **Psychology:** General. **Social sciences:** General. **Visual/performing arts:** Art, dramatic, music management, music performance. **Other:** Applied horticulture/horticultural business services, Building construction, finishing.

Most popular majors. Agriculture 10%, business/marketing 12%, education 7%, engineering/engineering technologies 8%, health sciences 19%, liberal arts 8%, trade and industry 21%.

Computing on campus. 225 workstations in dormitories, library, computer center, student center. Dormitories linked to campus network. Online course registration, online library, helpline available.

Student life. Freshman orientation: Mandatory. **Housing:** Coed dorms, special housing for disabled, apartments, wellness housing available. $25 deposit. **Activities:** Bands, choral groups, dance, drama, music ensembles, musical theater, radio station, student government, student newspaper, symphony orchestra, TV station, Habitat for Humanity, HOPE, multicultural club, Campus Crusade for Christ, Christian Student Fellowship.

Athletics. NJCAA. **Intercollegiate:** Basketball. **Intramural:** Basketball, soccer, softball. **Team name:** Hawks.

Student services. Adult student services, career counseling, student employment services, financial aid counseling, health services, minority student services, on-campus daycare, personal counseling, placement for graduates, veterans' counselor. **Physically disabled:** Services for visually, speech, hearing impaired. **Learning disabled:** Comprehensive services available. **Transfer:** Pre-admission transcript evaluation for new students. Transfer adviser for students transferring to 4-year colleges.

Contact. E-mail: admission@northeastcollege.com
Phone: (402) 844-7260 Toll-free number: (800) 348-9033
Fax: (402) 844-7400
Sandy Hilliges, Coordinator of Admissions Services, Northeast Community College, 801 East Benjamin Avenue, Norfolk, NE 68702-0469

Southeast Community College
Lincoln, Nebraska
www.southeast.edu **CB code: 1189**

- Public 2-year community college
- Commuter campus in small city

General. Founded in 1973. Regionally accredited. Extensive adult and continuing education programs, both credit and noncredit. Additional campuses in Beatrice and Milford. **Enrollment:** 8,136 degree-seeking undergraduates; 2,421 non-degree-seeking students. **Degrees:** 1,316 associate awarded. **Location:** 50 miles from Omaha. **Calendar:** Quarter, extensive summer session. **Full-time faculty:** 317 total. **Part-time faculty:** 326 total. **Special facilities:** Fire service training facility.

Student profile. Among degree-seeking undergraduates, 35% enrolled in a transfer program, 47% enrolled in a vocational program, 1,888 enrolled as first-time, first-year students.

Part-time:	31%	**Women:**	51%
Out-of-state:	2%	**25 or older:**	26%

Transfer out. Colleges most students transferred to 2008: University of Nebraska, Doane-Lincoln, College of St. Mary, Nebraska Wesleyan, University of Nebraska-Kearney.

Basis for selection. Open admission.

2008-2009 Annual costs. Tuition/fees: $2,162; $2,635 out-of-state. Per-credit charge: $47 in-state; $58 out-of-state. Books/supplies: $1,000. Personal expenses: $1,200.

Financial aid. Need-based: Need-based aid available for part-time students. Work-study available nights, weekends and for part-time students. **Non-need-based:** Scholarships awarded for academics.

Application procedures. Admission: No deadline. No application fee. Admission notification on a rolling basis. **Financial aid:** No deadline. FAFSA, institutional form required. Applicants notified on a rolling basis; must reply within 2 week(s) of notification.

Academics. Academic transfer courses (liberal arts) offered on Saturdays. **Special study options:** Cooperative education, distance learning, dual enrollment of high school students, independent study, internships, liberal arts/career combination, weekend college. License preparation in nursing, paramedic, physical therapy, radiology. **Credit/placement by examination:** AP, CLEP, institutional tests. 30 credit hours maximum toward associate degree. Most applicants required to take COMPASS or ASSET for placement purposes. ACT may be substituted for ASSET. **Support services:** GED preparation and test center, learning center, reduced course load, remedial instruction, study skills assistance, tutoring, writing center.

Majors. **Agriculture:** Business. **Business:** Administrative services, business admin, marketing, office/clerical, vehicle parts marketing. **Communications technology:** Radio/tv. **Computer sciences:** Information systems. **Construction:** General. **Engineering technology:** Architectural, architectural drafting, civil, drafting, electrical, manufacturing, quality control. **Family/consumer sciences:** Child care. **Health:** Clinical lab technology, health services, medical radiologic technology/radiation therapy, nursing (RN), respiratory therapy technology, surgical technology. **Liberal arts:** Arts/sciences. **Mechanic/repair:** Auto body, automotive, diesel, heating/ac/refrig. **Personal/culinary services:** Restaurant/catering. **Production:** Machine tool, welding. **Protective services:** Criminal justice, fire safety technology. **Science technology:** Biological. **Visual/performing arts:** Commercial/advertising art.

Computing on campus. 300 workstations in dormitories, library, computer center, student center. Dormitories wired for high-speed internet access and linked to campus network. Online course registration, online library, helpline, wireless network available.

Student life. **Freshman orientation:** Mandatory. Preregistration for classes offered. **Housing:** $100 fully refundable deposit. **Activities:** Choral groups, drama, radio station, student government, student newspaper, multicultural student organization.

Athletics. NJCAA. **Intercollegiate:** Baseball M, basketball, golf M, softball W, volleyball W. **Intramural:** Baseball M, basketball, softball W, table tennis, tennis, volleyball.

Student services. Career counseling, student employment services, on-campus daycare, personal counseling, placement for graduates, veterans' counselor. **Physically disabled:** Services for visually, speech, hearing impaired. **Transfer:** Transfer adviser, college fairs on campus for students transferring to 4-year colleges.

Contact. Phone: (402) 437-2600 Toll-free number: (800) 642-4075
Fax: (402) 437-2402
Robin Moore, Dean of Student Services, Southeast Community College, 8800 O Street, Lincoln, NE 68520

Vatterott College: Spring Valley
Omaha, Nebraska
www.vatterott-college.com

- For-profit 2-year community and technical college
- Large city

General. Accredited by ACCSCT. **Calendar:** Quarter.

Annual costs/financial aid. Program cost ranges: $15,350 to $23,800 (certificate/diploma); $33,850 to $35,650 (associate degree).

Contact. Phone: (402) 891-9411
Director of Admissions, 11818 I Street, Omaha, NE 68137

Western Nebraska Community College
Scottsbluff, Nebraska
www.wn.edu **CB code: 6648**

- Public 2-year community college
- Commuter campus in large town

General. Founded in 1926. Regionally accredited. Additional campuses at Sidney and Alliance. Advanced Technology Center of Nebraska located in Scottsbluff. **Enrollment:** 1,502 degree-seeking undergraduates; 1,438 non-degree-seeking students. **Degrees:** 194 associate awarded. **Location:** 100 miles from Cheyenne, Wyoming. **Calendar:** Semester, limited summer session. **Full-time faculty:** 72 total; 7% have terminal degrees, 4% minority, 49% women. **Part-time faculty:** 96 total; 5% have terminal degrees, 3% minority, 55% women. **Class size:** 78% < 20, 18% 20-39, less than 1% 40-49, less than 1% 50-99, 3% >100.

Student profile. Among degree-seeking undergraduates, 41% enrolled in a transfer program, 59% enrolled in a vocational program, 1% already have a bachelor's degree or higher, 458 enrolled as first-time, first-year students, 47 transferred in from other institutions.

Part-time:	37%	**Hispanic American:**	15%
Out-of-state:	8%	**Native American:**	1%
Women:	64%	**International:**	3%
African American:	2%	**25 or older:**	38%
Asian American:	1%	**Live on campus:**	7%

Transfer out. 53% of students enrolled in the transfer program go on to 4-year colleges. **Colleges most students transferred to 2008:** Chadron State College, University of Nebraska-Lincoln, University of Wyoming.

Basis for selection. Open admission, but selective for some programs. Special requirements for practical nursing, Associate Degree-Nursing, and radiologic technologies programs. ASSET or COMPASS required unless SAT or ACT scores submitted. **Adult students:** ECOMPASS used for proper course placement in writing, mathematics, and classes with a reading prerequisite; ACT, SAT, or ASSET accepted in lieu of eCOMPASS. **Learning Disabled:** Students should contact the Director of Counseling to discuss the process required to request assistance and arrange for reasonable accommodations.

High school preparation. Recommended units include English 4, mathematics 4, social studies 3, history 3, science 4 (laboratory 2) and foreign language 1.

2008-2009 Annual costs. Tuition/fees: $2,370; $2,730 out-of-state. Per-credit charge: $66 in-state; $78 out-of-state. Room/board: $4,950. Books/supplies: $1,080. Personal expenses: $2,069.

2008-2009 Financial aid. **Need-based:** 287 full-time freshmen applied for aid; 230 were judged to have need; 228 of these received aid. Average need met was 88%. Average scholarship/grant was $4,559; average loan $2,650. 73% of total undergraduate aid awarded as scholarships/grants, 27% as loans/jobs. Need-based aid available for part-time students. Work-study available nights, weekends and for part-time students. **Non-need-based:** Awarded to 455 full-time undergraduates, including 260 freshmen. Scholarships awarded for academics, art, athletics, leadership, music/drama, state residency.

Application procedures. **Admission:** No deadline. No application fee. Application must be submitted online. Admission notification on a rolling basis. **Financial aid:** Priority date 3/1; no closing date. FAFSA required. Applicants notified on a rolling basis starting 4/1.

Academics. **Special study options:** Cooperative education, cross-registration, distance learning, double major, dual enrollment of high school students, ESL, independent study, internships, liberal arts/career combination, student-designed major. Radiological technology program at Regional West Medical Center, respiratory therapy technician and surgical technician in partnership with Southeast Community College. License preparation in aviation, nursing, paramedic, real estate. **Credit/placement by examination:** AP, CLEP, IB, institutional tests. 25 credit hours maximum toward associate degree. **Support services:** GED preparation and test center, learning center, pre-admission summer program, reduced course load, remedial instruction, study skills assistance, tutoring, writing center.

Majors. **Biology:** General, ecology. **Business:** General, accounting, administrative services, business admin, office/clerical. **Communications:** Journalism. **Computer sciences:** General, computer science, programming. **Conservation:** Forestry. **Construction:** Lineworker. **Education:** General, art, early childhood, elementary, music, physical, secondary. **Engineering:** General. **Family/consumer sciences:** Food/nutrition. **Foreign languages:** French, Spanish. **Health:** Athletic training, medical radiologic technology/radiation therapy, medical records technology, nursing (RN), predental, premedicine, prenursing, prepharmacy, preveterinary. **History:** General. **Legal studies:** Prelaw. **Liberal arts:** Arts/sciences. **Math:** General. **Mechanic/repair:** Aircraft, aircraft powerplant, auto body, automotive. **Parks/recreation:** Health/fitness. **Personal/culinary services:** Cosmetic. **Physical sciences:** Chemistry, physics. **Production:** Welding. **Protective services:** Criminal justice. **Psychology:** General. **Public administration:** Social work. **Social sciences:** Anthropology, economics, geography, political science, sociology. **Visual/performing arts:** Art.

Most popular majors. Business/marketing 17%, education 17%, health sciences 20%, liberal arts 20%, trade and industry 7%.

Computing on campus. 454 workstations in dormitories, library, computer center. Dormitories wired for high-speed internet access and linked to campus network. Commuter students can connect to campus network. Online course registration, online library, helpline, wireless network available.

Student life. **Freshman orientation:** Available. Preregistration for classes offered. 6 hours held the weekday before classes begin. **Policies:** All buildings are smoke-free. **Housing:** Coed dorms, wellness housing available. $150 fully refundable deposit, deadline 8/15. **Activities:** Jazz band, choral groups, drama, literary magazine, music ensembles, musical theater, student government, student newspaper, Campus Ventures, College Republicans, Student Ambassadors, United Leaders for Cultural Diversity, student senate, student council.

Athletics. NJCAA. **Intercollegiate:** Baseball M, basketball, soccer, volleyball W. **Intramural:** Basketball, football (non-tackle), table tennis, volleyball. **Team name:** Cougars.

Student services. Adult student services, alcohol/substance abuse counseling, career counseling, student employment services, financial aid counseling, minority student services, on-campus daycare, personal counseling, placement for graduates, veterans' counselor. **Physically disabled:** Services for visually, speech, hearing impaired. **Transfer:** Pre-admission transcript evaluation for new students. Transfer adviser, college fairs on campus for students transferring to 4-year colleges.

Contact. E-mail: ali@wncc.edu
Phone: (308) 635-6010 Toll-free number: (800) 348-4435 ext. 6010
Fax: (308) 635-6100
Ali Jay, Enrollment Management Director, Western Nebraska Community College, 1601 East 27th Street, Scottsbluff, NE 69361

Nevada

Career College of Northern Nevada
Reno, Nevada
www.ccnn.edu **CB code: 3202**

- For-profit 2-year career college
- Commuter campus in large city
- Interview required

General. Accredited by ACCSCT. **Enrollment:** 286 degree-seeking undergraduates. **Degrees:** 61 associate awarded. **Calendar:** Quarter, extensive summer session. **Full-time faculty:** 10 total. **Part-time faculty:** 12 total. **Class size:** 82% < 20, 18% 20-39.

Student profile. Among degree-seeking undergraduates, 100% enrolled in a vocational program, 286 enrolled as first-time, first-year students.

Out-of-state:	2%	**Women:**	76%

Basis for selection. Open admission. Must pass Wonderlic or CPaT test. **Homeschooled:** State high school equivalency certificate required.

2008-2009 Annual costs. Tuition for associate programs ranges from $20,055 to $26,250; diploma programs, $11,655 to $15,960. Fees are $210 to $672; books range from $650 to $2,650. Books/supplies: $1,500. Personal expenses: $1,832.

Financial aid. All financial aid based on need.

Application procedures. Admission: No deadline. $25 fee. Application must be submitted on paper. Admission notification on a rolling basis. **Financial aid:** Closing date 5/30. FAFSA required. Applicants notified on a rolling basis.

Academics. Special study options: Accelerated study, cooperative education, internships, liberal arts/career combination. **Credit/placement by examination:** CLEP. **Support services:** Remedial instruction, study skills assistance, tutoring.

Majors. Engineering technology: Electrical. **Health:** Insurance coding, insurance specialist, medical assistant, medical secretary. **Legal studies:** Paralegal.

Most popular majors. Computer/information sciences 14%, engineering/engineering technologies 19%, health sciences 62%, legal studies 6%.

Computing on campus. 78 workstations in computer center, student center.

Student life. Freshman orientation: Mandatory. Preregistration for classes offered. Held Saturday morning before classes begin.

Student services. Adult student services, career counseling, financial aid counseling, placement for graduates.

Contact. E-mail: mbuendia@ccnn4u.com
Phone: (775) 856-2266
Maria Buendia, Director of Admissions, Career College of Northern Nevada, 1195 A Corporate Boulevard, Reno, NV 89502-2331

College of Southern Nevada
Las Vegas, Nevada
www.csn.edu **CB code: 4136**

- Public 2-year community college
- Commuter campus in very large city

General. Founded in 1971. Regionally accredited. Branch campuses at Henderson and North Las Vegas. Health science center in West Las Vegas. **Enrollment:** 31,091 degree-seeking undergraduates; 10,297 non-degree-seeking students. **Degrees:** 9 bachelor's, 1,678 associate awarded. **ROTC:** Army. **Location:** 6 miles from downtown. **Calendar:** Semester, limited summer session. **Full-time faculty:** 505 total; 46% women. **Part-time faculty:** 996 total; 55% women. **Special facilities:** Planetarium, ornamental horticulture demonstration facilities, culinary facilities, telecommunications/multimedia center, automotive technology center, occupational therapy labs.

Student profile. Among degree-seeking undergraduates, 7,540 enrolled as first-time, first-year students.

Part-time:	75%	**Women:**	50%
Out-of-state:	2%	**25 or older:**	54%

Transfer out. Colleges most students transferred to 2008: University of Nevada Las Vegas.

Basis for selection. Open admission, but selective for some programs. Special requirements for nursing, dental hygiene, and health professions programs. Associate degree and certification required for BS dental hygiene program.

2008-2009 Annual costs. Tuition/fees: $1,921; $7,733 out-of-state. Per-credit charge: $60 in-state; $120 out-of-state. Discounted tuition for residents of western states participating in Western Undergraduate Exchange: Alaska, Arizona, California, Colorado, Hawaii, Idaho, Montana, Nevada, New Mexico, North Dakota, Oregon, South Dakota, Utah, Washington, Wyoming. Books/supplies: $900. Personal expenses: $1,800.

2007-2008 Financial aid. Need-based: 68% of total undergraduate aid awarded as scholarships/grants, 32% as loans/jobs. Work-study available nights, weekends and for part-time students. **Non-need-based:** Scholarships awarded for state residency.

Application procedures. Admission: No deadline. $5 fee, may be waived for applicants with need. Admission notification on a rolling basis. **Financial aid:** Priority date 5/1, closing date 6/30. FAFSA required. Applicants notified on a rolling basis starting 7/15; must reply within 2 week(s) of notification.

Academics. Special study options: Cooperative education, cross-registration, distance learning, double major, dual enrollment of high school students, ESL, honors, independent study, internships, liberal arts/career combination, student-designed major, weekend college. Bachelor's degree programs available on campus. License preparation in aviation, dental hygiene, nursing, occupational therapy, paramedic, physical therapy, radiology, real estate. **Credit/placement by examination:** CLEP, institutional tests. 15 credit hours maximum toward associate degree. **Support services:** GED preparation and test center, learning center, remedial instruction, study skills assistance, tutoring, writing center.

Majors. Agriculture: Landscaping, ornamental horticulture. **Architecture:** Technology. **Biology:** General, anatomy. **Business:** General, accounting, administrative services, banking/financial services, business admin, hospitality admin, hospitality/recreation, management information systems, office management, real estate, sales/distribution. **Communications:** General. **Communications technology:** Animation/special effects, computer typography, graphic/printing. **Computer sciences:** Computer graphics, data processing, database management, information systems, LAN/WAN management, networking, programming, systems analysis, webmaster. **Education:** Deaf/hearing impaired, early childhood, kindergarten/preschool. **Engineering:** Electrical, software. **Engineering technology:** General, CAD/CADD, drafting, electrical, environmental, mechanical, surveying, water quality. **Health:** Acupuncture, clinical lab assistant, clinical lab technology, dental hygiene, EMT paramedic, medical records technology, nursing (RN), optician, orthotics/prosthetics, physical therapy assistant. **Legal studies:** Legal secretary, paralegal. **Liberal arts:** Arts/sciences. **Mechanic/repair:** Automotive, heating/ac/refrig. **Personal/culinary services:** Chef training. **Production:** Welding. **Protective services:** Corrections, criminal justice, fire safety technology, firefighting, police science, security services. **Psychology:** General. **Social sciences:** General. **Visual/performing arts:** Art, commercial photography, commercial/advertising art, studio arts.

Computing on campus. 650 workstations in library, computer center. Commuter students can connect to campus network. Online course registration, online library, helpline, wireless network available.

Student life. Freshman orientation: Mandatory. Orientation is mandatory for degree-seeking students only. **Activities:** Jazz band, choral groups, dance, drama, literary magazine, music ensembles, musical theater, student government, student newspaper.

Athletics. NJCAA. **Intercollegiate:** Baseball M, softball W. **Team name:** Coyotes.

Student services. Adult student services, career counseling, student employment services, financial aid counseling, on-campus daycare, personal counseling, placement for graduates, veterans' counselor, women's services. **Physically disabled:** Services for visually, speech, hearing impaired. **Transfer:** Re-entry adviser, pre-admission transcript evaluation for new students. Transfer center, transfer adviser, college fairs on campus for students transferring to 4-year colleges.

Contact. E-mail: admrec@csn.edu
Phone: (702) 651-4060 Fax: (702) 651-4811
Patricia Zozaya, Registrar, College of Southern Nevada, 6375 West Charleston Boulevard, Las Vegas, NV 89146-1164

High-Tech Institute
Las Vegas, Nevada
www.hightechinstitute.edu

- For-profit 2-year technical college
- Commuter campus in very large city
- Interview required

General. Accredited by ACCSCT. **Enrollment:** 509 undergraduates. **Degrees:** 119 associate awarded. **Calendar:** Semester, extensive summer session. **Full-time faculty:** 23 total; 26% have terminal degrees, 44% minority, 91% women. **Class size:** 100% 20-39.

Basis for selection. Open admission, but selective for some programs.

Financial aid. All financial aid based on need.

Application procedures. Admission: No deadline. $50 fee, may be waived for applicants with need. Application must be submitted on paper. Admission notification on a rolling basis. **Financial aid:** FAFSA, institutional form required.

Academics. Special study options: Accelerated study, distance learning. Bachelor's degree programs available on campus. **Credit/placement by examination:** CLEP. **Support services:** GED preparation, learning center, study skills assistance, tutoring.

Majors. Health: Dental assistant, insurance coding, massage therapy, medical assistant, pharmacy assistant, surgical technology. **Protective services:** Law enforcement admin.

Computing on campus. 65 workstations in library, computer center. Online library, helpline available.

Student life. Freshman orientation: Mandatory.

Student services. Career counseling, student employment services, financial aid counseling, personal counseling, placement for graduates. **Physically disabled:** Services for visually impaired.

Contact. Phone: (702) 385-6700 Toll-free number: (866) 385-6700
Fax: (702) 388-4463
Kelly Folliard, Director of Admissions, High-Tech Institute, 2320 South Rancho Drive, Las Vegas, NV 89102

Kaplan College: Las Vegas
Las Vegas, Nevada
www.kaplancollege.com **CB code: 3167**

- For-profit 2-year career college
- Commuter campus in very large city
- Interview required

General. Accredited by ACCSCT. **Enrollment:** 371 degree-seeking undergraduates. **Degrees:** 24 associate awarded. **Calendar:** Continuous. **Full-time faculty:** 15 total. **Part-time faculty:** 15 total.

Basis for selection. Open admission, but selective for some programs. Clean legal record required for pharmacy technician, practical nursing and criminal justice programs. Wonderlic SLE exam required for all applicants; cut-off scores vary by program; Ability to Benefit students must also pass the Wonderlic ATB test. **Adult students:** All students must take a Wonderlic Scholastic Level Exam.

2008-2009 Annual costs. Cost of full programs: associate degree programs $28,354, diploma programs $14,424, including fees and books. Personal expenses: $380.

Application procedures. Admission: No deadline. No application fee. **Financial aid:** No deadline. FAFSA, institutional form required.

Academics. Credit/placement by examination: CLEP. **Support services:** GED preparation, study skills assistance, tutoring.

Majors. Health: Insurance coding, office assistant, pharmacy assistant. **Protective services:** Law enforcement admin.

Computing on campus. 90 workstations in library, computer center. Online library available.

Student life. Freshman orientation: Available. Orientation ranges from one week to a few days before the start of class. It is held on campus and all new students are encouraged to attend. **Activities:** Student government.

Student services. Adult student services, career counseling, student employment services, financial aid counseling, placement for graduates.

Contact. Phone: (702) 368-2338 Toll-free number: (888) 727-7863
Fax: (702) 368-3853
Queena Fuller, Director of Admissions, Kaplan College: Las Vegas, 3315 Spring Mountain Road, Las Vegas, NV 89102

Las Vegas College
Las Vegas, Nevada
lasvegas-college.com **CB code: 2149**

- For-profit 2-year business and health science college
- Commuter campus in very large city
- Interview required

General. Founded in 1979. Accredited by ACICS. **Enrollment:** 639 degree-seeking undergraduates. **Degrees:** 55 associate awarded. **Calendar:** Quarter, extensive summer session. **Full-time faculty:** 10 total. **Part-time faculty:** 40 total. **Special facilities:** Court reporting laboratory.

Basis for selection. Open admission.

2008-2009 Annual costs. Books/supplies: $300. Personal expenses: $124.

Financial aid. All financial aid based on need. Need-based aid available for part-time students. Work-study available nights and weekends.

Application procedures. Admission: No deadline. No application fee. Admission notification on a rolling basis. **Financial aid:** FAFSA required. Applicants notified on a rolling basis; must reply within 2 week(s) of notification.

Academics. Special study options: Accelerated study, independent study. **Credit/placement by examination:** CLEP. **Support services:** Reduced course load, study skills assistance, tutoring.

Majors. Business: Administrative services, business admin. **Health:** Medical assistant. **Legal studies:** Court reporting, paralegal.

Most popular majors. Business/marketing 40%, legal studies 60%.

Computing on campus. 55 workstations in library, computer center.

Student life. Freshman orientation: Available. **Activities:** Student government.

Student services. Adult student services, career counseling, services for economically disadvantaged, student employment services, financial aid counseling, placement for graduates, veterans' counselor. **Transfer:** Re-entry adviser, pre-admission transcript evaluation for new students.

Contact. E-mail: spetty@cci.edu
Phone: (702) 567-1920
Niki Smith, Director of Admissions, Las Vegas College, 170 North Stephanie Street, Las Vegas, NV 89014

Le Cordon Bleu College of Culinary Arts
Las Vegas, Nevada
www.VegasCulinary.com

- For-profit 2-year culinary school
- Commuter campus in very large city

General. Accredited by ACCSCT. **Enrollment:** 539 degree-seeking undergraduates. **Degrees:** 230 associate awarded. **Calendar:** Continuous. **Full-time faculty:** 50 total. **Part-time faculty:** 10 total. **Special facilities:** 10 kitchens, student-run restaurant open to general public.

Basis for selection. Open admission.

Application procedures. Admission: No deadline. $50 fee. Admission notification on a rolling basis.

Academics. **Special study options:** Accelerated study. **Credit/placement by examination:** CLEP. **Support services:** Learning center, tutoring.

Majors. **Personal/culinary services:** Chef training.

Student life. **Freshman orientation:** Mandatory. **Housing:** Apartments, wellness housing available. **Activities:** Student newspaper.

Student services. Career counseling, student employment services, financial aid counseling. **Transfer:** Re-entry adviser, pre-admission transcript evaluation for new students. Transfer center for students transferring to 4-year colleges.

Contact. E-mail: info@vegasculinary.com
Phone: (702) 365-7690 Toll-free number: (866) 450-2433
Fax: (702) 851-5299
Jeff Jenson, Vice President of Admissions, Le Cordon Bleu College of Culinary Arts, 1451 Center Crossing Road, Las Vegas, NV 89144

Truckee Meadows Community College

Reno, Nevada
www.tmcc.edu **CB code: 1096**

- Public 2-year community and technical college
- Commuter campus in large city

General. Founded in 1971. Regionally accredited. Classes offered at over 30 sites in Reno-Sparks area. **Enrollment:** 10,005 degree-seeking undergraduates; 3,092 non-degree-seeking students. **Degrees:** 680 associate awarded. **ROTC:** Army. **Location:** 9 miles from downtown. **Calendar:** Semester, limited summer session. **Full-time faculty:** 183 total; 10% minority, 48% women. **Part-time faculty:** 494 total; 13% minority, 56% women. **Class size:** 32% < 20, 65% 20-39, 2% 40-49, less than 1% 50-99.

Student profile. Among degree-seeking undergraduates, 61% enrolled in a transfer program, 39% enrolled in a vocational program, 1% already have a bachelor's degree or higher, 1,493 enrolled as first-time, first-year students, 329 transferred in from other institutions.

Part-time:	70%	**Asian American:**	7%
Out-of-state:	9%	**Hispanic American:**	15%
Women:	57%	**Native American:**	2%
African American:	3%	**International:**	1%

Transfer out. 45% of students enrolled in the transfer program go on to 4-year colleges. **Colleges most students transferred to 2008:** University of Nevada-Reno, University of Nevada-Las Vegas.

Basis for selection. Open admission. High school diploma or GED required if student under 18 years of age. Competitive admission to nursing, dental assistant, and radiological technician programs. **Learning Disabled:** Applicants must contact Disabled Students Office. Accommodations provided according to documentation.

2008-2009 Annual costs. Tuition/fees: $1,921; $7,547 out-of-state. Per-credit charge: $57. Discounted tuition (Good Neighbor rates) available for nonresident students residing in certain counties bordering Nevada. Books/supplies: $1,092. Personal expenses: $1,298.

2007-2008 Financial aid. **Need-based:** 60% of total undergraduate aid awarded as scholarships/grants, 40% as loans/jobs. Work-study available nights, weekends and for part-time students. **Non-need-based:** Scholarships awarded for academics, art, leadership, minority status, music/drama, state residency. **Additional information:** Institutional grants to state residents, short-term emergency loans available. Work-study applications must reply within 10 days of notification.

Application procedures. **Admission:** No deadline. $10 fee. Admission notification on a rolling basis. Application fee is paid at time of registration for first class. **Financial aid:** Closing date 6/30. FAFSA, institutional form required. Applicants notified by 5/15.

Academics. **Special study options:** Cooperative education, distance learning, dual enrollment of high school students, ESL, honors, internships, liberal arts/career combination, weekend college. License preparation in dental hygiene, nursing, radiology, real estate. **Credit/placement by examination:** AP, CLEP, institutional tests. 15 credit hours maximum toward associate degree. **Support services:** GED preparation and test center, learning center, reduced course load, remedial instruction, study skills assistance, tutoring, writing center.

Majors. **Architecture:** Landscape. **Business:** General, accounting, administrative services, business admin, office management, office technology, real estate. **Computer sciences:** General, data processing, programming. **Conservation:** Environmental studies. **Construction:** Carpentry, maintenance, masonry, pipefitting, power transmission. **Education:** Early childhood, elementary, secondary. **Engineering technology:** Architectural, drafting, solar energy. **Family/consumer sciences:** Child care, institutional food production. **Health:** Dental assistant, dental hygiene, medical radiologic technology/radiation therapy, medical secretary, nursing (RN), radiologic technology/medical imaging, substance abuse counseling. **Legal studies:** Legal secretary, paralegal. **Mechanic/repair:** Automotive, diesel, heating/ac/refrig. **Military:** General. **Parks/recreation:** Facilities management. **Protective services:** Corrections, criminal justice, firefighting, juvenile corrections, law enforcement admin, police science. **Social sciences:** Anthropology. **Visual/performing arts:** Design, dramatic.

Most popular majors. Health sciences 15%, liberal arts 55%, physical sciences 9%, security/protective services 6%.

Computing on campus. 558 workstations in library, computer center. Helpline, repair service available.

Student life. **Freshman orientation:** Available. Preregistration for classes offered. **Housing:** Housing available 2 miles away at University of Nevada: Reno, for students enrolled for 12 or more credits. **Activities:** Concert band, choral groups, drama, literary magazine, music ensembles, student government, student newspaper, symphony orchestra, social organization for handicapped students.

Student services. Adult student services, career counseling, student employment services, financial aid counseling, health services, on-campus daycare, personal counseling, placement for graduates, veterans' counselor. **Physically disabled:** Services for visually, speech, hearing impaired. **Transfer:** Re-entry adviser for new students. Transfer adviser, college fairs on campus for students transferring to 4-year colleges.

Contact. E-mail: admissions@tmcc.edu
Phone: (775) 673-7042 Fax: (775) 673-7028
Ty Moore, Director of Admissions/Registrar, Truckee Meadows Community College, 7000 Dandini Boulevard, Reno, NV 89512

Western Nevada College

Carson City, Nevada
www.wnc.edu **CB code: 4972**

- Public 2-year community college
- Commuter campus in small city

General. Founded in 1971. Regionally accredited. Three campuses and 6 teaching centers. **Enrollment:** 3,267 degree-seeking undergraduates. **Degrees:** 418 associate awarded. **Location:** 30 miles from Reno. **Calendar:** Semester, limited summer session. **Full-time faculty:** 77 total. **Part-time faculty:** 288 total. **Special facilities:** Observatory, fitness center, baseball field. **Partnerships:** Formal partnerships with selected high schools for dual credit.

Transfer out. **Colleges most students transferred to 2008:** University of Nevada-Reno.

Basis for selection. Open admission, but selective for some programs. SAT and ACT scores accepted, but not required, for math and English placement. Special requirements for nursing and surgical tech programs.

2008-2009 Annual costs. Tuition/fees: $1,921; $7,647 out-of-state. Per-credit charge: $60. Discounted tuition (Good Neighbor rates) available for nonresident students residing in certain counties bordering Nevada. Books/supplies: $1,100. Personal expenses: $1,200.

2007-2008 Financial aid. **Need-based:** 53% of total undergraduate aid awarded as scholarships/grants, 47% as loans/jobs. Need-based aid available for part-time students. Work-study available nights and weekends. **Non-need-based:** Scholarships awarded for academics, state residency.

Application procedures. **Admission:** No deadline. $15 fee. No notification sent to applicants except by request. **Financial aid:** Priority date 4/1; no closing date. FAFSA required. Applicants notified on a rolling basis.

Academics. **Special study options:** Accelerated study, cooperative education, distance learning, double major, dual enrollment of high school students, ESL, honors, independent study, internships. Bachelor's degree programs available on campus. License preparation in nursing, paramedic, real estate. **Credit/placement by examination:** AP, CLEP, institutional tests. 30 credit hours maximum toward associate degree. **Support services:** GED preparation and test center, learning center, remedial instruction, study skills assistance, tutoring.

Majors. Biology: Biophysics. **Business:** Accounting, business admin, management science, office technology, real estate. **Communications technology:** Graphics. **Computer sciences:** General, LAN/WAN management, webmaster. **Conservation:** General. **Education:** Early childhood. **Engineering:** General. **Engineering technology:** Drafting, electrical. **Health:** Nursing (RN). **Legal studies:** Paralegal. **Liberal arts:** Arts/sciences. **Math:** General. **Mechanic/repair:** Automotive. **Physical sciences:** Chemistry, physics. **Production:** Machine tool, welding. **Protective services:** Corrections, police science.

Most popular majors. Business/marketing 12%, health sciences 12%, liberal arts 55%.

Computing on campus. 678 workstations in library, computer center, student center. Commuter students can connect to campus network. Online course registration, online library, student web hosting, wireless network available.

Student life. Freshman orientation: Available. Preregistration for classes offered. **Activities:** Bands, choral groups, dance, drama, musical theater, student government, student newspaper.

Athletics. NJCAA. **Intercollegiate:** Baseball M. **Team name:** Wildcats.

Student services. Adult student services, alcohol/substance abuse counseling, career counseling, services for economically disadvantaged, student employment services, financial aid counseling, health services, on-campus daycare, personal counseling, placement for graduates, veterans' counselor, women's services. **Physically disabled:** Services for visually, speech, hearing impaired. **Learning disabled:** Comprehensive services available. **Transfer:** Pre-admission transcript evaluation for new students. Transfer center, transfer adviser for students transferring to 4-year colleges.

Contact. E-mail: wncc_aro@wnc.nevada.edu
Phone: (775) 445-3277 Fax: (775) 887-3147
Dianne Hilliard, Director, Admissions and Records, Western Nevada College, 2201 West College Parkway, Carson City, NV 89703-7399

Two-Year Colleges

New Hampshire

Great Bay Community College

Stratham, New Hampshire
www.greatbay.edu
CB member
CB code: 3661

- Public 2-year community and technical college
- Commuter campus in small town

General. Founded in 1945. Regionally accredited. **Enrollment:** 2,136 degree-seeking undergraduates. **Degrees:** 165 associate awarded. **Location:** 45 miles from Boston. **Calendar:** Semester, limited summer session. **Full-time faculty:** 34 total. **Part-time faculty:** 89 total. **Special facilities:** Biotechnology lab.

Transfer out. Colleges most students transferred to 2008: University of New Hampshire, Southern New Hampshire University, Keene State College, Plymouth State University, Granite State College.

Basis for selection. Open admission, but selective for some programs. Selective admission to allied health and automotive programs. National League for Nursing Pre-Admission Assessment for Registered Nursing required for applicants to RN program. ACT-PEP Nursing Fundamentals Test required for admission to associate degree nursing program as advanced standing students. Career Guidance Placement Test given to technical majors on selected basis. Interview required for allied health and education applicants. **Adult students:** SAT/ACT scores not required.

High school preparation. Recommended units include English 4, mathematics 2, social studies 2 and science 2. High school vocational and college-preparatory courses recommended. For mechanical-technical majors, algebra I and II and geometry recommended. For associate nursing applicants and surgical technology, biology, chemistry, algebra I required. For vet tech, algebra, biology and chemistry are required. For business management, typing or keyboarding skills required.

2008-2009 Annual costs. Tuition/fees: $5,400; $12,150 out-of-state. Per-credit charge: $175 in-state; $400 out-of-state. New England Regional tuition: $262 per credit hour. Books/supplies: $600.

2007-2008 Financial aid. All financial aid based on need. Need-based aid available for part-time students. Work-study available nights, weekends and for part-time students.

Application procedures. Admission: No deadline. $10 fee, may be waived for applicants with need, free for online applicants. Admission notification on a rolling basis. **Financial aid:** No deadline. FAFSA, institutional form required. Applicants notified on a rolling basis; must reply within 2 week(s) of notification.

Academics. Special study options: Accelerated study, distance learning, double major, dual enrollment of high school students, ESL, independent study, internships, liberal arts/career combination. License preparation in nursing. **Credit/placement by examination:** CLEP, institutional tests. **Support services:** GED preparation, learning center, pre-admission summer program, reduced course load, remedial instruction, study skills assistance, tutoring, writing center.

Majors. Biology: Biotechnology. **Business:** General, accounting, administrative services, business admin, hospitality admin. **Computer sciences:** Information systems, programming, web page design. **Education:** Social science. **Engineering technology:** Drafting. **Family/consumer sciences:** Child care. **Health:** Massage therapy, nursing (RN), surgical technology, veterinary technology/assistant. **Liberal arts:** Arts/sciences. **Mechanic/repair:** Automotive. **Protective services:** Law enforcement admin.

Computing on campus. 140 workstations in library, computer center. Online library, helpline, wireless network available.

Student life. Freshman orientation: Available. **Activities:** Literary magazine, student government, student senate, Phi Theta Kappa.

Student services. Career counseling, student employment services, placement for graduates. **Learning disabled:** Comprehensive services available. **Transfer:** Pre-admission transcript evaluation for new students. Transfer adviser, college fairs on campus for students transferring to 4-year colleges.

Contact. E-mail: lshennett@ccsnh.edu
Phone: (603) 772-1194 Toll-free number: (800) 522-1194
Fax: (603) 772-1198
Laurilee Shennett, Admissions Coordinator, Great Bay Community College, 277 Portsmouth Avenue, Stratham, NH 03885

Lakes Region Community College

Laconia, New Hampshire
www.lrcc.edu
CB code: 3850

- Public 2-year community and technical college
- Commuter campus in small city

General. Founded in 1967. Regionally accredited. Numerous satellite programs at various locations. **Enrollment:** 900 degree-seeking undergraduates. **Degrees:** 165 associate awarded. **Location:** 95 miles from Boston, 25 miles from Concord. **Calendar:** Semester, limited summer session. **Full-time faculty:** 45 total. **Part-time faculty:** 20 total. **Special facilities:** Student operated restaurant.

Student profile.

Out-of-state:	25%	**25 or older:**	50%

Basis for selection. Open admission, but selective for some programs.

High school preparation. College-preparatory program recommended. Required and recommended units include English 4, mathematics 2-3, social studies 2 and science 4.

2008-2009 Annual costs. Tuition/fees: $5,370; $12,120 out-of-state. Per-credit charge: $175 in-state; $400 out-of-state. New England regional tuition per-credit-hour charge: $262. Books/supplies: $500.

Application procedures. Admission: No deadline. $10 fee, may be waived for applicants with need, free for online applicants. Admission notification on a rolling basis beginning on or about 10/1. Must reply by May 1 or within 4 week(s) if notified thereafter. **Financial aid:** Priority date 5/1; no closing date.

Academics. Special study options: Cooperative education, distance learning, double major, honors, independent study, internships, liberal arts/career combination. License preparation in nursing. **Credit/placement by examination:** CLEP, IB, institutional tests. 12 credit hours maximum toward associate degree. **Support services:** Learning center, reduced course load, remedial instruction, study skills assistance, tutoring.

Majors. Business: Accounting, business admin, hospitality/recreation. **Communications technology:** Graphic/printing. **Computer sciences:** General, data processing, programming. **Construction:** Electrician. **Education:** Early childhood. **Interdisciplinary:** Gerontology. **Liberal arts:** Arts/sciences. **Mechanic/repair:** Automotive, marine. **Personal/culinary services:** Culinary arts. **Protective services:** Fire safety technology, fire services admin, firefighting. **Public administration:** Human services, social work. **Visual/performing arts:** Commercial/advertising art, studio arts.

Computing on campus. 100 workstations in library, computer center. Online course registration, wireless network available.

Student life. Freshman orientation: Mandatory, $30 fee. Preregistration for classes offered. **Activities:** Literary magazine, student government.

Athletics. Intramural: Soccer, table tennis, volleyball. **Team name:** Centurions.

Student services. Career counseling, student employment services, financial aid counseling, personal counseling, placement for graduates, veterans' counselor. **Physically disabled:** Services for hearing impaired. **Learning disabled:** Comprehensive services available. **Transfer:** Pre-admission transcript evaluation for new students. Transfer adviser, college fairs on campus for students transferring to 4-year colleges.

Contact. E-mail: wfraser@ccsnh.edu
Phone: (603) 524-3207 ext. 767 Toll-free number: (800) 357-2992
Fax: (603) 524-8084
Wayne Fraser, Director of Admissions, Lakes Region Community College, 379 Belmont Road, Laconia, NH 03246-9204

Lebanon College

Lebanon, New Hampshire
www.lebanoncollege.edu

- Private 2-year health science and community college
- Large town

General. Regionally accredited. **Calendar:** Trimester.

Annual costs/financial aid. Tuition/fees (projected): $8,050.

Contact. Phone: (603) 448-2445 ext. 103
15 Hanover Street, Lebanon, NH 03766

Manchester Community College

Manchester, New Hampshire **CB member**
www.manchestercommunitycollege.edu **CB code: 3660**

- Public 2-year community and technical college
- Commuter campus in small city

General. Founded in 1945. Regionally accredited. Many opportunities for internships, co-ops and clinicals; strong support for immigrants and first generation college students. **Enrollment:** 2,174 degree-seeking undergraduates. **Degrees:** 165 associate awarded. **Location:** 50 miles from Boston. **Calendar:** Semester, limited summer session. **Full-time faculty:** 70 total. **Part-time faculty:** 125 total. **Special facilities:** Wide variety of service learning opportunities. **Partnerships:** Formal partnerships with local businesses.

Basis for selection. Open admission, but selective for some programs. Special requirements for nursing program. Ford automotive program students must be sponsored by Ford dealership. NLN pre-admission test required for nursing applicants. ACCUPLACER required for all other applicants. Interview recommended for all; required for human services; portfolio recommended for graphic design; essay required for exercise science and nursing programs. **Learning Disabled:** A Disabilities Counselor is available for students with learning and other disabilities.

High school preparation. Recommended units include English 4, mathematics 3 and science 2. Chemistry, algebra, geometry and biology required for some programs.

2008-2009 Annual costs. Tuition/fees: $5,430; $12,180 out-of-state. Per-credit charge: $175 in-state; $400 out-of-state. New England Regional tuition: $262 per credit hour. Books/supplies: $550.

Financial aid. All financial aid based on need. Need-based aid available for part-time students. Work-study available nights, weekends and for part-time students. **Additional information:** 100% of direct educational expenses met for all financial aid applicants.

Application procedures. Admission: No deadline. $10 fee, may be waived for applicants with need, free for online applicants. Admission notification on a rolling basis. **Financial aid:** Priority date 5/1; no closing date. FAFSA, institutional form required. Applicants notified on a rolling basis starting 4/15; must reply within 2 week(s) of notification.

Academics. Special study options: Cooperative education, cross-registration, distance learning, double major, ESL, external degree, independent study, internships, liberal arts/career combination, student-designed major. License preparation in nursing, real estate. **Credit/placement by examination:** CLEP, institutional tests. 32 credit hours maximum toward associate degree. **Support services:** Learning center, reduced course load, remedial instruction, study skills assistance, tutoring, writing center.

Majors. Area/ethnic studies: American. **Business:** Accounting, administrative services, business admin, management science, marketing, office management. **Communications technology:** Desktop publishing, graphics. **Computer sciences:** General. **Construction:** Maintenance. **Education:** Early childhood. **Health:** Medical assistant, medical records technology, nursing (RN), prenursing. **Liberal arts:** Arts/sciences. **Mechanic/repair:** Automotive, heating/ac/refrig. **Parks/recreation:** Exercise sciences. **Production:** Welding. **Visual/performing arts:** Commercial/advertising art, interior design.

Computing on campus. 75 workstations in library, computer center. Online library, helpline, wireless network available.

Student life. Freshman orientation: Available, $25 fee. Preregistration for classes offered. **Activities:** Literary magazine, student government, honor society, community service club, Alternative Spring Break, international club, student senate.

Athletics. Intercollegiate: Basketball M, volleyball. **Intramural:** Basketball, skiing, soccer, volleyball.

Student services. Career counseling, services for economically disadvantaged, financial aid counseling, minority student services, on-campus daycare. **Physically disabled:** Services for visually, hearing impaired. **Transfer:** Pre-admission transcript evaluation for new students. Transfer adviser, college fairs on campus for students transferring to 4-year colleges.

Contact. E-mail: jpoirier@ccsnh.edu
Phone: (603) 668-6706 ext. 208 Toll-free number: (800) 924-3445 ext. 208
Fax: (603) 668-5354
Larissa Baia, AVP Enrollment Management, Manchester Community College, 1066 Front Street, Manchester, NH 03102-8518

Nashua Community College

Nashua, New Hampshire **CB member**
www.nashuacc.edu **CB code: 3643**

- Public 2-year community and technical college
- Commuter campus in small city
- Interview required

General. Founded in 1967. Regionally accredited. Clinical labs for nursing students off-campus at Southern New Hampshire Medical Center. **Enrollment:** 1,783 degree-seeking undergraduates. **Degrees:** 205 associate awarded. **Location:** 20 miles from Lowell, Massachusetts. **Calendar:** Semester, limited summer session. **Full-time faculty:** 43 total. **Part-time faculty:** 93 total.

Student profile.

Part-time:	63%	Women:	54%

Transfer out. Colleges most students transferred to 2008: University of Southern New Hampshire, University of New Hampshire, Keene State College, Plymouth State College.

Basis for selection. Open admission, but selective for some programs. Prerequisite courses, references, interview, exam required to apply for Nursing program. Clean driving record to apply for Honda program. Essay and interview with Program Coordinator required for Restaurant Management.

High school preparation. One unit algebra required for business and technical programs, 2 for computer/engineering technology.

2008-2009 Annual costs. Tuition/fees: $5,730; $12,480 out-of-state. Per-credit charge: $175 in-state; $400 out-of-state. New England regional tuition: $262 per credit hour. Books/supplies: $500. Personal expenses: $500.

2007-2008 Financial aid. All financial aid based on need. Need-based aid available for part-time students. Work-study available nights and for part-time students.

Application procedures. Admission: No deadline. $10 fee, may be waived for applicants with need, free for online applicants. Application must be submitted on paper. Admission notification on a rolling basis. Application priority date of 12/31 for nursing applicants. **Financial aid:** Priority date 5/1; no closing date. FAFSA required. Applicants notified on a rolling basis starting 3/1; must reply within 2 week(s) of notification.

Academics. Special study options: Distance learning, dual enrollment of high school students, ESL, independent study, internships, student-designed major, weekend college. License preparation in aviation, nursing. **Credit/placement by examination:** AP, CLEP, institutional tests. 48 credit hours maximum toward associate degree. **Support services:** Learning center, pre-admission summer program, reduced course load, remedial instruction, study skills assistance, tutoring, writing center.

Majors. Business: Accounting, business admin. **Computer sciences:** General, applications programming, computer science, data entry, data processing, information systems, networking, webmaster. **Education:** Early childhood. **Engineering:** Electrical. **Engineering technology:** Drafting, electrical, manufacturing, robotics. **Health:** Nursing (RN). **Legal studies:** Paralegal. **Liberal arts:** Arts/sciences. **Mechanic/repair:** Aircraft, auto body, automotive, electronics/electrical, industrial. **Public administration:** Human services.

Computing on campus. 150 workstations in library, computer center. Student web hosting, wireless network available.

Student life. Freshman orientation: Mandatory, $30 fee. Preregistration for classes offered. One-day session. **Housing:** Student housing available near campus. **Activities:** Drama, literary magazine, student government, student newspaper, Phi Theta Kappa, Rotoract.

Athletics. Intramural: Basketball, soccer, volleyball.

Student services. Adult student services, career counseling, services for economically disadvantaged, student employment services, financial aid counseling, personal counseling, placement for graduates, veterans' counselor. **Transfer:** Pre-admission transcript evaluation for new students. Transfer adviser, college fairs on campus for students transferring to 4-year colleges.

Contact. E-mail: nashua@ccsnh.edu
Phone: (603) 882-6923 ext. 1461 Fax: (603) 882-8690
Patricia Goodman, VP of Student Services, Nashua Community College, 505 Amherst Street, Nashua, NH 03063-1026

NHTI-Concord's Community College

Concord, New Hampshire
www.nhti.edu **CB code: 3647**

- Public 2-year community and technical college
- Commuter campus in large town

General. Founded in 1965. Regionally accredited. **Enrollment:** 3,000 degree-seeking undergraduates. **Degrees:** 519 associate awarded. **Location:** 75 miles from Boston. **Calendar:** Semester, extensive summer session. **Full-time faculty:** 100 total. **Part-time faculty:** 100 total. **Special facilities:** Planetarium, wellness center.

Student profile.

Out-of-state:	2%	**Live on campus:**	23%
25 or older:	33%		

Transfer out. Colleges most students transferred to 2008: University of New Hampshire, Southern New Hampshire University, Plymouth State College, Keene State College, Granite State College.

Basis for selection. Open admission, but selective for some programs. Requirements vary by program. Nursing and allied health programs require special testing and interviews. National League for Nursing Pre-Nursing Test, special challenge test for practical nursing required. Interview required for health program applicants, recommended for others. **Adult students:** Institutional assessment test is required of all students. **Homeschooled:** Transcript of courses and grades required. Must submit portfolio of work approved by school district.

High school preparation. Recommended units include English 4, mathematics 3 and science 2. High school academic subject requirements vary according to program. Strong background in mathematics and natural sciences recommended.

2008-2009 Annual costs. Tuition/fees: $5,760; $12,510 out-of-state. Per-credit charge: $175 in-state; $400 out-of-state. New England Regional tuition: $262 per credit hour. Room/board: $7,440. Books/supplies: $600. Personal expenses: $1,600.

2008-2009 Financial aid. All financial aid based on need. Need-based aid available for part-time students. Work-study available nights, weekends and for part-time students. **Additional information:** 60% of students who apply receive some form of financial aid. State school; all financial aid need-based, primarily from federal sources. No scholarships awarded.

Application procedures. Admission: No deadline. $10 fee, may be waived for applicants with need. Admission notification on a rolling basis. Must reply by May 1 or within 4 week(s) if notified thereafter. Applicants must make a $100 deposit within 30 days of acceptance. **Financial aid:** Priority date 5/1; no closing date. FAFSA, institutional form required. Applicants notified on a rolling basis starting 6/1; must reply within 2 week(s) of notification.

Academics. Special study options: Distance learning, double major, ESL, internships. License preparation in dental hygiene, nursing, paramedic, radiology, real estate. **Credit/placement by examination:** AP, CLEP, IB, institutional tests. **Support services:** Learning center, pre-admission summer program, reduced course load, remedial instruction, study skills assistance, tutoring, writing center.

Majors. Business: Accounting, business admin, hospitality admin, hospitality/recreation, marketing, tourism promotion, tourism/travel. **Communications technology:** General. **Computer sciences:** General. **Education:** General, early childhood. **Engineering technology:** Architectural, civil, computer, electrical, manufacturing. **Health:** Dental hygiene, EMT paramedic, medical radiologic technology/radiation therapy, mental health services, nursing (RN), substance abuse counseling. **Legal studies:** Paralegal. **Liberal arts:** Arts/sciences. **Parks/recreation:** Sports admin. **Protective services:** Law enforcement admin. **Public administration:** Human services. **Social sciences:** General.

Most popular majors. Business/marketing 15%, computer/information sciences 7%, engineering/engineering technologies 14%, health sciences 39%, liberal arts 8%, security/protective services 7%.

Computing on campus. 225 workstations in dormitories, library, computer center. Wireless network available.

Student life. Freshman orientation: Mandatory, $25 fee. Preregistration for classes offered. Held before start of fall and spring semesters. **Housing:** Coed dorms, single-sex dorms, wellness housing available. $300 deposit. **Activities:** Drama, literary magazine, student government, student newspaper, student senate, campus pride, outing club, Phi Theta Kappa, student nurses association, Roentga Ray society, alternative spring break, criminal justice club, Christian Fellowship.

Athletics. Intercollegiate: Baseball M, basketball, soccer, softball W, volleyball. **Intramural:** Basketball, football (non-tackle) M, volleyball. **Team name:** Capitals.

Student services. Career counseling, financial aid counseling, health services, on-campus daycare, personal counseling, placement for graduates, veterans' counselor. **Physically disabled:** Services for visually, speech, hearing impaired. **Learning disabled:** Comprehensive services available. **Transfer:** Pre-admission transcript evaluation for new students. Transfer adviser, college fairs on campus for students transferring to 4-year colleges.

Contact. E-mail: nhtiadm@nhctc.edu
Phone: (603) 271-7134 Toll-free number: (800) 247-0179
Fax: (603) 271-7139
Francis Meyer, Director of Admissions, NHTI-Concord's Community College, 31 College Drive, Concord, NH 03301

River Valley Community College

Claremont, New Hampshire
www.rivervalley.edu **CB code: 3684**

- Public 2-year technical college
- Large town

General. Founded in 1967. Regionally accredited. Restaurant management program includes one year in Switzerland with study at Les Roches International School of Hotel Management. **Enrollment:** 325 degree-seeking undergraduates. **Degrees:** 122 associate awarded. **Location:** 50 miles from Concord. **Calendar:** Semester, limited summer session. **Full-time faculty:** 32 total. **Part-time faculty:** 70 total.

Basis for selection. Open admission, but selective for some programs. ACCUPLACER test used for placement. Special requirements for nursing program.

High school preparation. Typing required for medical assistant, chemistry required for nursing and medical laboratory programs. Algebra recommended for all applicants.

2008-2009 Annual costs. Tuition/fees: $5,340; $12,090 out-of-state. Per-credit charge: $175 in-state; $400 out-of-state. New England Regional tuition: $262 per credit hour. Books/supplies: $550. Personal expenses: $1,100.

Financial aid. All financial aid based on need. Need-based aid available for part-time students.

Application procedures. Admission: No deadline. $10 fee. Admission notification on a rolling basis. **Financial aid:** Closing date 4/1. FAFSA required. Applicants notified on a rolling basis; must reply within 2 week(s) of notification.

Academics. Special study options: Accelerated study, cooperative education, double major, independent study, internships. Joint associate degree program in restaurant management with Les Roches, 2-2 program in teacher education with Keene State College. **Credit/placement by examination:** CLEP, institutional tests. 16 credit hours maximum toward associate degree. **Support services:** Learning center, reduced course load, tutoring.

Majors. Business: General, accounting, office technology. **Engineering technology:** Computer systems, manufacturing. **Health:** Clinical lab technology, nursing (RN), occupational therapy assistant, physical therapy assistant, respiratory therapy technology. **Liberal arts:** Arts/sciences. **Parks/recreation:** General. **Public administration:** Human services.

Most popular majors. Health sciences 87%.

Computing on campus. 45 workstations in library, computer center.

Student life. Activities: Student government.

Student services. Student employment services, health services, on-campus daycare, personal counseling, placement for graduates, veterans' counselor.

Contact. Phone: (603) 542-7744 Fax: (603) 543-1844
Chuck Kusselow, Director of Admissions, River Valley Community College, One College Drive, Claremont, NH 03743-9707

White Mountains Community College

Berlin, New Hampshire
www.wmcc.edu **CB code: 3646**

- Public 2-year community and technical college
- Commuter campus in large town

General. Founded in 1966. Regionally accredited. **Enrollment:** 666 degree-seeking undergraduates; 377 non-degree-seeking students. **Degrees:** 93 associate awarded. **Location:** 110 miles from Concord; 100 miles from Portland, Maine. **Calendar:** Semester, limited summer session. **Full-time faculty:** 29 total. **Part-time faculty:** 53 total.

Student profile. Among degree-seeking undergraduates, 158 enrolled as first-time, first-year students.

Part-time:	49%	**Asian American:**	1%
Women:	69%	**Native American:**	1%

Basis for selection. School record, class rank, counselor recommendations, test results, interview considered. NLN PreAdmission Exam-RN required for nursing students. All others participate in ASSET test. Interview recommended.

2008-2009 Annual costs. Tuition/fees: $5,370; $12,120 out-of-state. Per-credit charge: $175 in-state; $400 out-of-state. New England Regional tuition: $262 per credit hour. Books/supplies: $500. Personal expenses: $1,500.

Financial aid. All financial aid based on need. Need-based aid available for part-time students.

Application procedures. Admission: Priority date 5/1; no deadline. $10 fee, may be waived for applicants with need, free for online applicants. Admission notification on a rolling basis beginning on or about 12/1. **Financial aid:** Priority date 5/1; no closing date. FAFSA, institutional form required. Applicants notified on a rolling basis starting 5/1; must reply within 2 week(s) of notification.

Academics. Special study options: Cooperative education, distance learning, double major, dual enrollment of high school students, independent study, internships, student-designed major. Bachelor's degree programs available on campus. **Credit/placement by examination:** CLEP, institutional tests. 32 credit hours maximum toward associate degree. **Support services:** Learning center, reduced course load, remedial instruction, study skills assistance, tutoring.

Majors. Business: Accounting, administrative services, business admin, office technology, office/clerical, restaurant/food services. **Computer sciences:** General. **Conservation:** Environmental studies, forestry, management/policy. **Education:** Early childhood, multi-level teacher. **Engineering technology:** Computer systems, surveying. **Health:** Nursing (RN). **Liberal arts:** Arts/sciences. **Mechanic/repair:** Automotive, diesel. **Personal/culinary services:** Chef training, restaurant/catering. **Protective services:** Law enforcement admin. **Public administration:** Human services.

Computing on campus. 45 workstations in library, computer center. Online course registration, online library available.

Student life. Freshman orientation: Mandatory, $30 fee. **Activities:** Student government.

Student services. Adult student services, career counseling, student employment services, financial aid counseling, on-campus daycare, personal counseling, veterans' counselor. **Physically disabled:** Services for visually, hearing impaired. **Transfer:** Transfer adviser for students transferring to 4-year colleges.

Contact. E-mail: wmcc@ccsnh.edu
Phone: (603) 752-1113 Toll-free number: (800) 445-4525
Fax: (603) 752-6335
Mark Desmarais, Admissions Director, White Mountains Community College, 2020 Riverside Drive, Berlin, NH 03570

Two-Year Colleges

New Jersey

Assumption College for Sisters
Mendham, New Jersey
www.acs350.org **CB code: 2009**

- Private 2-year junior and liberal arts college for women affiliated with Roman Catholic Church
- Residential campus in small town
- Application essay required

General. Founded in 1953. Regionally accredited. **Enrollment:** 26 degree-seeking undergraduates; 7 non-degree-seeking students. **Degrees:** 14 associate awarded. **Location:** 35 miles from New York City. **Calendar:** Semester, limited summer session. **Part-time faculty:** 13 total; 23% have terminal degrees, 77% women. **Class size:** 100% < 20.

Student profile. Among degree-seeking undergraduates, 8 enrolled as first-time, first-year students.

Women:	100%	**International:**	92%
Hispanic American:	4%		

Basis for selection. Interview, recommendations, school achievement record, test scores, commitment to obligations of religious vocation as well as acceptance of applicant by a religious community important.

High school preparation. 16 units required. Required and recommended units include English 4, mathematics 2-3, history 2, science 2-3, foreign language 2, visual/performing arts 1 and academic electives 4.

2009-2010 Annual costs. Tuition/fees: $5,000. Per-credit charge: $150.

Application procedures. Admission: No deadline. $50 fee, may be waived for applicants with need. Admission notification on a rolling basis. **Financial aid:** No deadline.

Academics. Special study options: ESL. **Credit/placement by examination:** AP, CLEP, SAT. **Support services:** Reduced course load, remedial instruction, study skills assistance, tutoring.

Majors. Liberal arts: Arts/sciences.

Computing on campus. 21 workstations in library, computer center, student center. Online library, helpline, repair service, wireless network available.

Student life. Freshman orientation: Mandatory. **Policies:** Students reside with their religious congregations or with the Sisters of Christian Charity. Religious observance required.

Student services. Transfer: Pre-admission transcript evaluation for new students. Transfer adviser for students transferring to 4-year colleges.

Contact. E-mail: deanregistrar@acs350.org
Phone: (973) 543-6528 ext. 228 Fax: (973) 543-1738
Sr. Gerardine Tantsits, Academic Dean/Registrar, Assumption College for Sisters, 350 Bernardsville Road, Mendham, NJ 07945-2923

Atlantic Cape Community College
Mays Landing, New Jersey **CB member**
www.atlantic.edu **CB code: 2024**

- Public 2-year culinary school and community college
- Commuter campus in small town

General. Founded in 1964. Regionally accredited. Instruction and student/academic support services delivered at all 3 campuses (Mays Landing, Atlantic City, Cape May). **Enrollment:** 6,578 degree-seeking undergraduates; 429 non-degree-seeking students. **Degrees:** 719 associate awarded. **Location:** 15 miles from Atlantic City, 49 miles from Philadelphia. **Calendar:** Semester, limited summer session. **Full-time faculty:** 98 total; 13% have terminal degrees, 11% minority, 57% women. **Part-time faculty:** 310 total; 36% have terminal degrees, 11% minority, 54% women. **Special facilities:** Gourmet student-run restaurant.

Student profile. Among degree-seeking undergraduates, 1,463 enrolled as first-time, first-year students, 196 transferred in from other institutions.

Part-time:	46%	**Asian American:**	9%
Women:	62%	**Hispanic American:**	13%
African American:	13%	**25 or older:**	33%

Transfer out. Colleges most students transferred to 2008: Richard Stockton State College of New Jersey, Rowan University, Rutgers University.

Basis for selection. Open admission, but selective for some programs. Admission to allied health and nursing programs based upon entrance exam scores and GPA. ACCUPLACER exam used for placement only. All students must take college basic skills exam after completing 12th credit or when they officially matriculate. Students who score 500 on SAT Verbal, and 470 on SAT Math exempt from basic skills testing. **Homeschooled:** Students must be in certified homeschooling program. Letter from certifying school district approving courses required. **Learning Disabled:** Required to notify the registrar of disabilty.

2008-2009 Annual costs. Tuition/fees: $3,222; $5,874 out-of-district; $11,178 out-of-state. Per-credit charge: $88 in-district; $177 out-of-district; $354 out-of-state. Books/supplies: $1,400.

2007-2008 Financial aid. Need-based: 752 full-time freshmen applied for aid; 644 were judged to have need; 598 of these received aid. Average need met was 44%. Average scholarship/grant was $4,963; average loan $2,311. 82% of total undergraduate aid awarded as scholarships/grants, 18% as loans/jobs. Need-based aid available for part-time students. Work-study available for part-time students. **Non-need-based:** Awarded to 156 full-time undergraduates, including 107 freshmen. **Additional information:** Installment plan available for culinary arts majors. Employees of Atlantic City casinos may attend ACCC at in-county rates regardless of residence.

Application procedures. Admission: No deadline. $35 fee, may be waived for applicants with need. Admission notification on a rolling basis. Applicants must make arrangements to take College Basic Skills Placement Test unless SAT scores qualify them for exemption. May enroll part-time, non-matriculate with permission. **Financial aid:** Priority date 5/1; no closing date. FAFSA, institutional form required. Applicants notified on a rolling basis starting 5/1.

Academics. 8 associate degrees available through distance education: in liberal arts, history, psychology, business, computer information systems, humanities, general studies, and literature. **Special study options:** Cooperative education, distance learning, double major, dual enrollment of high school students, ESL, independent study, internships, liberal arts/career combination. Bachelor's degree programs available on campus. License preparation in nursing, real estate. **Credit/placement by examination:** AP, CLEP, institutional tests. 32 credit hours maximum toward associate degree. Total of 32 transfer credits may be awarded through combination of: college course transfer, articulation agreements, CLEP, Ponsi/ACE and/or Tech-Prep. **Support services:** GED test center, learning center, pre-admission summer program, reduced course load, remedial instruction, study skills assistance, tutoring, writing center.

Majors. Business: Accounting, administrative services, business admin, hotel/motel admin, management information systems. **Computer sciences:** Data processing, programming. **Health:** Nursing (RN), respiratory therapy technology. **Legal studies:** Paralegal. **Liberal arts:** Arts/sciences. **Personal/culinary services:** Chef training, institutional food service. **Protective services:** Police science. **Public administration:** Human services. **Other:** Math science: biology, chemisrty, math, Technical studies.

Most popular majors. Business/marketing 20%, health sciences 11%, liberal arts 54%, security/protective services 6%.

Computing on campus. 635 workstations in library, computer center, student center. Online course registration, online library, helpline, wireless network available.

Student life. Freshman orientation: Available. Preregistration for classes offered. Online orentation available. **Activities:** Choral groups, drama, international student organizations, literary magazine, music ensembles, radio station, student government, student newspaper, human services club, African American coalition, Jewish Association of Students, Phi Theta Kappa, Alpha and Omega Christian clubs, Shades of Brown of Atlantic City, special interest clubs.

Athletics. NJCAA. **Intercollegiate:** Archery, basketball M, golf, softball W. **Intramural:** Basketball, bowling, soccer, softball, volleyball. **Team name:** Buccaneers.

Student services. Adult student services, career counseling, student employment services, health services, on-campus daycare, personal counseling, placement for graduates, veterans' counselor. **Physically disabled:** Services for visually, speech, hearing impaired. **Transfer:** Pre-admission transcript evaluation for new students. Transfer adviser, college fairs on campus for students transferring to 4-year colleges.

Contact. E-mail: accadmit@atlantic.edu
Phone: (609) 343-5000 Fax: (609) 343-4921
Regina Skinner, Director, Admission and College Recruitment, Atlantic Cape Community College, 5100 Black Horse Pike, Mays Landing, NJ 08330

Bergen Community College

Paramus, New Jersey — **CB member**
www.bergen.edu — **CB code: 2032**

- Public 2-year community college
- Commuter campus in large town

General. Founded in 1965. Regionally accredited. Center for Deaf Education with counselors and specialized equipment. **Enrollment:** 13,389 degree-seeking undergraduates; 1,894 non-degree-seeking students. **Degrees:** 1,377 associate awarded. **Location:** 12 miles from New York City. **Calendar:** Semester, extensive summer session. **Full-time faculty:** 303 total; 13% minority, 54% women. **Part-time faculty:** 453 total; 15% minority, 51% women.

Student profile. Among degree-seeking undergraduates, 77% enrolled in a transfer program, 23% enrolled in a vocational program, 3,316 enrolled as first-time, first-year students.

Part-time:	40%	**Hispanic American:**	28%
Women:	51%	**International:**	8%
African American:	6%	**25 or older:**	33%
Asian American:	10%		

Transfer out. Colleges most students transferred to 2008: Montclair State University, William Paterson University, Rutgers University, Ramapo College.

Basis for selection. Open admission, but selective for some programs. Admission to allied health programs based on academic record and specific courses taken. Priority given to county residents. High school diploma not required for students over 18 years old. **Learning Disabled:** Students must provide documentation of disability to Office of Specialized Services.

High school preparation. Math, biology, chemistry required for most allied health programs.

2009-2010 Annual costs. Tuition/fees (projected): $4,742; $8,033 out-of-district; $8,333 out-of-state. Per-credit charge: $103 in-district; $213 out-of-district; $223 out-of-state. General Fee (15% of tuition) payable by all students each semester or session. Fee is non-refundable and based on number of credits taken.

2007-2008 Financial aid. Need-based: 82% of total undergraduate aid awarded as scholarships/grants, 18% as loans/jobs.

Application procedures. Admission: No deadline. No application fee. Admission notification on a rolling basis. Application closing date for nursing and dental hygiene March 1. **Financial aid:** No deadline. FAFSA required. Applicants notified on a rolling basis starting 6/1.

Academics. Special study options: Cooperative education, distance learning, dual enrollment of high school students, ESL, honors, internships, study abroad. **Credit/placement by examination:** AP, CLEP, institutional tests. **Support services:** Learning center, pre-admission summer program, reduced course load, remedial instruction, tutoring, writing center.

Majors. Agriculture: Horticulture. **Area/ethnic studies:** Women's. **Biology:** General, biotechnology. **Business:** Accounting technology, administrative services, banking/financial services, hotel/motel admin, marketing, sales/distribution, special products marketing. **Communications:** General, journalism. **Communications technology:** Animation/special effects, radio/tv, recording arts. **Computer sciences:** General, applications programming, computer graphics, information technology, system admin. **Conservation:** Environmental science. **Education:** General, early childhood. **Engineering:** General. **Engineering technology:** General, drafting, electrical, manufacturing, mechanical drafting. **Foreign languages:** General. **Health:** Clinical lab technology, dental hygiene, health services, medical assistant, medical radiologic technology/radiation therapy, nursing (RN), physical therapy assistant, respiratory therapy technology, sonography, veterinary technology/assistant. **History:** General. **Legal studies:** Paralegal. **Liberal arts:** Arts/sciences. **Math:** General. **Personal/culinary services:** Chef training, restaurant/catering. **Philosophy/religion:** Philosophy, religion. **Physical sciences:** General, chemistry, physics. **Protective services:** Corrections, police science. **Psychology:** General. **Social sciences:** Economics, sociology. **Visual/performing arts:** General, commercial/advertising art, film/cinema, theater arts management. **Other:** Legal nurse consultant, Music business.

Most popular majors. Health sciences 21%, liberal arts 62%.

Student life. Freshman orientation: Available. Preregistration for classes offered. **Activities:** Choral groups, dance, drama, literary magazine, music ensembles, musical theater, student government, student newspaper, TV station.

Athletics. NJCAA. **Intercollegiate:** Baseball M, basketball, cross-country, golf M, soccer M, softball W, tennis M, track and field, volleyball W, wrestling M. **Team name:** Bulldogs.

Student services. Career counseling, student employment services, financial aid counseling, health services, on-campus daycare, personal counseling, placement for graduates, veterans' counselor. **Physically disabled:** Services for visually, speech, hearing impaired. **Transfer:** Transfer adviser, college fairs on campus for students transferring to 4-year colleges.

Contact. E-mail: admsoffice@bergen.edu
Phone: (201) 447-7195 Fax: (201) 670-7973
Office of Enrollment Services, Bergen Community College, 400 Paramus Road, Paramus, NJ 07652-1595

Brookdale Community College

Lincroft, New Jersey — **CB member**
www.brookdalecc.edu — **CB code: 2181**

- Public 2-year community college
- Commuter campus in small city

General. Founded in 1967. Regionally accredited. **Enrollment:** 14,642 degree-seeking undergraduates. **Degrees:** 1,768 associate awarded. **ROTC:** Army, Air Force. **Location:** 5 miles from Red Bank, 25 miles from New Brunswick. **Calendar:** Semester, extensive summer session. **Full-time faculty:** 228 total. **Part-time faculty:** 624 total.

Student profile.

Out-of-state:	1%	**25 or older:**	38%

Transfer out. Colleges most students transferred to 2008: Monmouth University, Rutgers University, Kean University.

Basis for selection. Open admission, but selective for some programs. Special requirements for health sciences programs and automative technology programs. Applicants without high school diploma or GED may be admitted. Must take equivalent of GED after specific number of credits in specific distribution. ACCUPLACER used for placement for all degree-seeking students who have reached their 12th credit. Group interview required for nursing, medical laboratory technology, respiratory therapy applicants, radiologic technology.

High school preparation. One unit high school or college algebra, 1 chemistry, 1 biology required for allied health programs.

2008-2009 Annual costs. Tuition/fees: $4,018; $7,258 out-of-district; $8,008 out-of-state. Per-credit charge: $108 in-district; $216 out-of-district; $241 out-of-state. Books/supplies: $1,000. Personal expenses: $1,195.

Financial aid. Need-based: Need-based aid available for part-time students. **Non-need-based:** Scholarships awarded for athletics.

Application procedures. Admission: No deadline. $25 fee. Admission notification on a rolling basis. **Financial aid:** Priority date 5/1; no closing date. FAFSA, institutional form required. Applicants notified on a rolling basis starting 5/1; must reply within 2 week(s) of notification.

Academics. Special study options: Cooperative education, distance learning, ESL, honors, independent study, internships, study abroad, weekend college. License preparation in dental hygiene, nursing. **Credit/placement by examination:** AP, CLEP, institutional tests. **Support services:** GED preparation and test center, learning center, pre-admission summer program, reduced course load, remedial instruction, tutoring, writing center.

Majors. Business: General, accounting, administrative services, business admin, fashion, marketing. **Communications technology:** General, graphic/printing. **Computer sciences:** General. **Education:** General, teacher assistance. **Engineering:** General. **Engineering technology:** Electrical. **Health:** Clinical lab technology, dental hygiene, medical radiologic technology/radiation therapy, nursing (RN), respiratory therapy technology. **Legal studies:** Paralegal. **Liberal arts:** Arts/sciences. **Personal/culinary services:** Culinary arts. **Protective services:** Police science. **Public administration:** Social

Two-Year Colleges

work. **Social sciences:** General. **Visual/performing arts:** Art, interior design, photography, studio arts.

Computing on campus. 1,100 workstations in library, computer center. Commuter students can connect to campus network. Helpline available.

Student life. Freshman orientation: Available. Preregistration for classes offered. **Activities:** Dance, drama, film society, literary magazine, musical theater, radio station, student government, student newspaper, TV station.

Athletics. NJCAA. **Intercollegiate:** Baseball M, basketball, cross-country, soccer, softball W, tennis. **Intramural:** Basketball, golf M, volleyball. **Team name:** Blues.

Student services. Career counseling, student employment services, health services, on-campus daycare, personal counseling, placement for graduates, veterans' counselor. **Physically disabled:** Services for visually, speech, hearing impaired. **Transfer:** Transfer adviser for students transferring to 4-year colleges.

Contact. Phone: (732) 224-2375 Fax: (732) 224-2271
Bruce Marich, Director of Admissions, Brookdale Community College, 765 Newman Springs Road, Lincroft, NJ 07738

Burlington County College

Pemberton, New Jersey — **CB member**
www.bcc.edu — **CB code: 2180**

- Public 2-year community college
- Commuter campus in small town

General. Founded in 1966. Regionally accredited. Credit courses offered at main campus in Pemberton, Mount Laurel Campus, Willingboro Center, Mount Holly Center, educational centers at Bordentown Regional High School and McGuire AFB, as well as various other county high schools. **Enrollment:** 7,322 degree-seeking undergraduates; 1,366 non-degree-seeking students. **Degrees:** 770 associate awarded. **Location:** 30 miles from Philadelphia, 80 miles from New York City. **Calendar:** Semester, limited summer session. **Full-time faculty:** 55 total; 14% minority, 47% women. **Part-time faculty:** 403 total; 17% minority, 54% women. **Class size:** 27% < 20, 66% 20-39, 2% 40-49, 5% 50-99. **Special facilities:** Sculpture garden, outdoor amphitheatre, small business science and high technology incubators, NASA laboratory. **Partnerships:** Formal partnerships with Police Academy, Global Corporate College.

Student profile. Among degree-seeking undergraduates, 58% enrolled in a transfer program, 26% enrolled in a vocational program, 1% already have a bachelor's degree or higher, 2,036 enrolled as first-time, first-year students, 377 transferred in from other institutions.

Part-time:	44%	**Asian American:**	4%
Out-of-state:	1%	**Hispanic American:**	6%
Women:	59%	**International:**	1%
African American:	20%	**25 or older:**	31%

Transfer out. Colleges most students transferred to 2008: Rutgers University, Richard Stockton College of New Jersey, Rowan University, Drexel University, Rider University.

Basis for selection. Open admission, but selective for some programs. Academic high school background required of nursing program applicants.

2008-2009 Annual costs. Tuition/fees: $2,895; $3,375 out-of-district; $5,325 out-of-state. Per-credit charge: $78 in-district; $94 out-of-district; $159 out-of-state. Books/supplies: $1,200. Personal expenses: $3,438.

Financial aid. All financial aid based on need. Need-based aid available for part-time students. Work-study available nights, weekends and for part-time students.

Application procedures. Admission: No deadline. $20 fee, may be waived for applicants with need, free for online applicants. Admission notification on a rolling basis. **Financial aid:** No deadline. FAFSA required. Applicants notified on a rolling basis.

Academics. Special study options: Cooperative education, distance learning, double major, dual enrollment of high school students, ESL, independent study, study abroad, weekend college. Bachelor's degree programs available on campus. License preparation in dental hygiene, nursing, radiology, real estate. **Credit/placement by examination:** AP, CLEP, institutional tests. 30 credit hours maximum toward associate degree. **Support services:** GED preparation and test center, learning center, pre-admission summer program, reduced course load, remedial instruction, study skills assistance, tutoring, writing center.

Majors. Biology: Biotechnology. **Business:** General, accounting, accounting technology, business admin, management information systems, restaurant/food services, sales/distribution. **Communications technology:** Animation/special effects, photo/film/video, recording arts. **Computer sciences:** Computer graphics, computer science, data processing, information systems. **Engineering technology:** Automotive, CAD/CADD, civil, construction, electrical. **Foreign languages:** Sign language interpretation. **Health:** Dental hygiene, medical radiologic technology/radiation therapy, medical records technology, nursing (RN), sonography. **Legal studies:** Paralegal. **Liberal arts:** Arts/sciences. **Physical sciences:** General. **Protective services:** Firefighting, police science. **Public administration:** Human services. **Science technology:** Chemical. **Visual/performing arts:** Fashion design, graphic design, photography. **Other:** Hearing instrument science, Technical studies.

Most popular majors. Health sciences 15%, liberal arts 69%, security/protective services 6%.

Computing on campus. 1,600 workstations in library, computer center, student center. Commuter students can connect to campus network. Online library, helpline, wireless network available.

Student life. Freshman orientation: Available. Preregistration for classes offered. **Activities:** Concert band, choral groups, dance, drama, international student organizations, literary magazine, music ensembles, musical theater, radio station, student government, minority student union, veterans club, Phi Theta Kappa, student nurses association, Collegiate Republicans, Young Democrats, Circle K, students for ecological action, Christian student club.

Athletics. NJCAA. **Intercollegiate:** Baseball M, basketball, golf M, soccer, softball W. **Team name:** Barons.

Student services. Adult student services, career counseling, services for economically disadvantaged, student employment services, financial aid counseling, health services, minority student services, placement for graduates, veterans' counselor. **Physically disabled:** Services for visually, speech, hearing impaired. **Transfer:** Transfer center, transfer adviser, college fairs on campus for students transferring to 4-year colleges.

Contact. Phone: (609) 894-9311 ext. 1282 Fax: (609) 894-0764
Mary Lou Mascarin, Executive Director, Enrollment Management and Marketing, Burlington County College, 601 Pemberton-Browns Mills Road, Pemberton, NJ 08068-1599

Camden County College

Blackwood, New Jersey — **CB member**
www.camdencc.edu — **CB code: 2121**

- Public 2-year community college
- Commuter campus in large town

General. Founded in 1966. Regionally accredited. Additional locations in Camden and Cherry Hill. **Enrollment:** 13,115 degree-seeking undergraduates. **Degrees:** 1,317 associate awarded. **Location:** 15 miles from Philadelphia, 13 miles from Camden. **Calendar:** Semester, extensive summer session. **Full-time faculty:** 142 total. **Part-time faculty:** 598 total. **Special facilities:** Integrated manufacturing building, laser technology institute for education and research, computer graphics laboratories.

Student profile.

Out-of-state:	2%	**25 or older:**	41%

Transfer out. Colleges most students transferred to 2008: Rowan University, Rutgers University-Camden, Temple University, Widener University.

Basis for selection. Open admission, but selective for some programs. Special requirements for allied health, dental, and nursing programs. SAT or ACT required for admission to certain selective programs. Psychological Corporation Pre-Nursing examination, entrance examination for School of Nursing or National League for Nursing, Pre-Nursing and Guidance examination required of nursing applicants. Mechanical aptitude test required for General Motors automotive service education program applicants. Dental Hygiene Aptitude Test required of students entering dental hygiene program. Interview recommended for various health programs and the General Motors programs.

2008-2009 Annual costs. Tuition/fees: $3,210; $3,330 out-of-state. Per-credit charge: $88 in-state; $92 out-of-state. Books/supplies: $650.

Financial aid. Need-based: Need-based aid available for part-time students. Work-study available for part-time students.

Application procedures. **Admission:** No deadline. No application fee. Admission notification on a rolling basis beginning on or about 2/3. **Financial aid:** Closing date 7/1. FAFSA, institutional form required. Applicants notified on a rolling basis starting 7/1.

Academics. Strong program in robotics, laser/electro optics technology, and computer graphics. **Special study options:** Cooperative education, cross-registration, distance learning, dual enrollment of high school students, ESL, honors, independent study, internships, liberal arts/career combination, weekend college. General Motors automotive service education program. **Credit/placement by examination:** CLEP, institutional tests. 30 credit hours maximum toward associate degree. New Jersey College Basic Skills placement test required. **Support services:** Learning center, pre-admission summer program, reduced course load, remedial instruction, study skills assistance, tutoring.

Majors. **Business:** Accounting, banking/financial services, business admin, management information systems, marketing, sales/distribution. **Computer sciences:** General, computer graphics. **Engineering:** Science. **Engineering technology:** Drafting, electrical. **Foreign languages:** Sign language interpretation. **Health:** Clinical lab technology, dental assistant, dental hygiene, nursing (RN), optician, respiratory therapy technology, veterinary technology/assistant. **Liberal arts:** Arts/sciences. **Protective services:** Fire safety technology, police science. **Public administration:** Social work. **Visual/performing arts:** Photography.

Computing on campus. 800 workstations in library, computer center.

Student life. **Freshman orientation:** Available. **Activities:** Concert band, choral groups, drama, literary magazine, radio station, student government, student newspaper.

Athletics. NJCAA. **Intercollegiate:** Baseball M, basketball, soccer, softball W. **Intramural:** Racquetball W.

Student services. Career counseling, student employment services, health services, on-campus daycare, placement for graduates, veterans' counselor. **Physically disabled:** Services for visually, speech, hearing impaired. **Transfer:** Transfer adviser, college fairs on campus for students transferring to 4-year colleges.

Contact. Phone: (856) 227-7200 ext. 4200 Toll-free number: (888) 228-2466 Fax: (856) 374-4917
Sharon Wedington, Admissions Director, Camden County College, Box 200, Blackwood, NJ 08012

County College of Morris

Randolph, New Jersey — **CB member**
www.ccm.edu — **CB code: 2124**

- Public 2-year community college
- Commuter campus in large town

General. Founded in 1965. Regionally accredited. Courses available at off-campus sites. **Enrollment:** 6,922 degree-seeking undergraduates. **Degrees:** 1,124 associate awarded. **Location:** 40 miles from New York City. **Calendar:** Semester, extensive summer session. **Full-time faculty:** 166 total. **Part-time faculty:** 373 total. **Special facilities:** Planetarium.

Student profile. Among degree-seeking undergraduates, 673 transferred in from other institutions.

Out-of-state:	1%	**25 or older:**	25%

Transfer out. **Colleges most students transferred to 2008:** Montclair State University, William Paterson University of New Jersey, Rutgers University, Kean University, Fairleigh Dickinson University, New Jersey Institute of Technology.

Basis for selection. Open admission, but selective for some programs. Restricted admissions to nursing, medical lab technology, radiography, respiratory therapy, and veterinary technology on space-available basis. Applicants who are not native speakers of English required to take LOEP test (Levels of English Proficiency) for placement. SAT required for honors programs. Students who submit SAT section scores of 500 exempt from basic skills placement test. Audition required for music programs. **Learning Disabled:** Students may apply to Horizons program if they want accommodations.

High school preparation. 16 units recommended. Some programs require 2 to 4 units math and 1 to 2 units laboratory science.

2008-2009 Annual costs. Tuition/fees: $3,530; $6,500 out-of-district; $8,900 out-of-state. Per-credit charge: $99 in-district; $198 out-of-district; $278 out-of-state. Tuition reciprocity agreements with neighboring counties allow some out-of-county residents to pay in-county rates. Books/supplies: $900. Personal expenses: $1,220.

Financial aid. **Need-based:** Need-based aid available for part-time students. Work-study available for part-time students. **Non-need-based:** Scholarships awarded for athletics.

Application procedures. **Admission:** No deadline. $30 fee. Admission notification on a rolling basis. **Financial aid:** Priority date 3/1; no closing date. FAFSA required. Applicants notified on a rolling basis starting 5/1.

Academics. **Special study options:** Accelerated study, cooperative education, distance learning, double major, dual enrollment of high school students, ESL, exchange student, external degree, honors, independent study, internships, liberal arts/career combination, study abroad, teacher certification program, weekend college. License preparation in aviation, nursing, radiology. **Credit/placement by examination:** AP, CLEP, institutional tests. **Support services:** GED preparation, learning center, pre-admission summer program, reduced course load, remedial instruction, study skills assistance, tutoring, writing center.

Majors. **Agriculture:** Business. **Business:** Business admin, management information systems. **Communications:** Journalism. **Communications technology:** General. **Computer sciences:** General. **Education:** Biology, chemistry, drama/dance, early childhood, French, German, history, physics, Spanish. **Engineering:** Science. **Engineering technology:** Electrical. **Health:** Clinical lab technology, nursing (RN), respiratory therapy technology. **Liberal arts:** Arts/sciences. **Math:** General. **Parks/recreation:** Health/fitness. **Personal/culinary services:** Restaurant/catering. **Protective services:** Police science. **Public administration:** General. **Science technology:** Biological. **Social sciences:** General. **Transportation:** Aviation. **Visual/performing arts:** General.

Computing on campus. 475 workstations in library, computer center. Commuter students can connect to campus network. Online course registration, online library, helpline, wireless network available.

Student life. **Freshman orientation:** Available. Preregistration for classes offered. Half-day sessions held 1 week prior to start of academic year. **Activities:** Bands, choral groups, dance, drama, international student organizations, literary magazine, music ensembles, musical theater, radio station, student government, student newspaper, symphony orchestra, Phi Theta Kappa, united Latino organization, student ambassadors, black student union, Asian students association, Jewish students association, campus Christian fellowship, IEEE.

Athletics. NJCAA. **Intercollegiate:** Baseball M, basketball, golf, ice hockey M, soccer, softball W, tennis. **Intramural:** Badminton, basketball, bowling, soccer W, softball, tennis, volleyball. **Team name:** Titans.

Student services. Adult student services, alcohol/substance abuse counseling, career counseling, services for economically disadvantaged, student employment services, financial aid counseling, health services, minority student services, on-campus daycare, personal counseling, placement for graduates, veterans' counselor, women's services. **Physically disabled:** Services for visually, hearing impaired. **Learning disabled:** Comprehensive services available. **Transfer:** Pre-admission transcript evaluation for new students. Transfer adviser, college fairs on campus for students transferring to 4-year colleges.

Contact. E-mail: admis@ccm.edu
Phone: (973) 328-5100 Fax: (973) 328-5199
Bette Simmons, Director of Admissions, County College of Morris, 214 Center Grove Road, Randolph, NJ 07869-2086

Cumberland County College

Vineland, New Jersey — **CB member**
www.cccnj.edu — **CB code: 2118**

- Public 2-year community college
- Commuter campus in small city

General. Founded in 1963. Regionally accredited. **Enrollment:** 3,301 degree-seeking undergraduates. **Degrees:** 410 associate awarded. **Location:** 35 miles from Philadelphia. **Calendar:** Semester, extensive summer session. **Full-time faculty:** 49 total. **Part-time faculty:** 200 total. **Class size:** 47% < 20, 46% 20-39, 6% 40-49, less than 1% 50-99. **Special facilities:** Fine and performing arts center, conference center.

Student profile. Among degree-seeking undergraduates, 74% enrolled in a transfer program, 26% enrolled in a vocational program.

Transfer out. **Colleges most students transferred to 2008:** Rowan University, Stockton State College, Rutgers University, University of Delaware.

Basis for selection. Open admission, but selective for some programs. Special requirements for nursing program; National League for Nursing pre-entrance examination required.

High school preparation. College-preparatory program recommended.

2008-2009 Annual costs. Tuition/fees: $3,480; $6,150 out-of-district; $11,490 out-of-state. Per-credit charge: $89 in-district; $178 out-of-district; $356 out-of-state. Books/supplies: $1,300. Personal expenses: $2,006.

2007-2008 Financial aid. Need-based: Need-based aid available for part-time students. Work-study available for part-time students. **Non-need-based:** Scholarships awarded for academics.

Application procedures. Admission: No deadline. $25 fee, may be waived for applicants with need. Admission notification on a rolling basis. **Financial aid:** No deadline. FAFSA required. Applicants notified on a rolling basis; must reply within 3 week(s) of notification.

Academics. Special study options: Accelerated study, distance learning, double major, dual enrollment of high school students, ESL, honors, independent study. Clay College for Ceramics program. Project Assist for students with learning disabilities. Bachelor's degree programs available on campus. License preparation in nursing, radiology. **Credit/placement by examination:** CLEP, institutional tests. 32 credit hours maximum toward associate degree. **Support services:** GED preparation and test center, learning center, pre-admission summer program, reduced course load, remedial instruction, study skills assistance, tutoring, writing center.

Majors. Agriculture: General, ornamental horticulture. **Biology:** Biomedical sciences. **Business:** Accounting, administrative services, business admin, hospitality/recreation, management information systems, marketing, office management, operations, tourism/travel. **Communications:** Journalism, radio/tv. **Computer sciences:** General, computer science, information technology, LAN/WAN management, networking, vendor certification. **Construction:** Site management. **Education:** Art, early childhood, multi-level teacher. **Engineering:** General. **Engineering technology:** General, construction, electrical. **Health:** Health services, medical radiologic technology/radiation therapy, medical records admin, nursing (RN), respiratory therapy assistant. **Interdisciplinary:** Biological/physical sciences, math/computer science. **Legal studies:** Paralegal. **Liberal arts:** Arts/sciences, humanities. **Math:** General. **Protective services:** Corrections, criminal justice, emergency management/homeland security, forensics, police science. **Public administration:** Social work. **Social sciences:** General. **Visual/performing arts:** Acting, art, ceramics, cinematography, commercial/advertising art, dramatic, graphic design, studio arts. **Other:** Cyber security, Healthcare, Paralegal studies-Spanish, Philosophy/Religion, Psychosocial rehabilitation, Technology studies.

Most popular majors. Business/marketing 9%, health sciences 13%, liberal arts 47%, public administration/social services 12%, social sciences 8%.

Computing on campus. 200 workstations in library, computer center, student center. Commuter students can connect to campus network. Online course registration, online library, helpline, wireless network available.

Student life. Freshman orientation: Mandatory. Preregistration for classes offered. **Policies:** Comprehensive support center for learning disabled students. **Activities:** Choral groups, drama, literary magazine, student government, student newspaper, symphony orchestra, multicultural club, Latin American club, African American club.

Athletics. NJCAA. **Intercollegiate:** Baseball M, basketball, cross-country, softball W, track and field. **Intramural:** Cross-country. **Team name:** Dukes, Lady Dukes.

Student services. Career counseling, services for economically disadvantaged, student employment services, financial aid counseling, personal counseling, placement for graduates. **Physically disabled:** Services for visually, speech, hearing impaired. **Learning disabled:** Comprehensive services available. **Transfer:** Pre-admission transcript evaluation for new students. Transfer adviser, college fairs on campus for students transferring to 4-year colleges.

Contact. Phone: (609) 691-8986 Fax: (609) 691-6157
Maud Fried-Goodnight, Executive Director of Enrollment and Student Support Services, Cumberland County College, PO Box 1500, Vineland, NJ 08362-9912

Essex County College

Newark, New Jersey
www.essex.edu **CB code: 2237**

- Public 2-year community college
- Commuter campus in large city

General. Founded in 1966. Regionally accredited. Classes also given at West Caldwell campus and several locations in Essex County and Newark. **Enrollment:** 11,061 degree-seeking undergraduates; 1,258 non-degree-seeking students. **Degrees:** 907 associate awarded. **Location:** 12 miles from New York City. **Calendar:** Semester, limited summer session. **Full-time faculty:** 143 total; 48% minority, 46% women. **Part-time faculty:** 489 total; 56% minority, 45% women. **Special facilities:** Police academy, Africana Institute.

Student profile. Among degree-seeking undergraduates, 75% enrolled in a transfer program, 25% enrolled in a vocational program, 1% already have a bachelor's degree or higher, 3,119 enrolled as first-time, first-year students, 395 transferred in from other institutions.

Part-time:	39%	**Asian American:**	3%
Out-of-state:	2%	**Hispanic American:**	21%
Women:	61%	**International:**	9%
African American:	50%	**25 or older:**	42%

Transfer out. 80% of students enrolled in the transfer program go on to 4-year colleges. **Colleges most students transferred to 2008:** Rutgers University at Newark, Montclair University, Kean University, New Jersey Institute of Technology.

Basis for selection. Open admission, but selective for some programs. Special requirements for allied health programs. Priority given to allied health program applications received by April 15. National League for Nursing test required of nursing students. Interview recommended for nursing, ophthalmic science, physical therapy programs. **Adult students:** Companion Placement Test required.

2008-2009 Annual costs. Tuition/fees: $3,765; $6,615 out-of-district; $6,615 out-of-state. Per-credit charge: $95 in-district; $190 out-of-district; $190 out-of-state. Books/supplies: $1,000. Personal expenses: $1,061.

Financial aid. Need-based: Need-based aid available for part-time students.

Application procedures. Admission: No deadline. $25 fee, may be waived for applicants with need. Admission notification on a rolling basis. **Financial aid:** Priority date 6/30; no closing date. FAFSA, institutional form required. Applicants notified on a rolling basis starting 6/15; must reply within 3 week(s) of notification.

Academics. Special study options: Cooperative education, cross-registration, double major, dual enrollment of high school students, ESL, honors, independent study, internships, teacher certification program. Cross-registration with other institutions in Council of Higher Education in Newark; civil construction engineering program with New Jersey Institute of Technology; criminal justice program with Rutgers: State University of New Jersey. License preparation in nursing, physical therapy, radiology. **Credit/placement by examination:** AP, CLEP, institutional tests. 30 credit hours maximum toward associate degree. Maximum credits accepted must be 30 credits less than number required for degree at Essex County College; may not include more than half credits required in major field. **Support services:** GED preparation and test center, learning center, reduced course load, remedial instruction, study skills assistance, tutoring, writing center.

Majors. Biology: General. **Business:** Accounting, accounting technology, administrative services, business admin, hospitality admin, office technology, tourism/travel. **Communications:** Journalism, media studies. **Computer sciences:** General, programming. **Education:** General, elementary, kindergarten/preschool, music, physical, secondary. **Engineering:** General, civil, electrical. **Engineering technology:** Architectural, civil, construction, electrical, manufacturing, surveying. **Health:** Dental hygiene, EMT paramedic, health care admin, health services, medical radiologic technology/radiation therapy, medical secretary, nursing (RN), optician, physical therapy assistant, premedicine, respiratory therapy technology. **Legal studies:** Paralegal. **Liberal arts:** Arts/sciences. **Math:** General. **Physical sciences:** Chemistry. **Protective services:** Criminal justice, firefighting, law enforcement admin, police science. **Public administration:** Human services, social work. **Science technology:** Chemical. **Social sciences:** General. **Visual/performing arts:** Art, commercial/advertising art, dramatic, studio arts, theater design.

Most popular majors. Business/marketing 19%, education 14%, health sciences 21%, liberal arts 14%, security/protective services 6%, social sciences 8%.

Computing on campus. 870 workstations in library, computer center. Commuter students can connect to campus network. Online course registration available.

Student life. Freshman orientation: Available. Preregistration for classes offered. **Activities:** Choral groups, drama, music ensembles, musical theater, student government, student newspaper, French club, Islamic student organization, Latin student union, Distributive Education Club of America, criminal justice organization, black student association, social science club, fashion entertainment board, Phi Theta Kappa.

Athletics. NJCAA. **Intercollegiate:** Basketball, soccer M, track and field. **Intramural:** Basketball, table tennis, volleyball. **Team name:** Wolverines.

Student services. Alcohol/substance abuse counseling, career counseling, student employment services, financial aid counseling, on-campus daycare, personal counseling, placement for graduates, veterans' counselor, women's services. **Physically disabled:** Services for visually, speech, hearing impaired. **Transfer:** Transfer center, transfer adviser, college fairs on campus for students transferring to 4-year colleges.

Contact. Phone: (973) 877-3100 Fax: (973) 623-6449
Marva Mack, Director of Admissions, Essex County College, 303 University Avenue, Newark, NJ 07102

Gloucester County College

Sewell, New Jersey — **CB member**
www.gccnj.edu — **CB code: 2281**

- Public 2-year community college
- Commuter campus in large town

General. Founded in 1966. Regionally accredited. **Enrollment:** 5,698 degree-seeking undergraduates. **Degrees:** 668 associate awarded. **Location:** 12 miles from Camden, 16 miles from Philadelphia. **Calendar:** Semester, limited summer session. **Full-time faculty:** 69 total. **Part-time faculty:** 239 total. **Special facilities:** Satellite downlink dish, learning resource center, 60-station computer room for multimedia course delivery and Internet access, interactive television (ITV) distance learning classroom.

Student profile.

Out-of-state:	1%	25 or older:	55%

Transfer out. Colleges most students transferred to 2008: Rowan University, Rutgers University, Richard Stockton College of New Jersey, Drexel University.

Basis for selection. Open admission, but selective for some programs. Special requirements for certain programs including allied health and automotive technology programs. Special-need students, deaf or hearing-impaired evaluated for support college can offer. Institutional placement tests may be used. **Homeschooled:** Eligible, but admission determined on individual basis.

High school preparation. Biology and chemistry required for nursing applicants. Algebra also required for respiratory therapy, nuclear medicine, and diagnostic medical sonography applicants.

2008-2009 Annual costs. Tuition/fees: $2,985; $3,090 out-of-district; $5,610 out-of-state. Per-credit charge: $80 in-district; $84 out-of-district; $168 out-of-state. Books/supplies: $1,000. Personal expenses: $800.

2007-2008 Financial aid. All financial aid based on need. 69% of total undergraduate aid awarded as scholarships/grants, 31% as loans/jobs. Need-based aid available for part-time students. Work-study available nights and for part-time students.

Application procedures. Admission: No deadline. $20 fee, may be waived for applicants with need. Admission notification on a rolling basis beginning on or about 2/28. Application closing dates for selective admission programs vary per program. **Financial aid:** Priority date 5/1; no closing date. FAFSA, institutional form required. Applicants notified on a rolling basis starting 3/20.

Academics. Through New Jersey Virtual Community College Consortium, students can take online courses from any New Jersey community college and receive GCC credit at no extra cost. **Special study options:** Cooperative education, distance learning, dual enrollment of high school students, internships. License preparation in nursing. **Credit/placement by examination:** CLEP, institutional tests. 16 credit hours maximum toward associate degree. **Support services:** GED preparation and test center, learning center, pre-admission summer program, reduced course load, study skills assistance, tutoring.

Majors. Biology: General. **Business:** General, accounting, administrative services, business admin, finance, hospitality admin, marketing, office management, office technology, office/clerical, sales/distribution. **Communications:** General, journalism. **Computer sciences:** General, computer graphics, computer science, data processing, LAN/WAN management, web page design. **Education:** General, early childhood, multi-level teacher, physical, special. **Engineering:** General, science. **Engineering technology:** Civil, drafting, surveying. **Health:** Medical secretary, nuclear medical technology, nursing (RN), respiratory therapy technology, sonography. **History:** General. **Interdisciplinary:** Biological/physical sciences, math/computer science. **Legal studies:** Legal secretary, paralegal. **Liberal arts:** Arts/sciences. **Math:** General. **Mechanic/repair:** Automotive. **Parks/recreation:** Exercise sciences, health/fitness. **Physical sciences:** General, chemistry. **Protective services:** Police science. **Psychology:** General. **Social sciences:** Political science, sociology. **Visual/performing arts:** Art, commercial/advertising art, dramatic.

Computing on campus. 750 workstations in library, computer center. Online course registration, online library available.

Student life. Freshman orientation: Available. **Activities:** Choral groups, drama, literary magazine, musical theater, radio station, student government, student newspaper, student activities board, student government association, human services club, Equal Opportunity club, Phi Theta Kappa, paralegal club.

Athletics. NJCAA. **Intercollegiate:** Baseball M, basketball, cross-country, soccer, softball W, tennis, track and field, wrestling M. **Intramural:** Golf, volleyball.

Student services. Career counseling, services for economically disadvantaged, student employment services, financial aid counseling, health services, on-campus daycare, veterans' counselor. **Physically disabled:** Services for visually, speech, hearing impaired. **Transfer:** Pre-admission transcript evaluation for new students. Transfer adviser, college fairs on campus for students transferring to 4-year colleges.

Contact. Phone: (856) 415-2209 Fax: (856) 468-8498
Judith Atkinson, Director of Admissions, Gloucester County College, 1400 Tanyard Road, Sewell, NJ 08080

Hudson County Community College

Jersey City, New Jersey — **CB member**
www.hccc.edu — **CB code: 2291**

- Public 2-year community college
- Commuter campus in large city

General. Founded in 1974. Regionally accredited. **Enrollment:** 7,525 degree-seeking undergraduates. **Degrees:** 534 associate awarded. **Location:** 10 miles from New York City. **Calendar:** Semester, limited summer session. **Full-time faculty:** 84 total. **Part-time faculty:** 281 total. **Special facilities:** Culinary arts classroom, conference center.

Student profile.

Out-of-state:	2%	25 or older:	45%

Transfer out. Colleges most students transferred to 2008: New Jersey City University, St. Peter's College.

Basis for selection. Open admission. High school diploma required if applicant is less than 18 years of age.

2008-2009 Annual costs. Tuition/fees: $3,753; $6,543 out-of-district; $9,333 out-of-state. Per-credit charge: $93 in-district; $186 out-of-district; $279 out-of-state. Books/supplies: $800. Personal expenses: $1,500.

2007-2008 Financial aid. All financial aid based on need. Need-based aid available for part-time students.

Application procedures. Admission: No deadline. $15 fee, may be waived for applicants with need. Application must be submitted on paper. Admission notification on a rolling basis. **Financial aid:** Priority date 7/15; no closing date. FAFSA required. Applicants notified on a rolling basis starting 6/1; must reply within 1 week(s) of notification.

Academics. Students may earn second degree by completing 24 additional credits, including all requirements for second major. **Special study options:** Cross-registration, distance learning, dual enrollment of high school students, ESL, honors, independent study, internships, liberal arts/career combination, teacher certification program, weekend college. License preparation in nursing, paramedic. **Credit/placement by examination:** AP, CLEP, IB, institutional tests. 12 credit hours maximum toward associate degree. **Support services:** Pre-admission summer program, reduced course load, remedial instruction, study skills assistance, tutoring, writing center.

Majors. Business: Accounting, administrative services, business admin, hospitality admin, management information systems. **Computer sciences:** Computer science, data processing. **Education:** Early childhood. **Engineering:** Science. **Engineering technology:** Computer systems, electrical. **Family/consumer sciences:** Child care. **Health:** Medical assistant, medical records technology, respiratory therapy technology. **History:** General. **Legal studies:** Paralegal. **Liberal arts:** Arts/sciences. **Math:** General. **Personal/**

Two-Year Colleges

culinary services:** Chef training, culinary arts, mortuary science. **Physical sciences:** Chemistry. **Protective services:** Criminal justice. **Social sciences:** Sociology.

Most popular majors. Business/marketing 14%, computer/information sciences 6%, health sciences 18%, legal studies 8%, liberal arts 54%.

Computing on campus. 645 workstations in library, computer center. Commuter students can connect to campus network. Online library, wireless network available.

Student life. Freshman orientation: Mandatory. Preregistration for classes offered. **Activities:** Drama, film society, international student organizations, literary magazine, student government, student newspaper, South Asian society, black history and art society, law club, French club, Hispanos Unidos para el Progreso, women's awareness organization, hospitality club, health information and technology club, medical assisting club.

Student services. Adult student services, career counseling, student employment services, financial aid counseling, personal counseling, placement for graduates, veterans' counselor. **Physically disabled:** Services for visually, speech, hearing impaired. **Transfer:** Pre-admission transcript evaluation for new students. Transfer center, transfer adviser, college fairs on campus for students transferring to 4-year colleges.

Contact. E-mail: admissions@hccc.edu
Phone: (201) 714-7200 Fax: (201) 714-2136
Nelson Vieira, Director of Admissions, Hudson County Community College, 70 Sip Avenue, 1st Floor, Jersey City, NJ 07306

Mercer County Community College

Trenton, New Jersey — **CB member**
www.mccc.edu — **CB code: 2444**

- Public 2-year community college
- Commuter campus in small city

General. Founded in 1966. Regionally accredited. Courses also available at downtown Trenton location. External degree program for military service members. **Enrollment:** 8,138 degree-seeking undergraduates. **Degrees:** 807 associate awarded. **Location:** 35 miles from Philadelphia, 60 miles from New York City. **Calendar:** Semester, extensive summer session. **Full-time faculty:** 138 total. **Part-time faculty:** 395 total. **Class size:** 45% < 20, 53% 20-39, less than 1% 40-49, 1% 50-99. **Special facilities:** CAD laboratory, computer graphics laboratory, greenhouse complex, mortuary science lab.

Student profile.

Out-of-state:	2%	**25 or older:**	29%

Transfer out. Colleges most students transferred to 2008: The College of New Jersey, Rider University, Rutgers University, Rowan University, Thomas Edison State College.

Basis for selection. Open admission. Applicants without high school diploma or GED must be 18 or older and have completed the New Jersey Basic Skills Placement Examination. Designation of provisional status dependent on skills scores and/or high school units. Interview required for nursing and funeral service programs; recommended for all others.

2008-2009 Annual costs. Tuition/fees: $3,345; $4,485 out-of-district; $6,765 out-of-state. Per-credit charge: $112 in-district; $150 out-of-district; $226 out-of-state. Books/supplies: $920. Personal expenses: $1,700.

2007-2008 Financial aid. Need-based: Need-based aid available for part-time students. Work-study available nights and for part-time students. **Non-need-based:** Scholarships awarded for academics, athletics, state residency.

Application procedures. Admission: No deadline. No application fee. Admission notification on a rolling basis. **Financial aid:** No deadline. FAFSA required. Applicants notified on a rolling basis.

Academics. Cross-registration with area hospitals for nursing. **Special study options:** Cooperative education, cross-registration, distance learning, double major, dual enrollment of high school students, ESL, external degree, independent study, internships, liberal arts/career combination, weekend college. License preparation in aviation, nursing, occupational therapy, physical therapy, radiology. **Credit/placement by examination:** AP, CLEP, institutional tests. 45 credit hours maximum toward associate degree. **Support services:** GED preparation and test center, learning center, preadmission summer program, reduced course load, remedial instruction, study skills assistance, tutoring, writing center.

Majors. Agriculture: Ornamental horticulture, plant sciences. **Architecture:** Technology. **Biology:** General. **Business:** General, accounting, administrative services, business admin, management information systems. **Communications technology:** General. **Computer sciences:** Networking. **Engineering technology:** Architectural, civil, electrical. **Health:** Clinical lab technology, medical radiologic technology/radiation therapy, nursing (RN), physical therapy assistant, respiratory therapy technology. **Legal studies:** Paralegal. **Liberal arts:** Arts/sciences. **Math:** General. **Mechanic/repair:** Aircraft, automotive. **Personal/culinary services:** Culinary arts, mortuary science. **Protective services:** Fire safety technology, police science. **Public administration:** Human services. **Science technology:** Biological. **Transportation:** Aviation, aviation management, flight attendant. **Visual/performing arts:** General, commercial/advertising art.

Most popular majors. Business/marketing 18%, health sciences 20%, liberal arts 21%, security/protective services 6%, visual/performing arts 8%.

Computing on campus. 1,100 workstations in library, computer center. Commuter students can connect to campus network. Online course registration, online library, helpline, wireless network available.

Student life. Freshman orientation: Available. Preregistration for classes offered. **Activities:** Bands, choral groups, dance, drama, international student organizations, literary magazine, music ensembles, musical theater, radio station, student government, student newspaper, TV station, Christian Fellowship, bilingual club, African-American student organization, Fuerza Latina, ecology club, educational opportunity fund club, gay/straight alliance.

Athletics. NJCAA. **Intercollegiate:** Baseball M, basketball, soccer, softball W, tennis, track and field. **Intramural:** Basketball, softball, volleyball. **Team name:** Vikings.

Student services. Adult student services, career counseling, services for economically disadvantaged, student employment services, financial aid counseling, minority student services, personal counseling, placement for graduates, veterans' counselor. **Physically disabled:** Services for visually, speech, hearing impaired. **Transfer:** Transfer center, transfer adviser, college fairs on campus for students transferring to 4-year colleges.

Contact. E-mail: admiss@mccc.edu
Phone: (609) 570-3795 Fax: (609) 570-3861
Joan Guggenheim, Registrar, Enrollment Services, Mercer County Community College, Box B, Trenton, NJ 08690-1099

Middlesex County College

Edison, New Jersey — **CB member**
www.middlesexcc.edu — **CB code: 2441**

- Public 2-year community college
- Commuter campus in small city

General. Founded in 1964. Regionally accredited. **Enrollment:** 12,406 undergraduates. **Degrees:** 1,059 associate awarded. **ROTC:** Army. **Location:** 5 miles from New Brunswick, 30 miles from New York City. **Calendar:** Semester, extensive summer session. **Full-time faculty:** 198 total. **Part-time faculty:** 500 total. **Class size:** 23% < 20, 77% 20-39, less than 1% 40-49, less than 1% >100. **Special facilities:** Ecological walking path.

Student profile.

Out-of-state:	2%	**25 or older:**	35%

Transfer out. Colleges most students transferred to 2008: Rutgers State University, New Jersey Institute of Technology, Montclair State University, Kean University, Farleigh Dickinson University.

Basis for selection. Open admission, but selective for some programs. Special requirements for dental hygiene, nursing, radiography, respiratory care, psychosocial rehabilitation and treatment, medical laboratory technology, automotive technology programs. Allied Health Aptitude Test required for radiography education, dental hygiene and respiratory care applicants. National League of Nursing Exam (NLN) required for nursing applicants. **Learning Disabled:** Must submit separate application to Project Connections Office to be eligible for learning disabilities program.

High school preparation. Recommended units include English 4, mathematics 3, social studies 2, history 2, science 3 (laboratory 3) and foreign language 2. Math and science units required for some programs.

2008-2009 Annual costs. Tuition/fees: $3,645; $6,375 out-of-district; $6,375 out-of-state. Per-credit charge: $91 in-district; $182 out-of-district; $182 out-of-state. Out-of-county and out-of-state students pay additional $915 in required fees. Books/supplies: $1,162. Personal expenses: $1,643.

Financial aid. **Need-based:** Need-based aid available for part-time students. Work-study available for part-time students.

Application procedures. **Admission:** Priority date 8/1; no deadline. $25 fee, may be waived for applicants with need. Admission notification on a rolling basis. **Financial aid:** Priority date 4/1; no closing date. FAFSA, institutional form required. Applicants notified on a rolling basis starting 5/4.

Academics. **Special study options:** Cooperative education, cross-registration, distance learning, double major, dual enrollment of high school students, ESL, independent study, internships, study abroad. License preparation in dental hygiene, nursing. **Credit/placement by examination:** CLEP, institutional tests. 45 credit hours maximum toward associate degree. **Support services:** Learning center, pre-admission summer program, reduced course load, remedial instruction, tutoring.

Majors. **Business:** Accounting, business admin, fashion, office management. **Communications:** General, journalism. **Computer sciences:** General, computer graphics, programming. **Education:** General, teacher assistance. **Engineering:** Civil, science. **Engineering technology:** Civil, electrical, manufacturing, surveying. **Health:** Clinical lab technology, dental hygiene, nursing (RN), pharmacy assistant, respiratory therapy technology. **Legal studies:** Paralegal. **Mechanic/repair:** Automotive. **Parks/recreation:** Health/fitness. **Physical sciences:** Chemistry, physics. **Protective services:** Corrections, firefighting, law enforcement admin. **Science technology:** Biological. **Social sciences:** Political science, sociology. **Visual/performing arts:** Commercial photography, commercial/advertising art, dance, dramatic, music performance, studio arts.

Computing on campus. 1,255 workstations in library, computer center. Commuter students can connect to campus network. Online library, helpline available.

Student life. **Freshman orientation:** Available. Preregistration for classes offered. One-day program scheduled 1 week prior to start of classes. **Activities:** Jazz band, choral groups, dance, drama, literary magazine, music ensembles, musical theater, radio station, student government, student newspaper, Third World student association, Hispanic club, foreign student association.

Athletics. NJCAA. **Intercollegiate:** Baseball M, basketball, cross-country, golf, soccer, softball W, track and field, wrestling M. **Team name:** Blue Colts.

Student services. Alcohol/substance abuse counseling, career counseling, student employment services, financial aid counseling, health services, minority student services, on-campus daycare, personal counseling, placement for graduates, veterans' counselor. **Physically disabled:** Services for visually, speech, hearing impaired. **Transfer:** Transfer adviser, college fairs on campus for students transferring to 4-year colleges.

Contact. E-mail: admissions@middlesexcc.edu
Phone: (732) 906-4243 Toll-free number: (888) 968-4622
Fax: (732) 956-7728
Aretha Watson, Assistant Dean Admissions, Middlesex County College, 2600 Woodbridge Avenue, Edison, NJ 08818-3050

Ocean County College

Toms River, New Jersey
www.ocean.edu **CB code: 2630**

- Public 2-year community college
- Commuter campus in small city

General. Founded in 1964. Regionally accredited. Off-campus sites at 13 locations in Ocean County. **Enrollment:** 8,610 degree-seeking undergraduates. **Degrees:** 1,055 associate awarded. **Location:** 60 miles from Philadelphia, 80 miles from New York City. **Calendar:** Semester, extensive summer session. **Full-time faculty:** 107 total; 8% minority, 62% women. **Part-time faculty:** 378 total; 7% minority, 52% women. **Special facilities:** Planetarium, fine arts theater. **Partnerships:** Formal partnerships through Jump Start program that allows high school juniors/seniors to enroll for college credits.

Student profile. Among degree-seeking undergraduates, 334 transferred in from other institutions.

Transfer out. **Colleges most students transferred to 2008:** Georgian Court College, Richard Stockton College of New Jersey, Rutgers University, Rowan University, Kean University.

Basis for selection. Open admission, but selective for some programs. Admission to nursing, medical laboratory technology, honors programs based on test scores and academic record. SAT or ACT required of nursing and honors program applicants. Score report by May 30. **Learning Disabled:** Students invited to share learning disability needs with Disability Resource Center, which then makes appropriate accommodations.

High school preparation. Algebra, chemistry, biology required of nursing applicants.

2008-2009 Annual costs. Tuition/fees: $4,440; $5,460 out-of-district; $7,860 out-of-state. Per-credit charge: $120 in-district; $154 out-of-district; $234 out-of-state. Books/supplies: $1,000. Personal expenses: $2,500.

2008-2009 Financial aid. All financial aid based on need. 62% of total undergraduate aid awarded as scholarships/grants, 38% as loans/jobs. Need-based aid available for part-time students.

Application procedures. **Admission:** No deadline. No application fee. Admission notification on a rolling basis beginning on or about 11/1. **Financial aid:** Priority date 5/31; no closing date. FAFSA required. Applicants notified on a rolling basis starting 7/15; must reply within 1 week(s) of notification.

Academics. **Special study options:** Combined bachelor's/graduate degree, distance learning, dual enrollment of high school students, ESL, honors, independent study, internships, liberal arts/career combination, study abroad. Bachelor's degree programs available on campus. License preparation in aviation, nursing. **Credit/placement by examination:** AP, CLEP, institutional tests. 30 credit hours maximum toward associate degree. **Support services:** GED test center, learning center, reduced course load, remedial instruction, study skills assistance, tutoring, writing center.

Honors college/program. For liberal arts students only; admission based on GPA, test scores, class rank, interview.

Majors. **Agriculture:** Horticulture. **Business:** General, business admin. **Communications:** Broadcast journalism, journalism. **Communications technology:** General, photo/film/video. **Computer sciences:** General, computer science, LAN/WAN management. **Conservation:** Environmental science. **Engineering:** General. **Engineering technology:** Civil, environmental, surveying. **Family/consumer sciences:** Child care. **Foreign languages:** Sign language interpretation. **Health:** Histologic assistant, nursing (RN). **Legal studies:** Paralegal. **Liberal arts:** Arts/sciences. **Protective services:** Fire safety technology, police science. **Public administration:** Human services, social work. **Science technology:** Biological. **Visual/performing arts:** Art. **Other:** Visual communications technology.

Computing on campus. 500 workstations in library, computer center. Commuter students can connect to campus network. Online library, helpline available.

Student life. **Freshman orientation:** Available. Preregistration for classes offered. **Activities:** Bands, choral groups, dance, drama, literary magazine, musical theater, radio station, student government, student newspaper, TV station, Circle K, student life program board, Phi Theta Kappa, veterans club, student health organization, Organization for Black Unity, women's network, South Asian American student association, students learning about politics club, sign language society.

Athletics. NJCAA. **Intercollegiate:** Baseball M, basketball, golf, soccer, softball W, swimming, tennis. **Intramural:** Basketball, swimming, volleyball. **Team name:** Vikings.

Student services. Alcohol/substance abuse counseling, career counseling, services for economically disadvantaged, student employment services, financial aid counseling, health services, minority student services, on-campus daycare, personal counseling, placement for graduates, veterans' counselor, women's services. **Physically disabled:** Services for visually, speech, hearing impaired. **Learning disabled:** Comprehensive services available. **Transfer:** Re-entry adviser, pre-admission transcript evaluation for new students. Transfer adviser, college fairs on campus for students transferring to 4-year colleges.

Contact. E-mail: mfennessy@ocean.edu
Phone: (732) 255-0304 Fax: (732) 255-0444
Mary Fennessy, Director of Admissions and Records, Ocean County College, College Drive, Toms River, NJ 08754-2001

Passaic County Community College

Paterson, New Jersey **CB member**
www.pccc.edu **CB code: 2694**

- Public 2-year community college
- Commuter campus in small city

General. Founded in 1968. Regionally accredited. **Enrollment:** 7,902 degree-seeking undergraduates. **Degrees:** 373 associate awarded. **Location:** 15 miles

from New York City. **Calendar:** Semester, limited summer session. **Full-time faculty:** 99 total. **Part-time faculty:** 328 total. **Class size:** 59% < 20, 40% 20-39, less than 1% 40-49. **Special facilities:** 2 art galleries, playhouse, poetry center.

Transfer out. Colleges most students transferred to 2008: William Paterson University, Rutgers University, Montclair State University, Bergen County College, Kean University.

Basis for selection. Open admission, but selective for some programs. Special requirements for nursing and other allied health programs. Interview recommended.

2008-2009 Annual costs. Tuition/fees: $3,410; $6,065 out-of-state. Per-credit charge: $89 in-state; $177 out-of-state. Additional course fees up to maximum of $790 per year (excluding nursing and radiography). Books/supplies: $839. Personal expenses: $978.

2007-2008 Financial aid. Need-based: Need-based aid available for part-time students. **Non-need-based:** Scholarships awarded for academics. **Additional information:** Limited scholarship funds available for low income students eligible for federal or state aid.

Application procedures. Admission: No deadline. No application fee. Admission notification on a rolling basis. Early admissions available to high school students based on decisions made by high school guidance counselor and college's director of admissions. **Financial aid:** Priority date 8/1; no closing date. FAFSA, CSS PROFILE required. Applicants notified on a rolling basis starting 8/1; must reply within 2 week(s) of notification.

Academics. Special study options: Cooperative education, cross-registration, distance learning, double major, dual enrollment of high school students, ESL, honors, independent study, internships, liberal arts/career combination, student-designed major, study abroad, weekend college. License preparation in nursing. **Credit/placement by examination:** AP, CLEP, institutional tests. 12 credit hours maximum toward associate degree. New Jersey Basic Skills test required for placement. **Support services:** Learning center, reduced course load, remedial instruction, study skills assistance, tutoring, writing center.

Majors. Business: General, accounting, administrative services, management information systems, marketing, sales/distribution. **Communications:** General. **Computer sciences:** General, applications programming. **Education:** Early childhood. **Engineering:** Science. **Engineering technology:** Electrical. **Health:** Medical radiologic technology/radiation therapy, nursing (RN), respiratory therapy technology. **Liberal arts:** Arts/sciences. **Math:** General. **Protective services:** Police science. **Psychology:** General. **Public administration:** Human services. **Social sciences:** Sociology.

Computing on campus. 900 workstations in computer center.

Student life. Freshman orientation: Mandatory. Preregistration for classes offered. **Activities:** International student organizations, student government, student newspaper, Latin American club, Newman Club, Organization of African Ancestry, earth awareness, fashion awareness, veterans club, Phi Theta Kappa, photography club, Arabic club, poetry club.

Athletics. NJCAA. **Intercollegiate:** Basketball, soccer M. **Intramural:** Basketball M, volleyball W. **Team name:** Panthers.

Student services. Adult student services, career counseling, services for economically disadvantaged, student employment services, financial aid counseling, minority student services, on-campus daycare, personal counseling, placement for graduates, veterans' counselor, women's services. **Transfer:** Transfer adviser, college fairs on campus for students transferring to 4-year colleges.

Contact. Phone: (973) 684-6868 Fax: (973) 684-6778
Patrick Noonan, Director of Admission, Passaic County Community College, One College Boulevard, Paterson, NJ 07505-1179

Raritan Valley Community College

Somerville, New Jersey — **CB member**
www.raritanval.edu — **CB code: 2867**

- Public 2-year community college
- Commuter campus in large town

General. Founded in 1966. Regionally accredited. **Enrollment:** 5,824 degree-seeking undergraduates; 1,286 non-degree-seeking students. **Degrees:** 617 associate awarded. **ROTC:** Army, Air Force. **Location:** 36 miles from New York City. **Calendar:** Semester, extensive summer session. **Full-time faculty:** 105 total; 38% have terminal degrees, 10% minority, 58% women. **Part-time faculty:** 311 total; 22% have terminal degrees, 13% minority, 51% women. **Special facilities:** Planetarium, professional theater. **Partnerships:** Formal partnership with area high schools for articulated credit program.

Student profile. Among degree-seeking undergraduates, 52% enrolled in a transfer program, 48% enrolled in a vocational program, 3% already have a bachelor's degree or higher, 1,458 enrolled as first-time, first-year students, 424 transferred in from other institutions.

Part-time:	44%	**Asian American:**	6%
Out-of-state:	1%	**Hispanic American:**	10%
Women:	53%	**International:**	2%
African American:	8%		

Transfer out. Colleges most students transferred to 2008: Rutgers State University, Kean University, Montclair State University, College of New Jersey, Rider University.

Basis for selection. Open admission, but selective for some programs. Special requirements for nursing program; interview recommended. Matriculated students must take New Jersey Basic Skills Placement Test. **Home-schooled:** Must provide home school portfolio.

2008-2009 Annual costs. Tuition/fees: $3,610. Per-credit charge: $91. Books/supplies: $800. Personal expenses: $1,000.

2008-2009 Financial aid. Need-based: Average scholarship/grant was $2,497; average loan $3,139. 82% of total undergraduate aid awarded as scholarships/grants, 18% as loans/jobs. Need-based aid available for part-time students. Work-study available for part-time students. **Non-need-based:** Scholarships awarded for academics.

Application procedures. Admission: No deadline. $25 fee, may be waived for applicants with need. Admission notification on a rolling basis. **Financial aid:** No deadline. FAFSA required. Applicants notified on a rolling basis starting 4/1.

Academics. Special study options: Accelerated study, cooperative education, distance learning, double major, dual enrollment of high school students, ESL, external degree, honors, independent study, weekend college. Service learning. Bachelor's degree programs available on campus. License preparation in nursing. **Credit/placement by examination:** AP, CLEP, institutional tests. 45 credit hours maximum toward associate degree. **Support services:** GED test center, learning center, pre-admission summer program, remedial instruction, study skills assistance, tutoring, writing center.

Majors. Biology: Biotechnology. **Business:** General, accounting technology, business admin, marketing. **Communications:** Digital media. **Communications technology:** Animation/special effects. **Computer sciences:** Data processing, information technology. **Education:** General, early childhood, elementary, secondary. **Engineering:** Science. **Engineering technology:** Automotive, construction, heat/ac/refrig, manufacturing. **Health:** Nursing (RN), optician. **Legal studies:** Paralegal. **Liberal arts:** Arts/sciences. **Mechanic/repair:** Diesel. **Protective services:** Law enforcement admin. **Visual/performing arts:** Dance, interior design, studio arts, theater design.

Computing on campus. 844 workstations in library, computer center, student center. Commuter students can connect to campus network. Online course registration, online library, helpline, wireless network available.

Student life. Freshman orientation: Available. Preregistration for classes offered. **Activities:** Dance, drama, international student organizations, student government, student newspaper, Club Black; Latino, Asian, Caucasian Kollaboration; students for environmental awareness; BLGT club; Christian Fellowship; Islamic culture association; performing artist club; Latino/Latin pride club; social justice club.

Athletics. NJCAA. **Intercollegiate:** Baseball M, basketball, golf, soccer M, softball W. **Intramural:** Basketball, softball W, volleyball. **Team name:** Golden Lions.

Student services. Adult student services, alcohol/substance abuse counseling, career counseling, student employment services, financial aid counseling, on-campus daycare, personal counseling, placement for graduates, veterans' counselor. **Physically disabled:** Services for visually, hearing impaired. **Transfer:** Re-entry adviser, pre-admission transcript evaluation for new students. Transfer center, transfer adviser, college fairs on campus for students transferring to 4-year colleges.

Contact. E-mail: registrar@raritanval.edu
Phone: (908) 526-1200 Fax: (908) 704-3442
Mary O'Malley, Executive Director, Enrollment Services, Raritan Valley Community College, PO Box 3300, Somerville, NJ 08876-1265

Salem Community College
Carneys Point, New Jersey **CB member**
www.salemcc.edu **CB code: 2868**

- Public 2-year community college
- Commuter campus in small town

General. Founded in 1972. Regionally accredited. **Enrollment:** 898 degree-seeking undergraduates; 401 non-degree-seeking students. **Degrees:** 144 associate awarded. **Location:** 25 miles from Philadelphia. **Calendar:** Semester, limited summer session. **Full-time faculty:** 26 total; 15% have terminal degrees, 8% minority, 50% women. **Part-time faculty:** 64 total. **Special facilities:** Glass art and scientific glass technology laboratories, computer graphic arts lab.

Student profile. Among degree-seeking undergraduates, 295 enrolled as first-time, first-year students.

Part-time:	30%	**Hispanic American:**	4%
Out-of-state:	10%	**Native American:**	1%
Women:	60%	**International:**	2%
African American:	15%	**25 or older:**	28%
Asian American:	1%		

Transfer out. Colleges most students transferred to 2008: Rowan University, Wilmington College, Gloucester County College, Rutgers University, Cumberland County College.

Basis for selection. Open admission, but selective for some programs. Licensed Practical Nursing applicants must complete 6 prerequisite courses with C+ or higher grade in each course. In addition to 5 of the 6 Licensed Practical Nursing prerequisites, Registered Nursing applicants must complete 4 more prerequisites with C+ or higher grade in each course. Both programs require high school diploma or GED. Interview suggested for scientific glassblowing and glass art programs. **Learning Disabled:** Students must file release form and documentation of disability to be granted special accommodations.

2008-2009 Annual costs. Tuition/fees: $3,515; $3,815 out-of-state. Per-credit charge: $87 in-state; $97 out-of-state. Books/supplies: $975. Personal expenses: $1,150.

2007-2008 Financial aid. Need-based: Need-based aid available for part-time students. Work-study available for part-time students. **Non-need-based:** Scholarships awarded for academics, athletics, state residency.

Application procedures. Admission: No deadline. $25 fee, may be waived for applicants with need. Application must be submitted on paper. Admission notification on a rolling basis. **Financial aid:** Priority date 6/1; no closing date. FAFSA, institutional form required. Applicants notified on a rolling basis starting 4/1; must reply within 2 week(s) of notification.

Academics. Special study options: Cooperative education, distance learning, double major, dual enrollment of high school students, ESL, honors, independent study, internships, teacher certification program. License preparation in nursing. **Credit/placement by examination:** AP, CLEP, institutional tests. 30 credit hours maximum toward associate degree. **Support services:** GED preparation and test center, learning center, pre-admission summer program, reduced course load, remedial instruction, study skills assistance, tutoring, writing center.

Majors. Biology: Biotechnology. **Business:** Business admin. **Communications:** Journalism. **Computer sciences:** Computer graphics, computer science. **Education:** General, early childhood. **Engineering technology:** Energy systems, industrial. **Health:** Health services, nursing (RN). **History:** General. **Liberal arts:** Arts/sciences, humanities. **Math:** General. **Parks/recreation:** Health/fitness. **Physical sciences:** Chemistry, physics. **Protective services:** Forensics. **Psychology:** General. **Public administration:** Community org/advocacy. **Social sciences:** General, criminology, political science, sociology. **Visual/performing arts:** Industrial design. **Other:** Food processing technology, Glass art, Scientific glass technology.

Most popular majors. Business/marketing 11%, health sciences 23%, liberal arts 60%.

Computing on campus. 300 workstations in library, computer center. Commuter students can connect to campus network. Online library, helpline available.

Student life. Freshman orientation: Available. Preregistration for classes offered. Held at beginning of semester. **Activities:** Choral groups, drama, student government, Chi Alpha Epsilon, Educational Opportunity Fund Students, institutional diversity committee, Phi Theta Kappa, multicultural club.

Athletics. NJCAA. **Intercollegiate:** Baseball M, basketball, golf M, soccer W, softball W. **Team name:** Oaks.

Student services. Adult student services, career counseling, services for economically disadvantaged, student employment services, financial aid counseling, minority student services, personal counseling, veterans' counselor. **Physically disabled:** Services for visually, speech, hearing impaired. **Transfer:** Re-entry adviser, pre-admission transcript evaluation for new students. Transfer center, transfer adviser, college fairs on campus for students transferring to 4-year colleges.

Contact. E-mail: sccinfo@salemcc.edu
Phone: (856) 351-2703 Fax: (856) 299-9193
Lynn Fishlock, Director of Admissions and Records, Salem Community College, 460 Hollywood Avenue, Carneys Point, NJ 08069-2799

Sussex County Community College
Newton, New Jersey **CB member**
www.sussex.edu **CB code: 2711**

- Public 2-year community college
- Commuter campus in small town

General. Founded in 1981. Regionally accredited. Extension sites at Sussex County Technical School, several area high schools, and other locations. **Enrollment:** 3,118 degree-seeking undergraduates; 631 non-degree-seeking students. **Degrees:** 400 associate awarded. **Location:** 70 miles from New York City. **Calendar:** Semester, limited summer session. **Full-time faculty:** 45 total. **Part-time faculty:** 240 total. **Special facilities:** 10 computer laboratories (including graphic design). **Partnerships:** Formal partnerships with Oracle database administration training program, Unix operating system training program, Cisco network training program.

Student profile. Among degree-seeking undergraduates, 960 enrolled as first-time, first-year students.

Part-time:	34%	**Hispanic American:**	5%
Out-of-state:	12%	**Native American:**	1%
Women:	55%	**International:**	1%
African American:	2%	**25 or older:**	24%
Asian American:	1%		

Transfer out. Colleges most students transferred to 2008: Montclair State University, William Paterson University of New Jersey, Rutgers University, Ramapo College of New Jersey, Centenary College.

Basis for selection. Open admission, but selective for some programs. Special requirements for the nursing program. Incoming freshmen must pass ACCUPLACER placement test for admission to program of study; those failing any part of test must satisfactorily complete remedial study in appropriate areas before being admitted to program.

2008-2009 Annual costs. Tuition/fees: $3,285; $5,955 out-of-state. Per-credit charge: $89 in-state; $178 out-of-state. Residents of Wayne, Monroe and Pike County (PA): $123 per credit hour. Books/supplies: $900. Personal expenses: $1,244.

Financial aid. All financial aid based on need. Need-based aid available for part-time students.

Application procedures. Admission: No deadline. $15 fee, may be waived for applicants with need. Application must be submitted on paper. Admission notification on a rolling basis. **Financial aid:** Closing date 6/1. FAFSA, institutional form required. Applicants notified on a rolling basis; must reply within 2 week(s) of notification.

Academics. Special study options: Distance learning, double major, dual enrollment of high school students, ESL, honors, independent study, internships, teacher certification program. Bachelor's degree programs available on campus. License preparation in nursing, paramedic. **Credit/placement by examination:** CLEP, IB, institutional tests. 30 credit hours maximum toward associate degree. **Support services:** GED preparation and test center, learning center, reduced course load, remedial instruction, study skills assistance, tutoring, writing center.

Majors. Biology: General. **Business:** Accounting, business admin. **Communications:** Journalism. **Computer sciences:** General, applications programming. **Conservation:** Environmental studies. **Education:** Early childhood, elementary, secondary. **Engineering:** General. **Engineering technology:** Automotive. **Health:** Clinical lab technology, health services, predental, premedicine, prepharmacy, respiratory therapy technology, veterinary technology/assistant. **Interdisciplinary:** Biological/physical sciences. **Legal studies:** Paralegal. **Liberal arts:** Arts/sciences. **Math:** General. **Mechanic/repair:** Automotive. **Physical sciences:** Chemistry. **Protective services:** Criminal justice, firefighting. **Psychology:** General. **Public administration:** Social work. **Social sciences:** General. **Visual/performing arts:** Art, commercial/advertising art, studio arts.

Computing on campus. 250 workstations in library, computer center, student center. Online library, wireless network available.

Student life. **Freshman orientation:** Available. Preregistration for classes offered. Half-day program held 2 days before start of classes. **Activities:** Concert band, campus ministries, choral groups, dance, drama, international student organizations, literary magazine, music ensembles, musical theater, opera, student government, student newspaper, symphony orchestra, TV station, student ambassadors, humanities club, arts club, broadcasting club, criminal justice club, law and justice society, Phi Theta Kappa, AIDS Brigade, lifestyles and diversity group, psychology club.

Athletics. NJCAA. **Intercollegiate:** Baseball M, basketball M, soccer, softball W. **Intramural:** Archery, badminton, basketball, soccer, softball, table tennis, volleyball. **Team name:** Skylanders.

Student services. Adult student services, career counseling, student employment services, financial aid counseling, personal counseling, placement for graduates, veterans' counselor, women's services. **Physically disabled:** Services for visually, speech, hearing impaired. **Transfer:** Pre-admission transcript evaluation for new students. Transfer adviser, college fairs on campus for students transferring to 4-year colleges.

Contact. E-mail: tpoltersdorf@sussex.edu
Phone: (973) 300-2216 Fax: (973) 579-5226
Todd Poltersdorf, Director of Admissions, Sussex County Community College, One College Hill Road, Newton, NJ 07860

Union County College
Cranford, New Jersey
www.ucc.edu **CB code: 2921**

- Public 2-year community college
- Commuter campus in large town

General. Founded in 1933. Regionally accredited. Branch campuses in Elizabeth, Plainfield, and Scotch Plains. **Enrollment:** 10,217 degree-seeking undergraduates; 1,649 non-degree-seeking students. **Degrees:** 770 associate awarded. **ROTC:** Air Force. **Location:** 20 miles from New York City. **Calendar:** Semester, extensive summer session. **Full-time faculty:** 180 total; 32% have terminal degrees, 21% minority, 58% women. **Part-time faculty:** 281 total; 17% have terminal degrees, 28% minority, 46% women. **Special facilities:** Observatory.

Student profile. Among degree-seeking undergraduates, 79% enrolled in a transfer program, 21% enrolled in a vocational program, 2,534 enrolled as first-time, first-year students, 449 transferred in from other institutions.

Part-time:	47%	**Hispanic American:**	28%
Out-of-state:	3%	**Native American:**	1%
Women:	65%	**International:**	2%
African American:	24%	**25 or older:**	34%
Asian American:	5%		

Transfer out. 54% of students enrolled in the transfer program go on to 4-year colleges. **Colleges most students transferred to 2008:** Kean University, Rutgers University, Montclair State University, Jersey City State University.

Basis for selection. Open admission, but selective for some programs. Special requirements for allied health and nursing programs. SAT required of dental hygiene program applicants; score report required by April. Essay, interview recommended for nursing, interpreter for the deaf programs.

High school preparation. 19 units recommended. Recommended units include English 4, mathematics 3, history 3, science 2 (laboratory 2), foreign language 2 and academic electives 5. Chemistry and biology required of health program applicants. Trigonometry, geometry, algebra, physics and chemistry required of engineering and physical science applicants. Level 3 proficiency in American Sign Language required of interpreter for the deaf program applicants. Algebra and geometry recommended for business majors.

2008-2009 Annual costs. Tuition/fees: $3,510; $6,210 out-of-district; $6,210 out-of-state. Per-credit charge: $90 in-district; $180 out-of-district; $180 out-of-state. Books/supplies: $2,100. Personal expenses: $1,500.

2007-2008 Financial aid. All financial aid based on need. 80% of total undergraduate aid awarded as scholarships/grants, 20% as loans/jobs. Need-based aid available for part-time students. Work-study available nights, weekends and for part-time students.

Application procedures. **Admission:** No deadline. $35 fee. Admission notification on a rolling basis. **Financial aid:** Priority date 5/1; no closing date. FAFSA, institutional form required. Must reply within 2 week(s) of notification.

Academics. **Special study options:** Accelerated study, cross-registration, distance learning, dual enrollment of high school students, ESL, honors, internships, liberal arts/career combination, weekend college. Dual admissions agreements with Rutgers University, Montclair State University, New Jersey Institute of Technology, New Jersey City University, Kean University, Fairleigh Dickinson University. License preparation in dental hygiene, nursing, paramedic, physical therapy, radiology. **Credit/placement by examination:** AP, CLEP, institutional tests. 32 credit hours maximum toward associate degree. **Support services:** GED preparation and test center, learning center, reduced course load, remedial instruction, study skills assistance, tutoring, writing center.

Majors. **Biology:** General. **Business:** General, accounting technology, administrative services, business admin, hospitality admin, marketing. **Communications:** Media studies. **Communications technology:** Animation/special effects, recording arts. **Computer sciences:** Computer science, information technology. **Engineering:** General. **Engineering technology:** Civil, electromechanical, mechanical. **Foreign languages:** American Sign Language, sign language interpretation, translation. **Health:** Dental hygiene, EMT paramedic, medical radiologic technology/radiation therapy, nuclear medical technology, nursing (RN), physical therapy assistant, radiologic technology/medical imaging, respiratory therapy technology, sonography, vocational rehab counseling. **Interdisciplinary:** Gerontology. **Legal studies:** Paralegal. **Liberal arts:** Arts/sciences. **Mechanic/repair:** Automotive. **Parks/recreation:** Sports admin. **Physical sciences:** Chemistry. **Protective services:** Emergency management/homeland security, fire safety technology, law enforcement admin. **Public administration:** Human services. **Visual/performing arts:** Music. **Other:** Emergency health science, Technical studies.

Most popular majors. Business/marketing 18%, health sciences 26%, liberal arts 35%, security/protective services 7%.

Computing on campus. 1,024 workstations in library, computer center, student center. Commuter students can connect to campus network. Online library, helpline, wireless network available.

Student life. **Freshman orientation:** Available. **Activities:** Drama, international student organizations, literary magazine, radio station, student government, student newspaper, Catholic student organization, Christian Fellowship, student volunteer organization, Phi Theta Kappa, Phi Beta, Union of African Students, gerontology club, French club, Spanish club.

Athletics. NJCAA. **Intercollegiate:** Baseball M, basketball, golf, soccer M, volleyball W. **Team name:** Owls; Lady Owls.

Student services. Alcohol/substance abuse counseling, career counseling, services for economically disadvantaged, student employment services, financial aid counseling, minority student services, personal counseling, placement for graduates, veterans' counselor. **Physically disabled:** Services for visually, speech, hearing impaired. **Transfer:** Re-entry adviser, pre-admission transcript evaluation for new students. Transfer adviser, college fairs on campus for students transferring to 4-year colleges.

Contact. Phone: (908) 709-7500 Fax: (908) 709-7125
JoAnn Davis-Wayne, Registrar, Union County College, 1033 Springfield Avenue, Cranford, NJ 07016-1599

Warren County Community College
Washington, New Jersey
www.warren.edu **CB code: 2722**

- Public 2-year community college
- Commuter campus in small town

General. Founded in 1981. Regionally accredited. **Enrollment:** 1,810 degree-seeking undergraduates. **Degrees:** 159 associate awarded. **Location:** 10 miles from Phillipsburg. **Calendar:** Semester, extensive summer session. **Full-time faculty:** 23 total; 17% have terminal degrees, 4% minority, 56% women. **Part-time faculty:** 82 total.

Student profile.

Out-of-state:	3%	**25 or older:**	40%

Transfer out. **Colleges most students transferred to 2008:** Centenary College, Rutgers-New Brunswick, East Stroudsburg University.

Basis for selection. Open admission, but selective for some programs. Interview recommended.

High school preparation. High school diploma or GED strongly recommended.

2008-2009 Annual costs. Tuition/fees: $3,443; $3,743 out-of-district; $4,343 out-of-state. Per-credit charge: $91 in-district; $101 out-of-district; $121 out-of-state. Books/supplies: $700. Personal expenses: $900.

2008-2009 Financial aid. All financial aid based on need. Need-based aid available for part-time students. Work-study available nights, weekends and for part-time students.

Application procedures. Admission: No deadline. $25 fee, may be waived for applicants with need. Application must be submitted on paper. Admission notification on a rolling basis. Early admission students ages 16-18 must provide written permission from parent/guardian and high school official. **Financial aid:** Closing date 7/8. FAFSA, institutional form required. Applicants notified on a rolling basis; must reply within 2 week(s) of notification.

Academics. Special study options: Cooperative education, cross-registration, distance learning, double major, dual enrollment of high school students, ESL, independent study, internships, liberal arts/career combination, weekend college. Bachelor's degree programs available on campus. License preparation in dental hygiene, nursing, real estate. **Credit/placement by examination:** AP, CLEP, IB, institutional tests. Challenge exams. **Support services:** GED preparation, learning center, pre-admission summer program, reduced course load, remedial instruction, tutoring, writing center.

Majors. Biology: General. **Business:** General, accounting, entrepreneurial studies. **Computer sciences:** General. **Conservation:** General, environmental studies. **Education:** General, early childhood. **Health:** Health services, nursing (RN). **Interdisciplinary:** Natural sciences. **Legal studies:** General, paralegal, prelaw. **Liberal arts:** Arts/sciences. **Physical sciences:** Chemistry. **Protective services:** Criminal justice. **Social sciences:** General. **Visual/performing arts:** Studio arts.

Most popular majors. Business/marketing 10%, education 15%, liberal arts 45%.

Computing on campus. 100 workstations in library, computer center. Online library, wireless network available.

Student life. Freshman orientation: Mandatory. Preregistration for classes offered. **Activities:** Literary magazine, student government, student newspaper, Phi Theta Kappa Honor Society, criminal justice association.

Athletics. Team name: Golden Eagles.

Student services. Adult student services, career counseling, student employment services, financial aid counseling, personal counseling, placement for graduates, veterans' counselor. **Physically disabled:** Services for visually, speech, hearing impaired. **Learning disabled:** Comprehensive services available. **Transfer:** Transfer adviser, college fairs on campus for students transferring to 4-year colleges.

Contact. Phone: (908) 835-9222 Fax: (908) 689-5824
Shannon Horwath, Associate Director of Admissions, Warren County Community College, Route 57 West, Washington, NJ 07882-4343

Two-Year Colleges

New Mexico

Central New Mexico Community College

Albuquerque, New Mexico — **CB member**
www.cnm.edu — **CB code: 3387**

- Public 2-year community and technical college
- Commuter campus in very large city

General. Founded in 1965. Regionally accredited. **Enrollment:** 21,669 degree-seeking undergraduates; 3,201 non-degree-seeking students. **Degrees:** 1,296 associate awarded. **ROTC:** Army, Naval, Air Force. **Calendar:** Trimester, extensive summer session. **Full-time faculty:** 331 total; 18% minority, 53% women. **Part-time faculty:** 666 total; 58% minority, 54% women.

Student profile. Among degree-seeking undergraduates, 3,718 enrolled as first-time, first-year students, 1,706 transferred in from other institutions.

Part-time:	66%	**Asian American:**	2%
Out-of-state:	1%	**Hispanic American:**	42%
Women:	58%	**Native American:**	8%
African American:	4%	**25 or older:**	48%

Basis for selection. Open admission. Submitting test scores for placement is optional.

2008-2009 Annual costs. Tuition/fees: $1,064; $1,304 out-of-district; $4,880 out-of-state. Per-credit charge: $41 in-district; $51 out-of-district; $200 out-of-state. In-district students do not pay tuition for technical courses, only arts and sciences courses. Non-residents pay in-state rates during summer term. Non-residents pay in-state rates for 6 or fewer credit hours during all terms. Books/supplies: $772.

2007-2008 Financial aid. Need-based: 38% of total undergraduate aid awarded as scholarships/grants, 62% as loans/jobs. Need-based aid available for part-time students. Work-study available for part-time students. **Non-need-based:** Scholarships awarded for academics, state residency.

Application procedures. Admission: No deadline. No application fee. Admission notification on a rolling basis. **Financial aid:** Priority date 5/1; no closing date. FAFSA required. Applicants notified on a rolling basis starting 5/1.

Academics. Special study options: Cooperative education, distance learning, double major, dual enrollment of high school students, ESL, internships, liberal arts/career combination. Apprenticeships. License preparation in aviation, dental hygiene, nursing, paramedic, radiology, real estate. **Credit/placement by examination:** AP, CLEP, institutional tests. **Support services:** GED preparation and test center, learning center, remedial instruction, study skills assistance, tutoring, writing center.

Majors. Biology: Biotechnology. **Business:** Accounting, administrative services, banking/financial services, business admin, hospitality admin. **Computer sciences:** Data processing, information systems, systems analysis. **Education:** Elementary, technology/industrial arts. **Engineering:** General, environmental. **Engineering technology:** Architectural drafting, electrical, electrical drafting, laser/optical, manufacturing, surveying. **Family/consumer sciences:** Child care. **Health:** Clinical lab technology, medical radiologic technology/radiation therapy, medical records admin, nursing (RN), respiratory therapy technology, sonography, veterinary technology/assistant. **Legal studies:** Paralegal. **Liberal arts:** Arts/sciences. **Mechanic/repair:** Aircraft powerplant. **Parks/recreation:** General. **Personal/culinary services:** Chef training, cosmetic. **Protective services:** Criminal justice, fire safety technology. **Transportation:** Airline/commercial pilot.

Most popular majors. Business/marketing 19%, engineering/engineering technologies 6%, health sciences 22%, liberal arts 29%.

Computing on campus. Commuter students can connect to campus network. Online course registration, online library, student web hosting, wireless network available.

Student life. Freshman orientation: Mandatory. Preregistration for classes offered. **Activities:** Drama, literary magazine, student government, student newspaper.

Student services. Adult student services, career counseling, services for economically disadvantaged, student employment services, financial aid counseling, health services, minority student services, placement for graduates. **Physically disabled:** Services for visually, speech, hearing impaired. **Transfer:** Transfer adviser for students transferring to 4-year colleges.

Contact. Phone: (505) 224-3160 Fax: (505) 224-3237
Jane Campbell, Registrar/Director of Enrollment Services, Central New Mexico Community College, 525 Buena Vista SE, Albuquerque, NM 87106

Clovis Community College

Clovis, New Mexico — **CB member**
www.clovis.edu — **CB code: 4921**

- Public 2-year community and junior college
- Commuter campus in large town

General. Founded in 1990. Regionally accredited. **Enrollment:** 1,687 degree-seeking undergraduates; 2,070 non-degree-seeking students. **Degrees:** 183 associate awarded. **Location:** 200 miles from Albuquerque, 100 miles from Lubbock, Texas. **Calendar:** Semester, limited summer session. **Full-time faculty:** 48 total; 6% have terminal degrees, 6% minority, 69% women. **Part-time faculty:** 145 total; 8% have terminal degrees, 12% minority, 64% women. **Class size:** 60% < 20, 40% 20-39, less than 1% 40-49. **Special facilities:** Art collection representing multiple cultures of New Mexico.

Student profile. Among degree-seeking undergraduates, 60% enrolled in a transfer program, 40% enrolled in a vocational program, 5% already have a bachelor's degree or higher, 247 enrolled as first-time, first-year students, 202 transferred in from other institutions.

Part-time:	58%	**Women:**	32%
Out-of-state:	9%	**25 or older:**	47%

Transfer out. Colleges most students transferred to 2008: Eastern New Mexico University, New Mexico State University, University of New Mexico, Texas Tech University, West Texas A&M University.

Basis for selection. Open admission, but selective for some programs. Nursing and radiologic technology are selective; criteria include GPA, performance in related science courses. Test of Adult Basic Education (TABE) or ACCUPLACER required for vocational programs. **Learning Disabled:** Students with learning disabilities are encouraged but not required to register with the Office of Special Services. Students so registered may obtain special diagnostic services and modifications to include assistance with testing, note taking, and intervention with instructors.

2008-2009 Annual costs. Tuition/fees: $808; $856 out-of-district; $1,552 out-of-state. Per-credit charge: $29 in-district; $31 out-of-district; $60 out-of-state. Books/supplies: $800. Personal expenses: $1,800.

2007-2008 Financial aid. Need-based: 67% of total undergraduate aid awarded as scholarships/grants, 33% as loans/jobs. Need-based aid available for part-time students. Work-study available nights, weekends and for part-time students. **Non-need-based:** Scholarships awarded for academics, state residency. **Additional information:** Public and private funds have made possible the creation of an endowment in excess of $1,000,000 to assist nursing students.

Application procedures. Admission: No deadline. No application fee. Admission notification on a rolling basis. **Financial aid:** Priority date 9/1; no closing date. FAFSA required. Applicants notified on a rolling basis starting 4/15.

Academics. Special study options: Cooperative education, distance learning, double major, dual enrollment of high school students, ESL, independent study, internships, teacher certification program, weekend college. License preparation in aviation, nursing, paramedic, radiology. **Credit/placement by examination:** AP, CLEP, institutional tests. 32 credit hours maximum toward associate degree. **Support services:** GED preparation and test center, learning center, remedial instruction, study skills assistance, tutoring, writing center.

Majors. Business: General, accounting, administrative services, business admin, management information systems, office management, office technology. **Computer sciences:** General, computer graphics, computer science, information technology, networking, programming, systems analysis. **Education:** General, early childhood, teacher assistance. **Engineering:** Electrical. **Engineering technology:** Drafting. **Health:** Medical radiologic technology/radiation therapy, medical secretary. **Interdisciplinary:** Natural sciences. **Legal studies:** General, legal secretary. **Liberal arts:** Arts/sciences. **Math:** General. **Mechanic/repair:** Automotive, electronics/electrical, heating/ac/refrig, industrial. **Personal/culinary services:** Cosmetic. **Protective services:** Criminal justice. **Psychology:** General. **Transportation:** Aviation. **Visual/performing arts:** Commercial/advertising art, studio arts.

Most popular majors. Business/marketing 7%, health sciences 34%, liberal arts 41%.

Computing on campus. 260 workstations in library, computer center, student center. Online course registration, helpline, wireless network available.

Student life. **Freshman orientation:** Available. Preregistration for classes offered. 3 hours prior to semester. **Activities:** Choral groups, drama, literary magazine, musical theater, student government, Hispanic advisory council, Phi Theta Kappa, social committee, international awareness organization, student ambassadors.

Athletics. **Intramural:** Racquetball.

Student services. Adult student services, career counseling, services for economically disadvantaged, student employment services, financial aid counseling, minority student services, on-campus daycare, personal counseling, placement for graduates, veterans' counselor. **Physically disabled:** Services for visually, speech, hearing impaired. **Transfer:** Re-entry adviser for new students. Transfer adviser, college fairs on campus for students transferring to 4-year colleges.

Contact. E-mail: admissions@clovis.edu
Phone: (575) 769-4025 Fax: (575) 769-4190
Rosie Corrie, Director of Admissions/Registrar, Clovis Community College, 417 Schepps Boulevard, Clovis, NM 88101-8381

Dona Ana Community College of New Mexico State University

Las Cruces, New Mexico
www.dacc.nmsu.edu **CB code: 6296**

- Public 2-year branch campus and community college
- Commuter campus in small city

General. Founded in 1973. Regionally accredited. Access to New Mexico State University facilities and activities. **Enrollment:** 8,588 degree-seeking undergraduates. **Degrees:** 651 associate awarded. **ROTC:** Army, Air Force. **Location:** 42 miles from El Paso, Texas. **Calendar:** Semester, limited summer session. **Full-time faculty:** 130 total. **Part-time faculty:** 321 total.

Basis for selection. Open admission, but selective for some programs. Applicants to radiology technology, EMT-paramedic, and respiratory care programs selected on basis of COMPASS scores, Health Occupations Aptitude Test scores, resume, 3 letters of recommendation, clinical observation, and interview. Applicants to nursing program selected on basis of Nursing entrance exam scores and completion of requirements. COMPASS required for placement if ACT or SAT not taken.

2008-2009 Annual costs. Tuition/fees: $1,200; $1,440 out-of-district; $3,600 out-of-state. Per-credit charge: $50 in-district; $60 out-of-district; $150 out-of-state. Room/board: $5,976. Books/supplies: $664. Personal expenses: $1,215.

Financial aid. **Need-based:** Need-based aid available for part-time students.

Application procedures. **Admission:** No deadline. $15 fee, may be waived for applicants with need. Admission notification on a rolling basis. February 15th application deadline for radiology technology, EMT-paramedic, nursing, and respiratory care programs. **Financial aid:** Priority date 3/1; no closing date. FAFSA required. Applicants notified on a rolling basis starting 5/1.

Academics. **Special study options:** Combined bachelor's/graduate degree, cooperative education, cross-registration, distance learning, double major, dual enrollment of high school students, ESL, independent study, internships. License preparation in dental hygiene, nursing, paramedic, radiology. **Credit/placement by examination:** CLEP, institutional tests. 30 credit hours maximum toward associate degree. **Support services:** GED preparation and test center, learning center, pre-admission summer program, remedial instruction, study skills assistance, tutoring.

Majors. **Agriculture:** Landscaping. **Business:** Administrative services, business admin, fashion, hospitality admin, marketing, office management. **Computer sciences:** Computer graphics, computer science, data processing. **Construction:** Electrician, lineworker, maintenance. **Education:** General, early childhood. **Engineering:** Electrical. **Engineering technology:** Drafting, electrical. **Health:** EMT paramedic, medical radiologic technology/radiation therapy, medical secretary, nursing (RN), respiratory therapy technology. **Legal studies:** Legal secretary, paralegal. **Liberal arts:** Library assistant. **Mechanic/repair:** Automotive, electronics/electrical, heating/ac/refrig. **Protective services:** Firefighting.

Computing on campus. 460 workstations in library, computer center. Commuter students can connect to campus network. Online course registration, online library, helpline, repair service, wireless network available.

Student life. **Freshman orientation:** Available. **Housing:** Coed dorms, single-sex dorms, special housing for disabled, apartments available. Housing available on adjacent New Mexico State University campus. **Activities:** Student government, student newspaper, Vocational Industrial Clubs of America, Distributive Education Clubs of America, Phi Theta Kappa, fraternities and sororities available through New Mexico State University.

Student services. Adult student services, career counseling, student employment services, health services, personal counseling, placement for graduates, veterans' counselor. **Physically disabled:** Services for visually, speech, hearing impaired. **Transfer:** Transfer adviser, college fairs on campus for students transferring to 4-year colleges.

Contact. Phone: (575) 527-7710 Fax: (575) 527-7515
Becky Ordunez, Coordinator, Admissions, Dona Ana Community College of New Mexico State University, MSC-3DA, Las Cruces, NM 88003-8001

Eastern New Mexico University: Roswell Campus

Roswell, New Mexico **CB member**
www.roswell.enmu.edu **CB code: 4662**

- Public 2-year branch campus and community college
- Commuter campus in large town

General. Founded in 1958. Regionally accredited. **Enrollment:** 2,249 degree-seeking undergraduates; 1,434 non-degree-seeking students. **Degrees:** 269 associate awarded. **Location:** 200 miles from Albuquerque. **Calendar:** Semester, limited summer session. **Full-time faculty:** 77 total. **Part-time faculty:** 183 total. **Class size:** 80% < 20, 18% 20-39, less than 1% 40-49, less than 1% 50-99, less than 1% >100. **Special facilities:** Instructional television, online and on-site classes available from main campus, allowing students to continue upper-division classes without travel.

Student profile. Among degree-seeking undergraduates, 36% enrolled in a transfer program, 67% enrolled in a vocational program, 1% already have a bachelor's degree or higher, 581 enrolled as first-time, first-year students, 159 transferred in from other institutions.

Part-time:	56%	**25 or older:**	62%
Women:	63%	**Live on campus:**	4%

Transfer out. 7% of students enrolled in the transfer program go on to 4-year colleges. **Colleges most students transferred to 2008:** Eastern New Mexico University-Portales, New Mexico State University, University of New Mexico, New Mexico Highlands University.

Basis for selection. Open admission, but selective for some programs. Students must pass university skills placement test to enroll in math or English courses. Remedial reading course required if test not passed. Student may be exempt based on ACT scores. Some Health Services programs require completion of a pre-admission series of courses, have minimum course grades and GPAs. **Adult students:** Some programs require completion of placement testing as prerequisite. **Homeschooled:** ACT score of 15 or more and high school transcript with graduation date required. **Learning Disabled:** Services based on need and disability documentation. Students requiring special services asked to provide information on needs as soon as possible to avoid delays in receiving service.

2008-2009 Annual costs. Tuition/fees: $1,159; $4,121 out-of-state. Per-credit charge: $44 in-state; $167 out-of-state. Room/board: $7,524. Books/supplies: $1,200. Personal expenses: $3,000.

2007-2008 Financial aid. **Need-based:** Need-based aid available for part-time students. Work-study available nights, weekends and for part-time students.

Application procedures. **Admission:** No deadline. No application fee. Admission notification on a rolling basis. **Financial aid:** Priority date 4/1; no closing date. FAFSA required. Applicants notified on a rolling basis starting 7/1; must reply within 3 week(s) of notification.

Academics. **Special study options:** Combined bachelor's/graduate degree, distance learning, dual enrollment of high school students, independent study, internships, liberal arts/career combination. Bachelor's degree programs available on campus. License preparation in aviation, nursing, occupational therapy, paramedic. **Credit/placement by examination:** CLEP, IB, institutional tests. 30 credit hours maximum toward associate degree. Credits earned through CLEP and Advanced Placement must be mutually exclusive. **Support services:** GED preparation and test center, learning center, remedial instruction, study skills assistance, tutoring, writing center.

Majors. **Business:** General, accounting, administrative services. **Communications technology:** Animation/special effects. **Computer sciences:** General. **Education:** General, teacher assistance. **Engineering technology:** Architectural, drafting. **Family/consumer sciences:** Child care. **Health:** EMT paramedic, medical assistant, medical records technology, occupational therapy assistant, phlebotomy, respiratory therapy assistant. **Legal studies:** Paralegal. **Liberal arts:** Arts/sciences. **Mechanic/repair:** Automotive, avionics, electronics/electrical. **Production:** Welding. **Protective services:** Criminal justice, fire safety technology, police science. **Public administration:** Social work. **Transportation:** Aviation, aviation management.

Most popular majors. Business/marketing 12%, health sciences 22%, liberal arts 19%, trade and industry 31%.

Computing on campus. 50 workstations in library, computer center. Dormitories wired for high-speed internet access. Online course registration, wireless network available.

Student life. **Freshman orientation:** Available. Preregistration for classes offered. One-day program before classes commence. **Housing:** Coed dorms, apartments available. $150 deposit, deadline 8/1. **Activities:** Concert band, choral groups, drama, student government, art club, ski club, computer club, Spanish club, science club, Student Nurses Association, residence hall council, psychology club, electronics club, occupational therapy assistants.

Athletics. **Intramural:** Basketball M, football (non-tackle) M, racquetball, softball W, tennis, volleyball, weight lifting M.

Student services. Career counseling, services for economically disadvantaged, student employment services, financial aid counseling, health services, on-campus daycare, personal counseling, placement for graduates, veterans' counselor. **Physically disabled:** Services for visually, speech, hearing impaired. **Transfer:** College fairs on campus for students transferring to 4-year colleges.

Contact. E-mail: admissions@roswell.enmu.edu
Phone: (575) 624-7149 Toll-free number: (800) 243-6687 ext. 149
Fax: (575) 624-7144
Ida Stover, Director of Admissions and Records, Eastern New Mexico University: Roswell Campus, Box 6000, Roswell, NM 88202-6000

IIA College: Albuquerque

Albuquerque, New Mexico
www.iia.edu

- For-profit 2-year branch campus and career college
- Commuter campus in large city
- Interview required

General. Accredited by ACICS. Campuses in Phoenix, Mesa, and Tucson, AZ and Albuquerque, NM. **Enrollment:** 141 degree-seeking undergraduates; 141 non-degree-seeking students. **Degrees:** 35 associate awarded. **Location:** Located within the city limits of Albuquerque, New Mexico. **Calendar:** Continuous, extensive summer session. **Full-time faculty:** 6 total; 33% have terminal degrees, 50% women. **Part-time faculty:** 5 total; 20% have terminal degrees, 40% women.

Basis for selection. Open admission, but selective for some programs.

2009-2010 Annual costs. Tuition/fees (projected): $11,750. Tuition shown is an average, actual tuition and fees may vary by program.

Financial aid. All financial aid based on need.

Application procedures. **Admission:** No deadline. $250 fee. Application must be submitted on paper. Admission notification on a rolling basis. **Financial aid:** No deadline. FAFSA, institutional form required.

Academics. **Special study options:** Accelerated study, distance learning. Bachelor's degree programs available on campus. **Credit/placement by examination:** CLEP, institutional tests. **Support services:** GED preparation, learning center.

Majors. **Business:** Accounting, business admin. **Health:** Health care admin. **Legal studies:** Paralegal. **Protective services:** Law enforcement admin.

Most popular majors. Business/marketing 37%, legal studies 60%.

Computing on campus. Commuter students can connect to campus network. Online library available.

Student life. **Freshman orientation:** Mandatory.

Student services. Career counseling, financial aid counseling, placement for graduates. **Transfer:** Pre-admission transcript evaluation for new students.

Contact. E-mail: pdabous@iia.edu
Phone: (505) 880-2877 Toll-free number: (888) 744-6340
Fax: (505) 352-0199
Patrick Dabous, Regional Director of Admissions, IIA College: Albuquerque, 4201 Central Avenue NW, Suite J, Albuquerque, NM 87105-1649

Luna Community College

Las Vegas, New Mexico
www.luna.edu **CB code: 2591**

- Public 2-year community and technical college
- Large town

General. Regionally accredited. **Enrollment:** 739 degree-seeking undergraduates. **Degrees:** 102 associate awarded. **Calendar:** Semester. **Full-time faculty:** 31 total. **Part-time faculty:** 127 total.

Basis for selection. Open admission, but selective for some programs and for out-of-state students.

2008-2009 Annual costs. Tuition/fees: $718; $1,006 out-of-district; $1,942 out-of-state. Per-credit charge: $28 in-district; $40 out-of-district; $79 out-of-state. Books/supplies: $500. Personal expenses: $572.

Application procedures. **Admission:** No deadline. No application fee. Admission notification on a rolling basis.

Academics. **Credit/placement by examination:** CLEP.

Majors. **Business:** General, accounting, business admin, office management. **Computer sciences:** General. **Education:** Early childhood. **Engineering:** Electrical. **Engineering technology:** Drafting. **Health:** Clinical lab technology.

Student life. **Freshman orientation:** Mandatory. Preregistration for classes offered.

Contact. E-mail: tmares@luna.edu
Phone: (505) 454-2550
Moses Marquez, Director of Admissions, Luna Community College, 366 Luna Drive, Las Vegas, NM 87701

Mesalands Community College

Tucumcari, New Mexico
www.mesalands.edu **CB code: 3618**

- Public 2-year community and technical college
- Commuter campus in small town

General. Regionally accredited. **Enrollment:** 407 degree-seeking undergraduates; 537 non-degree-seeking students. **Degrees:** 30 associate awarded. **Location:** 175 miles from Albuquerque, 110 miles from Amarillo, Texas. **Calendar:** Semester, extensive summer session. **Full-time faculty:** 15 total. **Part-time faculty:** 24 total. **Special facilities:** Museum, foundry.

Student profile. Among degree-seeking undergraduates, 75% enrolled in a transfer program, 25% enrolled in a vocational program, 144 enrolled as first-time, first-year students.

Part-time:	25%	**Women:**	39%
Out-of-state:	10%		

Basis for selection. Open admission. **Homeschooled:** Ability to Benefit Test or GED required.

2008-2009 Annual costs. Tuition/fees: $1,496; $2,426 out-of-state. Per-credit charge: $40 in-state; $71 out-of-state. Personal expenses: $1,427.

Financial aid. **Need-based:** Need-based aid available for part-time students. Work-study available nights and for part-time students. **Non-need-based:** Scholarships awarded for academics, athletics, leadership, minority status, music/drama, state residency.

Application procedures. **Admission:** No deadline. No application fee. Admission notification on a rolling basis. **Financial aid:** Priority date 4/1; no closing date. FAFSA required. Applicants notified on a rolling basis starting 4/1; must reply within 3 week(s) of notification.

Academics. **Special study options:** Distance learning, dual enrollment of high school students, ESL, independent study, internships. Bachelor's degree programs available on campus. **Credit/placement by examination:** AP, CLEP, institutional tests. 18 credit hours maximum toward associate degree. **Support services:** GED preparation and test center, learning center, remedial instruction, study skills assistance, tutoring.

Majors. **Agriculture:** General. **Business:** Business admin. **Computer sciences:** General. **Construction:** General. **Education:** General. **Engineering:** General. **Liberal arts:** Arts/sciences. **Physical sciences:** Geology, paleontology. **Protective services:** Law enforcement admin.

Computing on campus. 75 workstations in library, computer center. Online course registration, wireless network available.

Student life. **Freshman orientation:** Available. Preregistration for classes offered. **Activities:** Student government.

Athletics. **Intercollegiate:** Rodeo.

Student services. Adult student services, career counseling, financial aid counseling. **Physically disabled:** Services for visually, hearing impaired.

Contact. Phone: (575) 461-4413
Mesalands Community College, 911 South Tenth Street, Tucumcari, NM 88401

Navajo Technical College
Crownpoint, New Mexico
www.navajotech.edu

- Public 2-year community and technical college
- Commuter campus in rural community

General. **Enrollment:** 300 full-time, degree-seeking students. **Degrees:** 40 associate awarded. **Location:** 28 miles from Thoreau, 71 miles from Farmigton. **Calendar:** Semester, limited summer session. **Full-time faculty:** 36 total; 36% women. **Part-time faculty:** 18 total; 44% women. **Class size:** 94% < 20, 6% 20-39. **Special facilities:** Navajo Culture and Visitors Center; Culinary Arts and Hospitality Center. **Partnerships:** Formal partnerships with TeraGrid, SC08, Navajo Head Start, University of New Mexico, New Mexico Computing Applications Center, Navajo Rural Systemic Initiative, Navajo Workforce Development, Office of Dine Youth, Lewis and Clark University (Illinois), Southern University (Louisiana), National Museum of the American Indian, UNM Telemedicine Consortium, New Mexico State University's Extension Program, Sandia National Laboratories.

Student profile. Among full-time, degree-seeking students, 2% enrolled in a transfer program, 62% enrolled in a vocational program, 1% already have a bachelor's degree or higher.

Out-of-state:	17%	**25 or older:**	42%
Native American:	100%		

Transfer out. 33% of students enrolled in the transfer program go on to 4-year colleges.

Basis for selection. Open admission. ACCUPLACER required for all students to identify any remedial education requirements. **Adult students:** SAT/ACT scores not required.

2008-2009 Annual costs. Tuition/fees: $840. Figures quoted are for members of federally recognized tribes. Non-members pay $1680 in tuition. Room/board: $4,056. Books/supplies: $800.

2007-2008 Financial aid. **Need-based:** 96% of total undergraduate aid awarded as scholarships/grants, 4% as loans/jobs. Need-based aid available for part-time students. **Non-need-based:** Scholarships awarded for academics.

Application procedures. **Admission:** No application fee. Admission notification on a rolling basis. **Financial aid:** No deadline. FAFSA, institutional form required. Applicants notified on a rolling basis starting 8/5; must reply by 11/30 or within 4 week(s) of notification.

Academics. **Special study options:** Accelerated study, double major, dual enrollment of high school students, honors, independent study, internships, teacher certification program. License preparation in nursing. **Credit/placement by examination:** CLEP. **Support services:** GED preparation, remedial instruction, study skills assistance, tutoring.

Majors. **Agriculture:** General. **Business:** Accounting. **Computer sciences:** General. **Education:** Early childhood. **Engineering technology:** CAD/CADD. **Health:** Veterinary technology/assistant. **Legal studies:** Paralegal. **Public administration:** General. **Other:** Professional assistant.

Most popular majors. Computer/information sciences 61%, education 9%, natural resources/environmental science 17%, public administration/social services 13%.

Computing on campus. 40 workstations in library, computer center, student center. Commuter students can connect to campus network. Online course registration, online library, helpline, repair service, wireless network available.

Student life. **Freshman orientation:** Mandatory. Preregistration for classes offered. 3 day event held one week before classes start. **Housing:** Guaranteed on-campus for all undergraduates. Single-sex dorms, apartments available. **Activities:** Campus ministries, dance, student government, student newspaper, child care services, behavioral health services, counseling, Native American Church, student senate council.

Athletics. NJCAA. **Intercollegiate:** Cross-country, rodeo. **Intramural:** Basketball, cross-country, softball, volleyball. **Team name:** Hawks.

Student services. Adult student services, alcohol/substance abuse counseling, career counseling, services for economically disadvantaged, student employment services, financial aid counseling, on-campus daycare, personal counseling, placement for graduates, veterans' counselor. **Physically disabled:** Services for visually, speech, hearing impaired. **Learning disabled:** Comprehensive services available.

Contact. E-mail: rdamon@navajotech.edu
Phone: (505) 786-4326 Fax: (505) 786-5644
Delores Becenti, Registrar, Navajo Technical College, PO Box 849, Crownpoint, NM 87313

New Mexico Junior College
Hobbs, New Mexico
www.nmjc.edu **CB code: 4553**

- Public 2-year community and technical college
- Commuter campus in large town

General. Founded in 1965. Regionally accredited. **Enrollment:** 2,978 degree-seeking undergraduates. **Degrees:** 276 associate awarded. **Location:** 110 miles from Roswell, NM; 100 miles from Lubbock, Texas. **Calendar:** Semester, extensive summer session. **Full-time faculty:** 73 total. **Part-time faculty:** 120 total. **Special facilities:** Western Heritage Museum, Cowboy Hall of Fame.

Student profile. Among degree-seeking undergraduates, 4% enrolled in a transfer program.

Out-of-state:	10%	**Live on campus:**	8%
25 or older:	51%		

Transfer out. **Colleges most students transferred to 2008:** College of the Southwest, Eastern New Mexico University, Texas Tech University, University of New Mexico, New Mexico State University.

Basis for selection. Open admission, but selective for some programs. Special requirements for nursing, law enforcement, and automotive service education programs. Applicants admitted without high school diploma or GED must pass GED before completion of degree program. Interview required for nursing, medical laboratory technician, automotive service education programs. **Homeschooled:** Transcript of courses and grades required.

High school preparation. 18 units recommended. Recommended units include English 4, mathematics 3, social studies 4, science 2 and academic electives 5.

2008-2009 Annual costs. Tuition/fees: $1,146; $1,578 out-of-district; $1,698 out-of-state. Per-credit charge: $29 in-district; $47 out-of-district; $52 out-of-state. Room/board: $3,800. Books/supplies: $700. Personal expenses: $1,575.

Financial aid. **Need-based:** Need-based aid available for part-time students. Work-study available nights and weekends. **Non-need-based:** Scholarships awarded for academics, art, athletics, leadership, music/drama.

Application procedures. **Admission:** No deadline. No application fee. Admission notification on a rolling basis. **Financial aid:** Priority date 6/1; no closing date. FAFSA required. Applicants notified on a rolling basis; must reply within 2 week(s) of notification.

Academics. **Special study options:** Cooperative education, cross-registration, distance learning, dual enrollment of high school students, ESL, honors, internships, weekend college. License preparation in nursing, real estate. **Credit/placement by examination:** AP, CLEP, institutional tests. 30 credit hours maximum toward associate degree. **Support services:** GED preparation and test center, learning center, pre-admission summer program, reduced course load, remedial instruction, study skills assistance, tutoring, writing center.

Majors. **Biology:** General. **Business:** General, accounting, administrative services, banking/financial services, business admin, office management, office technology, real estate. **Communications:** General. **Computer sciences:** General, applications programming, computer graphics, programming. **Education:** General, early childhood, elementary, middle, physical, secondary. **Engineering:** General. **Engineering technology:** Drafting, hazardous materials. **Foreign languages:** Spanish. **Health:** Athletic training, clinical lab assistant, clinical lab technology, EMT paramedic, medical radiologic technology/radiation therapy, predental, premedicine, prepharmacy. **Legal studies:** Legal secretary, paralegal, prelaw. **Liberal arts:** Arts/sciences. **Math:** General. **Mechanic/repair:** Automotive. **Personal/culinary services:** Cosmetic. **Physical sciences:** Chemistry, physics. **Protective services:** Criminal justice, police science. **Psychology:** General. **Social sciences:** General. **Visual/performing arts:** Commercial/advertising art, studio arts.

Most popular majors. Agriculture 6%, business/marketing 11%, education 13%, health sciences 24%, liberal arts 10%, mathematics 7%, trade and industry 13%.

Computing on campus. 275 workstations in dormitories, library, computer center, student center. Dormitories wired for high-speed internet access. Commuter students can connect to campus network. Helpline available.

Student life. **Freshman orientation:** Mandatory. Preregistration for classes offered. **Housing:** Single-sex dorms, special housing for disabled, wellness housing available. **Activities:** Bands, choral groups, drama, music ensembles, musical theater, student government, Young Republicans, Young Democrats, student nurses, ambassadors.

Athletics. NJCAA. **Intercollegiate:** Baseball M, basketball, golf M. **Intramural:** Badminton, basketball, bowling, golf, handball, racquetball, skiing, soccer, softball, swimming, table tennis, tennis, volleyball. **Team name:** Thunderbirds.

Student services. Career counseling, student employment services, financial aid counseling, health services, personal counseling, placement for graduates, veterans' counselor. **Physically disabled:** Services for visually, speech, hearing impaired. **Transfer:** Pre-admission transcript evaluation for new students. Transfer adviser, college fairs on campus for students transferring to 4-year colleges.

Contact. Phone: (575) 392-5113 Fax: (575) 392-0322
Michele Clingman, Dean of Enrollment Management, New Mexico Junior College, 5317 Lovington Highway, Hobbs, NM 88240

New Mexico Military Institute

Roswell, New Mexico — **CB member**
www.nmmi.edu — **CB code: 4534**

- Public 2-year junior and military college
- Residential campus in large town

General. Founded in 1891. Regionally accredited. **Enrollment:** 446 degree-seeking undergraduates. **Degrees:** 107 associate awarded. **ROTC:** Army. **Location:** 200 miles from Albuquerque; 200 miles from El Paso, Texas. **Calendar:** Semester, limited summer session. **Full-time faculty:** 70 total; 19% have terminal degrees, 44% women. **Class size:** 64% < 20, 34% 20-39, 3% 40-49.

Student profile. Among degree-seeking undergraduates, 346 enrolled as first-time, first-year students, 12 transferred in from other institutions.

Women:	17%	**Live on campus:**	100%

Transfer out. **Colleges most students transferred to 2008:** University of New Mexico, New Mexico State University, Texas A&M University, University of Colorado.

Basis for selection. 2.0 GPA, 19 ACT or 920 SAT (exclusive of writing) for participation in Advanced Army ROTC. 17 ACT or 800 SAT (exclusive of Writing) for Basic Army ROTC program. Preference given to in-state applicants. Maximum age of 22 for enrollment. Students cannot be married or have children.

High school preparation. 21 units recommended. Recommended units include English 4, mathematics 3, social studies 1, history 2, science 2 (laboratory 2), foreign language 2 and academic electives 5. Computer science 0.5 unit recommended.

2008-2009 Annual costs. Tuition/fees: $4,871; $8,421 out-of-state. Room/board: $3,830. Books/supplies: $700. Personal expenses: $1,000.

2007-2008 Financial aid. **Need-based:** 93% of total undergraduate aid awarded as scholarships/grants, 7% as loans/jobs. **Non-need-based:** Scholarships awarded for academics, alumni affiliation, athletics, ROTC, state residency.

Application procedures. **Admission:** No deadline. $85 fee, may be waived for applicants with need, free for online applicants. Admission notification on a rolling basis beginning on or about 9/1. Advanced Army ROTC applicants must pass Army physical examination. **Financial aid:** Priority date 4/1; no closing date. FAFSA required. Applicants notified on a rolling basis starting 5/1; must reply within 3 week(s) of notification.

Academics. **Special study options:** Dual enrollment of high school students. **Credit/placement by examination:** CLEP, institutional tests. 30 credit hours maximum toward associate degree. **Support services:** Learning center, remedial instruction, tutoring.

Majors. **Liberal arts:** Arts/sciences.

Computing on campus. 100 workstations in dormitories, library, computer center, student center. Dormitories linked to campus network. Helpline, repair service available.

Student life. **Freshman orientation:** Mandatory. **Housing:** Guaranteed on-campus for all undergraduates. Single-sex dorms available. $350 nonrefundable deposit. All students must live in college housing. **Activities:** Bands, campus ministries, choral groups, film society, music ensembles, student government, student newspaper, symphony orchestra, TV station.

Athletics. NJCAA. **Intercollegiate:** Baseball M, basketball M, fencing, football (tackle) M, golf, rifle, tennis, track and field. **Intramural:** Fencing, football (tackle) M, handball, racquetball, skiing, soccer, softball, swimming, tennis, track and field, volleyball. **Team name:** Broncos.

Student services. Career counseling, health services, personal counseling. **Transfer:** Pre-admission transcript evaluation for new students.

Contact. E-mail: admissions@nmmi.edu
Phone: (505) 624-8435 Toll-free number: (800) 421-5376
Fax: (505) 624-8058
Maj. Sonya Rodriguez, Director of Admissions & Financial Aid, New Mexico Military Institute, 101 West College Boulevard, Roswell, NM 88201-5173

New Mexico State University at Alamogordo

Alamogordo, New Mexico
nmsu.edu/ — **CB code: 4012**

- Public 2-year branch campus college
- Commuter campus in large town

General. Founded in 1958. Regionally accredited. **Enrollment:** 2,020 degree-seeking undergraduates. **Degrees:** 173 associate awarded. **ROTC:** Air Force. **Location:** 65 miles from Las Cruces, 85 miles from El Paso, Texas. **Calendar:** Semester, limited summer session. **Full-time faculty:** 51 total. **Part-time faculty:** 65 total. **Special facilities:** Planetarium.

Student profile. Among degree-seeking undergraduates, 75% enrolled in a transfer program, 15% enrolled in a vocational program. Of all enrolled students, 5% already have a bachelor's degree or higher.

Out-of-state:	6%	**25 or older:**	55%

Transfer out. **Colleges most students transferred to 2008:** New Mexico State University.

Basis for selection. Open admission, but selective for some programs. Special requirements for nursing and medical technologies programs; essay and interview required.

2008-2009 Annual costs. Tuition/fees: $1,440; $1,608 out-of-district; $4,056 out-of-state. Per-credit charge: $58 in-district; $65 out-of-district; $167 out-of-state. Books/supplies: $664. Personal expenses: $1,458.

2008-2009 Financial aid. **Need-based:** Need-based aid available for part-time students. **Non-need-based:** Scholarships awarded for academics, state residency.

Application procedures. Admission: No deadline. $20 fee. Admission notification on a rolling basis. **Financial aid:** Priority date 3/1; no closing date. FAFSA, institutional form required. Applicants notified by 6/1.

Academics. Special study options: Combined bachelor's/graduate degree, cooperative education, cross-registration, distance learning, double major, dual enrollment of high school students, honors, independent study, liberal arts/career combination, weekend college. License preparation in nursing, paramedic. **Credit/placement by examination:** AP, CLEP, institutional tests. 30 credit hours maximum toward associate degree. **Support services:** GED preparation and test center, learning center, reduced course load, remedial instruction, study skills assistance, tutoring, writing center.

Majors. Business: General, administrative services, management information systems. **Communications technology:** Photo/film/video. **Computer sciences:** Data processing, information systems, web page design. **Education:** General, early childhood, teacher assistance. **Engineering:** General, computer. **Engineering technology:** Electrical. **Health:** Clinical lab assistant, clinical lab technology. **Legal studies:** Paralegal. **Liberal arts:** Arts/sciences. **Protective services:** Criminal justice, firefighting, forensics. **Public administration:** Social work. **Visual/performing arts:** Art, commercial/advertising art, design.

Most popular majors. Business/marketing 17%, education 6%, health sciences 11%, liberal arts 52%.

Computing on campus. 203 workstations in library, computer center, student center. Commuter students can connect to campus network. Online course registration, online library, helpline, repair service available.

Student life. Freshman orientation: Available. **Activities:** Jazz band, choral groups, drama, music ensembles, student government.

Athletics. Intramural: Softball, table tennis, volleyball.

Student services. Career counseling, student employment services, financial aid counseling, personal counseling, placement for graduates, veterans' counselor. **Physically disabled:** Services for visually, speech, hearing impaired. **Transfer:** Transfer adviser, college fairs on campus for students transferring to 4-year colleges.

Contact. Phone: (505) 439-3700
Kathy Fuller, Admissions Coordinator, New Mexico State University at Alamogordo, 2400 North Scenic Drive, Alamogordo, NM 88310

New Mexico State University at Carlsbad

Carlsbad, New Mexico
artemis.nmsu.edu/ **CB code: 4547**

- Public 2-year branch campus and community college
- Commuter campus in large town

General. Founded in 1950. Regionally accredited. **Enrollment:** 854 degree-seeking undergraduates; 1,004 non-degree-seeking students. **Degrees:** 98 associate awarded. **Location:** 165 miles from El Paso, Texas. **Calendar:** Semester, limited summer session. **Full-time faculty:** 26 total; 19% have terminal degrees, 4% minority, 65% women. **Part-time faculty:** 50 total; 6% have terminal degrees, 16% minority, 56% women. **Class size:** 68% < 20, 32% 20-39, less than 1% 40-49.

Student profile. Among degree-seeking undergraduates, 25% enrolled in a transfer program, 10% enrolled in a vocational program, 260 enrolled as first-time, first-year students, 62 transferred in from other institutions.

Part-time:	37%	**Asian American:**	1%
Out-of-state:	2%	**Hispanic American:**	47%
Women:	72%	**Native American:**	1%
African American:	3%	**25 or older:**	33%

Transfer out. Colleges most students transferred to 2008: New Mexico State University.

Basis for selection. Open admission, but selective for some programs. Special admission process for nursing applicants; ACT and prerequisite courses required. **Homeschooled:** Copy of document verifying registration as home-schooled student and academic transcript outlining 9th-12th grade courses and grades required.

High school preparation. 10 units recommended. Recommended units include English 4, mathematics 3, science 2 and foreign language 1.

2008-2009 Annual costs. Tuition/fees: $964; $1,420 out-of-district; $2,812 out-of-state. Per-credit charge: $36 in-district; $55 out-of-district; $113 out-of-state.

2007-2008 Financial aid. Need-based: 74% of total undergraduate aid awarded as scholarships/grants, 26% as loans/jobs. Need-based aid available for part-time students. **Non-need-based:** Scholarships awarded for academics, state residency.

Application procedures. Admission: No deadline. $15 fee, may be waived for applicants with need. Admission notification on a rolling basis. **Financial aid:** Priority date 3/1; no closing date. FAFSA required. Applicants notified on a rolling basis starting 5/1; must reply within 4 week(s) of notification.

Academics. Special study options: Distance learning, double major, dual enrollment of high school students, ESL, independent study, internships, student-designed major, weekend college. Bachelor's degree programs available on campus. License preparation in nursing. **Credit/placement by examination:** AP, CLEP, institutional tests. 30 credit hours maximum toward associate degree. **Support services:** GED preparation and test center, learning center, reduced course load, remedial instruction, study skills assistance, tutoring, writing center.

Majors. Business: General, administrative services, office/clerical. **Education:** General, early childhood, teacher assistance. **Engineering:** General. **Health:** Nursing (RN), prenursing. **Interdisciplinary:** Natural sciences. **Production:** Welding. **Protective services:** Criminal justice. **Public administration:** Human services. **Other:** Applied science, Heritage interpretation.

Most popular majors. Business/marketing 10%, education 7%, health sciences 19%, library sciences 45%, public administration/social services 9%, security/protective services 6%.

Computing on campus. 365 workstations in library, computer center. Commuter students can connect to campus network. Online course registration, online library, helpline, wireless network available.

Student life. Freshman orientation: Available. **Activities:** Choral groups, drama, literary magazine, student government, student newspaper, Student Nursing Association, Criminal Justice Association, Associated Students (student government), RetroActive, Phi Theta Kappa.

Athletics. Team name: Aggies.

Student services. Career counseling, services for economically disadvantaged, student employment services, financial aid counseling, health services, personal counseling, veterans' counselor. **Physically disabled:** Services for visually, speech, hearing impaired. **Transfer:** Transfer adviser, college fairs on campus for students transferring to 4-year colleges.

Contact. E-mail: blindst@cavern.nmsu.edu
Phone: (575) 234-9223 Fax: (575) 885-4951
Michael Cleary, Vice President for Student Services, New Mexico State University at Carlsbad, 1500 University Drive, Carlsbad, NM 88220

New Mexico State University at Grants

Grants, New Mexico
www.grants.nmsu.edu **CB code: 0461**

- Public 2-year branch campus and community college
- Commuter campus in small town

General. Founded in 1968. Regionally accredited. **Enrollment:** 1,200 undergraduates. **Degrees:** 75 associate awarded. **Location:** 75 miles from Albuquerque. **Calendar:** Semester, limited summer session. **Full-time faculty:** 16 total. **Part-time faculty:** 46 total. **Special facilities:** Judicial district law library.

Basis for selection. Open admission.

High school preparation. 15 units recommended. Recommended units include English 3, mathematics 3, social studies 1 and science 1.

2008-2009 Annual costs. Tuition/fees: $1,320; $1,440 out-of-district; $2,904 out-of-state. Per-credit charge: $55 in-district; $60 out-of-district; $121 out-of-state. Books/supplies: $400.

Financial aid. Need-based: Need-based aid available for part-time students. Work-study available nights, weekends and for part-time students.

Application procedures. Admission: Closing date 8/28. $15 fee, may be waived for applicants with need. Admission notification on a rolling basis beginning on or about 8/3. **Financial aid:** Priority date 3/5; no closing date. FAFSA, institutional form required. Applicants notified on a rolling basis starting 6/15; must reply by 8/28.

Academics. **Special study options:** Distance learning, double major, dual enrollment of high school students, student-designed major, weekend college. Bachelor's degree programs available on campus. License preparation in nursing. **Credit/placement by examination:** CLEP, institutional tests. 30 credit hours maximum toward associate degree. **Support services:** GED preparation and test center, learning center, reduced course load, remedial instruction, tutoring.

Majors. **Business:** General, office management. **Computer sciences:** Programming. **Education:** General. **Engineering technology:** Electrical. **Legal studies:** Paralegal. **Mechanic/repair:** Automotive. **Protective services:** Law enforcement admin. **Public administration:** Human services. **Visual/performing arts:** Art.

Computing on campus. 230 workstations in computer center. Online library available.

Student life. **Freshman orientation:** Available. Preregistration for classes offered. **Activities:** Student government, student newspaper.

Athletics. **Team name:** Aggies.

Student services. Adult student services, career counseling, student employment services, personal counseling, veterans' counselor. **Transfer:** Preadmission transcript evaluation for new students. Transfer adviser, college fairs on campus for students transferring to 4-year colleges.

Contact. E-mail: ilutz@grants.nmsu.edu
Phone: (505) 287-7981 Toll-free number: (888) 450-6678
Fax: (505) 287-2329
Irene Lutz, Campus Student Services Officer, New Mexico State University at Grants, 1500 North Third Street, Grants, NM 87020

Northern New Mexico College

Espanola, New Mexico
www.nnmc.edu **CB code: 0425**

- Public 2-year community and teachers college
- Commuter campus in small town

General. Founded in 1909. Regionally accredited. Additional center in Tierra Amarilla. **Enrollment:** 2,139 degree-seeking undergraduates. **Degrees:** 15 bachelor's, 107 associate awarded. **Location:** 24 miles from Santa Fe. **Calendar:** Semester, limited summer session. **Full-time faculty:** 54 total. **Part-time faculty:** 132 total.

Student profile.

Out-of-state:	1%	**Live on campus:**	1%
25 or older:	39%		

Basis for selection. Open admission, but selective for some programs and for out-of-state students. Nursing, radiography, barbering, and cosmetology programs require separate applications subsequent to admission. 2-year nursing program requires 2.5 GPA and preadmission test. Limited number of out-of-state applicants considered. Four-year programs: applicants must complete 35 credits of general education common core plus 10 additional credits with 2.5 minimum GPA before applying to specific four-year program. Tests administered before or after admission for course placement purposes only, except for those admitted under ability to benefit. **Homeschooled:** Transcript of courses and grades, state high school equivalency certificate required. Applicant must be at least 16.

2008-2009 Annual costs. Tuition/fees: $1,099; $2,298 out-of-state. Per-credit charge: $37 in-state; $87 out-of-state. Upper division courses $87 per credit hour for in-state students, $367 per credit hour for out-of-state students. Room/board: $3,395. Books/supplies: $600. Personal expenses: $1,740.

Financial aid. All financial aid based on need.

Application procedures. **Admission:** Closing date 8/21. No application fee. Application must be submitted on paper. Admission notification on a rolling basis. **Financial aid:** Priority date 3/1; no closing date. FAFSA required. Applicants notified on a rolling basis starting 6/1; must reply within 2 week(s) of notification.

Academics. **Special study options:** Distance learning, dual enrollment of high school students, internships, liberal arts/career combination, teacher certification program. Bachelor's degree programs available on campus. License preparation in nursing, radiology. **Credit/placement by examination:** AP, CLEP, IB, institutional tests. 15 credit hours maximum toward associate degree, 30 toward bachelor's. **Support services:** GED preparation and test center, learning center, remedial instruction, study skills assistance, tutoring, writing center.

Majors. **Area/ethnic studies:** Regional. **Business:** General, accounting, administrative services, business admin, management information systems. **Computer sciences:** General. **Conservation:** General, forestry, management/policy. **Construction:** Electrician, maintenance, pipefitting. **Education:** Early childhood, elementary. **Engineering technology:** Drafting, electrical. **Health:** Medical radiologic technology/radiation therapy, substance abuse counseling. **Interdisciplinary:** Biological/physical sciences. **Liberal arts:** Arts/sciences, library assistant. **Personal/culinary services:** Cosmetic. **Physical sciences:** General. **Production:** Furniture, welding, woodworking. **Protective services:** Criminal justice. **Public administration:** Human services, social work. **Visual/performing arts:** General, art, design, fiber arts, studio arts.

Computing on campus. 24 workstations in library, computer center. Commuter students can connect to campus network.

Student life. **Freshman orientation:** Mandatory. Preregistration for classes offered. Three hour sessions held on Tuesdays prior to term. **Housing:** Single-sex dorms, wellness housing available. **Activities:** Choral groups, drama, music ensembles, student government, Phi Theta Kappa.

Athletics. **Intramural:** Basketball, softball.

Student services. Career counseling, student employment services, financial aid counseling, personal counseling, placement for graduates, veterans' counselor. **Physically disabled:** Services for visually, speech, hearing impaired. **Transfer:** Pre-admission transcript evaluation for new students. Transfer adviser, college fairs on campus for students transferring to 4-year colleges.

Contact. E-mail: mikec@nnmc.edu
Phone: (505) 747-2112 Fax: (505) 747-5449
Frank Orona, Director of Admissions, Northern New Mexico College, 921 Paseo de Onate, Espanola, NM 87532

San Juan College

Farmington, New Mexico **CB member**
www.sanjuancollege.edu **CB code: 4732**

- Public 2-year community college
- Commuter campus in large town

General. Founded in 1956. Regionally accredited. **Enrollment:** 5,139 degree-seeking undergraduates; 3,010 non-degree-seeking students. **Degrees:** 424 associate awarded. **Location:** 183 miles from Albuquerque. **Calendar:** Semester, limited summer session. **Full-time faculty:** 100 total; 8% minority, 48% women. **Part-time faculty:** 244 total. **Special facilities:** Planetarium, Southwestern books and materials collection, geographic information system, art gallery and 800-seat performance hall, fire tower for specialized training, commercial truck driving training range, drilling rig, clean room for instrumentation training, plant operations equipment, jet simulator.

Student profile. Among degree-seeking undergraduates, 26% enrolled in a transfer program, 27% enrolled in a vocational program, 850 enrolled as first-time, first-year students.

Part-time:	58%	**Asian American:**	1%
Women:	64%	**Hispanic American:**	12%
African American:	1%	**Native American:**	33%

Basis for selection. Open admission. **Homeschooled:** Transcript of courses and grades required. Minimum score on ACCUPLACER showing ability to benefit required.

High school preparation. 13 units recommended. Recommended units include English 4, mathematics 3, social studies 3, science 2 and foreign language 1.

2009-2010 Annual costs. Tuition/fees (projected): $768; $1,680 out-of-state. Per-credit charge: $32 in-state; $70 out-of-state. Books/supplies: $900. Personal expenses: $900.

2007-2008 Financial aid. **Need-based:** 57% of total undergraduate aid awarded as scholarships/grants, 43% as loans/jobs. Need-based aid available for part-time students. Work-study available nights, weekends and for part-time students. **Non-need-based:** Scholarships awarded for academics, state residency.

Application procedures. **Admission:** No deadline. No application fee. Admission notification on a rolling basis. **Financial aid:** No deadline. FAFSA required. Applicants notified on a rolling basis starting 7/1; must reply within 2 week(s) of notification.

Academics. **Special study options:** Combined bachelor's/graduate degree, cooperative education, distance learning, dual enrollment of high school students, ESL, external degree, honors, independent study, internships, liberal arts/career combination, teacher certification program. Bachelor's degree programs available on campus. License preparation in aviation, dental hygiene, nursing, physical therapy. **Credit/placement by examination:** CLEP, institutional tests. 30 credit hours maximum toward associate degree. **Support services:** GED preparation and test center, learning center, reduced course load, remedial instruction, study skills assistance, tutoring, writing center.

Majors. Agriculture: Business, landscaping. **Biology:** General. **Business:** Accounting technology, administrative services, business admin. **Computer sciences:** Data processing. **Construction:** Carpentry. **Engineering:** General. **Engineering technology:** Drafting, industrial, instrumentation, solar energy, surveying. **Health:** Clinical lab technology, dental hygiene, EMT paramedic, medical records technology, nursing (RN), physical therapy assistant, premedicine, surgical technology, veterinary technology/assistant. **Legal studies:** Paralegal. **Liberal arts:** Arts/sciences. **Math:** General. **Mechanic/repair:** Auto body, automotive, diesel, industrial. **Parks/recreation:** General. **Personal/culinary services:** Cosmetic. **Physical sciences:** General, chemistry, geology, physics. **Production:** Machine shop technology, welding. **Protective services:** Firefighting, police science. **Public administration:** General, social work. **Transportation:** Airline/commercial pilot. **Visual/performing arts:** Commercial/advertising art, dramatic. **Other:** Manufacturing Technology Semiconductor Emphasis, Microcomputer Applications in Buiness.

Most popular majors. Business/marketing 7%, engineering/engineering technologies 8%, family/consumer sciences 6%, health sciences 24%, liberal arts 29%, trade and industry 16%.

Computing on campus. 952 workstations in library, computer center, student center. Commuter students can connect to campus network. Online course registration, helpline, wireless network available.

Student life. Freshman orientation: Mandatory. Preregistration for classes offered. One-day session held prior to beginning of semester. **Activities:** Bands, choral groups, dance, drama, film society, music ensembles, musical theater, radio station, student government, student newspaper, TV station, Native American club, Student Ambassadors, Phi Theta Kappa honor society.

Athletics. Intramural: Archery, badminton, baseball M, basketball, bowling, cross-country, golf, handball, racquetball, skiing, softball, table tennis, tennis, volleyball.

Student services. Career counseling, student employment services, financial aid counseling, minority student services, on-campus daycare, personal counseling, placement for graduates, veterans' counselor. **Physically disabled:** Services for visually, speech, hearing impaired. **Transfer:** Transfer adviser, college fairs on campus for students transferring to 4-year colleges.

Contact. E-mail: betzj@sanjuancollege.edu
Phone: (505) 566-3300 Fax: (505) 566-3500
Jon Betz, Director of Admissions, San Juan College, 4601 College Boulevard, Farmington, NM 87402-4699

Santa Fe Community College

Santa Fe, New Mexico — **CB member**
www.sfccnm.edu — **CB code: 4816**

- Public 2-year community college
- Commuter campus in small city

General. Founded in 1983. Regionally accredited. **Enrollment:** 2,069 degree-seeking undergraduates; 3,183 non-degree-seeking students. **Degrees:** 222 associate awarded. **Location:** 50 miles from Albuquerque. **Calendar:** Semester, limited summer session. **Full-time faculty:** 59 total. **Part-time faculty:** 257 total. **Class size:** 76% < 20, 24% 20-39, less than 1% 40-49. **Special facilities:** Planetarium, art galleries, fine arts studios, fitness center, swimming pools, child development center. **Partnerships:** Formal partnerships with businesses and state agencies.

Student profile. Among degree-seeking undergraduates, 20% enrolled in a transfer program, 80% enrolled in a vocational program, 30% already have a bachelor's degree or higher, 304 enrolled as first-time, first-year students.

Part-time:	69%	**Hispanic American:**	48%
Women:	65%	**Native American:**	4%
African American:	2%	**International:**	1%
Asian American:	1%		

Transfer out. 20% of students enrolled in the transfer program go on to 4-year colleges. **Colleges most students transferred to 2008:** University of New Mexico, New Mexico State University.

Basis for selection. Open admission. Selective admissions to nursing program. Essay and interview required for international students;. **Home-schooled:** State high school equivalency certificate required.

2008-2009 Annual costs. Tuition/fees: $1,113; $1,434 out-of-district; $2,469 out-of-state. Per-credit charge: $32 in-district; $43 out-of-district; $78 out-of-state. Books/supplies: $600. Personal expenses: $1,500.

2007-2008 Financial aid. Need-based: Need-based aid available for part-time students. Work-study available nights, weekends and for part-time students. **Non-need-based:** Scholarships awarded for academics, state residency.

Application procedures. Admission: No deadline. No application fee. Admission notification on a rolling basis. **Financial aid:** Priority date 5/1; no closing date. FAFSA, institutional form required. Applicants notified on a rolling basis starting 7/15; must reply within 4 week(s) of notification.

Academics. Special study options: Accelerated study, cooperative education, cross-registration, distance learning, double major, dual enrollment of high school students, ESL, honors, independent study, internships, liberal arts/career combination, teacher certification program, weekend college. Bachelor's degree programs available on campus. License preparation in nursing, paramedic, real estate. **Credit/placement by examination:** AP, CLEP, institutional tests. 30 credit hours maximum toward associate degree. Maximum of 9 credit hours can be earned through challenge examinations. **Support services:** GED preparation and test center, reduced course load, remedial instruction, study skills assistance, tutoring, writing center.

Majors. Biology: General. **Business:** Accounting, banking/financial services, business admin. **Computer sciences:** General. **Conservation:** Environmental studies. **Education:** General, kindergarten/preschool. **Engineering:** General. **Engineering technology:** Construction, drafting. **Foreign languages:** Sign language interpretation, Spanish. **Health:** Dental assistant, nursing (RN), respiratory therapy technology. **Legal studies:** Paralegal. **Liberal arts:** Arts/sciences. **Parks/recreation:** Health/fitness. **Personal/culinary services:** Chef training. **Physical sciences:** General. **Protective services:** Criminal justice. **Psychology:** General. **Public administration:** Human services, social work. **Visual/performing arts:** Art, art history/conservation, arts management, design, interior design. **Other:** Exercise science.

Most popular majors. Biological/life sciences 10%, business/marketing 22%, education 6%, health sciences 23%, liberal arts 8%, public administration/social services 6%, visual/performing arts 6%.

Computing on campus. 200 workstations in library, computer center, student center. Commuter students can connect to campus network. Online course registration, online library, helpline, wireless network available.

Student life. Freshman orientation: Mandatory. Preregistration for classes offered. **Activities:** Choral groups, dance, drama, international student organizations, literary magazine, music ensembles, musical theater, radio station, student government, TV station, Phi Theta Kappa, Native American student association, student nursing association, student council, Movimiento Estudiantil Chiemo de Aztlan, fine arts club, Los Tournants, sign language interpreters club, student ambassadors.

Student services. Adult student services, career counseling, services for economically disadvantaged, student employment services, financial aid counseling, on-campus daycare, personal counseling, placement for graduates, veterans' counselor, women's services. **Physically disabled:** Services for visually, speech, hearing impaired. **Transfer:** Transfer adviser, college fairs on campus for students transferring to 4-year colleges.

Contact. E-mail: enroll@sfccnm.edu
Phone: (505) 428-1278 Fax: (505) 428-1468
Amy Tilley, Director of Admissions, Santa Fe Community College, 6401 Richards Avenue, Santa Fe, NM 87508-4887

Southwestern Indian Polytechnic Institute

Albuquerque, New Mexico — **CB member**
www.sipi.bia.edu — **CB code: 7047**

- Public 2-year community and technical college
- Residential campus in large city

General. Founded in 1971. Regionally accredited. National Indian community college serving American Indians from federally recognized Indian tribes from across the United States. **Enrollment:** 470 degree-seeking undergraduates. **Degrees:** 54 associate awarded. **Calendar:** Trimester, extensive summer session. **Full-time faculty:** 20 total.

Student profile. Among degree-seeking undergraduates, 51% enrolled in a vocational program, 143 enrolled as first-time, first-year students, 33 transferred in from other institutions.

Part-time:	23%	**Native American:**	100%
Women:	57%		

Transfer out. Colleges most students transferred to 2008: University of New Mexico, New Mexico State University, New Mexico Highlands University, Fort Lewis College.

Basis for selection. Open admission, but selective for some programs. ACT, COMPASS, and TABE required for placement. Applicants must have valid membership in U.S. federally recognized Indian tribe. **Homeschooled:** Transcript of courses and grades, state high school equivalency certificate required.

2008-2009 Annual costs. Required fees: full-time Lodge student $280, full-time commuter $225, part-time $150. Tuition-free to Native Americans. Books/supplies: $1,200. Personal expenses: $1,400.

2007-2008 Financial aid. Need-based: Need-based aid available for part-time students. Work-study available nights and weekends. **Non-need-based:** Scholarships awarded for academics, leadership, minority status. **Additional information:** Students with valid membership in recognized Indian tribe attend tuition-free.

Application procedures. Admission: Closing date 8/1 (receipt date). No application fee. Admission notification on a rolling basis. **Financial aid:** Closing date 3/1. FAFSA required. Applicants notified on a rolling basis starting 9/30.

Academics. Special study options: Cooperative education, distance learning, double major, honors, liberal arts/career combination. **Credit/placement by examination:** AP, CLEP, institutional tests. **Support services:** GED preparation, learning center, remedial instruction, study skills assistance, tutoring.

Majors. Agriculture: Agribusiness operations, agronomy, soil science. **Business:** General, accounting technology, business admin, hospitality admin, hospitality/recreation, office technology. **Computer sciences:** General, computer science, LAN/WAN management. **Conservation:** General, environmental science, management/policy. **Education:** Early childhood. **Engineering technology:** Electrical, environmental, manufacturing, surveying. **Family/consumer sciences:** Institutional food production. **Health:** Optician, optometric assistant. **Liberal arts:** Arts/sciences. **Personal/culinary services:** General, culinary arts. **Social sciences:** Cartography.

Most popular majors. Business/marketing 23%, computer/information sciences 10%, education 9%, health sciences 10%, liberal arts 33%, personal/culinary services 6%.

Computing on campus. 15 workstations in dormitories, library, computer center, student center. Dormitories linked to campus network. Wireless network available.

Student life. Freshman orientation: Mandatory. Held week prior to start of classes. **Policies:** Zero tolerance policy on alcohol and drugs. **Housing:** Single-sex dorms available. $55 fully refundable deposit. **Activities:** Dance, natural resources club, Native American political action council, Phi Theta Kappa, student senate, dance club, AISES, inter-tribal pow-wow club, music and art club, Four Winds and Golden Eagle Lodge Council.

Athletics. Intramural: Basketball, softball, volleyball, weight lifting. **Team name:** Eagles.

Student services. Alcohol/substance abuse counseling, chaplain/spiritual director, career counseling, student employment services, financial aid counseling, health services, personal counseling, placement for graduates. **Transfer:** Transfer adviser, college fairs on campus for students transferring to 4-year colleges.

Contact. E-mail: jcarpio@sipi.bia.edu
Phone: (505) 346-2324 Toll-free number: (800) 586-7474
Fax: (505) 346-2373
Joseph Carpio, Registrar, Southwestern Indian Polytechnic Institute, 9169 Coors Road NW, Albuquerque, NM 87184

New York

Adirondack Community College

Queensbury, New York **CB member**
www.sunyacc.edu **CB code: 2017**

- Public 2-year community college
- Commuter campus in large town

General. Founded in 1960. Regionally accredited. **Enrollment:** 2,804 degree-seeking undergraduates. **Degrees:** 425 associate awarded. **Location:** 50 miles from Albany, 1 mile from Glens Falls. **Calendar:** Semester, limited summer session. **Full-time faculty:** 91 total. **Part-time faculty:** 142 total. **Special facilities:** Solar botany lab, challenge course, fitness trail, pond preserve, arboretum, weather station, forensic science lab.

Student profile.

Out-of-state:	1%	**25 or older:**	32%

Transfer out. Colleges most students transferred to 2008: SUNY Plattsburgh, Siena College, SUNY Albany, College of Saint Rose, SUNY Oneonta.

Basis for selection. Open admission, but selective for some programs. Minimum high school average of 80 or minimum GPA of 2.5 for acceptance into nursing program. If submitted, SAT or ACT and SAT Subject Tests used for placement and counseling. Essay and interview recommended. **Homeschooled:** Must take and pass GED or successfuly complete ability to benefit test.

High school preparation. 22 units recommended. Recommended units include English 4, mathematics 3, social studies 4, history 2, science 3, foreign language 1 and academic electives 5. Allied health programs require Regents biology, chemistry examinations. Engineering requires Regents biology, chemistry and mathematics through pre-calculus. Computer science, mechanical and electrical technology require mathematics through advanced algebra. Forestry requires Regents biology, chemistry, and mathematics through intermediate algebra.

2008-2009 Annual costs. Tuition/fees: $3,357; $6,487 out-of-state. Per-credit charge: $131 in-state; $262 out-of-state. Books/supplies: $1,200. Personal expenses: $990.

Financial aid. All financial aid based on need. Need-based aid available for part-time students.

Application procedures. Admission: Priority date 3/15; deadline 8/1. $40 fee, may be waived for applicants with need. Application must be submitted on paper. Admission notification on a rolling basis beginning on or about 1/15. **Financial aid:** Priority date 4/15; no closing date. FAFSA, institutional form required. Applicants notified on a rolling basis starting 5/1.

Academics. Special study options: Distance learning, double major, dual enrollment of high school students, independent study, internships, liberal arts/career combination, study abroad. Bachelor's degree programs available on campus. License preparation in nursing. **Credit/placement by examination:** AP, CLEP, IB, institutional tests. 34 credit hours maximum toward associate degree. **Support services:** GED preparation, learning center, reduced course load, remedial instruction, study skills assistance, tutoring, writing center.

Majors. Business: Accounting, business admin, hospitality/recreation, marketing, tourism promotion. **Communications:** Broadcast journalism, media studies. **Computer sciences:** General, computer science, data processing, information systems, programming. **Engineering:** General. **Engineering technology:** Drafting, electrical. **Health:** Nursing (RN), radiologic technology/medical imaging. **Liberal arts:** Arts/sciences. **Personal/culinary services:** Culinary arts. **Protective services:** Corrections, police science. **Other:** Adventure sports.

Most popular majors. Business/marketing 18%, health sciences 18%, liberal arts 46%, security/protective services 6%.

Computing on campus. 350 workstations in library, computer center, student center. Online library available.

Student life. Freshman orientation: Available. **Activities:** Concert band, choral groups, dance, drama, literary magazine, music ensembles, musical theater, radio station, student government, TV station.

Athletics. NJCAA. **Intercollegiate:** Baseball M, basketball, bowling, golf M, soccer, softball W, volleyball W. **Intramural:** Badminton, basketball, football (non-tackle), skiing, softball, volleyball. **Team name:** Timberwolves.

Student services. Adult student services, career counseling, student employment services, financial aid counseling, on-campus daycare, personal counseling, placement for graduates, veterans' counselor. **Physically disabled:** Services for visually, speech, hearing impaired. **Transfer:** Transfer adviser, college fairs on campus for students transferring to 4-year colleges.

Contact. E-mail: info@acc.sunyacc.edu
Phone: (518) 743-2264 Fax: (518) 832-7602
Sara Jane Linehan, Director of Enrollment Management, Adirondack Community College, 640 Bay Road, Queensbury, NY 12804

American Academy McAllister Institute of Funeral Service

New York, New York
www.funeraleducation.org **CB code: 0774**

- Private 2-year school of mortuary science
- Commuter campus in very large city

General. Founded in 1926. **Enrollment:** 286 degree-seeking undergraduates. **Degrees:** 49 associate awarded. **Calendar:** Semester, extensive summer session. **Full-time faculty:** 3 total. **Part-time faculty:** 23 total. **Class size:** 67% 20-39, 33% 40-49.

Student profile.

Out-of-state:	26%	**25 or older:**	39%

Basis for selection. Open admission. Interview recommended.

2009-2010 Annual costs. Tuition/fees: $11,370. Books/supplies: $709. Personal expenses: $2,635.

Financial aid. All financial aid based on need.

Application procedures. Admission: Closing date 8/10. $50 fee. Admission notification on a rolling basis. **Financial aid:** FAFSA required. Applicants notified on a rolling basis starting 7/1; must reply by 9/1 or within 3 week(s) of notification.

Academics. Special study options: Cross-registration. **Credit/placement by examination:** CLEP. **Support services:** Tutoring.

Majors. Personal/culinary services: Mortuary science.

Computing on campus. 12 workstations in library.

Student life. Activities: Student government.

Student services. Personal counseling, placement for graduates. **Transfer:** Transfer adviser for students transferring to 4-year colleges.

Contact. E-mail: info@funeraleducation.org
Phone: (212) 757-1190 Fax: (212) 765-5923
Norman Provost, Director of Admissions/Bursar, American Academy McAllister Institute of Funeral Service, 619 West 54th Street, New York, NY 10019-3602

American Academy of Dramatic Arts

New York, New York
www.aada.org **CB code: 2603**

- Private 2-year junior and performing arts college
- Commuter campus in very large city
- Application essay, interview required

General. Founded in 1884. Regionally accredited. Offers practical conservatory and training. Additional campus in Hollywood, CA. **Enrollment:** 205 degree-seeking undergraduates. **Degrees:** 104 associate awarded. **Location:** Midtown Manhattan. **Calendar:** Semester, limited summer session. **Full-time faculty:** 7 total; 43% have terminal degrees, 57% women. **Part-time faculty:** 19 total; 21% have terminal degrees, 16% minority. **Class**

size: 100% < 20. **Special facilities:** 3 theaters, dance studio, costume department, property/production areas, audio/visual center, state-of-the-art television studio.

Student profile. Among degree-seeking undergraduates, 2% already have a bachelor's degree or higher, 55 enrolled as first-time, first-year students, 43 transferred in from other institutions.

Out-of-state:	87%	**Hispanic American:**	5%
Women:	63%	**International:**	26%
African American:	3%	**25 or older:**	14%
Asian American:	1%		

Basis for selection. Dramatic ability or potential, academic qualifications, maturity and motivation very important. Audition required; regional audition/interview may be arranged. **Homeschooled:** Transcript of courses and grades, interview, letter of recommendation (nonparent) required.

2009-2010 Annual costs. Tuition/fees: $27,500. Books/supplies: $1,650. Personal expenses: $1,100.

2007-2008 Financial aid. All financial aid based on need. **Additional information:** Need-based incentive grants of $200-$500 for first-year students available. Merit awards of $500-$1,500. Scholarships of $500-$3,000 available for second year. Scholarships of $500-$5,000 available for post-degree third year.

Application procedures. Admission: No deadline. $50 fee. Admission notification on a rolling basis. **Financial aid:** No deadline. FAFSA, institutional form required. Applicants notified on a rolling basis.

Academics. 2-year professional actor training program offered with associate of occupational studies degree. Third year, available by faculty invitation, forms showcase Academy Company. **Special study options:** Students may study 1 year at each of 2 campuses. **Credit/placement by examination:** CLEP. **Support services:** Tutoring.

Majors. Visual/performing arts: Acting.

Most popular majors. Visual/performing arts 95%.

Computing on campus. 6 workstations in library.

Student life. Freshman orientation: Mandatory. **Activities:** Drama, student government, student newspaper, various arts-related organizations available.

Student services. Career counseling, student employment services, placement for graduates.

Contact. E-mail: admissions-ny@aada.org
Phone: (212) 686-9244 Toll-free number: (800) 463-8990
Fax: (212) 685-8093
Karen Higginbotham, Director of Admissions, American Academy of Dramatic Arts, 120 Madison Avenue, New York, NY 10016

Art Institute of New York City

New York, New York — **CB member**
www.ainyc.artinstitutes.edu — **CB code: 3106**

- For-profit 2-year culinary school and technical college
- Commuter campus in very large city
- Application essay, interview required

General. Accredited by ACICS. **Enrollment:** 1,442 degree-seeking undergraduates. **Degrees:** 251 associate awarded. **Calendar:** Quarter, extensive summer session. **Full-time faculty:** 75 total. **Part-time faculty:** 22 total.

Basis for selection. Open admission. Accuplacer may be used in placement for certain programs of study. **Homeschooled:** Transcript of courses and grades, state high school equivalency certificate required.

2008-2009 Annual costs. Tuition/fees: $26,784. Per-credit charge: $509. Students in nonculinary programs (e.g., graphic design, fashion design, video production, advertising) do not pay $2,352 in additional fees. Fees may vary within culinary programs. Books/supplies: $650.

Application procedures. Admission: No deadline. $50 fee. Admission notification on a rolling basis.

Academics. Special study options: Internships. **Credit/placement by examination:** AP, CLEP. **Support services:** Learning center, remedial instruction, study skills assistance.

Majors. Personal/culinary services: Culinary arts. **Visual/performing arts:** Cinematography, fashion design, graphic design, interior design, multimedia.

Computing on campus. 40 workstations in library, computer center. Online library, helpline, repair service available.

Student life. Freshman orientation: Mandatory. Preregistration for classes offered. Scheduled prior to class start or in first week. **Activities:** Film society, student newspaper.

Student services. Adult student services, career counseling, student employment services, financial aid counseling, personal counseling, placement for graduates. **Transfer:** Re-entry adviser, pre-admission transcript evaluation for new students.

Contact. E-mail: mgrillo@aii.edu
Phone: (212) 226-5500 Toll-free number: (800) 654-2433
Fax: (212) 625-6065
Mary Ann Grillo, Senior Director of Admissions, Art Institute of New York City, 75 Varick Street, 16th Floor, New York, NY 10013-1917

ASA Institute of Business and Computer Technology

Brooklyn, New York
www.asa.edu

- For-profit 2-year career college
- Commuter campus in very large city
- Interview required

General. Regionally accredited; also accredited by ACICS. **Enrollment:** 3,583 degree-seeking undergraduates; 14 non-degree-seeking students. **Degrees:** 932 associate awarded. **Location:** Located in New York City. **Calendar:** Semester, extensive summer session. **Full-time faculty:** 53 total. **Part-time faculty:** 162 total. **Class size:** 49% < 20, 45% 20-39, 6% 40-49, less than 1% 50-99.

Student profile. Among degree-seeking undergraduates, 1,294 enrolled as first-time, first-year students, 283 transferred in from other institutions.

Part-time:	3%	**Hispanic American:**	39%
Out-of-state:	1%	**Native American:**	1%
Women:	73%	**International:**	7%
African American:	43%	**25 or older:**	53%
Asian American:	5%		

Basis for selection. Open admission. Candidates accorded individual consideration through assessment testing results.

2009-2010 Annual costs. Tuition/fees (projected): $11,499. Per-credit charge: $470. Books/supplies: $1,500. Personal expenses: $4,985.

2007-2008 Financial aid. Need-based: 56% of total undergraduate aid awarded as scholarships/grants, 44% as loans/jobs. Need-based aid available for part-time students. Work-study available nights and weekends. **Non-need-based:** Scholarships awarded for academics, alumni affiliation, leadership, state residency.

Application procedures. Admission: No deadline. $25 fee. Application must be submitted on paper. **Financial aid:** No deadline. FAFSA required. Applicants notified on a rolling basis starting 7/6; must reply by 10/6.

Academics. Special study options: Accelerated study, distance learning, ESL, internships. **Credit/placement by examination:** AP, CLEP. **Support services:** GED preparation, learning center, reduced course load, remedial instruction, study skills assistance, tutoring, writing center.

Majors. Business: Accounting/business management, business admin. **Computer sciences:** Networking, programming. **Health:** Medical assistant, medical records technology, pharmacy assistant. **Legal studies:** General. **Protective services:** Criminal justice.

Most popular majors. Business/marketing 18%, computer/information sciences 7%, health sciences 71%.

Computing on campus. 700 workstations in dormitories, library, computer center. Online library, helpline available.

Student life. Freshman orientation: Mandatory. **Activities:** Drama, literary magazine, student government.

Athletics. NJCAA. **Intercollegiate:** Basketball, soccer M.

Student services. Adult student services, career counseling, services for economically disadvantaged, student employment services, financial aid counseling, personal counseling, placement for graduates.

Contact. E-mail: admissions@asa.edu
Phone: (718) 522-9073 Toll-free number: (877) 867-5327
Fax: (718) 532-1432
Victoria Kostyukov, Vice President of Marketing and Admissions, ASA Institute of Business and Computer Technology, 151 Lawrence Street, Brooklyn, NY 11201

Bramson ORT College

Forest Hills, New York
www.bramsonort.org **CB code: 0944**

- Private 2-year junior and technical college affiliated with Jewish faith
- Commuter campus in very large city

General. Founded in 1977. Regionally accredited. Extensions in Brooklyn and Manhattan. **Enrollment:** 650 undergraduates. **Degrees:** 139 associate awarded. **Calendar:** Semester, extensive summer session. **Part-time faculty:** 89 total. **Special facilities:** Ophthalmic laboratory.

Basis for selection. High school diploma and placement examination required. English and mathematics placement tests required. Interview recommended.

2008-2009 Annual costs. Tuition/fees: $9,760. Per-credit charge: $395.

Application procedures. Admission: No deadline. $50 fee. Admission notification on a rolling basis. **Financial aid:** No deadline. Institutional form required. Applicants notified on a rolling basis; must reply within 3 week(s) of notification.

Academics. Special study options: Accelerated study, double major, ESL, internships. **Credit/placement by examination:** CLEP, institutional tests. 50% of total hours needed for degree may be maximum of earned by examination. **Support services:** Learning center, pre-admission summer program, reduced course load, remedial instruction, tutoring.

Majors. Business: Accounting, administrative services, business admin, financial planning, management information systems. **Computer sciences:** General, applications programming, data processing, programming. **Engineering:** Electrical.

Computing on campus. 87 workstations in library, computer center.

Student life. Activities: Student government, student newspaper.

Student services. Adult student services, career counseling, student employment services, personal counseling, placement for graduates, veterans' counselor. **Physically disabled:** Services for visually, speech, hearing impaired.

Contact. Phone: (718) 261-5800 Fax: (718) 575-5118
Aleksandra Kagan, Admissions Coordinator, Bramson ORT College, 6930 Austin Street, Forest Hills, NY 11375

Broome Community College

Binghamton, New York **CB member**
www.sunybroome.edu **CB code: 2048**

- Public 2-year community college
- Commuter campus in small city

General. Founded in 1946. Regionally accredited. SUNY institution. **Enrollment:** 5,414 degree-seeking undergraduates; 1,211 non-degree-seeking students. **Degrees:** 995 associate awarded. **Location:** 3 miles from downtown. **Calendar:** Semester, extensive summer session. **Full-time faculty:** 168 total. **Part-time faculty:** 238 total. **Class size:** 67% < 20, 31% 20-39, less than 1% 40-49, less than 1% 50-99, less than 1% >100. **Special facilities:** College-operated ice rink.

Student profile. Among degree-seeking undergraduates, 49% enrolled in a transfer program, 51% enrolled in a vocational program, 1,287 enrolled as first-time, first-year students.

Part-time:	24%	**Hispanic American:**	3%
Out-of-state:	4%	**Native American:**	1%
Women:	55%	**International:**	3%
African American:	4%	**25 or older:**	28%
Asian American:	2%		

Transfer out. Colleges most students transferred to 2008: Binghamton University, Rochester Institute of Technology, State University of New York Cortland, State University of New York Utica-Rome, Ithaca College.

Basis for selection. Open admission, but selective for some programs. Entry into certain health sciences programs (nursing, physical therapy assistant, medical lab technology, medical assistant, radiologic technology, health information technology, dental hygiene) limited on space-available basis. Interview recommended for computer science and health science programs. **Homeschooled:** Provide either 1) letter from superintendent of the school district in which student resides attesting to completion of program meeting requirements of Section 100.10 of the Regulations of the Commissioner of Education or 2) a passing score on GED (and diploma itself when available). Also may be admitted on ability-to-benefit basis.

2008-2009 Annual costs. Tuition/fees: $3,547; $6,709 out-of-state. Per-credit charge: $132 in-state; $264 out-of-state. Books/supplies: $1,400. Personal expenses: $938.

2008-2009 Financial aid. Need-based: Need-based aid available for part-time students. Work-study available nights.

Application procedures. Admission: No deadline. No application fee. Admission notification on a rolling basis. Health Science students should apply and have all transcripts sent by March 15 prior to the fall semester. **Financial aid:** Priority date 3/1; no closing date. FAFSA required. Applicants notified on a rolling basis starting 3/15; must reply within 2 week(s) of notification.

Academics. Special study options: Cooperative education, distance learning, dual enrollment of high school students, ESL, exchange student, honors, independent study, internships, student-designed major, study abroad, weekend college. License preparation in dental hygiene, nursing, paramedic, physical therapy, radiology, real estate. **Credit/placement by examination:** AP, CLEP, institutional tests. Contact division dean for assessment of experiential learning or portfolio assessment. **Support services:** Learning center, reduced course load, remedial instruction, study skills assistance, tutoring, writing center.

Majors. Business: Accounting technology, business admin, executive assistant, financial planning, hotel/motel admin, international finance. **Communications:** General. **Computer sciences:** General, data processing, information systems. **Engineering:** Science. **Engineering technology:** Civil, computer, electrical, industrial, mechanical, quality control. **Family/consumer sciences:** Child care. **Health:** Clinical lab technology, dental hygiene, EMT paramedic, medical assistant, medical radiologic technology/radiation therapy, medical records technology, nursing (RN), physical therapy assistant, substance abuse counseling. **Legal studies:** Paralegal. **Liberal arts:** Arts/sciences. **Protective services:** Corrections, firefighting, police science.

Most popular majors. Business/marketing 17%, engineering/engineering technologies 8%, health sciences 19%, liberal arts 40%, security/protective services 6%.

Computing on campus. 500 workstations in library, computer center. Commuter students can connect to campus network. Online course registration, helpline, wireless network available.

Student life. Freshman orientation: Available. Preregistration for classes offered. **Activities:** Bands, campus ministries, choral groups, dance, drama, international student organizations, music ensembles, musical theater, student government, student newspaper, black student union, Phi Theta Kappa, Ski Extreme, writing club, chess club, Alpha Beta Gamma, computer club, music association.

Athletics. NJCAA. **Intercollegiate:** Baseball M, basketball, cheerleading, cross-country, golf M, ice hockey M, lacrosse M, soccer, tennis M, volleyball W. **Intramural:** Badminton, basketball, bowling, golf, soccer, tennis, volleyball. **Team name:** Hornets.

Student services. Adult student services, career counseling, services for economically disadvantaged, student employment services, financial aid counseling, health services, on-campus daycare, personal counseling, placement for graduates, veterans' counselor. **Physically disabled:** Services for visually, speech, hearing impaired. **Transfer:** Transfer adviser, college fairs on campus for students transferring to 4-year colleges.

Contact. Phone: (607) 778-5001 Toll-free number: (800) 836-0689
Fax: (607) 778-5310
Janae Schmidt, Director of Admissions, Broome Community College, Box 1017, Binghamton, NY 13902

Bryant & Stratton College: Albany

Albany, New York
www.bryantstratton.edu **CB code: 2018**

- For-profit 2-year business college
- Commuter campus in small city
- Application essay, interview required

General. Founded in 1854. Regionally accredited. **Enrollment:** 686 degree-seeking undergraduates; 3 non-degree-seeking students. **Degrees:** 175 associate awarded. **Location:** 2 miles from Albany, 28 miles from Saratoga. **Calendar:** Semester, extensive summer session. **Full-time faculty:** 16 total; 38% have terminal degrees, 12% minority, 31% women. **Part-time faculty:** 41 total; 17% have terminal degrees, 10% minority, 54% women.

Student profile. Among degree-seeking undergraduates, 141 enrolled as first-time, first-year students.

Part-time:	32%	**25 or older:**	51%
Women:	77%		

Basis for selection. High school record, entrance examination score, personal interview and personal essay considered. Portfolio recommended.

High school preparation. Business courses recommended. Mathematics concentration preferred.

2008-2009 Annual costs. Tuition/fees: $13,740. Tuition may vary depending on program.

2007-2008 Financial aid. All financial aid based on need. Need-based aid available for part-time students. Work-study available nights, weekends and for part-time students.

Application procedures. Admission: No deadline. No application fee. Admission notification on a rolling basis. Must reply by May 1 or within 4 week(s) if notified thereafter. **Financial aid:** No deadline. FAFSA required. Applicants notified on a rolling basis.

Academics. Special study options: Distance learning, double major, independent study, internships. **Credit/placement by examination:** CLEP. 31 credit hours maximum toward associate degree. **Support services:** Learning center, reduced course load, remedial instruction, tutoring, writing center.

Majors. Business: Accounting, administrative services, business admin, human resources. **Computer sciences:** General. **Health:** Medical assistant. **Legal studies:** Paralegal. **Protective services:** Law enforcement admin.

Most popular majors. Business/marketing 40%, computer/information sciences 7%, health sciences 23%, legal studies 14%, security/protective services 16%.

Computing on campus. 100 workstations in library, computer center.

Student life. Freshman orientation: Mandatory.

Student services. Alcohol/substance abuse counseling, career counseling, student employment services, financial aid counseling, personal counseling, placement for graduates, veterans' counselor. **Physically disabled:** Services for visually impaired. **Transfer:** Pre-admission transcript evaluation for new students. Transfer adviser, college fairs on campus for students transferring to 4-year colleges.

Contact. Phone: (518) 437-1802 ext. 203 Fax: (518) 437-1049
Robert Ferrell, Director of Admissions, Bryant & Stratton College: Albany, 1259 Central Avenue, Albany, NY 12205

Bryant & Stratton College: Amherst

Amherst, New York
www.bryantstratton.edu **CB code: 3331**

- For-profit 2-year business college
- Small town

General. Regionally accredited. **Calendar:** Continuous.

Annual costs/financial aid. Tuition/fees (2008-2009): $13,080. Tuition varies by program. Books/supplies: $1,200.

Contact. Phone: (716) 691-0012
40 Hazelwood Drive, Amherst, NY 14228-2230

Bryant & Stratton College: Buffalo

Buffalo, New York
www.bryantstratton.edu **CB code: 2058**

- For-profit 2-year business and career college
- Large city
- Interview required

General. Founded in 1854. Regionally accredited. Branch campuses in Amherst and Orchard Park. **Enrollment:** 693 degree-seeking undergraduates. **Degrees:** 84 associate awarded. **Calendar:** Semester, extensive summer session. **Full-time faculty:** 11 total; 9% have terminal degrees, 73% women. **Part-time faculty:** 56 total; 2% have terminal degrees, 54% women.

Student profile. Among degree-seeking undergraduates, 29 transferred in from other institutions.

Transfer out. Colleges most students transferred to 2008: Erie Community College.

Basis for selection. Open admission. **Learning Disabled:** Students with special needs are invited to discuss their needs with their student services advisor prior to registration. Students requesting accommodations are required to provide current documentation in order to determine reasonable accommodations where appropriate.

2008-2009 Annual costs. Tuition/fees: $13,740. Per-credit charge: $458. Books/supplies: $1,200. Personal expenses: $1,350.

Application procedures. Admission: No deadline. $25 fee, may be waived for applicants with need. Admission notification on a rolling basis. CPAt entrance exam. **Financial aid:** No deadline. Applicants notified on a rolling basis.

Academics. Special study options: Distance learning, internships, weekend college. Bachelor's degree programs available on campus. **Credit/placement by examination:** AP, CLEP, institutional tests. 45 credit hours maximum toward associate degree. **Support services:** Learning center, remedial instruction, study skills assistance, tutoring, writing center.

Majors. Business: General, administrative services. **Computer sciences:** General. **Health:** Medical assistant.

Computing on campus. 130 workstations in library, computer center. Online library available.

Student life. Freshman orientation: Mandatory. Preregistration for classes offered. **Activities:** Radio station, student government, student newspaper, numerous special interest clubs.

Athletics. Intramural: Bowling, skiing, softball, swimming.

Student services. Career counseling, student employment services, personal counseling, placement for graduates. **Physically disabled:** Services for visually, hearing impaired. **Transfer:** Re-entry adviser, pre-admission transcript evaluation for new students. Transfer adviser, college fairs on campus for students transferring to 4-year colleges.

Contact. E-mail: mbrobinson@bryantstratton.edu
Phone: (716) 884-9120 Fax: (716) 884-0091
Philip Struebel, Director of Admissions, Bryant & Stratton College: Buffalo, 465 Main Street, Suite 400, Buffalo, NY 14203

Bryant & Stratton College: Henrietta

Rochester, New York
www.bryantstratton.edu

- For-profit 2-year business college
- Commuter campus in small city

General. Calendar: Semester.

Annual costs/financial aid. Tuition/fees (2008-2009): $13,740.

Contact. Phone: (585) 292-5627
Admissions Director, 1225 Jefferson Road, Rochester, NY 14623

Bryant & Stratton College: Rochester
Rochester, New York
www.bryantstratton.edu **CB code: 7327**

- For-profit 2-year business college
- Commuter campus in large city
- Interview required

General. Founded in 1973. Regionally accredited. Second campus in Rochester. Degree program runs 4 consecutive semesters. **Enrollment:** 700 degree-seeking undergraduates. **Degrees:** 252 associate awarded. **Calendar:** Continuous, extensive summer session. **Full-time faculty:** 20 total. **Part-time faculty:** 65 total.

Basis for selection. Character, previous scholastic record, and counselor recommendation important. CPAt required for admission.

2008-2009 Annual costs. Tuition/fees: $13,740. Per-credit charge: $458. Books/supplies: $1,000.

Application procedures. Admission: No deadline. $35 fee, may be waived for applicants with need. Admission notification on a rolling basis. **Financial aid:** No deadline. FAFSA required. Applicants notified on a rolling basis.

Academics. Special study options: Accelerated study, distance learning, double major, internships. **Credit/placement by examination:** CLEP. **Support services:** Learning center, reduced course load, study skills assistance, tutoring.

Majors. Business: Accounting, administrative services, business admin, customer service, office technology. **Computer sciences:** Information technology, webmaster. **Health:** Office admin. **Legal studies:** Legal secretary, paralegal. **Visual/performing arts:** Design.

Computing on campus. 10 workstations in computer center. Commuter students can connect to campus network.

Student life. Freshman orientation: Available. Preregistration for classes offered. **Activities:** Student government, professional interest clubs.

Athletics. Team name: Bobcats.

Student services. Career counseling, financial aid counseling, personal counseling, placement for graduates. **Transfer:** Pre-admission transcript evaluation for new students. Transfer adviser for students transferring to 4-year colleges.

Contact. Phone: (585) 292-5627
Maria Scalise, Director of Admissions, Bryant & Stratton College: Rochester, 1225 Jefferson Road, Rochester, NY 14623

Bryant & Stratton College: Southtowns
Orchard Park, New York
www.bryantstratton.edu **CB code: 3328**

- For-profit 2-year business college
- Commuter campus in large town

General. Regionally accredited. **Enrollment:** 419 degree-seeking undergraduates. **Degrees:** 2 associate awarded. **Location:** 11 miles from downtown Buffalo. **Calendar:** Continuous, extensive summer session. **Full-time faculty:** 7 total. **Part-time faculty:** 25 total.

Basis for selection. Open admission.

2008-2009 Annual costs. Tuition/fees: $13,740. Tuition costs vary by program. Books/supplies: $1,200.

Application procedures. Admission: No deadline. $25 fee.

Academics. Special study options: Distance learning, double major. **Credit/placement by examination:** CLEP. **Support services:** Learning center, study skills assistance, tutoring.

Majors. Business: Business admin. **Computer sciences:** General.

Computing on campus. Online library available.

Student life. Freshman orientation: Mandatory. Preregistration for classes offered. **Activities:** Student government, student newspaper.

Student services. Career counseling, student employment services, financial aid counseling. **Physically disabled:** Services for visually, hearing impaired. **Transfer:** Pre-admission transcript evaluation for new students.

Contact. E-mail: prkehr@bryantstratton.edu
Phone: (716) 677-9500 Fax: (716) 677-9599
Paul Kehr, Director of Admissions, Bryant & Stratton College: Southtowns, 200 Redtail, Orchard Park, NY 14127

Bryant & Stratton College: Syracuse
Syracuse, New York
www.bryantstratton.edu **CB code: 0654**

- For-profit 2-year business college
- Commuter campus in small city

General. Founded in 1854. Regionally accredited. **Enrollment:** 723 degree-seeking undergraduates; 1 non-degree-seeking students. **Degrees:** 190 associate awarded. **Location:** 75 miles from Rochester. **Calendar:** Trimester, extensive summer session. **Full-time faculty:** 19 total. **Part-time faculty:** 46 total. **Class size:** 54% < 20, 46% 20-39.

Student profile. Among degree-seeking undergraduates, 234 enrolled as first-time, first-year students.

Part-time:	32%	**25 or older:**	45%
Out-of-state:	2%	**Live on campus:**	10%
Women:	73%		

Basis for selection. Open admission.

2008-2009 Annual costs. Tuition/fees: $13,775. Per-credit charge: $458. Total room and board is $7,140 for triple-occupancy residence. Books/supplies: $700.

2008-2009 Financial aid. All financial aid based on need. Work-study available nights, weekends and for part-time students.

Application procedures. Admission: No deadline. No application fee. Application must be submitted on paper. Admission notification on a rolling basis. **Financial aid:** No deadline. FAFSA required. Applicants notified on a rolling basis starting 10/1.

Academics. Special study options: Cross-registration, distance learning, honors, internships. **Credit/placement by examination:** AP, CLEP. **Support services:** Learning center, reduced course load, remedial instruction, study skills assistance, tutoring.

Majors. Business: Accounting, administrative services, business admin, hotel/motel admin, marketing, office management, sales/distribution, tourism promotion, tourism/travel. **Computer sciences:** General. **Health:** Medical assistant, medical secretary. **Legal studies:** Legal secretary. **Protective services:** Police science.

Most popular majors. Business/marketing 61%, health sciences 35%.

Computing on campus. 230 workstations in dormitories, library, computer center. Dormitories wired for high-speed internet access and linked to campus network. Commuter students can connect to campus network. Online library available.

Student life. Freshman orientation: Mandatory. **Housing:** Single-sex dorms available. $100 fully refundable deposit. **Activities:** Student newspaper.

Athletics. NJCAA. **Intercollegiate:** Soccer. **Team name:** Bobcats.

Student services. Career counseling, student employment services, financial aid counseling, personal counseling, placement for graduates. **Physically disabled:** Services for visually, speech, hearing impaired. **Transfer:** Re-entry adviser, pre-admission transcript evaluation for new students. Transfer adviser, college fairs on campus for students transferring to 4-year colleges.

Contact. Phone: (315) 472-6603 Fax: (315) 474-4383
Andy Cunningham, Director of Admissions, Bryant & Stratton College: Syracuse, 953 James Street, Syracuse, NY 13203

Bryant & Stratton College: Syracuse North
Liverpool, New York
www.bryantstratton.edu

- For-profit 2-year business college
- Commuter campus in small town
- Interview required

General. **Enrollment:** 530 degree-seeking undergraduates. **Degrees:** 146 associate awarded. **Location:** 5 miles from Syracuse. **Calendar:** Semester, extensive summer session. **Full-time faculty:** 11 total; 9% have terminal degrees, 9% minority, 54% women. **Part-time faculty:** 76 total; 3% minority, 54% women.

Transfer out. **Colleges most students transferred to 2008:** Onondaga Community College.

Basis for selection. Open admission. ACCUPLACER used for placement/counseling; students with minimum SAT (exclusive of Writing) 956 or 20 ACT not required to take ACCUPLACER.

2008-2009 Annual costs. Tuition/fees: $13,080.

2007-2008 Financial aid. All financial aid based on need. 166 full-time freshmen applied for aid; 134 were judged to have need; 134 of these received aid. Average need met was 90%. Average scholarship/grant was $9,732; average loan $3,500. 55% of total undergraduate aid awarded as scholarships/grants, 45% as loans/jobs. Need-based aid available for part-time students. Work-study available nights and for part-time students.

Application procedures. **Admission:** No deadline. $35 fee. Admission notification on a rolling basis. **Financial aid:** No deadline. FAFSA, institutional form required.

Academics. **Special study options:** Internships. **Credit/placement by examination:** AP, CLEP. **Support services:** GED preparation, learning center, study skills assistance.

Majors. **Business:** General, accounting, administrative services. **Computer sciences:** Information technology. **Legal studies:** Paralegal. **Visual/performing arts:** Graphic design.

Student life. **Freshman orientation:** Available.

Athletics. NJCAA. **Intercollegiate:** Cross-country, soccer. **Team name:** Bobcats.

Student services. Career counseling, financial aid counseling, placement for graduates.

Contact. Phone: (315) 652-6500
Heather Macknick, Admissions Director, Bryant & Stratton College: Syracuse North, 8687 Carling Road, Liverpool, NY 13090

Business Informatics Center

Valley Stream, New York
www.thecollegeforbusiness.com

- For-profit 2-year business and community college
- Commuter campus in large town
- Interview required

General. Accredited by ACCSCT. **Enrollment:** 150 degree-seeking undergraduates. **Degrees:** 50 associate awarded. **Calendar:** Quarter. **Full-time faculty:** 10 total. **Part-time faculty:** 5 total. **Class size:** 92% <20, 8% 20-39.

Transfer out. **Colleges most students transferred to 2008:** Briarcliff College, Katharine Gibbs.

Basis for selection. Open admission.

2008-2009 Annual costs. Tuition/fees: $11,580.

Application procedures. **Admission:** No deadline. $50 fee, may be waived for applicants with need. Admission notification on a rolling basis. **Financial aid:** No deadline.

Academics. **Credit/placement by examination:** AP, CLEP, institutional tests. **Support services:** Tutoring.

Majors. **Business:** Office technology. **Legal studies:** Court reporting.

Most popular majors. Business/marketing 77%, legal studies 23%.

Computing on campus. 50 workstations in library, computer center.

Student life. **Freshman orientation:** Mandatory. **Activities:** Student government.

Student services. Financial aid counseling, placement for graduates. **Transfer:** Transfer center for students transferring to 4-year colleges.

Contact. Phone: (516) 561-0050
Hank Meaney, Admissions Director, Business Informatics Center, 134 South Central Avenue, Valley Stream, NY 11580-5431

Cayuga County Community College

Auburn, New York
www.cayuga-cc.edu **CB code: 2010**

- Public 2-year community college
- Commuter campus in large town

General. Founded in 1953. Regionally accredited. **Enrollment:** 2,606 degree-seeking undergraduates; 1,302 non-degree-seeking students. **Degrees:** 510 associate awarded. **Location:** 30 miles from Syracuse. **Calendar:** Semester, limited summer session. **Full-time faculty:** 59 total; 20% have terminal degrees, 3% minority, 49% women. **Part-time faculty:** 143 total; less than 1% minority, 59% women. **Class size:** 55% < 20, 45% 20-39, less than 1% 40-49, less than 1% 50-99. **Special facilities:** Nature trail, multitrack recording studio and video-editing suites, NASA Institute for the Application of Geospatial Technology.

Student profile. Among degree-seeking undergraduates, 43% enrolled in a transfer program, 23% enrolled in a vocational program, 518 enrolled as first-time, first-year students.

Part-time:	24%	**Asian American:**	1%
Out-of-state:	1%	**Hispanic American:**	2%
Women:	60%	**Native American:**	1%
African American:	3%	**25 or older:**	34%

Transfer out. 47% of students enrolled in the transfer program go on to 4-year colleges. **Colleges most students transferred to 2008:** SUNY Oswego, SUNY Cortland, SUNY Brockport, Rochester Institute of Technology, SUNY Institute of Technology.

Basis for selection. Open admission, but selective for some programs. Special requirements for nursing; interview required. All new students with no prior college credits must take placement test in English and math. **Homeschooled:** Must be able to document completion of high school or equivalent through: 1) official final high school transcript from student's school district indicating graduation or 2) letter on district letterhead from relevant district superintendent certifying that student has documented satisfactory completion of equivalent of 4-year high school program of study or 3) GED achieved by the State Education Department written exam or 4) taking college's placement test; and if Ability to Benefit scores set by college met/exceeded, may matriculate and be considered for financial aid and work toward satisfying 24-credit option prescribed by New York State Education Department.

High school preparation. Recommended units include English 4, mathematics 2, social studies 3 and science 1.

2008-2009 Annual costs. Tuition/fees: $3,763; $7,153 out-of-state. Per-credit charge: $132 in-state; $264 out-of-state. Books/supplies: $1,000. Personal expenses: $939.

2007-2008 Financial aid. All financial aid based on need. Need-based aid available for part-time students. Work-study available nights, weekends and for part-time students.

Application procedures. **Admission:** No deadline. No application fee. Admission notification on a rolling basis. **Financial aid:** Closing date 5/1. FAFSA required. Applicants notified on a rolling basis starting 3/15.

Academics. **Special study options:** Accelerated study, distance learning, double major, dual enrollment of high school students, honors, independent study, internships, liberal arts/career combination, study abroad, weekend college. License preparation in nursing. **Credit/placement by examination:** AP, CLEP, institutional tests. 30 credit hours maximum toward associate degree. **Support services:** Learning center, pre-admission summer program, reduced course load, remedial instruction, study skills assistance, tutoring, writing center.

Majors. **Biology:** General. **Business:** Accounting technology, business admin. **Communications:** Broadcast journalism, radio/tv. **Communications technology:** General, photo/film/video, recording arts. **Computer sciences:** General, computer science, web page design. **Education:** Early childhood. **Engineering technology:** Computer hardware, electrical, mechanical, telecommunications. **Health:** Nursing (RN). **Liberal arts:** Arts/sciences. **Math:** General. **Physical sciences:** Chemistry, geology. **Protective services:** Corrections, police science. **Visual/performing arts:** Art, studio arts.

Most popular majors. Business/marketing 17%, health sciences 8%, legal studies 15%, liberal arts 46%.

Computing on campus. 450 workstations in library, computer center. Online library, wireless network available.

Student life. Freshman orientation: Available. Held week before classes begin. **Activities:** Choral groups, drama, musical theater, radio station, student government, student newspaper, TV station, honor fraternity, business society, nursing club, multicultural association, criminal justice club, alumni association, diversity club.

Athletics. NJCAA. **Intercollegiate:** Basketball, lacrosse, soccer. **Intramural:** Racquetball, skiing, volleyball. **Team name:** Spartans.

Student services. Chaplain/spiritual director, career counseling, student employment services, financial aid counseling, health services, on-campus daycare, personal counseling, placement for graduates, veterans' counselor. **Learning disabled:** Comprehensive services available. **Transfer:** Pre-admission transcript evaluation for new students. Transfer adviser, college fairs on campus for students transferring to 4-year colleges.

Contact. E-mail: admissions@cayuga-cc.edu
Phone: (315) 255-1743 ext. 2241 Fax: (315) 255-2117
Bruce Blodgett, Director of Admissions, Cayuga County Community College, 197 Franklin Street, Auburn, NY 13021-3099

City University of New York: Borough of Manhattan Community College

New York, New York — **CB member**
www.bmcc.cuny.edu — **CB code: 2063**

- Public 2-year community college
- Commuter campus in very large city

General. Founded in 1963. Regionally accredited. **Enrollment:** 21,118 degree-seeking undergraduates; 740 non-degree-seeking students. **Degrees:** 2,175 associate awarded. **Calendar:** Semester, limited summer session. **Full-time faculty:** 393 total. **Part-time faculty:** 804 total. **Special facilities:** 2 theaters, media center, gymnasium with intercollegiate-size swimming pool.

Student profile. Among degree-seeking undergraduates, 4,949 enrolled as first-time, first-year students.

Part-time:	35%	**Asian American:**	11%
Out-of-state:	1%	**Hispanic American:**	33%
Women:	59%	**International:**	9%
African American:	33%	**25 or older:**	32%

Transfer out. Colleges most students transferred to 2008: Baruch College, Hunter College, City College, Brooklyn College, New York City College of Technology.

Basis for selection. Open admission, but selective for some programs. Special requirements for associate degree programs in nursing; admission to clinical sequence of AAS degree programs competitive, based on college GPA. High school academic units recommended for admission must be acquired before graduation.

High school preparation. 16 units recommended. Recommended units include English 4, mathematics 3, social studies 4, science 2 (laboratory 2) and foreign language 2. One unit of fine arts recommended.

2008-2009 Annual costs. Tuition/fees: $3,118; $6,018 out-of-state. Per-credit charge: $120 in-state; $190 out-of-state. Books/supplies: $938.

2007-2008 Financial aid. All financial aid based on need. 3,586 full-time freshmen applied for aid; 3,342 were judged to have need; 3,145 of these received aid. 82% of total undergraduate aid awarded as scholarships/grants, 18% as loans/jobs. Need-based aid available for part-time students.

Application procedures. Admission: Priority date 4/1; no deadline. $65 fee, may be waived for applicants with need. Admission notification on a rolling basis beginning on or about 3/1. **Financial aid:** Priority date 4/15, closing date 5/1. FAFSA, institutional form required. Applicants notified on a rolling basis starting 8/1; must reply within 2 week(s) of notification.

Academics. Special study options: Cooperative education, cross-registration, distance learning, dual enrollment of high school students, ESL, exchange student, honors, independent study, internships, student-designed major, study abroad, weekend college. License preparation in nursing. **Credit/placement by examination:** CLEP. 32 credit hours maximum toward associate degree. **Support services:** GED preparation and test center, learning center, pre-admission summer program, remedial instruction, study skills assistance, tutoring, writing center.

Majors. Business: Accounting, administrative services, business admin, office management. **Communications technology:** General. **Computer sciences:** Data processing, networking, programming. **Education:** Early childhood. **Engineering:** General, science. **Health:** EMT paramedic, health care admin, nursing (RN), respiratory therapy technology. **Liberal arts:** Arts/sciences. **Math:** General. **Public administration:** Human services. **Visual/performing arts:** Multimedia.

Most popular majors. Business/marketing 37%, health sciences 12%, liberal arts 32%.

Computing on campus. 1,200 workstations in library, computer center, student center. Commuter students can connect to campus network. Online course registration, online library, wireless network available.

Student life. Freshman orientation: Available. **Activities:** Jazz band, choral groups, dance, drama, music ensembles, musical theater, student government, student newspaper, numerous organizations.

Athletics. NJCAA. **Intercollegiate:** Baseball, basketball, soccer M, volleyball. **Intramural:** Basketball, cricket, football (non-tackle), soccer, table tennis, triathlon, volleyball. **Team name:** Panthers.

Student services. Alcohol/substance abuse counseling, career counseling, student employment services, financial aid counseling, health services, on-campus daycare, personal counseling, placement for graduates, veterans' counselor, women's services. **Physically disabled:** Services for visually, speech, hearing impaired. **Transfer:** Pre-admission transcript evaluation for new students. Transfer center, transfer adviser, college fairs on campus for students transferring to 4-year colleges.

Contact. E-mail: ebarrios@bmcc.cuny.edu
Phone: (212) 220-1265 Fax: (212) 220-2366
Eugenio Barrios, Director of Admissions, City University of New York: Borough of Manhattan Community College, 199 Chambers Street, New York, NY 10007-1097

City University of New York: Bronx Community College

Bronx, New York — **CB member**
www.bcc.cuny.edu — **CB code: 2051**

- Public 2-year community college
- Commuter campus in very large city

General. Founded in 1957. Regionally accredited. **Enrollment:** 8,556 degree-seeking undergraduates. **Degrees:** 717 associate awarded. **Calendar:** Semester, limited summer session. **Full-time faculty:** 271 total. **Part-time faculty:** 289 total. **Special facilities:** Hall of Fame for Great Americans.

Transfer out. Colleges most students transferred to 2008: Lehman College, City College, Baruch College, Hunter College, John Jay College of Criminal Justice.

Basis for selection. Open admission. Units recommended for admission must be acquired before graduation from any CUNY community college.

High school preparation. College-preparatory program recommended. 9 units recommended. Recommended units include English 3, mathematics 2 and science 1.

2008-2009 Annual costs. Tuition/fees: $3,104; $6,004 out-of-state. Per-credit charge: $120 in-state; $190 out-of-state. Books/supplies: $759. Personal expenses: $2,100.

Financial aid. All financial aid based on need. Need-based aid available for part-time students. Work-study available nights and weekends.

Application procedures. Admission: Priority date 1/15; deadline 8/15 (postmark date). $60 fee. Admission notification on a rolling basis. **Financial aid:** Closing date 7/15. FAFSA required. Applicants notified on a rolling basis starting 8/1.

Academics. Special study options: Cooperative education, cross-registration, distance learning, double major, dual enrollment of high school students, ESL, external degree, honors, independent study, internships, liberal arts/career combination, student-designed major, study abroad, weekend college. License preparation in nursing. **Credit/placement by examination:** AP, CLEP, IB, institutional tests. 30 credit hours maximum toward associate degree. **Support services:** GED preparation and test center, learning center, pre-admission summer program, reduced course load, remedial instruction, study skills assistance, tutoring, writing center.

Majors. Agriculture: Horticultural science. **Business:** General, accounting, administrative services, management information systems, office technology. **Computer sciences:** Computer science, data processing. **Education:** Teacher assistance. **Engineering technology:** Electrical. **Health:** Clinical lab technology, medical assistant, medical radiologic technology/radiation therapy, nuclear medical technology, nursing (RN). **Legal studies:** Paralegal. **Liberal arts:** Arts/sciences. **Visual/performing arts:** Commercial/advertising art.

Most popular majors. Business/marketing 21%, computer/information sciences 6%, health sciences 14%, liberal arts 27%, public administration/social services 15%.

Computing on campus. 490 workstations in library, computer center, student center. Commuter students can connect to campus network. Online course registration, wireless network available.

Student life. Freshman orientation: Available. Preregistration for classes offered. **Activities:** Choral groups, dance, drama, literary magazine, music ensembles, radio station, student government, student newspaper.

Athletics. Intercollegiate: Baseball M, basketball, soccer M, track and field. **Team name:** BCC Broncos.

Student services. Career counseling, student employment services, financial aid counseling, health services, on-campus daycare, personal counseling, placement for graduates, veterans' counselor. **Physically disabled:** Services for visually, speech impaired. **Transfer:** Transfer adviser, college fairs on campus for students transferring to 4-year colleges.

Contact. E-mail: admission@bcc.cuny.edu
Phone: (718) 289-5895 Fax: (718) 289-6352
Alba Cancetty, Director of Admissions, City University of New York: Bronx Community College, 2155 University Avenue, Bronx, NY 10453

City University of New York: Hostos Community College

Bronx, New York — **CB member**
www.hostos.cuny.edu — **CB code: 2303**

- Public 2-year community college
- Commuter campus in very large city

General. Founded in 1970. Regionally accredited. Bilingual Spanish/English liberal arts program. **Enrollment:** 4,715 degree-seeking undergraduates; 817 non-degree-seeking students. **Degrees:** 437 associate awarded. **Calendar:** Semester, limited summer session. **Full-time faculty:** 165 total; 58% have terminal degrees, 54% minority, 50% women. **Part-time faculty:** 194 total; 29% have terminal degrees, 66% minority, 46% women. **Class size:** 35% < 20, 62% 20-39, 3% 40-49.

Student profile. Among degree-seeking undergraduates, 35% enrolled in a transfer program, 63% enrolled in a vocational program, 2% already have a bachelor's degree or higher, 905 enrolled as first-time, first-year students, 584 transferred in from other institutions.

Part-time:	37%	**Women:**	71%
Out-of-state:	2%	**25 or older:**	39%

Transfer out. Colleges most students transferred to 2008: CUNY Lehman College, CUNY City College, CUNY John Jay College.

Basis for selection. Open admission, but selective for some programs. Admission to allied health programs based on Freshman Skills Assessment and subsequent performance in courses.

High school preparation. 16 units recommended. Recommended units include English 4, mathematics 3, social studies 4, science 2 and foreign language 2. 2 fine arts required. High school biology, chemistry, math required of allied health applicants.

2008-2009 Annual costs. Tuition/fees: $3,155; $6,055 out-of-state. Per-credit charge: $120 in-state; $190 out-of-state. Books/supplies: $692. Personal expenses: $2,667.

Financial aid. Need-based: Need-based aid available for part-time students. Work-study available for part-time students.

Application procedures. Admission: Closing date 8/15 (postmark date). $60 fee, may be waived for applicants with need. Admission notification on a rolling basis. **Financial aid:** Priority date 7/1; no closing date. FAFSA, institutional form required. Applicants notified on a rolling basis; must reply within 3 week(s) of notification.

Academics. Special study options: Cooperative education, distance learning, dual enrollment of high school students, ESL, honors, independent study, internships, liberal arts/career combination, student-designed major, study abroad, weekend college. Serrano scholars program. License preparation in dental hygiene, nursing, radiology. **Credit/placement by examination:** CLEP, institutional tests. **Support services:** GED preparation and test center, learning center, pre-admission summer program, remedial instruction, study skills assistance, tutoring, writing center.

Majors. Business: General, accounting, administrative services, business admin, office technology. **Computer sciences:** Data processing. **Education:** Early childhood. **Engineering:** Chemical, civil, electrical. **Health:** Community health, dental hygiene, medical radiologic technology/radiation therapy, medical secretary, nursing (RN). **Interdisciplinary:** Gerontology. **Legal studies:** Paralegal. **Liberal arts:** Arts/sciences. **Math:** General. **Physical sciences:** Forensic chemistry. **Protective services:** Criminal justice. **Public administration:** General. **Other:** Digital music.

Most popular majors. Business/marketing 12%, education 10%, family/consumer sciences 6%, health sciences 20%, liberal arts 41%.

Computing on campus. 1,000 workstations in library, computer center, student center. Commuter students can connect to campus network. Online course registration, online library, helpline, wireless network available.

Student life. Freshman orientation: Mandatory. Preregistration for classes offered. Held once a week each semester. **Activities:** Marching band, dance, drama, student government, student newspaper, TV station, Puerto Rican club, Christian club, black student union, Dominican association, South American student union, Ecuadorian student association, dental hygiene club, nursing club, Mexican club, Cuban club.

Athletics. NJCAA. **Intercollegiate:** Baseball M, basketball, soccer, volleyball W. **Intramural:** Basketball, volleyball W. **Team name:** Caimans.

Student services. Alcohol/substance abuse counseling, chaplain/spiritual director, career counseling, services for economically disadvantaged, student employment services, financial aid counseling, health services, on-campus daycare, personal counseling, placement for graduates, veterans' counselor, women's services. **Physically disabled:** Services for visually, speech, hearing impaired. **Learning disabled:** Comprehensive services available. **Transfer:** Re-entry adviser, pre-admission transcript evaluation for new students. Transfer adviser, college fairs on campus for students transferring to 4-year colleges.

Contact. E-mail: admissions@hostos.cuny.edu
Phone: (718) 518-4405 Fax: (718) 518-6643
Roland Velez, Director of Admissions/Recruitment, City University of New York: Hostos Community College, 500 Grand Concourse, Bronx, NY 10451

City University of New York: Kingsborough Community College

Brooklyn, New York — **CB member**
www.kbcc.cuny.edu — **CB code: 2358**

- Public 2-year community college
- Commuter campus in very large city

General. Founded in 1963. Regionally accredited. **Enrollment:** 11,870 degree-seeking undergraduates; 3,809 non-degree-seeking students. **Degrees:** 1,714 associate awarded. **Location:** 10 miles from midtown. **Calendar:** Semester, extensive summer session. **Full-time faculty:** 305 total; 65% have terminal degrees, 22% minority, 52% women. **Part-time faculty:** 505 total; 11% have terminal degrees, 17% minority, 51% women. **Class size:** 28% < 20, 63% 20-39, 8% 40-49. **Special facilities:** Private beach on campus. **Partnerships:** Formal partnership with College Now program for high school seniors.

Student profile. Among degree-seeking undergraduates, 60% enrolled in a transfer program, 40% enrolled in a vocational program, 2,386 enrolled as first-time, first-year students, 1,432 transferred in from other institutions.

Part-time:	27%	**Asian American:**	12%
Out-of-state:	1%	**Hispanic American:**	14%
Women:	57%	**International:**	6%
African American:	33%	**25 or older:**	24%

Transfer out. Colleges most students transferred to 2008: City University of New York: Brooklyn College, Long Island University, Pace University, City University of New York: College of Staten Island, City University of New York: Baruch College.

Basis for selection. Open admission. Units recommended for admission must be acquired before graduation from any CUNY community college.

High school preparation. 16 units recommended. Recommended units include English 4, mathematics 3, social studies 4, science 2 and foreign language 2. One unit fine arts.

2008-2009 Annual costs. Tuition/fees: $3,150; $6,050 out-of-state. Per-credit charge: $120 in-state; $190 out-of-state. Books/supplies: $1,016. Personal expenses: $2,706.

Financial aid. All financial aid based on need. Need-based aid available for part-time students.

Application procedures. Admission: Closing date 8/15. $65 fee, may be waived for applicants with need. Admission notification on a rolling basis beginning on or about 3/31. **Financial aid:** Closing date 4/30. FAFSA required. Applicants notified on a rolling basis; must reply within 2 week(s) of notification.

Academics. Special study options: Accelerated study, cross-registration, dual enrollment of high school students, ESL, honors, independent study, internships, student-designed major. My Turn Program for senior citizens, New Start Program for students academically dismissed from 4-year institutions. License preparation in nursing. **Credit/placement by examination:** AP, CLEP, institutional tests. 16 credit hours maximum toward associate degree. **Support services:** GED preparation, learning center, pre-admission summer program, reduced course load, remedial instruction, tutoring, writing center.

Majors. Biology: General. **Business:** Accounting, business admin, fashion, office management, tourism promotion, tourism/travel. **Communications:** Broadcast journalism, journalism. **Computer sciences:** Computer science, data processing. **Education:** Early childhood, elementary, teacher assistance. **Engineering:** General. **Health:** Community health services, mental health services, nursing (RN), physical therapy assistant, prenursing, surgical technology. **Legal studies:** Legal secretary. **Liberal arts:** Arts/sciences. **Math:** General. **Parks/recreation:** General, exercise sciences. **Physical sciences:** Chemistry, physics. **Visual/performing arts:** General, commercial/advertising art, studio arts.

Most popular majors. Biological/life sciences 6%, business/marketing 20%, education 6%, health sciences 14%, liberal arts 37%.

Computing on campus. 900 workstations in library, computer center. Online course registration available.

Student life. Freshman orientation: Available. **Activities:** Bands, choral groups, dance, drama, film society, literary magazine, music ensembles, musical theater, opera, radio station, student government, student newspaper, symphony orchestra, over 60 ethnic, academic, religious, and political groups.

Athletics. NJCAA. **Intercollegiate:** Baseball M, basketball, soccer M, softball W, tennis, track and field, volleyball W. **Intramural:** Basketball, bowling, football (non-tackle), racquetball, soccer, softball, swimming, table tennis, tennis, volleyball, weight lifting.

Student services. Adult student services, career counseling, student employment services, health services, on-campus daycare, personal counseling, placement for graduates, veterans' counselor. **Physically disabled:** Services for visually, speech, hearing impaired. **Transfer:** Transfer adviser for students transferring to 4-year colleges.

Contact. E-mail: info@kbcc.cuny.edu
Phone: (718) 368-4600 Fax: (718) 368-5356
Robert Ingenito, Admissions Information Center Director, City University of New York: Kingsborough Community College, 2001 Oriental Boulevard, Brooklyn, NY 11235

City University of New York: LaGuardia Community College

Long Island City, New York
www.lagcc.cuny.edu **CB code: 2246**

- Public 2-year community college
- Commuter campus in very large city

General. Founded in 1970. Regionally accredited. **Enrollment:** 13,195 degree-seeking undergraduates; 1,878 non-degree-seeking students. **Degrees:** 1,495 associate awarded. **Calendar:** Semester, limited summer session. **Full-time faculty:** 277 total; 50% have terminal degrees, 40% minority, 55% women. **Part-time faculty:** 825 total; 12% have terminal degrees, 38% minority, 52% women. **Class size:** 27% < 20, 72% 20-39, less than 1% 40-49, less than 1% 50-99. **Special facilities:** LaGuardia and Wagner archives.

Student profile. Among degree-seeking undergraduates, 55% enrolled in a transfer program, 41% enrolled in a vocational program, 2,629 enrolled as first-time, first-year students, 1,482 transferred in from other institutions.

Part-time:	38%	**Asian American:**	15%
Out-of-state:	1%	**Hispanic American:**	34%
Women:	61%	**International:**	11%
African American:	16%	**25 or older:**	34%

Transfer out. 54% of students enrolled in the transfer program go on to 4-year colleges. **Colleges most students transferred to 2008:** Borough of Manhattan Community College, Queensborough Community College, John Jay College, Hunter College, Kingsborough Community College.

Basis for selection. Open admission. **Adult students:** SAT/ACT scores not required. **Homeschooled:** Transcript of courses and grades required. Submit a letter from their school district superintendent confirming that all high school graduation requirements of the district have been met. **Learning Disabled:** Students encouraged to contact the office for Students with Disabilities before completing the application to ensure accommodations are addressed throughout the application and matriculation process.

High school preparation. 13 units recommended. Recommended units include English 4, mathematics 2, social studies 2, science 1 and academic electives 4.

2008-2009 Annual costs. Tuition/fees: $3,142; $6,042 out-of-state. Per-credit charge: $120 in-state; $190 out-of-state. Books/supplies: $1,016. Personal expenses: $1,686.

2007-2008 Financial aid. All financial aid based on need. 2,607 full-time freshmen applied for aid; 2,494 were judged to have need; 2,395 of these received aid. Average need met was 48%. Average scholarship/grant was $3,580. 94% of total undergraduate aid awarded as scholarships/grants, 6% as loans/jobs. Need-based aid available for part-time students. Work-study available nights, weekends and for part-time students.

Application procedures. Admission: Priority date 3/15; no deadline. $65 fee, may be waived for applicants with need. Admission notification on a rolling basis. **Financial aid:** Priority date 4/15; no closing date. FAFSA, institutional form required. Applicants notified on a rolling basis starting 3/1; must reply within 4 week(s) of notification.

Academics. Special study options: Accelerated study, cooperative education, cross-registration, distance learning, dual enrollment of high school students, ESL, independent study, internships, liberal arts/career combination, student-designed major. Summer program with Vassar College. License preparation in nursing, paramedic. **Credit/placement by examination:** AP, CLEP, institutional tests. 10 credit hours maximum toward associate degree. **Support services:** GED preparation and test center, learning center, pre-admission summer program, reduced course load, remedial instruction, tutoring, writing center.

Majors. Business: Accounting, administrative services, business admin, tourism promotion. **Computer sciences:** General, computer science, data processing, programming. **Education:** Bilingual. **Engineering:** General, civil, electrical, mechanical. **Family/consumer sciences:** Child care, institutional food production. **Health:** EMT paramedic, health services, occupational therapy assistant, physical therapy assistant, veterinary technology/assistant. **Interdisciplinary:** Gerontology. **Legal studies:** Legal secretary, paralegal. **Liberal arts:** Arts/sciences. **Personal/culinary services:** Mortuary science. **Visual/performing arts:** Commercial photography, studio arts.

Most popular majors. Business/marketing 30%, computer/information sciences 10%, education 6%, health sciences 13%, liberal arts 21%, personal/culinary services 11%.

Computing on campus. 1,180 workstations in library, computer center. Online course registration, helpline available.

Student life. Freshman orientation: Available. Preregistration for classes offered. **Activities:** Dance, drama, radio station, student government, student newspaper, Muslim, Christian, Buddhist, Phi Theta Kappa.

Athletics. Intramural: Basketball, bowling, football (non-tackle) M, football (tackle) M, handball, soccer, softball, swimming, table tennis, volleyball.

Student services. Adult student services, career counseling, student employment services, health services, on-campus daycare, personal counseling, placement for graduates, veterans' counselor. **Physically disabled:** Services for visually, speech, hearing impaired. **Transfer:** Transfer center, transfer adviser, college fairs on campus for students transferring to 4-year colleges.

Contact. E-mail: admissions@lagcc.cuny.edu
Phone: (718) 482-7206 Fax: (718) 609-2013
Reine Sarmiento, Senior Director of Admissions, City University of New York: LaGuardia Community College, 31-10 Thomson Avenue, Long Island City, NY 11101

City University of New York: Queensborough Community College

Bayside, New York
www.qcc.cuny.edu **CB code: 2751**

- Public 2-year community college
- Commuter campus in very large city

General. Founded in 1958. Regionally accredited. **Enrollment:** 11,798 degree-seeking undergraduates. **Degrees:** 1,220 associate awarded. **Location:** 10 miles from midtown Manhattan. **Calendar:** Semester, limited summer session. **Full-time faculty:** 304 total. **Part-time faculty:** 481 total. **Special facilities:** Resource center for Holocaust studies, observatory, art museum. **Partnerships:** Formal partnership with Verizon for Next Step associate degree program in telecommunication technology for Verizon employees.

Student profile.

Out-of-state:	1%	25 or older:	32%

Transfer out. Colleges most students transferred to 2008: CUNY Queens College, St. John's University.

Basis for selection. Open admission. Units recommended for admission must be acquired before graduation from CUNY.

High school preparation. 15 units recommended. Recommended units include English 4, mathematics 3, social studies 2, science 2 (laboratory 2) and academic electives 4.

2008-2009 Annual costs. Tuition/fees: $3,136; $6,036 out-of-state. Per-credit charge: $120 in-state; $190 out-of-state. Books/supplies: $500. Personal expenses: $2,100.

Application procedures. Admission: No deadline. $65 fee, may be waived for applicants with need. Admission notification on a rolling basis. **Financial aid:** No deadline. FAFSA, institutional form required. Applicants notified on a rolling basis starting 7/15.

Academics. Special study options: Cooperative education, dual enrollment of high school students, ESL, independent study, internships, liberal arts/career combination, student-designed major. External education for homebound students, honors program for high school seniors. License preparation in nursing. **Credit/placement by examination:** AP, CLEP, institutional tests. **Support services:** Learning center, pre-admission summer program, remedial instruction, tutoring.

Majors. Biology: General. **Business:** General, accounting, administrative services, business admin, office management. **Communications technology:** General, recording arts. **Computer sciences:** General, data processing, information systems, programming. **Engineering:** Computer. **Engineering technology:** Drafting, electrical. **Health:** Clinical lab technology, environmental health, nursing (RN). **History:** General. **Liberal arts:** Arts/sciences. **Physical sciences:** Chemistry. **Psychology:** General. **Social sciences:** Political science, sociology. **Visual/performing arts:** General, art, dance, dramatic, music history, photography.

Computing on campus. 143 workstations in library, computer center. Online course registration, helpline, wireless network available.

Student life. Freshman orientation: Available. Preregistration for classes offered. **Activities:** Bands, choral groups, dance, drama, film society, music ensembles, musical theater, student government, student newspaper, symphony orchestra, architecture club, Asian society, biology club, Chi Alpha Christian, drama society, future teachers society, Hillel club, Muslim student association, Newman club.

Athletics. NJCAA. **Intercollegiate:** Baseball M, basketball, cross-country, soccer M, softball W, tennis, track and field, volleyball. **Intramural:** Badminton, basketball, soccer, softball, swimming, table tennis, tennis, track and field, volleyball. **Team name:** Tigers.

Student services. Adult student services, career counseling, student employment services, health services, on-campus daycare, personal counseling, placement for graduates, veterans' counselor. **Physically disabled:** Services for visually, speech, hearing impaired. **Transfer:** Transfer adviser, college fairs on campus for students transferring to 4-year colleges.

Contact. Phone: (718) 281-5000 Fax: (718) 281-5189
Winston Yarde, Director of Admissions, City University of New York: Queensborough Community College, Springfield Boulevard & 56th Avenue, Bayside, NY 11364-1497

Clinton Community College

Plattsburgh, New York
www.clinton.edu **CB code: 2135**

- Public 2-year community college
- Commuter campus in large town

General. Founded in 1966. Regionally accredited. SUNY institution. **Enrollment:** 1,387 degree-seeking undergraduates. **Degrees:** 303 associate awarded. **Location:** 60 miles from Montreal, Canada, 30 miles from Burlington, Vermont. **Calendar:** Semester, limited summer session. **Full-time faculty:** 54 total. **Part-time faculty:** 93 total. **Class size:** 15% < 20, 83% 20-39, 2% 50-99. **Special facilities:** Science and technology center. **Partnerships:** Formal partnership with area high schools in collaboration with College Advancement Program (CAP).

Transfer out. Colleges most students transferred to 2008: SUNY at Plattsburgh.

Basis for selection. Open admission, but selective for some programs. Special requirements for nursing, including essay. Test scores may exempt students from taking placement test. **Homeschooled:** State high school equivalency certificate required. Recommend completing GED, must take ability to benefit test.

High school preparation. Recommended units include English 4, mathematics 3, social studies 4, history 4, science 2 (laboratory 2) and foreign language 2. Chemistry required for nursing.

2008-2009 Annual costs. Tuition/fees: $3,684; $8,784 out-of-state. Per-credit charge: $141 in-state; $350 out-of-state. Books/supplies: $800. Personal expenses: $634.

2008-2009 Financial aid. All financial aid based on need. Need-based aid available for part-time students. Work-study available for part-time students.

Application procedures. Admission: No deadline. No application fee. Admission notification on a rolling basis. **Financial aid:** Priority date 6/9; no closing date. FAFSA required. Applicants notified on a rolling basis starting 5/9; must reply within 2 week(s) of notification.

Academics. Special study options: Cross-registration, distance learning, dual enrollment of high school students, independent study, internships, liberal arts/career combination, student-designed major. Semester in Albany, basic skills program. License preparation in nursing. **Credit/placement by examination:** AP, CLEP, IB, institutional tests. 30 credit hours maximum toward associate degree. **Support services:** GED preparation, reduced course load, remedial instruction, study skills assistance, tutoring, writing center.

Majors. Business: Accounting, business admin. **Computer sciences:** General, data processing, information systems, networking. **Engineering technology:** Electrical, industrial. **Health:** Nursing (RN). **Liberal arts:** Arts/sciences. **Math:** General. **Protective services:** Law enforcement admin. **Public administration:** Human services. **Other:** Wind energy and turbine technology.

Computing on campus. 350 workstations in library, computer center. Dormitories wired for high-speed internet access and linked to campus network. Commuter students can connect to campus network. Online library, helpline, wireless network available.

Student life. Freshman orientation: Mandatory. Preregistration for classes offered. Held day before classes begin each semester. **Housing:** Guaranteed on-campus for freshmen. Coed dorms, special housing for disabled available. $200 nonrefundable deposit. **Activities:** Choral groups, drama, student government, student newspaper, nursing, laboratory technology, art clubs, business club, Native American club, Global Awareness, criminal justice, student activities board, student senate.

Athletics. NJCAA. **Intercollegiate:** Baseball M, basketball, soccer, softball W. **Intramural:** Golf, racquetball, tennis. **Team name:** Cougars.

Student services. Adult student services, alcohol/substance abuse counseling, career counseling, student employment services, financial aid counseling, health services, on-campus daycare, personal counseling, placement for graduates, veterans' counselor. **Physically disabled:** Services for visually, speech, hearing impaired. **Learning disabled:** Comprehensive services available. **Transfer:** Pre-admission transcript evaluation for new students. Transfer adviser, college fairs on campus for students transferring to 4-year colleges.

Contact. E-mail: admissions@clinton.edu
Phone: (518) 562-4170 Toll-free number: (800) 552-1160
Fax: (518) 562-4380
Karen Burnam, Director of Admissions/Financial Aid, Clinton Community College, 136 Clinton Point Drive, Plattsburgh, NY 12901-4297

Cochran School of Nursing-St. John's Riverside Hospital

Yonkers, New York
www.cochranschoolofnursing.us **CB code: 2894**

- Private 2-year nursing college
- Commuter campus in small city
- Application essay, interview required

General. Founded in 1894. Access to all clinical facilities at St. John's Riverside Hospital. **Enrollment:** 332 degree-seeking undergraduates. **Degrees:** 113 associate awarded. **Location:** 20 miles from New York City. **Calendar:** Semester, limited summer session. **Full-time faculty:** 16 total; 100% have terminal degrees, 25% minority, 94% women. **Part-time faculty:** 7 total; 100% have terminal degrees, 14% minority, 100% women. **Class size:** 20% < 20, 73% 20-39, 7% 40-49.

Student profile. Among degree-seeking undergraduates, 25% already have a bachelor's degree or higher, 89 transferred in from other institutions.

Part-time:	58%	**Asian American:**	18%
Women:	92%	**Hispanic American:**	12%
African American:	39%	**25 or older:**	73%

Transfer out. Colleges most students transferred to 2008: Mercy College, College of New Rochelle, College of Mount St. Vincent, Adelphi University.

Basis for selection. School achievement record, test scores, interview most important. Completion of prerequisite with C+ grade or better. **Learning Disabled:** Must submit necessary documentation of disabilities at time of admission to disability officer.

High school preparation. 16 units required. Required and recommended units include English 4, mathematics 4, social studies 2, history 2, science 2 and foreign language 2. Math units should include 1 algebra, science units should include 1 biology and 1 chemistry. 2 units of laboratory recommended.

2009-2010 Annual costs. Tuition/fees (projected): $10,195. Per-credit charge: $512. Books/supplies: $1,800.

2008-2009 Financial aid. All financial aid based on need. 74% of total undergraduate aid awarded as scholarships/grants, 26% as loans/jobs. Need-based aid available for part-time students.

Application procedures. Admission: Closing date 10/30. $35 fee. Application must be submitted on paper. Admission notification on a rolling basis. **Financial aid:** No deadline. FAFSA required. Applicants notified on a rolling basis.

Academics. Special testing program facilitates career goals of LPNs who want to become RNs. **Special study options:** Accelerated study, combined bachelor's/graduate degree, liberal arts/career combination. License preparation in nursing. **Credit/placement by examination:** AP, CLEP, IB, institutional tests. 27 credit hours maximum toward associate degree. **Support services:** Learning center, tutoring.

Majors. Health: Nursing (RN).

Computing on campus. 22 workstations in library, computer center, student center. Online library available.

Student life. Freshman orientation: Mandatory. **Housing:** Wellness housing available. **Activities:** Student government, student newspaper.

Student services. Adult student services, career counseling, health services, personal counseling. **Transfer:** Pre-admission transcript evaluation for new students. College fairs on campus for students transferring to 4-year colleges.

Contact. E-mail: admissions@cochranschoolofnursing.us
Phone: (914) 964-4296 Fax: (914) 964-4796
Kathy Vitola, Admissions Counselor, Cochran School of Nursing-St. John's Riverside Hospital, 967 North Broadway, Yonkers, NY 10701

College of Westchester

White Plains, New York
www.cw.edu **CB code: 1023**

- For-profit 2-year business and career college
- Commuter campus in large town
- Application essay, interview required

General. Founded in 1915. Regionally accredited. **Enrollment:** 981 degree-seeking undergraduates; 22 non-degree-seeking students. **Degrees:** 232 associate awarded. **Location:** 30 miles from New York City. **Calendar:** Semester, extensive summer session. **Full-time faculty:** 32 total. **Part-time faculty:** 60 total. **Class size:** 67% < 20, 33% 20-39. **Partnerships:** Formal partnerships with local corporations and businesses for internship and co-op work experience programs.

Student profile. Among degree-seeking undergraduates, 402 enrolled as first-time, first-year students.

Part-time:	6%	**Women:**	58%
Out-of-state:	3%	**25 or older:**	77%

Basis for selection. Interview, prior academic performance, recommendations most important. Activities considered. Test scores considered when available. Institution-administered assessments used for both admissions and academic placement.

High school preparation. College-preparatory program recommended. Recommended units include English 4 and mathematics 3.

2008-2009 Annual costs. Tuition/fees: $19,800. Per-credit charge: $630. Books/supplies: $990.

Financial aid. Need-based: Need-based aid available for part-time students. Work-study available nights and weekends. **Non-need-based:** Scholarships awarded for academics, alumni affiliation.

Application procedures. Admission: No deadline. $40 fee, may be waived for applicants with need. Admission notification on a rolling basis. **Financial aid:** No deadline. FAFSA, institutional form required. Applicants notified on a rolling basis starting 1/7; must reply within 2 week(s) of notification.

Academics. Special study options: Accelerated study, cooperative education, distance learning, double major, honors, internships, weekend college. **Credit/placement by examination:** AP, CLEP, SAT, institutional tests. **Support services:** Learning center, pre-admission summer program, reduced course load, remedial instruction, study skills assistance, tutoring.

Majors. Business: Accounting, administrative services, business admin, e-commerce, management information systems, office management, office technology, office/clerical, purchasing. **Computer sciences:** General, applications programming, computer graphics, computer science, data processing, information systems, LAN/WAN management, programming, systems analysis, web page design. **Engineering:** Software. **Health:** Office admin. **Visual/performing arts:** Commercial/advertising art.

Computing on campus. 290 workstations in library, computer center, student center. Commuter students can connect to campus network. Online library, helpline, repair service, wireless network available.

Student life. Freshman orientation: Mandatory. Preregistration for classes offered. **Activities:** Student government, student newspaper, accounting society, management and marketing club, office technology club, computer club, multimedia club, Alpha Beta honor society, women's business issues club, public speaking club.

Student services. Adult student services, career counseling, student employment services, financial aid counseling, personal counseling, placement for graduates. **Transfer:** Pre-admission transcript evaluation for new students. Transfer adviser for students transferring to 4-year colleges.

Contact. E-mail: admissions@cw.edu
Phone: (914) 948-4442 ext. 318 Toll-free number: (800) 333-4924
Fax: (914) 948-5441
Anthony Peluso, Director of Admissions, College of Westchester, 325 Central Park Avenue, White Plains, NY 10602

Columbia-Greene Community College
Hudson, New York
www.sunycgcc.edu **CB code: 2138**

- Public 2-year community college
- Commuter campus in small town

General. Founded in 1966. Regionally accredited. SUNY institution. **Enrollment:** 1,426 degree-seeking undergraduates; 413 non-degree-seeking students. **Degrees:** 305 associate awarded. **Location:** 40 miles from Albany. **Calendar:** Semester, limited summer session. **Full-time faculty:** 48 total; 6% minority. **Part-time faculty:** 75 total. **Class size:** 57% < 20, 41% 20-39, 1% 40-49, less than 1% 50-99. **Special facilities:** 4 art galleries, Hudson River biological field station.

Student profile. Among degree-seeking undergraduates, 33% enrolled in a transfer program, 68% enrolled in a vocational program, 469 enrolled as first-time, first-year students, 116 transferred in from other institutions.

Part-time:	30%	**Asian American:**	1%
Out-of-state:	1%	**Hispanic American:**	5%
Women:	64%	**Native American:**	1%
African American:	5%	**25 or older:**	28%

Transfer out. 45% of students enrolled in the transfer program go on to 4-year colleges. **Colleges most students transferred to 2008:** SUNY Albany, SUNY New Paltz, College of St. Rose.

Basis for selection. Open admission, but selective for some programs. Admission to some programs based on school achievement record, test scores, and recommendations. Interview recommended. **Adult students:** SAT/ACT scores not required. **Homeschooled:** Transcript of courses and grades, interview required.

High school preparation. Recommended units include English 3, mathematics 3, science 3 and foreign language 3.

2008-2009 Annual costs. Tuition/fees: $3,496; $6,712 out-of-state. Per-credit charge: $134 in-state; $268 out-of-state. Books/supplies: $1,200. Personal expenses: $950.

2007-2008 Financial aid. Need-based: 51% of total undergraduate aid awarded as scholarships/grants, 49% as loans/jobs. Need-based aid available for part-time students. Work-study available nights, weekends and for part-time students. **Non-need-based:** Scholarships awarded for academics, state residency.

Application procedures. Admission: No deadline. $30 fee, may be waived for applicants with need. Admission notification on a rolling basis. **Financial aid:** Priority date 5/1; no closing date. FAFSA, institutional form required. Applicants notified on a rolling basis starting 7/1; must reply within 2 week(s) of notification.

Academics. Special study options: Cooperative education, cross-registration, distance learning, dual enrollment of high school students, honors, independent study, internships, student-designed major. License preparation in aviation, nursing. **Credit/placement by examination:** AP, CLEP, institutional tests. 30 credit hours maximum toward associate degree. **Support services:** Learning center, pre-admission summer program, remedial instruction, study skills assistance, tutoring, writing center.

Honors college/program. Program offers the opportunity to work closely with faculty, conduct research, and participate in seminars and conferences with an interdisciplinary focus.

Majors. Biology: General. **Business:** Accounting, administrative services, business admin, office management, office technology. **Computer sciences:** General, applications programming, computer science, LAN/WAN management. **Conservation:** Environmental science. **Education:** Multi-level teacher, physical. **Health:** Massage therapy, nursing (RN). **Liberal arts:** Arts/sciences. **Math:** General. **Mechanic/repair:** Automotive. **Protective services:** Criminal justice, law enforcement admin. **Public administration:** Social work. **Social sciences:** General. **Visual/performing arts:** Studio arts.

Computing on campus. 150 workstations in library, computer center. Commuter students can connect to campus network. Online library, wireless network available.

Student life. Freshman orientation: Available. Preregistration for classes offered. Held 1 week prior to start of fall classes. **Activities:** Choral groups, dance, drama, music ensembles, musical theater, radio station, student government, International Rotary Club, minority alliance group, College Union Board.

Athletics. NJCAA. **Intercollegiate:** Baseball M, basketball, bowling, soccer W, softball W. **Intramural:** Basketball, bowling, fencing, table tennis, tennis, volleyball. **Team name:** Twins.

Student services. Adult student services, alcohol/substance abuse counseling, career counseling, student employment services, health services, on-campus daycare, personal counseling, placement for graduates, veterans' counselor. **Physically disabled:** Services for visually, hearing impaired. **Transfer:** Transfer adviser, college fairs on campus for students transferring to 4-year colleges.

Contact. E-mail: pepitone@sunycgcc.edu
Phone: (518) 828-4181 ext. 5513 Fax: (518) 828-8543
Christine Pepitone, Director of Admissions, Columbia-Greene Community College, 4400 Route 23, Hudson, NY 12534

Corning Community College
Corning, New York
www.corning-cc.edu **CB code: 2106**

- Public 2-year community college
- Commuter campus in large town

General. Founded in 1956. Regionally accredited. SUNY institution. **Enrollment:** 3,189 degree-seeking undergraduates. **Degrees:** 641 associate awarded. **Location:** 70 miles from Binghamton. **Calendar:** Semester, limited summer session. **Full-time faculty:** 93 total. **Part-time faculty:** 123 total. **Class size:** 67% < 20, 31% 20-39, less than 1% 40-49, less than 1% 50-99, less than 1% >100. **Special facilities:** 200-acre nature center, criminal justice complex, observatory with historic working model of Hale telescope, planetarium.

Student profile.

Out-of-state:	4%	**25 or older:**	43%

Transfer out. Colleges most students transferred to 2008: Elmira College, Mansfield University, SUNY Cortland, SUNY Binghamton, SUNY Buffalo.

Basis for selection. Open admission, but selective for some programs. Applicants without diploma or GED evaluated on individual basis. **Adult students:** SAT/ACT scores not required. **Homeschooled:** Ability to Benefit testing required. **Learning Disabled:** Students should contact disability services to arrange accommodations, including accommodations for placement tests.

High school preparation. Recommended units include English 4, mathematics 1, social studies 4, science 1 (laboratory 1). 4 math and 4 science required of engineering science applicants; 1 algebra and 1 biology required of nursing applicants.

2008-2009 Annual costs. Tuition/fees: $3,850; $7,320 out-of-state. Per-credit charge: $145 in-state; $290 out-of-state. Books/supplies: $900. Personal expenses: $550.

Financial aid. All financial aid based on need. Need-based aid available for part-time students. Work-study available weekends and for part-time students.

Application procedures. Admission: No deadline. $25 fee, may be waived for applicants with need. Admission notification on a rolling basis. **Financial aid:** Priority date 4/1; no closing date. FAFSA required. Applicants notified on a rolling basis starting 4/15; must reply within 2 week(s) of notification.

Academics. Special study options: Distance learning, double major, dual enrollment of high school students, honors, independent study, internships, study abroad, weekend college. License preparation in nursing, paramedic, real estate. **Credit/placement by examination:** AP, CLEP, institutional tests. 30 credit hours maximum toward associate degree. **Support services:** Learning center, reduced course load, remedial instruction, study skills assistance, tutoring, writing center.

Majors. Business: Accounting, administrative services, business admin. **Computer sciences:** General, computer graphics, computer science, programming. **Education:** Early childhood, elementary, health, physical. **Engineering:** Science. **Engineering technology:** Electrical, manufacturing. **Health:** EMT paramedic, nursing (RN), substance abuse counseling. **Interdisciplinary:** Biological/physical sciences. **Legal studies:** Paralegal. **Liberal arts:** Arts/sciences. **Math:** General. **Mechanic/repair:** Automotive, computer. **Parks/recreation:** Health/fitness. **Physical sciences:** General, optics. **Production:** Machine tool. **Protective services:** Corrections, criminal justice, fire safety technology, law enforcement admin. **Public administration:** Human services. **Science technology:** Chemical. **Social sciences:** General.

Computing on campus. 360 workstations in library, computer center. Wireless network available.

Student life. Freshman orientation: Available, $56 fee. One-day transition course offered in January, end of August. **Activities:** Choral groups, drama, literary magazine, music ensembles, radio station, student government, student newspaper, human services club, law society, Christian club, College Republicans, Phi Theta Kappa, nursing society, multicultural society.

Athletics. NJCAA. **Intercollegiate:** Baseball M, basketball, golf, soccer, softball W, volleyball W. **Intramural:** Badminton, basketball, soccer, volleyball. **Team name:** Red Barons.

Student services. Adult student services, alcohol/substance abuse counseling, chaplain/spiritual director, career counseling, services for economically disadvantaged, student employment services, financial aid counseling, health services, personal counseling, placement for graduates. **Physically disabled:** Services for visually, speech, hearing impaired. **Transfer:** Transfer center, transfer adviser, college fairs on campus for students transferring to 4-year colleges.

Contact. E-mail: admissions@corning-cc.edu
Phone: (607) 962-9151 Toll-free number: (800) 358-7171 ext. 151
Fax: (607) 962-9582
Craig Topple, Director of Admissions, Corning Community College, One Academic Drive, Corning, NY 14830

Dutchess Community College

Poughkeepsie, New York — **CB member**
www.sunydutchess.edu — **CB code: 2198**

- Public 2-year community college
- Commuter campus in large town

General. Founded in 1957. Regionally accredited. Extension programs at 6 sites. **Enrollment:** 6,434 degree-seeking undergraduates. **Degrees:** 865 associate awarded. **Location:** 70 miles from New York City. **Calendar:** Semester, limited summer session. **Full-time faculty:** 131 total; 23% have terminal degrees, 12% minority, 53% women. **Part-time faculty:** 292 total; 49% women. **Special facilities:** Biological experimentation site on Hudson River. **Partnerships:** Formal partnership with Verizon.

Student profile. Among degree-seeking undergraduates, 64% enrolled in a transfer program, 36% enrolled in a vocational program, 2,771 enrolled as first-time, first-year students.

Out-of-state:	1%	**25 or older:**	29%

Transfer out. Colleges most students transferred to 2008: State University of New York at Paltz, Marist College, Mount St. Mary's College, State University of New York at Albany.

Basis for selection. Open admission, but selective for some programs. Special requirements for nursing and engineering programs. **Homeschooled:** Students must pass entrance test unless they have local diploma or diploma from accredited school.

High school preparation. Recommended units include English 4, mathematics 3, social studies 4, science 3 and foreign language 2.

2008-2009 Annual costs. Tuition/fees: $3,292; $6,167 out-of-state. Per-credit charge: $120 in-state; $240 out-of-state. Books/supplies: $1,200. Personal expenses: $1,400.

2007-2008 Financial aid. Need-based: 85% of total undergraduate aid awarded as scholarships/grants, 15% as loans/jobs. Need-based aid available for part-time students. Work-study available for part-time students.

Application procedures. Admission: No deadline. No application fee. Admission notification on a rolling basis. **Financial aid:** Priority date 5/1; no closing date. FAFSA, institutional form required. Applicants notified on a rolling basis starting 5/15; must reply within 2 week(s) of notification.

Academics. Special study options: Cooperative education, cross-registration, distance learning, dual enrollment of high school students, ESL, honors, independent study, internships, liberal arts/career combination, weekend college. Combined degree in education with SUNY at New Paltz. License preparation in aviation, dental hygiene, nursing, paramedic. **Credit/placement by examination:** AP, CLEP, institutional tests. 40 credit hours maximum toward associate degree. **Support services:** GED preparation and test center, learning center, pre-admission summer program, reduced course load, remedial instruction, study skills assistance, tutoring, writing center.

Majors. Business: Accounting, administrative services, business admin, office technology, sales/distribution, tourism promotion, tourism/travel, travel services. **Communications:** General. **Computer sciences:** General, computer science. **Education:** Biology, chemistry, early childhood, elementary, English, French, German, kindergarten/preschool, mathematics, middle, science, secondary, social studies, Spanish, teacher assistance. **Engineering:** Electrical, science. **Engineering technology:** Architectural, construction, electrical, manufacturing. **Family/consumer sciences:** Child care. **Health:** Clinical lab technology, EMT paramedic, health services, mental health services, nursing (RN), physical therapy assistant. **Legal studies:** Legal secretary, paralegal. **Liberal arts:** Arts/sciences, humanities. **Math:** General. **Parks/recreation:** General, exercise sciences, facilities management. **Physical sciences:** General. **Protective services:** Criminal justice. **Visual/performing arts:** Commercial/advertising art, dramatic.

Most popular majors. Business/marketing 21%, education 10%, health sciences 11%, liberal arts 30%, security/protective services 8%.

Computing on campus. 1,000 workstations in library, computer center. Online course registration, online library, helpline, repair service, wireless network available.

Student life. Freshman orientation: Available. Preregistration for classes offered. **Activities:** Jazz band, choral groups, dance, drama, film society, international student organizations, literary magazine, music ensembles, musical theater, radio station, student government, student newspaper, TV station, foreign student organization, special interest clubs.

Athletics. NJCAA. **Intercollegiate:** Baseball M, basketball M, bowling M, golf M, soccer M, softball W, tennis, volleyball W. **Intramural:** Archery, badminton, basketball, bowling, fencing, racquetball, soccer, softball, tennis, volleyball, weight lifting. **Team name:** Falcons.

Student services. Adult student services, career counseling, services for economically disadvantaged, student employment services, financial aid counseling, health services, minority student services, on-campus daycare, personal counseling, placement for graduates, veterans' counselor. **Physically disabled:** Services for visually, speech, hearing impaired. **Transfer:** Pre-admission transcript evaluation for new students. Transfer adviser, college fairs on campus for students transferring to 4-year colleges.

Contact. E-mail: admissions@sunydutchess.edu
Phone: (845) 431-8010 Toll-free number: (800) 378-9707
Fax: (845) 431-8605
Rita Banner, Director of Admissions, Dutchess Community College, 53 Pendell Road, Poughkeepsie, NY 12601-1595

Elmira Business Institute

Elmira, New York
www.ebi-college.com — **CB code: 3332**

- For-profit 2-year business and technical college
- Commuter campus in large town
- Interview required

General. Accredited by ACICS. **Enrollment:** 150 degree-seeking undergraduates. **Degrees:** 46 associate awarded. **Calendar:** Trimester. **Full-time faculty:** 7 total; 86% women. **Part-time faculty:** 21 total; 76% women.

Student profile.

Out-of-state:	23%	**Hispanic American:**	1%
African American:	13%	**25 or older:**	80%

Basis for selection. Open admission. High school diploma or GED required along with a career planning session. **Homeschooled:** State high school equivalency certificate required.

2008-2009 Annual costs. Tuition/fees: $9,800. Per-credit charge: $320. Tuition varies by program.

2007-2008 Financial aid. All financial aid based on need. Need-based aid available for part-time students.

Application procedures. Admission: No deadline. No application fee. **Financial aid:** Closing date 5/1. FAFSA, institutional form required.

Academics. Special study options: Internships, weekend college. **Credit/placement by examination:** CLEP, institutional tests. **Support services:** Reduced course load, remedial instruction, tutoring.

Majors. Business: Accounting. **Health:** Clinical lab assistant, insurance coding, medical assistant, medical records admin, medical records technology, medical secretary, medical transcription. **Legal studies:** Legal secretary, paralegal.

Computing on campus. 100 workstations in library, computer center.

Student life. **Freshman orientation:** Mandatory.

Student services. Career counseling, financial aid counseling, personal counseling, placement for graduates. **Transfer:** Pre-admission transcript evaluation for new students. College fairs on campus for students transferring to 4-year colleges.

Contact. E-mail: lroan@ebi-college.com
Phone: (607) 733-7177 Toll-free number: (800) 843-1812
Fax: (607) 733-7178
Lisa Roan, Director of Admissions, Elmira Business Institute, 303 North Main Street, Elmira, NY 14901

Elmira Business Institute: Vestal

Vestal, New York
www.ebi-college.com

- For-profit 2-year business and technical college
- Commuter campus in small city
- Interview required

General. Accredited by ACICS. **Enrollment:** 119 degree-seeking undergraduates. **Degrees:** 52 associate awarded. **Calendar:** Trimester, extensive summer session. **Full-time faculty:** 5 total. **Part-time faculty:** 15 total.

Student profile.

African American:	22%	**Hispanic American:**	3%

Transfer out. **Colleges most students transferred to 2008:** Broome Community College.

Basis for selection. Open admission. Career planning session is required. **Homeschooled:** Statement describing homeschool structure and mission required. Must have a letter from school superintendent or principal.

2008-2009 Annual costs. Tuition/fees: $9,800. Per-credit charge: $320. Tuition varies by program.

Financial aid. All financial aid based on need. Need-based aid available for part-time students.

Application procedures. **Admission:** No deadline. No application fee. **Financial aid:** No deadline. FAFSA, institutional form required. Applicants notified on a rolling basis.

Academics. **Credit/placement by examination:** CLEP, institutional tests. **Support services:** Reduced course load, remedial instruction, study skills assistance, tutoring.

Majors. **Business:** Accounting technology. **Health:** Clinical lab assistant, insurance coding.

Computing on campus. Online library available.

Student life. **Freshman orientation:** Mandatory.

Student services. **Transfer:** Pre-admission transcript evaluation for new students.

Contact. Phone: (607) 729-8915
Lisa Roan, Director, Elmira Business Institute: Vestal, 4100 Vestal Road, Vestal, NY 13850

Erie Community College: City Campus

Buffalo, New York — **CB member**
www.ecc.edu — **CB code: 2213**

- Public 2-year community college
- Commuter campus in large city

General. Founded in 1971. Regionally accredited. SUNY institution. Main campus located in Buffalo. Additional campuses in Williamsville and Orchard Park. **Enrollment:** 2,894 degree-seeking undergraduates; 404 non-degree-seeking students. **Degrees:** 395 associate awarded. **ROTC:** Army. **Calendar:** Semester, limited summer session. **Full-time faculty:** 92 total; 17% minority, 58% women. **Part-time faculty:** 427 total; 11% minority, 46% women. **Special facilities:** Natatorium (City Campus), athletic fields (North and South campus), vehicle training technology center, corporate training facility. **Partnerships:** Formal partnerships with Ford Motor Company, Daimler Chrysler, Verizon.

Student profile. Among degree-seeking undergraduates, 46% enrolled in a transfer program, 54% enrolled in a vocational program, 1% already have a bachelor's degree or higher, 763 enrolled as first-time, first-year students, 96 transferred in from other institutions.

Part-time:	21%	**Asian American:**	2%
Out-of-state:	1%	**Hispanic American:**	9%
Women:	62%	**Native American:**	1%
African American:	43%	**25 or older:**	40%

Transfer out. **Colleges most students transferred to 2008:** SUNY College at Buffalo, SUNY College at Fredonia, SUNY College at Brockport, SUNY Buffalo.

Basis for selection. Open admission, but selective for some programs. Special requirements for nursing and radiologic technology programs; interview required. Students scoring 500 or higher on SAT Critical Reading waived from English placement test; students scoring 500 or higher on SAT Math waived from Math placement test. Minimum age is 17 for international students. **Homeschooled:** Applicants follow same criteria as applicants with GED.

2008-2009 Annual costs. Tuition/fees: $3,690; $6,877 out-of-state. Per-credit charge: $133 in-state; $266 out-of-state. Books/supplies: $1,000. Personal expenses: $900.

Financial aid. All financial aid based on need. Need-based aid available for part-time students. Work-study available weekends and for part-time students.

Application procedures. **Admission:** Priority date 8/1; no deadline. $25 fee. Admission notification on a rolling basis. **Financial aid:** Priority date 6/1; no closing date. FAFSA required. Applicants notified on a rolling basis starting 4/1; must reply within 2 week(s) of notification.

Academics. **Special study options:** Cooperative education, cross-registration, distance learning, double major, dual enrollment of high school students, ESL, exchange student, honors, independent study, internships, liberal arts/career combination, student-designed major, study abroad, teacher certification program, weekend college. Dual admissions with 4-year institutions. License preparation in nursing, paramedic, radiology. **Credit/placement by examination:** AP, CLEP, institutional tests. **Support services:** GED preparation and test center, learning center, pre-admission summer program, reduced course load, remedial instruction, study skills assistance, tutoring, writing center.

Majors. **Business:** Administrative services, business admin, office management. **Computer sciences:** Information technology. **Construction:** Maintenance. **Education:** Physical. **Family/consumer sciences:** Child care. **Health:** Community health services, medical radiologic technology/radiation therapy, nursing (RN), substance abuse counseling. **Legal studies:** Paralegal. **Liberal arts:** Arts/sciences, humanities. **Personal/culinary services:** Chef training. **Protective services:** Law enforcement admin, police science. **Public administration:** General, human services.

Most popular majors. Business/marketing 14%, family/consumer sciences 11%, health sciences 18%, legal studies 6%, liberal arts 34%, security/protective services 6%.

Computing on campus. 386 workstations in library, computer center. Commuter students can connect to campus network. Online course registration, online library, helpline, repair service, student web hosting, wireless network available.

Student life. **Freshman orientation:** Mandatory, $50 fee. Preregistration for classes offered. **Activities:** Bands, choral groups, dance, drama, literary magazine, music ensembles, musical theater, radio station, student government, student newspaper, Latino student association, honors association, Phi Theta Kappa, multilingual club, Black Student Union.

Athletics. NJCAA. **Intercollegiate:** Baseball M, basketball, bowling, cheerleading M, cross-country, diving, football (tackle) M, golf, ice hockey M, lacrosse W, soccer, softball W, swimming, track and field, volleyball W. **Team name:** Kats.

Student services. Adult student services, career counseling, services for economically disadvantaged, student employment services, financial aid counseling, health services, minority student services, on-campus daycare, personal counseling, placement for graduates, veterans' counselor, women's services. **Physically disabled:** Services for visually, speech, hearing impaired. **Transfer:** Pre-admission transcript evaluation for new students. Transfer adviser, college fairs on campus for students transferring to 4-year colleges.

Contact. E-mail: cheatom@ecc.edu
Phone: (716) 851-1155 Fax: (716) 270-2821
Petrina Hill-Cheatom, Director of Admissions, Erie Community College: City Campus, 121 Ellicott Street, Buffalo, NY 14203-2698

Erie Community College: North Campus
Williamsville, New York
www.ecc.edu **CB code: 2228**

- Public 2-year community college
- Commuter campus in small city

General. Founded in 1946. Regionally accredited. SUNY institution. Main campus located in Buffalo. Additional campuses in Williamsville and Orchard Park. **Enrollment:** 5,461 degree-seeking undergraduates; 788 non-degree-seeking students. **Degrees:** 801 associate awarded. **ROTC:** Army. **Location:** 10 miles from Buffalo. **Calendar:** Semester, limited summer session. **Full-time faculty:** 177 total; 8% minority, 52% women. **Part-time faculty:** 430 total; 7% minority, 45% women. **Special facilities:** Natatorium (City Campus), athletic fields (North and South Campus), vehicle training center, corporate training facility. **Partnerships:** Formal partnerships with Ford Motor Company, Daimler Chrysler, Verizon.

Student profile. Among degree-seeking undergraduates, 39% enrolled in a transfer program, 61% enrolled in a vocational program, 1% already have a bachelor's degree or higher, 1,375 enrolled as first-time, first-year students, 267 transferred in from other institutions.

Part-time:	24%	**Hispanic American:**	2%
Out-of-state:	1%	**Native American:**	1%
Women:	49%	**International:**	1%
African American:	13%	**25 or older:**	32%
Asian American:	2%		

Transfer out. Colleges most students transferred to 2008: SUNY College at Buffalo, SUNY College at Fredonia, SUNY College at Brockport, SUNY Buffalo.

Basis for selection. Open admission, but selective for some programs. Special requirements for nursing and occupational therapy programs; interview required. Students scoring 500 or higher on SAT Critical Reading waived from English placement test; students scoring 500 or higher on SAT Math waived from Math placement test. International students must be at least 17 years of age. **Homeschooled:** Applicants follow same criteria as applicants with GED.

2008-2009 Annual costs. Tuition/fees: $3,690; $6,877 out-of-state. Per-credit charge: $133 in-state; $266 out-of-state. Books/supplies: $1,000. Personal expenses: $900.

2007-2008 Financial aid. All financial aid based on need. Need-based aid available for part-time students. Work-study available weekends and for part-time students.

Application procedures. Admission: Priority date 8/1; no deadline. $25 fee. Admission notification on a rolling basis. **Financial aid:** Priority date 6/1; no closing date. FAFSA required. Applicants notified on a rolling basis starting 4/1; must reply within 2 week(s) of notification.

Academics. Special study options: Cooperative education, cross-registration, distance learning, double major, dual enrollment of high school students, ESL, exchange student, honors, independent study, internships, liberal arts/career combination, student-designed major, study abroad, teacher certification program, weekend college. Dual admissions with 4-year institutions. License preparation in dental hygiene, nursing, paramedic. **Credit/placement by examination:** AP, CLEP, institutional tests. **Support services:** GED preparation and test center, learning center, pre-admission summer program, reduced course load, remedial instruction, study skills assistance, tutoring, writing center.

Majors. Business: Business admin, construction management, office management. **Computer sciences:** General, information technology. **Education:** Physical. **Engineering:** General. **Engineering technology:** Civil, electrical, industrial, mechanical. **Health:** Clinical lab technology, dental hygiene, dietician assistant, medical records technology, nursing (RN), occupational therapy assistant, office admin, optician, respiratory therapy technology. **Liberal arts:** Arts/sciences, humanities. **Personal/culinary services:** Chef training, restaurant/catering. **Protective services:** Law enforcement admin, police science.

Most popular majors. Business/marketing 17%, health sciences 23%, liberal arts 33%, personal/culinary services 6%, security/protective services 13%.

Computing on campus. 436 workstations in library, computer center. Commuter students can connect to campus network. Online course registration, online library, helpline, repair service, student web hosting, wireless network available.

Student life. Freshman orientation: Mandatory, $50 fee. Preregistration for classes offered. **Activities:** Bands, choral groups, dance, drama, literary magazine, music ensembles, musical theater, radio station, student government, student newspaper, Latino student association, honors association, Phi Theta Kappa, multilingual club, Black Student Union.

Athletics. NJCAA. **Intercollegiate:** Baseball M, basketball, bowling, cheerleading M, cross-country, diving, football (tackle) M, golf, ice hockey M, lacrosse W, soccer, softball W, swimming, track and field, volleyball W. **Team name:** Kats.

Student services. Adult student services, career counseling, services for economically disadvantaged, student employment services, financial aid counseling, health services, minority student services, on-campus daycare, personal counseling, placement for graduates, veterans' counselor, women's services. **Physically disabled:** Services for visually, speech, hearing impaired. **Transfer:** Pre-admission transcript evaluation for new students. Transfer adviser, college fairs on campus for students transferring to 4-year colleges.

Contact. E-mail: cheatom@ecc.edu
Phone: (716) 851-1455 Fax: (716) 270-2961
Petrina Hill-Cheatom, Director of Admissions, Erie Community College: North Campus, 6205 Main Street, Williamsville, NY 14221-7095

Erie Community College: South Campus
Orchard Park, New York
www.ecc.edu **CB code: 2211**

- Public 2-year community college
- Commuter campus in large town

General. Founded in 1974. Regionally accredited. SUNY institution. Main campus located in Buffalo. Additional campuses in Williamsville and Orchard Park. **Enrollment:** 3,289 degree-seeking undergraduates; 867 non-degree-seeking students. **Degrees:** 578 associate awarded. **ROTC:** Army. **Location:** 10 miles from Buffalo. **Calendar:** Semester, limited summer session. **Full-time faculty:** 102 total; 8% minority, 41% women. **Part-time faculty:** 298 total; 3% minority, 35% women. **Special facilities:** Natatorium (City Campus), athletic fields (North & South Campus), vehicle training technology center, corporate training facility. **Partnerships:** Formal partnerships with Ford Motor Company, DaimlerChrysler, Verizon.

Student profile. Among degree-seeking undergraduates, 59% enrolled in a transfer program, 41% enrolled in a vocational program, 1% already have a bachelor's degree or higher, 971 enrolled as first-time, first-year students, 93 transferred in from other institutions.

Part-time:	21%	**Asian American:**	1%
Out-of-state:	2%	**Hispanic American:**	3%
Women:	42%	**Native American:**	1%
African American:	6%	**25 or older:**	21%

Transfer out. Colleges most students transferred to 2008: SUNY at Buffalo, SUNY College at Fredonia, SUNY College at Brockport, SUNY College at Buffalo.

Basis for selection. Open admission, but selective for some programs. Special requirements for dental laboratory technician program; interview required. Students scoring 500 or higher on SAT Critical Reading waived from English placement test; students scoring 500 or higher on SAT Math waived from Math placement test. Minimum age is 17 for international students. **Homeschooled:** Applicants follow same criteria as applicants with GED.

2008-2009 Annual costs. Tuition/fees: $3,690; $6,877 out-of-state. Per-credit charge: $133 in-state; $266 out-of-state. Books/supplies: $1,000. Personal expenses: $900.

Financial aid. All financial aid based on need. Need-based aid available for part-time students. Work-study available weekends and for part-time students.

Application procedures. Admission: Priority date 8/1; no deadline. $25 fee. Admission notification on a rolling basis. **Financial aid:** Priority date 6/1; no closing date. FAFSA required. Applicants notified on a rolling basis starting 4/1; must reply within 2 week(s) of notification.

Academics. Special study options: Cooperative education, cross-registration, distance learning, double major, dual enrollment of high school students, ESL, exchange student, honors, independent study, internships, liberal arts/career combination, student-designed major, study abroad, teacher certification program, weekend college. Dual admissions with 4-year institutions. License preparation in paramedic. **Credit/placement by examination:** AP, CLEP, institutional tests. **Support services:** GED preparation and test center, learning center, pre-admission summer program, reduced course load, remedial instruction, study skills assistance, tutoring, writing center.

Majors. Business: Business admin, office management. **Communications:** General. **Communications technology:** Graphic/printing. **Computer sciences:** Information technology. **Education:** Physical. **Engineering technology:** Architectural, CAD/CADD, computer systems, industrial. **Health:** Dental lab technology. **Liberal arts:** Arts/sciences, humanities. **Mechanic/repair:** Auto body, automotive, communications systems. **Parks/recreation:** Facilities management. **Protective services:** Fire services admin. **Public administration:** General, human services.

Most popular majors. Business/marketing 13%, communications/journalism 6%, engineering/engineering technologies 7%, liberal arts 49%, trade and industry 13%.

Computing on campus. 438 workstations in library, computer center. Commuter students can connect to campus network. Online course registration, online library, helpline, repair service, student web hosting, wireless network available.

Student life. Freshman orientation: Mandatory, $50 fee. Preregistration for classes offered. **Activities:** Bands, choral groups, dance, drama, literary magazine, music ensembles, musical theater, radio station, student government, student newspaper, Latino student association, honors association, Phi Theta Kappa, multilingual club, Black Student Union.

Athletics. NJCAA. **Intercollegiate:** Baseball M, basketball, bowling, cheerleading M, cross-country, diving, football (tackle) M, golf, ice hockey M, lacrosse W, soccer, softball W, swimming, track and field, volleyball W. **Team name:** Kats.

Student services. Adult student services, career counseling, services for economically disadvantaged, student employment services, financial aid counseling, health services, minority student services, on-campus daycare, personal counseling, placement for graduates, veterans' counselor, women's services. **Physically disabled:** Services for visually, speech, hearing impaired. **Transfer:** Pre-admission transcript evaluation for new students. Transfer adviser, college fairs on campus for students transferring to 4-year colleges.

Contact. E-mail: cheatom@ecc.edu
Phone: (716) 851-1655 Fax: (716) 851-1687
Petrina Hill-Cheatom, Director of Admissions, Erie Community College: South Campus, 4041 Southwestern Boulevard, Orchard Park, NY 14127-2199

Everest College: Rochester

Rochester, New York
www.everest.edu — **CB code: 2770**

- For-profit 2-year business and health science college
- Commuter campus in large city

General. Founded in 1863. Accredited by ACICS. **Calendar:** Quarter.

Contact. Phone: (585) 266-0430 ext. 101
Director of Admissions, 1630 Portland Avenue, Rochester, NY 14621-3007

Finger Lakes Community College

Canandaigua, New York
www.flcc.edu — **CB code: 2134**

- Public 2-year community college
- Commuter campus in small town

General. Founded in 1965. Regionally accredited. SUNY institution. **Enrollment:** 3,941 degree-seeking undergraduates; 1,809 non-degree-seeking students. **Degrees:** 746 associate awarded. **ROTC:** Army. **Location:** 25 miles from Rochester. **Calendar:** Semester, extensive summer session. **Full-time faculty:** 112 total; 3% minority, 47% women. **Part-time faculty:** 201 total; 55% women. **Class size:** 61% < 20, 38% 20-39, less than 1% 40-49, less than 1% 50-99. **Special facilities:** Outdoor classrooms, nature trails, music recording studio, performing arts center. **Partnerships:** Formal partnerships with local hospitals for nursing clinics; more informally for cooperative studies and placement of interns.

Student profile. Among degree-seeking undergraduates, 65% enrolled in a transfer program, 35% enrolled in a vocational program, 1,396 enrolled as first-time, first-year students.

Part-time:	21%	**Asian American:**	1%
Out-of-state:	1%	**Hispanic American:**	2%
Women:	55%	**25 or older:**	27%
African American:	7%		

Transfer out. Colleges most students transferred to 2008: SUNY at Brockport, SUNY at Geneseo, St. John Fisher College, Nazareth College of Rochester, Rochester Institute of Technology.

Basis for selection. Open admission, but selective for some programs. Admission to nursing program based on high school curriculum and GPA. Competitive admission to therapeutic massage/integrated health care program. Interview recommended for all; portfolio recommended for graphic arts program. **Homeschooled:** Student must submit certification of high school equivalent program provided by superintendent of school district in which student resides.

High school preparation. 1 each biology, chemistry, and algebra required of nursing applicants. Students without high school diploma or GED must pass federally approved Ability to Benefit test prior to acceptance. 1 biology required for therapeutic massage/integrated health care applicants.

2008-2009 Annual costs. Tuition/fees: $3,642; $6,888 out-of-state. Per-credit charge: $123 in-state; $246 out-of-state. Books/supplies: $900. Personal expenses: $958.

2007-2008 Financial aid. All financial aid based on need. 1,031 full-time freshmen applied for aid; 813 were judged to have need; 811 of these received aid. 64% of total undergraduate aid awarded as scholarships/grants, 36% as loans/jobs. Need-based aid available for part-time students. Work-study available nights, weekends and for part-time students.

Application procedures. Admission: No deadline. No application fee. Admission notification on a rolling basis beginning on or about 11/1. Must reply by May 1 or within 4 week(s) if notified thereafter. Application closing date for Nursing and Therapeutic Massage programs is February 1. **Financial aid:** Priority date 4/1; no closing date. FAFSA, institutional form required. Applicants notified on a rolling basis starting 3/1; must reply within 2 week(s) of notification.

Academics. Special study options: Cooperative education, cross-registration, distance learning, double major, dual enrollment of high school students, ESL, honors, independent study, internships. Credit-bearing travel opportunities. License preparation in nursing, paramedic. **Credit/placement by examination:** AP, CLEP, IB, institutional tests. 32 credit hours maximum toward associate degree. **Support services:** GED preparation, learning center, pre-admission summer program, reduced course load, remedial instruction, study skills assistance, tutoring, writing center.

Majors. Agriculture: Ornamental horticulture. **Biology:** Biotechnology. **Business:** General, accounting, administrative services, banking/financial services, business admin, e-commerce, hospitality/recreation, hotel/motel admin, marketing, sales/distribution, tourism promotion, tourism/travel. **Communications:** General, broadcast journalism. **Communications technology:** Recording arts. **Computer sciences:** General, computer science, information systems, programming. **Conservation:** General, environmental studies, fisheries, management/policy. **Education:** Elementary, physical. **Engineering:** General, science. **Engineering technology:** Architectural, mechanical. **Health:** Athletic training, massage therapy, nursing (RN), substance abuse counseling. **Legal studies:** Paralegal. **Liberal arts:** Arts/sciences. **Parks/recreation:** Sports admin. **Physical sciences:** Chemistry. **Protective services:** Criminal justice. **Public administration:** Human services. **Science technology:** Biological. **Social sciences:** General. **Visual/performing arts:** Commercial/advertising art, dramatic, studio arts.

Most popular majors. Business/marketing 17%, health sciences 15%, liberal arts 30%, natural resources/environmental science 9%, visual/performing arts 8%.

Computing on campus. 460 workstations in library, computer center, student center. Commuter students can connect to campus network. Online course registration, online library, helpline, student web hosting, wireless network available.

Student life. Freshman orientation: Available. Preregistration for classes offered. One-day program with faculty and student leaders. **Policies:** Student code of conduct policy, grievance procedures, procedures for services for students with disabilities. **Activities:** Bands, choral groups, drama, music ensembles, musical theater, radio station, student government, student newspaper, TV station, Phi Theta Kappa International Honor Society, Sigma Alpha Pi, nursing club, social science/human services club, legal society, College Republicans, College Democrats, Finger Lakes Environmental Action, radio club, Ghost of Ben Franklin (editorial paper).

Athletics. NJCAA. **Intercollegiate:** Baseball M, basketball, cross-country, lacrosse, soccer, softball W, track and field. **Intramural:** Badminton, basketball, football (non-tackle) M, soccer, softball, tennis, volleyball, weight lifting.

Student services. Adult student services, alcohol/substance abuse counseling, career counseling, services for economically disadvantaged, student employment services, financial aid counseling, health services, legal services, on-campus daycare, personal counseling, placement for graduates, veterans' counselor. **Physically disabled:** Services for visually, speech, hearing impaired. **Transfer:** Pre-admission transcript evaluation for new students. Transfer center, transfer adviser, college fairs on campus for students transferring to 4-year colleges.

Contact. E-mail: admissions@flcc.edu
Phone: (585) 394-3500 ext. 7278 Fax: (585) 394-5005
Bonnie Ritts, Admissions Office, Finger Lakes Community College, 4355 Lake Shore Drive, Canandaigua, NY 14424-8395

Fulton-Montgomery Community College

Johnstown, New York
www.fmcc.suny.edu **CB code: 2254**

- Public 2-year community college
- Commuter campus in large town

General. Founded in 1963. Regionally accredited. **Enrollment:** 1,887 degree-seeking undergraduates. **Degrees:** 325 associate awarded. **Location:** 40 miles from Albany, 200 miles from New York City. **Calendar:** Semester, extensive summer session. **Full-time faculty:** 53 total. **Part-time faculty:** 48 total. **Class size:** 46% <20, 46% 20-39, 7% 40-49, 1% 50-99. **Special facilities:** Regional history study center, BOCES facility co-located on campus.

Transfer out. Colleges most students transferred to 2008: State University of New York at Plattsburgh, College of Saint Rose, SUNY College at Oneonta, University at Albany.

Basis for selection. Open admission, but selective for some programs. Admission for nursing and radiologic technology programs based on high school GPA, class rank, and any college experience. Must meet program prerequisites. Focal Skills Test for ESL Placement and COMPASS used for placement. Interview recommended. **Homeschooled:** Applicants applying for financial aid may be required to complete Ability to Benefit Test. Applicants from accredited home school who have received or will receive diploma may not be required to take test.

2008-2009 Annual costs. Tuition/fees: $3,518; $6,662 out-of-state. Per-credit charge: $131 in-state; $262 out-of-state. Books/supplies: $500.

2007-2008 Financial aid. Need-based: Need-based aid available for part-time students. Work-study available nights, weekends and for part-time students. **Non-need-based:** Scholarships awarded for academics.

Application procedures. Admission: No deadline. No application fee. Admission notification on a rolling basis. **Financial aid:** Priority date 6/1; no closing date. FAFSA required. Applicants notified on a rolling basis starting 6/15; must reply within 2 week(s) of notification.

Academics. Career-oriented individual studies program offered. Can complete bachelor's degree online through Empire State College (SUNY) or Franklin University (OH); advising for both programs available on campus. **Special study options:** Accelerated study, cooperative education, cross-registration, distance learning, double major, dual enrollment of high school students, ESL, external degree, honors, independent study, internships, student-designed major, study abroad. 1+1 agreements with SUNY Agricultural and Technical Colleges at Canton and Cobleskill; automotive program at Career Education Center, Johnstown; EMT-Paramedic with SUNY Herkimer County Community College. Bachelor's degree programs available on campus. License preparation in nursing, radiology. **Credit/placement by examination:** AP, CLEP, institutional tests. 30 credit hours maximum toward associate degree. **Support services:** Learning center, reduced course load, remedial instruction, study skills assistance, tutoring, writing center.

Majors. Business: General, accounting technology, administrative services, business admin. **Communications:** General, journalism. **Communications technology:** Graphic/printing. **Computer sciences:** General, information systems. **Construction:** General. **Engineering:** General. **Engineering technology:** Computer, electrical. **Family/consumer sciences:** Child care. **Health:** Medical radiologic technology/radiation therapy, nursing (RN), office admin. **Liberal arts:** Arts/sciences, humanities. **Mechanic/repair:** Automotive. **Parks/recreation:** Health/fitness. **Personal/culinary services:** Restaurant/catering. **Protective services:** Criminal justice. **Public administration:** Community org/advocacy. **Visual/performing arts:** Art, commercial/advertising art.

Computing on campus. 400 workstations in library, computer center, student center. Commuter students can connect to campus network. Helpline available.

Student life. Freshman orientation: Available. Preregistration for classes offered. One-day orientation held one or two days before classes begin. **Activities:** Choral groups, drama, musical theater, student government, student newspaper, Phi Theta Kappa, Alpha Omega, international student union, business club, fencing club.

Athletics. NJCAA. **Intercollegiate:** Baseball M, basketball, soccer, softball W, volleyball W. **Intramural:** Basketball M, volleyball. **Team name:** Raiders.

Student services. Adult student services, student employment services, on-campus daycare, personal counseling, veterans' counselor. **Physically disabled:** Services for visually, speech, hearing impaired. **Transfer:** Pre-admission transcript evaluation for new students. Transfer center, college fairs on campus for students transferring to 4-year colleges.

Contact. E-mail: geninfo@fmcc.suny.edu
Phone: (518) 736-5300 Fax: (518) 762-4334
Laura LaPorte, Associate Dean of Enrollment Management, Fulton-Montgomery Community College, 2805 State Highway 67, Johnstown, NY 12095

Genesee Community College

Batavia, New York
www.genesee.edu **CB code: 2272**

- Public 2-year community college
- Commuter campus in large town

General. Founded in 1966. Regionally accredited. SUNY institution. Mall-type campus, suited to disabled. Off-campus sites in Orleans, Wyoming, and Livingston counties. **Enrollment:** 3,903 degree-seeking undergraduates; 2,769 non-degree-seeking students. **Degrees:** 612 associate awarded. **Location:** 35 miles from Buffalo, 35 miles from Rochester. **Calendar:** Semester, limited summer session. **Full-time faculty:** 81 total. **Part-time faculty:** 262 total. **Special facilities:** Nature preserve, arts center, technology building.

Student profile. Among degree-seeking undergraduates, 1,204 enrolled as first-time, first-year students.

Part-time:	24%	**Hispanic American:**	2%
Out-of-state:	1%	**Native American:**	1%
Women:	65%	**International:**	3%
African American:	6%	**25 or older:**	31%
Asian American:	1%		

Transfer out. Colleges most students transferred to 2008: SUNY Brockport, SUNY Buffalo, SUNY Geneseo, Rochester Institute of Technology, St. John Fisher.

Basis for selection. Open admission, but selective for some programs. Admission to nursing, physical therapist assistant, paralegal, and respiratory care programs based on academic achievement, test scores, interview, and school and community activities. ACT and COMPASS used for placement. Although SAT not used as placement test, students scoring above 500 on each part exempted from remedial courses. Portfolio recommended for digital art program.

High school preparation. Recommended units include English 4, mathematics 3, social studies 4, science 3 and foreign language 2. Additional units of math and science recommended for students planning to transfer to 4-year programs. 18 units, including biology and chemistry, required for nursing applicants. 18 units, including biology and physics, required for physical therapist assistant applicants.

2008-2009 Annual costs. Tuition/fees: $3,690; $4,580 out-of-state. Per-credit charge: $140 in-state; $160 out-of-state. Books/supplies: $955. Personal expenses: $850.

2007-2008 Financial aid. Need-based: Need-based aid available for part-time students. Work-study available nights, weekends and for part-time students.

Application procedures. Admission: No deadline. No application fee. Admission notification on a rolling basis beginning on or about 11/15. **Financial aid:** Priority date 3/1, closing date 5/1. FAFSA required. Applicants notified on a rolling basis starting 4/15; must reply within 2 week(s) of notification.

Academics. Special study options: Cooperative education, cross-registration, distance learning, double major, dual enrollment of high school

students, ESL, honors, independent study, internships, liberal arts/career combination. License preparation in nursing, physical therapy. **Credit/placement by examination:** AP, CLEP, IB, institutional tests. 31 credit hours maximum toward associate degree. **Support services:** GED preparation, learning center, reduced course load, remedial instruction, study skills assistance, tutoring, writing center.

Majors. Biology: Biotechnology. **Business:** Accounting, accounting technology, administrative services, business admin, customer service, fashion, retailing, tourism/travel. **Communications:** General. **Computer sciences:** Information systems, networking, webmaster. **Conservation:** Environmental studies. **Education:** Teacher assistance. **Engineering:** Science. **Engineering technology:** Drafting. **Health:** Medical secretary, nursing (RN), occupational therapy assistant, physical therapy assistant, recreational therapy, respiratory therapy technology, substance abuse counseling. **Legal studies:** Paralegal. **Liberal arts:** Arts/sciences, humanities. **Parks/recreation:** Health/fitness, sports admin. **Protective services:** Law enforcement admin. **Public administration:** Community org/advocacy. **Visual/performing arts:** Art, dramatic, theater design. **Other:** Economic crime investigation, Multimedia.

Most popular majors. Business/marketing 19%, health sciences 20%, liberal arts 32%, public administration/social services 8%, security/protective services 9%.

Computing on campus. 350 workstations in dormitories, library, computer center, student center. Dormitories wired for high-speed internet access and linked to campus network. Commuter students can connect to campus network. Online course registration, online library, helpline, wireless network available.

Student life. Freshman orientation: Mandatory. Preregistration for classes offered. Day-long orientation before classes begin. **Activities:** Choral groups, drama, film society, international student organizations, literary magazine, musical theater, radio station, student government, student newspaper, Intervarsity Christian Fellowship, Native American student organization, African American interest group, student parents, Enjoying Children Through Recreation and Education, Phi Theta Kappa, Distribution Education Clubs of America, adult student group, Habitat for Humanity.

Athletics. NJCAA. **Intercollegiate:** Baseball M, basketball, diving, lacrosse M, soccer, softball W, swimming, volleyball W. **Intramural:** Badminton, basketball, football (non-tackle), golf, skiing, soccer, softball, table tennis, tennis, volleyball. **Team name:** Cougars.

Student services. Adult student services, career counseling, student employment services, financial aid counseling, health services, on-campus daycare, personal counseling, placement for graduates, veterans' counselor. **Physically disabled:** Services for visually, speech, hearing impaired. **Transfer:** Re-entry adviser for new students. Transfer center, transfer adviser, college fairs on campus for students transferring to 4-year colleges.

Contact. E-mail: tmlanemartin@genesee.edu
Phone: (585) 345-6800 Toll-free number: (866) 225-5422
Fax: (585) 345-6810
Tanya Lane-Martin, Director of Admissions, Genesee Community College, One College Road, Batavia, NY 14020-9704

Helene Fuld College of Nursing

New York, New York
www.helenefuld.edu **CB code: 2327**

- Private 2-year nursing and junior college
- Commuter campus in very large city

General. Founded in 1945. Regionally accredited. One-year, full-time associate degree program accredited by National League for Nursing Accrediting Commission and Middle States Association of Colleges and Schools. Career ladder for LPNs. Part-time accredited study also offered. All applicants must be licensed practical nurses. **Enrollment:** 403 degree-seeking undergraduates. **Degrees:** 205 associate awarded. **Location:** Uptown. **Calendar:** Quarter, limited summer session. **Full-time faculty:** 17 total. **Part-time faculty:** 23 total. **Class size:** 6% < 20, 47% 20-39, 29% 40-49, 18% 50-99.

Basis for selection. Must be licensed practical nurse with 1 year work experience, PN licensure required. Require satisfactory performance on preentrance exams on practical nursing equivalent, mathematics, and English and completion of a prerequisite chemistry and mathematics course. After all entrance requirements fulfilled, including successful completion of testing, 18 credits granted for practical nursing. ATI testing required for entrance to nursing program.

2008-2009 Annual costs. Tuition/fees: $14,118. Per-credit charge: $252. Books/supplies: $1,861.

Financial aid. All financial aid based on need. Need-based aid available for part-time students.

Application procedures. Admission: No deadline. $110 fee. Admission notification on a rolling basis. **Financial aid:** No deadline. FAFSA required. Applicants notified on a rolling basis.

Academics. Special study options: Accelerated study, liberal arts/career combination. License preparation in nursing. **Credit/placement by examination:** CLEP, institutional tests. **Support services:** Learning center, reduced course load, study skills assistance, tutoring.

Majors. Health: Nursing (RN).

Computing on campus. 24 workstations in library, computer center. Commuter students can connect to campus network.

Student life. Freshman orientation: Mandatory. Preregistration for classes offered. 2 weeks before term starts. **Activities:** Student government.

Student services. Adult student services, career counseling, financial aid counseling, personal counseling. **Transfer:** Pre-admission transcript evaluation for new students. College fairs on campus for students transferring to 4-year colleges.

Contact. Phone: (212) 616-7200
Gladys Pineda, Assistant Director of Student Services, Helene Fuld College of Nursing, 24 East 120th Street, New York, NY 10035

Herkimer County Community College

Herkimer, New York
www.herkimer.edu **CB code: 2316**

- Public 2-year community college
- Commuter campus in small town

General. Founded in 1966. Regionally accredited. **Enrollment:** 2,653 degree-seeking undergraduates. **Degrees:** 511 associate awarded. **ROTC:** Army. **Location:** 10 miles from Utica, 55 miles from Syracuse. **Calendar:** Semester, limited summer session. **Full-time faculty:** 75 total. **Part-time faculty:** 75 total. **Class size:** 43% < 20, 55% 20-39, less than 1% 40-49, less than 1% 50-99. **Special facilities:** 500-acre nature center, natural history museum, archeology museum.

Student profile.

Out-of-state:	1%	**Live on campus:**	25%
25 or older:	23%		

Transfer out. Colleges most students transferred to 2008: SUNY Institute of Technology, SUNY Oneonta, SUNY Brockport, SUNY Oswego, SUNY Cortland.

Basis for selection. Open admission, but selective for some programs. SAT and ACT scores may be used to waive required college placement test. ASSET scores used to help determine placement into developmental courses. Interview recommended for emergency medical technician, occupational/physical therapy assistant programs. **Homeschooled:** Transcript of courses and grades, letter of recommendation (nonparent) required.

High school preparation. Physical/occupational therapist assistant applicants should contact admissions office to review high school course requirements.

2008-2009 Annual costs. Tuition/fees: $3,550; $6,020 out-of-state. Per-credit charge: $120 in-state; $233 out-of-state. Apartment-style dorms with a la carte meal service available. Books/supplies: $1,000. Personal expenses: $670.

Financial aid. Need-based: Need-based aid available for part-time students. Work-study available nights, weekends and for part-time students.

Application procedures. Admission: Priority date 7/1; deadline 8/26. No application fee. Admission notification on a rolling basis. **Financial aid:** Closing date 4/1. FAFSA required. Applicants notified on a rolling basis starting 4/1; must reply within 2 week(s) of notification.

Academics. Special study options: Distance learning, dual enrollment of high school students, ESL, honors, independent study, internships, liberal arts/career combination. License preparation in paramedic. **Credit/placement by examination:** AP, CLEP, institutional tests. 32 credit hours maximum toward associate degree. **Support services:** GED preparation, learning center, reduced course load, remedial instruction, study skills assistance, tutoring.

Honors college/program. Applicants need high school average of 88. Students must maintain GPA of 3.5.

Majors. **Biology:** General. **Business:** General, accounting, administrative services, business admin, entrepreneurial studies, fashion, human resources, international, logistics, marketing, office management, office technology, office/clerical, tourism/travel. **Communications:** Broadcast journalism, media studies. **Communications technology:** General. **Computer sciences:** Data processing, networking, webmaster. **Education:** Early childhood, physical, teacher assistance. **Engineering technology:** Construction. **Health:** Art therapy, EMT paramedic, health care admin, medical secretary, occupational therapy assistant, physical therapy assistant. **Legal studies:** Legal secretary, paralegal. **Liberal arts:** Arts/sciences. **Math:** General. **Parks/recreation:** Health/fitness. **Protective services:** Criminal justice, forensics, law enforcement admin. **Public administration:** Human services. **Social sciences:** General. **Visual/performing arts:** Art, arts management, photography, studio arts.

Computing on campus. 239 workstations in library, computer center. Dormitories linked to campus network. Commuter students can connect to campus network. Online library, helpline available.

Student life. **Freshman orientation:** Mandatory. Preregistration for classes offered. **Housing:** Coed dorms available. $500 deposit. **Activities:** Pep band, dance, drama, literary magazine, musical theater, radio station, student government, student newspaper, TV station, Students for a Better World, social issues club, Students Against Drunk Driving, Campus Christian Fellowship, cultural exchange club, black student union, Phi Theta Kappa.

Athletics. NJCAA. **Intercollegiate:** Baseball M, basketball, cross-country, diving, field hockey W, lacrosse, soccer, softball W, swimming, tennis, track and field, volleyball W. **Intramural:** Badminton, baseball M, basketball, bowling, lacrosse, soccer, softball, swimming, tennis, volleyball. **Team name:** Generals.

Student services. Adult student services, alcohol/substance abuse counseling, career counseling, student employment services, financial aid counseling, health services, on-campus daycare, personal counseling, placement for graduates, veterans' counselor. **Physically disabled:** Services for visually, hearing impaired. **Transfer:** Re-entry adviser, pre-admission transcript evaluation for new students. Transfer adviser, college fairs on campus for students transferring to 4-year colleges.

Contact. E-mail: admissions@herkimer.edu
Phone: (315) 866-0300 ext. 8278 Toll-free number: (888) 464-4222 ext. 8278 Fax: (315) 866-0062
Robert Palmieri, Director of Admissions, Herkimer County Community College, 100 Reservoir Road, Herkimer, NY 13350-1598

Hudson Valley Community College

Troy, New York — CB member
www.hvcc.edu — CB code: 2300

- Public 2-year community college
- Commuter campus in small city

General. Founded in 1953. Regionally accredited. SUNY institution. **Enrollment:** 12,787 degree-seeking undergraduates. **Degrees:** 1,711 associate awarded. **ROTC:** Army, Air Force. **Location:** 10 miles from Albany. **Calendar:** Semester, limited summer session. **Full-time faculty:** 272 total. **Part-time faculty:** 398 total. **Special facilities:** Language laboratory, computer laboratories.

Basis for selection. Open admission, but selective for some programs. Admission to some programs based on school achievement record and test scores. Interview also considered for some programs.

High school preparation. Requirements vary for selective programs.

2008-2009 Annual costs. Tuition/fees: $3,614; $9,414 out-of-state. Per-credit charge: $120 in-state; $360 out-of-state. Books/supplies: $550. Personal expenses: $800.

Application procedures. **Admission:** No deadline. $30 fee, may be waived for applicants with need. Admission notification on a rolling basis. **Financial aid:** Priority date 5/30; no closing date. FAFSA required. Applicants notified on a rolling basis starting 5/1; must reply within 2 week(s) of notification.

Academics. **Special study options:** Accelerated study, cooperative education, cross-registration, distance learning, double major, internships, student-designed major. License preparation in dental hygiene, nursing, paramedic, radiology. **Credit/placement by examination:** CLEP. 30 credit hours maximum toward associate degree. **Support services:** GED preparation, learning center, pre-admission summer program, reduced course load, remedial instruction, tutoring.

Majors. **Business:** General, accounting, administrative services, business admin, finance, insurance, international, office technology, real estate. **Computer sciences:** Data processing, networking. **Conservation:** Environmental studies. **Construction:** Carpentry, maintenance. **Education:** Physical. **Engineering:** General, science. **Engineering technology:** Civil, drafting, electrical. **Family/consumer sciences:** Child care. **Health:** Clinical lab science, clinical lab technology, dental hygiene, medical radiologic technology/radiation therapy, medical secretary, nursing (RN), physician assistant, respiratory therapy technology, substance abuse counseling. **Mechanic/repair:** Electronics/electrical, heating/ac/refrig. **Personal/culinary services:** Mortuary science. **Physical sciences:** Chemistry. **Protective services:** Forensics. **Public administration:** Community org/advocacy, social work. **Social sciences:** General.

Computing on campus. 1,000 workstations in library, computer center.

Student life. **Activities:** Drama, radio station, student government, student newspaper, TV station.

Athletics. NJCAA. **Intercollegiate:** Baseball M, basketball, bowling, cross-country, football (tackle) M, golf, ice hockey M, lacrosse M, soccer, softball W, tennis, track and field, volleyball W. **Intramural:** Baseball M, basketball, bowling, cross-country, field hockey W, golf, ice hockey, lacrosse, racquetball, skiing, soccer, softball, table tennis, tennis, track and field, volleyball, wrestling M.

Student services. Adult student services, career counseling, student employment services, health services, on-campus daycare, personal counseling, placement for graduates, veterans' counselor. **Physically disabled:** Services for visually, speech, hearing impaired.

Contact. E-mail: admissions@hvcc.edu
Phone: (518) 629-7309 Toll-free number: (877) 325-4822
Fax: (518) 629-4576
Mary Bauer, Director of Admissions, Hudson Valley Community College, 80 Vandenburgh Avenue, Troy, NY 12180

Institute of Design and Construction

Brooklyn, New York
www.idc.edu — CB code: 0677

- Private 2-year junior and technical college
- Commuter campus in very large city

General. Founded in 1947. Regionally accredited. Classes and seminars available for candidates preparing for Architects Registration Exam. **Enrollment:** 121 degree-seeking undergraduates. **Degrees:** 20 associate awarded. **Calendar:** Semester. **Part-time faculty:** 27 total.

Basis for selection. Open admission. Interview recommended.

High school preparation. Recommended units include English 4, mathematics 3 and science 1. One unit of drafting or architecture recommended.

2008-2009 Annual costs. Tuition/fees: $7,800. Per-credit charge: $260. Books/supplies: $800. Personal expenses: $400.

Application procedures. **Admission:** No deadline. $30 fee, may be waived for applicants with need. Admission notification on a rolling basis. **Financial aid:** No deadline. FAFSA, institutional form required. Applicants notified on a rolling basis starting 3/1; must reply within 4 week(s) of notification.

Academics. Work and study plan available. Students can spend 2 full-time semesters in accelerated study, then complete degree through part-time evening study while working during day as junior drafters. Credits transferable to Pratt Institute and New York Institute of Technology. **Special study options:** Double major. Work and study program. **Credit/placement by examination:** CLEP, institutional tests. 12 credit hours maximum toward associate degree. **Support services:** Learning center, reduced course load, remedial instruction, tutoring.

Majors. **Construction:** Maintenance. **Engineering technology:** Architectural, drafting. **Visual/performing arts:** Interior design.

Computing on campus. 17 workstations in library, computer center.

Student services. Career counseling, student employment services, personal counseling, placement for graduates, veterans' counselor. **Transfer:** Transfer adviser for students transferring to 4-year colleges.

Contact. Phone: (718) 855-3661 ext. 16 Fax: (718) 852-5889
Kevin Giannetti, Director of Admissions, Institute of Design and Construction, 141 Willoughby Street, Brooklyn, NY 11201-5380

Island Drafting and Technical Institute
Amityville, New York
www.idti.edu **CB code: 3048**

- For-profit 2-year technical and career college
- Commuter campus in large town
- Interview required

General. Accredited by ACCSCT. **Enrollment:** 139 degree-seeking undergraduates. **Degrees:** 93 associate awarded. **Location:** 25 miles from New York City. **Calendar:** Semester, extensive summer session. **Full-time faculty:** 5 total. **Part-time faculty:** 11 total.

Basis for selection. Open admission. School-administered test for CADD/ Architecture students.

High school preparation. Recommended units include English 2 and mathematics 2.

2008-2009 Annual costs. Tuition/fees: $13,100. Per-credit charge: $425. Books/supplies: $600.

Financial aid. All financial aid based on need.

Application procedures. Admission: No deadline. $25 fee, may be waived for applicants with need. Application must be submitted on paper. Admission notification on a rolling basis. **Financial aid:** No deadline. Applicants notified on a rolling basis.

Academics. Special study options: Liberal arts/career combination. **Credit/ placement by examination:** CLEP. **Support services:** Study skills assistance.

Majors. Computer sciences: Computer graphics. **Engineering:** Electrical. **Engineering technology:** Drafting, electrical. **Mechanic/repair:** Electronics/ electrical.

Computing on campus. 100 workstations in library, computer center.

Student life. Freshman orientation: Mandatory.

Student services. Alcohol/substance abuse counseling, career counseling, student employment services, financial aid counseling, personal counseling, placement for graduates, veterans' counselor.

Contact. E-mail: admissions@idti.edu
Phone: (631) 691-8733 Fax: (631) 691-8738
Steve Rothenberg, Admissions, Island Drafting and Technical Institute, 128 Broadway, Amityville, NY 11701-2704

ITT Technical Institute: Albany
Albany, New York
www.itt-tech.edu **CB code: 2689**

- For-profit 2-year technical college
- Commuter campus in large city

General. Accredited by ACICS. **Calendar:** Quarter.

Annual costs/financial aid. Books/supplies: $3,300.

Contact. Phone: (518) 452-9300
Director of Recruitment, 13 Airline Drive, Albany, NY 12205

ITT Technical Institute: Getzville
Getzville, New York
www.itt-tech.edu **CB code: 2704**

- For-profit 2-year technical college
- Commuter campus in rural community

General. Accredited by ACICS. **Calendar:** Quarter.

Contact. Phone: (716) 689-2200
Director of Recruitment, 2295 Millersport Highway, Getzville, NY 14068

ITT Technical Institute: Liverpool
Liverpool, New York
www.itt-tech.edu **CB code: 2725**

- For-profit 2-year technical college
- Commuter campus in small town

General. Accredited by ACICS. **Calendar:** Quarter.

Annual costs/financial aid. Books/supplies: $3,300.

Contact. Phone: (315) 461-8000
Director of Recruitment, 235 Greenfield Parkway, Liverpool, NY 13088

Jamestown Business College
Jamestown, New York
www.jamestownbusinesscollege.edu **CB code: 2346**

- For-profit 2-year business and junior college
- Commuter campus in large town

General. Founded in 1886. Regionally accredited. **Enrollment:** 263 degree-seeking undergraduates. **Degrees:** 97 associate awarded. **Location:** 80 miles from Buffalo, 60 miles from Erie, Pennsylvania. **Calendar:** Quarter, limited summer session. **Full-time faculty:** 8 total; 12% have terminal degrees, 12% minority, 75% women. **Part-time faculty:** 8 total; 12% minority, 62% women. **Class size:** 30% < 20, 70% 20-39.

Student profile.

Out-of-state:	18%	**25 or older:**	45%

Basis for selection. Class rank and academic record important. School and community activities considered. College uses the Comparative Guidance and Placement program in the admission process. Interview recommended.

2008-2009 Annual costs. Tuition/fees: $10,200. Books/supplies: $1,025. Personal expenses: $1,756.

2007-2008 Financial aid. Need-based: 65% of total undergraduate aid awarded as scholarships/grants, 35% as loans/jobs. Need-based aid available for part-time students. **Non-need-based:** Scholarships awarded for academics.

Application procedures. Admission: No deadline. $25 fee. Admission notification on a rolling basis. **Financial aid:** No deadline. FAFSA required. Applicants notified on a rolling basis starting 2/15.

Academics. Credit/placement by examination: CLEP, institutional tests. **Support services:** Reduced course load, study skills assistance, tutoring.

Majors. Business: Accounting, administrative services, business admin, marketing. **Computer sciences:** General, data processing. **Health:** Medical secretary. **Legal studies:** Legal secretary.

Computing on campus. 100 workstations in library, computer center. Commuter students can connect to campus network. Online library, wireless network available.

Student life. Freshman orientation: Mandatory.

Athletics. Intramural: Baseball, basketball, bowling, softball, volleyball.

Student services. Adult student services, career counseling, student employment services, personal counseling, placement for graduates, veterans' counselor. **Transfer:** Pre-admission transcript evaluation for new students. Transfer adviser for students transferring to 4-year colleges.

Contact. E-mail: admissions@jamestownbusinesscollege.edu
Phone: (716) 664-5100 Fax: (716) 664-3144
Brenda Salemme, Director of Admissions, Jamestown Business College, 7 Fairmount Avenue, Jamestown, NY 14702-0429

Jamestown Community College
Jamestown, New York
www.sunyjcc.edu **CB code: 2335**

- Public 2-year community college
- Commuter campus in large town

General. Founded in 1950. Regionally accredited. SUNY institution. Branch campus at Olean for Cattaraugus County. Extensions in Dunkirk, Allegany, Warren, PA. Bachelor's degree program through Franklin University. **Enrollment:** 3,220 degree-seeking undergraduates; 304 non-degree-seeking students. **Degrees:** 640 associate awarded. **Location:** 70 miles from Buffalo and Erie, Pennsylvania. **Calendar:** Semester, extensive summer session. **Full-time faculty:** 80 total; 2% minority. **Part-time faculty:** 318 total; 3% minority. **Class size:** 52% < 20, 48% 20-39, less than 1% 50-99. **Special facilities:** Natural history institute.

Student profile. Among degree-seeking undergraduates, 6% enrolled in a transfer program, 1,106 enrolled as first-time, first-year students.

Part-time:	24%	**Hispanic American:**	3%
Out-of-state:	8%	**Native American:**	2%
Women:	57%	**25 or older:**	26%
African American:	2%		

Transfer out. Colleges most students transferred to 2008: SUNY Fredonia, St. Bonaventure University, SUNY College at Buffalo, Houghton College.

Basis for selection. Open admission, but selective for some programs. Preference given to area students in highly subscribed programs. Competitive admission to nursing, occupational therapy assistant, with school achievement record very important. ACT and ASSET scores used for placement.

2008-2009 Annual costs. Tuition/fees: $4,000; $7,500 out-of-state. Per-credit charge: $146 in-state; $264 out-of-state. Books/supplies: $1,000. Personal expenses: $600.

2008-2009 Financial aid. Need-based: 901 full-time freshmen applied for aid; 708 were judged to have need; 705 of these received aid. 74% of total undergraduate aid awarded as scholarships/grants, 26% as loans/jobs. Need-based aid available for part-time students. Work-study available nights, weekends and for part-time students. **Non-need-based:** Awarded to 172 full-time undergraduates, including 103 freshmen. Scholarships awarded for academics, alumni affiliation, art, athletics, music/drama, state residency.

Application procedures. Admission: No deadline. $40 fee, may be waived for applicants with need, free for online applicants. Admission notification on a rolling basis. Must reply by May 1 or within 2 week(s) if notified thereafter. **Financial aid:** Priority date 3/1; no closing date. FAFSA required. Applicants notified on a rolling basis starting 4/15.

Academics. Strong liberal arts tradition, with a balance between transfer and career-oriented programs. **Special study options:** Cross-registration, distance learning, dual enrollment of high school students, honors, independent study, internships, liberal arts/career combination, study abroad, Washington semester, weekend college. License preparation in nursing. **Credit/placement by examination:** AP, CLEP, institutional tests. 36 credit hours maximum toward associate degree. **Support services:** Learning center, pre-admission summer program, reduced course load, remedial instruction, study skills assistance, tutoring.

Majors. Business: Accounting technology, banking/financial services, business admin, marketing, office management. **Computer sciences:** Data processing, programming. **Conservation:** Forestry. **Engineering:** General. **Engineering technology:** Electrical, mechanical. **Health:** Clinical lab technology, nursing (RN), occupational therapy assistant. **Liberal arts:** Arts/sciences, humanities. **Mechanic/repair:** Small engine. **Protective services:** Criminal justice, police science. **Public administration:** Human services. **Social sciences:** General. **Transportation:** Airline/commercial pilot. **Visual/performing arts:** Studio arts.

Most popular majors. Business/marketing 12%, health sciences 17%, liberal arts 25%, mathematics 7%, security/protective services 9%, social sciences 14%.

Computing on campus. 800 workstations in library, computer center, student center. Dormitories wired for high-speed internet access and linked to campus network. Commuter students can connect to campus network. Online course registration, online library, wireless network available.

Student life. Freshman orientation: Mandatory. **Housing:** $200 nonrefundable deposit, deadline 3/8. Coed housing available. **Activities:** Bands, choral groups, dance, drama, music ensembles, musical theater, radio station, student government, Earth Awareness, InterVarsity Christian Fellowship, Early Childhood Educators, Political Awareness, nursing club, humanities club, criminal justice club.

Athletics. NJCAA. **Intercollegiate:** Baseball M, basketball, cross-country, diving, golf, soccer, softball W, swimming, volleyball W, wrestling M. **Intramural:** Basketball, bowling, softball, table tennis, tennis, volleyball. **Team name:** Jayhawks.

Student services. Adult student services, alcohol/substance abuse counseling, career counseling, services for economically disadvantaged, student employment services, financial aid counseling, health services, personal counseling, placement for graduates, veterans' counselor. **Physically disabled:** Services for visually, speech, hearing impaired. **Transfer:** Transfer adviser, college fairs on campus for students transferring to 4-year colleges.

Contact. E-mail: admissions@mail.sunyjcc.edu
Phone: (716) 338-1000 ext. 1001 Toll-free number: (800) 388-8557
Fax: (716) 338-1450
Wendy Present, Director, Admissions and Recruitment, Jamestown Community College, 525 Falconer Street, Jamestown, NY 14702-0020

Jefferson Community College

Watertown, New York
www.sunyjefferson.edu **CB code: 2345**

- Public 2-year community college
- Commuter campus in large town

General. Founded in 1961. Regionally accredited. **Enrollment:** 2,407 degree-seeking undergraduates. **Degrees:** 487 associate awarded. **Location:** 70 miles from Syracuse. **Calendar:** Semester, limited summer session. **Full-time faculty:** 77 total. **Part-time faculty:** 98 total.

Student profile.

Out-of-state:	1%	**25 or older:**	37%

Transfer out. Colleges most students transferred to 2008: SUNY Empire State College, SUNY Oswego, SUNY Potsdam.

Basis for selection. Open admission, but selective for some programs. Admission to some programs based on grades, class rank, test scores, school recommendation, personal interview. Waiting list available for nursing program. Interview recommended for engineering science, nursing programs.

High school preparation. Strong background in math and science required for engineering science, computer science, nursing, and science laboratory technologies programs.

2008-2009 Annual costs. Tuition/fees: $3,601; $5,501 out-of-state. Per-credit charge: $132 in-state; $195 out-of-state. Books/supplies: $1,150. Personal expenses: $936.

2008-2009 Financial aid. All financial aid based on need. Need-based aid available for part-time students. Work-study available for part-time students.

Application procedures. Admission: No deadline. No application fee. Admission notification on a rolling basis. **Financial aid:** Priority date 4/1, closing date 8/15. FAFSA, institutional form required. Applicants notified on a rolling basis starting 4/15; must reply within 2 week(s) of notification.

Academics. Students in engineering science, computer science, and computer information systems programs required to purchase or lease microcomputers. **Special study options:** Cooperative education, distance learning, double major, dual enrollment of high school students, honors, independent study, internships, student-designed major, weekend college. Bachelor's degree programs available on campus. **Credit/placement by examination:** AP, CLEP, IB, institutional tests. 30 credit hours maximum toward associate degree. **Support services:** Learning center, reduced course load, remedial instruction, study skills assistance, tutoring.

Majors. Agriculture: Animal husbandry. **Business:** Accounting technology, administrative services, business admin, tourism promotion. **Computer sciences:** General, computer science, information systems. **Engineering:** General. **Health:** EMT paramedic, medical secretary, nursing (RN). **Legal studies:** Paralegal. **Liberal arts:** Arts/sciences. **Protective services:** Fire services admin, law enforcement admin. **Public administration:** Community org/advocacy.

Most popular majors. Business/marketing 19%, health sciences 6%, liberal arts 52%, security/protective services 9%.

Computing on campus. 354 workstations in library, computer center, student center. Online library, helpline, wireless network available.

Student life. Freshman orientation: Available. Half-day program held in August and January. **Housing:** Privately owned apartments available. **Activities:** Bands, choral groups, drama, literary magazine, music ensembles, student government, student newspaper, veterans club, multicultural club, human services club, environmental club, European excursion club, business club, office technology association, political clubs, Brothers and Sisters in Christ.

Athletics. NJCAA. **Intercollegiate:** Baseball M, basketball, golf, lacrosse, soccer, softball W, tennis W, volleyball W. **Intramural:** Badminton, basketball, soccer, softball, volleyball. **Team name:** Cannoneers.

Student services. Adult student services, chaplain/spiritual director, career counseling, student employment services, financial aid counseling, health services, on-campus daycare, personal counseling, placement for graduates, veterans' counselor. **Physically disabled:** Services for visually, speech, hearing impaired. **Transfer:** Transfer adviser, college fairs on campus for students transferring to 4-year colleges.

Contact. E-mail: admissions@sunyjefferson.edu
Phone: (315) 786-2277 Fax: (315) 786-2459
Rosanne Weir, Director of Admissions, Jefferson Community College, 1220 Coffeen Street, Watertown, NY 13601

Katharine Gibbs School: Melville

Melville, New York
www.gibbslongisland.com **CB code: 1039**

- For-profit 2-year junior college
- Small town

General. Founded in 1911. Accredited by ACICS. **Location:** 40 miles from New York City. **Calendar:** Quarter.

Annual costs/financial aid. Costs vary by program. Per-credit-hour charge $290; business program $283 per-credit-hour. Books/supplies: $700.

Contact. Phone: (631) 370-3300
Director of Admissions, 320 South Service Road, Melville, NY 11747

Long Island Business Institute

Commack, New York
www.libi.edu **CB code: 3334**

- For-profit 2-year business college
- Commuter campus in large town
- Application essay, interview required

General. Accredited by ACICS. Main campus in Flushing, Queens. Branch campus in Commack. **Enrollment:** 589 degree-seeking undergraduates; 15 non-degree-seeking students. **Degrees:** 173 associate awarded. **Calendar:** Semester, extensive summer session. **Full-time faculty:** 20 total; 5% have terminal degrees, 60% minority, 60% women. **Part-time faculty:** 76 total; 1% have terminal degrees, 40% minority, 62% women. **Class size:** 70% < 20, 30% 20-39.

Student profile. Among degree-seeking undergraduates, 1% already have a bachelor's degree or higher, 180 enrolled as first-time, first-year students.

Part-time:	37%	**Hispanic American:**	21%
Women:	78%	**Native American:**	1%
African American:	7%	**International:**	3%
Asian American:	34%	**25 or older:**	73%

Transfer out. Colleges most students transferred to 2008: St. Joseph's College, Mercy College, Briarcliffe College.

Basis for selection. Open admission, but selective for some programs. Prospective students should demonstrate an understanding and interest in a program of study through an admissions interview. **Adult students:** SAT/ACT scores not required. **Homeschooled:** State high school equivalency certificate required. **Learning Disabled:** Students must provide to the designated campus professional a recent, appropriate evaluation from a licensed medical professional familiar with the disability, and make a follow-up appointment to discuss accommodations.

2008-2009 Annual costs. Tuition/fees: $10,200. Per-credit charge: $325. Tuition varies by program. Books/supplies: $700. Personal expenses: $1,750.

2008-2009 Financial aid. Need-based: 141 full-time freshmen applied for aid; 141 were judged to have need; 141 of these received aid. Average need met was 87%. Average scholarship/grant was $3,300; average loan $3,000. 70% of total undergraduate aid awarded as scholarships/grants, 30% as loans/jobs. Need-based aid available for part-time students. Work-study available nights and for part-time students. **Non-need-based:** Scholarships awarded for academics.

Application procedures. Admission: No deadline. $50 fee. Admission notification on a rolling basis. **Financial aid:** No deadline. FAFSA required. Must reply within 2 week(s) of notification.

Academics. Special study options: ESL, independent study, internships. **Credit/placement by examination:** CLEP, institutional tests. Limited to 50% of specific curriculum total credit hours. **Support services:** Learning center, remedial instruction, tutoring.

Majors. Business: Accounting, business admin, office management. **Health:** Medical secretary. **Legal studies:** Court reporting.

Most popular majors. Business/marketing 61%, health sciences 20%, legal studies 20%.

Computing on campus. 275 workstations in library, computer center. Online library, wireless network available.

Student life. Freshman orientation: Mandatory. Held 2 days prior to each semester start and lasts approximately 4 hours. **Activities:** Student newspaper.

Student services. Career counseling, student employment services, financial aid counseling, placement for graduates. **Transfer:** Pre-admission transcript evaluation for new students.

Contact. E-mail: admissions@libi.edu
Phone: (631) 499-7100 Fax: (631) 499-7114
Robert Nazar, Director of Admissions, Long Island Business Institute, 6500 Jericho Turnpike, Commack, NY 11725

Long Island Business Institute: Flushing

Flushing, New York
www.libi.edu

- For-profit 2-year business college
- Commuter campus in very large city

General. Accredited by ACICS. **Calendar:** Semester.

Annual costs/financial aid. Tuition/fees (2008-2009): $10,200. Books/supplies: $400. Need-based financial aid available to full-time and part-time students.

Contact. Phone: (718) 939-5100
Director of Admissions, 37-12 Prince Street, Flushing, NY 11354

Long Island College Hospital School of Nursing

Brooklyn, New York
www.futurenurselich.org **CB code: 2377**

- Private 2-year nursing college
- Commuter campus in very large city

General. Founded in 1883. **Calendar:** Semester.

Annual costs/financial aid. Tuition/fees (2008-2009): $16,295. Freshmen typically take a combination of nursing courses at $350 per credit hour and liberal arts and sciences courses at $370 per credit hour. Books/supplies: $1,100. Personal expenses: $1,863.

Contact. Phone: (718) 780-1071
Manager of Student Services, 350 Henry Street, 7th Floor, Brooklyn, NY 11201

Maria College

Albany, New York **CB member**
www.mariacollege.edu **CB code: 2434**

- Private 2-year junior college
- Commuter campus in small city
- SAT or ACT (ACT writing optional), application essay, interview required

General. Founded in 1958. Regionally accredited. **Enrollment:** 738 degree-seeking undergraduates. **Degrees:** 125 associate awarded. **ROTC:** Army, Naval, Air Force. **Location:** 150 miles from New York City and Boston. **Calendar:** Semester, limited summer session. **Full-time faculty:** 35 total. **Part-time faculty:** 55 total. **Class size:** 79% < 20, 15% 20-39, less than 1% 40-49, 6% 50-99.

Transfer out. Colleges most students transferred to 2008: College of Saint Rose, State University at Albany, Hudson Valley Community College, The Sage Colleges, Schenectady County Community College.

Basis for selection. School achievement record, test scores, interviews, recommendations important. Test required for students with scores on SAT Verbal less than 480, Math less than 490, or ACT Composite less than 19. Dual interview required for Nursing (ADN) and Occupational Therapy Assistant. **Adult students:** SAT/ACT scores not required. Applicants who did not take SAT or ACT may be required to take an admissions test, which may be waived based on prior college credit. **Homeschooled:** Transcript of courses and grades, state high school equivalency certificate, interview, letter of recommendation (nonparent) required. SAT or ACT scores or applicant must take College admissions test for placement purposes. **Learning Disabled:** Must provide documentation regarding specific diagnosis and services/accommodations being requested. Documentation must be within 3 years of acceptance. Must meet with the Dean of Student Services for coordination of support services.

High school preparation. 21 units required. Required and recommended units include English 4, mathematics 2-3, social studies 4, science 2-3 (laboratory 3). Requirements vary with program.

2008-2009 Annual costs. Tuition/fees: $9,100. Per-credit charge: $325. Books/supplies: $600. Personal expenses: $500.

2008-2009 Financial aid. All financial aid based on need. 48% of total undergraduate aid awarded as scholarships/grants, 52% as loans/jobs. Need-based aid available for part-time students. Work-study available nights, weekends and for part-time students.

Application procedures. Admission: Closing date 8/15 (receipt date). $35 fee, may be waived for applicants with need. Application must be submitted on paper. Admission notification on a rolling basis. Must reply by May 1 or within 4 week(s) if notified thereafter. Tuition deposit deadline 30 days after acceptance. High school seniors have until May 1. **Financial aid:** No deadline. FAFSA required. Applicants notified on a rolling basis starting 2/1; must reply within 2 week(s) of notification.

Academics. Special study options: Accelerated study, cross-registration, distance learning, dual enrollment of high school students, independent study, internships, liberal arts/career combination, weekend college. Advanced placement program in nursing for licensed practical nurse and New York State LPN to ADN Nursing Bridge Course. License preparation in nursing, occupational therapy. **Credit/placement by examination:** AP, CLEP, IB, SAT, ACT, institutional tests. 16 credit hours maximum toward associate degree. **Support services:** Learning center, pre-admission summer program, reduced course load, remedial instruction, study skills assistance, tutoring.

Majors. Business: General, accounting, business admin. **Computer sciences:** General. **Education:** Early childhood, teacher assistance. **Health:** Nursing (RN), occupational therapy assistant. **Legal studies:** Paralegal. **Liberal arts:** Arts/sciences. **Science technology:** Biological.

Most popular majors. Education 7%, health sciences 76%, liberal arts 11%.

Computing on campus. 72 workstations in library, computer center. Commuter students can connect to campus network. Online course registration, online library, wireless network available.

Student life. Freshman orientation: Mandatory. Preregistration for classes offered. Held one day prior to the beginning of the semester.

Student services. Adult student services, alcohol/substance abuse counseling, chaplain/spiritual director, career counseling, student employment services, financial aid counseling, personal counseling, placement for graduates. **Physically disabled:** Services for visually impaired. **Transfer:** Reentry adviser, pre-admission transcript evaluation for new students. Transfer adviser, college fairs on campus for students transferring to 4-year colleges.

Contact. E-mail: laurieg@mariacollege.edu
Phone: (518) 438-3111 ext. 217 Fax: (518) 453-1366
Laurie Gilmore, Director of Admissions, Maria College, 700 New Scotland Avenue, Albany, NY 12208

Mildred Elley

Albany, New York
www.mildred-elley.edu **CB code: 3335**

- For-profit 2-year career college
- Commuter campus in very large city
- Interview required

General. Accredited by ACICS. **Enrollment:** 427 degree-seeking undergraduates. **Degrees:** 102 associate awarded. **Location:** 147 miles from New York City. **Calendar:** Semester, extensive summer session. **Full-time faculty:** 30 total. **Part-time faculty:** 18 total. **Class size:** 92% < 20, 8% 20-39.

Student profile. Among degree-seeking undergraduates, 100% enrolled in a vocational program, 1% already have a bachelor's degree or higher, 169 transferred in from other institutions.

Basis for selection. Open admission, but selective for some programs. Additional requirements for Massage Therapy and Practical Nursing programs. **Homeschooled:** Transcript of courses and grades, state high school equivalency certificate required.

2008-2009 Annual costs. Tuition/fees: $10,920. Per-credit charge: $354. Books/supplies: $800.

Financial aid. All financial aid based on need. Need-based aid available for part-time students. Work-study available nights and for part-time students.

Application procedures. Admission: No deadline. $25 fee, may be waived for applicants with need. Application must be submitted on paper. Admission notification on a rolling basis. **Financial aid:** No deadline. FAFSA required.

Academics. Special study options: Accelerated study, cooperative education, double major, independent study, internships, weekend college. License preparation in nursing. **Credit/placement by examination:** AP, CLEP, institutional tests. **Support services:** GED preparation, learning center, remedial instruction, study skills assistance, tutoring, writing center.

Majors. Business: Business admin. **Computer sciences:** General, information systems. **Health:** Massage therapy, medical assistant. **Legal studies:** General, paralegal. **Visual/performing arts:** Design.

Most popular majors. Business/marketing 38%, computer/information sciences 22%, health sciences 21%, legal studies 20%.

Computing on campus. PC or laptop required. 120 workstations in library, computer center, student center. Commuter students can connect to campus network. Online library, helpline, repair service, wireless network available.

Student life. Freshman orientation: Mandatory. Preregistration for classes offered.

Student services. Adult student services, alcohol/substance abuse counseling, career counseling, financial aid counseling, legal services, personal counseling, placement for graduates, veterans' counselor, women's services. **Transfer:** Re-entry adviser, pre-admission transcript evaluation for new students. College fairs on campus for students transferring to 4-year colleges.

Contact. E-mail: admissions@mildred-elley.edu
Phone: (518) 786-3171 Toll-free number: (800) 622-6327
Fax: (518) 786-0011
George Chakmakas, Admissions Director, Mildred Elley, 855 Central Avenue, Albany, NY 12206-1513

Mohawk Valley Community College

Utica, New York
www.mvcc.edu **CB code: 2414**

- Public 2-year community college
- Commuter campus in small city

General. Founded in 1946. Regionally accredited. SUNY institution. Branch campus in Rome, New York. **Enrollment:** 4,857 degree-seeking undergraduates; 1,327 non-degree-seeking students. **Degrees:** 736 associate awarded. **ROTC:** Army. **Location:** 55 miles from Syracuse, 95 miles from Albany. **Calendar:** Semester, limited summer session. **Full-time faculty:** 139 total; 19% have terminal degrees, 9% minority, 40% women. **Part-time faculty:** 242 total; 2% minority, 49% women. **Class size:** 49% < 20, 46% 20-39, 4% 40-49, 1% 50-99. **Special facilities:** Human cadaver lab, welding facilities, airframe and powerplant hangar facilities. **Partnerships:** Formal partnership with Verizon for NEXT STEP, a virtual university program for Verizon employees to earn an associate in telecommunications.

Two-Year Colleges

Student profile. Among degree-seeking undergraduates, 43% enrolled in a transfer program, 57% enrolled in a vocational program, 1,556 enrolled as first-time, first-year students, 251 transferred in from other institutions.

Part-time:	21%	**Native American:**	1%
Women:	54%	**International:**	1%
African American:	7%	**25 or older:**	25%
Asian American:	2%	**Live on campus:**	11%
Hispanic American:	4%		

Transfer out. Colleges most students transferred to 2008: SUNY Institute of Technology (Utica/Rome), Utica College, SUNY College at Oneonta, SUNY College at Oswego, SUNY Albany.

Basis for selection. Open admission, but selective for some programs. Applicants' records reviewed for completion of program-specific prerequisites to determine regular or underprepared acceptance to program. Interview recommended for all, required for airframe & powerplant tech applicants. **Homeschooled:** State high school equivalency certificate required. Must pass ability-to-benefit test prior to acceptance if the state high school equivalency certificate letter is not provided. **Learning Disabled:** Learning-disabled applicants should forward copy of IEP to Coordinator of Disabilities Services.

High school preparation. College-preparatory program recommended. 15 units recommended. Recommended units include English 4, mathematics 2, social studies 4, science 2, foreign language 1 and academic electives 2. Requirements vary for admission to nursing and certain other programs.

2008-2009 Annual costs. Tuition/fees: $3,664; $6,914 out-of-state. Per-credit charge: $120 in-state; $240 out-of-state. Room/board: $7,500. Books/supplies: $1,350. Personal expenses: $820.

2008-2009 Financial aid. Need-based: Need-based aid available for part-time students. Work-study available nights, weekends and for part-time students.

Application procedures. Admission: No deadline. No application fee. Admission notification on a rolling basis beginning on or about 12/1. Within 30 days of date of acceptance due to limited housing availability on campus. **Financial aid:** Priority date 4/15; no closing date. FAFSA, institutional form required. Applicants notified on a rolling basis starting 3/1; must reply within 2 week(s) of notification.

Academics. Special study options: Cross-registration, distance learning, double major, dual enrollment of high school students, ESL, honors, independent study, internships, student-designed major. License preparation in nursing. **Credit/placement by examination:** AP, CLEP, institutional tests. 45 credit hours maximum toward associate degree. Each department has its own policy. **Support services:** Learning center, reduced course load, remedial instruction, study skills assistance, tutoring, writing center.

Majors. Business: Accounting technology, administrative services, banking/financial services, business admin, entrepreneurial studies, hotel/motel admin. **Communications:** Advertising. **Computer sciences:** General, programming, webmaster. **Construction:** Maintenance. **Education:** Elementary, secondary. **Engineering:** General. **Engineering technology:** Civil, drafting, electrical, heat/ac/refrig, mechanical, surveying. **Family/consumer sciences:** Institutional food production. **Health:** EMT paramedic, medical assistant, medical radiologic technology/radiation therapy, medical records technology, nursing (RN), respiratory therapy technology, substance abuse counseling. **Interdisciplinary:** Nutrition sciences. **Liberal arts:** Arts/sciences, humanities. **Mechanic/repair:** Aircraft, communications systems, electronics/electrical. **Parks/recreation:** Facilities management. **Personal/culinary services:** Restaurant/catering. **Production:** Welding. **Protective services:** Fire services admin, law enforcement admin. **Public administration:** General, community org/advocacy. **Science technology:** Chemical. **Visual/performing arts:** Art, commercial photography, commercial/advertising art, dramatic. **Other:** Liberal arts and sciences/psychology, Semiconductor manufacturing technology.

Most popular majors. Business/marketing 15%, engineering/engineering technologies 8%, health sciences 18%, liberal arts 27%, public administration/social services 6%, security/protective services 8%, visual/performing arts 10%.

Computing on campus. 125 workstations in library, computer center. Dormitories wired for high-speed internet access. Commuter students can connect to campus network. Online course registration, online library, helpline, wireless network available.

Student life. Freshman orientation: Mandatory, $40 fee. Preregistration for classes offered. Two-hour commuter orientation and 3-day dorm student orientation in January and August. **Housing:** Coed dorms, special housing for disabled, cooperative housing, wellness housing available. $100 fully refundable deposit. Pets allowed in dorm rooms. All halls nonsmoking; 1 residence hall has extended quiet hours. Limited visitation suites available. On-campus housing is on first-come, first-served basis. **Activities:** Concert band, dance, drama, international student organizations, musical theater, student government, student newspaper, Black Student Union, chemical dependency club, education club, international club, Kidz-N-Coaches, Latino student union, respiratory care club, returning adult student association, student congress/program board, student nurses organization.

Athletics. NJCAA. **Intercollegiate:** Baseball M, basketball, bowling, cross-country, golf, ice hockey M, lacrosse M, soccer, softball W, tennis, track and field, volleyball W. **Intramural:** Basketball, football (non-tackle), racquetball, soccer, softball, tennis, volleyball, weight lifting. **Team name:** Hawks.

Student services. Adult student services, alcohol/substance abuse counseling, career counseling, student employment services, financial aid counseling, health services, on-campus daycare, personal counseling, placement for graduates, veterans' counselor. **Physically disabled:** Services for visually, speech, hearing impaired. **Transfer:** Pre-admission transcript evaluation for new students. Transfer center, transfer adviser, college fairs on campus for students transferring to 4-year colleges.

Contact. E-mail: admissions@mvcc.edu
Phone: (315) 792-5354 Toll-free number: (800) 733-6822
Fax: (315) 792-5527
Denis Kennelty, Director of Admissions, Mohawk Valley Community College, 1101 Sherman Drive, Utica, NY 13501-5394

Monroe Community College

Rochester, New York — **CB member**
www.monroecc.edu — **CB code: 2429**

- Public 2-year community college
- Commuter campus in large city

General. Founded in 1961. Regionally accredited. SUNY institution. Off-campus extension centers in 2 area high schools, branch campus in downtown Rochester. Applied technology center. **Enrollment:** 16,250 degree-seeking undergraduates; 1,864 non-degree-seeking students. **Degrees:** 2,306 associate awarded. **ROTC:** Army, Naval, Air Force. **Location:** 4 miles from downtown. **Calendar:** Semester, limited summer session. **Full-time faculty:** 317 total; 20% have terminal degrees, 13% minority, 52% women. **Part-time faculty:** 590 total; 8% have terminal degrees, 10% minority, 51% women. **Class size:** 35% < 20, 59% 20-39, 4% 40-49, 2% 50-99, less than 1% >100. **Special facilities:** Human ecology habitat, human performance laboratory, electronic learning center. **Partnerships:** Formal partnerships with Xerox, Kodak, Frontier, Wegman's.

Student profile. Among degree-seeking undergraduates, 76% enrolled in a transfer program, 24% enrolled in a vocational program, 2% already have a bachelor's degree or higher, 4,585 enrolled as first-time, first-year students, 1,124 transferred in from other institutions.

Part-time:	33%	**Hispanic American:**	6%
Out-of-state:	1%	**Native American:**	1%
Women:	54%	**International:**	1%
African American:	17%	**25 or older:**	34%
Asian American:	4%	**Live on campus:**	2%

Transfer out. 55% of students enrolled in the transfer program go on to 4-year colleges. **Colleges most students transferred to 2008:** SUNY College at Brockport, Rochester Institute of Technology, St. John Fisher College, SUNY College at Geneseo, Nazareth College.

Basis for selection. Open admission, but selective for some programs. Admissions to certain programs based on high school records, with preference given to county residents. Applicants to engineering and computer science must have precalculus, chemistry and physics. **Homeschooled:** Transcript of courses and grades required. Must meet Federal Ability to Benefit guidelines on placement exam if not issued a regular high school diploma.

High school preparation. Recommended units include English 4, mathematics 4, social studies 4 and science 4. Individual programs have specific math and science requirements.

2008-2009 Annual costs. Tuition/fees: $3,290; $6,190 out-of-state. Per-credit charge: $121 in-state; $242 out-of-state. Room only: $5,555. Books/supplies: $1,000.

2007-2008 Financial aid. All financial aid based on need. 50% of total undergraduate aid awarded as scholarships/grants, 50% as loans/jobs. Need-based aid available for part-time students. Work-study available nights, weekends and for part-time students.

Application procedures. Admission: Priority date 3/1; no deadline. $20 fee, may be waived for applicants with need. Admission notification on a

rolling basis. Application deadline for healthcare programs: 1/31 for fall term, 10/31 for spring term. Applicants to nursing program are encouraged to apply 1 year prior to registration. **Financial aid:** Priority date 3/30; no closing date. FAFSA required. Applicants notified on a rolling basis starting 3/15; must reply within 2 week(s) of notification.

Academics. Special study options: Accelerated study, cooperative education, cross-registration, distance learning, dual enrollment of high school students, ESL, exchange student, honors, independent study, internships, liberal arts/career combination, weekend college. License preparation in aviation, dental hygiene, nursing, paramedic, radiology. **Credit/placement by examination:** AP, CLEP, institutional tests. 30 credit hours maximum toward associate degree. **Support services:** Learning center, pre-admission summer program, reduced course load, remedial instruction, study skills assistance, tutoring, writing center.

Majors. Architecture: Landscape. **Biology:** General. **Business:** General, accounting, administrative services, international, marketing, sales/distribution, tourism promotion, tourism/travel. **Communications:** General, advertising. **Communications technology:** General. **Computer sciences:** General, computer science. **Construction:** General. **Education:** Music. **Engineering:** Science. **Engineering technology:** Civil, construction, electrical, manufacturing. **Health:** Dental hygiene, medical records technology, nursing (RN), physics/radiologic health. **History:** General. **Liberal arts:** Arts/sciences. **Math:** General. **Mechanic/repair:** Automotive, heating/ac/refrig. **Parks/recreation:** Health/fitness. **Personal/culinary services:** Culinary arts. **Physical sciences:** Chemistry, optics, physics. **Protective services:** Corrections, criminal justice, fire safety technology, police science. **Public administration:** Human services. **Science technology:** Biological. **Social sciences:** General, political science. **Visual/performing arts:** Commercial/advertising art, interior design, music performance, photography, studio arts.

Most popular majors. Business/marketing 59%, health sciences 12%.

Computing on campus. 150 workstations in library, computer center, student center. Dormitories wired for high-speed internet access and linked to campus network. Commuter students can connect to campus network. Helpline available.

Student life. Freshman orientation: Available. Orientation held 1 week prior to beginning of semester. **Housing:** Coed dorms available. **Activities:** Bands, choral groups, drama, literary magazine, musical theater, radio station, student government, student newspaper, symphony orchestra, Christian, Jewish, and Christian Science groups; Latin American, Italian-American, black, and international student organizations; veterans and handicapped student clubs; honor society.

Athletics. NJCAA. **Intercollegiate:** Baseball M, basketball, diving, golf M, ice hockey M, lacrosse M, soccer, softball W, swimming, tennis, volleyball W. **Intramural:** Archery, basketball, bowling, cheerleading W, cross-country, diving, lacrosse, racquetball, rugby M, skiing, soccer, softball, swimming, tennis, volleyball, water polo M. **Team name:** Tribunes.

Student services. Adult student services, career counseling, student employment services, financial aid counseling, health services, on-campus daycare, personal counseling, placement for graduates, veterans' counselor. **Physically disabled:** Services for visually, hearing impaired. **Transfer:** Transfer center, transfer adviser, college fairs on campus for students transferring to 4-year colleges.

Contact. Phone: (585) 292-2200 Fax: (585) 292-3680
Andrew Freeman, Director of Admissions, Monroe Community College, Office of Admissions-Monroe Community College, Rochester, NY 14692-8908

Nassau Community College

Garden City, New York — **CB member**
www.ncc.edu — **CB code: 2563**

- Public 2-year community college
- Commuter campus in large town

General. Founded in 1959. Regionally accredited. SUNY institution. Students may attend some courses at off-campus locations. Partnerships with local businesses and industry to provide on-site training to employees. **Enrollment:** 21,631 degree-seeking undergraduates. **Degrees:** 2,689 associate awarded. **ROTC:** Army. **Location:** 25 miles from New York City. **Calendar:** Semester, extensive summer session. **Full-time faculty:** 555 total. **Part-time faculty:** 922 total. **Class size:** 100% 20-39.

Transfer out. Colleges most students transferred to 2008: Hofstra University, Adelphi University, SUNY Old Westbury, SUNY Stony Brook, Dowling College.

Basis for selection. Open admission, but selective for some programs. Class rank and fulfillment of mathematics and science requirements important for admission to accounting, business, engineering, nursing, allied health, mortuary science, civil technology, computer information systems, computer science, electrical technology, paralegal, and telecommunications technology programs. Students without high school diploma or equivalent may apply for GED after successful completion of 24 college credits. SAT scores may result in exemption from placement testing. Interview required for allied health programs; audition required for music program; portfolio review required for fashion apparel design program. **Adult students:** Placement test in reading, English, and math required unless applicant has prior associate or bachelor's degree or prior college credit for English composition and college-level math. **Homeschooled:** Transcript of courses and grades required. **Learning Disabled:** Students must submit a copy of their I.E.P. in order to get services through our Center for Students with Disabilities.

High school preparation. Recommended units include English 4, mathematics 4, social studies 4, science 4 (laboratory 4), foreign language 3 and academic electives 4.

2008-2009 Annual costs. Tuition/fees: $3,832; $7,384 out-of-state. Per-credit charge: $148 in-state; $296 out-of-state. Books/supplies: $1,152. Personal expenses: $1,440.

2007-2008 Financial aid. Need-based: Need-based aid available for part-time students. Work-study available nights, weekends and for part-time students. **Non-need-based:** Scholarships awarded for academics, minority status.

Application procedures. Admission: Closing date 8/11 (receipt date). $40 fee. Admission notification on a rolling basis beginning on or about 11/15. **Financial aid:** Priority date 6/7; no closing date. FAFSA required. Applicants notified on a rolling basis; must reply within 1 week(s) of notification.

Academics. Special study options: Cooperative education, cross-registration, distance learning, ESL, honors, internships, study abroad, weekend college. Cooperative programs with SUNY College of Technology at Utica-Rome and SUNY at New Paltz, New York State Chiropractic College, Fashion Institute of Technology, Adelphi University; joint admissions with SUNY at Stony Brook and SUNY College at Old Westbury. License preparation in nursing, physical therapy, radiology, real estate. **Credit/placement by examination:** AP, CLEP, IB, institutional tests. 33 credit hours maximum toward associate degree. **Support services:** GED preparation and test center, learning center, reduced course load, remedial instruction, study skills assistance, tutoring, writing center.

Honors college/program. Honors applicants must rank in the top 20% of their graduating class and have 3 years of Regents math, English, science and high grades in each.

Majors. Area/ethnic studies: African. **Business:** Accounting, administrative services, business admin, fashion, management information systems, sales/distribution. **Communications:** General, media studies. **Computer sciences:** General, computer science, programming. **Education:** Early childhood, elementary, middle, secondary. **Engineering:** General, electrical. **Engineering technology:** Civil, computer systems, electrical. **Family/consumer sciences:** Food/nutrition. **Foreign languages:** American Sign Language. **Health:** Clinical lab science, medical radiologic technology/radiation therapy, medical secretary, nursing (RN), physical therapy assistant, respiratory therapy technology, surgical technology. **Legal studies:** Legal secretary, paralegal. **Liberal arts:** Arts/sciences. **Math:** General. **Personal/culinary services:** Embalming, food service, mortuary science, restaurant/catering. **Protective services:** Law enforcement admin. **Transportation:** General. **Visual/performing arts:** Art, commercial/advertising art, graphic design, interior design, music performance, photography. **Other:** Computer repair tech.

Most popular majors. Business/marketing 11%, family/consumer sciences 6%, health sciences 11%, liberal arts 57%.

Computing on campus. 1,300 workstations in library, computer center. Commuter students can connect to campus network. Online library available.

Student life. Freshman orientation: Available. Full-day program. **Activities:** Bands, choral groups, dance, drama, literary magazine, music ensembles, musical theater, radio station, student government, student newspaper, symphony orchestra, TV station, Haraya Caribbean students organizations, Asian American society, Irish American club, NYPIRG, women center, Association Catholic Community, Jewish students organization, organization of Latinos, multicultural club, Intervarsity Christian Fellowship.

Athletics. NJCAA. **Intercollegiate:** Baseball M, basketball, bowling, cross-country, football (tackle) M, golf, lacrosse, soccer, softball W, tennis, track and field, volleyball W, wrestling M. **Intramural:** Badminton, baseball M, basketball, football (non-tackle) M, handball, judo, racquetball, soccer, softball, swimming, table tennis, tennis, volleyball. **Team name:** Lions.

Student services. Adult student services, career counseling, student employment services, financial aid counseling, health services, minority student services, on-campus daycare, personal counseling, placement for graduates, veterans' counselor, women's services. **Physically disabled:** Services for visually, speech, hearing impaired. **Transfer:** Pre-admission transcript evaluation for new students. Transfer center, transfer adviser, college fairs on campus for students transferring to 4-year colleges.

Contact. E-mail: admissions@ncc.edu
Phone: (516) 572-7345 Fax: (516) 572-9743
Tika Esler, Associate Dean of Admissions, Nassau Community College, One Education Drive, Garden City, NY 11530

New York Career Institute
New York, New York
www.nyci.com **CB code: 5324**

- For-profit 2-year junior college
- Commuter campus in very large city
- Interview required

General. Accredited by New York State Board of Regents. **Enrollment:** 629 degree-seeking undergraduates. **Degrees:** 49 associate awarded. **Calendar:** Trimester, extensive summer session. **Full-time faculty:** 9 total; 22% have terminal degrees, 11% minority, 67% women. **Part-time faculty:** 22 total; 23% have terminal degrees, 32% minority, 27% women.

Student profile. Among degree-seeking undergraduates, 79 transferred in from other institutions.

Part-time:	17%	**Women:**	89%

Basis for selection. Open admission. CPAt examination performance important for all students who enter without college credit in English and/or mathematics. All applicants take English and math placement examinations (CPAt).

2008-2009 Annual costs. Full-time tuition and fees for Court Reporting, Paralegal, and Medical daytime programs $11,250; for court reporting night program $10,650. Tuition for paralegal and medical evening programs $360 per credit hour. Books/supplies: $800. Personal expenses: $4,000.

Financial aid. All financial aid based on need. Need-based aid available for part-time students. Work-study available nights.

Application procedures. Admission: No deadline. $50 fee. Admission notification on a rolling basis. **Financial aid:** No deadline. Applicants notified on a rolling basis.

Academics. Special study options: Internships. **Credit/placement by examination:** AP, CLEP, institutional tests. **Support services:** Remedial instruction, study skills assistance.

Majors. Health: Medical records admin, medical secretary. **Legal studies:** Court reporting, legal secretary, paralegal.

Computing on campus. Online library, repair service available.

Student life. Freshman orientation: Mandatory.

Student services. Career counseling, student employment services, financial aid counseling, personal counseling, placement for graduates. **Transfer:** Pre-admission transcript evaluation for new students.

Contact. E-mail: cmcmahon@nyci.edu
Phone: (212) 962-0002 Fax: (212) 385-7574
Larry Steiglitz, Director of Admissions, New York Career Institute, 11 Park Place, New York, NY 10007

Niagara County Community College
Sanborn, New York **CB member**
www.niagaracc.suny.edu **CB code: 2568**

- Public 2-year community college
- Commuter campus in rural community

General. Founded in 1962. Regionally accredited. SUNY institution. **Enrollment:** 4,583 degree-seeking undergraduates; 2,095 non-degree-seeking students. **Degrees:** 865 associate awarded. **ROTC:** Army. **Location:** 10 miles from Niagara Falls. **Calendar:** Semester, limited summer session. **Full-time faculty:** 117 total; 31% have terminal degrees, 7% minority, 51% women. **Part-time faculty:** 283 total; 9% have terminal degrees, 5% minority, 60% women. **Special facilities:** Biofeedback laboratory.

Student profile. Among degree-seeking undergraduates, 40% enrolled in a transfer program, 38% enrolled in a vocational program, 1,370 enrolled as first-time, first-year students, 114 transferred in from other institutions.

Part-time:	25%	**Hispanic American:**	1%
Out-of-state:	1%	**Native American:**	2%
Women:	59%	**International:**	1%
African American:	7%	**25 or older:**	27%
Asian American:	1%	**Live on campus:**	3%

Transfer out. Colleges most students transferred to 2008: Buffalo State College, Niagara University, SUNY Buffalo, Brockport, Fredonia.

Basis for selection. Open admission, but selective for some programs. Admission to nursing, physical therapist assistant, radiologic technology, and surgical technology programs based on school achievement record and test scores, on a space-available basis. SAT/ACT reviewed for placement if submitted. Interview recommended.

High school preparation. 1 drafting required for drafting applicants; 1 biology or chemistry required for nursing applicants; 3 mathematics for engineering technology; 1 biology, 1 chemistry and 2 mathematics for physical therapist assistant; 1 chemistry, 1 biology, 2 mathematics for radiologic technology; 1 biology for surgical technician; 2 mathematics for business administration.

2008-2009 Annual costs. Tuition/fees: $3,634; $6,946 out-of-state. Per-credit charge: $138 in-state; $276 out-of-state. Books/supplies: $700. Personal expenses: $650.

2007-2008 Financial aid. All financial aid based on need. 53% of total undergraduate aid awarded as scholarships/grants, 47% as loans/jobs. Need-based aid available for part-time students. Work-study available nights and for part-time students. **Additional information:** Assistance offered placing students in part-time employment. Students can charge books, food coupons, or $100 advance against anticipated financial aid.

Application procedures. Admission: Closing date 8/31. No application fee. Admission notification on a rolling basis beginning on or about 8/1. Must reply by May 1 or within 4 week(s) if notified thereafter. **Financial aid:** Priority date 4/1; no closing date. FAFSA required. Applicants notified on a rolling basis starting 5/1; must reply within 2 week(s) of notification.

Academics. Orientation program for Distance Learning students. **Special study options:** Cooperative education, cross-registration, distance learning, double major, dual enrollment of high school students, honors, independent study, internships, study abroad. License preparation in nursing. **Credit/placement by examination:** AP, CLEP, IB, institutional tests. 30 credit hours maximum toward associate degree. **Support services:** Learning center, pre-admission summer program, reduced course load, remedial instruction, study skills assistance, tutoring, writing center.

Majors. Business: Accounting, administrative services, business admin, hospitality admin, retailing. **Communications:** General, digital media. **Computer sciences:** General, computer science. **Conservation:** Environmental studies. **Education:** Elementary. **Engineering technology:** CAD/CADD, mechanical. **Health:** Medical assistant, medical radiologic technology/radiation therapy, nursing (RN), physical therapy assistant, surgical technology. **Liberal arts:** Arts/sciences, humanities. **Parks/recreation:** Health/fitness. **Personal/culinary services:** Chef training. **Protective services:** Criminalistics, law enforcement admin. **Public administration:** Human services. **Visual/performing arts:** Dramatic, studio arts. **Other:** Gaming and casino management, Science technologies/technicians.

Most popular majors. Business/marketing 15%, health sciences 21%, liberal arts 29%, security/protective services 9%, visual/performing arts 7%.

Computing on campus. 500 workstations in library, computer center, student center. Dormitories wired for high-speed internet access and linked to campus network. Commuter students can connect to campus network. Online course registration, online library, helpline, student web hosting, wireless network available.

Student life. Freshman orientation: Available. One-day orientation in August. **Housing:** Guaranteed on-campus for all undergraduates. Coed dorms available. **Activities:** Jazz band, choral groups, dance, drama, music ensembles, musical theater, radio station, student government, student newspaper, disabled student association, comeback club, African American student association, Native American club, nursing club, human services club, international club, women's studies club.

Athletics. NJCAA. **Intercollegiate:** Baseball M, basketball, golf, soccer, softball W, volleyball W, wrestling M. **Intramural:** Basketball. **Team name:** Trailblazers.

Student services. Adult student services, alcohol/substance abuse counseling, career counseling, student employment services, financial aid counseling, health services, on-campus daycare, personal counseling, placement for graduates, veterans' counselor. **Physically disabled:** Services for visually, speech, hearing impaired. **Transfer:** Pre-admission transcript evaluation for new students. Transfer adviser, college fairs on campus for students transferring to 4-year colleges.

Contact. E-mail: admissions@niagaracc.suny.edu
Phone: (716) 614-6200 Fax: (716) 614-6820
Kathy Saunders, Director of Admissions, Niagara County Community College, 3111 Saunders Settlement Road, Sanborn, NY 14132-9460

North Country Community College

Saranac Lake, New York
www.nccc.edu **CB code: 2571**

- Public 2-year community college
- Commuter campus in small town

General. Founded in 1967. Regionally accredited. SUNY institution. Campuses in Saranac Lake, Malone, and Ticonderoga. **Enrollment:** 1,031 degree-seeking undergraduates. **Degrees:** 216 associate awarded. **Location:** 150 miles from Albany, 50 miles from Plattsburgh. **Calendar:** Semester, limited summer session. **Full-time faculty:** 43 total; 19% have terminal degrees, 2% minority, 51% women. **Part-time faculty:** 105 total; 6% have terminal degrees, 1% minority, 60% women. **Class size:** 75% < 20, 24% 20-39, 1% 40-49. **Partnerships:** Formal partnerships with local high schools through College Bridge Program.

Student profile.

Out-of-state:	2%	**Live on campus:**	6%
25 or older:	26%		

Transfer out. Colleges most students transferred to 2008: SUNY Colleges at Plattsburgh, Potsdam, Cobleskill, Geneseo; SUNY at Buffalo.

Basis for selection. Open admission, but selective for some programs. Special requirements for nursing, radiologic technology, and massage therapy. SAT or ACT and placement tests recommended for competitive programs. **Homeschooled:** Must complete and score in appropriate ranges on College Board Descriptive Tests System in math, English, and reading.

High school preparation. 16 units recommended. Recommended units include English 4, mathematics 3, social studies 4, science 3 (laboratory 1) and foreign language 3. 5 units of math and science recommended (3 math and 2 science or 2 math and 3 science).

2008-2009 Annual costs. Tuition/fees: $4,385; $9,695 out-of-state. Per-credit charge: $160 in-state; $390 out-of-state. Room/board: $8,500. Books/supplies: $800. Personal expenses: $800.

2007-2008 Financial aid. All financial aid based on need. Need-based aid available for part-time students. Work-study available nights, weekends and for part-time students.

Application procedures. Admission: Priority date 2/1; deadline 9/1 (receipt date). No application fee. Admission notification on a rolling basis. Must reply by May 1 or within 4 week(s) if notified thereafter. **Financial aid:** Priority date 4/1; no closing date. FAFSA required. Applicants notified on a rolling basis starting 4/1; must reply within 3 week(s) of notification.

Academics. 23-42 credit hours required in major, 62-70 required for graduation depending on field of study. **Special study options:** Distance learning, double major, dual enrollment of high school students, internships, liberal arts/career combination, student-designed major. License preparation in nursing, radiology. **Credit/placement by examination:** AP, CLEP, institutional tests. 31 credit hours maximum toward associate degree. **Support services:** Learning center, reduced course load, remedial instruction, study skills assistance, tutoring.

Majors. Business: General, business admin, office/clerical. **Computer sciences:** Computer graphics. **Health:** Health services, massage therapy, medical radiologic technology/radiation therapy, nursing (RN). **Interdisciplinary:** Biological/physical sciences. **Liberal arts:** Arts/sciences. **Parks/recreation:** Facilities management. **Protective services:** Criminal justice.

Most popular majors. Business/marketing 20%, health sciences 25%, liberal arts 28%, security/protective services 12%.

Computing on campus. 200 workstations in dormitories, library, computer center, student center. Dormitories linked to campus network. Commuter students can connect to campus network. Online library, helpline, wireless network available.

Student life. Freshman orientation: Mandatory. Preregistration for classes offered. Day-long session held 1 day prior to start of classes. **Housing:** Coed dorms, wellness housing available. $250 nonrefundable deposit. **Activities:** Drama, literary magazine, music ensembles, student government, student newspaper.

Athletics. NJCAA. **Intercollegiate:** Basketball M, ice hockey M, soccer, softball W. **Intramural:** Badminton, basketball, bowling, golf, soccer, softball, swimming, volleyball, weight lifting. **Team name:** Saints.

Student services. Adult student services, alcohol/substance abuse counseling, career counseling, student employment services, financial aid counseling, personal counseling, placement for graduates. **Physically disabled:** Services for visually, speech, hearing impaired. **Learning disabled:** Comprehensive services available. **Transfer:** Pre-admission transcript evaluation for new students. Transfer adviser, college fairs on campus for students transferring to 4-year colleges.

Contact. E-mail: info@nccc.edu
Phone: (518) 891-2915 ext. 233 Toll-free number: (888) 879-6222
Fax: (518) 891-0898
Edwin Trathen, Vice President for Enrollment and Student Services, North Country Community College, 23 Santanoni Avenue, Saranac Lake, NY 12983

Olean Business Institute

Olean, New York
www.obi.edu **CB code: 0630**

- For-profit 2-year business college
- Commuter campus in large town

General. Founded in 1961. Accredited by ACICS. **Enrollment:** 100 degree-seeking undergraduates. **Degrees:** 15 associate awarded. **Location:** 90 miles from Buffalo, 90 miles from Erie, Pennsylvania. **Calendar:** Semester, limited summer session. **Full-time faculty:** 8 total; 100% women. **Part-time faculty:** 4 total; 75% women.

Student profile.

25 or older:	53%	**Live on campus:**	2%

Basis for selection. Open admission. Interview recommended.

2009-2010 Annual costs. Tuition/fees (projected): $10,450. Books/supplies: $700.

Application procedures. Admission: No deadline. $25 fee, may be waived for applicants with need. Admission notification on a rolling basis. **Financial aid:** Priority date 5/1; no closing date. FAFSA required. Applicants notified on a rolling basis.

Academics. Academic offerings intended to provide student with as much work-field knowledge and experience as possible. **Special study options:** Internships. **Credit/placement by examination:** CLEP, institutional tests. **Support services:** Learning center, reduced course load, remedial instruction, tutoring.

Majors. Business: General, accounting, accounting/business management, administrative services, business admin, management science, office management, office technology. **Computer sciences:** Data entry, data processing, word processing. **Health:** Medical records admin, medical secretary, office admin. **Legal studies:** Paralegal.

Computing on campus. 75 workstations in dormitories, library, computer center.

Student life. Housing: Single-sex dorms available. Student housing available near campus. **Activities:** Student government.

Student services. Adult student services, career counseling, student employment services, personal counseling, placement for graduates. **Transfer:** Transfer adviser for students transferring to 4-year colleges.

Contact. E-mail: cenglish@obi.edu
Phone: (716) 372-7978 Fax: (716) 372-2120
Carl English, Director of Admissions, Olean Business Institute, 301 North Union Street, Olean, NY 14760

Onondaga Community College
Syracuse, New York
www.sunyocc.edu
CB member
CB code: 2627

- Public 2-year community college
- Commuter campus in small city

General. Founded in 1962. Regionally accredited. SUNY institution. **Enrollment:** 7,539 degree-seeking undergraduates; 3,173 non-degree-seeking students. **Degrees:** 870 associate awarded. **ROTC:** Army, Air Force. **Location:** 4 miles from downtown Syracuse. **Calendar:** Semester, extensive summer session. **Full-time faculty:** 162 total; 9% minority, 52% women. **Part-time faculty:** 420 total; 6% minority, 48% women. **Special facilities:** Children's learning center, county library branch, applied technology center. **Partnerships:** Formal partnerships with Syracuse City Schools, Manufacturers Association of Central New York.

Student profile. Among degree-seeking undergraduates, 66% enrolled in a transfer program, 44% enrolled in a vocational program, 1,779 enrolled as first-time, first-year students, 320 transferred in from other institutions.

Part-time:	25%	**Hispanic American:**	3%
Out-of-state:	3%	**Native American:**	2%
Women:	51%	**25 or older:**	29%
African American:	10%	**Live on campus:**	7%
Asian American:	2%		

Transfer out. Colleges most students transferred to 2008: SUNY Oswego, SUNY Cortland, Le Moyne College, Syracuse University.

Basis for selection. Open admission, but selective for some programs. Admission to some programs based on high school GPA, test scores, and specific program prerequisites. Mandatory developmental skills courses required as condition of acceptance for students lacking adequate academic background. School achievement record, test scores, special talents considered for placement only. Interview, recommendations required for some programs. Interview required for graphic arts, radio-television; recommended for nursing, physical therapist assistant. Audition required for music; portfolio required for art, recommended for photography. **Homeschooled:** Submit diplomas from school districts of record, transcripts if available.

High school preparation. 15 units recommended. Recommended units include English 4, mathematics 3, science 3 and foreign language 2. Algebra, biology, chemistry required of respiratory care, surgical technology, nursing applicants. 4 math required for engineering, science, computer science and physical therapy assistant applicants. Language required for humanities.

2008-2009 Annual costs. Tuition/fees: $3,762; $7,154 out-of-state. Per-credit charge: $132 in-state; $264 out-of-state. Books/supplies: $1,230. Personal expenses: $700.

2007-2008 Financial aid. All financial aid based on need. Need-based aid available for part-time students. Work-study available for part-time students.

Application procedures. Admission: Closing date 8/31. $40 fee, may be waived for applicants with need. Admission notification on a rolling basis. **Financial aid:** Priority date 2/15; no closing date. FAFSA required. Applicants notified on a rolling basis starting 4/15; must reply within 4 week(s) of notification.

Academics. Special study options: Accelerated study, cooperative education, cross-registration, distance learning, double major, dual enrollment of high school students, ESL, honors, independent study, internships, liberal arts/career combination, New York semester, study abroad. License preparation in nursing. **Credit/placement by examination:** AP, CLEP, institutional tests. 30 credit hours maximum toward associate degree. **Support services:** GED preparation, learning center, pre-admission summer program, reduced course load, remedial instruction, study skills assistance, tutoring, writing center.

Majors. Architecture: Interior. **Business:** General, accounting, administrative services, hotel/motel admin, labor relations. **Communications:** Broadcast journalism. **Computer sciences:** General, computer science. **Engineering:** Computer, electrical, science. **Engineering technology:** Construction, electrical. **Health:** Medical records technology, nursing assistant, physical therapy assistant, recreational therapy, respiratory therapy technology. **Interdisciplinary:** Math/computer science. **Liberal arts:** Arts/sciences, humanities. **Mechanic/repair:** Automotive. **Parks/recreation:** Facilities management. **Personal/culinary services:** Culinary arts. **Protective services:** Criminal justice, fire safety technology. **Public administration:** Human services. **Visual/performing arts:** Art, commercial/advertising art, interior design, photography.

Most popular majors. Business/marketing 13%, engineering/engineering technologies 6%, health sciences 8%, liberal arts 27%, security/protective services 10%, visual/performing arts 7%.

Computing on campus. PC or laptop required. 1,000 workstations in library, computer center, student center. Dormitories wired for high-speed internet access and linked to campus network. Commuter students can connect to campus network. Online course registration, helpline, repair service, student web hosting, wireless network available.

Student life. Freshman orientation: Available. Preregistration for classes offered. Programs held for half day in fall and spring prior to start of classes. **Policies:** Dorms are alcohol free. **Housing:** Coed dorms, wellness housing available. $300 nonrefundable deposit. Suite-style housing available. **Activities:** Bands, choral groups, drama, film society, international student organizations, music ensembles, musical theater, radio station, student government, student newspaper, international students, minority, veterans, interreligious, older/returning student clubs.

Athletics. NJCAA. **Intercollegiate:** Baseball M, basketball, cross-country, lacrosse M, softball W, tennis, volleyball W. **Intramural:** Basketball, bowling, fencing, golf, lacrosse M, skiing, skin diving, softball W, swimming, tennis, volleyball. **Team name:** Lazers.

Student services. Chaplain/spiritual director, career counseling, services for economically disadvantaged, student employment services, financial aid counseling, health services, minority student services, on-campus daycare, personal counseling, placement for graduates, veterans' counselor. **Physically disabled:** Services for visually, speech, hearing impaired. **Transfer:** Pre-admission transcript evaluation for new students. Transfer adviser, college fairs on campus for students transferring to 4-year colleges.

Contact. E-mail: admissions@sunyocc.edu
Phone: (315) 498-2000 Fax: (315) 498-2107
Katherine Perry, Director of Admissions, Onondaga Community College, 4585 West Seneca Turnpike, Syracuse, NY 13215-4585

Orange County Community College
Middletown, New York
www.orange.cc.ny.us
CB member
CB code: 2625

- Public 2-year community college
- Commuter campus in large town

General. Founded in 1950. Regionally accredited. **Enrollment:** 6,763 degree-seeking undergraduates. **Degrees:** 655 associate awarded. **ROTC:** Army. **Location:** 25 miles from Newburgh, 60 miles from New York City. **Calendar:** Semester, limited summer session. **Full-time faculty:** 141 total. **Part-time faculty:** 340 total.

Student profile.

Out-of-state:	2%	**25 or older:**	27%

Transfer out. Colleges most students transferred to 2008: SUNY at New Paltz, Mount St. Mary's College, Marist College, Dominican College of Blauvelt.

Basis for selection. Open admission, but selective for some programs. Admission to allied health and nursing programs based on academic record, assessment scores and, to some extent, residency.

High school preparation. Regents biology required for physical therapist assistant, occupational therapy assistant, radiologic technologist and dental hygienist. Regents chemistry required for dental hygiene.

2008-2009 Annual costs. Tuition/fees: $3,648; $6,948 out-of-state. Per-credit charge: $138 in-state; $276 out-of-state. Books/supplies: $850. Personal expenses: $925.

Financial aid. Need-based: Need-based aid available for part-time students.

Application procedures. Admission: No deadline. $30 fee, may be waived for applicants with need. Admission notification on a rolling basis. February 1 application closing date for allied health/nursing program. Notification by March 15, must reply within 2 weeks. **Financial aid:** Priority date 5/1; no closing date. FAFSA, institutional form required. Applicants notified on a rolling basis starting 5/1; must reply within 4 week(s) of notification.

Academics. Agreement with Franklin University (Ohio) for bachelor's completion program. **Special study options:** Cooperative education, distance learning, dual enrollment of high school students, ESL, honors, independent study, internships, weekend college. License preparation in dental hygiene, nursing, real estate. **Credit/placement by examination:** AP, CLEP, institutional tests. 30 credit hours maximum toward associate degree. **Support services:** GED preparation and test center, learning center, reduced course load, remedial instruction, study skills assistance, tutoring, writing center.

Majors. Business: General, accounting, administrative services, business admin, e-commerce, finance, office technology, sales/distribution. **Communications:** General. **Computer sciences:** General, data processing. **Education:** General, elementary. **Engineering:** General. **Engineering technology:** Architectural, electrical. **Family/consumer sciences:** Child care. **Foreign languages:** General, French, Spanish. **Health:** Clinical lab science, clinical lab technology, dental hygiene, health services, medical radiologic technology/radiation therapy, occupational therapy assistant, physical therapy assistant. **Interdisciplinary:** Global studies. **Liberal arts:** Arts/sciences. **Math:** General. **Parks/recreation:** Exercise sciences, facilities management. **Protective services:** Criminal justice, police science. **Public administration:** Human services.

Computing on campus. 300 workstations in library, computer center, student center. Online library available.

Student life. Freshman orientation: Available. Preregistration for classes offered. **Activities:** Bands, choral groups, dance, drama, music ensembles, musical theater, radio station, student government, student newspaper, black and Latino organization, Helping Hands, social service organization, Habitat for Humanity.

Athletics. NJCAA. **Intercollegiate:** Baseball M, basketball, golf, soccer, softball W, swimming, tennis, volleyball W. **Intramural:** Football (non-tackle), racquetball, soccer M, softball, tennis, volleyball. **Team name:** Colts.

Student services. Adult student services, alcohol/substance abuse counseling, career counseling, services for economically disadvantaged, student employment services, financial aid counseling, health services, on-campus daycare, personal counseling, placement for graduates, veterans' counselor. **Physically disabled:** Services for visually, speech, hearing impaired. **Transfer:** Transfer adviser, college fairs on campus for students transferring to 4-year colleges.

Contact. Phone: (845) 341-4030 Fax: (845) 342-8662
Michael Roe, Director of Admissions, Orange County Community College, 115 South Street, Middletown, NY 10940-0115

Phillips Beth Israel School of Nursing

New York, New York
www.futurenursebi.org **CB code: 2031**

- Private 2-year nursing college
- Commuter campus in very large city
- Application essay, interview required

General. Founded in 1904. **Enrollment:** 285 degree-seeking undergraduates. **Degrees:** 100 associate awarded. **Calendar:** Semester, limited summer session. **Full-time faculty:** 9 total; 11% have terminal degrees, 22% minority, 100% women. **Part-time faculty:** 27 total; 4% have terminal degrees, 52% minority, 89% women. **Class size:** 12% < 20, 68% 20-39, 21% 40-49.

Student profile. Among degree-seeking undergraduates, 45% already have a bachelor's degree or higher, 10 enrolled as first-time, first-year students, 108 transferred in from other institutions.

Part-time:	86%	**Asian American:**	19%
Out-of-state:	8%	**Hispanic American:**	10%
Women:	80%	**International:**	3%
African American:	18%	**25 or older:**	60%

Transfer out. Colleges most students transferred to 2008: Pace University, New York University.

Basis for selection. Academic achievement, aptitude test scores, personal interview, recommendations, and prior experience of primary consideration. 55th percentile score on National League for Nursing's Preadmission Examination-RN mandatory (65th percentile score recommended). Standing in top half of high school class recommended. High school minimum average of 75 percent required, college GPA of 2.5 or better, GED minimum score of 250. **Homeschooled:** Statement describing homeschool structure and mission, transcript of courses and grades, state high school equivalency certificate required.

High school preparation. College-preparatory program recommended. 16 units required. Required units include English 4, mathematics 2, social studies 2, science 2 (laboratory 2). Chemistry and biology required.

2009-2010 Annual costs. Tuition/fees: $17,250. Per-credit charge: $360. Books/supplies: $1,600.

2008-2009 Financial aid. Need-based: 2 full-time freshmen applied for aid; 2 were judged to have need; 2 of these received aid. Average need met was 100%. Average scholarship/grant was $3,170; average loan $7,500. 34% of total undergraduate aid awarded as scholarships/grants, 66% as loans/jobs. Need-based aid available for part-time students.

Application procedures. Admission: Closing date 4/1 (postmark date). $50 fee. Application must be submitted on paper. Admission notification on a rolling basis beginning on or about 2/1. **Financial aid:** Closing date 6/1. FAFSA, institutional form required. Applicants notified by 8/1; must reply within 3 week(s) of notification.

Academics. Special study options: Weekend college. License preparation in nursing. **Credit/placement by examination:** AP, CLEP, institutional tests. 24 credit hours maximum toward associate degree. **Support services:** Learning center, pre-admission summer program, reduced course load, remedial instruction, study skills assistance, tutoring.

Majors. Health: Nursing (RN).

Computing on campus. 15 workstations in library, computer center. Commuter students can connect to campus network. Online course registration available.

Student life. Freshman orientation: Mandatory. 2 full days the week before classes start. **Activities:** Choral groups, student government, student newspaper, National Student Nurses Association Chapter.

Student services. Alcohol/substance abuse counseling, career counseling, financial aid counseling, health services, personal counseling. **Physically disabled:** Services for visually, speech, hearing impaired. **Transfer:** Pre-admission transcript evaluation for new students. Transfer adviser, college fairs on campus for students transferring to 4-year colleges.

Contact. E-mail: bstern@chpnet.org
Phone: (212) 614-6108 Fax: (212) 614-6109
Bernice Pass-Stern, Assistant Dean, Phillips Beth Israel School of Nursing, 776 Sixth Avenue, Fourth Floor, New York, NY 10001

Plaza College

Jackson Heights, New York
www.plazacollege.edu **CB code: 0545**

- For-profit 2-year business and junior college
- Commuter campus in very large city
- Application essay, interview required

General. Founded in 1916. Regionally accredited. **Enrollment:** 705 degree-seeking undergraduates. **Degrees:** 38 bachelor's, 125 associate awarded. **Calendar:** Semester, extensive summer session. **Full-time faculty:** 15 total. **Part-time faculty:** 33 total.

Basis for selection. Essay, interview, and test scores most important. Student must pass entrance examination. CPAT and college-administered writing test required of all students.

2009-2010 Annual costs. Tuition/fees (projected): $10,300. Per-credit charge: $400. 3 semesters required in academic year; costs quoted for 2 of 3 semesters. Books/supplies: $1,100. Personal expenses: $5,102.

Application procedures. Admission: No deadline. $100 fee, may be waived for applicants with need, free for online applicants. Admission notification on a rolling basis. **Financial aid:** No deadline. FAFSA, institutional form required. Applicants notified on a rolling basis.

Academics. Special study options: Accelerated study, internships. Bachelor's degree programs available on campus. **Credit/placement by examination:** CLEP, institutional tests. 30 credit hours maximum toward associate degree. **Support services:** Learning center, reduced course load, remedial instruction, study skills assistance, tutoring, writing center.

Majors. Business: Accounting, business admin. **Computer sciences:** Information systems. **Health:** Medical assistant.

Most popular majors. Business/marketing 48%, health sciences 52%.

Computing on campus. 200 workstations in library, computer center, student center. Online library, wireless network available.

Student life. Freshman orientation: Mandatory. Preregistration for classes offered.

Student services. Career counseling, financial aid counseling, personal counseling, placement for graduates. **Physically disabled:** Services for visually, speech, hearing impaired. **Transfer:** Transfer adviser for students transferring to 4-year colleges.

Contact. E-mail: plazainfo@plazacollege.edu
Phone: (718) 779-1430 Fax: (718) 779-7423
Rose Ann Black, Dean of Admissions, Plaza College, 74-09 37th Avenue, Jackson Heights, NY 11372

Professional Business College
New York, New York
www.pbcny.edu

- Private 2-year business college
- Very large city

General. Regionally accredited; also accredited by ACICS. **Enrollment:** 600 undergraduates. **Degrees:** 152 associate awarded. **Calendar:** Trimester.

Basis for selection. Applicants required to have high school diploma or its equivalent. Limited number of students who are not high school graduates, but who qualify for admission under "ability to benefit" (atb) guidelines. Ability-to-benefit students required to achieve a satisfactory score on the Career Programs Assessment test (CPAt).

2008-2009 Annual costs. Tuition/fees: $8,510.

Application procedures. Admission: No deadline.

Academics. Credit/placement by examination: CLEP.

Majors. Business: Accounting, business admin, office technology.

Contact. E-mail: dbrusca@pbcny.edu
Professional Business College, 125 Canal St., New York, NY 10002

Rockland Community College
Suffern, New York — **CB member**
www.sunyrockland.edu — **CB code: 2767**

- Public 2-year community college
- Commuter campus in large town

General. Founded in 1959. Regionally accredited. SUNY institution. Extension sites/centers located throughout county. **Enrollment:** 6,422 degree-seeking undergraduates. **Degrees:** 757 associate awarded. **Location:** 35 miles from New York City. **Calendar:** Semester, extensive summer session. **Full-time faculty:** 125 total. **Part-time faculty:** 250 total.

Student profile.

Out-of-state:	2%	**25 or older:**	35%

Transfer out. Colleges most students transferred to 2008: SUNY New Paltz, Ramapo College, Dominican College.

Basis for selection. Open admission. Students required to take assessment examination before enrolling full-time.

High school preparation. 18 units recommended. Recommended units include English 4, mathematics 2, social studies 4, history 4, science 2, foreign language 1 and academic electives 4.

2008-2009 Annual costs. Tuition/fees: $3,642; $6,942 out-of-state. Per-credit charge: $137 in-state; $274 out-of-state. Books/supplies: $1,200. Personal expenses: $600.

2007-2008 Financial aid. Need-based: Need-based aid available for part-time students. Work-study available nights and weekends.

Application procedures. Admission: Priority date 8/1; no deadline. $25 fee, may be waived for applicants with need. Admission notification on a rolling basis. **Financial aid:** Priority date 5/31; no closing date. FAFSA, institutional form required. Applicants notified on a rolling basis starting 6/1; must reply within 3 week(s) of notification.

Academics. Special study options: Cross-registration, distance learning, double major, dual enrollment of high school students, ESL, honors, independent study, internships, liberal arts/career combination, student-designed major, study abroad, weekend college. **Credit/placement by examination:** AP, CLEP, IB. 45 credit hours maximum toward associate degree. **Support services:** Learning center, remedial instruction, study skills assistance, tutoring, writing center.

Honors college/program. Mentor/Talented honors program. Business honors degree requires minimum combined SAT score of 1100 (exclusive of Writing) and at least 90 average; interviews, auditions and portfolios recommended.

Majors. Business: General, accounting, accounting technology, administrative services, business admin, hospitality admin, tourism/travel. **Communications:** General. **Computer sciences:** Computer graphics, data processing, programming. **Education:** Elementary. **Engineering technology:** Electrical. **Family/consumer sciences:** Food/nutrition, institutional food production. **Health:** EMT paramedic, medical assistant, medical records technology, nursing (RN), occupational therapy assistant, respiratory therapy technology. **Legal studies:** Paralegal. **Liberal arts:** Arts/sciences. **Mechanic/repair:** Automotive. **Protective services:** Criminal justice, fire safety technology. **Public administration:** Human services. **Social sciences:** General. **Visual/performing arts:** Commercial photography, commercial/advertising art, dramatic, photography, studio arts.

Most popular majors. Business/marketing 15%, computer/information sciences 9%, health sciences 18%, liberal arts 48%.

Computing on campus. 177 workstations in computer center.

Student life. Freshman orientation: Available. Preregistration for classes offered. **Activities:** Jazz band, choral groups, dance, drama, literary magazine, musical theater, radio station, student government, student newspaper, symphony orchestra, TV station, special interest clubs.

Athletics. NJCAA. **Intercollegiate:** Baseball M, basketball, bowling, golf M, soccer, softball W, table tennis, tennis, volleyball W. **Intramural:** Basketball, bowling, racquetball, soccer, softball, table tennis, track and field, volleyball. **Team name:** Hawks.

Student services. Adult student services, alcohol/substance abuse counseling, chaplain/spiritual director, career counseling, services for economically disadvantaged, student employment services, financial aid counseling, health services, minority student services, on-campus daycare, personal counseling, placement for graduates, veterans' counselor. **Physically disabled:** Services for visually, speech, hearing impaired. **Transfer:** Pre-admission transcript evaluation for new students. Transfer adviser, college fairs on campus for students transferring to 4-year colleges.

Contact. E-mail: info@sunyrockland.edu
Phone: (845) 574-4462 Toll-free number: (800) 722-7666
Fax: (845) 574-4433
Lorraine Glynn, Director of Admissions, Rockland Community College, 145 College Road, Suffern, NY 10901

St. Elizabeth College of Nursing
Utica, New York
www.secon.edu — **CB code: 2847**

- Private 2-year nursing college affiliated with Roman Catholic Church
- Commuter campus in small city
- SAT or ACT (ACT writing optional), application essay, interview required

General. Regionally accredited. **Enrollment:** 225 degree-seeking undergraduates. **Degrees:** 73 associate awarded. **Location:** 40 miles from Albany, 50 miles from Syracuse. **Calendar:** Semester. **Full-time faculty:** 18 total. **Part-time faculty:** 1 total.

Student profile.

Out-of-state:	1%	**25 or older:**	52%

Basis for selection. Rigor of secondary record, test scores most important. SAT Subject Tests recommended. **Adult students:** SAT/ACT scores not required. **Homeschooled:** Strong math and science background required, including coursework in chemistry, biology and equivalent of Math Level 1 and 2. **Learning Disabled:** Written documentation of disability required in order to set up special testing.

High school preparation. Required and recommended units include English 4, mathematics 2-3, social studies 4, history 4, science 2 (laboratory 2) and foreign language 1.

2008-2009 Annual costs. Tuition/fees: $12,400. Per-credit charge: $300. Books/supplies: $1,700. Personal expenses: $1,300.

2008-2009 Financial aid. Need-based: Need-based aid available for part-time students.

Application procedures. Admission: Priority date 5/30; deadline 6/30 (receipt date). $65 fee, may be waived for applicants with need. Admission notification on a rolling basis. Must reply by May 1 or within 2 week(s) if notified thereafter. Admission application fee $25 if submitted before 2/1. **Financial aid:** No deadline. FAFSA required. Applicants notified on a rolling basis starting 1/1; must reply within 2 week(s) of notification.

Academics. One 6-week summer session at end of first year. **Special study options:** Combined bachelor's/graduate degree, distance learning, liberal arts/career combination, weekend college. Articulation agreements with upper division BSN colleges. License preparation in nursing. **Credit/placement by examination:** CLEP, institutional tests. **Support services:** Remedial instruction, study skills assistance, tutoring.

Majors. Health: Nursing (RN).

Computing on campus. 20 workstations in library, computer center. Commuter students can connect to campus network. Online library, repair service available.

Student life. Freshman orientation: Mandatory. Preregistration for classes offered. Held week prior to classes. **Housing:** Option of staying on campus at affiliated college available. **Activities:** Student government, National League of Nursing.

Student services. Alcohol/substance abuse counseling, chaplain/spiritual director, financial aid counseling, health services, on-campus daycare. **Transfer:** Pre-admission transcript evaluation for new students. Transfer adviser for students transferring to 4-year colleges.

Contact. E-mail: conadmis@stemc.org
Phone: (315) 798-88189 Fax: (315) 798-8271
Donna Ernst, Recruitment Director, St. Elizabeth College of Nursing, 2215 Genesee Street, Utica, NY 13501

St. Joseph's College of Nursing

Syracuse, New York
www.sjhsyr.org/nursing **CB code: 2825**

- Private 2-year nursing college affiliated with Roman Catholic Church
- Commuter campus in small city
- SAT or ACT (ACT writing optional), application essay, interview required

General. Founded in 1898. Practice in a variety of settings including medical/surgical, maternity, pediatrics, oncology, psychiatry, ambulatory care clinics, and home care and outpatient experiences. **Enrollment:** 289 degree-seeking undergraduates. **Degrees:** 103 associate awarded. **Calendar:** Semester, limited summer session. **Full-time faculty:** 26 total; 92% women. **Part-time faculty:** 8 total; 12% have terminal degrees, 100% women. **Class size:** 57% 20-39, 29% 40-49, 14% 50-99. **Special facilities:** Cardiovascular lab, electro-physiology lab, home care, outpatient services, 462-bed teaching hospital.

Student profile. Among degree-seeking undergraduates, 9 enrolled as first-time, first-year students.

Part-time:	47%	**25 or older:**	49%
Out-of-state:	1%	**Live on campus:**	30%
Women:	91%		

Transfer out. Colleges most students transferred to 2008: SUNY New York Upstate Medical University, SUNY College of Technology at Utica-Rome, Le Moyne College.

Basis for selection. High school record, SAT/ACT test scores or pre-entrance examination, and personal interview very important. **Adult students:** SAT/ACT scores not required. **Homeschooled:** Transcript of courses and grades, state high school equivalency certificate, letter of recommendation (nonparent) required.

High school preparation. College-preparatory program recommended. 13 units required. Required and recommended units include English 4, mathematics 2-3, social studies 4 and science 3-4. Science units must be in biology and chemistry; advanced biology and/or physics recommended.

2008-2009 Annual costs. Tuition/fees: $12,948. Tuition includes liberal arts component of degree taken at other institution. Room only: $3,700. Books/supplies: $1,000. Personal expenses: $1,272.

2007-2008 Financial aid. All financial aid based on need. 20% of total undergraduate aid awarded as scholarships/grants, 80% as loans/jobs. Need-based aid available for part-time students.

Application procedures. Admission: No deadline. $50 fee, may be waived for applicants with need. Application must be submitted on paper. Admission notification on a rolling basis. **Financial aid:** Priority date 3/1; no closing date. FAFSA required. Applicants notified on a rolling basis starting 6/15.

Academics. Weekend program meets every other Friday, Saturday and Sunday year-round for 2 years. **Special study options:** Liberal arts/career combination, weekend college. License preparation in nursing. **Credit/placement by examination:** AP, CLEP. **Support services:** Reduced course load, study skills assistance, tutoring.

Majors. Health: Nursing (RN).

Computing on campus. 31 workstations in dormitories, library, computer center. Dormitories wired for high-speed internet access and linked to campus network. Commuter students can connect to campus network. Online library, helpline, wireless network available.

Student life. Freshman orientation: Mandatory. Preregistration for classes offered. 5 days one week prior to start of classes. **Housing:** Guaranteed on-campus for all undergraduates. Coed dorms, wellness housing available. $200 fully refundable deposit. **Activities:** Student government.

Student services. Adult student services, alcohol/substance abuse counseling, chaplain/spiritual director, career counseling, student employment services, financial aid counseling, health services, personal counseling, placement for graduates, veterans' counselor. **Physically disabled:** Services for visually, speech, hearing impaired. **Transfer:** Pre-admission transcript evaluation for new students. Transfer adviser, college fairs on campus for students transferring to 4-year colleges.

Contact. E-mail: rhonda.reader@sjhsyr.org
Phone: (315) 448-5040 Fax: (315) 448-5745
Rhonda Reader, Assistant Dean of Admissions, St. Joseph's College of Nursing, 206 Prospect Avenue, Syracuse, NY 13203

St. Vincent Catholic Medical Centers

Fresh Meadows, New York
www.svcmc.org/body.cfm?id=758 **CB code: 3400**

- Private 2-year nursing college affiliated with Roman Catholic Church
- Commuter campus in very large city
- Application essay, interview required

General. Founded in 1969. **Enrollment:** 153 degree-seeking undergraduates. **Degrees:** 67 associate awarded. **Location:** 10 miles from Manhattan. **Calendar:** Semester. **Full-time faculty:** 9 total. **Part-time faculty:** 10 total.

Basis for selection. Test scores, high school achievement, interview, and personal essay considered. National League for Nursing test required.

High school preparation. 11 units required. Required units include English 4, mathematics 2, social studies 3 and science 2.

2008-2009 Annual costs. Tuition/fees: $7,020. Per-credit charge: $468. Books/supplies: $900. Personal expenses: $2,400.

2007-2008 Financial aid. Need-based: 36% of total undergraduate aid awarded as scholarships/grants, 64% as loans/jobs.

Application procedures. Admission: Closing date 4/1. $45 fee. Admission notification on a rolling basis. Must reply by May 1 or within 3 week(s) if notified thereafter. **Financial aid:** No deadline. FAFSA required. Applicants notified on a rolling basis; must reply within 2 week(s) of notification.

Academics. Special study options: License preparation in nursing. **Credit/placement by examination:** CLEP.

Majors. Health: Nursing (RN).

Student services. Health services, personal counseling.

Contact. Phone: (718) 357-0500 ext. 131 Fax: (718) 357-4683
Nancy Wolinski, Chairperson, Admissions Committee, St. Vincent Catholic Medical Centers, 175-05 Horace Harding Expressway, Fresh Meadows, NY 11356

Schenectady County Community College

Schenectady, New York
www.sunysccc.edu **CB code: 2879**

- Public 2-year community college
- Commuter campus in small city

General. Founded in 1968. Regionally accredited. SUNY institution. **Enrollment:** 2,578 degree-seeking undergraduates. **Degrees:** 452 associate awarded. **ROTC:** Air Force. **Location:** 150 miles from New York City, 20 miles from Albany. **Calendar:** Semester, limited summer session. **Full-time faculty:** 68 total. **Part-time faculty:** 142 total. **Special facilities:** Child care center.

Transfer out. Colleges most students transferred to 2008: SUNY Albany, College of Saint Rose, Siena College, Sage College of Albany.

Basis for selection. Open admission, but selective for some programs. Special requirements for music program. Interview recommended for all; audition required for music, music merchandising programs. **Home-schooled:** Letter from school district superintendent where they reside attesting to home school equivalency of public system.

High school preparation. Certain programs have specific mathematics and science prerequisites.

2008-2009 Annual costs. Tuition/fees: $3,263; $6,293 out-of-state. Per-credit charge: $134 in-state; $260 out-of-state. Books/supplies: $800. Personal expenses: $900.

2007-2008 Financial aid. All financial aid based on need. Need-based aid available for part-time students. Work-study available for part-time students.

Application procedures. Admission: No deadline. No application fee. Admission notification on a rolling basis. **Financial aid:** Priority date 5/1; no closing date. FAFSA required. Applicants notified on a rolling basis starting 4/15; must reply by 8/31.

Academics. 25-32 credit hours required in major depending on program. 60-66 credit hours required for graduation depending on program. **Special study options:** Cooperative education, cross-registration, distance learning, dual enrollment of high school students, ESL, honors, independent study, internships, liberal arts/career combination, teacher certification program. License preparation in aviation. **Credit/placement by examination:** AP, CLEP, institutional tests. 30 credit hours maximum toward associate degree. **Support services:** GED preparation and test center, learning center, reduced course load, remedial instruction, tutoring.

Majors. Business: General, tourism promotion, travel services. **Computer sciences:** General, computer science, programming. **Education:** Early childhood, multi-level teacher. **Engineering technology:** Telecommunications. **Interdisciplinary:** Accounting/computer science, math/computer science. **Liberal arts:** Arts/sciences. **Personal/culinary services:** Food service, restaurant/catering. **Physical sciences:** General. **Protective services:** Criminal justice, security services. **Social sciences:** General. **Transportation:** Aviation, aviation management.

Computing on campus. 400 workstations in library, computer center, student center.

Student life. Freshman orientation: Available. Preregistration for classes offered. **Activities:** Bands, choral groups, drama, literary magazine, music ensembles, student government, Black and Latino student alliance, Christian Fellowship, human services club, disabled student awareness committee, culinary club.

Athletics. NJCAA. **Intercollegiate:** Baseball M, basketball, bowling, softball W. **Team name:** The Royals.

Student services. Adult student services, alcohol/substance abuse counseling, career counseling, services for economically disadvantaged, student employment services, financial aid counseling, minority student services, on-campus daycare, personal counseling, placement for graduates, veterans' counselor. **Physically disabled:** Services for visually, speech, hearing impaired. **Transfer:** Transfer adviser, college fairs on campus for students transferring to 4-year colleges.

Contact. E-mail: sampsondg@gw.sunysccc.edu
Phone: (518) 381-1366 Fax: (518) 346-0379
David Sampson, Director of Admissions, Schenectady County Community College, 78 Washington Avenue, Schenectady, NY 12305

State University of New York College of Agriculture and Technology at Cobleskill

Cobleskill, New York
www.cobleskill.edu
CB code: 2524

- Public 2-year agricultural and technical college
- Residential campus in small town

General. Founded in 1911. Regionally accredited. **Enrollment:** 2,588 degree-seeking undergraduates; 31 non-degree-seeking students. **Degrees:** 203 bachelor's, 361 associate awarded. **Location:** 35 miles from Albany, 29 miles from Oneonta. **Calendar:** Semester, limited summer session. **Full-time faculty:** 101 total; 36% have terminal degrees, 9% minority, 37% women. **Part-time faculty:** 74 total; 5% have terminal degrees, 4% minority, 51% women. **Class size:** 39% < 20, 48% 20-39, 7% 40-49, 6% 50-99, less than 1% >100. **Special facilities:** Arboretum, 14 greenhouses, livestock pavilion, 350-acre farm, modern chemical and biological technology laboratories, student-operated restaurant, fish hatchery, ski area, equestrian center, child care and development center. **Partnerships:** Formal partnership with John Deere Company for agricultural engineering.

Student profile. Among degree-seeking undergraduates, 978 enrolled as first-time, first-year students, 194 transferred in from other institutions.

Part-time:	3%	**Hispanic American:**	5%
Out-of-state:	7%	**International:**	3%
Women:	48%	**25 or older:**	9%
African American:	8%	**Live on campus:**	59%
Asian American:	1%		

Transfer out. Colleges most students transferred to 2008: Cornell University, College of St. Rose, SUNY Albany, SUNY Oneonta, SUNY Plattsburgh.

Basis for selection. Strength of high school curriculum most important. GPA, SAT/ACT scores considered. Letters of recommendation, interview recommended. SAT or ACT optional for associate degree students, depending on degree. SAT required for bachelor degree seeking students. **Home-schooled:** Transcript of courses and grades, letter of recommendation (nonparent) required. Letter of certification from local high school required.

High school preparation. 10 units required; 16 recommended. Required and recommended units include English 3-4, mathematics 2-3, social studies 1, history 1, science 2-3 (laboratory 2-3) and foreign language 1. Additional recommendations for some programs.

2008-2009 Annual costs. Tuition/fees: $5,499; $11,759 out-of-state. Per-credit charge: $181 in-state; $442 out-of-state. Room/board: $9,010. Books/supplies: $1,000. Personal expenses: $1,092.

2007-2008 Financial aid. Need-based: 937 full-time freshmen applied for aid; 731 were judged to have need; 710 of these received aid. Average need met was 68%. Average scholarship/grant was $4,227; average loan $3,337. 53% of total undergraduate aid awarded as scholarships/grants, 47% as loans/jobs. Need-based aid available for part-time students. Work-study available nights and weekends. **Non-need-based:** Awarded to 655 full-time undergraduates, including 312 freshmen. Scholarships awarded for academics, alumni affiliation, leadership, state residency. **Additional information:** Application deadline for scholarships March 15. Separate application required, available through admissions office.

Application procedures. Admission: Priority date 5/1; no deadline. $40 fee, may be waived for applicants with need. Admission notification on a rolling basis beginning on or about 11/1. Must reply by May 1 or within 2 week(s) if notified thereafter. **Financial aid:** Closing date 2/15. FAFSA required. Applicants notified on a rolling basis; must reply within 2 week(s) of notification.

Academics. Special study options: Cross-registration, distance learning, ESL, honors, independent study, internships, study abroad, weekend college. **Credit/placement by examination:** AP, CLEP, institutional tests. 33 credit hours maximum toward associate degree, 60 toward bachelor's. **Support services:** Learning center, pre-admission summer program, reduced course load, remedial instruction, study skills assistance, tutoring, writing center.

Majors. Agriculture: General, agribusiness operations, agronomy, animal sciences, mechanization, ornamental horticulture, poultry. **Business:** Accounting technology, business admin, hotel/motel admin, travel services. **Communications:** General. **Computer sciences:** General, information systems. **Conservation:** General, fisheries. **Family/consumer sciences:** Child care, institutional food production. **Health:** EMT paramedic. **Liberal arts:** Arts/sciences, humanities. **Mechanic/repair:** Diesel. **Personal/culinary services:** Chef training, restaurant/catering. **Public administration:** Social work. **Science technology:** Biological, chemical. **Visual/performing arts:** Commercial/advertising art. **Other:** Agricultural engineering technology, Health science studies.

Most popular majors. Agriculture 21%, business/marketing 23%, family/consumer sciences 9%, liberal arts 15%, personal/culinary services 8%.

Computing on campus. 270 workstations in dormitories, library, computer center, student center. Dormitories wired for high-speed internet access and linked to campus network. Commuter students can connect to campus network. Online course registration, online library, helpline, repair service, student web hosting, wireless network available.

Student life. Freshman orientation: Mandatory. Preregistration for classes offered. 2-day academic and social program held first week of classes. **Housing:** Guaranteed on-campus for freshmen. Coed dorms, single-sex dorms, special housing for disabled, wellness housing available. $55 fully refundable deposit. Designated quiet study, sophomore experience, upper-class experience. **Activities:** Jazz band, campus ministries, drama, international student organizations, student government, student newspaper, Phi Theta Kappa, activities team, community club, Student Christian Fellowship, student medical response team, X-Pressions of Kolor, black and Latino alliance.

Athletics. NCAA. **Intercollegiate:** Baseball M, basketball, cross-country, diving, golf, lacrosse M, soccer, softball W, swimming, tennis, track and field, volleyball W. **Intramural:** Bowling, football (non-tackle), soccer, softball. **Team name:** Tigers.

Student services. Adult student services, alcohol/substance abuse counseling, chaplain/spiritual director, career counseling, student employment services, financial aid counseling, health services, on-campus daycare, personal counseling, placement for graduates, veterans' counselor. **Physically disabled:** Services for visually, speech, hearing impaired. **Learning disabled:** Comprehensive services available. **Transfer:** Pre-admission transcript evaluation for new students. Transfer adviser, college fairs on campus for students transferring to 4-year colleges.

Contact. E-mail: admissions@cobleskill.edu
Phone: (518) 255-5525 Toll-free number: (800) 295-8988
Fax: (518) 255-6769
Christopher Tacea, Director of Admissions and Marketing, State University of New York College of Agriculture and Technology at Cobleskill, Knapp Hall, Cobleskill, NY 12043

State University of New York College of Agriculture and Technology at Morrisville

Morrisville, New York
www.morrisville.edu **CB code: 2527**

- Public 2-year agricultural and technical college
- Residential campus in small town

General. Founded in 1908. Regionally accredited. Students wishing to enroll in Morrisville programs not offered at the Norwich Campus may take general education or elective courses that can be applied to Morrisville State College (main campus) associate or bachelor's degree programs. **Enrollment:** 3,125 degree-seeking undergraduates; 213 non-degree-seeking students. **Degrees:** 132 bachelor's, 453 associate awarded. **ROTC:** Army. **Location:** 30 miles from Syracuse and Utica. **Calendar:** Semester, limited summer session. **Full-time faculty:** 147 total; 87% have terminal degrees, 9% minority, 48% women. **Part-time faculty:** 88 total; 81% have terminal degrees, 3% minority, 56% women. **Class size:** 45% < 20, 48% 20-39, 2% 40-49, 4% 50-99, less than 1% >100. **Special facilities:** Arboretum, archery range, Helyar Pond, 2 ice arenas, Nelson Farms, observatory, walking trail, wildlife museum, dairy facilities, equestrian center.

Student profile. Among degree-seeking undergraduates, 1,132 enrolled as first-time, first-year students, 290 transferred in from other institutions.

Part-time:	9%	**25 or older:**	21%
Out-of-state:	7%	**Live on campus:**	62%
Women:	50%		

Transfer out. Colleges most students transferred to 2008: Cornell University, Rochester Institute of Technology, Clarkson, State University of New York.

Basis for selection. High school record most important. SAT required for bachelor's degree applicants, SAT or ACT required for students seeking academic scholarship. Essays or interviews not required, but students welcome to submit essay or visit for interview. **Homeschooled:** State high school equivalency certificate required. GED required for students without supporting documentation.

High school preparation. Recommended units include English 4, mathematics 3, social studies 4 and science 3. Requirements depend on program. Math and science preparation important for technical majors.

2008-2009 Annual costs. Tuition/fees: $5,375; $11,635 out-of-state. Per-credit charge: $181 in-state; $442 out-of-state. Room/board: $8,510. Books/supplies: $1,000. Personal expenses: $1,150.

2007-2008 Financial aid. Need-based: 43% of total undergraduate aid awarded as scholarships/grants, 57% as loans/jobs. Need-based aid available for part-time students. Work-study available nights, weekends and for part-time students. **Non-need-based:** Scholarships awarded for academics.

Application procedures. Admission: No deadline. $40 fee, may be waived for applicants with need. Admission notification on a rolling basis beginning on or about 11/1. Housing deposit refundable only through June 1. **Financial aid:** Priority date 2/1; no closing date. FAFSA required. Applicants notified on a rolling basis starting 3/1; must reply within 3 week(s) of notification.

Academics. Think-Pad university in partnership with IBM. **Special study options:** Accelerated study, cooperative education, distance learning, double major, dual enrollment of high school students, ESL, exchange student, honors, internships, liberal arts/career combination, student-designed major, study abroad, weekend college. Joint program with SUNY Forest Technology School at Wanakena, 2-2 transfer program with SUNY College of Environmental Science and Forestry. License preparation in nursing. **Credit/placement by examination:** AP, CLEP, institutional tests. 21 credit hours maximum toward associate degree. **Support services:** Learning center, pre-admission summer program, reduced course load, remedial instruction, study skills assistance, tutoring.

Majors. Agriculture: General, agribusiness operations, animal husbandry, animal sciences, aquaculture, business, business technology, dairy, dairy husbandry, equestrian studies, equine science, equipment technology, farm/ranch, floriculture, greenhouse operations, horticultural science, horticulture, landscaping, livestock, mechanization, nursery operations, ornamental horticulture, power machinery. **Architecture:** Landscape, technology. **Biology:** General, conservation, marine. **Business:** General, accounting, accounting technology, accounting/business management, accounting/finance, administrative services, business admin, office management, office technology, restaurant/food services, tourism promotion, tourism/travel, travel services. **Communications:** Journalism. **Computer sciences:** General, applications programming, computer science, information technology, programming. **Conservation:** General, environmental science, environmental studies, fisheries, forest management, forest sciences, forest technology, forestry, management/policy, wood science. **Construction:** General, building inspection, carpentry, maintenance. **Engineering:** General, architectural, computer, computer hardware, construction, electrical, mechanics, polymer, science, software. **Engineering technology:** General, architectural, architectural drafting, automotive, CAD/CADD, computer hardware, computer systems, construction, electrical, manufacturing, mechanical, plastics. **Family/consumer sciences:** Food/nutrition. **Health:** Clinical lab technology, massage therapy, nursing (RN), prenursing. **Interdisciplinary:** Nutrition sciences. **Liberal arts:** Arts/sciences, humanities. **Math:** General. **Mechanic/repair:** Auto body, automotive, diesel, electronics/electrical, heavy equipment. **Parks/recreation:** Exercise sciences, facilities management, health/fitness, sports admin. **Personal/culinary services:** Food service. **Physical sciences:** Chemistry, physics. **Production:** Furniture, woodworking. **Psychology:** General. **Social sciences:** General.

Most popular majors. Agriculture 24%, business/marketing 13%, health sciences 14%, interdisciplinary studies 8%, liberal arts 15%, trade and industry 12%.

Computing on campus. 140 workstations in dormitories, library, computer center, student center. Dormitories linked to campus network. Commuter students can connect to campus network. Online library, helpline, repair service, wireless network available.

Student life. Freshman orientation: Mandatory, $75 fee. **Housing:** Guaranteed on-campus for all undergraduates. Coed dorms, special housing for disabled, wellness housing available. $50 fully refundable deposit, deadline 5/1. Special interest housing available. **Activities:** Bands, choral groups, dance, drama, literary magazine, music ensembles, musical theater, radio station, student government, student newspaper, Newman Society, Latin American student organization, African student union/black alliance.

Athletics. NCAA. **Intercollegiate:** Basketball, diving, equestrian, field hockey W, football (tackle) M, ice hockey M, lacrosse, soccer, softball W, swimming, volleyball W, wrestling M. **Intramural:** Archery, badminton, basketball, diving, equestrian, golf, handball, racquetball, rifle, soccer, swimming, table tennis, tennis, volleyball, wrestling M. **Team name:** Mustangs.

Student services. Adult student services, alcohol/substance abuse counseling, chaplain/spiritual director, career counseling, services for economically disadvantaged, student employment services, financial aid counseling, health services, minority student services, on-campus daycare, personal counseling, placement for graduates, veterans' counselor, women's services. **Physically disabled:** Services for visually, speech, hearing impaired. **Transfer:** Pre-admission transcript evaluation for new students. Transfer center, transfer adviser, college fairs on campus for students transferring to 4-year colleges.

Contact. E-mail: admissions@morrisville.edu
Phone: (315) 684-6046 Toll-free number: (800) 258-0111
Fax: (315) 684-6427
Thomas VerDow, Dean of Enrollment Management, State University of New York College of Agriculture and Technology at Morrisville, PO Box 901, Morrisville, NY 13408-0901

State University of New York College of Technology at Alfred

Alfred, New York
www.alfredstate.edu **CB code: 2522**

- Public 2-year liberal arts and technical college
- Residential campus in rural community

General. Founded in 1908. Regionally accredited. School of Applied Technology located in Wellsville. **Enrollment:** 3,177 degree-seeking undergraduates; 105 non-degree-seeking students. **Degrees:** 186 bachelor's, 696 associate awarded. **ROTC:** Army. **Location:** 75 miles from Rochester, 90 miles from Buffalo. **Calendar:** Semester, limited summer session. **Full-time faculty:** 161 total. **Part-time faculty:** 29 total. **Class size:** 50% < 20, 46% 20-39, 2% 40-49, 2% 50-99. **Special facilities:** 750-acre working farm.

Student profile. Among degree-seeking undergraduates, 22% enrolled in a vocational program, 1,434 enrolled as first-time, first-year students, 239 transferred in from other institutions.

Part-time:	7%	**25 or older:**	17%
Out-of-state:	7%	**Live on campus:**	80%
Women:	35%		

Basis for selection. School achievement record most important, test scores, class rank, school and community service considered. Letters of recommendation and personal essay recommended but not required. SAT or ACT recommended. SAT or ACT required for students applying for baccalaureate degree programs. Interview recommended.

High school preparation. Recommended units include English 4, mathematics 4, social studies 4 and science 4. Course requirements vary depending on program.

2008-2009 Annual costs. Tuition/fees: $5,498; $8,358 out-of-state. Per-credit charge: $181 in-state; $300 out-of-state. Room/board: $8,660. Books/supplies: $1,200. Personal expenses: $750.

2007-2008 Financial aid. Need-based: Need-based aid available for part-time students. Work-study available nights, weekends and for part-time students. **Non-need-based:** Scholarships awarded for academics, alumni affiliation, job skills, minority status.

Application procedures. Admission: No deadline. $40 fee, may be waived for applicants with need. Admission notification on a rolling basis beginning on or about 11/1. Must reply by May 1 or within 4 week(s) if notified thereafter. Early application recommended for Applied Technology programs. **Financial aid:** No deadline. FAFSA required. Applicants notified on a rolling basis starting 3/1; must reply within 3 week(s) of notification.

Academics. Special study options: Cooperative education, cross-registration, distance learning, ESL, honors, independent study, internships, liberal arts/career combination, student-designed major, study abroad. Bachelor's degree programs available on campus. License preparation in nursing. **Credit/placement by examination:** AP, CLEP, IB, SAT, ACT, institutional tests. 30 credit hours maximum toward associate degree, 60 toward bachelor's. **Support services:** Learning center, reduced course load, remedial instruction, study skills assistance, tutoring, writing center.

Majors. Agriculture: Agronomy, animal sciences, business, dairy. **Architecture:** Landscape. **Biology:** General. **Business:** Accounting, business admin, entrepreneurial studies, finance, marketing. **Computer sciences:** General, computer science. **Conservation:** Environmental science, urban forestry. **Construction:** Carpentry, electrician, masonry, plumbing. **Engineering:** General. **Engineering technology:** Architectural, CAD/CADD, computer, computer hardware, construction, electrical, electromechanical, mechanical, robotics, surveying. **Health:** Medical records technology, nursing (RN), veterinary technology/assistant. **Legal studies:** Court reporting. **Liberal arts:** Arts/sciences. **Mechanic/repair:** Auto body, automotive, diesel, electronics/electrical, heating/ac/refrig, heavy equipment. **Parks/recreation:** Sports admin. **Personal/culinary services:** Baking, culinary arts. **Production:** Machine tool, welding. **Public administration:** Human services. **Visual/performing arts:** Interior design. **Other:** Motorsports technology.

Most popular majors. Agriculture 7%, business/marketing 11%, engineering/engineering technologies 29%, health sciences 11%, social sciences 9%, trade and industry 17%.

Computing on campus. 1,200 workstations in dormitories, library, computer center. Dormitories wired for high-speed internet access and linked to campus network. Commuter students can connect to campus network. Online course registration, online library, helpline, repair service, student web hosting, wireless network available.

Student life. Freshman orientation: Available, $100 fee. Preregistration for classes offered. Students have option of spending the night on campus. Current students assigned as orientation advisers. **Housing:** Guaranteed on-campus for all undergraduates. Coed dorms, fraternity/sorority housing, wellness housing available. $50 deposit. Extended stay, computer lifestyle, quiet study, over 21 or over 24, single-room options available. **Activities:** Bands, choral groups, dance, drama, literary magazine, music ensembles, musical theater, radio station, student government, student newspaper, symphony orchestra, Sustainability club, international club, Black student union, Alfred State Response Team, cultural life committee, student senate, political alliance club, Bacchus Peer Education Network.

Athletics. NJCAA. **Intercollegiate:** Baseball M, basketball, cross-country, football (tackle) M, lacrosse M, soccer, softball W, swimming, track and field, volleyball W, wrestling M. **Intramural:** Basketball, football (non-tackle), golf, handball, soccer, softball, tennis, volleyball. **Team name:** Pioneers.

Student services. Adult student services, alcohol/substance abuse counseling, chaplain/spiritual director, career counseling, services for economically disadvantaged, student employment services, financial aid counseling, health services, minority student services, personal counseling, placement for graduates, veterans' counselor. **Physically disabled:** Services for visually, hearing impaired. **Transfer:** Transfer center, transfer adviser, college fairs on campus for students transferring to 4-year colleges.

Contact. E-mail: admissions@alfredstate.edu
Phone: (607) 587-4215 Toll-free number: (800) 425-3733 ext. 1
Fax: (607) 587-4299
Deborah Goodrich, Associate Vice President for Enrollment Management, State University of New York College of Technology at Alfred, Huntington Administration Building, Alfred, NY 14802-1196

State University of New York College of Technology at Canton

Canton, New York
www.canton.edu **CB code: 2523**

- Public 2-year technical college
- Residential campus in small town

General. Founded in 1906. Regionally accredited. **Enrollment:** 2,647 degree-seeking undergraduates; 323 non-degree-seeking students. **Degrees:** 85 bachelor's, 467 associate awarded. **ROTC:** Army, Air Force. **Location:** 135 miles from Syracuse, 120 miles from Montreal, Canada. **Calendar:** Semester, limited summer session. **Full-time faculty:** 108 total; 43% have terminal degrees, 8% minority, 42% women. **Part-time faculty:** 64 total; 5% have terminal degrees, 2% minority, 48% women. **Class size:** 37% < 20, 51% 20-39, 7% 40-49, 4% 50-99. **Special facilities:** Cross-country trails. **Partnerships:** Formal partnership with Polaris.

Student profile. Among degree-seeking undergraduates, 829 enrolled as first-time, first-year students, 260 transferred in from other institutions.

Part-time:	13%	**Native American:**	2%
Out-of-state:	3%	**International:**	6%
Women:	51%	**25 or older:**	21%
African American:	10%	**Live on campus:**	35%
Hispanic American:	4%		

Transfer out. Colleges most students transferred to 2008: SUNY College at Potsdam, Clarkson University, SUNY Institute of Technology at Utica/Rome, Rochester Institute of Technology, SUNY College at Plattsburgh.

Basis for selection. High school record most important. Admission requirements vary according to program of study. Some enrolled freshmen must complete ACCUPLACER placement test on campus before classes begin. Students notified of testing dates and whether they need ACCUPLACER. SAT or ACT required of bachelor's degree program applicants. SAT, ACT, SAT Subject Test scores received on rolling basis. Interview recommended. **Homeschooled:** Transcript of courses and grades required. Applicants must do 1 of following: present letter from superintendent from school district they reside in indicating completion of program equivalent to high school diploma; take GED exam; take 5 Regents Exams indicated in SUNY policy; complete 24 credit-hour program to earn GED. **Learning Disabled:** Students with documented needs should request accommodations through coordinator of Accommodative Services.

High school preparation. Required and recommended units include English 4, mathematics 3, social studies 4, history 3, science 3 (laboratory 1-2) and foreign language 1. Required high school courses vary with major. Engineering science technologies, health, and life sciences stress math and science; business technologies stress algebra.

2008-2009 Annual costs. Tuition/fees: $5,514; $8,374 out-of-state. Per-credit charge: $181 in-state; $300 out-of-state. Room/board: $8,970. Books/supplies: $1,200. Personal expenses: $1,000.

2007-2008 Financial aid. Need-based: 66% of total undergraduate aid awarded as scholarships/grants, 34% as loans/jobs. Need-based aid available for part-time students. Work-study available nights, weekends and for part-time students. **Non-need-based:** Scholarships awarded for academics, alumni affiliation, leadership, minority status, state residency.

Application procedures. Admission: Priority date 3/1; no deadline. $40 fee, may be waived for applicants with need. Admission notification on a rolling basis beginning on or about 11/1. Must reply by May 1 or within 4 week(s) if notified thereafter. **Financial aid:** Priority date 3/15; no closing date. FAFSA required. Applicants notified on a rolling basis starting 2/15; must reply within 4 week(s) of notification.

Academics. Special study options: Cross-registration, distance learning, dual enrollment of high school students, independent study, internships, liberal arts/career combination, student-designed major. Criminal justice students can complete Police Academy during spring semester of senior year. License preparation in dental hygiene, nursing, physical therapy. **Credit/placement by examination:** AP, CLEP, IB, institutional tests. Student must take at least 15 credit hours at SUNY Canton to earn an Associate Degree and 30 hours to earn a Bachelor's Degree. Maximum of 30 hours for prior work and/or life experience is for Bachelor's Degree. Maximum hours for an Associate Degree is 15 credits. **Support services:** Learning center, reduced course load, remedial instruction, study skills assistance, tutoring, writing center.

Majors. Business: Accounting technology, administrative services, business admin. **Computer sciences:** Information systems. **Construction:** Maintenance. **Education:** Early childhood. **Engineering:** General. **Engineering technology:** Civil, construction, electrical, heat/ac/refrig, mechanical. **Health:** Dental hygiene, nursing (RN), physical therapy assistant, veterinary technology/assistant. **Liberal arts:** Arts/sciences. **Mechanic/repair:** Automotive. **Personal/culinary services:** Mortuary science. **Protective services:** Police science.

Most popular majors. Business/marketing 13%, engineering/engineering technologies 11%, health sciences 26%, liberal arts 18%, security/protective services 15%, trade and industry 6%.

Computing on campus. 300 workstations in library. Dormitories wired for high-speed internet access. Online library, helpline, wireless network available.

Student life. Freshman orientation: Mandatory, $60 fee. Preregistration for classes offered. 2-day orientation for resident students and 1-day for commuters. **Policies:** All full-time students must live in college housing unless requirement waived by Residence Life office. **Housing:** Guaranteed on-campus for freshmen. Coed dorms, special housing for disabled, fraternity/sorority housing, wellness housing available. $105 nonrefundable deposit, deadline 5/1. Pets allowed in dorm rooms. Some all-male or all-female floors and wings available. **Activities:** Campus ministries, choral groups, dance, drama, international student organizations, literary magazine, radio station, student government, student newspaper, Newman Club, Chinese culture club, Brother 2 Brother, Afro Latin Society, Caribbean United, African student union, Native American Organization, Habitat for Humanity, Peer Educators.

Athletics. NAIA. **Intercollegiate:** Baseball M, basketball, cross-country, soccer, softball W, volleyball W. **Intramural:** Basketball, football (non-tackle), soccer, table tennis, tennis, volleyball. **Team name:** Kangaroos.

Student services. Adult student services, alcohol/substance abuse counseling, chaplain/spiritual director, career counseling, services for economically disadvantaged, student employment services, financial aid counseling, health services, minority student services, personal counseling, placement for graduates, veterans' counselor. **Physically disabled:** Services for visually, speech, hearing impaired. **Learning disabled:** Comprehensive services available. **Transfer:** Pre-admission transcript evaluation for new students. Transfer adviser, college fairs on campus for students transferring to 4-year colleges.

Contact. E-mail: admissions@canton.edu
Phone: (315) 386-7123 Toll-free number: (800) 388-7123
Fax: (315) 386-7929
Jonathan Kent, Director of Admissions, State University of New York College of Technology at Canton, 34 Cornell Drive, Canton, NY 13617-1098

State University of New York College of Technology at Delhi

Delhi, New York
www.delhi.edu **CB code: 2525**

- Public 2-year liberal arts and technical college
- Residential campus in rural community

General. Founded in 1913. Regionally accredited. Students can also earn Bachelor degrees in selected programs at remote sites and online. **Enrollment:** 2,751 degree-seeking undergraduates; 220 non-degree-seeking students. **Degrees:** 74 bachelor's, 498 associate awarded. **Location:** 70 miles from Albany and Binghamton. **Calendar:** Semester, limited summer session. **Full-time faculty:** 115 total. **Part-time faculty:** 64 total. **Class size:** 48% < 20, 44% 20-39, 3% 40-49, 3% 50-99, less than 1% >100. **Special facilities:** Demonstration forest and arboretum, student-operated restaurant, veterinary science laboratories, golf course, CAD laboratory, architecture laboratories.

Student profile. Among degree-seeking undergraduates, 1,016 enrolled as first-time, first-year students, 414 transferred in from other institutions.

Part-time:	9%	**Hispanic American:**	8%
Out-of-state:	2%	**International:**	2%
Women:	44%	**25 or older:**	16%
African American:	11%	**Live on campus:**	60%
Asian American:	2%		

Basis for selection. Special requirements for 4-year programs. Enrollment limits in some programs. Admissable students then waitlisted or given the opportunity to withdraw. SAT/ACT required for 4-year program applicants. Interview recommended. **Homeschooled:** Transcript of courses and grades, state high school equivalency certificate required.

High school preparation. College-preparatory program recommended. 18 units recommended. Recommended units include English 4, mathematics 2, social studies 4, science 2 (laboratory 2) and foreign language 2. Requirements vary by program.

2008-2009 Annual costs. Tuition/fees: $5,648; $8,508 out-of-state. Out-of-state tuition for bachelor's program: $12,870; per-credit-hour $536. Room/board: $9,204. Books/supplies: $1,300. Personal expenses: $1,410.

2007-2008 Financial aid. Need-based: 45% of total undergraduate aid awarded as scholarships/grants, 55% as loans/jobs. Need-based aid available for part-time students.

Application procedures. Admission: Priority date 8/1; no deadline. $40 fee, may be waived for applicants with need. Admission notification on a rolling basis beginning on or about 11/1. Must reply by May 1 or within 4 week(s) if notified thereafter. **Financial aid:** Priority date 2/15; no closing date. FAFSA required. Applicants notified on a rolling basis starting 3/1; must reply within 2 week(s) of notification.

Academics. Special study options: Cross-registration, distance learning, double major, ESL, honors, internships. Bachelor's degree programs available on campus. License preparation in nursing. **Credit/placement by examination:** AP, CLEP, IB, institutional tests. 50 credit hours maximum toward associate degree, 50 toward bachelor's. Maximum of 50 percent of credits required for degree may be earned by combination of transfer, life experience and credit by examination. **Support services:** Learning center, reduced course load, remedial instruction, study skills assistance, tutoring, writing center.

Majors. Agriculture: Animal sciences, horticultural science, horticulture, landscaping, ornamental horticulture, turf management. **Architecture:** Landscape, technology. **Business:** Accounting, administrative services, business admin, management information systems, tourism promotion, tourism/travel. **Computer sciences:** Data processing. **Construction:** Carpentry, electrician, masonry. **Education:** Physical. **Engineering:** Science. **Engineering technology:** Architectural, construction, drafting. **Family/consumer sciences:** Institutional food production. **Health:** Nursing (RN), veterinary technology/assistant. **Legal studies:** Legal secretary. **Liberal arts:** Arts/sciences. **Mechanic/repair:** Automotive, heating/ac/refrig. **Parks/recreation:** Facilities management. **Personal/culinary services:** Chef training, culinary arts, restaurant/catering. **Social sciences:** General.

Most popular majors. Business/marketing 13%, health sciences 19%, liberal arts 17%, personal/culinary services 6%, trade and industry 24%.

Computing on campus. 230 workstations in library, computer center. Dormitories wired for high-speed internet access and linked to campus network. Commuter students can connect to campus network. Online course registration, helpline, repair service, student web hosting, wireless network available.

Student life. **Freshman orientation:** Available, $75 fee. Preregistration for classes offered. **Housing:** Guaranteed on-campus for freshmen. Coed dorms, apartments, wellness housing available. $100 deposit. **Activities:** Bands, campus ministries, choral groups, dance, drama, international student organizations, literary magazine, musical theater, radio station, student government, student newspaper, TV station, Delhi Interfaith Council, black student union, Latin student association, West Indian coalition.

Athletics. NAIA, NJCAA. **Intercollegiate:** Basketball, cross-country, golf, lacrosse M, soccer, softball W, swimming, tennis, track and field, volleyball W. **Intramural:** Basketball, bowling, boxing, football (non-tackle) M, handball, racquetball, soccer, softball, swimming, table tennis, tennis, volleyball. **Team name:** Broncos.

Student services. Adult student services, alcohol/substance abuse counseling, chaplain/spiritual director, career counseling, services for economically disadvantaged, student employment services, financial aid counseling, health services, minority student services, on-campus daycare, personal counseling, placement for graduates, veterans' counselor, women's services. **Physically disabled:** Services for visually, hearing impaired. **Learning disabled:** Comprehensive services available. **Transfer:** Transfer adviser, college fairs on campus for students transferring to 4-year colleges.

Contact. E-mail: enroll@delhi.edu
Phone: (607) 746-4550 Toll-free number: (800) 963-3544
Fax: (607) 746-4104
Robert Mazzei, Director of Admissions, State University of New York College of Technology at Delhi, 2 Main Street, Delhi, NY 13753-1190

Suffolk County Community College

Selden, New York **CB member**
www.sunysuffolk.edu **CB code: 2827**

- Public 2-year community college
- Commuter campus in large town

General. Founded in 1959. Regionally accredited. 3 campuses in Suffolk County: Brentwood, Selden, Riverhead. Downtown center in Sayville dedicated to nursing, downtown center in Riverhead dedicated to culinary arts. **Enrollment:** 22,839 degree-seeking undergraduates. **Degrees:** 2,788 associate awarded. **Location:** 60 miles from New York City. **Calendar:** Semester, extensive summer session. **Full-time faculty:** 355 total. **Part-time faculty:** 1,113 total. **Special facilities:** Planetarium.

Student profile.

Out-of-state:	2%	25 or older:	51%

Transfer out. **Colleges most students transferred to 2008:** SUNY Stony Brook, Hofstra University, St. Joseph's College, C.W. Post, Dowling College.

Basis for selection. Open admission, but selective for some programs. Admission tests may be used for admission or placement in certain programs in conjunction with high school record. Portfolio required for visual arts program; interview recommended for broadcast telecommunications, fine arts, health career, and paralegal assistant programs. Audition recommended for performing arts programs.

High school preparation. Special course requirements vary by program.

2008-2009 Annual costs. Tuition/fees: $3,736; $7,112 out-of-state. Books/supplies: $900. Personal expenses: $1,048.

2007-2008 Financial aid. **Need-based:** Need-based aid available for part-time students. Work-study available nights, weekends and for part-time students. **Non-need-based:** Scholarships awarded for academics, art, leadership, minority status, music/drama.

Application procedures. **Admission:** No deadline. $35 fee, may be waived for applicants with need. Admission notification on a rolling basis. **Financial aid:** Priority date 4/15, closing date 6/1. FAFSA required. Applicants notified on a rolling basis starting 4/15; must reply within 2 week(s) of notification.

Academics. **Special study options:** Cooperative education, distance learning, dual enrollment of high school students, ESL, honors, independent study, internships, study abroad, weekend college. Joint admissions with other SUNY units and private institutions. License preparation in nursing. **Credit/placement by examination:** AP, CLEP, IB, institutional tests. 30 credit hours maximum toward associate degree. **Support services:** GED preparation and test center, learning center, pre-admission summer program, reduced course load, remedial instruction, study skills assistance, tutoring, writing center.

Majors. **Architecture:** Environmental design, interior. **Area/ethnic studies:** Women's. **Biology:** General. **Business:** General, accounting, administrative services, business admin, finance, human resources, insurance, management science, marketing, office management, office technology, real estate, sales/distribution. **Communications:** General, broadcast journalism. **Communications technology:** General. **Computer sciences:** General, computer graphics, computer science, information systems, information technology, webmaster. **Conservation:** Environmental science, environmental studies. **Education:** Early childhood, secondary. **Engineering:** Electrical, science. **Engineering technology:** Architectural, construction, drafting, electrical, heat/ac/refrig. **Family/consumer sciences:** Food/nutrition. **Foreign languages:** Sign language interpretation. **Health:** Medical assistant, nursing (RN), occupational therapy assistant, optician, physical therapy assistant, substance abuse counseling, veterinary technology/assistant. **History:** General. **Legal studies:** Paralegal. **Liberal arts:** Arts/sciences. **Math:** General. **Mechanic/repair:** Automotive. **Personal/culinary services:** Culinary arts. **Physical sciences:** Astronomy, chemistry, geology, meteorology, physics, planetary. **Protective services:** Firefighting. **Psychology:** General. **Public administration:** Human services. **Social sciences:** General, economics, political science. **Visual/performing arts:** Commercial/advertising art, dramatic, interior design, studio arts, theater design.

Computing on campus. 1,785 workstations in library, computer center, student center. Commuter students can connect to campus network. Online course registration, online library, helpline, wireless network available.

Student life. **Freshman orientation:** Available. Preregistration for classes offered. **Activities:** Bands, choral groups, drama, literary magazine, music ensembles, musical theater, radio station, student government, student newspaper, over 60 clubs available.

Athletics. NJCAA. **Intercollegiate:** Baseball M, basketball, bowling M, cross-country, golf M, lacrosse M, soccer M, softball, tennis, track and field, triathlon W. **Intramural:** Basketball, bowling, softball.

Student services. Adult student services, career counseling, services for economically disadvantaged, student employment services, financial aid counseling, health services, minority student services, on-campus daycare, personal counseling, placement for graduates, veterans' counselor. **Physically disabled:** Services for visually, speech, hearing impaired. **Transfer:** Preadmission transcript evaluation for new students. Transfer adviser, college fairs on campus for students transferring to 4-year colleges.

Contact. E-mail: admissions@sunysuffolk.edu
Phone: (631) 451-4000 Fax: (631) 451-4415
Kate Rowe, College Dean of Enrollment Management, Suffolk County Community College, 533 College Road, Selden, NY 11784

Sullivan County Community College

Loch Sheldrake, New York
www.sullivan.suny.edu **CB code: 2855**

- Public 2-year community college
- Commuter campus in small town

General. Founded in 1962. Regionally accredited. **Enrollment:** 1,354 degree-seeking undergraduates. **Degrees:** 218 associate awarded. **Location:** 100 miles from New York City, 90 miles from Binghamton. **Calendar:** 4-1-4, limited summer session. **Full-time faculty:** 50 total. **Part-time faculty:** 52 total. **Special facilities:** Complete kitchen, dining room for hospitality programs, mini-travel agency for travel and tourism program, color and black and white darkrooms, computer graphics labs, child development center.

Student profile.

Out-of-state:	5%	25 or older:	43%

Basis for selection. Open admission, but selective for some programs. Special requirements for nursing program and university parallel business administration program. Out-of-county applicants must have 68 or better high school grade point average. SAT or ACT recommended for placement and counseling. Interview recommended.

High school preparation. Liberal arts applicants entering science programs should have 3 each in math and science. Computer science applicants, 3 math and 1 chemistry or physics. Nursing applicants, 1 laboratory biology. Engineering science, 3.5 math and 1 chemistry or physics.

2008-2009 Annual costs. Tuition/fees: $3,904; $7,432 out-of-state. Per-credit charge: $138 in-state; $176 out-of-state. Books/supplies: $1,000. Personal expenses: $700.

Financial aid. **Need-based:** Need-based aid available for part-time students. **Additional information:** 60% of students hold part-time jobs locally.

Application procedures. Admission: No deadline. No application fee. Admission notification on a rolling basis. Recommended priority application date for nursing department is December 1. **Financial aid:** Priority date 4/15; no closing date. FAFSA required. Applicants notified on a rolling basis starting 5/15; must reply within 2 week(s) of notification.

Academics. Practical experience in class laboratory situations emphasized in technical programs. **Special study options:** Dual enrollment of high school students, exchange student, honors, independent study, internships, study abroad. Joint admissions with SUNY New Paltz in elementary education. **Credit/placement by examination:** AP, CLEP, institutional tests. 31 credit hours maximum toward associate degree. **Support services:** Learning center, reduced course load, remedial instruction, tutoring.

Majors. Business: General, accounting, business admin, insurance, management information systems, office management, office technology, sales/distribution. **Communications:** General, broadcast journalism. **Computer sciences:** General, data processing. **Conservation:** General, forestry. **Education:** Early childhood, elementary. **Engineering:** General, science. **Engineering technology:** Surveying. **Family/consumer sciences:** Child care, institutional food production. **Health:** Nursing (RN), predental, premedicine, prepharmacy, preveterinary, substance abuse counseling. **History:** General. **Legal studies:** Paralegal, prelaw. **Liberal arts:** Arts/sciences. **Math:** General. **Parks/recreation:** Facilities management. **Personal/culinary services:** Cosmetic. **Philosophy/religion:** Philosophy. **Protective services:** Criminal justice, police science. **Psychology:** General. **Public administration:** Human services. **Social sciences:** General, sociology. **Visual/performing arts:** Commercial photography, commercial/advertising art.

Computing on campus. 80 workstations in library, computer center.

Student life. Freshman orientation: Mandatory. Preregistration for classes offered. **Policies:** 45 percent of students are county residents. **Housing:** College-approved housing adjacent to campus. **Activities:** Drama, radio station, student government, black student union, Latin student union.

Athletics. NJCAA. **Intercollegiate:** Basketball M, golf, softball W, volleyball W. **Intramural:** Archery, badminton, basketball, bowling, equestrian, golf, handball, racquetball, skiing, soccer, softball, swimming, table tennis, tennis, volleyball. **Team name:** Generals.

Student services. Adult student services, career counseling, student employment services, health services, on-campus daycare, personal counseling, placement for graduates, veterans' counselor. **Transfer:** Transfer adviser, college fairs on campus for students transferring to 4-year colleges.

Contact. Phone: (845) 434-5750 ext. 4287 Toll-free number: (800) 577-5243 Fax: (845) 434-0923
Sari Rosenheck, Director of Admissions and Registration Services, Sullivan County Community College, 112 College Road, Loch Sheldrake, NY 12759-5151

Swedish Institute

New York, New York
www.swedishinstitute.edu

- For-profit 2-year health science college
- Very large city
- Interview required

General. Accredited by ACCSCT. **Enrollment:** 575 degree-seeking undergraduates. **Degrees:** 230 associate awarded; master's offered. **Calendar:** Trimester. **Full-time faculty:** 20 total. **Part-time faculty:** 40 total.

Basis for selection. GPA, recommendations considered.

2008-2009 Annual costs. Tuition/fees: $8,420. Students generally attend 3 semesters/year.

Financial aid. All financial aid based on need. Need-based aid available for part-time students.

Application procedures. Admission: No deadline. $50 fee. **Financial aid:** No deadline. FAFSA, institutional form required.

Academics. Credit/placement by examination: CLEP, institutional tests. **Support services:** Reduced course load, study skills assistance, tutoring.

Majors. Health: Asian bodywork therapy, massage therapy.

Computing on campus. 7 workstations in library, computer center.

Contact. E-mail: admissions@swedishinstitute.edu
Phone: (212) 924-5900 Fax: (212) 924-7600
Swedish Institute, 226 West 26th Street, 5th Floor, New York, NY 10001-6700

Technical Career Institutes

New York, New York
www.tcicollege.edu **CB code: 2755**

- For-profit 2-year junior and technical college
- Commuter campus in very large city
- Interview required

General. Founded in 1909. Regionally accredited. **Enrollment:** 4,051 degree-seeking undergraduates. **Degrees:** 669 associate awarded. **Location:** Downtown. **Calendar:** Semester, extensive summer session. **Full-time faculty:** 67 total. **Part-time faculty:** 95 total.

Basis for selection. Open admission. Students without GED/high school diploma must pass CPAt to be admitted. **Homeschooled:** Transcript of courses and grades, state high school equivalency certificate required.

High school preparation. High school algebra 1 unit, general science 1 required for engineering technology program. Geometry, trigonometry, physics preferred for engineering program.

2008-2009 Annual costs. Tuition/fees: $10,565. Per-credit charge: $420. Required fees $250/year for second-year students. Books/supplies: $800. Personal expenses: $1,280.

Application procedures. Admission: No deadline. No application fee. Admission notification on a rolling basis beginning on or about 3/1. **Financial aid:** No deadline. FAFSA, institutional form required. Applicants notified on a rolling basis.

Academics. Special study options: Cooperative education, distance learning, ESL, honors, independent study, internships. **Credit/placement by examination:** CLEP, institutional tests. **Support services:** Learning center, reduced course load, remedial instruction, tutoring.

Majors. Business: Accounting, administrative services, office technology. **Computer sciences:** General, LAN/WAN management. **Engineering technology:** Construction, electrical. **Mechanic/repair:** Electronics/electrical, heating/ac/refrig.

Computing on campus. 350 workstations in library, computer center, student center.

Student life. Activities: Choral groups, music ensembles, student government, student newspaper, student chapter of Institute of Electrical and Electronics Engineering, Tau Alpha Pi honor fraternity, American Society of Heating, Refrigeration, and Air Conditioning Engineers, chess club, Future Business Leaders, photography club, Society of Women Engineers, Dare to Dream Volunteer Project.

Athletics. NJCAA. **Intercollegiate:** Basketball M.

Student services. Career counseling, student employment services, personal counseling, placement for graduates, veterans' counselor. **Transfer:** Transfer adviser for students transferring to 4-year colleges.

Contact. E-mail: admissions@tcicollege.edu
Phone: (212) 594-4001 Toll-free number: (800) 878-8246
Fax: (212) 629-3937
Aldwyn Cook, Director of Admissions, Technical Career Institutes, 320 West 31st Street, New York, NY 10001

Tompkins Cortland Community College

Dryden, New York
www.TC3.edu **CB code: 2904**

- Public 2-year community college
- Commuter campus in small town

General. Founded in 1968. Regionally accredited. SUNY institution. **Enrollment:** 2,954 degree-seeking undergraduates; 315 non-degree-seeking students. **Degrees:** 504 associate awarded. **Location:** 45 miles from Syracuse, 12 miles from Ithaca. **Calendar:** Semester, extensive summer session. **Full-time faculty:** 71 total. **Part-time faculty:** 210 total. **Class size:** 63% < 20, 37% 20-39, less than 1% 50-99.

Two-Year Colleges

Student profile. Among degree-seeking undergraduates, 66% enrolled in a transfer program, 34% enrolled in a vocational program, 924 enrolled as first-time, first-year students, 299 transferred in from other institutions.

Part-time:	18%	**Hispanic American:**	3%
Out-of-state:	1%	**International:**	3%
Women:	54%	**25 or older:**	17%
African American:	7%	**Live on campus:**	21%
Asian American:	1%		

Transfer out. Colleges most students transferred to 2008: SUNY Cortland, Ithaca College, Cornell University, Binghamton University, Oswego State University.

Basis for selection. Open admission, but selective for some programs. Special requirements for nursing and aviation science students. Nursing requires high school average of B or better, plus math and science prerequisites, and ACT. Aviation science requires student to be ready for pre-calculus math. Interview required for aviation science, recommended for nursing. **Homeschooled:** Letter of recommendation (nonparent) required. Completion of an IHIP pursuant to section 100.10 of the Regulations of the Commissions of Education required.

High school preparation. College-preparatory program recommended.

2008-2009 Annual costs. Tuition/fees: $4,040; $7,780 out-of-state. Per-credit charge: $132 in-state; $274 out-of-state. Books/supplies: $1,000.

2007-2008 Financial aid. Need-based: Need-based aid available for part-time students. Work-study available nights, weekends and for part-time students. **Non-need-based:** Scholarships awarded for academics.

Application procedures. Admission: No deadline. $15 fee, may be waived for applicants with need, free for online applicants. Admission notification on a rolling basis. **Financial aid:** Priority date 4/15; no closing date. FAFSA, institutional form required. Applicants notified on a rolling basis starting 3/15; must reply within 4 week(s) of notification.

Academics. Special study options: Cooperative education, cross-registration, distance learning, dual enrollment of high school students, ESL, honors, independent study, internships, liberal arts/career combination, study abroad. License preparation in nursing, real estate. **Credit/placement by examination:** AP, CLEP, IB, institutional tests. 47 credit hours maximum toward associate degree. **Support services:** GED preparation, learning center, reduced course load, remedial instruction, study skills assistance, tutoring, writing center.

Majors. Biology: Biotechnology. **Business:** Accounting technology, business admin, hotel/motel admin, international, labor relations, retailing. **Communications:** General, advertising, broadcast journalism. **Communications technology:** Radio/tv. **Computer sciences:** General, computer support specialist, information systems, webmaster. **Conservation:** General. **Construction:** General. **Education:** Early childhood, kindergarten/preschool, secondary. **Engineering:** General. **Engineering technology:** Electrical, mechanical. **Family/consumer sciences:** Child care. **Health:** Nursing (RN), substance abuse counseling. **Legal studies:** Paralegal. **Liberal arts:** Arts/sciences, humanities. **Mechanic/repair:** Avionics. **Parks/recreation:** Facilities management, sports admin. **Protective services:** Forensics, police science. **Public administration:** Community org/advocacy. **Visual/performing arts:** Commercial/advertising art, photography.

Most popular majors. Business/marketing 22%, health sciences 11%, liberal arts 34%, security/protective services 8%.

Computing on campus. 400 workstations in library, computer center, student center. Dormitories wired for high-speed internet access and linked to campus network. Commuter students can connect to campus network. Online course registration, online library, helpline, wireless network available.

Student life. Freshman orientation: Available. Preregistration for classes offered. Held prior to each semester. Multiple sessions offered: new students, international students, and adult students. **Policies:** All campus organizations must apply for recognition, must have staff advisor, and are funded by the activity fee through faculty-student association and student government. **Housing:** Special housing for disabled, apartments available. $250 fully refundable deposit, deadline 5/15. **Activities:** Choral groups, dance, drama, film society, literary magazine, radio station, student government, student advisoryboard, Students Acting for a Greener Earth, drama club, outdoor adventure club, nursing club, accounting & business association, Phi Theta Kappa-Alpha Gamma Nu Chapter, Gay Straight Alliance, Chi Alpha Christian Fellowship, Black student union.

Athletics. NJCAA. **Intercollegiate:** Baseball M, basketball, golf, lacrosse M, soccer, softball W, volleyball W. **Intramural:** Badminton, basketball, bowling, football (non-tackle), golf, handball, lacrosse, racquetball, skiing, soccer, softball, squash, swimming, table tennis, tennis, volleyball, water polo, weight lifting, wrestling. **Team name:** Panthers.

Student services. Adult student services, career counseling, services for economically disadvantaged, student employment services, financial aid counseling, health services, minority student services, on-campus daycare, personal counseling, placement for graduates, veterans' counselor. **Physically disabled:** Services for visually, speech, hearing impaired. **Transfer:** Re-entry adviser, pre-admission transcript evaluation for new students. Transfer center, transfer adviser, college fairs on campus for students transferring to 4-year colleges.

Contact. E-mail: admissions@tc3.edu
Phone: (607) 844-6580 Toll-free number: (888) 567-8211
Fax: (607) 844-6541
Sandy Drumluk, Director of Admissions, Tompkins Cortland Community College, 170 North Street, Dryden, NY 13053-0139

Trocaire College

Buffalo, New York
www.trocaire.edu **CB code: 2856**

- Private 2-year junior college affiliated with Roman Catholic Church
- Commuter campus in large city

General. Founded in 1958. Regionally accredited. Affiliated with Sisters of Mercy, Buffalo Diocese. **Enrollment:** 1,056 degree-seeking undergraduates. **Degrees:** 199 associate awarded. **Calendar:** Semester, limited summer session. **Full-time faculty:** 55 total. **Part-time faculty:** 81 total. **Class size:** 79% < 20, 21% 20-39.

Basis for selection. Open admission, but selective for some programs. Special requirements for health-related fields.

High school preparation. 16 units required. Laboratory science and mathematics required for some programs.

2008-2009 Annual costs. Tuition/fees: $11,614. Per-credit charge: $457. Books/supplies: $1,000. Personal expenses: $700.

Financial aid. Need-based: Need-based aid available for part-time students. **Non-need-based:** Scholarships awarded for academics, alumni affiliation.

Application procedures. Admission: No deadline. $25 fee, may be waived for applicants with need. Admission notification on a rolling basis. Must reply by May 1 or within 4 week(s) if notified thereafter. **Financial aid:** Closing date 4/15. FAFSA required. Applicants notified on a rolling basis starting 3/1; must reply within 2 week(s) of notification.

Academics. Special study options: Cross-registration, dual enrollment of high school students, independent study, internships. License preparation in nursing, radiology. **Credit/placement by examination:** CLEP, institutional tests. 30 credit hours maximum toward associate degree. **Support services:** Learning center, reduced course load, remedial instruction, study skills assistance, tutoring.

Majors. Business: Administrative services, business admin, office management, sales/distribution. **Education:** Early childhood. **Health:** Massage therapy, medical assistant, medical radiologic technology/radiation therapy, medical records technology, nursing (RN), surgical technology. **Legal studies:** Legal secretary. **Liberal arts:** Arts/sciences.

Most popular majors. Business/marketing 16%, education 7%, health sciences 71%.

Computing on campus. 114 workstations in library, computer center, student center. Helpline available.

Student life. Freshman orientation: Mandatory. **Activities:** Student government.

Student services. Adult student services, career counseling, student employment services, health services, personal counseling, placement for graduates, veterans' counselor. **Physically disabled:** Services for visually, hearing impaired. **Transfer:** Pre-admission transcript evaluation for new students. Transfer center, transfer adviser, college fairs on campus for students transferring to 4-year colleges.

Contact. E-mail: info@trocaire.edu
Phone: (716) 827-2545 Fax: (716) 828-6107
Maria Povlock, Director of Admissions, Trocaire College, 360 Choate Avenue, Buffalo, NY 14220

Ulster County Community College
Stone Ridge, New York
www.sunyulster.edu **CB code: 2938**

- Public 2-year community college
- Commuter campus in small town

General. Founded in 1963. Regionally accredited. SUNY institution. **Enrollment:** 2,287 degree-seeking undergraduates; 1,196 non-degree-seeking students. **Degrees:** 369 associate awarded. **Location:** 8 miles from Kingston. **Calendar:** Semester, extensive summer session. **Full-time faculty:** 64 total. **Part-time faculty:** 138 total. **Class size:** 54% < 20, 42% 20-39, 4% 40-49. **Special facilities:** Computer art graphics laboratory, small-business incubator, Mid-Hudson Health and Safety Institute. **Partnerships:** SUNY Ulster is a Cisco Regional Academy and member of the Microsoft IT Academy program.

Student profile. Among degree-seeking undergraduates, 84% enrolled in a transfer program, 16% enrolled in a vocational program, 590 enrolled as first-time, first-year students, 142 transferred in from other institutions.

Part-time:	31%	**Hispanic American:**	7%
Women:	58%	**Native American:**	1%
African American:	5%	**25 or older:**	31%
Asian American:	2%		

Transfer out. 56% of students enrolled in the transfer program go on to 4-year colleges. **Colleges most students transferred to 2008:** SUNY New Paltz, SUNY Albany, Marist College, Mount St. Mary's College, College of Saint Rose.

Basis for selection. Open admission, but selective for some programs. Special requirements for nursing and honors programs, with school achievement record very important. SAT or ACT recommended for all applicants. Interview required for nursing, honors program, early admissions applicants; recommended for others. Portfolio recommended for graphic arts.

High school preparation. 18 units recommended. Recommended units include English 4 and social studies 4. 3 math and 3 science, including chemistry and physics, required of engineering applicants. 4 English, 3 math, 3 language required of honors program applicants.

2008-2009 Annual costs. Tuition/fees: $3,951; $7,371 out-of-state. Per-credit charge: $130 in-state; $260 out-of-state. Books/supplies: $1,000. Personal expenses: $800.

2008-2009 Financial aid. Need-based: Need-based aid available for part-time students.

Application procedures. Admission: No deadline. No application fee. Admission notification on a rolling basis. **Financial aid:** Priority date 6/1; no closing date. FAFSA required. Applicants notified on a rolling basis starting 6/1; must reply within 2 week(s) of notification.

Academics. Special study options: Cooperative education, cross-registration, distance learning, double major, dual enrollment of high school students, ESL, honors, independent study, internships, student-designed major. License preparation in nursing, paramedic. **Credit/placement by examination:** AP, CLEP, institutional tests. 30 credit hours maximum toward associate degree. **Support services:** Learning center, pre-admission summer program, reduced course load, remedial instruction, study skills assistance, tutoring, writing center.

Majors. Business: General, accounting technology, business admin, entrepreneurial studies, managerial economics, office/clerical. **Communications:** General. **Computer sciences:** General, computer science, system admin. **Conservation:** Environmental studies. **Education:** Biology, chemistry, elementary, English, kindergarten/preschool, mathematics, middle, science, social studies, Spanish. **Engineering:** General. **Engineering technology:** Drafting, industrial. **Health:** EMT paramedic, nursing (RN), substance abuse counseling, veterinary technology/assistant. **Legal studies:** Legal secretary. **Liberal arts:** Arts/sciences, humanities. **Math:** General. **Parks/recreation:** General. **Protective services:** Emergency management/homeland security, law enforcement admin. **Public administration:** Community org/advocacy. **Social sciences:** General. **Visual/performing arts:** General, commercial/advertising art, dramatic. **Other:** Microcomputer for business.

Most popular majors. Business/marketing 6%, education 8%, health sciences 21%, liberal arts 42%, security/protective services 6%.

Computing on campus. 243 workstations in library, computer center, student center.

Student life. Freshman orientation: Available. Preregistration for classes offered. **Activities:** Bands, choral groups, drama, music ensembles, musical theater, student government, TV station, child care club, environmental awareness club, business club, improv club, Phi Theta Kappa, LGBTA, vet tech club, tomorrow's teachers, psychology club, nursing club.

Athletics. NJCAA. **Intercollegiate:** Baseball M, basketball M, golf, soccer, softball W, tennis, volleyball W. **Intramural:** Basketball M. **Team name:** Senators.

Student services. Adult student services, career counseling, services for economically disadvantaged, student employment services, financial aid counseling, health services, on-campus daycare, personal counseling, placement for graduates, veterans' counselor. **Physically disabled:** Services for visually, speech, hearing impaired. **Transfer:** Transfer adviser, college fairs on campus for students transferring to 4-year colleges.

Contact. E-mail: admissions@sunyulster.edu
Phone: (845) 687-5022 Toll-free number: (800) 724-5022
Fax: (845) 687-5090
Susan Weatherly, Director of Admissions, Ulster County Community College, Cottekill Road, Stone Ridge, NY 12484

Utica School of Commerce
Utica, New York
www.uscny.edu **CB code: 0343**

- For-profit 2-year business college
- Commuter campus in small city
- Interview required

General. Founded in 1896. Regionally accredited. Branch campuses in Oneonta and Canastota. **Enrollment:** 414 degree-seeking undergraduates. **Degrees:** 67 associate awarded. **Location:** 50 miles from Syracuse. **Calendar:** Semester, extensive summer session. **Full-time faculty:** 47 total. **Part-time faculty:** 64 total. **Special facilities:** Museum of business education.

Student profile. Among degree-seeking undergraduates, 95 enrolled as first-time, first-year students.

Part-time:	28%	**Women:**	76%
Out-of-state:	1%	**25 or older:**	30%

Transfer out. Colleges most students transferred to 2008: SUNY College of Technology, St. Rose College, SUNY at Oneonta.

Basis for selection. Open admission. Admissions interview required. High School diploma or GED required.

2008-2009 Annual costs. Tuition/fees: $11,220. Per-credit charge: $450. Books/supplies: $1,185.

Financial aid. All financial aid based on need.

Application procedures. Admission: No deadline. No application fee. Admission notification on a rolling basis. Must reply by May 1 or within 3 week(s) if notified thereafter. **Financial aid:** No deadline. FAFSA, institutional form required. Applicants notified on a rolling basis.

Academics. Special study options: Accelerated study, dual enrollment of high school students, liberal arts/career combination. Joint admissions with SUNY Institute of Technology. **Credit/placement by examination:** CLEP, institutional tests. 30 credit hours maximum toward associate degree. **Support services:** Learning center, reduced course load, remedial instruction, tutoring.

Majors. Business: General, accounting, administrative services, business admin, executive assistant, management information systems, nonprofit/public, retailing, sales/distribution. **Computer sciences:** General, data processing, programming, word processing. **Health:** Health care admin, medical records technology, medical secretary. **Legal studies:** Legal secretary.

Most popular majors. Business/marketing 81%, computer/information sciences 19%.

Computing on campus. 168 workstations in library, computer center.

Student life. Freshman orientation: Mandatory. **Activities:** Student government, student newspaper, future secretaries association, accounting association.

Student services. Career counseling, student employment services, personal counseling, placement for graduates, veterans' counselor. **Physically disabled:** Services for visually, hearing impaired. **Transfer:** Transfer adviser, college fairs on campus for students transferring to 4-year colleges.

Contact. E-mail: admissions@uscny.edu
Phone: (315) 733-2307 Toll-free number: (800) 321-4872
Fax: (315) 733-9281
Director of Admissions, Utica School of Commerce, 201 Bleecker Street, Utica, NY 13501

Utica School of Commerce: Canastota

Utica, New York
www.uscny.edu **CB code: 3340**

- For-profit 2-year business college
- Commuter campus in small town

General. Regionally accredited. **Calendar:** Semester.

Annual costs/financial aid. Tuition/fees (2008-2009): $11,220.

Contact. Director of Admissions, 201 Bleecker Street, Utica, NY 13501

Utica School of Commerce: Oneonta

Oneonta, New York
www.uscny.edu **CB code: 3341**

- For-profit 2-year branch campus and business college
- Small city

General. Regionally accredited. **Location:** 70 miles from Albany. **Calendar:** Quarter.

Annual costs/financial aid. Tuition/fees (2008-2009): $11,220.

Contact. Phone: (607) 732-7003
17 Elm Street, Oneonta, NY 13820

Villa Maria College of Buffalo

Buffalo, New York **CB member**
www.villa.edu **CB code: 2962**

- Private 2-year visual arts and liberal arts college affiliated with Roman Catholic Church
- Commuter campus in large city
- Interview required

General. Founded in 1960. Regionally accredited. **Enrollment:** 473 degree-seeking undergraduates; 15 non-degree-seeking students. **Degrees:** 6 bachelor's, 99 associate awarded. **Location:** 2 miles from downtown. **Calendar:** Semester, limited summer session. **Full-time faculty:** 33 total; 36% have terminal degrees, 6% minority, 54% women. **Part-time faculty:** 44 total; 20% have terminal degrees, 2% minority, 41% women. **Class size:** 85% < 20, 14% 20-39, less than 1% 50-99. **Special facilities:** Interior design resource center, education resource center, recording studio, digital photography lab.

Student profile. Among degree-seeking undergraduates, 60% enrolled in a vocational program, 4% already have a bachelor's degree or higher, 132 enrolled as first-time, first-year students, 73 transferred in from other institutions.

Part-time:	19%	**Hispanic American:**	3%
Out-of-state:	1%	**Native American:**	1%
Women:	68%	**25 or older:**	25%
African American:	27%	**Live on campus:**	5%
Asian American:	1%		

Transfer out. 50% of students enrolled in the transfer program go on to 4-year colleges. **Colleges most students transferred to 2008:** SUNY at Buffalo, Buffalo State College, Medaille College, D'Youville College, Canisius College.

Basis for selection. Open admission, but selective for some programs. Admissions based on academic records, learning experience, and assessment and advisement program results where applicable. Interview, recommendations also considered. Physical therapist assistant program requires 3.5 GPA. Audition required for music programs; portfolio recommended for fine arts, interior design, photography programs. **Homeschooled:** Statement describing homeschool structure and mission, transcript of courses and grades, interview required. Letter required verifying completion of all requirements from the school district in which home schooled individual resides. **Learning Disabled:** Must submit all documentation to Coordinator for Students with Disabilities prior to admission and must take VMCAPP.

High school preparation. Recommended units include English 4, mathematics 3, social studies 4, history 4 and science 3. General physics with lab required for physical therapist assistant applicants.

2008-2009 Annual costs. Tuition/fees: $13,990. Per-credit charge: $455. Books/supplies: $2,500. Personal expenses: $700.

2007-2008 Financial aid. Need-based: 100 full-time freshmen applied for aid; 84 were judged to have need; 84 of these received aid. Average need met was 88%. Average scholarship/grant was $5,224; average loan $3,240. 37% of total undergraduate aid awarded as scholarships/grants, 63% as loans/jobs. Need-based aid available for part-time students. **Non-need-based:** Awarded to 42 full-time undergraduates, including 68 freshmen. Scholarships awarded for academics, alumni affiliation, art, leadership, minority status, music/drama.

Application procedures. Admission: No deadline. No application fee. Admission notification on a rolling basis. **Financial aid:** No deadline. FAFSA required. Applicants notified on a rolling basis starting 2/15; must reply within 2 week(s) of notification.

Academics. Implemented Adviser/Advisee Action Plan provides early identification of students encountering difficulty with scheduling, finances, academic skills, personal problems, and employment. **Special study options:** Cooperative education, cross-registration, double major, dual enrollment of high school students, internships, liberal arts/career combination, study abroad. Evening modules for adult students, member Western New York Consortium of Institutions of Higher Education. Bachelor's degree programs available on campus. **Credit/placement by examination:** AP, CLEP, institutional tests. **Support services:** Learning center, pre-admission summer program, reduced course load, remedial instruction, study skills assistance, tutoring.

Majors. Business: Business admin. **Computer sciences:** General. **Education:** General, early childhood. **Health:** Physical therapy assistant. **Liberal arts:** Arts/sciences, humanities. **Visual/performing arts:** Commercial/advertising art, interior design, jazz, music management, music performance, photography, studio arts.

Most popular majors. Business/marketing 18%, communication technologies 11%, education 11%, health sciences 15%, liberal arts 9%, visual/performing arts 35%.

Computing on campus. 100 workstations in library, computer center. Commuter students can connect to campus network. Online library available.

Student life. Freshman orientation: Mandatory, $50 fee. Preregistration for classes offered. One-day program for first-time students and their parents; half day for transfer students. **Housing:** Apartments available. $300 fully refundable deposit. **Activities:** Jazz band, campus ministries, choral groups, literary magazine, music ensembles, student government, student newspaper, Helping Adults' New Dreams Succeed, Students Actively Striving for Success, Students Against Destructive Decision Making, Multicultural Club.

Student services. Adult student services, alcohol/substance abuse counseling, chaplain/spiritual director, career counseling, services for economically disadvantaged, student employment services, financial aid counseling, health services, minority student services, personal counseling, placement for graduates, veterans' counselor. **Transfer:** Pre-admission transcript evaluation for new students. Transfer center, transfer adviser, college fairs on campus for students transferring to 4-year colleges.

Contact. E-mail: admissions@villa.edu
Phone: (716) 896-0700 ext. 1805 Fax: (716) 896-0705
Kevin Donovan, Director of Admissions, Villa Maria College of Buffalo, 240 Pine Ridge Road, Buffalo, NY 14225-3999

Westchester Community College

Valhalla, New York **CB member**
www.sunywcc.edu **CB code: 2972**

- Public 2-year community college
- Commuter campus in large town

General. Founded in 1946. Regionally accredited. SUNY institution. **Enrollment:** 11,091 degree-seeking undergraduates; 1,522 non-degree-seeking students. **Degrees:** 1,034 associate awarded. **Location:** 30 miles from New York City, 6 miles from White Plains. **Calendar:** Semester, extensive summer session. **Full-time faculty:** 167 total; 28% have terminal degrees, 12% minority, 52% women. **Part-time faculty:** 310 total; 19% minority, 56% women. **Special facilities:** On-campus child care center.

Student profile. Among degree-seeking undergraduates, 2,496 enrolled as first-time, first-year students, 1,029 transferred in from other institutions.

Part-time:	42%	**Women:**	54%
Out-of-state:	1%	**25 or older:**	36%

Transfer out. Colleges most students transferred to 2008: SUNY Purchase, CUNY Baruch, Mercy College, Iona College, CUNY Lehman.

Basis for selection. Open admission, but selective for some programs. Competitive programs in allied health curricula. High school diploma or GED required of applicants 18 years of age or younger. Interview recommended. **Homeschooled:** Statement describing homeschool structure and mission required. Students must submit letter from superintendent of district in which they reside certifying that home instruction program is equivalent of high school program.

2008-2009 Annual costs. Tuition/fees: $3,913; $9,239 out-of-state. Per-credit charge: $148 in-state; $370 out-of-state. Books/supplies: $1,200. Personal expenses: $600.

2007-2008 Financial aid. Need-based: 89% of total undergraduate aid awarded as scholarships/grants, 11% as loans/jobs. Need-based aid available for part-time students. Work-study available nights, weekends and for part-time students. **Non-need-based:** Scholarships awarded for academics.

Application procedures. Admission: No deadline. $25 fee, may be waived for applicants with need. Application must be submitted on paper. Admission notification on a rolling basis beginning on or about 2/1. **Financial aid:** No deadline. FAFSA, institutional form required. Applicants notified on a rolling basis; must reply within 4 week(s) of notification.

Academics. Extensive ESL program. **Special study options:** Accelerated study, cooperative education, cross-registration, distance learning, double major, ESL, honors, independent study, internships, liberal arts/career combination, student-designed major, study abroad. Cambridge University summer program; Italian language study program in Italy. License preparation in nursing, paramedic, radiology, real estate. **Credit/placement by examination:** AP, CLEP, IB, institutional tests. 32 credit hours maximum toward associate degree. **Support services:** Learning center, reduced course load, remedial instruction, study skills assistance, tutoring, writing center.

Majors. Business: Accounting, administrative services, business admin, international, marketing, merchandising, office/clerical, sales/distribution. **Communications:** General. **Computer sciences:** General, computer science, information systems, LAN/WAN management. **Education:** Early childhood. **Engineering:** General, science. **Engineering technology:** Civil, electrical. **Family/consumer sciences:** Child care, food/nutrition, institutional food production. **Health:** EMT paramedic, medical radiologic technology/radiation therapy, nursing (RN), nursing assistant, respiratory therapy technology, substance abuse counseling. **Legal studies:** Paralegal. **Liberal arts:** Arts/sciences. **Mechanic/repair:** Automotive. **Personal/culinary services:** Culinary arts, restaurant/catering. **Physical sciences:** General. **Protective services:** Corrections, police science. **Public administration:** Social work. **Social sciences:** General. **Visual/performing arts:** General, dramatic, music performance.

Computing on campus. 2,260 workstations in library, computer center, student center. Online library, helpline, wireless network available.

Student life. Freshman orientation: Available. Held last week in August for fall semester, usually 2-day event. **Activities:** Choral groups, dance, drama, literary magazine, musical theater, radio station, student government, student newspaper, TV station, international friendship club, black student union, Brazilian club, Haitian club, El Club Hispano Americano, Irish society, Jamaican club, Il Club Italiano, French club, Amnesty International.

Athletics. NJCAA. **Intercollegiate:** Baseball M, basketball, bowling, golf M, soccer M, softball W, volleyball W. **Intramural:** Basketball M, soccer M, softball, volleyball. **Team name:** Westcos.

Student services. Adult student services, alcohol/substance abuse counseling, career counseling, student employment services, financial aid counseling, health services, minority student services, on-campus daycare, personal counseling, placement for graduates, veterans' counselor, women's services. **Physically disabled:** Services for visually, speech, hearing impaired. **Transfer:** Pre-admission transcript evaluation for new students. Transfer center, transfer adviser, college fairs on campus for students transferring to 4-year colleges.

Contact. E-mail: admissions@sunywcc.edu
Phone: (914) 606-6735 Fax: (914) 606-6540
Teresita Wisell, Director of Admissions, Westchester Community College, 75 Grasslands Road, Valhalla, NY 10595

Wood Tobe-Coburn School

New York, New York
www.woodtobecoburn.com **CB code: 2913**

- For-profit 2-year career college
- Commuter campus in very large city

General. Founded in 1879. Regionally accredited. **Calendar:** Semester.

Annual costs/financial aid. Tuition/fees (2008-2009): $16,360. Books/supplies: $1,165. Personal expenses: $2,110.

Contact. Phone: (212) 686-9040
Director of Admissions, 8 East 40th Street, New York, NY 10016-0190

North Carolina

Alamance Community College
Graham, North Carolina
www.alamancecc.edu **CB code: 5790**

- Public 2-year community college
- Commuter campus in large town

General. Founded in 1958. Regionally accredited. **Enrollment:** 3,740 degree-seeking undergraduates; 991 non-degree-seeking students. **Degrees:** 371 associate awarded. **Location:** 4 miles from Burlington, 30 miles from Greensboro. **Calendar:** Semester, extensive summer session. **Full-time faculty:** 102 total; 7% have terminal degrees, 11% minority, 53% women. **Part-time faculty:** 284 total; 2% have terminal degrees, 9% minority, 49% women. **Class size:** 86% < 20, 14% 20-39.

Student profile. Among degree-seeking undergraduates, 20% enrolled in a transfer program, 80% enrolled in a vocational program, 4% already have a bachelor's degree or higher, 637 enrolled as first-time, first-year students, 924 transferred in from other institutions.

Part-time:	64%	**Asian American:**	2%
Out-of-state:	1%	**Hispanic American:**	5%
Women:	66%	**Native American:**	1%
African American:	22%	**25 or older:**	54%

Transfer out. Colleges most students transferred to 2008: University of North Carolina System.

Basis for selection. Open admission, but selective for some programs. Special requirements for Dental and Nursing. SAT or ACT score may waive required testing for placement. Portfolio recommended for advertising design, commercial art majors. **Learning Disabled:** Disabilities must be documented with special needs counselor. Contact Student Development Office.

High school preparation. 21 units recommended. Recommended units include English 4, mathematics 3, social studies 2, history 1, science 3 (laboratory 1), foreign language 2 and academic electives 6. Biology, chemistry required for nursing.

2008-2009 Annual costs. Tuition/fees: $1,290; $7,029 out-of-state. Per-credit charge: $42 in-state; $233 out-of-state. Books/supplies: $800. Personal expenses: $800.

2007-2008 Financial aid. Need-based: 240 full-time freshmen applied for aid; 214 were judged to have need; 190 of these received aid. Average need met was 30%. Average scholarship/grant was $3,000. 96% of total undergraduate aid awarded as scholarships/grants, 4% as loans/jobs. Need-based aid available for part-time students. Work-study available nights and for part-time students. **Non-need-based:** Awarded to 148 full-time undergraduates, including 100 freshmen. Scholarships awarded for academics, state residency.

Application procedures. Admission: No deadline. No application fee. Admission notification on a rolling basis. **Financial aid:** Priority date 5/15; no closing date. FAFSA required. Applicants notified on a rolling basis starting 3/15; must reply within 2 week(s) of notification.

Academics. Special study options: Cooperative education, distance learning, double major, dual enrollment of high school students, ESL, independent study, internships, weekend college. License preparation in nursing. **Credit/placement by examination:** AP, CLEP, IB, institutional tests. 18 credit hours maximum toward associate degree. Maximum 25% of hours for degree by examination. **Support services:** GED preparation and test center, learning center, reduced course load, remedial instruction, study skills assistance, tutoring.

Majors. Agriculture: Horticultural science, horticulture. **Biology:** Biotechnology. **Business:** General, accounting, administrative services, banking/financial services, business admin, management science, office management, sales/distribution. **Computer sciences:** Information systems. **Education:** Early childhood. **Engineering:** Electrical. **Engineering technology:** Drafting. **Health:** Clinical lab assistant, clinical lab technology, medical records admin, medical secretary, nursing (RN). **Legal studies:** Legal secretary. **Liberal arts:** Arts/sciences. **Mechanic/repair:** Electronics/electrical, heating/ac/refrig, industrial. **Personal/culinary services:** Culinary arts. **Protective services:** Criminal justice, firefighting, law enforcement admin.

Most popular majors. Business/marketing 21%, health sciences 21%, liberal arts 20%.

Computing on campus. 152 workstations in library, computer center, student center. Wireless network available.

Student life. Freshman orientation: Available. Preregistration for classes offered. General orientation available; some programs have additional orientations. **Activities:** Student government, student newspaper, ethnic student association, marketing club, Phi Beta Lambda (service organization), criminal justice club, early childhood education club, Phi Theta Kappa, nursing club, medical assisting club, Sigma Psi, animal care club, biotechnology, college transfer student club.

Student services. Career counseling, student employment services, financial aid counseling, health services, on-campus daycare, personal counseling, placement for graduates, veterans' counselor. **Physically disabled:** Services for visually, speech, hearing impaired. **Transfer:** Pre-admission transcript evaluation for new students. Transfer adviser, college fairs on campus for students transferring to 4-year colleges.

Contact. E-mail: accadmissions@alamancecc.edu
Phone: (336) 506-4270 Fax: (336) 506-4264
Elizabeth Brehler, Director of Enrollment Management, Alamance Community College, Box 8000, Graham, NC 27253

Asheville-Buncombe Technical Community College
Asheville, North Carolina **CB member**
www.abtech.edu **CB code: 5033**

- Public 2-year community and technical college
- Commuter campus in small city

General. Founded in 1959. Regionally accredited. Certain credit courses offered at the Madison Campus during evening hours. **Enrollment:** 4,077 degree-seeking undergraduates. **Degrees:** 575 associate awarded. **Location:** 115 miles from Charlotte. **Calendar:** Semester. **Full-time faculty:** 154 total; 6% have terminal degrees, 1% minority, 58% women. **Part-time faculty:** 482 total; 5% have terminal degrees, 8% minority, 52% women.

Student profile.

Out-of-state:	1%	**25 or older:**	48%

Basis for selection. Open admission, but selective for some programs. Computerized Placement Test (CPT) administered by college. SAT and/or ACT scores may be used in lieu of CPT for English and math placement. For allied health programs, tests used to earn admission through point system. Provisional or unconditional admission to individual programs will be determined by scores on the test requirements. Placement interview required of all entering students; interview required for all medical programs.

High school preparation. 8 units recommended. Recommended units include English 4, mathematics 2 and science 2. Algebra I and algebra II or geometry for engineering; algebra I, chemistry and biology for nursing, medical laboratory and dental programs; algebra I for radiologic technology; biology and 1 mathematics for practical nursing.

2008-2009 Annual costs. Tuition/fees: $1,375; $7,497 out-of-state. Per-credit charge: $42 in-state; $234 out-of-state. Books/supplies: $980. Personal expenses: $7,367.

Financial aid. Non-need-based: Scholarships awarded for academics, leadership.

Application procedures. Admission: No deadline. No application fee. **Financial aid:** Priority date 3/15, closing date 3/31. FAFSA required. Applicants notified on a rolling basis starting 5/1; must reply within 2 week(s) of notification.

Academics. Special study options: Cooperative education, cross-registration, distance learning, double major, dual enrollment of high school students, independent study, internships, liberal arts/career combination. License preparation in real estate. **Credit/placement by examination:** CLEP, institutional tests. **Support services:** GED preparation and test center, learning center, pre-admission summer program, reduced course load, remedial instruction, tutoring.

Majors. Business: Accounting, administrative services, business admin, management information systems, office technology, office/clerical, operations, sales/distribution. **Computer sciences:** Applications programming. **Engineering technology:** Civil, drafting, electrical, surveying. **Family/consumer sciences:** Child care, institutional food production. **Health:** Clinical lab technology, dental hygiene, EMT paramedic, medical radiologic technology/

radiation therapy, nursing (RN). **Liberal arts:** Arts/sciences. **Mechanic/repair:** Automotive, heating/ac/refrig. **Protective services:** Police science. **Public administration:** Social work. **Transportation:** Flight attendant.

Computing on campus. 300 workstations in library, computer center.

Student life. Activities: Drama, literary magazine, student government, student newspaper.

Student services. Career counseling, student employment services, on-campus daycare, personal counseling, placement for graduates, veterans' counselor. **Physically disabled:** Services for visually, speech, hearing impaired. **Transfer:** Transfer adviser, college fairs on campus for students transferring to 4-year colleges.

Contact. E-mail: admissions@abtech.edu
Phone: (828) 254-1921 ext. 144 Fax: (828) 251-6718
Scott Douglas, Director, Enrollment Management, Asheville-Buncombe Technical Community College, 340 Victoria Road, Asheville, NC 28801-4897

Beaufort County Community College

Washington, North Carolina
www.beaufortccc.edu **CB code: 7307**

- Public 2-year community college
- Commuter campus in rural community

General. Founded in 1967. Regionally accredited. **Enrollment:** 865 full-time, degree-seeking students. **Degrees:** 149 associate awarded. **Location:** 23 miles from Greenville. **Calendar:** Semester, limited summer session. **Full-time faculty:** 61 total. **Part-time faculty:** 147 total. **Special facilities:** Wachovia Partnership East hub site.

Transfer out. Colleges most students transferred to 2008: East Carolina University.

Basis for selection. Open admission, but selective for some programs. Special admission requirements for allied health programs and basic law enforcement training. **Homeschooled:** Statement describing homeschool structure and mission required. Must provide proof that the home school is registered with the appropriate state agencies.

High school preparation. One unit chemistry required for nursing and medical technology applicants.

2008-2009 Annual costs. Tuition/fees: $1,408; $7,530 out-of-state. Per-credit charge: $42 in-state; $233 out-of-state. Some programs require insurance and uniforms. Books/supplies: $1,200. Personal expenses: $2,247.

2008-2009 Financial aid. Need-based: Need-based aid available for part-time students. **Non-need-based:** Scholarships awarded for academics.

Application procedures. Admission: No deadline. No application fee. **Financial aid:** Priority date 6/1; no closing date. FAFSA required. Applicants notified on a rolling basis starting 5/1; must reply within 2 week(s) of notification.

Academics. Special study options: Cooperative education, distance learning, dual enrollment of high school students, ESL, internships, liberal arts/career combination. Bachelor's degree programs available on campus. License preparation in nursing, real estate. **Credit/placement by examination:** AP, CLEP, institutional tests. **Support services:** GED preparation and test center, learning center, remedial instruction, study skills assistance, tutoring.

Majors. Agriculture: Mechanization. **Business:** Accounting, administrative services, business admin. **Computer sciences:** Applications programming, information systems, networking, programming, vendor certification. **Construction:** Electrician. **Education:** General, early childhood. **Engineering technology:** Drafting, electrical. **Family/consumer sciences:** Child care, child development. **Health:** Clinical lab technology, medical secretary, nursing (RN), office admin. **Liberal arts:** Arts/sciences. **Mechanic/repair:** Automotive, diesel, heavy equipment. **Production:** Welding. **Protective services:** Criminal justice. **Public administration:** Human services. **Science technology:** Biological.

Computing on campus. Commuter students can connect to campus network. Online library, wireless network available.

Student life. Freshman orientation: Available. Preregistration for classes offered. **Activities:** Student government.

Student services. Career counseling, services for economically disadvantaged, student employment services, financial aid counseling, personal counseling, placement for graduates, veterans' counselor. **Transfer:** Preadmission transcript evaluation for new students. Transfer adviser, college fairs on campus for students transferring to 4-year colleges.

Contact. E-mail: garyb@beaufortccc.edu
Phone: (252) 940-6237 Fax: (252) 940-6393
Gary Burbage, Director of Admissions and Recruitment, Beaufort County Community College, Box 1069, Washington, NC 27889

Bladen Community College

Dublin, North Carolina
www.bladencc.edu **CB code: 3082**

- Public 2-year community college
- Commuter campus in rural community

General. Founded in 1967. Regionally accredited. **Enrollment:** 1,323 degree-seeking undergraduates. **Degrees:** 102 associate awarded. **Location:** 35 miles from Fayetteville. **Calendar:** Semester, limited summer session. **Full-time faculty:** 50 total; 6% have terminal degrees, 22% minority, 64% women. **Part-time faculty:** 60 total; 7% have terminal degrees, 27% minority, 48% women. **Class size:** 82% < 20, 18% 20-39.

Transfer out. Colleges most students transferred to 2008: University of North Carolina-Wilmington, University of North Carolina-Pembroke, Fayetteville State University, East Carolina University, North Carolina State University.

Basis for selection. Open admission, but selective for some programs. Practical nursing program requires submission of appropriate test results and completion of high school biology and algebra courses with grade of C or better. ADN program requires biology and algebra, plus general chemistry. Biology and chemistry must be within last 5 years for ADN.

High school preparation. 26 units recommended. Recommended units include English 4, mathematics 3, social studies 1, history 2, science 3 (laboratory 1), foreign language 2, computer science 1 and academic electives 10.

2008-2009 Annual costs. Tuition/fees: $1,326; $7,065 out-of-state. Per-credit charge: $42 in-state; $233 out-of-state. Books/supplies: $800. Personal expenses: $725.

Financial aid. Need-based: Need-based aid available for part-time students. Work-study available nights and for part-time students.

Application procedures. Admission: Priority date 8/15; no deadline. No application fee. Admission notification on a rolling basis beginning on or about 6/15. **Financial aid:** Priority date 6/1; no closing date. FAFSA required. Applicants notified on a rolling basis starting 8/1; must reply within 2 week(s) of notification.

Academics. Special study options: Cooperative education, distance learning, double major, dual enrollment of high school students, ESL, independent study, internships, liberal arts/career combination, weekend college. Bachelor's degree programs available on campus. **Credit/placement by examination:** CLEP, institutional tests. 10 credit hours maximum toward associate degree. **Support services:** GED preparation and test center, learning center, reduced course load, remedial instruction, study skills assistance, tutoring, writing center.

Majors. Agriculture: Agribusiness operations, business. **Biology:** Biotechnology. **Business:** Business admin, office technology, office/clerical. **Computer sciences:** General, applications programming, programming. **Education:** General. **Engineering technology:** Electrical, industrial. **Health:** Nursing (RN). **Liberal arts:** Arts/sciences. **Mechanic/repair:** Electronics/electrical. **Personal/culinary services:** Cosmetic. **Production:** Welding. **Protective services:** Law enforcement admin.

Computing on campus. 100 workstations in library, computer center, student center. Online course registration, helpline, wireless network available.

Student life. Freshman orientation: Mandatory. Preregistration for classes offered. **Activities:** Drama, literary magazine, student government, student newspaper.

Athletics. Team name: Eagles.

Student services. Adult student services, alcohol/substance abuse counseling, career counseling, services for economically disadvantaged, student employment services, financial aid counseling, minority student services, personal counseling, placement for graduates, veterans' counselor. **Physically disabled:** Services for visually, speech, hearing impaired. **Transfer:**

Pre-admission transcript evaluation for new students. Transfer center, transfer adviser, college fairs on campus for students transferring to 4-year colleges.

Contact. E-mail: ywilloughby@bladencc.edu
Phone: (910) 879-5593 Fax: (910) 879-5564
Jeffrey Kornegay, Vice President of Student Services, Bladen Community College, Box 266, Dublin, NC 28332-0266

Blue Ridge Community College
Flat Rock, North Carolina
www.blueridge.edu **CB code: 5644**

- Public 2-year community and technical college
- Commuter campus in large town

General. Founded in 1969. Regionally accredited. **Enrollment:** 2,146 degree-seeking undergraduates. **Degrees:** 145 associate awarded. **Location:** 25 miles from Asheville. **Calendar:** Semester, limited summer session. **Full-time faculty:** 56 total. **Part-time faculty:** 232 total. **Class size:** 81% < 20, 19% 20-39, less than 1% 40-49.

Student profile.

Out-of-state:	2%	25 or older:	29%

Basis for selection. Open admission, but selective for some programs. Mathematics and science requirements for allied health programs in surgical technology, pharmacy technology, nursing.

High school preparation. 3 units of science, one of which must be lab, required for allied health programs only.

2008-2009 Annual costs. Tuition/fees: $1,355; $7,094 out-of-state. Per-credit charge: $42 in-state; $233 out-of-state. Books/supplies: $750.

2007-2008 Financial aid. Need-based: Need-based aid available for part-time students. Work-study available nights and for part-time students. **Non-need-based:** Scholarships awarded for academics, athletics, leadership, minority status, state residency.

Application procedures. Admission: No deadline. No application fee. Admission notification on a rolling basis. **Financial aid:** Priority date 6/30; no closing date. FAFSA, institutional form required. Applicants notified on a rolling basis starting 2/1; must reply within 4 week(s) of notification.

Academics. Special study options: Cooperative education, distance learning, double major, dual enrollment of high school students, ESL, study abroad, teacher certification program. Bachelor's degree programs available on campus. License preparation in nursing, paramedic, physical therapy, real estate. **Credit/placement by examination:** CLEP, institutional tests. Maximum of 50% of credit hours by examination may be counted toward degree. **Support services:** GED preparation and test center, learning center, reduced course load, remedial instruction, study skills assistance, tutoring.

Majors. Agriculture: Horticulture. **Business:** General, administrative services, sales/distribution, tourism promotion. **Computer sciences:** Information systems, programming. **Conservation:** General. **Engineering:** Electrical. **Engineering technology:** Drafting, electrical. **Family/consumer sciences:** Child care. **Foreign languages:** Sign language interpretation. **Health:** Nursing (RN), surgical technology. **Liberal arts:** Arts/sciences.

Most popular majors. Business/marketing 14%, computer/information sciences 26%, health sciences 12%, liberal arts 23%.

Computing on campus. 200 workstations in library, computer center. Commuter students can connect to campus network. Online course registration, helpline available.

Student life. Freshman orientation: Mandatory. Preregistration for classes offered. **Activities:** Drama, literary magazine, student government, Circle-K, Rotaract, Phi Theta Kappa, National Vocational-Technical Honor Society.

Athletics. NJCAA. **Intercollegiate:** Bowling M, volleyball W. **Team name:** Bears.

Student services. Adult student services, career counseling, student employment services, financial aid counseling, on-campus daycare, personal counseling, placement for graduates, veterans' counselor. **Physically disabled:** Services for visually, speech, hearing impaired. **Transfer:** Preadmission transcript evaluation for new students. Transfer adviser, college fairs on campus for students transferring to 4-year colleges.

Contact. E-mail: kirstenb@blueridge.edu
Phone: (828) 694-1800 Fax: (828) 694-1693
Marcia Stoneman, Dean for Student Services, Blue Ridge Community College, 180 West Campus Drive, Flat Rock, NC 28731-9624

Brunswick Community College
Supply, North Carolina
www.brunswickcc.edu **CB code: 7314**

- Public 2-year community college
- Commuter campus in small town

General. Founded in 1979. Regionally accredited. **Enrollment:** 1,164 degree-seeking undergraduates. **Degrees:** 194 associate awarded. **Location:** 25 miles from Wilmington, 30 miles from Myrtle Beach, South Carolina. **Calendar:** Semester, limited summer session. **Full-time faculty:** 40 total. **Part-time faculty:** 130 total. **Class size:** 81% < 20, 18% 20-39, 1% 40-49.

Student profile.

Out-of-state:	3%	25 or older:	45%

Transfer out. Colleges most students transferred to 2008: University of North Carolina at Wilmington.

Basis for selection. Open admission, but selective for some programs. Phlebotomy, basic law enforcement technology, practical nursing, associate degree nursing, and health information technology program applicants must have completed specific course work before they are considered. Limited slots. May also enter based on test scores. **Adult students:** SAT/ACT scores not required. **Learning Disabled:** Requests for any accommodations should be made at least 2 weeks prior to beginning of applicant's first semester.

2008-2009 Annual costs. Tuition/fees: $1,442; $7,564 out-of-state. Per-credit charge: $42 in-state; $233 out-of-state. Books/supplies: $1,000. Personal expenses: $800.

2008-2009 Financial aid. Need-based: Need-based aid available for part-time students. Work-study available nights, weekends and for part-time students. **Non-need-based:** Scholarships awarded for academics, state residency. **Additional information:** Attendance required at financial aid orientation session for those receiving federal student aid.

Application procedures. Admission: No deadline. No application fee. Admission notification on a rolling basis. **Financial aid:** Priority date 6/1, closing date 6/15. FAFSA, institutional form required. Applicants notified on a rolling basis starting 3/1; must reply by 6/15 or within 2 week(s) of notification.

Academics. Special study options: Cooperative education, distance learning, double major, dual enrollment of high school students, ESL, internships. License preparation in nursing, paramedic, real estate. **Credit/placement by examination:** AP, CLEP, SAT, institutional tests. No limits on credit by examination hours that may be applied toward an associate degree. **Support services:** GED preparation and test center, learning center, reduced course load, remedial instruction, study skills assistance, tutoring.

Majors. Agriculture: Aquaculture, horticultural science, turf management. **Business:** Administrative services, business admin, small business admin. **Computer sciences:** Information systems, programming. **Education:** Early childhood. **Health:** Medical records technology, nursing (RN). **Liberal arts:** Arts/sciences. **Personal/culinary services:** Cosmetic.

Most popular majors. Agriculture 11%, business/marketing 11%, computer/information sciences 6%, education 9%, health sciences 8%, liberal arts 46%.

Computing on campus. 146 workstations in library, computer center. Wireless network available.

Student life. Freshman orientation: Available. Preregistration for classes offered. **Policies:** All facilities are nonsmoking. Smoking allowed in designated outdoor areas only. **Activities:** Jazz band, dance, drama, radio station, student government, student newspaper, National Technical Honor Society, Phi Theta Kappa, science club, journalism club, drama club, art club.

Athletics. NJCAA. **Intercollegiate:** Baseball M, basketball, softball W, volleyball W. **Team name:** Dolphins.

Student services. Alcohol/substance abuse counseling, career counseling, student employment services, financial aid counseling, personal counseling, placement for graduates, veterans' counselor. **Physically disabled:** Services for visually, speech, hearing impaired. **Transfer:** Pre-admission transcript evaluation for new students. Transfer adviser, college fairs on campus for students transferring to 4-year colleges.

Contact. E-mail: coxc@brunswickcc.edu
Phone: (910) 755-7324 Toll-free number: (800) 754-1050 ext. 324
Fax: (910) 754-9609
Christen Cox, Admissions Counselor, Brunswick Community College, Box 30, Supply, NC 28462

Caldwell Community College and Technical Institute

Hudson, North Carolina
www.cccti.edu **CB code: 5146**

- Public 2-year community and technical college
- Commuter campus in small town

General. Founded in 1964. Regionally accredited. **Enrollment:** 3,074 degree-seeking undergraduates; 876 non-degree-seeking students. **Degrees:** 379 associate awarded. **Location:** 70 miles from Charlotte. **Calendar:** Semester, limited summer session. **Full-time faculty:** 130 total. **Part-time faculty:** 290 total. **Class size:** 68% < 20, 31% 20-39, 1% 40-49, less than 1% 50-99, less than 1% >100.

Student profile. Among degree-seeking undergraduates, 699 enrolled as first-time, first-year students.

Part-time:	56%	**Women:**	59%
Out-of-state:	2%	**25 or older:**	43%

Basis for selection. Open admission, but selective for some programs. Limited number of applicants admitted to health science programs, interview required.

2008-2009 Annual costs. Tuition/fees: $1,292; $7,031 out-of-state. Per-credit charge: $42 in-state; $233 out-of-state. Books/supplies: $1,100. Personal expenses: $1,350.

2008-2009 Financial aid. All financial aid based on need. Need-based aid available for part-time students. Work-study available for part-time students.

Application procedures. Admission: No deadline. No application fee. Admission notification on a rolling basis. **Financial aid:** Priority date 6/1; no closing date. FAFSA required. Applicants notified on a rolling basis starting 6/30.

Academics. Special study options: Cooperative education, distance learning, dual enrollment of high school students, independent study. Bachelor's degree programs available on campus. License preparation in aviation, nursing, physical therapy, real estate. **Credit/placement by examination:** AP, CLEP, institutional tests. 16 credit hours maximum toward associate degree. **Support services:** GED preparation and test center, learning center, reduced course load, remedial instruction, study skills assistance, tutoring, writing center.

Majors. Business: Accounting, administrative services, business admin. **Computer sciences:** Applications programming, data processing, programming. **Education:** Early childhood. **Engineering technology:** Drafting, electrical. **Health:** Cardiovascular technology, medical radiologic technology/radiation therapy, medical secretary, nuclear medical technology, nursing (RN), physical therapy assistant, sonography, speech-language pathology assistant. **Legal studies:** Paralegal. **Liberal arts:** Arts/sciences. **Math:** General. **Mechanic/repair:** Industrial. **Transportation:** Aviation management. **Visual/performing arts:** Art.

Most popular majors. Business/marketing 22%, computer/information sciences 12%, health sciences 37%, liberal arts 16%.

Computing on campus. 750 workstations in library, computer center. Commuter students can connect to campus network. Helpline available.

Student life. Freshman orientation: Available. Preregistration for classes offered. 2-day session held prior to beginning of fall semester. **Activities:** Choral groups, drama, literary magazine, student government, TV station, Ebony Kinship, special interest clubs, Phi Theta Kappa, Alpha Omega (non-denominational religious organization).

Athletics. NJCAA. **Intercollegiate:** Basketball, volleyball W. **Team name:** Cobras.

Student services. Career counseling, services for economically disadvantaged, student employment services, financial aid counseling, personal counseling, placement for graduates, veterans' counselor. **Physically disabled:** Services for visually, speech, hearing impaired. **Transfer:** Transfer adviser, college fairs on campus for students transferring to 4-year colleges.

Contact. Phone: (828) 726-2200 Fax: (828) 726-2709
Carolyn Woodard, Director, Enrollment Management Services, Caldwell Community College and Technical Institute, 2855 Hickory Boulevard, Hudson, NC 28638-2672

Cape Fear Community College

Wilmington, North Carolina
www.cfcc.edu **CB code: 5094**

- Public 2-year community college
- Commuter campus in small city

General. Founded in 1959. Regionally accredited. Campuses at Burgaw and North Campus, 7 miles from downtown Wilmington. **Enrollment:** 6,799 degree-seeking undergraduates; 1,068 non-degree-seeking students. **Degrees:** 356 associate awarded. **Location:** 125 miles from Raleigh. **Calendar:** Semester, limited summer session. **Full-time faculty:** 251 total. **Part-time faculty:** 214 total.

Student profile. Among degree-seeking undergraduates, 35% enrolled in a transfer program, 65% enrolled in a vocational program, 1,821 enrolled as first-time, first-year students, 2,145 transferred in from other institutions.

Part-time:	46%	**Women:**	54%
Out-of-state:	8%	**25 or older:**	38%

Transfer out. Colleges most students transferred to 2008: University of North Carolina at Wilmington.

Basis for selection. Open admission, but selective for some programs. Special requirements for nursing and allied health programs: Psychological Corporation Pre-Nursing Examination and interview required. **Home-schooled:** A copy of approval from North Carolina Department of Non-Public Instruction required or similar documents from states other than North Carolina. **Learning Disabled:** Students must register with Disability Services.

2008-2009 Annual costs. Tuition/fees: $1,491; $7,603 out-of-state. Per-credit charge: $42 in-state; $233 out-of-state. Books/supplies: $1,230. Personal expenses: $3,307.

2007-2008 Financial aid. Need-based: 70% of total undergraduate aid awarded as scholarships/grants, 30% as loans/jobs. Need-based aid available for part-time students. Work-study available nights and for part-time students. **Non-need-based:** Scholarships awarded for academics, athletics, job skills, leadership, music/drama, religious affiliation.

Application procedures. Admission: No deadline. No application fee. Admission notification on a rolling basis. **Financial aid:** Priority date 6/1; no closing date. FAFSA required. Applicants notified on a rolling basis starting 4/1; must reply within 2 week(s) of notification.

Academics. Special study options: Cooperative education, distance learning, dual enrollment of high school students, ESL, independent study, internships. Bachelor's degree programs available on campus. License preparation in dental hygiene, nursing, occupational therapy, paramedic, radiology, real estate. **Credit/placement by examination:** AP, CLEP, IB, institutional tests. **Support services:** GED preparation and test center, learning center, remedial instruction, study skills assistance, tutoring.

Majors. Agriculture: Landscaping. **Architecture:** Interior, landscape, urban/community planning. **Business:** Accounting technology, administrative services, business admin, executive assistant, hospitality admin, hotel/motel admin, restaurant/food services. **Computer sciences:** Information technology. **Conservation:** General. **Construction:** Electrician. **Education:** General. **Engineering technology:** Architectural, computer systems, electrical, instrumentation, mechanical. **Family/consumer sciences:** Child care, institutional food production. **Health:** Dental hygiene, medical radiologic technology/radiation therapy, nursing (RN), occupational therapy assistant, sonography. **Legal studies:** Paralegal. **Liberal arts:** Arts/sciences. **Mechanic/repair:** Automotive. **Personal/culinary services:** General, cosmetic, culinary arts, restaurant/catering. **Physical sciences:** Oceanography. **Production:** Machine shop technology, welding. **Protective services:** Police science. **Visual/performing arts:** Cinematography, interior design.

Most popular majors. Health sciences 14%, liberal arts 59%.

Computing on campus. 80 workstations in library, computer center. Online course registration, helpline, wireless network available.

Student life. Freshman orientation: Available. Preregistration for classes offered. Half-day program held in August and December. **Activities:** Choral groups, student government, student newspaper, Phi Theta Kappa Honor Society.

Athletics. NJCAA. **Intercollegiate:** Basketball M, golf, volleyball W. **Intramural:** Cheerleading, soccer. **Team name:** Sea Devils.

Student services. Alcohol/substance abuse counseling, career counseling, student employment services, financial aid counseling, on-campus daycare, personal counseling, placement for graduates, veterans' counselor. **Physically disabled:** Services for visually, speech, hearing impaired. **Transfer:** Pre-admission transcript evaluation for new students. Transfer adviser, college fairs on campus for students transferring to 4-year colleges.

Contact. E-mail: admissions@cfcc.edu
Phone: (910) 362-7557 Fax: (910) 362-7080
Linda Kasyan, Director of Enrollment Management, Cape Fear Community College, 411 North Front Street, Wilmington, NC 28401-3910

Carolinas College of Health Sciences
Charlotte, North Carolina
www.carolinascollege.edu **CB code: 6211**

- Public 2-year health science and junior college
- Commuter campus in very large city
- SAT or ACT required

General. Regionally accredited. Institution supported by public hospital system. **Enrollment:** 528 degree-seeking undergraduates. **Degrees:** 118 associate awarded. **Calendar:** Semester, limited summer session. **Full-time faculty:** 47 total. **Part-time faculty:** 24 total. **Class size:** 40% < 20, 57% 20-39, 3% 40-49.

Transfer out. Colleges most students transferred to 2008: Queens College, University of North Carolina at Charlotte, Winston-Salem State University, Central Piedmont Community College, Mercy School of Nursing.

Basis for selection. Open admission, but selective for some programs. Selection based on SAT/ACT test scores and high school GPA. Only students with permanent resident status will be considered for enrollment.

High school preparation. 15 units required. Required units include English 4, mathematics 1, social studies 2, history 2, science 2 (laboratory 2) and foreign language 2. Algebra, biology, chemistry required.

2008-2009 Annual costs. Tuition/fees: $6,895. Per-credit charge: $210. Tuition varies by program. Books/supplies: $946.

2007-2008 Financial aid. Need-based: Need-based aid available for part-time students. Work-study available for part-time students. **Non-need-based:** Scholarships awarded for academics.

Application procedures. Admission: Priority date 12/1; deadline 3/1 (receipt date). $50 fee. Application must be submitted on paper. Admission notification on a rolling basis beginning on or about 1/1. Must reply by May 1 or within 4 week(s) if notified thereafter. Application deadlines vary by program. **Financial aid:** Priority date 5/1; no closing date. FAFSA, institutional form required. Applicants notified on a rolling basis starting 5/1.

Academics. Post-bachelor's certificate in Medical Technology available. **Special study options:** Distance learning, independent study, liberal arts/career combination. Bachelor's degree programs available on campus. License preparation in nursing. **Credit/placement by examination:** AP, CLEP, IB, institutional tests. 25 credit hours maximum toward associate degree. **Support services:** Learning center, tutoring.

Majors. Health: Medical radiologic technology/radiation therapy, nursing (RN).

Computing on campus. 30 workstations in computer center. Online library, wireless network available.

Student life. Freshman orientation: Mandatory. Preregistration for classes offered. **Housing:** Apartments owned by health care system available. **Activities:** Student government.

Student services. Alcohol/substance abuse counseling, chaplain/spiritual director, career counseling, student employment services, financial aid counseling, health services, personal counseling, placement for graduates, veterans' counselor. **Transfer:** Pre-admission transcript evaluation for new students. College fairs on campus for students transferring to 4-year colleges.

Contact. E-mail: cchsinformation@carolinas.org
Phone: (704) 355-5583 Fax: (704) 355-9336
Rhoda Rillorta, Admissions Officer, Carolinas College of Health Sciences, PO Box 32861, Charlotte, NC 28232

Carteret Community College
Morehead City, North Carolina
www.carteret.edu **CB code: 5092**

- Public 2-year community and technical college
- Commuter campus in small town

General. Founded in 1963. Regionally accredited. Aquaculture technology and marine technical trades programs. **Enrollment:** 1,418 degree-seeking undergraduates. **Degrees:** 154 associate awarded. **Location:** 150 miles from Raleigh, 87 miles from Wilmington. **Calendar:** Semester, limited summer session. **Full-time faculty:** 95 total; 43% have terminal degrees, 5% minority, 48% women. **Part-time faculty:** 84 total; 36% have terminal degrees, 12% minority, 67% women. **Special facilities:** Carteret County historical research center, center for marine science and technology, North Carolina marine technical education center. **Partnerships:** Formal partnerships with the North Carolina State Department of Public Instruction and the North Carolina Community College System.

Student profile. Among degree-seeking undergraduates, 33% enrolled in a transfer program, 67% enrolled in a vocational program, 10% already have a bachelor's degree or higher, 220 enrolled as first-time, first-year students.

Part-time:	55%	**Asian American:**	1%
Out-of-state:	2%	**Hispanic American:**	3%
Women:	69%	**25 or older:**	48%
African American:	10%		

Transfer out. Colleges most students transferred to 2008: University of North Carolina at Wilmington, East Carolina University, North Carolina State University, Pitt Community College, Cape Fear Community College.

Basis for selection. Open admission, but selective for some programs. Personal information sessions required for allied health science program. SAT required of radiologic technology and respiratory therapy applicants; score report due by January 1. **Homeschooled:** Transcript of courses and grades required. **Learning Disabled:** Students requesting academic accommodations must present proper documentation and follow the procedures to request reasonable accommodations.

High school preparation. College-preparatory program recommended. Extensive science and mathematics recommended for allied health programs, particularly respiratory therapy, radiography, and nursing.

2008-2009 Annual costs. Tuition/fees: $1,395; $7,517 out-of-state. Per-credit charge: $42 in-state; $233 out-of-state. Tuition is set by the NC Legislature and the NC Community College System. Fees are set by the CCC Board of Trustees. Tuition and fees are subject to change each year, and without notice. Books/supplies: $950. Personal expenses: $1,081.

2007-2008 Financial aid. Need-based: 75% of total undergraduate aid awarded as scholarships/grants, 25% as loans/jobs. Need-based aid available for part-time students. **Non-need-based:** Scholarships awarded for academics, leadership, minority status, state residency. **Additional information:** Institutional student loan program administered by college. Student may charge up to $600 for books, supplies and tuition per quarter. Repayment due by 11th week of semester.

Application procedures. Admission: No deadline. No application fee. Admission notification on a rolling basis. **Financial aid:** No deadline. FAFSA, institutional form required. Applicants notified on a rolling basis starting 7/1; must reply within 2 week(s) of notification.

Academics. Special study options: Cooperative education, cross-registration, distance learning, double major, dual enrollment of high school students, ESL, independent study, internships, liberal arts/career combination, teacher certification program. License preparation in nursing, paramedic, radiology, real estate. **Credit/placement by examination:** AP, CLEP, institutional tests. **Support services:** GED preparation and test center, learning center, pre-admission summer program, reduced course load, remedial instruction, study skills assistance, tutoring, writing center.

Majors. Agriculture: Greenhouse operations, horticultural science, horticulture. **Biology:** Biotechnology. **Business:** General, administrative services, hotel/motel admin, office/clerical. **Communications:** Photojournalism. **Communications technology:** Photo/film/video. **Computer sciences:** General, information technology, LAN/WAN management, web page design, webmaster. **Education:** General, teacher assistance. **Family/consumer sciences:** Child development. **Health:** EMT ambulance attendant, massage therapy, medical radiologic technology/radiation therapy, office admin, predental, premedicine, prenursing, prepharmacy, preveterinary, radiologic technology/medical imaging, recreational therapy, respiratory therapy technology. **Legal studies:** Legal secretary, paralegal. **Liberal arts:** Arts/

sciences. **Math:** General. **Personal/culinary services:** Restaurant/catering. **Protective services:** Criminal justice, police science. **Psychology:** General. **Visual/performing arts:** General, interior design, photography.

Most popular majors. Business/marketing 70%, health sciences 25%.

Computing on campus. 225 workstations in library, computer center, student center. Commuter students can connect to campus network. Online course registration, online library, helpline, student web hosting, wireless network available.

Student life. **Freshman orientation:** Available. Preregistration for classes offered. **Activities:** Choral groups, drama, literary magazine, student government, student newspaper, Psi Beta (honorary society for psychology majors), Phi Beta Lambda (business organization), Sigma Kappa Delta (honorary society for English majors), Phi Theta Kappa - Beta Delta Pi (honors fraternity).

Student services. Adult student services, alcohol/substance abuse counseling, career counseling, services for economically disadvantaged, student employment services, financial aid counseling, personal counseling, placement for graduates, veterans' counselor. **Physically disabled:** Services for visually, speech, hearing impaired. **Transfer:** Pre-admission transcript evaluation for new students. Transfer center, transfer adviser, college fairs on campus for students transferring to 4-year colleges.

Contact. E-mail: admissions@carteret.edu
Phone: (252) 222-6154 Fax: (252) 222-6265
Margie Ward, Admissions Officer, Carteret Community College, 3505 Arendell Street, Morehead City, NC 28557-2989

Catawba Valley Community College

Hickory, North Carolina
www.cvcc.edu **CB code: 5098**

- Public 2-year community college
- Commuter campus in large town

General. Founded in 1960. Regionally accredited. **Enrollment:** 3,740 degree-seeking undergraduates; 969 non-degree-seeking students. **Degrees:** 459 associate awarded. **Location:** 50 miles from Charlotte. **Calendar:** Semester, limited summer session. **Full-time faculty:** 144 total; 4% minority, 49% women. **Part-time faculty:** 339 total; 8% minority, 58% women. **Class size:** 70% < 20, 30% 20-39, less than 1% 40-49, less than 1% 50-99, less than 1% >100.

Student profile. Among degree-seeking undergraduates, 943 enrolled as first-time, first-year students, 697 transferred in from other institutions.

Part-time:	58%	**Asian American:**	7%
Women:	59%	**Hispanic American:**	4%
African American:	10%	**25 or older:**	45%

Basis for selection. Open admission, but selective for some programs. Special requirements for nursing, emergency medical science, surgical technology, respiratory care, health information technology, dental hygiene, speech-language pathology assistant, advertising and graphic design, electroneurodiagnostic technology, polysomnography, radiography. Interview required for health program applicants, advertising and graphic design applicants, and photography applicants; recommended for all others. **Homeschooled:** Transcript of courses and grades, state high school equivalency certificate required.

2008-2009 Annual costs. Tuition/fees: $1,366; $7,488 out-of-state. Per-credit charge: $42 in-state; $233 out-of-state. Books/supplies: $1,150. Personal expenses: $3,280.

2007-2008 Financial aid. **Need-based:** 444 full-time freshmen applied for aid; 292 were judged to have need; 247 of these received aid. 78% of total undergraduate aid awarded as scholarships/grants, 22% as loans/jobs. Need-based aid available for part-time students. **Non-need-based:** Awarded to 658 full-time undergraduates, including 479 freshmen. Scholarships awarded for academics, leadership, music/drama.

Application procedures. **Admission:** No deadline. No application fee. Admission notification on a rolling basis. **Financial aid:** Closing date 3/15. FAFSA required. Applicants notified on a rolling basis starting 5/15.

Academics. **Special study options:** Cooperative education, distance learning, double major, dual enrollment of high school students, ESL, honors, independent study, student-designed major, teacher certification program, weekend college. License preparation in dental hygiene, nursing, paramedic, real estate. **Credit/placement by examination:** AP, CLEP, IB, institutional tests. Maximum of 65% of total credit hours required for degree may be obtained by examination. **Support services:** GED preparation and test center, learning center, reduced course load, remedial instruction, study skills assistance, tutoring, writing center.

Majors. **Agriculture:** Horticultural science, turf management. **Architecture:** Technology. **Business:** Accounting technology, banking/financial services, business admin, customer service, e-commerce, management information systems, office management, operations, real estate. **Communications technology:** Photo/film/video. **Computer sciences:** Information systems, information technology, LAN/WAN management, programming. **Education:** Early childhood. **Engineering:** Industrial. **Engineering technology:** Architectural, computer, electrical, electromechanical, mechanical. **Health:** Dental hygiene, EMT paramedic, health services, medical radiologic technology/radiation therapy, medical records technology, nursing (RN), office admin, respiratory therapy technology. **Liberal arts:** Arts/sciences. **Mechanic/repair:** Automotive. **Production:** Furniture. **Protective services:** Criminal justice, fire safety technology, forensics. **Visual/performing arts:** Commercial/advertising art. **Other:** Cyber crime technology.

Most popular majors. Business/marketing 17%, health sciences 31%, liberal arts 26%.

Computing on campus. 1,360 workstations in library, computer center. Commuter students can connect to campus network. Online course registration, online library, repair service, wireless network available.

Student life. **Freshman orientation:** Available. Available for degree-seeking students. **Activities:** Choral groups, drama, international student organizations, music ensembles, student government, student newspaper, Phi Theta Kappa, association of nursing students, Certifiable club, Rotaract club, Student American Dental Hygiene Association, Students in Free Enterprise, theater arts club, student photographic society club, Seeds of Service, Hmong student association.

Athletics. NJCAA. **Intercollegiate:** Basketball M, volleyball W. **Team name:** Buccaneers.

Student services. Career counseling, services for economically disadvantaged, student employment services, financial aid counseling, personal counseling, placement for graduates, veterans' counselor, women's services. **Physically disabled:** Services for visually, hearing impaired. **Transfer:** Pre-admission transcript evaluation for new students. Transfer adviser, college fairs on campus for students transferring to 4-year colleges.

Contact. Phone: (828) 327-7000 Fax: (828) 327-7276
Laurie Wegner, Director of Admissions, Catawba Valley Community College, 2550 Highway 70 SE, Hickory, NC 28602

Central Carolina Community College

Sanford, North Carolina
www.cccc.edu **CB code: 5147**

- Public 2-year community college
- Commuter campus in large town

General. Founded in 1958. Regionally accredited. **Enrollment:** 3,934 degree-seeking undergraduates. **Degrees:** 305 associate awarded. **Location:** 45 miles from Raleigh. **Calendar:** Semester, limited summer session. **Full-time faculty:** 356 total. **Part-time faculty:** 145 total. **Class size:** 82% < 20, 17% 20-39, less than 1% 40-49, less than 1% 50-99.

Student profile.

Out-of-state:	2%	**25 or older:**	49%

Transfer out. **Colleges most students transferred to 2008:** ECU, NCSU, UNC-G, UNC-W, ASU.

Basis for selection. Open admission, but selective for some programs. Special requirements for veterinary technician, nursing education, radio-television broadcasting, laser electro-optic, electronics and instrumentation technology, cosmetology, medical assisting programs. ACT/SAT scores may exempt student from placement tests. **Homeschooled:** Must be registered with local county Board of Education and NC Non-public Education office; must submit documentation of successful completion of NC Competency Exam, copies of transcript and high school diploma. **Learning Disabled:** Students must sign up with special populations office and request accommodations and services.

High school preparation. Strong background in mathematics, biology, and chemistry required for veterinary technician and nursing education option programs.

2008-2009 Annual costs. Tuition/fees: $1,348; $7,087 out-of-state. Per-credit charge: $42 in-state; $233 out-of-state. Books/supplies: $666.

Financial aid. **Need-based:** Need-based aid available for part-time students. Work-study available nights and for part-time students. **Non-need-based:** Scholarships awarded for academics.

Application procedures. **Admission:** No deadline. No application fee. Admission notification on a rolling basis. **Financial aid:** Priority date 3/15, closing date 5/1. FAFSA, institutional form required. Applicants notified on a rolling basis starting 7/1; must reply within 2 week(s) of notification.

Academics. **Special study options:** Distance learning, dual enrollment of high school students, honors, independent study, internships, liberal arts/career combination. License preparation in dental hygiene, nursing. **Credit/placement by examination:** CLEP, institutional tests. Placement interview required. **Support services:** GED preparation, learning center, reduced course load, remedial instruction, study skills assistance, tutoring, writing center.

Majors. **Business:** Accounting, administrative services, business admin, office/clerical. **Computer sciences:** Applications programming, information systems, networking, programming. **Education:** General, early childhood. **Engineering:** Civil, computer. **Engineering technology:** Architectural, civil, drafting, electrical, manufacturing, robotics, surveying. **Family/consumer sciences:** Child care. **Health:** Licensed practical nurse, medical assistant, medical secretary, nursing (RN), veterinary technology/assistant. **Legal studies:** Legal secretary, paralegal. **Liberal arts:** Arts/sciences. **Mechanic/repair:** Automotive, industrial. **Personal/culinary services:** Aesthetician, cosmetic, cosmetology. **Protective services:** Criminal justice. **Public administration:** Human services. **Science technology:** Biological.

Most popular majors. Business/marketing 32%, computer/information sciences 6%, education 15%, health sciences 29%, liberal arts 6%.

Computing on campus. Online library, helpline available.

Student life. **Freshman orientation:** Mandatory. **Activities:** Radio station, student government, Student Nurses Association, Student Ambassador Program, Veterinary Medical Technician Student Organization.

Athletics. NJCAA. **Intercollegiate:** Basketball M, golf, softball, volleyball. **Intramural:** Basketball M, bowling, golf, softball, tennis M, volleyball.

Student services. Career counseling, student employment services, financial aid counseling, personal counseling, placement for graduates, veterans' counselor. **Physically disabled:** Services for visually, speech, hearing impaired. **Transfer:** Transfer adviser for students transferring to 4-year colleges.

Contact. E-mail: khoyle@cccc.edu
Phone: (919) 775-5401 Toll-free number: (800) 682-8353
Fax: (919) 718-7379
Ken Hoyle, Vice President of Student Services, Central Carolina Community College, 1105 Kelly Drive, Sanford, NC 27330

Central Piedmont Community College

Charlotte, North Carolina — **CB member**
www.cpcc.edu — **CB code: 5102**

- Public 2-year community college
- Commuter campus in very large city

General. Founded in 1963. Regionally accredited. **Enrollment:** 15,380 degree-seeking undergraduates; 3,226 non-degree-seeking students. **Degrees:** 908 associate awarded. **Location:** 247 miles from Atlanta. **Calendar:** Semester, extensive summer session. **Full-time faculty:** 342 total. **Part-time faculty:** 819 total.

Student profile. Among degree-seeking undergraduates, 56% enrolled in a transfer program, 44% enrolled in a vocational program, 5% already have a bachelor's degree or higher, 2,568 enrolled as first-time, first-year students.

Part-time:	58%	**Women:**	57%
Out-of-state:	2%	**25 or older:**	45%

Basis for selection. Open admission, but selective for some programs. Placement test scores used for admission to some programs with specific requirements.

High school preparation. Recommended units include English 4, mathematics 3, social studies 3 and science 3.

2008-2009 Annual costs. Tuition/fees: $1,458; $7,197 out-of-state. Per-credit charge: $42 in-state; $233 out-of-state. Books/supplies: $1,194. Personal expenses: $2,798.

Financial aid. **Need-based:** Need-based aid available for part-time students. **Non-need-based:** Scholarships awarded for academics, minority status.

Application procedures. **Admission:** No deadline. No application fee. Admission notification on a rolling basis. **Financial aid:** Priority date 4/1, closing date 6/1. FAFSA required. Applicants notified on a rolling basis.

Academics. **Special study options:** Cooperative education, cross-registration, distance learning, double major, dual enrollment of high school students, ESL, honors, independent study, internships, study abroad, weekend college. **Credit/placement by examination:** AP, CLEP, institutional tests. **Support services:** GED preparation and test center, learning center, reduced course load, remedial instruction, study skills assistance, tutoring, writing center.

Majors. **Agriculture:** Horticulture, turf management. **Business:** Accounting technology, administrative services, business admin, hospitality admin, international, management information systems, real estate, retailing, tourism/travel. **Communications technology:** Graphic/printing. **Computer sciences:** Database management, information technology, LAN/WAN management, programming, webmaster. **Construction:** Electrician. **Education:** Early childhood. **Engineering technology:** Architectural, civil, electrical, industrial management, mechanical, occupational safety, surveying. **Family/consumer sciences:** Child care. **Foreign languages:** Sign language interpretation. **Health:** Cardiovascular technology, clinical lab assistant, cytotechnology, dental hygiene, medical assistant, medical records technology, mental health services, nursing (RN), physical therapy assistant, respiratory therapy technology, substance abuse counseling. **Legal studies:** Legal secretary, paralegal. **Liberal arts:** Arts/sciences. **Mechanic/repair:** Automotive, diesel, heating/ac/refrig. **Parks/recreation:** Facilities management. **Personal/culinary services:** Chef training. **Production:** Machine shop technology, welding. **Protective services:** Corrections, fire safety technology. **Visual/performing arts:** Commercial/advertising art, interior design.

Most popular majors. Business/marketing 8%, health sciences 18%, liberal arts 49%.

Computing on campus. 2,591 workstations in library, computer center, student center. Commuter students can connect to campus network. Online course registration, helpline, wireless network available.

Student life. **Freshman orientation:** Available. **Activities:** Bands, campus ministries, choral groups, dance, drama, film society, international student organizations, literary magazine, music ensembles, musical theater, opera, radio station, student government, student newspaper, symphony orchestra, TV station, Afro-American Cultural Club, Baptist Student Union, Chess Club, Phi Theta Kappa.

Athletics. NJCAA. **Intramural:** Soccer.

Student services. Adult student services, chaplain/spiritual director, career counseling, student employment services, financial aid counseling, personal counseling, placement for graduates, veterans' counselor, women's services. **Physically disabled:** Services for visually, speech, hearing impaired. **Transfer:** Re-entry adviser, pre-admission transcript evaluation for new students. Transfer adviser, college fairs on campus for students transferring to 4-year colleges.

Contact. Phone: (704) 330-2722 Fax: (704) 330-6007
Linda McComb, Associate Dean of Admissions/Registration/Records, Central Piedmont Community College, Box 35009, Charlotte, NC 28235-5009

Coastal Carolina Community College

Jacksonville, North Carolina
www.coastalcarolina.edu — **CB code: 5134**

- Public 2-year community college
- Commuter campus in large town

General. Founded in 1964. Regionally accredited. Off-campus classes available at Camp Lejeune Marine Corps Base and New River Marine Corps Air Station. **Enrollment:** 3,913 degree-seeking undergraduates; 222 non-degree-seeking students. **Degrees:** 528 associate awarded. **Location:** 100 miles from Raleigh. **Calendar:** Semester, limited summer session. **Full-time faculty:** 127 total; 13% have terminal degrees, 9% minority, 56% women. **Part-time faculty:** 158 total; 11% have terminal degrees, 10% minority, 63% women. **Class size:** 67% < 20, 33% 20-39.

Student profile. Among degree-seeking undergraduates, 915 enrolled as first-time, first-year students, 780 transferred in from other institutions.

Part-time:	52%	**Hispanic American:**	9%
Out-of-state:	31%	**Native American:**	1%
Women:	65%	**International:**	1%
African American:	18%	**25 or older:**	44%
Asian American:	4%		

Transfer out. Colleges most students transferred to 2008: University of North Carolina - Wilmington, East Carolina University, North Carolina State University.

Basis for selection. Open admission, but selective for some programs. Admission to limited enrollment programs based on examination. **Adult students:** SAT/ACT scores not required. **Homeschooled:** Transcript of courses and grades required.

High school preparation. 20 units recommended. Recommended units include English 4, mathematics 3, social studies 2, history 1, science 3 (laboratory 1) and academic electives 6. Recommended units may vary by college.

2008-2009 Annual costs. Tuition/fees: $1,290; $7,029 out-of-state. Per-credit charge: $42 in-state; $233 out-of-state. Books/supplies: $1,382. Personal expenses: $1,934.

2007-2008 Financial aid. Need-based: Need-based aid available for part-time students. Work-study available nights, weekends and for part-time students. **Non-need-based:** Scholarships awarded for academics, state residency.

Application procedures. Admission: No deadline. No application fee. Admission notification on a rolling basis beginning on or about 2/15. **Financial aid:** Priority date 5/15; no closing date. FAFSA, institutional form required. Applicants notified on a rolling basis starting 5/15; must reply within 2 week(s) of notification.

Academics. Special study options: Cooperative education, distance learning, dual enrollment of high school students, independent study, internships, liberal arts/career combination. License preparation in dental hygiene, nursing, paramedic. **Credit/placement by examination:** AP, CLEP, IB, institutional tests. 30 credit hours maximum toward associate degree. **Support services:** GED preparation and test center, learning center, reduced course load, remedial instruction, tutoring.

Majors. Business: Accounting technology, administrative services, business admin, information resources management. **Computer sciences:** Information systems. **Education:** Early childhood. **Engineering technology:** Architectural. **Health:** Clinical lab technology, dental hygiene, EMT paramedic, nursing (RN). **Legal studies:** Paralegal. **Liberal arts:** Arts/sciences. **Mechanic/repair:** Electronics/electrical, heating/ac/refrig. **Protective services:** Fire safety technology, police science.

Most popular majors. Business/marketing 6%, health sciences 17%, liberal arts 57%.

Computing on campus. 720 workstations in library, computer center, student center. Commuter students can connect to campus network. Online library, helpline available.

Student life. Freshman orientation: Available. Preregistration for classes offered. Orientation sessions available throughout the month prior to start of each term. **Activities:** Concert band, choral groups, drama, music ensembles, student government, Phi Theta Kappa, Star of Life, Association of Nursing Students, social science club, Practical Nursing Students, fine arts society, Extreme Science, SGA, Fellowship of Christian Athletes.

Athletics. Intercollegiate: Soccer W.

Student services. Adult student services, alcohol/substance abuse counseling, career counseling, services for economically disadvantaged, student employment services, financial aid counseling, minority student services, personal counseling, placement for graduates, veterans' counselor. **Physically disabled:** Services for visually, speech, hearing impaired. **Transfer:** Transfer adviser, college fairs on campus for students transferring to 4-year colleges.

Contact. E-mail: herringd@coastalcarolina.edu
Phone: (910) 938-6332 Fax: (910) 455-2767
Don Herring, Division Chair for Admissions, Coastal Carolina Community College, 444 Western Boulevard, Jacksonville, NC 28546-6877

College of the Albemarle
Elizabeth City, North Carolina
www.albemarle.cc.nc.us **CB code: 5133**

- Public 2-year branch campus and community college
- Commuter campus in large town

General. Founded in 1960. Regionally accredited. Multi-campus institution with campuses in: Elizabeth City, Dare County, and Edenton-Chowan. **Enrollment:** 1,795 degree-seeking undergraduates. **Degrees:** 176 associate awarded. **ROTC:** Army. **Location:** 45 miles from Norfolk, Virginia. **Calendar:** Semester, limited summer session. **Full-time faculty:** 81 total; 6% have terminal degrees, 10% minority. **Part-time faculty:** 119 total; 8% have terminal degrees, 20% minority. **Special facilities:** Community theater, civic auditorium.

Student profile.

Out-of-state:	1%	**25 or older:**	43%

Transfer out. Colleges most students transferred to 2008: Elizabeth City State University, East Carolina University, North Carolina State University, UNC-Chapel Hill, UNC-Wilmington.

Basis for selection. Open admission, but selective for some programs. All degree-seeking students required to take placement test. Students may waive placement test if scores for SAT or ACT are acceptable. Limited enrollment programs have additional admissions criteria. Admission limited to fall semester for associate degree in nursing, practical nursing, associate degree nursing, electrical/electronics technology, AC/HR, machining technology, surgical technology, medical assisting, and phlebotomy. New students admitted to cosmetology program as spaces become available. Interview required for allied health programs.

High school preparation. Recommended units include English 4, mathematics 3, social studies 3, history 3, science 3 and academic electives 6.

2008-2009 Annual costs. Tuition/fees: $1,414; $7,535 out-of-state. Per-credit charge: $42 in-state; $233 out-of-state. Books/supplies: $1,000.

2007-2008 Financial aid. Need-based: Need-based aid available for part-time students. **Non-need-based:** Scholarships awarded for academics, art, leadership, minority status, music/drama, state residency. **Additional information:** Separate application must be submitted for COA Private Scholarships.

Application procedures. Admission: No deadline. No application fee. Application must be submitted on paper. Admission notification on a rolling basis. Application deadline for allied health January 15 prior to fall semester. **Financial aid:** Priority date 3/15; no closing date. FAFSA required. Applicants notified on a rolling basis starting 5/1; must reply within 2 week(s) of notification.

Academics. Special study options: Cooperative education, distance learning, double major, dual enrollment of high school students, ESL, honors, independent study, internships, liberal arts/career combination. Agreement with Elizabeth City State University to offer the first 2 years of Elementary Education. License preparation in nursing, real estate. **Credit/placement by examination:** AP, CLEP, institutional tests. 30 credit hours maximum toward associate degree. Credit by examination not granted until examinee has enrolled at COA and passed 12 credit hours with 2.0 or better grade point average. **Support services:** GED preparation and test center, learning center, reduced course load, remedial instruction, study skills assistance, tutoring, writing center.

Majors. Architecture: Technology. **Business:** Administrative services, business admin, office/clerical. **Computer sciences:** General, applications programming, information systems, networking, programming. **Conservation:** Fisheries. **Education:** General, early childhood. **Engineering:** Computer. **Engineering technology:** Electrical, heat/ac/refrig. **Health:** Clinical lab science, medical assistant, medical secretary, nursing (RN), office admin. **Legal studies:** Prelaw. **Liberal arts:** Arts/sciences. **Production:** Machine shop technology. **Protective services:** Law enforcement admin. **Visual/performing arts:** Art, dramatic.

Computing on campus. 475 workstations in library, computer center. Commuter students can connect to campus network. Online library, wireless network available.

Student life. Freshman orientation: Available. Preregistration for classes offered. Monthly information sessions held for all COA programs. **Activities:** Bands, drama, literary magazine, musical theater, student government, student newspaper, Phi Theta Kappa, Environmental club, Literacy Round Table, Nursing club, SADD.

Athletics. Intramural: Archery, badminton, baseball, basketball, bowling, football (non-tackle), golf, racquetball, sailing, soccer, softball, swimming, tennis, volleyball.

Student services. Adult student services, career counseling, services for economically disadvantaged, student employment services, financial aid counseling, personal counseling, placement for graduates, veterans' counselor. **Physically disabled:** Services for visually, speech, hearing impaired. **Transfer:** Pre-admission transcript evaluation for new students. College fairs on campus for students transferring to 4-year colleges.

Contact. Phone: (252) 335-0821 ext. 2290 Fax: (252) 335-2011
Kenneth Krentz, Assistant Dean for Admissions and Testing, College of the Albemarle, 1208 North Road Street, Elizabeth City, NC 27906-2327

Craven Community College

New Bern, North Carolina
www.cravencc.edu **CB code: 5148**

- Public 2-year community college
- Commuter campus in large town
- Interview required

General. Founded in 1965. Regionally accredited. Campuses in New Bern and Havelock. **Enrollment:** 2,695 degree-seeking undergraduates. **Degrees:** 323 associate awarded. **Location:** 100 miles from Raleigh, 45 miles from Greenville. **Calendar:** Semester, limited summer session. **Full-time faculty:** 81 total. **Part-time faculty:** 253 total. **Class size:** 69% < 20, 31% 20-39, less than 1% 40-49.

Student profile.

Out-of-state:	17%	**25 or older:**	50%

Transfer out. Colleges most students transferred to 2008: East Carolina University, University of North Carolina at Wilmington, North Carolina State University, Mount Olive College.

Basis for selection. Open admission, but selective for some programs. Tests in math, English and reading required for placement for degree-seeking students. Admission to nursing program based on school achievement record and test scores.

High school preparation. 20 units recommended. Recommended units include English 4, mathematics 3, social studies 1, history 1, science 3 (laboratory 1), foreign language 2 and academic electives 6.

2008-2009 Annual costs. Tuition/fees: $1,340; $7,079 out-of-state. Per-credit charge: $42 in-state; $233 out-of-state. Books/supplies: $700. Personal expenses: $1,056.

2007-2008 Financial aid. All financial aid based on need.

Application procedures. Admission: No deadline. No application fee. Admission notification on a rolling basis. **Financial aid:** Priority date 3/31; no closing date. FAFSA required. Applicants notified on a rolling basis starting 6/1.

Academics. Level 2 CRLA tutoring center. **Special study options:** Accelerated study, cooperative education, distance learning, double major, dual enrollment of high school students, independent study, internships, liberal arts/career combination, student-designed major, study abroad. Bachelor's degree programs available on campus. License preparation in aviation, nursing. **Credit/placement by examination:** AP, CLEP, institutional tests. 20 credit hours maximum toward associate degree. **Support services:** GED preparation and test center, learning center, reduced course load, remedial instruction, study skills assistance, tutoring, writing center.

Majors. Business: Accounting, business admin, management information systems, sales/distribution. **Computer sciences:** Applications programming, networking. **Education:** Teacher assistance. **Engineering technology:** Electrical, manufacturing. **Family/consumer sciences:** Child care. **Health:** Medical assistant, medical secretary, nursing (RN), office admin. **Legal studies:** Legal secretary. **Liberal arts:** Arts/sciences. **Mechanic/repair:** Automotive, heating/ac/refrig, industrial. **Protective services:** Law enforcement admin.

Computing on campus. 500 workstations in library, computer center.

Student life. Freshman orientation: Available. Preregistration for classes offered. **Activities:** Concert band, choral groups, drama, film society, literary magazine, music ensembles, student government, student newspaper, Phi Beta Lambda (business), cosmetology club, nursing club, accounting club, banking and marketing club, Spanish club, Bible club, criminal justice club, electronics club, learning community club.

Athletics. Intramural: Baseball M, basketball, bowling, football (non-tackle) M, golf, soccer, tennis, volleyball. **Team name:** Panthers.

Student services. Career counseling, student employment services, financial aid counseling, personal counseling, placement for graduates, veterans' counselor. **Physically disabled:** Services for visually, speech, hearing impaired. **Transfer:** Pre-admission transcript evaluation for new students. Transfer center, transfer adviser, college fairs on campus for students transferring to 4-year colleges.

Contact. Phone: (252) 638-7227 Fax: (252) 638-4649
Wanda Thomas, Director of Admissions and Counseling Services, Craven Community College, 800 College Court, New Bern, NC 28562

Davidson County Community College

Lexington, North Carolina
www.davidsonccc.edu **CB code: 5170**

- Public 2-year community college
- Commuter campus in large town

General. Founded in 1958. Regionally accredited. Davie Campus in Mocksville has 3 buildings and an emergency services training facility on 45 acres. **Enrollment:** 2,912 degree-seeking undergraduates. **Degrees:** 369 associate awarded. **Location:** 30 miles from Greensboro. **Calendar:** Semester, limited summer session. **Full-time faculty:** 98 total. **Part-time faculty:** 125 total. **Class size:** 59% < 20, 39% 20-39, less than 1% 40-49, less than 1% 50-99.

Student profile.

Out-of-state:	1%	**25 or older:**	46%

Transfer out. Colleges most students transferred to 2008: University of North Carolina-Greensboro, University of North Carolina-Charlotte, High Point University, Winston-Salem State University, Catawba College.

Basis for selection. Open admission, but selective for some programs. Admissions to nursing program under points system; based on test scores and grades. ASSET required unless acceptable test scores submitted.

High school preparation. Recommended units include English 4, mathematics 3, social studies 2, history 2, science 3 and foreign language 2.

2008-2009 Annual costs. Tuition/fees: $1,370; $7,109 out-of-state. Per-credit charge: $42 in-state; $233 out-of-state. Books/supplies: $1,000. Personal expenses: $600.

2007-2008 Financial aid. Need-based: Need-based aid available for part-time students. **Non-need-based:** Scholarships awarded for academics, leadership.

Application procedures. Admission: No deadline. No application fee. Admission notification on a rolling basis. Nursing program deadline 1/31, Allied Health program deadlines 3/15 to 5/15. **Financial aid:** Closing date 3/31. FAFSA, institutional form required. Applicants notified on a rolling basis starting 7/1; must reply within 2 week(s) of notification.

Academics. Special study options: Distance learning, dual enrollment of high school students, ESL, independent study. License preparation in nursing, paramedic, real estate. **Credit/placement by examination:** AP, CLEP, institutional tests. Students must complete 25% of hours required for graduation in residence. **Support services:** GED preparation and test center, learning center, pre-admission summer program, reduced course load, remedial instruction, study skills assistance, tutoring, writing center.

Majors. Biology: Zoology. **Business:** Accounting, business admin, human resources. **Computer sciences:** Information technology, networking, programming. **Education:** Early childhood. **Engineering technology:** Electrical. **Health:** Clinical lab technology, EMT paramedic, medical assistant, medical records technology, nursing (RN). **Legal studies:** Paralegal. **Liberal arts:** Arts/sciences. **Mechanic/repair:** Automotive. **Protective services:** Criminal justice, fire safety technology. **Other:** Community spanish interpreter.

Computing on campus. 450 workstations in library, computer center. Commuter students can connect to campus network. Helpline available.

Student life. Freshman orientation: Available. Preregistration for classes offered. **Activities:** Literary magazine, student government, criminal justice club, association of nursing students, Phi Theta Kappa, Rotaract, spanish club, cosmetology club, Christian organization, computer system technology association, future educators club.

Athletics. Intramural: Basketball, golf.

Student services. Career counseling, student employment services, financial aid counseling, on-campus daycare, personal counseling, placement for graduates, veterans' counselor. **Physically disabled:** Services for visually, speech, hearing impaired. **Transfer:** Pre-admission transcript evaluation for new students. Transfer adviser, college fairs on campus for students transferring to 4-year colleges.

Contact. E-mail: admissions@davidsonccc.edu
Phone: (336) 249-8186 ext. 6731 Fax: (336) 224-0240
Lori Blevins, Director of Admissions, Davidson County Community College, PO Box 1287, Lexington, NC 27293-1287

Durham Technical Community College

Durham, North Carolina
www.durhamtech.edu **CB code: 5172**

- Public 2-year community and technical college
- Commuter campus in small city

General. Founded in 1958. Regionally accredited. Most programs are structured to begin in fall and continue for 5 or 6 consecutive semesters. Satellite sites in northern Durham and Orange Counties. **Enrollment:** 3,050 degree-seeking undergraduates. **Degrees:** 299 associate awarded. **Location:** 25 miles from Raleigh, 50 miles from Greensboro. **Calendar:** Semester, limited summer session. **Full-time faculty:** 150 total. **Part-time faculty:** 390 total.

Transfer out. Colleges most students transferred to 2008: University of North Carolina - Chapel Hill, North Carolina Central University, North Carolina State University.

Basis for selection. Open admission, but selective for some programs. Placement testing required. ASSET and COMPASS used. Admission to some allied health programs based on placement test and completion of prerequisite courses. **Homeschooled:** Documentation of state recognition of home school required.

High school preparation. Algebra, chemistry, and biology required for allied health programs. Algebra and science courses recommended for most associate degree programs.

2008-2009 Annual costs. Tuition/fees: $1,340; $7,079 out-of-state. Per-credit charge: $42 in-state; $233 out-of-state. Personal expenses: $562.

Financial aid. Need-based: Need-based aid available for part-time students. Work-study available nights and for part-time students. **Non-need-based:** Scholarships awarded for academics, minority status, state residency. **Additional information:** Special funds available to single parents for tuition, fees, books, supplies and child care expenses.

Application procedures. Admission: Closing date 8/8 (receipt date). No application fee. Admission notification on a rolling basis. **Financial aid:** FAFSA required. Applicants notified on a rolling basis starting 1/31; must reply within 3 week(s) of notification.

Academics. Special study options: Distance learning, dual enrollment of high school students, ESL, weekend college. License preparation in nursing, occupational therapy, paramedic, real estate. **Credit/placement by examination:** AP, CLEP, institutional tests. Maximum of 10% of total curriculum hours of credit by examination may be counted toward degree. **Support services:** GED preparation and test center, learning center, remedial instruction, study skills assistance, tutoring.

Majors. Architecture: Technology. **Biology:** Biotechnology. **Business:** Accounting, administrative services, business admin, operations. **Computer sciences:** Applications programming, data processing, information technology, networking, programming, security, systems analysis. **Education:** Early childhood, teacher assistance. **Engineering:** Electrical. **Engineering technology:** Architectural, drafting, electrical. **Health:** Dental lab technology, environmental health, medical records admin, medical secretary, nursing (RN), occupational health, occupational therapy assistant, office admin, optician, respiratory therapy assistant, respiratory therapy technology. **Legal studies:** Paralegal. **Liberal arts:** Arts/sciences. **Mechanic/repair:** Automotive, electronics/electrical.

Student life. Freshman orientation: Available. Preregistration for classes offered. **Activities:** Drama, literary magazine, student government.

Student services. Career counseling, services for economically disadvantaged, financial aid counseling, minority student services, personal counseling, veterans' counselor. **Physically disabled:** Services for visually, speech, hearing impaired. **Transfer:** College fairs on campus for students transferring to 4-year colleges.

Contact. E-mail: admissions@durhamtech.edu
Phone: (919) 686-3333 Fax: (919) 686-3669
Penny Augustine, Director of Admissions & Student Records, Durham Technical Community College, 1637 Lawson Street, Durham, NC 27703

Edgecombe Community College

Tarboro, North Carolina **CB member**
www.edgecombe.edu **CB code: 5199**

- Public 2-year community college
- Commuter campus in large town

General. Founded in 1967. Regionally accredited. Branch campus in Rocky Mount. **Enrollment:** 2,579 degree-seeking undergraduates. **Degrees:** 210 associate awarded. **Location:** 75 miles from Raleigh. **Calendar:** Semester, limited summer session. **Full-time faculty:** 79 total; 11% have terminal degrees, 48% minority. **Part-time faculty:** 115 total; 7% have terminal degrees, 34% minority. **Class size:** 77% < 20, 20% 20-39, 2% 40-49, less than 1% 50-99. **Special facilities:** Wildlife preserve.

Student profile.

Out-of-state:	1%	**25 or older:**	46%

Transfer out. Colleges most students transferred to 2008: East Carolina University, Pitt Community College, NC Wesleyan College, North Carolina Agricultural and Technical State University.

Basis for selection. Open admission, but selective for some programs. Special requirements for allied health programs and networking technology. TEAS Nursing Test required for nursing applicants.

2008-2009 Annual costs. Tuition/fees: $1,284; $7,023 out-of-state. Per-credit charge: $42 in-state; $220 out-of-state. Books/supplies: $750. Personal expenses: $1,800.

2008-2009 Financial aid. All financial aid based on need. 79% of total undergraduate aid awarded as scholarships/grants, 21% as loans/jobs. Need-based aid available for part-time students.

Application procedures. Admission: No deadline. No application fee. Admission notification on a rolling basis. **Financial aid:** No deadline. FAFSA, institutional form required. Applicants notified on a rolling basis starting 8/15; must reply within 3 week(s) of notification.

Academics. Special study options: Cooperative education, distance learning, double major, dual enrollment of high school students, ESL, independent study. License preparation in nursing, radiology. **Credit/placement by examination:** AP, CLEP, institutional tests. 24 credit hours maximum toward associate degree. **Support services:** GED preparation and test center, learning center, reduced course load, remedial instruction, study skills assistance, tutoring.

Majors. Business: Accounting, administrative services, business admin. **Computer sciences:** General, information systems, networking. **Education:** Early childhood, teacher assistance. **Engineering:** Manufacturing. **Engineering technology:** Electrical, manufacturing, plastics. **Family/consumer sciences:** Child care. **Health:** Medical assistant, medical radiologic technology/radiation therapy, medical records technology, nursing (RN), respiratory therapy technology. **Liberal arts:** Arts/sciences. **Personal/culinary services:** Mortuary science. **Protective services:** Criminal justice.

Most popular majors. Business/marketing 13%, education 14%, health sciences 48%, liberal arts 13%.

Computing on campus. 120 workstations in library, computer center. Online library, helpline available.

Student life. Activities: Drama, student government.

Athletics. Team name: Eagles.

Student services. Alcohol/substance abuse counseling, career counseling, student employment services, financial aid counseling, minority student services, personal counseling, placement for graduates, veterans' counselor. **Physically disabled:** Services for visually, hearing impaired. **Transfer:** Pre-admission transcript evaluation for new students. Transfer adviser, college fairs on campus for students transferring to 4-year colleges.

Contact. Phone: (252) 823-5166 ext. 254 Fax: (252) 823-6817
Ginny McLendon, Dean of Enrollment Management, Edgecombe Community College, 2009 West Wilson Street, Tarboro, NC 27886

Fayetteville Technical Community College
Fayetteville, North Carolina
www.faytechcc.edu **CB code: 5208**

- Public 2-year community and technical college
- Commuter campus in large city

General. Founded in 1961. Regionally accredited. Offers the only funeral services curriculum in North Carolina community college system. Offers Imaging 3-D program. **Enrollment:** 8,195 degree-seeking undergraduates; 2,330 non-degree-seeking students. **Degrees:** 860 associate awarded. **Location:** 60 miles from Raleigh. **Calendar:** Semester, limited summer session. **Full-time faculty:** 300 total; 7% have terminal degrees, 25% minority, 58% women. **Part-time faculty:** 519 total; 39% minority, 60% women. **Class size:** 65% < 20, 33% 20-39, 1% 40-49, less than 1% 50-99. **Special facilities:** Center for applied technology; virtual college center; horticulture educational center. **Partnerships:** Formal partnership with GoArmyEd.

Student profile. Among degree-seeking undergraduates, 16% enrolled in a transfer program, 84% enrolled in a vocational program, 4% already have a bachelor's degree or higher, 1,877 enrolled as first-time, first-year students, 635 transferred in from other institutions.

Part-time:	63%	**Women:**	73%
Out-of-state:	11%	**25 or older:**	87%

Transfer out. Colleges most students transferred to 2008: Forsyth Technical Community College, Central Piedmont Community College, Wilson Technical Community College, Pitt Community College, Catawba Community College.

Basis for selection. Open admission, but selective for some programs. Admission of health applicants based on transcripts, academic average, interview, and institutional assessment of reading, writing, and math. Group interview required for health and paralegal programs. **Learning Disabled:** Documentation of disability required if applicant desires any academic accommodations.

High school preparation. Engineering and College Transfer programs require 2 algebra. Health programs require up to 2 algebra, 1 biology, and 1 chemistry.

2008-2009 Annual costs. Tuition/fees: $1,404; $7,586 out-of-state. Per-credit charge: $42 in-state; $233 out-of-state. Books/supplies: $1,750. Personal expenses: $3,800.

2007-2008 Financial aid. Need-based: 53% of total undergraduate aid awarded as scholarships/grants, 47% as loans/jobs. Need-based aid available for part-time students. Work-study available for part-time students.

Application procedures. Admission: No deadline. No application fee. Admission notification on a rolling basis. Deadline for health program applicants is January 30. Applicants admitted to these programs must reply immediately upon notification. **Financial aid:** Priority date 6/1, closing date 7/15. FAFSA required. Applicants notified on a rolling basis starting 4/1.

Academics. Tutoring is a limited offering available to students enrolled in vocational education programs. **Special study options:** Cooperative education, distance learning, double major, dual enrollment of high school students, ESL, independent study, liberal arts/career combination, student-designed major, weekend college. License preparation in dental hygiene, nursing, paramedic, physical therapy, radiology, real estate. **Credit/placement by examination:** AP, CLEP, institutional tests. **Support services:** GED preparation and test center, learning center, pre-admission summer program, reduced course load, remedial instruction, study skills assistance, tutoring.

Majors. Agriculture: Horticulture. **Architecture:** Technology. **Business:** Accounting, banking/financial services, business admin, e-commerce, hotel/motel admin, human resources, marketing, office management, operations. **Computer sciences:** Information systems, information technology, networking, programming, security, web page design. **Construction:** General, electrician. **Education:** General, early childhood, elementary, special. **Engineering technology:** Architectural, civil, electrical, surveying. **Foreign languages:** Translation. **Health:** Dental hygiene, EMT paramedic, management/clinical assistant, medical radiologic technology/radiation therapy, medical records technology, nuclear medical technology, nursing (RN), office admin, physical therapy assistant, radiologic technology/medical imaging, respiratory therapy technology, speech-language pathology assistant, surgical technology. **Legal studies:** Paralegal. **Liberal arts:** Arts/sciences. **Mechanic/repair:** Automotive, heating/ac/refrig. **Personal/culinary services:** Chef training, mortuary science. **Production:** Machine shop technology. **Protective services:** Criminal justice, emergency management/homeland security, fire safety technology, forensics. **Public administration:** General. **Science technology:** Biological. **Visual/performing arts:** Commercial/advertising art. **Other:** Occupational technology, Postal service technology.

Most popular majors. Business/marketing 14%, education 9%, health sciences 26%, liberal arts 26%.

Computing on campus. 200 workstations in library, computer center, student center. Online course registration, online library, helpline, student web hosting available.

Student life. Freshman orientation: Mandatory. Preregistration for classes offered. Two hours, held the first day of new student registration. **Activities:** Drama, international student organizations, student government, student newspaper, TV station, African-American Heritage Club, Democratic club, Latino cultural organization, Parents for Higher Education, Students Against Destructive Decisions, Republican Club.

Athletics. Intramural: Basketball, bowling, football (non-tackle), golf, softball, tennis, volleyball.

Student services. Alcohol/substance abuse counseling, career counseling, financial aid counseling, on-campus daycare, personal counseling, placement for graduates, veterans' counselor. **Physically disabled:** Services for visually, speech, hearing impaired. **Transfer:** Transfer adviser, college fairs on campus for students transferring to 4-year colleges.

Contact. E-mail: kelleyj@faytechcc.edu
Phone: (910) 678-8274 Fax: (910) 678-8407
James Kelley, Director of Admissions, Fayetteville Technical Community College, PO Box 35236, Fayetteville, NC 28303-0236

Forsyth Technical Community College
Winston-Salem, North Carolina **CB member**
www.forsythtech.edu **CB code: 5234**

- Public 2-year community and technical college
- Commuter campus in small city

General. Founded in 1964. Regionally accredited. **Enrollment:** 6,749 degree-seeking undergraduates; 1,119 non-degree-seeking students. **Degrees:** 760 associate awarded. **Location:** 32 miles from Greensboro, 85 miles from Charlotte. **Calendar:** Semester, extensive summer session. **Full-time faculty:** 183 total. **Part-time faculty:** 750 total.

Student profile. Among degree-seeking undergraduates, 1,455 enrolled as first-time, first-year students.

Part-time:	53%	**Asian American:**	1%
Out-of-state:	1%	**Hispanic American:**	4%
Women:	64%	**Native American:**	1%
African American:	26%		

Transfer out. Colleges most students transferred to 2008: Winston-Salem State University, Gardner-Webb University, High Point University, Appalachian State University, North Carolina A&T State University.

Basis for selection. Open admission, but selective for some programs. Admission to health program based on school record and test scores. Health information session attendance required. SAT or ACT used for admission to health and developmental programs and for placement in other programs. **Homeschooled:** NCDPI registration information or similar information from the respective state's department of education authorizing the home school to provide instruction.

High school preparation. Algebra I required for allied health and engineering programs. Biology and chemistry required for allied health programs.

2008-2009 Annual costs. Tuition/fees: $1,476; $7,598 out-of-state. Per-credit charge: $42 in-state; $233 out-of-state. Books/supplies: $904. Personal expenses: $1,150.

2007-2008 Financial aid. Need-based: Need-based aid available for part-time students. Work-study available nights and for part-time students. **Non-need-based:** Scholarships awarded for academics, state residency. **Additional information:** Apply for aid as close to January 1 as possible for best consideration.

Application procedures. Admission: No deadline. No application fee. Admission notification on a rolling basis. **Financial aid:** Priority date 6/1; no closing date. FAFSA, institutional form required. Applicants notified on a rolling basis starting 7/1; must reply within 2 week(s) of notification.

Academics. Special study options: Cooperative education, cross-registration, distance learning, double major, dual enrollment of high school students, ESL, exchange student, external degree, honors, independent study, internships, liberal arts/career combination, student-designed major. License preparation in dental hygiene, nursing, radiology, real estate. **Credit/placement by examination:** AP, CLEP, institutional tests. **Support services:** GED preparation and test center, learning center, pre-admission summer program, reduced course load, remedial instruction, study skills assistance, tutoring, writing center.

Majors. Agriculture: Horticulture. **Business:** Accounting, business admin, finance, office/clerical. **Computer sciences:** Applications programming, data entry. **Education:** Early childhood, science. **Engineering technology:** Architectural, drafting, electrical, robotics. **Health:** Licensed practical nurse, medical assistant, medical radiologic technology/radiation therapy, nuclear medical technology, nursing (RN), respiratory therapy technology, sonography. **Legal studies:** Paralegal. **Liberal arts:** Arts/sciences. **Protective services:** Law enforcement admin.

Computing on campus. 400 workstations in library, computer center. Online library, wireless network available.

Student life. Freshman orientation: Mandatory. Preregistration for classes offered. **Activities:** Student government, student newspaper, Circle-K, Afro-American Society, minority male mentoring program, women's center.

Athletics. Intercollegiate: Basketball M, softball. **Intramural:** Basketball, bowling, golf, softball, volleyball. **Team name:** Tech Tigers.

Student services. Adult student services, alcohol/substance abuse counseling, career counseling, services for economically disadvantaged, student employment services, financial aid counseling, health services, minority student services, personal counseling, placement for graduates, veterans' counselor, women's services. **Physically disabled:** Services for visually, speech, hearing impaired. **Transfer:** Transfer adviser, college fairs on campus for students transferring to 4-year colleges.

Contact. E-mail: admissions@forsythtech.edu
Phone: (336) 734-7253 Fax: (336) 734-7291
Jewel Cherry, Dean of Enrollment Management, Forsyth Technical Community College, 2100 Silas Creek Parkway, Winston-Salem, NC 27103

Gaston College
Dallas, North Carolina
www.gaston.cc.nc.us **CB code: 5262**

- Public 2-year community college
- Commuter campus in small town

General. Founded in 1963. Regionally accredited. Branch campus at Lincolnton. **Enrollment:** 2,040 full-time, degree-seeking students. **Degrees:** 497 associate awarded. **Location:** 25 miles from Charlotte. **Calendar:** Semester, limited summer session. **Full-time faculty:** 138 total. **Part-time faculty:** 386 total.

Student profile.

Out-of-state:	1%	**25 or older:**	54%

Basis for selection. Open admission, but selective for some programs. Admission to health services programs, including nursing, based on ACT scores and interview. Basic literacy must be demonstrated, after admission, in order to take certain courses. ACT required for health services programs. Interview recommended for emergency medical technician, medical assistant, nursing programs; audition recommended for music programs; portfolio recommended for art programs.

2008-2009 Annual costs. Tuition/fees: $1,300; $7,039 out-of-state. Per-credit charge: $42 in-state; $233 out-of-state. Books/supplies: $1,000. Personal expenses: $1,000.

Financial aid. Need-based: Work-study available for part-time students. **Non-need-based:** Scholarships awarded for academics, state residency. **Additional information:** Grants/scholarships available for women pursuing nontraditional roles.

Application procedures. Admission: No deadline. No application fee. Admission notification on a rolling basis. **Financial aid:** Priority date 3/15; no closing date. FAFSA, institutional form required. Applicants notified on a rolling basis.

Academics. Special study options: Cooperative education, cross-registration, distance learning, double major, dual enrollment of high school students, ESL, independent study, internships, weekend college. **Credit/placement by examination:** CLEP, institutional tests. 18 credit hours maximum toward associate degree. **Support services:** GED preparation and test center, learning center, reduced course load, remedial instruction, study skills assistance, tutoring, writing center.

Majors. Architecture: Technology. **Business:** Accounting, administrative services, business admin. **Communications:** Broadcast journalism. **Computer sciences:** Applications programming, information technology, programming. **Education:** Early childhood. **Engineering technology:** Architectural, biomedical, civil, computer, electrical, industrial. **Health:** Dietetic technician, EMT paramedic, massage therapy, medical assistant, medical secretary, nursing (RN), office admin, veterinary technology/assistant. **Legal studies:** Legal secretary, paralegal. **Liberal arts:** Arts/sciences. **Personal/culinary services:** Cosmetic. **Protective services:** Fire safety technology. **Public administration:** Social work.

Computing on campus. 233 workstations in library, computer center.

Student life. Freshman orientation: Available. **Activities:** Literary magazine, music ensembles, radio station, student government.

Student services. Adult student services, career counseling, student employment services, financial aid counseling, on-campus daycare, placement for graduates, veterans' counselor. **Physically disabled:** Services for visually, speech, hearing impaired. **Transfer:** Transfer adviser, college fairs on campus for students transferring to 4-year colleges.

Contact. E-mail: wray.michelle@gaston.edu
Phone: (704) 922-6214 Fax: (704) 922-2344
Michelle Wray, Director of Admissions/Enrollment Management, Gaston College, 201 Highway 321 South, Dallas, NC 28034-1499

Guilford Technical Community College
Jamestown, North Carolina
www.gtcc.edu **CB code: 5275**

- Public 2-year community college
- Commuter campus in large city

General. Founded in 1958. Regionally accredited. Campuses in Greensboro and High Point. **Enrollment:** 7,501 degree-seeking undergraduates. **Degrees:** 736 associate awarded. **ROTC:** Army, Naval, Air Force. **Location:** 2 miles from Greensboro, 5 miles from High Point. **Calendar:** Semester, limited summer session. **Full-time faculty:** 248 total. **Part-time faculty:** 269 total. **Special facilities:** Observatory.

Student profile.

Out-of-state:	2%	**25 or older:**	43%

Transfer out. Colleges most students transferred to 2008: University of North Carolina-Greensboro, University of North Carolina-Charlotte, North Carolina A&T, University of North Carolina-Chapel Hill, North Carolina State University.

Basis for selection. Open admission, but selective for some programs. Admission to allied health programs is highly competitive. Each program has specific requirements that must be met to be considered for admission. **Learning Disabled:** Contact Disability Access Services office.

High school preparation. Allied health programs have specific course requirements that vary according to program.

2008-2009 Annual costs. Tuition/fees: $1,417; $7,156 out-of-state. Per-credit charge: $42 in-state; $233 out-of-state. Books/supplies: $900. Personal expenses: $1,151.

2007-2008 Financial aid. Need-based: 67% of total undergraduate aid awarded as scholarships/grants, 33% as loans/jobs. Need-based aid available for part-time students. Work-study available for part-time students.

Application procedures. Admission: No deadline. No application fee. Admission notification on a rolling basis. Applicants for limited enrollment programs (nursing, aviation maintenance/mechanic, dental hygiene, dental assistant, medical assistant, surgical technology cosmetology, emergency medical science) advised to apply before December 31. **Financial aid:** Priority date 3/15; no closing date. FAFSA required. Applicants notified on a rolling basis starting 7/1; must reply within 2 week(s) of notification.

Academics. Special study options: Cooperative education, cross-registration, distance learning, dual enrollment of high school students, ESL, independent study, internships. License preparation in aviation, dental hygiene, nursing, paramedic, physical therapy, real estate. **Credit/placement by examination:** AP, CLEP, IB, institutional tests. 60 credit hours maximum toward associate degree. **Support services:** GED preparation and test center, learning center, reduced course load, remedial instruction, study skills assistance, tutoring, writing center.

Majors. **Agriculture:** Turf management. **Business:** Accounting technology, business admin, executive assistant, human resources, management information systems. **Communications technology:** Recording arts. **Computer sciences:** Information systems. **Construction:** Electrician, maintenance. **Education:** General, early childhood. **Engineering technology:** Architectural, civil, electrical, mechanical, plastics, surveying. **Health:** Dental hygiene, EMT paramedic, medical assistant, mental health services, nursing (RN), physical therapy assistant, substance abuse counseling, surgical technology. **Legal studies:** Paralegal. **Liberal arts:** Arts/sciences. **Mechanic/repair:** Automotive, avionics, heating/ac/refrig. **Personal/culinary services:** Cosmetic. **Production:** Machine shop technology. **Protective services:** Criminal justice, fire safety technology. **Science technology:** Chemical. **Transportation:** Airline/commercial pilot. **Visual/performing arts:** Commercial/advertising art, music management.

Computing on campus. 130 workstations in library, computer center. Online library, helpline, repair service, wireless network available.

Student life. **Freshman orientation:** Available. **Activities:** Drama, student government, student newspaper, American Muslim student association, Ambassadors for Christ, international student association, market place of ideas (political), Nurses Christian Fellowship, veterans and students organization, Black student union, single parent club, students in free enterprise.

Athletics. NJCAA. **Intercollegiate:** Basketball M, volleyball W. **Team name:** Titans.

Student services. Career counseling, student employment services, financial aid counseling, on-campus daycare, personal counseling, placement for graduates, veterans' counselor. **Physically disabled:** Services for visually, speech, hearing impaired. **Transfer:** Transfer adviser, college fairs on campus for students transferring to 4-year colleges.

Contact. E-mail: jmgroome@gtcc.edu
Phone: (336) 334-4822 ext. 5350 Fax: (336) 819-2022
Jesse Cross, Director of Admissions, Guilford Technical Community College, PO Box 309, Jamestown, NC 27282

Halifax Community College

Weldon, North Carolina
www.hcc.cc.nc.us **CB code: 0621**

- Public 2-year community college
- Small town

General. Founded in 1967. Regionally accredited. **Enrollment:** 974 degree-seeking undergraduates. **Degrees:** 120 associate awarded. **Location:** 83 miles from Raleigh. **Calendar:** Semester, limited summer session. **Full-time faculty:** 65 total. **Part-time faculty:** 99 total. **Special facilities:** Performing arts auditorium.

Basis for selection. Open admission, but selective for some programs. Special requirements for nursing and allied health programs.

High school preparation. High school chemistry or equivalent and developmental mathematics required for nursing applicants.

2008-2009 Annual costs. Tuition/fees: $1,462; $7,584 out-of-state. Per-credit charge: $42 in-state; $233 out-of-state. Books/supplies: $500. Personal expenses: $896.

Application procedures. **Admission:** No deadline. No application fee. Admission notification on a rolling basis. **Financial aid:** Priority date 6/1; no closing date. Applicants notified on a rolling basis starting 8/1; must reply within 2 week(s) of notification.

Academics. **Special study options:** Dual enrollment of high school students, independent study, internships. **Credit/placement by examination:** CLEP, institutional tests. **Support services:** Learning center, reduced course load, remedial instruction, tutoring.

Majors. **Business:** Accounting, business admin, office management, office technology, office/clerical. **Communications:** Advertising. **Computer sciences:** General. **Conservation:** Wood science. **Education:** Early childhood, multi-level teacher, teacher assistance. **Engineering technology:** Electrical. **Health:** Clinical lab technology, medical secretary, nursing (RN), phlebotomy. **Liberal arts:** Arts/sciences. **Mechanic/repair:** Industrial. **Production:** Welding. **Public administration:** Human services, social work. **Visual/performing arts:** Commercial/advertising art, interior design.

Most popular majors. Business/marketing 11%, engineering/engineering technologies 18%, health sciences 29%, liberal arts 15%, security/protective services 14%, visual/performing arts 8%.

Computing on campus. 100 workstations in computer center.

Student life. **Freshman orientation:** Available. Preregistration for classes offered. **Activities:** Student government, student newspaper.

Student services. Career counseling, student employment services, personal counseling, placement for graduates, veterans' counselor. **Transfer:** Transfer adviser, college fairs on campus for students transferring to 4-year colleges.

Contact. E-mail: vassorc@halifax.hcc.cc.nc.us
Phone: (252) 536-7220 Fax: (252) 538-4311
Cathy Vassor, Director of Admissions, Halifax Community College, Drawer 809, Weldon, NC 27890

Haywood Community College

Clyde, North Carolina
www.haywood.edu **CB code: 5289**

- Public 2-year community and technical college
- Commuter campus in rural community

General. Founded in 1965. Regionally accredited. **Enrollment:** 1,453 degree-seeking undergraduates. **Degrees:** 193 associate awarded. **Location:** 25 miles from Asheville. **Calendar:** Semester, extensive summer session. **Full-time faculty:** 70 total. **Part-time faculty:** 135 total. **Class size:** 85% < 20, 14% 20-39, less than 1% 40-49.

Student profile.

Out-of-state:	14%	**25 or older:**	39%

Transfer out. **Colleges most students transferred to 2008:** Western Carolina University, Appalachian State University, University of North Carolina - Asheville.

Basis for selection. Open admission, but selective for some programs. Completion of Accuplacer, SAT score of 500 or higher on each section, ACT composite score of 21 or higher, or official transcript with "C" or better in college-level English and algebra required. Admission to nursing program based on admission test scores, high school record, GPA, prerequisite courses, and health occupations aptitude examination. Informational interview required for electrical engineering technology, manufacturing engineering technology, cosmetology, and professional crafts programs. **Learning Disabled:** Accommodations made upon request.

High school preparation. Algebra, biology and chemistry required for nursing. Algebra recommended for electrical and manufacturing engineering, microcomputer systems and college transfer.

2008-2009 Annual costs. Tuition/fees: $1,394; $7,516 out-of-state. Per-credit charge: $42 in-state; $233 out-of-state. Books/supplies: $1,000. Personal expenses: $1,656.

2007-2008 Financial aid. **Need-based:** Need-based aid available for part-time students. Work-study available for part-time students. **Non-need-based:** Scholarships awarded for academics. **Additional information:** Complete FAFSA by priority filing date for consideration for institutional scholarships.

Application procedures. **Admission:** No deadline. No application fee. Admission notification on a rolling basis. **Financial aid:** Priority date 4/1; no closing date. FAFSA, institutional form required. Applicants notified on a rolling basis starting 4/15; must reply within 2 week(s) of notification.

Academics. **Special study options:** Cooperative education, distance learning, dual enrollment of high school students, independent study, internships. **Credit/placement by examination:** CLEP, institutional tests. 18 credit hours maximum toward associate degree. **Support services:** GED preparation and test center, learning center, reduced course load, remedial instruction, tutoring.

Majors. **Agriculture:** Horticulture. **Business:** Accounting, administrative services, business admin. **Computer sciences:** Applications programming, networking. **Conservation:** Fisheries, forest resources, forestry, wildlife, wood science. **Construction:** Electrician, maintenance. **Engineering:** Computer. **Engineering technology:** Electrical, industrial management. **Family/consumer sciences:** Child care. **Health:** Medical assistant, nursing (RN). **Liberal arts:** Arts/sciences. **Mechanic/repair:** Automotive. **Personal/culinary services:** Cosmetic. **Production:** Woodworking. **Protective services:** Criminal justice. **Visual/performing arts:** Ceramics, fiber arts, metal/jewelry.

Most popular majors. Agriculture 6%, business/marketing 10%, engineering/engineering technologies 7%, family/consumer sciences 6%, health sciences 10%, liberal arts 15%, natural resources/environmental science 19%, trade and industry 8%, visual/performing arts 8%.

Computing on campus. 10 workstations in library.

Student life. **Freshman orientation:** Available. Preregistration for classes offered. **Activities:** Student government, Phi Theta Kappa, Phi Beta Lambda.

Athletics. **Intramural:** Basketball, bowling, football (non-tackle), softball, volleyball.

Student services. Career counseling, student employment services, financial aid counseling, on-campus daycare, personal counseling, placement for graduates, veterans' counselor. **Physically disabled:** Services for visually, speech, hearing impaired. **Transfer:** Transfer adviser for students transferring to 4-year colleges.

Contact. E-mail: drowland@haywood.cc.nc.us
Phone: (828) 627-4505 Toll-free number: (866) 468-6422
Fax: (828) 627-4513
Jennifer Herrera, Director of Enrollment Management, Haywood Community College, 185 Freelander Drive, Clyde, NC 28721-9454

Isothermal Community College

Spindale, North Carolina
www.isothermal.edu **CB code: 5319**

- Public 2-year community college
- Commuter campus in small town

General. Founded in 1964. Regionally accredited. **Enrollment:** 1,652 degree-seeking undergraduates; 672 non-degree-seeking students. **Degrees:** 202 associate awarded. **Location:** 65 miles from Charlotte, 48 miles from Asheville. **Calendar:** Semester, extensive summer session. **Full-time faculty:** 74 total. **Part-time faculty:** 60 total. **Class size:** 73% < 20, 27% 20-39.

Student profile. Among degree-seeking undergraduates, 44% enrolled in a transfer program, 56% enrolled in a vocational program, 274 enrolled as first-time, first-year students, 106 transferred in from other institutions.

Part-time:	41%	**Hispanic American:**	2%
Women:	62%	**25 or older:**	44%
African American:	14%		

Basis for selection. Open admission. **Homeschooled:** Copy of license to operate as provided by the state required.

2008-2009 Annual costs. Tuition/fees: $1,298; $7,037 out-of-state. Per-credit charge: $42 in-state; $233 out-of-state. Books/supplies: $728. Personal expenses: $666.

2007-2008 Financial aid. Need-based: Need-based aid available for part-time students. Work-study available nights and for part-time students. **Non-need-based:** Scholarships awarded for academics, job skills, leadership, minority status, music/drama, state residency.

Application procedures. Admission: No deadline. No application fee. Admission notification on a rolling basis. **Financial aid:** Priority date 5/31; no closing date. FAFSA, institutional form required. Applicants notified on a rolling basis starting 4/30; must reply within 4 week(s) of notification.

Academics. Special study options: Cooperative education, distance learning, dual enrollment of high school students, ESL, honors, independent study. Bachelor's degree programs available on campus. License preparation in nursing, real estate. **Credit/placement by examination:** AP, CLEP, institutional tests. 12 credit hours maximum toward associate degree. **Support services:** GED preparation and test center, learning center, pre-admission summer program, reduced course load, remedial instruction, tutoring.

Majors. Business: Banking/financial services, business admin, e-commerce, marketing, office management, operations. **Communications technology:** Radio/tv. **Computer sciences:** Applications programming, information systems, information technology, networking, programming, security. **Construction:** General, electrician. **Education:** Early childhood, elementary. **Engineering technology:** Computer, electrical, mechanical, mechanical drafting, plastics. **Health:** Nursing (RN), office admin. **Legal studies:** Paralegal. **Liberal arts:** Arts/sciences. **Mechanic/repair:** Auto body. **Personal/culinary services:** Cosmetic. **Production:** Machine shop technology, welding. **Protective services:** Criminal justice. **Visual/performing arts:** Commercial/advertising art, music. **Other:** Manufacturing technology.

Most popular majors. Business/marketing 12%, computer/information sciences 6%, education 7%, engineering/engineering technologies 20%, health sciences 24%, liberal arts 18%, trade and industry 6%.

Computing on campus. 44 workstations in library, computer center. Wireless network available.

Student life. Freshman orientation: Available. Preregistration for classes offered. **Activities:** Choral groups, drama, literary magazine, radio station, student government, student newspaper, TV station, Afro-American club, Phi Theta Kappa, Phi Beta Lambda.

Athletics. Intramural: Basketball, football (non-tackle), volleyball.

Student services. Career counseling, health services, placement for graduates, veterans' counselor. **Transfer:** College fairs on campus for students transferring to 4-year colleges.

Contact. Phone: (828) 286-3636 ext. 288 Fax: (828) 286-8109
Maggie Killoran, Director, Enrollment Management, Isothermal Community College, PO Box 804, Spindale, NC 28160-0804

James Sprunt Community College

Kenansville, North Carolina
www.jamessprunt.edu **CB code: 6256**

- Public 2-year community college
- Commuter campus in rural community

General. Founded in 1964. Regionally accredited. **Enrollment:** 926 degree-seeking undergraduates; 286 non-degree-seeking students. **Degrees:** 163 associate awarded. **Location:** 75 miles from Raleigh, 45 miles from Wilmington. **Calendar:** Semester, limited summer session. **Full-time faculty:** 51 total; 4% have terminal degrees, 10% minority, 63% women. **Part-time faculty:** 53 total; 2% have terminal degrees, 13% minority, 40% women. **Class size:** 82% < 20, 17% 20-39, less than 1% 40-49, less than 1% 50-99.

Student profile. Among degree-seeking undergraduates, 29% enrolled in a transfer program, 70% enrolled in a vocational program, 1% already have a bachelor's degree or higher, 223 enrolled as first-time, first-year students, 258 transferred in from other institutions.

Part-time:	41%	**Asian American:**	1%
Out-of-state:	1%	**Hispanic American:**	3%
Women:	69%	**25 or older:**	49%
African American:	41%		

Transfer out. 83% of students enrolled in the transfer program go on to 4-year colleges. **Colleges most students transferred to 2008:** University of North Carolina at Wilmington, East Carolina University, Mount Olive College, North Carolina State University, Fayetteville State University.

Basis for selection. Open admission, but selective for some programs. Admission to nursing programs based on test scores and high school or transfer courses. 2.0 GPA in biology, chemistry, and algebra required. SAT or ACT accepted in lieu of academic placement tests. Nursing Entrance Test (NET) required for nursing applicants. Credit may be awarded for graphic arts classes based on portfolio. **Homeschooled:** Letter from State Board of Education giving approval for home school. **Learning Disabled:** Submit letter from professional stating disabilities.

2008-2009 Annual costs. Tuition/fees: $1,414; $7,536 out-of-state. Per-credit charge: $42 in-state; $233 out-of-state. Books/supplies: $1,500. Personal expenses: $1,200.

2007-2008 Financial aid. All financial aid based on need. 59 full-time freshmen applied for aid; 59 were judged to have need; 59 of these received aid. Average need met was 60%. Average scholarship/grant was $2,500; average loan $3,000. 79% of total undergraduate aid awarded as scholarships/grants, 21% as loans/jobs. Need-based aid available for part-time students. Work-study available nights and for part-time students.

Application procedures. Admission: No deadline. No application fee. Admission notification on a rolling basis. **Financial aid:** Priority date 6/1; no closing date. FAFSA, institutional form required. Applicants notified on a rolling basis starting 7/15; must reply within 2 week(s) of notification.

Academics. Special study options: Cooperative education, distance learning, double major, dual enrollment of high school students, ESL, independent study, internships, liberal arts/career combination. License preparation in nursing. **Credit/placement by examination:** AP, CLEP, institutional tests. 16 credit hours maximum toward associate degree. **Support services:** GED preparation and test center, learning center, pre-admission summer program, reduced course load, remedial instruction, study skills assistance, tutoring.

Majors. Agriculture: Agribusiness operations, animal husbandry. **Business:** Accounting, administrative services, business admin, office management. **Computer sciences:** Information technology. **Education:** Early childhood, elementary. **Family/consumer sciences:** Child development. **Health:** Medical assistant, nursing (RN). **Liberal arts:** Arts/sciences. **Personal/**

culinary services: Cosmetic. **Protective services:** Police science. **Visual/performing arts:** Commercial/advertising art.

Most popular majors. Business/marketing 10%, education 26%, health sciences 19%, liberal arts 34%, security/protective services 6%.

Computing on campus. 261 workstations in library, computer center.

Student life. Freshman orientation: Available. Preregistration for classes offered. **Activities:** Student government, student newspaper, Phi Theta Kappa, student nurses association, National Vocational-Technical Honor Society, ambassador program, criminal justice club.

Athletics. Intercollegiate: Softball, tennis, volleyball.

Student services. Career counseling, services for economically disadvantaged, student employment services, financial aid counseling, personal counseling, placement for graduates, veterans' counselor. **Physically disabled:** Services for visually, hearing impaired. **Transfer:** Pre-admission transcript evaluation for new students. Transfer adviser, college fairs on campus for students transferring to 4-year colleges.

Contact. E-mail: lgrady@jamessprunt.edu
Phone: (910) 296-2500 Fax: (910) 296-1222
Lea Grady, Admissions Specialist, James Sprunt Community College, PO Box 398, Kenansville, NC 28349-0398

Johnston Community College

Smithfield, North Carolina — **CB member**
www.johnstoncc.edu — **CB code: 0727**

- Public 2-year community and technical college
- Commuter campus in large town

General. Founded in 1969. Regionally accredited. **Enrollment:** 4,178 degree-seeking undergraduates. **Degrees:** 314 associate awarded. **Location:** 30 miles from Raleigh. **Calendar:** Semester, limited summer session. **Full-time faculty:** 135 total. **Part-time faculty:** 243 total. **Class size:** 57% < 20, 42% 20-39, less than 1% 40-49, less than 1% 50-99, less than 1% >100.

Student profile. Among degree-seeking undergraduates, 55% enrolled in a transfer program, 45% enrolled in a vocational program, 964 enrolled as first-time, first-year students.

Out-of-state:	1%	**Hispanic American:**	5%
African American:	20%	**Native American:**	1%
Asian American:	1%		

Transfer out. Colleges most students transferred to 2008: East Carolina University, University of North Carolina at Wilmington, North Carolina State University.

Basis for selection. Open admission, but selective for some programs. Admission to health programs based on test scores, high school record and related completed courses. PSB required for admission to nursing and radiologic technology programs. Placement interview required for all applicants; interview required for health programs.

2008-2009 Annual costs. Tuition/fees: $1,441; $7,563 out-of-state. Per-credit charge: $42 in-state; $233 out-of-state. Books/supplies: $1,152. Personal expenses: $1,619.

2007-2008 Financial aid. All financial aid based on need. Need-based aid available for part-time students. Work-study available for part-time students.

Application procedures. Admission: Priority date 8/1; no deadline. No application fee. Admission notification on a rolling basis. **Financial aid:** Priority date 5/31; no closing date. FAFSA, institutional form required. Applicants notified on a rolling basis starting 6/1; must reply within 2 week(s) of notification.

Academics. Special study options: Cross-registration, distance learning, double major, dual enrollment of high school students, internships. **Credit/placement by examination:** AP, CLEP, institutional tests. **Support services:** GED preparation and test center, learning center, pre-admission summer program, reduced course load, remedial instruction, tutoring.

Majors. Business: Accounting, administrative services, business admin, office/clerical. **Computer sciences:** Programming. **Education:** Early childhood. **Health:** Cardiopulmonary technology, medical assistant, medical radiologic technology/radiation therapy, medical secretary, radiologic technology/medical imaging. **Legal studies:** Paralegal. **Liberal arts:** Arts/sciences. **Mechanic/repair:** Diesel, heating/ac/refrig. **Protective services:** Law enforcement admin, police science. **Visual/performing arts:** Commercial/advertising art.

Most popular majors. Business/marketing 16%, computer/information sciences 9%, education 8%, health sciences 21%, liberal arts 26%, visual/performing arts 8%.

Computing on campus. 115 workstations in library, computer center. Commuter students can connect to campus network.

Student life. Freshman orientation: Mandatory. **Activities:** Jazz band, choral groups, student government.

Athletics. NJCAA. **Intercollegiate:** Basketball M, golf M. **Team name:** Jaguars.

Student services. Chaplain/spiritual director, career counseling, student employment services, financial aid counseling, minority student services, on-campus daycare, personal counseling, placement for graduates, veterans' counselor. **Physically disabled:** Services for visually, speech, hearing impaired. **Transfer:** Pre-admission transcript evaluation for new students. College fairs on campus for students transferring to 4-year colleges.

Contact. Phone: (919) 209-2128 Fax: (919) 989-7862
Joan McLendon, Director of Admissions and Counseling, Johnston Community College, PO Box 2350, Smithfield, NC 27577

King's College

Charlotte, North Carolina
www.kingscollegecharlotte.edu — **CB code: 5361**

- For-profit 2-year career college
- Large city
- Interview required

General. Accredited by ACICS. **Enrollment:** 596 degree-seeking undergraduates. **Degrees:** 173 associate awarded. **Calendar:** Semester. **Full-time faculty:** 16 total. **Part-time faculty:** 9 total.

Basis for selection. Interview required, class rank and standardized test scores important.

2008-2009 Annual costs. Tuition/fees: $12,720. Room/board: $6,200. Books/supplies: $1,300.

Application procedures. Admission: No deadline. $50 fee. Admission notification on a rolling basis.

Academics. Credit/placement by examination: CLEP.

Majors. Business: Accounting, administrative services, tourism/travel. **Computer sciences:** Applications programming. **Health:** Medical secretary. **Legal studies:** Legal secretary, paralegal. **Visual/performing arts:** Commercial/advertising art.

Student life. Freshman orientation: Mandatory. Held on the day prior to the start of classes. **Policies:** Dress code observed; no alcoholic beverages or drugs on campus. **Housing:** Single-sex dorms available. **Activities:** Student government, Sigma Chi Kappa, Lambda Epsilon Chi.

Student services. Career counseling, financial aid counseling, placement for graduates.

Contact. Phone: (704) 372-0266 Toll-free number: (800) 768-2255
Fax: (704) 348-2029
Diane Ryon, Director of Admissions, King's College , 322 Lamar Avenue, Charlotte, NC 28204

Lenoir Community College

Kinston, North Carolina
www.lenoircc.edu — **CB code: 5378**

- Public 2-year community college
- Commuter campus in large town

General. Founded in 1958. Regionally accredited. Extension campuses in Jones and Greene Counties. **Enrollment:** 2,967 degree-seeking undergraduates. **Degrees:** 270 associate awarded. **Location:** 75 miles from Raleigh, 25 miles from Greenville. **Calendar:** Semester, extensive summer session. **Full-time faculty:** 105 total. **Part-time faculty:** 240 total. **Class size:** 73% < 20, 26% 20-39, 1% 40-49, less than 1% 50-99. **Special facilities:** Facility for local history, genealogy collection.

Transfer out. **Colleges most students transferred to 2008:** East Carolina University.

Basis for selection. Open admission, but selective for some programs. Special requirements for allied health programs. Interview required for surgical technology program.

High school preparation. Recommended units include English 4, mathematics 2, social studies 2, history 1, science 2 (laboratory 1). One biology, 1 chemistry required for registered nursing program.

2008-2009 Annual costs. Tuition/fees: $1,447; $7,569 out-of-state. Per-credit charge: $42 in-state; $233 out-of-state. Books/supplies: $1,400. Personal expenses: $540.

Financial aid. **Need-based:** Need-based aid available for part-time students. Work-study available nights and for part-time students. **Non-need-based:** Scholarships awarded for academics, athletics, leadership, state residency.

Application procedures. **Admission:** No deadline. No application fee. Admission notification on a rolling basis. Separate application required for allied health programs. January 31 deadline for nursing and April 30 for surgical technology. **Financial aid:** Priority date 7/1, closing date 8/15. Institutional form required. Applicants notified on a rolling basis starting 8/1; must reply within 2 week(s) of notification.

Academics. **Special study options:** Cooperative education, distance learning, dual enrollment of high school students, honors, liberal arts/career combination, study abroad, weekend college. License preparation in aviation, nursing, paramedic, real estate. **Credit/placement by examination:** CLEP, IB, institutional tests. **Support services:** GED preparation and test center, learning center, pre-admission summer program, reduced course load, remedial instruction, tutoring.

Majors. **Agriculture:** Horticulture. **Business:** Accounting, administrative services, business admin, e-commerce, executive assistant, management information systems. **Computer sciences:** Data processing, programming. **Conservation:** Water/wetlands/marine. **Education:** General, art, biology, chemistry, early childhood, elementary, health, history, physical, social science, teacher assistance. **Engineering:** General. **Engineering technology:** Electrical, mechanical. **Family/consumer sciences:** Child care. **Health:** Massage therapy, medical assistant, medical secretary, nursing (RN), radiologic technology/medical imaging. **Legal studies:** Court reporting. **Liberal arts:** Arts/sciences. **Math:** General. **Mechanic/repair:** Automotive, electronics/electrical. **Personal/culinary services:** Culinary arts. **Production:** Machine shop technology, welding. **Psychology:** General. **Public administration:** Social work. **Transportation:** Airline/commercial pilot, aviation management. **Visual/performing arts:** Commercial/advertising art, studio arts.

Computing on campus. 100 workstations in library, computer center, student center. Commuter students can connect to campus network. Online course registration available.

Student life. **Freshman orientation:** Available. Preregistration for classes offered. **Activities:** Choral groups, radio station, student government, student newspaper, Phi Theta Kappa, various clubs related to major fields of study.

Athletics. NJCAA. **Intercollegiate:** Baseball M, basketball M, volleyball W. **Intramural:** Basketball M. **Team name:** Lancers.

Student services. Adult student services, career counseling, student employment services, financial aid counseling, health services, personal counseling, placement for graduates, veterans' counselor. **Transfer:** Pre-admission transcript evaluation for new students. Transfer adviser, college fairs on campus for students transferring to 4-year colleges.

Contact. E-mail: bspence@lenoircc.edu
Phone: (252) 527-6223 ext. 309 Fax: (252) 233-6879 ext. 323
Myra Poole, Director of Enrollment Management, Lenoir Community College, Box 188, Kinston, NC 28502-0188

Louisburg College

Louisburg, North Carolina — **CB member**
www.louisburg.edu — **CB code: 5369**

- Private 2-year junior college affiliated with United Methodist Church
- Residential campus in small town
- SAT or ACT (ACT writing optional) required

General. Founded in 1787. Regionally accredited. **Enrollment:** 586 degree-seeking undergraduates. **Degrees:** 56 associate awarded. **Location:** 30 miles from Raleigh. **Calendar:** Semester, limited summer session. **Full-time faculty:** 35 total. **Part-time faculty:** 20 total.

Student profile.

Out-of-state:	20%	**Live on campus:**	80%
25 or older:	3%		

Transfer out. **Colleges most students transferred to 2008:** North Carolina State University, East Carolina University, Appalachian State University, University of North Carolina at Wilmington, University of North Carolina at Greensboro, University of North Carolina at Chapel Hill.

Basis for selection. School achievement most important, followed by test scores and recommendations. Interview recommended for some applicants. Students more than one year out of high school not required to submit test scores. **Learning Disabled:** Comprehensive tutorial program available for learning-disabled students. Interested students must contact the Learning Partners program for testing and consideration.

High school preparation. 20 units recommended. Recommended units include English 4, mathematics 3, social studies 3, science 2 and foreign language 2.

2008-2009 Annual costs. Tuition/fees: $13,185. Room/board: $8,244. Books/supplies: $900.

2007-2008 Financial aid. **Need-based:** 50% of total undergraduate aid awarded as scholarships/grants, 50% as loans/jobs. Work-study available nights and weekends. **Additional information:** Job location and development program helps students obtain work in the community.

Application procedures. **Admission:** No deadline. $25 fee, may be waived for applicants with need. Admission notification on a rolling basis. Must reply by May 1 or within 2 week(s) if notified thereafter. **Financial aid:** Priority date 3/1; no closing date. FAFSA, institutional form required. Applicants notified on a rolling basis starting 3/15.

Academics. **Special study options:** Cooperative education, dual enrollment of high school students, independent study. Louisburg Learning Partners for Students with Learning Differences. **Credit/placement by examination:** AP, CLEP, IB, institutional tests. 30 credit hours maximum toward associate degree. **Support services:** Learning center, pre-admission summer program, reduced course load, remedial instruction, study skills assistance, tutoring, writing center.

Majors. **Biology:** General. **Business:** General, business admin. **Communications:** General. **Computer sciences:** General. **Education:** General, biology, chemistry, early childhood, elementary, history, mathematics, physical, science, secondary. **Engineering:** General. **Health:** Athletic training, premedicine, prepharmacy. **History:** General. **Liberal arts:** Arts/sciences. **Math:** General. **Parks/recreation:** General, exercise sciences, facilities management. **Physical sciences:** Chemistry. **Psychology:** General. **Public administration:** Social work. **Social sciences:** General, sociology. **Visual/performing arts:** Art, dance, dramatic.

Most popular majors. Liberal arts 92%.

Computing on campus. 75 workstations in library, computer center. Dormitories linked to campus network. Online library available.

Student life. **Freshman orientation:** Mandatory. Preregistration for classes offered. **Policies:** Non-resident undergraduates under 21 must live at home. **Housing:** Guaranteed on-campus for all undergraduates. Single-sex dorms available. $200 deposit. **Activities:** Choral groups, dance, drama, literary magazine, music ensembles, musical theater, radio station, student government, student newspaper, Christian Life Council, Young Democrats, Young Republicans, Spanish club, Workers Actively Volunteering Energetic Services, peace group, French club, Phi Theta Kappa, Appalachian Trail White Water Club, ecological concerns club.

Athletics. NJCAA. **Intercollegiate:** Baseball M, basketball, cheerleading, golf, soccer, softball W, volleyball W. **Intramural:** Basketball, football (tackle), soccer, softball, table tennis, tennis, volleyball. **Team name:** Hurricanes.

Student services. Adult student services, alcohol/substance abuse counseling, chaplain/spiritual director, career counseling, student employment services, financial aid counseling, health services, personal counseling, veterans' counselor. **Learning disabled:** Comprehensive services available. **Transfer:** Transfer adviser, college fairs on campus for students transferring to 4-year colleges.

Contact. E-mail: admissions@louisburg.edu
Phone: (919) 497-3222 Toll-free number: (800) 775-0208
Fax: (919) 496-1788
Tracey Sala, Vice President of Enrollment Management, Louisburg College, 501 North Main Street, Louisburg, NC 27549

Martin Community College
Williamston, North Carolina — **CB member**
www.martincc.edu — **CB code: 5445**

- Public 2-year community and technical college
- Commuter campus in small town

General. Founded in 1967. Regionally accredited. **Enrollment:** 689 degree-seeking undergraduates. **Degrees:** 73 associate awarded. **Location:** 30 miles from Greenville, 100 miles from Raleigh. **Calendar:** Semester, limited summer session. **Full-time faculty:** 25 total. **Part-time faculty:** 30 total. **Special facilities:** Equine arena, bull riding, rodeos.

Student profile. Among degree-seeking undergraduates, 83 enrolled as first-time, first-year students.

Part-time:	52%	**Women:**	67%
Out-of-state:	1%	**25 or older:**	58%

Transfer out. Colleges most students transferred to 2008: East Carolina University.

Basis for selection. Open admission, but selective for some programs. Limited enrollment in physical therapy assistant program. Selection based on high school record, placement test results, completion of required courses and interview. Selection of Dental Assisting applications includes high school record, completion of required courses, and an interview. COMPASS required of some students. Interview required for physical therapist assistant applicants and dental assisting applicants. **Homeschooled:** Statement describing homeschool structure and mission, transcript of courses and grades required.

High school preparation. 22 units recommended. Recommended units include English 4, mathematics 3, social studies 2, history 1, science 3 (laboratory 1) and academic electives 9.

2008-2009 Annual costs. Tuition/fees: $1,298; $7,037 out-of-state. Per-credit charge: $42 in-state; $233 out-of-state. Books/supplies: $1,050. Personal expenses: $400.

Financial aid. Need-based: Need-based aid available for part-time students. Work-study available nights and for part-time students. **Non-need-based:** Scholarships awarded for academics.

Application procedures. Admission: No deadline. No application fee. Admission notification on a rolling basis. Closing date for physical therapist assistant program applicants May 15. **Financial aid:** Priority date 5/1; no closing date. FAFSA required. Applicants notified on a rolling basis starting 5/1.

Academics. Special study options: Cooperative education, distance learning, double major, dual enrollment of high school students, ESL, independent study, internships, liberal arts/career combination, teacher certification program. License preparation in real estate. **Credit/placement by examination:** AP, CLEP, institutional tests. No more than half of credits required in program of study may be earned through credit by exam (including CLEP). **Support services:** GED preparation and test center, learning center, reduced course load, remedial instruction, study skills assistance, tutoring.

Majors. Agriculture: Equestrian studies. **Business:** Accounting technology, business admin, executive assistant, management information systems. **Computer sciences:** Information systems. **Construction:** Electrician. **Education:** General, early childhood, elementary, secondary. **Health:** Medical assistant, medical secretary, physical therapy assistant. **Liberal arts:** Arts/sciences. **Mechanic/repair:** Automotive, heating/ac/refrig. **Personal/culinary services:** Cosmetic.

Computing on campus. 31 workstations in library, computer center. Commuter students can connect to campus network.

Student life. Freshman orientation: Available. Offered on registration day. **Activities:** Student government, physical therapist assistant club, Phi Theta Kappa, equine club, medical assisting club, Alpha Beta Gamma.

Athletics. Team name: Screaming Eagles.

Student services. Career counseling, services for economically disadvantaged, student employment services, financial aid counseling, on-campus daycare, personal counseling, placement for graduates, veterans' counselor. **Transfer:** Pre-admission transcript evaluation for new students. Transfer adviser, college fairs on campus for students transferring to 4-year colleges.

Contact. E-mail: jbussell@martincc.edu
Phone: (252) 792-1521 ext. 268 Fax: (252) 792-0826
Jim Bussell, Admissions Officer, Martin Community College, 1161 Kehukee Park Road, Williamston, NC 27892-9988

Mayland Community College
Spruce Pine, North Carolina — **CB member**
www.mayland.edu — **CB code: 0795**

- Public 2-year community college
- Commuter campus in rural community

General. Founded in 1971. Regionally accredited. **Enrollment:** 1,551 degree-seeking undergraduates. **Degrees:** 111 associate awarded. **Location:** 50 miles from Asheville. **Calendar:** Semester, limited summer session. **Full-time faculty:** 47 total. **Part-time faculty:** 50 total. **Class size:** 71% < 20, 29% 20-39. **Special facilities:** Child development center, interactive TV facility.

Transfer out. Colleges most students transferred to 2008: Appalachian State University, University of North Carolina-Asheville, Western Carolina University, Mars Hill College, East Tennessee State University.

Basis for selection. Open admission, but selective for some programs. Placement assessment required of all degree-seeking students. Admission to associate degree nursing program and practical nursing program based on competitive ranking system. Medical assisting admissions based on completion of requirements and timely application. **Homeschooled:** Transcript of courses and grades required.

2008-2009 Annual costs. Tuition/fees: $1,560; $7,682 out-of-state. Per-credit charge: $42 in-state; $233 out-of-state. Books/supplies: $750. Personal expenses: $1,087.

2008-2009 Financial aid. Need-based: Need-based aid available for part-time students.

Application procedures. Admission: No deadline. No application fee. Admission notification on a rolling basis beginning on or about 3/1. Application by February 28 required for nursing program. **Financial aid:** Priority date 3/15; no closing date. FAFSA, institutional form required. Applicants notified on a rolling basis starting 6/15.

Academics. Special study options: Cooperative education, cross-registration, distance learning, double major, dual enrollment of high school students, independent study, internships, liberal arts/career combination. Bachelor's degree programs available on campus. License preparation in nursing, real estate. **Credit/placement by examination:** AP, CLEP, institutional tests. Maximum 25% of program hours can be earned via credit by examination. **Support services:** GED preparation and test center, learning center, pre-admission summer program, reduced course load, remedial instruction, study skills assistance, tutoring, writing center.

Majors. Agriculture: Horticulture. **Business:** Accounting, administrative services, business admin. **Computer sciences:** Systems analysis. **Education:** General, early childhood. **Engineering:** Electrical. **Health:** Medical secretary, nursing (RN). **Liberal arts:** Arts/sciences. **Personal/culinary services:** Cosmetic.

Most popular majors. Business/marketing 28%, education 7%, engineering/engineering technologies 7%, health sciences 31%, liberal arts 19%.

Computing on campus. 150 workstations in library, computer center. Commuter students can connect to campus network. Online course registration, online library, helpline, student web hosting available.

Student life. Freshman orientation: Mandatory. Preregistration for classes offered. One-hour class each semester. **Activities:** Literary magazine, student government, Phi Theta Kappa, National Nursing Association, early childhood students' association.

Student services. Career counseling, services for economically disadvantaged, student employment services, financial aid counseling, on-campus daycare, personal counseling, placement for graduates, veterans' counselor. **Physically disabled:** Services for visually, speech, hearing impaired. **Transfer:** Pre-admission transcript evaluation for new students. Transfer adviser, college fairs on campus for students transferring to 4-year colleges.

Contact. Phone: (828) 765-7351 Toll-free number: (800) 462-9526
Fax: (828) 765-0728
Monica Boyd, Director of Enrollment Management, Mayland Community College, Box 547, Spruce Pine, NC 28777

McDowell Technical Community College

Marion, North Carolina
www.mcdowelltech.edu **CB code: 0789**

- Public 2-year community and technical college
- Commuter campus in small town

General. Founded in 1964. Regionally accredited. **Enrollment:** 1,004 degree-seeking undergraduates. **Degrees:** 118 associate awarded. **Location:** 35 miles from Asheville. **Calendar:** Semester, limited summer session. **Full-time faculty:** 35 total; 57% women. **Part-time faculty:** 72 total; 3% minority, 49% women. **Special facilities:** Color and black/white photography laboratories.

Student profile.

Out-of-state:	2%	**25 or older:**	58%

Basis for selection. Open admission, but selective for some programs. Special requirements for allied health programs. Interview required for some allied health programs. **Adult students:** Must take required placement tests. **Homeschooled:** Transcript of courses and grades required.

2008-2009 Annual costs. Tuition/fees: $1,400; $7,522 out-of-state. Per-credit charge: $42 in-state; $233 out-of-state. Books/supplies: $1,000. Personal expenses: $4,212.

2007-2008 Financial aid. All financial aid based on need. Need-based aid available for part-time students. Work-study available nights and for part-time students.

Application procedures. Admission: No deadline. No application fee. Application must be submitted on paper. Admission notification on a rolling basis. **Financial aid:** Priority date 3/15; no closing date. FAFSA, institutional form required. Applicants notified on a rolling basis starting 7/1.

Academics. Special study options: Cooperative education, distance learning, double major, dual enrollment of high school students, independent study, internships, liberal arts/career combination. Bachelor's degree programs available on campus. License preparation in nursing. **Credit/placement by examination:** CLEP, institutional tests. 20 credit hours maximum toward associate degree. **Support services:** GED preparation and test center, learning center, reduced course load, remedial instruction, tutoring.

Majors. Business: General, accounting, office/clerical. **Communications technology:** Graphic/printing. **Computer sciences:** Applications programming, programming. **Education:** General. **Health:** Nursing (RN). **Liberal arts:** Arts/sciences. **Mechanic/repair:** Electronics/electrical, industrial. **Visual/performing arts:** Commercial photography, commercial/advertising art.

Most popular majors. Business/marketing 13%, computer/information sciences 6%, education 16%, health sciences 25%, liberal arts 14%, trade and industry 20%.

Computing on campus. 80 workstations in library, computer center.

Student life. Freshman orientation: Available. Preregistration for classes offered. Two-hour orientation held one day prior to registration day. **Activities:** Student government.

Student services. Adult student services, career counseling, student employment services, on-campus daycare, personal counseling, placement for graduates, veterans' counselor. **Physically disabled:** Services for visually, speech, hearing impaired. **Transfer:** Transfer adviser for students transferring to 4-year colleges.

Contact. E-mail: rickw@mcdowelltech.edu
Phone: (828) 652-0632 Fax: (828) 652-1014
Rick Wilson, Director of Admissions, McDowell Technical Community College, 54 College Drive, Marion, NC 28752

Miller-Motte Technical College: Cary

Cary, North Carolina
www.mmccary.net

- For-profit 2-year technical college
- Small city

General. Regionally accredited; also accredited by ACICS. **Enrollment:** 465 degree-seeking undergraduates. **Degrees:** 68 associate awarded. **Location:** 10 miles from downtown Raleigh. **Calendar:** Quarter. **Full-time faculty:** 16 total. **Part-time faculty:** 19 total.

2008-2009 Annual costs. Tuition/fees: $10,440. Per-credit charge: $232.

Application procedures. Admission: No deadline. $35 fee. **Financial aid:** No deadline.

Academics. Credit/placement by examination: CLEP.

Majors. Health: Massage therapy, medical assistant, surgical technology.

Contact. Alison Mecca, Admissions Director, Miller-Motte Technical College: Cary, 2205 Walnut Street, Cary, NC 27518

Mitchell Community College

Statesville, North Carolina **CB member**
www.mitchellcc.edu **CB code: 5412**

- Public 2-year community college
- Commuter campus in large town

General. Founded in 1852. Regionally accredited. **Enrollment:** 2,982 degree-seeking undergraduates. **Degrees:** 210 associate awarded. **Location:** 40 miles from Charlotte, 40 miles from Winston-Salem. **Calendar:** Semester, limited summer session. **Full-time faculty:** 66 total. **Part-time faculty:** 80 total.

Student profile.

Out-of-state:	8%	**25 or older:**	40%

Transfer out. Colleges most students transferred to 2008: University of North Carolina-Charlotte, Appalachian State University, Gardner-Webb University, Lenoir-Rhyne University.

Basis for selection. Open admission, but selective for some programs. All applicants must take college placement tests to determine readiness for college-level studies. Nursing program applicants must meet minimum admissions requirements; interview and essay required.

2008-2009 Annual costs. Tuition/fees: $1,328; $7,067 out-of-state. Per-credit charge: $42 in-state; $233 out-of-state. Books/supplies: $900. Personal expenses: $1,448.

Financial aid. Need-based: Need-based aid available for part-time students. Work-study available for part-time students.

Application procedures. Admission: No deadline. No application fee. Admission notification on a rolling basis. **Financial aid:** No deadline. FAFSA, institutional form required. Applicants notified on a rolling basis starting 3/1; must reply within 2 week(s) of notification.

Academics. Special study options: Cooperative education, distance learning, dual enrollment of high school students, independent study, weekend college. License preparation in nursing, paramedic, real estate. **Credit/placement by examination:** AP, CLEP, institutional tests. 20 credit hours maximum toward associate degree. **Support services:** GED preparation and test center, learning center, reduced course load, remedial instruction, tutoring.

Majors. Business: Accounting, administrative services, business admin, operations. **Computer sciences:** Information systems, programming. **Education:** Early childhood, teacher assistance. **Engineering:** Electrical. **Engineering technology:** Construction, drafting, electrical, industrial management, manufacturing. **Health:** Nursing (RN), predental, premedicine, prepharmacy, preveterinary. **Legal studies:** Prelaw. **Liberal arts:** Arts/sciences. **Mechanic/repair:** Industrial. **Production:** Machine shop technology. **Protective services:** Police science. **Public administration:** Human services. **Visual/performing arts:** Studio arts.

Most popular majors. Business/marketing 15%, computer/information sciences 13%, engineering/engineering technologies 6%, health sciences 26%, liberal arts 18%, personal/culinary services 8%.

Computing on campus. 45 workstations in library, computer center.

Student life. Freshman orientation: Available. Usually held immediately prior to fall semester for approximately 2.5 hours. **Activities:** Concert band, choral groups, literary magazine, student government, Circle-K, Christian Student Fellowship, Ebony Kinship.

Student services. Chaplain/spiritual director, career counseling, student employment services, financial aid counseling, personal counseling, placement for graduates, veterans' counselor. **Physically disabled:** Services for visually, hearing impaired. **Transfer:** College fairs on campus for students transferring to 4-year colleges.

Contact. E-mail: kmoore@mitchellcc.edu
Phone: (704) 878-3243 Fax: (704) 878-0872
Brenda Sawyer, Director of Admissions and Records, Mitchell Community College, 500 West Broad Street, Statesville, NC 28677

Montgomery Community College
Troy, North Carolina
www.montgomery.edu **CB code: 0785**

- Public 2-year community college
- Commuter campus in small town

General. Founded in 1967. Regionally accredited. **Enrollment:** 732 degree-seeking undergraduates; 71 non-degree-seeking students. **Degrees:** 105 associate awarded. **Location:** 50 miles from Greensboro, 62 miles from Charlotte. **Calendar:** Semester, limited summer session. **Full-time faculty:** 40 total. **Part-time faculty:** 32 total. **Special facilities:** Rifle/pistol firing range.

Student profile. Among degree-seeking undergraduates, 17% enrolled in a transfer program, 17% enrolled in a vocational program, 120 enrolled as first-time, first-year students.

Part-time:	44%	**Women:**	65%
Out-of-state:	1%	**25 or older:**	55%

Transfer out. Colleges most students transferred to 2008: Pfeiffer University, Gardner-Webb University, University of North Carolina at Greensboro.

Basis for selection. Open admission, but selective for some programs. Special requirements for nursing program. Secondary school record and test scores considered. **Homeschooled:** Home school must provide copy of "Notification of intent to operate" card from NC Department of Non-Public Education.

High school preparation. 28 units recommended. Recommended units include English 4, mathematics 3, social studies 3, science 3 (laboratory 1) and academic electives 15.

2008-2009 Annual costs. Tuition/fees: $1,410; $7,532 out-of-state. Per-credit charge: $42 in-state; $233 out-of-state. Books/supplies: $1,100. Personal expenses: $1,200.

Financial aid. Need-based: Need-based aid available for part-time students. Work-study available nights and for part-time students. **Non-need-based:** Scholarships awarded for academics, minority status, state residency.

Application procedures. Admission: No deadline. No application fee. Admission notification on a rolling basis. Practical Nursing Program applicants must apply by October 15 for following fall program. **Financial aid:** Priority date 7/15; no closing date. FAFSA, institutional form required. Applicants notified on a rolling basis starting 6/1.

Academics. Special study options: Distance learning, double major, dual enrollment of high school students. License preparation in nursing. **Credit/placement by examination:** AP, CLEP, institutional tests. 16 credit hours maximum toward associate degree. **Support services:** GED preparation and test center, learning center, reduced course load, remedial instruction, tutoring.

Majors. Business: Accounting, business admin, office management. **Computer sciences:** Information systems, information technology. **Conservation:** Forest technology. **Construction:** Electrician. **Education:** Early childhood. **Health:** Medical assistant. **Liberal arts:** Arts/sciences. **Mechanic/repair:** Gunsmithing. **Protective services:** Criminal justice. **Visual/performing arts:** Crafts.

Most popular majors. Business/marketing 19%, education 10%, health sciences 18%, liberal arts 20%, natural resources/environmental science 17%, trade and industry 8%.

Computing on campus. 90 workstations in library, computer center. Commuter students can connect to campus network.

Student life. Freshman orientation: Available. **Activities:** Student government, gunsmithing society, forestry club, business technologies club, practical nursing club, medical assisting club.

Student services. Career counseling, student employment services, financial aid counseling, on-campus daycare, personal counseling, veterans' counselor. **Physically disabled:** Services for visually, speech, hearing impaired. **Transfer:** Transfer adviser, college fairs on campus for students transferring to 4-year colleges.

Contact. E-mail: fryek@montgomery.edu
Phone: (910) 576-6222 ext. 240 Toll-free number: (800) 839-6222
Fax: (910) 576-2176
Karen Frye, Admissions Officer, Montgomery Community College, 1011 Page Street, Troy, NC 27371-0787

Nash Community College
Rocky Mount, North Carolina **CB member**
www.nashcc.edu **CB code: 5881**

- Public 2-year community college
- Commuter campus in small city

General. Founded in 1967. Regionally accredited. **Enrollment:** 2,991 degree-seeking undergraduates. **Degrees:** 214 associate awarded. **Location:** 55 miles from Raleigh. **Calendar:** Semester, limited summer session. **Full-time faculty:** 75 total. **Part-time faculty:** 150 total. **Class size:** 54% < 20, 46% 20-39. **Partnerships:** Formal partnership with high schools to provide students opportunity to earn college credit.

Student profile.

Out-of-state:	1%	**25 or older:**	52%

Transfer out. Colleges most students transferred to 2008: University of North Carolina system universities.

Basis for selection. Open admission, but selective for some programs. Special requirements for nursing, physical therapy assistant, phlebotomy, cosmetology programs. **Adult students:** College recommends ASSET or COMPASS placement test if student does not have SAT scores.

High school preparation. Appropriate biology courses required for nursing and physical therapist assistant programs.

2008-2009 Annual costs. Tuition/fees: $1,380; $7,119 out-of-state. Per-credit charge: $42 in-state; $233 out-of-state. Books/supplies: $900. Personal expenses: $2,000.

Financial aid. Need-based: Need-based aid available for part-time students. **Non-need-based:** Scholarships awarded for academics.

Application procedures. Admission: No deadline. No application fee. Admission notification on a rolling basis. **Financial aid:** Priority date 6/30; no closing date. FAFSA, institutional form required. Applicants notified on a rolling basis starting 7/15.

Academics. Special study options: Accelerated study, distance learning, dual enrollment of high school students, ESL, liberal arts/career combination. License preparation in nursing, paramedic, physical therapy, real estate. **Credit/placement by examination:** CLEP, IB, institutional tests. **Support services:** GED preparation and test center, learning center, reduced course load, remedial instruction, study skills assistance, tutoring.

Majors. Architecture: Technology. **Business:** Accounting, administrative services, business admin, hotel/motel admin, management information systems. **Computer sciences:** Information systems. **Construction:** Lineworker. **Education:** General, early childhood, teacher assistance. **Engineering:** Electrical. **Engineering technology:** Architectural, computer, electrical, industrial safety. **Family/consumer sciences:** Child care. **Health:** Licensed practical nurse, medical secretary, nursing (RN). **Legal studies:** Legal secretary. **Liberal arts:** Arts/sciences. **Personal/culinary services:** Culinary arts. **Protective services:** Police science.

Most popular majors. Business/marketing 18%, computer/information sciences 8%, engineering/engineering technologies 16%, health sciences 21%, liberal arts 21%, social sciences 7%.

Computing on campus. 110 workstations in library, computer center. Online library available.

Student life. Freshman orientation: Available. Preregistration for classes offered. **Activities:** Student government.

Student services. Career counseling, services for economically disadvantaged, student employment services, financial aid counseling, placement for graduates, veterans' counselor. **Physically disabled:** Services for visually, speech, hearing impaired. **Transfer:** Pre-admission transcript evaluation for new students. Transfer adviser, college fairs on campus for students transferring to 4-year colleges.

Contact. Phone: (252) 443-4011 ext. 300 Fax: (252) 443-0828
Dot Gardner, Admissions Officer, Nash Community College, Box 7488, Rocky Mount, NC 27804-0488

Pamlico Community College

Grantsboro, North Carolina
www.pamlicocc.edu **CB code: 0864**

- Public 2-year community college
- Commuter campus in rural community

General. Founded in 1962. Regionally accredited. **Enrollment:** 471 degree-seeking undergraduates. **Degrees:** 39 associate awarded. **Location:** 20 miles from New Bern. **Calendar:** Semester, limited summer session. **Full-time faculty:** 19 total. **Part-time faculty:** 16 total.

Basis for selection. Open admission.

2008-2009 Annual costs. Tuition/fees: $1,295; $7,034 out-of-state. Per-credit charge: $42 in-state; $233 out-of-state. Books/supplies: $380. Personal expenses: $1,630.

2008-2009 Financial aid. **Need-based:** 99% of total undergraduate aid awarded as scholarships/grants, 1% as loans/jobs. **Additional information:** Jobs Training Partner Act and Displaced Homemaker Programs cover tuition, books, fees.

Application procedures. **Admission:** No deadline. No application fee. Admission notification on a rolling basis. **Financial aid:** Priority date 3/15; no closing date. FAFSA required. Applicants notified on a rolling basis.

Academics. **Special study options:** Dual enrollment of high school students, independent study, internships. **Credit/placement by examination:** CLEP, institutional tests. **Support services:** Learning center, reduced course load, remedial instruction, tutoring.

Majors. **Business:** Accounting, business admin, office/clerical. **Conservation:** General. **Education:** General, early childhood. **Engineering:** Electrical. **Engineering technology:** Electrical.

Computing on campus. 40 workstations in library.

Student life. **Freshman orientation:** Available. **Activities:** Student government, student newspaper.

Athletics. **Intramural:** Basketball, softball, table tennis, tennis, volleyball.

Student services. Career counseling, student employment services, health services, personal counseling, placement for graduates, veterans' counselor.

Contact. E-mail: jgibbs@pamlicocc.edu
Phone: (252) 249-1851 Fax: (252) 249-2377
Jamie Gibbs, Dean of Student Enrollment Services, Pamlico Community College, PO Box 185, Grantsboro, NC 28529

Piedmont Community College

Roxboro, North Carolina
www.piedmontcc.edu **CB code: 5518**

- Public 2-year community college
- Small town

General. Founded in 1970. Regionally accredited. Branch campus in Caswell County. Correctional education offered at Hillsborough, Yanceyville, and Roxboro. **Enrollment:** 2,691 degree-seeking undergraduates. **Degrees:** 206 associate awarded. **Location:** 30 miles from Durham, 45 miles from Chapel Hill. **Calendar:** Semester, limited summer session. **Full-time faculty:** 80 total. **Part-time faculty:** 70 total. **Special facilities:** 4-mile nature trail.

Student profile. Among degree-seeking undergraduates, 714 enrolled as first-time, first-year students.

Out-of-state:	5%	**25 or older:**	51%

Basis for selection. Open admission, but selective for some programs. Admission for nursing based on test scores, interview and recommendations. Nursing applicants must provide health data.

2008-2009 Annual costs. Tuition/fees: $1,305; $7,044 out-of-state. Per-credit charge: $42 in-state; $233 out-of-state. Books/supplies: $1,200. Personal expenses: $750.

Application procedures. **Admission:** No deadline. No application fee. Admission notification on a rolling basis. Certain certificate programs do not require high school diploma. **Financial aid:** Priority date 4/15; no closing date. FAFSA required. Applicants notified on a rolling basis; must reply within 2 week(s) of notification.

Academics. **Special study options:** Cooperative education, cross-registration, distance learning, double major, dual enrollment of high school students, independent study, internships, weekend college. License preparation in nursing. **Credit/placement by examination:** CLEP, institutional tests. Maximum of 50% of coursework may be completed through credit by examination. **Support services:** GED preparation and test center, learning center, reduced course load, remedial instruction, study skills assistance, tutoring.

Majors. **Business:** General, accounting, administrative services, business admin, international, office technology. **Computer sciences:** Applications programming, programming. **Health:** Medical secretary, nursing (RN). **Legal studies:** Legal secretary. **Liberal arts:** Arts/sciences. **Mechanic/repair:** Electronics/electrical, gunsmithing. **Personal/culinary services:** General, cosmetic. **Protective services:** Criminal justice. **Public administration:** Social work. **Visual/performing arts:** Cinematography, studio arts.

Computing on campus. 140 workstations in library, computer center.

Student life. **Freshman orientation:** Available. **Activities:** Dance, drama, student government, student newspaper, Phi Theta Kappa, Student Nursing Association, gunsmithing club, taxidermy club, cosmetology club, criminal justice club, CARE.

Athletics. **Team name:** Pacers.

Student services. Career counseling, services for economically disadvantaged, student employment services, financial aid counseling, on-campus daycare, personal counseling, placement for graduates, veterans' counselor. **Physically disabled:** Services for visually, hearing impaired. **Transfer:** Transfer adviser for students transferring to 4-year colleges.

Contact. Phone: (336) 599-1181 Fax: (336) 597-3817
Shelia Williamson, Coordinator of Admissions, Piedmont Community College, 1715 College Drive, Roxboro, NC 27573-1197

Pitt Community College

Greenville, North Carolina **CB member**
www.pittcc.edu **CB code: 5556**

- Public 2-year community and technical college
- Commuter campus in small city

General. Founded in 1961. Regionally accredited. **Enrollment:** 5,813 degree-seeking undergraduates. **Degrees:** 697 associate awarded. **ROTC:** Army. **Location:** 85 miles from Raleigh. **Calendar:** Semester, limited summer session. **Full-time faculty:** 181 total. **Part-time faculty:** 394 total. **Class size:** 66% < 20, 34% 20-39, less than 1% 40-49, less than 1% 50-99.

Student profile.

Out-of-state:	2%	**25 or older:**	39%

Transfer out. **Colleges most students transferred to 2008:** East Carolina University, University of North Carolina at Wilmington, Barton College.

Basis for selection. Open admission, but selective for some programs. Special admission requirements for some allied health programs. SAT and/or ACT may be used in lieu of the college's placement test for placement into English and math courses.

2008-2009 Annual costs. Tuition/fees: $1,430; $7,552 out-of-state. Per-credit charge: $42 in-state; $233 out-of-state. Books/supplies: $800.

2007-2008 Financial aid. **Need-based:** 69% of total undergraduate aid awarded as scholarships/grants, 31% as loans/jobs. Need-based aid available for part-time students. Work-study available nights and for part-time students. **Non-need-based:** Scholarships awarded for academics, athletics, ROTC.

Application procedures. **Admission:** No deadline. No application fee. Admission notification on a rolling basis. **Financial aid:** Priority date 3/15; no closing date. FAFSA required. Applicants notified on a rolling basis starting 2/1.

Academics. **Special study options:** Cooperative education, distance learning, double major, dual enrollment of high school students, ESL, internships. License preparation in nursing, occupational therapy, paramedic, radiology, real estate. **Credit/placement by examination:** CLEP, institutional tests. 40 credit hours maximum toward associate degree. Credit by examination can not be included in the 25% residency requirement. **Support services:** GED preparation and test center, learning center, remedial instruction, tutoring.

Majors. Business: Accounting, business admin, e-commerce, human resources, marketing, office management, operations, sales/distribution, training/development. **Computer sciences:** Applications programming, information systems, vendor certification. **Construction:** Electrician. **Education:** Early childhood. **Engineering technology:** Architectural, electrical, industrial management, manufacturing. **Health:** Health services, medical assistant, medical radiologic technology/radiation therapy, medical records technology, medical secretary, mental health services, nuclear medical technology, nursing (RN), occupational therapy assistant, office admin, respiratory therapy assistant, respiratory therapy technology, sonography. **Legal studies:** Paralegal. **Liberal arts:** Arts/sciences. **Mechanic/repair:** Automotive, electronics/electrical, heating/ac/refrig. **Personal/culinary services:** Cosmetic, mortuary science. **Production:** Machine shop technology, welding. **Protective services:** Criminal justice, police science. **Science technology:** Biological. **Visual/performing arts:** Commercial/advertising art.

Most popular majors. Business/marketing 10%, computer/information sciences 10%, engineering/engineering technologies 10%, health sciences 33%, liberal arts 20%, trade and industry 15%.

Computing on campus. 50 workstations in library, computer center. Helpline available.

Student life. Freshman orientation: Available. Preregistration for classes offered. **Activities:** Student government, Gamma Beta Phi, student government association, Southern Organization of Human Services Organization, Society of Advancement of Management, Delta Epsilon Chi, multicultural/international Club, Students Monitoring Students.

Athletics. NJCAA. **Intercollegiate:** Baseball M, golf M, softball W, volleyball W. **Intramural:** Basketball, football (non-tackle), volleyball. **Team name:** Bulldogs.

Student services. Adult student services, alcohol/substance abuse counseling, career counseling, services for economically disadvantaged, student employment services, financial aid counseling, on-campus daycare, personal counseling, veterans' counselor. **Physically disabled:** Services for visually, speech, hearing impaired. **Transfer:** Transfer adviser, college fairs on campus for students transferring to 4-year colleges.

Contact. E-mail: pittadm@pcc.pitt.cc.nc.us
Phone: (252) 321-4245 Fax: (252) 321-4612
Joanne Ceres, Director of Admissions, Pitt Community College, PO Drawer 7007, Greenville, NC 27835-7007

Randolph Community College

Asheboro, North Carolina
www.randolph.edu **CB code: 5585**

- Public 2-year community and technical college
- Commuter campus in large town

General. Founded in 1962. Regionally accredited. **Enrollment:** 3,177 degree-seeking undergraduates. **Degrees:** 219 associate awarded. **Location:** 65 miles from Charlotte, 26 miles from Greensboro. **Calendar:** Semester, limited summer session. **Full-time faculty:** 50 total. **Part-time faculty:** 151 total.

Transfer out. 5% of students enrolled in the transfer program go on to 4-year colleges. **Colleges most students transferred to 2008:** University of North Carolina-Greensboro, High Point University, Guilford College, University of North Carolina-Charlotte.

Basis for selection. Open admission, but selective for some programs. Admission to nursing and radiography program based primarily on competitive admission. **Homeschooled:** Transcript of courses and grades required. Copy of certificate of home school operation or a Notice of Intent (to operate a home school) is required to have been sent to the North Carolina Non-Public Education Office.

High school preparation. College-preparatory program recommended.

2008-2009 Annual costs. Tuition/fees: $1,320; $7,059 out-of-state. Per-credit charge: $42 in-state; $233 out-of-state. Books/supplies: $1,011. Personal expenses: $3,104.

2007-2008 Financial aid. Need-based: Work-study available nights and for part-time students. **Non-need-based:** Scholarships awarded for academics, leadership, minority status, state residency.

Application procedures. Admission: No deadline. No application fee. Admission notification on a rolling basis. **Financial aid:** No deadline. FAFSA required. Applicants notified on a rolling basis.

Academics. Special study options: Cooperative education, distance learning, double major, dual enrollment of high school students, ESL, internships, liberal arts/career combination, weekend college. **Credit/placement by examination:** AP, CLEP, IB, institutional tests. 16 credit hours maximum toward associate degree. **Support services:** GED preparation and test center, learning center, remedial instruction, study skills assistance, tutoring, writing center.

Majors. Business: Accounting, administrative services, business admin, management information systems. **Communications technology:** Photo/film/video. **Computer sciences:** Networking. **Construction:** Electrician. **Engineering technology:** Electrical, manufacturing. **Family/consumer sciences:** Child care. **Foreign languages:** Sign language interpretation. **Health:** EMT paramedic, nursing (RN). **Interdisciplinary:** Historic preservation. **Liberal arts:** Arts/sciences. **Mechanic/repair:** Automotive. **Protective services:** Police science. **Visual/performing arts:** Commercial photography, commercial/advertising art, interior design, photography, studio arts.

Most popular majors. Business/marketing 44%, health sciences 11%, liberal arts 12%, security/protective services 6%, visual/performing arts 22%.

Computing on campus. Online course registration, online library, wireless network available.

Student life. Freshman orientation: Mandatory. 30 minute overview of policies and procedures. **Activities:** Student government, student newspaper.

Athletics. Team name: Armadillos.

Student services. Adult student services, career counseling, student employment services, financial aid counseling, personal counseling, placement for graduates, veterans' counselor. **Physically disabled:** Services for visually, speech, hearing impaired. **Transfer:** Pre-admission transcript evaluation for new students. Transfer adviser, college fairs on campus for students transferring to 4-year colleges.

Contact. E-mail: masmith@randolph.edu
Phone: (336) 633-0239 Fax: (336) 629-9547
Brandi Hagerman, Director of Admissions/Registrar, Randolph Community College, PO Box 1009, Asheboro, NC 27204-1009

Richmond Community College

Hamlet, North Carolina **CB member**
www.richmondcc.edu **CB code: 5588**

- Public 2-year community college
- Commuter campus in small town

General. Founded in 1964. Regionally accredited. **Enrollment:** 1,700 degree-seeking undergraduates. **Degrees:** 250 associate awarded. **Location:** 75 miles from Charlotte. **Calendar:** Semester, limited summer session. **Full-time faculty:** 60 total. **Part-time faculty:** 140 total. **Special facilities:** Health science building with exam rooms and simulation areas.

Student profile. Among degree-seeking undergraduates, 15% enrolled in a transfer program, 47% enrolled in a vocational program, 2% already have a bachelor's degree or higher, 250 transferred in from other institutions.

Out-of-state:	2%	**25 or older:**	45%

Transfer out. Colleges most students transferred to 2008: UNC-Pembroke, Gardner-Webb University, UNC-Charlotte, Fayetteville State.

Basis for selection. Open admission, but selective for some programs. Admission to nursing program based on academic record and completion of admission requirements, interview required. **Homeschooled:** Transcript of courses and grades required.

2008-2009 Annual costs. Tuition/fees: $1,422; $7,544 out-of-state. Per-credit charge: $42 in-state; $233 out-of-state. Books/supplies: $600. Personal expenses: $900.

Financial aid. Need-based: Need-based aid available for part-time students. Work-study available nights and for part-time students. **Non-need-based:** Scholarships awarded for academics, leadership.

Application procedures. Admission: No deadline. No application fee. Admission notification on a rolling basis. **Financial aid:** No deadline. FAFSA, institutional form required. Applicants notified on a rolling basis starting 7/8; must reply within 2 week(s) of notification.

Academics. **Special study options:** Cooperative education, cross-registration, distance learning, double major, dual enrollment of high school students, ESL, independent study, internships, student-designed major, teacher certification program. License preparation in nursing. **Credit/placement by examination:** AP, CLEP, institutional tests. 15 credit hours maximum toward associate degree. Interview required for placement and counseling. **Support services:** GED preparation and test center, learning center, reduced course load, remedial instruction, study skills assistance, tutoring.

Majors. **Business:** Accounting, administrative services, business admin, management information systems. **Computer sciences:** Information systems, networking. **Engineering:** Electrical. **Engineering technology:** Electrical, manufacturing. **Family/consumer sciences:** Child care. **Health:** Medical assistant, mental health services, nursing (RN). **Liberal arts:** Arts/sciences. **Public administration:** Social work.

Computing on campus. 250 workstations in library, computer center.

Student life. **Freshman orientation:** Mandatory. **Activities:** Drama, student government, student newspaper.

Athletics. **Team name:** Panthers.

Student services. Career counseling, student employment services, financial aid counseling, health services, personal counseling, placement for graduates, veterans' counselor. **Physically disabled:** Services for visually, hearing impaired. **Transfer:** Transfer adviser, college fairs on campus for students transferring to 4-year colleges.

Contact. Phone: (910) 410-1736 Fax: (910) 582-7102
Wanda Watts, Director of Admissions and Registrar, Richmond Community College, Box 1189, Hamlet, NC 28345

Roanoke-Chowan Community College

Ahoskie, North Carolina
www.roanokechowan.edu **CB code: 5564**

- Public 2-year community college
- Commuter campus in small town

General. Founded in 1967. Regionally accredited. **Enrollment:** 998 degree-seeking undergraduates. **Degrees:** 76 associate awarded. **Location:** 60 miles from Greenville, 65 miles from Norfolk, Virginia. **Calendar:** Semester, limited summer session. **Full-time faculty:** 37 total. **Part-time faculty:** 52 total. **Class size:** 70% < 20, 29% 20-39, 2% 40-49. **Special facilities:** Arboretum/environmental science outdoor laboratory.

Basis for selection. Open admission, but selective for out-of-state students. Admission to nursing program based on interview and test scores.

2008-2009 Annual costs. Tuition/fees: $1,445; $7,567 out-of-state. Per-credit charge: $42 in-state; $233 out-of-state. Books/supplies: $800. Personal expenses: $1,555.

2007-2008 Financial aid. **Need-based:** Need-based aid available for part-time students. **Non-need-based:** Scholarships awarded for academics.

Application procedures. **Admission:** No deadline. No application fee. Admission notification on a rolling basis. **Financial aid:** Priority date 3/15; no closing date. FAFSA required. Applicants notified on a rolling basis starting 7/1.

Academics. **Special study options:** Cooperative education, distance learning, dual enrollment of high school students, independent study, internships, liberal arts/career combination. License preparation in nursing, real estate. **Credit/placement by examination:** CLEP, institutional tests. **Support services:** GED preparation and test center, learning center, reduced course load, remedial instruction, study skills assistance, tutoring.

Majors. **Architecture:** Technology. **Business:** Administrative services, business admin, management information systems. **Computer sciences:** Information systems. **Conservation:** Environmental science. **Education:** Early childhood, teacher assistance. **Engineering technology:** Industrial. **Family/consumer sciences:** Child care. **Health:** Mental health services, nursing (RN), substance abuse counseling. **Interdisciplinary:** Global studies. **Liberal arts:** Arts/sciences. **Protective services:** Criminal justice.

Most popular majors. Business/marketing 56%, education 8%, health sciences 22%, liberal arts 6%, security/protective services 6%.

Computing on campus. 200 workstations in library, computer center. Online library available.

Student life. **Freshman orientation:** Available. Preregistration for classes offered. Held week before fall semester registration. **Activities:** Student government.

Athletics. **Intercollegiate:** Basketball M. **Intramural:** Basketball, softball, volleyball.

Student services. Career counseling, services for economically disadvantaged, student employment services, financial aid counseling, personal counseling, placement for graduates, veterans' counselor. **Physically disabled:** Services for visually, speech, hearing impaired. **Transfer:** Transfer adviser for students transferring to 4-year colleges.

Contact. Phone: (252) 862-1200 Fax: (252) 862-1355
Sandra Copeland, Director of Admissions/Counseling, Roanoke-Chowan Community College, 109 Community College Road, Ahoskie, NC 27910-9522

Robeson Community College

Lumberton, North Carolina
www.robeson.edu **CB code: 5594**

- Public 2-year community college
- Commuter campus in large town

General. Founded in 1965. Regionally accredited. **Enrollment:** 2,289 degree-seeking undergraduates. **Degrees:** 180 associate awarded. **Location:** 30 miles from Fayetteville. **Calendar:** Semester, limited summer session. **Full-time faculty:** 69 total. **Part-time faculty:** 75 total.

Basis for selection. Open admission, but selective for some programs. Special requirements for allied health programs. Interview recommended.

2008-2009 Annual costs. Tuition/fees: $1,324; $7,526 out-of-state. Per-credit charge: $42 in-state; $233 out-of-state. Books/supplies: $1,300. Personal expenses: $75.

2007-2008 Financial aid. **Need-based:** 99% of total undergraduate aid awarded as scholarships/grants, 1% as loans/jobs. Need-based aid available for part-time students.

Application procedures. **Admission:** Closing date 8/1. No application fee. Admission notification on a rolling basis. **Financial aid:** Priority date 5/15; no closing date. FAFSA required. Applicants notified on a rolling basis starting 7/31.

Academics. **Special study options:** Distance learning, double major, dual enrollment of high school students. **Credit/placement by examination:** CLEP, institutional tests. 40 credit hours maximum toward associate degree. **Support services:** Learning center, reduced course load, remedial instruction, tutoring.

Majors. **Business:** Business admin. **Computer sciences:** Information technology. **Engineering technology:** Electrical. **Health:** EMT paramedic, nursing (RN), radiologic technology/medical imaging, respiratory therapy technology, surgical technology. **Personal/culinary services:** Culinary arts. **Protective services:** Criminal justice.

Student life. **Activities:** Choral groups, literary magazine, student government, student newspaper.

Student services. Adult student services, career counseling, student employment services, health services, personal counseling, placement for graduates, veterans' counselor. **Physically disabled:** Services for hearing impaired. **Transfer:** Transfer adviser, college fairs on campus for students transferring to 4-year colleges.

Contact. E-mail: jrevels@robeson.cc.nc.us
Phone: (910) 272-3700 ext. 3347 Fax: (910) 618-5686
Judith Revels, Director of Admissions, Robeson Community College, PO Box 1420, Lumberton, NC 28359

Rockingham Community College

Wentworth, North Carolina
www.rockinghamcc.edu **CB code: 5582**

- Public 2-year community college
- Commuter campus in rural community

General. Founded in 1963. Regionally accredited. **Enrollment:** 1,812 degree-seeking undergraduates; 313 non-degree-seeking students. **Degrees:** 169 associate awarded. **Location:** 26 miles from Greensboro. **Calendar:** Semester, extensive summer session. **Full-time faculty:** 64 total. **Part-time faculty:** 45 total.

Student profile. Among degree-seeking undergraduates, 452 enrolled as first-time, first-year students.

Part-time:	50%	**Asian American:**	1%
Out-of-state:	1%	**Hispanic American:**	2%
Women:	65%	**Native American:**	1%
African American:	20%		

Transfer out. Colleges most students transferred to 2008: University of North Carolina at Greensboro, North Carolina A&T University.

Basis for selection. Open admission, but selective for some programs. All allied health programs and some other programs require all or some of the following: qualifying high school and college GPA, placement testing, specific high school courses, professional certification, other exams. Interview required for nursing and occupational therapy assistant programs. **Homeschooled:** Need complete record of all courses taken in grades 9-12.

High school preparation. Recommended units include English 4, mathematics 3, social studies 2, history 1, science 3 (laboratory 1) and foreign language 2.

2008-2009 Annual costs. Tuition/fees: $1,440; $7,561 out-of-state. Per-credit charge: $42 in-state; $233 out-of-state. Books/supplies: $1,500. Personal expenses: $4,100.

2007-2008 Financial aid. Need-based: Need-based aid available for part-time students. **Non-need-based:** Scholarships awarded for academics, art, job skills, leadership, minority status, state residency.

Application procedures. Admission: No deadline. No application fee. Admission notification on a rolling basis. **Financial aid:** Priority date 3/15; no closing date. FAFSA, institutional form required. Applicants notified on a rolling basis starting 5/30; must reply within 2 week(s) of notification.

Academics. Special study options: Cooperative education, distance learning, dual enrollment of high school students, independent study, student-designed major. Preengineering program leading to transfer to North Carolina State University, North Carolina Agricultural and Technical State University, or University of North Carolina at Charlotte. License preparation in nursing. **Credit/placement by examination:** AP, CLEP, institutional tests. **Support services:** GED preparation and test center, learning center, reduced course load, remedial instruction, study skills assistance, tutoring.

Majors. Agriculture: Horticultural science. **Business:** Accounting, business admin, office technology, office/clerical. **Computer sciences:** Information systems. **Education:** Early childhood. **Engineering:** Electrical. **Health:** Medical secretary, nursing (RN), respiratory therapy technology. **Liberal arts:** Arts/sciences. **Mechanic/repair:** Electronics/electrical. **Production:** Furniture. **Protective services:** Law enforcement admin. **Visual/performing arts:** Studio arts.

Most popular majors. Business/marketing 17%, education 9%, health sciences 30%, liberal arts 27%, security/protective services 9%.

Computing on campus. 200 workstations in library, computer center.

Student life. Freshman orientation: Mandatory. **Activities:** Student government, student newspaper, Phi Theta Kappa, nature study club, astronomy club, science fiction club, trips and outings clubs, cultural diversity awareness club.

Athletics. NJCAA. **Intercollegiate:** Baseball M, basketball M, cheerleading M, golf M, softball W, volleyball W. **Intramural:** Basketball, table tennis, tennis, volleyball. **Team name:** Eagles.

Student services. Career counseling, student employment services, on-campus daycare, personal counseling, placement for graduates. **Physically disabled:** Services for visually, hearing impaired. **Transfer:** Transfer adviser, college fairs on campus for students transferring to 4-year colleges.

Contact. E-mail: dunnm@rockinghamcc.edu
Phone: (336) 342-4261 ext. 2114 Fax: (336) 342-1809
Leigh Hawkins, Admissions Director, Rockingham Community College, Box 38, Wentworth, NC 27375-0038

Rowan-Cabarrus Community College

Salisbury, North Carolina
www.rowancabarrus.edu **CB code: 5589**

- Public 2-year community and technical college
- Commuter campus in large town

General. Founded in 1961. Regionally accredited. **Enrollment:** 5,876 degree-seeking undergraduates. **Degrees:** 412 associate awarded. **Location:** 40 miles from Charlotte. **Calendar:** Semester, extensive summer session. **Full-time faculty:** 153 total. **Part-time faculty:** 190 total. **Class size:** 58% < 20, 39% 20-39, 2% 40-49, less than 1% 50-99.

Transfer out. Colleges most students transferred to 2008: University of North Carolina-Charlotte, Pfeiffer University, Catawba College.

Basis for selection. Open admission, but selective for some programs. Interview required for allied health programs.

2008-2009 Annual costs. Tuition/fees: $1,324; $7,063 out-of-state. Per-credit charge: $42 in-state; $230 out-of-state.

2008-2009 Financial aid. Need-based: Need-based aid available for part-time students. Work-study available nights and for part-time students. **Non-need-based:** Scholarships awarded for academics, job skills, state residency.

Application procedures. Admission: No deadline. No application fee. Admission notification on a rolling basis. **Financial aid:** Priority date 3/15, closing date 8/1. FAFSA required. Applicants notified on a rolling basis starting 5/1; must reply within 3 week(s) of notification.

Academics. Special study options: Cooperative education, distance learning, dual enrollment of high school students, ESL, liberal arts/career combination, teacher certification program. License preparation in nursing, radiology, real estate. **Credit/placement by examination:** CLEP, institutional tests. 75 credit hours maximum toward associate degree. Student must complete 25% of credits required for graduation in resident classes. **Support services:** GED preparation and test center, learning center, reduced course load, remedial instruction, tutoring, writing center.

Majors. Business: Accounting, business admin, office technology. **Computer sciences:** Information systems, programming. **Education:** Early childhood. **Engineering technology:** Biomedical, drafting, electrical, industrial. **Health:** Nursing (RN), radiologic technology/medical imaging. **Legal studies:** Paralegal. **Mechanic/repair:** Industrial. **Protective services:** Criminal justice, fire safety technology.

Student life. Freshman orientation: Available. Fall and spring orientation. **Activities:** Student government.

Student services. Career counseling, student employment services, on-campus daycare, personal counseling, placement for graduates, veterans' counselor. **Physically disabled:** Services for visually, speech, hearing impaired. **Learning disabled:** Comprehensive services available. **Transfer:** Pre-admission transcript evaluation for new students. College fairs on campus for students transferring to 4-year colleges.

Contact. Phone: (704) 216-3602 Fax: (704) 633-6804
Gail Cummins, Director, Admissions and Recruitment, Rowan-Cabarrus Community College, Box 1595, Salisbury, NC 28145

Sampson Community College

Clinton, North Carolina
www.sampsoncc.edu **CB code: 0505**

- Public 2-year community college
- Commuter campus in small town

General. Founded in 1965. Regionally accredited. **Enrollment:** 1,278 degree-seeking undergraduates. **Degrees:** 104 associate awarded. **Location:** 30 miles from Fayetteville. **Calendar:** Semester, limited summer session. **Full-time faculty:** 55 total. **Part-time faculty:** 57 total.

Student profile. Among degree-seeking undergraduates, 469 enrolled as first-time, first-year students.

Part-time:	58%	**Women:**	73%
Out-of-state:	1%	**25 or older:**	47%

Transfer out. Colleges most students transferred to 2008: Fayetteville State University, UNC-Wilmington, Campbell University, Mt. Olive College, East Carolina University.

Basis for selection. Open admission, but selective for some programs. Special requirements for nursing and practical nursing; secondary school record and test scores important. Interview required for nursing programs.

High school preparation. 15 units recommended. Recommended units include English 4, mathematics 3, social studies 3, science 4 and foreign language 2. Algebra, chemistry and biology required for nursing programs.

2008-2009 Annual costs. Tuition/fees: $1,421; $7,543 out-of-state. Per-credit charge: $42 in-state; $233 out-of-state. Books/supplies: $600. Personal expenses: $900.

Financial aid. Need-based: Need-based aid available for part-time students. **Non-need-based:** Scholarships awarded for academics, state residency. **Additional information:** Short-term loans available to students waiting for federal aid to be approved. Covers tuition, fees and books only.

Application procedures. Admission: No deadline. No application fee. Admission notification on a rolling basis. **Financial aid:** Priority date 7/1; no closing date. FAFSA required. Applicants notified on a rolling basis starting 7/15; must reply within 2 week(s) of notification.

Academics. Special study options: Cooperative education, distance learning, dual enrollment of high school students, independent study, internships, liberal arts/career combination, weekend college. License preparation in nursing, real estate. **Credit/placement by examination:** AP, CLEP, institutional tests. 15 credit hours maximum toward associate degree. **Support services:** GED preparation and test center, learning center, pre-admission summer program, reduced course load, remedial instruction, study skills assistance, tutoring.

Majors. Agriculture: Horticulture, ornamental horticulture. **Business:** Accounting, administrative services, business admin, office/clerical. **Computer sciences:** General, applications programming, information systems. **Construction:** Carpentry. **Education:** General, early childhood. **Health:** Licensed practical nurse, nursing (RN). **Mechanic/repair:** Industrial. **Personal/culinary services:** Cosmetic.

Computing on campus. 110 workstations in library, computer center.

Student life. Freshman orientation: Mandatory. Preregistration for classes offered. **Activities:** Student government, student newspaper.

Athletics. Intercollegiate: Golf M. **Intramural:** Basketball M. **Team name:** Vikings.

Student services. Adult student services, career counseling, student employment services, financial aid counseling, personal counseling, placement for graduates, veterans' counselor. **Physically disabled:** Services for visually, speech, hearing impaired. **Transfer:** Pre-admission transcript evaluation for new students. Transfer adviser, college fairs on campus for students transferring to 4-year colleges.

Contact. Phone: (910) 592-8084 Fax: (910) 592-8048
Oscar Rodriguez, Director of Admissions, Sampson Community College, PO Box 318, Clinton, NC 28329

Sandhills Community College

Pinehurst, North Carolina
www.sandhills.edu **CB code: 5649**

- Public 2-year community college
- Commuter campus in large town

General. Founded in 1963. Regionally accredited. **Enrollment:** 3,947 degree-seeking undergraduates. **Degrees:** 371 associate awarded. **Location:** 41 miles from Fayetteville, 71 miles from Raleigh. **Calendar:** Semester, limited summer session. **Full-time faculty:** 120 total. **Part-time faculty:** 130 total. **Class size:** 51% < 20, 46% 20-39, 1% 40-49, 2% 50-99. **Special facilities:** Student maintained 30-acre garden, culinary arts lab.

Student profile.

Out-of-state:	1%	**25 or older:**	39%

Transfer out. Colleges most students transferred to 2008: University of North Carolina-Chapel Hill, University of North Carolina-Charlotte, University of North Carolina-Pembroke, North Carolina State University, Appalachian State University.

Basis for selection. Open admission, but selective for some programs. Placement testing required for all students who wish to enroll in curriculum programs and all non-degree seeking students who enroll in English, mathematics, or other restricted courses. Students with a minimum SAT score of 500 Writing, 500 Critical Reading, 500 Math or ACT score of 21 Writing, 21 Reading, 21 Math may be placed into college level English and math classes without taking a placement test. Accuplacer placement test administered and accepted, ASSET and COMPASS tests accepted. All test scores are valid for 3 years from the original test date. Transfer credits from another college may also allow placement test exemptions. **Homeschooled:** Transcript of courses and grades required. Copy of state registration required. **Learning Disabled:** Students with learning disabilities recommended to take classes in Continuing Education Program first.

2008-2009 Annual costs. Tuition/fees: $1,330; $7,069 out-of-state. Per-credit charge: $42 in-state; $233 out-of-state. Books/supplies: $547. Personal expenses: $1,080.

2007-2008 Financial aid. Need-based: 82% of total undergraduate aid awarded as scholarships/grants, 18% as loans/jobs. Need-based aid available for part-time students. **Non-need-based:** Scholarships awarded for academics. **Additional information:** Scholarships available, limited loan capability.

Application procedures. Admission: No deadline. No application fee. Admission notification on a rolling basis. **Financial aid:** Priority date 6/1; no closing date. FAFSA required. Applicants notified on a rolling basis starting 2/1; must reply by 8/1 or within 4 week(s) of notification.

Academics. Weekend support services held at satellite campus. **Special study options:** Cooperative education, distance learning, double major, dual enrollment of high school students, ESL, honors, independent study, internships, liberal arts/career combination, teacher certification program. Third and fourth year courses offered on campus evenings by St. Andrews Presbyterian College and UNC Pembroke, distance learning classes through Franklin University. License preparation in nursing, paramedic, radiology, real estate. **Credit/placement by examination:** AP, CLEP, institutional tests. **Support services:** GED preparation and test center, learning center, reduced course load, remedial instruction, study skills assistance, tutoring.

Majors. Agriculture: Landscaping, turf management. **Architecture:** Technology. **Biology:** General. **Business:** Accounting, administrative services, business admin, e-commerce, hotel/motel admin, restaurant/food services. **Computer sciences:** General, applications programming, computer science, information systems, programming, webmaster. **Education:** Biology, chemistry, early childhood, elementary, history, science, secondary, social science, social studies, teacher assistance. **Engineering technology:** Architectural, civil, computer, drafting, surveying. **Family/consumer sciences:** Child care. **Health:** Clinical lab technology, EMT ambulance attendant, EMT paramedic, massage therapy, medical radiologic technology/radiation therapy, medical records admin, nursing (RN), predental, premedicine, prenursing, prepharmacy, preveterinary, respiratory therapy technology, substance abuse counseling, surgical technology. **Legal studies:** Prelaw. **Liberal arts:** Arts/sciences. **Math:** General. **Mechanic/repair:** Automotive. **Personal/culinary services:** Cosmetic, culinary arts. **Protective services:** Criminal justice. **Psychology:** General. **Public administration:** Social work. **Social sciences:** General. **Visual/performing arts:** Art.

Most popular majors. Business/marketing 8%, computer/information sciences 6%, health sciences 42%, liberal arts 11%, trade and industry 11%.

Computing on campus. 400 workstations in library, computer center. Commuter students can connect to campus network.

Student life. Freshman orientation: Mandatory. Preregistration for classes offered. 2-hour information session, course planning, and registration. **Activities:** Bands, choral groups, music ensembles, student government, student newspaper, symphony orchestra, Minority Students for Academic and Cultural Enrichment, Circle-K, Young Democrats, Young Republicans, Phi Theta Kappa, Student Government Association.

Student services. Alcohol/substance abuse counseling, career counseling, student employment services, financial aid counseling, personal counseling, placement for graduates, veterans' counselor. **Physically disabled:** Services for visually, hearing impaired. **Transfer:** Pre-admission transcript evaluation for new students. Transfer adviser, college fairs on campus for students transferring to 4-year colleges.

Contact. E-mail: farmerdj@sandhills.edu
Phone: (910) 692-6185 Toll-free number: (800) 338-3944
Fax: (910) 695-3981
DJ Farmer, Admissions Director, Sandhills Community College, 3395 Airport Road, Pinehurst, NC 28374

Shepherds Theological Seminary

Cary, North Carolina
www.shepherdsseminary.org

- Private 2-year seminary college
- Small city

General. Regionally accredited. **Enrollment:** 5 degree-seeking undergraduates. **Calendar:** Semester. **Full-time faculty:** 2 total. **Part-time faculty:** 6 total.

Application procedures. Admission: Closing date 8/15.

Academics. Credit/placement by examination: CLEP.

Majors. Other: Church ministry.

Contact. E-mail: info@shepherdsseminary.org
Toll-free number: (800) 672-3060
Randall McKinion, Registrar, Shepherds Theological Seminary, 6051 Tryon Road, Cary, NC 27518

South College
Asheville, North Carolina
www.southcollegenc.edu **CB code: 0508**

- For-profit 2-year health science and technical college
- Commuter campus in small city
- Interview required

General. Founded in 1905. Candidate for regional accreditation; also accredited by ACICS. **Enrollment:** 141 degree-seeking undergraduates. **Degrees:** 1 bachelor's, 50 associate awarded. **Location:** 4 miles from downtown. **Calendar:** Quarter, extensive summer session. **Full-time faculty:** 13 total. **Part-time faculty:** 33 total. **Class size:** 91% < 20, 9% 20-39.

Transfer out. Colleges most students transferred to 2008: Asheville-Buncombe Technical Community College, Blue Ridge Community College, Mars Hill College, Montreat College.

Basis for selection. Open admission, but selective for some programs. College-administered exam required of all applicants. Scores used for admission and program placement. **Homeschooled:** Copy of homeschool diploma required.

2008-2009 Annual costs. Tuition/fees: $13,200. Per-credit charge: $350. Books/supplies: $1,050. Personal expenses: $1,080.

2007-2008 Financial aid. Need-based: 40% of total undergraduate aid awarded as scholarships/grants, 60% as loans/jobs. Need-based aid available for part-time students. Work-study available for part-time students.

Application procedures. Admission: No deadline. $50 fee, may be waived for applicants with need. Admission notification on a rolling basis. **Financial aid:** No deadline. FAFSA required. Applicants notified on a rolling basis.

Academics. Special study options: Accelerated study, cooperative education, double major, internships, liberal arts/career combination. Bachelor's degree programs available on campus. License preparation in physical therapy, radiology. **Credit/placement by examination:** CLEP, institutional tests. Varies with program, but no more than 60% of any program. **Support services:** Reduced course load, study skills assistance, tutoring.

Majors. Business: Accounting, administrative services, business admin, office technology. **Computer sciences:** General. **Health:** Medical assistant. **Legal studies:** Paralegal. **Protective services:** Law enforcement admin.

Computing on campus. 28 workstations in library, computer center.

Student life. Freshman orientation: Mandatory. Orientation is held prior to each quarter.

Student services. Career counseling, student employment services, financial aid counseling, personal counseling, placement for graduates, veterans' counselor. **Transfer:** Pre-admission transcript evaluation for new students.

Contact. Phone: (828) 277-5521 Fax: (828) 277-6151
Duff Moore, Director of Admissions, South College, 29 Turtle Creek Drive, Asheville, NC 28803

South Piedmont Community College
Polkton, North Carolina
www.spcc.edu **CB code: 0457**

- Public 2-year community college
- Commuter campus in small city

General. Founded in 1962. Regionally accredited. Multiple campus locations near Charlotte. **Enrollment:** 2,310 degree-seeking undergraduates. **Degrees:** 100 associate awarded. **Location:** 60 miles from Charlotte. **Calendar:** Semester, limited summer session. **Full-time faculty:** 75 total. **Part-time faculty:** 200 total. **Partnerships:** Formal partnership with local high schools.

Student profile.

Out-of-state:	1%	**25 or older:**	57%

Basis for selection. Open admission, but selective for some programs. Special requirements for health technology programs. **Homeschooled:** Students should have state certification number, successful completion of competency exam, registered with local board of education, copy of transcript and diploma.

2008-2009 Annual costs. Tuition/fees: $1,372; $7,111 out-of-state. Per-credit charge: $56 in-state; $248 out-of-state. Books/supplies: $650. Personal expenses: $900.

2008-2009 Financial aid. Need-based: 98% of total undergraduate aid awarded as scholarships/grants, 2% as loans/jobs. Need-based aid available for part-time students. Work-study available nights and weekends. **Additional information:** Small amount of nonfederal scholarship aid available.

Application procedures. Admission: No deadline. No application fee. Admission notification on a rolling basis. **Financial aid:** No deadline. FAFSA required. Applicants notified on a rolling basis.

Academics. Special study options: Cooperative education, cross-registration, distance learning, dual enrollment of high school students, independent study, internships. **Credit/placement by examination:** CLEP, institutional tests. **Support services:** GED preparation and test center, learning center, reduced course load, remedial instruction, study skills assistance, tutoring.

Majors. Business: Accounting, administrative services, business admin, office/clerical. **Computer sciences:** General, applications programming, information systems, networking, programming. **Education:** General. **Engineering technology:** Drafting, electrical, manufacturing. **Family/consumer sciences:** Child care. **Health:** Health services, massage therapy, medical assistant, medical records technology, nursing (RN), sonography. **Legal studies:** Legal secretary, paralegal. **Liberal arts:** Arts/sciences. **Mechanic/repair:** Heating/ac/refrig. **Protective services:** Criminal justice. **Public administration:** Human services. **Visual/performing arts:** Commercial/advertising art.

Computing on campus. 200 workstations in library, computer center.

Student life. Freshman orientation: Available. Preregistration for classes offered. **Activities:** Student government, student newspaper, Phi Beta Lambda business organization, criminal justice student association, social services club, Phi Theta Kappa.

Athletics. Team name: Patriots.

Student services. Alcohol/substance abuse counseling, career counseling, student employment services, financial aid counseling, personal counseling, placement for graduates, veterans' counselor. **Physically disabled:** Services for visually, hearing impaired. **Transfer:** Transfer adviser for students transferring to 4-year colleges.

Contact. E-mail: a-russell@spcc.edu
Phone: (704) 272-5324 Toll-free number: (800) 766-0319
Fax: (704) 272-5303
John Curtis, Director, Admissions/ Enrollment, South Piedmont Community College, PO Box 126, Polkton, NC 28135

Southeastern Community College
Whiteville, North Carolina
www.sccnc.edu **CB code: 5651**

- Public 2-year community college
- Commuter campus in small town

General. Founded in 1964. Regionally accredited. **Enrollment:** 1,630 degree-seeking undergraduates. **Degrees:** 182 associate awarded. **Location:** 45 miles from Wilmington. **Calendar:** Semester, limited summer session. **Full-time faculty:** 81 total; 2% have terminal degrees, 11% minority, 58% women. **Part-time faculty:** 130 total; 4% have terminal degrees, 18% minority, 52% women. **Class size:** 64% < 20, 33% 20-39, 2% 40-49, less than 1% 50-99. **Special facilities:** Outdoor natural resources lab of 23 acres of hardwood and pine forest, signed nature trail, butterfly garden. **Partnerships:** Formal partnership with Columbus County School System.

Student profile.

Out-of-state:	1%	25 or older:	45%

Transfer out. **Colleges most students transferred to 2008:** University of North Carolina at Wilmington, University of North Carolina at Pembroke, Fayetteville State University, East Carolina University.

Basis for selection. Open admission, but selective for some programs. Basic law Enforcement Training: Age 21 and Reading test requirements. Allied Health: Reading, Math, CNA 1 certification, points requirements. SAT may be substituted for placement test. **Homeschooled:** Transcript of courses and grades required. Documentation from state showing authorization. **Learning Disabled:** Applicant must provide proof of disability from specialist, and list of required accommodations from specialist, and list of requested accommodations from student.

High school preparation. Recommended units include English 6, mathematics 6, social studies 6 and science 6.

2008-2009 Annual costs. Tuition/fees: $1,329; $7,068 out-of-state. Per-credit charge: $42 in-state; $233 out-of-state. Books/supplies: $910. Personal expenses: $972.

2007-2008 Financial aid. **Need-based:** Need-based aid available for part-time students. Work-study available for part-time students. **Non-need-based:** Scholarships awarded for academics, athletics, leadership, music/drama, state residency.

Application procedures. **Admission:** No deadline. No application fee. Admission notification on a rolling basis. **Financial aid:** Priority date 4/1; no closing date. FAFSA required. Applicants notified on a rolling basis starting 6/1; must reply within 2 week(s) of notification.

Academics. **Special study options:** Cooperative education, distance learning, double major, dual enrollment of high school students, honors, independent study, internships, liberal arts/career combination. License preparation in nursing, real estate. **Credit/placement by examination:** AP, CLEP, institutional tests. **Support services:** GED preparation and test center, learning center, reduced course load, remedial instruction, study skills assistance, tutoring, writing center.

Majors. **Biology:** Biotechnology. **Business:** General, accounting technology, accounting/finance, banking/financial services, business admin, finance, marketing, office technology, office/clerical. **Communications:** General. **Communications technology:** Radio/tv. **Computer sciences:** General, information technology, networking, web page design, word processing. **Conservation:** Environmental science, forest technology. **Education:** Early childhood, elementary, secondary. **Engineering technology:** Electrical. **Family/consumer sciences:** Child care. **Health:** Clinical lab technology, nursing (RN). **Interdisciplinary:** Biological/physical sciences. **Liberal arts:** Arts/sciences. **Mechanic/repair:** Industrial. **Parks/recreation:** Facilities management. **Personal/culinary services:** Cosmetic. **Visual/performing arts:** Art.

Most popular majors. Business/marketing 8%, education 6%, health sciences 42%, visual/performing arts 16%.

Computing on campus. 115 workstations in library, computer center.

Student life. **Freshman orientation:** Mandatory, $42 fee. Preregistration for classes offered. College Student Success is a required one credit class with 16 contact hours, 4 of which are online. Topics covered are college life, college skills, and personal awareness. **Activities:** Concert band, choral groups, drama, literary magazine, student government, student newspaper, Student Ambassadors.

Athletics. NJCAA. **Intercollegiate:** Baseball M, volleyball W. **Team name:** Rams.

Student services. Adult student services, career counseling, services for economically disadvantaged, student employment services, financial aid counseling, on-campus daycare, personal counseling, placement for graduates, veterans' counselor. **Physically disabled:** Services for visually, speech, hearing impaired. **Transfer:** Pre-admission transcript evaluation for new students. Transfer adviser, college fairs on campus for students transferring to 4-year colleges.

Contact. E-mail: start@sccnc.edu
Phone: (910) 642-7141 ext. 249 Fax: (910) 642-1267
Sylvia Tart, Director of Student Records/Registrar, Southeastern Community College, 4564 Chadbourn Highway, Whiteville, NC 28472-0151

Southwestern Community College

Sylva, North Carolina
www.southwesterncc.edu **CB code: 5667**

- Public 2-year community college
- Commuter campus in rural community

General. Founded in 1964. Regionally accredited. Five off-campus sites serve two adjoining counties. **Enrollment:** 900 full-time, degree-seeking students. **Degrees:** 252 associate awarded. **Location:** 48 miles from Asheville. **Calendar:** Semester, limited summer session. **Full-time faculty:** 73 total. **Part-time faculty:** 121 total. **Class size:** 80% < 20, 20% 20-39.

Student profile.

Out-of-state:	1%	25 or older:	46%

Transfer out. **Colleges most students transferred to 2008:** Western Carolina University.

Basis for selection. Open admission, but selective for some programs. Admission to allied health programs based on test scores, academic record, interview, and recommendations. Interview required for allied health applicants; recommended for all others.

High school preparation. Algebra, biology, and chemistry required for allied health program applicants.

2008-2009 Annual costs. Tuition/fees: $1,324; $7,063 out-of-state. Per-credit charge: $42 in-state; $233 out-of-state. Books/supplies: $750. Personal expenses: $1,238.

Financial aid. **Need-based:** Need-based aid available for part-time students. Work-study available for part-time students.

Application procedures. **Admission:** No deadline. No application fee. Admission notification on a rolling basis. **Financial aid:** Priority date 4/30; no closing date. FAFSA required. Applicants notified on a rolling basis starting 5/1; must reply within 2 week(s) of notification.

Academics. **Special study options:** Cooperative education, double major, dual enrollment of high school students, ESL, independent study, internships, liberal arts/career combination. License preparation in nursing, paramedic, physical therapy, radiology, real estate. **Credit/placement by examination:** CLEP, institutional tests. **Support services:** GED preparation and test center, learning center, reduced course load, remedial instruction, tutoring.

Majors. **Business:** Accounting, administrative services, business admin, marketing. **Computer sciences:** General, networking, programming. **Education:** General, early childhood, trade/industrial. **Engineering:** Computer, electrical, surveying. **Engineering technology:** Electrical. **Family/consumer sciences:** Child care. **Health:** Clinical lab science, clinical lab technology, EMT paramedic, medical radiologic technology/radiation therapy, medical records technology, mental health services, nursing (RN), physical therapy assistant, respiratory therapy assistant, respiratory therapy technology, sonography, substance abuse counseling. **Legal studies:** Paralegal. **Liberal arts:** Arts/sciences. **Mechanic/repair:** Automotive. **Parks/recreation:** General. **Personal/culinary services:** Cosmetic, culinary arts. **Protective services:** Criminal justice. **Visual/performing arts:** Commercial/advertising art.

Most popular majors. Business/marketing 7%, health sciences 35%, liberal arts 22%, security/protective services 10%.

Computing on campus. 200 workstations in computer center. Commuter students can connect to campus network.

Student life. **Freshman orientation:** Mandatory. Preregistration for classes offered. One-day live orientation held on Jackson Campus at beginning of Fall Semester for all students enrolling for first time. New students enrolling in Spring or Summer semesters take on-line orientation program. **Activities:** Literary magazine, student government, Phi Theta Kappa, Native American Society, Spanish Club.

Student services. Career counseling, services for economically disadvantaged, student employment services, financial aid counseling, on-campus daycare, personal counseling, placement for graduates, veterans' counselor. **Physically disabled:** Services for visually, speech, hearing impaired. **Transfer:** Pre-admission transcript evaluation for new students. Transfer adviser for students transferring to 4-year colleges.

Contact. Phone: (828) 586-4091 ext. 352 Toll-free number: (800) 447-4091 Fax: (828) 586-3129
Phil Weast, Dean of Student Services, Southwestern Community College, 447 College Drive, Sylva, NC 28779

Stanly Community College
Albemarle, North Carolina
www.stanly.edu **CB code: 0496**

- Public 2-year community college
- Commuter campus in large town

General. Founded in 1971. Regionally accredited. **Enrollment:** 3,090 degree-seeking undergraduates. **Degrees:** 253 associate awarded. **Location:** 30 miles from Charlotte. **Calendar:** Semester, limited summer session. **Full-time faculty:** 88 total. **Part-time faculty:** 167 total.

Transfer out. **Colleges most students transferred to 2008:** University of North Carolina at Charlotte, Pfeiffer University.

Basis for selection. Open admission, but selective for some programs. Special requirements for nursing, radiography, respiratory therapy, and medical lab assistant majors. **Learning Disabled:** Written verification of disability, no more than five years old, required at least 60 days prior to enrollment.

2008-2009 Annual costs. Tuition/fees: $1,376; $7,115 out-of-state. Per-credit charge: $42 in-state; $233 out-of-state. Books/supplies: $900. Personal expenses: $1,050.

2007-2008 Financial aid. All financial aid based on need. Need-based aid available for part-time students. Work-study available for part-time students.

Application procedures. **Admission:** No deadline. No application fee. Admission notification on a rolling basis. **Financial aid:** Closing date 4/15. FAFSA, institutional form required. Applicants notified on a rolling basis starting 6/1; must reply within 2 week(s) of notification.

Academics. **Special study options:** Distance learning, dual enrollment of high school students, ESL, weekend college. **Credit/placement by examination:** AP, CLEP, institutional tests. **Support services:** GED preparation and test center, remedial instruction, study skills assistance, tutoring.

Majors. **Business:** Accounting, business admin, human resources. **Computer sciences:** Computer graphics, information systems, information technology, LAN/WAN management, networking, security. **Education:** Early childhood, elementary, special. **Engineering technology:** Biomedical, computer, electrical. **Health:** Clinical lab assistant, EMT paramedic, medical assistant, nursing (RN), radiologic technology/medical imaging, respiratory therapy technology. **Liberal arts:** Arts/sciences. **Personal/culinary services:** Cosmetic. **Protective services:** Criminal justice.

Most popular majors. Business/marketing 13%, computer/information sciences 11%, education 13%, engineering/engineering technologies 9%, health sciences 21%, liberal arts 12%, security/protective services 13%, social sciences 7%.

Computing on campus. 100 workstations in library, computer center, student center. Commuter students can connect to campus network. Online library, helpline, wireless network available.

Student life. **Freshman orientation:** Available. Preregistration for classes offered. **Activities:** Student government.

Athletics. NJCAA. **Intercollegiate:** Softball W, volleyball W. **Team name:** Eagles.

Student services. Adult student services, alcohol/substance abuse counseling, career counseling, services for economically disadvantaged, student employment services, financial aid counseling, minority student services, personal counseling, placement for graduates, veterans' counselor, women's services. **Transfer:** Pre-admission transcript evaluation for new students. Transfer adviser, college fairs on campus for students transferring to 4-year colleges.

Contact. E-mail: sccadmissions@stanly.edu
Phone: (704) 991-0226 Fax: (704) 991-0255
Ronnie Hinson, Dean of Students, Stanly Community College, 141 College Drive, Albemarle, NC 28001

Surry Community College
Dobson, North Carolina
www.surry.edu **CB code: 5656**

- Public 2-year community college
- Commuter campus in rural community

General. Founded in 1964. Regionally accredited. **Enrollment:** 1,578 full-time, degree-seeking students. **Degrees:** 347 associate awarded. **Location:** 40 miles from Winston-Salem. **Calendar:** Semester, extensive summer session. **Full-time faculty:** 100 total. **Part-time faculty:** 220 total. **Special facilities:** Working vineyard and wine-making facilities.

Transfer out. **Colleges most students transferred to 2008:** Appalachian State University, Gardner-Webb University, Lees-McRae University, University of North Carolina-Greensboro, Winston-Salem State University.

Basis for selection. Open admission, but selective for some programs. Competitive admission to associate degree nursing program (RN) and practical nursing program (LPN) based primarily on academic standing; test scores considered. Special admissions also required for Physical Therapy Assistant includes prerequisites, Teas testing and interviews. Portfolio required for admission to advertising and graphic design programs. **Home-schooled:** Proof of home school registration from the state of NC required.

2008-2009 Annual costs. Tuition/fees: $1,420; $7,542 out-of-state. Per-credit charge: $42 in-state; $233 out-of-state. Books/supplies: $1,200. Personal expenses: $1,000.

2007-2008 Financial aid. **Need-based:** Need-based aid available for part-time students. Work-study available nights and for part-time students. **Non-need-based:** Scholarships awarded for academics.

Application procedures. **Admission:** No deadline. No application fee. Admission notification on a rolling basis. **Financial aid:** Priority date 5/1; no closing date. FAFSA, institutional form required. Applicants notified on a rolling basis starting 6/1; must reply within 2 week(s) of notification.

Academics. **Special study options:** Accelerated study, cooperative education, distance learning, double major, dual enrollment of high school students, ESL, independent study, internships, weekend college. Bachelor's degree programs available on campus. License preparation in nursing, paramedic, physical therapy, real estate. **Credit/placement by examination:** AP, CLEP, institutional tests. **Support services:** GED preparation and test center, learning center, reduced course load, remedial instruction, study skills assistance, tutoring.

Majors. **Agriculture:** Horticulture. **Business:** Accounting, business admin, office/clerical. **Computer sciences:** Information systems. **Construction:** Carpentry, site management. **Education:** Early childhood, early childhood special. **Engineering:** Computer, electrical. **Engineering technology:** Drafting. **Foreign languages:** Translation. **Health:** Medical assistant, nursing (RN), office admin. **Legal studies:** Paralegal. **Liberal arts:** Arts/sciences. **Mechanic/repair:** Automotive, heating/ac/refrig, industrial, industrial electronics. **Personal/culinary services:** Cosmetic. **Protective services:** Law enforcement admin. **Visual/performing arts:** Commercial/advertising art.

Computing on campus. 500 workstations in library, computer center. Online library, helpline, wireless network available.

Student life. **Freshman orientation:** Mandatory. Preregistration for classes offered. **Activities:** Choral groups, literary magazine, radio station, student government, student newspaper.

Athletics. NJCAA. **Intercollegiate:** Baseball M, basketball M, volleyball W. **Team name:** Knights.

Student services. Adult student services, career counseling, services for economically disadvantaged, student employment services, financial aid counseling, personal counseling, placement for graduates, veterans' counselor. **Physically disabled:** Services for visually, hearing impaired. **Transfer:** Transfer adviser, college fairs on campus for students transferring to 4-year colleges.

Contact. E-mail: childressj@surry.edu
Phone: (336) 386-3392 Fax: (336) 386-8951
Jamie Childress, Associate Vice President for Student Services, Surry Community College, 630 South Main Street, Dobson, NC 27017

Tri-County Community College
Murphy, North Carolina
www.tricountycc.edu **CB code: 5785**

- Public 2-year community college
- Commuter campus in rural community

General. Founded in 1964. Regionally accredited. **Enrollment:** 648 degree-seeking undergraduates; 411 non-degree-seeking students. **Degrees:** 105 associate awarded. **Location:** 110 miles from Asheville, 96 miles from Chattanooga, Tennessee. **Calendar:** Semester, extensive summer session. **Full-time faculty:** 37 total. **Part-time faculty:** 42 total. **Class size:** 22% < 20, 57% 20-39, 20% 40-49, 1% 50-99.

Student profile. Among degree-seeking undergraduates, 54% enrolled in a transfer program, 79% enrolled in a vocational program, 1% already have a bachelor's degree or higher, 152 enrolled as first-time, first-year students.

Part-time:	35%	**Women:**	54%
Out-of-state:	9%	**25 or older:**	54%

Transfer out. 80% of students enrolled in the transfer program go on to 4-year colleges. **Colleges most students transferred to 2008:** Western Carolina University, Southwestern Community College.

Basis for selection. Open admission. **Learning Disabled:** Tutoring is available.

2008-2009 Annual costs. Tuition/fees: $1,319; $7,058 out-of-state. Per-credit charge: $42 in-state; $233 out-of-state. Books/supplies: $300. Personal expenses: $450.

2007-2008 Financial aid. All financial aid based on need. 400 full-time freshmen applied for aid; 350 were judged to have need; 350 of these received aid. Average need met was 50%. Average scholarship/grant was $2,500. 98% of total undergraduate aid awarded as scholarships/grants, 2% as loans/jobs. Need-based aid available for part-time students.

Application procedures. Admission: No deadline. No application fee. Admission notification on a rolling basis. **Financial aid:** Priority date 6/30; no closing date. FAFSA required. Applicants notified on a rolling basis starting 6/1; must reply within 4 week(s) of notification.

Academics. Special study options: Double major, dual enrollment of high school students, independent study, internships. License preparation in nursing, paramedic, real estate. **Credit/placement by examination:** AP, CLEP, institutional tests. 6 credit hours maximum toward associate degree. **Support services:** GED preparation and test center, learning center, reduced course load, remedial instruction, study skills assistance, tutoring.

Majors. Business: Accounting, administrative services, business admin. **Computer sciences:** Information systems. **Construction:** Electrician. **Engineering technology:** Surveying. **Health:** EMT paramedic, medical assistant, nursing (RN). **Liberal arts:** Arts/sciences. **Mechanic/repair:** Automotive, electronics/electrical.

Most popular majors. Business/marketing 24%, liberal arts 43%, trade and industry 35%.

Computing on campus. 42 workstations in library, computer center, student center. Online library available.

Student life. Freshman orientation: Mandatory. Preregistration for classes offered. **Activities:** Student government, student newspaper, honor society.

Student services. Adult student services, career counseling, services for economically disadvantaged, student employment services, financial aid counseling, on-campus daycare, personal counseling, placement for graduates, veterans' counselor. **Physically disabled:** Services for visually, hearing impaired. **Transfer:** Pre-admission transcript evaluation for new students. College fairs on campus for students transferring to 4-year colleges.

Contact. E-mail: jchambers@tricountycc.edu
Phone: (828) 837-6810 Toll-free number: (828) 835-4225
Fax: (828) 837-3266
Jason Chambers, Director of Admissions, Tri-County Community College, 4600 Highway 64 East, Murphy, NC 28906

Vance-Granville Community College

Henderson, North Carolina — **CB member**
www.vgcc.edu — **CB code: 0617**

- Public 2-year community college
- Commuter campus in large town

General. Founded in 1969. Regionally accredited. 4 rural counties served with satellite campuses in Warrenton, Butner and Louisburg. **Enrollment:** 3,948 degree-seeking undergraduates. **Degrees:** 339 associate awarded. **Location:** 42 miles from Raleigh. **Calendar:** Semester, limited summer session. **Full-time faculty:** 141 total. **Part-time faculty:** 232 total.

Basis for selection. Open admission, but selective for some programs. Admission to nursing, radiologic technology, and medical assisting is based on academic record, health education aptitude test, and other criteria. Interview recommended for nursing, radiologic technology programs.

2008-2009 Annual costs. Tuition/fees: $1,408; $7,530 out-of-state. Per-credit charge: $42 in-state; $233 out-of-state. Books/supplies: $800. Personal expenses: $400.

2007-2008 Financial aid. Need-based: Need-based aid available for part-time students. **Non-need-based:** Scholarships awarded for academics.

Application procedures. Admission: No deadline. No application fee. Admission notification on a rolling basis. Application deadlines apply and may vary for Allied Health programs. College placement examinations required of all students, unless acceptable scores on SAT/ACT or special students. **Financial aid:** Closing date 3/15. FAFSA required. Applicants notified on a rolling basis starting 5/1; must reply within 2 week(s) of notification.

Academics. Special study options: Cooperative education, distance learning, double major, dual enrollment of high school students, ESL, independent study, internships. License preparation in nursing, radiology, real estate. **Credit/placement by examination:** CLEP, institutional tests. **Support services:** GED preparation and test center, learning center, pre-admission summer program, reduced course load, remedial instruction, study skills assistance, tutoring.

Majors. Business: Accounting, administrative services, business admin, office technology. **Computer sciences:** Information technology, networking, security, web page design. **Education:** General, early childhood, teacher assistance. **Engineering:** Electrical. **Engineering technology:** Electrical. **Family/consumer sciences:** Child care. **Health:** Medical assistant, medical radiologic technology/radiation therapy, nursing (RN), recreational therapy. **Liberal arts:** Arts/sciences. **Mechanic/repair:** Electronics/electrical. **Parks/recreation:** General. **Personal/culinary services:** Culinary arts. **Protective services:** Law enforcement admin. **Public administration:** Human services. **Science technology:** Biological.

Most popular majors. Business/marketing 17%, computer/information sciences 9%, education 14%, health sciences 21%, liberal arts 8%, security/protective services 7%.

Computing on campus. 48 workstations in library, computer center.

Student life. Freshman orientation: Available. **Activities:** Drama, student government, departmental clubs.

Student services. Adult student services, career counseling, student employment services, financial aid counseling, on-campus daycare, personal counseling, placement for graduates, veterans' counselor. **Physically disabled:** Services for visually, hearing impaired. **Transfer:** Transfer adviser for students transferring to 4-year colleges.

Contact. Phone: (252) 492-2061 Fax: (252) 430-0460
Kathy Ktul, Registrar/Director of Admissions, Vance-Granville Community College, Box 917, Henderson, NC 27536

Wake Technical Community College

Raleigh, North Carolina
www.waketech.edu — **CB code: 5928**

- Public 2-year community and technical college
- Commuter campus in small city

General. Founded in 1958. Regionally accredited. **Enrollment:** 13,775 degree-seeking undergraduates. **Degrees:** 985 associate awarded. **Location:** 10 miles from Raleigh. **Calendar:** Semester, extensive summer session. **Full-time faculty:** 310 total. **Part-time faculty:** 630 total.

Student profile. Among degree-seeking undergraduates, 40% enrolled in a transfer program, 60% enrolled in a vocational program, 11% already have a bachelor's degree or higher.

Transfer out. Colleges most students transferred to 2008: North Carolina State University, University of North Carolina at Chapel Hill, East Carolina University, University of North Carolina at Greensboro, Appalachian State University.

Basis for selection. Open admission, but selective for some programs. Admission to health programs based on standardized test scores, post-secondary coursework. Placement tests required of all degree and diploma students with SAT scores below 480 verbal or math, or below ACT math 20, reading 19, and writing 19. Interview recommended. **Homeschooled:** Must include transcript and test scores.

High school preparation. Recommended units include English 4 and mathematics 4. 1 chemistry required for health sciences associate degree programs.

2008-2009 Annual costs. Tuition/fees: $1,320; $7,059 out-of-state. Per-credit charge: $42 in-state; $233 out-of-state. Books/supplies: $1,000. Personal expenses: $1,350.

Two-Year Colleges

Financial aid. **Need-based:** Need-based aid available for part-time students. Work-study available for part-time students. **Non-need-based:** Scholarships awarded for academics, job skills, leadership, state residency.

Application procedures. **Admission:** No deadline. No application fee. Admission notification on a rolling basis. **Financial aid:** Priority date 3/15; no closing date. FAFSA, institutional form required. Applicants notified on a rolling basis starting 4/1; must reply within 2 week(s) of notification.

Academics. **Special study options:** Cooperative education, distance learning, double major, dual enrollment of high school students, ESL, honors, liberal arts/career combination. License preparation in dental hygiene, nursing, paramedic, radiology, real estate. **Credit/placement by examination:** AP, CLEP, IB, institutional tests. 25% of degree requirement must be taken in residence. **Support services:** GED preparation and test center, learning center, pre-admission summer program, reduced course load, remedial instruction, study skills assistance, tutoring, writing center.

Majors. **Architecture:** Landscape. **Business:** General, accounting, administrative services, hospitality/recreation. **Computer sciences:** General, applications programming, computer graphics, programming. **Conservation:** General. **Construction:** Power transmission. **Education:** Early childhood. **Engineering technology:** Architectural, civil, drafting, electrical, manufacturing, robotics, surveying. **Health:** Clinical lab technology, dental hygiene, EMT paramedic, medical assistant, medical radiologic technology/radiation therapy, medical records technology, medical secretary, nursing (RN), surgical technology. **Interdisciplinary:** Global studies. **Legal studies:** Legal secretary. **Liberal arts:** Arts/sciences. **Mechanic/repair:** Electronics/electrical, industrial. **Personal/culinary services:** Culinary arts. **Protective services:** Police science. **Public administration:** Human services.

Most popular majors. Business/marketing 22%, computer/information sciences 15%, engineering/engineering technologies 17%, health sciences 15%, liberal arts 25%.

Computing on campus. 62 workstations in library, computer center, student center. Online course registration, helpline, wireless network available.

Student life. **Freshman orientation:** Available. Held on first day of class. **Activities:** Choral groups, drama, radio station, student government, student newspaper.

Athletics. NJCAA. **Intercollegiate:** Golf, soccer M, volleyball W. **Team name:** Eagles.

Student services. Career counseling, student employment services, financial aid counseling, health services, personal counseling, placement for graduates, veterans' counselor. **Physically disabled:** Services for visually, speech, hearing impaired. **Transfer:** Transfer adviser, college fairs on campus for students transferring to 4-year colleges.

Contact. Phone: (919) 866-5500 Fax: (919) 661-0117
Susan Bloomfield, Director of Admissions, Wake Technical Community College, 9101 Fayetteville Road, Raleigh, NC 27603

Wayne Community College

Goldsboro, North Carolina
www.waynecc.edu **CB code: 5926**

- Public 2-year community college
- Commuter campus in large town
- Interview required

General. Founded in 1957. Regionally accredited. **Enrollment:** 2,885 degree-seeking undergraduates. **Degrees:** 350 associate awarded. **Location:** 55 miles from Raleigh. **Calendar:** Semester, limited summer session. **Full-time faculty:** 121 total. **Part-time faculty:** 154 total.

Student profile.

Out-of-state:	16%	**25 or older:**	45%

Transfer out. **Colleges most students transferred to 2008:** East Carolina University, Mount Olive College, Campbell University, North Carolina State.

Basis for selection. Open admission, but selective for some programs. Admission to allied health programs based on placement test, academic record, interview.

High school preparation. 14 units recommended. Recommended units include English 4, mathematics 3, social studies 1, history 1, science 3 (laboratory 1) and foreign language 2.

2008-2009 Annual costs. Tuition/fees: $1,324; $7,063 out-of-state. Per-credit charge: $42 in-state; $233 out-of-state. Books/supplies: $800. Personal expenses: $400.

2007-2008 Financial aid. **Need-based:** Need-based aid available for part-time students. Work-study available nights and for part-time students. **Non-need-based:** Scholarships awarded for academics, job skills.

Application procedures. **Admission:** No deadline. No application fee. Admission notification on a rolling basis. **Financial aid:** Priority date 3/15; no closing date. FAFSA, institutional form required. Applicants notified on a rolling basis starting 6/1; must reply within 2 week(s) of notification.

Academics. **Special study options:** Accelerated study, cooperative education, distance learning, double major, dual enrollment of high school students, internships, weekend college. License preparation in aviation, dental hygiene, nursing, occupational therapy, paramedic, real estate. **Credit/placement by examination:** AP, CLEP, institutional tests. **Support services:** GED preparation and test center, learning center, reduced course load, remedial instruction, study skills assistance, tutoring, writing center.

Majors. **Agriculture:** Agribusiness operations, poultry, turf management. **Business:** General, accounting, administrative services, business admin, sales/distribution. **Conservation:** Forest resources. **Family/consumer sciences:** Child care. **Health:** Dental hygiene, licensed practical nurse, medical assistant, medical secretary, mental health services, nursing (RN). **Interdisciplinary:** Biological/physical sciences. **Legal studies:** Legal secretary. **Liberal arts:** Arts/sciences. **Mechanic/repair:** Aircraft. **Parks/recreation:** Facilities management. **Protective services:** Police science. **Public administration:** Human services.

Computing on campus. 400 workstations in library, computer center. Online course registration available.

Student life. **Freshman orientation:** Mandatory. Preregistration for classes offered. **Policies:** Student government organizes sports program. **Activities:** Concert band, choral groups, student government, student newspaper.

Athletics. **Intramural:** Basketball, bowling, golf, softball, table tennis, tennis, volleyball. **Team name:** Bisons.

Student services. Adult student services, career counseling, student employment services, financial aid counseling, health services, minority student services, on-campus daycare, personal counseling, placement for graduates, veterans' counselor, women's services. **Physically disabled:** Services for visually, speech, hearing impaired. **Transfer:** Transfer center, transfer adviser, college fairs on campus for students transferring to 4-year colleges.

Contact. E-mail: msm@waynecc.edu
Phone: (919) 735-5151 ext. 238 Fax: (919) 736-9425
Susan Sasser, Director of Admissions and Records, Wayne Community College, PO Box 8002, Goldsboro, NC 27533-8002

Western Piedmont Community College

Morganton, North Carolina
www.wpcc.edu **CB code: 5922**

- Public 2-year community college
- Commuter campus in large town

General. Founded in 1964. Regionally accredited. **Enrollment:** 2,030 degree-seeking undergraduates. **Degrees:** 357 associate awarded. **Location:** 60 miles from Charlotte. **Calendar:** Semester, extensive summer session. **Full-time faculty:** 74 total; 7% have terminal degrees, 5% minority, 57% women. **Part-time faculty:** 306 total; 1% have terminal degrees, 6% minority, 55% women. **Special facilities:** Greenhouses, fitness and nature trails, alpine climbing tower, Senator Sam J. Ervin Jr. library and museum.

Student profile.

Out-of-state:	20%	**25 or older:**	51%

Transfer out. **Colleges most students transferred to 2008:** Appalachian State University, Gardner-Webb University, Western Carolina University, Lenoir-Rhyne College, Lees McRae.

Basis for selection. Open admission, but selective for some programs. Special requirements for health programs.

2008-2009 Annual costs. Tuition/fees: $1,287; $7,026 out-of-state. Per-credit charge: $42 in-state; $233 out-of-state. Books/supplies: $1,168. Personal expenses: $2,482.

2007-2008 Financial aid. **Need-based:** Need-based aid available for part-time students. Work-study available for part-time students. **Non-need-based:** Scholarships awarded for academics.

Application procedures. Admission: No deadline. No application fee. Admission notification on a rolling basis. Application closing date for nursing, medical laboratory applicants is January 1 for fall admission. **Financial aid:** Priority date 6/1; no closing date. FAFSA required. Applicants notified on a rolling basis starting 6/15; must reply within 2 week(s) of notification.

Academics. Special study options: Cooperative education, distance learning, dual enrollment of high school students. License preparation in nursing. **Credit/placement by examination:** AP, CLEP, IB, institutional tests. 15 credit hours maximum toward associate degree. **Support services:** GED preparation and test center, learning center, reduced course load, remedial instruction, tutoring.

Majors. Agriculture: Horticulture. **Business:** Accounting, administrative services, business admin, office technology, office/clerical, operations, sales/distribution. **Computer sciences:** Computer science, data processing, information systems, systems analysis. **Conservation:** General. **Construction:** Maintenance. **Education:** Early childhood. **Engineering:** General, civil, electrical, mechanical. **Engineering technology:** Construction. **Family/consumer sciences:** Child care. **Health:** Clinical lab assistant, medical assistant, nursing (RN), office admin, recreational therapy. **Interdisciplinary:** Natural sciences. **Legal studies:** Paralegal. **Liberal arts:** Arts/sciences. **Protective services:** Criminal justice. **Visual/performing arts:** Interior design, studio arts.

Most popular majors. Business/marketing 21%, health sciences 24%, liberal arts 26%, security/protective services 9%.

Computing on campus. 280 workstations in library, computer center. Commuter students can connect to campus network. Online library, wireless network available.

Student life. Freshman orientation: Available. Preregistration for classes offered. **Activities:** Drama, student government, Phi Beta Lambda, Phi Theta Kappa, African American Students Association, Students for Christ.

Athletics. Team name: Pioneers.

Student services. Adult student services, career counseling, services for economically disadvantaged, student employment services, financial aid counseling, personal counseling, placement for graduates, veterans' counselor. **Physically disabled:** Services for visually, speech, hearing impaired. **Transfer:** Transfer adviser, college fairs on campus for students transferring to 4-year colleges.

Contact. E-mail: swilliams@wpcc.edu
Phone: (828) 438-6051 Fax: (828) 438-6065
Susan Williams, Director of Admissions, Western Piedmont Community College, 1001 Burkemont Avenue, Morganton, NC 28655-4504

Wilkes Community College

Wilkesboro, North Carolina
www.wilkescc.edu **CB code: 5921**

- Public 2-year community college
- Commuter campus in small town

General. Founded in 1965. Regionally accredited. **Enrollment:** 2,060 degree-seeking undergraduates. **Degrees:** 279 associate awarded. **Location:** 50 miles from Winston-Salem. **Calendar:** Semester, limited summer session. **Full-time faculty:** 83 total. **Part-time faculty:** 156 total. **Class size:** 80% < 20, 19% 20-39, 1% 40-49, less than 1% 50-99. **Special facilities:** Community center.

Student profile.

Out-of-state:	1%	**25 or older:**	39%

Transfer out. Colleges most students transferred to 2008: Appalachian State University, Gardner-Webb University, Winston-Salem State University.

Basis for selection. Open admission, but selective for some programs. Special requirements for nursing program.

High school preparation. 20 units recommended. Recommended units include English 4, mathematics 4, social studies 3, history 2, science 3 (laboratory 1), foreign language 2 and academic electives 2.

2008-2009 Annual costs. Tuition/fees: $1,340; $7,079 out-of-state. Per-credit charge: $42 in-state; $233 out-of-state. Books/supplies: $1,200. Personal expenses: $500.

2007-2008 Financial aid. Need-based: Need-based aid available for part-time students. Work-study available nights and for part-time students. **Non-need-based:** Scholarships awarded for academics, art, job skills, leadership, minority status, music/drama, state residency.

Application procedures. Admission: No deadline. No application fee. Admission notification on a rolling basis. **Financial aid:** Priority date 5/1; no closing date. FAFSA required. Applicants notified on a rolling basis starting 4/1; must reply by 8/1.

Academics. Special study options: Cooperative education, distance learning, double major, dual enrollment of high school students, ESL, independent study, internships. Bachelor's degree programs available on campus. License preparation in nursing, paramedic, real estate. **Credit/placement by examination:** AP, CLEP, IB, institutional tests. 16 credit hours maximum toward associate degree. **Support services:** GED preparation and test center, learning center, pre-admission summer program, reduced course load, remedial instruction, study skills assistance, tutoring, writing center.

Majors. Agriculture: Horticulture. **Business:** Accounting, business admin, marketing, office management. **Communications technology:** Radio/tv. **Computer sciences:** Computer graphics, information systems, information technology, LAN/WAN management, programming. **Construction:** General, electrician. **Education:** Early childhood, elementary. **Engineering technology:** Architectural, computer, electrical, industrial. **Health:** Health services, medical assistant, nursing (RN). **Liberal arts:** Arts/sciences. **Mechanic/repair:** Automotive, diesel. **Personal/culinary services:** Baking, chef training. **Protective services:** Criminal justice.

Most popular majors. Business/marketing 18%, education 7%, engineering/engineering technologies 11%, health sciences 16%, liberal arts 26%, trade and industry 9%.

Computing on campus. 150 workstations in library, computer center, student center.

Student life. Freshman orientation: Mandatory. Preregistration for classes offered. **Activities:** Choral groups, drama, literary magazine, music ensembles, musical theater, radio station, student government, student newspaper, Baptist student union, Ye Hosts food service club, camera club, Phi Theta Kappa, Association of Information Technology Professionals, Rotaract, human services club, medical assisting club, student government association, Student Ambassadors.

Athletics. NJCAA. **Intercollegiate:** Baseball M, basketball, volleyball W. **Intramural:** Basketball, table tennis, tennis, volleyball. **Team name:** Cougars.

Student services. Adult student services, career counseling, services for economically disadvantaged, student employment services, financial aid counseling, minority student services, personal counseling, placement for graduates, veterans' counselor. **Physically disabled:** Services for visually, speech, hearing impaired. **Transfer:** Pre-admission transcript evaluation for new students. Transfer adviser, college fairs on campus for students transferring to 4-year colleges.

Contact. E-mail: mac.warren@wilkescc.edu
Phone: (336) 838-6135 Fax: (336) 838-6547
Scott Johnson, Director of Admissions, Wilkes Community College, 1328 South Collegiate Drive, Wilkesboro, NC 28697-0120

Wilson Community College

Wilson, North Carolina
www.wilsoncc.edu **CB code: 5930**

- Public 2-year community college
- Commuter campus in large town

General. Founded in 1958. Regionally accredited. **Enrollment:** 1,483 degree-seeking undergraduates; 370 non-degree-seeking students. **Degrees:** 197 associate awarded. **Location:** 50 miles from Raleigh. **Calendar:** Semester, limited summer session. **Full-time faculty:** 55 total. **Part-time faculty:** 193 total. **Class size:** 64% < 20, 33% 20-39, 2% 40-49, less than 1% 50-99. **Special facilities:** Student services green building featuring sustainable energy technologies such as a vertical axis wind turbine and photovoltaic solar panels.

Student profile. Among degree-seeking undergraduates, 14% enrolled in a transfer program, 260 enrolled as first-time, first-year students.

Part-time:	54%	**Asian American:**	1%
Out-of-state:	1%	**Hispanic American:**	2%
Women:	70%	**25 or older:**	56%
African American:	47%		

Basis for selection. Open admission, but selective for some programs. Admission for nursing based on test scores, high school record, skills, and experience. Health requirement for emergency medical technology. Interview recommended.

High school preparation. High school diploma not required for certificate programs.

2008-2009 Annual costs. Tuition/fees: $1,408; $7,530 out-of-state. Per-credit charge: $42 in-state; $233 out-of-state. Books/supplies: $1,000. Personal expenses: $5,814.

Financial aid. Need-based: Need-based aid available for part-time students. **Non-need-based:** Scholarships awarded for academics.

Application procedures. Admission: No deadline. No application fee. Admission notification on a rolling basis beginning on or about 1/1. Applicants accepted to nursing program must reply by May 1. **Financial aid:** Priority date 3/15; no closing date. FAFSA, institutional form required. Applicants notified on a rolling basis.

Academics. Special program assistance for hearing-impaired students. **Special study options:** Cooperative education, distance learning, double major, dual enrollment of high school students, ESL, liberal arts/career combination. License preparation in nursing. **Credit/placement by examination:** AP, CLEP, institutional tests. 50 credit hours maximum toward associate degree. **Support services:** GED preparation and test center, learning center, reduced course load, remedial instruction, tutoring.

Majors. Business: Accounting, business admin, office management. **Computer sciences:** Information technology, networking, programming, security. **Education:** Early childhood, elementary, special. **Engineering technology:** Mechanical. **Foreign languages:** Sign language interpretation, translation. **Health:** Nursing (RN), surgical technology. **Legal studies:** Paralegal. **Liberal arts:** Arts/sciences. **Protective services:** Criminal justice, fire safety technology.

Most popular majors. Business/marketing 19%, computer/information sciences 6%, education 24%, foreign language 6%, health sciences 12%, liberal arts 14%, security/protective services 12%.

Computing on campus. 33 workstations in library, computer center. Online course registration, helpline available.

Student life. Freshman orientation: Available. Preregistration for classes offered. **Activities:** Choral groups, student government.

Student services. Career counseling, services for economically disadvantaged, student employment services, placement for graduates, veterans' counselor. **Physically disabled:** Services for hearing impaired. **Transfer:** Transfer adviser, college fairs on campus for students transferring to 4-year colleges.

Contact. E-mail: lmansfield@wilsoncc.edu
Phone: (252) 246-1285 Fax: (252) 246-1384
Leonard Mansfield, Director of Admissions and Registration, Wilson Community College, Box 4305, Wilson, NC 27893-0305

North Dakota

Bismarck State College

Bismarck, North Dakota
www.bismarckstate.edu **CB code: 6041**

- Public 2-year community college
- Commuter campus in small city

General. Founded in 1939. Regionally accredited. **Enrollment:** 3,788 degree-seeking undergraduates. **Degrees:** 737 associate awarded. **Location:** 200 miles from Fargo. **Calendar:** Semester, limited summer session. **Full-time faculty:** 110 total. **Part-time faculty:** 160 total.

Student profile. Among degree-seeking undergraduates, 50% enrolled in a transfer program, 37% enrolled in a vocational program, 874 enrolled as first-time, first-year students, 312 transferred in from other institutions.

Part-time:	34%	**25 or older:**	30%
Out-of-state:	11%	**Live on campus:**	11%
Women:	46%		

Basis for selection. Open admission, but selective for some programs. Test scores required for selective admission programs in air conditioning, heating and refrigeration, automotive technology, automotive collision technology, carpentry, electronics technology, line worker (electrical), power plant technology, process plant technology, welding, hotel restaurant management, commercial art. Interview recommended for some programs; portfolio recommended for graphic arts program. **Adult students:** Students aged 25 or older must submit COMPASS assessment scores in the areas of English, math, and reading.

High school preparation. Recommended units include English 4, mathematics 3, social studies 3, science 3 and foreign language 2.

2008-2009 Annual costs. Tuition/fees: $3,933; $9,551 out-of-state. Per-credit charge: $112 in-state; $299 out-of-state. Full-time annual tuition for residents of Minnesota: $4,075. Full-time annual tuition for residents of South Dakota, Montana, Manitoba, Saskatchewan: $4,205. Room/board: $4,525. Books/supplies: $750. Personal expenses: $1,900.

Financial aid. All financial aid based on need. Need-based aid available for part-time students. Work-study available nights, weekends and for part-time students.

Application procedures. Admission: No deadline. $35 fee. Admission notification on a rolling basis beginning on or about 1/1. **Financial aid:** Priority date 3/15; no closing date. FAFSA required. Applicants notified on a rolling basis starting 6/1; must reply within 3 week(s) of notification.

Academics. Academic advising focus over the summer with 20+ sessions offered to students who are enrolling for the following fall session. Online academic support services available. **Special study options:** Combined bachelor's/graduate degree, cooperative education, distance learning, dual enrollment of high school students, internships, liberal arts/career combination. Bachelor's degree programs available on campus. License preparation in nursing, paramedic. **Credit/placement by examination:** AP, CLEP, institutional tests. 30 credit hours maximum toward associate degree. **Support services:** Learning center, remedial instruction, study skills assistance, tutoring, writing center.

Majors. Agriculture: Business, farm/ranch. **Business:** General, administrative services, hospitality admin, office technology, transportation. **Communications:** Public relations. **Computer sciences:** Networking, web page design. **Construction:** Carpentry, lineworker. **Education:** Teacher assistance. **Engineering technology:** General, electrical, industrial, nuclear. **Health:** Clinical lab technology, EMT paramedic, licensed practical nurse, medical secretary, nursing (RN), surgical technology. **Legal studies:** Legal secretary. **Liberal arts:** Arts/sciences. **Mechanic/repair:** Auto body, automotive, heating/ac/refrig, industrial. **Production:** Welding. **Protective services:** Criminal justice. **Public administration:** Human services. **Visual/performing arts:** Commercial/advertising art.

Computing on campus. 450 workstations in library, computer center, student center. Dormitories wired for high-speed internet access. Commuter students can connect to campus network. Online course registration, online library, helpline, wireless network available.

Student life. Freshman orientation: Available. Preregistration for classes offered. **Housing:** Coed dorms, single-sex dorms, wellness housing available. $100 partly refundable deposit. **Activities:** Bands, choral groups, dance, drama, literary magazine, music ensembles, musical theater, student government, student newspaper.

Athletics. NJCAA. **Intercollegiate:** Baseball M, basketball, golf, tennis, volleyball W. **Intramural:** Basketball, bowling, golf, soccer, softball, table tennis, volleyball. **Team name:** Mystics.

Student services. Adult student services, alcohol/substance abuse counseling, career counseling, student employment services, financial aid counseling, minority student services, personal counseling, placement for graduates, veterans' counselor. **Physically disabled:** Services for visually, speech, hearing impaired. **Transfer:** Pre-admission transcript evaluation for new students. Transfer adviser, college fairs on campus for students transferring to 4-year colleges.

Contact. E-mail: BSC.Admissions@bsc.nodak.edu
Phone: (701) 224-5429 Toll-free number: (800) 445-5073
Fax: (701) 224-5643
Karla Gabriel, Dean of Admissions and Enrollment Services, Bismarck State College, PO Box 5587, Bismarck, ND 58506-5587

Cankdeska Cikana Community College

Fort Totten, North Dakota
www.littlehoop.edu **CB code: 1306**

- Public 2-year community college
- Residential campus in rural community

General. Founded in 1974. Regionally accredited. **Enrollment:** 181 degree-seeking undergraduates. **Degrees:** 20 associate awarded. **Location:** 13 miles from Devils Lake. **Calendar:** Semester, limited summer session. **Full-time faculty:** 13 total.

Basis for selection. Open admission.

2008-2009 Annual costs. Tuition/fees: $3,040. Per-credit charge: $98. Books/supplies: $700. Personal expenses: $3,000.

2007-2008 Financial aid. All financial aid based on need. Need-based aid available for part-time students.

Application procedures. Admission: No deadline. No application fee. **Financial aid:** Closing date 8/20. FAFSA, institutional form required. Applicants notified on a rolling basis.

Academics. Special study options: Cooperative education, independent study. **Credit/placement by examination:** CLEP. **Support services:** Learning center, remedial instruction, tutoring.

Majors. Agriculture: General. **Area/ethnic studies:** Native American. **Business:** General, administrative services, auditing, business admin, office technology. **Computer sciences:** General, applications programming. **Education:** Early childhood. **Health:** Prenursing. **Mechanic/repair:** Automotive.

Computing on campus. 30 workstations in computer center.

Student life. Activities: Drama, student government, Indian organization.

Athletics. Intercollegiate: Basketball, bowling, volleyball.

Student services. Career counseling, on-campus daycare, personal counseling. **Transfer:** College fairs on campus for students transferring to 4-year colleges.

Contact. Phone: (701) 766-1342 Fax: (701) 766-4077
Ermen Brown, Registrar, Cankdeska Cikana Community College, Box 269, Fort Totten, ND 58335

Fort Berthold Community College

New Town, North Dakota
www.fbcc.bia.edu **CB code: 7304**

- Public 2-year community college
- Small town

General. Founded in 1973. Regionally accredited. Affiliated with American Indian Higher Education Consortium. **Enrollment:** 133 degree-seeking undergraduates; 54 non-degree-seeking students. **Degrees:** 22 associate awarded.

Location: 80 miles from Minot, 150 miles from Bismarck. **Calendar:** Semester, limited summer session. **Full-time faculty:** 20 total. **Part-time faculty:** 40 total.

Student profile. Among degree-seeking undergraduates, 82 enrolled as first-time, first-year students.

Part-time:	32%	**Women:**	66%

Transfer out. 19% of students enrolled in the transfer program go on to 4-year colleges.

Basis for selection. Open admission.

2008-2009 Annual costs. Tuition/fees: $3,340. Per-credit charge: $110. Books/supplies: $400. Personal expenses: $800.

2007-2008 Financial aid. **Need-based:** 30 full-time freshmen applied for aid; 30 were judged to have need; 30 of these received aid.

Application procedures. **Admission:** No deadline. No application fee.

Academics. **Special study options:** Double major, independent study. **Credit/placement by examination:** CLEP. **Support services:** GED preparation and test center, remedial instruction, tutoring.

Majors. **Business:** Business admin. **Construction:** General. **Health:** Medical secretary.

Student life. **Activities:** Drama, student government.

Athletics. **Intercollegiate:** Basketball, cross-country.

Student services. Adult student services, personal counseling, veterans' counselor. **Transfer:** Transfer adviser for students transferring to 4-year colleges.

Contact. E-mail: taulau@fbcc.bia.edu
Phone: (701) 627-4738 ext. 286 Fax: (701) 627-4790
Twila Aulaumea, Registrar/Admissions Director, Fort Berthold Community College, Box 490, New Town, ND 58763

Lake Region State College

Devils Lake, North Dakota
www.lrsc.edu **CB code: 6163**

- Public 2-year community and technical college
- Commuter campus in small town

General. Founded in 1941. Regionally accredited. Satellite center at Grand Forks Air Force Base. **Enrollment:** 627 degree-seeking undergraduates; 1,030 non-degree-seeking students. **Degrees:** 177 associate awarded. **Location:** 90 miles from Grand Forks, 400 miles from Minneapolis-St. Paul. **Calendar:** Semester, limited summer session. **Full-time faculty:** 29 total. **Part-time faculty:** 157 total. **Partnerships:** Formal partnership with CISCO.

Student profile. Among degree-seeking undergraduates, 53% enrolled in a transfer program, 47% enrolled in a vocational program, 1% already have a bachelor's degree or higher, 64 transferred in from other institutions.

Part-time:	34%	**25 or older:**	28%
Out-of-state:	10%	**Live on campus:**	20%
Women:	61%		

Transfer out. 40% of students enrolled in the transfer program go on to 4-year colleges. **Colleges most students transferred to 2008:** Mayville State University, Minot State University, University of North Dakota, North Dakota State University, Valley City State University.

Basis for selection. Open admission, but selective for some programs. Special requirements for peace officer training program, nursing, sign language, interpretive studies, speech language pathology assistant, wind turbine technician. **Adult students:** SAT/ACT scores not required if applicant over 24. New adult students must take a Compass test. **Homeschooled:** Transcript of courses and grades required.

High school preparation. College-preparatory program recommended. Recommended units include English 4, mathematics 3, social studies 3, science 3 (laboratory 2) and foreign language 2.

2008-2009 Annual costs. Tuition/fees: $3,908; $3,908 out-of-state. Per-credit charge: $128 in-state; $122 out-of-state. Room/board: $4,608.

2008-2009 Financial aid. **Need-based:** Average need met was 76%. Average scholarship/grant was $3,290; average loan $2,873. 40% of total undergraduate aid awarded as scholarships/grants, 60% as loans/jobs. Need-based aid available for part-time students. Work-study available nights, weekends and for part-time students. **Non-need-based:** Scholarships awarded for academics, athletics, leadership, minority status, music/drama.

Application procedures. **Admission:** No deadline. $35 fee. Admission notification on a rolling basis. **Financial aid:** Priority date 3/15; no closing date. FAFSA required. Applicants notified on a rolling basis starting 5/15; must reply within 2 week(s) of notification.

Academics. **Special study options:** Combined bachelor's/graduate degree, cooperative education, distance learning, dual enrollment of high school students, ESL, honors, internships, liberal arts/career combination. Bachelor's degree programs available on campus. License preparation in nursing. **Credit/placement by examination:** AP, CLEP, institutional tests. **Support services:** GED preparation and test center, learning center, reduced course load, remedial instruction, study skills assistance, tutoring, writing center.

Majors. **Business:** Accounting, accounting technology, administrative services, business admin, executive assistant, fashion, management information systems, market research, office management, office/clerical, sales/distribution, small business admin. **Computer sciences:** General, computer science, data processing, networking, vendor certification. **Education:** Voc/tech. **Engineering:** Electrical. **Family/consumer sciences:** Child care. **Health:** Licensed practical nurse, medical secretary. **Legal studies:** Legal secretary, paralegal. **Liberal arts:** Arts/sciences. **Mechanic/repair:** Automotive, avionics, diesel, electronics/electrical. **Protective services:** Police science. **Transportation:** General. **Other:** Wind turbine technology.

Computing on campus. 305 workstations in dormitories, library, computer center, student center. Dormitories wired for high-speed internet access and linked to campus network. Commuter students can connect to campus network. Online course registration, online library, helpline, wireless network available.

Student life. **Freshman orientation:** Mandatory, $10 fee. Preregistration for classes offered. Summer orientation available. Mandatory session the day before classes start. **Policies:** Alcohol not allowed on campus. **Housing:** Single-sex dorms, special housing for disabled, apartments, wellness housing available. $50 nonrefundable deposit, deadline 9/1. **Activities:** Campus ministries, choral groups, drama, international student organizations, literary magazine, musical theater, student government, symphony orchestra, Delta Epsilon Chi, Skills USA, Students Other than Average, business club, legal assistant club, simulator maintenance technician club, Campus Crusade for Christ, Phi Theta Kappa.

Athletics. NJCAA. **Intercollegiate:** Basketball. **Intramural:** Archery, basketball, bowling, football (non-tackle), golf, ice hockey, soccer, softball, swimming, table tennis, volleyball. **Team name:** Royals.

Student services. Adult student services, career counseling, services for economically disadvantaged, student employment services, financial aid counseling, on-campus daycare, personal counseling, placement for graduates, veterans' counselor. **Physically disabled:** Services for speech, hearing impaired. **Learning disabled:** Comprehensive services available. **Transfer:** Transfer adviser, college fairs on campus for students transferring to 4-year colleges.

Contact. E-mail: lrsc.admissions@lrsc.edu
Phone: (701) 662-1514 Toll-free number: (800) 443-1313 ext. 1514
Fax: (701) 662-1581
Laurel Goulding, Vice President of Student Services, Lake Region State College, 1801 College Drive North, Devils Lake, ND 58301-1598

Minot State University: Bottineau Campus

Bottineau, North Dakota
www.msub.edu **CB code: 1540**

- Public 2-year branch campus and junior college
- Residential campus in small town

General. Founded in 1907. Regionally accredited. **Enrollment:** 638 degree-seeking undergraduates. **Degrees:** 87 associate awarded. **Location:** 80 miles from Minot. **Calendar:** Semester, limited summer session. **Full-time faculty:** 27 total; 7% have terminal degrees, 22% women. **Part-time faculty:** 38 total; 3% have terminal degrees, 71% women. **Special facilities:** Headquarters for North Dakota Forest Service, outdoor laboratories on state and federally owned refuges, forests, and parklands. **Partnerships:** Formal partnerships with high schools where students have taken CISCO and A+ modules for certification to transfer into information technology - network engineering program.

Student profile.

Out-of-state:	7%	Live on campus:	22%
25 or older:	39%		

Basis for selection. Open admission. **Adult students:** SAT/ACT scores not required if applicant over 25.

2008-2009 Annual costs. Tuition/fees: $3,802; $5,362 out-of-state. Room/board: $4,122. Books/supplies: $900. Personal expenses: $1,900.

Financial aid. Need-based: Need-based aid available for part-time students. Work-study available nights, weekends and for part-time students. **Non-need-based:** Scholarships awarded for academics, alumni affiliation, athletics, music/drama.

Application procedures. Admission: No deadline. $35 fee. Admission notification on a rolling basis. **Financial aid:** Priority date 4/15; no closing date. FAFSA required. Applicants notified on a rolling basis starting 6/1; must reply within 2 week(s) of notification.

Academics. Special study options: Cooperative education, distance learning, double major, dual enrollment of high school students, independent study, internships, liberal arts/career combination. License preparation in nursing. **Credit/placement by examination:** CLEP, institutional tests. **Support services:** Learning center, reduced course load, remedial instruction, study skills assistance, tutoring.

Majors. Agriculture: Greenhouse operations, landscaping, turf management. **Biology:** General. **Business:** Accounting technology, administrative services. **Communications:** Advertising. **Computer sciences:** Webmaster. **Conservation:** General, urban forestry, wildlife. **Education:** Teacher assistance. **Engineering technology:** Environmental, water quality. **Health:** Medical assistant, medical secretary, nursing (RN). **History:** General. **Liberal arts:** Arts/sciences.

Most popular majors. Agriculture 18%, health sciences 23%, liberal arts 56%.

Computing on campus. 80 workstations in library, computer center, student center. Dormitories wired for high-speed internet access. Online course registration, online library, repair service, wireless network available.

Student life. Freshman orientation: Mandatory. Preregistration for classes offered. Two sessions offered. **Housing:** Guaranteed on-campus for all undergraduates. Single-sex dorms, wellness housing available. $75 nonrefundable deposit. **Activities:** Jazz band, campus ministries, drama, music ensembles, student government, student newspaper.

Athletics. NJCAA. **Intercollegiate:** Baseball M, basketball, football (tackle) M, ice hockey M, softball W, volleyball W. **Intramural:** Badminton, basketball, bowling, football (non-tackle), racquetball, skiing, soccer, softball, volleyball. **Team name:** Lumberjacks and Ladyjacks.

Student services. Adult student services, alcohol/substance abuse counseling, career counseling, student employment services, financial aid counseling, health services, personal counseling, veterans' counselor. **Learning disabled:** Comprehensive services available. **Transfer:** Transfer adviser, college fairs on campus for students transferring to 4-year colleges.

Contact. E-mail: jessica.migler@misu.nodak.edu
Phone: (701) 228-5426 Toll-free number: (800) 542-6866
Fax: (701) 228-5499
Paula Berg, Associate Dean, Minot State University: Bottineau Campus, 105 Simrall Boulevard, Bottineau, ND 58318-1198

North Dakota State College of Science

Wahpeton, North Dakota
www.ndscs.nodak.edu **CB code: 6476**

- Public 2-year junior and technical college
- Residential campus in small town

General. Founded in 1903. Regionally accredited. **Enrollment:** 2,545 undergraduates. **Degrees:** 572 associate awarded. **Location:** 50 miles from Fargo, 200 miles from Sioux Falls, South Dakota. **Calendar:** Semester, limited summer session. **Full-time faculty:** 123 total; 4% have terminal degrees. **Part-time faculty:** 90 total. **Class size:** 57% < 20, 36% 20-39, 5% 40-49, 2% 50-99. **Partnerships:** Formal partnerships with Caterpillar Corporation and John Deere.

Student profile. 621 enrolled as first-time, first-year students.

Out-of-state:	28%	Live on campus:	52%
25 or older:	20%		

Transfer out. Colleges most students transferred to 2008: Minnesota State University Moorhead, North Dakota State University, University of North Dakota, Northwest Technical College-Moorhead, Valley City State University.

Basis for selection. Open admission, but selective for some programs. Special requirements for allied health programs. **Adult students:** SAT/ACT scores not required if applicant over 25.

High school preparation. Chemistry, English and anatomy & physiology required for dental hygiene.

2008-2009 Annual costs. Tuition/fees: $3,888; $9,512 out-of-state. Per-credit charge: $112 in-state; $299 out-of-state. Full-time tuition for Minnesota residents: $4,075. Full-time tuition for South Dakota, Montana, Saskatchewan, Manitoba residents: $4,209. Room/board: $4,598. Books/supplies: $900. Personal expenses: $2,190.

2008-2009 Financial aid. Need-based: Need-based aid available for part-time students. Work-study available nights, weekends and for part-time students. **Non-need-based:** Scholarships awarded for academics, athletics, job skills, music/drama, state residency.

Application procedures. Admission: No deadline. $35 fee, may be waived for applicants with need. Admission notification on a rolling basis. **Financial aid:** Priority date 4/15; no closing date. FAFSA, institutional form required. Applicants notified on a rolling basis starting 6/1; must reply within 2 week(s) of notification.

Academics. Special study options: Cooperative education, distance learning, dual enrollment of high school students, ESL, internships, liberal arts/career combination, student-designed major. License preparation in dental hygiene, nursing, occupational therapy. **Credit/placement by examination:** AP, CLEP, institutional tests. 32 credit hours maximum toward associate degree. **Support services:** Learning center, pre-admission summer program, reduced course load, remedial instruction, study skills assistance, tutoring, writing center.

Majors. Agriculture: Agribusiness operations, business, power machinery, supplies. **Architecture:** Technology. **Business:** General, administrative services, banking/financial services, business admin, executive assistant, finance, office management, office/clerical, restaurant/food services. **Computer sciences:** Applications programming, data entry, information systems, LAN/WAN management, web page design. **Construction:** General, electrician. **Engineering technology:** Architectural, architectural drafting, automotive, civil, civil drafting, computer hardware, construction, electrical, heat/ac/refrig, software. **Family/consumer sciences:** Institutional food production. **Health:** Dental hygiene, insurance coding, licensed practical nurse, medical records technology, medical transcription, mental health services, occupational therapy assistant, office admin, office assistant, pharmacy assistant. **Liberal arts:** Arts/sciences. **Mechanic/repair:** Auto body, automotive, diesel, electronics/electrical, heating/ac/refrig, small engine. **Personal/culinary services:** Baking, culinary arts, restaurant/catering. **Production:** Machine tool, welding.

Most popular majors. Health sciences 37%, liberal arts 19%, trade and industry 24%.

Computing on campus. 550 workstations in dormitories, library, computer center, student center. Dormitories wired for high-speed internet access and linked to campus network. Commuter students can connect to campus network. Online course registration, online library, helpline, wireless network available.

Student life. Freshman orientation: Mandatory, $25 fee. Preregistration for classes offered. Orientation held the day before classes start. **Housing:** Guaranteed on-campus for freshmen. Coed dorms, single-sex dorms, special housing for disabled, apartments available. $40 deposit. **Activities:** Bands, choral groups, drama, music ensembles, student government, Intervarsity Christian Fellowship.

Athletics. NJCAA. **Intercollegiate:** Basketball, football (tackle) M, volleyball W. **Intramural:** Basketball, racquetball, softball, volleyball. **Team name:** Wildcats.

Student services. Alcohol/substance abuse counseling, career counseling, student employment services, financial aid counseling, health services, on-campus daycare, personal counseling, placement for graduates, veterans' counselor. **Physically disabled:** Services for visually, hearing impaired. **Transfer:** Pre-admission transcript evaluation for new students. Transfer adviser, college fairs on campus for students transferring to 4-year colleges.

Contact. E-mail: ndscs.admissions@ndscs.edu
Phone: (701) 671-2202 Toll-free number: (800) 342-4325 ext. 32202
Fax: (701) 671-2201
Karen Reilly, Director of Enrollment Services and Records, North Dakota State College of Science, 800 North 6th Street, Wahpeton, ND 58076

Rasmussen College: Bismarck
Bismarck, North Dakota
www.rasmussen.edu

- For-profit 2-year career college
- Commuter campus in small city

General. **Enrollment:** 400 undergraduates. **Degrees:** 2 bachelor's, 72 associate awarded. **Calendar:** Quarter, extensive summer session.

Basis for selection. Open admission.

2008-2009 Annual costs. Tuition/fees: $15,750. Per-credit charge: $350.

Financial aid. Need-based: Need-based aid available for part-time students.

Application procedures. Admission: No deadline. $60 fee. Admission notification on a rolling basis. **Financial aid:** No deadline. FAFSA, institutional form required. Applicants notified on a rolling basis.

Academics. Special study options: Distance learning, double major, honors, independent study, internships. **Credit/placement by examination:** AP, CLEP, institutional tests. 45 credit hours maximum toward associate degree, 90 toward bachelor's. Credit limited to specific programs, and to courses for which examinations are available. 50% of the student's program must be completed through coursework at institution. **Support services:** Learning center, remedial instruction, study skills assistance, tutoring, writing center.

Majors. Business: Accounting, administrative services, business admin. **Health:** Clinical lab technology, massage therapy, medical records technology, medical secretary, medical transcription. **Other:** Criminal justice.

Computing on campus. 100 workstations in library, computer center, student center. Online course registration, online library, helpline, wireless network available.

Student life. Freshman orientation: Mandatory.

Student services. Adult student services, career counseling, services for economically disadvantaged, student employment services, financial aid counseling, placement for graduates.

Contact. E-mail: mike.heitkamp@rasmussen.edu
Phone: (701) 530-9600 Toll-free number: (877) 530-9600
Fax: (701) 530-9604
Mike Heitkamp, Director of Admissions, Rasmussen College: Bismarck, 1701 East Century Avenue, Bismarck, ND 58503

Sitting Bull College
Fort Yates, North Dakota
www.sittingbull.edu **CB code: 0310**

- Public 2-year community college
- Residential campus in small town

General. Founded in 1971. Regionally accredited. **Enrollment:** 310 degree-seeking undergraduates. **Degrees:** 7 associate awarded. **Location:** 75 miles from Bismarck, 60 miles from Mobridge, South Dakota. **Calendar:** Semester, limited summer session. **Full-time faculty:** 22 total. **Part-time faculty:** 25 total.

Transfer out. Colleges most students transferred to 2008: Northern State College, Black Hills State College, Minot State University, United Tribes Technical College.

Basis for selection. Open admission. TABE (Test of Adult Basic Education) required of students without 2-year college degree. High school students may enroll with approval of Vice President of academic affairs and parents. Letters of recommendation from high school counselor or principal required. **Adult students:** Compass Test required for placement in Math and English.

2008-2009 Annual costs. Tuition/fees: $3,140. Per-credit charge: $100. Books/supplies: $1,000. Personal expenses: $1,170.

2007-2008 Financial aid. Need-based: Need-based aid available for part-time students.

Application procedures. Admission: No deadline. $25 fee. Admission notification on a rolling basis. **Financial aid:** Priority date 5/1; no closing date. FAFSA, institutional form required. Applicants notified on a rolling basis starting 7/15; must reply within 6 week(s) of notification.

Academics. Special study options: Cooperative education, dual enrollment of high school students, independent study. Bachelor's degree programs available on campus. **Credit/placement by examination:** CLEP. **Support services:** GED preparation and test center, learning center, remedial instruction, study skills assistance, tutoring.

Majors. Agriculture: Agribusiness operations. **Area/ethnic studies:** Native American. **Business:** Business admin, entrepreneurial studies, office technology, small business admin. **Computer sciences:** Applications programming. **Conservation:** Environmental science, wildlife. **Construction:** Carpentry. **Education:** Early childhood, elementary, multi-level teacher. **Health:** Licensed practical nurse. **Public administration:** Human services.

Computing on campus. Online course registration, wireless network available.

Student life. Housing: Very limited housing available for single parents or married students. **Activities:** Student government, cultural club, Phi Beta Lambda, rodeo club.

Athletics. Team name: Suns.

Student services. Career counseling, student employment services, personal counseling, placement for graduates, veterans' counselor. **Transfer:** Transfer adviser for students transferring to 4-year colleges.

Contact. E-mail: melodya@sbci.edu
Phone: (701) 854-8000 ext. 8020 Fax: (701) 854-3403
Melody Azure, Director of Admissions/Registrar, Sitting Bull College, 1341 92nd Street, Fort Yates, ND 58538

Turtle Mountain Community College
Belcourt, North Dakota
www.tm.edu **CB code: 0352**

- Public 2-year community college
- Commuter campus in rural community

General. Regionally accredited. **Enrollment:** 604 degree-seeking undergraduates. **Degrees:** 5 bachelor's, 46 associate awarded. **Calendar:** Semester. **Full-time faculty:** 33 total. **Part-time faculty:** 24 total.

Basis for selection. Open admission, but selective for some programs. Special requirements for Bachelor of Science Elementary Education program.

2008-2009 Annual costs. Tuition/fees: $2,000. Room and board for dependent students $3,664, for independent students $6,374. Room/board: $3,664. Books/supplies: $400.

2007-2008 Financial aid. Need-based: 99% of total undergraduate aid awarded as scholarships/grants, 1% as loans/jobs.

Application procedures. Admission: No deadline. No application fee. Admission notification on a rolling basis. **Financial aid:** Priority date 4/15, closing date 5/1. FAFSA required.

Academics. Special study options: Bachelor's degree programs available on campus. **Credit/placement by examination:** CLEP.

Majors. Business: Business admin. **Computer sciences:** Computer science. **Construction:** General. **Education:** Early childhood. **Health:** Insurance coding.

Student life. Activities: Student government.

Contact. E-mail: jlafontaine@tm.edu
Phone: (701) 477-7862 Fax: (701) 477-7892
Joni LaFontaine, Admissions/Records Officer, Turtle Mountain Community College, PO Box 340, Belcourt, ND 58316

United Tribes Technical College
Bismarck, North Dakota
www.uttc.edu **CB code: 4915**

- Private 2-year technical college
- Residential campus in small city

General. Regionally accredited. Native American college. **Enrollment:** 363 degree-seeking undergraduates. **Degrees:** 84 associate awarded. **Location:** One mile from Bismarck. **Calendar:** Semester, limited summer session. **Full-time faculty:** 50 total. **Part-time faculty:** 10 total. **Special facilities:** Elementary school on campus.

Basis for selection. Open admission, but selective for some programs. Some programs have limited enrollment and/or more stringent academic, medical, and legal requirements. Admittance priority given to those who are members of recognized tribe. **Homeschooled:** Statement describing homeschool structure and mission, transcript of courses and grades, state high school equivalency certificate required.

2008-2009 Annual costs. Tuition/fees: $3,115. Per-credit charge: $88. Room/board: $3,000. Books/supplies: $800. Personal expenses: $2,060.

2008-2009 Financial aid. Need-based: Need-based aid available for part-time students. Work-study available nights and weekends.

Application procedures. Admission: Closing date 8/17. No application fee. Application must be submitted on paper. Admission notification on a rolling basis. **Financial aid:** Priority date 5/29; no closing date. FAFSA required. Applicants notified on a rolling basis starting 5/29; must reply within 2 week(s) of notification.

Academics. Special study options: Accelerated study, distance learning. **Credit/placement by examination:** CLEP. **Support services:** Learning center, remedial instruction, study skills assistance, tutoring.

Majors. Business: Administrative services, business admin. **Education:** General. **Health:** Licensed practical nurse. **Protective services:** Law enforcement admin.

Computing on campus. 40 workstations in computer center. Commuter students can connect to campus network. Online course registration, repair service available.

Student life. Freshman orientation: Mandatory. Preregistration for classes offered. **Housing:** Coed dorms, single-sex dorms, wellness housing available. **Activities:** Student newspaper.

Athletics. NJCAA. **Intercollegiate:** Basketball, cross-country. **Team name:** Thunderbirds.

Student services. Adult student services, alcohol/substance abuse counseling, chaplain/spiritual director, career counseling, financial aid counseling, health services, on-campus daycare, personal counseling, placement for graduates, women's services. **Transfer:** Pre-admission transcript evaluation for new students.

Contact. E-mail: vgillette@uttc.edu
Phone: (701) 255-3285 ext. 1334 Toll-free number: (800) 643-8882
Fax: (701) 530-0640
Vivian Gillette, Director of Admissions, United Tribes Technical College, 3315 University Drive, Bismarck, ND 58504

Williston State College

Williston, North Dakota
www.wsc.nodak.edu **CB code: 6905**

- Public 2-year junior college
- Commuter campus in large town

General. Founded in 1957. Regionally accredited. Baccalaureate, post-baccalaureate programs from other campuses available on-campus, all via interactive video network. **Enrollment:** 399 degree-seeking undergraduates. **Degrees:** 190 associate awarded. **Location:** 250 miles from Bismarck, 130 miles from Minot. **Calendar:** Semester, limited summer session. **Full-time faculty:** 26 total. **Part-time faculty:** 65 total. **Class size:** 100% < 20.

Student profile.

Out-of-state:	12%	**Live on campus:**	20%
25 or older:	28%		

Transfer out. 42% of students enrolled in the transfer program go on to 4-year colleges. **Colleges most students transferred to 2008:** University of North Dakota, Minot State University, Dickinson State University, North Dakota State University, Montana State University.

Basis for selection. Open admission, but selective for some programs. Special requirements for practical nursing and physical therapist assistant programs. Immunization records required for applicants born after 1956.

High school preparation. 15 units recommended. Recommended units include English 4, mathematics 3, social studies 3, science 3 (laboratory 1) and foreign language 1.

2008-2009 Annual costs. Tuition/fees: $3,378; $4,687 out-of-state. Per-credit charge: $101 in-state; $151 out-of-state. Tuition for Minnesota residents: $3,532. Tuition for South Dakota, Montana, and Canadian residents: $2,618. Room/board: $3,218. Books/supplies: $600. Personal expenses: $500.

2007-2008 Financial aid. Need-based: 124 full-time freshmen applied for aid; 106 were judged to have need; 103 of these received aid. Average need met was 96%. Average scholarship/grant was $3,065; average loan $3,260. 43% of total undergraduate aid awarded as scholarships/grants, 57% as loans/jobs. Need-based aid available for part-time students. Work-study available nights and for part-time students. **Non-need-based:** Awarded to 159 full-time undergraduates, including 75 freshmen. Scholarships awarded for academics, athletics, music/drama.

Application procedures. Admission: No deadline. $35 fee. Admission notification on a rolling basis. **Financial aid:** Priority date 3/15; no closing date. FAFSA required. Applicants notified on a rolling basis starting 5/15.

Academics. Special study options: Cooperative education, cross-registration, distance learning, double major, dual enrollment of high school students, internships, liberal arts/career combination, student-designed major. Bachelor's degree programs available on campus. License preparation in aviation, nursing, physical therapy. **Credit/placement by examination:** AP, CLEP, institutional tests. 15 credit hours maximum toward associate degree. **Support services:** GED preparation and test center, learning center, reduced course load, remedial instruction, study skills assistance, tutoring, writing center.

Majors. Business: Accounting technology, administrative services, entrepreneurial studies, marketing. **Computer sciences:** Data processing, system admin, systems analysis, vendor certification, web page design. **Education:** Teacher assistance. **Health:** Massage therapy, medical records technology, medical transcription, nursing (RN), physical therapy assistant, speech-language pathology assistant. **Liberal arts:** Arts/sciences. **Mechanic/repair:** Automotive, diesel. **Transportation:** Airline/commercial pilot.

Most popular majors. Health sciences 39%, liberal arts 45%.

Computing on campus. 70 workstations in library, computer center. Dormitories linked to campus network. Online course registration, online library, wireless network available.

Student life. Freshman orientation: Available. Preregistration for classes offered. Activities take place on the day prior to first day of fall semester. **Housing:** Coed dorms, single-sex dorms, apartments, wellness housing available. $100 fully refundable deposit. Separate housing for athletes. **Activities:** Choral groups, drama, literary magazine, music ensembles, student government, Campus Crusade.

Athletics. NJCAA. **Intercollegiate:** Baseball M, basketball, volleyball W. **Intramural:** Basketball, softball, volleyball. **Team name:** Tetons.

Student services. Alcohol/substance abuse counseling, career counseling, student employment services, financial aid counseling, minority student services, personal counseling, placement for graduates, veterans' counselor. **Physically disabled:** Services for visually, speech, hearing impaired. **Transfer:** Pre-admission transcript evaluation for new students. Transfer adviser, college fairs on campus for students transferring to 4-year colleges.

Contact. E-mail: wsc.admission@wsc.nodak.edu
Phone: (701) 774-4210 Toll-free number: (888) 863-9455
Fax: (701) 774-4211
Keith Dawson, Director for Admission & Records, Williston State College, 1410 University Avenue, Williston, ND 58802-1326

Ohio

Academy of Court Reporting: Akron
Akron, Ohio
CB code: 3250

- For-profit 2-year college of court reporting
- Commuter campus in small city

General. Accredited by ACICS. **Location:** 30 miles from Cleveland. **Calendar:** Continuous.

Annual costs/financial aid. Tuition/fees (2008-2009): $14,850. Tuition includes required textbooks. Books/supplies: $1,500. Personal expenses: $1,000.

Contact. Phone: (330) 867-4030
Director of Admissions, 2930 West Market Street, Akron, OH 44333

Academy of Court Reporting: Cincinnati
Cincinnati, Ohio

- For-profit 2-year business college
- Large city

General. Accredited by ACICS. **Enrollment:** 334 degree-seeking undergraduates. **Degrees:** 32 associate awarded. **Calendar:** Quarter. **Full-time faculty:** 1 total. **Part-time faculty:** 34 total.

Basis for selection. Open admission, but selective for some programs.

2008-2009 Annual costs. Tuition/fees: $14,850. Per-credit charge: $325. Tuition includes required textbooks. Books/supplies: $1,500.

Application procedures. Admission: No deadline. $25 fee.

Academics. Credit/placement by examination: CLEP.

Majors. Legal studies: Court reporting, paralegal.

Contact. Phone: (513) 723-0520
Sheila Woods, Director of Admissions, Academy of Court Reporting: Cincinnati, 830 Main Street, Suite 1000, Cincinnati, OH 45202

Academy of Court Reporting: Cleveland
Cleveland, Ohio
CB code: 2173

- For-profit 2-year technical college
- Commuter campus in very large city

General. Accredited by ACICS. **Calendar:** Quarter.

Annual costs/financial aid. Tuition/fees (2008-2009): $14,850. Tuition includes required textbooks. Books/supplies: $1,500. Need-based financial aid available to full-time and part-time students.

Contact. Phone: (216) 861-3222
Director of Admissions, 2044 Euclid Avenue, Cleveland, OH 44115

Academy of Court Reporting: Columbus
Columbus, Ohio
CB code: 3344

- For-profit 2-year junior college
- Commuter campus in very large city

General. Accredited by ACICS. **Calendar:** Continuous.

Annual costs/financial aid. Tuition/fees (2008-2009): $14,850. Tuition includes required textbooks. Books/supplies: $1,500.

Contact. Phone: (614) 221-7770
Director of Admissions, 150 East Gay Street, 15th Floor, Columbus, OH 43215

Antonelli College
Cincinnati, Ohio
www.antonellicollege.edu
CB code: 0611

- For-profit 2-year visual arts and technical college
- Commuter campus in large city
- Interview required

General. Founded in 1947. Accredited by ACCSCT. **Enrollment:** 400 degree-seeking undergraduates. **Degrees:** 135 associate awarded. **Location:** 55 miles from Dayton; 90 miles from Lexington, Kentucky. **Calendar:** Quarter. **Full-time faculty:** 16 total. **Part-time faculty:** 24 total. **Special facilities:** Computer graphics laboratory, complete darkroom and commercial studio facilities.

Student profile.

Out-of-state:	25%	**Live on campus:**	11%
25 or older:	25%		

Basis for selection. Interview and portfolio reviewed to determine interest, motivation, and ability. Portfolio required for commercial art program.

Application procedures. Admission: No deadline. $100 fee. Admission notification on a rolling basis. **Financial aid:** No deadline. FAFSA required. Applicants notified on a rolling basis.

Academics. Special study options: Internships. **Credit/placement by examination:** CLEP, institutional tests. **Support services:** Pre-admission summer program, reduced course load, tutoring.

Majors. Computer sciences: General, information systems. **Visual/performing arts:** Commercial photography, commercial/advertising art, interior design, photography.

Most popular majors. Health sciences 29%, visual/performing arts 66%.

Computing on campus. 44 workstations in library, computer center.

Student life. Freshman orientation: Available. **Housing:** Off-campus coeducational dormitory housing available at nearby College of Mount St. Joseph. **Activities:** Student newspaper, Alpha Beta Kappa honor society.

Athletics. Intramural: Softball.

Student services. Adult student services, career counseling, student employment services, personal counseling, placement for graduates, veterans' counselor. **Transfer:** Pre-admission transcript evaluation for new students.

Contact. Phone: (513) 241-4338 Toll-free number: (800) 505-4338
Fax: (513) 241-9396
Shawnya Moore, Registrar, Antonelli College, 124 East Seventh Street, Cincinnati, OH 45202

Art Institute of Cincinnati
Cincinnati, Ohio
www.aic-arts.edu
CB code: 3181

- For-profit 2-year visual arts college
- Commuter campus in large city
- Application essay, interview required

General. Accredited by ACCSCT. **Enrollment:** 70 degree-seeking undergraduates. **Degrees:** 35 associate awarded. **Location:** 12 miles from downtown. **Calendar:** Quarter. **Full-time faculty:** 8 total. **Part-time faculty:** 5 total.

Basis for selection. Admission determined by applicant's artistic ability. Portfolio, letter of recommendation from art teacher required. **Homeschooled:** Portfolio presentation of at least 10 pieces of art with variety of media and subject matter.

High school preparation. Required and recommended units include English 2-3, mathematics 1, social studies 1, history 1, science 1 and foreign language 1.

2008-2009 Annual costs. Tuition/fees: $14,047. Total program cost $40,221 (8 quarters). Books/supplies: $1,515.

2007-2008 Financial aid. **Non-need-based:** Scholarships awarded for academics, art.

Application procedures. **Admission:** No deadline. $100 fee. Application must be submitted on paper. Admission notification on a rolling basis. **Financial aid:** No deadline. FAFSA required. Applicants notified on a rolling basis starting 9/1; must reply within 1 week(s) of notification.

Academics. **Credit/placement by examination:** CLEP. **Support services:** Study skills assistance.

Majors. **Computer sciences:** Computer graphics. **Visual/performing arts:** Design.

Computing on campus. Online library, student web hosting available.

Student life. **Freshman orientation:** Mandatory.

Student services. Financial aid counseling, personal counseling, placement for graduates. **Transfer:** Pre-admission transcript evaluation for new students.

Contact. E-mail: aic@theartinstituteofcincinnati.com
Phone: (513) 751-1206 Fax: (513) 751-1209
Cyndi Mendell, Vice President, Admissions, Art Institute of Cincinnati, 1171 East Kemper Road, Cincinnati, OH 45246

Art Institute of Ohio: Cincinnati

Cincinnati, Ohio
www.artinstitutes.edu/cincinnati/

- For-profit 2-year culinary school, branch campus and visual arts college
- Commuter campus in very large city
- Application essay, interview required

General. Regionally accredited; also accredited by ACICS. **Enrollment:** 688 degree-seeking undergraduates. **Degrees:** 75 associate awarded. **Calendar:** Quarter, extensive summer session. **Full-time faculty:** 19 total. **Part-time faculty:** 58 total; 7% minority, 53% women. **Class size:** 62% < 20, 38% 20-39, less than 1% 40-49.

Student profile. Among degree-seeking undergraduates, 3% already have a bachelor's degree or higher, 180 enrolled as first-time, first-year students, 180 transferred in from other institutions.

Part-time:	41%	**Asian American:**	2%
Women:	61%	**Hispanic American:**	2%
African American:	21%	**25 or older:**	21%

Basis for selection. 1.5 GPA required. **Homeschooled:** Transcript of courses and grades required.

2008-2009 Annual costs. Tuition/fees: $21,552. Books/supplies: $2,353. Personal expenses: $4,753.

Application procedures. **Admission:** No deadline. $50 fee, may be waived for applicants with need. Application must be submitted on paper. Admission notification on a rolling basis.

Academics. **Special study options:** Distance learning. **Credit/placement by examination:** AP, CLEP, SAT, ACT, institutional tests. 8 credit hours maximum toward associate degree. **Support services:** Reduced course load, remedial instruction, tutoring.

Majors. **Business:** Fashion. **Personal/culinary services:** Chef training. **Visual/performing arts:** Cinematography, graphic design, interior design, multimedia.

Most popular majors. Visual/performing arts 96%.

Student life. **Freshman orientation:** Available. **Housing:** Apartments available. $200 partly refundable deposit, deadline 9/7.

Student services. Career counseling, financial aid counseling, personal counseling, placement for graduates. **Physically disabled:** Services for visually, speech, hearing impaired. **Transfer:** Pre-admission transcript evaluation for new students.

Contact. E-mail: jdrennen@aii.edu
Fax: (513) 833-2411
Joe Drennen, Director of Admissions, Art Institute of Ohio: Cincinnati, 8845 Governor's Hill Drive, Cincinnati, OH 45249-3317

ATS Institute of Technology

Highland Heights, Ohio
www.atsinstitute.com

- For-profit 2-year nursing and technical college
- Very large city

General. Accredited by ACICS. **Enrollment:** 440 undergraduates. **Degrees:** 98 associate awarded. **Calendar:** Semester. **Full-time faculty:** 3 total. **Part-time faculty:** 21 total.

Basis for selection. Open admission, but selective for some programs. Selective admissions to allied health programs.

2008-2009 Annual costs. Books/supplies: $900.

Application procedures. **Admission:** No deadline. $30 fee. **Financial aid:** FAFSA required. Applicants notified on a rolling basis.

Academics. **Special study options:** Accelerated study. License preparation in nursing. **Credit/placement by examination:** CLEP.

Majors. **Health:** Nursing (RN).

Contact. E-mail: info@atsinstitute.com
Phone: (440) 449-1700 Fax: (440) 442-9876
Yelena Bykov, Academic Director, ATS Institute of Technology, 325 Alpha Park, Highland Heights, OH 44143

Aultman College of Nursing and Health Sciences

Canton, Ohio
www.aultmancollege.org

- Private 2-year health science and nursing college
- Commuter campus in small city
- SAT or ACT required

General. Candidate for regional accreditation. **Enrollment:** 237 degree-seeking undergraduates. **Degrees:** 67 associate awarded. **Calendar:** Semester, limited summer session. **Full-time faculty:** 12 total; 100% women. **Part-time faculty:** 1 total; 100% women.

Basis for selection. Academic GPA and test scores very important.

High school preparation. College-preparatory program required. Required units include mathematics 1 and science 1.

2008-2009 Annual costs. Tuition/fees: $12,615.

Application procedures. **Admission:** Closing date 8/1 (receipt date). $30 fee. Admission notification on a rolling basis. **Financial aid:** Priority date 5/1, closing date 10/1.

Academics. **Special study options:** Independent study. License preparation in nursing. **Credit/placement by examination:** CLEP, institutional tests. **Support services:** Remedial instruction, study skills assistance, tutoring.

Majors. **Health:** Nursing (RN).

Computing on campus. 35 workstations in library, computer center. Online library, wireless network available.

Student life. **Freshman orientation:** Mandatory. **Activities:** Student government, student newspaper.

Student services. Financial aid counseling, health services.

Contact. E-mail: mspeedy@aultman.com
Phone: (330) 363-5075
Michelle Speedy, Admissions Director, Aultman College of Nursing and Health Sciences, 2600 Sixth St. SW, Canton, OH 44710

Belmont Technical College

St. Clairsville, Ohio
www.btc.edu **CB code: 1072**

- Public 2-year community and technical college
- Commuter campus in small town
- Interview required

General. Founded in 1969. Regionally accredited. **Enrollment:** 1,798 undergraduates. **Degrees:** 227 associate awarded. **Location:** 15 miles from Wheeling, West Virginia. **Calendar:** Quarter, limited summer session. **Full-time faculty:** 45 total. **Part-time faculty:** 120 total. **Class size:** 79% < 20, 20% 20-39, less than 1% 40-49, less than 1% 50-99.

Student profile.

Out-of-state:	15%	25 or older:	45%

Transfer out. Colleges most students transferred to 2008: Wheeling Jesuit University, Ohio University Eastern Campus, West Liberty State College.

Basis for selection. Open admission, but selective for some programs. Admission to registered nursing and LPN programs predicated on completion of remediation with grade of C or better and completion of selected general courses with C or better, based on ACCUPLACER placement test scores. Applicants for paramedic program must take admissions test on campus. ACT scores accepted for placement if provided. Interview required for nursing and paramedic applicants after admission to program, recommended for all others. **Homeschooled:** State high school equivalency certificate required.

2008-2009 Annual costs. Tuition/fees: $3,784; $6,585 out-of-state. Per-credit charge: $61 in-state; $123 out-of-state. Books/supplies: $1,200. Personal expenses: $1,617.

2007-2008 Financial aid. Need-based: Need-based aid available for part-time students. **Non-need-based:** Scholarships awarded for state residency.

Application procedures. Admission: No deadline. No application fee. Admission notification on a rolling basis. **Financial aid:** No deadline. FAFSA required. Applicants notified on a rolling basis starting 6/1; must reply within 2 week(s) of notification.

Academics. Special study options: Cross-registration, distance learning, double major, dual enrollment of high school students, internships, student-designed major, weekend college. **Credit/placement by examination:** AP, CLEP, institutional tests. **Support services:** GED test center, learning center, reduced course load, remedial instruction, study skills assistance, tutoring, writing center.

Majors. Business: General, accounting, office/clerical. **Computer sciences:** General, computer graphics, programming. **Education:** Early childhood. **Engineering:** Civil, electrical. **Health:** EMT paramedic, health services, medical assistant, nursing (RN). **Interdisciplinary:** Historic preservation. **Mechanic/repair:** Heating/ac/refrig.

Most popular majors. Business/marketing 15%, computer/information sciences 11%, engineering/engineering technologies 18%, health sciences 10%, security/protective services 6%, social sciences 7%.

Computing on campus. Online library, wireless network available.

Student life. Freshman orientation: Available. Preregistration for classes offered. **Activities:** Phi Theta Kappa.

Athletics. Intercollegiate: Football (non-tackle).

Student services. Adult student services, career counseling, student employment services, financial aid counseling, on-campus daycare, personal counseling, placement for graduates, veterans' counselor. **Physically disabled:** Services for visually, hearing impaired. **Transfer:** Pre-admission transcript evaluation for new students. Transfer adviser, college fairs on campus for students transferring to 4-year colleges.

Contact. E-mail: info@btc.edu
Phone: (740) 695-9500 ext. 1158 Fax: (740) 699-3049
Michael Sterling, Director of Admissions, Belmont Technical College, 120 Fox Shannon Place, St. Clairsville, OH 43950

Bohecker College
Ravenna, Ohio
www.boheckers.com **CB code: 2195**

- For-profit 2-year business college
- Large town

General. Accredited by ACICS. **Enrollment:** 450 degree-seeking undergraduates. **Degrees:** 148 associate awarded. **Calendar:** Five 10-week sessions per calendar year. **Full-time faculty:** 15 total. **Part-time faculty:** 45 total.

Basis for selection. Test score on CPAt most important.

2008-2009 Annual costs. Tuition/fees: $8,868.

Financial aid. All financial aid based on need. Need-based aid available for part-time students.

Application procedures. Admission: No deadline. No application fee. Admission notification on a rolling basis. **Financial aid:** FAFSA required. Applicants notified on a rolling basis.

Academics. Credit/placement by examination: CLEP.

Majors. Business: Accounting, business admin. **Engineering technology:** Heat/ac/refrig. **Health:** Health care admin. **Legal studies:** Paralegal.

Student life. Freshman orientation: Mandatory. Held right before start of classes.

Contact. E-mail: sonyah@marcogrp.com
Phone: (330) 297-7319 Toll-free number: (800) 794-2856
Fax: (330) 296-2159
Bohecker College, 326 East Main Street, Ravenna, OH 44266

Bowling Green State University: Firelands College
Huron, Ohio
www.firelands.bgsu.edu **CB code: 0749**

- Public 2-year branch campus college
- Commuter campus in small town

General. Founded in 1967. Regionally accredited. **Enrollment:** 1,697 degree-seeking undergraduates. **Degrees:** 206 associate awarded. **Location:** 50 miles from Cleveland, 60 miles from Toledo. **Calendar:** Semester, limited summer session. **Full-time faculty:** 48 total. **Part-time faculty:** 54 total. **Class size:** 54% < 20, 45% 20-39, less than 1% 40-49. **Special facilities:** Arboretum.

Basis for selection. Open admission. **Homeschooled:** Home school program must be accredited.

High school preparation. 16 units recommended. Recommended units include English 4, mathematics 3, social studies 3, science 3 (laboratory 2) and foreign language 2. One visual or performing arts recommended.

2008-2009 Annual costs. Tuition/fees: $4,228; $11,536 out-of-state. Books/supplies: $1,140. Personal expenses: $2,600.

2007-2008 Financial aid. All financial aid based on need. Need-based aid available for part-time students. Work-study available for part-time students. **Additional information:** Scholarship application deadline May 1. Technology computer loan program available. Based on need, students may receive computer on semester by semester loan basis.

Application procedures. Admission: Priority date 2/1; deadline 7/15 (receipt date). $40 fee, may be waived for applicants with need. Admission notification on a rolling basis. **Financial aid:** Priority date 3/1; no closing date. FAFSA required. Applicants notified on a rolling basis starting 4/15; must reply within 2 week(s) of notification.

Academics. Upper-division program in nursing available for registered nurses who hold associate degree or have completed 3-year diploma program. Satellite associate degree registered nursing program from Lorain County Community College. Upper division programs available in liberal studies, general studies in business, applied health science, early childhood studies, criminal justice, manufacturing technology, visual communication technology. **Special study options:** Cross-registration, distance learning, dual enrollment of high school students, independent study, internships, liberal arts/career combination, student-designed major, teacher certification program. Satellite associate degree registered nurse program from Lorain County Community College. Bachelor's degree programs available on campus. License preparation in nursing. **Credit/placement by examination:** AP, CLEP, institutional tests. 15 credit hours maximum toward associate degree. **Support services:** Learning center, reduced course load, remedial instruction, tutoring.

Majors. Business: General, accounting, administrative services, business admin, operations. **Communications technology:** General. **Computer sciences:** Programming. **Engineering:** Electrical. **Engineering technology:** General, computer, electrical, manufacturing. **Health:** Medical radiologic technology/radiation therapy, medical records technology, nursing (RN), respiratory therapy technology. **Interdisciplinary:** Biological/physical sciences. **Liberal arts:** Arts/sciences. **Protective services:** Criminal justice. **Public administration:** Human services. **Social sciences:** General.

Most popular majors. Business/marketing 10%, health sciences 25%, liberal arts 21%.

Computing on campus. 300 workstations in library, computer center. Commuter students can connect to campus network. Online library, helpline, wireless network available.

Student life. Freshman orientation: Available. **Activities:** Drama, student government, student newspaper, allied health club, Campus Fellowship, theater group, writing center, Model United Nations, peace and justice club, virtual communication technology organization, women's resource group.

Athletics. Intramural: Basketball, football (non-tackle) M, table tennis, volleyball.

Student services. Adult student services, career counseling, student employment services, financial aid counseling, personal counseling, placement for graduates. **Physically disabled:** Services for visually, hearing impaired. **Transfer:** Transfer adviser, college fairs on campus for students transferring to 4-year colleges.

Contact. E-mail: fireadm@bgsu.edu
Phone: (419) 433-5560 ext. 20607 Fax: (419) 372-0604
Debralee Divers, Director of Admissions and Financial Aid, Bowling Green State University: Firelands College, One University Drive, Huron, OH 44839

Bradford School
Columbus, Ohio
www.bradfordschoolcolumbus.edu **CB code: 3952**

- For-profit 2-year business and technical college
- Commuter campus in very large city

General. Founded in 1911. Accredited by ACICS. **Enrollment:** 608 degree-seeking undergraduates. **Degrees:** 247 associate awarded. **Calendar:** Semester, extensive summer session. **Full-time faculty:** 16 total. **Part-time faculty:** 11 total.

Basis for selection. Open admission. Interview required to ensure interest in business, health care or culinary education.

2008-2009 Annual costs. Tuition/fees: $13,200. Room only: $5,960.

Application procedures. Admission: No deadline. $50 fee. Admission notification on a rolling basis.

Academics. Credit/placement by examination: CLEP.

Majors. Business: Accounting, office management. **Computer sciences:** LAN/WAN management, programming. **Health:** Veterinary technology/assistant. **Legal studies:** Legal secretary, paralegal.

Student life. Housing: Single-sex dorms available.

Student services. Career counseling, financial aid counseling, placement for graduates.

Contact. E-mail: bradfordcols@bradfordschoolcolumbus.edu
Phone: (614) 416-6200 Toll-free number: (800) 678-7981
Fax: (614) 416-6210
Raeann Lee, Director of Admissions, Bradford School, 2469 Stelzer Road, Columbus, OH 43219

Brown Mackie College: Akron
Akron, Ohio
www.brownmackie.edu **CB code: 3266**

- For-profit 2-year business college
- Commuter campus in small city

General. Accredited by ACICS. **Calendar:** Quarter.

Annual costs/financial aid. Tuition/fees (2008-2009): $11,250. Books/supplies: $1,000. Personal expenses: $2,664.

Contact. Phone: (330) 733-8766
Director of Admissions, 755 White Pond Drive, Suite 101, Akron, OH 44320

Brown Mackie College: Cincinnati
Cincinnati, Ohio
www.brownmackie.edu **CB code: 0297**

- For-profit 2-year business and nursing college
- Commuter campus in large city

General. Founded in 1927. Accredited by ACICS. **Location:** 10 miles from downtown. **Calendar:** Quarter.

Annual costs/financial aid. Books/supplies: $1,275. Personal expenses: $2,700. Need-based financial aid available to full-time and part-time students.

Contact. Phone: (513) 771-2424
Director of Admissions, 1011 Glendale-Milford Road, Cincinnati, OH 45215

Brown Mackie College: Findlay
Findlay, Ohio
www.brownmackie.edu

- For-profit 2-year business and junior college
- Commuter campus in small city

General. Accredited by ACICS. **Location:** 20 miles Bowling Green, 48 miles from Toledo. **Calendar:** Quarter.

Annual costs/financial aid. Tuition/fees: $14,490. Books/supplies: $1,850. Personal expenses: $2,700. Need-based financial aid available to full-time and part-time students.

Contact. Phone: (419) 423-2211
Sr. Admissions Director, 1700 Fostoria Avenue, Suite 100, Findlay, OH 45840

Brown Mackie College: North Canton
Canton, Ohio
www.brownmackie.edu

- For-profit 2-year career college
- Commuter campus in small city

General. Accredited by ACICS. **Calendar:** Continuous.

Annual costs/financial aid. Tuition/fees (2008-2009): $11,250. Books/supplies: $1,000.

Contact. Phone: (330) 494-1214
Director of Admissions, 4300 Munson Street Northwest, Canton, OH 44718-3674

Bryant & Stratton College: Cleveland
Cleveland, Ohio
www.bryantstratton.edu **CB code: 0814**

- For-profit 2-year technical college
- Commuter campus in very large city
- Interview required

General. Founded in 1929. Regionally accredited. **Enrollment:** 712 degree-seeking undergraduates. **Degrees:** 12 bachelor's, 86 associate awarded. **Location:** Downtown. **Calendar:** Trimester, extensive summer session. **Full-time faculty:** 18 total. **Part-time faculty:** 36 total. **Class size:** 79% < 20, 21% 20-39.

Transfer out. Colleges most students transferred to 2008: ITT Technical Institute, Cuyahoga Community College, Myer University, Cleveland State University.

Basis for selection. Open admission. Institutional test scores and interview most important. Passing scores on entrance exams required. CPAt entrance exam required. If ACT or SAT scores high enough, may be submitted in lieu of CPAt.

2008-2009 Annual costs. Tuition/fees: $13,775. Per-credit charge: $458. Books/supplies: $1,800. Personal expenses: $1,530.

2007-2008 Financial aid. Need-based: Need-based aid available for part-time students. Work-study available nights. **Non-need-based:** Scholarships awarded for academics.

Application procedures. Admission: No deadline. No application fee. Admission notification on a rolling basis. **Financial aid:** No deadline. FAFSA, institutional form required. Applicants notified on a rolling basis starting 5/1; must reply within 2 week(s) of notification.

Academics. Special study options: Distance learning, double major, independent study, internships, liberal arts/career combination. Bachelor's degree programs available on campus. **Credit/placement by examination:** AP, CLEP, institutional tests. 26 credit hours maximum toward associate degree. **Support services:** Learning center, reduced course load, remedial instruction, study skills assistance, tutoring, writing center.

Majors. Business: General, administrative services. **Computer sciences:** Information technology. **Engineering technology:** CAD/CADD, electrical.

Most popular majors. Architecture 38%, computer/information sciences 38%, engineering/engineering technologies 25%.

Computing on campus. 106 workstations in library, computer center. Online library available.

Student life. Freshman orientation: Available. Preregistration for classes offered. Three-hour session 1 week prior to start of semester. **Activities:** Literary magazine, student government, student newspaper.

Athletics. Intramural: Softball. **Team name:** Bobcats.

Student services. Adult student services, alcohol/substance abuse counseling, career counseling, student employment services, financial aid counseling, personal counseling, placement for graduates. **Transfer:** Pre-admission transcript evaluation for new students. Transfer adviser, college fairs on campus for students transferring to 4-year colleges.

Contact. E-mail: stkampa@bryantstratton.edu
Phone: (216) 771-1700 Fax: (216) 771-7787
Brian Wilson, Director of Admissions, Bryant & Stratton College: Cleveland, 1700 East 13th Street, Cleveland, OH 44114-3203

Central Ohio Technical College

Newark, Ohio
www.cotc.edu **CB code: 7331**

- Public 2-year technical college
- Commuter campus in large town

General. Founded in 1971. Regionally accredited. Campus shared with Ohio State University: Newark campus. Off-campus evening classes are taught in Mount Vernon and Coshocton. Students can take classes at Ohio State Newark. **Enrollment:** 3,110 undergraduates. **Degrees:** 413 associate awarded. **Location:** 45 miles from Columbus. **Calendar:** Quarter, limited summer session. **Full-time faculty:** 64 total. **Part-time faculty:** 206 total. **Class size:** 73% < 20, 26% 20-39, less than 1% 40-49.

Student profile.

Out-of-state:	1%	**Live on campus:**	1%
25 or older:	52%		

Transfer out. Colleges most students transferred to 2008: Franklin University, Mount Vernon Nazarene, Ohio State University.

Basis for selection. Open admission, but selective for some programs. Degree-seeking applicants must be 18 years or older and meet minimum scores on the COTC COMPASS test or ACT or meet COTC waiver eligibility of all 3 COMPASS tests due to applicant transferring from another college. **Homeschooled:** Must have COMPASS scores of 32 writing, 62 reading and 25 pre-algebra or 14 ACT English and 15 ACT Math.

High school preparation. 1 chemistry, 1 algebra and 1 biology required for medical sonography, nursing and surgical technology; 1 chemistry, 1 algebra, 1 math beyond algebra I, 1 biology required for radiographic.

2008-2009 Annual costs. Tuition/fees: $3,600; $6,300 out-of-state. Per-credit charge: $76 in-state; $151 out-of-state. Books/supplies: $1,251. Personal expenses: $2,178.

2007-2008 Financial aid. Need-based: Need-based aid available for part-time students. Work-study available nights, weekends and for part-time students. **Non-need-based:** Scholarships awarded for academics.

Application procedures. Admission: Priority date 6/15; no deadline. $20 fee, may be waived for applicants with need. Admission notification on a rolling basis. **Financial aid:** Priority date 3/1; no closing date. FAFSA required. Applicants notified on a rolling basis starting 5/1; must reply within 3 week(s) of notification.

Academics. Special study options: Cooperative education, double major, dual enrollment of high school students, ESL, internships, weekend college. License preparation in nursing, paramedic, radiology. **Credit/placement by examination:** CLEP, IB, institutional tests. 55 credit hours maximum toward associate degree. **Support services:** Learning center, reduced course load, remedial instruction, study skills assistance, tutoring.

Majors. Business: Accounting, administrative services, business admin, human resources. **Communications technology:** Desktop publishing. **Computer sciences:** Applications programming, data entry, web page design. **Education:** Early childhood. **Engineering technology:** Architectural drafting, CAD/CADD, civil drafting, electrical, electromechanical. **Health:** Medical radiologic technology/radiation therapy, nursing (RN), sonography, surgical technology. **Protective services:** Criminal justice, forensics, law enforcement admin. **Public administration:** Human services, social work.

Most popular majors. Business/marketing 9%, health sciences 63%, public administration/social services 6%, security/protective services 7%.

Computing on campus. 40 workstations in library, computer center. Commuter students can connect to campus network. Online course registration, helpline, wireless network available.

Student life. Freshman orientation: Mandatory. Preregistration for classes offered. Three-hour program. **Housing:** Apartments available. **Activities:** Choral groups, drama, music ensembles, student government, student newspaper, Phi Theta Kappa, theatre arts association, student nurses organization, criminal justice club, rad tech club, Habitat for Humanity College Chapter, ski club, Students in Free Enterpise.

Athletics. NJCAA. **Intercollegiate:** Baseball M, basketball, cross-country, golf, soccer M, softball W, volleyball. **Intramural:** Badminton, basketball, bowling, football (non-tackle), softball, table tennis, tennis, volleyball.

Student services. Career counseling, student employment services, financial aid counseling, minority student services, on-campus daycare, personal counseling, placement for graduates, veterans' counselor. **Physically disabled:** Services for visually, speech, hearing impaired. **Transfer:** Transfer adviser, college fairs on campus for students transferring to 4-year colleges.

Contact. E-mail: kquick@cotc.tec.oh.us
Phone: (740) 366-9222 Fax: (740) 366-5047
John Merrin, Coordinator of Admissions, Central Ohio Technical College, 1179 University Drive, Newark, OH 43055

Chatfield College

St. Martin, Ohio
www.chatfield.edu **CB code: 1143**

- Private 2-year liberal arts college affiliated with Roman Catholic Church
- Commuter campus in rural community

General. Founded in 1970. Regionally accredited. **Enrollment:** 248 degree-seeking undergraduates. **Degrees:** 21 associate awarded. **Location:** 40 miles from Cincinnati. **Calendar:** Semester, limited summer session. **Full-time faculty:** 1 total. **Part-time faculty:** 61 total. **Class size:** 95% < 20, 5% 20-39.

Student profile. Among degree-seeking undergraduates, 78 enrolled as first-time, first-year students.

Part-time:	42%	**African American:**	37%
Women:	79%	**25 or older:**	40%

Transfer out. Colleges most students transferred to 2008: Wilmington College, Xavier University, Mount St. Joseph, Northern Kentucky University.

Basis for selection. Open admission. Interview recommended. **Homeschooled:** Official documentation of home school program required.

High school preparation. 16 units recommended. Recommended units include English 4, mathematics 3, social studies 3, science 3 and foreign language 2. Computer science recommended.

2008-2009 Annual costs. Tuition/fees: $9,190. Books/supplies: $650. Personal expenses: $1,922.

Financial aid. Need-based: Need-based aid available for part-time students. Work-study available for part-time students. **Non-need-based:** Scholarships awarded for academics, leadership. **Additional information:** Institutional grants/scholarships given primarily to first-year students to reduce debt load during initial year.

Application procedures. Admission: No deadline. $10 fee. Admission notification on a rolling basis. **Financial aid:** Priority date 5/1, closing date 8/3. FAFSA, institutional form required. Applicants notified on a rolling basis starting 4/1; must reply within 2 week(s) of notification.

Academics. Special study options: Cooperative education, cross-registration, dual enrollment of high school students, independent study, internships, liberal arts/career combination. Cooperative programs leading to bachelor's in business and liberal studies with 2 local institutions. Third-year option: student can complete junior year at school through arrangements with several regional 4-year colleges. **Credit/placement by examination:** CLEP, institutional tests. **Support services:** Learning center, remedial instruction, study skills assistance, tutoring, writing center.

Majors. Business: Business admin. **Education:** Early childhood. **Liberal arts:** Arts/sciences. **Public administration:** Human services.

Computing on campus. 26 workstations in library, computer center.

Student life. Freshman orientation: Available. **Activities:** Student newspaper.

Student services. Adult student services, career counseling, financial aid counseling, personal counseling. **Transfer:** Transfer adviser, college fairs on campus for students transferring to 4-year colleges.

Contact. E-mail: admissions@chatfield.edu
Phone: (513) 875-3344 Fax: (513) 875-3912
Brian Wright, Director of Admissions, Chatfield College, 20918 State Route 251, St. Martin, OH 45118

Cincinnati State Technical and Community College
Cincinnati, Ohio
www.cincinnatistate.edu **CB code: 1984**

- Public 2-year community and technical college
- Commuter campus in large city

General. Founded in 1966. Regionally accredited. **Enrollment:** 7,325 degree-seeking undergraduates; 820 non-degree-seeking students. **Degrees:** 983 associate awarded. **ROTC:** Army. **Location:** 5 miles from downtown. **Calendar:** Five 10-week terms. Extensive summer session. **Full-time faculty:** 173 total; 11% have terminal degrees, 15% minority, 57% women. **Part-time faculty:** 444 total. **Class size:** 67% < 20, 32% 20-39, less than 1% 40-49. **Special facilities:** Aviation maintenance facility, culinary facility, television studio.

Student profile. Among degree-seeking undergraduates, 16% enrolled in a transfer program, 84% enrolled in a vocational program, 5% already have a bachelor's degree or higher, 1,859 enrolled as first-time, first-year students.

Part-time:	55%	**Asian American:**	1%
Out-of-state:	11%	**Hispanic American:**	1%
Women:	54%	**International:**	1%
African American:	23%	**25 or older:**	45%

Transfer out. Colleges most students transferred to 2008: University of Cincinnati, Northern Kentucky University, Wilmington College, College of Mount St. Joseph, Xavier University.

Basis for selection. Open admission, but selective for some programs. Health technology programs require biology and chemistry courses to have been taken in last 7 years. COMPASS test required for placement. **Homeschooled:** Statement describing homeschool structure and mission, transcript of courses and grades required.

High school preparation. Specific course prerequisites for some programs.

2008-2009 Annual costs. Tuition/fees: $3,867; $7,476 out-of-state. Per-credit charge: $80 in-state; $160 out-of-state. Books/supplies: $3,000. Personal expenses: $1,260.

2007-2008 Financial aid. Need-based: 54% of total undergraduate aid awarded as scholarships/grants, 46% as loans/jobs. Need-based aid available for part-time students. Work-study available nights, weekends and for part-time students. **Non-need-based:** Scholarships awarded for academics, athletics, state residency.

Application procedures. Admission: No deadline. No application fee. Admission notification on a rolling basis. **Financial aid:** Priority date 2/15; no closing date. FAFSA required. Applicants notified on a rolling basis starting 3/15; must reply within 4 week(s) of notification.

Academics. Special study options: Cooperative education, cross-registration, distance learning, double major, dual enrollment of high school students, ESL, honors, independent study, internships, student-designed major. Bachelor's degree programs available on campus. License preparation in aviation, nursing, occupational therapy, paramedic, real estate. **Credit/placement by examination:** AP, CLEP, IB, institutional tests. 55 credit hours maximum toward associate degree. **Support services:** GED preparation and test center, reduced course load, remedial instruction, study skills assistance, tutoring, writing center.

Majors. Agriculture: Landscaping, turf management. **Business:** Accounting, accounting technology, business admin, executive assistant, finance, hotel/motel admin, international, marketing, office management, office/clerical, purchasing, real estate, restaurant/food services. **Communications technology:** Desktop publishing. **Computer sciences:** General, applications programming, networking. **Education:** Deaf/hearing impaired, early childhood. **Engineering technology:** Aerospace, architectural, automotive, biomedical, civil, computer, computer systems, construction, electrical, electromechanical, environmental, industrial, laser/optical, manufacturing, mechanical, occupational safety, plastics, surveying. **Family/consumer sciences:** Child care, institutional food production. **Foreign languages:** Sign language interpretation. **Health:** Clinical lab assistant, clinical lab technology, dietetic technician, EMT paramedic, massage therapy, medical records technology, nursing (RN), occupational therapy assistant, respiratory therapy technology, sonography, surgical technology, ward clerk. **Legal studies:** Legal secretary. **Liberal arts:** Arts/sciences. **Mechanic/repair:** Aircraft, automotive, computer. **Personal/culinary services:** Chef training, restaurant/catering. **Production:** Machine tool. **Protective services:** Firefighting. **Visual/performing arts:** Cinematography, commercial/advertising art.

Most popular majors. Business/marketing 17%, engineering/engineering technologies 22%, health sciences 21%, liberal arts 16%, personal/culinary services 7%.

Computing on campus. 175 workstations in library, computer center, student center. Commuter students can connect to campus network. Online course registration, online library, helpline, wireless network available.

Student life. Freshman orientation: Available. Preregistration for classes offered. Day and evening sessions held for 2-3 hours before start of classes. **Activities:** Drama, student government, TV station, United African American Association, international students, Phi Theta Kappa, adult learners on campus, environmental club, students in free enterprise.

Athletics. NJCAA. **Intercollegiate:** Basketball, golf, soccer. **Team name:** Surge.

Student services. Adult student services, alcohol/substance abuse counseling, career counseling, services for economically disadvantaged, student employment services, financial aid counseling, on-campus daycare, personal counseling, veterans' counselor. **Physically disabled:** Services for visually, speech, hearing impaired. **Transfer:** College fairs on campus for students transferring to 4-year colleges.

Contact. E-mail: adm@cincinnatistate.edu
Phone: (513) 861-7700 Fax: (513) 569-1562
Gabriele Boeckermann, Director of Admission, Cincinnati State Technical and Community College, 3520 Central Parkway, Cincinnati, OH 45223-2690

Clark State Community College
Springfield, Ohio
www.clarkstate.edu **CB code: 0777**

- Public 2-year community college
- Commuter campus in small city

General. Founded in 1966. Regionally accredited. **Enrollment:** 1,250 full-time, degree-seeking students. **Degrees:** 300 associate awarded. **Location:** 30 miles from Dayton, 45 miles from Columbus. **Calendar:** Quarter, limited summer session. **Full-time faculty:** 65 total. **Part-time faculty:** 440 total. **Special facilities:** Performing arts center.

Student profile.

Out-of-state:	1%	25 or older:	45%

Transfer out. **Colleges most students transferred to 2008:** Wright State University.

Basis for selection. Open admission, but selective for some programs. Nursing and allied health applicants must have high school chemistry; allied health must also have algebra or equivalent with grade of 2.0 or better. Mathematics placement test with score of 12 or better required for nursing.

High school preparation. 15 units recommended. Recommended units include English 4, mathematics 3, social studies 3, science 3 and foreign language 2. Chemistry required for nursing and medical technology. Algebra required for medical technology. 2 math units required for engineering programs.

2008-2009 Annual costs. Tuition/fees: $3,485; $6,432 out-of-state. Per-credit charge: $66 in-state; $131 out-of-state. Books/supplies: $1,200. Personal expenses: $550.

Financial aid. **Need-based:** Work-study available nights, weekends and for part-time students.

Application procedures. **Admission:** No deadline. $15 fee. Admission notification on a rolling basis. Early admission open to high school juniors and seniors. Placement test, high school approval, and 3.0 GPA required. **Financial aid:** Priority date 6/15; no closing date. FAFSA required. Applicants notified on a rolling basis.

Academics. **Special study options:** Accelerated study, cooperative education, cross-registration, distance learning, double major, dual enrollment of high school students, honors, independent study, internships, liberal arts/career combination, student-designed major, study abroad, weekend college. Bachelor's degree programs available on campus. License preparation in nursing, paramedic, physical therapy, real estate. **Credit/placement by examination:** AP, CLEP, institutional tests. 24 credit hours maximum toward associate degree. **Support services:** Learning center, pre-admission summer program, reduced course load, remedial instruction, tutoring, writing center.

Majors. **Agriculture:** Business, horticulture. **Business:** Accounting technology, business admin, human resources, logistics, marketing. **Computer sciences:** Applications programming, networking. **Education:** Early childhood, kindergarten/preschool. **Engineering:** Agricultural. **Engineering technology:** Drafting, industrial, mechanical. **Health:** Clinical lab technology, EMT paramedic, medical assistant, medical secretary, nursing (RN), physical therapy assistant. **Legal studies:** Court reporting, legal secretary. **Liberal arts:** Arts/sciences. **Protective services:** Corrections, law enforcement admin. **Public administration:** Social work. **Visual/performing arts:** Commercial/advertising art.

Most popular majors. Business/marketing 18%, health sciences 30%, liberal arts 24%, public administration/social services 8%, security/protective services 7%.

Computing on campus. Commuter students can connect to campus network. Online course registration, online library, helpline, wireless network available.

Student life. **Freshman orientation:** Available. Preregistration for classes offered. **Activities:** Campus ministries, choral groups, dance, drama, student government, student newspaper, professional and technological fraternities and sororities, minority student forum, Phi Theta Kappa, social work club.

Athletics. NJCAA. **Intercollegiate:** Baseball M, basketball, softball W, volleyball W. **Intramural:** Basketball, volleyball. **Team name:** Eagles.

Student services. Chaplain/spiritual director, career counseling, services for economically disadvantaged, student employment services, financial aid counseling, health services, minority student services, on-campus daycare, personal counseling, placement for graduates, veterans' counselor. **Physically disabled:** Services for visually, speech, hearing impaired. **Transfer:** Transfer adviser, college fairs on campus for students transferring to 4-year colleges.

Contact. Phone: (937) 328-6028 Fax: (937) 328-3853
Corey Holliday, Director of Admissions, Clark State Community College, Box 570, Springfield, OH 45501-0570

Cleveland Institute of Electronics

Cleveland, Ohio
www.cie-wc.edu **CB code: 0802**

- For-profit 2-year technical college
- Very large city

General. Founded in 1934. Accredited by DETC. Curriculum completed entirely through distance learning with no classroom attendance. **Enrollment:** 1,856 undergraduates. **Degrees:** 60 associate awarded. **Calendar:** Continuous. **Full-time faculty:** 6 total. **Part-time faculty:** 75 total.

Basis for selection. Open admission.

2008-2009 Annual costs. Tuition/fees: $3,770. Associate degree tuition $1,885 per 6-month term. Books/supplies: $1,000.

2008-2009 Financial aid. All financial aid based on need.

Application procedures. **Admission:** No deadline. No application fee. Admission notification on a rolling basis. High school students permitted to enroll with signed approval of parents and guidance counselors (if students are minors). **Financial aid:** No deadline. FAFSA required.

Academics. **Special study options:** Accelerated study, distance learning, independent study. **Credit/placement by examination:** CLEP.

Majors. **Computer sciences:** Programming. **Engineering technology:** Electrical. **Mechanic/repair:** Electronics/electrical.

Computing on campus. Online course registration available.

Student life. **Activities:** Student newspaper.

Student services. Student employment services, veterans' counselor.

Contact. E-mail: instruct@cie-wc.edu
Phone: (216) 781-9400 Toll-free number: (800) 243-6446
Fax: (216) 781-0331
Keith Conn, Admissions Director, Cleveland Institute of Electronics, 1776 East 17th Street, Cleveland, OH 44114-3679

Columbus State Community College

Columbus, Ohio
www.cscc.edu **CB code: 1148**

- Public 2-year community and technical college
- Commuter campus in very large city

General. Founded in 1967. Regionally accredited. Courses offered at 10 off-campus centers. **Enrollment:** 13,060 degree-seeking undergraduates. **Degrees:** 1,591 associate awarded. **ROTC:** Army, Air Force. **Location:** 2 miles from downtown. **Calendar:** Quarter, extensive summer session. **Full-time faculty:** 280 total. **Part-time faculty:** 1,170 total. **Class size:** 56% < 20, 43% 20-39, less than 1% 40-49, less than 1% 50-99, less than 1% >100. **Special facilities:** College-owned building for aviation maintenance program at Bolton Field Airport.

Student profile. Among degree-seeking undergraduates, 60% enrolled in a transfer program, 25% enrolled in a vocational program.

Transfer out. **Colleges most students transferred to 2008:** Ohio State University.

Basis for selection. Open admission, but selective for some programs. Select applicant populations such as underage, international, felon, and dismissed transfer students may be required to submit documentation to determine admission status. Some technology programs have special admission requirements. COMPASS required for placement. English as a Second Language applicants required to complete ESL placement test. Placement testing required for all students who plan to take courses that have an English, math, and/or reading prerequisite. Interview required for chef apprenticeship and some health and human service techology programs. **Homeschooled:** Some academic programs may require completion of GED. Recommend completing COMPASS Ability to Benefit Placement Test if applying for financial aid. **Learning Disabled:** Students must provide documentation and register with Disability Services to receive services.

High school preparation. Algebra required for transfer programs and engineering, health, and business technology programs. Chemistry and biology required for health programs.

2008-2009 Annual costs. Tuition/fees: $3,555; $7,875 out-of-state. Per-credit charge: $70 in-state; $166 out-of-state. Books/supplies: $1,050. Personal expenses: $168.

Financial aid. **Need-based:** Need-based aid available for part-time students. Work-study available nights, weekends and for part-time students. **Non-need-based:** Scholarships awarded for athletics, state residency.

Application procedures. **Admission:** No deadline. No application fee. Application must be submitted online. Admission notification on a rolling basis. Many health programs admit qualified students on space-available basis; students advised to apply early. **Financial aid:** Priority date 7/24; no closing date. FAFSA required. Applicants notified on a rolling basis starting 4/1.

Academics. Special study options: Cooperative education, cross-registration, distance learning, double major, dual enrollment of high school students, ESL, honors, independent study, internships, liberal arts/career combination, student-designed major, study abroad, teacher certification program, weekend college. Bachelor's degree programs available on campus. License preparation in dental hygiene, nursing, paramedic, real estate. **Credit/placement by examination:** AP, CLEP, IB, institutional tests. **Support services:** GED preparation and test center, learning center, reduced course load, remedial instruction, study skills assistance, tutoring, writing center.

Majors. Architecture: Landscape. **Business:** Accounting, accounting technology, administrative services, business admin, entrepreneurial studies, hospitality admin, hospitality/recreation, human resources, logistics, marketing, office management, office/clerical, purchasing, real estate, sales/distribution, tourism promotion, tourism/travel. **Communications technology:** General, graphic/printing. **Computer sciences:** General, applications programming, computer graphics, information systems, programming. **Conservation:** Environmental studies. **Education:** Early childhood. **Engineering technology:** Aerospace, architectural, automotive, civil, construction, electrical, electromechanical, industrial, mechanical, quality control, surveying. **Family/consumer sciences:** Aging, child development. **Foreign languages:** Sign language interpretation. **Health:** Clinical lab assistant, dental hygiene, dental lab technology, EMT paramedic, health services, medical radiologic technology/radiation therapy, medical records admin, medical records technology, medical secretary, mental health services, nuclear medical technology, nursing (RN), respiratory therapy technology, substance abuse counseling, surgical technology, veterinary technology/assistant. **Interdisciplinary:** Gerontology. **Legal studies:** Legal secretary, paralegal. **Liberal arts:** Arts/sciences. **Mechanic/repair:** Aircraft, automotive, electronics/electrical, heating/ac/refrig. **Parks/recreation:** Exercise sciences, sports admin. **Personal/culinary services:** Chef training, culinary arts. **Production:** Cabinetmaking/millwright, sheet metal, welding. **Protective services:** Corrections, fire safety technology, firefighting, law enforcement admin, police science. **Public administration:** General. **Transportation:** General. **Visual/performing arts:** Commercial photography.

Computing on campus. Commuter students can connect to campus network. Online course registration, online library, helpline, wireless network available.

Student life. Freshman orientation: Available. **Housing:** Students may live in residence halls of other local colleges if space is available. **Activities:** Concert band, choral groups, dance, drama, international student organizations, literary magazine, music ensembles, musical theater, student government, student newspaper.

Athletics. NJCAA. **Intercollegiate:** Basketball, golf M, volleyball W. **Intramural:** Basketball, volleyball. **Team name:** Cougars.

Student services. Adult student services, alcohol/substance abuse counseling, career counseling, services for economically disadvantaged, student employment services, financial aid counseling, minority student services, on-campus daycare, personal counseling, placement for graduates, veterans' counselor. **Physically disabled:** Services for visually, speech, hearing impaired. **Learning disabled:** Comprehensive services available. **Transfer:** Transfer adviser, college fairs on campus for students transferring to 4-year colleges.

Contact. Phone: (614) 287-2669 Toll-free number: (800) 621-6407 ext. 2669 Fax: (614) 287-6019
Tari Blaney, Director of Admissions, Columbus State Community College, 550 East Spring Street, Columbus, OH 43216-1609

Cuyahoga Community College: Eastern Campus

Highland Hills, Ohio
www.tri-c.edu — **CB code: 1978**

- Public 2-year branch campus and community college
- Commuter campus in large city

General. Founded in 1971. Regionally accredited. **Location:** 3 miles from Cleveland. **Calendar:** Semester.

Annual costs/financial aid. Tuition/fees (2008-2009): $2,416; $3,194 out-of-district; $6,541 out-of-state. Books/supplies: $900. Personal expenses: $1,504. Need-based financial aid available to full-time and part-time students.

Contact. Phone: (216) 987-2024
Director of Admissions, 4250 Richmond Road, Highland Hills, OH 44122

Cuyahoga Community College: Metropolitan Campus

Cleveland, Ohio — **CB member**
www.tri-c.edu — **CB code: 1159**

- Public 2-year community college
- Commuter campus in very large city

General. Founded in 1963. Regionally accredited. Additional campuses in Highland Hills, Westlake and Parma. **Enrollment:** 10,339 degree-seeking undergraduates; 13,405 non-degree-seeking students. **Degrees:** 1,793 associate awarded. **ROTC:** Naval, Air Force. **Location:** Downtown. **Calendar:** Semester, limited summer session. **Full-time faculty:** 322 total; 22% have terminal degrees, 19% minority, 59% women. **Part-time faculty:** 1,193 total; 8% have terminal degrees, 17% minority, 51% women. **Class size:** 60% < 20, 37% 20-39, 2% 40-49, less than 1% 50-99, less than 1% >100. **Special facilities:** Technology center.

Student profile. Among degree-seeking undergraduates, 22% enrolled in a transfer program, 78% enrolled in a vocational program, 2,126 enrolled as first-time, first-year students, 738 transferred in from other institutions.

Part-time:	54%	**Hispanic American:**	4%
Women:	62%	**International:**	2%
African American:	32%	**25 or older:**	49%
Asian American:	2%		

Transfer out. 62% of students enrolled in the transfer program go on to 4-year colleges. **Colleges most students transferred to 2008:** Cleveland State University, Baldwin-Wallace College, Kent State University, University of Akron.

Basis for selection. Open admission, but selective for some programs. Special requirements for some health technology programs (SAT or ACT required). English placement test required.

2008-2009 Annual costs. Tuition/fees: $2,416; $3,194 out-of-district; $6,541 out-of-state. Per-credit charge: $73 in-district; $99 out-of-district; $210 out-of-state. Books/supplies: $1,400. Personal expenses: $1,320.

2008-2009 Financial aid. Need-based: Average need met was 100%. Average scholarship/grant was $5,987; average loan $2,931. 82% of total undergraduate aid awarded as scholarships/grants, 18% as loans/jobs. Need-based aid available for part-time students. Work-study available nights, weekends and for part-time students. **Non-need-based:** Scholarships awarded for academics, art, athletics, leadership, minority status, music/drama.

Application procedures. Admission: No deadline. No application fee. Admission notification on a rolling basis. **Financial aid:** No deadline. FAFSA, institutional form required. Applicants notified on a rolling basis starting 5/8.

Academics. Special study options: Cooperative education, cross-registration, distance learning, dual enrollment of high school students, ESL, honors, independent study. **Credit/placement by examination:** AP, CLEP, institutional tests. 30 credit hours maximum toward associate degree. **Support services:** GED preparation and test center, learning center, reduced course load, remedial instruction, study skills assistance, tutoring, writing center.

Majors. Agriculture: Horticulture. **Business:** General, accounting, administrative services, business admin, entrepreneurial studies, hospitality admin, management information systems, real estate. **Communications technology:** General. **Computer sciences:** General. **Education:** Early childhood. **Engineering technology:** Architectural, drafting, electrical. **Family/consumer sciences:** Child care. **Foreign languages:** Sign language interpretation. **Health:** Clinical lab technology, dental assistant, dental hygiene, dental lab technology, EMT paramedic, health services, medical assistant, medical records admin, medical records technology, nursing (RN), occupational therapy assistant, optician, pharmacy assistant, physical therapy assistant, surgical technology. **Legal studies:** Court reporting, paralegal. **Liberal arts:** Arts/sciences. **Mechanic/repair:** Automotive. **Personal/culinary services:** Culinary arts. **Protective services:** Corrections, fire safety technology, police science. **Visual/performing arts:** Commercial/advertising art, photography.

Most popular majors. Business/marketing 12%, health sciences 31%, liberal arts 37%.

Computing on campus. 1,000 workstations in library, computer center, student center. Online course registration, online library, helpline available.

Student life. Freshman orientation: Mandatory. Preregistration for classes offered. **Activities:** Bands, choral groups, dance, drama, musical theater, student government, student newspaper, Hillel, Afro-American society, veterans service fraternity, Young Socialist Alliance, Student Coalition Against Racism, National Education Association, Hispanic club, Phi Theta Kappa.

Athletics. NJCAA. **Intercollegiate:** Baseball M, basketball, cross-country, soccer, softball W, track and field, volleyball W, wrestling M. **Intramural:** Baseball M, basketball, bowling, gymnastics, handball, racquetball, softball, tennis, volleyball, weight lifting. **Team name:** Challengers.

Student services. Adult student services, alcohol/substance abuse counseling, career counseling, student employment services, financial aid counseling, health services, minority student services, on-campus daycare, personal counseling, placement for graduates, veterans' counselor, women's services. **Physically disabled:** Services for visually, speech, hearing impaired. **Learning disabled:** Comprehensive services available. **Transfer:** Transfer adviser, college fairs on campus for students transferring to 4-year colleges.

Contact. E-mail: customerservice@tri-c.edu
Phone: (216) 987-4200 Fax: (216) 696-2567
Rena Mason, Director of Admissions, Cuyahoga Community College: Metropolitan Campus, 2900 Community College Avenue, Cleveland, OH 44115-2878

Cuyahoga Community College: Western Campus

Parma, Ohio
www.tri-c.edu **CB code: 1985**

- Public 2-year community college
- Commuter campus in small city

General. Founded in 1966. Regionally accredited. **Location:** 15 miles from Cleveland. **Calendar:** Semester.

Annual costs/financial aid. Tuition/fees (2008-2009): $2,416; $3,194 out-of-district; $6,541 out-of-state. Books/supplies: $900. Personal expenses: $1,504. Need-based financial aid available to full-time and part-time students.

Contact. Phone: (216) 987-5150
Director of Admissions and Records, 11000 Pleasant Valley Road, Parma, OH 44130

Davis College

Toledo, Ohio
www.daviscollege.edu **CB code: 2155**

- For-profit 2-year junior college
- Commuter campus in large city
- Interview required

General. Founded in 1858. Regionally accredited. **Enrollment:** 477 degree-seeking undergraduates; 8 non-degree-seeking students. **Degrees:** 100 associate awarded. **Location:** 6 miles from downtown, 45 miles from Detroit. **Calendar:** Quarter, limited summer session. **Full-time faculty:** 15 total; 80% women. **Part-time faculty:** 12 total; 42% women. **Class size:** 81% < 20, 19% 20-39.

Student profile. Among degree-seeking undergraduates, 51 enrolled as first-time, first-year students, 144 transferred in from other institutions.

Part-time:	57%	**African American:**	38%
Out-of-state:	3%	**Hispanic American:**	2%
Women:	84%	**25 or older:**	56%

Transfer out. Colleges most students transferred to 2008: Lourdes College, Spring Arbor University, University of Toledo, Owens Community College, Monroe Community College.

Basis for selection. Character and personal qualities very important; CPAt score, interview, talent and ability important. School and College Ability Tests (CPAt) required. Portfolio required for some graphic design degree programs. **Homeschooled:** State high school equivalency certificate required.

2008-2009 Annual costs. Tuition/fees: $11,145. Per-credit charge: $237. Books/supplies: $1,350. Personal expenses: $2,073.

2007-2008 Financial aid. All financial aid based on need. 28 full-time freshmen applied for aid; 28 were judged to have need; 27 of these received aid. Average need met was 89%. 36% of total undergraduate aid awarded as scholarships/grants, 64% as loans/jobs. Need-based aid available for part-time students. Work-study available nights and weekends.

Application procedures. Admission: Closing date 9/1 (receipt date). $30 fee. Admission notification on a rolling basis. **Financial aid:** No deadline. FAFSA required. Applicants notified on a rolling basis.

Academics. Special study options: Distance learning, internships, liberal arts/career combination. **Credit/placement by examination:** CLEP, institutional tests. 16 credit hours maximum toward associate degree. **Support services:** Reduced course load, remedial instruction, tutoring.

Majors. Business: Accounting, accounting technology, administrative services, business admin, fashion, human resources, insurance, marketing. **Computer sciences:** Networking, webmaster. **Education:** Early childhood. **Health:** Insurance coding, medical assistant, medical secretary, medical transcription. **Legal studies:** Legal secretary. **Visual/performing arts:** Graphic design, interior design. **Other:** Sports and recreation marketing.

Most popular majors. Business/marketing 31%, computer/information sciences 8%, health sciences 45%, visual/performing arts 10%.

Computing on campus. 106 workstations in library, computer center. Wireless network available.

Student life. Freshman orientation: Mandatory. **Activities:** Student newspaper.

Student services. Career counseling, student employment services, financial aid counseling, personal counseling, placement for graduates, veterans' counselor. **Transfer:** Pre-admission transcript evaluation for new students.

Contact. E-mail: dstern@daviscollege.edu
Phone: (419) 473-2700 Toll-free number: (800) 477-7021
Fax: (419) 473-2472
Dana Stern, Senior Career Coordinator, Davis College, 4747 Monroe Street, Toledo, OH 43623

Edison State Community College

Piqua, Ohio
www.edisonohio.edu **CB code: 1191**

- Public 2-year community college
- Commuter campus in large town

General. Founded in 1973. Regionally accredited. **Enrollment:** 2,249 degree-seeking undergraduates; 1,090 non-degree-seeking students. **Degrees:** 324 associate awarded. **Location:** 30 miles from Dayton. **Calendar:** Semester, extensive summer session. **Full-time faculty:** 50 total; 22% have terminal degrees, 4% minority, 50% women. **Part-time faculty:** 162 total; 7% have terminal degrees, 6% minority, 51% women. **Class size:** 75% < 20, 24% 20-39, less than 1% 40-49, less than 1% 50-99. **Partnerships:** Formal partnership with Tech Prep.

Student profile. Among degree-seeking undergraduates, 21% enrolled in a transfer program, 79% enrolled in a vocational program, 1% already have a bachelor's degree or higher, 590 enrolled as first-time, first-year students, 131 transferred in from other institutions.

Part-time:	57%	**Asian American:**	1%
Out-of-state:	1%	**Hispanic American:**	1%
Women:	67%	**25 or older:**	40%
African American:	3%		

Transfer out. 73% of students enrolled in the transfer program go on to 4-year colleges. **Colleges most students transferred to 2008:** Ohio State University, Sinclair Community College, Bowling Green State University, Miami University, Wright State University.

Basis for selection. Open admission, but selective for some programs. Special admissions requirements for nursing, health care, early childhood education, human services programs. Degree-seeking students without recent ACT or SAT scores must complete COMPASS or ASSET for placement.

High school preparation. College-preparatory program recommended. Recommended units include English 4, mathematics 3, social studies 3, science 3 and foreign language 2. 1 fine arts recommended.

2008-2009 Annual costs. Tuition/fees: $3,450; $6,420 out-of-state. Per-credit charge: $99 in-state; $198 out-of-state. Books/supplies: $1,300. Personal expenses: $756.

Financial aid. **Need-based:** Need-based aid available for part-time students. Work-study available nights and weekends. **Non-need-based:** Scholarships awarded for academics, art, athletics.

Application procedures. **Admission:** No deadline. $20 fee, may be waived for applicants with need. Admission notification on a rolling basis. **Financial aid:** Priority date 5/2; no closing date. FAFSA, institutional form required. Applicants notified on a rolling basis starting 5/15.

Academics. **Special study options:** Combined bachelor's/graduate degree, cross-registration, distance learning, double major, dual enrollment of high school students, independent study, internships, student-designed major, weekend college. License preparation in nursing, physical therapy, real estate. **Credit/placement by examination:** AP, CLEP, institutional tests. 30 credit hours maximum toward associate degree. DANTE, DSST and professional exams recommended by American Council on Education accepted. **Support services:** Learning center, pre-admission summer program, reduced course load, remedial instruction, study skills assistance, tutoring, writing center.

Majors. **Business:** General, accounting, administrative services, business admin, communications, executive assistant, finance, human resources, labor relations, logistics, marketing, office management, operations, real estate, sales/distribution. **Computer sciences:** General, computer graphics, information technology, LAN/WAN management, networking, programming, security, system admin, web page design, webmaster. **Education:** General, early childhood. **Engineering:** General, electrical. **Engineering technology:** Computer, electrical, industrial, manufacturing, mechanical, mechanical drafting, plastics, quality control. **Family/consumer sciences:** Child care, child development. **Health:** Medical assistant, medical records admin, medical secretary, medical transcription, nursing (RN), office admin, physical therapy assistant, prenursing, receptionist. **Legal studies:** Legal secretary, paralegal. **Liberal arts:** Arts/sciences. **Mechanic/repair:** Electronics/electrical. **Production:** Welding. **Protective services:** Police science. **Public administration:** Human services. **Visual/performing arts:** Art, commercial/advertising art, design, dramatic.

Most popular majors. Business/marketing 14%, health sciences 21%, liberal arts 19%, visual/performing arts 24%.

Computing on campus. 67 workstations in library, student center. Commuter students can connect to campus network. Online course registration, online library, helpline, wireless network available.

Student life. **Freshman orientation:** Available. **Activities:** Drama, student government, Phi Theta Kappa, photo society, writers club, student ambassadors, theater group, international club, digital media club, arts league, society of human resource management, Campus Crusade for Christ.

Athletics. NJCAA. **Intercollegiate:** Basketball, volleyball W. **Team name:** Chargers.

Student services. Adult student services, career counseling, student employment services, financial aid counseling, health services, on-campus daycare, personal counseling, placement for graduates, veterans' counselor. **Physically disabled:** Services for visually, speech, hearing impaired. **Transfer:** Pre-admission transcript evaluation for new students. Transfer adviser, college fairs on campus for students transferring to 4-year colleges.

Contact. E-mail: info@edisonohio.edu
Phone: (937) 778-7868 Toll-free number: (800) 922-3722 ext. 7868
Fax: (937) 778-1920
Velina Bogart, Coordinator of Admissions, Edison State Community College, 1973 Edison Drive, Piqua, OH 45356-9253

ETI Technical College of Niles
Niles, Ohio
www.eticollege.edu **CB code: 3149**

- For-profit 2-year technical college
- Commuter campus in large city
- Interview required

General. Accredited by ACCSCT. **Enrollment:** 188 degree-seeking undergraduates. **Degrees:** 80 associate awarded. **Location:** 50 miles from Cleveland and Pittsburgh. **Calendar:** Semester. **Full-time faculty:** 5 total. **Part-time faculty:** 16 total.

Student profile. Among degree-seeking undergraduates, 86 enrolled as first-time, first-year students.

Part-time:	12%	**Women:**	70%

Basis for selection. Open admission, but selective for some programs.

2008-2009 Annual costs. Tuition/fees: $7,600. Per-credit charge: $236. Full-time tuition varies by program: $7,475-$7,997. Books/supplies: $1,600. Personal expenses: $2,140.

2008-2009 Financial aid. **Need-based:** 32% of total undergraduate aid awarded as scholarships/grants, 68% as loans/jobs. Need-based aid available for part-time students.

Application procedures. **Admission:** No deadline. $50 fee. Admission notification on a rolling basis. **Financial aid:** No deadline. FAFSA required. Applicants notified on a rolling basis; must reply within 16 week(s) of notification.

Academics. **Special study options:** Internships. License preparation in real estate. **Credit/placement by examination:** CLEP. **Support services:** GED preparation, tutoring.

Majors. **Business:** Accounting, administrative services. **Computer sciences:** Information technology, web page design. **Engineering technology:** Electrical. **Health:** Insurance coding, medical assistant, medical secretary, medical transcription. **Legal studies:** Legal secretary, paralegal.

Most popular majors. Business/marketing 13%, engineering/engineering technologies 10%, health sciences 66%, legal studies 11%.

Student life. **Freshman orientation:** Available. **Activities:** Student government.

Student services. Career counseling, financial aid counseling, placement for graduates.

Contact. E-mail: etiadmissionsdir@hotmail.com
Phone: (330) 652-9919 Fax: (330) 652-4399
Diane Marsteller, Director of Admissions, ETI Technical College of Niles, 2076 Youngstown Warren Road, Niles, OH 44446-4398

Gallipolis Career College
Gallipolis, Ohio
www.gallipoliscareercollege.com **CB code: 2469**

- For-profit 2-year business and technical college
- Commuter campus in small town
- Interview required

General. Accredited by ACICS. **Enrollment:** 147 degree-seeking undergraduates. **Degrees:** 29 associate awarded. **Location:** 45 miles from Huntington, West Virginia. **Calendar:** Quarter, extensive summer session. **Full-time faculty:** 2 total; 50% women. **Part-time faculty:** 13 total. **Class size:** 89% < 20, 11% 20-39.

Student profile.

Out-of-state:	3%	**25 or older:**	60%

Transfer out. **Colleges most students transferred to 2008:** University of Rio Grande.

Basis for selection. Open admission. Testing for counseling/placement purposes only.

2008-2009 Annual costs. Tuition/fees: $9,650. Per-credit charge: $200. Books/supplies: $1,400. Personal expenses: $4,000.

2007-2008 Financial aid. All financial aid based on need. 67% of total undergraduate aid awarded as scholarships/grants, 33% as loans/jobs. Need-based aid available for part-time students.

Application procedures. **Admission:** No deadline. $50 fee. Application must be submitted on paper. Admission notification on a rolling basis. **Financial aid:** No deadline. FAFSA, institutional form required.

Academics. **Special study options:** Double major, independent study, internships. License preparation in real estate. **Credit/placement by examination:** CLEP. 16 credit hours maximum toward associate degree. **Support services:** Remedial instruction, tutoring.

Majors. **Business:** Accounting, administrative services, business admin. **Computer sciences:** General. **Health:** Medical secretary.

Most popular majors. Business/marketing 23%, computer/information sciences 27%.

Computing on campus. 36 workstations in library, computer center.

Student life. **Freshman orientation:** Available. Preregistration for classes offered. **Activities:** Student newspaper.

Student services. Career counseling, student employment services, financial aid counseling, placement for graduates. **Transfer:** Pre-admission transcript evaluation for new students.

Contact. Phone: (740) 446-4367 ext. 12 Toll-free number: (800) 214-0452 Fax: (740) 446-4124
Bo Shirey, Director of Admissions, Gallipolis Career College, 1176 Jackson Pike, Suite 312, Gallipolis, OH 45631

Good Samaritan College of Nursing and Health Science

Cincinnati, Ohio
www.gscollege.edu **CB code: 1259**

- Private 2-year nursing college
- Commuter campus in very large city
- SAT or ACT (ACT writing optional) required

General. Hospital-based program. **Enrollment:** 304 degree-seeking undergraduates. **Degrees:** 94 associate awarded. **Calendar:** Semester, limited summer session. **Full-time faculty:** 24 total; 4% have terminal degrees, 17% minority, 92% women. **Part-time faculty:** 8 total; 88% women.

Student profile. Among degree-seeking undergraduates, 8% already have a bachelor's degree or higher, 14 enrolled as first-time, first-year students, 18 transferred in from other institutions.

Part-time:	59%	**Asian American:**	1%
Women:	93%	**Hispanic American:**	2%
African American:	11%		

Basis for selection. Test scores very important. COMPASS and ATI critical thinking used for advising only. **Adult students:** SAT/ACT scores not required if out of high school 5 year(s) or more.

High school preparation. College-preparatory program recommended. 14 units required. Required and recommended units include English 4, mathematics 4, social studies 3, history 2, science 3, foreign language 2 and computer science 1.

2008-2009 Annual costs. Tuition/fees: $17,080. Per-credit charge: $390. Second year tuition $12,660, fees $550. Books/supplies: $1,254.

Application procedures. **Admission:** No deadline. $40 fee. Admission notification on a rolling basis.

Academics. **Credit/placement by examination:** CLEP. **Support services:** Learning center, study skills assistance, tutoring.

Majors. **Health:** Nursing (RN).

Most popular majors. Health sciences 94%.

Student life. **Freshman orientation:** Mandatory.

Contact. E-mail: mose_cartier@trihealth.com
Phone: (513) 872-2743
Mose Cartier, Admissions Director, Good Samaritan College of Nursing and Health Science, 375 Dixmyth Avenue, Cincinnati, OH 45220

Hocking College

Nelsonville, Ohio
www.hocking.edu **CB code: 1822**

- Public 2-year technical college
- Commuter campus in small town

General. Founded in 1968. Regionally accredited. Courses available at Perry Campus, New Lexington High School, Logan Hocking High School, Miller High School, Sauber Center, Great Oaks Career Center, Tri County Career Center, 5 prisons (classes available for inmates and employees). Courses also available online. Co-ops with several trade associations. **Enrollment:** 4,235 degree-seeking undergraduates; 1,446 non-degree-seeking students. **Degrees:** 657 associate awarded. **ROTC:** Army, Air Force. **Location:** 15 miles from Athens, 55 miles from Columbus. **Calendar:** Quarter, limited summer session. **Full-time faculty:** 177 total; 8% have terminal degrees, 1% minority, 50% women. **Part-time faculty:** 189 total; 1% have terminal degrees, 2% minority, 42% women. **Class size:** 59% < 20, 35% 20-39, 4% 40-49, 2% 50-99, less than 1% >100. **Special facilities:** Nature center, living history village, college-operated inn, land lab, firing range, burn building, college operated travel agency, early learning center, fish hatchery. **Partnerships:** Formal partnerships with local career centers.

Student profile. Among degree-seeking undergraduates, 1,313 enrolled as first-time, first-year students, 504 transferred in from other institutions.

Part-time:	24%	**25 or older:**	23%
Out-of-state:	2%	**Live on campus:**	8%
Women:	50%		

Transfer out. 14% of students enrolled in the transfer program go on to 4-year colleges. **Colleges most students transferred to 2008:** Ohio University, Rio Grande University, Franklin University.

Basis for selection. Open admission, but selective for some programs. Special admissions requirements to nursing program (based on test scores), physical therapist assistant program (based on grades), and radiologic and surgical/operating room technology (based on test scores and grades). Some programs have additional admission requirements. Interview recommended. **Homeschooled:** Applicants to health and public safety technology must have GED before classes begin. **Learning Disabled:** Documentation required for services in the Access Center - Office of Disability Services.

High school preparation. Recommended units include English 4, mathematics 3 and science 3. 1 algebra, 1 biology highly recommended for recreation/wildlife and forestry applicants.

2008-2009 Annual costs. Tuition/fees: $3,546; $7,092 out-of-state. Per-credit charge: $68 in-state; $167 out-of-state. Books/supplies: $1,200. Personal expenses: $550.

2007-2008 Financial aid. **Need-based:** 1,094 full-time freshmen applied for aid; 892 were judged to have need; 892 of these received aid. 51% of total undergraduate aid awarded as scholarships/grants, 49% as loans/jobs. Need-based aid available for part-time students. Work-study available nights, weekends and for part-time students. **Non-need-based:** Awarded to 451 full-time undergraduates, including 230 freshmen. Scholarships awarded for academics, minority status, state residency.

Application procedures. **Admission:** No deadline. $15 fee. Admission notification on a rolling basis. **Financial aid:** Priority date 2/28; no closing date. FAFSA, institutional form required. Applicants notified on a rolling basis starting 4/15.

Academics. Self paced online courses available. Enrollment possible any day college is in session. **Special study options:** Accelerated study, combined bachelor's/graduate degree, cooperative education, cross-registration, distance learning, double major, dual enrollment of high school students, ESL, independent study, internships, student-designed major, study abroad. Bachelor's degree programs available on campus. License preparation in nursing, paramedic, physical therapy, radiology, real estate. **Credit/placement by examination:** AP, CLEP, institutional tests. 60 credit hours maximum toward associate degree. **Support services:** GED test center, learning center, pre-admission summer program, reduced course load, remedial instruction, study skills assistance, tutoring, writing center.

Majors. **Agriculture:** Equestrian studies. **Architecture:** Landscape. **Biology:** Biomedical sciences. **Business:** General, accounting technology, administrative services, hotel/motel admin. **Communications technology:** Radio/tv. **Computer sciences:** Networking, programming. **Conservation:** General, fisheries, forest management, management/policy, wildlife. **Construction:** Carpentry, electrician. **Education:** Teacher assistance. **Engineering:** Materials science. **Engineering technology:** Construction, drafting, electrical, energy systems. **Health:** EMT paramedic, massage therapy, medical assistant, medical records technology, nursing (RN), optician, physical therapy assistant. **Parks/recreation:** Sports admin. **Personal/culinary services:** Chef training. **Protective services:** Corrections, firefighting, police science. **Public administration:** Human services. **Visual/performing arts:** Art, theater design.

Most popular majors. Agriculture 6%, business/marketing 12%, health sciences 25%, natural resources/environmental science 19%, security/protective services 16%.

Computing on campus. 863 workstations in dormitories, library, computer center, student center. Dormitories wired for high-speed internet access and linked to campus network. Commuter students can connect to campus network. Online course registration, online library, helpline, repair service, wireless network available.

Student life. **Freshman orientation:** Mandatory, $20 fee. Preregistration for classes offered. **Policies:** All students have full use of student center. Clubs must be sanctioned by college. **Housing:** Coed dorms, wellness housing available. $100 partly refundable deposit. **Activities:** Campus ministries, dance, drama, literary magazine, radio station, student government, student newspaper, Phi Theta Kappa, Kappa Beta Delta, SIFE, Unity Board, technology based clubs, Hocking Heights hall council.

Athletics. Intramural: Basketball, football (non-tackle), golf, soccer, softball, swimming, table tennis, tennis, volleyball, weight lifting, wrestling.

Student services. Adult student services, alcohol/substance abuse counseling, chaplain/spiritual director, career counseling, student employment services, financial aid counseling, health services, legal services, on-campus daycare, personal counseling, placement for graduates, veterans' counselor, women's services. **Physically disabled:** Services for visually, speech, hearing impaired. **Transfer:** Pre-admission transcript evaluation for new students. Transfer center, transfer adviser, college fairs on campus for students transferring to 4-year colleges.

Contact. E-mail: admissions@hocking.edu
Phone: (740) 753-7049 Toll-free number: (800) 282-4163
Fax: (740) 753-7065
Lynn Hull, Dean of Enrollment Services, Hocking College, 3301 Hocking Parkway, Nelsonville, OH 45764-9704

Hondros College
Westerville, Ohio
www.hondros.edu **CB code: 3255**

- For-profit 2-year business, nursing and technical college
- Commuter campus in very large city
- Interview required

General. Accredited by ACICS. Additional campuses in Cincinnati and Dayton. **Enrollment:** 633 degree-seeking undergraduates. **Degrees:** 30 associate awarded. **Location:** 10 miles from Columbus. **Calendar:** Quarter, extensive summer session. **Part-time faculty:** 150 total.

Transfer out. Colleges most students transferred to 2008: University of Phoenix, Devry University.

Basis for selection. Open admission, but selective for some programs. Special requirements for allied health related programs. **Adult students:** SAT/ACT scores not required. **Homeschooled:** State high school equivalency certificate required.

2008-2009 Annual costs. Tuition/fees: $8,425. Per-credit charge: $185.

Application procedures. Admission: No deadline. $25 fee. Admission notification on a rolling basis.

Academics. Special study options: Distance learning, liberal arts/career combination. License preparation in real estate. **Credit/placement by examination:** CLEP.

Majors. Business: Real estate, selling. **Health:** Nursing (RN). **Visual/performing arts:** Music.

Most popular majors. Business/marketing 66%, health sciences 33%.

Computing on campus. 10 workstations in library, computer center. Online library, helpline available.

Student life. Freshman orientation: Mandatory.

Student services. Student employment services. **Transfer:** Re-entry adviser, pre-admission transcript evaluation for new students.

Contact. E-mail: degreeadmissions@hondros.edu
Phone: (888) 466-3767 Toll-free number: (888) 466-3767
Fax: (614) 508-7280
Zachary Selby, Admissions Manager, Hondros College, 4140 Executive Parkway, Westerville, OH 43081-3855

International College of Broadcasting
Dayton, Ohio
www.icbcollege.com **CB code: 3047**

- For-profit 2-year technical college
- Commuter campus in small city

General. Accredited by ACCSCT. **Enrollment:** 105 degree-seeking undergraduates. **Degrees:** 50 associate awarded. **Location:** 50 miles from Cincinnati, 70 miles from Columbus. **Calendar:** Semester, limited summer session. **Full-time faculty:** 10 total. **Part-time faculty:** 4 total.

Student profile.

Out-of-state:	3%	**25 or older:**	20%

Basis for selection. Open admission. Tour of the campus and interview required before admission.

2008-2009 Annual costs. Tuition/fees: $10,395. Per-credit charge: $362. Personal expenses: $2,862.

Financial aid. Need-based: Need-based aid available for part-time students.

Application procedures. Admission: No deadline. $100 fee. **Financial aid:** No deadline. FAFSA required. Applicants notified on a rolling basis starting 11/1.

Academics. Credit/placement by examination: CLEP. **Support services:** Reduced course load.

Majors. Communications: General. **Visual/performing arts:** General.

Computing on campus. Wireless network available.

Contact. E-mail: zenaicb@aol.com
Phone: (937) 258-8251 ext. 202 Fax: (937) 258-8714
Dean Grandfield, Director of Admissions, International College of Broadcasting, 6 South Smithville Road, Dayton, OH 45431

ITT Technical Institute: Dayton
Dayton, Ohio
www.itt-tech.edu **CB code: 7312**

- For-profit 2-year technical college
- Commuter campus in small city

General. Founded in 1935. Accredited by ACICS. **Location:** 5 miles from downtown. **Calendar:** Quarter.

Contact. Phone: (937) 454-2267
Director of Recruitment, 3325 Stop Eight Road, Dayton, OH 45414

ITT Technical Institute: Hilliard
Hilliard, Ohio

- For-profit 2-year business and technical college
- Large town

General. Accredited by ACICS. **Calendar:** Quarter.

Contact. 3781 Park Mill Run Drive, Suite 1, Hilliard, OH 43026

ITT Technical Institute: Norwood
Norwood, Ohio
www.itt-tech.edu **CB code: 2739**

- For-profit 2-year technical college
- Commuter campus in large town

General. Accredited by ACICS. **Calendar:** Quarter.

Contact. Phone: (513) 531-8300
Director of Recruitment, 4750 Wesley Avenue, Norwood, OH 45212

ITT Technical Institute: Strongsville
Strongsville, Ohio
www.itt-tech.edu **CB code: 2773**

- For-profit 2-year technical college
- Commuter campus in large town

General. Accredited by ACICS. **Calendar:** Quarter.

Contact. Phone: (440) 234-9091
Director of Recruitment, 14955 Sprague Road, Strongsville, OH 44136

ITT Technical Institute: Youngstown

Youngstown, Ohio
www.itt-tech.edu **CB code: 0418**

- For-profit 2-year technical college
- Commuter campus in small city

General. Founded in 1967. Accredited by ACICS. **Location:** 60 miles from Cleveland, 60 miles from Pittsburgh. **Calendar:** Quarter.

Contact. Phone: (330) 270-1600
Director of Recruitment, 1030 North Meridian Road, Youngstown, OH 44509

James A. Rhodes State College

Lima, Ohio
www.rhodesstate.edu **CB code: 0754**

- Public 2-year nursing and technical college
- Commuter campus in large town

General. Founded in 1971. Regionally accredited. **Enrollment:** 3,369 degree-seeking undergraduates; 296 non-degree-seeking students. **Degrees:** 427 associate awarded. **Location:** 75 miles from Dayton, 75 miles from Toledo. **Calendar:** Quarter, limited summer session. **Full-time faculty:** 65 total; 3% minority, 71% women. **Part-time faculty:** 173 total; 5% minority, 58% women. **Class size:** 62% < 20, 32% 20-39, 4% 40-49, 2% 50-99. **Partnerships:** Formal partnerships with Central Ohio Regional Healthcare Alliance, Tech Prep/PSEOP, Ford Training Center, Lima City High School, Allen County Health Partners, Agile Manufacturing, West Ohio Manufacturing Consortium.

Student profile. Among degree-seeking undergraduates, 5% enrolled in a transfer program, 90% enrolled in a vocational program.

Part-time:	42%	**Hispanic American:**	1%
Out-of-state:	1%	**25 or older:**	41%
Women:	73%	**Live on campus:**	1%
African American:	8%		

Transfer out. Colleges most students transferred to 2008: Bowling Green State University, University of Toledo, Ohio State University, Wright State University, University of Cincinnati.

Basis for selection. Open admission, but selective for some programs. Special requirements for health programs (ACT required); interview recommended. **Homeschooled:** Transcript of courses and grades required. **Learning Disabled:** Students must self-disclose; accommodations are available.

High school preparation. Recommended units include English 4, mathematics 3, social studies 3 and science 3.

2008-2009 Annual costs. Tuition/fees: $4,229; $8,382 out-of-state. Per-credit charge: $76 in-state; $168 out-of-state. Books/supplies: $945. Personal expenses: $473.

2007-2008 Financial aid. Need-based: Need-based aid available for part-time students. Work-study available nights, weekends and for part-time students. **Non-need-based:** Scholarships awarded for academics.

Application procedures. Admission: No deadline. $25 fee ($25 out-of-state). Admission notification on a rolling basis. **Financial aid:** Priority date 2/15; no closing date. FAFSA required. Applicants notified on a rolling basis starting 5/1; must reply within 2 week(s) of notification.

Academics. Associate of Technical Studies degree program offered, integrating technology and business. **Special study options:** Combined bachelor's/graduate degree, cooperative education, cross-registration, distance learning, double major, dual enrollment of high school students, independent study, internships, liberal arts/career combination, student-designed major. License preparation in dental hygiene, nursing, occupational therapy, paramedic, physical therapy, radiology, real estate. **Credit/placement by examination:** AP, CLEP, institutional tests. 15 credit hours maximum toward associate degree. ASSET required for placement for all new students. Maximum 45 credit hours, 15 each from life experiences (non-academic learning); knowledge (by exam) and work training/experience. **Support services:** Learning center, pre-admission summer program, reduced course load, remedial instruction, study skills assistance, tutoring.

Majors. Business: General, accounting, administrative services, business admin, finance, management information systems, marketing, office management. **Computer sciences:** General, LAN/WAN management, networking, programming, security, web page design. **Education:** Early childhood. **Engineering technology:** General, civil, electrical, environmental, industrial, industrial safety, manufacturing, mechanical, quality control. **Family/consumer sciences:** Family/community services. **Health:** Dental assistant, EMT paramedic, medical assistant, medical radiologic technology/radiation therapy, medical secretary, nursing (RN), occupational therapy assistant, office assistant, phlebotomy, physical therapy assistant, radiologic technology/medical imaging, respiratory therapy assistant. **Legal studies:** Legal secretary, paralegal. **Protective services:** Corrections, law enforcement admin, police science. **Public administration:** Human services.

Most popular majors. Business/marketing 7%, computer/information sciences 7%, engineering/engineering technologies 14%, health sciences 58%.

Computing on campus. 332 workstations in library, computer center. Commuter students can connect to campus network. Online course registration, helpline, repair service, student web hosting available.

Student life. Freshman orientation: Mandatory. Preregistration for classes offered. Orientation programs held before each quarter begins; specific dates and times mailed after application is made. **Activities:** Campus ministries, choral groups, drama, music ensembles, student government, academic area organizations, political party clubs, special interest clubs, fellowship and bible study.

Athletics. Intercollegiate: Golf M. **Intramural:** Baseball M, basketball, bowling, football (non-tackle), softball, volleyball. **Team name:** Barons.

Student services. Career counseling, student employment services, financial aid counseling, on-campus daycare, placement for graduates, veterans' counselor. **Physically disabled:** Services for visually, speech, hearing impaired. **Transfer:** Pre-admission transcript evaluation for new students. College fairs on campus for students transferring to 4-year colleges.

Contact. E-mail: admissions@rhodesstate.edu
Phone: (419) 995-8320 Fax: (419) 995-8098
Traci Cox, Director of Admissions, Student Advising and Development, James A. Rhodes State College, 4240 Campus Drive, PS 148, Lima, OH 45804-3597

Jefferson Community College

Steubenville, Ohio
www.jcc.edu **CB code: 2264**

- Public 2-year community and technical college
- Commuter campus in large town

General. Founded in 1966. Regionally accredited. **Enrollment:** 1,597 degree-seeking undergraduates; 147 non-degree-seeking students. **Degrees:** 161 associate awarded. **Location:** 30 miles from Pittsburgh. **Calendar:** Semester, limited summer session. **Full-time faculty:** 32 total. **Part-time faculty:** 145 total. **Class size:** 75% < 20, 25% 20-39, less than 1% 40-49.

Student profile. Among degree-seeking undergraduates, 32% enrolled in a transfer program, 68% enrolled in a vocational program, 380 enrolled as first-time, first-year students.

Part-time:	44%	**Women:**	61%
Out-of-state:	18%		

Transfer out. Colleges most students transferred to 2008: Franciscan University of Steubenville, Franklin University, West Liberty State College, Kent State University.

Basis for selection. Open admission, but selective for some programs. Special requirements for all allied health technologies programs. ACT required for admission to radiology, medical laboratory, medical assisting, and dental assisting technologies. **Homeschooled:** Final transcript showing successful home school completion signed and dated by home school principal required.

2008-2009 Annual costs. Tuition/fees: $2,700; $2,880 out-of-district; $3,690 out-of-state. Per-credit charge: $90 in-district; $93 out-of-district; $120 out-of-state. Residents of 5 neighboring West Virginia counties eligible for in-state, out-of-district tuition rates. Books/supplies: $700. Personal expenses: $400.

Financial aid. All financial aid based on need. Need-based aid available for part-time students. Work-study available nights, weekends and for part-time students.

Application procedures. Admission: No deadline. $20 fee. Admission notification on a rolling basis. **Financial aid:** Priority date 7/1; no closing date. FAFSA, institutional form required. Applicants notified on a rolling basis starting 6/15.

Academics. **Special study options:** Distance learning, double major, dual enrollment of high school students, external degree, honors, independent study, internships, weekend college. License preparation in paramedic, radiology, real estate. **Credit/placement by examination:** AP, CLEP, institutional tests. 42 credit hours maximum toward associate degree. **Support services:** GED preparation and test center, learning center, pre-admission summer program, remedial instruction, study skills assistance, tutoring, writing center.

Majors. **Biology:** General. **Business:** General, accounting, administrative services, banking/financial services, business admin, e-commerce, management information systems, office management. **Computer sciences:** General, applications programming, computer science, data processing, information systems, systems analysis. **Construction:** Maintenance, power transmission. **Education:** Early childhood. **Engineering:** General, science, systems. **Engineering technology:** Construction, drafting, electrical, manufacturing, robotics. **Family/consumer sciences:** Child care. **Health:** Clinical lab assistant, clinical lab technology, dental assistant, EMT paramedic, medical assistant, medical radiologic technology/radiation therapy, medical secretary, respiratory therapy technology, ward clerk. **Interdisciplinary:** Biological/physical sciences, math/computer science. **Legal studies:** Legal secretary. **Liberal arts:** Arts/sciences. **Mechanic/repair:** Electronics/electrical, industrial. **Physical sciences:** Chemistry, physics. **Protective services:** Police science. **Psychology:** General.

Most popular majors. Business/marketing 16%, engineering/engineering technologies 16%, family/consumer sciences 10%, health sciences 32%, liberal arts 21%.

Computing on campus. 260 workstations in library, computer center. Online library, wireless network available.

Student life. **Freshman orientation:** Mandatory. **Housing:** Students may live in dormitory of local university on space-available basis. **Activities:** Drama, student government, student newspaper.

Athletics. **Intramural:** Baseball M, basketball, bowling, football (non-tackle), softball, table tennis, tennis, volleyball.

Student services. Adult student services, career counseling, student employment services, financial aid counseling, health services, on-campus daycare, personal counseling, placement for graduates, veterans' counselor. **Physically disabled:** Services for visually, hearing impaired. **Transfer:** Re-entry adviser, pre-admission transcript evaluation for new students. Transfer center, transfer adviser, college fairs on campus for students transferring to 4-year colleges.

Contact. E-mail: cmascellino@jcc.edu
Phone: (740) 264-5591 ext. 106 Toll-free number: (800) 682-6553 ext. 106
Fax: (740) 266-2944
Chuck Mascellino, Director of Admissions, Jefferson Community College, 4000 Sunset Boulevard, Steubenville, OH 43952

Kent State University: Ashtabula

Ashtabula, Ohio
www.ashtabula.kent.edu **CB code: 1485**

- Public 2-year branch campus college
- Commuter campus in large town

General. Founded in 1958. Regionally accredited. Off-site courses available. **Enrollment:** 1,488 degree-seeking undergraduates; 165 non-degree-seeking students. **Degrees:** 143 associate awarded. **ROTC:** Army, Air Force. **Location:** 50 miles from Cleveland. **Calendar:** Semester, limited summer session. **Full-time faculty:** 48 total; 12% minority, 58% women. **Part-time faculty:** 58 total; 5% minority, 62% women. **Class size:** 60% < 20, 35% 20-39, 2% 40-49, 2% 50-99, less than 1% >100. **Special facilities:** Interactive television link with all county high schools.

Student profile. Among degree-seeking undergraduates, 262 enrolled as first-time, first-year students, 109 transferred in from other institutions.

Part-time:	44%	**Asian American:**	1%
Out-of-state:	1%	**Hispanic American:**	2%
Women:	70%	**25 or older:**	49%
African American:	5%		

Transfer out. **Colleges most students transferred to 2008:** Lakeland Community College, Mount Union College, University of Akron.

Basis for selection. Open admission, but selective for some programs. Special requirements for nursing, human services, physical therapy assisting progams.

High school preparation. College-preparatory program recommended. 16 units recommended. Recommended units include English 4, mathematics 3, social studies 3, science 3 (laboratory 2) and foreign language 2. One art unit recommended.

2008-2009 Annual costs. Tuition/fees: $4,770; $12,202 out-of-state. Per-credit charge: $217 in-state; $555 out-of-state. Books/supplies: $990. Personal expenses: $1,900.

2008-2009 Financial aid. **Need-based:** 188 full-time freshmen applied for aid; 169 were judged to have need; 169 of these received aid. Average need met was 49%. Average scholarship/grant was $5,511; average loan $2,786. 39% of total undergraduate aid awarded as scholarships/grants, 61% as loans/jobs. Need-based aid available for part-time students. **Non-need-based:** Awarded to 17 full-time undergraduates, including 8 freshmen. Scholarships awarded for academics, alumni affiliation, art, athletics, job skills, leadership, minority status, music/drama, ROTC, state residency.

Application procedures. **Admission:** No deadline. $30 fee, may be waived for applicants with need. Admission notification on a rolling basis beginning on or about 10/1. **Financial aid:** Priority date 3/1; no closing date. FAFSA required. Applicants notified on a rolling basis starting 3/15; must reply within 2 week(s) of notification.

Academics. **Special study options:** Accelerated study, distance learning, double major, dual enrollment of high school students, independent study, internships, student-designed major. Bachelor's degree programs available on campus. License preparation in nursing. **Credit/placement by examination:** AP, CLEP, SAT, ACT, institutional tests. 12 credit hours maximum toward associate degree. **Support services:** Learning center, remedial instruction, tutoring.

Majors. **Business:** General, accounting technology, administrative services. **Computer sciences:** Applications programming. **Education:** Early childhood. **Engineering technology:** Electrical, mechanical. **Health:** Health care admin, nursing (RN), physical therapy assistant, preop/surgical nursing. **Liberal arts:** Arts/sciences. **Protective services:** Criminal justice.

Most popular majors. Business/marketing 15%, computer/information sciences 6%, health sciences 53%, liberal arts 17%.

Computing on campus. 82 workstations in library, computer center. Online course registration, online library, helpline, student web hosting available.

Student life. **Freshman orientation:** Available. Preregistration for classes offered. **Activities:** Dance, drama, radio station, student government, student newspaper, world affairs club, social issues club.

Athletics. **Intramural:** Basketball, football (non-tackle), softball W, volleyball, weight lifting. **Team name:** Golden Flashes.

Student services. Adult student services, career counseling, student employment services, on-campus daycare, personal counseling, placement for graduates, veterans' counselor. **Physically disabled:** Services for visually impaired. **Transfer:** Transfer adviser for students transferring to 4-year colleges.

Contact. E-mail: sanford@ashtabula.kent.edu
Phone: (440) 964-4217 Toll-free number: (800) 988-5368
Fax: (440) 964-4269
Kelly Sanford, Admissions Counselor, Kent State University: Ashtabula, 3325 West 13th Street, Ashtabula, OH 44004

Kent State University: East Liverpool

East Liverpool, Ohio
www.kenteliv.kent.edu **CB code: 0328**

- Public 2-year branch campus college
- Commuter campus in large town

General. Founded in 1965. Regionally accredited. **Enrollment:** 835 degree-seeking undergraduates; 123 non-degree-seeking students. **Degrees:** 98 associate awarded. **ROTC:** Army, Air Force. **Location:** 45 miles from Youngstown, 40 miles from Pittsburgh. **Calendar:** Semester, extensive summer session. **Full-time faculty:** 26 total; 15% minority, 50% women. **Part-time faculty:** 35 total; 57% women. **Class size:** 69% < 20, 29% 20-39, 2% 40-49, less than 1% 50-99.

Student profile. Among degree-seeking undergraduates, 120 enrolled as first-time, first-year students, 53 transferred in from other institutions.

Part-time:	44%	**African American:**	3%
Out-of-state:	3%	**25 or older:**	42%
Women:	75%		

Transfer out. **Colleges most students transferred to 2008:** Youngstown State University, Jefferson Community College, West Virginia Northern Community College, Hannah Mullins School of Nursing.

Basis for selection. Open admission, but selective for some programs. Special requirements for nursing, occupational therapy, and physical therapy applicants. Interview recommended.

High school preparation. College-preparatory program recommended. 16 units recommended. Recommended units include English 4, mathematics 3, social studies 3, science 3 (laboratory 2) and foreign language 2. One unit algebra, 1 unit chemistry, 1 unit biology required for nursing applicants. One unit algebra, 1 unit biology required for physical therapy and occupational therapy. One art unit recommended for all.

2008-2009 Annual costs. Tuition/fees: $4,770; $12,202 out-of-state. Per-credit charge: $217 in-state; $555 out-of-state. Books/supplies: $550. Personal expenses: $1,315.

2008-2009 Financial aid. **Need-based:** 88 full-time freshmen applied for aid; 76 were judged to have need; 76 of these received aid. Average need met was 49%. Average scholarship/grant was $5,936; average loan $2,899. 40% of total undergraduate aid awarded as scholarships/grants, 60% as loans/jobs. Need-based aid available for part-time students. Work-study available for part-time students. **Non-need-based:** Awarded to 17 full-time undergraduates, including 11 freshmen. Scholarships awarded for academics, alumni affiliation, art, athletics, leadership, minority status, music/drama, ROTC, state residency.

Application procedures. **Admission:** Priority date 8/1; no deadline. $30 fee, may be waived for applicants with need. Admission notification on a rolling basis beginning on or about 10/1. All new applicants must complete basic skills assessment tests. **Financial aid:** Priority date 3/1; no closing date. FAFSA required. Applicants notified on a rolling basis starting 3/15; must reply within 2 week(s) of notification.

Academics. **Special study options:** Accelerated study, distance learning, double major, dual enrollment of high school students, independent study, internships, student-designed major. Bachelor's degree programs available on campus. License preparation in nursing. **Credit/placement by examination:** AP, CLEP, SAT, ACT, institutional tests. 14 credit hours maximum toward associate degree. **Support services:** Learning center, pre-admission summer program, reduced course load, remedial instruction, study skills assistance, tutoring, writing center.

Honors college/program. 3.5 GPA, 24 ACT, recommendation, interview, placement exam required. Various course offerings plus Freshman Year Colloquium to replace university composition requirement.

Majors. **Business:** General, accounting technology. **Computer sciences:** Applications programming. **Health:** Nursing (RN), occupational therapy assistant, physical therapy assistant. **Legal studies:** Paralegal. **Liberal arts:** Arts/sciences. **Protective services:** Criminal justice.

Most popular majors. Health sciences 82%.

Computing on campus. 114 workstations in library, computer center. Online course registration, online library, helpline, student web hosting available.

Student life. **Freshman orientation:** Available. Preregistration for classes offered. **Activities:** Literary magazine, student government, student newspaper.

Athletics. **Team name:** Golden Flashes.

Student services. Career counseling, student employment services, placement for graduates, veterans' counselor. **Learning disabled:** Comprehensive services available. **Transfer:** Transfer adviser, college fairs on campus for students transferring to 4-year colleges.

Contact. E-mail: admissions@eliv.kent.edu
Phone: (330) 385-3805 Fax: (330) 382-7562
Nancy Dellavecchia, Director, Kent State University: East Liverpool, 400 East Fourth Street, East Liverpool, OH 43920

Kent State University: Geauga
Burton, Ohio
www.geauga.kent.edu

- Public 2-year branch campus college
- Rural community

General. Regionally accredited. **Enrollment:** 1,337 degree-seeking undergraduates; 107 non-degree-seeking students. **Degrees:** 40 associate awarded. **Calendar:** Semester. **Full-time faculty:** 22 total; 4% have terminal degrees, 18% minority, 73% women. **Part-time faculty:** 71 total; 1% have terminal degrees, 20% minority, 48% women. **Class size:** 79% < 20, 21% 20-39.

Student profile. Among degree-seeking undergraduates, 155 enrolled as first-time, first-year students, 112 transferred in from other institutions.

Part-time:	42%	**Asian American:**	1%
Out-of-state:	1%	**Hispanic American:**	1%
Women:	63%	**Native American:**	1%
African American:	9%	**25 or older:**	42%

Basis for selection. Open admission, but selective for some programs. Special requirements for nursing progams. **Homeschooled:** Transcript of courses and grades required.

High school preparation. College-preparatory program recommended. 16 units recommended. Recommended units include English 4, mathematics 3, social studies 3, science 3 (laboratory 2) and foreign language 2.

2008-2009 Annual costs. Tuition/fees: $4,770; $12,202 out-of-state. Per-credit charge: $217 in-state; $555 out-of-state. Books/supplies: $1,030. Personal expenses: $1,500.

2008-2009 Financial aid. **Need-based:** 97 full-time freshmen applied for aid; 78 were judged to have need; 78 of these received aid. Average need met was 47%. Average scholarship/grant was $4,588; average loan $2,851. 31% of total undergraduate aid awarded as scholarships/grants, 69% as loans/jobs. Need-based aid available for part-time students. **Non-need-based:** Awarded to 6 full-time undergraduates, including 3 freshmen. Scholarships awarded for academics, alumni affiliation, art, athletics, leadership, minority status, music/drama, ROTC, state residency.

Application procedures. **Admission:** No deadline. $30 fee, may be waived for applicants with need. Admission notification on a rolling basis beginning on or about 10/1. **Financial aid:** Priority date 3/1; no closing date. FAFSA required. Must reply within 2 week(s) of notification.

Academics. **Special study options:** Accelerated study, distance learning, double major, dual enrollment of high school students, internships, student-designed major, teacher certification program. **Credit/placement by examination:** AP, CLEP, institutional tests. **Support services:** Learning center, pre-admission summer program, reduced course load, remedial instruction, study skills assistance, tutoring, writing center.

Honors college/program. 3.5 GPA, 24 ACT, recommendation, interview, placement exam required. Various course offerings, freshman year colloquium to replace university composition requirement.

Majors. **Agriculture:** Horticultural science. **Engineering technology:** Computer systems, industrial. **Health:** EMT paramedic. **Liberal arts:** Arts/sciences.

Most popular majors. Computer/information sciences 20%, engineering/engineering technologies 8%, health sciences 28%, liberal arts 43%.

Computing on campus. Online course registration, online library, helpline, student web hosting available.

Student life. **Freshman orientation:** Available. Preregistration for classes offered.

Athletics. **Team name:** Golden Flashes.

Student services. **Transfer:** Transfer adviser, college fairs on campus for students transferring to 4-year colleges.

Contact. E-mail: info@geauga.kent.edu
Phone: (440) 834-4187
Nancy Dellavecchia, Director, Admissions, Kent State University: Geauga, Office of Admissions, Burton, OH 44021

Kent State University: Salem

Salem, Ohio
www.salem.kent.edu **CB code: 0683**

- Public 2-year branch campus college
- Commuter campus in large town

General. Founded in 1962. Regionally accredited. **Enrollment:** 1,201 degree-seeking undergraduates; 109 non-degree-seeking students. **Degrees:** 29 bachelor's, 96 associate awarded. **ROTC:** Army, Air Force. **Location:** 25 miles from Youngstown, 40 miles from Canton. **Calendar:** Semester, limited summer session. **Full-time faculty:** 41 total; 15% minority, 58% women. **Part-time faculty:** 57 total; 4% minority, 63% women. **Class size:** 66% < 20, 33% 20-39, less than 1% 40-49, less than 1% 50-99. **Special facilities:** Writers' workshop, science and math lab, academic center.

Student profile. Among degree-seeking undergraduates, 190 enrolled as first-time, first-year students, 82 transferred in from other institutions.

Part-time:	30%	**Asian American:**	1%
Out-of-state:	1%	**Hispanic American:**	1%
Women:	70%	**25 or older:**	39%
African American:	2%		

Transfer out. Colleges most students transferred to 2008: Youngstown State University, Stark State College of Technology, University of Akron, Ohio State University, ITT Technical Institute.

Basis for selection. Open admission, but selective for some programs. Radiologic technology program requires 2.5 GPA, completion of certain courses, SAT/ACT. Nursing program requires 2.5 GPA, SAT/ACT.

High school preparation. College-preparatory program recommended. 16 units recommended. Recommended units include English 4, mathematics 3, social studies 3, science 3 (laboratory 2) and foreign language 2. One visual or performing arts may be substituted for 1 foreign language.

2008-2009 Annual costs. Tuition/fees: $4,770; $12,202 out-of-state. Per-credit charge: $217 in-state; $555 out-of-state. Books/supplies: $700. Personal expenses: $1,500.

2008-2009 Financial aid. Need-based: 145 full-time freshmen applied for aid; 119 were judged to have need; 119 of these received aid. Average need met was 51%. Average scholarship/grant was $5,096; average loan $2,899. 40% of total undergraduate aid awarded as scholarships/grants, 60% as loans/jobs. Need-based aid available for part-time students. **Non-need-based:** Scholarships awarded for academics, alumni affiliation, art, athletics, leadership, minority status, music/drama, ROTC.

Application procedures. Admission: Priority date 8/1; no deadline. $30 fee, may be waived for applicants with need. Admission notification on a rolling basis beginning on or about 10/1. **Financial aid:** Priority date 3/1; no closing date. FAFSA required. Applicants notified on a rolling basis starting 3/15; must reply within 2 week(s) of notification.

Academics. Special study options: Accelerated study, cooperative education, cross-registration, distance learning, double major, dual enrollment of high school students, independent study, internships, study abroad, teacher certification program, weekend college. Bachelor's degree programs available on campus. **Credit/placement by examination:** AP, CLEP, SAT, ACT, institutional tests. 24 credit hours maximum toward associate degree. **Support services:** Learning center, remedial instruction, study skills assistance, tutoring, writing center.

Honors college/program. 17 students admitted each year. Minimum 3.3 GPA and 23 ACT score required. Full tuition scholarships awarded renewable for 1 additional year.

Majors. Agriculture: Horticulture. **Business:** General, administrative services. **Computer sciences:** Applications programming. **Education:** Elementary. **Engineering technology:** Industrial. **Health:** Health care admin, medical radiologic technology/radiation therapy, nuclear medical technology. **Liberal arts:** Arts/sciences. **Protective services:** Criminal justice.

Most popular majors. Agriculture 11%, business/marketing 14%, education 24%, health sciences 42%, liberal arts 6%.

Computing on campus. 118 workstations in library, computer center. Commuter students can connect to campus network. Online course registration, student web hosting available.

Student life. Freshman orientation: Available. Preregistration for classes offered. **Activities:** Choral groups, drama, music ensembles, student government, student newspaper, professional business and engineering clubs, art club, nontraditional student club, ski club, Women of Wonder, horticulture, criminal justice club, psychology club.

Athletics. Intramural: Basketball, racquetball, skiing, table tennis, tennis, volleyball. **Team name:** Golden Flashes.

Student services. Adult student services, career counseling, financial aid counseling, personal counseling, placement for graduates, veterans' counselor. **Physically disabled:** Services for visually, hearing impaired. **Learning disabled:** Comprehensive services available. **Transfer:** Transfer adviser for students transferring to 4-year colleges.

Contact. E-mail: ask-us@salem.kent.edu
Phone: (330) 332-0361 Toll-free number: (800) 988-5368
Fax: (330) 332-9256
Michelle Schuster, Director, Enrollment Management and Student Services, Kent State University: Salem, 2491 State Route 45 South, Salem, OH 44460

Two-Year Colleges

Kent State University: Stark

Canton, Ohio
www.stark.kent.edu **CB code: 0585**

- Public 2-year branch campus college
- Commuter campus in small city

General. Founded in 1946. Regionally accredited. **Enrollment:** 3,601 degree-seeking undergraduates; 271 non-degree-seeking students. **Degrees:** 90 associate awarded. **ROTC:** Army, Air Force. **Location:** 14 miles from Akron, 60 miles from Cleveland. **Calendar:** Semester, limited summer session. **Full-time faculty:** 100 total; 11% minority, 51% women. **Part-time faculty:** 107 total; 4% minority, 41% women. **Class size:** 44% < 20, 45% 20-39, 7% 40-49, 4% 50-99.

Student profile. Among degree-seeking undergraduates, 695 enrolled as first-time, first-year students, 322 transferred in from other institutions.

Part-time:	30%	**Hispanic American:**	1%
Women:	62%	**Native American:**	1%
African American:	6%	**25 or older:**	30%
Asian American:	1%		

Basis for selection. Open admission, but selective for some programs. Special requirements for honors college, art, music, education, nursing, business. Essay required for honors college, early admission; audition required for music programs; portfolio required for art programs.

High school preparation. College-preparatory program recommended. 16 units recommended. Recommended units include English 4, mathematics 3, social studies 3, science 3 (laboratory 2) and foreign language 2. One unit of fine arts may be substituted for 1 unit of foreign language; math units should be in algebra I & II and geometry.

2008-2009 Annual costs. Tuition/fees: $4,770; $12,202 out-of-state. Per-credit charge: $217 in-state; $555 out-of-state. Books/supplies: $1,140. Personal expenses: $1,826.

2008-2009 Financial aid. Need-based: 479 full-time freshmen applied for aid; 395 were judged to have need; 395 of these received aid. Average need met was 49%. Average scholarship/grant was $4,578; average loan $2,717. 37% of total undergraduate aid awarded as scholarships/grants, 63% as loans/jobs. Need-based aid available for part-time students. Work-study available for part-time students. **Non-need-based:** Awarded to 67 full-time undergraduates, including 32 freshmen. Scholarships awarded for academics, alumni affiliation, art, athletics, leadership, minority status, music/drama, ROTC, state residency.

Application procedures. Admission: No deadline. $30 fee, may be waived for applicants with need. Admission notification on a rolling basis beginning on or about 10/1. Early admission available to high school juniors or seniors in top 15% of class with 24 ACT and 3.4 GPA through Ohio PSEO Program. **Financial aid:** Priority date 3/1; no closing date. FAFSA required. Applicants notified on a rolling basis starting 3/15; must reply within 2 week(s) of notification.

Academics. Special study options: Accelerated study, distance learning, double major, dual enrollment of high school students, honors, independent study, internships, student-designed major. Access program for senior citizens, video conference advising. Bachelor's degree programs available on campus. **Credit/placement by examination:** AP, CLEP, SAT, ACT, institutional tests. 24 credit hours maximum toward associate degree. **Support services:** Learning center, reduced course load, remedial instruction, study skills assistance, tutoring, writing center.

Honors college/program. 3.2 GPA, essay, 24 ACT required.

Majors. Liberal arts: Arts/sciences. **Protective services:** Criminal justice.

Most popular majors. Liberal arts 93%, security/protective services 7%.

Computing on campus. 145 workstations in library, computer center, student center. Commuter students can connect to campus network. Online course registration, online library, helpline, student web hosting available.

Student life. Freshman orientation: Mandatory. **Activities:** Bands, campus ministries, choral groups, dance, drama, literary magazine, music ensembles, musical theater, student government, political science forum, Academy of Life Sciences, student education association, Pan African student alliance.

Athletics. Team name: Golden Flashes.

Student services. Chaplain/spiritual director, career counseling, student employment services, financial aid counseling, personal counseling, veterans' counselor. **Physically disabled:** Services for visually, speech, hearing impaired. **Transfer:** Transfer adviser for students transferring to 4-year colleges.

Contact. E-mail: admit@stark.kent.edu
Phone: (330) 499-9600 Fax: (330) 494-0301
Deborah Speck, Director of Admissions, Kent State University: Stark, 6000 Frank Avenue NW, Canton, OH 44720-7599

Kent State University: Trumbull

Warren, Ohio
www.trumbull.kent.edu **CB code: 0593**

- Public 2-year branch campus college
- Commuter campus in small city

General. Founded in 1954. Regionally accredited. **Enrollment:** 1,883 degree-seeking undergraduates; 141 non-degree-seeking students. **Degrees:** 100 associate awarded. **ROTC:** Army, Air Force. **Location:** 2 miles from downtown. **Calendar:** Semester, limited summer session. **Full-time faculty:** 58 total; 16% minority, 34% women. **Part-time faculty:** 59 total; 3% minority, 44% women. **Class size:** 54% < 20, 44% 20-39, 2% 40-49.

Student profile. Among degree-seeking undergraduates, 306 enrolled as first-time, first-year students, 116 transferred in from other institutions.

Part-time:	38%	**Asian American:**	1%
Women:	63%	**Hispanic American:**	2%
African American:	11%	**25 or older:**	45%

Basis for selection. Open admission, but selective for some programs. Interview recommended.

High school preparation. College-preparatory program recommended. 16 units recommended. Recommended units include English 4, mathematics 3, social studies 3, science 3 (laboratory 2) and foreign language 2. 1 art recommended.

2008-2009 Annual costs. Tuition/fees: $4,770; $12,202 out-of-state. Per-credit charge: $217 in-state; $555 out-of-state. Books/supplies: $990. Personal expenses: $1,900.

2008-2009 Financial aid. Need-based: 209 full-time freshmen applied for aid; 180 were judged to have need; 180 of these received aid. Average need met was 50%. Average scholarship/grant was $5,279; average loan $3,010. 36% of total undergraduate aid awarded as scholarships/grants, 64% as loans/jobs. Need-based aid available for part-time students. **Non-need-based:** Awarded to 16 full-time undergraduates, including 5 freshmen. Scholarships awarded for academics, alumni affiliation, art, athletics, leadership, minority status, music/drama, ROTC, state residency.

Application procedures. Admission: No deadline. $30 fee, may be waived for applicants with need. Admission notification on a rolling basis beginning on or about 10/1. International students must apply through main campus at Kent. Current high school students eligible for part-time early admission with a 3.5 GPA, 26 ACT, and letter of recommendation. **Financial aid:** Priority date 3/1; no closing date. FAFSA required. Applicants notified on a rolling basis starting 3/15; must reply within 2 week(s) of notification.

Academics. Special study options: Accelerated study, distance learning, double major, dual enrollment of high school students, honors, independent study, internships, student-designed major, weekend college. **Credit/placement by examination:** AP, CLEP, IB, SAT, ACT, institutional tests. 6 credit hours maximum toward associate degree. **Support services:** Learning center, pre-admission summer program, reduced course load, remedial instruction, tutoring.

Majors. Biology: General. **Business:** General, accounting technology, administrative services, office technology, office/clerical. **Computer sciences:** Applications programming. **Engineering technology:** Electrical, industrial, mechanical, plastics. **Legal studies:** Paralegal. **Liberal arts:** Arts/sciences. **Protective services:** Criminal justice.

Most popular majors. Business/marketing 26%, computer/information sciences 28%, liberal arts 25%, security/protective services 6%.

Computing on campus. 265 workstations in library, computer center. Online course registration, online library, helpline, student web hosting available.

Student life. Freshman orientation: Available. Preregistration for classes offered. **Activities:** Drama, student government, student newspaper, nontraditional student and minority student organizations, independent black/minority coalition, Christian Fellowship, environmental council, alcohol, drugs and AIDS awareness programs.

Athletics. NJCAA. **Team name:** Golden Flashes.

Student services. Adult student services, career counseling, student employment services, health services, personal counseling, placement for graduates, veterans' counselor. **Physically disabled:** Services for visually, speech, hearing impaired. **Transfer:** Transfer adviser, college fairs on campus for students transferring to 4-year colleges.

Contact. E-mail: info@trumbull.kent.edu
Phone: (330) 847-0571 Fax: (330) 847-6571
Randi Schneider, Director of Enrollment Management, Kent State University: Trumbull, 4314 Mahoning Avenue, NW, Warren, OH 44483-1998

Kent State University: Tuscarawas

New Philadelphia, Ohio
www.tusc.kent.edu **CB code: 1434**

- Public 2-year branch campus college
- Commuter campus in large town

General. Founded in 1962. Regionally accredited. **Enrollment:** 1,773 degree-seeking undergraduates; 233 non-degree-seeking students. **Degrees:** 201 associate awarded. **ROTC:** Army, Air Force. **Location:** 80 miles from Cleveland. **Calendar:** Semester, limited summer session. **Full-time faculty:** 48 total; 17% minority, 50% women. **Part-time faculty:** 55 total; 53% women. **Class size:** 50% < 20, 42% 20-39, 4% 40-49, 4% 50-99. **Partnerships:** Formal partnership with Buckeye Career Center engaged in Tech Prep program.

Student profile. Among degree-seeking undergraduates, 352 enrolled as first-time, first-year students, 157 transferred in from other institutions.

Part-time:	38%	**Asian American:**	1%
Out-of-state:	1%	**Hispanic American:**	1%
Women:	60%	**25 or older:**	36%
African American:	2%		

Basis for selection. Open admission, but selective for some programs and for out-of-state students. Special requirements for nursing program. **Adult students:** Test scores not required for placement if applicant is over 21 years of age.

High school preparation. College-preparatory program recommended. 16 units recommended. Recommended units include English 4, mathematics 3, social studies 3, science 3 (laboratory 2) and foreign language 2. One arts unit recommended.

2008-2009 Annual costs. Tuition/fees: $4,770; $12,202 out-of-state. Per-credit charge: $217 in-state; $555 out-of-state. Books/supplies: $700. Personal expenses: $1,500.

2008-2009 Financial aid. Need-based: 241 full-time freshmen applied for aid; 218 were judged to have need; 218 of these received aid. Average need met was 49%. Average scholarship/grant was $4,891; average loan $2,881. 40% of total undergraduate aid awarded as scholarships/grants, 60% as loans/jobs. Need-based aid available for part-time students. Work-study available nights, weekends and for part-time students. **Non-need-based:** Scholarships awarded for academics, alumni affiliation, art, athletics, leadership, minority status, music/drama, ROTC.

Application procedures. **Admission:** No deadline. $30 fee, may be waived for applicants with need. Admission notification on a rolling basis. **Financial aid:** Closing date 3/1. FAFSA required. Applicants notified on a rolling basis starting 3/15; must reply within 2 week(s) of notification.

Academics. **Special study options:** Accelerated study, distance learning, double major, dual enrollment of high school students, honors, independent study, internships, student-designed major. License preparation in nursing. **Credit/placement by examination:** AP, CLEP, SAT, ACT, institutional tests. 15 credit hours maximum toward associate degree. **Support services:** Learning center, reduced course load, remedial instruction, study skills assistance, tutoring, writing center.

Majors. **Business:** General, accounting technology, administrative services. **Computer sciences:** Applications programming. **Education:** Early childhood. **Engineering technology:** Industrial, mechanical, plastics. **Health:** Nursing (RN). **Liberal arts:** Arts/sciences. **Protective services:** Criminal justice.

Most popular majors. Business/marketing 8%, computer/information sciences 9%, engineering/engineering technologies 16%, health sciences 29%, liberal arts 31%.

Computing on campus. 300 workstations in library, computer center. Online course registration, online library, helpline, student web hosting available.

Student life. **Freshman orientation:** Mandatory. Preregistration for classes offered. **Activities:** Choral groups.

Athletics. **Intramural:** Basketball M, volleyball. **Team name:** Golden Flashes.

Student services. Career counseling, student employment services, on-campus daycare. **Physically disabled:** Services for visually, hearing impaired. **Transfer:** Transfer adviser for students transferring to 4-year colleges.

Contact. E-mail: info@tusc.kent.edu
Phone: (330) 339-3391 ext. 47425 Fax: (330) 339-3321
Denise Testa, Director of Enrollment Management, Kent State University: Tuscarawas, 330 University Drive Northeast, New Philadelphia, OH 44663-9403

Lakeland Community College

Kirtland, Ohio — **CB member**
www.lakelandcc.edu — **CB code: 1422**

- Public 2-year community college
- Commuter campus in large town

General. Founded in 1967. Regionally accredited. **Enrollment:** 8,924 degree-seeking undergraduates. **Degrees:** 818 associate awarded. **Location:** 15 miles from Cleveland. **Calendar:** Semester, extensive summer session. **Full-time faculty:** 120 total. **Part-time faculty:** 525 total. **Special facilities:** Planetarium, observatory, licensed preschool program laboratory.

Student profile. Among degree-seeking undergraduates, 43% enrolled in a transfer program, 57% enrolled in a vocational program.

Out-of-state:	1%	**25 or older:**	42%

Transfer out. **Colleges most students transferred to 2008:** Cleveland State University, University of Akron, Kent State University, Ohio State University, John Carroll University.

Basis for selection. Open admission, but selective for some programs. Admissions to health technology programs based on test scores and school achievement record.

High school preparation. Recommended units include English 4, mathematics 3, social studies 3, science 3 and foreign language 2. Health technology programs require algebra, biology, chemistry.

2008-2009 Annual costs. Tuition/fees: $2,726; $3,333 out-of-district; $7,095 out-of-state. Per-credit charge: $79 in-district; $99 out-of-district; $225 out-of-state. Books/supplies: $1,200.

2007-2008 Financial aid. **Need-based:** 41% of total undergraduate aid awarded as scholarships/grants, 59% as loans/jobs. Need-based aid available for part-time students. Work-study available nights, weekends and for part-time students. **Non-need-based:** Scholarships awarded for academics, art, athletics, job skills, leadership, minority status, music/drama, state residency. **Additional information:** Loans available for tuition and books.

Application procedures. **Admission:** No deadline. $15 fee, may be waived for applicants with need. Admission notification on a rolling basis. **Financial aid:** Priority date 3/1; no closing date. FAFSA, institutional form required. Applicants notified on a rolling basis starting 5/1.

Academics. **Special study options:** Accelerated study, cooperative education, cross-registration, distance learning, dual enrollment of high school students, ESL, independent study, internships, liberal arts/career combination, weekend college. Bachelor's degree programs available on campus. License preparation in dental hygiene, nursing, paramedic, radiology, real estate. **Credit/placement by examination:** AP, CLEP, institutional tests. 44 credit hours maximum toward associate degree. **Support services:** Learning center, reduced course load, remedial instruction, study skills assistance, tutoring.

Majors. **Biology:** Biotechnology. **Business:** Accounting, administrative services, business admin, e-commerce, hospitality admin, management information systems, small business admin, tourism promotion, tourism/travel. **Computer sciences:** Information systems, LAN/WAN management, programming, web page design. **Education:** Early childhood. **Engineering technology:** Civil, electrical, electrical drafting, manufacturing, mechanical, nuclear. **Family/consumer sciences:** Child care. **Health:** Clinical lab technology, dental hygiene, histologic technology, medical radiologic technology/radiation therapy, nursing (RN), ophthalmic lab technology, optician, respiratory therapy technology, surgical technology. **Legal studies:** Paralegal. **Liberal arts:** Arts/sciences. **Protective services:** Corrections, firefighting, police science, security services. **Public administration:** Human services. **Science technology:** Biological, nuclear power. **Visual/performing arts:** Commercial/advertising art.

Computing on campus. 500 workstations in library, computer center, student center. Commuter students can connect to campus network. Online course registration, online library, helpline, repair service, wireless network available.

Student life. **Freshman orientation:** Available. **Activities:** Bands, choral groups, drama, international student organizations, music ensembles, Model UN, radio station, student government, student newspaper, TV station, Access Unlimited, minority student union, Newman Catholic student association, La Tertulia.

Athletics. NJCAA. **Intercollegiate:** Baseball M, basketball, golf M, soccer M, softball W, volleyball W. **Intramural:** Basketball, racquetball, skiing, softball, tennis, volleyball. **Team name:** Lakers.

Student services. Adult student services, career counseling, student employment services, financial aid counseling, health services, on-campus daycare, personal counseling, placement for graduates, veterans' counselor, women's services. **Physically disabled:** Services for visually, speech, hearing impaired. **Transfer:** Transfer center, transfer adviser, college fairs on campus for students transferring to 4-year colleges.

Contact. E-mail: tcooper@lakelandcc.edu
Phone: (440) 525-7100 Toll-free number: (800) 589-8520
Fax: (440) 525-7651
Tracey Cooper, Director of Admissions/Registrar, Lakeland Community College, 7700 Clocktower Drive, Kirtland, OH 44094-5198

Lorain County Community College

Elyria, Ohio
www.lorainccc.edu — **CB code: 1417**

- Public 2-year community college
- Commuter campus in small city

General. Founded in 1963. Regionally accredited. **Location:** 26 miles south of Cleveland. **Calendar:** Semester.

Annual costs/financial aid. Tuition/fees (2008-2009): $2,400; $2,890 out-of-district; $5,838 out-of-state. Books/supplies: $955. Need-based financial aid available to full-time and part-time students.

Contact. Phone: (440) 366-4032
Director of Enrollment Services, 1005 Abbe Road North, Elyria, OH 44035-1691

Marion Technical College

Marion, Ohio
www.mtc.edu — **CB code: 0699**

- Public 2-year technical college
- Commuter campus in large town

General. Founded in 1971. Regionally accredited. Common campus and some shared facilities with Ohio State University: Marion. **Enrollment:** 1,079 full-time, degree-seeking students. **Degrees:** 176 associate awarded. **Location:** 45 miles from Columbus. **Calendar:** Quarter, limited summer session. **Full-time faculty:** 40 total. **Part-time faculty:** 5 total.

Student profile.

Out-of-state:	1%	**25 or older:**	45%

Basis for selection. Open admission, but selective for some programs. Selective programs include medical assisting, phlebotomy, human and social services, medical administrative assistant, medical lab technician, nursing, PTA, radiology. Application to program additional to application to college. Programs accept on rolling basis once minimum criteria are met. ACT scores required of nursing, human and social services applicants and recommended for PTA and med lab technician applicants for admissions, placement and counseling; recommended for other applicants for counseling. Interview required for health technologies, human and social services, law enforcement academy. **Adult students:** ACT may be required for limited enrollment programs. **Homeschooled:** Transcript of courses and grades, interview required. Appropriate standardized test or other documentation as defined by policy. **Learning Disabled:** Students must meet with Student Resource Center for assessment of special accommodations.

High school preparation. Recommended units include English 4, mathematics 2, social studies 1, science 2 and foreign language 2. Algebra, biology, and chemistry required for health technology applicants. Algebra and physics recommended for engineering applicants.

2008-2009 Annual costs. Tuition/fees: $3,660; $5,568 out-of-state. Per-credit charge: $83 in-state; $237 out-of-state. Books/supplies: $1,200. Personal expenses: $900.

2008-2009 Financial aid. Need-based: Need-based aid available for part-time students. Work-study available for part-time students. **Non-need-based:** Scholarships awarded for academics, leadership, minority status.

Application procedures. Admission: Priority date 6/1; no deadline. $20 fee, may be waived for applicants with need. Admission notification on a rolling basis. **Financial aid:** Closing date 6/1. FAFSA, institutional form required. Applicants notified on a rolling basis.

Academics. Special study options: Accelerated study, cooperative education, cross-registration, distance learning, double major, dual enrollment of high school students, independent study, internships, liberal arts/career combination, student-designed major. License preparation in nursing, physical therapy, radiology, real estate. **Credit/placement by examination:** AP, CLEP, institutional tests. Maximum of 48 quarter hours of credit may be earned through exam, life experience or combination. **Support services:** Learning center, reduced course load, remedial instruction, tutoring.

Majors. Business: General, accounting, accounting technology, administrative services, business admin, e-commerce, executive assistant, human resources, marketing, office management, office technology, real estate. **Computer sciences:** General, applications programming, data entry, information technology, LAN/WAN management, networking, programming, vendor certification, web page design, webmaster, word processing. **Engineering technology:** Electrical, electromechanical, manufacturing, mechanical, quality control, telecommunications. **Health:** Clinical lab technology, medical radiologic technology/radiation therapy, medical secretary, nursing (RN), physical therapy assistant. **Legal studies:** Paralegal. **Protective services:** Law enforcement admin. **Public administration:** Human services. **Other:** Industrial Mechanical Maintenance.

Computing on campus. 229 workstations in computer center.

Student life. Freshman orientation: Available. Held week or two before classes begin. **Activities:** Campus ministries, choral groups, drama, literary magazine, student government, joint activities committee, Campus Christian Fellowship, program of outdoor pursuits club, cultural arts program, student organized clubs/organizations, indoor rock climbing, wellness and conditioning, aerobics center, Beta Nu Pi honorary society (Phi Theta Kappa local chapter).

Athletics. Intercollegiate: Basketball, cheerleading M, golf, soccer, volleyball W. **Intramural:** Badminton, basketball, cross-country, football (non-tackle), racquetball, skiing, softball, table tennis, tennis, volleyball.

Student services. Adult student services, career counseling, student employment services, financial aid counseling, personal counseling, placement for graduates, veterans' counselor. **Physically disabled:** Services for visually, speech, hearing impaired. **Transfer:** College fairs on campus for students transferring to 4-year colleges.

Contact. E-mail: enroll@mtc.edu
Phone: (740) 389-4636 ext. 260 Fax: (740) 389-6136
Joel Liles, Director of Admission and Career Services, Marion Technical College, 1467 Mount Vernon Avenue, Marion, OH 43302-5694

Miami University: Hamilton Campus

Hamilton, Ohio
www.ham.muohio.edu **CB code: 1526**

- Public 2-year branch campus college
- Commuter campus in small city

General. Founded in 1968. Regionally accredited. Degrees earned on Hamilton campus conferred by main (Oxford) campus. **Enrollment:** 3,491 degree-seeking undergraduates; 81 non-degree-seeking students. **Degrees:** 29 bachelor's, 133 associate awarded. **ROTC:** Naval, Air Force. **Location:** 25 miles from Cincinnati. **Calendar:** Semester, limited summer session. **Full-time faculty:** 84 total. **Part-time faculty:** 140 total. **Class size:** 67% < 20, 24% 20-39, 6% 40-49, 3% 50-99. **Special facilities:** Botanical conservatory.

Student profile. Among degree-seeking undergraduates, 796 enrolled as first-time, first-year students.

Part-time:	22%	**25 or older:**	26%
Women:	53%		

Basis for selection. Open admission, but selective for some programs. Open admission policy with additional application required for competitive nursing program. Test scores required for consideration in nursing and teacher education programs. **Homeschooled:** Applicants must present GED scores or credentials that demonstrate equivalent levels of academic achievement, ability and performance to that of state-chartered diploma at least 8 weeks before classes begin.

High school preparation. 16 units recommended. Recommended units include English 4, mathematics 3, social studies 2, history 1, science 3, foreign language 2 and visual/performing arts 1.

2008-2009 Annual costs. Tuition/fees: $4,314; $17,945 out-of-state. Per-credit charge: $180 in-state; $748 out-of-state. Books/supplies: $580. Personal expenses: $1,732.

2008-2009 Financial aid. Need-based: Need-based aid available for part-time students. Work-study available nights, weekends and for part-time students. **Non-need-based:** Scholarships awarded for academics, athletics, leadership, minority status, state residency. **Additional information:** Special gift funds for needy, multicultural students who enter with appropriate academic record. Separate application required for scholarships; closing date January 31.

Application procedures. Admission: No deadline. $35 fee, may be waived for applicants with need. Admission notification on a rolling basis. Nursing application deadline for Fall admission 2/1. **Financial aid:** Priority date 2/15; no closing date. FAFSA required. Applicants notified on a rolling basis starting 4/1.

Academics. Some graduate coursework available. **Special study options:** Cooperative education, cross-registration, distance learning, double major, dual enrollment of high school students, ESL, honors, independent study, internships, liberal arts/career combination, student-designed major, study abroad, teacher certification program. Bachelor's degree programs available on campus. License preparation in nursing, real estate. **Credit/placement by examination:** AP, CLEP, IB, institutional tests. 32 credit hours maximum toward associate degree, 32 toward bachelor's. **Support services:** Learning center, reduced course load, remedial instruction, study skills assistance, tutoring, writing center.

Majors. Business: Accounting technology, business admin, marketing, office management, real estate. **Computer sciences:** General, computer support specialist, networking. **Education:** Kindergarten/preschool. **Engineering technology:** Computer systems, electrical, mechanical. **Health:** Nursing (RN). **Protective services:** Law enforcement admin. **Other:** Computer and electrical engineering technology, Software development and support.

Computing on campus. 300 workstations in library, computer center, student center. Commuter students can connect to campus network. Online course registration, online library, helpline, wireless network available.

Student life. Freshman orientation: Available. **Activities:** Choral groups, drama, musical theater, student government, campus activities committee, student nursing association, minority action committee, Campus Crusade for Christ, athletic club, Organization for Wiser and Worldwide Learners.

Athletics. Intramural: Basketball, bowling, skiing, soccer, softball, table tennis, tennis, volleyball, weight lifting. **Team name:** Harriers.

Student services. Career counseling, student employment services, financial aid counseling, minority student services, on-campus daycare, personal counseling, placement for graduates, veterans' counselor. **Physically disabled:** Services for visually, speech, hearing impaired. **Transfer:** Pre-admission transcript evaluation for new students.

Contact. Phone: (513) 785-3111 Fax: (513) 785-1807
Archie Nelson, Director of Admission and Financial Aid, Miami University: Hamilton Campus, 1601 University Boulevard, Hamilton, OH 45011-3399

Miami University: Middletown Campus

Middletown, Ohio
www.mid.muohio.edu **CB code: 1509**

- Public 2-year branch campus and community college
- Commuter campus in large town

General. Founded in 1963. Regionally accredited. Degrees earned on Middletown campus conferred by main (Oxford) campus. **Enrollment:** 2,400 degree-seeking undergraduates. **ROTC:** Naval, Air Force. **Location:** 30 miles from Cincinnati, 20 miles from Dayton. **Calendar:** Semester, extensive summer session. **Full-time faculty:** 80 total. **Part-time faculty:** 150 total. **Special facilities:** Nature trail.

Student profile.

Out-of-state:	1%	**25 or older:**	28%

Basis for selection. Open admission, but selective for some programs. Special requirements for allied health programs. Interview recommended for nursing program. **Homeschooled:** Submit curriculum and description of resources used during last 4 years.

High school preparation. 16 units recommended. Recommended units include English 4, mathematics 3, social studies 3, science 3, foreign language 2 and academic electives 1. One fine arts also recommended.

2008-2009 Annual costs. Tuition/fees: $4,314; $17,945 out-of-state. Per-credit charge: $180 in-state; $748 out-of-state. Students paying by the credit hour pay $15.25 general fee per credit hour. Books/supplies: $1,195. Personal expenses: $4,088.

Financial aid. All financial aid based on need. Need-based aid available for part-time students. Work-study available for part-time students.

Application procedures. Admission: Priority date 8/1; no deadline. $35 fee, may be waived for applicants with need. Admission notification on a rolling basis beginning on or about 3/1. **Financial aid:** Priority date 2/15; no closing date. FAFSA required. Applicants notified on a rolling basis.

Academics. Special study options: Cooperative education, cross-registration, distance learning, double major, dual enrollment of high school students, independent study, internships, liberal arts/career combination, student-designed major, study abroad, teacher certification program. License preparation in nursing. **Credit/placement by examination:** AP, CLEP, IB, institutional tests. 30 credit hours maximum toward bachelor's degree. **Support services:** Learning center, pre-admission summer program, reduced course load, remedial instruction, study skills assistance, tutoring, writing center.

Majors. Biology: Molecular, zoology. **Business:** General, accounting, administrative services, business admin, finance, office management, office/clerical. **Communications:** General. **Computer sciences:** General, applications programming, systems analysis. **Engineering technology:** Computer systems, electrical. **Foreign languages:** Spanish. **Health:** Nursing (RN). **History:** General. **Liberal arts:** Arts/sciences, humanities. **Math:** General. **Philosophy/religion:** Philosophy. **Physical sciences:** Chemistry, physics. **Psychology:** General. **Social sciences:** Anthropology, geography, political science, sociology.

Computing on campus. 170 workstations in library, computer center. Commuter students can connect to campus network. Online course registration, online library, helpline, student web hosting available.

Student life. Freshman orientation: Mandatory. Full-day program, choice of 5 days ranging from June 4 through August 11. **Activities:** Drama, literary magazine, student government, student newspaper.

Athletics. Intercollegiate: Baseball M, basketball, golf, tennis, volleyball W. **Intramural:** Basketball, golf, racquetball, soccer, softball, table tennis, tennis, volleyball. **Team name:** Thunder Hawks.

Student services. Adult student services, career counseling, student employment services, financial aid counseling, minority student services, on-campus daycare, personal counseling, placement for graduates, veterans' counselor. **Physically disabled:** Services for visually, speech, hearing impaired. **Transfer:** College fairs on campus for students transferring to 4-year colleges.

Contact. E-mail: mlflynn@muohio.edu
Phone: (513) 727-3216 Fax: (513) 727-3223
Stacey Adams, Director of Admission and Financial Aid, Miami University: Middletown Campus, 4200 East University Boulevard, Middletown, OH 45042

Miami-Jacobs Career College

Dayton, Ohio
www.miamijacobs.edu **CB code: 1528**

- For-profit 2-year junior college
- Commuter campus in small city
- Application essay, interview required

General. Founded in 1860. Accredited by ACICS. Center for information technology provides high-end software training preparation for certification. **Enrollment:** 248 degree-seeking undergraduates. **Degrees:** 176 associate awarded. **Location:** Downtown. **Calendar:** Quarter, extensive summer session. **Full-time faculty:** 10 total. **Part-time faculty:** 75 total. **Special facilities:** Antique typewriter museum.

Basis for selection. Interview, essay, recommendations most important. Wonderlic exam required.

2008-2009 Annual costs. Tuition/fees: $11,010. Per-credit charge: $305. Personal expenses: $2,500.

Financial aid. All financial aid based on need. Need-based aid available for part-time students.

Application procedures. Admission: No deadline. $20 fee. Admission notification on a rolling basis. **Financial aid:** No deadline. FAFSA, institutional form required. Applicants notified on a rolling basis.

Academics. College has dress code and attendance policy establishing patterns and habits to be carried over into employment setting. **Special study options:** Accelerated study, cross-registration, distance learning, double major, dual enrollment of high school students, independent study, internships, weekend college. **Credit/placement by examination:** AP, CLEP, institutional tests. 45 credit hours maximum toward associate degree. **Support services:** Pre-admission summer program, reduced course load, remedial instruction, tutoring.

Majors. Business: Accounting, administrative services, office management, office technology, office/clerical. **Computer sciences:** General, applications programming, data processing, information systems, information technology, networking, programming. **Engineering:** Software. **Health:** Massage therapy, medical assistant, medical records technology, medical secretary, medical transcription, respiratory therapy technology, surgical technology. **Legal studies:** Court reporting. **Protective services:** Law enforcement admin.

Computing on campus. 180 workstations in computer center.

Student life. Freshman orientation: Mandatory. Preregistration for classes offered.

Student services. Adult student services, career counseling, student employment services, financial aid counseling, personal counseling, placement for graduates, veterans' counselor. **Transfer:** Transfer adviser for students transferring to 4-year colleges.

Contact. E-mail: careeradvocate@miamijacobs.edu
Phone: (937) 222-7337
Mike Montgomery, Director of Admissions, Miami-Jacobs Career College, 110 North Patterson Boulevard, Dayton, OH 45402

National College: Cincinnati

Cincinnati, Ohio

- For-profit 2-year branch campus college
- Large city

General. Regionally accredited; also accredited by ACICS. **Enrollment:** 427 degree-seeking undergraduates. **Degrees:** 87 associate awarded. **Calendar:** Quarter. **Full-time faculty:** 3 total. **Part-time faculty:** 56 total.

Basis for selection. Open admission.

2008-2009 Annual costs. Tuition/fees: $9,585. Per-credit charge: $212.

Application procedures. Admission: No deadline. $30 fee.

Academics. Credit/placement by examination: CLEP.

Majors. Business: Accounting/business management, administrative services, business admin. **Engineering technology:** Computer systems. **Health:** Pharmacy assistant, surgical technology. **Other:** Information systems engineering.

Contact. Phone: (513) 761-1291
Larry Steele, Vice President of Admissions, National College: Cincinnati, 6871 Steger Drive, Cincinnati, OH 45237

National College: Dayton
Kettering, Ohio

- For-profit 2-year business and technical college
- Large city

General. Accredited by ACICS. **Enrollment:** 394 degree-seeking undergraduates. **Degrees:** 77 associate awarded. **Calendar:** Quarter. **Full-time faculty:** 4 total. **Part-time faculty:** 40 total.

Basis for selection. Open admission.

2008-2009 Annual costs. Tuition/fees: $9,585. Per-credit charge: $212. Books and supplies $130 per class.

Application procedures. Admission: No deadline. $30 fee. **Financial aid:** No deadline.

Academics. Credit/placement by examination: CLEP.

Contact. Phone: (937) 299-9450
Larry Steele, Vice President of Admissions, National College: Dayton, 1837 Woodman Center Drive, Kettering, OH 45420

National College: Stow
Stow, Ohio

- For-profit 2-year branch campus college
- Large town

General. Regionally accredited; also accredited by ACICS. **Enrollment:** 203 degree-seeking undergraduates. **Calendar:** Quarter. **Full-time faculty:** 6 total. **Part-time faculty:** 29 total.

Basis for selection. Open admission.

2008-2009 Annual costs. Tuition/fees: $9,585. Per-credit charge: $212.

Application procedures. Admission: No deadline. $30 fee.

Academics. Credit/placement by examination: CLEP.

Majors. Business: Accounting/business management, administrative services, business admin. **Engineering technology:** Computer systems. **Health:** Medical assistant, medical records technology, pharmacy assistant. **Other:** Information systems engineering.

Contact. Larry Steele, Vice President of Admissions, National College: Stow, 3855 Fishercreek Road, Stow, OH 44224

National College: Youngstown
Youngstown, Ohio

- For-profit 2-year branch campus college
- Small city

General. Regionally accredited; also accredited by ACICS. **Enrollment:** 399 degree-seeking undergraduates. **Calendar:** Quarter. **Full-time faculty:** 3 total. **Part-time faculty:** 34 total.

Basis for selection. Open admission.

2008-2009 Annual costs. Tuition/fees: $9,585. Per-credit charge: $212.

Application procedures. Admission: No deadline. $30 fee. **Financial aid:** No deadline.

Academics. Credit/placement by examination: CLEP.

Majors. Business: Business admin. **Engineering technology:** Computer systems. **Health:** Medical records technology, office assistant, physical therapy assistant. **Other:** Information systems engineering.

Contact. Larry Steele, Vice President of Admissions, National College: Youngstown, 3487 Belmont Avenue, Youngstown, OH 44505

National Institute of Technology
Cuyahoga Falls, Ohio
www.nationalinstituteoftechnology.edu

- For-profit 2-year health science and technical college
- Commuter campus in small city

General. Accredited by ACCSCT. **Calendar:** Continuous.

Annual costs/financial aid. Program cost for associate degree in medical assisting $24,055; associate in dental assisting, $24,495; associate in registered nursing, $24,592; associate in criminal justice, $24,395; associate in business administration, $24,115; associate in electronics, $24,115; associate in computer information systems, $24,115; diploma in medical billing and coding, $14,735; diploma in dental assisting, $18,435.

Contact. Phone: (330) 923-9959 ext. 14
Director of Admissions, 2545 Bailey Road, Cuyahoga Falls, OH 44221

North Central State College
Mansfield, Ohio
www.ncstatecollege.edu **CB code: 0721**

- Public 2-year technical college
- Commuter campus in small city

General. Founded in 1961. Regionally accredited. **Enrollment:** 3,250 degree-seeking undergraduates. **Degrees:** 420 associate awarded. **Location:** 70 miles from Cleveland and Columbus. **Calendar:** Quarter, limited summer session. **Full-time faculty:** 71 total. **Part-time faculty:** 123 total. **Special facilities:** Wooded hiking trails.

Student profile.

Out-of-state:	1%	**25 or older:**	53%

Transfer out. Colleges most students transferred to 2008: Ashland University, Mount Vernon Nazarene College, University of Cincinnati, Franklin University.

Basis for selection. Open admission, but selective for some programs. ACT scores used for admission to physical therapist assistant and radiology programs; score report by September 15. Interview recommended for all health and public service programs.

High school preparation. One algebra and 1 chemistry required for nursing, physical therapist assistant, respiratory therapy, radiologic technology and pharmacy technology programs.

2008-2009 Annual costs. Tuition/fees: $3,634; $6,694 out-of-state. Per-credit charge: $68 in-state; $136 out-of-state. Books/supplies: $705. Personal expenses: $726.

Financial aid. All financial aid based on need. Need-based aid available for part-time students.

Application procedures. Admission: No deadline. No application fee. Admission notification on a rolling basis. **Financial aid:** Priority date 4/1; no closing date. FAFSA required. Applicants notified on a rolling basis starting 5/30; must reply within 1 week(s) of notification.

Academics. Special study options: Distance learning, dual enrollment of high school students, independent study, internships, student-designed major, weekend college. **Credit/placement by examination:** CLEP, institutional tests. **Support services:** GED preparation, learning center, reduced course load, remedial instruction, study skills assistance, tutoring, writing center.

Majors. Business: General, accounting, administrative services, business admin, operations. **Communications:** Digital media. **Communications technology:** Animation/special effects, radio/tv. **Computer sciences:** General, applications programming, programming. **Education:** Early childhood, teacher assistance. **Engineering technology:** Computer, drafting, electrical, heat/ac/refrig, mechanical. **Health:** Health services, medical radiologic technology/

radiation therapy, mental health services, nursing (RN), physical therapy assistant, radiologic technology/medical imaging, respiratory therapy technology. **Legal studies:** Legal secretary, paralegal. **Mechanic/repair:** Electronics/electrical, heating/ac/refrig. **Production:** Tool and die. **Protective services:** Criminal justice, law enforcement admin, police science.

Computing on campus. 144 workstations in library, computer center.

Student life. Freshman orientation: Available. Two- or three-hour evening program held prior to beginning of each quarter. **Activities:** Choral groups, student government, student newspaper.

Athletics. Intramural: Basketball, bowling, football (non-tackle), golf, softball, table tennis, tennis, volleyball. **Team name:** Mavericks.

Student services. Career counseling, student employment services, financial aid counseling, on-campus daycare, personal counseling, placement for graduates, veterans' counselor. **Physically disabled:** Services for visually, speech, hearing impaired. **Transfer:** College fairs on campus for students transferring to 4-year colleges.

Contact. E-mail: admissions@ncstatecollege.edu
Phone: (419) 755-4761 Toll-free number: (888) 755-4899
Fax: (419) 755-4757
Nikia Fletcher, Director of Admissions/Enrollment Services, North Central State College, 2441 Kenwood Circle, PO Box 698, Mansfield, OH 44901-0698

Northwest State Community College
Archbold, Ohio
www.northweststate.edu **CB code: 1235**

- Public 2-year community and technical college
- Commuter campus in small town

General. Founded in 1968. Regionally accredited. **Enrollment:** 1,840 degree-seeking undergraduates. **Degrees:** 305 associate awarded. **Location:** 45 miles from Toledo. **Calendar:** Semester, limited summer session. **Full-time faculty:** 50 total. **Part-time faculty:** 194 total. **Class size:** 68% < 20, 32% 20-39, less than 1% 40-49. **Special facilities:** Childcare center.

Student profile.

Out-of-state:	2%	**25 or older:**	46%

Basis for selection. Open admission, but selective for some programs. Special requirements for nursing program; interview required. COMPASS test required for all new students for placement in math, English, reading.

High school preparation. Recommended units include English 4, mathematics 3, social studies 3 and science 3. College-preparatory program preferred.

2008-2009 Annual costs. Tuition/fees: $4,140; $7,410 out-of-state. Per-credit charge: $130 in-state; $239 out-of-state. Personal expenses: $750.

Financial aid. Need-based: Need-based aid available for part-time students. **Non-need-based:** Scholarships awarded for academics.

Application procedures. Admission: No deadline. $20 fee. Admission notification on a rolling basis. **Financial aid:** Priority date 6/1; no closing date. FAFSA, institutional form required. Applicants notified on a rolling basis starting 4/1.

Academics. Special study options: Cooperative education, distance learning, dual enrollment of high school students, independent study, internships, student-designed major, weekend college. Bachelor's degree programs available on campus. License preparation in nursing, real estate. **Credit/placement by examination:** CLEP, institutional tests. 40 credit hours maximum toward associate degree. **Support services:** Learning center, remedial instruction, tutoring.

Majors. Business: General, accounting, administrative services, business admin, finance, marketing, office technology. **Computer sciences:** LAN/WAN management, programming. **Education:** General. **Engineering technology:** Drafting, electrical, industrial management, mechanical, plastics, quality control. **Family/consumer sciences:** Child development, family studies. **Health:** Medical secretary, nursing (RN). **Legal studies:** Legal secretary, paralegal. **Liberal arts:** Arts/sciences. **Production:** Machine tool, sheet metal, tool and die. **Protective services:** Corrections, criminal justice, law enforcement admin, police science. **Public administration:** Social work. **Visual/performing arts:** Design.

Computing on campus. 400 workstations in library, computer center. Online library, wireless network available.

Student life. Freshman orientation: Available. Preregistration for classes offered. **Activities:** Student government, Student Nurses Association, Phi Theta Kappa, Campus Crusade for Christ, student body organization.

Athletics. Intramural: Basketball, bowling, football (non-tackle), softball, table tennis, volleyball. **Team name:** Pacers.

Student services. Adult student services, career counseling, student employment services, financial aid counseling, on-campus daycare, personal counseling, placement for graduates, veterans' counselor. **Physically disabled:** Services for visually, hearing impaired. **Transfer:** Transfer adviser, college fairs on campus for students transferring to 4-year colleges.

Contact. E-mail: admissions@northweststate.edu
Phone: (419) 267-5511 ext. 320 Fax: (419) 267-5604
Kathy Thompson, Director of Admissions, Northwest State Community College, 22600 State Route 34, Archbold, OH 43502

Ohio Business College
Lorain, Ohio
www.ohiobusinesscollege.edu **CB code: 2470**

- For-profit 2-year branch campus and business college
- Commuter campus in small city

General. Founded in 1903. Accredited by ACICS. **Location:** 35 miles from Cleveland. **Calendar:** Quarter.

Annual costs/financial aid. Tuition/fees (2008-2009): $9,705. Books/supplies: $1,080. Need-based financial aid available to full-time and part-time students.

Contact. Phone: (440) 277-0021
Admissions Manager, 1907 North Ridge Road, Lorain, OH 44055

Ohio Business College: Sandusky
Sandusky, Ohio
www.ohiobusinesscollege.edu **CB code: 3260**

- For-profit 2-year business college
- Commuter campus in small city

General. Accredited by ACICS. **Location:** 60 miles from Cleveland and Toledo. **Calendar:** Quarter.

Annual costs/financial aid. Tuition/fees (2008-2009): $9,585. Books/supplies: $1,200. Need-based financial aid available to full-time and part-time students.

Contact. Phone: (419) 627-8345
Director of Admissions, 5202 Timber Commons Drive, Sandusky, OH 44870

Ohio College of Massotherapy
Akron, Ohio
www.ocm.edu **CB code: 2985**

- For-profit 2-year health science college
- Commuter campus in very large city

General. Accredited by ACCSCT. **Enrollment:** 167 degree-seeking undergraduates. **Degrees:** 42 associate awarded. **Calendar:** Continuous. **Part-time faculty:** 18 total. **Special facilities:** Massage and spa clinic.

Basis for selection. Open admission. **Homeschooled:** State high school equivalency certificate required.

Application procedures. Admission: Closing date 8/21. $25 fee. **Financial aid:** Priority date 10/1; no closing date.

Academics. Special study options: Distance learning. **Credit/placement by examination:** CLEP. **Support services:** Reduced course load, tutoring.

Majors. Health: Massage therapy.

Computing on campus. 4 workstations in computer center.

Student life. Freshman orientation: Mandatory.

Contact. E-mail: admissions@ocm.edu
Phone: (330) 665-1084 Fax: (330) 665-5021
Jeff Morrow, Admissions/Marketing Manager, Ohio College of Massotherapy, 225 Heritage Woods Drive, Akron, OH 44321

Ohio Institute of Health Careers: Columbus

Columbus, Ohio
www.ohioinstituteofhealthcareers.edu

- For-profit 2-year health science college
- Very large city
- Interview required

General. Accredited by ACCSCT. **Enrollment:** 240 degree-seeking undergraduates. **Calendar:** Continuous. **Full-time faculty:** 15 total. **Part-time faculty:** 15 total.

Basis for selection. Open admission.

Application procedures. Admission: No deadline. $40 fee.

Academics. Credit/placement by examination: CLEP.

Majors. Health: Massage therapy, medical assistant.

Contact. Phone: (614) 891-5030 Toll-free number: (800) 954-4274
Duane Landrum, Admissions Director, Ohio Institute of Health Careers: Columbus, 1880 East Dublin-Granville Road, Suite 100, Columbus, OH 43229

Ohio Institute of Health Careers: Elyria

Sheffield Village, Ohio
www.ohiobusinesscollege.edu

- For-profit 2-year health science college
- Small city

General. Accredited by ACCSCT. **Enrollment:** 420 degree-seeking undergraduates. **Degrees:** 71 associate awarded. **Calendar:** Quarter. **Full-time faculty:** 9 total. **Part-time faculty:** 10 total.

Basis for selection. Open admission.

Application procedures. Admission: No deadline. $32 fee.

Academics. Credit/placement by examination: CLEP.

Majors. Business: Accounting, administrative services, business admin, human resources. **Computer sciences:** Data entry, web page design. **Health:** Medical assistant, office assistant. **Legal studies:** Legal secretary.

Contact. Fax: (440) 934-3105
John Tobin, Admissions Director, Ohio Institute of Health Careers: Elyria, 5095 Waterford Drive, Sheffield Village, OH 44035-0701

Ohio Institute of Photography and Technology

Dayton, Ohio
www.oipt.com **CB code: 3380**

- For-profit 2-year technical college
- Commuter campus in very large city
- Interview required

General. Founded in 1971. Accredited by ACCSCT. **Enrollment:** 813 degree-seeking undergraduates. **Degrees:** 217 associate awarded. **Location:** 55 miles from Cincinnati, 80 miles from Columbus. **Calendar:** Quarter, extensive summer session. **Full-time faculty:** 19 total; 10% have terminal degrees, 10% minority, 58% women. **Part-time faculty:** 25 total; 4% have terminal degrees, 12% minority, 52% women. **Special facilities:** Photographic laboratories and computer laboratory for digital imaging.

Student profile. Among degree-seeking undergraduates, 100% enrolled in a vocational program, 131 enrolled as first-time, first-year students.

Part-time:	9%	**Women:**	72%
Out-of-state:	19%	**25 or older:**	33%

Basis for selection. Open admission, but selective for some programs. CPAt exam and interview required. Minimum CPAt score of 150 required for pharmacy technician students. Essay and portfolio recommended.

2008-2009 Annual costs. Tuition/fees: $21,093. Tuition listed reflects the Photographic Technology program. Tuition varies by program. Books/supplies: $1,350. Personal expenses: $1,701.

Financial aid. Need-based: Need-based aid available for part-time students.

Application procedures. Admission: No deadline. $20 fee. Admission notification on a rolling basis. **Financial aid:** No deadline. FAFSA, institutional form required. Applicants notified on a rolling basis starting 3/1.

Academics. Training directed toward technical and professional aspects of photography. **Special study options:** Double major, independent study, internships. **Credit/placement by examination:** AP, CLEP. **Support services:** GED preparation, reduced course load, tutoring.

Majors. Health: Office admin. **Protective services:** Law enforcement admin. **Visual/performing arts:** Commercial photography, graphic design, photography.

Computing on campus. 36 workstations in library. Online library available.

Student life. Freshman orientation: Available. Preregistration for classes offered. Held for 3 hours, prior to first day of classes.

Student services. Adult student services, career counseling, student employment services, financial aid counseling, placement for graduates. **Transfer:** Pre-admission transcript evaluation for new students. Transfer adviser for students transferring to 4-year colleges.

Contact. E-mail: info@oipt.com
Phone: (937) 294-6155 Toll-free number: (800) 932-9698
Fax: (937) 294-2259
Todd Harlow, Director of Admissions, Ohio Institute of Photography and Technology, 2029 Edgefield Road, Dayton, OH 45439

Ohio State University Agricultural Technical Institute

Wooster, Ohio
www.ati.osu.edu **CB code: 1009**

- Public 2-year agricultural and branch campus college
- Residential campus in large town

General. Founded in 1971. Regionally accredited. **Enrollment:** 782 degree-seeking undergraduates. **Degrees:** 190 associate awarded. **Location:** 30 miles from Akron, 60 miles from Cleveland. **Calendar:** Quarter, limited summer session. **Full-time faculty:** 34 total; 97% have terminal degrees, 6% minority, 29% women. **Part-time faculty:** 29 total; 7% minority, 31% women. **Class size:** 56% < 20, 39% 20-39, 2% 40-49, 3% 50-99. **Special facilities:** 18 hole public golf course, 1800-acre farm operation/enterprise laboratory, horticulture complex including greenhouses, conservatory and display gardens.

Student profile. Among degree-seeking undergraduates, 55% enrolled in a transfer program, 45% enrolled in a vocational program, 1% already have a bachelor's degree or higher, 375 enrolled as first-time, first-year students.

Out-of-state:	3%	**Live on campus:**	51%
25 or older:	9%		

Basis for selection. Open admission, but selective for out-of-state students. Out-of-state applicants evaluated on basis of GPA, class rank, curriculum, principal/counselor recommendations, and SAT or ACT scores. **Adult students:** Test scores not required for out-of-state applicants over 21 years of age. **Homeschooled:** Statement describing homeschool structure and mission, transcript of courses and grades, interview required. SAT or ACT required.

High school preparation. Recommended units include English 4, mathematics 4, social studies 3, science 3 (laboratory 3), foreign language 3 and academic electives 1. Science units should include biology and chemistry. Physics recommended for engineering technology majors. One unit of visual or performing arts recommended.

2008-2009 Annual costs. Tuition/fees: $5,859; $19,098 out-of-state. Books/supplies: $1,383. Personal expenses: $3,420.

2008-2009 Financial aid. All financial aid based on need. Need-based aid available for part-time students. Work-study available nights, weekends and for part-time students.

Application procedures. Admission: Priority date 7/1; deadline 8/9 (postmark date). $40 fee, may be waived for applicants with need. Admission notification on a rolling basis beginning on or about 11/1. Must reply by May 1 or within 6 week(s) if notified thereafter. **Financial aid:** Priority date 3/1; no closing date. FAFSA required. Applicants notified on a rolling basis starting 5/1; must reply within 4 week(s) of notification.

Academics. One-quarter of occupational internship required. **Special study options:** Cross-registration, double major, dual enrollment of high school students, independent study, internships, student-designed major, study abroad. **Credit/placement by examination:** AP, CLEP, SAT, ACT, institutional tests. 45 credit hours maximum toward associate degree. **Support services:** Learning center, reduced course load, remedial instruction, study skills assistance, tutoring, writing center.

Majors. Agriculture: General, agronomy, animal husbandry, business, communications, crop production, dairy, equine science, equipment technology, floriculture, greenhouse operations, horticultural science, horticulture, landscaping, nursery operations, ornamental horticulture, plant sciences, power machinery, soil science, turf management. **Business:** Business admin, restaurant/food services. **Conservation:** General, environmental studies. **Construction:** Power transmission. **Education:** Agricultural. **Engineering technology:** Construction, hydraulics. **Personal/culinary services:** Restaurant/catering.

Most popular majors. Agriculture 85%, education 6%.

Computing on campus. 85 workstations in dormitories, library, computer center. Dormitories wired for high-speed internet access. Commuter students can connect to campus network. Online course registration, online library, helpline, repair service, wireless network available.

Student life. Freshman orientation: Mandatory, $75 fee. **Policies:** Resident freshmen under 21 required to live on campus. **Housing:** Apartments, wellness housing available. $100 nonrefundable deposit. **Activities:** Campus ministries, student government, Phi Theta Kappa.

Athletics. Intramural: Basketball, football (tackle), racquetball, softball, volleyball.

Student services. Adult student services, career counseling, student employment services, health services, minority student services, personal counseling, placement for graduates. **Physically disabled:** Services for visually, speech, hearing impaired.

Contact. E-mail: ati@osu.edu
Phone: (330) 287-1327 Toll-free number: (800) 647-8283
Fax: (330) 287-1333
Tim Kracker, Coordinator of Admissions, Ohio State University Agricultural Technical Institute, 1328 Dover Road, Wooster, OH 44691

Ohio Technical College

Cleveland, Ohio
www.ohiotechnicalcollege.com **CB code: 2999**

- For-profit 2-year technical college
- Very large city

General. Accredited by ACCSCT. **Enrollment:** 801 degree-seeking undergraduates. **Degrees:** 60 associate awarded. **Calendar:** Continuous. **Full-time faculty:** 192 total.

Basis for selection. Applicants must pass Wonderlic test to be admitted.

2008-2009 Annual costs. Tuition for full associate programs range from $25,000 to $29,400; full diploma programs range from $18,400 to $26,280; full certificate programs range from $2,700 to $4,500. Fees are $100. Personal expenses: $1,837.

2007-2008 Financial aid. Need-based: 35% of total undergraduate aid awarded as scholarships/grants, 65% as loans/jobs.

Application procedures. Admission: $100 fee. **Financial aid:** No deadline.

Academics. Credit/placement by examination: CLEP.

Majors. Mechanic/repair: General. **Transportation:** General.

Contact. E-mail: info@ohiotechnicalcollege.com
Phone: (216) 881-1700 Toll-free number: (800) 322-7000
Fax: (216) 881-9145
Tom King, President, Ohio Technical College, 1374 East 51st Street, Cleveland, OH 44103-1269

Ohio Valley College of Technology

East Liverpool, Ohio
www.ovct.edu **CB code: 5852**

- For-profit 2-year business and technical college
- Commuter campus in large town
- Interview required

General. Founded in 1886. Accredited by ACICS. **Enrollment:** 147 degree-seeking undergraduates. **Degrees:** 67 associate awarded. **Location:** 30 miles from Youngstown, 35 miles from Pittsburgh. **Calendar:** Semester, extensive summer session. **Full-time faculty:** 4 total. **Part-time faculty:** 7 total.

Student profile. Among degree-seeking undergraduates, 42 enrolled as first-time, first-year students.

Part-time:	10%	**Women:**	86%
Out-of-state:	13%	**25 or older:**	75%

Basis for selection. CPAt scores most important.

2008-2009 Annual costs. Tuition/fees: $8,185.

Financial aid. All financial aid based on need. Need-based aid available for part-time students.

Application procedures. Admission: No deadline. $95 fee. Admission notification on a rolling basis. **Financial aid:** Priority date 10/1; no closing date. FAFSA required. Applicants notified on a rolling basis; must reply within 6 week(s) of notification.

Academics. Special study options: Double major, internships. **Credit/placement by examination:** CLEP, institutional tests. **Support services:** Reduced course load, remedial instruction.

Majors. Business: General, accounting, administrative services, office/clerical. **Computer sciences:** General, data processing. **Health:** Dental assistant, medical assistant, medical secretary.

Computing on campus. 20 workstations in computer center.

Student life. Activities: Student government.

Student services. Student employment services, personal counseling, placement for graduates. **Transfer:** Transfer adviser for students transferring to 4-year colleges.

Contact. E-mail: info@ovct.edu
Phone: (330) 385-1070 Fax: (330) 385-4606
Scott Rogers, Director of Admissions, Ohio Valley College of Technology, 16808 St. Clair Avenue, PO Box 7000, East Liverpool, OH 43920

Owens Community College: Toledo

Toledo, Ohio
www.owens.edu **CB code: 1643**

- Public 2-year community college
- Commuter campus in large city

General. Founded in 1966. Regionally accredited. Branch campus in Findlay. **Enrollment:** 9,636 degree-seeking undergraduates; 11,650 non-degree-seeking students. **Degrees:** 1,199 associate awarded. **ROTC:** Army, Air Force. **Location:** 6 miles from downtown. **Calendar:** Semester, limited summer session. **Full-time faculty:** 206 total; 15% have terminal degrees, 6% minority, 52% women. **Part-time faculty:** 1,420 total; 7% have terminal degrees, 8% minority, 53% women. **Class size:** 77% < 20, 21% 20-39, less than 1% 40-49, less than 1% 50-99, less than 1% >100.

Student profile. Among degree-seeking undergraduates, 3,630 enrolled as first-time, first-year students, 130 transferred in from other institutions.

Part-time:	52%	**Asian American:**	1%
Out-of-state:	3%	**Hispanic American:**	5%
Women:	63%	**International:**	4%
African American:	13%	**25 or older:**	45%

Transfer out. Colleges most students transferred to 2008: Bowling Green State University, Lourdes College, University of Findlay, University of Toledo.

Basis for selection. Open admission, but selective for some programs. Admission to health technologies, Peace Officer Academy, and early childhood education requires high school transcripts and test scores. ACT required for select health technology programs.

High school preparation. 19 units recommended. Recommended units include English 4, science 3 (laboratory 3).

2008-2009 Annual costs. Tuition/fees: $2,972; $5,552 out-of-state. Per-credit charge: $108 in-state; $323 out-of-state. Books/supplies: $1,400. Personal expenses: $1,458.

2008-2009 Financial aid. Need-based: Average scholarship/grant was $5,452; average loan $3,199. 56% of total undergraduate aid awarded as scholarships/grants, 44% as loans/jobs. Need-based aid available for part-time students. Work-study available nights, weekends and for part-time students. **Non-need-based:** Scholarships awarded for academics, alumni affiliation, athletics, leadership, state residency. **Additional information:** Other types of financial aid available: federal family education loan program, private foundation loan (SCHELL).

Application procedures. Admission: No deadline. No application fee. Admission notification on a rolling basis. February 1 application deadline for dental hygiene and physical therapist assistant programs. **Financial aid:** Priority date 3/31; no closing date. FAFSA required. Applicants notified by 2/7.

Academics. Special study options: Cooperative education, distance learning, double major, dual enrollment of high school students, ESL, honors, independent study, internships, student-designed major, weekend college. License preparation in dental hygiene, nursing, paramedic, radiology, real estate. **Credit/placement by examination:** AP, CLEP, institutional tests. No limit placed upon number of credit hours student may obtain via proficiency exams as long as student has met graduation residency requirement. **Support services:** GED preparation and test center, learning center, preadmission summer program, reduced course load, remedial instruction, study skills assistance, tutoring, writing center.

Majors. Agriculture: Business, landscaping, mechanization. **Area/ethnic studies:** African-American, Canadian, women's. **Biology:** General, biotechnology. **Business:** General, accounting technology, banking/financial services, business admin, executive assistant, international, office management, operations, restaurant/food services, retailing. **Communications:** General. **Communications technology:** General, desktop publishing. **Computer sciences:** Applications programming, information technology. **Education:** General, early childhood, multi-level teacher. **Engineering:** General. **Engineering technology:** Architectural, architectural drafting, automotive, biomedical, computer, construction, electrical, electromechanical, environmental, hydraulics, industrial, manufacturing, mechanical, quality control, surveying. **Foreign languages:** General. **Health:** Dental hygiene, dietetics, health care admin, management/clinical assistant, massage therapy, medical radiologic technology/radiation therapy, medical records technology, medical secretary, nuclear medical technology, nursing (RN), occupational therapy assistant, physical therapy assistant, radiologic technology/medical imaging, sonography, surgical technology. **History:** General. **Math:** General. **Military:** General. **Physical sciences:** Chemistry. **Production:** Tool and die, welding. **Protective services:** Corrections, fire safety technology, firefighting, law enforcement admin, police science, security services. **Psychology:** General. **Public administration:** General, social work. **Social sciences:** Sociology. **Visual/performing arts:** Arts management, commercial photography, commercial/advertising art, dramatic, music history, music management, music performance. **Other:** Design/drafting, Fine art concentration, Gender studies.

Most popular majors. Business/marketing 26%, engineering/engineering technologies 10%, health sciences 35%, liberal arts 6%, security/protective services 8%.

Computing on campus. 1,345 workstations in library, computer center. Commuter students can connect to campus network. Online course registration, online library, helpline, wireless network available.

Student life. Freshman orientation: Available. Preregistration for classes offered. **Activities:** Jazz band, choral groups, dance, drama, international student organizations, literary magazine, music ensembles, student government, student newspaper, Bible study club, College Republicans, environmental club, Japanese club, ski club, students in free enterprise, Rotoract Club, Toastmasters.

Athletics. NJCAA. **Intercollegiate:** Baseball M, basketball, soccer, softball W, volleyball W. **Intramural:** Basketball, bowling, football (non-tackle), golf, skiing, softball, table tennis, tennis, volleyball, weight lifting. **Team name:** Express.

Student services. Adult student services, career counseling, services for economically disadvantaged, student employment services, financial aid counseling, health services, on-campus daycare, personal counseling, placement for graduates, veterans' counselor. **Physically disabled:** Services for visually, hearing impaired. **Transfer:** Pre-admission transcript evaluation for new students. Transfer adviser, college fairs on campus for students transferring to 4-year colleges.

Contact. Phone: (567) 661-7225 Toll-free number: (800) 466-9367 ext. 7777 Fax: (567) 661-7734
Jennifer Irelan, Director Enrollment Services, Owens Community College: Toledo, PO Box 10000, Toledo, OH 43699-1947

Remington College: Cleveland
Cleveland, Ohio
www.remingtoncollege.edu **CB code: 3154**

- For-profit 2-year technical and career college
- Very large city

General. Accredited by ACCSCT. **Location:** 8 miles from Cleveland. **Calendar:** Continuous.

Annual costs/financial aid. Associate degree programs annual tuition $19,500 plus $50 fees. 8-month diploma program full tuition $13,900 plus $50 fees. Tuition includes textbooks and supplies.

Contact. Phone: (216) 475-7520
Director of Recruitment, 14445 Broadway Avenue, Cleveland, OH 44125

Remington College: Cleveland West
North Olmsted, Ohio
www.remingtoncollege.edu/clevelandwest/ **CB code: 4200**

- For-profit 2-year technical and career college
- Large town

General. Accredited by ACCSCT. **Enrollment:** 350 undergraduates. **Degrees:** 35 associate awarded. **Location:** 10 miles from Cleveland. **Calendar:** Quarter. **Full-time faculty:** 15 total. **Part-time faculty:** 15 total.

Basis for selection. Open admission, but selective for some programs. Selective admissions to allied health programs.

2008-2009 Annual costs. Associate degree programs annual tuition $19,500 plus $50 fees. 8-month diploma program full tuition $13,900 plus $50 fees. Tuition includes textbooks and supplies.

Application procedures. Admission: No deadline. $50 fee.

Academics. Special study options: Internships. **Credit/placement by examination:** CLEP. **Support services:** GED test center, tutoring.

Majors. Business: Business admin. **Computer sciences:** Networking. **Protective services:** Criminal justice, law enforcement admin, police science.

Contact. Phone: (440) 777-2560
James Malley, Director of Admissions, Remington College: Cleveland West, 26350 Brookpark Road, North Olmsted, OH 44070

RETS Tech Center
Centerville, Ohio
www.retstechcenter.com **CB code: 1610**

- For-profit 2-year junior and technical college
- Commuter campus in large town

General. Founded in 1953. Accredited by ACCSCT. **Location:** 15 miles from Dayton. **Calendar:** Semester.

Annual costs/financial aid. Costs are charged per entire associate degree or diploma program and vary with specific program. Associate programs range from $17,015 to $24,785. Diploma programs range from $8,400 to $17,085. Books/supplies: $950. Personal expenses: $945. Need-based financial aid available to full-time and part-time students.

Contact. Phone: (937) 433-3410
Director, 555 East Alex Bell Road, Centerville, OH 45459-9627

Rosedale Bible College
Irwin, Ohio
www.rosedale.edu **CB code: 3936**

- Private 2-year Bible and junior college affiliated with Mennonite Church
- Residential campus in rural community

General. Accredited by ABHE. **Enrollment:** 67 degree-seeking undergraduates. **Degrees:** 17 associate awarded. **Location:** 20 miles from Columbus. **Calendar:** Semester. **Part-time faculty:** 10 total; 10% have terminal degrees, 20% women. **Class size:** 71% < 20, 29% 20-39.

Basis for selection. Loyal devotion to Christ most important. **Homeschooled:** Transcript of courses and grades required.

2008-2009 Annual costs. Tuition/fees: $7,175. Per-credit charge: $230. Room/board: $5,000. Books/supplies: $500.

Application procedures. Admission: No deadline. $50 fee. Admission notification on a rolling basis. **Financial aid:** FAFSA, institutional form required. Applicants notified on a rolling basis.

Academics. Special study options: Double major, dual enrollment of high school students, independent study, study abroad. **Credit/placement by examination:** CLEP. **Support services:** Reduced course load.

Majors. Theology: Bible.

Computing on campus. 12 workstations in library, computer center. Wireless network available.

Student life. Freshman orientation: Mandatory. Preregistration for classes offered. **Policies:** Religious observance required. **Housing:** Guaranteed on-campus for all undergraduates. Single-sex dorms, apartments available. **Activities:** Choral groups, drama, student government, student newspaper.

Athletics. Intramural: Basketball, soccer, table tennis, volleyball.

Student services. Chaplain/spiritual director, financial aid counseling, health services. **Transfer:** Pre-admission transcript evaluation for new students.

Contact. E-mail: admissions@rosedale.edu
Phone: (740) 857-1311 Fax: (877) 857-1312
Elizabeth Diller, Enrollment Services Coordinator, Rosedale Bible College, 2270 Rosedale Road, Irwin, OH 43029

Samuel Stephen College
Chillicothe, Ohio
www.samuelstephencollege.edu **CB code: 2468**

- For-profit 2-year business college
- Commuter campus in large town

General. Founded in 1962. Accredited by ACICS. **Location:** 45 miles from Columbus, 90 miles from Cincinnati. **Calendar:** Quarter.

Annual costs/financial aid. Tuition/fees (2008-2009): $9,590. Need-based financial aid available to full-time and part-time students.

Contact. Phone: (740) 774-6300
Admissions Representative, 1410 Industrial Drive, Chillicothe, OH 45601

School of Advertising Art
Kettering, Ohio
www.saacollege.com

- For-profit 2-year visual arts and technical college
- Commuter campus in small city
- Interview required

General. Accredited by ACCSCT. **Enrollment:** 143 degree-seeking undergraduates. **Degrees:** 47 associate awarded. **Location:** 5 miles from downtown. **Calendar:** Quarter. **Full-time faculty:** 8 total; 25% minority, 25% women. **Part-time faculty:** 2 total; 50% women. **Class size:** 100% 20-39.

Student profile.

Out-of-state:	2%	**25 or older:**	3%

Transfer out. Colleges most students transferred to 2008: Art Institute of Pittsburgh, Art Institute of Atlanta, Columbus College of Art and Design, American Inter-Continental University of London.

Basis for selection. Portfolio and creative potential most important. Portfolio of 8 to 12 pieces of own artwork required. Depending on GPA and attendance, personal essay and 2 letters of recommendation may be required. **Homeschooled:** Proof of completion of high school requirements required.

High school preparation. Recommended units include English 4. 3 art units recommended.

2009-2010 Annual costs. Tuition/fees (projected): $24,433. Per-credit charge: $350. Books/supplies: $1,380. Personal expenses: $500.

2007-2008 Financial aid. Need-based: 2% of total undergraduate aid awarded as scholarships/grants, 98% as loans/jobs. **Non-need-based:** Scholarships awarded for academics, art, leadership.

Application procedures. Admission: No deadline. No application fee. Admission notification on a rolling basis. Students may pay discounted enrollment fee of $50 (normal fee is $100) if they elect to enroll by January 1. Conditional acceptance notification given at time of portfolio review and remains pending until final high school transcripts received. **Financial aid:** No deadline. FAFSA required. Applicants notified on a rolling basis starting 4/1; must reply by 7/1 or within 1 week(s) of notification.

Academics. Credit/placement by examination: CLEP. **Support services:** Study skills assistance, tutoring.

Majors. Communications: Advertising. **Computer sciences:** Computer graphics, webmaster. **Visual/performing arts:** Commercial/advertising art.

Computing on campus. PC or laptop required. Student web hosting, wireless network available.

Student life. Freshman orientation: Mandatory. Four-hour session held on a Saturday in the spring. **Activities:** Student government.

Student services. Career counseling, financial aid counseling, personal counseling, placement for graduates. **Transfer:** Re-entry adviser, pre-admission transcript evaluation for new students. Transfer adviser for students transferring to 4-year colleges.

Contact. E-mail: keith@saacollege.com
Phone: (937) 294-0592 ext. 102 Toll-free number: (877) 300-9326 ext. 102
Fax: (937) 294-5869
Keith McPherson, Director of Admissions, School of Advertising Art, 1725 East David Road, Kettering, OH 45440-1612

Sinclair Community College
Dayton, Ohio **CB member**
www.sinclair.edu **CB code: 1720**

- Public 2-year community college
- Commuter campus in small city

General. Founded in 1887. Regionally accredited. Member of the League for Innovation. College offers both transfer and technical academic programs. **Enrollment:** 19,053 degree-seeking undergraduates; 4,206 non-degree-seeking students. **Degrees:** 1,683 associate awarded. **ROTC:** Army, Air Force. **Location:** 50 miles from Cincinnati, 80 miles from Columbus. **Calendar:** Quarter, extensive summer session. **Full-time faculty:** 480 total. **Part-time faculty:** 690 total. **Class size:** 54% < 20, 45% 20-39, less than 1% 40-49, less than 1% 50-99, less than 1% >100. **Special facilities:** Art galleries, theater, center for corporate and community events. **Partnerships:** Formal partnerships with eight area high schools.

Student profile. Among degree-seeking undergraduates, 3,698 enrolled as first-time, first-year students, 586 transferred in from other institutions.

Part-time:	57%	**Asian American:**	2%
Out-of-state:	2%	**Hispanic American:**	2%
Women:	58%	**Native American:**	1%
African American:	17%	**25 or older:**	47%

Transfer out. Colleges most students transferred to 2008: Wright State University, University of Cincinnati, University of Dayton, Capital University, Park College, Ohio State University.

Basis for selection. Open admission, but selective for some programs. Admission to allied health programs, paralegal program, tool and machining program, early childhood education all based on placement test scores and/or high school grades and specific program criteria. Interview required for some allied health programs.

2008-2009 Annual costs. Tuition/fees: $2,026; $3,308 out-of-district; $6,526 out-of-state. Per-credit charge: $42 in-district; $70 out-of-district; $142 out-of-state. Books/supplies: $810. Personal expenses: $2,000.

2008-2009 Financial aid. Need-based: Need-based aid available for part-time students. Work-study available nights, weekends and for part-time students. **Non-need-based:** Scholarships awarded for academics, athletics, state residency.

Application procedures. Admission: No deadline. $20 fee. Admission notification on a rolling basis. Closing dates for allied health programs vary by program. **Financial aid:** Priority date 5/1, closing date 8/1. FAFSA, institutional form required. Applicants notified on a rolling basis.

Academics. Special study options: Cooperative education, cross-registration, distance learning, dual enrollment of high school students, ESL, honors, independent study, internships, liberal arts/career combination, student-designed major. License preparation in aviation, dental hygiene, nursing, occupational therapy, paramedic, physical therapy, radiology, real estate. **Credit/placement by examination:** AP, CLEP, IB, institutional tests. 45 credit hours maximum toward associate degree. **Support services:** Learning center, pre-admission summer program, reduced course load, remedial instruction, study skills assistance, tutoring, writing center.

Majors. Architecture: Technology. **Area/ethnic studies:** African-American. **Biology:** General, biotechnology. **Business:** General, accounting, administrative services, banking/financial services, business admin, hospitality admin, labor relations, labor studies, logistics, purchasing, real estate, retailing, sales/distribution, tourism promotion, tourism/travel. **Communications:** General. **Computer sciences:** General, applications programming, webmaster. **Education:** Elementary, multiple handicapped, music, physical, secondary, special. **Engineering:** General. **Engineering technology:** Architectural, automotive, CAD/CADD, civil, drafting, electrical, electromechanical, environmental, manufacturing, mechanical, plastics, robotics, surveying. **Family/consumer sciences:** Child care, food/nutrition, institutional food production. **Foreign languages:** Sign language interpretation. **Health:** Dental hygiene, dietetic technician, EMT paramedic, health services, licensed practical nurse, massage therapy, medical radiologic technology/radiation therapy, medical records technology, mental health services, occupational therapy assistant, physical therapy assistant, radiologic technology/medical imaging, respiratory therapy assistant, respiratory therapy technology, surgical technology. **History:** General. **Legal studies:** Legal secretary, paralegal. **Liberal arts:** Arts/sciences. **Math:** General. **Mechanic/repair:** Automotive, heating/ac/refrig. **Parks/recreation:** Health/fitness. **Personal/culinary services:** Culinary arts. **Physical sciences:** Chemistry, geology, physics. **Production:** Tool and die. **Protective services:** Corrections, criminal justice, fire safety technology, police science. **Psychology:** General. **Public administration:** General, human services, social work. **Social sciences:** Geography, sociology, urban studies. **Transportation:** Aviation management. **Visual/performing arts:** General, commercial/advertising art, dance, dramatic, interior design, music history, music performance, studio arts, theater design.

Most popular majors. Business/marketing 17%, computer/information sciences 6%, engineering/engineering technologies 10%, health sciences 27%, liberal arts 12%, visual/performing arts 6%.

Computing on campus. 1,000 workstations in library, computer center, student center. Commuter students can connect to campus network. Online course registration, helpline available.

Student life. Freshman orientation: Mandatory. Required for degree and certificate-seeking students. **Activities:** Bands, choral groups, dance, drama, music ensembles, musical theater, opera, student government, student newspaper, African American cultural club, Native American cultural club, Latinos Unidos en Sinclair club, Phi Theta Kappa honorary club, Rowdy Tartan pep club, social issues club, Appalachian club, College Republican's club, international students' club, think tank.

Athletics. NJCAA. **Intercollegiate:** Baseball M, basketball, golf, tennis, volleyball W. **Team name:** Tartans.

Student services. Adult student services, alcohol/substance abuse counseling, chaplain/spiritual director, career counseling, services for economically disadvantaged, student employment services, financial aid counseling, personal counseling, placement for graduates, veterans' counselor, women's services. **Physically disabled:** Services for visually, speech, hearing impaired. **Transfer:** Pre-admission transcript evaluation for new students. Transfer adviser for students transferring to 4-year colleges.

Contact. E-mail: admit@sinclair.edu
Phone: (937) 512-3000 Toll-free number: (800) 315-3000
Fax: (937) 512-2393
Greg Potts, Director and Systems Manager for Outreach Services, Sinclair Community College, 444 West Third Street, Dayton, OH 45402-1460

Southeastern Business College: Jackson

Jackson, Ohio
www.southeasternbusinesscollege.com **CB code: 3264**

- For-profit 2-year business college
- Commuter campus in large town

General. Accredited by ACICS. **Calendar:** Quarter.

Annual costs/financial aid. Books/supplies: $1,200. Need-based financial aid available to full-time and part-time students.

Contact. Phone: (740) 286-1554
Director/Registrar, 504 McCarty Lane, Jackson, OH 45640

Southeastern Business College: Lancaster

Lancaster, Ohio
www.careersohio.com **CB code: 3263**

- For-profit 2-year business and technical college
- Residential campus in large town

General. Accredited by ACICS. **Location:** 25 miles from Columbus. **Calendar:** Quarter.

Annual costs/financial aid. Books/supplies: $1,380. Personal expenses: $2,460. Need-based financial aid available to full-time and part-time students.

Contact. Phone: (740) 687-6126
Admissions, 1522 Sheridan Drive, Lancaster, OH 43130-1303

Southeastern Business College: New Boston

New Boston, Ohio
www.southeasternbusinesscollege.com

- For-profit 2-year branch campus and business college
- Commuter campus in rural community

General. Accredited by ACICS. **Calendar:** Quarter.

Annual costs/financial aid. Need-based financial aid available to full-time and part-time students.

Contact. Phone: (740) 456-4124
Admissions Representative, 3879 Rhodes Avenue, New Boston, OH 45662

Southern State Community College

Hillsboro, Ohio
www.sscc.edu **CB code: 1752**

- Public 2-year community college
- Commuter campus in small town

General. Founded in 1975. Regionally accredited. **Enrollment:** 2,584 degree-seeking undergraduates. **Degrees:** 319 associate awarded. **Location:** 60 miles from Cincinnati, 55 miles from Columbus. **Calendar:** Quarter, limited summer session. **Full-time faculty:** 52 total; 17% have terminal degrees, 52% women. **Part-time faculty:** 96 total; 3% have terminal degrees, 52% women. **Class size:** 66% < 20, 32% 20-39, less than 1% 40-49, less than 1% 50-99.

Student profile. Among degree-seeking undergraduates, 51% enrolled in a transfer program, 49% enrolled in a vocational program, 804 enrolled as first-time, first-year students, 138 transferred in from other institutions.

Part-time:	44%	**Asian American:**	1%
Women:	72%	**Hispanic American:**	1%
African American:	1%	**25 or older:**	43%

Transfer out. 19% of students enrolled in the transfer program go on to 4-year colleges.

Basis for selection. Open admission, but selective for some programs. Special requirements for nursing, respiratory therapy, EMT programs. Interview required for nursing program. **Learning Disabled:** If modifications requested, appointment with Disabilities Service Coordinator required.

2008-2009 Annual costs. Tuition/fees: $3,390; $6,528 out-of-state. Per-credit charge: $81 in-state; $162 out-of-state. Books/supplies: $1,500.

2007-2008 Financial aid. Need-based: 57% of total undergraduate aid awarded as scholarships/grants, 43% as loans/jobs. Need-based aid available for part-time students. Work-study available for part-time students. **Non-need-based:** Scholarships awarded for academics, art, athletics, music/drama.

Application procedures. Admission: No deadline. No application fee. Admission notification on a rolling basis. **Financial aid:** Priority date 7/1, closing date 9/1. FAFSA, institutional form required. Applicants notified by 4/15; must reply within 2 week(s) of notification.

Academics. Special study options: Cross-registration, distance learning, dual enrollment of high school students, liberal arts/career combination, student-designed major. License preparation in nursing, paramedic, real estate. **Credit/placement by examination:** AP, CLEP, institutional tests. 45 credit hours maximum toward associate degree. **Support services:** GED preparation and test center, learning center, remedial instruction, study skills assistance, tutoring.

Majors. Agriculture: General. **Business:** General, accounting technology, administrative services, business admin, real estate. **Computer sciences:** Applications programming, programming, systems analysis. **Education:** Early childhood, teacher assistance. **Engineering technology:** CAD/CADD, computer systems, drafting, electrical. **Health:** EMT paramedic, medical assistant, nursing (RN), respiratory therapy technology, substance abuse counseling. **Liberal arts:** Arts/sciences. **Protective services:** Corrections, police science. **Public administration:** Human services.

Most popular majors. Business/marketing 21%, computer/information sciences 6%, health sciences 32%, liberal arts 26%.

Computing on campus. 375 workstations in library, computer center. Commuter students can connect to campus network. Online course registration, online library, helpline, wireless network available.

Student life. Freshman orientation: Mandatory. Preregistration for classes offered. **Activities:** Bands, choral groups, drama.

Athletics. Intercollegiate: Basketball, soccer M, softball W, volleyball W. **Team name:** Patriots.

Student services. Career counseling, student employment services, financial aid counseling, on-campus daycare, placement for graduates. **Physically disabled:** Services for visually, speech, hearing impaired. **Transfer:** Transfer adviser, college fairs on campus for students transferring to 4-year colleges.

Contact. E-mail: info@sscc.edu
Phone: (937) 393-3431 ext. 2607 Fax: (937) 393-6682
Wendy Johnson, Director of Admissions, Southern State Community College, 100 Hobart Drive, Hillsboro, OH 45133

Southwestern College: Dayton

Dayton, Ohio
www.swcollege.net **CB code: 2483**

- For-profit 2-year business college
- Commuter campus in small city

General. Accredited by ACICS. **Enrollment:** 800 degree-seeking undergraduates. **Degrees:** 29 associate awarded. **Calendar:** Quarter, extensive summer session. **Full-time faculty:** 20 total. **Part-time faculty:** 20 total. **Class size:** 76% < 20, 24% 20-39.

Basis for selection. Open admission. Applicants not holding high school diploma or GED must take Wonderlic exam.

2008-2009 Annual costs. Tuition/fees: $10,000. Books/supplies: $825.

Financial aid. All financial aid based on need. Need-based aid available for part-time students.

Application procedures. Admission: No deadline. No application fee. Admission notification on a rolling basis. **Financial aid:** No deadline. FAFSA required.

Academics. Special study options: Liberal arts/career combination. **Credit/placement by examination:** CLEP. **Support services:** GED preparation, tutoring.

Majors. Business: Business admin. **Computer sciences:** General. **Health:** Medical secretary. **Protective services:** Law enforcement admin.

Computing on campus. 44 workstations in library, computer center.

Student life. Freshman orientation: Mandatory.

Student services. Career counseling, financial aid counseling, on-campus daycare, personal counseling, placement for graduates.

Contact. Phone: (937) 224-0061
Bill Furlong, Director, Southwestern College: Dayton, 111 West 1st Street, Dayton, OH 45402

Southwestern College: Franklin

Franklin, Ohio
www.swcollege.net **CB code: 3268**

- For-profit 2-year technical and career college
- Large town

General. Accredited by ACICS. **Enrollment:** 280 degree-seeking undergraduates. **Degrees:** 25 associate awarded. **Calendar:** Quarter, extensive summer session. **Full-time faculty:** 5 total. **Part-time faculty:** 10 total.

Basis for selection. Open admission. **Homeschooled:** Interview required.

2008-2009 Annual costs. Tuition/fees: $10,825. Books/supplies: $750.

Application procedures. Admission: No deadline. $20 fee. Application must be submitted on paper. Admission notification on a rolling basis.

Academics. Credit/placement by examination: CLEP.

Majors. Business: Business admin, office technology. **Computer sciences:** General. **Health:** Medical secretary. **Protective services:** Law enforcement admin.

Student life. Activities: Student government, student newspaper.

Student services. Transfer: Re-entry adviser, pre-admission transcript evaluation for new students. Transfer adviser for students transferring to 4-year colleges.

Contact. E-mail: lpaletta@swcollege.net
Phone: (937) 746-6633 ext. 45103 Fax: (937) 746-6754
Laura Paletta, Director of Admissions, Southwestern College: Franklin, 201 East Second Street, Franklin, OH 45005

Southwestern College: Tri-County

Cincinnati, Ohio
www.swcollege.net **CB code: 2478**

- For-profit 2-year career college
- Small city
- Interview required

General. Accredited by ACICS. **Enrollment:** 668 degree-seeking undergraduates. **Degrees:** 25 associate awarded. **Calendar:** Quarter, extensive summer session. **Full-time faculty:** 28 total. **Part-time faculty:** 40 total.

Basis for selection. Open admission. **Homeschooled:** High school diploma or GED required. Non-high school graduates will be accepted if they pass the Ability-to-Benefit exam; must obtain GED prior to graduation from college.

2009-2010 Annual costs. Tuition/fees (projected): $11,400. Books/supplies: $900. Personal expenses: $1,701.

2007-2008 Financial aid. All financial aid based on need.

Application procedures. Admission: No deadline. $100 fee. Application must be submitted on paper. Admission notification on a rolling basis. **Financial aid:** No deadline. FAFSA required.

Academics. Credit/placement by examination: CLEP. **Support services:** GED preparation, tutoring.

Majors. Business: Business admin. **Health:** Medical assistant. **Protective services:** Law enforcement admin.

Computing on campus. Online library available.

Student life. Freshman orientation: Available.

Contact. E-mail: rkimble@swcollege.net
Phone: (513) 874-0432
Roy Kimble, Director of Admissions, Southwestern College: Tri-County, 149 Northland Boulevard, Cincinnati, OH 45246

Southwestern College: Vine Street Campus

Cincinnati, Ohio
www.swcollege.net **CB code: 3267**

- For-profit 2-year business and health science college
- Large city
- Interview required

General. Accredited by ACICS. **Enrollment:** 420 degree-seeking undergraduates. **Degrees:** 24 associate awarded. **Location:** Downtown. **Calendar:** Quarter, extensive summer session. **Full-time faculty:** 12 total; 50% have terminal degrees, 50% minority, 58% women. **Part-time faculty:** 8 total; 25% have terminal degrees, 25% minority, 38% women.

Transfer out. Colleges most students transferred to 2008: Southwestern College: Tri-County Campus.

Basis for selection. Open admission. **Homeschooled:** Interview required. Applicants without high school diploma or GED must pass an ATB exam. **Learning Disabled:** Recommend applicants with high school IEP to inform Education department, but not required.

2009-2010 Annual costs. Tuition/fees (projected): $10,600. Per-credit charge: $275. Books/supplies: $900. Personal expenses: $2,500.

Financial aid. All financial aid based on need. Need-based aid available for part-time students.

Application procedures. Admission: No deadline. $20 fee. **Financial aid:** FAFSA required.

Academics. Special study options: Independent study, internships. **Credit/placement by examination:** CLEP. **Support services:** GED preparation, remedial instruction, study skills assistance, tutoring.

Majors. Business: General. **Health:** Medical secretary. **Social sciences:** Criminology.

Most popular majors. Business/marketing 33%, health sciences 33%, social sciences 33%.

Computing on campus. 65 workstations in library, computer center. Online library available.

Student life. Freshman orientation: Mandatory.

Contact. Phone: (513) 421-3212 Fax: (513) 421-8325
Roy Kimble, Director of Admission, Southwestern College: Vine Street Campus, 632 Vine Street, Cincinnati, OH 45202

Stark State College of Technology

North Canton, Ohio
www.starkstate.edu **CB code: 1688**

- Public 2-year technical college
- Commuter campus in small city

General. Founded in 1970. Regionally accredited. **Enrollment:** 9,395 degree-seeking undergraduates. **Degrees:** 811 associate awarded. **Location:** 50 miles from Cleveland. **Calendar:** Semester, limited summer session. **Full-time faculty:** 146 total. **Part-time faculty:** 460 total.

Student profile.

Out-of-state:	1%	**25 or older:**	50%

Basis for selection. Open admission, but selective for some programs. Special requirements for allied health programs. **Learning Disabled:** All students should meet with disability services coordinator.

High school preparation. College-preparatory program recommended. Recommended units include English 4, mathematics 4, social studies 3, science 3 and foreign language 1.

2008-2009 Annual costs. Tuition/fees: $3,810; $5,610 out-of-state. Per-credit charge: $103 in-state; $163 out-of-state. Books/supplies: $900.

Financial aid. All financial aid based on need. Need-based aid available for part-time students. Work-study available nights, weekends and for part-time students.

Application procedures. Admission: Priority date 6/1; no deadline. $65 fee. Admission notification on a rolling basis. **Financial aid:** Priority date 5/1; no closing date. FAFSA, institutional form required. Applicants notified on a rolling basis starting 4/1; must reply within 4 week(s) of notification.

Academics. Special study options: Accelerated study, cooperative education, cross-registration, distance learning, double major, dual enrollment of high school students, independent study, internships, liberal arts/career combination, student-designed major, weekend college. License preparation in dental hygiene, nursing, paramedic. **Credit/placement by examination:** CLEP, institutional tests. 12 credit hours maximum toward associate degree. **Support services:** Learning center, pre-admission summer program, reduced course load, remedial instruction, study skills assistance, tutoring, writing center.

Majors. Architecture: Environmental design, urban/community planning. **Business:** General, accounting, accounting technology, accounting/business management, accounting/finance, administrative services, business admin, communications, construction management, e-commerce, executive assistant, hospitality admin, international, logistics, management information systems, market research, marketing, office management, office technology, operations, sales/distribution, taxation. **Computer sciences:** General, applications programming, computer graphics, computer science, data entry, data processing, database management, information systems, information technology, networking, programming, security, systems analysis, web page design, webmaster, word processing. **Conservation:** Environmental studies. **Education:** Early childhood. **Engineering:** Architectural, civil, electrical, environmental, software. **Engineering technology:** Architectural, civil, construction, electrical, manufacturing, surveying. **Family/consumer sciences:** Aging. **Health:** Clinical lab assistant, clinical lab technology, dental hygiene, massage therapy, medical assistant, medical records technology, nursing (RN), occupational therapy assistant, office assistant, physical therapy assistant, respiratory therapy assistant, respiratory therapy technology. **Legal studies:** Court reporting, legal secretary. **Liberal arts:** Arts/sciences. **Math:** General. **Mechanic/repair:** Automotive, electronics/electrical, heating/ac/refrig, industrial. **Protective services:** Firefighting. **Public administration:** Human services. **Social sciences:** General.

Computing on campus. 500 workstations in computer center, student center. Commuter students can connect to campus network. Online course registration, helpline, wireless network available.

Student life. Freshman orientation: Available. Preregistration for classes offered. Half-day prior to all semesters. Evening sessions are 2 hours. **Activities:** Literary magazine, student newspaper, Bible study group, Minority Awareness Association, Phi Theta Kappa.

Athletics. Team name: Spartans.

Student services. Adult student services, chaplain/spiritual director, career counseling, services for economically disadvantaged, student employment services, financial aid counseling, minority student services, on-campus daycare, personal counseling, placement for graduates, veterans' counselor. **Physically disabled:** Services for visually, speech, hearing impaired. **Learning disabled:** Comprehensive services available. **Transfer:** Pre-admission transcript evaluation for new students. Transfer adviser, college fairs on campus for students transferring to 4-year colleges.

Contact. E-mail: info@starkstate.edu
Phone: (330) 494-6170 ext. 4228 Toll-free number: (800) 797-8275
Fax: (330) 497-6313
Wallace Hoffer, Dean of Student Services, Stark State College of Technology, 6200 Frank Avenue NW, North Canton, OH 44720

Stautzenberger College

Maumee, Ohio
www.sctoday.edu **CB code: 2487**

- For-profit 2-year business and technical college
- Commuter campus in large city
- Interview required

General. Founded in 1928. Accredited by ACICS. **Enrollment:** 850 degree-seeking undergraduates. **Degrees:** 120 associate awarded. **Location:** 50 miles from Detroit, 120 miles from Cleveland. **Calendar:** Quarter, extensive summer session. **Full-time faculty:** 8 total. **Part-time faculty:** 60 total. **Class size:** 85% < 20, 15% 20-39. **Special facilities:** Veterinary technician labs, medical assisting labs, massage therapy clinic. **Partnerships:** Formal partnership with Microsoft IT Academy.

Basis for selection. Open admission. Campus visit and completion of Program Questionaire required. **Learning Disabled:** Any special accommodations must be requested in writing with appropriate documentation. Approval needed before acceptance.

2008-2009 Annual costs. Tuition ranges from $210 to $375 per credit hour; required fees, $270. Books/supplies: $1,050. Personal expenses: $2,619.

Financial aid. All financial aid based on need. Need-based aid available for part-time students.

Application procedures. Admission: No deadline. $25 fee. Application must be submitted on paper. Admission notification on a rolling basis. **Financial aid:** No deadline. FAFSA required. Applicants notified on a rolling basis.

Academics. Special study options: Distance learning, double major, internships, weekend college. License preparation in real estate. **Credit/placement by examination:** CLEP. **Support services:** Learning center, study skills assistance, tutoring.

Majors. Business: Accounting technology, entrepreneurial studies, office technology. **Computer sciences:** Data entry, LAN/WAN management, web page design. **Health:** Insurance coding, massage therapy, medical assistant, medical secretary, medical transcription, receptionist, veterinary technology/assistant. **Legal studies:** Court reporting, paralegal. **Other:** Personal fitness trainer.

Computing on campus. 200 workstations in library, computer center.

Student life. Freshman orientation: Available.

Student services. Financial aid counseling, placement for graduates, veterans' counselor. **Transfer:** Pre-admission transcript evaluation for new students.

Contact. E-mail: admissions@stautzenberger.com
Phone: (419) 866-0261 Toll-free number: (800) 552-5099
Fax: (419) 867-9821
Karen Fitzgerald, Director of Admission, Stautzenberger College, 1796 Indian Wood Circle, Maumee, OH 43537

Stautzenberger College: Strongsville
Brecksville, Ohio
www.LearnWhatYouLove.com

- For-profit 2-year career college
- Large town
- Interview required

General. Accredited by ACICS. **Enrollment:** 399 degree-seeking undergraduates. **Degrees:** 33 associate awarded. **Location:** 15 miles from Cleveland. **Calendar:** Quarter, extensive summer session. **Full-time faculty:** 8 total; 88% have terminal degrees, 75% women. **Part-time faculty:** 33 total. **Class size:** 77% < 20, 23% 20-39.

Transfer out. Colleges most students transferred to 2008: Cuyahoga Community College, Stautzenberger College Toledo, Lorain County Community College.

Basis for selection. Open admission. **Homeschooled:** Interview required.

2008-2009 Annual costs. Tuition/fees: $9,540. Per-credit charge: $210. Books/supplies: $300.

2007-2008 Financial aid. All financial aid based on need. 41% of total undergraduate aid awarded as scholarships/grants, 59% as loans/jobs. Need-based aid available for part-time students.

Application procedures. Admission: No deadline. $25 fee. Admission notification on a rolling basis. **Financial aid:** No deadline. FAFSA required. Applicants notified on a rolling basis.

Academics. Special study options: Internships. **Credit/placement by examination:** CLEP. **Support services:** Reduced course load, study skills assistance, tutoring.

Majors. Health: Veterinary technology/assistant. **Legal studies:** Paralegal.

Computing on campus. Online library, wireless network available.

Student life. Freshman orientation: Mandatory.

Student services. Transfer: Pre-admission transcript evaluation for new students.

Contact. E-mail: rsgreen@LearnWhatYouLove.com
Phone: (440) 838-0960
Carlee Polisena, Director of Admissions, Stautzenberger College: Strongsville, 8001 Katherine Boulevard, Brecksville, OH 44141

Technology Education College
Columbus, Ohio
www.teccollege.com **CB code: 3035**

- For-profit 2-year health science, technical and career college
- Commuter campus in very large city
- Application essay, interview required

General. Accredited by ACCSCT. **Enrollment:** 250 degree-seeking undergraduates. **Degrees:** 100 associate awarded. **Calendar:** Quarter, extensive summer session. **Full-time faculty:** 25 total. **Part-time faculty:** 10 total.

Basis for selection. Open admission.

2008-2009 Annual costs. Tuition varies per program, but averages $11,952 per academic year.

Financial aid. All financial aid based on need. Need-based aid available for part-time students. Work-study available nights.

Application procedures. Admission: No deadline. $20 fee. Admission notification on a rolling basis. **Financial aid:** No deadline. FAFSA, institutional form required. Applicants notified on a rolling basis.

Academics. Credit/placement by examination: CLEP. **Support services:** GED preparation, learning center, study skills assistance, tutoring.

Majors. Engineering technology: CAD/CADD. **Health:** Medical assistant. **Protective services:** Police science.

Computing on campus. 100 workstations in library, computer center, student center. Online library, helpline available.

Student life. Freshman orientation: Mandatory.

Student services. Career counseling, student employment services, financial aid counseling, personal counseling, placement for graduates.

Contact. Phone: (614) 456-4600 Toll-free number: (800) 838-3233
Fax: (614) 456-4640
Chris Brown, Director of Admissions, Technology Education College, 2745 Winchester Pike, Columbus, OH 43232

Terra State Community College
Fremont, Ohio
www.terra.edu **CB code: 0365**

- Public 2-year community and technical college
- Commuter campus in large town

General. Founded in 1968. Regionally accredited. **Enrollment:** 2,464 degree-seeking undergraduates. **Degrees:** 229 associate awarded. **Location:** 33 miles from Toledo, 86 miles from Columbus. **Calendar:** Semester, limited summer session. **Full-time faculty:** 50 total. **Part-time faculty:** 150 total.

Transfer out. Colleges most students transferred to 2008: Bowling Green State University, University of Toledo, Owens Community College, Ohio State University, Tiffin University.

Basis for selection. Open admission.

High school preparation. Recommended units include English 4, mathematics 3, social studies 3 and science 3. Algebra recommended for engineering and computer programming applicants.

2008-2009 Annual costs. Tuition/fees: $3,610; $5,657 out-of-state. Per-credit charge: $108 in-state; $176 out-of-state. Books/supplies: $1,350. Personal expenses: $890.

Financial aid. Need-based: Need-based aid available for part-time students. Work-study available for part-time students. **Non-need-based:** Scholarships awarded for academics.

Application procedures. Admission: No deadline. No application fee. Admission notification on a rolling basis. **Financial aid:** Priority date 5/1;

no closing date. FAFSA, institutional form required. Applicants notified on a rolling basis starting 5/15.

Academics. Special study options: Accelerated study, cooperative education, distance learning, double major, dual enrollment of high school students, honors, independent study, internships, student-designed major, study abroad, weekend college. Bachelor's degree programs available on campus. License preparation in real estate. **Credit/placement by examination:** AP, CLEP, institutional tests. **Support services:** GED test center, learning center, reduced course load, remedial instruction, study skills assistance, tutoring, writing center.

Majors. Biology: General. **Business:** General, accounting, administrative services, business admin, finance, marketing, office management, office/clerical, real estate. **Communications:** General. **Computer sciences:** General, computer graphics, information systems, programming. **Education:** General, early childhood. **Engineering:** Mechanical, polymer. **Engineering technology:** Architectural, construction, drafting, electrical, manufacturing, plastics, robotics, surveying. **Foreign languages:** Comparative lit, sign language interpretation. **Health:** Medical secretary. **Interdisciplinary:** Natural sciences. **Liberal arts:** Arts/sciences. **Mechanic/repair:** Automotive, heating/ac/refrig. **Physical sciences:** Chemistry, physics. **Production:** Machine tool, welding. **Protective services:** Police science. **Visual/performing arts:** Commercial/advertising art.

Computing on campus. 299 workstations in library, computer center. Online course registration, online library available.

Student life. Freshman orientation: Mandatory, $16 fee. **Activities:** Jazz band, choral groups, music ensembles, student government, Phi Theta Kappa, Koinonia, Society of Plastic Engineers.

Athletics. NJCAA. **Intramural:** Basketball, bowling, football (non-tackle) M, softball, table tennis, tennis, volleyball. **Team name:** Thunder-Cats.

Student services. Career counseling, student employment services, on-campus daycare, placement for graduates, veterans' counselor. **Physically disabled:** Services for visually, speech, hearing impaired. **Transfer:** Re-entry adviser, pre-admission transcript evaluation for new students. Transfer center, transfer adviser, college fairs on campus for students transferring to 4-year colleges.

Contact. E-mail: admissions@terra.edu
Phone: (419) 559-2349 Toll-free number: (866) 288-3772 ext. 2349
Fax: (419) 334-9035
Terra State Community College, 2830 Napoleon Road, Fremont, OH 43420-9600

Tri-State College
North Lima, Ohio
www.tristatecollege.edu

- For-profit 2-year health science and community college
- Small city

General. Regionally accredited; also accredited by ACCSCT. **Enrollment:** 40 degree-seeking undergraduates. **Calendar:** Semester. **Full-time faculty:** 2 total. **Part-time faculty:** 8 total.

Basis for selection. Open admission.

Application procedures. Admission: No deadline.

Academics. Credit/placement by examination: CLEP.

Majors. Health: Massage therapy.

Contact. E-mail: diane@tristatecollege.edu
Phone: (330) 629-9998
Emily Schaff, Admissions Administrative Assistant, Tri-State College, 9159 Market Street, Suite 26, North Lima, OH 44452

Trumbull Business College
Warren, Ohio
www.tbc-trumbullbusiness.com **CB code: 3270**

- For-profit 2-year business college
- Commuter campus in large town

General. Accredited by ACICS. **Enrollment:** 322 degree-seeking undergraduates. **Degrees:** 72 associate awarded. **Calendar:** Quarter.

Basis for selection. Open admission. **Homeschooled:** Transcript of courses and grades required.

2008-2009 Annual costs. Tuition/fees: $12,171. Per-credit charge: $252.

Financial aid. Need-based: Need-based aid available for part-time students.

Application procedures. Admission: No deadline. $75 fee. Admission notification on a rolling basis. **Financial aid:** FAFSA required.

Academics. Credit/placement by examination: AP, CLEP.

Majors. Business: Accounting, business admin, office technology. **Computer sciences:** General, applications programming. **Health:** Medical assistant, medical secretary.

Computing on campus. 100 workstations in library, computer center.

Student life. Freshman orientation: Mandatory.

Student services. Career counseling, financial aid counseling, placement for graduates.

Contact. E-mail: admissions@tbc-trumbullbusiness.com
Phone: (330) 369-3200
Shawn Swaney, Director of Admissions, Trumbull Business College, 3200 Ridge Road, Warren, OH 44484

University of Akron: Wayne College
Orrville, Ohio
www.wayne.uakron.edu **CB code: 1892**

- Public 2-year branch campus and junior college
- Commuter campus in small town

General. Founded in 1972. Regionally accredited. **Enrollment:** 1,700 degree-seeking undergraduates. **Degrees:** 91 associate awarded. **ROTC:** Army, Air Force. **Location:** 35 miles from Akron. **Calendar:** Semester, limited summer session. **Full-time faculty:** 29 total. **Part-time faculty:** 118 total. **Class size:** 65% < 20, 31% 20-39, 3% 40-49, less than 1% 50-99. **Special facilities:** Nature trail, arboretum, wetlands, mock hazardous spill facility, distance learning room.

Transfer out. Colleges most students transferred to 2008: Ashland University, Kent State, Cleveland State, Ohio State, Ohio University.

Basis for selection. Open admission. **Adult students:** SAT/ACT scores not required if applicant over 21. **Homeschooled:** Recommend completion of GED.

High school preparation. Recommended units include English 4, mathematics 3, social studies 3, science 3 and foreign language 2.

2008-2009 Annual costs. Tuition/fees: $5,331; $12,854 out-of-state. Books/supplies: $600. Personal expenses: $1,465.

Financial aid. Need-based: Need-based aid available for part-time students. Work-study available nights and weekends. **Non-need-based:** Scholarships awarded for academics, art, athletics, leadership, minority status, music/drama, state residency. **Additional information:** All financial aid processed through University of Akron.

Application procedures. Admission: No deadline. $30 fee, may be waived for applicants with need. Admission notification on a rolling basis. **Financial aid:** Closing date 3/15. FAFSA, institutional form required. Applicants notified on a rolling basis starting 4/15.

Academics. First 2 years of general bachelor's degree classes available for students who plan to continue at University of Akron or other colleges and universities. Paraprofessional and technical programs (associates and certificates) available in business, industry, public services occupation areas. **Special study options:** Cooperative education, cross-registration, distance learning, dual enrollment of high school students, honors, independent study, internships, liberal arts/career combination, student-designed major, weekend college. **Credit/placement by examination:** AP, CLEP, institutional tests. **Support services:** Learning center, remedial instruction, study skills assistance, tutoring, writing center.

Majors. Business: General, accounting, administrative services, business admin, management information systems, marketing, office management, office technology. **Computer sciences:** Applications programming, data processing, networking. **Health:** Environmental health, health care admin, medical assistant, medical radiologic technology/radiation therapy, medical secretary, respiratory therapy technology, surgical technology. **Legal studies:**

Legal secretary. **Liberal arts:** Arts/sciences. **Public administration:** Social work.

Most popular majors. Business/marketing 57%, health sciences 6%, liberal arts 20%, security/protective services 13%.

Computing on campus. 140 workstations in library, computer center, student center. Commuter students can connect to campus network. Online course registration, helpline available.

Student life. **Freshman orientation:** Mandatory. **Activities:** Literary magazine, student government, student newspaper.

Athletics. NJCAA. **Intercollegiate:** Basketball, cheerleading M, golf M, volleyball W. **Intramural:** Basketball, racquetball, volleyball W. **Team name:** Warriors.

Student services. Adult student services, career counseling, student employment services, financial aid counseling, personal counseling, placement for graduates, veterans' counselor. **Physically disabled:** Services for visually, speech, hearing impaired. **Learning disabled:** Comprehensive services available. **Transfer:** Pre-admission transcript evaluation for new students. Transfer adviser, college fairs on campus for students transferring to 4-year colleges.

Contact. E-mail: wayneadmissions@uakron.edu
Phone: (330) 683-2010 Toll-free number: (800) 221-8308 ext. 8900
Fax: (330) 684-8989
Alicia Broadus, Coordinator of Admissions, University of Akron: Wayne College, 1901 Smucker Road, Orrville, OH 44667-9758

University of Cincinnati: Clermont College

Batavia, Ohio
www.ucclermont.edu **CB code: 3073**

- Public 2-year branch campus college
- Commuter campus in small town

General. Founded in 1972. Regionally accredited. College serves Clermont, Brown, and eastern Hamilton counties. One of 2 open-access regional campuses of the University of Cincinnati. **Enrollment:** 2,886 degree-seeking undergraduates; 355 non-degree-seeking students. **Degrees:** 281 associate awarded. **ROTC:** Army. **Location:** 17 miles from Cincinnati. **Calendar:** Quarter, limited summer session. **Full-time faculty:** 66 total; 36% have terminal degrees, 11% minority, 53% women. **Part-time faculty:** 146 total. **Partnerships:** Formal partnerships with Barnes Aerospace, Tech Prep Consortium.

Student profile. Among degree-seeking undergraduates, 788 enrolled as first-time, first-year students.

Part-time:	34%	**Asian American:**	1%
Out-of-state:	1%	**Hispanic American:**	1%
Women:	59%	**International:**	1%
African American:	2%	**25 or older:**	35%

Transfer out. **Colleges most students transferred to 2008:** Northern Kentucky University, University of Cincinnati, Wilmington College.

Basis for selection. Open admission, but selective for some programs. **Homeschooled:** All existing school records and formal documentation of high school curriculum required. Course content descriptions, copy of superintendent release form, notarized statement from parent, and precollege curriculum form completed and signed by parent may also be required. Appointment involving student, teacher, and admissions representative may be encouraged.

High school preparation. 16 units recommended. Recommended units include English 4, mathematics 3, social studies 2, science 2, foreign language 2 and academic electives 2. 1 fine arts recommended.

2008-2009 Annual costs. Tuition/fees: $4,542; $11,394 out-of-state. Per-credit charge: $127 in-state; $317 out-of-state.

2008-2009 Financial aid. **Need-based:** Need-based aid available for part-time students. Work-study available nights, weekends and for part-time students. **Non-need-based:** Scholarships awarded for academics, state residency. **Additional information:** All financial aid applications and awards administered through Uptown campus except in-house loans and scholarships.

Application procedures. **Admission:** No deadline. $40 fee, may be waived for applicants with need. Admission notification on a rolling basis. **Financial aid:** No deadline. FAFSA required. Applicants notified on a rolling basis.

Academics. **Special study options:** Cooperative education, cross-registration, distance learning, double major, dual enrollment of high school students, honors, independent study, internships, student-designed major, study abroad, weekend college. Bachelor's degree programs available on campus. License preparation in aviation, nursing, paramedic, real estate. **Credit/placement by examination:** AP, CLEP, IB, institutional tests. 50% of hours needed for degree may be earned by examination. **Support services:** GED test center, learning center, reduced course load, remedial instruction, study skills assistance, tutoring.

Majors. **Architecture:** Urban/community planning. **Biology:** General. **Business:** General, accounting technology, administrative services, business admin, office management, office technology. **Communications:** Digital media. **Computer sciences:** General, applications programming, computer graphics, data entry, data processing, information technology, networking, programming, vendor certification, web page design. **Education:** Early childhood, elementary, kindergarten/preschool, middle, secondary. **Engineering technology:** CAD/CADD, computer systems. **Health:** EMT ambulance attendant, EMT paramedic, nursing (RN), predental, premedicine, prenursing, prepharmacy, preveterinary, respiratory therapy technology, surgical technology. **Legal studies:** Legal secretary, paralegal, prelaw. **Liberal arts:** Arts/sciences. **Physical sciences:** Chemistry. **Protective services:** Corrections, criminal justice, forensics, law enforcement admin, security services. **Psychology:** General. **Public administration:** Social work. **Social sciences:** Urban studies. **Transportation:** Aviation, flight instructor.

Most popular majors. Business/marketing 28%, education 13%, health sciences 9%, legal studies 9%, liberal arts 11%, security/protective services 10%.

Computing on campus. 77 workstations in library, computer center, student center. Commuter students can connect to campus network. Online course registration, online library, helpline, wireless network available.

Student life. **Freshman orientation:** Mandatory. Preregistration for classes offered. Programs held each quarter for 2-3 hours. **Activities:** Campus ministries, dance, student government, student newspaper, student tribunal, Christian Fellowship, foreign language club, Young Democrats, Circle K (Kiwanis).

Athletics. USCAA. **Intercollegiate:** Basketball, cheerleading M, golf M, softball W, tennis, volleyball W. **Intramural:** Volleyball. **Team name:** Cougars.

Student services. Alcohol/substance abuse counseling, chaplain/spiritual director, career counseling, services for economically disadvantaged, student employment services, financial aid counseling, personal counseling, placement for graduates, veterans' counselor, women's services. **Physically disabled:** Services for visually, speech, hearing impaired. **Transfer:** Transfer adviser, college fairs on campus for students transferring to 4-year colleges.

Contact. E-mail: clc.admissions@uc.edu
Phone: (513) 732-5294 Toll-free number: (866) 446-2822
Fax: (513) 732-5303
John Fisher, Director of Enrollment Services, University of Cincinnati: Clermont College, 4200 Clermont College Drive, Batavia, OH 45103

University of Cincinnati: Raymond Walters College

Cincinnati, Ohio
www.rwc.uc.edu **CB code: 0354**

- Public 2-year branch campus college
- Commuter campus in large city

General. Founded in 1967. Regionally accredited. **Enrollment:** 3,859 degree-seeking undergraduates. **Degrees:** 13 bachelor's, 451 associate awarded. **ROTC:** Army, Naval, Air Force. **Location:** 15 miles from downtown. **Calendar:** Quarter, limited summer session. **Full-time faculty:** 155 total. **Part-time faculty:** 151 total. **Class size:** 41% < 20, 58% 20-39, less than 1% 40-49, less than 1% 50-99. **Partnerships:** Formal partnerships with GEAE Sharonville, Ford, GM, Ethicon Blue Ash, Soft Skills & IT Training, Ford, Sara Lee, 30 small companies.

Transfer out. **Colleges most students transferred to 2008:** University of Cincinnati, Xavier University, Northern Kentucky University, College of Mount St. Joseph.

Basis for selection. Open admission, but selective for some programs. Most health programs require lab science in biology and chemistry with grade of C or higher within the last 6 years. SAT/ACT required for high school seniors applying to nursing and dental hygiene. TOEFL or ability to benefit test required of non-native English speakers for placement. **Homeschooled:** Students should have 17 ACT or 870 SAT (exclusive of Writing), copy of curriculum, and high school transcript.

High school preparation. Recommended units include English 4, mathematics 3, social studies 2, history 2, science 2 and foreign language 2.

2008-2009 Annual costs. Tuition/fees: $5,232; $13,566 out-of-state. Per-credit charge: $146 in-state; $377 out-of-state. Books/supplies: $700.

Financial aid. All financial aid based on need. Need-based aid available for part-time students. Work-study available for part-time students. **Additional information:** All financial aid applications and awards administered through main campus.

Application procedures. **Admission:** No deadline. $40 fee, may be waived for applicants with need. Admission notification on a rolling basis. **Financial aid:** Priority date 3/15; no closing date. FAFSA required. Applicants notified on a rolling basis starting 3/15; must reply within 2 week(s) of notification.

Academics. **Special study options:** Accelerated study, cooperative education, cross-registration, distance learning, double major, dual enrollment of high school students, independent study, internships, liberal arts/career combination, student-designed major, study abroad, teacher certification program, weekend college. Bachelor's degree programs available on campus. License preparation in dental hygiene, nursing, paramedic, radiology, real estate. **Credit/placement by examination:** AP, CLEP, IB, institutional tests. Students must complete at least 45 credits at school to receive degree. CLEP credit by evaluation and credit by portfolio may be available. **Support services:** Learning center, pre-admission summer program, reduced course load, remedial instruction, study skills assistance, tutoring, writing center.

Majors. **Biology:** General. **Business:** General, accounting technology, administrative services, business admin, executive assistant, financial planning, office/clerical, real estate, sales/distribution. **Communications:** General, digital media. **Communications technology:** Graphics. **Computer sciences:** General, computer graphics, information technology, web page design, webmaster. **Education:** General, early childhood, elementary, middle, secondary. **Family/consumer sciences:** Food/nutrition. **Health:** Clinical nutrition, community health, dental hygiene, dietetics, EMT paramedic, health services, insurance specialist, medical radiologic technology/radiation therapy, medical secretary, medical transcription, nuclear medical technology, nursing (RN), office assistant, predental, premedicine, prepharmacy, preveterinary, radiation protection, radiologic technology/medical imaging, veterinary technology/assistant, vocational rehab counseling. **Interdisciplinary:** Nutrition sciences. **Legal studies:** Legal secretary, prelaw. **Liberal arts:** Arts/sciences. **Mechanic/repair:** Automotive, computer. **Personal/culinary services:** Mortuary science. **Physical sciences:** Chemistry. **Protective services:** Criminal justice. **Public administration:** Social work. **Science technology:** Biological, chemical. **Social sciences:** Economics, urban studies. **Visual/performing arts:** Design, graphic design.

Most popular majors. Business/marketing 18%, computer/information sciences 16%, education 6%, health sciences 39%.

Computing on campus. 275 workstations in computer center. Commuter students can connect to campus network. Online course registration, online library, helpline available.

Student life. **Freshman orientation:** Available, $30 fee. Preregistration for classes offered. One-day program. **Policies:** Student organization members must be in good academic standing. **Activities:** Student government, student newspaper, campus ministry, international student club.

Athletics. **Intramural:** Golf.

Student services. Adult student services, career counseling, student employment services, financial aid counseling, minority student services, on-campus daycare, placement for graduates. **Physically disabled:** Services for visually, hearing impaired. **Transfer:** Pre-admission transcript evaluation for new students. College fairs on campus for students transferring to 4-year colleges.

Contact. Phone: (513) 745-5700 Fax: (513) 745-5768
Chris Powers, Director, Enrollment Services, University of Cincinnati: Raymond Walters College, 9555 Plainfield Road, Cincinnati, OH 45236-1096

University of Northwestern Ohio

Lima, Ohio
www.unoh.edu **CB code: 0816**

- Private 2-year business and technical college
- Residential campus in large town

General. Founded in 1920. Regionally accredited. **Enrollment:** 3,616 degree-seeking undergraduates. **Degrees:** 74 bachelor's, 640 associate awarded. **Location:** 75 miles from Toledo, 90 miles from Columbus. **Calendar:** Differs by program, extensive summer session. **Full-time faculty:** 93 total. **Part-time faculty:** 44 total.

Student profile.

Out-of-state:	21%	**Live on campus:**	65%
25 or older:	18%		

Transfer out. **Colleges most students transferred to 2008:** Lima Technical College, Ohio State University, Wright State University, Bowling Green State University.

Basis for selection. Students with 1.5 GPA or lower admitted conditionally. **Homeschooled:** Statement describing homeschool structure and mission required. **Learning Disabled:** Students must self-disclose personal needs and provide IEP.

2008-2009 Annual costs. Tuition/fees: $9,063. Per-credit charge: $195. $245 per credit hour charge for virtual classes. Room only: $2,700. Books/supplies: $1,798. Personal expenses: $1,818.

2007-2008 Financial aid. **Need-based:** 36% of total undergraduate aid awarded as scholarships/grants, 64% as loans/jobs. Need-based aid available for part-time students. Work-study available nights and for part-time students. **Non-need-based:** Scholarships awarded for academics, job skills, minority status.

Application procedures. **Admission:** No deadline. $50 fee. Admission notification on a rolling basis. **Financial aid:** Priority date 4/1; no closing date. FAFSA required. Applicants notified on a rolling basis starting 4/30; must reply within 2 week(s) of notification.

Academics. Students wanting credit for life experience must register for 1-hour course in portfolio development. **Special study options:** Accelerated study, cooperative education, distance learning, double major, weekend college. Bachelor's degree programs available on campus. **Credit/placement by examination:** AP, CLEP, institutional tests. 25 credit hours maximum toward associate degree. **Support services:** Learning center, remedial instruction, tutoring.

Majors. **Agriculture:** Business. **Business:** Accounting, administrative services, business admin, marketing, office technology, tourism/travel. **Computer sciences:** General, applications programming. **Health:** Medical assistant, medical secretary, pharmacy assistant. **Legal studies:** Legal secretary, paralegal. **Mechanic/repair:** Automotive, diesel, heating/ac/refrig.

Most popular majors. Business/marketing 6%, trade and industry 73%.

Computing on campus. 212 workstations in library, computer center, student center. Commuter students can connect to campus network. Online course registration available.

Student life. **Freshman orientation:** Available. Held 4 to 6 weeks before quarter or session begins. **Housing:** Guaranteed on-campus for all undergraduates. Single-sex dorms, special housing for disabled, apartments, wellness housing available. $100 deposit. **Activities:** Student government, student newspaper, TV station.

Athletics. **Intramural:** Bowling, volleyball.

Student services. Adult student services, career counseling, student employment services, financial aid counseling, minority student services, personal counseling, placement for graduates, veterans' counselor. **Physically disabled:** Services for visually, hearing impaired. **Transfer:** Pre-admission transcript evaluation for new students.

Contact. E-mail: info@unoh.edu
Phone: (419) 998-3120 Fax: (419) 229-6926
Rick Morrison, Director of Admissions, University of Northwestern Ohio, 1441 North Cable Road, Lima, OH 45805

Vatterott College: Cleveland

Broadview Heights, Ohio
www.vatterott-college.edu

- For-profit 2-year technical college
- Commuter campus in large town

General. Accredited by ACCSCT. **Enrollment:** 243 degree-seeking undergraduates. **Degrees:** 47 associate awarded. **Calendar:** Semester. **Full-time faculty:** 13 total. **Part-time faculty:** 4 total.

Basis for selection. Open admission.

2008-2009 Annual costs. Program cost ranges: $18,400 to $19,600 (certificate/diploma); $32,250 (associate degree). Books/supplies: $1,877.

2008-2009 Financial aid. Need-based: 35% of total undergraduate aid awarded as scholarships/grants, 65% as loans/jobs.

Application procedures. Admission: No deadline. No application fee. **Financial aid:** No deadline.

Academics. Credit/placement by examination: CLEP.

Majors. Computer sciences: System admin. **Construction:** Building inspection.

Contact. E-mail: cleveland@vatterott-college.edu
Phone: (440) 526-1660 Toll-free number: (800) 864-5644
Fax: (440) 526-1933
Karen Fisher, Director of Admissions, Vatterott College: Cleveland, 5025 East Royalton Road, Broadview Heights, OH 44147

Virginia Marti College of Art and Design

Lakewood, Ohio
www.vmcad.edu **CB code: 0396**

- For-profit 2-year visual arts and business college
- Commuter campus in large city
- Application essay, interview required

General. Founded in 1966. Accredited by ACCSCT. **Enrollment:** 260 undergraduates. **Degrees:** 83 associate awarded. **Location:** 7 miles from Cleveland. **Calendar:** Quarter, extensive summer session. **Full-time faculty:** 10 total. **Part-time faculty:** 52 total.

Basis for selection. School achievement record, admission test scores and interview considered. Essay questions and letter of recommendation reviewed. Career Ability Placement Survey (CAPS) required for admission. Portfolio recommended for graphic design, interior design, digital media and fashion design majors; in lieu of portfolio, preliminary art courses required in first quarter. **Homeschooled:** Transcript of courses and grades required. **Learning Disabled:** Provide high school IEP for review of special needs.

2008-2009 Annual costs. Tuition/fees: $19,215. Per-credit charge: $345. Books/supplies: $1,800. Personal expenses: $1,746.

Financial aid. All financial aid based on need.

Application procedures. Admission: No deadline. $50 fee. Admission notification on a rolling basis. **Financial aid:** No deadline. FAFSA required. Applicants notified on a rolling basis.

Academics. Special study options: Dual enrollment of high school students, independent study, internships, study abroad. **Credit/placement by examination:** CLEP, institutional tests. **Support services:** Remedial instruction, study skills assistance, tutoring.

Majors. Business: Fashion. **Computer sciences:** Computer science. **Visual/performing arts:** Art, art history/conservation, commercial/advertising art, design, fashion design, illustration, interior design, photography.

Computing on campus. 28 workstations in library, computer center. Commuter students can connect to campus network. Online course registration, wireless network available.

Student life. Freshman orientation: Mandatory. Two-four hour program held 1 week prior to start of classes. **Policies:** Students participate in yearly fashion shows; competitions; trips to New York, France, and Italy. **Activities:** Student government, Student chapters of American Institute of Graphic Artists, Fashion Group International, American Society of Interior Designers.

Student services. Career counseling, student employment services, placement for graduates, veterans' counselor. **Transfer:** Pre-admission transcript evaluation for new students. Transfer adviser for students transferring to 4-year colleges.

Contact. E-mail: qmarti@vmcad.edu
Phone: (216) 221-8584 ext. 106 Toll-free number: (800) 473-4350
Quinn Marti, Director of Admissions, Virginia Marti College of Art and Design, 11724 Detroit Avenue, Lakewood, OH 44107

Washington State Community College

Marietta, Ohio
www.wscc.edu **CB code: 0381**

- Public 2-year community college
- Commuter campus in large town

General. Founded in 1971. Regionally accredited. **Enrollment:** 2,096 degree-seeking undergraduates. **Degrees:** 304 associate awarded. **Location:** 112 miles from Columbus. **Calendar:** Quarter, limited summer session. **Full-time faculty:** 61 total. **Part-time faculty:** 116 total.

Student profile.

Out-of-state:	12%	**25 or older:**	46%

Basis for selection. Open admission, but selective for some programs. Special requirements for medical laboratory technology, nursing, physical therapist assistant, radiology, respiratory therapy programs. ACT required for nursing, radiologic technology programs. 3/28 scores submission deadline for nursing program. Interview required for programs with selective admission.

2008-2009 Annual costs. Tuition/fees: $3,555; $6,975 out-of-state. Per-credit charge: $76 in-state; $152 out-of-state. Books/supplies: $705. Personal expenses: $4,145.

Application procedures. Admission: No deadline. No application fee. Admission notification on a rolling basis. **Financial aid:** No deadline. FAFSA, institutional form required. Applicants notified on a rolling basis starting 5/15; must reply within 2 week(s) of notification.

Academics. Special study options: Distance learning, double major, dual enrollment of high school students, independent study, internships, student-designed major. License preparation in nursing, radiology. **Credit/placement by examination:** CLEP, institutional tests. 60 credit hours maximum toward associate degree. **Support services:** Learning center, pre-admission summer program, reduced course load, remedial instruction, tutoring.

Majors. Business: General, accounting, business admin, e-commerce, marketing. **Communications:** Broadcast journalism, media studies. **Communications technology:** Animation/special effects. **Computer sciences:** Computer graphics, data processing, programming. **Education:** General, elementary, multi-level teacher, secondary. **Engineering:** General, electrical. **Engineering technology:** Drafting, electrical. **Health:** Clinical lab assistant, medical radiologic technology/radiation therapy, medical transcription, nursing (RN), physical therapy assistant, respiratory therapy technology. **Interdisciplinary:** Natural sciences. **Liberal arts:** Arts/sciences. **Math:** General. **Mechanic/repair:** Automotive, diesel, heating/ac/refrig. **Protective services:** Corrections, law enforcement admin. **Public administration:** Human services. **Science technology:** Biological.

Student life. Freshman orientation: Available. Preregistration for classes offered. **Activities:** Choral groups, music ensembles, student government, student newspaper, veterans club, Phi Theta Kappa honor fraternity.

Student services. Adult student services, career counseling, student employment services, financial aid counseling, personal counseling, placement for graduates, veterans' counselor. **Physically disabled:** Services for visually, hearing impaired. **Transfer:** Transfer adviser, college fairs on campus for students transferring to 4-year colleges.

Contact. E-mail: admissions@wscc.edu
Phone: (740) 568-1900 Fax: (740) 373-7496
Kristen Meeks, Assistant Director of Admissions, Washington State Community College, 710 Colegate Drive, Marietta, OH 45750

Wright State University: Lake Campus

Celina, Ohio
www.wright.edu/lake **CB code: 1947**

- Public 2-year branch campus college
- Commuter campus in small town

General. Founded in 1969. Regionally accredited. **Enrollment:** 653 degree-seeking undergraduates; 312 non-degree-seeking students. **Degrees:** 59 associate awarded. **Location:** 70 miles from Dayton. **Calendar:** Quarter, limited summer session. **Full-time faculty:** 25 total; 76% women. **Part-time faculty:** 50 total. **Class size:** 76% < 20, 24% 20-39.

Student profile. Among degree-seeking undergraduates, 6% enrolled in a transfer program, 2% already have a bachelor's degree or higher, 169 enrolled as first-time, first-year students, 46 transferred in from other institutions.

Part-time:	23%	**Hispanic American:**	1%
Women:	62%	**Native American:**	1%
African American:	2%	**25 or older:**	17%
Asian American:	1%		

Basis for selection. Open admission, but selective for some programs. Special requirements for engineering and education programs. SAT/ACT required for all students but only used for placement in selective programs.

High school preparation. 16 units recommended. Recommended units include English 4, mathematics 3, social studies 3, science 3 (laboratory 3) and foreign language 2. One unit of art recommended.

2008-2009 Annual costs. Tuition/fees: $4,893; $11,619 out-of-state. Per-credit charge: $148 in-state; $354 out-of-state.

2007-2008 Financial aid. Need-based: 99 full-time freshmen applied for aid; 81 were judged to have need; 80 of these received aid. Average need met was 64%. Average scholarship/grant was $3,932; average loan $3,215. 31% of total undergraduate aid awarded as scholarships/grants, 69% as loans/jobs. Need-based aid available for part-time students. Work-study available nights, weekends and for part-time students. **Non-need-based:** Awarded to 64 full-time undergraduates, including 21 freshmen. Scholarships awarded for academics, alumni affiliation, art, athletics, leadership, minority status, music/drama, ROTC.

Application procedures. Admission: No deadline. $30 fee. Admission notification on a rolling basis. **Financial aid:** Priority date 2/15; no closing date. FAFSA required. Applicants notified on a rolling basis starting 3/15.

Academics. Bachelor's degrees awarded through main campus. **Special study options:** Cooperative education, cross-registration, distance learning, double major, dual enrollment of high school students, honors, independent study, internships, student-designed major. Bachelor's degree programs available on campus. **Credit/placement by examination:** CLEP, IB, institutional tests. **Support services:** Learning center, pre-admission summer program, reduced course load, remedial instruction, tutoring.

Majors. Biology: General. **Business:** General, business admin, management information systems. **Communications:** General. **Computer sciences:** Information systems. **Engineering technology:** General, drafting, manufacturing. **History:** General. **Liberal arts:** Arts/sciences. **Physical sciences:** Chemistry. **Psychology:** General. **Public administration:** Social work. **Social sciences:** Sociology.

Most popular majors. Business/marketing 32%, computer/information sciences 31%, liberal arts 7%, psychology 14%.

Computing on campus. 105 workstations in computer center. Commuter students can connect to campus network. Online course registration, online library, helpline, repair service, wireless network available.

Student life. Freshman orientation: Available. **Activities:** Drama, student government, student newspaper, Business Professionals of America, Student Manufacturing Engineers.

Athletics. NCAA. **Intercollegiate:** Basketball, golf M, volleyball W. **Team name:** Raiders.

Student services. Adult student services, career counseling, financial aid counseling, on-campus daycare, personal counseling, placement for graduates, veterans' counselor. **Physically disabled:** Services for visually, hearing impaired.

Contact. E-mail: discoverlakecampus@wright.edu
Phone: (419) 586-0324 Toll-free number: (800) 237-1477
Fax: (419) 586-0358
BJ Hobbler, Student Services Officer, Wright State University: Lake Campus, 7600 State Route 703, Celina, OH 45822-2952

Zane State College

Zanesville, Ohio
www.zanestate.edu **CB code: 1535**

- Public 2-year technical college
- Commuter campus in large town

General. Founded in 1969. Regionally accredited. **Enrollment:** 1,942 degree-seeking undergraduates; 269 non-degree-seeking students. **Degrees:** 362 associate awarded. **Location:** 60 miles from Columbus. **Calendar:** Quarter, limited summer session. **Full-time faculty:** 46 total. **Part-time faculty:** 101 total. **Special facilities:** Natural resource center.

Student profile. Among degree-seeking undergraduates, 10% enrolled in a transfer program, 465 enrolled as first-time, first-year students.

Part-time:	40%	**African American:**	4%
Women:	63%	**Native American:**	1%

Transfer out. Colleges most students transferred to 2008: Ohio University, Ohio State University, Muskingum College, Franklin University.

Basis for selection. Open admission, but selective for some programs. Special requirements for allied health programs.

High school preparation. 15 units recommended. Recommended units include English 4, mathematics 3, social studies 4 and science 4.

2008-2009 Annual costs. Tuition/fees: $3,825; $7,650 out-of-state. Per-credit charge: $75 in-state; $160 out-of-state. Books/supplies: $1,500.

Financial aid. Need-based: Need-based aid available for part-time students.

Application procedures. Admission: No deadline. $20 fee. Application must be submitted on paper. Admission notification on a rolling basis. **Financial aid:** Priority date 5/1, closing date 7/15. FAFSA required. Must reply by 9/1.

Academics. Special study options: Cross-registration, distance learning, dual enrollment of high school students, internships, student-designed major. **Credit/placement by examination:** AP, CLEP, institutional tests. All new freshmen must take assessment tests for English and math. **Support services:** Learning center, reduced course load, remedial instruction, study skills assistance, tutoring, writing center.

Majors. Business: Accounting, administrative services, business admin, marketing, sales/distribution. **Computer sciences:** General, computer science, information systems. **Conservation:** Management/policy. **Engineering technology:** Drafting, electrical. **Family/consumer sciences:** Child care. **Health:** Clinical lab technology, health services, medical assistant, medical radiologic technology/radiation therapy, occupational therapy assistant, physical therapy assistant. **Legal studies:** Paralegal. **Mechanic/repair:** Automotive. **Personal/culinary services:** Culinary arts. **Production:** Tool and die. **Public administration:** Social work.

Most popular majors. Business/marketing 40%, computer/information sciences 19%, engineering/engineering technologies 9%, health sciences 29%, parks/recreation 7%.

Computing on campus. Online library, wireless network available.

Student life. Freshman orientation: Mandatory. **Activities:** Student government.

Athletics. Intramural: Golf M.

Student services. Adult student services, career counseling, student employment services, financial aid counseling, personal counseling, placement for graduates, veterans' counselor. **Transfer:** Pre-admission transcript evaluation for new students. Transfer adviser for students transferring to 4-year colleges.

Contact. E-mail: pyoung@zanestate.edu
Phone: (740) 454-2501 ext. 1225 Toll-free number: (800) 686-8324 ext. 1226 Fax: (740) 454-0035
Paul Young, Director of Admissions, Zane State College, 1555 Newark Road, Zanesville, OH 43701-2626

Oklahoma

Carl Albert State College
Poteau, Oklahoma
www.carlalbert.edu **CB code: 1474**

- Public 2-year community and junior college
- Commuter campus in large town

General. Founded in 1932. Regionally accredited. **Enrollment:** 2,480 degree-seeking undergraduates. **Degrees:** 460 associate awarded. **Location:** 35 miles from Fort Smith, Arkansas. **Calendar:** Semester, limited summer session. **Full-time faculty:** 40 total. **Part-time faculty:** 8 total.

Transfer out. Colleges most students transferred to 2008: Northeastern State University, University of Arkansas, Southeastern State University, University of Central Oklahoma.

Basis for selection. Open admission, but selective for some programs. Nursing, radiographic technology, and physical therapy assistant programs employ selective enrollment.

High school preparation. 15 units recommended. Recommended units include English 4, mathematics 3, social studies 1, history 2, science 2 (laboratory 2) and academic electives 1. One social science unit should be in American history.

2008-2009 Annual costs. Tuition/fees: $2,250; $5,220 out-of-state. Per-credit charge: $51 in-state; $150 out-of-state. Room/board: $3,384. Books/supplies: $750. Personal expenses: $1,678.

Financial aid. All financial aid based on need. Need-based aid available for part-time students. Work-study available nights and for part-time students.

Application procedures. Admission: No deadline. No application fee. Admission notification on a rolling basis. **Financial aid:** No deadline. FAFSA, institutional form required. Applicants notified on a rolling basis.

Academics. Special study options: Distance learning, dual enrollment of high school students, honors, independent study, liberal arts/career combination. Bachelor's degree programs available on campus. License preparation in nursing, physical therapy, radiology. **Credit/placement by examination:** AP, CLEP, institutional tests. 18 credit hours maximum toward associate degree. **Support services:** GED test center, learning center, remedial instruction, study skills assistance, tutoring.

Majors. Biology: General, zoology. **Business:** General, accounting, administrative services, business admin. **Communications:** Journalism. **Computer sciences:** Computer science. **Education:** Elementary, secondary. **Health:** Nursing (RN), physical therapy assistant, premedicine, prepharmacy, preveterinary. **Legal studies:** Prelaw. **Math:** General. **Parks/recreation:** Health/fitness. **Protective services:** Criminal justice. **Psychology:** General. **Social sciences:** General, sociology. **Visual/performing arts:** Art, dramatic.

Most popular majors. Business/marketing 17%, education 19%, family/consumer sciences 8%, health sciences 23%, social sciences 13%.

Computing on campus. 50 workstations in library, computer center. Dormitories wired for high-speed internet access. Commuter students can connect to campus network. Online library available.

Student life. Freshman orientation: Mandatory. Preregistration for classes offered. One-day session held at beginning of semester offered online. **Housing:** Single-sex dorms available. Scholar's housing available. **Activities:** Choral groups, dance, drama, music ensembles, musical theater, radio station, student government, student newspaper, African-American awareness, American Indian student association, Young Democrats, Young Republicans.

Athletics. NJCAA. **Intercollegiate:** Baseball M, basketball M, cheerleading M. **Team name:** Vikings.

Student services. Chaplain/spiritual director, career counseling, services for economically disadvantaged, financial aid counseling, on-campus daycare, veterans' counselor. **Physically disabled:** Services for hearing impaired. **Transfer:** Pre-admission transcript evaluation for new students. Transfer adviser, college fairs on campus for students transferring to 4-year colleges.

Contact. E-mail: ddickerson@carlalbert.edu
Phone: (918) 647-1300 Fax: (918) 647-1306
Dee Ann Dickerson, Registrar, Carl Albert State College, 1507 South McKenna, Poteau, OK 74953-5208

Connors State College
Warner, Oklahoma
www.connorsstate.edu **CB code: 6117**

- Public 2-year community and junior college
- Commuter campus in rural community

General. Founded in 1908. Regionally accredited. Main campus in Warner. Branch campus in Muskogee. **Enrollment:** 1,747 degree-seeking undergraduates; 605 non-degree-seeking students. **Degrees:** 387 associate awarded. **Location:** 20 miles from Muskogee, 65 miles from Tulsa. **Calendar:** Semester, extensive summer session. **Full-time faculty:** 50 total. **Part-time faculty:** 60 total. **Class size:** 64% < 20, 32% 20-39, 3% 40-49, 1% 50-99. **Special facilities:** 1300 acre wetlands and nature preserve.

Student profile. Among degree-seeking undergraduates, 85% enrolled in a transfer program, 15% enrolled in a vocational program, 10% already have a bachelor's degree or higher, 581 enrolled as first-time, first-year students.

Part-time:	30%	**Hispanic American:**	2%
Out-of-state:	4%	**Native American:**	29%
Women:	70%	**25 or older:**	42%
African American:	11%	**Live on campus:**	10%

Transfer out. Colleges most students transferred to 2008: Northeastern State University, Oklahoma State University.

Basis for selection. Open admission, but selective for some programs. Special requirements for nursing and equine programs; interview required. **Adult students:** SAT/ACT scores not required if applicant over 21. Must complete secondary assessment. **Homeschooled:** The student's equivalent public high school class must have graduated; must take ACT; proficiency in subject area curricula required. **Learning Disabled:** Students with documented disabilities must complete designated paperwork in the office of the Vice President for Student Services.

High school preparation. Recommended units include English 4, mathematics 4, history 3, science 3 (laboratory 3), visual/performing arts 2 and academic electives 3.

2008-2009 Annual costs. Tuition/fees: $2,598; $6,225 out-of-state. Per-credit charge: $66 in-state; $187 out-of-state. Apartment-style housing. Room/board: $6,692. Books/supplies: $1,200.

2008-2009 Financial aid. Need-based: Need-based aid available for part-time students. **Non-need-based:** Scholarships awarded for academics, alumni affiliation, athletics, leadership, state residency.

Application procedures. Admission: No deadline. No application fee. Admission notification on a rolling basis. High school diploma required of applicants younger than 18. **Financial aid:** Priority date 2/28, closing date 5/1. FAFSA, institutional form required. Applicants notified on a rolling basis starting 4/1; must reply within 2 week(s) of notification.

Academics. Special study options: Distance learning, dual enrollment of high school students, internships, liberal arts/career combination. License preparation in nursing. **Credit/placement by examination:** AP, CLEP, institutional tests. 18 credit hours maximum toward associate degree. **Support services:** Learning center, remedial instruction, tutoring.

Majors. Agriculture: Equestrian studies. **Biology:** General. **Business:** General, accounting, business admin. **Communications:** General, journalism. **Computer sciences:** General, data processing. **Education:** General, early childhood, elementary, physical, secondary. **Engineering:** General. **Family/consumer sciences:** General, business, child care. **Health:** Nursing (RN), predental, premedicine, prepharmacy, preveterinary. **History:** General. **Interdisciplinary:** Math/computer science. **Legal studies:** Prelaw. **Liberal arts:** Arts/sciences. **Math:** General. **Physical sciences:** Chemistry, physics. **Protective services:** Police science. **Psychology:** General. **Public administration:** Social work. **Social sciences:** General, sociology. **Visual/performing arts:** Art, music history.

Computing on campus. 217 workstations in dormitories, library, computer center. Dormitories wired for high-speed internet access and linked to campus network. Online library, wireless network available.

Student life. **Freshman orientation:** Available. Preregistration for classes offered. **Housing:** Single-sex dorms, apartments, wellness housing available. $55 deposit. **Activities:** Drama, student government, student newspaper, Phi Theta Kappa, Mu Alpha Theta, Aggie club, black student society, Indian club, business club, English club, psychology club.

Athletics. NJCAA. **Intercollegiate:** Baseball M, basketball, rodeo, softball W. **Intramural:** Basketball, softball, tennis. **Team name:** Cowboys.

Student services. Career counseling, health services, on-campus daycare, personal counseling, veterans' counselor. **Transfer:** Pre-admission transcript evaluation for new students. College fairs on campus for students transferring to 4-year colleges.

Contact. Phone: (918) 463-2931 ext. 6300 Fax: (918) 463-6327
Ronald Ramming, Dean of Enrollment Services, Connors State College, RR 1, Box 1000, Warner, OK 74469-9700

Eastern Oklahoma State College

Wilburton, Oklahoma
www.eosc.edu **CB code: 6189**

- Public 2-year community college
- Commuter campus in small town

General. Founded in 1908. Regionally accredited. **Enrollment:** 1,589 degree-seeking undergraduates. **Degrees:** 290 associate awarded. **Location:** 90 miles from Tulsa. **Calendar:** Semester, limited summer session. **Full-time faculty:** 49 total. **Part-time faculty:** 55 total. **Class size:** 22% < 20, 61% 20-39, 16% 40-49, less than 1% 50-99, less than 1% >100. **Special facilities:** Oklahoma Miner Training Institute, Center for Correction Officer Studies.

Student profile.

Out-of-state:	2%	**Live on campus:**	20%
25 or older:	65%		

Transfer out. **Colleges most students transferred to 2008:** East Central State University, Northeastern State University, Southeastern Oklahoma State University.

Basis for selection. Open admission, but selective for some programs. Special requirements for nursing program; interview required.

High school preparation. 12 units recommended. Recommended units include English 4, mathematics 3, social studies 2 and science 2. 1 citizenship or government.

2008-2009 Annual costs. Tuition/fees: $2,835; $6,452 out-of-state. Per-credit charge: $68 in-state; $189 out-of-state. Room/board: $4,624. Books/supplies: $578. Personal expenses: $500.

2007-2008 Financial aid. All financial aid based on need. 70% of total undergraduate aid awarded as scholarships/grants, 30% as loans/jobs. Need-based aid available for part-time students.

Application procedures. **Admission:** No deadline. $10 fee. Admission notification on a rolling basis. **Financial aid:** Priority date 3/1; no closing date. FAFSA, institutional form required. Applicants notified on a rolling basis starting 5/1; must reply within 2 week(s) of notification.

Academics. **Special study options:** Cooperative education, distance learning, dual enrollment of high school students, honors, internships. License preparation in nursing. **Credit/placement by examination:** AP, CLEP, institutional tests. 30 credit hours maximum toward associate degree. **Support services:** Learning center, remedial instruction, tutoring.

Majors. **Agriculture:** General, agronomy, animal sciences, business, farm/ranch, food science, horticultural science, horticulture, ornamental horticulture, products processing, soil science. **Biology:** General, bacteriology, entomology. **Business:** General, accounting, administrative services, business admin, management information systems, office/clerical. **Communications:** Journalism. **Computer sciences:** General, computer science, programming, systems analysis. **Conservation:** General, environmental studies, forestry, wildlife. **Education:** Agricultural, art, biology, business, chemistry, computer, drama/dance, elementary, health, history, mathematics, music, physical, physics, science, secondary, social science, social studies, speech. **Engineering:** General. **Family/consumer sciences:** Child care. **Health:** Medical secretary, nursing (RN), predental, premedicine, prenursing, prepharmacy, preveterinary. **History:** General. **Interdisciplinary:** Biological/physical sciences. **Legal studies:** Legal secretary, prelaw. **Math:** General. **Parks/recreation:** Facilities management, health/fitness. **Physical sciences:** Chemistry, physics. **Protective services:** Criminal justice, law enforcement admin. **Psychology:** General. **Social sciences:** General, sociology. **Visual/performing arts:** Dramatic.

Most popular majors. Agriculture 18%, business/marketing 20%, education 6%, legal studies 8%, liberal arts 16%, psychology 16%.

Computing on campus. 250 workstations in dormitories, library, computer center. Dormitories linked to campus network. Commuter students can connect to campus network. Online library, helpline, wireless network available.

Student life. **Freshman orientation:** Mandatory, $12 fee. Preregistration for classes offered. **Housing:** Coed dorms, single-sex dorms, special housing for disabled, apartments available. $50 deposit, deadline 8/15. **Activities:** Choral groups, drama, music ensembles, musical theater, radio station, student government, student newspaper, campus religious organizations, Afro-American and Native American clubs, professional clubs.

Athletics. NJCAA. **Intercollegiate:** Baseball M, basketball, cheerleading, rodeo, softball W. **Intramural:** Basketball, handball, racquetball, softball, swimming, table tennis, tennis, volleyball. **Team name:** Mountaineers.

Student services. Adult student services, chaplain/spiritual director, career counseling, student employment services, financial aid counseling, personal counseling, placement for graduates, veterans' counselor. **Physically disabled:** Services for visually, speech, hearing impaired. **Transfer:** Pre-admission transcript evaluation for new students. Transfer adviser, college fairs on campus for students transferring to 4-year colleges.

Contact. Phone: (918) 465-2361 Fax: (918) 465-2431
Donna Rice, Registrar, Eastern Oklahoma State College, 1301 West Main Street, Wilburton, OK 74578-4999

Murray State College

Tishomingo, Oklahoma
www.mscok.edu **CB code: 6421**

- Public 2-year junior college
- Commuter campus in small town

General. Founded in 1908. Regionally accredited. **Enrollment:** 1,914 degree-seeking undergraduates; 305 non-degree-seeking students. **Degrees:** 398 associate awarded. **Location:** 32 miles from Ardmore. **Calendar:** Semester, limited summer session. **Full-time faculty:** 40 total. **Part-time faculty:** 45 total.

Student profile.

Part-time:	41%	**Women:**	69%

Basis for selection. Open admission, but selective for some programs. Special requirements for nursing and vet tech programs.

High school preparation. 15 units recommended. Recommended units include English 4, mathematics 3, social studies 1, history 2, science 2 (laboratory 2) and academic electives 3. Recommend 1 unit in citizenship.

2008-2009 Annual costs. Tuition/fees: $2,840; $6,650 out-of-state. Per-credit charge: $81 in-state; $208 out-of-state. Room/board: $5,100. Books/supplies: $600. Personal expenses: $1,984.

Application procedures. **Admission:** No deadline. No application fee. Admission notification on a rolling basis beginning on or about 4/15. **Financial aid:** Priority date 4/15; no closing date. Applicants notified on a rolling basis starting 5/1.

Academics. **Special study options:** Honors. License preparation in nursing. **Credit/placement by examination:** CLEP. **Support services:** Learning center, remedial instruction, tutoring.

Majors. **Business:** Administrative services, business admin. **Computer sciences:** General, computer science. **Education:** Elementary. **Family/consumer sciences:** Child care. **Health:** Preveterinary. **History:** General. **Interdisciplinary:** Behavioral sciences. **Liberal arts:** Arts/sciences. **Math:** General. **Visual/performing arts:** General.

Most popular majors. Business/marketing 11%, health sciences 22%, liberal arts 57%, social sciences 6%.

Computing on campus. Commuter students can connect to campus network. Helpline available.

Student life. **Freshman orientation:** Mandatory. **Housing:** Coed dorms available. $50 deposit. **Activities:** Drama, music ensembles, student government.

Athletics. NJCAA. **Intercollegiate:** Baseball M, basketball. **Intramural:** Baseball M, basketball. **Team name:** Aggies.

Student services. Career counseling, veterans' counselor. **Transfer:** College fairs on campus for students transferring to 4-year colleges.

Contact. Phone: (580) 371-2371 ext. 108 Fax: (580) 371-9844
Ann Beck, Registrar and Director of Admissions, Murray State College, One Murray Campus, Tishomingo, OK 73460

Northeastern Oklahoma Agricultural and Mechanical College

Miami, Oklahoma — **CB member**
www.neo.edu — **CB code: 6484**

- Public 2-year community and junior college
- Commuter campus in large town

General. Founded in 1919. Regionally accredited. Extension courses offered in neighboring towns and on the Internet. **Enrollment:** 1,698 degree-seeking undergraduates; 109 non-degree-seeking students. **Degrees:** 302 associate awarded. **ROTC:** Air Force. **Location:** 76 miles from Tulsa. **Calendar:** Semester, limited summer session. **Full-time faculty:** 71 total; 11% have terminal degrees, 11% minority, 56% women. **Part-time faculty:** 47 total; 15% minority, 53% women. **Class size:** 56% < 20, 42% 20-39, less than 1% 40-49, less than 1% 50-99. **Special facilities:** College farm, equine center, music hall, activity center.

Student profile. Among degree-seeking undergraduates, 70% enrolled in a transfer program, 30% enrolled in a vocational program, 1% already have a bachelor's degree or higher, 657 enrolled as first-time, first-year students, 177 transferred in from other institutions.

Part-time:	21%	**Hispanic American:**	2%
Out-of-state:	17%	**Native American:**	19%
Women:	59%	**International:**	2%
African American:	8%	**Live on campus:**	31%
Asian American:	1%		

Transfer out. Colleges most students transferred to 2008: Oklahoma State University, Missouri Southern State University, Pittsburg State University, Northeastern State University, Rogers State University.

Basis for selection. Open admission. **Adult students:** Students over the age of 21 must complete placement testing before enrolling in college level classes. **Homeschooled:** Transcript of courses and grades required.

High school preparation. 15 units recommended. Recommended units include English 4, mathematics 3, history 3, science 2 (laboratory 2) and academic electives 3. History and citizenship skills, including 1 unit of U.S. history and 2 additional units from the subjects of history, economics, geography, government, or non-Western culture.

2008-2009 Annual costs. Tuition/fees: $2,442; $6,263 out-of-state. Per-credit charge: $58 in-state; $185 out-of-state. Room/board: $3,858. Books/supplies: $800. Personal expenses: $1,000.

2007-2008 Financial aid. Need-based: Need-based aid available for part-time students. Work-study available nights, weekends and for part-time students. **Non-need-based:** Scholarships awarded for academics, art, athletics, leadership, music/drama, state residency.

Application procedures. Admission: No deadline. No application fee. Admission notification on a rolling basis. **Financial aid:** Priority date 4/1; no closing date. FAFSA required. Applicants notified on a rolling basis starting 4/1; must reply by 8/30 or within 2 week(s) of notification.

Academics. Special study options: Combined bachelor's/graduate degree, distance learning, double major, dual enrollment of high school students, independent study, internships. Bachelor's degree programs available on campus. License preparation in nursing, physical therapy. **Credit/placement by examination:** AP, CLEP, institutional tests. 36 credit hours maximum toward associate degree. **Support services:** GED preparation and test center, learning center, reduced course load, remedial instruction, study skills assistance, tutoring, writing center.

Majors. Agriculture: General, equestrian studies, farm/ranch. **Area/ethnic studies:** Native American. **Biology:** General. **Business:** Accounting, administrative services, business admin, marketing. **Communications:** Radio/tv. **Computer sciences:** General, programming. **Conservation:** Forestry. **Education:** Early childhood. **Engineering technology:** CAD/CADD. **Health:** Athletic training, clinical lab technology, medical secretary, nursing (RN), physical therapy assistant, predental, premedicine, prenursing, prepharmacy, preveterinary. **Legal studies:** Legal secretary. **Math:** General. **Parks/recreation:** Health/fitness. **Physical sciences:** General. **Protective services:** Criminal justice. **Psychology:** General. **Social sciences:** General. **Visual/performing arts:** Art, dramatic.

Most popular majors. Agriculture 14%, business/marketing 8%, education 10%, health sciences 29%, liberal arts 17%, psychology 6%.

Computing on campus. 85 workstations in dormitories, library, computer center. Dormitories linked to campus network. Commuter students can connect to campus network. Online library, helpline, wireless network available.

Student life. Freshman orientation: Mandatory, $81 fee. Preregistration for classes offered. **Policies:** Single students under the age of 21 who reside more than 50 miles from campus are required to live on campus. **Housing:** Guaranteed on-campus for all undergraduates. Single-sex dorms, special housing for disabled, apartments, wellness housing available. $75 fully refundable deposit. **Activities:** Bands, choral groups, dance, drama, music ensembles, musical theater, student government, TV station, Ministerial Alliance, Baptist student union, Aggie Society, Collegiates for Christ, Young Democrats, Young Republicans, Phi Theta Kappa, Afro-American Society, Native American student association, Masquers.

Athletics. NJCAA. **Intercollegiate:** Baseball M, basketball, football (tackle) M, golf, rodeo, soccer, softball W, volleyball W. **Intramural:** Baseball, basketball, bowling, football (tackle) M, soccer, softball, swimming, volleyball. **Team name:** Norsemen.

Student services. Alcohol/substance abuse counseling, career counseling, services for economically disadvantaged, financial aid counseling, health services, personal counseling, veterans' counselor. **Physically disabled:** Services for visually, hearing impaired. **Transfer:** Transfer adviser, college fairs on campus for students transferring to 4-year colleges.

Contact. E-mail: neoadmission@neo.edu
Phone: (918) 540-6210 Toll-free number: (888) 464-6636
Fax: (918) 540-6946
Amy Ishmael, Vice President of Enrollment Management and Student Records, Northeastern Oklahoma Agricultural and Mechanical College, 200 I Street Northeast, Miami, OK 74354-6497

Northern Oklahoma College

Tonkawa, Oklahoma — **CB member**
www.north-ok.edu — **CB code: 6486**

- Public 2-year community college
- Commuter campus in small town

General. Founded in 1901. Regionally accredited. **Enrollment:** 3,804 degree-seeking undergraduates. **Degrees:** 546 associate awarded. **Location:** 90 miles from Oklahoma City; 70 miles from Wichita, Kansas. **Calendar:** Semester, limited summer session. **Full-time faculty:** 66 total. **Part-time faculty:** 94 total. **Special facilities:** Museum of science and history, observatory, arboretum.

Student profile.

Out-of-state:	1%	**Live on campus:**	17%

Transfer out. Colleges most students transferred to 2008: Oklahoma State University, Northwestern Oklahoma State University, Oklahoma University, University of Central Oklahoma.

Basis for selection. Open admission, but selective for out-of-state students. Out-of-state applicants must have high school diploma and rank in top half of class or have 19 ACT. ACT required for students under 21 years old for placement. Students with below 19 ACT in English, math, and reading must take placement tests. **Adult students:** Placement testing required.

High school preparation. High school units mandated by state law may vary with program.

2008-2009 Annual costs. Tuition/fees: $2,303; $5,813 out-of-state. Per-credit charge: $53 in-state; $170 out-of-state. Room/board: $3,790. Books/supplies: $600. Personal expenses: $1,200.

Financial aid. Need-based: Need-based aid available for part-time students.

Application procedures. Admission: No deadline. $25 fee. Application must be submitted on paper. Admission notification on a rolling basis. **Financial aid:** Priority date 6/1; no closing date. FAFSA, institutional form required. Applicants notified on a rolling basis starting 4/1.

Academics. Special study options: Distance learning, dual enrollment of high school students, honors, independent study, internships, liberal arts/

career combination. **Credit/placement by examination:** CLEP, institutional tests. 30 credit hours maximum toward associate degree. **Support services:** Learning center, remedial instruction, tutoring.

Majors. **Agriculture:** Agribusiness operations. **Area/ethnic studies:** Native American. **Biology:** General, zoology. **Business:** General, accounting, business admin, office management. **Communications:** Broadcast journalism, journalism, public relations. **Computer sciences:** General, web page design. **Education:** Elementary, physical, secondary. **Engineering technology:** Drafting. **Health:** Medical radiologic technology/radiation therapy, nursing (RN), premedicine, prepharmacy, respiratory therapy technology, surgical technology. **Legal studies:** Prelaw. **Liberal arts:** Arts/sciences. **Math:** General. **Physical sciences:** Chemistry, physics. **Protective services:** Law enforcement admin. **Social sciences:** General. **Visual/performing arts:** Art, music management.

Computing on campus. 200 workstations in dormitories, library, computer center. Dormitories wired for high-speed internet access and linked to campus network. Commuter students can connect to campus network. Online course registration, online library, student web hosting, wireless network available.

Student life. **Freshman orientation:** Mandatory. **Housing:** Single-sex dorms, apartments available. $60 deposit. **Activities:** Bands, choral groups, drama, literary magazine, music ensembles, musical theater, opera, radio station, student government, student newspaper, symphony orchestra, TV station.

Athletics. NJCAA. **Intercollegiate:** Baseball M, basketball, soccer, softball W. **Intramural:** Basketball, racquetball, softball, tennis, volleyball. **Team name:** Mavericks.

Student services. Career counseling, financial aid counseling, health services, personal counseling, veterans' counselor. **Physically disabled:** Services for visually, speech, hearing impaired. **Transfer:** College fairs on campus for students transferring to 4-year colleges.

Contact. E-mail: rick.edgington@north-ok.edu
Phone: (580) 628-6221 Toll-free number: (888) 429-5715
Fax: (580) 628-6371
Rick Edgington, Associate Vice President, Northern Oklahoma College, Box 310, Tonkawa, OK 74653-0310

Oklahoma City Community College

Oklahoma City, Oklahoma — **CB member**
www.occc.edu — **CB code: 0270**

- Public 2-year community college
- Commuter campus in large city

General. Founded in 1969. Regionally accredited. **Enrollment:** 11,027 degree-seeking undergraduates; 1,586 non-degree-seeking students. **Degrees:** 1,039 associate awarded. **Calendar:** Semester, extensive summer session. **Full-time faculty:** 148 total. **Part-time faculty:** 411 total. **Class size:** 33% < 20, 59% 20-39, 7% 40-49, less than 1% 50-99. **Special facilities:** Olympic-size swimming pool, diving well.

Student profile. Among degree-seeking undergraduates, 55% enrolled in a transfer program, 45% enrolled in a vocational program, 2% already have a bachelor's degree or higher, 2,397 enrolled as first-time, first-year students.

Part-time:	62%	**Hispanic American:**	8%
Out-of-state:	1%	**Native American:**	6%
Women:	58%	**International:**	4%
African American:	9%	**25 or older:**	41%
Asian American:	5%		

Transfer out. **Colleges most students transferred to 2008:** University of Central Oklahoma, University of Oklahoma-OU Health Science Center, Oklahoma State University, University of Oklahoma, Oklahoma City University.

Basis for selection. Open admission, but selective for some programs. Special requirements for nursing, occupational therapy and physical therapy programs; reading test required. **Homeschooled:** If under the age of 21, official high school transcript and ACT scores required.

High school preparation. 15 units recommended. Recommended units include English 4, mathematics 3, history 2, science 2 (laboratory 2), foreign language 3 and academic electives 1. History recommendation includes 1 unit of American history and 2 units of citizenship skills or other history.

2008-2009 Annual costs. Tuition/fees: $2,521; $6,721 out-of-state. Per-credit charge: $61 in-state; $201 out-of-state. Books/supplies: $1,500. Personal expenses: $700.

2007-2008 Financial aid. **Need-based:** 392 full-time freshmen applied for aid; 327 were judged to have need; 327 of these received aid. Average need met was 63%. Average scholarship/grant was $2,288; average loan $2,250. 57% of total undergraduate aid awarded as scholarships/grants, 43% as loans/jobs. Need-based aid available for part-time students. Work-study available nights, weekends and for part-time students. **Non-need-based:** Awarded to 1,377 full-time undergraduates, including 176 freshmen. Scholarships awarded for academics, alumni affiliation, art, leadership, music/drama, state residency.

Application procedures. **Admission:** No deadline. $25 fee, may be waived for applicants with need. Application must be submitted on paper. Admission notification on a rolling basis. **Financial aid:** Priority date 4/15; no closing date. FAFSA required. Applicants notified on a rolling basis starting 2/15.

Academics. **Special study options:** Accelerated study, distance learning, double major, dual enrollment of high school students, ESL, honors, independent study, internships, liberal arts/career combination, student-designed major, weekend college. License preparation in nursing, occupational therapy, paramedic, physical therapy, real estate. **Credit/placement by examination:** AP, CLEP, IB, institutional tests. 45 credit hours maximum toward associate degree. Credit will not be transcripted until 12 resident hours have been completed. **Support services:** GED preparation and test center, learning center, reduced course load, remedial instruction, study skills assistance, tutoring, writing center.

Majors. **Biology:** General, bioinformatics, biotechnology. **Business:** General, finance, office/clerical, real estate, tourism promotion, tourism/travel. **Communications:** Broadcast journalism, journalism. **Communications technology:** Desktop publishing, graphics, photo/film/video. **Computer sciences:** General, computer science, data processing, programming, security, systems analysis, web page design. **Education:** General, multi-level teacher, secondary. **Engineering:** General. **Engineering technology:** Drafting, electrical, manufacturing. **Family/consumer sciences:** Child care. **Foreign languages:** French, Spanish, translation. **Health:** EMT paramedic, nursing (RN), occupational therapy assistant, physical therapy assistant. **History:** General. **Legal studies:** Legal secretary, prelaw. **Liberal arts:** Arts/sciences. **Math:** General. **Mechanic/repair:** General. **Physical sciences:** Chemistry, physics. **Psychology:** General. **Social sciences:** Sociology. **Transportation:** Aviation. **Visual/performing arts:** Commercial/advertising art, studio arts, theater design.

Computing on campus. 2,000 workstations in library, computer center, student center. Commuter students can connect to campus network. Online course registration, online library, helpline, wireless network available.

Student life. **Freshman orientation:** Available. Preregistration for classes offered. Held the week prior to classes for 3 hours on days, evenings and weekends. **Activities:** Campus ministries, choral groups, drama, literary magazine, music ensembles, student government, student newspaper, Phi Theta Kappa, Chi Alpha, Christians on Campus, African-American student association, Asian cultural exchange, Native American cultural awareness organization, Young Democrats, deaf student association.

Athletics. **Intramural:** Baseball M, basketball, golf, soccer, softball, volleyball.

Student services. Career counseling, student employment services, financial aid counseling, on-campus daycare, personal counseling, placement for graduates, veterans' counselor. **Physically disabled:** Services for visually, speech, hearing impaired. **Transfer:** Transfer adviser, college fairs on campus for students transferring to 4-year colleges.

Contact. E-mail: admissions@occc.edu
Phone: (405) 682-6222 Fax: (405) 682-7817
Jon Horinek, Director of Recruitment and Admissions, Oklahoma City Community College, 7777 South May Avenue, Oklahoma City, OK 73159

Oklahoma State University Institute of Technology: Okmulgee

Okmulgee, Oklahoma
www.osuit.edu — **CB code: 3382**

- Public 2-year branch campus and technical college
- Commuter campus in large town

General. Founded in 1946. Regionally accredited. **Enrollment:** 2,100 degree-seeking undergraduates. **Degrees:** 57 bachelor's, 488 associate awarded. **Location:** 35 miles from Tulsa. **Calendar:** Trimester, extensive summer session. **Full-time faculty:** 130 total. **Part-time faculty:** 25 total.

Student profile.

Out-of-state:	9%	**Live on campus:**	35%
25 or older:	33%		

Basis for selection. Open admission, but selective for some programs. Special requirements for multimedia and engineering technologies programs.

High school preparation. Recommended units include English 4, mathematics 3, social studies 2, science 2, foreign language 3 and academic electives 1.

2008-2009 Annual costs. Tuition/fees: $3,705; $9,015 out-of-state. Per-credit charge: $92 in-state; $269 out-of-state. Room/board: $5,180. Books/supplies: $1,050.

2007-2008 Financial aid. Need-based: Need-based aid available for part-time students. Work-study available nights, weekends and for part-time students.

Application procedures. Admission: No deadline. $15 fee. Admission notification on a rolling basis. **Financial aid:** Priority date 4/1; no closing date. FAFSA, institutional form required. Applicants notified on a rolling basis.

Academics. Special study options: Cooperative education, distance learning, double major, dual enrollment of high school students, internships, liberal arts/career combination. Bachelor's degree programs available on campus. License preparation in nursing. **Credit/placement by examination:** AP, CLEP, institutional tests. **Support services:** Learning center, remedial instruction, tutoring.

Majors. Agriculture: Business. **Business:** General, accounting, administrative services, business admin, hospitality/recreation, management information systems. **Communications technology:** Graphic/printing. **Computer sciences:** General, applications programming, computer graphics, networking, programming. **Construction:** Electrician, maintenance, pipefitting, power transmission. **Education:** General. **Engineering:** Civil, electrical. **Engineering technology:** Biomedical, civil, construction, drafting, electrical, manufacturing. **Health:** Medical secretary, medical transcription, orthotics/prosthetics. **Legal studies:** Legal secretary. **Mechanic/repair:** Auto body, automotive, diesel, heating/ac/refrig, watch/jewelry. **Personal/culinary services:** Culinary arts. **Visual/performing arts:** Commercial/advertising art, photography.

Computing on campus. 50 workstations in dormitories, library, computer center. Dormitories wired for high-speed internet access and linked to campus network. Online library, helpline, repair service, wireless network available.

Student life. Freshman orientation: Available. **Housing:** Guaranteed on-campus for all undergraduates. Coed dorms, single-sex dorms, apartments available. $100 deposit. Housing for parents with dependent children available. **Activities:** Film society, student government, student newspaper, Baptist student union, black student society, Native American student association, Junior Ambassadors.

Athletics. NAIA. **Intercollegiate:** Rodeo. **Intramural:** Basketball, bowling, football (non-tackle), handball, racquetball, soccer, softball, table tennis, volleyball. **Team name:** Cowboys.

Student services. Alcohol/substance abuse counseling, career counseling, student employment services, financial aid counseling, health services, on-campus daycare, personal counseling, placement for graduates, veterans' counselor. **Physically disabled:** Services for visually, speech, hearing impaired. **Transfer:** Pre-admission transcript evaluation for new students. College fairs on campus for students transferring to 4-year colleges.

Contact. E-mail: admissions@okstate.edu
Phone: (918) 293-4680 Toll-free number: (800) 722-4471 ext. 4680
Fax: (918) 293-4643
Mary Graves, Director of Retention & Career Services, Oklahoma State University Institute of Technology: Okmulgee, 1801 East Fourth Street, Okmulgee, OK 74447-3901

Oklahoma State University: Oklahoma City

Oklahoma City, Oklahoma
www.osuokc.edu **CB code: 1436**

- Public 2-year branch campus and technical college
- Commuter campus in very large city

General. Founded in 1961. Regionally accredited. **Enrollment:** 5,742 degree-seeking undergraduates. **Degrees:** 188 associate awarded. **Location:** 5 miles from downtown. **Calendar:** Semester, extensive summer session. **Full-time faculty:** 71 total. **Part-time faculty:** 226 total. **Special facilities:** Horticulture center, precision driving training center, child development center, golf maintenance training facility, learning resource center, power transmission distribution pole yard.

Transfer out. Colleges most students transferred to 2008: University of Central Oklahoma, Oklahoma State University: Stillwater, University of Oklahoma.

Basis for selection. Open admission, but selective for some programs. Special requirements for nursing program and emergency responder bachelor program. Interviews required for nursing program.

High school preparation. 15 units recommended. Recommended units include English 4, mathematics 3, social studies 1, history 2, (laboratory 2) and academic electives 3.

2008-2009 Annual costs. Tuition/fees: $2,930; $7,790 out-of-state. Per-credit charge: $76 in-state; $238 out-of-state. Books/supplies: $1,080.

2007-2008 Financial aid. All financial aid based on need. Need-based aid available for part-time students.

Application procedures. Admission: No deadline. No application fee in-state; $15 out-of-state. Admission notification on a rolling basis. **Financial aid:** Priority date 7/15; no closing date. FAFSA required. Applicants notified on a rolling basis starting 8/1; must reply within 2 week(s) of notification.

Academics. Special study options: Cooperative education, distance learning, double major, dual enrollment of high school students, honors, independent study, liberal arts/career combination, weekend college. Fire/police/EMS training available. Bachelor's degree programs available on campus. License preparation in nursing, paramedic, radiology. **Credit/placement by examination:** CLEP, institutional tests. 30 credit hours maximum toward associate degree. Credit granted for Fundamentals of Nursing (6 hours), Adult Nursing (8 hours). **Support services:** GED preparation and test center, learning center, remedial instruction, study skills assistance, tutoring, writing center.

Majors. Agriculture: Horticulture, turf management. **Business:** Accounting technology, accounting/finance, business admin, construction management, management science, office technology. **Computer sciences:** Applications programming, computer graphics. **Education:** Bilingual. **Engineering technology:** General, architectural drafting, civil, construction, electrical. **Family/consumer sciences:** Child care. **Foreign languages:** Sign language interpretation, sign language linguistics. **Health:** Cardiovascular technology, EMT paramedic, environmental health, health care admin, health services, nursing (RN), radiologic technology/medical imaging, sonography, substance abuse counseling, veterinary technology/assistant. **Protective services:** Firefighting, police science. **Visual/performing arts:** Commercial/advertising art. **Other:** Emergency management, Power transmission distribution technology, Public service.

Computing on campus. 372 workstations in library, computer center, student center. Commuter students can connect to campus network. Online course registration, repair service, wireless network available.

Student life. Freshman orientation: Mandatory. Preregistration for classes offered. **Activities:** Student government, student newspaper, Students Offering Support, Phi Theta Kappa, Project Second Chance, Native American Students, student government association, Hispanic student association, College Republicans, Young Democrats, Deaf/Hearing student association, student nursing association.

Student services. Adult student services, career counseling, student employment services, financial aid counseling, on-campus daycare, personal counseling, placement for graduates, veterans' counselor. **Physically disabled:** Services for visually, speech, hearing impaired. **Transfer:** Transfer center, transfer adviser, college fairs on campus for students transferring to 4-year colleges.

Contact. E-mail: jkubier@osuokc.edu
Phone: (405) 945-3224 Toll-free number: (800) 560-4099
Fax: (405) 945-3277
Jeanne Kubier, Director of Admissions, Oklahoma State University: Oklahoma City, 900 North Portland, Oklahoma City, OK 73107-6195

Platt College: Oklahoma City Central

Oklahoma City, Oklahoma
www.plattcollege.org

- For-profit 2-year branch campus and health science college
- Small city
- Interview required

Two-Year Colleges

General. Accredited by ACCSCT. **Enrollment:** 200 degree-seeking undergraduates. **Degrees:** 70 associate awarded. **Calendar:** Continuous. **Full-time faculty:** 40 total. **Part-time faculty:** 2 total.

Basis for selection. Open admission, but selective for some programs. Entrance exam required for Practical Nursing and Surgical Technologist Programs.

2008-2009 Annual costs. Tuition varies by program. Full-time tuition ranges from $10,200 to $23,600. Required fees $100.

Application procedures. Admission: No deadline. $100 fee. Admission notification on a rolling basis. **Financial aid:** FAFSA required.

Academics. Credit/placement by examination: CLEP.

Majors. Health: Licensed practical nurse.

Student life. Freshman orientation: Mandatory.

Student services. Adult student services, alcohol/substance abuse counseling, career counseling, financial aid counseling, personal counseling, placement for graduates.

Contact. E-mail: angiem@plattcollege.org
Phone: (405) 946-7799 Fax: (405) 943-2150
Kim Lamb, Director of Admissions, Platt College: Oklahoma City Central, 309 South Ann Arbor, Oklahoma City, OK 73128

Platt College: Tulsa
Tulsa, Oklahoma
www.plattcollege.org

- For-profit 2-year health science college
- Commuter campus in large city
- Interview required

General. Accredited by ACCSCT. **Enrollment:** 75 degree-seeking undergraduates. **Degrees:** 110 associate awarded. **Calendar:** Continuous. **Full-time faculty:** 35 total. **Part-time faculty:** 20 total. **Class size:** 100% < 20.

Basis for selection. Open admission, but selective for some programs. High school diploma or GED required for some programs. Others require successful completion of entrance exams. Nursing programs requires additional interview with Director of Nursing. **Homeschooled:** State high school equivalency certificate required.

2008-2009 Annual costs. Tuition varies by program. Full-time tuition ranges from $10,300 to $23,600, depending on program. Required fees $100.

Financial aid. All financial aid based on need. Need-based aid available for part-time students.

Application procedures. Admission: No deadline. $100 fee. **Financial aid:** No deadline. FAFSA required.

Academics. Special study options: Liberal arts/career combination. Bachelor's degree programs available on campus. License preparation in nursing. **Credit/placement by examination:** CLEP. **Support services:** Remedial instruction, tutoring.

Majors. Health: Licensed practical nurse, nursing (RN).

Computing on campus. 35 workstations in library, computer center. Online library, wireless network available.

Student life. Freshman orientation: Mandatory. Preregistration for classes offered. Held for 5 hours on first day of classes.

Student services. Student employment services, financial aid counseling, placement for graduates. **Transfer:** Pre-admission transcript evaluation for new students.

Contact. E-mail: stephanieh@plattcollege.org
Phone: (918) 663-9000 Fax: (918) 622-1240
Admission Director, Platt College: Tulsa, 3801 South Sheridan, Tulsa, OK 74145-1132

Redlands Community College
El Reno, Oklahoma
www.redlandscc.edu **CB code: 7324**

- Public 2-year community college
- Commuter campus in large town

General. Founded in 1938. Regionally accredited. **Enrollment:** 2,463 degree-seeking undergraduates. **Degrees:** 255 associate awarded. **Location:** 25 miles from Oklahoma City. **Calendar:** Semester, limited summer session. **Full-time faculty:** 36 total. **Part-time faculty:** 102 total. **Class size:** 72% < 20, 26% 20-39, less than 1% 40-49, less than 1% 50-99, less than 1% >100. **Special facilities:** Applied agricultural research center, ranch, working farm and equine centers, viticulture and enology programs.

Student profile. Among degree-seeking undergraduates, 45% enrolled in a transfer program, 28% enrolled in a vocational program, 1% already have a bachelor's degree or higher, 422 enrolled as first-time, first-year students, 211 transferred in from other institutions.

Part-time:	64%	**Hispanic American:**	3%
Out-of-state:	3%	**Native American:**	7%
Women:	65%	**25 or older:**	39%
African American:	6%	**Live on campus:**	4%
Asian American:	2%		

Transfer out. Colleges most students transferred to 2008: University of Central Oklahoma, Southwestern Oklahoma State University, Oklahoma State University, University of Oklahoma, University of Science and Arts of Oklahoma.

Basis for selection. Open admission, but selective for some programs. Competitive admissions to nursing and honors programs. Students without ACT scores or with ACT below 19 required to take COMPASS placement test offered on campus. Interviews required for nursing program admission.

High school preparation. College-preparatory program recommended. Recommended units include English 4, mathematics 3, social studies 2, science 2 and foreign language 1.

2008-2009 Annual costs. Tuition/fees: $2,903; $5,153 out-of-state. Per-credit charge: $97 in-state; $172 out-of-state. Books/supplies: $960. Personal expenses: $1,500.

2007-2008 Financial aid. Need-based: Average need met was 95%. Average scholarship/grant was $3,197; average loan $2,765. 52% of total undergraduate aid awarded as scholarships/grants, 48% as loans/jobs. Need-based aid available for part-time students. Work-study available nights, weekends and for part-time students. **Non-need-based:** Scholarships awarded for academics, athletics, leadership.

Application procedures. Admission: No deadline. $25 fee, may be waived for applicants with need. Admission notification on a rolling basis. **Financial aid:** Priority date 7/1; no closing date. FAFSA required. Applicants notified on a rolling basis starting 6/1; must reply within 6 week(s) of notification.

Academics. Special study options: Accelerated study, cooperative education, cross-registration, distance learning, double major, dual enrollment of high school students, honors, independent study, internships, liberal arts/career combination. License preparation in nursing, paramedic. **Credit/placement by examination:** AP, CLEP, institutional tests. 32 credit hours maximum toward associate degree. **Support services:** Learning center, reduced course load, remedial instruction, study skills assistance, tutoring.

Majors. Agriculture: General, agronomy, equestrian studies. **Business:** Business admin. **Computer sciences:** General. **Education:** General. **Family/consumer sciences:** Child care, child development. **Health:** EMT paramedic, health services, nursing (RN), veterinary technology/assistant. **Math:** General. **Parks/recreation:** Exercise sciences, health/fitness. **Physical sciences:** General. **Protective services:** Police science. **Psychology:** General. **Social sciences:** General. **Visual/performing arts:** Art. **Other:** Applied technology.

Most popular majors. Agriculture 7%, business/marketing 14%, family/consumer sciences 6%, health sciences 19%, liberal arts 30%, security/protective services 9%.

Computing on campus. 180 workstations in dormitories, library, computer center. Dormitories wired for high-speed internet access. Commuter students can connect to campus network. Online library, helpline, wireless network available.

Student life. Freshman orientation: Available. Preregistration for classes offered. Class held the Thursday and Friday prior to start of Fall semester. **Housing:** Apartments, wellness housing available. $200 partly refundable deposit. Limited housing for agriculture students at working ranch available. **Activities:** Choral groups, Model UN, student government, nursing student association, Aggie club, Phi Theta Kappa, Young Democrats, College Republicans, art club, Students in Free Enterprise, fencing club, photography club.

Athletics. NJCAA. **Intercollegiate:** Baseball M, basketball, golf W, volleyball W. **Intramural:** Cheerleading. **Team name:** Cougars.

Student services. Adult student services, career counseling, services for economically disadvantaged, student employment services, financial aid counseling, placement for graduates, veterans' counselor. **Transfer:** Transfer adviser, college fairs on campus for students transferring to 4-year colleges.

Contact. E-mail: studentservices@redlandscc.edu
Phone: (405) 262-2552 ext. 1417 Toll-free
number: (866) 415-6367 ext. 1417 Fax: (405) 422-1239
Tricia Hobson, Director of Enrollment Management, Redlands Community College, 1300 South Country Club Road, El Reno, OK 73036

Rose State College
Midwest City, Oklahoma
www.rose.edu **CB code: 1462**

- Public 2-year community college
- Commuter campus in small city

General. Founded in 1968. Regionally accredited. **Enrollment:** 6,581 degree-seeking undergraduates; 1,501 non-degree-seeking students. **Degrees:** 712 associate awarded. **Location:** 5 miles from Oklahoma City. **Calendar:** Semester, extensive summer session. **Full-time faculty:** 121 total; 16% have terminal degrees, 9% minority, 62% women. **Part-time faculty:** 285 total; 10% have terminal degrees, 13% minority, 56% women. **Class size:** 54% < 20, 43% 20-39, 2% 40-49, less than 1% 50-99, less than 1% >100. **Special facilities:** Regional history center, 1400-seat performing arts theater, wetlands project.

Student profile. Among degree-seeking undergraduates, 75% enrolled in a transfer program, 25% enrolled in a vocational program, 1,285 enrolled as first-time, first-year students, 817 transferred in from other institutions.

Part-time:	59%	**Asian American:**	3%
Out-of-state:	1%	**Hispanic American:**	5%
Women:	62%	**Native American:**	10%
African American:	18%	**25 or older:**	41%

Transfer out. Colleges most students transferred to 2008: Oklahoma State University, Southwestern Oklahoma State University, University of Oklahoma, University of Central Oklahoma.

Basis for selection. Open admission, but selective for some programs. Interview required for health science programs. **Adult students:** COMPASS Placement test required. **Homeschooled:** Peer class must have graduated. **Learning Disabled:** If students indicate disability, they are referred to disability counselor.

High school preparation. 15 units required. Required units include English 4, mathematics 3, social studies 1, history 2, science 2 (laboratory 2) and academic electives 3. Electives may include English, lab science, math, history/citizenship skills, computer science or foreign language.

2008-2009 Annual costs. Tuition/fees: $2,534; $7,394 out-of-state. Per-credit charge: $65 in-state; $227 out-of-state. Books/supplies: $1,250.

2007-2008 Financial aid. Need-based: 43% of total undergraduate aid awarded as scholarships/grants, 57% as loans/jobs. Need-based aid available for part-time students. Work-study available nights, weekends and for part-time students. **Non-need-based:** Scholarships awarded for academics, athletics.

Application procedures. Admission: Closing date 8/20 (receipt date). No application fee. Admission notification on a rolling basis. **Financial aid:** Priority date 6/1; no closing date. FAFSA required. Applicants notified on a rolling basis starting 3/1; must reply within 4 week(s) of notification.

Academics. Special study options: Accelerated study, cooperative education, cross-registration, distance learning, double major, honors, independent study, internships, liberal arts/career combination, weekend college. Bachelor's degree programs available on campus. License preparation in dental hygiene, nursing, radiology. **Credit/placement by examination:** AP, CLEP, IB, institutional tests. 50 credit hours maximum toward associate degree. **Support services:** GED preparation and test center, learning center, reduced course load, remedial instruction, study skills assistance, tutoring, writing center.

Majors. Biology: General. **Business:** General, accounting technology, business admin, e-commerce, human resources, small business admin. **Communications:** Broadcast journalism, digital media, journalism. **Computer sciences:** General, LAN/WAN management, networking, web page design, webmaster. **Conservation:** Environmental science. **Construction:** Carpentry, masonry, plumbing. **Education:** Multi-level teacher. **Engineering:** General. **Engineering technology:** Drafting, electrical, heat/ac/refrig, telecommunications, water quality. **Family/consumer sciences:** General, child care, child development. **Foreign languages:** General. **Health:** Athletic training, clinical lab assistant, clinical lab technology, dental assistant, dental hygiene, EMT paramedic, medical records technology, nursing (RN), predental, premedicine, prenursing, prepharmacy, radiologic technology/medical imaging, respiratory therapy assistant, respiratory therapy technology. **History:** General. **Legal studies:** Court reporting, paralegal. **Liberal arts:** Arts/sciences, library assistant. **Math:** General. **Mechanic/repair:** Auto body, automotive, heating/ac/refrig. **Parks/recreation:** Health/fitness. **Physical sciences:** Chemistry, geology, physics. **Protective services:** Police science. **Psychology:** General. **Public administration:** Social work. **Social sciences:** General, political science, sociology. **Transportation:** Aviation. **Visual/performing arts:** Art, dramatic.

Most popular majors. Business/marketing 15%, education 6%, health sciences 29%, liberal arts 25%.

Computing on campus. 150 workstations in library, computer center, student center. Commuter students can connect to campus network. Online course registration, online library, helpline, student web hosting, wireless network available.

Student life. Freshman orientation: Mandatory. Preregistration for classes offered. **Activities:** Jazz band, choral groups, dance, drama, music ensembles, student government, student newspaper, Phi Theta Kappa, criminal justice club, black student association, broadcasting club, drama club, Oklahoma Intercollegiate Legislature, American Indian association.

Athletics. NJCAA. **Intercollegiate:** Baseball M, softball W. **Intramural:** Bowling, cheerleading, soccer, swimming, table tennis, tennis, volleyball. **Team name:** Raiders.

Student services. Adult student services, alcohol/substance abuse counseling, career counseling, student employment services, financial aid counseling, on-campus daycare, personal counseling, placement for graduates, veterans' counselor. **Physically disabled:** Services for visually, speech, hearing impaired. **Learning disabled:** Comprehensive services available. **Transfer:** Pre-admission transcript evaluation for new students. Transfer center, transfer adviser, college fairs on campus for students transferring to 4-year colleges.

Contact. Phone: (405) 733-7312 Toll-free number: (866) 621-0987
Fax: (405) 736-0309
M. Mechelle Aitson-Roessler, Registrar/Director of Admissions, Rose State College, 6420 SE 15th Street, Midwest City, OK 73110

Seminole State College
Seminole, Oklahoma
www.ssc.cc.ok.us **CB code: 0316**

- Public 2-year community and junior college
- Commuter campus in small town

General. Founded in 1931. Regionally accredited. **Enrollment:** 1,400 full-time, degree-seeking students. **Degrees:** 277 associate awarded. **Location:** 55 miles from Oklahoma City. **Calendar:** Semester, extensive summer session. **Full-time faculty:** 45 total. **Part-time faculty:** 53 total.

Student profile.

Out-of-state:	3%	**Live on campus:**	3%

Basis for selection. Open admission, but selective for some programs. Additional requirements for admission to A.D. Nursing Program and MLT Program include 19 ACT and score of 15 on Nelson Denny Reading Test.

High school preparation. 15 units recommended. Recommended units include English 4, mathematics 3, social studies 2, history 2, science 2 and academic electives 2.

2008-2009 Annual costs. Tuition/fees: $2,849; $6,665 out-of-state. Per-credit charge: $58 in-state; $185 out-of-state. Room/board: $5,850. Books/supplies: $350. Personal expenses: $920.

2008-2009 Financial aid. Non-need-based: Scholarships awarded for academics, athletics, state residency.

Application procedures. Admission: No deadline. $15 fee. Admission notification on a rolling basis. **Financial aid:** Priority date 7/15; no closing date. FAFSA, institutional form required. Applicants notified on a rolling basis starting 3/1; must reply within 4 week(s) of notification.

Academics. Special study options: Dual enrollment of high school students, honors. Bachelor's degree programs available on campus. **Credit/placement by examination:** CLEP, institutional tests. 30 credit hours maximum toward associate degree. **Support services:** Learning center, remedial instruction, tutoring, writing center.

Majors. **Business:** Business admin, office management, office/clerical. **Computer sciences:** Computer science. **Education:** General, elementary. **Health:** Clinical lab technology, nursing (RN). **Interdisciplinary:** Behavioral sciences. **Liberal arts:** Arts/sciences. **Math:** General. **Parks/recreation:** Health/fitness. **Social sciences:** General. **Visual/performing arts:** Art.

Most popular majors. Business/marketing 20%, computer/information sciences 10%, health sciences 10%, liberal arts 60%.

Computing on campus. 310 workstations in dormitories, library, computer center, student center. Dormitories wired for high-speed internet access and linked to campus network. Commuter students can connect to campus network. Helpline, repair service available.

Student life. **Freshman orientation:** Mandatory. Preregistration for classes offered. **Housing:** Coed dorms, single-sex dorms available. $50 deposit. **Activities:** Concert band, student government, student newspaper, student government, Native American student association, Baptist student union.

Athletics. NJCAA. **Intercollegiate:** Baseball M, basketball, golf, softball W, tennis, volleyball. **Intramural:** Baseball M, basketball. **Team name:** Trojans.

Student services. Career counseling, services for economically disadvantaged, financial aid counseling, personal counseling, veterans' counselor. **Physically disabled:** Services for visually, speech, hearing impaired. **Transfer:** Transfer adviser, college fairs on campus for students transferring to 4-year colleges.

Contact. E-mail: c.lindley@sscok.edu
Phone: (405) 382-9950 ext. 230 Fax: (405) 382-9524
Chris Lindley, Director of Enrollment Management, Seminole State College, 2701 Boren Boulevard, Seminole, OK 74868

Tulsa Community College

Tulsa, Oklahoma **CB member**
www.tulsacc.edu **CB code: 6839**

- Public 2-year community college
- Commuter campus in large city

General. Founded in 1968. Regionally accredited. 4 branch campuses located in Tulsa. **Enrollment:** 12,162 degree-seeking undergraduates. **Degrees:** 2,042 associate awarded. **Calendar:** Semester, extensive summer session. **Full-time faculty:** 294 total. **Part-time faculty:** 826 total. **Class size:** 60% < 20, 19% 20-39, 5% 40-49, 7% 50-99, 9% >100.

Student profile.

Out-of-state:	2%	**25 or older:**	59%

Transfer out. **Colleges most students transferred to 2008:** University of Oklahoma, Oklahoma State University, Northeastern Oklahoma State University, Tulsa University, University of Central Oklahoma.

Basis for selection. Open admission, but selective for some programs. Special requirements for health-related, legal assistant, and management programs. Interview required for health, legal assistant, and nursing programs. **Adult students:** ACT or Accuplacer CPT required for placement.

High school preparation. 15 units recommended. Recommended units include English 4, mathematics 3, social studies 1, history 2, science 2 (laboratory 2) and academic electives 3.

2008-2009 Annual costs. Tuition/fees: $2,709; $7,376 out-of-state. Per-credit charge: $62 in-state; $218 out-of-state. Books/supplies: $600. Personal expenses: $900.

Financial aid. **Need-based:** Need-based aid available for part-time students. Work-study available nights, weekends and for part-time students. **Non-need-based:** Scholarships awarded for academics, art, leadership, music/drama, state residency.

Application procedures. **Admission:** No deadline. $20 fee. Admission notification on a rolling basis. **Financial aid:** Priority date 8/1; no closing date. FAFSA, institutional form required. Applicants notified on a rolling basis starting 4/1; must reply within 2 week(s) of notification.

Academics. Many short-period intensive courses within conventional semesters. **Special study options:** Cross-registration, distance learning, dual enrollment of high school students, ESL, honors, independent study, internships, weekend college. **Credit/placement by examination:** CLEP, institutional tests. 30 credit hours maximum toward associate degree. **Support services:** Learning center, remedial instruction, study skills assistance, tutoring, writing center.

Majors. **Agriculture:** Horticultural science. **Business:** General, accounting, administrative services, business admin, fashion, finance, hospitality admin, hospitality/recreation, human resources, insurance, management information systems, managerial economics, office technology, real estate, tourism/travel. **Communications:** Journalism. **Communications technology:** General. **Computer sciences:** General, applications programming, programming. **Education:** General, physical. **Engineering:** General. **Engineering technology:** Civil, drafting, electrical. **Family/consumer sciences:** Child care. **Foreign languages:** French, German, Italian, Japanese, Russian, sign language interpretation, Spanish. **Health:** Clinical lab assistant, clinical lab technology, dental hygiene, medical assistant, medical radiologic technology/radiation therapy, medical secretary, occupational therapy assistant, physical therapy assistant, respiratory therapy technology. **History:** General. **Legal studies:** Legal secretary, paralegal. **Liberal arts:** Library science. **Math:** General. **Mechanic/repair:** Avionics, electronics/electrical, heating/ac/refrig. **Philosophy/religion:** Philosophy. **Physical sciences:** Astronomy, chemistry, geology, physics. **Protective services:** Criminal justice, fire safety technology, police science. **Psychology:** General. **Social sciences:** General, economics, geography, political science, sociology. **Transportation:** Aviation management. **Visual/performing arts:** Dramatic, interior design.

Computing on campus. 2,306 workstations in library, computer center. Online course registration, online library available.

Student life. **Freshman orientation:** Available. **Activities:** Bands, choral groups, drama, music ensembles, student government, student newspaper.

Athletics. **Intramural:** Basketball, soccer, softball, table tennis, tennis, volleyball.

Student services. Career counseling, student employment services, health services, on-campus daycare, personal counseling, placement for graduates, veterans' counselor. **Physically disabled:** Services for visually, hearing impaired. **Transfer:** College fairs on campus for students transferring to 4-year colleges.

Contact. E-mail: theck@tulsacc.edu
Phone: (918) 595-7000 Fax: (918) 595-7000
Traci Heck, Director of Admissions and Records, Tulsa Community College, 6111 East Skelly Drive, Tulsa, OK 74135

Tulsa Welding School

Tulsa, Oklahoma
www.weldingschool.com **CB code: 2958**

- For-profit 2-year technical college
- Commuter campus in very large city
- Interview required

General. Accredited by ACCSCT. **Enrollment:** 730 degree-seeking undergraduates. **Degrees:** 20 associate awarded. **Calendar:** Continuous. **Full-time faculty:** 16 total. **Part-time faculty:** 1 total.

Student profile.

Out-of-state:	41%	**25 or older:**	36%

Basis for selection. Open admission. **Homeschooled:** Applicants must pass ATB test.

2008-2009 Annual costs. Tuition and fees vary by program from $8,355 to $14,690.

Financial aid. All financial aid based on need.

Application procedures. **Admission:** No deadline. No application fee. Admission notification on a rolling basis. Must have high school diploma or GED or pass Ability To Benefit test. **Financial aid:** FAFSA required.

Academics. **Credit/placement by examination:** CLEP.

Majors. **Production:** Welding.

Computing on campus. 3 workstations in library.

Student life. **Freshman orientation:** Mandatory. Preregistration for classes offered.

Student services. Career counseling, student employment services, financial aid counseling, personal counseling, placement for graduates. **Physically disabled:** Services for hearing impaired.

Contact. E-mail: tws@ionet.net
Phone: (918) 587-6789 ext. 240 Toll-free number: (800) 331-2934 ext. 221
Fax: (918) 587-8170
Mike Thurber, Director of Admissions, Tulsa Welding School, 2545 East 11th Street, Tulsa, OK 74104-3909

Vatterott College
Oklahoma City, Oklahoma
www.vatterott-college.com **CB code: 2899**

- For-profit 2-year technical and career college
- Residential campus in very large city

General. Accredited by ACCSCT. **Enrollment:** 260 degree-seeking undergraduates. **Degrees:** 80 associate awarded. **Calendar:** Continuous. **Full-time faculty:** 22 total. **Part-time faculty:** 16 total. **Class size:** 75% < 20, 25% 20-39.

Student profile. Among degree-seeking undergraduates, 100% enrolled in a vocational program.

Basis for selection. Open admission. Program-specific institutional entrance exams are administered.

2008-2009 Annual costs. Program cost ranges: $17,200 to $22,000 (certificate/diploma); $24,250 to $32,050 (associate degree).

2007-2008 Financial aid. All financial aid based on need.

Application procedures. Admission: No deadline. No application fee. **Financial aid:** No deadline. FAFSA required.

Academics. Credit/placement by examination: CLEP. **Support services:** Learning center, remedial instruction, study skills assistance, tutoring.

Majors. Computer sciences: General, information technology, LAN/WAN management, programming. **Mechanic/repair:** Heating/ac/refrig.

Computing on campus. 125 workstations in library, computer center.

Student life. Freshman orientation: Mandatory.

Student services. Career counseling, financial aid counseling.

Contact. Phone: (405) 945-0088 Fax: (405) 945-0788
David Haynes, Director of Admissions, Vatterott College, 4621 NW 23rd Street, Oklahoma City, OK 73127

Vatterott College: Tulsa
Tulsa, Oklahoma
www.vatterott-college.edu **CB code: 3637**

- For-profit 2-year branch campus and technical college
- Commuter campus in large city
- Interview required

General. Accredited by ACCSCT. **Enrollment:** 145 degree-seeking undergraduates. **Degrees:** 65 associate awarded. **Calendar:** Continuous. **Full-time faculty:** 16 total; 19% women. **Part-time faculty:** 1 total; 100% women. **Special facilities:** Extensive HVAC lab.

Basis for selection. High school diploma or GED required.

2008-2009 Annual costs. Program cost ranges: $18,400 to $22,000 (certificate/diploma); $24,250 to $33,850 (associate degree).

Application procedures. Admission: No deadline. No application fee.

Academics. Credit/placement by examination: CLEP, institutional tests. **Support services:** Study skills assistance, tutoring.

Majors. Computer sciences: LAN/WAN management, web page design. **Health:** Office assistant. **Mechanic/repair:** Computer, electronics/electrical, heating/ac/refrig.

Computing on campus. 20 workstations in library, computer center.

Student life. Freshman orientation: Available. **Activities:** Student newspaper.

Student services. Transfer: Pre-admission transcript evaluation for new students. College fairs on campus for students transferring to 4-year colleges.

Contact. E-mail: tulsa@vatterott-college.edu
Phone: (918) 835-8288 Toll-free number: (888) 857-4016
Fax: (918) 835-9698
Director of Admissions, Vatterott College: Tulsa, 4343 South 118th East Avenue, Tulsa, OK 74146

Western Oklahoma State College
Altus, Oklahoma **CB member**
www.wosc.edu **CB code: 6020**

- Public 2-year community college
- Commuter campus in large town

General. Founded in 1926. Regionally accredited. **Enrollment:** 720 full-time, degree-seeking students. **Degrees:** 273 associate awarded. **Location:** 60 miles from Lawton, 140 miles from Oklahoma City. **Calendar:** Semester, limited summer session. **Full-time faculty:** 46 total; 4% have terminal degrees. **Part-time faculty:** 56 total. **Class size:** 78% < 20, 20% 20-39, less than 1% 40-49, 1% 50-99.

Transfer out. Colleges most students transferred to 2008: Southwestern Oklahoma State University, Cameron University, Oklahoma State University, University of Central Oklahoma, University of Oklahoma.

Basis for selection. Open admission. SAT or ACT required for applicants under 21 for placement; no minimum score required. **Adult students:** ACT required for adults who don't have high school diploma or GED. Must demonstrate proficiency in English, math, science, and reading through COMPASS or ACT subtest scores. **Homeschooled:** Transcript of courses and grades, letter of recommendation (nonparent) required. Must have ACT or SAT. High school class must have graduated and must satisfy curricular requirements.

High school preparation. 15 units recommended. Recommended units include English 4, mathematics 3, history 3, science 2 and academic electives 3. 2 fine arts recommended.

2008-2009 Annual costs. Tuition/fees: $2,684; $6,164 out-of-state. Per-credit charge: $57 in-state; $173 out-of-state. Room/board: $3,750. Books/supplies: $1,000. Personal expenses: $1,200.

2007-2008 Financial aid. Need-based: Need-based aid available for part-time students. Work-study available nights, weekends and for part-time students. **Non-need-based:** Scholarships awarded for academics, alumni affiliation, art, athletics, leadership, music/drama, state residency.

Application procedures. Admission: No deadline. $15 fee. Admission notification on a rolling basis. **Financial aid:** Priority date 3/1; no closing date. FAFSA, institutional form required. Applicants notified on a rolling basis; must reply within 3 week(s) of notification.

Academics. Special study options: Distance learning, dual enrollment of high school students, honors, liberal arts/career combination. Cooperative agreements with local technology centers. Students may co-enroll and earn college credits for votech courses. License preparation in aviation, nursing, radiology. **Credit/placement by examination:** AP, CLEP, institutional tests. 30 credit hours maximum toward associate degree. **Support services:** Learning center, remedial instruction, study skills assistance, tutoring.

Majors. Biology: General. **Business:** General, administrative services, business admin, management science, office technology, office/clerical. **Computer sciences:** General, computer science, information systems, programming. **Conservation:** Wildlife. **Education:** General, physical, social studies. **Engineering:** General. **Engineering technology:** Construction, drafting, manufacturing. **Family/consumer sciences:** Child care. **Foreign languages:** Spanish. **Health:** EMT paramedic, medical radiologic technology/radiation therapy, medical records admin, medical secretary, nursing (RN). **History:** General. **Liberal arts:** Arts/sciences. **Math:** General. **Mechanic/repair:** Auto body, automotive, diesel, electronics/electrical. **Parks/recreation:** Health/fitness. **Protective services:** Corrections, firefighting, police science. **Psychology:** General. **Social sciences:** General, political science, sociology. **Transportation:** Aviation, aviation management. **Visual/performing arts:** Art.

Most popular majors. Health sciences 16%, liberal arts 11%.

Computing on campus. 50 workstations in library. Dormitories wired for high-speed internet access and linked to campus network. Commuter students can connect to campus network. Online course registration, online library, helpline, wireless network available.

Student life. Freshman orientation: Mandatory. Preregistration for classes offered. **Housing:** Coed dorms, wellness housing available. $50 deposit. **Activities:** Bands, choral groups, drama, music ensembles, musical theater, radio station, student government, student newspaper, Baptist student union, Wesley Foundation, tutoring club, College Democrats, College Republicans, Fellowship of Christians.

Athletics. NJCAA. **Intercollegiate:** Baseball M, basketball, softball W. **Intramural:** Basketball, volleyball. **Team name:** Pioneers.

Student services. Career counseling, financial aid counseling, health services, personal counseling, veterans' counselor. **Transfer:** Transfer adviser, college fairs on campus for students transferring to 4-year colleges.

Contact. E-mail: tanya.wingate@wosc.edu
Phone: (580) 477-2000 Fax: (580) 477-7723
Lana Scott, Director of Admission and Registrar, Western Oklahoma State College, 2801 North Main Street, Altus, OK 73521

Oregon

Blue Mountain Community College

Pendleton, Oregon
www.bluecc.edu **CB code: 4025**

- Public 2-year community college
- Commuter campus in large town

General. Founded in 1962. Regionally accredited. Located in agricultural area. **Enrollment:** 700 full-time, degree-seeking students. **Degrees:** 160 associate awarded. **Location:** 200 miles from Portland. **Calendar:** Quarter, limited summer session. **Full-time faculty:** 60 total. **Part-time faculty:** 140 total. **Class size:** 74% < 20, 25% 20-39, less than 1% 40-49, less than 1% 50-99.

Student profile.

Out-of-state:	6%	**25 or older:**	55%

Transfer out. Colleges most students transferred to 2008: Eastern Oregon University, Oregon State University, University of Oregon.

Basis for selection. Open admission, but selective for some programs. Admission to nursing program based on prerequisite course work, GPA, security check, point system. Dental Assisting students admitted based on prerequisites and GPA.

2008-2009 Annual costs. Tuition/fees: $3,417; $9,357 out-of-state. Per-credit charge: $66 in-state; $198 out-of-state. Washington, Idaho, Nevada, Montana, and California state residents pay in-state tuition. Books/supplies: $1,425. Personal expenses: $1,965.

Financial aid. Need-based: Need-based aid available for part-time students. Work-study available nights, weekends and for part-time students. **Non-need-based:** Scholarships awarded for athletics, music/drama.

Application procedures. Admission: No deadline. No application fee. Admission notification on a rolling basis. **Financial aid:** Priority date 3/30; no closing date. FAFSA required. Applicants notified on a rolling basis starting 4/1; must reply within 2 week(s) of notification.

Academics. Learning disabilities diagnostician available. **Special study options:** Cooperative education, cross-registration, distance learning, double major, dual enrollment of high school students, ESL, liberal arts/career combination. Bachelor's degree programs available on campus. License preparation in nursing. **Credit/placement by examination:** AP, CLEP, institutional tests. 15 credit hours maximum toward associate degree. **Support services:** GED preparation and test center, learning center, reduced course load, remedial instruction, study skills assistance, tutoring.

Majors. Agriculture: Animal husbandry, business, crop production, farm/ranch, production. **Business:** Accounting technology, administrative services, business admin, marketing. **Education:** Early childhood, teacher assistance. **Engineering technology:** Civil, drafting, electrical. **Family/consumer sciences:** Family/community services. **Health:** Medical secretary, nursing (RN). **Liberal arts:** Arts/sciences. **Mechanic/repair:** Industrial. **Parks/recreation:** Health/fitness. **Public administration:** Human services.

Computing on campus. 200 workstations in library, computer center. Commuter students can connect to campus network. Online course registration, online library, wireless network available.

Student life. Freshman orientation: Available, $10 fee. Preregistration for classes offered. Half-day session in fall prior to classes. **Activities:** Jazz band, choral groups, drama, music ensembles, musical theater, student government, multicultural club, MECHA, Native American club.

Athletics. Intercollegiate: Baseball M, basketball, rodeo, softball W, volleyball W. **Team name:** Timberwolves.

Student services. Alcohol/substance abuse counseling, career counseling, services for economically disadvantaged, student employment services, financial aid counseling, personal counseling, placement for graduates, veterans' counselor. **Physically disabled:** Services for visually, speech, hearing impaired. **Learning disabled:** Comprehensive services available. **Transfer:** Pre-admission transcript evaluation for new students. Transfer center, transfer adviser, college fairs on campus for students transferring to 4-year colleges.

Contact. E-mail: getinfo@bluecc.edu
Phone: (541) 278-5759 Fax: (541) 278-5871
Theresa Bosworth, Director of Admissions, Records & Testing/Registrar, Blue Mountain Community College, 2411 Northwest Carden Avenue, Pendleton, OR 97801

Central Oregon Community College

Bend, Oregon
www.cocc.edu **CB code: 4090**

- Public 2-year community college
- Commuter campus in small city

General. Founded in 1949. Regionally accredited. **Enrollment:** 4,430 degree-seeking undergraduates; 803 non-degree-seeking students. **Degrees:** 316 associate awarded. **ROTC:** Army. **Location:** 150 miles from Portland, 120 miles from Salem. **Calendar:** Quarter, limited summer session. **Full-time faculty:** 95 total; 36% have terminal degrees, 4% minority, 50% women. **Part-time faculty:** 125 total; 2% minority, 57% women. **Class size:** 32% < 20, 66% 20-39, 1% 40-49, 2% 50-99. **Special facilities:** Exercise physiology laboratory, dental clinic.

Student profile. Among degree-seeking undergraduates, 63% enrolled in a transfer program, 37% enrolled in a vocational program, 7% already have a bachelor's degree or higher, 935 enrolled as first-time, first-year students, 612 transferred in from other institutions.

Part-time:	53%	**Hispanic American:**	5%
Out-of-state:	5%	**Native American:**	3%
Women:	57%	**25 or older:**	40%
African American:	1%	**Live on campus:**	2%
Asian American:	2%		

Transfer out. Colleges most students transferred to 2008: Oregon State University, University of Oregon, Southern Oregon University, Portland State University.

Basis for selection. Open admission, but selective for some programs. Special requirements for nursing, emergency medical services. Limited enrollment (first-come first-served basis, with fall term only start date) for medical assistant, dental assistant, and massage therapy. **Homeschooled:** High school diploma or GED not required if student is 18 or older.

2009-2010 Annual costs. Tuition/fees (projected): $2,958; $3,993 out-of-district; $8,088 out-of-state. Per-credit charge: $63 in-district; $86 out-of-district; $176 out-of-state. Residents of WA, ID, NV and CA pay the in-state, out-of-district tuition. Emergency Medical Services, Aviation, Nursing, Culinary and Massage Therapy programs carry additional fees. Room/board: $7,326. Books/supplies: $1,050. Personal expenses: $2,601.

2008-2009 Financial aid. Need-based: 369 full-time freshmen applied for aid; 301 were judged to have need; 291 of these received aid. Average need met was 83%. Average scholarship/grant was $5,701; average loan $3,221. 46% of total undergraduate aid awarded as scholarships/grants, 54% as loans/jobs. Need-based aid available for part-time students. Work-study available for part-time students. **Non-need-based:** Awarded to 62 full-time undergraduates, including 17 freshmen. Scholarships awarded for academics, state residency. **Additional information:** Institution-sponsored short-term loans. Extensive part-time student employment.

Application procedures. Admission: Priority date 6/15; no deadline. $25 fee, may be waived for applicants with need. Admission notification on a rolling basis. **Financial aid:** No deadline. FAFSA required. Applicants notified on a rolling basis starting 3/30; must reply within 4 week(s) of notification.

Academics. Special study options: Cooperative education, distance learning, double major, dual enrollment of high school students, ESL, independent study, internships, student-designed major, study abroad. Bachelor's degree programs available on campus. License preparation in aviation, nursing, paramedic, physical therapy. **Credit/placement by examination:** AP, CLEP, IB, institutional tests. Credit for prior training or certification varies by program. **Support services:** GED preparation, learning center, pre-admission summer program, reduced course load, remedial instruction, study skills assistance, tutoring, writing center.

Majors. Agriculture: General, horticultural science. **Architecture:** Landscape. **Biology:** General. **Business:** Accounting, administrative services, business admin, customer service, hospitality/recreation, management information systems, marketing. **Communications:** General. **Computer sciences:**

General, computer science, computer support specialist, networking. **Conservation:** General, forest technology, forestry. **Education:** General. **Engineering:** General. **Engineering technology:** CAD/CADD, drafting, industrial, manufacturing. **Foreign languages:** General. **Health:** EMT paramedic, massage therapy, medical records technology, nursing (RN), premedicine, prepharmacy, radiologic technology/medical imaging. **History:** General. **Legal studies:** Prelaw. **Liberal arts:** Arts/sciences, humanities. **Math:** General. **Parks/recreation:** General, health/fitness. **Physical sciences:** General, chemistry, geology, physics. **Protective services:** Criminal justice, firefighting. **Psychology:** General. **Social sciences:** General, anthropology, criminology, economics, political science, sociology. **Transportation:** Airline/commercial pilot. **Visual/performing arts:** General, studio arts.

Most popular majors. Health sciences 20%, liberal arts 57%, security/protective services 9%.

Computing on campus. 650 workstations in dormitories, library, computer center, student center. Dormitories wired for high-speed internet access and linked to campus network. Commuter students can connect to campus network. Online course registration, online library, helpline, wireless network available.

Student life. **Freshman orientation:** Available, $25 fee. Preregistration for classes offered. **Housing:** Coed dorms available. $250 partly refundable deposit. **Activities:** Bands, campus ministries, choral groups, drama, music ensembles, student government, student newspaper, symphony orchestra.

Athletics. **Intramural:** Basketball, cross-country, football (non-tackle), golf, soccer, softball, table tennis, track and field, volleyball, weight lifting. **Team name:** Bobcats.

Student services. Adult student services, alcohol/substance abuse counseling, career counseling, services for economically disadvantaged, student employment services, financial aid counseling, health services, minority student services, personal counseling, placement for graduates, veterans' counselor, women's services. **Physically disabled:** Services for visually, speech, hearing impaired. **Transfer:** Pre-admission transcript evaluation for new students. Transfer adviser, college fairs on campus for students transferring to 4-year colleges.

Contact. E-mail: welcome@cocc.edu
Phone: (541) 383-7500 Fax: (541) 383-7506
Aimee Metcalf, Director, Admissions and Records, Central Oregon Community College, 2600 Northwest College Way, Bend, OR 97701-5998

Chemeketa Community College
Salem, Oregon
www.chemeketa.edu **CB code: 4745**

- Public 2-year community and junior college
- Commuter campus in small city

General. Founded in 1962. Regionally accredited. **Enrollment:** 8,016 degree-seeking undergraduates. **Degrees:** 361 associate awarded. **Location:** 45 miles from Portland. **Calendar:** Quarter, extensive summer session. **Full-time faculty:** 223 total. **Part-time faculty:** 524 total. **Class size:** 43% < 20, 52% 20-39, 4% 40-49, less than 1% 50-99, less than 1% >100. **Special facilities:** Planetarium, vineyard and winemaking facility. **Partnerships:** Formal partnerships with local high schools.

Student profile.

Out-of-state:	5%	25 or older:	60%

Transfer out. **Colleges most students transferred to 2008:** University of Oregon, Oregon State University, Western Oregon University, Eastern Oregon University, Portland State University.

Basis for selection. Open admission, but selective for some programs. Interview required for limited enrollment programs; preparatory courses may be required.

2008-2009 Annual costs. Tuition/fees: $3,038; $9,698 out-of-state. Per-credit charge: $61 in-state; $209 out-of-state. International students have additional required fees. Individual courses may have extra fees. Books/supplies: $1,200. Personal expenses: $300.

2007-2008 Financial aid. All financial aid based on need. Need-based aid available for part-time students. Work-study available nights, weekends and for part-time students.

Application procedures. **Admission:** No deadline. No application fee. Admission notification on a rolling basis. **Financial aid:** Priority date 4/1; no closing date. FAFSA required. Applicants notified on a rolling basis starting 6/30; must reply within 2 week(s) of notification.

Academics. **Special study options:** Accelerated study, cooperative education, distance learning, double major, dual enrollment of high school students, ESL, independent study, internships, study abroad, teacher certification program, weekend college. License preparation in dental hygiene, nursing, paramedic. **Credit/placement by examination:** AP, CLEP, IB, institutional tests. 12 credit hours maximum toward associate degree. **Support services:** GED preparation and test center, learning center, pre-admission summer program, remedial instruction, study skills assistance, tutoring, writing center.

Majors. **Agriculture:** Agribusiness operations, horticultural science. **Biology:** General, anatomy, botany, pharmacology, zoology. **Business:** Accounting, administrative services, business admin, hospitality admin, management information systems, management science, office management, office technology, operations, real estate, tourism/travel. **Communications:** Journalism. **Communications technology:** Graphic/printing. **Computer sciences:** General, applications programming, programming. **Conservation:** Forest management, forest sciences, forestry. **Construction:** Building inspection, maintenance. **Education:** Bilingual, early childhood, elementary, health, physical, secondary, teacher assistance, technology/industrial arts. **Engineering:** General, electrical. **Engineering technology:** Civil, construction, drafting, electrical. **Family/consumer sciences:** General, child care, family studies. **Foreign languages:** Sign language interpretation. **Health:** Dental assistant, dental hygiene, EMT ambulance attendant, EMT paramedic, health care admin, health services, medical records admin, medical records technology, medical secretary, medical transcription, nursing (RN), office admin, office assistant, office computer specialist, predental, premedicine, prenursing, prepharmacy, speech-language pathology assistant, substance abuse counseling. **History:** General, American. **Interdisciplinary:** Gerontology. **Legal studies:** Legal secretary, prelaw. **Liberal arts:** Arts/sciences. **Math:** General, geometry. **Mechanic/repair:** Automotive, industrial. **Parks/recreation:** General. **Philosophy/religion:** Philosophy. **Physical sciences:** Chemistry, geology, physics. **Protective services:** Criminal justice, fire safety technology, firefighting, law enforcement admin, police science. **Psychology:** General. **Public administration:** Community org/advocacy, human services, social work. **Social sciences:** Anthropology, economics, geography, political science, sociology. **Visual/performing arts:** Art, design, theater design.

Computing on campus. 1,000 workstations in library, computer center. Commuter students can connect to campus network. Online course registration, online library, helpline, wireless network available.

Student life. **Freshman orientation:** Available. Preregistration for classes offered. **Activities:** Choral groups, dance, literary magazine, student government, student newspaper, TV station, sexual minority students organization, Christian student organization, LDS club, College Republicans, Democratic students, Phi Theta Kappa, Latino development network.

Athletics. NJCAA. **Intercollegiate:** Baseball M, basketball, softball W, volleyball W. **Intramural:** Softball W, tennis. **Team name:** The Storm.

Student services. Adult student services, alcohol/substance abuse counseling, career counseling, student employment services, financial aid counseling, minority student services, on-campus daycare, placement for graduates. **Physically disabled:** Services for visually, speech, hearing impaired. **Learning disabled:** Comprehensive services available. **Transfer:** Pre-admission transcript evaluation for new students. Transfer adviser, college fairs on campus for students transferring to 4-year colleges.

Contact. E-mail: admissions@chemeketa.edu
Phone: (503) 399-5006 Fax: (503) 399-3918
Melissa Frey, Enrollment Services Coordinator, Chemeketa Community College, Admissions Office, Salem, OR 97305-1453

Clackamas Community College
Oregon City, Oregon
www.clackamas.edu **CB code: 4111**

- Public 2-year community college
- Commuter campus in small city

General. Founded in 1966. Regionally accredited. **Enrollment:** 2,135 full-time, degree-seeking students. **Degrees:** 559 associate awarded. **ROTC:** Air Force. **Location:** 15 miles from Portland. **Calendar:** Quarter, extensive summer session. **Full-time faculty:** 157 total; 8% have terminal degrees, 8% minority, 46% women. **Part-time faculty:** 429 total; 9% minority, 51% women. **Class size:** 67% < 20, 32% 20-39, 1% 40-49. **Special facilities:** Environmental learning center, observatory. **Partnerships:** Formal partnerships with Intel Microelectronics and Portland General Electric/Pacificorps.

Student profile.

Out-of-state:	2%	25 or older:	47%

Transfer out. **Colleges most students transferred to 2008:** Portland State University, Oregon State University, University of Oregon.

Basis for selection. Open admission, but selective for some programs. Special prerequisite requirements for nursing, dental assistant, medical technician, and water quality programs. Special admission process for accelerated degree and CCC/PSU co-admittance programs.

2008-2009 Annual costs. Tuition/fees: $3,015; $9,360 out-of-state. Per-credit charge: $62 in-state; $203 out-of-state. In-state tuition applies to residents of Oregon, Washington, Idaho, Nevada and California. Books/supplies: $1,200. Personal expenses: $900.

2007-2008 Financial aid. **Need-based:** Need-based aid available for part-time students. Work-study available nights, weekends and for part-time students. **Non-need-based:** Scholarships awarded for academics, art, athletics, leadership, music/drama. **Additional information:** Institutional tuition rebate guarantee. Frozen tuition rates for new fall students who graduate within 3 years. Any tuition increase levied by college during those 3 years will be refunded to student upon graduation.

Application procedures. **Admission:** No deadline. No application fee. Admission notification on a rolling basis. **Financial aid:** Priority date 4/10; no closing date. FAFSA, institutional form required. Applicants notified on a rolling basis starting 3/15; must reply within 3 week(s) of notification.

Academics. Some occupational technologies offered as self-paced programs. **Special study options:** Accelerated study, cooperative education, cross-registration, distance learning, double major, dual enrollment of high school students, ESL, honors, independent study, internships, liberal arts/career combination, study abroad. License preparation in nursing, paramedic. **Credit/placement by examination:** AP, CLEP, institutional tests. 12 credit hours maximum toward associate degree. **Support services:** GED preparation and test center, learning center, reduced course load, remedial instruction, study skills assistance, tutoring.

Majors. **Agriculture:** Horticulture, landscaping, ornamental horticulture. **Business:** Accounting, administrative services, business admin, e-commerce, marketing, office management, operations, sales/distribution. **Communications technology:** General. **Computer sciences:** Applications programming, networking, web page design, webmaster. **Construction:** General. **Education:** Early childhood. **Engineering:** Industrial. **Engineering technology:** Architectural drafting, CAD/CADD, construction, drafting, electrical, electrical drafting, industrial, manufacturing, water quality. **Family/consumer sciences:** Child care. **Health:** Nursing (RN). **Liberal arts:** Arts/sciences. **Mechanic/repair:** Auto body, automotive, electronics/electrical. **Production:** Machine shop technology, welding. **Protective services:** Corrections, firefighting, police science. **Public administration:** Community org/advocacy, social work. **Other:** Music technology.

Computing on campus. 500 workstations in library, computer center. Commuter students can connect to campus network. Online course registration, helpline available.

Student life. **Freshman orientation:** Available. One-day program during week before classes begin. **Activities:** Jazz band, choral groups, drama, literary magazine, music ensembles, student government, student newspaper, environmental group, Baptist student ministries, foreign language clubs, Campus Crusade for Christ, nursing organization, Chatino club, service club, computer club, rainbow club, speech/forensics club.

Athletics. NJCAA. **Intercollegiate:** Baseball M, basketball, cross-country, soccer W, softball W, track and field, volleyball W, wrestling M. **Intramural:** Basketball, racquetball, soccer W, tennis, volleyball W. **Team name:** Cougars.

Student services. Adult student services, alcohol/substance abuse counseling, career counseling, student employment services, financial aid counseling, minority student services, on-campus daycare, personal counseling, placement for graduates, veterans' counselor, women's services. **Physically disabled:** Services for visually, speech, hearing impaired. **Transfer:** Transfer adviser, college fairs on campus for students transferring to 4-year colleges.

Contact. E-mail: pattyw@clackamas.edu
Phone: (503) 657-6958 ext. 2263 Fax: (503) 722-5864
Tara Sprehe, Registrar, Clackamas Community College, 19600 Molalla Avenue, Oregon City, OR 97045

Clatsop Community College

Astoria, Oregon
www.clatsopcollege.com **CB code: 4089**

- Public 2-year community college
- Commuter campus in large town

General. Founded in 1958. Regionally accredited. Vessel fire fighting training program available. **Enrollment:** 634 degree-seeking undergraduates. **Degrees:** 85 associate awarded. **Location:** 100 miles from Portland. **Calendar:** Quarter, limited summer session. **Full-time faculty:** 39 total. **Part-time faculty:** 66 total. **Class size:** 83% < 20, 15% 20-39, less than 1% 40-49, 1% 50-99, less than 1% >100. **Special facilities:** 51-foot commercial fishing vessel.

Student profile.

Out-of-state:	13%	**25 or older:**	42%

Basis for selection. Open admission, but selective for some programs. Special admissions requirements for nursing program applicants and international students.

2008-2009 Annual costs. Tuition/fees: $3,150; $6,030 out-of-state. Per-credit charge: $64 in-state; $128 out-of-state. Books/supplies: $1,200. Personal expenses: $648.

2007-2008 Financial aid. **Need-based:** Need-based aid available for part-time students. Work-study available for part-time students. **Non-need-based:** Scholarships awarded for academics.

Application procedures. **Admission:** No deadline. $15 fee. Admission notification on a rolling basis. **Financial aid:** Priority date 5/1; no closing date. FAFSA, institutional form required. Applicants notified on a rolling basis starting 2/1.

Academics. **Special study options:** Cooperative education, distance learning, double major, dual enrollment of high school students, student-designed major, teacher certification program. License preparation in nursing. **Credit/placement by examination:** CLEP, institutional tests. 24 credit hours maximum toward associate degree. **Support services:** GED preparation and test center, learning center, reduced course load, remedial instruction, study skills assistance, tutoring, writing center.

Majors. **Business:** Accounting, business admin, management information systems, office management, office technology. **Computer sciences:** Applications programming, networking. **Health:** Medical assistant, medical secretary, nursing (RN). **Legal studies:** Legal secretary. **Liberal arts:** Arts/sciences. **Protective services:** Criminal justice, firefighting.

Most popular majors. Business/marketing 7%, health sciences 23%, liberal arts 64%.

Computing on campus. 80 workstations in library, computer center, student center.

Student life. **Freshman orientation:** Mandatory. Preregistration for classes offered. **Activities:** Concert band, dance, drama, student government.

Athletics. **Intramural:** Volleyball M.

Student services. Career counseling, services for economically disadvantaged, student employment services, financial aid counseling, personal counseling, veterans' counselor. **Physically disabled:** Services for visually, speech, hearing impaired. **Transfer:** Pre-admission transcript evaluation for new students. Transfer center, transfer adviser, college fairs on campus for students transferring to 4-year colleges.

Contact. Phone: (503) 338-2411 Toll-free number: (866) 252-8768
Fax: (503) 325-5738
Kristen Lee, Coordinator of Admissions, Clatsop Community College, 1653 Jerome Avenue, Astoria, OR 97103

Everest College: Portland

Portland, Oregon
www.everest-college.com **CB code: 2152**

- Private 2-year branch campus and business college
- Very large city

General. Accredited by ACICS. **Calendar:** Quarter.

Contact. Phone: (503) 222-3225 ext. 102
425 SW Washington Street, Portland, OR 97204

Heald College: Portland

Portland, Oregon
www.heald.edu

- Private 2-year business and technical college
- Very large city

General. **Enrollment:** 377 degree-seeking undergraduates. **Degrees:** 5 associate awarded. **Calendar:** Quarter. **Full-time faculty:** 6 total. **Part-time faculty:** 19 total.

Basis for selection. Open admission.

2008-2009 Annual costs. Tuition/fees: $11,550. Books/supplies: $1,500.

Application procedures. **Admission:** No deadline. No application fee. Admission notification on a rolling basis. **Financial aid:** No deadline.

Academics. **Credit/placement by examination:** CLEP.

Majors. **Business:** Business admin. **Computer sciences:** General. **Health:** Medical assistant, medical secretary.

Student life. **Freshman orientation:** Available.

Contact. Phone: (503) 229-0492
Jack Kempt, Director of Admissions, Heald College: Portland, 625 SW Broadway, Portland, OR 97205

Klamath Community College
Klamath Falls, Oregon
www.klamathcc.edu **CB code: 4127**

- Public 2-year community college
- Commuter campus in small city

General. Regionally accredited. **Enrollment:** 850 degree-seeking undergraduates. **Degrees:** 40 associate awarded. **Calendar:** Quarter, limited summer session. **Full-time faculty:** 20 total. **Part-time faculty:** 75 total.

Basis for selection. Open admission.

2009-2010 Annual costs. Tuition/fees (projected): $3,075; $6,585 out-of-state. Per-credit charge: $65 in-state; $143 out-of-state.

Application procedures. **Admission:** No deadline. No application fee. **Financial aid:** No deadline. FAFSA required.

Academics. **Special study options:** Bachelor's degree programs available on campus. **Credit/placement by examination:** CLEP, institutional tests. **Support services:** GED preparation and test center, learning center, remedial instruction, study skills assistance, tutoring, writing center.

Majors. **Agriculture:** Business. **Business:** Accounting technology, business admin, marketing. **Computer sciences:** LAN/WAN management. **Conservation:** Environmental science. **Education:** Early childhood, teacher assistance. **Health:** Nursing assistant, office assistant. **Liberal arts:** Arts/sciences.

Computing on campus. Commuter students can connect to campus network. Online library, wireless network available.

Student life. **Freshman orientation:** Available.

Student services. Financial aid counseling, personal counseling. **Physically disabled:** Services for visually, hearing impaired. **Transfer:** College fairs on campus for students transferring to 4-year colleges.

Contact. E-mail: wood@klamathcc.edu
Phone: (541) 882-3521 Fax: (541) 880-2297
Jason Wood, Student Services Offices, Klamath Community College, 7390 South 6th Street, Klamath Falls, OR 97603

Lane Community College
Eugene, Oregon **CB member**
www.lanecc.edu **CB code: 4407**

- Public 2-year community college
- Commuter campus in small city

General. Founded in 1964. Regionally accredited. Outreach centers in downtown Eugene, Cottage Grove, and Florence. **Enrollment:** 7,574 degree-seeking undergraduates. **Degrees:** 636 associate awarded. **Location:** 110 miles from Portland. **Calendar:** Quarter, extensive summer session. **Full-time faculty:** 231 total. **Part-time faculty:** 324 total. **Partnerships:** Formal partnerships with professional technical advisory groups.

Student profile.

Out-of-state:	2%	**25 or older:**	40%

Transfer out. **Colleges most students transferred to 2008:** University of Oregon, Oregon State University.

Basis for selection. Open admission, but selective for some programs. Special requirements for allied health and flight technology programs. Sequential Tests of Educational Progress required for dental applicants, School and College Ability Tests for nursing applicants, Nelson-Denny Reading Test for dental and medical assistant applicants.

2008-2009 Annual costs. Tuition/fees: $3,729; $12,031 out-of-state. Per-credit charge: $76 in-state; $260 out-of-state. Books/supplies: $1,086. Personal expenses: $1,035.

2007-2008 Financial aid. **Need-based:** 63% of total undergraduate aid awarded as scholarships/grants, 37% as loans/jobs. Need-based aid available for part-time students. Work-study available nights and weekends. **Non-need-based:** Scholarships awarded for art, athletics, minority status, music/drama.

Application procedures. **Admission:** No deadline. No application fee. Admission notification on a rolling basis. **Financial aid:** Closing date 2/15. FAFSA required. Applicants notified on a rolling basis starting 6/1; must reply within 2 week(s) of notification.

Academics. **Special study options:** Accelerated study, cooperative education, cross-registration, distance learning, double major, dual enrollment of high school students, ESL, independent study, internships, liberal arts/career combination, study abroad, weekend college. License preparation in aviation, nursing. **Credit/placement by examination:** CLEP, institutional tests. **Support services:** GED preparation and test center, learning center, pre-admission summer program, reduced course load, remedial instruction, study skills assistance, tutoring, writing center.

Majors. **Business:** Accounting, administrative services, office management, real estate. **Communications:** Broadcast journalism, journalism. **Communications technology:** General. **Computer sciences:** Data processing, programming, systems analysis, web page design. **Construction:** Electrician, maintenance. **Engineering technology:** Construction, drafting, electrical. **Family/consumer sciences:** Child care. **Health:** Dental hygiene, EMT paramedic, nursing (RN), respiratory therapy technology, substance abuse counseling. **Legal studies:** Legal secretary. **Liberal arts:** Arts/sciences. **Mechanic/repair:** Aircraft, auto body, automotive, diesel, electronics/electrical, heating/ac/refrig. **Parks/recreation:** Health/fitness. **Personal/culinary services:** Culinary arts. **Production:** Machine tool. **Protective services:** Criminal justice. **Public administration:** Community org/advocacy. **Transportation:** Aviation. **Visual/performing arts:** Commercial/advertising art.

Most popular majors. Business/marketing 7%, computer/information sciences 7%, health sciences 17%, liberal arts 51%, trade and industry 9%.

Computing on campus. 800 workstations in library, computer center. Commuter students can connect to campus network. Helpline available.

Student life. **Freshman orientation:** Available. Preregistration for classes offered. Each field of study has its own orientation. Program also available for undecided majors. **Activities:** Bands, choral groups, dance, drama, literary magazine, music ensembles, musical theater, radio station, student government, student newspaper, OSPIRG, campus ministry, women's center, associate student group.

Athletics. **Intercollegiate:** Baseball M, basketball, cross-country, track and field, volleyball W. **Intramural:** Badminton, basketball, golf, skiing, soccer, volleyball.

Student services. Adult student services, chaplain/spiritual director, career counseling, student employment services, financial aid counseling, health services, minority student services, on-campus daycare, personal counseling, placement for graduates, veterans' counselor, women's services. **Physically disabled:** Services for visually, speech, hearing impaired. **Transfer:** Pre-admission transcript evaluation for new students. Transfer adviser, college fairs on campus for students transferring to 4-year colleges.

Contact. E-mail: garretth@lanecc.edu
Phone: (541) 463-3100 Fax: (541) 463-3995
Helen Garrett, Director of Admissions, Lane Community College, 4000 East 30th Avenue, Eugene, OR 97405

Linn-Benton Community College
Albany, Oregon **CB member**
www.linnbenton.edu **CB code: 4413**

- Public 2-year community college
- Commuter campus in large town

General. Founded in 1966. Regionally accredited. Courses available at off-campus centers in Corvallis, Lebanon, and Sweet Home. **Enrollment:** 5,079 degree-seeking undergraduates; 215 non-degree-seeking students. **Degrees:** 474 associate awarded. **ROTC:** Army, Air Force. **Location:** 70 miles from Portland, 45 miles from Eugene. **Calendar:** Quarter, limited summer session. **Full-time faculty:** 166 total; 7% minority, 57% women. **Part-time faculty:** 309 total; 7% minority, 66% women. **Class size:** 60% < 20, 37% 20-39, 2% 40-49, less than 1% 50-99. **Special facilities:** Stables, riding arena.

Student profile. Among degree-seeking undergraduates, 1,413 enrolled as first-time, first-year students, 448 transferred in from other institutions.

Part-time:	47%	**Women:**	53%

Transfer out. **Colleges most students transferred to 2008:** Oregon State University, Western Oregon University, University of Oregon, Portland State University, Southern Oregon University.

Basis for selection. Open admission, but selective for some programs. Special requirements for nursing, dental assistant, veterinary technology, pharmacy technology, phlebotomy, public safety dispatcher, and radiologic technology programs. High school diploma or GED required of applicants under 18.

2008-2009 Annual costs. Tuition/fees: $3,112; $7,657 out-of-state. Per-credit charge: $65 in-state; $166 out-of-state. Books/supplies: $1,260. Personal expenses: $4,551.

2007-2008 Financial aid. **Need-based:** 646 full-time freshmen applied for aid; 538 were judged to have need; 511 of these received aid. Average need met was 60%. Average scholarship/grant was $4,172; average loan $2,799. 56% of total undergraduate aid awarded as scholarships/grants, 44% as loans/jobs. Need-based aid available for part-time students. Work-study available nights, weekends and for part-time students. **Non-need-based:** Awarded to 337 full-time undergraduates, including 135 freshmen. Scholarships awarded for academics, art, job skills, leadership, music/drama, state residency.

Application procedures. **Admission:** Priority date 7/14; deadline 10/4 (receipt date). $25 fee. Admission notification on a rolling basis beginning on or about 7/1. **Financial aid:** Priority date 4/1; no closing date. FAFSA required. Applicants notified on a rolling basis starting 4/15; must reply within 2 week(s) of notification.

Academics. **Special study options:** Cooperative education, cross-registration, distance learning, dual enrollment of high school students, ESL, independent study, internships, student-designed major, study abroad. Evening degree program. License preparation in nursing, paramedic, radiology, real estate. **Credit/placement by examination:** AP, CLEP, institutional tests. 24 credit hours maximum toward associate degree. **Support services:** GED preparation and test center, learning center, remedial instruction, study skills assistance, tutoring, writing center.

Majors. **Agriculture:** General, animal sciences, business, dairy, equestrian studies, equine science, horticultural science. **Biology:** General. **Business:** Accounting technology, administrative services, business admin, office management. **Communications:** Journalism. **Computer sciences:** General, applications programming, system admin. **Construction:** Carpentry, electrician, painting, pipefitting. **Education:** General, elementary, physical, secondary, teacher assistance. **Engineering:** General. **Engineering technology:** Drafting, electrical, water quality. **Family/consumer sciences:** General, child care. **Foreign languages:** Spanish. **Health:** Medical assistant, medical records admin, medical secretary, nursing (RN), office assistant, predental, premedicine, prenursing, prepharmacy, preveterinary. **History:** General. **Interdisciplinary:** Biological/physical sciences. **Legal studies:** Legal secretary, paralegal, prelaw. **Liberal arts:** Arts/sciences. **Math:** General. **Mechanic/repair:** General, automotive, diesel, electronics/electrical, heavy equipment, industrial. **Personal/culinary services:** Chef training, restaurant/catering. **Physical sciences:** Chemistry, physics. **Protective services:** Criminal justice, police science. **Psychology:** General. **Social sciences:** General, anthropology, economics, geography, political science, sociology. **Visual/performing arts:** Art, commercial/advertising art, dramatic, photography.

Most popular majors. Business/marketing 13%, engineering/engineering technologies 6%, health sciences 14%, liberal arts 42%.

Computing on campus. 500 workstations in library, computer center, student center. Commuter students can connect to campus network. Online course registration, online library, helpline, wireless network available.

Student life. **Freshman orientation:** Mandatory. Two-hour program. Orientation also available on-line. **Activities:** Concert band, choral groups, dance, drama, student government, student newspaper, Pacific party, Campus Crusade for Christ, Baha'i, Christians on Campus, Chi Alpha Radical Reality, Phi Theta Kappa, campus family co-op, student ambassadors, livestock judging.

Athletics. **Intercollegiate:** Baseball M, basketball, equestrian, volleyball W. **Intramural:** Basketball, bowling, tennis. **Team name:** Roadrunners.

Student services. Adult student services, career counseling, services for economically disadvantaged, student employment services, financial aid counseling, minority student services, on-campus daycare, personal counseling, placement for graduates, veterans' counselor. **Physically disabled:** Services for visually, speech, hearing impaired. **Transfer:** Transfer center, transfer adviser, college fairs on campus for students transferring to 4-year colleges.

Contact. E-mail: admissions@linnbenton.edu
Phone: (541) 917-4811 Fax: (541) 917-4868
Christine Baker, Admissions Outreach Coordinator, Linn-Benton Community College, 6500 SW Pacific Boulevard, Albany, OR 97321-3779

Mt. Hood Community College

Gresham, Oregon
www.mhcc.cc.or.us **CB code: 4508**

- Public 2-year community college
- Commuter campus in small city

General. Founded in 1965. Regionally accredited. **Enrollment:** 7,245 degree-seeking undergraduates; 554 non-degree-seeking students. **Degrees:** 816 associate awarded. **Location:** 12 miles from Portland. **Calendar:** Quarter, limited summer session. **Full-time faculty:** 157 total; 100% have terminal degrees, 6% minority, 54% women. **Part-time faculty:** 404 total; 7% minority, 58% women. **Special facilities:** Planetarium, solar observatory.

Student profile. Among degree-seeking undergraduates, 32% enrolled in a transfer program, 33% enrolled in a vocational program, 6% already have a bachelor's degree or higher, 2,091 enrolled as first-time, first-year students.

Part-time:	57%	**Asian American:**	7%
Out-of-state:	1%	**Hispanic American:**	7%
Women:	59%	**Native American:**	1%
African American:	4%	**25 or older:**	49%

Transfer out. 18% of students enrolled in the transfer program go on to 4-year colleges. **Colleges most students transferred to 2008:** Portland State University, Oregon State University, Eastern Oregon University, Concordia University, University of Phoenix.

Basis for selection. Open admission, but selective for some programs. SAT scores may be used in place of in-house placement test. Special requirements for nursing and graphic design programs. Allied health programs require 2.5 GPA. Interview required for cosmetology and most health services.

High school preparation. Requirements for health programs include 1 algebra, 1 biology, and 1 chemistry.

2009-2010 Annual costs. Tuition/fees (projected): $3,673; $9,991 out-of-state. Per-credit charge: $69 in-state; $209 out-of-state. Books/supplies: $1,011. Personal expenses: $1,971.

2007-2008 Financial aid. **Need-based:** Need-based aid available for part-time students. **Non-need-based:** Scholarships awarded for academics.

Application procedures. **Admission:** No deadline. $25 fee. Application must be submitted on paper. Admission notification on a rolling basis. Most health services majors must apply between November 1 and March 30 for fall admission. Application fee for these programs $15. Application deadlines and priority dates vary by program. **Financial aid:** No deadline. FAFSA, institutional form required. Applicants notified on a rolling basis starting 2/15; must reply within 4 week(s) of notification.

Academics. **Special study options:** Accelerated study, cooperative education, distance learning, double major, dual enrollment of high school students, ESL, exchange student, external degree, honors, independent study, internships, study abroad, weekend college. Bachelor's degree programs available on campus. License preparation in dental hygiene, nursing, paramedic, physical therapy. **Credit/placement by examination:** CLEP, institutional tests. 45 credit hours maximum toward associate degree. College placement test required for chemistry, math, writing, or reading courses. **Support services:** GED preparation and test center, learning center, pre-admission summer program, reduced course load, remedial instruction, tutoring.

Majors. **Agriculture:** Horticulture. **Business:** General, accounting, administrative services, hospitality admin, tourism/travel. **Communications:** Broadcast journalism, journalism. **Communications technology:** Graphic/printing. **Computer sciences:** General. **Conservation:** Fisheries, forestry, management/policy. **Education:** Early childhood. **Engineering technology:** Architectural, civil. **Health:** Dental hygiene, health services, medical assistant, medical records admin, occupational therapy assistant, physical therapy assistant, respiratory therapy technology, surgical technology. **Legal studies:** Legal secretary. **Mechanic/repair:** Automotive, electronics/ electrical. **Personal/culinary services:** Cosmetic, mortuary science. **Protective services:** Firefighting. **Transportation:** Aviation. **Visual/performing arts:** Commercial/advertising art, dramatic.

Most popular majors. Health sciences 23%, liberal arts 46%.

Student life. Freshman orientation: Available. Preregistration for classes offered. **Activities:** Bands, choral groups, dance, drama, music ensembles, musical theater, radio station, student government, student newspaper, symphony orchestra, TV station, Asian cultures appreciation, Campus Agnostics of America, Campus Ambassadors, Chako-Kumtux club, human services student support club, Latino club, Latter-day Saint student association, radio interest group, science club, writers club.

Athletics. NCAA. **Intercollegiate:** Baseball M, basketball, cross-country, golf M, tennis, track and field, volleyball W. **Intramural:** Archery, badminton M, basketball, bowling, cross-country, golf, racquetball, skiing, soccer, softball, swimming, tennis, track and field, volleyball, wrestling M. **Team name:** Saints.

Student services. Career counseling, student employment services, financial aid counseling, health services, minority student services, on-campus daycare, personal counseling, placement for graduates, veterans' counselor. **Physically disabled:** Services for visually, speech, hearing impaired. **Transfer:** Transfer adviser, college fairs on campus for students transferring to 4-year colleges.

Contact. Phone: (503) 491-7391 Fax: (503) 491-6006
Patricia Martin, Associate Dean, Enrollment Services, Mt. Hood Community College, 26000 Southeast Stark Street, Gresham, OR 97030

Pioneer Pacific College

Wilsonville, Oregon
www.pioneerpacific.edu **CB code: 0492**

- For-profit 2-year career college
- Commuter campus in large town
- Interview required

General. Accredited by ACICS. Additional campuses include the Health Career Institute in Wilsonville, learning site in Clackamas, branch campus in Springfield, Oregon Culinary Institute in Portland. **Enrollment:** 364 degree-seeking undergraduates; 465 non-degree-seeking students. **Degrees:** 30 bachelor's, 195 associate awarded. **Location:** 20 miles from Portland. **Calendar:** Continuous, extensive summer session. **Full-time faculty:** 48 total. **Part-time faculty:** 49 total. **Class size:** 94% < 20, 6% 20-39.

Student profile. Among degree-seeking undergraduates, 260 enrolled as first-time, first-year students.

Part-time:	32%	**Women:**	67%
Out-of-state:	1%	**25 or older:**	67%

Transfer out. Colleges most students transferred to 2008: University of Phoenix, Clackamas Community College.

Basis for selection. Open admission, but selective for some programs.

2009-2010 Annual costs. Tuition/fees (projected): $10,993. Per-credit charge: $420. Costs vary by program from $7,840 to $27,835. Certain programs have additional lab fees. Personal expenses: $3,619.

Financial aid. All financial aid based on need. Need-based aid available for part-time students.

Application procedures. Admission: No deadline. $50 fee. Application must be submitted on paper. Admission notification on a rolling basis. **Financial aid:** No deadline. FAFSA required. Applicants notified on a rolling basis starting 2/27.

Academics. Special study options: Accelerated study, honors, internships, liberal arts/career combination. Externships. Bachelor's degree programs available on campus. **Credit/placement by examination:** CLEP, institutional tests. **Support services:** Study skills assistance, tutoring.

Majors. Business: Accounting, business admin, marketing. **Computer sciences:** Information systems, webmaster. **Health:** Health care admin, medical assistant. **Legal studies:** Paralegal. **Personal/culinary services:** Chef training. **Protective services:** Criminal justice.

Most popular majors. Business/marketing 19%, computer/information sciences 19%, health sciences 37%, legal studies 13%, security/protective services 11%.

Computing on campus. 250 workstations in library, computer center. Online library, wireless network available.

Student life. Freshman orientation: Mandatory.

Student services. Career counseling, student employment services, financial aid counseling, placement for graduates. **Transfer:** Pre-admission transcript evaluation for new students.

Contact. E-mail: inquiries@pioneerpacific.edu
Phone: (503) 682-3903 Toll-free number: (866) 772-4636
Fax: (503) 682-1514
Vickie Church, Director of Admissions, Pioneer Pacific College, 27501 Southwest Parkway Avenue, Wilsonville, OR 97070

Pioneer Pacific College: Springfield

Springfield, Oregon
www.pioneerpacific.edu

- For-profit 2-year branch campus and career college
- Commuter campus in small city
- Interview required

General. Accredited by ACICS. Multi-campus institution with main campus in Wilsonville, Health Career Institute in Wilsonville, learning site in Clackamas, branch campus in Springfield, and Oregon Culinary Institute in Portland. **Enrollment:** 240 degree-seeking undergraduates; 203 non-degree-seeking students. **Degrees:** 143 associate awarded. **Location:** 10 miles from Eugene. **Calendar:** Continuous, extensive summer session. **Full-time faculty:** 19 total. **Part-time faculty:** 23 total. **Class size:** 80% < 20, 20% 20-39.

Student profile. Among degree-seeking undergraduates, 214 enrolled as first-time, first-year students.

Part-time:	25%	**25 or older:**	67%
Women:	70%		

Transfer out. Colleges most students transferred to 2008: Clackamas Community College, Chemeketa Community College, University of Phoenix, Lane Community College, Portland Community College.

Basis for selection. Open admission, but selective for some programs.

2009-2010 Annual costs. Tuition/fees (projected): $10,993. Costs vary by program from $7,840 to $27,835. Certain programs have additional lab fees. Personal expenses: $3,619.

Application procedures. Admission: No deadline. $50 fee. Application must be submitted on paper. Admission notification on a rolling basis. **Financial aid:** No deadline. FAFSA required. Applicants notified on a rolling basis starting 3/15.

Academics. Special study options: Accelerated study, honors, internships. **Credit/placement by examination:** CLEP. **Support services:** Study skills assistance, tutoring.

Majors. Business: Accounting, business admin, marketing. **Computer sciences:** Information systems. **Health:** Health care admin, medical assistant. **Protective services:** Criminal justice.

Most popular majors. Business/marketing 20%, computer/information sciences 20%, health sciences 38%, security/protective services 22%.

Computing on campus. 120 workstations in computer center. Online library available.

Student life. Freshman orientation: Mandatory.

Student services. Career counseling, student employment services, financial aid counseling, placement for graduates.

Contact. E-mail: inquiries@pioneerpacific.edu
Phone: (541) 684-4644 Toll-free number: (866) 772-4636
Fax: (541) 684-0665
Vickie Church, Director of Admissions, Pioneer Pacific College: Springfield, 3800 Sports Way, Springfield, OR 97477

Portland Community College

Portland, Oregon **CB member**
www.pcc.edu **CB code: 4617**

- Public 2-year community college
- Commuter campus in very large city

General. Founded in 1961. Regionally accredited. 3 comprehensive campuses; classes offered at several centers throughout district. **Enrollment:** 26,436 degree-seeking undergraduates. **Degrees:** 1,757 associate awarded. **Location:** 5 miles from downtown. **Calendar:** Quarter, extensive summer session. **Full-time faculty:** 413 total; 11% minority, 55% women. **Part-time faculty:** 1,013 total; 10% minority, 57% women.

Student profile. Among degree-seeking undergraduates, 58% enrolled in a transfer program, 42% enrolled in a vocational program.

Out-of-state:	4%	**25 or older:**	52%

Transfer out. Colleges most students transferred to 2008: Portland State University, University of Oregon, Oregon State University.

Basis for selection. Open admission, but selective for some programs. Enrollment in certain programs or courses may require prerequisite course work or permission by a department representative.

High school preparation. High school diploma required for some allied health programs.

2008-2009 Annual costs. Tuition/fees: $3,425; $9,185 out-of-state. Per-credit charge: $70 in-state; $198 out-of-state. Books/supplies: $1,320. Personal expenses: $1,140.

2007-2008 Financial aid. All financial aid based on need. 36% of total undergraduate aid awarded as scholarships/grants, 64% as loans/jobs. Need-based aid available for part-time students. Work-study available nights, weekends and for part-time students.

Application procedures. Admission: No deadline. $25 fee. **Financial aid:** Priority date 3/1; no closing date. FAFSA required. Applicants notified on a rolling basis starting 6/1; must reply within 3 week(s) of notification.

Academics. Special study options: Cooperative education, distance learning, double major, dual enrollment of high school students, ESL, internships, study abroad, weekend college. License preparation in aviation, dental hygiene, nursing, paramedic, radiology, real estate. **Credit/placement by examination:** AP, CLEP, institutional tests. 45 credit hours maximum toward associate degree. **Support services:** GED preparation and test center, learning center, reduced course load, remedial instruction, study skills assistance, tutoring, writing center.

Majors. Agriculture: Landscaping. **Business:** General, accounting, administrative services, business admin, office management, office technology, real estate. **Construction:** Building inspection. **Education:** Early childhood. **Engineering technology:** Civil, computer systems, construction, drafting, electrical, manufacturing. **Family/consumer sciences:** Child care. **Foreign languages:** Sign language interpretation. **Health:** Clinical lab technology, dental hygiene, dental lab technology, EMT paramedic, medical radiologic technology/radiation therapy, medical records admin, substance abuse counseling, veterinary technology/assistant. **Interdisciplinary:** Gerontology. **Legal studies:** Legal secretary, paralegal. **Liberal arts:** Arts/sciences. **Mechanic/repair:** Aircraft, aircraft powerplant, auto body, automotive, diesel, heating/ac/refrig. **Parks/recreation:** Health/fitness. **Protective services:** Criminal justice, fire safety technology. **Visual/performing arts:** Commercial/advertising art, interior design, music performance.

Most popular majors. Business/marketing 8%, health sciences 16%, liberal arts 58%, trade and industry 7%.

Computing on campus. 3,100 workstations in library, computer center, student center. Commuter students can connect to campus network. Online course registration, online library, helpline, wireless network available.

Student life. Freshman orientation: Mandatory. Online orientation available. **Activities:** Bands, choral groups, dance, drama, international student organizations, literary magazine, music ensembles, musical theater, student government, student newspaper.

Athletics. NJCAA. **Intercollegiate:** Basketball. **Intramural:** Basketball, bowling, cross-country, golf, racquetball, soccer, softball, swimming, tennis, volleyball. **Team name:** Panthers.

Student services. Career counseling, services for economically disadvantaged, student employment services, financial aid counseling, minority student services, on-campus daycare, personal counseling, placement for graduates, veterans' counselor, women's services. **Physically disabled:** Services for visually, speech, hearing impaired. **Learning disabled:** Comprehensive services available. **Transfer:** Pre-admission transcript evaluation for new students. Transfer center, transfer adviser, college fairs on campus for students transferring to 4-year colleges.

Contact. Phone: (503) 977-4519 Fax: (503) 977-4740
Veronica Garcia, Dean of Enrollment Services, Portland Community College, Box 19000, Portland, OR 97280-0990

Rogue Community College
Grants Pass, Oregon
www.roguecc.edu **CB code: 4653**

- Public 2-year community college
- Commuter campus in large town

General. Founded in 1970. Regionally accredited. Branch campuses in Medford and White City, learning centers in Medford and Cave Junction. **Enrollment:** 3,232 degree-seeking undergraduates; 1,394 non-degree-seeking students. **Degrees:** 282 associate awarded. **Location:** 30 miles from Medford, 240 miles from Portland. **Calendar:** Quarter, limited summer session. **Full-time faculty:** 78 total; 1% minority, 54% women. **Part-time faculty:** 277 total; 2% minority, 53% women. **Class size:** 54% < 20, 44% 20-39, 2% 40-49, less than 1% 50-99. **Special facilities:** Outdoor concert bowl.

Student profile. Among degree-seeking undergraduates, 81% enrolled in a transfer program, 19% enrolled in a vocational program, 9% already have a bachelor's degree or higher, 817 enrolled as first-time, first-year students.

Part-time:	57%	**Hispanic American:**	7%
Women:	59%	**Native American:**	3%
African American:	1%	**25 or older:**	48%
Asian American:	2%		

Transfer out. 17% of students enrolled in the transfer program go on to 4-year colleges. **Colleges most students transferred to 2008:** Southern Oregon University, Oregon State University, Portland State, University of Oregon.

Basis for selection. Open admission, but selective for some programs. Special requirements for nursing, respiratory therapy, emergency medical technology, human services, and mental health technician. ASSET or COMPASS test required prior to registration for placement purposes. Interview recommended for allied health, nursing programs.

2008-2009 Annual costs. Tuition/fees: $3,390; $4,065 out-of-state. Per-credit charge: $68 in-state; $83 out-of-state. Washington, Idaho, Nevada, and California residents pay in-state tuition. Books/supplies: $1,500. Personal expenses: $1,350.

2007-2008 Financial aid. Need-based: 209 full-time freshmen applied for aid; 160 were judged to have need; 160 of these received aid. Average need met was 78%. Average scholarship/grant was $3,495; average loan $2,469. 66% of total undergraduate aid awarded as scholarships/grants, 34% as loans/jobs. Need-based aid available for part-time students. **Non-need-based:** Awarded to 215 full-time undergraduates, including 76 freshmen.

Application procedures. Admission: No deadline. No application fee. Admission notification on a rolling basis. **Financial aid:** Priority date 5/1; no closing date. FAFSA, institutional form required. Applicants notified on a rolling basis; must reply within 2 week(s) of notification.

Academics. Special study options: Cooperative education, distance learning, double major, dual enrollment of high school students, ESL, independent study, study abroad. License preparation in nursing, paramedic. **Credit/placement by examination:** AP, CLEP, institutional tests. **Support services:** GED preparation and test center, learning center, remedial instruction, study skills assistance, tutoring, writing center.

Majors. Business: General, business admin. **Construction:** General. **Engineering technology:** Construction, electrical, manufacturing. **Family/consumer sciences:** Child care. **Health:** EMT paramedic, nursing (RN), office computer specialist, substance abuse counseling. **Liberal arts:** Arts/sciences. **Mechanic/repair:** Automotive, diesel. **Production:** Welding. **Protective services:** Fire safety technology, police science. **Public administration:** Social work.

Most popular majors. Business/marketing 8%, health sciences 18%, liberal arts 58%.

Computing on campus. 115 workstations in library, computer center. Commuter students can connect to campus network. Online course registration available.

Student life. Freshman orientation: Available. Preregistration for classes offered. **Activities:** Bands, choral groups, drama, literary magazine, musical theater, student government, student newspaper, Latino club.

Athletics. Intramural: Basketball, volleyball.

Student services. Career counseling, services for economically disadvantaged, student employment services, financial aid counseling, on-campus daycare, personal counseling, placement for graduates, veterans' counselor. **Physically disabled:** Services for visually, speech, hearing impaired. **Transfer:** Pre-admission transcript evaluation for new students. Transfer adviser, college fairs on campus for students transferring to 4-year colleges.

Contact. E-mail: csullivan@roguecc.edu
Phone: (541) 956-7427
Claudia Sullivan, Director of Enrollment Services, Rogue Community College, 3345 Redwood Highway, Grants Pass, OR 97527

Southwestern Oregon Community College

Coos Bay, Oregon
www.socc.edu **CB code: 4729**

- Public 2-year culinary school and community college
- Commuter campus in large town

General. Founded in 1961. Regionally accredited. **Enrollment:** 1,600 degree-seeking undergraduates. **Degrees:** 223 associate awarded. **Location:** 125 miles from Eugene, 225 miles from Portland. **Calendar:** Quarter, limited summer session. **Full-time faculty:** 80 total. **Part-time faculty:** 195 total. **Special facilities:** Culinary institute, small business development center, university center.

Student profile.

Out-of-state:	17%	**Live on campus:**	17%
25 or older:	34%		

Transfer out. Colleges most students transferred to 2008: Oregon State University, Southern Oregon University, University of Oregon, Linfield College, Eastern Oregon University.

Basis for selection. Open admission, but selective for some programs. Separate application process for nursing students. Background check required for emergency response and EMTs.

2008-2009 Annual costs. Tuition/fees: $3,660. Per-credit charge: $62. Room/board: $6,160. Books/supplies: $1,200. Personal expenses: $540.

2007-2008 Financial aid. Need-based: Need-based aid available for part-time students. Work-study available for part-time students. **Non-need-based:** Scholarships awarded for art, athletics, leadership, music/drama.

Application procedures. Admission: No deadline. $30 fee, may be waived for applicants with need. Admission notification on a rolling basis. **Financial aid:** Priority date 2/28, closing date 6/30. FAFSA required. Applicants notified on a rolling basis starting 5/1; must reply within 3 week(s) of notification.

Academics. Special study options: Combined bachelor's/graduate degree, cooperative education, distance learning, double major, dual enrollment of high school students, ESL, honors, independent study, internships, liberal arts/career combination. Bachelor's degree programs available on campus. License preparation in nursing. **Credit/placement by examination:** AP, CLEP, institutional tests. **Support services:** GED preparation and test center, learning center, reduced course load, remedial instruction, study skills assistance, tutoring, writing center.

Majors. Agriculture: Turf management. **Business:** Accounting technology, administrative services, banking/financial services, business admin, entrepreneurial studies, management information systems, office management, sales/distribution. **Computer sciences:** Applications programming, computer science, information systems, webmaster. **Conservation:** Environmental studies. **Education:** Teacher assistance. **Engineering:** General. **Family/consumer sciences:** Child care, family studies. **Health:** Licensed practical nurse, medical assistant, substance abuse counseling. **Interdisciplinary:** Biological/physical sciences. **Liberal arts:** Arts/sciences. **Math:** General. **Personal/culinary services:** Culinary arts. **Production:** Welding. **Protective services:** Corrections, criminal justice, firefighting, police science. **Public administration:** Social work.

Most popular majors. Business/marketing 10%, health sciences 8%, liberal arts 58%, security/protective services 8%.

Computing on campus. 338 workstations in dormitories, library, computer center. Dormitories wired for high-speed internet access and linked to campus network. Commuter students can connect to campus network. Online course registration, online library, helpline, wireless network available.

Student life. Freshman orientation: Available. Preregistration for classes offered. **Housing:** Guaranteed on-campus for freshmen. Single-sex dorms, special housing for disabled, apartments, wellness housing available. $250 partly refundable deposit. **Activities:** Bands, choral groups, drama, literary magazine, music ensembles, student government, student newspaper, Rotaract, Phi Theta Kappa, student ambassadors.

Athletics. NJCAA. **Intercollegiate:** Baseball M, basketball, cross-country, golf, soccer, softball W, track and field, volleyball W, wrestling M. **Intramural:** Basketball. **Team name:** Lakers.

Student services. Adult student services, alcohol/substance abuse counseling, career counseling, services for economically disadvantaged, student employment services, financial aid counseling, health services, on-campus daycare, personal counseling, placement for graduates, veterans' counselor. **Physically disabled:** Services for visually, speech, hearing impaired. **Learning disabled:** Comprehensive services available. **Transfer:** Transfer center, college fairs on campus for students transferring to 4-year colleges.

Contact. E-mail: admissions@socc.edu
Phone: (541) 888-7636 Toll-free number: (800) 962-2838 ext. 7636
Fax: (541) 888-7247
Tom Nicholls, Director of Enrollment Management, Southwestern Oregon Community College, 1988 Newmark Avenue, Coos Bay, OR 97420-2956

Treasure Valley Community College

Ontario, Oregon
www.tvcc.cc **CB code: 4825**

- Public 2-year community college
- Commuter campus in small town

General. Founded in 1961. Regionally accredited. **Enrollment:** 2,122 degree-seeking undergraduates; 229 non-degree-seeking students. **Degrees:** 219 associate awarded. **Location:** 60 miles from Boise, Idaho. **Calendar:** Quarter, extensive summer session. **Full-time faculty:** 56 total; 4% minority, 50% women. **Part-time faculty:** 84 total; 21% minority, 44% women. **Class size:** 51% < 20, 44% 20-39, 3% 40-49, 2% 50-99.

Student profile. Among degree-seeking undergraduates, 77% enrolled in a transfer program, 23% enrolled in a vocational program, 847 enrolled as first-time, first-year students, 84 transferred in from other institutions.

Part-time:	44%	**Hispanic American:**	19%
Out-of-state:	70%	**Native American:**	1%
Women:	62%	**25 or older:**	38%
African American:	1%	**Live on campus:**	6%
Asian American:	2%		

Transfer out. Colleges most students transferred to 2008: Eastern Oregon University, Boise State University, Oregon State University, University of Oregon.

Basis for selection. Open admission, but selective for some programs. Special requirements for nursing program. **Homeschooled:** Transcript of courses and grades, state high school equivalency certificate required.

2008-2009 Annual costs. Tuition/fees: $3,600; $4,050 out-of-state. Per-credit charge: $68 in-state; $78 out-of-state. Room/board: $6,660. Books/supplies: $1,050. Personal expenses: $1,500.

2007-2008 Financial aid. Need-based: 829 full-time freshmen applied for aid; 655 were judged to have need; 525 of these received aid. Average need met was 34%. Average scholarship/grant was $3,637; average loan $2,511. 54% of total undergraduate aid awarded as scholarships/grants, 46% as loans/jobs. Need-based aid available for part-time students. Work-study available for part-time students. **Non-need-based:** Scholarships awarded for academics, athletics, leadership, music/drama, state residency.

Application procedures. Admission: No deadline. No application fee. Admission notification on a rolling basis. **Financial aid:** Priority date 4/1; no closing date. FAFSA required. Applicants notified on a rolling basis starting 5/1.

Academics. Special study options: Cooperative education, distance learning, dual enrollment of high school students, ESL, independent study, internships. Elementary education program with Eastern Oregon State College and satellite program with Boise State University. License preparation in nursing, paramedic, real estate. **Credit/placement by examination:** AP, CLEP, institutional tests. 45 credit hours maximum toward associate degree. **Support services:** GED preparation and test center, learning center, preadmission summer program, reduced course load, remedial instruction, study skills assistance, tutoring, writing center.

Majors. Agriculture: Agronomy, animal sciences, business, economics, farm/ranch. **Biology:** General. **Business:** General, business admin, management information systems, office management, office/clerical. **Communications:** General. **Computer sciences:** General, computer science. **Conservation:** Management/policy, wildlife. **Education:** Bilingual, elementary, secondary.

Engineering: General. **Engineering technology:** Computer, drafting. **Foreign languages:** General. **Health:** Athletic training, medical secretary, medical transcription, nursing (RN), predental, premedicine, preveterinary. **History:** General. **Legal studies:** Legal secretary, paralegal, prelaw. **Liberal arts:** Arts/sciences. **Math:** General. **Physical sciences:** Chemistry, geology, physics. **Production:** Welding. **Protective services:** Criminal justice, fire safety technology, firefighting, law enforcement admin, police science. **Psychology:** General. **Public administration:** Social work. **Social sciences:** General, political science. **Visual/performing arts:** General, art.

Most popular majors. Agriculture 7%, business/marketing 12%, education 13%, health sciences 18%, liberal arts 30%, psychology 6%.

Computing on campus. 250 workstations in dormitories, library, computer center, student center. Dormitories wired for high-speed internet access and linked to campus network. Commuter students can connect to campus network. Online course registration, online library, helpline, wireless network available.

Student life. Freshman orientation: Available. Preregistration for classes offered. Online orientation available. **Housing:** Coed dorms, wellness housing available. $200 partly refundable deposit. **Activities:** Bands, choral groups, drama, music ensembles, musical theater, student government, Young Republicans, LDS student association.

Athletics. Intercollegiate: Baseball M, basketball, cross-country, golf, rodeo, soccer, tennis, track and field, volleyball. **Intramural:** Basketball, softball, volleyball. **Team name:** Chukars.

Student services. Financial aid counseling, on-campus daycare, personal counseling, veterans' counselor, women's services. **Transfer:** Pre-admission transcript evaluation for new students. Transfer adviser, college fairs on campus for students transferring to 4-year colleges.

Contact. E-mail: admissions@tvcc.cc
Phone: (541) 881-8822 ext. 228 Fax: (541) 881-2721
Stephanie Oester, Director of Admissions, Treasure Valley Community College, 650 College Boulevard, Ontario, OR 97914

Umpqua Community College

Roseburg, Oregon
www.umpqua.edu **CB code: 4862**

- Public 2-year community college
- Commuter campus in large town

General. Founded in 1964. Regionally accredited. **Enrollment:** 1,444 degree-seeking undergraduates; 1,137 non-degree-seeking students. **Degrees:** 237 associate awarded. **Location:** 60 miles from Eugene. **Calendar:** Quarter, limited summer session. **Full-time faculty:** 56 total; 46% women. **Part-time faculty:** 103 total; 2% minority, 44% women. **Class size:** 50% < 20, 47% 20-39, 1% 40-49, 1% 50-99.

Student profile. Among degree-seeking undergraduates, 52% enrolled in a transfer program, 48% enrolled in a vocational program, 2% already have a bachelor's degree or higher, 405 enrolled as first-time, first-year students.

Part-time:	41%	**Asian American:**	1%
Out-of-state:	25%	**Hispanic American:**	4%
Women:	60%	**Native American:**	2%
African American:	1%	**25 or older:**	42%

Transfer out. Colleges most students transferred to 2008: Oregon State University, University of Oregon, Northwest Christian College, Western Oregon University, Southern Oregon University.

Basis for selection. Open admission, but selective for some programs. Special requirements for nursing program. COMPASS placement test and/or ACT ASSET test used for placement only. **Homeschooled:** High school release required.

2009-2010 Annual costs. Tuition/fees (projected): $3,195; $8,775 out-of-state. Per-credit charge: $63 in-state; $186 out-of-state. Books/supplies: $1,200. Personal expenses: $1,200.

2007-2008 Financial aid. Need-based: 230 full-time freshmen applied for aid; 106 were judged to have need; 103 of these received aid. Need-based aid available for part-time students. **Non-need-based:** Awarded to 75 full-time undergraduates, including 28 freshmen. Scholarships awarded for academics, athletics.

Application procedures. Admission: No deadline. $25 fee. Application must be submitted on paper. Admission notification on a rolling basis. **Financial aid:** Priority date 3/1; no closing date. FAFSA required. Applicants notified on a rolling basis starting 5/1; must reply within 2 week(s) of notification.

Academics. Special study options: Cooperative education, distance learning, double major, ESL, independent study, internships, student-designed major. Bachelor's degree programs available on campus. License preparation in aviation, nursing, paramedic. **Credit/placement by examination:** AP, CLEP, SAT, institutional tests. 45 credit hours maximum toward associate degree. 24 hours of credit by exam may be counted toward 1-year certificate program. **Support services:** GED preparation and test center, learning center, remedial instruction, study skills assistance, tutoring.

Majors. Business: General, accounting, administrative services. **Computer sciences:** Information systems. **Education:** General, early childhood. **Engineering technology:** Civil. **Health:** EMT paramedic, medical secretary, nursing (RN). **Legal studies:** Legal secretary. **Liberal arts:** Arts/sciences. **Mechanic/repair:** Automotive, electronics/electrical. **Personal/culinary services:** Cosmetic. **Protective services:** Firefighting. **Public administration:** Human services. **Transportation:** Airline/commercial pilot. **Other:** Viticulture and enology.

Most popular majors. Business/marketing 8%, health sciences 28%, liberal arts 38%, trade and industry 6%.

Computing on campus. 200 workstations in library, computer center, student center. Commuter students can connect to campus network. Online course registration, helpline, wireless network available.

Student life. Freshman orientation: Mandatory. Preregistration for classes offered. Held the Thursday or Friday prior to beginning of term. **Activities:** Bands, choral groups, drama, music ensembles, musical theater, student government, student newspaper.

Athletics. Intercollegiate: Basketball, volleyball W. **Intramural:** Cheerleading W. **Team name:** Riverhawks.

Student services. Career counseling, student employment services, on-campus daycare, personal counseling, placement for graduates, veterans' counselor. **Physically disabled:** Services for visually, hearing impaired. **Transfer:** Pre-admission transcript evaluation for new students. Transfer center, transfer adviser, college fairs on campus for students transferring to 4-year colleges.

Contact. E-mail: lavera.nordling@umpqua.edu
Phone: (541) 440-7743 Toll-free number: (800) 820-5161
Fax: (541) 440-4612
David Farrington, Director of Enrollment Services, Umpqua Community College, 1140 College Road, Roseburg, OR 97470-0226

Western Culinary Institute

Portland, Oregon
www.wci.edu

- For-profit 2-year culinary school
- Commuter campus in very large city

General. Accredited by ACCSCT. **Enrollment:** 577 undergraduates. **Degrees:** 399 associate awarded. **Calendar:** Continuous. **Full-time faculty:** 26 total. **Part-time faculty:** 3 total.

Basis for selection. Open admission.

2008-2009 Annual costs. Full programs range from $18,050 to $41,050.

Application procedures. Admission: No deadline. $50 fee. Admission notification on a rolling basis.

Academics. Credit/placement by examination: CLEP.

Majors. Business: Hospitality admin. **Personal/culinary services:** Baking, chef training.

Contact. Phone: (503) 223-2245 Toll-free number: (888) 848-3202
Jon Alberts, Western Culinary Institute, 921 SW Morrison Street, Suite 400, Portland, OR 97205

Pennsylvania

Allied Medical and Technical Institute
Forty Fort, Pennsylvania
www.alliedteched.edu **CB code: 3190**

- For-profit 2-year technical college
- Small town

General. Accredited by ACCSCT. **Enrollment:** 402 undergraduates. **Degrees:** 14 associate awarded. **Calendar:** Continuous. **Full-time faculty:** 2 total. **Part-time faculty:** 20 total.

Basis for selection. Admissions based on secondary school record and institutional entrance exam.

2008-2009 Annual costs. Cost of full programs ranges from $10,870 to $22,240 depending on program.

Application procedures. Admission: No deadline.

Academics. Credit/placement by examination: CLEP.

Majors. Business: General. **Health:** Office assistant. **Personal/culinary services:** General.

Contact. Phone: (570) 288-8400
Heather Contardi, Admissions Director, Allied Medical and Technical Institute, 166 Slocum Avenue, Forty Fort, PA 18704-2936

Antonelli Institute of Art and Photography
Erdenheim, Pennsylvania
www.antonelli.edu **CB code: 0971**

- For-profit 2-year visual arts and junior college
- Commuter campus in large town
- Interview required

General. Founded in 1938. Accredited by ACCSCT. **Enrollment:** 219 degree-seeking undergraduates; 3 non-degree-seeking students. **Degrees:** 89 associate awarded. **Location:** 1 mile from Philadelphia. **Calendar:** Semester, limited summer session. **Full-time faculty:** 13 total; 8% women. **Part-time faculty:** 4 total; 25% women. **Class size:** 100% < 20. **Special facilities:** Wet black and white darkroom, computer graphics labs, digital photo labs.

Student profile. Among degree-seeking undergraduates, 100% enrolled in a vocational program, 2% already have a bachelor's degree or higher, 114 enrolled as first-time, first-year students, 2 transferred in from other institutions.

Out-of-state:	21%	**Hispanic American:**	3%
Women:	64%	**25 or older:**	4%
African American:	5%	**Live on campus:**	48%
Asian American:	1%		

Transfer out. 5% of students enrolled in the transfer program go on to 4-year colleges. **Colleges most students transferred to 2008:** Brooks Institute, Arcadia University, Chestnut Hill College.

Basis for selection. Emphasis placed on interview, recommendations, and samples of art and photography or portfolio. Although not required, student portfolios will be evaluated. **Homeschooled:** Transcript of courses and grades, interview required. Documentation of high school graduation/equivalency from local school district, state department of education or recognized home school organization required. If these items are not available, a GED will be required.

2008-2009 Annual costs. Tuition/fees: $19,325. Per-credit charge: $640. Annual tuition for graphic design/commercial art students is $17,200; for photography students $19,200. Room only: $7,500. Books/supplies: $6,400. Personal expenses: $3,740.

2007-2008 Financial aid. All financial aid based on need. Average need met was 42%. Average scholarship/grant was $6,200; average loan $3,500. 23% of total undergraduate aid awarded as scholarships/grants, 77% as loans/jobs. Need-based aid available for part-time students. Work-study available nights.

Application procedures. Admission: No deadline. $25 fee, may be waived for applicants with need. Admission notification on a rolling basis. **Financial aid:** No deadline. FAFSA required. Applicants notified on a rolling basis; must reply within 2 week(s) of notification.

Academics. Credit/placement by examination: CLEP.

Majors. Visual/performing arts: Commercial photography, commercial/advertising art, design, photography.

Computing on campus. 60 workstations in library, computer center. Online library, wireless network available.

Student life. Freshman orientation: Mandatory. Preregistration for classes offered. **Housing:** Coed dorms, apartments, wellness housing available. $375 fully refundable deposit. Dormitory facilities available from local apartments.

Athletics. Intramural: Volleyball.

Student services. Career counseling, student employment services, financial aid counseling, personal counseling, placement for graduates. **Transfer:** Pre-admission transcript evaluation for new students. Transfer adviser for students transferring to 4-year colleges.

Contact. E-mail: admissions@antonelli.edu
Phone: (800) 722-7871 Toll-free number: (800) 722-7871
Fax: (215) 836-2794
Anthony DeTore, Director of Admissions, Antonelli Institute of Art and Photography, 300 Montgomery Avenue, Erdenheim, PA 19038-8242

Art Institute of York
York, Pennsylvania
www.aiba.artinstitutes.edu **CB code: 1548**

- For-profit 2-year visual arts and technical college
- Commuter campus in large town

General. Founded in 1952. Accredited by ACCSCT. **Location:** 20 miles from Harrisburg, 90 miles from Philadelphia. **Calendar:** Quarter.

Annual costs/financial aid. Tuition/fees (2008-2009): $17,460. Books/supplies: $1,250. Personal expenses: $2,610.

Contact. Phone: (800) 864-7725
Director of Admissions, 1409 Williams Road, York, PA 17402

Berks Technical Institute
Wyomissing, Pennsylvania
www.berks.edu **CB code: 3198**

- For-profit 2-year business and technical college
- Commuter campus in small city

General. Accredited by ACCSCT. **Enrollment:** 566 degree-seeking undergraduates. **Degrees:** 214 associate awarded. **Location:** 64 miles from Philadelphia. **Calendar:** Quarter. **Full-time faculty:** 29 total. **Part-time faculty:** 27 total. **Class size:** 89% < 20, 11% 20-39.

Basis for selection. Test scores very important; interview and school record important. **Learning Disabled:** Meeting with dean of education and department head if deemed necessary by dean of education.

2008-2009 Annual costs. Approximate cost for diploma program, $9,600 to $17,000; for degree program, $21,000 to $30,000. Books/supplies: $992.

Financial aid. All financial aid based on need. Need-based aid available for part-time students.

Application procedures. Admission: No deadline. $50 fee. Admission notification on a rolling basis. **Financial aid:** No deadline. FAFSA required. Applicants notified on a rolling basis; must reply within 2 week(s) of notification.

Academics. Special study options: Internships. **Credit/placement by examination:** CLEP. **Support services:** Learning center, reduced course load, remedial instruction, study skills assistance, tutoring, writing center.

Majors. Business: Accounting, business admin. **Computer sciences:** General, computer graphics, computer science, networking, programming. **Engineering technology:** Drafting. **Health:** Medical assistant, medical secretary. **Legal studies:** Paralegal. **Protective services:** Law enforcement admin. **Visual/performing arts:** Commercial/advertising art.

Computing on campus. 200 workstations in library, computer center. Repair service available.

Student life. Freshman orientation: Mandatory.

Student services. Financial aid counseling, placement for graduates. **Transfer:** Pre-admission transcript evaluation for new students. Transfer adviser for students transferring to 4-year colleges.

Contact. E-mail: platham@berks.edu
Phone: (610) 372-1722 Toll-free number: (800) 490-6992
Ginny Carpenter, Director of Admissions, Berks Technical Institute, 2205 Ridgewood Road, Wyomissing, PA 19610

Bidwell Training Center

Pittsburgh, Pennsylvania
www.bidwell-training.org **CB code: 3199**

- For-profit 1-year business and health science college
- Commuter campus in large city

General. Accredited by ACCSCT. **Calendar:** Continuous.

Annual costs/financial aid. Tuition per year ranges from $7,000 to $10,000, including all fees. Programs offered at no cost to Pennsylvania residents. Need-based financial aid available for full-time students.

Contact. Phone: (412) 323-4000 ext. 156
Director of Student Services, 1815 Metropolitan Street, Pittsburgh, PA 15233

Bradford School: Pittsburgh

Pittsburgh, Pennsylvania
www.bradfordpittsburgh.edu **CB code: 2206**

- For-profit 2-year junior college
- Commuter campus in very large city

General. Accredited by ACICS. **Calendar:** Semester.

Annual costs/financial aid. Need-based financial aid available for full-time students.

Contact. Phone: (412) 391-6710
Director of Admissions, 125 West Station Square Drive, Pittsburgh, PA 15219

Bucks County Community College

Newtown, Pennsylvania **CB member**
www.bucks.edu **CB code: 2066**

- Public 2-year community college
- Commuter campus in large town

General. Founded in 1964. Regionally accredited. Credit courses available at several off-campus locations. **Enrollment:** 10,084 degree-seeking undergraduates. **Degrees:** 755 associate awarded. **Location:** 35 miles from Philadelphia. **Calendar:** Semester, limited summer session. **Full-time faculty:** 166 total. **Part-time faculty:** 435 total. **Class size:** 99% < 20, less than 1% 50-99. **Partnerships:** Formal partnerships with Bucks County Technical High School, Eastern Center for Arts & Technology, Middle Bucks Institute of Technology, Northern Montgomery County Technical Career Center, Upper Bucks County Area Vocational Technical High School, Western Center for Technical Studies.

Student profile.

Out-of-state:	1%	**25 or older:**	36%

Transfer out. Colleges most students transferred to 2008: Temple University, Holy Family University, Pennsylvania State University, Drexel University.

Basis for selection. Open admission, but selective for some programs. Admissions to nursing, fine arts, chef apprenticeship and fine woodworking programs based on GPA and satisfaction of prerequisites. Admission to music program based on above, plus audition. Admission to art program based on above, plus portfolio. College's own test administered for placement purposes, after admission. Interview required for chef apprentice, fine arts, fine woodworking, and nursing programs. Audition required for music program; portfolio required for art, fine woodworking programs; essay required for chef apprentice program. **Adult students:** Students over 65 exempt from placement tests. **Homeschooled:** Final official transcript certified by state required. **Learning Disabled:** Special testing accommodations can be provided for the entrance assessment test for students with learning disabilities.

2008-2009 Annual costs. Tuition/fees: $3,584; $6,734 out-of-district; $9,884 out-of-state. Per-credit charge: $95 in-district; $190 out-of-district; $285 out-of-state. Books/supplies: $1,350. Personal expenses: $1,350.

2008-2009 Financial aid. Need-based: 69% of total undergraduate aid awarded as scholarships/grants, 31% as loans/jobs. Need-based aid available for part-time students. Work-study available nights, weekends and for part-time students. **Non-need-based:** Scholarships awarded for academics.

Application procedures. Admission: Closing date 5/1 (postmark date). $30 fee. Application must be submitted on paper. Admission notification on a rolling basis. **Financial aid:** Closing date 5/1. FAFSA required. Applicants notified on a rolling basis starting 6/1; must reply within 2 week(s) of notification.

Academics. Special study options: Cooperative education, distance learning, dual enrollment of high school students, ESL, external degree, honors, independent study, internships, student-designed major, weekend college. Bachelor's degree programs available on campus. License preparation in nursing, occupational therapy, physical therapy, radiology, real estate. **Credit/placement by examination:** AP, CLEP, institutional tests. 30 credit hours maximum toward associate degree. **Support services:** GED preparation and test center, learning center, reduced course load, remedial instruction, study skills assistance, tutoring, writing center.

Majors. Area/ethnic studies: American. **Biology:** General. **Business:** General, accounting, administrative services, business admin, hospitality admin, hotel/motel admin, marketing, office management, office/clerical, operations, restaurant/food services, retailing, small business admin, tourism/travel. **Communications:** General, digital media, journalism. **Communications technology:** Animation/special effects, graphic/printing. **Computer sciences:** General, computer graphics, computer science, data processing, information systems, information technology, networking, programming. **Conservation:** Environmental science. **Education:** General, biology, chemistry, early childhood, health, mathematics, physical, teacher assistance. **Engineering:** General. **Family/consumer sciences:** Institutional food production. **Health:** Health services, management/clinical assistant, medical assistant, nursing (RN), office assistant. **Legal studies:** Legal secretary, paralegal. **Liberal arts:** Arts/sciences, humanities. **Math:** General. **Parks/recreation:** Health/fitness, sports admin. **Personal/culinary services:** Baking, chef training, culinary arts, restaurant/catering. **Physical sciences:** Chemistry. **Production:** Woodworking. **Protective services:** Correctional facilities, corrections, criminal justice, firefighting, police science. **Psychology:** General. **Public administration:** Social work. **Social sciences:** General. **Visual/performing arts:** General, cinematography, commercial/advertising art, dramatic, graphic design, studio arts.

Most popular majors. Business/marketing 19%, education 14%, health sciences 14%, liberal arts 13%, visual/performing arts 6%.

Computing on campus. 450 workstations in library, computer center. Commuter students can connect to campus network. Online course registration, online library, helpline, wireless network available.

Student life. Freshman orientation: Available. **Activities:** Bands, choral groups, dance, drama, film society, literary magazine, music ensembles, student government, student newspaper, TV station, wide variety of service, social, and recreational programs.

Athletics. NJCAA. **Intercollegiate:** Baseball M, basketball M, equestrian, golf, soccer, tennis, volleyball W. **Intramural:** Baseball M, basketball M, bowling W, equestrian, skiing, softball, volleyball. **Team name:** Centurions.

Student services. Adult student services, alcohol/substance abuse counseling, career counseling, services for economically disadvantaged, student employment services, financial aid counseling, minority student services, on-campus daycare, personal counseling, veterans' counselor, women's services. **Physically disabled:** Services for visually, speech, hearing impaired. **Learning disabled:** Comprehensive services available. **Transfer:** Pre-admission transcript evaluation for new students. Transfer center, transfer adviser, college fairs on campus for students transferring to 4-year colleges.

Contact. E-mail: admissions@bucks.edu
Phone: (215) 968-8100 Fax: (215) 968-8110
Marlene Barlow, Director of Admissions, Bucks County Community College, 275 Swamp Road, Newtown, PA 18940

Butler County Community College

Butler, Pennsylvania
www.bc3.edu **CB code: 2069**

- Public 2-year community college
- Commuter campus in large town

General. Founded in 1965. Regionally accredited. Classes offered in Cranberry township, Mercer, and Lawrence counties. **Enrollment:** 3,837 degree-seeking undergraduates. **Degrees:** 391 associate awarded. **Location:** 35 miles from Pittsburgh. **Calendar:** Semester, limited summer session. **Full-time faculty:** 64 total; 16% have terminal degrees, 53% women. **Part-time faculty:** 271 total; 1% have terminal degrees, 40% women. **Special facilities:** Environmental education center, cultural center/theater, meteorology lab, computer forensics lab. **Partnerships:** Formal partnerships with American Management Association, Workforce & Economic Development Network of PA, Backflow Management, Inc., Carnegie Mellon University, 13 regional fire schools, 12 local high schools.

Student profile. Among degree-seeking undergraduates, 70% enrolled in a transfer program, 30% enrolled in a vocational program.

Part-time:	48%	**Women:**	62%
Out-of-state:	1%	**25 or older:**	37%

Transfer out. 75% of students enrolled in the transfer program go on to 4-year colleges. **Colleges most students transferred to 2008:** Slippery Rock University of Pennsylvania, Clarion University of Pennsylvania, Indiana University of Pennsylvania.

Basis for selection. Open admission, but selective for some programs. Admission to nursing, medical assistant, physical therapist assistant, massage therapy, and metrology programs based on high school record.

2008-2009 Annual costs. Tuition/fees: $2,790; $4,980 out-of-district; $7,170 out-of-state. Per-credit charge: $73 in-district; $146 out-of-district; $219 out-of-state.

2007-2008 Financial aid. Need-based: 48% of total undergraduate aid awarded as scholarships/grants, 52% as loans/jobs. Need-based aid available for part-time students. Work-study available for part-time students. **Non-need-based:** Scholarships awarded for academics, state residency.

Application procedures. Admission: No deadline. $25 fee, may be waived for applicants with need. Application must be submitted on paper. Admission notification on a rolling basis. **Financial aid:** Priority date 4/15; no closing date. FAFSA required. Applicants notified on a rolling basis starting 5/1; must reply within 2 week(s) of notification.

Academics. Special study options: Cooperative education, distance learning, independent study, internships. License preparation in nursing, physical therapy. **Credit/placement by examination:** AP, CLEP, institutional tests. 45 credit hours maximum toward associate degree. **Support services:** GED preparation, learning center, pre-admission summer program, reduced course load, remedial instruction, study skills assistance, tutoring, writing center.

Majors. Biology: General. **Business:** Accounting technology, administrative services, business admin, human resources, marketing, sales/distribution, tourism promotion. **Communications:** Organizational. **Computer sciences:** Applications programming, security, web page design. **Education:** General, kindergarten/preschool. **Engineering:** General. **Engineering technology:** Architectural drafting, civil, computer systems, electrical, instrumentation, manufacturing, mechanical drafting. **Family/consumer sciences:** Institutional food production. **Health:** Health care admin, nursing (RN), office assistant, physical therapy assistant. **Legal studies:** Legal secretary. **Math:** General. **Mechanic/repair:** Heating/ac/refrig. **Parks/recreation:** General, sports admin. **Personal/culinary services:** Cosmetic. **Physical sciences:** General. **Production:** Machine shop technology. **Protective services:** Law enforcement admin, police science. **Psychology:** General. **Visual/performing arts:** Graphic design.

Most popular majors. Business/marketing 21%, engineering/engineering technologies 10%, health sciences 25%, liberal arts 12%, security/protective services 6%.

Computing on campus. 108 workstations in library, computer center. Online course registration available.

Student life. Freshman orientation: Available. **Activities:** Drama, literary magazine, student government, student newspaper, Christian outreach organization.

Athletics. NJCAA. **Intercollegiate:** Baseball M, basketball, cheerleading, golf M, softball W, volleyball W. **Intramural:** Basketball, golf, table tennis, volleyball, weight lifting. **Team name:** Pioneers.

Student services. Adult student services, career counseling, services for economically disadvantaged, student employment services, financial aid counseling, on-campus daycare, personal counseling, placement for graduates, veterans' counselor. **Physically disabled:** Services for visually, hearing impaired. **Transfer:** Pre-admission transcript evaluation for new students. Transfer adviser, college fairs on campus for students transferring to 4-year colleges.

Contact. E-mail: pattie.bajuszik@bc3.edu
Phone: (724) 287-8711 ext. 8346 Toll-free number: (888) 826-2829
Fax: (724) 287-3460
Pattie Bajuszik, Director of Admissions, Butler County Community College, PO Box 1203, Butler, PA 16003-1203

Cambria-Rowe Business College

Johnstown, Pennsylvania
www.crbc.net **CB code: 2210**

- For-profit 2-year business college
- Commuter campus in small city

General. Founded in 1891. Accredited by ACICS. **Enrollment:** 186 degree-seeking undergraduates. **Degrees:** 87 associate awarded. **Location:** 60 miles from Pittsburgh. **Calendar:** Quarter, extensive summer session. **Full-time faculty:** 10 total.

Transfer out. Colleges most students transferred to 2008: Saint Francis University, Mount Aloysius College.

Basis for selection. Students must pass entrance exam. High school transcript, GED scores reviewed. Interview recommended. **Homeschooled:** Transcript of courses and grades required.

2008-2009 Annual costs. Tuition/fees: $9,500. Depending on choice of laptop, fees could be as much as $1,140. Books/supplies: $1,000.

Financial aid. Need-based: Need-based aid available for part-time students. **Non-need-based:** Scholarships awarded for academics, leadership.

Application procedures. Admission: No deadline. $15 fee. Students notified within 2 weeks of receipt of application. **Financial aid:** Closing date 8/1. FAFSA required. Applicants notified on a rolling basis.

Academics. Special study options: Accelerated study, liberal arts/career combination. **Credit/placement by examination:** CLEP, institutional tests. **Support services:** Pre-admission summer program, reduced course load, tutoring.

Majors. Business: General, accounting, administrative services, business admin. **Health:** Medical secretary, medical transcription. **Legal studies:** Legal secretary.

Computing on campus. PC or laptop required. Online library, repair service, wireless network available.

Student life. Freshman orientation: Mandatory. Preregistration for classes offered. Usually held 3 weeks prior to start date.

Student services. Adult student services, career counseling, student employment services, financial aid counseling, personal counseling, placement for graduates. **Transfer:** Transfer adviser for students transferring to 4-year colleges.

Contact. E-mail: admissions@crbc.net
Phone: (814) 536-5168 Fax: (814) 536-5160
Amanda Artim, Director of Admissions, Cambria-Rowe Business College, 221 Central Avenue, Johnstown, PA 15902

Cambria-Rowe Business College: Indiana

Indiana, Pennsylvania
www.crbc.net **CB code: 3274**

- For-profit 2-year business and technical college
- Commuter campus in small town
- Interview required

General. Accredited by ACICS. **Enrollment:** 108 degree-seeking undergraduates. **Degrees:** 47 associate awarded. **Calendar:** Quarter. **Full-time faculty:** 8 total; 25% have terminal degrees, 100% women.

Student profile. Among degree-seeking undergraduates, 41 enrolled as first-time, first-year students.

Part-time:	3%	**Women:**	91%
Out-of-state:	2%		

Basis for selection. Admissions based on high school transcript or GED scores and passing grade on entrance examination administered by school.

2009-2010 Annual costs. Tuition/fees (projected): $9,840. Per-credit charge: $265. Depending on choice of laptop, fees could be as much as $1,140. Books/supplies: $1,100.

Financial aid. Need-based: Need-based aid available for part-time students.

Application procedures. Admission: No deadline. $15 fee. Admission notification on a rolling basis. **Financial aid:** No deadline. FAFSA required. Applicants notified on a rolling basis.

Academics. Special study options: Double major. **Credit/placement by examination:** AP, CLEP, institutional tests. **Support services:** Tutoring.

Majors. Business: Accounting, administrative services, business admin, management information systems. **Computer sciences:** Computer support specialist. **Health:** Medical secretary.

Most popular majors. Business/marketing 62%, health sciences 38%.

Computing on campus. PC or laptop required. Online library, repair service, wireless network available.

Student life. Freshman orientation: Mandatory.

Student services. Transfer: Pre-admission transcript evaluation for new students.

Contact. E-mail: sbell-leger@crbc.net
Phone: (724) 463-0222 Toll-free number: (800) 639-2273
Stacey Bell-Leger, Admissions Representative, Cambria-Rowe Business College: Indiana, 422 South 13th Street, Indiana, PA 15701

Career Training Academy

New Kensington, Pennsylvania
www.careerta.com **CB code: 3205**

- For-profit 2-year career college
- Commuter campus in small town

General. Accredited by ACCSCT. **Location:** 18 miles from Pittsburgh. **Calendar:** Quarter.

Annual costs/financial aid. Tuition ranges from $7,750 to $19,750 depending on program; required fees range from $253 to $1,378. Books and supplies range from $777 to $3,390. Need-based financial aid available for full-time students.

Contact. Phone: (724) 337-1000
Director of Admissions, 950 Fifth Avenue, New Kensington, PA 15068

Career Training Academy: Monroeville

Monroeville, Pennsylvania
www.careerta.edu **CB code: 3207**

- For-profit 2-year branch campus college
- Commuter campus in small city

General. Accredited by ACCSCT. **Location:** 10 miles from Pittsburgh. **Calendar:** Continuous.

Annual costs/financial aid. Tuition ranges from $7,750 to $19,750 depending on program; required fees range from $253 to $1,378. Books and supplies range from $777 to $3,390. Personal expenses: $2,889. Need-based financial aid available to full-time and part-time students.

Contact. Phone: (412) 372-3900
Director of Admissions, 4314 Old William Penn Highway #103, Monroeville, PA 15146

Career Training Academy: Pittsburgh

Pittsburgh, Pennsylvania
www.careerta.edu

- For-profit 2-year branch campus college
- Small city

General. Regionally accredited; also accredited by ACCSCT. **Enrollment:** 64 degree-seeking undergraduates. **Degrees:** 13 associate awarded. **Calendar:** Continuous. **Full-time faculty:** 8 total. **Part-time faculty:** 4 total.

2008-2009 Annual costs. Tuition ranges from $7,750 to $19,750 depending on program; required fees range from $253 to $1,378. Books and supplies range from $777 to $3,390.

Application procedures. Admission: No deadline.

Academics. Credit/placement by examination: CLEP.

Majors. Health: Insurance specialist, massage therapy, medical assistant.

Contact. E-mail: admissions3@careerta.edu
Phone: (412) 367-4000
Career Training Academy: Pittsburgh, 1500 Shoppes at Northway, Pittsburgh, PA 15237

CHI Institute: Broomall

Broomall, Pennsylvania
www.chitraining.com **CB code: 3398**

- For-profit 2-year technical and career college
- Large town

General. Accredited by ACCSCT. **Location:** 7 miles from Philadelphia. **Calendar:** Quarter.

Annual costs/financial aid. Tuition ranges from $14,440 to $22,640 per 18-month associate degree program, inclusive of books and fees. Need-based financial aid available to full-time and part-time students.

Contact. Phone: (610) 355-3300
Director of Admissions, 1991 Sproul Road, Suite 42, Broomall, PA 19008

CHI Institute: Franklin Mills

Philadelphia, Pennsylvania
www.chitraining.com **CB code: 3386**

- For-profit 2-year technical college
- Commuter campus in large town

General. Founded in 1981. Accredited by ACCSCT. **Location:** 5 miles from Philadelphia. **Calendar:** Continuous.

Annual costs/financial aid. Costs vary by program. Books/supplies: $765.

Contact. Phone: (215) 357-5100
Admissions Director, 125 Franklin Mills Boulevard, Philadelphia, PA 19154

Commonwealth Technical Institute

Johnstown, Pennsylvania
www.hgac.org **CB code: 3125**

- Private 2-year technical college
- Residential campus in small city

General. Accredited by ACCSCT. Specially geared toward students with disabilities. **Enrollment:** 74 degree-seeking undergraduates. **Degrees:** 50 associate awarded. **Calendar:** Semester. **Full-time faculty:** 34 total.

Transfer out. Colleges most students transferred to 2008: Cambria County Area Community College.

Basis for selection. Open admission.

2008-2009 Annual costs. Tuition/fees: $11,224. Room/board: $9,516.

2007-2008 Financial aid. All financial aid based on need. Need-based aid available for part-time students. Work-study available nights and weekends.

Application procedures. Admission: No deadline. No application fee. Admission notification on a rolling basis. **Financial aid:** No deadline. FAFSA required. Applicants notified on a rolling basis.

Academics. Credit/placement by examination: CLEP. **Support services:** Remedial instruction, tutoring.

Majors. Business: Accounting. **Engineering technology:** Architectural drafting, computer systems, mechanical drafting. **Health:** Dental lab technology, medical secretary. **Personal/culinary services:** Chef training.

Computing on campus. Dormitories wired for high-speed internet access.

Student life. Housing: Single-sex dorms, special housing for disabled, wellness housing available. **Activities:** Choral groups, student government.

Athletics. Intramural: Basketball, volleyball.

Student services. Alcohol/substance abuse counseling, financial aid counseling, health services, personal counseling, veterans' counselor. **Physically disabled:** Services for visually, speech, hearing impaired.

Contact. Phone: (814) 255-8237
Ann Yurcisin, Director of Admissions, Commonwealth Technical Institute, 727 Goucher Street, Johnstown, PA 15905-3902

Community College of Allegheny County

Pittsburgh, Pennsylvania — **CB member**
www.ccac.edu — **CB code: 2122**

- Public 2-year community college
- Commuter campus in very large city

General. Founded in 1966. Regionally accredited. Campuses located in and around Pittsburgh. **Enrollment:** 17,406 degree-seeking undergraduates. **Degrees:** 1,728 associate awarded. **Calendar:** Semester, extensive summer session. **Full-time faculty:** 272 total. **Part-time faculty:** 1,071 total. **Class size:** 56% < 20, 43% 20-39, less than 1% 40-49, less than 1% 50-99, less than 1% >100.

Student profile.

Out-of-state:	1%	**25 or older:**	52%

Transfer out. Colleges most students transferred to 2008: University of Pittsburgh, Robert Morris University, Duquesne University, Point Park University, Carlow College.

Basis for selection. Open admission, but selective for some programs. Special requirements for some health-related, culinary arts, and automotive programs. COMPASS used for placement. Audition recommended for music program.

2008-2009 Annual costs. Tuition/fees: $2,819; $5,399 out-of-district; $7,949 out-of-state. Per-credit charge: $85 in-district; $171 out-of-district; $256 out-of-state. If county does not have community college, tuition is $2,970 per year. Nursing and allied health courses subject to additional fees. Books/supplies: $750. Personal expenses: $3,737.

2007-2008 Financial aid. Need-based: Need-based aid available for part-time students. Work-study available nights, weekends and for part-time students. **Non-need-based:** Scholarships awarded for academics, minority status.

Application procedures. Admission: No deadline. No application fee. Admission notification on a rolling basis. **Financial aid:** Priority date 5/1; no closing date. FAFSA required. Applicants notified on a rolling basis starting 5/1.

Academics. Special study options: Cross-registration, distance learning, dual enrollment of high school students, ESL, external degree, honors, independent study, liberal arts/career combination, study abroad. License preparation in nursing. **Credit/placement by examination:** AP, CLEP, institutional tests. 30 credit hours maximum toward associate degree. **Support services:** GED preparation and test center, learning center, reduced course load, remedial instruction, study skills assistance, tutoring, writing center.

Majors. Agriculture: Horticulture, landscaping, turf management. **Biology:** General. **Business:** Accounting technology, administrative services, banking/financial services, business admin, entrepreneurial studies, human resources, management information systems, marketing. **Communications:** Journalism. **Construction:** General, electrician, maintenance, painting, power transmission. **Education:** Elementary, teacher assistance. **Engineering technology:** Automotive, civil, electrical, environmental, hydraulics, robotics. **Family/consumer sciences:** Child development. **Foreign languages:** General. **Health:** Cardiovascular technology, clinical lab technology, medical assistant, medical radiologic technology/radiation therapy, medical records technology, mental health services, nuclear medical technology, nursing (RN), occupational therapy assistant, pharmacy assistant, physical therapy assistant, respiratory therapy technology, sonography, surgical technology. **Liberal arts:** Arts/sciences, humanities. **Math:** General. **Mechanic/repair:** Business machine, heating/ac/refrig. **Parks/recreation:** Health/fitness. **Personal/culinary services:** Chef training, restaurant/catering. **Physical sciences:** Chemistry, physics. **Production:** Welding. **Protective services:** Corrections, fire safety technology, police science. **Psychology:** General. **Public administration:** Social work. **Science technology:** Chemical. **Social sciences:** General, sociology. **Transportation:** Airline/commercial pilot, aviation management. **Visual/performing arts:** Art, commercial/advertising art.

Most popular majors. Business/marketing 12%, health sciences 36%, liberal arts 26%, trade and industry 7%.

Computing on campus. 3,700 workstations in library, computer center. Commuter students can connect to campus network. Helpline available.

Student life. Freshman orientation: Available. **Activities:** Jazz band, choral groups, drama, music ensembles, student government, student newspaper.

Athletics. NJCAA. **Intercollegiate:** Baseball M, basketball, bowling, golf, ice hockey M, softball W, tennis, volleyball W.

Student services. Adult student services, career counseling, student employment services, health services, on-campus daycare, personal counseling, placement for graduates, veterans' counselor. **Physically disabled:** Services for visually, speech, hearing impaired. **Transfer:** Transfer adviser for students transferring to 4-year colleges.

Contact. Phone: (412) 323-2323
Mary Lou Kennedy, Director of Admissions, Community College of Allegheny County, 800 Allegheny Avenue, Pittsburgh, PA 15233

Community College of Beaver County

Monaca, Pennsylvania — **CB member**
www.ccbc.edu — **CB code: 2126**

- Public 2-year community college
- Commuter campus in small town

General. Founded in 1966. Regionally accredited. **Enrollment:** 1,859 degree-seeking undergraduates. **Degrees:** 372 associate awarded. **Location:** 30 miles from Pittsburgh. **Calendar:** Semester, limited summer session. **Full-time faculty:** 51 total. **Part-time faculty:** 115 total. **Class size:** 58% < 20, 41% 20-39, less than 1% 40-49. **Special facilities:** Student-monitored control tower for aviation, computerized mannequins/patient simulators for nursing.

Student profile.

Out-of-state:	5%	**25 or older:**	31%

Transfer out. Colleges most students transferred to 2008: Slippery Rock State University, Geneva College, Robert Morris College, Edinboro State University.

Basis for selection. Open admission, but selective for some programs. NLN Pre-Admission PN test given for admission into nursing program. Interview recommended.

2008-2009 Annual costs. Tuition/fees: $3,255; $6,300 out-of-district; $9,345 out-of-state. Per-credit charge: $87 in-district; $173 out-of-district; $260 out-of-state. Academic enhancement fees, ranging from $25 to $600 per course, apply in programs requiring specialized technology and equipment; $10 per-credit-hour fee for courses that include a lab. Books/supplies: $1,000. Personal expenses: $1,200.

2007-2008 Financial aid. Need-based: Need-based aid available for part-time students. Work-study available nights, weekends and for part-time students. **Non-need-based:** Scholarships awarded for academics, athletics, state residency.

Application procedures. Admission: Priority date 6/1; no deadline. No application fee. Application must be submitted on paper. Admission notification on a rolling basis. Application deadline January 20 for nursing, must reply within 3 weeks of notification. **Financial aid:** Priority date 5/1, closing date 7/1. FAFSA, institutional form required. Applicants notified on a rolling basis starting 8/5; must reply within 2 week(s) of notification.

Academics. Special study options: Cross-registration, distance learning, double major, dual enrollment of high school students, independent study, internships, liberal arts/career combination. License preparation in aviation, nursing, radiology. **Credit/placement by examination:** AP, CLEP, institutional tests. 45 credit hours maximum toward associate degree. **Support services:** GED preparation and test center, learning center, reduced course load, remedial instruction, study skills assistance, tutoring, writing center.

Majors. Agriculture: Landscaping. **Business:** Accounting technology, business admin, human resources, management information systems, marketing. **Communications:** Digital media. **Communications technology:** General. **Computer sciences:** Applications programming, networking. **Education:** Teacher assistance. **Engineering:** Materials. **Engineering technology:** Aerospace, heat/ac/refrig. **Health:** Health aide, medical secretary, nursing (RN). **Interdisciplinary:** Biological/physical sciences. **Liberal arts:** Arts/sciences, humanities. **Personal/culinary services:** Chef training. **Production:** Machine tool, welding. **Protective services:** Police science. **Social sciences:** General. **Transportation:** Air traffic control, aviation management. **Visual/performing arts:** Studio arts.

Most popular majors. Business/marketing 13%, health sciences 19%, liberal arts 10%, security/protective services 17%, trade and industry 28%.

Computing on campus. 220 workstations in library, computer center, student center. Online library available.

Student life. Freshman orientation: Available. Preregistration for classes offered. **Activities:** Drama, literary magazine, student government, student newspaper.

Athletics. NJCAA. **Intercollegiate:** Basketball M, softball W, volleyball W. **Intramural:** Basketball M, golf, softball, table tennis, volleyball. **Team name:** Titans.

Student services. Adult student services, career counseling, services for economically disadvantaged, financial aid counseling, on-campus daycare, personal counseling, veterans' counselor. **Physically disabled:** Services for visually, speech, hearing impaired. **Transfer:** Transfer adviser, college fairs on campus for students transferring to 4-year colleges.

Contact. E-mail: dan.slater@ccbc.edu
Phone: (724) 775-8561 ext. 330 Toll-free number: (800) 335-0222 ext. 330
Fax: (724) 728-7599
Daniel Slater, Registrar, Community College of Beaver County, One Campus Drive, Monaca, PA 15061-2588

Community College of Philadelphia

Philadelphia, Pennsylvania — **CB member**
www.ccp.edu — **CB code: 2682**

- Public 2-year community college
- Commuter campus in very large city

General. Founded in 1965. Regionally accredited. Regional centers located in northeast, northwest, and west Philadelphia. Many additional temporary facilities located throughout city. **Enrollment:** 17,327 degree-seeking undergraduates. **Degrees:** 1,634 associate awarded. **ROTC:** Army. **Calendar:** Semester, extensive summer session. **Full-time faculty:** 409 total; 25% minority, 49% women. **Part-time faculty:** 684 total; 32% minority, 47% women. **Class size:** 36% < 20, 64% 20-39, less than 1% 40-49.

Student profile. Among degree-seeking undergraduates, 78% enrolled in a transfer program, 22% enrolled in a vocational program, 3,847 enrolled as first-time, first-year students, 534 transferred in from other institutions.

Part-time:	67%	**Asian American:**	7%
Out-of-state:	1%	**Hispanic American:**	7%
Women:	67%	**25 or older:**	50%
African American:	46%		

Transfer out. Colleges most students transferred to 2008: Temple University, Drexel University, St. Joseph's University, Holy Family College, Chestnut Hill College.

Basis for selection. Open admission, but selective for some programs. Special requirements for health, music, art and some technical programs. Audition required for music program; portfolio required for art program.

High school preparation. One chemistry, 2 math required of health program applicants.

2008-2009 Annual costs. Tuition/fees: $4,410; $8,160 out-of-district; $11,910 out-of-state. Per-credit charge: $115 in-district; $230 out-of-district; $345 out-of-state. Books/supplies: $750. Personal expenses: $856.

2007-2008 Financial aid. All financial aid based on need. 54% of total undergraduate aid awarded as scholarships/grants, 46% as loans/jobs. Need-based aid available for part-time students. Work-study available nights, weekends and for part-time students.

Application procedures. Admission: No deadline. $20 fee. Admission notification on a rolling basis. **Financial aid:** Closing date 5/1. FAFSA, institutional form required. Applicants notified on a rolling basis.

Academics. Special study options: Accelerated study, distance learning, dual enrollment of high school students, ESL, honors, internships, study abroad, weekend college. License preparation in dental hygiene, nursing, radiology, real estate. **Credit/placement by examination:** AP, CLEP, institutional tests. 30 credit hours maximum toward associate degree. **Support services:** GED preparation and test center, learning center, pre-admission summer program, reduced course load, remedial instruction, tutoring.

Majors. Area/ethnic studies: Women's. **Business:** General, accounting, administrative services, business admin, fashion, international marketing, office/clerical, operations, real estate, sales/distribution. **Communications technology:** Recording arts. **Computer sciences:** General, applications programming, networking, programming, security, system admin, webmaster. **Education:** General, business, secondary. **Engineering:** General. **Engineering technology:** Architectural, biomedical, CAD/CADD, computer, computer systems, construction, electrical, environmental. **Family/consumer sciences:** Child care, institutional food production. **Foreign languages:** Sign language interpretation. **Health:** Clinical lab technology, dental hygiene, health services admin, medical assistant, medical radiologic technology/radiation therapy, medical records technology, mental health services, nursing (RN), respiratory therapy technology. **Legal studies:** Paralegal. **Liberal arts:** Arts/sciences. **Math:** General. **Personal/culinary services:** Chef training, restaurant/catering. **Physical sciences:** General. **Protective services:** Fire safety technology, forensics, police science. **Public administration:** Human services. **Science technology:** Chemical. **Social sciences:** Geography. **Visual/performing arts:** Art, commercial photography, commercial/advertising art, dramatic, music performance.

Most popular majors. Business/marketing 17%, health sciences 13%, liberal arts 35%, public administration/social services 7%.

Computing on campus. 994 workstations in library, student center. Commuter students can connect to campus network. Helpline available.

Student life. Freshman orientation: Available. Preregistration for classes offered. **Activities:** Jazz band, choral groups, dance, drama, music ensembles, radio station, student government, student newspaper, TV station, Christian Coalition, Newman club, Black Student Congress, Latin American student organization, Phi Theta Kappa, Muslim student association, Vietnamese student organization, Asian-American association.

Athletics. Intercollegiate: Baseball M, basketball, cross-country, soccer M, softball W, volleyball W. **Intramural:** Basketball, soccer, softball, tennis, track and field, volleyball. **Team name:** Colonials.

Student services. Adult student services, career counseling, student employment services, financial aid counseling, health services, on-campus daycare, personal counseling, placement for graduates, women's services. **Physically disabled:** Services for visually, speech, hearing impaired. **Transfer:** Transfer adviser, college fairs on campus for students transferring to 4-year colleges.

Contact. E-mail: admissions@ccp.edu
Phone: (215) 751-8010
Luke Kasim, Director of Recruitment and Admissions, Community College of Philadelphia, 1700 Spring Garden Street, Philadelphia, PA 19130-3991

Consolidated School of Business: Lancaster

Lancaster, Pennsylvania
www.csb.edu — **CB code: 2240**

- For-profit 2-year business college
- Commuter campus in small city
- Interview required

General. Founded in 1986. Accredited by ACICS. Additional campus in York. **Enrollment:** 156 degree-seeking undergraduates. **Degrees:** 65 associate awarded. **Location:** 85 miles from Philadelphia, 35 miles from Harrisburg. **Calendar:** Continuous. **Full-time faculty:** 13 total. **Part-time faculty:** 5 total.

Two-Year Colleges

Basis for selection. Open admission.

High school preparation. Recommended computer application coursework for accelerated or advanced placement.

2008-2009 Annual costs. Tuition/fees: $11,500. Books/supplies: $1,500.

Financial aid. Need-based: Need-based aid available for part-time students.

Application procedures. Admission: No deadline. $25 fee. Admission notification on a rolling basis. **Financial aid:** No deadline. FAFSA required. Applicants notified on a rolling basis.

Academics. Programs consist of 3 core elements: business English, computer applications and approximately 34 credit hours of specialty courses. Curriculum developed with area employer's input to maximize job placement. **Special study options:** Accelerated study, internships. **Credit/placement by examination:** CLEP. **Support services:** Study skills assistance, tutoring.

Majors. Business: Accounting, accounting technology, administrative services, business admin, executive assistant, office technology. **Computer sciences:** Data entry, data processing, web page design, webmaster, word processing. **Health:** Insurance coding, insurance specialist, management/clinical assistant, medical records admin, medical secretary, medical transcription, office admin, office assistant, office computer specialist, receptionist, ward clerk. **Legal studies:** Legal secretary.

Computing on campus. 125 workstations in library.

Student life. Freshman orientation: Mandatory.

Student services. Adult student services, career counseling, student employment services, financial aid counseling, placement for graduates. **Physically disabled:** Services for speech, hearing impaired. **Transfer:** Pre-admission transcript evaluation for new students.

Contact. E-mail: admissions@csb.edu
Phone: (717) 394-6211 Toll-free number: (800) 541-8298
Fax: (717) 394-6213
Derena Cedeno, Director of Admissions, Consolidated School of Business: Lancaster, 2124 Ambassador Circle, Lancaster, PA 17603

Consolidated School of Business: York

York, Pennsylvania
www.csb.edu **CB code: 2242**

- For-profit 2-year business college
- Commuter campus in small city
- Interview required

General. Founded in 1986. Accredited by ACICS. Additional campus in Lancaster. **Enrollment:** 112 degree-seeking undergraduates. **Degrees:** 64 associate awarded. **Location:** 28 miles from Harrisburg, 33 miles from Baltimore. **Calendar:** Continuous. **Full-time faculty:** 13 total. **Part-time faculty:** 2 total.

Basis for selection. Open admission. Interview and tour must be completed before acceptance issued. All financial aid matters must be satisfied before classes begin.

2008-2009 Annual costs. Tuition/fees: $11,850. Books/supplies: $1,500.

Financial aid. Need-based: Need-based aid available for part-time students.

Application procedures. Admission: No deadline. $25 fee. Admission notification on a rolling basis. **Financial aid:** No deadline. FAFSA required. Applicants notified on a rolling basis.

Academics. Programs consist of 3 core elements: business English, computer applications and approximately 34 credit hours of specialty courses. Curriculum developed with area employers' input to maximize job placement. **Special study options:** Accelerated study, internships. **Credit/placement by examination:** CLEP. **Support services:** Study skills assistance, tutoring.

Majors. Business: Accounting, accounting technology, administrative services, business admin, executive assistant, office technology, tourism promotion, tourism/travel, travel services. **Computer sciences:** Data processing, LAN/WAN management, web page design, webmaster, word processing. **Health:** Insurance coding, insurance specialist, management/clinical assistant, medical secretary, medical transcription, office computer specialist, receptionist, ward clerk. **Legal studies:** Legal secretary, paralegal.

Student life. Freshman orientation: Mandatory.

Student services. Adult student services, career counseling, student employment services, placement for graduates. **Transfer:** Pre-admission transcript evaluation for new students.

Contact. E-mail: admissions@csb.edu
Phone: (717) 764-9550 Toll-free number: (800) 520-0691
Derena Cedeno, Director of Admissions, Consolidated School of Business: York, York City Business and Industry Park, York, PA 17404

Dean Institute of Technology

Pittsburgh, Pennsylvania
www.deantech.edu **CB code: 2199**

- For-profit 2-year technical college
- Commuter campus in large city
- Interview required

General. Founded in 1948. Accredited by ACCSCT. **Enrollment:** 205 degree-seeking undergraduates. **Degrees:** 52 associate awarded. **Location:** 2 miles from downtown. **Calendar:** Quarter, extensive summer session. **Full-time faculty:** 10 total. **Part-time faculty:** 10 total.

Student profile. Among degree-seeking undergraduates, 65 enrolled as first-time, first-year students.

Part-time:	33%	**Women:**	3%
Out-of-state:	2%		

Transfer out. 91% of students enrolled in the transfer program go on to 4-year colleges. **Colleges most students transferred to 2008:** Point Park College.

Basis for selection. Open admission.

2009-2010 Annual costs. Tuition/fees (projected): $19,350. Per-credit charge: $215. Books/supplies: $709. Personal expenses: $1,440.

Financial aid. Need-based: Need-based aid available for part-time students.

Application procedures. Admission: No deadline. $50 fee. Admission notification on a rolling basis. Must reply by May 1 or within 3 week(s) if notified thereafter. **Financial aid:** Closing date 8/1. FAFSA required. Applicants notified on a rolling basis; must reply within 8 week(s) of notification.

Academics. Special study options: Cooperative education. **Credit/placement by examination:** CLEP, institutional tests. 12 credit hours maximum toward associate degree. **Support services:** Tutoring.

Majors. Construction: Power transmission. **Mechanic/repair:** Heating/ac/refrig.

Computing on campus. 30 workstations in computer center.

Student services. Career counseling, personal counseling, placement for graduates, veterans' counselor. **Transfer:** Transfer adviser for students transferring to 4-year colleges.

Contact. E-mail: info@deantech.edu
Phone: (412) 531-4433 Fax: (412) 531-4435
Richard Ali, Admissions Director, Dean Institute of Technology, 1501 West Liberty Avenue, Pittsburgh, PA 15226

Delaware County Community College

Media, Pennsylvania **CB member**
www.dccc.edu **CB code: 2125**

- Public 2-year community college
- Commuter campus in large town

General. Founded in 1967. Regionally accredited. **Location:** 20 miles from Philadelphia. **Calendar:** Semester.

Contact. Phone: (610) 359-5050
Director of Admissions and Enrollment Services, 901 South Media Line Road, Media, PA 19063

Douglas Education Center
Monessen, Pennsylvania
www.douglas-school.com **CB code: 3288**

- For-profit 2-year visual arts and business college
- Small town
- Interview required

General. Accredited by ACICS. **Enrollment:** 285 degree-seeking undergraduates. **Degrees:** 108 associate awarded. **Location:** 25 miles from Pittsburgh. **Calendar:** Semester, extensive summer session. **Full-time faculty:** 9 total. **Part-time faculty:** 21 total.

Basis for selection. Open admission. Portfolios recommended.

2008-2009 Annual costs. All-inclusive associate, certificate and diploma programs in art, business, cosmetology and medical fields available from $3,290 to $39,825. Books and supplies range from $190 to $2,240.

2008-2009 Financial aid. All financial aid based on need. Need-based aid available for part-time students. Work-study available nights, weekends and for part-time students.

Application procedures. Admission: $50 fee. Admission notification on a rolling basis. **Financial aid:** No deadline. Applicants notified on a rolling basis.

Academics. Special study options: Accelerated study, double major, internships, liberal arts/career combination. **Credit/placement by examination:** CLEP. **Support services:** GED preparation, learning center, reduced course load, remedial instruction, study skills assistance, tutoring.

Majors. Business: Business admin, executive assistant. **Communications technology:** Animation/special effects. **Computer sciences:** Computer graphics, webmaster. **Health:** Medical assistant, medical secretary, office admin, office assistant. **Visual/performing arts:** General, commercial/advertising art.

Student life. Freshman orientation: Available.

Student services. Adult student services, alcohol/substance abuse counseling, career counseling, services for economically disadvantaged, student employment services, financial aid counseling, placement for graduates. **Transfer:** Pre-admission transcript evaluation for new students. Transfer center for students transferring to 4-year colleges.

Contact. E-mail: dec@douglas-school.com
Phone: (724) 684-3684 ext. 100 Toll-free number: (800) 416-6013 ext. 100
Sherry Walters, Director of Enrollment Services, Douglas Education Center, 130 Seventh Street, Monessen, PA 15062

DuBois Business College
DuBois, Pennsylvania
www.dbcollege.com **CB code: 3886**

- For-profit 2-year business and technical college
- Commuter campus in large town
- Interview required

General. Founded in 1885. Accredited by ACICS. **Enrollment:** 254 degree-seeking undergraduates. **Degrees:** 125 associate awarded. **Location:** 100 miles from Pittsburgh. **Calendar:** Quarter, extensive summer session. **Full-time faculty:** 15 total. **Part-time faculty:** 2 total. **Partnerships:** Formal partnerships with 32 Tech Prep high schools.

Student profile.

Out-of-state:	1%	**Live on campus:**	40%
25 or older:	40%		

Basis for selection. Open admission.

High school preparation. Courses in shorthand, accounting, computer, typing, law, psychology, and speech recommended.

2008-2009 Annual costs. Tuition/fees: $9,450. Per-credit charge: $194. Books/supplies: $2,500.

Application procedures. Admission: No deadline. $25 fee, may be waived for applicants with need. Admission notification on a rolling basis. Must reply by May 1 or within 5 week(s) if notified thereafter. **Financial aid:** Closing date 8/1. FAFSA required. Applicants notified on a rolling basis.

Academics. Special study options: Cooperative education, double major, internships, liberal arts/career combination, study abroad. **Credit/placement by examination:** AP, CLEP, institutional tests. **Support services:** Reduced course load, remedial instruction, tutoring.

Majors. Business: General, accounting, administrative services, business admin. **Health:** Medical secretary. **Legal studies:** Legal secretary.

Computing on campus. 100 workstations in library, computer center.

Student life. Freshman orientation: Mandatory. **Housing:** Single-sex dorms available. $225 deposit. **Activities:** Student government, student newspaper, student association.

Athletics. Intercollegiate: Volleyball. **Intramural:** Volleyball.

Student services. Adult student services, career counseling, student employment services, financial aid counseling, personal counseling, placement for graduates, veterans' counselor. **Physically disabled:** Services for visually, speech, hearing impaired. **Transfer:** Transfer adviser for students transferring to 4-year colleges.

Contact. E-mail: admissions@dbcollege.com
Phone: (814) 371-6920 Toll-free number: (800) 692-6213
Fax: (814) 371-3974
Lisa Doty, Director of Admissions, DuBois Business College, One Beaver Drive, DuBois, PA 15801

DuBois Business College: Huntingdon
Huntingdon, Pennsylvania
www.dbcollege.com **CB code: 3290**

- For-profit 2-year business college
- Small town

General. Accredited by ACICS. **Enrollment:** 50 degree-seeking undergraduates. **Degrees:** 14 associate awarded. **Calendar:** Continuous. **Full-time faculty:** 5 total. **Part-time faculty:** 2 total.

Basis for selection. Open admission.

2008-2009 Annual costs. Tuition/fees: $9,450. Per-credit charge: $194. Books/supplies: $2,500.

Application procedures. Admission: No deadline. $25 fee. Admission notification on a rolling basis. **Financial aid:** Closing date 8/1.

Academics. Credit/placement by examination: CLEP.

Majors. Business: General, accounting. **Health:** Medical secretary. **Legal studies:** Legal secretary.

Contact. Phone: (814) 371-6920
Jeannine Coursen, Director, DuBois Business College: Huntingdon, 1001 Moore Street, Huntingdon, PA 16652

DuBois Business College: Oil City
Oil City, Pennsylvania
www.dbcollege.com **CB code: 3292**

- For-profit 2-year branch campus and business college
- Large town

General. Accredited by ACICS. **Enrollment:** 80 degree-seeking undergraduates. **Degrees:** 42 associate awarded. **Location:** 90 miles from Pittsburgh. **Calendar:** Quarter. **Full-time faculty:** 4 total. **Part-time faculty:** 1 total.

Basis for selection. Open admission.

2008-2009 Annual costs. Tuition/fees: $9,450. Per-credit charge: $194. Books/supplies: $2,500.

Application procedures. Admission: No deadline. $25 fee. Admission notification on a rolling basis. **Financial aid:** FAFSA required.

Academics. Credit/placement by examination: CLEP.

Majors. **Business:** Accounting, administrative services. **Computer sciences:** Information systems. **Health:** Medical secretary. **Legal studies:** Legal secretary.

Contact. Phone: (814) 677-1322
Lisa Doty, Director of Admissions, DuBois Business College: Oil City, 701 East Third Street, Oil City, PA 16301

Erie Business Center

Erie, Pennsylvania
www.eriebc.edu **CB code: 2215**

- For-profit 2-year business college
- Commuter campus in small city

General. Founded in 1884. Accredited by ACICS. **Location:** 95 miles from Cleveland. **Calendar:** Trimester.

Annual costs/financial aid. Tuition/fees (2008-2009): $11,230. Books/supplies: $800. Need-based financial aid available to full-time and part-time students.

Contact. Phone: (814) 456-7504 ext. 102
Admissions Administrator, 246 West Ninth Street, Erie, PA 16501

Erie Business Center South

New Castle, Pennsylvania
www.eriebc.edu/newcastle **CB code: 2577**

- For-profit 2-year branch campus and business college
- Commuter campus in small city
- Application essay, interview required

General. Accredited by ACICS. **Enrollment:** 52 degree-seeking undergraduates. **Degrees:** 27 associate awarded. **Location:** 60 miles from Pittsburgh. **Calendar:** Trimester. **Full-time faculty:** 2 total; 100% have terminal degrees. **Part-time faculty:** 2 total; 50% have terminal degrees, 50% women. **Partnerships:** Formal partnerships with Laurel HIgh School, Lincoln High School, Neshannock High School, West Middlesex High School, Beaver Falls High School, Union High School, Seneca Valley High School.

Transfer out. **Colleges most students transferred to 2008:** Thiel College, Slippery Rock University, Edinboro University.

Basis for selection. Open admission. **Homeschooled:** Transcript of courses and grades, state high school equivalency certificate, interview required.

2008-2009 Annual costs. Tuition/fees: $5,820. Per-credit charge: $184. Books/supplies: $1,400. Personal expenses: $1,107.

Application procedures. **Admission:** No deadline. $25 fee.

Academics. **Special study options:** Internships. **Credit/placement by examination:** CLEP. **Support services:** Reduced course load, tutoring.

Majors. **Business:** Accounting, business admin, marketing, tourism/travel. **Computer sciences:** General. **Health:** Medical records admin, medical transcription. **Legal studies:** Legal secretary.

Computing on campus. Online library available.

Student life. **Freshman orientation:** Mandatory. Preregistration for classes offered. **Activities:** Student government, student newspaper.

Student services. Career counseling, student employment services, financial aid counseling, placement for graduates. **Transfer:** Pre-admission transcript evaluation for new students. Transfer adviser for students transferring to 4-year colleges.

Contact. E-mail: hallr@eriebcs.com
Phone: (724) 658-9066 Toll-free number: (800) 722-6227
Fax: (724) 658-3083
Karen Musolino, Admissions Coordinator, Erie Business Center South, 170 Cascade Galleria, New Castle, PA 16101

Erie Institute of Technology

Erie, Pennsylvania
www.erieit.org **CB code: 2284**

- For-profit 2-year technical college
- Small city

General. Accredited by ACCSCT. **Calendar:** Semester.

Annual costs/financial aid. Tuition/fees (2008-2009): $10,625. Books/supplies: $400. Personal expenses: $30.

Contact. Phone: (814) 868-9900
Director of Admissions, 940 Millcreek Mall, Erie, PA 16565

Everest Institute: Pittsburgh

Pittsburgh, Pennsylvania
CB code: 2201

- For-profit 2-year business college
- Large city

General. Accredited by ACICS. **Calendar:** Semester.

Contact. Phone: (412) 261-4520
Director of Admissions, 100 Forbes Avenue, Suite 1200, Pittsburgh, PA 15222

Harcum College

Bryn Mawr, Pennsylvania **CB member**
www.harcum.edu **CB code: 2287**

- Private 2-year junior college
- Commuter campus in large town
- Application essay required

General. Founded in 1915. Regionally accredited. **Enrollment:** 949 degree-seeking undergraduates. **Degrees:** 237 associate awarded. **Location:** 10 miles from Philadelphia. **Calendar:** Semester, limited summer session. **Full-time faculty:** 36 total. **Part-time faculty:** 106 total. **Class size:** 87% < 20, 12% 20-39, less than 1% 40-49. **Special facilities:** Veterinary services building, physical therapist assistant lab, dental clinic, nursing lab, radiology lab.

Student profile.

Out-of-state:	10%	**Live on campus:**	17%
25 or older:	40%		

Transfer out. **Colleges most students transferred to 2008:** Cabrini College, West Chester University, Temple University, Rosemont College, Widener University.

Basis for selection. School record of primary importance. Writing sample required. 750 SAT (exclusive of Writing) and/or 2.0 GPA required. Nursing, dental hygiene, physical therapy assistant, veterinary technology require 900 SAT (exclusive of Writing) and 2.5 GPA. ACCUPLACER exam used for placement. Interview required of dental hygiene, radiology technician, nursing and neurodiognostic technician programs; recommended for all others. **Adult students:** SAT/ACT scores not required if out of high school 3 year(s) or more. **Learning Disabled:** Must provide documentation of disability to ensure proper accommodations are made.

High school preparation. Recommended units include English 4, mathematics 2, social studies 2, history 2, science 2 and academic electives 2. Required units for veterinary technnology, dental hygiene, and physical therapy assistant programs include 2 algebra, geometry, biology, chemistry. 1 unit biology and algebra required for dental assisting program. 2 algebra, biology, and chemistry required for medical laboratory technology.

2008-2009 Annual costs. Tuition/fees: $17,510. Per-credit charge: $550. Room/board: $7,680. Books/supplies: $1,200. Personal expenses: $2,792.

2008-2009 Financial aid. **Need-based:** 50% of total undergraduate aid awarded as scholarships/grants, 50% as loans/jobs. Need-based aid available for part-time students. Work-study available nights, weekends and for part-time students. **Non-need-based:** Scholarships awarded for academics, leadership.

Application procedures. **Admission:** Priority date 5/1; no deadline. $40 fee, may be waived for applicants with need. Admission notification on a rolling basis. **Financial aid:** Priority date 4/15, closing date 5/1. FAFSA, institutional form required. Applicants notified on a rolling basis starting 3/1; must reply within 3 week(s) of notification.

Academics. 86% of academic programs offered have internship/practicum component. **Special study options:** Accelerated study, cooperative education, distance learning, double major, dual enrollment of high school students, ESL, independent study, internships, liberal arts/career combination, study abroad. License preparation in dental hygiene, nursing, physical therapy, radiology. **Credit/placement by examination:** AP, CLEP, institutional tests. 20 credit hours maximum toward associate degree. Maximum of 30 credits total for transfer credits, life experience, challenge examination, and CLEP. **Support services:** Learning center, pre-admission summer program, reduced course load, remedial instruction, study skills assistance, tutoring.

Majors. **Agriculture:** Animal sciences. **Business:** General, business admin, fashion, sales/distribution. **Education:** Early childhood. **Health:** Clinical lab technology, dental assistant, dental hygiene, health services, physical therapy assistant, radiologic technology/medical imaging, veterinary technology/assistant. **Liberal arts:** Arts/sciences. **Protective services:** Law enforcement admin. **Psychology:** General. **Visual/performing arts:** Fashion design, interior design.

Most popular majors. Business/marketing 8%, education 9%, health sciences 63%, visual/performing arts 14%.

Computing on campus. 86 workstations in dormitories, library, computer center, student center. Dormitories wired for high-speed internet access. Commuter students can connect to campus network. Online course registration, online library, helpline, repair service, wireless network available.

Student life. **Freshman orientation:** Available. Preregistration for classes offered. One-day introduction to campus services, separate evening orientation for Lifelong Learners. **Housing:** Guaranteed on-campus for all undergraduates. Coed dorms, special housing for disabled available. $200 deposit. **Activities:** International student organizations, literary magazine, student government, student newspaper, ebony club, Campus Ambassadors, animal technician student organization, Phi Theta Kappa, peer mentors, community service club, dental assisting club, Association for the Education of Young Children, physical therapy assistant club.

Athletics. NJCAA. **Intercollegiate:** Basketball, volleyball W. **Team name:** Bears.

Student services. Adult student services, alcohol/substance abuse counseling, career counseling, services for economically disadvantaged, student employment services, financial aid counseling, health services, minority student services, on-campus daycare, personal counseling, placement for graduates, veterans' counselor, women's services. **Physically disabled:** Services for visually, speech, hearing impaired. **Transfer:** Re-entry adviser, pre-admission transcript evaluation for new students. Transfer center, transfer adviser, college fairs on campus for students transferring to 4-year colleges.

Contact. E-mail: journey@harcum.edu
Phone: (610) 526-6050 Toll-free number: (800) 345-2600
Fax: (610) 526-6147
Nicola DiFronzo-Heitzer, Dean of Admissions, Harcum College, 750 Montgomery Avenue, Bryn Mawr, PA 19010-3476

Harrisburg Area Community College

Harrisburg, Pennsylvania — **CB member**
www.hacc.edu — **CB code: 2309**

- Public 2-year community college
- Commuter campus in small city

General. Founded in 1964. Regionally accredited. County high schools utilized for credit-course offerings. Availability varies by semester. **Enrollment:** 11,703 degree-seeking undergraduates; 8,183 non-degree-seeking students. **Degrees:** 1,620 associate awarded. **ROTC:** Army. **Location:** 90 miles from Philadelphia, 180 miles from New York City. **Calendar:** Semester, limited summer session. **Full-time faculty:** 340 total; 15% have terminal degrees, 13% minority, 60% women. **Part-time faculty:** 827 total; less than 1% have terminal degrees, 6% minority, 57% women. **Class size:** 53% < 20, 45% 20-39, 2% 40-49, less than 1% 50-99.

Student profile. Among degree-seeking undergraduates, 27% enrolled in a transfer program, 73% enrolled in a vocational program, 1,947 enrolled as first-time, first-year students, 1,546 transferred in from other institutions.

Part-time:	66%	**Women:**	71%
Out-of-state:	1%	**25 or older:**	42%

Transfer out. 68% of students enrolled in the transfer program go on to 4-year colleges. **Colleges most students transferred to 2008:** Penn State University, Shippensburg University, Millersville University, Elizabethtown College, York College.

Basis for selection. Open admission, but selective for some programs. Special requirements for allied health programs and chef apprenticeship. ACT required for allied health programs, score report by February 1. Interview required for allied health, and chef apprenticeship programs; essay required for chef apprenticeship program. **Homeschooled:** Statement describing homeschool structure and mission, transcript of courses and grades, letter of recommendation (nonparent) required.

2009-2010 Annual costs. Tuition/fees (projected): $3,960; $6,510 out-of-district; $9,360 out-of-state. Per-credit charge: $97 in-district; $178 out-of-district; $268 out-of-state. Books/supplies: $1,657. Personal expenses: $1,600.

2007-2008 Financial aid. **Need-based:** 1,456 full-time freshmen applied for aid; 1,020 were judged to have need; 949 of these received aid. Average need met was 51%. Average scholarship/grant was $1,826; average loan $2,906. 27% of total undergraduate aid awarded as scholarships/grants, 73% as loans/jobs. Need-based aid available for part-time students. Work-study available for part-time students. **Non-need-based:** Awarded to 100 full-time undergraduates, including 8 freshmen. Scholarships awarded for academics. **Additional information:** Federal work study community service positions available.

Application procedures. **Admission:** No deadline. $35 fee, may be waived for applicants with need. Admission notification on a rolling basis. Must reply by May 1 or within 5 week(s) if notified thereafter. **Financial aid:** Priority date 3/15; no closing date. FAFSA, institutional form required. Applicants notified on a rolling basis starting 6/1.

Academics. **Special study options:** Distance learning, double major, dual enrollment of high school students, ESL, honors, independent study, internships, student-designed major, study abroad, weekend college. Dual admissions with 6 United Negro College Fund institutions, with Penn State Harrisburg Capital College, and with Cheney University of Pennsylvania. License preparation in dental hygiene, nursing, paramedic, radiology, real estate. **Credit/placement by examination:** AP, CLEP, IB, institutional tests. 30 credit hours maximum toward associate degree. **Support services:** GED preparation and test center, learning center, pre-admission summer program, reduced course load, remedial instruction, study skills assistance, tutoring, writing center.

Majors. **Agriculture:** Agribusiness operations, landscaping. **Biology:** General. **Business:** General, accounting technology, accounting/business management, administrative services, banking/financial services, business admin, hospitality admin, hotel/motel admin, real estate, restaurant/food services, retailing, sales/distribution, small business admin, tourism/travel. **Communications:** Media studies. **Computer sciences:** General, computer science, information technology, networking, web page design. **Conservation:** Environmental science, environmental studies. **Construction:** General, building inspection, electrician, lineworker. **Education:** Early childhood, elementary, secondary. **Engineering:** General. **Engineering technology:** Architectural, civil, construction, electrical, mechanical. **Family/consumer sciences:** Institutional food production. **Health:** Cardiovascular technology, clinical lab technology, dental hygiene, dietetics, EMT paramedic, health care admin, health services admin, medical assistant, medical records technology, nuclear medical technology, nursing (RN), radiologic technology/medical imaging, respiratory therapy technology, sonography, surgical technology. **Legal studies:** Court reporting, paralegal. **Math:** General. **Mechanic/repair:** Automotive, computer, heating/ac/refrig, industrial. **Personal/culinary services:** Chef training. **Physical sciences:** General, chemistry. **Protective services:** Criminalistics, firefighting, law enforcement admin, police science. **Psychology:** General. **Public administration:** Human services, social work. **Social sciences:** General, international relations. **Visual/performing arts:** General, art, crafts, design, dramatic, graphic design, music management, photography.

Most popular majors. Business/marketing 23%, education 9%, health sciences 24%, liberal arts 8%, security/protective services 6%, visual/performing arts 7%.

Computing on campus. 280 workstations in library, computer center, student center. Commuter students can connect to campus network. Online course registration, online library, helpline, wireless network available.

Student life. **Freshman orientation:** Mandatory. Preregistration for classes offered. **Activities:** Jazz band, choral groups, drama, literary magazine, music ensembles, musical theater, student government, student newspaper, Allies, African American student association, Christian student fellowship, international awareness, Student Environmental Action Coalition, Students for a Free Tibet, Phi Beta Lambda.

Athletics. **Intercollegiate:** Basketball, soccer M, tennis, volleyball W. **Intramural:** Basketball, soccer, swimming, tennis, volleyball.

Student services. Career counseling, student employment services, financial aid counseling, minority student services, on-campus daycare, personal counseling, placement for graduates, veterans' counselor. **Physically disabled:** Services for visually, hearing impaired. **Transfer:** Pre-admission transcript evaluation for new students. Transfer adviser, college fairs on campus for students transferring to 4-year colleges.

Contact. E-mail: admit@hacc.edu
Phone: (717) 780-2400 Toll-free number: (800) 222-4222
Fax: (717) 236-7674
Jennifer Bucher, Director of Admissions, Harrisburg Area Community College, One HACC Drive, Cooper 206, Harrisburg, PA 17110-2999

Hussian School of Art
Philadelphia, Pennsylvania
www.hussianart.edu **CB code: 7309**

- For-profit 2-year visual arts and technical college
- Commuter campus in very large city
- Interview required

General. Founded in 1946. Accredited by ACCSCT. **Enrollment:** 136 degree-seeking undergraduates. **Degrees:** 35 associate awarded. **Calendar:** Semester. **Full-time faculty:** 3 total; 33% women. **Part-time faculty:** 23 total; 13% have terminal degrees, 4% minority, 22% women. **Class size:** 31% < 20, 69% 20-39. **Special facilities:** Computer graphics facilities.

Student profile. Among degree-seeking undergraduates, 51 enrolled as first-time, first-year students, 1 transferred in from other institutions.

Out-of-state:	10%	**Asian American:**	1%
Women:	26%	**Hispanic American:**	7%
African American:	17%	**25 or older:**	2%

Basis for selection. Personal interview and portfolio review required for acceptance; talent, ability and potential most important. Portfolio required.

High school preparation. High school art or other art training required.

2009-2010 Annual costs. Tuition/fees (projected): $12,550. Supply costs estimated at $375 for required Freshman Supply Kit; consumable supply estimate at $350 additional for the freshman year. Books/supplies: $800. Personal expenses: $2,538.

Application procedures. Admission: No deadline. $25 fee, may be waived for applicants with need. Admission notification on a rolling basis. **Financial aid:** No deadline. FAFSA, institutional form required. Applicants notified on a rolling basis starting 2/15; must reply within 3 week(s) of notification.

Academics. Second-semester freshmen must earn GPA of 2.0 or above to continue in good standing. **Special study options:** Internships. **Credit/placement by examination:** CLEP. **Support services:** Pre-admission summer program.

Majors. Visual/performing arts: Commercial/advertising art, graphic design.

Computing on campus. PC or laptop required. 60 workstations in computer center. Wireless network available.

Student life. Freshman orientation: Available. Preregistration for classes offered. Morning program held 2 weeks prior to official start of classes.

Student services. Career counseling, financial aid counseling, placement for graduates. **Transfer:** Pre-admission transcript evaluation for new students.

Contact. E-mail: info@hussianart.edu
Phone: (215) 574-9600 ext. 201 Fax: (215) 574-9800
Lynne Wartman, Admissions Director, Hussian School of Art, The Bourse, Suite 300, 111 South Independence Mall East, Philadelphia, PA 19106

ITT Technical Institute: Bensalem
Bensalem, Pennsylvania
www.itt-tech.edu

- For-profit 2-year technical college
- Small city

General. Accredited by ACICS. **Calendar:** Quarter.

Contact. Phone: (215) 244-8871
Director of Recruitment, 3330 Tillman Drive, Bensalem, PA 19020

ITT Technical Institute: King of Prussia
King of Prussia, Pennsylvania

- For-profit 2-year visual arts and technical college
- Large town

General. Accredited by ACICS. **Calendar:** Quarter.

Contact. 760 Moore Road, Suite 150, King of Prussia, PA 19406-1212

ITT Technical Institute: Monroeville
Monroeville, Pennsylvania
www.itt-tech.edu **CB code: 2735**

- For-profit 2-year technical college
- Commuter campus in large town

General. Accredited by ACICS. **Calendar:** Quarter.

Contact. Phone: (412) 856-5920
Director of Recruitment, 105 Mall Boulevard, Suite 200E, Monroeville, PA 15146

ITT Technical Institute: Pittsburgh
Pittsburgh, Pennsylvania
www.itt-tech.edu **CB code: 2745**

- For-profit 2-year technical college
- Commuter campus in large city

General. Accredited by ACICS. **Calendar:** Quarter.

Contact. Phone: (412) 937-9150
Director of Recruitment, 10 Parkway Center, Pittsburgh, PA 15220

JNA Institute of Culinary Arts
Philadelphia, Pennsylvania
www.culinaryarts.com **CB code: 3049**

- For-profit 2-year technical college
- Commuter campus in very large city

General. Accredited by ACCSCT. **Enrollment:** 60 degree-seeking undergraduates. **Degrees:** 40 associate awarded. **Calendar:** Quarter, extensive summer session. **Full-time faculty:** 10 total. **Part-time faculty:** 3 total. **Special facilities:** Student-operated restaurant and catering services.

Student profile.

Out-of-state:	12%	**25 or older:**	38%

Basis for selection. Open admission.

2008-2009 Annual costs. Tuition for 15-month associate program, $17,000; 6-month professional cooking diploma program, $8,500. Required fees $75 for both programs. Books and supplies are $225 for the diploma program and $1,050 for the associate program.

Application procedures. Admission: No deadline. No application fee. **Financial aid:** FAFSA required.

Academics. Special study options: Internships. **Credit/placement by examination:** AP, CLEP.

Majors. Personal/culinary services: Culinary arts.

Student life. Freshman orientation: Mandatory.

Student services. Alcohol/substance abuse counseling, career counseling, student employment services, financial aid counseling, legal services, placement for graduates.

Contact. E-mail: admissions@culinaryarts.edu
Phone: (215) 468-8800 Toll-free number: (877) 872-3197
John English, Director of Admissions, JNA Institute of Culinary Arts, 1212 South Broad Street, Philadelphia, PA 19146

Johnson College

Scranton, Pennsylvania — **CB member**
www.johnson.edu — **CB code: 1542**

- Private 2-year technical college
- Commuter campus in small city
- Application essay required

General. Founded in 1912. Accredited by ACCSCT. **Enrollment:** 394 degree-seeking undergraduates. **Degrees:** 125 associate awarded. **Location:** 117 miles from Philadelphia, 125 miles from New York City. **Calendar:** Semester, limited summer session. **Full-time faculty:** 25 total. **Part-time faculty:** 5 total. **Class size:** 44% < 20, 56% 20-39. **Special facilities:** Materials test laboratory, veterinary hospital. **Partnerships:** Formal partnerships with tech prep programs.

Student profile.

Out-of-state:	2%	**Live on campus:**	10%
25 or older:	13%		

Transfer out. Colleges most students transferred to 2008: State University of New York Utica/Rome.

Basis for selection. Open admission, but selective for some programs. Limited admissions to veterinary technology and radiologic technology programs.

High school preparation. 3 units required. Required units include English 2 and mathematics 1. One year chemistry and biology with C or higher required for veterinary science technology majors. One year chemistry or biology and one year algebra II or geometry with C or higher required for radiologic technology.

2008-2009 Annual costs. Tuition/fees: $14,530. Per-credit charge: $375. Room only: $3,612. Books/supplies: $1,500. Personal expenses: $4,500.

Financial aid. Need-based: Need-based aid available for part-time students. Work-study available nights, weekends and for part-time students. **Non-need-based:** Scholarships awarded for academics.

Application procedures. Admission: Closing date 8/1 (receipt date). $30 fee, may be waived for applicants with need, free for online applicants. Admission notification on a rolling basis. Must reply within 30 days. **Financial aid:** Priority date 4/28; no closing date. FAFSA, institutional form required. Applicants notified on a rolling basis starting 4/15; must reply within 2 week(s) of notification.

Academics. Extensive shop and laboratory facilities. **Special study options:** Internships. License preparation in radiology. **Credit/placement by examination:** AP, CLEP, institutional tests. 9 credit hours maximum toward associate degree. **Support services:** Learning center, pre-admission summer program, reduced course load, remedial instruction, study skills assistance, tutoring.

Majors. Business: Logistics. **Computer sciences:** Networking. **Construction:** Carpentry. **Engineering technology:** Architectural drafting, biomedical, electrical. **Health:** Radiologic technology/medical imaging, veterinary technology/assistant. **Mechanic/repair:** General, automotive, diesel, electronics/electrical, industrial. **Production:** Machine tool.

Most popular majors. Computer/information sciences 11%, engineering/engineering technologies 22%, health sciences 27%, trade and industry 40%.

Computing on campus. 52 workstations in library, computer center. Repair service available.

Student life. Freshman orientation: Mandatory, $125 fee. **Housing:** Apartments available. $300 fully refundable deposit, deadline 6/1. **Activities:** Student government, Social Force.

Athletics. Intercollegiate: Basketball, bowling, cross-country, golf. **Intramural:** Basketball, football (non-tackle) M, skiing, soccer, softball, table tennis, volleyball. **Team name:** Jaguars.

Student services. Career counseling, student employment services, financial aid counseling, personal counseling, placement for graduates, veterans' counselor. **Physically disabled:** Services for visually, hearing impaired. **Transfer:** Pre-admission transcript evaluation for new students. Transfer adviser, college fairs on campus for students transferring to 4-year colleges.

Contact. E-mail: admit@johnson.edu
Phone: (570) 702-8911 Toll-free number: (800) 293-9675
Fax: (570) 348-2181
Melissa Ide, Director of Enrollment Management, Johnson College, 3427 North Main Avenue, Scranton, PA 18508

Kaplan Career Institute: Harrisburg

Harrisburg, Pennsylvania
www.kci-harrisburg.com — **CB code: 3212**

- For-profit 2-year health science and technical college
- Commuter campus in small city

General. Accredited by ACICS. **Calendar:** Differs by program.

Annual costs/financial aid. Books/supplies: $2,040. Personal expenses: $2,862.

Contact. Phone: (717) 564-4112
Director of Admissions, 5650 Derry Street, Harrisburg, PA 17111-4112

Kaplan Career Institute: Pittsburgh

Pittsburgh, Pennsylvania
www.icmschool.com — **CB code: 3823**

- For-profit 2-year business and health science college
- Commuter campus in large city
- Application essay, interview required

General. Accredited by ACICS. **Enrollment:** 827 degree-seeking undergraduates. **Degrees:** 158 associate awarded. **Calendar:** Quarter, extensive summer session. **Full-time faculty:** 24 total; 33% have terminal degrees, 8% minority, 58% women. **Part-time faculty:** 32 total; 41% have terminal degrees, 6% minority, 38% women. **Special facilities:** Firearms training simulator.

Basis for selection. Wonderlic required.

2008-2009 Annual costs. Tuition/fees: $17,080. Tuition costs include books and supplies. Books/supplies: $305.

Financial aid. All financial aid based on need. Need-based aid available for part-time students. Work-study available nights and for part-time students.

Application procedures. Admission: No deadline. $20 fee, may be waived for applicants with need. Admission notification on a rolling basis. **Financial aid:** Closing date 4/30. FAFSA, institutional form required. Applicants notified on a rolling basis.

Academics. Special study options: Double major, internships. License preparation in occupational therapy. **Credit/placement by examination:** CLEP. 11 credit hours maximum toward associate degree. **Support services:** Reduced course load, study skills assistance, tutoring.

Majors. Business: Accounting, administrative services, business admin, fashion. **Computer sciences:** General, applications programming, information technology, LAN/WAN management, programming, security, systems analysis, webmaster. **Engineering:** Computer. **Health:** Medical assistant, medical secretary, occupational therapy assistant. **Legal studies:** Legal secretary. **Protective services:** Corrections, criminal justice, law enforcement admin, police science, security services.

Computing on campus. 225 workstations in library, computer center. Online library, helpline, repair service available.

Student life. Freshman orientation: Mandatory. Preregistration for classes offered.

Student services. Career counseling, student employment services, financial aid counseling, personal counseling, placement for graduates.

Contact. E-mail: rsabo@kaplan.edu
Phone: (412) 261-2647 Toll-free number: (800) 441-5222
Fax: (412) 261-0998
Rebekah Sabo, Director of Admissions, Kaplan Career Institute: Pittsburgh, 10 Wood Street, Pittsburgh, PA 15222

Keystone Technical Institute
Harrisburg, Pennsylvania
www.kti.edu **CB code: 3188**

- For-profit 2-year health science and technical college
- Commuter campus in small city
- Interview required

General. Accredited by ACCSCT. **Enrollment:** 57 degree-seeking undergraduates. **Degrees:** 89 associate awarded. **Location:** 206 miles from Philadelphia, 200 miles from Washington, DC. **Calendar:** Continuous. **Full-time faculty:** 10 total. **Part-time faculty:** 6 total.

Basis for selection. All applicants must tour campus. **Homeschooled:** For state grants, applicants must submit either accredited diploma or certification from local superintendent of compliance with Home Education Act. **Learning Disabled:** Provide copy of independent educational program.

2008-2009 Annual costs. Tuition and fees vary by program. Books/supplies: $1,430. Personal expenses: $1,000.

Financial aid. All financial aid based on need. Need-based aid available for part-time students. Work-study available nights.

Application procedures. Admission: No deadline. $20 fee. Admission notification on a rolling basis. **Financial aid:** Priority date 8/1; no closing date. FAFSA required. Applicants notified on a rolling basis.

Academics. Special study options: Dual enrollment of high school students, honors, internships. License preparation in radiology. **Credit/placement by examination:** AP, CLEP. **Support services:** Study skills assistance, tutoring.

Majors. Computer sciences: Data entry, data processing. **Family/consumer sciences:** Child care. **Health:** Asian bodywork therapy, Chinese medicine/herbology, dental assistant, massage therapy, medical assistant, medical records admin, medical records technology, medical secretary, medical transcription, movement therapy. **Legal studies:** Paralegal. **Personal/culinary services:** Chef training, culinary arts.

Most popular majors. Health sciences 76%, legal studies 15%.

Computing on campus. 65 workstations in library. Online library, helpline, repair service available.

Student life. Freshman orientation: Mandatory. Preregistration for classes offered. Held first day of class for all new students.

Student services. Adult student services, alcohol/substance abuse counseling, career counseling, services for economically disadvantaged, student employment services, financial aid counseling, on-campus daycare, placement for graduates. **Transfer:** Re-entry adviser, pre-admission transcript evaluation for new students. Transfer adviser, college fairs on campus for students transferring to 4-year colleges.

Contact. E-mail: info@kti.edu
Phone: (717) 545-4747
William Stradley, Admissions Director, Keystone Technical Institute, 2301 Academy Drive, Harrisburg, PA 17112-1012

Lackawanna College
Scranton, Pennsylvania
www.lackawanna.edu **CB code: 2373**

- Private 2-year junior college
- Commuter campus in small city
- Interview required

General. Founded in 1894. Regionally accredited. **Enrollment:** 1,322 degree-seeking undergraduates; 172 non-degree-seeking students. **Degrees:** 222 associate awarded. **ROTC:** Army, Air Force. **Location:** 150 miles from New York City, 120 miles from Philadelphia. **Calendar:** Semester, limited summer session. **Full-time faculty:** 25 total; 8% have terminal degrees, 36% women. **Part-time faculty:** 141 total; 6% have terminal degrees, 49% women. **Class size:** 75% < 20, 25% 20-39. **Partnerships:** Formal partnerships with Tobyhanna Army Depot and Cinram Corporation; IT Security Pipeline Program and Misericordia University.

Student profile. Among degree-seeking undergraduates, 604 enrolled as first-time, first-year students, 99 transferred in from other institutions.

Part-time:	23%	**Asian American:**	2%
Out-of-state:	9%	**Hispanic American:**	6%
Women:	49%	**25 or older:**	27%
African American:	16%	**Live on campus:**	18%

Transfer out. Colleges most students transferred to 2008: Marywood University, Keystone College, College Misericordia, East Stroudsburg University, Bloomsburg University.

Basis for selection. Open admission. **Homeschooled:** Transcript of courses and grades, state high school equivalency certificate, interview required. **Learning Disabled:** Submit current documentation of disability for arrangement of accommodations.

High school preparation. 11 units recommended. Recommended units include English 4, mathematics 3, social studies 1 and science 3.

2008-2009 Annual costs. Tuition/fees: $10,560. Per-credit charge: $350. Room/board: $6,800. Books/supplies: $1,500. Personal expenses: $1,280.

2008-2009 Financial aid. Need-based: Average need met was 55%. Average scholarship/grant was $5,867; average loan $3,379. 42% of total undergraduate aid awarded as scholarships/grants, 58% as loans/jobs. Need-based aid available for part-time students. Work-study available nights, weekends and for part-time students. **Non-need-based:** Scholarships awarded for academics, athletics, leadership.

Application procedures. Admission: Priority date 8/31; no deadline. $30 fee, may be waived for applicants with need. Admission notification on a rolling basis. Must reply by May 1 or within 4 week(s) if notified thereafter. **Financial aid:** Priority date 5/1; no closing date. FAFSA, institutional form required. Applicants notified on a rolling basis starting 5/1.

Academics. Online tutoring on evenings and weekends. **Special study options:** Cooperative education, distance learning, double major, dual enrollment of high school students, ESL, honors, independent study, internships. Bachelor's degree programs available on campus. License preparation in nursing, paramedic. **Credit/placement by examination:** AP, CLEP, IB, institutional tests. 30 credit hours maximum toward associate degree. **Support services:** GED preparation and test center, learning center, preadmission summer program, reduced course load, remedial instruction, study skills assistance, tutoring, writing center.

Majors. Biology: General. **Business:** General, accounting, administrative services, banking/financial services, business admin. **Communications:** Media studies. **Computer sciences:** General. **Conservation:** Environmental studies. **Education:** General, early childhood. **Engineering technology:** Industrial. **Health:** EMT paramedic, sonography, surgical technology. **Liberal arts:** Arts/sciences, humanities. **Mechanic/repair:** Industrial electronics. **Protective services:** Criminal justice, police science. **Public administration:** Human services. **Social sciences:** General.

Most popular majors. Business/marketing 36%, education 10%, health sciences 23%, liberal arts 11%, security/protective services 17%.

Computing on campus. 300 workstations in dormitories, library, computer center. Dormitories wired for high-speed internet access and linked to campus network. Commuter students can connect to campus network. Online library, helpline available.

Student life. Freshman orientation: Mandatory. Two day program, scheduled the weekend before the start of classes. **Housing:** Guaranteed on-campus for freshmen. Single-sex dorms available. $250 fully refundable deposit. **Activities:** Choral groups, drama, literary magazine, student government, student newspaper, spiritual study group, student government association, diversity club and social justice center.

Athletics. NJCAA. **Intercollegiate:** Baseball M, basketball, cheerleading M, cross-country, football (tackle) M, golf, soccer W, softball W, volleyball W. **Team name:** FIghting Falcons.

Student services. Adult student services, career counseling, services for economically disadvantaged, student employment services, financial aid counseling, personal counseling, placement for graduates, veterans' counselor. **Transfer:** Re-entry adviser, pre-admission transcript evaluation for new students. Transfer adviser, college fairs on campus for students transferring to 4-year colleges.

Contact. E-mail: adminfo@lackawanna.edu
Phone: (570) 961-7814 Toll-free number: (877) 346-3552
Fax: (570) 961-7843
Brian Costanzo, Director of Admissions, Lackawanna College, 501 Vine Street, Scranton, PA 18509

Lansdale School of Business
North Wales, Pennsylvania
www.lsb.edu **CB code: 5853**

- For-profit 2-year career college
- Commuter campus in small town

General. Accredited by ACICS. **Location:** 25 miles from Philadelphia. **Calendar:** Semester.

Annual costs/financial aid. 17-month associate degree program: $18,970 tuition; $75 required fees; $271 per-credit-hour charge; $2,100 books and supplies estimate. Computer lab fees vary by program.

Contact. Phone: (215) 699-5700
Director of Admissions, 201 Church Road, North Wales, PA 19454

Laurel Business Institute
Uniontown, Pennsylvania
www.laurel.edu **CB code: 2329**

- For-profit 2-year technical and career college
- Commuter campus in large town
- Application essay, interview required

General. Founded in 1985. Accredited by ACICS. **Enrollment:** 316 degree-seeking undergraduates. **Degrees:** 122 associate awarded. **Location:** 50 miles from Pittsburgh. **Calendar:** Trimester, extensive summer session. **Full-time faculty:** 23 total. **Part-time faculty:** 17 total. **Class size:** 95% < 20, 5% 20-39. **Special facilities:** Microsoft testing center, Prometric testing site. **Partnerships:** Formal partnership with Nemacolin Woodlands resort.

Student profile. Among degree-seeking undergraduates, 100% enrolled in a vocational program, 1% already have a bachelor's degree or higher, 112 enrolled as first-time, first-year students, 2 transferred in from other institutions.

Part-time:	2%	**African American:**	5%
Out-of-state:	1%	**25 or older:**	85%
Women:	81%		

Transfer out. 2% of students enrolled in the transfer program go on to 4-year colleges. **Colleges most students transferred to 2008:** Robert Morris University, Point Park College, California University of PA, Carlow University, University of Phoenix.

Basis for selection. Test scores, high school grades or GED, and personal interview most important.

2008-2009 Annual costs. Tuition/fees: $8,055. Per-credit charge: $225. Books/supplies: $970.

2008-2009 Financial aid. All financial aid based on need. Need-based aid available for part-time students. Work-study available for part-time students.

Application procedures. Admission: No deadline. $55 fee. Application must be submitted on paper. Admission notification on a rolling basis. **Financial aid:** Closing date 8/1. FAFSA, institutional form required. Applicants notified on a rolling basis; must reply within 4 week(s) of notification.

Academics. Special study options: Accelerated study, double major, dual enrollment of high school students, honors, internships. **Credit/placement by examination:** AP, CLEP, institutional tests. 24 credit hours maximum toward associate degree. **Support services:** Reduced course load, tutoring.

Majors. Business: Accounting, administrative services, business admin. **Computer sciences:** Computer science, networking. **Family/consumer sciences:** Child care. **Health:** Insurance coding, massage therapy, medical assistant, medical transcription, nursing assistant, office assistant, pharmacy assistant, respiratory therapy technology. **Legal studies:** Legal secretary. **Personal/culinary services:** Cosmetic.

Most popular majors. Business/marketing 23%, computer/information sciences 14%, education 12%, family/consumer sciences 6%, health sciences 28%, personal/culinary services 19%.

Computing on campus. 50 workstations in library, computer center. Online library available.

Student life. Freshman orientation: Mandatory. **Policies:** Attendance required in all classes. Excessive absences will result in points being deducted from final grade. **Activities:** Student newspaper, Phi Beta Lambda.

Student services. Student employment services, placement for graduates. **Physically disabled:** Services for visually, speech impaired. **Transfer:** Pre-admission transcript evaluation for new students.

Contact. E-mail: ddecker@laurel.edu
Phone: (724) 439-4900 Fax: (724) 439-3607
Douglas Decker, Admissions Director, Laurel Business Institute, 11 East Penn Street, Uniontown, PA 15401

Laurel Technical Institute
Sharon, Pennsylvania
www.biop.edu **CB code: 2466**

- For-profit 2-year business and technical college
- Commuter campus in large town
- Interview required

General. Accredited by ACICS. Branch campus located in Meadville. **Enrollment:** 190 degree-seeking undergraduates. **Degrees:** 42 associate awarded. **Location:** 50 miles from Pittsburgh; 15 miles from Youngstown, Ohio. **Calendar:** Quarter, extensive summer session. **Full-time faculty:** 3 total. **Part-time faculty:** 6 total. **Class size:** 76% < 20, 24% 20-39.

Student profile.

Out-of-state:	7%	**25 or older:**	45%

Basis for selection. All applicants must take CPAt for skill assessment and placement. If SAT or ACT submitted, CPAt requirement may be waived.

High school preparation. Recommended units include English 3, mathematics 3 and science 2. Accounting, business, computer and English preferred.

2008-2009 Annual costs. Books/supplies: $1,500.

Financial aid. Non-need-based: Scholarships awarded for academics.

Application procedures. Admission: No deadline. $50 fee. Admission notification on a rolling basis. **Financial aid:** Closing date 7/31. Institutional form required.

Academics. Special study options: Internships. **Credit/placement by examination:** CLEP, institutional tests. 15 credit hours maximum toward associate degree. **Support services:** Study skills assistance.

Majors. Business: Accounting, accounting technology, accounting/business management, administrative services, business admin, executive assistant, marketing, office technology. **Computer sciences:** General, data entry, data processing, information technology, word processing. **Health:** Insurance coding, insurance specialist, medical records admin, medical records technology, medical secretary, office admin, office assistant, office computer specialist, receptionist. **Legal studies:** Legal secretary.

Most popular majors. Business/marketing 15%, computer/information sciences 15%.

Computing on campus. 35 workstations in computer center.

Student life. Freshman orientation: Mandatory. Orientation takes place the first day of each quarter. **Activities:** Student government, student newspaper.

Student services. Career counseling, financial aid counseling, placement for graduates. **Transfer:** Pre-admission transcript evaluation for new students.

Contact. Phone: (724) 983-0700 Fax: (724) 983-8355
Diane Heathcote, Admissions Officer, Laurel Technical Institute, 335 Boyd Drive, Sharon, PA 16146

Lehigh Carbon Community College
Schnecksville, Pennsylvania
www.lccc.edu **CB code: 2381**

- Public 2-year community college
- Commuter campus in small town

General. Founded in 1966. Regionally accredited. 3 campuses enable students from northern rural areas as well as city dwellers residing south of main campus to take classes close to home. **Enrollment:** 6,280 degree-seeking undergraduates; 705 non-degree-seeking students. **Degrees:** 643 associate awarded. **ROTC:** Army. **Location:** 8 miles from Allentown, 50 miles from Philadelphia. **Calendar:** Semester, limited summer session. **Full-time faculty:** 89 total; 17% have terminal degrees, 2% minority, 38% women. **Part-time faculty:** 381 total; 6% minority, 50% women. **Class size:** 55% < 20, 45% 20-39.

Student profile. Among degree-seeking undergraduates, 65% enrolled in a transfer program, 35% enrolled in a vocational program, 2,021 enrolled as first-time, first-year students, 226 transferred in from other institutions.

Part-time:	54%	**25 or older:**	35%
Women:	63%		

Transfer out. 70% of students enrolled in the transfer program go on to 4-year colleges. **Colleges most students transferred to 2008:** Kutztown University, DeSales University, Cedar Crest College, Albright College, Penn State University.

Basis for selection. Open admission, but selective for some programs. Special requirements for aviation, allied health, nursing and veterinary technician programs. COMPASS used for course placement. High school diploma or GED required of applicants to allied health and professional pilot programs, and applicants under the age of 18. Interview required for allied health, aviation, medical assistant, veterinary technician programs. **Home-schooled:** Personal interview encouraged.

High school preparation. Special requirements for allied health programs and nursing.

2009-2010 Annual costs. Tuition/fees (projected): $2,976; $5,712 out-of-district; $8,448 out-of-state. Per-credit charge: $85 in-district; $179 out-of-district; $273 out-of-state. Books/supplies: $1,500. Personal expenses: $1,200.

2007-2008 Financial aid. Need-based: Need-based aid available for part-time students. Work-study available nights and for part-time students. **Non-need-based:** Scholarships awarded for academics, state residency.

Application procedures. Admission: No deadline. $30 fee. Admission notification on a rolling basis. **Financial aid:** No deadline. FAFSA required. Applicants notified on a rolling basis starting 5/5; must reply within 2 week(s) of notification.

Academics. Special study options: Cooperative education, cross-registration, distance learning, dual enrollment of high school students, ESL, external degree, honors, independent study, internships, study abroad. Bachelor's degree programs available on campus. License preparation in aviation, nursing, occupational therapy, physical therapy. **Credit/placement by examination:** AP, CLEP, institutional tests. 18 credit hours maximum toward associate degree. **Support services:** GED preparation and test center, learning center, pre-admission summer program, reduced course load, remedial instruction, study skills assistance, tutoring, writing center.

Honors college/program. Top 10% of sponsoring school district, with 1200 SAT, skills assessment score of 90 or above in reading and writing, and 70 or above in algebra required.

Majors. Agriculture: Horticultural science. **Biology:** General, biotechnology. **Business:** Accounting technology, business admin, construction management, human resources, operations, resort management, restaurant/food services. **Communications:** General. **Communications technology:** Animation/special effects, recording arts. **Computer sciences:** Information systems, networking, programming, security, systems analysis, web page design. **Education:** General, early childhood, Montessori teacher, special, teacher assistance. **Engineering:** General, mechanical. **Engineering technology:** Computer, construction, drafting, electrical, manufacturing. **Health:** Medical assistant, medical records technology, nursing (RN), occupational therapy assistant, physical therapy assistant, veterinary technology/assistant. **Legal studies:** Paralegal. **Liberal arts:** Arts/sciences, humanities. **Math:** General. **Mechanic/repair:** Avionics, heating/ac/refrig, industrial electronics. **Parks/recreation:** Sports admin. **Personal/culinary services:** Culinary arts. **Physical sciences:** General. **Protective services:** Criminal justice, law enforcement admin. **Psychology:** General. **Public administration:** Human services. **Science technology:** Chemical. **Social sciences:** General. **Visual/performing arts:** Art, commercial/advertising art, fashion design, interior design. **Other:** Aviation science, Mechanical technology.

Most popular majors. Business/marketing 18%, education 17%, health sciences 17%, liberal arts 17%, security/protective services 6%.

Computing on campus. 830 workstations in library, computer center. Commuter students can connect to campus network. Online course registration, online library, wireless network available.

Student life. Freshman orientation: Available. Morning or afternoon sessions at 3 separate campuses 1 week before classes. Lasts about 2 hours. **Policies:** Must follow student bill of rights and responsibilities. **Activities:** Choral groups, drama, literary magazine, radio station, student government, multicultural student association, political society, justice society, returning adult program, entertainment club, student government association, business honor society, teacher education student association, nursing student organization.

Athletics. Intercollegiate: Baseball, basketball, cheerleading, golf, soccer M, softball W, volleyball W. **Intramural:** Baseball, basketball, bowling, field hockey W, football (non-tackle), golf, racquetball, soccer, softball, table tennis, tennis, track and field M, volleyball, weight lifting. **Team name:** Cougars.

Student services. Adult student services, career counseling, services for economically disadvantaged, student employment services, financial aid counseling, minority student services, on-campus daycare, personal counseling, placement for graduates, veterans' counselor. **Physically disabled:** Services for visually, speech, hearing impaired. **Transfer:** Pre-admission transcript evaluation for new students. Transfer adviser, college fairs on campus for students transferring to 4-year colleges.

Contact. E-mail: tellme@lccc.edu
Phone: (610) 799-1575 Toll-free number: (800) 414-3975
Fax: (610) 799-1629
Mary Theresa Taglang, Director of Admissions, Lehigh Carbon Community College, 4525 Education Park Drive, Schnecksville, PA 18078

Lincoln Technical Institute: Allentown

Allentown, Pennsylvania
www.lincolntech.com **CB code: 2741**

- For-profit 2-year technical college
- Commuter campus in small city
- Interview required

General. Founded in 1946. Accredited by ACCSCT. **Enrollment:** 536 degree-seeking undergraduates. **Degrees:** 42 associate awarded. **Location:** 60 miles from Philadelphia. **Calendar:** Continuous. **Full-time faculty:** 23 total. **Part-time faculty:** 4 total.

Basis for selection. Open admission.

2008-2009 Annual costs. Total program costs range from $12,180 to $29,230. Cost of books included in tuition.

Application procedures. Admission: No deadline. $25 fee, may be waived for applicants with need. **Financial aid:** No deadline.

Academics. Credit/placement by examination: AP, CLEP.

Majors. Engineering technology: Drafting, electrical.

Student life. Freshman orientation: Mandatory. **Housing:** Wellness housing available. **Activities:** TV station.

Contact. Phone: (610) 398-5300 Fax: (610) 395-2706
Mark Garner, Director of Admissions, Lincoln Technical Institute: Allentown, 5151 Tilghman Street, Allentown, PA 18104

Lincoln Technical Institute: Northeast Philadelphia

Philadelphia, Pennsylvania
www.lincolntech.com

- For-profit 2-year technical college
- Very large city

General. Accredited by ACICS. **Enrollment:** 315 degree-seeking undergraduates. **Degrees:** 14 associate awarded. **Calendar:** Continuous. **Full-time faculty:** 15 total. **Part-time faculty:** 6 total.

Basis for selection. Open admission.

2008-2009 Annual costs. Cost of diploma programs ranges from $12,000 to $17,000; associate degree programs range from $22,180 to $26,265. Program cost includes books, uniforms, and fees.

Application procedures. Admission: No deadline. No application fee.

Academics. Credit/placement by examination: CLEP. **Support services:** Tutoring.

Majors. Computer sciences: System admin. **Health:** Office assistant.

Computing on campus. Online library available.

Student life. Freshman orientation: Mandatory.

Contact. Phone: (215) 969-0869 Fax: (215) 969-3457
Janie Muschlitz, Regional Director of Admissions, Lincoln Technical Institute: Northeast Philadelphia, 2180 Hornig Road, Philadelphia, PA 19116

Lincoln Technical Institute: Philadelphia

Philadelphia, Pennsylvania
www.lincolntech.com **CB code: 9010**

- For-profit 2-year technical college
- Very large city

General. Accredited by ACCSCT. **Enrollment:** 366 full-time, degree-seeking students. **Degrees:** 293 associate awarded. **Calendar:** Quarter. **Full-time faculty:** 17 total.

Basis for selection. Open admission.

2008-2009 Annual costs. Cost of diploma programs ranges from $11,600 to $13,840; associate degree programs, $23,090 to $28,000. Cost of books and tools included in tuition.

Application procedures. Admission: No deadline. $25 fee. Admission notification on a rolling basis.

Academics. Credit/placement by examination: CLEP.

Majors. Mechanic/repair: General, automotive, diesel.

Contact. E-mail: dcunningham@lincolntech.com
Phone: (215) 335-0800
Pat Fittipaldi, Director of Admissions, Lincoln Technical Institute: Philadelphia, 9191 Torresdale Avenue, Philadelphia, PA 19136

Luzerne County Community College

Nanticoke, Pennsylvania
www.luzerne.edu **CB code: 2382**

- Public 2-year community college
- Commuter campus in large town

General. Founded in 1966. Regionally accredited. **Enrollment:** 6,188 degree-seeking undergraduates; 357 non-degree-seeking students. **Degrees:** 771 associate awarded. **ROTC:** Air Force. **Location:** 8 miles from Wilkes-Barre. **Calendar:** Semester, extensive summer session. **Full-time faculty:** 108 total. **Part-time faculty:** 380 total.

Student profile. Among degree-seeking undergraduates, 54% enrolled in a transfer program, 47% enrolled in a vocational program, 1,633 enrolled as first-time, first-year students.

Part-time:	47%	**Asian American:**	1%
Women:	59%	**Hispanic American:**	3%
African American:	3%	**25 or older:**	35%

Transfer out. 58% of students enrolled in the transfer program go on to 4-year colleges. **Colleges most students transferred to 2008:** Bloomsburg University, Wilkes University, King's College, College Misericordia.

Basis for selection. Open admission, but selective for some programs. High school record, college record, test scores considered for admission to health sciences programs. Nurse Entrance Test required of nursing applicants. Interview recommended for health sciences program. **Home-schooled:** Transcript of courses and grades, state high school equivalency certificate required. **Learning Disabled:** Comprehensive services for special needs students at no cost providing the students present the required documentation.

High school preparation. One algebra, 1 chemistry, 1 biology required of nursing, respiratory therapy, surgical technology, and dental hygiene applicants.

2008-2009 Annual costs. Tuition/fees: $2,940; $5,640 out-of-district; $8,340 out-of-state. Per-credit charge: $80 in-district; $160 out-of-district; $240 out-of-state. Books/supplies: $1,200.

2007-2008 Financial aid. Need-based: 49% of total undergraduate aid awarded as scholarships/grants, 51% as loans/jobs. Need-based aid available for part-time students.

Application procedures. Admission: No deadline. $40 fee. Admission notification on a rolling basis. **Financial aid:** Priority date 4/15; no closing date. FAFSA, institutional form required. Applicants notified on a rolling basis starting 7/1.

Academics. Special study options: Cooperative education, distance learning, dual enrollment of high school students, ESL, external degree, honors, independent study, internships, liberal arts/career combination, weekend college. **Credit/placement by examination:** AP, CLEP, institutional tests. 30 credit hours maximum toward associate degree. **Support services:** GED preparation and test center, learning center, pre-admission summer program, reduced course load, remedial instruction, study skills assistance, tutoring, writing center.

Majors. Agriculture: Horticulture, landscaping. **Business:** General, accounting, accounting technology, administrative services, banking/financial services, business admin, hospitality admin, management information systems, real estate, tourism/travel. **Communications:** Advertising, digital media, journalism, radio/tv. **Communications technology:** Recording arts. **Computer sciences:** General, applications programming, computer graphics, security, web page design. **Construction:** Electrician, maintenance. **Education:** General, teacher assistance. **Engineering technology:** Architectural drafting, CAD/CADD, computer systems, electrical, nuclear, robotics. **Family/consumer sciences:** Institutional food production. **Health:** Dental assistant, dental hygiene, EMT paramedic, insurance specialist, nursing (RN), office admin, prepharmacy, respiratory therapy technology, surgical technology. **Interdisciplinary:** Biological/physical sciences. **Legal studies:** Court reporting, paralegal. **Liberal arts:** Arts/sciences, humanities. **Math:** General. **Mechanic/repair:** Automotive, communications systems, heating/ac/refrig, small engine. **Parks/recreation:** Health/fitness. **Personal/culinary services:** Chef training, mortuary science, restaurant/catering. **Protective services:** Criminal justice, fire safety technology. **Public administration:** Human services. **Science technology:** Biological. **Social sciences:** General. **Transportation:** Airline/commercial pilot, aviation management. **Visual/performing arts:** Graphic design, illustration, photography.

Most popular majors. Business/marketing 14%, education 9%, engineering/engineering technologies 7%, health sciences 26%, liberal arts 10%, security/protective services 6%.

Computing on campus. 150 workstations in library, computer center, student center. Commuter students can connect to campus network. Online course registration, online library, helpline, wireless network available.

Student life. Freshman orientation: Mandatory. Preregistration for classes offered. **Activities:** Drama, international student organizations, literary magazine, radio station, student government, student newspaper, TV station, Circle K, Brothers and Sisters in Christ, ACLU, NAACP, Amnesty International, NOW, GLBTA.

Athletics. Intercollegiate: Baseball M, basketball, cross-country, golf, softball W, volleyball W. **Intramural:** Badminton, basketball, football (non-tackle), volleyball. **Team name:** Trailblazers.

Student services. Adult student services, career counseling, student employment services, health services, personal counseling, placement for graduates, veterans' counselor. **Physically disabled:** Services for visually, hearing impaired. **Transfer:** Pre-admission transcript evaluation for new students. Transfer adviser, college fairs on campus for students transferring to 4-year colleges.

Contact. E-mail: admissions@luzerne.edu
Phone: (570) 740-0337 Fax: (570) 740-0238
Francis Curry, Director of Admissions, Luzerne County Community College, 1333 South Prospect Street, Nanticoke, PA 18634-3899

Manor College

Jenkintown, Pennsylvania
www.manor.edu **CB code: 2260**

- Private 2-year junior college affiliated with Ukrainian Catholic Church
- Commuter campus in small town
- SAT or ACT with writing, interview required

General. Founded in 1947. Regionally accredited. **Enrollment:** 802 degree-seeking undergraduates; 156 non-degree-seeking students. **Degrees:** 158 associate awarded. **Location:** 15 miles from Philadelphia. **Calendar:** Semester, limited summer session. **Full-time faculty:** 24 total; 25% have terminal degrees, 79% women. **Part-time faculty:** 94 total; 43% have terminal degrees, 11% minority, 52% women. **Class size:** 74% < 20, 26% 20-39. **Special facilities:** Ukrainian heritage studies center and museum, dental health center, law library, veterinary technology radiology lab, surgical suite, Civil War library.

Student profile. Among degree-seeking undergraduates, 61% enrolled in a transfer program, 39% enrolled in a vocational program, 3% already have a bachelor's degree or higher, 156 enrolled as first-time, first-year students, 159 transferred in from other institutions.

Part-time:	43%	**Asian American:**	3%
Out-of-state:	5%	**Hispanic American:**	4%
Women:	81%	**Live on campus:**	3%
African American:	22%		

Transfer out. 68% of students enrolled in the transfer program go on to 4-year colleges. **Colleges most students transferred to 2008:** Holy Family University, LaSalle University, Temple University, Drexel University, Thomas Jefferson University.

Basis for selection. Class rank, GPA, course selection, recommendation of counselor or teacher, SAT/ACT scores, interview with admissions counselor most important. Institutional entrance test required of all applicants except those holding bachelor's degree. **Adult students:** SAT/ACT scores not required if applicant over 21. **Homeschooled:** Statement describing homeschool structure and mission, transcript of courses and grades, state high school equivalency certificate, interview, letter of recommendation (nonparent) required. GED. **Learning Disabled:** IEP required of all with diagnosed disability.

High school preparation. College-preparatory program recommended. 16 units required. Required and recommended units include English 4, mathematics 2, social studies 2, science 1-2 (laboratory 1-2) and academic electives 6. Biology with laboratory, chemistry with laboratory, 3 math courses required of all allied health science applicants.

2008-2009 Annual costs. Tuition/fees: $12,156. Per-credit charge: $255. Tuition for allied health program: $12,328; $348 per credit hour. Room/board: $5,772. Books/supplies: $1,008. Personal expenses: $2,430.

2008-2009 Financial aid. Need-based: Average need met was 32%. Average scholarship/grant was $4,850; average loan $3,520. 52% of total undergraduate aid awarded as scholarships/grants, 48% as loans/jobs. Need-based aid available for part-time students. **Non-need-based:** Scholarships awarded for academics, alumni affiliation, art.

Application procedures. Admission: Closing date 8/15 (postmark date). $25 fee, may be waived for applicants with need. Application must be submitted on paper. Admission notification 9/1. Admission notification on a rolling basis beginning on or about 10/15. Must reply by May 1 or within 2 week(s) if notified thereafter. **Financial aid:** Priority date 4/1; no closing date. FAFSA required. Applicants notified on a rolling basis starting 3/1; must reply within 2 week(s) of notification.

Academics. Special study options: Accelerated study, distance learning, double major, dual enrollment of high school students, ESL, honors, independent study, internships. License preparation in real estate. **Credit/placement by examination:** AP, CLEP, institutional tests. 30 credit hours maximum toward associate degree. **Support services:** Learning center, pre-admission summer program, reduced course load, remedial instruction, study skills assistance, tutoring, writing center.

Majors. Business: Accounting, business admin, international, marketing. **Communications:** General. **Computer sciences:** Applications programming. **Education:** Early childhood, elementary. **Health:** Dental assistant, dental hygiene, health services, prenursing, preveterinary, veterinary technology/assistant. **Legal studies:** Paralegal. **Liberal arts:** Arts/sciences. **Psychology:** General.

Most popular majors. Business/marketing 17%, education 7%, health sciences 56%, liberal arts 8%.

Computing on campus. 111 workstations in dormitories, library, computer center. Dormitories wired for high-speed internet access and linked to campus network. Commuter students can connect to campus network. Online library, helpline, wireless network available.

Student life. Freshman orientation: Mandatory, $25 fee. Preregistration for classes offered. Three 1-day orientations are held annually in January and August. Registration is held after orientation if the student has not already registered. **Policies:** Alcohol and drug policy strictly reinforced; mandatory meningitis vaccines and completed health record forms are required to live in the residence hall. **Housing:** Guaranteed on-campus for all undergraduates. Coed dorms, wellness housing available. $100 fully refundable deposit, deadline 9/1. **Activities:** Campus ministries, dance, drama, international student organizations, literary magazine, music ensembles, Model UN, student government, Students United for Nature, Black cultural awareness club, Rotaract, music ministry, student senate, Admissions Ambassadors, Yellow Ribbon Supporters.

Athletics. NJCAA. **Intercollegiate:** Basketball, soccer. **Team name:** Blue Jays.

Student services. Adult student services, alcohol/substance abuse counseling, chaplain/spiritual director, career counseling, student employment services, financial aid counseling, health services, personal counseling, placement for graduates. **Physically disabled:** Services for hearing impaired. **Transfer:** Pre-admission transcript evaluation for new students. Transfer center, transfer adviser, college fairs on campus for students transferring to 4-year colleges.

Contact. E-mail: ftadmiss@manor.edu
Phone: (215) 884-2216 Fax: (215) 576-6564
I. Jerry Czenstuch, Vice President for Enrollment Management, Manor College, 700 Fox Chase Road, Jenkintown, PA 19046-3319

McCann School of Business and Technology: Dickson City

Dickson City, Pennsylvania
www.mccannschool.com

- For-profit 2-year business and technical college
- Commuter campus in small city
- Interview required

General. Accredited by ACICS. **Enrollment:** 395 degree-seeking undergraduates. **Degrees:** 120 associate awarded. **Calendar:** Quarter, extensive summer session. **Full-time faculty:** 40 total.

Student profile. Among degree-seeking undergraduates, 100% enrolled in a vocational program, 1% already have a bachelor's degree or higher.

Part-time:	49%	**Women:**	62%

Basis for selection. Evidence of high school diploma or equivalent required; interview; must earn certain score on entrance examination.

2008-2009 Annual costs. Costs vary by program of study; average annual tuition, $7,848; per-credit-hour charge, $218.

Application procedures. Admission: No deadline. $40 fee, may be waived for applicants with need. Admission notification on a rolling basis. **Financial aid:** No deadline. FAFSA required.

Academics. Credit/placement by examination: CLEP. **Support services:** Reduced course load, remedial instruction, tutoring.

Majors. Business: Marketing. **Computer sciences:** General, networking. **Education:** Early childhood, teacher assistance. **Health:** Massage therapy, medical assistant, medical secretary, receptionist, surgical technology. **Legal studies:** Paralegal.

Student life. Freshman orientation: Mandatory. **Activities:** Student council, business club, medical club, early childhood club.

Student services. Career counseling, student employment services, financial aid counseling, placement for graduates.

Contact. Phone: (570) 307-2000
Melissa Sweetz, Director of Admissions, McCann School of Business and Technology: Dickson City, 2227 Scranton Carbondale Highway, Dickson City, PA 18519

McCann School of Business and Technology: Hazleton

Hazleton, Pennsylvania
www.mccannschool.edu **CB code: 3887**

- For-profit 2-year business and technical college
- Commuter campus in large town
- Interview required

General. Founded in 1897. Accredited by ACICS. **Enrollment:** 505 degree-seeking undergraduates. **Degrees:** 160 associate awarded. **Location:** 35 miles from Wilkes Barre. **Calendar:** Quarter, extensive summer session. **Full-time faculty:** 11 total. **Part-time faculty:** 28 total.

Student profile. Among degree-seeking undergraduates, 505 enrolled as first-time, first-year students.

Basis for selection. Open admission.

2008-2009 Annual costs. Costs vary by program of study; average annual tuition, $7,848; per-credit-hour charge, $218. Books/supplies: $1,500. Personal expenses: $1,600.

Application procedures. **Admission:** No deadline. $40 fee, may be waived for applicants with need. Application must be submitted on paper. Admission notification on a rolling basis. **Financial aid:** No deadline. FAFSA required. Applicants notified on a rolling basis.

Academics. **Special study options:** Distance learning, double major. **Credit/placement by examination:** CLEP. **Support services:** Reduced course load, remedial instruction, tutoring.

Majors. **Business:** Accounting, administrative services, business admin, hospitality/recreation, marketing, office/clerical. **Computer sciences:** General, applications programming, computer support specialist, LAN/WAN management. **Education:** Early childhood, teacher assistance. **Health:** Medical secretary. **Legal studies:** Legal secretary, paralegal.

Computing on campus. 80 workstations in library, computer center.

Student life. **Freshman orientation:** Mandatory. **Activities:** Student government, student newspaper, Circle-K.

Student services. Adult student services, career counseling, student employment services, financial aid counseling, placement for graduates, veterans' counselor. **Transfer:** Transfer adviser for students transferring to 4-year colleges.

Contact. E-mail: msm@mccannschool.edu
Phone: (570) 454-6172 Fax: (570) 454-6286
Michael Mazalusky, Director of Admissions, McCann School of Business and Technology: Hazleton, 370 Maplewood Drive, Hazleton, PA 18202

McCann School of Business and Technology: Pottsville

Pottsville, Pennsylvania
www.mccannschool.edu **CB code: 3296**

- For-profit 2-year branch campus and technical college
- Small town

General. Accredited by ACICS. **Enrollment:** 510 degree-seeking undergraduates. **Degrees:** 86 associate awarded. **Calendar:** Quarter. **Full-time faculty:** 7 total. **Part-time faculty:** 30 total. **Special facilities:** On-site massage therapy training center.

Basis for selection. Open admission.

2008-2009 Annual costs. Costs vary by program of study; average annual tuition, $7,848; per-credit-hour charge, $218.

Application procedures. **Admission:** No deadline. $40 fee.

Academics. **Special study options:** Distance learning, dual enrollment of high school students, internships. **Credit/placement by examination:** CLEP.

Majors. **Business:** Accounting, administrative services, business admin. **Computer sciences:** General. **Education:** Early childhood. **Legal studies:** Paralegal. **Protective services:** Criminal justice, police science, security services.

Contact. Phone: (570) 622-7622 Fax: (570) 622-7770
Shannon Brennan, Director, McCann School of Business and Technology: Pottsville, 2650 Woodglen Road, Pottsville, PA 17901

McCann School of Business and Technology: Sunbury

Sunbury, Pennsylvania
www.mccannschool.edu **CB code: 3298**

- For-profit 2-year branch campus and technical college
- Commuter campus in small town

General. Accredited by ACICS. **Enrollment:** 749 degree-seeking undergraduates. **Degrees:** 123 associate awarded. **Calendar:** Quarter. **Full-time faculty:** 17 total. **Part-time faculty:** 41 total.

Basis for selection. Open admission.

2008-2009 Annual costs. Costs vary by program of study; average annual tuition, $7,848; per-credit-hour charge, $218.

Application procedures. **Admission:** No deadline. $40 fee. **Financial aid:** No deadline.

Academics. **Special study options:** Distance learning, dual enrollment of high school students, internships. **Credit/placement by examination:** CLEP.

Majors. **Business:** Accounting, administrative services, marketing. **Computer sciences:** General. **Health:** Massage therapy, medical records technology, medical secretary, respiratory therapy assistant, surgical technology. **Legal studies:** Paralegal. **Personal/culinary services:** Cosmetic. **Protective services:** Law enforcement admin.

Contact. E-mail: lisa.davis@mccannschool.edu
Phone: (570) 286-3058
Lisa Davis, Director of Admissions, McCann School of Business and Technology: Sunbury, 1147 North 4th Street, Sunbury, PA 17801

Metropolitan Career Center Computer Technology Institute

Philadelphia, Pennsylvania
www.careersinit.org

- Private 2-year technical college
- Very large city

General. Accredited by ACCSCT. **Enrollment:** 174 degree-seeking undergraduates. **Degrees:** 29 associate awarded. **Calendar:** Continuous. **Full-time faculty:** 6 total. **Part-time faculty:** 4 total.

Basis for selection. Applicants 18 years or older (or with an official dropout slip from high school) must have high school diploma or GED, score at least 9.0 in both verbal and quantitative on standardized achievement test.

2008-2009 Annual costs. Full program cost is $18,050 and includes all fees and supplies.

2007-2008 Financial aid. **Need-based:** 60% of total undergraduate aid awarded as scholarships/grants, 40% as loans/jobs.

Application procedures. **Admission:** No deadline. $50 fee. **Financial aid:** No deadline.

Academics. **Credit/placement by examination:** CLEP.

Majors. **Computer sciences:** Programming.

Contact. E-mail: bgrossman@mccworks.org
Phone: (215) 568-9215 Fax: (215) 568-3511
Brett Grossman, Admissions Director, Metropolitan Career Center Computer Technology Institute, 100 South Broad Street, Suite 830, Philadelphia, PA 19110

Montgomery County Community College

Blue Bell, Pennsylvania **CB member**
www.mc3.edu **CB code: 2445**

- Public 2-year community college
- Commuter campus in large town

General. Founded in 1964. Regionally accredited. Campus in Pottstown serves students in western part of the county. Several off-campus sites: Lansdale, Willow Grove Naval Air Station. **Enrollment:** 12,142 degree-seeking undergraduates. **Degrees:** 1,041 associate awarded. **Location:** 20 miles from Philadelphia. **Calendar:** Semester, extensive summer session. **Full-time faculty:** 191 total; 8% minority, 57% women. **Part-time faculty:** 501 total; 7% minority, 54% women. **Class size:** 50% < 20, 50% 20-39. **Special facilities:** Dental hygiene clinic.

Student profile. Among degree-seeking undergraduates, 61% enrolled in a transfer program, 39% enrolled in a vocational program, 4,371 enrolled as first-time, first-year students, 417 transferred in from other institutions.

Part-time:	54%	**Asian American:**	6%
Out-of-state:	1%	**Hispanic American:**	3%
Women:	57%	**International:**	2%
African American:	12%	**25 or older:**	36%

Transfer out. 68% of students enrolled in the transfer program go on to 4-year colleges. **Colleges most students transferred to 2008:** Temple University, Gwynedd-Mercy College, West Chester University, Penn State.

Basis for selection. Open admission, but selective for some programs. Special requirements for allied health and automotive technology programs. ACT or SAT required for allied health applicants; report score by August 1. County residents given priority. High school transcript required for students less than 5 years out of high school. **Homeschooled:** Transcript of courses and grades required. Must provide approved curriculum and portfolio. **Learning Disabled:** Recommend meeting with Director of Services for Students with Disabilities. Require current documentation from students of accommodations needed.

High school preparation. Biology, chemistry, and algebra required of nursing and medical laboratory technician applicants, chemistry of dental hygiene applicants.

2009-2010 Annual costs. Tuition/fees (projected): $3,270; $6,240 out-of-district; $9,210 out-of-state. Per-credit charge: $89 in-district; $178 out-of-district; $267 out-of-state. Books/supplies: $1,300. Personal expenses: $1,640.

2007-2008 Financial aid. Need-based: 1,052 full-time freshmen applied for aid; 828 were judged to have need; 697 of these received aid. Average need met was 15%. Average scholarship/grant was $2,037; average loan $1,637. 60% of total undergraduate aid awarded as scholarships/grants, 40% as loans/jobs. Need-based aid available for part-time students. Work-study available nights, weekends and for part-time students. **Non-need-based:** Awarded to 1,159 full-time undergraduates, including 510 freshmen. Scholarships awarded for academics.

Application procedures. Admission: No deadline. $25 fee, may be waived for applicants with need, free for online applicants. Admission notification on a rolling basis. **Financial aid:** Priority date 5/1; no closing date. FAFSA required. Applicants notified on a rolling basis starting 2/1.

Academics. Special study options: Accelerated study, cooperative education, distance learning, dual enrollment of high school students, ESL, honors, independent study, internships, student-designed major, study abroad, teacher certification program, weekend college. Bachelor's degree programs available on campus. License preparation in dental hygiene, nursing, radiology, real estate. **Credit/placement by examination:** AP, CLEP, institutional tests. 30 credit hours maximum toward associate degree. **Support services:** GED preparation, learning center, reduced course load, remedial instruction, study skills assistance, tutoring.

Majors. Biology: General, biotechnology. **Business:** General, accounting, accounting technology, administrative services, business admin, communications, hospitality/recreation, management information systems, real estate, sales/distribution, travel services. **Communications:** General. **Communications technology:** Recording arts. **Computer sciences:** General, information systems, networking. **Conservation:** Environmental science. **Education:** Elementary, physical, secondary, teacher assistance. **Engineering:** Science. **Engineering technology:** General, automotive, CAD/CADD, electrical, mechanical. **Family/consumer sciences:** Child care. **Health:** Clinical lab technology, dental hygiene, medical radiologic technology/radiation therapy, mental health services, nursing (RN), surgical technology. **Liberal arts:** Arts/sciences, humanities. **Math:** General. **Personal/culinary services:** Baking, chef training. **Physical sciences:** General. **Protective services:** Fire safety technology, police science, security services. **Social sciences:** General. **Visual/performing arts:** Art, commercial/advertising art. **Other:** Digital broadcasting, Digital design, Web development.

Most popular majors. Business/marketing 15%, health sciences 19%, liberal arts 43%.

Computing on campus. 1,235 workstations in library, student center. Commuter students can connect to campus network. Online course registration, online library, helpline, wireless network available.

Student life. Freshman orientation: Available. Preregistration for classes offered. One day, week before semester starts. 3 days offered at Central campus. 2 days offered at West campus. **Housing:** Housing for up to 8 foreign students (F1 visas) available. **Activities:** Jazz band, choral groups, dance, drama, film society, international student organizations, literary magazine, music ensembles, radio station, student government, student newspaper, TV station, African-American club, Writers' club, Meridian club, Christian fellowship club, Hola club, S-Flag, ACE club, Indo American club, College Democrats, Young Republicans.

Athletics. NJCAA. **Intercollegiate:** Baseball M, basketball, soccer, softball W. **Intramural:** Badminton, baseball M, basketball, bowling, cross-country, football (non-tackle) M, judo, racquetball, soccer, softball, table tennis, tennis, volleyball, weight lifting. **Team name:** Mustangs.

Student services. Career counseling, student employment services, financial aid counseling, health services, minority student services, on-campus daycare, personal counseling, placement for graduates, veterans' counselor. **Physically disabled:** Services for visually, speech, hearing impaired. **Transfer:** Pre-admission transcript evaluation for new students. Transfer center, transfer adviser, college fairs on campus for students transferring to 4-year colleges.

Contact. E-mail: admissionsregistration@mc3.edu
Phone: (215) 641-6551 Fax: (215) 641-6681
Penny Sawyer, Director of Admissions, Montgomery County Community College, 340 DeKalb Pike, Blue Bell, PA 19422

New Castle School of Trades
Pulaski, Pennsylvania
www.ncstrades.com **CB code: 2404**

- For-profit 2-year technical college
- Commuter campus in rural community
- Interview required

General. Accredited by ACCSCT. **Enrollment:** 385 degree-seeking undergraduates. **Degrees:** 195 associate awarded. **Location:** 10 miles from Youngstown, Ohio. **Calendar:** Differs by program. **Full-time faculty:** 25 total. **Part-time faculty:** 20 total.

Basis for selection. Secondary school record and Wonderlic test scores most important. Wonderlic exam used for admission.

2008-2009 Annual costs. Tuition varies by program from $4,838 to $16,950. Costs include fees. Books and tool expenses up to $2,672.

2007-2008 Financial aid. Need-based: Need-based aid available for part-time students.

Application procedures. Admission: No deadline. $25 fee. Admission notification on a rolling basis.

Academics. Credit/placement by examination: CLEP. **Support services:** Study skills assistance, tutoring.

Majors. Engineering technology: Construction, electrical. **Mechanic/repair:** Automotive.

Student life. Freshman orientation: Available. Preregistration for classes offered.

Student services. Career counseling, financial aid counseling, personal counseling, placement for graduates.

Contact. E-mail: ncstrades@aol.com
Phone: (724) 964-8811 Toll-free number: (800) 837-8299
Fax: (724) 964-8177
Jim Catheline, Director of Admissions, New Castle School of Trades, 4164 US 422, Pulaski, PA 16143-9721

Newport Business Institute: Lower Burrell
Lower Burrell, Pennsylvania
www.nbi.edu **CB code: 2413**

- For-profit 2-year business college
- Commuter campus in small town
- Interview required

General. Accredited by ACICS. **Enrollment:** 61 degree-seeking undergraduates. **Degrees:** 34 associate awarded. **Location:** 15 miles from Pittsburgh. **Calendar:** Quarter. **Full-time faculty:** 7 total. **Part-time faculty:** 1 total. **Special facilities:** All students receive a laptop to use while enrolled. **Partnerships:** Formal partnerships with Microsoft Testing Center, Prometrics Testing Center.

Basis for selection. Open admission.

2008-2009 Annual costs. Tuition/fees: $10,950. Books/supplies: $1,350.

Financial aid. Need-based: Need-based aid available for part-time students. **Non-need-based:** Scholarships awarded for academics, leadership.

Application procedures. Admission: No deadline. $25 fee, may be waived for applicants with need. Admission notification on a rolling basis. **Financial aid:** No deadline. FAFSA required. Applicants notified on a rolling basis starting 5/1.

Academics. Special study options: Liberal arts/career combination. Bachelor's degree programs available on campus. **Credit/placement by examination:** CLEP. **Support services:** Tutoring.

Majors. Business: Accounting, accounting technology, accounting/business management, administrative services, business admin, customer service, executive assistant, hospitality admin, hospitality/recreation, hotel/

motel admin, office technology, office/clerical, receptionist, resort management, retailing, small business admin, tourism/travel, travel services. **Computer sciences:** Data entry, data processing, database management, web page design, word processing. **Health:** Insurance coding, insurance specialist, medical records admin, medical secretary, medical transcription, office admin, office assistant, office computer specialist, receptionist. **Visual/ performing arts:** Music.

Most popular majors. Business/marketing 60%, computer/information sciences 34%, health sciences 16%.

Computing on campus. PC or laptop required. 2 workstations in computer center. Helpline, repair service, wireless network available.

Student life. **Freshman orientation:** Mandatory. Preregistration for classes offered. **Activities:** Student newspaper.

Student services. Adult student services, career counseling, student employment services, financial aid counseling, placement for graduates. **Transfer:** Pre-admission transcript evaluation for new students.

Contact. E-mail: admissions1@nbi.edu
Phone: (724) 339-7542 Toll-free number: (800) 752-7695
Fax: (724) 339-2950
Don Acker, Assistant Director of Admissions, Newport Business Institute: Lower Burrell, 945 Greensburg Road, Lower Burrell, PA 15068

Newport Business Institute: Williamsport

Williamsport, Pennsylvania
www.newportbusiness.com **CB code: 2551**

- For-profit 2-year business and career college
- Commuter campus in small city
- Interview required

General. Accredited by ACICS. **Enrollment:** 69 degree-seeking undergraduates. **Degrees:** 51 associate awarded. **Calendar:** Quarter. **Full-time faculty:** 6 total; 17% have terminal degrees, 67% women.

Student profile. Among degree-seeking undergraduates, 100% enrolled in a vocational program, 1% already have a bachelor's degree or higher, 32 enrolled as first-time, first-year students, 4 transferred in from other institutions.

Women:	96%	**African American:**	10%

Basis for selection. Open admission.

2008-2009 Annual costs. Tuition/fees: $10,350. Per-credit charge: $275. Books/supplies: $1,200.

Application procedures. **Admission:** No deadline. $25 fee. Admission notification on a rolling basis. **Financial aid:** No deadline. FAFSA required. Applicants notified on a rolling basis.

Academics. **Special study options:** Distance learning, internships. **Credit/ placement by examination:** CLEP.

Majors. **Business:** Business admin, executive assistant. **Health:** Medical secretary. **Legal studies:** Legal secretary.

Most popular majors. Business/marketing 33%, health sciences 47%, legal studies 20%.

Computing on campus. PC or laptop required. Wireless network available.

Student life. **Freshman orientation:** Mandatory.

Student services. Financial aid counseling, personal counseling, placement for graduates. **Transfer:** Pre-admission transcript evaluation for new students.

Contact. E-mail: admissions1_nbi@comcast.net
Phone: (570) 326-2869 Fax: (570) 326-2136
Mary Weaver, Director, Newport Business Institute: Williamsport, 941 West Third Street, Williamsport, PA 17701

Northampton Community College

Bethlehem, Pennsylvania **CB member**
www.northampton.edu **CB code: 2573**

- Public 2-year community college
- Commuter campus in small city

General. Founded in 1966. Regionally accredited. Branch campus at Monroe County. Off-campus sites in southside Bethlehem, Lehigh Valley Industrial Park IV, Shohola, and Tobyhanna. Individualized transfer study program. **Enrollment:** 10,032 degree-seeking undergraduates; 252 non-degree-seeking students. **Degrees:** 965 associate awarded. **Location:** 60 miles from Philadelphia, 90 miles from New York City. **Calendar:** Semester, limited summer session. **Full-time faculty:** 115 total; 46% have terminal degrees, 16% minority, 61% women. **Part-time faculty:** 556 total; 15% have terminal degrees, 9% minority, 54% women. **Special facilities:** Electrotechnology applications center. **Partnerships:** Formal partnerships with General Motors, Daimler Chrysler.

Student profile. Among degree-seeking undergraduates, 61% enrolled in a transfer program, 39% enrolled in a vocational program, 4% already have a bachelor's degree or higher, 2,512 enrolled as first-time, first-year students, 433 transferred in from other institutions.

Part-time:	55%	**Hispanic American:**	11%
Out-of-state:	2%	**International:**	1%
Women:	61%	**25 or older:**	36%
African American:	8%	**Live on campus:**	3%
Asian American:	2%		

Transfer out. 70% of students enrolled in the transfer program go on to 4-year colleges. **Colleges most students transferred to 2008:** East Stroudsburg University, Kutztown University, DeSales University, Cedar Crest College, Moravian College.

Basis for selection. Open admission, but selective for some programs. Special requirements for allied health, veterinary technician, and culinary arts programs. Interview required for radiography, veterinary technology, and diagnostic medical sonography programs; portfolio required for communication design, fine arts programs; audition required for theater program.

High school preparation. Biology, chemistry, and algebra requirements for allied health, veterinary technician, and culinary arts programs.

2008-2009 Annual costs. Tuition/fees: $3,090; $5,340 out-of-district; $7,590 out-of-state. Per-credit charge: $75 in-district; $150 out-of-district; $225 out-of-state. Room/board: $6,658. Books/supplies: $1,300. Personal expenses: $3,372.

2008-2009 Financial aid. **Need-based:** 71% of total undergraduate aid awarded as scholarships/grants, 29% as loans/jobs. Need-based aid available for part-time students. Work-study available nights, weekends and for part-time students. **Non-need-based:** Scholarships awarded for academics, alumni affiliation, art, leadership, minority status, music/drama.

Application procedures. **Admission:** No deadline. $25 fee, may be waived for applicants with need. Admission notification on a rolling basis. **Financial aid:** Priority date 3/31; no closing date. FAFSA, institutional form required. Applicants notified on a rolling basis starting 6/1; must reply within 2 week(s) of notification.

Academics. **Special study options:** Accelerated study, cooperative education, distance learning, double major, dual enrollment of high school students, ESL, honors, internships, student-designed major, study abroad, teacher certification program. Bachelor's degree programs available on campus. License preparation in dental hygiene, nursing, radiology, real estate. **Credit/ placement by examination:** AP, CLEP, institutional tests. 30 credit hours maximum toward associate degree. **Support services:** GED preparation, learning center, reduced course load, remedial instruction, study skills assistance, tutoring, writing center.

Majors. **Biology:** General, biotechnology. **Business:** General, accounting technology, administrative services, business admin, construction management, hotel/motel admin, marketing, restaurant/food services. **Communications:** General, journalism. **Communications technology:** Radio/tv. **Computer sciences:** Computer science, networking, programming, security. **Construction:** Electrician. **Education:** General, teacher assistance. **Engineering:** General. **Engineering technology:** Architectural, CAD/CADD, electrical, electromechanical, quality control. **Health:** Athletic training, dental hygiene, medical secretary, nursing (RN), radiologic technology/medical imaging, sonography, surgical technology, veterinary technology/assistant. **Legal studies:** Legal secretary, paralegal. **Liberal arts:** Arts/sciences. **Math:** General. **Mechanic/repair:** Automotive, computer, heating/ac/refrig, industrial electronics. **Parks/recreation:** Sports admin. **Personal/culinary services:** Chef training, mortuary science. **Physical sciences:** Chemistry, physics. **Protective services:** Criminal justice, fire services admin. **Public administration:** Social work. **Science technology:** Chemical. **Visual/ performing arts:** Acting, graphic design, interior design, studio arts.

Most popular majors. Business/marketing 15%, education 7%, health sciences 21%, liberal arts 14%, security/protective services 6%.

Computing on campus. 1,700 workstations in dormitories, library, computer center, student center. Dormitories wired for high-speed internet access and linked to campus network. Commuter students can connect to campus network. Online course registration, online library, helpline, student web hosting, wireless network available.

Student life. Freshman orientation: Available. Preregistration for classes offered. 1/2 day program offered over 2 weeks in summer. **Housing:** Coed dorms, apartments available. $150 deposit. **Activities:** Choral groups, dance, drama, film society, international student organizations, radio station, student government, student newspaper.

Athletics. NJCAA. **Intercollegiate:** Baseball M, basketball, golf, soccer M, softball W, tennis, volleyball W. **Intramural:** Basketball, football (non-tackle), soccer, volleyball. **Team name:** Spartans.

Student services. Adult student services, alcohol/substance abuse counseling, career counseling, services for economically disadvantaged, financial aid counseling, health services, minority student services, on-campus daycare, personal counseling, placement for graduates. **Physically disabled:** Services for visually, speech, hearing impaired. **Learning disabled:** Comprehensive services available. **Transfer:** Pre-admission transcript evaluation for new students. Transfer center, transfer adviser, college fairs on campus for students transferring to 4-year colleges.

Contact. E-mail: adminfo@northampton.edu
Phone: (610) 861-5500 Fax: (610) 861-4560
James McCarthy, Director of Admissions, Northampton Community College, 3835 Green Pond Road, Bethlehem, PA 18020

Oakbridge Academy of Arts

Lower Burrell, Pennsylvania
www.oaa.edu **CB code: 2984**

- For-profit 2-year visual arts college
- Commuter campus in large town
- Interview required

General. Accredited by ACCSCT. **Enrollment:** 49 degree-seeking undergraduates. **Degrees:** 23 associate awarded. **Location:** 21 miles from Pittsburgh. **Calendar:** Quarter, extensive summer session. **Full-time faculty:** 2 total. **Part-time faculty:** 9 total.

Student profile. Among degree-seeking undergraduates, 24 enrolled as first-time, first-year students.

Transfer out. Colleges most students transferred to 2008: Art Institute of Pittsburgh.

Basis for selection. Open admission. Portfolio review recommended for visual design and photography programs. **Homeschooled:** Transcript of courses and grades, state high school equivalency certificate required. **Learning Disabled:** Reading test.

2008-2009 Annual costs. Tuition/fees: $10,650. Books/supplies: $1,000. Personal expenses: $4,123.

Financial aid. All financial aid based on need. Need-based aid available for part-time students.

Application procedures. Admission: No deadline. $25 fee. Application must be submitted on paper. Admission notification on a rolling basis. **Financial aid:** Closing date 5/1. FAFSA required. Applicants notified on a rolling basis; must reply by 5/1.

Academics. Special study options: Internships. **Credit/placement by examination:** AP, CLEP. **Support services:** Tutoring.

Majors. Communications: Advertising. **Visual/performing arts:** General, commercial photography, commercial/advertising art, design, drawing, graphic design, painting, photography.

Computing on campus. PC or laptop required. 20 workstations in computer center. Wireless network available.

Student life. Freshman orientation: Mandatory. Preregistration for classes offered. **Activities:** Student government.

Student services. Placement for graduates. **Transfer:** Pre-admission transcript evaluation for new students.

Contact. E-mail: admissions@oaa.edu
Phone: (724) 335-5336 Toll-free number: (800) 734-5601
Fax: (724) 335-5336
Robert Gaydosh, Admissions Coordinator, Oakbridge Academy of Arts, 1250 Greensburg Road, Lower Burrell, PA 15068

Orleans Technical Institute - Center City Campus

Philadelphia, Pennsylvania
www.orleanstech.edu **CB code: 3127**

- Private 2-year technical and career college
- Commuter campus in very large city
- Interview required

General. Accredited by ACCSCT. **Enrollment:** 82 full-time, degree-seeking students. **Degrees:** 12 associate awarded. **Calendar:** Continuous, limited summer session. **Full-time faculty:** 8 total. **Part-time faculty:** 9 total.

Student profile.

African American:	20%	**Hispanic American:**	4%

Transfer out. Colleges most students transferred to 2008: Community College of Philadelphia.

Basis for selection. Open admission.

2008-2009 Annual costs. Tuition for full associate program (3 years, including internship) is $33,000. Books/supplies: $1,221.

Financial aid. Need-based: Need-based aid available for part-time students.

Application procedures. Admission: No deadline. $125 fee. Admission notification on a rolling basis. **Financial aid:** No deadline. FAFSA, institutional form required. Applicants notified on a rolling basis.

Academics. Credit/placement by examination: CLEP, institutional tests. **Support services:** Tutoring.

Majors. Business: Business admin.

Student life. Freshman orientation: Mandatory.

Student services. Adult student services, career counseling, financial aid counseling, personal counseling, placement for graduates. **Physically disabled:** Services for visually impaired. **Transfer:** Re-entry adviser, pre-admission transcript evaluation for new students.

Contact. E-mail: bellod@jevs.org
Phone: (215) 728-4426 Fax: (215) 745-1689
Debbie Bello, Director, Orleans Technical Institute - Center City Campus, 2770 Red Lion Road, Philadelphia, PA 19114

Pace Institute

Reading, Pennsylvania
www.paceinstitute.com **CB code: 2438**

- For-profit 2-year junior college
- Large city

General. Accredited by ACICS. **Enrollment:** 193 degree-seeking undergraduates. **Degrees:** 41 associate awarded. **Calendar:** Continuous. **Full-time faculty:** 5 total. **Part-time faculty:** 18 total. **Class size:** 93% < 20, 7% 20-39.

Basis for selection. Open admission.

2008-2009 Annual costs. Tuition varies by program from $7,458 to $22,242 annually.

Application procedures. Admission: No deadline. $10 fee, may be waived for applicants with need.

Academics. Special study options: Accelerated study, internships. **Credit/placement by examination:** CLEP.

Majors. Business: Accounting, administrative services, business admin, fashion, tourism/travel. **Computer sciences:** Programming. **Engineering:** Electrical. **Health:** Medical secretary. **Legal studies:** Paralegal.

Contact. E-mail: pace4u2@aol.com
Phone: (610) 375-1212
Ryan DeGeorge, Admissions Team Leader, Pace Institute, 606 Court Street, Reading, PA 19601

Penn Commercial Business and Technical School

Washington, Pennsylvania
www.penncommercial.edu **CB code: 3300**

- For-profit 2-year business and technical college
- Small city

General. Accredited by ACICS. **Enrollment:** 390 degree-seeking undergraduates. **Degrees:** 91 associate awarded. **Calendar:** Continuous. **Full-time faculty:** 18 total. **Part-time faculty:** 30 total.

Basis for selection. Open admission, but selective for some programs.

2008-2009 Annual costs. Tuition and fees range from $3,124 to $19,000 per academic year depending on program. Books/supplies: $945. Personal expenses: $2,438.

Application procedures. Admission: No deadline. $25 fee. Admission notification on a rolling basis. **Financial aid:** No deadline.

Academics. Credit/placement by examination: CLEP.

Majors. Business: General, administrative services, business admin. **Computer sciences:** Information technology, networking. **Engineering technology:** Computer systems, drafting, heat/ac/refrig. **Health:** Medical secretary, office assistant. **Legal studies:** Legal secretary. **Mechanic/repair:** General.

Contact. E-mail: pcadmissions@penncommercial.edu
Phone: (724) 222-5330 ext. 1 Fax: (724) 225-3561
Michael Joyce, Admissions Director, Penn Commercial Business and Technical School, 242 Oak Spring Road, Washington, PA 15301

Pennco Tech

Bristol, Pennsylvania
www.penncotech.com **CB code: 0380**

- For-profit 2-year technical college
- Large town
- Interview required

General. Founded in 1973. Accredited by ACCSCT. Branch campus in Blackwood, New Jersey. **Enrollment:** 360 full-time, degree-seeking students. **Degrees:** 58 associate awarded. **Location:** 18 miles from Philadelphia. **Calendar:** Modular, year-round calendar. Limited summer session. **Full-time faculty:** 70 total. **Part-time faculty:** 10 total.

Basis for selection. Institution's entrance examination and campus interview most important.

2008-2009 Annual costs. Tuition ranges from $6,500 to $29,900 depending on program. Books/supplies: $850.

Application procedures. Admission: No deadline. $100 fee. Admission notification on a rolling basis. **Financial aid:** No deadline. Applicants notified on a rolling basis.

Academics. Credit/placement by examination: CLEP, institutional tests. 30 credit hours maximum toward associate degree. **Support services:** Tutoring.

Majors. Business: Hospitality admin. **Computer sciences:** Programming. **Engineering:** Electrical. **Mechanic/repair:** Auto body, automotive.

Student life. Housing: Single-sex dorms available. **Activities:** Choral groups, TV station.

Student services. Career counseling, student employment services, on-campus daycare, personal counseling, placement for graduates.

Contact. E-mail: admissions@penncotech.com
Phone: (215) 824-3200 Toll-free number: (800) 575-9399
Glenn Slater, Director of Admissions, Pennco Tech, 3815 Otter Street, Bristol, PA 19007

Pennsylvania Culinary Institute

Pittsburgh, Pennsylvania
www.paculinary.com **CB code: 2440**

- For-profit 2-year culinary school and technical college
- Residential campus in large city
- Interview required

General. Founded in 1986. Accredited by ACCSCT. **Enrollment:** 1,092 full-time, degree-seeking students. **Degrees:** 527 associate awarded. **Location:** 300 miles from Philadelphia. **Calendar:** Semester, extensive summer session. **Full-time faculty:** 40 total.

Student profile.

Out-of-state:	49%	**Live on campus:**	25%
25 or older:	21%		

Basis for selection. Interview, high school diploma or GED, Wonderlic reading assessment important. SAT or ACT recommended. Wonderlic assessment required of all students who do not provide qualified SAT or ACT scores. **Homeschooled:** State high school equivalency certificate required.

2008-2009 Annual costs. Total costs vary by program: Culinary Arts $41,885; Patisserie & Baking $37,485; Hospitality & Restaurant Management $35,518. Books/supplies: $3,074.

2008-2009 Financial aid. All financial aid based on need.

Application procedures. Admission: No deadline. $50 fee. Admission notification on a rolling basis. **Financial aid:** No deadline. FAFSA, institutional form required. Applicants notified on a rolling basis.

Academics. Special study options: Internships. **Credit/placement by examination:** AP, CLEP, institutional tests. **Support services:** Learning center, remedial instruction, study skills assistance, tutoring.

Majors. Personal/culinary services: Culinary arts.

Computing on campus. 80 workstations in library, computer center. Online library available.

Student life. Freshman orientation: Mandatory. Approximately 2 hours, held day before classes start. **Housing:** Guaranteed on-campus for all undergraduates. Coed dorms available. $200 deposit. **Activities:** Student government, student newspaper.

Student services. Alcohol/substance abuse counseling, career counseling, student employment services, financial aid counseling, personal counseling, placement for graduates. **Transfer:** Pre-admission transcript evaluation for new students.

Contact. E-mail: info@paculinary.com
Phone: (412) 566-2433 Toll-free number: (800) 432-2433
Fax: (412) 566-2434
George Morey, Director of Admissions, Pennsylvania Culinary Institute, 717 Liberty Avenue, Pittsburgh, PA 15222

Pennsylvania Highlands Community College

Johnstown, Pennsylvania
www.pennhighlands.edu **CB code: 2484**

- Public 2-year community college
- Commuter campus in large town

General. Regionally accredited. **Enrollment:** 972 degree-seeking undergraduates; 263 non-degree-seeking students. **Degrees:** 142 associate awarded. **Location:** 70 miles from Pittsburgh. **Calendar:** Semester, extensive summer session. **Full-time faculty:** 24 total. **Part-time faculty:** 81 total.

Student profile. Among degree-seeking undergraduates, 24% enrolled in a transfer program, 76% enrolled in a vocational program, 248 enrolled as first-time, first-year students.

Part-time:	32%	**Asian American:**	1%
Women:	59%	**Hispanic American:**	1%
African American:	3%		

Transfer out. Colleges most students transferred to 2008: University of Pittsburgh at Johnstown, Indiana University of Pennsylvania, Mount Aloysius College, Penn State University, Saint Francis University.

Basis for selection. Open admission.

2008-2009 Annual costs. Tuition/fees: $3,270; $5,860 out-of-district; $8,450 out-of-state. Per-credit charge: $86 in-district; $172 out-of-district; $258 out-of-state. Students in Blair, Bedford and Somerset counties pay tuition of $3,890 per year. Students outside Cambria County pay additional fee of $210 per year. Books/supplies: $900.

Financial aid. **Need-based:** Need-based aid available for part-time students. Work-study available nights and for part-time students. **Non-need-based:** Scholarships awarded for academics, state residency.

Application procedures. **Admission:** No deadline. $20 fee, may be waived for applicants with need. Application must be submitted on paper. Admission notification on a rolling basis. **Financial aid:** Closing date 4/1. FAFSA required. Applicants notified on a rolling basis; must reply by 8/1.

Academics. **Special study options:** Cooperative education, distance learning, dual enrollment of high school students, honors, independent study, internships. **Credit/placement by examination:** CLEP, institutional tests. **Support services:** Learning center, reduced course load, remedial instruction, study skills assistance, tutoring.

Majors. **Biology:** Biotechnology. **Business:** Accounting technology, administrative services, business admin, restaurant/food services. **Communications:** General. **Computer sciences:** Database management, networking, security, web page design. **Construction:** Lineworker. **Education:** General, teacher assistance. **Engineering technology:** Architectural, electrical, environmental, manufacturing. **Family/consumer sciences:** Aging. **Health:** Medical transcription. **Legal studies:** Court reporting. **Liberal arts:** Arts/sciences. **Protective services:** Corrections, law enforcement admin. **Public administration:** Human services. **Other:** Health and medical administrative services.

Most popular majors. Business/marketing 29%, computer/information sciences 12%, education 8%, engineering/engineering technologies 7%, health sciences 18%, liberal arts 10%, public administration/social services 9%.

Computing on campus. 250 workstations in library, computer center, student center.

Student life. **Freshman orientation:** Available. Preregistration for classes offered. **Activities:** Literary magazine.

Student services. Career counseling, services for economically disadvantaged, student employment services, financial aid counseling, placement for graduates. **Transfer:** Pre-admission transcript evaluation for new students. College fairs on campus for students transferring to 4-year colleges.

Contact. E-mail: jmaul@pennhighlands.edu
Phone: (814) 262-6446 Toll-free number: (888) 385-7325
Fax: (814) 262-6420
Jeff Maul, Director of Admissions, Pennsylvania Highlands Community College, 101 Community College Way, Johnstown, PA 15904

Pennsylvania Institute of Health and Technology

Mount Braddock, Pennsylvania
www.wvci.edu **CB code: 3214**

- For-profit 2-year business college
- Small town
- Interview required

General. Accredited by ACICS. **Enrollment:** 127 degree-seeking undergraduates. **Degrees:** 78 associate awarded. **Calendar:** Continuous. **Full-time faculty:** 5 total. **Part-time faculty:** 4 total.

Basis for selection. Open admission.

2008-2009 Annual costs. Cost of entire associate degree program: $20,700; diploma program: $12,000.

Application procedures. **Admission:** No deadline. $25 fee.

Academics. **Credit/placement by examination:** CLEP.

Majors. **Business:** General, administrative services. **Health:** Medical secretary.

Contact. Phone: (724) 437-4600 Fax: (724) 437-6053
Mary Jo Barnhart, Director of Student Services, Pennsylvania Institute of Health and Technology, Route 119 North and Mount Braddock Road, Mount Braddock, PA 15465

Pennsylvania Institute of Technology

Media, Pennsylvania
www.pit.edu **CB code: 2675**

- Private 2-year technical college
- Commuter campus in small town
- Application essay, interview required

General. Founded in 1953. Regionally accredited. **Enrollment:** 768 degree-seeking undergraduates; 7 non-degree-seeking students. **Degrees:** 79 associate awarded. **Location:** 13 miles from Philadelphia, 15 miles from Wilmington, Delaware. **Calendar:** Semester, extensive summer session. **Full-time faculty:** 21 total. **Part-time faculty:** 26 total. **Class size:** 99% < 20, less than 1% 20-39. **Partnerships:** Formal partnerships with Tech Prep in high schools.

Student profile. Among degree-seeking undergraduates, 324 enrolled as first-time, first-year students.

Part-time:	24%	**25 or older:**	42%
Women:	63%		

Basis for selection. Open admission, but selective for some programs. Selective admissions to Practical Nursing program. Interview and essay used for placement purposes only.

2009-2010 Annual costs. Tuition/fees (projected): $10,350. Per-credit charge: $315. Books/supplies: $900.

Financial aid. **Need-based:** Need-based aid available for part-time students. Work-study available nights, weekends and for part-time students. **Non-need-based:** Scholarships awarded for academics, leadership.

Application procedures. **Admission:** No deadline. $25 fee, may be waived for applicants with need. Admission notification on a rolling basis. **Financial aid:** Closing date 8/1. FAFSA, institutional form required. Applicants notified on a rolling basis starting 7/1.

Academics. Curricula designed to prepare students for positions in industry through combination of general education and job specific courses. **Special study options:** Accelerated study, cooperative education, double major, dual enrollment of high school students, independent study, internships. **Credit/placement by examination:** AP, CLEP, institutional tests. 60 credit hours maximum toward associate degree. **Support services:** Learning center, reduced course load, remedial instruction, tutoring.

Majors. **Business:** Administrative services, business admin. **Computer sciences:** Computer science, networking. **Engineering technology:** Architectural, civil, electrical. **Health:** Medical secretary.

Most popular majors. Business/marketing 18%, computer/information sciences 56%, engineering/engineering technologies 26%.

Computing on campus. 80 workstations in library, computer center, student center. Commuter students can connect to campus network. Online library available.

Student life. **Freshman orientation:** Mandatory. Orientation lasts several days, held 1 week before start of classes. **Activities:** Radio station, student government, student newspaper, amateur radio club.

Athletics. **Intramural:** Basketball M, softball M, volleyball.

Student services. Adult student services, career counseling, student employment services, personal counseling, placement for graduates, veterans' counselor. **Physically disabled:** Services for speech, hearing impaired. **Transfer:** Transfer adviser, college fairs on campus for students transferring to 4-year colleges.

Contact. E-mail: info@pit.edu
Phone: (610) 565-7900 Fax: (610) 892-1510
Angela Cassetta, Director of Admissions, Pennsylvania Institute of Technology, 800 Manchester Avenue, Media, PA 19063-4098

Pennsylvania School of Business

Allentown, Pennsylvania
www.pennschoolofbusiness.edu-search.com
CB code: 3044

- For-profit 2-year business and technical college
- Small city

General. Accredited by ACCSCT. **Calendar:** Continuous.

Annual costs/financial aid. Tuition for associate-degree programs: network technician (6 semesters): $27,000; personal computer administration (5 semesters): $22,500. Books/supplies: $800. Need-based financial aid available to full-time and part-time students.

Contact. Phone: (610) 841-3333
Director of Admissions, 406 West Hamilton Street, Allentown, PA 18101

Pittsburgh Institute of Aeronautics

Pittsburgh, Pennsylvania
www.pia.edu **CB code: 0652**

- Private 2-year technical college
- Commuter campus in large city

General. Founded in 1929. Accredited by ACCSCT. Located in active county airport. **Enrollment:** 249 degree-seeking undergraduates. **Degrees:** 104 associate awarded. **Location:** 8 miles from Pittsburgh. **Calendar:** Quarter, extensive summer session. **Full-time faculty:** 20 total; 5% minority, 10% women. **Part-time faculty:** 2 total. **Special facilities:** Modern aviation maintenance, aviation electronics, electronic systems laboratories.

Student profile. Among degree-seeking undergraduates, 100% enrolled in a vocational program, 5% already have a bachelor's degree or higher.

Out-of-state:	35%	**25 or older:**	25%

Transfer out. 15% of students enrolled in the transfer program go on to 4-year colleges.

Basis for selection. Open admission.

2009-2010 Annual costs. Tuition/fees (projected): $14,705. Books/supplies: $1,025. Personal expenses: $400.

Application procedures. Admission: No deadline. $150 fee. Admission notification on a rolling basis. **Financial aid:** Priority date 5/1; no closing date. FAFSA required. Applicants notified on a rolling basis.

Academics. Special study options: License preparation in aviation. **Credit/placement by examination:** CLEP, institutional tests. **Support services:** Remedial instruction, tutoring.

Majors. Engineering: Electrical. **Engineering technology:** Aerospace, electrical, mechanical. **Mechanic/repair:** Aircraft, electronics/electrical.

Computing on campus. 35 workstations in computer center. Commuter students can connect to campus network.

Student life. Housing: Referral housing available. **Activities:** Student government, student newspaper.

Student services. Adult student services, career counseling, student employment services, financial aid counseling, placement for graduates, veterans' counselor. **Transfer:** Pre-admission transcript evaluation for new students.

Contact. E-mail: admissions@pia.edu
Phone: (412) 346-2100 Toll-free number: (800) 444-1440
Fax: (412) 466-0513
Suzanne Markle, Director of Admissions, Pittsburgh Institute of Aeronautics, Box 10897, Pittsburgh, PA 15236-0897

Pittsburgh Institute of Mortuary Science

Pittsburgh, Pennsylvania
www.pims.edu **CB code: 7030**

- Private 2-year technical college
- Commuter campus in large city

General. Founded in 1939. Accredited by American Board of Funeral Services Education, Inc. **Enrollment:** 85 full-time, degree-seeking students. **Degrees:** 45 associate awarded. **Calendar:** Trimester, extensive summer session. **Full-time faculty:** 2 total. **Part-time faculty:** 19 total. **Special facilities:** Preparation center, specialized library.

Transfer out. Colleges most students transferred to 2008: Point Park University.

Basis for selection. Open admission. **Homeschooled:** Transcript of courses and grades, state high school equivalency certificate required. **Learning Disabled:** Diagnosis documentation within 3 years of enrollment required.

2008-2009 Annual costs. Tuition/fees: $14,780. Books/supplies: $866.

2007-2008 Financial aid. Need-based: Need-based aid available for part-time students.

Application procedures. Admission: Priority date 9/1; no deadline. $40 fee. Admission notification on a rolling basis. **Financial aid:** No deadline. FAFSA required. Applicants notified on a rolling basis.

Academics. Four-pronged approach to funeral service management via natural sciences, social sciences, mortuary sciences, and business studies. Students with previous associate degrees will earn diploma or another associate degree in embalming and funeral directing. **Special study options:** Distance learning. **Credit/placement by examination:** CLEP, institutional tests. 48 credit hours maximum toward associate degree. **Support services:** Reduced course load, tutoring.

Majors. Personal/culinary services: Mortuary science.

Computing on campus. 10 workstations in library, computer center.

Student life. Freshman orientation: Mandatory. Generally held week before start of classes. **Housing:** Housing available at local funeral homes. **Activities:** Student government.

Student services. Alcohol/substance abuse counseling, career counseling, student employment services, financial aid counseling, personal counseling, placement for graduates, veterans' counselor. **Transfer:** Pre-admission transcript evaluation for new students. Transfer adviser for students transferring to 4-year colleges.

Contact. E-mail: pims5808@aol.com
Phone: (412) 362-8500 Toll-free number: (800) 933-5808
Fax: (412) 362-1684
Karen Rocco, Registrar, Pittsburgh Institute of Mortuary Science, 5808 Baum Boulevard, Pittsburgh, PA 15206-3706

Pittsburgh Technical Institute

Oakdale, Pennsylvania
www.pti.edu **CB code: 0382**

- For-profit 2-year technical and career college
- Commuter campus in large town
- Interview required

General. Founded in 1946. Locations in Oakdale and at the Regional Learning Alliance. Evening certificate and on-line/on-site degrees for adult students ages 22+ through PTI Center for Certification and Adult Learning. **Enrollment:** 2,072 degree-seeking undergraduates; 1 non-degree-seeking students. **Degrees:** 575 associate awarded. **Location:** 12 miles from Pittsburgh. **Calendar:** Quarter, extensive summer session. **Full-time faculty:** 73 total; 37% women. **Part-time faculty:** 44 total; 48% women. **Class size:** 52% < 20, 48% 20-39. **Special facilities:** MILO Range Pro training system; A/V Suite with 2 video shooting studios, control room and 4 recording booths; fully integrated 2-room house complete with functioning home theater, security, surveillance and lighting systems; Forensic Recovery of Evidence Device (FRED) for computer security analysis; Surgical Technology and Medical Assisting/Office laboratories featuring laparoscopic camera with light source and monitor, anatomical model for simulating surgery, functional anesthesia machine; hospitality lab; therapeutic massage lab.

Student profile. Among degree-seeking undergraduates, 1,013 enrolled as first-time, first-year students.

Out-of-state:	20%	**25 or older:**	17%
Women:	33%		

Transfer out. Colleges most students transferred to 2008: Robert Morris University, Point Park University, University of Phoenix.

Basis for selection. Open admission, but selective for some programs. Upper 50% of class or passing score on CPAt required for computer programming. Criminal background check required for safety and security administration, home and commercial systems integration, and HVAC technology. Upper 80% of class or passing score on COMPASS and portfolio review required for graphic design and multimedia technologies. Criminal background check and dexterity test required for surgical technology. International students must complete application in English, show official certification of fund sources and amounts, and submit letter certifying sponsorship.

2008-2009 Annual costs. Tuition and supply costs vary by program. Tuition does not increase if student maintains continuous and consistent enrollment.

2007-2008 Financial aid. Need-based: 53% of total undergraduate aid awarded as scholarships/grants, 47% as loans/jobs. Need-based aid available for part-time students.

Application procedures. Admission: No deadline. No application fee. Admission notification on a rolling basis. **Financial aid:** No deadline. FAFSA, institutional form required. Applicants notified on a rolling basis.

Academics. All associate degree programs and selected certificate programs include industry-based internship. Tutoring services available at no charge in all courses during the day and by appointment. **Special study options:** Distance learning, double major, internships. PTI Plus Program provides students the opportunity to take cross-curricular courses in addition to their required course load if they maintain a 3.0 GPA and 90% attendance. No tuition is assessed for PTI Plus courses. **Credit/placement by examination:** CLEP, institutional tests. **Support services:** Learning center, remedial instruction, study skills assistance, tutoring, writing center.

Majors. Business: Accounting, business admin, hotel/motel admin, sales/distribution, tourism promotion. **Computer sciences:** Computer graphics, programming, web page design. **Engineering technology:** Architectural drafting, computer systems, electrical, mechanical drafting. **Health:** Management/clinical assistant, office assistant, surgical technology. **Mechanic/repair:** Electronics/electrical. **Protective services:** Security services.

Most popular majors. Business/marketing 26%, computer/information sciences 24%, engineering/engineering technologies 23%, health sciences 8%, visual/performing arts 14%.

Computing on campus. 844 workstations in library, computer center, student center. Commuter students can connect to campus network. Online library, helpline, wireless network available.

Student life. Freshman orientation: Mandatory. Held every January, April, June and September. **Housing:** Apartments available. $350 fully refundable deposit. **Activities:** Drama, student newspaper.

Athletics. Intramural: Basketball, softball, volleyball.

Student services. Adult student services, alcohol/substance abuse counseling, career counseling, student employment services, financial aid counseling, personal counseling, placement for graduates. **Transfer:** Preadmission transcript evaluation for new students. Transfer adviser, college fairs on campus for students transferring to 4-year colleges.

Contact. E-mail: james@pti.edu
Phone: (412) 809-5100 Toll-free number: (800) 784-9675
Fax: (412) 809-5388
Marylu Zuk, Vice President of Enrollment Management, Pittsburgh Technical Institute, 1111 McKee Road, Oakdale, PA 15071-3205

PJA School

Upper Darby, Pennsylvania
www.pjaschool.com **CB code: 2887**

- For-profit 2-year business and career college
- Commuter campus in very large city
- Application essay, interview required

General. Accredited by ACCSCT. **Enrollment:** 250 degree-seeking undergraduates. **Degrees:** 64 associate awarded. **Location:** 4 miles from Philadelphia. **Calendar:** Semester, extensive summer session. **Full-time faculty:** 6 total. **Part-time faculty:** 15 total. **Class size:** 43% < 20, 57% 20-39. **Special facilities:** Law library.

Student profile.

Out-of-state:	6%	**25 or older:**	58%

Transfer out. 75% of students enrolled in the transfer program go on to 4-year colleges.

Basis for selection. Test scores, essay, interview, talents, and character most important. Student must pass institutional exam for admission. **Adult students:** SAT/ACT scores not required. Applicant must pass institutional test for admission.

2008-2009 Annual costs. Tuition/fees: $10,830. Books and materials included in cost of tuition. Personal expenses: $2,067.

Financial aid. All financial aid based on need. Need-based aid available for part-time students. **Additional information:** Interest-free payment plan available.

Application procedures. Admission: No deadline. $50 fee. Application must be submitted on paper. Admission notification on a rolling basis. **Financial aid:** No deadline. FAFSA, institutional form required. Applicants notified on a rolling basis.

Academics. Special study options: Accelerated study, double major, independent study, internships, liberal arts/career combination, weekend college. Bachelor's degree programs available on campus. **Credit/placement by examination:** AP, CLEP, institutional tests. No more than 20% of credits required for degree may be awarded for prior work or life experience. **Support services:** Learning center, reduced course load, remedial instruction, study skills assistance, tutoring.

Majors. Business: General, accounting. **Legal studies:** Paralegal.

Most popular majors. Business/marketing 20%, interdisciplinary studies 20%, legal studies 61%.

Computing on campus. 120 workstations in library, computer center, student center.

Student life. Freshman orientation: Mandatory. Preregistration for classes offered.

Student services. Adult student services, career counseling, student employment services, financial aid counseling, personal counseling, placement for graduates, veterans' counselor.

Contact. E-mail: dgentile@pjaschool.com
Phone: (610) 789-6700 Toll-free number: (800) 746-4752
Fax: (610) 789-5208
Dina Gentile, Director of Admissions, PJA School, 7900 West Chester Pike, Upper Darby, PA 19082

Reading Area Community College

Reading, Pennsylvania
www.racc.edu **CB code: 2743**

- Public 2-year community college
- Commuter campus in small city

General. Founded in 1971. Regionally accredited. **Enrollment:** 4,250 degree-seeking undergraduates. **Degrees:** 400 associate awarded. **Location:** 55 miles from Philadelphia. **Calendar:** Semester, limited summer session. **Full-time faculty:** 67 total. **Part-time faculty:** 176 total. **Class size:** 44% < 20, 56% 20-39, less than 1% 40-49, less than 1% 50-99. **Special facilities:** Arts center, training and technology center.

Student profile.

Out-of-state:	1%	**25 or older:**	40%

Transfer out. Colleges most students transferred to 2008: Albright College, Kutztown University, Alvernia College, West Chester University, Penn State-Berks.

Basis for selection. Open admission, but selective for some programs. Special requirements for nursing, radiology, respiratory therapy and clinical portion of medical laboratory technician program. Interview, science background considered. Interview recommended.

High school preparation. 16 units required for nursing program, including 4 English, 3 social studies, 2 math (1 must be algebra), and 2 science with related laboratory or equivalent.

2008-2009 Annual costs. Tuition/fees: $3,510; $5,730 out-of-district; $7,950 out-of-state. Per-credit charge: $74 in-district; $148 out-of-district; $222 out-of-state. Books/supplies: $500. Personal expenses: $1,200.

2007-2008 Financial aid. Need-based: 44% of total undergraduate aid awarded as scholarships/grants, 56% as loans/jobs.

Application procedures. Admission: Closing date 8/15 (receipt date). No application fee. Admission notification on a rolling basis. **Financial aid:** Priority date 7/1; no closing date. FAFSA, institutional form required. Applicants notified on a rolling basis starting 4/15; must reply within 2 week(s) of notification.

Academics. Special study options: Cooperative education, cross-registration, distance learning, dual enrollment of high school students, ESL, honors, independent study, internships, student-designed major. License preparation in nursing. **Credit/placement by examination:** AP, CLEP, institutional tests. 45 credit hours maximum toward associate degree. **Support services:** GED preparation and test center, learning center, pre-admission summer program, reduced course load, remedial instruction, tutoring.

Majors. Biology: General. **Business:** General, accounting, administrative services, banking/financial services, business admin, entrepreneurial studies, human resources, management information systems, office management, office technology, office/clerical, operations, tourism promotion. **Computer sciences:** Data processing, networking, programming. **Education:** General, business, early childhood, elementary, middle, secondary. **Engineering:** General, electrical. **Engineering technology:** Electrical. **Family/consumer sciences:** Child care. **Health:** Clinical lab science, health services, licensed practical nurse, medical radiologic technology/radiation therapy, medical secretary, nursing (RN), predental, premedicine, prepharmacy, respiratory therapy technology. **Interdisciplinary:** Gerontology. **Legal studies:** Legal secretary, prelaw. **Liberal arts:** Arts/sciences. **Mechanic/repair:** Industrial. **Personal/culinary services:** Culinary arts. **Physical sciences:** Chemistry. **Protective services:** Law enforcement admin, police science. **Psychology:** General. **Public administration:** General, social work. **Social sciences:** General, criminology.

Most popular majors. Business/marketing 18%, education 7%, health sciences 23%, liberal arts 16%, psychology 10%, security/protective services 7%.

Computing on campus. 90 workstations in library, computer center. Online course registration available.

Student life. Freshman orientation: Mandatory. Preregistration for classes offered. **Activities:** Choral groups, international student organizations, radio station, student government, student newspaper, TV station.

Athletics. Intercollegiate: Basketball M, cross-country, soccer M, volleyball W. **Intramural:** Basketball M. **Team name:** Ravens.

Student services. Career counseling, student employment services, on-campus daycare, personal counseling, placement for graduates, veterans' counselor. **Physically disabled:** Services for visually, hearing impaired. **Transfer:** Transfer adviser, college fairs on campus for students transferring to 4-year colleges.

Contact. E-mail: admissions@racc.edu
Phone: (610) 607-6224 Toll-free number: (800) 626-1665
Fax: (610) 607-6238
Maria Mitchell, Associate Vice-President, Enrollment Management/Student Services, Reading Area Community College, 10 South Second Street, Reading, PA 19603-1706

Rosedale Technical Institute

Pittsburgh, Pennsylvania
www.rosedaletech.org **CB code: 3025**

- Private 2-year technical and career college
- Large city
- Interview required

General. Accredited by ACCSCT. **Enrollment:** 227 degree-seeking undergraduates. **Degrees:** 65 associate awarded. **Calendar:** Continuous, extensive summer session. **Full-time faculty:** 14 total. **Part-time faculty:** 5 total.

Basis for selection. High school diploma or equivalency required. General knowledge test used in admissions process, and interview is required. Applicants to automotive and diesel programs must be eligible for valid driver's license prior to graduation. Wonderlic exam required for admissions.

2008-2009 Annual costs. Tuition/fees: $11,610.

Application procedures. Admission: No deadline. $20 fee. Admission notification on a rolling basis. **Financial aid:** Closing date 8/1. FAFSA required.

Academics. Credit/placement by examination: CLEP. **Support services:** Learning center, study skills assistance, tutoring.

Majors. Mechanic/repair: General.

Computing on campus. 25 workstations in library, computer center. Online library, wireless network available.

Student life. Freshman orientation: Mandatory. Generally held 2 weeks prior to the start of classes.

Student services. Career counseling, student employment services, financial aid counseling, legal services, personal counseling, placement for graduates.

Contact. E-mail: admissions@rosedaletech.org
Phone: (412) 521-6200 Toll-free number: (800) 521-6262
Debbie Bier, Director of Admissions, Rosedale Technical Institute, 215 Beecham Drive, Pittsburgh, PA 15205-9791

Sanford-Brown Institute: Monroeville

Monroeville, Pennsylvania
www.wshb-monroeville.com **CB code: 2939**

- For-profit 2-year business and health science college
- Large town

General. Accredited by ACCSCT. **Calendar:** Courses begin every 3 months.

Annual costs/financial aid. Tuition ranges from $13,950 to $38,610 and includes books, registration and lab fees. Need-based financial aid available to full-time and part-time students.

Contact. Phone: (412) 373-6400
Director of Admission, One Monroeville Center, Suite 125, Monroeville, PA 15146

Sanford-Brown Institute: Pittsburgh

Pittsburgh, Pennsylvania
www.westernschoolpitt.com **CB code: 2933**

- For-profit 2-year technical college
- Very large city

General. Accredited by ACCSCT. **Location:** Downtown. **Calendar:** Continuous.

Annual costs/financial aid. Tuition ranges from $10,030 to $38,760 and includes books, registration and lab fees. Need-based financial aid available for full-time students.

Contact. Phone: (800) 333-6607
Director of Admissions, 421 Seventh Avenue, Pittsburgh, PA 15219

South Hills School of Business & Technology

State College, Pennsylvania
www.southhills.edu **CB code: 2467**

- For-profit 2-year business and technical college
- Commuter campus in large town
- Interview required

General. Founded in 1970. Regionally accredited; also accredited by ACICS. Free brush-up classes and career services for graduates. Branch campuses in Altoona, Lewistown, and Philipsburg. **Enrollment:** 652 degree-seeking undergraduates; 9 non-degree-seeking students. **Degrees:** 203 associate awarded. **Location:** 125 miles from Pittsburgh, 200 miles from Philadelphia. **Calendar:** Quarter, limited summer session. **Full-time faculty:** 39 total; 3% have terminal degrees, 64% women. **Part-time faculty:** 33 total; 46% women.

Student profile. Among degree-seeking undergraduates, 327 enrolled as first-time, first-year students.

Part-time:	9%	**Women:**	65%
Out-of-state:	1%	**25 or older:**	26%

Transfer out. Colleges most students transferred to 2008: St. Francis University, Lock Haven University, Mount Aloysius, Pennsylvania State University.

Basis for selection. Open admission, but selective for some programs. **Adult students:** SAT tests required for all students applying for the Diagnostic Medical Sonography program only. **Homeschooled:** Transcript of courses and grades required.

High school preparation. Recommended units include English 4, mathematics 3, social studies 4 and science 3.

2009-2010 Annual costs. Tuition/fees (projected): $13,573. Per-credit charge: $356. Books/supplies: $2,400.

2008-2009 Financial aid. All financial aid based on need. Average loan was $3,750. 59% of total undergraduate aid awarded as scholarships/grants, 41% as loans/jobs. Need-based aid available for part-time students.

Application procedures. Admission: No deadline. $25 fee. Admission notification on a rolling basis. **Financial aid:** Closing date 6/30. FAFSA required. Applicants notified on a rolling basis starting 7/5.

Academics. **Special study options:** Double major, internships. Technical preparatory program. **Credit/placement by examination:** AP, CLEP. 9 credit hours maximum toward associate degree. **Support services:** Pre-admission summer program, study skills assistance, tutoring.

Majors. **Business:** Accounting, marketing. **Computer sciences:** Computer science. **Engineering technology:** Industrial. **Health:** Medical records technology, medical secretary, sonography. **Legal studies:** Legal secretary. **Visual/performing arts:** Graphic design.

Most popular majors. Business/marketing 37%, computer/information sciences 29%, health sciences 25%.

Computing on campus. 383 workstations in library, computer center, student center. Commuter students can connect to campus network. Online library, wireless network available.

Student life. **Freshman orientation:** Mandatory. One-day program. **Activities:** Student government, student newspaper.

Student services. Career counseling, student employment services, financial aid counseling, placement for graduates. **Transfer:** Pre-admission transcript evaluation for new students. Transfer adviser, college fairs on campus for students transferring to 4-year colleges.

Contact. E-mail: admissions@southhills.edu
Phone: (814) 234-7755 Toll-free number: (888) 282-7427
Fax: (814) 234-0926
Vickey Warshaw, Director of Admissions, South Hills School of Business & Technology, 480 Waupelani Drive, State College, PA 16801-4516

South Hills School of Business & Technology: Altoona

Altoona, Pennsylvania
www.southhills.edu **CB code: 2176**

- For-profit 2-year business and technical college
- Commuter campus in small city
- Interview required

General. Accredited by ACICS. Free brush-up classes and career services assistance for graduates. Campuses in State College, Lewistown, and Philipsburg. **Enrollment:** 125 degree-seeking undergraduates. **Degrees:** 57 associate awarded. **Calendar:** Quarter, limited summer session. **Full-time faculty:** 10 total; 50% women. **Part-time faculty:** 2 total; 50% women.

Basis for selection. Open admission, but selective for some programs. **Homeschooled:** Transcript of courses and grades required. **Learning Disabled:** Documentation of disability required for student file.

High school preparation. Recommended units include English 4, mathematics 3, social studies 4 and science 3.

2009-2010 Annual costs. Tuition/fees: $13,623. Per-credit charge: $374. Books/supplies: $1,500.

Financial aid. All financial aid based on need. Need-based aid available for part-time students.

Application procedures. **Admission:** No deadline. $25 fee. Admission notification on a rolling basis. **Financial aid:** Closing date 6/30. FAFSA required. Applicants notified on a rolling basis starting 7/1.

Academics. **Credit/placement by examination:** CLEP.

Majors. **Business:** Accounting, accounting technology, administrative services, business admin, management information systems, marketing, office management, office/clerical, retailing. **Computer sciences:** Computer science. **Engineering technology:** General. **Health:** Medical records technology, medical secretary, office computer specialist. **Legal studies:** Legal secretary.

Most popular majors. Business/marketing 55%, computer/information sciences 29%, health sciences 16%.

Computing on campus. 100 workstations in library. Commuter students can connect to campus network. Online library, repair service, wireless network available.

Student life. **Freshman orientation:** Mandatory. One-day orientation program. **Housing:** Off-campus housing information available upon request. **Activities:** Student government.

Student services. Career counseling, student employment services, financial aid counseling, placement for graduates.

Contact. E-mail: admisssions@southhills.edu
Phone: (814) 944-6134 Toll-free number: (888) 282-7427
Fax: (814) 944-4684
Holly Emerick, Director of Admissions, South Hills School of Business & Technology: Altoona, 508 58th Street, Altoona, PA 16602

Thaddeus Stevens College of Technology

Lancaster, Pennsylvania
www.stevenscollege.edu **CB code: 0560**

- Public 2-year technical and career college
- Residential campus in small city

General. Founded in 1905. Regionally accredited. **Enrollment:** 800 degree-seeking undergraduates. **Degrees:** 230 associate awarded. **Location:** 60 miles from Philadelphia, 30 miles from Harrisburg. **Calendar:** Semester, limited summer session. **Full-time faculty:** 40 total. **Part-time faculty:** 10 total.

Student profile. Among degree-seeking undergraduates, 100% enrolled in a vocational program.

25 or older:	8%	**Live on campus:**	50%

Transfer out. 10% of students enrolled in the transfer program go on to 4-year colleges.

Basis for selection. Priority given to orphans and financially needy students. Admission based on school achievement record and institutional placement examination (COMPASS). Students must score proficient or higher on the PSSA exams administered in their junior year of high school. Interview recommended for associate of specialized technology program. **Homeschooled:** Transcript of courses and grades required.

High school preparation. 14 units required. Required and recommended units include English 4, mathematics 2-4 and science 2-6. Algebra required for entry to some associate degree programs.

2008-2009 Annual costs. Tuition/fees: $5,950. Per-credit charge: $135. Room/board: $6,500. Books/supplies: $275. Personal expenses: $300.

Financial aid. **Additional information:** Tuition and room and board costs waived for students with adjusted family income of $18,500 or less. Tuition and other costs also waived for orphans.

Application procedures. **Admission:** Priority date 1/1; deadline 7/30 (postmark date). $25 fee, may be waived for applicants with need. Admission notification on a rolling basis beginning on or about 9/1. Must reply by May 1 or within 4 week(s) if notified thereafter. Applicant must reply within 30 days of receiving notification of decision. **Financial aid:** Priority date 3/15; no closing date. Applicants notified on a rolling basis starting 7/15.

Academics. **Special study options:** Cooperative education, dual enrollment of high school students. **Credit/placement by examination:** CLEP, ACT, institutional tests. **Support services:** Learning center, pre-admission summer program, reduced course load, remedial instruction, study skills assistance, tutoring.

Majors. **Architecture:** Technology. **Business:** Business admin. **Communications technology:** Graphic/printing. **Computer sciences:** Networking. **Construction:** Carpentry, masonry, plumbing, power transmission. **Engineering:** Mechanical. **Engineering technology:** CAD/CADD, drafting, heat/ac/refrig, mechanical. **Mechanic/repair:** Auto body, automotive, heating/ac/refrig. **Production:** Cabinetmaking/millwright, furniture, machine shop technology, machine tool, sheet metal, tool and die, welding, woodworking.

Computing on campus. 32 workstations in library, computer center. Dormitories linked to campus network. Wireless network available.

Student life. **Freshman orientation:** Mandatory. **Housing:** Single-sex dorms available. **Activities:** Campus ministries, student government, student newspaper, Bible study group, dormitory council, outdoor club.

Athletics. NJCAA. **Intercollegiate:** Basketball M, cross-country, football (tackle) M, track and field, wrestling M. **Intramural:** Basketball, bowling, boxing M, cheerleading W, football (non-tackle), softball, table tennis. **Team name:** Bulldogs.

Student services. Adult student services, career counseling, student employment services, health services, personal counseling, placement for graduates. **Transfer:** Transfer adviser for students transferring to 4-year colleges.

Contact. E-mail: admissions@stevenscollege.edu
Phone: (717) 299-7701 Toll-free number: (800) 842-3832
Fax: (717) 391-6929
Erin Nelsen, Director of Enrollment Services, Thaddeus Stevens College of Technology, 750 East King Street, Lancaster, PA 17602

Tri-State Business Institute
Erie, Pennsylvania
www.tsbi.edu **CB code: 2502**

- For-profit 2-year business college
- Small city

General. Accredited by ACICS. **Calendar:** Quarter.

Annual costs/financial aid. Tuition ranges from $7,425 to $14,019; required fees, including books, from $1,380 to $1,920 per academic year, depending on program.

Contact. Phone: (814) 838-7673
Enrollment Coordinator, 5757 West Twenty-Sixth Street, Erie, PA 16506

Triangle Tech: Bethlehem
Bethlehem, Pennsylvania
www.triangle-tech.edu

- For-profit 2-year branch campus and technical college
- Commuter campus in small city
- Interview required

General. Regionally accredited; also accredited by ACCSCT. **Enrollment:** 98 degree-seeking undergraduates; 6 non-degree-seeking students. **Degrees:** 58 associate awarded. **Calendar:** Semester, extensive summer session. **Full-time faculty:** 8 total. **Part-time faculty:** 1 total; 100% women.

Student profile. Among degree-seeking undergraduates, 100% enrolled in a vocational program, 2% already have a bachelor's degree or higher, 44 enrolled as first-time, first-year students, 3 transferred in from other institutions.

Out-of-state:	14%	**Hispanic American:**	10%
Women:	4%	**25 or older:**	29%
African American:	8%		

Transfer out. 5% of students enrolled in the transfer program go on to 4-year colleges.

Basis for selection. Open admission. School tour required. **Homeschooled:** State high school equivalency certificate required.

High school preparation. Recommended units include mathematics 3.

2008-2009 Annual costs. Tuition/fees: $13,547. Per-credit charge: $367.

2007-2008 Financial aid. Need-based: 142 full-time freshmen applied for aid; 131 were judged to have need; 131 of these received aid. Average need met was 35%. Average scholarship/grant was $4,609; average loan $1,997. 40% of total undergraduate aid awarded as scholarships/grants, 60% as loans/jobs. Need-based aid available for part-time students. Work-study available nights.

Application procedures. Admission: No deadline. No application fee. Admission notification on a rolling basis. **Financial aid:** No deadline. FAFSA required. Applicants notified on a rolling basis.

Academics. Credit/placement by examination: CLEP, institutional tests. **Support services:** Learning center, remedial instruction, study skills assistance, tutoring.

Majors. Construction: General, carpentry, electrician.

Computing on campus. 27 workstations in library, computer center.

Student life. Freshman orientation: Mandatory. Preregistration for classes offered.

Student services. Transfer: Re-entry adviser, pre-admission transcript evaluation for new students. Transfer center, transfer adviser, college fairs on campus for students transferring to 4-year colleges.

Contact. Phone: (610) 691-1300 Fax: (610) 691-7525
Jason Vallozzi, Director of Admissions, Triangle Tech: Bethlehem, 31 South Commerce Way, Lehigh Valley Industrial Park IV, Bethlehem, PA 18017

Triangle Tech: DuBois
DuBois, Pennsylvania
www.triangle-tech.edu **CB code: 7133**

- For-profit 2-year technical college
- Commuter campus in large town
- Interview required

General. Accredited by ACCSCT. **Enrollment:** 236 degree-seeking undergraduates. **Degrees:** 132 associate awarded. **Location:** 145 miles from Pittsburgh. **Calendar:** Semester, extensive summer session. **Full-time faculty:** 17 total; 35% women. **Class size:** 100% < 20.

Student profile. Among degree-seeking undergraduates, 100% enrolled in a vocational program, 140 enrolled as first-time, first-year students.

Women:	5%	**Native American:**	1%
African American:	2%	**25 or older:**	16%
Hispanic American:	1%		

Transfer out. 1% of students enrolled in the transfer program go on to 4-year colleges.

Basis for selection. Open admission. **Homeschooled:** State high school equivalency certificate required.

High school preparation. Recommended units include English 4 and mathematics 4.

2008-2009 Annual costs. Tuition/fees: $13,605. Per-credit charge: $367. Books/supplies: $1,685. Personal expenses: $1,608.

2007-2008 Financial aid. All financial aid based on need. 136 full-time freshmen applied for aid; 136 were judged to have need; 136 of these received aid. Average need met was 100%. Average scholarship/grant was $3,375; average loan $2,825. 48% of total undergraduate aid awarded as scholarships/grants, 52% as loans/jobs. Need-based aid available for part-time students.

Application procedures. Admission: No deadline. No application fee. Admission notification on a rolling basis. **Financial aid:** No deadline. FAFSA, institutional form required. Applicants notified on a rolling basis.

Academics. Special study options: Dual enrollment of high school students. **Credit/placement by examination:** AP, CLEP. **Support services:** Learning center, remedial instruction, study skills assistance, tutoring.

Majors. Construction: Carpentry, electrician. **Engineering technology:** Architectural drafting, mechanical drafting. **Production:** Welding.

Most popular majors. Engineering/engineering technologies 21%, trade and industry 79%.

Computing on campus. 53 workstations in library, computer center.

Student life. Freshman orientation: Mandatory. Orientation held Thursday before classes begin, approximately 1-1/2 hours in length. **Activities:** Student government.

Student services. Career counseling, student employment services, financial aid counseling, placement for graduates. **Transfer:** Pre-admission transcript evaluation for new students.

Contact. E-mail: scraig@triangle-tech.edu
Phone: (814) 371-2090 Toll-free number: (800) 874-8324
Fax: (814) 371-9227
Jason Vallozzi, Director of Admissions, Triangle Tech: DuBois, PO Box 551, DuBois, PA 15801-0551

Triangle Tech: Erie
Erie, Pennsylvania
www.triangle-tech.edu **CB code: 1572**

- For-profit 2-year technical college
- Commuter campus in small city
- Interview required

General. Founded in 1976. Accredited by ACCSCT. **Enrollment:** 144 degree-seeking undergraduates. **Degrees:** 90 associate awarded. **Location:** 100 miles from Pittsburgh and Cleveland. **Calendar:** Semester, extensive summer session. **Full-time faculty:** 13 total; 15% women. **Part-time faculty:** 1 total; 100% women.

Student profile. Among degree-seeking undergraduates, 42 enrolled as first-time, first-year students.

Out-of-state:	12%	**25 or older:**	41%
Women:	3%		

Basis for selection. Open admission.

2008-2009 Annual costs. Tuition/fees: $13,497. Per-credit charge: $367. Books/supplies: $1,150. Personal expenses: $1,608.

2007-2008 Financial aid. Need-based: 44% of total undergraduate aid awarded as scholarships/grants, 56% as loans/jobs. Need-based aid available for part-time students.

Application procedures. Admission: No deadline. $75 fee. Admission notification on a rolling basis. **Financial aid:** FAFSA required. Applicants notified on a rolling basis.

Academics. Credit/placement by examination: AP, CLEP, institutional tests. **Support services:** Remedial instruction, study skills assistance, tutoring.

Majors. Construction: Carpentry, electrician. **Engineering technology:** Architectural drafting, mechanical drafting.

Computing on campus. 50 workstations in computer center.

Student life. Freshman orientation: Mandatory. Preregistration for classes offered. **Activities:** Student government, student newspaper.

Student services. Career counseling, student employment services, financial aid counseling, personal counseling, placement for graduates. **Transfer:** Re-entry adviser, pre-admission transcript evaluation for new students. Transfer adviser for students transferring to 4-year colleges.

Contact. Phone: (814) 453-6016 Fax: (814) 454-2818
Jason Vallozzi, Director of Admissions, Triangle Tech: Erie, 2000 Liberty Street, Erie, PA 16502-2594

Triangle Tech: Greensburg

Greensburg, Pennsylvania
www.triangle-tech.edu **CB code: 0658**

- For-profit 2-year technical college
- Commuter campus in large town
- Interview required

General. Founded in 1944. Accredited by ACCSCT. **Enrollment:** 209 degree-seeking undergraduates; 9 non-degree-seeking students. **Degrees:** 179 associate awarded. **Location:** 40 miles from Pittsburgh. **Calendar:** Semester, extensive summer session. **Full-time faculty:** 20 total; 5% have terminal degrees, 15% women. **Part-time faculty:** 3 total. **Class size:** 89% < 20, 11% 20-39.

Student profile. Among degree-seeking undergraduates, 100% enrolled in a vocational program, 100 enrolled as first-time, first-year students.

Women:	4%	**Native American:**	1%
African American:	2%	**25 or older:**	42%

Transfer out. 1% of students enrolled in the transfer program go on to 4-year colleges.

Basis for selection. Open admission.

2008-2009 Annual costs. Tuition/fees: $13,478. Per-credit charge: $367. Books/supplies: $1,176. Personal expenses: $1,608.

2007-2008 Financial aid. Need-based: 318 full-time freshmen applied for aid; 318 were judged to have need; 318 of these received aid. Average need met was 35%. Average scholarship/grant was $8,721; average loan $4,363. 48% of total undergraduate aid awarded as scholarships/grants, 52% as loans/jobs. Need-based aid available for part-time students. **Non-need-based:** Awarded to 35 full-time undergraduates, including 31 freshmen.

Application procedures. Admission: No deadline. No application fee. Admission notification on a rolling basis. **Financial aid:** No deadline. FAFSA, institutional form required. Applicants notified on a rolling basis starting 1/1.

Academics. Credit/placement by examination: AP, CLEP, institutional tests. **Support services:** Learning center, remedial instruction, study skills assistance, tutoring.

Majors. Construction: Carpentry, electrician. **Engineering technology:** Architectural drafting, heat/ac/refrig, mechanical drafting.

Most popular majors. Engineering/engineering technologies 39%, trade and industry 61%.

Computing on campus. 52 workstations in library, computer center.

Student life. Freshman orientation: Mandatory. Preregistration for classes offered. **Activities:** Student government.

Student services. Career counseling, student employment services, personal counseling, placement for graduates, veterans' counselor. **Transfer:** Re-entry adviser, pre-admission transcript evaluation for new students. Transfer adviser for students transferring to 4-year colleges.

Contact. Phone: (724) 832-1050 Toll-free number: (800) 874-8324
Fax: (724) 834-0325
Jason Vallozzi, Director of Admissions, Triangle Tech: Greensburg, 222 East Pittsburgh Street, Suite A, Greensburg, PA 15601-3304

Triangle Tech: Pittsburgh

Pittsburgh, Pennsylvania
www.triangle-tech.edu **CB code: 0734**

- For-profit 2-year technical college
- Commuter campus in large city
- Interview required

General. Founded in 1944. Accredited by ACCSCT. **Enrollment:** 247 degree-seeking undergraduates. **Degrees:** 154 associate awarded. **Location:** 5 miles from downtown. **Calendar:** Semester, extensive summer session. **Full-time faculty:** 22 total. **Part-time faculty:** 4 total. **Class size:** 92% < 20, 8% 20-39.

Student profile. Among degree-seeking undergraduates, 100% enrolled in a vocational program, 136 enrolled as first-time, first-year students.

Out-of-state:	1%	**25 or older:**	41%
Women:	4%		

Transfer out. 1% of students enrolled in the transfer program go on to 4-year colleges. **Colleges most students transferred to 2008:** Point Park College, Robert Morris College, Edinboro University, Slippery Rock University, University of Pittsburgh.

Basis for selection. Open admission, but selective for some programs. Must have high school diploma or GED. Applicants must take TABE test for placement. **Homeschooled:** Transcript of courses and grades, state high school equivalency certificate required.

2008-2009 Annual costs. Tuition/fees: $13,558. Per-credit charge: $367. Books/supplies: $1,315. Personal expenses: $1,608.

2007-2008 Financial aid. Need-based: 377 full-time freshmen applied for aid; 377 were judged to have need; 377 of these received aid. Average need met was 32%. Average scholarship/grant was $5,839; average loan $4,890. 45% of total undergraduate aid awarded as scholarships/grants, 55% as loans/jobs. Need-based aid available for part-time students. Work-study available nights. **Non-need-based:** Awarded to 35 full-time undergraduates, including 31 freshmen. Scholarships awarded for academics, state residency.

Application procedures. Admission: No deadline. $75 fee. Admission notification on a rolling basis. **Financial aid:** No deadline. FAFSA, institutional form required. Applicants notified on a rolling basis.

Academics. Credit/placement by examination: CLEP, institutional tests. 36 credit hours maximum toward associate degree. **Support services:** Learning center, remedial instruction, study skills assistance, tutoring.

Majors. Construction: Carpentry, electrician, power transmission. **Engineering technology:** Drafting. **Mechanic/repair:** Heating/ac/refrig. **Production:** Welding.

Computing on campus. 46 workstations in library, computer center. Online library available.

Student life. Freshman orientation: Mandatory. Held approximately 5 days prior to start; approximately 2-and-one-half hours long. **Activities:** Student government.

Student services. Career counseling, student employment services, financial aid counseling, personal counseling, placement for graduates. **Transfer:** Pre-admission transcript evaluation for new students. College fairs on campus for students transferring to 4-year colleges.

Contact. E-mail: info@triangle-tech.edu
Phone: (412) 359-1000 Toll-free number: (800) 874-8324
Fax: (412) 359-1012
Jason Vallozzi, Director of Admissions, Triangle Tech: Pittsburgh, 1940 Perrysville Avenue, Pittsburgh, PA 15214-3897

Triangle Tech: Sunbury

Sunbury, Pennsylvania
www.triangle-tech.edu

- For-profit 2-year technical college
- Commuter campus in large town
- Interview required

General. Accredited by ACCSCT. **Enrollment:** 111 degree-seeking undergraduates. **Degrees:** 41 associate awarded. **Calendar:** Semester. **Full-time faculty:** 13 total; 8% women. **Part-time faculty:** 1 total. **Class size:** 100% < 20.

Student profile. Among degree-seeking undergraduates, 59 enrolled as first-time, first-year students.

Basis for selection. High school GPA important. Test scores and recommendations considered.

2008-2009 Annual costs. Tuition/fees: $13,670. Per-credit charge: $367. Books/supplies: $1,034. Personal expenses: $1,608.

2007-2008 Financial aid. Need-based: 68 full-time freshmen applied for aid; 68 were judged to have need; 68 of these received aid. Average need met was 96%. Average scholarship/grant was $4,846; average loan $3,414. 41% of total undergraduate aid awarded as scholarships/grants, 59% as loans/jobs. Work-study available nights. **Non-need-based:** Awarded to 11 full-time undergraduates, including 8 freshmen.

Application procedures. Admission: No deadline. No application fee. Admission notification on a rolling basis. **Financial aid:** No deadline. FAFSA, institutional form required.

Academics. Credit/placement by examination: AP, CLEP, institutional tests. **Support services:** Tutoring.

Majors. Construction: General, carpentry. **Engineering technology:** Electrical. **Production:** Welding.

Computing on campus. 27 workstations in library, computer center.

Student life. Freshman orientation: Mandatory.

Student services. Adult student services, student employment services, financial aid counseling, placement for graduates.

Contact. E-mail: jdrumm@triangle-tech.edu
Phone: (570) 988-0700 Toll-free number: (800) 874-8324
Fax: (570) 988-4641
John Mazzarese, Vice President of Admissions, Triangle Tech: Sunbury, 191 Performance Road, Sunbury, PA 17801

University of Pittsburgh at Titusville

Titusville, Pennsylvania
www.upt.pitt.edu **CB code: 2937**

- Public 2-year branch campus and liberal arts college
- Residential campus in small town
- SAT or ACT (ACT writing optional) required

General. Founded in 1963. Regionally accredited. **Enrollment:** 537 degree-seeking undergraduates; 26 non-degree-seeking students. **Degrees:** 49 associate awarded. **Location:** 100 miles from Pittsburgh, 50 miles from Erie. **Calendar:** Semester, limited summer session. **Full-time faculty:** 20 total. **Part-time faculty:** 40 total. **Class size:** 70% < 20, 28% 20-39, less than 1% 40-49, 2% 50-99.

Student profile. Among degree-seeking undergraduates, 63% enrolled in a transfer program, 201 enrolled as first-time, first-year students, 28 transferred in from other institutions.

Part-time:	20%	**Hispanic American:**	2%
Out-of-state:	4%	**Native American:**	1%
Women:	66%	**25 or older:**	10%
African American:	18%	**Live on campus:**	25%
Asian American:	2%		

Transfer out. Colleges most students transferred to 2008: Clarion University, Edinboro University, Indiana University of Pennsylvania, Penn State University, Mercyhurst College.

Basis for selection. Decisions based on academic performance. Applicants deserving additional consideration referred to Admissions Committee. SAT recommended. Essay, interview recommended. **Homeschooled:** Math/English placement tests required. **Learning Disabled:** Students with disabilities asked to provide comprehensive documentation to Disability Resources and Services representative to establish eligibility for accommodations.

High school preparation. College-preparatory program recommended. 15 units required. Required and recommended units include English 4, mathematics 2, science 1 (laboratory 1), foreign language 3 and academic electives 7. One unit lab science required.

2008-2009 Annual costs. Tuition/fees: $10,430; $19,050 out-of-state. Per-credit charge: $404 in-state; $763 out-of-state. Room/board: $8,076. Books/supplies: $800. Personal expenses: $1,600.

2008-2009 Financial aid. Need-based: Average need met was 78%. Average scholarship/grant was $10,500; average loan $3,500. 55% of total undergraduate aid awarded as scholarships/grants, 45% as loans/jobs. Need-based aid available for part-time students. Work-study available nights and weekends. **Non-need-based:** Scholarships awarded for academics, athletics, state residency.

Application procedures. Admission: No deadline. $45 fee, may be waived for applicants with need. Admission notification on a rolling basis beginning on or about 11/1. **Financial aid:** Priority date 3/1; no closing date. FAFSA required. Applicants notified on a rolling basis; must reply within 2 week(s) of notification.

Academics. Special study options: Combined bachelor's/graduate degree, cross-registration, dual enrollment of high school students, internships, study abroad. Bachelor's degree programs available on campus. License preparation in nursing, real estate. **Credit/placement by examination:** AP, CLEP, SAT, ACT, institutional tests. 6 credit hours maximum toward associate degree. **Support services:** Learning center, reduced course load, remedial instruction, study skills assistance, tutoring.

Majors. Business: General, accounting, management information systems. **Family/consumer sciences:** General. **Health:** Nursing (RN), physical therapy assistant. **Interdisciplinary:** Natural sciences. **Liberal arts:** Arts/sciences.

Most popular majors. Biological/life sciences 7%, business/marketing 9%, health sciences 49%, liberal arts 13%, public administration/social services 18%.

Computing on campus. 62 workstations in dormitories, library, computer center, student center. Dormitories wired for high-speed internet access and linked to campus network. Commuter students can connect to campus network. Online course registration, online library, helpline, student web hosting, wireless network available.

Student life. Freshman orientation: Mandatory, $60 fee. Preregistration for classes offered. **Policies:** Organizations must complete 1 community service and fundraising activity per year to receive student activity funding. **Housing:** Guaranteed on-campus for all undergraduates. Coed dorms, special housing for disabled, wellness housing available. $100 fully refundable deposit. Townhouse apartments without cooking facilities available. **Activities:** Choral groups, dance, drama, student government, diversity club, Students in Free Enterprise, commuter student association, Alpha Omega Christian fellowship, Phi Theta Kappa, student activities board, chemistry club, travel club, student physical therapy association.

Athletics. USCAA. **Intercollegiate:** Basketball, golf M, volleyball W. **Intramural:** Basketball, bowling, football (non-tackle), racquetball, skiing, soccer, softball, swimming, table tennis, tennis, volleyball. **Team name:** Panthers.

Student services. Adult student services, alcohol/substance abuse counseling, chaplain/spiritual director, career counseling, student employment services, financial aid counseling, health services, minority student services, personal counseling, placement for graduates. **Physically disabled:** Services for visually impaired. **Transfer:** Pre-admission transcript evaluation for new students. Transfer adviser, college fairs on campus for students transferring to 4-year colleges.

Contact. E-mail: uptadm@pitt.edu
Phone: (814) 827-4427 Toll-free number: (888) 878-0462
Fax: (814) 827-4519
John Mumford, Executive Director of Enrollment Management, University of Pittsburgh at Titusville, UPT Admissions Office, Titusville, PA 16354-0287

Valley Forge Military Academy & College

Wayne, Pennsylvania
www.vfmac.edu
CB member
CB code: 2955

- Private 2-year junior and military college
- Residential campus in small city
- SAT or ACT (ACT writing optional) required

General. Founded in 1928. Regionally accredited. One of only 5 military junior colleges in nation offering Army ROTC early commissioning program leading to commission as second lieutenant in U.S. Army Reserve at end of second year. Regimental marching band, drum and bugle corps, regimental choir. **Enrollment:** 217 degree-seeking undergraduates. **Degrees:** 57 associate awarded. **ROTC:** Army, Air Force. **Location:** 15 miles from Philadelphia. **Calendar:** Semester, limited summer session. **Full-time faculty:** 13 total. **Part-time faculty:** 8 total. **Special facilities:** Motorized artillery unit, mounted cavalry troop, aviation training.

Student profile. Among degree-seeking undergraduates, 100% enrolled in a transfer program.

Out-of-state:	69%	**Live on campus:**	100%

Transfer out. Colleges most students transferred to 2008: Lehigh University, Villanova University, Drexel University, The Citadel, George Mason University.

Basis for selection. School achievement record, test scores, and personal character most important. TOEFL score accepted in lieu of SAT or ACT scores for international students. Interview recommended. **Homeschooled:** Statement describing homeschool structure and mission, transcript of courses and grades, interview, letter of recommendation (nonparent) required.

High school preparation. Required and recommended units include English 4, mathematics 3, science 3 and foreign language 2.

2008-2009 Annual costs. Tuition/fees: $26,441. Room/board: $8,535. Books/supplies: $1,000.

2007-2008 Financial aid. Need-based: Work-study available nights, weekends and for part-time students. **Non-need-based:** Scholarships awarded for academics, alumni affiliation, athletics, music/drama, ROTC, state residency. **Additional information:** Students enrolled in advanced military science program can receive up to $5,000 from the Army. In addition, competitively awarded ROTC scholarships pay average of another $14,100 per school year for direct educational expenses.

Application procedures. Admission: Closing date 8/1 (receipt date). $25 fee, may be waived for applicants with need. Admission notification on a rolling basis. Must reply by May 1 or within 2 week(s) if notified thereafter. **Financial aid:** Closing date 5/1. FAFSA, institutional form required. Applicants notified on a rolling basis starting 5/15; must reply within 2 week(s) of notification.

Academics. Special study options: Cross-registration, dual enrollment of high school students, ESL, study abroad. **Credit/placement by examination:** AP, CLEP, SAT, ACT, institutional tests. 15 credit hours maximum toward associate degree. **Support services:** Reduced course load, remedial instruction, writing center.

Majors. Business: General. **Engineering:** General, science. **Liberal arts:** Arts/sciences. **Protective services:** Criminal justice.

Computing on campus. PC or laptop required. 44 workstations in library, computer center. Dormitories wired for high-speed internet access and linked to campus network. Helpline, repair service, wireless network available.

Student life. Freshman orientation: Mandatory. Preregistration for classes offered. 3-day orientation with placement testing. **Policies:** Religious observance required. **Housing:** Guaranteed on-campus for all undergraduates. Single-sex dorms, wellness housing available. $1,000 partly refundable deposit, deadline 5/1. **Activities:** Bands, choral groups, drama, music ensembles, radio station, student government, student newspaper, Catholic Fellowship, Jewish Fellowship, Christian Fellowship, Muslim Fellowship, Young Republicans.

Athletics. Intercollegiate: Basketball M, cross-country M, equestrian M, football (tackle) M, lacrosse M, rifle M, soccer M, tennis M, wrestling M. **Intramural:** Baseball M, basketball M, fencing M, football (tackle) M, golf M, judo M, rugby M, soccer M, softball M, volleyball M, water polo M, weight lifting M. **Team name:** Trojans.

Student services. Chaplain/spiritual director, career counseling, financial aid counseling, health services, personal counseling, placement for graduates. **Transfer:** Pre-admission transcript evaluation for new students. Transfer adviser for students transferring to 4-year colleges.

Contact. E-mail: admission@vfmac.edu
Phone: (610) 989-1300 Toll-free number: (800) 234-8362
Fax: (610) 688-1545
Gerald Hale, Director of Enrollment Management, Valley Forge Military Academy & College, 1001 Eagle Road, Wayne, PA 19087

Vet Tech Institute

Pittsburgh, Pennsylvania
www.vettechinstitute.edu
CB code: 7134

- For-profit 2-year health science and technical college
- Commuter campus in large city

General. Accredited by ACCSCT. Veterinary technician AVMA accredited. **Enrollment:** 320 degree-seeking undergraduates. **Degrees:** 162 associate awarded. **Calendar:** Semester. **Full-time faculty:** 9 total. **Part-time faculty:** 2 total. **Special facilities:** Animal tech rooms, on-site kennel.

Transfer out. Colleges most students transferred to 2008: Point Park College.

Basis for selection. Satisfactory performance on school admission test required. Essay, interview recommended.

2008-2009 Annual costs. Tuition/fees: $29,250.

Financial aid. Need-based: Work-study available nights. **Non-need-based:** Scholarships awarded for academics.

Application procedures. Admission: No deadline. $50 fee. Admission notification on a rolling basis. **Financial aid:** No deadline. FAFSA required. Applicants notified on a rolling basis.

Academics. Special study options: Internships. **Credit/placement by examination:** AP, CLEP. **Support services:** Tutoring.

Majors. Health: Veterinary technology/assistant.

Computing on campus. 38 workstations in library, computer center.

Student life. Freshman orientation: Mandatory.

Student services. Career counseling, placement for graduates.

Contact. E-mail: admissions@vettechinstitute.edu
Phone: (412) 391-7021 Toll-free number: (800) 570-0693
Fax: (412) 232-4348
Terry Taylor, Senior Admissions Coordinator, Vet Tech Institute, 125 Seventh Street, Pittsburgh, PA 15222-3400

Westmoreland County Community College

Youngwood, Pennsylvania
www.wccc.edu
CB code: 2968

- Public 2-year community college
- Commuter campus in small town

General. Founded in 1970. Regionally accredited. **Enrollment:** 5,584 degree-seeking undergraduates; 830 non-degree-seeking students. **Degrees:** 556 associate awarded. **Location:** 30 miles from Pittsburgh. **Calendar:** Semester, limited summer session. **Full-time faculty:** 88 total; 4% minority, 52% women. **Part-time faculty:** 399 total; 2% minority, 53% women. **Class size:** 77% < 20, 23% 20-39. **Special facilities:** Culinary arts kitchens, greenhouse, student lounges, theater.

Student profile. Among degree-seeking undergraduates, 27% enrolled in a transfer program, 73% enrolled in a vocational program, 1,783 enrolled as first-time, first-year students.

Part-time:	48%	**Hispanic American:**	1%
Women:	63%	**25 or older:**	41%
African American:	3%		

Transfer out. Colleges most students transferred to 2008: University of Pittsburgh, Indiana University of Pennsylvania, California University of Pennsylvania, Seton Hill University, St. Vincent College.

Basis for selection. Open admission, but selective for some programs. Allied Health program applicants required to take Comparative Guidance and Placement test, submit application by November 30 of the year prior to enrollment, and satisfactory results from pre-entrance physicals. Interview recommended.

2008-2009 Annual costs. Tuition/fees: $2,580; $4,860 out-of-district; $7,140 out-of-state. Per-credit charge: $76 in-district; $152 out-of-district; $228 out-of-state. Books/supplies: $750.

Financial aid. Need-based: Need-based aid available for part-time students. Work-study available nights and for part-time students. **Non-need-based:** Scholarships awarded for academics.

Application procedures. Admission: No deadline. $10 fee, may be waived for applicants with need. Admission notification on a rolling basis. **Financial aid:** No deadline. FAFSA, institutional form required. Applicants notified on a rolling basis starting 5/1.

Academics. Special study options: Cooperative education, cross-registration, distance learning, double major, honors, independent study, internships, student-designed major, study abroad. Bachelor's degree programs available on campus. License preparation in dental hygiene, nursing, radiology, real estate. **Credit/placement by examination:** AP, CLEP, institutional tests. 30 credit hours maximum toward associate degree. **Support services:** GED preparation and test center, learning center, remedial instruction, study skills assistance, tutoring.

Majors. Agriculture: Floriculture, horticultural science, horticulture, turf management. **Business:** Accounting technology, administrative services, banking/financial services, business admin, executive assistant, hotel/motel admin, human resources, marketing, real estate, retailing, tourism/travel. **Communications technology:** Photo/film/video. **Computer sciences:** Computer science, database management, networking, programming, security, web page design. **Education:** Teacher assistance. **Engineering technology:** Architectural drafting, computer, computer hardware, electrical, environmental, manufacturing, mechanical, mechanical drafting. **Health:** Dental hygiene, dietetic technician, medical secretary, nursing (RN), radiologic technology/medical imaging. **Legal studies:** Paralegal. **Liberal arts:** Arts/sciences. **Mechanic/repair:** Heating/ac/refrig, industrial. **Personal/culinary services:** Baking, chef training, restaurant/catering. **Production:** Machine shop technology, machine tool, welding. **Protective services:** Criminal justice, fire safety technology. **Public administration:** Human services. **Science technology:** Biological. **Visual/performing arts:** Commercial/advertising art, photography.

Most popular majors. Business/marketing 26%, computer/information sciences 9%, family/consumer sciences 8%, health sciences 28%, security/protective services 9%.

Computing on campus. 600 workstations in library, computer center. Commuter students can connect to campus network. Online course registration, online library, helpline, student web hosting, wireless network available.

Student life. Freshman orientation: Available. **Policies:** All clubs required to complete 10 hours of community service per semester and send two representatives to each student government meeting (twice a month). **Activities:** Choral groups, drama, literary magazine, musical theater, student government, student newspaper, cultural awareness coalition, Reach Out club, Republican club, human services club, Veteran's club.

Athletics. NJCAA. **Intercollegiate:** Baseball M, basketball, bowling, golf, softball W, volleyball W. **Intramural:** Baseball M, basketball, bowling, golf, skiing, soccer, softball, table tennis, volleyball. **Team name:** Wolfpack.

Student services. Career counseling, services for economically disadvantaged, student employment services, financial aid counseling, on-campus daycare, personal counseling, placement for graduates, veterans' counselor. **Physically disabled:** Services for visually, speech, hearing impaired. **Transfer:** Pre-admission transcript evaluation for new students. Transfer adviser, college fairs on campus for students transferring to 4-year colleges.

Contact. E-mail: tatarj@wccc.edu
Phone: (724) 925-4077 Toll-free number: (800) 262-2103 ext. 4077
Fax: (724) 925-5802
Janice Grabowski, Director of Admissions, Westmoreland County Community College, 145 Pavilion Lane, Youngwood, PA 15697

Williamson Free School of Mechanical Trades

Media, Pennsylvania
www.williamson.edu **CB code: 0765**

- Private 2-year technical college for men affiliated with nondenominational tradition
- Residential campus in large town
- Interview required

General. Founded in 1888. Accredited by ACCSCT. Discipline-oriented school that prepares students through academic instruction and hands-on training in a structured environment; scholarship-only students. **Enrollment:** 237 degree-seeking undergraduates. **Degrees:** 73 associate awarded. **Location:** 14 miles from Philadelphia, 14 miles from Wilmington, Delaware. **Calendar:** Semester. **Full-time faculty:** 19 total. **Part-time faculty:** 13 total. **Special facilities:** Natural arboretum.

Student profile.

Out-of-state:	15%	**Live on campus:**	100%

Basis for selection. Family economic need, high school performance, letters of character reference, interview important. First consideration given to applicants with 2.0 or better average in math, science, and English. Applicant must have reached 16th birthday (but not passed 20th birthday) prior to June of year of admission. Armed Services Vocational Aptitude Battery (ASVAB) required by March 24th. Essay recommended.

High school preparation. 7 units required. Required units include English 3, mathematics 2 and science 2. Math units must include algebra I and geometry. Science units should include chemistry and physics.

2008-2009 Annual costs. All students receive full scholarships covering tuition, room and board, and textbooks. Required fees vary by program and year, average $1,052.

Application procedures. Admission: Closing date 2/28 (postmark date). No application fee. Admission notification 4/30. Must reply by 5/23. **Financial aid:** No deadline.

Academics. Special study options: Cooperative education, internships. **Credit/placement by examination:** CLEP, institutional tests. **Support services:** Pre-admission summer program, tutoring.

Majors. Agriculture: Horticulture. **Construction:** Maintenance.

Computing on campus. 35 workstations in library, computer center.

Student life. Freshman orientation: Mandatory. Takes place first 3 days of school and includes shop orientation, rules, classroom schedules and math testing. **Policies:** Student life carefully structured, including prescribed daily schedule, dress code, required chapel, and clearly defined privileges and responsibilities. Religious observance required. **Housing:** Guaranteed on-campus for all undergraduates. **Activities:** Jazz band, choral groups, student government, student newspaper, Campus Crusade for Christ, Bible study groups.

Athletics. NJCAA. **Intercollegiate:** Baseball M, basketball M, cross-country M, football (tackle) M, lacrosse M, soccer M, wrestling M. **Intramural:** Archery M, volleyball M. **Team name:** Mechanics.

Student services. Alcohol/substance abuse counseling, career counseling, student employment services, health services, personal counseling, placement for graduates.

Contact. E-mail: jmerillat@williamson.edu
Phone: (610) 566-1776 ext. 235 Fax: (610) 566-6502
Jason Merillat, Director of Enrollments, Williamson Free School of Mechanical Trades, 106 South New Middletown Road, Media, PA 19063

Yorktowne Business Institute

York, Pennsylvania
www.ybi.edu **CB code: 2553**

- For-profit 2-year business and health science college
- Commuter campus in small city
- Application essay, interview required

General. Founded in 1976. Accredited by ACICS. **Enrollment:** 250 undergraduates. **Degrees:** 68 associate awarded. **Location:** 100 miles from Philadelphia, 50 miles from Baltimore. **Calendar:** Trimester, extensive summer session. **Part-time faculty:** 32 total. **Special facilities:** Culinary arts center with teaching kitchens and student-run restaurant.

Basis for selection. Open admission, but selective for some programs.

2008-2009 Annual costs. Tuition $18,750 for business and medical programs, $28,470 for culinary program. Fees vary and are charged on a per term basis. Books/supplies: $2,900. Personal expenses: $1,656.

Financial aid. Need-based: Need-based aid available for part-time students.

Application procedures. Admission: No deadline. No application fee. Admission notification on a rolling basis. **Financial aid:** Priority date 5/1; no closing date. FAFSA required.

Academics. Special study options: Double major. Bachelor's degree programs available on campus. **Credit/placement by examination:** CLEP. **Support services:** Reduced course load, tutoring.

Majors. Business: Accounting, administrative services, business admin, hospitality admin, hospitality/recreation, tourism promotion. **Computer sciences:** General, data processing. **Health:** Dental assistant, medical assistant, medical records technology, medical secretary. **Legal studies:** Legal secretary, paralegal. **Personal/culinary services:** Culinary arts.

Computing on campus. 100 workstations in library, computer center.

Student services. Career counseling, student employment services, personal counseling, placement for graduates, veterans' counselor. **Transfer:** Pre-admission transcript evaluation for new students.

Contact. E-mail: admissions@ybi.edu
Phone: (717) 846-5000 Toll-free number: (800) 840-1004
Fax: (717) 848-4584
Jane Regan, Director of Admissions, Yorktowne Business Institute, West 7th Avenue, York, PA 17404-2034

YTI Career Institute: Lancaster

Lancaster, Pennsylvania
www.yti.edu

- For-profit 2-year business and technical college
- Small city

General. Accredited by ACCSCT. **Enrollment:** 312 degree-seeking undergraduates. **Degrees:** 197 associate awarded. **Calendar:** Quarter. **Full-time faculty:** 66 total. **Part-time faculty:** 18 total.

Basis for selection. Open admission, but selective for some programs. Medical Office Assistant and Medical Assistant programs require criminal background check and health information form completed by certified physician to include documentation for Hepatitis B and TB immunizations. Dental Assisting Program requires verification of Hepatitis B vaccination. Criminal Justice and First Response program requires background/record check, valid driver's license, and applicants must be at least 18 years of age at time of matriculation. COMPASS used for placement.

2008-2009 Annual costs. Diploma programs: $15,100 to $21,320; associate degree programs: $28,560 to $39,970. Additional supply costs of $1,430 to $2,660 may apply, depending on program.

Application procedures. Admission: No deadline. $50 fee.

Academics. Special study options: Internships. License preparation in radiology. **Credit/placement by examination:** CLEP.

Majors. Health: Medical assistant. **Personal/culinary services:** Restaurant/catering. **Protective services:** Law enforcement admin.

Contact. E-mail: thomas.driscoll@yti.edu
Phone: (717) 295-1100 Toll-free number: (866) 984-5262
Fax: (717) 295-1135
Thomas Driscoll, Director of Admissions, YTI Career Institute: Lancaster, 3050 Hempland Road, Lancaster, PA 17601

YTI Career Institute: York

York, Pennsylvania
www.yti.edu **CB code: 2943**

- For-profit 2-year career college
- Commuter campus in small city

General. Candidate for regional accreditation; also accredited by ACCSCT. **Enrollment:** 387 degree-seeking undergraduates. **Degrees:** 327 associate awarded. **Calendar:** Quarter, extensive summer session. **Full-time faculty:** 37 total. **Part-time faculty:** 13 total.

Student profile.

Out-of-state:	8%	**25 or older:**	15%

Basis for selection. Open admission, but selective for some programs. Medical Office Assistant and Medical Assistant programs require criminal background check and health information form completed by certified physician to include documentation for Hepatitis B and TB immunizations. Dental Assisting Program requires verification of Hepatitis B vaccination. Criminal Justice and First Response program requires background/record check, valid driver's license, and applicants must be at least 18 years of age at time of matriculation. COMPASS used for placement.

2009-2010 Annual costs. Depending on program, cost of full diploma and associate programs range from $10,800 - $35,000; books and supplies, $1,100 - $2,970 additional charge. Books/supplies: $1,500.

Application procedures. Admission: No deadline. $50 fee, may be waived for applicants with need. Admission notification on a rolling basis.

Academics. Special study options: Cooperative education, internships. **Credit/placement by examination:** CLEP, institutional tests. **Support services:** Remedial instruction, study skills assistance, tutoring.

Majors. Business: Accounting, business admin, hospitality admin, marketing. **Computer sciences:** Systems analysis. **Engineering technology:** CAD/CADD, electrical. **Health:** Medical assistant. **Personal/culinary services:** Culinary arts. **Protective services:** Law enforcement admin, police science, security services.

Computing on campus. 250 workstations in library, computer center. Commuter students can connect to campus network. Helpline, repair service, wireless network available.

Student life. Freshman orientation: Mandatory. Preregistration for classes offered. **Housing:** Apartments available.

Student services. Adult student services, career counseling, student employment services, financial aid counseling, placement for graduates. **Transfer:** Re-entry adviser, pre-admission transcript evaluation for new students. Transfer adviser for students transferring to 4-year colleges.

Contact. Phone: (717) 757-1100 Toll-free number: (800) 227-9675
Fax: (717) 757-4964
Frank Vella, Director of Admissions, YTI Career Institute: York, 1405 Williams Road, York, PA 17402

Puerto Rico

Centro de Estudios Multidisciplinarios
San Juan, Puerto Rico
www.cempr.edu

- Private 2-year health science college
- Large city

General. Accredited by ACCSCT. **Calendar:** Quarter.

Contact. Phone: (787) 765-4210
Director of Admissions, PO Box 191317, San Juan, PR 00926-1931

Colegio de las Ciencias Artes y Television
Bayamon, Puerto Rico
www.ccat.edu

- Private 2-year liberal arts and technical college
- Small city

General. Accredited by ACCSCT. **Calendar:** Semester.

Contact. Phone: (787) 779-2500
P.O. Box 10774, San Juan, PR 00922

Columbia Centro Universitario: Yauco
Yauco, Puerto Rico
www.columbiaco.edu **CB code: 3215**

- For-profit 2-year business and nursing college
- Commuter campus in large town
- Interview required

General. Regionally accredited. **Enrollment:** 544 degree-seeking undergraduates. **Degrees:** 22 bachelor's, 90 associate awarded. **Calendar:** Continuous. **Full-time faculty:** 15 total; 7% have terminal degrees. **Part-time faculty:** 35 total; 11% have terminal degrees.

Student profile. Among degree-seeking undergraduates, 135 enrolled as first-time, first-year students.

Part-time:	36%	Women:	81%

Basis for selection. Open admission, but selective for some programs. **Homeschooled:** Transcript of courses and grades, state high school equivalency certificate, interview required.

2008-2009 Annual costs. Tuition/fees: $4,360. Per-credit charge: $160.

2007-2008 Financial aid. All financial aid based on need. 53% of total undergraduate aid awarded as scholarships/grants, 47% as loans/jobs. Need-based aid available for part-time students. Work-study available weekends.

Application procedures. Admission: $50 fee. Application must be submitted on paper. **Financial aid:** FAFSA, institutional form required.

Academics. Special study options: Combined bachelor's/graduate degree. Bachelor's degree programs available on campus. License preparation in nursing. **Credit/placement by examination:** CLEP. **Support services:** Learning center, study skills assistance, tutoring.

Majors. Business: Business admin, office technology. **Computer sciences:** Programming. **Health:** Nursing (RN).

Student life. Freshman orientation: Available. **Activities:** Drama.

Student services. Personal counseling, placement for graduates. **Transfer:** Pre-admission transcript evaluation for new students.

Contact. E-mail: rpadilla@columbiaco.edu
Phone: (787) 743-4041 Toll-free number: (800) 981-4877
Fax: (787) 744-7031
Rosario Padilla, Director, Columbia Centro Universitario: Yauco, Box 3062, Yauco, PR 00698-3062

EDIC College
Caguas, Puerto Rico
www.ediccollege.com

- For-profit 2-year health science and technical college
- Large city

General. Regionally accredited. **Calendar:** Semester.

Contact. Phone: (787) 744-8519 ext. 229
Box 9120, Caguas, PR 00726-9120

Huertas Junior College
Caguas, Puerto Rico **CB member**
www.huertas.edu **CB code: 3406**

- For-profit 2-year junior and technical college
- Commuter campus in small city

General. Founded in 1945. Accredited by ACICS. **Enrollment:** 1,774 degree-seeking undergraduates; 4 non-degree-seeking students. **Degrees:** 306 associate awarded. **Location:** 25 miles from San Juan, 32 miles from Navanjito. **Calendar:** Semester, extensive summer session. **Full-time faculty:** 24 total; 4% have terminal degrees, 100% minority, 58% women. **Part-time faculty:** 88 total; 8% have terminal degrees, 100% minority, 54% women. **Class size:** 69% < 20, 29% 20-39, 1% 40-49.

Student profile. Among degree-seeking undergraduates, 373 enrolled as first-time, first-year students, 446 transferred in from other institutions.

Part-time:	17%	Women:	56%

Transfer out. Colleges most students transferred to 2008: Banca Institute, EDIC College, Liceo of Arts and Technology, Mech Tech.

Basis for selection. Open admission. **Learning Disabled:** Students with learning disabilities are referred to counseling office for assistance.

High school preparation. Required units include science 3. Students with work experience present a letter from their employer indicating domain of knowledge and skills related to program.

2008-2009 Annual costs. Books/supplies: $700.

2008-2009 Financial aid. All financial aid based on need. 373 full-time freshmen applied for aid; 316 were judged to have need; 316 of these received aid. Average scholarship/grant was $6,249; average loan $3,500. 98% of total undergraduate aid awarded as scholarships/grants, 2% as loans/jobs. Need-based aid available for part-time students.

Application procedures. Admission: No deadline. $25 fee. Application must be submitted on paper. Admission notification on a rolling basis. **Financial aid:** No deadline. FAFSA, institutional form required. Applicants notified on a rolling basis.

Academics. Special study options: Cooperative education. **Credit/placement by examination:** CLEP. **Support services:** Learning center, study skills assistance, tutoring.

Majors. Business: Accounting, administrative services, business admin. **Computer sciences:** Computer science. **Health:** Dental assistant, medical records admin, medical records technology, pharmacy assistant, respiratory therapy technology. **Mechanic/repair:** Electronics/electrical, heating/ac/refrig.

Computing on campus. 50 workstations in computer center.

Student life. Freshman orientation: Mandatory. Program held in first 2 weeks of classes.

Student services. Career counseling, student employment services, health services, personal counseling, placement for graduates, veterans' counselor. **Physically disabled:** Services for hearing impaired. **Transfer:** Transfer adviser for students transferring to 4-year colleges.

Contact. E-mail: admisiones@huertas.edu
Phone: (787) 743-1242 Fax: (787) 743-0203
Barbara Hassim, Director of Admissions, Huertas Junior College, PO Box 8429, Caguas, PR 00726

Humacao Community College
Humacao, Puerto Rico
CB code: 2313

- Private 2-year business and community college
- Commuter campus in small city
- Interview required

General. Founded in 1956. Accredited by ACICS. **Enrollment:** 769 degree-seeking undergraduates. **Degrees:** 159 associate awarded. **Location:** 42 miles from San Juan. **Calendar:** Trimester. **Full-time faculty:** 17 total; 53% women. **Part-time faculty:** 14 total; 57% women.

Student profile. Among degree-seeking undergraduates, 42% enrolled in a transfer program, 1% already have a bachelor's degree or higher, 238 enrolled as first-time, first-year students, 42 transferred in from other institutions.

Part-time:	25%	**25 or older:**	38%
Women:	64%		

Transfer out. Colleges most students transferred to 2008: Turabo University, University of Puerto Rico (all campuses), Inter American University of Puerto Rico (all campuses), Huertas Junior College.

Basis for selection. Open admission. **Homeschooled:** Transcript of courses and grades, state high school equivalency certificate required.

High school preparation. 15 units recommended. Recommended units include English 3, mathematics 3, social studies 3, science 3 and academic electives 3.

2009-2010 Annual costs. Tuition/fees (projected): $4,602. Per-credit charge: $108. Books/supplies: $1,152. Personal expenses: $1,350.

2007-2008 Financial aid. All financial aid based on need. 98% of total undergraduate aid awarded as scholarships/grants, 2% as loans/jobs. Need-based aid available for part-time students. Work-study available nights and for part-time students.

Application procedures. Admission: No deadline. $17 fee. Application must be submitted on paper. Admission notification on a rolling basis. **Financial aid:** Priority date 1/1, closing date 6/30. FAFSA, institutional form required. Applicants notified on a rolling basis starting 3/4.

Academics. Special study options: Internships. **Credit/placement by examination:** AP, CLEP. 9 credit hours maximum toward associate degree. **Support services:** Learning center, remedial instruction, tutoring.

Majors. Business: Administrative services, business admin. **Computer sciences:** Information systems. **Engineering technology:** Electrical, heat/ac/refrig. **Health:** Medical secretary, pharmacy assistant.

Most popular majors. Business/marketing 28%, computer/information sciences 14%, engineering/engineering technologies 18%, health sciences 40%.

Computing on campus. 104 workstations in library, computer center, student center. Online library available.

Student life. Freshman orientation: Mandatory. Preregistration for classes offered. Counseling and Orientation Department holds group meetings (75 participants per session) for all freshmen. Usually held during the first four weeks of each term, these meetings have a duration of approximately 90 minutes. **Activities:** Student government.

Student services. Adult student services, alcohol/substance abuse counseling, career counseling, student employment services, financial aid counseling, personal counseling, placement for graduates. **Transfer:** Pre-admission transcript evaluation for new students. Transfer adviser for students transferring to 4-year colleges.

Contact. E-mail: admisiones_hcc@yahoo.com
Phone: (787) 852-1430 ext. 31 Fax: (787) 850-1577
Carolina Flores, Admissions Director, Humacao Community College, PO Box 9139, Humacao, PR 00792-9139

ICPR Junior College
San Juan, Puerto Rico
www.icprjc.edu
CB member
CB code: 7315

- For-profit 2-year business and junior college
- Commuter campus in large city

General. Founded in 1946. Regionally accredited. **Calendar:** Trimester.

Annual costs/financial aid. Books/supplies: $954. Personal expenses: $2,556.

Contact. Phone: (787) 763-1010
Director of Admissions, PO Box 190304, San Juan, PR 00919-0304

Ponce Paramedical College
Ponce, Puerto Rico
www.popac.edu

- For-profit 2-year health science and junior college
- Small city

General. Accredited by ACCSCT. **Calendar:** Differs by program.

Contact. Phone: (787) 848-1589 ext. 413
Director of Admissions, Calle Acacia L-1213, Urb. Villa Flores, Ponce, PR 00731

Universal Technology College of Puerto Rico
Aguadilla, Puerto Rico
www.unitecpr.edu/

- Private 2-year health science and career college
- Commuter campus in small city

General. Accredited by ACCSCT. **Calendar:** Semester.

Annual costs/financial aid. Books/supplies: $450. Personal expenses: $250. Need-based financial aid available to full-time and part-time students.

Contact. Phone: (787) 882-2065 ext. 308
Admissions Coordinator, Apartado 1955, Victoria Station, Aguadilla, PR 00605

Rhode Island

Community College of Rhode Island

Warwick, Rhode Island **CB member**
www.ccri.edu **CB code: 3733**

- Public 2-year community college
- Commuter campus in small city

General. Founded in 1964. Regionally accredited. Additional campuses in Lincoln, Providence, and Newport. **Enrollment:** 16,007 degree-seeking undergraduates; 1,605 non-degree-seeking students. **Degrees:** 1,223 associate awarded. **ROTC:** Army. **Location:** 10 miles from Providence. **Calendar:** Semester, extensive summer session. **Full-time faculty:** 311 total; 61% women. **Part-time faculty:** 450 total; 47% women. **Class size:** 37% < 20, 63% 20-39, less than 1% 40-49. **Special facilities:** Observatory.

Student profile. Among degree-seeking undergraduates, 3,754 enrolled as first-time, first-year students, 552 transferred in from other institutions.

Part-time:	60%	**Asian American:**	3%
Out-of-state:	6%	**Hispanic American:**	13%
Women:	62%	**Native American:**	1%
African American:	8%	**25 or older:**	40%

Transfer out. Colleges most students transferred to 2008: Rhode Island College, University of Rhode Island, New England Institute of Technology, Johnson and Wales University, Roger Williams University.

Basis for selection. Open admission, but selective for some programs. Placement testing in mathematics and English required; testing in chemistry may be required for programs with limited enrollment.

High school preparation. Some programs may require mathematics and science background. Special considerations for nursing and allied health applicants.

2008-2009 Annual costs. Tuition/fees: $3,090; $8,216 out-of-state. Per-credit charge: $128 in-state; $378 out-of-state. Books/supplies: $935. Personal expenses: $1,251.

Financial aid. Need-based: Need-based aid available for part-time students. Work-study available nights, weekends and for part-time students. **Non-need-based:** Scholarships awarded for athletics.

Application procedures. Admission: No deadline. $20 fee, may be waived for applicants with need. Admission notification on a rolling basis beginning on or about 1/1. Application closing date and admitted student reply deadline is the first week of fall semester in September and first week of spring semester in January. After the first week of each semester, applicants are processed for the following semester. **Financial aid:** Priority date 3/1; no closing date. FAFSA, institutional form required. Applicants notified on a rolling basis starting 5/1; must reply within 2 week(s) of notification.

Academics. Special study options: Cooperative education, cross-registration, distance learning, double major, dual enrollment of high school students, ESL, honors, internships, study abroad, weekend college. License preparation in dental hygiene, nursing, occupational therapy, physical therapy, radiology, real estate. **Credit/placement by examination:** AP, CLEP. 30 credit hours maximum toward associate degree. **Support services:** GED preparation and test center, learning center, reduced course load, remedial instruction, study skills assistance, tutoring, writing center.

Majors. Biology: Biotechnology. **Business:** General, accounting, administrative services, banking/financial services, business admin, customer service, marketing. **Computer sciences:** General, applications programming, networking, webmaster. **Education:** Kindergarten/preschool, special. **Engineering:** General, surveying. **Engineering technology:** Computer, computer hardware, electrical, mechanical, telecommunications. **Family/consumer sciences:** Aging. **Health:** Clinical lab technology, dental hygiene, histologic assistant, massage therapy, medical secretary, nursing (RN), occupational therapy assistant, physical therapy assistant, radiologic technology/medical imaging, respiratory therapy technology, sonography, substance abuse counseling. **Interdisciplinary:** Biological/physical sciences. **Legal studies:** Legal secretary, paralegal. **Liberal arts:** Arts/sciences. **Protective services:** Firefighting, police science. **Public administration:** Social work. **Science technology:** Chemical. **Visual/performing arts:** Art, dramatic, jazz, theater design.

Most popular majors. Business/marketing 11%, health sciences 32%, liberal arts 32%, security/protective services 8%.

Computing on campus. 1,200 workstations in library, computer center, student center. Commuter students can connect to campus network. Online course registration, online library, helpline, wireless network available.

Student life. Freshman orientation: Mandatory. Preregistration for classes offered. **Activities:** Bands, choral groups, dance, drama, music ensembles, student government, student newspaper, Black American student association, Latin American student organization, Spanish club, German club, Portuguese club, French club, South East Asian club, organization for students with disabilities, minority mentoring program, Distributive Education Club of America.

Athletics. NJCAA. **Intercollegiate:** Baseball M, basketball, cross-country, golf, soccer, softball W, tennis, track and field, volleyball W. **Intramural:** Basketball, cross-country, table tennis, volleyball, water polo. **Team name:** Knights.

Student services. Adult student services, alcohol/substance abuse counseling, chaplain/spiritual director, career counseling, services for economically disadvantaged, student employment services, financial aid counseling, health services, minority student services, on-campus daycare, personal counseling, placement for graduates, veterans' counselor, women's services. **Physically disabled:** Services for visually, speech, hearing impaired. **Transfer:** Re-entry adviser, pre-admission transcript evaluation for new students. Transfer adviser, college fairs on campus for students transferring to 4-year colleges.

Contact. E-mail: webadmission@ccri.edu
Phone: (401) 825-2003 Fax: (401) 825-2394
Terri Kless, Director of Enrollment Services, Community College of Rhode Island, 400 East Avenue, Warwick, RI 02886-1807

Two-Year Colleges

South Carolina

Aiken Technical College
Aiken, South Carolina
www.atc.edu **CB code: 5037**

- Public 2-year community and technical college
- Commuter campus in small city

General. Founded in 1972. Regionally accredited. **Enrollment:** 2,655 degree-seeking undergraduates. **Degrees:** 215 associate awarded. **Location:** 8 miles from Aiken, 10 miles from Augusta, Georgia. **Calendar:** Semester, extensive summer session. **Full-time faculty:** 61 total; 25% minority, 51% women. **Part-time faculty:** 103 total. **Class size:** 49% < 20, 51% 20-39.

Student profile. Among degree-seeking undergraduates, 14% enrolled in a transfer program, 86% enrolled in a vocational program, 315 transferred in from other institutions.

Out-of-state:	13%	**25 or older:**	42%

Transfer out. Colleges most students transferred to 2008: Augusta State University, Lander University, University of South Carolina.

Basis for selection. Open admission, but selective for some programs. Test scores considered if submitted. Special requirements for all health programs. **Adult students:** SAT/ACT scores not required.

High school preparation. 18 units recommended. Recommended units include English 4, mathematics 4, social studies 2, history 2, science 2, foreign language 2 and academic electives 2.

2008-2009 Annual costs. Tuition/fees: $3,356; $3,716 out-of-district; $9,644 out-of-state. Books/supplies: $450. Personal expenses: $900.

2007-2008 Financial aid. Need-based: Need-based aid available for part-time students. Work-study available nights, weekends and for part-time students. **Non-need-based:** Scholarships awarded for academics, athletics, leadership, minority status, state residency.

Application procedures. Admission: Priority date 7/1; no deadline. No application fee. Admission notification on a rolling basis. **Financial aid:** Priority date 5/1, closing date 6/30. FAFSA required. Applicants notified on a rolling basis starting 4/1; must reply within 2 week(s) of notification.

Academics. Special study options: Accelerated study, cooperative education, cross-registration, distance learning, double major, dual enrollment of high school students, ESL, independent study, internships, liberal arts/career combination. License preparation in aviation, nursing, radiology, real estate. **Credit/placement by examination:** AP, CLEP, institutional tests. **Support services:** Learning center, pre-admission summer program, reduced course load, remedial instruction, study skills assistance, tutoring, writing center.

Majors. Business: Accounting, administrative services, business admin, sales/distribution. **Computer sciences:** Data processing. **Education:** Voc/tech. **Engineering:** Computer, electrical. **Engineering technology:** Computer, electrical, electromechanical, mechanical drafting. **Health:** Medical radiologic technology/radiation therapy, nursing (RN). **Liberal arts:** Arts/sciences. **Mechanic/repair:** Industrial. **Production:** Machine tool. **Protective services:** Criminal justice. **Public administration:** Human services, social work. **Science technology:** Nuclear power.

Most popular majors. Business/marketing 15%, family/consumer sciences 6%, health sciences 27%, interdisciplinary studies 19%, liberal arts 15%, public administration/social services 7%.

Computing on campus. 1,005 workstations in library, computer center, student center. Online course registration, online library, helpline, repair service available.

Student life. Freshman orientation: Available. **Activities:** Campus ministries, student government, Phi Theta Kappa Honor Society.

Athletics. NJCAA. **Intercollegiate:** Basketball M, softball W. **Intramural:** Basketball, softball, table tennis, volleyball. **Team name:** Knights.

Student services. Adult student services, alcohol/substance abuse counseling, career counseling, services for economically disadvantaged, student employment services, financial aid counseling, minority student services, personal counseling, placement for graduates, veterans' counselor. **Physically disabled:** Services for visually, speech, hearing impaired. **Transfer:** Pre-admission transcript evaluation for new students. Transfer adviser, college fairs on campus for students transferring to 4-year colleges.

Contact. Phone: (803) 593-9954 ext. 1247 Fax: (803) 593-6526
Dawn Butts, Director of Admissions and Records, Aiken Technical College, PO Drawer 696, Aiken, SC 29802

Central Carolina Technical College
Sumter, South Carolina
www.cctech.edu **CB code: 5665**

- Public 2-year community and technical college
- Commuter campus in large town

General. Founded in 1963. Regionally accredited. Branch campuses in Clarendon, Kershaw, and Lee Counties. Additional facility located at Shaw Air Force Base. **Enrollment:** 2,924 degree-seeking undergraduates; 282 non-degree-seeking students. **Degrees:** 216 associate awarded. **Location:** 45 miles from Columbia. **Calendar:** Semester, limited summer session. **Full-time faculty:** 81 total. **Part-time faculty:** 154 total. **Special facilities:** South Carolina Environmental Training Center.

Student profile. Among degree-seeking undergraduates, 569 enrolled as first-time, first-year students, 244 transferred in from other institutions.

Part-time:	65%	**25 or older:**	40%
Women:	72%		

Transfer out. 52% of students enrolled in the transfer program go on to 4-year colleges. **Colleges most students transferred to 2008:** Unversity of South Carolina, Clemson University, Lander University, Limestone, Francis Marion University.

Basis for selection. Open admission, but selective for some programs. Test scores required for placement. Associate degree nursing program: minimum SAT Verbal 510 and Math 510 or ACT 22 composite or TEAS minimum of 74 composite. LPN program: minimum SAT Verbal 470 and Math 460 or ACT Composite 19 or TEAS 67. Interview required for nursing program.

2008-2009 Annual costs. Tuition/fees: $3,020; $3,548 out-of-district; $5,372 out-of-state. Books/supplies: $900.

2007-2008 Financial aid. All financial aid based on need. Need-based aid available for part-time students. Work-study available nights and for part-time students.

Application procedures. Admission: No deadline. No application fee. Admission notification on a rolling basis. **Financial aid:** Priority date 4/1; no closing date. FAFSA required. Applicants notified on a rolling basis; must reply within 2 week(s) of notification.

Academics. Special study options: Cooperative education, distance learning, dual enrollment of high school students, independent study, internships. License preparation in nursing. **Credit/placement by examination:** AP, CLEP, IB, institutional tests. 15 credit hours maximum toward associate degree. **Support services:** GED test center, learning center, reduced course load, remedial instruction, study skills assistance, tutoring, writing center.

Majors. Business: Accounting, administrative services, management science. **Computer sciences:** Programming. **Conservation:** Management/policy. **Engineering technology:** Drafting. **Health:** Nursing (RN), surgical technology. **Legal studies:** Paralegal. **Liberal arts:** Arts/sciences.

Most popular majors. Business/marketing 16%, family/consumer sciences 11%, health sciences 32%, liberal arts 18%, natural resources/environmental science 6%, security/protective services 7%.

Computing on campus. 125 workstations in library, computer center. Commuter students can connect to campus network. Online course registration, online library, helpline available.

Student life. Freshman orientation: Available. Preregistration for classes offered. **Activities:** Phi Theta Kappa, Earth club, computer club.

Student services. Career counseling, services for economically disadvantaged, student employment services, financial aid counseling, personal counseling, placement for graduates, veterans' counselor, women's services. **Physically disabled:** Services for visually, speech, hearing impaired. **Transfer:** Pre-admission transcript evaluation for new students. College fairs on campus for students transferring to 4-year colleges.

Contact. Phone: (803) 778-6605 Toll-free number: (800) 221-8711 ext. 205 Fax: (803) 778-6696
Barbara Wright, Director of Admissions and Student Services, Central Carolina Technical College, 506 North Guignard Drive, Sumter, SC 29150-2499

Clinton Junior College
Rock Hill, South Carolina
www.clintonjuniorcollege.edu

- Private 2-year junior and liberal arts college
- Residential campus in small city

General. Regionally accredited. **Enrollment:** 114 degree-seeking undergraduates. **Degrees:** 33 associate awarded. **Calendar:** Semester. **Full-time faculty:** 12 total. **Part-time faculty:** 16 total.

Student profile. Among degree-seeking undergraduates, 7 transferred in from other institutions.

Out-of-state:	10%	**Live on campus:**	90%
25 or older:	4%		

Basis for selection. Open admission. **Homeschooled:** Statement describing homeschool structure and mission, transcript of courses and grades required.

2008-2009 Annual costs. Tuition/fees: $3,950.

Application procedures. **Admission:** No deadline. $25 fee. Institutional placement test given after enrollment. **Financial aid:** No deadline.

Academics. **Credit/placement by examination:** CLEP.

Majors. **Business:** General. **Education:** Early childhood. **Liberal arts:** Arts/sciences. **Physical sciences:** General. **Theology:** Bible.

Student life. **Activities:** Student government.

Contact. E-mail: rcopeland@clintonjuniorcollege.edu
Phone: (803) 327-7402 ext. 242
Robert Copeland, Vice President for Student Affairs, Clinton Junior College, 1029 Crawford Road, Rock Hill, SC 29730

Denmark Technical College
Denmark, South Carolina
www.denmarktech.edu **CB code: 5744**

- Public 2-year technical college
- Residential campus in small town

General. Founded in 1948. Regionally accredited. **Enrollment:** 1,400 degree-seeking undergraduates. **Degrees:** 133 associate awarded. **ROTC:** Army. **Location:** 55 miles from Columbia. **Calendar:** Semester, extensive summer session. **Full-time faculty:** 45 total. **Part-time faculty:** 10 total.

Student profile.

Out-of-state:	3%	**Live on campus:**	50%

Basis for selection. Open admission. Interview recommended.

High school preparation. Recommended units include English 4, mathematics 4, social studies 2, science 2 and foreign language 2. College preparatory program required for AA and AS transfer college programs.

2008-2009 Annual costs. Tuition/fees: $2,378; $4,466 out-of-state. Room/board: $3,386. Books/supplies: $1,100. Personal expenses: $2,000.

Financial aid. **Need-based:** Need-based aid available for part-time students.

Application procedures. **Admission:** No deadline. $10 fee, may be waived for applicants with need. Admission notification on a rolling basis. **Financial aid:** No deadline. FAFSA required. Applicants notified on a rolling basis starting 6/1; must reply within 2 week(s) of notification.

Academics. **Special study options:** Cooperative education, cross-registration, independent study, internships. License preparation in nursing. **Credit/placement by examination:** AP, CLEP, institutional tests. **Support services:** GED preparation, learning center, reduced course load, remedial instruction, tutoring.

Majors. **Business:** General. **Health:** Licensed practical nurse. **Liberal arts:** Arts/sciences. **Mechanic/repair:** Electronics/electrical. **Public administration:** Human services.

Computing on campus. 85 workstations in library. Dormitories wired for high-speed internet access and linked to campus network. Commuter students can connect to campus network. Wireless network available.

Student life. **Freshman orientation:** Mandatory. Preregistration for classes offered. **Housing:** Single-sex dorms available. **Activities:** Choral groups, student government, student newspaper, Student Christian Association.

Athletics. **Intercollegiate:** Basketball. **Intramural:** Basketball. **Team name:** Panthers and Lady Panthers.

Student services. Career counseling, student employment services, health services, personal counseling, placement for graduates, veterans' counselor. **Learning disabled:** Comprehensive services available. **Transfer:** College fairs on campus for students transferring to 4-year colleges.

Contact. E-mail: thomast@denmarktech.edu
Phone: (803) 793-5176 Fax: (803) 793-5942
Tonya Thomas, Dean of Enrollment Management, Denmark Technical College, 1126 Solomon Blatt Boulevard, Denmark, SC 29042

Florence-Darlington Technical College
Florence, South Carolina **CB member**
www.fdtc.edu **CB code: 5207**

- Public 2-year community and technical college
- Commuter campus in small city

General. Founded in 1964. Regionally accredited. **Enrollment:** 4,505 degree-seeking undergraduates. **Degrees:** 376 associate awarded. **Location:** 80 miles from Columbia, 50 miles from Myrtle Beach. **Calendar:** Semester, limited summer session. **Full-time faculty:** 105 total. **Part-time faculty:** 192 total. **Partnerships:** Formal partnerships with local, regional, and national corporations which enhance student opportunities for training.

Transfer out. **Colleges most students transferred to 2008:** Francis Marion University, Clemson University, University of South Carolina.

Basis for selection. Open admission, but selective for some programs. Computerized Placement Test administered as alternative to SAT or ACT for placement for most programs. RSAT, NLN, HOAE or HOBET required for some allied health programs. Interview required for allied health, nursing programs. **Homeschooled:** GED may be required.

High school preparation. Recommended units include English 4, mathematics 3, social studies 2, history 1, science 2 (laboratory 2), foreign language 2 and academic electives 2. Algebra I, algebra II, biology, and chemistry required for most health programs.

2008-2009 Annual costs. Tuition/fees: $3,190; $3,452 out-of-district; $5,286 out-of-state. Books/supplies: $900. Personal expenses: $2,338.

2007-2008 Financial aid. **Need-based:** 79% of total undergraduate aid awarded as scholarships/grants, 21% as loans/jobs. Need-based aid available for part-time students. Work-study available for part-time students. **Non-need-based:** Scholarships awarded for academics.

Application procedures. **Admission:** Priority date 7/15; deadline 8/10. No application fee. Admission notification on a rolling basis beginning on or about 1/1. **Financial aid:** Priority date 5/1; no closing date. FAFSA required. Applicants notified on a rolling basis starting 7/1; must reply within 2 week(s) of notification.

Academics. **Special study options:** Cooperative education, cross-registration, distance learning, dual enrollment of high school students, independent study, internships, liberal arts/career combination. Cooperative program with Greenville Technical College for physical therapy, Fayetteville Technical College for funeral services. License preparation in dental hygiene, nursing, physical therapy. **Credit/placement by examination:** AP, CLEP, IB, institutional tests. Student may receive credit for up to 50% of the course work required by his or her major. **Support services:** GED preparation, learning center, reduced course load, remedial instruction, tutoring.

Majors. **Business:** Accounting, administrative services, entrepreneurial studies, sales/distribution. **Computer sciences:** Data processing. **Education:** Voc/tech. **Engineering technology:** Civil, drafting, electrical. **Health:** Clinical lab technology, dental hygiene, medical radiologic technology/radiation therapy, medical records technology, nursing (RN), physical therapy assistant, respiratory therapy technology. **Legal studies:** Paralegal. **Liberal arts:** Arts/sciences. **Mechanic/repair:** Automotive, heating/ac/refrig. **Personal/**

culinary services: Mortuary science. **Physical sciences:** General. **Protective services:** Criminal justice. **Public administration:** Social work.

Computing on campus. 128 workstations in library, computer center. Commuter students can connect to campus network.

Student life. Freshman orientation: Mandatory. Preregistration for classes offered. **Activities:** Music ensembles, student government, student newspaper.

Athletics. NJCAA. **Intercollegiate:** Baseball M, softball W. **Team name:** Stingers.

Student services. Career counseling, services for economically disadvantaged, student employment services, financial aid counseling, on-campus daycare, personal counseling, placement for graduates, veterans' counselor. **Physically disabled:** Services for hearing impaired. **Transfer:** Transfer adviser for students transferring to 4-year colleges.

Contact. E-mail: admissions@fdtc.edu
Phone: (843) 661-8324 Toll-free number: (800) 228-5745
Fax: (843) 661-8041
Elaine Hodges, Director of Admissions, Florence-Darlington Technical College, PO Box 100548, Florence, SC 29501-0548

Forrest Junior College

Anderson, South Carolina
www.forrestcollege.edu **CB code: 7138**

- For-profit 2-year business and junior college
- Commuter campus in large town
- Application essay, interview required

General. Accredited by ACICS. Majority of students are working adults with children. Free child care provided. **Enrollment:** 98 degree-seeking undergraduates. **Degrees:** 10 associate awarded. **Location:** 30 miles from Greenville. **Calendar:** Quarter, extensive summer session. **Full-time faculty:** 3 total; 33% have terminal degrees, 100% women. **Part-time faculty:** 20 total; 75% have terminal degrees, 35% minority, 75% women.

Student profile. Among degree-seeking undergraduates, 7 enrolled as first-time, first-year students.

Part-time:	10%	**25 or older:**	60%
Women:	94%		

Transfer out. 20% of students enrolled in the transfer program go on to 4-year colleges. **Colleges most students transferred to 2008:** Greenville Technical College, Piedmont Technical College, Lander University, Strayer University, Webster University.

Basis for selection. Open admission, but selective for some programs. Audition, portfolio recommended. **Homeschooled:** Transcript of courses and grades, state high school equivalency certificate required.

2008-2009 Annual costs. Tuition/fees: $9,290. Per-credit charge: $197.

2008-2009 Financial aid. All financial aid based on need. Need-based aid available for part-time students. Work-study available nights, weekends and for part-time students.

Application procedures. Admission: No deadline. $50 fee. Admission notification on a rolling basis. **Financial aid:** No deadline. FAFSA required. Applicants notified on a rolling basis starting 4/30; must reply by 5/31 or within 4 week(s) of notification.

Academics. Special study options: Cooperative education, double major, ESL, independent study, internships, liberal arts/career combination, weekend college. **Credit/placement by examination:** AP, CLEP, institutional tests. **Support services:** Reduced course load, tutoring.

Majors. Business: General, accounting, administrative services, business admin, communications, human resources, managerial economics, marketing, office management, office technology, office/clerical. **Computer sciences:** General, information systems. **Education:** Early childhood, sales/marketing, teacher assistance. **Family/consumer sciences:** Child care. **Health:** Clinical lab assistant, clinical lab technology, medical assistant, medical records admin, medical records technology, medical secretary, medical transcription. **Legal studies:** Legal secretary, paralegal. **Personal/culinary services:** General.

Computing on campus. 52 workstations in library, computer center. Online library, repair service available.

Student life. Freshman orientation: Mandatory. Preregistration for classes offered. **Activities:** Literary magazine, student government, student newspaper.

Student services. Adult student services, career counseling, student employment services, financial aid counseling, on-campus daycare, placement for graduates. **Transfer:** Pre-admission transcript evaluation for new students.

Contact. E-mail: janieturmon@forrestcollege.edu
Phone: (864) 225-7653 ext. 210 Fax: (864) 261-7471
Janie Turmon, Admissions Officer, Forrest Junior College, 601 East River Street, Anderson, SC 29624

Golf Academy of America: The Carolinas

Myrtle Beach, South Carolina
www.golfacademy.edu **CB code: 3223**

- For-profit 2-year golf academy
- Large town

General. Accredited by ACICS. **Calendar:** Continuous.

Annual costs/financial aid. Tuition/fees (2008-2009): $13,350. Books/supplies: $700. Personal expenses: $1,552.

Contact. Phone: (480) 905-9288
Admissions Director, 7373 North Scottsdale Road, Suite B-100, Scottsdale, AZ 82253

Greenville Technical College

Greenville, South Carolina
www.gvltec.edu **CB code: 5278**

- Public 2-year community and technical college
- Commuter campus in large city

General. Founded in 1962. Regionally accredited. Classes and some programs offered at satellite campuses in Greenville County. **Enrollment:** 12,848 degree-seeking undergraduates; 1,566 non-degree-seeking students. **Degrees:** 1,034 associate awarded. **Calendar:** Semester, extensive summer session. **Full-time faculty:** 341 total; 8% have terminal degrees, 12% minority, 59% women. **Part-time faculty:** 481 total; 16% have terminal degrees, 15% minority, 64% women.

Student profile. Among degree-seeking undergraduates, 26% enrolled in a transfer program, 74% enrolled in a vocational program, 2,669 enrolled as first-time, first-year students.

Part-time:	52%	**Asian American:**	2%
Out-of-state:	1%	**Hispanic American:**	4%
Women:	62%	**Live on campus:**	3%
African American:	25%		

Transfer out. 86% of students enrolled in the transfer program go on to 4-year colleges.

Basis for selection. Open admission, but selective for some programs. Weighted admissions requirements for registered nursing, licensed practical nursing, certain allied health programs. Interview required for allied health sciences, nursing, photography, and aircraft mechanic applicants and recommended for all others. Portfolio required for visual arts program. **Learning Disabled:** Contact Student Disability Services early in admission process for appropriate accommodations. Self-identification and documentation required.

High school preparation. Algebra, biology, and chemistry are required for most health care program applicants.

2008-2009 Annual costs. Tuition/fees: $3,396; $3,680 out-of-district; $6,912 out-of-state. Books/supplies: $998. Personal expenses: $671.

2007-2008 Financial aid. Need-based: 32% of total undergraduate aid awarded as scholarships/grants, 68% as loans/jobs. Need-based aid available for part-time students. Work-study available nights, weekends and for part-time students. **Non-need-based:** Scholarships awarded for academics, state residency.

Application procedures. Admission: No deadline. $35 fee. Admission notification on a rolling basis. **Financial aid:** Priority date 5/1; no closing date. FAFSA required. Applicants notified on a rolling basis starting 6/15; must reply within 2 week(s) of notification.

Academics. **Special study options:** Accelerated study, cooperative education, distance learning, dual enrollment of high school students, ESL, honors, independent study, internships, liberal arts/career combination, teacher certification program, weekend college. License preparation in aviation, dental hygiene, nursing, occupational therapy, paramedic, physical therapy, radiology, real estate. **Credit/placement by examination:** AP, CLEP, IB, institutional tests. Credits for work experience evaluated and awarded by program department head. Courses requiring research cannot be completed by exam. **Support services:** Learning center, reduced course load, remedial instruction, study skills assistance, tutoring, writing center.

Honors college/program. Require 3.5 GPA and interview with head of department.

Majors. **Biology:** Biotechnology. **Business:** Accounting, administrative services, business admin, purchasing, sales/distribution. **Computer sciences:** Data processing. **Engineering technology:** Architectural, construction, electrical, mechanical, mechanical drafting. **Family/consumer sciences:** Child care. **Health:** Clinical lab technology, dental hygiene, EMT paramedic, medical radiologic technology/radiation therapy, medical records technology, nursing (RN), occupational therapy assistant, physical therapy assistant, respiratory therapy technology, sonography. **Legal studies:** Paralegal. **Liberal arts:** Arts/sciences. **Mechanic/repair:** Automotive, industrial. **Personal/culinary services:** Chef training. **Production:** Machine tool. **Protective services:** Criminal justice. **Public administration:** Social work. **Social sciences:** Cartography.

Most popular majors. Business/marketing 13%, health sciences 40%, liberal arts 19%.

Computing on campus. 1,186 workstations in library, computer center. Dormitories wired for high-speed internet access. Commuter students can connect to campus network. Online library, wireless network available.

Student life. **Freshman orientation:** Mandatory. Preregistration for classes offered. **Housing:** $150 fully refundable deposit. College-affiliated housing available on Barton campus. **Activities:** Campus ministries, drama, international student organizations, student government, student newspaper, Campus Crusade for Christ, human services organization, Spanish club, national technical honor society, Phi Theta Kappa, critics choice club.

Student services. Adult student services, alcohol/substance abuse counseling, chaplain/spiritual director, career counseling, services for economically disadvantaged, student employment services, financial aid counseling, on-campus daycare, personal counseling, placement for graduates, veterans' counselor. **Physically disabled:** Services for visually, speech, hearing impaired. **Transfer:** Pre-admission transcript evaluation for new students. Transfer adviser for students transferring to 4-year colleges.

Contact. E-mail: carolyn.watkins@gvltec.edu
Phone: (864) 250-8109 Toll-free number: (800) 922-1183
Fax: (864) 250-8534
Carolyn Watkins, Dean of Admissions, Greenville Technical College, PO Box 5616, Greenville, SC 29606-5616

Horry-Georgetown Technical College

Conway, South Carolina
www.hgtc.edu **CB code: 5305**

- Public 2-year community and technical college
- Commuter campus in large town

General. Founded in 1965. Regionally accredited. **Enrollment:** 5,603 degree-seeking undergraduates; 584 non-degree-seeking students. **Degrees:** 498 associate awarded. **Location:** 4 miles from Conway, 8 miles from Myrtle Beach. **Calendar:** Semester, extensive summer session. **Full-time faculty:** 138 total. **Part-time faculty:** 187 total. **Special facilities:** Art gallery, golf course.

Student profile. Among degree-seeking undergraduates, 1,053 enrolled as first-time, first-year students, 2,758 transferred in from other institutions.

Part-time:	59%	**Asian American:**	1%
Out-of-state:	10%	**Hispanic American:**	2%
Women:	68%	**International:**	1%
African American:	24%		

Transfer out. **Colleges most students transferred to 2008:** Coastal Carolina University.

Basis for selection. Open admission, but selective for some programs. Special requirements for engineering, technology, allied health, science programs.

2008-2009 Annual costs. Tuition/fees: $3,194; $4,026 out-of-district; $5,034 out-of-state. Books/supplies: $1,000. Personal expenses: $1,615.

2008-2009 Financial aid. **Need-based:** 59% of total undergraduate aid awarded as scholarships/grants, 41% as loans/jobs. Need-based aid available for part-time students. **Non-need-based:** Scholarships awarded for academics, state residency. **Additional information:** Participates in South Carolina lottery tuition assistance program. Full-time technical college students who are state residents receive assistance for tuition not covered by federal or need-based grants.

Application procedures. **Admission:** No deadline. $25 fee, may be waived for applicants with need. Admission notification on a rolling basis. **Financial aid:** Priority date 4/1, closing date 6/30. FAFSA required. Applicants notified on a rolling basis starting 4/1.

Academics. **Special study options:** Distance learning, double major, dual enrollment of high school students, exchange student, independent study, internships. License preparation in dental hygiene, nursing, radiology, real estate. **Credit/placement by examination:** CLEP, institutional tests. **Support services:** Learning center, reduced course load, remedial instruction, study skills assistance, tutoring.

Majors. **Agriculture:** Horticulture, turf management. **Business:** General, accounting, administrative services, hotel/motel admin. **Computer sciences:** Data processing. **Conservation:** Forest technology. **Education:** Voc/tech. **Engineering:** Electrical. **Engineering technology:** Civil, construction, electrical. **Family/consumer sciences:** Child care. **Health:** Dental hygiene, EMT paramedic, medical radiologic technology/radiation therapy, nursing (RN), pharmacy assistant. **Legal studies:** Paralegal. **Liberal arts:** Arts/sciences. **Mechanic/repair:** Heating/ac/refrig, industrial electronics. **Personal/culinary services:** Chef training. **Production:** Machine tool. **Protective services:** Criminal justice. **Public administration:** Social work. **Visual/performing arts:** Design.

Most popular majors. Business/marketing 16%, engineering/engineering technologies 6%, family/consumer sciences 11%, health sciences 26%, liberal arts 17%, security/protective services 6%.

Computing on campus. 900 workstations in library, computer center, student center. Commuter students can connect to campus network. Online course registration, online library, helpline, wireless network available.

Student life. **Freshman orientation:** Available. Preregistration for classes offered. **Activities:** Choral groups.

Student services. Career counseling, financial aid counseling, on-campus daycare, personal counseling, placement for graduates, veterans' counselor.

Contact. E-mail: admissions@hgtc.edu
Phone: (843) 349-5277 Fax: (843) 349-7501
George Swindoll, Assistant Vice President for Enrollment Development and Registration, Horry-Georgetown Technical College, PO Box 261966, Conway, SC 29528

Midlands Technical College

Columbia, South Carolina **CB member**
www.midlandstech.edu **CB code: 5584**

- Public 2-year technical college
- Commuter campus in large city

General. Founded in 1974. Regionally accredited. Additional campuses include Airport Campus, Beltline Campus, Batesburg-Leesville Center, Enterprise Campus/Center and Harbison Center. **Enrollment:** 10,706 degree-seeking undergraduates; 527 non-degree-seeking students. **Degrees:** 695 associate awarded. **ROTC:** Army, Naval, Air Force. **Location:** 10 miles from Columbia. **Calendar:** Semester, limited summer session. **Full-time faculty:** 221 total; 58% women. **Part-time faculty:** 526 total. **Class size:** 51% < 20, 49% 20-39, less than 1% 40-49. **Partnerships:** Formal partnerships with middle schools.

Student profile. Among degree-seeking undergraduates, 2,302 enrolled as first-time, first-year students.

Part-time:	52%	**Asian American:**	2%
Out-of-state:	2%	**Hispanic American:**	2%
Women:	62%	**Native American:**	1%
African American:	36%	**25 or older:**	38%

Transfer out. **Colleges most students transferred to 2008:** University of South Carolina.

Basis for selection. Open admission, but selective for some programs. High school record, SAT/ACT or college placement test scores, and interviews considered for nursing/health science applicants. Admission cut-off scores established for full admission into each program. Students falling below cut-off scores may enter in developmental studies. National League for Nursing Test required of nursing applicants in place of SAT or ACT. Interview, orientation required for health science and nursing programs. **Homeschooled:** Must be an approved Home School Association in South Carolina. If home schooler is applying for concurrent admission they must have a letter of permission from the home school association and a letter of permission from their parent/guardian.

2008-2009 Annual costs. Tuition/fees: $3,360; $4,176 out-of-district; $9,840 out-of-state. Books/supplies: $1,240. Personal expenses: $1,200.

2007-2008 Financial aid. Need-based: Average need met was 65%. Average scholarship/grant was $3,896; average loan $3,087. 57% of total undergraduate aid awarded as scholarships/grants, 43% as loans/jobs. Need-based aid available for part-time students.

Application procedures. Admission: Priority date 7/20; no deadline. No application fee. Admission notification on a rolling basis. **Financial aid:** Priority date 4/15; no closing date. FAFSA required. Applicants notified on a rolling basis; must reply within 2 week(s) of notification.

Academics. Special study options: Cooperative education, distance learning, dual enrollment of high school students, ESL, liberal arts/career combination. License preparation in nursing, physical therapy, radiology. **Credit/placement by examination:** AP, CLEP, institutional tests. **Support services:** GED preparation, learning center, remedial instruction, study skills assistance, tutoring, writing center.

Majors. Business: Accounting, administrative services, business admin. **Computer sciences:** Computer science, data processing, information systems. **Engineering technology:** Architectural, civil, electrical, mechanical drafting. **Health:** Clinical lab technology, dental assistant, dental hygiene, medical radiologic technology/radiation therapy, medical records technology, nuclear medical technology, nursing (RN), pharmacy assistant, physical therapy assistant, respiratory therapy technology. **Legal studies:** Court reporting, paralegal. **Liberal arts:** Arts/sciences. **Mechanic/repair:** Automotive, heating/ac/refrig. **Protective services:** Criminal justice. **Public administration:** Social work. **Visual/performing arts:** Commercial/advertising art.

Most popular majors. Business/marketing 20%, health sciences 21%, interdisciplinary studies 6%, liberal arts 30%.

Computing on campus. 46 workstations in library, computer center, student center. Commuter students can connect to campus network. Online course registration, online library, helpline, wireless network available.

Student life. Freshman orientation: Available. Preregistration for classes offered. **Activities:** Campus ministries, drama, international student organizations, literary magazine, student government, student newspaper, Campus Crusade for Christ, student human services organization, African American student organization.

Athletics. Intramural: Baseball, bowling, equestrian, football (non-tackle), softball, volleyball.

Student services. Adult student services, career counseling, services for economically disadvantaged, student employment services, financial aid counseling, placement for graduates, veterans' counselor. **Physically disabled:** Services for visually, speech, hearing impaired. **Learning disabled:** Comprehensive services available. **Transfer:** Re-entry adviser, pre-admission transcript evaluation for new students. Transfer adviser, college fairs on campus for students transferring to 4-year colleges.

Contact. E-mail: mtcinfo@midlandstech.edu
Phone: (803) 738-8324 Toll-free number: (800) 922-8038
Fax: (803) 738-7784
Sylvia Littlejohn, Director of Enrollment Services, Midlands Technical College, PO Box 2408, Columbia, SC 29202

Miller-Motte Technical College

North Charleston, South Carolina
www.miller-motte.net

- For-profit 2-year branch campus and technical college
- Small city

General. Accredited by ACICS. **Enrollment:** 745 degree-seeking undergraduates. **Degrees:** 147 associate awarded. **Calendar:** Quarter. **Full-time faculty:** 14 total. **Part-time faculty:** 40 total.

Basis for selection. Open admission. **Adult students:** SAT/ACT scores not required. **Homeschooled:** Transcript of courses and grades, interview required.

2008-2009 Annual costs. Tuition/fees: $10,575. Per-credit charge: $235. Fees vary according to programs from $6-$27 per credit hour.

2007-2008 Financial aid. Need-based: 27% of total undergraduate aid awarded as scholarships/grants, 73% as loans/jobs.

Application procedures. Admission: No deadline. $35 fee. **Financial aid:** FAFSA, institutional form required. Applicants notified on a rolling basis.

Academics. Credit/placement by examination: CLEP. **Support services:** Tutoring.

Majors. Business: Accounting/business management, business admin. **Health:** Massage therapy, medical assistant, surgical technology. **Legal studies:** Paralegal.

Contact. Phone: (843) 574-0101 Toll-free number: (877) 617-4740
Fax: (843) 329-4992
Jean Vokes, Director of Admissions, Miller-Motte Technical College, 8085 Rivers Avenue, Suite E, North Charleston, SC 29406

Northeastern Technical College

Cheraw, South Carolina
www.netc.edu **CB code: 5095**

- Public 2-year community and technical college
- Commuter campus in small town

General. Founded in 1969. Regionally accredited. High percentage of non-traditional students. **Enrollment:** 917 degree-seeking undergraduates; 93 non-degree-seeking students. **Degrees:** 110 associate awarded. **Location:** 89 miles from Columbia. **Calendar:** Semester, extensive summer session. **Full-time faculty:** 30 total; 7% have terminal degrees, 3% minority, 57% women. **Part-time faculty:** 100 total; 3% have terminal degrees, 20% minority, 53% women.

Student profile. Among degree-seeking undergraduates, 46% enrolled in a transfer program, 1% already have a bachelor's degree or higher, 259 enrolled as first-time, first-year students.

Part-time:	52%	**Women:**	72%
Out-of-state:	1%	**25 or older:**	87%

Transfer out. Colleges most students transferred to 2008: Francis Marion University, Clemson University, Coastal Carolina University, Florence-Darlington Technical College, University of South Carolina.

Basis for selection. Open admission, but selective for some programs. Special requirements for nursing program, including high school math and science courses and SAT (exclusive of Writing) combined score of 960. Interview recommended. **Homeschooled:** Must be under auspices of school district or an approved homeschool agency.

High school preparation. Algebra I and II, chemistry with laboratory required for nursing applicants.

2008-2009 Annual costs. Tuition/fees: $3,270; $3,486 out-of-district; $5,886 out-of-state. Books/supplies: $1,200. Personal expenses: $1,800.

Application procedures. Admission: Closing date 8/14. $25 fee, may be waived for applicants with need. Admission notification on a rolling basis. **Financial aid:** No deadline. FAFSA required. Applicants notified on a rolling basis; must reply within 8 week(s) of notification.

Academics. Special study options: Cross-registration, distance learning, dual enrollment of high school students, independent study, liberal arts/career combination. **Credit/placement by examination:** AP, CLEP, institutional tests. Credit by examination limited to 50% of semester hours required for degree. ASSET and English language proficiency required for placement. **Support services:** Remedial instruction, tutoring, writing center.

Majors. Business: Accounting, administrative services, business admin, office technology, office/clerical. **Computer sciences:** Data processing. **Education:** General. **Engineering technology:** Electrical. **Health:** Licensed practical nurse. **Liberal arts:** Arts/sciences.

Most popular majors. Business/marketing 30%, engineering/engineering technologies 11%, liberal arts 30%, public administration/social services 7%, trade and industry 27%.

Computing on campus. 125 workstations in library, computer center. Online library available.

Student life. Freshman orientation: Available. Preregistration for classes offered. Four early orientations held in the summer. **Activities:** Student government, service-leadership organization.

Student services. Career counseling, student employment services, personal counseling, placement for graduates, veterans' counselor. **Transfer:** Transfer adviser for students transferring to 4-year colleges.

Contact. E-mail: mnewton@netc.edu
Phone: (843) 921-6900 Fax: (843) 921-1476
Mary Newton, Dean of Students, Northeastern Technical College, Drawer 1007, Cheraw, SC 29520

Orangeburg-Calhoun Technical College
Orangeburg, South Carolina
www.octech.edu **CB code: 5527**

- Public 2-year community and technical college
- Commuter campus in large town

General. Founded in 1968. Regionally accredited. **Enrollment:** 2,290 degree-seeking undergraduates. **Degrees:** 258 associate awarded. **ROTC:** Army. **Location:** 75 miles from Charleston, 45 miles from Columbia. **Calendar:** Semester, extensive summer session. **Full-time faculty:** 85 total. **Part-time faculty:** 70 total.

Student profile.

African American:	60%	**25 or older:**	41%
Hispanic American:	1%		

Basis for selection. Open admission, but selective for some programs. ASSET used for placement. SAT or ACT may be submitted in place of ASSET. Admission to nursing and allied health programs based on school achievement record and test scores.

High school preparation. 24 units recommended. Recommended units include English 4, mathematics 3, social studies 3, history 2, science 2, foreign language 3 and academic electives 7.

2008-2009 Annual costs. Tuition/fees: $3,078; $3,798 out-of-district; $4,518 out-of-state. Books/supplies: $800. Personal expenses: $2,123.

Financial aid. All financial aid based on need. Need-based aid available for part-time students.

Application procedures. Admission: No deadline. $15 fee, may be waived for applicants with need. Admission notification on a rolling basis beginning on or about 1/1. $15 application processing fee due upon notification of acceptance. **Financial aid:** Priority date 6/4; no closing date. FAFSA, institutional form required. Applicants notified on a rolling basis starting 5/1; must reply within 2 week(s) of notification.

Academics. Special study options: Cooperative education, cross-registration, distance learning, double major, dual enrollment of high school students, independent study, liberal arts/career combination. License preparation in nursing, radiology, real estate. **Credit/placement by examination:** CLEP, institutional tests. 60% of hours needed for degree may be earned by examination. **Support services:** GED preparation and test center, learning center, pre-admission summer program, reduced course load, remedial instruction, study skills assistance, tutoring, writing center.

Majors. Business: General, accounting, administrative services. **Computer sciences:** Data processing, programming. **Conservation:** Forest resources. **Engineering technology:** Drafting, electrical. **Health:** Clinical lab assistant, clinical lab technology, medical radiologic technology/radiation therapy, nursing (RN). **Legal studies:** Paralegal. **Liberal arts:** Arts/sciences. **Mechanic/repair:** Automotive, electronics/electrical. **Protective services:** Criminal justice.

Computing on campus. 100 workstations in library, computer center, student center. Commuter students can connect to campus network. Online course registration, online library, helpline, repair service, wireless network available.

Student life. Freshman orientation: Available. Preregistration for classes offered. **Activities:** Student government, honor fraternities, curriculum clubs.

Student services. Adult student services, career counseling, services for economically disadvantaged, student employment services, financial aid counseling, minority student services, personal counseling, placement for graduates, veterans' counselor. **Physically disabled:** Services for visually, speech, hearing impaired. **Transfer:** Pre-admission transcript evaluation for new students. Transfer adviser, college fairs on campus for students transferring to 4-year colleges.

Contact. E-mail: felderb@octech.edu
Phone: (803) 535-1218 Fax: (803) 535-1388
Bobbie Felder, Dean of Students, Orangeburg-Calhoun Technical College, 3250 St. Matthews Road, Orangeburg, SC 29118-8222

Piedmont Technical College
Greenwood, South Carolina
www.ptc.edu **CB code: 5550**

- Public 2-year community and technical college
- Commuter campus in small city

General. Founded in 1966. Regionally accredited. Serves 7-county region of the state (satellite campus in each county offering Internet classes, traditional classes and interactive televised classes with main campus). **Enrollment:** 3,960 degree-seeking undergraduates. **Degrees:** 508 associate awarded. **Location:** 75 miles from Columbia, 50 miles from Greenville. **Calendar:** Semester, extensive summer session. **Full-time faculty:** 100 total. **Part-time faculty:** 145 total. **Class size:** 72% < 20, 28% 20-39, less than 1% 40-49, less than 1% 50-99. **Special facilities:** Engineering lab, South Carolina Center for Funeral Service Education, technologically advanced nursing labs equipped with SIMS man Bruce.

Student profile.

Out-of-state:	1%	**25 or older:**	45%

Transfer out. Colleges most students transferred to 2008: Lander University, Clemson University, University of South Carolina, South Carolina State University.

Basis for selection. Open admission, but selective for some programs. Students with SAT Verbal of at least 480 and SAT Math of at least 440 or ACT Composite of at least 20 do not need to take institutional placement tests.

2008-2009 Annual costs. Tuition/fees: $3,126; $3,534 out-of-district; $4,734 out-of-state. In Service Area, not fully supporting tuition, $3,288. Books/supplies: $850. Personal expenses: $200.

Financial aid. All financial aid based on need. Need-based aid available for part-time students. Work-study available nights, weekends and for part-time students.

Application procedures. Admission: No deadline. No application fee. Admission notification on a rolling basis. **Financial aid:** Priority date 5/1; no closing date. FAFSA required. Applicants notified on a rolling basis starting 6/1; must reply within 2 week(s) of notification.

Academics. Special study options: Cooperative education, distance learning, double major, dual enrollment of high school students, independent study, internships, liberal arts/career combination, weekend college. Bachelor's degree programs available on campus. License preparation in nursing, real estate. **Credit/placement by examination:** CLEP, IB, institutional tests. 24 credit hours maximum toward associate degree. **Support services:** GED preparation, learning center, pre-admission summer program, reduced course load, remedial instruction, study skills assistance, tutoring, writing center.

Majors. Business: General, administrative services. **Computer sciences:** Data processing. **Education:** Voc/tech. **Engineering technology:** Construction, drafting, electrical, surveying. **Health:** Cardiovascular technology, medical radiologic technology/radiation therapy, nursing (RN), respiratory therapy technology. **Interdisciplinary:** Global studies. **Liberal arts:** Arts/sciences. **Mechanic/repair:** Automotive, electronics/electrical, heating/ac/refrig, industrial electronics. **Personal/culinary services:** Mortuary science. **Production:** Machine tool, welding. **Protective services:** Criminal justice. **Public administration:** Social work.

Most popular majors. Business/marketing 25%, engineering/engineering technologies 9%, health sciences 13%, liberal arts 13%, security/protective services 10%, trade and industry 26%.

Computing on campus. 250 workstations in computer center, student center. Commuter students can connect to campus network. Online library, helpline, repair service available.

Student life. Freshman orientation: Available. Preregistration for classes offered. **Activities:** Alpha Delta Omega, Christian sudent union, computer club, horticulture club, Kappa Beta Delta, Lambda Chi Nu, Phi Theta Kappa, psychology club, rad tech club, student nurses association.

Student services. Adult student services, career counseling, services for economically disadvantaged, student employment services, financial aid counseling, minority student services, personal counseling, placement for graduates, veterans' counselor. **Transfer:** Pre-admission transcript evaluation for new students. Transfer adviser, college fairs on campus for students transferring to 4-year colleges.

Contact. E-mail: king.m@ptc.edu
Phone: (864) 941-8369 Toll-free number: (800) 868-5528
Fax: (864) 941-8555
Zeolean Kinard, Dean of Enrollment Management, Piedmont Technical College, PO Box 1467, Greenwood, SC 29648

Spartanburg Community College

Spartanburg, South Carolina **CB member**
www.sccsc.edu **CB code: 5668**

- Public 2-year community and technical college
- Commuter campus in small city
- Interview required

General. Founded in 1961. Regionally accredited. Satellite campuses located in Greer and Gaffney. **Enrollment:** 4,678 degree-seeking undergraduates. **Degrees:** 383 associate awarded. **Location:** 4 miles from downtown. **Calendar:** Semester, limited summer session. **Full-time faculty:** 114 total; 57% women. **Part-time faculty:** 170 total; 55% women. **Class size:** 65% < 20, 35% 20-39. **Special facilities:** Horticultural arboretum. **Partnerships:** Formal partnership with Ford Asset Program (auto mechanic training program).

Student profile. Among degree-seeking undergraduates, 30% enrolled in a transfer program, 70% enrolled in a vocational program, 10% already have a bachelor's degree or higher.

Out-of-state:	2%	**25 or older:**	38%

Transfer out. 82% of students enrolled in the transfer program go on to 4-year colleges. **Colleges most students transferred to 2008:** Clemson University, University of South Carolina Upstate, University of South Carolina at Columbia, Wofford College, Spartanburg Methodist College.

Basis for selection. Open admission, but selective for some programs. Test of Adult Basic Education required for admissions. Programmer's Aptitude Test required for computer programming and data processing. Admission to some health science programs limited usually based on size of class. Essay recommended. **Homeschooled:** Transcript of courses and grades required. State Department approval of the applicable home school association.

High school preparation. College-preparatory program recommended. 21 units required. Required units include English 4, mathematics 2, social studies 2, history 2, science 2 (laboratory 2), foreign language 1 and academic electives 6. One biology and/or chemistry and 1 algebra required for most health programs. Algebra required for all engineering and computer programs.

2008-2009 Annual costs. Tuition/fees: $3,314; $4,134 out-of-district; $7,048 out-of-state. Books/supplies: $1,000. Personal expenses: $2,619.

2007-2008 Financial aid. Need-based: 98% of total undergraduate aid awarded as scholarships/grants, 2% as loans/jobs. Need-based aid available for part-time students. Work-study available for part-time students. **Additional information:** Participates in South Carolina lottery tuition assistance program. Full-time technical college students who are state residents receive assistance for tuition not covered by federal or need-based grants.

Application procedures. Admission: No deadline. No application fee. Admission notification on a rolling basis. **Financial aid:** Priority date 2/28, closing date 5/1. FAFSA required. Applicants notified on a rolling basis starting 5/1.

Academics. Special study options: Cooperative education, distance learning, double major, dual enrollment of high school students, ESL, independent study. License preparation in dental hygiene, nursing, occupational therapy, physical therapy, radiology. **Credit/placement by examination:** AP, CLEP, institutional tests. **Support services:** GED preparation and test center, learning center, remedial instruction, tutoring, writing center.

Majors. Agriculture: Horticulture. **Business:** Accounting, administrative services, business admin, hospitality admin, hotel/motel admin, marketing, restaurant/food services. **Computer sciences:** General. **Education:** Voc/tech. **Engineering technology:** General, civil, electrical, mechanical. **Health:** Clinical lab technology, medical radiologic technology/radiation therapy, nursing (RN), predental, respiratory therapy technology. **Liberal arts:** Arts/sciences. **Mechanic/repair:** Automotive, industrial electronics. **Production:** Machine tool.

Most popular majors. Business/marketing 23%, health sciences 24%, liberal arts 12%, trade and industry 16%.

Computing on campus. 1,500 workstations in library, computer center, student center. Commuter students can connect to campus network. Online course registration, helpline, repair service, wireless network available.

Student life. Freshman orientation: Available. Preregistration for classes offered. **Activities:** Drama, student government, student newspaper.

Student services. Adult student services, career counseling, student employment services, financial aid counseling, personal counseling, placement for graduates, veterans' counselor, women's services. **Physically disabled:** Services for visually, speech, hearing impaired. **Transfer:** Transfer adviser, college fairs on campus for students transferring to 4-year colleges.

Contact. E-mail: Admissions, SCC@sccsc.edu
Phone: (864) 592-4800 Toll-free number: (866) 592-4700
Fax: (864) 592-4642
Kathy McKinzie, Director of Enrollment Services, Spartanburg Community College, Box 4386, Spartanburg, SC 29305-4386

Spartanburg Methodist College

Spartanburg, South Carolina **CB member**
www.smcsc.edu **CB code: 5627**

- Private 2-year junior and liberal arts college affiliated with United Methodist Church
- Residential campus in small city
- SAT or ACT with writing required

General. Founded in 1911. Regionally accredited. **Enrollment:** 727 degree-seeking undergraduates; 23 non-degree-seeking students. **Degrees:** 195 associate awarded. **ROTC:** Army. **Location:** 30 miles from Greenville, 60 miles from Charlotte, North Carolina. **Calendar:** Semester, limited summer session. **Full-time faculty:** 28 total; 21% have terminal degrees, 11% minority, 57% women. **Part-time faculty:** 17 total; 29% have terminal degrees, 12% minority, 59% women. **Class size:** 29% <.20, 69% 20-39, 2% 40-49, less than 1% >100.

Student profile. Among degree-seeking undergraduates, 100% enrolled in a transfer program, 445 enrolled as first-time, first-year students, 25 transferred in from other institutions.

Part-time:	2%	**Hispanic American:**	4%
Out-of-state:	7%	**International:**	1%
Women:	48%	**25 or older:**	2%
African American:	29%	**Live on campus:**	71%
Asian American:	1%		

Transfer out. 90% of students enrolled in the transfer program go on to 4-year colleges. **Colleges most students transferred to 2008:** University of South Carolina Upstate, Clemson University, University of South Carolina, Lander University, College of Charleston.

Basis for selection. High school GPA, SAT/ACT scores, and class rank very important. Audition, essay, interview recommended. **Adult students:** SAT/ACT scores not required if applicant over 21. **Homeschooled:** Applicants need complete high school academic transcript. Recommend students be supervised through accredited home school association to provide curriculum and academic oversight throughout high school program.

High school preparation. Recommended units include English 4, mathematics 4, social studies 2, history 1, science 3, foreign language 1 and academic electives 7. One computer science recommended.

2008-2009 Annual costs. Tuition/fees: $11,731. Per-credit charge: $312. Room/board: $6,741. Books/supplies: $1,200.

2008-2009 Financial aid. Need-based: Need-based aid available for part-time students. Work-study available nights, weekends and for part-time students. **Non-need-based:** Scholarships awarded for academics, athletics, job skills, leadership, music/drama, religious affiliation, state residency.

Application procedures. Admission: No deadline. $20 fee, may be waived for applicants with need. Admission notification on a rolling basis beginning on or about 9/1. Housing deposit refundable until June 1. Applicant notified of decision within a week. **Financial aid:** Priority date 6/30, closing date 8/22. FAFSA required. Applicants notified on a rolling basis starting 3/1; must reply within 2 week(s) of notification.

Academics. **Special study options:** Dual enrollment of high school students, ESL, honors, independent study, liberal arts/career combination, study abroad. **Credit/placement by examination:** AP, CLEP, SAT, ACT, institutional tests. 15 credit hours maximum toward associate degree. **Support services:** Learning center, pre-admission summer program, reduced course load, remedial instruction, study skills assistance, tutoring, writing center.

Majors. **Liberal arts:** Arts/sciences. **Protective services:** Law enforcement admin.

Most popular majors. Liberal arts 94%, security/protective services 6%.

Computing on campus. 45 workstations in dormitories, library, computer center, student center. Dormitories wired for high-speed internet access and linked to campus network. Commuter students can connect to campus network. Online library, helpline, wireless network available.

Student life. **Freshman orientation:** Mandatory, $25 fee. Preregistration for classes offered. One session in mid-July, one session in early August, one session on move-in weekend (mid August). **Policies:** No alcohol, drugs, or firearms allowed on campus. All campus buildings smoke free. **Housing:** Guaranteed on-campus for freshmen. Coed dorms, single-sex dorms, special housing for disabled, wellness housing available. $100 fully refundable deposit, deadline 11/30. **Activities:** Jazz band, campus ministries, choral groups, dance, drama, literary magazine, music ensembles, student government, student newspaper, computer programming club, Psi Omega Theatre Fraternity, People Organizing People Successfully, Presbyterian Student Association, Wesly Fellowship, Campus Crusade for Christ, Sigma Kappa Delta, Phi Theta Kappa, Psi Beta.

Athletics. NJCAA. **Intercollegiate:** Baseball M, basketball, cheerleading, cross-country, golf, soccer, softball W, tennis, volleyball W, wrestling M. **Intramural:** Basketball, football (non-tackle) M, softball, table tennis, tennis, volleyball. **Team name:** Pioneers.

Student services. Adult student services, alcohol/substance abuse counseling, chaplain/spiritual director, career counseling, services for economically disadvantaged, student employment services, financial aid counseling, health services, personal counseling, placement for graduates, veterans' counselor. **Physically disabled:** Services for visually, speech, hearing impaired. **Transfer:** Pre-admission transcript evaluation for new students. Transfer center, transfer adviser, college fairs on campus for students transferring to 4-year colleges.

Contact. E-mail: admiss@smcsc.edu
Phone: (864) 587-4213 Toll-free number: (800) 772-7286
Fax: (864) 587-4355
Daniel Philbeck, Vice President for Enrollment Management, Spartanburg Methodist College, 1000 Powell Mill Road, Spartanburg, SC 29301-5899

Technical College of the Lowcountry

Beaufort, South Carolina
www.tcl.edu **CB code: 5047**

- Public 2-year community and technical college
- Commuter campus in small town

General. Founded in 1972. Regionally accredited. **Enrollment:** 1,900 degree-seeking undergraduates. **Degrees:** 122 associate awarded. **Location:** 45 miles from Hilton Head, 45 miles from Savannah, Georgia. **Calendar:** Semester, extensive summer session. **Full-time faculty:** 55 total. **Part-time faculty:** 60 total.

Basis for selection. Open admission, but selective for some programs. SAT or ACT required for placement and counseling. Nursing students are encouraged to have a personal interview and must submit NET test results. Interview recommended for nursing program. **Adult students:** After admission all students take either COMPASS or ASSET for placement.

2008-2009 Annual costs. Tuition/fees: $3,270; $7,082 out-of-state.

Financial aid. All financial aid based on need. Need-based aid available for part-time students. **Additional information:** State lottery aid may be available to South Carolina residents who take 6 credit hours or more.

Application procedures. **Admission:** No deadline. $25 fee. Admission notification on a rolling basis. **Financial aid:** No deadline. FAFSA required.

Academics. **Special study options:** Cooperative education, cross-registration, distance learning, double major, dual enrollment of high school students, ESL, independent study, internships. **Credit/placement by examination:** AP, CLEP, institutional tests. **Support services:** GED preparation and test center, learning center, pre-admission summer program, reduced course load, remedial instruction, study skills assistance, tutoring, writing center.

Majors. **Agriculture:** Horticulture. **Business:** General, accounting, administrative services, hospitality/recreation, office management. **Computer sciences:** General, data processing, programming. **Engineering:** Electrical. **Engineering technology:** Construction. **Family/consumer sciences:** Child care. **Health:** Nursing (RN). **Legal studies:** Paralegal. **Liberal arts:** Arts/sciences. **Mechanic/repair:** Heating/ac/refrig. **Personal/culinary services:** Cosmetic. **Protective services:** Criminal justice, law enforcement admin.

Computing on campus. 400 workstations in library, computer center, student center. Online library, helpline available.

Student life. **Freshman orientation:** Available. Preregistration for classes offered. One-day session at start of fall semester. **Activities:** Student government, Phi Theta Kappa, Rotaract Club, professional societies.

Student services. Career counseling, student employment services, financial aid counseling, personal counseling, placement for graduates, veterans' counselor.

Contact. E-mail: mgallion@tcl.edu
Phone: (843) 525-8208 Toll-free number: (800) 768-8252
Fax: (843) 525-8285
Melanie Gallion, Director of Admissions, Technical College of the Lowcountry, 921 South Ribaut Road, Beaufort, SC 29901-1288

Tri-County Technical College

Pendleton, South Carolina
www.tctc.edu **CB code: 5789**

- Public 2-year community and technical college
- Commuter campus in small town

General. Founded in 1962. Regionally accredited. **Enrollment:** 5,730 degree-seeking undergraduates. **Degrees:** 414 associate awarded. **ROTC:** Army, Air Force. **Location:** 5 miles from Clemson. **Calendar:** Semester, limited summer session. **Full-time faculty:** 130 total. **Part-time faculty:** 200 total. **Special facilities:** Amphitheater. **Partnerships:** Formal partnerships with 7 area school districts, local businesses and industries, National Drop-out Prevention Center at Clemson, the Anderson and Oconee County Business and Education Partnerships, the Career Center and Technology Center, and Tri-County Tech in a Partnership for Academic and Career Education (business and education consortium to initiate Tech Prep/School-to-Work programs).

Student profile.

Out-of-state:	2%	**25 or older:**	85%

Transfer out. **Colleges most students transferred to 2008:** Clemson University.

Basis for selection. Open admission, but selective for some programs. SAT used only for admission to nursing: 450 verbal and 420 math score required.

High school preparation. High school unit or college course in chemistry, biology, and algebra taken within past 5 years required for nursing, medical laboratory, practical nursing, surgical technology, dental assisting, and veterinary technology.

2008-2009 Annual costs. Tuition/fees: $3,060; $3,384 out-of-district; $6,786 out-of-state. Books/supplies: $650.

Financial aid. **Need-based:** Need-based aid available for part-time students. Work-study available nights and for part-time students. **Non-need-based:** Scholarships awarded for academics, state residency. **Additional information:** Deadline for application to institutional scholarships April 2.

Application procedures. **Admission:** No deadline. $30 fee. Application must be submitted on paper. Admission notification on a rolling basis. **Financial aid:** Priority date 6/30; no closing date. FAFSA required. Applicants notified on a rolling basis starting 6/15; must reply within 2 week(s) of notification.

Academics. Electronic engineering majors may transfer to any 4-year college accredited by the Technology Accreditation Commission of the Accreditation Board for Engineering and Technology. **Special study options:** Cooperative education, distance learning, dual enrollment of high school students, ESL, internships, liberal arts/career combination, student-designed major. License preparation in dental hygiene, nursing, real estate. **Credit/placement by examination:** AP, CLEP, institutional tests. Credit available from documented work experience, course waiver, noncollective organization training programs, technical advanced placement. **Support services:** GED preparation, learning center, reduced course load, remedial instruction, study skills assistance, tutoring, writing center.

Majors. **Business:** Accounting, administrative services, business admin. **Communications:** Broadcast journalism. **Computer sciences:** General, data processing, programming. **Engineering technology:** Drafting, electrical. **Family/consumer sciences:** Clothing/textiles. **Health:** Clinical lab technology, nursing (RN), veterinary technology/assistant. **Liberal arts:** Arts/sciences. **Mechanic/repair:** Heating/ac/refrig, industrial.

Computing on campus. 700 workstations in library, computer center. Online course registration, online library, helpline available.

Student life. **Freshman orientation:** Available. Preregistration for classes offered. **Activities:** International student organizations, student government, student newspaper, minority student association, criminal justice club, gospel choir, North American Veterinary Technician Association, student nurses association, forensics team, South Carolina Society of Clinical Laboratory Science.

Athletics. NJCAA. **Intercollegiate:** Golf M, soccer M. **Team name:** Lynx.

Student services. Alcohol/substance abuse counseling, career counseling, services for economically disadvantaged, student employment services, financial aid counseling, minority student services, placement for graduates, veterans' counselor. **Transfer:** Transfer adviser, college fairs on campus for students transferring to 4-year colleges.

Contact. E-mail: infocent@tctc.edu
Phone: (864) 646-1550 Fax: (864) 646-1890
Renae Frazier, Director of Admissions, Tri-County Technical College, Box 587, Pendleton, SC 29670

Trident Technical College
Charleston, South Carolina
www.tridenttech.edu **CB code: 5049**

- Public 2-year community and technical college
- Commuter campus in large city

General. Founded in 1964. Regionally accredited. 3 campuses: Palmer Campus in downtown Charleston, Main Campus in North Charleston and Berkeley Campus in Moncks Corner. **Enrollment:** 11,840 degree-seeking undergraduates; 923 non-degree-seeking students. **Degrees:** 708 associate awarded. **Location:** 15 miles from downtown. **Calendar:** Semester, extensive summer session. **Full-time faculty:** 298 total; 11% minority, 54% women. **Part-time faculty:** 371 total; 16% minority, 59% women. **Class size:** 55% < 20, 42% 20-39, 2% 40-49, less than 1% 50-99, less than 1% >100.

Student profile. Among degree-seeking undergraduates, 2,280 enrolled as first-time, first-year students, 725 transferred in from other institutions.

Part-time:	54%	**Asian American:**	2%
Out-of-state:	2.5%	**Hispanic American:**	2%
Women:	63%	**25 or older:**	44%
African American:	27%		

Basis for selection. Open admission, but selective for some programs. Selective admisssion for nursing students. **Learning Disabled:** Student should provide current medical, psychological, and/or psychiatric documentation providing a diagnosis and describing how his/her disability affects his/her ability to function in a collegiate, adult learning environment. Documentation indicating what accommodations the student received in high school and/or at another college may also be helpful.

2008-2009 Annual costs. Tuition/fees: $3,330; $3,696 out-of-district; $6,380 out-of-state. Books/supplies: $1,150. Personal expenses: $1,226.

Financial aid. **Need-based:** Need-based aid available for part-time students. Work-study available nights, weekends and for part-time students.

Application procedures. **Admission:** Closing date 8/4 (postmark date). $25 fee. Admission notification on a rolling basis. Applicants to early admissions program must rank in upper half of high school class and must have combined SAT score (exclusive of Writing) of 800 or ACT composite score of 17. **Financial aid:** No deadline. FAFSA required. Applicants notified on a rolling basis; must reply within 6 week(s) of notification.

Academics. **Special study options:** Accelerated study, cooperative education, cross-registration, distance learning, double major, dual enrollment of high school students, ESL, independent study, internships. **Credit/placement by examination:** AP, CLEP, IB, institutional tests. **Support services:** Learning center, reduced course load, remedial instruction, study skills assistance, tutoring, writing center.

Majors. **Agriculture:** Horticultural science, horticulture. **Business:** General, accounting, administrative services, business admin, customer service, e-commerce, entrepreneurial studies, hospitality admin, hotel/motel admin, logistics, marketing, office management, restaurant/food services, tourism/travel, transportation. **Communications:** Broadcast journalism. **Communications technology:** General. **Computer sciences:** Data processing, information systems, programming. **Construction:** Electrician. **Education:** Voc/tech. **Engineering technology:** Architectural, civil, electrical, manufacturing, robotics. **Family/consumer sciences:** Child care. **Health:** Clinical lab technology, dental hygiene, medical radiologic technology/radiation therapy, nursing (RN), occupational therapy assistant, physical therapy assistant, respiratory therapy technology. **Legal studies:** Paralegal. **Liberal arts:** Arts/sciences. **Mechanic/repair:** General, aircraft, aircraft powerplant, automotive, industrial. **Personal/culinary services:** Culinary arts. **Physical sciences:** General. **Protective services:** Fire services admin, law enforcement admin. **Public administration:** Human services. **Transportation:** General, aviation. **Visual/performing arts:** Commercial/advertising art, graphic design.

Most popular majors. Business/marketing 10%, health sciences 28%, liberal arts 33%.

Computing on campus. 3,000 workstations in library, computer center, student center. Online library, wireless network available.

Student life. **Freshman orientation:** Available. Preregistration for classes offered. 45-minute ongoing service. **Activities:** International student organizations, student government, student newspaper, Phi Theta Kappa international honor society, Alpha Mu Gamma, Asian Studies, Black Student Association, Campus Crusade for Christ, La Sociedad Hispanoamericana, Society of Student Leaders.

Student services. Adult student services, alcohol/substance abuse counseling, career counseling, services for economically disadvantaged, student employment services, financial aid counseling, personal counseling, placement for graduates, veterans' counselor. **Physically disabled:** Services for visually, hearing impaired. **Transfer:** Pre-admission transcript evaluation for new students. Transfer adviser, college fairs on campus for students transferring to 4-year colleges.

Contact. E-mail: admissions@tridenttech.edu
Phone: (843) 574-6125 Toll-free number: (877) 349-7184
Fax: (843) 574-6483
Clara Martin, Director of Admissions, Trident Technical College, Box 118067, AM-M, Charleston, SC 29423-8067

University of South Carolina at Lancaster
Lancaster, South Carolina
usclancaster.sc.edu **CB code: 5849**

- Public 2-year branch campus and junior college
- Commuter campus in large town

General. Founded in 1959. Regionally accredited. **Enrollment:** 1,119 degree-seeking undergraduates; 547 non-degree-seeking students. **Degrees:** 143 associate awarded. **ROTC:** Army. **Location:** 50 miles from Columbia, 40 miles from Charlotte, North Carolina. **Calendar:** Semester, limited summer session. **Full-time faculty:** 55 total; 66% have terminal degrees, 11% minority, 44% women. **Part-time faculty:** 35 total; 20% have terminal degrees, 11% minority, 60% women. **Special facilities:** Health sciences facilities, diabetic education center.

Student profile. Among degree-seeking undergraduates, 358 enrolled as first-time, first-year students, 61 transferred in from other institutions.

Part-time:	30%	**Women:**	63%
Out-of-state:	2%	**25 or older:**	20%

Transfer out. 90% of students enrolled in the transfer program go on to 4-year colleges. **Colleges most students transferred to 2008:** University of South Carolina-Columbia, Winthrop University, Clemson University, York Technical College.

Basis for selection. Open admission. SAT or ACT required in admissions process but applicants with scores below required levels will be admitted provisionally. **Adult students:** SAT/ACT scores not required if applicant over 25. **Homeschooled:** Transcript of courses and grades required.

High school preparation. College-preparatory program recommended. 23 units recommended. Recommended units include English 4, mathematics 3, social studies 3, history 1, science 3 (laboratory 3), foreign language 2 and academic electives 4. One unit physical education/ ROTC required.

2008-2009 Annual costs. Tuition/fees: $5,264; $12,680 out-of-state. Per-credit charge: $206 in-state; $515 out-of-state. Books/supplies: $600. Personal expenses: $950.

Application procedures. **Admission:** Priority date 7/30; no deadline. $40 fee, may be waived for applicants with need. Admission notification on a rolling basis. **Financial aid:** Priority date 4/15; no closing date. FAFSA required. Applicants notified on a rolling basis starting 6/1; must reply within 2 week(s) of notification.

Academics. Special study options: Accelerated study, combined bachelor's/graduate degree, cross-registration, distance learning, dual enrollment of high school students, honors, independent study, internships, liberal arts/career combination. Bachelor's degree programs available on campus. License preparation in nursing. **Credit/placement by examination:** AP, CLEP, IB, institutional tests. 30 credit hours maximum toward associate degree. **Support services:** Learning center, study skills assistance, tutoring, writing center.

Majors. Business: Administrative services, business admin. **Health:** Nursing (RN). **Liberal arts:** Arts/sciences. **Protective services:** Criminal justice. **Visual/performing arts:** Art.

Computing on campus. 110 workstations in library, computer center. Commuter students can connect to campus network. Online course registration, repair service, wireless network available.

Student life. Freshman orientation: Mandatory, $50 fee. Preregistration for classes offered. 2-day program. **Activities:** Campus ministries, drama, literary magazine, student government, student newspaper, Black awareness group, adult group for education, Campus Crusade for Christ.

Athletics. NJCAA. **Intercollegiate:** Baseball M, soccer W, tennis. **Intramural:** Basketball, table tennis, volleyball. **Team name:** Lancers.

Student services. Adult student services, career counseling, student employment services, financial aid counseling, health services, personal counseling, veterans' counselor. **Transfer:** Pre-admission transcript evaluation for new students. College fairs on campus for students transferring to 4-year colleges.

Contact. Phone: (803) 313-7073 Fax: (803) 313-7116
Karen Faile, Director of Enrollment Management, University of South Carolina at Lancaster, Box 889, Lancaster, SC 29721

University of South Carolina at Sumter
Sumter, South Carolina
www.uscsumter.edu **CB code: 5821**

- Public 2-year branch campus college
- Commuter campus in small city
- SAT or ACT (ACT writing optional) required

General. Founded in 1966. Regionally accredited. **Enrollment:** 870 degree-seeking undergraduates; 375 non-degree-seeking students. **Degrees:** 91 associate awarded. **ROTC:** Army. **Location:** 40 miles from Columbia, 98 miles from Charleston. **Calendar:** Semester, limited summer session. **Full-time faculty:** 54 total. **Part-time faculty:** 29 total. **Class size:** 68% < 20, 30% 20-39, 2% 40-49. **Partnerships:** Formal partnerships with high schools (college-level courses for eligible high school students.).

Student profile. Among degree-seeking undergraduates, 245 enrolled as first-time, first-year students.

Part-time:	25%	**Women:**	60%
Out-of-state:	1%	**25 or older:**	28%

Transfer out. Colleges most students transferred to 2008: Central Carolina Technical College, College of Charleston, Midlands Technical College.

Basis for selection. Entering freshmen must have 2.25 GPA. Class rank and test scores also important. All freshmen required to take foreign language tests. Placement in mathematics may require additional testing. Interview required for academically marginal. **Adult students:** SAT/ACT scores not required if applicant over 23. **Homeschooled:** Official transcripts, SAT/ACT and a GPR converted to the South Carolina Uniform grading scale if home schooled in South Carolina. **Learning Disabled:** Must submit recent documentation.

High school preparation. 20 units required. Required and recommended units include English 4, mathematics 3-4, social studies 3, history 2, science 3 (laboratory 3), foreign language 2-3 and academic electives 4. 1 physical education required, 1 computer science recommended.

2008-2009 Annual costs. Tuition/fees: $5,264; $12,680 out-of-state. Per-credit charge: $206 in-state; $515 out-of-state. Books/supplies: $932. Personal expenses: $2,053.

2008-2009 Financial aid. All financial aid based on need. Need-based aid available for part-time students. Work-study available nights, weekends and for part-time students.

Application procedures. Admission: Priority date 8/1; no deadline. $40 fee, may be waived for applicants with need. Admission notification on a rolling basis. **Financial aid:** Priority date 4/15; no closing date. FAFSA required. Applicants notified on a rolling basis starting 4/16; must reply within 2 week(s) of notification.

Academics. Special study options: Combined bachelor's/graduate degree, cross-registration, distance learning, dual enrollment of high school students, independent study, liberal arts/career combination, student-designed major, teacher certification program. Bachelor's degree programs available on campus. **Credit/placement by examination:** AP, CLEP, institutional tests. 30 credit hours maximum toward associate degree. **Support services:** Learning center, remedial instruction, study skills assistance, tutoring, writing center.

Majors. Liberal arts: Arts/sciences.

Computing on campus. 195 workstations in library, computer center, student center. Commuter students can connect to campus network. Online course registration, online library, student web hosting, wireless network available.

Student life. Freshman orientation: Mandatory. Preregistration for classes offered. **Activities:** Choral groups, drama, literary magazine, music ensembles, student government, student newspaper, African-American club, Baptist Student clubs, campus activities board, Circle K, student art guild, student education association, student nursing organization, environmental club.

Athletics. NJCAA. **Intercollegiate:** Baseball M. **Intramural:** Baseball M, basketball, bowling, football (non-tackle), golf, handball, racquetball, soccer M, softball, table tennis, tennis, volleyball, weight lifting.

Student services. Adult student services, chaplain/spiritual director, career counseling, services for economically disadvantaged, student employment services, financial aid counseling, personal counseling, veterans' counselor. **Physically disabled:** Services for visually, speech, hearing impaired.

Contact. E-mail: kbritton@uscsumter.edu
Phone: (803) 938-3762 Fax: (803) 938-3901
Keith Britton, Director of Admissions, University of South Carolina at Sumter, 200 Miller Road, Sumter, SC 29150-2498

University of South Carolina at Union
Union, South Carolina
uscunion.sc.edu **CB code: 5846**

- Public 2-year branch campus college
- Commuter campus in small town
- SAT or ACT required

General. Founded in 1965. Regionally accredited. Off-campus site at Laurens offers full range of courses. **Enrollment:** 250 degree-seeking undergraduates. **Degrees:** 70 associate awarded. **Location:** 30 miles from Spartanburg, 60 miles from Columbia. **Calendar:** Semester, limited summer session. **Full-time faculty:** 8 total. **Part-time faculty:** 15 total.

Student profile. Among degree-seeking undergraduates, 1% already have a bachelor's degree or higher, 200 transferred in from other institutions.

Out-of-state:	1%	**25 or older:**	40%

Transfer out. 75% of students enrolled in the transfer program go on to 4-year colleges.

Basis for selection. Secondary school record most important. Standardized test scores and class rank also important. Students with high school diploma or GED but without required high school curriculum units may be admitted into Opportunity Program based on school achievement record and SAT or ACT scores. Institutional placement tests in mathematics and writing required of all freshmen. **Adult students:** SAT/ACT scores not required.

High school preparation. 20 units required. Required units include English 4, mathematics 3, social studies 3, science 3 (laboratory 3), foreign language 2 and academic electives 4.

2008-2009 Annual costs. Tuition/fees: $5,264; $12,680 out-of-state. Per-credit charge: $206 in-state; $515 out-of-state. Books/supplies: $744. Personal expenses: $1,307.

Financial aid. All financial aid based on need. Work-study available nights, weekends and for part-time students.

Application procedures. **Admission:** No deadline. $40 fee, may be waived for applicants with need. Admission notification on a rolling basis beginning on or about 6/1. **Financial aid:** Priority date 4/15; no closing date. FAFSA required. Applicants notified on a rolling basis starting 7/15; must reply within 2 week(s) of notification.

Academics. Upper division courses leading to bachelor's degree in interdisciplinary studies available. Degree awarded by Columbia campus. **Special study options:** Cross-registration, distance learning, dual enrollment of high school students, independent study, internships, student-designed major. Bachelor's degree programs available on campus. **Credit/placement by examination:** AP, CLEP, institutional tests. **Support services:** Pre-admission summer program, reduced course load, remedial instruction, tutoring.

Majors. **Liberal arts:** Arts/sciences.

Student life. **Freshman orientation:** Mandatory. Preregistration for classes offered. **Activities:** Drama, literary magazine, student government, student newspaper, Afro-American and political groups, student media association, computer club, history club, art club, travel club, music club, biology club.

Athletics. **Intercollegiate:** Basketball M, softball W. **Intramural:** Baseball M, basketball, bowling, gymnastics, racquetball, skiing, softball, table tennis, tennis, volleyball.

Student services. Adult student services, career counseling, student employment services, on-campus daycare, personal counseling. **Transfer:** College fairs on campus for students transferring to 4-year colleges.

Contact. Phone: (864) 429-8728 Fax: (864) 427-3682
Terry Young, Director of Enrollment Services, University of South Carolina at Union, PO Drawer 729, Union, SC 29379

University of South Carolina: Salkehatchie Regional Campus

Allendale, South Carolina
uscsalkehatchie.sc.edu **CB code: 5847**

- Public 2-year branch campus college
- Commuter campus in rural community
- SAT or ACT required

General. Founded in 1965. Regionally accredited. **Enrollment:** 700 degree-seeking undergraduates. **Degrees:** 62 associate awarded. **ROTC:** Army, Naval, Air Force. **Location:** 75 miles from Columbia, 75 miles from Charleston. **Calendar:** Semester, limited summer session. **Full-time faculty:** 25 total. **Part-time faculty:** 40 total.

Student profile.

Out-of-state:	1%	**25 or older:**	26%

Transfer out. **Colleges most students transferred to 2008:** University of South Carolina-Columbia, University of South Carolina-Aiken.

Basis for selection. Secondary schoool record and class rank most important. Standardized test scores also important. **Adult students:** SAT/ACT scores not required if applicant over 25.

High school preparation. Required units include English 4, mathematics 3, social studies 3, history 1, science 2 (laboratory 2), foreign language 2 and academic electives 2.

2008-2009 Annual costs. Tuition/fees: $5,264; $12,680 out-of-state. Per-credit charge: $206 in-state; $515 out-of-state. Books/supplies: $1,036. Personal expenses: $1,746.

2007-2008 Financial aid. **Need-based:** Need-based aid available for part-time students. Work-study available nights, weekends and for part-time students. **Non-need-based:** Scholarships awarded for academics.

Application procedures. **Admission:** Priority date 8/19; no deadline. $40 fee, may be waived for applicants with need. Admission notification on a rolling basis. **Financial aid:** Priority date 4/30; no closing date. FAFSA required. Applicants notified on a rolling basis starting 6/1.

Academics. **Special study options:** Cross-registration, dual enrollment of high school students, independent study, student-designed major, study abroad. Bachelor's degree programs available on campus. **Credit/placement by examination:** CLEP, IB, institutional tests. 15 credit hours maximum toward associate degree. **Support services:** Learning center, pre-admission summer program, reduced course load, tutoring.

Majors. **Liberal arts:** Arts/sciences.

Computing on campus. 102 workstations in library, computer center.

Student life. **Freshman orientation:** Mandatory. Preregistration for classes offered. **Activities:** Student government, minority student organization.

Athletics. NJCAA. **Intercollegiate:** Baseball M, basketball M, soccer, softball W. **Team name:** Indians.

Student services. Career counseling, financial aid counseling, personal counseling, veterans' counselor. **Physically disabled:** Services for visually, hearing impaired.

Contact. Phone: (803) 584-3446 Toll-free number: (800) 922-5500
Fax: (803) 584-3884
Jane Brewer, Dean for Student Services, University of South Carolina: Salkehatchie Regional Campus, PO Box 617, Allendale, SC 29810

Williamsburg Technical College

Kingstree, South Carolina
www.wiltech.edu **CB code: 5892**

- Public 2-year community and technical college
- Commuter campus in small town

General. Founded in 1969. Regionally accredited. **Enrollment:** 588 degree-seeking undergraduates. **Degrees:** 56 associate awarded. **Location:** 75 miles from Charleston, 40 miles from Florence. **Calendar:** Semester, extensive summer session. **Full-time faculty:** 20 total. **Part-time faculty:** 25 total. **Class size:** 90% < 20, 10% 20-39. **Partnerships:** Formal partnerships with Tupperware, Firestone and Williamsburg County school district.

Student profile.

African American:	72%	**25 or older:**	52%
Hispanic American:	1%		

Transfer out. **Colleges most students transferred to 2008:** Francis Marion University, Coker College, Limestone College, University of South Carolina, Coastal Carolina University.

Basis for selection. Open admission. Academically weak students must enroll in Applied Studies Program.

High school preparation. 25 units recommended. Recommended units include English 4, mathematics 4, social studies 3, history 1, science 3, foreign language 1 and academic electives 7. Recommend one unit physical education/JROTC. 1 unit computer technology, 6 or more units in occupational area will substitute for one science.

2008-2009 Annual costs. Tuition/fees: $2,942; $3,062 out-of-district; $5,642 out-of-state. Books/supplies: $1,000. Personal expenses: $3,780.

Financial aid. **Need-based:** Need-based aid available for part-time students. Work-study available nights, weekends and for part-time students. **Non-need-based:** Scholarships awarded for academics, leadership, minority status, state residency. **Additional information:** Tuition waivers for children of war veterans.

Application procedures. **Admission:** No deadline. $10 fee, may be waived for applicants with need. Admission notification on a rolling basis. **Financial aid:** Priority date 4/15; no closing date. FAFSA required. Applicants notified on a rolling basis starting 7/1; must reply within 4 week(s) of notification.

Academics. **Special study options:** Distance learning, double major, dual enrollment of high school students, honors, independent study, internships, liberal arts/career combination, student-designed major. License preparation in nursing. **Credit/placement by examination:** CLEP, institutional tests. 18 credit hours maximum toward associate degree. **Support services:** Learning center, pre-admission summer program, remedial instruction, study skills assistance, tutoring.

Majors. **Business:** General, administrative services, information resources management, office management. **Computer sciences:** General. **Education:** Early childhood, teacher assistance. **Engineering:** Electrical. **Engineering technology:** Drafting. **Liberal arts:** Arts/sciences. **Mechanic/repair:** General, heating/ac/refrig. **Production:** Machine tool.

Computing on campus. 60 workstations in library, computer center. Online library, wireless network available.

Student life. **Freshman orientation:** Available. **Activities:** Student government.

Student services. Career counseling, services for economically disadvantaged, financial aid counseling, personal counseling, placement for graduates, veterans' counselor. **Physically disabled:** Services for hearing impaired. **Transfer:** Pre-admission transcript evaluation for new students. College fairs on campus for students transferring to 4-year colleges.

Contact. E-mail: wrighta@wiltech.edu
Phone: (843) 355-4162 Toll-free number: (800) 768-2021 ext. 4162
Fax: (843) 355-4289
Alexis Wright, Admissions Director, Williamsburg Technical College, 601 Martin Luther King Jr. Avenue, Kingstree, SC 29556-4197

York Technical College
Rock Hill, South Carolina
www.yorktech.com **CB code: 5989**

- Public 2-year community and technical college
- Commuter campus in large town

General. Founded in 1962. Regionally accredited. Member of Charlotte Area Consortium of Colleges and Universities. **Enrollment:** 4,248 degree-seeking undergraduates. **Degrees:** 360 associate awarded. **Location:** 70 miles from Columbia, 14 miles from Charlotte, North Carolina. **Calendar:** Semester, extensive summer session. **Full-time faculty:** 120 total. **Part-time faculty:** 147 total. **Special facilities:** Center for Manufacturing Productivity.

Student profile. Among degree-seeking undergraduates, 24% enrolled in a transfer program, 76% enrolled in a vocational program, 2,057 transferred in from other institutions. Of all enrolled students, 10% already have a bachelor's degree or higher.

Out-of-state:	5%	**25 or older:**	65%

Transfer out. Colleges most students transferred to 2008: Winthrop University, Clemson University, University of South Carolina.

Basis for selection. Open admission, but selective for some programs. Additional qualification criteria required for admission to limited enrollment Health Science programs. All students whose goal is a Health Science degree program are encouraged to prepare for college level coursework and take the SAT or ACT. COMPASS, SAT, or ACT scores may be used for placement. **Homeschooled:** Applicants must have graduated from approved South Carolina Homeschool Association or a homeschool recognized by the Department of Education in its home state. **Learning Disabled:** Students with disabilities who wish to receive special testing accommodations should contact Special Resources Office in Student Services.

High school preparation. College prep chemistry required for dental hygiene and nursing programs.

2008-2009 Annual costs. Tuition/fees: $3,244; $3,592 out-of-district; $7,288 out-of-state. Books/supplies: $900.

2007-2008 Financial aid. Need-based: Need-based aid available for part-time students. Work-study available nights and for part-time students. **Non-need-based:** Scholarships awarded for academics, leadership, state residency.

Application procedures. Admission: No deadline. No application fee. Application must be submitted online. Admission notification on a rolling basis. **Financial aid:** Priority date 6/1; no closing date. FAFSA required. Applicants notified on a rolling basis starting 3/1.

Academics. Special study options: Cooperative education, distance learning, dual enrollment of high school students, ESL, liberal arts/career combination. License preparation in dental hygiene, nursing, paramedic, radiology, real estate. **Credit/placement by examination:** AP, CLEP, institutional tests. At least 25% of semester credit hours required for program completion must be earned through instruction at York Technical College. **Support services:** Learning center, pre-admission summer program, reduced course load, remedial instruction, study skills assistance, tutoring, writing center.

Majors. Business: General, accounting, administrative services, business admin, human resources, logistics. **Computer sciences:** Applications programming, LAN/WAN management, programming. **Construction:** General. **Education:** Early childhood. **Engineering technology:** Computer, computer systems, drafting, electrical, heat/ac/refrig, mechanical, mechanical drafting. **Health:** Clinical lab technology, dental hygiene, medical radiologic technology/radiation therapy, nursing (RN), radiologic technology/medical imaging. **Legal studies:** Paralegal. **Liberal arts:** Arts/sciences. **Mechanic/repair:** General, automotive, electronics/electrical, heating/ac/refrig, industrial. **Production:** Machine tool, tool and die, welding. **Protective services:** Fire services admin, police science.

Most popular majors. Business/marketing 34%, engineering/engineering technologies 10%, family/consumer sciences 9%, health sciences 16%, liberal arts 15%.

Computing on campus. 180 workstations in library, computer center. Commuter students can connect to campus network. Online library, wireless network available.

Student life. Freshman orientation: Mandatory. Preregistration for classes offered. **Activities:** Student government, student newspaper, Jacobin Society, Phi Theta Kappa, Christian Fellowship, Students With Vision.

Student services. Career counseling, student employment services, financial aid counseling, on-campus daycare, personal counseling, placement for graduates, veterans' counselor, women's services. **Physically disabled:** Services for visually, hearing impaired. **Transfer:** Transfer adviser, college fairs on campus for students transferring to 4-year colleges.

Contact. E-mail: admissionsoffice@yorktech.com
Phone: (803) 327-8008 Toll-free number: (800) 922-8324
Fax: (803) 327-7237
Kenny Aldridge, Admissions Department Manager, York Technical College, 452 South Anderson Road, Rock Hill, SC 29730

South Dakota

Kilian Community College

Sioux Falls, South Dakota
www.kilian.edu **CB code: 6149**

- Private 2-year community college
- Commuter campus in small city

General. Founded in 1976. Regionally accredited. **Enrollment:** 286 degree-seeking undergraduates; 44 non-degree-seeking students. **Degrees:** 54 associate awarded. **Location:** 180 miles from Omaha, Nebraska, 240 miles from Minneapolis-St. Paul. **Calendar:** Trimester, limited summer session. **Full-time faculty:** 5 total; 20% have terminal degrees, 80% women. **Part-time faculty:** 28 total; 7% minority, 50% women. **Class size:** 88% < 20, 12% 20-39.

Student profile. Among degree-seeking undergraduates, 53% enrolled in a transfer program, 47% enrolled in a vocational program, 1% already have a bachelor's degree or higher, 41 enrolled as first-time, first-year students, 25 transferred in from other institutions.

Part-time:	83%	**Asian American:**	1%
Out-of-state:	16%	**Hispanic American:**	3%
Women:	74%	**Native American:**	8%
African American:	8%	**25 or older:**	55%

Transfer out. Colleges most students transferred to 2008: Presentation College, University of Sioux Falls, Colorado Technical University, University of South Dakota, South Dakota State University.

Basis for selection. Open admission. Non-native speaking applicants, must take a COMPASS ESL assessment and receive at least a level 3. Students graduating from non-US high schools must have a 12-year, translated high school diploma and a minimum score of 3 on the COMPASS ESL assessment. **Adult students:** SAT/ACT scores not required. **Learning Disabled:** Must provide documentation to the Director of the Student Success Center prior to enrolling in classes.

2008-2009 Annual costs. Tuition/fees: $8,469. Per-credit charge: $229. Books/supplies: $1,020. Personal expenses: $725.

2007-2008 Financial aid. Need-based: 17 full-time freshmen applied for aid; 17 were judged to have need; 17 of these received aid. Average loan was $1,166. 38% of total undergraduate aid awarded as scholarships/grants, 62% as loans/jobs. Need-based aid available for part-time students. Work-study available nights and for part-time students. **Non-need-based:** Awarded to 7 full-time undergraduates, including 5 freshmen. Scholarships awarded for academics, leadership, minority status.

Application procedures. Admission: No deadline. $25 fee. Admission notification on a rolling basis. **Financial aid:** No deadline. FAFSA, institutional form required. Applicants notified on a rolling basis starting 7/1; must reply within 2 week(s) of notification.

Academics. Special study options: Cross-registration, distance learning, double major, dual enrollment of high school students, ESL, internships. Bachelor's degree programs available on campus. **Credit/placement by examination:** AP, CLEP, institutional tests. 18 credit hours maximum toward associate degree. **Support services:** GED test center, learning center, remedial instruction, study skills assistance, tutoring, writing center.

Majors. Business: Accounting, business admin, executive assistant. **Computer sciences:** Information systems, LAN/WAN management, vendor certification. **Education:** General. **Health:** Medical secretary, substance abuse counseling. **History:** General. **Liberal arts:** Arts/sciences. **Protective services:** Law enforcement admin. **Psychology:** General. **Public administration:** Social work. **Social sciences:** Sociology.

Most popular majors. Business/marketing 16%, health sciences 25%, liberal arts 31%, public administration/social services 13%, security/protective services 7%.

Computing on campus. 48 workstations in computer center, student center. Online library available.

Student life. Freshman orientation: Available. 2-3 hour program held the week before classes begin. **Activities:** Student newspaper.

Student services. Adult student services, career counseling, financial aid counseling, personal counseling. **Transfer:** Pre-admission transcript evaluation for new students. Transfer adviser for students transferring to 4-year colleges.

Contact. E-mail: mklockman@kilian.edu
Phone: (605) 221-3100 Toll-free number: (800) 888-1147
Fax: (605) 336-2606
Mary Klockman, Director of Admissions, Kilian Community College, 300 East 6th Street, Sioux Falls, SD 57103-7020

Lake Area Technical Institute

Watertown, South Dakota
www.lakeareatech.edu **CB code: 0717**

- Public 2-year technical college
- Commuter campus in large town

General. Founded in 1965. Regionally accredited. **Enrollment:** 1,259 degree-seeking undergraduates. **Degrees:** 290 associate awarded. **Location:** 90 miles from Sioux Falls. **Calendar:** Semester, limited summer session. **Full-time faculty:** 85 total. **Part-time faculty:** 10 total.

Basis for selection. Open admission, but selective for some programs. Testing requirements vary by program. Interview required for medical laboratory technician, physical therapy assistant, practical nursing, occupational therapy assistant programs.

High school preparation. 3 units mathematics/science required. 1 Latin and typing recommended.

2008-2009 Annual costs. Approximate program costs $4,000 - $7,000 per year, depending on course of study; includes tuition, books and supplies. Books/supplies: $550. Personal expenses: $750.

Financial aid. All financial aid based on need. Need-based aid available for part-time students.

Application procedures. Admission: No deadline. $20 fee. Admission notification on a rolling basis. **Financial aid:** Priority date 4/15; no closing date. FAFSA required. Applicants notified on a rolling basis starting 5/1.

Academics. Special study options: Internships. **Credit/placement by examination:** CLEP, institutional tests. **Support services:** Learning center, pre-admission summer program, reduced course load, tutoring.

Majors. Agriculture: General, agribusiness operations. **Business:** Accounting, banking/financial services, business admin, finance. **Computer sciences:** General, data processing, programming. **Engineering:** Civil, mechanical. **Engineering technology:** Drafting. **Health:** Clinical lab technology, nursing (RN), occupational therapy assistant, physical therapy assistant. **Mechanic/repair:** General, aircraft, aircraft powerplant, automotive, diesel, electronics/electrical. **Production:** Tool and die, welding.

Computing on campus. 70 workstations in library, computer center.

Student life. Freshman orientation: Available. **Activities:** Student government, student newspaper.

Athletics. Intercollegiate: Rodeo. **Intramural:** Basketball, bowling, softball, volleyball.

Student services. Career counseling, student employment services, health services, on-campus daycare, personal counseling, placement for graduates, veterans' counselor. **Transfer:** Transfer adviser for students transferring to 4-year colleges.

Contact. Phone: (605) 882-5284 Toll-free number: (800) 657-4344
Fax: (605) 882-6299
Kim Bellum, Dean of Curriculum Coordinator, Lake Area Technical Institute, PO Box 730, Watertown, SD 57201

Mitchell Technical Institute

Mitchell, South Dakota
www.mitchelltech.com **CB code: 7038**

- Public 2-year culinary school and technical college
- Residential campus in large town

General. Founded in 1968. Regionally accredited. **Enrollment:** 633 degree-seeking undergraduates; 114 non-degree-seeking students. **Degrees:** 207 associate awarded. **Location:** 70 miles from Sioux Falls. **Calendar:** Semester, limited summer session. **Full-time faculty:** 47 total; 6% minority, 36%

women. **Part-time faculty:** 5 total; 20% women. **Class size:** 40% < 20, 60% 20-39. **Special facilities:** Satellite communications earth station, day care center, utilities field.

Student profile. Among degree-seeking undergraduates, 342 enrolled as first-time, first-year students, 28 transferred in from other institutions.

Part-time:	3%	**Women:**	32%
Out-of-state:	7%		

Basis for selection. Open admission, but selective for some programs. Admission decisions based on high school GPA and ACT score. TABE test used for placement. Interview recommended.

High school preparation. 16 units recommended. Recommended units include English 4, mathematics 2, social studies 2 and science 2.

2009-2010 Annual costs. Tuition/fees: $4,600. Books/supplies: $700. Personal expenses: $750.

2007-2008 Financial aid. Need-based: Need-based aid available for part-time students.

Application procedures. Admission: No deadline. $35 fee. Admission notification on a rolling basis. **Financial aid:** No deadline. FAFSA required. Applicants notified on a rolling basis; must reply within 3 week(s) of notification.

Academics. Special study options: Cooperative education, distance learning, dual enrollment of high school students, independent study, internships. License preparation in radiology. **Credit/placement by examination:** AP, CLEP, institutional tests. 12 credit hours maximum toward associate degree. **Support services:** Learning center, pre-admission summer program, reduced course load, remedial instruction, study skills assistance, tutoring.

Majors. Architecture: Technology. **Computer sciences:** General. **Health:** Clinical lab technology, medical radiologic technology/radiation therapy, medical transcription, office assistant. **Mechanic/repair:** Electronics/electrical, heating/ac/refrig.

Computing on campus. 80 workstations in library, computer center. Commuter students can connect to campus network. Repair service, wireless network available.

Student life. Freshman orientation: Mandatory. Preregistration for classes offered. **Activities:** Student government, student newspaper.

Athletics. Intercollegiate: Rodeo. **Intramural:** Basketball, bowling, volleyball. **Team name:** Mavericks.

Student services. Adult student services, career counseling, services for economically disadvantaged, student employment services, financial aid counseling, on-campus daycare, personal counseling, placement for graduates, veterans' counselor, women's services. **Physically disabled:** Services for visually, speech, hearing impaired. **Transfer:** Transfer adviser for students transferring to 4-year colleges.

Contact. E-mail: questions@mitchelltech.edu
Phone: (605) 995-3025 Toll-free number: (800) 684-1969
Fax: (605) 996-3299
Tim Edwards, Director of Student Services, Mitchell Technical Institute, 821 North Capital Street, Mitchell, SD 57301

Sisseton Wahpeton College
Sisseton, South Dakota
www.swc.tc **CB code: 3403**

- Public 2-year community and technical college
- Commuter campus in rural community

General. Founded in 1979. Regionally accredited. Member of American Indian Higher Education Consortium. Dakota language and culture resource. **Enrollment:** 225 degree-seeking undergraduates; 2 non-degree-seeking students. **Degrees:** 21 associate awarded. **Location:** 48 miles from Watertown, 85 miles from Fargo, North Dakota. **Calendar:** Semester, limited summer session. **Full-time faculty:** 26 total; 27% minority, 58% women. **Part-time faculty:** 7 total; 57% minority, 43% women. **Special facilities:** Indians in North America book collection, Song to the Great Spirit building, institute for excellence in Dakota language.

Student profile. Among degree-seeking undergraduates, 29% enrolled in a vocational program, 56 enrolled as first-time, first-year students.

Part-time:	23%	**Women:**	74%
Out-of-state:	5%		

Transfer out. Colleges most students transferred to 2008: University of Minnesota, North Dakota State University, University of North Dakota, South Dakota State University, University of South Dakota.

Basis for selection. Open admission. If student is member of recognized Native American tribe, must submit certification of tribal membership. **Adult students:** COMPASS test is given to all new/returning students. **Homeschooled:** State high school equivalency certificate required.

High school preparation. 16 units recommended. Recommended units include English 4, mathematics 4 and science 8.

2008-2009 Annual costs. Tuition/fees: $3,790. Per-credit charge: $110. Books/supplies: $440. Personal expenses: $1,680.

Application procedures. Admission: Closing date 7/1. No application fee. Admission notification on a rolling basis beginning on or about 7/1. **Financial aid:** No deadline. FAFSA required. Applicants notified on a rolling basis.

Academics. Special study options: Distance learning, double major, dual enrollment of high school students, independent study, internships, liberal arts/career combination. Bachelor's degree programs available on campus. **Credit/placement by examination:** CLEP, institutional tests. **Support services:** GED preparation and test center, learning center, remedial instruction, tutoring.

Majors. Area/ethnic studies: Native American. **Business:** Accounting, business admin, hospitality admin. **Computer sciences:** General. **Construction:** Carpentry. **Education:** Early childhood. **Family/consumer sciences:** Food/nutrition. **Health:** Nursing (RN), substance abuse counseling. **Interdisciplinary:** Natural sciences. **Liberal arts:** Arts/sciences. **Physical sciences:** Planetary.

Most popular majors. Area/ethnic studies 14%, business/marketing 19%, computer/information sciences 14%, education 10%, health sciences 24%, liberal arts 14%.

Computing on campus. 136 workstations in library, computer center, student center. Wireless network available.

Student life. Freshman orientation: Mandatory. Preregistration for classes offered. 2-day program. **Activities:** Student government.

Student services. Career counseling, personal counseling. **Transfer:** Transfer adviser for students transferring to 4-year colleges.

Contact. E-mail: dredday@swc.tc
Phone: (605) 698-3966 Fax: (605) 698-3132
Darlene Redday, Admissions Officer/Registrar, Sisseton Wahpeton College, BIA 700, Box 689, Agency Village, SD 57262-0689

Southeast Technical Institute
Sioux Falls, South Dakota
www.southeasttech.edu **CB code: 7054**

- Public 2-year technical college
- Commuter campus in small city

General. Founded in 1969. Regionally accredited. **Enrollment:** 2,093 degree-seeking undergraduates; 45 non-degree-seeking students. **Degrees:** 534 associate awarded. **Location:** 220 miles from Minneapolis-St. Paul, 200 miles from Omaha, Nebraska. **Calendar:** Semester, limited summer session. **Full-time faculty:** 83 total; 2% have terminal degrees. **Part-time faculty:** 44 total; 9% have terminal degrees.

Student profile. Among degree-seeking undergraduates, 100% enrolled in a vocational program, 5% already have a bachelor's degree or higher, 633 enrolled as first-time, first-year students, 317 transferred in from other institutions.

Part-time:	21%	**Hispanic American:**	1%
Out-of-state:	9%	**Native American:**	2%
Women:	44%	**25 or older:**	16%
African American:	2%	**Live on campus:**	1%
Asian American:	1%		

Transfer out. **Colleges most students transferred to 2008:** University of Sioux Falls, Bellevue University, Colorado Technical University.

Basis for selection. Open admission, but selective for some programs. Additional testing and background checks required for all health and criminal justice programs. ACT recommended for those programs that are not open admissions. **Homeschooled:** Statement describing homeschool structure and mission, transcript of courses and grades, interview required. ACT and institutional entrance exam required.

High school preparation. 18 units recommended. Recommended units include English 4, mathematics 2, social studies 2, science 2 and academic electives 8.

2008-2009 Annual costs. Tuition/fees: $3,817. Per-credit charge: $78. $450 per semester laptop fee required for some students. Students able to keep laptop after paying for 4 semesters of the lease. Books/supplies: $900. Personal expenses: $1,350.

Financial aid. All financial aid based on need. Need-based aid available for part-time students.

Application procedures. **Admission:** No deadline. No application fee. Admission notification on a rolling basis. Must reply by May 1 or within 4 week(s) if notified thereafter. **Financial aid:** Priority date 5/1; no closing date. FAFSA required. Applicants notified on a rolling basis starting 5/1; must reply within 3 week(s) of notification.

Academics. **Special study options:** Accelerated study, double major. Bachelor's degree programs available on campus. License preparation in nursing, real estate. **Credit/placement by examination:** AP, CLEP, IB, institutional tests. 30 credit hours maximum toward associate degree. **Support services:** GED preparation and test center, learning center, reduced course load, remedial instruction, study skills assistance, tutoring.

Majors. **Agriculture:** Greenhouse operations, horticulture, landscaping, nursery operations, turf management. **Biology:** Biomedical sciences. **Business:** Accounting, banking/financial services, business admin, marketing. **Communications:** Advertising. **Communications technology:** Animation/special effects, graphic/printing. **Computer sciences:** General, applications programming, LAN/WAN management, networking, programming. **Construction:** Site management. **Engineering technology:** Architectural, biomedical, civil, computer hardware, construction, drafting, electrical, heat/ac/refrig, mechanical, mechanical drafting, surveying. **Health:** Cardiovascular technology, electroencephalograph technology, nuclear medical technology, sonography. **Mechanic/repair:** General, auto body, automotive, diesel, electronics/electrical, heating/ac/refrig. **Production:** Machine shop technology, machine tool. **Protective services:** Law enforcement admin. **Visual/performing arts:** Commercial/advertising art.

Most popular majors. Business/marketing 40%, health sciences 25%, trade and industry 23%.

Computing on campus. PC or laptop required. 88 workstations in library, computer center. Commuter students can connect to campus network. Online course registration, online library, helpline, repair service, student web hosting, wireless network available.

Student life. **Freshman orientation:** Available. Preregistration for classes offered. **Housing:** Apartments available. $100 fully refundable deposit, deadline 7/1. **Activities:** Student government.

Athletics. **Intramural:** Basketball, bowling, football (non-tackle), volleyball.

Student services. Career counseling, student employment services, financial aid counseling, on-campus daycare, personal counseling, placement for graduates. **Physically disabled:** Services for visually, speech, hearing impaired. **Transfer:** Pre-admission transcript evaluation for new students. College fairs on campus for students transferring to 4-year colleges.

Contact. E-mail: jim.rokusek@southeasttech.edu
Phone: (605) 367-7624 Toll-free number: (800) 247-0789
Fax: (605) 367-4372
Jim Rokusek, Director of Student Services, Southeast Technical Institute, 2320 North Career Avenue, Sioux Falls, SD 57107

Western Dakota Technical Institute

Rapid City, South Dakota
www.wdt.edu **CB code: 6393**

- Public 2-year technical college
- Commuter campus in small city

General. Founded in 1978. Regionally accredited. **Enrollment:** 924 degree-seeking undergraduates. **Degrees:** 161 associate awarded. **Location:** 3 miles from downtown. **Calendar:** Semester, limited summer session. **Full-time faculty:** 60 total. **Part-time faculty:** 20 total. **Special facilities:** 500-acre operating ranch for agricultural production students.

Student profile.

Out-of-state:	8%	**25 or older:**	41%

Transfer out. **Colleges most students transferred to 2008:** Black Hills State University.

Basis for selection. Open admission, but selective for some programs. Special requirements for nursing, law enforcement, surgical technology, phlebotomy and paralegal programs. Applicants may be placed on waiting lists for programs reaching capacity. Institution requires Test of Adult Basic Education or equivalent unless other recent test results indicate ability to benefit from instruction. Interview, recommendations required for law enforcement, practical nursing, surgical technology and phlebotomy programs.

High school preparation. Recommended units include English 4 and mathematics 2.

2008-2009 Annual costs. Tuition/fees: $3,885. Per-credit charge: $78. Total program cost ranges from $4,850- $13,150 depending on course of study. Books/supplies: $816. Personal expenses: $1,353.

Financial aid. **Need-based:** Need-based aid available for part-time students. Work-study available nights, weekends and for part-time students.

Application procedures. **Admission:** Closing date 8/1 (postmark date). $20 fee. Admission notification on a rolling basis. **Financial aid:** Priority date 4/20; no closing date. FAFSA required. Applicants notified on a rolling basis starting 6/30; must reply within 2 week(s) of notification.

Academics. **Special study options:** Distance learning, dual enrollment of high school students, internships. License preparation in nursing. **Credit/placement by examination:** CLEP, institutional tests. 35 credit hours maximum toward associate degree. **Support services:** Learning center, pre-admission summer program, reduced course load, remedial instruction, study skills assistance, tutoring.

Majors. **Agriculture:** General, agribusiness operations, business, farm/ranch. **Business:** Accounting, marketing. **Construction:** Electrician, power transmission. **Engineering:** Geotechnical. **Engineering technology:** Architectural drafting, electromechanical. **Health:** Medical transcription. **Legal studies:** Paralegal. **Mechanic/repair:** Automotive, electronics/electrical, industrial. **Protective services:** Police science.

Computing on campus. 210 workstations in library, computer center. Commuter students can connect to campus network. Online course registration, helpline, repair service, wireless network available.

Student life. **Freshman orientation:** Mandatory. Preregistration for classes offered. 1-day session held prior to start of classes. **Policies:** Regular attendance required. Must make commitment to attend classes/labs 5 days a week from 8AM to 3PM. **Activities:** Student government, student newspaper, minority club, single-parent club.

Student services. Adult student services, alcohol/substance abuse counseling, career counseling, services for economically disadvantaged, student employment services, financial aid counseling, minority student services, on-campus daycare, personal counseling, placement for graduates, veterans' counselor, women's services. **Physically disabled:** Services for visually, speech, hearing impaired. **Transfer:** Pre-admission transcript evaluation for new students. Transfer adviser for students transferring to 4-year colleges.

Contact. E-mail: admissions@wdt.edu
Phone: (605) 718-2411 Toll-free number: (800) 544-8765
Fax: (605) 394-2204
Jill Elder, Admissions Coordinator, Western Dakota Technical Institute, 800 Mickelson Drive, Rapid City, SD 57703

Tennessee

Chattanooga State Technical Community College
Chattanooga, Tennessee
www.chattanoogastate.edu **CB code: 1084**

- Public 2-year community and technical college
- Commuter campus in small city

General. Founded in 1963. Regionally accredited. Credit-bearing courses offered at various off-campus locations. **Enrollment:** 6,759 degree-seeking undergraduates. **Degrees:** 652 associate awarded. **Location:** 129 miles from Nashville. **Calendar:** Semester, limited summer session. **Full-time faculty:** 210 total; 9% minority, 57% women. **Part-time faculty:** 408 total.

Student profile. Among degree-seeking undergraduates, 32% enrolled in a transfer program.

Transfer out. Colleges most students transferred to 2008: Austin Peay State University, East Tennessee State University, Middle Tennessee State University, Tennessee Tech University, University of Tennessee at Chattanooga.

Basis for selection. Open admission, but selective for some programs. Special requirements for allied health program. National standardized dental assisting and dental hygiene tests required of applicants to these programs. Interview required for allied health, nursing programs. **Adult students:** SAT/ACT scores not required if applicant over 21. Placement Test. **Homeschooled:** Transcript of courses and grades required. Students are required to register with their local department/board of education or present affiliation with accredited home school agency.

High school preparation. 19 units recommended. Recommended units include English 4, mathematics 3, social studies 1, history 1, science 2 (laboratory 1), foreign language 2 and visual/performing arts 1. College preparatory program required for students choosing transfer majors.

2008-2009 Annual costs. Tuition/fees: $2,797; $10,297 out-of-state. Per-credit charge: $107 in-state; $431 out-of-state.

2008-2009 Financial aid. Need-based: Need-based aid available for part-time students. Work-study available nights, weekends and for part-time students. **Non-need-based:** Scholarships awarded for state residency.

Application procedures. Admission: Priority date 8/15; no deadline. $15 fee. Admission notification on a rolling basis. **Financial aid:** Priority date 4/1; no closing date. FAFSA required. Applicants notified on a rolling basis starting 4/1; must reply within 2 week(s) of notification.

Academics. Special study options: Accelerated study, cooperative education, cross-registration, distance learning, double major, dual enrollment of high school students, honors, independent study, internships, student-designed major, weekend college. Bachelor's degree programs available on campus. License preparation in dental hygiene, nursing, paramedic, radiology, real estate. **Credit/placement by examination:** AP, CLEP, IB, institutional tests. Final 20 hours must be taken in residency; maximun of 40 hours may be awarded by combination of credit by exam and credit for experience. **Support services:** GED preparation and test center, learning center, pre-admission summer program, reduced course load, remedial instruction, study skills assistance, tutoring, writing center.

Honors college/program. ACT Composite score 25 or higher; SAT score 1130-1160; HS GPA of 3.5 or higher; College GPA of 3.5 or higher based on min. of 12 hours of college-level courses. Designated Honors courses restricted to eligible students.

Majors. Business: Accounting, management science, office/clerical. **Communications:** Advertising. **Computer sciences:** Information systems, programming. **Education:** Early childhood. **Engineering:** Civil, mechanical. **Health:** Dental hygiene, medical radiologic technology/radiation therapy, medical records admin, physical therapy assistant, respiratory therapy technology. **Legal studies:** Court reporting, paralegal. **Liberal arts:** Arts/sciences. **Visual/performing arts:** Commercial/advertising art.

Computing on campus. 1,200 workstations in library, computer center, student center. Commuter students can connect to campus network. Online course registration, online library, helpline, wireless network available.

Student life. Freshman orientation: Mandatory, $10 fee. Preregistration for classes offered. 5-hour sessions begin in July and end in August for the fall term. **Activities:** Jazz band, choral groups, drama, music ensembles, radio station, student government, student newspaper, TV station, Baptist student union.

Athletics. NJCAA. **Intercollegiate:** Baseball M, basketball. **Intramural:** Racquetball, soccer, softball, table tennis, tennis. **Team name:** Tigers.

Student services. Adult student services, alcohol/substance abuse counseling, career counseling, services for economically disadvantaged, student employment services, financial aid counseling, minority student services, on-campus daycare, personal counseling, placement for graduates, veterans' counselor. **Physically disabled:** Services for visually, speech, hearing impaired. **Learning disabled:** Comprehensive services available. **Transfer:** Transfer adviser, college fairs on campus for students transferring to 4-year colleges.

Contact. E-mail: admissions@chattanoogastate.edu
Phone: (423) 697-4401 Fax: (423) 697-4709
Diane Norris, Director, Chattanooga State Technical Community College, 4501 Amnicola Highway, Chattanooga, TN 37406

Cleveland State Community College
Cleveland, Tennessee
www.clevelandstatecc.edu **CB code: 2848**

- Public 2-year community college
- Commuter campus in small city

General. Founded in 1967. Regionally accredited. **Enrollment:** 2,273 degree-seeking undergraduates; 1,062 non-degree-seeking students. **Degrees:** 277 associate awarded. **Location:** 30 miles from Chattanooga, 80 miles from Knoxville. **Calendar:** Semester, limited summer session. **Full-time faculty:** 69 total; 14% have terminal degrees, 9% minority, 54% women. **Part-time faculty:** 108 total; 15% have terminal degrees, 6% minority, 56% women. **Class size:** 48% < 20, 43% 20-39, less than 1% 40-49, 5% 50-99, 2% >100. **Special facilities:** Observatory.

Student profile. Among degree-seeking undergraduates, 39% enrolled in a transfer program, 34% enrolled in a vocational program, 639 enrolled as first-time, first-year students, 202 transferred in from other institutions.

Part-time:	39%	**Women:**	62%
Out-of-state:	1%	**25 or older:**	39%

Transfer out. Colleges most students transferred to 2008: University of Tennessee-Chattanooga, University of Tennessee-Knoxville, Tennessee Technological University, Lee University.

Basis for selection. Open admission, but selective for some programs. Program admission required for nursing and medical office assistant. **Adult students:** SAT/ACT scores not required if applicant over 21. California Critical Thinking and Skills Test (CCTST), COMPASS testing for degree-seeking students 21 and over who do not have current ACT/SAT scores (scores less than 3 years old) for placement in Developmental Studies. **Homeschooled:** Transcript of courses and grades required.

High school preparation. 14 units required. Required units include English 4, mathematics 3, social studies 1, history 1, science 2 (laboratory 1), foreign language 2 and visual/performing arts 1. College-preparatory program required for transfer programs: 14 total academic units, 4 English, 2 foreign language, 3 mathematics, 1 social science, 2 science, 1 US history, 1 visual or performing arts. Same units recommended for career/technical programs.

2008-2009 Annual costs. Tuition/fees: $2,769; $10,269 out-of-state. Per-credit charge: $107 in-state; $431 out-of-state. Books/supplies: $1,000. Personal expenses: $900.

2007-2008 Financial aid. Need-based: 448 full-time freshmen applied for aid; 280 were judged to have need; 269 of these received aid. Average need met was 77%. Average scholarship/grant was $4,247; average loan $2,679. 71% of total undergraduate aid awarded as scholarships/grants, 29% as loans/jobs. Need-based aid available for part-time students. **Non-need-based:** Awarded to 405 full-time undergraduates, including 242 freshmen. Scholarships awarded for athletics, minority status.

Application procedures. Admission: No deadline. $10 fee. Admission notification on a rolling basis. **Financial aid:** Priority date 6/15; no closing date. FAFSA, institutional form required. Applicants notified on a rolling basis starting 7/1; must reply within 2 week(s) of notification.

Academics. Special study options: Cooperative education, cross-registration, distance learning, double major, dual enrollment of high school

students, honors, independent study, internships, study abroad. License preparation in nursing. **Credit/placement by examination:** AP, CLEP, institutional tests. 15 credit hours maximum toward associate degree. Students scoring above 32 on the English portion of the enhanced ACT receive 6 credits of English composition. AP credit awarded is determined on an individual basis by the relevant department for grades of 3 or higher. **Support services:** GED test center, learning center, reduced course load, remedial instruction, study skills assistance, tutoring.

Majors. **Business:** Administrative services, business admin. **Education:** General. **Engineering technology:** Industrial. **Family/consumer sciences:** Child development. **Health:** Nursing (RN). **Liberal arts:** Arts/sciences. **Public administration:** General. **Other:** General Technology.

Most popular majors. Business/marketing 19%, health sciences 22%, liberal arts 41%.

Computing on campus. 650 workstations in library, computer center, student center. Commuter students can connect to campus network. Online course registration, online library, helpline, wireless network available.

Student life. **Freshman orientation:** Available. Preregistration for classes offered. Half-day program includes campus tour, career and academic counseling, placement assessment, and registration. **Activities:** Campus ministries, choral groups, literary magazine, student government, student newspaper, Baptist Student Union, Circle-K, Phi Theta Kappa, Professional Secretaries International, Adult Student League.

Athletics. NJCAA. **Intercollegiate:** Baseball M, basketball, cheerleading, softball W. **Intramural:** Badminton, golf, table tennis, tennis, volleyball. **Team name:** Cougars.

Student services. Adult student services, career counseling, student employment services, financial aid counseling, minority student services, personal counseling, placement for graduates, veterans' counselor. **Physically disabled:** Services for visually, speech, hearing impaired. **Transfer:** Reentry adviser, pre-admission transcript evaluation for new students. Transfer adviser, college fairs on campus for students transferring to 4-year colleges.

Contact. E-mail: mburnette@clevelandstatecc.edu
Phone: (423) 478-6212 Toll-free number: (800) 604-2722
Fax: (423) 478-6255
Midge Burnette, Director of Admissions and Records, Cleveland State Community College, 3535 Adkisson Drive, Cleveland, TN 37320-3570

Columbia State Community College
Columbia, Tennessee
www.columbiastate.edu **CB code: 1081**

- Public 2-year community college
- Commuter campus in large town

General. Founded in 1966. Regionally accredited. **Enrollment:** 4,828 degree-seeking undergraduates. **Degrees:** 472 associate awarded. **Location:** 40 miles from Nashville. **Calendar:** Semester, limited summer session. **Full-time faculty:** 106 total. **Part-time faculty:** 140 total. **Class size:** 34% < 20, 21% 20-39, 9% 40-49, 16% 50-99, 20% >100.

Basis for selection. Open admission, but selective for some programs. Special requirements for allied health sciences.

High school preparation. Recommended units include English 4, mathematics 3, social studies 1, history 1, science 2 (laboratory 1) and foreign language 2. One visual and performing arts recommended.

2008-2009 Annual costs. Tuition/fees: $2,747; $10,247 out-of-state. Per-credit charge: $107 in-state; $431 out-of-state. Personal expenses: $625.

Financial aid. **Need-based:** Need-based aid available for part-time students. **Non-need-based:** Scholarships awarded for academics, athletics, state residency.

Application procedures. **Admission:** Closing date 8/22. $10 fee. Admission notification on a rolling basis. **Financial aid:** Closing date 3/15. FAFSA, institutional form required. Applicants notified on a rolling basis starting 5/15; must reply within 2 week(s) of notification.

Academics. **Special study options:** Cooperative education, distance learning, dual enrollment of high school students. **Credit/placement by examination:** AP, CLEP. 30 credit hours maximum toward associate degree. **Support services:** Learning center, remedial instruction, study skills assistance, tutoring.

Majors. **Agriculture:** Business. **Biology:** General. **Business:** General, accounting, administrative services. **Communications:** Journalism. **Computer sciences:** General. **Education:** Early childhood, elementary. **Engineering:** General. **Engineering technology:** Electrical. **Health:** Clinical lab technology, dental hygiene, medical radiologic technology/radiation therapy, predental, premedicine, prepharmacy, respiratory therapy technology, veterinary technology/assistant. **History:** General. **Legal studies:** Prelaw. **Liberal arts:** Arts/sciences. **Math:** General. **Parks/recreation:** Health/fitness. **Physical sciences:** Chemistry, physics. **Psychology:** General. **Social sciences:** Economics, geography, sociology. **Visual/performing arts:** Art.

Most popular majors. Business/marketing 6%, health sciences 29%, liberal arts 58%.

Computing on campus. 60 workstations in library, computer center.

Student life. **Activities:** Choral groups, drama, student government, Baptist Student Union, Students in Free Enterprise, Circle K Club, Collegiate Secretaries International, computer club, Geste, Gamma Beta Phi, returning adults organization.

Athletics. NJCAA. **Intercollegiate:** Baseball M, basketball, softball W. **Intramural:** Basketball, softball M, table tennis, volleyball. **Team name:** Chargers, Lady Chargers.

Student services. Career counseling, health services, personal counseling, placement for graduates, veterans' counselor. **Physically disabled:** Services for visually, hearing impaired. **Transfer:** College fairs on campus for students transferring to 4-year colleges.

Contact. E-mail: scruggs@columbiastate.edu
Phone: (931) 540-2545 Fax: (931) 540-2535
Pauletta Burns, Director of Admissions/Registrar, Columbia State Community College, 1665 Hampshire Pike, Columbia, TN 38401

Draughons Junior College: Clarksville
Clarksville, Tennessee
www.draughons.edu **CB code: 3225**

- For-profit 2-year business and career college
- Small city

General. Accredited by ACICS. **Calendar:** Continuous.

Annual costs/financial aid. Tuition/fees (2008-2009): $12,150. Books/supplies: $2,250.

Contact. Phone: (931) 552-7600
Campus Director, 1860 Wilma Rudolph Boulevard, Clarksville, TN 37040

Draughons Junior College: Murfreesboro
Murfreesboro, Tennessee
www.draughons.edu

- For-profit 2-year junior college
- Commuter campus in very large city

General. Accredited by ACICS. **Location:** 25 miles from Nashville. **Calendar:** Quarter.

Annual costs/financial aid. Tuition/fees (2008-2009): $12,150. Books/supplies: $2,250.

Contact. Phone: (615) 217-9347
Director of Admissions, 415 Golden Bear Court, Murfreesboro, TN 37128

Draughons Junior College: Nashville
Nashville, Tennessee
www.draughons.edu **CB code: 7325**

- For-profit 2-year junior and career college
- Commuter campus in very large city

General. Founded in 1884. Accredited by ACICS. **Location:** 2 miles from downtown. **Calendar:** Quarter.

Annual costs/financial aid. Tuition/fees (2008-2009): $12,150. Books/supplies: $2,250. Need-based financial aid available to full-time and part-time students.

Contact. Phone: (615) 361-7555
Director of Admissions, 340 Plus Park at Pavilion Boulevard, Nashville, TN 37217

Dyersburg State Community College
Dyersburg, Tennessee
www.dscc.edu **CB code: 7323**

- Public 2-year community college
- Commuter campus in large town

General. Founded in 1967. Regionally accredited. **Enrollment:** 2,170 degree-seeking undergraduates; 579 non-degree-seeking students. **Degrees:** 183 associate awarded. **Location:** 78 miles from Memphis. **Calendar:** Semester, limited summer session. **Full-time faculty:** 52 total; 27% have terminal degrees, 14% minority, 62% women. **Part-time faculty:** 120 total. **Class size:** 46% < 20, 52% 20-39, 1% 40-49, less than 1% 50-99.

Student profile. Among degree-seeking undergraduates, 41% enrolled in a transfer program, 634 enrolled as first-time, first-year students.

Part-time:	41%	**African American:**	21%
Out-of-state:	1%	**Hispanic American:**	1%
Women:	75%	**25 or older:**	39%

Transfer out. Colleges most students transferred to 2008: University of Tennessee-Martin, University of Memphis, Middle Tennessee State University.

Basis for selection. Open admission, but selective for some programs. Acceptance into nursing program is based on point system, taking into consideration National League of Nursing test score, GPA, science courses completed with grade of C or above, and required courses that have been successfully completed. High school students who meet specific admission requirements may enroll as first time freshmen. **Learning Disabled:** Students are encouraged to self-identify with the college's ADA coordinator.

High school preparation. 14 units recommended. Recommended units include English 4, mathematics 3, social studies 2, history 1, science 2 and foreign language 2.

2008-2009 Annual costs. Tuition/fees: $2,777; $10,277 out-of-state. Per-credit charge: $107 in-state; $431 out-of-state. Books/supplies: $1,000. Personal expenses: $990.

2007-2008 Financial aid. Need-based: Need-based aid available for part-time students. Work-study available nights and for part-time students. **Non-need-based:** Scholarships awarded for academics, alumni affiliation, athletics, job skills, leadership, minority status, music/drama, state residency.

Application procedures. Admission: Priority date 8/1; no deadline. $10 fee. Admission notification on a rolling basis. **Financial aid:** Priority date 3/1; no closing date. FAFSA required. Applicants notified on a rolling basis starting 3/1; must reply within 2 week(s) of notification.

Academics. Special study options: Cooperative education, distance learning, dual enrollment of high school students, honors, independent study, internships, liberal arts/career combination. **Credit/placement by examination:** AP, CLEP, institutional tests. 24 credit hours maximum toward associate degree. **Support services:** GED preparation and test center, learning center, reduced course load, remedial instruction, study skills assistance, tutoring.

Majors. Biology: General. **Business:** Business admin. **Computer sciences:** Information systems. **Education:** General. **Engineering technology:** Electrical. **Family/consumer sciences:** Child development. **Health:** Medical records technology, nursing (RN). **Liberal arts:** Arts/sciences. **Math:** General. **Protective services:** Police science. **Psychology:** General. **Social sciences:** General.

Most popular majors. Business/marketing 21%, education 21%, health sciences 39%.

Computing on campus. 542 workstations in library, computer center, student center. Commuter students can connect to campus network. Online course registration, online library, helpline, wireless network available.

Student life. Freshman orientation: Available. Preregistration for classes offered. Half-day programs with pre-registration. **Activities:** Campus ministries, choral groups, drama, music ensembles, student government, student newspaper, American Chemical Society Affiliates, business and office systems association, student nurses association, Minority Association for Successful Students, astronomy club, advanced technology association, music club, Phi Theta Kappa, psychology club.

Athletics. NJCAA. **Intercollegiate:** Baseball M, basketball, softball W. **Intramural:** Basketball, volleyball. **Team name:** Eagles.

Student services. Adult student services, alcohol/substance abuse counseling, career counseling, services for economically disadvantaged, student employment services, financial aid counseling, minority student services, personal counseling, placement for graduates, veterans' counselor, women's services. **Physically disabled:** Services for visually, speech, hearing impaired. **Transfer:** Pre-admission transcript evaluation for new students. Transfer adviser, college fairs on campus for students transferring to 4-year colleges.

Contact. E-mail: enroll@dscc.edu
Phone: (731) 286-3330 Fax: (731) 286-3325
J Gullett, Assistant Vice President for Academic Affairs, Dyersburg State Community College, 1510 Lake Road, Dyersburg, TN 38024

Electronic Computer Programming College
Chattanooga, Tennessee
www.ecpconline.com **CB code: 2267**

- For-profit 2-year technical college
- Large city

General. Accredited by ACCSCT. **Calendar:** Quarter.

Contact. Phone: (423) 624-0077
Director of Admissions, 3805 Brainerd Road, Chattanooga, TN 37411

Fountainhead College of Technology
Knoxville, Tennessee
www.fountainheadcollege.edu **CB code: 0446**

- For-profit 2-year technical and career college
- Commuter campus in small city
- Interview required

General. Founded in 1947. Accredited by ACCSCT. **Enrollment:** 119 degree-seeking undergraduates. **Degrees:** 79 bachelor's, 125 associate awarded. **Location:** 200 miles from Nashville, 200 miles from Atlanta. **Calendar:** Semester, extensive summer session. **Full-time faculty:** 30 total.

Transfer out. 37% of students enrolled in the transfer program go on to 4-year colleges.

Basis for selection. Open admission, but selective for some programs. Institutional aptitude test required. Test scores, interview important. Institutional aptitude test required for admissions.

2009-2010 Annual costs. Tuition/fees (projected): $14,800. Books/supplies: $1,300.

Financial aid. All financial aid based on need.

Application procedures. Admission: No deadline. $100 fee. Admission notification on a rolling basis. **Financial aid:** No deadline. FAFSA required. Applicants notified on a rolling basis.

Academics. Special study options: Bachelor's degree programs available on campus. **Credit/placement by examination:** CLEP, institutional tests. 27 credit hours maximum toward associate degree. **Support services:** Tutoring.

Majors. Engineering technology: Electrical. **Health:** Medical records admin.

Computing on campus. PC or laptop required. 200 workstations in computer center. Online library, wireless network available.

Student life. Freshman orientation: Mandatory. Preregistration for classes offered.

Student services. Career counseling, student employment services, financial aid counseling, personal counseling, placement for graduates.

Contact. E-mail: info@fountainheadcollege.com
Phone: (865) 688-9422 Toll-free number: (888) 218-7335
Fax: (865) 688-2419
Christopher Hill, Director of Administration, Fountainhead College of Technology, 3203 Tazewell Pike, Knoxville, TN 37918

High-Tech Institute
Nashville, Tennessee
www.hightechinstitute.edu

- For-profit 2-year technical and career college
- Very large city

General. Accredited by ACCSCT. **Calendar:** Continuous.

Contact. Phone: (615) 232-3700
Director of Admissions, 560 Royal Parkway, Nashville, TN 37214

Huntington College of Health Sciences
Knoxville, Tennessee
www.hchs.edu **CB code: 3945**

- For-profit 2-year health science college
- Small city

General. Accredited by DETC. **Enrollment:** 343 degree-seeking undergraduates; 84 non-degree-seeking students. **Degrees:** 7 associate awarded; master's offered. **Calendar:** Continuous, extensive summer session. **Part-time faculty:** 21 total.

Student profile. Among degree-seeking undergraduates, 170 enrolled as first-time, first-year students.

Basis for selection. Open admission, but selective for some programs. **Homeschooled:** Transcript of courses and grades required.

2008-2009 Annual costs. Tuition/fees: $5,150. Books/supplies: $1,350.

Application procedures. Admission: No deadline. No application fee. **Financial aid:** No deadline.

Academics. Special study options: Accelerated study, distance learning, external degree, internships. **Credit/placement by examination:** CLEP.

Majors. Health: Clinical nutrition.

Student life. Activities: Student newspaper.

Contact. E-mail: studentservices@hchs.edu
Phone: (865) 524-8079 Toll-free number: (800) 290-4226
Fax: (865) 524-8339
Cheryl Freeman, Registrar, Director of Student Services, Huntington College of Health Sciences, 1204D Kenesaw, Knoxville, TN 37919-7736

Jackson State Community College
Jackson, Tennessee
www.jscc.edu **CB code: 2266**

- Public 2-year community college
- Commuter campus in small city

General. Founded in 1965. Regionally accredited. **Enrollment:** 4,381 degree-seeking undergraduates. **Degrees:** 470 associate awarded. **ROTC:** Army. **Location:** 80 miles from Memphis, 130 miles from Nashville. **Calendar:** Semester, limited summer session. **Full-time faculty:** 110 total. **Part-time faculty:** 190 total. **Class size:** 36% < 20, 62% 20-39, 2% 40-49, less than 1% 50-99, less than 1% >100.

Student profile. Among degree-seeking undergraduates, 48% enrolled in a transfer program, 52% enrolled in a vocational program, 897 enrolled as first-time, first-year students.

Part-time:	51%	**Asian American:**	1%
Out-of-state:	1%	**Hispanic American:**	2%
Women:	67%	**25 or older:**	38%
African American:	17%		

Transfer out. Colleges most students transferred to 2008: Union University, University of Memphis, University of Tennessee at Martin, Middle Tennessee State University, Lambuth University.

Basis for selection. Open admission, but selective for some programs. Special requirements for nursing, medical laboratory technology, radiology, respiratory care, physical therapy assistant, and emergency medical technician programs. Interview required for allied health, nursing programs. **Adult students:** SAT/ACT scores not required if applicant over 21. Compass test if degree-seeking first-time adult students.

High school preparation. 14 units recommended. Recommended units include English 4, mathematics 3, social studies 1, history 1, science 2 (laboratory 1), foreign language 2 and visual/performing arts 1.

2008-2009 Annual costs. Tuition/fees: $2,759; $10,259 out-of-state. Per-credit charge: $107 in-state; $431 out-of-state. Books/supplies: $1,000. Personal expenses: $908.

2007-2008 Financial aid. Need-based: 683 full-time freshmen applied for aid; 542 were judged to have need; 523 of these received aid. Average need met was 82%. Average scholarship/grant was $3,438; average loan $3,150. 98% of total undergraduate aid awarded as scholarships/grants, 2% as loans/jobs. Need-based aid available for part-time students. Work-study available nights, weekends and for part-time students. **Non-need-based:** Awarded to 756 full-time undergraduates, including 405 freshmen. Scholarships awarded for academics, art, athletics, job skills, leadership, minority status, music/drama.

Application procedures. Admission: Priority date 7/1; no deadline. $10 fee. Admission notification on a rolling basis. **Financial aid:** Priority date 3/15; no closing date. FAFSA, institutional form required. Applicants notified on a rolling basis starting 6/1; must reply within 2 week(s) of notification.

Academics. Special study options: Distance learning, double major, dual enrollment of high school students, honors, internships, liberal arts/career combination, weekend college. Bachelor's degree programs available on campus. License preparation in nursing, paramedic, physical therapy, radiology, real estate. **Credit/placement by examination:** AP, CLEP, institutional tests. 21 credit hours maximum toward associate degree. Must complete additional 15 college credit hours before credit by examination is awarded. **Support services:** GED preparation and test center, learning center, reduced course load, remedial instruction, study skills assistance, tutoring, writing center.

Majors. Agriculture: Business. **Biology:** General. **Business:** Accounting, business admin. **Communications:** General. **Computer sciences:** General. **Education:** General, early childhood. **Engineering:** General. **Engineering technology:** Industrial. **Health:** Clinical lab technology, medical radiologic technology/radiation therapy, nursing (RN), physical therapy assistant, premedicine, prenursing, respiratory therapy technology. **History:** General. **Legal studies:** Prelaw. **Liberal arts:** Arts/sciences. **Math:** General. **Parks/recreation:** Health/fitness. **Philosophy/religion:** Philosophy. **Physical sciences:** General, chemistry. **Protective services:** Police science. **Psychology:** General. **Public administration:** General, social work. **Social sciences:** Political science, sociology. **Visual/performing arts:** Art, commercial/advertising art.

Most popular majors. Business/marketing 10%, health sciences 46%, liberal arts 36%.

Computing on campus. 871 workstations in library, student center. Commuter students can connect to campus network. Online course registration, online library, helpline, wireless network available.

Student life. Freshman orientation: Available. **Activities:** Choral groups, drama, music ensembles, student government.

Athletics. NJCAA. **Intercollegiate:** Baseball M, basketball, softball W. **Team name:** Generals.

Student services. Career counseling, student employment services, financial aid counseling, health services, personal counseling, placement for graduates, veterans' counselor. **Physically disabled:** Services for visually, speech, hearing impaired. **Transfer:** College fairs on campus for students transferring to 4-year colleges.

Contact. E-mail: awinchester@jscc.edu
Phone: (731) 425-8844 Fax: (731) 425-9559
Andrea Winchester, Interim Director of Admissions, Jackson State Community College, 2046 North Parkway, Jackson, TN 38301-3797

John A. Gupton College
Nashville, Tennessee
www.guptoncollege.com **CB code: 0539**

- Private 2-year school of mortuary science
- Commuter campus in large city

General. Founded in 1946. Regionally accredited. **Calendar:** Semester.

Annual costs/financial aid. Tuition/fees (2008-2009): $7,680. Room: $3,600. Books/supplies: $900. Need-based financial aid available to full-time and part-time students.

Contact. Phone: (615) 327-3927
Registrar, 1616 Church Street, Nashville, TN 37203-2920

Miller-Motte Technical College: Chattanooga
Chattanooga, Tennessee
www.miller-motte.com/chattanoogawelcome.html

- For-profit 2-year technical college
- Commuter campus in large city

General. Accredited by ACICS. **Calendar:** Quarter.

Contact. Phone: (423) 510-9675
Director of Admissions, 6020 Shallowford Road, Suite 100, Chattanooga, TN 37421

Miller-Motte Technical College: Clarksville
Clarksville, Tennessee
www.miller-motte.com **CB code: 3228**

- For-profit 2-year business and health science college
- Commuter campus in small city
- Interview required

General. Accredited by ACICS. **Enrollment:** 558 degree-seeking undergraduates. **Degrees:** 73 associate awarded. **Location:** 45 miles from Nashville. **Calendar:** Quarter, extensive summer session. **Full-time faculty:** 10 total. **Part-time faculty:** 46 total. **Special facilities:** Simulated operating rooms, medical laboratories, simulated doctor's exam room.

Student profile.

Out-of-state:	50%	**25 or older:**	60%

Transfer out. Colleges most students transferred to 2008: Austin Peay University, Hopkinsville Community College.

Basis for selection. Open admission, but selective for some programs. 2 years experience or 2-year/4-year degree and interview with department head required for entrance into network administration certificate program. **Learning Disabled:** Letter of request for any accommodation required.

2008-2009 Annual costs. Tuition/fees: $11,170. Per-credit charge: $231. Required fees vary by program. Books/supplies: $1,200. Personal expenses: $1,350.

Financial aid. All financial aid based on need. Need-based aid available for part-time students. Work-study available nights, weekends and for part-time students.

Application procedures. Admission: No deadline. No application fee. Application must be submitted on paper. Admission notification on a rolling basis. **Financial aid:** No deadline. FAFSA, institutional form required. Applicants notified on a rolling basis.

Academics. Special study options: Weekend college. **Credit/placement by examination:** CLEP, institutional tests. 40 credit hours maximum toward associate degree. No more than 50% of required credit hours in a major and/or entire program. **Support services:** Reduced course load, remedial instruction, study skills assistance, tutoring.

Majors. Business: Accounting, business admin. **Computer sciences:** General. **Health:** Massage therapy, medical assistant, phlebotomy, surgical technology. **Legal studies:** Paralegal.

Most popular majors. Business/marketing 7%, computer/information sciences 22%, engineering/engineering technologies 6%, health sciences 46%, legal studies 15%.

Computing on campus. 75 workstations in library, computer center. Online library available.

Student life. Freshman orientation: Mandatory. Preregistration for classes offered. **Activities:** Student government.

Student services. Adult student services, career counseling, student employment services, financial aid counseling, placement for graduates, veterans' counselor. **Transfer:** Re-entry adviser, pre-admission transcript evaluation for new students.

Contact. E-mail: gcastleberry@miller-motte.com
Phone: (931) 553-0071 Toll-free number: (800) 558-0071
Kayle Kilgore, Director of Admissions, Miller-Motte Technical College: Clarksville, 1820 Business Park Drive, Clarksville, TN 37040

Motlow State Community College
Lynchburg, Tennessee
www.mscc.cc.tn.us **CB code: 1543**

- Public 2-year community college
- Commuter campus in rural community

General. Founded in 1969. Regionally accredited. **Enrollment:** 3,741 degree-seeking undergraduates; 641 non-degree-seeking students. **Degrees:** 400 associate awarded. **Location:** 65 miles from Nashville. **Calendar:** Semester, limited summer session. **Full-time faculty:** 76 total; 67% women. **Part-time faculty:** 144 total. **Class size:** 38% < 20, 57% 20-39, 3% 40-49, 2% >100.

Student profile. Among degree-seeking undergraduates, 1,327 enrolled as first-time, first-year students, 4,386 transferred in from other institutions.

Part-time:	37%	**Women:**	62%
Out-of-state:	1%	**25 or older:**	29%

Transfer out. Colleges most students transferred to 2008: Middle Tennessee State University, Tennessee Technological University.

Basis for selection. Open admission, but selective for some programs. Students entering into the college's Nursing Program have different admissions criteria. Interview required for nursing program. **Adult students:** SAT/ACT scores not required if applicant over 21. **Homeschooled:** Transcript of courses and grades required.

High school preparation. 16 units recommended. Recommended units include English 4, mathematics 3, social studies 2, history 1, science 2 (laboratory 1) and foreign language 2.

2008-2009 Annual costs. Tuition/fees: $2,765; $10,265 out-of-state. Per-credit charge: $107 in-state; $431 out-of-state. Books/supplies: $1,200. Personal expenses: $1,000.

2007-2008 Financial aid. Need-based: Need-based aid available for part-time students. Work-study available for part-time students. **Non-need-based:** Scholarships awarded for academics, alumni affiliation, art, athletics, leadership, state residency.

Application procedures. Admission: $10 fee. Admission notification on a rolling basis. **Financial aid:** No deadline. FAFSA required. Applicants notified on a rolling basis starting 3/15.

Academics. Special study options: Accelerated study, cooperative education, distance learning, double major, dual enrollment of high school students, honors, independent study, internships, weekend college. License preparation in nursing. **Credit/placement by examination:** AP, CLEP, institutional tests. Maximum number of credits by examination that may be earned is limited to 25% of total number of credits needed for graduation. **Support services:** Learning center, reduced course load, remedial instruction, study skills assistance, tutoring, writing center.

Majors. Business: Business admin. **Education:** General, elementary, secondary. **Health:** Nursing (RN). **Liberal arts:** Arts/sciences.

Most popular majors. Business/marketing 6%, health sciences 13%, liberal arts 78%.

Computing on campus. 250 workstations in library, computer center. Commuter students can connect to campus network. Online course registration, online library, helpline, repair service, wireless network available.

Student life. Freshman orientation: Mandatory. Preregistration for classes offered. **Activities:** Choral groups, drama, literary magazine, music ensembles, student government, student newspaper, Baptist Student Union, African American Student Association, outing club, communications club, law and government club, literary club, Phi Theta Kappa, psychology club, Tennessee Association of Student Nurses.

Athletics. NJCAA. **Intercollegiate:** Baseball M, basketball, softball W. **Intramural:** Baseball M, basketball, bowling, softball. **Team name:** Bucks.

Student services. Adult student services, alcohol/substance abuse counseling, career counseling, student employment services, financial aid counseling, health services, personal counseling, placement for graduates, veterans' counselor. **Physically disabled:** Services for visually impaired. **Transfer:**

Pre-admission transcript evaluation for new students. College fairs on campus for students transferring to 4-year colleges.

Contact. E-mail: galsup@mscc.edu
Phone: (931) 393-1529 Toll-free number: (800) 654-4877
Fax: (931) 393-1971
Greer Alsup, Director of Admissions and Records, Motlow State Community College, Box 8500, Lynchburg, TN 37352-8500

Nashville Auto-Diesel College

Nashville, Tennessee
www.nadcedu.com **CB code: 3098**

- For-profit 1-year technical college
- Commuter campus in large city
- Interview required

General. Accredited by ACCSCT. **Enrollment:** 2,956 degree-seeking undergraduates. **Degrees:** 105 associate awarded. **Calendar:** Continuous, extensive summer session. **Full-time faculty:** 75 total. **Class size:** 100% 20-39.

Student profile.

Out-of-state:	90%	**Live on campus:**	30%
25 or older:	1%		

Basis for selection. Secondary school record, interview, test scores most important. State proficiency tests used in admission decisions.

2008-2009 Annual costs. Tuition/fees: $14,195. Full program costs range from $21,400 to $32,600 for diploma programs; $27,400 to $34,900 for associate programs. Room/board: $5,502. Books/supplies: $987.

Financial aid. All financial aid based on need. Work-study available nights and weekends.

Application procedures. Admission: No deadline. $100 fee. Admission notification on a rolling basis. **Financial aid:** No deadline. FAFSA required. Applicants notified on a rolling basis.

Academics. Credit/placement by examination: AP, CLEP, institutional tests. **Support services:** Study skills assistance, tutoring.

Majors. Mechanic/repair: General, auto body, automotive, diesel, heavy equipment.

Computing on campus. 46 workstations in library, computer center. Dormitories wired for high-speed internet access. Online library available.

Student life. Freshman orientation: Mandatory. **Housing:** Single-sex dorms available. $200 deposit.

Student services. Career counseling, student employment services, financial aid counseling, placement for graduates, veterans' counselor. **Physically disabled:** Services for visually impaired.

Contact. E-mail: admissions@nadcedu.com
Phone: (615) 226-3990 Toll-free number: (800) 228-6232
Fax: (615) 262-8466
Cary Oliver, Vice President, Nashville Auto-Diesel College, 1524 Gallatin Road, Nashville, TN 37206

Nashville State Community College

Nashville, Tennessee
www.nscc.edu **CB code: 0850**

- Public 2-year community and technical college
- Commuter campus in very large city

General. Founded in 1969. Regionally accredited. **Enrollment:** 7,716 degree-seeking undergraduates. **Degrees:** 506 associate awarded. **Location:** 6 miles from Nashville, 200 miles from Memphis. **Calendar:** Semester, limited summer session. **Full-time faculty:** 138 total. **Part-time faculty:** 275 total. **Special facilities:** Television production studio.

Student profile. Among degree-seeking undergraduates, 52% enrolled in a transfer program, 48% enrolled in a vocational program.

Out-of-state:	2%	**Hispanic American:**	2%
African American:	30%	**International:**	2%
Asian American:	3%	**25 or older:**	49%

Transfer out. Colleges most students transferred to 2008: Middle Tennessee University, Tennessee State University, Tennessee Technical University.

Basis for selection. Open admission, but selective for some programs. Selective admissions for some programs. Test scores used for placement. Interview required for automotive services technology, occupational therapy assistant, surgical technology programs. **Adult students:** Degree-seeking students over 21 with no previous college-level English and / or Math are required to take the COMPASS placement exam. **Homeschooled:** Transcript of courses and grades required. Transcript of home schooled student should be official copy from organization as defined by state law (T.C.A. 49-50-801) and must have certification of registration with superintendent of local education agency where student would have attended.

High school preparation. Recommended units include English 4, mathematics 3, social studies 2, history 2, science 2 (laboratory 1), foreign language 2 and visual/performing arts 1. One visual/performing art recommended. Business technologies majors: 1 unit bookkeeping or accounting recommended. Engineering technologies majors: additional math and science recommended.

2008-2009 Annual costs. Tuition/fees: $2,731; $10,231 out-of-state. Per-credit charge: $107 in-state; $431 out-of-state. Books/supplies: $1,000. Personal expenses: $544.

2008-2009 Financial aid. Need-based: Need-based aid available for part-time students. Work-study available nights, weekends and for part-time students. **Non-need-based:** Scholarships awarded for academics, minority status.

Application procedures. Admission: No deadline. $5 fee. Automotive services technology applicants must have automobile dealer sponsorship prior to acceptance. **Financial aid:** Priority date 3/1; no closing date. FAFSA, institutional form required. Applicants notified on a rolling basis starting 6/1; must reply within 2 week(s) of notification.

Academics. Special study options: Cooperative education, distance learning, double major, dual enrollment of high school students, ESL, honors, internships, student-designed major, study abroad. **Credit/placement by examination:** AP, CLEP, institutional tests. 20 credit hours maximum toward associate degree. **Support services:** GED preparation, learning center, reduced course load, remedial instruction, study skills assistance, tutoring, writing center.

Majors. Business: Accounting, business admin. **Communications technology:** General. **Computer sciences:** General. **Education:** Early childhood. **Engineering technology:** Architectural, civil, construction, electrical. **Foreign languages:** Sign language interpretation. **Health:** Medical secretary. **Legal studies:** Legal secretary. **Mechanic/repair:** Automotive. **Personal/culinary services:** Culinary arts. **Protective services:** Police science. **Visual/performing arts:** Commercial/advertising art, photography.

Computing on campus. 518 workstations in library, computer center. Commuter students can connect to campus network. Online course registration, online library, helpline, wireless network available.

Student life. Freshman orientation: Available. **Activities:** International student organizations, literary magazine, student government, student newspaper, Black student organization.

Student services. Adult student services, career counseling, student employment services, personal counseling, placement for graduates, veterans' counselor. **Physically disabled:** Services for visually, hearing impaired. **Transfer:** Pre-admission transcript evaluation for new students. College fairs on campus for students transferring to 4-year colleges.

Contact. Phone: (615) 353-3215 Toll-free number: (800) 272-7363
Fax: (615) 353-3243
Laura Potter, Director of Admissions, Nashville State Community College, 120 White Bridge Road, Nashville, TN 37209-4515

National College: Bartlett

Bartlett, Tennessee

- For-profit 2-year branch campus college
- Large town

General. Regionally accredited; also accredited by ACICS. **Enrollment:** 243 degree-seeking undergraduates. **Calendar:** Quarter. **Full-time faculty:** 2 total. **Part-time faculty:** 36 total.

2008-2009 Annual costs. Tuition/fees: $9,585. Per-credit charge: $212.

Application procedures. Admission: No deadline. $30 fee.

Academics. Credit/placement by examination: CLEP.

Majors. Business: Accounting/business management, administrative services, business admin. **Engineering technology:** Computer systems. **Health:** Medical assistant, medical records technology, pharmacy assistant.

Contact. Phone: (901) 213-1681
Larry Steele, Vice President of Admissions, National College: Bartlett, 5760 Stage Road, Bartlett, TN 38134

National College: Bristol

Bristol, Tennessee
www.ncbt.edu **CB code: 3247**

- For-profit 2-year business college
- Commuter campus in large town

General. Accredited by ACICS. Eight campuses in Virginia. **Enrollment:** 300 degree-seeking undergraduates. **Degrees:** 55 associate awarded. **Calendar:** Quarter, limited summer session. **Full-time faculty:** 1 total. **Part-time faculty:** 32 total.

Basis for selection. Open admission. Interview recommended.

2008-2009 Annual costs. Tuition/fees: $9,585. Per-credit charge: $212. Books/supplies: $1,200.

Financial aid. All financial aid based on need. Need-based aid available for part-time students.

Application procedures. Admission: No deadline. $30 fee, may be waived for applicants with need. Admission notification on a rolling basis. **Financial aid:** No deadline. FAFSA required. Applicants notified on a rolling basis starting 9/1.

Academics. Special study options: Double major, internships. **Credit/placement by examination:** CLEP, institutional tests. **Support services:** Tutoring.

Majors. Business: Accounting, administrative services, business admin, office management. **Computer sciences:** Computer science. **Health:** Medical assistant.

Computing on campus. 35 workstations in library, computer center.

Student life. Freshman orientation: Mandatory.

Student services. Career counseling, personal counseling.

Contact. E-mail: market@educorp.edu
Phone: (423) 878-4440
Larry Steele, Vice President of Admissions, National College: Bristol, 1328 Highway 11W, Bristol, TN 37620

National College: Knoxville

Knoxville, Tennessee
www.ncbt.edu

- For-profit 2-year business and technical college
- Large city

General. Accredited by ACICS. **Enrollment:** 395 degree-seeking undergraduates. **Degrees:** 51 associate awarded. **Calendar:** Quarter. **Full-time faculty:** 4 total. **Part-time faculty:** 37 total.

Basis for selection. Open admission. Interview recommended.

2008-2009 Annual costs. Tuition/fees: $9,540. Per-credit charge: $212.

Application procedures. Admission: No deadline. $30 fee. **Financial aid:** No deadline.

Academics. Credit/placement by examination: CLEP.

Majors. Business: Accounting, administrative services, business admin. **Health:** Medical assistant, medical records admin, pharmacy assistant, surgical technology.

Contact. Phone: (865) 539-2011
Larry Steele, Vice President of Admissions, National College: Knoxville, 8415 Kingston Pike, Knoxville, TN 37919

National College: Madison

Madison, Tennessee

- For-profit 2-year branch campus college
- Large town

General. Regionally accredited; also accredited by ACICS. **Enrollment:** 239 degree-seeking undergraduates. **Degrees:** 3 associate awarded. **Calendar:** Quarter. **Full-time faculty:** 1 total. **Part-time faculty:** 31 total.

2008-2009 Annual costs. Tuition/fees: $9,585. Per-credit charge: $212.

Application procedures. Admission: No deadline. $30 fee. **Financial aid:** No deadline.

Academics. Credit/placement by examination: CLEP.

Majors. Business: Accounting/business management, administrative services, business admin, hospitality admin, tourism/travel. **Engineering technology:** Computer systems. **Health:** Medical assistant, medical records technology, pharmacy assistant.

Contact. Phone: (615) 612-3015
Larry Steele, Vice President of Admissions, National College: Madison, 900 Madison Square, Madison, TN 37115

National College: Memphis

Memphis, Tennessee

- For-profit 2-year branch campus college
- Very large city

General. Regionally accredited; also accredited by ACICS. **Enrollment:** 329 degree-seeking undergraduates. **Degrees:** 3 associate awarded. **Calendar:** Quarter. **Full-time faculty:** 3 total. **Part-time faculty:** 30 total.

Basis for selection. Open admission.

2008-2009 Annual costs. Tuition/fees: $9,585. Per-credit charge: $212.

Application procedures. Admission: No deadline. $30 fee. **Financial aid:** No deadline.

Academics. Credit/placement by examination: CLEP.

Majors. Business: Accounting/business management, administrative services, business admin. **Engineering technology:** Computer systems. **Health:** Medical assistant, medical records technology, pharmacy assistant, surgical technology.

Contact. Phone: (901) 363-9046
Larry Steel, Vice President of Admissions, National College: Memphis, 3545 Lamar Avenue, Suite 1, Memphis, TN 38118

National College: Nashville

Nashville, Tennessee
www.ncbt.edu **CB code: 3227**

- For-profit 2-year business and technical college
- Commuter campus in large city

General. Accredited by ACICS. **Enrollment:** 298 degree-seeking undergraduates. **Degrees:** 61 associate awarded. **Calendar:** Quarter. **Full-time faculty:** 1 total. **Part-time faculty:** 19 total.

Basis for selection. Open admission. Interview recommended.

2008-2009 Annual costs. Tuition/fees: $9,540. Per-credit charge: $212. Books/supplies: $900. Personal expenses: $3,259.

Financial aid. All financial aid based on need. Need-based aid available for part-time students.

Application procedures. **Admission:** No deadline. $30 fee. **Financial aid:** No deadline. FAFSA required.

Academics. **Special study options:** Liberal arts/career combination. **Credit/placement by examination:** CLEP.

Majors. **Business:** Accounting, administrative services, business admin. **Computer sciences:** General. **Health:** Medical assistant, medical secretary.

Student life. **Freshman orientation:** Mandatory. Preregistration for classes offered.

Contact. E-mail: market@educorp.edu
Phone: (615) 333-3344
Larry Steele, Vice President of Admissions, National College: Nashville, PO Box 6400, Roanoke, VA 24017

Northeast State Technical Community College

Blountville, Tennessee
www.NortheastState.edu **CB code: 0453**

- Public 2-year community and technical college
- Commuter campus in small city

General. Founded in 1965. Regionally accredited. **Location:** 12 miles from Johnson City, 10 miles from Kingsport. **Calendar:** Semester.

Annual costs/financial aid. Tuition/fees (2008-2009): $2,787; $10,287 out-of-state. Need-based financial aid available to full-time and part-time students.

Contact. Phone: (423) 323-0253
Admissions Director, Box 246, Blountville, TN 37617-0246

Nossi College of Art

Goodlettsville, Tennessee
www.nossi.com **CB code: 3118**

- Private 2-year visual arts and technical college
- Commuter campus in large town
- Interview required

General. Accredited by ACCSCT. **Enrollment:** 425 degree-seeking undergraduates. **Degrees:** 12 bachelor's, 98 associate awarded. **Location:** 20 miles from Nashville. **Calendar:** Semester, extensive summer session. **Part-time faculty:** 20 total.

Basis for selection. Interview and talent most important. Portfolio required for commercial art program. **Adult students:** SAT/ACT scores not required.

2008-2009 Annual costs. Tuition for first year (3 semesters) $10,500; required fees $240. Books/supplies: $1,800.

Financial aid. **Need-based:** Need-based aid available for part-time students.

Application procedures. **Admission:** No deadline. $100 fee.

Academics. **Credit/placement by examination:** CLEP.

Majors. **Visual/performing arts:** General, commercial photography, commercial/advertising art.

Computing on campus. 40 workstations in library, computer center.

Student life. **Freshman orientation:** Mandatory.

Student services. Alcohol/substance abuse counseling, career counseling, student employment services, financial aid counseling, personal counseling, placement for graduates.

Contact. E-mail: admissions@nossi.com
Phone: (615) 851-1088 ext. 17 Toll-free number: (887) 860-1601
Fax: (615) 851-1087
Mary Alexander, Director of Admissions, Nossi College of Art, 907 Rivergate Parkway, Building E-6, Goodlettsville, TN 37072

Pellissippi State Technical Community College

Knoxville, Tennessee
www.pstcc.edu **CB code: 0319**

- Public 2-year community and technical college
- Commuter campus in small city

General. Founded in 1974. Regionally accredited. **Enrollment:** 8,742 degree-seeking undergraduates. **Degrees:** 682 associate awarded. **ROTC:** Army. **Location:** 178 miles from Nashville, 388 miles from Memphis. **Calendar:** Semester, extensive summer session. **Full-time faculty:** 185 total. **Part-time faculty:** 287 total. **Class size:** 46% < 20, 52% 20-39, 2% 40-49, less than 1% 50-99, less than 1% >100.

Student profile.

Out-of-state:	1%	**25 or older:**	40%

Transfer out. **Colleges most students transferred to 2008:** University of Tennessee in Knoxville, East Tennessee State University, Tennessee Technological University, Maryville College, Middle Tennessee State University.

Basis for selection. Open admission. Credit may be awarded for course-work taken at international colleges or universities. ACT/SAT scores for placement purposes. **Adult students:** SAT/ACT scores not required if applicant over 21. Institutional placement test required of students 21 and older who have not had college-level math or English. **Learning Disabled:** Accommodations for testing/programs are provided on a case-by-case basis with supporting documentation.

High school preparation. 14 units recommended. Recommended units include English 4, mathematics 3, social studies 1, history 1, science 1 (laboratory 1) and foreign language 2. 1 U.S. history and one visual and performing arts required.

2008-2009 Annual costs. Tuition/fees: $2,799; $10,299 out-of-state. Per-credit charge: $107 in-state; $431 out-of-state. Books/supplies: $800. Personal expenses: $1,500.

2008-2009 Financial aid. **Need-based:** Need-based aid available for part-time students. Work-study available nights, weekends and for part-time students. **Non-need-based:** Scholarships awarded for academics, art, minority status, music/drama.

Application procedures. **Admission:** Closing date 8/20 (postmark date). $100 fee, may be waived for applicants with need. Admission notification on a rolling basis beginning on or about 9/1. **Financial aid:** Priority date 5/1; no closing date. FAFSA required. Applicants notified on a rolling basis starting 7/15; must reply within 2 week(s) of notification.

Academics. **Special study options:** Cooperative education, distance learning, double major, dual enrollment of high school students, ESL, honors, independent study, internships, liberal arts/career combination, weekend college. **Credit/placement by examination:** AP, CLEP, IB, institutional tests. 36 credit hours maximum toward associate degree. **Support services:** GED preparation and test center, learning center, pre-admission summer program, reduced course load, remedial instruction, study skills assistance, tutoring, writing center.

Majors. **Business:** Accounting technology, administrative services, business admin, e-commerce. **Computer sciences:** Computer science, information systems, web page design. **Engineering technology:** CAD/CADD, civil, electrical, mechanical. **Family/consumer sciences:** Child development. **Legal studies:** Paralegal. **Liberal arts:** Arts/sciences. **Public administration:** Community org/advocacy. **Social sciences:** Cartography. **Visual/performing arts:** Cinematography, commercial/advertising art, interior design.

Most popular majors. Business/marketing 9%, liberal arts 59%, visual/performing arts 9%.

Computing on campus. 1,290 workstations in library, computer center, student center. Commuter students can connect to campus network. Online course registration, online library, helpline, repair service, wireless network available.

Student life. **Freshman orientation:** Available. Preregistration for classes offered. **Activities:** Jazz band, campus ministries, choral groups, drama, international student organizations, literary magazine, music ensembles, musical theater, student government, student newspaper, Association of Information Technology Professionals, Institute of Electrical and Electronics Engineers, paralegal association, Active Black Students Association, Students In Free Enterprise, Phi Theta Kappa.

Athletics. Intramural: Archery, basketball, football (non-tackle), golf, soccer, softball, tennis, volleyball.

Student services. Career counseling, student employment services, personal counseling, placement for graduates, veterans' counselor. **Physically disabled:** Services for visually, speech, hearing impaired. **Transfer:** Transfer adviser, college fairs on campus for students transferring to 4-year colleges.

Contact. E-mail: latouzeau@pstcc.edu
Phone: (865) 694-6570 Fax: (865) 539-7217
Leigh Anne Touzeau, Assistant Vice President, Enrollment Services, Pellissippi State Technical Community College, Box 22990, Knoxville, TN 37933-0990

Remington College: Memphis

Memphis, Tennessee
www.remingtoncollege.edu **CB code: 3159**

- For-profit 2-year business and technical college
- Commuter campus in very large city
- Interview required

General. Accredited by ACCSCT. **Enrollment:** 450 degree-seeking undergraduates. **Degrees:** 10 bachelor's, 50 associate awarded. **Calendar:** Quarter, extensive summer session. **Full-time faculty:** 55 total. **Part-time faculty:** 10 total. **Class size:** 81% < 20, 19% 20-39.

Basis for selection. All applicants must pass college administered entrance exam prior to acceptance.

2008-2009 Annual costs. Costs of entire programs leading to certificate, associate degree, bachelor's degree range from $13,500 to $37,000; includes books and supplies.

Financial aid. All financial aid based on need. Need-based aid available for part-time students.

Application procedures. Admission: No deadline. $50 fee. Admission notification on a rolling basis. **Financial aid:** No deadline. FAFSA, institutional form required. Applicants notified on a rolling basis; must reply within 2 week(s) of notification.

Academics. Special study options: Cooperative education, independent study, liberal arts/career combination. Bachelor's degree programs available on campus. **Credit/placement by examination:** CLEP, institutional tests. 48 credit hours maximum toward associate degree, 96 toward bachelor's. **Support services:** Tutoring.

Majors. Business: Office technology. **Computer sciences:** LAN/WAN management. **Engineering technology:** Electrical. **Protective services:** Criminal justice.

Computing on campus. Commuter students can connect to campus network. Helpline, repair service, wireless network available.

Student life. Freshman orientation: Mandatory. 3-hour session held Saturday two weeks before quarter begins. **Activities:** Student newspaper.

Student services. Adult student services, career counseling, student employment services, financial aid counseling, placement for graduates. **Transfer:** Pre-admission transcript evaluation for new students.

Contact. Phone: (901) 345-1000 Fax: (901) 396-8310
Micheal Coker, Asst. Director of Admissions, Remington College: Memphis, 2710 Nonconnah Boulevard, Memphis, TN 38132

Remington College: Nashville

Nashville, Tennessee
www.remingtoncollege.edu

- For-profit 2-year health science, technical and career college
- Very large city

General. Accredited by ACCSCT. **Calendar:** Quarter.

Annual costs/financial aid. Costs of entire programs leading to certificate, associate degree, bachelor's degree range from $13,950 to $39,950 including books and supplies.

Contact. 441 Donelson Pike, Suite 150, Nashville, TN 37214

Roane State Community College

Harriman, Tennessee
www.roanestate.edu **CB code: 1656**

- Public 2-year community and junior college
- Commuter campus in small town

General. Founded in 1971. Regionally accredited. **Enrollment:** 4,417 degree-seeking undergraduates; 1,114 non-degree-seeking students. **Degrees:** 623 associate awarded. **ROTC:** Army, Air Force. **Location:** 40 miles from Knoxville. **Calendar:** Semester, limited summer session. **Full-time faculty:** 136 total; 11% minority, 52% women. **Part-time faculty:** 197 total; 4% minority, 55% women. **Class size:** 48% < 20, 49% 20-39, 2% 40-49, less than 1% 50-99. **Special facilities:** Observatory.

Student profile. Among degree-seeking undergraduates, 42% enrolled in a transfer program, 58% enrolled in a vocational program, 1,070 enrolled as first-time, first-year students.

Part-time:	37%	**African American:**	2%
Out-of-state:	1%	**Hispanic American:**	1%
Women:	69%	**25 or older:**	37%

Transfer out. Colleges most students transferred to 2008: University of Tennessee-Knoxville, Tennessee Technological University, Middle Tennessee State University, East Tennessee State University.

Basis for selection. Open admission, but selective for some programs. All health science AAS programs require minimum ACT score of 20 and 2.5 GPA for 8 hours general course work. Additional requirements for nursing program: minimum 2.75 GPA for 12 hours general course work and pre-admissions test. Interview required for some health programs; audition required for some music programs. **Adult students:** SAT/ACT scores not required if applicant over 21. Those who do not submit SAT/ACT scores must undergo placement assessment. **Homeschooled:** State high school equivalency certificate required.

High school preparation. 20 units recommended. Recommended units include English 4, mathematics 3, social studies 1, history 1, science 2 and foreign language 2.

2008-2009 Annual costs. Tuition/fees: $2,788; $10,288 out-of-state. Per-credit charge: $107 in-state; $431 out-of-state. Books/supplies: $1,000. Personal expenses: $8,143.

2007-2008 Financial aid. Need-based: Need-based aid available for part-time students. Work-study available nights, weekends and for part-time students. **Non-need-based:** Scholarships awarded for academics, art, athletics, leadership, music/drama, state residency.

Application procedures. Admission: No deadline. $10 fee. Admission notification on a rolling basis. **Financial aid:** Priority date 4/1; no closing date. FAFSA, institutional form required. Applicants notified on a rolling basis starting 5/1.

Academics. Special study options: Accelerated study, cooperative education, distance learning, double major, dual enrollment of high school students, honors, independent study, internships, liberal arts/career combination, study abroad, teacher certification program, weekend college. License preparation in dental hygiene, nursing, occupational therapy, paramedic, physical therapy, radiology. **Credit/placement by examination:** AP, CLEP, institutional tests. 18 credit hours maximum toward associate degree. **Support services:** GED test center, learning center, remedial instruction, study skills assistance, tutoring, writing center.

Majors. Biology: General. **Business:** Business admin, management science. **Education:** General. **Family/consumer sciences:** Child development. **Health:** Dental hygiene, environmental health, medical radiologic technology/radiation therapy, medical records technology, nursing (RN), occupational therapy assistant, optician, physical therapy assistant, respiratory therapy technology. **Legal studies:** Paralegal. **Math:** General. **Protective services:** Police science. **Social sciences:** Cartography. **Other:** General technology.

Most popular majors. Business/marketing 9%, health sciences 35%, liberal arts 39%, science technologies 9%.

Computing on campus. 600 workstations in library, computer center, student center. Commuter students can connect to campus network. Online course registration, helpline, wireless network available.

Student life. Freshman orientation: Mandatory. Preregistration for classes offered. One half-day orientation. **Activities:** Jazz band, campus ministries, choral groups, dance, drama, international student organizations, music ensembles, musical theater, student government, student newspaper, Coffee House Writers Workshop, College Republican Club, Life Enablers, Oak Ridge

Institute for Contined Learning, Phi Theta Kappa, Playmakers, SADD, Students in Free Enterprise, Tao Astronomical Society, Southwest Field Trip.

Athletics. NJCAA. **Intercollegiate:** Baseball M, basketball, softball W. **Intramural:** Basketball, cheerleading W, football (non-tackle) M, softball. **Team name:** Raiders.

Student services. Career counseling, student employment services, financial aid counseling, health services, minority student services, personal counseling, placement for graduates, veterans' counselor. **Physically disabled:** Services for visually, speech, hearing impaired. **Transfer:** Transfer adviser, college fairs on campus for students transferring to 4-year colleges.

Contact. E-mail: admissions@roanestate.edu
Phone: (865) 882-4523 Toll-free number: (866) 462-7722 ext. 4523
Fax: (865) 882-4562
Maria Gonzales, Director of Admissions, Roane State Community College, 276 Patton Lane, Harriman, TN 37748

Southwest Tennessee Community College
Memphis, Tennessee
www.southwest.tn.edu **CB code: 0274**

- Public 2-year community college
- Commuter campus in very large city

General. Founded in 1970. Regionally accredited. **Enrollment:** 10,464 degree-seeking undergraduates; 963 non-degree-seeking students. **Degrees:** 713 associate awarded. **ROTC:** Army, Air Force. **Calendar:** Semester, extensive summer session. **Full-time faculty:** 249 total. **Part-time faculty:** 184 total. **Class size:** 47% < 20, 53% 20-39.

Student profile. Among degree-seeking undergraduates, 26% enrolled in a transfer program, 74% enrolled in a vocational program, 2,182 enrolled as first-time, first-year students.

Part-time:	51%	**Asian American:**	2%
Out-of-state:	2%	**Hispanic American:**	2%
Women:	65%	**International:**	1%
African American:	60%	**25 or older:**	44%

Transfer out. Colleges most students transferred to 2008: University of Memphis, Christian Brothers University.

Basis for selection. Open admission, but selective for some programs. Special requirements for admission to nursing, dietetic technician, laboratory phlebotomy, medical assistant, medical laboratory technician, physical therapist assistant, radiologic technology, paramedic programs. **Adult students:** SAT/ACT scores not required if applicant over 21. ACT COMPASS exam required for placement. **Learning Disabled:** Require documentation of disability to be shown to disability counselor.

High school preparation. 15 units recommended. Recommended units include English 4, mathematics 3, social studies 1, history 1, science 2 (laboratory 1), foreign language 2 and visual/performing arts 1.

2008-2009 Annual costs. Tuition/fees: $2,791; $10,291 out-of-state. Per-credit charge: $107 in-state; $431 out-of-state. Personal expenses: $1,400.

Financial aid. All financial aid based on need. Need-based aid available for part-time students. Work-study available nights, weekends and for part-time students. **Additional information:** State grants available to eligible students who apply by 4/1.

Application procedures. Admission: No deadline. $10 fee. Admission notification on a rolling basis. **Financial aid:** Priority date 3/15; no closing date. FAFSA required. Applicants notified on a rolling basis starting 6/1; must reply within 4 week(s) of notification.

Academics. Special study options: Cooperative education, distance learning, double major, dual enrollment of high school students, ESL, honors, independent study, internships, liberal arts/career combination, student-designed major, study abroad, weekend college. On-site extension courses at business, industry and government installations. License preparation in nursing, paramedic, physical therapy, radiology, real estate. **Credit/placement by examination:** AP, CLEP, institutional tests. **Support services:** GED preparation and test center, learning center, pre-admission summer program, reduced course load, remedial instruction, study skills assistance, tutoring.

Majors. Agriculture: Horticulture. **Biology:** Biotechnology. **Business:** General, accounting, administrative services, business admin, finance, hotel/motel admin, management information systems, office technology. **Computer sciences:** General, computer science. **Construction:** Maintenance. **Education:** General, early childhood. **Engineering technology:** Architectural, computer, electrical. **Family/consumer sciences:** Child care, family studies, food/nutrition, institutional food production. **Health:** Clinical lab technology, dietician assistant, EMT paramedic, medical radiologic technology/radiation therapy, medical transcription, nursing (RN), physical therapy assistant. **Legal studies:** Court reporting, paralegal. **Liberal arts:** Arts/sciences. **Mechanic/repair:** General, automotive, electronics/electrical, industrial. **Physical sciences:** General. **Protective services:** Firefighting, police science. **Social sciences:** Geography. **Visual/performing arts:** Commercial/advertising art.

Most popular majors. Business/marketing 28%, health sciences 21%, liberal arts 32%.

Computing on campus. 269 workstations in library, computer center. Commuter students can connect to campus network. Online course registration, online library, helpline, wireless network available.

Student life. Freshman orientation: Available. Preregistration for classes offered. **Activities:** Bands, choral groups, drama, music ensembles, student government, student newspaper, NAACP, Baptist Student Union, Human Key Society, National Student Support Council for Africa, Black Student Association, Phi Theta Kappa Honor Society, Police Science Association, science club, Radiologic Technology Student Association, Collegiate Secretaries.

Athletics. NJCAA. **Intercollegiate:** Baseball M, basketball, softball W. **Team name:** Saluqis.

Student services. Adult student services, chaplain/spiritual director, career counseling, services for economically disadvantaged, student employment services, financial aid counseling, on-campus daycare, personal counseling, placement for graduates, veterans' counselor. **Physically disabled:** Services for visually, speech, hearing impaired. **Transfer:** Re-entry adviser, pre-admission transcript evaluation for new students. Transfer center, transfer adviser, college fairs on campus for students transferring to 4-year colleges.

Contact. Phone: (901) 333-5924 Toll-free number: (877) 717-7822
Fax: (901) 333-4473
Vanessa Dowdy, Associate Director of Recruitment, Southwest Tennessee Community College, PO Box 780, Memphis, TN 38101-0780

Vatterott College: Memphis
Memphis, Tennessee
www.vatterott-college.edu

- For-profit 2-year technical college
- Commuter campus in large city

General. Accredited by ACCSCT. **Calendar:** Continuous.

Annual costs/financial aid. Program cost ranges: $14,350 to $20,800 (certificate/diploma); $26,650 to $32,050 (associate degree).

Contact. Phone: (901) 761-5730
Director of Admissions, 2655 Dividend Drive, Memphis, TN 38132

Volunteer State Community College
Gallatin, Tennessee
www.volstate.edu **CB code: 1881**

- Public 2-year community and junior college
- Commuter campus in small city

General. Founded in 1970. Regionally accredited. **Enrollment:** 5,667 degree-seeking undergraduates; 1,574 non-degree-seeking students. **Degrees:** 591 associate awarded. **Location:** 25 miles from Nashville. **Calendar:** Semester, limited summer session. **Full-time faculty:** 143 total; 16% have terminal degrees, 14% minority, 51% women. **Part-time faculty:** 245 total; 9% minority, 61% women. **Class size:** 58% < 20, 41% 20-39, 1% 40-49, less than 1% 50-99. **Partnerships:** Formal partnerships with GAP Inc.

Student profile. Among degree-seeking undergraduates, 44% enrolled in a transfer program, 56% enrolled in a vocational program, 1,429 enrolled as first-time, first-year students, 474 transferred in from other institutions.

Part-time:	40%	**Asian American:**	1%
Out-of-state:	1%	**International:**	1%
Women:	63%	**25 or older:**	34%
African American:	10%		

Transfer out. **Colleges most students transferred to 2008:** Middle Tennessee State University, Austin Peay State University, Tennessee State University, Tennessee Technical University,.

Basis for selection. Open admission, but selective for some programs. Allied health students screened into programs after completing designated amount of college coursework. Screening based on GPA and interview. Test scores where required in selective programs must be received by August 30. Interview required for allied health program. **Adult students:** SAT/ACT scores not required if applicant over 21. Unless exempt by ACT scores, must take COMPASS or ASSET Placement test. **Homeschooled:** Transcript must be an official copy from an affiliated organization as defined by state law or be accompanied by a certification of registration with the superintendent of the local education agency, which the student would otherwise attend.

High school preparation. 14 units recommended. Recommended units include English 4, mathematics 3, social studies 1, history 1, science 2 (laboratory 1) and foreign language 2. 1 visual and/or performing arts also required.

2008-2009 Annual costs. Tuition/fees: $2,767; $10,267 out-of-state. Per-credit charge: $107 in-state; $431 out-of-state. Books/supplies: $950. Personal expenses: $400.

2007-2008 Financial aid. **Need-based:** Need-based aid available for part-time students. Work-study available for part-time students. **Non-need-based:** Scholarships awarded for academics, art, athletics, leadership, minority status, music/drama, religious affiliation, state residency.

Application procedures. **Admission:** Priority date 7/31; deadline 8/28 (receipt date). $10 fee. Admission notification on a rolling basis. **Financial aid:** Priority date 4/15; no closing date. FAFSA, institutional form required. Applicants notified on a rolling basis; must reply within 2 week(s) of notification.

Academics. **Special study options:** Cooperative education, distance learning, double major, dual enrollment of high school students, ESL, honors, independent study. Bachelor's degree programs available on campus. License preparation in dental hygiene, paramedic, physical therapy, radiology, real estate. **Credit/placement by examination:** AP, CLEP, institutional tests. 36 credit hours maximum toward associate degree. Maximum 12 hours of credit by examination in specific allied health programs. **Support services:** GED test center, learning center, pre-admission summer program, reduced course load, remedial instruction, study skills assistance, tutoring, writing center.

Majors. **Business:** Business admin. **Family/consumer sciences:** Child development. **Health:** Clinical lab technology, medical radiologic technology/radiation therapy, medical records technology, ophthalmic technology, physical therapy assistant, respiratory therapy technology. **Legal studies:** Paralegal. **Liberal arts:** Arts/sciences. **Protective services:** Firefighting. **Public administration:** Community org/advocacy.

Most popular majors. Business/marketing 12%, health sciences 25%, liberal arts 58%.

Computing on campus. 800 workstations in library, computer center. Commuter students can connect to campus network. Online course registration, online library, helpline, wireless network available.

Student life. **Freshman orientation:** Mandatory. Preregistration for classes offered. One-day program held multiple times prior to registration both on campus and online. **Activities:** Campus ministries, choral groups, drama, literary magazine, radio station, student government, student newspaper, African-American Student Union, returning women's organization, College Democrats, College Republicans.

Athletics. NJCAA. **Intercollegiate:** Baseball M, basketball, softball W. **Team name:** Pioneers.

Student services. Career counseling, services for economically disadvantaged, financial aid counseling, health services, personal counseling, placement for graduates, veterans' counselor. **Physically disabled:** Services for visually, speech, hearing impaired. **Transfer:** Pre-admission transcript evaluation for new students. Transfer adviser, college fairs on campus for students transferring to 4-year colleges.

Contact. E-mail: admissions@volstate.edu
Phone: (615) 452-8600 ext. 3688 Toll-free
number: (888) 335-8722 ext. 3688 Fax: (615) 230-4875
Tim Amyx, Director of Admissions, Volunteer State Community College, 1480 Nashville Pike, Gallatin, TN 37066

Walters State Community College

Morristown, Tennessee — **CB member**
www.ws.edu — **CB code: 1893**

- Public 2-year culinary school and community college
- Commuter campus in small city

General. Founded in 1970. Regionally accredited. Degree programs and a variety of courses at sites throughout 10-county service delivery area with facilities located in Greeneville, Sevierville, and Tazewell. Instructional alternatives include interactive television, web-based, video streaming, and telecourses. **Enrollment:** 4,526 degree-seeking undergraduates; 1,299 non-degree-seeking students. **Degrees:** 622 associate awarded. **ROTC:** Army. **Location:** 45 miles from Knoxville. **Calendar:** Semester, limited summer session. **Full-time faculty:** 138 total; 20% have terminal degrees, 7% minority, 56% women. **Part-time faculty:** 188 total; 15% have terminal degrees, 4% minority, 57% women. **Special facilities:** Observatory, training restaurant, exposition center, industrial technology manufacturing laboratory with complete computer integrated manufacturing (CIM), work center and coordinate measuring machine (MM), public safety law enforcement training center, greenhouse, production horticulture lab, arboretum, center for workforce education.

Student profile. Among degree-seeking undergraduates, 53% enrolled in a transfer program, 47% enrolled in a vocational program, 1% already have a bachelor's degree or higher, 1,209 enrolled as first-time, first-year students, 243 transferred in from other institutions.

Part-time:	34%	**25 or older:**	35%
Women:	63%		

Transfer out. **Colleges most students transferred to 2008:** University of Tennessee-Knoxville, East Tennessee State University, Carson Newman College.

Basis for selection. Open admission, but selective for some programs. Special requirements for education programs, allied health, public safety. International students must submit application 60 days prior to start of term. Placement test required for applicants with ACT scores below 18. **Adult students:** SAT/ACT scores not required if applicant over 21. Required to take placement assessment prior to enrollment.

High school preparation. College-preparatory program recommended. 14 units required. Required units include English 4, mathematics 3, social studies 1, history 1, science 2 (laboratory 1), foreign language 2 and visual/performing arts 1. College-preparatory program required for 2-year transfer program: 1 unit biological science, 4 English, 2 foreign language, 3 mathematics, 1 physical science, 2 social science, 1 visual or performing arts. Same preparation recommended for all students.

2008-2009 Annual costs. Tuition/fees: $2,775; $10,275 out-of-state. Per-credit charge: $107 in-state; $431 out-of-state. Books/supplies: $1,200. Personal expenses: $1,400.

2007-2008 Financial aid. **Need-based:** 948 full-time freshmen applied for aid; 644 were judged to have need; 615 of these received aid. Average need met was 78%. Average scholarship/grant was $3,874; average loan $2,329. 81% of total undergraduate aid awarded as scholarships/grants, 19% as loans/jobs. Need-based aid available for part-time students. Work-study available for part-time students. **Non-need-based:** Awarded to 1,292 full-time undergraduates, including 612 freshmen. Scholarships awarded for academics, athletics, minority status, music/drama, state residency.

Application procedures. **Admission:** No deadline. $10 fee. Application must be submitted on paper. Admission notification on a rolling basis. **Financial aid:** Priority date 5/1; no closing date. FAFSA required. Applicants notified on a rolling basis.

Academics. **Special study options:** Distance learning, dual enrollment of high school students, ESL, honors, liberal arts/career combination, weekend college. Bachelor's degree programs available on campus. License preparation in nursing, paramedic, physical therapy. **Credit/placement by examination:** AP, CLEP, institutional tests. 40 credit hours maximum toward associate degree. **Support services:** GED test center, learning center, reduced course load, remedial instruction, study skills assistance, tutoring, writing center.

Majors. **Agriculture:** Ornamental horticulture. **Business:** Business admin, management information systems. **Computer sciences:** Web page design. **Education:** General. **Engineering technology:** Industrial. **Family/consumer sciences:** Child development. **Health:** EMT paramedic, medical records technology, nursing (RN), physical therapy assistant, respiratory therapy technology. **Liberal arts:** Arts/sciences. **Protective services:** Police science. **Other:** Information technology.

Most popular majors. Business/marketing 12%, health sciences 33%, liberal arts 49%.

Computing on campus. 900 workstations in library, computer center, student center. Commuter students can connect to campus network. Online course registration, online library, helpline, wireless network available.

Student life. Freshman orientation: Mandatory. Preregistration for classes offered. **Activities:** Bands, choral groups, dance, drama, literary magazine, music ensembles, student government, student newspaper.

Athletics. NJCAA. **Intercollegiate:** Baseball M, basketball, golf, softball W. **Intramural:** Basketball, soccer, softball. **Team name:** Senators.

Student services. Adult student services, alcohol/substance abuse counseling, chaplain/spiritual director, career counseling, student employment services, financial aid counseling, health services, minority student services, personal counseling, placement for graduates, veterans' counselor. **Physically disabled:** Services for visually, speech, hearing impaired. **Transfer:** Re-entry adviser for new students. Transfer center, transfer adviser, college fairs on campus for students transferring to 4-year colleges.

Contact. E-mail: kim.gunnin@ws.edu
Phone: (423) 585-2685 Toll-free number: (800) 225-4770
Fax: (423) 585-6786
Mike Campbell, Assistant Vice President for Student Affairs, Walters State Community College, 500 South Davy Crockett Parkway, Morristown, TN 37813-6899

West Tennessee Business College
Jackson, Tennessee
www.wtbc.com

- For-profit 2-year business and health science college
- Commuter campus in small city

General. Accredited by ACICS. **Location:** 90 miles from Memphis. **Calendar:** Continuous.

Annual costs/financial aid. Program costs vary by program. Total cost of medical/clinical assistant program: $11,470.

Contact. Phone: (731) 668-7240
Admissions Director, 1186 Highway 45 Bypass, Jackson, TN 38301

Texas

Alvin Community College

Alvin, Texas
www.alvincollege.edu **CB code: 6005**

- Public 2-year community and liberal arts college
- Residential campus in large town

General. Founded in 1948. Regionally accredited. **Enrollment:** 2,817 degree-seeking undergraduates. **Degrees:** 410 associate awarded. **Location:** 32 miles from Houston. **Calendar:** Semester, extensive summer session. **Full-time faculty:** 98 total. **Part-time faculty:** 164 total. **Special facilities:** Radio station, recording studio, indoor firing range for law enforcement program, Nolan Ryan exhibit.

Transfer out. Colleges most students transferred to 2008: University of Houston-Clear Lake, University of Houston, Texas A&M, Sam Houston State University, Southwest Texas State University.

Basis for selection. Open admission, but selective for some programs. Texas Academic Skills Program test required by Texas law. Special requirements for nursing, respiratory therapy, criminal justice, court reporting, musical theater, EMT, diagnostic cardiovascular sonography programs. Interview required for court reporting, medical laboratory technology, nursing, respiratory therapy programs; audition required for music, musical theater programs.

High school preparation. 25 units recommended. Recommended units include English 4, mathematics 4, social studies 4, science 3, foreign language 3 and academic electives 7.

2009-2010 Annual costs. Tuition/fees (projected): $1,216; $2,056 out-of-district; $3,616 out-of-state. Per-credit charge: $30 in-district; $58 out-of-district; $110 out-of-state.

Financial aid. All financial aid based on need. Need-based aid available for part-time students. Work-study available nights, weekends and for part-time students.

Application procedures. Admission: No deadline. No application fee. Admission notification on a rolling basis. **Financial aid:** Priority date 6/30; no closing date. FAFSA required. Applicants notified on a rolling basis; must reply within 2 week(s) of notification.

Academics. Special study options: Cooperative education, cross-registration, distance learning, dual enrollment of high school students, ESL, honors, internships, liberal arts/career combination, study abroad. License preparation in nursing, paramedic. **Credit/placement by examination:** CLEP, institutional tests. **Support services:** GED preparation and test center, learning center, reduced course load, remedial instruction, study skills assistance, tutoring, writing center.

Majors. Biology: General. **Business:** General, business admin, executive assistant. **Communications:** Radio/tv. **Computer sciences:** Programming. **Education:** Early childhood, physical. **Engineering technology:** Electrical. **Family/consumer sciences:** Child development. **Health:** Cardiovascular technology, EMT paramedic, mental health services, nursing (RN), respiratory therapy technology. **Legal studies:** Paralegal. **Liberal arts:** Arts/sciences. **Math:** General. **Parks/recreation:** Health/fitness. **Physical sciences:** General. **Protective services:** Corrections, criminal justice. **Science technology:** Chemical. **Visual/performing arts:** Art, dramatic, music performance.

Computing on campus. 600 workstations in library, computer center. Online course registration, online library, wireless network available.

Student life. Freshman orientation: Mandatory. Preregistration for classes offered. **Housing:** Housing provided for scholarship athletes. **Activities:** Bands, choral groups, drama, literary magazine, music ensembles, musical theater, radio station, student government, student newspaper, TV station, Newman Association, Phi Theta Kappa, Pan American College Forum, Baptist student union.

Athletics. NJCAA. **Intercollegiate:** Baseball M, softball W. **Team name:** Dolphins.

Student services. Career counseling, student employment services, financial aid counseling, on-campus daycare, personal counseling, placement for graduates, veterans' counselor. **Physically disabled:** Services for visually, speech, hearing impaired. **Transfer:** Transfer adviser, college fairs on campus for students transferring to 4-year colleges.

Contact. E-mail: admiss@alvincollege.edu
Phone: (281) 756-3531 Fax: (281) 756-3843
Stephanie Stockstill, Director of Admissions/Academic Advising, Alvin Community College, 3110 Mustang Road, Alvin, TX 77511-4898

Amarillo College

Amarillo, Texas
www.actx.edu **CB code: 6006**

- Public 2-year community college
- Commuter campus in small city

General. Founded in 1929. Regionally accredited. **Location:** 300 miles from Dallas, 300 miles from Denver. **Calendar:** Semester.

Annual costs/financial aid. Tuition/fees (2008-2009): $1,763; $2,273 out-of-district; $3,353 out-of-state. Books/supplies: $996. Personal expenses: $1,302.

Contact. Phone: (806) 371-5030
Registrar and Director of Admissions, Box 447, Amarillo, TX 79178

Angelina College

Lufkin, Texas
www.angelina.edu **CB code: 6025**

- Public 2-year community college
- Commuter campus in large town

General. Founded in 1966. Regionally accredited. Teaching centers located in 5 contiguous counties. Branch campus located in Jasper. **Enrollment:** 4,934 degree-seeking undergraduates. **Degrees:** 313 associate awarded. **ROTC:** Army. **Location:** 125 miles from Houston. **Calendar:** Semester, extensive summer session. **Full-time faculty:** 99 total; 9% have terminal degrees, 7% minority, 59% women. **Part-time faculty:** 220 total; 6% have terminal degrees, 9% minority, 61% women. **Class size:** 72% < 20, 28% 20-39. **Special facilities:** Computer-aided design laboratory, performing arts center.

Student profile. Among degree-seeking undergraduates, 1,386 enrolled as first-time, first-year students, 312 transferred in from other institutions.

Part-time:	65%	**Hispanic American:**	8%
Women:	65%	**International:**	1%
African American:	9%		

Transfer out. Colleges most students transferred to 2008: Stephen F. Austin State University, Sam Houston State University.

Basis for selection. Open admission, but selective for some programs. Special requirements for nursing, respiratory care, EMS, pharmacy, and radiologic technology programs; interview required. General Aptitude Test Battery required of nursing applicants. All students must take Texas Higher Education Assessment Test or ACCUPLACER before enrolling. **Adult students:** Physical education requirements waived for veterans, adults 25 and over, and some part-time students. **Homeschooled:** Transcript of courses and grades required. **Learning Disabled:** May have to take different test based on disability.

2008-2009 Annual costs. Tuition/fees: $1,200; $1,800 out-of-district; $2,550 out-of-state. Per-credit charge: $33 in-district; $53 out-of-district; $78 out-of-state. Students taking 1-3 credits pay higher per-credit-hour charge. Room/board: $5,550. Books/supplies: $1,070. Personal expenses: $1,920.

2007-2008 Financial aid. All financial aid based on need. 983 full-time freshmen applied for aid; 918 were judged to have need; 888 of these received aid. Average need met was 69%. Average scholarship/grant was $2,404. 97% of total undergraduate aid awarded as scholarships/grants, 3% as loans/jobs. Need-based aid available for part-time students. Work-study available nights and for part-time students.

Application procedures. Admission: No deadline. No application fee. Admission notification on a rolling basis. **Financial aid:** Priority date 7/15; no closing date. FAFSA, institutional form required. Applicants notified on a rolling basis starting 7/15.

Academics. **Special study options:** Accelerated study, cooperative education, distance learning, dual enrollment of high school students, internships, liberal arts/career combination. License preparation in nursing, paramedic, radiology, real estate. **Credit/placement by examination:** AP, CLEP, IB, institutional tests. 15 credit hours maximum toward associate degree. **Support services:** GED test center, learning center, reduced course load, remedial instruction, study skills assistance, tutoring.

Majors. **Biology:** General. **Business:** General, accounting, administrative services, business admin. **Communications:** General. **Computer sciences:** General, data processing. **Education:** General, elementary, health. **Engineering:** General. **Engineering technology:** Drafting, electrical, electromechanical, environmental. **Family/consumer sciences:** Child development. **Health:** Clinical lab technology, EMT paramedic, nursing (RN), predental, premedicine, prepharmacy, preveterinary, radiologic technology/medical imaging, respiratory therapy technology, substance abuse counseling. **Interdisciplinary:** Science/society. **Legal studies:** Paralegal, prelaw. **Math:** General. **Physical sciences:** Physics. **Production:** Machine tool, welding. **Protective services:** Criminal justice. **Public administration:** Human services, social work. **Visual/performing arts:** Art, design, dramatic, music management, piano/organ, voice/opera. **Other:** Pre-physical therapy/pre-occupational therapy.

Most popular majors. Business/marketing 15%, engineering/engineering technologies 11%, health sciences 30%, security/protective services 14%.

Computing on campus. 200 workstations in library, computer center, student center. Online course registration, online library available.

Student life. **Freshman orientation:** Mandatory. Preregistration for classes offered. **Housing:** Coed dorms, wellness housing available. $100 fully refundable deposit, deadline 7/15. Apartments for single mothers. **Activities:** Bands, choral groups, dance, drama, music ensembles, musical theater, student government, student newspaper, Baptist student union.

Athletics. NJCAA. **Intercollegiate:** Baseball M, basketball, cheerleading M, softball W. **Intramural:** Golf, volleyball. **Team name:** Roadrunners.

Student services. Adult student services, career counseling, services for economically disadvantaged, student employment services, financial aid counseling, health services, personal counseling, placement for graduates, veterans' counselor. **Physically disabled:** Services for visually, speech, hearing impaired. **Transfer:** Pre-admission transcript evaluation for new students. Transfer adviser, college fairs on campus for students transferring to 4-year colleges.

Contact. E-mail: registrar@angelina.edu
Phone: (936) 639-5212 Fax: (936) 633-5455
Jeremy Thomas, Director of Admissions & Enrollment Services, Angelina College, PO Box 1768, Lufkin, TX 75902-1768

ATI Career Training Center: Dallas

Dallas, Texas
www.aticareertraining.edu

- For-profit 2-year technical college
- Very large city

General. Accredited by ACCSCT. **Calendar:** Semester.

Annual costs/financial aid. Total cost of programs vary: Professional Massage Therapy: $10,400 for 20-week program; Pharmacy Technician: $13,200 for 30-36 week program; Medical Assisting, Dental Assisting, or Business Administration Technology: $16,700 each for 40-week program; Network Administration: $22,938 for 60-week program. Need-based financial aid available for full-time students.

Contact. Phone: (214) 902-8191
Director of Admissions, 10003 Technology Boulevard, West, Dallas, TX 75220

Austin Community College

Austin, Texas **CB member**
www.austincc.edu **CB code: 6759**

- Public 2-year community college
- Commuter campus in very large city

General. Founded in 1972. Regionally accredited. 8 campuses serving greater Austin, 10 instructional centers in surrounding towns. **Enrollment:** 35,798 undergraduates. **Degrees:** 1,121 associate awarded. **ROTC:** Army, Air Force. **Location:** 85 miles from San Antonio. **Calendar:** Semester, extensive summer session. **Full-time faculty:** 526 total; 26% minority, 56% women. **Part-time faculty:** 1,316 total; 18% minority, 46% women. **Class size:** 43% < 20, 57% 20-39, less than 1% 40-49. **Special facilities:** Water-quality monitoring well. **Partnerships:** Formal partnerships with Sustainability Project, Semiconductor Manufacturing Program, Seton Health.

Transfer out. **Colleges most students transferred to 2008:** University of Texas at Austin, Texas State University.

Basis for selection. Open admission, but selective for some programs. Special requirements for health sciences programs. Students may submit SAT or ACT test scores for exemption from Texas Academic Skills Program (TASP) requirements. **Adult students:** SAT/ACT scores not required. Texas Success Initiative test may be required.

2008-2009 Annual costs. Tuition/fees: $1,608; $4,248 out-of-district; $8,988 out-of-state. Per-credit charge: $39 in-district; $127 out-of-district; $285 out-of-state. Books/supplies: $1,000. Personal expenses: $2,000.

2007-2008 Financial aid. **Need-based:** 565 full-time freshmen applied for aid; 494 were judged to have need; 494 of these received aid. 32% of total undergraduate aid awarded as scholarships/grants, 68% as loans/jobs. Need-based aid available for part-time students.

Application procedures. **Admission:** No deadline. No application fee. No notification. Applications accepted at all times for any future semester enrollment. **Financial aid:** Closing date 4/1. FAFSA, institutional form required. Applicants notified on a rolling basis starting 6/1; must reply within 2 week(s) of notification.

Academics. **Special study options:** Accelerated study, distance learning, dual enrollment of high school students, ESL, honors, independent study, internships, study abroad, teacher certification program, weekend college. License preparation in dental hygiene, nursing, occupational therapy, paramedic, physical therapy, radiology, real estate. **Credit/placement by examination:** AP, CLEP, institutional tests. 30 credit hours maximum toward associate degree. **Support services:** GED preparation and test center, learning center, reduced course load, remedial instruction, study skills assistance, tutoring.

Majors. **Biology:** General. **Business:** General, accounting technology, administrative services, banking/financial services, business admin, hospitality admin, international, marketing, real estate. **Communications:** Radio/tv. **Communications technology:** Animation/special effects. **Computer sciences:** General, networking, programming. **Construction:** Carpentry. **Education:** Health, middle. **Engineering:** General. **Engineering technology:** Drafting, electrical, environmental, heat/ac/refrig, quality control, surveying. **Family/consumer sciences:** Child development. **Foreign languages:** General, French, German, Japanese, Latin, Russian, sign language interpretation, Spanish. **Health:** Clinical lab technology, dental hygiene, EMT paramedic, nursing (RN), occupational therapy assistant, physical therapy assistant, predental, premedicine, prepharmacy, preveterinary, radiologic technology/medical imaging, recreational therapy, sonography, substance abuse counseling, surgical technology. **History:** General. **Legal studies:** Paralegal. **Math:** General. **Mechanic/repair:** Automotive, watch/jewelry. **Parks/recreation:** Health/fitness. **Personal/culinary services:** Chef training. **Philosophy/religion:** Philosophy. **Physical sciences:** General, chemistry, geology, physics. **Production:** Welding. **Protective services:** Corrections, fire safety technology, police science. **Psychology:** General. **Public administration:** Human services, social work. **Science technology:** Biological. **Social sciences:** Anthropology, economics, geography, political science, sociology. **Visual/performing arts:** Art, commercial photography, commercial/advertising art, dance, dramatic, music management.

Most popular majors. Business/marketing 15%, engineering/engineering technologies 9%, health sciences 30%, visual/performing arts 7%.

Computing on campus. 307 workstations in library, computer center. Commuter students can connect to campus network. Online course registration, online library, helpline available.

Student life. **Freshman orientation:** Mandatory. Preregistration for classes offered. **Policies:** No alcohol, no drugs, no hazing. **Activities:** Jazz band, dance, drama, literary magazine, music ensembles, student government, student newspaper, Phi Theta Kappa, Hispanic student association, Biomass, Peer Players, Austin Society for Semi-Conductor Electronics Technicians, Campus Crusade for Christ, Toastmasters, American Drafting Design Association, associate degree student nursing association, black student alliance.

Student services. Alcohol/substance abuse counseling, career counseling, services for economically disadvantaged, student employment services, financial aid counseling, minority student services, on-campus daycare, placement for graduates, veterans' counselor. **Physically disabled:** Services for visually, speech, hearing impaired. **Transfer:** Transfer center, transfer adviser, college fairs on campus for students transferring to 4-year colleges.

Contact. E-mail: admission@austincc.edu
Phone: (512) 223-7503 Fax: (512) 223-7175
Linda Kluck, Director of Admissions and Records, Austin Community College, PO Box 15306, Austin, TX 78681-5306

Blinn College
Brenham, Texas
www.blinn.edu **CB code: 6043**

- Public 2-year community college
- Commuter campus in large town

General. Founded in 1883. Regionally accredited. Campuses located at Brenham, Bryan, Sealy and Schulenburg. **Enrollment:** 13,640 degree-seeking undergraduates. **Degrees:** 832 associate awarded. **Location:** 79 miles from Houston, 90 miles from Austin. **Calendar:** Semester, limited summer session. **Full-time faculty:** 222 total. **Part-time faculty:** 348 total. **Special facilities:** College-operated museum, state park, city-operated historical museums, observatory, ice cream factory, George Bush library, children's museum, natural science center, art museums.

Student profile. Among degree-seeking undergraduates, 65% enrolled in a transfer program, 26% enrolled in a vocational program, 2% already have a bachelor's degree or higher, 3,234 enrolled as first-time, first-year students, 7,835 transferred in from other institutions.

Part-time:	40%	**25 or older:**	14%
Out-of-state:	1%	**Live on campus:**	10%
Women:	50%		

Transfer out. Colleges most students transferred to 2008: Texas A&M-College Station, Sam Houston State University, Texas State University, University of Texas at Austin, University of Houston.

Basis for selection. Open admission, but selective for some programs. Special requirements for registered nursing program, dental hygiene, physical therapy, various other allied health and some technology-based programs. TASP test required for all per Texas state law. **Homeschooled:** Transcript of courses and grades required.

2008-2009 Annual costs. Tuition/fees: $1,890; $2,760 out-of-district; $5,040 out-of-state. Per-credit charge: $35 in-district; $64 out-of-district; $140 out-of-state. Room/board: $4,940. Books/supplies: $1,018. Personal expenses: $1,350.

2008-2009 Financial aid. Need-based: Need-based aid available for part-time students.

Application procedures. Admission: No deadline. No application fee. Admission notification on a rolling basis. **Financial aid:** Priority date 6/1; no closing date. FAFSA, institutional form required. Applicants notified on a rolling basis starting 7/1.

Academics. All campuses offer academic support services. **Special study options:** Cross-registration, distance learning, dual enrollment of high school students, ESL, liberal arts/career combination, teacher certification program. License preparation in dental hygiene, nursing, paramedic, physical therapy, radiology, real estate. **Credit/placement by examination:** AP, CLEP, IB, institutional tests. 12 credit hours maximum toward associate degree. THEA (Texas Higher Education Assessment) test used for placement; students submitting sufficient score on TAKS, SAT or ACT exempt (Education students must take THEA). **Support services:** GED preparation and test center, learning center, pre-admission summer program, reduced course load, remedial instruction, study skills assistance, tutoring, writing center.

Majors. Agriculture: General. **Biology:** General. **Business:** Accounting, office/clerical, small business admin. **Computer sciences:** System admin. **Education:** Multi-level teacher. **Family/consumer sciences:** Child care. **Foreign languages:** General, French, German, sign language interpretation, Spanish. **Health:** Medical radiologic technology/radiation therapy, nursing (RN). **History:** General. **Legal studies:** Paralegal. **Liberal arts:** Arts/sciences. **Math:** General. **Parks/recreation:** Exercise sciences. **Philosophy/religion:** Philosophy. **Physical sciences:** Chemistry, physics. **Protective services:** Criminal justice, firefighting. **Psychology:** General. **Social sciences:** General. **Visual/performing arts:** Design, dramatic.

Most popular majors. Biological/life sciences 10%, business/marketing 20%, English 7%, health sciences 15%, liberal arts 7%, security/protective services 7%.

Computing on campus. 500 workstations in library, computer center. Dormitories wired for high-speed internet access and linked to campus network. Commuter students can connect to campus network. Online course registration, online library, helpline, wireless network available.

Student life. Freshman orientation: Available. Preregistration for classes offered. Held 3-4 times during summer, parents welcome. **Policies:** Student classroom attendance policy, full-time student status for residence halls. **Housing:** Single-sex dorms, special housing for disabled, apartments, wellness housing available. $200 fully refundable deposit. **Activities:** Bands, campus ministries, choral groups, dance, drama, international student organizations, music ensembles, musical theater, student government, College Republicans, Young Democrats, Bahai Club, Baptist Student Ministries, Catholic Student Organization, Wesley Foundation, Blinn College Lion's Club, Ebony and Ivory, Hispanic Organization, Kappa Kappa Psi, Chi Alpha.

Athletics. NJCAA. **Intercollegiate:** Baseball M, basketball, cheerleading, football (tackle) M, softball W, volleyball W. **Intramural:** Basketball, softball, volleyball. **Team name:** Buccaneers.

Student services. Career counseling, financial aid counseling, personal counseling, veterans' counselor. **Physically disabled:** Services for visually, speech, hearing impaired. **Transfer:** Transfer adviser, college fairs on campus for students transferring to 4-year colleges.

Contact. E-mail: recruit@blinn.edu
Phone: (979) 830-4140 Fax: (979) 830-4009
Julie Maass, Dean of Admissions/Registrar, Blinn College, 902 College Avenue, Brenham, TX 77833

Bradford School of Business
Houston, Texas
www.bradfordschoolhouston.edu

- For-profit 2-year technical college
- Very large city
- Interview required

General. Regionally accredited; also accredited by ACICS. **Enrollment:** 53 degree-seeking undergraduates. **Degrees:** 3 associate awarded. **Calendar:** Semester. **Full-time faculty:** 7 total. **Part-time faculty:** 7 total.

Basis for selection. Interviews required.

2008-2009 Annual costs. Tuition/fees: $13,800. Lab fees vary depending upon program selected.

Application procedures. Admission: No deadline. $50 fee.

Academics. Credit/placement by examination: CLEP. **Support services:** Learning center, tutoring.

Majors. Business: Accounting. **Health:** Veterinary technology/assistant. **Legal studies:** Legal secretary.

Contact. E-mail: mortiz@bradfordschoolhouston.edu
Phone: (713) 629-1500
Elbert Hamilton, Director of Education, Bradford School of Business, 4669 Southwest Freeway, Houston, TX 77027

Brazosport College
Lake Jackson, Texas
www.brazosport.edu **CB code: 6054**

- Public 2-year community college
- Commuter campus in large town

General. Founded in 1948. Regionally accredited. **Enrollment:** 3,883 degree-seeking undergraduates. **Degrees:** 5 bachelor's, 218 associate awarded. **Location:** 50 miles from Houston. **Calendar:** Semester, extensive summer session. **Full-time faculty:** 80 total. **Part-time faculty:** 85 total. **Class size:** 49% < 20, 50% 20-39, 1% 40-49. **Special facilities:** Chemical unit operations laboratory, music performance hall, child care center, center for business and industry training.

Student profile.

Out-of-state:	1%	**25 or older:**	32%

Transfer out. Colleges most students transferred to 2008: University of Houston, Sam Houston State University, Texas A&M University, Stephen F. Austin State University, University of Texas.

Basis for selection. Open admission, but selective for some programs. Special requirements for nursing and applied technology programs.

2008-2009 Annual costs. Tuition/fees: $1,392; $2,022 out-of-district; $3,432 out-of-state. Per-credit charge: $31 in-district; $52 out-of-district; $99 out-of-state. Books/supplies: $910. Personal expenses: $2,504.

2007-2008 Financial aid. Need-based: 85% of total undergraduate aid awarded as scholarships/grants, 15% as loans/jobs. Need-based aid available for part-time students. Work-study available for part-time students. **Non-need-based:** Scholarships awarded for academics, art, job skills, leadership, music/drama, state residency.

Application procedures. Admission: Closing date 8/22. No application fee. Admission notification on a rolling basis. **Financial aid:** Priority date 7/1; no closing date. FAFSA, institutional form required. Applicants notified on a rolling basis starting 5/1.

Academics. Special study options: Cooperative education, distance learning, dual enrollment of high school students, ESL, honors, internships. Bachelor's degree programs available on campus. License preparation in nursing, paramedic. **Credit/placement by examination:** CLEP, institutional tests. 24 credit hours maximum toward associate degree. Minimum of 6 semester credit hours must be earned in residence before credit posted on transcript. **Support services:** GED preparation and test center, learning center, remedial instruction, study skills assistance, tutoring.

Majors. Agriculture: General. **Biology:** General. **Business:** General, accounting, administrative services, business admin, finance, purchasing. **Communications:** General. **Computer sciences:** General, programming. **Construction:** Electrician, pipefitting. **Education:** General, elementary, health, secondary. **Engineering:** General. **Engineering technology:** Construction, drafting, electrical. **Family/consumer sciences:** General, child care. **Foreign languages:** General. **Health:** Nursing (RN). **History:** General. **Legal studies:** General, paralegal. **Liberal arts:** Arts/sciences, library science. **Math:** General. **Mechanic/repair:** Automotive, heating/ac/refrig. **Physical sciences:** General, chemistry, physics, planetary. **Protective services:** Police science. **Psychology:** General. **Public administration:** General. **Social sciences:** Economics, political science, sociology. **Theology:** Theology. **Visual/performing arts:** Art, dramatic.

Computing on campus. 40 workstations in library, computer center. Online course registration, wireless network available.

Student life. Freshman orientation: Mandatory. Preregistration for classes offered. Half-hour video presentation. **Activities:** Bands, choral groups, drama, music ensembles, student government, student newspaper, Baptist student ministry, Phi Theta Kappa.

Athletics. Intramural: Archery, basketball, bowling, fencing, football (non-tackle), golf, soccer, softball, table tennis, tennis, volleyball.

Student services. Career counseling, student employment services, financial aid counseling, on-campus daycare, personal counseling, placement for graduates, veterans' counselor. **Physically disabled:** Services for visually impaired. **Transfer:** Transfer adviser, college fairs on campus for students transferring to 4-year colleges.

Contact. E-mail: regist@brazosport.edu
Phone: (979) 230-3216 Fax: (979) 230-3376
Patricia Leyendecker, Director of Admissions and Registrar, Brazosport College, 500 College Drive, Lake Jackson, TX 77566

Brookhaven College

Farmers Branch, Texas
www.brookhavencollege.edu **CB code: 6070**

- Public 2-year community college
- Commuter campus in large town

General. Founded in 1965. Regionally accredited. **Enrollment:** 8,817 degree-seeking undergraduates. **Degrees:** 432 associate awarded. **Location:** 12 miles from downtown Dallas. **Calendar:** Semester, limited summer session. **Full-time faculty:** 128 total. **Part-time faculty:** 588 total.

Basis for selection. Open admission. Observes TASP guidelines.

2008-2009 Annual costs. Tuition/fees: $1,170; $2,160 out-of-district; $3,450 out-of-state. Per-credit charge: $39 in-district; $72 out-of-district. Books/supplies: $1,200. Personal expenses: $920.

Financial aid. Additional information: Some tuition waivers available based upon state residency.

Application procedures. Admission: No deadline. No application fee. Admission notification on a rolling basis. **Financial aid:** Priority date 6/1; no closing date. FAFSA required. Applicants notified on a rolling basis.

Academics. Special study options: Cooperative education, distance learning, dual enrollment of high school students, ESL, honors, internships, study abroad, weekend college. License preparation in nursing, paramedic, radiology, real estate. **Credit/placement by examination:** CLEP, IB. At least 25% of credit hours required for graduation must be taken by instruction and not by credit-by-exam. **Support services:** GED preparation, remedial instruction, study skills assistance, tutoring, writing center.

Majors. Business: General, accounting, apparel, business admin, e-commerce, entrepreneurial studies, executive assistant, fashion, management information systems, marketing, office management, office technology. **Computer sciences:** Information systems, programming. **Education:** Early childhood. **Engineering technology:** Electrical. **Family/consumer sciences:** Child care. **Health:** Nursing (RN), radiologic technology/medical imaging. **Legal studies:** Legal secretary. **Mechanic/repair:** Automotive. **Transportation:** General. **Visual/performing arts:** Commercial/advertising art, design.

Most popular majors. Business/marketing 12%, health sciences 17%, liberal arts 55%, trade and industry 7%.

Computing on campus. Commuter students can connect to campus network. Helpline, wireless network available.

Student life. Freshman orientation: Mandatory. **Activities:** Choral groups, drama, film society, music ensembles, musical theater, student newspaper.

Athletics. NJCAA. **Intercollegiate:** Baseball M, golf M, soccer M, tennis. **Intramural:** Soccer. **Team name:** Bears.

Student services. Adult student services, career counseling, student employment services, health services, personal counseling, placement for graduates, veterans' counselor. **Physically disabled:** Services for visually, speech impaired. **Transfer:** College fairs on campus for students transferring to 4-year colleges.

Contact. E-mail: bhcadmissions@dcccd.edu
Phone: (972) 860-4883 Fax: (972) 860-4886
Thoa Vo, Director of Admissions, Brookhaven College, 3939 Valley View Lane, Farmers Branch, TX 75244-4997

Cedar Valley College

Lancaster, Texas
www.cedarvalleycollege.edu **CB code: 6148**

- Public 2-year community college
- Commuter campus in large town

General. Founded in 1974. Regionally accredited. One of seven colleges in the Dallas County Community College District. **Enrollment:** 4,400 degree-seeking undergraduates. **Degrees:** 264 associate awarded. **Location:** 10 miles from Dallas. **Calendar:** Semester, limited summer session. **Full-time faculty:** 61 total. **Part-time faculty:** 140 total. **Special facilities:** Veterinary technology facilities, commercial music facilities including recording studios. **Partnerships:** Formal partnerships with Vartec, Owens Corning, University of North Texas, Upward Bound.

Transfer out. Colleges most students transferred to 2008: University of Texas at Arlington, Texas A&M at Commerce, University of North Texas.

Basis for selection. Open admission. Student must be graduate of accredited high school, or at least 18 years of age, or be admitted by individual approval. **Homeschooled:** Interview required.

2008-2009 Annual costs. Tuition/fees: $1,170; $2,160 out-of-district; $3,450 out-of-state. Per-credit charge: $39 in-district; $72 out-of-district. Books/supplies: $800. Personal expenses: $1,045.

Application procedures. Admission: No deadline. No application fee. Application must be submitted on paper. Admission notification on a rolling basis. **Financial aid:** Priority date 5/1; no closing date. FAFSA required. Applicants notified on a rolling basis.

Academics. Special study options: Cooperative education, distance learning, dual enrollment of high school students, liberal arts/career combination, student-designed major, study abroad, weekend college. License preparation in real estate. **Credit/placement by examination:** CLEP, institutional tests. 45 credit hours maximum toward associate degree. **Support services:** GED preparation, learning center, reduced course load, remedial instruction, study skills assistance, tutoring, writing center.

Majors. Business: Accounting/business management, administrative services, business admin, management information systems, marketing, office management, office technology, real estate. **Communications technology:** Recording arts. **Computer sciences:** Data processing, networking, programming. **Health:** Veterinary technology/assistant. **Mechanic/repair:** Heating/

ac/refrig. **Protective services:** Law enforcement admin. **Visual/performing arts:** Design, music performance.

Computing on campus. 400 workstations in library, computer center, student center. Commuter students can connect to campus network. Online course registration, helpline, repair service, wireless network available.

Student life. Freshman orientation: Mandatory. 1-day program includes assessment testing. **Activities:** Jazz band, choral groups, drama, music ensembles, musical theater, student government, student newspaper, student government, Sierra club, Christian student union, Latin American student organization, Phi Theta Kappa, student ambassadors, preprofessional club, art club, veterinary technology club.

Athletics. NJCAA. **Intercollegiate:** Baseball M, basketball M. **Intramural:** Cheerleading W, football (non-tackle) M, golf, soccer W, volleyball W. **Team name:** Suns.

Student services. Career counseling, services for economically disadvantaged, student employment services, financial aid counseling, health services, personal counseling, placement for graduates, veterans' counselor. **Physically disabled:** Services for visually, speech, hearing impaired. **Transfer:** Pre-admission transcript evaluation for new students. College fairs on campus for students transferring to 4-year colleges.

Contact. E-mail: cdw3310@dcccd.edu
Phone: (972) 860-8201 Fax: (972) 860-8001
Carolyn Boswell-Ward, Director of Admissions and Registrar, Cedar Valley College, 3030 North Dallas Avenue, Lancaster, TX 75134

Central Texas College

Killeen, Texas
www.ctcd.edu **CB code: 6130**

- Public 2-year community and technical college
- Commuter campus in small city

General. Founded in 1965. Regionally accredited. **Enrollment:** 18,488 degree-seeking undergraduates. **Degrees:** 2,494 associate awarded. **ROTC:** Army. **Location:** 5 miles from Killeen, 60 miles from Austin. **Calendar:** Semester, extensive summer session. **Full-time faculty:** 158 total. **Part-time faculty:** 807 total. **Special facilities:** Planetarium, space theater. **Partnerships:** Formal partnerships with Killeen and Copperas Cove ISDs (school to career facilitator program).

Student profile.

Out-of-state:	3%	**Live on campus:**	2%
25 or older:	60%		

Transfer out. Colleges most students transferred to 2008: University of Mary Hardin-Baylor, Tarleton State University, Texas State University, University of North Texas, Texas Tech.

Basis for selection. Open admission, but selective for some programs. Observes TASP requirements. Special requirements for registered nursing, paramedic, EMT, aviation science programs. Interview required for medical laboratory technician, nursing programs; audition recommended for music; portfolio recommended for art. **Homeschooled:** Transcript of courses and grades required.

High school preparation. 22 units recommended. Recommended units include English 4, mathematics 3, social studies 1.5, history 1, science 2 (laboratory 1) and academic electives 1. 0.5 economics, 0.5 speech, 1 technology applications, 1 physical education, 0.5 foundations of personal fitness, 0.5 health, 5.5 electives recommended.

2008-2009 Annual costs. Tuition/fees: $1,380; $1,680 out-of-district; $4,140 out-of-state. Per-credit charge: $36 in-district; $46 out-of-district; $130 out-of-state. Room/board: $3,300. Books/supplies: $1,200. Personal expenses: $500.

Financial aid. All financial aid based on need. Need-based aid available for part-time students. Work-study available nights, weekends and for part-time students.

Application procedures. Admission: No deadline. No application fee. Application must be submitted on paper. Admission notification on a rolling basis. **Financial aid:** Closing date 7/1. FAFSA, institutional form required. Applicants notified on a rolling basis starting 3/1; must reply within 4 week(s) of notification.

Academics. Special study options: Cross-registration, distance learning, dual enrollment of high school students, ESL, independent study, internships, liberal arts/career combination. License preparation in aviation, nursing, paramedic, real estate. **Credit/placement by examination:** AP, CLEP, IB, institutional tests. 48 credit hours maximum toward associate degree. **Support services:** GED preparation and test center, learning center, reduced course load, remedial instruction, study skills assistance, tutoring.

Majors. Agriculture: Farm/ranch. **Biology:** General. **Business:** General, administrative services, business admin, hospitality admin, office management, real estate, tourism promotion. **Communications:** Broadcast journalism. **Communications technology:** Graphic/printing. **Computer sciences:** General, computer science, data processing, information systems, networking, programming. **Education:** General. **Engineering:** General. **Engineering technology:** Drafting. **Family/consumer sciences:** Child care. **Foreign languages:** General. **Health:** Clinical lab assistant, clinical lab technology, nursing (RN), premedicine, substance abuse counseling. **Interdisciplinary:** Biological/physical sciences. **Legal studies:** General, paralegal, prelaw. **Liberal arts:** Arts/sciences. **Math:** General. **Mechanic/repair:** General, auto body, automotive, diesel, electronics/electrical, heating/ac/refrig. **Personal/culinary services:** Culinary arts. **Physical sciences:** Chemistry, geology, physics. **Protective services:** Law enforcement admin. **Social sciences:** General. **Visual/performing arts:** Art.

Most popular majors. Interdisciplinary studies 70%, military 9%.

Computing on campus. 600 workstations in library, computer center. Online course registration, online library, helpline available.

Student life. Freshman orientation: Available. Preregistration for classes offered. **Housing:** Coed dorms, apartments available. $100 nonrefundable deposit, deadline 8/1. **Activities:** Choral groups, drama, radio station, student government, student newspaper, TV station.

Student services. Adult student services, alcohol/substance abuse counseling, career counseling, services for economically disadvantaged, student employment services, financial aid counseling, on-campus daycare, placement for graduates, veterans' counselor. **Physically disabled:** Services for visually, speech, hearing impaired. **Transfer:** Pre-admission transcript evaluation for new students. Transfer center, transfer adviser, college fairs on campus for students transferring to 4-year colleges.

Contact. E-mail: admissions@ctcd.edu
Phone: (254) 526-1696 Toll-free number: (800) 792-3348 ext. 1696
Fax: (254) 526-1481
Dottie Kyle, Director, Admissions and Recruitment, Central Texas College, Box 1800, Killeen, TX 76540

Cisco Junior College

Cisco, Texas
www.cjc.edu **CB code: 6096**

- Public 2-year junior college
- Commuter campus in small town

General. Founded in 1940. Regionally accredited. **Enrollment:** 3,421 degree-seeking undergraduates; 338 non-degree-seeking students. **Degrees:** 221 associate awarded. **Location:** 100 miles from Fort Worth. **Calendar:** Semester, limited summer session. **Full-time faculty:** 73 total. **Part-time faculty:** 93 total.

Student profile. Among degree-seeking undergraduates, 1,395 enrolled as first-time, first-year students.

Part-time:	48%	**Hispanic American:**	18%
Out-of-state:	8%	**International:**	1%
Women:	61%	**25 or older:**	90%
African American:	9%	**Live on campus:**	28%
Asian American:	1%		

Basis for selection. Open admission.

2008-2009 Annual costs. Tuition/fees: $1,960; $2,440 out-of-district; $2,746 out-of-state. Room cost $100 more per semester for women. Room/board: $3,100. Books/supplies: $800. Personal expenses: $1,986.

Application procedures. Admission: No deadline. No application fee. Admission notification on a rolling basis. **Financial aid:** Priority date 8/15; no closing date. FAFSA required. Applicants notified on a rolling basis starting 8/15.

Academics. Special study options: Dual enrollment of high school students. **Credit/placement by examination:** CLEP. 22 credit hours maximum toward associate degree. **Support services:** GED test center, remedial instruction, tutoring.

Two-Year Colleges

Majors. **Agriculture:** Animal sciences, business. **Biology:** General. **Business:** General, accounting. **Communications:** General. **Computer sciences:** General. **Education:** General. **Engineering:** General. **Engineering technology:** Drafting. **Foreign languages:** French, Spanish. **Health:** Medical records technology. **History:** General. **Legal studies:** Prelaw. **Math:** General. **Mechanic/repair:** General. **Physical sciences:** Chemistry. **Psychology:** General. **Public administration:** Social work. **Social sciences:** General, economics, sociology. **Visual/performing arts:** Art, dramatic.

Student life. **Housing:** Single-sex dorms available. **Activities:** Bands, choral groups, drama, music ensembles, student government, student newspaper.

Athletics. **Intercollegiate:** Baseball W, basketball, football (tackle) M, golf, rodeo, soccer W, volleyball W. **Intramural:** Basketball, track and field. **Team name:** Wranglers.

Student services. Health services, personal counseling.

Contact. Phone: (254) 442-5000 Fax: (254) 442-5000
Olin Odom, Dean of Enrollment Management, Cisco Junior College, 101 College Heights, Cisco, TX 76437

Clarendon College
Clarendon, Texas
www.clarendoncollege.edu **CB code: 6097**

- Public 2-year community college
- Residential campus in rural community

General. Founded in 1898. Regionally accredited. **Enrollment:** 1,151 degree-seeking undergraduates; 91 non-degree-seeking students. **Degrees:** 97 associate awarded. **Location:** 60 miles from Amarillo. **Calendar:** Semester, limited summer session. **Full-time faculty:** 31 total; 3% have terminal degrees, 42% women. **Part-time faculty:** 52 total; 8% have terminal degrees, 67% women. **Class size:** 73% < 20, 24% 20-39, 1% 40-49, less than 1% 50-99, less than 1% >100. **Partnerships:** Formal partnership with Tech Prep.

Student profile. Among degree-seeking undergraduates, 12% enrolled in a vocational program, 501 enrolled as first-time, first-year students, 65 transferred in from other institutions.

Part-time:	53%	**Hispanic American:**	18%
Out-of-state:	8%	**Native American:**	1%
Women:	49%	**International:**	1%
African American:	8%	**Live on campus:**	24%
Asian American:	1%		

Transfer out. **Colleges most students transferred to 2008:** West Texas A&M University, Texas Tech University, Texas A&M University, Tarleton State University, Midwestern State University.

Basis for selection. Open admission, but selective for some programs. Special requirements for certain technical programs and vocational nursing. Interview before May 1 required for ranch and feedlot operations program. 3 personal references, interview required for vocational nursing program. **Homeschooled:** Transcript of courses and grades required. A request for admission by Individual Approval should be submitted to the Admissions Office.

High school preparation. 24 units recommended. Recommended units include English 4, mathematics 4, social studies 2, history 2, science 4, foreign language 2, academic electives 3.5. 0.5 health, 0.5 economics, 1 computer, 0.5 speech recommended.

2008-2009 Annual costs. Tuition/fees: $2,370; $2,940 out-of-district; $3,510 out-of-state. Room/board: $3,450. Books/supplies: $1,000. Personal expenses: $3,894.

2007-2008 Financial aid. **Need-based:** 48% of total undergraduate aid awarded as scholarships/grants, 52% as loans/jobs. Need-based aid available for part-time students. Work-study available nights, weekends and for part-time students. **Non-need-based:** Scholarships awarded for academics, art, athletics, leadership, music/drama, state residency.

Application procedures. **Admission:** Priority date 8/15; no deadline. No application fee. Admission notification on a rolling basis. **Financial aid:** Priority date 8/1; no closing date. FAFSA, institutional form required. Applicants notified on a rolling basis starting 5/15; must reply by 8/15 or within 2 week(s) of notification.

Academics. **Special study options:** Cross-registration, distance learning, dual enrollment of high school students, internships, liberal arts/career combination, student-designed major. License preparation in nursing. **Credit/placement by examination:** AP, CLEP. 30 credit hours maximum toward associate degree. **Support services:** GED test center, remedial instruction, tutoring.

Majors. **Agriculture:** General, agronomy, animal sciences, business, economics, equestrian studies, farm/ranch. **Biology:** General. **Business:** General, accounting, finance, management science, marketing, office technology. **Communications:** General. **Computer sciences:** General. **Conservation:** Environmental science. **Education:** General, elementary, secondary. **Engineering:** General. **Engineering technology:** Computer systems. **Foreign languages:** General. **Health:** EMT paramedic, health services, nursing (RN), predental, premedicine, prepharmacy, preveterinary. **History:** General. **Legal studies:** Prelaw. **Liberal arts:** Arts/sciences. **Math:** General. **Parks/recreation:** General, exercise sciences, health/fitness. **Philosophy/religion:** Religion. **Physical sciences:** Chemistry, geology, physics. **Protective services:** Criminal justice. **Psychology:** General. **Public administration:** Social work. **Social sciences:** Economics, political science, sociology. **Visual/performing arts:** Art, commercial/advertising art, dramatic.

Most popular majors. Agriculture 16%, business/marketing 18%, computer/information sciences 10%, education 8%, health sciences 10%, liberal arts 18%, security/protective services 7%.

Computing on campus. 221 workstations in library, computer center. Dormitories wired for high-speed internet access. Commuter students can connect to campus network. Online course registration, online library, wireless network available.

Student life. **Freshman orientation:** Mandatory, $40 fee. Preregistration for classes offered. Full-semester, two-hour hybrid course with both in-class and on-line components. **Housing:** Guaranteed on-campus for freshmen. Coed dorms, single-sex dorms, special housing for disabled available. $100 partly refundable deposit. **Activities:** Jazz band, choral groups, drama, music ensembles, student government, multicultural club, student ambassadors, Block & Bridle, rodeo club.

Athletics. NJCAA. **Intercollegiate:** Baseball M, basketball, cheerleading, cross-country, rodeo, softball W, volleyball W. **Intramural:** Basketball, football (non-tackle), golf, rodeo, table tennis, volleyball. **Team name:** Bulldogs.

Student services. Career counseling, financial aid counseling. **Physically disabled:** Services for visually, speech, hearing impaired. **Transfer:** College fairs on campus for students transferring to 4-year colleges.

Contact. E-mail: admissions@clarendoncollege.edu
Phone: (806) 874-3571 Toll-free number: (800) 687-9737
Fax: (806) 874-3201
Brandi Havens, Director of Admissions and Registrar, Clarendon College, PO Box 968, Clarendon, TX 79226

Coastal Bend College
Beeville, Texas
www.coastalbend.edu **CB code: 6055**

- Public 2-year community college
- Commuter campus in large town

General. Founded in 1965. Regionally accredited. In addition to main campus in Beeville, there are campuses in Alice, Kingsville, and Pleasanton. **Enrollment:** 3,450 degree-seeking undergraduates. **Degrees:** 214 associate awarded. **Location:** 60 miles from Corpus Christi, 90 miles from San Antonio. **Calendar:** Semester, limited summer session. **Full-time faculty:** 94 total; 4% have terminal degrees, 36% minority, 53% women. **Part-time faculty:** 88 total; 2% have terminal degrees, 42% minority, 61% women. **Partnerships:** Formal partnerships with national corporations to provide truck driver training, with local businesses to provide training for employees, and with high schools and tech prep programs.

Student profile. Among degree-seeking undergraduates, 68% enrolled in a transfer program, 32% enrolled in a vocational program, 1% already have a bachelor's degree or higher, 1,126 enrolled as first-time, first-year students, 167 transferred in from other institutions.

Part-time:	59%	**Asian American:**	1%
Out-of-state:	1%	**Hispanic American:**	65%
Women:	64%	**25 or older:**	60%
African American:	4%	**Live on campus:**	5%

Transfer out. 36% of students enrolled in the transfer program go on to 4-year colleges. **Colleges most students transferred to 2008:** Texas A&M-Corpus Christi, Texas A&M-Kingsville, Southwest Texas State University, Texas A&M-College Station, University of Texas.

Basis for selection. Open admission, but selective for some programs. Texas requires that all students satisfy Texas THEA test requirements before being enrolled in college-level courses in public college or university. Scores not used in admission decisions. Special requirements for dental hygiene and vocational nursing programs. **Adult students:** SAT/ACT scores not required. **Homeschooled:** Transcript of courses and grades required. Transcript must be notarized.

2008-2009 Annual costs. Tuition/fees: $1,820; $3,590 out-of-district; $4,040 out-of-state. Meal ticket (a la carte) food service available. Room only; $1,560. Books/supplies: $600. Personal expenses: $1,500.

2007-2008 Financial aid. Need-based: Need-based aid available for part-time students. **Non-need-based:** Scholarships awarded for academics, leadership.

Application procedures. Admission: No deadline. No application fee. Admission notification on a rolling basis. **Financial aid:** Priority date 4/1; no closing date. FAFSA, institutional form required. Applicants notified on a rolling basis starting 5/1; must reply within 2 week(s) of notification.

Academics. Special study options: Cooperative education, cross-registration, distance learning, dual enrollment of high school students, independent study, internships, liberal arts/career combination, weekend college. License preparation in dental hygiene, nursing, radiology. **Credit/placement by examination:** CLEP, institutional tests. 30 credit hours maximum toward associate degree. ACCUPLACER, ASSET, COMPASS, MAPS tests may be used instead of THEA. **Support services:** GED preparation and test center, learning center, remedial instruction, study skills assistance, tutoring.

Majors. Biology: General. **Business:** General, accounting, administrative services, business admin, office technology, office/clerical. **Communications:** General. **Computer sciences:** General, computer science, data processing, programming. **Conservation:** General. **Education:** General, elementary, secondary. **Engineering:** General. **Engineering technology:** Drafting. **Family/consumer sciences:** General, child care. **Foreign languages:** Spanish. **Health:** Dental hygiene, medical records technology, medical secretary, nursing (RN), predental, premedicine, prepharmacy, preveterinary. **History:** General. **Legal studies:** Prelaw. **Liberal arts:** Arts/sciences. **Math:** General. **Physical sciences:** Chemistry, geology, physics. **Protective services:** Corrections, criminal justice, police science. **Psychology:** General. **Social sciences:** Political science, sociology. **Visual/performing arts:** General, commercial/advertising art, studio arts.

Computing on campus. 700 workstations in library, computer center. Dormitories wired for high-speed internet access and linked to campus network. Commuter students can connect to campus network. Online course registration, online library, helpline, wireless network available.

Student life. Freshman orientation: Mandatory. Preregistration for classes offered. Half-day program, parents welcome. **Housing:** Single-sex dorms, apartments available. $250 partly refundable deposit, deadline 8/15. **Activities:** Student government, Baptist Student Union, Newman Club.

Athletics. NJCAA. **Intercollegiate:** Basketball, volleyball W. **Intramural:** Archery, badminton, basketball, bowling, cross-country, golf, soccer, softball, swimming, table tennis, tennis, track and field, volleyball, weight lifting. **Team name:** Cougars.

Student services. Career counseling, services for economically disadvantaged, student employment services, financial aid counseling, on-campus daycare, personal counseling, placement for graduates, veterans' counselor. **Physically disabled:** Services for visually, speech, hearing impaired. **Transfer:** Pre-admission transcript evaluation for new students. Transfer adviser, college fairs on campus for students transferring to 4-year colleges.

Contact. E-mail: register@coastalbend.edu
Phone: (361) 354-2254 Toll-free number: (800) 722-2838 ext. 2254
Fax: (361) 354-2554
Alicia Ulloa, Registrar and Director Admissions, Coastal Bend College, 3800 Charco Road, Beeville, TX 78102

College of the Mainland

Texas City, Texas
www.com.edu — **CB code: 6133**

- Public 2-year community and technical college
- Commuter campus in large town

General. Founded in 1966. Regionally accredited. **Enrollment:** 3,561 degree-seeking undergraduates. **Degrees:** 259 associate awarded. **Location:** 25 miles from Houston. **Calendar:** Semester, extensive summer session. **Full-time faculty:** 100 total. **Part-time faculty:** 105 total.

Student profile.

Out-of-state:	1%	**25 or older:**	44%

Transfer out. Colleges most students transferred to 2008: University of Houston-Clear Lake.

Basis for selection. Open admission, but selective for some programs. Special requirements for nursing program.

2008-2009 Annual costs. Tuition/fees: $1,282; $2,302 out-of-district; $3,262 out-of-state. Books/supplies: $800. Personal expenses: $1,087.

Financial aid. All financial aid based on need. Need-based aid available for part-time students. Work-study available nights, weekends and for part-time students.

Application procedures. Admission: No deadline. No application fee. Admission notification on a rolling basis. **Financial aid:** No deadline. FAFSA, institutional form required. Applicants notified on a rolling basis.

Academics. Special study options: Cooperative education, cross-registration, distance learning, double major, dual enrollment of high school students, independent study, internships, weekend college. License preparation in nursing, paramedic, real estate. **Credit/placement by examination:** CLEP, institutional tests. 24 credit hours maximum toward associate degree. **Support services:** GED preparation and test center, learning center, remedial instruction, tutoring, writing center.

Majors. Biology: General. **Business:** General, accounting, administrative services, banking/financial services, business admin, labor relations, marketing, office management, office technology, office/clerical, real estate. **Communications:** Journalism. **Computer sciences:** General, programming. **Education:** Elementary, secondary. **Engineering:** General. **Engineering technology:** Drafting, electrical. **Family/consumer sciences:** Child care. **Health:** Licensed practical nurse. **History:** General. **Interdisciplinary:** Biological/physical sciences. **Liberal arts:** Arts/sciences. **Math:** General. **Mechanic/repair:** Diesel, heating/ac/refrig. **Physical sciences:** Chemistry, planetary. **Protective services:** Fire safety technology, police science. **Psychology:** General. **Public administration:** General, social work. **Social sciences:** General, economics, political science, sociology. **Visual/performing arts:** General, dramatic, studio arts.

Computing on campus. 100 workstations in library, computer center. Online course registration, wireless network available.

Student life. Freshman orientation: Mandatory. Preregistration for classes offered. **Activities:** Bands, choral groups, drama, literary magazine, music ensembles, musical theater, student government, Phi Beta Kappa, Students for Christ, COM Amigos, Organization of African-American Culture, biology club.

Athletics. Intramural: Basketball, football (non-tackle) M, racquetball, soccer, softball, tennis, volleyball. **Team name:** Ducks.

Student services. Career counseling, student employment services, financial aid counseling, on-campus daycare, personal counseling, placement for graduates, veterans' counselor. **Physically disabled:** Services for visually, speech, hearing impaired. **Transfer:** Transfer adviser, college fairs on campus for students transferring to 4-year colleges.

Contact. Phone: (409) 938-1211 ext. 264 Fax: (409) 938-3126
Kelly Musick, Director of Admissions and Records, College of the Mainland, 1200 Amburn Road, Texas City, TX 77591

Collin County Community College District

Plano, Texas — **CB member**
www.ccccd.edu — **CB code: 1951**

- Public 2-year community college
- Commuter campus in large city

General. Founded in 1985. Regionally accredited. **Enrollment:** 20,695 degree-seeking undergraduates; 305 non-degree-seeking students. **Degrees:** 1,180 associate awarded. **ROTC:** Army. **Location:** 25 miles from Dallas. **Calendar:** Semester, extensive summer session. **Full-time faculty:** 293 total; 14% minority, 56% women. **Part-time faculty:** 839 total; 22% minority, 59% women. **Class size:** 33% < 20, 64% 20-39, 3% 40-49, less than 1% 50-99. **Special facilities:** Regional fire training facility. **Partnerships:** Formal partnership with Cisco to provide Certified Network Professional Certification.

Student profile. Among degree-seeking undergraduates, 4,198 enrolled as first-time, first-year students.

Part-time:	59%	**Hispanic American:**	13%
Out-of-state:	9%	**Native American:**	1%
Women:	57%	**International:**	1%
African American:	10%	**25 or older:**	33%
Asian American:	10%		

Transfer out. Colleges most students transferred to 2008: University of Texas at Dallas, University of North Texas, Texas A&M University, University of Texas at Austin, Texas Tech University.

Basis for selection. Open admission, but selective for some programs. Special requirements for programs in nursing, dental hygiene, emergency medical services, firefighter, respiratory care, interpreter prep, honors institute, center for advanced study in mathematics and natural sciences. **Homeschooled:** If under 18 years must provide written parental/guardian permission.

High school preparation. 17 units recommended. Recommended units include English 4, mathematics 3, social studies 2, history 2, science 2 (laboratory 2) and foreign language 2.

2008-2009 Annual costs. Tuition/fees: $1,114; $1,534 out-of-district; $3,184 out-of-state. Per-credit charge: $37 in-district; $51 out-of-district; $106 out-of-state. Books/supplies: $810. Personal expenses: $1,444.

2007-2008 Financial aid. Need-based: 984 full-time freshmen applied for aid; 802 were judged to have need; 642 of these received aid. Average need met was 32%. Average scholarship/grant was $3,650; average loan $2,773. 57% of total undergraduate aid awarded as scholarships/grants, 43% as loans/jobs. Need-based aid available for part-time students. Work-study available nights, weekends and for part-time students. **Non-need-based:** Awarded to 555 full-time undergraduates, including 259 freshmen. Scholarships awarded for academics, art, athletics, music/drama.

Application procedures. Admission: No deadline. No application fee. Admission notification on a rolling basis. **Financial aid:** Priority date 6/1, closing date 6/30. FAFSA, institutional form required. Applicants notified on a rolling basis starting 5/1; must reply within 2 week(s) of notification.

Academics. Special study options: Cooperative education, distance learning, dual enrollment of high school students, ESL, honors, internships, teacher certification program, weekend college. Learning communities; service learning opportunities; dual admissions agreements with University of North Texas, University of Texas at Dallas, Southern Methodist University, Texas Women?s University, Texas Tech University, Texas A&M University-Commerce, Baylor University, Texas A&M, Dallas Baptist University, Austin College. License preparation in dental hygiene, nursing. **Credit/placement by examination:** CLEP, institutional tests. 18 credit hours maximum toward associate degree. 6 hours traditional credit must be completed in residence before examination credit awarded. **Support services:** Learning center, remedial instruction, study skills assistance, tutoring, writing center.

Honors college/program. Students with GPA of 3.5 or over admitted to Honors Institute.

Majors. Business: Business admin, hospitality admin, office technology, real estate, sales/distribution. **Communications technology:** Animation/special effects. **Computer sciences:** General, networking, programming, web page design. **Engineering technology:** Drafting, electrical, electrical drafting, telecommunications. **Family/consumer sciences:** Child development. **Foreign languages:** Sign language interpretation. **Health:** Dental hygiene, EMT paramedic, nursing (RN), respiratory therapy technology. **Legal studies:** Paralegal. **Mechanic/repair:** Electronics/electrical. **Protective services:** Fire safety technology. **Science technology:** Biological. **Visual/performing arts:** Commercial/advertising art, interior design, music management.

Computing on campus. 1,980 workstations in library, computer center. Online course registration, helpline, repair service, wireless network available.

Student life. Freshman orientation: Available. One-day program; online section available for distance learning students. **Housing:** Apartments available. **Activities:** Jazz band, campus ministries, choral groups, dance, drama, international student organizations, literary magazine, music ensembles, Model UN, musical theater, student government, American Sign Language club, black student association, nursing student association, hospitality and culinary arts student society, Latter-day Saints student association, Muslim student association, College Republicans.

Athletics. NJCAA. **Intercollegiate:** Basketball, tennis. **Team name:** Cougars.

Student services. Adult student services, alcohol/substance abuse counseling, career counseling, student employment services, financial aid counseling, on-campus daycare, personal counseling, placement for graduates. **Physically disabled:** Services for visually, speech, hearing impaired. **Transfer:** Transfer adviser, college fairs on campus for students transferring to 4-year colleges.

Contact. E-mail: tfields@ccccd.edu
Phone: (972) 881-5710 Fax: (972) 881-5175
Stephanie Meinhardt, Registrar/ Director of Admissions, Collin County Community College District, 2800 East Spring Creek Parkway, Plano, TX 75074

Commonwealth Institute of Funeral Service

Houston, Texas
www.commonwealthinst.org **CB code: 7031**

- Private 2-year school of mortuary science
- Commuter campus in very large city

General. Founded in 1988. Accredited by American Board of Funeral Service Education, Inc. **Enrollment:** 97 degree-seeking undergraduates. **Degrees:** 43 associate awarded. **Location:** 15 miles from downtown. **Calendar:** Quarter. **Full-time faculty:** 6 total. **Part-time faculty:** 8 total. **Class size:** 50% < 20, 50% 50-99.

Student profile.

Out-of-state:	20%	**25 or older:**	49%

Basis for selection. Class rank and standardized test scores most important. SAT or ACT recommended. TASP required.

2008-2009 Annual costs. Tuition/fees: $6,290. Per-credit charge: $143. Books/supplies: $1,183. Personal expenses: $1,102.

Financial aid. All financial aid based on need. Need-based aid available for part-time students.

Application procedures. Admission: $50 fee. Admission notification on a rolling basis beginning on or about 8/28. Application deadline is 3 days after announced enrollment date. **Financial aid:** Priority date 7/20; no closing date. FAFSA required. Applicants notified on a rolling basis starting 7/12.

Academics. Credit/placement by examination: CLEP. **Support services:** Tutoring.

Majors. Personal/culinary services: Mortuary science.

Computing on campus. 15 workstations in library, computer center.

Student life. Housing: Some local funeral homes provide student employees accommodations while attending college. **Activities:** Student government.

Student services. Career counseling, student employment services, financial aid counseling, personal counseling, placement for graduates, veterans' counselor. **Transfer:** Re-entry adviser, pre-admission transcript evaluation for new students. Transfer adviser for students transferring to 4-year colleges.

Contact. Phone: (281) 873-0262 Fax: (281) 873-5232
Patricia Moreno, Registrar, Commonwealth Institute of Funeral Service, 415 Barren Springs Drive, Houston, TX 77090-5913

Court Reporting Institute of Dallas

Dallas, Texas
www.crid.com **CB code: 3231**

- For-profit 2-year technical college
- Very large city

General. Accredited by ACICS. **Enrollment:** 950 degree-seeking undergraduates. **Degrees:** 16 associate awarded. **Calendar:** Quarter. **Full-time faculty:** 15 total. **Part-time faculty:** 10 total.

Basis for selection. Open admission. **Adult students:** SAT/ACT scores not required.

2008-2009 Annual costs. Program cost ranges: $32,600 to $41,400 (associate degree). Books/supplies: $700.

Application procedures. **Admission:** No deadline. $100 fee.

Academics. **Credit/placement by examination:** CLEP.

Majors. **Legal studies:** Court reporting.

Student life. **Activities:** Student newspaper.

Contact. E-mail: rwatts@crid.com
Phone: (214) 350-9722 Toll-free number: (866) 382-1284
Joe Mehlmann, Director, Court Reporting Institute of Dallas, 1341 West Mockingbird Lane, Suite 200E, Dallas, TX 75247

Court Reporting Institute of Houston
Houston, Texas
www.crid.com

- For-profit 2-year technical college
- Commuter campus in very large city
- Application essay, interview required

General. Accredited by ACICS. **Enrollment:** 294 degree-seeking undergraduates. **Degrees:** 5 associate awarded. **Calendar:** Quarter. **Full-time faculty:** 6 total. **Part-time faculty:** 16 total.

Basis for selection. Open admission. **Homeschooled:** Transcript of courses and grades required.

2008-2009 Annual costs. Program cost ranges: $32,600 to $48,000 (associate degree).

Application procedures. **Admission:** No deadline. No application fee.

Academics. **Credit/placement by examination:** CLEP.

Student life. **Freshman orientation:** Mandatory. Preregistration for classes offered. One week before classes start; 2 hours long. **Activities:** Student newspaper.

Contact. E-mail: ono.moore@vatterott-college.edu
Phone: (713) 996-8300 Toll-free number: (866) 996-8300
Fax: (713) 996-8360
Ono Moore, Director of Admissions, Court Reporting Institute of Houston, 13101 Northwest Freeway, Suite 100, Houston, TX 77040

Culinary Institute Alain & Marie LeNotre
Houston, Texas
www.culinaryinstitute.edu

- For-profit 2-year culinary school and junior college
- Very large city

General. Regionally accredited; also accredited by ACCSCT. **Enrollment:** 96 degree-seeking undergraduates. **Calendar:** Five 10-week terms. **Full-time faculty:** 8 total. **Part-time faculty:** 12 total.

Basis for selection. Open admission.

Academics. **Credit/placement by examination:** CLEP.

Majors. **Personal/culinary services:** Baking, chef training.

Contact. E-mail: admission@culinaryinstitute.edu
Phone: (713) 692-0077
Jean-Luc Hauviller, Assistant Director of Admissions, Culinary Institute Alain & Marie LeNotre, 7070 Allensby Street, Houston, TX 77022

Dallas Institute of Funeral Service
Dallas, Texas
www.dallasinstitute.edu **CB code: 7032**

- Private 2-year school of mortuary science
- Commuter campus in very large city

General. Regionally accredited. 15-month AAS in funeral service program and 6-month funeral director's program (Texas, Louisiana, and Missouri students only). **Enrollment:** 132 degree-seeking undergraduates. **Degrees:** 64 associate awarded. **Calendar:** Quarter, limited summer session. **Full-time faculty:** 5 total; 20% minority, 20% women. **Part-time faculty:** 4 total; 25% have terminal degrees, 50% women. **Special facilities:** On-campus embalming facilities.

Student profile. Among degree-seeking undergraduates, 100% enrolled in a vocational program, 11% already have a bachelor's degree or higher, 45 enrolled as first-time, first-year students.

Women:	55%	**Hispanic American:**	11%
African American:	33%		

Basis for selection. Open admission.

2008-2009 Annual costs. Tuition is $3,000 per quarter, which includes required textbooks for the quarter?s studies, laboratory supplies, activities fees, graduation fee, Practice National Board Exam, and National Board Exam (or State Board Exam for FD?s) fee. AAS in Funeral Service Program tuition is $15,000 for 15-month program. Funeral Director?s Program tuition is $6,000 for 6-month program. Students pursuing less than a full quarter of studies will be charged $200 per quarter hour or $3,000, whichever is less. Personal expenses: $1,190.

Application procedures. **Admission:** Closing date 8/15. $50 fee. Admission notification on a rolling basis. Application deadline is 30 days prior to enrollment. **Financial aid:** No deadline. Applicants notified on a rolling basis.

Academics. **Special study options:** Distance learning. **Credit/placement by examination:** AP, CLEP, IB. **Support services:** Study skills assistance, tutoring.

Majors. **Personal/culinary services:** Mortuary science.

Computing on campus. 25 workstations in library, computer center. Wireless network available.

Student services. **Physically disabled:** Services for visually, hearing impaired.

Contact. Phone: (214) 388-5466 Fax: (214) 388-0316
Terry Parrish, Director of Admissions, Dallas Institute of Funeral Service, 3909 South Buckner Boulevard, Dallas, TX 75227-4314

Del Mar College
Corpus Christi, Texas
www.delmar.edu **CB code: 6160**

- Public 2-year community college
- Commuter campus in large city

General. Founded in 1935. Regionally accredited. Courses taught at 7 off-campus sites in the Coastal Bend Region. Center for Early Learning provides day-care on campus. **Enrollment:** 11,310 degree-seeking undergraduates. **Degrees:** 895 associate awarded. **ROTC:** Army. **Location:** 155 miles from San Antonio. **Calendar:** Semester, extensive summer session. **Full-time faculty:** 314 total; 18% have terminal degrees, 28% minority, 50% women. **Part-time faculty:** 268 total. **Partnerships:** Formal partnerships with Corpus Christi Army Depot, University of the Incarnate Word.

Student profile. Among degree-seeking undergraduates, 54% enrolled in a transfer program, 45% enrolled in a vocational program, 1,735 enrolled as first-time, first-year students.

Part-time:	71%	**Asian American:**	2%
Out-of-state:	1%	**Hispanic American:**	58%
Women:	59%	**25 or older:**	38%
African American:	3%		

Transfer out. **Colleges most students transferred to 2008:** Texas A&M University (College Station, Corpus Christi, Kingsville); University of Texas (Austin, San Antonio).

Basis for selection. Open admission, but selective for some programs. Admissions criteria for health science programs vary by program. Interview required for health science programs. **Homeschooled:** Transcript of courses and grades required. Must provide notarized transcript with date of graduation.

High school preparation. 24 units recommended. Recommended units include English 4, mathematics 3, social studies 1, history 2, science 2, foreign language 2 and academic electives 10.

2008-2009 Annual costs. Tuition/fees: $2,124; $5,124 out-of-district; $6,234 out-of-state. Per-credit charge: $37 in-district; $137 out-of-district; $174 out-of-state. Books/supplies: $1,000. Personal expenses: $1,000.

2007-2008 Financial aid. All financial aid based on need. 75% of total undergraduate aid awarded as scholarships/grants, 25% as loans/jobs. Need-based aid available for part-time students. Work-study available nights, weekends and for part-time students.

Application procedures. Admission: No deadline. No application fee. Application must be submitted on paper. Admission notification on a rolling basis. **Financial aid:** Priority date 5/1; no closing date. FAFSA required. Applicants notified on a rolling basis starting 7/1; must reply within 2 week(s) of notification.

Academics. Short semester courses, accelerated associate degree program. **Special study options:** Accelerated study, combined bachelor's/graduate degree, cooperative education, distance learning, dual enrollment of high school students, ESL, honors, independent study, internships, teacher certification program. License preparation in aviation, dental hygiene, nursing, occupational therapy, paramedic, physical therapy, radiology, real estate. **Credit/placement by examination:** AP, CLEP, IB, institutional tests. 30 credit hours maximum toward associate degree. Credit may not be earned by examination for most performance-oriented courses. **Support services:** GED preparation and test center, learning center, remedial instruction, study skills assistance, tutoring, writing center.

Majors. Biology: General. **Business:** General, accounting technology, administrative services, business admin, finance, hotel/motel admin, logistics, management information systems, marketing. **Communications:** Advertising, journalism, radio/tv. **Communications technology:** Photo/film/video. **Computer sciences:** Applications programming, security. **Construction:** Maintenance. **Education:** Art, bilingual, Deaf/hearing impaired, developmentally delayed, early childhood special, elementary, English, foreign languages, history, middle, special. **Engineering technology:** Architectural, drafting, occupational safety. **Family/consumer sciences:** Child care, child development. **Foreign languages:** General, sign language interpretation. **Health:** Clinical lab technology, dental assistant, dental hygiene, EMT paramedic, marriage/family therapy, medical records technology, medical secretary, nuclear medical technology, nursing (RN), occupational therapy assistant, pharmacy assistant, physical therapy assistant, radiologic technology/medical imaging, respiratory therapy technology, sonography, substance abuse counseling, surgical technology. **History:** General. **Legal studies:** Court reporting, paralegal. **Liberal arts:** Arts/sciences. **Math:** General. **Mechanic/repair:** Aircraft, aircraft powerplant, automotive, communications systems, diesel, heating/ac/refrig. **Parks/recreation:** Health/fitness. **Personal/culinary services:** Chef training, food service, restaurant/catering. **Physical sciences:** Chemical physics, chemistry. **Production:** Machine tool, welding. **Protective services:** Criminal justice, fire safety technology, police science. **Psychology:** General. **Public administration:** Social work. **Science technology:** Chemical. **Social sciences:** Political science, sociology. **Visual/performing arts:** Art, dramatic, music performance, music theory/composition.

Most popular majors. Business/marketing 12%, education 6%, health sciences 37%, liberal arts 13%, trade and industry 6%.

Computing on campus. 2,570 workstations in library, computer center, student center. Commuter students can connect to campus network. Online course registration, online library, helpline, wireless network available.

Student life. Freshman orientation: Available. Preregistration for classes offered. 2-hour session held 6 weeks prior to scheduled registration. **Activities:** Bands, campus ministries, choral groups, dance, drama, international student organizations, literary magazine, music ensembles, opera, student government, student newspaper, Newman Club, Latter-day Saints, Baptist student union, InterCambio club, students with disabilities.

Athletics. Intramural: Badminton, basketball, bowling, cross-country, golf, racquetball, sailing, softball, swimming, table tennis, tennis, track and field, volleyball. **Team name:** Vikings.

Student services. Adult student services, career counseling, student employment services, financial aid counseling, on-campus daycare, personal counseling, placement for graduates, veterans' counselor. **Physically disabled:** Services for visually, speech, hearing impaired. **Transfer:** College fairs on campus for students transferring to 4-year colleges.

Contact. E-mail: reginfo@delmar.edu
Phone: (361) 698-1255 Toll-free number: (800) 652-3357
Fax: (361) 698-1595
Frances Jordan, Assistant Dean of Enrollment Services and Registrar, Del Mar College, 101 Baldwin Boulevard, Corpus Christi, TX 78404-3897

Eastfield College

Mesquite, Texas
www.efc.dcccd.edu **CB code: 6201**

- Public 2-year community and liberal arts college
- Commuter campus in small city

General. Founded in 1970. Regionally accredited. **Enrollment:** 10,025 degree-seeking undergraduates; 242 non-degree-seeking students. **Degrees:** 427 associate awarded. **Location:** 1 mile from Dallas. **Calendar:** Semester, limited summer session. **Full-time faculty:** 111 total; 35% minority, 39% women. **Part-time faculty:** 316 total; 28% minority, 49% women. **Class size:** 74% < 20, 24% 20-39, 1% 40-49, less than 1% 50-99, less than 1% >100. **Special facilities:** Automotive diagnostic center.

Student profile. Among degree-seeking undergraduates, 40% enrolled in a transfer program, 27% enrolled in a vocational program, 1,670 enrolled as first-time, first-year students, 188 transferred in from other institutions.

Part-time:	76%	**Asian American:**	4%
Out-of-state:	1%	**Hispanic American:**	33%
Women:	60%	**25 or older:**	36%
African American:	22%		

Transfer out. Colleges most students transferred to 2008: University of Texas-Arlington, University of Texas-Dallas, University of North Texas, Texas A&M-Commerce, Southern Methodist University.

Basis for selection. Open admission. Interview recommended for international students.

High school preparation. 22 units recommended. Recommended units include English 4, mathematics 3, social studies 1, history 1, science 2, academic electives 5.5. 0.5 health education; 0.5 speech; 1 history, geography or science; 1 technical applications; 1 history or geography recommended.

2008-2009 Annual costs. Tuition/fees: $1,170; $2,160 out-of-district; $3,450 out-of-state. Per-credit charge: $39 in-district; $72 out-of-district. Books/supplies: $400. Personal expenses: $935.

Financial aid. Need-based: Need-based aid available for part-time students. Work-study available nights, weekends and for part-time students.

Application procedures. Admission: No deadline. No application fee. Admission notification on a rolling basis. **Financial aid:** Priority date 5/1; no closing date. FAFSA, institutional form required. Applicants notified on a rolling basis starting 4/15.

Academics. Special study options: Cooperative education, distance learning, dual enrollment of high school students, ESL, honors, independent study, weekend college. **Credit/placement by examination:** CLEP, IB, institutional tests. 15 credit hours maximum toward associate degree. **Support services:** GED preparation, learning center, pre-admission summer program, remedial instruction, tutoring.

Majors. Business: General, administrative services, business admin, management information systems, office management, office technology. **Communications technology:** Graphic/printing. **Computer sciences:** General, applications programming, computer science, data processing, networking, programming. **Engineering technology:** CAD/CADD, electrical. **Family/consumer sciences:** Child development. **Foreign languages:** Sign language interpretation. **Health:** Mental health services, substance abuse counseling. **Liberal arts:** Arts/sciences. **Mechanic/repair:** Auto body, automotive, heating/ac/refrig. **Protective services:** Criminal justice. **Public administration:** Social work.

Most popular majors. Business/marketing 10%, engineering/engineering technologies 6%, liberal arts 60%, trade and industry 6%.

Computing on campus. 152 workstations in library, computer center. Online library available.

Student life. Freshman orientation: Available. Online and on-campus orientations offered. **Policies:** Student code of conduct in effect. **Activities:** Bands, choral groups, dance, drama, music ensembles, musical theater, student government, student newspaper, Fellowship of Christian Athletes, Latter-day Saint student association, multicultural club, Vital Signers, piano club, poetry club, automotive club, jazz dance club.

Athletics. NJCAA. **Intercollegiate:** Baseball M, basketball M, golf M, soccer W, volleyball W. **Intramural:** Archery, basketball M, bowling, golf M, gymnastics, tennis, volleyball. **Team name:** Harvesters.

Student services. Career counseling, student employment services, health services, personal counseling, placement for graduates, veterans' counselor. **Physically disabled:** Services for visually, speech, hearing impaired. **Transfer:** College fairs on campus for students transferring to 4-year colleges.

Contact. E-mail: efc@dcccd.edu
Phone: (972) 860-7100 Fax: (972) 860-8306
Linda Richardson, Dean of Admissions and Testing, Eastfield College, 3737 Motley Drive, Mesquite, TX 75150

El Centro College

Dallas, Texas
www.elcentrocollege.edu **CB code: 6199**

- Public 2-year community college
- Commuter campus in very large city

General. Founded in 1966. Regionally accredited. **Enrollment:** 5,984 degree-seeking undergraduates; 1,175 non-degree-seeking students. **Degrees:** 531 associate awarded. **ROTC:** Army. **Location:** Downtown. **Calendar:** Semester, limited summer session. **Full-time faculty:** 122 total; 38% minority, 66% women. **Part-time faculty:** 275 total; 38% minority, 56% women. **Class size:** 64% < 20, 34% 20-39, 1% 40-49, less than 1% 50-99. **Special facilities:** Outdoor amphitheater, art studios, interior design and fashion design studios, allied health laboratories. **Partnerships:** Formal partnerships with regional CISCO training center, many local businesses, and area high schools.

Student profile. Among degree-seeking undergraduates, 58% enrolled in a transfer program, 42% enrolled in a vocational program, 4% already have a bachelor's degree or higher, 963 enrolled as first-time, first-year students, 1,148 transferred in from other institutions.

Part-time:	77%	**Hispanic American:**	32%
Out-of-state:	2%	**Native American:**	1%
Women:	71%	**International:**	2%
African American:	32%	**25 or older:**	50%
Asian American:	4%		

Transfer out. Colleges most students transferred to 2008: University of Texas at Arlington, University of North Texas, University of Texas at Dallas, Southern Methodist University.

Basis for selection. Open admission, but selective for some programs. Specific application requirements for nursing, some allied health, and food and hospitality programs. Interview recommended for international students.

2008-2009 Annual costs. Tuition/fees: $1,170; $2,160 out-of-district; $3,450 out-of-state. Per-credit charge; $39 in-district; $72 out-of-district. Books/supplies: $600. Personal expenses: $600.

Financial aid. Need-based: Need-based aid available for part-time students. **Additional information:** Interview required for financial aid applicants.

Application procedures. Admission: No deadline. No application fee. Admission notification on a rolling basis beginning on or about 6/1. **Financial aid:** Priority date 5/1; no closing date. FAFSA required. Applicants notified on a rolling basis; must reply within 2 week(s) of notification.

Academics. Special study options: Accelerated study, combined bachelor's/graduate degree, cooperative education, cross-registration, distance learning, double major, dual enrollment of high school students, ESL, external degree, honors, internships, liberal arts/career combination, teacher certification program. License preparation in nursing, paramedic, radiology. **Credit/placement by examination:** AP, CLEP, IB, institutional tests. 45 credit hours maximum toward associate degree. **Support services:** GED preparation, learning center, reduced course load, remedial instruction, study skills assistance, tutoring.

Majors. Business: Accounting, business admin, executive assistant, management information systems. **Computer sciences:** Data processing, information systems, programming. **Education:** Teacher assistance. **Health:** Cardiovascular technology, clinical lab technology, medical radiologic technology/radiation therapy, medical records admin, medical records technology, nursing (RN), respiratory therapy technology, sonography. **Legal studies:** Paralegal. **Liberal arts:** Arts/sciences. **Personal/culinary services:** Baking, chef training. **Science technology:** Biological. **Visual/performing arts:** Fashion design, interior design.

Most popular majors. Health sciences 58%, legal studies 10%, liberal arts 15%.

Computing on campus. 832 workstations in library, computer center, student center. Commuter students can connect to campus network. Online course registration, online library, helpline, wireless network available.

Student life. Freshman orientation: Mandatory. Preregistration for classes offered. **Activities:** Choral groups, drama, music ensembles, musical theater, student government, Phi Theta Kappa, organization of Latin American students, El Centro computer society, international college association, Disabled and Realizing Excellence, teacher education preparatory program, Circle-K, association of black college students.

Athletics. Intramural: Basketball, volleyball, weight lifting.

Student services. Adult student services, career counseling, services for economically disadvantaged, student employment services, financial aid counseling, health services, minority student services, personal counseling, placement for graduates, veterans' counselor. **Physically disabled:** Services for visually, hearing impaired. **Transfer:** Transfer adviser, college fairs on campus for students transferring to 4-year colleges.

Contact. E-mail: rgarza@dcccd.edu
Phone: (214) 860-2311 Fax: (214) 860-2233
Rebecca Garza, Director of Admissions/Registrar, El Centro College, 801 Main Street, Dallas, TX 75202

El Paso Community College

El Paso, Texas **CB member**
www,epcc.edu **CB code: 6203**

- Public 2-year community college
- Commuter campus in very large city

General. Founded in 1969. Regionally accredited. Comprised of five campuses in greater El Paso. **Enrollment:** 23,350 degree-seeking undergraduates. **Degrees:** 1,984 associate awarded. **ROTC:** Army. **Location:** 240 miles from Albuquerque, New Mexico. **Calendar:** Semester, extensive summer session. **Full-time faculty:** 396 total. **Part-time faculty:** 934 total. **Special facilities:** Advanced technology center. **Partnerships:** Formal partnerships with local high schools for Tech Prep programs and with hospitals for health programs.

Student profile.

Out-of-state:	6%	**25 or older:**	37%

Transfer out. Colleges most students transferred to 2008: University of Texas at El Paso, New Mexico State University.

Basis for selection. Open admission, but selective for some programs. Observes TASP requirements. Nelson-Denny Reading Test, institutional math test and minimum GPA required for admission to health programs.

2008-2009 Annual costs. Tuition/fees: $1,700; $2,442 out-of-state. Per-credit charge: $47 in-state; $71 out-of-state. Per-credit-hour costs listed are for each additional credit-hour beyond one credit-hour for in-state students, and beyond six credit-hours for out-of-state students. Books/supplies: $545. Personal expenses: $1,223.

2007-2008 Financial aid. Need-based: 90% of total undergraduate aid awarded as scholarships/grants, 10% as loans/jobs. Work-study available nights, weekends and for part-time students. **Non-need-based:** Scholarships awarded for academics, athletics.

Application procedures. Admission: No deadline. $15 fee, may be waived for applicants with need. Admission notification on a rolling basis. **Financial aid:** Priority date 5/1; no closing date. FAFSA, institutional form required. Applicants notified on a rolling basis starting 7/1; must reply within 2 week(s) of notification.

Academics. Special study options: Cooperative education, cross-registration, distance learning, double major, dual enrollment of high school students, ESL, honors, independent study, internships, teacher certification program, weekend college. License preparation in dental hygiene, nursing, physical therapy, radiology. **Credit/placement by examination:** AP, CLEP, IB, institutional tests. 45 credit hours maximum toward associate degree. **Support services:** GED preparation and test center, learning center, remedial instruction, study skills assistance, tutoring, writing center.

Majors. Area/ethnic studies: Women's. **Biology:** General. **Business:** General, accounting, administrative services, business admin, fashion, finance, hospitality/recreation, international, management science, office/clerical, operations, real estate, tourism promotion, tourism/travel. **Communications:** General, journalism. **Communications technology:** General. **Computer sciences:** General, computer science, information systems, programming, systems analysis. **Education:** Elementary, physical, secondary, special, technology/industrial arts. **Engineering:** General. **Engineering technology:** Drafting, electrical. **Family/consumer sciences:** Child care, family studies, institutional food production. **Foreign languages:** General, sign language interpretation. **Health:** Clinical lab technology, dental assistant, dental hygiene, dietetics, medical assistant, medical radiologic technology/radiation therapy, medical records technology, mental health services, nursing (RN), optician, physical therapy assistant, predental, premedicine, prepharmacy, preveterinary, respiratory therapy technology, substance abuse counseling, surgical technology. **History:** General. **Legal studies:** Court reporting, paralegal. **Liberal arts:** Arts/sciences. **Math:** General. **Mechanic/repair:** Electronics/electrical, heating/ac/refrig. **Parks/recreation:** Health/fitness. **Personal/**

culinary services: Culinary arts. **Physical sciences:** Chemistry, geology, physics. **Protective services:** Corrections, criminal justice, fire safety technology. **Psychology:** General. **Social sciences:** General, political science, sociology. **Visual/performing arts:** Art, cinematography, commercial photography, commercial/advertising art, dramatic, fashion design, interior design, photography.

Computing on campus. 2,000 workstations in library, computer center. Wireless network available.

Student life. Freshman orientation: Mandatory. **Activities:** Jazz band, choral groups, dance, drama, film society, literary magazine, music ensembles, radio station, student government, student newspaper, TV station, Phi Theta Kappa, African-American coalition, art student society, architecture club, social science club.

Athletics. NJCAA. **Intercollegiate:** Baseball M, softball W. **Intramural:** Basketball, bowling, cross-country, soccer, softball, table tennis, tennis, track and field, volleyball, weight lifting. **Team name:** Tejanos/Tejanas.

Student services. Career counseling, student employment services, health services, personal counseling, placement for graduates, veterans' counselor, women's services. **Physically disabled:** Services for visually, speech, hearing impaired. **Transfer:** Transfer adviser, college fairs on campus for students transferring to 4-year colleges.

Contact. Phone: (915) 831-2580 Fax: (915) 831-2161
Daryle Hendry, Director of Admissions, El Paso Community College, Box 20500, El Paso, TX 79998

Everest College: Arlington
Arlington, Texas
www.everest-college.com

- For-profit 2-year business and technical college
- Commuter campus in large city

General. Accredited by ACICS. **Enrollment:** 169 degree-seeking undergraduates. **Degrees:** 94 associate awarded. **Location:** 10 miles from Dallas. **Calendar:** Differs by program, extensive summer session. **Full-time faculty:** 6 total. **Part-time faculty:** 32 total.

Basis for selection. Open admission, but selective for some programs. High school record important.

2008-2009 Annual costs. Total cost of programs vary: Business Administration and Criminal Justice, $30,528; estimated books and supplies, $4,050. Medical Insurance Billing/Coding, Pharmacy Technician, Medical Assistant, $13,203; estimated books and equipment $311-$1,037. Books/supplies: $680.

Application procedures. Admission: No deadline. $25 fee.

Academics. Credit/placement by examination: CLEP.

Majors. Business: Business admin. **Protective services:** Security management.

Student life. Freshman orientation: Mandatory.

Student services. Adult student services, career counseling, financial aid counseling, placement for graduates.

Contact. E-mail: tevans@cci.edu
Phone: (817) 652-7790 Toll-free number: (888) 741-4270
Fax: (817) 649-6033
Terri Evans, Director of Admissions, Everest College: Arlington, 2801 East Division Street, Suite 250, Arlington, TX 76011

Everest College: Dallas
Dallas, Texas
www.everest-college.com

- For-profit 2-year business and technical college
- Commuter campus in very large city

General. Accredited by ACICS. **Calendar:** Differs by program.

Contact. Phone: (214) 234-4850
Director of Admissions, 6060 North Central Expressway, Suite 101, Dallas, TX 75206

Everest College: Fort Worth
Forth Worth, Texas
www.everest-college.com

- For-profit 2-year business and technical college
- Very large city

General. Accredited by ACICS.

Contact. Phone: (817) 838-3000
5237 North Riverside Drive, Suite 100, Forth Worth, TX 76137

Frank Phillips College
Borger, Texas
www.fpctx.edu **CB code: 6222**

- Public 2-year community and junior college
- Commuter campus in large town

General. Founded in 1948. Regionally accredited. Guaranteed transfer program. Contract training provided on site or at on-campus location for Occupational Safety and Health Administration mandated certification. **Enrollment:** 755 degree-seeking undergraduates; 489 non-degree-seeking students. **Degrees:** 75 associate awarded. **Location:** 60 miles from Amarillo. **Calendar:** Semester, extensive summer session. **Full-time faculty:** 30 total; 7% have terminal degrees. **Part-time faculty:** 40 total; 5% have terminal degrees. **Class size:** 31% < 20, 68% 20-39, 1% 40-49.

Student profile. Among degree-seeking undergraduates, 69% enrolled in a transfer program, 31% enrolled in a vocational program, 1% already have a bachelor's degree or higher, 179 enrolled as first-time, first-year students, 32 transferred in from other institutions.

Part-time:	32%	**Native American:**	3%
Out-of-state:	4%	**International:**	2%
Women:	57%	**25 or older:**	32%
African American:	5%	**Live on campus:**	20%
Hispanic American:	21%		

Transfer out. 80% of students enrolled in the transfer program go on to 4-year colleges. **Colleges most students transferred to 2008:** West Texas A&M University, Texas A&M University.

Basis for selection. Open admission. SAT/ACT, COMPASS, ASSET, TAKS, or ACCUPLACER may be used in lieu of THEA. Veterans receive preferential admission. Texas Success Initiative guidelines followed. **Homeschooled:** Transcript of courses and grades required.

2008-2009 Annual costs. Tuition/fees: $2,333; $2,963 out-of-district; $3,173 out-of-state. Per-credit charge: $64 in-district; $106 out-of-district; $120 out-of-state. Room/board: $4,150. Books/supplies: $605. Personal expenses: $985.

2007-2008 Financial aid. Need-based: Need-based aid available for part-time students. Work-study available nights, weekends and for part-time students. **Non-need-based:** Scholarships awarded for academics, athletics, music/drama, state residency. **Additional information:** Some Texas fire department and police department personnel, active duty military personnel, children of military missing in action may qualify for reduced or waived tuition. Out-of-state tuition waived for students living in Oklahoma counties adjacent to Texas.

Application procedures. Admission: No deadline. No application fee. Admission notification on a rolling basis. **Financial aid:** No deadline. FAFSA, institutional form required. Applicants notified on a rolling basis; must reply within 2 week(s) of notification.

Academics. Special study options: Cooperative education, distance learning, dual enrollment of high school students, internships, liberal arts/career combination. License preparation in nursing. **Credit/placement by examination:** AP, CLEP, IB, institutional tests. 24 credit hours maximum toward associate degree. **Support services:** GED preparation and test center, learning center, pre-admission summer program, reduced course load, remedial instruction, study skills assistance, tutoring, writing center.

Majors. Agriculture: Equestrian studies, farm/ranch, range science. **Biology:** General. **Business:** General, accounting, administrative services, business admin. **Computer sciences:** General. **Construction:** Pipefitting, power transmission. **Education:** General, elementary, secondary. **Engineering technology:** Manufacturing. **Health:** Medical secretary. **History:** General. **Legal studies:** Legal secretary. **Liberal arts:** Arts/sciences. **Math:** General. **Philosophy/religion:** Philosophy. **Physical sciences:** Chemistry, physics. **Psychology:** General. **Social sciences:** General, political science, sociology.

Computing on campus. 59 workstations in dormitories, library, student center. Dormitories wired for high-speed internet access. Online course registration, wireless network available.

Student life. **Freshman orientation:** Mandatory. Preregistration for classes offered. Session available at start of and during semester. **Housing:** Single-sex dorms, apartments, wellness housing available. $135 fully refundable deposit, deadline 8/1. **Activities:** Choral groups, drama, music ensembles, student government, rodeo club, agriculture club, Phi Theta Kappa, cosmetology club, licensed vocational nursing club, Circle K, business club, art club, computer club, Future Educators Association.

Athletics. NJCAA. **Intercollegiate:** Baseball M, basketball, softball W, volleyball W. **Intramural:** Basketball, bowling, cheerleading, racquetball, softball, table tennis, tennis, volleyball. **Team name:** Plainsmen.

Student services. Adult student services, alcohol/substance abuse counseling, career counseling, services for economically disadvantaged, student employment services, financial aid counseling, personal counseling, placement for graduates, veterans' counselor. **Transfer:** Re-entry adviser, preadmission transcript evaluation for new students. Transfer adviser, college fairs on campus for students transferring to 4-year colleges.

Contact. E-mail: admissions@fpctx.edu
Phone: (806) 457-4200 ext. 740 Fax: (806) 457-4225
Beth Raper, Director of Enrollment Management, Frank Phillips College, Box 5118, Borger, TX 79008-5118

Galveston College
Galveston, Texas
www.gc.edu **CB code: 6255**

- Public 2-year community college
- Commuter campus in small city

General. Founded in 1967. Regionally accredited. **Enrollment:** 1,790 degree-seeking undergraduates; 439 non-degree-seeking students. **Degrees:** 156 associate awarded. **Location:** 50 miles from Houston. **Calendar:** Semester, limited summer session. **Full-time faculty:** 37 total; 22% have terminal degrees, 22% minority, 43% women. **Part-time faculty:** 96 total; 2% have terminal degrees, 24% minority, 53% women. **Class size:** 76% < 20, 24% 20-39, less than 1% >100. **Special facilities:** Center for health related technology. **Partnerships:** Formal partnerships with UTMB in health career profession.

Student profile. Among degree-seeking undergraduates, 60% enrolled in a transfer program, 40% enrolled in a vocational program, 233 enrolled as first-time, first-year students, 317 transferred in from other institutions.

Part-time:	73%	**Asian American:**	3%
Out-of-state:	4%	**Hispanic American:**	25%
Women:	66%	**International:**	1%
African American:	20%	**25 or older:**	44%

Transfer out. **Colleges most students transferred to 2008:** University of Houston-Clear Lake.

Basis for selection. Open admission, but selective for some programs. Health occupations majors have special admission requirements.

2008-2009 Annual costs. Tuition/fees: $1,414; $2,314 out-of-state. Per-credit charge: $30 in-state; $60 out-of-state. Books/supplies: $876. Personal expenses: $1,380.

2007-2008 Financial aid. All financial aid based on need. Need-based aid available for part-time students. Work-study available for part-time students.

Application procedures. **Admission:** No deadline. No application fee. Application must be submitted on paper. Admission notification on a rolling basis. **Financial aid:** Priority date 6/9; no closing date. FAFSA required. Applicants notified on a rolling basis starting 6/1.

Academics. **Special study options:** Cooperative education, distance learning, dual enrollment of high school students, independent study, internships, weekend college. License preparation in dental hygiene, nursing, paramedic, radiology, real estate. **Credit/placement by examination:** CLEP. 24 credit hours maximum toward associate degree. **Support services:** GED test center, learning center, remedial instruction, tutoring.

Majors. **Biology:** General, marine. **Business:** Accounting, administrative services, business admin, entrepreneurial studies, marketing, office/clerical. **Computer sciences:** General, computer science, information systems, programming. **Education:** Elementary, physical. **Engineering:** General. **Family/consumer sciences:** Family studies. **Foreign languages:** Spanish. **Health:** EMT paramedic, health care admin, medical radiologic technology/radiation therapy, medical records technology, medical secretary, nuclear medical technology, nursing (RN), predental, premedicine, preveterinary. **History:** General. **Interdisciplinary:** Biological/physical sciences. **Legal studies:** Prelaw. **Liberal arts:** Arts/sciences. **Math:** General. **Personal/culinary services:** Culinary arts. **Physical sciences:** Chemistry, geology, physics. **Protective services:** Criminal justice, fire safety technology. **Psychology:** General. **Public administration:** Social work. **Social sciences:** Anthropology, economics, geography, political science, sociology. **Visual/performing arts:** Art, dramatic.

Computing on campus. 170 workstations in library, computer center, student center. Commuter students can connect to campus network. Online library, helpline, wireless network available.

Student life. **Freshman orientation:** Mandatory. Preregistration for classes offered. **Housing:** Special housing for scholarship athletes. **Activities:** Choral groups, drama, music ensembles, student government, student newspaper, student activities council, journalism club, African American club, Campus Crusade for Christ, Hispanic student organization, single parents organization, environmental awareness club, Phi Theta Kappa, nuclear medicine club, student nurses association.

Athletics. NJCAA. **Intercollegiate:** Baseball M, softball W, volleyball W. **Intramural:** Bowling, golf, tennis. **Team name:** Whitecaps.

Student services. Career counseling, student employment services, on-campus daycare, personal counseling, placement for graduates, veterans' counselor. **Physically disabled:** Services for visually, speech, hearing impaired. **Transfer:** Transfer adviser, college fairs on campus for students transferring to 4-year colleges.

Contact. E-mail: calcala@gc.edu
Phone: (409) 944-1230 Fax: (409) 944-1501
Acala Cynthia, Director of Admissions/Registrar, Galveston College, 4015 Avenue Q, Galveston, TX 77550-7447

Grayson County College
Denison, Texas **CB member**
www.grayson.edu **CB code: 6254**

- Public 2-year community and technical college
- Commuter campus in large town

General. Founded in 1963. Regionally accredited. **Location:** 7 miles from Sherman, 75 miles from Dallas. **Calendar:** Semester.

Annual costs/financial aid. Tuition/fees (2008-2009): $1,350; $1,920 out-of-district; $3,390 out-of-state. Room/board: $3,567. Books/supplies: $594. Personal expenses: $1,412. Need-based financial aid available to full-time and part-time students.

Contact. Phone: (903) 465-8604
Director of Admissions and Records, 6101 Grayson Drive, Denison, TX 75020

Hallmark College of Aeronautics
San Antonio, Texas
www.hallmarkcollege.edu **CB code: 3166**

- For-profit 2-year technical and career college
- Commuter campus in very large city
- Interview required

General. Accredited by ACCSCT. Located at San Antonio International Airport. **Enrollment:** 166 degree-seeking undergraduates. **Degrees:** 104 associate awarded. **Calendar:** Continuous, extensive summer session. **Full-time faculty:** 9 total; 22% minority, 11% women.

Student profile. Among degree-seeking undergraduates, 1% enrolled in a transfer program, 98% enrolled in a vocational program, 1% already have a bachelor's degree or higher, 166 enrolled as first-time, first-year students.

Out-of-state:	3%	**25 or older:**	51%

Transfer out. 1% of students enrolled in the transfer program go on to 4-year colleges. **Colleges most students transferred to 2008:** Texas State Technical College, Palo Alto College.

Basis for selection. Aviation entrance test and interview required. **Homeschooled:** Transcript of courses and grades, interview required.

2008-2009 Annual costs. Tuition for combined associate program in airframe technology or powerplant technology: $29,400. Costs include books, equipment and supplies. Registration fee: $100. Course fees vary. International students pay additional 8%.

Application procedures. Admission: No deadline. $110 fee. Admission notification on a rolling basis. **Financial aid:** No deadline. FAFSA required. Applicants notified on a rolling basis.

Academics. Special study options: Accelerated study, honors, liberal arts/career combination. License preparation in aviation. **Credit/placement by examination:** AP, CLEP. 49 credit hours maximum toward associate degree. **Support services:** Tutoring.

Majors. Mechanic/repair: Aircraft, aircraft powerplant, avionics.

Computing on campus. Online library available.

Student life. Freshman orientation: Mandatory.

Student services. Career counseling, student employment services, financial aid counseling, placement for graduates. **Transfer:** Pre-admission transcript evaluation for new students.

Contact. E-mail: slava.ross@hallmarkcollege.edu
Phone: (210) 826-1000 Toll-free number: (888) 656-9300
Fax: (210) 826-3707
Slava Ross, Director of Admissions, Hallmark College of Aeronautics, 8901 Wetmore Road, San Antonio, TX 78230

Hallmark College of Technology
San Antonio, Texas
www.hallmarkcollege.edu **CB code: 2307**

- For-profit 2-year technical and career college
- Commuter campus in very large city
- Interview required

General. Founded in 1969. Accredited by ACCSCT. Additional campus focusing on aeronautics (Hallmark College of Aeronautics) located on property of San Antonio Airport. **Enrollment:** 438 degree-seeking undergraduates. **Degrees:** 306 associate awarded. **Location:** 5 miles from San Antonio, 80 miles from Austin. **Calendar:** Continuous, extensive summer session. **Full-time faculty:** 23 total; 17% have terminal degrees, 39% minority, 22% women. **Part-time faculty:** 14 total; 7% have terminal degrees, 29% minority, 36% women. **Class size:** 65% < 20, 35% 20-39.

Student profile. Among degree-seeking undergraduates, 100% enrolled in a vocational program, 1% already have a bachelor's degree or higher, 438 enrolled as first-time, first-year students.

Women:	29%	25 or older:	60%

Basis for selection. Standardized test scores, interview, high school diploma or GED required. **Homeschooled:** Transcript of courses and grades, interview required. Student must be approved by the Acceptance Committee for admissions after meeting all entrance requirements.

2008-2009 Annual costs. Costs for associate programs range from $19,566 to $30,800; additional registration fee $110 for all programs.

Application procedures. Admission: No deadline. $110 fee. Admission notification on a rolling basis. **Financial aid:** No deadline. FAFSA required. Applicants notified on a rolling basis.

Academics. Special study options: Accelerated study. License preparation in aviation. **Credit/placement by examination:** AP, CLEP. 36 credit hours maximum toward associate degree. **Support services:** Remedial instruction, study skills assistance, tutoring.

Majors. Business: Office technology. **Computer sciences:** Networking. **Engineering technology:** Electrical. **Health:** Medical assistant.

Computing on campus. 193 workstations in library, computer center. Online library, wireless network available.

Student life. Freshman orientation: Mandatory. **Activities:** Student newspaper.

Student services. Career counseling, student employment services, financial aid counseling, placement for graduates. **Transfer:** Pre-admission transcript evaluation for new students.

Contact. E-mail: sross@hallmarkcollege.com
Phone: (210) 690-9000 Toll-free number: (800) 880-6600
Fax: (210) 697-8225
Sonia Ross, Director of Admissions, Hallmark College of Technology, Hallmark College, San Antonio, TX 78230-1737

Hill College
Hillsboro, Texas
www.hillcollege.edu **CB code: 6285**

- Public 2-year community and junior college
- Commuter campus in small town

General. Founded in 1923. Regionally accredited. **Enrollment:** 3,712 degree-seeking undergraduates. **Degrees:** 220 associate awarded. **Location:** 64 miles from Dallas. **Calendar:** Semester, limited summer session. **Full-time faculty:** 79 total. **Part-time faculty:** 116 total. **Special facilities:** History complex including gun museum and Civil War research center.

Student profile.

Out-of-state:	1%	Live on campus:	14%

Transfer out. Colleges most students transferred to 2008: Tarleton State University, Tarrant County Junior College, University of Texas at Arlington.

Basis for selection. Open admission, but selective for some programs. Observes TASP guidelines. THEA Test or Approved State Alternative Test required for academic students unless exempted by state. Special requirements for nursing program. **Homeschooled:** Transcript of courses and grades required.

2008-2009 Annual costs. Tuition/fees: $1,620; $2,100 out-of-district; $2,500 out-of-state. Room/board: $2,950. Books/supplies: $2,000. Personal expenses: $1,440.

2008-2009 Financial aid. Need-based: Need-based aid available for part-time students. Work-study available for part-time students. **Non-need-based:** Scholarships awarded for academics, athletics, music/drama.

Application procedures. Admission: No deadline. No application fee. Application must be submitted on paper. Admission notification on a rolling basis. **Financial aid:** Closing date 7/1. FAFSA, institutional form required. Applicants notified on a rolling basis.

Academics. Special study options: Combined bachelor's/graduate degree, cooperative education, distance learning, dual enrollment of high school students, honors, independent study, internships, liberal arts/career combination. Bachelor's degree programs available on campus. **Credit/placement by examination:** AP, CLEP. 24 credit hours maximum toward associate degree. **Support services:** GED test center, learning center, reduced course load, remedial instruction, study skills assistance, tutoring.

Majors. Agriculture: Business. **Biology:** General, botany. **Business:** Administrative services, business admin, office management, office technology, office/clerical, real estate. **Communications:** General, journalism. **Computer sciences:** General, applications programming, computer science, data processing, programming. **Education:** General. **Engineering:** General. **Engineering technology:** Drafting, electrical, robotics. **Family/consumer sciences:** Institutional food production. **Foreign languages:** General. **Health:** Licensed practical nurse. **Interdisciplinary:** Biological/physical sciences. **Legal studies:** Prelaw. **Liberal arts:** Arts/sciences. **Math:** General. **Mechanic/repair:** Auto body, heating/ac/refrig. **Parks/recreation:** Health/fitness. **Physical sciences:** Chemistry, geology, physics. **Protective services:** Criminal justice, fire services admin, law enforcement admin, police science, security services. **Psychology:** General. **Visual/performing arts:** General, art, commercial/advertising art.

Most popular majors. Business/marketing 11%, education 14%, engineering/engineering technologies 6%, liberal arts 43%.

Computing on campus. 65 workstations in library, computer center. Online library, helpline available.

Student life. Freshman orientation: Mandatory. Preregistration for classes offered. **Housing:** Single-sex dorms, wellness housing available. $50 deposit. International students must live in dormitories. **Activities:** Bands, choral groups, drama, film society, music ensembles, student government, Circle K, Young Democrats, Young Republicans, Baptist Student Union, student council.

Athletics. NJCAA. **Intercollegiate:** Baseball M, basketball, soccer W, softball W, volleyball W. **Intramural:** Volleyball.

Student services. Adult student services, career counseling, services for economically disadvantaged, student employment services, financial aid counseling, personal counseling, placement for graduates, veterans' counselor. **Physically disabled:** Services for visually, speech, hearing impaired. **Transfer:** Transfer adviser, college fairs on campus for students transferring to 4-year colleges.

Contact. Phone: (254) 582-2555 Fax: (254) 582-7591
Pat Davis, Director of Admissions, Hill College, Box 619, Hillsboro, TX 76645

Houston Community College System
Houston, Texas **CB member**
www.hccs.edu **CB code: 0929**

- Public 2-year community college
- Commuter campus in very large city

General. Founded in 1971. Regionally accredited. Multi-campus college enrolling a large number of international students. Students may attend the campus of their choice. **Enrollment:** 32,836 degree-seeking undergraduates; 15,333 non-degree-seeking students. **Degrees:** 2,352 associate awarded. **ROTC:** Army, Air Force. **Location:** 51 miles from Galveston, 164 miles from Austin. **Calendar:** Semester, extensive summer session. **Full-time faculty:** 829 total; 43% minority, 51% women. **Part-time faculty:** 2,049 total; 57% minority, 51% women. **Class size:** 50% < 20, 49% 20-39, less than 1% 40-49, less than 1% 50-99. **Special facilities:** 300-seat Heinen Theatre, a registered National Landmark, HCC Public Safety Institute. **Partnerships:** Formal partnerships with local high schools for tech-prep and school-to-work programs; contract training agreements with industry.

Student profile. Among degree-seeking undergraduates, 8,126 enrolled as first-time, first-year students, 2,592 transferred in from other institutions.

Part-time:	66%	**Asian American:**	11%
Women:	58%	**Hispanic American:**	28%
African American:	24%	**International:**	13%

Basis for selection. Open admission, but selective for some programs. High school transcript, assessment, personal interview required for admission to some health programs. According to Texas state law, students must take TASP (Texas Academic Skills Program) test or TASP alternative. Some students may qualify for TASP exemptions. International students must demonstrate English proficiency by taking TASP (or accepted alternative) and CELSA. Interview required for health careers. **Adult students:** If a student has not previously taken an approved Texas State Initiative (TSI) test or other required placement test and is not exempt or waived from testing requirements, they must test prior to enrollment.

2008-2009 Annual costs. Tuition/fees: $1,674; $3,294 out-of-district; $3,894 out-of-state.

2007-2008 Financial aid. Need-based: Need-based aid available for part-time students. Work-study available nights and weekends.

Application procedures. Admission: No deadline. No application fee. **Financial aid:** No deadline. Applicants notified on a rolling basis starting 6/1; must reply within 2 week(s) of notification.

Academics. Special study options: Cooperative education, distance learning, dual enrollment of high school students, ESL, honors, independent study, internships, study abroad, weekend college. Alternative teacher certification program. License preparation in aviation, dental hygiene, nursing, occupational therapy, paramedic, physical therapy, radiology, real estate. **Credit/placement by examination:** AP, CLEP, IB, institutional tests. 24 credit hours maximum toward associate degree. **Support services:** GED preparation and test center, learning center, remedial instruction, tutoring.

Majors. Agriculture: Horticulture, turf management. **Business:** Accounting, banking/financial services, business admin, communications, fashion, hotel/motel admin, international, logistics, marketing, office technology, real estate, tourism/travel. **Communications technology:** Animation/special effects, graphic/printing, radio/tv. **Computer sciences:** Applications programming, networking, programming, system admin. **Engineering technology:** Computer, construction, drafting, instrumentation, manufacturing, petroleum. **Family/consumer sciences:** Child development. **Foreign languages:** Sign language interpretation. **Health:** Cardiovascular technology, clinical lab technology, dental hygiene, EMT paramedic, histologic assistant, medical records technology, mental health services, nuclear medical technology, nursing (RN), occupational therapy assistant, radiologic technology/medical imaging, respiratory therapy technology. **Legal studies:** Paralegal. **Mechanic/repair:** Aircraft, aircraft powerplant, automotive. **Parks/recreation:** Health/fitness. **Personal/culinary services:** Baking, chef training, cosmetic. **Production:** Machine shop technology. **Protective services:** Fire safety technology, police science. **Public administration:** General. **Science technology:** Biological, chemical. **Social sciences:** Cartography. **Visual/performing arts:** Cinematography, fashion design, interior design, music management, music performance, music theory/composition.

Most popular majors. Business/marketing 8%, health sciences 11%, liberal arts 66%.

Computing on campus. 4,121 workstations in library, computer center. Online course registration, helpline available.

Student life. Freshman orientation: Mandatory. Various locations. **Activities:** Drama, international student organizations, literary magazine, student government, student newspaper, TV station, International Student Association, Vietnamese Student Association, United Student Council, Black Student Union, Association of Latin American Students, Phi Theta Kappa.

Athletics. Intramural: Basketball M, football (non-tackle) M, golf, soccer, softball, volleyball W.

Student services. Alcohol/substance abuse counseling, career counseling, services for economically disadvantaged, student employment services, financial aid counseling, minority student services, on-campus daycare, personal counseling, placement for graduates, veterans' counselor, women's services. **Physically disabled:** Services for visually, speech, hearing impaired. **Transfer:** College fairs on campus for students transferring to 4-year colleges.

Contact. Phone: (713) 718-8500 Fax: (713) 718-2111
Mary Lemburg, Registrar, Houston Community College System, 3100 Main, Houston, TX 77266-7517

Howard College
Big Spring, Texas
www.howardcollege.edu **CB code: 6277**

- Public 2-year community college
- Commuter campus in large town

General. Founded in 1945. Regionally accredited. **Enrollment:** 3,415 degree-seeking undergraduates; 158 non-degree-seeking students. **Degrees:** 221 associate awarded. **Location:** 105 miles from Lubbock, 40 miles from Midland. **Calendar:** Semester, limited summer session. **Full-time faculty:** 128 total; 6% have terminal degrees, 12% minority, 56% women. **Part-time faculty:** 112 total; 14% minority, 64% women. **Special facilities:** Rodeo arena, arts center, coliseum.

Student profile. Among degree-seeking undergraduates, 66% enrolled in a transfer program, 34% enrolled in a vocational program, 1% already have a bachelor's degree or higher, 546 enrolled as first-time, first-year students.

Part-time:	65%	**25 or older:**	28%
Out-of-state:	2%	**Live on campus:**	8%
Women:	62%		

Transfer out. Colleges most students transferred to 2008: Texas Tech University, Angelo State University, Tarleton State University, University of Texas-Permian Basin, Texas A&M University.

Basis for selection. Open admission, but selective for some programs. Special requirements for health, cosmetology programs. Interview required for dental hygiene, degree and licensed vocational nursing, cosmetology programs.

2008-2009 Annual costs. Tuition/fees: $1,712; $2,132 out-of-district; $2,832 out-of-state. Room/board: $3,600. Books/supplies: $800. Personal expenses: $1,330.

Financial aid. Need-based: Need-based aid available for part-time students. Work-study available for part-time students. **Non-need-based:** Scholarships awarded for academics, art, athletics, leadership, music/drama.

Application procedures. Admission: No deadline. No application fee. Admission notification on a rolling basis. **Financial aid:** Priority date 4/1; no closing date. FAFSA, institutional form required. Applicants notified on a rolling basis starting 7/15; must reply within 2 week(s) of notification.

Academics. Special study options: Cooperative education, cross-registration, distance learning, dual enrollment of high school students, ESL, liberal arts/career combination, weekend college. License preparation in dental hygiene, nursing, occupational therapy, paramedic, physical therapy, radiology, real estate. **Credit/placement by examination:** CLEP, institutional tests. 18 credit hours maximum toward associate degree. **Support services:** GED preparation and test center, learning center, pre-admission summer

Two-Year Colleges

program, reduced course load, remedial instruction, study skills assistance, tutoring, writing center.

Majors. **Agriculture:** General, business. **Biology:** General. **Business:** General, accounting, office/clerical. **Communications:** Journalism. **Computer sciences:** General. **Education:** General. **Family/consumer sciences:** Child care. **Foreign languages:** General, sign language interpretation. **Health:** Athletic training, dental hygiene, dental lab technology, EMT ambulance attendant, medical assistant, medical records admin, medical records technology, nursing (RN), physical therapy assistant, predental, premedicine, respiratory therapy technology, substance abuse counseling. **Legal studies:** Paralegal. **Liberal arts:** Arts/sciences. **Math:** General. **Parks/recreation:** Health/fitness. **Physical sciences:** Chemistry, physics. **Protective services:** Corrections, forensics, law enforcement admin. **Psychology:** General. **Social sciences:** General. **Visual/performing arts:** General, art, dramatic.

Most popular majors. Business/marketing 15%, health sciences 24%, liberal arts 43%, security/protective services 6%.

Computing on campus. 100 workstations in dormitories, library, computer center. Dormitories wired for high-speed internet access and linked to campus network. Commuter students can connect to campus network. Online course registration, online library, helpline, wireless network available.

Student life. **Freshman orientation:** Available. Preregistration for classes offered. **Housing:** Single-sex dorms, wellness housing available. **Activities:** Bands, choral groups, dance, drama, music ensembles, musical theater, student government.

Athletics. NJCAA. **Intercollegiate:** Baseball M, basketball, cheerleading, rodeo, softball W. **Intramural:** Basketball, bowling, golf, handball, racquetball, softball, table tennis, tennis, volleyball. **Team name:** Hawks.

Student services. Adult student services, career counseling, services for economically disadvantaged, student employment services, financial aid counseling, health services, on-campus daycare, personal counseling, placement for graduates, veterans' counselor. **Physically disabled:** Services for hearing impaired. **Transfer:** Transfer adviser, college fairs on campus for students transferring to 4-year colleges.

Contact. E-mail: dmerrick@howardcollege.edu
Phone: (432) 264-5000 Fax: (432) 264-5072
Donna Merrick, Registrar, Howard College, 1001 Birdwell Lane, Big Spring, TX 79720

International Academy of Design and Technology: San Antonio

San Antonio, Texas
www.iadtsanantonio.com

- For-profit 2-year technical college
- Very large city

General. Regionally accredited. **Calendar:** Quarter.

Contact. Phone: (210) 530-9449
4511 Horizon Hill Boulevard, San Antonio, TX 78229

ITT Technical Institute: Arlington

Arlington, Texas
www.itt-tech.edu **CB code: 3572**

- For-profit 2-year technical college
- Commuter campus in large city

General. Founded in 1982. Accredited by ACICS. **Location:** 11 miles from Fort Worth, 18 miles from Dallas. **Calendar:** Quarter.

Contact. Phone: (817) 794-5100
Director of Recruitment, 551 Ryan Plaza Drive, Arlington, TX 76011

ITT Technical Institute: Austin

Austin, Texas
www.itt-tech.edu **CB code: 2692**

- For-profit 2-year technical college
- Commuter campus in large city

General. Accredited by ACICS. **Calendar:** Quarter.

Contact. Phone: (512) 467-6800
Director of Recruitment, 6330 Highway 290 East, Austin, TX 78723

ITT Technical Institute: Houston

Houston, Texas
www.itt-tech.edu **CB code: 3573**

- For-profit 2-year technical college
- Commuter campus in very large city

General. Founded in 1983. Accredited by ACICS. **Calendar:** Quarter.

Contact. Phone: (713) 952-2294
Director of Recruitment, 2950 South Gessner, Houston, TX 77063-3751

ITT Technical Institute: Houston North

Houston, Texas
www.itt-tech.edu **CB code: 2712**

- For-profit 2-year technical college
- Commuter campus in very large city

General. Accredited by ACICS. **Calendar:** Quarter.

Contact. Phone: (281) 873-0512
Director of Recruitment, 15621 Blue Ash Drive, Houston, TX 77090-5818

ITT Technical Institute: Houston South

Webster, Texas
www.itt-tech.edu **CB code: 2715**

- For-profit 2-year technical college
- Commuter campus in very large city

General. Accredited by ACICS. **Calendar:** Quarter.

Contact. Director of Recruitment, 1001 Magnolia Avenue, Webster, TX 77598

ITT Technical Institute: Richardson

Richardson, Texas
www.itt-tech.edu **CB code: 2747**

- For-profit 2-year technical college
- Commuter campus in small city

General. Accredited by ACICS. **Location:** 12 miles from Dallas. **Calendar:** Quarter.

Contact. Phone: (972) 690-9100
Director of Recruitment, 2101 Waterview Parkway, Richardson, TX 75080

ITT Technical Institute: San Antonio

San Antonio, Texas
www.itt-tech.edu **CB code: 2328**

- For-profit 2-year technical college
- Commuter campus in very large city

General. Founded in 1988. Accredited by ACICS. **Location:** 200 miles from Houston, 75 miles from Austin. **Calendar:** Quarter.

Contact. Phone: (210) 694-4612
Director of Recruitment, 5700 Northwest Parkway, San Antonio, TX 78249

Jacksonville College

Jacksonville, Texas
www.jacksonville-college.edu **CB code: 6317**

- Private 2-year junior and liberal arts college affiliated with Baptist faith
- Commuter campus in large town

General. Founded in 1899. Regionally accredited. Owned and operated by the Baptist Missionary Association of Texas and affiliated with the Southern

Baptists of Texas Convention. **Enrollment:** 275 degree-seeking undergraduates. **Degrees:** 39 associate awarded. **Location:** 120 miles from Dallas, 25 miles from Tyler. **Calendar:** Semester, limited summer session. **Full-time faculty:** 13 total. **Part-time faculty:** 15 total. **Class size:** 67% < 20, 32% 20-39, 1% >100.

Student profile. Among degree-seeking undergraduates, 100% enrolled in a transfer program, 1% already have a bachelor's degree or higher.

Out-of-state:	6%	**Live on campus:**	32%

Transfer out. Colleges most students transferred to 2008: University of Texas at Tyler, Stephen F. Austin State University, Dallas Baptist University, East Texas Baptist University.

Basis for selection. Open admission. Interview recommended. **Homeschooled:** Must take ACT, SAT, or THEA.

2008-2009 Annual costs. Tuition/fees: $6,596. Per-credit charge: $200. Room/board: $2,961. Books/supplies: $910. Personal expenses: $1,310.

2008-2009 Financial aid. Need-based: Need-based aid available for part-time students. **Non-need-based:** Scholarships awarded for academics, athletics, leadership, music/drama, religious affiliation, state residency.

Application procedures. Admission: Priority date 8/15; no deadline. $15 fee. Application must be submitted on paper. Admission notification on a rolling basis beginning on or about 1/15. **Financial aid:** Priority date 8/1; no closing date. FAFSA, institutional form required. Applicants notified on a rolling basis.

Academics. Special study options: Dual enrollment of high school students. **Credit/placement by examination:** AP, CLEP, institutional tests. **Support services:** Reduced course load, remedial instruction, tutoring.

Majors. Liberal arts: Arts/sciences.

Computing on campus. 45 workstations in dormitories, library, computer center. Dormitories wired for high-speed internet access and linked to campus network. Commuter students can connect to campus network. Wireless network available.

Student life. Freshman orientation: Available. Preregistration for classes offered. **Housing:** Single-sex dorms, apartments available. $80 deposit. **Activities:** Concert band, choral groups, drama, music ensembles, student government, student newspaper, ministerial alliance, mission band.

Athletics. NJCAA. **Intercollegiate:** Basketball. **Intramural:** Basketball, football (non-tackle), softball, table tennis, tennis, volleyball. **Team name:** Jaguars.

Student services. Chaplain/spiritual director, career counseling, financial aid counseling, health services, personal counseling. **Transfer:** Transfer adviser, college fairs on campus for students transferring to 4-year colleges.

Contact. E-mail: admissions@jacksonville-college.edu
Phone: (903) 586-2518 Toll-free number: (800) 256-8522
Fax: (903) 586-0743
Danny Morris, Director of Admissions, Jacksonville College, 105 B.J. Albritton Drive, Jacksonville, TX 75766-4759

Kilgore College

Kilgore, Texas — **CB member**
www.kilgore.edu — **CB code: 6341**

- Public 2-year community college
- Commuter campus in large town

General. Founded in 1935. Regionally accredited. **Enrollment:** 5,513 degree-seeking undergraduates. **Degrees:** 516 associate awarded. **Location:** 120 miles from Dallas, 60 miles from Shreveport, Louisiana. **Calendar:** Semester, extensive summer session. **Full-time faculty:** 135 total; 11% have terminal degrees, 10% minority, 53% women. **Part-time faculty:** 132 total; 6% have terminal degrees, 12% minority, 56% women. **Class size:** 42% < 20, 52% 20-39, 5% 40-49, less than 1% 50-99. **Special facilities:** Experimental farm, oil museum.

Student profile. Among degree-seeking undergraduates, 56% enrolled in a transfer program, 44% enrolled in a vocational program, 1% already have a bachelor's degree or higher, 1,173 enrolled as first-time, first-year students.

Part-time:	52%	**Hispanic American:**	8%
Out-of-state:	3%	**International:**	2%
Women:	63%	**25 or older:**	31%
African American:	19%	**Live on campus:**	10%
Asian American:	1%		

Transfer out. Colleges most students transferred to 2008: University of Texas at Tyler, University of North Texas, Stephen F. Austin State University, Texas A&M University, University of Texas at Austin.

Basis for selection. Open admission, but selective for some programs. For health occupation programs and some public service programs, standardized test scores, secondary school record, essay used as admissions criteria.

2008-2009 Annual costs. Tuition/fees: $1,320; $2,790 out-of-district; $3,810 out-of-state. Per-credit charge: $22 in-district; $71 out-of-district; $105 out-of-state. Room/board: $3,630. Books/supplies: $1,000. Personal expenses: $1,200.

2007-2008 Financial aid. Need-based: Need-based aid available for part-time students. Work-study available for part-time students. **Non-need-based:** Scholarships awarded for academics, alumni affiliation, art, athletics, job skills, leadership, music/drama, state residency. **Additional information:** State of Texas grants and loans available for honor graduates with unmet needs and for non-traditional students.

Application procedures. Admission: Priority date 8/15; no deadline. No application fee. Admission notification on a rolling basis. **Financial aid:** Priority date 6/1, closing date 7/15. FAFSA, institutional form required. Applicants notified on a rolling basis starting 3/1; must reply within 2 week(s) of notification.

Academics. Special study options: Cooperative education, distance learning, dual enrollment of high school students, ESL, internships. License preparation in nursing. **Credit/placement by examination:** AP, CLEP, institutional tests. 14 credit hours maximum toward associate degree. **Support services:** GED preparation and test center, learning center, pre-admission summer program, reduced course load, remedial instruction, study skills assistance, tutoring, writing center.

Majors. Agriculture: General. **Biology:** General. **Business:** General, accounting, business admin, e-commerce, executive assistant, management information systems, operations, real estate. **Communications:** General, journalism. **Computer sciences:** General, programming, systems analysis. **Education:** General, art, biology, chemistry, health, health occupations, history, social science. **Engineering:** General, chemical, civil. **Engineering technology:** Civil, drafting, electrical, metallurgical, occupational safety. **Family/consumer sciences:** Child care. **Foreign languages:** French, German, Spanish. **Health:** Clinical lab technology, EMT paramedic, medical assistant, medical radiologic technology/radiation therapy, nursing (RN), physical therapy assistant, surgical technology. **History:** General. **Legal studies:** Court reporting, legal secretary, paralegal, prelaw. **Liberal arts:** Arts/sciences. **Math:** General. **Mechanic/repair:** Auto body, automotive, diesel, electronics/electrical. **Parks/recreation:** Health/fitness. **Physical sciences:** Chemistry, physics. **Production:** Machine tool. **Protective services:** Criminal justice, law enforcement admin, police science. **Psychology:** General. **Social sciences:** Sociology. **Visual/performing arts:** Art, commercial photography, commercial/advertising art, dance, dramatic.

Most popular majors. Business/marketing 15%, engineering/engineering technologies 11%, health sciences 36%, liberal arts 16%.

Computing on campus. 350 workstations in library, computer center, student center. Online course registration available.

Student life. Freshman orientation: Mandatory. Preregistration for classes offered. **Housing:** Single-sex dorms available. $100 deposit, deadline 8/15. **Activities:** Bands, choral groups, dance, drama, music ensembles, musical theater, radio station, student government, student newspaper, TV station, church organizations, rodeo club, physical therapy club.

Athletics. NJCAA. **Intercollegiate:** Basketball, football (tackle) M. **Intramural:** Badminton, bowling, handball, racquetball, softball, swimming, tennis, volleyball. **Team name:** Rangers.

Student services. Career counseling, student employment services, health services, on-campus daycare, personal counseling, placement for graduates, veterans' counselor. **Physically disabled:** Services for visually, speech, hearing impaired. **Transfer:** Pre-admission transcript evaluation for new students. College fairs on campus for students transferring to 4-year colleges.

Contact. Phone: (903) 983-8209 Fax: (903) 983-8607
Eloise Ashley, Director of Admissions, Kilgore College, 1100 Broadway, Kilgore, TX 75662-3299

Lamar Institute of Technology
Beaumont, Texas
www.lit.edu

- Public 2-year technical college
- Commuter campus in small city

General. LIT students have access to Lamar University dormitories, recreational sports center, and library as part of intercomponent service agreement. **Enrollment:** 2,718 degree-seeking undergraduates. **Degrees:** 406 associate awarded. **Location:** 80 miles from Houston. **Calendar:** Semester, limited summer session. **Full-time faculty:** 68 total. **Part-time faculty:** 94 total. **Class size:** 63% < 20, 35% 20-39, 1% 40-49, less than 1% 50-99.

Student profile.

Out-of-state:	2%	**Live on campus:**	3%
25 or older:	35%		

Basis for selection. Open admission, but selective for some programs. Special requirements for various allied health programs (dental hygiene, sonography, health information technology, radiology, respiratory care).

2008-2009 Annual costs. Tuition/fees: $3,810; $12,090 out-of-state. Per-credit charge: $86 in-state; $362 out-of-state.

2008-2009 Financial aid. Need-based: 67% of total undergraduate aid awarded as scholarships/grants, 33% as loans/jobs.

Application procedures. Admission: No deadline. No application fee. Admission notification on a rolling basis. **Financial aid:** Priority date 4/1; no closing date.

Academics. Credit/placement by examination: CLEP, IB, SAT, ACT, institutional tests.

Majors. Business: Accounting technology, administrative services, business admin, real estate. **Computer sciences:** General. **Engineering technology:** Computer systems, drafting, heat/ac/refrig, instrumentation, occupational safety. **Health:** Dental hygiene, EMT paramedic, medical radiologic technology/radiation therapy, medical records technology, respiratory therapy technology, sonography. **Mechanic/repair:** Diesel, industrial. **Personal/culinary services:** Institutional food service. **Production:** Machine tool, welding. **Protective services:** Fire safety technology, forensics. **Public administration:** General. **Science technology:** Chemical.

Most popular majors. Business/marketing 17%, computer/information sciences 6%, engineering/engineering technologies 26%, health sciences 26%, science technologies 13%.

Computing on campus. 150 workstations in library, computer center. Dormitories wired for high-speed internet access and linked to campus network. Online course registration, online library, wireless network available.

Student life. Freshman orientation: Available. Preregistration for classes offered. **Housing:** Single-sex dorms, wellness housing available. Access to dormitories located on Lamar University campus.

Student services. Alcohol/substance abuse counseling, career counseling, services for economically disadvantaged, student employment services, financial aid counseling, health services, placement for graduates, veterans' counselor. **Physically disabled:** Services for visually, hearing impaired.

Contact. Phone: (409) 880-8321 Toll-free number: (800) 950-6989
Fax: (409) 880-1711
Vivian Jefferson, Dean of Student Services, Lamar Institute of Technology, PO Box 10043, Beaumont, TX 77705

Lamar State College at Orange
Orange, Texas
www.lsco.edu **CB code: 1694**

- Public 2-year junior and liberal arts college
- Commuter campus in small city

General. Regionally accredited. **Enrollment:** 1,823 degree-seeking undergraduates; 324 non-degree-seeking students. **Degrees:** 146 associate awarded. **Location:** 92 miles from Houston. **Calendar:** Semester, limited summer session. **Full-time faculty:** 52 total; 14% have terminal degrees, 8% minority, 67% women. **Part-time faculty:** 49 total; 16% have terminal degrees, 12% minority, 67% women. **Partnerships:** Formal partnership with CISCO.

Student profile. Among degree-seeking undergraduates, 44% enrolled in a transfer program, 56% enrolled in a vocational program, 391 enrolled as first-time, first-year students, 156 transferred in from other institutions.

Part-time:	44%	**Asian American:**	1%
Out-of-state:	9%	**Hispanic American:**	4%
Women:	77%	**Native American:**	1%
African American:	22%	**25 or older:**	35%

Transfer out. Colleges most students transferred to 2008: Lamar University, Texas A&M-College Station, Sam Houston State University, Lamar State College-Port Arthur.

Basis for selection. Open admission, but selective for some programs. Nursing program competitive; high school record and test scores may be evaluated for admission. Interview required for students without high school diploma or GED, to determine if applicant can benefit from available educational programs.

High school preparation. 12 units recommended. Recommended units include English 4, mathematics 3, history 2 and science 3.

2008-2009 Annual costs. Tuition/fees: $3,400; $11,830 out-of-state. Per-credit charge: $84 in-state; $365 out-of-state. Books/supplies: $650. Personal expenses: $1,592.

2007-2008 Financial aid. All financial aid based on need. Need-based aid available for part-time students. Work-study available for part-time students.

Application procedures. Admission: No deadline. No application fee. Admission notification on a rolling basis. **Financial aid:** Priority date 4/1; no closing date. FAFSA, institutional form required. Applicants notified on a rolling basis starting 5/15; must reply within 2 week(s) of notification.

Academics. Special study options: Distance learning, dual enrollment of high school students, internships, liberal arts/career combination, teacher certification program. License preparation in nursing, paramedic. **Credit/placement by examination:** CLEP. 15 credit hours maximum toward associate degree. **Support services:** GED test center, learning center, remedial instruction, study skills assistance, tutoring.

Majors. Biology: General. **Business:** General, accounting technology, administrative services, business admin. **Computer sciences:** General, data processing, programming. **Education:** General. **Engineering technology:** Electrical, environmental. **Health:** Clinical lab technology, EMT paramedic, medical secretary, nursing (RN). **Liberal arts:** Arts/sciences. **Math:** General. **Protective services:** Corrections, criminal justice. **Psychology:** General. **Science technology:** Chemical. **Social sciences:** Sociology.

Computing on campus. 150 workstations in library, computer center, student center. Commuter students can connect to campus network. Online library, helpline, wireless network available.

Student life. Freshman orientation: Available. Preregistration for classes offered. **Activities:** Student government.

Athletics. Intramural: Basketball, racquetball, volleyball.

Student services. Career counseling, financial aid counseling, placement for graduates, veterans' counselor. **Physically disabled:** Services for visually, hearing impaired.

Contact. Phone: (409) 882-3364 Fax: (409) 882-3055
Kerry Olson, Director of Admissions and Financial Aid, Lamar State College at Orange, 410 Front Street, Orange, TX 77630

Lamar State College at Port Arthur
Port Arthur, Texas
www.lamarpa.edu **CB code: 6589**

- Public 2-year community and technical college
- Commuter campus in small city

General. Regionally accredited. **Enrollment:** 1,985 degree-seeking undergraduates. **Degrees:** 194 associate awarded. **Location:** 90 miles from Houston. **Calendar:** Semester, limited summer session. **Full-time faculty:** 62 total. **Part-time faculty:** 53 total. **Partnerships:** Formal partnerships with Microsoft and Novell (authorized training center).

Student profile. Among degree-seeking undergraduates, 7% enrolled in a transfer program, 45% enrolled in a vocational program, 2% already have a bachelor's degree or higher.

Transfer out. **Colleges most students transferred to 2008:** Lamar University.

Basis for selection. Open admission, but selective for some programs. Special requirements for nursing programs only.

2008-2009 Annual costs. Tuition/fees: $4,117; $12,547 out-of-state. Books/supplies: $950. Personal expenses: $1,723.

Financial aid. All financial aid based on need. Need-based aid available for part-time students. Work-study available nights, weekends and for part-time students.

Application procedures. **Admission:** No deadline. No application fee. Admission notification on a rolling basis. **Financial aid:** Priority date 4/1; no closing date. FAFSA, institutional form required. Applicants notified on a rolling basis starting 4/15; must reply within 2 week(s) of notification.

Academics. **Special study options:** Cooperative education, cross-registration, distance learning, double major, dual enrollment of high school students, ESL, external degree, honors, independent study, internships, liberal arts/career combination, weekend college. License preparation in nursing. **Credit/placement by examination:** CLEP, institutional tests. SAT used for math placement if submitted. **Support services:** Learning center, pre-admission summer program, reduced course load, remedial instruction, study skills assistance, tutoring.

Majors. **Business:** Accounting, administrative services, business admin. **Computer sciences:** General. **Engineering technology:** Electrical, instrumentation. **Family/consumer sciences:** General, child care. **Health:** Medical secretary, nursing (RN), substance abuse counseling, surgical technology. **Legal studies:** Legal secretary. **Mechanic/repair:** Automotive, heating/ac/refrig. **Personal/culinary services:** Cosmetic. **Protective services:** Criminal justice.

Computing on campus. 50 workstations in library, student center. Online course registration, online library available.

Student life. **Freshman orientation:** Available. Preregistration for classes offered. Held 1 day in July and 1 in August. **Activities:** Campus ministries, choral groups, drama, musical theater, student government, association of family and consumer sciences, criminal justice association, Epsilon Delta Phi, legal assistant student school organization, historical society, Phi Theta Kappa.

Athletics. NJCAA. **Intercollegiate:** Basketball M, softball W. **Team name:** Seahawks.

Student services. Adult student services, career counseling, services for economically disadvantaged, student employment services, financial aid counseling, on-campus daycare, personal counseling, placement for graduates, veterans' counselor. **Physically disabled:** Services for visually, speech, hearing impaired. **Transfer:** Pre-admission transcript evaluation for new students. College fairs on campus for students transferring to 4-year colleges.

Contact. E-mail: Connie.Nicholas@lamarpa.edu
Phone: (409) 984-6168 Toll-free number: (800) 477-5872 ext. 6168
Fax: (409) 984-6025
Connie Nicholas, Registrar, Lamar State College at Port Arthur, Box 310, Port Arthur, TX 77641-0310

Laredo Community College

Laredo, Texas **CB member**
www.laredo.edu **CB code: 6362**

- Public 2-year community college
- Commuter campus in large city

General. Founded in 1946. Regionally accredited. Two-campus institution. **Enrollment:** 7,825 degree-seeking undergraduates. **Degrees:** 628 associate awarded. **ROTC:** Army. **Location:** 150 miles from San Antonio, 140 miles from Corpus Christi. **Calendar:** Semester, extensive summer session. **Full-time faculty:** 198 total; 12% have terminal degrees, 75% minority, 40% women. **Part-time faculty:** 112 total; 7% have terminal degrees, 81% minority, 42% women. **Special facilities:** Environmental science center, special collections relating to regional history.

Student profile. Among degree-seeking undergraduates, 120 transferred in from other institutions.

Part-time:	63%	**25 or older:**	30%
Out-of-state:	8%	**Live on campus:**	2%
Women:	57%		

Transfer out. **Colleges most students transferred to 2008:** Texas A&M International University, University of Texas at San Antonio.

Basis for selection. Open admission, but selective for some programs. Special requirements for nursing and allied health programs.

2008-2009 Annual costs. Tuition/fees: $2,016; $3,216 out-of-district; $4,416 out-of-state. Per-credit charge: $40 in-district; $80 out-of-district; $200 out-of-state. Room/board: $4,374. Books/supplies: $1,250. Personal expenses: $1,354.

Application procedures. **Admission:** No deadline. No application fee. Admission notification on a rolling basis. **Financial aid:** Priority date 5/1; no closing date. FAFSA, institutional form required. Applicants notified on a rolling basis.

Academics. Mandatory assessment program provides effective educational services for students. **Special study options:** Accelerated study, cooperative education, cross-registration, distance learning, dual enrollment of high school students, ESL, exchange student, honors, liberal arts/career combination, teacher certification program, weekend college. License preparation in nursing, occupational therapy, paramedic, physical therapy, radiology, real estate. **Credit/placement by examination:** AP, CLEP, institutional tests. 30 credit hours maximum toward associate degree. **Support services:** GED preparation and test center, learning center, remedial instruction, tutoring.

Majors. **Agriculture:** General. **Biology:** General, bacteriology, botany, marine. **Business:** General, accounting, administrative services, fashion, finance, marketing, office management, office technology, office/clerical, real estate, sales/distribution. **Communications:** General, broadcast journalism. **Computer sciences:** General, computer science, information systems, programming. **Construction:** Power transmission. **Education:** General, agricultural, art, bilingual, biology, business, chemistry, computer, early childhood, elementary, English, family/consumer sciences, foreign languages, health, history, mathematics, music, physical, physics, reading, Spanish, special, speech. **Engineering:** General, aerospace, agricultural, architectural, electrical, petroleum. **Engineering technology:** Civil. **Family/consumer sciences:** General, child care. **Foreign languages:** General, Spanish. **Health:** Clinical lab technology, EMT paramedic, medical assistant, medical radiologic technology/radiation therapy, medical secretary, mental health services, nursing (RN), occupational health, occupational therapy assistant, physical therapy assistant, predental, premedicine, prepharmacy, preveterinary. **History:** General. **Interdisciplinary:** Math/computer science. **Liberal arts:** Arts/sciences. **Math:** General. **Mechanic/repair:** Electronics/electrical. **Philosophy/religion:** Philosophy. **Physical sciences:** Chemistry, geology, physics. **Protective services:** Criminal justice, fire safety technology. **Psychology:** General. **Public administration:** Human services, social work. **Social sciences:** General, economics, political science, sociology. **Visual/performing arts:** Art, dramatic.

Computing on campus. 514 workstations in library, computer center. Dormitories wired for high-speed internet access. Online course registration, online library, repair service available.

Student life. **Freshman orientation:** Available. Preregistration for classes offered. **Housing:** Coed dorms available. $100 fully refundable deposit. **Activities:** Bands, choral groups, dance, drama, literary magazine, music ensembles, musical theater, opera, student government, student newspaper, symphony orchestra, TV station.

Athletics. NJCAA. **Intercollegiate:** Baseball M, tennis, volleyball W. **Intramural:** Baseball M, basketball, bowling, football (tackle) M, golf, handball, racquetball, softball, tennis, volleyball. **Team name:** Palominos.

Student services. Alcohol/substance abuse counseling, chaplain/spiritual director, career counseling, services for economically disadvantaged, student employment services, financial aid counseling, health services, on-campus daycare, personal counseling, placement for graduates, veterans' counselor. **Physically disabled:** Services for visually, speech, hearing impaired. **Transfer:** Transfer adviser, college fairs on campus for students transferring to 4-year colleges.

Contact. E-mail: admissions@laredo.edu
Phone: (956) 721-5117 Fax: (956) 721-5493
Felix Gamez, Director of Admissions and Records, Laredo Community College, West End Washington Street, Laredo, TX 78040-4395

Lee College

Baytown, Texas **CB member**
www.lee.edu **CB code: 6363**

- Public 2-year community college
- Commuter campus in small city

General. Founded in 1934. Regionally accredited. **Enrollment:** 5,841 degree-seeking undergraduates. **Degrees:** 618 associate awarded. **Location:** 25 miles from Houston. **Calendar:** Semester, limited summer session. **Full-time faculty:** 165 total. **Part-time faculty:** 200 total.

Basis for selection. Open admission, but selective for some programs. Observes TASP guidelines. Special requirements for allied health programs.

2008-2009 Annual costs. Tuition/fees: $1,302; $2,052 out-of-district; $3,102 out-of-state. Per-credit charge: $25 in-district; $50 out-of-district; $85 out-of-state. Books/supplies: $1,200. Personal expenses: $1,354.

Financial aid. Need-based: Need-based aid available for part-time students. Work-study available for part-time students. **Non-need-based:** Scholarships awarded for academics, art, athletics, job skills, music/drama.

Application procedures. Admission: No deadline. No application fee. Admission notification on a rolling basis. **Financial aid:** Priority date 4/1; no closing date. FAFSA required. Applicants notified on a rolling basis starting 6/1.

Academics. Special study options: Cooperative education, distance learning, dual enrollment of high school students, ESL, honors, independent study, internships, weekend college. **Credit/placement by examination:** CLEP, institutional tests. 30 credit hours maximum toward associate degree. **Support services:** GED preparation and test center, learning center, remedial instruction, tutoring.

Majors. Business: Accounting, administrative services, business admin, office/clerical. **Communications technology:** Graphic/printing. **Computer sciences:** General, data processing, information systems, programming. **Construction:** Pipefitting. **Engineering technology:** Drafting, electrical. **Foreign languages:** General. **Health:** EMT paramedic, medical records technology, substance abuse counseling. **Interdisciplinary:** Natural sciences. **Legal studies:** Paralegal. **Liberal arts:** Arts/sciences. **Math:** General. **Mechanic/repair:** Electronics/electrical, heating/ac/refrig. **Parks/recreation:** Health/fitness. **Physical sciences:** General. **Protective services:** Police science. **Visual/performing arts:** Dramatic.

Computing on campus. 500 workstations in library, computer center, student center. Online course registration, online library, helpline, wireless network available.

Student life. Freshman orientation: Available. Preregistration for classes offered. **Activities:** Bands, choral groups, drama, literary magazine, music ensembles, student government, Baptist student union, awareness club, Phi Theta Kappa, nursing students association, environmental science club, cosmetology club, digital information society, student honors council.

Athletics. NJCAA. **Intercollegiate:** Basketball M, tennis W, volleyball W. **Intramural:** Basketball, bowling, football (non-tackle), softball, table tennis, volleyball. **Team name:** Rebels.

Student services. Adult student services, career counseling, student employment services, financial aid counseling, personal counseling, placement for graduates, veterans' counselor. **Physically disabled:** Services for hearing impaired. **Transfer:** Transfer adviser for students transferring to 4-year colleges.

Contact. E-mail: admissions@lee.edu
Phone: (281) 425-6393 Fax: (281) 425-6831
Becki Griffith, Registrar, Lee College, Box 818, Baytown, TX 77522

Lincoln College of Technology: Grand Prairie

Grand Prairie, Texas
www.lincolntech.com

- For-profit 2-year technical college
- Large city

General. Regionally accredited; also accredited by ACCSCT. **Calendar:** Semester. **Full-time faculty:** 72 total. **Part-time faculty:** 10 total.

Academics. Credit/placement by examination: CLEP.

Majors. Engineering technology: Automotive.

Contact. Lincoln College of Technology: Grand Prairie, 2915 Alouette Drive, Grand Prairie, TX 75052

Lon Morris College

Jacksonville, Texas
www.lonmorris.edu **CB code: 6369**

- Private 2-year junior and liberal arts college affiliated with United Methodist Church
- Residential campus in large town
- SAT or ACT (ACT writing optional) required

General. Founded in 1873. Regionally accredited. **Enrollment:** 340 degree-seeking undergraduates. **Degrees:** 68 associate awarded. **ROTC:** Army, Naval, Air Force. **Location:** 100 miles from Dallas, 25 miles from Tyler. **Calendar:** Semester, limited summer session. **Full-time faculty:** 25 total; 24% have terminal degrees, 8% minority, 68% women. **Part-time faculty:** 20 total; 45% have terminal degrees, 5% minority, 50% women. **Class size:** 39% < 20, 58% 20-39, 3% 40-49.

Student profile.

Out-of-state:	7%	Live on campus:	67%

Transfer out. Colleges most students transferred to 2008: Stephen F. Austin State University, University of Texas at Tyler, Schreiner University, Southwestern University.

Basis for selection. School achievement record, minimum GPA of 2.0, recommendation, ACT/SAT scores important. Audition required for choral, drama; interview recommended for academically weak; portfolio recommended for art. **Homeschooled:** Transcript of courses and grades required. **Learning Disabled:** Students with learning disabilities SAT/ACT exempt.

High school preparation. 9 units recommended. Recommended units include English 4, social studies 2, science 2 and foreign language 1.

2008-2009 Annual costs. Tuition/fees: $13,500. Room/board: $6,130. Books/supplies: $617. Personal expenses: $2,295.

2008-2009 Financial aid. All financial aid based on need. Need-based aid available for part-time students. Work-study available nights, weekends and for part-time students.

Application procedures. Admission: No deadline. $35 fee, may be waived for applicants with need. Admission notification on a rolling basis. **Financial aid:** Priority date 5/1; no closing date. FAFSA, institutional form required. Applicants notified on a rolling basis starting 2/15; must reply within 2 week(s) of notification.

Academics. Special study options: Distance learning, dual enrollment of high school students, ESL, independent study, study abroad. **Credit/placement by examination:** AP, CLEP, IB, SAT, ACT, institutional tests. 30 credit hours maximum toward associate degree. **Support services:** Learning center, pre-admission summer program, reduced course load, remedial instruction, study skills assistance, tutoring, writing center.

Majors. Biology: General. **Business:** General, accounting. **Computer sciences:** Computer science. **Education:** General. **Foreign languages:** Spanish. **Health:** Predental, premedicine, prenursing, prepharmacy, preveterinary. **History:** General. **Legal studies:** Prelaw. **Liberal arts:** Arts/sciences. **Math:** General. **Philosophy/religion:** Philosophy, religion. **Physical sciences:** Astronomy, chemistry, physics. **Protective services:** Criminal justice. **Psychology:** General. **Social sciences:** General, economics, political science, sociology. **Visual/performing arts:** General, art, art history/conservation, dramatic, music history, music performance, music theory/composition, piano/organ, studio arts, theater design, voice/opera.

Most popular majors. Liberal arts 81%, visual/performing arts 19%.

Computing on campus. 50 workstations in library, computer center. Dormitories wired for high-speed internet access and linked to campus network. Commuter students can connect to campus network. Online course registration, online library available.

Student life. Freshman orientation: Mandatory. Preregistration for classes offered. Held the week before classes begin. Students have opportunity to pay bills and move into dorms. **Housing:** Single-sex dorms, wellness housing available. $100 deposit. **Activities:** Bands, choral groups, dance, drama, literary magazine, music ensembles, musical theater, ecology club, poetry and literary group, midnight club, Christian service organization, Disciples on Campus, Christian worship group, international club, student senate, LMC Chamber, student activity association.

Athletics. NJCAA. **Intercollegiate:** Baseball M, basketball, cheerleading, golf, soccer, softball W. **Intramural:** Baseball M, basketball, football (non-tackle), soccer, softball, swimming, table tennis, tennis, volleyball. **Team name:** Bearcats.

Student services. Chaplain/spiritual director, career counseling, student employment services, financial aid counseling, health services, personal counseling. **Physically disabled:** Services for visually, speech, hearing impaired. **Learning disabled:** Comprehensive services available. **Transfer:** Pre-admission transcript evaluation for new students. Transfer adviser, college fairs on campus for students transferring to 4-year colleges.

Contact. E-mail: kmarquis@lonmorris.edu
Phone: (903) 589-4005 Toll-free number: (800) 259-5753
Fax: (903) 589-4006
Kris Marquis, Director of Admissions/Student Financial Aid, Lon Morris College, 800 College Avenue, Jacksonville, TX 75766

Lone Star College System

The Woodlands, Texas
www.nhmccd.edu **CB code: 6508**

- Public 2-year community college
- Commuter campus in very large city

General. Founded in 1972. Regionally accredited. Includes 5 colleges: Cy-Fair College, Kingwood College, North Harris College, Montgomery College, Tomball College. **Enrollment:** 51,718 degree-seeking undergraduates. **Degrees:** 2,259 associate awarded. **Location:** 40 miles from Houston. **Calendar:** Semester, extensive summer session. **Full-time faculty:** 2,155 total. **Part-time faculty:** 643 total. **Class size:** 47% < 20, 53% 20-39, less than 1% 40-49, less than 1% 50-99, less than 1% >100.

Student profile.

Out-of-state:	1%	**25 or older:**	30%

Transfer out. Colleges most students transferred to 2008: University of Houston, Sam Houston State University, Texas A&M-College Station, University of Texas-Austin.

Basis for selection. Open admission, but selective for some programs. Placement testing required in reading, writing, and math. Special requirements for nursing, respiratory therapy, occupational therapy, physical therapist assistant program, veterinary technician, diagnostic medical imagery, cosmetology.

2008-2009 Annual costs. Tuition/fees: $1,360; $2,860 out-of-district; $3,310 out-of-state. Per-credit charge: $36 in-district; $86 out-of-district; $101 out-of-state. Books/supplies: $600. Personal expenses: $1,600.

2007-2008 Financial aid. Need-based: Need-based aid available for part-time students. Work-study available nights and weekends. **Non-need-based:** Scholarships awarded for academics.

Application procedures. Admission: No deadline. No application fee. Admission notification on a rolling basis. **Financial aid:** Priority date 4/1; no closing date. FAFSA, institutional form required. Applicants notified on a rolling basis starting 4/1.

Academics. Special study options: Cooperative education, distance learning, double major, dual enrollment of high school students, ESL, honors, independent study, internships, study abroad, teacher certification program, weekend college. Bachelor's degree programs available on campus. License preparation in dental hygiene, nursing, occupational therapy, paramedic, physical therapy, radiology, real estate. **Credit/placement by examination:** AP, CLEP, IB, institutional tests. 42 credit hours maximum toward associate degree. **Support services:** GED preparation and test center, learning center, pre-admission summer program, reduced course load, remedial instruction, study skills assistance, tutoring, writing center.

Majors. Architecture: Technology. **Business:** Accounting, administrative services, business admin, hospitality admin. **Computer sciences:** General. **Education:** Early childhood, instructional media, kindergarten/preschool, middle. **Engineering technology:** Industrial, telecommunications. **Family/consumer sciences:** Child care. **Foreign languages:** Sign language interpretation. **Health:** Dental hygiene, EMT paramedic, medical radiologic technology/radiation therapy, medical records technology, medical secretary, nursing (RN), occupational therapy assistant, pharmacy assistant, physical therapy assistant, respiratory therapy technology, sonography, substance abuse counseling, veterinary technology/assistant. **Legal studies:** Paralegal. **Liberal arts:** Arts/sciences. **Mechanic/repair:** Automotive, heating/ac/refrig. **Personal/culinary services:** Cosmetic. **Production:** Welding. **Protective services:** Firefighting. **Science technology:** Biological. **Social sciences:** Cartography. **Visual/performing arts:** Interior design.

Most popular majors. Health sciences 21%, liberal arts 66%.

Computing on campus. 500 workstations in library, computer center, student center. Commuter students can connect to campus network. Online course registration, online library, helpline, wireless network available.

Student life. Freshman orientation: Available. Preregistration for classes offered. Available on campus and online. **Activities:** Bands, choral groups, dance, drama, international student organizations, literary magazine, music ensembles, musical theater, radio station, student government, student newspaper, symphony orchestra, TV station, Phi Theta Kappa, honors student association, student nurses association, African American society, Latin American student association, Asian student association, Campus Crusade for Christ, Muslim student organization, Show of Hands (deaf students).

Athletics. Intercollegiate: Baseball M. **Intramural:** Badminton, basketball, bowling, football (non-tackle), golf, racquetball, soccer, softball, table tennis, tennis, volleyball.

Student services. Adult student services, career counseling, services for economically disadvantaged, student employment services, financial aid counseling, minority student services, on-campus daycare, personal counseling, placement for graduates, veterans' counselor. **Physically disabled:** Services for visually, speech, hearing impaired. **Transfer:** Transfer adviser, college fairs on campus for students transferring to 4-year colleges.

Contact. Phone: (832) 813-6500
Glen Wood, Director of Records and Reporting, Lone Star College System, 5000 Research Forest Drive, The Woodlands, TX 77381-4356

McLennan Community College

Waco, Texas **CB member**
www.mclennan.edu **CB code: 6429**

- Public 2-year community and junior college
- Commuter campus in small city

General. Founded in 1965. Regionally accredited. **Enrollment:** 7,899 degree-seeking undergraduates. **Degrees:** 549 associate awarded. **ROTC:** Air Force. **Location:** 100 miles from Dallas and Austin. **Calendar:** Semester, extensive summer session. **Full-time faculty:** 191 total. **Part-time faculty:** 195 total.

Basis for selection. Open admission, but selective for some programs. Observes TASP guidelines in testing for placement. Admission to health careers programs is competitive.

2008-2009 Annual costs. Tuition/fees: $2,100; $2,460 out-of-district; $3,900 out-of-state. Per-credit charge: $61 in-district; $73 out-of-district; $121 out-of-state. Books/supplies: $725. Personal expenses: $1,596.

2007-2008 Financial aid. Need-based: 57% of total undergraduate aid awarded as scholarships/grants, 43% as loans/jobs. Need-based aid available for part-time students. **Non-need-based:** Scholarships awarded for athletics.

Application procedures. Admission: No deadline. No application fee. Admission notification on a rolling basis. **Financial aid:** Priority date 6/1; no closing date. FAFSA required. Applicants notified on a rolling basis starting 5/1.

Academics. Special study options: Distance learning, dual enrollment of high school students, honors, internships, study abroad, teacher certification program. Bachelor's degree programs available on campus. **Credit/placement by examination:** CLEP, institutional tests. 24 credit hours maximum toward associate degree. **Support services:** Learning center, reduced course load, remedial instruction, tutoring, writing center.

Majors. Business: General, accounting, office technology, real estate. **Communications:** General. **Computer sciences:** General, data processing, programming. **Family/consumer sciences:** Child care. **Foreign languages:** Sign language interpretation. **Health:** Clinical lab technology, EMT paramedic, medical radiologic technology/radiation therapy, medical records technology, medical secretary, mental health services, respiratory therapy technology, substance abuse counseling. **Interdisciplinary:** Gerontology. **Legal studies:** Legal secretary, paralegal. **Protective services:** Law enforcement admin.

Computing on campus. 425 workstations in library, computer center, student center. Commuter students can connect to campus network. Online library, helpline, wireless network available.

Student life. Freshman orientation: Mandatory. **Activities:** Bands, choral groups, dance, drama, international student organizations, music ensembles, musical theater, student government.

Athletics. NJCAA. **Intercollegiate:** Baseball M, basketball, golf M, softball W. **Team name:** Highlanders/Highlassies.

Student services. Adult student services, career counseling, student employment services, health services, on-campus daycare, personal counseling, placement for graduates, veterans' counselor. **Physically disabled:** Services for visually, hearing impaired. **Transfer:** Transfer adviser, college fairs on campus for students transferring to 4-year colleges.

Contact. Phone: (254) 299-8628 Fax: (254) 299-8694
Karen Clark, Director of Admissions, McLennan Community College, 1400 College Drive, Waco, TX 76708

Midland College

Midland, Texas
www.midland.edu **CB code: 6459**

- Public 2-year community college
- Commuter campus in small city
- Interview required

General. Founded in 1969. Regionally accredited. **Enrollment:** 3,509 degree-seeking undergraduates. **Degrees:** 414 associate awarded. **Location:** 300 miles from El Paso, 300 miles from Dallas. **Calendar:** Semester, extensive summer session. **Full-time faculty:** 131 total. **Part-time faculty:** 187 total. **Class size:** 29% < 20, 71% 20-39.

Student profile.

Out-of-state:	1%	**Live on campus:**	2%
25 or older:	60%		

Transfer out. Colleges most students transferred to 2008: University of Texas of the Permian Basin, Texas A&M University, Angelo State University, West Texas A&M University, Texas Tech University.

Basis for selection. Open admission, but selective for some programs. Observes TASP requirements. Special requirements for allied health science programs.

2008-2009 Annual costs. Tuition/fees: $1,710; $2,310 out-of-district; $3,240 out-of-state. Per-credit charge: $43 in-district; $63 out-of-district; $94 out-of-state. Additional $48 charge per credit hour for baccalaureate program. Room/board: $3,900. Books/supplies: $666. Personal expenses: $1,450.

2007-2008 Financial aid. Need-based: 92% of total undergraduate aid awarded as scholarships/grants, 8% as loans/jobs. Need-based aid available for part-time students. Work-study available for part-time students. **Non-need-based:** Scholarships awarded for academics, athletics, minority status, music/drama, state residency.

Application procedures. Admission: Priority date 9/1; no deadline. No application fee. Admission notification on a rolling basis. **Financial aid:** Priority date 4/2, closing date 6/1. FAFSA required. Applicants notified on a rolling basis starting 5/15; must reply within 2 week(s) of notification.

Academics. Special study options: Cooperative education, cross-registration, distance learning, dual enrollment of high school students, ESL, honors, internships, liberal arts/career combination, Washington semester. Bachelor's degree programs available on campus. License preparation in aviation, nursing, paramedic, radiology, real estate. **Credit/placement by examination:** AP, CLEP, IB, institutional tests. 12 credit hours maximum toward associate degree. **Support services:** GED preparation and test center, learning center, reduced course load, remedial instruction, study skills assistance, tutoring, writing center.

Majors. Biology: General. **Business:** General, accounting, administrative services, business admin, entrepreneurial studies, management information systems, management science, managerial economics, office technology, office/clerical. **Communications:** General, broadcast journalism, journalism. **Communications technology:** Graphic/printing. **Computer sciences:** General, computer graphics, data processing, information systems, programming. **Conservation:** Environmental science. **Education:** Physical, teacher assistance. **Engineering:** Petroleum. **Engineering technology:** Drafting, electrical. **Family/consumer sciences:** Child care. **Foreign languages:** General, French, Spanish. **Health:** EMT ambulance attendant, EMT paramedic, medical radiologic technology/radiation therapy, medical records technology, nursing (RN), predental, premedicine, prepharmacy, respiratory therapy technology, substance abuse counseling, veterinary technology/assistant. **History:** General. **Legal studies:** Legal secretary, paralegal, prelaw. **Math:** General. **Mechanic/repair:** Automotive, electronics/electrical, heating/ac/refrig. **Parks/recreation:** Exercise sciences. **Physical sciences:** Chemistry, geology, physics. **Production:** Welding. **Protective services:** Fire safety technology, firefighting, law enforcement admin, police science. **Psychology:** General. **Public administration:** Social work. **Social sciences:** General, economics, political science, sociology. **Transportation:** Airline/commercial pilot. **Visual/performing arts:** Art, dramatic, music performance.

Computing on campus. 274 workstations in library, computer center, student center. Dormitories wired for high-speed internet access and linked to campus network. Online course registration, repair service, wireless network available.

Student life. Freshman orientation: Available. Preregistration for classes offered. 3-hour session held 5 times throughout year. **Housing:** Coed dorms, single-sex dorms, apartments available. $100 deposit, deadline 7/1. **Activities:** Bands, choral groups, drama, literary magazine, music ensembles, student government, student newspaper, several religious groups, ethnic and service clubs, clubs related to majors.

Athletics. NJCAA. **Intercollegiate:** Basketball, golf M, softball W. **Intramural:** Basketball, bowling, football (non-tackle), soccer M, table tennis, tennis, volleyball. **Team name:** Chaparrals.

Student services. Career counseling, student employment services, on-campus daycare, personal counseling, placement for graduates, veterans' counselor. **Physically disabled:** Services for visually, speech, hearing impaired. **Transfer:** Transfer center, transfer adviser, college fairs on campus for students transferring to 4-year colleges.

Contact. E-mail: rhaines@midland.edu
Phone: (432) 685-4502 Fax: (432) 685-4623
Ryan Gibbs, Admissions Director, Midland College, 3600 North Garfield, Midland, TX 79705

Mountain View College

Dallas, Texas
www.mvc.dcccd.edu **CB code: 6438**

- Public 2-year community college
- Commuter campus in very large city

General. Founded in 1970. Regionally accredited. **Location:** 8 miles from downtown. **Calendar:** Semester.

Annual costs/financial aid. Tuition/fees (2008-2009): $1,170; $2,160 out-of-district; $3,450 out-of-state. Books/supplies: $1,200. Personal expenses: $1,664. Need-based financial aid available to full-time and part-time students.

Contact. Phone: (214) 860-8600
Director of Admissions, 4849 West Illinois Avenue, Dallas, TX 75211-6599

Navarro College

Corsicana, Texas
www.navarrocollege.edu **CB code: 6465**

- Public 2-year community and junior college
- Commuter campus in large town

General. Founded in 1946. Regionally accredited. **Enrollment:** 8,328 degree-seeking undergraduates. **Degrees:** 514 associate awarded. **Location:** 50 miles from Dallas. **Calendar:** Semester, extensive summer session. **Full-time faculty:** 137 total. **Part-time faculty:** 351 total. **Special facilities:** Arts, science and technology center; IMAX theater.

Student profile. Among degree-seeking undergraduates, 63% enrolled in a transfer program, 37% enrolled in a vocational program, 1,677 enrolled as first-time, first-year students.

Part-time:	56%	**Women:**	62%
Out-of-state:	1%	**Live on campus:**	10%

Basis for selection. Open admission, but selective for some programs. Special requirements for health professions programs. Portfolio required for art.

2008-2009 Annual costs. Tuition/fees: $1,480; $2,380 out-of-district; $3,234 out-of-state. Room/board: $4,290. Books/supplies: $1,300. Personal expenses: $2,245.

Application procedures. Admission: No deadline. No application fee. Admission notification on a rolling basis. **Financial aid:** Priority date 6/1; no closing date. FAFSA required. Applicants notified on a rolling basis starting 7/1; must reply within 2 week(s) of notification.

Academics. Special study options: Distance learning, dual enrollment of high school students, ESL, honors, independent study, internships, liberal arts/career combination. Bachelor's degree programs available on campus. License preparation in paramedic. **Credit/placement by examination:** CLEP, institutional tests. 30 credit hours maximum toward associate degree. CLEP credit awarded only after successful completion of 12 credit hours in residence. **Support services:** GED preparation and test center, learning center, reduced course load, remedial instruction, tutoring.

Majors. Agriculture: Business, farm/ranch. **Biology:** General. **Business:** General, accounting, administrative services, business admin, management information systems, office technology, real estate, taxation. **Communications:** General, broadcast journalism, journalism. **Communications technology:** Graphic/printing. **Computer sciences:** General. **Education:** General, elementary, physical, secondary. **Engineering:** General. **Engineering technology:** Drafting. **Family/consumer sciences:** Child care, clothing/textiles. **Foreign languages:** Linguistics. **Health:** EMT paramedic, licensed practical nurse, medical radiologic technology/radiation therapy, predental, premedicine, prepharmacy, preveterinary. **Interdisciplinary:** Biological/physical sciences. **Liberal arts:** Arts/sciences. **Math:** General. **Physical sciences:** Chemistry, physics. **Protective services:** Criminal justice, fire safety technology, police science. **Psychology:** General. **Social sciences:** General. **Transportation:** Aviation. **Visual/performing arts:** Art, commercial/advertising art, dramatic, music performance, voice/opera.

Computing on campus. Dormitories wired for high-speed internet access and linked to campus network. Online course registration, wireless network available.

Student life. Freshman orientation: Available. Preregistration for classes offered. **Housing:** Single-sex dorms available. $200 deposit. **Activities:** Bands, choral groups, drama, music ensembles, student government, religious organizations, honorary and special interest clubs.

Athletics. NJCAA. **Intercollegiate:** Baseball M, basketball M, cheerleading, football (tackle) M, soccer W, softball W, tennis, volleyball W. **Intramural:** Softball. **Team name:** Bulldogs.

Student services. Career counseling, student employment services, personal counseling, placement for graduates, veterans' counselor. **Transfer:** Pre-admission transcript evaluation for new students. Transfer adviser, college fairs on campus for students transferring to 4-year colleges.

Contact. E-mail: admissions@navarrocollege.edu
Phone: (903) 875-7348 Toll-free number: (800) 628-2776
Fax: (903) 875-7353
David Edwards, Registrar, Navarro College, 3200 West Seventh Avenue, Corsicana, TX 75110

North Central Texas College

Gainesville, Texas
www.nctc.edu **CB code: 6245**

- Public 2-year community college
- Commuter campus in large town

General. Founded in 1924. Regionally accredited. **Enrollment:** 7,444 degree-seeking undergraduates. **Degrees:** 350 associate awarded. **ROTC:** Air Force. **Location:** 70 miles from Dallas. **Calendar:** Semester, extensive summer session. **Full-time faculty:** 117 total. **Part-time faculty:** 251 total. **Special facilities:** Planetarium, experimental farm, cattle center, horse arena.

Student profile.

Out-of-state:	9%	**Live on campus:**	3%
25 or older:	40%		

Basis for selection. Open admission, but selective for some programs. Observes TASP guidelines. Special requirements for some health professions programs.

High school preparation. 16 units recommended. Recommended units include English 4, mathematics 2, social studies 2 and science 2.

2008-2009 Annual costs. Tuition/fees: $1,350; $2,310 out-of-district; $3,450 out-of-state. Per-credit charge: $35 in-district; $67 out-of-district; $105 out-of-state. Room/board: $3,528. Books/supplies: $1,050. Personal expenses: $1,300.

Financial aid. All financial aid based on need. Need-based aid available for part-time students. Work-study available nights and for part-time students.

Application procedures. Admission: No deadline. No application fee. Admission notification on a rolling basis. High school transcript, proof of state residency, pre-TASP placement required for certain courses of study. **Financial aid:** Priority date 5/1; no closing date. FAFSA required. Applicants notified on a rolling basis starting 6/1; must reply within 4 week(s) of notification.

Academics. Special study options: Cross-registration, distance learning, dual enrollment of high school students. **Credit/placement by examination:** AP, CLEP, institutional tests. 18 credit hours maximum toward associate degree. **Support services:** Learning center, remedial instruction, tutoring.

Majors. Agriculture: Equestrian studies, farm/ranch. **Business:** General, administrative services, office technology, office/clerical. **Computer sciences:** General, data processing. **Engineering technology:** Drafting, electrical. **Health:** EMT paramedic, nursing (RN), occupational health, occupational therapy assistant. **Interdisciplinary:** Biological/physical sciences. **Legal studies:** Legal secretary, paralegal. **Mechanic/repair:** Diesel. **Protective services:** Criminal justice, police science. **Social sciences:** Criminology. **Visual/performing arts:** Commercial photography.

Computing on campus. 60 workstations in dormitories, library, computer center, student center. Dormitories linked to campus network. Commuter students can connect to campus network. Online course registration, online library, helpline available.

Student life. Freshman orientation: Mandatory. One-day program throughout summer and when classes commence. **Housing:** Coed dorms, special housing for disabled, wellness housing available. $150 deposit. **Activities:** Choral groups, dance, drama, literary magazine, music ensembles, student government, Baptist student union, Future Farmers of America, honor society, Young Republicans, nursing student association, criminal justice club, Methodist student organization, computer club.

Athletics. NJCAA. **Intercollegiate:** Baseball M, rodeo, tennis W, volleyball W. **Intramural:** Badminton, basketball, bowling, equestrian, golf, racquetball, softball, table tennis, tennis, track and field, volleyball. **Team name:** Lions.

Student services. Adult student services, career counseling, student employment services, personal counseling, veterans' counselor, women's services. **Transfer:** Transfer adviser for students transferring to 4-year colleges.

Contact. E-mail: admissions@nctc.edu
Phone: (940) 668-4222 ext. 222 Fax: (940) 668-6049
Melinda Carroll, Director of Admissions, North Central Texas College, 1525 West California Street, Gainesville, TX 76240

North Lake College

Irving, Texas **CB member**
www.northlakecollege.edu **CB code: 6519**

- Public 2-year community and liberal arts college
- Commuter campus in small city

General. Founded in 1977. Regionally accredited. **Enrollment:** 7,985 degree-seeking undergraduates. **Degrees:** 404 associate awarded. **Location:** 15 miles from Dallas. **Calendar:** Semester, limited summer session. **Full-time faculty:** 102 total; 22% have terminal degrees, 28% minority, 44% women. **Part-time faculty:** 449 total; 1% have terminal degrees, 22% minority, 42% women. **Class size:** 59% < 20, 36% 20-39, 3% 40-49, less than 1% 50-99, less than 1% >100. **Special facilities:** Natatorium, pool.

Student profile.

Out-of-state:	3%	**25 or older:**	40%

Transfer out. Colleges most students transferred to 2008: University of Texas at Arlington, University of North Texas, University of Texas at Dallas.

Basis for selection. Open admission. **Homeschooled:** Transcript of courses and grades, interview required. Must take placement test.

High school preparation. College-preparatory program recommended.

2008-2009 Annual costs. Tuition/fees: $1,170; $2,160 out-of-district; $3,450 out-of-state. Per-credit charge: $39 in-district; $72 out-of-district. Books/supplies: $600.

Financial aid. Need-based: Need-based aid available for part-time students. **Non-need-based:** Scholarships awarded for academics, minority status, state residency.

Application procedures. Admission: No deadline. No application fee. Admission notification on a rolling basis. **Financial aid:** Priority date 3/1, closing date 5/1. FAFSA required. Applicants notified on a rolling basis starting 7/1.

Academics. **Special study options:** Accelerated study, cooperative education, cross-registration, distance learning, double major, dual enrollment of high school students, ESL, honors, independent study, internships, liberal arts/career combination, study abroad, teacher certification program. License preparation in nursing, real estate. **Credit/placement by examination:** AP, CLEP. 15 credit hours maximum toward associate degree. **Support services:** GED preparation and test center, learning center, remedial instruction, study skills assistance, tutoring, writing center.

Majors. **Architecture:** Technology. **Business:** Accounting, administrative services, business admin, management science, office management, office technology, real estate. **Communications:** General. **Communications technology:** Graphics, photo/film/video. **Computer sciences:** General, applications programming, computer science, information systems, information technology, networking, programming, security, systems analysis, web page design. **Construction:** Carpentry, power transmission. **Education:** Adult literacy, elementary, ESL, kindergarten/preschool, music, teacher assistance. **Engineering technology:** General, electrical. **Liberal arts:** Arts/sciences. **Math:** General, applied, computational, statistics. **Psychology:** General. **Visual/performing arts:** Cinematography.

Computing on campus. 1,100 workstations in library, computer center, student center. Online course registration, online library, wireless network available.

Student life. **Freshman orientation:** Mandatory. Preregistration for classes offered. **Activities:** Jazz band, choral groups, dance, drama, film society, international student organizations, literary magazine, music ensembles, musical theater, opera, student government, student newspaper, association of black collegians, environmental club, Christians on Campus, Phi Theta Kappa, single parents association, Estamos Unidos, South Asian student organization, student ambassadors, anime club.

Athletics. NJCAA. **Intercollegiate:** Baseball, basketball, cheerleading M, gymnastics, swimming, volleyball, weight lifting. **Intramural:** Baseball, basketball, cheerleading W, soccer, swimming. **Team name:** Blazers.

Student services. Alcohol/substance abuse counseling, career counseling, services for economically disadvantaged, student employment services, financial aid counseling, health services, minority student services, personal counseling, placement for graduates, veterans' counselor. **Physically disabled:** Services for visually, hearing impaired. **Transfer:** Pre-admission transcript evaluation for new students. Transfer center, transfer adviser, college fairs on campus for students transferring to 4-year colleges.

Contact. Phone: (972) 273-3183 Fax: (972) 273-3112
Stephen Twenge, Director of Admissions and Registration, North Lake College, 5001 North MacArthur Boulevard, Irving, TX 75038-3899

Northeast Texas Community College
Mount Pleasant, Texas
www.ntcc.edu **CB code: 6531**

- Public 2-year community college
- Commuter campus in large town

General. Founded in 1984. Regionally accredited. **Location:** 60 miles from Texarkana, 118 miles from Dallas. **Calendar:** Semester.

Annual costs/financial aid. Tuition/fees (2008-2009): $1,800; $2,640 out-of-district; $3,956 out-of-state. Room/board: $3,820. Books/supplies: $1,075. Personal expenses: $2,020. Need-based financial aid available to full-time and part-time students.

Contact. Phone: (903) 572-1911 ext. 263
Director of Admissions, Box 1307, Mount Pleasant, TX 75456-1307

Northwest Vista College
San Antonio, Texas
www.accd.edu/nvc **CB code: 6517**

- Public 2-year community college
- Commuter campus in very large city

General. Regionally accredited. **Enrollment:** 11,961 degree-seeking undergraduates. **Degrees:** 622 associate awarded. **Location:** 16 miles from downtown. **Calendar:** Semester, extensive summer session. **Full-time faculty:** 155 total. **Part-time faculty:** 374 total.

Transfer out. **Colleges most students transferred to 2008:** University of Texas at San Antonio, Texas State University, Palo Alto College, San Antonio College, St. Philip's College.

Basis for selection. Open admission. **Homeschooled:** Transcript of courses and grades required.

High school preparation. 22 units recommended. Recommended units include English 4, mathematics 3, social studies 5, history 1, science 3, foreign language 2 and academic electives 3.

2008-2009 Annual costs. Tuition/fees: $1,772; $3,092 out-of-district; $5,732 out-of-state.

Financial aid. **Need-based:** Need-based aid available for part-time students. Work-study available nights, weekends and for part-time students. **Non-need-based:** Scholarships awarded for academics, leadership.

Application procedures. **Admission:** Priority date 4/23; deadline 8/19. No application fee. **Financial aid:** Priority date 4/1; no closing date. FAFSA required. Applicants notified on a rolling basis starting 5/15; must reply within 2 week(s) of notification.

Academics. **Special study options:** Cross-registration, distance learning, dual enrollment of high school students, ESL, internships, liberal arts/career combination, teacher certification program, weekend college. **Credit/placement by examination:** CLEP, institutional tests. 32 credit hours maximum toward associate degree. **Support services:** Learning center, remedial instruction, study skills assistance, tutoring, writing center.

Majors. **Biology:** General. **Business:** Business admin. **Communications:** General, journalism, media studies. **Communications technology:** General. **Computer sciences:** General, computer science, networking, programming. **Education:** General. **Foreign languages:** General. **Health:** Health services. **History:** General. **Interdisciplinary:** Behavioral sciences. **Legal studies:** Prelaw. **Liberal arts:** Arts/sciences. **Math:** General. **Parks/recreation:** Exercise sciences, health/fitness. **Physical sciences:** Chemistry. **Psychology:** General. **Public administration:** Social work. **Science technology:** Biological. **Social sciences:** General, economics, political science, sociology.

Computing on campus. 3,500 workstations in library, computer center, student center. Commuter students can connect to campus network. Online course registration, online library, helpline, wireless network available.

Student life. **Freshman orientation:** Mandatory. Preregistration for classes offered. **Activities:** Campus ministries, dance, drama, film society, literary magazine, student government, student newspaper.

Athletics. **Team name:** Wildcats.

Student services. Career counseling, student employment services, financial aid counseling, health services, personal counseling, placement for graduates, veterans' counselor. **Physically disabled:** Services for visually, speech, hearing impaired. **Learning disabled:** Comprehensive services available. **Transfer:** Pre-admission transcript evaluation for new students. Transfer center, transfer adviser, college fairs on campus for students transferring to 4-year colleges.

Contact. E-mail: nvc-admissions@mail.accd.edu
Phone: (210) 486-4700 Fax: (210) 486-4170
Elaine Lang, Director of Enrollment Services, Northwest Vista College, 3535 North Ellison Drive, San Antonio, TX 78251-4217

Odessa College
Odessa, Texas
www.odessa.edu **CB code: 6540**

- Public 2-year community college
- Commuter campus in small city

General. Founded in 1946. Regionally accredited. Extension centers in Pecos, Monahans, Andrews, Crane, Kermit, McCamey, Seminole. **Enrollment:** 3,177 degree-seeking undergraduates; 1,512 non-degree-seeking students. **Degrees:** 298 associate awarded. **Location:** 140 miles from Lubbock, 290 miles from El Paso. **Calendar:** Semester, extensive summer session. **Full-time faculty:** 120 total. **Part-time faculty:** 150 total. **Special facilities:** College-owned and operated NPR radio station.

Student profile. Among degree-seeking undergraduates, 634 enrolled as first-time, first-year students.

Part-time:	66%	**Hispanic American:**	51%
Out-of-state:	1%	**Native American:**	1%
Women:	66%	**25 or older:**	33%
African American:	5%	**Live on campus:**	5%
Asian American:	1%		

Basis for selection. Open admission, but selective for some programs. Allied health programs require successful completion of placement exams, supporting applications, and interviews. Requirements for other selective programs vary. **Homeschooled:** Transcript of courses and grades required.

2009-2010 Annual costs. Tuition/fees: $1,740; $2,340 out-of-district; $3,240 out-of-state. Room/board: $4,687. Books/supplies: $1,360. Personal expenses: $1,175.

2007-2008 Financial aid. Need-based: Need-based aid available for part-time students. Work-study available nights and for part-time students. **Non-need-based:** Scholarships awarded for academics, athletics, music/drama.

Application procedures. Admission: No deadline. No application fee. Admission notification on a rolling basis. **Financial aid:** Priority date 5/1; no closing date. FAFSA required. Applicants notified on a rolling basis starting 6/15.

Academics. Special study options: Cooperative education, cross-registration, distance learning, dual enrollment of high school students, independent study, internships, liberal arts/career combination. License preparation in nursing, paramedic, physical therapy, radiology. **Credit/placement by examination:** AP, CLEP, institutional tests. 15 credit hours maximum toward associate degree. **Support services:** GED preparation and test center, learning center, reduced course load, remedial instruction, study skills assistance, tutoring, writing center.

Majors. Biology: General. **Business:** General, administrative services, business admin. **Communications:** Radio/tv. **Computer sciences:** Computer science, information systems, programming. **Construction:** Carpentry, maintenance. **Education:** General, teacher assistance. **Engineering technology:** Drafting, occupational safety, petroleum. **Family/consumer sciences:** Child care. **Foreign languages:** General. **Health:** Clinical lab science, EMT paramedic, medical radiologic technology/radiation therapy, medical secretary, nursing (RN), physical therapy assistant, respiratory therapy technology, substance abuse counseling, surgical technology. **Legal studies:** Legal secretary, paralegal. **Liberal arts:** Arts/sciences. **Math:** General. **Mechanic/repair:** Automotive, diesel, electronics/electrical, heating/ac/refrig. **Personal/culinary services:** Chef training, cosmetic. **Physical sciences:** Chemistry, geology. **Production:** Machine tool, welding. **Protective services:** Fire safety technology, firefighting, police science. **Psychology:** General. **Social sciences:** General. **Visual/performing arts:** Art, commercial photography.

Computing on campus. 775 workstations in dormitories, library, computer center, student center. Dormitories wired for high-speed internet access and linked to campus network. Commuter students can connect to campus network. Online course registration, online library, student web hosting, wireless network available.

Student life. Freshman orientation: Available. Preregistration for classes offered. **Housing:** Apartments available. $200 partly refundable deposit. **Activities:** Bands, choral groups, drama, music ensembles, radio station, student government, Baptist student union, black organization of successful students, student alliance of Latinos succeeding academically, changing attitudes helping others overcome the situation.

Athletics. NJCAA. **Intercollegiate:** Baseball M, basketball, cross-country, golf M, rodeo, softball W. **Intramural:** Racquetball, softball, table tennis, tennis, volleyball. **Team name:** Wranglers.

Student services. Chaplain/spiritual director, career counseling, student employment services, financial aid counseling, on-campus daycare, personal counseling, placement for graduates, veterans' counselor. **Physically disabled:** Services for visually, hearing impaired. **Transfer:** Pre-admission transcript evaluation for new students. Transfer adviser, college fairs on campus for students transferring to 4-year colleges.

Contact. E-mail: thilliard@odessa.edu
Phone: (432) 335-6432 Fax: (432) 335-6636
Tracy Hilliard, Associate Director of Admissions, Odessa College, 201 West University, Odessa, TX 79764-7127

Palo Alto College

San Antonio, Texas
www.accd.edu/pac

CB member
CB code: 3730

- Public 2-year community college
- Commuter campus in very large city

General. Founded in 1987. Regionally accredited. **Enrollment:** 7,880 degree-seeking undergraduates. **Degrees:** 498 associate awarded. **Calendar:** Semester, limited summer session. **Full-time faculty:** 133 total. **Part-time faculty:** 356 total. **Special facilities:** FAA aviation education resource center. **Partnerships:** Formal partnership with a car/truck manufacturing company for occupational training.

Student profile.

Out-of-state:	1%	**25 or older:**	33%

Transfer out. Colleges most students transferred to 2008: University of Texas at San Antonio, St. Mary's University, Our Lady of the Lake University, University of the Incarnate Word.

Basis for selection. Open admission. SLEP used for placement of non-native speakers.

2008-2009 Annual costs. Tuition/fees: $1,802; $3,122 out-of-district; $5,762 out-of-state. Books/supplies: $500.

2007-2008 Financial aid. All financial aid based on need. 81% of total undergraduate aid awarded as scholarships/grants, 19% as loans/jobs. Need-based aid available for part-time students.

Application procedures. Admission: No deadline. No application fee. Admission notification on a rolling basis. **Financial aid:** Priority date 4/1, closing date 6/1. FAFSA required. Applicants notified on a rolling basis starting 5/31.

Academics. Special study options: Cooperative education, distance learning, dual enrollment of high school students, ESL, honors, internships, liberal arts/career combination, weekend college. Bachelor's degree programs available on campus. License preparation in aviation. **Credit/placement by examination:** CLEP, institutional tests. 32 credit hours maximum toward associate degree. **Support services:** GED preparation, learning center, remedial instruction, study skills assistance, tutoring, writing center.

Majors. Agriculture: Agribusiness operations, animal sciences, horticultural science, landscaping, ornamental horticulture, turf management. **Area/ethnic studies:** Hispanic-American/Latino/Chicano, Latin American. **Biology:** General. **Business:** Accounting, administrative services, banking/financial services, business admin, entrepreneurial studies, fashion, logistics, office management, office technology. **Communications:** General, advertising, journalism. **Computer sciences:** General, computer science, information systems, programming. **Conservation:** Environmental science. **Education:** General. **Engineering:** General, environmental. **Engineering technology:** Environmental. **Family/consumer sciences:** Food/nutrition. **Foreign languages:** General. **Health:** Health services, nursing assistant. **History:** General. **Interdisciplinary:** Biological/physical sciences. **Liberal arts:** Arts/sciences. **Math:** General. **Parks/recreation:** Exercise sciences. **Philosophy/religion:** Philosophy. **Physical sciences:** General, chemistry, physics. **Protective services:** Law enforcement admin. **Psychology:** General. **Public administration:** Social work. **Social sciences:** Anthropology, economics, political science, sociology. **Transportation:** Aviation. **Visual/performing arts:** Art, studio arts.

Computing on campus. Commuter students can connect to campus network. Online course registration, online library, wireless network available.

Student life. Freshman orientation: Mandatory. Preregistration for classes offered. **Activities:** Jazz band, campus ministries, choral groups, dance, drama, music ensembles, student government, student newspaper, international club, veterinary technician association, Phi Theta Kappa.

Athletics. NJCAA. **Intercollegiate:** Cross-country, diving, swimming. **Intramural:** Weight lifting. **Team name:** Palominos.

Student services. Adult student services, career counseling, services for economically disadvantaged, student employment services, financial aid counseling, health services, on-campus daycare, personal counseling, veterans' counselor. **Physically disabled:** Services for visually, speech, hearing impaired. **Learning disabled:** Comprehensive services available. **Transfer:** Transfer center, transfer adviser, college fairs on campus for students transferring to 4-year colleges.

Contact. Phone: (210) 921-5270 Fax: (210) 921-5310
Rachel Marez, Director of Enrollment Management, Palo Alto College, 1400 West Villaret Boulevard, San Antonio, TX 78224-2499

Panola College

Carthage, Texas
www.panola.edu

CB code: 6572

- Public 2-year community and junior college
- Commuter campus in small town

General. Founded in 1947. Regionally accredited. Additional campuses in Marshall and Center. Panola offers a wide variety of online and interactive television classes there as well as at area high schools. **Enrollment:** 1,985 degree-seeking undergraduates; 27 non-degree-seeking students. **Degrees:** 188 associate awarded. **Location:** 40 miles from Shreveport, Louisiana, 150 miles from Dallas. **Calendar:** Semester, limited summer session. **Full-time faculty:** 60 total; 12% have terminal degrees, 10% minority, 55% women. **Part-time faculty:** 54 total; 4% have terminal degrees, 2% minority, 48% women. **Class size:** 69% < 20, 29% 20-39, 2% 40-49.

Student profile. Among degree-seeking undergraduates, 15% enrolled in a transfer program, 85% enrolled in a vocational program, 2% already have a bachelor's degree or higher, 379 enrolled as first-time, first-year students, 180 transferred in from other institutions.

Part-time:	52%	**Hispanic American:**	6%
Women:	66%	**International:**	1%
African American:	18%	**25 or older:**	33%
Asian American:	1%	**Live on campus:**	10%

Transfer out. Colleges most students transferred to 2008: Stephen F. Austin State University, University of Texas at Tyler, Texas A&M Commerce, East Texas Baptist University.

Basis for selection. Open admission, but selective for some programs. Institution observes Texas Success Initiative guidelines. Departmental admission required prior to registration for some occupational/vocational programs of study. Early admissions for dual credit, tech prep. Interview required for some health program applicants. Auditions required for some fine arts scholarships.

High school preparation. Recommended units include English 4, mathematics 3, social studies 4, science 3, foreign language 2, academic electives 5.5.

2008-2009 Annual costs. Tuition/fees: $1,620; $2,490 out-of-district; $3,210 out-of-state. Room/board: $4,160. Books/supplies: $1,400. Personal expenses: $2,870.

2007-2008 Financial aid. Need-based: 96% of total undergraduate aid awarded as scholarships/grants, 4% as loans/jobs. Need-based aid available for part-time students. Work-study available nights, weekends and for part-time students. **Non-need-based:** Scholarships awarded for academics, alumni affiliation, art, athletics, leadership, music/drama.

Application procedures. Admission: No deadline. No application fee. **Financial aid:** Priority date 6/1; no closing date. FAFSA, institutional form required. Applicants notified on a rolling basis starting 6/1.

Academics. Special study options: Distance learning, dual enrollment of high school students, liberal arts/career combination. License preparation in nursing, occupational therapy. **Credit/placement by examination:** AP, CLEP. 12 credit hours maximum toward associate degree. **Support services:** GED preparation and test center, learning center, remedial instruction, study skills assistance, tutoring.

Majors. Business: General, administrative services, management information systems, office technology. **Computer sciences:** General. **Education:** General, early childhood. **Engineering technology:** Industrial. **Health:** Medical records technology, nursing (RN), occupational therapy assistant. **Liberal arts:** Arts/sciences. **Other:** Multi-/Interdisciplinary studies.

Most popular majors. Engineering/engineering technologies 12%, health sciences 31%, liberal arts 52%.

Computing on campus. 376 workstations in dormitories, library, computer center, student center. Dormitories wired for high-speed internet access and linked to campus network. Commuter students can connect to campus network. Online course registration, online library, helpline, wireless network available.

Student life. Freshman orientation: Available. Preregistration for classes offered. **Housing:** Coed dorms, apartments, wellness housing available. $150 partly refundable deposit, deadline 7/15. **Activities:** Bands, campus ministries, choral groups, dance, drama, literary magazine, music ensembles, musical theater, student government, student newspaper, Young Republicans, Excel club, forensics club, chemistry club, Phi Theta Kappa, computer club, nursing club, biology club, Circle K.

Athletics. NJCAA. **Intercollegiate:** Baseball M, basketball, rodeo, volleyball W. **Intramural:** Basketball, football (non-tackle), racquetball, softball, volleyball. **Team name:** Ponies and Fillies.

Student services. Alcohol/substance abuse counseling, career counseling, services for economically disadvantaged, financial aid counseling, personal counseling, veterans' counselor. **Physically disabled:** Services for visually, speech, hearing impaired. **Transfer:** College fairs on campus for students transferring to 4-year colleges.

Contact. E-mail: bsimpson@panola.edu
Phone: (903) 693-2038 Fax: (903) 693-2031
Barbara Simpson, Registrar/Director of Admissions, Panola College, 1109 West Panola Street, Carthage, TX 75633

Paris Junior College

Paris, Texas
www.parisjc.edu
CB member
CB code: 6573

- Public 2-year community and junior college
- Commuter campus in large town

General. Founded in 1924. Regionally accredited. **Enrollment:** 4,733 degree-seeking undergraduates. **Degrees:** 287 associate awarded. **Location:** 110 miles from Dallas. **Calendar:** Semester, limited summer session. **Full-time faculty:** 108 total. **Part-time faculty:** 125 total. **Special facilities:** Regional archives, collection of historical documents and artifacts of region, biological field laboratory with nature trails.

Student profile. Among degree-seeking undergraduates, 80% enrolled in a transfer program, 20% enrolled in a vocational program, 950 enrolled as first-time, first-year students.

Part-time:	60%	**Hispanic American:**	7%
Out-of-state:	13%	**Native American:**	2%
Women:	62%	**25 or older:**	40%
African American:	12%	**Live on campus:**	12%
Asian American:	1%		

Basis for selection. Open admission, but selective for some programs. Special admission to nursing program; interview required.

2008-2009 Annual costs. Tuition/fees: $1,350; $2,250 out-of-district; $3,450 out-of-state. Room/board: $4,132. Books/supplies: $500.

2007-2008 Financial aid. Need-based: Need-based aid available for part-time students. **Non-need-based:** Scholarships awarded for athletics, music/drama.

Application procedures. Admission: No deadline. No application fee. Admission notification on a rolling basis. **Financial aid:** No deadline. FAFSA required. Applicants notified on a rolling basis starting 6/1.

Academics. Special study options: Accelerated study, cross-registration, distance learning, dual enrollment of high school students. License preparation in nursing, paramedic, radiology. **Credit/placement by examination:** CLEP, institutional tests. **Support services:** GED preparation and test center, learning center, reduced course load, remedial instruction, tutoring.

Majors. Biology: General. **Business:** General, accounting, administrative services, business admin, office management, office technology, real estate. **Communications:** Journalism. **Computer sciences:** Data processing. **Construction:** Carpentry. **Education:** General. **Engineering technology:** Drafting, electrical. **Foreign languages:** General, French, German, Spanish. **Health:** Licensed practical nurse, medical records technology, predental, premedicine, prepharmacy, preveterinary. **History:** General. **Legal studies:** Prelaw. **Liberal arts:** Arts/sciences. **Math:** General. **Mechanic/repair:** Heating/ac/refrig, watch/jewelry. **Physical sciences:** Chemistry, physics. **Production:** Welding. **Psychology:** General. **Social sciences:** Political science, sociology. **Visual/performing arts:** Dramatic, metal/jewelry, studio arts.

Computing on campus. Dormitories wired for high-speed internet access and linked to campus network. Commuter students can connect to campus network.

Student life. Freshman orientation: Available. Preregistration for classes offered. **Housing:** Single-sex dorms, apartments available. **Activities:** Campus ministries, choral groups, drama, music ensembles, student government, student newspaper, Baptist student union, Afro-American club, honorary business fraternity, honorary scholastic fraternity.

Athletics. NJCAA. **Intercollegiate:** Baseball M, basketball, golf M, softball W, volleyball W. **Team name:** Dragons.

Student services. Career counseling, services for economically disadvantaged, student employment services, financial aid counseling, health services, personal counseling, placement for graduates, veterans' counselor.

Contact. Phone: (903) 785-7661 Fax: (903) 784-9370
Shelia Reese, Director of Admissions, Paris Junior College, 2400 Clarksville Street, Paris, TX 75460

Ranger College

Ranger, Texas
www.rangercollege.edu **CB code: 6608**

- Public 2-year junior college
- Rural community

General. Founded in 1926. Regionally accredited. **Enrollment:** 776 degree-seeking undergraduates. **Degrees:** 28 associate awarded. **Location:** 85 miles from Fort Worth, 65 miles from Abilene. **Calendar:** Semester, limited summer session. **Full-time faculty:** 27 total. **Part-time faculty:** 26 total.

Basis for selection. Open admission, but selective for some programs. Observe all TSI guidelines. Special requirements for vocational nursing program candidates include additional applications and testing.

2008-2009 Annual costs. Tuition/fees: $2,252; $2,432 out-of-state. Room/board: $3,452. Books/supplies: $1,000.

2007-2008 Financial aid. All financial aid based on need. Need-based aid available for part-time students.

Application procedures. Admission: No deadline. No application fee. Application must be submitted on paper. Candidates accepted into the vocational nursing program will receive notification and must reply by the date indicated. **Financial aid:** Priority date 6/1, closing date 7/24. FAFSA required. Applicants notified on a rolling basis; must reply within 2 week(s) of notification.

Academics. Special study options: Distance learning, dual enrollment of high school students, honors. 2-2 programs in education, business administration, computer systems, and information sciences with Tarleton State University. License preparation in nursing. **Credit/placement by examination:** CLEP, institutional tests. 12 credit hours maximum toward associate degree. **Support services:** GED test center, learning center, reduced course load, remedial instruction.

Majors. Business: Administrative services. **Computer sciences:** General. **Liberal arts:** Arts/sciences. **Production:** Welding.

Computing on campus. 30 workstations in library, computer center.

Student life. Freshman orientation: Mandatory. **Housing:** Single-sex dorms available. **Activities:** Bands, dance, music ensembles, student government, student newspaper.

Athletics. NJCAA. **Intercollegiate:** Baseball M, basketball, cheerleading, golf, rodeo, soccer, softball W, volleyball W. **Team name:** Rangers.

Student services. Career counseling, student employment services, health services, personal counseling, placement for graduates, veterans' counselor. **Transfer:** Transfer adviser for students transferring to 4-year colleges.

Contact. Phone: (254) 647-3234 ext. 215 Fax: (254) 647-3739
Roseatta Stephens, Registrar, Ranger College, 1100 College Circle, Ranger, TX 76470

Remington College: Dallas

Garland, Texas
www.educationamerica.com **CB code: 3232**

- For-profit 2-year junior and technical college
- Small city

General. Accredited by ACICS. **Calendar:** Continuous.

Annual costs/financial aid. Associate degree programs annual tuition $19,500 plus $50 fees. 8-month diploma program full tuition $13,900 plus $50 fees. Tuition includes textbooks and supplies. Personal expenses: $3,360.

Contact. Phone: (972) 686-7878
1800 Eastgate Drive, Garland, TX 75041

Remington College: Fort Worth

Fort Worth, Texas
www.remingtoncollege.edu **CB code: 3151**

- For-profit 2-year technical and career college
- Large city

General. Accredited by ACCSCT. **Location:** 7 miles from downtown. **Calendar:** Continuous.

Annual costs/financial aid. Associate degree programs annual tuition $19,500 plus $50 fees. 8-month diploma program full tuition $13,900 plus $50 fees. Tuition includes textbooks and supplies.

Contact. Phone: (817) 451-0017
Director of Recruitment, 300 East Loop 820, Fort Worth, TX 76112

Remington College: Houston

Houston, Texas
www.remingtoncollege.edu **CB code: 3152**

- For-profit 2-year technical college
- Commuter campus in very large city

General. Accredited by ACCSCT. **Calendar:** Quarter.

Annual costs/financial aid. Associate degree programs annual tuition $19,500 plus $50 fees. 8-month diploma program full tuition $13,900 plus $50 fees. Tuition includes textbooks and supplies. Personal expenses: $1,764. Need-based financial aid available to full-time and part-time students.

Contact. Phone: (281) 899-1240
Director of Recruitment, 3110 Hayes Road, Suite 380, Houston, TX 77082

Remington College: North Houston

Houston, Texas
www.remingtoncollege.edu

- For-profit 2-year health science and technical college
- Very large city

General. Accredited by ACCSCT. **Calendar:** Quarter.

Annual costs/financial aid. Associate degree programs annual tuition $19,500 plus $50 fees. 8-month diploma program full tuition $13,900 plus $50 fees. Tuition includes textbooks and supplies.

Contact. Phone: (281) 885-4450
11310 Greens Crossing, Suite 200, Houston, TX 77067

Richland College

Dallas, Texas
www.rlc.dcccd.edu **CB code: 6607**

- Public 2-year community college
- Commuter campus in very large city

General. Founded in 1972. Regionally accredited. **Enrollment:** 12,177 degree-seeking undergraduates. **Degrees:** 861 associate awarded. **Location:** 15 miles from downtown. **Calendar:** Semester, extensive summer session. **Full-time faculty:** 148 total. **Part-time faculty:** 515 total. **Special facilities:** Planetarium, laser light theater, horticulture demonstration garden, meditation labyrinth.

Student profile.

Out-of-state:	2%	25 or older:	39%

Basis for selection. Open admission. Students required by legislative mandate to take TASP test or alternative assessment before enrolling in college-level courses. **Homeschooled:** Require completed application, concurrent enrollment permission form, student information profile sheet, student health history form, authorization to release test scores, official home school transcripts.

2008-2009 Annual costs. Tuition/fees: $1,170; $2,160 out-of-district; $3,450 out-of-state. Per-credit charge: $39 in-district; $72 out-of-district. Books/supplies: $350. Personal expenses: $935.

2008-2009 Financial aid. Need-based: 68% of total undergraduate aid awarded as scholarships/grants, 32% as loans/jobs. Need-based aid available for part-time students. Work-study available nights and for part-time students. **Non-need-based:** Scholarships awarded for art, leadership, music/drama.

Application procedures. Admission: No deadline. No application fee. Admission notification on a rolling basis. **Financial aid:** Priority date 5/2, closing date 7/31. FAFSA required. Applicants notified on a rolling basis starting 6/1; must reply within 2 week(s) of notification.

Academics. **Special study options:** Cooperative education, cross-registration, distance learning, dual enrollment of high school students, ESL, honors, independent study, internships, study abroad, teacher certification program, weekend college. License preparation in real estate. **Credit/placement by examination:** AP, CLEP, institutional tests. 45 credit hours maximum toward associate degree. **Support services:** Learning center, remedial instruction, study skills assistance, tutoring.

Majors. **Agriculture:** Horticultural science, horticulture. **Business:** Accounting, administrative services, business admin, entrepreneurial studies, management information systems, real estate, tourism/travel. **Communications technology:** General. **Computer sciences:** General, applications programming. **Education:** Bilingual, teacher assistance. **Engineering technology:** Electrical, manufacturing. **Health:** Insurance coding, medical informatics, medical records technology. **Liberal arts:** Arts/sciences.

Computing on campus. 210 workstations in library, computer center. Commuter students can connect to campus network. Online course registration, online library, wireless network available.

Student life. **Freshman orientation:** Mandatory. Sessions held online. **Activities:** Bands, campus ministries, choral groups, dance, drama, music ensembles, musical theater, student government, student newspaper, TV station, Spanish heritage association, arts club, Educators of America, Sierra Student Coalition, German film club.

Athletics. NJCAA. **Intercollegiate:** Baseball M, basketball M, soccer, volleyball W. **Intramural:** Basketball, bowling, cross-country, football (non-tackle), golf, soccer, softball, tennis, volleyball. **Team name:** Thunder Ducks.

Student services. Adult student services, career counseling, services for economically disadvantaged, student employment services, financial aid counseling, health services, personal counseling, placement for graduates, veterans' counselor, women's services. **Physically disabled:** Services for visually, speech, hearing impaired. **Transfer:** Transfer adviser, college fairs on campus for students transferring to 4-year colleges.

Contact. Phone: (972) 238-6106 Fax: (972) 238-6346
Mary Darin, Director of Admissions, Richland College, 12800 Abrams Road, Dallas, TX 75243-2199

St. Philip's College

San Antonio, Texas
www.accd.edu/spc
CB member
CB code: 6642

- Public 2-year community college
- Commuter campus in very large city

General. Founded in 1898. Regionally accredited. Some courses held at off-campus sites throughout San Antonio. **Enrollment:** 7,617 degree-seeking undergraduates; 2,718 non-degree-seeking students. **Degrees:** 733 associate awarded. **ROTC:** Army. **Location:** 1 mile from downtown. **Calendar:** Semester, extensive summer session. **Full-time faculty:** 219 total; 10% have terminal degrees, 45% minority, 42% women. **Part-time faculty:** 375 total; 6% have terminal degrees, 50% minority, 43% women. **Class size:** 61% < 20, 38% 20-39, less than 1% 40-49. **Special facilities:** Restaurant on campus run by hospitality students, human patient simulator for nursing and allied health students. **Partnerships:** Formal partnerships with Boeing and Dee Howard for aircraft technology training.

Student profile. Among degree-seeking undergraduates, 48% enrolled in a transfer program, 52% enrolled in a vocational program, 1,520 enrolled as first-time, first-year students.

Part-time:	63%	**Asian American:**	2%
Out-of-state:	1%	**Hispanic American:**	52%
Women:	56%	**25 or older:**	50%
African American:	18%		

Transfer out. **Colleges most students transferred to 2008:** University of Texas at San Antonio, Texas State University.

Basis for selection. Open admission, but selective for some programs. Special requirements for nursing and certain allied health programs. PTASP or ACCUPLACER may be taken at entry in lieu of TASP, SAT, or ACT scores for placement. **Adult students:** Students age 65 and older do not have to test if they are auditing classes. **Homeschooled:** Transcript of courses and grades required.

2008-2009 Annual costs. Tuition/fees: $1,802; $3,122 out-of-district; $5,762 out-of-state. Per-credit charge: $51 in-district; $95 out-of-district; $183 out-of-state. Books/supplies: $900. Personal expenses: $2,185.

2007-2008 Financial aid. All financial aid based on need. 70% of total undergraduate aid awarded as scholarships/grants, 30% as loans/jobs. Need-based aid available for part-time students. Work-study available nights, weekends and for part-time students.

Application procedures. **Admission:** No deadline. No application fee. **Financial aid:** No deadline. FAFSA required.

Academics. **Special study options:** Accelerated study, cooperative education, cross-registration, distance learning, double major, dual enrollment of high school students, ESL, honors, independent study, internships, study abroad, teacher certification program, weekend college. License preparation in aviation, nursing, occupational therapy, physical therapy, radiology, real estate. **Credit/placement by examination:** AP, CLEP, institutional tests. 32 credit hours maximum toward associate degree. **Support services:** GED preparation and test center, learning center, pre-admission summer program, reduced course load, remedial instruction, study skills assistance, tutoring, writing center.

Majors. **Architecture:** Interior. **Biology:** General, biomedical sciences. **Business:** Accounting, accounting technology, administrative services, business admin, construction management, hospitality admin, tourism/travel. **Communications technology:** General. **Computer sciences:** Data entry, data processing, information systems, LAN/WAN management, programming, webmaster. **Construction:** Carpentry, electrician, maintenance. **Education:** General, teacher assistance. **Engineering:** General. **Engineering technology:** Biomedical, computer hardware, construction, drafting, electrical, heat/ac/refrig, instrumentation. **Family/consumer sciences:** Child care, institutional food production. **Foreign languages:** General, Spanish. **Health:** Clinical lab technology, medical radiologic technology/radiation therapy, medical records admin, medical records technology, medical secretary, nursing (RN), occupational therapy assistant, physical therapy assistant, predental, premedicine, prenursing, respiratory therapy technology. **History:** General. **Legal studies:** Legal secretary, paralegal, prelaw. **Liberal arts:** Arts/sciences. **Math:** General. **Mechanic/repair:** Aircraft, aircraft powerplant, auto body, automotive, communications systems, diesel, electronics/electrical, heating/ac/refrig. **Parks/recreation:** Health/fitness. **Personal/culinary services:** Chef training, culinary arts, restaurant/catering. **Philosophy/religion:** Philosophy. **Physical sciences:** Chemistry, geology. **Production:** Machine tool, welding. **Protective services:** Law enforcement admin. **Psychology:** General. **Public administration:** Social work. **Social sciences:** Economics, political science, sociology, urban studies. **Visual/performing arts:** Art, dramatic, studio arts. **Other:** Railroad operation mechanic.

Most popular majors. Business/marketing 10%, engineering/engineering technologies 7%, health sciences 34%, liberal arts 13%, personal/culinary services 6%, social sciences 6%, trade and industry 9%.

Computing on campus. 1,000 workstations in library, computer center. Commuter students can connect to campus network. Online course registration, online library, helpline, repair service available.

Student life. **Freshman orientation:** Mandatory. Preregistration for classes offered. **Activities:** Jazz band, campus ministries, choral groups, dance, drama, literary magazine, music ensembles, musical theater, student government, student newspaper, Black Educational Network, Los Unidos, African-American Men on the Move, Campus Crusade for Christ.

Athletics. **Intramural:** Basketball, swimming, table tennis, tennis, volleyball, weight lifting. **Team name:** Tigers.

Student services. Adult student services, chaplain/spiritual director, career counseling, services for economically disadvantaged, student employment services, financial aid counseling, health services, on-campus daycare, personal counseling, placement for graduates, veterans' counselor, women's services. **Physically disabled:** Services for visually, hearing impaired. **Transfer:** Transfer center, transfer adviser, college fairs on campus for students transferring to 4-year colleges.

Contact. E-mail: angarza2@mail.accd.edu
Phone: (210) 486-2300 Fax: (210) 486-2836
Burton Crow, Dean of Enrollment Management, St. Philip's College, 1801 Martin Luther King Drive, San Antonio, TX 78203

San Antonio College

San Antonio, Texas
www.accd.edu/sac
CB member
CB code: 6645

- Public 2-year community college
- Commuter campus in very large city

General. Founded in 1925. Regionally accredited. **Enrollment:** 21,766 undergraduates. **Degrees:** 900 associate awarded. **ROTC:** Army, Air Force.

Location: Downtown. **Calendar:** Semester, extensive summer session. **Full-time faculty:** 396 total. **Part-time faculty:** 655 total. **Special facilities:** Planetarium.

Transfer out. Colleges most students transferred to 2008: University of Texas at San Antonio.

Basis for selection. Open admission, but selective for some programs. Nursing requires 2.5 GPA, satisfactory completion of human anatomy/ physiology and ethics. Mortuary science program requires admissions interview, proof of complete hepatitis B vaccination series (or submit a waiver/ declination form), and counseling card. Dental assisting requires complete dental assisting technology program application, proof of advisement, formal admission to college, and counseling card. **Adult students:** Texas Higher Education Assessment required.

2008-2009 Annual costs. Tuition/fees: $1,666; $2,986 out-of-district; $5,626 out-of-state. Per-credit charge: $51 in-district; $95 out-of-district; $183 out-of-state. Books/supplies: $1,200. Personal expenses: $2,571.

2007-2008 Financial aid. All financial aid based on need. Need-based aid available for part-time students. Work-study available nights, weekends and for part-time students. **Additional information:** Leveraging Educational Assistance Partnership (LEAP), public student incentive grant, towards excellence access and success grants (Texas and Texas II grants) available.

Application procedures. Admission: Closing date 8/25. No application fee. Application must be submitted online. Admission notification on a rolling basis. Nursing applicants must apply by January 15. **Financial aid:** Priority date 3/1; no closing date. FAFSA required. Applicants notified by 7/1.

Academics. Special study options: Cooperative education, cross-registration, distance learning, double major, dual enrollment of high school students, ESL, honors, internships, liberal arts/career combination, study abroad, teacher certification program, weekend college. Internet courses, premedical/predental program, alternative teacher certification program, basic skills enrichment program, distance education through Virtual College of Texas, teaching academy program. License preparation in dental hygiene, nursing, paramedic, real estate. **Credit/placement by examination:** AP, CLEP, IB, institutional tests. 32 credit hours maximum toward associate degree. Student must earn 6 credits at college before credit by examination may be posted on transcript. No credit by examination may be earned for course already completed in classroom. **Support services:** GED preparation and test center, learning center, reduced course load, remedial instruction, study skills assistance, tutoring, writing center.

Majors. Business: Accounting technology, business admin. **Communications:** Journalism, radio/tv. **Computer sciences:** Programming, security. **Education:** Teacher assistance. **Engineering:** General. **Engineering technology:** Architectural, civil, electrical, occupational safety, telecommunications. **Family/consumer sciences:** Child development. **Foreign languages:** Sign language interpretation. **Health:** Medical assistant, nursing (RN), substance abuse counseling. **Interdisciplinary:** Global studies. **Legal studies:** Paralegal. **Math:** General. **Personal/culinary services:** Mortuary science. **Protective services:** Corrections, criminal justice, fire safety technology, police science, security management. **Psychology:** General. **Public administration:** General. **Visual/performing arts:** Graphic design.

Computing on campus. 325 workstations in library, computer center, student center. Commuter students can connect to campus network. Online course registration, online library, helpline, wireless network available.

Student life. Freshman orientation: Mandatory. Preregistration for classes offered. **Housing:** Special program places students in homes of elderly residents who have spare rooms and need assistance. **Activities:** Bands, choral groups, dance, drama, film society, international student organizations, literary magazine, music ensembles, musical theater, radio station, student government, student newspaper, symphony orchestra, TV station, Baptist student center, Catholic student center, Methodist student center, Church of Christ student center, black student alliance, United Mexican-American Students, College Republicans, Young Democrats, Young Socialist Alliance.

Athletics. Intramural: Basketball, bowling, cheerleading, cross-country, fencing, golf, racquetball, soccer, softball, swimming, table tennis, tennis, triathlon, volleyball, water polo. **Team name:** Rangers.

Student services. Adult student services, alcohol/substance abuse counseling, chaplain/spiritual director, career counseling, services for economically disadvantaged, student employment services, financial aid counseling, health services, on-campus daycare, personal counseling, placement for graduates, veterans' counselor, women's services. **Physically disabled:** Services for visually, speech, hearing impaired. **Transfer:** Pre-admission transcript evaluation for new students. Transfer center, transfer adviser, college fairs on campus for students transferring to 4-year colleges.

Contact. E-mail: sac-ar@mail.accd.edu
Phone: (210) 486-0700 Toll-free number: (800) 944-7575
Fax: (210) 486-1543
J. Martin Ortega, Director of Admissions and Records, San Antonio College, 1300 San Pedro Avenue, San Antonio, TX 78212-4299

San Jacinto College

Pasadena, Texas
www.sanjac.edu **CB code: 6694**

- Public 2-year community and technical college
- Commuter campus in very large city

General. Founded in 1960. Regionally accredited. Campuses in Houston and Pasadena and multiple extension centers. Aerospace and Biotechnology Academy (NASA-Johnson Space Center). **Enrollment:** 24,635 degree-seeking undergraduates; 199 non-degree-seeking students. **Degrees:** 1,836 associate awarded. **ROTC:** Air Force. **Location:** 20 miles from Houston. **Calendar:** Semester, limited summer session. **Full-time faculty:** 438 total; 19% have terminal degrees, 18% minority, 52% women. **Part-time faculty:** 634 total; 9% have terminal degrees, 30% minority, 56% women. **Class size:** 49% < 20, 49% 20-39, 2% 40-49, less than 1% 50-99. **Special facilities:** Nature preserve (North Campus). **Partnerships:** Formal partnerships with NASA Space Center Houston, Partnership for Innovation in Biotechnology and Life Sciences, Boeing for Reduced Gravity Student Flight Program, University of Houston-College of Engineering for Aerospace Workforce Innovation Network.

Student profile. Among degree-seeking undergraduates, 73% enrolled in a transfer program, 27% enrolled in a vocational program, 5,803 enrolled as first-time, first-year students, 11,261 transferred in from other institutions.

Part-time:	61%	**Women:**	57%
Out-of-state:	1%	**25 or older:**	32%

Basis for selection. Open admission, but selective for some programs. Special requirements for health science program. Psychological Services Bureau test and interview required of nursing applicants. SAT or ACT score used for nursing, medical laboratory technology, radiography, and respiratory programs. In some selective programs, specific courses taken successfully within San Jacinto district may obviate need for qualifying SAT/ACT scores. Interview recommended for nursing program, and EMT programs. **Learning Disabled:** Students should meet with Special Populations counselor after registering for classes.

2009-2010 Annual costs. Tuition/fees (projected): $1,376; $2,176 out-of-district; $3,776 out-of-state. Per-credit charge: $33 in-district; $58 out-of-district; $108 out-of-state.

2007-2008 Financial aid. All financial aid based on need. 1,817 full-time freshmen applied for aid; 1,615 were judged to have need; 916 of these received aid. Average scholarship/grant was $1,427; average loan $2,715. 68% of total undergraduate aid awarded as scholarships/grants, 32% as loans/ jobs. Need-based aid available for part-time students. Work-study available nights, weekends and for part-time students.

Application procedures. Admission: No deadline. No application fee. Application must be submitted online. Admission notification on a rolling basis. **Financial aid:** Priority date 7/1; no closing date. FAFSA, institutional form required. Applicants notified on a rolling basis starting 4/1; must reply within 4 week(s) of notification.

Academics. Special study options: Accelerated study, cooperative education, cross-registration, distance learning, double major, dual enrollment of high school students, ESL, honors, internships, teacher certification program, weekend college. License preparation in aviation, nursing, paramedic, radiology, real estate. **Credit/placement by examination:** AP, CLEP, institutional tests. Freshman College Composition CLEP subject examination must be accompanied by essay. **Support services:** GED preparation and test center, learning center, pre-admission summer program, remedial instruction, study skills assistance, tutoring, writing center.

Majors. Biology: General, biotechnology. **Business:** General, accounting, administrative services, business admin, fashion, hospitality/recreation, international, management information systems, office technology, real estate. **Communications:** Journalism. **Communications technology:** Graphic/ printing. **Computer sciences:** LAN/WAN management, programming. **Construction:** Power transmission. **Engineering:** Mechanics. **Engineering technology:** Construction, drafting, instrumentation, occupational safety. **Family/ consumer sciences:** Child development, institutional food production. **Foreign languages:** General. **Health:** Clinical lab science, clinical lab technology, dietician assistant, EMT paramedic, medical assistant, medical radiologic technology/radiation therapy, medical records technology, medical secretary, nursing (RN), optometric assistant, physical therapy assistant, radiologic technology/medical imaging, respiratory therapy technology, surgical technology. **History:** General. **Legal studies:** Paralegal. **Math:** General. **Mechanic/repair:** Auto body, automotive, heating/ac/refrig. **Parks/recreation:** Health/fitness. **Personal/culinary services:** Chef training, food prep. **Physical sciences:** General, chemistry, geology, physics. **Production:** Welding. **Protective services:** Fire safety technology, firefighting, police science. **Psychology:** General. **Public administration:** General. **Science technology:** Chemical. **Social sciences:** General, sociology. **Theology:** Bible. **Transportation:** Airline/commercial pilot, aviation management. **Visual/performing arts:** Art, commercial/advertising art, dramatic, film/cinema.

Most popular majors. Biological/life sciences 7%, business/marketing 18%, health sciences 21%, liberal arts 15%, social sciences 8%.

Computing on campus. 200 workstations in library, computer center. Online course registration, helpline, repair service, wireless network available.

Student life. Freshman orientation: Available. 4-hour sessions scheduled several times prior to beginning of semester. **Policies:** Student conduct code. **Activities:** Jazz band, choral groups, dance, drama, literary magazine, music ensembles, musical theater, student government, student newspaper, Phi Theta Kappa honor society, Latin American student organization, College Republicans, College Democrats, Phi Beta Lambda business, Texas student education association, student government association.

Athletics. NJCAA. **Intercollegiate:** Baseball M, basketball, volleyball W. **Intramural:** Badminton, basketball, racquetball, softball, swimming, tennis, volleyball, weight lifting. **Team name:** Ravens / Gators / Coyotes.

Student services. Alcohol/substance abuse counseling, career counseling, student employment services, financial aid counseling, on-campus daycare, personal counseling, placement for graduates, veterans' counselor. **Transfer:** Transfer adviser, college fairs on campus for students transferring to 4-year colleges.

Contact. E-mail: information@sjcd.edu
Phone: (281) 998-6150 Fax: (281) 478-2720
Wanda Simpson, Director of Enrollment Services, San Jacinto College, 8060 Spencer Highway, Pasadena, TX 77505-5999

South Plains College
Levelland, Texas
www.southplainscollege.edu **CB code: 6695**

- Public 2-year community and junior college
- Commuter campus in large town

General. Founded in 1957. Regionally accredited. Continuing education and workforce development programs available. **Enrollment:** 6,970 degree-seeking undergraduates; 1,911 non-degree-seeking students. **Degrees:** 473 associate awarded. **Location:** 30 miles from Lubbock. **Calendar:** Semester, extensive summer session. **Full-time faculty:** 268 total. **Part-time faculty:** 186 total. **Special facilities:** Audio/video recording studio.

Student profile. Among degree-seeking undergraduates, 70% enrolled in a transfer program, 30% enrolled in a vocational program, 2% already have a bachelor's degree or higher, 1,436 enrolled as first-time, first-year students.

Part-time:	39%	**25 or older:**	21%
Out-of-state:	3%	**Live on campus:**	10%
Women:	52%		

Transfer out. 42% of students enrolled in the transfer program go on to 4-year colleges. **Colleges most students transferred to 2008:** Texas Tech University, San Angelo State University, West Texas A&M University, Eastern New Mexico State University.

Basis for selection. Open admission, but selective for some programs. State law requires TASP exam before student may enroll in college-level course work. Special requirements for allied health, cosmetology, law enforcement academy programs. Interview required for health care.

2008-2009 Annual costs. Tuition/fees: $1,892; $2,552 out-of-district; $3,032 out-of-state. Room/board: $3,200. Books/supplies: $580. Personal expenses: $1,100.

Financial aid. Need-based: Need-based aid available for part-time students. **Non-need-based:** Scholarships awarded for academics, art, athletics, leadership, music/drama, state residency.

Application procedures. Admission: No deadline. No application fee. Admission notification on a rolling basis. **Financial aid:** Priority date 6/1; no closing date. FAFSA required. Applicants notified on a rolling basis starting 6/30; must reply within 2 week(s) of notification.

Academics. Special study options: Distance learning, dual enrollment of high school students, internships. License preparation in nursing, occupational therapy, paramedic, physical therapy, radiology, real estate. **Credit/placement by examination:** AP, CLEP, institutional tests. 15 credit hours maximum toward associate degree. **Support services:** GED preparation, learning center, remedial instruction, study skills assistance, tutoring.

Majors. Agriculture: Business. **Biology:** General. **Business:** Accounting, administrative services, business admin, fashion, office management, real estate. **Communications:** General, broadcast journalism, journalism. **Communications technology:** Graphic/printing. **Computer sciences:** General, computer science, data processing. **Construction:** Power transmission. **Education:** General. **Engineering:** General. **Engineering technology:** Drafting. **Family/consumer sciences:** General, child care. **Foreign languages:** French, Spanish. **Health:** Athletic training, EMT paramedic, health services, medical radiologic technology/radiation therapy, medical records technology, medical secretary, nursing (RN), predental, premedicine, prenursing, preop/surgical nursing, prepharmacy, preveterinary, respiratory therapy technology. **History:** General. **Interdisciplinary:** Behavioral sciences. **Legal studies:** Legal secretary, paralegal. **Liberal arts:** Arts/sciences. **Math:** General. **Mechanic/repair:** Auto body, automotive, diesel, electronics/electrical, heating/ac/refrig. **Parks/recreation:** Health/fitness. **Physical sciences:** Chemistry, geology, physics. **Protective services:** Fire safety technology, firefighting, law enforcement admin. **Psychology:** General. **Public administration:** Human services. **Social sciences:** Criminology, political science, sociology. **Visual/performing arts:** Cinematography, commercial/advertising art, design, dramatic.

Computing on campus. 2,000 workstations in library, computer center, student center. Dormitories linked to campus network. Commuter students can connect to campus network. Online course registration, online library, wireless network available.

Student life. Freshman orientation: Mandatory. Preregistration for classes offered. **Housing:** Single-sex dorms, special housing for disabled, apartments available. $100 deposit. **Activities:** Bands, choral groups, dance, drama, literary magazine, music ensembles, musical theater, radio station, student government, student newspaper, TV station.

Athletics. NJCAA. **Intercollegiate:** Basketball, cheerleading, cross-country, rodeo, track and field. **Intramural:** Basketball, racquetball, softball, table tennis, volleyball. **Team name:** Texans/Lady Texans.

Student services. Career counseling, student employment services, financial aid counseling, health services, minority student services, personal counseling, placement for graduates, veterans' counselor. **Physically disabled:** Services for visually, hearing impaired. **Transfer:** Transfer adviser, college fairs on campus for students transferring to 4-year colleges.

Contact. E-mail: arangel@southplainscollege.edu
Phone: (806) 894-9611 ext. 2373 Fax: (806) 897-3167
Andrea Rangel, Dean of Admissions and Records, South Plains College, 1401 South College Avenue, Levelland, TX 79336

South Texas College
McAllen, Texas
www.southtexascollege.edu **CB code: 6654**

- Public 2-year community and technical college
- Commuter campus in small city

General. Regionally accredited. **Enrollment:** 21,425 degree-seeking undergraduates; 241 non-degree-seeking students. **Degrees:** 57 bachelor's, 1,799 associate awarded. **Calendar:** Semester, extensive summer session. **Full-time faculty:** 461 total; 59% minority, 43% women. **Part-time faculty:** 325 total; 75% minority, 54% women.

Student profile. Among degree-seeking undergraduates, 2,389 enrolled as first-time, first-year students.

Part-time:	67%	**Women:**	59%

Basis for selection. Open admission, but selective for some programs. Special requirements for nursing program. **Homeschooled:** Transcript of courses and grades required.

2008-2009 Annual costs. Tuition/fees: $2,510; $3,023 out-of-district; $6,800 out-of-state. Books/supplies: $1,000. Personal expenses: $1,200.

2007-2008 Financial aid. All financial aid based on need. 99% of total undergraduate aid awarded as scholarships/grants, 1% as loans/jobs. Need-based aid available for part-time students. Work-study available nights, weekends and for part-time students.

Application procedures. Admission: No deadline. No application fee. Application must be submitted on paper. **Financial aid:** Priority date 3/1; no closing date. FAFSA required. Applicants notified on a rolling basis starting 4/15.

Academics. Special study options: Cooperative education, distance learning, dual enrollment of high school students, ESL, weekend college. Bachelor's degree programs available on campus. **Credit/placement by examination:** CLEP, institutional tests. **Support services:** Learning center, remedial instruction, study skills assistance, tutoring, writing center.

Majors. Architecture: Technology. **Biology:** General. **Business:** Accounting, banking/financial services, business admin, marketing, office management. **Computer sciences:** General, applications programming, computer science, computer support specialist, database management, networking, security, web page design, webmaster. **Conservation:** Environmental studies. **Education:** Early childhood, elementary, middle, secondary. **Engineering:** General. **Engineering technology:** Drafting. **Family/consumer sciences:** Child development. **Health:** EMT paramedic, medical records technology, nursing assistant, occupational therapy assistant, office assistant, pharmacy assistant, physical therapy assistant, radiologic technology/medical imaging. **History:** General. **Interdisciplinary:** Intercultural. **Legal studies:** Legal secretary, paralegal. **Liberal arts:** Arts/sciences. **Math:** General. **Mechanic/repair:** Automotive, diesel, heating/ac/refrig. **Personal/culinary services:** General, restaurant/catering. **Philosophy/religion:** Philosophy. **Physical sciences:** Chemistry, physics. **Production:** General. **Protective services:** Law enforcement admin. **Public administration:** Human services. **Social sciences:** General, political science. **Visual/performing arts:** General, studio arts.

Computing on campus. Online course registration available.

Student life. Freshman orientation: Mandatory. Preregistration for classes offered. **Activities:** Drama, student government.

Athletics. Intramural: Basketball, football (non-tackle), football (tackle), softball, volleyball. **Team name:** Jaguars.

Student services. Career counseling, student employment services, financial aid counseling, personal counseling, placement for graduates, veterans' counselor. **Physically disabled:** Services for visually, speech, hearing impaired. **Learning disabled:** Comprehensive services available. **Transfer:** Transfer center, transfer adviser, college fairs on campus for students transferring to 4-year colleges.

Contact. Phone: (956) 618-8311
Matthew Hebbard, Director of Admissions and Registrar, South Texas College, 3201 West Pecan Boulevard, McAllen, TX 78502

Southwest Institute of Technology
Austin, Texas
www.switaustin.com **CB code: 2471**

- For-profit 2-year technical college
- Commuter campus in large city

General. Accredited by ACCSCT. **Enrollment:** 32 degree-seeking undergraduates. **Degrees:** 21 associate awarded. **Calendar:** Quarter. **Full-time faculty:** 4 total. **Part-time faculty:** 3 total. **Class size:** 100% < 20.

Basis for selection. Open admission. Interview recommended.

2008-2009 Annual costs. Tuition/fees: $19,419. Per-credit charge: $325. Books/supplies: $1,526.

2008-2009 Financial aid. All financial aid based on need. Work-study available nights and weekends.

Application procedures. Admission: No deadline. $100 fee, may be waived for applicants with need. **Financial aid:** No deadline. FAFSA, institutional form required.

Academics. Special study options: Cooperative education. **Credit/placement by examination:** CLEP. **Support services:** Learning center, tutoring.

Majors. Engineering: Electrical.

Computing on campus. Repair service available.

Student life. Freshman orientation: Mandatory.

Student services. Career counseling, student employment services, financial aid counseling, placement for graduates, veterans' counselor.

Contact. Phone: (512) 892-2640
Dick Roose, Director of Admissions, Southwest Institute of Technology, 5424 Highway 290 West, Suite 200, Austin, TX 78735

Southwest Texas Junior College
Uvalde, Texas
www.swtjc.edu **CB code: 6666**

- Public 2-year community and junior college
- Commuter campus in large town

General. Founded in 1946. Regionally accredited. **Enrollment:** 1,899 full-time, degree-seeking students. **Degrees:** 432 associate awarded. **Location:** 80 miles from San Antonio, 70 miles from Del Rio. **Calendar:** Semester, limited summer session. **Full-time faculty:** 114 total. **Part-time faculty:** 102 total.

Student profile.

Out-of-state:	10%	**Live on campus:**	9%

Basis for selection. Open admission.

2008-2009 Annual costs. Tuition/fees: $1,931; $2,816 out-of-district; $3,341 out-of-state. Per-credit charge: $43 in-district; $73 out-of-district; $90 out-of-state. Additional fees for off-campus classes may apply. Room/board: $3,100. Books/supplies: $900. Personal expenses: $745.

Financial aid. Need-based: Need-based aid available for part-time students.

Application procedures. Admission: No deadline. No application fee. Admission notification on a rolling basis. **Financial aid:** Priority date 6/15; no closing date. FAFSA required. Applicants notified on a rolling basis starting 5/1; must reply within 2 week(s) of notification.

Academics. Special study options: Dual enrollment of high school students. License preparation in aviation, nursing. **Credit/placement by examination:** CLEP. TASP required of all students for placement and counseling. **Support services:** GED preparation and test center, learning center, remedial instruction, study skills assistance, tutoring, writing center.

Majors. Agriculture: General, agribusiness operations, business, farm/ranch. **Business:** Administrative services, management information systems, office technology. **Computer sciences:** General, data processing. **Education:** General. **Health:** Licensed practical nurse, nursing (RN). **Liberal arts:** Arts/sciences.

Computing on campus. 150 workstations in dormitories, library, computer center. Dormitories wired for high-speed internet access and linked to campus network. Commuter students can connect to campus network. Online library, helpline available.

Student life. Freshman orientation: Mandatory. Preregistration for classes offered. **Housing:** Coed dorms, single-sex dorms available. **Activities:** Drama, literary magazine, radio station, student government, student newspaper.

Athletics. Intercollegiate: Rodeo. **Intramural:** Baseball M, basketball, golf, racquetball, softball, swimming, tennis, volleyball.

Student services. Adult student services, chaplain/spiritual director, career counseling, services for economically disadvantaged, student employment services, financial aid counseling, health services, minority student services, on-campus daycare, personal counseling, placement for graduates, veterans' counselor. **Physically disabled:** Services for visually, hearing impaired. **Transfer:** Pre-admission transcript evaluation for new students. Transfer adviser, college fairs on campus for students transferring to 4-year colleges.

Contact. E-mail: luana.rodriguez@swtjc.cc.tx.us
Phone: (830) 278-4401 Fax: (830) 591-7396
Joe Barker, Dean of Admissions/Student Services, Southwest Texas Junior College, Garner Field Road, Uvalde, TX 78801

Tarrant County College
Fort Worth, Texas **CB member**
www.tccd.edu **CB code: 6834**

- Public 2-year community and liberal arts college
- Commuter campus in very large city

General. Founded in 1965. Regionally accredited. Tarrant County College has four campuses located within Tarrant County: South and Northwest Campuses in Fort Worth; Northeast Campus in Hurst; and Southeast Campus in Arlington. **Enrollment:** 39,597 undergraduates. **Degrees:** 2,145 associate awarded. **ROTC:** Army, Air Force. **Calendar:** Semester, extensive summer session. **Full-time faculty:** 574 total; 18% have terminal degrees, 23% minority, 55% women. **Part-time faculty:** 965 total; 12% have terminal degrees, 19% minority, 49% women.

Student profile.

Out-of-state:	1%	**25 or older:**	45%

Transfer out. Colleges most students transferred to 2008: University of Texas at Arlington, University of North Texas, Texas Woman's University, Texas Tech University, Texas State University.

Basis for selection. Open admission, but selective for some programs. Special requirements for nursing and allied health programs, honors program, and certain automotive programs; must submit separate application and meet highly selective admission criteria. Placement testing required of all first-time college students and for those entering certain English, math, and reading-based courses. Interview and essay may be required for selective admission programs. **Homeschooled:** Transcript of courses and grades required.

2009-2010 Annual costs. Tuition/fees (projected): $1,500; $2,190 out-of-district; $4,950 out-of-state. Per-credit charge: $50 in-district; $73 out-of-district; $165 out-of-state. Books/supplies: $1,341. Personal expenses: $1,733.

2007-2008 Financial aid. Need-based: Need-based aid available for part-time students. **Non-need-based:** Scholarships awarded for academics.

Application procedures. Admission: No deadline. No application fee. Admission notification on a rolling basis. There is a deadline for International applicants. Applicants 18 years of age or older without high school diploma may be admitted on individual basis. **Financial aid:** Priority date 5/1; no closing date. FAFSA, institutional form required. Applicants notified on a rolling basis starting 5/1; must reply within 2 week(s) of notification.

Academics. Core curriculum guaranteed to transfer to any Texas public university. **Special study options:** Distance learning, double major, dual enrollment of high school students, ESL, honors, liberal arts/career combination. Limited Saturday classes available. License preparation in aviation, dental hygiene, nursing, paramedic, physical therapy, radiology, real estate. **Credit/placement by examination:** AP, CLEP, institutional tests. 18 credit hours maximum toward associate degree. **Support services:** GED preparation and test center, learning center, reduced course load, remedial instruction, study skills assistance, tutoring, writing center.

Majors. Agriculture: Horticulture. **Business:** General, accounting, administrative services, business admin, entrepreneurial studies, fashion, hospitality admin, operations, real estate, sales/distribution, tourism/travel. **Communications technology:** General, graphic/printing. **Computer sciences:** General, programming. **Engineering technology:** Architectural, drafting, electrical. **Family/consumer sciences:** Child care, institutional food production. **Foreign languages:** Sign language interpretation. **Health:** Dental hygiene, EMT paramedic, medical radiologic technology/radiation therapy, medical records technology, mental health services, nursing (RN), physical therapy assistant, respiratory therapy technology. **Legal studies:** Paralegal. **Mechanic/repair:** Aircraft, auto body, automotive, electronics/electrical, heating/ac/refrig. **Protective services:** Criminal justice, fire safety technology, firefighting, police science. **Public administration:** General.

Computing on campus. 3,000 workstations in library, computer center, student center. Commuter students can connect to campus network. Online course registration, online library available.

Student life. Freshman orientation: Available. Preregistration for classes offered. 1-2 hours, held intermittently. **Activities:** Bands, choral groups, dance, drama, literary magazine, music ensembles, student government, student newspaper.

Athletics. Intramural: Basketball M, table tennis.

Student services. Adult student services, career counseling, services for economically disadvantaged, student employment services, financial aid counseling, health services, personal counseling, placement for graduates. **Physically disabled:** Services for visually, speech, hearing impaired. **Transfer:** College fairs on campus for students transferring to 4-year colleges.

Contact. E-mail: suzanne.carter@tccd.edu
Phone: (817) 515-8223 Fax: (817) 515-5283
Suzanne Carter, Director of Admissions Services, Tarrant County College, 1500 Houston Street, Fort Worth, TX 76102-6599

Temple College
Temple, Texas
www.templejc.edu **CB code: 6818**

- Public 2-year community college
- Commuter campus in small city

General. Founded in 1926. Regionally accredited. **Enrollment:** 4,970 degree-seeking undergraduates; 208 non-degree-seeking students. **Degrees:** 329 associate awarded. **Location:** 65 miles from Austin. **Calendar:** Semester, limited summer session. **Full-time faculty:** 123 total; 20% have terminal degrees, 15% minority, 55% women. **Part-time faculty:** 138 total; 7% have terminal degrees, 12% minority, 51% women. **Class size:** 57% < 20, 42% 20-39, less than 1% 40-49, less than 1% 50-99. **Special facilities:** Health sciences simulation center. **Partnerships:** Formal partnerships with area high schools for tech prep programs.

Student profile. Among degree-seeking undergraduates, 652 enrolled as first-time, first-year students, 348 transferred in from other institutions.

Part-time:	61%	**Women:**	66%
Out-of-state:	1%	**25 or older:**	32%

Transfer out. Colleges most students transferred to 2008: Texas A&M University, Tarleton State University, Texas State University, University of Texas at Austin, University of Mary Hardin-Baylor.

Basis for selection. Open admission, but selective for some programs. Limited enrollment in allied health programs; interview required. **Homeschooled:** Transcript of courses and grades required.

High school preparation. College-preparatory program recommended. 23 units recommended. Recommended units include English 4, mathematics 3, social studies 2, history 2, science 3, foreign language 2 and academic electives 7.

2008-2009 Annual costs. Tuition/fees: $2,100; $3,300 out-of-district; $5,280 out-of-state. Per-credit charge: $70 in-district; $110 out-of-district; $176 out-of-state. Books/supplies: $1,236. Personal expenses: $1,481.

2007-2008 Financial aid. All financial aid based on need. Need-based aid available for part-time students. Work-study available nights and for part-time students.

Application procedures. Admission: No deadline. No application fee. **Financial aid:** Priority date 6/1; no closing date. FAFSA required. Applicants notified on a rolling basis starting 5/1; must reply within 4 week(s) of notification.

Academics. Special study options: Accelerated study, cooperative education, distance learning, dual enrollment of high school students, ESL, honors, internships. License preparation in dental hygiene, nursing, paramedic. **Credit/placement by examination:** AP, CLEP, IB, institutional tests. 32 credit hours maximum toward associate degree. Last 18 hours or total 32 hours earned in residence may not be earned through credit by examination. **Support services:** GED preparation, learning center, remedial instruction, study skills assistance, tutoring, writing center.

Majors. Biology: General. **Business:** General, office management. **Computer sciences:** General, data entry, LAN/WAN management, programming, system admin, webmaster. **Education:** Elementary, teacher assistance. **Engineering:** General. **Engineering technology:** Drafting. **Family/consumer sciences:** Child development. **Health:** Dental hygiene, EMT paramedic, nursing (RN), respiratory therapy technology, sonography. **Liberal arts:** Arts/sciences. **Math:** General. **Mechanic/repair:** Computer, electronics/electrical. **Protective services:** Criminal justice. **Public administration:** Social work. **Science technology:** Biological. **Social sciences:** Cartography. **Visual/performing arts:** Art.

Most popular majors. Business/marketing 13%, health sciences 25%, liberal arts 43%.

Computing on campus. 150 workstations in dormitories, library, computer center, student center. Dormitories wired for high-speed internet access and linked to campus network. Commuter students can connect to campus network. Online library, helpline, repair service, wireless network available.

Student life. Freshman orientation: Available. Preregistration for classes offered. Held prior to fall semester; 4 hours over 2 days. **Housing:** Apartments available. Privately run student apartments on campus. **Activities:** Bands, campus ministries, choral groups, dance, drama, literary magazine, music ensembles, musical theater, student government, symphony orchestra, black American cultural club, society of Latin American cultures, College Republicans, Young Democrats, literary club.

Athletics. NJCAA. **Intercollegiate:** Baseball M, basketball, softball W, tennis, volleyball W. **Intramural:** Basketball, bowling, football (non-tackle), golf, racquetball, soccer, softball, swimming, table tennis, tennis, volleyball. **Team name:** Leopards.

Student services. Adult student services, career counseling, services for economically disadvantaged, student employment services, financial aid counseling, personal counseling, placement for graduates, veterans' counselor. **Physically disabled:** Services for visually, hearing impaired. **Learning disabled:** Comprehensive services available. **Transfer:** Pre-admission transcript evaluation for new students. Transfer adviser for students transferring to 4-year colleges.

Contact. E-mail: carey.rose@templejc.edu
Phone: (254) 298-8300 Toll-free number: (800) 460-4636
Fax: (254) 298-8288
Carey Rose, Director of Admission and Records, Temple College, 2600 South First Street, Temple, TX 76504-7435

Texarkana College

Texarkana, Texas
www.texarkanacollege.edu **CB code: 6819**

- Public 2-year community college
- Commuter campus in small city

General. Founded in 1927. Regionally accredited. **Enrollment:** 4,654 degree-seeking undergraduates. **Degrees:** 454 associate awarded. **Location:** 80 miles from Shreveport, Louisiana, 180 miles from Dallas. **Calendar:** Semester, limited summer session. **Full-time faculty:** 96 total. **Part-time faculty:** 131 total. **Special facilities:** 365-acre farm.

Student profile.

Out-of-state:	30%	**Live on campus:**	3%
25 or older:	38%		

Transfer out. Colleges most students transferred to 2008: Texas A&M at Texarkana, Southern Arkansas University.

Basis for selection. Open admission. Interview recommended for nursing program.

2008-2009 Annual costs. Tuition/fees: $1,110; $1,770 out-of-district; $2,270 out-of-state. Per-credit charge: $34 in-district; $56 out-of-district; $73 out-of-state. Arkansas and Oklahoma residents pay out-of-district rates. Books/supplies: $750. Personal expenses: $1,200.

Financial aid. Need-based: Need-based aid available for part-time students. Work-study available nights, weekends and for part-time students. **Non-need-based:** Scholarships awarded for academics, athletics.

Application procedures. Admission: No deadline. No application fee. Admission notification on a rolling basis. **Financial aid:** Priority date 6/1; no closing date. FAFSA, institutional form required. Applicants notified on a rolling basis starting 3/1.

Academics. Special study options: Cooperative education, cross-registration, distance learning, dual enrollment of high school students, internships, liberal arts/career combination. License preparation in nursing, paramedic, real estate. **Credit/placement by examination:** AP, CLEP. 14 credit hours maximum toward associate degree. **Support services:** GED test center, learning center, remedial instruction, tutoring.

Majors. Agriculture: General. **Biology:** General. **Business:** General, administrative services, business admin, marketing. **Communications:** Journalism. **Computer sciences:** General. **Engineering:** General. **Engineering technology:** Drafting, electrical. **Family/consumer sciences:** Child development. **Foreign languages:** General. **Health:** EMT paramedic, nursing (RN), substance abuse counseling. **History:** General. **Liberal arts:** Humanities. **Math:** General. **Physical sciences:** Chemistry, physics. **Protective services:** Criminal justice, law enforcement admin. **Social sciences:** General, political science. **Visual/performing arts:** Art, dramatic.

Most popular majors. Business/marketing 11%, health sciences 32%, liberal arts 31%.

Computing on campus. 500 workstations in library, computer center. Dormitories wired for high-speed internet access.

Student life. Freshman orientation: Available. Preregistration for classes offered. **Housing:** Coed dorms available. **Activities:** Concert band, choral groups, drama, literary magazine, musical theater, radio station, student government, student newspaper.

Athletics. NJCAA. **Intercollegiate:** Baseball M, softball W. **Intramural:** Archery, badminton, basketball, bowling, handball, racquetball, sailing, skin diving, swimming, tennis, volleyball. **Team name:** Bulldogs.

Student services. Career counseling, student employment services, personal counseling, veterans' counselor.

Contact. E-mail: admissions@texarkanacollege.edu
Phone: (903) 832-5565 ext. 3358 Fax: (903) 832-5030
Tom Elder, Director of Admissions and Registrar, Texarkana College, 2500 North Robison Road, Texarkana, TX 75599

Texas Culinary Academy

Austin, Texas
www.tca.edu

- For-profit 2-year culinary school and technical college
- Very large city

General. Accredited by ACICS. **Enrollment:** 948 degree-seeking undergraduates. **Degrees:** 452 associate awarded. **Calendar:** Semester. **Full-time faculty:** 36 total. **Part-time faculty:** 11 total.

Basis for selection. Open admission, but selective for some programs.

2009-2010 Annual costs. Tuition/fees: $38,750. Books/supplies: $3,355.

Application procedures. Admission: No deadline. $100 fee.

Academics. Credit/placement by examination: CLEP.

Majors. Personal/culinary services: Chef training.

Contact. E-mail: info@tca.edu
Phone: (512) 837-2665 Toll-free number: (888) 553-3433
Texas Culinary Academy, 11400 Burnet Road, Suite 2100, Austin, TX 78758

Texas State Technical College: Harlingen

Harlingen, Texas
www.harlingen.tstc.edu **CB code: 6843**

- Public 2-year technical college
- Commuter campus in small city

General. Founded in 1969. Regionally accredited. **Enrollment:** 1,703 degree-seeking undergraduates. **Degrees:** 308 associate awarded. **Location:** 25 miles from Brownsville, 30 miles from South Padre Island. **Calendar:** Semester, extensive summer session. **Full-time faculty:** 152 total; 7% have terminal degrees, 66% minority, 38% women. **Part-time faculty:** 28 total; 7% have terminal degrees, 43% minority, 50% women. **Special facilities:** Computer labs with digital imaging technology, semi-conductor technology training center.

Transfer out. Colleges most students transferred to 2008: University of Texas at Brownsville, University of Texas-Pan American, University of Texas-San Antonio, South Texas College, Texas Southmost College.

Basis for selection. Open admission, but selective for some programs. Competitive admissions for dental assisting, surgical technology, dental hygiene, and health information technology programs. Associate degree candidates required to take state-mandated Texas Academic Skills Program. Results used only for placement. SAT/ACT scores may be substituted. **Homeschooled:** Statement describing homeschool structure and mission required.

2008-2009 Annual costs. Tuition/fees: $2,830; $6,400 out-of-state. Per-credit charge: $66 in-state; $185 out-of-state. Room/board: $3,160. Books/supplies: $900. Personal expenses: $2,449.

2008-2009 Financial aid. Need-based: Need-based aid available for part-time students.

Application procedures. Admission: No deadline. No application fee. Admission notification on a rolling basis. **Financial aid:** Closing date 4/30. FAFSA, institutional form required. Applicants notified on a rolling basis starting 6/30; must reply within 2 week(s) of notification.

Academics. Special study options: Cooperative education, distance learning, dual enrollment of high school students, ESL, independent study, internships, liberal arts/career combination, teacher certification program, weekend college. License preparation in aviation, dental hygiene, paramedic. **Credit/placement by examination:** AP, CLEP, institutional tests. **Support services:**

GED preparation and test center, learning center, remedial instruction, study skills assistance, tutoring.

Majors. Agriculture: Business technology. **Business:** Administrative services. **Computer sciences:** Networking, programming. **Education:** Teacher assistance. **Engineering technology:** Biomedical, computer systems, construction, drafting, electrical, electromechanical, telecommunications. **Health:** Dental hygiene, dental lab technology, EMT paramedic, medical assistant, medical records technology, surgical technology. **Legal studies:** Legal secretary. **Mechanic/repair:** Aircraft, auto body, heating/ac/refrig. **Personal/culinary services:** Institutional food service. **Production:** Tool and die. **Science technology:** Chemical.

Computing on campus. 1,750 workstations in library, computer center. Online library, helpline available.

Student life. Freshman orientation: Available. Preregistration for classes offered. **Housing:** Guaranteed on-campus for all undergraduates. Coed dorms, special housing for disabled, apartments, wellness housing available. $100 deposit. **Activities:** Dance, literary magazine, student government, student newspaper, Baptist student union, Hispanic club.

Athletics. Intramural: Baseball, basketball, football (tackle), racquetball, soccer, softball, table tennis, tennis, volleyball, weight lifting.

Student services. Alcohol/substance abuse counseling, career counseling, student employment services, financial aid counseling, health services, on-campus daycare, personal counseling, placement for graduates, veterans' counselor, women's services. **Physically disabled:** Services for visually, speech, hearing impaired. **Transfer:** Transfer adviser, college fairs on campus for students transferring to 4-year colleges.

Contact. E-mail: blanca.guerra@harlingen.tstc.edu
Phone: (956) 364-4320 Toll-free number: (800) 852-8784
Fax: (956) 364-5117
Blanca Guerra, Director of Admissions and Records, Texas State Technical College: Harlingen, 1902 North Loop 499, Harlingen, TX 78550-3697

Texas State Technical College: Marshall

Marshall, Texas
www.marshall.tstc.edu

- Public 2-year technical college
- Large town

General. Regionally accredited. **Enrollment:** 471 degree-seeking undergraduates. **Degrees:** 128 associate awarded. **Location:** 150 miles from Dallas, 230 miles from Houston. **Calendar:** Semester, extensive summer session. **Full-time faculty:** 34 total. **Part-time faculty:** 19 total.

Basis for selection. Open admission. Admission tests used only for placement.

2008-2009 Annual costs. Tuition/fees: $2,830; $6,400 out-of-state. Per-credit charge: $66 in-state; $185 out-of-state. Room only: $2,390.

Application procedures. Admission: No deadline. No application fee. Admission notification on a rolling basis. **Financial aid:** Priority date 6/1; no closing date. FAFSA required.

Academics. Credit/placement by examination: CLEP.

Majors. Business: E-commerce. **Communications technology:** General. **Computer sciences:** A.i./robotics, LAN/WAN management, networking. **Engineering technology:** Industrial, telecommunications. **Health:** Environmental health.

Student life. Freshman orientation: Mandatory, $15 fee. **Activities:** Student newspaper.

Contact. Phone: (903) 935-1010
Susan Carter, Director of Admissions, Texas State Technical College: Marshall, 2400 East End Boulevard South, Marshall, TX 75672

Texas State Technical College: Waco

Waco, Texas
www.waco.tstc.edu **CB code: 6328**

- Public 2-year technical college
- Residential campus in small city

General. Founded in 1965. Regionally accredited. **Enrollment:** 5,224 degree-seeking undergraduates. **Degrees:** 649 associate awarded. **Location:** 90 miles from Dallas, 99 miles from Austin. **Calendar:** Semester, extensive summer session. **Full-time faculty:** 239 total. **Part-time faculty:** 32 total. **Special facilities:** Advanced manufacturing center, 8,600-foot runway at TSTC-Waco airport, institutionally owned and operated 18-hole golf course.

Basis for selection. Open admission. Accuplacer or THEA test required prior to enrollment; used for placement purposes only. Aircraft pilot training, dental assistant technology, and pharmacy technician students must provide updated immunization data to be admitted and to register. Aircraft pilot training students must provide a current Class II Medical certificate to be eligible to register; fall start only. Interview required for students who indicate felony charges. **Homeschooled:** Transcript of courses and grades required.

2008-2009 Annual costs. Tuition/fees: $2,834; $6,404 out-of-state. Per-credit charge: $66 in-state; $185 out-of-state. Room/board: $4,800. Books/supplies: $751. Personal expenses: $1,899.

2007-2008 Financial aid. All financial aid based on need. 54% of total undergraduate aid awarded as scholarships/grants, 46% as loans/jobs. Need-based aid available for part-time students. Work-study available for part-time students.

Application procedures. Admission: No deadline. No application fee. Admission notification on a rolling basis. **Financial aid:** Priority date 6/1; no closing date. FAFSA required. Applicants notified on a rolling basis starting 5/15.

Academics. Special study options: Cooperative education, distance learning, double major, dual enrollment of high school students. License preparation in aviation, dental hygiene. **Credit/placement by examination:** AP, CLEP, IB, institutional tests. 24 credit hours maximum toward associate degree. **Support services:** GED test center, learning center, remedial instruction, study skills assistance, tutoring.

Majors. Agriculture: Turf management. **Business:** Operations. **Communications technology:** General, graphic/printing. **Computer sciences:** General, computer science, data processing, information systems, programming. **Construction:** Maintenance, power transmission. **Engineering technology:** Drafting, electrical. **Family/consumer sciences:** Institutional food production. **Health:** Clinical lab science. **Mechanic/repair:** General, aircraft, auto body, automotive, avionics, diesel, electronics/electrical, heating/ac/refrig, industrial. **Physical sciences:** General. **Transportation:** Aviation. **Visual/performing arts:** Cinematography, commercial/advertising art.

Computing on campus. 1,000 workstations in library, computer center, student center. Dormitories wired for high-speed internet access and linked to campus network. Commuter students can connect to campus network. Helpline, student web hosting, wireless network available.

Student life. Freshman orientation: Mandatory, $10 fee. Preregistration for classes offered. Held prior to semester. **Housing:** Coed dorms, special housing for disabled, apartments, wellness housing available. $150 fully refundable deposit. Duplexes and houses available to married students or students with families. **Activities:** Campus ministries, student government, student newspaper.

Athletics. Intramural: Basketball, football (non-tackle), golf, racquetball, softball, volleyball. **Team name:** Tornadoes.

Student services. Adult student services, career counseling, student employment services, financial aid counseling, health services, on-campus daycare, personal counseling, placement for graduates, veterans' counselor, women's services. **Physically disabled:** Services for visually, speech, hearing impaired. **Transfer:** Pre-admission transcript evaluation for new students. Transfer adviser for students transferring to 4-year colleges.

Contact. Phone: (254) 867-2361 Toll-free number: (800) 792-8784 ext. 2361 Fax: (254) 867-2250
Dawn Khoury, Director of Admissions and Records, Texas State Technical College: Waco, 3801 Campus Drive, Waco, TX 76705

Texas State Technical College: West Texas

Sweetwater, Texas
www.westtexas.tstc.edu **CB code: 3137**

- Public 2-year technical college
- Commuter campus in large town

General. Founded in 1970. Regionally accredited. **Enrollment:** 1,071 degree-seeking undergraduates. **Degrees:** 183 associate awarded. **Location:** 50 miles from Abilene. **Calendar:** Semester, limited summer session. **Full-time faculty:** 147 total; 16% minority, 53% women. **Part-time faculty:** 40 total; 5% minority, 35% women. **Special facilities:** Robotics lab, Cisco Academy, Microsoft Academy. **Partnerships:** Formal partnership with Florida Power

& Light Energy for development of TSTC West Texas' Wind Energy Technology Program.

Student profile.

Out-of-state:	1%	**Live on campus:**	16%
25 or older:	44%		

Basis for selection. Open admission, but selective for some programs. Standardized test scores, if submitted, may be used in placement and counseling. SAT and ACT scores, if high enough, may exempt applicant from THEA testing requirements. Base score on placement test considered for nursing program.

2008-2009 Annual costs. Tuition/fees: $2,830; $6,400 out-of-state. Per-credit charge: $66 in-state; $185 out-of-state. Room/board: $4,250. Books/supplies: $1,100. Personal expenses: $650.

2007-2008 Financial aid. Need-based: Need-based aid available for part-time students. Work-study available nights, weekends and for part-time students. **Non-need-based:** Scholarships awarded for academics, leadership.

Application procedures. Admission: Priority date 8/1; no deadline. No application fee. Admission notification on a rolling basis. **Financial aid:** Priority date 5/1; no closing date. FAFSA, institutional form required. Applicants notified on a rolling basis starting 7/1.

Academics. Special study options: Cooperative education, cross-registration, distance learning, dual enrollment of high school students, internships, liberal arts/career combination. 1-1 and 1-1-2 electronics technology programs with numerous area institutions. License preparation in aviation, nursing, paramedic. **Credit/placement by examination:** AP, CLEP, institutional tests. Varies per program and individual student. **Support services:** GED test center, learning center, reduced course load, remedial instruction, study skills assistance, tutoring.

Majors. Business: Management information systems. **Communications technology:** General. **Computer sciences:** Networking, programming, web page design. **Conservation:** Environmental science. **Engineering technology:** Construction, drafting, electrical, robotics. **Health:** EMT paramedic, licensed practical nurse, medical records technology, substance abuse counseling. **Mechanic/repair:** Aircraft, automotive, diesel. **Personal/culinary services:** Chef training. **Production:** Machine tool. **Visual/performing arts:** Design.

Computing on campus. 50 workstations in library, student center. Dormitories wired for high-speed internet access. Commuter students can connect to campus network. Online library, helpline, wireless network available.

Student life. Freshman orientation: Mandatory, $15 fee. Preregistration for classes offered. Held day before start of classes. **Housing:** Coed dorms, special housing for disabled, apartments, wellness housing available. $150 deposit. Pets allowed in dorm rooms. **Activities:** Student government, student newspaper, Mexican American club, Baptist student union, technical students association, data processing management association, Business Professionals of America, society of manufacturing engineers, Vocational Industrial Clubs of America.

Athletics. Intramural: Basketball, bowling, golf, softball, swimming, table tennis, tennis, volleyball W.

Student services. Career counseling, services for economically disadvantaged, student employment services, financial aid counseling, health services, personal counseling, placement for graduates, veterans' counselor, women's services. **Physically disabled:** Services for hearing impaired. **Transfer:** Transfer adviser, college fairs on campus for students transferring to 4-year colleges.

Contact. E-mail: maria.aguirre@tstc.edu
Phone: (325) 235-7300 Toll-free number: (800) 592-8784
Fax: (325) 235-7416
Maria Aguirre-Acuna, Director of Admissions & Records, Texas State Technical College: West Texas, 300 Homer K Taylor Drive, Sweetwater, TX 79556

Trinity Valley Community College
Athens, Texas
www.tvcc.edu **CB code: 6271**

- Public 2-year community college
- Commuter campus in large town

General. Founded in 1946. Regionally accredited. **Location:** 70 miles from Dallas. **Calendar:** Semester.

Annual costs/financial aid. Tuition/fees (2008-2009): $1,200; $1,800 out-of-district; $2,550 out-of-state. Room/board: $3,706. Books/supplies: $435. Personal expenses: $980. Need-based financial aid available to full-time and part-time students.

Contact. Phone: (903) 675-6357
Director of School Relations, 100 Cardinal Drive, Athens, TX 75751

Tyler Junior College
Tyler, Texas
www.tjc.edu **CB code: 6833**

- Public 2-year junior college
- Commuter campus in small city

General. Founded in 1926. Regionally accredited. **Enrollment:** 9,685 degree-seeking undergraduates. **Degrees:** 924 associate awarded. **Location:** 85 miles from Dallas, 85 miles from Shreveport, Louisiana. **Calendar:** Semester, extensive summer session. **Full-time faculty:** 272 total. **Part-time faculty:** 199 total. **Class size:** 48% < 20, 46% 20-39, 4% 40-49, 1% 50-99, less than 1% >100. **Special facilities:** Planetarium, conservatory.

Student profile.

Out-of-state:	2%	**Live on campus:**	1%
25 or older:	28%		

Transfer out. Colleges most students transferred to 2008: Stephen F. Austin State University, Texas A&M University, University of Texas at Tyler.

Basis for selection. Open admission, but selective for some programs. Admission to allied health programs based on test scores. High school units mandated by state law may vary by program. Texas Higher Education Assessment (THEA) required by Texas law for all incoming students. Interview required for some allied health programs, recommended for others. **Homeschooled:** Must complete equivalent of accepted high school diploma.

2008-2009 Annual costs. Tuition/fees: $1,730; $2,780 out-of-district; $3,530 out-of-state. Per-credit charge: $23 in-district; $58 out-of-district; $93 out-of-state. Room/board: $4,150. Books/supplies: $1,000. Personal expenses: $1,866.

2008-2009 Financial aid. Need-based: Need-based aid available for part-time students. Work-study available for part-time students. **Non-need-based:** Scholarships awarded for academics, alumni affiliation, art, athletics, leadership, music/drama.

Application procedures. Admission: No deadline. No application fee. Admission notification on a rolling basis. **Financial aid:** Priority date 6/1; no closing date. FAFSA, institutional form required. Applicants notified on a rolling basis starting 3/1; must reply within 2 week(s) of notification.

Academics. Special study options: Accelerated study, cooperative education, cross-registration, distance learning, dual enrollment of high school students, ESL, honors, internships, liberal arts/career combination, weekend college. License preparation in dental hygiene, nursing, paramedic, radiology, real estate. **Credit/placement by examination:** AP, CLEP, IB, institutional tests. **Support services:** GED preparation and test center, learning center, remedial instruction, study skills assistance, tutoring.

Honors college/program. SAT 1070 (exclusive of Writing), minimum 500 Math and Verbal; ACT 23, minimum 19 in each area.

Majors. Agriculture: General, farm/ranch. **Biology:** General. **Business:** General, accounting technology, administrative services, business admin, managerial economics, marketing, office management. **Communications:** Journalism. **Communications technology:** Graphic/printing. **Computer sciences:** General, applications programming, information systems, web page design. **Construction:** Electrician, maintenance. **Education:** General. **Engineering:** General. **Engineering technology:** Civil drafting, drafting, electrical, surveying. **Family/consumer sciences:** General, child care. **Foreign languages:** General, French, sign language interpretation, Spanish. **Health:** Clinical lab assistant, dental hygiene, EMT ambulance attendant, EMT paramedic, medical radiologic technology/radiation therapy, medical records technology, medical secretary, nursing (RN), office admin, ophthalmic lab technology, predental, premedicine, prenursing, prepharmacy, preveterinary, radiologic technology/medical imaging, respiratory therapy technology, sonography, substance abuse counseling, surgical technology. **History:** General. **Interdisciplinary:** Natural sciences. **Legal studies:** Legal secretary, paralegal, prelaw. **Liberal arts:** Arts/sciences. **Math:** General. **Mechanic/repair:** Automotive, heating/ac/refrig. **Parks/recreation:** Exercise sciences, health/fitness. **Physical sciences:** Chemistry, geology, physics. **Protective services:** Criminal justice, fire safety technology, police science. **Psychology:**

General. **Public administration:** Human services. **Social sciences:** General, sociology. **Visual/performing arts:** General, art, commercial/advertising art, dance, dramatic, interior design, music performance, studio arts.

Computing on campus. 95 workstations in library, computer center, student center. Dormitories wired for high-speed internet access. Commuter students can connect to campus network. Online course registration, online library, helpline, repair service, student web hosting, wireless network available.

Student life. **Freshman orientation:** Mandatory, $50 fee. Preregistration for classes offered. 2-day orientation program in summer. **Housing:** Single-sex dorms available. $200 partly refundable deposit. **Activities:** Bands, campus ministries, choral groups, dance, drama, international student organizations, literary magazine, music ensembles, musical theater, student government, student newspaper, symphony orchestra, TV station, Wesleyan Ministries, Phi Theta Kappa, Hispanic student organization.

Athletics. NAIA, NJCAA. **Intercollegiate:** Baseball M, basketball, cheerleading, football (tackle) M, golf, soccer M, tennis, volleyball W. **Intramural:** Badminton, basketball, football (tackle) M, handball, racquetball, softball, table tennis, tennis, volleyball M. **Team name:** Apaches.

Student services. Adult student services, alcohol/substance abuse counseling, chaplain/spiritual director, career counseling, services for economically disadvantaged, student employment services, financial aid counseling, health services, personal counseling, placement for graduates, veterans' counselor, women's services. **Physically disabled:** Services for visually, speech, hearing impaired. **Transfer:** College fairs on campus for students transferring to 4-year colleges.

Contact. E-mail: admissions@tjc.edu
Phone: (903) 510-2523 Toll-free number: (800) 687-5680 ext. 2523
Fax: (903) 510-2161
Nidia Arellano, Director of Admissions, Tyler Junior College, Box 9020, Tyler, TX 75711-9020

Vernon College
Vernon, Texas
www.vernoncollege.edu **CB code: 6913**

- Public 2-year community and junior college
- Commuter campus in large town

General. Founded in 1970. Regionally accredited. **Location:** 50 miles from Wichita Falls. **Calendar:** Semester.

Annual costs/financial aid. Tuition/fees (2008-2009): $2,100; $2,925 out-of-district; $4,260 out-of-state. Room/board: $3,270. Books/supplies: $1,000. Personal expenses: $1,238. Need-based financial aid available to full-time and part-time students.

Contact. Phone: (940) 552-6291
Dean of Admissions and Financial Aid/Registrar, 4400 College Drive, Vernon, TX 76384-4092

Victoria College
Victoria, Texas
www.victoriacollege.edu **CB code: 6915**

- Public 2-year community college
- Commuter campus in small city

General. Founded in 1925. Regionally accredited. **Enrollment:** 3,989 degree-seeking undergraduates. **Degrees:** 299 associate awarded. **Location:** 110 miles from San Antonio, 125 miles from Austin. **Calendar:** Semester, limited summer session. **Full-time faculty:** 101 total. **Part-time faculty:** 81 total.

Student profile. Among degree-seeking undergraduates, 60% enrolled in a transfer program, 40% enrolled in a vocational program, 2% already have a bachelor's degree or higher, 669 enrolled as first-time, first-year students, 194 transferred in from other institutions.

Part-time:	67%	**Asian American:**	2%
Women:	66%	**Hispanic American:**	33%
African American:	5%	**International:**	1%

Basis for selection. Open admission, but selective for some programs. Special requirements for allied health programs; interview required.

High school preparation. 24 units recommended. Recommended units include English 4, mathematics 3, social studies 2.5, history 1, science 3, foreign language 2, academic electives 3.5. 0.5 economics, 1 fine arts, 0.5 speech, 1 technical applications recommended.

2008-2009 Annual costs. Tuition/fees: $1,620; $2,340 out-of-district; $2,700 out-of-state. Books/supplies: $2,090. Personal expenses: $2,502.

Financial aid. **Need-based:** Work-study available for part-time students. **Non-need-based:** Scholarships awarded for academics, art, minority status, music/drama.

Application procedures. **Admission:** No deadline. No application fee. Admission notification on a rolling basis beginning on or about 7/1. **Financial aid:** Priority date 4/15; no closing date. FAFSA, institutional form required. Applicants notified on a rolling basis.

Academics. **Special study options:** Distance learning, dual enrollment of high school students. 2+2 plans with University of Texas-San Antonio, University of Houston-Victoria, Texas A&M-Corpus Christi, University of Texas-Brownsville. **Credit/placement by examination:** AP, CLEP, IB, institutional tests. **Support services:** GED preparation and test center, learning center, remedial instruction, tutoring.

Majors. **Business:** Administrative services, business admin. **Computer sciences:** General, information systems, networking, programming, system admin, web page design, webmaster. **Engineering technology:** Electrical, instrumentation. **Health:** Clinical lab technology, EMT paramedic, nursing (RN), respiratory therapy technology. **Legal studies:** Paralegal. **Liberal arts:** Arts/sciences.

Most popular majors. Business/marketing 7%, health sciences 43%, library sciences 39%.

Computing on campus. 500 workstations in library, computer center, student center. Commuter students can connect to campus network. Online course registration, online library, helpline, wireless network available.

Student life. **Freshman orientation:** Mandatory, $100 fee. Summer 2-day orientation sessions; online orientation also available. **Activities:** Bands, campus ministries, choral groups, drama, international student organizations, literary magazine, music ensembles, student government, student newspaper.

Athletics. **Intramural:** Basketball, volleyball. **Team name:** Pirates.

Student services. Career counseling, services for economically disadvantaged, student employment services, financial aid counseling, personal counseling, veterans' counselor. **Physically disabled:** Services for visually impaired. **Transfer:** College fairs on campus for students transferring to 4-year colleges.

Contact. E-mail: registrar@victoriacollege.edu
Phone: (361) 572-6408 Fax: (361) 582-2525
LaVern Dentler, Registrar, Victoria College, 2200 East Red River, Victoria, TX 77901

Virginia College at Austin
Austin, Texas
www.vc.edu/austin

- For-profit 2-year business and technical college
- Commuter campus in very large city

General. Accredited by ACICS. **Calendar:** Continuous.

Contact. Phone: (512) 371-3500
Director of Admissions, 6301 East Highway 290, Austin, TX 78723

Wade College
Dallas, Texas
www.wadecollege.edu **CB code: 1537**

- For-profit 2-year junior and career college
- Commuter campus in very large city
- Application essay, interview required

General. Founded in 1965. Regionally accredited. **Enrollment:** 242 degree-seeking undergraduates. **Degrees:** 106 associate awarded. **Location:** 2 miles from downtown Dallas. **Calendar:** Trimester, extensive summer session. **Full-time faculty:** 8 total. **Part-time faculty:** 10 total. **Class size:** 77% < 20, 23% 20-39.

Student profile. Among degree-seeking undergraduates, 10% enrolled in a transfer program, 90% enrolled in a vocational program, 3% already have a bachelor's degree or higher.

Basis for selection. Open admission.

2008-2009 Annual costs. Tuition/fees: $9,390. Room only: $4,000.

2007-2008 Financial aid. All financial aid based on need. Need-based aid available for part-time students. Work-study available nights, weekends and for part-time students.

Application procedures. Admission: No deadline. No application fee. Application must be submitted on paper. Admission notification on a rolling basis. **Financial aid:** No deadline. FAFSA required. Applicants notified on a rolling basis; must reply within 4 week(s) of notification.

Academics. Special study options: Accelerated study, cooperative education, double major. **Credit/placement by examination:** CLEP, IB. **Support services:** Learning center, reduced course load, study skills assistance, tutoring.

Majors. Business: Fashion, sales/distribution. **Computer sciences:** Computer graphics. **Family/consumer sciences:** Clothing/textiles. **Visual/ performing arts:** Design, fashion design, interior design.

Most popular majors. Business/marketing 45%, visual/performing arts 55%.

Computing on campus. 65 workstations in library, computer center. Online library, wireless network available.

Student life. Freshman orientation: Mandatory. **Housing:** Apartments available. $200 fully refundable deposit.

Student services. Adult student services, career counseling, student employment services, financial aid counseling, placement for graduates, veterans' counselor. **Transfer:** Re-entry adviser, pre-admission transcript evaluation for new students. Transfer adviser for students transferring to 4-year colleges.

Contact. E-mail: rmartin@wadecollege.edu
Phone: (214) 658-8800 Toll-free number: (800) 624-4850
Fax: (214) 637-0827
Renee Martin, Director of Admissions and Marketing, Wade College, Dallas Market Center, PO Box 421149, Dallas, TX 75342

Weatherford College
Weatherford, Texas
www.wc.edu **CB code: 6931**

- Public 2-year community college
- Commuter campus in large town

General. Founded in 1869. Regionally accredited. Off-campus courses held in Mineral Wells, Decatur, Aledo, Bridgeport, Granbury, Jacksboro, Springtown, Azle. **Enrollment:** 4,396 degree-seeking undergraduates; 377 non-degree-seeking students. **Degrees:** 582 associate awarded. **ROTC:** Air Force. **Location:** 25 miles from Fort Worth. **Calendar:** Semester, extensive summer session. **Full-time faculty:** 98 total. **Part-time faculty:** 104 total. **Special facilities:** 300-acre college farm. **Partnerships:** Formal partnerships with tech prep program and dual credit articulation agreements.

Student profile. Among degree-seeking undergraduates, 55% enrolled in a transfer program, 45% enrolled in a vocational program, 1% already have a bachelor's degree or higher, 920 enrolled as first-time, first-year students.

Part-time:	51%	**Hispanic American:**	10%
Out-of-state:	3%	**Native American:**	1%
Women:	63%	**International:**	1%
African American:	2%	**25 or older:**	50%
Asian American:	1%	**Live on campus:**	5%

Transfer out. Colleges most students transferred to 2008: Tarleton State University, University of North Texas, University of Texas at Arlington, Texas Tech University.

Basis for selection. Open admission, but selective for some programs. Nursing school, fire science requires entrance examination. Peace officer requires physical, drug testing, background check.

2008-2009 Annual costs. Tuition/fees: $1,770; $2,550 out-of-district; $3,930 out-of-state. Per-credit charge: $59 in-district; $85 out-of-district; $131 out-of-state. Room/board: $7,180. Books/supplies: $1,000. Personal expenses: $1,297.

Financial aid. All financial aid based on need. Work-study available nights, weekends and for part-time students.

Application procedures. Admission: No deadline. No application fee. Admission notification on a rolling basis. **Financial aid:** Priority date 7/3; no closing date. FAFSA required. Applicants notified on a rolling basis; must reply within 2 week(s) of notification.

Academics. Special study options: Cooperative education, distance learning, dual enrollment of high school students, ESL, honors, internships, liberal arts/career combination, teacher certification program, weekend college. License preparation in nursing, paramedic, radiology, real estate. **Credit/ placement by examination:** AP, CLEP, institutional tests. 30 credit hours maximum toward associate degree. Credit earned by examination does not reduce resident requirement of 15 semester hours of class completed at college. **Support services:** GED preparation and test center, learning center, remedial instruction, study skills assistance, tutoring.

Majors. Agriculture: Business, farm/ranch. **Business:** General, accounting, administrative services, human resources, marketing, office/clerical, operations. **Communications:** General. **Computer sciences:** General, data processing, programming. **Engineering technology:** Electrical. **Family/ consumer sciences:** Child care. **Health:** EMT paramedic, licensed practical nurse, phlebotomy, predental, premedicine, prenursing, prepharmacy, respiratory therapy assistant, respiratory therapy technology. **Liberal arts:** Arts/ sciences. **Personal/culinary services:** Cosmetic. **Protective services:** Corrections, police science. **Social sciences:** Sociology.

Computing on campus. 300 workstations in library, computer center. Dormitories linked to campus network. Commuter students can connect to campus network. Online course registration available.

Student life. Freshman orientation: Mandatory. Half-day sessions held before registration. **Housing:** Special housing for disabled, apartments, wellness housing available. $100 deposit, deadline 8/15. **Activities:** Jazz band, choral groups, dance, drama, music ensembles, musical theater, student government, black awareness student organization, Hispanic student organization, Baptist student union, international student organization, Wesleyan foundation, Baptist student ministries, A Better Life Through Education, disabled club.

Athletics. NJCAA. **Intercollegiate:** Baseball M, basketball, cheerleading, rodeo, tennis W. **Intramural:** Badminton, basketball, golf, softball, tennis, volleyball. **Team name:** Coyotes.

Student services. Adult student services, career counseling, services for economically disadvantaged, student employment services, financial aid counseling, personal counseling, placement for graduates, veterans' counselor. **Physically disabled:** Services for visually, speech, hearing impaired. **Transfer:** Pre-admission transcript evaluation for new students. Transfer adviser, college fairs on campus for students transferring to 4-year colleges.

Contact. Phone: (817) 598-6241 Toll-free number: (800) 287-5471
Fax: (817) 598-6205
Ralph Willingham, Director of Admissions, Weatherford College, 225 College Park Drive, Weatherford, TX 76086

Western Technical College
El Paso, Texas
www.wtc-ep.edu **CB code: 2941**

- For-profit 2-year technical college
- Commuter campus in very large city

General. Accredited by ACCSCT. Two campuses: main campus downtown, branch campus in NE section. **Enrollment:** 268 degree-seeking undergraduates. **Degrees:** 168 associate awarded. **Calendar:** Continuous. **Full-time faculty:** 32 total. **Part-time faculty:** 15 total.

Basis for selection. Open admission, but selective for some programs. Some programs require CPAT or other entrance requirements.

Financial aid. All financial aid based on need. Need-based aid available for part-time students.

Application procedures. Admission: No deadline. No application fee. **Financial aid:** No deadline. FAFSA required. Applicants notified on a rolling basis.

Academics. Credit/placement by examination: CLEP. **Support services:** GED preparation, remedial instruction, tutoring.

Majors. Mechanic/repair: General.

Computing on campus. 200 workstations in library, computer center, student center. Online library, wireless network available.

Contact. Phone: (915) 532-3737
Bill Terrell, Director of Admissions, Western Technical College, 9624 Plaza Circle, El Paso, TX 79927

Western Technical College: Diana Drive
El Paso, Texas
www.wtc-ep.edu

- For-profit 2-year technical college
- Very large city
- Interview required

General. Accredited by ACCSCT. **Enrollment:** 248 degree-seeking undergraduates. **Degrees:** 75 associate awarded. **Calendar:** Continuous. **Full-time faculty:** 35 total. **Part-time faculty:** 12 total.

Basis for selection. Open admission, but selective for some programs. Assessment test and various minimum scores required for following programs: medical assisting, health technology, computer technology, electronics technology, automotive technology, refrigeration technology, combination welding.

Application procedures. Admission: No deadline. No application fee. **Financial aid:** No deadline.

Academics. Credit/placement by examination: AP, CLEP.

Majors. Mechanic/repair: Automotive, heating/ac/refrig.

Contact. Phone: (915) 566-9621 Toll-free number: (800) 522-2072
Bill Terrell, Director of Admissions, Western Technical College: Diana Drive, 9451 Diana Drive, El Paso, TX 79924

Western Texas College
Snyder, Texas
www.wtc.edu **CB code: 6951**

- Public 2-year community and junior college
- Commuter campus in large town

General. Founded in 1969. Regionally accredited. **Enrollment:** 2,002 degree-seeking undergraduates. **Degrees:** 110 associate awarded. **Location:** 80 miles from Lubbock. **Calendar:** Semester, extensive summer session. **Full-time faculty:** 32 total. **Part-time faculty:** 46 total. **Class size:** 83% < 20, 16% 20-39, less than 1% 40-49, less than 1% 50-99.

Student profile.

Out-of-state:	3%	**Live on campus:**	15%
25 or older:	32%		

Transfer out. Colleges most students transferred to 2008: Texas Tech University, Angelo State University, University of Texas, Texas A&M University.

Basis for selection. Open admission, but selective for some programs. Institutional placement tests may be submitted in place of SAT/ACT. Special requirements for nursing program. Interview recommended.

2008-2009 Annual costs. Tuition/fees: $1,980; $2,420 out-of-district; $3,150 out-of-state. Per-credit charge: $39 in-district; $58 out-of-district; $83 out-of-state. Room/board: $4,900. Books/supplies: $500. Personal expenses: $900.

2008-2009 Financial aid. Need-based: Need-based aid available for part-time students. Work-study available nights and weekends. **Non-need-based:** Scholarships awarded for academics, art, athletics, leadership, music/drama, state residency.

Application procedures. Admission: No deadline. No application fee. Application must be submitted on paper. Admission notification on a rolling basis beginning on or about 11/5. **Financial aid:** Closing date 8/1. FAFSA, institutional form required. Applicants notified on a rolling basis starting 5/1; must reply within 2 week(s) of notification.

Academics. Special study options: Distance learning, dual enrollment of high school students, honors, independent study, internships. License preparation in nursing, paramedic. **Credit/placement by examination:** AP, CLEP, institutional tests. 12 credit hours maximum toward associate degree. **Support services:** GED preparation and test center, learning center, pre-admission summer program, reduced course load, remedial instruction, tutoring.

Majors. Agriculture: Animal sciences, greenhouse operations, horticulture, landscaping, nursery operations. **Biology:** General. **Business:** General, accounting, administrative services, business admin. **Communications:** Journalism. **Computer sciences:** General, computer science, data processing, LAN/WAN management, programming. **Education:** General, early childhood. **Engineering:** General. **Foreign languages:** General. **Health:** EMT paramedic, predental, premedicine, prenursing, prepharmacy, preveterinary. **History:** General. **Legal studies:** Prelaw. **Liberal arts:** Arts/sciences. **Math:** General. **Parks/recreation:** Facilities management, health/fitness. **Philosophy/religion:** Philosophy. **Physical sciences:** Chemistry, geology, physics. **Production:** Welding. **Protective services:** Corrections, law enforcement admin, police science. **Psychology:** General. **Social sciences:** General, economics, geography, international relations, political science, sociology. **Visual/performing arts:** Art, ceramics, dramatic, drawing, metal/jewelry, painting, photography, sculpture.

Computing on campus. 70 workstations in dormitories, library, computer center, student center. Dormitories wired for high-speed internet access and linked to campus network. Online library available.

Student life. Freshman orientation: Available. Preregistration for classes offered. **Housing:** Guaranteed on-campus for all undergraduates. Single-sex dorms, apartments available. $50 deposit. **Activities:** Drama, literary magazine, musical theater, student government, TV station, Baptist student union, Phi Theta Kappa.

Athletics. NJCAA. **Intercollegiate:** Baseball M, cheerleading M, cross-country, rodeo, softball W, volleyball W. **Intramural:** Basketball, bowling, diving, golf, handball, racquetball, softball, swimming, volleyball, weight lifting. **Team name:** Westerners.

Student services. Adult student services, alcohol/substance abuse counseling, career counseling, services for economically disadvantaged, student employment services, financial aid counseling, personal counseling, placement for graduates, veterans' counselor. **Transfer:** Pre-admission transcript evaluation for new students. Transfer adviser, college fairs on campus for students transferring to 4-year colleges.

Contact. E-mail: cmadrid@wtc.edu
Phone: (325) 573-8511 ext. 372 Toll-free number: (888) 468-6982
Fax: (325) 573-9321
Nellie Leatherwood, Director of Admissions, Western Texas College, 6200 College Avenue, Snyder, TX 79549

Westwood College: Dallas
Dallas, Texas
www.westwoodcollege.com

- For-profit 2-year technical college
- Commuter campus in very large city

General. Accredited by ACICS. **Calendar:** Continuous.

Contact. Phone: (214) 570-0100
Director of Admissions, 8390 LBJ Freeway, Dallas, TX 75243

Westwood College: Fort Worth
Fort Worth, Texas
www.westwood.edu/location/texas/fort-worth.asp

- For-profit 2-year health science and technical college
- Commuter campus in very large city

General. Accredited by ACICS. **Enrollment:** 472 degree-seeking undergraduates. **Degrees:** 67 associate awarded. **Calendar:** Continuous. **Full-time faculty:** 6 total. **Part-time faculty:** 45 total.

Student profile.

African American:	16%	**Hispanic American:**	28%
Asian American:	3%	**Native American:**	1%

Basis for selection. Personal career assessment, application/evaluation, and entrance assessment required.

High school preparation. College-preparatory program required.

Application procedures. **Admission:** No deadline. $25 fee. **Financial aid:** No deadline.

Academics. **Special study options:** Accelerated study, internships. **Credit/placement by examination:** CLEP, institutional tests. **Support services:** Learning center, reduced course load, study skills assistance, tutoring.

Majors. **Computer sciences:** Networking. **Engineering technology:** Architectural drafting.

Computing on campus. 200 workstations in library, computer center. Helpline, wireless network available.

Student life. **Freshman orientation:** Mandatory.

Student services. Career counseling, student employment services, financial aid counseling, placement for graduates.

Contact. Phone: (817) 547-9600 Toll-free number: (866) 533-9998
Fax: (817) 547-9602
John Roberts, Director of Admissions, Westwood College: Fort Worth, 4232 North Freeway, Fort Worth, TX 76137

Westwood College: Houston South

Houston, Texas
www.westwood.edu

- For-profit 2-year technical college
- Commuter campus in very large city
- Application essay, interview required

General. Accredited by ACCSCT. **Enrollment:** 440 degree-seeking undergraduates. **Degrees:** 73 associate awarded. **Calendar:** Continuous. **Full-time faculty:** 12 total. **Part-time faculty:** 27 total.

Student profile. Among degree-seeking undergraduates, 100% enrolled in a vocational program, 1% already have a bachelor's degree or higher.

Basis for selection. Interview and documentation of prior education important; must demonstrate proficiency in basic college-level skills. SAT or ACT recommended. SAT/ACT test scores accepted. If student has not taken either we will administer ACCUPLACER (for Degree Programs) and Wonderlic (SLE) assessments for entry. **Homeschooled:** State high school equivalency certificate required. Provide copy of applicant's certificate of a home school program if applicant's home state recognizes the home school. Documentation of the state's recognition must be evident in applicant's records. **Learning Disabled:** All reasonable accommodations will be made for documented disabilities.

2008-2009 Annual costs. Cost per term differs by program and ranges from $3,088-$4,609. One-time cost of toolkits $100-$490.

2007-2008 Financial aid. **Need-based:** Need-based aid available for part-time students.

Application procedures. **Admission:** Closing date 8/6 (receipt date). $25 fee, may be waived for applicants with need. **Financial aid:** No deadline. FAFSA, institutional form required.

Academics. **Special study options:** Accelerated study, distance learning, independent study, internships. **Credit/placement by examination:** AP, CLEP, institutional tests. **Support services:** Learning center, reduced course load, remedial instruction, study skills assistance, tutoring.

Majors. **Engineering:** Computer. **Engineering technology:** CAD/CADD. **Visual/performing arts:** Graphic design, multimedia.

Computing on campus. Online library, wireless network available.

Student life. **Freshman orientation:** Mandatory. **Activities:** Student newspaper.

Student services. Adult student services, alcohol/substance abuse counseling, career counseling, services for economically disadvantaged, student employment services, financial aid counseling, legal services, minority student services, placement for graduates, veterans' counselor. **Transfer:** Reentry adviser, pre-admission transcript evaluation for new students.

Contact. E-mail: tlevinthal@westwood.edu
Phone: (866) 340-3677 Toll-free number: (866) 340-3677
Fax: (713) 219-2088
Tara Levinthal, Director of Admissions, Westwood College: Houston South, 7322 Southwest Freeway, Houston, TX 77074

Wharton County Junior College

Wharton, Texas
www.wcjc.edu **CB code: 6939**

- Public 2-year junior college
- Commuter campus in small town

General. Founded in 1946. Regionally accredited. **Enrollment:** 6,115 degree-seeking undergraduates. **Degrees:** 346 associate awarded. **Location:** 60 miles from Houston. **Calendar:** Semester, limited summer session. **Full-time faculty:** 142 total; 78% have terminal degrees, 18% minority, 61% women. **Part-time faculty:** 116 total; 78% have terminal degrees, 27% minority, 54% women.

Student profile. Among degree-seeking undergraduates, 29% enrolled in a transfer program, 71% enrolled in a vocational program, 1% already have a bachelor's degree or higher, 1,337 enrolled as first-time, first-year students, 427 transferred in from other institutions.

Part-time:	57%	**Hispanic American:**	26%
Out-of-state:	2%	**International:**	4%
Women:	58%	**25 or older:**	18%
African American:	9%	**Live on campus:**	3%
Asian American:	5%		

Transfer out. **Colleges most students transferred to 2008:** Texas A&M University, University of Houston, Sam Houston State University, Texas State University, University of Texas.

Basis for selection. Open admission, but selective for some programs. Test scores and school achievement record important factors for admission into nursing, dental hygiene, physical therapy, and radiology programs. Audition required for music scholarship applicants.

High school preparation. Recommended units include English 4, mathematics 3, science 3 and foreign language 2.

2009-2010 Annual costs. Tuition/fees: $1,620; $2,580 out-of-state. Per-credit charge: $32 in-state; $64 out-of-state. Annual out-of-district fees $1,560. Room/board: $3,550. Books/supplies: $875. Personal expenses: $1,500.

Financial aid. **Need-based:** Need-based aid available for part-time students. **Non-need-based:** Scholarships awarded for academics, athletics, music/drama.

Application procedures. **Admission:** Priority date 7/1; no deadline. No application fee. Application must be submitted on paper. Admission notification on a rolling basis beginning on or about 2/1. **Financial aid:** Closing date 6/1. FAFSA required. Applicants notified on a rolling basis starting 8/1; must reply by 8/15.

Academics. **Special study options:** Cooperative education, cross-registration, distance learning, dual enrollment of high school students, internships, teacher certification program. License preparation in dental hygiene, nursing, paramedic, physical therapy, radiology. **Credit/placement by examination:** AP, CLEP, institutional tests. 16 credit hours maximum toward associate degree. **Support services:** GED preparation and test center, learning center, remedial instruction, tutoring.

Majors. **Agriculture:** Business technology. **Biology:** General. **Business:** Administrative services, business admin. **Communications technology:** Graphics. **Computer sciences:** General, networking. **Education:** Early childhood, elementary. **Engineering technology:** Drafting, electrical. **Family/consumer sciences:** Child development. **Health:** Clinical lab technology, dental hygiene, EMT paramedic, medical records technology, mental health services, nursing (RN), physical therapy assistant, radiologic technology/medical imaging. **History:** General. **Legal studies:** Paralegal. **Liberal arts:** Arts/sciences. **Math:** General. **Mechanic/repair:** Automotive. **Physical sciences:** Chemistry, physics. **Protective services:** Police science. **Psychology:** General. **Science technology:** Chemical. **Social sciences:** Criminology, sociology. **Visual/performing arts:** Art, dramatic.

Computing on campus. 500 workstations in library, computer center, student center. Online course registration, online library available.

Student life. **Freshman orientation:** Available. Preregistration for classes offered. **Housing:** Single-sex dorms available. $100 deposit, deadline 7/1. **Activities:** Bands, choral groups, dance, drama, music ensembles, musical theater, student government.

Athletics. NJCAA. **Intercollegiate:** Baseball M, rodeo, volleyball W. **Team name:** Pioneers.

Student services. Career counseling, personal counseling, placement for graduates. **Physically disabled:** Services for visually, speech, hearing impaired. **Transfer:** Transfer adviser, college fairs on campus for students transferring to 4-year colleges.

Contact. E-mail: registrar@wcjc.edu
Phone: (979) 532-4560 ext. 6303 Toll-free number: (800) 561-9252
Fax: (979) 532-6494
Karen Preisler, Director of Admissions/Registrar, Wharton County Junior College, 911 Boling Highway, Wharton, TX 77488-0080

Utah

Careers Unlimited
Orem, Utah
www.ucdh.edu/

- For-profit 2-year health science college
- Commuter campus in large city

General. Accredited by ACCSCT. Three-year bachelor's degree program offered. **Enrollment:** 114 degree-seeking undergraduates. **Degrees:** 30 bachelor's, 20 associate awarded. **Calendar:** Semester. **Full-time faculty:** 7 total; 14% have terminal degrees, 14% minority, 71% women. **Part-time faculty:** 10 total. **Special facilities:** 53 dental operatories, 10 x-ray/operative rooms.

Basis for selection. Open admission.

2008-2009 Annual costs. Cost of entire bachelor's degree program in dental hygiene: $45,675 plus $4, 275 in fees.

Application procedures. Admission: No deadline. $50 fee. Admission notification on a rolling basis.

Academics. Special study options: Bachelor's degree programs available on campus. **Credit/placement by examination:** CLEP.

Majors. Health: Dental hygiene.

Contact. E-mail: admissions@ucdh.edu
Phone: (801) 226-1081
Keely Spencer, Director of Admissions, Careers Unlimited, 1176 South 1480 West, Orem, UT 84058

College of Eastern Utah
Price, Utah
www.ceu.edu **CB code: 4040**

- Public 2-year community college
- Commuter campus in small town

General. Founded in 1938. Regionally accredited. **Enrollment:** 1,100 full-time, degree-seeking students. **Degrees:** 375 associate awarded. **Location:** 65 miles from Provo, 125 miles from Salt Lake City. **Calendar:** Semester, limited summer session. **Full-time faculty:** 89 total. **Part-time faculty:** 76 total. **Class size:** 80% < 20, 17% 20-39, 2% 40-49, less than 1% 50-99, less than 1% >100. **Special facilities:** Observatory, prehistoric museum.

Student profile.

Out-of-state:	6%	**Live on campus:**	15%
25 or older:	26%		

Basis for selection. Open admission, but selective for some programs. Admission to nursing program based on test scores and prerequisites.

2008-2009 Annual costs. Tuition/fees: $2,242; $4,142 out-of-state. Room/board: $4,120. Books/supplies: $750. Personal expenses: $1,179.

Financial aid. Need-based: Need-based aid available for part-time students. Work-study available nights and weekends. **Non-need-based:** Scholarships awarded for academics, art, athletics, leadership, minority status, music/drama, religious affiliation, state residency.

Application procedures. Admission: Priority date 3/1; no deadline. $25 fee. Admission notification on a rolling basis. **Financial aid:** Priority date 2/1; no closing date. FAFSA, institutional form required. Applicants notified on a rolling basis starting 3/15; must reply within 2 week(s) of notification.

Academics. Special study options: Cooperative education, distance learning, double major, dual enrollment of high school students, ESL. **Credit/placement by examination:** AP, CLEP, institutional tests. 32 credit hours maximum toward associate degree. **Support services:** GED preparation and test center, learning center, remedial instruction, study skills assistance, tutoring, writing center.

Majors. Business: Administrative services, business admin. **Computer sciences:** Computer graphics, systems analysis. **Construction:** Carpentry. **Education:** Early childhood. **Family/consumer sciences:** Child care. **Liberal arts:** Arts/sciences. **Mechanic/repair:** Diesel. **Personal/culinary services:** Cosmetic.

Computing on campus. 150 workstations in dormitories, library, computer center, student center. Dormitories linked to campus network. Commuter students can connect to campus network. Online course registration, online library, helpline available.

Student life. Freshman orientation: Mandatory. Preregistration for classes offered. **Housing:** Coed dorms, single-sex dorms available. $100 deposit. **Activities:** Bands, choral groups, dance, drama, literary magazine, music ensembles, musical theater, radio station, student government, student newspaper, religious clubs, Catholic Newman club, theater club, Native American club, recreation club, leadership club, business club.

Athletics. NJCAA. **Intercollegiate:** Baseball M, basketball, golf M, volleyball W. **Intramural:** Basketball M, racquetball, tennis. **Team name:** Eagles.

Student services. Adult student services, alcohol/substance abuse counseling, career counseling, services for economically disadvantaged, student employment services, financial aid counseling, health services, personal counseling, placement for graduates, veterans' counselor, women's services. **Physically disabled:** Services for visually, speech, hearing impaired. **Transfer:** Transfer adviser for students transferring to 4-year colleges.

Contact. E-mail: jan.young@ceu.edu
Phone: (435) 613-5226 Fax: (435) 613-5814
Todd Olsen, Director of Admissions and Scholarships, College of Eastern Utah, 451 East 400 North, Price, UT 84501

Eagle Gate College: Layton
Layton, Utah
www.eaglegatecollege.edu

- For-profit 2-year business and technical college
- Small city

General. Accredited by ACICS. **Enrollment:** 190 full-time, degree-seeking students. **Degrees:** 95 associate awarded. **Location:** 15 miles from Sallt Lake City, 5 miles from Ogden. **Calendar:** Five ten-week terms.

Basis for selection. Open admission. **Homeschooled:** Statement describing homeschool structure and mission, state high school equivalency certificate required.

Application procedures. Admission: No deadline. $40 fee.

Academics. Special study options: Bachelor's degree programs available on campus. **Credit/placement by examination:** CLEP. **Support services:** Learning center, tutoring, writing center.

Majors. Business: Accounting, business admin. **Computer sciences:** Web page design. **Health:** Insurance coding, medical assistant, pharmacy assistant. **Legal studies:** Paralegal. **Protective services:** Law enforcement admin. **Visual/performing arts:** Graphic design.

Contact. E-mail: admissions@eaglegatecollege.edu
Phone: (801) 546-7500 ext. 7512 Toll-free number: (800) 429-4513
Fax: (801) 593-6654
Angie McMillan, Director of Admissions, Eagle Gate College: Layton, 915 North 400 West Layton, Layton, UT 84041

Eagle Gate College: Murray
Murray, Utah
www.eaglegatecollege.edu

- For-profit 2-year business and technical college
- Large town

General. Accredited by ACICS. **Enrollment:** 125 full-time, degree-seeking students. **Degrees:** 75 associate awarded. **Calendar:** Five ten-week terms.

Basis for selection. Open admission.

Application procedures. Admission: No deadline. $40 fee. Admission notification on a rolling basis.

Academics. Credit/placement by examination: CLEP.

Majors. **Business:** Accounting/finance, business admin. **Computer sciences:** General. **Health:** Dental assistant, insurance coding, medical assistant, pharmacy assistant. **Protective services:** Law enforcement admin. **Visual/performing arts:** Graphic design.

Contact. Phone: (801) 281-7700
Eagle Gate College: Murray, 5588 South Green Street, Murray, UT 84123

Eagle Gate College: Salt Lake City
Salt Lake City, Utah
www.eaglegatecollege.edu

- For-profit 2-year business and technical college
- Small city

General. Accredited by ACICS. **Enrollment:** 70 full-time, degree-seeking students. **Degrees:** 15 associate awarded. **Calendar:** Five ten-week terms.

Basis for selection. Open admission.

Application procedures. **Admission:** No deadline. $40 fee. Admission notification on a rolling basis.

Academics. **Credit/placement by examination:** CLEP.

Majors. **Health:** Medical assistant. **Legal studies:** Paralegal. **Visual/performing arts:** Commercial/advertising art.

Contact. Phone: (801) 287-9640
Eagle Gate College: Salt Lake City, 405 South Main Street, Suite 130, Salt Lake City, UT 84111

Everest College: Salt Lake City
West Valley City, Utah
www.cci.edu **CB code: 5341**

- For-profit 2-year business and junior college
- Commuter campus in small city

General. Founded in 1981. Accredited by ACICS. **Location:** 5 miles from Salt Lake City. **Calendar:** Quarter.

Contact. Phone: (801) 485-0221
Admissions Director, 3280 W 3500 S, West Valley City, UT 84119-2668

LDS Business College
Salt Lake City, Utah
www.ldsbc.edu **CB code: 4412**

- Private 2-year business and junior college affiliated with Church of Jesus Christ of Latter-day Saints
- Commuter campus in small city
- Interview required

General. Founded in 1886. Regionally accredited. **Enrollment:** 1,373 degree-seeking undergraduates. **Degrees:** 296 associate awarded. **ROTC:** Army, Air Force. **Calendar:** Semester, limited summer session. **Full-time faculty:** 19 total; 16% have terminal degrees, 32% women. **Part-time faculty:** 81 total; 2% have terminal degrees, 52% women. **Class size:** 37% < 20, 53% 20-39, 8% 40-49, 3% 50-99.

Student profile. Among degree-seeking undergraduates, 285 enrolled as first-time, first-year students, 178 transferred in from other institutions.

Part-time:	26%	**Asian American:**	2%
Out-of-state:	50%	**Hispanic American:**	7%
Women:	50%	**International:**	18%
African American:	1%	**25 or older:**	23%

Transfer out. **Colleges most students transferred to 2008:** Brigham Young University, University of Utah, Utah State University.

Basis for selection. Open admission. Color board required for placement in interior design program. SAT/ACT recommended for counseling, used as pre-test and placement in English or math. **Adult students:** Students who have not taken ACT or SAT must take COMPASS for placement in English and math. **Homeschooled:** Students must submit ACT or GED if not from accredited program. Students qualify for admission after reaching age 17. **Learning Disabled:** Must submit documentation under ADA.

2009-2010 Annual costs. Tuition/fees (projected): $2,800. Per-credit charge: $117. Students who are not members of The Church of Jesus Christ of Latter-Day Saints pay tuition of $5,600 per academic year, $235 per-credit-hour. Books/supplies: $1,026. Personal expenses: $1,500.

2007-2008 Financial aid. **Need-based:** Need-based aid available for part-time students. **Non-need-based:** Scholarships awarded for academics, leadership.

Application procedures. **Admission:** No deadline. $30 fee. Admission notification on a rolling basis. **Financial aid:** Priority date 7/1; no closing date. FAFSA required. Applicants notified on a rolling basis starting 3/1; must reply within 3 week(s) of notification.

Academics. **Special study options:** Cooperative education, dual enrollment of high school students, internships. **Credit/placement by examination:** AP, CLEP, IB, institutional tests. 30 credit hours maximum toward associate degree. **Support services:** Reduced course load, study skills assistance, tutoring.

Majors. **Business:** General, accounting, administrative services, business admin, executive assistant, office management. **Computer sciences:** Information technology. **Health:** Medical records admin, medical secretary, office admin, office assistant. **Legal studies:** Legal secretary. **Visual/performing arts:** Interior design.

Most popular majors. Business/marketing 9%, liberal arts 32%.

Computing on campus. 350 workstations in dormitories, library, computer center. Dormitories linked to campus network. Helpline available.

Student life. **Freshman orientation:** Available. Preregistration for classes offered. Full-day session held Friday before start of classes. **Policies:** Religious observance required. **Housing:** $100 fully refundable deposit. **Activities:** Choral groups, student government, Latter-Day Saint student association, men's association, women's association, service-learning council.

Student services. Career counseling, student employment services, financial aid counseling, health services, personal counseling, placement for graduates. **Transfer:** Transfer adviser, college fairs on campus for students transferring to 4-year colleges.

Contact. E-mail: admissions@ldsbc.edu
Phone: (801) 524-8145 Toll-free number: (800) 999-5767
Fax: (801) 524-1900
Renae Richards, Director of Enrollment Management, LDS Business College, 95 North 300 West, Salt Lake City, UT 84101-3500

Provo College
Provo, Utah
www.provocollege.edu **CB code: 3021**

- For-profit 2-year junior college
- Small city

General. Accredited by ACCSCT. **Enrollment:** 175 full-time, degree-seeking students. **Degrees:** 145 associate awarded. **Calendar:** Quarter. **Full-time faculty:** 60 total.

Basis for selection. Open admission.

2008-2009 Annual costs. $675 per credit hour for nursing program. Books/supplies: $600. Personal expenses: $2,088.

Application procedures. **Admission:** No deadline. $25 fee. Admission notification on a rolling basis.

Academics. **Credit/placement by examination:** CLEP.

Majors. **Business:** Accounting, administrative services, business admin, hospitality/recreation. **Computer sciences:** General, programming. **Health:** Dental assistant, medical secretary, physical therapy assistant. **Visual/performing arts:** General, commercial/advertising art.

Contact. Phone: (801) 375-1861 Toll-free number: (800) 748-4834
Fax: (801) 375-9728
Director of Admissions, Provo College, 1450 West 820 North, Provo, UT 84601

Salt Lake Community College
Salt Lake City, Utah **CB member**
www.slcc.edu **CB code: 4864**

- Public 2-year community and technical college
- Commuter campus in very large city

General. Founded in 1948. Regionally accredited. 5 campus locations, 8 teaching centers. **Enrollment:** 27,916 degree-seeking undergraduates. **Degrees:** 2,902 associate awarded. **ROTC:** Army, Air Force. **Location:** 5 miles from downtown. **Calendar:** Semester, extensive summer session. **Full-time faculty:** 350 total; 10% minority, 49% women. **Part-time faculty:** 1,059 total; 3% minority, 40% women. **Class size:** 55% < 20, 44% 20-39, 1% 40-49, less than 1% 50-99.

Student profile.

Out-of-state:	6%	**25 or older:**	40%

Transfer out. Colleges most students transferred to 2008: University of Utah, Utah State University, Weber State University, Westminster College.

Basis for selection. Open admission, but selective for some programs. Admission for flight technology programs based on testing; admissions for health sciences based on school records, testing and prerequisite courses.

High school preparation. 27 units recommended. Recommended units include English 4, mathematics 2, social studies 3, science 2 and academic electives 11. Biological science recommended for health science programs. Algebra recommended for preengineering and electronics.

2008-2009 Annual costs. Tuition/fees: $2,660; $8,374 out-of-state. Books/supplies: $1,730. Personal expenses: $1,740.

2007-2008 Financial aid. Need-based: Need-based aid available for part-time students. Work-study available nights, weekends and for part-time students. **Non-need-based:** Scholarships awarded for academics, alumni affiliation, art, athletics, leadership, minority status, music/drama.

Application procedures. Admission: No deadline. $35 fee. Admission notification on a rolling basis. **Financial aid:** Priority date 5/1; no closing date. FAFSA, institutional form required. Applicants notified on a rolling basis starting 5/1; must reply within 4 week(s) of notification.

Academics. Special study options: Cooperative education, distance learning, dual enrollment of high school students, ESL, exchange student, study abroad. Bachelor's degree programs available on campus. License preparation in aviation, dental hygiene, nursing. **Credit/placement by examination:** AP, CLEP, IB, SAT, ACT, institutional tests. 50 credit hours maximum toward associate degree. **Support services:** GED preparation and test center, learning center, pre-admission summer program, reduced course load, remedial instruction, study skills assistance, tutoring, writing center.

Majors. Agriculture: Landscaping. **Biology:** General. **Business:** General, accounting technology, business admin, finance, marketing, restaurant/food services. **Communications:** General, digital media. **Communications technology:** Animation/special effects, photo/film/video, radio/tv. **Computer sciences:** General, computer science. **Construction:** Carpentry, electrician, maintenance, pipefitting, plumbing, site management. **Education:** Early childhood special, kindergarten/preschool. **Engineering:** Electrical, manufacturing, materials, mechanical. **Engineering technology:** Architectural drafting, civil drafting, computer, computer systems, drafting, environmental, instrumentation, manufacturing, mechanical, surveying, telecommunications. **Family/consumer sciences:** Family studies. **Foreign languages:** Sign language interpretation. **Health:** Dental hygiene, medical radiologic technology/radiation therapy, nursing (RN), occupational therapy assistant, physical therapy assistant. **History:** General. **Interdisciplinary:** Global studies. **Legal studies:** Paralegal. **Liberal arts:** Humanities. **Math:** General. **Mechanic/repair:** Auto body, automotive, avionics, diesel, electronics/electrical, heating/ac/refrig. **Parks/recreation:** Sports admin. **Personal/culinary services:** Chef training, cosmetic. **Physical sciences:** Chemistry, geology, physics. **Production:** Ironworking, machine tool, welding. **Protective services:** Criminal justice. **Psychology:** General. **Public administration:** Social work. **Science technology:** Biological, chemical, radiologic. **Social sciences:** Economics, geography, political science, sociology. **Transportation:** Airline/commercial pilot. **Visual/performing arts:** Design, photography, theater design.

Most popular majors. Business/marketing 9%, health sciences 15%, liberal arts 50%.

Computing on campus. 2,400 workstations in library, computer center, student center. Commuter students can connect to campus network. Online course registration, helpline, wireless network available.

Student life. Freshman orientation: Available, $3 fee. Preregistration for classes offered. One-day program. **Activities:** Bands, choral groups, dance, drama, literary magazine, radio station, student government, student newspaper, TV station, Circle-K, Latter-Day Saints student association, Hispanos Unidos, African-American student association, American Indian club, Asian club, Polynesian club, American Sign Language club, professional societies.

Athletics. NJCAA. **Intercollegiate:** Baseball M, basketball, softball W, volleyball W. **Team name:** Bruins.

Student services. Alcohol/substance abuse counseling, career counseling, services for economically disadvantaged, student employment services, financial aid counseling, health services, minority student services, on-campus daycare, personal counseling, placement for graduates, veterans' counselor. **Physically disabled:** Services for visually, speech, hearing impaired. **Transfer:** Transfer center, transfer adviser, college fairs on campus for students transferring to 4-year colleges.

Contact. E-mail: futurestudents@slcc.edu
Phone: (801) 957-4298 Fax: (801) 957-4961
Eric Weber, Dean of Student Enrollment Services, Salt Lake Community College, 4600 South Redwood Road, Salt Lake City, UT 84130-0808

Snow College
Ephraim, Utah
www.snow.edu **CB code: 4727**

- Public 2-year community and junior college
- Residential campus in small town

General. Founded in 1888. Regionally accredited. Collaborative program with Julliard in music, theater arts, and dance. **Enrollment:** 3,798 degree-seeking undergraduates. **Degrees:** 676 associate awarded. **Location:** 120 miles from Salt Lake City, 70 miles from Provo. **Calendar:** Semester, limited summer session. **Full-time faculty:** 121 total; 4% minority, 26% women. **Part-time faculty:** 127 total. **Class size:** 72% < 20, 24% 20-39, 2% 40-49, less than 1% 50-99, less than 1% >100.

Student profile. Among degree-seeking undergraduates, 8% enrolled in a vocational program, 1,359 enrolled as first-time, first-year students, 53 transferred in from other institutions.

Part-time:	40%	**25 or older:**	13%
Out-of-state:	6%	**Live on campus:**	10%
Women:	52%		

Transfer out. 70% of students enrolled in the transfer program go on to 4-year colleges. **Colleges most students transferred to 2008:** Utah State University, Salt Lake Community College, Utah Valley State College, Southern Utah University.

Basis for selection. Open admission. Auditions recommended for fine arts. **Homeschooled:** State high school equivalency certificate required.

High school preparation. 15 units recommended. Recommended units include English 4, mathematics 2, social studies 3, science 3 (laboratory 3).

2008-2009 Annual costs. Tuition/fees: $2,346; $8,228 out-of-state. Room/board: $3,000. Books/supplies: $530. Personal expenses: $900.

2007-2008 Financial aid. Need-based: 431 full-time freshmen applied for aid; 253 were judged to have need; 253 of these received aid. Average scholarship/grant was $1,929; average loan $1,608. Work-study available for part-time students. **Non-need-based:** Awarded to 447 full-time undergraduates, including 201 freshmen. Scholarships awarded for academics, alumni affiliation, athletics, leadership, music/drama, state residency.

Application procedures. Admission: Priority date 6/1; no deadline. $30 fee. Application must be submitted on paper. Admission notification on a rolling basis beginning on or about 12/1. Applications received after May 15 will be on a space-available basis. **Financial aid:** Priority date 3/1, closing date 7/15. FAFSA, institutional form required. Applicants notified on a rolling basis starting 8/1; must reply within 1 week(s) of notification.

Academics. Special study options: Cooperative education, distance learning, dual enrollment of high school students, ESL, honors, independent study. **Credit/placement by examination:** AP, CLEP, institutional tests. 45 credit hours maximum toward associate degree. **Support services:** GED test center, learning center, reduced course load, remedial instruction, study skills assistance, tutoring, writing center.

Majors. Agriculture: Agribusiness operations, animal sciences, business, farm/ranch. **Biology:** General, bacteriology, botany, pharmacology, physiology, zoology. **Business:** General, accounting, business admin, managerial economics. **Communications:** Journalism. **Computer sciences:** General, computer science, information systems. **Conservation:** General, forestry, management/policy, wildlife. **Construction:** General. **Education:** General, business, early childhood, elementary, ESL, family/consumer sciences, health, physical, secondary, special. **Engineering:** General. **Engineering technology:** Drafting. **Family/consumer sciences:** General, child care, clothing/textiles, family/community services, food/nutrition. **Foreign languages:** General, French, Japanese, Spanish. **Health:** Clinical lab science, EMT paramedic, licensed practical nurse, predental, premedicine, prenursing, prepharmacy, preveterinary, veterinary technology/assistant. **History:** General. **Interdisciplinary:** Biological/physical sciences, natural sciences. **Legal studies:** Prelaw. **Math:** General, statistics. **Mechanic/repair:** General. **Parks/recreation:** General, health/fitness. **Personal/culinary services:** Barbering, chef training, cosmetic, cosmetology, culinary arts. **Philosophy/religion:** Philosophy. **Physical sciences:** Chemistry, geology, physics. **Protective services:** Law enforcement admin. **Psychology:** General. **Public administration:** Social work. **Social sciences:** General, anthropology, economics, geography, political science, sociology. **Visual/performing arts:** General, art, dance.

Most popular majors. Business/marketing 11%, education 7%, health sciences 17%, liberal arts 31%, visual/performing arts 9%.

Computing on campus. 450 workstations in library, computer center, student center. Dormitories wired for high-speed internet access. Online course registration, helpline, wireless network available.

Student life. **Freshman orientation:** Available. Begins 2 days prior to fall semester. **Housing:** Coed dorms, single-sex dorms, apartments available. $200 partly refundable deposit, deadline 6/1. **Activities:** Bands, choral groups, dance, drama, literary magazine, music ensembles, musical theater, radio station, student government, student newspaper, symphony orchestra, Latter-Day Saints student association, associated women students, associated men students, Badgers Against Alcohol & Drugs, Polynesian club, ski club, Spanish club, international club.

Athletics. NJCAA. **Intercollegiate:** Basketball, football (tackle) M, softball W, volleyball W. **Intramural:** Basketball, football (non-tackle) M, golf, racquetball, soccer, softball, tennis, volleyball. **Team name:** Badgers.

Student services. Adult student services, alcohol/substance abuse counseling, career counseling, services for economically disadvantaged, financial aid counseling, health services, on-campus daycare, personal counseling, veterans' counselor. **Physically disabled:** Services for visually, hearing impaired. **Learning disabled:** Comprehensive services available. **Transfer:** Pre-admission transcript evaluation for new students. Transfer adviser, college fairs on campus for students transferring to 4-year colleges.

Contact. E-mail: hsrelations@snow.edu
Phone: (435) 283-7150 Toll-free number: (800) 848-3399
Fax: (435) 283-6879
Tim Dolan, Director of Admissions, Snow College, 150 East College Avenue, Ephraim, UT 84627

Utah Career College

West Jordan, Utah
www.utahcollege.edu **CB code: 2892**

- For-profit 2-year technical and career college
- Commuter campus in small city
- Interview required

General. Accredited by ACCSCT. **Enrollment:** 603 degree-seeking undergraduates. **Degrees:** 152 associate awarded. **Location:** 8 miles from Salt Lake City. **Calendar:** Quarter, extensive summer session. **Full-time faculty:** 20 total. **Part-time faculty:** 55 total.

Transfer out. **Colleges most students transferred to 2008:** Salt Lake Community College.

Basis for selection. Open admission, but selective for some programs. Interview and institutional testing required for placement. **Homeschooled:** GED certificate and documentation required.

2008-2009 Annual costs. Tuition/fees: $16,200. Per-credit charge: $360. Nursing program courses $458 per credit hour.

2008-2009 Financial aid. All financial aid based on need. Need-based aid available for part-time students.

Application procedures. **Admission:** No deadline. $50 fee. Application must be submitted on paper. Admission notification on a rolling basis. **Financial aid:** No deadline. FAFSA, institutional form required. Applicants notified on a rolling basis starting 7/1; must reply within 2 week(s) of notification.

Academics. **Special study options:** Distance learning, liberal arts/career combination. Bachelor's degree programs available on campus. **Credit/placement by examination:** AP, CLEP. Credits for prior work experience and examination may not exceed 75% of total credits required to complete student's program. **Support services:** Reduced course load, study skills assistance, tutoring.

Majors. **Business:** Accounting, business admin. **Computer sciences:** Information technology. **Health:** Licensed practical nurse, massage therapy, medical assistant, medical records admin, pharmacy assistant, veterinary technology/assistant. **Legal studies:** Paralegal. **Parks/recreation:** Exercise sciences.

Most popular majors. Health sciences 85%.

Computing on campus. 90 workstations in library, computer center.

Student life. **Freshman orientation:** Mandatory. Preregistration for classes offered. **Policies:** Drug- and alcohol-free campus.

Student services. Career counseling, student employment services, financial aid counseling, placement for graduates, veterans' counselor. **Transfer:** Re-entry adviser, pre-admission transcript evaluation for new students.

Contact. E-mail: admissions@utahcollege.edu
Phone: (801) 304-4224 Toll-free number: (866) 304-4224
Fax: (801) 304-4229
Cori Perkins, Director of Admissions, Utah Career College, 1902 West 7800 South, West Jordan, UT 84088

Vermont

Community College of Vermont

Waterbury, Vermont
www.ccv.edu
CB member
CB code: 3286

- Public 2-year community and liberal arts college
- Commuter campus in small town

General. Founded in 1970. Regionally accredited. Courses offered in 12 locations statewide and online. **Enrollment:** 3,869 degree-seeking undergraduates. **Degrees:** 457 associate awarded. **Calendar:** Semester, extensive summer session. **Part-time faculty:** 650 total.

Student profile.

Out-of-state:	4%	**25 or older:**	60%

Transfer out. Colleges most students transferred to 2008: University of Vermont, Johnson State College.

Basis for selection. Open admission. Skill assessments administered by college required for placement purposes. International students must provide TOEFL score. Recommendation required if applicant has neither high school diploma nor GED. **Adult students:** SAT/ACT scores not required.

2008-2009 Annual costs. Tuition/fees: $5,830; $11,560 out-of-state. Per-credit charge: $191 in-state; $382 out-of-state. New England Board of Higher Education rate for students from other New England states: 150% of Vermont resident tuition. Available to degree candidates in academic areas not offered by educational institutions in their home states.

2008-2009 Financial aid. All financial aid based on need. Need-based aid available for part-time students. Work-study available nights.

Application procedures. Admission: No deadline. No application fee. Admission notification on a rolling basis. **Financial aid:** No deadline. FAFSA, institutional form required. Applicants notified on a rolling basis starting 9/1; must reply within 3 week(s) of notification.

Academics. Special study options: Cooperative education, cross-registration, distance learning, double major, dual enrollment of high school students, ESL, external degree, independent study, internships, liberal arts/career combination, student-designed major, study abroad, weekend college. **Credit/placement by examination:** AP, CLEP, institutional tests. 50 credit hours maximum toward associate degree. **Support services:** Learning center, reduced course load, remedial instruction, study skills assistance, tutoring, writing center.

Majors. Business: General. **Communications:** Media studies. **Education:** General. **Health:** Health services. **Liberal arts:** Arts/sciences. **Mechanic/repair:** General.

Most popular majors. Business/marketing 22%, education 6%, liberal arts 58%, public administration/social services 7%.

Computing on campus. 300 workstations in library, computer center. Online course registration, online library, wireless network available.

Student life. Freshman orientation: Available. Preregistration for classes offered. **Activities:** Choral groups, student government.

Student services. Adult student services, career counseling, student employment services, financial aid counseling, placement for graduates, veterans' counselor. **Physically disabled:** Services for visually, speech, hearing impaired. **Transfer:** Transfer adviser, college fairs on campus for students transferring to 4-year colleges.

Contact. Phone: (802) 241-3535 Toll-free number: (800) 228-6686
Fax: (802) 254-3473
Susan Henry, Admissions Director, Community College of Vermont, PO BOX 120, Waterbury, VT 05676-0120

Landmark College

Putney, Vermont
www.landmark.edu
CB code: 0081

- Private 2-year liberal arts college
- Residential campus in small town
- Application essay, interview required

General. Founded in 1983. Regionally accredited. College exclusively for bright students with dyslexia, attention disorders, or specific learning disabilities. We also offer professional development workshops and consultancies. **Enrollment:** 486 degree-seeking undergraduates. **Degrees:** 100 associate awarded. **Location:** 8 miles from Brattleboro, 23 miles from Keene, New Hampshire. **Calendar:** Semester, limited summer session. **Full-time faculty:** 93 total; 12% have terminal degrees, 1% minority, 62% women. **Part-time faculty:** 3 total; 33% have terminal degrees, 33% minority, 33% women. **Class size:** 100% < 20, less than 1% 20-39. **Special facilities:** Fine arts building, ropes course.

Student profile. Among degree-seeking undergraduates, 100% enrolled in a transfer program, 131 enrolled as first-time, first-year students, 107 transferred in from other institutions.

Out-of-state:	95%	**Hispanic American:**	6%
Women:	28%	**International:**	2%
African American:	5%	**25 or older:**	3%
Asian American:	3%	**Live on campus:**	95%

Transfer out. 76% of students enrolled in the transfer program go on to 4-year colleges.

Basis for selection. Successful applicants are highly motivated, have average-to-superior intellectual ability and diagnosis of dyslexia, attentional disorder (ADHD), or specific learning disability. WAIS III or Woodcock Johnson Cognitive assessment required. Nelson-Denny reading scores required. **Learning Disabled:** Students must have a diagnosed learning disability and must submit the results of cognitive and achievement testing.

High school preparation. Recommended units include English 4, mathematics 3, social studies 3, history 3, science 3, foreign language 1, visual/performing arts 1 and academic electives 1.

2009-2010 Annual costs. Tuition/fees: $45,800. Notebook computer and software required; approximate cost through school $1,500. Room/board: $8,100. Books/supplies: $1,200. Personal expenses: $750.

2008-2009 Financial aid. Need-based: 74% of total undergraduate aid awarded as scholarships/grants, 26% as loans/jobs. Need-based aid available for part-time students. Work-study available nights, weekends and for part-time students. **Non-need-based:** Scholarships awarded for academics, art, leadership, minority status, music/drama. **Additional information:** Students encouraged to apply to their state departments of vocational rehabilitation for additional financial assistance.

Application procedures. Admission: Priority date 5/15; no deadline. $75 fee, may be waived for applicants with need. Application must be submitted on paper. Admission notification on a rolling basis beginning on or about 12/1. **Financial aid:** Priority date 3/15; no closing date. FAFSA required. Applicants notified on a rolling basis starting 4/15; must reply within 2 week(s) of notification.

Academics. Special study options: Internships, study abroad. **Credit/placement by examination:** AP, CLEP, SAT, ACT, institutional tests. **Support services:** Learning center, pre-admission summer program, reduced course load, remedial instruction, study skills assistance, writing center.

Majors. Business: Business admin. **Liberal arts:** Arts/sciences.

Most popular majors. Business/marketing 9%, liberal arts 91%.

Computing on campus. PC or laptop required. 50 workstations in dormitories, library, student center. Dormitories wired for high-speed internet access and linked to campus network. Online library, helpline, repair service, wireless network available.

Student life. Freshman orientation: Mandatory. **Policies:** Alcohol not permitted on campus. All new students must live on campus. Others may petition to live off-campus. **Housing:** Guaranteed on-campus for all undergraduates. Coed dorms, special housing for disabled, wellness housing available. **Activities:** Jazz band, choral groups, dance, drama, literary magazine, music ensembles, radio station, student government, Phi Theta Kappa honor society, Society for Social Justice.

Athletics. Intercollegiate: Baseball, basketball, cross-country, soccer, softball W. **Intramural:** Basketball, volleyball. **Team name:** Landsharks.

Student services. Adult student services, alcohol/substance abuse counseling, career counseling, financial aid counseling, health services, personal counseling, placement for graduates, women's services. **Learning disabled:** Comprehensive services available. **Transfer:** Transfer center, transfer adviser, college fairs on campus for students transferring to 4-year colleges.

Contact. E-mail: admissions@landmark.edu
Phone: (802) 387-6718 Fax: (802) 387-6868
Dale Herold, Vice President for Enrollment Management, Landmark College, River Road South, Putney, VT 05346

New England Culinary Institute

Montpelier, Vermont
www.neci.edu **CB code: 3405**

- For-profit 2-year culinary school
- Residential campus in small town
- Application essay required

General. Founded in 1980. Accredited by ACCSCT. Branch campus located in Essex, VT. **Enrollment:** 628 degree-seeking undergraduates. **Degrees:** 30 bachelor's, 155 associate awarded. **Location:** 39 miles from Burlington. **Calendar:** Differs by program, extensive summer session. **Full-time faculty:** 60 total. **Part-time faculty:** 10 total. **Special facilities:** Gourmet restaurant, bakeshop, cafeteria, catering business, American cuisine restaurant. **Partnerships:** Formal partnership with the Council of Independent Restaurants of America.

Basis for selection. High school achievement record, essay or personal statement demonstrating understanding of and passion for the industry. Advanced placement standing available to students through school testing. Interview may be required and a tour is always recommended. **Homeschooled:** Personal interview may be required. **Learning Disabled:** Recommend a shadow experience if there is question regarding ability to succeed in the program.

High school preparation. Transcript must demonstrate proficiency in English and mathematics. Foreign language and culinary arts training highly desirable.

2008-2009 Annual costs. Tuition/fees: $25,681. Costs vary with program. Required fees include books, knife kit, library and room deposit. Room/board: $8,776. Books/supplies: $664.

2008-2009 Financial aid. Need-based: Work-study available nights and weekends. **Non-need-based:** Scholarships awarded for academics, alumni affiliation, job skills.

Application procedures. Admission: No deadline. $50 fee. Admission notification on a rolling basis. **Financial aid:** No deadline. FAFSA required. Applicants notified on a rolling basis.

Academics. Special study options: Accelerated study, distance learning, dual enrollment of high school students, internships. Bachelor's degree programs available on campus. **Credit/placement by examination:** AP, CLEP, IB. **Support services:** Learning center, study skills assistance, tutoring.

Majors. Business: Hospitality admin, restaurant/food services. **Personal/culinary services:** Baking, chef training, culinary arts, food prep, food service, restaurant/catering.

Computing on campus. PC or laptop required. 40 workstations in library, computer center. Dormitories wired for high-speed internet access. Commuter students can connect to campus network.

Student life. Freshman orientation: Mandatory. Orientation and registration held 2-3 days prior to first day of classes. **Housing:** Coed dorms, single-sex dorms, apartments, wellness housing available. Students have own bedroom and share kitchen, living room and bathroom space in apartment-style housing units. **Activities:** Student government, student newspaper.

Student services. Career counseling, student employment services, financial aid counseling, placement for graduates, veterans' counselor.

Contact. E-mail: admissions@neci.edu
Phone: (802) 223-6324 Toll-free number: (877) 223-6324
Fax: (802) 225-3280
Ted Wiechman, Director of Admissions, New England Culinary Institute, 56 College Street, Montpelier, VT 05602

New England Culinary Institute: Essex Junction

Essex Junction, Vermont
www.neci.edu **CB code: 3100**

- For-profit 2-year culinary school and business college
- Small city

General. Accredited by ACCSCT. **Location:** 8 miles from Burlington. **Calendar:** Quarter.

Annual costs/financial aid. Tuition/fees (2008-2009): $25,682. Costs will vary by program. Room/board: $8,776. Books/supplies: $1,000. Need-based financial aid available for full-time students.

Contact. Phone: (802) 872-3400
Admissions Director, 5 Franklin Street, Essex Junction, VT 05452

Virginia

Advanced Technology Institute
Virginia Beach, Virginia
www.auto.edu

- For-profit 2-year technical college
- Commuter campus in large city

General. Accredited by ACCSCT. **Calendar:** Continuous.

Annual costs/financial aid. Total program cost varies by program: $15,800 - $33,600.

Contact. Phone: (757) 490-1241
Director of Admissions, 5700 Southern Boulevard, Virginia Beach, VA 23462

Aviation Institute of Maintenance: Virginia Beach
Chesapeake, Virginia
www.aviationmaintenance.edu

- For-profit 2-year technical college
- Large city

General. Accredited by ACCSCT. **Calendar:** Differs by program.

Annual costs/financial aid. Tuition/fees (2008-2009): $10,800.

Contact. Phone: (757) 363-2121
Director of Admissions, 2211 South Military Highway, Chesapeake, VA 23320

Blue Ridge Community College
Weyers Cave, Virginia
www.brcc.edu **CB code: 5083**

- Public 2-year community college
- Commuter campus in rural community

General. Founded in 1965. Regionally accredited. **Enrollment:** 4,466 degree-seeking undergraduates. **Degrees:** 498 associate awarded. **Location:** 12 miles from Harrisonburg, 15 miles from Staunton. **Calendar:** Semester, limited summer session. **Full-time faculty:** 67 total. **Part-time faculty:** 98 total. **Special facilities:** Arboretum. **Partnerships:** Tech Prep Consortium.

Student profile.

Out-of-state:	3%	**25 or older:**	34%

Transfer out. Colleges most students transferred to 2008: James Madison University, Mary Baldwin College, Old Dominion University, Eastern Mennonite University, Bridgewater College.

Basis for selection. Open admission, but selective for some programs. Special requirements for veterinary assistant technology and nursing programs; interview required.

High school preparation. 8 units recommended. Recommended units include English 4, mathematics 2, social studies 1 and science 1.

2008-2009 Annual costs. Tuition/fees: $2,678; $7,842 out-of-state. Per-credit charge: $82 in-state; $264 out-of-state. Out of state students pay an additional $90 capital outlay fee. Books/supplies: $600. Personal expenses: $900.

2007-2008 Financial aid. Need-based: Need-based aid available for part-time students. **Non-need-based:** Scholarships awarded for academics, job skills, leadership, minority status.

Application procedures. Admission: No deadline. No application fee. Admission notification on a rolling basis. Closing date for veterinary assistant technology is January 1. Nursing clinical component application deadline is January 31. **Financial aid:** Priority date 5/1; no closing date. FAFSA, institutional form required. Applicants notified on a rolling basis starting 5/30; must reply within 2 week(s) of notification.

Academics. Special study options: Accelerated study, cross-registration, distance learning, double major, dual enrollment of high school students, ESL, honors, independent study, internships, study abroad. Bachelor's degree programs available on campus. License preparation in nursing. **Credit/placement by examination:** AP, CLEP, institutional tests. Credit cannot duplicate earned course credits, nor courses audited or failed. **Support services:** Learning center, remedial instruction, tutoring.

Majors. Agriculture: Animal sciences. **Business:** Accounting, administrative services, business admin. **Computer sciences:** General, information systems, programming, systems analysis. **Engineering technology:** Electrical. **Health:** Health services, nursing (RN), veterinary technology/assistant. **Liberal arts:** Arts/sciences. **Public administration:** Human services.

Computing on campus. 285 workstations in library, computer center, student center. Online course registration, online library, wireless network available.

Student life. Freshman orientation: Mandatory. Preregistration for classes offered. **Activities:** Student government, Phi Theta Kappa, Christian Fellowship, special interest groups.

Athletics. Intramural: Basketball M.

Student services. Career counseling, student employment services, financial aid counseling, minority student services, personal counseling, placement for graduates, veterans' counselor, women's services. **Physically disabled:** Services for visually, speech, hearing impaired. **Transfer:** Transfer adviser, college fairs on campus for students transferring to 4-year colleges.

Contact. Phone: (540) 234-9261 ext. 2287 Toll-free number: (888) 750-2722 ext. 2287 Fax: (540) 453-2437
Mary Wayland, Dean of Academic Support Services, Blue Ridge Community College, Box 80, Weyers Cave, VA 24486-9989

Bryant & Stratton College: Richmond
Richmond, Virginia
www.bryantstratton.edu **CB code: 4762**

- For-profit 2-year career college
- Commuter campus in small city

General. Enrollment: 572 degree-seeking undergraduates. **Degrees:** 122 bachelor's, 14 associate awarded. **Calendar:** Semester, extensive summer session. **Full-time faculty:** 12 total; 50% women. **Part-time faculty:** 37 total; 65% women. **Class size:** 84% < 20, 16% 20-39.

Student profile. Among degree-seeking undergraduates, 219 enrolled as first-time, first-year students.

Part-time:	49%	**Women:**	84%

Basis for selection. Open admission, but selective for some programs.

2008-2009 Annual costs. Tuition/fees: $13,775. Annual tuition for bachelor's degree may vary by program. Books/supplies: $800. Personal expenses: $1,384.

2007-2008 Financial aid. All financial aid based on need. 33% of total undergraduate aid awarded as scholarships/grants, 67% as loans/jobs. Need-based aid available for part-time students.

Application procedures. Admission: No deadline. **Financial aid:** No deadline. FAFSA required.

Academics. Special study options: Distance learning, double major, independent study, internships. **Credit/placement by examination:** CLEP, institutional tests. 30 credit hours maximum toward associate degree, 60 toward bachelor's. Up to 50% of total credit hours required for graduation, including 50% of the total required hours in major study areas, may be earned through combination of transfer credits and proficiency evaluations. **Support services:** Study skills assistance, tutoring.

Majors. Business: Accounting, administrative services, business admin, human resources. **Computer sciences:** Information technology. **Health:** Medical assistant, medical secretary. **Legal studies:** Paralegal. **Protective services:** Criminal justice.

Computing on campus. 100 workstations in library, computer center. Commuter students can connect to campus network. Online course registration, online library, wireless network available.

Student life. Freshman orientation: Mandatory. Preregistration for classes offered. Day and evening sessions, the day before classes begin. **Activities:** Student government.

Student services. Career counseling, financial aid counseling, placement for graduates, veterans' counselor. **Physically disabled:** Services for hearing impaired.

Contact. Phone: (804) 745-2444 Toll-free number: (800) 735-2420
Fax: (804) 745-6884
David Mayle, Director of Admissions, Bryant & Stratton College: Richmond, 8141 Hull Street Road, Richmond, VA 23235

Bryant & Stratton College: Virginia Beach

Virginia Beach, Virginia
www.bryantstratton.edu **CB code: 4761**

- For-profit 2-year business and junior college
- Commuter campus in large city
- Interview required

General. Founded in 1952. Regionally accredited. **Enrollment:** 567 degree-seeking undergraduates; 26 non-degree-seeking students. **Degrees:** 24 bachelor's, 91 associate awarded. **Location:** 10 miles from Norfolk. **Calendar:** Semester, extensive summer session. **Full-time faculty:** 13 total; 54% have terminal degrees, 38% minority, 31% women. **Part-time faculty:** 32 total; 31% have terminal degrees, 56% minority, 50% women. **Class size:** 89% < 20, 11% 20-39.

Student profile. Among degree-seeking undergraduates, 133 enrolled as first-time, first-year students, 41 transferred in from other institutions.

Part-time:	54%	**25 or older:**	59%
Women:	79%		

Transfer out. Colleges most students transferred to 2008: Tidewater Community College, Strayer University, University of Phoenix.

Basis for selection. Open admission. Personal interview most important. TOEFL used for non-native English speakers.

High school preparation. Recommended units include English 4, mathematics 2, social studies 3, science 2, foreign language 2 and academic electives 1.

2008-2009 Annual costs. Tuition/fees: $13,775. Per-credit charge: $458. Books/supplies: $1,600. Personal expenses: $1,600.

2008-2009 Financial aid. Need-based: Need-based aid available for part-time students. Work-study available nights and for part-time students.

Application procedures. Admission: No deadline. $35 fee, may be waived for applicants with need. Admission notification on a rolling basis. **Financial aid:** No deadline. FAFSA required. Applicants notified on a rolling basis.

Academics. Free tutoring and extensive academic advising available. Portfolio projects in all classes. **Special study options:** Cooperative education, double major, independent study, internships, liberal arts/career combination, weekend college. **Credit/placement by examination:** AP, CLEP, institutional tests. 30 credit hours maximum toward associate degree, 60 toward bachelor's. **Support services:** Learning center, reduced course load, remedial instruction, study skills assistance, tutoring, writing center.

Majors. Business: Accounting, administrative services, business admin, human resources. **Computer sciences:** General. **Health:** Medical assistant, office assistant. **Legal studies:** General. **Protective services:** Law enforcement admin.

Most popular majors. Business/marketing 43%, computer/information sciences 9%, health sciences 13%, legal studies 19%, security/protective services 16%.

Computing on campus. 100 workstations in library, computer center.

Student life. Freshman orientation: Mandatory. Preregistration for classes offered. Held week classes start, 2 to 3 hours. **Activities:** Student government, student newspaper, Alpha Beta Gamma, Phi Beta Lambda, law society, medical club, computer club, Society for the Advancement of Management.

Student services. Adult student services, career counseling, student employment services, on-campus daycare, personal counseling, placement for graduates, veterans' counselor. **Transfer:** Pre-admission transcript evaluation for new students.

Contact. E-mail: dmsoutherland@bryantstratton.edu
Phone: (757) 499-7900 Fax: (757) 499-9977
Deana Southerland, Director of Admissions, Bryant & Stratton College: Virginia Beach, 301 Centre Pointe Drive, Virginia Beach, VA 23462-4417

Central Virginia Community College

Lynchburg, Virginia **CB member**
www.cvcc.va.us **CB code: 5141**

- Public 2-year community college
- Commuter campus in small city

General. Founded in 1966. Regionally accredited. **Enrollment:** 3,187 degree-seeking undergraduates. **Degrees:** 280 associate awarded. **Location:** 120 miles from Richmond. **Calendar:** Semester, limited summer session. **Full-time faculty:** 62 total. **Part-time faculty:** 183 total.

Transfer out. Colleges most students transferred to 2008: Lynchburg College, Virginia Polytechnic Institute and State University, Longwood College, Old Dominion University.

Basis for selection. Open admission, but selective for some programs. Allied health program applicants must have 2 interviews with program head and meet specific criteria. Only 15 applicants accepted into each program each year. Interview required for health program.

2008-2009 Annual costs. Tuition/fees: $2,675; $7,839 out-of-state. Per-credit charge: $82 in-state; $254 out-of-state. Out of state students pay an additional $90 capital outlay fee. Books/supplies: $600. Personal expenses: $1,550.

2008-2009 Financial aid. Need-based: Work-study available for part-time students. **Non-need-based:** Scholarships awarded for academics, alumni affiliation. **Additional information:** Payment plan available.

Application procedures. Admission: Priority date 9/5; no deadline. No application fee. Admission notification on a rolling basis. **Financial aid:** Priority date 3/15; no closing date. FAFSA required. Applicants notified on a rolling basis starting 5/1; must reply within 2 week(s) of notification.

Academics. GPA of 2.0 required to graduate. System-wide core curriculum to ensure ease of transfer. **Special study options:** Cooperative education, distance learning, dual enrollment of high school students, ESL, independent study, internships, study abroad, weekend college. Bachelor's degree programs available on campus. License preparation in dental hygiene, paramedic, radiology, real estate. **Credit/placement by examination:** AP, CLEP, IB, institutional tests. 45 credit hours maximum toward associate degree. **Support services:** Learning center, reduced course load, remedial instruction, study skills assistance, tutoring.

Majors. Business: General, accounting, administrative services, business admin, finance, management information systems. **Computer sciences:** Information systems. **Education:** General. **Engineering technology:** Architectural, civil, electrical. **Health:** Clinical lab technology, physics/radiologic health. **Liberal arts:** Arts/sciences. **Protective services:** Law enforcement admin. **Visual/performing arts:** Commercial/advertising art.

Computing on campus. 230 workstations in library, computer center. Commuter students can connect to campus network. Online library available.

Student life. Freshman orientation: Mandatory, $65 fee. **Activities:** Drama, literary magazine, student government, student newspaper, Black Student Union, art club, honor society, Students Together For Environmental Protection, data processing management association, Spanish club, medical lab club, respiratory club, radiology club.

Athletics. Intramural: Softball, volleyball.

Student services. Career counseling, student employment services, financial aid counseling, personal counseling, placement for graduates, veterans' counselor. **Physically disabled:** Services for visually, speech, hearing impaired. **Transfer:** Transfer adviser, college fairs on campus for students transferring to 4-year colleges.

Contact. Phone: (434) 832-7633 Toll-free number: (800) 562-3060
Fax: (434) 832-7793
Geoffrey Hicks, Chief Academic Officer, Central Virginia Community College, 3506 Wards Road, Lynchburg, VA 24502-2498

Centura College: Chesapeake
Chesapeake, Virginia

- For-profit 2-year business and health science college
- Commuter campus in large city

General. Accredited by ACCSCT. **Enrollment:** 184 degree-seeking undergraduates. **Degrees:** 100 associate awarded. **Calendar:** Continuous. **Full-time faculty:** 30 total. **Part-time faculty:** 10 total.

Basis for selection. Open admission.

2008-2009 Annual costs. Tuition/fees: $11,060. Annual tuition and fees vary by program.

Application procedures. **Admission:** No deadline.

Academics. **Special study options:** Accelerated study. **Credit/placement by examination:** CLEP.

Majors. **Business:** Business admin, office technology. **Computer sciences:** LAN/WAN management. **Health:** Medical assistant, medical secretary. **Legal studies:** Paralegal.

Contact. E-mail: admdirttc@tidewatertech.edu
Fax: (757) 548-1196
Monica Lamb, Director of Admission, Centura College: Chesapeake, 932 Ventures Way, Chesapeake, VA 23320-2882

Centura College: Newport News
Newport News, Virginia

- For-profit 2-year business and technical college
- Commuter campus in small city

General. Accredited by ACCSCT. **Enrollment:** 241 degree-seeking undergraduates. **Degrees:** 134 associate awarded. **Calendar:** Continuous. **Full-time faculty:** 15 total. **Part-time faculty:** 22 total.

Basis for selection. Open admission.

2008-2009 Annual costs. Tuition/fees: $11,060. Annual tuition and fees vary by program.

Application procedures. **Admission:** No deadline. $25 fee, may be waived for applicants with need.

Academics. **Credit/placement by examination:** CLEP.

Majors. **Business:** Business admin. **Computer sciences:** Networking. **Health:** Massage therapy, medical assistant.

Contact. E-mail: admdirttp@tidewatertech.edu
Phone: (757) 874-2121 Fax: (757) 874-3857
Victoria Whitehead, Director of Admissions, Centura College: Newport News, 616 Denbigh Boulevard, Newport News, VA 23608

Centura College: Norfolk
Norfolk, Virginia

- For-profit 2-year branch campus and career college
- Commuter campus in large city

General. Accredited by ACCSCT. **Enrollment:** 370 full-time, degree-seeking students. **Degrees:** 42 associate awarded. **Calendar:** Continuous. **Full-time faculty:** 17 total. **Part-time faculty:** 10 total.

Basis for selection. Open admission. **Homeschooled:** State high school equivalency certificate required.

2008-2009 Annual costs. Tuition/fees: $11,060. Annual tuition and fees reported are representative and will vary depending on program.

2008-2009 Financial aid. **Need-based:** 24% of total undergraduate aid awarded as scholarships/grants, 76% as loans/jobs.

Application procedures. **Admission:** No deadline. $25 fee, may be waived for applicants with need.

Academics. **Special study options:** Bachelor's degree programs available on campus. License preparation in dental hygiene, nursing, radiology. **Credit/placement by examination:** CLEP. **Support services:** Tutoring.

Majors. **Health:** Medical assistant, office assistant.

Student life. **Freshman orientation:** Available. **Activities:** Student newspaper.

Contact. E-mail: admdirttn@tidetech.com
Phone: (757) 853-2121 Toll-free number: (877) 604-2121
Fax: (757) 852-9017
Nida Rogers, Admissions Director, Centura College: Norfolk, 7020 North Military Highway, Norfolk, VA 23518-4202

Centura College: Richmond
Richmond, Virginia

- For-profit 2-year business and health science college
- Commuter campus in small city

General. Accredited by ACCSCT. **Enrollment:** 120 degree-seeking undergraduates. **Degrees:** 98 associate awarded. **Calendar:** Continuous. **Full-time faculty:** 6 total. **Part-time faculty:** 25 total.

Basis for selection. Open admission.

2008-2009 Annual costs. Tuition/fees: $11,060. Annual tuition and fees will vary by program.

Application procedures. **Admission:** No deadline.

Academics. **Credit/placement by examination:** CLEP.

Majors. **Computer sciences:** LAN/WAN management. **Health:** Massage therapy, medical assistant. **Legal studies:** Paralegal.

Contact. E-mail: admdirbtr@betatech.edu
Phone: (804) 330-0111
Paula Bowne, Admissions Director, Centura College: Richmond, 7914 Midlothian Turnpike, Richmond, VA 23608

Centura College: Richmond Westend
Richmond, Virginia

- For-profit 2-year business and health science college
- Commuter campus in small city

General. Accredited by ACCSCT. **Enrollment:** 118 degree-seeking undergraduates. **Degrees:** 44 associate awarded. **Calendar:** Continuous. **Full-time faculty:** 5 total. **Part-time faculty:** 17 total.

Basis for selection. Open admission.

2008-2009 Annual costs. Tuition/fees: $11,060. Annual tuition and fees vary by program.

Application procedures. **Admission:** No deadline. $25 fee.

Academics. **Credit/placement by examination:** CLEP.

Majors. **Business:** Business admin. **Computer sciences:** General. **Health:** Medical assistant.

Contact. E-mail: admdirbtw@betatech.edu
Phone: (804) 672-2300
Synthia Munn, Director of Admissions, Centura College: Richmond Westend, 7001 West Broad Street, Richmond, VA 23294

Centura College: Virginia Beach
Virginia Beach, Virginia

- For-profit 2-year technical college
- Commuter campus in small city

General. Accredited by ACCSCT. **Enrollment:** 189 degree-seeking undergraduates. **Degrees:** 103 associate awarded. **Calendar:** Modules begin every 5 weeks. **Full-time faculty:** 6 total. **Part-time faculty:** 30 total.

Basis for selection. Open admission, but selective for some programs.

2008-2009 Annual costs. Tuition/fees: $11,060. Annual tuition and fees reported are representative and will vary depending on program.

Application procedures. Admission: No deadline. $25 fee.

Academics. Special study options: Accelerated study, distance learning. **Credit/placement by examination:** CLEP.

Majors. Business: General. **Computer sciences:** Networking. **Health:** Management/clinical assistant, massage therapy, office assistant. **Legal studies:** Paralegal. **Protective services:** Law enforcement admin.

Contact. E-mail: directorttv@tidetech.com
Phone: (757) 340-2121 Fax: (757) 340-9704
Paul Spirelis, Director of Admissions, Centura College: Virginia Beach, 2697 Dean Drive, Suite 100, Virginia Beach, VA 23452

Dabney S. Lancaster Community College

Clifton Forge, Virginia
www.dslcc.edu **CB code: 5139**

- Public 2-year community college
- Commuter campus in small town

General. Founded in 1967. Regionally accredited. **Enrollment:** 529 degree-seeking undergraduates; 743 non-degree-seeking students. **Degrees:** 90 associate awarded. **Location:** 55 miles from Roanoke. **Calendar:** Semester, extensive summer session. **Full-time faculty:** 20 total. **Part-time faculty:** 90 total. **Class size:** 88% < 20, 11% 20-39, less than 1% 40-49. **Special facilities:** Modern sawmill.

Student profile. Among degree-seeking undergraduates, 197 enrolled as first-time, first-year students.

Part-time:	40%	**Women:**	50%
Out-of-state:	8%		

Basis for selection. Open admission, but selective for some programs. Special requirements for nursing program. High school diploma or GED required of applicants under 18. Interview required for nursing program.

High school preparation. Course recommendations vary according to planned curriculum.

2008-2009 Annual costs. Tuition/fees: $2,636; $7,800 out-of-state. Per-credit charge: $82 in-state; $254 out-of-state. Out of state students pay an additional $90 capital outlay fee. Books/supplies: $580. Personal expenses: $1,680.

Financial aid. All financial aid based on need. Need-based aid available for part-time students.

Application procedures. Admission: No deadline. No application fee. Admission notification on a rolling basis beginning on or about 2/1. **Financial aid:** Priority date 3/15; no closing date. FAFSA, institutional form required. Applicants notified on a rolling basis starting 4/15; must reply within 2 week(s) of notification.

Academics. Special study options: Cooperative education, distance learning, double major, dual enrollment of high school students, independent study, internships. Bachelor's degree programs available on campus. **Credit/placement by examination:** CLEP, institutional tests. **Support services:** Learning center, pre-admission summer program, reduced course load, remedial instruction, study skills assistance, tutoring, writing center.

Majors. Business: Administrative services, business admin, communications, office management, office/clerical. **Communications technology:** Graphic/printing. **Computer sciences:** General. **Conservation:** Forestry. **Engineering technology:** Electrical. **Liberal arts:** Arts/sciences. **Personal/culinary services:** Food prep. **Protective services:** Criminal justice, police science.

Most popular majors. Education 9%, health sciences 36%, liberal arts 12%, natural resources/environmental science 15%, security/protective services 6%.

Computing on campus. 60 workstations in library, computer center. Helpline, wireless network available.

Student life. Freshman orientation: Mandatory. Preregistration for classes offered. **Activities:** Choral groups, drama, literary magazine, student government, student newspaper, various social, religious and service clubs available.

Athletics. Intramural: Basketball, softball, volleyball.

Student services. Career counseling, student employment services, personal counseling, placement for graduates, veterans' counselor. **Physically disabled:** Services for visually, speech, hearing impaired. **Transfer:** Transfer adviser, college fairs on campus for students transferring to 4-year colleges.

Contact. Phone: (540) 863-2815 Fax: (540) 863-2915
Mary Wilson, Director of Student Services, Dabney S. Lancaster Community College, Box 1000, Clifton Forge, VA 24422

Danville Community College

Danville, Virginia
www.dcc.vccs.edu **CB code: 5163**

- Public 2-year community college
- Commuter campus in small city

General. Founded in 1967. Regionally accredited. **Enrollment:** 2,106 degree-seeking undergraduates. **Degrees:** 281 associate awarded. **Location:** 45 miles from Greensboro, North Carolina. **Calendar:** Semester, limited summer session. **Full-time faculty:** 150 total. **Part-time faculty:** 200 total. **Class size:** 71% < 20, 28% 20-39, 1% 50-99.

Student profile.

Out-of-state:	2%	**25 or older:**	52%

Transfer out. Colleges most students transferred to 2008: Averett University, Virginia Polytechnic Institute, Radford University.

Basis for selection. Open admission, but selective for some programs. Special requirements for nursing program.

High school preparation. Recommended units include English 4 and mathematics 1.

2008-2009 Annual costs. Tuition/fees: $2,617; $7,781 out-of-state. Per-credit charge: $82 in-state; $254 out-of-state. Out of state students pay an additional $90 capital outlay fee. Books/supplies: $700. Personal expenses: $1,328.

2007-2008 Financial aid. All financial aid based on need. Need-based aid available for part-time students. Work-study available for part-time students.

Application procedures. Admission: Priority date 8/20; no deadline. No application fee. Admission notification on a rolling basis beginning on or about 1/15. **Financial aid:** Priority date 6/1; no closing date. FAFSA required. Applicants notified on a rolling basis starting 5/1; must reply within 2 week(s) of notification.

Academics. System-wide core curriculum to ensure ease of transfer. **Special study options:** Accelerated study, cooperative education, distance learning, double major, dual enrollment of high school students, honors, independent study, internships. Bachelor's degree programs available on campus. License preparation in dental hygiene, nursing, real estate. **Credit/placement by examination:** AP, CLEP, institutional tests. **Support services:** GED preparation and test center, learning center, pre-admission summer program, reduced course load, remedial instruction, study skills assistance, tutoring.

Majors. Business: General, accounting, administrative services, business admin, executive assistant, receptionist. **Communications technology:** Graphic/printing. **Computer sciences:** General, computer science, programming. **Engineering:** General. **Engineering technology:** Drafting, manufacturing. **Family/consumer sciences:** Child development. **Health:** Dental hygiene, medical secretary, office assistant, respiratory therapy assistant. **Interdisciplinary:** Biological/physical sciences, science/society. **Liberal arts:** Arts/sciences, humanities. **Mechanic/repair:** Heating/ac/refrig. **Protective services:** Law enforcement admin.

Most popular majors. Business/marketing 40%, education 15%, liberal arts 33%, security/protective services 11%.

Computing on campus. 425 workstations in library, computer center. Online course registration, online library available.

Student life. Freshman orientation: Mandatory. Preregistration for classes offered. Two 1-day summer sessions to choose from. **Activities:** Choral groups, student government, African-American culture club, Christian Students Fellowship, graphics club, International Association of Administrative Professionals, Phi Theta Kappa, National Vocational-Technical Honor Society, gospel club, Lambda Alpha Epsilon.

Athletics. **Team name:** Knights.

Student services. Adult student services, chaplain/spiritual director, career counseling, student employment services, financial aid counseling, on-campus daycare, personal counseling, placement for graduates, veterans' counselor, women's services. **Physically disabled:** Services for visually, speech, hearing impaired. **Transfer:** College fairs on campus for students transferring to 4-year colleges.

Contact. E-mail: ethornton@dcc.vccs.edu
Phone: (434) 797-8467 Toll-free number: (800) 560-4291
Fax: (434) 797-8451
Peter Castiglione, Director of Student Development and Enrollment Management, Danville Community College, 1008 South Main Street, Danville, VA 24541

Eastern Shore Community College

Melfa, Virginia
www.es.vccs.edu **CB code: 5844**

- Public 2-year community college
- Commuter campus in rural community

General. Founded in 1971. Regionally accredited. **Enrollment:** 582 degree-seeking undergraduates. **Degrees:** 89 associate awarded. **Location:** 70 miles from Norfolk. **Calendar:** Semester, limited summer session. **Full-time faculty:** 20 total. **Part-time faculty:** 55 total.

Transfer out. 78% of students enrolled in the transfer program go on to 4-year colleges.

Basis for selection. Open admission. Practical Nursing program has prerequisites for admission. Students must take the PSB nursing aptitude test and meet state requirements for screening. **Learning Disabled:** ESCC honors all reasonable, documented requests for accommodations. In order to obtain special accommodations, a student must meet with a counselor prior to classes.

High school preparation. 18 units recommended. Recommended units include English 4, mathematics 3, social studies 2 and science 2.

2008-2009 Annual costs. Tuition/fees: $2,645; $7,809 out-of-state. Per-credit charge: $82 in-state; $254 out-of-state. Out of state students pay an additional $90 capital outlay fee. Books/supplies: $500. Personal expenses: $1,196.

Financial aid. All financial aid based on need. Need-based aid available for part-time students. **Additional information:** ESCC is a member of the Servicemembers Opportunity Colleges (SOC) program. This is a worldwide network of colleges and universities working with the Armed Forces dedicated to helping service people and their families get college degrees.

Application procedures. **Admission:** No deadline. No application fee. Admission notification on a rolling basis. **Financial aid:** Priority date 5/1; no closing date. FAFSA required. Applicants notified on a rolling basis starting 6/1; must reply within 2 week(s) of notification.

Academics. **Special study options:** Cross-registration, distance learning, dual enrollment of high school students, ESL. Bachelor's degree programs available on campus. License preparation in real estate. **Credit/placement by examination:** AP, CLEP, institutional tests. 30 credit hours maximum toward associate degree. Students who do not achieve minimum scores on institutional placement tests must enroll in developmental courses. **Support services:** GED preparation and test center, learning center, reduced course load, remedial instruction, study skills assistance, tutoring.

Majors. **Business:** Business admin, office/clerical. **Computer sciences:** General. **Education:** General, science. **Engineering:** Electrical. **Liberal arts:** Arts/sciences. **Mechanic/repair:** Electronics/electrical.

Computing on campus. 53 workstations in library, computer center. Online course registration, online library, helpline, wireless network available.

Student life. **Freshman orientation:** Available. Preregistration for classes offered. **Activities:** Campus ministries, student government, Phi Theta Kappa, Phi Beta Lambda, ACTS.

Student services. Career counseling, student employment services, financial aid counseling, health services, personal counseling, placement for graduates, veterans' counselor. **Physically disabled:** Services for visually, hearing impaired. **Transfer:** Transfer adviser for students transferring to 4-year colleges.

Contact. E-mail: bsmith@es.vccs.edu
Phone: (757) 789-1731 Fax: (757) 789-1737
P Smith, Dean of Student Services, Eastern Shore Community College, 29300 Lankford Highway, Melfa, VA 23410-9755

ECPI Technical College: Richmond

Richmond, Virginia
www.ecpi.edu **CB code: 3145**

- For-profit 2-year technical college
- Small city

General. Accredited by ACCSCT. **Calendar:** Continuous.

Annual costs/financial aid. Tuition/fees (2008-2009): $10,650. Personal expenses: $2,072.

Contact. Phone: (804) 359-3535
Director of Admissions, 800 Moorefield Park Drive, Richmond, VA 23236

ECPI Technical College: Roanoke

Roanoke, Virginia
www.ecpitech.edu **CB code: 3147**

- For-profit 2-year technical college
- Commuter campus in small city
- Interview required

General. Accredited by ACCSCT. **Enrollment:** 347 degree-seeking undergraduates. **Degrees:** 5 bachelor's, 70 associate awarded. **Calendar:** Continuous, extensive summer session. **Full-time faculty:** 12 total. **Part-time faculty:** 20 total.

Student profile.

Out-of-state:	5%	**25 or older:**	40%

Basis for selection. Interview important; program-specific admissions tests required. No special considerations given.

2008-2009 Annual costs. Tuition/fees: $10,650. Personal expenses: $2,072.

Financial aid. **Need-based:** Need-based aid available for part-time students.

Application procedures. **Admission:** No deadline. $50 fee. Admission notification on a rolling basis. **Financial aid:** No deadline. FAFSA required. Applicants notified on a rolling basis.

Academics. **Special study options:** Accelerated study, distance learning. Bachelor's degree programs available on campus. **Credit/placement by examination:** AP, CLEP. 15 credit hours maximum toward associate degree, 30 toward bachelor's. **Support services:** Remedial instruction, tutoring.

Majors. **Business:** Accounting, administrative services, office technology, office/clerical, taxation. **Communications technology:** General. **Computer sciences:** General, applications programming, computer science, data entry, data processing, information systems, information technology, LAN/WAN management, networking, programming, security, system admin, systems analysis, web page design, webmaster, word processing. **Engineering:** Electrical. **Engineering technology:** Computer hardware, computer systems, electrical, telecommunications. **Health:** Health care admin, medical assistant, medical records admin, medical records technology, medical secretary, medical transcription. **Mechanic/repair:** Communications systems, computer, electronics/electrical, industrial electronics.

Computing on campus. 180 workstations in library, computer center. Online library available.

Student services. Career counseling, student employment services, financial aid counseling, placement for graduates, veterans' counselor.

Contact. Phone: (540) 563-8080
Carol Rouch, Director, ECPI Technical College: Roanoke, 5234 Airport Road, Roanoke, VA 24012

Everest College: Arlington

Arlington, Virginia

- For-profit 2-year branch campus and business college
- Large city

General. Accredited by ACICS. **Calendar:** Quarter.

Contact. Phone: (703) 248-8887
Director of Admissions, 801 North Quincy Street, Arlington, VA 22207

Everest College: Tysons Corner
McLean, Virginia
www.parks-college.com

- For-profit 2-year branch campus college
- Large city

General. Accredited by ACICS. **Calendar:** Quarter.

Contact. Phone: (703) 288-3131
Director of Admissions, 1430 Spring Hill Road, Suite 200, McLean, VA 22102

Germanna Community College
Locust Grove, Virginia
www.germanna.edu **CB code: 5276**

- Public 2-year community college
- Commuter campus in rural community

General. Founded in 1969. Regionally accredited. Off-campus sites in high schools; dual enrollment courses offered at area high schools. **Enrollment:** 4,157 degree-seeking undergraduates. **Degrees:** 444 associate awarded. **Location:** 15 miles from Culpeper, 18 miles from Fredericksburg. **Calendar:** Semester, limited summer session. **Full-time faculty:** 66 total; 62% women. **Part-time faculty:** 255 total; 52% women. **Class size:** 40% < 20, 60% 20-39, less than 1% 50-99. **Special facilities:** Art exhibits, local history collection.

Student profile. Among degree-seeking undergraduates, 64% enrolled in a transfer program, 36% enrolled in a vocational program.

Out-of-state:	1%	**25 or older:**	29%

Transfer out. 65% of students enrolled in the transfer program go on to 4-year colleges. **Colleges most students transferred to 2008:** University of Mary Washington, Old Dominion University, Radford University, Virginia Commonwealth University, Virginia Tech.

Basis for selection. Open admission, but selective for some programs. Special requirements for nursing program with local applicants given preference. **Adult students:** SAT scores, GCC placement tests, or proof of college transcripts required. **Homeschooled:** Transcript of courses and grades required. Provide current copy of signed home school agreement between appropriate school system and authorizing parent or guardian. Provide written recommendation from home school teacher or tutor.

2008-2009 Annual costs. Tuition/fees: $2,638; $7,802 out-of-state. Per-credit charge: $82 in-state; $254 out-of-state. An indirect cost fee of $31 per credit hour is charged to all out-of-state distance learning students. Books/supplies: $800. Personal expenses: $2,770.

2007-2008 Financial aid. Need-based: Need-based aid available for part-time students. Work-study available for part-time students. **Non-need-based:** Scholarships awarded for academics.

Application procedures. Admission: No deadline. No application fee. Admission notification on a rolling basis. Nursing program applications must be completed by February 1. **Financial aid:** Priority date 4/1; no closing date. FAFSA required. Applicants notified on a rolling basis starting 5/15; must reply within 2 week(s) of notification.

Academics. Systemwide core curriculum to ensure ease of transfer. **Special study options:** Accelerated study, distance learning, double major, dual enrollment of high school students, ESL, independent study, internships, liberal arts/career combination. Bachelor's degree programs available on campus. License preparation in dental hygiene, nursing. **Credit/placement by examination:** AP, CLEP, institutional tests. 8 credit hours maximum toward associate degree. **Support services:** GED test center, reduced course load, remedial instruction, study skills assistance, tutoring.

Majors. Biology: General. **Business:** General, business admin. **Computer sciences:** Information technology. **Education:** General, elementary. **Health:** Dental hygiene, nursing (RN), radiologic technology/medical imaging. **Liberal arts:** Arts/sciences. **Protective services:** Police science. **Psychology:** General.

Most popular majors. Biological/life sciences 10%, business/marketing 22%, education 7%, health sciences 16%, liberal arts 41%.

Computing on campus. 90 workstations in library, computer center. Online course registration, online library, helpline, wireless network available.

Student life. Freshman orientation: Mandatory. Preregistration for classes offered. **Activities:** Student government, Black studies, student Christian associations.

Athletics. Team name: Grizzly Bears.

Student services. Career counseling, student employment services, financial aid counseling, personal counseling, placement for graduates, veterans' counselor. **Physically disabled:** Services for visually, hearing impaired. **Transfer:** Transfer adviser, college fairs on campus for students transferring to 4-year colleges.

Contact. Phone: (540) 423-9122 Fax: (540) 423-9158
Rita Dunston, Registrar, Germanna Community College, 2130 Germanna Highway, Locust Grove, VA 22508-2102

J. Sargeant Reynolds Community College
Richmond, Virginia
www.reynolds.edu **CB code: 5676**

- Public 2-year community college
- Commuter campus in very large city

General. Founded in 1972. Regionally accredited. **Enrollment:** 8,750 degree-seeking undergraduates. **Degrees:** 765 associate awarded. **ROTC:** Army. **Location:** Downtown. **Calendar:** Semester, extensive summer session. **Full-time faculty:** 135 total. **Part-time faculty:** 482 total. **Special facilities:** Hospitality development center, distance education center. **Partnerships:** Formal partnerships with local medical facilities.

Student profile.

Out-of-state:	3%	**25 or older:**	44%

Transfer out. Colleges most students transferred to 2008: Virginia Commonwealth University, Old Dominion University.

Basis for selection. Open admission, but selective for some programs. Special requirements for nursing, health technology, engineering, legal assisting programs; interview recommended.

High school preparation. College preparatory units recommended for applicants to college transfer programs. Recommended units vary per program of study and include up to 4 English, 4 mathematics, 2 lab science, 2 foreign language, 2 social studies.

2008-2009 Annual costs. Tuition/fees: $2,810; $7,974 out-of-state. Per-credit charge: $82 in-state; $254 out-of-state. Out of state students pay an additional $90 capital outlay fee. Books/supplies: $1,000. Personal expenses: $900.

Financial aid. Need-based: Need-based aid available for part-time students. Work-study available nights, weekends and for part-time students. **Non-need-based:** Scholarships awarded for academics.

Application procedures. Admission: No deadline. No application fee. Admission notification on a rolling basis beginning on or about 1/15. **Financial aid:** Priority date 6/30; no closing date. FAFSA required. Applicants notified on a rolling basis starting 7/15; must reply within 2 week(s) of notification.

Academics. Special study options: Cooperative education, distance learning, double major, dual enrollment of high school students, ESL, independent study, internships, weekend college. License preparation in dental hygiene, nursing, paramedic, real estate. **Credit/placement by examination:** AP, CLEP, IB, institutional tests. 53 credit hours maximum toward associate degree. Essay required for composition and literature subject exams (CLEP). **Support services:** Learning center, pre-admission summer program, reduced course load, remedial instruction, study skills assistance, tutoring, writing center.

Majors. Agriculture: Horticulture, landscaping, turf management. **Architecture:** Technology. **Business:** Accounting, business admin, hospitality admin, office technology, office/clerical. **Computer sciences:** General, computer science, information systems, programming. **Education:** Early childhood, teacher assistance. **Engineering:** General. **Engineering technology:** Architectural, civil, construction, electrical. **Family/consumer sciences:** Child care, institutional food production. **Health:** Clinical lab technology, dental lab technology, nursing (RN), occupational therapy assistant, optician, respiratory therapy technology. **Interdisciplinary:** Biological/physical sciences, math/computer science, natural sciences. **Legal studies:** Legal secretary, paralegal. **Liberal arts:** Arts/sciences. **Math:** General. **Mechanic/repair:** Auto body, automotive. **Personal/culinary services:** Baking, chef training, culinary arts, restaurant/catering. **Protective services:** Criminal justice, firefighting. **Public administration:** Community org/advocacy. **Social sciences:** General. **Other:** Social sciences studies.

Computing on campus. 1,100 workstations in library, computer center, student center. Commuter students can connect to campus network. Online course registration, helpline, repair service, wireless network available.

Student life. Freshman orientation: Available. Preregistration for classes offered. **Activities:** Music ensembles, student government, TV station, culinary arts, horticultural club, music club, PAVE club, Phi Beta Lambda, Phi Theta Kappa, photography club, sign language club, Student Virginia Education Association, sustainable agriculture club.

Student services. Career counseling, student employment services, financial aid counseling, veterans' counselor. **Physically disabled:** Services for visually, speech, hearing impaired. **Transfer:** Transfer adviser, college fairs on campus for students transferring to 4-year colleges.

Contact. E-mail: kpettis-walden@reynolds.edu
Phone: (804) 523-5029 Fax: (804) 371-3650
Karen Pettis-Walden, Director of Admissions and Records, J. Sargeant Reynolds Community College, Box 85622, Richmond, VA 23285-5622

John Tyler Community College

Chester, Virginia — **CB member**
www.jtcc.edu — **CB code: 5342**

- Public 2-year community college
- Commuter campus in small city

General. Founded in 1965. Regionally accredited. **Enrollment:** 4,989 degree-seeking undergraduates; 3,819 non-degree-seeking students. **Degrees:** 520 associate awarded. **ROTC:** Army. **Location:** 16 miles from Richmond. **Calendar:** Semester, extensive summer session. **Full-time faculty:** 72 total; 35% have terminal degrees. **Part-time faculty:** 310 total; 16% have terminal degrees. **Partnerships:** Formal partnership with Virgina Power.

Student profile. Among degree-seeking undergraduates, 35% enrolled in a transfer program, 30% enrolled in a vocational program, 1,109 enrolled as first-time, first-year students.

Part-time:	60%	**Women:**	67%
Out-of-state:	2%	**25 or older:**	43%

Basis for selection. Open admission, but selective for some programs. Special requirements for nursing, funeral services and police science programs.

High school preparation. Required units include English 4 and mathematics 4. Biology and/or chemistry required for allied health programs.

2008-2009 Annual costs. Tuition/fees: $2,635; $7,799 out-of-state. Per-credit charge: $82 in-state; $254 out-of-state. Out of state students pay an additional $90 capital outlay fee.

2007-2008 Financial aid. Need-based: Need-based aid available for part-time students. Work-study available nights, weekends and for part-time students. **Non-need-based:** Scholarships awarded for academics, state residency.

Application procedures. Admission: Priority date 8/1; no deadline. No application fee. Admission notification on a rolling basis. High school students may attend with written approval of school principal. **Financial aid:** Priority date 5/15, closing date 7/15. FAFSA required. Applicants notified on a rolling basis starting 6/15.

Academics. Students seeking associate degree must complete 25 percent of core courses at college. **Special study options:** Cooperative education, distance learning, dual enrollment of high school students, internships, weekend college. 2-2 transfer programs in various engineering technology disciplines and business education; 1-3 transfer certificate in art. License preparation in nursing. **Credit/placement by examination:** AP, CLEP, IB, institutional tests. **Support services:** Learning center, remedial instruction, study skills assistance, tutoring.

Majors. Business: General, administrative services. **Computer sciences:** General, programming, systems analysis. **Education:** Teacher assistance. **Engineering:** Architectural, civil, electrical, environmental, mechanical. **Engineering technology:** Architectural, civil, electrical, manufacturing, mechanical. **Family/consumer sciences:** Child care. **Health:** Nursing (RN). **Liberal arts:** Arts/sciences. **Personal/culinary services:** Mortuary science. **Public administration:** Human services. **Visual/performing arts:** Studio arts.

Most popular majors. Business/marketing 11%, education 6%, engineering/engineering technologies 15%, health sciences 22%, liberal arts 34%, personal/culinary services 8%.

Computing on campus. 165 workstations in library, student center. Commuter students can connect to campus network. Online course registration, online library available.

Student life. Freshman orientation: Mandatory. Preregistration for classes offered. **Activities:** Drama, student government, student nurses association, data processing club, human services organization, business honor society, funeral services student organization, biology club, art club.

Student services. Adult student services, alcohol/substance abuse counseling, career counseling, financial aid counseling, personal counseling, veterans' counselor. **Physically disabled:** Services for visually, speech, hearing impaired. **Transfer:** Transfer adviser, college fairs on campus for students transferring to 4-year colleges.

Contact. E-mail: admissionsandrecords@jtcc.edu
Phone: (804) 706-5220 Toll-free number: (800) 552-3490
Fax: (804) 796-4362
Joy James, Coordinator of Admission, John Tyler Community College, 13101 Jefferson Davis Highway, Chester, VA 23831-5316

Lord Fairfax Community College

Middletown, Virginia
www.lfcc.edu — **CB code: 5381**

- Public 2-year community college
- Commuter campus in small town

General. Founded in 1969. Regionally accredited. Additional locations in Fauquier, Middletown and the Luray-Page County Center. **Enrollment:** 3,827 degree-seeking undergraduates. **Degrees:** 471 associate awarded. **Calendar:** Semester, limited summer session. **Full-time faculty:** 66 total. **Part-time faculty:** 215 total.

Student profile. Among degree-seeking undergraduates, 47% enrolled in a transfer program, 11% enrolled in a vocational program.

Transfer out. Colleges most students transferred to 2008: George Mason University, James Madison University, Old Dominion University, Shenandoah University, University of Mary Washington.

Basis for selection. Open admission.

2008-2009 Annual costs. Tuition/fees: $2,647; $7,811 out-of-state. Per-credit charge: $82 in-state; $254 out-of-state. Out-of-state students pay an additional $45 capital outlay fee per 15 credit hours. Books/supplies: $800.

2007-2008 Financial aid. All financial aid based on need. Need-based aid available for part-time students.

Application procedures. Admission: No deadline. No application fee. Admission notification on a rolling basis. **Financial aid:** Priority date 5/1; no closing date. FAFSA required. Applicants notified on a rolling basis starting 6/1.

Academics. Special study options: Distance learning, double major, dual enrollment of high school students, ESL, honors, independent study. Bachelor's degree programs available on campus. **Credit/placement by examination:** AP, CLEP, institutional tests. **Support services:** Learning center, reduced course load, remedial instruction, tutoring.

Majors. Business: Accounting, administrative services, business admin, management information systems, marketing, office management. **Communications:** General. **Computer sciences:** General, database management, networking, webmaster. **Education:** General. **Engineering:** General, civil, electrical, mechanical. **Engineering technology:** Electrical. **Health:** Dental hygiene, nursing (RN). **Interdisciplinary:** Biological/physical sciences. **Liberal arts:** Arts/sciences. **Philosophy/religion:** Philosophy, religion.

Computing on campus. Online course registration, online library available.

Student life. Freshman orientation: Mandatory. Preregistration for classes offered. **Activities:** Drama, musical theater, student government, special interest and program-related organizations, ambassadors club, honor society.

Athletics. **Intercollegiate:** Soccer. **Team name:** Cannons.

Student services. Adult student services, career counseling, services for economically disadvantaged, financial aid counseling, veterans' counselor. **Physically disabled:** Services for visually, speech, hearing impaired. **Transfer:** Transfer center, transfer adviser, college fairs on campus for students transferring to 4-year colleges.

Contact. E-mail: admissions@lfcc.edu
Phone: (540) 868-7105 Toll-free number: (800) 906-5322 ext. 7105
Fax: (540) 868-7005
Karen Bucher, Director of Enrollment Management, Lord Fairfax Community College, 173 Skirmisher Lane, Middletown, VA 22645

Miller-Motte Technical College: Lynchburg

Lynchburg, Virginia
www.miller-motte.com

- For-profit 2-year technical college
- Commuter campus in small city
- Interview required

General. Accredited by ACICS. **Enrollment:** 335 degree-seeking undergraduates. **Degrees:** 100 associate awarded. **Location:** 60 miles from Charlottesville, 180 miles from Richmond. **Calendar:** Quarter. **Full-time faculty:** 6 total; 17% minority, 100% women. **Part-time faculty:** 32 total; 6% have terminal degrees, 6% minority, 81% women. **Special facilities:** College-operated massage therapy clinic, aesthetics clinic.

Student profile. Among degree-seeking undergraduates, 70 transferred in from other institutions.

Basis for selection. Open admission. **Homeschooled:** Statement describing homeschool structure and mission required.

2008-2009 Annual costs. Tuition/fees: $6,750. Per-credit charge: $225.

Financial aid. All financial aid based on need. Need-based aid available for part-time students. Work-study available nights and for part-time students.

Application procedures. **Admission:** No deadline. $35 fee. Application must be submitted on paper. Admission notification on a rolling basis. **Financial aid:** No deadline. FAFSA required. Applicants notified on a rolling basis.

Academics. **Special study options:** Cooperative education, dual enrollment of high school students. **Credit/placement by examination:** AP, CLEP, institutional tests. Students are encouraged to test out of introductory classes if they feel they have the necessary experience. There is a $100 nonrefundable examination fee. Students are not encouraged to test out of advanced classes leading to the associate degree. **Support services:** Learning center, study skills assistance, tutoring.

Majors. **Business:** Management science. **Computer sciences:** General. **Health:** Massage therapy, medical assistant, office assistant, pharmacy assistant, surgical technology.

Computing on campus. 75 workstations in library, computer center.

Student life. **Freshman orientation:** Available. Preregistration for classes offered.

Student services. Student employment services, financial aid counseling.

Contact. Phone: (434) 239-5222 Toll-free number: (877) 333-6622
Fax: (434) 239-1069
Miller-Motte Technical College: Lynchburg, 1011 Creekside Lane, Lynchburg, VA 24502

Mountain Empire Community College

Big Stone Gap, Virginia
www.mecc.edu **CB code: 5451**

- Public 2-year community college
- Commuter campus in small town

General. Founded in 1970. Regionally accredited. **Enrollment:** 1,983 degree-seeking undergraduates. **Degrees:** 188 associate awarded. **Location:** 40 miles from Bristol. **Calendar:** Semester, limited summer session. **Full-time faculty:** 47 total. **Part-time faculty:** 113 total.

Student profile.

Out-of-state:	4%	**25 or older:**	40%

Transfer out. **Colleges most students transferred to 2008:** University of Virginia's College at Wise, Radford University, Virginia Polytechnic Institute and State University, East Tennessee State University.

Basis for selection. Open admission, but selective for some programs. Nursing students must meet admission test score, plus biology, chemistry and algebra I required. Respiratory therapy students must meet admission test score, plus algebra I and biology required. High school diploma or GED required for practical nursing, nursing and respiratory care programs.

High school preparation. Recommended units include English 4, mathematics 1 and social studies 2. 1 algebra, 1 biology, 1 chemistry required for nursing program; 1 algebra, 1 biology required for respiratory care program.

2008-2009 Annual costs. Tuition/fees: $2,675; $7,839 out-of-state. Per-credit charge: $82 in-state; $254 out-of-state. Out of state students pay an additional $90 capital outlay fee. Books/supplies: $860.

2007-2008 Financial aid. **Need-based:** Need-based aid available for part-time students. Work-study available for part-time students. **Non-need-based:** Scholarships awarded for academics, state residency. **Additional information:** The college does not participate in loan programs. All financial aid is in form of grants, scholarships, or work study.

Application procedures. **Admission:** No deadline. No application fee. Admission notification on a rolling basis beginning on or about 1/1. **Financial aid:** Priority date 5/1; no closing date. FAFSA required. Applicants notified on a rolling basis starting 1/1.

Academics. System-wide core curriculum to ensure ease of transfer. **Special study options:** Accelerated study, distance learning, double major, dual enrollment of high school students, independent study, internships, liberal arts/career combination, student-designed major. Bachelor's degree programs available on campus. **Credit/placement by examination:** AP, CLEP, IB, institutional tests. 16 credit hours maximum toward associate degree. Maximum 25% of credits awarded for work and/or life experience. **Support services:** Learning center, pre-admission summer program, reduced course load, remedial instruction, tutoring.

Majors. **Agriculture:** Soil science. **Biology:** General. **Business:** General, accounting, business admin, office management, office/clerical. **Computer sciences:** General, information systems, information technology, networking, word processing. **Conservation:** General, environmental science, forestry. **Education:** General. **Engineering:** Electrical, manufacturing. **Engineering technology:** CAD/CADD, computer hardware, electrical, manufacturing. **Health:** EMT paramedic, medical secretary, medical transcription, nursing (RN), predental, premedicine, prepharmacy, preveterinary, respiratory therapy technology. **Legal studies:** Legal secretary, paralegal, prelaw. **Liberal arts:** Arts/sciences. **Math:** General. **Mechanic/repair:** Electronics/electrical. **Protective services:** Corrections, criminal justice, law enforcement admin. **Public administration:** Social work.

Most popular majors. Business/marketing 17%, computer/information sciences 16%, education 12%, health sciences 10%, legal studies 6%, liberal arts 26%.

Computing on campus. 400 workstations in library, computer center.

Student life. **Freshman orientation:** Mandatory. Preregistration for classes offered. **Activities:** Drama, student government, student newspaper, service, business, nursing organizations available.

Athletics. **Intramural:** Archery, badminton, basketball, bowling, softball, table tennis, tennis, volleyball. **Team name:** Red Fox Fliers.

Student services. Career counseling, student employment services, financial aid counseling, health services, personal counseling, placement for graduates, veterans' counselor. **Transfer:** Pre-admission transcript evaluation for new students. Transfer adviser for students transferring to 4-year colleges.

Contact. E-mail: khall@me.vccs.edu
Phone: (276) 523-2400 Fax: (276) 523-8297
Kristy Hall, Director of Enrollment Services, Mountain Empire Community College, 3441 Mountain Empire Road, Big Stone Gap, VA 24219

National College: Bluefield

Bluefield, Virginia
www.ncbt.edu **CB code: 3246**

- For-profit 2-year business college
- Commuter campus in small city

General. Accredited by ACICS. **Enrollment:** 194 degree-seeking undergraduates. **Degrees:** 30 associate awarded. **Calendar:** Quarter. **Full-time faculty:** 11 total. **Part-time faculty:** 6 total.

Basis for selection. Open admission. Interview recommended.

2008-2009 Annual costs. Tuition/fees: $9,585. Per-credit charge: $212. Books/supplies: $1,200.

Financial aid. All financial aid based on need. Need-based aid available for part-time students.

Application procedures. Admission: No deadline. $30 fee, may be waived for applicants with need. Admission notification on a rolling basis. **Financial aid:** No deadline. FAFSA required. Applicants notified on a rolling basis starting 9/1.

Academics. Special study options: Double major, internships, liberal arts/career combination. **Credit/placement by examination:** CLEP, institutional tests. **Support services:** Tutoring.

Majors. Business: Accounting, administrative services, business admin, office management. **Computer sciences:** Computer science. **Health:** Medical assistant.

Computing on campus. 35 workstations in computer center.

Student life. Freshman orientation: Mandatory. Preregistration for classes offered.

Student services. Career counseling, personal counseling.

Contact. E-mail: tharris@national-college.edu
Phone: (540) 326-3621 Fax: (276) 650-2516
Larry Steele, Vice President of Admissions, National College: Bluefield, PO Box 6400, Roanoke, VA 24017

National College: Charlottesville
Charlottesville, Virginia
www.ncbt.edu **CB code: 3248**

- For-profit 2-year business college
- Commuter campus in small city
- Interview required

General. Accredited by ACICS. **Enrollment:** 199 degree-seeking undergraduates. **Degrees:** 24 associate awarded. **Calendar:** Quarter, limited summer session. **Full-time faculty:** 5 total. **Part-time faculty:** 14 total.

Basis for selection. Open admission.

2008-2009 Annual costs. Tuition/fees: $9,585. Per-credit charge: $212. Books/supplies: $1,200.

Financial aid. All financial aid based on need. Need-based aid available for part-time students.

Application procedures. Admission: No deadline. $30 fee, may be waived for applicants with need. Admission notification on a rolling basis. **Financial aid:** No deadline. FAFSA required. Applicants notified on a rolling basis.

Academics. Special study options: Double major, internships, liberal arts/career combination. **Credit/placement by examination:** CLEP, institutional tests. **Support services:** Tutoring.

Majors. Business: Accounting, administrative services, business admin. **Computer sciences:** Computer science. **Health:** Medical assistant.

Computing on campus. 35 workstations in library, computer center.

Student life. Freshman orientation: Mandatory. Preregistration for classes offered.

Contact. Phone: (804) 295-0136 Toll-free number: (800) 664-1886
Fax: (804) 979-8061
Larry Steele, Vice President of Admissions, National College: Charlottesville, PO Box 6400, Roanoke, VA 24017

National College: Danville
Danville, Virginia
www.ncbt.edu **CB code: 3249**

- For-profit 2-year branch campus and business college
- Commuter campus in small city

General. Accredited by ACICS. **Enrollment:** 343 degree-seeking undergraduates. **Degrees:** 36 associate awarded. **Calendar:** Quarter, limited summer session. **Full-time faculty:** 3 total. **Part-time faculty:** 59 total.

Basis for selection. Open admission. Interview recommended.

2008-2009 Annual costs. Tuition/fees: $9,585. Per-credit charge: $212. Books/supplies: $1,200.

Financial aid. All financial aid based on need. Need-based aid available for part-time students.

Application procedures. Admission: No deadline. $30 fee, may be waived for applicants with need. Admission notification on a rolling basis. **Financial aid:** No deadline. FAFSA required. Applicants notified on a rolling basis starting 9/1.

Academics. Special study options: Double major, internships. **Credit/placement by examination:** CLEP, institutional tests. **Support services:** Tutoring.

Majors. Business: Accounting, administrative services, business admin. **Computer sciences:** Computer science. **Health:** Medical assistant.

Computing on campus. 35 workstations in library, computer center.

Student life. Freshman orientation: Mandatory. Preregistration for classes offered.

Student services. Career counseling, student employment services, personal counseling, placement for graduates.

Contact. E-mail: market@educorp.edu
Phone: (804) 793-6822
Larry Steele, Director of Admissions, National College: Danville, PO Box 6400, Roanoke, VA 24017

National College: Harrisonburg
Harrisonburg, Virginia
www.national-college.edu **CB code: 3173**

- For-profit 2-year business college
- Commuter campus in large town

General. Accredited by ACICS. **Enrollment:** 352 degree-seeking undergraduates. **Degrees:** 39 associate awarded. **Calendar:** Quarter, limited summer session. **Full-time faculty:** 12 total. **Part-time faculty:** 11 total.

Basis for selection. Open admission. Interview recommended.

2008-2009 Annual costs. Tuition/fees: $9,585. Per-credit charge: $212. Books/supplies: $1,200.

Financial aid. All financial aid based on need. Need-based aid available for part-time students.

Application procedures. Admission: No deadline. $30 fee, may be waived for applicants with need. Admission notification on a rolling basis. **Financial aid:** No deadline. FAFSA required. Applicants notified on a rolling basis starting 9/1.

Academics. Special study options: Double major, internships. **Credit/placement by examination:** CLEP, institutional tests. **Support services:** Tutoring.

Majors. Business: Accounting, administrative services, business admin, office management. **Computer sciences:** Computer science. **Health:** Medical assistant.

Computing on campus. 35 workstations in library, computer center.

Student life. Freshman orientation: Mandatory.

Student services. Career counseling, personal counseling.

Contact. E-mail: market@national-college.edu
Phone: (540) 432-0943 Fax: (540) 432-1133
Larry Steele, Director of Admissions, National College: Harrisonburg, PO Box 6400, Roanoke, VA 24017

National College: Lynchburg
Lynchburg, Virginia
www.national-college.edu **CB code: 3172**

- For-profit 2-year business college
- Commuter campus in small city

General. Accredited by ACICS. **Enrollment:** 302 degree-seeking undergraduates. **Degrees:** 41 associate awarded. **Calendar:** Quarter, limited summer session. **Full-time faculty:** 1 total. **Part-time faculty:** 31 total.

Basis for selection. Open admission. Interview recommended.

2008-2009 Annual costs. Tuition/fees: $9,585. Per-credit charge: $212. Books/supplies: $1,200.

Financial aid. All financial aid based on need. Need-based aid available for part-time students.

Application procedures. Admission: No deadline. $30 fee, may be waived for applicants with need. Admission notification on a rolling basis. **Financial aid:** No deadline. FAFSA required. Applicants notified on a rolling basis starting 9/1.

Academics. Special study options: Double major, internships. **Credit/placement by examination:** CLEP, institutional tests. **Support services:** Tutoring.

Majors. Business: Accounting, administrative services, business admin. **Computer sciences:** General, computer science. **Health:** Medical assistant.

Computing on campus. 35 workstations in library, computer center.

Student life. Freshman orientation: Mandatory. Preregistration for classes offered.

Student services. Career counseling, student employment services, financial aid counseling, personal counseling, placement for graduates, veterans' counselor.

Contact. E-mail: market@national-college.edu
Phone: (804) 239-3500 Toll-free number: (800) 664-1886
Larry Steele, Vice President of Admissions, National College: Lynchburg, PO Box 6400, Roanoke, VA 24017

National College: Martinsville
Martinsville, Virginia
www.national-college.edu **CB code: 3171**

- Private 2-year business and junior college
- Commuter campus in small city

General. Accredited by ACICS. **Enrollment:** 382 degree-seeking undergraduates. **Degrees:** 28 associate awarded. **Calendar:** Quarter, limited summer session. **Full-time faculty:** 5 total. **Part-time faculty:** 28 total.

Basis for selection. Open admission.

2008-2009 Annual costs. Tuition/fees: $9,585. Per-credit charge: $212. Books/supplies: $1,200.

Financial aid. All financial aid based on need. Need-based aid available for part-time students.

Application procedures. Admission: No deadline. $30 fee, may be waived for applicants with need. Admission notification on a rolling basis. **Financial aid:** No deadline. FAFSA required. Applicants notified on a rolling basis.

Academics. Special study options: Double major, internships. **Credit/placement by examination:** CLEP, institutional tests. **Support services:** Tutoring.

Majors. Business: Accounting, administrative services, business admin. **Computer sciences:** Computer science.

Computing on campus. 35 workstations in library, computer center.

Student life. Freshman orientation: Mandatory. Preregistration for classes offered.

Student services. Career counseling, student employment services, personal counseling.

Contact. Phone: (540) 632-5621
Larry Steele, Admissions Vice President, National College: Martinsville, PO Box 6400, Roanoke, VA 24017

New River Community College
Dublin, Virginia
www.nr.edu **CB code: 5513**

- Public 2-year community college
- Commuter campus in rural community

General. Founded in 1966. Regionally accredited. **Enrollment:** 2,889 degree-seeking undergraduates. **Degrees:** 356 associate awarded. **ROTC:** Naval. **Location:** 50 miles from Roanoke. **Calendar:** Semester, limited summer session. **Full-time faculty:** 55 total. **Part-time faculty:** 136 total. **Class size:** 57% < 20, 36% 20-39, 5% 40-49, 1% 50-99, less than 1% >100.

Transfer out. Colleges most students transferred to 2008: Radford University, Virginia Tech, Old Dominion University.

Basis for selection. Open admission. Interview required for nursing program. **Adult students:** SAT/ACT scores not required.

2008-2009 Annual costs. Tuition/fees: $2,647; $7,811 out-of-state. Per-credit charge: $82 in-state; $254 out-of-state. Out of state students pay an additional $90 capital outlay fee. Books/supplies: $700. Personal expenses: $1,200.

2007-2008 Financial aid. Need-based: 12% of total undergraduate aid awarded as scholarships/grants, 88% as loans/jobs. Need-based aid available for part-time students.

Application procedures. Admission: No deadline. No application fee. Admission notification on a rolling basis. **Financial aid:** Priority date 4/15; no closing date. FAFSA, institutional form required. Applicants notified on a rolling basis starting 6/1.

Academics. Special study options: Cooperative education, distance learning, dual enrollment of high school students, teacher certification program. License preparation in real estate. **Credit/placement by examination:** AP, CLEP, IB, institutional tests. **Support services:** GED preparation and test center, learning center, remedial instruction, study skills assistance, tutoring, writing center.

Majors. Business: Accounting, administrative services, business admin, logistics, office technology. **Computer sciences:** Computer graphics, information technology, programming. **Education:** General, early childhood. **Engineering:** General, computer. **Engineering technology:** Architectural, drafting, electrical, instrumentation. **Health:** Medical secretary. **Interdisciplinary:** Biological/physical sciences, gerontology. **Legal studies:** Legal secretary, paralegal. **Liberal arts:** Arts/sciences. **Mechanic/repair:** Automotive. **Production:** Machine shop technology. **Protective services:** Forensics, law enforcement admin. **Public administration:** Human services.

Computing on campus. Commuter students can connect to campus network. Online course registration, online library, repair service, wireless network available.

Student life. Freshman orientation: Available. Preregistration for classes offered. **Activities:** Concert band, choral groups, literary magazine, music ensembles, TV station, Black Awareness Association, Phi Beta Lambda, Phi Theta Kappa.

Athletics. Intramural: Baseball M, basketball, cheerleading, soccer, softball, table tennis, tennis, volleyball. **Team name:** Knights.

Student services. Career counseling, student employment services, financial aid counseling, on-campus daycare, personal counseling, placement for graduates, veterans' counselor. **Physically disabled:** Services for visually, speech, hearing impaired. **Learning disabled:** Comprehensive services available. **Transfer:** Transfer adviser, college fairs on campus for students transferring to 4-year colleges.

Contact. E-mail: nrtaylm@nr.edu
Phone: (540) 674-3603 Toll-free number: (866) 462-6722
Fax: (540) 674-3644
Margaret Taylor, Coordinator of Admissions and Records, New River Community College, Drawer 1127, Dublin, VA 24084

Northern Virginia Community College

Annandale, Virginia **CB member**
www.nvcc.edu **CB code: 5515**

- Public 2-year community college
- Commuter campus in small city

General. Founded in 1965. Regionally accredited. 6 campuses in Alexandria, Annandale, Loudoun County, Manassas, Springfield (medical education), Woodbridge. **Enrollment:** 34,202 degree-seeking undergraduates. **Degrees:** 2,973 associate awarded. **Location:** 12 miles from Washington, DC. **Calendar:** Semester, limited summer session. **Full-time faculty:** 569 total. **Part-time faculty:** 1,207 total.

Transfer out. Colleges most students transferred to 2008: George Mason University.

Basis for selection. Open admission, but selective for some programs. Admission to health and veterinary technology programs based on academic prerequisites, placement tests, and space availability. Interview recommended for allied health, animal science, dental hygiene, nursing programs.

2008-2009 Annual costs. Tuition/fees: $3,018; $8,262 out-of-state. Per-credit charge: $90 in-state; $265 out-of-state. Out of state students pay an additional $90 capital outlay fee. Books/supplies: $850. Personal expenses: $2,159.

Financial aid. Non-need-based: Scholarships awarded for academics, state residency.

Application procedures. Admission: No deadline. No application fee. Admission notification on a rolling basis. **Financial aid:** Priority date 3/1; no closing date. FAFSA, institutional form required. Applicants notified on a rolling basis starting 5/15; must reply within 2 week(s) of notification.

Academics. Systemwide core curriculum to ensure ease of transfer. **Special study options:** Cooperative education, distance learning, double major, dual enrollment of high school students, ESL, honors, independent study, internships, liberal arts/career combination, student-designed major, study abroad, weekend college. Old Dominion University Teletechnet degree programs. **Credit/placement by examination:** AP, CLEP, IB, institutional tests. Maximum of 75% of credit hours required for program may be awarded through CLEP. 25% of requirements must be completed at institution. **Support services:** Learning center, reduced course load, remedial instruction, tutoring, writing center.

Majors. Agriculture: Horticultural science. **Business:** Accounting, business admin, international, management information systems, office management, purchasing, real estate, tourism/travel. **Communications:** General. **Computer sciences:** General, computer science, programming. **Education:** Art, early childhood. **Engineering:** Civil. **Engineering technology:** Architectural, civil, drafting, electrical. **Family/consumer sciences:** Institutional food production. **Health:** Clinical lab assistant, clinical lab technology, dental hygiene, EMT paramedic, medical radiologic technology/radiation therapy, medical records technology, physical therapy assistant, respiratory therapy technology, substance abuse counseling, veterinary technology/assistant. **Interdisciplinary:** Biological/physical sciences, biopsychology, gerontology. **Legal studies:** Paralegal. **Liberal arts:** Arts/sciences. **Math:** General. **Mechanic/repair:** Aircraft, automotive, electronics/electrical, heating/ac/refrig. **Parks/recreation:** Facilities management. **Protective services:** Fire safety technology, fire services admin, law enforcement admin, security services. **Psychology:** General. **Public administration:** Human services. **Transportation:** Aviation. **Visual/performing arts:** Commercial photography, commercial/advertising art, interior design, photography, studio arts.

Computing on campus. 2,000 workstations in library, computer center.

Student life. Activities: Bands, choral groups, dance, drama, international student organizations, music ensembles, musical theater, student government, student newspaper, symphony orchestra, TV station, honor societies, African American student organizations, religious groups, Korean and Vietnamese student organizations, data processing management club, art association, physical therapist assistants club, Omega Engineering Students.

Athletics. Intramural: Basketball, football (tackle), soccer, volleyball.

Student services. Career counseling, veterans' counselor. **Physically disabled:** Services for visually, hearing impaired. **Transfer:** Transfer adviser, college fairs on campus for students transferring to 4-year colleges.

Contact. Phone: (703) 323-3000
Northern Virginia Community College, 4001 Wakefield Chapel Road, Annandale, VA 22003-3796

Patrick Henry Community College

Martinsville, Virginia
www.ph.vccs.edu **CB code: 5549**

- Public 2-year community college
- Commuter campus in large town

General. Founded in 1962. Regionally accredited. **Enrollment:** 2,948 degree-seeking undergraduates. **Degrees:** 130 associate awarded. **Location:** 50 miles from Roanoke, 50 miles from Greensboro, North Carolina. **Calendar:** Semester, limited summer session. **Full-time faculty:** 50 total. **Part-time faculty:** 113 total. **Special facilities:** Southern history collection, Virginia literature collection, fine arts theater.

Student profile.

Out-of-state:	1%	**25 or older:**	50%

Basis for selection. Open admission. High school diploma or GED required for some programs.

2008-2009 Annual costs. Tuition/fees: $2,640; $7,804 out-of-state. Per-credit charge: $82 in-state; $254 out-of-state. Out of state students pay an additional $90 capital outlay fee. Books/supplies: $500. Personal expenses: $840.

Financial aid. Need-based: Need-based aid available for part-time students.

Application procedures. Admission: Priority date 8/1; no deadline. No application fee. Admission notification on a rolling basis beginning on or about 2/1. Deadline for nursing applicants March 1. **Financial aid:** Priority date 6/1; no closing date. FAFSA required. Applicants notified on a rolling basis starting 6/15.

Academics. System-wide core curriculum to ensure ease of transfer. **Special study options:** Cooperative education, distance learning, double major, dual enrollment of high school students, independent study, internships, teacher certification program, weekend college. Bachelor's degree programs available on campus. License preparation in nursing. **Credit/placement by examination:** CLEP, institutional tests. 12 credit hours maximum toward associate degree. **Support services:** Learning center, pre-admission summer program, reduced course load, remedial instruction, study skills assistance, tutoring, writing center.

Majors. Business: Accounting, business admin. **Computer sciences:** General, programming. **Engineering technology:** Drafting. **Legal studies:** Paralegal. **Liberal arts:** Arts/sciences.

Computing on campus. 500 workstations in library, computer center. Commuter students can connect to campus network. Online library, helpline, repair service available.

Student life. Activities: Choral groups, drama, musical theater, student government, student newspaper, TV station, Black student association, Phi Theta Kappa, campus awareness network, nurses association.

Athletics. Intercollegiate: Baseball M, basketball M, soccer M, softball M. **Intramural:** Basketball, football (tackle) M, soccer, softball, table tennis, tennis, volleyball. **Team name:** Patriots.

Student services. Adult student services, career counseling, student employment services, personal counseling, placement for graduates, veterans' counselor. **Physically disabled:** Services for visually, speech, hearing impaired. **Transfer:** Transfer adviser, college fairs on campus for students transferring to 4-year colleges.

Contact. E-mail: ttisdale@ph.vccs.edu
Phone: (276) 656-0325 Toll-free number: (800) 232-7997
Fax: (276) 656-0352
Graham Valentine, Admissions Counselor, Patrick Henry Community College, Box 5311, Martinsville, VA 24115-5311

Paul D. Camp Community College

Franklin, Virginia
www.pc.vccs.edu **CB code: 5557**

- Public 2-year community college
- Commuter campus in small town

General. Founded in 1970. Regionally accredited. Campuses in Franklin and Suffolk, site in Smithsfield. **Enrollment:** 746 degree-seeking undergraduates. **Degrees:** 124 associate awarded. **Location:** 50 miles from Norfolk.

Calendar: Semester, limited summer session. **Full-time faculty:** 23 total. **Part-time faculty:** 60 total. **Class size:** 87% < 20, 11% 20-39, 2% 40-49.

Transfer out. Colleges most students transferred to 2008: Old Dominion University, Christopher Newport University, Norfolk State University.

Basis for selection. Open admission, but selective for some programs. Limited enrollment to nursing programs. **Homeschooled:** Student must provide Admissions and Records Office current copy of signed home school agreement between appropriate school system and authorizing parent or guardian.

High school preparation. Recommended units include English 4, mathematics 2, social studies 2, history 2, science 2 (laboratory 2) and foreign language 1.

2008-2009 Annual costs. Tuition/fees: $2,585; $7,749 out-of-state. Per-credit charge: $82 in-state; $254 out-of-state. Out of state students pay an additional $90 capital outlay fee. Books/supplies: $500. Personal expenses: $900.

Financial aid. Need-based: Need-based aid available for part-time students. Work-study available nights and for part-time students.

Application procedures. Admission: Priority date 8/1; no deadline. No application fee. Admission notification on a rolling basis. **Financial aid:** Priority date 6/1; no closing date. FAFSA required. Applicants notified on a rolling basis starting 8/1; must reply within 2 week(s) of notification.

Academics. Special study options: Cross-registration, distance learning, dual enrollment of high school students, honors, independent study, internships. License preparation in nursing, real estate. **Credit/placement by examination:** AP, CLEP, institutional tests. 52 credit hours maximum toward associate degree. **Support services:** Learning center, pre-admission summer program, reduced course load, remedial instruction, study skills assistance, tutoring.

Majors. Business: Administrative services, business admin, office management. **Computer sciences:** General. **Education:** General. **Engineering technology:** Drafting, electrical. **Health:** Nursing (RN). **Interdisciplinary:** Biological/physical sciences. **Mechanic/repair:** Electronics/electrical. **Protective services:** Police science.

Most popular majors. Business/marketing 22%, computer/information sciences 13%, interdisciplinary studies 6%, liberal arts 37%, security/protective services 18%.

Computing on campus. 100 workstations in library, computer center. Online course registration, online library available.

Student life. Freshman orientation: Mandatory. Preregistration for classes offered. **Activities:** Student government, student newspaper, honor societies, Circle K.

Athletics. Intramural: Volleyball.

Student services. Career counseling, student employment services, personal counseling, placement for graduates, veterans' counselor. **Transfer:** Pre-admission transcript evaluation for new students. College fairs on campus for students transferring to 4-year colleges.

Contact. Phone: (757) 569-6700 Fax: (757) 569-6795
Monette Williams, Director of Student Development Services, Paul D. Camp Community College, 100 North College Drive, Franklin, VA 23851-0737

Piedmont Virginia Community College

Charlottesville, Virginia — **CB member**
www.pvcc.edu — **CB code: 5561**

- Public 2-year community college
- Commuter campus in large town

General. Founded in 1969. Regionally accredited. **Enrollment:** 3,138 degree-seeking undergraduates. **Degrees:** 265 associate awarded. **ROTC:** Army, Air Force. **Location:** 70 miles from Richmond. **Calendar:** Semester, limited summer session. **Full-time faculty:** 62 total. **Part-time faculty:** 198 total. **Class size:** 54% < 20, 45% 20-39, 1% 40-49. **Partnerships:** Formal partnerships with local businesses, including nursing/retirement home and hospitals.

Student profile.

Out-of-state:	5%	**25 or older:**	35%

Transfer out. Colleges most students transferred to 2008: University of Virginia, James Madison University, Virginia Commonwealth University, Virginia Polytech and State University, Old Dominion University.

Basis for selection. Open admission, but selective for some programs. Special requirements for nursing program; interview recommended. **Homeschooled:** Students must meet with Dean of Student Services prior to enrolling.

2008-2009 Annual costs. Tuition/fees: $2,645; $7,829 out-of-state. Per-credit charge: $82 in-state; $254 out-of-state. Out of state students pay an additional $90 capital outlay fee. Books/supplies: $950. Personal expenses: $1,908.

2007-2008 Financial aid. Need-based: Need-based aid available for part-time students. Work-study available nights, weekends and for part-time students. **Non-need-based:** Scholarships awarded for academics.

Application procedures. Admission: No deadline. No application fee. Application must be submitted online. Admission notification on a rolling basis. Accepted applicants to nursing program must reply within 10 days. **Financial aid:** No deadline. FAFSA required. Applicants notified on a rolling basis starting 4/1.

Academics. System-wide core curriculum to ensure ease of transfer. **Special study options:** Accelerated study, cooperative education, distance learning, dual enrollment of high school students, ESL, honors, independent study, internships, weekend college. License preparation in aviation, nursing, paramedic, real estate. **Credit/placement by examination:** AP, CLEP, institutional tests. Must obtain 25% of degree requirement credits at PVCC. **Support services:** Learning center, reduced course load, remedial instruction, study skills assistance, tutoring, writing center.

Majors. Business: General, business admin. **Computer sciences:** General. **Construction:** Carpentry, electrician, lineworker, masonry, plumbing. **Education:** General. **Engineering:** General. **Engineering technology:** Electrical, industrial, mechanical. **Health:** EMT paramedic, nursing (RN). **Interdisciplinary:** Biological/physical sciences. **Liberal arts:** Arts/sciences. **Protective services:** Police science. **Science technology:** Biological. **Visual/performing arts:** General.

Most popular majors. Business/marketing 21%, education 8%, engineering/engineering technologies 7%, health sciences 28%, liberal arts 28%.

Computing on campus. 124 workstations in library, computer center. Online course registration, online library, helpline, wireless network available.

Student life. Freshman orientation: Mandatory. Preregistration for classes offered. Six-week student development program for first-time students in their first semester. **Activities:** Choral groups, dance, drama, international student organizations, music ensembles, student government, student newspaper, Black student alliance, Phi Theta Kappa, Christian Fellowship Organization, Ambassadors club, engineering club, Masquers club, chemistry club.

Athletics. Intramural: Golf, soccer, tennis.

Student services. Adult student services, career counseling, services for economically disadvantaged, student employment services, financial aid counseling, personal counseling, placement for graduates, veterans' counselor. **Physically disabled:** Services for visually, speech, hearing impaired. **Transfer:** Transfer adviser, college fairs on campus for students transferring to 4-year colleges.

Contact. E-mail: admissions@pvcc.edu
Phone: (434) 961-6551 Fax: (434) 961-5425
Lorraine Conca, Registrar, Piedmont Virginia Community College, 501 College Drive, Charlottesville, VA 22902-7589

Rappahannock Community College

Glenns, Virginia
www.rappahannock.edu — **CB code: 5590**

- Public 2-year community college
- Commuter campus in rural community

General. Founded in 1970. Regionally accredited. **Enrollment:** 1,612 degree-seeking undergraduates. **Degrees:** 164 associate awarded. **Location:** 60 miles from Richmond. **Calendar:** Semester, limited summer session. **Full-time faculty:** 30 total. **Part-time faculty:** 100 total.

Transfer out. Colleges most students transferred to 2008: Old Dominion University.

Basis for selection. Open admission. In-house test used for assessment purposes.

2008-2009 Annual costs. Tuition/fees: $2,615; $7,779 out-of-state. Per-credit charge: $82 in-state; $254 out-of-state. Out of state students pay an additional $90 capital outlay fee. Books/supplies: $690. Personal expenses: $1,500.

Financial aid. Need-based: Need-based aid available for part-time students.

Application procedures. Admission: No deadline. No application fee. Admission notification on a rolling basis. **Financial aid:** Priority date 5/15; no closing date. FAFSA, institutional form required. Applicants notified on a rolling basis starting 6/30.

Academics. Special study options: Cooperative education, cross-registration, distance learning, double major, dual enrollment of high school students, independent study, internships, liberal arts/career combination. Bachelor's degree programs available on campus. License preparation in nursing. **Credit/placement by examination:** AP, CLEP, institutional tests. **Support services:** Learning center, reduced course load, remedial instruction, study skills assistance, tutoring.

Majors. Business: Accounting, accounting/business management, business admin. **Computer sciences:** Information systems. **Education:** General. **Engineering technology:** General, electrical, electromechanical. **Health:** Nursing (RN). **Liberal arts:** Arts/sciences. **Protective services:** Criminal justice.

Computing on campus. 48 workstations in library, computer center. Online course registration, online library available.

Student life. Freshman orientation: Mandatory. Preregistration for classes offered. **Activities:** Student government, Phi Theta Kappa Honors Society.

Athletics. Intramural: Baseball M, basketball M, bowling, softball W, table tennis, tennis, volleyball.

Student services. Adult student services, career counseling, services for economically disadvantaged, student employment services, financial aid counseling, personal counseling, placement for graduates, veterans' counselor. **Physically disabled:** Services for visually, speech, hearing impaired. **Transfer:** Transfer adviser, college fairs on campus for students transferring to 4-year colleges.

Contact. Phone: (804) 758-6700 Fax: (804) 758-3852
Felicia Packett, Registrar, Rappahannock Community College, 12745 College Drive, Glenns, VA 23149-2616

Richard Bland College

Petersburg, Virginia — **CB member**
www.rbc.edu — **CB code: 5574**

- Public 2-year junior and liberal arts college
- Commuter campus in small city
- Application essay required

General. Founded in 1960. Regionally accredited. General education program prepares students to transfer with junior status to a wide variety of public and private institutions located in Virginia. Affiliated with The College of William and Mary. Only two-year residential college in Virginia. **Enrollment:** 1,310 degree-seeking undergraduates; 324 non-degree-seeking students. **Degrees:** 174 associate awarded. **ROTC:** Army. **Location:** 3 miles from Petersburg, 25 miles from Richmond. **Calendar:** Semester, limited summer session. **Full-time faculty:** 33 total; 48% have terminal degrees, 12% minority, 58% women. **Part-time faculty:** 28 total; 7% have terminal degrees, 11% minority, 54% women. **Special facilities:** Nature trail, Civil War sites.

Student profile. Among degree-seeking undergraduates, 597 enrolled as first-time, first-year students.

Part-time:	23%	**Hispanic American:**	3%
Out-of-state:	2%	**Native American:**	1%
Women:	63%	**25 or older:**	9%
African American:	27%	**Live on campus:**	15%
Asian American:	3%		

Transfer out. 53% of students enrolled in the transfer program go on to 4-year colleges. **Colleges most students transferred to 2008:** Virginia Commonwealth University, College of William and Mary, James Madison University, Longwood University, Virginia Tech.

Basis for selection. Academic record most important; test scores, essay also important; recommendations, extracurricular activities, interview considered. 2.0 GPA required for all commuter students, 2.5 GPA for residential students. Students who wish to live on campus must have at least a 2.5 GPA to be considered. Commuter students must have a 2.0 GPA or higher to be considered. SAT or ACT recommended. All incoming students who have not completed college-level course work in English and/or mathematics must take the COMPASS placement tests. Interview recommended depending on GPA. **Homeschooled:** Transcript of courses and grades required. GED or SAT required. SAT scores must be equal to or greater than the mean score for current RBC students. **Learning Disabled:** Students eligible for ADA should contact the Division of Student Affairs one month prior to the start of classes to request services.

High school preparation. 13 units required. Required units include English 4, mathematics 3, history 2, science 2 and foreign language 2.

2008-2009 Annual costs. Tuition/fees: $3,048; $11,638 out-of-state. Per-credit charge: $100 in-state; $456 out-of-state. Room only: $8,400. Books/supplies: $1,000. Personal expenses: $1,200.

2007-2008 Financial aid. Need-based: Need-based aid available for part-time students. **Non-need-based:** Scholarships awarded for academics.

Application procedures. Admission: Priority date 5/15; deadline 8/15 (receipt date). $20 fee, may be waived for applicants with need. Admission notification on a rolling basis beginning on or about 2/1. Students are admitted before completing high school, cannot be considered as full-time first-time. They are considered as part of the dual enrollment program. **Financial aid:** Priority date 5/1; no closing date. FAFSA, institutional form required. Applicants notified by 6/1; must reply within 2 week(s) of notification.

Academics. Special study options: Dual enrollment of high school students. Educational trips abroad during spring break and summer session for academic credit. **Credit/placement by examination:** AP, CLEP, institutional tests. 30 credit hours maximum toward associate degree. **Support services:** Reduced course load, remedial instruction, study skills assistance, tutoring, writing center.

Majors. Liberal arts: Arts/sciences.

Computing on campus. 100 workstations in dormitories, library, computer center, student center. Dormitories wired for high-speed internet access and linked to campus network. Commuter students can connect to campus network. Online library, wireless network available.

Student life. Freshman orientation: Available. Preregistration for classes offered. One-day program. **Policies:** Campus-wide honor code observed. **Housing:** Coed dorms available. $500 nonrefundable deposit, deadline 5/15. **Activities:** Campus ministries, choral groups, dance, drama, international student organizations, literary magazine, student government, student newspaper, Spanish club, Gay Lesbian Bisexual Transgender Alliance, Student Ambassadors, wellness club.

Athletics. Intramural: Basketball, cheerleading W, softball, tennis, volleyball.

Student services. Financial aid counseling. **Physically disabled:** Services for visually, speech, hearing impaired. **Transfer:** Pre-admission transcript evaluation for new students. Transfer adviser, college fairs on campus for students transferring to 4-year colleges.

Contact. E-mail: admit@rbc.edu
Phone: (804) 862-6249 Fax: (804) 862-6490
Randy Dean, Assistant Provost for Student Activities, Richard Bland College, 11301 Johnson Road, Petersburg, VA 23805

Southside Virginia Community College

Alberta, Virginia
www.sv.vccs.edu — **CB code: 5660**

- Public 2-year community college
- Commuter campus in rural community
- Interview required

General. Founded in 1970. Regionally accredited. Additional campuses at John H. Daniel Campus, Keysville, VA; Campus Without Walls, Emporia, VA. **Enrollment:** 2,661 degree-seeking undergraduates. **Degrees:** 328 associate awarded. **ROTC:** Army. **Location:** 70 miles from Richmond. **Calendar:** Semester, limited summer session. **Full-time faculty:** 84 total. **Part-time faculty:** 214 total. **Special facilities:** Nature trail, fitness trail.

Student profile.

Out-of-state:	1%	25 or older:	36%

Transfer out. **Colleges most students transferred to 2008:** Longwood University, Old Dominion University, Saint Paul's College, Virginia Commonwealth University.

Basis for selection. Open admission, but selective for some programs. National League for Nursing Pre-Admissions Examination required for nursing applicants. Psychological Services Bureau Revised Aptitude for Practical Nursing Examination required for practical nursing applicants. **Home-schooled:** If not enrolled in program leading to completion credential, student should obtain GED.

2008-2009 Annual costs. Tuition/fees: $2,660; $7,824 out-of-state. Per-credit charge: $82 in-state; $254 out-of-state. Out of state students pay an additional $90 capital outlay fee. Books/supplies: $1,040. Personal expenses: $2,340.

2007-2008 Financial aid. **Need-based:** 98% of total undergraduate aid awarded as scholarships/grants, 2% as loans/jobs. Need-based aid available for part-time students. Work-study available nights and for part-time students. **Non-need-based:** Scholarships awarded for academics.

Application procedures. **Admission:** No deadline. No application fee. Admission notification on a rolling basis. **Financial aid:** Priority date 6/1, closing date 8/1. FAFSA required. Applicants notified on a rolling basis starting 6/15.

Academics. System-wide core curriculum to ensure ease of transfer. **Special study options:** Cross-registration, distance learning, dual enrollment of high school students, honors, internships, study abroad. Cooperative programs in respiratory therapy with J. Sargeant Reynolds Community College, medical laboratory program with Central Virginia Community College. Bachelor's degree programs available on campus. License preparation in nursing. **Credit/placement by examination:** AP, CLEP, institutional tests. 45 credit hours maximum toward associate degree. **Support services:** GED preparation and test center, reduced course load, remedial instruction, study skills assistance, tutoring.

Majors. **Business:** Administrative services, business admin, management science. **Computer sciences:** General. **Education:** General. **Engineering technology:** Drafting, electrical. **Health:** Clinical lab technology, nursing (RN), respiratory therapy technology. **Interdisciplinary:** Biological/physical sciences. **Liberal arts:** Arts/sciences. **Protective services:** Police science. **Public administration:** Human services.

Most popular majors. Business/marketing 18%, health sciences 22%, liberal arts 47%, security/protective services 10%.

Computing on campus. 200 workstations in library, computer center.

Student life. **Freshman orientation:** Mandatory, $78 fee. Preregistration for classes offered. **Activities:** Choral groups, drama, music ensembles, student government, Phi Theta Kappa, Criminal Justice Organization, Phi Beta Lambda, Lambda Alpha Epsilon, Alpha Delta Omega.

Athletics. **Intramural:** Basketball, softball, table tennis, tennis, volleyball.

Student services. Career counseling, financial aid counseling, personal counseling, veterans' counselor. **Transfer:** Pre-admission transcript evaluation for new students. College fairs on campus for students transferring to 4-year colleges.

Contact. E-mail: rhina.jones@sv.vccs.edu
Phone: (434) 949-1000 Fax: (434) 949-7863
Brent Richey, Dean of Admissions, Records and Institutional Research, Southside Virginia Community College, 109 Campus Drive, Alberta, VA 23821

Southwest Virginia Community College

Richlands, Virginia
www.sw.edu **CB code: 5659**

- Public 2-year community college
- Commuter campus in small town

General. Founded in 1967. Regionally accredited. **Enrollment:** 2,494 degree-seeking undergraduates; 1,490 non-degree-seeking students. **Degrees:** 296 associate awarded. **Location:** 45 miles from Bluefield and Bristol. **Calendar:** Semester, extensive summer session. **Full-time faculty:** 69 total; 1% minority, 39% women. **Part-time faculty:** 177 total. **Class size:** 83% < 20, 14% 20-39, 2% 40-49, 2% 50-99. **Special facilities:** Community center.

Student profile. Among degree-seeking undergraduates, 41% enrolled in a transfer program, 59% enrolled in a vocational program, 1% already have a bachelor's degree or higher, 727 enrolled as first-time, first-year students, 103 transferred in from other institutions.

Part-time:	49%	Women:	58%
Out-of-state:	12%	25 or older:	55%

Transfer out. 51% of students enrolled in the transfer program go on to 4-year colleges. **Colleges most students transferred to 2008:** Virginia Tech, Radford University, University of Virginia at Wise, East Tennessee State University.

Basis for selection. Open admission, but selective for some programs. Special requirements for engineering and health programs. Students are required to take COMPASS, ASSET or some other placement test with the scores used to determine if students will need to take developmental English, mathematics or reading. Interview required for full-time.

High school preparation. Subject and unit requirements vary with degree programs.

2008-2009 Annual costs. Tuition/fees: $2,630; $7,794 out-of-state. Per-credit charge: $82 in-state; $254 out-of-state. Out of state students pay an additional $72 capital outlay fee for 24 credit hours. Books/supplies: $1,000. Personal expenses: $1,700.

2008-2009 Financial aid. All financial aid based on need. Need-based aid available for part-time students. Work-study available for part-time students.

Application procedures. **Admission:** No deadline. No application fee. Admission notification on a rolling basis. Applicants for nursing and allied health programs must apply by January 15 and reply within 2 weeks of acceptance. No deferred admission for these programs. **Financial aid:** Priority date 5/30; no closing date. FAFSA, institutional form required. Applicants notified on a rolling basis starting 7/1.

Academics. **Special study options:** Accelerated study, cooperative education, distance learning, double major, dual enrollment of high school students, honors, independent study, internships. Bachelor's degree programs available on campus. **Credit/placement by examination:** AP, CLEP. **Support services:** Learning center, pre-admission summer program, reduced course load, remedial instruction, study skills assistance, tutoring, writing center.

Majors. **Business:** General, accounting, administrative services, business admin, managerial economics. **Computer sciences:** General. **Conservation:** Environmental studies. **Education:** General, early childhood. **Engineering:** General, electrical. **Engineering technology:** General, CAD/CADD, mining, software. **Health:** EMT paramedic, health services, medical radiologic technology/radiation therapy, medical secretary, nursing (RN), radiologic technology/medical imaging, respiratory therapy assistant. **Liberal arts:** Arts/sciences. **Protective services:** Corrections, police science. **Public administration:** Human services.

Most popular majors. Business/marketing 7%, education 12%, health sciences 35%, liberal arts 33%.

Computing on campus. 150 workstations in library, computer center. Commuter students can connect to campus network. Online course registration, online library, wireless network available.

Student life. **Freshman orientation:** Mandatory, $88 fee. Preregistration for classes offered. **Activities:** Jazz band, choral groups, international student organizations, literary magazine, music ensembles, student government, student newspaper, Intervoice Club, Black Student Union, Phi Theta Kappa, Lion's Club, Phi Beta Lambda, Lambda Alpha Epsilon, Helping Minds, Campus Crusade for Christ, Young Republicans, Young Democrats.

Athletics. **Intercollegiate:** Baseball M, basketball M, cheerleading M. **Intramural:** Baseball M, basketball M, racquetball. **Team name:** Eagles.

Student services. Career counseling, services for economically disadvantaged, student employment services, financial aid counseling, health services, minority student services, personal counseling, placement for graduates, veterans' counselor. **Physically disabled:** Services for visually, speech, hearing impaired. **Transfer:** Transfer adviser, college fairs on campus for students transferring to 4-year colleges.

Contact. E-mail: admissions@sw.edu
Phone: (276) 964-7238 Toll-free number: (800) 822-7822
Fax: (276) 964-7716
Jim Farris, Director of Admissions and Counseling, Southwest Virginia Community College, PO Box SVCC, Richlands, VA 24641-1101

TESST College of Technology: Alexandria
Alexandria, Virginia
www.tesst.com

- For-profit 2-year technical college
- Small city

General. Accredited by ACCSCT. **Calendar:** Semester.

Contact. Phone: (703) 354-1005
Executive Director, 6315 Bren Mar Drive, Alexandria, VA 22312

Thomas Nelson Community College
Hampton, Virginia
www.tncc.edu **CB code: 5793**

- Public 2-year community college
- Commuter campus in small city

General. Founded in 1967. Regionally accredited. **Enrollment:** 7,571 degree-seeking undergraduates. **Degrees:** 761 associate awarded. **ROTC:** Army. **Location:** 20 miles from Norfolk, 35 miles from Virginia Beach. **Calendar:** Semester, extensive summer session. **Full-time faculty:** 109 total. **Part-time faculty:** 335 total.

Transfer out. Colleges most students transferred to 2008: Christopher Newport University, Old Dominion University, Norfolk State University, Hampton University.

Basis for selection. Open admission, but selective for some programs. Special requirements for nursing program. **Homeschooled:** Must be 18 or have GED.

High school preparation. Nursing program requires specific high school units.

2008-2009 Annual costs. Tuition/fees: $2,626; $7,790 out-of-state. Per-credit charge: $82 in-state; $264 out-of-state. Out of state students pay an additional $90 capital outlay fee. Books/supplies: $800. Personal expenses: $1,600.

2008-2009 Financial aid. Need-based: Need-based aid available for part-time students. Work-study available nights and for part-time students.

Application procedures. Admission: No deadline. No application fee. Application must be submitted online. Admission notification on a rolling basis. **Financial aid:** Priority date 5/1; no closing date. FAFSA, institutional form required. Applicants notified on a rolling basis starting 6/1; must reply within 2 week(s) of notification.

Academics. System-wide core curriculum to ensure ease of transfer, 2-2 program available. **Special study options:** Accelerated study, cooperative education, cross-registration, distance learning, dual enrollment of high school students, ESL, honors, independent study, internships, weekend college. License preparation in nursing. **Credit/placement by examination:** AP, CLEP, institutional tests. SAT Critical Reading or ACT English tests may be substituted for institutional placement examinations if scores high enough. **Support services:** Learning center, remedial instruction, study skills assistance, tutoring, writing center.

Majors. Business: Accounting, business admin, management science, office management. **Computer sciences:** General, computer graphics, computer science, information systems, networking, programming. **Education:** Early childhood. **Engineering:** General, electrical. **Engineering technology:** CAD/CADD, electrical. **Health:** Licensed practical nurse. **Interdisciplinary:** Natural sciences. **Liberal arts:** Arts/sciences. **Mechanic/repair:** Automotive. **Protective services:** Fire services admin, law enforcement admin. **Public administration:** General, human services, social work. **Social sciences:** General. **Visual/performing arts:** Commercial/advertising art, photography, studio arts.

Computing on campus. Online library available.

Student life. Freshman orientation: Available. **Activities:** Choral groups, dance, drama, international student organizations, student government, Digital Arts Society, philosophy and religion club, science club, Phi Theta Kappa.

Athletics. Intramural: Baseball M, basketball. **Team name:** Gators.

Student services. Career counseling, student employment services, financial aid counseling, personal counseling, placement for graduates, veterans' counselor. **Physically disabled:** Services for visually, speech, hearing impaired. **Transfer:** Transfer center, transfer adviser, college fairs on campus for students transferring to 4-year colleges.

Contact. E-mail: admissions@tncc.edu
Phone: (757) 825-2800 Fax: (757) 825-2763
Vicki Richmond, Associate Vice President for Enrollment Services, Thomas Nelson Community College, Box 9407, Hampton, VA 23670

Tidewater Community College
Norfolk, Virginia **CB member**
www.tcc.vccs.edu **CB code: 5226**

- Public 2-year community college
- Commuter campus in large city

General. Founded in 1968. Regionally accredited. Multi-location institution with campuses at Portsmouth, Virginia Beach, Chesapeake, and Norfolk. **Enrollment:** 22,852 degree-seeking undergraduates. **Degrees:** 2,204 associate awarded. **Calendar:** Semester, extensive summer session. **Full-time faculty:** 325 total; 16% minority, 47% women. **Part-time faculty:** 894 total. **Class size:** 45% < 20, 54% 20-39, less than 1% 40-49, less than 1% 50-99. **Special facilities:** Visual arts center, observatory.

Student profile. Among degree-seeking undergraduates, 2,169 transferred in from other institutions.

Out-of-state:	10%	**25 or older:**	53%

Transfer out. Colleges most students transferred to 2008: Old Dominion University, Norfolk State University, Virginia Wesleyan College, Christopher Newport University.

Basis for selection. Open admission, but selective for some programs. Special requirements for health science programs. ACT required for placement for students enrolling in English or mathematics courses. Interview required for medical technologies and other limited enrollment programs. **Homeschooled:** Transcript of courses and grades, letter of recommendation (nonparent) required.

2008-2009 Annual costs. Tuition/fees: $2,846; $8,010 out-of-state. Per-credit charge: $82 in-state; $254 out-of-state. Out of state students pay an additional $90 capital outlay fee. Books/supplies: $1,200. Personal expenses: $710.

2007-2008 Financial aid. All financial aid based on need. Need-based aid available for part-time students.

Application procedures. Admission: No deadline. No application fee. Admission notification on a rolling basis. **Financial aid:** Priority date 4/1; no closing date. FAFSA required. Applicants notified on a rolling basis starting 4/1.

Academics. System-wide core curriculum to ensure ease of transfer. **Special study options:** Cooperative education, cross-registration, distance learning, double major, dual enrollment of high school students, ESL, honors, independent study, internships, study abroad, weekend college. Member Virginia Tidewater Consortium of Higher Education. License preparation in real estate. **Credit/placement by examination:** AP, CLEP, institutional tests. **Support services:** GED preparation and test center, learning center, reduced course load, remedial instruction, study skills assistance, tutoring, writing center.

Majors. Agriculture: Business technology, horticulture. **Business:** Accounting, administrative services, banking/financial services, business admin, hospitality admin, real estate, sales/distribution. **Computer sciences:** General, networking, systems analysis. **Conservation:** Environmental studies. **Education:** General, early childhood, teacher assistance. **Engineering:** General, industrial. **Engineering technology:** CAD/CADD, civil, drafting, electromechanical, occupational safety, quality control. **Foreign languages:** American Sign Language. **Health:** EMT paramedic, medical radiologic technology/radiation therapy, medical records technology, nursing (RN), occupational therapy assistant, physical therapy assistant, respiratory therapy technology. **Interdisciplinary:** Biological/physical sciences. **Legal studies:** Paralegal. **Liberal arts:** Arts/sciences. **Mechanic/repair:** Automotive, industrial. **Parks/recreation:** General, facilities management. **Personal/culinary services:** Culinary arts. **Production:** Welding. **Protective services:** Firefighting. **Public administration:** General. **Social sciences:** General. **Transportation:** Truck/bus/commercial vehicle. **Visual/performing arts:** Commercial/advertising art, graphic design, interior design, multimedia, photography, studio arts.

Most popular majors. Biological/life sciences 8%, business/marketing 21%, engineering/engineering technologies 8%, health sciences 11%, liberal arts 22%, social sciences 14%.

Computing on campus. Commuter students can connect to campus network. Online course registration, online library, wireless network available.

Two-Year Colleges

Student life. Freshman orientation: Available. Preregistration for classes offered. 3-hour sessions held on each campus. **Activities:** Choral groups, drama, music ensembles, student government, student newspaper, honorary societies, Black Student Alliance, Inter-Varsity Christian Fellowship, student nurses association.

Athletics. Intramural: Basketball. **Team name:** Storm.

Student services. Adult student services, career counseling, student employment services, financial aid counseling, personal counseling, placement for graduates, veterans' counselor, women's services. **Physically disabled:** Services for visually, speech, hearing impaired. **Transfer:** Transfer adviser, college fairs on campus for students transferring to 4-year colleges.

Contact. E-mail: tcc@tcc.vccs.edu
Phone: (757) 822-1100 Fax: (757) 822-1247
Michael Summers, Vice President for Academic and Student Affairs, Tidewater Community College, 7000 College Drive/Portsmouth Campus, Portsmouth, VA 23703

Virginia Highlands Community College

Abingdon, Virginia
www.vhcc.edu **CB code: 5927**

- Public 2-year community college
- Commuter campus in small town

General. Founded in 1967. Regionally accredited. **Enrollment:** 2,650 degree-seeking undergraduates. **Degrees:** 225 associate awarded. **Location:** 120 miles from Roanoke. **Calendar:** Semester, extensive summer session. **Full-time faculty:** 45 total. **Part-time faculty:** 149 total. **Special facilities:** Greenhouse.

Student profile.

Out-of-state:	11%	**25 or older:**	36%

Transfer out. Colleges most students transferred to 2008: East Tennessee State University, Virginia Tech, Radford University, Old Dominion University, University of Virginia at Wise.

Basis for selection. Open admission, but selective for some programs. COMPASS required for placement. Paramedic, nursing, radiography, physical therapy, dental hygiene, and medical laboratory technology programs have special requirements. **Learning Disabled:** Developmental courses are to be taken by students who test below set standards on COMPASS and/or ASSET test.

High school preparation. 12 units recommended. Recommended units include English 4, mathematics 2, social studies 4, science 1 (laboratory 1).

2008-2009 Annual costs. Tuition/fees: $2,675; $7,839 out-of-state. Per-credit charge: $82 in-state; $254 out-of-state. Out of state students pay an additional $90 capital outlay fee. Books/supplies: $750. Personal expenses: $1,272.

2007-2008 Financial aid. Need-based: 90% of total undergraduate aid awarded as scholarships/grants, 10% as loans/jobs. Work-study available for part-time students.

Application procedures. Admission: No deadline. No application fee. Admission notification on a rolling basis. **Financial aid:** No deadline. FAFSA, institutional form required. Applicants notified on a rolling basis starting 5/1.

Academics. Special study options: Cooperative education, distance learning, double major, dual enrollment of high school students, independent study, internships, liberal arts/career combination. License preparation in nursing, paramedic, real estate. **Credit/placement by examination:** AP, CLEP, institutional tests. 45 credit hours maximum toward associate degree. **Support services:** Learning center, pre-admission summer program, reduced course load, remedial instruction, tutoring.

Majors. Agriculture: Farm/ranch. **Business:** Accounting, administrative services, business admin, office management. **Computer sciences:** General, data processing. **Education:** General, drama/dance. **Engineering technology:** Drafting, electrical. **Health:** Clinical lab assistant, dental hygiene, medical radiologic technology/radiation therapy, nursing (RN), physical therapy assistant. **Interdisciplinary:** Biological/physical sciences. **Legal studies:** Legal secretary. **Liberal arts:** Arts/sciences. **Protective services:** Police science. **Public administration:** Social work.

Computing on campus. 230 workstations in library, computer center, student center. Online course registration, wireless network available.

Student life. Freshman orientation: Mandatory, $68 fee. Preregistration for classes offered. **Activities:** Choral groups, drama, music ensembles, musical theater, student government, student newspaper, IMPACT club, law enforcement club, Roteract club, College Republicans, College Democrats, anglers' club, VATNP (nursing) club, National Honors Society, Christian club.

Athletics. Intramural: Basketball.

Student services. Career counseling, services for economically disadvantaged, student employment services, financial aid counseling, personal counseling, placement for graduates, veterans' counselor. **Physically disabled:** Services for visually, speech, hearing impaired. **Transfer:** Transfer adviser, college fairs on campus for students transferring to 4-year colleges.

Contact. E-mail: dbarrett@vhcc.edu
Phone: (276) 739-2460 Fax: (276) 739-2591
David Matlock, Director of Admissions, Records and Financial Aid, Virginia Highlands Community College, PO Box 828, Abingdon, VA 24212-0828

Virginia Western Community College

Roanoke, Virginia
www.virginiawestern.edu **CB code: 5868**

- Public 2-year community college
- Commuter campus in small city

General. Founded in 1966. Regionally accredited. **Enrollment:** 4,665 degree-seeking undergraduates. **Degrees:** 479 associate awarded. **Location:** 3 miles from downtown. **Calendar:** Semester, extensive summer session. **Full-time faculty:** 102 total. **Part-time faculty:** 428 total. **Special facilities:** Arboretum.

Transfer out. Colleges most students transferred to 2008: Virginia Tech, Radford University, Old Dominion University, Roanoke College, Hollins University.

Basis for selection. Open admission, but selective for some programs. Special requirements for health programs and communication design program. Interview required for health technologies. **Adult students:** SAT/ACT scores not required. **Learning Disabled:** Student Support Services/REACH program to provide accommodations for students with learning disabilities.

2008-2009 Annual costs. Tuition/fees: $2,663; $7,827 out-of-state. Per-credit charge: $82 in-state; $254 out-of-state. Out of state students pay an additional $90 capital outlay fee. Books/supplies: $550. Personal expenses: $1,200.

Financial aid. Need-based: Need-based aid available for part-time students. **Non-need-based:** Scholarships awarded for academics, state residency.

Application procedures. Admission: No deadline. No application fee. Admission notification on a rolling basis. **Financial aid:** No deadline. FAFSA required. Applicants notified on a rolling basis starting 4/1.

Academics. Special study options: Distance learning, dual enrollment of high school students, external degree, honors, independent study, internships, liberal arts/career combination, study abroad, weekend college. License preparation in dental hygiene, nursing, radiology, real estate. **Credit/placement by examination:** AP, CLEP, IB, institutional tests. **Support services:** Learning center, reduced course load, remedial instruction, study skills assistance, tutoring, writing center.

Majors. Agriculture: Horticultural science, horticulture, landscaping. **Business:** General, accounting, administrative services, banking/financial services, business admin, management information systems, office technology, real estate. **Communications technology:** General. **Computer sciences:** General, computer science. **Education:** General, early childhood, social science. **Engineering:** General. **Engineering technology:** Architectural, civil, electrical. **Family/consumer sciences:** Child care. **Health:** Dental hygiene, health services, medical radiologic technology/radiation therapy, medical secretary, mental health services, nursing (RN). **Interdisciplinary:** Biological/physical sciences, natural sciences. **Legal studies:** Legal secretary, paralegal. **Liberal arts:** Arts/sciences. **Math:** General. **Mechanic/repair:** General, heating/ac/refrig. **Personal/culinary services:** General. **Protective services:** Criminal justice, police science. **Public administration:** Human services. **Social sciences:** General. **Visual/performing arts:** Commercial/advertising art, studio arts.

Computing on campus. 100 workstations in library, computer center. Online course registration, helpline, wireless network available.

Student life. **Freshman orientation:** Mandatory. Preregistration for classes offered. **Activities:** Choral groups, drama, student government, student newspaper, minority student alliance, Christian Fellowship.

Athletics. **Intramural:** Basketball, cheerleading W.

Student services. Adult student services, alcohol/substance abuse counseling, career counseling, services for economically disadvantaged, student employment services, financial aid counseling, minority student services, personal counseling, placement for graduates, veterans' counselor. **Physically disabled:** Services for visually, speech, hearing impaired. **Learning disabled:** Comprehensive services available. **Transfer:** Transfer center, transfer adviser, college fairs on campus for students transferring to 4-year colleges.

Contact. E-mail: mpatterson@vw.vccs.edu
Phone: (540) 857-7231 Fax: (540) 857-6102
Meg Patterson, Admissions and Records Coordinator/Registrar, Virginia Western Community College, Box 14007, Roanoke, VA 24038

Wytheville Community College

Wytheville, Virginia
www.wcc.vccs.edu **CB code: 5917**

- Public 2-year community college
- Commuter campus in small town

General. Founded in 1962. Regionally accredited. **Enrollment:** 1,926 degree-seeking undergraduates. **Degrees:** 329 associate awarded. **Location:** 74 miles from Roanoke. **Calendar:** Semester, limited summer session. **Full-time faculty:** 38 total; 5% minority, 71% women. **Part-time faculty:** 131 total; 5% minority, 62% women.

Student profile. Among degree-seeking undergraduates, 28 transferred in from other institutions.

Out-of-state:	4%	**25 or older:**	44%

Basis for selection. Open admission, but selective for some programs. Limited admissions to allied health programs. High school transcripts required of all allied health applicants. Interview required for allied health, police science. **Homeschooled:** Statement describing homeschool structure and mission required.

2008-2009 Annual costs. Tuition/fees: $2,615; $7,779 out-of-state. Per-credit charge: $82 in-state; $254 out-of-state. Out of state students pay an additional $90 capital outlay fee. Books/supplies: $840. Personal expenses: $250.

2007-2008 Financial aid. All financial aid based on need. Need-based aid available for part-time students.

Application procedures. **Admission:** No deadline. No application fee. Admission notification on a rolling basis. **Financial aid:** Priority date 4/1; no closing date. FAFSA, institutional form required. Applicants notified on a rolling basis starting 5/1; must reply within 4 week(s) of notification.

Academics. **Special study options:** Distance learning, dual enrollment of high school students, honors, independent study, internships. License preparation in dental hygiene, nursing, physical therapy, radiology. **Credit/placement by examination:** AP, CLEP, institutional tests. **Support services:** Remedial instruction, tutoring.

Majors. **Business:** Accounting, administrative services, business admin, managerial economics. **Computer sciences:** Information systems. **Construction:** Carpentry, electrician, plumbing. **Education:** General. **Engineering:** Computer. **Engineering technology:** Drafting, electrical. **Family/consumer sciences:** Child care. **Health:** Clinical lab technology, dental hygiene, nursing (RN), physical therapy assistant, radiologic technology/medical imaging, respiratory therapy technology. **Interdisciplinary:** Biological/physical sciences. **Liberal arts:** Arts/sciences. **Protective services:** Police science.

Most popular majors. Education 10%, health sciences 33%, liberal arts 6%, security/protective services 13%.

Computing on campus. 133 workstations in library, computer center, student center.

Student life. **Activities:** Concert band, drama, student government, student newspaper.

Athletics. **Intramural:** Basketball, softball, table tennis, tennis, volleyball.

Student services. Career counseling, student employment services, personal counseling, placement for graduates, veterans' counselor. **Physically disabled:** Services for visually, hearing impaired. **Transfer:** College fairs on campus for students transferring to 4-year colleges.

Contact. E-mail: wcdixxs@wcc.vccs.edu
Phone: (276) 223-4700 Toll-free number: (800) 468-1195
Fax: (276) 223-4860
Sherry Dix, Registrar, Wytheville Community College, 1000 East Main Street, Wytheville, VA 24382

Washington

Bates Technical College

Tacoma, Washington
www.bates.ctc.edu
CB code: 4152

- Public 2-year technical college
- Small city

General. **Enrollment:** 1,437 degree-seeking undergraduates. **Degrees:** 165 associate awarded. **Calendar:** Quarter, extensive summer session. **Full-time faculty:** 143 total.

Basis for selection. Open admission. COMPASS required for admission. **Adult students:** SAT/ACT scores not required.

2008-2009 Annual costs. Programs range in costs from $4,245 to $5,606; cost includes tuition and fees. Books/supplies: $1,116.

Financial aid. All financial aid based on need. Need-based aid available for part-time students. Work-study available nights and for part-time students.

Application procedures. **Admission:** No deadline. $59 fee. Application must be submitted on paper. **Financial aid:** No deadline. FAFSA, institutional form required. Applicants notified on a rolling basis starting 9/7.

Academics. **Special study options:** Cooperative education, distance learning, dual enrollment of high school students, ESL, independent study, internships, teacher certification program. License preparation in dental hygiene, nursing. **Credit/placement by examination:** CLEP, IB. **Support services:** GED preparation and test center, learning center, reduced course load, remedial instruction, study skills assistance, tutoring.

Majors. **Architecture:** Technology. **Biology:** Biotechnology. **Business:** Accounting technology, administrative services, marketing, retailing. **Communications technology:** General, radio/tv. **Computer sciences:** Computer support specialist, database management, information technology, networking, programming, web page design, webmaster. **Construction:** General, carpentry, electrician, maintenance, metal building assembly. **Education:** Early childhood. **Engineering:** Architectural, civil, electrical, mechanical, surveying, textile. **Engineering technology:** General, architectural drafting, biomedical, civil drafting, computer, electrical, electrical drafting, electromechanical, industrial safety, mechanical, surveying. **Family/consumer sciences:** Institutional food production. **Health:** Dental assistant, dental lab technology, licensed practical nurse. **Legal studies:** Legal secretary. **Mechanic/repair:** General, auto body, automotive, communications systems, diesel, electronics/electrical, heating/ac/refrig, heavy equipment, industrial electronics, small engine. **Personal/culinary services:** General, cosmetic, culinary arts. **Production:** Cabinetmaking/millwright, machine tool, sheet metal, welding. **Protective services:** Fire safety technology, fire services admin, firefighting. **Science technology:** Biological. **Other:** Boat building, Wireless and advanced communications technology.

Computing on campus. Commuter students can connect to campus network. Online library available.

Student life. **Freshman orientation:** Available. Preregistration for classes offered.

Student services. Career counseling, financial aid counseling, on-campus daycare.

Contact. E-mail: registration@bates.ctc.edu
Phone: (253) 680-7002
Steve Ashpole, Admissions Director, Bates Technical College, 1101 South Yakima Avenue, Tacoma, WA 98405

Bellevue Community College

Bellevue, Washington
www.bcc.ctc.edu
CB code: 4029

- Public 2-year community college
- Commuter campus in small city

General. Founded in 1965. Regionally accredited. **Enrollment:** 5,017 degree-seeking undergraduates. **Degrees:** 1,491 associate awarded. **Location:** 12 miles from Seattle. **Calendar:** Quarter, limited summer session. **Full-time faculty:** 162 total. **Part-time faculty:** 543 total. **Special facilities:** Planetarium, National Workforce Center for Emerging Technologies, greenhouses, observatory, scanning electron microscope.

Transfer out. **Colleges most students transferred to 2008:** University of Washington, Washington State University, Central Washington University, Seattle University, Western Washington University.

Basis for selection. Open admission, but selective for some programs. Interview, essay, 2 letters of recommendation, transcripts required of applicants to allied health programs, including radiologic technology, diagnostic ultrasound, radiation therapy. **Homeschooled:** Must be at least 18 years old. **Learning Disabled:** Student may request reasonable classroom accommodations through Disability Support Services Office. Student must provide documentation from appropriate professional.

High school preparation. Allied health programs have special requirements.

2008-2009 Annual costs. Tuition/fees: $3,105; $8,319 out-of-state. Per-credit charge: $153 in-state; $433 out-of-state. Books/supplies: $924. Personal expenses: $1,968.

2007-2008 Financial aid. **Need-based:** Need-based aid available for part-time students. Work-study available nights, weekends and for part-time students. **Non-need-based:** Scholarships awarded for academics, athletics.

Application procedures. **Admission:** No deadline. $30 fee. Admission notification on a rolling basis. **Financial aid:** Priority date 4/16; no closing date. FAFSA, institutional form required. Applicants notified on a rolling basis starting 8/1.

Academics. **Special study options:** Distance learning, dual enrollment of high school students, ESL, honors, independent study, internships, study abroad. Bachelor's degree programs available on campus. **Credit/placement by examination:** AP, CLEP, institutional tests. 15 credit hours maximum toward associate degree. **Support services:** GED preparation and test center, learning center, remedial instruction, tutoring, writing center.

Majors. **Business:** Accounting, accounting technology, administrative services, business admin, marketing, office management, real estate. **Computer sciences:** General, computer graphics, database management, networking, programming, security, web page design. **Education:** Early childhood. **Health:** Medical radiologic technology/radiation therapy, nuclear medical technology, nursing (RN), sonography. **Liberal arts:** Arts/sciences. **Parks/recreation:** General. **Protective services:** Fire safety technology, fire services admin, firefighting, law enforcement admin. **Visual/performing arts:** Interior design.

Most popular majors. Business/marketing 12%, computer/information sciences 8%, health sciences 8%, liberal arts 64%.

Computing on campus. 244 workstations in library, computer center. Commuter students can connect to campus network. Online course registration, online library, helpline, student web hosting, wireless network available.

Student life. **Freshman orientation:** Available. Quarterly, prior to start of term. **Activities:** Jazz band, choral groups, dance, drama, literary magazine, music ensembles, musical theater, radio station, student government, student newspaper, TV station.

Athletics. NAIA, NJCAA. **Intercollegiate:** Baseball M, basketball, cross-country, golf M, soccer, softball W, tennis, track and field, volleyball W. **Intramural:** Badminton, basketball, racquetball, soccer W, softball W, table tennis, tennis, volleyball. **Team name:** Bulldogs.

Student services. Career counseling, services for economically disadvantaged, student employment services, financial aid counseling, health services, minority student services, on-campus daycare, personal counseling, placement for graduates, veterans' counselor, women's services. **Physically disabled:** Services for visually, speech, hearing impaired. **Transfer:** Transfer center, transfer adviser, college fairs on campus for students transferring to 4-year colleges.

Contact. E-mail: admissions@bcc.ctc.edu
Phone: (425) 564-2222 Fax: (425) 564-4065
Robin Young, Director of Admissions, Bellevue Community College, 3000 Landerholm Circle SE, Bellevue, WA 98007-6484

Bellingham Technical College

Bellingham, Washington **CB member**
www.btc.ctc.edu **CB code: 3499**

- Public 2-year technical college
- Commuter campus in small city

General. Regionally accredited. **Enrollment:** 1,698 degree-seeking undergraduates. **Degrees:** 270 associate awarded. **Location:** 90 miles from Seattle. **Calendar:** Quarter, limited summer session. **Full-time faculty:** 66 total; 6% minority, 50% women. **Part-time faculty:** 116 total. **Class size:** 84% < 20, 15% 20-39, less than 1% 40-49, less than 1% 50-99.

Student profile.

Out-of-state:	1%	**25 or older:**	52%

Basis for selection. Open admission.

2008-2009 Annual costs. Tuition/fees: $3,420. Books/supplies: $2,029. Personal expenses: $1,623.

Financial aid. All financial aid based on need. Need-based aid available for part-time students. Work-study available for part-time students.

Application procedures. Admission: No deadline. $35 fee. Application must be submitted on paper. Admission notification on a rolling basis. **Financial aid:** Priority date 4/30; no closing date. FAFSA required. Applicants notified on a rolling basis starting 7/1; must reply within 2 week(s) of notification.

Academics. Special study options: Distance learning, ESL, internships. License preparation in nursing, paramedic, real estate. **Credit/placement by examination:** CLEP, institutional tests. **Support services:** GED preparation and test center, learning center, remedial instruction, study skills assistance, tutoring.

Majors. Business: Accounting technology, executive assistant, human resources, marketing, operations. **Computer sciences:** Data entry, networking. **Conservation:** Fisheries. **Construction:** Electrician, maintenance. **Education:** Voc/tech. **Engineering technology:** Biomedical, civil, computer systems, instrumentation, manufacturing, mechanical, surveying. **Health:** Dental hygiene, EMT paramedic, insurance coding, medical radiologic technology/radiation therapy, nursing (RN), radiologic technology/medical imaging. **Legal studies:** Legal secretary. **Mechanic/repair:** Appliance, auto body, automotive, communications systems, diesel, heating/ac/refrig, industrial. **Personal/culinary services:** Chef training. **Production:** Machine tool, welding. **Other:** Process technology.

Computing on campus. 14 workstations in library. Commuter students can connect to campus network. Online course registration, online library, wireless network available.

Student life. Freshman orientation: Available. Orientation is held quarterly for new students within the month prior to students' start date. **Activities:** Student government.

Student services. Adult student services, career counseling, services for economically disadvantaged, financial aid counseling, minority student services, veterans' counselor. **Physically disabled:** Services for visually, speech, hearing impaired. **Transfer:** Pre-admission transcript evaluation for new students.

Contact. E-mail: admissions@btc.ctc.edu
Phone: (360) 785-8345 Fax: (360) 676-2798
Erin Runestrand, Director of Admissions, Bellingham Technical College, 3028 Lindbergh Avenue, Bellingham, WA 98225

Big Bend Community College

Moses Lake, Washington
www.bigbend.edu **CB code: 4024**

- Public 2-year community college
- Commuter campus in large town

General. Founded in 1962. Regionally accredited. **Enrollment:** 1,238 degree-seeking undergraduates; 655 non-degree-seeking students. **Degrees:** 319 associate awarded. **Location:** 107 miles from Spokane, 170 miles from Seattle. **Calendar:** Quarter, limited summer session. **Full-time faculty:** 55 total; 9% have terminal degrees, 7% minority, 34% women. **Part-time faculty:** 91 total; 2% have terminal degrees, 26% minority, 53% women. **Partnerships:** Formal partnership with high schools for Tech Prep programs.

Student profile. Among degree-seeking undergraduates, 56% enrolled in a transfer program, 44% enrolled in a vocational program, 1% already have a bachelor's degree or higher, 330 enrolled as first-time, first-year students, 81 transferred in from other institutions.

Part-time:	24%	**Hispanic American:**	27%
Out-of-state:	5%	**Native American:**	2%
Women:	57%	**25 or older:**	47%
African American:	1%	**Live on campus:**	5%
Asian American:	1%		

Transfer out. Colleges most students transferred to 2008: Central Washington University, Eastern Washington University, Washington State University.

Basis for selection. Open admission, but selective for some programs. Special admission criteria for aviation and nursing programs.

2008-2009 Annual costs. Tuition/fees: $2,820; $3,216 out-of-state. Per-credit charge: $79 in-state; $92 out-of-state. Room only: $2,790. Books/supplies: $984. Personal expenses: $1,560.

2007-2008 Financial aid. All financial aid based on need. 73% of total undergraduate aid awarded as scholarships/grants, 27% as loans/jobs. Need-based aid available for part-time students. Work-study available nights, weekends and for part-time students.

Application procedures. Admission: No deadline. $30 fee. Admission notification on a rolling basis. **Financial aid:** Priority date 4/15; no closing date. FAFSA, institutional form required. Applicants notified on a rolling basis starting 5/15; must reply within 2 week(s) of notification.

Academics. Special study options: Cooperative education, distance learning, dual enrollment of high school students, liberal arts/career combination. Bachelor's degree programs available on campus. License preparation in aviation, nursing. **Credit/placement by examination:** AP, CLEP, institutional tests. 45 credit hours maximum toward associate degree. **Support services:** GED preparation and test center, learning center, reduced course load, remedial instruction, study skills assistance, tutoring, writing center.

Majors. Agriculture: Production. **Business:** General, accounting technology, office management. **Computer sciences:** General, programming. **Construction:** Electrician. **Education:** Teacher assistance. **Health:** Medical assistant, nursing (RN), office admin. **Liberal arts:** Arts/sciences. **Mechanic/repair:** Aircraft, automotive, industrial. **Physical sciences:** General. **Production:** Welding. **Transportation:** Airline/commercial pilot.

Most popular majors. Business/marketing 6%, health sciences 12%, liberal arts 67%, trade and industry 7%.

Computing on campus. 432 workstations in dormitories, library, computer center, student center. Dormitories wired for high-speed internet access and linked to campus network. Online course registration, student web hosting, wireless network available.

Student life. Freshman orientation: Available. Preregistration for classes offered. Half-day fall student advising and registration sessions held throughout the summer. Full-day student orientation held in September. **Housing:** Coed dorms, wellness housing available. $200 partly refundable deposit. **Activities:** Choral groups, music ensembles, student government.

Athletics. Intercollegiate: Baseball M, basketball, softball W, volleyball W. **Team name:** Vikings.

Student services. Career counseling, services for economically disadvantaged, student employment services, financial aid counseling, minority student services, on-campus daycare, personal counseling, placement for graduates, veterans' counselor. **Physically disabled:** Services for visually, hearing impaired. **Transfer:** Transfer adviser, college fairs on campus for students transferring to 4-year colleges.

Contact. E-mail: admissions@bigbend.edu
Phone: (509) 793-2061 Toll-free number: (877) 745-1212
Fax: (509) 762-6243
Candy Lacher, Associate Vice President of Student Services, Big Bend Community College, 7662 Chanute Street, Moses Lake, WA 98837-3299

Cascadia Community College

Bothell, Washington
www.cascadia.edu **CB code: 2859**

- Public 2-year community college
- Commuter campus in large town

General. Commitment to themes of global perspective and sustainability infused into most courses. **Enrollment:** 1,724 degree-seeking undergraduates. **Degrees:** 250 associate awarded. **Location:** 15 miles from Seattle. **Calendar:** Quarter, extensive summer session. **Full-time faculty:** 34 total; 29% have terminal degrees, 53% women. **Part-time faculty:** 103 total; 70% women.

Basis for selection. Open admission. All students taking credit classes required to assess their current skill levels in English and Math with the COMPASS placement test.

2008-2009 Annual costs. Tuition/fees: $2,850; $8,064 out-of-state.

2007-2008 Financial aid. Need-based: Work-study available nights, weekends and for part-time students.

Application procedures. Admission: No deadline. No application fee. **Financial aid:** Priority date 4/16; no closing date. FAFSA, institutional form required.

Academics. Special study options: Distance learning, dual enrollment of high school students, ESL, independent study, internships, study abroad. **Credit/placement by examination:** AP, CLEP, IB, institutional tests. 45 credit hours maximum toward associate degree. **Support services:** GED preparation, learning center, remedial instruction, study skills assistance, tutoring, writing center.

Majors. Biology: General. **Computer sciences:** General. **Conservation:** Environmental science. **Education:** Elementary. **Physical sciences:** Atmospheric physics, chemistry, geology, physics. **Other:** Environmental technologies and sustainable practices.

Computing on campus. Commuter students can connect to campus network. Online library, helpline, wireless network available.

Student life. Freshman orientation: Mandatory. Preregistration for classes offered. Student orientation, advising, and Rrgistration sessions last approximately two hours and are offered several times before each quarter begins. Students given assistance in selecting courses, building schedules, registering for classes, and are also introduced to web registration as well as other online services. **Activities:** Film society, international student organizations, literary magazine, student government, Students in Service, Campus Crusade for Christ, Access Futures.

Athletics. Team name: Kodiaks.

Student services. Adult student services, career counseling, services for economically disadvantaged, student employment services, financial aid counseling, personal counseling, veterans' counselor. **Physically disabled:** Services for visually, speech, hearing impaired. **Transfer:** Pre-admission transcript evaluation for new students. Transfer center, transfer adviser, college fairs on campus for students transferring to 4-year colleges.

Contact. E-mail: admissions@cascadia.edu
Phone: (425) 352-8860 Fax: (425) 352-8137
Erin Blakeney, Associate Dean for Admissions and Retention, Cascadia Community College, 18345 Campus Way, NE, Bothell, WA 98011

Centralia College

Centralia, Washington
www.centralia.edu **CB code: 4045**

- Public 2-year community college
- Commuter campus in large town

General. Founded in 1925. Regionally accredited. **Enrollment:** 1,927 degree-seeking undergraduates. **Degrees:** 342 associate awarded. **Location:** 90 miles from Seattle, 90 miles from Portland, Oregon. **Calendar:** Quarter, extensive summer session. **Full-time faculty:** 54 total; 46% women. **Part-time faculty:** 115 total. **Class size:** 50% < 20, 43% 20-39, 5% 40-49, 2% 50-99.

Student profile.

Out-of-state:	1%	**25 or older:**	53%

Transfer out. Colleges most students transferred to 2008: Western Washington University, Washington State University, The Evergreen State College, Saint Martin's College, Central Washington University.

Basis for selection. Open admission, but selective for some programs. Special requirements for nursing program, includes prerequisites and grade point average criteria. **Homeschooled:** Transcript of courses and grades required.

High school preparation. 16 units recommended. Recommended units include English 4, mathematics 3, social studies 2, history 1, science 2 (laboratory 1), foreign language 2 and academic electives 1.

2008-2009 Annual costs. Tuition/fees: $3,002; $3,397 out-of-state. Per-credit charge: $76 in-state; $89 out-of-state. Books/supplies: $924. Personal expenses: $3,030.

2007-2008 Financial aid. Need-based: Need-based aid available for part-time students. Work-study available for part-time students. **Non-need-based:** Scholarships awarded for academics, alumni affiliation, art, athletics, leadership, minority status, music/drama.

Application procedures. Admission: Priority date 9/1; no deadline. No application fee. Admission notification on a rolling basis beginning on or about 12/1. **Financial aid:** Priority date 5/1, closing date 9/1. FAFSA, institutional form required. Applicants notified on a rolling basis starting 7/10; must reply within 2 week(s) of notification.

Academics. Special study options: Cooperative education, cross-registration, distance learning, double major, dual enrollment of high school students, ESL, honors, independent study, internships, liberal arts/career combination, student-designed major, study abroad, weekend college. Bachelor's degree programs available on campus. License preparation in nursing, paramedic, real estate. **Credit/placement by examination:** AP, CLEP, IB, institutional tests. 45 credit hours maximum toward associate degree. **Support services:** GED preparation and test center, learning center, reduced course load, remedial instruction, study skills assistance, tutoring, writing center.

Honors college/program. Selective application process after completion of 30 college credits. Limited to 20 students per year.

Majors. Biology: General, botany. **Business:** General, accounting, business admin, marketing, office technology, office/clerical, receptionist, sales/distribution. **Communications:** Broadcast journalism, journalism, radio/tv. **Communications technology:** Graphics, radio/tv. **Computer sciences:** General, computer science, data processing, information systems, LAN/WAN management, networking, programming. **Conservation:** Wildlife. **Construction:** Building inspection, maintenance, site management. **Education:** General, early childhood, teacher assistance. **Engineering:** General. **Engineering technology:** Civil, electrical, surveying. **Foreign languages:** General, French, German, Spanish. **Health:** Nursing (RN), polarity therapy, sonography. **History:** General. **Legal studies:** Legal secretary, paralegal. **Liberal arts:** Arts/sciences. **Math:** General. **Mechanic/repair:** Diesel, electronics/electrical. **Parks/recreation:** Health/fitness. **Physical sciences:** General, chemistry, geology, physics, planetary. **Production:** Welding. **Protective services:** Forensics, law enforcement admin, police science. **Psychology:** General. **Social sciences:** General, anthropology, economics, political science, sociology. **Visual/performing arts:** General, art, commercial/advertising art, dramatic, graphic design, music theory/composition, studio arts.

Most popular majors. Health sciences 7%, liberal arts 70%, trade and industry 8%.

Computing on campus. 150 workstations in library, computer center, student center. Online course registration, online library, helpline, wireless network available.

Student life. Freshman orientation: Available, $20 fee. Preregistration for classes offered. Held 2 days prior to fall quarter. **Activities:** Bands, choral groups, drama, literary magazine, music ensembles, musical theater, radio station, student government, student newspaper, symphony orchestra, TV station, honors club, international student club, Rotaract.

Athletics. Intercollegiate: Baseball M, basketball, golf W, softball W, volleyball W. **Team name:** Trailblazers.

Student services. Adult student services, career counseling, services for economically disadvantaged, student employment services, financial aid counseling, minority student services, on-campus daycare, personal counseling, placement for graduates, veterans' counselor. **Physically disabled:** Services for visually, speech, hearing impaired. **Transfer:** Re-entry adviser, pre-admission transcript evaluation for new students. Transfer center, transfer adviser, college fairs on campus for students transferring to 4-year colleges.

Contact. E-mail: admissions@centralia.edu
Phone: (360) 736-9391 ext. 221 Fax: (360) 330-7503
Michael Grubiak, VP, Student Services, Centralia College, 600 Centralia College Boulevard, Centralia, WA 98531

Clark College

Vancouver, Washington
www.clark.edu **CB code: 4055**

- Public 2-year community college
- Commuter campus in small city

General. Founded in 1933. Regionally accredited. **Enrollment:** 6,098 degree-seeking undergraduates; 4,508 non-degree-seeking students. **Degrees:** 1,004 associate awarded. **ROTC:** Army, Air Force. **Location:** 8 miles from Portland, Oregon. **Calendar:** Quarter, extensive summer session. **Full-time faculty:** 179 total; 15% have terminal degrees. **Part-time faculty:** 391 total; 8% have terminal degrees. **Class size:** 43% < 20, 51% 20-39, 6% 40-49, less than 1% 50-99, less than 1% >100. **Special facilities:** Environmental education center, arboretum. **Partnerships:** Formal partnerships with Toyota T-10 and Cisco; industry partnerships to train students in specific equipment use.

Student profile. Among degree-seeking undergraduates, 55% enrolled in a transfer program, 45% enrolled in a vocational program, 2% already have a bachelor's degree or higher, 1,143 enrolled as first-time, first-year students.

Part-time:	55%	**Asian American:**	5%
Out-of-state:	3%	**Hispanic American:**	5%
Women:	60%	**Native American:**	1%
African American:	2%	**25 or older:**	27%

Transfer out. Colleges most students transferred to 2008: Washington State University-Vancouver, Portland State University, University of Washington, Western Washington University, Central Washington.

Basis for selection. Open admission, but selective for some programs. Submit application for admissions and statement of intent. GPA requirements vary by program. ASSET required for placement in math and English. Interview required for dental hygiene, nursing, and pharmacy technician applicants.

2008-2009 Annual costs. Tuition/fees: $2,962; $3,357 out-of-state. Per-credit charge: $81 in-state; $94 out-of-state. Books/supplies: $924. Personal expenses: $1,884.

2007-2008 Financial aid. Need-based: Need-based aid available for part-time students. Work-study available nights, weekends and for part-time students. **Non-need-based:** Scholarships awarded for academics, alumni affiliation, art, athletics, job skills, leadership, minority status, music/drama, religious affiliation, ROTC, state residency.

Application procedures. Admission: Priority date 7/24; no deadline. No application fee. Admission notification on a rolling basis. **Financial aid:** Priority date 5/1; no closing date. FAFSA, institutional form required. Applicants notified on a rolling basis starting 5/1; must reply within 2 week(s) of notification.

Academics. Special study options: Combined bachelor's/graduate degree, cooperative education, cross-registration, distance learning, dual enrollment of high school students, ESL, honors, independent study, internships, liberal arts/career combination, study abroad. Bachelor's degree programs available on campus. License preparation in dental hygiene, nursing, radiology. **Credit/placement by examination:** AP, CLEP, IB, institutional tests. 30 credit hours maximum toward associate degree. **Support services:** GED preparation and test center, learning center, reduced course load, remedial instruction, study skills assistance, tutoring, writing center.

Majors. Agriculture: Horticulture, landscaping. **Business:** Accounting technology, business admin, executive assistant, human resources, office technology, retailing, selling. **Communications technology:** Graphics. **Computer sciences:** Data entry, networking, programming, webmaster. **Education:** Early childhood. **Engineering technology:** Construction, electrical, manufacturing, surveying, telecommunications. **Health:** Dental hygiene, EMT paramedic, medical assistant, medical secretary, nursing (RN), radiologic technology/medical imaging, substance abuse counseling. **Legal studies:** Paralegal. **Liberal arts:** Arts/sciences. **Mechanic/repair:** Automotive, diesel. **Parks/recreation:** Sports admin. **Personal/culinary services:** Baking, chef training. **Production:** Machine tool, welding.

Most popular majors. Business/marketing 12%, health sciences 16%, liberal arts 59%.

Computing on campus. 923 workstations in library, computer center, student center. Online course registration, online library, helpline, wireless network available.

Student life. Freshman orientation: Available. Preregistration for classes offered. Sessions held during quarterly registration period. Online orientation option available. **Activities:** Bands, choral groups, dance, drama, international student organizations, literary magazine, music ensembles, musical theater, student government, student newspaper, symphony orchestra, American Sign Language, Clark College Feminists, manga anime club, club for social action, Generation for Truth prayer club, international club, Japanese language club, Queer Penguins and Allies, multicultural student union, Students for Political Action Now.

Athletics. Intercollegiate: Basketball, cross-country, soccer, track and field, volleyball W. **Intramural:** Basketball, fencing, football (non-tackle), soccer, softball, table tennis, volleyball. **Team name:** Penguins.

Student services. Adult student services, alcohol/substance abuse counseling, career counseling, services for economically disadvantaged, student employment services, financial aid counseling, health services, legal services, minority student services, on-campus daycare, personal counseling, placement for graduates, veterans' counselor, women's services. **Physically disabled:** Services for visually, speech, hearing impaired. **Transfer:** Transfer adviser, college fairs on campus for students transferring to 4-year colleges.

Contact. E-mail: admissionrequest@clark.edu
Phone: (360) 992-2107 Fax: (360) 992-2867
Sheryl Anderson, Director of Admissions, Clark College, 1933 Fort Vancouver Way, Vancouver, WA 98663

Clover Park Technical College

Lakewood, Washington
www.cptc.edu **CB code: 3971**

- Public 2-year technical college
- Commuter campus in small city

General. Regionally accredited. **Enrollment:** 1,301 degree-seeking undergraduates. **Degrees:** 307 associate awarded. **Location:** 10 miles from Tacoma, 40 miles from Seattle. **Calendar:** Quarter, extensive summer session. **Full-time faculty:** 92 total. **Part-time faculty:** 159 total. **Class size:** 70% < 20, 27% 20-39, 2% 40-49, 1% 50-99.

Basis for selection. Open admission, but selective for some programs. Some programs have test score minimums and/or course prerequisite requirements.

2008-2009 Annual costs. Tuition/fees: $3,591. Per-credit charge: $60. Students in programs with high computer usage will pay a $45 per quarter computer use fee. Books/supplies: $1,200. Personal expenses: $1,950.

2007-2008 Financial aid. All financial aid based on need. Need-based aid available for part-time students. Work-study available nights and weekends.

Application procedures. Admission: No deadline. $43 fee. Admission notification on a rolling basis. **Financial aid:** Priority date 6/15, closing date 8/25. FAFSA, institutional form required. Applicants notified on a rolling basis.

Academics. Special study options: Cooperative education, distance learning, dual enrollment of high school students, ESL, internships. License preparation in aviation, nursing. **Credit/placement by examination:** CLEP, institutional tests. 15 credit hours maximum toward associate degree. 25 percent of total approved hours may be awarded for prior work and/or life experience. **Support services:** GED preparation and test center, tutoring.

Majors. Agriculture: Landscaping. **Business:** Accounting technology, marketing, office management. **Communications technology:** Graphic/printing, radio/tv. **Computer sciences:** LAN/WAN management, networking, programming, security, web page design. **Education:** Early childhood, teacher assistance. **Engineering technology:** Architectural, environmental, mechanical. **Health:** Clinical lab assistant, dental assistant, health services, licensed practical nurse, massage therapy, pharmacy assistant, surgical technology. **Legal studies:** Legal secretary. **Mechanic/repair:** Aircraft powerplant, automotive, avionics, business machine, heating/ac/refrig, heavy equipment. **Personal/culinary services:** Aesthetician. **Production:** Machine tool. **Transportation:** Airline/commercial pilot. **Visual/performing arts:** Interior design.

Most popular majors. Computer/information sciences 14%, education 8%, health sciences 34%, trade and industry 15%.

Computing on campus. 94 workstations in library. Online library available.

Student life. Freshman orientation: Available. **Activities:** Student government.

Student services. Adult student services, career counseling, services for economically disadvantaged, student employment services, financial aid counseling, minority student services, on-campus daycare, veterans' counselor. **Physically disabled:** Services for visually, speech, hearing impaired.

Contact. Phone: (253) 589-5678 Fax: (253) 589-5852
Judy MacDougall, Director of Enrollment Services, Clover Park Technical College, 4500 Steilacoom Boulevard, SW, Lakewood, WA 98499-4098

Columbia Basin College

Pasco, Washington
www.columbiabasin.edu
CB code: 4077

- Public 2-year community college
- Commuter campus in small city

General. Founded in 1955. Regionally accredited. **Enrollment:** 5,904 degree-seeking undergraduates. **Degrees:** 812 associate awarded. **Location:** 130 miles from Spokane, 200 miles from Seattle. **Calendar:** Quarter, limited summer session. **Full-time faculty:** 119 total. **Part-time faculty:** 227 total. **Special facilities:** Performing arts theater, health science building, observatory, math and science working atrium, regional medical library, tutor and writing center, research farm.

Student profile.

Out-of-state:	1%	**25 or older:**	58%

Transfer out. Colleges most students transferred to 2008: Washington State University.

Basis for selection. Open admission, but selective for some programs. Special application process and requirements for nursing, dental hygiene, radiologic technology, paramedic, medical assistant, automotive technology and surgical technician programs. Applicants not graduates of regionally accredited high schools or those without a GED must submit Washington Pre-College Test, SAT, or ACT scores.

High school preparation. College-preparatory program required. 11 units recommended. Recommended units include English 3, mathematics 2, social studies 3, science 2 and foreign language 1.

2008-2009 Annual costs. Tuition/fees: $2,936; $3,995 out-of-state. Books/supplies: $924. Personal expenses: $1,524.

2008-2009 Financial aid. Need-based: Need-based aid available for part-time students. Work-study available nights, weekends and for part-time students. **Non-need-based:** Scholarships awarded for academics, athletics, state residency.

Application procedures. Admission: No deadline. $28 fee, may be waived for applicants with need. Application must be submitted on paper. Admission notification on a rolling basis. **Financial aid:** Priority date 4/10; no closing date. FAFSA, institutional form required. Applicants notified on a rolling basis starting 6/15; must reply within 2 week(s) of notification.

Academics. Special study options: Cross-registration, distance learning, dual enrollment of high school students, ESL, internships, liberal arts/career combination, weekend college. Bachelor's degree programs available on campus. License preparation in dental hygiene, nursing, paramedic, radiology. **Credit/placement by examination:** CLEP, IB, institutional tests. 30 credit hours maximum toward associate degree. **Support services:** GED preparation and test center, learning center, reduced course load, remedial instruction, study skills assistance, tutoring, writing center.

Majors. Agriculture: Agribusiness operations, business. **Business:** Accounting, administrative services, management information systems, office management, purchasing, sales/distribution. **Computer sciences:** General, computer science, data processing, programming. **Construction:** Carpentry. **Education:** General, early childhood. **Engineering technology:** Electrical. **Family/consumer sciences:** Child care. **Health:** Clinical lab technology, dental hygiene, EMT paramedic, licensed practical nurse, medical records admin, medical transcription. **Interdisciplinary:** Biological/physical sciences, math/computer science. **Legal studies:** Paralegal. **Liberal arts:** Arts/sciences. **Mechanic/repair:** Auto body, automotive, diesel. **Physical sciences:** General. **Protective services:** Firefighting, law enforcement admin, police science. **Public administration:** Human services. **Visual/performing arts:** General, commercial/advertising art.

Most popular majors. Health sciences 7%, liberal arts 77%.

Computing on campus. 680 workstations in library, computer center. Online course registration, online library, wireless network available.

Student life. Freshman orientation: Mandatory. **Activities:** Bands, choral groups, drama, music ensembles, musical theater, student government, student newspaper.

Athletics. NJCAA. **Intercollegiate:** Baseball M, basketball, golf, soccer, softball W, volleyball W. **Intramural:** Basketball, bowling, soccer M, softball, volleyball. **Team name:** Hawks.

Student services. Adult student services, career counseling, student employment services, minority student services, personal counseling, placement for graduates, veterans' counselor, women's services. **Physically disabled:** Services for visually, speech, hearing impaired. **Learning disabled:** Comprehensive services available. **Transfer:** Transfer adviser, college fairs on campus for students transferring to 4-year colleges.

Contact. E-mail: dkorstad@columbiabasin.edu
Phone: (509) 547-0511 Fax: (509) 546-0401
Patricia Campbell, Director of Admissions and Registration, Columbia Basin College, 2600 North 20th Avenue, Pasco, WA 99301

Edmonds Community College

Lynnwood, Washington
www.edcc.edu
CB member
CB code: 4307

- Public 2-year community college
- Commuter campus in small city

General. Founded in 1967. Regionally accredited. **Enrollment:** 7,823 degree-seeking undergraduates. **Degrees:** 789 associate awarded. **Location:** 15 miles from Seattle. **Calendar:** Quarter, extensive summer session. **Full-time faculty:** 145 total. **Part-time faculty:** 348 total. **Special facilities:** Center for Business and Employment Development, golf course.

Transfer out. Colleges most students transferred to 2008: University of Washington, Central Washington University, Western Washington University, Washington State University.

Basis for selection. Open admission, but selective for some programs. Interview recommended for international studies, travel tourism majors; audition required for music performance majors. **Learning Disabled:** SSD is available to provide appropriate accommodation.

2008-2009 Annual costs. Tuition/fees: $2,960; $8,174 out-of-state. Books/supplies: $900. Personal expenses: $1,824.

Financial aid. Need-based: Need-based aid available for part-time students. Work-study available nights and for part-time students. **Non-need-based:** Scholarships awarded for athletics.

Application procedures. Admission: No deadline. $18 fee, may be waived for applicants with need. Admission notification on a rolling basis. TOEFL optional for students whose first language is not English. **Financial aid:** Priority date 5/1; no closing date. FAFSA, institutional form required. Applicants notified on a rolling basis starting 6/1; must reply within 4 week(s) of notification.

Academics. Special study options: Cooperative education, cross-registration, distance learning, dual enrollment of high school students, ESL, exchange student, honors, independent study, internships, study abroad, weekend college. **Credit/placement by examination:** CLEP, institutional tests. 15 credit hours maximum toward associate degree. **Support services:** GED preparation and test center, learning center, remedial instruction, tutoring, writing center.

Majors. Agriculture: Business technology, landscaping, nursery operations. **Business:** Accounting technology, business admin, construction management, hospitality admin, human resources, international, office management, office/clerical, travel services. **Computer sciences:** Computer graphics, data processing, database management, networking, security, web page design, webmaster. **Education:** Early childhood, elementary. **Engineering:** Chemical, electrical, mechanical. **Engineering technology:** General, electrical, occupational safety. **Health:** Community health services, medical radiologic technology/radiation therapy, medical records technology, mental health services, nursing (RN), substance abuse counseling, vocational rehab counseling. **Legal studies:** Legal secretary, paralegal. **Liberal arts:** Arts/sciences. **Personal/culinary services:** Chef training. **Protective services:** Fire services admin. **Science technology:** Chemical. **Visual/performing arts:** Commercial photography.

Computing on campus. 1,129 workstations in library, computer center. Commuter students can connect to campus network. Online course registration available.

Student life. Freshman orientation: Available. Students receive brief orientation prior to placement test. **Housing:** Host families available for international students. **Activities:** Jazz band, choral groups, dance, drama, international student organizations, literary magazine, music ensembles, student government, student newspaper, Phi Theta Kappa, Design and Invention Club, I-Hope Club, DESI Club, Baptist Collegiate Ministry, Black Student Association, American Indian Student Association, Gay and Lesbian Alliance, Digital Production Club.

Athletics. **Intercollegiate:** Baseball M, basketball, golf, soccer, softball W, volleyball W. **Intramural:** Basketball M, bowling, golf, table tennis, volleyball. **Team name:** Tritons.

Student services. Adult student services, career counseling, student employment services, financial aid counseling, minority student services, on-campus daycare, personal counseling, placement for graduates, women's services. **Physically disabled:** Services for visually, speech, hearing impaired. **Transfer:** Transfer center, transfer adviser, college fairs on campus for students transferring to 4-year colleges.

Contact. E-mail: admiss@edcc.edu
Phone: (425) 640-1459 Fax: (425) 640-1159
Nanci Froemming, Office Manager, Enrollment Services, Edmonds Community College, 20000 68th Avenue West, Lynnwood, WA 98036-5912

Everest College: Vancouver
Vancouver, Washington
www.everest-college.com

- For-profit 2-year business college
- Large city

General. Accredited by ACICS. **Calendar:** Quarter.

Contact. Phone: (360) 254-3282
Admissions Director, 120 NE 136th Avenue, Suite 130, Vancouver, WA 98684

Everett Community College
Everett, Washington
www.everettcc.edu **CB code: 4303**

- Public 2-year community college
- Commuter campus in small city

General. Founded in 1941. Regionally accredited. **Enrollment:** 4,041 degree-seeking undergraduates; 4,099 non-degree-seeking students. **Degrees:** 745 associate awarded. **Location:** 30 miles from Seattle. **Calendar:** Quarter, limited summer session. **Full-time faculty:** 135 total; 18% have terminal degrees, 14% minority, 56% women. **Part-time faculty:** 234 total. **Class size:** 47% < 20, 46% 20-39, 5% 40-49, 2% 50-99. **Partnerships:** Formal partnership with Boeing.

Student profile. Among degree-seeking undergraduates, 53% enrolled in a transfer program, 47% enrolled in a vocational program, 3% already have a bachelor's degree or higher, 753 enrolled as first-time, first-year students, 254 transferred in from other institutions.

Part-time:	46%	**Hispanic American:**	5%
Out-of-state:	1%	**Native American:**	2%
Women:	60%	**International:**	1%
African American:	3%	**25 or older:**	35%
Asian American:	7%		

Transfer out. 51% of students enrolled in the transfer program go on to 4-year colleges. **Colleges most students transferred to 2008:** Western Washington University, University of Washington, Central Washington University, Washington State University.

Basis for selection. Open admission, but selective for some programs. Special requirements for nursing, fire science, and criminal justice. Interview recommended for nursing.

High school preparation. College-preparatory program recommended. 16 units recommended. Recommended units include English 4, mathematics 3, social studies 3, history 2, science 2 and foreign language 2.

2008-2009 Annual costs. Tuition/fees: $2,835; $8,049 out-of-state. Per-credit charge: $76 in-state; $248 out-of-state. Books/supplies: $924. Personal expenses: $1,590.

2007-2008 Financial aid. All financial aid based on need. Need-based aid available for part-time students. Work-study available nights, weekends and for part-time students.

Application procedures. **Admission:** No deadline. No application fee. Admission notification on a rolling basis. **Financial aid:** Priority date 5/5; no closing date. FAFSA, institutional form required. Applicants notified on a rolling basis starting 4/15; must reply within 4 week(s) of notification.

Academics. Offers direct-transfer associate degrees that assure full transfer to most Washington and Oregon universities. Transfer degrees for specific majors at designated universities can be designed by the student and faculty advisor. **Special study options:** Cooperative education, distance learning, dual enrollment of high school students, ESL, independent study, internships, study abroad. Bachelor's degree programs available on campus. License preparation in aviation, nursing, paramedic. **Credit/placement by examination:** AP, CLEP, IB, institutional tests. 45 credit hours maximum toward associate degree. **Support services:** GED preparation and test center, learning center, reduced course load, remedial instruction, study skills assistance, tutoring, writing center.

Majors. **Agriculture:** Animal sciences. **Area/ethnic studies:** Asian. **Biology:** General. **Business:** General, accounting, administrative services, business admin, management information systems, office/clerical. **Communications:** General, advertising, journalism. **Computer sciences:** General, computer graphics, computer science, information systems, networking, programming, webmaster. **Conservation:** General, environmental science. **Education:** General, early childhood. **Engineering:** General. **Engineering technology:** General, CAD/CADD, manufacturing. **Foreign languages:** General, comparative lit, French, German, Japanese, Russian, Spanish. **Health:** Dental hygiene, medical assistant, nursing (RN), predental, premedicine, prepharmacy, preveterinary. **History:** General. **Interdisciplinary:** Natural sciences. **Legal studies:** Prelaw. **Liberal arts:** Arts/sciences. **Math:** General. **Mechanic/repair:** Aircraft powerplant. **Personal/culinary services:** Cosmetology. **Philosophy/religion:** Philosophy. **Physical sciences:** Astronomy, atmospheric science, chemistry, geology, oceanography, physics. **Protective services:** Corrections, firefighting, law enforcement admin. **Psychology:** General. **Public administration:** Human services. **Social sciences:** General, anthropology, economics, geography, political science, sociology. **Visual/performing arts:** General, art, commercial/advertising art, dramatic, music performance, photography, studio arts.

Most popular majors. Business/marketing 12%, health sciences 14%, liberal arts 60%.

Computing on campus. 900 workstations in library, computer center, student center. Online course registration, wireless network available.

Student life. **Freshman orientation:** Mandatory. Preregistration for classes offered. One-day program of placement testing, orientation and advising sessions. **Housing:** Housing in private homes available for foreign students. **Activities:** Choral groups, drama, literary magazine, music ensembles, musical theater, student government, student newspaper, 25 student clubs.

Athletics. **Intercollegiate:** Baseball M, basketball, cross-country, soccer, softball W, volleyball W. **Intramural:** Basketball, bowling, golf, soccer, softball, tennis, volleyball, weight lifting. **Team name:** Trojans.

Student services. Adult student services, career counseling, services for economically disadvantaged, student employment services, financial aid counseling, minority student services, on-campus daycare, personal counseling, placement for graduates, veterans' counselor, women's services. **Physically disabled:** Services for visually, speech, hearing impaired. **Transfer:** Transfer adviser, college fairs on campus for students transferring to 4-year colleges.

Contact. E-mail: admissions@everettcc.edu
Phone: (425) 388-9219 Fax: (425) 388-9173
Linda Baca, Admissions Manager, Everett Community College, 2000 Tower Street, Everett, WA 98201-1352

Grays Harbor College
Aberdeen, Washington
www.ghc.edu **CB code: 4332**

- Public 2-year community college
- Commuter campus in large town

General. Founded in 1930. Regionally accredited. **Enrollment:** 641 degree-seeking undergraduates; 1,850 non-degree-seeking students. **Degrees:** 242 associate awarded. **Location:** 100 miles from Seattle. **Calendar:** Quarter, limited summer session. **Full-time faculty:** 64 total; 2% minority, 39% women. **Part-time faculty:** 89 total; 4% minority, 60% women. **Class size:** 77% < 20, 22% 20-39, less than 1% 40-49, less than 1% 50-99. **Special facilities:** 4-acre lake linked to Grays Harbor estuary and fish hatcheries, 440 seat theater. **Partnerships:** Formal partnerships with local businesses for internships and short-term training.

Student profile. Among degree-seeking undergraduates, 24% enrolled in a transfer program, 38% enrolled in a vocational program, 162 enrolled as first-time, first-year students.

Part-time:	29%	**Hispanic American:**	5%
Out-of-state:	1%	**Native American:**	7%
Women:	63%	**25 or older:**	51%
Asian American:	2%		

Transfer out. Colleges most students transferred to 2008: Washington State University, Evergreen State College, Western Washington University, Central Washington University, Eastern Washington University.

Basis for selection. Open admission, but selective for some programs. High school diploma or GED required of applicants under 18 years of age. Limited admission to nursing program.

2008-2009 Annual costs. Tuition/fees: $3,167; $8,381 out-of-state. Books/supplies: $750. Personal expenses: $2,178.

2007-2008 Financial aid. Need-based: 94% of total undergraduate aid awarded as scholarships/grants, 6% as loans/jobs. Need-based aid available for part-time students. Work-study available nights and for part-time students. **Non-need-based:** Scholarships awarded for academics, art, athletics, music/drama.

Application procedures. Admission: Priority date 9/1; no deadline. No application fee. Admission notification on a rolling basis. **Financial aid:** Priority date 5/1; no closing date. FAFSA, institutional form required. Applicants notified on a rolling basis starting 5/15.

Academics. Special study options: Accelerated study, cooperative education, distance learning, double major, dual enrollment of high school students, ESL, independent study, internships, study abroad, teacher certification program. Bachelor's degree programs available on campus. License preparation in nursing. **Credit/placement by examination:** AP, CLEP, institutional tests. 45 credit hours maximum toward associate degree. **Support services:** GED preparation and test center, learning center, reduced course load, remedial instruction, study skills assistance, tutoring, writing center.

Majors. Business: Accounting technology, business admin, office management. **Computer sciences:** Data processing. **Conservation:** General, wildlife. **Construction:** Carpentry. **Education:** Teacher assistance. **Health:** Nursing (RN). **Liberal arts:** Arts/sciences. **Mechanic/repair:** Automotive, diesel. **Physical sciences:** General. **Production:** Welding. **Protective services:** Police science. **Public administration:** Human services.

Most popular majors. Business/marketing 10%, health sciences 14%, liberal arts 67%, trade and industry 7%.

Computing on campus. 382 workstations in library, computer center, student center. Online course registration, online library, student web hosting, wireless network available.

Student life. Freshman orientation: Mandatory. Preregistration for classes offered. Offered online or face to face. **Activities:** Bands, choral groups, drama, music ensembles, musical theater, student government, student newspaper, symphony orchestra, Native American Student Association, the Tyee Honorary Service Club, Human Services Student Association, AGAPE Christian ministry, Foreign Language and Culture, Student Nurses Association.

Athletics. Intercollegiate: Baseball M, basketball, golf, softball W, volleyball W. **Team name:** Chokers.

Student services. Adult student services, career counseling, services for economically disadvantaged, student employment services, financial aid counseling, minority student services, on-campus daycare, personal counseling, placement for graduates, veterans' counselor. **Physically disabled:** Services for visually, speech, hearing impaired. **Transfer:** Pre-admission transcript evaluation for new students. Transfer adviser, college fairs on campus for students transferring to 4-year colleges.

Contact. E-mail: bdell@ghc.edu
Phone: (360) 538-4026 Toll-free number: (800) 562-4830
Fax: (360) 538-4293
Nancy DeVerse, Associate Dean for Student Services/Registrar, Grays Harbor College, 1620 Edward P Smith Drive, Aberdeen, WA 98520

Green River Community College
Auburn, Washington
www.greenriver.edu **CB code: 4337**

- Public 2-year community college
- Commuter campus in large town

General. Founded in 1965. Regionally accredited. **Enrollment:** 4,962 degree-seeking undergraduates. **Degrees:** 991 associate awarded. **Location:** 35 miles from Seattle. **Calendar:** Quarter, limited summer session. **Full-time faculty:** 145 total. **Part-time faculty:** 297 total.

Basis for selection. Open admission, but selective for some programs. Special requirements for health occupation programs. Interview required for occupational therapy.

2008-2009 Annual costs. Tuition/fees: $3,113; $3,545 out-of-state. Books/supplies: $939. Personal expenses: $1,170.

2008-2009 Financial aid. All financial aid based on need. Need-based aid available for part-time students.

Application procedures. Admission: No deadline. No application fee. Admission notification on a rolling basis. **Financial aid:** Priority date 4/15; no closing date. FAFSA, institutional form required. Applicants notified on a rolling basis starting 6/30; must reply within 2 week(s) of notification.

Academics. Special study options: Cooperative education, cross-registration, distance learning, dual enrollment of high school students, ESL, independent study, internships, study abroad. **Credit/placement by examination:** AP, CLEP, institutional tests. **Support services:** GED preparation and test center, learning center, reduced course load, remedial instruction, tutoring, writing center.

Majors. Business: Accounting, marketing, office technology, office/clerical, real estate. **Computer sciences:** Information systems. **Conservation:** Forest resources. **Construction:** Carpentry. **Education:** Early childhood. **Engineering technology:** Drafting, electrical, hazardous materials. **Health:** Medical secretary, occupational therapy assistant, physical therapy assistant. **Legal studies:** Court reporting, legal secretary. **Liberal arts:** Arts/sciences. **Mechanic/repair:** Auto body. **Protective services:** Police science. **Transportation:** General, aviation. **Visual/performing arts:** General.

Computing on campus. 210 workstations in library, computer center.

Student life. Freshman orientation: Available. **Housing:** Apartments available. **Activities:** Jazz band, choral groups, dance, drama, music ensembles, radio station, student government, student newspaper, Asian Student Union, Black Student Union, Native American Student Association, Los Latinos Unidos, Phi Theta Kappa, Teachers of Tomorrow, Skills USA, forestry club, court reporting club, American Society of Mechanical Engineers.

Athletics. NJCAA. **Intercollegiate:** Baseball M, basketball, golf, soccer, softball W, tennis, volleyball W. **Intramural:** Badminton, baseball M, basketball, soccer, softball, tennis, volleyball. **Team name:** Gators.

Student services. Career counseling, services for economically disadvantaged, student employment services, financial aid counseling, health services, minority student services, on-campus daycare, personal counseling, placement for graduates, veterans' counselor, women's services. **Physically disabled:** Services for visually, hearing impaired. **Transfer:** Transfer center, transfer adviser, college fairs on campus for students transferring to 4-year colleges.

Contact. Phone: (253) 833-9111 ext. 2500 Fax: (253) 288-3454
Denise Bennatts, Registrar, Green River Community College, 12401 SE 320th Street, Auburn, WA 98092

Highline Community College
Des Moines, Washington
www.highline.edu **CB code: 4348**

- Public 2-year community college
- Commuter campus in small city

General. Founded in 1961. Regionally accredited. **Enrollment:** 6,387 degree-seeking undergraduates. **Degrees:** 826 associate awarded. **ROTC:** Army, Air Force. **Location:** 18 miles from Seattle. **Calendar:** Quarter, limited summer session. **Full-time faculty:** 150 total. **Part-time faculty:** 185 total.

Student profile. Among degree-seeking undergraduates, 57% enrolled in a transfer program, 32% enrolled in a vocational program, 1% already have a bachelor's degree or higher.

Basis for selection. Open admission, but selective for some programs. School achievement record considered for health programs. College and work experience also considered for nursing.

High school preparation. Health occupation programs require chemistry and algebra.

2008-2009 Annual costs. Tuition/fees: $2,805; $3,184 out-of-state. Per-credit charge: $76 in-state; $89 out-of-state. Books/supplies: $618. Personal expenses: $1,644.

2007-2008 Financial aid. Need-based: Need-based aid available for part-time students.

Application procedures. Admission: No deadline. $24 fee. Admission notification on a rolling basis. **Financial aid:** Priority date 5/31; no closing date. FAFSA required. Applicants notified on a rolling basis starting 6/1.

Academics. Special study options: Accelerated study, cooperative education, cross-registration, distance learning, double major, dual enrollment of high school students, ESL, honors, independent study, internships, student-designed major. **Credit/placement by examination:** CLEP, institutional tests. **Support services:** GED preparation and test center, learning center, pre-admission summer program, reduced course load, remedial instruction, tutoring.

Majors. Business: General, accounting, administrative services, business admin, fashion, hospitality/recreation, international, office/clerical, sales/distribution, tourism/travel. **Communications:** General, journalism. **Computer sciences:** General. **Education:** General, teacher assistance. **Engineering:** General. **Engineering technology:** Drafting, manufacturing. **Family/consumer sciences:** General, child care, food/nutrition. **Foreign languages:** General, French, German, linguistics. **Health:** Dental assistant, health care admin, medical assistant, medical transcription, nursing (RN), respiratory therapy technology. **History:** General. **Legal studies:** General, paralegal, prelaw. **Liberal arts:** Arts/sciences, library assistant. **Math:** General. **Parks/recreation:** Health/fitness. **Physical sciences:** Astronomy, geology. **Psychology:** General. **Public administration:** Human services. **Social sciences:** General, anthropology, economics, geography, sociology. **Transportation:** General, aviation. **Visual/performing arts:** General, art, commercial/advertising art, dramatic, multimedia.

Most popular majors. Business/marketing 6%, computer/information sciences 6%, health sciences 9%, liberal arts 66%.

Computing on campus. 100 workstations in library, computer center, student center.

Student life. Activities: Bands, choral groups, drama, literary magazine, music ensembles, student government, student newspaper, TV station, Indian and international student clubs, political forum, paralegal and arts societies, respiratory care club, academic honor society, campus crusade for Christ.

Athletics. NJCAA. **Intercollegiate:** Basketball, cross-country, soccer, softball W, track and field, volleyball W, wrestling M. **Team name:** Thunderbirds.

Student services. Adult student services, career counseling, student employment services, health services, minority student services, on-campus daycare, personal counseling, placement for graduates, veterans' counselor, women's services. **Physically disabled:** Services for visually, speech, hearing impaired. **Transfer:** Transfer adviser, college fairs on campus for students transferring to 4-year colleges.

Contact. E-mail: lwesterg@highline.edu
Phone: (206) 878-3710 ext. 3559 Fax: (206) 870-3782
Laura Westergard, Assistant Registrar, Highline Community College, 2400 South 240th Street, Des Moines, WA 98198-9800

Lake Washington Technical College

Kirkland, Washington
www.lwtc.edu **CB code: 1453**

- Public 2-year technical college
- Commuter campus in large town

General. Founded in 1949. Regionally accredited. **Location:** 10 miles from Seattle. **Calendar:** Quarter.

Annual costs/financial aid. $77 per credit hour (1-5 credits); $38 per credit hour (more than 5 credits). No difference between resident and non-resident rate. Books/supplies: $1,182. Personal expenses: $1,590. Need-based financial aid available to full-time and part-time students.

Contact. Phone: (425) 739-8104
Director of Admissions, 11605 132nd Avenue, NE, Kirkland, WA 98034

Lower Columbia College

Longview, Washington
www.lowercolumbia.edu **CB code: 4402**

- Public 2-year community college
- Commuter campus in small city

General. Founded in 1934. Regionally accredited. **Enrollment:** 1,313 degree-seeking undergraduates; 3,291 non-degree-seeking students. **Degrees:** 365 associate awarded. **Location:** 50 miles from Portland, Oregon, 120 miles from Seattle. **Calendar:** Quarter, limited summer session. **Full-time faculty:** 76 total; 5% minority, 38% women. **Part-time faculty:** 98 total; 3% minority, 67% women. **Class size:** 60% < 20, 36% 20-39, 2% 40-49, 2% 50-99, less than 1% >100. **Special facilities:** Fine and performing arts center.

Student profile. Among degree-seeking undergraduates, 37% enrolled in a transfer program, 63% enrolled in a vocational program, 2% already have a bachelor's degree or higher, 185 enrolled as first-time, first-year students.

Part-time:	33%	**Asian American:**	3%
Out-of-state:	1%	**Hispanic American:**	7%
Women:	64%	**Native American:**	3%
African American:	2%	**25 or older:**	56%

Transfer out. 20% of students enrolled in the transfer program go on to 4-year colleges. **Colleges most students transferred to 2008:** Washington State University-Vancouver, Washington State University-Pullman, Central Washington University, Eastern Washington University, Western Washington University.

Basis for selection. Open admission, but selective for some programs. Special requirements for nursing program and medical assistant program.

2008-2009 Annual costs. Tuition/fees: $3,144; $3,867 out-of-state. Per-credit charge: $82 in-state; $104 out-of-state. Full-time "border county" tuition for students in Oregon's Clatsop, Multnomah, Washington, and Columbia counties: $3,157. Books/supplies: $1,110. Personal expenses: $1,800.

2007-2008 Financial aid. Need-based: 64% of total undergraduate aid awarded as scholarships/grants, 36% as loans/jobs. Need-based aid available for part-time students. Work-study available for part-time students.

Application procedures. Admission: No deadline. $14 fee. Admission notification on a rolling basis. **Financial aid:** Priority date 5/1; no closing date. Institutional form, CSS PROFILE required. Applicants notified on a rolling basis starting 4/21; must reply within 2 week(s) of notification.

Academics. Comprehensive tutoring and other support services available in LCC's Learning Commons. **Special study options:** Cooperative education, cross-registration, distance learning, dual enrollment of high school students, ESL, independent study, internships, liberal arts/career combination, student-designed major, teacher certification program. Bachelor's degree programs available on campus. License preparation in nursing. **Credit/placement by examination:** AP, CLEP, institutional tests. **Support services:** GED preparation and test center, learning center, reduced course load, remedial instruction, study skills assistance, tutoring, writing center.

Majors. Business: Accounting, accounting technology, administrative services, business admin, office technology, office/clerical. **Computer sciences:** General, computer science, data entry, data processing, networking, programming. **Education:** Elementary, teacher assistance. **Engineering:** General. **Engineering technology:** Electrical. **Family/consumer sciences:** Child development. **Health:** Licensed practical nurse, medical assistant, medical secretary, nursing (RN), nursing assistant, substance abuse counseling. **Legal studies:** Legal secretary, paralegal. **Liberal arts:** Arts/sciences. **Mechanic/repair:** Auto body, automotive, diesel, heavy equipment, industrial, industrial electronics. **Production:** Welding. **Protective services:** Law enforcement admin. **Other:** Contemporary musicianship and audio production.

Computing on campus. 450 workstations in library, computer center, student center. Online course registration, online library, helpline, wireless network available.

Student life. Freshman orientation: Available. **Housing:** Apartments normally available in local community. **Activities:** Bands, choral groups, dance, drama, international student organizations, literary magazine, music ensembles, musical theater, student government, theater club, student nurses organization, services and relations club, campus entertainment, diesel mechanics club, Phi Theta Kappa.

Athletics. NJCAA. **Intercollegiate:** Baseball M, basketball, soccer W, softball W, volleyball W. **Team name:** Red Devils.

Student services. Adult student services, career counseling, services for economically disadvantaged, student employment services, financial aid counseling, on-campus daycare, personal counseling, placement for graduates, veterans' counselor. **Physically disabled:** Services for visually, speech, hearing impaired. **Transfer:** Re-entry adviser, pre-admission transcript evaluation for new students. Transfer center, transfer adviser, college fairs on campus for students transferring to 4-year colleges.

Contact. E-mail: entry@lowercolumbia.edu
Phone: (360) 442-2311 Toll-free number: (866) 900-2311
Fax: (360) 442-2379
Lynn Lawrence, Registrar, Lower Columbia College, 1600 Maple Street, Longview, WA 98632-0310

North Seattle Community College

Seattle, Washington
www.northseattle.edu **CB code: 4554**

- Public 2-year community college
- Commuter campus in very large city

General. Founded in 1970. Regionally accredited. Associate degree programs available via distance learning; Watch Technology Institute, specializing in watch repair, is one of only 3 certified programs in the country and the only college on the West Coast that offers this curriculum. **Enrollment:** 2,055 degree-seeking undergraduates; 4,286 non-degree-seeking students. **Degrees:** 498 associate awarded. **Location:** 8 miles from downtown. **Calendar:** Quarter, limited summer session. **Full-time faculty:** 94 total; 6% have terminal degrees, 28% minority, 58% women. **Part-time faculty:** 201 total; 1% have terminal degrees, 13% minority, 60% women. **Class size:** 41% < 20, 57% 20-39, 1% 40-49, less than 1% 50-99. **Special facilities:** Wetlands, wellness center, observatory. **Partnerships:** Formal partnerships with Rolex Watch USA, Comcast, Lennox / HVAC, Northwest Hospital, City of Seattle Municipal Court.

Student profile. Among degree-seeking undergraduates, 61% enrolled in a transfer program, 39% enrolled in a vocational program, 22% already have a bachelor's degree or higher, 666 enrolled as first-time, first-year students.

Part-time:	51%	**Asian American:**	14%
Out-of-state:	2%	**Hispanic American:**	7%
Women:	55%	**Native American:**	2%
African American:	9%	**25 or older:**	58%

Transfer out. Colleges most students transferred to 2008: University of Washington, Seattle University, Seattle Pacific University, Washington State University, Western Washington University.

Basis for selection. Open admission. Applicants with deficient English or Math skills are required to take remedial courses to qualify for college level work.

2008-2009 Annual costs. Tuition/fees: $2,969; $8,183 out-of-state. Per-credit charge: $76 in-state; $248 out-of-state. Books/supplies: $972. Personal expenses: $1,674.

2007-2008 Financial aid. Need-based: Need-based aid available for part-time students. Work-study available weekends and for part-time students.

Application procedures. Admission: No deadline. No application fee. Admission notification on a rolling basis. **Financial aid:** Priority date 4/30, closing date 8/31. FAFSA, institutional form required. Applicants notified on a rolling basis starting 7/1; must reply within 2 week(s) of notification.

Academics. Special study options: Cooperative education, cross-registration, distance learning, dual enrollment of high school students, ESL, independent study, internships, liberal arts/career combination, study abroad. License preparation in nursing, paramedic, radiology, real estate. **Credit/placement by examination:** AP, CLEP, IB, institutional tests. 45 credit hours maximum toward associate degree. **Support services:** GED preparation and test center, learning center, reduced course load, remedial instruction, study skills assistance, tutoring, writing center.

Majors. Business: General, accounting technology, administrative services, office management, office technology, office/clerical, real estate. **Communications technology:** General. **Computer sciences:** Networking. **Education:** General, early childhood. **Engineering technology:** Biomedical, civil drafting, electrical. **Health:** Licensed practical nurse, medical assistant, nursing (RN), office assistant, pharmacy assistant, radiologic technology/medical imaging. **Mechanic/repair:** Heating/ac/refrig, industrial electronics, watch/jewelry. **Visual/performing arts:** General, art, dramatic, studio arts. **Other:** Nanotechnology.

Most popular majors. Business/marketing 21%, health sciences 14%, liberal arts 49%, physical sciences 6%.

Computing on campus. 2,000 workstations in library, computer center, student center. Commuter students can connect to campus network. Online course registration, online library, helpline, student web hosting, wireless network available.

Student life. Freshman orientation: Available. Preregistration for classes offered. Students can select from in-person or on-line orientations. **Activities:** Bands, choral groups, drama, international student organizations, literary magazine, music ensembles, radio station, student government, student newspaper, symphony orchestra, TV station, Phi Theta Kappa, Black student union, Indonesian community club, Vietnamese student association, art group, student leadership, Muslim student association, bio-med club, golf club.

Athletics. Intercollegiate: Basketball. **Intramural:** Basketball. **Team name:** Storm.

Student services. Adult student services, career counseling, services for economically disadvantaged, student employment services, financial aid counseling, minority student services, on-campus daycare, personal counseling, placement for graduates, veterans' counselor, women's services. **Physically disabled:** Services for visually, speech, hearing impaired. **Transfer:** Transfer adviser, college fairs on campus for students transferring to 4-year colleges.

Contact. E-mail: nsccregistration@sccd.ctc.edu
Phone: (206) 527-3663 Fax: (206) 527-3671
Betsy Abts, Registrar / Director of Admissions, North Seattle Community College, 9600 College Way North, Seattle, WA 98103

Northwest Aviation College

Auburn, Washington
www.NorthwestAviationCollege.edu **CB code: 3115**

- For-profit 2-year technical college
- Commuter campus in large town

General. Accredited by ACCSCT. Designated as 14 CFR Part 141 flight school, INS approved for issuance of I-20 for M1 and F1 visa. VA approved. **Enrollment:** 22 degree-seeking undergraduates. **Location:** 7 miles from Seattle. **Calendar:** Quarter, extensive summer session. **Full-time faculty:** 4 total; 25% minority, 25% women. **Part-time faculty:** 6 total; 17% minority. **Class size:** 100% < 20.

Student profile. Among degree-seeking undergraduates, 100% enrolled in a vocational program, 5% already have a bachelor's degree or higher, 5 enrolled as first-time, first-year students, 1 transferred in from other institutions.

Part-time:	36%	**Women:**	23%
Out-of-state:	14%	**25 or older:**	50%

Transfer out. Colleges most students transferred to 2008: Embry-Riddle Aeronautical University.

Basis for selection. Open admission. **Homeschooled:** Students must demonstrate the Ability to Benefit by submission of official test score from an independently administered test such as GED, ASSET, COMPASS.

High school preparation. College-preparatory program recommended.

2008-2009 Annual costs. Program costs for Associate program in Aviation Flight Technology: $60,233; Certificate programs for Professional Pilot 1: $51,111; Professional Pilot 2: $56,083; Professional Pilot 3: $69,912. All costs include tuition, books, materials, aircraft rental.

Application procedures. Admission: No deadline. $50 fee. Application must be submitted on paper. Admission notification on a rolling basis.

Academics. Special study options: Accelerated study, independent study. License preparation in aviation. **Credit/placement by examination:** CLEP, institutional tests. 60 credit hours maximum toward associate degree. **Support services:** Reduced course load, study skills assistance, tutoring.

Majors. Transportation: Airline/commercial pilot.

Computing on campus. 4 workstations in student center. Online library available.

Student life. Freshman orientation: Available. Preregistration for classes offered.

Student services. Adult student services, career counseling, student employment services, financial aid counseling. **Transfer:** Pre-admission transcript evaluation for new students. Transfer adviser for students transferring to 4-year colleges.

Contact. E-mail: spratt@afsnac.com
Phone: (253) 854-4960 Fax: (253) 931-0768
Shawn Pratt, Assistant Director of Education, Northwest Aviation College, 506 23rd Street, NE, Auburn, WA 98002

Northwest Indian College
Bellingham, Washington
www.nwic.edu **CB code: 3973**

- Public 2-year community college
- Commuter campus in small town

General. Regionally accredited. **Enrollment:** 467 degree-seeking undergraduates. **Degrees:** 49 associate awarded. **Location:** 8 miles from Bellingham. **Calendar:** Quarter, limited summer session. **Full-time faculty:** 22 total. **Part-time faculty:** 45 total.

Transfer out. Colleges most students transferred to 2008: Western Washington University, University of Washington, Lewis-Clark State College.

Basis for selection. Open admission.

2008-2009 Annual costs. Tuition/fees: $2,796; $7,332 out-of-state. Per-credit charge: $74 in-state; $200 out-of-state. Eligibility to pay resident costs based on tribal enrollment verification. Books/supplies: $800.

Financial aid. Need-based: Need-based aid available for part-time students. **Non-need-based:** Scholarships awarded for academics.

Application procedures. Admission: No deadline. No application fee. Application must be submitted on paper. Admission notification on a rolling basis. **Financial aid:** No deadline. FAFSA, institutional form required. Applicants notified on a rolling basis.

Academics. Special study options: Cooperative education, distance learning, dual enrollment of high school students, independent study, internships, student-designed major. Bachelor's degree programs available on campus. **Credit/placement by examination:** CLEP, institutional tests. **Support services:** GED preparation and test center, learning center, reduced course load, remedial instruction, study skills assistance, tutoring, writing center.

Majors. Area/ethnic studies: Native American. **Computer sciences:** Information technology. **Education:** Early childhood, Native American. **Other:** Chemical dependency studies, Life sciences, Native environmental science.

Most popular majors. Area/ethnic studies 25%, health sciences 10%, liberal arts 65%.

Computing on campus. 90 workstations in dormitories, library, computer center, student center. Dormitories wired for high-speed internet access and linked to campus network. Online course registration, helpline, repair service, wireless network available.

Student life. Freshman orientation: Available. Preregistration for classes offered. First days of fall quarter. **Housing:** Guaranteed on-campus for all undergraduates. Coed dorms available. $200 fully refundable deposit. **Activities:** Drama, student government, student newspaper, service learning center, culture club.

Athletics. Intercollegiate: Basketball, cross-country. **Intramural:** Basketball. **Team name:** Eagles.

Student services. Adult student services, alcohol/substance abuse counseling, career counseling, services for economically disadvantaged, student employment services, financial aid counseling, minority student services, on-campus daycare. **Transfer:** Pre-admission transcript evaluation for new students. Transfer adviser, college fairs on campus for students transferring to 4-year colleges.

Contact. E-mail: admissions@nwic.edu
Phone: (360) 676-2772 ext. 4269 Toll-free number: (866) 676-2772 ext. 4269 Fax: (360) 392-4333
Crystal Bagby, Associate Dean of Student Life, Northwest Indian College, 2522 Kwina Road, Bellingham, WA 98226-9217

Northwest School of Wooden Boatbuilding
Port Hadlock, Washington
www.nwboatschool.org **CB code: 3116**

- Private 1-year technical and maritime college
- Commuter campus in large town

General. Accredited by ACCSCT. **Location:** 60 miles from Seattle. **Calendar:** Quarter.

Annual costs/financial aid. Twelve month programs offered at a cost of $14,800. Estimated cost of tools $1,075; nine month diploma program $11,625; six month diploma program $7,850. Books/supplies: $1,000.

Contact. Phone: (360) 385-4948
42 North Water Street, Port Hadlock, WA 98339

Olympic College
Bremerton, Washington **CB member**
www.olympic.edu **CB code: 4583**

- Public 2-year community and liberal arts college
- Commuter campus in large town

General. Founded in 1946. Regionally accredited. Campuses at Shelton and Poulsbo. Classes also offered off-campus at Naval Base Kitsap, Bremerton and Bangor, and some local high schools. **Enrollment:** 3,111 degree-seeking undergraduates; 3,512 non-degree-seeking students. **Degrees:** 905 associate awarded. **Location:** 30 miles from Seattle, 35 miles from Tacoma. **Calendar:** Quarter, extensive summer session. **Full-time faculty:** 118 total. **Part-time faculty:** 401 total. **Partnerships:** Formal partnerships with Puget Sound Naval Shipyard, Running Start (high schools), West Sound Technical (cosmetology), US Navy, Service Corps of Retired Executives, the NW Women's Business Center, and Kitsap Regional Library.

Student profile. Among degree-seeking undergraduates, 598 enrolled as first-time, first-year students, 773 transferred in from other institutions.

Part-time:	46%	**Women:**	60%
Out-of-state:	17%	**25 or older:**	48%

Transfer out. Colleges most students transferred to 2008: University of Washington, Central Washington University, Washington State University, Western Washington University.

Basis for selection. Open admission, but selective for some programs. Admissions to registered nursing, licensed practical nursing, medical office assistant program based on several requirements including prerequisites, academic GPA, and test scores. English and math placement assessment is administered to degree/certificate-seeking applicants or for those who wish to enroll in English or math classes. Nursing and health occupation programs require students to attend a pre-application orientation. **Adult students:** SAT/ACT scores not required. **Homeschooled:** Transcript of courses and grades required.

2008-2009 Annual costs. Tuition/fees: $2,910; $3,305 out-of-state. Per-credit charge: $76 in-state; $89 out-of-state. Books/supplies: $924. Personal expenses: $1,524.

2008-2009 Financial aid. Need-based: Need-based aid available for part-time students. Work-study available nights and for part-time students. **Non-need-based:** Scholarships awarded for academics, state residency.

Application procedures. Admission: No deadline. No application fee. Admission notification on a rolling basis. **Financial aid:** Priority date 3/1; no closing date. FAFSA, institutional form required. Applicants notified on a rolling basis starting 6/1; must reply within 2 week(s) of notification.

Academics. Special study options: Combined bachelor's/graduate degree, cooperative education, cross-registration, distance learning, dual enrollment of high school students, ESL, independent study, internships, liberal arts/career combination, study abroad. 2-2 program with Old Dominion University permits completion of bachelor degree on premises at Olympic College, programs with Western Washington University and St. Martin's College. Running Start Program available for high school juniors/seniors with 2.5 GPA. Special articulation for professional/technical programs to transfer to Evergreen State College, Old Dominion, University of Washington-Tacoma in Business Management. Bachelor of Science in Nursing through UWT. Bachelor's degree programs available on campus. License preparation in nursing, physical therapy. **Credit/placement by examination:** AP, CLEP, IB, institutional tests. Credit awarded by exam, experiential credit, or CLEP varies by degree program. **Support services:** GED preparation and test center, learning center, remedial instruction, study skills assistance, tutoring, writing center.

Majors. Business: General, accounting technology, administrative services, business admin. **Communications:** General. **Communications technology:** Animation/special effects. **Computer sciences:** Computer science, networking, programming, security. **Construction:** Electrician, plumbing. **Education:** General, early childhood. **Engineering:** General. **Engineering technology:** Drafting, electrical, industrial. **Health:** Licensed practical nurse, medical assistant, nursing (RN). **Legal studies:** Legal secretary. **Liberal**

Two-Year Colleges

arts: Arts/sciences. **Mechanic/repair:** Automotive, marine. **Personal/culinary services:** Barbering, chef training, cosmetic. **Physical sciences:** Chemistry, geology, physics. **Production:** Welding. **Protective services:** Fire services admin, firefighting, police science. **Social sciences:** Anthropology, political science, sociology. **Visual/performing arts:** General, art.

Computing on campus. 670 workstations in library, computer center, student center. Commuter students can connect to campus network. Online course registration, online library, helpline, student web hosting, wireless network available.

Student life. Freshman orientation: Available. Preregistration for classes offered. In-person or online. In-person orientation takes place before advising. **Policies:** Student code of conduct. **Housing:** Apartments available for out-of-region students. **Activities:** Bands, choral groups, drama, music ensembles, musical theater, opera, student government, student newspaper, symphony orchestra, Phi Theta Kappa.

Athletics. NJCAA. **Intercollegiate:** Baseball M, basketball, golf, soccer, softball W, volleyball W, weight lifting. **Intramural:** Golf, soccer, weight lifting. **Team name:** Rangers.

Student services. Adult student services, career counseling, services for economically disadvantaged, student employment services, financial aid counseling, minority student services, on-campus daycare, personal counseling, placement for graduates, veterans' counselor, women's services. **Physically disabled:** Services for visually, speech, hearing impaired. **Transfer:** Reentry adviser for new students. Transfer adviser, college fairs on campus for students transferring to 4-year colleges.

Contact. E-mail: prospect@olympic.edu
Phone: (360) 475-7479 Toll-free number: (800) 259-6718 ext. 7479
Fax: (360) 475-7202
Jennifer Fyllingness, Director of Admissions and Outreach, Olympic College, 1600 Chester Avenue, Bremerton, WA 98337-1699

Peninsula College
Port Angeles, Washington
www.pc.ctc.edu **CB code: 4615**

- Public 2-year community college
- Commuter campus in large town

General. Founded in 1961. Regionally accredited. **Enrollment:** 928 degree-seeking undergraduates; 4,199 non-degree-seeking students. **Degrees:** 228 associate awarded. **Location:** 75 miles from Seattle. **Calendar:** Quarter, limited summer session. **Full-time faculty:** 56 total; 29% have terminal degrees, 11% minority. **Part-time faculty:** 98 total; 5% minority. **Class size:** 82% < 20, 17% 20-39, less than 1% 40-49, less than 1% 50-99. **Special facilities:** Marine laboratory, dam removal project.

Student profile. Among degree-seeking undergraduates, 216 enrolled as first-time, first-year students.

Part-time:	39%	**Women:**	62%
Out-of-state:	1%	**25 or older:**	41%

Basis for selection. Open admission, but selective for some programs. Special requirements for nursing program. ASSET required for full-time applicants for placement only. Admission to college does not guarantee admission to all courses or vocational education programs. Additional applications may be necessary. **Adult students:** SAT/ACT scores not required.

2008-2009 Annual costs. Tuition/fees: $2,847; $3,246 out-of-state. Per-credit charge: $79 in-state; $92 out-of-state. Books/supplies: $900. Personal expenses: $1,548.

2007-2008 Financial aid. Need-based: Need-based aid available for part-time students. **Non-need-based:** Scholarships awarded for academics, athletics, job skills.

Application procedures. Admission: No deadline. No application fee. Admission notification on a rolling basis. **Financial aid:** Priority date 4/1; no closing date. FAFSA, institutional form required. Applicants notified on a rolling basis starting 6/1; must reply within 2 week(s) of notification.

Academics. Special study options: Distance learning, double major, dual enrollment of high school students, ESL, honors, internships, liberal arts/career combination, study abroad. Bachelor's degree programs available on campus. License preparation in dental hygiene, nursing. **Credit/placement by examination:** AP, CLEP, institutional tests. 10 credit hours maximum toward associate degree. Must complete minimum 30 quarter hours of credit in residency with 2.75 GPA. **Support services:** GED preparation and test center, learning center, reduced course load, remedial instruction, study skills assistance, tutoring, writing center.

Majors. Business: Accounting, accounting technology, administrative services, business admin, marketing, office management. **Communications:** Journalism. **Computer sciences:** General, applications programming, data processing, networking, vendor certification, web page design. **Conservation:** Fisheries. **Education:** Early childhood. **Engineering technology:** Surveying. **Family/consumer sciences:** Child care. **Health:** Home attendant, medical assistant, medical secretary, nursing (RN), substance abuse counseling. **Liberal arts:** Arts/sciences. **Mechanic/repair:** Automotive, diesel, electronics/electrical. **Production:** Welding. **Protective services:** Corrections, law enforcement admin.

Most popular majors. Health sciences 17%, liberal arts 64%, natural resources/environmental science 7%.

Computing on campus. 79 workstations in library, computer center, student center. Online course registration, online library, wireless network available.

Student life. Freshman orientation: Available. **Activities:** Jazz band, choral groups, dance, drama, literary magazine, music ensembles, student government, student newspaper, Christian Collegiate Fellowship, Communications Careers Club, Native American Nations, Phi Theta Kappa, Phi Beta Lambda, IT club, Basketball Club, German Club.

Athletics. Intercollegiate: Basketball, soccer M, softball W. **Intramural:** Basketball, bowling, football (non-tackle) M, golf, soccer, softball, tennis, volleyball. **Team name:** Pirates.

Student services. Adult student services, career counseling, services for economically disadvantaged, student employment services, financial aid counseling, on-campus daycare, personal counseling, placement for graduates, veterans' counselor. **Physically disabled:** Services for visually, hearing impaired. **Transfer:** Pre-admission transcript evaluation for new students. Transfer adviser, college fairs on campus for students transferring to 4-year colleges.

Contact. E-mail: admissions@pcadmin.ctc.edu
Phone: (877) 452-9277 Toll-free number: (877) 452-9277
Fax: (360) 417-6581
Cindy Lauderback, Enrollment Service Manager, Peninsula College, 1502 East Lauridsen Boulevard, Port Angeles, WA 98362

Pierce College
Lakewood, Washington
www.pierce.ctc.edu **CB code: 4103**

- Public 2-year community college
- Commuter campus in small city

General. Founded in 1967. Regionally accredited. Colleges in Puyallup and Lakewood and education centers at Fort Lewis, McChord Air Force Base, McNeil Island, Cedar Creek, Western State Hospital and Rainier School. **Enrollment:** 9,939 degree-seeking undergraduates. **Degrees:** 1,445 associate awarded. **ROTC:** Army. **Location:** 10 miles from downtown. **Calendar:** Quarter, limited summer session. **Full-time faculty:** 138 total. **Part-time faculty:** 389 total. **Class size:** 82% < 20, 17% 20-39, 1% 40-49, less than 1% 50-99. **Special facilities:** Bird refuge, international house (video conferencing center for international/cross-cultural communications). **Partnerships:** Formal partnership with the Institute of Real Estate Management (IREM).

Student profile.

Out-of-state:	1%	**25 or older:**	48%

Transfer out. Colleges most students transferred to 2008: University of Washington (Seattle), University of Washington (Tacoma), Western Washington University, Central Washington University.

Basis for selection. Open admission, but selective for some programs. Admissions to dental hygiene and veterinary technology programs based on college course work, high school GPA, and/or related work experience. Running Start students must test at college level in English prior to admission. Students required to take ASSET or COMPASS placement tests to register for math, English, or reading courses. **Adult students:** SAT/ACT scores not required. Placement testing required for English and Quantitative courses. **Learning Disabled:** Accommodations for placement testing.

High school preparation. Algebra, biology, and chemistry required of veterinary technology applicants. Dental hygiene applicants have special mathematics/science requirements.

2008-2009 Annual costs. Tuition/fees: $3,071; $3,530 out-of-state. Per-credit charge: $76 in-state; $89 out-of-state. Books/supplies: $924. Personal expenses: $1,476.

Financial aid. **Need-based:** Need-based aid available for part-time students. Work-study available for part-time students. **Non-need-based:** Scholarships awarded for academics, athletics, music/drama.

Application procedures. **Admission:** No deadline. No application fee. Admission notification on a rolling basis. March 1 closing date for veterinary technology applications, February 1 for dental hygiene. High school students admitted early through Running Start Program. Must test at college level prior to admission. **Financial aid:** Priority date 4/15; no closing date. FAFSA, institutional form required. Applicants notified on a rolling basis starting 4/15.

Academics. **Special study options:** Cooperative education, cross-registration, distance learning, double major, dual enrollment of high school students, ESL, independent study, internships, student-designed major, study abroad, weekend college. License preparation in dental hygiene, nursing, real estate. **Credit/placement by examination:** AP, CLEP, institutional tests. 65 credit hours maximum toward associate degree. Credit by exam does not count toward degree residency requirement. **Support services:** GED preparation and test center, learning center, pre-admission summer program, reduced course load, remedial instruction, study skills assistance, tutoring, writing center.

Majors. **Agriculture:** Animal sciences, landscaping. **Business:** General, accounting, administrative services, business admin, office management, office/clerical. **Computer sciences:** Data processing, programming. **Construction:** Site management. **Education:** Business, early childhood, teacher assistance. **Engineering technology:** Electrical. **Family/consumer sciences:** Child care. **Foreign languages:** Translation. **Health:** Clinical lab assistant, dental hygiene, medical secretary, mental health services, substance abuse counseling, veterinary technology/assistant. **Legal studies:** Legal secretary, paralegal. **Liberal arts:** Arts/sciences. **Protective services:** Criminal justice, fire safety technology. **Visual/performing arts:** Commercial/advertising art.

Computing on campus. 600 workstations in library, computer center. Online course registration, helpline, wireless network available.

Student life. **Freshman orientation:** Available. 2-hour orientation offered quarterly and throughout summer. **Activities:** Bands, choral groups, drama, literary magazine, music ensembles, musical theater, student government, student newspaper, ethnic and foreign student associations, religious organizations, special interest clubs, Phi Theta Kappa, Barrier Breakers (disabled students).

Athletics. **Intercollegiate:** Baseball M, basketball, soccer M, softball W, volleyball W. **Intramural:** Cheerleading. **Team name:** Raiders.

Student services. Adult student services, career counseling, services for economically disadvantaged, student employment services, financial aid counseling, minority student services, on-campus daycare, personal counseling, veterans' counselor, women's services. **Physically disabled:** Services for visually, speech, hearing impaired. **Transfer:** Transfer center, transfer adviser, college fairs on campus for students transferring to 4-year colleges.

Contact. E-mail: cburbank@pierce.ctc.edu
Phone: (253) 964-6501 Fax: (253) 964-6427
Anne White, Registrar, Pierce College, 9401 Farwest Drive SW, Lakewood, WA 98498-1999

Renton Technical College

Renton, Washington
www.RTC.edu **CB code: 0790**

- Public 2-year technical college
- Commuter campus in large town

General. Founded in 1942. Regionally accredited. **Enrollment:** 791 degree-seeking undergraduates. **Degrees:** 169 associate awarded. **Location:** 10 miles from Seattle. **Calendar:** Quarter, extensive summer session. **Full-time faculty:** 87 total. **Part-time faculty:** 134 total. **Special facilities:** Technology resource center.

Basis for selection. Open admission. ACT, ASSET and SLEP scores required for all applicants for placement purposes. Interview recommended. **Adult students:** Students must complete on-campus assessment.

2008-2009 Annual costs. Tuition/fees: $3,105. Books/supplies: $690.

2007-2008 Financial aid. All financial aid based on need. Need-based aid available for part-time students.

Application procedures. **Admission:** No deadline. $25 fee, may be waived for applicants with need. Application must be submitted on paper. Admission notification on a rolling basis. **Financial aid:** Priority date 5/1; no closing date. FAFSA, institutional form required. Applicants notified on a rolling basis.

Academics. Many programs have co-op component. **Special study options:** Cooperative education, distance learning, dual enrollment of high school students, ESL, external degree, internships, liberal arts/career combination, student-designed major. License preparation in nursing, real estate. **Credit/placement by examination:** CLEP. 30 credit hours maximum toward associate degree. **Support services:** GED preparation and test center, learning center, remedial instruction, study skills assistance, tutoring.

Majors. **Business:** Accounting, administrative services, office management, office/clerical. **Computer sciences:** Applications programming, computer science, networking, programming. **Construction:** Carpentry. **Education:** Business, early childhood, teacher assistance, voc/tech. **Engineering:** Electrical. **Engineering technology:** CAD/CADD, drafting, surveying. **Family/consumer sciences:** Child care. **Health:** Dental assistant, insurance coding, licensed practical nurse, massage therapy, medical assistant, medical records admin, medical secretary, pharmacy assistant, surgical technology. **Legal studies:** Legal secretary. **Mechanic/repair:** Auto body, automotive, electronics/electrical, heating/ac/refrig, industrial, musical instruments. **Personal/culinary services:** Culinary arts. **Production:** Machine shop technology.

Computing on campus. 150 workstations in library, computer center, student center. Online library available.

Student life. **Freshman orientation:** Available. **Activities:** Student newspaper.

Student services. Career counseling, student employment services, financial aid counseling, on-campus daycare, personal counseling, placement for graduates. **Physically disabled:** Services for visually, speech, hearing impaired. **Transfer:** Pre-admission transcript evaluation for new students. Transfer adviser for students transferring to 4-year colleges.

Contact. E-mail: briverman@rtc.edu
Phone: (425) 235-5840 Fax: (425) 235-7832
Jon Pozega, Vice President Student Services, Renton Technical College, 3000 NE Fourth Street, Renton, WA 98056-4195

Seattle Central Community College

Seattle, Washington
www.seattlecentral.org **CB code: 4741**

- Public 2-year community college
- Commuter campus in very large city

General. Founded in 1966. Regionally accredited. **Calendar:** Quarter.

Annual costs/financial aid. Tuition/fees (2008-2009): $2,910; $8,124 out-of-state. Books/supplies: $720. Personal expenses: $1,896. Need-based financial aid available to full-time and part-time students.

Contact. Phone: (206) 587-5450
Admissions Director, 1701 Broadway, Seattle, WA 98122

Shoreline Community College

Shoreline, Washington
www.shoreline.edu **CB code: 4738**

- Public 2-year community college
- Commuter campus in small city

General. Founded in 1964. Regionally accredited. Courses available at Lake Forest Park campus. **Enrollment:** 5,823 degree-seeking undergraduates. **Degrees:** 709 associate awarded. **Location:** 10 miles from Seattle. **Calendar:** Quarter, limited summer session. **Full-time faculty:** 149 total. **Part-time faculty:** 232 total.

Transfer out. **Colleges most students transferred to 2008:** University of Washington, Western Washington University.

Basis for selection. Open admission, but selective for some programs. SAT, ACT, or ASSET required for English and math placement unless student has taken college-level English or math with grades of C or better. Nursing and dental hygiene programs use competitive admissions process.

2008-2009 Annual costs. Tuition/fees: $2,881; $5,268 out-of-state. Books/supplies: $924. Personal expenses: $3,516.

2007-2008 Financial aid. **Need-based:** 63% of total undergraduate aid awarded as scholarships/grants, 37% as loans/jobs. Work-study available nights, weekends and for part-time students. **Additional information:** Tuition and/or fee waiver for students with need on space-available basis.

Application procedures. **Admission:** No deadline. No application fee. Admission notification on a rolling basis beginning on or about 2/1. **Financial aid:** Priority date 4/1; no closing date. FAFSA, institutional form required. Applicants notified on a rolling basis starting 8/1; must reply within 3 week(s) of notification.

Academics. **Special study options:** Cooperative education, cross-registration, distance learning, dual enrollment of high school students, ESL, independent study, internships, study abroad. Senior College for senior citizens. **Credit/placement by examination:** CLEP, IB. **Support services:** GED preparation and test center, learning center, remedial instruction, tutoring.

Majors. **Biology:** Biotechnology. **Business:** Accounting technology, business admin, fashion, international, logistics, marketing, sales/distribution, small business admin. **Communications:** Broadcast journalism. **Communications technology:** Graphic/printing. **Computer sciences:** General, data processing, database management, networking, web page design. **Education:** Early childhood, special, teacher assistance. **Engineering:** General, civil, mechanical. **Engineering technology:** CAD/CADD, civil, drafting, industrial, manufacturing, mechanical. **Family/consumer sciences:** Food/nutrition. **Health:** Clinical lab assistant, dental hygiene, dietetics, medical records technology, nursing (RN). **Liberal arts:** Arts/sciences. **Mechanic/repair:** Automotive. **Personal/culinary services:** Cosmetic. **Physical sciences:** General, oceanography. **Production:** Machine tool. **Protective services:** Law enforcement admin. **Science technology:** Biological. **Visual/performing arts:** Cinematography, commercial/advertising art, design, music management, music performance, photography, theater design. **Other:** Digital/Audio engineering, Emergency dispatcher, Speech language pathology assistant.

Most popular majors. Health sciences 20%, liberal arts 57%.

Computing on campus. 450 workstations in library, computer center. Commuter students can connect to campus network. Online library, helpline, wireless network available.

Student life. **Freshman orientation:** Mandatory. Preregistration for classes offered. Two to three hours, prior to each quarter. **Activities:** Bands, choral groups, drama, literary magazine, music ensembles, musical theater, opera, student government, student newspaper, International club, Black Student Union, arts and entertainment board, women's club, Cambodian club, Vietnamese club, DEC, Phi Theta Kappa, Student Body Association.

Athletics. NJCAA. **Intercollegiate:** Baseball M, basketball, soccer, softball W, tennis, volleyball W. **Intramural:** Archery, basketball, bowling, diving, fencing, golf, racquetball, skiing, soccer, softball W, swimming, tennis, volleyball. **Team name:** Dolphins.

Student services. Adult student services, career counseling, student employment services, financial aid counseling, minority student services, on-campus daycare, personal counseling, placement for graduates, veterans' counselor, women's services. **Physically disabled:** Services for visually, hearing impaired. **Transfer:** Transfer adviser, college fairs on campus for students transferring to 4-year colleges.

Contact. E-mail: sccadmis@ctc.edu
Phone: (206) 546-4621 Fax: (206) 546-5835
Chris Melton, Registrar, Shoreline Community College, 16101 Greenwood Avenue North, Seattle, WA 98133

Skagit Valley College
Mount Vernon, Washington
www.skagit.edu **CB code: 4699**

- Public 2-year community college
- Commuter campus in large town

General. Founded in 1926. Regionally accredited. 2 campuses: Mount Vernon (main campus) and Oak Harbor on Whidbey Island. **Enrollment:** 2,207 full-time, degree-seeking students. **Degrees:** 535 associate awarded. **Location:** 60 miles from Seattle, 90 miles from Vancouver, British Columbia. **Calendar:** Quarter, extensive summer session. **Full-time faculty:** 125 total. **Part-time faculty:** 120 total. **Partnerships:** Contract programs with Washington businesses, Tech Prep, College in the High School.

Student profile.

Out-of-state:	4%	**Live on campus:**	2%
25 or older:	56%		

Transfer out. **Colleges most students transferred to 2008:** Everett Community College, Whatcom Community College, Western Washington University, Edmonds Community College, University of Washington.

Basis for selection. Open admission. High school diploma required for some programs.

2008-2009 Annual costs. Tuition/fees: $2,905; $3,300 out-of-state. Per-credit charge: $76 in-state; $89 out-of-state. Room only: $3,420. Books/supplies: $900.

Financial aid. All financial aid based on need. Need-based aid available for part-time students. Work-study available nights, weekends and for part-time students.

Application procedures. **Admission:** No deadline. No application fee. Admission notification on a rolling basis. **Financial aid:** Priority date 3/1; no closing date. FAFSA, institutional form required. Applicants notified on a rolling basis starting 7/1; must reply within 2 week(s) of notification.

Academics. **Special study options:** Cooperative education, cross-registration, distance learning, dual enrollment of high school students, ESL, external degree, honors, independent study, internships, study abroad, weekend college. License preparation in nursing. **Credit/placement by examination:** CLEP, IB, institutional tests. 15 credit hours maximum toward associate degree. **Support services:** GED preparation and test center, learning center, pre-admission summer program, reduced course load, remedial instruction, study skills assistance, tutoring, writing center.

Majors. **Agriculture:** Business, dairy, horticulture. **Business:** Accounting, administrative services, business admin, hospitality/recreation. **Communications:** General. **Computer sciences:** General, applications programming, information systems, programming. **Conservation:** General. **Education:** Early childhood. **Engineering:** Electrical. **Engineering technology:** Electrical. **Health:** Licensed practical nurse, nursing (RN), prenursing. **Legal studies:** Paralegal. **Liberal arts:** Arts/sciences. **Mechanic/repair:** Automotive, diesel, electronics/electrical. **Personal/culinary services:** Culinary arts. **Protective services:** Firefighting. **Public administration:** Human services. **Visual/performing arts:** Commercial/advertising art.

Most popular majors. Business/marketing 7%, computer/information sciences 7%, liberal arts 68%.

Computing on campus. 250 workstations in library, computer center. Commuter students can connect to campus network. Online course registration, helpline, repair service, student web hosting available.

Student life. **Freshman orientation:** Available. Preregistration for classes offered. Orientation/registration/testing before start of each quarter. Evening and day orientation at beginning of each quarter. **Housing:** Apartments available. $180 deposit. **Activities:** Bands, choral groups, dance, drama, literary magazine, music ensembles, musical theater, radio station, student government, student newspaper, symphony orchestra, Calling All Color, nurses club, firefighters club, Campus Christian Fellowship, sailing club, Delta Epsilon Chi, ski club, horticultural club, Phi Theta Kappa, international club.

Athletics. **Intercollegiate:** Baseball M, basketball, golf, soccer, softball W, tennis, volleyball W. **Intramural:** Badminton, baseball M, basketball, bowling, golf, sailing, soccer, softball, tennis, volleyball. **Team name:** Cardinals.

Student services. Adult student services, career counseling, services for economically disadvantaged, student employment services, financial aid counseling, health services, minority student services, on-campus daycare, personal counseling, placement for graduates, veterans' counselor, women's services. **Physically disabled:** Services for visually, speech, hearing impaired. **Transfer:** Re-entry adviser, pre-admission transcript evaluation for new students. Transfer center, transfer adviser, college fairs on campus for students transferring to 4-year colleges.

Contact. E-mail: admissions@skagit.edu
Phone: (360) 416-7697 Toll-free number: (877) 385-5360
Fax: (360) 416-7890
Karen Bates, Recruitment and Admissions, Skagit Valley College, 2405 East College Way, Mount Vernon, WA 98273

South Puget Sound Community College
Olympia, Washington
www.spscc.ctc.edu **CB code: 4578**

- Public 2-year community college
- Commuter campus in small city

General. Founded in 1962. Regionally accredited. **Enrollment:** 2,930 degree-seeking undergraduates; 2,460 non-degree-seeking students. **Degrees:** 563

associate awarded. **ROTC:** Air Force. **Location:** 60 miles from Seattle. **Calendar:** Quarter, limited summer session. **Full-time faculty:** 96 total; 15% minority, 52% women. **Part-time faculty:** 242 total; 37% minority, 57% women.

Student profile. Among degree-seeking undergraduates, 46% enrolled in a transfer program, 39% enrolled in a vocational program, 6% already have a bachelor's degree or higher, 424 enrolled as first-time, first-year students.

Part-time:	44%	**Asian American:**	5%
Out-of-state:	3%	**Hispanic American:**	6%
Women:	61%	**Native American:**	2%
African American:	3%	**25 or older:**	41%

Transfer out. Colleges most students transferred to 2008: Evergreen State College, University of Washington, Washington State University, Western Washington State University.

Basis for selection. Open admission, but selective for some programs. Special requirements for nursing, dental assisting, fire protection. **Adult students:** CASAS required for Adult Basic Education.

2008-2009 Annual costs. Tuition/fees: $2,824; $3,283 out-of-state. Per-credit charge: $75 in-state; $89 out-of-state. Books/supplies: $900. Personal expenses: $2,844.

2007-2008 Financial aid. Need-based: 80% of total undergraduate aid awarded as scholarships/grants, 20% as loans/jobs. Need-based aid available for part-time students. **Non-need-based:** Scholarships awarded for academics, athletics.

Application procedures. Admission: Closing date 9/5. No application fee. Admission notification on a rolling basis beginning on or about 12/1. Early applicants register in mid-July for fall quarter. **Financial aid:** Priority date 5/1, closing date 6/27. FAFSA, institutional form required. Applicants notified on a rolling basis starting 7/10; must reply within 2 week(s) of notification.

Academics. Special study options: Cooperative education, cross-registration, distance learning, dual enrollment of high school students, ESL, honors, independent study, internships, study abroad, weekend college. License preparation in nursing. **Credit/placement by examination:** AP, CLEP, IB, institutional tests. 45 credit hours maximum toward associate degree. **Support services:** GED preparation and test center, learning center, remedial instruction, study skills assistance, tutoring, writing center.

Majors. Agriculture: Horticulture, ornamental horticulture. **Business:** General, accounting, administrative services, hospitality admin, office/clerical. **Computer sciences:** Applications programming, data processing, information systems. **Education:** Early childhood. **Engineering technology:** Drafting, electrical. **Health:** Dental assistant, medical assistant, medical secretary, nursing assistant. **Legal studies:** Legal secretary, paralegal. **Liberal arts:** Arts/sciences. **Personal/culinary services:** Culinary arts. **Production:** Welding. **Protective services:** Firefighting.

Most popular majors. Business/marketing 13%, health sciences 13%, liberal arts 59%.

Computing on campus. 117 workstations in library, computer center, student center. Commuter students can connect to campus network. Online course registration, wireless network available.

Student life. Freshman orientation: Available. **Activities:** Choral groups, drama, international student organizations, music ensembles, musical theater, student government, student newspaper.

Athletics. Intercollegiate: Basketball, soccer M, softball W. **Team name:** Clippers.

Student services. Adult student services, career counseling, services for economically disadvantaged, student employment services, financial aid counseling, minority student services, on-campus daycare, personal counseling, placement for graduates, veterans' counselor. **Physically disabled:** Services for visually, speech, hearing impaired. **Transfer:** Transfer adviser, college fairs on campus for students transferring to 4-year colleges.

Contact. E-mail: enrollmentservices@spscc.ctc.edu
Phone: (360) 754-7711 ext. 5241 Fax: (360) 596-5907
Lyn Sharp, Director of Admissions and Registration, South Puget Sound Community College, 2011 Mottman Road, SW, Olympia, WA 98512-6218

South Seattle Community College

Seattle, Washington
www.southseattle.edu **CB code: 4759**

- Public 2-year community college
- Commuter campus in very large city

General. Founded in 1969. Regionally accredited. Culturally diverse campus with over 35 languages spoken. **Enrollment:** 3,667 degree-seeking undergraduates. **Degrees:** 464 associate awarded. **Location:** 10 minutes from downtown. **Calendar:** Quarter, limited summer session. **Full-time faculty:** 80 total; 11% have terminal degrees, 26% minority, 40% women. **Part-time faculty:** 240 total; 21% minority, 47% women. **Special facilities:** College operated bakery and restaurants, arboretum; Seattle Chinese Garden.

Student profile.

Out-of-state:	1%	**25 or older:**	63%

Transfer out. Colleges most students transferred to 2008: University of Washington.

Basis for selection. Open admission, but selective for some programs. COMPASS, ESL COMPASS tests used for placement and counseling. **Learning Disabled:** Referred to Educational Support Services Office.

2008-2009 Annual costs. Tuition/fees: $2,910; $8,124 out-of-state. Books/supplies: $924. Personal expenses: $1,590.

2007-2008 Financial aid. Need-based: 94% of total undergraduate aid awarded as scholarships/grants, 6% as loans/jobs. Need-based aid available for part-time students. Work-study available for part-time students. **Non-need-based:** Scholarships awarded for academics, state residency.

Application procedures. Admission: No deadline. No application fee. Admission notification on a rolling basis. **Financial aid:** Priority date 4/16; no closing date. FAFSA, institutional form required. Applicants notified on a rolling basis starting 7/1.

Academics. Special study options: Cross-registration, distance learning, dual enrollment of high school students, ESL, independent study, internships, study abroad. Concurrent enrollment agreements with other colleges in vicinity; university partners offer bachelor's degrees on campus. License preparation in aviation, nursing. **Credit/placement by examination:** CLEP, IB, institutional tests. Credit awarded for CLEP applies only to electives category of Associate of Arts degree. **Support services:** GED preparation and test center, learning center, remedial instruction, study skills assistance, tutoring, writing center.

Majors. Agriculture: Greenhouse operations, horticultural science, landscaping, nursery operations, ornamental horticulture. **Architecture:** Landscape. **Area/ethnic studies:** Asian. **Biology:** General. **Business:** General, accounting, administrative services, hospitality admin, office management, office technology, restaurant/food services. **Computer sciences:** General, computer graphics, information systems, LAN/WAN management, programming, security, system admin, web page design, webmaster. **Construction:** Electrician. **Engineering:** General, software. **Engineering technology:** CAD/CADD, civil, drafting, mechanical. **Health:** Licensed practical nurse, premedicine, prenursing, prepharmacy. **Liberal arts:** Arts/sciences. **Mechanic/repair:** Aircraft, aircraft powerplant, auto body, automotive, diesel, heavy equipment. **Personal/culinary services:** Baking, chef training, culinary arts, food prep, restaurant/catering. **Physical sciences:** Atmospheric science, chemistry. **Production:** Welding. **Transportation:** Aviation, truck/bus/commercial vehicle.

Computing on campus. 700 workstations in library, computer center, student center. Online course registration, online library, wireless network available.

Student life. Freshman orientation: Available. **Policies:** Enrollment in 10 or more credits and 2.5 cumulative GPA required to serve as student government representative. **Activities:** Choral groups, international student organizations, literary magazine, student government, student newspaper, Vietnamese student club, Black student union, Latino club, Gay Straight Alliance, engineering club, Aviation Technician Association, International Student club, nursing club.

Athletics. Intramural: Basketball. **Team name:** Storm.

Student services. Adult student services, career counseling, services for economically disadvantaged, student employment services, financial aid counseling, minority student services, on-campus daycare, placement for graduates, veterans' counselor, women's services. **Physically disabled:** Services for visually, speech, hearing impaired. **Transfer:** Pre-admission transcript evaluation for new students. Transfer center, transfer adviser, college fairs on campus for students transferring to 4-year colleges.

Contact. E-mail: ssccadmissions@sccd.ctc.edu
Phone: (206) 768-7943 Fax: (206) 764-7947
Vanessa Reed, Director of Student Outreach, Admissions and Recruitment, South Seattle Community College, 6000 16th Avenue, SW, Seattle, WA 98106-1499

Spokane Community College
Spokane, Washington
www.scc.spokane.edu **CB code: 4739**

- Public 2-year community college
- Commuter campus in small city

General. Founded in 1963. Regionally accredited. **Enrollment:** 6,211 degree-seeking undergraduates; 794 non-degree-seeking students. **Degrees:** 1,055 associate awarded. **ROTC:** Army, Naval, Air Force. **Location:** 2 miles from downtown. **Calendar:** Quarter, limited summer session. **Full-time faculty:** 196 total. **Part-time faculty:** 213 total. **Special facilities:** Nursery, floral shop, automotive repair service center, cosmetology center.

Student profile. Among degree-seeking undergraduates, 25% enrolled in a transfer program, 46% enrolled in a vocational program, 4% already have a bachelor's degree or higher, 2,121 enrolled as first-time, first-year students.

Part-time:	29%	**Women:**	60%
Out-of-state:	4%	**25 or older:**	54%

Transfer out. Colleges most students transferred to 2008: Eastern Washington University, Washington State University.

Basis for selection. Open admission, but selective for some programs. Admission to college does not guarantee acceptance into every program. ASSET used for placement. **Homeschooled:** If under 18, must be deemed able to benefit from curricular offerings of college. Required to take ASSET or COMPASS tests and must place at college level.

2008-2009 Annual costs. Tuition/fees: $2,876; $3,410 out-of-state. Per-credit charge: $76 in-state; $102 out-of-state. Books/supplies: $780. Personal expenses: $3,012.

2008-2009 Financial aid. Non-need-based: Scholarships awarded for athletics.

Application procedures. Admission: No deadline. $15 fee, may be waived for applicants with need. Admission notification on a rolling basis beginning on or about 1/1. **Financial aid:** No deadline. FAFSA, institutional form required. Applicants notified on a rolling basis; must reply within 2 week(s) of notification.

Academics. Special study options: Cooperative education, cross-registration, distance learning, dual enrollment of high school students, ESL, independent study, internships, student-designed major, study abroad. License preparation in nursing, paramedic. **Credit/placement by examination:** AP, CLEP, institutional tests. 60 credit hours maximum toward associate degree. **Support services:** Learning center, reduced course load, remedial instruction, study skills assistance, tutoring, writing center.

Majors. Agriculture: Business, greenhouse operations, horticulture, nursery operations, soil science, turf management. **Business:** General, accounting, administrative services, banking/financial services, business admin, management information systems, marketing, office management, office technology, office/clerical, selling, vehicle parts marketing. **Computer sciences:** Applications programming, data processing, information systems. **Conservation:** Forest resources, forestry, water/wetlands/marine, wildlife. **Construction:** Carpentry, power transmission. **Engineering technology:** Architectural, civil, construction, electrical, hydraulics, robotics. **Health:** Cardiovascular technology, clinical lab technology, dental assistant, EMT paramedic, medical secretary, optician, pharmacy assistant, recreational therapy, respiratory therapy technology, surgical technology, ward clerk. **Legal studies:** Legal secretary, paralegal, prelaw. **Liberal arts:** Arts/sciences. **Mechanic/repair:** Aircraft, auto body, diesel, electronics/electrical, heating/ac/refrig, industrial. **Parks/recreation:** Facilities management. **Personal/culinary services:** Cosmetic, culinary arts. **Protective services:** Corrections, fire services admin, law enforcement admin, police science, security services.

Computing on campus. 913 workstations in library, computer center, student center. Online course registration available.

Student life. Freshman orientation: Available. Preregistration for classes offered. **Activities:** Drama, literary magazine, student government, student newspaper.

Athletics. Intercollegiate: Baseball M, basketball, cross-country, golf, soccer, softball W, tennis, track and field, volleyball W. **Team name:** Big Foot.

Student services. Adult student services, career counseling, services for economically disadvantaged, student employment services, financial aid counseling, minority student services, on-campus daycare, personal counseling, placement for graduates, veterans' counselor. **Physically disabled:** Services for visually, speech, hearing impaired. **Transfer:** College fairs on campus for students transferring to 4-year colleges.

Contact. Phone: (509) 533-8860 Toll-free number: (800) 248-5644
Fax: (509) 533-8860
Doug Jones, Dean of Student Services for Enrollment Services, Spokane Community College, 1810 North Greene Street, Spokane, WA 99217-5399

Spokane Falls Community College
Spokane, Washington
www.spokanefalls.edu **CB code: 4752**

- Public 2-year community college
- Commuter campus in small city
- Interview required

General. Founded in 1967. Regionally accredited. **Enrollment:** 5,783 degree-seeking undergraduates. **Degrees:** 937 associate awarded. **ROTC:** Army. **Location:** 4 miles from downtown. **Calendar:** Quarter, limited summer session. **Full-time faculty:** 180 total. **Part-time faculty:** 416 total. **Special facilities:** Theater, performing arts center, 60-foot Foucault pendulum.

Transfer out. Colleges most students transferred to 2008: Spokane Community Colleges, Big Bend Community College.

Basis for selection. Open admission, but selective for some programs. Admission to college does not guarantee acceptance to every program. ASSET test required for placement.

2008-2009 Annual costs. Tuition/fees: $2,876; $3,410 out-of-state. Per-credit charge: $76 in-state; $102 out-of-state. Books/supplies: $924. Personal expenses: $3,110.

Financial aid. All financial aid based on need. Need-based aid available for part-time students.

Application procedures. Admission: No deadline. $15 fee. Admission notification on a rolling basis. **Financial aid:** Priority date 4/1; no closing date. FAFSA, institutional form required. Applicants notified on a rolling basis starting 5/15; must reply within 2 week(s) of notification.

Academics. Special study options: Cooperative education, cross-registration, distance learning, dual enrollment of high school students, ESL, honors, independent study, internships, study abroad, weekend college. License preparation in aviation, physical therapy. **Credit/placement by examination:** AP, CLEP, institutional tests. 60 credit hours maximum toward associate degree. **Support services:** GED preparation and test center, learning center, remedial instruction, study skills assistance, tutoring, writing center.

Majors. Architecture: Interior. **Business:** General, accounting, administrative services, banking/financial services, business admin, fashion, international, management information systems, marketing, office management, office/clerical, tourism/travel. **Communications:** Journalism. **Communications technology:** General. **Computer sciences:** General, computer graphics, computer science, information systems, web page design. **Education:** General, early childhood, special, teacher assistance. **Engineering:** General. **Engineering technology:** Architectural, drafting, electrical. **Foreign languages:** General, sign language interpretation. **Health:** Athletic training, clinical lab technology, health services, medical assistant, medical records technology, nursing (RN), occupational therapy assistant, orthotics/prosthetics, physical therapy assistant, prenursing, substance abuse counseling, vocational rehab counseling. **Legal studies:** Paralegal. **Liberal arts:** Arts/sciences. **Math:** General. **Mechanic/repair:** Automotive. **Parks/recreation:** Sports admin. **Protective services:** Firefighting, law enforcement admin. **Transportation:** General. **Visual/performing arts:** Commercial photography, commercial/advertising art, interior design.

Most popular majors. Health sciences 9%, liberal arts 74%.

Computing on campus. 400 workstations in library, computer center.

Student life. Freshman orientation: Mandatory. Preregistration for classes offered. **Policies:** Student conduct code. **Activities:** Bands, choral groups, drama, literary magazine, music ensembles, opera, student government, student newspaper, symphony orchestra.

Athletics. Intercollegiate: Baseball M, basketball, cross-country, golf, soccer, softball W, tennis, track and field. **Intramural:** Basketball, soccer, table tennis, tennis, volleyball.

Student services. Adult student services, career counseling, services for economically disadvantaged, student employment services, financial aid counseling, health services, minority student services, on-campus daycare, personal counseling, placement for graduates, veterans' counselor, women's services. **Physically disabled:** Services for visually, hearing impaired. **Transfer:** Transfer adviser, college fairs on campus for students transferring to 4-year colleges.

Contact. Phone: (509) 533-3305 Toll-free number: (888) 509-7944
Fax: (509) 533-3237
Vice President of Student Services, Spokane Falls Community College, 3410 West Fort George Wright Drive, Spokane, WA 99224

Tacoma Community College
Tacoma, Washington
www.tacomacc.edu
CB member
CB code: 4826

- Public 2-year community college
- Commuter campus in small city

General. Founded in 1965. Regionally accredited. Programs offered at Tacoma Campus and Gig Harbor Center. **Enrollment:** 6,090 degree-seeking undergraduates. **Degrees:** 701 associate awarded. **Location:** 30 miles from Seattle, 30 miles from Olympia. **Calendar:** Quarter, limited summer session. **Full-time faculty:** 139 total. **Part-time faculty:** 330 total.

Student profile.

Part-time:	41%	**Women:**	65%
Out-of-state:	1%	**25 or older:**	49%

Transfer out. Colleges most students transferred to 2008: University of Washington.

Basis for selection. Open admission. **Adult students:** Accuplacer assessment required for students intending to enroll in 6 or more credits; students taking math or English; students enrolling in a degree or certificate program. **Learning Disabled:** Students who wish to receive accommodations need to present documentation to the college.

High school preparation. College-preparatory program recommended. 23 units recommended. Recommended units include English 4, mathematics 3, social studies 4, history 3, science 3 (laboratory 1), foreign language 2, computer science 1, visual/performing arts 1 and academic electives 1.

2008-2009 Annual costs. Tuition/fees: $2,932; $3,328 out-of-state. Books/supplies: $800.

Financial aid. All financial aid based on need. Need-based aid available for part-time students. Work-study available nights, weekends and for part-time students.

Application procedures. Admission: No deadline. No application fee. Admission notification on a rolling basis. **Financial aid:** Priority date 3/26; no closing date. FAFSA, institutional form required. Applicants notified on a rolling basis starting 7/20; must reply within 4 week(s) of notification.

Academics. Special study options: Distance learning, dual enrollment of high school students, ESL, internships, study abroad. Concurrent enrollment with nearby community colleges. Bachelor's degree programs available on campus. License preparation in nursing, paramedic, radiology. **Credit/placement by examination:** AP, CLEP, IB, institutional tests. 45 credit hours maximum toward associate degree. **Support services:** GED preparation and test center, learning center, reduced course load, remedial instruction, study skills assistance, tutoring, writing center.

Majors. Computer sciences: General. **Education:** Teacher assistance. **Health:** EMT paramedic. **Liberal arts:** Arts/sciences. **Protective services:** Corrections.

Computing on campus. 185 workstations in library, computer center, student center. Commuter students can connect to campus network. Online course registration, online library, helpline, wireless network available.

Student life. Freshman orientation: Mandatory. Preregistration for classes offered. **Housing:** Homestay Program available for international students. **Activities:** Jazz band, choral groups, international student organizations, literary magazine, music ensembles, student government, student newspaper.

Athletics. Intercollegiate: Baseball M, basketball, soccer, volleyball W. **Team name:** Titans.

Student services. Adult student services, career counseling, services for economically disadvantaged, student employment services, financial aid counseling, minority student services, on-campus daycare, personal counseling, veterans' counselor. **Physically disabled:** Services for visually, speech, hearing impaired. **Transfer:** Pre-admission transcript evaluation for new students. Transfer adviser, college fairs on campus for students transferring to 4-year colleges.

Contact. Phone: (253) 566-5001 Fax: (253) 566-6011
Mary McCabe, Registrar, Tacoma Community College, 6501 South 19th Street, Tacoma, WA 98466-9971

Walla Walla Community College
Walla Walla, Washington
www.wwcc.edu
CB code: 4963

- Public 2-year community and technical college
- Commuter campus in large town

General. Founded in 1967. Regionally accredited. Academic and vocational courses offered at educational center at Clarkston, Washington and Department of Corrections at the Washington State Penitentiary. **Enrollment:** 2,841 degree-seeking undergraduates; 3,079 non-degree-seeking students. **Degrees:** 494 associate awarded. **Location:** 158 miles from Spokane, 262 miles from Seattle. **Calendar:** Quarter, limited summer session. **Full-time faculty:** 129 total. **Part-time faculty:** 173 total. **Class size:** 78% < 20, 19% 20-39, less than 1% 40-49, 2% 50-99. **Special facilities:** Enology (winemaking), viticulture, culinary and John Deere facilities. **Partnerships:** Formal partnerships with John Deere & Company training center, Cisco Corporation.

Student profile. Among degree-seeking undergraduates, 37% enrolled in a transfer program, 62% enrolled in a vocational program, 4% already have a bachelor's degree or higher, 631 enrolled as first-time, first-year students.

Part-time:	35%	**Women:**	59%
Out-of-state:	20%	**25 or older:**	45%

Transfer out. Colleges most students transferred to 2008: Washington State University, Lewis & Clark College, Walla Walla University, Eastern Washington University, University of Idaho.

Basis for selection. Open admission, but selective for some programs. Special requirements for health science and vocational programs. COMPASS or ASSET placement tests used for English, reading, math. TOEFL score of 500 or higher needed to demonstrate English proficiency. **Learning Disabled:** Flexible procedures; early registration.

High school preparation. Recommended units include English 4, mathematics 4 and science 3.

2008-2009 Annual costs. Tuition/fees: $2,970; $4,069 out-of-state. Per-credit charge: $92 in-state; $105 out-of-state. Books/supplies: $924. Personal expenses: $1,800.

2007-2008 Financial aid. Need-based: 61% of total undergraduate aid awarded as scholarships/grants, 39% as loans/jobs. Need-based aid available for part-time students. Work-study available nights and for part-time students. **Non-need-based:** Scholarships awarded for academics, athletics, leadership, music/drama.

Application procedures. Admission: No deadline. No application fee. Admission notification on a rolling basis. **Financial aid:** Priority date 3/1; no closing date. FAFSA, institutional form required. Applicants notified on a rolling basis starting 6/1; must reply within 2 week(s) of notification.

Academics. Special study options: Cooperative education, distance learning, dual enrollment of high school students, ESL, external degree, honors, independent study, internships, liberal arts/career combination. License preparation in nursing, paramedic. **Credit/placement by examination:** AP, CLEP, institutional tests. 23 credit hours maximum toward associate degree. **Support services:** GED preparation and test center, learning center, preadmission summer program, reduced course load, remedial instruction, study skills assistance, tutoring, writing center.

Majors. Agriculture: Business, equipment technology, mechanization, production, turf management. **Business:** Accounting technology, banking/financial services, business admin, executive assistant, office management, retailing. **Communications technology:** Desktop publishing. **Computer sciences:** Data entry, data processing, information systems, networking, web page design, webmaster. **Construction:** Carpentry. **Education:** Early childhood, teacher assistance. **Engineering technology:** Civil. **Health:** Medical secretary, nursing (RN). **Legal studies:** Legal secretary. **Liberal arts:** Arts/sciences. **Mechanic/repair:** General, auto body, automotive, computer, heating/ac/refrig. **Parks/recreation:** Facilities management. **Personal/culinary services:** Chef training, cosmetic, cosmetology. **Production:** Machine tool, welding. **Protective services:** Corrections, criminal justice, firefighting.

Most popular majors. Agriculture 10%, business/marketing 6%, health sciences 22%, liberal arts 39%, trade and industry 10%.

Computing on campus. 716 workstations in library, computer center, student center. Commuter students can connect to campus network. Online course registration, online library, helpline, repair service, student web hosting, wireless network available.

Student life. Freshman orientation: Mandatory. **Activities:** Jazz band, choral groups, dance, drama, international student organizations, music ensembles, musical theater, student government, student newspaper, Warriors for Christ, ecology club.

Athletics. NJCAA. **Intercollegiate:** Baseball M, basketball, cheerleading W, golf, rodeo, soccer, softball W, volleyball W. **Intramural:** Basketball, softball, volleyball. **Team name:** Warriors.

Student services. Adult student services, career counseling, services for economically disadvantaged, student employment services, financial aid counseling, minority student services, on-campus daycare, personal counseling, placement for graduates, veterans' counselor, women's services. **Physically disabled:** Services for visually, speech, hearing impaired. **Transfer:** Reentry adviser, pre-admission transcript evaluation for new students. Transfer center, transfer adviser, college fairs on campus for students transferring to 4-year colleges.

Contact. E-mail: admissions@wwcc.edu
Phone: (509) 527-4283 Toll-free number: (877) 992-9922
Fax: (509) 527-3661
Sally Wagoner, Director of Admissions and Registrar, Walla Walla Community College, 500 Tausick Way, Walla Walla, WA 99362-9972

Wenatchee Valley College

Wenatchee, Washington
www.wvc.edu **CB code: 4942**

- Public 2-year community college
- Commuter campus in small city

General. Founded in 1939. Regionally accredited. Washington State University and Central Washington University have branch facilities on campus. **Enrollment:** 2,477 degree-seeking undergraduates. **Degrees:** 529 associate awarded. **Location:** 145 miles from Seattle, 170 miles from Spokane. **Calendar:** Quarter, limited summer session. **Full-time faculty:** 81 total. **Part-time faculty:** 175 total. **Class size:** 55% < 20, 43% 20-39, 1% 40-49, less than 1% 50-99, less than 1% >100.

Student profile.

Out-of-state:	2%	**25 or older:**	51%

Transfer out. Colleges most students transferred to 2008: Central Washington University, Washington State University, Eastern Washington University, University of Washington, Western Washington University.

Basis for selection. Open admission, but selective for some programs. Allied health applicants must submit supplemental application form that details work completed in specific program prerequisites. **Homeschooled:** Statement describing homeschool structure and mission, transcript of courses and grades, interview required. Applicants must be affiliated with their local school district. **Learning Disabled:** Students are encouraged to meet with our Special Populations Coordinator at 509-682-6854.

2008-2009 Annual costs. Tuition/fees: $2,922; $3,318 out-of-state. Per-credit charge: $76 in-state; $89 out-of-state. Books/supplies: $900. Personal expenses: $1,548.

Financial aid. Need-based: Need-based aid available for part-time students. Work-study available for part-time students. **Non-need-based:** Scholarships awarded for academics, athletics, leadership.

Application procedures. Admission: No deadline. No application fee. Admission notification on a rolling basis. **Financial aid:** Closing date 3/1. FAFSA required. Applicants notified by 7/2; must reply within 3 week(s) of notification.

Academics. Special study options: Accelerated study, cooperative education, cross-registration, distance learning, double major, dual enrollment of high school students, ESL, independent study, internships, liberal arts/career combination, student-designed major. Bachelor's degree programs available on campus. License preparation in nursing, paramedic, radiology. **Credit/placement by examination:** AP, CLEP, institutional tests. 15 credit hours maximum toward associate degree. At least 15 credits must be completed in residence before credits earned by examination will be applied. **Support services:** GED preparation and test center, remedial instruction, study skills assistance, tutoring, writing center.

Majors. Agriculture: Production, products processing. **Business:** Accounting technology, business admin, office management. **Computer sciences:** Networking, programming. **Conservation:** General. **Education:** Early childhood. **Health:** Clinical lab assistant, nursing (RN), radiologic technology/medical imaging, sonography, substance abuse counseling. **Liberal arts:** Arts/sciences. **Mechanic/repair:** Automotive, heating/ac/refrig, industrial electronics. **Protective services:** Police science.

Most popular majors. Health sciences 19%, liberal arts 69%.

Computing on campus. 75 workstations in library, computer center, student center. Online course registration, online library, helpline, student web hosting, wireless network available.

Student life. Freshman orientation: Available. **Activities:** Jazz band, choral groups, dance, drama, music ensembles, student government, student newspaper, professional associations, Inter-Varsity Fellowship.

Athletics. NJCAA. **Intercollegiate:** Baseball M, basketball, soccer, softball W, volleyball W. **Intramural:** Basketball. **Team name:** Knights.

Student services. Adult student services, career counseling, services for economically disadvantaged, student employment services, financial aid counseling, minority student services, on-campus daycare, personal counseling, veterans' counselor. **Physically disabled:** Services for visually, speech, hearing impaired. **Learning disabled:** Comprehensive services available. **Transfer:** Re-entry adviser, pre-admission transcript evaluation for new students. Transfer adviser, college fairs on campus for students transferring to 4-year colleges.

Contact. Phone: (509) 682-6806 Toll-free number: (877) 982-4698
Fax: (509) 682-6801
William Maxwell, Director of Enrollment Services, Wenatchee Valley College, 1300 Fifth Street, Wenatchee, WA 98801-1799

Whatcom Community College

Bellingham, Washington **CB member**
www.whatcom.ctc.edu **CB code: 1275**

- Public 2-year community college
- Commuter campus in small city

General. Founded in 1970. Regionally accredited. **Enrollment:** 4,367 degree-seeking undergraduates. **Degrees:** 611 associate awarded. **Location:** 90 miles from Seattle, 60 miles from Vancouver, Canada. **Calendar:** Quarter, limited summer session. **Full-time faculty:** 75 total. **Part-time faculty:** 172 total. **Class size:** 18% < 20, 77% 20-39, less than 1% 40-49, 4% 50-99.

Transfer out. Colleges most students transferred to 2008: Western Washington University, University of Washington, Washington State University, Central Washington University, Eastern Washington University.

Basis for selection. Open admission.

High school preparation. Recommended units include English 4, mathematics 4, social studies 3, science 2 (laboratory 1), foreign language 3 and academic electives 1. One Fine Arts.

2008-2009 Annual costs. Tuition/fees: $2,799; $8,013 out-of-state. Per-credit charge: $78 in-state; $250 out-of-state. Books/supplies: $1,080. Personal expenses: $2,238.

2007-2008 Financial aid. Need-based: 74% of total undergraduate aid awarded as scholarships/grants, 26% as loans/jobs. Need-based aid available for part-time students. Work-study available nights and for part-time students. **Non-need-based:** Scholarships awarded for academics, athletics, state residency.

Application procedures. Admission: Priority date 6/23; no deadline. No application fee. Admission notification on a rolling basis. **Financial aid:** No deadline. FAFSA, institutional form required. Applicants notified on a rolling basis starting 7/1; must reply within 3 week(s) of notification.

Academics. Special study options: Accelerated study, cooperative education, distance learning, dual enrollment of high school students, ESL, honors, independent study, internships, student-designed major, study abroad. License preparation in nursing. **Credit/placement by examination:** AP, CLEP, institutional tests. 15 credit hours maximum toward associate degree. **Support services:** GED preparation and test center, learning center, reduced course load, remedial instruction, study skills assistance, tutoring, writing center.

Majors. Business: General, accounting. **Computer sciences:** Computer science, data processing, systems analysis. **Education:** General, early childhood, teacher assistance. **Health:** Massage therapy, medical assistant, nursing (RN), physical therapy assistant. **Legal studies:** Paralegal. **Liberal arts:** Arts/sciences. **Protective services:** Police science. **Visual/performing arts:** Commercial/advertising art.

Most popular majors. Health sciences 13%, liberal arts 79%.

Computing on campus. 294 workstations in library, computer center, student center. Online course registration, online library available.

Student life. Freshman orientation: Available. **Activities:** Jazz band, choral groups, drama, film society, student government, student newspaper, Phi Theta Kappa, Anime Anonymous, Deaf Students Fellowship, health & wellness club, international friendship club, snow club, Gay/Straight Alliance (GSA), multicultural club.

Athletics. Intercollegiate: Basketball, soccer M, volleyball W. **Intramural:** Badminton, basketball, soccer, tennis, volleyball. **Team name:** Orcas.

Student services. Adult student services, alcohol/substance abuse counseling, career counseling, student employment services, financial aid counseling, on-campus daycare, personal counseling, veterans' counselor. **Physically disabled:** Services for visually, speech, hearing impaired. **Learning disabled:** Comprehensive services available. **Transfer:** Re-entry adviser for new students. Transfer center, transfer adviser, college fairs on campus for students transferring to 4-year colleges.

Contact. E-mail: admit@whatcom.ctc.edu
Phone: (360) 383-3000 Fax: (360) 383-4000
Michael Singletary, Registrar, Whatcom Community College, 237 West Kellogg Road, Bellingham, WA 98226

Yakima Valley Community College

Yakima, Washington
www.yvcc.edu **CB code: 4993**

- Public 2-year community college
- Commuter campus in small city

General. Founded in 1928. Regionally accredited. Additional campus in Grandview. **Enrollment:** 2,807 degree-seeking undergraduates. **Degrees:** 627 associate awarded. **Location:** 150 miles from Seattle. **Calendar:** Quarter, extensive summer session. **Full-time faculty:** 124 total. **Part-time faculty:** 237 total.

Student profile.

Out-of-state:	10%	**Live on campus:**	2%
25 or older:	49%		

Transfer out. Colleges most students transferred to 2008: Central Washington University, Washington State University.

Basis for selection. Open admission, but selective for some programs. Special requirements for allied health programs. ACT/ASSET required for placement and advising of degree seeking students and for math/English placement. Previous college/university transcripts showing successful completion of English and math courses may replace ASSET. Essay required for radiologic technology.

High school preparation. College-preparatory program recommended.

2008-2009 Annual costs. Tuition/fees: $2,963; $3,359 out-of-state. Per-credit charge: $76 in-state; $89 out-of-state. Books/supplies: $720. Personal expenses: $1,575.

2007-2008 Financial aid. Need-based: Need-based aid available for part-time students. Work-study available nights, weekends and for part-time students. **Non-need-based:** Scholarships awarded for academics, athletics.

Application procedures. Admission: Priority date 5/26; no deadline. $20 fee. Admission notification on a rolling basis. **Financial aid:** Priority date 5/1; no closing date. FAFSA required. Applicants notified on a rolling basis starting 8/1; must reply within 2 week(s) of notification.

Academics. Special study options: Cooperative education, distance learning, dual enrollment of high school students, ESL, internships, liberal arts/career combination, weekend college. Bachelor's degree programs available on campus. License preparation in dental hygiene, nursing, radiology. **Credit/placement by examination:** AP, CLEP, IB, institutional tests. 45 credit hours maximum toward associate degree. **Support services:** GED preparation and test center, learning center, remedial instruction, study skills assistance, tutoring, writing center.

Majors. Agriculture: General, business, food processing, products processing, supplies. **Business:** General, accounting, accounting technology, administrative services, business admin, e-commerce, entrepreneurial studies, marketing, office management. **Communications technology:** Graphic/printing. **Computer sciences:** General, information systems, web page design. **Construction:** Electrician. **Education:** General, early childhood. **Engineering:** General. **Engineering technology:** Drafting, instrumentation. **Family/consumer sciences:** Child care. **Health:** Dental hygiene, insurance coding, licensed practical nurse, medical assistant, medical radiologic technology/radiation therapy, medical secretary, nursing (RN), pharmacy assistant, substance abuse counseling, surgical technology, veterinary technology/assistant. **Liberal arts:** Arts/sciences. **Mechanic/repair:** Automotive. **Protective services:** Criminal justice, fire services admin, firefighting, law enforcement admin. **Visual/performing arts:** Design.

Most popular majors. Business/marketing 12%, education 8%, health sciences 23%, liberal arts 52%.

Computing on campus. 300 workstations in dormitories, library, computer center, student center. Dormitories wired for high-speed internet access. Online course registration, wireless network available.

Student life. Freshman orientation: Available. Preregistration for classes offered. **Housing:** Single-sex dorms, wellness housing available. $200 deposit. **Activities:** Jazz band, choral groups, drama, music ensembles, musical theater, student government, student newspaper, Mecha, Veterans, Tiin Ma, International Club, Phi Theta Kappa, Action, Auto, allied health clubs.

Athletics. NJCAA. **Intercollegiate:** Baseball M, basketball, soccer W, softball W, volleyball W, wrestling. **Intramural:** Basketball. **Team name:** Yaks.

Student services. Career counseling, services for economically disadvantaged, financial aid counseling, health services, minority student services, on-campus daycare, personal counseling, veterans' counselor, women's services. **Physically disabled:** Services for visually, speech, hearing impaired. **Transfer:** Transfer adviser, college fairs on campus for students transferring to 4-year colleges.

Contact. E-mail: admis@yvcc.edu
Phone: (509) 574-4712 Fax: (509) 574-4649
Denise Anderson, Registrar and Director for Enrollment Services, Yakima Valley Community College, PO Box 22520, Yakima, WA 98907-2520

West Virginia

Blue Ridge Community and Technical College

Martinsburg, West Virginia
www.blueridgectc.edu **CB member**

- Public 2-year community and technical college
- Commuter campus in small city

General. Regionally accredited. **Enrollment:** 1,126 degree-seeking undergraduates; 1,340 non-degree-seeking students. **Degrees:** 169 associate awarded. **Location:** Downtown. **Calendar:** Semester, limited summer session. **Full-time faculty:** 27 total; 4% minority, 70% women. **Part-time faculty:** 64 total; 12% have terminal degrees, 58% women. **Class size:** 77% < 20, 19% 20-39, 3% 40-49, 1% 50-99, less than 1% >100.

Student profile. Among degree-seeking undergraduates, 22% enrolled in a transfer program, 78% enrolled in a vocational program, 1% already have a bachelor's degree or higher, 327 enrolled as first-time, first-year students.

Part-time:	40%	**Women:**	61%
Out-of-state:	7%	**25 or older:**	40%

Transfer out. Colleges most students transferred to 2008: Shepherd University.

Basis for selection. Open admission. **Adult students:** Students without ACT/SAT may take the ACCUPLACER in-house. **Homeschooled:** Transcript of courses and grades required.

High school preparation. Recommended units include English 4, mathematics 4, social studies 2, history 1, science 3 (laboratory 3), foreign language 2 and visual/performing arts 1.

2008-2009 Annual costs. Tuition/fees: $3,072; $5,520 out-of-state. Per-credit charge: $128 in-state; $230 out-of-state. Books/supplies: $1,000. Personal expenses: $2,000.

Application procedures. Admission: No deadline. $25 fee, may be waived for applicants with need. Application must be submitted on paper. Admission notification on a rolling basis.

Academics. Special study options: Dual enrollment of high school students, ESL, independent study, liberal arts/career combination. License preparation in dental hygiene, nursing, paramedic, real estate. **Credit/placement by examination:** AP, CLEP, institutional tests. **Support services:** GED test center, learning center, reduced course load, remedial instruction, tutoring, writing center.

Majors. Business: General, business admin, office technology. **Computer sciences:** Information systems. **Engineering technology:** Automotive, electromechanical, occupational safety. **Health:** EMT paramedic, medical assistant, nursing (RN), surgical technology. **Legal studies:** Paralegal. **Liberal arts:** Arts/sciences. **Mechanic/repair:** Automotive, heating/ac/refrig. **Personal/culinary services:** Restaurant/catering. **Protective services:** Criminal justice, fire safety technology, firefighting. **Other:** Electric distribution technology, Occupational development, Technical studies.

Most popular majors. Business/marketing 14%, engineering/engineering technologies 7%, health sciences 21%, liberal arts 39%, security/protective services 7%.

Computing on campus. 106 workstations in library, computer center, student center. Online course registration, online library, helpline, student web hosting, wireless network available.

Student life. Freshman orientation: Mandatory, $25 fee. Preregistration for classes offered. **Activities:** Campus ministries, student government.

Athletics. Team name: Bruins.

Student services. Adult student services, career counseling, student employment services, financial aid counseling, placement for graduates, veterans' counselor. **Physically disabled:** Services for visually, speech, hearing impaired. **Learning disabled:** Comprehensive services available. **Transfer:** Pre-admission transcript evaluation for new students. College fairs on campus for students transferring to 4-year colleges.

Contact. E-mail: ewoolast@blueridgectc.edu
Phone: (304) 260-4380 ext. 2103 Fax: (304) 260-4376
Leslie See, Director of Enrollment, Blue Ridge Community and Technical College, 400 West Stephen Street, Martinsburg, WV 25401

Eastern West Virginia Community and Technical College

Moorefield, West Virginia
www.eastern.wvnet.edu **CB code: 3837**

- Public 2-year community and technical college
- Commuter campus in rural community

General. Regionally accredited. **Enrollment:** 420 degree-seeking undergraduates; 110 non-degree-seeking students. **Degrees:** 26 associate awarded. **Location:** 55 miles from Winchester, Virginia. **Calendar:** Semester, limited summer session. **Part-time faculty:** 36 total.

Student profile. Among degree-seeking undergraduates, 75 enrolled as first-time, first-year students.

Part-time:	76%	**25 or older:**	70%
Women:	74%		

Transfer out. Colleges most students transferred to 2008: Shepherd College, West Virginia University, Potomac State College.

Basis for selection. Open admission. Degree-seeking students required to take ACCUPLACER. **Homeschooled:** Applicants advised to take GED.

2008-2009 Annual costs. Tuition/fees: $1,920; $6,822 out-of-state.

Financial aid. Need-based: Need-based aid available for part-time students.

Application procedures. Admission: No deadline. No application fee. Application must be submitted on paper. Admission notification on a rolling basis. **Financial aid:** Priority date 6/1; no closing date. FAFSA, institutional form required. Applicants notified on a rolling basis; must reply within 2 week(s) of notification.

Academics. Special study options: Distance learning, dual enrollment of high school students, external degree, internships, student-designed major. License preparation in nursing. **Credit/placement by examination:** AP, CLEP, institutional tests. **Support services:** GED preparation, reduced course load, remedial instruction, study skills assistance, tutoring.

Majors. Business: Administrative services, business admin. **Computer sciences:** Information systems. **Liberal arts:** Arts/sciences. **Mechanic/repair:** Industrial.

Computing on campus. Online library available.

Student life. Freshman orientation: Mandatory. General orientation program is 3 hours long. Second program required for students taking online courses.

Student services. Adult student services, career counseling, services for economically disadvantaged, financial aid counseling, veterans' counselor. **Physically disabled:** Services for visually, hearing impaired. **Transfer:** College fairs on campus for students transferring to 4-year colleges.

Contact. E-mail: askeast@eastern.wvnet.edu
Phone: (304) 434-8000 Toll-free number: (877) 982-2322
Fax: (304) 434-7000
Robert Eagle, Dean of Learner Support Services, Eastern West Virginia Community and Technical College, 1929 State Road 55, Moorefield, WV 26836

Everest Institute: Cross Lanes

Cross Lanes, West Virginia
www.cci.edu **CB code: 1579**

- For-profit 2-year technical college
- Commuter campus in large town

General. Founded in 1968. Accredited by ACCSCT. **Location:** 12 miles from Charleston. **Calendar:** Quarter.

Contact. Phone: (304) 776-6290
Director of Admission, 5514 Big Tyler Road, Cross Lanes, WV 25313

Huntington Junior College
Huntington, West Virginia
www.huntingtonjuniorcollege.edu **CB code: 7310**

- For-profit 2-year junior college
- Commuter campus in small city

General. Founded in 1936. Regionally accredited. **Enrollment:** 800 degree-seeking undergraduates. **Degrees:** 18 associate awarded. **Location:** 45 miles from Charleston. **Calendar:** Quarter, extensive summer session. **Full-time faculty:** 25 total. **Part-time faculty:** 8 total.

Basis for selection. Open admission. Interview recommended.

2008-2009 Annual costs. Tuition/fees: $6,900. Tuition includes books.

Application procedures. Admission: No deadline. No application fee. Admission notification on a rolling basis. **Financial aid:** No deadline. Applicants notified on a rolling basis.

Academics. Special study options: Double major, internships. **Credit/placement by examination:** CLEP, institutional tests. **Support services:** Learning center, reduced course load, remedial instruction, study skills assistance, tutoring.

Majors. Business: General, accounting, administrative services. **Computer sciences:** General, database management, programming, web page design. **Foreign languages:** Classics. **Health:** Dental assistant, insurance coding, medical assistant. **Legal studies:** Court reporting, legal secretary.

Student life. Freshman orientation: Mandatory. Three-hour program held during the first day of class. **Activities:** Student government.

Student services. Career counseling, student employment services, financial aid counseling, personal counseling, placement for graduates.

Contact. E-mail: admissions@huntingtonjuniorcollege.edu
Phone: (304) 697-7550 Toll-free number: (800) 344-4522
Fax: (304) 697-7554
James Garrett, Director of Marketing and Education Services, Huntington Junior College, 900 Fifth Avenue, Huntington, WV 25701

Mountain State College
Parkersburg, West Virginia
www.mountainstate.org **CB code: 2389**

- For-profit 2-year business and technical college
- Commuter campus in large town
- Interview required

General. Founded in 1888. Accredited by ACICS. **Enrollment:** 85 full-time, degree-seeking students. **Degrees:** 45 associate awarded. **Location:** 81 miles from Charleston. **Calendar:** Quarter. **Full-time faculty:** 7 total. **Part-time faculty:** 4 total. **Special facilities:** Legal resource center, dependency resource center.

Basis for selection. Open admission. CPAT required for placement.

2008-2009 Annual costs. Books/supplies: $600.

Application procedures. Admission: No deadline. No application fee. Admission notification on a rolling basis. **Financial aid:** No deadline. FAFSA required. Applicants notified on a rolling basis.

Academics. Special study options: Accelerated study, cooperative education, double major, internships. **Credit/placement by examination:** CLEP. **Support services:** Tutoring.

Majors. Business: Accounting, administrative services, hospitality/recreation, tourism promotion, tourism/travel. **Computer sciences:** General, applications programming. **Health:** Health services, medical assistant, medical transcription, mental health services, substance abuse counseling. **Legal studies:** Legal secretary, paralegal.

Most popular majors. Business/marketing 16%, computer/information sciences 22%, health sciences 51%, legal studies 11%.

Computing on campus. 25 workstations in library, computer center.

Student life. Freshman orientation: Mandatory. Held the week prior to beginning of quarter. **Activities:** Student government.

Student services. Career counseling, student employment services, personal counseling, placement for graduates.

Contact. E-mail: adm@mountainstate.org
Phone: (304) 485-5487 Toll-free number: (800) 841-0201
Fax: (304) 485-3524
Director of Student Services, Mountain State College, Spring at 16th Street, Parkersburg, WV 26101-3993

New River Community and Technical College
Beckley, West Virginia
www.newriver.edu

- Public 2-year community and technical college
- Commuter campus in large town

General. Regionally accredited. **Enrollment:** 2,338 degree-seeking undergraduates. **Degrees:** 139 associate awarded. **Calendar:** Semester, limited summer session. **Full-time faculty:** 32 total. **Part-time faculty:** 125 total.

Student profile. Among degree-seeking undergraduates, 10% enrolled in a transfer program, 60% enrolled in a vocational program, 438 enrolled as first-time, first-year students, 438 transferred in from other institutions.

Part-time:	49%	**Women:**	67%

Transfer out. 50% of students enrolled in the transfer program go on to 4-year colleges.

Basis for selection. Open admission. **Adult students:** COMPASS required for placement.

2008-2009 Annual costs. Tuition/fees: $2,748; $6,150 out-of-state. Per-credit charge: $115 in-state; $256 out-of-state. Books/supplies: $600.

Application procedures. Admission: No deadline. No application fee.

Academics. Special study options: License preparation in nursing. **Credit/placement by examination:** CLEP, SAT, ACT, institutional tests. **Support services:** GED preparation, tutoring, writing center.

Majors. Agriculture: Aquaculture. **Biology:** Ecology. **Business:** General, accounting, banking/financial services, hospitality admin, marketing, tourism/travel. **Communications technology:** General. **Computer sciences:** General, information technology, LAN/WAN management. **Conservation:** Environmental science. **Education:** General, teacher assistance. **Health:** Medical assistant. **Legal studies:** Legal secretary. **Protective services:** Corrections, law enforcement admin. **Science technology:** Biological.

Student life. Freshman orientation: Available. Preregistration for classes offered. **Activities:** Student government, student newspaper.

Student services. Career counseling, financial aid counseling. **Physically disabled:** Services for visually, speech, hearing impaired.

Contact. Phone: (304) 255-5812 Fax: (304) 255-5889
Harry Faulk, Vice President/Chief Academic Officer, New River Community and Technical College, 167 Dye Drive, Beckley, WV 25801

Potomac State College of West Virginia University
Keyser, West Virginia
www.potomacstatecollege.edu **CB code: 5539**

- Public 2-year branch campus and junior college
- Commuter campus in small town

General. Founded in 1901. Regionally accredited. **Enrollment:** 1,263 degree-seeking undergraduates. **Degrees:** 6 bachelor's, 200 associate awarded. **Location:** 80 miles from Morgantown, 150 miles from Baltimore. **Calendar:** Semester, limited summer session. **Full-time faculty:** 40 total. **Part-time faculty:** 56 total. **Special facilities:** 2 fully operational farms.

Transfer out. Colleges most students transferred to 2008: West Virginia University, Fairmont State College, Frostburg State University.

Basis for selection. Open admission. English ACT score used in conjunction with high school GPA to place students in either college-level or remedial composition courses. Scores also used for math placement. Audition recommended for music applicants and for scholarship consideration.

2008-2009 Annual costs. Tuition/fees: $2,726; $8,674 out-of-state. Per-credit charge: $114 in-state; $361 out-of-state. Students residing in selected counties in bordering states receive reduced out-of-state tuition rates. Room/board: $6,814. Books/supplies: $750.

2007-2008 Financial aid. Need-based: Need-based aid available for part-time students. Work-study available nights and weekends. **Non-need-based:** Scholarships awarded for academics, athletics, leadership.

Application procedures. Admission: No deadline. No application fee. Admission notification on a rolling basis beginning on or about 9/15. **Financial aid:** Priority date 3/1; no closing date. FAFSA required. Applicants notified on a rolling basis starting 4/1; must reply within 2 week(s) of notification.

Academics. Special study options: Distance learning, double major, dual enrollment of high school students, honors, internships, study abroad. Bachelor's degree programs available on campus. **Credit/placement by examination:** AP, CLEP, institutional tests. 30 credit hours maximum toward associate degree. **Support services:** Learning center, reduced course load, remedial instruction, tutoring.

Majors. Agriculture: General, agronomy, animal sciences, horticultural science. **Biology:** General. **Business:** General, accounting, administrative services, business admin, entrepreneurial studies, management information systems, managerial economics. **Communications:** Journalism. **Computer sciences:** General, applications programming, data processing, information technology, programming. **Conservation:** General, forest management, forest resources, forest technology, forestry, wildlife, wood science. **Education:** General, elementary, physical, secondary. **Engineering:** General, civil, electrical, mechanical. **Foreign languages:** Spanish. **Health:** Predental, premedicine, prepharmacy, preveterinary. **History:** General. **Legal studies:** Prelaw. **Liberal arts:** Arts/sciences. **Math:** General. **Parks/recreation:** Facilities management. **Personal/culinary services:** General. **Physical sciences:** Chemistry, geology, physics. **Protective services:** Correctional facilities, criminal justice, law enforcement admin. **Psychology:** General. **Public administration:** Social work. **Social sciences:** Economics, political science, sociology.

Computing on campus. 100 workstations in library, computer center, student center. Dormitories wired for high-speed internet access. Helpline, repair service available.

Student life. Freshman orientation: Mandatory, $50 fee. Preregistration for classes offered. **Housing:** Coed dorms, single-sex dorms available. $150 deposit, deadline 8/15. **Activities:** Bands, campus ministries, choral groups, drama, music ensembles, student government, student newspaper, agriculture and forestry club, Circle K, equestrian club, criminal justice club, engineering club, peer advocates, life sciences club.

Athletics. NJCAA. **Intercollegiate:** Baseball M, basketball, golf, soccer, softball W, volleyball W. **Intramural:** Basketball. **Team name:** Catamounts.

Student services. Adult student services, career counseling, services for economically disadvantaged, student employment services, financial aid counseling, health services, minority student services, on-campus daycare, personal counseling, placement for graduates, veterans' counselor, women's services. **Physically disabled:** Services for visually, hearing impaired. **Transfer:** Pre-admission transcript evaluation for new students. Transfer adviser, college fairs on campus for students transferring to 4-year colleges.

Contact. E-mail: go2psc@mail.wvu.edu
Phone: (304) 788-6820 Toll-free number: (800) 262-7332
Fax: (304) 788-6939
Beth Little, Director of Enrollment Services, Potomac State College of West Virginia University, One Grand Central Park, Suite 2090, Keyser, WV 26726

Southern West Virginia Community and Technical College

Mount Gay, West Virginia **CB member**
www.southernwv.edu **CB code: 0770**

- Public 2-year community college
- Commuter campus in small town

General. Founded in 1971. Regionally accredited. Additional campuses in Williamson, Saulsville, Madison and Hamlin. **Enrollment:** 2,264 degree-seeking undergraduates. **Degrees:** 283 associate awarded. **Location:** 60 miles from Charleston. **Calendar:** Semester, limited summer session. **Full-time faculty:** 52 total. **Part-time faculty:** 116 total. **Special facilities:** Allied health and technology building.

Transfer out. Colleges most students transferred to 2008: Marshall University, West Virginia University, West Virginia State University, Mountain State University, Concord University.

Basis for selection. Open admission, but selective for some programs. Limited admissions to salon management/cosmetology, nursing, medical laboratory, radiologic technology, dental hygiene, paramedic science, respiratory technology, and surgical technology programs. Interview recommended. **Adult students:** Adult students may also take ACCUPLACER to determine placement in English and math. **Homeschooled:** Transcript of courses and grades required. **Learning Disabled:** Recommend meeting with disability counselor.

2008-2009 Annual costs. Tuition/fees: $1,920; $6,816 out-of-state. Per-credit charge: $80 in-state; $284 out-of-state. Books/supplies: $1,200. Personal expenses: $900.

2007-2008 Financial aid. Need-based: Need-based aid available for part-time students.

Application procedures. Admission: No deadline. No application fee. Admission notification on a rolling basis. Application for limited admissions programs must be submitted by January 31. **Financial aid:** No deadline. FAFSA required. Applicants notified on a rolling basis.

Academics. Special study options: Distance learning, dual enrollment of high school students, independent study, internships, teacher certification program. Fast Track courses. Bachelor's degree programs available on campus. License preparation in dental hygiene, nursing, paramedic, radiology. **Credit/placement by examination:** AP, CLEP, institutional tests. **Support services:** GED preparation, learning center, reduced course load, remedial instruction, tutoring.

Majors. Business: General, accounting, administrative services, business admin, entrepreneurial studies, hospitality admin, marketing, small business admin. **Communications technology:** General. **Computer sciences:** General, information technology. **Engineering technology:** Drafting, electrical, environmental. **Health:** Clinical lab technology, health services, medical radiologic technology/radiation therapy, nursing (RN). **Liberal arts:** Arts/sciences. **Protective services:** Forensics.

Most popular majors. Business/marketing 15%, computer/information sciences 10%, health sciences 40%, liberal arts 35%.

Computing on campus. 7 workstations in library. Online course registration, online library, helpline available.

Student life. Freshman orientation: Available. Preregistration for classes offered. Orientation courses offered to first-time freshman, or students with less than 30 credit hours. **Activities:** Drama, musical theater, student government, special interest clubs.

Student services. Career counseling, student employment services, financial aid counseling, on-campus daycare, personal counseling, placement for graduates, veterans' counselor. **Physically disabled:** Services for visually, speech, hearing impaired. **Transfer:** Transfer adviser, college fairs on campus for students transferring to 4-year colleges.

Contact. Phone: (304) 896-7443 Toll-free number: (866) 798-2821
Fax: (304) 792-7056
Teri Wells, Student Records Assistant, Southern West Virginia Community and Technical College, PO Box 2900, Mount Gay, WV 25637

Valley College

Martinsburg, West Virginia
www.vct.edu **CB code: 3176**

- For-profit 2-year business and career college
- Commuter campus in small city
- Interview required

General. Accredited by ACICS. Additional campuses in Princeton and Beckley. **Enrollment:** 90 degree-seeking undergraduates. **Degrees:** 14 associate awarded. **Location:** 20 miles from Winchester, Virginia. **Calendar:** Semester, extensive summer session. **Full-time faculty:** 3 total. **Part-time faculty:** 2 total. **Class size:** 100% < 20.

Transfer out. Colleges most students transferred to 2008: Mountain State University, Shepherd University.

Basis for selection. Admission based primarily on high school record, standardized test scores, and interview. Institutional test administered for students without ACT or SAT. **Homeschooled:** State high school equivalency certificate required.

2008-2009 Annual costs. Tuition/fees: $7,300. Per-credit charge: $225. Tuition varies according to program. Books/supplies: $1,185. Personal expenses: $7,653.

2007-2008 Financial aid. Need-based: Need-based aid available for part-time students.

Application procedures. Admission: No deadline. No application fee. Application must be submitted on paper. Admission notification on a rolling basis. **Financial aid:** No deadline. FAFSA, institutional form required. Applicants notified on a rolling basis.

Academics. Credit/placement by examination: CLEP. 29 credit hours maximum toward associate degree. **Support services:** Remedial instruction, study skills assistance.

Majors. Business: General, business admin, small business admin.

Computing on campus. 42 workstations in computer center.

Student life. Freshman orientation: Mandatory. Orientation held during first week of classes.

Student services. Career counseling, student employment services, financial aid counseling, placement for graduates. **Transfer:** Pre-admission transcript evaluation for new students.

Contact. E-mail: martinsburg@vct.edu
Phone: (304) 263-0979 Fax: (304) 263-2413
Gail Kennedy, Admissions Director, Valley College, 287 Aikens Center, Martinsburg, WV 25404

West Virginia Business College: Nutter Fort

Wheeling, West Virginia
www.wvbc.edu **CB code: 2546**

- For-profit 2-year business college
- Commuter campus in small city
- Interview required

General. Accredited by ACICS. **Enrollment:** 70 full-time, degree-seeking students. **Degrees:** 30 associate awarded. **Calendar:** Quarter. **Part-time faculty:** 14 total.

Transfer out. Colleges most students transferred to 2008: West Virginia Northern Community College, Belmont Technical College.

Basis for selection. Open admission, but selective for some programs. Score of a least 20 on college entrance evaluation required for acceptance directly into associate degree programs. Office administration/medical assistant associate degree programs require score of 25. Acceptance into any degree program guaranteed after completion of diploma program at WVBC.

2008-2009 Annual costs. Diploma program is $9,500. Associate degree program costs $18,000 for entire 2-year program. Cost of books, $2,500 - $4,000. Books/supplies: $2,124.

Application procedures. Admission: No deadline. $50 fee. Application must be submitted on paper.

Academics. Credit/placement by examination: CLEP. **Support services:** Reduced course load, tutoring.

Majors. Business: Accounting, administrative services, business admin. **Health:** Medical secretary. **Legal studies:** Legal secretary, paralegal.

Most popular majors. Business/marketing 11%, health sciences 11%, legal studies 78%.

Computing on campus. 16 workstations in library, computer center.

Student life. Freshman orientation: Mandatory, $125 fee. **Activities:** Student government.

Student services. Financial aid counseling, personal counseling, placement for graduates.

Contact. E-mail: kcarpenter@wvbc.edu
Phone: (304) 232-0361 Fax: (304) 232-0363
Karen Shaw, Director, West Virginia Business College: Nutter Fort, 1052 Main Street, Wheeling, WV 26003

West Virginia Business College: Wheeling

Wheeling, West Virginia
www.wvbc.edu

- For-profit 2-year business and career college
- Commuter campus in small city
- Interview required

General. Accredited by ACICS. **Enrollment:** 60 degree-seeking undergraduates. **Degrees:** 30 associate awarded. **Location:** 35 miles from Morgantown, 50 miles from Pittsburgh. **Calendar:** Quarter, extensive summer session. **Part-time faculty:** 15 total; 13% have terminal degrees, 13% minority, 60% women.

Basis for selection. Open admission. **Homeschooled:** State high school equivalency certificate required.

2008-2009 Annual costs. Diploma program is $9,500. Associate degree program costs $18,000 for entire 2-year program. Cost of books, $2,500 - $4,000. Books/supplies: $475.

Application procedures. Admission: No deadline. $75 fee. Application must be submitted on paper.

Academics. Credit/placement by examination: CLEP. 8 credit hours maximum toward associate degree. **Support services:** Study skills assistance, tutoring.

Majors. Business: Administrative services, business admin. **Legal studies:** Paralegal.

Computing on campus. Online library, wireless network available.

Student life. Activities: Student newspaper.

Student services. Career counseling, financial aid counseling, placement for graduates.

Contact. E-mail: info@wvbc.edu
Phone: (304) 624-7695 Toll-free number: (304) 232-0361
Fax: (304) 232-0363
Gary Gorby, General Manager, West Virginia Business College: Wheeling, 1052 Main Street, Wheeling, WV 26003

West Virginia Junior College

Morgantown, West Virginia
www.wvjc.edu **CB code: 3179**

- For-profit 2-year junior college
- Large town

General. Accredited by ACICS. **Enrollment:** 157 degree-seeking undergraduates. **Degrees:** 60 associate awarded. **Calendar:** Quarter. **Full-time faculty:** 3 total. **Part-time faculty:** 10 total.

Basis for selection. Open admission.

2008-2009 Annual costs. Personal expenses: $2,529.

Financial aid. Need-based: Need-based aid available for part-time students.

Application procedures. Admission: No deadline. $25 fee. Admission notification on a rolling basis. Prospective students meet with admissions counselor as part of application process. **Financial aid:** No deadline. FAFSA required. Applicants notified on a rolling basis.

Academics. Credit/placement by examination: CLEP.

Majors. Business: Business admin, office technology. **Computer sciences:** Information systems, information technology. **Health:** Insurance coding, medical assistant. **Legal studies:** General, paralegal.

Contact. E-mail: info@wvjc.edu
Phone: (304) 296-8282
Leann Cardozo, Academic Dean, West Virginia Junior College, 148 Willey Street, Morgantown, WV 26505

Two-Year Colleges

West Virginia Junior College: Bridgeport
Bridgeport, West Virginia
www.wvjcinfo.net

- For-profit 2-year business and health science college
- Large town

General. Accredited by ACICS. **Enrollment:** 220 degree-seeking undergraduates. **Degrees:** 105 associate awarded. **Location:** 120 miles from Charleston. **Calendar:** Quarter. **Full-time faculty:** 19 total.

Basis for selection. Open admission.

Application procedures. Admission: No deadline. Admission notification on a rolling basis.

Academics. Credit/placement by examination: CLEP.

Majors. Business: Business admin. **Computer sciences:** Information technology. **Health:** Dental assistant, medical assistant.

Contact. Phone: (304) 842-4007
West Virginia Junior College: Bridgeport, 176 Thompson Drive, Bridgeport, WV 26330

West Virginia Junior College: Charleston
Charleston, West Virginia
www.wvjc.com **CB code: 3180**

- For-profit 2-year junior and technical college
- Commuter campus in small city

General. Accredited by ACICS. **Enrollment:** 150 full-time, degree-seeking students. **Degrees:** 60 associate awarded. **Calendar:** Quarter, extensive summer session. **Full-time faculty:** 8 total. **Part-time faculty:** 9 total.

Basis for selection. Open admission.

Financial aid. Need-based: Need-based aid available for part-time students.

Application procedures. Admission: No deadline. Admission notification on a rolling basis. **Financial aid:** Applicants notified on a rolling basis.

Academics. Credit/placement by examination: AP, CLEP, institutional tests. **Support services:** Tutoring.

Majors. Business: Office management. **Computer sciences:** General. **Health:** Medical assistant.

Computing on campus. 130 workstations in library, computer center.

Student life. Freshman orientation: Mandatory. Preregistration for classes offered.

Student services. Adult student services, alcohol/substance abuse counseling, career counseling, financial aid counseling, placement for graduates. **Transfer:** Pre-admission transcript evaluation for new students.

Contact. Phone: (304) 345-2820
Bonnie Landon, Executive Director, West Virginia Junior College: Charleston, 1000 Virginia Street East, Charleston, WV 25301

West Virginia Northern Community College
Wheeling, West Virginia
www.wvncc.edu **CB code: 0674**

- Public 2-year community and technical college
- Commuter campus in large town

General. Founded in 1972. Regionally accredited. Additional campuses in New Martinsville and Weirton. **Enrollment:** 2,165 degree-seeking undergraduates; 759 non-degree-seeking students. **Degrees:** 248 associate awarded. **Location:** 45 miles from Pittsburgh. **Calendar:** Semester, limited summer session. **Full-time faculty:** 56 total; 14% have terminal degrees, 4% minority, 66% women. **Part-time faculty:** 122 total; 3% have terminal degrees, 2% minority, 45% women. **Partnerships:** Formal agreements with Northern Panhandle Technical Education and Training Partnership, Oglebay Institute Partnership, RESA 6, West Virginia Rehabilitation Center, National Retail Federation, Northern Panhandle Workforce Investment Board.

Student profile. Among degree-seeking undergraduates, 409 enrolled as first-time, first-year students.

Part-time:	38%	**African American:**	4%
Women:	71%	**Hispanic American:**	1%

Transfer out. Colleges most students transferred to 2008: West Liberty State College, Wheeling Jesuit University, West Virginia University, Bethany College, Ohio Eastern University.

Basis for selection. Open admission, but selective for some programs. Special requirements for health programs. Students without high school diploma or GED required to submit ACT.

High school preparation. Strong science and math background recommended for health science applicants.

2008-2009 Annual costs. Tuition/fees: $1,998; $6,510 out-of-state. Tuition for students residing in border counties is $4,590. Books/supplies: $600. Personal expenses: $1,153.

Financial aid. Need-based: Need-based aid available for part-time students.

Application procedures. Admission: No deadline. No application fee. Application must be submitted online. Admission notification on a rolling basis. Health science applicants must apply by January 10; late applicants evaluated after June 30 if space available. **Financial aid:** Priority date 3/15; no closing date. FAFSA, institutional form required. Applicants notified on a rolling basis starting 3/10.

Academics. Special study options: Accelerated study, distance learning, double major, dual enrollment of high school students, independent study, internships, liberal arts/career combination. 2+2 in education, business administration, criminal justice at West Liberty State College. 2+2 mental health and human services, social work, accounting/business administration, business studies, business administration option, and transfer agreement in early childhood education with Franciscan University of Steubenville. 2+2 in social work with West Virginia University. License preparation in nursing. **Credit/placement by examination:** AP, CLEP, institutional tests. 45 credit hours maximum toward associate degree. **Support services:** Learning center, remedial instruction, study skills assistance, tutoring.

Majors. Business: Accounting technology, administrative services, business admin, hospitality admin. **Computer sciences:** Programming. **Health:** Medical radiologic technology/radiation therapy, nursing (RN), respiratory therapy technology, surgical technology. **Liberal arts:** Arts/sciences. **Mechanic/repair:** Heating/ac/refrig. **Personal/culinary services:** Culinary arts. **Protective services:** Police science. **Other:** Technical studies.

Most popular majors. Business/marketing 20%, health sciences 39%, liberal arts 15%, public administration/social services 8%.

Computing on campus. 215 workstations in library, computer center. Commuter students can connect to campus network.

Student life. Freshman orientation: Mandatory. Preregistration for classes offered. Held during spring and early fall for about 3.5-4 hours. **Activities:** Student government, student newspaper, African American/multicultural organization.

Athletics. Intramural: Badminton, basketball, bowling, football (non-tackle), golf, soccer, softball, volleyball. **Team name:** Thundering Chickens.

Student services. Career counseling, student employment services, personal counseling, placement for graduates, veterans' counselor. **Physically disabled:** Services for visually, hearing impaired. **Transfer:** Transfer adviser, college fairs on campus for students transferring to 4-year colleges.

Contact. E-mail: info@wvncc.edu
Phone: (304) 233-5900 ext. 8848 Fax: (304) 232-8187
Janet Fike, Dean of Enrollment Management, West Virginia Northern Community College, 1704 Market Street, Wheeling, WV 26003

West Virginia State Community and Technical College
Institute, West Virginia
www.wvsctc.edu

- Public 2-year community and technical college
- Small town

General. Regionally accredited. Located on West Virginia State University campus. **Enrollment:** 1,737 degree-seeking undergraduates. **Degrees:** 255

associate awarded. **Location:** 8 miles from Charleston. **Calendar:** Semester, limited summer session. **Full-time faculty:** 39 total. **Part-time faculty:** 44 total. **Partnerships:** Formal partnerships with Charleston Area Medical Center, American Electric Power.

Basis for selection. Open admission, but selective for some programs. Special requirements for nursing and nuclear medicine technology programs. Nursing requirements include 3.0 GPA and 21 ACT or 1000 SAT, exclusive of Writing. Nuclear medicine technology requires interview with the program director or clinical coordinator and submission of SAT or ACT scores. Immunization records required if born after January 1, 1957. Statement of activities requested for students out of high school 6 months or longer. **Homeschooled:** Statement describing homeschool structure and mission, transcript of courses and grades required. Must provide detailed description of home school curriculum.

High school preparation. Recommended units include English 4, mathematics 4, social studies 4, science 3 (laboratory 2) and foreign language 2.

2008-2009 Annual costs. Tuition/fees: $2,898; $8,468 out-of-state. Per-credit charge: $121 in-state; $353 out-of-state. Books/supplies: $1,009. Personal expenses: $3,141.

2007-2008 Financial aid. Need-based: Work-study available nights, weekends and for part-time students. **Non-need-based:** Scholarships awarded for academics, state residency. **Additional information:** All students may apply for tuition waivers. Financial aid deadline enforced only if Federal financial aid is the only source of payment.

Application procedures. Admission: No deadline. No application fee. Admission notification on a rolling basis. **Financial aid:** Closing date 6/30.

Academics. Special study options: Double major, dual enrollment of high school students, honors, internships, study abroad. Bachelor's degree programs available on campus. License preparation in aviation, dental hygiene, nursing, occupational therapy, paramedic, real estate. **Credit/placement by examination:** CLEP, SAT, ACT, institutional tests. **Support services:** GED preparation and test center, remedial instruction, study skills assistance, tutoring, writing center.

Majors. Business: Accounting, accounting technology, administrative services, banking/financial services, business admin, finance, sales/distribution. **Communications:** General. **Computer sciences:** Computer science, information systems. **Engineering technology:** Architectural drafting, drafting, electrical, manufacturing. **Health:** EMT paramedic, mental health services, nuclear medical technology, nursing (RN). **Interdisciplinary:** Gerontology, science/society. **Liberal arts:** Arts/sciences. **Physical sciences:** Meteorology. **Protective services:** Police science. **Other:** Allied health & human technology, Occupational development, Technical studies.

Most popular majors. Business/marketing 18%, engineering/engineering technologies 15%, health sciences 22%, interdisciplinary studies 9%, liberal arts 29%.

Computing on campus. Dormitories wired for high-speed internet access and linked to campus network. Commuter students can connect to campus network. Online course registration, online library, helpline, wireless network available.

Student life. Housing: $125 nonrefundable deposit. **Activities:** Student newspaper.

Athletics. Team name: Yellow Jackets.

Student services. Transfer: College fairs on campus for students transferring to 4-year colleges.

Contact. E-mail: admissions@wvsctc.edu
Phone: (304) 766-3221 Toll-free number: (800) 987-2112
Fax: (304) 766-4104
Trina Sweeney, Director, West Virginia State Community and Technical College, PO Box 1000, Institute, WV 25112-1000

Wisconsin

Blackhawk Technical College
Janesville, Wisconsin
www.blackhawk.edu
CB code: 7319

- Public 2-year technical college
- Commuter campus in small city

General. Founded in 1912. Regionally accredited. **Enrollment:** 2,760 degree-seeking undergraduates. **Degrees:** 273 associate awarded. **Location:** 75 miles from Milwaukee and Chicago. **Calendar:** Semester, limited summer session. **Full-time faculty:** 100 total; 2% have terminal degrees, 7% minority, 55% women. **Part-time faculty:** 273 total; 6% minority, 48% women. **Class size:** 95% < 20, 4% 20-39, less than 1% 40-49, less than 1% 50-99.

Student profile. Among degree-seeking undergraduates, 100% enrolled in a vocational program, 3% already have a bachelor's degree or higher, 759 enrolled as first-time, first-year students.

Part-time:	52%	**Asian American:**	1%
Out-of-state:	1%	**Hispanic American:**	3%
Women:	59%	**Native American:**	1%
African American:	7%		

Basis for selection. Open admission, but selective for some programs. Applicants to nursing, dental hygiene, radiography, sonography, and physical therapist assistant programs must meet additional testing and course requirements. National League for Nursing, Pre-Nursing and Guidance examination required for nursing applicants.

2008-2009 Annual costs. Tuition/fees: $3,118; $18,034 out-of-state. Per-credit charge: $97 in-state; $594 out-of-state. Material fees vary by program; minimum $4 per course. $10 per credit fee for online courses. Books/supplies: $1,148. Personal expenses: $1,597.

2007-2008 Financial aid. Need-based: 59% of total undergraduate aid awarded as scholarships/grants, 41% as loans/jobs. Need-based aid available for part-time students. Work-study available nights and for part-time students.

Application procedures. Admission: Priority date 9/1; no deadline. $30 fee. Admission notification on a rolling basis beginning on or about 10/1. **Financial aid:** Priority date 4/30; no closing date. FAFSA required. Applicants notified on a rolling basis starting 3/15; must reply within 2 week(s) of notification.

Academics. Special study options: Accelerated study, distance learning, dual enrollment of high school students, ESL, independent study, internships, student-designed major. License preparation in aviation, nursing, physical therapy, radiology. **Credit/placement by examination:** CLEP. 30 credit hours maximum toward associate degree. **Support services:** GED preparation and test center, learning center, pre-admission summer program, reduced course load, remedial instruction, study skills assistance, tutoring.

Majors. Business: Accounting, administrative services, marketing, office management, operations. **Computer sciences:** LAN/WAN management, security, web page design. **Engineering:** Electrical. **Engineering technology:** Drafting, robotics. **Family/consumer sciences:** Institutional food production. **Health:** Medical radiologic technology/radiation therapy, medical secretary, nursing (RN), physical therapy assistant, sonography. **Legal studies:** Legal secretary. **Mechanic/repair:** Heating/ac/refrig. **Personal/culinary services:** Culinary arts. **Protective services:** Fire safety technology, police science.

Most popular majors. Business/marketing 29%, computer/information sciences 6%, education 10%, engineering/engineering technologies 7%, health sciences 28%, personal/culinary services 6%, security/protective services 14%.

Computing on campus. 58 workstations in library, computer center. Online course registration, helpline, wireless network available.

Student life. Freshman orientation: Available. **Activities:** Student government, student newspaper.

Student services. Alcohol/substance abuse counseling, career counseling, services for economically disadvantaged, student employment services, financial aid counseling, minority student services, on-campus daycare, personal counseling, placement for graduates, veterans' counselor. **Physically disabled:** Services for visually, speech, hearing impaired.

Contact. Phone: (608) 757-7665 Fax: (608) 743-4407
Barbara Erlandson, Student Services Manager, Blackhawk Technical College, Box 5009, Janesville, WI 53547-5009

Bryant & Stratton College: Milwaukee
Milwaukee, Wisconsin
www.bryantstratton.edu
CB code: 3617

- For-profit 2-year business and junior college
- Commuter campus in very large city

General. Founded in 1854. Regionally accredited. **Location:** 75 miles from Chicago. **Calendar:** Trimester.

Annual costs/financial aid. Tuition/fees (2008-2009): $14,555. Tuition and fees provided are for Associate degrees only. Bachelor's program tuition and fees may vary. Books/supplies: $750.

Contact. Phone: (414) 276-5200
Director of Admissions, 310 West Wisconsin Avenue, Suite 500, Milwaukee, WI 53203

Chippewa Valley Technical College
Eau Claire, Wisconsin
www.cvtc.edu
CB code: 0786

- Public 2-year technical college
- Commuter campus in small city

General. Founded in 1912. Regionally accredited. **Enrollment:** 5,624 degree-seeking undergraduates. **Degrees:** 819 associate awarded. **Location:** 90 miles from Minneapolis-St. Paul. **Calendar:** Semester, limited summer session. **Full-time faculty:** 241 total; 12% have terminal degrees, 2% minority, 54% women. **Part-time faculty:** 353 total; 1% minority, 39% women. **Special facilities:** Health Education Center with state-of the art equipment and lab facilities, NanoRite Facility. **Partnerships:** Formal partnerships with University Wisconsin Family Medicine Clinic, University Wisconsin: Marquette, Haas Manufacturing, ECASD (Eau Claire Area School District) Technology Charter, NanoRite, University Wisconsin:Stout, NWMOC, Workforce Resource, Job Service, ECAEDC- SmarttNet, Districts Mutual Insurance.

Transfer out. Colleges most students transferred to 2008: University of Wisconsin-Stout.

Basis for selection. Open admission, but selective for some programs. Additional testing and course requirements for applicants to nursing, dental hygiene, radiography, surgical technologist, medical assistant and physical therapist assistant programs. Interview required for alcohol abuse prevention and other drug abuse prevention associate programs, and fire protective service technician program.

High school preparation. Algebra and science requirements for some degree programs.

2008-2009 Annual costs. Tuition/fees: $3,086; $18,002 out-of-state. Per-credit charge: $97 in-state; $594 out-of-state. Material fees vary by program; minimum $4 per course. $10 per credit fee for online courses. Books/supplies: $853. Personal expenses: $1,370.

2007-2008 Financial aid. Need-based: Need-based aid available for part-time students. Work-study available nights, weekends and for part-time students.

Application procedures. Admission: Priority date 8/15; no deadline. $30 fee, may be waived for applicants with need. Admission notification on a rolling basis. **Financial aid:** Priority date 3/15; no closing date. FAFSA required. Applicants notified on a rolling basis starting 6/1; must reply within 2 week(s) of notification.

Academics. Special study options: Distance learning, double major, dual enrollment of high school students, ESL, external degree, independent study, internships, liberal arts/career combination, student-designed major, weekend college. License preparation in dental hygiene, nursing, paramedic, real estate. **Credit/placement by examination:** CLEP, institutional tests. 34 credit hours maximum toward associate degree. 50% of semester hours needed for degree may be earned as credit by examination. **Support services:** GED preparation and test center, learning center, reduced course load, remedial instruction, study skills assistance, tutoring.

Majors. **Agriculture:** General, agronomy, animal sciences, horticultural science, landscaping. **Business:** General, accounting, administrative services, hospitality/recreation, logistics, office technology, operations, restaurant/food services. **Computer sciences:** General, applications programming, programming. **Engineering:** Civil. **Engineering technology:** Civil, drafting, electrical, robotics. **Health:** Clinical lab assistant, clinical lab technology, dental hygiene, dialysis technology, medical radiologic technology/radiation therapy, medical records technology, nursing (RN), pharmacy assistant, physical therapy assistant, radiologic technology/medical imaging, respiratory therapy assistant, respiratory therapy technology, sonography, substance abuse counseling, surgical technology. **Legal studies:** Paralegal. **Mechanic/repair:** Auto body, automotive, diesel, electronics/electrical, heating/ac/refrig, industrial. **Personal/culinary services:** Restaurant/catering. **Production:** Machine tool, tool and die. **Protective services:** Firefighting, police science. **Other:** NanoScience technology, Paramedic technician.

Most popular majors. Business/marketing 30%, computer/information sciences 13%, health sciences 8%, security/protective services 19%, trade and industry 19%.

Computing on campus. 1,200 workstations in library, computer center. Commuter students can connect to campus network. Online course registration, helpline, wireless network available.

Student life. **Freshman orientation:** Mandatory. **Activities:** Student government, student newspaper, Student Impact, diversity student organization.

Athletics. **Intramural:** Basketball, skiing, softball, table tennis, tennis, volleyball.

Student services. Career counseling, student employment services, financial aid counseling, health services, minority student services, on-campus daycare, personal counseling, placement for graduates, veterans' counselor. **Physically disabled:** Services for visually, speech, hearing impaired. **Transfer:** Pre-admission transcript evaluation for new students. College fairs on campus for students transferring to 4-year colleges.

Contact. E-mail: mkeys@cvtc.edu
Phone: (715) 833-6246 Toll-free number: (800) 547-2882
Fax: (715) 833-6470
Sue Brehm, Director of Enrollment Services, Chippewa Valley Technical College, 620 West Clairemont Avenue, Eau Claire, WI 54701-6162

College of Menominee Nation

Keshena, Wisconsin
www.menominee.edu **CB code: 3974**

- Private 2-year community college
- Commuter campus in rural community

General. Regionally accredited. **Location:** 150 miles from Madison, 35 miles from Green Bay. **Calendar:** Semester.

Annual costs/financial aid. Tuition/fees (2008-2009): $6,100. Books/supplies: $1,190. Personal expenses: $1,380. Need-based financial aid available to full-time and part-time students.

Contact. Phone: (715) 799-5600 ext. 3053
Admissions Representative, N 172 State Highway 47/55, Keshena, WI 54135

Fox Valley Technical College

Appleton, Wisconsin **CB member**
www.fvtc.edu **CB code: 0747**

- Public 2-year technical college
- Commuter campus in small city

General. Founded in 1967. Regionally accredited. **Enrollment:** 4,667 degree-seeking undergraduates; 1,716 non-degree-seeking students. **Degrees:** 759 associate awarded. **Location:** 100 miles from Milwaukee. **Calendar:** Semester, limited summer session. **Full-time faculty:** 302 total. **Part-time faculty:** 30 total.

Student profile. Among degree-seeking undergraduates, 992 enrolled as first-time, first-year students.

Part-time:	51%	**Women:**	50%
Out-of-state:	1%	**25 or older:**	35%

Basis for selection. Open admission, but selective for some programs. Special requirements for nursing and criminal justice programs. ACT, ACCUPLACER, COMPASS required for placement.

2008-2009 Annual costs. Tuition/fees: $3,232; $18,148 out-of-state. Per-credit charge: $97 in-state; $594 out-of-state. Material fees vary by program; minimum $4 per course. $10 per credit fee for online courses. Books/supplies: $1,000. Personal expenses: $1,550.

2007-2008 Financial aid. **Need-based:** 40% of total undergraduate aid awarded as scholarships/grants, 60% as loans/jobs.

Application procedures. **Admission:** No deadline. $30 fee, may be waived for applicants with need. Admission notification on a rolling basis. **Financial aid:** Priority date 4/15; no closing date. FAFSA required. Applicants notified on a rolling basis.

Academics. **Special study options:** Accelerated study, distance learning, double major, dual enrollment of high school students, ESL, internships, student-designed major. License preparation in aviation, dental hygiene, nursing, occupational therapy, paramedic, physical therapy. **Credit/placement by examination:** AP, CLEP, institutional tests. 45 credit hours maximum toward associate degree. **Support services:** GED preparation and test center, reduced course load, remedial instruction, tutoring.

Majors. **Agriculture:** Agribusiness operations, business, horticulture, supplies. **Business:** General, accounting, administrative services, banking/financial services, hospitality admin, hospitality/recreation, human resources, office technology, restaurant/food services, tourism promotion, training/development. **Communications technology:** Graphic/printing. **Computer sciences:** Applications programming, data processing, information systems. **Conservation:** General. **Construction:** General. **Engineering technology:** Drafting, electrical, mechanical drafting. **Family/consumer sciences:** Child care, institutional food production. **Health:** Dental hygiene, nursing (RN), occupational therapy assistant, substance abuse counseling. **Legal studies:** Legal secretary, paralegal. **Mechanic/repair:** Aircraft, aircraft powerplant, auto body, automotive, avionics. **Parks/recreation:** Facilities management. **Personal/culinary services:** Baking, chef training, culinary arts. **Protective services:** Criminal justice, fire safety technology, police science. **Public administration:** Human services. **Transportation:** Airline/commercial pilot. **Visual/performing arts:** Interior design.

Computing on campus. 260 workstations in library, computer center, student center. Commuter students can connect to campus network. Online course registration, online library, helpline, repair service, wireless network available.

Student life. **Freshman orientation:** Mandatory. Held on various dates 2 months prior to beginning of semester. **Activities:** Student government, student newspaper, 28 curriculum-related clubs.

Athletics. NJCAA. **Intercollegiate:** Basketball M. **Intramural:** Basketball, bowling, football (non-tackle), golf, soccer, softball, table tennis, volleyball. **Team name:** Foxes.

Student services. Adult student services, alcohol/substance abuse counseling, career counseling, services for economically disadvantaged, student employment services, financial aid counseling, health services, minority student services, on-campus daycare, personal counseling, placement for graduates, veterans' counselor, women's services. **Physically disabled:** Services for visually, speech, hearing impaired.

Contact. E-mail: admissions@fvtc.edu
Phone: (920) 735-5645 Toll-free number: (800) 735-3882
Fax: (920) 735-2484
Melissa Kohlbeck, Associate Director, Enrollment Services, Fox Valley Technical College, 1825 North Bluemound Drive, Appleton, WI 54912-2277

Gateway Technical College

Kenosha, Wisconsin **CB member**
www.gtc.edu **CB code: 0761**

- Public 2-year technical college
- Commuter campus in small city

General. Founded in 1911. Regionally accredited. **Location:** 30 miles from Milwaukee, 60 miles from Chicago. **Calendar:** Semester.

Annual costs/financial aid. Tuition/fees (2008-2009): $3,430; $18,346 out-of-state. Materials fees vary by program; minimum $4 per course. Books/supplies: $910. Personal expenses: $1,461. Need-based financial aid available to full-time and part-time students.

Contact. Phone: (262) 564-2912
Director of Admissions, 3520 30th Avenue, Kenosha, WI 53144-1690

Lac Courte Oreilles Ojibwa Community College
Hayward, Wisconsin
www.lco.edu **CB code: 7351**

- Public 2-year community college
- Commuter campus in small town

General. Regionally accredited. Located on the Lac Courte Oreilles Reservation. **Enrollment:** 448 degree-seeking undergraduates. **Degrees:** 63 associate awarded. **Calendar:** Semester, limited summer session. **Full-time faculty:** 20 total. **Part-time faculty:** 50 total.

Student profile. Among degree-seeking undergraduates, 76 enrolled as first-time, first-year students, 4 transferred in from other institutions.

Part-time:	33%	**Women:**	67%

Transfer out. 20% of students enrolled in the transfer program go on to 4-year colleges.

Basis for selection. Open admission. **Homeschooled:** State high school equivalency certificate required.

2009-2010 Annual costs. Tuition/fees (projected): $4,075; $4,075 out-of-state. Per-credit charge: $140. Books/supplies: $300.

Application procedures. Admission: No deadline. $10 fee, may be waived for applicants with need. Application must be submitted on paper. Admission notification on a rolling basis. **Financial aid:** No deadline. FAFSA required. Applicants notified on a rolling basis.

Academics. Special study options: Cooperative education, distance learning, double major, independent study, liberal arts/career combination. **Credit/placement by examination:** AP, CLEP. **Support services:** GED preparation and test center, remedial instruction, study skills assistance, tutoring.

Majors. Area/ethnic studies: Native American. **Business:** Business admin, logistics, office management. **Computer sciences:** Systems analysis. **Health:** Medical assistant. **Liberal arts:** Arts/sciences. **Public administration:** Human services.

Computing on campus. Wireless network available.

Student life. Freshman orientation: Available. Preregistration for classes offered. **Activities:** Drama, student government.

Student services. Career counseling, financial aid counseling. **Transfer:** Transfer center, college fairs on campus for students transferring to 4-year colleges.

Contact. Phone: (715) 634-4790 ext. 104 Fax: (715) 634-7579
Annette Wiggins, Registrar, Lac Courte Oreilles Ojibwa Community College, 13466 West Trepania Road, Hayward, WI 54843

Lakeshore Technical College
Cleveland, Wisconsin **CB member**
www.gotoltc.edu **CB code: 0618**

- Public 2-year technical college
- Commuter campus in rural community

General. Founded in 1912. Regionally accredited. **Enrollment:** 2,238 degree-seeking undergraduates; 548 non-degree-seeking students. **Degrees:** 287 associate awarded. **Location:** 15 miles from Sheboygan, 65 miles from Milwaukee. **Calendar:** Semester, limited summer session. **Full-time faculty:** 100 total. **Part-time faculty:** 300 total. **Special facilities:** Wind turbine, photovoltaic panels (solar), emergency operations center. **Partnerships:** Formal partnerships with Tech Prep with all public schools and employers in Manitowoc and Sheboygan counties.

Student profile. Among degree-seeking undergraduates, 257 enrolled as first-time, first-year students.

Part-time:	62%	**Asian American:**	4%
Out-of-state:	1%	**Hispanic American:**	2%
Women:	60%	**25 or older:**	55%
African American:	1%		

Transfer out. Colleges most students transferred to 2008: Silver Lake College, Lakeland College.

Basis for selection. Open admission. All health-related, public safety and child care programs require background checks and physical examinations. International students whose first language is not English must have minimum 550 TOEFL. ASSET, COMPASS, ACCUPLACER are preferred placement exams, but will accept ACT/SAT. **Homeschooled:** State high school equivalency certificate required.

2008-2009 Annual costs. Tuition/fees: $3,045; $17,961 out-of-state. Per-credit charge: $97 in-state; $594 out-of-state. Materials fees vary by program; minimum $4 per course. $10 per credit fee for online courses. Books/supplies: $1,050. Personal expenses: $1,625.

2008-2009 Financial aid. All financial aid based on need. 55% of total undergraduate aid awarded as scholarships/grants, 45% as loans/jobs. Need-based aid available for part-time students. Work-study available nights and for part-time students.

Application procedures. Admission: No deadline. $30 fee, may be waived for applicants with need. Admission notification on a rolling basis. **Financial aid:** Priority date 6/1; no closing date. FAFSA, institutional form required. Applicants notified on a rolling basis starting 6/1; must reply within 3 week(s) of notification.

Academics. Special study options: Accelerated study, combined bachelor's/graduate degree, cross-registration, distance learning, double major, dual enrollment of high school students, ESL, honors, independent study, internships, student-designed major. License preparation in nursing, paramedic, real estate. **Credit/placement by examination:** AP, CLEP, institutional tests. **Support services:** GED preparation and test center, learning center, pre-admission summer program, reduced course load, remedial instruction, study skills assistance, tutoring.

Majors. Business: Accounting, administrative services, business admin, hospitality admin, logistics, marketing, office technology, operations, training/development, warehousing. **Communications technology:** Desktop publishing. **Computer sciences:** Computer support specialist, networking, webmaster. **Education:** Early childhood. **Engineering technology:** Drafting, electromechanical, mechanical drafting, quality control. **Health:** Clinical lab technology, EMT paramedic, medical radiologic technology/radiation therapy, medical secretary, nursing (RN). **Legal studies:** Court reporting, paralegal. **Protective services:** Police science. **Science technology:** Nuclear power. **Other:** Broadcast captioning, Wind energy technology.

Most popular majors. Business/marketing 33%, computer/information sciences 6%, education 7%, engineering/engineering technologies 9%, health sciences 20%, interdisciplinary studies 9%, legal studies 7%, security/protective services 6%.

Computing on campus. 950 workstations in library, computer center, student center. Online course registration, online library, helpline, wireless network available.

Student life. Freshman orientation: Available. Preregistration for classes offered. **Activities:** Student government, student newspaper.

Athletics. Intramural: Basketball, football (non-tackle), volleyball.

Student services. Adult student services, alcohol/substance abuse counseling, career counseling, services for economically disadvantaged, student employment services, financial aid counseling, health services, minority student services, on-campus daycare, personal counseling, placement for graduates. **Physically disabled:** Services for visually, speech, hearing impaired. **Transfer:** Re-entry adviser, pre-admission transcript evaluation for new students. Transfer adviser, college fairs on campus for students transferring to 4-year colleges.

Contact. E-mail: enroll@gotoltc.edu
Phone: (920) 693-1000 Toll-free number: (888) 468-6582
Fax: (920) 693-3561
Scott Lieburn, Manager Student Services, Lakeshore Technical College, 1290 North Avenue, Cleveland, WI 53015-9761

Madison Area Technical College
Madison, Wisconsin
http://matcmadison.edu **CB code: 1536**

- Public 2-year community and technical college
- Commuter campus in small city

General. Founded in 1912. Regionally accredited. Campuses in Fort Atkinson, Portage, Reedsburg, and Watertown. **Enrollment:** 14,650 degree-seeking undergraduates. **Degrees:** 1,304 associate awarded. **Calendar:** Semester, limited summer session. **Full-time faculty:** 400 total. **Part-time faculty:** 1,100 total. **Special facilities:** Satellite downlink.

Student profile.

Out-of-state:	2%	**25 or older:**	10%

Basis for selection. Open admission, but selective for some programs. School achievement record, class rank, test scores considered for all health occupation programs.

High school preparation. High school academic subject requirements for health and technical programs.

2008-2009 Annual costs. Tuition/fees: $3,161; $18,077 out-of-state. Per-credit charge: $97 in-state; $594 out-of-state. Material fees vary by program; minimum $4 per course. $10 per credit fee for online courses. Books/supplies: $760. Personal expenses: $1,340.

Application procedures. Admission: Priority date 11/20; no deadline. $30 fee, may be waived for applicants with need. Admission notification on a rolling basis. Early application recommended for programs with limited enrollment. **Financial aid:** Priority date 4/15; no closing date. FAFSA required. Applicants notified on a rolling basis starting 4/15.

Academics. Technical College offering a college transfer program, advanced technical certificates, apprenticeships, English as a second language, adult continuing education and basic skills education. **Special study options:** Accelerated study, cross-registration, distance learning, dual enrollment of high school students, ESL, external degree, internships. Bachelor's degree programs available on campus. License preparation in nursing. **Credit/placement by examination:** CLEP, institutional tests. 32 credit hours maximum toward associate degree. **Support services:** GED preparation, learning center, reduced course load, remedial instruction, study skills assistance, tutoring.

Majors. Agriculture: General, animal sciences, horticulture. **Business:** Accounting, administrative services, business admin, communications, fashion, finance, hospitality admin, hospitality/recreation, insurance, office management, real estate, tourism/travel. **Communications technology:** Graphic/printing. **Computer sciences:** General, programming. **Engineering technology:** Architectural, civil. **Family/consumer sciences:** Child care, food/nutrition. **Health:** Clinical lab technology, dental hygiene, EMT paramedic, medical assistant, medical radiologic technology/radiation therapy, medical records admin, medical secretary, mental health services, nursing (RN), occupational therapy assistant, respiratory therapy technology, veterinary technology/assistant. **Interdisciplinary:** Biological/physical sciences. **Legal studies:** Court reporting. **Liberal arts:** Arts/sciences. **Mechanic/repair:** Electronics/electrical. **Personal/culinary services:** Cosmetic, culinary arts. **Protective services:** Police science. **Science technology:** Biological. **Visual/performing arts:** Commercial photography, commercial/advertising art, design, interior design.

Most popular majors. Business/marketing 28%, computer/information sciences 7%, family/consumer sciences 6%, health sciences 19%, trade and industry 12%, visual/performing arts 7%.

Computing on campus. 470 workstations in library, computer center.

Student life. Freshman orientation: Available. **Policies:** Student life department promotes a variety of cultural diversity and activities and plays an active role in student government activities. **Activities:** Jazz band, choral groups, drama, music ensembles, student government, student newspaper.

Athletics. NJCAA. **Intercollegiate:** Baseball M, basketball, bowling, cross-country M, golf M, softball W, volleyball W, wrestling M. **Intramural:** Basketball, racquetball, soccer, swimming, table tennis, tennis, volleyball. **Team name:** Wolf Pack.

Student services. Career counseling, student employment services, health services, on-campus daycare, personal counseling, placement for graduates, veterans' counselor. **Physically disabled:** Services for visually, speech, hearing impaired. **Transfer:** Transfer adviser for students transferring to 4-year colleges.

Contact. Phone: (608) 246-6205 Fax: (608) 258-2329
Jennifer Hoege, Admissions Administrator, Madison Area Technical College, 3350 Anderson Street, Madison, WI 53704-2599

Madison Media Institute
Madison, Wisconsin
www.madisonmedia.edu

- For-profit 2-year visual arts and music college
- Large city

General. Accredited by ACCSCT. **Calendar:** Trimester.

Annual costs/financial aid. Tuition/fees (2008-2009): $13,790. Books/supplies: $420.

Contact. Phone: (800) 236-4997
Director of Admissions, 2702 Agriculture Drive, Madison, WI 53718

Mid-State Technical College
Wisconsin Rapids, Wisconsin — **CB member**
www.mstc.edu — **CB code: 0635**

- Public 2-year technical college
- Commuter campus in large town

General. Founded in 1967. Regionally accredited. Branch campuses in Marshfield and Stevens Point, outreach center in Adams. **Enrollment:** 2,970 undergraduates. **Degrees:** 316 associate awarded. **Location:** 20 miles from Stevens Point, 115 miles from Madison. **Calendar:** Semester, limited summer session. **Full-time faculty:** 95 total.

Student profile.

Out-of-state:	1%	**25 or older:**	15%

Basis for selection. Open admission, but selective for some programs. Students must take ACCUPLACER entrance exam. Certain programs have additional admission requirements. **Homeschooled:** Proof of completion of 12th grade is required.

High school preparation. Biology, anatomy, physiology, chemistry, medical terminology recommended for health programs. Information processing, general business, business law, economics, accounting recommended for business programs. Geometry, drafting, chemistry, advanced math recommended for technical and industrial programs.

2008-2009 Annual costs. Tuition/fees: $3,206; $18,122 out-of-state. Per-credit charge: $97 in-state; $594 out-of-state. Material fees vary by program; minimum $4 per course. Books/supplies: $986. Personal expenses: $1,500.

2007-2008 Financial aid. Need-based: Need-based aid available for part-time students. Work-study available nights, weekends and for part-time students. **Non-need-based:** Scholarships awarded for academics, leadership.

Application procedures. Admission: No deadline. $30 fee, may be waived for applicants with need. Admission notification on a rolling basis. **Financial aid:** No deadline. FAFSA required. Applicants notified on a rolling basis starting 5/30; must reply within 2 week(s) of notification.

Academics. Special study options: Accelerated study, cooperative education, distance learning, double major, dual enrollment of high school students, ESL, independent study, internships. License preparation in nursing, paramedic. **Credit/placement by examination:** AP, CLEP, institutional tests. 32 credit hours maximum toward associate degree. **Support services:** GED preparation and test center, learning center, reduced course load, remedial instruction, study skills assistance, tutoring.

Majors. Business: Accounting, administrative services, business admin, human resources, marketing, office management, office/clerical. **Computer sciences:** LAN/WAN management, networking, programming, web page design. **Conservation:** Urban forestry. **Education:** Early childhood. **Engineering technology:** Civil, computer systems, electrical, industrial, instrumentation, manufacturing. **Health:** EMT paramedic, nursing (RN), respiratory therapy assistant, respiratory therapy technology. **Mechanic/repair:** Electronics/electrical. **Protective services:** Corrections, firefighting, police science. **Other:** Paper & Chemical Technology.

Computing on campus. 600 workstations in library, computer center, student center. Online course registration, online library, helpline, wireless network available.

Student life. Freshman orientation: Available. **Activities:** Student government, student newspaper, animation/video game club, Association for Information Technology Professionals, Campus Crusade for Christ, civil technology club, criminal justice-corrections club, cosmetology and barbering club, electronics club, Law Enforcement Organization, student nurses' association, Student Society of Arborists.

Student services. Adult student services, alcohol/substance abuse counseling, career counseling, services for economically disadvantaged, student employment services, financial aid counseling, minority student services, personal counseling, placement for graduates, veterans' counselor, women's services. **Physically disabled:** Services for visually, speech, hearing impaired. **Learning disabled:** Comprehensive services available. **Transfer:** Pre-admission transcript evaluation for new students. Transfer adviser, college fairs on campus for students transferring to 4-year colleges.

Two-Year Colleges

Contact. E-mail: enrollment@mstc.edu
Phone: (715) 422-5444 Toll-free number: (888) 575-6782
Fax: (715) 422-5440
Jim Barrett, Director of Admissions, Mid-State Technical College, 500 32nd Street North, Wisconsin Rapids, WI 54494

Milwaukee Area Technical College

Milwaukee, Wisconsin
www.matc.edu
CB member
CB code: 1475

- Public 2-year junior and technical college
- Commuter campus in very large city

General. Founded in 1912. Regionally accredited. Campuses in Milwaukee, Oak Creek, Mequon, and West Allis. **Enrollment:** 15,942 degree-seeking undergraduates; 2,838 non-degree-seeking students. **Degrees:** 1,380 associate awarded. **Location:** 85 miles from Chicago. **Calendar:** Semester, limited summer session. **Full-time faculty:** 588 total; 9% have terminal degrees, 27% minority, 49% women. **Part-time faculty:** 768 total; 4% have terminal degrees, 19% minority, 51% women. **Class size:** 81% < 20, 19% 20-39.

Student profile. Among degree-seeking undergraduates, 15% enrolled in a transfer program, 85% enrolled in a vocational program, 10% already have a bachelor's degree or higher, 2,031 enrolled as first-time, first-year students, 453 transferred in from other institutions.

Part-time:	64%	**Asian American:**	4%
Out-of-state:	1%	**Hispanic American:**	9%
Women:	58%	**Native American:**	1%
African American:	28%	**25 or older:**	54%

Transfer out. 25% of students enrolled in the transfer program go on to 4-year colleges. **Colleges most students transferred to 2008:** University of Wisconsin-Milwaukee, Waukesha County Technical College, Cardinal Stritch University, Gateway Technical College, Alverno College.

Basis for selection. Open admission, but selective for some programs. Special requirements for health programs. ACCUPLACER required for placement. Institutionally administered reading, math, and English examinations required for all applicants if SAT or ACT not taken. **Homeschooled:** Must complete ACCUPLACER testing.

High school preparation. Specific subject requirements for some programs.

2008-2009 Annual costs. Tuition/fees: $3,216; $18,132 out-of-state. Per-credit charge: $97 in-state; $594 out-of-state. Material fees vary by program; minimum $4 per course. $10 per credit fee for online courses. Books/supplies: $1,312. Personal expenses: $1,824.

2007-2008 Financial aid. Need-based: Need-based aid available for part-time students. Work-study available for part-time students. **Non-need-based:** Scholarships awarded for academics.

Application procedures. Admission: Closing date 8/10 (postmark date). $30 fee. Admission notification on a rolling basis. **Financial aid:** Priority date 3/15; no closing date. FAFSA required. Applicants notified on a rolling basis starting 4/15.

Academics. Special study options: Accelerated study, cooperative education, distance learning, double major, dual enrollment of high school students, ESL, honors, independent study, internships, liberal arts/career combination, weekend college. Teacher education program with guaranteed admission to University of Wisconsin-Milwaukee. License preparation in aviation, dental hygiene, nursing. **Credit/placement by examination:** AP, CLEP, institutional tests. **Support services:** GED preparation and test center, learning center, reduced course load, remedial instruction, study skills assistance, tutoring, writing center.

Majors. Agriculture: Landscaping. **Business:** Accounting, administrative services, apparel, banking/financial services, business admin, e-commerce, hotel/motel admin, international marketing, logistics, marketing, operations, real estate, tourism/travel. **Communications technology:** Graphic/printing, graphics, radio/tv. **Computer sciences:** Computer graphics, computer support specialist, networking, programming, security, systems analysis. **Engineering:** Materials. **Engineering technology:** Architectural, biomedical, civil, computer systems, electrical, heat/ac/refrig, industrial, mechanical drafting, plastics, water quality. **Foreign languages:** Sign language interpretation. **Health:** Anesthesiologist assistant, cardiovascular technology, clinical lab technology, dental hygiene, dietetic technician, electroencephalograph technology, medical radiologic technology/radiation therapy, medical records technology, medical secretary, nursing (RN), occupational therapy assistant, physical therapy assistant, respiratory therapy technology, surgical technology. **Legal studies:** Legal secretary, paralegal. **Liberal arts:** Arts/sciences. **Mechanic/repair:** Automotive. **Personal/culinary services:** Mortuary science, restaurant/catering. **Production:** Welding. **Protective services:** Fire-fighting, police science. **Science technology:** Chemical. **Visual/performing arts:** Commercial photography, graphic design, interior design, music performance.

Most popular majors. Business/marketing 19%, computer/information sciences 6%, engineering/engineering technologies 6%, health sciences 33%, liberal arts 8%, security/protective services 7%.

Computing on campus. 275 workstations in library, computer center, student center. Online course registration, online library, helpline, wireless network available.

Student life. Freshman orientation: Mandatory. **Housing:** Certified housing available at nearby colleges and other facilities. **Activities:** Literary magazine, student government, student newspaper, TV station, student senate, student life committee, African American student club, American Culinary Federation, architectural technology club, Association of Information Technology Professionals, campus bible fellowship, criminal justice student organization, environmental club, Phi Theta Kappa Honor Society, paralegal association.

Athletics. NJCAA. **Intercollegiate:** Baseball M, basketball M, golf, soccer M, softball W, volleyball W. **Intramural:** Basketball, table tennis, volleyball. **Team name:** Lakestormers.

Student services. Alcohol/substance abuse counseling, career counseling, services for economically disadvantaged, student employment services, financial aid counseling, health services, legal services, minority student services, on-campus daycare, personal counseling, placement for graduates, veterans' counselor, women's services. **Physically disabled:** Services for visually, speech, hearing impaired. **Learning disabled:** Comprehensive services available. **Transfer:** Transfer center, transfer adviser, college fairs on campus for students transferring to 4-year colleges.

Contact. E-mail: adamss4@matc.edu
Phone: (414) 297-6370 Fax: (414) 297-7800
Sarah Adams, Registrar, Director, Enrollment Services, Milwaukee Area Technical College, 700 West State Street, Milwaukee, WI 53233-1443

Moraine Park Technical College

Fond du Lac, Wisconsin
www.morainepark.edu
CB code: 0667

- Public 2-year technical college
- Commuter campus in large town
- Interview required

General. Founded in 1967. Regionally accredited. Campus locations in Beaver Dam and West Bend. **Enrollment:** 3,711 degree-seeking undergraduates. **Degrees:** 471 associate awarded. **Location:** 60 miles from Milwaukee. **Calendar:** Semester, limited summer session. **Full-time faculty:** 150 total. **Part-time faculty:** 200 total.

Basis for selection. Open admission, but selective for some programs. Students without high school diploma may be admitted to certain job-entry preparation programs. ACT required of associate-degree-seeking nursing applicants.

High school preparation. 16 units recommended. Recommended units include English 3, mathematics 2, social studies 2 and science 2.

2008-2009 Annual costs. Tuition/fees: $3,043; $17,959 out-of-state. Per-credit charge: $97 in-state; $594 out-of-state. Material fees vary by program; minimum $4 per course. $10 per credit fee for online courses. Books/supplies: $900.

2007-2008 Financial aid. Need-based: Need-based aid available for part-time students. Work-study available nights and for part-time students. **Non-need-based:** Scholarships awarded for academics, job skills, leadership, minority status, state residency.

Application procedures. Admission: No deadline. $30 fee, may be waived for applicants with need. Admission notification on a rolling basis. Some programs may have application windows. Please check with admissions department or on the admissions Web page. Limited enrollment health care programs have varying application deadlines. **Financial aid:** Priority date 5/1; no closing date. FAFSA, institutional form required. Applicants notified on a rolling basis starting 6/15; must reply within 2 week(s) of notification.

Academics. Special study options: Accelerated study, distance learning, double major, dual enrollment of high school students, ESL, independent study, internships, weekend college. **Credit/placement by examination:**

CLEP, institutional tests. 30 credit hours maximum toward associate degree. **Support services:** GED preparation and test center, learning center, pre-admission summer program, reduced course load, remedial instruction, tutoring.

Majors. Business: Accounting, administrative services, marketing, office management, office technology, sales/distribution. **Communications technology:** Graphic/printing. **Computer sciences:** Applications programming, data processing. **Engineering technology:** Civil, drafting. **Family/consumer sciences:** Child care, family studies. **Health:** EMT paramedic, health services, medical records technology, medical secretary, nursing (RN), substance abuse counseling. **Legal studies:** Legal secretary. **Mechanic/repair:** Electronics/electrical, heating/ac/refrig. **Personal/culinary services:** Culinary arts. **Protective services:** Corrections, fire safety technology, police science.

Most popular majors. Business/marketing 24%, computer/information sciences 9%, engineering/engineering technologies 12%, health sciences 26%, trade and industry 9%.

Student life. Freshman orientation: Mandatory. **Activities:** Student government.

Student services. Career counseling, student employment services, health services, on-campus daycare, personal counseling, placement for graduates, veterans' counselor. **Physically disabled:** Services for visually, hearing impaired. **Transfer:** College fairs on campus for students transferring to 4-year colleges.

Contact. Phone: (920) 924-3408 Toll-free number: (800) 472-4554
Fax: (920) 924-3421
Richard Barnhouse, Admissions Director, Moraine Park Technical College, 235 North National Avenue, Fond du Lac, WI 54935-1940

Nicolet Area Technical College
Rhinelander, Wisconsin
www.nicoletcollege.edu **CB code: 0713**

- Public 2-year community and technical college
- Commuter campus in small town

General. Founded in 1967. Regionally accredited. **Location:** 225 miles from Milwaukee, 200 miles from Madison. **Calendar:** Semester.

Annual costs/financial aid. Tuition/fees (2008-2009): $3,023; $17,939 out-of-state. Material fees vary by program; minimum $4 per course. $10 per credit fee for online courses. Books/supplies: $760. Personal expenses: $1,249.

Contact. Phone: (715) 365-4451
Director of Enrollment Management, Box 518, Rhinelander, WI 54501

Northcentral Technical College
Wausau, Wisconsin
www.ntc.edu **CB code: 0735**

- Public 2-year community and technical college
- Commuter campus in small city

General. Founded in 1911. Regionally accredited. Regional campuses located in Antigo, Medford, Phillips, Wittenberg and Spencer. Public safety training center in Merrill. **Enrollment:** 2,917 degree-seeking undergraduates. **Degrees:** 456 associate awarded. **Location:** 200 miles from Milwaukee and Minneapolis-St. Paul, 150 miles from Madison. **Calendar:** Semester, limited summer session. **Full-time faculty:** 151 total. **Part-time faculty:** 8 total.

Basis for selection. Open admission, but selective for some programs. Special requirements for health programs including application portfolio. ACCUPLACER or ACT required for placement. **Homeschooled:** Transcript of courses and grades required.

High school preparation. 3 units each of math and science required for the following programs: radiography, nursing, dental hygiene. Math emphasis for technical programs, chemistry for nursing.

2008-2009 Annual costs. Tuition/fees: $3,062; $17,978 out-of-state. Per-credit charge: $97 in-state; $594 out-of-state. Materials fees vary by program; minimum $4 per course.

2007-2008 Financial aid. Need-based: Need-based aid available for part-time students. Work-study available nights and for part-time students.

Application procedures. Admission: No deadline. $30 fee, may be waived for applicants with need. Admission notification on a rolling basis. **Financial aid:** No deadline. FAFSA required. Applicants notified on a rolling basis.

Academics. Special study options: Accelerated study, distance learning, double major, dual enrollment of high school students, ESL, internships, student-designed major, weekend college. Bachelor's degree programs available on campus. License preparation in dental hygiene, nursing, paramedic, radiology. **Credit/placement by examination:** AP, CLEP, IB, institutional tests. 24 credit hours maximum toward associate degree. **Support services:** GED preparation and test center, learning center, pre-admission summer program, reduced course load, remedial instruction, study skills assistance, tutoring, writing center.

Majors. Architecture: Technology. **Business:** Accounting, administrative services, business admin, entrepreneurial studies, office technology, operations. **Communications technology:** Graphic/printing. **Computer sciences:** Computer support specialist, programming, systems analysis. **Construction:** General. **Engineering:** Electrical, mechanics. **Engineering technology:** Drafting, electrical. **Foreign languages:** Sign language interpretation. **Health:** Clinical lab assistant, clinical lab technology, dental hygiene, medical radiologic technology/radiation therapy, medical records technology, medical secretary, nursing (RN), radiologic technology/medical imaging, sonography, surgical technology. **Legal studies:** Legal secretary. **Mechanic/repair:** Auto body, automotive. **Production:** Machine tool, welding. **Protective services:** Police science.

Computing on campus. 1,200 workstations in library, computer center, student center. Commuter students can connect to campus network. Online course registration, online library, helpline, repair service, wireless network available.

Student life. Freshman orientation: Available. Preregistration for classes offered. **Housing:** Coed dorms available. **Activities:** Radio station, student government, student newspaper, Campus Crusade for Christ, international student club, multicultural student club.

Athletics. Intramural: Basketball, football (non-tackle), softball, volleyball. **Team name:** Timberwolves.

Student services. Adult student services, career counseling, services for economically disadvantaged, student employment services, financial aid counseling, health services, minority student services, on-campus daycare, personal counseling, placement for graduates. **Physically disabled:** Services for visually, speech, hearing impaired. **Transfer:** Pre-admission transcript evaluation for new students. Transfer adviser, college fairs on campus for students transferring to 4-year colleges.

Contact. E-mail: admissions@ntc.edu
Phone: (715) 675-3331 ext. 4482 Toll-free number: (888) 682-7144
Fax: (715) 675-0629
Erin McNally, Director of Admissions, Northcentral Technical College, 1000 West Campus Drive, Wausau, WI 54401

Northeast Wisconsin Technical College
Green Bay, Wisconsin **CB member**
www.nwtc.edu **CB code: 4190**

- Public 2-year community and technical college
- Commuter campus in small city

General. Founded in 1913. Regionally accredited. **Enrollment:** 5,860 degree-seeking undergraduates. **Degrees:** 912 associate awarded. **Location:** 129 miles from Milwaukee, 150 miles from Madison. **Calendar:** Semester, limited summer session. **Full-time faculty:** 240 total. **Part-time faculty:** 700 total.

Student profile. Among degree-seeking undergraduates, 60% enrolled in a vocational program, 240 transferred in from other institutions.

Transfer out. Colleges most students transferred to 2008: University of Wisconsin-Green Bay, University of Wisconsin-Oshkosh.

Basis for selection. Open admission, but selective for some programs. Special requirements for health programs. **Homeschooled:** State high school equivalency certificate required.

2008-2009 Annual costs. Tuition/fees: $3,075; $17,991 out-of-state. Per-credit charge: $97 in-state; $594 out-of-state. Material fees vary by program; minimum $4 per course. Books/supplies: $1,148. Personal expenses: $1,920.

2007-2008 Financial aid. **Need-based:** 52% of total undergraduate aid awarded as scholarships/grants, 48% as loans/jobs. Need-based aid available for part-time students. Work-study available nights and for part-time students.

Application procedures. **Admission:** Closing date 8/31 (receipt date). $30 fee, may be waived for applicants with need. Admission notification on a rolling basis beginning on or about 9/4. **Financial aid:** Priority date 4/1; no closing date. FAFSA required. Applicants notified on a rolling basis starting 5/1; must reply within 2 week(s) of notification.

Academics. **Special study options:** Accelerated study, distance learning, double major, ESL, honors, independent study, internships, liberal arts/career combination. License preparation in dental hygiene, nursing, paramedic, physical therapy, radiology, real estate. **Credit/placement by examination:** AP, CLEP, IB, institutional tests. 48 credit hours maximum toward associate degree. **Support services:** GED preparation and test center, learning center, reduced course load, remedial instruction, study skills assistance, tutoring.

Majors. **Agriculture:** Business, farm/ranch, food science. **Business:** General, accounting, administrative services, business admin, hospitality/recreation, logistics, office management, office technology, sales/distribution, tourism/travel. **Computer sciences:** General, data processing, networking, programming. **Engineering:** Civil. **Engineering technology:** Architectural, civil, drafting, electrical, industrial management. **Health:** Dental hygiene, health care admin, medical records admin, medical secretary, nursing (RN), physical therapy assistant, respiratory therapy technology. **Legal studies:** Paralegal. **Mechanic/repair:** Heating/ac/refrig, industrial. **Protective services:** Fire safety technology, police science. **Transportation:** General.

Most popular majors. Business/marketing 27%, computer/information sciences 7%, engineering/engineering technologies 14%, health sciences 27%, trade and industry 7%.

Computing on campus. Online course registration, online library, helpline, wireless network available.

Student life. **Freshman orientation:** Mandatory. 2-hour program in conjunction with registration. **Activities:** Student government, Asian American student association, African American student association, Native American student association, Hispanic student association, Students Taking Responsibility in Drug Education, Phi Theta Kappa International Honor Society.

Athletics. **Intramural:** Basketball, football (non-tackle), volleyball.

Student services. Adult student services, alcohol/substance abuse counseling, career counseling, services for economically disadvantaged, student employment services, health services, minority student services, personal counseling, placement for graduates, veterans' counselor. **Physically disabled:** Services for visually, speech, hearing impaired. **Transfer:** Re-entry adviser for new students.

Contact. Phone: (920) 498-5444 Toll-free number: (800) 422-6982 ext. 5444 Fax: (920) 498-6882
Christine Lemerande, Program Enrollment Supervisor, Northeast Wisconsin Technical College, 2740 West Mason Street, Green Bay, WI 54307-9042

Rasmussen College: Green Bay

Green Bay, Wisconsin
www.rasmussen.edu

- For-profit 2-year technical college
- Small city

General. Regionally accredited. **Enrollment:** 448 degree-seeking undergraduates. **Calendar:** Quarter. **Full-time faculty:** 3 total. **Part-time faculty:** 20 total.

Basis for selection. Open admission, but selective for some programs.

2009-2010 Annual costs. Regular courses: $350/credit; early childhood education courses: $280/credit; medical laboratory technician and networking courses: $395/credit; multimedia and web programming courses: $430/credit.

Application procedures. **Admission:** $60 fee.

Academics. **Credit/placement by examination:** CLEP.

Majors. **Business:** Accounting, business admin, management information systems, office management. **Computer sciences:** Webmaster. **Education:** Early childhood. **Health:** Clinical lab assistant, massage therapy, medical assistant, medical records technology, medical transcription, office admin, pharmacy assistant. **Legal studies:** Paralegal. **Protective services:** Police science.

Contact. Phone: (920) 593-8400
Juliana Klocek, Director of Admissions, Rasmussen College: Green Bay, 904 South Taylor Street, Suite 100, Green Bay, WI 54303-2349

Southwest Wisconsin Technical College

Fennimore, Wisconsin
www.swtc.edu — **CB code: 0900**

- Public 2-year technical college
- Commuter campus in rural community

General. Founded in 1967. Regionally accredited. **Enrollment:** 971 degree-seeking undergraduates; 2,137 non-degree-seeking students. **Degrees:** 180 associate awarded. **Location:** 75 miles from Madison, 38 miles from Dubuque, Iowa. **Calendar:** Semester, limited summer session. **Full-time faculty:** 94 total; 61% women.

Student profile. Among degree-seeking undergraduates, 463 enrolled as first-time, first-year students.

Part-time:	40%	**25 or older:**	37%
Women:	63%	**Live on campus:**	4%

Basis for selection. Open admission, but selective for some programs. Interview and Test of Adult Basic Education required for admission. Secondary school record not considered. Students may have admissions requirements based on admission test scores. Psychological Services Bureau Test required for nursing RN applicants, C-NET test required for LPN applicants.

2008-2009 Annual costs. Tuition/fees: $3,029; $17,945 out-of-state. Per-credit charge: $97 in-state; $594 out-of-state. Materials fees vary by program; minimum $4 per course. $10 per credit fee for online courses. Books/supplies: $1,148. Personal expenses: $1,600.

2007-2008 Financial aid. **Need-based:** 51% of total undergraduate aid awarded as scholarships/grants, 49% as loans/jobs. Work-study available nights and for part-time students.

Application procedures. **Admission:** No deadline. $30 fee. Admission notification on a rolling basis beginning on or about 9/1. Students notified of admission before July 1 must pay tuition deposit of $100 by July 1; students applying after that date must pay deposit as part of application process. **Financial aid:** Priority date 4/15; no closing date. FAFSA, institutional form required. Applicants notified on a rolling basis starting 5/15; must reply within 4 week(s) of notification.

Academics. **Special study options:** Accelerated study, distance learning, double major, dual enrollment of high school students, ESL, internships, student-designed major. License preparation in nursing, real estate. **Credit/placement by examination:** CLEP, institutional tests. **Support services:** GED preparation and test center, learning center, pre-admission summer program, reduced course load, remedial instruction, study skills assistance, tutoring, writing center.

Majors. **Agriculture:** Agribusiness operations, business. **Business:** Accounting, administrative services. **Computer sciences:** Networking, programming, systems analysis. **Education:** Teacher assistance. **Engineering technology:** Drafting, electrical. **Family/consumer sciences:** Child care, institutional food production. **Health:** Nursing (RN). **Legal studies:** Legal secretary. **Mechanic/repair:** Electronics/electrical. **Personal/culinary services:** Culinary arts. **Public administration:** Human services.

Computing on campus. 250 workstations in library, computer center. Dormitories wired for high-speed internet access. Online library, helpline, wireless network available.

Student life. **Freshman orientation:** Mandatory. Preregistration for classes offered. One-half day session held one day prior to beginning of classes. **Housing:** Special housing for disabled, apartments available. $300 partly refundable deposit, deadline 5/1. **Activities:** Student government, student newspaper, marketing and management association, Business Professionals of America, Vocational and Industrial Clubs of America, professional food preparers, Health Occupations Students of America, National Student Nursing Association, post-secondary agricultural students, cross-cultural communications club.

Athletics. **Intramural:** Basketball, softball, volleyball.

Student services. Alcohol/substance abuse counseling, career counseling, services for economically disadvantaged, student employment services, financial aid counseling, health services, minority student services, on-campus daycare, personal counseling, placement for graduates, women's services. **Physically disabled:** Services for visually, hearing impaired. **Transfer:** Transfer adviser for students transferring to 4-year colleges.

Contact. E-mail: studentservices@swtc.edu
Phone: (608) 822-3262 ext. 2354 Toll-free
number: (800) 362-3322 ext. 2354 Fax: (608) 822-6019
Paige Wegner, Director of Student Services, Southwest Wisconsin Technical College, 1800 Bronson Boulevard, Fennimore, WI 53809

University of Wisconsin-Baraboo/Sauk County

Baraboo, Wisconsin
www.baraboo.uwc.edu **CB code: 1996**

- Public 2-year branch campus and liberal arts college
- Commuter campus in large town
- SAT or ACT (ACT writing optional) required

General. Founded in 1968. Regionally accredited. **Enrollment:** 669 degree-seeking undergraduates. **Degrees:** 80 associate awarded. **Location:** 40 miles from Madison. **Calendar:** Semester, limited summer session. **Full-time faculty:** 20 total. **Part-time faculty:** 30 total. **Class size:** 57% < 20, 42% 20-39, less than 1% 40-49.

Student profile.

Out-of-state:	1%	**25 or older:**	17%

Transfer out. Colleges most students transferred to 2008: University of Wisconsin-Madison, University of Wisconsin-LaCrosse, University of Wisconsin-Stevens Point, University of Wisconsin-Whitewater, University of Wisconsin-Platteville.

Basis for selection. High school courses, rank in upper 75% of class, ACT or SAT test scores most important. Students in bottom 25% may be admitted based on individual record and circumstances. Students not admitted may be deferred and admitted following semester. Special attention given to returning adult, homeschooled, learning disabled, and minority students. ACT or SAT scores must be submitted but are used for advisory purposes only for most students. Interview required for those with borderline academic records and class rank and recommended for others with special circumstances. **Adult students:** SAT/ACT scores not required if applicant over 21. University of Wisconsin Placement Test required of all students not having had college credit English and/or math courses. **Homeschooled:** Transcript of courses and grades, interview required. Interview, portfolio of curriculum, method of assessment, work samples and experiences recommended. **Learning Disabled:** Interview recommended, recent professional testing required to create program accommodations for special needs.

High school preparation. 17 units required. Required and recommended units include English 4, mathematics 3-4, social studies 3, science 3-4 (laboratory 3-4), foreign language 2 and academic electives 4. Math must be college preparatory.

2008-2009 Annual costs. Tuition/fees: $4,644; $11,628 out-of-state. Per-credit charge: $178 in-state; $469 out-of-state. Minnesota reciprocity tuition: $167 per credit hour. Books/supplies: $680. Personal expenses: $2,660.

2007-2008 Financial aid. All financial aid based on need. Need-based aid available for part-time students. Work-study available nights and for part-time students.

Application procedures. Admission: Priority date 6/1; deadline 8/31 (receipt date). $35 fee, may be waived for applicants with need. Admission notification on a rolling basis beginning on or about 9/15. **Financial aid:** Priority date 4/15; no closing date. FAFSA, institutional form required. Applicants notified on a rolling basis starting 4/15; must reply within 3 week(s) of notification.

Academics. Required courses for associate degree available evenings over 4-year period. Bachelor's degree available on campus through University of Wisconsin Milwaukee. **Special study options:** Cross-registration, distance learning, dual enrollment of high school students, external degree, honors, independent study, internships, liberal arts/career combination, study abroad. Bachelor's degree programs available on campus. **Credit/placement by examination:** AP, CLEP, IB, institutional tests. **Support services:** Learning center, reduced course load, remedial instruction, study skills assistance, tutoring, writing center.

Majors. Liberal arts: Arts/sciences.

Computing on campus. 60 workstations in library, computer center, student center. Commuter students can connect to campus network. Online course registration, online library, wireless network available.

Student life. Freshman orientation: Mandatory, $200 fee. Preregistration for classes offered. Orientation in 3 parts over summer. **Policies:** Students participate actively in campus governance and committee work with faculty and staff. **Housing:** Privately owned apartments adjacent to campus. **Activities:** Bands, choral groups, drama, literary magazine, music ensembles, student government, student newspaper, Campus Crusade for Christ, Phi Theta Kappa, Wellness Alliance, business club, Native American club, cine club, UWB Ambassadors, green club, art club, Future Educators.

Athletics. NJCAA. **Intercollegiate:** Basketball M, soccer, tennis, volleyball W. **Intramural:** Basketball, cross-country, racquetball, softball, volleyball. **Team name:** Fighting Spirits.

Student services. Adult student services, alcohol/substance abuse counseling, career counseling, financial aid counseling, minority student services, personal counseling, veterans' counselor. **Physically disabled:** Services for visually, speech, hearing impaired. **Transfer:** Pre-admission transcript evaluation for new students. Transfer adviser, college fairs on campus for students transferring to 4-year colleges.

Contact. E-mail: apply@wisconsin.edu
Phone: (608) 355-5230 Fax: (608) 355-5289
Ruth Joyce, Assistant Dean for Student Services, University of Wisconsin-Baraboo/Sauk County, 1006 Connie Road, Baraboo, WI 53913-1098

University of Wisconsin-Barron County

Rice Lake, Wisconsin
www.barron.uwc.edu **CB code: 1772**

- Public 2-year branch campus and junior college
- Commuter campus in small town
- SAT or ACT (ACT writing optional) required

General. Founded in 1966. Regionally accredited. **Enrollment:** 624 degree-seeking undergraduates. **Degrees:** 54 associate awarded. **Location:** 80 miles from Minneapolis-St. Paul, 50 miles from Eau Claire. **Calendar:** Semester, limited summer session. **Full-time faculty:** 22 total. **Part-time faculty:** 16 total. **Special facilities:** Observatory, amphitheater.

Student profile.

Out-of-state:	2%	**25 or older:**	21%

Basis for selection. Rank in upper 75% of class ensures admission. Students in bottom 25% or those submitting GED scores evaluated on individual basis. ACT preferred. **Adult students:** SAT/ACT scores not required if applicant over 21.

High school preparation. 16 units required. Required units include English 4, mathematics 3, social studies 3 and science 2.

2008-2009 Annual costs. Tuition/fees: $4,693; $11,677 out-of-state. Per-credit charge: $178 in-state; $469 out-of-state. Minnesota reciprocity tuition: $167 per credit hour. Books/supplies: $150.

2007-2008 Financial aid. Need-based: Need-based aid available for part-time students.

Application procedures. Admission: Priority date 7/1; no deadline. $35 fee, may be waived for applicants with need. Admission notification on a rolling basis. **Financial aid:** Priority date 4/15; no closing date. FAFSA required. Applicants notified on a rolling basis starting 6/1.

Academics. Special study options: Cross-registration, dual enrollment of high school students, internships. **Credit/placement by examination:** AP, CLEP, institutional tests. **Support services:** Learning center, pre-admission summer program, reduced course load, remedial instruction, tutoring.

Majors. Liberal arts: Arts/sciences.

Computing on campus. 24 workstations in library, computer center.

Student life. Activities: Bands, choral groups, drama, music ensembles, musical theater, student government, student newspaper, Phi Theta Kappa.

Athletics. NJCAA. **Intercollegiate:** Baseball M, basketball, golf, soccer, volleyball W. **Intramural:** Basketball, table tennis, volleyball. **Team name:** Chargers.

Student services. Adult student services, career counseling, student employment services, health services, personal counseling, veterans' counselor. **Physically disabled:** Services for visually, speech, hearing impaired. **Transfer:** Transfer adviser, college fairs on campus for students transferring to 4-year colleges.

Contact. Phone: (715) 234-8024 Fax: (715) 234-8024
Dale Fenton, Director of Student Services, University of Wisconsin-Barron County, 1800 College Drive, Rice Lake, WI 54868

University of Wisconsin-Fond du Lac

Fond du Lac, Wisconsin
www.fdl.uwc.edu **CB code: 1942**

- Public 2-year junior college
- Commuter campus in large town
- SAT or ACT (ACT writing optional) required

General. Founded in 1968. Regionally accredited. **Enrollment:** 732 degree-seeking undergraduates. **Degrees:** 122 associate awarded. **Location:** 70 miles from Milwaukee. **Calendar:** Semester, limited summer session. **Full-time faculty:** 22 total. **Part-time faculty:** 18 total. **Special facilities:** Nature preserve, arboretum.

Student profile.

Out-of-state:	1%	**25 or older:**	30%

Transfer out. Colleges most students transferred to 2008: UW Oshkosh, UW Milwaukee, UW Madison, UW Stevens Point, UW Green Bay.

Basis for selection. Rank in upper 75% of class ensures admission. Students in bottom 25% will be considered. Students with Wisconsin GED score of 250 or higher ensured admission. Applicants admitted who rank in bottom 25% of class may have course credit restrictions during first semester or required to participate in summer school classes as condition of continued enrollment. ACT preferred. Interview required for students in bottom 25% of high school. **Adult students:** SAT/ACT scores not required if applicant over 21. **Homeschooled:** Transcript of courses and grades required.

High school preparation. 17 units required. Required units include English 4, mathematics 3, social studies 3, science 3 and academic electives 4.

2008-2009 Annual costs. Tuition/fees: $4,584; $11,568 out-of-state. Per-credit charge: $178 in-state; $469 out-of-state. Minnesota reciprocity tuition: $167 per credit hour. Books/supplies: $810. Personal expenses: $1,620.

2007-2008 Financial aid. Need-based: Need-based aid available for part-time students. Work-study available for part-time students. **Non-need-based:** Scholarships awarded for academics, leadership, music/drama.

Application procedures. Admission: Priority date 6/30; no deadline. $35 fee. Admission notification on a rolling basis. **Financial aid:** Priority date 4/15; no closing date. FAFSA required. Applicants notified on a rolling basis starting 6/1; must reply within 2 week(s) of notification.

Academics. Special study options: Accelerated study, cross-registration, distance learning, dual enrollment of high school students, independent study, liberal arts/career combination, study abroad, teacher certification program. Bachelor's degree programs available on campus. **Credit/placement by examination:** AP, CLEP, IB, institutional tests. 18 credit hours maximum toward associate degree. **Support services:** Learning center, pre-admission summer program, reduced course load, remedial instruction, study skills assistance, tutoring.

Majors. Liberal arts: Arts/sciences.

Computing on campus. 60 workstations in library, computer center. Commuter students can connect to campus network. Online course registration, online library, wireless network available.

Student life. Freshman orientation: Mandatory, $65 fee. **Housing:** Student housing available at nearby Marian College. **Activities:** Bands, choral groups, drama, literary magazine, music ensembles, musical theater, student government, student newspaper, symphony orchestra.

Athletics. NJCAA. **Intercollegiate:** Baseball M, basketball, golf, soccer, tennis, volleyball W. **Intramural:** Basketball M, bowling, football (non-tackle), volleyball. **Team name:** Falcons.

Student services. Career counseling, financial aid counseling, personal counseling, veterans' counselor. **Physically disabled:** Services for visually, speech, hearing impaired. **Transfer:** Transfer adviser for students transferring to 4-year colleges.

Contact. Phone: (920) 929-3606 Fax: (920) 929-3626
Tom Martin, Assistant Campus Dean for Student Services, University of Wisconsin-Fond du Lac, 400 University Drive, Fond du Lac, WI 54935-2998

University of Wisconsin-Fox Valley

Menasha, Wisconsin
www.uwfoxvalley.uwc.edu **CB code: 1889**

- Public 2-year liberal arts college
- Commuter campus in small city
- SAT or ACT (ACT writing optional) required

General. Founded in 1933. Regionally accredited. **Enrollment:** 1,650 degree-seeking undergraduates. **Degrees:** 130 associate awarded. **Location:** 90 miles from Milwaukee. **Calendar:** Semester, limited summer session. **Full-time faculty:** 50 total. **Part-time faculty:** 32 total. **Class size:** 100% < 20. **Special facilities:** Observatory, planetarium, earth science museum.

Basis for selection. Rank in upper 75% of class ensures admission. Students in bottom 25% may be placed on waiting list. Course unit requirements must be met. Wisconsin state law requires submission of ACT or SAT before registration. Scores not normally considered by college for admission, but may be required for students in bottom 25% of graduating class. Interview required for those in bottom 25% of class and those submitting GED scores. **Adult students:** SAT/ACT scores not required if applicant over 21. **Homeschooled:** Transcript of courses and grades required.

High school preparation. 17 units required. Required and recommended units include English 4, mathematics 3, social studies 3, science 3, foreign language 2 and academic electives 4. Math units must be in algebra, geometry, or higher level.

2008-2009 Annual costs. Tuition/fees: $4,502; $11,486 out-of-state. Per-credit charge: $178 in-state; $469 out-of-state. Minnesota reciprocity tuition: $167 per credit hour. Books/supplies: $455. Personal expenses: $810.

2007-2008 Financial aid. Need-based: Need-based aid available for part-time students. Work-study available nights, weekends and for part-time students.

Application procedures. Admission: Priority date 5/1; no deadline. $35 fee, may be waived for applicants with need. Admission notification on a rolling basis. **Financial aid:** Priority date 4/15; no closing date. FAFSA required. Applicants notified on a rolling basis starting 6/1; must reply within 3 week(s) of notification.

Academics. Enrollment includes admissions to all University of Wisconsin campuses. **Special study options:** Accelerated study, distance learning, dual enrollment of high school students, honors, independent study, study abroad. **Credit/placement by examination:** AP, CLEP, institutional tests. **Support services:** Learning center, reduced course load, remedial instruction, study skills assistance, tutoring, writing center.

Majors. Liberal arts: Arts/sciences.

Computing on campus. Online course registration, online library, student web hosting, wireless network available.

Student life. Freshman orientation: Mandatory, $135 fee. Day-long program. **Activities:** Bands, choral groups, dance, drama, film society, music ensembles, musical theater, radio station, student government, student newspaper, symphony orchestra, TV station.

Athletics. NJCAA. **Intercollegiate:** Basketball, golf, soccer, tennis, volleyball. **Team name:** Cyclones.

Student services. Adult student services, career counseling, on-campus daycare, veterans' counselor. **Physically disabled:** Services for visually, speech, hearing impaired. **Transfer:** Transfer adviser, college fairs on campus for students transferring to 4-year colleges.

Contact. Phone: (920) 832-2620 Fax: (920) 832-2850
Carla Rabe, Assistant Campus Dean for Student Services, University of Wisconsin-Fox Valley, 1478 Midway Road, Menasha, WI 54952-2850

University of Wisconsin-Manitowoc

Manitowoc, Wisconsin
www.manitowoc.uwc.edu **CB code: 1890**

- Public 2-year branch campus and liberal arts college
- Commuter campus in large town

General. Founded in 1933. Regionally accredited. **Enrollment:** 541 degree-seeking undergraduates. **Degrees:** 142 associate awarded. **Location:** 45 miles from Green Bay. **Calendar:** Semester, limited summer session. **Full-time faculty:** 20 total; 5% minority. **Part-time faculty:** 20 total. **Class size:** 26% < 20, 67% 20-39, 2% 40-49, 5% 50-99.

Student profile.

Out-of-state:	1%	**25 or older:**	27%

Transfer out. Colleges most students transferred to 2008: UW Green Bay, UW Oshkosh, UW Madison, UW Milwaukee, UW Stevens Point.

Basis for selection. Open admission, but selective for some programs. Rank in top 75% of high school class ensures admission. Students in bottom 25% will be considered but may require campus interview. Students not admitted for specific semester applied for will be admitted at later date. Interview required for applicants in bottom quarter of class. **Adult students:** SAT/ACT scores not required if applicant over 21. **Homeschooled:** Transcript of courses and grades required. 19 ACT required. **Learning Disabled:** Students must meet with campus coordinator for students with disabilities for information about support programs.

High school preparation. 17 units required. Required units include English 4, mathematics 3, social studies 3, science 3 and academic electives 4.

2008-2009 Annual costs. Tuition/fees: $4,946; $11,929 out-of-state. Per-credit charge: $178 in-state; $469 out-of-state. Books/supplies: $515. Personal expenses: $990.

2007-2008 Financial aid. All financial aid based on need. Need-based aid available for part-time students. Work-study available nights and for part-time students.

Application procedures. Admission: Priority date 7/1; no deadline. $44 fee, may be waived for applicants with need. Admission notification on a rolling basis beginning on or about 9/15. **Financial aid:** Priority date 3/1; no closing date. FAFSA, institutional form required. Applicants notified on a rolling basis starting 5/1; must reply within 2 week(s) of notification.

Academics. Special study options: Cross-registration, dual enrollment of high school students, independent study. Bachelor's degree programs available on campus. **Credit/placement by examination:** AP, CLEP, IB, institutional tests. 18 credit hours maximum toward associate degree. **Support services:** Learning center, reduced course load, remedial instruction, tutoring, writing center.

Majors. Liberal arts: Arts/sciences.

Computing on campus. 60 workstations in library, computer center. Commuter students can connect to campus network. Online course registration, online library, helpline, wireless network available.

Student life. Freshman orientation: Mandatory, $75 fee. Preregistration for classes offered. One day program. **Activities:** Bands, choral groups, drama, literary magazine, music ensembles, student government, student newspaper, symphony orchestra, College Democrats.

Athletics. NAIA, NJCAA. **Intercollegiate:** Basketball, golf, tennis, volleyball W. **Intramural:** Badminton, football (non-tackle). **Team name:** Blue Devils.

Student services. Adult student services, career counseling, financial aid counseling, on-campus daycare, personal counseling, veterans' counselor. **Physically disabled:** Services for visually, speech, hearing impaired. **Transfer:** Re-entry adviser for new students. Transfer adviser for students transferring to 4-year colleges.

Contact. E-mail: manadmit@uwc.edu
Phone: (920) 683-4707 Fax: (920) 683-4776
Julie DeZeeuw, Dean for Student Services, University of Wisconsin-Manitowoc, 705 Viebahn Street, Manitowoc, WI 54220-6699

University of Wisconsin-Marathon County

Wausau, Wisconsin
www.uwmc.uwc.edu **CB code: 1995**

- Public 2-year liberal arts college
- Commuter campus in small city
- SAT or ACT (ACT writing optional) required

General. Founded in 1933. Regionally accredited. Guaranteed transfer program to University of Wisconsin 4-year schools. **Enrollment:** 1,361 degree-seeking undergraduates. **Degrees:** 107 associate awarded. **Location:** 180 miles from Milwaukee, 180 miles from Minneapolis-St. Paul. **Calendar:** Semester, limited summer session. **Full-time faculty:** 48 total. **Part-time faculty:** 28 total. **Special facilities:** Planetarium, hiking and cross-country ski trails, indoor skating and curling rinks.

Student profile.

Out-of-state:	3%	**Live on campus:**	12%
25 or older:	28%		

Basis for selection. Rank in upper 75% of class ensures admission. Students in bottom 25% and those with GED admitted on basis of interview. **Adult students:** SAT/ACT scores not required if applicant over 21. **Learning Disabled:** Must provide official documentation for review of accommodations 90 days in advance.

High school preparation. 17 units required. Required and recommended units include English 4, mathematics 3-4, social studies 3-4, science 3-4 and foreign language 4. Math units must be algebra, geometry or other courses leading to calculus.

2008-2009 Annual costs. Tuition/fees: $4,507; $11,491 out-of-state. Per-credit charge: $178 in-state; $469 out-of-state. Minnesota reciprocity tuition: $167 per credit hour. Books/supplies: $700. Personal expenses: $810.

2007-2008 Financial aid. All financial aid based on need. Need-based aid available for part-time students. Work-study available nights and for part-time students.

Application procedures. Admission: Priority date 8/1; no deadline. $35 fee, may be waived for applicants with need. Admission notification on a rolling basis. **Financial aid:** Priority date 4/15; no closing date. FAFSA, institutional form required. Applicants notified on a rolling basis starting 6/1; must reply within 3 week(s) of notification.

Academics. Special study options: Cross-registration, dual enrollment of high school students, honors, independent study, internships, liberal arts/career combination, study abroad. Bachelor's degree programs available on campus. **Credit/placement by examination:** AP, CLEP, IB, institutional tests. 18 credit hours maximum toward associate degree. **Support services:** Learning center, pre-admission summer program, reduced course load, remedial instruction, study skills assistance, tutoring, writing center.

Majors. Liberal arts: Arts/sciences.

Computing on campus. 92 workstations in dormitories, library, computer center. Dormitories wired for high-speed internet access and linked to campus network. Online library, helpline available.

Student life. Freshman orientation: Available, $15 fee. Preregistration for classes offered. One-day program held week before start of fall classes. **Policies:** Zero tolerance alcohol and drug policy in residence hall. **Housing:** Coed dorms available. $100 deposit. **Activities:** Bands, choral groups, drama, literary magazine, music ensembles, musical theater, student government, student newspaper, symphony orchestra, Christian Fellowship, business club, computer club, drama club, international relations club, biology club, gay/lesbian/bisexual student association.

Athletics. NJCAA. **Intercollegiate:** Basketball, golf, soccer, tennis, volleyball W. **Intramural:** Archery, badminton, basketball, bowling, fencing, golf, handball, racquetball, skiing, skin diving, softball, swimming, table tennis, tennis, volleyball. **Team name:** Huskies.

Student services. Adult student services, career counseling, student employment services, personal counseling, veterans' counselor. **Physically disabled:** Services for visually, hearing impaired. **Transfer:** Transfer adviser, college fairs on campus for students transferring to 4-year colleges.

Contact. E-mail: uwmc@uwe.edu
Phone: (715) 261-6241 Toll-free number: (888) 367-8962
Fax: (715) 261-6331
Nolan Beck, Director of Student Services, University of Wisconsin-Marathon County, 518 South Seventh Avenue, Wausau, WI 54401-5396

University of Wisconsin-Marinette

Marinette, Wisconsin
www.marinette.uwc.edu **CB code: 1891**

- Public 2-year branch campus and liberal arts college
- Commuter campus in large town
- SAT or ACT (ACT writing optional), application essay required

General. Founded in 1946. Regionally accredited. **Enrollment:** 220 degree-seeking undergraduates. **Degrees:** 86 associate awarded. **Location:** 50 miles from Green Bay, 170 miles from Milwaukee. **Calendar:** Semester, limited summer session. **Full-time faculty:** 19 total; 90% have terminal degrees, 10% minority, 42% women. **Part-time faculty:** 20 total; 10% have terminal degrees, 45% women.

Student profile. Among degree-seeking undergraduates, 16 transferred in from other institutions.

Out-of-state:	22%	**25 or older:**	23%

Transfer out. Colleges most students transferred to 2008: UW-Green Bay, UW-Oshkosh, UW-Stevens Point, UW-Madison, Northern Michigan University.

Basis for selection. Class rank, GPA, courses, ACT scores, and involvement important. Applicants not meeting minimum standards may be accepted but required to take reduced course load and/or noncredit courses to remedy deficiencies. **Adult students:** SAT/ACT scores not required if applicant over 21. **Homeschooled:** Transcript of courses and grades required.

High school preparation. 17 units required. Required units include English 4, mathematics 3, social studies 3 and science 3. 4 electives of computer science, business, foreign language and/or fine arts required.

2008-2009 Annual costs. Tuition/fees: $4,536; $11,520 out-of-state. Per-credit charge: $178 in-state; $469 out-of-state. Minnesota reciprocity tuition: $178 per credit hour. Books/supplies: $860. Personal expenses: $1,650.

2007-2008 Financial aid. All financial aid based on need. Need-based aid available for part-time students. Work-study available nights and for part-time students.

Application procedures. Admission: Priority date 7/1; no deadline. $44 fee, may be waived for applicants with need. Admission notification on a rolling basis. Students may be conditionally admitted prior to receipt of ACT scores, but may not register for classes until scores are received. **Financial aid:** Priority date 4/15; no closing date. FAFSA required. Applicants notified on a rolling basis.

Academics. Special study options: Accelerated study, combined bachelor's/graduate degree, cross-registration, distance learning, dual enrollment of high school students, ESL, independent study, study abroad. Bachelor's degree programs available on campus. **Credit/placement by examination:** AP, CLEP, institutional tests. **Support services:** Reduced course load, remedial instruction, study skills assistance, tutoring, writing center.

Majors. Area/ethnic studies: Women's. **Liberal arts:** Arts/sciences.

Computing on campus. 80 workstations in library, computer center, student center. Online course registration, online library, helpline, wireless network available.

Student life. Freshman orientation: Mandatory, $50 fee. **Activities:** Bands, choral groups, drama, international student organizations, literary magazine, music ensembles, musical theater, student government, student newspaper, Phi Theta Kappa.

Athletics. NJCAA. **Intercollegiate:** Basketball, volleyball W. **Intramural:** Basketball, bowling, football (non-tackle), skiing, table tennis, volleyball. **Team name:** Buccaneers.

Student services. Adult student services, career counseling, services for economically disadvantaged, student employment services, financial aid counseling, minority student services, personal counseling, veterans' counselor. **Physically disabled:** Services for visually, speech, hearing impaired. **Transfer:** Transfer adviser, college fairs on campus for students transferring to 4-year colleges.

Contact. E-mail: ssinfo@uwc.edu
Phone: (715) 735-4301 Fax: (715) 735-4304
Cynthia Bailey, Assistant Campus Dean for Student Services, University of Wisconsin-Marinette, 750 West Bay Shore Street, Marinette, WI 54143

University of Wisconsin-Marshfield/Wood County

Marshfield, Wisconsin
www.marshfield.uwc.edu **CB code: 1997**

- Public 2-year branch campus college
- Commuter campus in large town
- SAT or ACT (ACT writing optional) required

General. Founded in 1964. Regionally accredited. Two-year transfer program prepares students for any four-year program in Wisconsin system. **Enrollment:** 617 degree-seeking undergraduates. **Degrees:** 55 associate awarded. **Location:** 138 miles from Madison. **Calendar:** Semester, limited summer session. **Full-time faculty:** 21 total. **Part-time faculty:** 21 total. **Class size:** 30% < 20, 67% 20-39, 1% 40-49, 2% 50-99.

Student profile.

Out-of-state:	1%	**25 or older:**	28%

Transfer out. Colleges most students transferred to 2008: University of Wisconsin Steven's Point, University of Wisconsin-Eau Claire, University of Wisconsin Madison.

Basis for selection. Rank in top 75% of class and 17 specified high school academic units ensure admission. Students in bottom 25% and/or with missing units may be placed on waiting list. Students not admitted for specific semester applied for may be admitted later. Placement tests required in math and English. **Adult students:** SAT/ACT scores not required if applicant over 21 or out of high school 3 years or more.

High school preparation. 17 units required. Required and recommended units include English 4, mathematics 3-4, social studies 3, science 3-4 and academic electives 4.

2008-2009 Annual costs. Tuition/fees: $4,572; $11,556 out-of-state. Per-credit charge: $178 in-state; $469 out-of-state. Minnesota reciprocity tuition: $167 per credit hour. Books/supplies: $500. Personal expenses: $1,022.

2007-2008 Financial aid. All financial aid based on need. Need-based aid available for part-time students. Work-study available nights, weekends and for part-time students.

Application procedures. Admission: No deadline. $35 fee. Admission notification on a rolling basis. **Financial aid:** Priority date 4/15; no closing date. FAFSA required. Applicants notified on a rolling basis starting 5/15; must reply within 3 week(s) of notification.

Academics. Special study options: Cross-registration, distance learning, dual enrollment of high school students, independent study, internships, study abroad. **Credit/placement by examination:** AP, CLEP, institutional tests. **Support services:** Pre-admission summer program, reduced course load, remedial instruction, study skills assistance, tutoring.

Majors. Liberal arts: Arts/sciences.

Computing on campus. 40 workstations in library, computer center, student center. Commuter students can connect to campus network. Online course registration available.

Student life. Freshman orientation: Mandatory, $55 fee. Preregistration for classes offered. One day in January and late August. **Activities:** Bands, choral groups, drama, literary magazine, music ensembles, musical theater, student government, student newspaper, symphony orchestra, Inter-Varsity Christian Fellowship, business club, nursing associaton, program board, honor fraternity, student education association.

Athletics. NJCAA. **Intercollegiate:** Basketball, golf, tennis, volleyball W. **Intramural:** Basketball, bowling, football (tackle) M, soccer, softball, tennis, volleyball. **Team name:** Marauders.

Student services. Adult student services, alcohol/substance abuse counseling, career counseling, student employment services, financial aid counseling, personal counseling, veterans' counselor. **Physically disabled:** Services for visually, speech, hearing impaired. **Transfer:** Transfer adviser, college fairs on campus for students transferring to 4-year colleges.

Contact. E-mail: msfadmit@uwc.edu
Phone: (715) 389-6500 Fax: (715) 384-1718
Jeff Meece, Director of Student Services, University of Wisconsin-Marshfield/Wood County, 2000 West Fifth Street, Marshfield, WI 54449

University of Wisconsin-Richland

Richland Center, Wisconsin
www.richland.uwc.edu **CB code: 1662**

- Public 2-year liberal arts college
- Commuter campus in small town
- SAT or ACT (ACT writing optional) required

General. Founded in 1967. Regionally accredited. **Enrollment:** 472 degree-seeking undergraduates. **Degrees:** 55 associate awarded. **Location:** 60 miles from Madison, 60 miles from LaCrosse. **Calendar:** Semester, limited summer session. **Full-time faculty:** 17 total. **Part-time faculty:** 12 total. **Class size:** 57% < 20, 43% 20-39.

Student profile. Among degree-seeking undergraduates, 100% enrolled in a transfer program.

Out-of-state:	1%	**Live on campus:**	40%
25 or older:	22%		

Transfer out. 95% of students enrolled in the transfer program go on to 4-year colleges. **Colleges most students transferred to 2008:** University of Wisconsin-LaCrosse, University of Wisconsin-Stevens Point, University of Wisconsin-Platteville, University of Wisconsin-Madison, University of Wisconsin-Eau Claire, University of Wisconsin-Whitewater.

Basis for selection. Rank in upper 75% of class ensures admission. Students in bottom 25% may be admitted on a discretionary category basis. Students not admitted for specific semester applied for will be admitted at later date. Test scores for matriculating students must be received prior to enrollment. Interview required for applicants in bottom 25% of class; recommended for all others. **Adult students:** SAT/ACT scores not required if applicant over 21. **Homeschooled:** 19 ACT required.

High school preparation. 17 units required. Required units include English 4, mathematics 3, social studies 3, science 3 and academic electives 4. 4 of the required units may be in foreign language, fine arts, computer science or other academic areas.

2008-2009 Annual costs. Tuition/fees: $4,836; $11,820 out-of-state. Per-credit charge: $178 in-state; $469 out-of-state. Minnesota reciprocity tuition: $185 per credit hour. Books/supplies: $860. Personal expenses: $1,650.

2007-2008 Financial aid. All financial aid based on need. 54% of total undergraduate aid awarded as scholarships/grants, 46% as loans/jobs. Need-based aid available for part-time students. Work-study available nights, weekends and for part-time students.

Application procedures. Admission: No deadline. $44 fee, may be waived for applicants with need. Admission notification on a rolling basis. **Financial aid:** Priority date 4/15; no closing date. FAFSA required. Applicants notified on a rolling basis starting 5/15; must reply within 3 week(s) of notification.

Academics. Associate of arts and science degree accepted throughout University of Wisconsin System as transfer tool; satisfies general education requirements of any system campus. Online writing lab available to students at all times. **Special study options:** Cross-registration, distance learning, dual enrollment of high school students, independent study, study abroad, teacher certification program. Bachelor's degree programs available on campus. **Credit/placement by examination:** AP, CLEP, IB, institutional tests. **Support services:** Reduced course load, remedial instruction, study skills assistance, tutoring, writing center.

Majors. Liberal arts: Arts/sciences.

Computing on campus. 60 workstations in dormitories, library, computer center. Dormitories wired for high-speed internet access and linked to campus network. Commuter students can connect to campus network. Online library, wireless network available.

Student life. Freshman orientation: Mandatory, $35 fee. Preregistration for classes offered. Orientation held during the first week of fall classes. **Housing:** Coed dorms, apartments available. $200 deposit. **Activities:** Concert band, choral groups, drama, international student organizations, literary magazine, music ensembles, musical theater, student government, student newspaper, Educators of the Future, Student Wisconsin Education Association, student senate, Gay-Straight Alliance, Campus Democrats, College Republicans, gamers club, InterVarsity Christian Fellowship, outdoor conservation club.

Athletics. Intercollegiate: Basketball, volleyball W. **Intramural:** Basketball, football (non-tackle), racquetball, softball, swimming, tennis, volleyball. **Team name:** Roadrunners.

Student services. Adult student services, alcohol/substance abuse counseling, career counseling, student employment services, financial aid counseling, personal counseling. **Transfer:** Transfer adviser, college fairs on campus for students transferring to 4-year colleges.

Contact. E-mail: rlninfo@uwc.edu
Phone: (608) 647-6186 ext. 3 Fax: (608) 647-2275
John Poole, Director of Student Services, University of Wisconsin-Richland, 1200 Highway 14 West, Richland Center, WI 53581

University of Wisconsin-Rock County

Janesville, Wisconsin
www.rock.uwc.edu **CB code: 1998**

- Public 2-year branch campus and liberal arts college
- Commuter campus in small city
- SAT or ACT (ACT writing optional) required

General. Founded in 1966. Regionally accredited. **Enrollment:** 1,046 degree-seeking undergraduates. **Degrees:** 99 associate awarded. **Location:** 40 miles from Madison. **Calendar:** Semester, limited summer session. **Full-time faculty:** 33 total. **Part-time faculty:** 17 total. **Class size:** 51% < 20, 46% 20-39, 2% 40-49, less than 1% 50-99.

Student profile.

Out-of-state:	1%	**25 or older:**	25%

Transfer out. Colleges most students transferred to 2008: University of Wisconsin-Whitewater, University of Wisconsin-Madison.

Basis for selection. Rank in upper 75% of class ensures admission. Students in bottom 25% and those with GED admitted under special conditions. SAT or ACT scores used for students with GED or in bottom 25% of class. Essays considered. **Adult students:** SAT/ACT scores not required if applicant over 21. **Homeschooled:** Transcript of courses and grades required.

High school preparation. 17 units recommended. Recommended units include English 4, mathematics 3, social studies 3, science 3 and academic electives 4.

2008-2009 Annual costs. Tuition/fees: $4,561; $11,545 out-of-state. Per-credit charge: $178 in-state; $469 out-of-state. Minnesota reciprocity tuition: $167 per credit hour. Books/supplies: $500. Personal expenses: $810.

2007-2008 Financial aid. All financial aid based on need. Need-based aid available for part-time students. Work-study available nights, weekends and for part-time students.

Application procedures. Admission: No deadline. $35 fee. Admission notification on a rolling basis. **Financial aid:** Priority date 4/15; no closing date. FAFSA, institutional form required. Applicants notified on a rolling basis starting 6/1; must reply within 3 week(s) of notification.

Academics. Special study options: Cross-registration, distance learning, dual enrollment of high school students, independent study, study abroad. Bachelor's degree programs available on campus. **Credit/placement by examination:** AP, CLEP, institutional tests. **Support services:** Learning center, reduced course load, remedial instruction, study skills assistance, tutoring, writing center.

Majors. Liberal arts: Arts/sciences.

Computing on campus. 50 workstations in library, computer center. Commuter students can connect to campus network.

Student life. Freshman orientation: Mandatory, $30 fee. Three-hour sessions held in May, June, July, and August. **Activities:** Bands, choral groups, dance, drama, literary magazine, music ensembles, student government, student newspaper, symphony orchestra, SGA, MSU, GLBSA, Future Educators, adult student organization.

Athletics. NJCAA. **Intercollegiate:** Soccer, tennis, volleyball W. **Intramural:** Badminton, basketball, soccer, softball, tennis, volleyball. **Team name:** Rattlers.

Student services. Adult student services, alcohol/substance abuse counseling, career counseling, services for economically disadvantaged, student employment services, financial aid counseling, minority student services, personal counseling, veterans' counselor. **Physically disabled:** Services for visually, hearing impaired. **Transfer:** Re-entry adviser for new students. Transfer adviser, college fairs on campus for students transferring to 4-year colleges.

Contact. E-mail: rckinfo@uwc.edu
Phone: (608) 758-6523 Fax: (608) 758-6579
Steve Ullrick, Assistant Campus Dean for Student Services, University of Wisconsin-Rock County, 2909 Kellogg Avenue, Janesville, WI 53546-5699

University of Wisconsin-Sheboygan

Sheboygan, Wisconsin
www.sheboygan.uwc.edu **CB code: 1994**

- Public 2-year community and junior college
- Commuter campus in small city
- SAT or ACT (ACT writing optional) required

General. Founded in 1933. Regionally accredited. Several collaborative degrees with 4-year institutions so students can earn bachelor's degree. **Enrollment:** 754 degree-seeking undergraduates. **Degrees:** 78 associate awarded. **Location:** 60 miles from Milwaukee, 50 miles from Green Bay. **Calendar:**

Semester, limited summer session. **Full-time faculty:** 22 total. **Part-time faculty:** 25 total.

Student profile.

Out-of-state:	1%	25 or older:	24%

Transfer out. Colleges most students transferred to 2008: University of Wisconsin-Milwaukee, University of Wisconsin-Green Bay, University of Wisconsin-Whitewater, University of Wisconsin-Madison, University of Wisconsin-Oshkosh.

Basis for selection. Admissions based on secondary school record and class rank. Standardized test scores also important. ACT preferred. Interview recommended. **Adult students:** SAT/ACT scores not required if applicant over 21.

High school preparation. 17 units required. Required units include English 4, mathematics 3, social studies 3 and science 3. Additional 4 units required from English, social science, math, natural science, foreign language, fine arts, or computer science.

2008-2009 Annual costs. Tuition/fees: $4,545; $11,529 out-of-state. Per-credit charge: $178 in-state; $469 out-of-state. Minnesota reciprocity tuition: $167 per credit hour. Books/supplies: $470. Personal expenses: $900.

2008-2009 Financial aid. Need-based: Need-based aid available for part-time students. **Non-need-based:** Scholarships awarded for academics, leadership, music/drama. **Additional information:** Scholarship deadline 2/28.

Application procedures. Admission: Priority date 6/30; no deadline. $35 fee, may be waived for applicants with need. Admission notification on a rolling basis. **Financial aid:** Priority date 4/15; no closing date. FAFSA, institutional form required. Applicants notified on a rolling basis starting 6/1; must reply within 2 week(s) of notification.

Academics. Special study options: Distance learning, dual enrollment of high school students, exchange student, honors, independent study, study abroad. Bachelor's degree programs available on campus. **Credit/placement by examination:** AP, CLEP, IB, institutional tests. **Support services:** GED test center, learning center, reduced course load, remedial instruction, study skills assistance, tutoring, writing center.

Majors. Liberal arts: Arts/sciences.

Computing on campus. 80 workstations in library, computer center. Commuter students can connect to campus network. Helpline available.

Student life. Freshman orientation: Mandatory, $75 fee. **Activities:** Bands, choral groups, drama, film society, literary magazine, musical theater, student government, student newspaper, TV station, Intervarsity Christian Fellowship, Circle K, 10% Society, Zoomers Club.

Athletics. NJCAA. **Intercollegiate:** Basketball, golf, tennis, volleyball W. **Intramural:** Badminton, basketball, football (tackle) M, soccer, softball, volleyball. **Team name:** Wombats.

Student services. Adult student services, career counseling, financial aid counseling, personal counseling, veterans' counselor. **Physically disabled:** Services for visually, speech, hearing impaired. **Transfer:** Preadmission transcript evaluation for new students. Transfer center, transfer adviser, college fairs on campus for students transferring to 4-year colleges.

Contact. E-mail: braffael@uwc.edu
Phone: (920) 459-6633 Fax: (920) 459-6662
Steve Ullrick, Assistant Campus Dean for Student Services, University of Wisconsin-Sheboygan, One University Drive, Sheboygan, WI 53081

University of Wisconsin-Washington County

West Bend, Wisconsin
www.washington.uwc.edu **CB code: 1993**

- Public 2-year branch campus and liberal arts college
- Commuter campus in large town
- SAT or ACT (ACT writing optional) required

General. Founded in 1968. Regionally accredited. **Enrollment:** 1,018 degree-seeking undergraduates. **Degrees:** 100 associate awarded. **Location:** 70 miles from Madison, 35 miles from Milwaukee. **Calendar:** Semester, limited summer session. **Full-time faculty:** 32 total. **Part-time faculty:** 20 total. **Special facilities:** Observatory.

Student profile.

Out-of-state:	2%	25 or older:	17%

Transfer out. Colleges most students transferred to 2008: University of Wisconsin-Milwaukee, University of Wisconsin-Oshkosh, University of Wisconsin-Whitewater, University of Wisconsin-Madison.

Basis for selection. Rank in top 75% of class ensures admission. Students in bottom 25% placed in discretionary category. Qualified students not admitted for specific semester applied for will be admitted at later date. ACT preferred. Interview required for applicants with GED or those ranking in bottom 25% of high school class. **Adult students:** SAT/ACT scores not required if applicant over 21. **Homeschooled:** Transcript of courses and grades required.

High school preparation. 17 units required. Required units include English 4, mathematics 3, social studies 3, science 3 and academic electives 4.

2008-2009 Annual costs. Tuition/fees: $4,618; $11,602 out-of-state. Per-credit charge: $178 in-state; $469 out-of-state. Minnesota reciprocity tuition: $167 per credit hour. Books/supplies: $552. Personal expenses: $930.

2007-2008 Financial aid. Need-based: Need-based aid available for part-time students. Work-study available weekends and for part-time students. **Non-need-based:** Scholarships awarded for academics.

Application procedures. Admission: Priority date 8/1; no deadline. $35 fee, may be waived for applicants with need. Admission notification on a rolling basis beginning on or about 11/1. **Financial aid:** Priority date 4/15; no closing date. FAFSA required. Applicants notified on a rolling basis starting 4/30; must reply within 3 week(s) of notification.

Academics. Special study options: Cross-registration, distance learning, dual enrollment of high school students, honors, independent study, internships, study abroad. Collaborative B.A. degree programs in organizational administration, information resources, communications, BSN in nursing, all in cooperation with University of Wisconsin-Milwaukee. Bachelor's degree programs available on campus. **Credit/placement by examination:** AP, CLEP, IB, institutional tests. **Support services:** Learning center, pre-admission summer program, reduced course load, remedial instruction, study skills assistance, tutoring, writing center.

Majors. Liberal arts: Arts/sciences.

Computing on campus. 78 workstations in library, computer center. Commuter students can connect to campus network. Wireless network available.

Student life. Freshman orientation: Mandatory, $50 fee. Preregistration for classes offered. **Activities:** Bands, choral groups, dance, drama, literary magazine, music ensembles, musical theater, student government, student newspaper, symphony orchestra, Phi Theta Kappa honorary society, Literary Guild, business club, Student Impact.

Athletics. NAIA. **Intercollegiate:** Basketball, golf, soccer, tennis, volleyball W. **Intramural:** Basketball, softball, volleyball. **Team name:** Wildcats.

Student services. Adult student services, career counseling, financial aid counseling, personal counseling, veterans' counselor. **Physically disabled:** Services for hearing impaired. **Transfer:** Pre-admission transcript evaluation for new students. Transfer center, transfer adviser, college fairs on campus for students transferring to 4-year colleges.

Contact. Phone: (262) 335-5201 Fax: (262) 335-5274
Martha Nelson, Assistant Campus Dean for Student Services, University of Wisconsin-Washington County, 400 University Drive, West Bend, WI 53095

University of Wisconsin-Waukesha

Waukesha, Wisconsin
www.waukesha.uwc.edu **CB code: 1999**

- Public 2-year branch campus and junior college
- Commuter campus in small city
- SAT or ACT (ACT writing optional) required

General. Founded in 1966. Regionally accredited. **Enrollment:** 1,764 degree-seeking undergraduates; 248 non-degree-seeking students. **Degrees:** 173 associate awarded. **Location:** 17 miles from Milwaukee. **Calendar:** Semester, limited summer session. **Full-time faculty:** 38 total. **Part-time faculty:** 52 total. **Special facilities:** 98-acre environmental studies field station.

Student profile. Among degree-seeking undergraduates, 11% enrolled in a transfer program, 1,309 enrolled as first-time, first-year students.

Part-time:	37%	**Women:**	48%
Out-of-state:	5%	**25 or older:**	29%

Transfer out. Colleges most students transferred to 2008: University of Wisconsin-Milwaukee, University of Wisconsin-Whitewater, University of Wisconsin-Madison.

Basis for selection. Rank in top 75% of class ensures admission. Students in bottom 25% and those with GED considered for admission based on interview; if ACT score 19 or higher admission granted. Interview recommended for applicants in bottom 25% of class. **Adult students:** SAT/ACT scores not required if applicant over 21.

High school preparation. 17 units required. Required and recommended units include English 4, mathematics 3, social studies 3, science 3, foreign language 2 and academic electives 4.

2008-2009 Annual costs. Tuition/fees: $4,560; $11,544 out-of-state. Per-credit charge: $178 in-state; $469 out-of-state. Minnesota reciprocity tuition: $175 per credit hour. Books/supplies: $500. Personal expenses: $1,000.

2008-2009 Financial aid. Need-based: Need-based aid available for part-time students. Work-study available nights, weekends and for part-time students. **Non-need-based:** Scholarships awarded for academics, art, leadership, minority status, music/drama.

Application procedures. Admission: Priority date 4/1; no deadline. $44 fee, may be waived for applicants with need. Admission notification on a rolling basis beginning on or about 8/1. **Financial aid:** Priority date 4/15; no closing date. FAFSA required. Applicants notified on a rolling basis starting 5/15; must reply within 3 week(s) of notification.

Academics. Special study options: Cross-registration, distance learning, dual enrollment of high school students, honors, independent study, study abroad. Bachelor's degree programs available on campus. **Credit/placement by examination:** AP, CLEP, institutional tests. CLEP general exams must be taken before 16 degree credits completed. **Support services:** Learning center, pre-admission summer program, reduced course load, remedial instruction, study skills assistance, tutoring, writing center.

Majors. Liberal arts: Arts/sciences.

Computing on campus. 90 workstations in library, computer center, student center. Commuter students can connect to campus network. Online course registration, wireless network available.

Student life. Freshman orientation: Mandatory, $100 fee. Held periodically throughout the summer and fall semester. **Activities:** Bands, choral groups, drama, literary magazine, music ensembles, musical theater, student government, student newspaper, multicultural student alliance, ecology club, philosophy club, Phi Theta Kappa honor society.

Athletics. NJCAA. **Intercollegiate:** Basketball, golf, soccer, tennis, volleyball W. **Team name:** Cougars.

Student services. Adult student services, career counseling, financial aid counseling, on-campus daycare, personal counseling, veterans' counselor. **Physically disabled:** Services for visually, speech, hearing impaired. **Transfer:** Transfer adviser, college fairs on campus for students transferring to 4-year colleges.

Contact. E-mail: becky.gill@uwc.edu
Phone: (262) 521-5040 Toll-free number: (888) 289-9285
Fax: (262) 521-5530
Deb Kusick, Admission Specialist, University of Wisconsin-Waukesha, 1500 University Drive, Waukesha, WI 53188

Waukesha County Technical College

Pewaukee, Wisconsin
www.wctc.edu **CB code: 0724**

- Public 2-year technical college
- Commuter campus in large town

General. Founded in 1923. Regionally accredited. **Enrollment:** 5,076 degree-seeking undergraduates; 2,536 non-degree-seeking students. **Degrees:** 517 associate awarded. **Location:** 15 miles from Milwaukee. **Calendar:** Semester, limited summer session. **Full-time faculty:** 184 total. **Part-time faculty:** 688 total.

Student profile. Among degree-seeking undergraduates, 100% enrolled in a vocational program, 6% already have a bachelor's degree or higher, 814 enrolled as first-time, first-year students.

Part-time:	61%	**Hispanic American:**	4%
Women:	53%	**Native American:**	1%
African American:	4%	**25 or older:**	47%
Asian American:	2%		

Basis for selection. Open admission, but selective for some programs. Individual programs may have additional requirements or prerequisites, and some programs may have wait lists. Some health occupations programs may require interviews and a general college preparatory background of prerequisites. **Homeschooled:** Transcript of courses and grades required.

2008-2009 Annual costs. Tuition/fees: $3,206; $18,122 out-of-state. Per-credit charge: $97 in-state; $594 out-of-state. Materials fees vary by program; minimum $4 per course. $10 per credit fee for online courses. Books/supplies: $927. Personal expenses: $2,820.

Financial aid. Need-based: Work-study available nights. **Non-need-based:** Scholarships awarded for academics.

Application procedures. Admission: No deadline. $30 fee, may be waived for applicants with need. Admission notification on a rolling basis. **Financial aid:** Priority date 3/31; no closing date. FAFSA, institutional form required. Applicants notified on a rolling basis.

Academics. Special study options: Cooperative education, distance learning, double major, dual enrollment of high school students, ESL, independent study, internships, student-designed major, study abroad. License preparation in dental hygiene, nursing, real estate. **Credit/placement by examination:** CLEP, institutional tests. **Support services:** GED preparation and test center, learning center, reduced course load, remedial instruction, study skills assistance, tutoring, writing center.

Majors. Business: Accounting, administrative services, financial planning, hospitality admin, international marketing, marketing, operations, real estate, retailing. **Communications technology:** Graphics. **Computer sciences:** Networking, programming, systems analysis. **Education:** Early childhood, teacher assistance. **Engineering:** Mechanical, mechanics. **Engineering technology:** Architectural drafting, electrical, mechanical drafting, telecommunications. **Family/consumer sciences:** Child care. **Health:** Dental hygiene, nursing (RN), surgical technology. **Mechanic/repair:** Automotive, computer. **Personal/culinary services:** Restaurant/catering. **Protective services:** Police science. **Public administration:** Human services. **Visual/performing arts:** Graphic design, interior design.

Computing on campus. Online course registration, online library, wireless network available.

Student life. Freshman orientation: Available. Preregistration for classes offered. **Activities:** Student government.

Student services. Adult student services, alcohol/substance abuse counseling, career counseling, services for economically disadvantaged, student employment services, financial aid counseling, health services, minority student services, on-campus daycare, personal counseling, placement for graduates. **Physically disabled:** Services for visually, speech, hearing impaired. **Transfer:** Pre-admission transcript evaluation for new students. College fairs on campus for students transferring to 4-year colleges.

Contact. Phone: (262) 691-5275 Fax: (262) 691-5593
Kathleen Kazda, Manager, Admissions & Assessment, Waukesha County Technical College, 800 Main Street, Pewaukee, WI 53072

Western Technical College

La Crosse, Wisconsin
www.westerntc.edu **CB code: 1087**

- Public 2-year community and technical college
- Residential campus in small city

General. Founded in 1912. Regionally accredited. **Enrollment:** 3,932 degree-seeking undergraduates; 532 non-degree-seeking students. **Degrees:** 520 associate awarded. **Location:** 200 miles from Milwaukee, 150 miles from Minneapolis-St. Paul. **Calendar:** Semester, limited summer session. **Full-time faculty:** 209 total. **Part-time faculty:** 143 total. **Class size:** 100% < 20.

Student profile. Among degree-seeking undergraduates, 29% enrolled in a vocational program, 5% already have a bachelor's degree or higher, 835 enrolled as first-time, first-year students, 66 transferred in from other institutions.

Part-time:	55%	**Women:**	58%

Basis for selection. Open admission, but selective for some programs. Standardized test scores required for admission into selected health programs. COMPASS required for placement if ACT scores not available. Interviews recommended for placement, portfolios recommended for commercial art applicants for placement.

High school preparation. Recommended units include English 3, mathematics 2, social studies 3 and science 2.

2008-2009 Annual costs. Tuition/fees: $3,164; $18,080 out-of-state. Per-credit charge: $97 in-state; $594 out-of-state. Materials fees vary by program; minimum $4.50 per course. Room/board: $3,896. Books/supplies: $1,050. Personal expenses: $1,680.

2007-2008 Financial aid. Need-based: 51% of total undergraduate aid awarded as scholarships/grants, 49% as loans/jobs. Need-based aid available for part-time students. Work-study available nights, weekends and for part-time students.

Application procedures. Admission: No deadline. $30 fee, may be waived for applicants with need. Admission notification on a rolling basis. **Financial aid:** Priority date 3/1; no closing date. FAFSA, institutional form required. Applicants notified on a rolling basis starting 4/1.

Academics. Special study options: Accelerated study, cooperative education, distance learning, double major, dual enrollment of high school students, ESL, honors, independent study, internships, liberal arts/career combination, student-designed major, weekend college. License preparation in dental hygiene, nursing, occupational therapy, paramedic, physical therapy, radiology, real estate. **Credit/placement by examination:** AP, CLEP, institutional tests. 45 credit hours maximum toward associate degree. **Support services:** GED preparation and test center, learning center, reduced course load, remedial instruction, study skills assistance, tutoring, writing center.

Majors. Agriculture: Business technology. **Architecture:** Technology. **Business:** Accounting, administrative services, business admin, finance, human resources, operations, sales/distribution. **Communications:** Media studies. **Communications technology:** General, desktop publishing. **Computer sciences:** Applications programming, data entry, data processing, LAN/WAN management, networking. **Education:** Teacher assistance. **Engineering technology:** Biomedical, computer, electrical, electromechanical, heat/ac/refrig, mechanical, mechanical drafting. **Family/consumer sciences:** Child care. **Health:** Clinical lab technology, dental hygiene, electroencephalograph technology, medical radiologic technology/radiation therapy, medical records technology, nursing (RN), occupational therapy assistant, physical therapy assistant, respiratory therapy technology. **Legal studies:** Paralegal. **Mechanic/repair:** Automotive, diesel. **Personal/culinary services:** Restaurant/catering. **Production:** Machine shop technology, tool and die. **Protective services:** Fire safety technology, police science. **Public administration:** Community org/advocacy. **Visual/performing arts:** Design, graphic design, interior design, music.

Most popular majors. Business/marketing 26%, communications/journalism 6%, computer/information sciences 7%, health sciences 32%, security/protective services 7%.

Computing on campus. 145 workstations in dormitories, library, computer center. Dormitories wired for high-speed internet access and linked to campus network. Commuter students can connect to campus network. Online course registration, online library, helpline, repair service available.

Student life. Freshman orientation: Available. Preregistration for classes offered. General school orientation held in August. **Housing:** Coed dorms available. **Activities:** Student government, student newspaper, TV station, multicultural club, Campus Crusade for Christ.

Athletics. NJCAA. **Intercollegiate:** Baseball M, basketball, volleyball W. **Intramural:** Basketball, volleyball. **Team name:** Cavaliers.

Student services. Adult student services, alcohol/substance abuse counseling, career counseling, services for economically disadvantaged, student employment services, financial aid counseling, health services, minority student services, on-campus daycare, personal counseling, placement for graduates, veterans' counselor, women's services. **Physically disabled:** Services for visually, speech, hearing impaired. **Transfer:** Pre-admission transcript evaluation for new students.

Contact. E-mail: wellsj@westerntc.edu
Phone: (608) 785-9476 Toll-free number: (800) 322-9982
Fax: (608) 785-9148
Jayne Wells, Admissions, Registration and Records, Western Technical College, PO Box 908, La Crosse, WI 54602-0908

Wisconsin Indianhead Technical College
Shell Lake, Wisconsin
www.witc.edu **CB code: 1580**

- Public 2-year technical college
- Commuter campus in rural community
- Interview required

General. Founded in 1972. Regionally accredited. 4 campuses covering 11 county area. **Enrollment:** 3,007 degree-seeking undergraduates; 482 non-degree-seeking students. **Degrees:** 330 associate awarded. **Calendar:** Semester, limited summer session. **Full-time faculty:** 152 total. **Part-time faculty:** 981 total.

Student profile. Among degree-seeking undergraduates, 99% enrolled in a vocational program, 572 enrolled as first-time, first-year students.

Part-time:	53%	**Asian American:**	1%
Out-of-state:	5%	**Hispanic American:**	1%
Women:	59%	**Native American:**	2%
African American:	1%	**25 or older:**	26%

Transfer out. Colleges most students transferred to 2008: University of Wisconsin.

Basis for selection. Open admission, but selective for some programs. Required ASSET scores: 44 for nursing program, 39 for other associate degree programs, 36 for technical diplomas. SAT or ACT can be used in lieu of ASSET assessment. Required ASSET scores: 44 for nursing program, 39 for other associate degree programs, 36 for technical diplomas. SAT or ACT can be used in lieu of ASSET assessment. **Homeschooled:** Must pass ability to benefit assessment.

2008-2009 Annual costs. Tuition/fees: $3,212; $18,128 out-of-state. Per-credit charge: $97 in-state; $594 out-of-state. Materials fees vary by program; minimum $4 per course. $10 per credit fee for online courses. Books/supplies: $808. Personal expenses: $1,128.

2007-2008 Financial aid. All financial aid based on need. Need-based aid available for part-time students. Work-study available nights, weekends and for part-time students.

Application procedures. Admission: No deadline. $30 fee. Admission notification on a rolling basis. **Financial aid:** Priority date 4/1; no closing date. FAFSA required. Applicants notified on a rolling basis starting 5/9; must reply by 9/1 or within 4 week(s) of notification.

Academics. Special study options: Accelerated study, distance learning, double major, internships. **Credit/placement by examination:** AP, CLEP, institutional tests. **Support services:** GED preparation and test center, learning center, pre-admission summer program, reduced course load, remedial instruction, tutoring.

Majors. Business: Accounting, administrative services, business admin, finance, marketing, operations, retailing. **Computer sciences:** General, networking, programming, web page design. **Education:** Early childhood, teacher assistance. **Engineering technology:** Architectural, computer systems, heat/ac/refrig, manufacturing, mechanical drafting. **Health:** Medical secretary, nursing (RN), occupational therapy assistant. **Mechanic/repair:** Communications systems, computer. **Protective services:** Corrections, police science. **Other:** Individual technical studies.

Most popular majors. Business/marketing 37%, computer/information sciences 7%, education 8%, engineering/engineering technologies 11%, health sciences 32%.

Computing on campus. 1,900 workstations in library, computer center, student center. Online course registration, online library, helpline, wireless network available.

Student life. Freshman orientation: Available. Preregistration for classes offered. **Activities:** Student government, student newspaper, technical student organizations, vocational student organizations.

Student services. Adult student services, career counseling, services for economically disadvantaged, student employment services, financial aid counseling, health services, minority student services, on-campus daycare, personal counseling, placement for graduates, veterans' counselor, women's services. **Physically disabled:** Services for hearing impaired. **Transfer:** College fairs on campus for students transferring to 4-year colleges.

Contact. Phone: (715) 468-2815 Toll-free number: (800) 243-9482
Fax: (715) 468-2819
Shane Evenson, Registrar, Wisconsin Indianhead Technical College, 505 Pine Ridge Drive, Shell Lake, WI 54871

Wyoming

Casper College
Casper, Wyoming
www.caspercollege.edu CB code: 4043

- Public 2-year community college
- Commuter campus in small city

General. Founded in 1945. Regionally accredited. **Enrollment:** 2,701 degree-seeking undergraduates; 1,410 non-degree-seeking students. **Degrees:** 556 associate awarded. **Location:** 280 miles from Denver. **Calendar:** Semester, limited summer session. **Full-time faculty:** 159 total; 27% have terminal degrees, 4% minority, 43% women. **Part-time faculty:** 118 total; 10% have terminal degrees, 2% minority, 48% women. **Class size:** 67% < 20, 30% 20-39, 2% 40-49, 2% 50-99. **Special facilities:** Wildlife museum, geological museum, family resource center, fitness center.

Student profile. Among degree-seeking undergraduates, 63% enrolled in a transfer program, 37% enrolled in a vocational program, 723 enrolled as first-time, first-year students, 210 transferred in from other institutions.

Part-time:	31%	**Hispanic American:**	3%
Out-of-state:	7%	**Native American:**	1%
Women:	62%	**International:**	1%
African American:	1%	**25 or older:**	38%
Asian American:	1%	**Live on campus:**	11%

Transfer out. 40% of students enrolled in the transfer program go on to 4-year colleges. **Colleges most students transferred to 2008:** University of Wyoming, University of North Dakota, Colorado State University, Montana State University, Black Hills State University.

Basis for selection. Open admission, but selective for some programs and for out-of-state students. 2.0 GPA required for out-of-state applicants. Selective admission for nursing, respiratory therapy, radiology; requirements vary by program. Audition recommended for music, theater, athletics and forensics; portfolio recommended for art. **Homeschooled:** Program must be accredited and recognized by state department of education as being equivalent to high school diploma.

High school preparation. College-preparatory program recommended. Recommended units include English 4, mathematics 3, social studies 3 and science 3.

2008-2009 Annual costs. Tuition/fees: $1,752; $4,872 out-of-state. Per-credit charge: $65 in-state; $195 out-of-state. Western Undergraduate Exchange students pay $93.50 per credit-hour and $2,244 per year for full-time students. Room/board: $3,980. Books/supplies: $888. Personal expenses: $2,250.

2008-2009 Financial aid. Need-based: Need-based aid available for part-time students. Work-study available nights, weekends and for part-time students. **Non-need-based:** Scholarships awarded for academics, art, athletics, leadership, music/drama, state residency.

Application procedures. Admission: Priority date 8/1; deadline 8/15 (postmark date). No application fee. Admission notification on a rolling basis beginning on or about 2/1. **Financial aid:** Priority date 3/15; no closing date. FAFSA required. Applicants notified on a rolling basis starting 4/1.

Academics. Special study options: Cooperative education, cross-registration, distance learning, dual enrollment of high school students, honors, independent study, internships. Bachelor's degree programs available on campus. License preparation in nursing, radiology. **Credit/placement by examination:** AP, CLEP, IB, institutional tests. 30 credit hours maximum toward associate degree. **Support services:** GED preparation and test center, learning center, remedial instruction, study skills assistance, tutoring, writing center.

Majors. Agriculture: General, animal husbandry, business, range science. **Area/ethnic studies:** Women's. **Biology:** General. **Business:** Accounting, accounting technology, administrative services, business admin, construction management, entrepreneurial studies, hospitality admin, management information systems, marketing, office technology, retailing. **Communications:** General. **Computer sciences:** Applications programming, information technology, networking, programming, vendor certification, web page design. **Conservation:** Environmental science, wildlife. **Construction:** General. **Education:** Art, kindergarten/preschool, music, physical, social studies, teacher assistance, technology/industrial arts. **Engineering:** General. **Engineering technology:** Drafting, electrical, manufacturing, mining, robotics, water quality. **Foreign languages:** General. **Health:** Athletic training, clinical lab technology, health services, medical transcription, nursing (RN), occupational therapy assistant, pharmacy assistant, predental, premedicine, prepharmacy, preveterinary, radiologic technology/medical imaging, respiratory therapy technology, substance abuse counseling. **History:** General. **Interdisciplinary:** Museum, nutrition sciences. **Legal studies:** Paralegal, prelaw. **Liberal arts:** Arts/sciences. **Math:** General. **Mechanic/repair:** Auto body, automotive, diesel, industrial. **Physical sciences:** Chemistry, geology, physics. **Production:** Machine tool, welding. **Protective services:** Criminal justice, firefighting, forensics. **Psychology:** General. **Public administration:** Social work. **Social sciences:** Anthropology, economics, international relations, political science, sociology. **Transportation:** Airline/commercial pilot. **Visual/performing arts:** Acting, art, dance, dramatic, graphic design, music performance, photography, studio arts, theater design. **Other:** Applied statistics.

Most popular majors. Business/marketing 6%, education 13%, health sciences 22%, liberal arts 13%, security/protective services 8%.

Computing on campus. 120 workstations in library, computer center. Dormitories wired for high-speed internet access and linked to campus network. Commuter students can connect to campus network. Helpline, wireless network available.

Student life. Freshman orientation: Mandatory. Preregistration for classes offered. One-day program, held 4 times in summer. **Housing:** Coed dorms, apartments, wellness housing available. $200 fully refundable deposit. **Activities:** Bands, campus ministries, choral groups, dance, drama, international student organizations, literary magazine, music ensembles, musical theater, student government, student newspaper, Latter-day Saints student association, Baptist student union, Phi Theta Kappa, Phi Rho Pi, student nurses association, Students in Free Enterprise, AG club, student activities board, Bakkai.

Athletics. NJCAA. **Intercollegiate:** Basketball, cheerleading, rodeo, volleyball W. **Intramural:** Basketball, bowling, football (non-tackle), racquetball, soccer, softball, tennis, volleyball. **Team name:** Thunderbirds.

Student services. Adult student services, alcohol/substance abuse counseling, career counseling, student employment services, financial aid counseling, health services, on-campus daycare, personal counseling, placement for graduates, veterans' counselor. **Physically disabled:** Services for visually, speech, hearing impaired. **Transfer:** Transfer adviser, college fairs on campus for students transferring to 4-year colleges.

Contact. E-mail: kfoltz@caspercollege.edu
Phone: (307) 268-2458 Toll-free number: (800) 442-2963
Fax: (307) 268-2611
Kyla Foltz, Admissions Coordinator, Casper College, 125 College Drive, Casper, WY 82601

Central Wyoming College
Riverton, Wyoming
www.cwc.edu CB code: 4115

- Public 2-year community college
- Commuter campus in large town

General. Founded in 1966. Regionally accredited. **Enrollment:** 1,150 degree-seeking undergraduates; 1,002 non-degree-seeking students. **Degrees:** 190 associate awarded. **Location:** 120 miles from Casper, 240 miles from Billings, MT. **Calendar:** Semester, limited summer session. **Full-time faculty:** 46 total; 72% have terminal degrees, 9% minority, 52% women. **Part-time faculty:** 85 total; 27% have terminal degrees, 19% minority, 54% women. **Class size:** 87% < 20, 13% 20-39, less than 1% 40-49. **Special facilities:** Rodeo arena, fine arts center, Microsoft training laboratory, Cisco training laboratory, Native American artifacts, canyon center, Wyoming PBS station.

Student profile. Among degree-seeking undergraduates, 64% enrolled in a transfer program, 36% enrolled in a vocational program, 373 enrolled as first-time, first-year students, 165 transferred in from other institutions.

Part-time:	40%	**Hispanic American:**	4%
Out-of-state:	14%	**Native American:**	14%
Women:	64%	**International:**	2%
African American:	1%	**25 or older:**	41%
Asian American:	1%	**Live on campus:**	10%

Transfer out. Colleges most students transferred to 2008: University of Wyoming, Colorado State University, Montana State University, University of Utah, Chadron.

Basis for selection. Open admission, but selective for some programs. Special admission to nursing program; minimum GPA and test scores required. COMPASS placement tests required for all first-time students who have not taken ACT or SAT. Certain music courses require audition.

2008-2009 Annual costs. Tuition/fees: $2,064; $5,184 out-of-state. Per-credit charge: $65 in-state; $195 out-of-state. Western Undergraduate Exchange students pay $2,448 or $102 per credit hour. Room/board: $4,322. Books/supplies: $1,000. Personal expenses: $1,500.

2008-2009 Financial aid. Need-based: 169 full-time freshmen applied for aid; 130 were judged to have need; 130 of these received aid. 72% of total undergraduate aid awarded as scholarships/grants, 28% as loans/jobs. Need-based aid available for part-time students. Work-study available nights, weekends and for part-time students. **Non-need-based:** Awarded to 265 full-time undergraduates, including 109 freshmen. Scholarships awarded for academics, alumni affiliation, art, athletics, leadership, minority status, music/drama, state residency.

Application procedures. Admission: No deadline. No application fee. Admission notification on a rolling basis beginning on or about 1/1. **Financial aid:** Priority date 4/15; no closing date. FAFSA, institutional form required. Applicants notified on a rolling basis starting 5/1; must reply within 2 week(s) of notification.

Academics. Special study options: Cooperative education, cross-registration, distance learning, double major, dual enrollment of high school students, external degree, honors, independent study, student-designed major, teacher certification program. Bachelor's degree programs available on campus. License preparation in dental hygiene, nursing, paramedic. **Credit/placement by examination:** AP, CLEP, institutional tests. 32 credit hours maximum toward associate degree. Some DANTES and APE exams accepted. **Support services:** GED preparation and test center, learning center, reduced course load, remedial instruction, study skills assistance, tutoring, writing center.

Majors. Agriculture: Business, equestrian studies, range science. **Area/ethnic studies:** Native American. **Biology:** General. **Business:** Accounting, accounting technology, administrative services, business admin, management information systems, office technology. **Communications:** Radio/tv. **Communications technology:** Radio/tv. **Computer sciences:** Computer graphics, computer science, web page design. **Conservation:** Environmental science. **Construction:** Carpentry. **Education:** Early childhood, elementary, secondary, teacher assistance. **Engineering:** General. **Engineering technology:** Computer systems. **Family/consumer sciences:** Child care. **Health:** Health services, medical transcription, nursing (RN). **Legal studies:** Prelaw. **Math:** General. **Mechanic/repair:** Automotive. **Parks/recreation:** General, facilities management. **Personal/culinary services:** Chef training. **Physical sciences:** General, geology. **Production:** Welding. **Protective services:** Emergency management/homeland security, firefighting, law enforcement admin. **Psychology:** General. **Public administration:** Human services. **Social sciences:** General. **Visual/performing arts:** Acting, art, dramatic, theater design. **Other:** Business Office systems, Western American studies.

Most popular majors. Business/marketing 10%, health sciences 15%, liberal arts 22%, security/protective services 6%, visual/performing arts 10%.

Computing on campus. 450 workstations in dormitories, library, computer center, student center. Dormitories wired for high-speed internet access and linked to campus network. Commuter students can connect to campus network. Online course registration, online library, wireless network available.

Student life. Freshman orientation: Mandatory. Preregistration for classes offered. **Housing:** Coed dorms, apartments available. $225 partly refundable deposit, deadline 5/1. **Activities:** Bands, choral groups, dance, drama, music ensembles, musical theater, radio station, student government, student newspaper, TV station, American Indian club, multicultural club, social science club, veterans club, Hispanic club, law and justice club, science club, Phi Theta Kappa, American Indian science and engineering society.

Athletics. NJCAA. **Intercollegiate:** Basketball, rodeo, volleyball W. **Intramural:** Badminton, basketball, skiing, soccer, softball, swimming, table tennis, tennis, volleyball, weight lifting. **Team name:** Rustlers.

Student services. Adult student services, alcohol/substance abuse counseling, career counseling, services for economically disadvantaged, student employment services, financial aid counseling, personal counseling, placement for graduates, veterans' counselor. **Physically disabled:** Services for visually, hearing impaired. **Transfer:** College fairs on campus for students transferring to 4-year colleges.

Contact. E-mail: admit@cwc.edu
Phone: (307) 855-2119 Toll-free number: (800) 865-0193
Fax: (307) 855-2093
Brenda Barlow, Admissions Office Assistant, Central Wyoming College, 2660 Peck Avenue, Riverton, WY 82501

Eastern Wyoming College
Torrington, Wyoming
ewc.wy.edu **CB code: 4700**

- Public 2-year community college
- Commuter campus in small town

General. Founded in 1948. Regionally accredited. **Enrollment:** 678 degree-seeking undergraduates; 782 non-degree-seeking students. **Degrees:** 101 associate awarded. **Location:** 190 miles from Denver. **Calendar:** Semester, limited summer session. **Full-time faculty:** 45 total; 18% have terminal degrees. **Part-time faculty:** 49 total. **Special facilities:** Veterinarian technology facility.

Student profile. Among degree-seeking undergraduates, 57% enrolled in a transfer program, 39% enrolled in a vocational program, 222 enrolled as first-time, first-year students.

Part-time:	32%	**Asian American:**	1%
Out-of-state:	13%	**Hispanic American:**	7%
Women:	62%	**International:**	1%
African American:	2%	**25 or older:**	35%

Transfer out. Colleges most students transferred to 2008: University of Wyoming, Chadron State College.

Basis for selection. Open admission. **Homeschooled:** Transcript of courses and grades required. ACT recommended but not required. Signed statement that student was homeschooled required for financial aid.

2008-2009 Annual costs. Tuition/fees: $2,072; $5,192 out-of-state. Per-credit charge: $65 in-state; $195 out-of-state. Students from Western Undergraduate Exchange pay $2,448 tuition plus $384 fees per year; $102 per credit hour. Room/board: $3,666. Books/supplies: $992. Personal expenses: $1,434.

Financial aid. Need-based: Need-based aid available for part-time students. Work-study available nights, weekends and for part-time students. **Non-need-based:** Scholarships awarded for academics, alumni affiliation, art, athletics, leadership, music/drama. **Additional information:** Installment payment plan on room and board contracts offered.

Application procedures. Admission: No deadline. No application fee. Admission notification on a rolling basis. **Financial aid:** Priority date 3/15; no closing date. FAFSA, institutional form required. Applicants notified on a rolling basis starting 1/1.

Academics. Special study options: Cross-registration, distance learning, dual enrollment of high school students, ESL, independent study, internships. License preparation on campus for welding and joining, veterinary technology, and cosmetology. Bachelor's degree programs available on campus. **Credit/placement by examination:** AP, CLEP, IB, institutional tests. 16 credit hours maximum toward associate degree. **Support services:** GED preparation and test center, learning center, reduced course load, remedial instruction, study skills assistance, tutoring.

Majors. Agriculture: General, agribusiness operations, animal sciences, economics, farm/ranch, range science. **Biology:** General, environmental. **Business:** Accounting, administrative services, business admin, office management. **Communications:** General. **Computer sciences:** Networking. **Conservation:** Wildlife. **Education:** Agricultural, business, early childhood, elementary, mathematics, music, physical, secondary. **Foreign languages:** General. **Health:** Predental, premedicine, prenursing, prepharmacy, preveterinary, veterinary technology/assistant. **History:** General. **Liberal arts:** Arts/sciences. **Math:** General, statistics. **Personal/culinary services:** Cosmetic. **Production:** Welding. **Protective services:** Correctional facilities, criminal justice, law enforcement admin, police science. **Psychology:** General. **Social sciences:** Economics, political science, sociology. **Visual/performing arts:** Art. **Other:** Pre-medical technology.

Most popular majors. Agriculture 6%, business/marketing 12%, education 13%, health sciences 18%, liberal arts 22%, personal/culinary services 9%, trade and industry 28%.

Computing on campus. 120 workstations in dormitories, library, student center. Dormitories wired for high-speed internet access. Online course registration available.

Student life. Freshman orientation: Available. Preregistration for classes offered. Held in fall 1 day prior to first day of classes. **Housing:** Coed dorms, wellness housing available. $100 fully refundable deposit. **Activities:** Campus ministries, choral groups, musical theater, student government, student newspaper.

Athletics. NJCAA. **Intercollegiate:** Basketball, golf, rodeo, volleyball W. **Intramural:** Basketball, bowling, handball, racquetball, rodeo, softball, tennis, volleyball, weight lifting. **Team name:** Lancers.

Student services. Adult student services, alcohol/substance abuse counseling, career counseling, student employment services, financial aid counseling, health services, personal counseling, placement for graduates, veterans' counselor. **Physically disabled:** Services for visually, speech, hearing impaired. **Transfer:** Re-entry adviser, pre-admission transcript evaluation for new students. Transfer adviser, college fairs on campus for students transferring to 4-year colleges.

Contact. E-mail: rex.cogdill@ewc.wy.edu
Phone: (307) 532-8230 Toll-free number: (800) 658-3195
Fax: (307) 532-8222
Rex Cogdill, Dean of Students, Eastern Wyoming College, 3200 West C Street, Torrington, WY 82240

Laramie County Community College

Cheyenne, Wyoming
www.lccc.wy.edu **CB code: 0360**

- Public 2-year community college
- Commuter campus in small city

General. Founded in 1968. Regionally accredited. Additional campus in Laramie, outreach center in Pine Bluffs. **Enrollment:** 3,165 degree-seeking undergraduates; 1,803 non-degree-seeking students. **Degrees:** 466 associate awarded. **ROTC:** Army, Air Force. **Location:** 4 miles from downtown, 100 miles from Denver. **Calendar:** Semester, limited summer session. **Full-time faculty:** 92 total; 9% have terminal degrees, 5% minority, 53% women. **Part-time faculty:** 226 total; 4% minority, 63% women. **Class size:** 76% < 20, 23% 20-39, less than 1% 40-49, less than 1% 50-99. **Special facilities:** Bureau of Land Management park, indoor arena, networking laboratory.

Student profile. Among degree-seeking undergraduates, 60% enrolled in a transfer program, 40% enrolled in a vocational program, 7% already have a bachelor's degree or higher, 391 enrolled as first-time, first-year students, 317 transferred in from other institutions.

Part-time:	44%	**Hispanic American:**	8%
Out-of-state:	10%	**Native American:**	1%
Women:	63%	**International:**	2%
African American:	2%	**25 or older:**	40%
Asian American:	1%	**Live on campus:**	8%

Transfer out. 50% of students enrolled in the transfer program go on to 4-year colleges. **Colleges most students transferred to 2008:** University of Wyoming.

Basis for selection. Open admission, but selective for some programs. Special requirements for nursing, radiography, equine studies, dental hygiene programs. Interview required for equine studies. **Homeschooled:** Students must complete institutional home schooler form and attach to transcript. **Learning Disabled:** Interview with Disability Resource Center coordinator to arrange accomodations.

2008-2009 Annual costs. Tuition/fees: $2,208; $5,328 out-of-state. Per-credit charge: $65 in-state; $195 out-of-state. Students from Western Undergraduate Exchange schools and Nebraska residents pay $3,000 in tuition and fees per year; $125 per credit hour. Room/board: $5,974. Books/supplies: $1,500.

2007-2008 Financial aid. Need-based: Need-based aid available for part-time students. **Non-need-based:** Scholarships awarded for academics, art, athletics, music/drama.

Application procedures. Admission: No deadline. $20 fee. Admission notification on a rolling basis. Nursing, radiology, and dental hygiene applications must be received by February 1. **Financial aid:** Priority date 4/1; no closing date. FAFSA, institutional form required. Applicants notified on a rolling basis starting 6/1; must reply within 2 week(s) of notification.

Academics. Special study options: Cooperative education, distance learning, dual enrollment of high school students, internships. License preparation in dental hygiene, nursing, paramedic, radiology. **Credit/placement by examination:** AP, CLEP, IB, institutional tests. 15 credit hours maximum toward associate degree. **Support services:** GED preparation and test center, learning center, remedial instruction, study skills assistance, tutoring.

Majors. Agriculture: General, agribusiness operations, business technology, equestrian studies, production. **Biology:** General. **Business:** General, accounting, business admin, entrepreneurial studies, management science. **Communications:** General, digital media, media studies. **Computer sciences:** General, computer science, information technology, programming, systems analysis, web page design. **Conservation:** Wildlife. **Construction:** General. **Education:** General, early childhood, physical, special. **Engineering:** General. **Engineering technology:** Civil, energy systems. **Foreign languages:** Spanish. **Health:** Dental hygiene, medical radiologic technology/radiation therapy, nursing (RN), physical therapy assistant, predental, premedicine, prepharmacy, preveterinary, radiologic technology/medical imaging, sonography, surgical technology. **History:** General. **Interdisciplinary:** Biological/physical sciences. **Legal studies:** Paralegal, prelaw. **Liberal arts:** Humanities. **Math:** General. **Mechanic/repair:** Auto body, automotive, diesel. **Philosophy/religion:** Religion. **Physical sciences:** Chemistry. **Protective services:** Corrections, emergency management/homeland security, law enforcement admin. **Psychology:** General. **Public administration:** General, human services. **Social sciences:** General, anthropology, economics, political science, sociology. **Visual/performing arts:** Art.

Most popular majors. Business/marketing 9%, education 11%, health sciences 31%, interdisciplinary studies 17%.

Computing on campus. Dormitories wired for high-speed internet access. Online course registration, helpline, wireless network available.

Student life. Freshman orientation: Available. Preregistration for classes offered. **Housing:** Coed dorms, wellness housing available. $100 deposit. **Activities:** Bands, choral groups, drama, international student organizations, literary magazine, music ensembles, musical theater, student government, student newspaper, TV station.

Athletics. NJCAA. **Intercollegiate:** Basketball M, equestrian, rodeo, soccer, volleyball W. **Team name:** Golden Eagles.

Student services. Adult student services, alcohol/substance abuse counseling, career counseling, services for economically disadvantaged, student employment services, financial aid counseling, health services, on-campus daycare, personal counseling, placement for graduates, veterans' counselor. **Physically disabled:** Services for visually, speech, hearing impaired. **Transfer:** College fairs on campus for students transferring to 4-year colleges.

Contact. E-mail: learnmore@lccc.wy.edu
Phone: (307) 778-1357 Toll-free number: (800) 522-2993 ext. 1357
Fax: (307) 778-1350
Holly Allison, Director of Admissions, Laramie County Community College, 1400 East College Drive, Cheyenne, WY 82007-3299

Northwest College

Powell, Wyoming
www.northwestcollege.edu **CB code: 4542**

- Public 2-year community college
- Residential campus in small town

General. Founded in 1946. Regionally accredited. **Enrollment:** 1,819 degree-seeking undergraduates. **Degrees:** 1,158 associate awarded. **Location:** 90 miles from Billings, Montana. **Calendar:** Semester, limited summer session. **Full-time faculty:** 78 total. **Part-time faculty:** 58 total. **Class size:** 85% < 20, 15% 20-39, less than 1% 40-49.

Student profile.

Out-of-state:	26%	**Live on campus:**	40%
25 or older:	24%		

Transfer out. Colleges most students transferred to 2008: University of Wyoming, Montana State University-Bozeman, Montana State University-Billings.

Basis for selection. Open admission, but selective for some programs and for out-of-state students. Admissions for out-of-state applicants based on high school GPA and test scores. Nursing, photography, and equestrian training programs require extra applications and qualifications. Placement tests in math and English required for all first-time freshmen. SAT or ACT required of out-of-state students. **Learning Disabled:** Individuals must identify needs in order to to procure services.

High school preparation. Recommended units include English 4, mathematics 2, social studies 2 and science 1.

2008-2009 Annual costs. Tuition/fees: $2,107; $5,227 out-of-state. Per-credit charge: $65 in-state; $195 out-of-state. Students from Western Undergraduate Exchange schools pay $2,352 tuition; $98 per credit hour. Room/board: $4,674. Books/supplies: $700. Personal expenses: $1,285.

2007-2008 Financial aid. Need-based: 64% of total undergraduate aid awarded as scholarships/grants, 36% as loans/jobs. Work-study available nights and for part-time students. **Non-need-based:** Scholarships awarded for academics, athletics. **Additional information:** Interview, essay recommended for scholarships.

Application procedures. **Admission:** No deadline. No application fee. Admission notification on a rolling basis. **Financial aid:** Priority date 5/1; no closing date. FAFSA, institutional form required. Applicants notified on a rolling basis starting 5/1; must reply within 2 week(s) of notification.

Academics. **Special study options:** Accelerated study, cooperative education, distance learning, double major, dual enrollment of high school students, honors, independent study, internships, liberal arts/career combination, study abroad, teacher certification program. Bachelor's degree programs available on campus. License preparation in nursing. **Credit/placement by examination:** CLEP, institutional tests. 16 credit hours maximum toward associate degree. **Support services:** GED preparation and test center, learning center, reduced course load, remedial instruction, study skills assistance, tutoring.

Majors. **Agriculture:** General, animal sciences, business, equestrian studies, range science, soil science. **Biology:** General. **Business:** General, administrative services, business admin, management information systems, managerial economics, office management, tourism promotion. **Communications:** General, journalism. **Communications technology:** Graphic/printing. **Computer sciences:** General, information systems. **Conservation:** Forestry, management/policy, wildlife. **Education:** General, agricultural, early childhood, elementary, secondary, special. **Engineering:** General. **Engineering technology:** Drafting. **Foreign languages:** General. **Health:** Predental, premedicine, prepharmacy, preveterinary. **History:** General. **Interdisciplinary:** Biological/physical sciences. **Legal studies:** Prelaw. **Liberal arts:** Arts/sciences. **Math:** General. **Parks/recreation:** Facilities management. **Physical sciences:** Chemistry, physics. **Psychology:** General. **Social sciences:** General, political science, sociology. **Visual/performing arts:** Commercial photography, commercial/advertising art, design, photography.

Computing on campus. 134 workstations in dormitories, library, computer center, student center. Commuter students can connect to campus network.

Student life. **Freshman orientation:** Available, $35 fee. Preregistration for classes offered. Held once in June, July, and August. **Housing:** Coed dorms, single-sex dorms, apartments available. $100 deposit. **Activities:** Bands, choral groups, dance, drama, literary magazine, music ensembles, musical theater, student government, student newspaper, symphony orchestra, Northwest Trail Blazers, civic service organization.

Athletics. NJCAA. **Intercollegiate:** Basketball, volleyball W, wrestling M. **Intramural:** Archery, badminton, baseball M, basketball, cross-country, field hockey W, golf, handball, racquetball, rifle M, sailing, skiing, soccer, softball, squash, swimming, table tennis, tennis, volleyball, wrestling M. **Team name:** Trappers.

Student services. Adult student services, alcohol/substance abuse counseling, chaplain/spiritual director, career counseling, student employment services, financial aid counseling, health services, minority student services, on-campus daycare, personal counseling, placement for graduates, veterans' counselor. **Physically disabled:** Services for visually, speech, hearing impaired. **Transfer:** Pre-admission transcript evaluation for new students. Transfer adviser, college fairs on campus for students transferring to 4-year colleges.

Contact. E-mail: admissions@northwestcollege.edu
Phone: (307) 754-6101 Toll-free number: (800) 560-4692
Fax: (307) 754-6249
Brad Hammond, Registrar, Northwest College, 231 West 6th Street, Powell, WY 82435

Sheridan College

Sheridan, Wyoming
www.sheridan.edu **CB code: 4536**

- Public 2-year community college
- Commuter campus in large town

General. Founded in 1948. Regionally accredited. **Enrollment:** 1,521 degree-seeking undergraduates; 2,494 non-degree-seeking students. **Degrees:** 226 associate awarded. **Location:** 130 miles from Casper; 130 miles from Billings, Montana. **Calendar:** Semester, limited summer session. **Full-time faculty:** 83 total; 19% have terminal degrees, 4% minority, 59% women. **Part-time faculty:** 81 total; 4% have terminal degrees, 2% minority, 62% women. **Class size:** 71% < 20, 29% 20-39, less than 1% 40-49, less than 1% 50-99. **Special facilities:** Geological museum, federal depository for government publications, observatory.

Student profile. Among degree-seeking undergraduates, 49% enrolled in a transfer program, 47% enrolled in a vocational program, 332 enrolled as first-time, first-year students, 351 transferred in from other institutions.

Part-time:	40%	**Hispanic American:**	3%
Out-of-state:	17%	**Native American:**	2%
Women:	62%	**International:**	1%
African American:	1%	**25 or older:**	34%
Asian American:	1%	**Live on campus:**	20%

Transfer out. **Colleges most students transferred to 2008:** University of Wyoming, Chadron State College, Black Hills State University, Montana State University.

Basis for selection. Open admission, but selective for some programs. Special admissions for nursing, dental hygiene, massage therapy; requirements vary by program.

High school preparation. One chemistry required of dental hygiene applicants.

2008-2009 Annual costs. Tuition/fees: $2,131; $5,251 out-of-state. Per-credit charge: $65 in-state; $195 out-of-state. Room/board: $4,300. Books/supplies: $900. Personal expenses: $1,800.

2007-2008 Financial aid. **Need-based:** Need-based aid available for part-time students. Work-study available nights, weekends and for part-time students. **Non-need-based:** Scholarships awarded for academics, art, athletics, leadership, music/drama, state residency.

Application procedures. **Admission:** No deadline. No application fee. Admission notification on a rolling basis. **Financial aid:** Priority date 3/1; no closing date. FAFSA, institutional form required. Applicants notified on a rolling basis; must reply within 3 week(s) of notification.

Academics. **Special study options:** Cooperative education, distance learning, double major, dual enrollment of high school students, ESL, independent study, internships, liberal arts/career combination. Bachelor's degree programs available on campus. License preparation in dental hygiene, nursing. **Credit/placement by examination:** AP, CLEP, institutional tests. 18 credit hours maximum toward associate degree. **Support services:** GED preparation and test center, learning center, reduced course load, remedial instruction, study skills assistance, tutoring, writing center.

Majors. **Agriculture:** Animal sciences, business, food science, horticultural science, production, range science, turf management. **Biology:** General. **Business:** General, administrative services, hospitality admin. **Computer sciences:** General, information systems, webmaster. **Education:** Elementary, secondary, teacher assistance. **Engineering:** General. **Engineering technology:** CAD/CADD, surveying. **Foreign languages:** General. **Health:** Dental hygiene, health services, massage therapy, nursing (RN), pharmacy assistant. **History:** General. **Interdisciplinary:** Biological/physical sciences. **Liberal arts:** Humanities. **Math:** General. **Mechanic/repair:** Diesel. **Parks/recreation:** Health/fitness. **Personal/culinary services:** Chef training. **Physical sciences:** General, chemistry. **Production:** Machine tool, welding. **Protective services:** Criminal justice. **Psychology:** General. **Social sciences:** General. **Visual/performing arts:** Art, dramatic.

Most popular majors. Business/marketing 9%, engineering/engineering technologies 6%, health sciences 19%, interdisciplinary studies 6%, liberal arts 21%, security/protective services 7%, trade and industry 9%, visual/performing arts 6%.

Computing on campus. 500 workstations in dormitories, library, student center. Dormitories wired for high-speed internet access and linked to campus network. Commuter students can connect to campus network. Online library, helpline, student web hosting, wireless network available.

Student life. **Freshman orientation:** Mandatory. Preregistration for classes offered. Online orientation. **Housing:** Coed dorms, single-sex dorms, special housing for disabled, apartments available. $60 fully refundable deposit. Apartments available for single parents. **Activities:** Bands, choral groups, drama, music ensembles, student government, student newspaper, TV station, art club, nursing clubs, dental auxiliary, multidiversity club.

Athletics. NJCAA. **Intercollegiate:** Basketball, cross-country, rodeo, volleyball W. **Intramural:** Basketball, bowling, soccer, softball, tennis, volleyball. **Team name:** Generals.

Student services. Adult student services, career counseling, student employment services, financial aid counseling, health services, personal counseling, placement for graduates. **Physically disabled:** Services for visually, speech, hearing impaired. **Transfer:** Pre-admission transcript evaluation for new students. Transfer adviser, college fairs on campus for students transferring to 4-year colleges.

Contact. E-mail: admissions@sheridan.edu
Phone: (307) 674-6446 ext. 2002 Toll-free number: (800) 913-9139 ext. 2002 Fax: (307) 674-3373
Zane Garstad, Director of Admissions, Sheridan College, PO Box 1500, Sheridan, WY 82801-1500

Western Wyoming Community College
Rock Springs, Wyoming
www.wwcc.wy.edu **CB code: 4957**

- Public 2-year community college
- Commuter campus in large town

General. Founded in 1959. Regionally accredited. **Enrollment:** 2,139 degree-seeking undergraduates; 757 non-degree-seeking students. **Degrees:** 285 associate awarded. **Location:** 180 miles from Salt Lake City. **Calendar:** Semester, limited summer session. **Full-time faculty:** 70 total; 21% have terminal degrees, 6% minority, 56% women. **Part-time faculty:** 149 total. **Class size:** 82% < 20, 18% 20-39. **Special facilities:** Dinosaur museum, natural history museum, wildlife exhibit.

Student profile. Among degree-seeking undergraduates, 57% enrolled in a transfer program, 22% enrolled in a vocational program, 491 enrolled as first-time, first-year students, 115 transferred in from other institutions.

Part-time:	53%	**25 or older:**	50%
Out-of-state:	20%	**Live on campus:**	43%
Women:	62%		

Transfer out. 66% of students enrolled in the transfer program go on to 4-year colleges. **Colleges most students transferred to 2008:** University of Wyoming, Utah State University, Idaho State University.

Basis for selection. Open admission, but selective for some programs. Admissions to nursing program based on academic performance, pre-entrance exam and prerequisite course completion. **Homeschooled:** If home school is not through an accredited institution, student needs to obtain GED.

High school preparation. Recommended units include English 4, mathematics 3, social studies 2, science 3 (laboratory 1) and foreign language 2.

2008-2009 Annual costs. Tuition/fees: $1,916; $5,036 out-of-state. Per-credit charge: $65 in-state; $195 out-of-state. Room/board: $3,900. Books/supplies: $800.

2008-2009 Financial aid. Need-based: 60% of total undergraduate aid awarded as scholarships/grants, 40% as loans/jobs. Need-based aid available for part-time students. Work-study available for part-time students. **Non-need-based:** Scholarships awarded for academics, art, athletics, music/drama, state residency.

Application procedures. Admission: No deadline. No application fee. Admission notification on a rolling basis. **Financial aid:** Priority date 4/1; no closing date. FAFSA required. Applicants notified on a rolling basis starting 2/15; must reply within 2 week(s) of notification.

Academics. Online tutoring provided through Smart Thinking at no charge to students. **Special study options:** Cooperative education, distance learning, dual enrollment of high school students, ESL, external degree, honors, independent study, internships. Bachelor's degree programs available on campus. License preparation in nursing. **Credit/placement by examination:** AP, CLEP, IB, institutional tests. 40 credit hours maximum toward associate degree. **Support services:** GED preparation and test center, learning center, remedial instruction, study skills assistance, tutoring.

Honors college/program. Competitive program, open to 20 students a year. Students participate in challenging courses and travel to cultural and educational events at the expense of the institution.

Majors. Biology: General, ecology, wildlife. **Business:** Accounting, administrative services, business admin, marketing, office technology. **Communications:** General, journalism. **Computer sciences:** General, computer science, data processing, information systems. **Conservation:** General, environmental studies, water/wetlands/marine, wildlife. **Education:** General, elementary, multi-level teacher, secondary. **Engineering:** General. **Engineering technology:** Instrumentation, mining. **Family/consumer sciences:** General. **Foreign languages:** Spanish. **Health:** Licensed practical nurse, medical assistant, medical secretary, predental, premedicine, prenursing, prepharmacy, preveterinary. **History:** General. **Legal studies:** Prelaw. **Math:** General. **Mechanic/repair:** Automotive, diesel, electronics/electrical, heavy equipment, industrial, industrial electronics. **Parks/recreation:** Exercise sciences. **Physical sciences:** Chemistry, geology. **Production:** Welding. **Protective services:** Law enforcement admin. **Psychology:** General. **Public administration:** Social work. **Social sciences:** General, anthropology, archaeology, criminology, economics, international relations, political science, sociology. **Visual/performing arts:** General, art, ceramics, dance, dramatic, studio arts, theater design.

Most popular majors. Education 6%, engineering/engineering technologies 6%, health sciences 16%, liberal arts 31%, psychology 6%, trade and industry 6%, visual/performing arts 7%.

Computing on campus. 210 workstations in dormitories, library, computer center, student center. Dormitories wired for high-speed internet access and linked to campus network. Commuter students can connect to campus network. Online course registration, online library, helpline, wireless network available.

Student life. Freshman orientation: Mandatory. Preregistration for classes offered. Program for students and parents. **Housing:** Coed dorms, special housing for disabled, apartments available. $150 partly refundable deposit. **Activities:** Bands, campus ministries, choral groups, dance, drama, international student organizations, music ensembles, musical theater, radio station, student government, student newspaper, Phi Theta Kappa, outdoor club, ambassadors, Students Without Borders.

Athletics. NJCAA. **Intercollegiate:** Basketball, cheerleading, soccer, volleyball W, wrestling M. **Intramural:** Basketball, football (non-tackle), softball, table tennis, tennis, volleyball. **Team name:** Mustangs.

Student services. Adult student services, alcohol/substance abuse counseling, career counseling, student employment services, financial aid counseling, on-campus daycare, personal counseling, placement for graduates, veterans' counselor. **Physically disabled:** Services for visually, hearing impaired. **Transfer:** Pre-admission transcript evaluation for new students. Transfer adviser, college fairs on campus for students transferring to 4-year colleges.

Contact. E-mail: admissions@wwcc.wy.edu
Phone: (307) 382-1648 Toll-free number: (800) 226-1181
Fax: (307) 382-1636
Joe Mueller, Director of Admissions, Western Wyoming Community College, Box 428, Rock Springs, WY 82902-0428

WyoTech: Laramie
Laramie, Wyoming
www.wyotech.edu **CB code: 7141**

- For-profit 2-year technical college
- Large town
- Interview required

General. Founded in 1966. Accredited by ACCSCT. **Enrollment:** 1,476 degree-seeking undergraduates. **Degrees:** 546 associate awarded. **Location:** 50 miles from Cheyenne, 70 miles from Ft. Collins, Colorado. **Calendar:** Differs by program. **Full-time faculty:** 61 total. **Part-time faculty:** 1 total.

Basis for selection. Open admission.

2008-2009 Annual costs. Tuition ranges from $23,700 to $32,400 depending on program. Books and tools loaned at no additional charge except for $100 refundable tool deposit. Room rent in institutional housing $250-$400 per month.

Financial aid. All financial aid based on need.

Application procedures. Admission: No deadline. No application fee. Admission notification on a rolling basis. **Financial aid:** No deadline. FAFSA required. Applicants notified on a rolling basis.

Academics. Special study options: Double major. **Credit/placement by examination:** CLEP. **Support services:** Tutoring.

Majors. Mechanic/repair: Auto body, automotive, diesel.

Computing on campus. 2 workstations in library.

Student life. Freshman orientation: Mandatory. **Housing:** Guaranteed on-campus for all undergraduates. Coed dorms, special housing for disabled, apartments available. $100 fully refundable deposit.

Athletics. Intramural: Basketball, bowling, football (non-tackle), softball M, volleyball, weight lifting.

Student services. Career counseling, student employment services, personal counseling, placement for graduates. **Physically disabled:** Services for visually, hearing impaired.

Contact. E-mail: admissions@wyotech.com
Phone: (307) 742-3776 Toll-free number: (800) 521-7158
Fax: (307) 742-4852
Angela Burke, Admissions Manager, WyoTech: Laramie, 4373 North Third Street, Laramie, WY 82072

American Samoa

American Samoa Community College

Pago Pago, American Samoa
www.amsamoa.edu **CB code: 0020**

- Public 2-year community college
- Commuter campus in large town

General. Founded in 1970. Regionally accredited. Only institution of higher education in American Samoa and only land grant institution in the South Pacific. Students seeking 4-year degrees often transfer to colleges in Hawaii or mainland United States. **Enrollment:** 1,826 degree-seeking undergraduates. **Degrees:** 249 associate awarded. **ROTC:** Army. **Location:** 9 miles from downtown. **Calendar:** Semester, limited summer session. **Full-time faculty:** 55 total; 13% have terminal degrees, 100% minority, 44% women. **Part-time faculty:** 33 total; 100% minority, 39% women.

Basis for selection. Open admission. Institutional placement exam may be required for applicants without SAT/ACT scores.

2008-2009 Annual costs. Per-credit charge: $65 in-state; $75 out-of-state. Books/supplies: $800. Personal expenses: $900.

Application procedures. Admission: No deadline. No application fee. Admission notification on a rolling basis. **Financial aid:** No deadline. FAFSA required. Applicants notified on a rolling basis; must reply within 3 week(s) of notification.

Academics. Special study options: Distance learning, independent study, teacher certification program. Bachelor's degree programs available on campus. License preparation in nursing. **Credit/placement by examination:** CLEP, institutional tests. Credit by examination for course credit may be taken only once. "E" grades for credit by examination will not be counted toward overall grade point average and cumulative grade point average. Credits earned by examination are not covered under federal financial aid. **Support services:** GED preparation, learning center, reduced course load, remedial instruction, study skills assistance, tutoring.

Majors. Agriculture: General, business. **Business:** Accounting, business admin, office management. **Conservation:** Management/policy. **Construction:** Maintenance. **Education:** General, multi-level teacher. **Engineering technology:** Architectural drafting, civil. **Family/consumer sciences:** General. **Health:** Health services, nursing assistant. **Legal studies:** Prelaw. **Liberal arts:** Arts/sciences. **Mechanic/repair:** Auto body, automotive, electronics/electrical. **Production:** Welding. **Protective services:** Criminal justice, forensics. **Public administration:** Human services. **Social sciences:** Political science. **Transportation:** Maritime/Merchant Marine. **Visual/performing arts:** Art. **Other:** Architectural drafting, Samoan studies.

Computing on campus. 104 workstations in library, computer center. Helpline, repair service available.

Student life. Freshman orientation: Available. Preregistration for classes offered. **Activities:** Bands, choral groups, dance, drama, music ensembles, musical theater, student government, student newspaper, Phi Theta Kappa, Polynesian club, Christian club, You Are Not Alone Coalition (emotional support for young people).

Athletics. Intramural: Basketball, golf, tennis, volleyball, weight lifting. **Team name:** Chiefs.

Student services. Career counseling, health services, personal counseling, veterans' counselor. **Transfer:** Transfer adviser for students transferring to 4-year colleges.

Contact. E-mail: admissions@amsamoa.edu
Phone: (684) 699-9155 ext. 411 Fax: (684) 699-1083
James Sutherland, Admissions Officer, American Samoa Community College, PO Box 2609, Pago Pago, AS 96799-2609

Guam

Guam Community College

Barrigada, Guam **CB member**
www.guamcc.edu **CB code: 2302**

- Public 2-year community and technical college
- Commuter campus in small city

General. Founded in 1977. Regionally accredited. Multicultural U.S. territory with island setting. **Enrollment:** 651 degree-seeking undergraduates. **Degrees:** 83 associate awarded. **ROTC:** Army. **Location:** 1,500 miles from Manila, Philippines; 3,600 miles from Honolulu. **Calendar:** Semester, limited summer session. **Full-time faculty:** 53 total. **Part-time faculty:** 74 total. **Special facilities:** Rare book collection of more than 400 volumes devoted to history of Guam, Micronesia, and the Pacific.

Transfer out. Colleges most students transferred to 2008: University of Guam.

Basis for selection. Open admission. **Homeschooled:** Official high school transcript required.

High school preparation. Recommended units include English 4, mathematics 3, social studies 3, science 2 and academic electives 9.

2008-2009 Annual costs. Tuition/fees: $3,592; $4,342 out-of-state. Per-credit charge: $110 in-state; $135 out-of-state. Books/supplies: $800. Personal expenses: $2,250.

Financial aid. Additional information: Tuition assistance available for students in nontraditional courses.

Application procedures. Admission: No deadline. No application fee. Application must be submitted on paper. Admission notification on a rolling basis. **Financial aid:** Priority date 5/1; no closing date. FAFSA, institutional form required. Applicants notified on a rolling basis starting 8/28; must reply within 2 week(s) of notification.

Academics. Special study options: Cooperative education, cross-registration, double major, dual enrollment of high school students, independent study, internships. **Credit/placement by examination:** AP, CLEP, institutional tests. 48 credit hours maximum toward associate degree. **Support services:** GED preparation and test center, learning center, remedial instruction, study skills assistance, tutoring.

Majors. Business: Accounting, office management, office technology, sales/distribution, tourism/travel. **Computer sciences:** Computer science. **Education:** Early childhood, teacher assistance. **Family/consumer sciences:** Institutional food production. **Health:** Medical assistant. **Liberal arts:** Arts/sciences. **Mechanic/repair:** Automotive. **Personal/culinary services:** Chef training. **Protective services:** Law enforcement admin. **Visual/performing arts:** Graphic design.

Computing on campus. 79 workstations in library, computer center, student center. Online library, repair service available.

Student life. Freshman orientation: Available. Held 1 week before start of semester. **Activities:** Student government, Habitat for Humanity, Health Occupational Students of America, Phi Theta Kappa, Postsecondary Tourism Association.

Student services. Adult student services, alcohol/substance abuse counseling, career counseling, services for economically disadvantaged, student employment services, financial aid counseling, health services, personal counseling, placement for graduates, veterans' counselor. **Physically disabled:** Services for visually, speech, hearing impaired. **Transfer:** Re-entry adviser for new students.

Contact. E-mail: pclymer@guamcc.edu
Phone: (671) 735-5531 Fax: (671) 734-5238
Patrick Clymer, Coordinator of Admissions and Registration, Guam Community College, PO Box 23069 GMF, Barrigada, GU 96921

Marshall Islands

College of the Marshall Islands

Majuro, Marshall Islands
www.cmi.edu **CB code: 7142**

- Public 2-year community and junior college
- Commuter campus in large town

General. Regionally accredited. Marine science center in Arrak is operated by the College of the Marshall Islands. **Enrollment:** 678 degree-seeking undergraduates; 11 non-degree-seeking students. **Degrees:** 62 associate awarded. **Location:** 2,280 miles from Honolulu. **Calendar:** Semester, limited summer session. **Full-time faculty:** 37 total. **Part-time faculty:** 20 total. **Class size:** 64% < 20, 36% 20-39. **Special facilities:** Nuclear institute, research and extension science station, public policy institute.

Student profile. Among degree-seeking undergraduates, 231 enrolled as first-time, first-year students.

Part-time:	43%	**Asian American:**	100%
Women:	52%		

Basis for selection. Minimum 2.0 high school GPA or 35 score on GED required. Applicants who do not meet minimum requirements may be admitted into Developmental Studies program.

2008-2009 Annual costs. Books/supplies: $600.

Application procedures. Admission: Closing date 7/15. $30 fee. Admission notification on a rolling basis. **Financial aid:** Priority date 7/1; no closing date. FAFSA required. Applicants notified on a rolling basis.

Academics. Special study options: Distance learning, double major, ESL, independent study, internships, teacher certification program. **Credit/placement by examination:** CLEP. **Support services:** Learning center, remedial instruction, study skills assistance, tutoring, writing center.

Majors. Business: Business admin. **Education:** Elementary. **Health:** Nursing (RN). **Liberal arts:** Arts/sciences.

Most popular majors. Business/marketing 23%, education 35%, health sciences 10%, liberal arts 32%.

Computing on campus. Online library, helpline, wireless network available.

Student life. Freshman orientation: Available. Preregistration for classes offered. **Housing:** Single-sex dorms available. **Activities:** Student government, student newspaper.

Student services. Health services, personal counseling. **Transfer:** Transfer center, transfer adviser for students transferring to 4-year colleges.

Contact. E-mail: cmiadmissions@cmi.edu
Phone: (625) 682-3 Fax: (625) 720-3
Rosita Capelle, Director of Admissions and Records, College of the Marshall Islands, Box 1258, Majuro, MH 96960

Micronesia

College of Micronesia-FSM

Kolonia, Micronesia
www.comfsm.fm **CB code: 0115**

- Public 2-year community college
- Commuter campus in small city

General. Founded in 1963. Regionally accredited. **Enrollment:** 2,462 degree-seeking undergraduates. **Degrees:** 215 associate awarded. **Calendar:** Semester, limited summer session. **Full-time faculty:** 110 total.

Student profile. Among degree-seeking undergraduates, 16% enrolled in a vocational program, 854 enrolled as first-time, first-year students.

Part-time:	24%	**Asian American:**	100%
Out-of-state:	7%	**25 or older:**	16%
Women:	52%	**Live on campus:**	20%

Transfer out. Colleges most students transferred to 2008: University of Hawaii at Hilo, University of Guam, Southwestern Adventist University, Chaminade University, Durham Community College.

Basis for selection. Minimum 2.0 high school GPA and institutional test scores required. **Homeschooled:** Transcript of courses and grades, letter of recommendation (nonparent) required. First-time students should pass the College of Micronesia-FSM Entrance Test in order to be eligible for admission into degree or certificate programs.

2008-2009 Annual costs. Tuition/fees: $3,050. Per-credit charge: $95. Room/board: $3,086. Books/supplies: $530.

2007-2008 Financial aid. All financial aid based on need. Work-study available nights and weekends.

Application procedures. Admission: Closing date 6/15. $10 fee. Admission notification on a rolling basis. **Financial aid:** No deadline. FAFSA, institutional form required. Applicants notified on a rolling basis.

Academics. Special study options: Cooperative education, distance learning, independent study, internships, liberal arts/career combination, teacher certification program. Bachelor's degree programs available on campus. **Credit/placement by examination:** CLEP. **Support services:** Learning center, remedial instruction, study skills assistance, tutoring, writing center.

Majors. Agriculture: General. **Biology:** Marine. **Business:** General, accounting. **Computer sciences:** General, computer science. **Education:** Elementary, multi-level teacher, special. **Liberal arts:** Arts/sciences.

Computing on campus. 6 workstations in dormitories, library, computer center, student center. Dormitories linked to campus network. Online library, repair service, wireless network available.

Student life. Freshman orientation: Mandatory. Preregistration for classes offered. Week-long orientation held beginning of fall semester. **Housing:** Single-sex dorms available. $50 nonrefundable deposit, deadline 6/15. On-campus housing for all undergraduates on space available basis. **Activities:** Choral groups, dance, drama, radio station, student government.

Athletics. Intercollegiate: Basketball, softball, track and field, volleyball. **Intramural:** Basketball, softball, volleyball. **Team name:** Sharks.

Student services. Alcohol/substance abuse counseling, career counseling, financial aid counseling, health services, personal counseling. **Transfer:** Pre-admission transcript evaluation for new students. Transfer center, transfer adviser for students transferring to 4-year colleges.

Contact. E-mail: oar@comfsm.fm
Phone: (691) 320-2480 ext. 150 Fax: (691) 320-2479
Joey Oducado, Admissions Coordinator, College of Micronesia-FSM, PO Box 159, Kolonia, FM 96941

Palau

Palau Community College

Koror, Palau
www.palau.edu **CB code: 7329**

- Public 2-year community and technical college
- Commuter campus in small city

General. Founded in 1969. Regionally accredited. **Enrollment:** 579 degree-seeking undergraduates. **Degrees:** 94 associate awarded. **Location:** 800 miles from Guam, 600 miles from Manila. **Calendar:** Semester, limited summer session. **Full-time faculty:** 28 total. **Part-time faculty:** 14 total.

Basis for selection. Open admission, but selective for some programs. To enter the associate of applied science degree program, a student must be a high school graduate with cumulative grade point average of 2.0 or possess a GED certificate; associate of science and associate of arts degree programs require a TOEFL score of 500 or better in addition to the above requirements; exceptions are degree programs in education and liberal arts, which require 2.5 cumulatve GPA.

2008-2009 Annual costs. Books/supplies: $1,000.

Financial aid. Need-based: Work-study available nights, weekends and for part-time students.

Application procedures. Admission: Closing date 8/29 (receipt date). $10 fee. Application must be submitted on paper. Admission notification on a rolling basis beginning on or about 4/30. **Financial aid:** Priority date 4/1; no closing date. FAFSA required. Applicants notified on a rolling basis starting 5/1.

Academics. Special study options: Double major, dual enrollment of high school students, internships. **Credit/placement by examination:** CLEP, institutional tests. **Support services:** Learning center, remedial instruction, study skills assistance, tutoring.

Majors. Agriculture: Plant breeding. **Business:** Administrative services, hospitality admin. **Conservation:** Environmental studies. **Construction:** Electrician. **Education:** Early childhood, elementary, special. **Engineering:** Electrical, mechanics. **Engineering technology:** Construction, electrical. **Liberal arts:** Arts/sciences, library science. **Mechanic/repair:** General, electronics/electrical, heating/ac/refrig. **Protective services:** Police science.

Computing on campus. 60 workstations in library, computer center, student center. Online library available.

Student life. Freshman orientation: Mandatory. Week-long program held prior to first week of classes each term designed to familiarize students with facility, programs, and services; includes administration of placement tests, academic advising, and registration. **Policies:** Possession, consumption, and storage of alcoholic beverages and illegal drugs are prohibited. **Housing:** Coed dorms, single-sex dorms available. **Activities:** Student government, Yapese, Chuukese, Kosrean, Pohnpeians, Palauans, and Marshallese ethnic clubs, Pacific writers club, agriculture science majors club.

Athletics. Intramural: Basketball M, softball, swimming, table tennis, volleyball, weight lifting M, wrestling M.

Student services. Alcohol/substance abuse counseling, career counseling, student employment services, financial aid counseling, health services, on-campus daycare, personal counseling, placement for graduates. **Physically disabled:** Services for visually impaired. **Transfer:** Pre-admission transcript evaluation for new students.

Contact. E-mail: dahliapcc@palaunet.com
Phone: (680) 488-2470 Fax: (680) 488-4468
Dahlia Katosang, Director of Admissions & Financial Aid, Palau Community College, PO Box 9, Koror, PW 96940

Bermuda

Bermuda College

Paget, Bermuda
www.bercol.bm **CB code: 2581**

- Public 2-year community college
- Commuter campus in small city

General. Calendar: Semester.

Annual costs/financial aid. Academic year 2008/2009 tuition is free to all qualified Bermudian students (i.e., those with minimum GPA of 2.0 and passport stamped by immigration office); required fees are charged according to number of credits taken. Non-Bermudians (i.e., those in Bermuda with work permit but not primarily to attend school) pay approximately $3,280 in tuition and fees, while international students (i.e., those granted permission to come to Bermuda solely for the purpose of attending Bermuda College) pay $3,280 plus additional fees. All costs are in Bermudian dollars (BMD). Books/supplies: $400.

Contact. Phone: (441) 236-9000 ext. 4343
Program Manager, PO Box PG 297, Paget, BM

Early Decision and Early Action table

The following table lists early decision and early action policies at 445 colleges, which are listed alphabetically by state or country. Colleges were asked to supply the deadline for student applications and the date by which the college will notify the applicant of a decision to admit, deny admission, or defer the application to the regular admission cycle. If a college offers two early decision cycles, both sets of dates are listed.

Some colleges support both a binding early decision plan and a nonbinding early action plan and report dates for both. Colleges with binding early decision plans were asked to give the number of students who applied for early decision and the number of those applicants admitted to the fall 2008 freshman class.

Institution	Early Applicants: Number applied	Early Applicants: Number admitted	Early Decision: Apply by	Early Decision: Notified by	Early Action: Apply by	Early Action: Notified by
Arizona						
Grand Canyon University						
Prescott College	16	15	12/1	12/15		
Arkansas						
Lyon College					10/31	11/15
Philander Smith College			11/1	11/15		
University of Arkansas					11/15	12/15
California						
American Jewish University			12/31	1/31		
Azusa Pacific University					12/1	1/15
Biola University					12/1	1/15
California Baptist University					12/1	12/20
California Institute of Technology					11/1	12/15
California Lutheran University	942	831			11/15	1/15
California Polytechnic State University: San Luis Obispo	3450	871	10/31	12/15		
California State University: Sacramento					11/30	
Chapman University	1853	1036			11/15	1/10
Claremont McKenna College	316	88	11/15 1/2	12/15 2/15		
Concordia University					12/1	12/15
Harvey Mudd College	103	35	11/15	12/15		
Hope International University			2/1			
Loyola Marymount University					11/1	12/21
Menlo College					12/1	12/15
Mills College					11/15	12/15

Institution	Early Applicants		Early Decision		Early Action	
	Number applied	Number admitted	Apply by	Notified by	Apply by	Notified by
Mount St. Mary's College	472	388			12/1	1/1
Northwestern Polytechnic University						
Notre Dame de Namur University					12/1	12/15
Occidental College	112	50	11/15	12/15		
Pitzer College			11/15	1/1		
Point Loma Nazarene University					12/1	1/15
Pomona College			11/15 12/28	12/15 2/15		
San Francisco Art Institute	25	23			11/30	12/15
Santa Clara University	2507	1698			11/1	12/31
Scripps College	81	39	11/1 1/1	12/15 2/15		
Soka University of America	51	29			10/15	12/1
St. Mary's College of California	1253	1071			11/15	1/12
Stanford University	4551	738			11/1	12/15
The Master's College					11/15	12/22
University of San Diego					11/15	1/31
University of San Francisco					11/15	1/16
University of the Pacific	1347	1014			11/15	1/15
University of the West			3/1			
Westmont College					11/1	12/20
Whittier College					12/1	12/30
Colorado						
CollegeAmerica: Fort Collins						
Colorado College	1717	753	11/15 1/1	12/20 2/10	11/15	1/15
University of Colorado at Boulder					12/15	2/15
University of Denver	1735	1386			11/1	1/15
Connecticut						
Connecticut College	301	195	11/15 1/1	12/15 2/15		
Fairfield University	3695	2151			11/15	1/1
Mitchell College			11/15	12/15		
Sacred Heart University	193	144	12/1	12/15		
Trinity College	417	282	11/15 1/1	12/15 2/15		
United States Coast Guard Academy	469	135			11/1	12/15
University of Connecticut					12/1	2/1
University of Hartford					11/15	12/1
Wesleyan University	650	296	11/15 1/1	12/15 2/15		
Yale University					11/1	12/15
District of Columbia						
American University	397	298	11/15	12/31		
Catholic University of America					11/15	12/15
George Washington University	1159	774	11/10 1/10	12/15 2/1		
Georgetown University					11/1	12/15
Howard University			11/1 2/15	12/24 12/24	11/1	12/15
Trinity Washington University					12/1	1/1

Institution	Early Applicants		Early Decision		Early Action	
	Number applied	Number admitted	Apply by	Notified by	Apply by	Notified by
Florida						
Flagler College	571	413	12/1 1/15	12/15 2/1		
Florida Southern College	155	141	12/1	12/15		
Jacksonville University					12/1	12/15
Palm Beach Atlantic University					12/1	12/15
Rollins College			11/15 1/15	12/15 2/1		
Stetson University	34	31	11/1	11/25		
University of Miami	8674	4156	11/1	12/15	11/1	2/1
University of North Florida	314	314			6/26	12/1
University of Tampa					11/15	12/15
Georgia						
Agnes Scott College					11/15	12/15
Emory University	1904	490	11/1 1/1	12/15 2/15		
Georgia College and State University					11/1	12/1
Georgia Southwestern State University			12/15	1/15		
Mercer University					11/1	11/15
Morehouse College					11/1	12/15
Oglethorpe University					12/5	12/20
Oxford College of Emory University	509	437			11/1	12/15
Spelman College			11/1	12/15	11/15	12/31
University of Georgia					10/15	12/15
Wesleyan College			11/15 1/15	12/15 2/15	2/15	3/15
Idaho						
College of Idaho	215	207			12/15	
Northwest Nazarene University	932	225			12/15	1/15
Illinois						
DePaul University					11/15	1/15
Illinois Institute of Technology					1/7	2/7
Knox College					12/1	12/31
Lake Forest College			12/1	12/20	12/1	1/20
Lakeview College of Nursing						
Moody Bible Institute			12/1	1/15	12/1	1/15
Northwestern University	1395	554	11/1	12/15		
School of the Art Institute of Chicago					1/2	2/15
Trinity College of Nursing and Health Sciences			12/1	12/15		
University of Chicago	4424	1449			11/1	12/15
University of Illinois at Urbana-Champaign					11/1	12/14
Wheaton College	1087	553			11/1	12/31
Indiana						
Butler University	3780	3224			12/1	12/20
DePauw University	1237	1225	11/1	1/1	12/1	2/15
Earlham College	895	792	12/1	12/15	1/1	2/1
Grace College					12/1	12/20
Hanover College	1264	954			12/1	12/20

Institution	Early Applicants: Number applied	Early Applicants: Number admitted	Early Decision: Apply by	Early Decision: Notified by	Early Action: Apply by	Early Action: Notified by
Saint Mary's College	115	104	11/15	12/15		
Taylor University	1168	887			12/1	12/20
University of Evansville	2248	2033			12/1	12/15
University of Notre Dame	4059	1712			11/1	12/20
Valparaiso University	790	765			11/1	12/1
Wabash College	63	47	11/15	12/15	12/15	1/31
Iowa						
Coe College					12/10	1/20
Cornell College			11/1 2/1	12/15 3/1	12/1	2/1
Grinnell College	200	137	11/15 1/2	12/15 2/1		
Wartburg College					12/1	
Kansas						
Sterling College					11/15	12/15
Tabor College			12/31			
Kentucky						
Bellarmine University					11/1	11/15
Centre College	839	668			12/1	1/15
Transylvania University	923	603			12/1	1/15
Louisiana						
Centenary College of Louisiana			12/1	12/15	1/15	1/15
Dillard University					12/1	12/30
Tulane University					11/1	12/15
Xavier University of Louisiana					1/15	2/15
Maine						
Bates College	549	250	11/15 1/1	12/20 2/15		
Bowdoin College	690	207	11/15 1/1	12/31 2/15		
Colby College	455	208	11/15 1/1	12/15 2/1		
College of the Atlantic	39	31	12/1 1/10	12/15 1/25		
Maine Maritime Academy			12/20	1/1		
St. Joseph's College					11/15	12/15
Thomas College	314	241			12/15	12/31
University of Maine					12/15	1/31
University of Maine at Farmington	106	106			11/15	1/15
University of Maine at Machias					12/15	12/31
University of New England					12/1	12/31
Maryland						
Baltimore International College					12/15	2/15
Goucher College	1238	957			12/1	2/15
Hood College	187	104			12/1	12/15
Johns Hopkins University			11/1	12/15		
Loyola College in Maryland					11/15	1/15
Maryland Institute College of Art			11/14	12/15		
McDaniel College	1213	1076			12/1	1/1
Mount St. Mary's University	485	420			12/1	12/15

Institution	Early Applicants		Early Decision		Early Action	
	Number applied	Number admitted	Apply by	Notified by	Apply by	Notified by
Salisbury University	2945	1944			12/1	1/15
St. Mary's College of Maryland	369	163	11/1 12/1	12/1 1/1		
University of Maryland: Baltimore County					11/1	12/15
University of Maryland: College Park					12/1	2/15
University of Maryland: Eastern Shore					11/15	12/1
Washington College	740	675	11/1	12/1	11/15	12/15
Massachusetts						
Amherst College	404	138	11/15	12/15		
Assumption College	1067	942			11/15	12/15
Babson College			11/1	12/10	11/1	1/1
Bay Path College	406	326			12/15	1/2
Bentley University	2571	1350	11/15	12/19	11/15	1/23
Berklee College of Music					11/1	1/31
Boston College	6697	2433			11/1	12/25
Boston University	836	340	11/1	12/15		
Brandeis University	1021	530	11/15 1/1	12/15 2/1	12/15	2/15
Bridgewater State College					11/15	12/15
Clark University	90	68	11/15	12/15		
College of the Holy Cross	522	291	12/15	1/15		
Curry College	110	32	12/1	12/15		
Emerson College	1745	825			11/1	12/15
Emmanuel College	15	12	11/1	12/1		
Framingham State College	372	211			11/15	12/15
Gordon College	516	484	11/15	12/15	12/1	1/1
Hampshire College	616	380	11/15	12/15	12/1	2/15
Lesley University					12/1	12/31
Massachusetts College of Art and Design	81	43			12/1	1/5
Massachusetts College of Liberal Arts	278	211			12/1	12/15
Massachusetts College of Pharmacy and Health Sciences	593	562			11/15	12/15
Massachusetts Institute of Technology	3919	522			11/1	12/20
Massachusetts Maritime Academy					11/1	12/15
Merrimack College	991	874			11/15	12/15
Montserrat College of Art	27	25			1/17	1/17
Mount Holyoke College	263	136	11/15 1/1	1/1 2/1		
Newbury College					12/1	1/1
Northeastern University					11/1	12/31
Simmons College	1666	934			12/1	1/20
Smith College	256	163	11/15 1/2	12/15 2/2		
Springfield College			12/1	2/1		
Stonehill College	1572	1099	11/1	12/15	11/1	1/15
Suffolk University	1582	916			11/20	12/22
Tufts University			11/1 1/1	12/15 2/1		
University of Massachusetts Amherst	6222	4992			11/1	12/15

Institution	Early Applicants: Number applied	Early Applicants: Number admitted	Early Decision: Apply by	Early Decision: Notified by	Early Action: Apply by	Early Action: Notified by
University of Massachusetts Dartmouth	66	40	11/15	12/15		
Wellesley College	208	107	11/1	12/15		
Wheaton College	195	167	11/15 1/15	12/15 2/15		
Wheelock College	192	180			12/1	12/20
Williams College	605	226	11/10	12/15		
Worcester Polytechnic Institute	1801	1509			11/15	12/15
Michigan						
Albion College					12/1	11/1
Cleary University						
Hillsdale College			11/15	12/1	1/1	1/20
Kalamazoo College			11/15	12/1	12/1	12/20
Michigan State University					10/6	11/6
Olivet College					12/1	1/15
University of Michigan					11/1	12/24
Minnesota						
Carleton College	375	207	11/15 1/15	12/15 2/15		
College of St. Benedict	1429	1147			11/15	12/15
Gustavus Adolphus College	708	626			11/1	11/20
Hamline University	1075	947			12/1	12/20
Macalester College	252	118	11/15 1/2	12/15 2/7		
Oak Hills Christian College						
St. John's University	1129	899			11/15	12/15
St. Olaf College	151	140	11/15 1/15	12/15 2/15		
Mississippi						
Millsaps College	808	657			1/8	
Mississippi College			12/1	12/15		
Missouri						
Cox College			11/1	12/1		
Washington University in St. Louis			11/15	12/15		
Nebraska						
Nebraska Wesleyan University	513	448			11/15	12/15
New Hampshire						
Colby-Sawyer College					12/1	
Daniel Webster College	18	16	11/15			
Dartmouth College	1428	399	11/1	12/15		
Magdalen College			1/1	1/15		
Rivier College					11/15	12/1
Southern New Hampshire University					11/15	12/15
St. Anselm College	79	60	11/15	12/1		
University of New Hampshire	5765	2831			11/15	1/15
New Jersey						
Bloomfield College	62	48			1/7	1/21
Caldwell College					1/1	1/15
Centenary College					12/15	

Institution	Early Applicants		Early Decision		Early Action	
	Number applied	Number admitted	Apply by	Notified by	Apply by	Notified by
Drew University	36	31	12/1 1/15	1/19 2/15		
Georgian Court University					11/15	12/30
Monmouth University	2660	2187			12/1	1/15
Ramapo College of New Jersey					11/15	12/15
Rider University	1614	655	11/15	12/15	11/15	12/15
Stevens Institute of Technology	399	278	11/15 1/15	12/15 2/15		
The College of New Jersey	450	258	11/15	12/15		
New York						
Adelphi University	1431	1203			12/1	12/31
Albany College of Pharmacy and Health Sciences	191	137	11/1	12/15		
Alfred University			12/1	12/15		
Bard College	782	511			11/1	1/1
Barnard College	392	187	11/15	12/15		
City University of New York: Baruch College			12/13	1/7		
Clarkson University	113	106	12/1	1/1		
Colgate University	741	378	11/15 1/15	12/15		
College of Mount St. Vincent	181	144			11/1	12/1
College of New Rochelle			11/1	12/15		
College of Saint Rose					12/1	12/15
Columbia University	2509	596	11/1	12/15		
Concordia College					11/15	12/15
Cooper Union for the Advancement of Science and Art	449	72	12/1 12/1	12/23 2/1		
Cornell University	3094	1145	11/1			
Elmira College	50	45	11/15 1/15	12/15 1/31		
Eugene Lang College The New School for Liberal Arts			11/15	12/15		
Fashion Institute of Technology					11/15	1/31
Five Towns College	12	8	12/1	1/15		
Fordham University					12/1	12/25
Hamilton College	612	223	11/15 1/1	12/15 2/15		
Hartwick College	115	95	11/15 1/15	12/10 1/24		
Hobart and William Smith Colleges			11/15 1/1	12/15 2/1		
Hofstra University	8349	3751			12/15	1/15
Iona College	1712	1390			12/1	12/21
Ithaca College			11/1	12/15		
Jewish Theological Seminary of America	26	18	11/15 1/15	12/15 2/15		
King's College					11/15	1/15
Laboratory Institute of Merchandising					11/15	12/15
Le Moyne College	56	40	12/1	12/15		
Manhattan College	56	41	11/15	12/15		
Manhattanville College			12/1	12/31		
Marist College	3743	1870	11/15	12/15	12/1	1/30
Mercy College					12/1	1/2

Institution	Early Applicants		Early Decision		Early Action	
	Number applied	Number admitted	Apply by	Notified by	Apply by	Notified by
Molloy College					12/1	1/15
Nazareth College of Rochester	765	686	11/15	12/15	12/15	1/15
New York University	2994	996	11/1	12/15		
Niagara University					10/1	12/1
North Country Community College			11/15	12/15		
Pace University	2453	1356			11/30	1/1
Pratt Institute					11/1	12/22
Rensselaer Polytechnic Institute	1288	641	11/1 12/15	12/5 1/16		
Rochester Institute of Technology	1461	970	12/1	1/15		
Russell Sage College			12/1	12/15	12/8	12/15
Sage College of Albany					12/1	12/15
Sarah Lawrence College	137	85	11/15 1/1	12/15 2/15		
School of Visual Arts					12/1	1/15
Siena College	4379	2807	12/1	12/15	12/1	1/1
Skidmore College	497	295	11/15 1/15	12/15 2/15		
St. John Fisher College	155	97	12/1	12/15		
St. Joseph's College of Nursing			11/15	12/15		
St. Lawrence University	245	200	11/15 1/15	12/15 2/10		
St. Thomas Aquinas College			12/15	3/1		
State University of New York College at Buffalo	52	33	11/15	12/15		
State University of New York College at Cortland			11/15	12/15		
State University of New York College at Fredonia	56	41	11/1	12/1		
State University of New York College at Geneseo	339	132	11/15	12/15		
State University of New York College at Old Westbury			11/1	12/15		
State University of New York College at Oneonta	2866	1418			11/15	12/15
State University of New York College at Plattsburgh	89	46	11/15	12/15		
State University of New York College of Environmental Science and Forestry	328	323			11/15	1/2
State University of New York Institute of Technology at Utica/Rome			11/1	12/1		
State University of New York at Albany					11/15	1/1
State University of New York at Buffalo	555	391	11/1	12/15		
State University of New York at New Paltz					11/15	12/15
State University of New York at Oswego	150	80	11/15	12/15		
State University of New York at Purchase	34	10	11/1	12/5		
State University of New York at Stony Brook	4066	1783			11/15	1/1
Syracuse University	826	639	11/15	12/15		
Union College	327	252	11/15 1/15	12/15 2/1		
University of Rochester	583	285	11/1	12/15		

Institution	Early Applicants: Number applied	Early Applicants: Number admitted	Early Decision: Apply by	Early Decision: Notified by	Early Action: Apply by	Early Action: Notified by
Vassar College	582	223	11/15 1/1	12/15 2/1		
Wagner College	90	57	12/1 1/1	12/15		
Webb Institute	17	6	10/15	12/15		
Wells College	550	410	12/15	1/15	12/15	2/1
North Carolina						
Carolinas College of Health Sciences			12/1	1/15		
Davidson College	549	222	11/15 1/2	12/15 2/1		
Duke University	1174	469	11/1	12/15		
Elon University	5426	2636	11/1	12/1	11/10	12/20
Greensboro College					12/15	1/15
Guilford College					1/15	2/15
High Point University			11/3	11/25	11/10	12/12
Meredith College	143	77	10/15	11/1		
North Carolina State University	10612	5738			11/1	1/31
Piedmont Baptist College			11/1	12/1	11/1	12/1
University of North Carolina at Asheville					11/15	12/15
University of North Carolina at Chapel Hill					11/1	1/15
University of North Carolina at Charlotte					10/15	12/1
University of North Carolina at Greensboro					1/15	
University of North Carolina at Wilmington					11/1	1/20
Wake Forest University	671	340	11/15	12/15	11/15	1/15
Warren Wilson College			11/15	12/1		
Western Carolina University	3374	2274	11/15	12/15	11/15	12/15
Ohio						
Case Western Reserve University	1709	1513			11/1	12/15
Cleveland State University					5/1	
College of Wooster	87	76	12/1 1/15	12/15 2/1		
Denison University	153	120	12/1	1/1		
Kenyon College	340	187	11/15 1/15	12/15 2/1		
Miami University: Oxford Campus	636	481	11/1	12/15	12/1	2/1
Oberlin College	341	225	11/15 1/2	12/20 2/1		
Ohio Wesleyan University	61	19	12/1	12/15	12/15	1/15
University of Akron	3130	1467			11/1	12/15
Ursuline College	53	18			11/15	2/15
Wittenberg University	1979	1695	11/15	12/15	12/1	1/1
Oregon						
Eastern Oregon University	144	112			12/1	1/15
George Fox University	292	287			12/1	12/15
Lewis & Clark College	1109	877			11/1	1/15
Linfield College	422	409			11/15	1/15
Oregon State University					11/1	12/15
Reed College	214	110	11/15 1/2	12/15 2/1		

Institution	Early Applicants		Early Decision		Early Action	
	Number applied	Number admitted	Apply by	Notified by	Apply by	Notified by
University of Oregon					11/1	12/15
Willamette University	540	481			12/1	1/15
Pennsylvania						
Allegheny College	86	61	11/15	12/15		
Bloomsburg University of Pennsylvania	151	151	11/15	12/15		5/1
Bryn Mawr College	130	69	11/15 1/1	12/15 2/1		
Bucknell University	567	370	11/15 1/15	12/15 2/15		
Carlow University	187	107			9/30	10/30
Carnegie Mellon University	855	249	11/1 12/1	12/15 1/15		
Chestnut Hill College			12/1	12/15		
Dickinson College	1517	1071	11/15 1/15	12/15 2/15	12/1	2/1
Duquesne University	1646	1064	11/1	12/15	12/1	1/15
Franklin & Marshall College	582	410	11/15 1/15	12/15 2/15		
Gettysburg College	472	305	11/15 1/15	12/15 2/15		
Grove City College	592	311	11/15	12/15		
Haverford College	215	109	11/15	12/15		
Juniata College	874	753	12/1	12/31	1/1	1/30
La Salle University	2116	1705			11/15	12/15
Lafayette College	436	245	2/15			
Lehigh University	939	543	11/15 1/15	12/15 2/15		
Lincoln Technical Institute: Allentown						
Moravian College	176	136	2/1	12/15		
Muhlenberg College	428	312	2/1	12/1		
Saint Joseph's University	3840	3642			11/15	12/25
Susquehanna University	173	143	11/15	12/1		
Swarthmore College	480	162	11/15 1/2	12/15 2/15		
University of Pennsylvania	3912	1147	11/1	12/15		
University of Scranton	3424	2741			11/15	12/15
Ursinus College	4695	2917	1/15	2/15	12/1	
Villanova University	5645	2061			11/1	12/20
Washington & Jefferson College	6609	2549	12/1	12/15	2/15	2/28
Westminster College					11/15	12/1
Puerto Rico						
University of Puerto Rico: Aguadilla					1/15	1/30
University of Puerto Rico: Mayaguez					1/30	2/15
Rhode Island						
Brown University	2453	555	11/1	12/15		
Bryant University	239	140	11/15 1/2	12/15 2/2		
Providence College					11/1	1/1
Rhode Island School of Design					12/15	1/31
Roger Williams University	2224	1799			11/1	12/15
Salve Regina University	1270	760			11/1	12/25

Institution	Early Applicants: Number applied	Early Applicants: Number admitted	Early Decision: Apply by	Early Decision: Notified by	Early Action: Apply by	Early Action: Notified by
University of Rhode Island	10237	5676			12/1	1/31
South Carolina						
College of Charleston					11/1	12/15
Erskine College					11/1	11/15
Furman University	639	424	11/15	12/15		
Medical University of South Carolina						
Presbyterian College	56	44	11/1	12/1	11/15	12/15
The Citadel			10/26			
University of South Carolina					10/1	12/20
Wofford College	587	376	11/15	12/1		
Tennessee						
Fisk University					12/1	12/31
Maryville College	408	356	11/15	12/1	10/1	10/15
Rhodes College	140	67	11/1 1/1	12/1 2/1		
University of the South	370	200	11/15 1/2	12/17 2/8		
Vanderbilt University	2936	1062	11/1 1/3	12/15 2/15		
Texas						
Austin Graduate School of Theology						
Baylor University					11/1	1/15
Rice University	674	229	11/1	12/15		
Southern Methodist University					11/1	12/31
Southwestern University	64	56	11/1	12/15		
Tarleton State University	431	253			11/30	
Texas Christian University					11/1	1/1
Trinity University			11/1	12/15	11/1	12/15
University of Dallas	365	344			12/1	1/15
Vermont						
Bennington College	75	45	11/15 1/5	12/15 2/15		
Champlain College	331	248	11/15 1/15	12/15 2/15		
Lyndon State College					11/1	12/15
Marlboro College			12/1	12/15	2/1	2/15
Middlebury College	927	252	11/1 12/15	12/15 2/15		
Norwich University			11/15	12/31		
St. Michael's College	1646	1214			11/1	1/1
Sterling College	34	29			12/15	1/15
University of Vermont	5331	3780			11/1	12/15
Virginia						
Christendom College	152	134			12/1	12/15
Christopher Newport University					12/1	1/1
College of William and Mary	900	470	11/1	12/1		
Emory & Henry College					12/1	1/1
George Mason University	2294	1763			11/1	12/19
Hampden-Sydney College	1353	911	11/15	12/15	1/15	2/15
Hampton University					12/1	12/15

Institution	Early Applicants		Early Decision		Early Action	
	Number applied	Number admitted	Apply by	Notified by	Apply by	Notified by
Hollins University	50	45	12/1	12/15		
James Madison University	6102	3917			11/1	1/15
Longwood University	1587	1169			12/1	1/1
Lynchburg College	205	107	11/15	12/15		
Mary Baldwin College			11/15	12/1		
Old Dominion University	5282	3201			12/1	1/15
Patrick Henry College					11/1	
Radford University	4653	2196			12/15	1/9
Randolph College					12/1	12/15
Randolph-Macon College	2446	1378			11/15	1/1
Roanoke College	123	41	12/1	12/15		
Stratford University: Falls Church						
Sweet Briar College	63	62	12/1	12/15		
University of Richmond	364	219	11/15 1/15	12/15 2/15		
University of Virginia's College at Wise					12/1	12/15
Virginia Military Institute	283	172	11/15	12/15		
Virginia Polytechnic Institute and State University			11/1	12/15		
Washington and Lee University	428	190	11/15 1/3	12/22 2/1		
Washington						
Gonzaga University					11/15	1/15
Seattle Pacific University	1052	990			11/15	1/5
Seattle University					11/15	12/22
University of Puget Sound	132	119	11/15 1/2	12/15 2/15		
Walla Walla University						
Whitman College	145	108	11/15 1/1	12/21 1/21		
Whitworth University					12/1	12/20
West Virginia						
Shepherd University					11/15	12/15
Wisconsin						
Beloit College	611	524			12/1	1/1
Lawrence University	732	607	11/15	12/1	12/1	1/15
Egypt						
American University in Cairo	1505	706			3/15	3/31
Lebanon						
American University of Beirut	288	288			11/30	1/15
Mexico						
Universidad de Monterrey						
Monaco						
International University of Monaco			1/2			
Switzerland						
Franklin College: Switzerland					12/1	1/15

Wait list table

Students who are wait listed have met a college's admission requirements, but will only be offered a place in the freshman class if space becomes available. The table that follows shows wait list outcomes for students who applied for admission to the freshman class of 2008-2009 at 308 colleges, which are listed alphabetically by state.

Institution	Total applied	Number placed on wait list	Number accepting place on wait list	Number on wait list admitted
Alabama				
Talladega College		50	50	15
Tuskegee University	2827	0		
Arkansas				
Hendrix College	1420	35	35	25
California				
Azusa Pacific University	4441	0		
California Institute of Technology	3957	556	339	12
California Lutheran University	2803	43	33	8
Chapman University	5356	471	134	46
Claremont McKenna College	3670	511	222	0
Deep Springs College	130	3	3	0
Harvey Mudd College	2190	448	197	0
Loyola Marymount University	9086	943	918	165
Occidental College	5790	885	334	17
Pepperdine University	6910	742	410	0
Point Loma Nazarene University	1810	323	282	154
San Francisco Conservatory of Music	272	52	41	27
Santa Clara University	10124	2138	870	56
Scripps College	1931	489	176	0
Soka University of America	355	13	13	5
Southern California Institute of Architecture	124	0		
St. Mary's College of California	3638	145	70	28
University of San Diego	10584	552	351	1
Westmont College	2078	436	173	22
Colorado				
Colorado College	5338	925	321	1
University of Colorado at Boulder	23004	1014	292	6
University of Denver	7144	1158	478	283
Connecticut				
Connecticut College	4716	1068	360	61
Eastern Connecticut State University	3383	297	188	61
Fairfield University	8732	2301	946	120
Quinnipiac University	14994	1787	900	210
Trinity College	5136	1289	460	4
University of Connecticut	21058	3304	1839	14
Wesleyan University	8250	1500	700	21

Institution	Total applied	Number placed on wait list	Number accepting place on wait list	Number on wait list admitted
District of Columbia				
American University	15413	1138	201	0
George Washington University	19430	2427	653	136
Georgetown University	18696	2294	1307	139
Florida				
Flagler College	2358	484	131	22
Florida State University	25485	1907	667	277
New College of Florida	1221	112	51	6
Rollins College	3485	570	330	49
University of Central Florida	28659	1172	436	26
University of Tampa	8408	723	510	109
Georgia				
Agnes Scott College	1593	30	25	18
Emory University	17446	1500	800	147
Georgia Institute of Technology	10258	184	98	92
University of Georgia	17207	1423	813	558
Illinois				
Bradley University	5932	74	42	21
Illinois State University	13549	363	173	17
Illinois Wesleyan University	3136	350	79	23
Knox College	2750	228	85	7
Northwestern University	25013	3135	1307	155
Robert Morris College: Chicago	3116	10	10	0
Trinity College of Nursing and Health Sciences		24	18	18
University of Chicago	12376	2445	1453	26
Wheaton College	2083	402	164	150
Indiana				
Butler University	5923	379	332	285
DePauw University	4064	76	73	73
Earlham College	1825	21	13	9
Wabash College	1394	59	53	5
Iowa				
Cornell College	2659	140	86	22
Grinnell College	3217	951	402	5
Mercy College of Health Sciences	597	0		
St. Luke's College	140	12	10	4
University of Iowa	15582	143	143	11
Wartburg College	2209	21	9	6
Kansas				
Benedictine College	2192	20	20	0
Kentucky				
Asbury College	1563	0		
Centre College	2176	139	38	0
Louisiana				
Tulane University	34125	2320	207	69
Xavier University of Louisiana	3516	0		

Institution	Total applied	Number placed on wait list	Number accepting place on wait list	Number on wait list admitted
Maine				
Bates College	5098	947	756	0
Colby College	4835	891	431	16
Husson University	1203	43	22	10
Kennebec Valley Community College	1858	85	85	22
Maryland				
Goucher College	4077	171	82	57
Hood College	1570	17	1	1
Johns Hopkins University	16011	4206	3476	46
Loyola College in Maryland	7623	1242	614	11
McDaniel College	2651	38	15	3
St. Mary's College of Maryland	2723	423	214	31
United States Naval Academy	10960			33
University of Maryland: Baltimore County	5820	171	171	74
Washington College	3413	567	245	147
Massachusetts				
Amherst College	7745	1832	806	37
Assumption College	3889	353	146	33
Babson College	4318	519	262	10
Boston College	30845	5000	2300	317
Boston University	38010	2991	1467	557
Brandeis University	7724	1469	404	75
Clark University	5299	240	81	15
College of the Holy Cross	7227	1236	382	33
Curry College	3944	96	72	35
Emerson College	6944	1449	560	228
Endicott College	4032	374	174	4
Franklin W. Olin College of Engineering	969	25	12	7
Hampshire College	3289	293	94	26
Lasell College	3222	24	11	9
Lesley University	2523	32	32	32
Massachusetts College of Pharmacy and Health Sciences	2768	92	92	51
Massachusetts Institute of Technology	13396	739	629	35
Mount Holyoke College	3127	554	324	14
New England Conservatory of Music	1080	104	69	18
Quinsigamond Community College	3881	504	504	50
Simmons College	3222	116	33	33
Smith College	3771	581	353	127
Stonehill College	6838	1420	587	241
Suffolk University	9171	308	134	17
University of Massachusetts Amherst	28931	3230	113	91
University of Massachusetts Lowell	5549	142	85	42
Wellesley College	4001	816	421	11
Westfield State College	5188	70	70	34
Wheaton College	3832	740	237	65
Williams College	7552	1066	438	42
Worcester Polytechnic Institute	5706	724	237	40
Michigan				
Hope College	2846	256	116	26

Institution	Total applied	Number placed on wait list	Number accepting place on wait list	Number on wait list admitted
Kalamazoo College	2059	234	60	37
Minnesota				
Bethel University	1945	65	65	5
Carleton College	4956	1531	363	8
College of St. Benedict	1737	108	11	10
College of St. Scholastica	1899	32	32	30
Dakota County Technical College	3304	275	275	180
Macalester College	5041	433	182	11
St. John's University	1557	7	3	0
St. Olaf College	3964	610	114	3
Missouri				
Bolivar Technical College		15	9	0
College of the Ozarks	2698	420	420	15
Research College of Nursing	227	5	5	5
Nebraska				
Creighton University	4740	110	110	44
New Hampshire				
Dartmouth College	16538			41
Rivier College	825	103	103	10
St. Anselm College	3835	696	321	248
New Jersey				
Princeton University	21370	1526	1061	148
Ramapo College of New Jersey	5556	487	273	230
Richard Stockton College of New Jersey	4511	444	398	96
Rider University	6829	56	27	27
Rowan University	7146	300	120	60
Seton Hall University	9775	1065	993	845
The College of New Jersey	9692	912	405	76
New Mexico				
St. John's College	323	13	13	6
New York				
Albany College of Pharmacy and Health Sciences	1186	138	83	51
Bard College	5459	542	250	0
Barnard College	4274	885	633	11
Clarkson University	3204	111	21	14
Cochran School of Nursing-St. John's Riverside Hospital		6	6	2
Colgate University	9416	1152	515	11
College of Mount St. Vincent	2224	115	104	2
Cooper Union for the Advancement of Science and Art	3055	65	59	8
Cornell University	33073	3444	2163	44
Elmira College	2090	66	63	5
Finger Lakes Community College	3603	41	41	6
Fordham University	23892	3701	1268	22
Hamilton College	5073	762	275	51
Hartwick College	2532	199	105	24
Helene Fuld College of Nursing	171	20	20	20
Hofstra University	20071	3808	934	831

Institution	Total applied	Number placed on wait list	Number accepting place on wait list	Number on wait list admitted
Iona College	6009	345	114	18
Juilliard School	2138	39	30	14
Laboratory Institute of Merchandising	1069	34	34	9
Le Moyne College	4212	164	73	60
Manhattan College	5511	404	128	8
Manhattan School of Music	963	1	0	
Marist College	9198	1696	465	39
Marymount Manhattan College	3065	28	28	16
Mohawk Valley Community College	3699	15	4	3
Monroe College	2612	125	63	38
Nazareth College of Rochester	2181	83	28	23
New York University	37245	1864	1037	543
Phillips Beth Israel School of Nursing	62	30	25	5
Pratt Institute	5010	221	150	20
Rensselaer Polytechnic Institute	11249	3497	1301	371
Rochester Institute of Technology	12725	376	344	344
Sarah Lawrence College	2785	600	200	60
Siena College	6490	1040	359	2
Skidmore College	7316	1786	1105	87
St. John Fisher College	3231	242	43	1
St. John's University	40970	2137	1933	502
St. Lawrence University	5419	658	186	17
State University of New York College at Oneonta	12571	255	224	224
State University of New York College at Plattsburgh	6909	140	47	8
State University of New York College at Potsdam	4326	80	80	9
State University of New York College of Environmental Science and Forestry	1568	83	74	10
State University of New York College of Technology at Canton	2361	40	38	25
State University of New York College of Technology at Delhi	5070	137	58	29
State University of New York Maritime College	1141	50	25	15
State University of New York at Binghamton	26666	840	730	87
State University of New York at Buffalo	19784	840	374	128
State University of New York at Stony Brook	25590	1244	529	8
Syracuse University	22079	3351	1550	504
Union College	5271	999	298	15
University of Rochester	11633	1096	390	0
Wagner College	3012	168	120	63
North Carolina				
Elon University	9434	2754	1215	90
University of North Carolina School of the Arts	695	10	9	3
University of North Carolina at Chapel Hill	21543	2328	1420	453
University of North Carolina at Wilmington	9311	232	101	0
Western Carolina University	7331	0		
Ohio				
Case Western Reserve University	7351	761	254	77
Denison University	5305	611	511	1

Tables and Indexes

Institution	Total applied	Number placed on wait list	Number accepting place on wait list	Number on wait list admitted
Kenyon College	4509	849	321	9
MedCentral College of Nursing	181	0		
Mercy College of Northwest Ohio	211	61	61	52
Miami University: Oxford Campus	15009	519	218	0
Oberlin College	7006	934	354	8
Ohio Wesleyan University	4238	33	12	6
University of Dayton	11610	811	72	21
Xavier University	6151	125	43	26
Oklahoma				
University of Oklahoma	9764	1704	1704	893
University of Tulsa	4713	293	293	158
Oregon				
Lewis & Clark College	5551	738	238	7
Linfield College	2066	0		
Reed College	3485	656	650	25
Willamette University	3501	133	61	20
Pennsylvania				
Allegheny College	4243	362	362	16
Bryn Mawr College	2150	246	174	7
Bucknell University	8024	2521	875	9
Carnegie Mellon University	13527	3139	320	0
Curtis Institute of Music	243	2	1	1
Dickinson College	5282	422	422	19
East Stroudsburg University of Pennsylvania	6137	65	26	14
Elizabethtown College	3315	103	30	13
Franklin & Marshall College	5632	1951	670	81
Grove City College	1847	642	185	42
Haverford College	3311	756	333	3
Hussian School of Art	116	2	2	2
Lafayette College	6357	1238	459	46
Laurel Business Institute	332	3	3	1
Lehigh University	12941	3154	1388	7
Manor College	514	14	8	5
Mansfield University of Pennsylvania	4076	13	13	10
Messiah College	2844	25	25	11
Millersville University of Pennsylvania	6689	1391	737	118
Misericordia University	1430	50	50	10
Moravian College	2098	114	49	27
Muhlenberg College	4846	1609	541	21
Penn State University Park	39089	1477	1434	647
Pennsylvania College of Technology	3002	199	102	54
Saint Joseph's University	7012	416	104	0
Slippery Rock University of Pennsylvania	5779	1908	630	340
St. Francis University	1533	18	6	6
St. Vincent College	1843	213	61	42
Susquehanna University	2777	221	195	21
Swarthmore College	6121			34
Temple University	18670	1245	500	500
University of Pennsylvania	22935	2907	2381	166
University of Pittsburgh	20685	684	300	43
University of Pittsburgh at Bradford	1032	12	12	12

Institution	Total applied	Number placed on wait list	Number accepting place on wait list	Number on wait list admitted
University of Scranton	7890	1661	582	54
University of the Sciences in Philadelphia	3836	650	600	75
Ursinus College	6192	679	260	8
Villanova University	15102	5425	2391	64
Washington & Jefferson College	6826	139	30	18
West Chester University of Pennsylvania	13353	850	319	35
Widener University	4690	64	64	28
Puerto Rico				
Conservatory of Music of Puerto Rico	104	3	3	3
Rhode Island				
Brown University	20633	1400	450	68
Bryant University	6253	1420	720	162
Providence College	8844	2531	932	176
Salve Regina University	5937	614	230	35
South Carolina				
Clemson University	15542	164	86	20
College of Charleston	9964	463	203	126
Furman University	4414	525	181	0
Presbyterian College	1403	15	11	3
Wofford College	2278	64	11	3
South Dakota				
Mitchell Technical Institute		64	64	15
Tennessee				
University of the South	2488	282	107	38
Vanderbilt University	16944	3109	1390	202
Texas				
Austin College	1525	31	19	16
Baylor University	25501	226	122	25
Rice University	9813	1607	808	8
Southern Methodist University	8270	806	415	80
Southwestern University	1923	23	4	0
St. Edward's University	2766	365	90	56
Texas A&M University	20887	981	357	260
Texas Christian University	12212	802	304	274
Vermont				
Bennington College	1057	32	25	21
Middlebury College	7823	1812	831	49
St. Michael's College	3618	438	186	14
University of Vermont	21062	3074	1214	6
Virginia				
Christendom College	271	2	2	0
Christopher Newport University	7174	330	160	86
College of William and Mary	11636	2921	1368	159
George Mason University	12943	1065	597	210
Hollins University	658	38	20	1
James Madison University	19245	1547	765	135
Jefferson College of Health Sciences	609	100	90	5
Radford University	7819	199	199	81

Institution	Total applied	Number placed on wait list	Number accepting place on wait list	Number on wait list admitted
Randolph-Macon College	3502	322	77	45
Roanoke College	3579	360	109	26
University of Mary Washington	4600	599	219	198
University of Richmond	7970	2523	810	140
University of Virginia	18363	3238	2159	60
Virginia Military Institute	1600	248	88	19
Virginia Polytechnic Institute and State University	20615	1716	1286	0
Washington and Lee University	6386	1227	441	68
Washington				
Gonzaga University	5026	271	58	25
Seattle Pacific University	2049	249	249	140
University of Puget Sound	5580	386	136	16
University of Washington	20224	1721	821	53
Washington State University	11983	1073	515	39
Western Washington University	9518	502	388	285
Whitworth University	5472	604	604	40
Wisconsin				
Beloit College	2248	187	80	33
Edgewood College	1244	30	30	30
Lawrence University	2618	236	54	34
Marquette University	15206	3012	1094	699
Northeast Wisconsin Technical College		1192	1134	374
University of Wisconsin-Eau Claire	8060	13	10	10
University of Wisconsin-Stevens Point	5423	475	475	6
United Kingdom				
Richmond, The American International University in London	1400	12	12	12

Indexes

College type

Liberal arts colleges

Four-year

Alabama
Andrew Jackson University
Athens State University
Birmingham-Southern College
Concordia College
Faulkner University
Huntingdon College
Judson College
Miles College
Oakwood University
Spring Hill College
Stillman College
Talladega College
Tuskegee University
University of Mobile
University of Montevallo

Alaska
Alaska Pacific University
University of Alaska
Southeast

Arizona
Art Institute of Tucson
College of the Humanities and Sciences
Prescott College
Southwestern College

Arkansas
Arkansas Baptist College
Arkansas Tech University
Ecclesia College
Henderson State University
Hendrix College
John Brown University
Lyon College
Ouachita Baptist University
Philander Smith College
University of the Ozarks
Williams Baptist College

California
American Jewish University
Antioch Southern California
Antioch University Los Angeles
Antioch University Santa Barbara
Bethany University
California Baptist University
California Institute of Integral Studies
California Lutheran University
California State University
Bakersfield
Chico
Monterey Bay
San Bernardino
Stanislaus
Chapman University
Claremont McKenna College
Concordia University
Dominican University of California
Fresno Pacific University
Harvey Mudd College
Hope International University
Humboldt State University
Humphreys College
International Academy of Design and Technology
Sacramento
The Master's College
Menlo College
Mills College
Monterey Institute of International Studies
Mount St. Mary's College
NewSchool of Architecture & Design
Notre Dame de Namur University
Occidental College
Pacific Union College
Patten University
Pepperdine University
Pitzer College
Point Loma Nazarene University
Pomona College
St. Mary's College of California
San Diego Christian College
San Jose State University
Scripps College
Simpson University
Soka University of America
Sonoma State University
Thomas Aquinas College
University of La Verne
University of Redlands
University of the West
Vanguard University of Southern California
Westmont College
Whittier College
William Jessup University

Colorado
Adams State College
Colorado Christian University
Colorado College
Fort Lewis College
Mesa State College
Metropolitan State College of Denver
Naropa University
Regis University
Teikyo Loretto Heights University
Western State College of Colorado

Connecticut
Albertus Magnus College
Charter Oak State College
Connecticut College
Eastern Connecticut State University
Holy Apostles College and Seminary
Mitchell College
Sacred Heart University
St. Joseph College
Trinity College
Wesleyan University

Delaware
Wesley College
Wilmington University

District of Columbia
Gallaudet University
Trinity Washington University
University of the District of Columbia

Florida
Ave Maria University
Beacon College
Bethune-Cookman University
Clearwater Christian College
Eckerd College
Edison State College
Edward Waters College
Everglades University: Orlando
Flagler College
Florida College
Florida Memorial University
Florida Southern College
Jacksonville University
New College of Florida
Palm Beach Atlantic University
Rollins College
St. John Vianney College Seminary
Southeastern University
University of Tampa
Warner University

Georgia
Agnes Scott College
Albany State University
Atlanta Christian College
Augusta State University
Berry College
Brenau University
Brewton-Parker College
Clayton State University
Columbus State University
Covenant College
Dalton State College
Emmanuel College
Fort Valley State University
Georgia College and State University
Georgia Southwestern State University
LaGrange College
Morehouse College
Oglethorpe University
Paine College
Piedmont College
Savannah State University
Shorter College
Spelman College
Thomas University
Toccoa Falls College
Truett-McConnell College
Wesleyan College

Hawaii
Brigham Young University-Hawaii
Hawaii Pacific University
University of Hawaii
West Oahu

Idaho
College of Idaho
Lewis-Clark State College
New Saint Andrews College

Illinois
Augustana College
Benedictine University
Blackburn College
Columbia College Chicago
Dominican University
Elmhurst College
Eureka College
Greenville College
Illinois College
Illinois Wesleyan University
Judson University
Knox College
Lake Forest College
MacMurray College
McKendree University
Monmouth College
North Central College
North Park University
Olivet Nazarene University
Principia College
Quincy University
Rockford College
St. Augustine College
Shimer College
Trinity Christian College
Trinity International University
University of Chicago
University of Illinois
Springfield
University of St. Francis
Wheaton College

Indiana
Anderson University
Bethel College
Calumet College of St. Joseph
DePauw University
Earlham College
Franklin College
Goshen College
Grace College
Hanover College
Holy Cross College
Huntington University
Indiana Wesleyan University
Manchester College
Marian College
Martin University
Oakland City University
Saint Joseph's College
Saint Mary's College
St. Mary-of-the-Woods College
Taylor University
University of Evansville
University of Indianapolis
University of St. Francis
University of Southern Indiana
Wabash College

Iowa
Briar Cliff University
Buena Vista University
Central College
Clarke College
Coe College
Cornell College
Divine Word College
Dordt College
Graceland University
Grand View University
Grinnell College
Iowa Wesleyan College
Loras College
Luther College
Maharishi University of Management
Morningside College
Mount Mercy College
Northwestern College
St. Ambrose University
Simpson College
Waldorf College
Wartburg College
William Penn University

Kansas
Baker University
Benedictine College
Bethany College
Bethel College
Central Christian College of Kansas
Friends University
Kansas Wesleyan University
McPherson College
MidAmerica Nazarene University
Newman University
Ottawa University
Southwestern College
Sterling College
Tabor College

Kentucky
Alice Lloyd College
Asbury College
Bellarmine University
Berea College
Brescia University
Centre College
Georgetown College
Kentucky Christian University
Kentucky State University
Kentucky Wesleyan College
Lindsey Wilson College
Mid-Continent University
Midway College
Pikeville College
St. Catharine College
Thomas More College
Transylvania University
Union College
University of the Cumberlands

Louisiana
Centenary College of Louisiana
Dillard University
Louisiana College
Loyola University New Orleans
Our Lady of Holy Cross College
St. Joseph Seminary College

Maine
Bates College
Bowdoin College
Colby College
College of the Atlantic
St. Joseph's College
Thomas College
Unity College
University of Maine
Farmington
Machias
University of Southern Maine

Maryland
College of Notre Dame of Maryland
Columbia Union College
Coppin State University
Goucher College
Hood College
Loyola College in Maryland
McDaniel College
Morgan State University
Mount St. Mary's University
National Labor College
St. John's College
St. Mary's College of Maryland
Salisbury University
Sojourner-Douglass College
University of Baltimore
Washington College

Massachusetts
American International College
Amherst College
Anna Maria College
Assumption College
Atlantic Union College
Bard College at Simon's Rock
Becker College
Bridgewater State College
Cambridge College

Clark University
College of the Holy Cross
Curry College
Eastern Nazarene College
Elms College
Emmanuel College
Endicott College
Fitchburg State College
Framingham State College
Gordon College
Hampshire College
Harvard College
Hellenic College/Holy Cross
Lasell College
Lesley University
Massachusetts College of Liberal Arts
Merrimack College
Mount Holyoke College
Mount Ida College
Newbury College
Nichols College
Pine Manor College
Regis College
Simmons College
Smith College
Springfield College
Stonehill College
Wellesley College
Westfield State College
Wheaton College
Wheelock College
Williams College
Worcester State College

Michigan

Adrian College
Albion College
Alma College
Aquinas College
Calvin College
Concordia University
Cornerstone University
Finlandia University
Grace Bible College
Hillsdale College
Hope College
Kalamazoo College
Madonna University
Marygrove College
Michigan Jewish Institute
Olivet College
Rochester College
Siena Heights University
Spring Arbor University

Minnesota

Augsburg College
Bethany Lutheran College
Bethel University
Brown College
Carleton College
College of St. Benedict
College of St. Catherine
College of St. Scholastica
Concordia College: Moorhead
Crown College
Gustavus Adolphus College
Hamline University
Macalester College
Northwestern College
St. John's University
St. Olaf College
Southwest Minnesota State University
University of Minnesota
Morris
University of St. Thomas

Mississippi

Belhaven College
Blue Mountain College
Millsaps College
Mississippi University for Women
Mississippi Valley State University
Rust College
Tougaloo College
William Carey University

Missouri

Avila University
Central Methodist University
College of the Ozarks
Columbia College
Culver-Stockton College
Drury University
Evangel University
Fontbonne University
Hannibal-LaGrange College
Lincoln University
Lindenwood University
Missouri Baptist University
Missouri Southern State University
Missouri Valley College
Missouri Western State University
Rockhurst University
Stephens College
Truman State University
Westminster College
William Jewell College
William Woods University

Montana

Carroll College
Montana State University
Northern
Rocky Mountain College
Salish Kootenai College
University of Great Falls
University of Montana
University of Montana: Western

Nebraska

Chadron State College
College of Saint Mary
Dana College
Doane College
Hastings College
Midland Lutheran College
Nebraska Wesleyan University
Peru State College
Union College
Wayne State College
York College

Nevada

Nevada State College
Sierra Nevada College

New Hampshire

Chester College of New England
Colby-Sawyer College
Daniel Webster College
Dartmouth College
Franklin Pierce University
Granite State College
Keene State College
Magdalen College
New England College
Rivier College
St. Anselm College
Thomas More College of Liberal Arts
University of New Hampshire at Manchester

New Jersey

Bloomfield College
Caldwell College
Centenary College
The College of New Jersey
College of St. Elizabeth
Drew University
Felician College
Georgian Court University
Kean University
Ramapo College of New Jersey
Richard Stockton College of New Jersey
Saint Peter's College
Somerset Christian College
Thomas Edison State College
William Paterson University of New Jersey

New Mexico

New Mexico Institute of Mining and Technology
St. John's College
University of the Southwest

New York

Bard College
Barnard College
Boricua College
Canisius College
Cazenovia College
City University of New York
Baruch College
Brooklyn College
College of Staten Island
Hunter College
Lehman College
Medgar Evers College
Queens College
York College
Colgate University
College of Mount St. Vincent
College of New Rochelle
College of Saint Rose
Columbia University
School of General Studies
Concordia College
D'Youville College
Daemen College
Dowling College
Elmira College
Eugene Lang College The New School for Liberal Arts
Excelsior College
Five Towns College
Hamilton College
Hartwick College
Hilbert College
Hobart and William Smith Colleges
Houghton College
Iona College
Ithaca College
Keuka College
King's College
Le Moyne College
Long Island University
Brooklyn Campus
C. W. Post Campus
Manhattan College
Manhattanville College
Marist College
Marymount Manhattan College
Medaille College
Medaille College: Amherst
Medaille College: Rochester
Mercy College
Metropolitan College of New York
Molloy College
Mount St. Mary College
Nazareth College of Rochester
Nyack College
Paul Smith's College
Roberts Wesleyan College
Russell Sage College
Sage College of Albany
St. Francis College
St. John Fisher College
St. Joseph's College
St. Joseph's College: Suffolk Campus
St. Lawrence University
St. Thomas Aquinas College
Sarah Lawrence College
Siena College
Skidmore College
State University of New York
College at Brockport
College at Buffalo
College at Cortland
College at Fredonia
College at Geneseo
College at Old Westbury
College at Oneonta
College at Plattsburgh
College at Potsdam
College of Environmental Science and Forestry
Empire State College
New Paltz
Touro College
Union College
Utica College
Vassar College
Wagner College
Wells College

North Carolina

Barton College
Belmont Abbey College
Bennett College
Brevard College
Campbell University
Catawba College
Chowan University
Davidson College
Elizabeth City State University
Elon University
Gardner-Webb University
Greensboro College
Guilford College
High Point University
Johnson C. Smith University
Lees-McRae College
Lenoir-Rhyne University
Livingstone College
Mars Hill College
Meredith College
Methodist University
Montreat College
Mount Olive College
North Carolina Wesleyan College
Peace College
Pfeiffer University
St. Andrews Presbyterian College
St. Augustine's College
Salem College
Shaw University
University of North Carolina
Asheville
Pembroke
Warren Wilson College
Wingate University

North Dakota

Jamestown College
Minot State University
Valley City State University

Ohio

Antioch University McGregor
Ashland University
Baldwin-Wallace College
Bluffton University
Cedarville University
Central State University
College of Mount St. Joseph
College of Wooster
Defiance College
Denison University
Heidelberg University
Hiram College
John Carroll University
Kenyon College
Lake Erie College
Laura and Alvin Siegal College of Judaic Studies
Lourdes College
Marietta College
Mount Union College
Muskingum College
Notre Dame College
Oberlin College
Ohio Dominican University
Ohio Wesleyan University
Otterbein College
Pontifical College Josephinum
Temple Baptist College
University of Rio Grande
Urbana University
Ursuline College
Walsh University
Wilberforce University
Wilmington College
Wittenberg University

Oklahoma

Bacone College
Cameron University
Hillsdale Free Will Baptist College
Langston University
Mid-America Christian University
Oklahoma Baptist University
Oklahoma Christian University
Oklahoma City University
Oklahoma Panhandle State University
Oklahoma Wesleyan University
Oral Roberts University
St. Gregory's University
Southeastern Oklahoma State University
Southern Nazarene University
Southwestern Christian University
University of Science and Arts of Oklahoma

Oregon

Art Institute of Portland
Concordia University
Corban College
Eastern Oregon University
Gutenberg College
Lewis & Clark College
Linfield College
Marylhurst University
Reed College
Southern Oregon University
Warner Pacific College
Western Oregon University
Willamette University

Pennsylvania

Albright College
Allegheny College
Alvernia University
Bloomsburg University of Pennsylvania
Bryn Athyn College of the New Church
Bryn Mawr College
Cabrini College
Carlow University
Cedar Crest College
Chatham University
Chestnut Hill College
Delaware Valley College
Dickinson College
Elizabethtown College
Franklin & Marshall College
Geneva College
Gettysburg College
Grove City College
Gwynedd-Mercy College
Haverford College
Holy Family University
Immaculata University
Juniata College
Keystone College
King's College
La Roche College
La Salle University
Lafayette College
Lebanon Valley College
Lincoln University
Lock Haven University of Pennsylvania
Lycoming College
Mansfield University of Pennsylvania
Mercyhurst College

Messiah College
Millersville University of Pennsylvania
Misericordia University
Moravian College
Mount Aloysius College
Muhlenberg College
Neumann College
Rosemont College
St. Francis University
St. Vincent College
Seton Hill University
Susquehanna University
Swarthmore College
Thiel College
University of Pittsburgh
  Greensburg
  Johnstown
University of Scranton
Ursinus College
Valley Forge Christian College
Washington & Jefferson College
Waynesburg University
Westminster College
Wilson College
York College of Pennsylvania

Puerto Rico

Atlantic College
Caribbean University
Inter American University of Puerto Rico
  Aguadilla Campus
  Arecibo Campus
Turabo University
Universidad Adventista de las Antillas
Universidad del Este
Universidad Metropolitana
University of Puerto Rico
  Aguadilla
  Cayey University College
  Humacao
University of the Sacred Heart

Rhode Island

Brown University
Bryant University
Providence College
Rhode Island College
Roger Williams University
Salve Regina University

South Carolina

Allen University
Anderson University
Benedict College
Bob Jones University
Charleston Southern University
Claflin University
Coker College
College of Charleston
Columbia College
Converse College
Erskine College
Francis Marion University
Furman University
Lander University
Limestone College
Morris College
Newberry College
North Greenville University
Presbyterian College
Southern Wesleyan University
University of South Carolina
  Aiken
  Beaufort
Voorhees College
Wofford College

South Dakota

Augustana College
Black Hills State University
Dakota Wesleyan University
Mount Marty College
Northern State University
Oglala Lakota College
Sinte Gleska University
University of Sioux Falls

Tennessee

Aquinas College
Austin Peay State University
Bethel College
Bryan College
Carson-Newman College
Crichton College
Cumberland University
Fisk University
Freed-Hardeman University
King College
Lambuth University
Lane College
Lee University
LeMoyne-Owen College
Lincoln Memorial University
Lipscomb University
Martin Methodist College
Maryville College
Milligan College
Rhodes College
South College
Southern Adventist University
Tennessee Wesleyan College
Trevecca Nazarene University
Tusculum College
Union University
Williamson Christian College

Texas

Austin College
College of Saint Thomas More
Concordia University Texas
East Texas Baptist University
Houston Baptist University
Howard Payne University
Huston-Tillotson University
Jarvis Christian College
Lubbock Christian University
McMurry University
Midwestern State University
Paul Quinn College
St. Edward's University
Schreiner University
Southwestern Adventist University
Southwestern Christian College
Southwestern University
Texas College
Texas Lutheran University
Trinity University
University of Dallas
University of North Texas
University of St. Thomas
University of the Incarnate Word
Wayland Baptist University
Wiley College

Utah

Dixie State College of Utah
Stevens-Henager College: Ogden
Westminster College

Vermont

Bennington College
Burlington College
Castleton State College
Champlain College
College of St. Joseph in Vermont
Goddard College
Green Mountain College
Johnson State College
Lyndon State College
Marlboro College
Middlebury College
St. Michael's College
Southern Vermont College
Sterling College

Virginia

Averett University
Bluefield College
Bridgewater College
Christendom College
Christopher Newport University
Eastern Mennonite University
Emory & Henry College
Ferrum College
Hampden-Sydney College
Hollins University
Lynchburg College
Mary Baldwin College
Patrick Henry College
Randolph College
Randolph-Macon College
Roanoke College
St. Paul's College
Southern Virginia University
Sweet Briar College
University of Mary Washington
University of Richmond
University of Virginia's College at Wise
Virginia Intermont College
Virginia Military Institute
Virginia Union University
Virginia University of Lynchburg
Virginia Wesleyan College
Washington and Lee University

Washington

Antioch University Seattle
Evergreen State College
Gonzaga University
Heritage University
Northwest University
Trinity Lutheran College
University of Puget Sound
Walla Walla University
Whitman College
Whitworth University

West Virginia

Alderson-Broaddus College
Bethany College
Bluefield State College
Concord University
Davis and Elkins College
Glenville State College
Ohio Valley University
Salem International University
University of Charleston
West Liberty State College
West Virginia State University
West Virginia Wesleyan College
Wheeling Jesuit University

Wisconsin

Alverno College
Beloit College
Carroll University
Carthage College
Concordia University Wisconsin
Edgewood College
Lakeland College
Lawrence University
Marian University
Mount Mary College
Northland College
Ripon College
St. Norbert College
Silver Lake College
University of Wisconsin
  Green Bay
  River Falls
  Superior
Viterbo University
Wisconsin Lutheran College

Northern Mariana Islands

Northern Marianas College

France

American University of Paris

Switzerland

Franklin College: Switzerland

United Kingdom

Richmond, The American International University in London

Two-year

Arkansas

Arkansas State University:
  Newport
National Park Community College

California

Deep Springs College
Feather River College
Fresno City College
Marymount College

Colorado

Colorado Mountain College

Florida

Florida National College

Georgia

Andrew College
Georgia Highlands College
Georgia Perimeter College
Oxford College of Emory University
Waycross College
Young Harris College

Hawaii

Hawaii Tokai International College
TransPacific Hawaii College

Illinois

Lincoln College
Springfield College in Illinois

Indiana

Ancilla College

Iowa

Kaplan University
  Cedar Rapids

Kansas

Donnelly College

Massachusetts

Dean College
Fisher College

Michigan

Montcalm Community College
Wayne County Community College

Minnesota

Itasca Community College

Missouri

Cottey College
Crowder College
Patricia Stevens College

New Jersey

Assumption College for Sisters

New York

State University of New York
  College of Technology at Alfred
  College of Technology at Delhi
Villa Maria College of Buffalo

Ohio

Chatfield College

Pennsylvania

University of Pittsburgh
  Titusville

Puerto Rico

Colegio de las Ciencias Artes y Television

South Carolina

Clinton Junior College
Spartanburg Methodist College

Texas

Alvin Community College
Eastfield College
Jacksonville College
Lamar State College at Orange
Lon Morris College
North Lake College
Tarrant County College

Vermont

Community College of Vermont
Landmark College

Virginia

Richard Bland College

Washington

Olympic College

Wisconsin

University of Wisconsin
  Baraboo/Sauk County
  Fox Valley
  Manitowoc
  Marathon County
  Marinette
  Richland
  Rock County
  Washington County

Upper-division colleges

Alabama

Athens State University
United States Sports Academy

California

Alliant International University
Antioch Southern California
  Antioch University Los Angeles
  Antioch University Santa Barbara
California Institute of Integral Studies
John F. Kennedy University
Monterey Institute of International Studies
Pacific Oaks College
Samuel Merritt University

Georgia

Medical College of Georgia

Illinois

Governors State University
Lakeview College of Nursing
Rosalind Franklin University of Medicine and Science
Rush University
Saint Anthony College of Nursing
St. Francis Medical Center College of Nursing
St. John's College
West Suburban College of Nursing
Western Illinois University: Quad Cities

Kansas

University of Kansas Medical Center

Louisiana

Louisiana State University Health Sciences Center

Maryland

University of Maryland
  Baltimore

Michigan

Walsh College of Accountancy and Business Administration

Minnesota

Northwestern Health Sciences University

Mississippi

University of Mississippi Medical Center

Missouri
Goldfarb School of Nursing at Barnes-Jewish College
Midwest University
St. Luke's College

Nebraska
University of Nebraska
Medical Center

Nevada
University of Southern Nevada

New Jersey
University of Medicine and Dentistry of New Jersey
School of Health Related Professions

New York
State University of New York
Downstate Medical Center
Upstate Medical University

North Dakota
Medcenter One College of Nursing

Pennsylvania
Thomas Jefferson University: College of Health Professions

Puerto Rico
Carlos Albizu University: San Juan

South Carolina
Medical University of South Carolina

Tennessee
University of Tennessee Health Science Center

Texas
Austin Graduate School of Theology
Texas A&M University
Baylor College of Dentistry
Texarkana
Texas Tech University Health Sciences Center
University of Houston
Clear Lake
Victoria
University of Texas
Health Science Center at Houston
Health Science Center at San Antonio
Medical Branch at Galveston
Southwestern Medical Center at Dallas

Virginia
Catholic Distance University

Washington
Antioch University Seattle
Bastyr University
City University of Seattle

Northern Mariana Islands
Northern Marianas College

Agricultural colleges

Four-year
Alabama Agricultural and Mechanical University, AL
Alcorn State University, MS
Clemson University, SC
Delaware Valley College, PA
Louisiana State University and Agricultural and Mechanical College, LA
Oklahoma Panhandle State University, OK
University of Puerto Rico
Utuado, PR

Two-year
Abraham Baldwin Agricultural College, GA
College of the Sequoias, CA
Nebraska College of Technical Agriculture, NE
Ohio State University
Agricultural Technical Institute, OH
State University of New York
College of Agriculture and Technology at Cobleskill, NY
College of Agriculture and Technology at Morrisville, NY

Arts/music colleges

Four-year
Academy of Art University, CA
American Academy of Art, IL
Art Academy of Cincinnati, OH
Art Center College of Design, CA
Art Center Design College, NM
Art Center Design College, AZ
Art Institute
of Atlanta, GA
of California: Orange County, CA
of California: San Diego, CA
of Charlotte, NC
of Colorado, CO
of Dallas, TX
of Houston, TX
of Las Vegas, NV
of Philadelphia, PA
of Phoenix, AZ
of Pittsburgh, PA
of Washington, VA
Art Institute of Boston at Lesley University, MA
Art Institute of California: Hollywood, CA
Art Institute of California: Inland Empire, CA
Art Institute of California: Sacramento, CA
Art Institute of California: San Francisco, CA
Art Institute of Fort Lauderdale, FL
Art Institute of Michigan, MI
Art Institute of Portland, OR
Art Institute of Seattle, WA
Art Institutes International Minnesota, MN
Berklee College of Music, MA
Boston Conservatory, MA
Brooks Institute, CA
Brooks Institute: Ventura, CA
California College of the Arts, CA
California Institute of the Arts, CA
Chester College of New England, NH
Cleveland Institute of Art, OH
Cleveland Institute of Music, OH
Cogswell Polytechnical College, CA
College for Creative Studies, MI
College of Visual Arts, MN
Collins College, AZ
Columbia College Chicago, IL
Columbus College of Art and Design, OH
Conservatory of Music of Puerto Rico, PR
Converse College, SC
Cooper Union for the Advancement of Science and Art, NY
Corcoran College of Art and Design, DC
Cornish College of the Arts, WA
Creative Center, NE
Curtis Institute of Music, PA
DigiPen Institute of Technology, WA
Eastman School of Music of the University of Rochester, NY
Escuela de Artes Plasticas de Puerto Rico, PR
Ex'pression College for Digital Arts, CA
Fashion Institute of Technology, NY
Five Towns College, NY
Harrington College of Design, IL
Illinois Institute of Art: Chicago, IL
Illinois Institute of Art: Schaumburg, IL
Institute of American Indian Arts, NM
Interior Designers Institute, CA
International Academy of Design and Technology: Chicago, IL
International Academy of Design and Technology: Detroit, MI
International Academy of Design and Technology: Henderson, NV
International Academy of Design and Technology: Nashville, TN
International Academy of Design and Technology: Schaumburg, IL
International Academy of Design and Technology: Tampa, FL
Johns Hopkins University: Peabody Conservatory of Music, MD
Juilliard School, NY
Kansas City Art Institute, MO
Kendall College of Art and Design of Ferris State University, MI
Laguna College of Art and Design, CA
Lawrence University, WI
Lyme Academy College of Fine Arts, CT
Maine College of Art, ME
Manhattan School of Music, NY
Mannes College The New School for Music, NY
Maryland Institute College of Art, MD
Massachusetts College of Art and Design, MA
Memphis College of Art, TN
Miami International University of Art and Design, FL
Milwaukee Institute of Art & Design, WI
Minneapolis College of Art and Design, MN
Montserrat College of Art, MA
Moore College of Art and Design, PA
New England Conservatory of Music, MA
New England Institute of Art, MA
New York School of Interior Design, NY
NewSchool of Architecture & Design, CA
Northwest College of Art, WA
O'More College of Design, TN
Oberlin College, OH
Oregon College of Art & Craft, OR
Otis College of Art and Design, CA
Pacific Northwest College of Art, OR
Paier College of Art, CT
Parsons Paris School of Design, FR
Parsons The New School for Design, NY
Pennsylvania College of Art and Design, PA
Platt College
Aurora, CO
San Diego, CA
Pratt Institute, NY
Rhode Island School of Design, RI
Rhodec International, MA
Ringling College of Art and Design, FL
Rocky Mountain College of Art & Design, CO
San Francisco Art Institute, CA
San Francisco Conservatory of Music, CA
Savannah College of Art and Design, GA
School of the Art Institute of Chicago, IL
School of the Museum of Fine Arts, MA
School of Visual Arts, NY
Southern California Institute of Architecture, CA
University of North Carolina School of the Arts, NC
University of the Arts, PA
VanderCook College of Music, IL
Visible School - Music and Worship Arts College, TN
Watkins College of Art, Design and Film, TN
Westwood College: Northlake, GA

Two-year
American Academy of Dramatic Arts, NY
American Academy of Dramatic Arts: West, CA
Antonelli College, OH
Antonelli Institute of Art and Photography, PA
Art Institute
of California: Los Angeles, CA
Art Institute of Cincinnati, OH
Art Institute of Ohio: Cincinnati, OH
Art Institute of York, PA
Delaware College of Art and Design, DE
Delta College of Arts & Technology, LA
Douglas Education Center, PA
Fashion Institute of Design and Merchandising
Los Angeles, CA
San Diego, CA
San Francisco, CA
Full Sail University, FL
Hussian School of Art, PA
Louisville Technical Institute, KY
Madison Media Institute, WI
Nossi College of Art, TN
Oakbridge Academy of Arts, PA
Platt College
Huntington Beach, CA
Los Angeles, CA
School of Advertising Art, OH
Villa Maria College of Buffalo, NY
Virginia Marti College of Art and Design, OH

Bible colleges

Four-year
Alaska Bible College, AK
Allegheny Wesleyan College, OH
American Baptist College of ABT Seminary, TN
American Indian College of the Assemblies of God, AZ
Apex School of Theology, NC
Appalachian Bible College, WV
Arlington Baptist College, TX
Atlanta Christian College, GA
Austin Graduate School of Theology, TX
Baptist Bible College, MO
Baptist Bible College of Pennsylvania, PA
Baptist College of Florida, FL
Baptist Missionary Association Theological Seminary, TX
Baptist University of the Americas, TX
Barclay College, KS
Bethany University, CA
Beulah Heights University, GA
Biola University, CA
Bob Jones University, SC
Boise Bible College, ID
Boston Baptist College, MA
Calvary Bible College and Theological Seminary, MO
Carolina Christian College, NC
Carver Bible College, GA
Central Baptist College, AR
Central Bible College, MO
Central Christian College of the Bible, MO
Clear Creek Baptist Bible College, KY
Colegio Biblico Pentecostal, PR
Colegio Pentecostal Mizpa, PR
College of Biblical Studies-Houston, TX
Columbia International University, SC
Criswell College, TX
Crossroads College, MN
Crown College, MN
Dallas Christian College, TX
Davis College, NY
Emmaus Bible College, IA
Eugene Bible College, OR
Faith Baptist Bible College and Theological Seminary, IA
Family of Faith College, OK
Florida Christian College, FL
Free Will Baptist Bible College, TN
Global University, MO
God's Bible School and College, OH
Grace Bible College, MI
Grace University, NE
Great Lakes Christian College, MI
Griggs University, MD
Heritage Christian University, AL
Hobe Sound Bible College, FL
Horizon College of San Diego, CA
Huntsville Bible College, AL
International Baptist College, AZ
John Wesley College, NC
Johnson Bible College, TN
Kentucky Christian University, KY
Kentucky Mountain Bible College, KY
The King's College and Seminary, CA
Kuyper College, MI
Lancaster Bible College, PA
Life Pacific College, CA
Lincoln Christian College and Seminary, IL
Lipscomb University, TN
Luther Rice University, GA
Magnolia Bible College, MS
Manhattan Christian College, KS
Maranatha Baptist Bible College, WI
Mid-Continent University, KY
Moody Bible Institute, IL
Multnomah University, OR
Nazarene Bible College, CO
Nebraska Christian College, NE

New Orleans Baptist Theological Seminary: Leavell College, LA
North Central University, MN
Northland Baptist Bible College, WI
Northwestern College, MN
Oak Hills Christian College, MN
Ohio Christian University, OH
Ozark Christian College, MO
Philadelphia Biblical University, PA
Piedmont Baptist College, NC
Roanoke Bible College, NC
St. Louis Christian College, MO
School of Urban Missions: New Orleans, LA
School of Urban Missions: Oakland, CA
Shasta Bible College and Graduate School, CA
Somerset Christian College, NJ
Southeastern Baptist College, MS
Southeastern Baptist Theological Seminary, NC
Southeastern Bible College, AL
Southern California Seminary, CA
Southern Methodist College, SC
Southwestern Assemblies of God University, TX
Southwestern Baptist Theological Seminary, TX
Southwestern Christian College, TX
Southwestern College, AZ
Tennessee Temple University, TN
Toccoa Falls College, GA
Tri-State Bible College, OH
Trinity Baptist College, FL
Trinity Bible College, ND
Trinity College of Florida, FL
Trinity Lutheran College, WA
Universidad FLET, FL
Virginia Baptist College, VA
Visible School - Music and Worship Arts College, TN
W.L. Bonner Bible College, SC
Washington Bible College, MD
Wesley College, MS
William Jessup University, CA
World Mission University, CA
Zion Bible College, MA

Two-year

California Christian College, CA
Rosedale Bible College, OH
Trinity Life Bible College, CA

Business colleges

Four-year

American University of Puerto Rico, PR
Aspen University, CO
Athens State University, AL
Babson College, MA
Baker College
- of Auburn Hills, MI
- of Cadillac, MI
- of Clinton Township, MI
- of Flint, MI
- of Jackson, MI
- of Muskegon, MI
- of Owosso, MI
- of Port Huron, MI

Baker College of Allen Park, MI
Baltimore International College, MD
Bay Path College, MA
Beckfield College, KY
Bellevue University, NE
Bentley University, MA
Berkeley College, NY
Berkeley College, NJ
Berkeley College of New York City, NY
Briarcliffe College, NY
Brown College, MN
Bryant & Stratton College
- Eastlake, OH

Bryant University, RI
California Coast University, CA
California College San Diego, CA
California State University
- Stanislaus, CA

California University of Management and Sciences, CA
Capitol College, MD
Central Pennsylvania College, PA
Chadron State College, NE
Champlain College, VT
City College: Fort Lauderdale, FL
City University of New York
- Baruch College, NY

Clarion University of Pennsylvania, PA
Cleary University, MI
CollegeAmerica
- Fort Collins, CO

Columbia Centro Universitario: Caguas, PR
Columbia Southern University, AL
Daniel Webster College, NH
Davenport University, MI
DeVry
- Devry College of New York, NY

DeVry University: Memphis, TN
DeVry University: Oklahoma City Center, OK
DeVry University: Sandy, UT
ECPI College of Technology: Newport News, VA
Electronic Data Processing College of Puerto Rico, PR
Electronic Data Processing College: San Sebastian, PR
Everest University: Brandon, FL
Everest University: Largo, FL
Everest University: North Orlando, FL
Everest University: Pompano Beach, FL
Everest University: South Orlando, FL
Everest University: Tampa, FL
Fashion Institute of Technology, NY
Franklin University, OH
Friends University, KS
Globe Institute of Technology, NY
Globe University, MN
Goldey-Beacom College, DE
Herzing College, AL
Herzing College, GA
Herzing College, WI
Hesser College, NH
Hickey College, MO
Hodges University, FL
Humphreys College, CA
Husson University, ME
Huston-Tillotson University, TX
Indiana Institute of Technology, IN
Instituto Tecnologico Autonomo de Mexico, MX
Instituto Tecnologico y de Estudios Superiores de Occidente, MX
International Business College, IN
International University of Monaco, MC
Iona College, NY
Jones College, FL
Kendall College, IL
King's College, PA
LA College International, CA
Lincoln University, CA
Loyola College in Maryland, MD
Macon State College, GA
Mayville State University, ND
Menlo College, CA
Merrimack College, MA
Metropolitan College of New York, NY
Michigan Jewish Institute, MI
Midstate College, IL
Miller-Motte Technical College, NC
Millsaps College, MS
Minnesota School of Business, MN
Minnesota School of Business: Blaine, MN
Minnesota School of Business: Plymouth, MN
Minnesota School of Business: Shakopee, MN
Missouri Western State University, MO
Monroe College, NY
Morrison University, NV
Mount Ida College, MA
National American University
- Rapid City, SD
- St. Paul, MN

National American University: Rio Rancho, NM
National College
- Roanoke Valley, VA

National College of Business and Technology: Arecibo, PR
National College of Business and Technology: Bayamon, PR
National College of Business and Technology: Rio Grande, PR
New England College, NH
Newbury College, MA
Nichols College, MA
Northwest Florida State College, FL
Northwestern Polytechnic University, CA
Northwood University
- Florida, FL

Northwood University: Michigan, MI
Northwood University: Texas, TX
Parsons Paris School of Design, FR
Peirce College, PA
Post University, CT
Potomac College, VA
Potomac College, DC
Presentation College, SD
Reinhardt College, GA
Restaurant School at Walnut Hill College, PA
Rockhurst University, MO
Sage College of Albany, NY
Sanford-Brown College: Milwaukee, WI
Sanford-Brown College: Vienna, VA
Savannah State University, GA
Silicon Valley University, CA
Silver Lake College, WI
South University: Montgomery, AL
South University: Savannah, GA
South University: Tampa, FL
South University: West Palm Beach, FL
Southeastern University, DC
Southern California Institute of Technology, CA
State University of New York
- College at Old Westbury, NY
- Institute of Technology at Utica/Rome, NY

Stevens-Henager College
- Murray, UT

Stevens-Henager College: Logan, UT
Stevens-Henager College: Orem, UT
Teikyo Loretto Heights University, CO
Thomas College, ME
Tiffin University, OH
Universidad Privada Boliviana, BO
University of Baltimore, MD
University of Management and Technology, VA
Virginia College at Huntsville, AL
Walsh College of Accountancy and Business Administration, MI
Webber International University, FL
Western International University, AZ
Westwood College of Technology
- Westwood College: Inland Empire, CA

Two-year

Academy of Court Reporting: Cincinnati, OH
AEC Southern Ohio College
- Brown Mackie College: Akron, OH
- Brown Mackie College: Findlay, OH

AIB College of Business, IA
Andover College, ME
Berks Technical Institute, PA
Bidwell Training Center, PA
Bohecker College, OH
Bradford School, OH
Brown Mackie College: Atlanta, GA
Brown Mackie College: Cincinnati, OH
Brown Mackie College: Fort Wayne, IN
Brown Mackie College: Hopkinsville, KY
Brown Mackie College: Merrillville, IN
Brown Mackie College: Miami, FL
Bryant & Stratton Business Institute
- Bryant & Stratton College: Albany, NY
- Bryant & Stratton College: Amherst, NY
- Bryant & Stratton College: Buffalo, NY
- Bryant & Stratton College: Rochester, NY
- Bryant & Stratton College: Southtowns, NY
- Bryant & Stratton College: Syracuse, NY

Bryant & Stratton College: Henrietta, NY
Bryant & Stratton College: Milwaukee, WI
Bryant & Stratton College: Syracuse North, NY
Bryant & Stratton College: Virginia Beach, VA
Business Informatics Center, NY
Cambria-Rowe Business College, PA
Cambria-Rowe Business College: Indiana, PA
Centura College: Chesapeake, VA
Centura College: Newport News, VA
Centura College: Richmond, VA
Centura College: Richmond Westend, VA
City College
- Gainesville, FL
- Miami, FL

Clemens College, CT
College of Business and Technology: Hialeah, FL
College of Court Reporting, IN
College of Office Technology, IL
College of Westchester, NY
Columbia College
- Columbia Centro Universitario: Yauco, PR

Concorde Career College: Kansas City, MO
Consolidated School of Business
- Lancaster, PA
- York, PA

Daymar College
- Louisville, KY
- Owensboro, KY

Delta School of Business & Technology, LA
Douglas Education Center, PA
Draughons Junior College: Clarksville, TN
DuBois Business College, PA
DuBois Business College
- Huntingdon, PA
- Oil City, PA

Duluth Business University, MN
Eagle Gate College: Layton, UT
Eagle Gate College: Murray, UT
Eagle Gate College: Salt Lake City, UT
Elmira Business Institute, NY
Elmira Business Institute: Vestal, NY
Empire College, CA
Erie Business Center, PA
Erie Business Center South, PA
Everest College: Arlington, TX
Everest College: Colorado Springs, CO
Fashion Careers College, CA
Fashion Institute of Design and Merchandising
- Los Angeles, CA
- San Diego, CA
- San Francisco, CA

Florida Career College: Miami, FL
Florida Career College: Pembroke Pines, FL
Florida Technical College
- Auburndale, FL

Forrest Junior College, SC
Gallipolis Career College, OH
Heald College
- Concord, CA
- Fresno, CA
- Roseville, CA
- Salinas, CA
- San Francisco, CA
- San Jose, CA
- Stockton, CA

Heald College: Portland, OR
Herzing College, FL
Hondros College, OH
Humacao Community College, PR
ICPR Junior College, PR
Indiana Business College
- Anderson, IN
- Columbus, IN
- Evansville, IN
- Fort Wayne, IN
- Indianapolis, IN
- Lafayette, IN
- Marion, IN
- Muncie, IN
- Terre Haute, IN

Indiana Business College: Elkhart, IN
Indiana Business College: Indianapolis Northwest, IN
International Business College: Indianapolis, IN
Jamestown Business College, NY
Kaplan Career Institute: Pittsburgh, PA
Kaplan College: Hagerstown, MD
Kaplan College: Hammond, IN
Kaplan College: Indianapolis, IN
Kaplan College: Sacramento, CA
Kaplan College: San Diego, CA

Keiser Career College: Greenacres, FL
Keiser Career College: Miami Lakes, FL
Keiser University, FL
Key College, FL
Las Vegas College, NV
Laurel Technical Institute, PA
LDS Business College, UT
Long Island Business Institute, NY
Long Island Business Institute: Flushing, NY
McCann School of Business and Technology: Dickson City, PA
McCann School of Business and Technology: Hazleton, PA
Metro Business College, MO
Metro Business College
Jefferson City, MO
Rolla, MO
Miller-Motte Technical College: Clarksville, TN
Minneapolis Business College, MN
Minnesota School of Business: Brooklyn Center, MN
Mountain State College, WV
MTI College, CA
National College
Bluefield, VA
Charlottesville, VA
Danville, VA
Danville, KY
Dayton, OH
Florence, KY
Harrisonburg, VA
Knoxville, TN
Lexington, KY
Louisville, KY
Lynchburg, VA
Martinsville, VA
Nashville, TN
Pikeville, KY
Richmond, KY
National College of Business & Technology
National College: Bristol, TN
New England College of Finance, MA
New England Culinary Institute
Essex Junction, VT
Newport Business Institute: Lower Burrell, PA
Newport Business Institute: Williamsport, PA
North Florida Institute: Orange Park, FL
Ohio Business College, OH
Ohio Business College: Sandusky, OH
Ohio Valley College of Technology, OH
Olean Business Institute, NY
Penn Commercial Business and Technical School, PA
Pennsylvania Institute of Health and Technology, PA
Pennsylvania School of Business, PA
PJA School, PA
Plaza College, NY
Professional Business College, NY
Remington College
Memphis, TN
Samuel Stephen College, OH
Sanford-Brown College, MO
Sanford-Brown Institute
Monroeville, PA
South Coast College, CA
South Hills School of Business & Technology, PA
South Hills School of Business & Technology: Altoona, PA
Southeastern Business College: Jackson, OH
Southeastern Business College: Lancaster, OH
Southeastern Business College: New Boston, OH
Southern Ohio College
Brown Mackie College: North Kentucky, KY
Southwestern College of Business
Southwestern College: Vine Street Campus, OH
Southwestern College: Dayton, OH
Stautzenberger College, OH
Stenotype Institute: Jacksonville, FL
Taylor Business Institute, IL
Tri-State Business Institute, PA
Trumbull Business College, OH
University of Northwestern Ohio, OH
Utica School of Commerce, NY
Utica School of Commerce: Canastota, NY
Utica School of Commerce: Oneonta, NY
Valley College, WV
Virginia College at Austin, TX
Virginia College at Pensacola, FL
Virginia College Gulf Coast, MS
Virginia Marti College of Art and Design, OH
West Tennessee Business College, TN
West Virginia Business College: Nutter Fort, WV
West Virginia Business College: Wheeling, WV
West Virginia Junior College: Bridgeport, WV
Yorktowne Business Institute, PA
YTI Career Institute: Lancaster, PA

Culinary schools

Four-year

Art Institute
of California: Orange County, CA
of Colorado, CO
of Houston, TX
of Las Vegas, NV
of Phoenix, AZ
of Washington, VA
Art Institute of California: Inland Empire, CA
Art Institute of California: Sacramento, CA
Art Institutes International Minnesota, MN
Baltimore International College, MD
Culinary Institute of America, NY
Kendall College, IL
Restaurant School at Walnut Hill College, PA

Two-year

Art Institute
of New York City, NY
Art Institute of Ohio: Cincinnati, OH
Atlantic Cape Community College, NJ
California Culinary Academy, CA
California School of Culinary Arts, CA
Clemens College, CT
Cooking & Hospitality Institute of Chicago, IL
Culinary Institute Alain & Marie LeNotre, TX
L'Ecole Culinaire, MO
Le Cordon Bleu College of Culinary Arts, NV
Le Cordon Bleu College of Culinary Arts, MN
Le Cordon Bleu College of Culinary Arts: Miami, FL
Mitchell Technical Institute, SD
New England Culinary Institute, VT
New England Culinary Institute
Essex Junction, VT
Orlando Culinary Academy, FL
Pennsylvania Culinary Institute, PA
Scottsdale Culinary Institute, AZ
Southwestern Oregon Community College, OR
Texas Culinary Academy, TX
Walters State Community College, TN
Western Culinary Institute, OR

Engineering colleges

Four-year

Capitol College, MD
Cogswell Polytechnical College, CA
Colorado School of Mines, CO
Cooper Union for the Advancement of Science and Art, NY
DigiPen Institute of Technology, WA
Franklin W. Olin College of Engineering, MA
Harvey Mudd College, CA
Illinois Institute of Technology, IL
Indiana Institute of Technology, IN
Instituto Tecnologico Autonomo de Mexico, MX
Instituto Tecnologico y de Estudios Superiores de Occidente, MX
Inter American University of Puerto Rico
Bayamon Campus, PR
Kettering University, MI
Lafayette College, PA
Manhattan College, NY
Missouri Technical School, MO
Montana Tech of the University of Montana, MT
Neumont University, UT
New Mexico Institute of Mining and Technology, NM
Northwestern Polytechnic University, CA
Rose-Hulman Institute of Technology, IN
South Dakota School of Mines and Technology, SD
Southern California Institute of Technology, CA
Southern Polytechnic State University, GA
Stevens Institute of Technology, NJ
Trine University, IN
Union College, NY
United States Coast Guard Academy, CT
Universidad del Valle de Guatemala, GT
Universidad Politecnica de Puerto Rico, PR
Universidad Privada Boliviana, BO
University of Management and Technology, VA
University of Pittsburgh
Johnstown, PA
Vaughn College of Aeronautics and Technology, NY
Webb Institute, NY
Wentworth Institute of Technology, MA
West Virginia University Institute of Technology, WV

Maritime colleges

Four-year

California Maritime Academy, CA
Maine Maritime Academy, ME
Massachusetts Maritime Academy, MA
State University of New York
Maritime College, NY
United States Coast Guard Academy, CT
United States Merchant Marine Academy, NY
Webb Institute, NY

Two-year

National Polytechnic College of Science, CA
Northwest School of Wooden Boatbuilding, WA
Northwestern Michigan College, MI

Military colleges

Four-year

The Citadel, SC
Massachusetts Maritime Academy, MA
North Georgia College & State University, GA
Norwich University, VT
United States Air Force Academy, CO
United States Merchant Marine Academy, NY
United States Military Academy, NY
United States Naval Academy, MD
Virginia Military Institute, VA

Two-year

Georgia Military College, GA
Marion Military Institute, AL
New Mexico Military Institute, NM
Valley Forge Military Academy & College, PA
Wentworth Military Junior College, MO

Nursing and health science colleges

Four-year

Albany College of Pharmacy and Health Sciences, NY
Allen College, IA
Aquinas College, TN
Baker College
of Cadillac, MI
Baker College of Allen Park, MI
Baptist College of Health Sciences, TN
Bastyr University, WA
Beckfield College, KY
Bellin College of Nursing, WI
Blessing-Rieman College of Nursing, IL
BryanLGH College of Health Sciences, NE
Bryant & Stratton College
Parma, OH
Cabarrus College of Health Sciences, NC
California Coast University, CA
California College San Diego, CA
California University of Management and Sciences, CA
Caribbean University, PR
Chamberlain College of Nursing, MO
Charles R. Drew University of Medicine and Science, CA
Clarkson College, NE
Coe College, IA
College of New Rochelle, NY
College of St. Catherine, MN
College of Saint Mary, NE
CollegeAmerica
Fort Collins, CO
Columbia College of Nursing, WI
Cox College, MO
Curry College, MA
D'Youville College, NY
ECPI College of Technology: Virginia Beach, VA
Electronic Data Processing College: San Sebastian, PR
Florida Hospital College of Health Sciences, FL
Globe University, MN
Goldfarb School of Nursing at Barnes-Jewish College, MO
Gwynedd-Mercy College, PA
Husson University, ME
Independence University, UT
Ithaca College, NY
Jefferson College of Health Sciences, VA
Kettering College of Medical Arts, OH
King College, TN
Lakeview College of Nursing, IL
Loma Linda University, CA
Louisiana State University Health Sciences Center, LA
Macon State College, GA
Massachusetts College of Pharmacy and Health Sciences, MA
Medcenter One College of Nursing, ND
MedCentral College of Nursing, OH
Medical College of Georgia, GA
Mercy College of Health Sciences, IA
Mercy College of Northwest Ohio, OH
Misericordia University, PA
Monroe College, NY
Mount Carmel College of Nursing, OH
Mountain State University, WV
National University of Health Sciences, IL
Nebraska Methodist College of Nursing and Allied Health, NE
Nevada State College, NV
New York Institute of Technology, NY
Northwestern Health Sciences University, MN
Oregon Health & Science University, OR
Our Lady of the Lake College, LA
Platt College
Aurora, CO
Presentation College, SD
Regis College, MA
Research College of Nursing, MO
Rosalind Franklin University of Medicine and Science, IL
Rush University, IL
St. Anselm College, NH
Saint Anthony College of Nursing, IL
St. Catharine College, KY
St. Francis Medical Center College of Nursing, IL
St. John's College, IL

St. Luke's College, MO
Samuel Merritt University, CA
Sanford-Brown College: Milwaukee, WI
South University: Montgomery, AL
South University: Savannah, GA
South University: Tampa, FL
South University: West Palm Beach, FL
Springfield College, MA
State University of New York
  Downstate Medical Center, NY
  Institute of Technology at Utica/Rome, NY
  Upstate Medical University, NY
Stevens-Henager College Murray, UT
Stevens-Henager College: Orem, UT
Texas A&M University
  Baylor College of Dentistry, TX
Thomas Jefferson University: College of Health Professions, PA
Trinity College of Nursing and Health Sciences, IL
University of Arkansas for Medical Sciences, AR
University of Findlay, OH
University of Kansas Medical Center, KS
University of Maryland
  Baltimore, MD
University of Medicine and Dentistry of New Jersey
  School of Health Related Professions, NJ
  School of Nursing, NJ
University of Mississippi Medical Center, MS
University of Nebraska
  Medical Center, NE
University of Tennessee Health Science Center, TN
University of Texas
  Health Science Center at Houston, TX
  Health Science Center at San Antonio, TX
  Medical Branch at Galveston, TX
  Southwestern Medical Center at Dallas, TX
University of the Sciences in Philadelphia, PA
West Coast University, CA
West Suburban College of Nursing, IL
Winston-Salem State University, NC

Two-year

ATI College of Health, FL
ATS Institute of Technology, OH
Aultman College of Nursing and Health Sciences, OH
Bidwell Training Center, PA
Blue Cliff College: Lafayette, LA
Boulder College of Massage Therapy, CO
Brown Mackie College: Atlanta, GA
Brown Mackie College: Cincinnati, OH
Bryman School, AZ
Camelot College, LA
Careers Unlimited, UT
Caritas Laboure College, MA
Carolinas College of Health Sciences, NC
Central Maine Medical Center College of Nursing and Health Professions, ME
Centro de Estudios Multidisciplinarios, PR
Centura College: Chesapeake, VA
Centura College: Richmond, VA
Centura College: Richmond Westend, VA
City College
  Gainesville, FL
  Miami, FL
Cochran School of Nursing-St. John's Riverside Hospital, NY
College of Business and Technology: Kendall, FL
Columbia College
  Columbia Centro Universitario: Yauco, PR
Concorde Career College
  Garden Grove, CA
Concorde Career College: Aurora, CO
Concorde Career College: Kansas City, MO
Concorde Career College: North Hollywood, CA
Concorde Career College: San Diego, CA
EDIC College, PR
Everest Institute, GA
Florida College of Natural Health
  Bradenton, FL
  Maitland, FL
Florida Keys Community College, FL
Fremont College, CA
Good Samaritan College of Nursing and Health Science, OH
Goodwin College, CT
Helene Fuld College of Nursing, NY
Herzing College, FL
High-Tech Institute, FL
Hondros College, OH
Huntington College of Health Sciences, TN
Indiana Business College
  Anderson, IN
  Columbus, IN
  Evansville, IN
  Fort Wayne, IN
  Indianapolis, IN
  Lafayette, IN
  Marion, IN
  Medical, IN
  Muncie, IN
  Terre Haute, IN
Indiana Business College: Elkhart, IN
Indiana Business College: Indianapolis Northwest, IN
James A. Rhodes State College, OH
Jefferson Davis Community College, AL
Kaplan Career Institute: Harrisburg, PA
Kaplan Career Institute: Pittsburgh, PA
Kaplan College: Indianapolis, IN
Kaplan College: Palm Springs, CA
Kaplan College: Salida, CA
Kaplan College: San Diego, CA
Keiser Career College: Greenacres, FL
Keiser Career College: Miami Lakes, FL
Keiser University, FL
Keystone Technical Institute, PA
Lakeland Academy Division of Herzing College, MN
Las Vegas College, NV
Lebanon College, NH
Long Island College Hospital School of Nursing, NY
Los Angeles County College of Nursing and Allied Health, CA
Metro Business College
  Jefferson City, MO
Miller-Motte Technical College: Clarksville, TN
Myotherapy Institute, NE
National Institute of Technology, OH
National Polytechnic College of Science, CA
North Florida Institute: Orange Park, FL
Ohio College of Massotherapy, OH
Ohio Institute of Health Careers: Columbus, OH
Ohio Institute of Health Careers: Elyria, OH
Phillips Beth Israel School of Nursing, NY
Platt College
  Tulsa, OK
Platt College: Oklahoma City Central, OK
Ponce Paramedical College, PR
Remington College: Nashville, TN
Remington College: North Houston, TX
St. Elizabeth College of Nursing, NY
St. Joseph's College of Nursing, NY
St. Luke's College, IA
St. Vincent Catholic Medical Centers, NY
St. Vincent's College, CT
Sanford-Brown College, MO
Sanford-Brown College
  Colorado Technical University: North Kansas City, MO
Sanford-Brown Institute
  Monroeville, PA
Sanford-Brown Institute: Tampa, FL
South College, NC
Southeast Missouri Hospital College of Nursing and Health Sciences, MO
Southern Ohio College
  Brown Mackie College: North Kentucky, KY
Southwestern College of Business
  Southwestern College: Vine Street Campus, OH
Southwestern College: Florence, KY
Spencerian College, KY
Swedish Institute, NY
Technology Education College, OH
Texas County Technical Institute, MO
Tri-State College, OH
Ultrasound Diagnostic School
  Sanford-Brown Institute: Jacksonville, FL
Universal Technology College of Puerto Rico, PR
Vatterott College, IA
Vet Tech Institute, PA
Virginia College at Montgomery, AL
Virginia College at Pensacola, FL
Virginia College Gulf Coast, MS
Wallace State Community College at Hanceville, AL
West Tennessee Business College, TN
West Virginia Junior College: Bridgeport, WV
Western Career College
  Pleasant Hill, CA
  San Leandro, CA
Western Career College: Citrus Heights, CA
Western Career College: Sacramento, CA
Western Career College: Stockton, CA
Westwood College: Fort Worth, TX
WyoTech: Long Beach, CA
Yorktowne Business Institute, PA

Schools of mortuary science

Four-year

Cincinnati College of Mortuary Science, OH

Two-year

American Academy McAllister Institute of Funeral Service, NY
Commonwealth Institute of Funeral Service, TX
Dallas Institute of Funeral Service, TX
John A. Gupton College, TN
Mid-America College of Funeral Service, IN

Seminary/rabbinical colleges

Four-year

Amridge University, AL
Austin Graduate School of Theology, TX
Baptist Bible College, MO
Baptist Bible College of Pennsylvania, PA
Baptist Missionary Association Theological Seminary, TX
Beis Medrash Heichal Dovid, NY
Beth Hamedrash Shaarei Yosher Institute, NY
Beth Hatalmud Rabbinical College, NY
Beth Medrash Govoha, NJ
Calvary Bible College and Theological Seminary, MO
Central Yeshiva Tomchei Tmimim-Lubavitch, NY
Colegio Biblico Pentecostal, PR
Conception Seminary College, MO
Criswell College, TX
Darkei Noam Rabbinical College, NY
Divine Word College, IA
Earlham College, IN
Erskine College, SC
Faith Baptist Bible College and Theological Seminary, IA
Faith Evangelical Seminary, WA
George Fox University, OR
Global University, MO
Hebrew Theological College, IL
Hellenic College/Holy Cross, MA
Holy Apostles College and Seminary, CT
Holy Trinity Orthodox Seminary, NY
International Baptist College, AZ
Jewish Theological Seminary of America, NY
Kehilath Yakov Rabbinical Seminary, NY
The King's College and Seminary, CA
Lincoln Christian College and Seminary, IL
Luther Rice University, GA
Machzikei Hadath Rabbinical College, NY
The Master's College, CA
Mesivta Torah Vodaath Seminary, NY
Michigan Theological Seminary, MI
Midwest University, MO
Mirrer Yeshiva Central Institute, NY
Mount Angel Seminary, OR
Multnomah University, OR
Ner Israel Rabbinical College, MD
New Orleans Baptist Theological Seminary: Leavell College, LA
Ohr Somayach Tanenbaum Education Center, NY
Piedmont Baptist College, NC
Pontifical College Josephinum, OH
Rabbi Jacob Joseph School, NJ
Rabbinical Academy Mesivta Rabbi Chaim Berlin, NY
Rabbinical College Beth Shraga, NY
Rabbinical College Bobover Yeshiva B'nei Zion, NY
Rabbinical College Ch'san Sofer of New York, NY
Rabbinical College of America, NJ
Rabbinical College of Long Island, NY
Rabbinical College of Ohr Shimon Yisroel, NY
Rabbinical College of Telshe, OH
Rabbinical Seminary Adas Yereim, NY
Rabbinical Seminary of America, NY
Sacred Heart Major Seminary, MI
St. Charles Borromeo Seminary - Overbrook, PA
St. John Vianney College Seminary, FL
St. Joseph Seminary College, LA
Shor Yoshuv Rabbinical College, NY
Southeastern Baptist Theological Seminary, NC
Southern California Seminary, CA
Southwestern Baptist Theological Seminary, TX
Talmudic College of Florida, FL
Talmudical Academy of New Jersey, NJ
Talmudical Institute of Upstate New York, NY
Talmudical Seminary Oholei Torah, NY
Talmudical Yeshiva of Philadelphia, PA
Telshe Yeshiva-Chicago, IL
Torah Temimah Talmudical Seminary, NY
U.T.A. Mesivta-Kiryas Jocl, NY
United Talmudical Seminary, NY
University of Dubuque, IA
Virginia University of Lynchburg, VA
Washington Bible College, MD
World Mission University, CA
Yeshiva and Kolel Bais Medrash Elyon, NY
Yeshiva and Kollel Harbotzas Torah, NY
Yeshiva Beth Yehuda-Yeshiva Gedolah of Greater Detroit, MI
Yeshiva College of the Nations Capital, MD
Yeshiva D'Monsey Rabbinical College, NY
Yeshiva Derech Chaim, NY
Yeshiva Gedolah Imrei Yosef D'Spinka, NY
Yeshiva Gedolah Rabbinical College, FL
Yeshiva Gedolah Zichron Moshe, NY
Yeshiva Karlin Stolin, NY
Yeshiva Mikdash Melech, NY

Tables and Indexes

Yeshiva of Nitra, NY
Yeshiva of the Telshe Alumni, NY
Yeshiva Ohr Elchonon Chabad/West Coast Talmudical Seminary, CA
Yeshiva Shaar Hatorah, NY
Yeshiva Shaarei Torah of Rockland, NY
Yeshiva Toras Chaim Talmudical Seminary, CO
Yeshivas Novominsk, NY
Yeshivath Beth Moshe, PA
Yeshivath Viznitz, NY

Two-year

Salvation Army College for Officer Training at Crestmont, CA
Shepherds Theological Seminary, NC

Teacher's colleges

Four-year

American Indian College of the Assemblies of God, AZ
Anderson University, SC
Arlington Baptist College, TX
Athens State University, AL
Augusta State University, GA
Austin College, TX
Baker University, KS
Baltimore Hebrew University, MD
Baptist College of Florida, FL
Black Hills State University, SD
Bloomfield College, NJ
Bridgewater State College, MA
California State University
  Monterey Bay, CA
Cambridge College, MA
Canisius College, NY
Chadron State College, NE
Clarion University of Pennsylvania, PA
College of St. Joseph in Vermont, VT
College of Saint Mary, NE
College of Saint Rose, NY
Concordia University, MI
Concordia University, OR
Concordia University Chicago, IL
Dalton State College, GA
Eastern Illinois University, IL
Edinboro University of Pennsylvania, PA
Fitchburg State College, MA
Florida Christian College, FL
Fort Valley State University, GA
Framingham State College, MA
Free Will Baptist Bible College, TN
Frostburg State University, MD
Glenville State College, WV
Great Basin College, NV
Heritage University, WA
Howard Payne University, TX
Jarvis Christian College, TX
Jones College, FL
Keene State College, NH
Kendall College, IL
Lander University, SC
Laura and Alvin Siegal College of Judaic Studies, OH
Lesley University, MA
Lyndon State College, VT
Manhattanville College, NY
Mayville State University, ND
National-Louis University, IL
Nevada State College, NV
New England College, NH
Northwestern Oklahoma State University, OK
Oglala Lakota College, SD
Pacific Oaks College, CA
Peru State College, NE
Piedmont College, GA
Plymouth State University, NH
Rabbinical College of Long Island, NY
Rabbinical College of Telshe, OH
Reinhardt College, GA
Rivier College, NH
St. Joseph's College, NY
Southeastern Oklahoma State University, OK
Southeastern University, FL
State University of New York
  College at Buffalo, NY
  College at Cortland, NY
  College at Plattsburgh, NY
  College at Potsdam, NY
Tennessee Wesleyan College, TN
Trinity Baptist College, FL
Union College, KY
University of Hawaii
  West Oahu, HI
University of Maine
  Farmington, ME
University of Montana: Western, MT
University of Puerto Rico
  Cayey University College, PR
University of the Southwest, NM
Valley City State University, ND
VanderCook College of Music, IL
Wayne State College, NE
West Virginia State University, WV
Western Oregon University, OR
Westfield State College, MA
Wheelock College, MA
Worcester State College, MA
York College, NE

Two-year

Northern New Mexico College, NM

Technical and career colleges

Four-year

Art Institute
  of Pittsburgh, PA
Art Institute of California: Hollywood, CA
Art Institute of Fort Lauderdale, FL
Art Institute of Seattle, WA
Art Institute of Tucson, AZ
Baker College
  of Auburn Hills, MI
  of Clinton Township, MI
  of Flint, MI
  of Jackson, MI
  of Muskegon, MI
  of Owosso, MI
  of Port Huron, MI
Bluefield State College, WV
Briarcliffe College, NY
Central Pennsylvania College, PA
Charter College, AK
City College: Fort Lauderdale, FL
City University of New York
  New York City College of Technology, NY
Clayton State University, GA
Coleman University, CA
CollegeAmerica
  Fort Collins, CO
Collins College, AZ
Colorado Technical University, CO
Columbia Centro Universitario: Caguas, PR
Design Institute of San Diego, CA
DeVry
  Devry College of New York, NY
DeVry University: Memphis, TN
DeVry University: Sandy, UT
ECPI College of Technology: Newport News, VA
ECPI College of Technology: Virginia Beach, VA
ECPI Technical College
  Glen Allen, VA
Electronic Data Processing College of Puerto Rico, PR
Ex'pression College for Digital Arts, CA
Fairmont State University, WV
Florida Career College: Lauderdale Lakes, FL
Hamilton Technical College, IA
Herzing College, LA
Herzing College, AL
Herzing College, GA
Hickey College, MO
International Academy of Design and Technology
  Sacramento, CA
International Academy of Design and Technology: Chicago, IL
International Academy of Design and Technology: Detroit, MI
International Academy of Design and Technology: Henderson, NV
International Academy of Design and Technology: Schaumburg, IL
International Academy of Design and Technology: Tampa, FL
LA College International, CA
Lewis-Clark State College, ID
Miller-Motte Technical College, NC
Minnesota School of Business, MN
Minnesota School of Business: Plymouth, MN
Minnesota School of Business: Shakopee, MN
Missouri Technical School, MO
Montana State University
  Billings, MT
Montana Tech of the University of Montana, MT
Mt. Sierra College, CA
National American University
  Rapid City, SD
National College of Business and Technology: Arecibo, PR
National College of Business and Technology: Bayamon, PR
National College of Business and Technology: Rio Grande, PR
National Education Center
  Spartan College of Aeronautics and Technology, OK
Neumont University, UT
New England Institute of Art, MA
New England Institute of Technology, RI
Peirce College, PA
Pennsylvania College of Technology, PA
Platt College
  Ontario, CA
  San Diego, CA
Rasmussen College: Fort Myers, FL
Rasmussen College: Lake Elmo/Woodbury, MN
Remington College: Largo, FL
Remington College: Tampa, FL
Sanford-Brown College: Vienna, VA
Silicon Valley College
  Western Career College: Emeryville, CA
Silicon Valley University, CA
State University of New York
  Farmingdale, NY
Stevens-Henager College: Logan, UT
University College of San Juan, PR
University of Arkansas
  Monticello, AR
University of Puerto Rico
  Aguadilla, PR
  Bayamon University College, PR
Utah Valley University, UT
Vaughn College of Aeronautics and Technology, NY
Vermont Technical College, VT
Virginia College, AL
Virginia College at Huntsville, AL
Wentworth Institute of Technology, MA
West Virginia University Institute of Technology, WV
Westwood College of Technology
  Westwood College: Denver South, CO
  Westwood College: Inland Empire, CA
  Westwood College: O'Hare Airport, IL
Westwood College: Anaheim, CA
Westwood College: Atlanta Midtown, GA
Westwood College: Chicago Loop, IL
Westwood College: Denver North, CO
Westwood College: DuPage, IL
Westwood College: Northlake, GA
Westwood College: South Bay, CA
Woodbury Institute of Champlain College, VT
World College, VA

Two-year

Academy of Court Reporting: Cleveland, OH
Advanced Technology Institute, VA
Aiken Technical College, SC
Albany Technical College, GA
Alexandria Technical College, MN
Allied Medical and Technical Institute, PA
Angley College, FL
Anoka Technical College, MN
Anthem College, AZ
Antonelli College, OH
Antonelli College
  Hattiesburg, MS
  Jackson, MS
Arizona Automotive Institute, AZ
Arkansas State University
  Mountain Home, AR
Art Institute
  of New York City, NY
Art Institute of California: Sunnyvale, CA
Art Institute of York, PA
Asheville-Buncombe Technical Community College, NC
Asnuntuck Community College, CT
Athens Technical College, GA
ATI Career Training Center
  Dallas, TX
  Ft. Lauderdale, FL
  Oakland Park, FL
ATI College of Health, FL
Atlanta Technical College, GA
ATS Institute of Technology, OH
Augusta Technical College, GA
Aviation Institute of Maintenance: Indianapolis, IN
Aviation Institute of Maintenance: Kansas City, MO
Aviation Institute of Maintenance: Virginia Beach, VA
Bainbridge College, GA
Bates Technical College, WA
Baton Rouge School of Computers, LA
Bel-Rea Institute of Animal Technology, CO
Bellingham Technical College, WA
Belmont Technical College, OH
Benjamin Franklin Institute of Technology, MA
Berks Technical Institute, PA
Big Sandy Community and Technical College, KY
Black River Technical College, AR
Blackhawk Technical College, WI
Blue Cliff College: Gulfport, MS
Blue Cliff College: Houma, LA
Blue Cliff College: Lafayette, LA
Blue Cliff College: Metairie, LA
Blue Cliff College: Shreveport, LA
Blue Ridge Community and Technical College, WV
Blue Ridge Community College, NC
Bluegrass Community and Technical College, KY
Bolivar Technical College, MO
Bradford School, OH
Bradford School of Business, TX
Bramson ORT College, NY
Brown Mackie College: Atlanta, GA
Brown Mackie College: Louisville, KY
Brown Mackie College: South Bend, IN
Bryan College: Los Angeles, CA
Bryan College: Sacramento, CA
Bryant & Stratton College: Cleveland, OH
Caldwell Community College and Technical Institute, NC
Cambria-Rowe Business College: Indiana, PA
Cambridge College, CO
Camelot College, LA
Capital Community College, CT
Carteret Community College, NC
CEI College
  Kaplan College: Panorama City, CA
Central Carolina Technical College, SC
Central Community College, NE
Central Florida College, FL
Central Georgia Technical College, GA
Central Lakes College, MN
Central Maine Community College, ME
Central New Mexico Community College, NM
Central Ohio Technical College, OH
Central Texas College, TX
Centura College: Newport News, VA
Centura College: Virginia Beach, VA
Century Community and Technical College, MN
Chattahoochee Technical College, GA
Chattanooga State Technical Community College, TN
CHI Institute: Broomall, PA
CHI Institute: Franklin Mills, PA
Chippewa Valley Technical College, WI
Cincinnati State Technical and Community College, OH

Cleveland Institute of Electronics, OH
Clover Park Technical College, WA
Coffeyville Community College, KS
Colegio de las Ciencias Artes y Television, PR
Coleman College: San Marcos, CA
College of Business and Technology: Flagler, FL
College of Business and Technology: Hialeah, FL
College of Court Reporting, IN
College of the Mainland, TX
CollegeAmerica
Denver, CO
Colorado School of Trades, CO
Columbus State Community College, OH
Columbus Technical College, GA
Commonwealth Technical Institute, PA
Community College of the Air Force, AL
Concorde Career College
Garden Grove, CA
Concorde Career College: San Bernardino, CA
Coosa Valley Technical College, GA
Court Reporting Institute of Dallas, TX
Court Reporting Institute of Houston, TX
Cowley County Community College, KS
Dakota County Technical College, MN
Daymar College: Paducah, KY
Daytona State College, FL
Dean Institute of Technology, PA
DeKalb Technical College, GA
Delaware Technical and Community College
Owens, DE
Stanton/Wilmington, DE
Terry, DE
Delta College of Arts & Technology, LA
Delta School of Business & Technology, LA
Denmark Technical College, SC
Dodge City Community College, KS
DuBois Business College, PA
Dunwoody College of Technology, MN
Durham Technical Community College, NC
Eagle Gate College: Layton, UT
Eagle Gate College: Murray, UT
Eagle Gate College: Salt Lake City, UT
Eastern Idaho Technical College, ID
Eastern Maine Community College, ME
Eastern West Virginia Community and Technical College, WV
ECPI Technical College
Richmond, VA
ECPI Technical College: Roanoke, VA
EDIC College, PR
Electronic Computer Programming College, TN
Elizabethtown Community and Technical College, KY
Elmira Business Institute, NY
Elmira Business Institute: Vestal, NY
Erie Institute of Technology, PA
ETI Technical College of Niles, OH

Everest College
Phoenix, AZ
Everest College: Arlington, TX
Everest College: Aurora, CO
Fayetteville Technical Community College, NC
Florence-Darlington Technical College, SC
Florida Career College: Hialeah, FL
Florida Career College: Miami, FL
Florida Career College: Pembroke Pines, FL
Florida Career College: West Palm Beach, FL
Florida Technical College
Deland, FL
Jacksonville, FL
Orlando, FL
Forsyth Technical Community College, NC
Fountainhead College of Technology, TN
Fox College, IL
Fox Valley Technical College, WI
Full Sail University, FL
Fullerton College, CA
Gadsden State Community College, AL
Gallipolis Career College, OH
Gateway Community and Technical College, KY
Gateway Community College, AZ
Gateway Technical College, WI
George C. Wallace State Community College
Selma, AL
Grayson County College, TX
Great Bay Community College, NH
Greenville Technical College, SC
Gretna Career College, LA
Griffin Technical College, GA
Guam Community College, GU
Gulf Coast College, FL
Gupton Jones College of Funeral Service, GA
Gwinnett Technical College, GA
Hallmark College of Aeronautics, TX
Hallmark College of Technology, TX
Hawkeye Community College, IA
Haywood Community College, NC
Hazard Community and Technical College, KY
Heald College
Fresno, CA
Hayward, CA
Honolulu, HI
Rancho Cordova, CA
Heald College: Portland, OR
Helena College of Technology of the University of Montana, MT
Hennepin Technical College, MN
Herzing College
Minneapolis Drafting School Division of , MN
Hibbing Community College, MN
High-Tech Institute, GA
High-Tech Institute, TN
High-Tech Institute, FL
High-Tech Institute, MO
High-Tech Institute, NV
High-Tech Institute, MN
Hocking College, OH
Hondros College, OH
Horry-Georgetown Technical College, SC
Huertas Junior College, PR
Hussian School of Art, PA
Indian Hills Community College, IA
Institute of Business & Medical Careers, CO

Institute of Design and Construction, NY
IntelliTec College, CO
IntelliTec College: Grand Junction, CO
International Academy of Design and Technology: San Antonio, TX
International College of Broadcasting, OH
Iowa Western Community College, IA
Island Drafting and Technical Institute, NY
Itawamba Community College, MS
ITI Technical College, LA
James A. Rhodes State College, OH
Jefferson College, MO
Jefferson Community and Technical College, KY
Jefferson Community College, OH
JNA Institute of Culinary Arts, PA
Johnson College, PA
Johnston Community College, NC
Kaplan Career Institute: Harrisburg, PA
Kaplan College: Denver, CO
Kaplan College: Hammond, IN
Kaplan College: Merrillville, IN
Kaplan College: Palm Springs, CA
Kaplan College: Phoenix, AZ
Kaplan College: Sacramento, CA
Kaplan College: Salida, CA
Kaplan College: Vista, CA
Kennebec Valley Community College, ME
Key College, FL
Keystone Technical Institute, PA
Lake Area Technical Institute, SD
Lake Region State College, ND
Lake Superior College, MN
Lake Washington Technical College, WA
Lakes Region Community College, NH
Lakeshore Technical College, WI
Lamar Institute of Technology, TX
Lamar State College at Port Arthur, TX
Lamson College, AZ
Laurel Business Institute, PA
Laurel Technical Institute, PA
Le Cordon Bleu College of Culinary Arts, GA
Lincoln College of Technology: Denver, CO
Lincoln College of Technology: Grand Prairie, TX
Lincoln College of Technology: Indianapolis, IN
Lincoln College of Technology: West Palm Beach, FL
Lincoln Technical Institute: Allentown, PA
Lincoln Technical Institute: Northeast Philadelphia, PA
Lincoln Technical Institute: Philadelphia, PA
Linn State Technical College, MO
Los Angeles Trade and Technical College, CA
Louisville Technical Institute, KY
Luna Community College, NM
Madison Area Technical College, WI
Manchester Community College, NH
Manhattan Area Technical College, KS
Marion Technical College, OH
Martin Community College, NC

Maysville Community and Technical College, KY
McCann School of Business
and Technology: Pottsville, PA
and Technology: Sunbury, PA
McCann School of Business and Technology: Dickson City, PA
McCann School of Business and Technology: Hazleton, PA
McDowell Technical Community College, NC
Mesabi Range Community and Technical College, MN
Mesalands Community College, NM
Metropolitan Career Center Computer Technology Institute, PA
Metropolitan Community College, NE
Mid-Plains Community College Area, NE
Mid-State Technical College, WI
Middle Georgia Technical College, GA
Midlands Technical College, SC
Miller-Motte Technical College, SC
Miller-Motte Technical College: Cary, NC
Miller-Motte Technical College: Chattanooga, TN
Miller-Motte Technical College: Lynchburg, VA
Milwaukee Area Technical College, WI
Minneapolis Business College, MN
Minneapolis Community and Technical College, MN
Minnesota State College - Southeast Technical, MN
Minnesota State Community and Technical College, MN
Minnesota West Community and Technical College, MN
Missouri College, MO
Mitchell Technical Institute, SD
Montana State University
College of Technology: Great Falls, MT
Moraine Park Technical College, WI
Morrison Institute of Technology, IL
Mountain State College, WV
MTI College, CA
Nashua Community College, NH
Nashville Auto-Diesel College, TN
Nashville State Community College, TN
National College
Dayton, OH
Knoxville, TN
Nashville, TN
National Institute of Technology, OH
National Park Community College, AR
Naugatuck Valley Community College, CT
Navajo Technical College, NM
New Castle School of Trades, PA
New Mexico Junior College, NM
New River Community and Technical College, WV
NHTI-Concord's Community College, NH
Nicolet Area Technical College, WI
North Arkansas College, AR
North Central Kansas Technical College, KS
North Central State College, OH

North Dakota State College of Science, ND
North Georgia Technical College, GA
North Metro Technical College, GA
Northcentral Technical College, WI
Northeast State Technical Community College, TN
Northeast Wisconsin Technical College, WI
Northeastern Technical College, SC
Northern Maine Community College, ME
Northland Community & Technical College, MN
Northland Pioneer College, AZ
Northwest Aviation College, WA
Northwest School of Wooden Boatbuilding, WA
Northwest State Community College, OH
Northwest Technical College, MN
Northwest Technical Institute, MN
Northwest-Shoals Community College, AL
Northwestern Business College, IL
Northwestern Connecticut Community College, CT
Northwestern Technical College, GA
Norwalk Community College, CT
Nossi College of Art, TN
Nunez Community College, LA
Ohio Institute of Photography and Technology, OH
Ohio Technical College, OH
Ohio Valley College of Technology, OH
Oklahoma State University
Institute of Technology:
Okmulgee, OK
Oklahoma City, OK
Orangeburg-Calhoun Technical College, SC
Orleans Technical Institute - Center City Campus, PA
Ouachita Technical College, AR
Owensboro Community and Technical College, KY
Ozarka College, AR
Ozarks Technical Community College, MO
Palau Community College, PW
Pellissippi State Technical Community College, TN
Penn Commercial Business and Technical School, PA
Pennco Tech, PA
Pennsylvania Culinary Institute, PA
Pennsylvania Institute of Technology, PA
Pennsylvania School of Business, PA
Piedmont Technical College, SC
Pima Community College, AZ
Pine Technical College, MN
Pinnacle Career Institute: Kansas City, MO
Pitt Community College, NC
Pittsburgh Institute of Aeronautics, PA
Pittsburgh Institute of Mortuary Science, PA
Pittsburgh Technical Institute, PA
Platt College
Huntington Beach, CA
Los Angeles, CA
Pratt Community College, KS
Prince Institute of Professional Studies, AL
Pulaski Technical College, AR

Quinebaug Valley Community College, CT
Rainy River Community College, MN
Randolph Community College, NC
Ranken Technical College, MO
Rasmussen College: Aurora, IL
Rasmussen College: Green Bay, WI
Rasmussen College: Rockford, IL
Redstone College, CO
Refrigeration School, AZ
Remington College
Baton Rouge, LA
Cleveland, OH
Colorado Springs, CO
Dallas, TX
Fort Worth, TX
Houston, TX
Little Rock, AR
Memphis, TN
Mobile, AL
Remington College: Cleveland West, OH
Remington College: Nashville, TN
Remington College: North Houston, TX
Remington College: Shreveport, LA
Renton Technical College, WA
RETS Tech Center, OH
Ridgewater College, MN
River Valley Community College, NH
Riverland Community College, MN
Rochester Community and Technical College, MN
Rosedale Technical Institute, PA
Rowan-Cabarrus Community College, NC
Sage College, CA
St. Cloud Technical College, MN
St. Paul College, MN
Salt Lake Community College, UT
San Jacinto College, TX
Sanford-Brown College
Colorado Technical University: North Kansas City, MO
Hazelwood, MO
Sanford-Brown Institute: Pittsburgh, PA
Savannah River College, GA
Savannah Technical College, GA
School of Advertising Art, OH
Scottsdale Culinary Institute, AZ
Shelton State Community College, AL
Silicon Valley College
Western Career College: San Jose, CA
Sisseton Wahpeton College, SD
Somerset Community College, KY
South Central College, MN
South College, NC
South Florida Community College, FL
South Hills School of Business & Technology, PA
South Hills School of Business & Technology: Altoona, PA
South Texas College, TX
Southeast Arkansas College, AR
Southeast Kentucky Community and Technical College, KY
Southeast Technical Institute, SD
Southeastern Business College: Lancaster, OH
Southeastern Technical College, GA
Southern Arkansas University Tech, AR
Southern Maine Community College, ME
Southern Union State Community College, AL
Southwest Georgia Technical College, GA
Southwest Institute of Technology, TX
Southwest Wisconsin Technical College, WI
Southwestern College of Business
Southwestern College: Franklin, OH
Southwestern Indian Polytechnic Institute, NM
Spartanburg Community College, SC
Spencerian College: Lexington, KY
Springfield Technical Community College, MA
Stark State College of Technology, OH
State University of New York
College of Agriculture and Technology at Cobleskill, NY
College of Agriculture and Technology at Morrisville, NY
College of Technology at Alfred, NY
College of Technology at Canton, NY
College of Technology at Delhi, NY
Stautzenberger College, OH
Stenotype Institute: Orlando, FL
Stevens-Henager College: Boise, ID
Technical Career Institutes, NY
Technical College of the Lowcountry, SC
Technology Education College, OH
Terra State Community College, OH
TESST College of Technology
Baltimore, MD
Beltsville, MD
TESST College of Technology: Alexandria, VA
TESST College of Technology: Towson, MD
Texas County Technical Institute, MO
Texas Culinary Academy, TX
Texas State Technical College
Harlingen, TX
Waco, TX
West Texas, TX
Texas State Technical College: Marshall, TX
Thaddeus Stevens College of Technology, PA
Three Rivers Community College, CT
Tri-County Technical College, SC
Triangle Tech
DuBois, PA
Erie, PA
Greensburg, PA
Pittsburgh, PA
Triangle Tech: Bethlehem, PA
Triangle Tech: Sunbury, PA
Trident Technical College, SC
Truckee Meadows Community College, NV
Tulsa Welding School, OK
United Tribes Technical College, ND
Universal Technical Institute, AZ
University of Arkansas
Community College at Hope, AR
University of Hawaii
Honolulu Community College, HI
University of Northwestern Ohio, OH
Utah Career College, UT
Valdosta Technical College, GA
Vatterott College, OK
Vatterott College, MO
Vatterott College, IA
Vatterott College
Tulsa, OK
Vatterott College: Cleveland, OH
Vatterott College: Joplin, MO
Vatterott College: Kansas City, MO
Vatterott College: Memphis, TN
Vatterott College: O'Fallon, MO
Vatterott College: Quincy, IL
Vatterott College: St. Joseph, MO
Vatterott College: Spring Valley, NE
Vatterott College: Springfield, MO
Vatterott College: Sunset Hills, MO
Vermilion Community College, MN
Vet Tech Institute, PA
Virginia College at Austin, TX
Virginia College at Mobile, AL
Wake Technical Community College, NC
Walla Walla Community College, WA
Washington County Community College, ME
Waukesha County Technical College, WI
West Central Technical College, GA
West Georgia Technical College, GA
West Kentucky Community and Technical College, KY
West Virginia Junior College: Charleston, WV
West Virginia Northern Community College, WV
West Virginia State Community and Technical College, WV
Western Career College
Pleasant Hill, CA
San Leandro, CA
Western Career College: Antioch, CA
Western Career College: Citrus Heights, CA
Western Career College: Sacramento, CA
Western Career College: Stockton, CA
Western Dakota Technical Institute, SD
Western Technical College, TX
Western Technical College, WI
Western Technical College: Diana Drive, TX
Westwood College of Technology
Westwood College: Los Angeles, CA
Westwood College: Dallas, TX
Westwood College: Fort Worth, TX
Westwood College: Houston South, TX
White Mountains Community College, NH
Williamsburg Technical College, SC
Williamson Free School of Mechanical Trades, PA
Wisconsin Indianhead Technical College, WI
WyoTech: Fremont, CA
WyoTech: Laramie, WY
WyoTech: Long Beach, CA
York County Community College, ME
York Technical College, SC
YTI Career Institute: Lancaster, PA
Zane State College, OH

Special characteristics

Colleges for men

Four-year
Conception Seminary College, MO
Divine Word College, IA
Hampden-Sydney College, VA
Holy Trinity Orthodox Seminary, NY
Morehouse College, GA
Mount Angel Seminary, OR
Ohr Somayach Tanenbaum Education Center, NY
Pontifical College Josephinum, OH
Rabbinical College of Telshe, OH
St. Charles Borromeo Seminary - Overbrook, PA
St. John Vianney College Seminary, FL
St. John's University, MN
St. Joseph Seminary College, LA
Talmudic College of Florida, FL
Talmudical Yeshiva of Philadelphia, PA
Telshe Yeshiva-Chicago, IL
Wabash College, IN
Yeshiva Mikdash Melech, NY
Yeshiva Ohr Elchonon Chabad/West Coast Talmudical Seminary, CA

Two-year
Deep Springs College, CA
Williamson Free School of Mechanical Trades, PA

Colleges for women

Four-year
Agnes Scott College, GA
Alverno College, WI
Barnard College, NY
Bay Path College, MA
Bennett College, NC
Brenau University, GA
Bryn Mawr College, PA
Carlow University, PA
Cedar Crest College, PA
Chatham University, PA
College of New Rochelle, NY
College of Notre Dame of Maryland, MD
College of St. Benedict, MN
College of St. Catherine, MN
College of St. Elizabeth, NJ
College of Saint Mary, NE
Columbia College, SC
Converse College, SC
Georgian Court University, NJ
Hollins University, VA
Judson College, AL
Lexington College, IL
Mary Baldwin College, VA
Meredith College, NC
Midway College, KY
Mills College, CA
Moore College of Art and Design, PA
Mount Holyoke College, MA
Mount Mary College, WI
Peace College, NC
Pine Manor College, MA
Russell Sage College, NY
St. Joseph College, CT
Saint Mary's College, IN
St. Mary-of-the-Woods College, IN
Salem College, NC
Scripps College, CA
Simmons College, MA
Smith College, MA
Spelman College, GA
Stephens College, MO
Sweet Briar College, VA
Trinity Washington University, DC
Ursuline College, OH
Wellesley College, MA
Wesleyan College, GA
Wilson College, PA

Two-year
Assumption College for Sisters, NJ
Cottey College, MO

Affiliated with a religion

African Methodist Episcopal Church

Four-year
Allen University, SC
Edward Waters College, FL
Wilberforce University, OH

African Methodist Episcopal Zion Church

Four-year
Livingstone College, NC

American Baptist Churches in the USA

Four-year
Alderson-Broaddus College, WV
Arkansas Baptist College, AR
Bacone College, OK
Benedict College, SC
Eastern University, PA
Florida Memorial University, FL
Franklin College, IN
Judson University, IL
Keuka College, NY
Linfield College, OR
Ottawa University, KS
University of Sioux Falls, SD

Assemblies of God

Four-year
American Indian College of the Assemblies of God, AZ
Bethany University, CA
Central Bible College, MO
Evangel University, MO
Global University, MO
Northwest University, WA
School of Urban Missions: Oakland, CA
Southeastern University, FL
Southwestern Assemblies of God University, TX
Valley Forge Christian College, PA
Vanguard University of Southern California, CA
Zion Bible College, MA

Baptist faith

Four-year
Arlington Baptist College, TX
Baptist Bible College, MO
Baptist Bible College of Pennsylvania, PA
Baptist College of Health Sciences, TN
Baptist Missionary Association Theological Seminary, TX
Baylor University, TX
Bluefield College, VA
Campbellsville University, KY
Cedarville University, OH
Central Baptist College, AR
Corban College, OR
Dallas Baptist University, TX
East Texas Baptist University, TX
Hardin-Simmons University, TX
Houston Baptist University, TX
Howard Payne University, TX
Judson College, AL
Liberty University, VA
Maranatha Baptist Bible College, WI
Mars Hill College, NC
Mercer University, GA
Missouri Baptist University, MO
Morris College, SC
Piedmont Baptist College, NC
Selma University, AL
Shaw University, NC
Southwestern College, AZ
Tennessee Temple University, TN
University of Mary Hardin-Baylor, TX
University of Mobile, AL
University of the Cumberlands, KY
Virginia Intermont College, VA
Virginia Union University, VA
William Carey University, MS
Wingate University, NC

Two-year
Jacksonville College, TX

Baptist General Conference

Four-year
Bethel University, MN
Oakland City University, IN

Brethren Church

Four-year
Ashland University, OH
Emmaus Bible College, IA
Grace College, IN

Christian and Missionary Alliance

Four-year
Crown College, MN
Nyack College, NY
Simpson University, CA
Toccoa Falls College, GA

Christian Church

Four-year
Atlanta Christian College, GA
Bethesda Christian University, CA
Central Christian College of the Bible, MO
Crossroads College, MN
Johnson Bible College, TN
Manhattan Christian College, KS
The Master's College, CA
Visible School - Music and Worship Arts College, TN

Christian Church (Disciples of Christ)

Four-year
Barton College, NC
Bethany College, WV
Chapman University, CA
Columbia College, MO
Culver-Stockton College, MO
Eureka College, IL
Hiram College, OH
Jarvis Christian College, TX
Lynchburg College, VA
Midway College, KY
Northwest Christian University, OR
Texas Christian University, TX
Transylvania University, KY
William Woods University, MO

Christian Methodist Episcopal Church

Four-year
Lane College, TN
Miles College, AL
Texas College, TX

Christian Reformed Church

Four-year
Calvin College, MI
Dordt College, IA

Church of Christ

Four-year
Abilene Christian University, TX
Amridge University, AL
Austin Graduate School of Theology, TX
Carolina Christian College, NC
Faulkner University, AL
Freed-Hardeman University, TN
Harding University, AR
Heritage Christian University, AL
Lincoln Christian College and Seminary, IL
Lipscomb University, TN
Lubbock Christian University, TX
Magnolia Bible College, MS
Ohio Valley University, WV
Oklahoma Christian University, OK
Pepperdine University, CA
Roanoke Bible College, NC
Rochester College, MI
York College, NE

Two-year
Crowley's Ridge College, AR

Church of God

Four-year
Anderson University, IN
Lee University, TN
Mid-America Christian University, OK
University of Findlay, OH
Warner Pacific College, OR
Warner University, FL

Church of Jesus Christ of Latter-day Saints

Four-year
Brigham Young University, UT
Brigham Young University-Hawaii, HI
Brigham Young University-Idaho, ID
Southern Virginia University, VA

Two-year
LDS Business College, UT

Church of the Brethren

Four-year
Bridgewater College, VA
Elizabethtown College, PA
Manchester College, IN
McPherson College, KS

Church of the Nazarene

Four-year
MidAmerica Nazarene University, KS
Mount Vernon Nazarene University, OH
Nazarene Bible College, CO
Northwest Nazarene University, ID
Olivet Nazarene University, IL
Point Loma Nazarene University, CA
Southern Nazarene University, OK
Trevecca Nazarene University, TN

Episcopal Church

Four-year
Bard College, NY
Clarkson College, NE
St. Augustine College, IL
St. Augustine's College, NC
St. Luke's College, MO
St. Paul's College, VA
University of the South, TN

Evangelical Free Church of America

Four-year
Trinity International University, IL

Evangelical Lutheran Church in America

Four-year
Augsburg College, MN
Augustana College, IL
Augustana College, SD
Bethany College, KS
California Lutheran University, CA
Capital University, OH
Carthage College, WI
Concordia College: Moorhead, MN
Finlandia University, MI
Grand View University, IA
Gustavus Adolphus College, MN
Lenoir-Rhyne University, NC
Luther College, IA
Muhlenberg College, PA
Newberry College, SC
Pacific Lutheran University, WA
Roanoke College, VA
St. Olaf College, MN
Susquehanna University, PA
Texas Lutheran University, TX
Thiel College, PA
Waldorf College, IA
Wartburg College, IA
Wittenberg University, OH

Evangelical Lutheran Synod

Four-year
Bethany Lutheran College, MN

Free Methodist Church of North America

Four-year
Central Christian College of Kansas, KS
Greenville College, IL
Roberts Wesleyan College, NY
Seattle Pacific University, WA
Spring Arbor University, MI

Free Will Baptists

Four-year

Free Will Baptist Bible College, TN
Mount Olive College, NC

General Association of Regular Baptist Churches

Four-year

Faith Baptist Bible College and Theological Seminary, IA

Interdenominational tradition

Four-year

Asbury College, KY
Azusa Pacific University, CA
Biola University, CA
College of the Ozarks, MO
Cornerstone University, MI
Ecclesia College, AR
God's Bible School and College, OH
Grace University, NE
Heritage University, WA
Hobe Sound Bible College, FL
John Brown University, AR
John Wesley College, NC
Messiah College, PA
Moody Bible Institute, IL
Multnomah University, OR
Oak Hills Christian College, MN
Patten University, CA
Regent University, VA
Taylor University, IN
Trinity College of Florida, FL
Williamson Christian College, TN

Jewish faith

Four-year

American Jewish University, CA
Gratz College, PA
Jewish Theological Seminary of America, NY
Laura and Alvin Siegal College of Judaic Studies, OH
Michigan Jewish Institute, MI
Ohr Somayach Tanenbaum Education Center, NY
Rabbinical College of Telshe, OH
Talmudic College of Florida, FL
Talmudical Yeshiva of Philadelphia, PA
Telshe Yeshiva-Chicago, IL
Yeshiva Mikdash Melech, NY
Yeshiva Ohr Elchonon Chabad/West Coast Talmudical Seminary, CA

Two-year

Bramson ORT College, NY

Lutheran Church

Four-year

Trinity Lutheran College, WA
Valparaiso University, IN

Lutheran Church - Missouri Synod

Four-year

Concordia College, NY
Concordia University, CA
Concordia University, NE
Concordia University, MI
Concordia University, OR
Concordia University Chicago, IL
Concordia University Texas, TX
Concordia University Wisconsin, WI
Concordia University: St. Paul, MN

Lutheran Church in America

Four-year

Wagner College, NY

Mennonite Brethren Church

Four-year

Fresno Pacific University, CA
Tabor College, KS

Mennonite Church

Four-year

Bethel College, KS
Bluffton University, OH
Eastern Mennonite University, VA
Goshen College, IN

Two-year

Hesston College, KS
Rosedale Bible College, OH

Missionary Church

Four-year

Bethel College, IN

Moravian Church in America

Four-year

Moravian College, PA
Salem College, NC

Nondenominational tradition

Four-year

Alaska Bible College, AK
Amberton University, TX
Appalachian Bible College, WV
Boise Bible College, ID
Calvary Bible College and Theological Seminary, MO
Clearwater Christian College, FL
Colorado Christian University, CO
Crichton College, TN
Dallas Christian College, TX
Davis College, NY
Friends University, KS
Gordon College, MA
King's College, NY
The King's College and Seminary, CA
Lancaster Bible College, PA
LeTourneau University, TX
Northwestern College, MN
Occidental College, CA
Oral Roberts University, OK
Ozark Christian College, MO
Palm Beach Atlantic University, FL
San Diego Christian College, CA
Southeastern Bible College, AL
Washington Bible College, MD
Westmont College, CA
Wheaton College, IL
William Jessup University, CA
World Mission University, CA

Two-year

Williamson Free School of Mechanical Trades, PA

Pentecostal Holiness Church

Four-year

Colegio Pentecostal Mizpa, PR
Emmanuel College, GA
Southwestern Christian University, OK

Presbyterian Church (USA)

Four-year

Agnes Scott College, GA
Alma College, MI
Arcadia University, PA
Austin College, TX
Belhaven College, MS
Bethel College, TN
Blackburn College, IL
Bloomfield College, NJ
Buena Vista University, IA
Carroll University, WI
Centre College, KY
Coe College, IA
Davidson College, NC
Davis and Elkins College, WV
Eckerd College, FL
Grove City College, PA
Hampden-Sydney College, VA
Hanover College, IN
Jamestown College, ND
King College, TN
Lafayette College, PA
Lake Forest College, IL
Lees-McRae College, NC
Lindenwood University, MO
Lyon College, AR
Macalester College, MN
Mary Baldwin College, VA
Maryville College, TN
Millikin University, IL
Missouri Valley College, MO
Monmouth College, IL
Muskingum College, OH
Peace College, NC
Pikeville College, KY
Presbyterian College, SC
Queens University of Charlotte, NC
Rhodes College, TN
St. Andrews Presbyterian College, NC
Schreiner University, TX
Sterling College, KS
Trinity University, TX
Tusculum College, TN
University of Dubuque, IA
University of the Ozarks, AR
University of Tulsa, OK
Warren Wilson College, NC
Waynesburg University, PA
Westminster College, PA
Westminster College, MO
Whitworth University, WA
Wilson College, PA

Reformed Church in America

Four-year

Central College, IA
Hope College, MI
Northwestern College, IA

Reformed Presbyterian Church of North America

Four-year

Geneva College, PA

Roman Catholic Church

Four-year

Albertus Magnus College, CT
Alvernia University, PA
Alverno College, WI
Anna Maria College, MA
Aquinas College, MI
Aquinas College, TN
Assumption College, MA
Ave Maria University, FL
Avila University, MO
Barry University, FL
Bayamon Central University, PR
Bellarmine University, KY
Belmont Abbey College, NC
Benedictine College, KS
Benedictine University, IL
Boston College, MA
Brescia University, KY
Briar Cliff University, IA
Cabrini College, PA
Caldwell College, NJ
Calumet College of St. Joseph, IN
Canisius College, NY
Cardinal Stritch University, WI
Carlow University, PA
Carroll College, MT
Catholic University of America, DC
Chaminade University of Honolulu, HI
Chestnut Hill College, PA
Christendom College, VA
Christian Brothers University, TN
Clarke College, IA
College of Mount St. Joseph, OH
College of Mount St. Vincent, NY
College of New Rochelle, NY
College of Notre Dame of Maryland, MD
College of St. Benedict, MN
College of St. Catherine, MN
College of St. Elizabeth, NJ
College of St. Joseph in Vermont, VT
College of Saint Mary, NE
College of Saint Rose, NY
College of St. Scholastica, MN
College of Saint Thomas More, TX
College of the Holy Cross, MA
Conception Seminary College, MO
Creighton University, NE
DePaul University, IL
DeSales University, PA
Divine Word College, IA
Dominican University, IL
Dominican University of California, CA
Duquesne University, PA
Edgewood College, WI
Elms College, MA
Emmanuel College, MA
Fairfield University, CT
Felician College, NJ
Fontbonne University, MO
Fordham University, NY
Franciscan University of Steubenville, OH
Gannon University, PA
Georgetown University, DC
Georgian Court University, NJ
Gonzaga University, WA
Gwynedd-Mercy College, PA
Hilbert College, NY
Holy Apostles College and Seminary, CT
Holy Cross College, IN
Holy Family University, PA
Holy Names University, CA
Immaculata University, PA
Iona College, NY
John Carroll University, OH
King's College, PA
La Roche College, PA
La Salle University, PA
Le Moyne College, NY
Lewis University, IL
Lexington College, IL
Loras College, IA
Lourdes College, OH
Loyola College in Maryland, MD
Loyola Marymount University, CA
Loyola University Chicago, IL
Loyola University New Orleans, LA
Madonna University, MI
Magdalen College, NH
Manhattan College, NY
Marian College, IN
Marian University, WI
Marquette University, WI
Marygrove College, MI
Marylhurst University, OR
Marymount University, VA
Marywood University, PA
Mercy College of Health Sciences, IA
Mercy College of Northwest Ohio, OH
Mercyhurst College, PA
Merrimack College, MA
Misericordia University, PA
Molloy College, NY
Mount Aloysius College, PA
Mount Angel Seminary, OR
Mount Carmel College of Nursing, OH
Mount Marty College, SD
Mount Mary College, WI
Mount Mercy College, IA
Mount St. Mary College, NY
Mount St. Mary's College, CA
Mount St. Mary's University, MD
Neumann College, PA
Newman University, KS
Niagara University, NY
Notre Dame College, OH
Notre Dame de Namur University, CA
Ohio Dominican University, OH
Our Lady of Holy Cross College, LA
Our Lady of the Lake College, LA
Our Lady of the Lake University of San Antonio, TX
Pontifical Catholic University of Puerto Rico, PR
Pontifical College Josephinum, OH
Presentation College, SD
Providence College, RI
Quincy University, IL
Regis College, MA
Regis University, CO
Rivier College, NH
Rockhurst University, MO
Rosemont College, PA
Sacred Heart Major Seminary, MI
Sacred Heart University, CT
St. Ambrose University, IA
St. Anselm College, NH
Saint Anthony College of Nursing, IL
Saint Bonaventure University, NY
St. Catharine College, KY
St. Charles Borromeo Seminary - Overbrook, PA
St. Edward's University, TX
St. Francis College, NY
St. Francis Medical Center College of Nursing, IL
St. Francis University, PA
St. Gregory's University, OK
St. John Fisher College, NY
St. John Vianney College Seminary, FL
St. John's College, IL
St. John's University, MN
St. John's University, NY
St. Joseph College, CT
St. Joseph Seminary College, LA
Saint Joseph's College, IN
St. Joseph's College, ME
Saint Joseph's University, PA
St. Leo University, FL
Saint Louis University, MO
Saint Martin's University, WA
Saint Mary's College, IN
St. Mary's College of California, CA
St. Mary's University, TX
St. Mary's University of Minnesota, MN

St. Mary-of-the-Woods College, IN
St. Michael's College, VT
St. Norbert College, WI
Saint Peter's College, NJ
Saint Thomas University, FL
St. Vincent College, PA
St. Xavier University, IL
Salve Regina University, RI
Santa Clara University, CA
Seattle University, WA
Seton Hall University, NJ
Seton Hill University, PA
Siena College, NY
Siena Heights University, MI
Silver Lake College, WI
Spalding University, KY
Spring Hill College, AL
Stonehill College, MA
Thomas Aquinas College, CA
Thomas More College, KY
Thomas More College of Liberal Arts, NH
Trinity Washington University, DC
Universidad Anahuac, MX
Universidad de Monterrey, MX
University of Dallas, TX
University of Dayton, OH
University of Detroit Mercy, MI
University of Great Falls, MT
University of Mary, ND
University of Notre Dame, IN
University of Portland, OR
University of St. Francis, IN
University of St. Francis, IL
University of St. Mary, KS
University of St. Thomas, TX
University of St. Thomas, MN
University of San Diego, CA
University of San Francisco, CA
University of Scranton, PA
University of the Incarnate Word, TX
University of the Sacred Heart, PR
Ursuline College, OH
Villanova University, PA
Viterbo University, WI
Walsh University, OH
West Suburban College of Nursing, IL
Wheeling Jesuit University, WV
Xavier University, OH
Xavier University of Louisiana, LA

Two-year

Ancilla College, IN
Assumption College for Sisters, NJ
Caritas Laboure College, MA
Chatfield College, OH
Donnelly College, KS
Marian Court College, MA
Marymount College, CA
St. Elizabeth College of Nursing, NY
St. Joseph's College of Nursing, NY
St. Vincent Catholic Medical Centers, NY
Springfield College in Illinois, IL
Trocaire College, NY
Villa Maria College of Buffalo, NY

Seventh-day Adventists

Four-year

Andrews University, MI
Atlantic Union College, MA
Columbia Union College, MD
Florida Hospital College of Health Sciences, FL
Griggs University, MD
Kettering College of Medical Arts, OH
La Sierra University, CA
Loma Linda University, CA
Oakwood University, AL
Pacific Union College, CA
Southern Adventist University, TN
Southwestern Adventist University, TX
Union College, NE
Universidad Adventista de las Antillas, PR
Walla Walla University, WA

Society of Friends (Quaker)

Four-year

Earlham College, IN
George Fox University, OR
Guilford College, NC
William Penn University, IA
Wilmington College, OH

Southern Baptist Convention

Four-year

Anderson University, SC
Baptist College of Florida, FL
Blue Mountain College, MS
Brewton-Parker College, GA
California Baptist University, CA
Carson-Newman College, TN
Charleston Southern University, SC
Chowan University, NC
Clear Creek Baptist Bible College, KY
Gardner-Webb University, NC
Georgetown College, KY
Hannibal-LaGrange College, MO
Louisiana College, LA
Mid-Continent University, KY
Mississippi College, MS
New Orleans Baptist Theological Seminary: Leavell College, LA
North Greenville University, SC
Oklahoma Baptist University, OK
Ouachita Baptist University, AR
Samford University, AL
Shorter College, GA
Southwest Baptist University, MO
Truett-McConnell College, GA
Union University, TN
Wayland Baptist University, TX
Williams Baptist College, AR

Ukrainian Catholic Church

Two-year

Manor College, PA

United Brethren in Christ

Four-year

Huntington University, IN

United Church of Christ

Four-year

Catawba College, NC
Chamberlain College of Nursing, MO
Defiance College, OH
Doane College, NE
Elmhurst College, IL
Elon University, NC
Fisk University, TN
Heidelberg University, OH
Lakeland College, WI
Northland College, WI
Pacific University, OR
Talladega College, AL
Williams College, MA

United Methodist Church

Four-year

Adrian College, MI
Albion College, MI
Albright College, PA
Allegheny College, PA
American University, DC
Baker University, KS
Baldwin-Wallace College, OH
Bennett College, NC
Bethune-Cookman University, FL
Birmingham-Southern College, AL
Brevard College, NC
Centenary College, NJ
Centenary College of Louisiana, LA
Central Methodist University, MO
Claflin University, SC
Clark Atlanta University, GA
Columbia College, SC
Cornell College, IA
Dakota Wesleyan University, SD
DePauw University, IN
Drew University, NJ
Duke University, NC
Emory & Henry College, VA
Emory University, GA
Ferrum College, VA
Florida Southern College, FL
Green Mountain College, VT
Greensboro College, NC
Hamline University, MN
Hendrix College, AR
High Point University, NC
Huntingdon College, AL
Iowa Wesleyan College, IA
Kansas Wesleyan University, KS
Kendall College, IL
Kentucky Wesleyan College, KY
LaGrange College, GA
Lambuth University, TN
Lebanon Valley College, PA
Lindsey Wilson College, KY
Lycoming College, PA
MacMurray College, IL
Martin Methodist College, TN
McKendree University, IL
McMurry University, TX
Methodist University, NC
Millsaps College, MS
Morningside College, IA
Mount Union College, OH
Nebraska Methodist College of Nursing and Allied Health, NE
Nebraska Wesleyan University, NE
North Carolina Wesleyan College, NC
North Central College, IL
Ohio Northern University, OH
Ohio Wesleyan University, OH
Oklahoma City University, OK
Otterbein College, OH
Pfeiffer University, NC
Philander Smith College, AR
Randolph College, VA
Randolph-Macon College, VA
Reinhardt College, GA
Rust College, MS
Shenandoah University, VA
Simpson College, IA
Southern Methodist University, TX
Southwestern College, KS
Southwestern University, TX
Tennessee Wesleyan College, TN
Texas Wesleyan University, TX
Union College, KY
University of Denver, CO
University of Evansville, IN
University of Indianapolis, IN
Virginia Wesleyan College, VA
Wesley College, DE
Wesleyan College, GA
West Virginia Wesleyan College, WV
Wiley College, TX
Willamette University, OR
Wofford College, SC

Two-year

Andrew College, GA
Lon Morris College, TX
Louisburg College, NC
Oxford College of Emory University, GA
Spartanburg Methodist College, SC
Young Harris College, GA

Wesleyan Church

Four-year

Houghton College, NY
Indiana Wesleyan University, IN
Oklahoma Wesleyan University, OK
Southern Wesleyan University, SC

Wisconsin Evangelical Lutheran Synod

Four-year

Martin Luther College, MN
Wisconsin Lutheran College, WI

Historically Black colleges

Four-year

Alabama Agricultural and Mechanical University, AL
Alabama State University, AL
Albany State University, GA
Alcorn State University, MS
Allen University, SC
Arkansas Baptist College, AR
Benedict College, SC
Bennett College, NC
Bluefield State College, WV
Bowie State University, MD
Central State University, OH
Cheyney University of Pennsylvania, PA
Claflin University, SC
Clark Atlanta University, GA
Coppin State University, MD
Delaware State University, DE
Dillard University, LA
Edward Waters College, FL
Elizabeth City State University, NC
Fisk University, TN
Florida Agricultural and Mechanical University, FL
Florida Memorial University, FL
Fort Valley State University, GA
Grambling State University, LA
Hampton University, VA
Harris-Stowe State University, MO
Howard University, DC
Huston-Tillotson University, TX
Jackson State University, MS
Jarvis Christian College, TX
Johnson C. Smith University, NC
Kentucky State University, KY
Lane College, TN
Langston University, OK
LeMoyne-Owen College, TN
Lincoln University, PA
Lincoln University, MO
Livingstone College, NC
Miles College, AL
Mississippi Valley State University, MS
Morehouse College, GA
Morgan State University, MD
Morris College, SC
Norfolk State University, VA
North Carolina Agricultural and Technical State University, NC
North Carolina Central University, NC
Oakwood University, AL
Paine College, GA
Philander Smith College, AR
Prairie View A&M University, TX
Rust College, MS
St. Augustine's College, NC
St. Paul's College, VA
Savannah State University, GA
Selma University, AL
Shaw University, NC
South Carolina State University, SC
Southern University
New Orleans, LA
Southern University and Agricultural and Mechanical College, LA
Spelman College, GA
Talladega College, AL
Tennessee State University, TN
Texas College, TX
Texas Southern University, TX
Tougaloo College, MS
Tuskegee University, AL
University of Arkansas
Pine Bluff, AR
University of Maryland
Eastern Shore, MD
University of the District of Columbia, DC
University of the Virgin Islands, VI
Virginia State University, VA
West Virginia State University, WV
Wilberforce University, OH
Wiley College, TX
Winston-Salem State University, NC
Xavier University of Louisiana, LA

Two-year

Bishop State Community College, AL
Coahoma Community College, MS
Denmark Technical College, SC
Hinds Community College, MS
Lawson State Community College, AL
St. Philip's College, TX
Southern University
Shreveport, LA

Hispanic serving colleges

Four-year

Adams State College, CO
American University of Puerto Rico, PR
Atlantic College, PR
Barry University, FL
Bayamon Central University, PR
Boricua College, NY
California State University
Bakersfield, CA
Dominguez Hills, CA
Fresno, CA
Los Angeles, CA
Monterey Bay, CA
Northridge, CA
San Bernardino, CA
Stanislaus, CA
Caribbean University, PR
Carlos Albizu University, FL

Tables and Indexes

City University of New York
  City College, NY
  John Jay College of Criminal Justice, NY
  Lehman College, NY
  New York City College of Technology, NY
Conservatory of Music of Puerto Rico, PR
Escuela de Artes Plasticas de Puerto Rico, PR
Florida International University, FL
Heritage University, WA
Inter American University of Puerto Rico
  Aguadilla Campus, PR
  Arecibo Campus, PR
  Bayamon Campus, PR
  Fajardo Campus, PR
  Guayama Campus, PR
  Metropolitan Campus, PR
  Ponce Campus, PR
  San German Campus, PR
Lexington College, IL
Mercy College, NY
Mount Angel Seminary, OR
Mount St. Mary's College, CA
New Jersey City University, NJ
New Mexico State University, NM
Occidental College, CA
Our Lady of the Lake University of San Antonio, TX
Pontifical Catholic University of Puerto Rico, PR
Robert Morris College: Chicago, IL
St. Augustine College, IL
St. Edward's University, TX
St. John Vianney College Seminary, FL
St. Mary's University, TX
Saint Peter's College, NJ
Saint Thomas University, FL
San Diego State University, CA
Sul Ross State University, TX
Texas A&M International University, TX
Texas A&M University
  Corpus Christi, TX
  Kingsville, TX
Turabo University, PR
Universidad Adventista de las Antillas, PR
Universidad del Este, PR
Universidad Metropolitana, PR
Universidad Politecnica de Puerto Rico, PR
University College of San Juan, PR
University of Houston
  Downtown, TX
University of La Verne, CA
University of Miami, FL
University of New Mexico, NM
University of Puerto Rico
  Aguadilla, PR
  Arecibo, PR
  Bayamon University College, PR
  Carolina Regional College, PR
  Cayey University College, PR
  Humacao, PR
  Mayaguez, PR
  Medical Sciences, PR
  Ponce, PR
  Rio Piedras, PR
  Utuado, PR
University of Texas
  Brownsville - Texas Southmost College, TX
  El Paso, TX
  Health Science Center at San Antonio, TX
  Pan American, TX
  San Antonio, TX
  of the Permian Basin, TX
University of the Incarnate Word, TX
University of the Sacred Heart, PR
Vaughn College of Aeronautics and Technology, NY
Western New Mexico University, NM
Whittier College, CA
Woodbury University, CA

Two-year

Allan Hancock College, CA
Arizona Western College, AZ
Bakersfield College, CA
Central Arizona College, AZ
Central New Mexico Community College, NM
Cerritos College, CA
Chaffey College, CA
Citrus College, CA
City Colleges of Chicago
  Harry S. Truman College, IL
  Malcolm X College, IL
  Richard J. Daley College, IL
  Wright College, IL
City University of New York
  Borough of Manhattan Community College, NY
  Bronx Community College, NY
  Hostos Community College, NY
  LaGuardia Community College, NY
Coastal Bend College, TX
Cochise College, AZ
College of the Desert, CA
College of the Sequoias, CA
Community College of Denver, CO
Del Mar College, TX
Dodge City Community College, KS
Dona Ana Community College of New Mexico State University, NM
East Los Angeles College, CA
Eastern New Mexico University: Roswell Campus, NM
El Camino College, CA
El Camino College: Compton Center, CA
El Paso Community College, TX
Evergreen Valley College, CA
Fresno City College, CA
Fullerton College, CA
Gavilan College, CA
Hartnell College, CA
Heald College
  Fresno, CA
  Salinas, CA
  San Jose, CA
  Stockton, CA
Hudson County Community College, NJ
Humacao Community College, PR
Imperial Valley College, CA
Laredo Community College, TX
Long Beach City College, CA
Los Angeles City College, CA
Los Angeles Harbor College, CA
Los Angeles Mission College, CA
Los Angeles Trade and Technical College, CA
Los Angeles Valley College, CA
MacCormac College, IL
Merced College, CA
Miami Dade College, FL
Morton College, IL
Mount San Antonio College, CA
New Mexico Junior College, NM
New Mexico State University
  Carlsbad, NM
  Grants, NM
Northern New Mexico College, NM
Odessa College, TX
Otero Junior College, CO
Oxnard College, CA
Palo Alto College, TX
Palo Verde College, CA
Pasadena City College, CA
Passaic County Community College, NJ
Phoenix College, AZ
Pima Community College, AZ
Porterville College, CA
Pueblo Community College, CO
Reedley College, CA
Rio Hondo College, CA
Riverside Community College, CA
St. Philip's College, TX
San Antonio College, TX
San Bernardino Valley College, CA
San Jose City College, CA
Santa Ana College, CA
Santa Fe Community College, NM
South Mountain Community College, AZ
South Plains College, TX
Southwest Texas Junior College, TX
Southwestern College, CA
Texas State Technical College
  Harlingen, TX
Trinidad State Junior College, CO
Ventura College, CA
Victoria College, TX
Waubonsee Community College, IL
West Hills College: Coalinga, CA

Tribal colleges

Four-year

Oglala Lakota College, SD
Salish Kootenai College, MT

Two-year

Bay Mills Community College, MI
Cankdeska Cikana Community College, ND
Chief Dull Knife College, MT
Dine College, AZ
Fond du Lac Tribal and Community College, MN
Fort Belknap College, MT
Fort Berthold Community College, ND
Fort Peck Community College, MT
Lac Courte Oreilles Ojibwa Community College, WI
Little Big Horn College, MT
Little Priest Tribal College, NE
Nebraska Indian Community College, NE
Sisseton Wahpeton College, SD
Sitting Bull College, ND
Southwestern Indian Polytechnic Institute, NM
Stone Child College, MT
Turtle Mountain Community College, ND
United Tribes Technical College, ND

Undergraduate enrollment size

Very small (fewer than 750)

Four-year

Alabama
Amridge University
Judson College
South University: Montgomery
Southeastern Bible College
Talladega College
United States Sports Academy

Alaska
Alaska Bible College
Alaska Pacific University

Arizona
American Indian College of the Assemblies of God
Art Institute of Tucson
Brown Mackie College: Tucson
College of the Humanities and Sciences
International Baptist College
International Import-Export Institute
Northcentral University
Prescott College
Southwestern College

Arkansas
Arkansas Baptist College
Central Baptist College
Ecclesia College
Lyon College
University of the Ozarks
Williams Baptist College

California
Alliant International University
American Jewish University
Antioch Southern California
  Antioch University Los Angeles
  Antioch University Santa Barbara
Bethany University
Bethesda Christian University
California College San Diego
California Institute of Integral Studies
California National University for Advanced Studies
California University of Management and Sciences
Charles R. Drew University of Medicine and Science
Cogswell Polytechnical College
Design Institute of San Diego
DeVry University
  Sherman Oaks
Golden Gate University
Harvey Mudd College
Holy Names University
Humphreys College
Interior Designers Institute
John F. Kennedy University
Life Pacific College
Lincoln University
Menlo College
Mt. Sierra College
National Hispanic University
NewSchool of Architecture & Design
Northwestern Polytechnic University
Pacific Oaks College
Pacific States University
Platt College
  San Diego
Samuel Merritt University
San Diego Christian College
San Francisco Art Institute
San Francisco Conservatory of Music
School of Urban Missions: Oakland
Soka University of America
Southern California Institute of Architecture
Thomas Aquinas College
West Coast University
Westwood College: South Bay
William Jessup University
Yeshiva Ohr Elchonon Chabad/West Coast Talmudical Seminary

Colorado
Aspen University
CollegeAmerica
  Colorado Springs
  Fort Collins
DeVry University
  Westminster
Jones International University
Naropa University
Rocky Mountain College of Art & Design
Westwood College of Technology
  Westwood College: Denver South

Connecticut
Holy Apostles College and Seminary
Lyme Academy College of Fine Arts
Paier College of Art

District of Columbia
Corcoran College of Art and Design
Potomac College
Southeastern University

Florida
Ave Maria University
Baptist College of Florida
Beacon College
Carlos Albizu University
Clearwater Christian College
Florida Christian College
Florida College
Jones College
Northwood University
  Florida
Rasmussen College: Pasco County
Remington College: Tampa
St. John Vianney College Seminary
Schiller International University
South University: West Palm Beach
Talmudic College of Florida
Trinity College of Florida
Universidad FLET
Webber International University

Georgia
Atlanta Christian College
Beulah Heights University
DeVry University
  Alpharetta
Emmanuel College
Life University
Medical College of Georgia
Thomas University
Truett-McConnell College
Wesleyan College

Idaho
Boise Bible College
New Saint Andrews College

Illinois
Blackburn College
Blessing-Rieman College of Nursing
Lakeview College of Nursing
Lexington College
Lincoln Christian College and Seminary
Midstate College
National University of Health Sciences
Rosalind Franklin University of Medicine and Science
Saint Anthony College of Nursing
St. Francis Medical Center College of Nursing
St. John's College
Shimer College
Trinity College of Nursing and Health Sciences
VanderCook College of Music
West Suburban College of Nursing
Western Illinois University: Quad Cities
Westwood College of Technology
  Westwood College: O'Hare Airport
Westwood College: DuPage

Indiana
DeVry University: Indianapolis
International Business College

Iowa
Allen College
Emmaus Bible College
Faith Baptist Bible College and Theological Seminary
Kaplan University
  Cedar Falls
  Mason City
Maharishi University of Management
Mercy College of Health Sciences
Waldorf College

Kansas
Barclay College
Bethany College
Bethel College
Central Christian College of Kansas
McPherson College
Sterling College
Tabor College
University of Kansas Medical Center
University of St. Mary

Kentucky
Beckfield College
Brescia University
Clear Creek Baptist Bible College
Kentucky Christian University
Kentucky Mountain Bible College

Louisiana
Herzing College
Louisiana State University Health Sciences Center
St. Joseph Seminary College
School of Urban Missions: New Orleans

Maine
College of the Atlantic
Maine College of Art
New England School of Communications
Thomas College
Unity College

Maryland
DeVry University: Bethesda
Johns Hopkins University: Peabody Conservatory of Music
St. John's College
Washington Bible College

Massachusetts
Atlantic Union College
Bard College at Simon's Rock
Boston Architectural College
Franklin W. Olin College of Engineering
Hellenic College/Holy Cross
Montserrat College of Art
New England Conservatory of Music
Pine Manor College
Rhodec International
School of the Museum of Fine Arts
Zion Bible College

Michigan
Cleary University
Finlandia University
Grace Bible College
Kuyper College
Michigan Jewish Institute
Sacred Heart Major Seminary

Minnesota
Bethany Lutheran College
College of Visual Arts
Crossroads College
DeVry University
  Edina
Minneapolis College of Art and Design
Minnesota School of Business: Plymouth
Minnesota School of Business: Rochester
Minnesota School of Business: Shakopee
Northwestern Health Sciences University
Oak Hills Christian College

Mississippi
Blue Mountain College
Magnolia Bible College

Missouri
Baptist Bible College
Calvary Bible College and Theological Seminary
Central Bible College
Conception Seminary College
Cox College
Goldfarb School of Nursing at Barnes-Jewish College
Kansas City Art Institute
Ozark Christian College
Research College of Nursing
St. Louis Christian College

Montana
University of Great Falls

Nebraska
BryanLGH College of Health Sciences
Clarkson College
College of Saint Mary
Creative Center
Nebraska Christian College
Nebraska Methodist College of Nursing and Allied Health
York College

Nevada
DeVry University: Henderson
Morrison University
Sierra Nevada College
University of Southern Nevada

New Hampshire
Chester College of New England
Daniel Webster College
Magdalen College
Thomas More College of Liberal Arts

New Jersey
Somerset Christian College

New Mexico
National American University: Rio Rancho
St. John's College
University of the Southwest

New York
Berkeley College
City University of New York: CUNY Online
Concordia College
Eastman School of Music of the University of Rochester
Holy Trinity Orthodox Seminary
Jewish Theological Seminary of America
Juilliard School
King's College
Manhattan School of Music
Mannes College The New School for Music
New York School of Interior Design
Ohr Somayach Tanenbaum Education Center
Russell Sage College
State University of New York
  Downstate Medical Center
  Upstate Medical University
Webb Institute
Wells College
Yeshiva Mikdash Melech

North Carolina
Bennett College
Brevard College
Carolina Christian College
DeVry University: Charlotte
John Wesley College
Miller-Motte Technical College
Peace College
Piedmont Baptist College
Roanoke Bible College
St. Andrews Presbyterian College
Salem College

North Dakota
Medcenter One College of Nursing

Ohio
Antioch University McGregor
Art Academy of Cincinnati
Bryant & Stratton College
  Eastlake
Cincinnati College of Mortuary Science
Cleveland Institute of Art
Cleveland Institute of Music
MedCentral College of Nursing
Rabbinical College of Telshe
Tri-State Bible College

Oklahoma
DeVry University: Oklahoma City Center
St. Gregory's University

Oregon
DeVry University: Portland
Eugene Bible College
Gutenberg College
Mount Angel Seminary
Multnomah University
Northwest Christian University
Oregon College of Art & Craft
Oregon Health & Science University
Pacific Northwest College of Art

Pennsylvania
Bryn Athyn College of the New Church
Curtis Institute of Music

Gratz College
Harrisburg University of Science and Technology
Lancaster Bible College
Moore College of Art and Design
Penn State
  Beaver
  Greater Allegheny
  Lehigh Valley
  New Kensington
  Shenango
  Wilkes-Barre
Pennsylvania College of Art and Design
Rosemont College
St. Charles Borromeo Seminary - Overbrook
Talmudical Yeshiva of Philadelphia
Wilson College

Puerto Rico

Colegio Pentecostal Mizpa
Conservatory of Music of Puerto Rico
Escuela de Artes Plasticas de Puerto Rico
University of Puerto Rico
  Medical Sciences

South Carolina

Allen University
Columbia International University
Converse College
Erskine College
Limestone College
Medical University of South Carolina

South Dakota

Dakota Wesleyan University

Tennessee

DeVry University: Memphis
Fisk University
Free Will Baptist Bible College
Johnson Bible College
Memphis College of Art
Tennessee Temple University
University of Tennessee Health Science Center
Visible School - Music and Worship Arts College
Williamson Christian College

Texas

Amberton University
Arlington Baptist College
Austin Graduate School of Theology
College of Saint Thomas More
Dallas Christian College
Huston-Tillotson University
Jarvis Christian College
Northwood University: Texas
Texas A&M University
  Baylor College of Dentistry
Texas College
Texas Tech University Health Sciences Center
University of Texas
  Medical Branch at Galveston
  Southwestern Medical Center at Dallas

Utah

DeVry University: Sandy
Stevens-Henager College
  Murray
Stevens-Henager College: Ogden
Stevens-Henager College: Orem

Vermont

Bennington College
Burlington College
College of St. Joseph in Vermont
Goddard College
Marlboro College
Southern Vermont College
Sterling College

Virginia

Bluefield College
Christendom College
DeVry University
  Arlington
Patrick Henry College
Randolph College
St. Paul's College
Southern Virginia University
Sweet Briar College
Virginia Intermont College
World College

Washington

Antioch University Seattle
Bastyr University
DeVry University
  Federal Way
Northwest College of Art

West Virginia

Alderson-Broaddus College
Davis and Elkins College
Ohio Valley University
Salem International University

Wisconsin

Columbia College of Nursing
DeVry University: Milwaukee
Northland College

France

American University of Paris
Parsons Paris School of Design

Switzerland

Franklin College: Switzerland

United Kingdom

Richmond, The American International University in London

Two-year

Alabama

Marion Military Institute
Prince Institute of Professional Studies
Virginia College at Mobile

Arizona

Arizona Automotive Institute
IIA College
  Mesa
  Phoenix
International Institute of the Americas
  IIA College: Tucson
Kaplan College: Phoenix
Lamson College
Paralegal Institute
Refrigeration School
Tohono O'odham Community College

California

Bryan College: Los Angeles
Coleman College: San Marcos
Concorde Career College
  Garden Grove
Concorde Career College: North Hollywood
Deep Springs College
Empire College
Fashion Institute of Design and Merchandising
  San Diego
Fremont College
Los Angeles County College of Nursing and Allied Health
Marymount College
National Polytechnic College of Science
Platt College
  Los Angeles
Professional Golfers Career College
Sage College
South Coast College
Western Career College
  Pleasant Hill
Western Career College: Stockton

Colorado

Bel-Rea Institute of Animal Technology
Boulder College of Massage Therapy
Cambridge College
Colorado School of Trades
Concorde Career College: Aurora
Denver Academy of Court Reporting
Everest College: Aurora
Everest College: Colorado Springs
IntelliTec College
IntelliTec College: Grand Junction
Kaplan College: Denver
Redstone College
Remington College
  Colorado Springs

Connecticut

Clemens College
St. Vincent's College

Delaware

Delaware College of Art and Design

Florida

Angley College
Central Florida College
City College
  Gainesville
City College: Casselberry
College of Business and Technology: Flagler
College of Business and Technology: Kendall
Florida Technical College
  Deland
  Orlando
Key College
North Florida Institute: Orange Park
Professional Golfers Career College: Orlando
Virginia College at Pensacola

Georgia

Andrew College
Everest Institute
Gupton Jones College of Funeral Service
Gwinnett College
Savannah River College
Young Harris College

Hawaii

Hawaii Tokai International College

Idaho

Stevens-Henager College: Boise

Illinois

College of Office Technology
Fox College
MacCormac College
Vatterott College: Quincy

Indiana

Ancilla College
College of Court Reporting
Indiana Business College
  Anderson
  Columbus
  Fort Wayne
  Lafayette
Indiana Business College: Indianapolis Northwest
Mid-America College of Funeral Service

Iowa

Kaplan University
  Cedar Rapids
St. Luke's College
Vatterott College

Kansas

Brown Mackie College
  Salina
Colby Community College
Donnelly College
Hesston College
North Central Kansas Technical College
Pratt Community College

Kentucky

Louisville Technical Institute
Southern Ohio College
  Brown Mackie College: North Kentucky
Southwestern College: Florence
Spencerian College: Lexington

Louisiana

Blue Cliff College: Lafayette
Blue Cliff College: Metairie
Blue Cliff College: Shreveport
Delta College of Arts & Technology
ITI Technical College
Remington College
  Baton Rouge
  Lafayette

Maine

Beal College
Central Maine Medical Center College of Nursing and Health Professions
Washington County Community College

Maryland

Kaplan College: Hagerstown

Massachusetts

Benjamin Franklin Institute of Technology
Caritas Laboure College
Marian Court College
New England College of Finance
Urban College of Boston

Michigan

Bay Mills Community College
Saginaw Chippewa Tribal College

Minnesota

Academy College
Duluth Business University
Herzing College
  Minneapolis Drafting School Division of
Le Cordon Bleu College of Culinary Arts
Minnesota School of Business: Brooklyn Center
Northwest Technical Institute
Rainy River Community College
Rasmussen College
  Eagan
  Mankato
Vermilion Community College

Mississippi

Antonelli College
  Hattiesburg
  Jackson
Blue Cliff College: Gulfport

Missouri

Bolivar Technical College
Concorde Career College: Kansas City
Metro Business College
  Jefferson City
Pinnacle Career Institute: Kansas City
Vatterott College: Joplin
Vatterott College: St. Joseph
Vatterott College: Springfield

Montana

Dawson Community College
Miles Community College
Stone Child College

Nebraska

Kaplan University: Omaha
Little Priest Tribal College
Nebraska College of Technical Agriculture
Nebraska Indian Community College

Nevada

Career College of Northern Nevada
High-Tech Institute
Kaplan College: Las Vegas
Las Vegas College
Le Cordon Bleu College of Culinary Arts

New Hampshire

White Mountains Community College

New Jersey

Assumption College for Sisters

New Mexico

IIA College
  Albuquerque
Mesalands Community College
Navajo Technical College
New Mexico Military Institute
Southwestern Indian Polytechnic Institute

New York

American Academy McAllister Institute of Funeral Service
American Academy of Dramatic Arts
Bramson ORT College
Bryant & Stratton Business Institute
  Bryant & Stratton College: Albany
  Bryant & Stratton College: Buffalo
  Bryant & Stratton College: Rochester
  Bryant & Stratton College: Southtowns
  Bryant & Stratton College: Syracuse
Bryant & Stratton College: Syracuse North
Cochran School of Nursing-St. John's Riverside Hospital
Elmira Business Institute
Elmira Business Institute: Vestal
Helene Fuld College of Nursing
Institute of Design and Construction
Jamestown Business College
Long Island Business Institute
Mildred Elley
New York Career Institute
Olean Business Institute
Phillips Beth Israel School of Nursing
Plaza College
Professional Business College
St. Elizabeth College of Nursing
St. Joseph's College of Nursing
Swedish Institute
Utica School of Commerce
Villa Maria College of Buffalo

North Carolina

Carolinas College of Health Sciences
King's College
Martin Community College
Miller-Motte Technical College: Cary

Montgomery Community College
Tri-County Community College

North Dakota
Cankdeska Cikana Community College
Fort Berthold Community College
Lake Region State College
Minot State University: Bottineau Campus
Rasmussen College: Bismarck

Ohio
Antonelli College
Art Institute of Cincinnati
Art Institute of Ohio: Cincinnati
ATS Institute of Technology
Aultman College of Nursing and Health Sciences
Bohecker College
Bradford School
Chatfield College
Davis College
ETI Technical College of Niles
Good Samaritan College of Nursing and Health Science
Hondros College
Miami-Jacobs Career College
Ohio College of Massotherapy
Ohio Institute of Health Careers: Columbus
Ohio Valley College of Technology
Remington College: Cleveland West
Technology Education College
Virginia Marti College of Art and Design
Wright State University: Lake Campus

Oklahoma
Platt College
- Tulsa

Tulsa Welding School
Vatterott College

Oregon
Heald College: Portland
Pioneer Pacific College
Pioneer Pacific College: Springfield
Western Culinary Institute

Pennsylvania
Allied Medical and Technical Institute
Antonelli Institute of Art and Photography
Cambria-Rowe Business College
Cambria-Rowe Business College: Indiana
Career Training Academy: Pittsburgh
Consolidated School of Business
- Lancaster

Dean Institute of Technology
DuBois Business College
DuBois Business College
- Huntingdon
- Oil City

Hussian School of Art
JNA Institute of Culinary Arts
Johnson College
Laurel Business Institute
Laurel Technical Institute
Lincoln Technical Institute: Allentown
Lincoln Technical Institute: Northeast Philadelphia
Lincoln Technical Institute: Philadelphia
McCann School of Business and Technology: Pottsville
McCann School of Business and Technology: Dickson City
McCann School of Business and Technology: Hazleton
New Castle School of Trades
Newport Business Institute: Williamsport
Oakbridge Academy of Arts
Orleans Technical Institute - Center City Campus
Pace Institute
Pennco Tech
Pennsylvania Institute of Health and Technology
Pittsburgh Institute of Aeronautics
Pittsburgh Institute of Mortuary Science
PJA School
South Hills School of Business & Technology
South Hills School of Business & Technology: Altoona
Triangle Tech
- DuBois
- Erie
- Greensburg
- Pittsburgh

Triangle Tech: Bethlehem
Triangle Tech: Sunbury
University of Pittsburgh
- Titusville

Vet Tech Institute
Williamson Free School of Mechanical Trades
Yorktowne Business Institute
YTI Career Institute: Lancaster
YTI Career Institute: York

Puerto Rico
Columbia College
- Columbia Centro
  - Universitario: Yauco

South Carolina
Clinton Junior College
Forrest Junior College
Spartanburg Methodist College
University of South Carolina
- Union

Williamsburg Technical College

South Dakota
Kilian Community College
Mitchell Technical Institute
Sisseton Wahpeton College

Tennessee
Fountainhead College of Technology
Huntington College of Health Sciences

Texas
Bradford School of Business
Dallas Institute of Funeral Service
Everest College: Arlington
Hallmark College of Aeronautics
Hallmark College of Technology
Jacksonville College
Lon Morris College
Southwest Institute of Technology
Wade College
Westwood College: Fort Worth
Westwood College: Houston South

Utah
Careers Unlimited
Eagle Gate College: Layton
Eagle Gate College: Murray
Eagle Gate College: Salt Lake City
Provo College

Vermont
Landmark College

Virginia
Bryant & Stratton College
- Richmond

Bryant & Stratton College: Virginia Beach
Centura College: Chesapeake
Centura College: Virginia Beach
Dabney S. Lancaster Community College
Miller-Motte Technical College: Lynchburg

Washington
Grays Harbor College
Northwest Aviation College

West Virginia
Eastern West Virginia Community and Technical College
Mountain State College
Valley College
West Virginia Business College: Nutter Fort
West Virginia Business College: Wheeling
West Virginia Junior College
West Virginia Junior College: Bridgeport
West Virginia Junior College: Charleston

Wisconsin
Lac Courte Oreilles Ojibwa Community College
University of Wisconsin
- Marinette
- Richland

Wyoming
Eastern Wyoming College

Marshall Islands
College of the Marshall Islands

Small (750-1,999)

Four-year

Alabama
Birmingham-Southern College
Huntingdon College
Oakwood University
Spring Hill College
University of Mobile
University of West Alabama

Alaska
University of Alaska
- Southeast

Arizona
Art Institute
- of Phoenix

Collins College
DeVry University
- Phoenix

Embry-Riddle Aeronautical University: Prescott Campus
University of Advancing Technology
Western International University

Arkansas
Hendrix College
John Brown University
Ouachita Baptist University
University of Arkansas
- for Medical Sciences

California
Art Center College of Design
Art Institute
- of California: Orange County

Art Institute of California: Hollywood
Brooks Institute
California College of the Arts
California Institute of Technology
California Institute of the Arts
California Maritime Academy
Claremont McKenna College
DeVry University
- Fremont
- Long Beach
- Pomona

Dominican University of California
La Sierra University
Loma Linda University
The Master's College
Mills College
Mount St. Mary's College
Notre Dame de Namur University
Occidental College
Otis College of Art and Design
Pitzer College
Pomona College
Scripps College
Simpson University
University of La Verne
Vanguard University of Southern California
Westmont College
Westwood College of Technology
- Westwood College: Inland Empire

Colorado
American Sentinel University
Colorado College
Johnson & Wales University: Denver
Nazarene Bible College
Regis University

Connecticut
Albertus Magnus College
Charter Oak State College
Connecticut College
Mitchell College
Post University
St. Joseph College
United States Coast Guard Academy

Delaware
Goldey-Beacom College

District of Columbia
Gallaudet University

Florida
Chipola College
DeVry University
- Miramar
- Orlando

Eckerd College
Edward Waters College
Florida Memorial University
Florida Southern College
Hodges University
Johnson & Wales University: North Miami
Lynn University
New College of Florida
Rasmussen College: Ocala
Ringling College of Art and Design
Rollins College
St. Leo University
Saint Thomas University
Warner University

Georgia
Agnes Scott College
Bauder College
Berry College
Brenau University
Brewton-Parker College
Covenant College
LaGrange College
Oglethorpe University
Paine College
Piedmont College
Reinhardt College
Shorter College
Toccoa Falls College

Hawaii
University of Hawaii
- West Oahu

Idaho
College of Idaho
Northwest Nazarene University

Illinois
Concordia University Chicago
DeVry University
- Addison
- Chicago
- Tinley Park

Dominican University
East-West University
Greenville College
Harrington College of Design
Illinois College
Illinois Institute of Art: Schaumburg
Judson University
Kendall College
Knox College
Lake Forest College
Monmouth College
National-Louis University
Quincy University
Rockford College
St. Augustine College
Trinity Christian College
Trinity International University
University of St. Francis

Indiana
Calumet College of St. Joseph
Earlham College
Franklin College
Goshen College
Grace College
Hanover College
Huntington University
Manchester College
Marian College
Martin University
Oakland City University
Rose-Hulman Institute of Technology
Saint Joseph's College
Saint Mary's College
St. Mary-of-the-Woods College
Taylor University
Trine University
University of St. Francis
Wabash College

Iowa
Briar Cliff University
Buena Vista University
Central College
Clarke College
Coe College
Cornell College
Dordt College
Graceland University
Grand View University
Grinnell College
Iowa Wesleyan College
Kaplan University
- Des Moines

Morningside College
Mount Mercy College
Northwestern College
Simpson College
University of Dubuque
Upper Iowa University
Wartburg College
William Penn University

Kansas
Baker University
Benedictine College
Kansas Wesleyan University
MidAmerica Nazarene University
Newman University
Southwestern College

Kentucky
Asbury College
Berea College
Campbellsville University
Centre College
Georgetown College
Kentucky Wesleyan College
Mid-Continent University
Midway College

Pikeville College
St. Catharine College
Spalding University
Thomas More College
Transylvania University
Union College
University of the Cumberlands

Louisiana

Centenary College of Louisiana
Dillard University
Louisiana College
Our Lady of Holy Cross College
Our Lady of the Lake College

Maine

Bates College
Bowdoin College
Colby College
St. Joseph's College
University of Maine
  Fort Kent
  Machias
  Presque Isle

Maryland

Columbia Union College
Goucher College
Hood College
Maryland Institute College of Art
McDaniel College
Mount St. Mary's University
St. Mary's College of Maryland
University of Maryland
  Baltimore
Washington College

Massachusetts

American International College
Amherst College
Anna Maria College
Babson College
Bay Path College
Becker College
Cambridge College
Elms College
Emmanuel College
Gordon College
Hampshire College
Lasell College
Lesley University
Massachusetts College of Art and Design
Massachusetts College of Liberal Arts
Massachusetts Maritime Academy
Mount Ida College
New England Institute of Art
Nichols College
Regis College
Wheaton College
Wheelock College
Williams College

Michigan

Adrian College
Albion College
Alma College
Andrews University
Aquinas College
College for Creative Studies
Cornerstone University
Kalamazoo College
Kendall College of Art and Design of Ferris State University
Marygrove College
Northwood University: Michigan
Olivet College
Siena Heights University
Walsh College of Accountancy and Business Administration

Minnesota

Art Institutes International
  Minnesota
Carleton College
Concordia University: St. Paul
Crown College
Hamline University
Macalester College
Martin Luther College
Minnesota School of Business
Minnesota School of Business: St. Cloud
Northwestern College
St. John's University
St. Mary's University of Minnesota
University of Minnesota
  Crookston
  Morris

Mississippi

Millsaps College
Mississippi University for Women
Tougaloo College
William Carey University

Missouri

Avila University
Central Methodist University
College of the Ozarks
Columbia College
Culver-Stockton College
DeVry University
  Kansas City
Drury University
Evangel University
Hannibal-LaGrange College
Harris-Stowe State University
Missouri Valley College
Rockhurst University
Stephens College
Westminster College
William Jewell College
William Woods University

Montana

Carroll College
Montana State University
  Northern
University of Montana: Western

Nebraska

Concordia University
Doane College
Nebraska Wesleyan University
Union College
University of Nebraska
  Medical Center

Nevada

Art Institute
  of Las Vegas
Nevada State College

New Hampshire

Colby-Sawyer College
Granite State College
New England College
Rivier College
St. Anselm College

New Jersey

College of St. Elizabeth
DeVry University: North Brunswick
Drew University
Felician College
Georgian Court University

New Mexico

New Mexico Highlands University
New Mexico Institute of Mining and Technology
Western New Mexico University

New York

Albany College of Pharmacy and Health Sciences
Bard College
Boricua College
Briarcliffe College
Cazenovia College
College of Mount St. Vincent
College of New Rochelle
Columbia University
  School of General Studies
Cooper Union for the Advancement of Science and Art
D'Youville College
Daemen College
DeVry
  Devry College of New York
Dominican College of Blauvelt
Elmira College
Eugene Lang College The New School for Liberal Arts
Five Towns College
Hamilton College
Hartwick College
Hilbert College
Houghton College
Keuka College
Laboratory Institute of Merchandising
Manhattanville College
Marymount Manhattan College
Medaille College
Nyack College
Polytechnic Institute of New York University
Roberts Wesleyan College
Sage College of Albany
Saint Bonaventure University
St. Joseph's College
St. Thomas Aquinas College
Sarah Lawrence College
State University of New York
  College of Environmental Science and Forestry
  Institute of Technology at Utica/Rome
  Maritime College
United States Merchant Marine Academy
Vaughn College of Aeronautics and Technology
Wagner College

North Carolina

Art Institute
  of Charlotte
Barton College
Belmont Abbey College
Catawba College
Chowan University
Davidson College
Greensboro College
Johnson C. Smith University
Lenoir-Rhyne University
Livingstone College
Mars Hill College
Meredith College
Methodist University
Montreat College
North Carolina Wesleyan College
Pfeiffer University
Queens University of Charlotte
St. Augustine's College
University of North Carolina
  School of the Arts
Warren Wilson College
Wingate University

North Dakota

Jamestown College
Mayville State University
Rasmussen College: Fargo
Valley City State University

Ohio

Bluffton University
Cincinnati Christian University
College of Mount St. Joseph
College of Wooster
Columbus College of Art and Design
Defiance College
Heidelberg University
Hiram College
Kenyon College
Lake Erie College
Lourdes College
Malone University
Marietta College
Mercy College of Northwest Ohio
Mount Vernon Nazarene University
Muskingum College
Ohio Christian University
Ohio State University
  Lima Campus
  Mansfield Campus
  Marion Campus
Ohio University
  Chillicothe Campus
  Eastern Campus
  Lancaster Campus
  Southern Campus at Ironton
  Zanesville Campus
Ohio Wesleyan University
Tiffin University
Union Institute & University
University of Rio Grande
Ursuline College
Wilmington College
Wittenberg University

Oklahoma

Bacone College
Mid-America Christian University
National Education Center
  Spartan College of Aeronautics and Technology
Northwestern Oklahoma State University
Oklahoma Baptist University
Oklahoma Christian University
Oklahoma Panhandle State University
Oklahoma Wesleyan University
Southern Nazarene University
University of Science and Arts of Oklahoma

Oregon

Concordia University
Corban College
George Fox University
Lewis & Clark College
Linfield College
Marylhurst University
Pacific University
Reed College
Warner Pacific College
Willamette University

Pennsylvania

Alvernia University
Bryn Mawr College
Cabrini College
Carlow University
Cedar Crest College
Central Pennsylvania College
Chatham University
Chestnut Hill College
Cheyney University of Pennsylvania
Delaware Valley College
DeVry University
  Fort Washington
Geneva College
Gwynedd-Mercy College
Haverford College
Juniata College
Keystone College
La Roche College
Lebanon Valley College
Lincoln University
Lycoming College
Moravian College
Mount Aloysius College
Penn State
  Brandywine
  Dubois
  Fayette, The Eberly Campus
  Hazleton
  Mont Alto
  Schuylkill
  Worthington Scranton
  York
Philadelphia Biblical University
St. Francis University
St. Vincent College
Seton Hill University
Swarthmore College
Thiel College
Thomas Jefferson University: College of Health Professions
University of Pittsburgh
  Bradford
  Greensburg
Ursinus College
Valley Forge Christian College
Washington & Jefferson College
Waynesburg University
Westminster College

Puerto Rico

Columbia Centro Universitario: Caguas
Universidad Adventista de las Antillas

South Carolina

Anderson University
Claflin University
Columbia College
Morris College
Newberry College
North Greenville University
Presbyterian College
South University: Columbia
Southern Wesleyan University
University of South Carolina
  Beaufort
Wofford College

South Dakota

Augustana College
Dakota State University
Mount Marty College
Northern State University
Oglala Lakota College
South Dakota School of Mines and Technology
University of Sioux Falls

Tennessee

Aquinas College
Baptist College of Health Sciences
Carson-Newman College
Christian Brothers University
Crichton College
Cumberland University
Freed-Hardeman University
King College
Lambuth University
Lane College
LeMoyne-Owen College
Lincoln Memorial University
Martin Methodist College
Maryville College
Milligan College
Rhodes College
Tennessee Wesleyan College
Trevecca Nazarene University
University of the South

Texas

Art Institute
  of Dallas
  of Houston
Austin College
College of Biblical Studies-Houston
Concordia University Texas
DeVry University
  Irving
DeVry University: Houston

East Texas Baptist University
Hardin-Simmons University
Howard Payne University
Lubbock Christian University
McMurry University
Our Lady of the Lake University of San Antonio
Schreiner University
Southwestern Adventist University
Southwestern Assemblies of God University
Southwestern University
Sul Ross State University
Texas A&M University
- Galveston
- Texarkana

Texas Lutheran University
Texas Wesleyan University
University of Dallas
University of Houston
- Victoria

University of St. Thomas
University of Texas
- Health Science Center at San Antonio

Wayland Baptist University
Wiley College

Utah

Independence University

Vermont

Castleton State College
Green Mountain College
Johnson State College
Lyndon State College
St. Michael's College
Vermont Technical College

Virginia

Art Institute
- of Washington

Averett University
Bridgewater College
Eastern Mennonite University
Emory & Henry College
Ferrum College
Hampden-Sydney College
Hollins University
Jefferson College of Health Sciences
Mary Baldwin College
Randolph-Macon College
Regent University
Roanoke College
Shenandoah University
University of Virginia's College at Wise
Virginia Military Institute
Virginia Union University
Virginia Wesleyan College
Washington and Lee University

Washington

City University of Seattle
Cornish College of the Arts
DigiPen Institute of Technology
Northwest University
Saint Martin's University
University of Washington Bothell
Walla Walla University
Whitman College

West Virginia

Bethany College
Bluefield State College
Glenville State College
University of Charleston
West Virginia University Institute of Technology
West Virginia Wesleyan College
Wheeling Jesuit University

Wisconsin

Beloit College
Edgewood College
Herzing College
Lawrence University
Maranatha Baptist Bible College
Marian University
Mount Mary College
Ripon College
Viterbo University
Wisconsin Lutheran College

Northern Mariana Islands

Northern Marianas College

Two-year

Alabama

Alabama Southern Community College
George C. Wallace State Community College
- Selma

Arizona

Bryman School
Chandler-Gilbert Community College
- Pecos

Dine College
Scottsdale Culinary Institute
Universal Technical Institute

Arkansas

Arkansas Northeastern College
Arkansas State University
- Mountain Home

Black River Technical College
Mid-South Community College
North Arkansas College
Ouachita Technical College
Ozarka College
Phillips Community College of the University of Arkansas
Rich Mountain Community College
Southeast Arkansas College
Southern Arkansas University Tech
University of Arkansas
- Community College at Batesville
- Community College at Hope
- Cossatot Community College of the

University of Arkansas Community College at Morrilton

California

Copper Mountain College
Fashion Institute of Design and Merchandising
- San Francisco

Feather River College
Lassen Community College
San Joaquin Valley College
Westwood College of Technology
- Westwood College: Los Angeles

Colorado

Institute of Business & Medical Careers
Lincoln College of Technology: Denver
Northeastern Junior College
Otero Junior College

Connecticut

Goodwin College
Middlesex Community College
Northwestern Connecticut Community College
Quinebaug Valley Community College

Florida

Florida Keys Community College
North Florida Community College
Southwest Florida College

Georgia

Le Cordon Bleu College of Culinary Arts
Northwestern Technical College
Oxford College of Emory University
South Georgia College
Southwest Georgia Technical College
West Georgia Technical College

Hawaii

University of Hawaii
- Kauai Community College
- Windward Community College

Idaho

Eastern Idaho Technical College

Illinois

Carl Sandburg College
Cooking & Hospitality Institute of Chicago
Highland Community College
Illinois Eastern Community Colleges
- Frontier Community College
- Lincoln Trail College
- Olney Central College

John Wood Community College
Northwestern Business College

Indiana

Brown Mackie College: Fort Wayne
Indiana Business College
- Indianapolis

Iowa

AIB College of Business
Clinton Community College
Iowa Lakes Community College
Muscatine Community College
Northwest Iowa Community College
Southwestern Community College

Kansas

Cloud County Community College
Coffeyville Community College
Garden City Community College
Labette Community College

Kentucky

Spencerian College

Louisiana

Nunez Community College
River Parishes Community College
South Louisiana Community College

Maine

Andover College
Eastern Maine Community College
Kennebec Valley Community College
Northern Maine Community College
York County Community College

Maryland

Garrett College

Massachusetts

Berkshire Community College
Dean College
Fisher College
Greenfield Community College

Michigan

Glen Oaks Community College
Gogebic Community College
Kirtland Community College
Montcalm Community College
West Shore Community College

Minnesota

Dunwoody College of Technology
Hibbing Community College
Itasca Community College
Mesabi Range Community and Technical College
Minnesota State College - Southeast Technical
Northwest Technical College
Rasmussen College
- Eden Prairie
- St. Cloud

Rasmussen College: Brooklyn Park

Mississippi

Southwest Mississippi Community College
Virginia College

Missouri

Linn State Technical College
Missouri State University: West Plains
North Central Missouri College
Ranken Technical College
Wentworth Military Junior College

Montana

Flathead Valley Community College
Helena College of Technology of the University of Montana

Nebraska

Mid-Plains Community College Area
Western Nebraska Community College

New Hampshire

Lakes Region Community College
Nashua Community College

New Jersey

Salem Community College
Warren County Community College

New Mexico

Clovis Community College
New Mexico State University
- Carlsbad
- Grants

New York

Art Institute
- of New York City

College of Westchester
Columbia-Greene Community College
North Country Community College
Sullivan County Community College

North Carolina

Beaufort County Community College
Bladen Community College
Carteret Community College
Isothermal Community College
James Sprunt Community College
Mayland Community College
McDowell Technical Community College
Richmond Community College
Rockingham Community College
Sampson Community College
Southeastern Community College
Wilson Community College

North Dakota

Williston State College

Ohio

Belmont Technical College
Cleveland Institute of Electronics
Jefferson Community College
Kent State University
- Ashtabula
- East Liverpool
- Salem
- Trumbull
- Tuscarawas

Kent State University: Geauga
Ohio Institute of Photography and Technology
Ohio State University
- Agricultural Technical Institute

Southwestern College of Business
- Southwestern College: Tri-County

Southwestern College: Dayton
Zane State College

Oklahoma

Connors State College
Murray State College
Northeastern Oklahoma Agricultural and Mechanical College

Oregon

Clatsop Community College
Klamath Community College
Umpqua Community College

Pennsylvania

Kaplan Career Institute: Pittsburgh
Lackawanna College
Manor College
Pennsylvania Culinary Institute
Pennsylvania Highlands Community College
Pennsylvania Institute of Technology
Thaddeus Stevens College of Technology

Puerto Rico

Huertas Junior College
Humacao Community College

South Carolina

Denmark Technical College
Northeastern Technical College
Technical College of the Lowcountry
University of South Carolina
- Lancaster
- Salkehatchie Regional Campus
- Sumter

South Dakota

Western Dakota Technical Institute

Texas

Clarendon College
Court Reporting Institute of Dallas
Frank Phillips College
Galveston College
Lamar State College at Orange
Lamar State College at Port Arthur
Panola College
Ranger College
Texas Culinary Academy
Texas State Technical College
- West Texas

Utah

LDS Business College

Virginia

Eastern Shore Community College
Paul D. Camp Community College
Richard Bland College

Washington

Big Bend Community College
Lower Columbia College

Northwest Indian College
Peninsula College

West Virginia

Blue Ridge Community and Technical College
West Virginia State Community and Technical College

Wisconsin

Southwest Wisconsin Technical College
University of Wisconsin
  Waukesha

Wyoming

Central Wyoming College
Sheridan College
WyoTech: Laramie

Guam

Guam Community College

Medium to large (2,000-7,499)

Four-year

Alabama

Alabama Agricultural and Mechanical University
Alabama State University
Athens State University
Auburn University at Montgomery
Faulkner University
Samford University
Tuskegee University
University of Alabama
  Huntsville
University of Montevallo
University of North Alabama

Alaska

University of Alaska
  Fairbanks

Arizona

Grand Canyon University

Arkansas

Arkansas Tech University
Harding University
Henderson State University
Southern Arkansas University
University of Arkansas
  Fort Smith
  Monticello
  Pine Bluff

California

Azusa Pacific University
Biola University
California Baptist University
California Lutheran University
California State University
  Monterey Bay
  Stanislaus
California State University: Channel Islands
Chapman University
Humboldt State University
Loyola Marymount University
National University
Pepperdine University
Point Loma Nazarene University
St. Mary's College of California
Santa Clara University
Stanford University
University of California: Merced
University of Redlands
University of San Diego
University of San Francisco
University of the Pacific

Colorado

Adams State College
Art Institute of Colorado
Colorado Christian University
Colorado School of Mines
Colorado State University
  Pueblo
Fort Lewis College
Mesa State College
United States Air Force Academy
University of Colorado
  Colorado Springs
University of Denver
Western State College of Colorado
Westwood College: Denver North

Connecticut

Eastern Connecticut State University
Fairfield University
Quinnipiac University
Sacred Heart University
Trinity College
University of Bridgeport
University of Hartford
University of New Haven
Wesleyan University
Western Connecticut State University
Yale University

Delaware

Delaware State University
Wesley College
Wilmington University

District of Columbia

American University
Catholic University of America
Georgetown University
Howard University
University of the District of Columbia

Florida

Art Institute of Fort Lauderdale
Barry University
Bethune-Cookman University
Embry-Riddle Aeronautical University
Flagler College
Florida Institute of Technology
Jacksonville University
Miami International University of Art and Design
Nova Southeastern University
Palm Beach Atlantic University
Southeastern University
Stetson University
University of Tampa

Georgia

Albany State University
Armstrong Atlantic State University
Augusta State University
Clark Atlanta University
Clayton State University
Columbus State University
Dalton State College
DeVry University
  Decatur
Emory University
Fort Valley State University
Georgia College and State University
Georgia Southwestern State University
Macon State College
Mercer University
Morehouse College
North Georgia College & State University
South University: Savannah
Southern Polytechnic State University
Spelman College

Hawaii

Brigham Young University-Hawaii
Hawaii Pacific University
University of Hawaii
  Hilo

Idaho

Lewis-Clark State College

Illinois

Augustana College
Aurora University
Benedictine University
Bradley University
Chicago State University
Elmhurst College
Governors State University
Illinois Institute of Art: Chicago
Illinois Institute of Technology
Illinois Wesleyan University
Lewis University
McKendree University
Millikin University
Moody Bible Institute
North Central College
North Park University
Olivet Nazarene University
Robert Morris College: Chicago
Roosevelt University
St. Xavier University
School of the Art Institute of Chicago
University of Chicago
University of Illinois
  Springfield
Wheaton College

Indiana

Anderson University
Butler University
DePauw University
Indiana Institute of Technology
Indiana University
  East
  Kokomo
  Northwest
  South Bend
  Southeast
Indiana Wesleyan University
Purdue University
  North Central
University of Evansville
University of Indianapolis
Valparaiso University

Iowa

Drake University
Luther College
St. Ambrose University

Kansas

Emporia State University
Friends University
Pittsburg State University
Washburn University

Kentucky

Bellarmine University
Kentucky State University
Morehead State University
Sullivan University

Louisiana

Grambling State University
Louisiana State University
  Alexandria
  Shreveport
Loyola University New Orleans
McNeese State University
Nicholls State University
Northwestern State University
Southern University and Agricultural and Mechanical College
Tulane University
University of Louisiana at Monroe
Xavier University of Louisiana

Maine

Husson University
University of Maine
  Augusta
  Farmington
University of New England
University of Southern Maine

Maryland

Bowie State University
Coppin State University
Frostburg State University
Johns Hopkins University
Loyola College in Maryland
Salisbury University
Stevenson University
United States Naval Academy
University of Baltimore
University of Maryland
  Eastern Shore

Massachusetts

Assumption College
Bentley University
Berklee College of Music
Brandeis University
Clark University
College of the Holy Cross
Curry College
Emerson College
Endicott College
Fitchburg State College
Framingham State College
Harvard College
Massachusetts College of Pharmacy and Health Sciences
Massachusetts Institute of Technology
Merrimack College
Mount Holyoke College
Salem State College
Simmons College
Smith College
Springfield College
Stonehill College
Suffolk University
Tufts University
University of Massachusetts
  Lowell
Wellesley College
Wentworth Institute of Technology
Western New England College
Westfield State College
Worcester Polytechnic Institute
Worcester State College

Michigan

Calvin College
Hope College
Kettering University
Lake Superior State University
Lawrence Technological University
Madonna University
Michigan Technological University
Spring Arbor University
University of Detroit Mercy
University of Michigan
  Dearborn
  Flint

Minnesota

Augsburg College
Bemidji State University
Bethel University
Capella University
College of St. Benedict
College of St. Catherine
College of St. Scholastica
Concordia College: Moorhead
Gustavus Adolphus College
Metropolitan State University
St. Olaf College
Southwest Minnesota State University
University of St. Thomas
Walden University

Mississippi

Alcorn State University
Belhaven College
Delta State University
Jackson State University
Mississippi College

Missouri

Fontbonne University
Grantham University
Lincoln University
Lindenwood University
Maryville University of Saint Louis
Missouri Baptist University
Missouri Southern State University
Missouri Western State University
Northwest Missouri State University
Southwest Baptist University
Truman State University
University of Missouri
  Kansas City
  Missouri University of Science and Technology
Washington University in St. Louis
Webster University

Montana

Montana State University
  Billings
Montana Tech of the University of Montana

Nebraska

Bellevue University
Chadron State College
Creighton University
University of Nebraska
  Kearney
Wayne State College

Nevada

Great Basin College

New Hampshire

Dartmouth College
Franklin Pierce University
Hesser College
Keene State College
Plymouth State University
Southern New Hampshire University

New Jersey

Berkeley College
Bloomfield College
Centenary College
The College of New Jersey
Fairleigh Dickinson University
  College at Florham
  Metropolitan Campus
Monmouth University
New Jersey City University
New Jersey Institute of Technology
Princeton University
Ramapo College of New Jersey
Richard Stockton College of New Jersey
Rider University
Rutgers, The State University of New Jersey
  Camden Regional Campus
  Newark Regional Campus
Saint Peter's College
Seton Hall University
Stevens Institute of Technology

New Mexico

Eastern New Mexico University

New York

Adelphi University
Barnard College
Berkeley College of New York City
Canisius College

City University of New York
- Medgar Evers College
- York College

Clarkson University
Colgate University
College of Saint Rose
Columbia University
Culinary Institute of America
Dowling College
Iona College
Ithaca College
Le Moyne College
Long Island University
- Brooklyn Campus
- C. W. Post Campus

Manhattan College
Marist College
Mercy College
Molloy College
Monroe College
Mount St. Mary College
Nazareth College of Rochester
New York Institute of Technology
Niagara University
Pace University
Parsons The New School for Design
Pratt Institute
Rensselaer Polytechnic Institute
St. Francis College
St. John Fisher College
St. Joseph's College: Suffolk Campus
St. Lawrence University
School of Visual Arts
Siena College
Skidmore College
State University of New York
- College at Brockport
- College at Cortland
- College at Fredonia
- College at Geneseo
- College at Old Westbury
- College at Oneonta
- College at Plattsburgh
- College at Potsdam
- Farmingdale
- New Paltz
- Oswego
- Purchase

Union College
United States Military Academy
University of Rochester
Utica College
Vassar College
Yeshiva University

North Carolina
Campbell University
Duke University
Elon University
Fayetteville State University
Gardner-Webb University
Guilford College
High Point University
Johnson & Wales University: Charlotte
Mount Olive College
Shaw University
University of North Carolina
- Asheville
- Pembroke

Wake Forest University
Western Carolina University

North Dakota
Dickinson State University
Minot State University
University of Mary

Ohio
Ashland University
Baldwin-Wallace College
Capital University
Case Western Reserve University
Cedarville University
Central State University
Denison University
DeVry University
- Columbus

John Carroll University
Mount Union College
Oberlin College
Ohio Dominican University
Ohio Northern University
Ohio State University
- Newark Campus

Shawnee State University
University of Dayton
University of Findlay
Walsh University
Xavier University

Oklahoma
Cameron University
East Central University
Langston University
Oklahoma City University
Oral Roberts University
Rogers State University
Southeastern Oklahoma State University
Southwestern Oklahoma State University
University of Tulsa

Oregon
Eastern Oregon University
Oregon Institute of Technology
Southern Oregon University
University of Portland
Western Oregon University

Pennsylvania
Albright College
Allegheny College
Arcadia University
Bucknell University
California University of Pennsylvania
Carnegie Mellon University
Clarion University of Pennsylvania
DeSales University
Dickinson College
Duquesne University
East Stroudsburg University of Pennsylvania
Eastern University
Edinboro University of Pennsylvania
Elizabethtown College
Franklin & Marshall College
Gannon University
Gettysburg College
Grove City College
Holy Family University
Immaculata University
King's College
La Salle University
Lafayette College
Lehigh University
Lock Haven University of Pennsylvania
Mansfield University of Pennsylvania
Marywood University
Mercyhurst College
Messiah College
Millersville University of Pennsylvania
Misericordia University
Muhlenberg College
Neumann College
Peirce College
Penn State
- Abington
- Altoona
- Berks
- Erie, The Behrend College
- Harrisburg

Pennsylvania College of Technology
Philadelphia University
Point Park University
Robert Morris University
Saint Joseph's University
Shippensburg University of Pennsylvania
Susquehanna University
University of Pittsburgh
- Johnstown

University of Scranton
University of the Arts
University of the Sciences in Philadelphia
Villanova University
Widener University
Wilkes University
York College of Pennsylvania

Puerto Rico
American University of Puerto Rico
Caribbean University
Inter American University of Puerto Rico
- Aguadilla Campus
- Bayamon Campus
- Fajardo Campus
- Guayama Campus
- Metropolitan Campus
- Ponce Campus
- San German Campus

Pontifical Catholic University of Puerto Rico
University of Puerto Rico
- Aguadilla
- Bayamon University College
- Carolina Regional College
- Cayey University College
- Humacao
- Ponce

University of the Sacred Heart

Rhode Island
Brown University
Bryant University
New England Institute of Technology
Providence College
Rhode Island College
Roger Williams University
Salve Regina University

South Carolina
Benedict College
The Citadel
Coastal Carolina University
Francis Marion University
Furman University
Lander University
South Carolina State University
University of South Carolina
- Aiken
- Upstate

Winthrop University

South Dakota
Black Hills State University
University of South Dakota

Tennessee
Belmont University
Bethel College
Lee University
Lipscomb University
Tennessee State University
Tusculum College
Union University
University of Tennessee
- Martin

Vanderbilt University

Texas
Abilene Christian University
Angelo State University
Dallas Baptist University
Houston Baptist University
LeTourneau University
Midwestern State University
Prairie View A&M University
Rice University
St. Edward's University
St. Mary's University
Southern Methodist University
Texas A&M University
- Commerce
- Corpus Christi
- Kingsville

Texas Christian University
Texas Southern University
Texas Woman's University
Trinity University
University of Houston
- Clear Lake

University of Mary Hardin-Baylor
University of Texas
- Tyler
- of the Permian Basin

University of the Incarnate Word
West Texas A&M University

Utah
Dixie State College of Utah
Southern Utah University
Westminster College

Vermont
Champlain College
Middlebury College

Virginia
Christopher Newport University
College of William and Mary
Hampton University
Longwood University
Lynchburg College
Marymount University
Norfolk State University
University of Mary Washington
University of Richmond
Virginia State University

Washington
Art Institute of Seattle
Evergreen State College
Gonzaga University
Pacific Lutheran University
Seattle Pacific University
Seattle University
University of Puget Sound
University of Washington Tacoma
Whitworth University

West Virginia
Concord University
Fairmont State University
Mountain State University
Shepherd University
West Liberty State College
West Virginia University at Parkersburg

Wisconsin
Alverno College
Cardinal Stritch University
Carroll University
Concordia University Wisconsin
Lakeland College
Milwaukee School of Engineering
St. Norbert College
University of Wisconsin
- Green Bay
- Parkside
- Platteville
- River Falls
- Superior

Virgin Islands, U.S.
University of the Virgin Islands

Canada
Acadia University

Egypt
American University in Cairo

Lebanon
American University of Beirut

United Arab Emirates
American University in Dubai

Two-year

Alabama
Bevill State Community College
Bishop State Community College
Central Alabama Community College
Enterprise-Ozark Community College
Gadsden State Community College
George C. Wallace State Community College
- George C. Wallace Community College at Dothan

Jefferson State Community College
Lawson State Community College
Northeast Alabama Community College
Northwest-Shoals Community College
Southern Union State Community College
Wallace State Community College at Hanceville

Arizona
Anthem College
Arizona Western College
Central Arizona College
Cochise College
Coconino County Community College
Eastern Arizona College
Estrella Mountain Community College
Glendale Community College
Mohave Community College
Northland Pioneer College

Arkansas
Northwest Arkansas Community College

California
Art Institute
- of California: Los Angeles

Barstow Community College
Berkeley City College
Canada College
Cerro Coso Community College
College of Alameda
College of Marin: Kentfield
College of the Redwoods
College of the Siskiyous
Columbia College
Crafton Hills College
El Camino College: Compton Center
Fashion Institute of Design and Merchandising
- Los Angeles

Gavilan College
Lake Tahoe Community College
Los Angeles Southwest College
Mendocino College
Merritt College
Palo Verde College
Porterville College
West Hills College: Coalinga
West Hills College: Lemoore

Colorado
Arapahoe Community College
Community College of Aurora
Community College of Denver
Pueblo Community College

Connecticut
Capital Community College
Gateway Community College
Housatonic Community College
Manchester Community College
Naugatuck Valley Community College
Norwalk Community College
Three Rivers Community College

Tunxis Community College

Delaware

Delaware Technical and Community College
- Owens
- Stanton/Wilmington
- Terry

Florida

Florida National College
Full Sail University
Gulf Coast Community College
Lake City Community College
Lake-Sumter Community College
Polk Community College
Saint Johns River Community College
South Florida Community College

Georgia

Abraham Baldwin Agricultural College
Albany Technical College
Ashworth University
Athens Technical College
Atlanta Metropolitan College
Atlanta Technical College
Augusta Technical College
Bainbridge College
Central Georgia Technical College
Chattahoochee Technical College
College of Coastal Georgia
Columbus Technical College
Darton College
DeKalb Technical College
East Georgia College
Georgia Highlands College
Georgia Military College
Gordon College
Griffin Technical College
Gwinnett Technical College
Middle Georgia Technical College
North Georgia Technical College
North Metro Technical College
Savannah Technical College
West Central Technical College

Hawaii

University of Hawaii
- Honolulu Community College
- Maui Community College

Idaho

North Idaho College

Illinois

Black Hawk College
Danville Area Community College
Elgin Community College
Heartland Community College
Illinois Eastern Community Colleges
- Wabash Valley College

Kankakee Community College
Kaskaskia College
Lake Land College
Lincoln Land Community College
Morton College
Richland Community College
Shawnee Community College
South Suburban College of Cook County
Southeastern Illinois College
Spoon River College
Waubonsee Community College

Indiana

Ivy Tech Community College: Richmond
Ivy Tech State College
- Ivy Tech Community College: Bloomington
- Ivy Tech Community College: Columbus
- Ivy Tech Community College: East Central
- Ivy Tech Community College: Kokomo
- Ivy Tech Community College: Lafayette
- Ivy Tech Community College: North Central
- Ivy Tech Community College: Northeast
- Ivy Tech Community College: Northwest
- Ivy Tech Community College: South Central
- Ivy Tech Community College: Southeast
- Ivy Tech Community College: Southwest
- Ivy Tech Community College: Wabash Valley

Iowa

Hawkeye Community College
Indian Hills Community College
Iowa Central Community College
Iowa Western Community College
North Iowa Area Community College
Northeast Iowa Community College
Scott Community College
Southeastern Community College North Campus
Western Iowa Tech Community College

Kansas

Barton County Community College
Cowley County Community College
Highland Community College
Hutchinson Community College
Kansas City Kansas Community College
Neosho County Community College

Kentucky

Big Sandy Community and Technical College
Elizabethtown Community and Technical College
Hazard Community and Technical College
Hopkinsville Community College
Madisonville Community College
Owensboro Community and Technical College
Somerset Community College
Southeast Kentucky Community and Technical College

Louisiana

Baton Rouge Community College
Bossier Parish Community College
Louisiana State University
- Eunice

Southern University
- Shreveport

Maine

Central Maine Community College
Southern Maine Community College

Maryland

Allegany College of Maryland
Baltimore City Community College
Carroll Community College
Cecil College
Chesapeake College
College of Southern Maryland
Frederick Community College
Hagerstown Community College
Harford Community College
Howard Community College
Wor-Wic Community College

Massachusetts

Bristol Community College
Bunker Hill Community College
Cape Cod Community College
Holyoke Community College
Massachusetts Bay Community College
Massasoit Community College
Mount Wachusett Community College
North Shore Community College
Northern Essex Community College
Quinsigamond Community College
Roxbury Community College
Springfield Technical Community College

Michigan

Bay de Noc Community College
Jackson Community College
Kellogg Community College
Lake Michigan College
Monroe County Community College
Muskegon Community College
North Central Michigan College
Northwestern Michigan College
St. Clair County Community College
Southwestern Michigan College

Minnesota

Alexandria Technical College
Anoka Technical College
Central Lakes College
Dakota County Technical College
Fond du Lac Tribal and Community College
Inver Hills Community College
Lake Superior College
Minnesota State Community and Technical College
North Hennepin Community College
Northland Community & Technical College
Ridgewater College
Riverland Community College
Rochester Community and Technical College
St. Cloud Technical College
St. Paul College
South Central College

Mississippi

East Mississippi Community College
Meridian Community College
Northwest Mississippi Community College

Missouri

Crowder College
East Central College
Jefferson College
Metropolitan Community College: Blue River
Metropolitan Community College: Longview
Metropolitan Community College: Maple Woods
Metropolitan Community College: Penn Valley
Mineral Area College
Moberly Area Community College
St. Charles Community College
State Fair Community College
Three Rivers Community College

Montana

Montana State University
- College of Technology: Great Falls

Nebraska

Central Community College
Metropolitan Community College
Northeast Community College

Nevada

Western Nevada College

New Hampshire

Great Bay Community College
NHTI-Concord's Community College

New Jersey

Atlantic Cape Community College
Burlington County College
Cumberland County College
Gloucester County College
Raritan Valley Community College
Sussex County Community College

New Mexico

Eastern New Mexico University: Roswell Campus
New Mexico Junior College
San Juan College
Santa Fe Community College

New York

Adirondack Community College
ASA Institute of Business and Computer Technology
Broome Community College
Cayuga County Community College
City University of New York
- Hostos Community College

Clinton Community College
Erie Community College
- City Campus
- North Campus
- South Campus

Finger Lakes Community College
Fulton-Montgomery Community College
Genesee Community College
Jamestown Community College
Jefferson Community College
Mohawk Valley Community College
Niagara County Community College
Orange County Community College
Rockland Community College
State University of New York
- College of Agriculture and Technology at Cobleskill
- College of Agriculture and Technology at Morrisville
- College of Technology at Alfred
- College of Technology at Canton
- College of Technology at Delhi

Technical Career Institutes
Tompkins Cortland Community College
Ulster County Community College

North Carolina

Alamance Community College
Asheville-Buncombe Technical Community College
Blue Ridge Community College
Caldwell Community College and Technical Institute
Cape Fear Community College
Catawba Valley Community College
Coastal Carolina Community College
Craven Community College
Forsyth Technical Community College
Gaston College
Haywood Community College
Johnston Community College
Lenoir Community College
Piedmont Community College
Randolph Community College
Rowan-Cabarrus Community College
South Piedmont Community College
Southwestern Community College
Stanly Community College
Surry Community College
Wayne Community College
Western Piedmont Community College

North Dakota

Bismarck State College
North Dakota State College of Science

Ohio

Bowling Green State University: Firelands College
Central Ohio Technical College
Cincinnati State Technical and Community College
Clark State Community College
Edison State Community College
Hocking College
James A. Rhodes State College
Kent State University
- Stark

Marion Technical College
Miami University
- Hamilton Campus

Northwest State Community College
Southern State Community College
University of Cincinnati
- Clermont College

Oklahoma

Oklahoma State University
- Institute of Technology: Okmulgee
- Oklahoma City

Redlands Community College
Rose State College
Seminole State College
Western Oklahoma State College

Oregon

Central Oregon Community College
Clackamas Community College
Linn-Benton Community College
Mt. Hood Community College
Rogue Community College
Southwestern Oregon Community College
Treasure Valley Community College

Pennsylvania

Butler County Community College
Community College of Beaver County
Lehigh Carbon Community College
Luzerne County Community College
Pittsburgh Technical Institute
Westmoreland County Community College

South Carolina

Aiken Technical College

Central Carolina Technical College
Horry-Georgetown Technical College
Orangeburg-Calhoun Technical College
Piedmont Technical College
Spartanburg Community College

South Dakota
Southeast Technical Institute

Tennessee
Cleveland State Community College
Dyersburg State Community College
Jackson State Community College
Motlow State Community College
Roane State Community College
Volunteer State Community College
Walters State Community College

Texas
Alvin Community College
Angelina College
Brazosport College
Cedar Valley College
Cisco Junior College
Coastal Bend College
El Centro College
Howard College
Kilgore College
Lee College
Midland College
Odessa College
Paris Junior College
South Plains College
Southwest Texas Junior College
Temple College
Texas State Technical College
  Harlingen
  Waco
Victoria College
Weatherford College
Wharton County Junior College

Utah
College of Eastern Utah
Snow College

Vermont
Community College of Vermont

Virginia
Blue Ridge Community College
Central Virginia Community College
Danville Community College
Germanna Community College
John Tyler Community College
Lord Fairfax Community College
Mountain Empire Community College
Southwest Virginia Community College
Virginia Highlands Community College
Wytheville Community College

Washington
Bellingham Technical College
Cascadia Community College
Centralia College
Clark College
Everett Community College
North Seattle Community College
Olympic College
Skagit Valley College
South Puget Sound Community College
Spokane Community College
Spokane Falls Community College
Tacoma Community College
Walla Walla Community College
Yakima Valley Community College

West Virginia
New River Community and Technical College
Southern West Virginia Community and Technical College
West Virginia Northern Community College

Wisconsin
Blackhawk Technical College
Chippewa Valley Technical College
Fox Valley Technical College
Lakeshore Technical College
Mid-State Technical College
Waukesha County Technical College
Western Technical College
Wisconsin Indianhead Technical College

Wyoming
Casper College
Laramie County Community College
Western Wyoming Community College

Micronesia
College of Micronesia-FSM

Large (7,500-14,499)

Four-year

Alabama
Columbia Southern University
Jacksonville State University
University of Alabama
  Birmingham
University of South Alabama

Alaska
University of Alaska
  Anchorage

Arkansas
Arkansas State University
University of Arkansas
University of Arkansas
  Little Rock
University of Central Arkansas

California
Academy of Art University
California State University
  Dominguez Hills
  East Bay
  San Bernardino
  San Marcos
Sonoma State University

Colorado
University of Colorado
  Denver
University of Northern Colorado

Connecticut
Central Connecticut State University
Southern Connecticut State University

District of Columbia
George Washington University

Florida
Embry-Riddle Aeronautical University: Worldwide Campus
Florida Agricultural and Mechanical University
Florida Gulf Coast University
University of Miami
University of North Florida
University of West Florida

Georgia
Georgia Institute of Technology
Georgia Southern University
Savannah College of Art and Design
University of West Georgia
Valdosta State University

Hawaii
University of Hawaii
  Manoa

Idaho
Brigham Young University-Idaho
Idaho State University
University of Idaho

Illinois
Columbia College Chicago
DeVry University: Online
Eastern Illinois University
Loyola University Chicago
Northeastern Illinois University
Northwestern University
Southern Illinois University
  Edwardsville
Western Illinois University

Indiana
Indiana State University
Indiana University-Purdue University Fort Wayne
Purdue University
  Calumet
University of Notre Dame
University of Southern Indiana

Iowa
University of Northern Iowa

Kansas
Wichita State University

Kentucky
Eastern Kentucky University
Murray State University
Northern Kentucky University
University of Louisville

Louisiana
Louisiana Tech University
Southeastern Louisiana University
University of Louisiana at Lafayette
University of New Orleans

Maine
University of Maine

Maryland
University of Maryland
  Baltimore County

Massachusetts
Boston College
Bridgewater State College
University of Massachusetts
  Boston
  Dartmouth

Michigan
Davenport University
Ferris State University
Northern Michigan University
Oakland University
Saginaw Valley State University

Minnesota
Minnesota State University
  Mankato
Saint Cloud State University
University of Minnesota
  Duluth
Winona State University

Mississippi
Mississippi State University
University of Mississippi
University of Southern Mississippi

Missouri
Missouri State University
Park University
Saint Louis University
Southeast Missouri State University
University of Central Missouri
University of Missouri
  St. Louis

Montana
Montana State University
  Bozeman

Nebraska
University of Nebraska
  Omaha

Nevada
University of Nevada
  Reno

New Hampshire
University of New Hampshire

New Jersey
Kean University
Montclair State University
Rowan University
William Paterson University of New Jersey

New Mexico
New Mexico State University

New York
City University of New York
  Baruch College
  Brooklyn College
  City College
  College of Staten Island
  Hunter College
  John Jay College of Criminal Justice
  Lehman College
  New York City College of Technology
  Queens College
Cornell University
Fashion Institute of Technology
Fordham University
Hofstra University
Rochester Institute of Technology
St. John's University
State University of New York
  Albany
  Binghamton
  College at Buffalo
  Empire State College
Syracuse University
Touro College

North Carolina
Appalachian State University
North Carolina Agricultural and Technical State University
University of North Carolina
  Greensboro
  Wilmington

North Dakota
North Dakota State University
University of North Dakota

Ohio
Bowling Green State University
Cleveland State University
Miami University
  Oxford Campus
Wright State University
Youngstown State University

Oklahoma
Northeastern State University
University of Central Oklahoma

Pennsylvania
Art Institute
  Online
  of Pittsburgh
Bloomsburg University of Pennsylvania
Drexel University
Indiana University of Pennsylvania
Kutztown University of Pennsylvania
Slippery Rock University of Pennsylvania
University of Pennsylvania
West Chester University of Pennsylvania

Puerto Rico
Turabo University
Universidad del Este
Universidad Metropolitana
University of Puerto Rico
  Mayaguez

Rhode Island
Johnson & Wales University: Providence
University of Rhode Island

South Carolina
Clemson University
College of Charleston

South Dakota
South Dakota State University

Tennessee
Austin Peay State University
Tennessee Technological University
University of Tennessee
  Chattanooga

Texas
Baylor University
Lamar University
Sam Houston State University
Stephen F. Austin State University
Tarleton State University
University of Houston
  Downtown
University of Texas
  Brownsville - Texas Southmost College
  Dallas

Utah
Utah State University
Western Governors University

Vermont
University of Vermont

Virginia
Radford University
University of Virginia

Washington
Central Washington University
Eastern Washington University
Western Washington University

West Virginia
Marshall University

Wisconsin
Marquette University
University of Wisconsin
  Eau Claire
  La Crosse
  Oshkosh
  Stevens Point
  Stout
  Whitewater

Wyoming
University of Wyoming

Canada
Memorial University of Newfoundland

Two-year

Alabama
Calhoun Community College

Arizona
Paradise Valley Community College
Phoenix College
Scottsdale Community College

Yavapai College

Arkansas
Pulaski Technical College

California
Butte College
Chabot College
Citrus College
Coastline Community College
College of San Mateo
College of the Desert
College of the Sequoias
Contra Costa College
Cosumnes River College
Cuesta College
Cuyamaca College
Cypress College
Evergreen Valley College
Folsom Lake College
Golden West College
Hartnell College
Imperial Valley College
Irvine Valley College
Laney College
Las Positas College
Los Angeles Harbor College
Los Angeles Mission College
Los Angeles Trade and Technical College
Los Medanos College
Merced College
Mission College
Monterey Peninsula College
Napa Valley College
Ohlone College
Oxnard College
Reedley College
San Bernardino Valley College
San Diego Miramar College
San Jose City College
Santiago Canyon College
Shasta College
Skyline College
Solano Community College
Taft College
Ventura College
Victor Valley College
West Los Angeles College
West Valley College
Yuba Community College District

Colorado
Front Range Community College
Pikes Peak Community College
Red Rocks Community College

Florida
Brevard Community College
Daytona State College
Manatee Community College
Seminole Community College

Georgia
Gainesville State College

Illinois
College of Lake County
Harper College
Illinois Central College
Moraine Valley Community College
Parkland College
Triton College

Indiana
Vincennes University

Iowa
Des Moines Area Community College
Kirkwood Community College

Louisiana
Delgado Community College

Michigan
Grand Rapids Community College
Henry Ford Community College
Lansing Community College
Macomb Community College
Mott Community College
Oakland Community College
Schoolcraft College

Minnesota
Century Community and Technical College
Hennepin Technical College
Minneapolis Community and Technical College
Normandale Community College

Mississippi
Hinds Community College
Mississippi Gulf Coast Community College

Nebraska
Southeast Community College

Nevada
Truckee Meadows Community College

New Jersey
Bergen Community College
County College of Morris
Essex County College
Hudson County Community College
Middlesex County College
Union County College

New York
City University of New York
- Bronx Community College
- Kingsborough Community College
- LaGuardia Community College
- Queensborough Community College

Dutchess Community College
Hudson Valley Community College
Onondaga Community College
Westchester Community College

North Carolina
Fayetteville Technical Community College
Wake Technical Community College

Ohio
Cuyahoga Community College
- Metropolitan Campus

Lakeland Community College
Owens Community College
- Toledo

Oklahoma
Oklahoma City Community College

Oregon
Chemeketa Community College

Pennsylvania
Harrisburg Area Community College
Montgomery County Community College
Northampton Community College

South Carolina
Greenville Technical College
Midlands Technical College
Trident Technical College

Tennessee
Chattanooga State Technical Community College
Nashville State Community College
Southwest Tennessee Community College

Texas
Blinn College
Brookhaven College
Del Mar College
Eastfield College
Laredo Community College
Navarro College
North Central Texas College
North Lake College
Northwest Vista College
St. Philip's College
Tyler Junior College

Virginia
J. Sargeant Reynolds Community College
Thomas Nelson Community College

Washington
Edmonds Community College
Highline Community College
Renton Technical College
South Seattle Community College

Wisconsin
Northeast Wisconsin Technical College

Very large (15,000 or more)

Four-year

Alabama
Auburn University
Troy University
University of Alabama

Arizona
Arizona State University
Northern Arizona University
University of Arizona
University of Phoenix

California
California Polytechnic State University: San Luis Obispo
California State Polytechnic University: Pomona
California State University
- Chico
- Fresno
- Fullerton
- Long Beach
- Los Angeles
- Northridge
- Sacramento

San Diego State University
San Francisco State University
San Jose State University
University of California
- Berkeley
- Davis
- Irvine
- Los Angeles
- Riverside
- San Diego
- Santa Barbara
- Santa Cruz

University of Southern California

Colorado
Colorado State University
Metropolitan State College of Denver
University of Colorado
- Boulder

Connecticut
University of Connecticut

Delaware
University of Delaware

District of Columbia
Strayer University

Florida
Florida Atlantic University
Florida International University
Florida State University
University of Central Florida
University of Florida
University of South Florida

Georgia
Georgia State University
Kennesaw State University
University of Georgia

Idaho
Boise State University

Illinois
DePaul University
Illinois State University
Northern Illinois University
Southern Illinois University
- Carbondale

University of Illinois
- Chicago
- Urbana-Champaign

Indiana
Ball State University
Indiana University
- Bloomington

Indiana University-Purdue University Indianapolis
Purdue University

Iowa
Ashford University
Iowa State University
University of Iowa

Kansas
Kansas State University
University of Kansas

Kentucky
University of Kentucky
Western Kentucky University

Louisiana
Louisiana State University and Agricultural and Mechanical College

Maryland
Towson University
University of Maryland
- College Park
- University College

Massachusetts
Boston University
Northeastern University
University of Massachusetts
- Amherst

Michigan
Central Michigan University
Eastern Michigan University
Grand Valley State University
Michigan State University
University of Michigan
Wayne State University
Western Michigan University

Minnesota
University of Minnesota
- Twin Cities

Missouri
University of Missouri
- Columbia

Nebraska
University of Nebraska
- Lincoln

Nevada
University of Nevada
- Las Vegas

New Jersey
Rutgers, The State University of New Jersey
- New Brunswick/Piscataway Campus

Thomas Edison State College

New Mexico
University of New Mexico

New York
Excelsior College
New York University
State University of New York
- Buffalo
- Stony Brook

North Carolina
East Carolina University
North Carolina State University
University of North Carolina
- Chapel Hill
- Charlotte

Ohio
Kent State University
Ohio State University
- Columbus Campus

Ohio University
University of Akron
University of Cincinnati
University of Toledo

Oklahoma
Oklahoma State University
University of Oklahoma

Oregon
Oregon State University
Portland State University
University of Oregon

Pennsylvania
Penn State
- University Park

Temple University
University of Pittsburgh

Puerto Rico
University of Puerto Rico
- Rio Piedras

South Carolina
University of South Carolina

Tennessee
Middle Tennessee State University
University of Memphis
University of Tennessee
- Knoxville

Texas
Texas A&M University
Texas State University: San Marcos
Texas Tech University
University of Houston
University of North Texas
University of Texas
- Arlington
- Austin
- Pan American
- San Antonio

Utah
Brigham Young University
University of Utah
Utah Valley University
Weber State University

Virginia
George Mason University
James Madison University
Liberty University
Old Dominion University
Virginia Commonwealth University
Virginia Polytechnic Institute and State University

Washington
University of Washington
Washington State University

West Virginia
American Public University System
West Virginia University

Wisconsin
University of Wisconsin
Madison
Milwaukee

Canada
McGill University
University of Alberta
University of British Columbia
University of Toronto

Germany
University of Karlsruhe

Republic of Korea
Yonsei University

Two-year

Arizona
Penn Foster College
Pima Community College
Rio Salado College

California
Allan Hancock College
American River College
Antelope Valley College
Bakersfield College
Cabrillo College
Cerritos College
Chaffey College
City College of San Francisco
College of the Canyons
De Anza College
Diablo Valley College
East Los Angeles College
El Camino College
Foothill College
Fresno City College
Fullerton College
Glendale Community College
Grossmont College
Long Beach City College
Los Angeles City College
Los Angeles Pierce College
Los Angeles Valley College
MiraCosta College
Modesto Junior College
Moorpark College
Mount San Antonio College
Mount San Jacinto College
Orange Coast College
Palomar College
Pasadena City College
Rio Hondo College
Riverside Community College
Sacramento City College
Saddleback College
San Diego City College
San Diego Mesa College
San Joaquin Delta College
Santa Ana College
Santa Barbara City College
Santa Monica College
Santa Rosa Junior College
Sierra College
Southwestern College

Florida
Broward College
Florida Community College at Jacksonville
Hillsborough Community College
Miami Dade College
Palm Beach Community College
St. Petersburg College
Santa Fe College
Valencia Community College

Georgia
Georgia Perimeter College

Illinois
College of DuPage

Indiana
Ivy Tech State College
Ivy Tech Community College: Central Indiana

Kansas
Johnson County Community College

Kentucky
Jefferson Community and Technical College

Maryland
Community College of Baltimore County
Montgomery College

Michigan
Wayne County Community College

Missouri
St. Louis Community College
Meramec

Nevada
College of Southern Nevada

New Mexico
Central New Mexico Community College

New York
City University of New York
Borough of Manhattan Community College
Monroe Community College
Suffolk County Community College

North Carolina
Central Piedmont Community College

Ohio
Columbus State Community College
Sinclair Community College

Oregon
Portland Community College

Pennsylvania
Community College of Philadelphia

Rhode Island
Community College of Rhode Island

Texas
Austin Community College
Central Texas College
Collin County Community College District
Houston Community College System
Lone Star College System
San Antonio College
San Jacinto College
South Texas College
Tarrant County College

Utah
Salt Lake Community College

Virginia
Tidewater Community College

Wisconsin
Milwaukee Area Technical College

Admission selectivity

Admit under 50% of applicants

Four-year

Alabama
Alabama Agricultural and Mechanical University
Alabama State University

Alaska
Alaska Pacific University

California
California Institute of Technology
California Institute of the Arts
California Polytechnic State University: San Luis Obispo
California State University
  Long Beach
Claremont McKenna College
Harvey Mudd College
Occidental College
Pepperdine University
Pitzer College
Pomona College
San Diego State University
San Francisco Conservatory of Music
Scripps College
Stanford University
University of California
  Berkeley
  Irvine
  Los Angeles
  San Diego
  Santa Barbara
University of Southern California

Colorado
Colorado Christian University
Colorado College
United States Air Force Academy

Connecticut
Connecticut College
Mitchell College
Quinnipiac University
Trinity College
United States Coast Guard Academy
Wesleyan University
Yale University

Delaware
Delaware State University

District of Columbia
George Washington University
Georgetown University
Howard University

Florida
Baptist College of Florida
Flagler College
Florida Atlantic University
Florida Christian College
Florida International University
Florida State University
Nova Southeastern University
Palm Beach Atlantic University
Trinity College of Florida
University of Central Florida
University of Florida
University of Miami
University of South Florida

Georgia
Agnes Scott College
Albany State University
Brenau University
Emory University
Fort Valley State University
Life University
Oglethorpe University
Paine College
Spelman College
Toccoa Falls College

Hawaii
Brigham Young University-Hawaii

Illinois
MacMurray College
Northwestern University
University of Chicago

Indiana
University of Notre Dame
University of St. Francis
Wabash College

Iowa
Allen College
Cornell College
Grinnell College

Kansas
Benedictine College
Newman University

Kentucky
Alice Lloyd College
Berea College
Kentucky State University
Spalding University

Louisiana
Dillard University
Tulane University

Maine
Bates College
Bowdoin College
Colby College

Maryland
Bowie State University
Coppin State University
Johns Hopkins University
Johns Hopkins University: Peabody Conservatory of Music
Morgan State University
United States Naval Academy
University of Maryland
  College Park

Massachusetts
Amherst College
Atlantic Union College
Babson College
Bentley University
Berklee College of Music
Boston College
Boston Conservatory
Brandeis University
College of the Holy Cross
Emerson College
Endicott College
Franklin W. Olin College of Engineering
Hampshire College
Harvard College
Massachusetts Institute of Technology
New England Conservatory of Music
New England Institute of Art
Northeastern University
Smith College
Stonehill College
Tufts University
Wellesley College
Wheaton College
Williams College

Michigan
College for Creative Studies
Marygrove College
University of Michigan

Minnesota
Carleton College
Macalester College

Mississippi
Delta State University
Mississippi University for Women
Mississippi Valley State University
Rust College

Missouri
College of the Ozarks
Lindenwood University
Missouri Valley College
Washington University in St. Louis

Nebraska
College of Saint Mary
Peru State College

New Hampshire
Chester College of New England
Dartmouth College
Thomas More College of Liberal Arts

New Jersey
Bloomfield College
The College of New Jersey
New Jersey City University
Princeton University
Ramapo College of New Jersey

New Mexico
New Mexico Institute of Mining and Technology

New York
Bard College
Barnard College
Boricua College
City University of New York
  Baruch College
  Brooklyn College
  City College
  Hunter College
  Lehman College
  Queens College
Colgate University
College of New Rochelle
Columbia University
  School of General Studies
Cooper Union for the Advancement of Science and Art
Cornell University
Fashion Institute of Technology
Fordham University
Hamilton College
Juilliard School
Manhattan School of Music
Mannes College The New School for Music
Marist College
Metropolitan College of New York
New York School of Interior Design
New York University
Pratt Institute
Rensselaer Polytechnic Institute
St. John's University
St. Lawrence University
Sarah Lawrence College
Skidmore College
State University of New York
  Binghamton
  College at Brockport
  College at Buffalo
  College at Cortland
  College at Geneseo
  College at Old Westbury
  College at Oneonta
  College at Plattsburgh
  College of Environmental Science and Forestry
  Farmingdale
  Institute of Technology at Utica/Rome
  New Paltz
  Oswego
  Purchase
  Stony Brook
Union College
United States Merchant Marine Academy
United States Military Academy
University of Rochester
Vassar College
Webb Institute

North Carolina
Barton College
Bennett College
Brevard College
Cabarrus College of Health Sciences
Davidson College
Duke University
Elizabeth City State University
Elon University
Johnson C. Smith University
University of North Carolina
  Chapel Hill
University of North Carolina
  School of the Arts
Wake Forest University

Ohio
Art Academy of Cincinnati
Central State University
Denison University
Kenyon College
Notre Dame College
Oberlin College
Ursuline College

Oklahoma
Langston University
National Education Center
  Spartan College of Aeronautics and Technology
Oklahoma Christian University
Oklahoma Wesleyan University
University of Tulsa

Oregon
Eastern Oregon University
Reed College
Warner Pacific College
Western Oregon University

Pennsylvania
Bryn Mawr College
Bucknell University
Carnegie Mellon University
Cheyney University of Pennsylvania
Curtis Institute of Music
Dickinson College
Franklin & Marshall College
Gettysburg College
Haverford College
Lafayette College
Lehigh University
Lincoln University
Muhlenberg College
Swarthmore College
University of Pennsylvania
Villanova University
Washington & Jefferson College
West Chester University of Pennsylvania

Puerto Rico
Bayamon Central University
Inter American University of Puerto Rico
  Bayamon Campus
  Fajardo Campus
  Metropolitan Campus
University of Puerto Rico
  Bayamon University College
  Carolina Regional College
  Cayey University College
  Humacao
  Ponce
  Rio Piedras

Rhode Island
Brown University
Bryant University
Providence College
Rhode Island School of Design

South Carolina
Claflin University
University of South Carolina
  Aiken

Tennessee
Baptist College of Health Sciences
Crichton College
Lane College
LeMoyne-Owen College
O'More College of Design
Rhodes College
Tennessee Temple University
Vanderbilt University

Texas
Abilene Christian University
Dallas Baptist University
Dallas Christian College
Hardin-Simmons University
Houston Baptist University
Rice University
Southern Methodist University
Southwestern Adventist University
University of Mary Hardin-Baylor
University of Texas
  Austin

Vermont
Middlebury College

Virginia
College of William and Mary
Jefferson College of Health Sciences
University of Richmond
University of Virginia
Washington and Lee University

Washington
Trinity Lutheran College
Whitman College

West Virginia
West Virginia University Institute of Technology

Wisconsin
Silver Lake College

Canada
University of British Columbia

Republic of Korea
Yonsei University

Two-year

Alabama
Marion Military Institute

California
American Academy of Dramatic Arts: West
Deep Springs College

Connecticut
St. Vincent's College

Georgia
Oxford College of Emory University

New York
Phillips Beth Israel School of Nursing
St. Joseph's College of Nursing

Pennsylvania
Manor College
Williamson Free School of Mechanical Trades

Admit 50 to 75% of applicants

Four-year

Alabama
Auburn University
Birmingham-Southern College
Faulkner University
Huntingdon College
Oakwood University
Spring Hill College
Troy University
Tuskegee University
University of Alabama
University of Mobile
University of Montevallo
University of West Alabama

Alaska
University of Alaska
  Fairbanks

Arizona
Northern Arizona University

Arkansas
Harding University
Henderson State University
John Brown University
Lyon College
Ouachita Baptist University
Southern Arkansas University
University of Arkansas
University of Arkansas
  Monticello
  Pine Bluff
University of Central Arkansas
Williams Baptist College

California
American Jewish University
Art Center College of Design
Azusa Pacific University
Bethany University
California Baptist University
California Lutheran University
California Maritime Academy
California State Polytechnic University: Pomona
California State University
  Bakersfield
  East Bay
  Fresno
  Fullerton
  Monterey Bay
  Northridge
  Sacramento
  San Marcos
  Stanislaus
Chapman University
Cogswell Polytechnical College
Concordia University
Design Institute of San Diego
Dominican University of California
Fresno Pacific University
Holy Names University
La Sierra University
Loyola Marymount University
The Master's College
Menlo College
Mills College
National Hispanic University
Otis College of Art and Design
San Diego Christian College
San Francisco Art Institute
San Francisco State University
San Jose State University
Santa Clara University
Simpson University
Soka University of America
Thomas Aquinas College
University of California
  Davis
  Santa Cruz
University of La Verne
University of Redlands
University of San Diego
University of San Francisco
University of the Pacific
Westmont College
Whittier College
William Jessup University
Woodbury University

Colorado
Adams State College
Colorado School of Mines
Fort Lewis College
Johnson & Wales University: Denver
Metropolitan State College of Denver
Regis University
University of Colorado
  Colorado Springs
  Denver
University of Denver

Connecticut
Central Connecticut State University
Eastern Connecticut State University
Fairfield University
Paier College of Art
Post University
Sacred Heart University
Southern Connecticut State University
University of Bridgeport
University of Connecticut
University of Hartford
University of New Haven
Western Connecticut State University

Delaware
University of Delaware

District of Columbia
American University
Corcoran College of Art and Design
Gallaudet University
Southeastern University
Trinity Washington University

Florida
Ave Maria University
Barry University
Beacon College
Bethune-Cookman University
Eckerd College
Florida Agricultural and Mechanical University
Florida College
Florida Gulf Coast University
Florida Southern College
Jacksonville University
Lynn University
New College of Florida
Northwood University
  Florida
Ringling College of Art and Design
Rollins College
St. Leo University
Stetson University
University of North Florida
University of Tampa
University of West Florida
Warner University
Webber International University

Georgia
Armstrong Atlantic State University
Augusta State University
Berry College
Clark Atlanta University
Columbus State University
Covenant College
Dalton State College
Emmanuel College
Georgia College and State University
Georgia Institute of Technology
Georgia Southern University
Georgia Southwestern State University
Georgia State University
Herzing College
Kennesaw State University
LaGrange College
Macon State College
Mercer University
Morehouse College
North Georgia College & State University
Piedmont College
Reinhardt College
Savannah College of Art and Design
Shorter College
Southern Polytechnic State University
University of Georgia
University of West Georgia
Valdosta State University
Wesleyan College

Hawaii
University of Hawaii
  Manoa
  West Oahu

Idaho
College of Idaho
Lewis-Clark State College
Northwest Nazarene University

Illinois
Augustana College
Blackburn College
Bradley University
DePaul University
Eastern Illinois University
Elmhurst College
Eureka College
Illinois College
Illinois Institute of Technology
Illinois State University
Illinois Wesleyan University
Judson University
Knox College
Lake Forest College
Lewis University
Lexington College
Loyola University Chicago
McKendree University
Monmouth College
North Central College
North Park University
Northeastern Illinois University
Northern Illinois University
Rockford College
St. Xavier University
Southern Illinois University
  Carbondale
Trinity International University
University of Illinois
  Chicago
  Urbana-Champaign
University of St. Francis
Western Illinois University
Westwood College: Chicago Loop
Wheaton College

Indiana
Anderson University
Ball State University
Butler University
Calumet College of St. Joseph
DePauw University
Franklin College
Goshen College
Hanover College
Indiana Institute of Technology
Indiana State University
Indiana University
  Bloomington
Indiana University-Purdue University Indianapolis
Marian College
Purdue University
Purdue University
  Calumet
Rose-Hulman Institute of Technology
Saint Joseph's College
St. Mary-of-the-Woods College
Trine University

Iowa
Briar Cliff University
Clarke College
Coe College
Drake University
Graceland University
Iowa Wesleyan College
Loras College
Mercy College of Health Sciences
Morningside College
University of Dubuque
Upper Iowa University
Waldorf College
Wartburg College
William Penn University

Kansas
Baker University
Bethany College
Bethel College
Central Christian College of Kansas
Friends University
MidAmerica Nazarene University
Ottawa University
Sterling College
University of St. Mary

Kentucky
Asbury College
Bellarmine University
Brescia University
Campbellsville University
Centre College
Eastern Kentucky University
Kentucky Christian University
Kentucky Wesleyan College
Mid-Continent University
Morehead State University
University of Louisville

Louisiana
Centenary College of Louisiana
Louisiana College
Louisiana State University and Agricultural and Mechanical College
Louisiana Tech University
Loyola University New Orleans
Southern University and Agricultural and Mechanical College
University of Louisiana at Lafayette
University of New Orleans
Xavier University of Louisiana

Maine
College of the Atlantic
Maine Maritime Academy
New England School of Communications
Unity College
University of Maine
  Farmington

Maryland
Baltimore International College
College of Notre Dame of Maryland
Frostburg State University
Goucher College
Loyola College in Maryland
Maryland Institute College of Art
St. Mary's College of Maryland
Salisbury University
Stevenson University
Towson University
University of Baltimore
University of Maryland
  Baltimore County
  Eastern Shore
Washington College

Massachusetts
Assumption College
Becker College
Boston University
Bridgewater State College
Clark University
Curry College
Emmanuel College
Fitchburg State College
Framingham State College
Gordon College
Lasell College
Lesley University
Massachusetts College of Art and Design
Massachusetts College of Pharmacy and Health Sciences
Massachusetts Maritime Academy
Montserrat College of Art
Mount Holyoke College
Mount Ida College
Newbury College
Nichols College
Pine Manor College
Regis College
Salem State College
Simmons College
Springfield College
University of Massachusetts
  Amherst
  Boston
  Dartmouth
Wentworth Institute of Technology
Western New England College
Westfield State College
Wheelock College
Worcester Polytechnic Institute
Worcester State College

Michigan
Adrian College
Alma College
Andrews University
Central Michigan University
Concordia University
Cornerstone University
Eastern Michigan University
Grace Bible College
Hillsdale College
Kalamazoo College
Kendall College of Art and Design of Ferris State University
Kettering University
Lawrence Technological University
Michigan State University
Michigan Technological University
Northwood University: Michigan
Olivet College
University of Detroit Mercy
University of Michigan
  Dearborn

Minnesota
Augsburg College
College of Visual Arts
Concordia University: St. Paul

Crossroads College
Gustavus Adolphus College
Minneapolis College of Art and Design
Minnesota State University
 Mankato
St. John's University
St. Mary's University of Minnesota
St. Olaf College
Southwest Minnesota State University
University of Minnesota
 Duluth
 Morris
 Twin Cities
Winona State University

Mississippi

Belhaven College
Blue Mountain College
Jackson State University
Mississippi College
Mississippi State University
University of Southern Mississippi

Missouri

Avila University
Central Methodist University
Columbia College
Culver-Stockton College
Drury University
Evangel University
Kansas City Art Institute
Maryville University of Saint Louis
Missouri Baptist University
Missouri State University
Research College of Nursing
Saint Louis University
Southwest Baptist University
Stephens College
University of Missouri
 Kansas City
 St. Louis
Webster University
William Jewell College

Montana

Montana State University
 Bozeman
Rocky Mountain College

Nebraska

Concordia University
Grace University
Nebraska Methodist College of Nursing and Allied Health
Union College
University of Nebraska
 Lincoln
York College

Nevada

University of Nevada
 Las Vegas

New Hampshire

Keene State College
Plymouth State University
St. Anselm College
University of New Hampshire
University of New Hampshire at Manchester

New Jersey

Caldwell College
Centenary College
Drew University
Fairleigh Dickinson University
 College at Florham
 Metropolitan Campus
Georgian Court University
Kean University
Monmouth University
Montclair State University
New Jersey Institute of Technology
Richard Stockton College of New Jersey
Rider University
Rowan University
Rutgers, The State University of New Jersey
 Camden Regional Campus
 New Brunswick/Piscataway Campus
 Newark Regional Campus
Saint Peter's College
Seton Hall University
Stevens Institute of Technology
William Paterson University of New Jersey

New Mexico

Eastern New Mexico University

New York

Adelphi University
Albany College of Pharmacy and Health Sciences
Cazenovia College
City University of New York
 John Jay College of Criminal Justice
College of Mount St. Vincent
College of Saint Rose
Concordia College
Daemen College
Elmira College
Eugene Lang College The New School for Liberal Arts
Hobart and William Smith Colleges
Hofstra University
Iona College
Ithaca College
Jewish Theological Seminary of America
Laboratory Institute of Merchandising
Le Moyne College
Manhattan College
Manhattanville College
Marymount Manhattan College
Medaille College
Mercy College
Molloy College
Monroe College
Nazareth College of Rochester
Niagara University
Pace University
Parsons The New School for Design
Polytechnic Institute of New York University
Roberts Wesleyan College
Rochester Institute of Technology
Russell Sage College
Sage College of Albany
St. Francis College
St. John Fisher College
St. Joseph's College
Siena College
State University of New York
 Albany
 Buffalo
 College at Fredonia
 College at Potsdam
Syracuse University
Touro College
Utica College
Wagner College
Wells College
Yeshiva University

North Carolina

Appalachian State University
Belmont Abbey College
Campbell University
Catawba College
East Carolina University
Gardner-Webb University
Greensboro College
Guilford College
High Point University
Johnson & Wales University: Charlotte
Lees-McRae College
Livingstone College
Mars Hill College
Meredith College
Methodist University
North Carolina Agricultural and Technical State University
North Carolina Central University
North Carolina State University
North Carolina Wesleyan College
Peace College
Pfeiffer University
Roanoke Bible College
St. Augustine's College
Salem College
University of North Carolina
 Asheville
 Greensboro
 Wilmington
Western Carolina University
Winston-Salem State University

North Dakota

Jamestown College
Minot State University

Ohio

Baldwin-Wallace College
Bluffton University
Case Western Reserve University
Cleveland State University
College of Mount St. Joseph
Columbus College of Art and Design
Defiance College
Franciscan University of Steubenville
Heidelberg University
Kent State University
Kettering College of Medical Arts
Lake Erie College
Laura and Alvin Siegal College of Judaic Studies
Malone University
MedCentral College of Nursing
Mercy College of Northwest Ohio
Mount Carmel College of Nursing
Ohio Dominican University
Ohio State University
 Columbus Campus
Ohio Wesleyan University
Tiffin University
University of Akron
University of Cincinnati
University of Dayton
University of Findlay
Wilberforce University
Wittenberg University

Oklahoma

Bacone College
Northeastern State University
Oklahoma Baptist University
Oral Roberts University
Rogers State University
University of Central Oklahoma

Oregon

Art Institute of Portland
Concordia University
Eugene Bible College
Lewis & Clark College
Multnomah University
Pacific Northwest College of Art

Pennsylvania

Albright College
Allegheny College
Arcadia University
Baptist Bible College of Pennsylvania
Bloomsburg University of Pennsylvania
Cabrini College
California University of Pennsylvania
Carlow University
Cedar Crest College
Chatham University
Chestnut Hill College
Clarion University of Pennsylvania
Delaware Valley College
DeSales University
Drexel University
East Stroudsburg University of Pennsylvania
Edinboro University of Pennsylvania
Elizabethtown College
Grove City College
Gwynedd-Mercy College
Holy Family University
Indiana University of Pennsylvania
Juniata College
Kutztown University of Pennsylvania
La Roche College
La Salle University
Lancaster Bible College
Lebanon Valley College
Lock Haven University of Pennsylvania
Lycoming College
Mansfield University of Pennsylvania
Mercyhurst College
Messiah College
Millersville University of Pennsylvania
Misericordia University
Moore College of Art and Design
Moravian College
Mount Aloysius College
Penn State
 Altoona
 Harrisburg
 University Park
Pennsylvania College of Art and Design
Philadelphia University
Point Park University
Restaurant School at Walnut Hill College
Robert Morris University
Rosemont College
St. Vincent College
Seton Hill University
Shippensburg University of Pennsylvania
Slippery Rock University of Pennsylvania
Susquehanna University
Temple University
Thiel College
University of Pittsburgh
University of Pittsburgh
 Bradford
 Greensburg
University of Scranton
University of the Sciences in Philadelphia
Ursinus College
Westminster College
Widener University
Wilson College
York College of Pennsylvania

Puerto Rico

Conservatory of Music of Puerto Rico
Escuela de Artes Plasticas de Puerto Rico
Inter American University of Puerto Rico
 Guayama Campus
 Ponce Campus
National College of Business and Technology: Arecibo
National College of Business and Technology: Rio Grande
Universidad Metropolitana

Rhode Island

Johnson & Wales University: Providence
Rhode Island College
Roger Williams University
Salve Regina University

South Carolina

Charleston Southern University
Clemson University
Coastal Carolina University
College of Charleston
Converse College
Erskine College
Francis Marion University
Furman University
Limestone College
North Greenville University
Presbyterian College
University of South Carolina
University of South Carolina
 Upstate
Winthrop University
Wofford College

South Dakota

Presentation College

Tennessee

Aquinas College
Belmont University
Bethel College
Carson-Newman College
Christian Brothers University
Cumberland University
Fisk University
Freed-Hardeman University
King College
Lambuth University
Lee University
Lipscomb University
Memphis College of Art
Middle Tennessee State University
Milligan College
Southern Adventist University
Tennessee State University
Trevecca Nazarene University
Tusculum College
University of Memphis
University of Tennessee
 Knoxville
University of the South

Texas

Baylor University
Concordia University Texas
East Texas Baptist University
Howard Payne University
Huston-Tillotson University
LeTourneau University
Lubbock Christian University
McMurry University
Midwestern State University
Northwood University: Texas
Our Lady of the Lake University of San Antonio
Prairie View A&M University
St. Edward's University
St. Mary's University
Sam Houston State University
Schreiner University
Southwestern University
Stephen F. Austin State University
Tarleton State University
Texas A&M International University
Texas A&M University
Texas A&M University
 Commerce
 Corpus Christi
Texas Christian University
Texas Lutheran University
Texas State University: San Marcos
Texas Tech University
Texas Wesleyan University
Texas Woman's University

Trinity University
University of North Texas
University of Texas
Dallas
University of the Incarnate Word

Utah

Brigham Young University
Southern Utah University

Vermont

Bennington College
Burlington College
Castleton State College
Champlain College
Green Mountain College
Marlboro College
St. Michael's College
Southern Vermont College
University of Vermont
Vermont Technical College

Virginia

Bluefield College
Christopher Newport University
Eastern Mennonite University
Emory & Henry College
George Mason University
Hampden-Sydney College
James Madison University
Longwood University
Lynchburg College
Mary Baldwin College
Old Dominion University
Radford University
Randolph-Macon College
Roanoke College
University of Mary Washington
Virginia Commonwealth University
Virginia Intermont College
Virginia Military Institute
Virginia Polytechnic Institute and State University
Virginia State University
Virginia Union University

Washington

Cornish College of the Arts
Pacific Lutheran University
Seattle University
University of Puget Sound
University of Washington
Washington State University
Western Washington University
Whitworth University

West Virginia

Alderson-Broaddus College
Appalachian Bible College
Glenville State College
Ohio Valley University
Shepherd University
University of Charleston
West Virginia State University
West Virginia Wesleyan College
Wheeling Jesuit University

Wisconsin

Beloit College
Carroll University
Concordia University Wisconsin
Lawrence University
Maranatha Baptist Bible College
Marquette University
Milwaukee School of Engineering
Mount Mary College
Northland College
University of Wisconsin
Eau Claire
Green Bay
La Crosse
Madison
Stevens Point
Stout
Superior
Whitewater

Virgin Islands, U.S.

University of the Virgin Islands

Canada

McGill University
Simon Fraser University
University of Toronto

Egypt

American University in Cairo

France

American University of Paris

Lebanon

American University of Beirut

Switzerland

Franklin College: Switzerland

Two-year

Arkansas

University of Arkansas Community College at Morrilton

California

Fashion Institute of Design and Merchandising
San Diego
San Francisco

Delaware

Delaware College of Art and Design

Georgia

Georgia Perimeter College
Gordon College
Young Harris College

Illinois

Lincoln College

Iowa

AIB College of Business
St. Luke's College

Massachusetts

Dean College
Marian Court College

New Mexico

New Mexico Military Institute

New York

American Academy of Dramatic Arts
State University of New York
College of Agriculture and Technology at Morrisville
College of Technology at Alfred
College of Technology at Delhi

North Carolina

Louisburg College

Ohio

Miami-Jacobs Career College

Pennsylvania

Antonelli Institute of Art and Photography

South Carolina

Spartanburg Methodist College

Admit over 75% of applicants

Four-year

Alabama

Auburn University at Montgomery
Heritage Christian University
Jacksonville State University
Judson College
Samford University
Southeastern Bible College
University of Alabama
Birmingham
Huntsville
University of North Alabama
University of South Alabama

Alaska

University of Alaska
Southeast

Arizona

American Indian College of the Assemblies of God
Arizona State University
Art Center Design College
DeVry University
Phoenix
Embry-Riddle Aeronautical University: Prescott Campus
Grand Canyon University
Prescott College
University of Arizona

Arkansas

Arkansas State University
Arkansas Tech University
Central Baptist College
Hendrix College
Philander Smith College
University of Arkansas
Little Rock
University of the Ozarks

California

Biola University
California College of the Arts
California State University
Chico
Dominguez Hills
Los Angeles
Charles R. Drew University of Medicine and Science
Golden Gate University
Hope International University
Humboldt State University
International Academy of Design and Technology
Sacramento
Lincoln University
Mount St. Mary's College
Mt. Sierra College
NewSchool of Architecture & Design
Notre Dame de Namur University
Pacific Union College
Point Loma Nazarene University
St. Mary's College of California
School of Urban Missions: Oakland
Sonoma State University
Southern California Institute of Architecture
University of California
Riverside
University of California: Merced
Vanguard University of Southern California

Colorado

Colorado State University
Colorado State University
Pueblo
Mesa State College
Naropa University
Rocky Mountain College of Art & Design
University of Colorado
Boulder
University of Northern Colorado
Western State College of Colorado
Westwood College of Technology
Westwood College: Denver South

Connecticut

Albertus Magnus College
Holy Apostles College and Seminary
Lyme Academy College of Fine Arts
St. Joseph College

District of Columbia

Catholic University of America

Florida

Clearwater Christian College
Embry-Riddle Aeronautical University
Everest University: South Orlando
Florida Institute of Technology
Hodges University
Johnson & Wales University: North Miami
St. John Vianney College Seminary
Saint Thomas University

Georgia

Atlanta Christian College
Brewton-Parker College

Hawaii

Chaminade University of Honolulu
Hawaii Pacific University

Idaho

Boise Bible College
Boise State University
Brigham Young University-Idaho
Idaho State University
New Saint Andrews College
University of Idaho

Illinois

Aurora University
Benedictine University
Concordia University Chicago
Dominican University
Greenville College
Midstate College
Millikin University
National-Louis University
Olivet Nazarene University
Principia College
Quincy University
Robert Morris College: Chicago
Roosevelt University
School of the Art Institute of Chicago
Shimer College
Southern Illinois University
Edwardsville
Trinity Christian College
University of Illinois
Springfield
VanderCook College of Music

Indiana

Bethel College
DeVry University: Indianapolis
Earlham College
Grace College
Holy Cross College
Huntington University
Indiana University
Kokomo
Northwest
South Bend
Southeast
Indiana University-Purdue University Fort Wayne
Indiana Wesleyan University
Manchester College
Purdue University
North Central
Saint Mary's College
Taylor University
University of Evansville
University of Indianapolis
University of Southern Indiana
Valparaiso University

Iowa

Buena Vista University
Central College
Divine Word College
Dordt College
Emmaus Bible College
Faith Baptist Bible College and Theological Seminary
Grand View University
Iowa State University
Luther College
Mount Mercy College
Northwestern College
St. Ambrose University
Simpson College
University of Iowa
University of Northern Iowa

Kansas

Barclay College
Emporia State University
Kansas State University
McPherson College
Pittsburg State University
Southwestern College
Tabor College
University of Kansas
Wichita State University

Kentucky

Georgetown College
Murray State University
Thomas More College
Transylvania University
University of Kentucky
University of the Cumberlands

Louisiana

Grambling State University
Louisiana State University
Alexandria
Shreveport
McNeese State University
New Orleans Baptist Theological Seminary: Leavell College
Nicholls State University
Northwestern State University
School of Urban Missions: New Orleans
Southeastern Louisiana University
University of Louisiana at Monroe

Maine

Husson University
Maine College of Art
St. Joseph's College
Thomas College
University of Maine
University of Maine
Fort Kent
Machias
University of New England
University of Southern Maine

Maryland

Capitol College
Hood College
McDaniel College
Mount St. Mary's University
St. John's College

Massachusetts

American International College
Anna Maria College
Bard College at Simon's Rock
Bay Path College
Elms College
Massachusetts College of Liberal Arts
Merrimack College
School of the Museum of Fine Arts
Suffolk University
University of Massachusetts
Lowell

Michigan

Albion College

Aquinas College
Calvin College
Finlandia University
Grand Valley State University
Great Lakes Christian College
Hope College
Kuyper College
Lake Superior State University
Madonna University
Northern Michigan University
Oakland University
Rochester College
Sacred Heart Major Seminary
Saginaw Valley State University
Siena Heights University
Spring Arbor University
University of Michigan
  Flint
Wayne State University
Western Michigan University

Minnesota

Bemidji State University
Bethany Lutheran College
Bethel University
College of St. Benedict
College of St. Catherine
College of St. Scholastica
Concordia College: Moorhead
Hamline University
Minnesota School of Business: St. Cloud
Minnesota State University
  Moorhead
Northwestern College
Oak Hills Christian College
Saint Cloud State University
University of Minnesota
  Crookston
University of St. Thomas

Mississippi

Alcorn State University
Millsaps College
Tougaloo College
University of Mississippi

Missouri

Central Bible College
Central Christian College of the Bible
Conception Seminary College
Fontbonne University
Harris-Stowe State University
Missouri Southern State University
Missouri Technical School
Northwest Missouri State University
Park University
Rockhurst University
Southeast Missouri State University
Truman State University
University of Central Missouri
University of Missouri
  Columbia
  Missouri University of Science and Technology
Westminster College
William Woods University

Montana

Carroll College
Montana State University
  Billings
Montana Tech of the University of Montana
University of Great Falls
University of Montana

Nebraska

BryanLGH College of Health Sciences
Creighton University
Doane College
Nebraska Wesleyan University
University of Nebraska
  Kearney
  Omaha

Nevada

Nevada State College
University of Nevada
  Reno

New Hampshire

Colby-Sawyer College
Franklin Pierce University
Magdalen College
New England College
Southern New Hampshire University

New Jersey

College of St. Elizabeth
Felician College

New Mexico

New Mexico State University
St. John's College

New York

Alfred University
Canisius College
City University of New York
  College of Staten Island
Clarkson University
Culinary Institute of America
D'Youville College
Dominican College of Blauvelt
Dowling College
Hartwick College
Hilbert College
Houghton College
Keuka College
King's College
Long Island University
  Brooklyn Campus
  C. W. Post Campus
Mount St. Mary College
New York Institute of Technology
Paul Smith's College
Saint Bonaventure University
St. Joseph's College: Suffolk Campus
St. Thomas Aquinas College
State University of New York
  Empire State College
  Maritime College
Vaughn College of Aeronautics and Technology

North Carolina

Lenoir-Rhyne University
Queens University of Charlotte
St. Andrews Presbyterian College
University of North Carolina
  Charlotte
  Pembroke

North Dakota

North Dakota State University
University of Mary
University of North Dakota
Valley City State University

Ohio

Ashland University
Bowling Green State University
Capital University
Cincinnati Christian University
Cleveland Institute of Art
College of Wooster
Hiram College
John Carroll University
Lourdes College
Marietta College
Miami University
  Oxford Campus
Mount Union College
Mount Vernon Nazarene University
Muskingum College
Ohio Christian University
Ohio Northern University
Ohio University
Otterbein College
Pontifical College Josephinum
Rabbinical College of Telshe
Walsh University
Wilmington College
Wright State University
Xavier University

Oklahoma

Cameron University
East Central University
Family of Faith College
Northwestern Oklahoma State University
Oklahoma City University
Oklahoma Panhandle State University
Oklahoma State University
St. Gregory's University
Southeastern Oklahoma State University
Southwestern Oklahoma State University
University of Oklahoma
University of Science and Arts of Oklahoma

Oregon

Corban College
George Fox University
Linfield College
Northwest Christian University
Oregon College of Art & Craft
Oregon Institute of Technology
Oregon State University
Pacific University
Portland State University
Southern Oregon University
University of Oregon
University of Portland
Willamette University

Pennsylvania

Alvernia University
Bryn Athyn College of the New Church
Duquesne University
Eastern University
Gannon University
Geneva College
Immaculata University
Keystone College
King's College
Marywood University
Neumann College
Penn State
  Abington
  Beaver
  Berks
  Brandywine
  Dubois
  Erie, The Behrend College
  Fayette, The Eberly Campus
  Greater Allegheny
  Hazleton
  Lehigh Valley
  Mont Alto
  New Kensington
  Schuylkill
  Shenango
  Wilkes-Barre
  Worthington Scranton
  York
Philadelphia Biblical University
St. Charles Borromeo Seminary - Overbrook
St. Francis University
Saint Joseph's University
Talmudical Yeshiva of Philadelphia
University of Pittsburgh
  Johnstown
Valley Forge Christian College
Waynesburg University
Wilkes University

Puerto Rico

Colegio Pentecostal Mizpa
Inter American University of Puerto Rico
  Arecibo Campus
  San German Campus
Pontifical Catholic University of Puerto Rico
Universidad Politecnica de Puerto Rico
University College of San Juan
University of Puerto Rico
  Aguadilla
  Mayaguez

Rhode Island

University of Rhode Island

South Carolina

Anderson University
The Citadel
Columbia College
Columbia International University
Morris College
Newberry College
South Carolina State University
Southern Wesleyan University

South Dakota

Augustana College
Black Hills State University
Dakota State University
Northern State University
South Dakota School of Mines and Technology
South Dakota State University
University of Sioux Falls
University of South Dakota

Tennessee

Austin Peay State University
East Tennessee State University
Maryville College
Tennessee Technological University
Tennessee Wesleyan College
Union University
University of Tennessee
  Chattanooga
  Martin

Texas

Angelo State University
Austin College
College of Saint Thomas More
Lamar University
Texas A&M University
  Galveston
University of Dallas
University of Houston
University of St. Thomas
University of Texas
  Arlington
  El Paso
  Pan American
  San Antonio
  Tyler
  of the Permian Basin
Wayland Baptist University

Utah

University of Utah
Utah State University
Westminster College

Vermont

College of St. Joseph in Vermont
Goddard College
Johnson State College
Sterling College

Virginia

Averett University
Bridgewater College
Christendom College
Ferrum College
Hollins University
Liberty University
Marymount University
Randolph College
Regent University
St. Paul's College
Shenandoah University
Southern Virginia University
Sweet Briar College
University of Virginia's College at Wise
Virginia Wesleyan College

Washington

Central Washington University
Eastern Washington University
Evergreen State College
Gonzaga University
Northwest University
Saint Martin's University
Seattle Pacific University
University of Washington Tacoma
Walla Walla University

West Virginia

Bethany College
Bluefield State College
Concord University
Davis and Elkins College
Fairmont State University
Marshall University
West Liberty State College
West Virginia University

Wisconsin

Alverno College
Cardinal Stritch University
Carthage College
Lakeland College
Marian University
Milwaukee Institute of Art & Design
Ripon College
St. Norbert College
University of Wisconsin
  Milwaukee
  Oshkosh
  Parkside
  Platteville
  River Falls
Viterbo University
Wisconsin Lutheran College

Wyoming

University of Wyoming

France

Parsons Paris School of Design

United Arab Emirates

American University in Dubai

Two-year

California

Fashion Institute of Design and Merchandising
  Los Angeles
Marymount College
Professional Golfers Career College
Santa Barbara Business College
Santa Barbara Business College
  Bakersfield
  Santa Maria
Santa Barbara Business College: Ventura

Georgia

Abraham Baldwin Agricultural College
Darton College
Gainesville State College
Georgia Highlands College
Savannah River College

Illinois

Northwestern Business College

Kentucky

Louisville Technical Institute

New Jersey

Assumption College for Sisters

New York
Bryant & Stratton Business Institute
Bryant & Stratton College: Rochester
Helene Fuld College of Nursing
State University of New York
College of Agriculture and Technology at Cobleskill
College of Technology at Canton

Ohio
Art Institute of Ohio: Cincinnati
Bohecker College
Davis College

Pennsylvania
Cambria-Rowe Business College: Indiana
Hussian School of Art
Laurel Business Institute
University of Pittsburgh
Titusville

Tennessee
Nossi College of Art

Vermont
Landmark College

Virginia
Richard Bland College

Open admission

Four-year

Alabama
Amridge University
Andrew Jackson University
Columbia Southern University
Huntsville Bible College
Miles College
Selma University
Talladega College

Alaska
Alaska Bible College
University of Alaska
Anchorage

Arizona
Art Institute of Tucson
Brown Mackie College: Tucson
College of the Humanities and Sciences
Collins College
International Baptist College
International Import-Export Institute
Northcentral University
University of Phoenix
Western International University

Arkansas
Arkansas Baptist College
Ecclesia College
University of Arkansas
Fort Smith

California
Academy of Art University
Art Institute
of California: Orange County
Art Institute of California: Hollywood
Bethesda Christian University
Brooks Institute: Ventura
California Coast University
California College San Diego
Coleman University
Humphreys College
Interior Designers Institute
John F. Kennedy University
LA College International
Life Pacific College
National University
Pacific States University
Platt College
San Diego
Southern California Institute of Technology
Southern California Seminary
University of the West
West Coast University
Yeshiva Ohr Elchonon
Chabad/West Coast Talmudical Seminary

Colorado
American Sentinel University
Aspen University
CollegeAmerica
Colorado Springs
Fort Collins
National American University
Denver
Nazarene Bible College

Delaware
Wilmington University

District of Columbia
Potomac College
University of the District of Columbia

Florida
Chipola College
City College: Fort Lauderdale
Edison State College
Edward Waters College
International Academy of Design and Technology: Orlando
International Academy of Design and Technology: Tampa
Jones College
Northwest Florida State College
Rasmussen College: Fort Myers
Rasmussen College: Ocala
Rasmussen College: Pasco County
Schiller International University
Southeastern University
Universidad FLET

Georgia
Bauder College
Luther Rice University
Thomas University

Illinois
American Academy of Art
Columbia College Chicago
East-West University
Illinois Institute of Art: Schaumburg
International Academy of Design and Technology: Chicago
International Academy of Design and Technology: Schaumburg
St. Augustine College

Indiana
Indiana University
East
International Business College
Martin University
Oakland City University

Iowa
Hamilton Technical College
Kaplan University
Cedar Falls
Davenport
Des Moines
Mason City

Kansas
University of Kansas Medical Center
Washburn University

Kentucky
Beckfield College
Clear Creek Baptist Bible College
Kentucky Mountain Bible College
Lindsey Wilson College
Midway College
Northern Kentucky University
Pikeville College
St. Catharine College
Union College
Western Kentucky University

Louisiana
Our Lady of the Lake College
St. Joseph Seminary College
Southern University
New Orleans
Southwest University

Maine
University of Maine
Augusta

Maryland
National Labor College
Sojourner-Douglass College
University of Maryland
University College

Massachusetts
Boston Architectural College
Cambridge College
Rhodec International
Zion Bible College

Michigan
Baker College
of Auburn Hills
of Cadillac
of Clinton Township
of Flint
of Jackson
of Muskegon
of Owosso
of Port Huron
Baker College of Allen Park
Cleary University
International Academy of Design and Technology: Detroit
Michigan Jewish Institute
Walsh College of Accountancy and Business Administration

Minnesota
Art Institutes International
Minnesota
Brown College
Capella University
Globe University
National American University
St. Paul
National American University: Roseville
Rasmussen College: Lake Elmo/Woodbury

Mississippi
Magnolia Bible College
University of Mississippi Medical Center
William Carey University

Missouri
Baptist Bible College
Calvary Bible College and Theological Seminary
Cox College
Global University
Grantham University
Hickey College
Lincoln University
Missouri Western State University
National American University
Kansas City

Montana
Salish Kootenai College
University of Montana: Western

Nebraska
Bellevue University
Chadron State College
Clarkson College
Wayne State College

Nevada
Art Institute
of Las Vegas
Great Basin College
International Academy of Design and Technology: Henderson
Morrison University

New Hampshire
Granite State College
Hesser College
Rivier College

New Jersey
Thomas Edison State College

New Mexico
National American University: Rio Rancho
University of the Southwest
Western New Mexico University

New York
City University of New York
Medgar Evers College
New York City College of Technology
City University of New York: CUNY Online
Excelsior College
Yeshiva Mikdash Melech

North Carolina
Apex School of Theology
Art Institute
of Charlotte
Carolina Christian College
Miller-Motte Technical College
Montreat College
Mount Olive College
Wingate University

North Dakota
Dickinson State University
Mayville State University
Rasmussen College: Fargo

Ohio
Bryant & Stratton College
Eastlake
Cincinnati College of Mortuary Science
Franklin University
God's Bible School and College
Ohio State University
Lima Campus
Mansfield Campus
Marion Campus
Newark Campus
Ohio University
Chillicothe Campus
Eastern Campus
Lancaster Campus
Southern Campus at Ironton
Zanesville Campus
Shawnee State University
Tri-State Bible College
University of Rio Grande
University of Toledo
Youngstown State University

Oklahoma
Mid-America Christian University
Southern Nazarene University

Oregon
Marylhurst University

Pennsylvania
Central Pennsylvania College
Peirce College
Pennsylvania College of Technology

Puerto Rico
American University of Puerto Rico
Atlantic College
Columbia Centro Universitario: Caguas
Inter American University of Puerto Rico
Aguadilla Campus
National College of Business and Technology: Bayamon
Turabo University
Universidad Adventista de las Antillas
Universidad del Este

Rhode Island
New England Institute of Technology

South Carolina
Allen University
Benedict College
Bob Jones University
Lander University
South University: Columbia

South Dakota
Dakota Wesleyan University
Mount Marty College
National American University
Rapid City
Oglala Lakota College

Tennessee
Free Will Baptist Bible College
International Academy of Design and Technology: Nashville
Martin Methodist College
Williamson Christian College

Texas
Arlington Baptist College
Art Institute
of Dallas
Baptist Missionary Association Theological Seminary
Baptist University of the Americas
College of Biblical Studies-Houston
Jarvis Christian College
Texas A&M University
Kingsville
Texas College
Texas Southern University
University of Houston
Downtown
University of Texas
Brownsville - Texas Southmost College
Wiley College

Utah
Dixie State College of Utah
Independence University
Stevens-Henager College
Murray
Stevens-Henager College: Ogden
Stevens-Henager College: Orem
Utah Valley University
Weber State University
Western Governors University

Virginia
National College
Roanoke Valley
Stratford University: Falls Church
Virginia University of Lynchburg
World College

Washington
Art Institute of Seattle
City University of Seattle
Faith Evangelical Seminary
Heritage University
International Academy of Design and Technology: Seattle

West Virginia
American Public University System
Mountain State University
West Virginia University at Parkersburg

Wisconsin
Edgewood College
Herzing College

Guam
University of Guam

Northern Mariana Islands
Northern Marianas College

Canada
University of Manitoba

Mexico
Instituto Tecnologico Autonomo de Mexico
Universidad de Monterrey

United Kingdom
Richmond, The American International University in London

Two-year

Alabama
Alabama Southern Community College
Bevill State Community College
Bishop State Community College
Calhoun Community College
Central Alabama Community College
Chattahoochee Valley Community College
Community College of the Air Force
Enterprise-Ozark Community College
Faulkner State Community College
Gadsden State Community College
George C. Wallace State Community College
George C. Wallace Community College at Dothan
Selma
Jefferson Davis Community College
Jefferson State Community College
Lawson State Community College
Lurleen B. Wallace Community College
Northeast Alabama Community College
Northwest-Shoals Community College
Prince Institute of Professional Studies
Remington College
Mobile
Shelton State Community College
Snead State Community College
Southern Union State Community College
Virginia College at Mobile
Wallace State Community College at Hanceville

Alaska
Ilisagvik College
Prince William Sound Community College

Arizona
Anthem College
Arizona Automotive Institute
Arizona Western College
Bryman School
Central Arizona College
Chandler-Gilbert Community College
Pecos
Cochise College
Coconino County Community College
Dine College
Eastern Arizona College
Estrella Mountain Community College
Everest College
Phoenix
Gateway Community College
Glendale Community College
IIA College
Mesa
Phoenix
International Institute of the Americas
IIA College: Tucson
Kaplan College: Phoenix
Lamson College
Mesa Community College
Mohave Community College
Northland Pioneer College
Paradise Valley Community College
Paralegal Institute
Penn Foster College
Phoenix College
Pima Community College
Refrigeration School
Rio Salado College
Scottsdale Community College
Scottsdale Culinary Institute
South Mountain Community College
Tohono O'odham Community College
Universal Technical Institute
Yavapai College

Arkansas
Arkansas Northeastern College
Arkansas State University
Beebe
Mountain Home
Arkansas State University: Newport
Crowley's Ridge College
East Arkansas Community College
Mid-South Community College
National Park Community College
North Arkansas College
Northwest Arkansas Community College
Ouachita Technical College
Ozarka College
Phillips Community College of the University of Arkansas
Pulaski Technical College
Rich Mountain Community College
South Arkansas Community College
Southeast Arkansas College
Southern Arkansas University Tech
University of Arkansas
Community College at Batesville
Community College at Hope
Cossatot Community College of the

California
Allan Hancock College
American River College
Antelope Valley College
Bakersfield College
Barstow Community College
Berkeley City College
Bryan College: Los Angeles
Butte College
Cabrillo College
California School of Culinary Arts
Canada College
CEI College
Kaplan College: Panorama City
Cerritos College
Cerro Coso Community College
Chabot College
Chaffey College
Citrus College
City College of San Francisco
Coastline Community College
College of Alameda
College of Marin: Kentfield
College of San Mateo
College of the Canyons
College of the Desert
College of the Redwoods
College of the Sequoias
College of the Siskiyous
Columbia College
Concorde Career College
Garden Grove
Contra Costa College
Copper Mountain College
Cosumnes River College
Crafton Hills College
Cuesta College
Cuyamaca College
Cypress College
De Anza College
Diablo Valley College
East Los Angeles College
El Camino College
El Camino College: Compton Center
Empire College
Evergreen Valley College
Feather River College
Folsom Lake College
Foothill College
Fremont College
Fresno City College
Fullerton College
Gavilan College
Glendale Community College
Golden West College
Grossmont College
Hartnell College
Heald College
Stockton
Imperial Valley College
Irvine Valley College
Lake Tahoe Community College
Laney College
Las Positas College
Lassen Community College
Long Beach City College
Los Angeles City College
Los Angeles Harbor College
Los Angeles Mission College
Los Angeles Pierce College
Los Angeles Southwest College
Los Angeles Trade and Technical College
Los Angeles Valley College
Los Medanos College
Mendocino College
Merced College
Merritt College
MiraCosta College
Mission College
Modesto Junior College
Monterey Peninsula College
Moorpark College
Mount San Antonio College
Mount San Jacinto College
Napa Valley College
National Polytechnic College of Science
Ohlone College
Orange Coast College
Oxnard College
Palo Verde College
Palomar College
Pasadena City College
Porterville College
Reedley College
Rio Hondo College
Riverside Community College
Sacramento City College
Saddleback College
San Bernardino Valley College
San Diego City College
San Diego Mesa College
San Diego Miramar College
San Joaquin Delta College
San Joaquin Valley College
San Jose City College
Santa Ana College
Santa Barbara City College
Santa Monica College
Santa Rosa Junior College
Santiago Canyon College
Shasta College
Sierra College
Skyline College
Solano Community College
South Coast College
Southwestern College
Taft College
Ventura College
Victor Valley College
West Hills College: Coalinga
West Hills College: Lemoore
West Los Angeles College
West Valley College
Westwood College of Technology
Westwood College: Los Angeles
Yuba Community College District

Colorado
Aims Community College
Arapahoe Community College
Boulder College of Massage Therapy
Colorado Mountain College
Colorado Northwestern Community College
Colorado School of Healing Arts
Colorado School of Trades
Community College of Aurora
Community College of Denver
Denver Academy of Court Reporting
Everest College: Aurora
Everest College: Colorado Springs
Front Range Community College
Institute of Business & Medical Careers
IntelliTec College
IntelliTec College: Grand Junction
Kaplan College: Denver
Lamar Community College
Lincoln College of Technology: Denver
Morgan Community College
Northeastern Junior College
Otero Junior College
Pikes Peak Community College
Pueblo Community College
Red Rocks Community College
Redstone College
Remington College
Colorado Springs
Trinidad State Junior College

Connecticut
Asnuntuck Community College
Briarwood College
Capital Community College
Gateway Community College
Goodwin College
Housatonic Community College
Manchester Community College
Middlesex Community College
Naugatuck Valley Community College
Northwestern Connecticut Community College
Norwalk Community College
Quinebaug Valley Community College
Three Rivers Community College
Tunxis Community College

Delaware
Delaware Technical and Community College
Owens
Stanton/Wilmington
Terry

Florida
Brevard Community College
Broward College
Central Florida College
Central Florida Community College
City College
Gainesville
College of Business and Technology: Flagler
College of Business and Technology: Kendall
Daytona State College
Florida College of Natural Health
Bradenton
Florida Community College at Jacksonville
Florida Keys Community College
Florida National College
Florida Technical College
Deland
Orlando
Full Sail University
Gulf Coast Community College
Herzing College
Hillsborough Community College
Indian River State College
Key College
Lake City Community College
Lake-Sumter Community College
Manatee Community College
Miami Dade College
North Florida Community College
North Florida Institute: Orange Park
Palm Beach Community College
Pasco-Hernando Community College
Pensacola Junior College
Polk Community College
Saint Johns River Community College
St. Petersburg College
Santa Fe College
Seminole Community College
South Florida Community College
Southwest Florida College
Tallahassee Community College
Valencia Community College
Virginia College at Pensacola

Georgia
Albany Technical College
Ashworth University
Athens Technical College
Atlanta Technical College
Augusta Technical College
Brown Mackie College: Atlanta
Central Georgia Technical College
Chattahoochee Technical College
College of Coastal Georgia
Columbus Technical College
Coosa Valley Technical College
DeKalb Technical College
Georgia Military College
Griffin Technical College
Gupton Jones College of Funeral Service
Gwinnett College
Gwinnett Technical College
Le Cordon Bleu College of Culinary Arts
Middle Georgia Technical College
North Georgia Technical College
North Metro Technical College
Northwestern Technical College
Savannah Technical College

South Georgia College
Southeastern Technical College
Southwest Georgia Technical College
West Central Technical College
West Georgia Technical College

Hawaii

Heald College
- Honolulu

University of Hawaii
- Hawaii Community College
- Honolulu Community College
- Kapiolani Community College
- Kauai Community College
- Leeward Community College
- Maui Community College
- Windward Community College

Idaho

College of Southern Idaho
Eastern Idaho Technical College
North Idaho College
Stevens-Henager College: Boise

Illinois

Black Hawk College
Black Hawk College: East Campus
Carl Sandburg College
City Colleges of Chicago
- Harold Washington College
- Harry S. Truman College
- Kennedy-King College
- Malcolm X College
- Olive-Harvey College
- Richard J. Daley College
- Wright College

College of DuPage
College of Lake County
College of Office Technology
Cooking & Hospitality Institute of Chicago
Danville Area Community College
Elgin Community College
Fox College
Harper College
Heartland Community College
Highland Community College
Illinois Central College
Illinois Eastern Community Colleges
- Frontier Community College
- Lincoln Trail College
- Olney Central College
- Wabash Valley College

Illinois Valley Community College
John A. Logan College
John Wood Community College
Joliet Junior College
Kankakee Community College
Kaskaskia College
Kishwaukee College
Lake Land College
Lewis and Clark Community College
Lincoln Land Community College
MacCormac College
McHenry County College
Moraine Valley Community College
Morrison Institute of Technology
Morton College
Oakton Community College
Parkland College
Prairie State College
Rasmussen College: Aurora
Rasmussen College: Rockford
Rend Lake College
Richland Community College
Rock Valley College
Rockford Business College
Sauk Valley Community College
Shawnee Community College
South Suburban College of Cook County
Southeastern Illinois College
Spoon River College
Taylor Business Institute
Triton College
Vatterott College: Quincy
Waubonsee Community College

Indiana

Ancilla College
Aviation Institute of Maintenance: Indianapolis
Brown Mackie College: Fort Wayne
Brown Mackie College: South Bend
College of Court Reporting
Indiana Business College: Elkhart
Ivy Tech Community College: Richmond
Ivy Tech State College
- Ivy Tech Community College: Bloomington
- Ivy Tech Community College: Central Indiana
- Ivy Tech Community College: Columbus
- Ivy Tech Community College: East Central
- Ivy Tech Community College: Kokomo
- Ivy Tech Community College: Lafayette
- Ivy Tech Community College: North Central
- Ivy Tech Community College: Northeast
- Ivy Tech Community College: Northwest
- Ivy Tech Community College: South Central
- Ivy Tech Community College: Southeast
- Ivy Tech Community College: Southwest
- Ivy Tech Community College: Wabash Valley

Kaplan College: Merrillville
Mid-America College of Funeral Service
National College: Indianapolis
Vincennes University

Iowa

Clinton Community College
Des Moines Area Community College
Ellsworth Community College
Hawkeye Community College
Indian Hills Community College
Iowa Central Community College
Iowa Lakes Community College
Iowa Western Community College
Kaplan University
- Cedar Rapids

Kirkwood Community College
Marshalltown Community College
Muscatine Community College
North Iowa Area Community College
Northeast Iowa Community College
Northwest Iowa Community College
Scott Community College
Southeastern Community College
- North Campus

Southwestern Community College
Vatterott College
Western Iowa Tech Community College

Kansas

Allen County Community College
Barton County Community College
Brown Mackie College
- Salina

Cloud County Community College
Coffeyville Community College
Colby Community College
Cowley County Community College
Dodge City Community College
Donnelly College
Fort Scott Community College
Garden City Community College
Hesston College
Highland Community College
Hutchinson Community College
Independence Community College
Johnson County Community College
Kansas City Kansas Community College
Labette Community College
Neosho County Community College
North Central Kansas Technical College
Pratt Community College
Seward County Community College

Kentucky

Ashland Community and Technical College
Big Sandy Community and Technical College
Daymar College
- Owensboro

Daymar College: Paducah
Elizabethtown Community and Technical College
Hazard Community and Technical College
Henderson Community College
Hopkinsville Community College
Jefferson Community and Technical College
Madisonville Community College
Maysville Community and Technical College
National College
- Danville
- Florence
- Lexington
- Louisville
- Pikeville
- Richmond

Owensboro Community and Technical College
Somerset Community College
Southeast Kentucky Community and Technical College
Southern Ohio College
- Brown Mackie College: North Kentucky

Southwestern College: Florence
Spencerian College
Spencerian College: Lexington
West Kentucky Community and Technical College

Louisiana

Baton Rouge Community College
Baton Rouge School of Computers
Blue Cliff College: Houma
Blue Cliff College: Lafayette
Blue Cliff College: Metairie
Blue Cliff College: Shreveport
Bossier Parish Community College
Camelot College
Delgado Community College
Delta College of Arts & Technology
Delta School of Business & Technology
Gretna Career College
ITI Technical College
Louisiana State University
- Eunice

Nunez Community College
Remington College
- Baton Rouge
- Lafayette

Remington College: Shreveport
River Parishes Community College
South Louisiana Community College
Southern University
- Shreveport

Maine

Andover College
Beal College
Central Maine Community College
Eastern Maine Community College
Kennebec Valley Community College
Southern Maine Community College
Washington County Community College
York County Community College

Maryland

Allegany College of Maryland
Anne Arundel Community College
Baltimore City Community College
Carroll Community College
Cecil College
Chesapeake College
College of Southern Maryland
Community College of Baltimore County
Frederick Community College
Garrett College
Hagerstown Community College
Harford Community College
Howard Community College
Kaplan College: Hagerstown
Montgomery College
Prince George's Community College
TESST College of Technology
- Baltimore
- Beltsville

Wor-Wic Community College

Massachusetts

Berkshire Community College
Bristol Community College
Bunker Hill Community College
Cape Cod Community College
Greenfield Community College
Holyoke Community College
Massachusetts Bay Community College
Massasoit Community College
Middlesex Community College
Mount Wachusett Community College
New England College of Finance
North Shore Community College
Northern Essex Community College
Quincy College
Quinsigamond Community College
Roxbury Community College
Springfield Technical Community College
Urban College of Boston

Michigan

Alpena Community College
Bay de Noc Community College
Bay Mills Community College
Glen Oaks Community College
Gogebic Community College
Grand Rapids Community College
Henry Ford Community College
Jackson Community College
Kalamazoo Valley Community College
Kellogg Community College
Kirtland Community College
Lake Michigan College
Lansing Community College
Macomb Community College
Monroe County Community College
Montcalm Community College
Mott Community College
Muskegon Community College
North Central Michigan College
Northwestern Michigan College
Oakland Community College
Saginaw Chippewa Tribal College
St. Clair County Community College
Schoolcraft College
Southwestern Michigan College
Washtenaw Community College
Wayne County Community College
West Shore Community College

Minnesota

Academy College
Alexandria Technical College
Anoka Technical College
Anoka-Ramsey Community College
Central Lakes College
Century Community and Technical College
Dakota County Technical College
Fond du Lac Tribal and Community College
Hennepin Technical College
Herzing College
- Minneapolis Drafting School Division of

Hibbing Community College
Inver Hills Community College
Itasca Community College
Lake Superior College
Lakeland Academy Division of Herzing College
Le Cordon Bleu College of Culinary Arts
Leech Lake Tribal College
Mesabi Range Community and Technical College
Minneapolis Community and Technical College
Minnesota State College - Southeast Technical
Minnesota State Community and Technical College
Minnesota West Community and Technical College
Normandale Community College
North Hennepin Community College
Northland Community & Technical College
Northwest Technical College
Northwest Technical Institute
Pine Technical College
Rainy River Community College
Rasmussen College
- Eagan
- Eden Prairie
- Mankato
- St. Cloud

Rasmussen College: Brooklyn Park
Ridgewater College
Riverland Community College

Tables and Indexes

Rochester Community and Technical College
St. Cloud Technical College
St. Paul College
South Central College
Vermilion Community College

Mississippi
Antonelli College
  Hattiesburg
  Jackson
Blue Cliff College: Gulfport
Coahoma Community College
Copiah-Lincoln Community College
East Central Community College
East Mississippi Community College
Hinds Community College
Holmes Community College
Itawamba Community College
Meridian Community College
Mississippi Delta Community College
Mississippi Gulf Coast Community College
Northeast Mississippi Community College
Northwest Mississippi Community College
Pearl River Community College
Southwest Mississippi Community College

Missouri
Aviation Institute of Maintenance: Kansas City
Bolivar Technical College
Concorde Career College: Kansas City
Crowder College
East Central College
High-Tech Institute
Jefferson College
Linn State Technical College
Metro Business College
Metro Business College
  Jefferson City
Metropolitan Community College: Blue River
Metropolitan Community College: Longview
Metropolitan Community College: Maple Woods
Metropolitan Community College: Penn Valley
Mineral Area College
Missouri College
Missouri State University: West Plains
Moberly Area Community College
North Central Missouri College
Ozarks Technical Community College
Patricia Stevens College
Pinnacle Career Institute: Kansas City
Ranken Technical College
St. Charles Community College
St. Louis Community College
  Florissant Valley
  Meramec
Sanford-Brown College
  Hazelwood
  St. Peters
Southeast Missouri Hospital College of Nursing and Health Sciences
State Fair Community College
Three Rivers Community College
Vatterott College: O'Fallon
Vatterott College: St. Joseph
Vatterott College: Springfield
Vatterott College: Sunset Hills
Wentworth Military Junior College

Montana
Chief Dull Knife College
Dawson Community College
Flathead Valley Community College
Fort Belknap College
Fort Peck Community College
Helena College of Technology of the University of Montana
Little Big Horn College
Miles Community College
Montana State University
  College of Technology: Great Falls
Stone Child College

Nebraska
Central Community College
Kaplan University
  Lincoln
Kaplan University: Omaha
Little Priest Tribal College
Metropolitan Community College
Mid-Plains Community College Area
Nebraska College of Technical Agriculture
Nebraska Indian Community College
Northeast Community College
Southeast Community College
Western Nebraska Community College

Nevada
Career College of Northern Nevada
College of Southern Nevada
High-Tech Institute
Kaplan College: Las Vegas
Las Vegas College
Le Cordon Bleu College of Culinary Arts
Truckee Meadows Community College
Western Nevada College

New Hampshire
Great Bay Community College
Lakes Region Community College
Manchester Community College
Nashua Community College
NHTI-Concord's Community College
River Valley Community College

New Jersey
Atlantic Cape Community College
Bergen Community College
Brookdale Community College
Burlington County College
Camden County College
County College of Morris
Cumberland County College
Essex County College
Gloucester County College
Hudson County Community College
Mercer County Community College
Middlesex County College
Ocean County College
Passaic County Community College
Raritan Valley Community College
Salem Community College
Sussex County Community College
Union County College
Warren County Community College

New Mexico
Central New Mexico Community College
Clovis Community College
Dona Ana Community College of New Mexico State University
Eastern New Mexico University: Roswell Campus
IIA College
  Albuquerque
Luna Community College
Mesalands Community College
Navajo Technical College
New Mexico Junior College
New Mexico State University
  Alamogordo
  Carlsbad
  Grants
Northern New Mexico College
San Juan College
Santa Fe Community College
Southwestern Indian Polytechnic Institute

New York
Adirondack Community College
American Academy McAllister Institute of Funeral Service
Art Institute
  of New York City
ASA Institute of Business and Computer Technology
Broome Community College
Bryant & Stratton Business Institute
  Bryant & Stratton College: Buffalo
  Bryant & Stratton College: Southtowns
  Bryant & Stratton College: Syracuse
Bryant & Stratton College: Syracuse North
Business Informatics Center
Cayuga County Community College
City University of New York
  Borough of Manhattan Community College
  Bronx Community College
  Hostos Community College
  Kingsborough Community College
  LaGuardia Community College
  Queensborough Community College
Clinton Community College
Columbia-Greene Community College
Corning Community College
Dutchess Community College
Elmira Business Institute
Elmira Business Institute: Vestal
Erie Community College
  City Campus
  North Campus
  South Campus
Finger Lakes Community College
Fulton-Montgomery Community College
Genesee Community College
Herkimer County Community College
Hudson Valley Community College
Institute of Design and Construction
Island Drafting and Technical Institute
Jamestown Community College
Jefferson Community College
Long Island Business Institute
Mildred Elley
Mohawk Valley Community College
Monroe Community College
Nassau Community College
New York Career Institute
Niagara County Community College
North Country Community College
Olean Business Institute
Onondaga Community College
Orange County Community College
Rockland Community College
Schenectady County Community College
Suffolk County Community College
Sullivan County Community College
Technical Career Institutes
Tompkins Cortland Community College
Trocaire College
Ulster County Community College
Utica School of Commerce
Villa Maria College of Buffalo
Westchester Community College

North Carolina
Alamance Community College
Asheville-Buncombe Technical Community College
Beaufort County Community College
Bladen Community College
Blue Ridge Community College
Brunswick Community College
Caldwell Community College and Technical Institute
Cape Fear Community College
Carolinas College of Health Sciences
Carteret Community College
Catawba Valley Community College
Central Carolina Community College
Central Piedmont Community College
Coastal Carolina Community College
College of the Albemarle
Craven Community College
Davidson County Community College
Durham Technical Community College
Edgecombe Community College
Fayetteville Technical Community College
Forsyth Technical Community College
Gaston College
Guilford Technical Community College
Halifax Community College
Haywood Community College
Isothermal Community College
James Sprunt Community College
Johnston Community College
Lenoir Community College
Martin Community College
Mayland Community College
McDowell Technical Community College
Mitchell Community College
Montgomery Community College
Nash Community College
Pamlico Community College
Piedmont Community College
Pitt Community College
Randolph Community College
Richmond Community College
Roanoke-Chowan Community College
Robeson Community College
Rockingham Community College
Rowan-Cabarrus Community College
Sampson Community College
Sandhills Community College
South College
South Piedmont Community College
Southeastern Community College
Southwestern Community College
Stanly Community College
Surry Community College
Tri-County Community College
Vance-Granville Community College
Wake Technical Community College
Wayne Community College
Western Piedmont Community College
Wilkes Community College
Wilson Community College

North Dakota
Bismarck State College
Cankdeska Cikana Community College
Fort Berthold Community College
Lake Region State College
Minot State University: Bottineau Campus
North Dakota State College of Science
Rasmussen College: Bismarck
Sitting Bull College
Turtle Mountain Community College
United Tribes Technical College
Williston State College

Ohio
Academy of Court Reporting: Cincinnati
ATS Institute of Technology
Belmont Technical College
Bowling Green State University: Firelands College
Bradford School
Bryant & Stratton College: Cleveland
Central Ohio Technical College
Chatfield College
Cincinnati State Technical and Community College
Clark State Community College
Cleveland Institute of Electronics
Columbus State Community College
Cuyahoga Community College
  Metropolitan Campus
Edison State Community College
ETI Technical College of Niles
Gallipolis Career College
Hocking College
Hondros College
International College of Broadcasting
James A. Rhodes State College
Jefferson Community College
Kent State University
  Ashtabula
  East Liverpool
  Salem
  Stark
  Trumbull
  Tuscarawas
Kent State University: Geauga
Lakeland Community College
Marion Technical College
Miami University
  Hamilton Campus
  Middletown Campus
National College
  Dayton
National College: Cincinnati
National College: Stow
National College: Youngstown
North Central State College
Northwest State Community College

Ohio College of Massotherapy
Ohio Institute of Health Careers: Columbus
Ohio Institute of Health Careers: Elyria
Ohio Institute of Photography and Technology
Ohio State University
- Agricultural Technical Institute

Owens Community College
- Toledo

Remington College: Cleveland West
Sinclair Community College
Southern State Community College
Southwestern College of Business
- Southwestern College: Franklin
- Southwestern College: Tri-County
- Southwestern College: Vine Street Campus

Southwestern College: Dayton
Stark State College of Technology
Stautzenberger College
Stautzenberger College: Strongsville
Technology Education College
Terra State Community College
Tri-State College
Trumbull Business College
University of Akron: Wayne College
University of Cincinnati
- Clermont College
- Raymond Walters College

Vatterott College: Cleveland
Washington State Community College
Wright State University: Lake Campus
Zane State College

Oklahoma

Carl Albert State College
Connors State College
Eastern Oklahoma State College
Murray State College
Northeastern Oklahoma Agricultural and Mechanical College
Northern Oklahoma College
Oklahoma City Community College
Oklahoma State University
- Institute of Technology: Okmulgee
- Oklahoma City

Platt College
- Tulsa

Platt College: Oklahoma City Central
Redlands Community College
Rose State College
Seminole State College
Tulsa Community College
Tulsa Welding School
Vatterott College
Western Oklahoma State College

Oregon

Blue Mountain Community College
Central Oregon Community College
Chemeketa Community College
Clackamas Community College
Clatsop Community College
Heald College: Portland
Klamath Community College
Lane Community College
Linn-Benton Community College
Mt. Hood Community College
Pioneer Pacific College
Pioneer Pacific College: Springfield
Portland Community College
Rogue Community College
Southwestern Oregon Community College
Treasure Valley Community College
Umpqua Community College
Western Culinary Institute

Pennsylvania

Bucks County Community College
Butler County Community College
Commonwealth Technical Institute
Community College of Allegheny County
Community College of Beaver County
Community College of Philadelphia
Consolidated School of Business
- Lancaster
- York

Dean Institute of Technology
Douglas Education Center
DuBois Business College
DuBois Business College
- Huntingdon
- Oil City

Erie Business Center South
Harrisburg Area Community College
JNA Institute of Culinary Arts
Johnson College
Lackawanna College
Lehigh Carbon Community College
Lincoln Technical Institute: Allentown
Lincoln Technical Institute: Northeast Philadelphia
Lincoln Technical Institute: Philadelphia
Luzerne County Community College
McCann School of Business
- and Technology: Pottsville
- and Technology: Sunbury

McCann School of Business and Technology: Hazleton
Montgomery County Community College
Newport Business Institute: Lower Burrell
Newport Business Institute: Williamsport
Northampton Community College
Oakbridge Academy of Arts
Orleans Technical Institute - Center City Campus
Pace Institute
Penn Commercial Business and Technical School
Pennsylvania Highlands Community College
Pennsylvania Institute of Health and Technology
Pennsylvania Institute of Technology
Pittsburgh Institute of Aeronautics
Pittsburgh Institute of Mortuary Science
Pittsburgh Technical Institute
Reading Area Community College
South Hills School of Business & Technology
South Hills School of Business & Technology: Altoona
Triangle Tech
- DuBois
- Erie
- Greensburg
- Pittsburgh

Triangle Tech: Bethlehem
Westmoreland County Community College
Yorktowne Business Institute
YTI Career Institute: Lancaster
YTI Career Institute: York

Puerto Rico

Columbia College
- Columbia Centro Universitario: Yauco

Huertas Junior College
Humacao Community College

Rhode Island

Community College of Rhode Island

South Carolina

Aiken Technical College
Central Carolina Technical College
Clinton Junior College
Denmark Technical College
Florence-Darlington Technical College
Forrest Junior College
Greenville Technical College
Horry-Georgetown Technical College
Midlands Technical College
Miller-Motte Technical College
Northeastern Technical College
Orangeburg-Calhoun Technical College
Piedmont Technical College
Spartanburg Community College
Technical College of the Lowcountry
Tri-County Technical College
Trident Technical College
University of South Carolina
- Lancaster

Williamsburg Technical College
York Technical College

South Dakota

Kilian Community College
Lake Area Technical Institute
Mitchell Technical Institute
Sisseton Wahpeton College
Southeast Technical Institute
Western Dakota Technical Institute

Tennessee

Chattanooga State Technical Community College
Cleveland State Community College
Columbia State Community College
Dyersburg State Community College
Fountainhead College of Technology
Huntington College of Health Sciences
Jackson State Community College
Miller-Motte Technical College: Clarksville
Motlow State Community College
Nashville State Community College
National College
- Knoxville
- Nashville

National College of Business & Technology
- National College: Bristol

National College: Memphis
Pellissippi State Technical Community College
Roane State Community College
Southwest Tennessee Community College
Volunteer State Community College
Walters State Community College

Texas

Alvin Community College
Angelina College
Austin Community College
Blinn College
Brazosport College
Brookhaven College
Cedar Valley College
Central Texas College
Cisco Junior College
Clarendon College
Coastal Bend College
College of the Mainland
Collin County Community College District
Court Reporting Institute of Dallas
Court Reporting Institute of Houston
Culinary Institute Alain & Marie LeNotre
Dallas Institute of Funeral Service
Del Mar College
Eastfield College
El Centro College
El Paso Community College
Everest College: Arlington
Frank Phillips College
Galveston College
Hill College
Houston Community College System
Howard College
Jacksonville College
Kilgore College
Lamar Institute of Technology
Lamar State College at Orange
Lamar State College at Port Arthur
Laredo Community College
Lee College
Lone Star College System
McLennan Community College
Midland College
Navarro College
North Central Texas College
North Lake College
Northwest Vista College
Odessa College
Palo Alto College
Panola College
Paris Junior College
Ranger College
Richland College
St. Philip's College
San Antonio College
San Jacinto College
South Plains College
South Texas College
Southwest Institute of Technology
Southwest Texas Junior College
Tarrant County College
Temple College
Texarkana College
Texas Culinary Academy
Texas State Technical College
- Harlingen
- Waco
- West Texas

Texas State Technical College: Marshall
Tyler Junior College
Victoria College
Wade College
Weatherford College
Western Technical College
Western Technical College: Diana Drive
Western Texas College
Wharton County Junior College

Utah

Careers Unlimited
College of Eastern Utah
Eagle Gate College: Layton
Eagle Gate College: Murray
Eagle Gate College: Salt Lake City
LDS Business College
Provo College
Salt Lake Community College
Snow College
Utah Career College

Vermont

Community College of Vermont

Virginia

Blue Ridge Community College
Bryant & Stratton College
- Richmond

Bryant & Stratton College: Virginia Beach
Central Virginia Community College
Centura College: Chesapeake
Centura College: Newport News
Centura College: Norfolk
Centura College: Richmond
Centura College: Richmond Westend
Centura College: Virginia Beach
Dabney S. Lancaster Community College
Danville Community College
Eastern Shore Community College
Germanna Community College
J. Sargeant Reynolds Community College
John Tyler Community College
Lord Fairfax Community College
Miller-Motte Technical College: Lynchburg
Mountain Empire Community College
National College
- Bluefield
- Charlottesville
- Danville
- Harrisonburg
- Lynchburg
- Martinsville

New River Community College
Northern Virginia Community College
Patrick Henry Community College
Paul D. Camp Community College
Piedmont Virginia Community College
Rappahannock Community College
Southside Virginia Community College
Southwest Virginia Community College
Thomas Nelson Community College
Tidewater Community College
Virginia Highlands Community College
Virginia Western Community College
Wytheville Community College

Washington

Bates Technical College
Bellevue Community College
Bellingham Technical College
Big Bend Community College
Cascadia Community College
Centralia College
Clark College
Clover Park Technical College
Columbia Basin College
Edmonds Community College
Everett Community College

Grays Harbor College
Green River Community College
Highline Community College
Lower Columbia College
North Seattle Community College
Northwest Aviation College
Northwest Indian College
Olympic College
Peninsula College
Pierce College
Renton Technical College
Shoreline Community College
Skagit Valley College
South Puget Sound Community College
South Seattle Community College
Spokane Community College
Spokane Falls Community College
Tacoma Community College
Walla Walla Community College
Wenatchee Valley College
Whatcom Community College
Yakima Valley Community College

West Virginia

Blue Ridge Community and Technical College
Eastern West Virginia Community and Technical College
Huntington Junior College
Mountain State College
New River Community and Technical College
Potomac State College of West Virginia University
Southern West Virginia Community and Technical College
West Virginia Business College: Nutter Fort
West Virginia Business College: Wheeling
West Virginia Junior College
West Virginia Junior College: Bridgeport
West Virginia Junior College: Charleston
West Virginia Northern Community College
West Virginia State Community and Technical College

Wisconsin

Blackhawk Technical College
Chippewa Valley Technical College
Fox Valley Technical College
Lac Courte Oreilles Ojibwa Community College
Lakeshore Technical College
Madison Area Technical College
Mid-State Technical College
Milwaukee Area Technical College
Moraine Park Technical College
Northcentral Technical College
Northeast Wisconsin Technical College
Rasmussen College: Green Bay
Southwest Wisconsin Technical College
University of Wisconsin Manitowoc
Waukesha County Technical College
Western Technical College
Wisconsin Indianhead Technical College

Wyoming

Casper College
Central Wyoming College
Eastern Wyoming College
Laramie County Community College
Northwest College
Sheridan College
Western Wyoming Community College
WyoTech: Laramie

American Samoa

American Samoa Community College

Guam

Guam Community College

Palau

Palau Community College

Admission/placement policies

No closing date

Four-year

Alabama
Amridge University
Andrew Jackson University
Athens State University
Birmingham-Southern College
Columbia Southern University
Faulkner University
Heritage Christian University
Jacksonville State University
Judson College
Oakwood University
Samford University
Selma University
South University: Montgomery
Talladega College
Troy University
United States Sports Academy
University of North Alabama
University of West Alabama

Alaska
University of Alaska
Southeast

Arizona
American Indian College of the Assemblies of God
Art Center Design College
Art Institute of Tucson
Brown Mackie College: Tucson
College of the Humanities and Sciences
Collins College
DeVry University
Phoenix
Embry-Riddle Aeronautical University: Prescott Campus
International Baptist College
International Import-Export Institute
Northcentral University
Northern Arizona University
University of Advancing Technology
University of Phoenix
Western International University

Arkansas
Arkansas Baptist College
Arkansas Tech University
Harding University
Henderson State University
John Brown University
Lyon College
Ouachita Baptist University
University of Arkansas
Fort Smith
Little Rock
Monticello
Pine Bluff
University of Central Arkansas
University of the Ozarks
Williams Baptist College

California
Academy of Art University
Alliant International University
Antioch Southern California
Antioch University Los Angeles
Antioch University Santa Barbara
Art Center College of Design
Art Institute
of California: Orange County
of California: San Diego
Art Institute of California: Hollywood
Art Institute of California: San Francisco
Brooks Institute
Brooks Institute: Ventura
California Baptist University
California Coast University
California College of the Arts
California College San Diego
California Institute of Integral Studies
California Maritime Academy
California National University for Advanced Studies
California State University
Bakersfield
Dominguez Hills
San Bernardino
Coleman University
Concordia University
Design Institute of San Diego
DeVry University
Fremont
Long Beach
Pomona
Sherman Oaks
Dominican University of California
Ex'pression College for Digital Arts
Golden Gate University
Hope International University
Humphreys College
Interior Designers Institute
International Academy of Design and Technology
Sacramento
John F. Kennedy University
The King's College and Seminary
LA College International
La Sierra University
Laguna College of Art and Design
Lincoln University
Loma Linda University
Loyola Marymount University
The Master's College
Menlo College
Mt. Sierra College
National Hispanic University
National University
NewSchool of Architecture & Design
Notre Dame de Namur University
Otis College of Art and Design
Pacific States University
Pacific Union College
Platt College
San Diego
Samuel Merritt University
San Francisco Art Institute
Simpson University
Southern California Institute of Technology
Thomas Aquinas College
University of La Verne
University of San Francisco
Vanguard University of Southern California
West Coast University
Westmont College
Westwood College: South Bay
Whittier College
Woodbury University
World Mission University
Yeshiva Ohr Elchonon Chabad/West Coast Talmudical Seminary

Colorado
Adams State College
American Sentinel University
Art Institute
of Colorado
Aspen University
CollegeAmerica
Colorado Springs
Fort Collins
Colorado Technical University
DeVry University
Westminster
Johnson & Wales University: Denver
Jones International University
Mesa State College
National American University
Denver
Nazarene Bible College
Platt College
Aurora
Rocky Mountain College of Art & Design
University of Northern Colorado
Westwood College of Technology
Westwood College: Denver South
Westwood College: Denver North

Connecticut
Albertus Magnus College
Charter Oak State College
Eastern Connecticut State University
Holy Apostles College and Seminary
Lyme Academy College of Fine Arts
Mitchell College
Paier College of Art
Post University
Sacred Heart University
St. Joseph College
University of Bridgeport
University of Hartford
University of New Haven
Western Connecticut State University

Delaware
Delaware State University
Goldey-Beacom College
Wesley College
Wilmington University

District of Columbia
Corcoran College of Art and Design
Gallaudet University
Potomac College
Southeastern University
Strayer University

Florida
Art Institute of Fort Lauderdale
Ave Maria University
Barry University
Bethune-Cookman University
Carlos Albizu University
Chipola College
City College: Fort Lauderdale
DeVry University
Miramar
Orlando
Eckerd College
Edward Waters College
Embry-Riddle Aeronautical University
Embry-Riddle Aeronautical University: Worldwide Campus
Everest University: Brandon
Everest University: Lakeland
Everest University: Largo
Everest University: North Orlando
Everest University: South Orlando
Everest University: Tampa
Florida Institute of Technology
Florida International University
Florida Memorial University
Florida Southern College
Hodges University
International Academy of Design and Technology: Orlando
International Academy of Design and Technology: Tampa
Jacksonville University
Johnson & Wales University: North Miami
Jones College
Lynn University
Miami International University of Art and Design
Northwest Florida State College
Northwood University
Florida
Nova Southeastern University
Palm Beach Atlantic University
Rasmussen College: Fort Myers
Rasmussen College: Ocala
Rasmussen College: Pasco County
Remington College: Tampa
Ringling College of Art and Design
Saint Thomas University
Schiller International University
South University: West Palm Beach
Stetson University
Talmudic College of Florida
Universidad FLET
University of Tampa
Warner University

Georgia
American InterContinental University
Art Institute
of Atlanta
Augusta State University
Bauder College
Beulah Heights University
Brenau University
Brewton-Parker College
Carver Bible College
Clayton State University
Covenant College
Dalton State College
DeVry University
Alpharetta
Decatur
Herzing College
LaGrange College
Oglethorpe University
Reinhardt College
Shorter College
South University: Savannah
Thomas University

Hawaii
Chaminade University of Honolulu
Hawaii Pacific University

Idaho
Idaho State University
Lewis-Clark State College

Illinois
American Academy of Art
Argosy University
Augustana College
Benedictine University
Blackburn College
Blessing-Rieman College of Nursing
Chicago State University
Columbia College Chicago
Concordia University Chicago
DeVry University
Addison
Chicago
Tinley Park
DeVry University: Online
Dominican University
East-West University
Eastern Illinois University
Elmhurst College
Governors State University
Harrington College of Design
Illinois Institute of Art: Chicago
Illinois Institute of Art: Schaumburg
Illinois Wesleyan University
International Academy of Design and Technology: Chicago
Judson University
Kendall College
Lewis University
Lexington College
Lincoln Christian College and Seminary
Loyola University Chicago
MacMurray College
McKendree University
Midstate College
Millikin University
Monmouth College
National-Louis University
North Central College
Quincy University
Robert Morris College: Chicago
Rockford College
St. Augustine College
St. John's College
St. Xavier University
Shimer College
Southern Illinois University
Carbondale
Telshe Yeshiva-Chicago
Trinity Christian College
Trinity International University
University of Illinois
Springfield
VanderCook College of Music
Western Illinois University
Western Illinois University: Quad Cities
Westwood College of Technology
Westwood College: O'Hare Airport
Westwood College: DuPage

Indiana
Calumet College of St. Joseph
DeVry University: Indianapolis
Franklin College
Indiana Institute of Technology
Indiana University
Bloomington
East
Northwest
South Bend
Southeast
International Business College
Manchester College
Martin University
Purdue University
Calumet
North Central
Saint Joseph's College
Saint Mary's College
Taylor University
University of Indianapolis
University of St. Francis
Wabash College

Iowa
Ashford University
Briar Cliff University
Buena Vista University
Central College
Clarke College
Drake University
Emmaus Bible College
Graceland University

- Hamilton Technical College
- Iowa Wesleyan College
- Kaplan University
  - Cedar Falls
  - Davenport
  - Des Moines
  - Mason City
- Loras College
- Luther College
- Maharishi University of Management
- Morningside College
- Northwestern College
- St. Ambrose University
- University of Dubuque
- Upper Iowa University
- Waldorf College
- Wartburg College
- William Penn University

Kansas

- Baker University
- Benedictine College
- Bethany College
- Bethel College
- Emporia State University
- Fort Hays State University
- Friends University
- Kansas State University
- Kansas Wesleyan University
- McPherson College
- Newman University
- Ottawa University
- Pittsburg State University
- Sterling College
- Tabor College
- University of Kansas Medical Center
- University of St. Mary
- Wichita State University

Kentucky

- Alice Lloyd College
- Asbury College
- Beckfield College
- Bellarmine University
- Brescia University
- Campbellsville University
- Kentucky Christian University
- Kentucky Mountain Bible College
- Kentucky State University
- Kentucky Wesleyan College
- Lindsey Wilson College
- Mid-Continent University
- Midway College
- Morehead State University
- St. Catharine College
- Spalding University
- Sullivan University
- Union College

Louisiana

- Herzing College
- Louisiana State University
  - Alexandria
- Louisiana Tech University
- Loyola University New Orleans
- McNeese State University
- New Orleans Baptist Theological Seminary: Leavell College
- Nicholls State University
- Our Lady of Holy Cross College
- St. Joseph Seminary College
- Southwest University
- University of Louisiana at Lafayette
- University of Louisiana at Monroe

Maine

- Maine College of Art
- New England School of Communications
- St. Joseph's College
- Thomas College
- Unity College
- University of Maine
- University of Maine
  - Farmington
  - Fort Kent
  - Presque Isle
- University of Southern Maine

Maryland

- Bowie State University
- Capitol College
- College of Notre Dame of Maryland
- DeVry University: Bethesda
- Frostburg State University
- Griggs University
- Hood College
- Mount St. Mary's University
- National Labor College
- St. John's College
- Sojourner-Douglass College
- Stevenson University
- University of Baltimore
- University of Maryland
  - University College

Massachusetts

- American International College
- Anna Maria College
- Bay Path College
- Becker College
- Bridgewater State College
- Cambridge College
- Elms College
- Fitchburg State College
- Framingham State College
- Gordon College
- Lasell College
- Lesley University
- Massachusetts College of Liberal Arts
- Massachusetts Maritime Academy
- Montserrat College of Art
- Mount Ida College
- New England Conservatory of Music
- New England Institute of Art
- Newbury College
- Nichols College
- Pine Manor College
- Regis College
- Rhodec International
- Salem State College
- School of the Museum of Fine Arts
- University of Massachusetts
  - Dartmouth
  - Lowell
- Wentworth Institute of Technology
- Western New England College
- Wheelock College
- Zion Bible College

Michigan

- Adrian College
- Alma College
- Andrews University
- Aquinas College
- Baker College
  - of Auburn Hills
  - of Cadillac
  - of Clinton Township
  - of Flint
  - of Jackson
  - of Muskegon
  - of Owosso
  - of Port Huron
- Baker College of Allen Park
- Cornerstone University
- Davenport University
- Eastern Michigan University
- Hope College
- International Academy of Design and Technology: Detroit
- Kendall College of Art and Design of Ferris State University
- Kettering University
- Kuyper College
- Lake Superior State University
- Lawrence Technological University
- Madonna University
- Michigan Jewish Institute
- Michigan State University
- Michigan Technological University
- Northern Michigan University
- Northwood University: Michigan
- Oakland University
- Olivet College
- Rochester College
- Saginaw Valley State University
- Siena Heights University
- University of Michigan
  - Dearborn
  - Flint
- Walsh College of Accountancy and Business Administration
- Wayne State University

Minnesota

- Art Institutes International Minnesota
- Bemidji State University
- Bethel University
- Brown College
- Capella University
- College of St. Benedict
- College of St. Catherine
- College of St. Scholastica
- College of Visual Arts
- Concordia College: Moorhead
- DeVry University
  - Edina
- Globe University
- Hamline University
- Minnesota School of Business
- Minnesota School of Business: St. Cloud
- Minnesota School of Business: Shakopee
- National American University
  - St. Paul
- Northwestern Health Sciences University
- Oak Hills Christian College
- St. John's University
- University of Minnesota
  - Crookston
  - Twin Cities
- University of St. Thomas
- Walden University

Mississippi

- Alcorn State University
- Belhaven College
- Blue Mountain College
- Delta State University
- Jackson State University
- Magnolia Bible College
- Millsaps College
- Mississippi College
- Mississippi State University
- Mississippi University for Women
- Rust College
- Tougaloo College
- University of Southern Mississippi
- William Carey University

Missouri

- Avila University
- Baptist Bible College
- Central Bible College
- Central Christian College of the Bible
- Central Methodist University
- Culver-Stockton College
- DeVry University
  - Kansas City
- Fontbonne University
- Global University
- Goldfarb School of Nursing at Barnes-Jewish College
- Grantham University
- Harris-Stowe State University
- Hickey College
- Kansas City Art Institute
- Lindenwood University
- Missouri Baptist University
- Missouri Southern State University
- Missouri Technical School
- Missouri Valley College
- National American University
  - Kansas City
- Northwest Missouri State University
- Research College of Nursing
- Rockhurst University
- Southwest Baptist University
- Stephens College
- Truman State University
- University of Central Missouri
- University of Missouri
  - Columbia
  - Kansas City
- Westminster College
- William Woods University

Montana

- Montana State University
  - Billings
  - Bozeman
  - Northern
- Montana Tech of the University of Montana
- Rocky Mountain College
- Salish Kootenai College
- University of Montana
- University of Montana: Western

Nebraska

- Bellevue University
- BryanLGH College of Health Sciences
- Chadron State College
- Clarkson College
- College of Saint Mary
- Creative Center
- Doane College
- Nebraska Methodist College of Nursing and Allied Health
- Peru State College
- Union College
- University of Nebraska
  - Kearney

Nevada

- Art Institute
  - of Las Vegas
- DeVry University: Henderson
- Great Basin College
- International Academy of Design and Technology: Henderson
- Morrison University
- Nevada State College
- Sierra Nevada College
- University of Nevada
  - Las Vegas
  - Reno

New Hampshire

- Chester College of New England
- Colby-Sawyer College
- Daniel Webster College
- Franklin Pierce University
- Granite State College
- Hesser College
- New England College
- Rivier College
- St. Anselm College
- Southern New Hampshire University
- Thomas More College of Liberal Arts

New Jersey

- Berkeley College
- Caldwell College
- Centenary College
- DeVry University: North Brunswick
- Fairleigh Dickinson University
  - College at Florham
  - Metropolitan Campus
- Felician College
- Rider University
- Rutgers, The State University of New Jersey
  - Newark Regional Campus
- Saint Peter's College
- Seton Hall University
- Thomas Edison State College
- University of Medicine and Dentistry of New Jersey
  - School of Health Related Professions
  - School of Nursing

New Mexico

- Art Center Design College
- Eastern New Mexico University
- National American University: Rio Rancho
- New Mexico Highlands University
- New Mexico State University
- St. John's College
- University of the Southwest
- Western New Mexico University

New York

- Adelphi University
- Albany College of Pharmacy and Health Sciences
- Alfred University
- Berkeley College
- Berkeley College of New York City
- Boricua College
- Briarcliffe College
- Cazenovia College
- City University of New York
  - Baruch College
  - Brooklyn College
  - City College
  - College of Staten Island
  - Medgar Evers College
  - New York City College of Technology
  - Queens College
- College of Mount St. Vincent
- College of New Rochelle
- Culinary Institute of America
- D'Youville College
- Daemen College
- Davis College
- DeVry
  - Devry College of New York
- Dominican College of Blauvelt
- Dowling College
- Excelsior College
- Five Towns College
- Hofstra University
- Houghton College
- Keuka College
- King's College
- Laboratory Institute of Merchandising
- Le Moyne College
- Long Island University
  - Brooklyn Campus
  - C. W. Post Campus
- Manhattan College
- Marymount Manhattan College
- Medaille College
- Mercy College
- Metropolitan College of New York
- Molloy College
- Monroe College
- Mount St. Mary College
- New York School of Interior Design
- Nyack College
- Ohr Somayach Tanenbaum Education Center
- Paul Smith's College

Polytechnic Institute of New York University
Rochester Institute of Technology
Russell Sage College
Sage College of Albany
St. Francis College
St. John Fisher College
St. John's University
St. Joseph's College
St. Joseph's College: Suffolk Campus
St. Thomas Aquinas College
School of Visual Arts
State University of New York
- Binghamton
- Buffalo
- College at Brockport
- College at Buffalo
- College at Cortland
- College at Fredonia
- College at Old Westbury
- College at Oneonta
- College at Plattsburgh
- College at Potsdam
- College of Environmental Science and Forestry
- Empire State College
- Farmingdale
- Institute of Technology at Utica/Rome
- Maritime College
- Oswego
- Stony Brook
- Upstate Medical University

Touro College
Utica College
Vaughn College of Aeronautics and Technology
Yeshiva Mikdash Melech
Yeshiva University

North Carolina

Appalachian State University
Art Institute
- of Charlotte

Barton College
Bennett College
Brevard College
Cabarrus College of Health Sciences
Campbell University
Carolina Christian College
Catawba College
Chowan University
DeVry University: Charlotte
Gardner-Webb University
Greensboro College
Johnson & Wales University: Charlotte
Lees-McRae College
Livingstone College
Mars Hill College
Meredith College
Methodist University
Miller-Motte Technical College
Mount Olive College
North Carolina Agricultural and Technical State University
North Carolina Wesleyan College
Peace College
Pfeiffer University
Piedmont Baptist College
Queens University of Charlotte
Roanoke Bible College
St. Andrews Presbyterian College
Salem College
University of North Carolina School of the Arts
Wingate University

North Dakota

Dickinson State University
Jamestown College
Mayville State University
Medcenter One College of Nursing
Minot State University
Rasmussen College: Fargo
University of Mary
University of North Dakota
Valley City State University

Ohio

Ashland University
Baldwin-Wallace College
Capital University
Cedarville University
Central State University
Cincinnati College of Mortuary Science
Cleveland Institute of Art
Columbus College of Art and Design
Defiance College
DeVry University
- Columbus

Franciscan University of Steubenville
Franklin University
God's Bible School and College
Hiram College
Kettering College of Medical Arts
Laura and Alvin Siegal College of Judaic Studies
Lourdes College
Mercy College of Northwest Ohio
Mount Carmel College of Nursing
Mount Union College
Notre Dame College
Ohio Christian University
Ohio Dominican University
Ohio University
- Chillicothe Campus
- Eastern Campus
- Lancaster Campus
- Southern Campus at Ironton
- Zanesville Campus

Otterbein College
Pontifical College Josephinum
Shawnee State University
Temple Baptist College
Tiffin University
Tri-State Bible College
Union Institute & University
University of Dayton
University of Rio Grande
University of Toledo
Urbana University
Ursuline College
Wilmington College
Wright State University

Oklahoma

Bacone College
Cameron University
DeVry University: Oklahoma City Center
East Central University
Langston University
Mid-America Christian University
National Education Center
- Spartan College of Aeronautics and Technology

Northeastern State University
Northwestern Oklahoma State University
Oklahoma Christian University
Oklahoma Panhandle State University
Oklahoma State University
Oklahoma Wesleyan University
Oral Roberts University
Rogers State University
St. Gregory's University
Southeastern Oklahoma State University
Southwestern Christian University
Southwestern Oklahoma State University
University of Central Oklahoma
University of Tulsa

Oregon

Art Institute of Portland
DeVry University: Portland
George Fox University
Marylhurst University
Northwest Christian University
Oregon College of Art & Craft
Pacific Northwest College of Art
Portland State University
Southern Oregon University
Warner Pacific College
Western Oregon University

Pennsylvania

Albright College
Alvernia University
Art Institute
- Online
- of Philadelphia
- of Pittsburgh

Bloomsburg University of Pennsylvania
Cabrini College
California University of Pennsylvania
Carlow University
Cedar Crest College
Central Pennsylvania College
Chestnut Hill College
Clarion University of Pennsylvania
Delaware Valley College
DeVry University
- Fort Washington

Eastern University
Edinboro University of Pennsylvania
Elizabethtown College
Gannon University
Geneva College
Gratz College
Harrisburg University of Science and Technology
Holy Family University
Immaculata University
Indiana University of Pennsylvania
King's College
Kutztown University of Pennsylvania
La Roche College
La Salle University
Lancaster Bible College
Lebanon Valley College
Lincoln University
Lock Haven University of Pennsylvania
Mansfield University of Pennsylvania
Marywood University
Mercyhurst College
Messiah College
Millersville University of Pennsylvania
Misericordia University
Mount Aloysius College
Neumann College
Peirce College
Penn State
- Abington
- Altoona
- Beaver
- Berks
- Brandywine
- Dubois
- Erie, The Behrend College
- Fayette, The Eberly Campus
- Greater Allegheny
- Harrisburg
- Hazleton
- Lehigh Valley
- Mont Alto
- New Kensington
- Schuylkill
- Shenango
- University Park
- Wilkes-Barre
- Worthington Scranton
- York

Pennsylvania College of Art and Design
Philadelphia Biblical University
Philadelphia University
Point Park University
Restaurant School at Walnut Hill College
Rosemont College
Shippensburg University of Pennsylvania
Slippery Rock University of Pennsylvania
Talmudical Yeshiva of Philadelphia
Thomas Jefferson University: College of Health Professions
University of Pittsburgh
University of Pittsburgh
- Bradford
- Greensburg
- Johnstown

University of the Arts
University of the Sciences in Philadelphia
Waynesburg University
West Chester University of Pennsylvania
Widener University
Wilkes University
Wilson College
York College of Pennsylvania

Puerto Rico

American University of Puerto Rico
Atlantic College
Caribbean University
Colegio Pentecostal Mizpa
Columbia Centro Universitario: Caguas
Inter American University of Puerto Rico
- Guayama Campus

Turabo University
Universidad Adventista de las Antillas
Universidad del Este
University of Puerto Rico
- Utuado

Rhode Island

Johnson & Wales University: Providence
New England Institute of Technology
Salve Regina University

South Carolina

Anderson University
Benedict College
Charleston Southern University
The Citadel
Columbia College
Converse College
Erskine College
Francis Marion University
Lander University
Morris College
Newberry College
South University: Columbia
University of South Carolina
- Beaufort
- Upstate

South Dakota

Augustana College
Dakota State University
National American University
- Rapid City

Northern State University
Oglala Lakota College
South Dakota School of Mines and Technology
South Dakota State University
University of Sioux Falls
University of South Dakota

Tennessee

Aquinas College
Bethel College
Christian Brothers University
Crichton College
Cumberland University
DeVry University: Memphis
Free Will Baptist Bible College
Freed-Hardeman University
International Academy of Design and Technology: Nashville
King College
Lambuth University
Lincoln Memorial University
Lipscomb University
Maryville College
Memphis College of Art
Rhodes College
South College
Trevecca Nazarene University
Tusculum College
Visible School - Music and Worship Arts College
Williamson Christian College

Texas

Amberton University
Arlington Baptist College
Art Institute
- of Dallas
- of Houston

Austin Graduate School of Theology
Baptist Missionary Association Theological Seminary
Baptist University of the Americas
Baylor University
College of Biblical Studies-Houston
College of Saint Thomas More
Concordia University Texas
Dallas Baptist University
DeVry University
- Irving

DeVry University: Houston
Hardin-Simmons University
Houston Baptist University
Howard Payne University
Jarvis Christian College
Northwood University: Texas
St. Mary's University
Southwestern Assemblies of God University
Stephen F. Austin State University
Sul Ross State University
Texas A&M University
- Galveston
- Kingsville
- Texarkana

Texas College
Texas Wesleyan University
University of Houston
- Victoria

University of Mary Hardin-Baylor
University of St. Thomas
University of Texas
- Arlington
- Southwestern Medical Center at Dallas
- Tyler

University of the Incarnate Word
Wayland Baptist University
West Texas A&M University
Wiley College

Utah

DeVry University: Sandy
Dixie State College of Utah
Independence University
Neumont University

- Stevens-Henager College
  - Murray
- Stevens-Henager College: Ogden
- Stevens-Henager College: Orem
- Utah State University
- Western Governors University
- Westminster College

Vermont

- Burlington College
- Castleton State College
- College of St. Joseph in Vermont
- Green Mountain College
- Johnson State College
- Lyndon State College
- Marlboro College
- Norwich University
- Southern Vermont College
- Vermont Technical College

Virginia

- Art Institute
  - of Washington
- Bridgewater College
- Christendom College
- DeVry University
  - Arlington
- Eastern Mennonite University
- ECPI College of Technology: Newport News
- ECPI College of Technology: Virginia Beach
- Emory & Henry College
- Hollins University
- Jefferson College of Health Sciences
- Liberty University
- Longwood University
- Lynchburg College
- Mary Baldwin College
- Marymount University
- St. Paul's College
- Stratford University: Falls Church
- Virginia Commonwealth University
- Virginia Intermont College
- Virginia Union University
- Virginia University of Lynchburg
- Virginia Wesleyan College
- World College

Washington

- Art Institute of Seattle
- Bastyr University
- Central Washington University
- City University of Seattle
- DeVry University
  - Federal Way
- DigiPen Institute of Technology
- Evergreen State College
- Faith Evangelical Seminary
- Heritage University
- International Academy of Design and Technology: Seattle
- Pacific Lutheran University
- Saint Martin's University
- Seattle University
- Trinity Lutheran College
- Walla Walla University
- Washington State University

West Virginia

- Alderson-Broaddus College
- American Public University System
- Appalachian Bible College
- Bethany College
- Bluefield State College
- Concord University
- Davis and Elkins College
- Glenville State College
- Marshall University
- Mountain State University
- Ohio Valley University
- Salem International University
- Shepherd University
- University of Charleston
- West Liberty State College
- West Virginia State University
- West Virginia University at Parkersburg
- West Virginia Wesleyan College
- Wheeling Jesuit University

Wisconsin

- Alverno College
- Beloit College
- Cardinal Stritch University
- Carroll University
- DeVry University: Milwaukee
- Herzing College
- Lakeland College
- Maranatha Baptist Bible College
- Marian University
- Milwaukee Institute of Art & Design
- Milwaukee School of Engineering
- Mount Mary College
- Northland College
- Ripon College
- St. Norbert College
- Silver Lake College
- University of Wisconsin
  - Eau Claire
  - Green Bay
  - La Crosse
  - Oshkosh
  - Platteville
  - River Falls
  - Stevens Point
  - Stout
  - Superior
- Viterbo University
- Wisconsin Lutheran College

Northern Mariana Islands

- Northern Marianas College

Canada

- Acadia University

Mexico

- Instituto Tecnologico Autonomo de Mexico

Switzerland

- Franklin College: Switzerland

United Kingdom

- Richmond, The American International University in London

Two-year

Alabama

- Alabama Southern Community College
- Bevill State Community College
- Bishop State Community College
- Calhoun Community College
- Chattahoochee Valley Community College
- Community College of the Air Force
- Enterprise-Ozark Community College
- Faulkner State Community College
- Gadsden State Community College
- George C. Wallace State Community College
  - George C. Wallace Community College at Dothan
  - Selma
- Jefferson Davis Community College
- Jefferson State Community College
- Lawson State Community College
- Lurleen B. Wallace Community College
- Northeast Alabama Community College
- Northwest-Shoals Community College
- Prince Institute of Professional Studies
- Remington College
  - Mobile
- Shelton State Community College
- Southern Union State Community College
- Virginia College at Mobile
- Wallace State Community College at Hanceville

Alaska

- Ilisagvik College
- Prince William Sound Community College

Arizona

- Anthem College
- Arizona Automotive Institute
- Arizona Western College
- Bryman School
- Central Arizona College
- Chandler-Gilbert Community College
  - Pecos
- Cochise College
- Coconino County Community College
- Dine College
- Eastern Arizona College
- Everest College
  - Phoenix
- Gateway Community College
- Glendale Community College
- IIA College
  - Mesa
  - Phoenix
- International Institute of the Americas
  - IIA College: Tucson
- Kaplan College: Phoenix
- Lamson College
- Mesa Community College
- Mohave Community College
- Northland Pioneer College
- Paradise Valley Community College
- Paralegal Institute
- Penn Foster College
- Phoenix College
- Pima Community College
- Refrigeration School
- Rio Salado College
- Scottsdale Community College
- Scottsdale Culinary Institute
- South Mountain Community College
- Tohono O'odham Community College
- Universal Technical Institute
- Yavapai College

Arkansas

- Arkansas Northeastern College
- Arkansas State University
  - Beebe
- Arkansas State University: Newport
- Black River Technical College
- Crowley's Ridge College
- East Arkansas Community College
- Mid-South Community College
- National Park Community College
- North Arkansas College
- Northwest Arkansas Community College
- Ouachita Technical College
- Ozarka College
- Phillips Community College of the University of Arkansas
- Pulaski Technical College
- Rich Mountain Community College
- South Arkansas Community College
- Southeast Arkansas College
- University of Arkansas
  - Community College at Batesville
  - Community College at Hope
  - Cossatot Community College of the
- University of Arkansas Community College at Morrilton

California

- Allan Hancock College
- American Academy of Dramatic Arts: West
- American River College
- Antelope Valley College
- Art Institute
  - of California: Los Angeles
- Bakersfield College
- Barstow Community College
- Berkeley City College
- Bryan College: Sacramento
- Butte College
- Cabrillo College
- California School of Culinary Arts
- Canada College
- CEI College
  - Kaplan College: Panorama City
- Cerritos College
- Cerro Coso Community College
- Chabot College
- Chaffey College
- Citrus College
- City College of San Francisco
- Coastline Community College
- College of Alameda
- College of Marin: Kentfield
- College of San Mateo
- College of the Canyons
- College of the Redwoods
- College of the Sequoias
- College of the Siskiyous
- Columbia College
- Concorde Career College: North Hollywood
- Contra Costa College
- Copper Mountain College
- Cosumnes River College
- Crafton Hills College
- Cuesta College
- Cuyamaca College
- Cypress College
- De Anza College
- Diablo Valley College
- East Los Angeles College
- El Camino College
- El Camino College: Compton Center
- Empire College
- Evergreen Valley College
- Fashion Careers College
- Fashion Institute of Design and Merchandising
  - Los Angeles
  - San Diego
  - San Francisco
- Feather River College
- Folsom Lake College
- Foothill College
- Fremont College
- Fresno City College
- Fullerton College
- Gavilan College
- Glendale Community College
- Golden West College
- Grossmont College
- Hartnell College
- Heald College
  - Concord
  - Fresno
  - Hayward
  - Rancho Cordova
  - Roseville
  - Salinas
  - San Francisco
  - San Jose
  - Stockton
- Imperial Valley College
- Irvine Valley College
- Kaplan College: Vista
- Lake Tahoe Community College
- Laney College
- Las Positas College
- Lassen Community College
- Long Beach City College
- Los Angeles Mission College
- Los Angeles Southwest College
- Los Angeles Trade and Technical College
- Los Angeles Valley College
- Los Medanos College
- Marymount College
- Mendocino College
- Merced College
- Merritt College
- MiraCosta College
- Mission College
- Modesto Junior College
- Monterey Peninsula College
- Moorpark College
- MTI College
- Napa Valley College
- National Polytechnic College of Science
- Ohlone College
- Orange Coast College
- Oxnard College
- Palo Verde College
- Palomar College
- Platt College
  - Los Angeles
- Porterville College
- Professional Golfers Career College
- Reedley College
- Rio Hondo College
- Riverside Community College
- Sacramento City College
- Saddleback College
- Sage College
- San Bernardino Valley College
- San Diego City College
- San Diego Mesa College
- San Diego Miramar College
- San Joaquin Delta College
- San Joaquin Valley College
- San Jose City College
- Santa Ana College
- Santa Barbara Business College
- Santa Barbara Business College
  - Bakersfield
  - Santa Maria
- Santa Barbara Business College: Ventura
- Santa Monica College
- Santa Rosa Junior College
- Shasta College
- Sierra College
- Skyline College
- Solano Community College
- Southwestern College
- Taft College
- Ventura College
- Victor Valley College
- West Hills College: Coalinga
- West Hills College: Lemoore
- West Los Angeles College
- West Valley College
- Western Career College
  - Pleasant Hill
- Western Career College: Stockton
- Westwood College of Technology
  - Westwood College: Los Angeles

WyoTech: Fremont
WyoTech: Long Beach
Yuba Community College District

Colorado

Aims Community College
Arapahoe Community College
Bel-Rea Institute of Animal Technology
Boulder College of Massage Therapy
Cambridge College
Colorado Mountain College
Colorado Northwestern Community College
Colorado School of Healing Arts
Colorado School of Trades
Community College of Aurora
Community College of Denver
Concorde Career College: Aurora
Denver Academy of Court Reporting
Everest College: Aurora
Everest College: Colorado Springs
Front Range Community College
Institute of Business & Medical Careers
IntelliTec College
IntelliTec College: Grand Junction
Kaplan College: Denver
Lincoln College of Technology: Denver
Morgan Community College
Northeastern Junior College
Otero Junior College
Pikes Peak Community College
Pueblo Community College
Red Rocks Community College
Redstone College
Remington College
  Colorado Springs
Trinidad State Junior College

Connecticut

Asnuntuck Community College
Briarwood College
Capital Community College
Clemens College
Goodwin College
Housatonic Community College
Manchester Community College
Naugatuck Valley Community College
Northwestern Connecticut Community College
Norwalk Community College
Quinebaug Valley Community College
Three Rivers Community College
Tunxis Community College

Delaware

Delaware College of Art and Design
Delaware Technical and Community College
  Owens
  Stanton/Wilmington
  Terry

Florida

Angley College
Broward College
Central Florida College
City College
  Miami
City College: Casselberry
College of Business and Technology: Flagler
Daytona State College
Florida College of Natural Health
  Bradenton
Florida Community College at Jacksonville
Florida Keys Community College
Florida National College
Florida Technical College
  Deland
  Orlando
Full Sail University
Gulf Coast Community College
Herzing College
Hillsborough Community College
Indian River State College
Key College
Lake City Community College
Lake-Sumter Community College
Manatee Community College
Miami Dade College
North Florida Community College
Pasco-Hernando Community College
Pensacola Junior College
Polk Community College
Professional Golfers Career College: Orlando
Saint Johns River Community College
St. Petersburg College
Santa Fe College
South Florida Community College
Southwest Florida College

Georgia

Athens Technical College
Atlanta Metropolitan College
Augusta Technical College
Darton College
East Georgia College
Georgia Highlands College
Gordon College
Griffin Technical College
Gupton Jones College of Funeral Service
Gwinnett College
Le Cordon Bleu College of Culinary Arts
Middle Georgia Technical College
North Georgia Technical College
North Metro Technical College
Northwestern Technical College
Oxford College of Emory University
Savannah River College
Savannah Technical College
South Georgia College
Southwest Georgia Technical College
Waycross College
West Central Technical College
West Georgia Technical College
Young Harris College

Hawaii

Heald College
  Honolulu
University of Hawaii
  Honolulu Community College
  Kauai Community College
  Maui Community College
  Windward Community College

Idaho

College of Southern Idaho
North Idaho College
Stevens-Henager College: Boise

Illinois

Black Hawk College
Black Hawk College: East Campus
Carl Sandburg College
City Colleges of Chicago
  Harold Washington College
  Harry S. Truman College
  Kennedy-King College
  Malcolm X College
  Olive-Harvey College
  Richard J. Daley College
  Wright College
College of DuPage
College of Lake County
College of Office Technology
Cooking & Hospitality Institute of Chicago
Danville Area Community College
Elgin Community College
Fox College
Harper College
Heartland Community College
Highland Community College
Illinois Central College
Illinois Eastern Community Colleges
  Frontier Community College
  Lincoln Trail College
  Olney Central College
  Wabash Valley College
Illinois Valley Community College
John A. Logan College
John Wood Community College
Joliet Junior College
Kankakee Community College
Kaskaskia College
Kishwaukee College
Lake Land College
Lewis and Clark Community College
Lincoln Land Community College
MacCormac College
McHenry County College
Moraine Valley Community College
Morrison Institute of Technology
Morton College
Northwestern Business College
Oakton Community College
Parkland College
Prairie State College
Rend Lake College
Richland Community College
Rock Valley College
Rockford Business College
Sauk Valley Community College
Shawnee Community College
South Suburban College of Cook County
Southeastern Illinois College
Spoon River College
Springfield College in Illinois
Taylor Business Institute
Triton College
Vatterott College: Quincy
Waubonsee Community College

Indiana

Ancilla College
Aviation Institute of Maintenance: Indianapolis
Brown Mackie College: Fort Wayne
Brown Mackie College: South Bend
Indiana Business College
  Anderson
  Columbus
  Evansville
  Fort Wayne
  Indianapolis
  Lafayette
  Marion
  Medical
  Muncie
  Terre Haute
Indiana Business College: Elkhart
Indiana Business College: Indianapolis Northwest
Ivy Tech Community College: Richmond
Ivy Tech State College
  Ivy Tech Community College: Bloomington
  Ivy Tech Community College: Central Indiana
  Ivy Tech Community College: Columbus
  Ivy Tech Community College: East Central
  Ivy Tech Community College: Kokomo
  Ivy Tech Community College: Lafayette
  Ivy Tech Community College: North Central
  Ivy Tech Community College: Northeast
  Ivy Tech Community College: Northwest
  Ivy Tech Community College: South Central
  Ivy Tech Community College: Southeast
  Ivy Tech Community College: Southwest
  Ivy Tech Community College: Wabash Valley
Kaplan College: Merrillville
Mid-America College of Funeral Service
National College: Indianapolis
Vincennes University

Iowa

Clinton Community College
Des Moines Area Community College
Ellsworth Community College
Hawkeye Community College
Indian Hills Community College
Iowa Central Community College
Iowa Lakes Community College
Iowa Western Community College
Kaplan University
  Cedar Rapids
Kirkwood Community College
Marshalltown Community College
Muscatine Community College
North Iowa Area Community College
Northeast Iowa Community College
Northwest Iowa Community College
Scott Community College
Southeastern Community College
  North Campus
Southwestern Community College
Vatterott College
Western Iowa Tech Community College

Kansas

Allen County Community College
Barton County Community College
Brown Mackie College
  Salina
Cloud County Community College
Coffeyville Community College
Colby Community College
Cowley County Community College
Dodge City Community College
Donnelly College
Fort Scott Community College
Garden City Community College
Hesston College
Highland Community College
Hutchinson Community College
Independence Community College
Johnson County Community College
Kansas City Kansas Community College
Labette Community College
Neosho County Community College
North Central Kansas Technical College
Pratt Community College
Seward County Community College

Kentucky

Ashland Community and Technical College
Big Sandy Community and Technical College
Daymar College
  Owensboro
Daymar College: Paducah
Elizabethtown Community and Technical College
Hazard Community and Technical College
Hopkinsville Community College
Jefferson Community and Technical College
Louisville Technical Institute
Maysville Community and Technical College
National College
  Danville
  Florence
  Lexington
  Louisville
  Pikeville
  Richmond
Somerset Community College
Southeast Kentucky Community and Technical College
Southern Ohio College
  Brown Mackie College: North Kentucky
Southwestern College: Florence
Spencerian College
Spencerian College: Lexington
West Kentucky Community and Technical College

Louisiana

Baton Rouge Community College
Baton Rouge School of Computers
Blue Cliff College: Houma
Blue Cliff College: Metairie
Blue Cliff College: Shreveport
Camelot College
Delgado Community College
Delta College of Arts & Technology
Delta School of Business & Technology
Gretna Career College
ITI Technical College
Nunez Community College
Remington College
  Baton Rouge
  Lafayette
River Parishes Community College
South Louisiana Community College
Southern University
  Shreveport

Maine

Andover College
Beal College
Central Maine Community College
Eastern Maine Community College
Kennebec Valley Community College
Northern Maine Community College

Tables and Indexes

Southern Maine Community College
York County Community College

Maryland

Allegany College of Maryland
Anne Arundel Community College
Baltimore City Community College
Carroll Community College
Cecil College
Chesapeake College
College of Southern Maryland
Community College of Baltimore County
Frederick Community College
Garrett College
Hagerstown Community College
Harford Community College
Howard Community College
Kaplan College: Hagerstown
Montgomery College
Prince George's Community College
TESST College of Technology
Baltimore
Wor-Wic Community College

Massachusetts

Bay State College
Benjamin Franklin Institute of Technology
Berkshire Community College
Bristol Community College
Cape Cod Community College
Caritas Laboure College
Dean College
Fisher College
Greenfield Community College
Holyoke Community College
Marian Court College
Massachusetts Bay Community College
Massasoit Community College
Middlesex Community College
Mount Wachusett Community College
New England College of Finance
North Shore Community College
Northern Essex Community College
Quincy College
Quinsigamond Community College
Roxbury Community College
Springfield Technical Community College
Urban College of Boston

Michigan

Alpena Community College
Glen Oaks Community College
Gogebic Community College
Henry Ford Community College
Jackson Community College
Kalamazoo Valley Community College
Kellogg Community College
Kirtland Community College
Lake Michigan College
Lansing Community College
Macomb Community College
Monroe County Community College
Montcalm Community College
Mott Community College
Muskegon Community College
North Central Michigan College
Northwestern Michigan College
Oakland Community College
Saginaw Chippewa Tribal College
Schoolcraft College
Southwestern Michigan College
Washtenaw Community College
West Shore Community College

Minnesota

Academy College
Alexandria Technical College
Anoka-Ramsey Community College
Central Lakes College
Century Community and Technical College
Dakota County Technical College
Duluth Business University
Dunwoody College of Technology
Fond du Lac Tribal and Community College
Hennepin Technical College
Herzing College
Minneapolis Drafting School Division of
Hibbing Community College
Inver Hills Community College
Lakeland Academy Division of Herzing College
Le Cordon Bleu College of Culinary Arts
Mesabi Range Community and Technical College
Minneapolis Community and Technical College
Minnesota School of Business: Brooklyn Center
Minnesota State College - Southeast Technical
Minnesota State Community and Technical College
Minnesota West Community and Technical College
Normandale Community College
North Hennepin Community College
Northland Community & Technical College
Northwest Technical College
Northwest Technical Institute
Pine Technical College
Rainy River Community College
Rasmussen College
Eagan
Eden Prairie
Mankato
St. Cloud
Rasmussen College: Brooklyn Park
Ridgewater College
St. Paul College
Vermilion Community College

Mississippi

Antonelli College
Hattiesburg
Jackson
Blue Cliff College: Gulfport
Coahoma Community College
Copiah-Lincoln Community College
East Central Community College
East Mississippi Community College
Hinds Community College
Itawamba Community College
Mississippi Delta Community College
Mississippi Gulf Coast Community College
Northeast Mississippi Community College
Northwest Mississippi Community College
Pearl River Community College
Southwest Mississippi Community College
Virginia College
Virginia College Gulf Coast

Missouri

Bolivar Technical College
Cottey College
Crowder College
East Central College
Jefferson College
Metro Business College
Metro Business College
Jefferson City
Metropolitan Community College: Blue River
Metropolitan Community College: Longview
Metropolitan Community College: Maple Woods
Metropolitan Community College: Penn Valley
Mineral Area College
Missouri College
Moberly Area Community College
North Central Missouri College
Ozarks Technical Community College
Patricia Stevens College
Pinnacle Career Institute: Kansas City
Ranken Technical College
St. Charles Community College
St. Louis Community College
Florissant Valley
Meramec
Sanford-Brown College
Hazelwood
St. Peters
Southeast Missouri Hospital College of Nursing and Health Sciences
State Fair Community College
Texas County Technical Institute
Three Rivers Community College
Vatterott College: St. Joseph
Vatterott College: Springfield
Vatterott College: Sunset Hills
Wentworth Military Junior College

Montana

Chief Dull Knife College
Dawson Community College
Flathead Valley Community College
Fort Belknap College
Helena College of Technology of the University of Montana
Little Big Horn College
Miles Community College
Montana State University
College of Technology: Great Falls
Stone Child College

Nebraska

Central Community College
Kaplan University
Lincoln
Kaplan University: Omaha
Little Priest Tribal College
Metropolitan Community College
Mid-Plains Community College Area
Nebraska Indian Community College
Northeast Community College
Southeast Community College
Western Nebraska Community College

Nevada

Career College of Northern Nevada
College of Southern Nevada
High-Tech Institute
Kaplan College: Las Vegas
Las Vegas College
Le Cordon Bleu College of Culinary Arts
Truckee Meadows Community College
Western Nevada College

New Hampshire

Great Bay Community College
Lakes Region Community College
Manchester Community College
Nashua Community College
NHTI-Concord's Community College
River Valley Community College
White Mountains Community College

New Jersey

Assumption College for Sisters
Atlantic Cape Community College
Bergen Community College
Brookdale Community College
Burlington County College
Camden County College
County College of Morris
Cumberland County College
Essex County College
Gloucester County College
Hudson County Community College
Mercer County Community College
Middlesex County College
Ocean County College
Passaic County Community College
Raritan Valley Community College
Salem Community College
Sussex County Community College
Union County College
Warren County Community College

New Mexico

Central New Mexico Community College
Clovis Community College
Dona Ana Community College of New Mexico State University
Eastern New Mexico University: Roswell Campus
IIA College
Albuquerque
Luna Community College
Mesalands Community College
New Mexico Junior College
New Mexico Military Institute
New Mexico State University
Alamogordo
Carlsbad
San Juan College
Santa Fe Community College

New York

American Academy of Dramatic Arts
Art Institute of New York City
ASA Institute of Business and Computer Technology
Bramson ORT College
Broome Community College
Bryant & Stratton Business Institute
Bryant & Stratton College: Albany
Bryant & Stratton College: Buffalo
Bryant & Stratton College: Rochester
Bryant & Stratton College: Southtowns
Bryant & Stratton College: Syracuse
Bryant & Stratton College: Syracuse North
Business Informatics Center
Cayuga County Community College
City University of New York
Borough of Manhattan Community College
LaGuardia Community College
Queensborough Community College
Clinton Community College
College of Westchester
Columbia-Greene Community College
Corning Community College
Dutchess Community College
Elmira Business Institute
Elmira Business Institute: Vestal
Erie Community College
City Campus
North Campus
South Campus
Finger Lakes Community College
Fulton-Montgomery Community College
Genesee Community College
Helene Fuld College of Nursing
Hudson Valley Community College
Institute of Design and Construction
Island Drafting and Technical Institute
Jamestown Business College
Jamestown Community College
Jefferson Community College
Long Island Business Institute
Mildred Elley
Mohawk Valley Community College
Monroe Community College
New York Career Institute
Olean Business Institute
Orange County Community College
Plaza College
Professional Business College
Rockland Community College
St. Joseph's College of Nursing
Schenectady County Community College
State University of New York
College of Agriculture and Technology at Cobleskill
College of Agriculture and Technology at Morrisville
College of Technology at Alfred
College of Technology at Canton
College of Technology at Delhi
Suffolk County Community College
Sullivan County Community College
Swedish Institute
Technical Career Institutes
Tompkins Cortland Community College
Trocaire College
Ulster County Community College
Utica School of Commerce
Villa Maria College of Buffalo
Westchester Community College

North Carolina

Alamance Community College
Asheville-Buncombe Technical Community College
Beaufort County Community College
Bladen Community College
Blue Ridge Community College
Brunswick Community College
Caldwell Community College and Technical Institute
Cape Fear Community College
Carteret Community College

Catawba Valley Community College
Central Carolina Community College
Central Piedmont Community College
Coastal Carolina Community College
College of the Albemarle
Craven Community College
Davidson County Community College
Edgecombe Community College
Fayetteville Technical Community College
Forsyth Technical Community College
Gaston College
Guilford Technical Community College
Halifax Community College
Haywood Community College
Isothermal Community College
James Sprunt Community College
Johnston Community College
King's College
Lenoir Community College
Louisburg College
Martin Community College
Mayland Community College
McDowell Technical Community College
Miller-Motte Technical College: Cary
Mitchell Community College
Montgomery Community College
Nash Community College
Pamlico Community College
Piedmont Community College
Pitt Community College
Randolph Community College
Richmond Community College
Roanoke-Chowan Community College
Rockingham Community College
Rowan-Cabarrus Community College
Sampson Community College
Sandhills Community College
South College
South Piedmont Community College
Southeastern Community College
Southwestern Community College
Stanly Community College
Surry Community College
Tri-County Community College
Vance-Granville Community College
Wake Technical Community College
Wayne Community College
Western Piedmont Community College
Wilkes Community College
Wilson Community College

North Dakota

Bismarck State College
Cankdeska Cikana Community College
Fort Berthold Community College
Lake Region State College
Minot State University: Bottineau Campus
North Dakota State College of Science
Rasmussen College: Bismarck
Sitting Bull College
Turtle Mountain Community College
Williston State College

Ohio

Academy of Court Reporting: Cincinnati
Antonelli College
Art Institute of Cincinnati
Art Institute of Ohio: Cincinnati
ATS Institute of Technology
Belmont Technical College
Bohecker College
Bradford School
Bryant & Stratton College: Cleveland
Central Ohio Technical College
Chatfield College
Cincinnati State Technical and Community College
Clark State Community College
Cleveland Institute of Electronics
Columbus State Community College
Cuyahoga Community College
- Metropolitan Campus

Edison State Community College
ETI Technical College of Niles
Gallipolis Career College
Good Samaritan College of Nursing and Health Science
Hocking College
Hondros College
International College of Broadcasting
James A. Rhodes State College
Jefferson Community College
Kent State University
- Ashtabula
- East Liverpool
- Salem
- Stark
- Trumbull
- Tuscarawas

Kent State University: Geauga
Lakeland Community College
Marion Technical College
Miami University
- Hamilton Campus
- Middletown Campus

Miami-Jacobs Career College
National College
- Dayton

National College: Cincinnati
National College: Stow
National College: Youngstown
North Central State College
Northwest State Community College
Ohio Institute of Health Careers: Columbus
Ohio Institute of Health Careers: Elyria
Ohio Institute of Photography and Technology
Ohio Valley College of Technology
Owens Community College
- Toledo

Remington College: Cleveland West
Rosedale Bible College
School of Advertising Art
Sinclair Community College
Southern State Community College
Southwestern College of Business
- Southwestern College: Franklin
- Southwestern College: Tri-County
- Southwestern College: Vine Street Campus

Southwestern College: Dayton
Stark State College of Technology
Stautzenberger College
Stautzenberger College: Strongsville
Technology Education College
Terra State Community College
Tri-State College
Trumbull Business College
University of Akron: Wayne College
University of Cincinnati
- Clermont College
- Raymond Walters College

University of Northwestern Ohio
Vatterott College: Cleveland
Virginia Marti College of Art and Design
Washington State Community College
Wright State University: Lake Campus
Zane State College

Oklahoma

Carl Albert State College
Connors State College
Eastern Oklahoma State College
Murray State College
Northeastern Oklahoma Agricultural and Mechanical College
Northern Oklahoma College
Oklahoma City Community College
Oklahoma State University Institute of Technology:
- Okmulgee
- Oklahoma City

Platt College
- Tulsa

Platt College: Oklahoma City Central
Redlands Community College
Seminole State College
Tulsa Community College
Tulsa Welding School
Vatterott College
Vatterott College
- Tulsa

Western Oklahoma State College

Oregon

Blue Mountain Community College
Central Oregon Community College
Chemeketa Community College
Clackamas Community College
Clatsop Community College
Heald College: Portland
Klamath Community College
Lane Community College
Mt. Hood Community College
Pioneer Pacific College
Pioneer Pacific College: Springfield
Portland Community College
Rogue Community College
Southwestern Oregon Community College
Treasure Valley Community College
Umpqua Community College
Western Culinary Institute

Pennsylvania

Allied Medical and Technical Institute
Antonelli Institute of Art and Photography
Berks Technical Institute
Butler County Community College
Cambria-Rowe Business College
Cambria-Rowe Business College: Indiana
Career Training Academy: Pittsburgh
Commonwealth Technical Institute
Community College of Allegheny County
Community College of Beaver County
Community College of Philadelphia
Consolidated School of Business
- Lancaster
- York

Dean Institute of Technology
DuBois Business College
DuBois Business College
- Huntingdon
- Oil City

Erie Business Center South
Harcum College
Harrisburg Area Community College
Hussian School of Art
JNA Institute of Culinary Arts
Kaplan Career Institute: Pittsburgh
Keystone Technical Institute
Lackawanna College
Laurel Business Institute
Laurel Technical Institute
Lehigh Carbon Community College
Lincoln Technical Institute: Allentown
Lincoln Technical Institute: Northeast Philadelphia
Lincoln Technical Institute: Philadelphia
Luzerne County Community College
McCann School of Business
- and Technology: Pottsville
- and Technology: Sunbury

McCann School of Business and Technology: Dickson City
McCann School of Business and Technology: Hazleton
Metropolitan Career Center Computer Technology Institute
Montgomery County Community College
New Castle School of Trades
Newport Business Institute: Lower Burrell
Newport Business Institute: Williamsport
Northampton Community College
Oakbridge Academy of Arts
Orleans Technical Institute - Center City Campus
Pace Institute
Penn Commercial Business and Technical School
Pennco Tech
Pennsylvania Culinary Institute
Pennsylvania Highlands Community College
Pennsylvania Institute of Health and Technology
Pennsylvania Institute of Technology
Pittsburgh Institute of Aeronautics
Pittsburgh Institute of Mortuary Science
Pittsburgh Technical Institute
PJA School
Rosedale Technical Institute
South Hills School of Business & Technology
South Hills School of Business & Technology: Altoona
Triangle Tech
- DuBois
- Erie
- Greensburg
- Pittsburgh

Triangle Tech: Bethlehem
Triangle Tech: Sunbury
University of Pittsburgh
- Titusville

Vet Tech Institute
Westmoreland County Community College
Yorktowne Business Institute
YTI Career Institute: Lancaster
YTI Career Institute: York

Puerto Rico

Huertas Junior College
Humacao Community College

Rhode Island

Community College of Rhode Island

South Carolina

Aiken Technical College
Central Carolina Technical College
Clinton Junior College
Denmark Technical College
Forrest Junior College
Greenville Technical College
Horry-Georgetown Technical College
Midlands Technical College
Miller-Motte Technical College
Orangeburg-Calhoun Technical College
Piedmont Technical College
Spartanburg Community College
Spartanburg Methodist College
Technical College of the Lowcountry
Tri-County Technical College
University of South Carolina
- Lancaster
- Salkehatchie Regional Campus
- Sumter
- Union

Williamsburg Technical College
York Technical College

South Dakota

Kilian Community College
Lake Area Technical Institute
Mitchell Technical Institute
Southeast Technical Institute

Tennessee

Chattanooga State Technical Community College
Cleveland State Community College
Dyersburg State Community College
Fountainhead College of Technology
Huntington College of Health Sciences
Jackson State Community College
Miller-Motte Technical College: Clarksville
Nashville Auto-Diesel College
Nashville State Community College
National College
- Knoxville
- Nashville

National College of Business & Technology
- National College: Bristol

National College: Bartlett
National College: Madison
National College: Memphis
Nossi College of Art
Remington College
- Memphis

Roane State Community College
Southwest Tennessee Community College
Walters State Community College

Texas

Alvin Community College
Angelina College
Austin Community College
Blinn College
Bradford School of Business
Brookhaven College
Cedar Valley College
Central Texas College
Cisco Junior College
Clarendon College

Coastal Bend College
College of the Mainland
Collin County Community College District
Court Reporting Institute of Dallas
Court Reporting Institute of Houston
Del Mar College
Eastfield College
El Centro College
El Paso Community College
Everest College: Arlington
Frank Phillips College
Galveston College
Hallmark College of Aeronautics
Hallmark College of Technology
Hill College
Houston Community College System
Howard College
Jacksonville College
Kilgore College
Lamar Institute of Technology
Lamar State College at Orange
Lamar State College at Port Arthur
Laredo Community College
Lee College
Lon Morris College
Lone Star College System
McLennan Community College
Midland College
Navarro College
North Central Texas College
North Lake College
Odessa College
Palo Alto College
Panola College
Paris Junior College
Ranger College
Richland College
St. Philip's College
San Jacinto College
South Plains College
South Texas College
Southwest Institute of Technology
Southwest Texas Junior College
Tarrant County College
Temple College
Texarkana College
Texas Culinary Academy
Texas State Technical College
- Harlingen
- Waco
- West Texas

Texas State Technical College: Marshall
Tyler Junior College
Victoria College
Wade College
Weatherford College
Western Technical College
Western Technical College: Diana Drive
Western Texas College
Westwood College: Fort Worth
Wharton County Junior College

Utah

Careers Unlimited
College of Eastern Utah
Eagle Gate College: Layton
Eagle Gate College: Murray
Eagle Gate College: Salt Lake City
LDS Business College
Provo College
Salt Lake Community College
Snow College
Utah Career College

Vermont

Community College of Vermont
Landmark College
New England Culinary Institute

Virginia

Blue Ridge Community College
Bryant & Stratton College Richmond
Bryant & Stratton College: Virginia Beach
Central Virginia Community College
Centura College: Chesapeake
Centura College: Newport News
Centura College: Norfolk
Centura College: Richmond
Centura College: Richmond Westend
Centura College: Virginia Beach
Dabney S. Lancaster Community College
Danville Community College
Eastern Shore Community College
ECPI Technical College: Roanoke
Germanna Community College
J. Sargeant Reynolds Community College
John Tyler Community College
Lord Fairfax Community College
Miller-Motte Technical College: Lynchburg
Mountain Empire Community College
National College
- Bluefield
- Charlottesville
- Danville
- Harrisonburg
- Lynchburg
- Martinsville

New River Community College
Northern Virginia Community College
Patrick Henry Community College
Paul D. Camp Community College
Piedmont Virginia Community College
Rappahannock Community College
Southside Virginia Community College
Southwest Virginia Community College
Thomas Nelson Community College
Tidewater Community College
Virginia Highlands Community College
Virginia Western Community College
Wytheville Community College

Washington

Bates Technical College
Bellevue Community College
Bellingham Technical College
Big Bend Community College
Cascadia Community College
Centralia College
Clark College
Clover Park Technical College
Columbia Basin College
Edmonds Community College
Everett Community College
Grays Harbor College
Green River Community College
Highline Community College
Lower Columbia College
North Seattle Community College
Northwest Aviation College
Northwest Indian College
Olympic College
Peninsula College
Pierce College
Renton Technical College
Shoreline Community College
Skagit Valley College
South Seattle Community College
Spokane Community College
Spokane Falls Community College
Tacoma Community College
Walla Walla Community College
Wenatchee Valley College
Whatcom Community College
Yakima Valley Community College

West Virginia

Blue Ridge Community and Technical College
Eastern West Virginia Community and Technical College
Huntington Junior College
Mountain State College
New River Community and Technical College
Potomac State College of West Virginia University
Southern West Virginia Community and Technical College
Valley College
West Virginia Business College: Nutter Fort
West Virginia Business College: Wheeling
West Virginia Junior College
West Virginia Junior College: Bridgeport
West Virginia Junior College: Charleston
West Virginia Northern Community College
West Virginia State Community and Technical College

Wisconsin

Blackhawk Technical College
Chippewa Valley Technical College
Fox Valley Technical College
Lac Courte Oreilles Ojibwa Community College
Lakeshore Technical College
Madison Area Technical College
Mid-State Technical College
Moraine Park Technical College
Northcentral Technical College
Southwest Wisconsin Technical College
University of Wisconsin
- Barron County
- Fond du Lac
- Fox Valley
- Manitowoc
- Marathon County
- Marinette
- Marshfield/Wood County
- Richland
- Rock County
- Sheboygan
- Washington County
- Waukesha

Waukesha County Technical College
Western Technical College
Wisconsin Indianhead Technical College

Wyoming

Central Wyoming College
Eastern Wyoming College
Laramie County Community College
Northwest College
Sheridan College
Western Wyoming Community College
WyoTech: Laramie

American Samoa

American Samoa Community College

Guam

Guam Community College

SAT Subject Tests required for admission

Four-year

California

California Institute of Technology
Fresno Pacific University*
Harvey Mudd College
Pomona College*
University of California*
- Berkeley
- Davis
- Irvine
- Los Angeles
- Riverside
- San Diego
- Santa Barbara
- Santa Cruz

University of California: Merced

Connecticut

Wesleyan University*
Yale University*

Kansas

Newman University*

Massachusetts

Amherst College*
Boston College*
Boston University
Brandeis University*
Franklin W. Olin College of Engineering
Harvard College
Massachusetts Institute of Technology
Tufts University*
Wellesley College*
Williams College

Minnesota

Winona State University*

Nebraska

University of Nebraska* Kearney

New Hampshire

Dartmouth College*

New Jersey

Princeton University

New York

Barnard College*
Columbia University
Hamilton College*
State University of New York College at Buffalo
Vassar College*
Webb Institute

North Carolina

Duke University*
North Carolina Agricultural and Technical State University

Ohio

Bowling Green State University*

Pennsylvania

Bryn Mawr College*
Haverford College
Swarthmore College*
University of Pennsylvania*

Rhode Island

Brown University*

Texas

Rice University*

Vermont

Middlebury College*

Virginia

Washington and Lee University

West Virginia

Alderson-Broaddus College*

Canada

University of Toronto

SAT Subject Tests recommended for admission

Four-year

Alabama

University of Mobile

California

Chapman University
Mills College
Occidental College
Simpson University*
Stanford University
University of the Pacific

Connecticut

Trinity College

Delaware

University of Delaware

District of Columbia

American University
Catholic University of America
George Washington University
Georgetown University
Howard University
Trinity Washington University*

Florida

Florida International University

Illinois

Northwestern University

Indiana

Indiana University Bloomington

Maryland

Johns Hopkins University

Massachusetts

Babson College

Michigan

Calvin College
Hillsdale College

Minnesota

Carleton College

Montana

University of Great Falls

New York

City University of New York Queens College
Clarkson University
Eastman School of Music of the University of Rochester*
Fordham University
Hofstra University
Mercy College
St. Joseph's College: Suffolk Campus
Skidmore College
State University of New York
- College at Old Westbury
- Stony Brook

North Carolina

Davidson College*

Ohio

Cedarville University*
Oberlin College

Oregon

Reed College

Pennsylvania

Cheyney University of Pennsylvania

* ACT accepted as an alternative to SAT Subject Tests

Lafayette College

Tennessee
Vanderbilt University

Virginia
George Mason University*
Hampden-Sydney College
University of Virginia

Canada
University of Alberta

Switzerland
Franklin College: Switzerland

Two-year

California
Deep Springs College

Georgia
Gordon College

New York
St. Elizabeth College of Nursing

Tables and Indexes

Colleges that offer ROTC

Air Force ROTC

Four-year

Alabama
Alabama State University
Auburn University
Auburn University at Montgomery
Birmingham-Southern College
Faulkner University
Huntingdon College
Miles College
Samford University
Spring Hill College
Troy University
Tuskegee University
University of Alabama
University of Alabama
Birmingham
University of Mobile
University of Montevallo
University of South Alabama
University of West Alabama

Alaska
Alaska Pacific University
University of Alaska
Anchorage

Arizona
Arizona State University
DeVry University
Phoenix
Embry-Riddle Aeronautical University: Prescott Campus
Northern Arizona University
Southwestern College
University of Arizona

Arkansas
John Brown University
University of Arkansas
University of Arkansas
Fort Smith

California
Biola University
California Baptist University
California Institute of Technology
California Lutheran University
California State University
Dominguez Hills
Fresno
Los Angeles
Northridge
Sacramento
San Bernardino
San Marcos
Chapman University
Claremont McKenna College
Harvey Mudd College
Holy Names University
The King's College and Seminary
Loyola Marymount University
Menlo College
National University
Occidental College
Pepperdine University
Pitzer College
Point Loma Nazarene University
Pomona College
St. Mary's College of California
Samuel Merritt University
San Diego Christian College
San Diego State University
San Francisco State University
San Jose State University
Santa Clara University
Scripps College
Sonoma State University
Stanford University
University of California
Berkeley
Davis
Irvine
Los Angeles
Riverside
Santa Cruz
University of Redlands
University of San Diego
University of San Francisco
University of Southern California
University of the Pacific
Vanguard University of Southern California
Westmont College
Whittier College

Colorado
Colorado Christian University
Colorado School of Mines
Colorado State University
Metropolitan State College of Denver
Regis University
University of Colorado
Boulder
Denver
University of Denver
University of Northern Colorado

Connecticut
Central Connecticut State University
Eastern Connecticut State University
Fairfield University
Quinnipiac University
Southern Connecticut State University
University of Connecticut
University of Hartford
Wesleyan University
Western Connecticut State University
Yale University

Delaware
Delaware State University
Goldey-Beacom College
University of Delaware
Wilmington University

District of Columbia
American University
Catholic University of America
George Washington University
Georgetown University
Howard University
University of the District of Columbia

Florida
Barry University
Bethune-Cookman University
Clearwater Christian College
Eckerd College
Embry-Riddle Aeronautical University
Florida Agricultural and Mechanical University
Florida Atlantic University
Florida College
Florida International University
Florida Southern College
Florida State University
Lynn University
St. Leo University
University of Central Florida
University of Miami
University of South Florida
University of Tampa
University of West Florida

Georgia
Agnes Scott College
Clayton State University
Emory University
Georgia Institute of Technology
Georgia State University
Kennesaw State University
Morehouse College
Oglethorpe University
Southern Polytechnic State University
Spelman College
University of Georgia
Valdosta State University

Hawaii
Brigham Young University-Hawaii
Chaminade University of Honolulu
Hawaii Pacific University
University of Hawaii
Manoa
West Oahu

Idaho
Lewis-Clark State College
Northwest Nazarene University
University of Idaho

Illinois
Elmhurst College
Governors State University
Illinois Institute of Technology
Judson University
Lewis University
Loyola University Chicago
McKendree University
North Central College
North Park University
Northeastern Illinois University
Northwestern University
St. Xavier University
Southern Illinois University
Carbondale
Southern Illinois University
Edwardsville
University of Chicago
University of Illinois
Chicago
Urbana-Champaign
Wheaton College

Indiana
Bethel College
Butler University
DePauw University
Holy Cross College
Indiana State University
Indiana University
Bloomington
South Bend
Southeast
Indiana University-Purdue University Indianapolis
Purdue University
Rose-Hulman Institute of Technology
Saint Mary's College
St. Mary-of-the-Woods College
Trine University
University of Notre Dame
Valparaiso University

Iowa
Coe College
Grand View University
Iowa State University
University of Iowa

Kansas
Baker University
Kansas State University
Manhattan Christian College
MidAmerica Nazarene University
University of Kansas
University of St. Mary
Washburn University

Kentucky
Asbury College
Bellarmine University
Centre College
Georgetown College
Kentucky State University
Northern Kentucky University
Spalding University
Thomas More College
Transylvania University
University of Kentucky
University of Louisville
Western Kentucky University

Louisiana
Dillard University
Louisiana State University and Agricultural and Mechanical College
Loyola University New Orleans
Northwestern State University
Our Lady of Holy Cross College
Our Lady of the Lake College
Southern University
New Orleans
Southern University and Agricultural and Mechanical College
Tulane University
University of New Orleans
Xavier University of Louisiana

Maine
University of Maine
Augusta
University of Southern Maine

Maryland
Bowie State University
Johns Hopkins University
Loyola College in Maryland
Salisbury University
Towson University
University of Maryland
Baltimore County
College Park

Massachusetts
American International College
Amherst College
Anna Maria College
Assumption College
Babson College
Bay Path College
Becker College
Bentley University
Boston College
Boston University
Brandeis University
Bridgewater State College
Clark University
College of the Holy Cross
Curry College
Elms College
Endicott College
Gordon College
Harvard College
Massachusetts College of Pharmacy and Health Sciences
Massachusetts Institute of Technology
Massachusetts Maritime Academy
Merrimack College
Mount Holyoke College
Northeastern University
Pine Manor College
Salem State College
Smith College
Springfield College
Tufts University
University of Massachusetts
Amherst
Boston
Lowell
Wellesley College
Wentworth Institute of Technology
Western New England College
Westfield State College
Williams College
Worcester Polytechnic Institute
Worcester State College

Michigan
Concordia University
Eastern Michigan University
Finlandia University
Lawrence Technological University
Michigan State University
Michigan Technological University
Oakland University
Spring Arbor University
University of Michigan
University of Michigan
Dearborn
Wayne State University

Minnesota
Augsburg College
Bethel University
College of St. Catherine
College of St. Scholastica
Concordia College: Moorhead
Concordia University: St. Paul
Hamline University
Macalester College
Minnesota State University
Moorhead
Northwestern College
University of Minnesota
Crookston
Duluth
Twin Cities
University of St. Thomas

Mississippi
Belhaven College
Jackson State University
Mississippi State University
Mississippi University for Women
University of Mississippi
University of Southern Mississippi
William Carey University

Missouri
Central Bible College
Central Methodist University
Columbia College
Fontbonne University
Harris-Stowe State University
Lincoln University
Saint Louis University
Southeast Missouri State University
Stephens College
University of Central Missouri
University of Missouri
Columbia
Missouri University of Science and Technology
St. Louis
Washington University in St. Louis
Webster University
Westminster College
William Woods University

Montana
Montana State University
Billings
Bozeman

Nebraska
Bellevue University
Clarkson College
College of Saint Mary
Concordia University
Creighton University
Doane College
Grace University
Nebraska Wesleyan University

University of Nebraska
Lincoln
Medical Center
Omaha
York College

New Hampshire

Colby-Sawyer College
Daniel Webster College
Franklin Pierce University
Keene State College
New England College
Plymouth State University
Rivier College
St. Anselm College
Southern New Hampshire University
University of New Hampshire
University of New Hampshire at Manchester

New Jersey

The College of New Jersey
Fairleigh Dickinson University
College at Florham
Metropolitan Campus
Kean University
Monmouth University
Montclair State University
New Jersey Institute of Technology
Princeton University
Ramapo College of New Jersey
Rutgers, The State University of New Jersey
Camden Regional Campus
New Brunswick/Piscataway Campus
Newark Regional Campus
Saint Peter's College
Stevens Institute of Technology
William Paterson University of New Jersey

New Mexico

National American University: Rio Rancho
New Mexico State University
University of New Mexico

New York

Adelphi University
Albany College of Pharmacy and Health Sciences
Cazenovia College
Clarkson University
College of Saint Rose
Columbia University
School of General Studies
Cornell University
Dowling College
Elmira College
Fordham University
Hamilton College
Iona College
Ithaca College
Jewish Theological Seminary of America
Le Moyne College
Manhattan College
Mercy College
Molloy College
Nazareth College of Rochester
New York Institute of Technology
Pace University
Polytechnic Institute of New York University
Rensselaer Polytechnic Institute
Roberts Wesleyan College
Rochester Institute of Technology
Russell Sage College
Sage College of Albany
St. Francis College
St. John Fisher College
St. Joseph's College: Suffolk Campus
St. Lawrence University
St. Thomas Aquinas College
Siena College
Skidmore College
State University of New York
Albany
Binghamton
College at Brockport
College at Cortland
College at Geneseo
College at Old Westbury
College at Potsdam
College of Environmental Science and Forestry
Stony Brook
Syracuse University
Union College
University of Rochester
Utica College
Vaughn College of Aeronautics and Technology
Wells College

North Carolina

Belmont Abbey College
Bennett College
Davidson College
Duke University
East Carolina University
Elon University
Fayetteville State University
Gardner-Webb University
Greensboro College
Guilford College
High Point University
Johnson C. Smith University
Meredith College
Methodist University
North Carolina Agricultural and Technical State University
North Carolina Central University
North Carolina State University
Peace College
Queens University of Charlotte
St. Augustine's College
Shaw University
University of North Carolina
Chapel Hill
Charlotte
Greensboro
Pembroke
Wingate University

North Dakota

Mayville State University
North Dakota State University
University of North Dakota

Ohio

Baldwin-Wallace College
Bowling Green State University
Capital University
Case Western Reserve University
Cedarville University
Central State University
Cleveland Institute of Art
College of Mount St. Joseph
Heidelberg University
Kent State University
Lourdes College
Malone University
Miami University
Oxford Campus
Mount Union College
Ohio Northern University
Ohio State University
Columbus Campus
Lima Campus
Mansfield Campus
Marion Campus
Newark Campus
Ohio University
Ohio University
Lancaster Campus
Ohio Wesleyan University
Otterbein College
University of Akron
University of Cincinnati
University of Dayton
University of Findlay
University of Toledo
Urbana University
Wilberforce University
Wittenberg University
Wright State University
Xavier University
Youngstown State University

Oklahoma

Langston University
Oklahoma Baptist University
Oklahoma Christian University
Oklahoma City University
Oklahoma State University
Oral Roberts University
Rogers State University
St. Gregory's University
Southern Nazarene University
University of Oklahoma
University of Tulsa

Oregon

Concordia University
Corban College
George Fox University
Linfield College
Oregon State University
Pacific University
Portland State University
University of Oregon
University of Portland
Warner Pacific College
Western Oregon University
Willamette University

Pennsylvania

Bloomsburg University of Pennsylvania
Bryn Mawr College
Cabrini College
California University of Pennsylvania
Carlow University
Carnegie Mellon University
Chatham University
Drexel University
Duquesne University
East Stroudsburg University of Pennsylvania
Eastern University
Keystone College
King's College
La Roche College
La Salle University
Marywood University
Mercyhurst College
Misericordia University
Penn State
Abington
Altoona
Brandywine
Hazleton
University Park
Wilkes-Barre
Worthington Scranton
Philadelphia Biblical University
Point Park University
Robert Morris University
Rosemont College
Saint Joseph's University
St. Vincent College
Seton Hill University
Swarthmore College
Temple University
Thomas Jefferson University: College of Health Professions
University of Pennsylvania
University of Pittsburgh
University of Pittsburgh Greensburg
University of Scranton
University of the Sciences in Philadelphia
Villanova University
Washington & Jefferson College
Widener University
Wilkes University

Puerto Rico

Bayamon Central University
Caribbean University
Inter American University of Puerto Rico
Aguadilla Campus
Bayamon Campus
Fajardo Campus
Metropolitan Campus
San German Campus
Pontifical Catholic University of Puerto Rico
Universidad Metropolitana
Universidad Politecnica de Puerto Rico
University of Puerto Rico
Mayaguez
Rio Piedras

South Carolina

Anderson University
Benedict College
Charleston Southern University
The Citadel
Clemson University
College of Charleston
South Carolina State University
Southern Wesleyan University
University of South Carolina

South Dakota

Dakota State University
South Dakota State University

Tennessee

Austin Peay State University
Belmont University
Carson-Newman College
Christian Brothers University
Free Will Baptist Bible College
LeMoyne-Owen College
Lipscomb University
Rhodes College
Tennessee State University
Tennessee Technological University
Tennessee Wesleyan College
University of Memphis
University of Tennessee
Knoxville
Vanderbilt University

Texas

Angelo State University
Baylor University
College of Saint Thomas More
Concordia University Texas
Dallas Baptist University
Houston Baptist University
Midwestern State University
Our Lady of the Lake University of San Antonio
Rice University
St. Edward's University
St. Mary's University
Southern Methodist University
Texas A&M University
Texas Christian University
Texas Lutheran University
Texas State University: San Marcos
Texas Tech University
Texas Wesleyan University
Texas Woman's University
Trinity University
University of Dallas
University of Houston
University of Houston Downtown
University of Mary Hardin-Baylor
University of North Texas
University of St. Thomas
University of Texas
Arlington
Austin
Dallas
El Paso
San Antonio
University of the Incarnate Word
Wayland Baptist University

Utah

Brigham Young University
University of Utah
Utah State University
Utah Valley University
Weber State University
Westminster College

Vermont

Lyndon State College
Norwich University
St. Michael's College

Virginia

George Mason University
James Madison University
Liberty University
Mary Baldwin College
University of Virginia
Virginia Military Institute
Virginia Polytechnic Institute and State University

Washington

Central Washington University
Saint Martin's University
Seattle Pacific University
Seattle University
University of Washington
Washington State University

West Virginia

Fairmont State University
Shepherd University
West Virginia University

Wisconsin

Alverno College
Carroll University
Carthage College
Maranatha Baptist Bible College
Marquette University
Milwaukee School of Engineering
University of Wisconsin
Madison
Milwaukee
Stout
Superior
Whitewater
Wisconsin Lutheran College

Wyoming

University of Wyoming

Two-year

Alabama

Bishop State Community College
Jefferson State Community College
Marion Military Institute
Shelton State Community College

Arizona

Coconino County Community College
Estrella Mountain Community College
Gateway Community College
Mesa Community College
Phoenix College
Pima Community College
Yavapai College

Arkansas

Northwest Arkansas Community College

California

Chabot College
College of San Mateo
College of the Sequoias
Cuyamaca College
De Anza College
Foothill College
Fresno City College
Irvine Valley College
Los Angeles City College

Los Angeles Mission College
MiraCosta College
Mission College
Mount San Antonio College
Mount San Jacinto College
Ohlone College
Riverside Community College
Sacramento City College
San Diego City College
Solano Community College
West Valley College

Colorado
Aims Community College
Arapahoe Community College
Front Range Community College

Connecticut
Capital Community College
Tunxis Community College

Delaware
Delaware Technical and Community College
Stanton/Wilmington

Florida
Brevard Community College
Broward College
Daytona State College
Miami Dade College
Santa Fe College
Tallahassee Community College

Hawaii
University of Hawaii
Honolulu Community College
Leeward Community College

Illinois
John A. Logan College
Lincoln Land Community College
Parkland College
Shawnee Community College

Indiana
Vincennes University

Iowa
Hawkeye Community College
Iowa Western Community College

Louisiana
Delgado Community College

Maryland
Prince George's Community College

Massachusetts
Holyoke Community College
Middlesex Community College
Quinsigamond Community College

Michigan
Lansing Community College

Minnesota
Anoka-Ramsey Community College
Century Community and Technical College
Inver Hills Community College
Normandale Community College
North Hennepin Community College

Mississippi
Northwest Mississippi Community College

Missouri
St. Louis Community College
Meramec

New Jersey
Brookdale Community College
Raritan Valley Community College
Union County College

New Mexico
Central New Mexico Community College
Dona Ana Community College of New Mexico State University
New Mexico State University
Alamogordo

New York
Hudson Valley Community College
Maria College
Monroe Community College
Onondaga Community College
Schenectady County Community College
State University of New York College of Technology at Canton

North Carolina
Guilford Technical Community College

Ohio
Columbus State Community College
Cuyahoga Community College
Metropolitan Campus
Hocking College
Kent State University
Ashtabula
East Liverpool
Salem
Stark
Trumbull
Tuscarawas
Miami University
Hamilton Campus
Middletown Campus
Owens Community College
Toledo
Sinclair Community College
University of Akron: Wayne College
University of Cincinnati
Raymond Walters College

Oklahoma
Northeastern Oklahoma Agricultural and Mechanical College

Oregon
Clackamas Community College
Linn-Benton Community College

Pennsylvania
Lackawanna College
Luzerne County Community College
Valley Forge Military Academy & College

South Carolina
Midlands Technical College
Tri-County Technical College
University of South Carolina
Salkehatchie Regional Campus

Tennessee
Roane State Community College
Southwest Tennessee Community College

Texas
Austin Community College
Houston Community College System
Lon Morris College
McLennan Community College
North Central Texas College
San Antonio College
San Jacinto College
Tarrant County College
Weatherford College

Utah
LDS Business College
Salt Lake Community College

Virginia
Piedmont Virginia Community College

Washington
Clark College
Highline Community College
South Puget Sound Community College
Spokane Community College

Wyoming
Laramie County Community College

Army ROTC

Four-year

Alabama
Alabama Agricultural and Mechanical University
Alabama State University
Auburn University
Auburn University at Montgomery
Birmingham-Southern College
Faulkner University
Huntingdon College
Jacksonville State University
Judson College
Miles College
Samford University
Spring Hill College
Talladega College
Troy University
Tuskegee University
University of Alabama
University of Alabama
Birmingham
Huntsville
University of Mobile
University of Montevallo
University of North Alabama
University of South Alabama

Alaska
University of Alaska
Fairbanks

Arizona
Arizona State University
Embry-Riddle Aeronautical University: Prescott Campus
Grand Canyon University
Northern Arizona University
University of Arizona

Arkansas
Arkansas State University
Arkansas Tech University
Central Baptist College
Henderson State University
Hendrix College
John Brown University
Ouachita Baptist University
Philander Smith College
University of Arkansas
University of Arkansas
Fort Smith
Little Rock
Monticello
Pine Bluff
University of Central Arkansas
Williams Baptist College

California
Azusa Pacific University
Biola University
California Baptist University
California Institute of Technology
California Lutheran University
California Polytechnic State University: San Luis Obispo
California State Polytechnic University: Pomona
California State University
Dominguez Hills
Fresno
Fullerton
Long Beach
Los Angeles
Northridge
Sacramento
San Bernardino
San Marcos
Chapman University
Claremont McKenna College
Harvey Mudd College
Holy Names University
The King's College and Seminary
Loyola Marymount University
Menlo College
National Hispanic University
National University
Occidental College
Pepperdine University
Pitzer College
Point Loma Nazarene University
Pomona College
St. Mary's College of California
Samuel Merritt University
San Diego Christian College
San Diego State University
San Francisco State University
San Jose State University
Santa Clara University
Scripps College
Simpson University
Sonoma State University
Stanford University
University of California
Berkeley
Davis
Irvine
Los Angeles
Riverside
Santa Barbara
Santa Cruz
University of La Verne
University of Redlands
University of San Diego
University of San Francisco
University of Southern California
Vanguard University of Southern California
Westmont College
Whittier College

Colorado
Colorado Christian University
Colorado College
Colorado School of Mines
Colorado State University
Colorado State University
Pueblo
Colorado Technical University
Metropolitan State College of Denver
Regis University
University of Colorado
Boulder
Colorado Springs
Denver
University of Denver
University of Northern Colorado

Connecticut
Central Connecticut State University
Eastern Connecticut State University
Fairfield University
Quinnipiac University
Sacred Heart University
Southern Connecticut State University
Trinity College
University of Bridgeport
University of Connecticut
University of Hartford
Western Connecticut State University
Yale University

Delaware
Delaware State University
University of Delaware
Wesley College
Wilmington University

District of Columbia
American University
Catholic University of America
George Washington University
Georgetown University
Howard University
Trinity Washington University
University of the District of Columbia

Florida
Barry University
Bethune-Cookman University
Clearwater Christian College
Eckerd College
Embry-Riddle Aeronautical University
Florida Agricultural and Mechanical University
Florida Atlantic University
Florida College
Florida Institute of Technology
Florida International University
Florida Memorial University
Florida Southern College
Florida State University
Northwest Florida State College
St. Leo University
Southeastern University
Stetson University
University of Central Florida
University of Miami
University of South Florida
University of Tampa
University of West Florida

Georgia
Agnes Scott College
Albany State University
Armstrong Atlantic State University
Augusta State University
Clark Atlanta University
Clayton State University
Columbus State University
Emory University
Fort Valley State University
Georgia College and State University
Georgia Institute of Technology
Georgia Southern University
Georgia State University
Kennesaw State University
Mercer University
Morehouse College
North Georgia College & State University
Paine College
Savannah College of Art and Design
Savannah State University
Southern Polytechnic State University
Spelman College
University of Georgia
University of West Georgia

Hawaii
Brigham Young University-Hawaii
Chaminade University of Honolulu
Hawaii Pacific University
University of Hawaii
Manoa
West Oahu

Idaho
Boise State University

Brigham Young University-Idaho
College of Idaho
Idaho State University
Lewis-Clark State College
Northwest Nazarene University
University of Idaho

Illinois
Aurora University
Benedictine University
Bradley University
Chicago State University
DePaul University
Eastern Illinois University
Elmhurst College
Governors State University
Illinois Institute of Technology
Illinois State University
Illinois Wesleyan University
Judson University
Lewis University
Loyola University Chicago
McKendree University
Monmouth College
North Central College
North Park University
Northeastern Illinois University
Northern Illinois University
Northwestern University
Olivet Nazarene University
Robert Morris College: Chicago
Southern Illinois University
  Carbondale
Southern Illinois University
  Edwardsville
University of Chicago
University of Illinois
  Chicago
  Urbana-Champaign
Western Illinois University
Wheaton College

Indiana
Ball State University
Bethel College
Butler University
DePauw University
Franklin College
Holy Cross College
Indiana State University
Indiana University
  Bloomington
  Kokomo
  Northwest
  South Bend
  Southeast
Indiana University-Purdue University Fort Wayne
Indiana University-Purdue University Indianapolis
Indiana Wesleyan University
Marian College
Purdue University
Purdue University
  Calumet
Rose-Hulman Institute of Technology
Saint Mary's College
St. Mary-of-the-Woods College
University of Indianapolis
University of Notre Dame
University of Southern Indiana
Valparaiso University

Iowa
Allen College
Briar Cliff University
Clarke College
Coe College
Drake University
Grand View University
Iowa State University
Loras College
University of Dubuque
University of Iowa
University of Northern Iowa

Kansas
Baker University
Benedictine College
Kansas State University
Manhattan Christian College
MidAmerica Nazarene University
Pittsburg State University
University of Kansas
University of St. Mary
Washburn University

Kentucky
Asbury College
Bellarmine University
Campbellsville University
Centre College
Eastern Kentucky University
Georgetown College
Kentucky Christian University
Kentucky State University
Kentucky Wesleyan College
Midway College
Morehead State University
Murray State University
Northern Kentucky University
Spalding University
Thomas More College
Transylvania University
Union College
University of Kentucky
University of Louisville
University of the Cumberlands
Western Kentucky University

Louisiana
Dillard University
Grambling State University
Louisiana College
Louisiana State University
  Alexandria
  Shreveport
Louisiana State University and Agricultural and Mechanical College
Louisiana Tech University
Loyola University New Orleans
Northwestern State University
Our Lady of Holy Cross College
Southeastern Louisiana University
Southern University
  New Orleans
Southern University and Agricultural and Mechanical College
Tulane University
University of Louisiana at Lafayette
University of Louisiana at Monroe
University of New Orleans
Xavier University of Louisiana

Maine
Colby College
Husson University
Maine Maritime Academy
New England School of Communications
St. Joseph's College
Unity College
University of Maine
University of Maine
  Augusta
University of New England
University of Southern Maine

Maryland
Bowie State University
Capitol College
College of Notre Dame of Maryland
Coppin State University
Goucher College
Hood College
Johns Hopkins University
Loyola College in Maryland
Maryland Institute College of Art
McDaniel College
Morgan State University
Mount St. Mary's University
Salisbury University
Stevenson University
Towson University
University of Baltimore
University of Maryland
  Baltimore County
  College Park

Massachusetts
American International College
Assumption College
Babson College
Bay Path College
Becker College
Bentley University
Boston College
Boston University
Brandeis University
Bridgewater State College
Clark University
College of the Holy Cross
Curry College
Elms College
Emmanuel College
Endicott College
Fitchburg State College
Framingham State College
Gordon College
Hampshire College
Harvard College
Massachusetts College of Pharmacy and Health Sciences
Massachusetts Institute of Technology
Massachusetts Maritime Academy
Mount Holyoke College
Nichols College
Northeastern University
Pine Manor College
Regis College
Salem State College
Simmons College
Smith College
Springfield College
Stonehill College
Suffolk University
Tufts University
University of Massachusetts
  Amherst
  Boston
  Dartmouth
Wellesley College
Wentworth Institute of Technology
Western New England College
Westfield State College
Wheaton College
Worcester Polytechnic Institute
Worcester State College
Zion Bible College

Michigan
Alma College
Calvin College
Central Michigan University
Concordia University
Eastern Michigan University
Ferris State University
Finlandia University
Grace Bible College
Hope College
Kalamazoo College
Kuyper College
Lawrence Technological University
Michigan State University
Michigan Technological University
Northern Michigan University
Spring Arbor University
University of Michigan
University of Michigan
  Dearborn
Wayne State University
Western Michigan University

Minnesota
Augsburg College
Bethany Lutheran College
Bethel University
College of St. Benedict
College of St. Catherine
Concordia College: Moorhead
Concordia University: St. Paul
Gustavus Adolphus College
Macalester College
Minnesota State University
  Mankato
  Moorhead
Northwestern College
Saint Cloud State University
St. John's University
St. Mary's University of Minnesota
University of Minnesota
  Twin Cities
University of St. Thomas
Winona State University

Mississippi
Alcorn State University
Belhaven College
Delta State University
Jackson State University
Millsaps College
Mississippi College
Mississippi State University
Mississippi University for Women
Mississippi Valley State University
Tougaloo College
University of Mississippi
University of Southern Mississippi
William Carey University

Missouri
Avila University
Calvary Bible College and Theological Seminary
Central Bible College
Central Methodist University
College of the Ozarks
Columbia College
Drury University
Evangel University
Fontbonne University
Harris-Stowe State University
Lincoln University
Lindenwood University
Maryville University of Saint Louis
Missouri Baptist University
Missouri State University
Missouri Valley College
Missouri Western State University
Northwest Missouri State University
Park University
Research College of Nursing
Rockhurst University
Saint Louis University
Southwest Baptist University
Stephens College
Truman State University
University of Central Missouri
University of Missouri
  Columbia
  Kansas City
  Missouri University of Science and Technology
  St. Louis
Washington University in St. Louis
Webster University
Westminster College
William Jewell College
William Woods University

Montana
Carroll College
Montana State University
  Billings
  Bozeman
University of Montana

Nebraska
Bellevue University
Chadron State College
Clarkson College
College of Saint Mary
Concordia University
Creighton University
Doane College
Nebraska Methodist College of Nursing and Allied Health
Nebraska Wesleyan University
University of Nebraska
  Lincoln
  Medical Center
  Omaha
Wayne State College
York College

Nevada
Sierra Nevada College
University of Nevada
  Las Vegas
  Reno

New Hampshire
Colby-Sawyer College
Daniel Webster College
Dartmouth College
Franklin Pierce University
Granite State College
New England College
Plymouth State University
Rivier College
St. Anselm College
Southern New Hampshire University
University of New Hampshire
University of New Hampshire at Manchester

New Jersey
Bloomfield College
Caldwell College
The College of New Jersey
Fairleigh Dickinson University
  College at Florham
  Metropolitan Campus
Kean University
Montclair State University
New Jersey Institute of Technology
Princeton University
Rider University
Rowan University
Rutgers, The State University of New Jersey
  Camden Regional Campus
  New Brunswick/Piscataway Campus
  Newark Regional Campus
Saint Peter's College
Seton Hall University
Stevens Institute of Technology

New Mexico
New Mexico State University
University of New Mexico

New York
Adelphi University
Albany College of Pharmacy and Health Sciences
Alfred University
Canisius College
Cazenovia College
City University of New York
  Baruch College
  Lehman College
  Queens College
Clarkson University
Colgate University
College of New Rochelle
College of Saint Rose
Columbia University
  School of General Studies
Cornell University
D'Youville College

Daemen College
Dowling College
Elmira College
Fordham University
Hamilton College
Hilbert College
Hofstra University
Houghton College
Iona College
Ithaca College
Jewish Theological Seminary of America
Le Moyne College
Long Island University
 Brooklyn Campus
 C. W. Post Campus
Manhattan College
Marist College
Medaille College
Mercy College
Molloy College
Monroe College
Nazareth College of Rochester
New York Institute of Technology
New York University
Niagara University
Pace University
Polytechnic Institute of New York University
Rensselaer Polytechnic Institute
Roberts Wesleyan College
Rochester Institute of Technology
Russell Sage College
Sage College of Albany
Saint Bonaventure University
St. Francis College
St. John Fisher College
St. John's University
St. Joseph's College: Suffolk Campus
St. Lawrence University
Siena College
Skidmore College
State University of New York
 Albany
 Binghamton
 Buffalo
 College at Brockport
 College at Buffalo
 College at Cortland
 College at Geneseo
 College at Old Westbury
 College at Plattsburgh
 College at Potsdam
 College of Environmental Science and Forestry
 Institute of Technology at Utica/Rome
 Maritime College
 Oswego
 Stony Brook
 Upstate Medical University
Syracuse University
Union College
University of Rochester
Utica College
Vaughn College of Aeronautics and Technology
Wagner College
Wells College

North Carolina

Appalachian State University
Belmont Abbey College
Bennett College
Campbell University
Catawba College
Davidson College
Duke University
East Carolina University
Elizabeth City State University
Elon University
Fayetteville State University
Gardner-Webb University
Greensboro College
Guilford College
High Point University
Johnson C. Smith University
Lenoir-Rhyne University
Livingstone College
Meredith College
Methodist University
North Carolina Agricultural and Technical State University
North Carolina Central University
North Carolina State University
North Carolina Wesleyan College
Peace College
Pfeiffer University
Queens University of Charlotte
St. Augustine's College
Salem College
Shaw University
University of North Carolina
 Chapel Hill
 Charlotte
 Greensboro
 Pembroke
Wake Forest University
Wingate University
Winston-Salem State University

North Dakota

Mayville State University
North Dakota State University
University of North Dakota

Ohio

Baldwin-Wallace College
Bowling Green State University
Capital University
Case Western Reserve University
Cedarville University
Central State University
Cleveland Institute of Art
Cleveland State University
College of Mount St. Joseph
Denison University
DeVry University
 Columbus
Franciscan University of Steubenville
Franklin University
Heidelberg University
John Carroll University
Kent State University
Lourdes College
Malone University
Miami University
 Oxford Campus
Mount Union College
Notre Dame College
Ohio Dominican University
Ohio Northern University
Ohio State University
 Columbus Campus
 Lima Campus
 Mansfield Campus
 Marion Campus
 Newark Campus
Ohio University
Ohio University
 Lancaster Campus
Ohio Wesleyan University
Otterbein College
Tiffin University
University of Akron
University of Cincinnati
University of Dayton
University of Findlay
University of Rio Grande
University of Toledo
Urbana University
Ursuline College
Wilberforce University
Wittenberg University
Wright State University
Xavier University
Youngstown State University

Oklahoma

Cameron University
Langston University
Northeastern State University
Oklahoma Christian University
Oklahoma City University
Oklahoma State University
Southern Nazarene University
University of Central Oklahoma
University of Oklahoma

Oregon

Corban College
Eastern Oregon University
Northwest Christian University
Oregon Institute of Technology
Oregon State University
Pacific University
Portland State University
University of Oregon
University of Portland
Warner Pacific College
Western Oregon University

Pennsylvania

Alvernia University
Arcadia University
Bloomsburg University of Pennsylvania
Bucknell University
Cabrini College
California University of Pennsylvania
Carlow University
Carnegie Mellon University
Cedar Crest College
Chatham University
Cheyney University of Pennsylvania
Clarion University of Pennsylvania
DeSales University
Dickinson College
Drexel University
Duquesne University
East Stroudsburg University of Pennsylvania
Eastern University
Edinboro University of Pennsylvania
Gannon University
Geneva College
Gettysburg College
Indiana University of Pennsylvania
Keystone College
King's College
Kutztown University of Pennsylvania
La Roche College
La Salle University
Lafayette College
Lebanon Valley College
Lehigh University
Lincoln University
Lock Haven University of Pennsylvania
Lycoming College
Marywood University
Millersville University of Pennsylvania
Misericordia University
Moravian College
Muhlenberg College
Neumann College
Penn State
 Abington
 Altoona
 Berks
 Brandywine
 Erie, The Behrend College
 Harrisburg
 Hazleton
 Lehigh Valley
 Mont Alto
 University Park
 Wilkes-Barre
 Worthington Scranton
Pennsylvania College of Technology
Point Park University
Robert Morris University
Rosemont College
St. Francis University
Saint Joseph's University
St. Vincent College
Seton Hill University
Shippensburg University of Pennsylvania
Slippery Rock University of Pennsylvania
Susquehanna University
Swarthmore College
Temple University
University of Pennsylvania
University of Pittsburgh
University of Pittsburgh
 Bradford
 Greensburg
University of Scranton
University of the Sciences in Philadelphia
Villanova University
Washington & Jefferson College
Waynesburg University
West Chester University of Pennsylvania
Westminster College
Widener University
Wilkes University
Wilson College
York College of Pennsylvania

Puerto Rico

American University of Puerto Rico
Bayamon Central University
Caribbean University
Inter American University of Puerto Rico
 Aguadilla Campus
 Arecibo Campus
 Bayamon Campus
 Guayama Campus
 Metropolitan Campus
 San German Campus
Pontifical Catholic University of Puerto Rico
Turabo University
Universidad del Este
Universidad Metropolitana
Universidad Politecnica de Puerto Rico
University of Puerto Rico
 Aguadilla
 Arecibo
 Bayamon University College
 Cayey University College
 Mayaguez
 Ponce
 Rio Piedras
 Utuado

Rhode Island

Brown University
Bryant University
Johnson & Wales University: Providence
Providence College
Rhode Island College
Roger Williams University
Salve Regina University
University of Rhode Island

South Carolina

Allen University
Anderson University
Benedict College
The Citadel
Claflin University
Clemson University
Coastal Carolina University
Columbia College
Converse College
Furman University
Lander University
Limestone College
Morris College
Newberry College
North Greenville University
Presbyterian College
South Carolina State University
Southern Wesleyan University
University of South Carolina
University of South Carolina Upstate
Winthrop University
Wofford College

South Dakota

Black Hills State University
Dakota State University
Mount Marty College
National American University Rapid City
South Dakota School of Mines and Technology
South Dakota State University
University of South Dakota

Tennessee

Austin Peay State University
Belmont University
Carson-Newman College
Christian Brothers University
Cumberland University
East Tennessee State University
Fisk University
Free Will Baptist Bible College
King College
Lambuth University
LeMoyne-Owen College
Lipscomb University
Middle Tennessee State University
Milligan College
Rhodes College
Tennessee Technological University
Tennessee Wesleyan College
Trevecca Nazarene University
University of Memphis
University of Tennessee
 Chattanooga
 Knoxville
 Martin
Vanderbilt University

Texas

Baylor University
College of Saint Thomas More
Concordia University Texas
Dallas Baptist University
Houston Baptist University
Huston-Tillotson University
Lubbock Christian University
Our Lady of the Lake University of San Antonio
Prairie View A&M University
Rice University
St. Edward's University
St. Mary's University
Sam Houston State University
Southern Methodist University
Southwestern Assemblies of God University
Stephen F. Austin State University
Tarleton State University
Texas A&M University
Texas A&M University
 Corpus Christi
 Kingsville
Texas Christian University
Texas Lutheran University
Texas Southern University
Texas State University: San Marcos
Texas Tech University
Texas Wesleyan University
Texas Woman's University
University of Dallas
University of Houston
University of Houston Downtown
University of North Texas
University of St. Thomas

University of Texas
Arlington
Austin
Brownsville - Texas Southmost College
Dallas
El Paso
Pan American
San Antonio
University of the Incarnate Word
Wayland Baptist University

Utah
Brigham Young University
Dixie State College of Utah
Southern Utah University
University of Utah
Utah State University
Utah Valley University
Weber State University
Westminster College

Vermont
Castleton State College
Champlain College
Johnson State College
Middlebury College
Norwich University
St. Michael's College
University of Vermont
Vermont Technical College

Virginia
Christopher Newport University
College of William and Mary
George Mason University
Hampden-Sydney College
Hampton University
James Madison University
Liberty University
Longwood University
Lynchburg College
Mary Baldwin College
Marymount University
Norfolk State University
Old Dominion University
Radford University
Randolph-Macon College
Regent University
St. Paul's College
Southern Virginia University
University of Mary Washington
University of Richmond
University of Virginia
Virginia Commonwealth University
Virginia Military Institute
Virginia Polytechnic Institute and State University
Virginia State University
Virginia Union University
Virginia Wesleyan College
Washington and Lee University

Washington
Central Washington University
DeVry University
Federal Way
Eastern Washington University
Gonzaga University
Northwest University
Pacific Lutheran University
Saint Martin's University
Seattle Pacific University
Seattle University
University of Puget Sound
University of Washington
Washington State University
Whitworth University

West Virginia
Fairmont State University
Marshall University
University of Charleston
West Liberty State College
West Virginia State University
West Virginia University
West Virginia University Institute of Technology

Wisconsin
Alverno College
Carroll University
Carthage College
Edgewood College
Maranatha Baptist Bible College
Marian University
Marquette University
Milwaukee School of Engineering
Mount Mary College
Ripon College
St. Norbert College
University of Wisconsin
Eau Claire
Green Bay
La Crosse
Madison
Milwaukee
Oshkosh
Parkside
River Falls
Stevens Point
Stout
Whitewater
Viterbo University
Wisconsin Lutheran College

Wyoming
University of Wyoming

Guam
University of Guam

Virgin Islands, U.S.
University of the Virgin Islands

Northern Mariana Islands
Northern Marianas College

Republic of Korea
Yonsei University

Two-year

Alabama
Bishop State Community College
Chattahoochee Valley Community College
Gadsden State Community College
Jefferson State Community College
Marion Military Institute
Northwest-Shoals Community College
Shelton State Community College

Arizona
Coconino County Community College
Gateway Community College
Mesa Community College
Paradise Valley Community College
Phoenix College
Pima Community College
Yavapai College

Arkansas
Arkansas State University
Mountain Home
Northwest Arkansas Community College
Ouachita Technical College

California
Chabot College
City College of San Francisco
College of San Mateo
Cuyamaca College
De Anza College
Diablo Valley College
El Camino College
Foothill College
Fresno City College
Los Angeles City College
Los Angeles Mission College
MiraCosta College
Mount San Jacinto College
Riverside Community College
Sacramento City College
San Diego City College
West Valley College

Colorado
Arapahoe Community College
Community College of Denver
Front Range Community College
Red Rocks Community College

Connecticut
Capital Community College
Tunxis Community College

Florida
Brevard Community College
Broward College
Daytona State College
Hillsborough Community College
Miami Dade College
Pasco-Hernando Community College
Pensacola Junior College
Polk Community College
Santa Fe College
South Florida Community College
Tallahassee Community College
Valencia Community College

Georgia
East Georgia College
Georgia Military College

Hawaii
University of Hawaii
Honolulu Community College
Leeward Community College
Windward Community College

Idaho
North Idaho College

Illinois
Carl Sandburg College
John A. Logan College
Kankakee Community College
Kishwaukee College
Lewis and Clark Community College
Lincoln Land Community College
Parkland College
Shawnee Community College
Spoon River College
Waubonsee Community College

Indiana
Vincennes University

Iowa
Hawkeye Community College
Iowa Western Community College

Kentucky
Elizabethtown Community and Technical College
Jefferson Community and Technical College

Louisiana
Delgado Community College

Maryland
Allegany College of Maryland
Prince George's Community College

Massachusetts
Holyoke Community College
Quinsigamond Community College
Roxbury Community College

Michigan
Lansing Community College
Washtenaw Community College

Minnesota
Anoka-Ramsey Community College
Lake Superior College
Normandale Community College
North Hennepin Community College

Mississippi
Hinds Community College

Missouri
St. Louis Community College
Florissant Valley
Meramec
State Fair Community College
Wentworth Military Junior College

Nevada
College of Southern Nevada
Truckee Meadows Community College

New Jersey
Brookdale Community College
Middlesex County College
Raritan Valley Community College

New Mexico
Central New Mexico Community College
Dona Ana Community College of New Mexico State University
New Mexico Military Institute

New York
Erie Community College
City Campus
North Campus
South Campus
Finger Lakes Community College
Herkimer County Community College
Hudson Valley Community College
Maria College
Mohawk Valley Community College
Monroe Community College
Nassau Community College
Niagara County Community College
Onondaga Community College
Orange County Community College
State University of New York
College of Agriculture and Technology at Morrisville
College of Technology at Alfred
College of Technology at Canton

North Carolina
College of the Albemarle
Guilford Technical Community College
Pitt Community College

Ohio
Cincinnati State Technical and Community College
Columbus State Community College
Hocking College
Kent State University
Ashtabula
East Liverpool
Salem
Stark
Trumbull
Tuscarawas
Owens Community College
Toledo
Sinclair Community College
University of Akron: Wayne College
University of Cincinnati
Clermont College
Raymond Walters College

Oregon
Central Oregon Community College
Linn-Benton Community College

Pennsylvania
Community College of Philadelphia
Harrisburg Area Community College
Lackawanna College
Lehigh Carbon Community College
Valley Forge Military Academy & College

Rhode Island
Community College of Rhode Island

South Carolina
Denmark Technical College
Midlands Technical College
Orangeburg-Calhoun Technical College
Spartanburg Methodist College
Tri-County Technical College
University of South Carolina
Lancaster
Salkehatchie Regional Campus
Sumter

Tennessee
Jackson State Community College
Pellissippi State Technical Community College
Roane State Community College
Southwest Tennessee Community College
Walters State Community College

Texas
Angelina College
Austin Community College
Central Texas College
Collin County Community College District
Del Mar College
El Centro College
El Paso Community College
Houston Community College System
Laredo Community College
Lon Morris College
St. Philip's College
San Antonio College
Tarrant County College

Utah
LDS Business College
Salt Lake Community College

Virginia
J. Sargeant Reynolds Community College
John Tyler Community College
Piedmont Virginia Community College
Richard Bland College
Southside Virginia Community College
Thomas Nelson Community College

Washington
Clark College
Highline Community College
Pierce College
Spokane Community College
Spokane Falls Community College

Wyoming
Laramie County Community College

American Samoa
American Samoa Community College

Guam
Guam Community College

Naval ROTC

Four-year

Alabama
Auburn University

Arizona
Southwestern College
University of Arizona

California
California Maritime Academy
California State University
San Marcos
The King's College and Seminary
National Hispanic University
National University
Point Loma Nazarene University
Samuel Merritt University
San Diego State University
San Francisco State University
Sonoma State University
Stanford University
University of California
Berkeley
Davis
Los Angeles
Santa Cruz
University of Redlands
University of San Diego
University of Southern California

Colorado
Regis University
University of Colorado
Boulder

District of Columbia
Catholic University of America
George Washington University
Georgetown University
University of the District of Columbia

Florida
Clearwater Christian College
Embry-Riddle Aeronautical University
Florida Agricultural and Mechanical University
Florida State University
Jacksonville University
University of North Florida
University of South Florida
University of Tampa

Georgia
Armstrong Atlantic State University
Clark Atlanta University
Clayton State University
Emory University
Georgia Institute of Technology
Georgia State University
Morehouse College
Savannah State University
Southern Polytechnic State University
Spelman College

Hawaii
Brigham Young University-Hawaii

Idaho
Lewis-Clark State College
University of Idaho

Illinois
Illinois Institute of Technology
Judson University
Loyola University Chicago
Northwestern University
University of Illinois
Chicago
Urbana-Champaign

Indiana
Bethel College
Indiana University
South Bend
Indiana University-Purdue University Indianapolis
Purdue University
Saint Mary's College
University of Notre Dame

Iowa
Iowa State University

Kansas
University of Kansas
Washburn University

Louisiana
Dillard University
Louisiana State University and Agricultural and Mechanical College
Louisiana Tech University
Loyola University New Orleans
Our Lady of Holy Cross College
Southern University
New Orleans
Southern University and Agricultural and Mechanical College
Tulane University
University of New Orleans
Xavier University of Louisiana

Maine
Husson University
Maine Maritime Academy
University of Maine
University of Maine
Augusta

Maryland
University of Maryland
College Park

Massachusetts
Babson College
Becker College
Boston College
Boston University
Clark University
College of the Holy Cross
Harvard College
Massachusetts College of Pharmacy and Health Sciences
Massachusetts Institute of Technology
Massachusetts Maritime Academy
Northeastern University
Tufts University
University of Massachusetts
Boston
Worcester Polytechnic Institute
Worcester State College

Michigan
Eastern Michigan University
Finlandia University
Lawrence Technological University
University of Michigan
University of Michigan
Dearborn

Minnesota
Augsburg College
Concordia University: St. Paul
Macalester College
University of Minnesota
Twin Cities
University of St. Thomas

Mississippi
Tougaloo College
University of Mississippi

Missouri
Columbia College
Lincoln University
Stephens College
University of Missouri
Columbia
Missouri University of Science and Technology
William Woods University

Montana
Montana State University
Billings

Nebraska
University of Nebraska
Lincoln
York College

New Hampshire
Rivier College

New Jersey
Montclair State University

New Mexico
National American University: Rio Rancho
University of New Mexico

New York
Albany College of Pharmacy and Health Sciences
City University of New York
Queens College
College of New Rochelle
College of Saint Rose
Columbia University
Cornell University
Dowling College
Eastman School of Music of the University of Rochester
Fordham University
Jewish Theological Seminary of America
Molloy College
New York University
Rensselaer Polytechnic Institute
Rochester Institute of Technology
Russell Sage College
St. John Fisher College
Siena College
State University of New York
College at Brockport
Maritime College
Union College
University of Rochester

North Carolina
Belmont Abbey College
Duke University
Guilford College
Lenoir-Rhyne University
North Carolina State University
Peace College
University of North Carolina
Chapel Hill

Ohio
Cleveland Institute of Art
Cleveland State University
Miami University
Oxford Campus
Ohio State University
Columbus Campus
Lima Campus
Mansfield Campus
Marion Campus
Newark Campus
Ohio University
Lancaster Campus

Oklahoma
University of Oklahoma

Oregon
Oregon State University
Warner Pacific College
Western Oregon University

Pennsylvania
Carlow University
Carnegie Mellon University
Chatham University
Drexel University
Duquesne University
Penn State
University Park
Saint Joseph's University
Swarthmore College
Temple University
Thomas Jefferson University: College of Health Professions
University of Pennsylvania
University of Pittsburgh
Villanova University
Widener University

Puerto Rico
Caribbean University
Inter American University of Puerto Rico
Bayamon Campus
Ponce Campus
Universidad Metropolitana

South Carolina
The Citadel
University of South Carolina

Tennessee
Belmont University
Christian Brothers University
Fisk University
Tennessee Wesleyan College
University of Memphis
Vanderbilt University

Texas
Houston Baptist University
Prairie View A&M University
Rice University
Texas A&M University
Texas A&M University
Galveston
University of Houston
University of Texas
Austin

Utah
University of Utah
Weber State University
Westminster College

Vermont
Norwich University

Virginia
George Mason University
Hampton University
Mary Baldwin College
Norfolk State University
Old Dominion University
University of Virginia
Virginia Military Institute
Virginia Polytechnic Institute and State University

Washington
Seattle Pacific University
Seattle University
University of Washington
Washington State University

Wisconsin
Marquette University
Milwaukee School of Engineering
Mount Mary College
University of Wisconsin
Madison
Wisconsin Lutheran College

Two-year

Arizona
Gateway Community College
Mesa Community College
Pima Community College

California
Contra Costa College
Diablo Valley College
Foothill College
Fullerton College
Los Angeles City College
Mission College
Riverside Community College
Sacramento City College

Connecticut
Capital Community College
Tunxis Community College

Florida
Florida Community College at Jacksonville
Pasco-Hernando Community College
Tallahassee Community College

Hawaii
University of Hawaii
Hawaii Community College

Illinois
Lincoln Land Community College
Parkland College
Shawnee Community College

Iowa
Hawkeye Community College

Minnesota
Anoka-Ramsey Community College
Lake Superior College
Normandale Community College
North Hennepin Community College

Mississippi
East Mississippi Community College

New Mexico
Central New Mexico Community College

New York
Maria College
Monroe Community College

North Carolina
Guilford Technical Community College

Ohio
Cuyahoga Community College
Metropolitan Campus
Miami University
Hamilton Campus
Middletown Campus
University of Cincinnati
Raymond Walters College

South Carolina
Midlands Technical College
University of South Carolina
Salkehatchie Regional Campus

Texas
Lon Morris College

Virginia
New River Community College

Washington
Spokane Community College

Colleges with NCAA sports

Baseball Division I

Alabama
Alabama Agricultural and Mechanical University M
Alabama State University M
Auburn University M
Jacksonville State University M
Samford University M
Troy University M
University of Alabama M
University of Alabama
  Birmingham M
University of South Alabama M

Arizona
Arizona State University M
University of Arizona M

Arkansas
Arkansas State University M
University of Arkansas M
University of Arkansas
  Little Rock M
  Pine Bluff M
University of Central Arkansas M

California
California Polytechnic State University: San Luis Obispo M
California State University
  Fresno M
  Fullerton M
  Long Beach M
  Northridge M
  Sacramento M
Loyola Marymount University M
Pepperdine University M
St. Mary's College of California M
San Diego State University M
San Jose State University M
Santa Clara University M
Stanford University M
University of California
  Berkeley M
  Davis M
  Irvine M
  Los Angeles M
  Riverside M
  Santa Barbara M
University of San Diego M
University of San Francisco M
University of Southern California M
University of the Pacific M

Colorado
United States Air Force Academy M
University of Northern Colorado M

Connecticut
Central Connecticut State University M
Fairfield University M
Quinnipiac University M
Sacred Heart University M
University of Connecticut M
University of Hartford M
Yale University M

Delaware
Delaware State University M
University of Delaware M

District of Columbia
George Washington University M
Georgetown University M

Florida
Bethune-Cookman University M
Florida Agricultural and Mechanical University M
Florida Atlantic University M
Florida Gulf Coast University M
Florida International University M
Florida State University M
Jacksonville University M
Stetson University M
University of Central Florida M
University of Florida M
University of Miami M
University of North Florida M
University of South Florida M

Georgia
Georgia Institute of Technology M
Georgia Southern University M
Georgia State University M
Kennesaw State University M
Mercer University M
Savannah State University M
University of Georgia M

Hawaii
University of Hawaii
  Manoa M

Illinois
Bradley University M
Chicago State University M
Eastern Illinois University M
Illinois State University M
Northern Illinois University M
Northwestern University M
Southern Illinois University
  Carbondale M
Southern Illinois University
  Edwardsville M
University of Illinois
  Chicago M
  Urbana-Champaign M
Western Illinois University M

Indiana
Ball State University M
Butler University M
Indiana State University M
Indiana University
  Bloomington M
Indiana University-Purdue University Fort Wayne M
Purdue University M
University of Evansville M
University of Notre Dame M
Valparaiso University M

Iowa
University of Iowa M
University of Northern Iowa M

Kansas
Kansas State University M
University of Kansas M
Wichita State University M

Kentucky
Eastern Kentucky University M
Morehead State University M
Murray State University M
University of Kentucky M
University of Louisville M
Western Kentucky University M

Louisiana
Centenary College of Louisiana M
Grambling State University M
Louisiana State University and Agricultural and Mechanical College M
Louisiana Tech University M
McNeese State University M
Nicholls State University M
Northwestern State University M
Southeastern Louisiana University M
Southern University and Agricultural and Mechanical College M
Tulane University M
University of Louisiana at Lafayette M
University of Louisiana at Monroe M
University of New Orleans M

Maine
University of Maine M

Maryland
Coppin State University M
Mount St. Mary's University M
Towson University M
United States Naval Academy M
University of Maryland
  Baltimore County M
  College Park M
  Eastern Shore M

Massachusetts
Boston College M
College of the Holy Cross M
Harvard College M
Northeastern University M
University of Massachusetts
  Amherst M

Michigan
Central Michigan University M
Eastern Michigan University M
Michigan State University M
Oakland University M
University of Michigan M
Western Michigan University M

Minnesota
University of Minnesota
  Twin Cities M

Mississippi
Alcorn State University M
Jackson State University M
Mississippi State University M
Mississippi Valley State University M
University of Mississippi M
University of Southern Mississippi M

Missouri
Missouri State University M
Saint Louis University M
Southeast Missouri State University M
University of Missouri
  Columbia M

Nebraska
Creighton University M
University of Nebraska
  Lincoln M

Nevada
University of Nevada
  Las Vegas M
  Reno M

New Hampshire
Dartmouth College M

New Jersey
Fairleigh Dickinson University
  Metropolitan Campus M
Monmouth University M
New Jersey Institute of Technology M
Princeton University M
Rider University M
Rutgers, The State University of New Jersey
  New Brunswick/Piscataway Campus M
Saint Peter's College M
Seton Hall University M

New Mexico
New Mexico State University M
University of New Mexico M

New York
Canisius College M
Cornell University M
Fordham University M
Hofstra University M
Iona College M
Le Moyne College M
Long Island University
  Brooklyn Campus M
Manhattan College M
Marist College M
New York Institute of Technology M
Niagara University M
Saint Bonaventure University M
St. John's University M
Siena College M
State University of New York
  Albany M
  Binghamton M
  Buffalo M
  Stony Brook M
United States Military Academy M
Wagner College M

North Carolina
Appalachian State University M
Campbell University M
Davidson College M
Duke University M
East Carolina University M
Elon University M
Gardner-Webb University M
High Point University M
North Carolina Agricultural and Technical State University M
North Carolina Central University M
North Carolina State University M
University of North Carolina
  Asheville M
  Chapel Hill M
  Charlotte M
  Greensboro M
  Wilmington M
Wake Forest University M
Western Carolina University M

North Dakota
North Dakota State University M
University of North Dakota M

Ohio
Bowling Green State University M
Cleveland State University M
Kent State University M
Miami University
  Oxford Campus M
Ohio State University
  Columbus Campus M
Ohio University M
University of Akron M
University of Cincinnati M
University of Dayton M
University of Toledo M
Wright State University M
Xavier University M
Youngstown State University M

Oklahoma
Oklahoma State University M
Oral Roberts University M
University of Oklahoma M

Oregon
Oregon State University M
University of Oregon M
University of Portland M

Pennsylvania
Bucknell University M
Duquesne University M
La Salle University M
Lafayette College M
Lehigh University M
Penn State
  University Park M
Saint Joseph's University M
Temple University M
University of Pennsylvania M
University of Pittsburgh M
Villanova University M

Rhode Island
Brown University M
Bryant University M
University of Rhode Island M

South Carolina
Charleston Southern University M
The Citadel M
Clemson University M
Coastal Carolina University M
College of Charleston M
Furman University M
Presbyterian College M
University of South Carolina M
University of South Carolina
  Upstate M
Winthrop University M
Wofford College M

South Dakota
South Dakota State University M

Tennessee
Austin Peay State University M
Belmont University M
East Tennessee State University M
Lipscomb University M
Middle Tennessee State University M
Tennessee Technological University M
University of Memphis M
University of Tennessee
  Knoxville M
  Martin M
Vanderbilt University M

Texas
Baylor University M
Dallas Baptist University M
Houston Baptist University M
Lamar University M
Prairie View A&M University M
Rice University M
Sam Houston State University M
Stephen F. Austin State University M
Texas A&M University M
Texas A&M University
  Corpus Christi M
Texas Christian University M
Texas Southern University M
Texas State University: San Marcos M
Texas Tech University M
University of Houston M
University of Texas
  Arlington M
  Austin M
  Pan American M
  San Antonio M

Utah
Brigham Young University M
Southern Utah University M
University of Utah M
Utah Valley University M

Vermont
University of Vermont M

Virginia
College of William and Mary M
George Mason University M
James Madison University M
Liberty University M
Longwood University M

Norfolk State University M
Old Dominion University M
Radford University M
University of Richmond M
University of Virginia M
Virginia Commonwealth University M
Virginia Military Institute M
Virginia Polytechnic Institute and State University M

Washington
Gonzaga University M
University of Washington M
Washington State University M

West Virginia
Marshall University M
West Virginia University M

Wisconsin
University of Wisconsin
Milwaukee M

Baseball Division II

Alabama
Miles College M
Tuskegee University M
University of Alabama
Huntsville M
University of Montevallo M
University of North Alabama M
University of West Alabama M

Arizona
Grand Canyon University M

Arkansas
Arkansas Tech University M
Harding University M
Henderson State University M
Ouachita Baptist University M
Southern Arkansas University M
University of Arkansas
Monticello M

California
California State Polytechnic University: Pomona M
California State University
Chico M
Dominguez Hills M
Los Angeles M
Monterey Bay M
San Bernardino M
Stanislaus M
San Francisco State University M
Sonoma State University M
University of California
San Diego M

Colorado
Colorado Christian University M
Colorado School of Mines M
Colorado State University
Pueblo M
Mesa State College M
Metropolitan State College of Denver M
Regis University M

Connecticut
Post University M
Southern Connecticut State University M
University of Bridgeport M
University of New Haven M

Delaware
Wilmington University M

Florida
Barry University M
Eckerd College M
Flagler College M
Florida Institute of Technology M
Florida Southern College M
Lynn University M
Nova Southeastern University M
Palm Beach Atlantic University M
Rollins College M
St. Leo University M
University of Tampa M
University of West Florida M

Georgia
Albany State University M
Armstrong Atlantic State University M
Augusta State University M
Clark Atlanta University M
Columbus State University M
Georgia College and State University M
Georgia Southwestern State University M
Morehouse College M
North Georgia College & State University M
Paine College M
University of West Georgia M
Valdosta State University M

Hawaii
Hawaii Pacific University M
University of Hawaii
Hilo M

Idaho
Northwest Nazarene University M

Illinois
Lewis University M
Quincy University M

Indiana
Oakland City University M
Saint Joseph's College M
University of Indianapolis M
University of Southern Indiana M

Iowa
Upper Iowa University M

Kansas
Emporia State University M
Fort Hays State University M
Newman University M
Pittsburg State University M
Washburn University M

Kentucky
Bellarmine University M
Kentucky State University M
Kentucky Wesleyan College M
Northern Kentucky University M

Maryland
Columbia Union College M

Massachusetts
American International College M
Assumption College M
Bentley University M
Merrimack College M
Stonehill College M
University of Massachusetts
Lowell M

Michigan
Grand Valley State University M
Hillsdale College M
Northwood University: Michigan M
Saginaw Valley State University M
Wayne State University M

Minnesota
Bemidji State University M
Concordia University: St. Paul M
Minnesota State University
Mankato M
Saint Cloud State University M
Southwest Minnesota State University M
University of Minnesota
Crookston M
Duluth M
Winona State University M

Mississippi
Delta State University M

Missouri
Drury University M
Lincoln University M
Missouri Southern State University M
Missouri Western State University M
Northwest Missouri State University M
Rockhurst University M
Southwest Baptist University M
Truman State University M
University of Central Missouri M
University of Missouri
Missouri University of Science and Technology M
St. Louis M

Montana
Montana State University
Billings M

Nebraska
University of Nebraska
Kearney M
Omaha M
Wayne State College M

New Hampshire
Franklin Pierce University M
St. Anselm College M
Southern New Hampshire University M

New Jersey
Bloomfield College M
Caldwell College M
Felician College M

New Mexico
Eastern New Mexico University M
New Mexico Highlands University M

New York
Adelphi University M
City University of New York
Queens College M
College of Saint Rose M
Concordia College M
Dominican College of Blauvelt M
Dowling College M
Long Island University
C. W. Post Campus M
Mercy College M
Molloy College M
Nyack College M
Pace University M
St. Thomas Aquinas College M

North Carolina
Barton College M
Belmont Abbey College M
Brevard College M
Catawba College M
Chowan University M
Elizabeth City State University M
Lenoir-Rhyne University M
Mars Hill College M
Mount Olive College M
Pfeiffer University M
St. Andrews Presbyterian College M
St. Augustine's College M
Shaw University M
University of North Carolina
Pembroke M
Wingate University M

North Dakota
University of Mary M

Ohio
Ashland University M
Tiffin University M
University of Findlay M

Oklahoma
Cameron University M
East Central University M
Northeastern State University M
Oklahoma Panhandle State University M
Southeastern Oklahoma State University M
Southwestern Oklahoma State University M
University of Central Oklahoma M

Oregon
Western Oregon University M

Pennsylvania
Bloomsburg University of Pennsylvania M
California University of Pennsylvania M
Chestnut Hill College M
Clarion University of Pennsylvania M
East Stroudsburg University of Pennsylvania M
Gannon University M
Indiana University of Pennsylvania M
Kutztown University of Pennsylvania M
Lock Haven University of Pennsylvania M
Mansfield University of Pennsylvania M
Mercyhurst College M
Millersville University of Pennsylvania M
Philadelphia University M
Seton Hill University M
Shippensburg University of Pennsylvania M
Slippery Rock University of Pennsylvania M
University of Pittsburgh
Johnstown M
University of the Sciences in Philadelphia M
West Chester University of Pennsylvania M

Puerto Rico
University of Puerto Rico
Cayey University College M
Mayaguez M
Rio Piedras M

South Carolina
Anderson University M
Benedict College M
Claflin University M
Erskine College M
Francis Marion University M
Lander University M
Limestone College M
Newberry College M
North Greenville University M
University of South Carolina
Aiken M

South Dakota
Augustana College M
Northern State University M

Tennessee
Carson-Newman College M
Christian Brothers University M
Lane College M
LeMoyne-Owen College M
Lincoln Memorial University M
Tusculum College M

Texas
Abilene Christian University M
Angelo State University M
St. Edward's University M
St. Mary's University M
Tarleton State University M
Texas A&M International University M
Texas A&M University
Kingsville M
University of Texas
of the Permian Basin M
University of the Incarnate Word M
West Texas A&M University M

Utah
Dixie State College of Utah M

Vermont
St. Michael's College M

Virginia
St. Paul's College M
Virginia State University M

Washington
Central Washington University M
Saint Martin's University M

West Virginia
Alderson-Broaddus College M
Bluefield State College M
Concord University M
Davis and Elkins College M
Fairmont State University M
Ohio Valley University M
Salem International University M
Shepherd University M
University of Charleston M
West Liberty State College M
West Virginia State University M
West Virginia Wesleyan College M
Wheeling Jesuit University M

Wisconsin
University of Wisconsin
Parkside M

Baseball Division III

Alabama
Birmingham-Southern College M
Huntingdon College M

Arkansas
Hendrix College M
University of the Ozarks M

California
California Institute of Technology M
California Lutheran University M
California State University
East Bay M
Chapman University M
Claremont McKenna College M
La Sierra University M
Menlo College M
Occidental College M
Pomona College M
University of La Verne M
University of Redlands M
Whittier College M

Connecticut
Albertus Magnus College M
Eastern Connecticut State University M
Mitchell College M
Trinity College M
United States Coast Guard Academy M
Wesleyan University M
Western Connecticut State University M

Delaware
Wesley College M

District of Columbia
Catholic University of America M
Gallaudet University M

Georgia
Emory University M
LaGrange College M
Oglethorpe University M
Piedmont College M

Illinois
Augustana College M
Aurora University M
Benedictine University M
Blackburn College M
Concordia University Chicago M
Dominican University M
Elmhurst College M
Eureka College M
Greenville College M
Illinois College M
Illinois Wesleyan University M
Knox College M
MacMurray College M
Millikin University M
Monmouth College M
North Central College M
North Park University M
Principia College M
Rockford College M
University of Chicago M
Wheaton College M

Indiana
Anderson University M
DePauw University M
Earlham College M
Franklin College M
Hanover College M
Manchester College M
Rose-Hulman Institute of Technology M
Trine University M
Wabash College M

Iowa
Buena Vista University M
Central College M
Coe College M
Cornell College M
Grinnell College M
Loras College M
Luther College M
Simpson College M
University of Dubuque M
Wartburg College M

Kentucky
Centre College M
Spalding University M
Thomas More College M
Transylvania University M

Louisiana
Louisiana College M

Maine
Bates College M
Bowdoin College M
Colby College M
Husson University M
St. Joseph's College M
Thomas College M
University of Maine
  Farmington M
  Presque Isle M
University of Southern Maine M

Maryland
Frostburg State University M
Johns Hopkins University M
McDaniel College M
St. Mary's College of Maryland M
Salisbury University M
Stevenson University M
Washington College M

Massachusetts
Amherst College M
Anna Maria College M
Babson College M
Becker College M
Brandeis University M
Bridgewater State College M
Clark University M
Curry College M
Elms College M
Emerson College M
Endicott College M
Fitchburg State College M
Framingham State College M
Gordon College M
Lasell College M
Massachusetts College of Liberal Arts M
Massachusetts Institute of Technology M
Massachusetts Maritime Academy M
Newbury College M
Nichols College M
Salem State College M
Springfield College M
Suffolk University M
Tufts University M
University of Massachusetts
  Boston M
  Dartmouth M
Wentworth Institute of Technology M
Western New England College M
Westfield State College M
Wheaton College M
Williams College M
Worcester Polytechnic Institute M
Worcester State College M

Michigan
Adrian College M
Albion College M
Alma College M
Calvin College M
Finlandia University M
Hope College M
Kalamazoo College M
Olivet College M

Minnesota
Augsburg College M
Bethany Lutheran College M
Bethel University M
Carleton College M
College of St. Scholastica M
Concordia College: Moorhead M
Crown College M
Gustavus Adolphus College M
Hamline University M
Macalester College M
Martin Luther College M
Northwestern College M
St. John's University M
St. Mary's University of Minnesota M
St. Olaf College M
University of Minnesota
  Morris M
University of St. Thomas M

Mississippi
Millsaps College M
Mississippi College M
Rust College M

Missouri
Fontbonne University M
Maryville University of Saint Louis M
Washington University in St. Louis M
Webster University M
Westminster College M

Nebraska
Nebraska Wesleyan University M

New Hampshire
Colby-Sawyer College M
Daniel Webster College M
Keene State College M
New England College M
Plymouth State University M
Rivier College M

New Jersey
Centenary College M
The College of New Jersey M
Drew University M
Fairleigh Dickinson University
  College at Florham M
Kean University M
Montclair State University M
New Jersey City University M
Ramapo College of New Jersey M
Richard Stockton College of New Jersey M
Rowan University M
Rutgers, The State University of New Jersey
  Camden Regional Campus M
  Newark Regional Campus M
Stevens Institute of Technology M
William Paterson University of New Jersey M

New York
Cazenovia College M
City University of New York
  Baruch College M
  City College M
  College of Staten Island M
  John Jay College of Criminal Justice M
  Lehman College M
Clarkson University M
College of Mount St. Vincent M
D'Youville College M
Hamilton College M
Hilbert College M
Ithaca College M
Keuka College M
Manhattanville College M
Medaille College M
Mount St. Mary College M
Polytechnic Institute of New York University M
Rensselaer Polytechnic Institute M
Rochester Institute of Technology M
St. John Fisher College M
St. Joseph's College M
St. Joseph's College: Suffolk Campus M
St. Lawrence University M
Skidmore College M
State University of New York
  College at Brockport M
  College at Cortland M
  College at Fredonia M
  College at Old Westbury M
  College at Oneonta M
  College at Plattsburgh M
  College of Agriculture and Technology at Cobleskill M
  Farmingdale M
  Institute of Technology at Utica/Rome M
  Maritime College M
  New Paltz M
  Oswego M
  Purchase M
Union College M
United States Merchant Marine Academy M
University of Rochester M
Utica College M
Vassar College M
Yeshiva University M

North Carolina
Greensboro College M
Guilford College M
Methodist University M
North Carolina Wesleyan College M

Ohio
Baldwin-Wallace College M
Bluffton University M
Capital University M
Case Western Reserve University M
College of Mount St. Joseph M
College of Wooster M
Defiance College M
Denison University M
Franciscan University of Steubenville M
Heidelberg University M
Hiram College M
John Carroll University M
Kenyon College M
Lake Erie College M
Marietta College M
Mount Union College M
Muskingum College M
Oberlin College M
Ohio Northern University M
Ohio Wesleyan University M
Otterbein College M
Wilmington College M
Wittenberg University M

Oregon
George Fox University M
Lewis & Clark College M
Linfield College M
Pacific University M
Willamette University M

Pennsylvania
Albright College M
Allegheny College M
Alvernia University M
Arcadia University M
Baptist Bible College of Pennsylvania M
Delaware Valley College M
DeSales University M
Dickinson College M
Eastern University M
Elizabethtown College M
Franklin & Marshall College M
Geneva College M
Gettysburg College M
Grove City College M
Gwynedd-Mercy College M
Haverford College M
Juniata College M
Keystone College M
King's College M
La Roche College M
Lancaster Bible College M
Lebanon Valley College M
Lincoln University M
Marywood University M
Messiah College M
Misericordia University M
Moravian College M
Mount Aloysius College M
Muhlenberg College M
Neumann College M
Penn State
  Altoona M
  Berks M
  Erie, The Behrend College M
  Harrisburg M
Philadelphia Biblical University M
St. Vincent College M
Susquehanna University M
Swarthmore College M
Thiel College M
University of Pittsburgh
  Bradford M
  Greensburg M
University of Scranton M
Ursinus College M
Washington & Jefferson College M
Waynesburg University M
Westminster College M
Widener University M
Wilkes University M
York College of Pennsylvania M

Rhode Island
Johnson & Wales University: Providence M
Rhode Island College M
Roger Williams University M
Salve Regina University M

South Dakota
Presentation College M

Tennessee
Maryville College M
Rhodes College M
University of the South M

Texas
Austin College M
Concordia University Texas M
East Texas Baptist University M
Hardin-Simmons University M
Howard Payne University M
LeTourneau University M
McMurry University M
Schreiner University M
Southwestern University M
Sul Ross State University M
Texas Lutheran University M
Trinity University M
University of Dallas M
University of Mary Hardin-Baylor M
University of Texas
  Dallas M
  Tyler M

Vermont
Castleton State College M
Lyndon State College M
Middlebury College M
Norwich University M
Southern Vermont College M

Virginia
Averett University M
Bridgewater College M
Christopher Newport University M
Eastern Mennonite University M
Emory & Henry College M
Ferrum College M
Hampden-Sydney College M
Lynchburg College M
Randolph-Macon College M
Roanoke College M
Shenandoah University M
University of Mary Washington M
Virginia Wesleyan College M
Washington and Lee University M

Washington
Pacific Lutheran University M
University of Puget Sound M
Whitman College M
Whitworth University M

West Virginia
Bethany College M

Wisconsin
Beloit College M
Carroll University M
Carthage College M
Concordia University Wisconsin M
Edgewood College M
Lakeland College M
Lawrence University M
Maranatha Baptist Bible College M
Marian University M
Milwaukee School of Engineering M
Northland College M
Ripon College M
St. Norbert College M

University of Wisconsin
- La Crosse M
- Oshkosh M
- Platteville M
- Stevens Point M
- Stout M
- Superior M
- Whitewater M

Wisconsin Lutheran College M

Basketball Division I

Alabama
Alabama Agricultural and Mechanical University
Alabama State University
Auburn University
Birmingham-Southern College W
Jacksonville State University
Samford University
Troy University
University of Alabama
University of Alabama
- Birmingham

University of South Alabama

Arizona
Arizona State University
Northern Arizona University
University of Arizona

Arkansas
Arkansas State University
University of Arkansas
University of Arkansas
- Little Rock
- Pine Bluff

University of Central Arkansas

California
California Polytechnic State University: San Luis Obispo
California State University
- Bakersfield
- Fresno
- Fullerton
- Long Beach W
- Northridge
- Sacramento

Loyola Marymount University
Pepperdine University
St. Mary's College of California
San Diego State University
San Jose State University
Santa Clara University
Stanford University
University of California
- Berkeley
- Davis
- Irvine
- Los Angeles
- Riverside
- Santa Barbara

University of San Diego
University of San Francisco
University of Southern California
University of the Pacific

Colorado
Colorado State University
United States Air Force Academy
University of Colorado
- Boulder

University of Denver
University of Northern Colorado W

Connecticut
Central Connecticut State University
Fairfield University
Quinnipiac University
Sacred Heart University
University of Connecticut
University of Hartford
Yale University

Delaware
Delaware State University
University of Delaware

District of Columbia
American University
George Washington University
Georgetown University
Howard University

Florida
Bethune-Cookman University
Florida Agricultural and Mechanical University
Florida Atlantic University
Florida Gulf Coast University
Florida International University
Florida State University
Jacksonville University
Stetson University
University of Central Florida
University of Florida
University of Miami
University of North Florida
University of South Florida

Georgia
Georgia Institute of Technology
Georgia Southern University
Georgia State University
Kennesaw State University
Mercer University
Savannah State University
University of Georgia

Hawaii
University of Hawaii
- Manoa

Idaho
Boise State University
Idaho State University
University of Idaho

Illinois
Bradley University
Chicago State University
DePaul University
Eastern Illinois University
Illinois State University
Loyola University Chicago
Northern Illinois University
Northwestern University
Southern Illinois University
- Carbondale

Southern Illinois University
- Edwardsville

University of Illinois
- Chicago
- Urbana-Champaign

Western Illinois University

Indiana
Ball State University
Butler University
Indiana State University
Indiana University
- Bloomington

Indiana University-Purdue University Fort Wayne
Indiana University-Purdue University Indianapolis
Purdue University
University of Evansville
University of Notre Dame
Valparaiso University

Iowa
Drake University
Iowa State University
University of Iowa
University of Northern Iowa

Kansas
Kansas State University
University of Kansas
Wichita State University

Kentucky
Eastern Kentucky University
Morehead State University
Murray State University
University of Kentucky
University of Louisville
Western Kentucky University

Louisiana
Centenary College of Louisiana
Grambling State University
Louisiana State University and Agricultural and Mechanical College
Louisiana Tech University
McNeese State University
Nicholls State University
Northwestern State University
Southeastern Louisiana University
Southern University and Agricultural and Mechanical College
Tulane University
University of Louisiana at Lafayette
University of Louisiana at Monroe
University of New Orleans

Maine
University of Maine

Maryland
Coppin State University
Loyola College in Maryland
Morgan State University
Mount St. Mary's University
Towson University
United States Naval Academy
University of Maryland
- Baltimore County
- College Park
- Eastern Shore

Massachusetts
Boston College
Boston University
College of the Holy Cross
Harvard College
Northeastern University
University of Massachusetts
- Amherst

Michigan
Central Michigan University
Eastern Michigan University
Michigan State University
Oakland University
University of Detroit Mercy
University of Michigan
Western Michigan University

Minnesota
University of Minnesota
- Twin Cities

Mississippi
Alcorn State University
Jackson State University
Mississippi State University
Mississippi Valley State University
University of Mississippi
University of Southern Mississippi

Missouri
Missouri State University
Saint Louis University
Southeast Missouri State University
University of Missouri
- Columbia
- Kansas City

Montana
Montana State University
- Bozeman

University of Montana

Nebraska
Creighton University
University of Nebraska
- Lincoln

Nevada
University of Nevada
- Las Vegas
- Reno

New Hampshire
Dartmouth College
University of New Hampshire

New Jersey
Fairleigh Dickinson University
- Metropolitan Campus

Monmouth University
New Jersey Institute of Technology
Princeton University
Rider University
Rutgers, The State University of New Jersey
- New Brunswick/Piscataway Campus

Saint Peter's College
Seton Hall University

New Mexico
New Mexico State University
University of New Mexico

New York
Barnard College W
Canisius College
Colgate University
Cornell University
Fordham University
Hofstra University
Iona College
Long Island University
- Brooklyn Campus

Manhattan College
Marist College
Niagara University
Saint Bonaventure University
St. Francis College
St. John's University
Siena College
State University of New York
- Albany
- Binghamton
- Buffalo
- Stony Brook

Syracuse University
United States Military Academy
Wagner College

North Carolina
Appalachian State University
Campbell University
Davidson College
Duke University
East Carolina University
Elon University
Gardner-Webb University
High Point University
North Carolina Agricultural and Technical State University
North Carolina Central University
North Carolina State University
University of North Carolina
- Asheville
- Chapel Hill
- Charlotte
- Greensboro
- Wilmington

Wake Forest University
Western Carolina University
Winston-Salem State University

North Dakota
North Dakota State University
University of North Dakota

Ohio
Bowling Green State University
Cleveland State University
Kent State University
Miami University
- Oxford Campus

Ohio State University
- Columbus Campus

Ohio University
University of Akron
University of Cincinnati
University of Dayton
University of Toledo
Wright State University
Xavier University
Youngstown State University

Oklahoma
Oklahoma State University
Oral Roberts University
University of Oklahoma
University of Tulsa

Oregon
Oregon State University
Portland State University
University of Oregon
University of Portland

Pennsylvania
Bucknell University
Drexel University
Duquesne University
La Salle University
Lafayette College
Lehigh University
Penn State
- University Park

Robert Morris University
St. Francis University
Saint Joseph's University
Temple University
University of Pennsylvania
University of Pittsburgh
Villanova University

Rhode Island
Brown University
Bryant University
Providence College
University of Rhode Island

South Carolina
Charleston Southern University
The Citadel M
Clemson University
Coastal Carolina University
College of Charleston
Furman University
Presbyterian College
South Carolina State University
University of South Carolina
University of South Carolina
- Upstate

Winthrop University
Wofford College

South Dakota
South Dakota State University
University of South Dakota

Tennessee
Austin Peay State University
Belmont University
East Tennessee State University
Lipscomb University
Middle Tennessee State University
Tennessee State University
Tennessee Technological University
University of Memphis
University of Tennessee
- Chattanooga
- Knoxville
- Martin

Vanderbilt University

Texas
Baylor University
Houston Baptist University
Lamar University
Prairie View A&M University
Rice University
Sam Houston State University
Southern Methodist University

Stephen F. Austin State University
Texas A&M University
Texas A&M University
Corpus Christi
Texas Christian University
Texas Southern University
Texas State University: San Marcos
Texas Tech University
University of Houston
University of North Texas
University of Texas
Arlington
Austin
El Paso
Pan American
San Antonio

Utah

Brigham Young University
Southern Utah University
University of Utah
Utah State University
Utah Valley University
Weber State University

Vermont

University of Vermont

Virginia

College of William and Mary
George Mason University
Hampton University
James Madison University
Liberty University
Longwood University
Norfolk State University
Old Dominion University
Radford University
University of Richmond
University of Virginia
Virginia Commonwealth University
Virginia Military Institute M
Virginia Polytechnic Institute and State University

Washington

Eastern Washington University
Gonzaga University
Seattle University
University of Washington
Washington State University

West Virginia

Marshall University
West Virginia University

Wisconsin

Marquette University
University of Wisconsin
Green Bay
Madison
Milwaukee

Wyoming

University of Wyoming

Basketball Division II

Alabama

Miles College
Tuskegee University
University of Alabama
Huntsville
University of Montevallo
University of North Alabama
University of West Alabama

Alaska

University of Alaska
Anchorage
Fairbanks

Arizona

Grand Canyon University

Arkansas

Arkansas Tech University
Harding University
Henderson State University
Ouachita Baptist University
Southern Arkansas University
University of Arkansas
Monticello

California

California State Polytechnic University: Pomona
California State University
Chico
Dominguez Hills
Los Angeles
Monterey Bay
San Bernardino
Stanislaus
Humboldt State University
Notre Dame de Namur University
San Francisco State University
Sonoma State University
University of California
San Diego

Colorado

Adams State College
Colorado Christian University
Colorado School of Mines
Colorado State University
Pueblo
Fort Lewis College
Mesa State College
Metropolitan State College of Denver
Regis University
University of Colorado
Colorado Springs
Western State College of Colorado

Connecticut

Post University
Southern Connecticut State University
University of Bridgeport
University of New Haven

Delaware

Goldey-Beacom College
Wilmington University

District of Columbia

University of the District of Columbia

Florida

Barry University
Eckerd College
Flagler College
Florida Institute of Technology
Florida Southern College
Lynn University
Nova Southeastern University
Palm Beach Atlantic University
Rollins College
St. Leo University
University of Tampa
University of West Florida

Georgia

Albany State University
Armstrong Atlantic State University
Augusta State University
Clark Atlanta University
Clayton State University
Columbus State University
Fort Valley State University
Georgia College and State University
Georgia Southwestern State University
Morehouse College M
North Georgia College & State University
Paine College
University of West Georgia
Valdosta State University

Hawaii

Brigham Young University-Hawaii
Chaminade University of Honolulu
Hawaii Pacific University
University of Hawaii
Hilo

Idaho

Northwest Nazarene University

Illinois

Lewis University
Quincy University

Indiana

Oakland City University
Saint Joseph's College
University of Indianapolis
University of Southern Indiana

Iowa

Upper Iowa University

Kansas

Emporia State University
Fort Hays State University
Newman University
Pittsburg State University
Washburn University

Kentucky

Bellarmine University
Kentucky State University
Kentucky Wesleyan College
Northern Kentucky University

Maryland

Bowie State University
Columbia Union College

Massachusetts

American International College
Assumption College
Bentley University
Merrimack College
Stonehill College
University of Massachusetts
Lowell

Michigan

Ferris State University
Grand Valley State University
Hillsdale College
Lake Superior State University
Michigan Technological University
Northern Michigan University
Northwood University: Michigan
Saginaw Valley State University
Wayne State University

Minnesota

Bemidji State University
Concordia University: St. Paul
Minnesota State University
Mankato
Moorhead
Saint Cloud State University
Southwest Minnesota State University
University of Minnesota
Crookston
Duluth
Winona State University

Mississippi

Delta State University

Missouri

Drury University
Lincoln University
Missouri Southern State University
Missouri Western State University
Northwest Missouri State University
Rockhurst University
Southwest Baptist University
Truman State University
University of Central Missouri
University of Missouri
Missouri University of Science and Technology
St. Louis

Montana

Montana State University
Billings

Nebraska

Chadron State College
University of Nebraska
Kearney
Omaha
Wayne State College

New Hampshire

Franklin Pierce University
St. Anselm College
Southern New Hampshire University

New Jersey

Bloomfield College
Caldwell College
Felician College
Georgian Court University W

New Mexico

Eastern New Mexico University
New Mexico Highlands University
Western New Mexico University

New York

Adelphi University
City University of New York
Queens College
College of Saint Rose
Concordia College
Dominican College of Blauvelt
Dowling College
Le Moyne College
Long Island University
C. W. Post Campus M
Mercy College
Molloy College
New York Institute of Technology
Nyack College
Pace University
St. Thomas Aquinas College

North Carolina

Barton College
Belmont Abbey College
Brevard College
Catawba College
Chowan University
Elizabeth City State University
Fayetteville State University
Johnson C. Smith University
Lees-McRae College
Lenoir-Rhyne University
Livingstone College
Mars Hill College
Mount Olive College
Pfeiffer University
Queens University of Charlotte
St. Andrews Presbyterian College
St. Augustine's College
Shaw University
University of North Carolina
Pembroke
Wingate University

North Dakota

University of Mary

Ohio

Ashland University
Central State University
Tiffin University
University of Findlay

Oklahoma

Cameron University
East Central University
Northeastern State University
Oklahoma Panhandle State University
Southeastern Oklahoma State University
Southwestern Oklahoma State University
University of Central Oklahoma

Oregon

Western Oregon University

Pennsylvania

Bloomsburg University of Pennsylvania
California University of Pennsylvania
Chestnut Hill College
Cheyney University of Pennsylvania
Clarion University of Pennsylvania
East Stroudsburg University of Pennsylvania
Edinboro University of Pennsylvania
Gannon University
Holy Family University
Indiana University of Pennsylvania
Kutztown University of Pennsylvania
Lock Haven University of Pennsylvania
Mansfield University of Pennsylvania
Mercyhurst College
Millersville University of Pennsylvania
Philadelphia University
Seton Hill University
Shippensburg University of Pennsylvania
Slippery Rock University of Pennsylvania
University of Pittsburgh
Johnstown
University of the Sciences in Philadelphia
West Chester University of Pennsylvania

Puerto Rico

University of Puerto Rico
Bayamon University College W
Cayey University College
Mayaguez
Rio Piedras

South Carolina

Anderson University
Benedict College
Claflin University
Converse College W
Erskine College
Francis Marion University
Lander University
Limestone College
Newberry College
North Greenville University
University of South Carolina
Aiken

South Dakota

Augustana College
Northern State University

Tennessee

Carson-Newman College
Christian Brothers University
Lane College
LeMoyne-Owen College
Lincoln Memorial University
Tusculum College

Texas

Abilene Christian University
Angelo State University
Dallas Baptist University M

Midwestern State University
St. Edward's University
St. Mary's University
Tarleton State University
Texas A&M International University
Texas A&M University
Commerce
Kingsville
Texas Woman's University W
University of Texas
of the Permian Basin
University of the Incarnate Word
West Texas A&M University

Utah

Dixie State College of Utah

Vermont

St. Michael's College

Virginia

St. Paul's College
Virginia State University
Virginia Union University

Washington

Central Washington University
Saint Martin's University
Seattle Pacific University
Western Washington University

West Virginia

Alderson-Broaddus College
Bluefield State College
Concord University
Davis and Elkins College
Fairmont State University
Glenville State College
Ohio Valley University
Salem International University
Shepherd University
University of Charleston
West Liberty State College
West Virginia State University
West Virginia Wesleyan College
Wheeling Jesuit University

Wisconsin

University of Wisconsin
Parkside

Basketball Division III

Alabama

Birmingham-Southern College M
Huntingdon College

Arkansas

Hendrix College
University of the Ozarks

California

California Institute of Technology
California Lutheran University
California State University
East Bay
Chapman University
Claremont McKenna College
La Sierra University
Menlo College
Occidental College
Pitzer College
Pomona College
University of California
Santa Cruz
University of La Verne
University of Redlands
Whittier College

Colorado

Colorado College

Connecticut

Albertus Magnus College
Connecticut College
Eastern Connecticut State University
Mitchell College
St. Joseph College W
Trinity College
United States Coast Guard Academy
Wesleyan University
Western Connecticut State University

Delaware

Wesley College

District of Columbia

Catholic University of America
Gallaudet University
Trinity Washington University W

Georgia

Agnes Scott College W
Emory University
LaGrange College
Oglethorpe University
Piedmont College
Spelman College W
Wesleyan College W

Illinois

Augustana College
Aurora University
Benedictine University
Blackburn College
Concordia University Chicago
Dominican University
Elmhurst College
Eureka College
Greenville College
Illinois College
Illinois Wesleyan University
Knox College
Lake Forest College
MacMurray College
Millikin University
Monmouth College
North Central College
North Park University
Principia College
Rockford College
University of Chicago
Wheaton College

Indiana

Anderson University
DePauw University
Earlham College
Franklin College
Hanover College
Manchester College
Rose-Hulman Institute of Technology
Saint Mary's College W
Trine University
Wabash College M

Iowa

Buena Vista University
Central College
Coe College
Cornell College
Grinnell College
Loras College
Luther College
Simpson College
University of Dubuque
Wartburg College

Kentucky

Centre College
Spalding University
Thomas More College
Transylvania University

Louisiana

Louisiana College

Maine

Bates College
Bowdoin College
Colby College
Husson University
Maine Maritime Academy
St. Joseph's College
Thomas College
University of Maine
Farmington
Presque Isle
University of New England
University of Southern Maine

Maryland

College of Notre Dame of Maryland W
Frostburg State University
Goucher College
Hood College
Johns Hopkins University
McDaniel College
St. Mary's College of Maryland
Salisbury University
Stevenson University
Washington College

Massachusetts

Amherst College
Anna Maria College
Babson College
Bay Path College W
Becker College
Brandeis University
Bridgewater State College
Clark University
Curry College
Elms College
Emerson College
Emmanuel College
Endicott College
Fitchburg State College
Framingham State College
Gordon College
Lasell College
Lesley University
Massachusetts College of Liberal Arts
Massachusetts Institute of Technology
Mount Holyoke College W
Mount Ida College
Newbury College
Nichols College
Pine Manor College W
Regis College
Salem State College
Simmons College W
Smith College W
Springfield College
Suffolk University
Tufts University
University of Massachusetts
Boston
Dartmouth
Wellesley College W
Wentworth Institute of Technology
Western New England College
Westfield State College
Wheaton College
Wheelock College
Williams College
Worcester Polytechnic Institute
Worcester State College

Michigan

Adrian College
Albion College
Alma College
Calvin College
Finlandia University
Hope College
Kalamazoo College
Olivet College

Minnesota

Augsburg College
Bethany Lutheran College
Bethel University
Carleton College
College of St. Benedict W
College of St. Catherine W
College of St. Scholastica
Concordia College: Moorhead
Crown College
Gustavus Adolphus College
Hamline University
Macalester College
Martin Luther College
Northwestern College
St. John's University M
St. Mary's University of Minnesota
St. Olaf College
University of Minnesota
Morris
University of St. Thomas

Mississippi

Millsaps College
Mississippi College
Rust College

Missouri

Baptist Bible College W
Fontbonne University
Maryville University of Saint Louis
Washington University in St. Louis
Webster University
Westminster College

Nebraska

Nebraska Wesleyan University

New Hampshire

Colby-Sawyer College
Daniel Webster College
Keene State College
New England College
Plymouth State University
Rivier College

New Jersey

Centenary College
The College of New Jersey
College of St. Elizabeth W
Drew University
Fairleigh Dickinson University
College at Florham
Kean University
Montclair State University
New Jersey City University
Ramapo College of New Jersey
Richard Stockton College of New Jersey
Rowan University
Rutgers, The State University of New Jersey
Camden Regional Campus
Newark Regional Campus
Stevens Institute of Technology
William Paterson University of New Jersey

New York

Alfred University
Bard College
Cazenovia College
City University of New York
Baruch College
Brooklyn College
City College
College of Staten Island
Hunter College
John Jay College of Criminal Justice
Lehman College
Medgar Evers College
New York City College of Technology
York College
Clarkson University
College of Mount St. Vincent
College of New Rochelle W
D'Youville College
Elmira College
Hamilton College
Hartwick College
Hilbert College
Hobart and William Smith Colleges
Ithaca College
Keuka College
Manhattanville College
Medaille College
Mount St. Mary College
Nazareth College of Rochester
New York University
Polytechnic Institute of New York University
Rensselaer Polytechnic Institute
Rochester Institute of Technology
Russell Sage College W
Sage College of Albany W
St. John Fisher College
St. Joseph's College: Suffolk Campus
St. Lawrence University
Skidmore College
State University of New York
College at Brockport
College at Buffalo
College at Cortland
College at Fredonia
College at Geneseo
College at Old Westbury
College at Oneonta
College at Plattsburgh
College at Potsdam
College of Agriculture and Technology at Cobleskill
College of Agriculture and Technology at Morrisville
Farmingdale
Institute of Technology at Utica/Rome
Maritime College M
New Paltz
Oswego
Purchase
Union College
United States Merchant Marine Academy
University of Rochester
Utica College
Vassar College
Wells College M
Yeshiva University

North Carolina

Greensboro College
Guilford College
Meredith College W
Methodist University
North Carolina Wesleyan College
Peace College W
Salem College W

Ohio

Baldwin-Wallace College
Bluffton University
Capital University
Case Western Reserve University
College of Mount St. Joseph
College of Wooster
Defiance College
Denison University
Franciscan University of Steubenville
Heidelberg University
Hiram College
John Carroll University
Kenyon College
Lake Erie College
Marietta College
Mount Union College
Muskingum College
Oberlin College
Ohio Northern University
Ohio Wesleyan University
Otterbein College
Wilmington College
Wittenberg University

Oregon

George Fox University
Lewis & Clark College
Linfield College
Pacific University

Willamette University

Pennsylvania
Albright College
Allegheny College
Alvernia University
Arcadia University
Baptist Bible College of Pennsylvania M
Bryn Mawr College W
Cabrini College
Carnegie Mellon University
Cedar Crest College W
Chatham University W
Delaware Valley College
DeSales University
Dickinson College
Eastern University
Elizabethtown College
Franklin & Marshall College
Geneva College W
Gettysburg College
Grove City College
Gwynedd-Mercy College
Haverford College
Immaculata University
Juniata College
Keystone College
King's College
La Roche College
Lancaster Bible College
Lebanon Valley College
Lincoln University
Lycoming College
Marywood University
Messiah College
Misericordia University
Moravian College
Mount Aloysius College
Muhlenberg College
Neumann College
Penn State
  Altoona
  Berks
  Erie, The Behrend College
  Harrisburg
Philadelphia Biblical University
Rosemont College W
St. Vincent College
Susquehanna University
Swarthmore College
Thiel College
University of Pittsburgh
  Bradford
  Greensburg
University of Scranton
Ursinus College
Washington & Jefferson College
Waynesburg University
Westminster College
Widener University
Wilkes University
Wilson College W
York College of Pennsylvania

Rhode Island
Johnson & Wales University: Providence
Rhode Island College
Roger Williams University
Salve Regina University

South Dakota
Presentation College

Tennessee
Maryville College
Rhodes College
University of the South

Texas
Austin College
Concordia University Texas
East Texas Baptist University
Hardin-Simmons University
Howard Payne University
LeTourneau University
McMurry University
Schreiner University
Southwestern University
Sul Ross State University
Texas Lutheran University
Trinity University
University of Dallas
University of Mary Hardin-Baylor
University of Texas
  Dallas
  Tyler

Vermont
Castleton State College
Green Mountain College
Johnson State College
Lyndon State College
Middlebury College
Norwich University
Southern Vermont College

Virginia
Averett University
Bridgewater College
Christopher Newport University
Eastern Mennonite University
Emory & Henry College
Ferrum College
Hampden-Sydney College M
Hollins University W
Lynchburg College
Mary Baldwin College W
Marymount University
Randolph College
Randolph-Macon College
Roanoke College
Shenandoah University
University of Mary Washington
Virginia Wesleyan College
Washington and Lee University

Washington
Pacific Lutheran University
University of Puget Sound
Whitman College
Whitworth University

West Virginia
Bethany College

Wisconsin
Alverno College W
Beloit College
Carroll University
Carthage College
Concordia University Wisconsin
Edgewood College
Lakeland College
Lawrence University
Maranatha Baptist Bible College
Marian University
Milwaukee School of Engineering
Mount Mary College W
Northland College
Ripon College
St. Norbert College
University of Wisconsin
  Eau Claire
  La Crosse
  Oshkosh
  Platteville
  River Falls
  Stevens Point
  Stout
  Superior
  Whitewater
Wisconsin Lutheran College

Bowling Division I

Alabama
Alabama Agricultural and Mechanical University W
Alabama State University W

Arkansas
Arkansas State University W
University of Arkansas
  Pine Bluff W

Connecticut
Sacred Heart University W

Delaware
Delaware State University W

District of Columbia
Howard University W

Florida
Bethune-Cookman University W
Florida Agricultural and Mechanical University W

Louisiana
Grambling State University W
Louisiana Tech University W
Southern University and Agricultural and Mechanical College W

Maryland
Coppin State University W
Morgan State University W
University of Maryland
  Eastern Shore W

Mississippi
Jackson State University W
Mississippi Valley State University W

Nebraska
University of Nebraska
  Lincoln W

New Jersey
Fairleigh Dickinson University
  Metropolitan Campus W
Saint Peter's College W

New York
Long Island University
  Brooklyn Campus W
St. Francis College W

North Carolina
North Carolina Agricultural and Technical State University W
North Carolina Central University W
Winston-Salem State University W

South Carolina
South Carolina State University W

Tennessee
Vanderbilt University W

Texas
Prairie View A&M University W
Sam Houston State University W
Texas Southern University W

Virginia
Hampton University W
Norfolk State University W

Bowling Division II

Arizona
Grand Canyon University W

Maryland
Bowie State University W

Minnesota
Minnesota State University
  Mankato W

Missouri
University of Central Missouri W

New York
Adelphi University W

North Carolina
Elizabeth City State University W
Fayetteville State University W
Johnson C. Smith University W
Livingstone College W
St. Augustine's College W
Shaw University W

Pennsylvania
Cheyney University of Pennsylvania W
Kutztown University of Pennsylvania W

Virginia
St. Paul's College W
Virginia State University W
Virginia Union University W

Bowling Division III

Illinois
Elmhurst College W

Michigan
Adrian College W

Missouri
Fontbonne University W

New Jersey
New Jersey City University W

New York
Medaille College W
State University of New York
  Institute of Technology at Utica/Rome W

Wisconsin
University of Wisconsin
  Whitewater W

Cross-country Division I

Alabama
Alabama Agricultural and Mechanical University W
Alabama State University
Auburn University
Birmingham-Southern College
Jacksonville State University
Samford University
Troy University
University of Alabama
University of Alabama
  Birmingham W
University of South Alabama

Arizona
Arizona State University
Northern Arizona University
University of Arizona

Arkansas
Arkansas State University
University of Arkansas
University of Arkansas
  Little Rock
  Pine Bluff W
University of Central Arkansas

California
California Polytechnic State University: San Luis Obispo
California State University
  Bakersfield W
  Fresno
  Fullerton
  Northridge
  Sacramento
Loyola Marymount University
Pepperdine University
St. Mary's College of California
San Diego State University W
San Jose State University
Santa Clara University
Stanford University
University of California
  Berkeley
  Davis
  Irvine
  Los Angeles
  Riverside
  Santa Barbara
University of San Diego
University of San Francisco
University of Southern California W
University of the Pacific W

Colorado
Colorado State University
United States Air Force Academy
University of Colorado
  Boulder
University of Northern Colorado

Connecticut
Central Connecticut State University
Fairfield University
Quinnipiac University
Sacred Heart University
University of Connecticut
University of Hartford
Yale University

Delaware
Delaware State University
University of Delaware

District of Columbia
American University
George Washington University
Georgetown University
Howard University

Florida
Bethune-Cookman University
Florida Agricultural and Mechanical University
Florida Atlantic University
Florida Gulf Coast University
Florida International University
Florida State University
Jacksonville University
Stetson University
University of Central Florida W
University of Florida
University of Miami
University of North Florida
University of South Florida

Georgia
Georgia Institute of Technology
Georgia Southern University W
Georgia State University
Kennesaw State University
Mercer University
Savannah State University
University of Georgia

Hawaii
University of Hawaii
  Manoa W

Idaho
Boise State University
Idaho State University
University of Idaho

Illinois
Bradley University
Chicago State University
DePaul University
Eastern Illinois University
Illinois State University
Loyola University Chicago
Northern Illinois University W
Northwestern University W
Southern Illinois University
  Carbondale
Southern Illinois University
  Edwardsville
University of Illinois
  Chicago
  Urbana-Champaign

Western Illinois University

Indiana
Ball State University W
Butler University
Indiana State University
Indiana University
    Bloomington
Indiana University-Purdue
    University Fort Wayne
Indiana University-Purdue
    University Indianapolis
Purdue University
University of Evansville
University of Notre Dame
Valparaiso University

Iowa
Drake University
Iowa State University
University of Iowa
University of Northern Iowa

Kansas
Kansas State University
University of Kansas
Wichita State University

Kentucky
Eastern Kentucky University
Morehead State University
Murray State University
University of Kentucky
University of Louisville
Western Kentucky University

Louisiana
Centenary College of Louisiana
Grambling State University
Louisiana State University and
    Agricultural and Mechanical
    College
Louisiana Tech University
McNeese State University
Nicholls State University
Northwestern State University
Southeastern Louisiana University
Southern University and
    Agricultural and Mechanical
    College
Tulane University
University of Louisiana at
    Lafayette
University of Louisiana at
    Monroe

Maine
University of Maine

Maryland
Coppin State University
Loyola College in Maryland
Morgan State University
Mount St. Mary's University
Towson University W
United States Naval Academy
University of Maryland
    Baltimore County
    College Park
    Eastern Shore

Massachusetts
Boston College
Boston University
College of the Holy Cross
Harvard College
Northeastern University
University of Massachusetts
    Amherst

Michigan
Central Michigan University
Eastern Michigan University
Michigan State University
Oakland University
University of Detroit Mercy
University of Michigan
Western Michigan University W

Minnesota
University of Minnesota
    Twin Cities

Mississippi
Alcorn State University
Jackson State University
Mississippi State University
Mississippi Valley State
    University
University of Mississippi
University of Southern
    Mississippi W

Missouri
Missouri State University W
Saint Louis University
Southeast Missouri State
    University
University of Missouri
    Columbia
    Kansas City

Montana
Montana State University
    Bozeman
University of Montana

Nebraska
Creighton University
University of Nebraska
    Lincoln

Nevada
University of Nevada
    Las Vegas W
    Reno W

New Hampshire
Dartmouth College
University of New Hampshire

New Jersey
Fairleigh Dickinson University
    Metropolitan Campus
Monmouth University
New Jersey Institute of
    Technology
Princeton University
Rider University
Rutgers, The State University of
    New Jersey
        New Brunswick/Piscataway
        Campus
Saint Peter's College
Seton Hall University

New Mexico
New Mexico State University
University of New Mexico

New York
Barnard College W
Canisius College
Colgate University
Cornell University
Fordham University
Hofstra University
Iona College
Long Island University
    Brooklyn Campus
Manhattan College
Marist College
Niagara University
Saint Bonaventure University
St. Francis College
St. John's University W
Siena College
State University of New York
    Albany
    Binghamton
    Buffalo
    Stony Brook
Syracuse University
United States Military Academy
Wagner College

North Carolina
Appalachian State University
Campbell University
Davidson College
Duke University
East Carolina University
Elon University
Gardner-Webb University
High Point University
North Carolina Agricultural and
    Technical State University
North Carolina Central University
North Carolina State University
University of North Carolina
    Asheville M
    Chapel Hill
    Charlotte
    Greensboro
    Wilmington
Wake Forest University
Western Carolina University
Winston-Salem State University

North Dakota
North Dakota State University
University of North Dakota

Ohio
Bowling Green State University
Cleveland State University W
Kent State University
Miami University
    Oxford Campus
Ohio State University
    Columbus Campus
Ohio University
University of Akron
University of Cincinnati
University of Dayton
University of Toledo
Wright State University
Xavier University
Youngstown State University

Oklahoma
Oklahoma State University
Oral Roberts University
University of Oklahoma
University of Tulsa

Oregon
Oregon State University W
Portland State University
University of Oregon
University of Portland

Pennsylvania
Bucknell University
Duquesne University
La Salle University
Lafayette College
Lehigh University
Penn State
    University Park
Robert Morris University
St. Francis University
Saint Joseph's University
Temple University
University of Pennsylvania
University of Pittsburgh
Villanova University

Rhode Island
Brown University
Bryant University
Providence College
University of Rhode Island

South Carolina
Charleston Southern University
The Citadel
Clemson University
Coastal Carolina University
College of Charleston
Furman University
Presbyterian College
South Carolina State University
University of South Carolina W
University of South Carolina
    Upstate M
Winthrop University
Wofford College

South Dakota
South Dakota State University
University of South Dakota

Tennessee
Austin Peay State University
Belmont University
East Tennessee State University
Lipscomb University
Middle Tennessee State
    University
Tennessee State University
Tennessee Technological
    University
University of Memphis
University of Tennessee
    Chattanooga
    Knoxville
    Martin
Vanderbilt University

Texas
Baylor University
Lamar University
Prairie View A&M University
Rice University
Sam Houston State University
Southern Methodist University W
Stephen F. Austin State University
Texas A&M University
Texas A&M University
    Corpus Christi
Texas Christian University
Texas State University: San
    Marcos
Texas Tech University
University of Houston
University of North Texas
University of Texas
    Arlington
    Austin
    El Paso
    Pan American
    San Antonio

Utah
Brigham Young University
Southern Utah University
University of Utah W
Utah State University
Utah Valley University
Weber State University

Vermont
University of Vermont

Virginia
College of William and Mary
George Mason University
Hampton University
James Madison University W
Liberty University
Longwood University
Norfolk State University
Radford University
University of Richmond
University of Virginia
Virginia Commonwealth
    University
Virginia Military Institute
Virginia Polytechnic Institute and
    State University

Washington
Eastern Washington University
Gonzaga University
Seattle University
University of Washington
Washington State University

West Virginia
Marshall University
West Virginia University W

Wisconsin
Marquette University
University of Wisconsin
    Green Bay
    Madison
    Milwaukee

Wyoming
University of Wyoming

Cross-country Division II

Alabama
Miles College
Tuskegee University
University of Alabama
    Huntsville
University of Montevallo W
University of North Alabama
University of West Alabama

Alaska
University of Alaska
    Anchorage
    Fairbanks

Arizona
Grand Canyon University

Arkansas
Arkansas Tech University W
Harding University
Henderson State University
Ouachita Baptist University W
Southern Arkansas University
University of Arkansas
    Monticello

California
California State Polytechnic
    University: Pomona
California State University
    Chico
    Dominguez Hills W
    Los Angeles W
    Monterey Bay
    San Bernardino W
    Stanislaus
Humboldt State University
Notre Dame de Namur University
San Francisco State University
Sonoma State University W
University of California
    San Diego

Colorado
Adams State College
Colorado Christian University
Colorado School of Mines
Colorado State University
    Pueblo W
Fort Lewis College
Mesa State College W
Metropolitan State College of
    Denver
Regis University
University of Colorado
    Colorado Springs
Western State College of
    Colorado

Connecticut
Post University
Southern Connecticut State
    University
University of Bridgeport
University of New Haven

Delaware
Goldey-Beacom College
Wilmington University

District of Columbia
University of the District of
    Columbia

Florida
Flagler College
Florida Institute of Technology
Florida Southern College
Nova Southeastern University
Palm Beach Atlantic University
Rollins College
St. Leo University
University of Tampa

University of West Florida

Georgia
Albany State University
Augusta State University W
Clark Atlanta University
Clayton State University
Columbus State University
Fort Valley State University
Georgia College and State University
Morehouse College M
North Georgia College & State University
Paine College
University of West Georgia
Valdosta State University

Hawaii
Brigham Young University-Hawaii
Chaminade University of Honolulu
Hawaii Pacific University
University of Hawaii
Hilo

Idaho
Northwest Nazarene University

Illinois
Lewis University

Indiana
Oakland City University
Saint Joseph's College
University of Indianapolis
University of Southern Indiana

Kansas
Emporia State University
Fort Hays State University
Newman University
Pittsburg State University

Kentucky
Bellarmine University
Kentucky State University
Kentucky Wesleyan College
Northern Kentucky University

Maryland
Bowie State University
Columbia Union College

Massachusetts
American International College
Assumption College
Bentley University
Merrimack College
Stonehill College
University of Massachusetts
Lowell

Michigan
Ferris State University
Grand Valley State University
Hillsdale College
Lake Superior State University
Michigan Technological University
Northern Michigan University W
Northwood University: Michigan
Saginaw Valley State University
Wayne State University

Minnesota
Bemidji State University W
Concordia University: St. Paul
Minnesota State University
Mankato
Moorhead
Saint Cloud State University
University of Minnesota
Duluth
Winona State University

Mississippi
Delta State University W

Missouri
Drury University
Lincoln University W
Missouri Southern State University
Northwest Missouri State University
Southwest Baptist University
Truman State University
University of Central Missouri
University of Missouri
Missouri University of Science and Technology

Montana
Montana State University
Billings

Nebraska
University of Nebraska
Kearney
Omaha W
Wayne State College

New Hampshire
Franklin Pierce University W
St. Anselm College
Southern New Hampshire University

New Jersey
Bloomfield College
Caldwell College W
Felician College
Georgian Court University W

New Mexico
Eastern New Mexico University
New Mexico Highlands University
Western New Mexico University

New York
Adelphi University
City University of New York
Queens College
College of Saint Rose
Concordia College
Dominican College of Blauvelt W
Dowling College
Le Moyne College
Long Island University
C. W. Post Campus
Mercy College
Molloy College
New York Institute of Technology
Nyack College
Pace University
St. Thomas Aquinas College

North Carolina
Barton College
Belmont Abbey College
Brevard College
Catawba College
Elizabeth City State University
Fayetteville State University
Johnson C. Smith University
Lees-McRae College
Lenoir-Rhyne University
Livingstone College
Mars Hill College
Mount Olive College
Pfeiffer University
Queens University of Charlotte
St. Andrews Presbyterian College
St. Augustine's College
Shaw University
University of North Carolina
Pembroke
Wingate University

North Dakota
University of Mary

Ohio
Ashland University
Central State University
Tiffin University
University of Findlay

Oklahoma
Cameron University M
East Central University
Oklahoma Panhandle State University
Southeastern Oklahoma State University W
Southwestern Oklahoma State University W
University of Central Oklahoma W

Oregon
Western Oregon University

Pennsylvania
Bloomsburg University of Pennsylvania
California University of Pennsylvania
Chestnut Hill College
Cheyney University of Pennsylvania
Clarion University of Pennsylvania W
East Stroudsburg University of Pennsylvania
Edinboro University of Pennsylvania
Gannon University
Holy Family University
Indiana University of Pennsylvania
Kutztown University of Pennsylvania
Lock Haven University of Pennsylvania
Mansfield University of Pennsylvania
Mercyhurst College
Millersville University of Pennsylvania
Philadelphia University
Seton Hill University
Shippensburg University of Pennsylvania
Slippery Rock University of Pennsylvania
University of Pittsburgh
Johnstown W
University of the Sciences in Philadelphia
West Chester University of Pennsylvania

Puerto Rico
University of Puerto Rico
Bayamon University College W
Cayey University College
Mayaguez
Rio Piedras

South Carolina
Anderson University
Benedict College
Claflin University
Converse College W
Erskine College
Francis Marion University
Lander University W
Limestone College
Newberry College
North Greenville University
University of South Carolina
Aiken W

South Dakota
Augustana College
Northern State University

Tennessee
Carson-Newman College
Christian Brothers University
Lane College
LeMoyne-Owen College
Lincoln Memorial University
Tusculum College

Texas
Abilene Christian University
Angelo State University
Dallas Baptist University
Midwestern State University W
St. Edward's University
St. Mary's University W
Tarleton State University
Texas A&M International University
Texas A&M University
Commerce
Kingsville
University of Texas of the Permian Basin
University of the Incarnate Word
West Texas A&M University

Utah
Dixie State College of Utah

Vermont
St. Michael's College

Virginia
St. Paul's College
Virginia State University
Virginia Union University

Washington
Central Washington University
Saint Martin's University
Seattle Pacific University
Western Washington University

West Virginia
Alderson-Broaddus College
Bluefield State College
Concord University
Davis and Elkins College
Fairmont State University
Glenville State College
Ohio Valley University
University of Charleston
West Liberty State College
West Virginia Wesleyan College
Wheeling Jesuit University

Wisconsin
University of Wisconsin
Parkside

Cross-country Division III

Alabama
Huntingdon College

Arkansas
Hendrix College
University of the Ozarks

California
California Institute of Technology
California Lutheran University
California State University
East Bay
Chapman University
Claremont McKenna College
Menlo College
Mills College W
Occidental College
Pitzer College
Pomona College
University of California
Santa Cruz W
University of La Verne
University of Redlands
Whittier College

Colorado
Colorado College

Connecticut
Albertus Magnus College M
Connecticut College
Eastern Connecticut State University
Mitchell College
St. Joseph College W
Trinity College
United States Coast Guard Academy
Wesleyan University

Delaware
Wesley College

District of Columbia
Catholic University of America

Georgia
Agnes Scott College W
Emory University
LaGrange College
Oglethorpe University
Piedmont College
Spelman College W
Wesleyan College W

Illinois
Augustana College
Aurora University
Benedictine University
Blackburn College
Concordia University Chicago
Dominican University
Elmhurst College
Eureka College
Greenville College
Illinois College
Illinois Wesleyan University
Knox College
Lake Forest College
Millikin University
Monmouth College
North Central College
North Park University
Principia College
Rockford College
University of Chicago
Wheaton College

Indiana
Anderson University
DePauw University
Earlham College
Franklin College
Hanover College
Manchester College
Rose-Hulman Institute of Technology
Saint Mary's College W
Trine University
Wabash College M

Iowa
Buena Vista University
Central College
Coe College
Cornell College
Grinnell College
Loras College
Luther College
Simpson College
University of Dubuque
Wartburg College

Kentucky
Centre College
Spalding University
Thomas More College
Transylvania University

Louisiana
Louisiana College

Maine
Bates College
Bowdoin College
Colby College
Maine Maritime Academy
St. Joseph's College
University of Maine
Farmington
Presque Isle
University of New England
University of Southern Maine

Maryland
Frostburg State University
Goucher College
Hood College
Johns Hopkins University
McDaniel College
Salisbury University
Stevenson University

Massachusetts
Amherst College
Anna Maria College M
Babson College
Bay Path College W
Brandeis University
Bridgewater State College
Clark University
Curry College W
Elms College
Emerson College
Emmanuel College
Endicott College
Fitchburg State College
Framingham State College
Gordon College
Lasell College
Lesley University
Massachusetts College of Liberal Arts
Massachusetts Institute of Technology
Massachusetts Maritime Academy
Mount Holyoke College W
Mount Ida College W
Newbury College
Pine Manor College W
Salem State College
Smith College W
Springfield College
Suffolk University
Tufts University
University of Massachusetts
  Boston
  Dartmouth
Wellesley College W
Western New England College
Westfield State College
Wheaton College
Williams College
Worcester Polytechnic Institute
Worcester State College

Michigan
Adrian College
Albion College
Alma College
Calvin College
Finlandia University
Hope College
Kalamazoo College
Olivet College

Minnesota
Augsburg College
Bethel University
Carleton College
College of St. Benedict W
College of St. Catherine W
College of St. Scholastica
Concordia College: Moorhead
Crown College
Gustavus Adolphus College
Hamline University
Macalester College
Martin Luther College
Northwestern College
St. John's University M
St. Mary's University of Minnesota
St. Olaf College
University of Minnesota
  Morris W
University of St. Thomas

Mississippi
Millsaps College
Mississippi College
Rust College

Missouri
Fontbonne University
Maryville University of Saint Louis
Washington University in St. Louis
Webster University W
Westminster College

Nebraska
Nebraska Wesleyan University

New Hampshire
Daniel Webster College
Keene State College
New England College
Rivier College

New Jersey
Centenary College
The College of New Jersey
Drew University
Fairleigh Dickinson University
  College at Florham
New Jersey City University
Ramapo College of New Jersey
Richard Stockton College of New Jersey
Rowan University
Rutgers, The State University of New Jersey
  Camden Regional Campus
  Newark Regional Campus
Stevens Institute of Technology

New York
Alfred University
Bard College
Cazenovia College
City University of New York
  Baruch College
  Brooklyn College
  City College M
  Hunter College
  John Jay College of Criminal Justice
  Lehman College
  Medgar Evers College
  New York City College of Technology
  York College
Clarkson University
College of Mount St. Vincent
College of New Rochelle W
D'Youville College W
Hamilton College
Hartwick College
Hilbert College
Hobart and William Smith Colleges
Ithaca College
Keuka College
Manhattanville College
Medaille College
Mount St. Mary College
Nazareth College of Rochester
New York University
Polytechnic Institute of New York University
Rensselaer Polytechnic Institute
Rochester Institute of Technology
St. Joseph's College W
St. Joseph's College: Suffolk Campus M
St. Lawrence University
State University of New York
  College at Brockport
  College at Buffalo
  College at Cortland
  College at Fredonia
  College at Geneseo
  College at Old Westbury
  College at Oneonta
  College at Plattsburgh
  College at Potsdam
  College of Agriculture and Technology at Cobleskill
  Farmingdale
  Institute of Technology at Utica/Rome
  Maritime College
  New Paltz
  Oswego
  Purchase
Union College
United States Merchant Marine Academy
University of Rochester
Utica College
Vassar College
Wells College
Yeshiva University

North Carolina
Greensboro College
Guilford College
Meredith College W
Methodist University
North Carolina Wesleyan College W
Peace College W
Salem College W

Ohio
Baldwin-Wallace College
Bluffton University
Capital University
Case Western Reserve University
College of Mount St. Joseph
College of Wooster
Defiance College
Denison University
Franciscan University of Steubenville
Heidelberg University
Hiram College
John Carroll University
Kenyon College
Lake Erie College
Marietta College
Mount Union College
Muskingum College
Oberlin College
Ohio Northern University
Ohio Wesleyan University
Otterbein College
Wilmington College
Wittenberg University

Oregon
George Fox University
Lewis & Clark College
Linfield College
Pacific University
Willamette University

Pennsylvania
Albright College
Allegheny College
Alvernia University
Arcadia University M
Baptist Bible College of Pennsylvania
Bryn Mawr College W
Cabrini College
Carnegie Mellon University
Cedar Crest College W
Chatham University W
Delaware Valley College
DeSales University
Dickinson College
Eastern University
Elizabethtown College
Franklin & Marshall College
Geneva College
Gettysburg College
Grove City College
Gwynedd-Mercy College
Haverford College
Immaculata University
Juniata College
Keystone College
King's College
La Roche College
Lancaster Bible College
Lebanon Valley College
Lincoln University
Lycoming College
Marywood University
Messiah College
Misericordia University
Moravian College
Mount Aloysius College
Muhlenberg College
Penn State
  Altoona
  Berks
  Erie, The Behrend College
  Harrisburg
Philadelphia Biblical University M
St. Vincent College
Susquehanna University
Swarthmore College
Thiel College
University of Pittsburgh
  Bradford
  Greensburg
University of Scranton
Ursinus College
Washington & Jefferson College
Waynesburg University
Westminster College
Widener University
York College of Pennsylvania

Rhode Island
Johnson & Wales University: Providence
Rhode Island College
Roger Williams University
Salve Regina University

South Dakota
Presentation College M

Tennessee
Maryville College
Rhodes College
University of the South

Texas
Concordia University Texas
East Texas Baptist University
Hardin-Simmons University
McMurry University
Schreiner University
Southwestern University
Sul Ross State University
Texas Lutheran University W
Trinity University
University of Dallas
University of Texas
  Dallas
  Tyler

Vermont
Castleton State College
Green Mountain College
Johnson State College
Lyndon State College
Middlebury College
Norwich University
Southern Vermont College

Virginia
Averett University
Bridgewater College
Christopher Newport University
Eastern Mennonite University
Emory & Henry College
Ferrum College
Hampden-Sydney College M
Lynchburg College
Mary Baldwin College W
Marymount University
Randolph College
Roanoke College
Shenandoah University
University of Mary Washington
Virginia Wesleyan College
Washington and Lee University

Washington
Pacific Lutheran University
University of Puget Sound
Whitman College
Whitworth University

West Virginia
Bethany College

Wisconsin
Alverno College W
Beloit College
Carroll University
Carthage College
Concordia University Wisconsin
Edgewood College
Lakeland College
Lawrence University
Maranatha Baptist Bible College
Marian University
Milwaukee School of Engineering
Mount Mary College W
Northland College
Ripon College
St. Norbert College
University of Wisconsin
  Eau Claire
  La Crosse
  Oshkosh
  Platteville
  River Falls
  Stevens Point
  Stout
  Superior
  Whitewater
Wisconsin Lutheran College

Fencing Division I

California
California State University
  Fullerton W
Stanford University

Colorado
United States Air Force Academy

Connecticut
Sacred Heart University
Yale University

Illinois
Northwestern University W

Indiana
University of Notre Dame

Massachusetts
Boston College
Harvard College

Michigan
University of Detroit Mercy

New Jersey
Fairleigh Dickinson University
  Metropolitan Campus W
New Jersey Institute of Technology
Princeton University

New York
Barnard College W
Columbia University M
Cornell University W
St. Francis College W
St. John's University

North Carolina
Duke University
University of North Carolina
Chapel Hill

Ohio
Cleveland State University
Ohio State University
Columbus Campus

Pennsylvania
Lafayette College
Penn State
University Park
Temple University W
University of Pennsylvania

Rhode Island
Brown University

Fencing Division II

California
University of California
San Diego

Michigan
Wayne State University

New York
City University of New York
Queens College W

Fencing Division III

California
California Institute of Technology

Maryland
Johns Hopkins University

Massachusetts
Brandeis University
Massachusetts Institute of Technology
Tufts University W
Wellesley College W

New Jersey
Drew University
Stevens Institute of Technology

New York
City University of New York
City College W
Hunter College
New York University
Vassar College
Yeshiva University M

Pennsylvania
Haverford College

Wisconsin
Lawrence University

Field hockey Division I

California
Stanford University W
University of California
Berkeley W
University of the Pacific W

Connecticut
Fairfield University W
Quinnipiac University W
Sacred Heart University W
University of Connecticut W
Yale University W

Delaware
University of Delaware W

District of Columbia
American University W
Georgetown University W

Illinois
Northwestern University W

Indiana
Ball State University W
Indiana University
Bloomington W

Iowa
University of Iowa W

Kentucky
University of Louisville W

Maine
University of Maine W

Maryland
Towson University W
University of Maryland
College Park W

Massachusetts
Boston College W
Boston University W
College of the Holy Cross W
Harvard College W
Northeastern University W
University of Massachusetts
Amherst W

Michigan
Central Michigan University W
Michigan State University W
University of Michigan W

Missouri
Saint Louis University W

New Hampshire
Dartmouth College W
University of New Hampshire W

New Jersey
Monmouth University W
Princeton University W
Rider University W
Rutgers, The State University of New Jersey
New Brunswick/Piscataway Campus W

New York
Barnard College W
Colgate University W
Cornell University W
Hofstra University W
Siena College W
State University of New York
Albany W
Syracuse University W

North Carolina
Appalachian State University W
Davidson College W
Duke University W
University of North Carolina
Chapel Hill W
Wake Forest University W

Ohio
Kent State University W
Miami University
Oxford Campus W
Ohio State University
Columbus Campus W
Ohio University W

Pennsylvania
Bucknell University W
Drexel University W
La Salle University W
Lafayette College W
Lehigh University W
Lock Haven University of Pennsylvania W
Penn State
University Park W
Robert Morris University W
St. Francis University W
Saint Joseph's University W
Temple University W
University of Pennsylvania W
Villanova University W
West Chester University of Pennsylvania W

Rhode Island
Brown University W
Bryant University W
Providence College W

Vermont
University of Vermont W

Virginia
College of William and Mary W
James Madison University W
Longwood University W
Old Dominion University W
Radford University W
University of Richmond W
University of Virginia W
Virginia Commonwealth University W

Field hockey Division II

Connecticut
Southern Connecticut State University W

Kentucky
Bellarmine University W

Massachusetts
American International College W
Assumption College W
Bentley University W
Merrimack College W
Stonehill College W
University of Massachusetts
Lowell W

New Hampshire
Franklin Pierce University W
St. Anselm College W

New York
Adelphi University W
Long Island University
C. W. Post Campus W

North Carolina
Catawba College W

Pennsylvania
Bloomsburg University of Pennsylvania W
East Stroudsburg University of Pennsylvania W
Indiana University of Pennsylvania W
Kutztown University of Pennsylvania W
Mansfield University of Pennsylvania W
Mercyhurst College W
Millersville University of Pennsylvania W
Philadelphia University W
Seton Hill University W
Shippensburg University of Pennsylvania W
Slippery Rock University of Pennsylvania W

Vermont
St. Michael's College W

Field hockey Division III

Arkansas
Hendrix College W

Connecticut
Connecticut College W
Eastern Connecticut State University W
Trinity College W
Wesleyan University W
Western Connecticut State University W

Delaware
Wesley College W

District of Columbia
Catholic University of America W

Indiana
DePauw University W
Earlham College W

Kentucky
Centre College W
Transylvania University W

Maine
Bates College W
Bowdoin College W
Colby College W
Husson University W
St. Joseph's College W
Thomas College W
University of Maine
Farmington W
University of New England W
University of Southern Maine W

Maryland
College of Notre Dame of Maryland W
Frostburg State University W
Goucher College W
Hood College W
Johns Hopkins University W
McDaniel College W
St. Mary's College of Maryland W
Salisbury University W
Stevenson University W
Washington College W

Massachusetts
Amherst College W
Anna Maria College W
Babson College W
Becker College W
Bridgewater State College W
Clark University W
Elms College W
Endicott College W
Fitchburg State College W
Framingham State College W
Gordon College W
Lasell College W
Massachusetts Institute of Technology W
Mount Holyoke College W
Nichols College W
Regis College W
Salem State College W
Simmons College W
Smith College W
Springfield College W
Tufts University W
University of Massachusetts
Dartmouth W
Wellesley College W
Western New England College W
Westfield State College W
Wheaton College W
Wheelock College W
Williams College W
Worcester Polytechnic Institute W
Worcester State College W

New Hampshire
Daniel Webster College W
Keene State College W
New England College W
Plymouth State University W

New Jersey
The College of New Jersey W
Drew University W
Fairleigh Dickinson University
College at Florham W
Kean University W
Montclair State University W
Ramapo College of New Jersey W
Richard Stockton College of New Jersey W
Rowan University W
Stevens Institute of Technology W
William Paterson University of New Jersey W

New York
Elmira College W
Hamilton College W
Hartwick College W
Hobart and William Smith Colleges W
Ithaca College W
Manhattanville College W
Nazareth College of Rochester W
Rensselaer Polytechnic Institute W
St. Lawrence University W
Skidmore College W
State University of New York
College at Brockport W
College at Cortland W
College at Geneseo W
College at Oneonta W
College of Agriculture and Technology at Morrisville W
New Paltz W
Oswego W
Union College W
University of Rochester W
Utica College W
Vassar College W
Wells College W
Yeshiva University W

Ohio
College of Wooster W
Denison University W
Kenyon College W
Oberlin College W
Ohio Wesleyan University W
Wittenberg University W

Pennsylvania
Albright College W
Alvernia University W
Arcadia University W
Bryn Mawr College W
Cabrini College W
Cedar Crest College W
Delaware Valley College W
DeSales University W
Dickinson College W
Eastern University W
Elizabethtown College W
Franklin & Marshall College W
Gettysburg College W
Gwynedd-Mercy College W
Haverford College W
Immaculata University W
Juniata College W
Keystone College W
King's College W
Lebanon Valley College W
Marywood University W
Messiah College W
Misericordia University W
Moravian College W
Muhlenberg College W
Neumann College W
Philadelphia Biblical University W
Rosemont College W
St. Vincent College W
Susquehanna University W
Swarthmore College W
University of Scranton W
Ursinus College W

Washington & Jefferson College W
Widener University W
Wilkes University W
Wilson College W
York College of Pennsylvania W

Rhode Island
Salve Regina University W

Tennessee
Rhodes College W
University of the South W

Vermont
Castleton State College W
Middlebury College W

Virginia
Bridgewater College W
Christopher Newport University W
Eastern Mennonite University W
Lynchburg College W
Randolph-Macon College W
Roanoke College W
Shenandoah University W
Sweet Briar College W
University of Mary Washington W
Virginia Wesleyan College W
Washington and Lee University W

Football (tackle) Division IA

Alabama
Auburn University M
Troy University M
University of Alabama M
University of Alabama
Birmingham M

Arizona
Arizona State University M
University of Arizona M

Arkansas
Arkansas State University M
University of Arkansas M

California
California State University
Fresno M
San Diego State University M
San Jose State University M
Stanford University M
University of California
Berkeley M
Los Angeles M
University of Southern California M

Colorado
Colorado State University M
United States Air Force Academy M
University of Colorado
Boulder M

Connecticut
University of Connecticut M

Florida
Florida Atlantic University M
Florida International University M
Florida State University M
University of Central Florida M
University of Florida M
University of Miami M
University of South Florida M

Georgia
Georgia Institute of Technology M
University of Georgia M

Hawaii
University of Hawaii
Manoa M

Idaho
Boise State University M
University of Idaho M

Illinois
Northern Illinois University M
Northwestern University M
University of Illinois
Urbana-Champaign M

Indiana
Ball State University M
Indiana University
Bloomington M
Purdue University M
University of Notre Dame M

Iowa
Iowa State University M
University of Iowa M

Kansas
Kansas State University M
University of Kansas M

Kentucky
University of Kentucky M
University of Louisville M
Western Kentucky University M

Louisiana
Louisiana State University and Agricultural and Mechanical College M
Louisiana Tech University M
Tulane University M
University of Louisiana at Lafayette M
University of Louisiana at Monroe M

Maryland
United States Naval Academy M
University of Maryland
College Park M

Massachusetts
Boston College M

Michigan
Central Michigan University M
Eastern Michigan University M
Michigan State University M
University of Michigan M
Western Michigan University M

Minnesota
University of Minnesota
Twin Cities M

Mississippi
Mississippi State University M
University of Mississippi M
University of Southern Mississippi M

Missouri
University of Missouri
Columbia M

Nebraska
University of Nebraska
Lincoln M

Nevada
University of Nevada
Las Vegas M
Reno M

New Jersey
Rutgers, The State University of New Jersey
New Brunswick/Piscataway Campus M

New Mexico
New Mexico State University M
University of New Mexico M

New York
Syracuse University M
United States Military Academy M

North Carolina
Duke University M
East Carolina University M
North Carolina State University M
University of North Carolina
Chapel Hill M
Wake Forest University M

Ohio
Bowling Green State University M
Kent State University M
Miami University
Oxford Campus M
Ohio State University
Columbus Campus M
Ohio University M
University of Akron M
University of Cincinnati M
University of Toledo M

Oklahoma
Oklahoma State University M
University of Oklahoma M
University of Tulsa M

Oregon
Oregon State University M
University of Oregon M

Pennsylvania
Penn State
University Park M
Temple University M
University of Pittsburgh M

South Carolina
Clemson University M
University of South Carolina M

Tennessee
Middle Tennessee State University M
University of Memphis M
University of Tennessee
Knoxville M
Vanderbilt University M

Texas
Baylor University M
Rice University M
Southern Methodist University M
Texas A&M University M
Texas Christian University M
Texas Tech University M
University of Houston M
University of North Texas M
University of Texas
Austin M
El Paso M

Utah
Brigham Young University M
University of Utah M
Utah State University M

Virginia
University of Virginia M
Virginia Polytechnic Institute and State University M

Washington
University of Washington M
Washington State University M

West Virginia
Marshall University M
West Virginia University M

Wisconsin
University of Wisconsin
Madison M

Wyoming
University of Wyoming M

Football (tackle) Division IAA

Alabama
Alabama Agricultural and Mechanical University M
Alabama State University M
Jacksonville State University M
Samford University M

Arizona
Northern Arizona University M

Arkansas
University of Arkansas
Pine Bluff M
University of Central Arkansas M

California
California Polytechnic State University: San Luis Obispo M
California State University
Sacramento M
University of California
Davis M
University of San Diego M

Colorado
University of Northern Colorado M

Connecticut
Central Connecticut State University M
Sacred Heart University M
Yale University M

Delaware
Delaware State University M
University of Delaware M

District of Columbia
Georgetown University M
Howard University M

Florida
Bethune-Cookman University M
Florida Agricultural and Mechanical University M
Jacksonville University M

Georgia
Georgia Southern University M
Savannah State University M

Idaho
Idaho State University M

Illinois
Eastern Illinois University M
Illinois State University M
Southern Illinois University
Carbondale M
Western Illinois University M

Indiana
Butler University M
Indiana State University M
Valparaiso University M

Iowa
Drake University M
University of Northern Iowa M

Kentucky
Eastern Kentucky University M
Morehead State University M
Murray State University M

Louisiana
Grambling State University M
McNeese State University M
Nicholls State University M
Northwestern State University M
Southeastern Louisiana University M
Southern University and Agricultural and Mechanical College M

Maine
University of Maine M

Maryland
Morgan State University M
Towson University M

Massachusetts
College of the Holy Cross M
Harvard College M
Northeastern University M
University of Massachusetts
Amherst M

Mississippi
Alcorn State University M
Jackson State University M
Mississippi Valley State University M

Missouri
Missouri State University M
Southeast Missouri State University M

Montana
Montana State University
Bozeman M
University of Montana M

New Hampshire
Dartmouth College M
University of New Hampshire M

New Jersey
Monmouth University M
Princeton University M

New York
Colgate University M
Cornell University M
Fordham University M
Hofstra University M
Iona College M
Marist College M
State University of New York
Albany M
Stony Brook M
Wagner College M

North Carolina
Appalachian State University M
Campbell University M
Davidson College M
Elon University M
Gardner-Webb University M
North Carolina Agricultural and Technical State University M
Western Carolina University M
Winston-Salem State University M

North Dakota
North Dakota State University M
University of North Dakota M

Ohio
University of Dayton M
Youngstown State University M

Oregon
Portland State University M

Pennsylvania
Bucknell University M
Duquesne University M
Lafayette College M
Lehigh University M
Robert Morris University M
St. Francis University M
University of Pennsylvania M
Villanova University M

Rhode Island
Brown University M
Bryant University M
University of Rhode Island M

South Carolina
Charleston Southern University M
The Citadel M
Coastal Carolina University M
Furman University M
Presbyterian College M

South Carolina State University M
Wofford College M

South Dakota
South Dakota State University M
University of South Dakota M

Tennessee
Austin Peay State University M
Tennessee State University M
Tennessee Technological University M
University of Tennessee
Chattanooga M
Martin M

Texas
Prairie View A&M University M
Sam Houston State University M
Stephen F. Austin State University M
Texas Southern University M
Texas State University: San Marcos M

Utah
Southern Utah University M
Weber State University M

Virginia
College of William and Mary M
Hampton University M
James Madison University M
Liberty University M
Norfolk State University M
University of Richmond M
Virginia Military Institute M

Washington
Eastern Washington University M

Football (tackle) Division II

Alabama
Miles College M
Tuskegee University M
University of North Alabama M
University of West Alabama M

Arkansas
Arkansas Tech University M
Harding University M
Henderson State University M
Ouachita Baptist University M
Southern Arkansas University M
University of Arkansas
Monticello M

California
Humboldt State University M

Colorado
Adams State College M
Colorado School of Mines M
Colorado State University
Pueblo M
Fort Lewis College M
Mesa State College M
Western State College of Colorado M

Connecticut
Southern Connecticut State University M

Georgia
Albany State University M
Clark Atlanta University M
Fort Valley State University M
Morehouse College M
University of West Georgia M
Valdosta State University M

Illinois
Quincy University M

Indiana
Saint Joseph's College M
University of Indianapolis M

Iowa
Upper Iowa University M

Kansas
Emporia State University M
Fort Hays State University M
Pittsburg State University M
Washburn University M

Kentucky
Kentucky State University M
Kentucky Wesleyan College M

Maryland
Bowie State University M

Massachusetts
American International College M
Assumption College M
Bentley University M
Merrimack College M
Stonehill College M

Michigan
Ferris State University M
Grand Valley State University M
Hillsdale College M
Michigan Technological University M
Northern Michigan University M
Northwood University: Michigan M
Saginaw Valley State University M
Wayne State University M

Minnesota
Bemidji State University M
Concordia University: St. Paul M
Minnesota State University
Mankato M
Moorhead M
Saint Cloud State University M
Southwest Minnesota State University M
University of Minnesota
Crookston M
Duluth M
Winona State University M

Mississippi
Delta State University M

Missouri
Lincoln University M
Missouri Southern State University M
Missouri Western State University M
Northwest Missouri State University M
Southwest Baptist University M
Truman State University M
University of Central Missouri M
University of Missouri
Missouri University of Science and Technology M

Nebraska
Chadron State College M
University of Nebraska
Kearney M
Omaha M
Wayne State College M

New Hampshire
St. Anselm College M

New Mexico
Eastern New Mexico University M
New Mexico Highlands University M
Western New Mexico University M

New York
Long Island University
C. W. Post Campus M
Pace University M

North Carolina
Brevard College M
Catawba College M
Chowan University M
Elizabeth City State University M
Fayetteville State University M
Johnson C. Smith University M
Lenoir-Rhyne University M
Livingstone College M
Mars Hill College M
North Carolina Central University M
St. Augustine's College M
Shaw University M
University of North Carolina
Pembroke M
Wingate University M

North Dakota
University of Mary M

Ohio
Ashland University M
Central State University M
Tiffin University M
University of Findlay M

Oklahoma
East Central University M
Northeastern State University M
Oklahoma Panhandle State University M
Southeastern Oklahoma State University M
Southwestern Oklahoma State University M
University of Central Oklahoma M

Oregon
Western Oregon University M

Pennsylvania
Bloomsburg University of Pennsylvania M
California University of Pennsylvania M
Cheyney University of Pennsylvania M
Clarion University of Pennsylvania M
East Stroudsburg University of Pennsylvania M
Edinboro University of Pennsylvania M
Gannon University M
Indiana University of Pennsylvania M
Kutztown University of Pennsylvania M
Lock Haven University of Pennsylvania M
Mercyhurst College M
Millersville University of Pennsylvania M
Seton Hill University M
Shippensburg University of Pennsylvania M
Slippery Rock University of Pennsylvania M
West Chester University of Pennsylvania M

South Carolina
Benedict College M
Newberry College M
North Greenville University M

South Dakota
Augustana College M
Northern State University M

Tennessee
Carson-Newman College M
Lane College M
Tusculum College M

Texas
Abilene Christian University M
Angelo State University M
Midwestern State University M
Tarleton State University M
Texas A&M University
Commerce M
Kingsville M
West Texas A&M University M

Utah
Dixie State College of Utah M

Virginia
St. Paul's College M
Virginia State University M
Virginia Union University M

Washington
Central Washington University M
Western Washington University M

West Virginia
Concord University M
Fairmont State University M
Glenville State College M
Shepherd University M
University of Charleston M
West Liberty State College M
West Virginia State University M
West Virginia Wesleyan College M

Football (tackle) Division III

Alabama
Birmingham-Southern College M
Huntingdon College M

California
California Lutheran University M
Chapman University M
Claremont McKenna College M
Menlo College M
Occidental College M
Pitzer College M
Pomona College M
University of La Verne M
University of Redlands M
Whittier College M

Colorado
Colorado College M

Connecticut
Trinity College M
United States Coast Guard Academy M
Wesleyan University M
Western Connecticut State University M

Delaware
Wesley College M

District of Columbia
Catholic University of America M
Gallaudet University M

Georgia
LaGrange College M

Illinois
Augustana College M
Aurora University M
Benedictine University M
Blackburn College M
Concordia University Chicago M
Elmhurst College M
Eureka College M
Greenville College M
Illinois College M
Illinois Wesleyan University M
Knox College M
Lake Forest College M
MacMurray College M
Millikin University M
Monmouth College M
North Central College M
North Park University M
Principia College M
Rockford College M
University of Chicago M
Wheaton College M

Indiana
Anderson University M
DePauw University M
Earlham College M
Franklin College M
Hanover College M
Manchester College M
Rose-Hulman Institute of Technology M
Trine University M
Wabash College M

Iowa
Buena Vista University M
Central College M
Coe College M
Cornell College M
Grinnell College M
Loras College M
Luther College M
Simpson College M
University of Dubuque M
Wartburg College M

Kentucky
Centre College M
Thomas More College M

Louisiana
Louisiana College M

Maine
Bates College M
Bowdoin College M
Colby College M
Husson University M
Maine Maritime Academy M

Maryland
Frostburg State University M
Johns Hopkins University M
McDaniel College M
Salisbury University M

Massachusetts
Amherst College M
Becker College M
Bridgewater State College M
Curry College M
Endicott College M
Fitchburg State College M
Framingham State College M
Massachusetts Institute of Technology M
Massachusetts Maritime Academy M
Mount Ida College M
Nichols College M
Springfield College M
Tufts University M
University of Massachusetts
Dartmouth M
Western New England College M
Westfield State College M
Williams College M
Worcester Polytechnic Institute M
Worcester State College M

Michigan
Adrian College M
Albion College M
Alma College M
Hope College M
Kalamazoo College M
Olivet College M

Minnesota
Augsburg College M
Bethel University M
Carleton College M
College of St. Scholastica M
Concordia College: Moorhead M
Crown College M

Gustavus Adolphus College M
Hamline University M
Macalester College M
Martin Luther College M
Northwestern College M
St. John's University M
St. Olaf College M
University of Minnesota
  Morris M
University of St. Thomas M

Mississippi
Millsaps College M
Mississippi College M

Missouri
Washington University in St. Louis M
Westminster College M

Nebraska
Nebraska Wesleyan University M

New Hampshire
Plymouth State University M

New Jersey
The College of New Jersey M
Fairleigh Dickinson University
  College at Florham M
Kean University M
Montclair State University M
Rowan University M
William Paterson University of New Jersey M

New York
Alfred University M
Hamilton College M
Hartwick College M
Hobart and William Smith Colleges M
Ithaca College M
Rensselaer Polytechnic Institute M
St. John Fisher College M
St. Lawrence University M
State University of New York
  College at Brockport M
  College at Buffalo M
  College at Cortland M
  College of Agriculture and Technology at Morrisville M
  Maritime College M
Union College M
United States Merchant Marine Academy M
University of Rochester M
Utica College M

North Carolina
Greensboro College M
Guilford College M
Methodist University M
North Carolina Wesleyan College M

Ohio
Baldwin-Wallace College M
Bluffton University M
Capital University M
Case Western Reserve University M
College of Mount St. Joseph M
College of Wooster M
Defiance College M
Denison University M
Heidelberg University M
Hiram College M
John Carroll University M
Kenyon College M
Lake Erie College M
Marietta College M
Mount Union College M
Muskingum College M
Oberlin College M
Ohio Northern University M
Ohio Wesleyan University M
Otterbein College M
Wilmington College M
Wittenberg University M

Oregon
Lewis & Clark College M
Linfield College M
Willamette University M

Pennsylvania
Albright College M
Allegheny College M
Carnegie Mellon University M
Delaware Valley College M
Dickinson College M
Franklin & Marshall College M
Geneva College M
Gettysburg College M
Grove City College M
Juniata College M
King's College M
Lebanon Valley College M
Lincoln University M
Lycoming College M
Moravian College M
Muhlenberg College M
St. Vincent College M
Susquehanna University M
Thiel College M
Ursinus College M
Washington & Jefferson College M
Waynesburg University M
Westminster College M
Widener University M
Wilkes University M

Rhode Island
Salve Regina University M

Tennessee
Maryville College M
Rhodes College M
University of the South M

Texas
Austin College M
East Texas Baptist University M
Hardin-Simmons University M
Howard Payne University M
McMurry University M
Sul Ross State University M
Texas Lutheran University M
Trinity University M
University of Mary Hardin-Baylor M

Vermont
Middlebury College M
Norwich University M

Virginia
Averett University M
Bridgewater College M
Christopher Newport University M
Emory & Henry College M
Ferrum College M
Hampden-Sydney College M
Randolph-Macon College M
Shenandoah University M
Washington and Lee University M

Washington
Pacific Lutheran University M
University of Puget Sound M
Whitworth University M

West Virginia
Bethany College M

Wisconsin
Beloit College M
Carroll University M
Carthage College M
Concordia University Wisconsin M
Lakeland College M
Lawrence University M
Maranatha Baptist Bible College M
Ripon College M
St. Norbert College M
University of Wisconsin
  Eau Claire M
  La Crosse M
  Oshkosh M
  Platteville M
  River Falls M
  Stevens Point M
  Stout M
  Whitewater M
Wisconsin Lutheran College M

Golf Division I

Alabama
Alabama Agricultural and Mechanical University M
Alabama State University
Auburn University
Birmingham-Southern College
Jacksonville State University
Samford University
Troy University
University of Alabama
University of Alabama
  Birmingham
University of South Alabama

Arizona
Arizona State University
Northern Arizona University W
University of Arizona

Arkansas
Arkansas State University
University of Arkansas
University of Arkansas
  Little Rock
  Pine Bluff
University of Central Arkansas

California
California Polytechnic State University: San Luis Obispo
California State University
  Bakersfield
  Fresno
  Long Beach
  Northridge
  Sacramento
Loyola Marymount University M
Pepperdine University
St. Mary's College of California M
San Diego State University
San Jose State University
Santa Clara University
Stanford University
University of California
  Berkeley
  Davis
  Irvine
  Los Angeles
  Riverside
  Santa Barbara M
University of San Diego M
University of San Francisco
University of Southern California
University of the Pacific M

Colorado
Colorado State University
United States Air Force Academy M
University of Colorado
  Boulder
University of Denver
University of Northern Colorado

Connecticut
Central Connecticut State University
Fairfield University
Quinnipiac University M
Sacred Heart University
University of Connecticut M
University of Hartford
Yale University

Delaware
University of Delaware M

District of Columbia
George Washington University M
Georgetown University

Florida
Bethune-Cookman University
Florida Agricultural and Mechanical University M
Florida Atlantic University
Florida Gulf Coast University
Florida International University W
Florida State University
Jacksonville University
Stetson University
University of Central Florida
University of Florida
University of Miami W
University of North Florida M
University of South Florida

Georgia
Augusta State University
Georgia Institute of Technology M
Georgia Southern University M
Georgia State University
Kennesaw State University
Mercer University
Savannah State University
University of Georgia

Hawaii
University of Hawaii
  Manoa

Idaho
Boise State University
Idaho State University W
University of Idaho

Illinois
Bradley University
Chicago State University
DePaul University M
Eastern Illinois University
Illinois State University
Loyola University Chicago
Northern Illinois University
Northwestern University
Southern Illinois University
  Carbondale
Southern Illinois University
  Edwardsville
University of Illinojs
  Urbana-Champaign
Western Illinois University

Indiana
Ball State University
Butler University
Indiana State University W
Indiana University
  Bloomington
Indiana University-Purdue University Fort Wayne
Indiana University-Purdue University Indianapolis
Purdue University
University of Evansville
University of Notre Dame

Iowa
Drake University
Iowa State University
University of Iowa
University of Northern Iowa

Kansas
Kansas State University
University of Kansas
Wichita State University

Kentucky
Eastern Kentucky University
Morehead State University M
Murray State University
University of Kentucky
University of Louisville
Western Kentucky University

Louisiana
Centenary College of Louisiana
Grambling State University
Louisiana State University and Agricultural and Mechanical College
Louisiana Tech University M
McNeese State University
Nicholls State University
Southeastern Louisiana University M
Southern University and Agricultural and Mechanical College
University of Louisiana at Lafayette M
University of Louisiana at Monroe
University of New Orleans M

Maryland
Loyola College in Maryland M
Mount St. Mary's University
Towson University
United States Naval Academy M
University of Maryland
  College Park

Massachusetts
Boston College
Boston University W
College of the Holy Cross
Harvard College

Michigan
Eastern Michigan University
Michigan State University
Oakland University
University of Detroit Mercy
University of Michigan
Western Michigan University W

Minnesota
University of Minnesota
  Twin Cities

Mississippi
Alcorn State University
Jackson State University
Mississippi State University
Mississippi Valley State University
University of Mississippi
University of Southern Mississippi

Missouri
Missouri State University
University of Missouri
  Columbia
  Kansas City

Montana
Montana State University
  Bozeman W
University of Montana W

Nebraska
Creighton University
University of Nebraska
  Lincoln

Nevada
University of Nevada
  Las Vegas
  Reno

New Hampshire
Dartmouth College

New Jersey
Fairleigh Dickinson University
  Metropolitan Campus
Monmouth University
Princeton University

Rider University M
Rutgers, The State University of New Jersey
New Brunswick/Piscataway Campus
Saint Peter's College M
Seton Hall University M

New Mexico
New Mexico State University
University of New Mexico

New York
Barnard College W
Canisius College M
Colgate University M
Cornell University M
Fordham University M
Hofstra University
Iona College M
Long Island University
Brooklyn Campus
Manhattan College M
Niagara University M
Saint Bonaventure University M
St. Francis College
St. John's University
Siena College
State University of New York
Albany W
Binghamton M
United States Military Academy M
Wagner College

North Carolina
Appalachian State University
Campbell University
Davidson College M
Duke University
East Carolina University
Elon University
Gardner-Webb University
High Point University
North Carolina Central University M
North Carolina State University
University of North Carolina
Chapel Hill
Charlotte M
Greensboro
Wilmington
Wake Forest University
Western Carolina University
Winston-Salem State University M

North Dakota
North Dakota State University
University of North Dakota

Ohio
Bowling Green State University
Cleveland State University
Kent State University
Miami University
Oxford Campus M
Ohio State University
Columbus Campus
Ohio University
University of Akron M
University of Cincinnati
University of Dayton
University of Toledo
Wright State University M
Xavier University
Youngstown State University

Oklahoma
Oklahoma State University
Oral Roberts University
University of Oklahoma
University of Tulsa

Oregon
Oregon State University
Portland State University W
University of Oregon
University of Portland

Pennsylvania
Bucknell University
Drexel University M
Duquesne University M
La Salle University M
Lafayette College M
Lehigh University
Penn State
University Park
Robert Morris University
St. Francis University
Saint Joseph's University M
Temple University M
University of Pennsylvania
Villanova University M

Rhode Island
Brown University
Bryant University M
University of Rhode Island M

South Carolina
Charleston Southern University
The Citadel W
Clemson University M
Coastal Carolina University
College of Charleston
Francis Marion University M
Furman University
Presbyterian College
South Carolina State University
University of South Carolina
University of South Carolina
Upstate
Winthrop University
Wofford College

South Dakota
South Dakota State University
University of South Dakota

Tennessee
Austin Peay State University
Belmont University
East Tennessee State University
Lipscomb University
Middle Tennessee State University
Tennessee State University
Tennessee Technological University
University of Memphis
University of Tennessee
Chattanooga
Knoxville
Martin M
Vanderbilt University

Texas
Baylor University
Houston Baptist University
Lamar University
Prairie View A&M University
Rice University M
Sam Houston State University
Southern Methodist University
Stephen F. Austin State University M
Texas A&M University
Texas A&M University
Corpus Christi W
Texas Christian University
Texas Southern University
Texas State University: San Marcos
Texas Tech University
University of Houston M
University of North Texas
University of Texas
Arlington M
Austin
El Paso
Pan American
San Antonio

Utah
Brigham Young University
Southern Utah University
University of Utah M
Utah State University M
Utah Valley University
Weber State University

Virginia
College of William and Mary
George Mason University M
Hampton University
James Madison University
Liberty University M
Longwood University
Old Dominion University
Radford University
University of Richmond
University of Virginia
Virginia Commonwealth University M
Virginia Polytechnic Institute and State University M

Washington
Eastern Washington University W
Gonzaga University
University of Washington
Washington State University

West Virginia
Marshall University

Wisconsin
Marquette University M
University of Wisconsin
Green Bay
Madison

Wyoming
University of Wyoming

Golf Division II

Alabama
University of Montevallo
University of North Alabama M

Arizona
Grand Canyon University

Arkansas
Arkansas Tech University
Harding University
Henderson State University
Ouachita Baptist University M
Southern Arkansas University
University of Arkansas
Monticello

California
California State University
Chico
Dominguez Hills M
Monterey Bay
San Bernardino M
Stanislaus M
Notre Dame de Namur University
Sonoma State University
University of California
San Diego M

Colorado
Adams State College W
Colorado Christian University
Colorado School of Mines M
Colorado State University
Pueblo
Fort Lewis College M
Mesa State College W
Regis University
University of Colorado
Colorado Springs M

Connecticut
Post University M
University of New Haven M

Delaware
Goldey-Beacom College M
Wilmington University M

Florida
Barry University
Eckerd College
Flagler College
Florida Institute of Technology
Florida Southern College
Lynn University
Nova Southeastern University
Rollins College
St. Leo University
University of Tampa M
University of West Florida

Georgia
Albany State University W
Armstrong Atlantic State University
Clayton State University M
Columbus State University M
Georgia College and State University M
Georgia Southwestern State University M
Morehouse College M
Paine College M
University of West Georgia
Valdosta State University M

Hawaii
Brigham Young University-Hawaii M
Chaminade University of Honolulu M
Hawaii Pacific University M
University of Hawaii
Hilo

Idaho
Northwest Nazarene University M

Illinois
Lewis University
Quincy University

Indiana
Oakland City University
Saint Joseph's College
University of Indianapolis
University of Southern Indiana

Iowa
Upper Iowa University

Kansas
Fort Hays State University
Newman University
Pittsburg State University M
Washburn University M

Kentucky
Bellarmine University
Kentucky State University M
Kentucky Wesleyan College
Northern Kentucky University

Massachusetts
American International College M
Assumption College M
Bentley University M
University of Massachusetts
Lowell M

Michigan
Ferris State University
Grand Valley State University
Northern Michigan University M
Northwood University: Michigan
Saginaw Valley State University M
Wayne State University M

Minnesota
Bemidji State University
Concordia University: St. Paul
Minnesota State University
Mankato
Moorhead W
Saint Cloud State University
Southwest Minnesota State University W
University of Minnesota
Crookston
Winona State University

Mississippi
Delta State University M

Missouri
Drury University
Lincoln University M
Missouri Southern State University M
Missouri Western State University
Northwest Missouri State University W
Rockhurst University
Southwest Baptist University M
Truman State University
University of Central Missouri M
University of Missouri
St. Louis

Montana
Montana State University
Billings

Nebraska
Chadron State College W
University of Nebraska
Kearney
Omaha W
Wayne State College

New Hampshire
Franklin Pierce University M
St. Anselm College M
Southern New Hampshire University M

New Jersey
Caldwell College M
Felician College M

New Mexico
Western New Mexico University

New York
Adelphi University M
College of Saint Rose M
Dominican College of Blauvelt M
Dowling College M
Le Moyne College M
Nyack College M
Pace University M
St. Thomas Aquinas College M

North Carolina
Barton College M
Belmont Abbey College
Brevard College
Catawba College
Chowan University M
Elizabeth City State University M
Fayetteville State University M
Johnson C. Smith University M
Lees-McRae College M
Lenoir-Rhyne University
Mars Hill College
Mount Olive College
Pfeiffer University
Queens University of Charlotte
St. Andrews Presbyterian College
St. Augustine's College M
University of North Carolina
Pembroke
Wingate University

North Dakota
University of Mary

Ohio
Ashland University
Central State University
Tiffin University
University of Findlay

Oklahoma
Cameron University
East Central University
Northeastern State University
Oklahoma Panhandle State University
Southeastern Oklahoma State University M

Southwestern Oklahoma State University
University of Central Oklahoma

Pennsylvania
California University of Pennsylvania
Chestnut Hill College
Clarion University of Pennsylvania
East Stroudsburg University of Pennsylvania W
Gannon University
Holy Family University M
Indiana University of Pennsylvania M
Kutztown University of Pennsylvania W
Mercyhurst College
Millersville University of Pennsylvania M
Philadelphia University M
Seton Hill University
University of Pittsburgh Johnstown
University of the Sciences in Philadelphia M
West Chester University of Pennsylvania

South Carolina
Anderson University
Benedict College
Erskine College
Lander University M
Limestone College
Newberry College
North Greenville University M
University of South Carolina Aiken M

South Dakota
Augustana College
Northern State University

Tennessee
Carson-Newman College M
Christian Brothers University
LeMoyne-Owen College M
Lincoln Memorial University
Tusculum College

Texas
Abilene Christian University M
Angelo State University W
Dallas Baptist University
Midwestern State University M
St. Edward's University
St. Mary's University
Tarleton State University W
Texas A&M International University M
Texas A&M University Commerce
University of the Incarnate Word
West Texas A&M University

Utah
Dixie State College of Utah M

Vermont
St. Michael's College M

Virginia
St. Paul's College M
Virginia State University M
Virginia Union University M

Washington
Saint Martin's University
Western Washington University

West Virginia
Bluefield State College M
Concord University
Davis and Elkins College M
Fairmont State University
Glenville State College
Ohio Valley University
Salem International University
Shepherd University M
University of Charleston M
West Liberty State College
West Virginia State University
West Virginia Wesleyan College M
Wheeling Jesuit University

Wisconsin
University of Wisconsin Parkside M

Golf Division III

Alabama
Huntingdon College

Arkansas
Hendrix College

California
California Lutheran University M
California State University East Bay
Chapman University M
Claremont McKenna College
La Sierra University M
Menlo College M
Occidental College
Pitzer College M
Pomona College M
University of California Santa Cruz W
University of La Verne M
University of Redlands
Whittier College M

Connecticut
Mitchell College M
Trinity College M
Wesleyan University M

Delaware
Wesley College M

Georgia
Emory University M
LaGrange College M
Oglethorpe University
Piedmont College
Spelman College W

Illinois
Augustana College
Aurora University
Benedictine University
Blackburn College M
Elmhurst College
Eureka College M
Illinois College
Illinois Wesleyan University
Knox College
MacMurray College M
Millikin University
Monmouth College
North Central College
North Park University
Rockford College M
Wheaton College

Indiana
Anderson University
DePauw University
Franklin College
Hanover College
Manchester College
Rose-Hulman Institute of Technology
Saint Mary's College W
Trine University
Wabash College M

Iowa
Buena Vista University
Central College
Coe College
Cornell College
Grinnell College
Loras College
Luther College
Simpson College
University of Dubuque
Wartburg College

Kentucky
Centre College
Spalding University M
Thomas More College
Transylvania University

Louisiana
Louisiana College M

Maine
Bates College
Bowdoin College
Husson University M
Maine Maritime Academy M
St. Joseph's College M
Thomas College M
University of Maine
Farmington M
Presque Isle M
University of New England M

Maryland
Frostburg State University M
Hood College
McDaniel College
Stevenson University

Massachusetts
Amherst College
Anna Maria College M
Babson College M
Becker College M
Brandeis University M
Elms College M
Emerson College M
Endicott College M
Massachusetts College of Liberal Arts M
Massachusetts Institute of Technology M
Mount Holyoke College W
Newbury College M
Nichols College M
Salem State College M
Springfield College M
Suffolk University M
Tufts University M
University of Massachusetts Dartmouth M
Wellesley College W
Wentworth Institute of Technology M
Western New England College M
Westfield State College
Williams College
Worcester State College M

Michigan
Adrian College
Albion College
Alma College
Calvin College
Finlandia University M
Hope College
Kalamazoo College
Olivet College

Minnesota
Augsburg College
Bethany Lutheran College
Bethel University
Carleton College
College of St. Benedict W
Concordia College: Moorhead
Crown College M
Gustavus Adolphus College
Macalester College
Martin Luther College M
Northwestern College
St. John's University M
St. Mary's University of Minnesota
St. Olaf College
University of Minnesota Morris
University of St. Thomas

Mississippi
Millsaps College
Mississippi College M

Missouri
Fontbonne University
Maryville University of Saint Louis
Washington University in St. Louis W
Webster University M
Westminster College

Nebraska
Nebraska Wesleyan University

New Hampshire
Daniel Webster College M

New Jersey
Centenary College M
Fairleigh Dickinson University College at Florham M
Rutgers, The State University of New Jersey
Camden Regional Campus M
Stevens Institute of Technology M

New York
Cazenovia College M
Clarkson University M
D'Youville College M
Elmira College
Hamilton College M
Hilbert College M
Hobart and William Smith Colleges
Ithaca College W
Keuka College M
Manhattanville College M
Nazareth College of Rochester
New York University
Polytechnic Institute of New York University M
Rensselaer Polytechnic Institute M
Sage College of Albany M
St. John Fisher College
St. Joseph's College: Suffolk Campus M
St. Lawrence University
Skidmore College M
State University of New York
College at Cortland W
College at Old Westbury M
College at Potsdam M
College of Agriculture and Technology at Cobleskill
Farmingdale M
Institute of Technology at Utica/Rome M
Oswego M
United States Merchant Marine Academy M
University of Rochester M
Utica College M
Vassar College W
Yeshiva University M

North Carolina
Greensboro College M
Guilford College M
Methodist University
North Carolina Wesleyan College M

Ohio
Baldwin-Wallace College
Capital University
College of Mount St. Joseph
College of Wooster M
Defiance College
Denison University
Heidelberg University
Hiram College
John Carroll University
Kenyon College M
Lake Erie College
Mount Union College
Muskingum College
Oberlin College M
Ohio Northern University
Ohio Wesleyan University M
Otterbein College
Wilmington College
Wittenberg University

Oregon
George Fox University
Lewis & Clark College
Linfield College
Pacific University
Willamette University

Pennsylvania
Albright College M
Allegheny College
Alvernia University M
Arcadia University M
Baptist Bible College of Pennsylvania M
Cabrini College M
Carnegie Mellon University M
Delaware Valley College M
DeSales University M
Dickinson College
Eastern University M
Elizabethtown College M
Franklin & Marshall College
Gettysburg College
Grove City College
Gwynedd-Mercy College M
Immaculata University M
Keystone College M
King's College M
La Roche College M
Lebanon Valley College M
Lycoming College M
Messiah College M
Moravian College M
Mount Aloysius College M
Muhlenberg College
Neumann College M
Penn State
Altoona
Berks M
Erie, The Behrend College
Harrisburg M
Philadelphia Biblical University M
St. Vincent College
Susquehanna University
Swarthmore College M
Thiel College
University of Pittsburgh
Bradford
Greensburg M
University of Scranton M
Ursinus College M
Washington & Jefferson College
Waynesburg University
Westminster College
Widener University M
Wilkes University M
York College of Pennsylvania M

Rhode Island
Johnson & Wales University: Providence M
Rhode Island College M

South Dakota
Presentation College

Tennessee
Rhodes College
University of the South

Texas
Concordia University Texas M
Hardin-Simmons University
LeTourneau University
McMurry University
Schreiner University

Southwestern University
Texas Lutheran University
Trinity University
University of Dallas M
University of Mary Hardin-Baylor
University of Texas
Dallas
Tyler

Vermont
Castleton State College M
Green Mountain College M
Middlebury College

Virginia
Averett University M
Bridgewater College M
Christopher Newport University M
Emory & Henry College M
Ferrum College M
Hampden-Sydney College M
Hollins University W
Lynchburg College M
Marymount University M
Randolph-Macon College M
Roanoke College M
Shenandoah University M
Virginia Wesleyan College M
Washington and Lee University M

Washington
Pacific Lutheran University
University of Puget Sound
Whitman College
Whitworth University

West Virginia
Bethany College

Wisconsin
Beloit College
Carroll University
Carthage College
Concordia University Wisconsin
Edgewood College
Lakeland College
Lawrence University M
Marian University
Milwaukee School of Engineering
Ripon College
St. Norbert College
University of Wisconsin
Eau Claire
Oshkosh W
Platteville W
River Falls W
Stevens Point W
Stout
Superior W
Whitewater W
Wisconsin Lutheran College

Gymnastics Division I

Alabama
Auburn University W
University of Alabama W

Alaska
University of Alaska
Anchorage W

Arizona
Arizona State University W
University of Arizona W

Arkansas
University of Arkansas W

California
California State University
Fullerton W
Sacramento W
San Jose State University W
Stanford University
University of California
Berkeley
Davis W
Los Angeles W

Colorado
United States Air Force Academy
University of Denver W

Connecticut
Yale University W

District of Columbia
George Washington University W

Florida
University of Florida W

Georgia
University of Georgia W

Idaho
Boise State University W

Illinois
Illinois State University W
Northern Illinois University W
University of Illinois
Chicago
Urbana-Champaign

Indiana
Ball State University W

Iowa
Iowa State University W
University of Iowa

Kentucky
University of Kentucky W

Louisiana
Centenary College of Louisiana W
Louisiana State University and Agricultural and Mechanical College W

Maryland
Towson University W
United States Naval Academy M
University of Maryland
College Park W

Michigan
Central Michigan University W
Eastern Michigan University W
Michigan State University W
University of Michigan
Western Michigan University W

Minnesota
University of Minnesota
Twin Cities

Missouri
Southeast Missouri State University W
University of Missouri
Columbia W

Nebraska
University of Nebraska
Lincoln

New Hampshire
University of New Hampshire W

New Jersey
Rutgers, The State University of New Jersey
New Brunswick/Piscataway Campus W

New York
Cornell University W
United States Military Academy M

North Carolina
North Carolina State University W
University of North Carolina
Chapel Hill W

Ohio
Bowling Green State University W
Kent State University W
Ohio State University
Columbus Campus

Oklahoma
University of Oklahoma

Oregon
Oregon State University W

Pennsylvania
Penn State
University Park
Temple University
University of Pennsylvania W
University of Pittsburgh W

Rhode Island
Brown University W

Utah
Brigham Young University W
Southern Utah University W
University of Utah W
Utah State University W

Virginia
College of William and Mary

Washington
University of Washington W

West Virginia
West Virginia University W

Gymnastics Division II

Connecticut
Southern Connecticut State University W
University of Bridgeport W

Pennsylvania
West Chester University of Pennsylvania W

Texas
Texas Woman's University W

Washington
Seattle Pacific University W

Gymnastics Division III

Massachusetts
Massachusetts Institute of Technology
Springfield College

Minnesota
Gustavus Adolphus College W
Hamline University W
Winona State University W

New York
Ithaca College W
State University of New York
College at Brockport W
College at Cortland W

Pennsylvania
Ursinus College W
Wilson College W

Rhode Island
Rhode Island College W

Wisconsin
University of Wisconsin
Eau Claire W
La Crosse W
Oshkosh W
Stout W
Whitewater W

Ice hockey Division I

Alabama
University of Alabama
Huntsville M

Alaska
University of Alaska
Anchorage M
Fairbanks M

Colorado
Colorado College M
United States Air Force Academy M
University of Denver M

Connecticut
Quinnipiac University M
Sacred Heart University M
University of Connecticut M
Yale University M

Indiana
University of Notre Dame M

Maine
University of Maine M

Massachusetts
American International College M
Bentley University M
Boston College M
Boston University M
College of the Holy Cross M
Harvard College M
Merrimack College M
Northeastern University M
University of Massachusetts
Amherst M
Lowell M

Michigan
Ferris State University M
Lake Superior State University M
Michigan State University M
Michigan Technological University M
Northern Michigan University M
University of Michigan M
Western Michigan University M

Minnesota
Bemidji State University M
Minnesota State University
Mankato M
Saint Cloud State University M
University of Minnesota
Duluth
Twin Cities M

Nebraska
University of Nebraska
Omaha M

New Hampshire
Dartmouth College M
University of New Hampshire M

New Jersey
Princeton University M

New York
Canisius College M
Clarkson University M
Colgate University M
Cornell University M
Niagara University M
Rensselaer Polytechnic Institute M
St. Lawrence University M
Union College M
United States Military Academy M

North Dakota
University of North Dakota M

Ohio
Bowling Green State University M
Miami University
Oxford Campus M
Ohio State University
Columbus Campus M

Pennsylvania
Mercyhurst College M
Robert Morris University M

Rhode Island
Brown University M
Providence College M

Vermont
University of Vermont M

Wisconsin
University of Wisconsin
Madison M

Ice hockey Division II

Massachusetts
Assumption College M
Stonehill College M

Minnesota
University of Minnesota
Crookston M

New Hampshire
Franklin Pierce University M
St. Anselm College M
Southern New Hampshire University M

Vermont
St. Michael's College M

Ice hockey Division III

Connecticut
Connecticut College M
Trinity College M
Wesleyan University M

Illinois
Lake Forest College M

Maine
Bowdoin College M
Colby College M
University of Southern Maine M

Massachusetts
Amherst College M
Babson College M
Becker College M
Curry College M
Fitchburg State College M
Framingham State College M
Massachusetts Institute of Technology M
Nichols College M
Salem State College M
Suffolk University M
Tufts University M
University of Massachusetts
Boston M
Dartmouth M
Wentworth Institute of Technology M
Western New England College M
Westfield State College M
Williams College M
Worcester State College M

Michigan
Adrian College M
Finlandia University M

Minnesota
Augsburg College M
Bethel University M
College of St. Scholastica M
Concordia College: Moorhead M
Gustavus Adolphus College M
Hamline University M
St. John's University M

St. Mary's University of Minnesota M
St. Olaf College M
University of St. Thomas M

New Hampshire

New England College M
Plymouth State University M

New York

Elmira College M
Hamilton College M
Hobart and William Smith Colleges M
Manhattanville College M
Skidmore College M
State University of New York
- Buffalo M
- College at Brockport M
- College at Cortland M
- College at Fredonia M
- College at Geneseo M
- College at Plattsburgh M
- College at Potsdam M
- College of Agriculture and Technology at Morrisville M
- Oswego M

Utica College M

Pennsylvania

Lebanon Valley College M
Neumann College M
University of Scranton M

Rhode Island

Johnson & Wales University: Providence M
Salve Regina University M

Vermont

Castleton State College M
Middlebury College M
Norwich University M

Wisconsin

Lawrence University M
Marian University M
Milwaukee School of Engineering M
Northland College M
St. Norbert College M
University of Wisconsin
- Eau Claire M
- River Falls M
- Stevens Point M
- Stout M
- Superior M

Lacrosse Division I

California

California State University Fresno W
St. Mary's College of California W
Stanford University W
University of California
- Berkeley W
- Davis W

Colorado

United States Air Force Academy M
University of Denver

Connecticut

Central Connecticut State University W
Fairfield University
Quinnipiac University
Sacred Heart University
University of Connecticut W
University of Hartford M
Yale University

Delaware

University of Delaware

District of Columbia

American University W
George Washington University W
Georgetown University
Howard University W

Illinois

Northwestern University W

Indiana

University of Notre Dame

Kentucky

Bellarmine University M
University of Louisville W

Maryland

Johns Hopkins University
Loyola College in Maryland
Mount St. Mary's University
Towson University
United States Naval Academy
University of Maryland
- Baltimore County
- College Park

Massachusetts

Boston College W
Boston University W
College of the Holy Cross
Harvard College
University of Massachusetts Amherst

Michigan

University of Detroit Mercy

New Hampshire

Dartmouth College
University of New Hampshire W

New Jersey

Monmouth University W
Princeton University
Rutgers, The State University of New Jersey
- New Brunswick/Piscataway Campus

New York

Barnard College W
Canisius College
Colgate University
Cornell University
Hobart and William Smith Colleges M
Hofstra University
Iona College W
Le Moyne College W
Long Island University
- Brooklyn Campus W

Manhattan College
Marist College
Niagara University W
Saint Bonaventure University W
St. John's University M
Siena College
State University of New York
- Albany
- Binghamton
- Stony Brook

Syracuse University
United States Military Academy M
Wagner College

North Carolina

Davidson College W
Duke University
University of North Carolina
- Chapel Hill

Ohio

Ohio State University
- Columbus Campus

University of Cincinnati W

Oregon

University of Oregon W

Pennsylvania

Bucknell University
Drexel University
Duquesne University W
La Salle University W
Lafayette College
Lehigh University
Penn State
- University Park

Robert Morris University
St. Francis University W
Saint Joseph's University
Temple University W
University of Pennsylvania
Villanova University

Rhode Island

Brown University
Bryant University
Providence College M

South Carolina

Presbyterian College

Tennessee

Vanderbilt University W

Vermont

University of Vermont

Virginia

College of William and Mary W
George Mason University W
James Madison University W
Longwood University W
Old Dominion University W
University of Richmond W
University of Virginia
Virginia Military Institute M
Virginia Polytechnic Institute and State University W

Lacrosse Division II

Arizona

Grand Canyon University M

California

Notre Dame de Namur University M

Colorado

Fort Lewis College W
Regis University W

Connecticut

Southern Connecticut State University W
University of New Haven W

Delaware

Wilmington University W

Florida

Florida Southern College M
Rollins College
St. Leo University M

Massachusetts

American International College
Assumption College
Bentley University
Merrimack College
Stonehill College W

New Hampshire

Franklin Pierce University
St. Anselm College
Southern New Hampshire University

New Jersey

Georgian Court University W

New York

Adelphi University
Dominican College of Blauvelt
Dowling College
Le Moyne College M
Long Island University
- C. W. Post Campus

Molloy College
New York Institute of Technology M
Pace University M
St. Thomas Aquinas College W

North Carolina

Belmont Abbey College
Catawba College M
Lees-McRae College
Mars Hill College M
Pfeiffer University
Queens University of Charlotte
St. Andrews Presbyterian College
Wingate University M

Pennsylvania

Bloomsburg University of Pennsylvania W
Chestnut Hill College W
East Stroudsburg University of Pennsylvania W
Edinboro University of Pennsylvania W
Gannon University W
Holy Family University W
Indiana University of Pennsylvania W
Kutztown University of Pennsylvania W
Lock Haven University of Pennsylvania W
Mercyhurst College
Millersville University of Pennsylvania W
Philadelphia University W
Seton Hill University
Shippensburg University of Pennsylvania W
Slippery Rock University of Pennsylvania W
West Chester University of Pennsylvania W

South Carolina

Converse College W
Erskine College W
Limestone College

Vermont

St. Michael's College

West Virginia

Wheeling Jesuit University M

Lacrosse Division III

Alabama

Birmingham-Southern College M

Arkansas

Hendrix College M

California

Claremont McKenna College W
Pitzer College W
Pomona College W
University of Redlands W
Whittier College

Colorado

Colorado College

Connecticut

Connecticut College M
Eastern Connecticut State University
Mitchell College M
St. Joseph College W
Trinity College
Wesleyan University
Western Connecticut State University

Delaware

Wesley College

District of Columbia

Catholic University of America
Trinity Washington University W

Indiana

Trine University

Maine

Bates College
Bowdoin College
Colby College
Maine Maritime Academy M
St. Joseph's College
Thomas College
University of Maine
- Farmington W

University of New England
University of Southern Maine

Maryland

College of Notre Dame of Maryland W
Frostburg State University W
Goucher College
Hood College
McDaniel College
St. Mary's College of Maryland
Salisbury University
Stevenson University
Washington College

Massachusetts

Amherst College
Anna Maria College
Babson College
Becker College
Bridgewater State College W
Clark University M
Curry College
Elms College W
Emerson College
Endicott College
Fitchburg State College W
Framingham State College W
Gordon College
Lasell College
Massachusetts Institute of Technology
Massachusetts Maritime Academy M
Mount Holyoke College W
Mount Ida College M
Nichols College
Pine Manor College W
Regis College W
Salem State College M
Simmons College W
Smith College W
Springfield College
Tufts University
University of Massachusetts
- Boston M
- Dartmouth

Wellesley College W
Wentworth Institute of Technology M
Western New England College
Westfield State College W
Wheaton College
Williams College
Worcester State College W

Michigan

Adrian College

Missouri

Fontbonne University

New Hampshire

Colby-Sawyer College W
Daniel Webster College M
Keene State College
New England College
Plymouth State University

New Jersey

Centenary College
The College of New Jersey W
Drew University
Fairleigh Dickinson University
- College at Florham

Kean University
Montclair State University

Ramapo College of New Jersey W
Richard Stockton College of New Jersey M
Rowan University W
Stevens Institute of Technology

New York
Alfred University
Cazenovia College
Clarkson University
College of Mount St. Vincent
Elmira College
Hamilton College
Hartwick College
Hobart and William Smith Colleges W
Ithaca College
Keuka College
Manhattanville College
Medaille College
Nazareth College of Rochester
Polytechnic Institute of New York University W
Rensselaer Polytechnic Institute
Rochester Institute of Technology
Sage College of Albany W
St. John Fisher College
St. Lawrence University
Skidmore College
State University of New York
Buffalo W
College at Brockport
College at Cortland
College at Fredonia W
College at Geneseo
College at Oneonta
College at Plattsburgh M
College at Potsdam
College of Agriculture and Technology at Cobleskill M
College of Agriculture and Technology at Morrisville
Farmingdale
Maritime College
New Paltz W
Oswego
Union College
United States Merchant Marine Academy M
University of Rochester W
Utica College
Vassar College
Wells College

North Carolina
Greensboro College
Guilford College
Methodist University W

Ohio
College of Mount St. Joseph
College of Wooster
Denison University
Kenyon College
Oberlin College
Ohio Wesleyan University
Wittenberg University

Oregon
Linfield College W
Pacific University W

Pennsylvania
Allegheny College W
Alvernia University
Arcadia University W
Bryn Mawr College W
Cabrini College
Cedar Crest College W
DeSales University M
Dickinson College
Eastern University
Elizabethtown College
Franklin & Marshall College
Gettysburg College
Gwynedd-Mercy College
Haverford College
Immaculata University
King's College
Lancaster Bible College W
Lycoming College
Marywood University
Messiah College
Misericordia University
Moravian College
Muhlenberg College
Neumann College
St. Vincent College
Susquehanna University
Swarthmore College
University of Scranton
Ursinus College
Washington & Jefferson College
Waynesburg University W
Widener University
Wilkes University W
Wilson College W
York College of Pennsylvania

Rhode Island
Rhode Island College W
Roger Williams University
Salve Regina University

Tennessee
University of the South

Texas
University of Dallas W

Vermont
Castleton State College
Green Mountain College W
Johnson State College M
Lyndon State College M
Middlebury College
Norwich University

Virginia
Bridgewater College W
Christopher Newport University
Ferrum College W
Hampden-Sydney College M
Hollins University W
Lynchburg College
Marymount University
Randolph-Macon College
Roanoke College
Shenandoah University
Sweet Briar College W
University of Mary Washington
Virginia Wesleyan College
Washington and Lee University

Washington
University of Puget Sound W

Wisconsin
Carthage College M

Rifle Division I

Alabama
Birmingham-Southern College W
Jacksonville State University M
University of Alabama
Birmingham W

Colorado
United States Air Force Academy

Georgia
Mercer University

Kentucky
Morehead State University
Murray State University
University of Kentucky

Maryland
United States Naval Academy

Mississippi
University of Mississippi W

Nebraska
University of Nebraska
Lincoln W

Nevada
University of Nevada
Reno

New York
United States Military Academy

North Carolina
North Carolina State University

Ohio
Ohio State University
Columbus Campus
University of Akron

South Carolina
The Citadel
Wofford College

Tennessee
Tennessee Technological University
University of Memphis
University of Tennessee
Martin W

Texas
Texas Christian University W
University of Texas
El Paso W

Virginia
Virginia Military Institute

West Virginia
West Virginia University

Rifle Division II

Alaska
University of Alaska
Fairbanks

Georgia
North Georgia College & State University

Pennsylvania
University of the Sciences in Philadelphia W

Rifle Division III

Connecticut
United States Coast Guard Academy M

Indiana
Rose-Hulman Institute of Technology

Massachusetts
Massachusetts Institute of Technology
Massachusetts Maritime Academy
Wentworth Institute of Technology W

New York
City University of New York
John Jay College of Criminal Justice
State University of New York
Maritime College

Rowing (crew) Division I

Alabama
University of Alabama W

California
California State University
Sacramento W
Loyola Marymount University W
St. Mary's College of California W
San Diego State University W
Santa Clara University W
Stanford University W
University of California
Berkeley W
Davis W
Irvine W
Los Angeles W
University of San Diego W
University of Southern California W

Connecticut
Fairfield University W
Sacred Heart University W
University of Connecticut W
Yale University W

Delaware
University of Delaware W

District of Columbia
George Washington University W
Georgetown University W

Florida
Jacksonville University W
Stetson University W
University of Central Florida W
University of Miami W

Indiana
Indiana University
Bloomington W
University of Notre Dame W

Iowa
Drake University W
University of Iowa W

Kansas
Kansas State University W
University of Kansas W

Kentucky
University of Louisville W

Maryland
Loyola College in Maryland W
United States Naval Academy W

Massachusetts
Boston College W
Boston University W
College of the Holy Cross W
Harvard College W
Massachusetts Institute of Technology W
Northeastern University W
University of Massachusetts
Amherst W

Michigan
Eastern Michigan University W
Michigan State University W
University of Michigan W

Minnesota
University of Minnesota
Twin Cities W

Nebraska
Creighton University W

New Hampshire
Dartmouth College W

New Jersey
Princeton University W
Rutgers, The State University of New Jersey
New Brunswick/Piscataway Campus W

New York
Barnard College W
Colgate University W
Cornell University W
Fordham University W
Iona College W
Marist College W
State University of New York
Buffalo W
Syracuse University W

North Carolina
Duke University W
University of North Carolina
Asheville W
Chapel Hill W

Ohio
Ohio State University
Columbus Campus W
University of Dayton W

Oklahoma
University of Oklahoma W
University of Tulsa W

Oregon
Oregon State University W

Pennsylvania
Bucknell University W
Drexel University W
Duquesne University W
La Salle University W
Lehigh University W
Robert Morris University W
Saint Joseph's University W
Temple University W
University of Pennsylvania W
Villanova University W

Rhode Island
Brown University W
University of Rhode Island W

South Carolina
Clemson University W

Tennessee
University of Tennessee
Knoxville W

Texas
Southern Methodist University W
University of Texas
Austin W

Virginia
George Mason University W
Old Dominion University W
University of Virginia W

Washington
Gonzaga University W
University of Washington W
Washington State University W

West Virginia
West Virginia University W

Wisconsin
University of Wisconsin
Madison W

Rowing (crew) Division II

California
Humboldt State University W
University of California
San Diego W

Florida
Barry University W
Florida Institute of Technology W
Nova Southeastern University W
Rollins College W
University of Tampa W

Massachusetts
Assumption College W

New Hampshire
Franklin Pierce University W

New York
Dowling College W

Oklahoma
University of Central Oklahoma W

Pennsylvania
Mercyhurst College W
Philadelphia University W

Washington
Seattle Pacific University W
Western Washington University W

West Virginia
University of Charleston W

Rowing (crew) Division III

California
Chapman University W
Mills College W

Connecticut
Connecticut College W
Trinity College W
United States Coast Guard Academy W
Wesleyan University W

Illinois
North Park University W

Maine
Bates College W
Colby College W

Maryland
Johns Hopkins University W
Washington College W

Massachusetts
Clark University W
Lesley University W
Massachusetts Maritime Academy W
Mount Holyoke College W
Simmons College W
Smith College W
Tufts University W
Wellesley College W
Williams College W
Worcester Polytechnic Institute W

New Jersey
Richard Stockton College of New Jersey W
Rutgers, The State University of New Jersey
Camden Regional Campus W

New York
Cazenovia College W
D'Youville College W
Hamilton College W
Hobart and William Smith Colleges W
Ithaca College W
Rochester Institute of Technology W
St. Lawrence University W
Skidmore College W
State University of New York Maritime College W
Union College W
United States Merchant Marine Academy W
Vassar College W

Ohio
Marietta College W

Oregon
Lewis & Clark College W
Willamette University W

Pennsylvania
Bryn Mawr College W
Franklin & Marshall College W

Virginia
University of Mary Washington W

Washington
Pacific Lutheran University W
University of Puget Sound W

Skiing Division I

Colorado
University of Colorado
Boulder
University of Denver

Massachusetts
Boston College
Harvard College
University of Massachusetts
Amherst

Montana
Montana State University
Bozeman

Nevada
University of Nevada
Reno

New Hampshire
Dartmouth College
University of New Hampshire

New Mexico
University of New Mexico

Rhode Island
Brown University W

Utah
University of Utah

Vermont
University of Vermont

Wisconsin
University of Wisconsin
Green Bay

Skiing Division II

Alaska
University of Alaska
Anchorage
Fairbanks

Michigan
Finlandia University
Michigan Technological University
Northern Michigan University

Minnesota
Saint Cloud State University W

New Hampshire
St. Anselm College

Vermont
St. Michael's College

Skiing Division III

Maine
Bates College
Bowdoin College
Colby College
University of Maine
Presque Isle

Massachusetts
Babson College
Massachusetts Institute of Technology
Smith College W
Williams College

Michigan
Finlandia University

Minnesota
College of St. Benedict W
College of St. Scholastica
Gustavus Adolphus College
St. John's University M
St. Olaf College

Nebraska
Clarkson College M

New Hampshire
Colby-Sawyer College
Plymouth State University

New York
Clarkson University W
St. Lawrence University

Vermont
Green Mountain College
Middlebury College

Washington
Whitman College

Wisconsin
Northland College

Soccer Division I

Alabama
Alabama Agricultural and Mechanical University
Alabama State University W
Auburn University W
Birmingham-Southern College
Jacksonville State University W
Samford University W
Troy University W
University of Alabama W
University of Alabama
Birmingham
University of South Alabama W

Arizona
Arizona State University W
Northern Arizona University W
University of Arizona W

Arkansas
Arkansas State University W
University of Arkansas W
University of Arkansas
Little Rock W
Pine Bluff W
University of Central Arkansas

California
California Polytechnic State University: San Luis Obispo
California State University
Bakersfield
Fresno W
Fullerton
Long Beach W
Northridge
Sacramento
Loyola Marymount University
Pepperdine University W
St. Mary's College of California
San Diego State University
San Jose State University
Santa Clara University
Stanford University
University of California
Berkeley
Davis
Irvine
Los Angeles
Riverside
Santa Barbara
University of San Diego
University of San Francisco
University of Southern California W
University of the Pacific W

Colorado
Colorado College W
United States Air Force Academy
University of Colorado
Boulder W
University of Denver
University of Northern Colorado W

Connecticut
Central Connecticut State University
Fairfield University
Quinnipiac University
Sacred Heart University
University of Connecticut
University of Hartford
Yale University

Delaware
Delaware State University W
University of Delaware

District of Columbia
American University
George Washington University
Georgetown University
Howard University

Florida
Florida Atlantic University
Florida Gulf Coast University
Florida International University
Florida State University W
Jacksonville University
Stetson University
University of Central Florida
University of Florida W
University of Miami W
University of North Florida
University of South Florida

Georgia
Georgia Southern University
Georgia State University
Kennesaw State University W
Mercer University
University of Georgia W

Hawaii
University of Hawaii
Manoa W

Idaho
Boise State University W
Idaho State University W
University of Idaho W

Illinois
Bradley University M
DePaul University
Eastern Illinois University
Illinois State University W
Loyola University Chicago
Northern Illinois University
Northwestern University
Southern Illinois University
Edwardsville
University of Illinois
Chicago M
Urbana-Champaign W
Western Illinois University

Indiana
Ball State University W
Butler University
Indiana State University W
Indiana University
Bloomington
Indiana University-Purdue University Fort Wayne
Indiana University-Purdue University Indianapolis
Purdue University W
University of Evansville
University of Notre Dame
Valparaiso University

Iowa
Drake University
Iowa State University W
University of Iowa W
University of Northern Iowa W

Kansas
University of Kansas W

Kentucky
Eastern Kentucky University W
Morehead State University W
Murray State University W
University of Kentucky
University of Louisville
Western Kentucky University W

Louisiana
Centenary College of Louisiana
Grambling State University W
Louisiana State University and Agricultural and Mechanical College W
Louisiana Tech University W
McNeese State University W
Nicholls State University W
Northwestern State University W
Southeastern Louisiana University W
Southern University and Agricultural and Mechanical College W
University of Louisiana at Lafayette W
University of Louisiana at Monroe W

Maine
University of Maine

Maryland
Loyola College in Maryland
Mount St. Mary's University
Towson University
United States Naval Academy
University of Maryland
Baltimore County
College Park

Massachusetts
Boston College
Boston University
College of the Holy Cross
Harvard College
Northeastern University
University of Massachusetts
Amherst

Michigan
Central Michigan University W
Eastern Michigan University W
Michigan State University
Oakland University
University of Detroit Mercy
University of Michigan
Western Michigan University

Minnesota
University of Minnesota
Twin Cities W

Mississippi
Alcorn State University W
Jackson State University W
Mississippi State University W
Mississippi Valley State University W
University of Mississippi W
University of Southern Mississippi W

Missouri
Missouri State University
Saint Louis University
Southeast Missouri State University W
University of Missouri
Columbia W
Kansas City M

Montana
University of Montana W

Nebraska
Creighton University

University of Nebraska
Lincoln W

Nevada
University of Nevada
Las Vegas
Reno W

New Hampshire
Dartmouth College
University of New Hampshire

New Jersey
Fairleigh Dickinson University
Metropolitan Campus
Monmouth University
New Jersey Institute of Technology
Princeton University
Rider University
Rutgers, The State University of New Jersey
New Brunswick/Piscataway Campus
Saint Peter's College
Seton Hall University

New Mexico
University of New Mexico

New York
Adelphi University M
Barnard College W
Canisius College
Colgate University
Cornell University
Fordham University
Hartwick College M
Hofstra University
Iona College
Long Island University
Brooklyn Campus
Manhattan College
Marist College
Niagara University
Saint Bonaventure University
St. Francis College M
St. John's University
Siena College
State University of New York
Albany
Binghamton
Buffalo
Stony Brook
Syracuse University
United States Military Academy
Wagner College W

North Carolina
Appalachian State University
Campbell University
Davidson College
Duke University
East Carolina University W
Elon University
Gardner-Webb University
High Point University
North Carolina State University
University of North Carolina
Asheville
Chapel Hill
Charlotte
Greensboro
Wilmington
Wake Forest University
Western Carolina University W

North Dakota
North Dakota State University W
University of North Dakota W

Ohio
Bowling Green State University
Cleveland State University
Kent State University W
Miami University
Oxford Campus W
Ohio State University
Columbus Campus
Ohio University W
University of Akron
University of Cincinnati
University of Dayton
University of Toledo W
Wright State University
Xavier University
Youngstown State University W

Oklahoma
Oklahoma State University W
Oral Roberts University
University of Oklahoma W
University of Tulsa

Oregon
Oregon State University
Portland State University W
University of Oregon W
University of Portland

Pennsylvania
Bucknell University
Drexel University
Duquesne University
La Salle University
Lafayette College
Lehigh University
Penn State
University Park
Robert Morris University
St. Francis University
Saint Joseph's University
Temple University
University of Pennsylvania
University of Pittsburgh
Villanova University

Rhode Island
Brown University
Bryant University
Providence College
University of Rhode Island

South Carolina
Charleston Southern University W
The Citadel W
Clemson University
Coastal Carolina University
College of Charleston
Furman University
Presbyterian College
South Carolina State University W
University of South Carolina
University of South Carolina
Upstate
Winthrop University
Wofford College

South Dakota
South Dakota State University W
University of South Dakota W

Tennessee
Austin Peay State University W
Belmont University
East Tennessee State University
Lipscomb University
Middle Tennessee State University W
Tennessee Technological University W
University of Memphis
University of Tennessee
Chattanooga W
Knoxville W
Martin W
Vanderbilt University W

Texas
Baylor University W
Houston Baptist University
Lamar University W
Prairie View A&M University W
Rice University W
Sam Houston State University W
Southern Methodist University
Stephen F. Austin State University W
Texas A&M University W
Texas Christian University W
Texas Southern University W
Texas State University: San Marcos W
Texas Tech University W
University of Houston W
University of North Texas W
University of Texas
Austin W
El Paso W
San Antonio W

Utah
Brigham Young University W
Southern Utah University W
University of Utah W
Utah State University W
Utah Valley University W
Weber State University W

Vermont
University of Vermont

Virginia
College of William and Mary
George Mason University
James Madison University
Liberty University
Longwood University
Old Dominion University
Radford University
University of Richmond
University of Virginia
Virginia Commonwealth University
Virginia Military Institute
Virginia Polytechnic Institute and State University

Washington
Eastern Washington University W
Gonzaga University
Seattle University
University of Washington
Washington State University W

West Virginia
Marshall University
West Virginia University

Wisconsin
Marquette University
University of Wisconsin
Green Bay
Madison
Milwaukee

Wyoming
University of Wyoming W

Soccer Division II

Alabama
University of Alabama
Huntsville
University of Montevallo
University of North Alabama W

Arizona
Grand Canyon University

Arkansas
Harding University
Ouachita Baptist University

California
California State Polytechnic University: Pomona
California State University
Chico
Dominguez Hills
Los Angeles
Monterey Bay
San Bernardino
Stanislaus
Humboldt State University
Notre Dame de Namur University
San Francisco State University
Sonoma State University
University of California
San Diego

Colorado
Adams State College W
Colorado Christian University
Colorado School of Mines
Colorado State University
Pueblo
Fort Lewis College
Mesa State College
Metropolitan State College of Denver
Regis University
University of Colorado
Colorado Springs M

Connecticut
Post University
Southern Connecticut State University
University of Bridgeport
University of New Haven

Delaware
Goldey-Beacom College
Wilmington University

District of Columbia
University of the District of Columbia M

Florida
Barry University
Eckerd College
Flagler College
Florida Institute of Technology
Florida Southern College
Lynn University
Nova Southeastern University
Palm Beach Atlantic University
Rollins College
St. Leo University
University of Tampa
University of West Florida

Georgia
Armstrong Atlantic State University W
Clayton State University
Columbus State University W
Georgia College and State University W
Georgia Southwestern State University
North Georgia College & State University
University of West Georgia W

Hawaii
Brigham Young University-Hawaii
Chaminade University of Honolulu
Hawaii Pacific University
University of Hawaii
Hilo

Idaho
Northwest Nazarene University

Illinois
Lewis University
Quincy University

Indiana
Oakland City University
Saint Joseph's College
University of Indianapolis
University of Southern Indiana

Iowa
Upper Iowa University

Kansas
Emporia State University W
Newman University
Washburn University W

Kentucky
Bellarmine University
Kentucky Wesleyan College
Northern Kentucky University

Maryland
Columbia Union College

Massachusetts
American International College
Assumption College
Bentley University
Merrimack College
Stonehill College
University of Massachusetts
Lowell

Michigan
Ferris State University W
Grand Valley State University W
Northern Michigan University W
Northwood University: Michigan
Saginaw Valley State University

Minnesota
Bemidji State University W
Concordia University: St. Paul W
Minnesota State University
Mankato W
Moorhead W
Saint Cloud State University W
Southwest Minnesota State University W
University of Minnesota
Crookston W
Duluth W
Winona State University W

Mississippi
Delta State University

Missouri
Drury University
Missouri Southern State University
Missouri Western State University W
Northwest Missouri State University W
Rockhurst University
Southwest Baptist University W
Truman State University
University of Central Missouri W
University of Missouri
Missouri University of Science and Technology
St. Louis

Montana
Montana State University
Billings

Nebraska
University of Nebraska
Omaha W
Wayne State College W

New Hampshire
Franklin Pierce University
St. Anselm College
Southern New Hampshire University

New Jersey
Bloomfield College
Caldwell College
Felician College
Georgian Court University W

New Mexico
Eastern New Mexico University
New Mexico Highlands University W

New York
Adelphi University W
City University of New York
Queens College
College of Saint Rose
Concordia College
Dominican College of Blauvelt
Dowling College
Le Moyne College

Long Island University
C. W. Post Campus
Mercy College
Molloy College
New York Institute of Technology
Nyack College
Pace University W
St. Thomas Aquinas College

North Carolina

Barton College
Belmont Abbey College
Brevard College
Catawba College
Chowan University
Lees-McRae College
Lenoir-Rhyne University
Mars Hill College
Mount Olive College
Pfeiffer University
Queens University of Charlotte
St. Andrews Presbyterian College
University of North Carolina
Pembroke
Wingate University

North Dakota

University of Mary

Ohio

Ashland University
Tiffin University
University of Findlay

Oklahoma

East Central University W
Northeastern State University
Southwestern Oklahoma State
University W
University of Central Oklahoma
W

Oregon

Western Oregon University W

Pennsylvania

Bloomsburg University of
Pennsylvania
California University of
Pennsylvania
Chestnut Hill College
Clarion University of
Pennsylvania W
East Stroudsburg University of
Pennsylvania
Edinboro University of
Pennsylvania W
Gannon University
Holy Family University
Indiana University of
Pennsylvania W
Kutztown University of
Pennsylvania
Lock Haven University of
Pennsylvania
Mansfield University of
Pennsylvania W
Mercyhurst College
Millersville University of
Pennsylvania
Philadelphia University
Seton Hill University
Shippensburg University of
Pennsylvania
Slippery Rock University of
Pennsylvania
University of Pittsburgh
Johnstown
West Chester University of
Pennsylvania

Puerto Rico

University of Puerto Rico
Mayaguez M
Rio Piedras M

South Carolina

Anderson University
Converse College W
Erskine College
Francis Marion University
Lander University
Limestone College
Newberry College
North Greenville University
University of South Carolina
Aiken

South Dakota

Augustana College W
Northern State University W

Tennessee

Carson-Newman College
Christian Brothers University
Lincoln Memorial University
Tusculum College

Texas

Abilene Christian University W
Angelo State University W
Dallas Baptist University W
Midwestern State University
St. Edward's University
St. Mary's University
Texas A&M International
University
Texas A&M University
Commerce W
Texas Woman's University W
University of Texas
of the Permian Basin
University of the Incarnate Word
West Texas A&M University

Utah

Dixie State College of Utah

Vermont

St. Michael's College

Washington

Central Washington University W
Saint Martin's University
Seattle Pacific University
Western Washington University

West Virginia

Alderson-Broaddus College
Concord University
Davis and Elkins College
Ohio Valley University
Salem International University
Shepherd University
University of Charleston
West Virginia Wesleyan College
Wheeling Jesuit University

Wisconsin

University of Wisconsin
Parkside

Soccer Division III

Alabama

Huntingdon College

Arkansas

Hendrix College
University of the Ozarks

California

California Institute of Technology
M
California Lutheran University
California State University
East Bay
Chapman University
Claremont McKenna College
La Sierra University
Menlo College
Mills College W
Occidental College
Pitzer College W
Pomona College
University of California
Santa Cruz
University of La Verne
University of Redlands
Whittier College

Colorado

Colorado College M

Connecticut

Albertus Magnus College
Connecticut College
Eastern Connecticut State
University
Mitchell College
St. Joseph College W
Trinity College
United States Coast Guard
Academy
Wesleyan University
Western Connecticut State
University

Delaware

Wesley College

District of Columbia

Catholic University of America
Gallaudet University
Trinity Washington University W

Georgia

Agnes Scott College W
Emory University
LaGrange College
Oglethorpe University
Piedmont College
Spelman College W
Wesleyan College W

Illinois

Augustana College
Aurora University
Benedictine University
Blackburn College
Concordia University Chicago
Dominican University
Elmhurst College
Eureka College
Greenville College
Illinois College
Illinois Wesleyan University
Knox College
Lake Forest College
MacMurray College
Millikin University
Monmouth College
North Central College
North Park University
Principia College
Rockford College
University of Chicago
Wheaton College

Indiana

Anderson University
DePauw University
Earlham College
Franklin College
Hanover College
Manchester College
Rose-Hulman Institute of
Technology
Saint Mary's College W
Trine University
Wabash College M

Iowa

Buena Vista University
Central College
Coe College
Cornell College
Grinnell College
Loras College
Luther College
Simpson College
University of Dubuque
Wartburg College

Kentucky

Centre College
Spalding University
Thomas More College
Transylvania University

Louisiana

Louisiana College

Maine

Bates College
Bowdoin College
Colby College
Husson University
Maine Maritime Academy
St. Joseph's College
Thomas College
University of Maine
Farmington
Presque Isle
University of New England
University of Southern Maine

Maryland

College of Notre Dame of
Maryland W
Frostburg State University
Goucher College
Hood College
Johns Hopkins University
McDaniel College
St. Mary's College of Maryland
Salisbury University
Stevenson University
Washington College

Massachusetts

Amherst College
Anna Maria College
Babson College
Bay Path College W
Becker College
Brandeis University
Bridgewater State College
Clark University
Curry College
Elms College
Emerson College
Emmanuel College
Endicott College
Fitchburg State College
Framingham State College
Gordon College
Lasell College
Lesley University
Massachusetts College of Liberal
Arts
Massachusetts Institute of
Technology
Massachusetts Maritime Academy
Mount Holyoke College W
Mount Ida College
Newbury College
Nichols College
Pine Manor College W
Regis College
Salem State College
Simmons College W
Smith College W
Springfield College
Suffolk University
Tufts University
University of Massachusetts
Boston
Dartmouth
Wellesley College W
Wentworth Institute of
Technology
Western New England College
Westfield State College
Wheaton College
Wheelock College W
Williams College
Worcester Polytechnic Institute
Worcester State College

Michigan

Adrian College
Albion College
Alma College
Calvin College
Finlandia University
Hope College
Kalamazoo College
Olivet College

Minnesota

Augsburg College
Bethany Lutheran College
Bethel University
Carleton College
College of St. Benedict W
College of St. Catherine W
College of St. Scholastica
Concordia College: Moorhead
Crown College
Gustavus Adolphus College
Hamline University
Macalester College
Martin Luther College
Northwestern College
St. John's University M
St. Mary's University of
Minnesota
St. Olaf College
University of Minnesota
Morris
University of St. Thomas

Mississippi

Millsaps College
Mississippi College
Rust College M

Missouri

Baptist Bible College
Fontbonne University
Maryville University of Saint
Louis
Washington University in St.
Louis
Webster University
Westminster College

Nebraska

Nebraska Wesleyan University

New Hampshire

Colby-Sawyer College
Daniel Webster College
Keene State College
New England College
Plymouth State University
Rivier College

New Jersey

Centenary College
The College of New Jersey
College of St. Elizabeth W
Drew University
Fairleigh Dickinson University
College at Florham
Kean University
Montclair State University
New Jersey City University
Ramapo College of New Jersey
Richard Stockton College of New
Jersey
Rowan University
Rutgers, The State University of
New Jersey
Camden Regional Campus
Newark Regional Campus
Stevens Institute of Technology
William Paterson University of
New Jersey

New York

Alfred University
Bard College
Cazenovia College
City University of New York
Baruch College M
Brooklyn College M
City College
College of Staten Island
Hunter College M
John Jay College of
Criminal Justice M
Medgar Evers College
New York City College of
Technology M
York College M

Clarkson University
College of Mount St. Vincent
D'Youville College
Elmira College
Hamilton College
Hartwick College W
Hilbert College
Hobart and William Smith Colleges
Ithaca College
Keuka College
Manhattanville College
Medaille College
Mount St. Mary College
Nazareth College of Rochester
New York University
Polytechnic Institute of New York University
Rensselaer Polytechnic Institute
Rochester Institute of Technology
Russell Sage College W
St. John Fisher College
St. Joseph's College: Suffolk Campus
St. Lawrence University
Skidmore College
State University of New York
College at Brockport
College at Buffalo
College at Cortland
College at Fredonia
College at Geneseo
College at Old Westbury
College at Oneonta
College at Plattsburgh
College at Potsdam
College of Agriculture and Technology at Cobleskill
College of Agriculture and Technology at Morrisville
Farmingdale
Institute of Technology at Utica/Rome
Maritime College
New Paltz
Oswego
Purchase
Union College
United States Merchant Marine Academy M
University of Rochester
Utica College
Vassar College
Wells College
Yeshiva University

North Carolina
Greensboro College
Guilford College
Meredith College W
Methodist University
North Carolina Wesleyan College
Peace College W
Salem College W

Ohio
Baldwin-Wallace College
Bluffton University
Capital University
Case Western Reserve University
College of Mount St. Joseph
College of Wooster
Defiance College
Denison University
Franciscan University of Steubenville
Heidelberg University
Hiram College
John Carroll University
Kenyon College
Lake Erie College
Marietta College
Mount Union College
Muskingum College
Oberlin College
Ohio Northern University
Ohio Wesleyan University
Otterbein College
Wilmington College
Wittenberg University

Oregon
George Fox University
Lewis & Clark College W
Linfield College
Pacific University
Willamette University

Pennsylvania
Albright College
Allegheny College
Alvernia University
Arcadia University
Bryn Mawr College W
Cabrini College
Carnegie Mellon University
Cedar Crest College W
Chatham University W
Delaware Valley College
DeSales University
Dickinson College
Eastern University
Elizabethtown College
Franklin & Marshall College
Geneva College
Gettysburg College
Grove City College
Gwynedd-Mercy College
Haverford College
Immaculata University
Juniata College
Keystone College
King's College
La Roche College
Lancaster Bible College
Lebanon Valley College
Lincoln University
Lycoming College
Marywood University
Messiah College
Misericordia University
Moravian College
Mount Aloysius College
Muhlenberg College
Neumann College
Penn State
Altoona
Berks
Erie, The Behrend College
Harrisburg
Philadelphia Biblical University
St. Vincent College
Susquehanna University
Swarthmore College
Thiel College
University of Pittsburgh
Bradford
Greensburg
University of Scranton
Ursinus College
Washington & Jefferson College
Waynesburg University
Westminster College
Widener University
Wilkes University
Wilson College W
York College of Pennsylvania

Rhode Island
Johnson & Wales University: Providence
Rhode Island College
Roger Williams University
Salve Regina University

South Dakota
Presentation College

Tennessee
Maryville College
Rhodes College
University of the South

Texas
Austin College
Concordia University Texas
East Texas Baptist University
Hardin-Simmons University
Howard Payne University
LeTourneau University
McMurry University
Schreiner University
Southwestern University
Texas Lutheran University
Trinity University
University of Dallas
University of Mary Hardin-Baylor
University of Texas
Dallas
Tyler

Vermont
Castleton State College
Green Mountain College
Johnson State College
Lyndon State College
Middlebury College
Norwich University
Southern Vermont College

Virginia
Averett University
Bridgewater College
Christopher Newport University
Eastern Mennonite University
Emory & Henry College
Ferrum College
Hampden-Sydney College M
Hollins University W
Lynchburg College
Mary Baldwin College W
Marymount University
Randolph College
Randolph-Macon College
Roanoke College
Shenandoah University
Sweet Briar College W
University of Mary Washington
Virginia Wesleyan College
Washington and Lee University

Washington
Pacific Lutheran University
University of Puget Sound
Whitman College
Whitworth University

West Virginia
Bethany College

Wisconsin
Alverno College W
Beloit College
Carroll University
Carthage College
Concordia University Wisconsin
Edgewood College
Lakeland College
Lawrence University
Maranatha Baptist Bible College
Marian University
Milwaukee School of Engineering
Mount Mary College W
Northland College
Ripon College
St. Norbert College
University of Wisconsin
Eau Claire W
La Crosse W
Oshkosh
Platteville
River Falls W
Stevens Point W
Stout W
Superior
Whitewater
Wisconsin Lutheran College

Softball Division I

Alabama
Alabama Agricultural and Mechanical University W
Alabama State University W
Auburn University W
Birmingham-Southern College W
Jacksonville State University W
Samford University W
Troy University W
University of Alabama W
University of Alabama Birmingham W
University of South Alabama W

Arizona
Arizona State University W
University of Arizona W

Arkansas
University of Arkansas W
University of Arkansas Pine Bluff W
University of Central Arkansas W

California
California Polytechnic State University: San Luis Obispo W
California State University
Bakersfield W
Fresno W
Fullerton W
Long Beach W
Northridge W
Sacramento W
Loyola Marymount University W
St. Mary's College of California W
San Diego State University W
San Jose State University W
Santa Clara University W
Stanford University W
University of California
Berkeley W
Davis W
Los Angeles W
Riverside W
Santa Barbara W
University of San Diego W
University of the Pacific W

Colorado
Colorado State University W
University of Northern Colorado W

Connecticut
Central Connecticut State University W
Fairfield University W
Quinnipiac University W
Sacred Heart University W
University of Connecticut W
University of Hartford W
Yale University W

Delaware
Delaware State University W
University of Delaware W

District of Columbia
George Washington University W
Georgetown University W
Howard University W

Florida
Bethune-Cookman University W
Florida Agricultural and Mechanical University W
Florida Atlantic University W
Florida Gulf Coast University W
Florida International University W
Florida State University W
Jacksonville University W
Stetson University W
University of Central Florida W
University of Florida W
University of North Florida W
University of South Florida W

Georgia
Georgia Institute of Technology W
Georgia Southern University W
Georgia State University W
Kennesaw State University W
Mercer University W
Savannah State University W
University of Georgia W

Hawaii
University of Hawaii Manoa W

Idaho
Boise State University W
Idaho State University W

Illinois
Bradley University W
DePaul University W
Eastern Illinois University W
Illinois State University W
Loyola University Chicago W
Northern Illinois University W
Northwestern University W
Southern Illinois University Carbondale W
Southern Illinois University Edwardsville W
University of Illinois
Chicago W
Urbana-Champaign W
Western Illinois University W

Indiana
Ball State University W
Butler University W
Indiana State University W
Indiana University Bloomington W
Indiana University-Purdue University Fort Wayne W
Indiana University-Purdue University Indianapolis W
Purdue University W
University of Evansville W
University of Notre Dame W
Valparaiso University W

Iowa
Drake University W
Iowa State University W
University of Iowa W
University of Northern Iowa W

Kansas
University of Kansas W
Wichita State University W

Kentucky
Eastern Kentucky University W
Morehead State University W
University of Kentucky W
University of Louisville W
Western Kentucky University W

Louisiana
Centenary College of Louisiana W
Grambling State University W
Louisiana State University and Agricultural and Mechanical College W
Louisiana Tech University W
McNeese State University W
Nicholls State University W
Northwestern State University W
Southeastern Louisiana University W
Southern University and Agricultural and Mechanical College W
University of Louisiana at Lafayette W
University of Louisiana at Monroe W

Maine
University of Maine W

Maryland
Coppin State University W

Morgan State University W
Mount St. Mary's University W
Towson University W
University of Maryland
Baltimore County W
College Park W
Eastern Shore W

Massachusetts
Boston College W
Boston University W
College of the Holy Cross W
Harvard College W
University of Massachusetts
Amherst W

Michigan
Central Michigan University W
Eastern Michigan University W
Michigan State University W
Oakland University W
University of Detroit Mercy W
University of Michigan W
Western Michigan University W

Minnesota
University of Minnesota
Twin Cities W

Mississippi
Alcorn State University W
Jackson State University W
Mississippi State University W
Mississippi Valley State
University W
University of Mississippi W
University of Southern
Mississippi W

Missouri
Missouri State University W
Saint Louis University W
Southeast Missouri State
University W
University of Missouri
Columbia W
Kansas City W

Nebraska
Creighton University W
University of Nebraska
Lincoln W

Nevada
University of Nevada
Las Vegas W
Reno W

New Hampshire
Dartmouth College W

New Jersey
Fairleigh Dickinson University
Metropolitan Campus W
Monmouth University W
Princeton University W
Rider University W
Rutgers, The State University of
New Jersey
New Brunswick/Piscataway
Campus W
Saint Peter's College W
Seton Hall University W

New Mexico
New Mexico State University W
University of New Mexico W

New York
Barnard College W
Canisius College W
Colgate University W
Cornell University W
Fordham University W
Hofstra University W
Iona College W
Long Island University
Brooklyn Campus W
Manhattan College W
Marist College W
Niagara University W
Saint Bonaventure University W
St. John's University W
Siena College W
State University of New York
Albany W
Binghamton W
Buffalo W
Stony Brook W
Syracuse University W
United States Military Academy
W
Wagner College W

North Carolina
Appalachian State University W
Campbell University W
East Carolina University W
Elon University W
Gardner-Webb University W
North Carolina Agricultural and
Technical State University W
North Carolina Central University
W
North Carolina State University
W
University of North Carolina
Chapel Hill W
Charlotte W
Greensboro W
Wilmington W
Western Carolina University W
Winston-Salem State University
W

North Dakota
North Dakota State University W
University of North Dakota W

Ohio
Bowling Green State University
W
Cleveland State University W
Kent State University W
Miami University
Oxford Campus W
Ohio State University
Columbus Campus W
Ohio University W
University of Akron W
University of Dayton W
University of Toledo W
Wright State University W
Youngstown State University W

Oklahoma
Oklahoma State University W
University of Oklahoma W
University of Tulsa W

Oregon
Oregon State University W
Portland State University W
University of Oregon W

Pennsylvania
Bucknell University W
Drexel University W
La Salle University W
Lafayette College W
Lehigh University W
Penn State
University Park W
Robert Morris University W
St. Francis University W
Saint Joseph's University W
Temple University W
University of Pennsylvania W
University of Pittsburgh W
Villanova University W

Rhode Island
Brown University W
Bryant University W
Providence College W
University of Rhode Island W

South Carolina
Charleston Southern University
W
Coastal Carolina University W
College of Charleston W
Furman University W
Presbyterian College W
South Carolina State University
W
University of South Carolina W
University of South Carolina
Upstate W
Winthrop University W

South Dakota
South Dakota State University W
University of South Dakota W

Tennessee
Austin Peay State University W
Belmont University W
East Tennessee State University
W
Lipscomb University W
Middle Tennessee State
University W
Tennessee State University W
Tennessee Technological
University W
University of Tennessee
Chattanooga W
Knoxville W
Martin W

Texas
Baylor University W
Houston Baptist University W
Prairie View A&M University W
Sam Houston State University W
Stephen F. Austin State University
W
Texas A&M University W
Texas A&M University
Corpus Christi W
Texas Southern University W
Texas State University: San
Marcos W
Texas Tech University W
University of Houston W
University of North Texas W
University of Texas
Arlington W
Austin W
El Paso W
San Antonio W

Utah
Brigham Young University W
Southern Utah University W
University of Utah W
Utah State University W
Utah Valley University W

Vermont
University of Vermont W

Virginia
George Mason University W
Hampton University W
James Madison University W
Liberty University W
Longwood University W
Norfolk State University W
Radford University W
University of Virginia W
Virginia Polytechnic Institute and
State University W

Washington
Seattle University W
University of Washington W

West Virginia
Marshall University W

Wisconsin
University of Wisconsin
Green Bay W
Madison W

Softball Division II

Alabama
Miles College W
Tuskegee University W
University of Alabama
Huntsville W
University of North Alabama W
University of West Alabama W

Arizona
Grand Canyon University W

Arkansas
Arkansas Tech University W
Henderson State University W
Ouachita Baptist University W
Southern Arkansas University W
University of Arkansas
Monticello W

California
California State University
Chico W
Dominguez Hills W
Monterey Bay W
San Bernardino W
Stanislaus W
Humboldt State University W
Notre Dame de Namur University
W
San Francisco State University W
Sonoma State University W
University of California
San Diego W

Colorado
Adams State College W
Colorado School of Mines W
Colorado State University
Pueblo W
Fort Lewis College W
Mesa State College W
Metropolitan State College of
Denver W
Regis University W
University of Colorado
Colorado Springs W

Connecticut
Post University W
Southern Connecticut State
University W
University of Bridgeport W
University of New Haven W

Delaware
Goldey-Beacom College W
Wilmington University W

Florida
Barry University W
Eckerd College W
Flagler College W
Florida Institute of Technology W
Florida Southern College W
Lynn University W
Nova Southeastern University W
Palm Beach Atlantic University
W
Rollins College W
St. Leo University W
University of Tampa W
University of West Florida W

Georgia
Albany State University W
Armstrong Atlantic State
University W
Augusta State University W
Clark Atlanta University W
Columbus State University W
Fort Valley State University W
Georgia College and State
University W
Georgia Southwestern State
University W
North Georgia College & State
University W
Paine College W
University of West Georgia W
Valdosta State University W

Hawaii
Brigham Young
University-Hawaii W
Chaminade University of
Honolulu W
Hawaii Pacific University W
University of Hawaii
Hilo W

Idaho
Northwest Nazarene University
W

Illinois
Lewis University W
Quincy University W

Indiana
Oakland City University W
Saint Joseph's College W
University of Indianapolis W
University of Southern Indiana W

Iowa
Upper Iowa University W

Kansas
Emporia State University W
Fort Hays State University W
Newman University W
Pittsburg State University W
Washburn University W

Kentucky
Bellarmine University W
Kentucky State University W
Kentucky Wesleyan College W
Northern Kentucky University W

Maryland
Bowie State University W
Columbia Union College W

Massachusetts
American International College
W
Assumption College W
Bentley University W
Merrimack College W
Stonehill College W
University of Massachusetts
Lowell W

Michigan
Ferris State University W
Grand Valley State University W
Hillsdale College W
Lake Superior State University W
Northwood University: Michigan
W
Saginaw Valley State University
W
Wayne State University W

Minnesota
Bemidji State University W
Concordia University: St. Paul W
Minnesota State University
Mankato W
Moorhead W
Saint Cloud State University W
Southwest Minnesota State
University W
University of Minnesota
Crookston W
Duluth W
Winona State University W

Mississippi
Delta State University W

Missouri
Drury University W
Lincoln University W
Missouri Southern State
University W
Missouri Western State University
W

Northwest Missouri State University W
Rockhurst University W
Southwest Baptist University W
Truman State University W
University of Central Missouri W
University of Missouri
Missouri University of Science and Technology W
St. Louis W

Montana

Montana State University
Billings W

Nebraska

Chadron State College W
University of Nebraska
Kearney W
Omaha W
Wayne State College W

New Hampshire

Franklin Pierce University W
St. Anselm College W
Southern New Hampshire University W

New Jersey

Bloomfield College W
Caldwell College W
Felician College W
Georgian Court University W

New Mexico

Eastern New Mexico University W
New Mexico Highlands University W
Western New Mexico University W

New York

Adelphi University W
City University of New York
Queens College W
College of Saint Rose W
Concordia College W
Dominican College of Blauvelt W
Dowling College W
Le Moyne College W
Long Island University
C. W. Post Campus W
Mercy College W
Molloy College W
New York Institute of Technology W
Nyack College W
Pace University W
St. Thomas Aquinas College W

North Carolina

Barton College W
Belmont Abbey College W
Brevard College W
Catawba College W
Chowan University W
Elizabeth City State University W
Fayetteville State University W
Johnson C. Smith University W
Lees-McRae College W
Lenoir-Rhyne University W
Livingstone College W
Mars Hill College W
Mount Olive College W
Pfeiffer University W
Queens University of Charlotte W
St. Andrews Presbyterian College W
St. Augustine's College W
Shaw University W
University of North Carolina
Pembroke W
Wingate University W

North Dakota

University of Mary W

Ohio

Ashland University W
Tiffin University W
University of Findlay W

Oklahoma

Cameron University W
East Central University W
Northeastern State University W
Oklahoma Panhandle State University W
Southeastern Oklahoma State University W
Southwestern Oklahoma State University W
University of Central Oklahoma W

Oregon

Western Oregon University W

Pennsylvania

Bloomsburg University of Pennsylvania W
California University of Pennsylvania W
Chestnut Hill College W
Clarion University of Pennsylvania W
East Stroudsburg University of Pennsylvania W
Edinboro University of Pennsylvania W
Gannon University W
Holy Family University W
Indiana University of Pennsylvania W
Kutztown University of Pennsylvania W
Lincoln University W
Lock Haven University of Pennsylvania W
Mansfield University of Pennsylvania W
Mercyhurst College W
Millersville University of Pennsylvania W
Philadelphia University W
Seton Hill University W
Shippensburg University of Pennsylvania W
Slippery Rock University of Pennsylvania W
University of the Sciences in Philadelphia W
West Chester University of Pennsylvania W

Puerto Rico

University of Puerto Rico
Cayey University College W
Mayaguez W
Rio Piedras W

South Carolina

Anderson University W
Benedict College W
Claflin University W
Erskine College W
Francis Marion University W
Lander University W
Limestone College W
Newberry College W
North Greenville University W
University of South Carolina
Aiken W

South Dakota

Augustana College W
Northern State University W

Tennessee

Carson-Newman College W
Christian Brothers University W
Lane College W
LeMoyne-Owen College W
Lincoln Memorial University W
Tusculum College W

Texas

Abilene Christian University W
Angelo State University W
Midwestern State University W
St. Edward's University W
St. Mary's University W
Tarleton State University W
Texas A&M University
Kingsville W
Texas Woman's University W
University of Texas
of the Permian Basin W
University of the Incarnate Word W
West Texas A&M University W

Utah

Dixie State College of Utah W

Vermont

St. Michael's College W

Virginia

St. Paul's College W
Virginia State University W
Virginia Union University W

Washington

Central Washington University W
Saint Martin's University W
Western Washington University W

West Virginia

Alderson-Broaddus College W
Bluefield State College W
Concord University W
Davis and Elkins College W
Fairmont State University W
Glenville State College W
Ohio Valley University W
Salem International University W
Shepherd University W
University of Charleston W
West Liberty State College W
West Virginia State University W
West Virginia Wesleyan College W
Wheeling Jesuit University W

Wisconsin

University of Wisconsin
Parkside W

Softball Division III

Alabama

Huntingdon College W

Arkansas

Hendrix College W
University of the Ozarks W

California

California Lutheran University W
California State University
East Bay W
Chapman University W
Claremont McKenna College W
La Sierra University W
Menlo College W
Occidental College W
Pitzer College W
Pomona College W
University of La Verne W
University of Redlands W
Whittier College W

Colorado

Colorado College W

Connecticut

Albertus Magnus College W
Eastern Connecticut State University W
Mitchell College W
St. Joseph College W
Trinity College W
United States Coast Guard Academy W
Wesleyan University W
Western Connecticut State University W

Delaware

Wesley College W

District of Columbia

Catholic University of America W
Gallaudet University W

Georgia

Agnes Scott College W
Emory University W
LaGrange College W
Piedmont College W
Spelman College W
Wesleyan College W

Illinois

Augustana College W
Aurora University W
Benedictine University W
Blackburn College W
Concordia University Chicago W
Dominican University W
Elmhurst College W
Eureka College W
Greenville College W
Illinois College W
Illinois Wesleyan University W
Knox College W
Lake Forest College W
MacMurray College W
Millikin University W
Monmouth College W
North Central College W
North Park University W
Rockford College W
University of Chicago W
Wheaton College W

Indiana

Anderson University W
DePauw University W
Franklin College W
Hanover College W
Manchester College W
Rose-Hulman Institute of Technology W
Saint Mary's College W
Trine University W

Iowa

Buena Vista University W
Central College W
Coe College W
Cornell College W
Grinnell College W
Loras College W
Luther College W
Simpson College W
University of Dubuque W
Wartburg College W

Kentucky

Centre College W
Spalding University W
Thomas More College W
Transylvania University W

Louisiana

Louisiana College W

Maine

Bates College W
Bowdoin College W
Colby College W
Husson University W
Maine Maritime Academy W
St. Joseph's College W
Thomas College W
University of Maine
Farmington W
Presque Isle W
University of New England W
University of Southern Maine W

Maryland

College of Notre Dame of Maryland W
Frostburg State University W
Hood College W
McDaniel College W
Salisbury University W
Stevenson University W
Washington College W

Massachusetts

Amherst College W
Anna Maria College W
Babson College W
Bay Path College W
Becker College W
Brandeis University W
Bridgewater State College W
Clark University W
Curry College W
Elms College W
Emerson College W
Emmanuel College W
Endicott College W
Fitchburg State College W
Framingham State College W
Gordon College W
Lasell College W
Lesley University W
Massachusetts College of Liberal Arts W
Massachusetts Institute of Technology W
Massachusetts Maritime Academy W
Mount Ida College W
Newbury College W
Nichols College W
Pine Manor College W
Regis College W
Salem State College W
Simmons College W
Smith College W
Springfield College W
Suffolk University W
Tufts University W
University of Massachusetts
Boston W
Dartmouth W
Wellesley College W
Wentworth Institute of Technology W
Western New England College W
Westfield State College W
Wheaton College W
Wheelock College W
Williams College W
Worcester Polytechnic Institute W
Worcester State College W

Michigan

Adrian College W
Albion College W
Alma College W
Calvin College W
Finlandia University W
Hope College W
Olivet College W

Minnesota

Augsburg College W
Bethany Lutheran College W
Bethel University W
Carleton College W
College of St. Benedict W
College of St. Catherine W
College of St. Scholastica W
Concordia College: Moorhead W
Crown College W
Gustavus Adolphus College W
Hamline University W
Macalester College W
Martin Luther College W
Northwestern College W
St. Mary's University of Minnesota W
St. Olaf College W

University of Minnesota
Morris W
University of St. Thomas W

Mississippi
Millsaps College W
Mississippi College W
Rust College W

Missouri
Fontbonne University W
Maryville University of Saint Louis W
Washington University in St. Louis W
Webster University W
Westminster College W

Nebraska
Nebraska Wesleyan University W

New Hampshire
Daniel Webster College W
Keene State College W
New England College W
Plymouth State University W
Rivier College W

New Jersey
Centenary College W
The College of New Jersey W
College of St. Elizabeth W
Drew University W
Fairleigh Dickinson University
College at Florham W
Kean University W
Montclair State University W
New Jersey City University W
Ramapo College of New Jersey W
Richard Stockton College of New Jersey W
Rowan University W
Rutgers, The State University of New Jersey
Camden Regional Campus W
Newark Regional Campus W
William Paterson University of New Jersey W

New York
Alfred University W
Cazenovia College W
City University of New York
Baruch College W
Brooklyn College W
College of Staten Island W
Hunter College W
John Jay College of Criminal Justice W
Lehman College W
New York City College of Technology W
York College W
College of Mount St. Vincent W
College of New Rochelle W
D'Youville College W
Elmira College W
Hamilton College W
Hilbert College W
Ithaca College W
Keuka College W
Manhattanville College W
Medaille College W
Mount St. Mary College W
Nazareth College of Rochester W
Polytechnic Institute of New York University W
Rensselaer Polytechnic Institute W
Rochester Institute of Technology W
Russell Sage College W
St. John Fisher College W
St. Joseph's College W
St. Joseph's College: Suffolk Campus W
St. Lawrence University W
Skidmore College W
State University of New York
College at Brockport W
College at Buffalo W
College at Cortland W
College at Fredonia W
College at Geneseo W
College at Old Westbury W
College at Oneonta W
College at Plattsburgh W
College at Potsdam W
College of Agriculture and Technology at Cobleskill W
College of Agriculture and Technology at Morrisville W
Farmingdale W
Institute of Technology at Utica/Rome W
Maritime College W
New Paltz W
Oswego W
Purchase W
Union College W
United States Merchant Marine Academy W
University of Rochester W
Utica College W
Wells College W

North Carolina
Greensboro College W
Guilford College W
Meredith College W
Methodist University W
North Carolina Wesleyan College W
Peace College W

Ohio
Baldwin-Wallace College W
Bluffton University W
Capital University W
Case Western Reserve University W
College of Mount St. Joseph W
College of Wooster W
Defiance College W
Denison University W
Franciscan University of Steubenville W
Heidelberg University W
Hiram College W
John Carroll University W
Kenyon College W
Lake Erie College W
Marietta College W
Mount Union College W
Muskingum College W
Oberlin College W
Ohio Northern University W
Ohio Wesleyan University W
Otterbein College W
Wilmington College W
Wittenberg University W

Oregon
George Fox University W
Lewis & Clark College W
Linfield College W
Pacific University W
Willamette University W

Pennsylvania
Albright College W
Allegheny College W
Alvernia University W
Arcadia University W
Baptist Bible College of Pennsylvania W
Cabrini College W
Cedar Crest College W
Chatham University W
Delaware Valley College W
DeSales University W
Dickinson College W
Eastern University W
Elizabethtown College W
Franklin & Marshall College W
Geneva College W
Gettysburg College W
Grove City College W
Gwynedd-Mercy College W
Haverford College W
Immaculata University W
Juniata College W
Keystone College W
King's College W
La Roche College W
Lebanon Valley College W
Lycoming College W
Marywood University W
Messiah College W
Misericordia University W
Moravian College W
Mount Aloysius College W
Muhlenberg College W
Neumann College W
Penn State
Altoona W
Berks W
Erie, The Behrend College W
Harrisburg W
Philadelphia Biblical University W
Rosemont College W
St. Vincent College W
Susquehanna University W
Swarthmore College W
Thiel College W
University of Pittsburgh
Bradford W
Greensburg W
University of Scranton W
Ursinus College W
Washington & Jefferson College W
Waynesburg University W
Westminster College W
Widener University W
Wilkes University W
Wilson College W
York College of Pennsylvania W

Rhode Island
Johnson & Wales University: Providence W
Rhode Island College W
Roger Williams University W
Salve Regina University W

South Dakota
Presentation College W

Tennessee
Maryville College W
Rhodes College W
University of the South W

Texas
Austin College W
Concordia University Texas W
East Texas Baptist University W
Hardin-Simmons University W
Howard Payne University W
LeTourneau University W
Schreiner University W
Sul Ross State University W
Texas Lutheran University W
Trinity University W
University of Dallas W
University of Mary Hardin-Baylor W
University of Texas
Dallas W
Tyler W

Vermont
Castleton State College W
Johnson State College W
Lyndon State College W
Middlebury College W
Norwich University W
Southern Vermont College W

Virginia
Averett University W
Bridgewater College W
Christopher Newport University W
Eastern Mennonite University W
Emory & Henry College W
Ferrum College W
Lynchburg College W
Mary Baldwin College W
Randolph College W
Randolph-Macon College W
Roanoke College W
Shenandoah University W
Sweet Briar College W
University of Mary Washington W
Virginia Wesleyan College W

Washington
Pacific Lutheran University W
University of Puget Sound W
Whitworth University W

West Virginia
Bethany College W

Wisconsin
Alverno College W
Beloit College W
Carroll University W
Carthage College W
Concordia University Wisconsin W
Edgewood College W
Lakeland College W
Lawrence University W
Maranatha Baptist Bible College W
Marian University W
Milwaukee School of Engineering W
Mount Mary College W
Northland College W
Ripon College W
St. Norbert College W
University of Wisconsin
Eau Claire W
La Crosse W
Oshkosh W
Platteville W
River Falls W
Stevens Point W
Stout W
Superior W
Whitewater W
Wisconsin Lutheran College W

Swimming and diving Division I

Alabama
Auburn University
University of Alabama

Arizona
Arizona State University
Northern Arizona University W
University of Arizona

Arkansas
University of Arkansas W
University of Arkansas
Little Rock W

California
California Polytechnic State University: San Luis Obispo
California State University
Bakersfield
Fresno W
Northridge
Loyola Marymount University W
Pepperdine University W
San Diego State University W
San Jose State University W
Stanford University
University of California
Berkeley
Davis
Irvine
Los Angeles W
Santa Barbara
University of San Diego W
University of Southern California
University of the Pacific

Colorado
Colorado State University W
United States Air Force Academy
University of Denver
University of Northern Colorado W

Connecticut
Central Connecticut State University W
Fairfield University
Sacred Heart University W
University of Connecticut
Yale University

Delaware
University of Delaware

District of Columbia
American University
George Washington University
Georgetown University
Howard University

Florida
Florida Agricultural and Mechanical University
Florida Atlantic University
Florida Gulf Coast University W
Florida International University W
Florida State University
University of Florida
University of Miami
University of North Florida W

Georgia
Georgia Institute of Technology
Georgia Southern University W
University of Georgia

Hawaii
University of Hawaii
Manoa

Idaho
Boise State University W
University of Idaho W

Illinois
Eastern Illinois University
Illinois State University W
Northwestern University
Southern Illinois University Carbondale
University of Illinois
Chicago
Urbana-Champaign W
Western Illinois University

Indiana
Ball State University
Butler University W
Indiana University
Bloomington
Indiana University-Purdue University Indianapolis
Purdue University
University of Evansville
University of Notre Dame
Valparaiso University

Iowa
Iowa State University W
University of Iowa
University of Northern Iowa W

Kansas
University of Kansas W

Kentucky
University of Kentucky

University of Louisville
Western Kentucky University

Louisiana
Centenary College of Louisiana
Louisiana State University and Agricultural and Mechanical College
University of New Orleans

Maine
University of Maine

Maryland
Loyola College in Maryland
Mount St. Mary's University W
Towson University
United States Naval Academy
University of Maryland
Baltimore County
College Park

Massachusetts
Boston College
Boston University
College of the Holy Cross
Harvard College
Northeastern University W
University of Massachusetts
Amherst

Michigan
Eastern Michigan University
Michigan State University
Oakland University
University of Michigan

Minnesota
University of Minnesota
Twin Cities

Missouri
Missouri State University
Saint Louis University
University of Missouri
Columbia

Nebraska
University of Nebraska
Lincoln W

Nevada
University of Nevada
Las Vegas
Reno W

New Hampshire
Dartmouth College
University of New Hampshire W

New Jersey
New Jersey Institute of Technology
Princeton University
Rider University
Rutgers, The State University of New Jersey
New Brunswick/Piscataway Campus W
Saint Peter's College
Seton Hall University

New Mexico
New Mexico State University W
University of New Mexico W

New York
Barnard College W
Canisius College
Colgate University
Cornell University
Fordham University
Iona College
Manhattan College
Marist College
Niagara University
Saint Bonaventure University
St. Francis College
Siena College W
State University of New York
Binghamton
Buffalo
Stony Brook
Syracuse University
United States Military Academy
Wagner College W

North Carolina
Campbell University W
Davidson College
Duke University
East Carolina University
Gardner-Webb University
North Carolina Agricultural and Technical State University W
North Carolina State University
University of North Carolina
Chapel Hill
Wilmington

North Dakota
University of North Dakota

Ohio
Bowling Green State University W
Cleveland State University
Miami University
Oxford Campus
Ohio State University
Columbus Campus
Ohio University W
University of Akron W
University of Cincinnati
University of Toledo W
Wright State University
Xavier University
Youngstown State University W

Oregon
Oregon State University W

Pennsylvania
Bucknell University
Drexel University
Duquesne University
La Salle University
Lafayette College
Lehigh University
Penn State
University Park
St. Francis University W
University of Pennsylvania
University of Pittsburgh
Villanova University

Rhode Island
Brown University
Bryant University
Providence College
University of Rhode Island W

South Carolina
Clemson University
College of Charleston
University of South Carolina

South Dakota
South Dakota State University
University of South Dakota

Tennessee
University of Tennessee
Knoxville
Vanderbilt University W

Texas
Rice University W
Southern Methodist University
Texas A&M University
Texas Christian University
University of Houston W
University of North Texas W
University of Texas
Austin

Utah
Brigham Young University
University of Utah

Vermont
University of Vermont W

Virginia
College of William and Mary
George Mason University
James Madison University W
Old Dominion University
Radford University W
University of Richmond W
University of Virginia
Virginia Military Institute
Virginia Polytechnic Institute and State University

Washington
Seattle University
University of Washington
Washington State University W

West Virginia
Marshall University W
West Virginia University

Wisconsin
University of Wisconsin
Green Bay
Madison
Milwaukee

Wyoming
University of Wyoming

Swimming and diving Division II

Alaska
University of Alaska
Fairbanks W

Arizona
Grand Canyon University

Arkansas
Henderson State University
Ouachita Baptist University

California
University of California
San Diego

Colorado
Colorado School of Mines
Mesa State College W

Connecticut
Southern Connecticut State University
University of Bridgeport W

Florida
Florida Southern College
Rollins College
St. Leo University
University of Tampa

Illinois
Lewis University

Indiana
University of Indianapolis

Massachusetts
Bentley University

Michigan
Grand Valley State University
Hillsdale College W
Northern Michigan University W
Wayne State University

Minnesota
Minnesota State University
Mankato
Moorhead W
Saint Cloud State University

Mississippi
Delta State University

Missouri
Drury University
Truman State University
University of Missouri
Missouri University of Science and Technology M

Nebraska
University of Nebraska
Kearney W
Omaha W

New York
Adelphi University
City University of New York
Queens College
College of Saint Rose
Le Moyne College
Long Island University
C. W. Post Campus W
Pace University

North Carolina
Catawba College
Lenoir-Rhyne University W
Mars Hill College
Pfeiffer University
Wingate University

Ohio
Ashland University
University of Findlay

Pennsylvania
Bloomsburg University of Pennsylvania
California University of Pennsylvania W
Clarion University of Pennsylvania
East Stroudsburg University of Pennsylvania W
Edinboro University of Pennsylvania
Gannon University
Indiana University of Pennsylvania
Kutztown University of Pennsylvania
Lock Haven University of Pennsylvania W
Mansfield University of Pennsylvania W
Millersville University of Pennsylvania W
Shippensburg University of Pennsylvania
Slippery Rock University of Pennsylvania W
West Chester University of Pennsylvania

Puerto Rico
University of Puerto Rico
Mayaguez
Rio Piedras

South Carolina
Converse College W
Limestone College

South Dakota
Northern State University W

Texas
University of Texas
of the Permian Basin
University of the Incarnate Word

Vermont
St. Michael's College

West Virginia
Fairmont State University
Salem International University M
West Virginia Wesleyan College
Wheeling Jesuit University

Swimming and diving Division III

Arkansas
Hendrix College

California
California Institute of Technology
California Lutheran University
California State University
East Bay W
Chapman University W
Claremont McKenna College
Mills College W
Occidental College
Pitzer College M
Pomona College
University of California
Santa Cruz
University of La Verne
University of Redlands
Whittier College

Colorado
Colorado College
Regis University M

Connecticut
Connecticut College M
Eastern Connecticut State University W
St. Joseph College W
Trinity College
United States Coast Guard Academy
Wesleyan University
Western Connecticut State University W

District of Columbia
Catholic University of America
Gallaudet University

Georgia
Agnes Scott College W
Emory University
LaGrange College W

Illinois
Augustana College
Benedictine University M
Eureka College
Illinois College W
Illinois Wesleyan University
Knox College
Lake Forest College
Millikin University
Monmouth College
North Central College
Principia College
University of Chicago
Wheaton College

Indiana
DePauw University
Rose-Hulman Institute of Technology
Saint Mary's College W
Wabash College M

Iowa
Coe College
Grinnell College
Loras College
Luther College
Simpson College W

Kentucky
Centre College
Transylvania University

Maine
Bates College
Bowdoin College
Colby College
Husson University W
St. Joseph's College
University of New England W

Maryland
College of Notre Dame of Maryland W
Frostburg State University
Goucher College
Hood College
Johns Hopkins University
McDaniel College
St. Mary's College of Maryland
Salisbury University
Washington College

Massachusetts
Amherst College
Babson College
Brandeis University
Bridgewater State College
Clark University
Elms College
Gordon College
Massachusetts Institute of Technology
Mount Holyoke College W
Regis College W
Simmons College W
Smith College W
Springfield College
Tufts University
University of Massachusetts
Dartmouth
Wellesley College W
Western New England College W
Westfield State College W
Wheaton College
Wheelock College W
Williams College
Worcester Polytechnic Institute

Michigan
Albion College
Alma College
Calvin College
Hope College
Kalamazoo College
Olivet College

Minnesota
Augsburg College W
Carleton College
College of St. Benedict W
College of St. Catherine W
Concordia College: Moorhead W
Gustavus Adolphus College
Hamline University
Macalester College
St. John's University M
St. Mary's University of Minnesota
St. Olaf College
University of Minnesota
Morris W
University of St. Thomas

Missouri
Washington University in St. Louis

New Hampshire
Colby-Sawyer College
Keene State College
Plymouth State University W

New Jersey
The College of New Jersey
College of St. Elizabeth W
Drew University
Fairleigh Dickinson University
College at Florham
Montclair State University
Ramapo College of New Jersey M
Rowan University
Stevens Institute of Technology
William Paterson University of New Jersey

New York
Alfred University
Cazenovia College
City University of New York
Baruch College
College of Staten Island
Hunter College W
John Jay College of Criminal Justice W
Lehman College
York College
Clarkson University
College of Mount St. Vincent W
College of New Rochelle W
Hamilton College
Hartwick College
Hobart and William Smith Colleges W
Ithaca College
Mount St. Mary College
Nazareth College of Rochester
New York University
Rensselaer Polytechnic Institute
Rochester Institute of Technology
St. Joseph's College W
St. Lawrence University
Skidmore College
State University of New York
College at Brockport
College at Buffalo
College at Cortland
College at Fredonia
College at Geneseo
College at Old Westbury
College at Oneonta
College at Potsdam
College of Agriculture and Technology at Cobleskill
College of Agriculture and Technology at Morrisville
Maritime College
New Paltz
Oswego
Purchase W
Union College
United States Merchant Marine Academy
University of Rochester
Utica College
Vassar College
Wells College

North Carolina
Greensboro College W
Guilford College W
Salem College W

Ohio
Baldwin-Wallace College
Case Western Reserve University
College of Wooster
Denison University
Hiram College
John Carroll University
Kenyon College
Mount Union College
Oberlin College
Ohio Northern University
Ohio Wesleyan University
Wilmington College
Wittenberg University

Oregon
Lewis & Clark College
Linfield College
Pacific University
Willamette University

Pennsylvania
Albright College
Allegheny College
Arcadia University
Bryn Mawr College W
Cabrini College
Carnegie Mellon University
Chatham University W
Dickinson College
Elizabethtown College
Franklin & Marshall College
Gettysburg College
Grove City College
Juniata College W
King's College
Lebanon Valley College
Lycoming College
Misericordia University
Penn State
Altoona
Erie, The Behrend College
St. Vincent College
Susquehanna University
Swarthmore College
University of Pittsburgh
Bradford
University of Scranton
Ursinus College
Washington & Jefferson College
Westminster College
Widener University
York College of Pennsylvania

Rhode Island
Roger Williams University

Tennessee
Rhodes College
University of the South

Texas
Austin College
McMurry University
Southwestern University
Trinity University

Vermont
Middlebury College
Norwich University

Virginia
Bridgewater College W
Emory & Henry College W
Hollins University W
Marymount University
Randolph College W
Randolph-Macon College W
Sweet Briar College W
University of Mary Washington
Washington and Lee University

Washington
Pacific Lutheran University
University of Puget Sound
Whitman College
Whitworth University

West Virginia
Bethany College

Wisconsin
Beloit College
Carroll University
Carthage College
Lawrence University
Ripon College
St. Norbert College W
University of Wisconsin
Eau Claire
La Crosse
Oshkosh
River Falls
Stevens Point
Whitewater

Tennis Division I

Alabama
Alabama Agricultural and Mechanical University
Alabama State University
Auburn University
Birmingham-Southern College
Jacksonville State University
Samford University
Troy University
University of Alabama
University of Alabama
Birmingham
University of South Alabama

Arizona
Arizona State University W
Northern Arizona University
University of Arizona

Arkansas
Arkansas State University W
University of Arkansas
University of Arkansas
Little Rock W
Pine Bluff
University of Central Arkansas W

California
California Polytechnic State University: San Luis Obispo
California State University
Bakersfield W
Fresno
Fullerton W
Long Beach W
Northridge W
Sacramento
Stanislaus W
Loyola Marymount University
Pepperdine University
St. Mary's College of California
San Diego State University
San Jose State University W
Santa Clara University
Stanford University
University of California
Berkeley
Davis
Irvine
Los Angeles
Riverside
Santa Barbara
University of San Diego
University of San Francisco
University of Southern California
University of the Pacific

Colorado
Colorado State University W
United States Air Force Academy
University of Colorado
Boulder W
University of Denver
University of Northern Colorado

Connecticut
Fairfield University
Quinnipiac University
Sacred Heart University
University of Connecticut
University of Hartford
Yale University

Delaware
Delaware State University
University of Delaware

District of Columbia
George Washington University
Georgetown University
Howard University

Florida
Bethune-Cookman University
Florida Agricultural and Mechanical University
Florida Atlantic University
Florida Gulf Coast University
Florida International University W
Florida State University
Jacksonville University
Stetson University
University of Central Florida
University of Florida
University of Miami
University of North Florida
University of South Florida

Georgia
Georgia Institute of Technology
Georgia Southern University
Georgia State University
Kennesaw State University
Mercer University
Savannah State University W
University of Georgia

Hawaii
University of Hawaii
Manoa

Idaho
Boise State University
Idaho State University
University of Idaho

Illinois
Bradley University
Chicago State University
DePaul University
Eastern Illinois University
Illinois State University
Northern Illinois University
Northwestern University
Southern Illinois University
Carbondale
Southern Illinois University
Edwardsville
University of Illinois
Chicago
Urbana-Champaign
Western Illinois University

Indiana
Ball State University
Butler University
Indiana State University
Indiana University
Bloomington
Indiana University-Purdue University Fort Wayne
Indiana University-Purdue University Indianapolis
Purdue University
University of Evansville W
University of Notre Dame
Valparaiso University

Iowa
Drake University
Iowa State University W
University of Iowa
University of Northern Iowa W

Kansas
Kansas State University W
University of Kansas W
Wichita State University

Kentucky
Eastern Kentucky University
Morehead State University
Murray State University
University of Kentucky
University of Louisville
Western Kentucky University

Louisiana
Centenary College of Louisiana
Grambling State University
Louisiana State University and Agricultural and Mechanical College
Louisiana Tech University W
McNeese State University W
Nicholls State University
Northwestern State University W
Southeastern Louisiana University
Southern University and Agricultural and Mechanical College
Tulane University W
University of Louisiana at Lafayette
University of Louisiana at Monroe W
University of New Orleans

Maryland
Coppin State University
Loyola College in Maryland
Morgan State University
Mount St. Mary's University

Towson University W
United States Naval Academy M
University of Maryland
Baltimore County
College Park
Eastern Shore

Massachusetts
Boston College
Boston University
College of the Holy Cross
Harvard College
University of Massachusetts
Amherst W

Michigan
Eastern Michigan University W
Michigan State University
Oakland University W
University of Detroit Mercy
University of Michigan
Western Michigan University

Minnesota
University of Minnesota
Twin Cities

Mississippi
Alcorn State University
Jackson State University
Mississippi State University
Mississippi Valley State University
University of Mississippi
University of Southern Mississippi

Missouri
Saint Louis University
Southeast Missouri State University W
University of Missouri
Columbia W
Kansas City

Montana
Montana State University
Bozeman
University of Montana

Nebraska
Creighton University
University of Nebraska
Lincoln

Nevada
University of Nevada
Las Vegas
Reno

New Hampshire
Dartmouth College

New Jersey
Fairleigh Dickinson University
Metropolitan Campus
Monmouth University
New Jersey Institute of Technology
Princeton University
Rider University
Rutgers, The State University of New Jersey
New Brunswick/Piscataway Campus W
Saint Peter's College
Seton Hall University W

New Mexico
New Mexico State University
University of New Mexico

New York
Barnard College W
Colgate University
Columbia University M
Cornell University
Fordham University
Hofstra University
Long Island University
Brooklyn Campus W
Manhattan College W
Marist College
Niagara University
Saint Bonaventure University
St. Francis College
St. John's University
Siena College
State University of New York
Albany W
Binghamton
Buffalo
Stony Brook
Syracuse University W
United States Military Academy
Wagner College

North Carolina
Appalachian State University
Campbell University
Davidson College
Duke University
East Carolina University
Elon University
Gardner-Webb University
High Point University M
North Carolina Agricultural and Technical State University W
North Carolina Central University
North Carolina State University
University of North Carolina
Asheville
Chapel Hill
Charlotte
Greensboro
Wilmington
Wake Forest University
Western Carolina University W
Winston-Salem State University

North Dakota
University of North Dakota W

Ohio
Bowling Green State University W
Cleveland State University
Miami University
Oxford Campus W
Ohio State University
Columbus Campus
University of Akron W
University of Cincinnati W
University of Dayton
University of Toledo
Wright State University
Xavier University
Youngstown State University

Oklahoma
Oklahoma State University
Oral Roberts University
University of Oklahoma
University of Tulsa

Oregon
Portland State University
University of Oregon
University of Portland

Pennsylvania
Bucknell University
Drexel University
Duquesne University
La Salle University
Lafayette College
Lehigh University
Penn State
University Park
Robert Morris University
St. Francis University
Saint Joseph's University
Temple University
University of Pennsylvania
University of Pittsburgh W
Villanova University

Rhode Island
Brown University
Bryant University
Providence College W
University of Rhode Island W

South Carolina
Charleston Southern University W
The Citadel M
Clemson University
Coastal Carolina University
College of Charleston
Furman University
Presbyterian College
South Carolina State University
University of South Carolina
University of South Carolina Upstate
Winthrop University
Wofford College

South Dakota
South Dakota State University
University of South Dakota W

Tennessee
Austin Peay State University
Belmont University
East Tennessee State University
Lipscomb University
Middle Tennessee State University
Tennessee State University
Tennessee Technological University
University of Memphis
University of Tennessee
Chattanooga
Knoxville
Martin
Vanderbilt University

Texas
Baylor University
Lamar University
Prairie View A&M University
Rice University
Sam Houston State University W
Southern Methodist University
Stephen F. Austin State University W
Texas A&M University
Texas A&M University
Corpus Christi
Texas Christian University
Texas State University: San Marcos W
Texas Tech University
University of Houston W
University of North Texas W
University of Texas
Arlington
Austin
El Paso W
Pan American
San Antonio

Utah
Brigham Young University
Southern Utah University W
University of Utah
Utah State University
Weber State University

Virginia
College of William and Mary
George Mason University
Hampton University
James Madison University
Liberty University
Longwood University
Norfolk State University
Old Dominion University
Radford University
University of Richmond
University of Virginia
Virginia Commonwealth University
Virginia Polytechnic Institute and State University

Washington
Eastern Washington University
Gonzaga University
University of Washington
Washington State University W

West Virginia
Marshall University W
West Virginia University W

Wisconsin
Marquette University
University of Wisconsin
Green Bay
Madison
Milwaukee W

Wyoming
University of Wyoming W

Tennis Division II

Alabama
Tuskegee University
University of Alabama
Huntsville
University of Montevallo W
University of North Alabama
University of West Alabama

Arizona
Grand Canyon University

Arkansas
Arkansas Tech University W
Harding University
Henderson State University W
Ouachita Baptist University
Southern Arkansas University W

California
California State Polytechnic University: Pomona
California State University
Los Angeles W
San Bernardino W
Notre Dame de Namur University W
Sonoma State University
University of California
San Diego

Colorado
Colorado Christian University
Colorado State University
Pueblo
Mesa State College
Metropolitan State College of Denver

Connecticut
Post University
University of New Haven W

Delaware
Goldey-Beacom College W

District of Columbia
University of the District of Columbia

Florida
Barry University
Eckerd College
Flagler College
Florida Institute of Technology
Florida Southern College
Lynn University
Nova Southeastern University W
Palm Beach Atlantic University
Rollins College
St. Leo University
University of Tampa W
University of West Florida

Georgia
Albany State University W
Armstrong Atlantic State University
Augusta State University
Clark Atlanta University W
Clayton State University W
Columbus State University
Fort Valley State University
Georgia College and State University
Georgia Southwestern State University
Morehouse College M
North Georgia College & State University
Valdosta State University

Hawaii
Brigham Young University-Hawaii
Chaminade University of Honolulu W
Hawaii Pacific University
University of Hawaii
Hilo

Illinois
Lewis University
Quincy University

Indiana
Oakland City University
Saint Joseph's College
University of Indianapolis
University of Southern Indiana

Iowa
Upper Iowa University W

Kansas
Emporia State University
Fort Hays State University W
Newman University
Washburn University

Kentucky
Bellarmine University
Kentucky Wesleyan College W
Northern Kentucky University

Maryland
Bowie State University W

Massachusetts
American International College
Assumption College
Bentley University
Merrimack College
Stonehill College

Michigan
Ferris State University
Grand Valley State University
Lake Superior State University
Michigan Technological University
Northwood University: Michigan
Saginaw Valley State University W
Wayne State University

Minnesota
Bemidji State University W
Minnesota State University
Mankato
Moorhead W
Saint Cloud State University
Southwest Minnesota State University W
University of Minnesota
Crookston W
Duluth W
Winona State University

Mississippi
Delta State University

Missouri
Drury University
Lincoln University W
Missouri Southern State University W
Missouri Western State University W

Northwest Missouri State University
Rockhurst University
Southwest Baptist University
Truman State University
University of Missouri
St. Louis

Montana
Montana State University
Billings

Nebraska
University of Nebraska
Kearney
Omaha W

New Hampshire
Franklin Pierce University
St. Anselm College
Southern New Hampshire University

New Jersey
Bloomfield College M
Caldwell College
Georgian Court University W

New Mexico
Eastern New Mexico University W
Western New Mexico University

New York
Adelphi University
City University of New York
Queens College
College of Saint Rose W
Concordia College
Dowling College
Le Moyne College
Long Island University
C. W. Post Campus W
Mercy College M
Molloy College W
Pace University
St. Thomas Aquinas College

North Carolina
Barton College
Brevard College
Catawba College
Chowan University
Elizabeth City State University W
Fayetteville State University W
Johnson C. Smith University
Lees-McRae College
Lenoir-Rhyne University
Livingstone College W
Mars Hill College
Mount Olive College
Pfeiffer University
Queens University of Charlotte
St. Augustine's College
Shaw University
University of North Carolina
Pembroke W
Wingate University

North Dakota
University of Mary

Ohio
Ashland University W
Central State University
Tiffin University
University of Findlay

Oklahoma
Cameron University
East Central University
Northeastern State University W
Southeastern Oklahoma State University
University of Central Oklahoma W

Pennsylvania
Bloomsburg University of Pennsylvania
California University of Pennsylvania W
Chestnut Hill College
Cheyney University of Pennsylvania W
Clarion University of Pennsylvania W
East Stroudsburg University of Pennsylvania
Holy Family University W
Indiana University of Pennsylvania W
Kutztown University of Pennsylvania
Mercyhurst College
Millersville University of Pennsylvania
Philadelphia University
Seton Hill University
Shippensburg University of Pennsylvania W
Slippery Rock University of Pennsylvania W
University of the Sciences in Philadelphia
West Chester University of Pennsylvania

Puerto Rico
University of Puerto Rico
Bayamon University College
Cayey University College
Mayaguez
Rio Piedras

South Carolina
Anderson University
Benedict College
Converse College W
Erskine College
Francis Marion University
Lander University
Limestone College
Newberry College
North Greenville University
Presbyterian College M
University of South Carolina
Aiken

South Dakota
Augustana College
Northern State University W

Tennessee
Carson-Newman College
Christian Brothers University
Lane College
LeMoyne-Owen College
Lincoln Memorial University
Tusculum College

Texas
Abilene Christian University
Dallas Baptist University
Midwestern State University
St. Edward's University
St. Mary's University
Tarleton State University W
University of the Incarnate Word

Utah
Dixie State College of Utah W

Vermont
St. Michael's College

Virginia
St. Paul's College
Virginia State University
Virginia Union University

West Virginia
Bluefield State College
Concord University
Fairmont State University
Salem International University M
Shepherd University
University of Charleston
West Liberty State College
West Virginia State University
West Virginia Wesleyan College

Tennis Division III

Alabama
Huntingdon College

Arkansas
Hendrix College
University of the Ozarks

California
California Institute of Technology
California Lutheran University
Chapman University
Claremont McKenna College
La Sierra University
Mills College W
Occidental College
Pitzer College M
Pomona College
University of California
Santa Cruz
University of La Verne
University of Redlands
Whittier College

Colorado
Colorado College

Connecticut
Albertus Magnus College
Connecticut College M
Mitchell College
St. Joseph College W
Trinity College
United States Coast Guard Academy M
Wesleyan University
Western Connecticut State University

Delaware
Wesley College

District of Columbia
Catholic University of America
Trinity Washington University W

Georgia
Agnes Scott College W
Emory University
LaGrange College
Oglethorpe University
Piedmont College
Spelman College W
Wesleyan College W

Illinois
Augustana College
Aurora University
Benedictine University W
Blackburn College W
Concordia University Chicago
Dominican University
Elmhurst College
Eureka College
Greenville College
Illinois College
Illinois Wesleyan University
Knox College
Lake Forest College
Millikin University W
Monmouth College
North Central College
Principia College
Rockford College
University of Chicago
Wheaton College

Indiana
Anderson University
DePauw University
Earlham College
Franklin College
Hanover College
Manchester College
Rose-Hulman Institute of Technology
Saint Mary's College W
Trine University
Wabash College M

Iowa
Buena Vista University
Central College
Coe College
Cornell College
Grinnell College
Loras College
Luther College
Simpson College
University of Dubuque
Wartburg College

Kentucky
Centre College
Thomas More College
Transylvania University

Louisiana
Louisiana College

Maine
Bates College
Bowdoin College
Colby College
Thomas College M
University of Southern Maine

Maryland
College of Notre Dame of Maryland W
Frostburg State University
Goucher College
Hood College
Johns Hopkins University
McDaniel College
St. Mary's College of Maryland
Salisbury University
Stevenson University
Washington College

Massachusetts
Amherst College
Anna Maria College
Babson College
Bay Path College W
Becker College
Brandeis University
Bridgewater State College
Clark University
Curry College
Emerson College
Emmanuel College W
Endicott College
Gordon College
Lesley University M
Massachusetts College of Liberal Arts W
Massachusetts Institute of Technology
Mount Holyoke College W
Newbury College
Nichols College
Pine Manor College W
Regis College W
Salem State College
Simmons College W
Smith College W
Springfield College
Suffolk University
Tufts University
University of Massachusetts
Boston
Dartmouth
Wellesley College W
Wentworth Institute of Technology
Western New England College
Wheaton College
Wheelock College M
Williams College
Worcester State College W

Michigan
Adrian College
Albion College
Alma College
Calvin College
Hope College
Kalamazoo College
Olivet College W

Minnesota
Bethany Lutheran College
Bethel University
Carleton College
College of St. Benedict W
College of St. Catherine W
College of St. Scholastica
Concordia College: Moorhead
Gustavus Adolphus College
Hamline University
Macalester College
Martin Luther College
Northwestern College
St. John's University M
St. Mary's University of Minnesota
St. Olaf College
University of Minnesota
Morris
University of St. Thomas

Mississippi
Millsaps College
Mississippi College
Rust College

Missouri
Fontbonne University
Maryville University of Saint Louis
Washington University in St. Louis
Webster University
Westminster College

Nebraska
Nebraska Wesleyan University

New Hampshire
Colby-Sawyer College
Plymouth State University W

New Jersey
The College of New Jersey
College of St. Elizabeth W
Drew University
Fairleigh Dickinson University
College at Florham
Kean University W
Ramapo College of New Jersey
Richard Stockton College of New Jersey W
Rutgers, The State University of New Jersey
Newark Regional Campus
Stevens Institute of Technology
William Paterson University of New Jersey W

New York
Alfred University
Bard College
City University of New York
Baruch College
Brooklyn College
City College
College of Staten Island
Hunter College
John Jay College of Criminal Justice
Lehman College
Medgar Evers College W
New York City College of Technology
York College M
College of Mount St. Vincent
College of New Rochelle W
Elmira College
Hamilton College
Hartwick College
Hobart and William Smith Colleges
Ithaca College

Keuka College
Manhattanville College
Mount St. Mary College
Nazareth College of Rochester
New York University
Polytechnic Institute of New York University
Rensselaer Polytechnic Institute
Rochester Institute of Technology
Russell Sage College W
Sage College of Albany M
St. John Fisher College
St. Joseph's College M
St. Joseph's College: Suffolk Campus W
St. Lawrence University
Skidmore College
State University of New York
- College at Brockport W
- College at Cortland W
- College at Fredonia W
- College at Geneseo W
- College at Oneonta
- College at Plattsburgh W
- College of Agriculture and Technology at Cobleskill
- Farmingdale
- New Paltz W
- Oswego
- Purchase

Union College
United States Merchant Marine Academy M
University of Rochester
Utica College
Vassar College
Wells College W
Yeshiva University

North Carolina

Greensboro College
Guilford College
Meredith College W
Methodist University
North Carolina Wesleyan College
Peace College W
Salem College W

Ohio

Baldwin-Wallace College
Bluffton University
Capital University
Case Western Reserve University
College of Mount St. Joseph
College of Wooster
Defiance College
Denison University
Heidelberg University
Hiram College
John Carroll University
Kenyon College
Marietta College
Mount Union College
Muskingum College
Oberlin College
Ohio Northern University
Ohio Wesleyan University
Otterbein College
Wilmington College
Wittenberg University

Oregon

George Fox University
Lewis & Clark College
Linfield College
Pacific University
Willamette University

Pennsylvania

Albright College
Allegheny College
Alvernia University
Arcadia University
Baptist Bible College of Pennsylvania W
Bryn Mawr College W
Cabrini College
Carnegie Mellon University
Cedar Crest College W
Chatham University W
DeSales University
Dickinson College
Eastern University
Elizabethtown College
Franklin & Marshall College
Geneva College W
Gettysburg College
Grove City College
Gwynedd-Mercy College
Haverford College
Immaculata University
Juniata College
Keystone College
King's College
La Roche College W
Lancaster Bible College
Lebanon Valley College
Lincoln University
Lycoming College
Marywood University
Messiah College
Misericordia University
Moravian College
Muhlenberg College
Neumann College
Penn State
- Altoona
- Berks
- Erie, The Behrend College
- Harrisburg

Philadelphia Biblical University
Rosemont College W
St. Vincent College
Susquehanna University
Swarthmore College
University of Pittsburgh
- Bradford W
- Greensburg M

University of Scranton
Ursinus College
Washington & Jefferson College
Waynesburg University
Westminster College
Wilkes University
York College of Pennsylvania

Rhode Island

Johnson & Wales University: Providence
Rhode Island College
Roger Williams University
Salve Regina University

Tennessee

Maryville College
Rhodes College
University of the South

Texas

Austin College
Concordia University Texas
Hardin-Simmons University
Howard Payne University
LeTourneau University
McMurry University
Schreiner University
Southwestern University
Sul Ross State University
Texas Lutheran University
Trinity University
University of Mary Hardin-Baylor
University of Texas
- Dallas
- Tyler

Vermont

Castleton State College
Johnson State College
Lyndon State College
Middlebury College
Norwich University M

Virginia

Averett University
Bridgewater College
Christopher Newport University
Emory & Henry College
Ferrum College
Hampden-Sydney College M
Hollins University W
Lynchburg College
Mary Baldwin College W
Randolph College
Randolph-Macon College
Roanoke College
Shenandoah University
Sweet Briar College W
University of Mary Washington
Virginia Wesleyan College
Washington and Lee University

Washington

Pacific Lutheran University
University of Puget Sound
Whitman College
Whitworth University

West Virginia

Bethany College

Wisconsin

Beloit College
Carroll University
Carthage College
Concordia University Wisconsin
Edgewood College W
Lakeland College
Lawrence University
Marian University
Milwaukee School of Engineering
Mount Mary College W
Ripon College
St. Norbert College
University of Wisconsin
- Eau Claire
- La Crosse
- Oshkosh
- River Falls W
- Stevens Point W
- Stout W
- Whitewater

Wisconsin Lutheran College

Track, indoor Division I

Alabama

Alabama State University
Auburn University
Jacksonville State University W
Samford University
Troy University W
University of Alabama
University of Alabama
- Birmingham W

University of South Alabama

Arizona

Arizona State University
Northern Arizona University
University of Arizona

Arkansas

Arkansas State University
University of Arkansas
University of Arkansas
- Little Rock
- Pine Bluff W

University of Central Arkansas

California

California Polytechnic State University: San Luis Obispo W
California State University
- Bakersfield
- Fresno W
- Fullerton W
- Long Beach
- Northridge
- Sacramento

San Diego State University W
Stanford University
University of California
- Berkeley
- Davis
- Irvine W
- Los Angeles
- Riverside
- Santa Barbara W

University of Southern California

Colorado

Colorado State University
United States Air Force Academy
University of Colorado
- Boulder

University of Northern Colorado

Connecticut

Central Connecticut State University
Quinnipiac University
Sacred Heart University
University of Connecticut
University of Hartford
Yale University

Delaware

Delaware State University
University of Delaware

District of Columbia

American University
Georgetown University
Howard University

Florida

Bethune-Cookman University
Florida Agricultural and Mechanical University
Florida Atlantic University W
Florida International University
Florida State University
Jacksonville University W
University of Central Florida W
University of Florida
University of Miami
University of North Florida
University of South Florida

Georgia

Georgia Institute of Technology
Georgia Southern University W
Georgia State University W
Kennesaw State University
Savannah State University
University of Georgia

Hawaii

University of Hawaii
- Manoa W

Idaho

Boise State University
Idaho State University
University of Idaho

Illinois

Bradley University W
Chicago State University
DePaul University
Eastern Illinois University
Illinois State University
Loyola University Chicago
Northern Illinois University W
Southern Illinois University
- Carbondale

Southern Illinois University
- Edwardsville

University of Illinois
- Chicago
- Urbana-Champaign

Western Illinois University

Indiana

Ball State University W
Butler University
Indiana State University
Indiana University
- Bloomington

Indiana University-Purdue University Fort Wayne W
Purdue University
University of Notre Dame
Valparaiso University

Iowa

Drake University
Iowa State University
University of Iowa
University of Northern Iowa

Kansas

Kansas State University
University of Kansas
Wichita State University

Kentucky

Eastern Kentucky University
Murray State University W
University of Kentucky
University of Louisville
Western Kentucky University

Louisiana

Grambling State University
Louisiana State University and Agricultural and Mechanical College
Louisiana Tech University
McNeese State University
Nicholls State University W
Northwestern State University
Southeastern Louisiana University
Southern University and Agricultural and Mechanical College
Tulane University W
University of Louisiana at Lafayette
University of Louisiana at Monroe

Maine

University of Maine

Maryland

Coppin State University
Loyola College in Maryland W
Morgan State University
Mount St. Mary's University
Towson University W
United States Naval Academy
University of Maryland
- Baltimore County
- College Park
- Eastern Shore

Massachusetts

Boston College
Boston University
College of the Holy Cross
Harvard College
Northeastern University
University of Massachusetts
- Amherst

Michigan

Central Michigan University
Eastern Michigan University
Michigan State University
Oakland University
University of Detroit Mercy
University of Michigan
Western Michigan University W

Minnesota

University of Minnesota
- Twin Cities

Mississippi

Jackson State University
Mississippi State University W
Mississippi Valley State University
University of Mississippi
University of Southern Mississippi

Missouri

Missouri State University W
Saint Louis University

Southeast Missouri State University
University of Missouri
Columbia
Kansas City

Montana
Montana State University
Bozeman
University of Montana

Nebraska
University of Nebraska
Lincoln

Nevada
University of Nevada
Las Vegas W
Reno W

New Hampshire
Dartmouth College
University of New Hampshire

New Jersey
Fairleigh Dickinson University
Metropolitan Campus
Monmouth University
New Jersey Institute of Technology
Princeton University
Rider University
Rutgers, The State University of New Jersey
New Brunswick/Piscataway Campus
Saint Peter's College
Seton Hall University

New Mexico
New Mexico State University W
University of New Mexico

New York
Barnard College W
Colgate University
Cornell University
Fordham University
Iona College
Long Island University
Brooklyn Campus
Manhattan College
Marist College
St. Francis College
St. John's University W
State University of New York
Albany
Binghamton
Buffalo
Stony Brook
Syracuse University
United States Military Academy
Wagner College

North Carolina
Appalachian State University
Campbell University
Davidson College
Duke University
East Carolina University
Elon University W
Gardner-Webb University
High Point University
North Carolina Agricultural and Technical State University
North Carolina Central University
North Carolina State University
University of North Carolina
Asheville
Chapel Hill
Charlotte
Wilmington
Wake Forest University
Western Carolina University
Winston-Salem State University

North Dakota
North Dakota State University
University of North Dakota

Ohio
Bowling Green State University W
Kent State University
Miami University
Oxford Campus W
Ohio State University
Columbus Campus
Ohio University W
University of Akron
University of Cincinnati W
University of Dayton W
University of Toledo W
Wright State University W
Xavier University
Youngstown State University

Oklahoma
Oklahoma State University
Oral Roberts University
University of Oklahoma
University of Tulsa

Oregon
Portland State University
University of Oregon
University of Portland

Pennsylvania
Bucknell University
Duquesne University W
La Salle University
Lafayette College
Lehigh University
Penn State
University Park
Robert Morris University
St. Francis University
Saint Joseph's University
Temple University
University of Pennsylvania
University of Pittsburgh
Villanova University

Rhode Island
Brown University
Bryant University
Providence College
University of Rhode Island

South Carolina
Charleston Southern University
The Citadel
Clemson University
Coastal Carolina University W
College of Charleston W
Furman University
South Carolina State University
University of South Carolina
University of South Carolina Upstate
Winthrop University
Wofford College

South Dakota
South Dakota State University
University of South Dakota

Tennessee
Austin Peay State University W
Belmont University
East Tennessee State University
Lipscomb University
Middle Tennessee State University
Tennessee State University
Tennessee Technological University W
University of Memphis
University of Tennessee
Chattanooga
Knoxville
Vanderbilt University W

Texas
Baylor University
Lamar University
Prairie View A&M University
Rice University
Sam Houston State University
Southern Methodist University W
Stephen F. Austin State University
Texas A&M University
Texas A&M University
Corpus Christi
Texas Christian University
Texas Southern University
Texas State University: San Marcos
Texas Tech University
University of Houston
University of North Texas
University of Texas
Arlington
Austin
El Paso
Pan American
San Antonio

Utah
Brigham Young University
Southern Utah University
University of Utah W
Utah State University
Utah Valley University
Weber State University

Vermont
University of Vermont

Virginia
College of William and Mary
George Mason University
Hampton University
James Madison University W
Liberty University
Norfolk State University
Radford University
University of Richmond
University of Virginia
Virginia Commonwealth University
Virginia Military Institute
Virginia Polytechnic Institute and State University

Washington
Eastern Washington University
Seattle University
University of Washington
Washington State University

West Virginia
Marshall University W
West Virginia University W

Wisconsin
Marquette University
University of Wisconsin
Madison
Milwaukee

Wyoming
University of Wyoming

Track, indoor Division II

Alabama
University of Alabama
Huntsville

Arkansas
Harding University

California
California State University
Dominguez Hills W
Los Angeles W
Stanislaus W
San Francisco State University W

Colorado
Adams State College
Colorado School of Mines
Colorado State University
Pueblo W
Mesa State College W
Metropolitan State College of Denver
University of Colorado
Colorado Springs
Western State College of Colorado

Connecticut
Southern Connecticut State University
University of New Haven

District of Columbia
University of the District of Columbia W

Georgia
Clayton State University
Morehouse College M

Idaho
Northwest Nazarene University

Illinois
Lewis University

Indiana
Saint Joseph's College
University of Indianapolis
University of Southern Indiana

Kansas
Emporia State University
Fort Hays State University
Pittsburg State University

Kentucky
Bellarmine University
Kentucky State University
Northern Kentucky University

Maryland
Bowie State University

Massachusetts
American International College
Assumption College
Bentley University
Stonehill College
University of Massachusetts
Lowell

Michigan
Ferris State University
Grand Valley State University
Hillsdale College
Lake Superior State University
Northern Michigan University W
Northwood University: Michigan
Saginaw Valley State University

Minnesota
Bemidji State University
Concordia University: St. Paul
Minnesota State University
Mankato
Moorhead
Saint Cloud State University
University of Minnesota
Duluth
Winona State University W

Missouri
Lincoln University
Missouri Southern State University
Northwest Missouri State University
Southwest Baptist University
Truman State University
University of Central Missouri
University of Missouri
Missouri University of Science and Technology

Montana
Montana State University
Billings

Nebraska
Chadron State College
University of Nebraska
Kearney
Omaha W
Wayne State College

New Mexico
New Mexico Highlands University W

New York
Adelphi University
City University of New York
Queens College
College of Saint Rose
Long Island University
C. W. Post Campus
Mercy College
St. Thomas Aquinas College

North Carolina
Elizabeth City State University W
Johnson C. Smith University
Lees-McRae College
Livingstone College
Queens University of Charlotte
St. Augustine's College

North Dakota
University of Mary

Ohio
Ashland University
Central State University
Tiffin University
University of Findlay

Oregon
Western Oregon University

Pennsylvania
Bloomsburg University of Pennsylvania
California University of Pennsylvania
Cheyney University of Pennsylvania
Clarion University of Pennsylvania W
East Stroudsburg University of Pennsylvania
Edinboro University of Pennsylvania W
Indiana University of Pennsylvania
Kutztown University of Pennsylvania
Lock Haven University of Pennsylvania
Mansfield University of Pennsylvania
Millersville University of Pennsylvania
Seton Hill University W
Shippensburg University of Pennsylvania
Slippery Rock University of Pennsylvania
University of Pittsburgh
Johnstown W
West Chester University of Pennsylvania

South Carolina
Anderson University
Claflin University

South Dakota
Augustana College
Northern State University

Tennessee
Carson-Newman College

Texas
Abilene Christian University
Dallas Baptist University
University of the Incarnate Word W
West Texas A&M University

Virginia
St. Paul's College
Virginia State University
Virginia Union University

Washington
Central Washington University
Saint Martin's University
Seattle Pacific University
Western Washington University

West Virginia
Alderson-Broaddus College
Concord University
West Virginia State University
Wheeling Jesuit University

Wisconsin
University of Wisconsin
Parkside

Track, indoor Division III

Alabama
Birmingham-Southern College

California
California Lutheran University W
Occidental College
University of La Verne

Colorado
Colorado College W

Connecticut
Connecticut College M
Eastern Connecticut State University
Trinity College
United States Coast Guard Academy
Wesleyan University

Delaware
Wesley College

District of Columbia
Catholic University of America

Georgia
Emory University

Illinois
Augustana College
Aurora University
Benedictine University
Concordia University Chicago
Elmhurst College
Greenville College
Illinois College
Illinois Wesleyan University
Knox College
Millikin University
Monmouth College
North Central College
North Park University
Principia College
Rockford College
University of Chicago
Wheaton College

Indiana
Anderson University
DePauw University
Earlham College
Franklin College
Hanover College
Manchester College
Rose-Hulman Institute of Technology
Trine University
Wabash College M

Iowa
Buena Vista University
Central College
Coe College
Cornell College
Grinnell College
Loras College
Luther College
Northwestern College W
Simpson College
University of Dubuque
Wartburg College

Kentucky
Centre College

Maine
Bates College
Bowdoin College
Colby College
University of Southern Maine

Maryland
Frostburg State University
Goucher College
Johns Hopkins University
McDaniel College
Salisbury University

Massachusetts
Amherst College
Brandeis University
Bridgewater State College
Emerson College W
Emmanuel College
Fitchburg State College
Gordon College
Massachusetts Institute of Technology
Mount Holyoke College W
Regis College W
Salem State College
Smith College W
Springfield College
Tufts University
University of Massachusetts
Boston
Dartmouth
Wellesley College W
Westfield State College
Wheaton College
Williams College
Worcester Polytechnic Institute
Worcester State College

Michigan
Adrian College
Albion College
Alma College
Calvin College

Minnesota
Augsburg College
Bethel University
Carleton College
College of St. Benedict W
College of St. Catherine W
College of St. Scholastica
Concordia College: Moorhead
Gustavus Adolphus College
Hamline University
Macalester College
Northwestern College M
St. John's University M
St. Mary's University of Minnesota
St. Olaf College
University of Minnesota
Morris
University of St. Thomas

Mississippi
Mississippi College

Missouri
Washington University in St. Louis

Nebraska
Nebraska Wesleyan University

New Hampshire
Keene State College

New Jersey
The College of New Jersey
Kean University
Montclair State University
New Jersey City University
Ramapo College of New Jersey
Richard Stockton College of New Jersey
Rowan University
Rutgers, The State University of New Jersey
Camden Regional Campus
Newark Regional Campus
Stevens Institute of Technology

New York
Alfred University
City University of New York
City College
Hunter College
Lehman College
Medgar Evers College
New York City College of Technology
York College
Hamilton College
Ithaca College
Manhattanville College
Nazareth College of Rochester
New York University
Polytechnic Institute of New York University M
Rensselaer Polytechnic Institute
Rochester Institute of Technology
St. Joseph's College: Suffolk Campus
St. Lawrence University
State University of New York
College at Brockport
College at Buffalo
College at Cortland
College at Fredonia
College at Geneseo
College at Oneonta
College at Plattsburgh
Farmingdale
Oswego
Union College
United States Merchant Marine Academy
University of Rochester

North Carolina
Methodist University

Ohio
Baldwin-Wallace College
Bluffton University
Capital University
Case Western Reserve University
College of Mount St. Joseph
College of Wooster
Defiance College
Denison University
Heidelberg University
Hiram College
John Carroll University
Kenyon College
Lake Erie College
Marietta College
Mount Union College
Muskingum College
Oberlin College
Ohio Northern University
Ohio Wesleyan University
Otterbein College
Wilmington College
Wittenberg University

Oregon
Lewis & Clark College
Linfield College
Willamette University

Pennsylvania
Albright College
Allegheny College
Bryn Mawr College W
Cabrini College
Carnegie Mellon University
Delaware Valley College
DeSales University
Dickinson College
Elizabethtown College
Franklin & Marshall College
Geneva College
Gettysburg College
Gwynedd-Mercy College
Haverford College
Juniata College
Keystone College
Lebanon Valley College
Lincoln University
Messiah College
Misericordia University
Moravian College
Muhlenberg College
Penn State
Erie, The Behrend College
Susquehanna University
Swarthmore College
Thiel College
Ursinus College
Washington & Jefferson College
Waynesburg University M
Westminster College
Widener University

Rhode Island
Rhode Island College

Tennessee
Rhodes College
University of the South

Texas
Hardin-Simmons University
McMurry University
Texas Lutheran University W
Trinity University

Vermont
Middlebury College

Virginia
Bridgewater College
Christopher Newport University
Eastern Mennonite University
Lynchburg College
Roanoke College
University of Mary Washington
Virginia Wesleyan College
Washington and Lee University

Washington
Pacific Lutheran University W
University of Puget Sound
Whitworth University

West Virginia
Bethany College

Wisconsin
Beloit College
Carroll University
Carthage College
Concordia University Wisconsin
Edgewood College
Lawrence University
Milwaukee School of Engineering
Ripon College
St. Norbert College
University of Wisconsin
Eau Claire
La Crosse
Oshkosh
Platteville
River Falls
Stevens Point
Stout
Superior
Whitewater
Wisconsin Lutheran College

Track, outdoor Division I

Alabama
Alabama Agricultural and Mechanical University
Alabama State University
Auburn University
Jacksonville State University W
Samford University
Troy University
University of Alabama
University of Alabama
Birmingham W
University of South Alabama

Arizona
Arizona State University
Northern Arizona University
University of Arizona

Arkansas
Arkansas State University
University of Arkansas
University of Arkansas
Little Rock
Pine Bluff
University of Central Arkansas

California
California Polytechnic State University: San Luis Obispo
California State University
Bakersfield
Fresno
Fullerton
Long Beach
Northridge
Sacramento
Loyola Marymount University
Pepperdine University
San Diego State University W
Santa Clara University
Stanford University
University of California
Berkeley
Davis
Irvine
Los Angeles
Riverside
Santa Barbara
University of San Diego W
University of San Francisco
University of Southern California

Colorado
Colorado State University
United States Air Force Academy
University of Colorado
Boulder
University of Northern Colorado

Connecticut
Central Connecticut State University
Quinnipiac University
Sacred Heart University
University of Connecticut
University of Hartford
Yale University

Delaware
Delaware State University
University of Delaware

District of Columbia
American University
Georgetown University
Howard University

Florida
Bethune-Cookman University
Florida Agricultural and Mechanical University
Florida Atlantic University W
Florida International University
Florida State University
Jacksonville University W
University of Central Florida W
University of Florida
University of Miami
University of North Florida
University of South Florida

Georgia
Georgia Institute of Technology
Georgia Southern University W

Georgia State University
Kennesaw State University
Savannah State University
University of Georgia

Hawaii

University of Hawaii
Manoa W

Idaho

Boise State University
Idaho State University
University of Idaho

Illinois

Bradley University W
Chicago State University
DePaul University
Eastern Illinois University
Illinois State University
Loyola University Chicago
Northern Illinois University W
Southern Illinois University
Carbondale
Southern Illinois University
Edwardsville
University of Illinois
Chicago
Urbana-Champaign
Western Illinois University

Indiana

Ball State University W
Butler University
Indiana State University
Indiana University
Bloomington
Indiana University-Purdue
University Fort Wayne W
Purdue University
University of Notre Dame
Valparaiso University

Iowa

Drake University
Iowa State University
University of Iowa
University of Northern Iowa

Kansas

Kansas State University
University of Kansas
Wichita State University

Kentucky

Eastern Kentucky University
Morehead State University
Murray State University W
University of Kentucky
University of Louisville
Western Kentucky University

Louisiana

Grambling State University
Louisiana State University and
Agricultural and Mechanical
College
Louisiana Tech University
McNeese State University
Nicholls State University W
Northwestern State University
Southeastern Louisiana University
Southern University and
Agricultural and Mechanical
College
Tulane University
University of Louisiana at
Lafayette
University of Louisiana at
Monroe

Maine

University of Maine

Maryland

Coppin State University
Loyola College in Maryland W
Morgan State University
Mount St. Mary's University
Towson University W
United States Naval Academy
University of Maryland
Baltimore County
College Park
Eastern Shore

Massachusetts

Boston College
Boston University
College of the Holy Cross
Harvard College
Northeastern University
University of Massachusetts
Amherst

Michigan

Central Michigan University
Eastern Michigan University
Michigan State University
Oakland University
University of Detroit Mercy
University of Michigan
Western Michigan University W

Minnesota

University of Minnesota
Twin Cities

Mississippi

Alcorn State University
Jackson State University
Mississippi State University
Mississippi Valley State
University
University of Mississippi
University of Southern
Mississippi

Missouri

Missouri State University W
Saint Louis University
Southeast Missouri State
University
University of Missouri
Columbia
Kansas City

Montana

Montana State University
Bozeman
University of Montana

Nebraska

University of Nebraska
Lincoln

Nevada

University of Nevada
Las Vegas W
Reno W

New Hampshire

Dartmouth College
University of New Hampshire

New Jersey

Fairleigh Dickinson University
Metropolitan Campus
Monmouth University
New Jersey Institute of
Technology
Princeton University
Rider University
Rutgers, The State University of
New Jersey
New Brunswick/Piscataway
Campus
Saint Peter's College
Seton Hall University

New Mexico

New Mexico State University W
University of New Mexico

New York

Barnard College W
Colgate University
Columbia University M
Cornell University
Fordham University
Iona College
Long Island University
Brooklyn Campus
Manhattan College
Marist College
St. Francis College
St. John's University W
State University of New York
Albany
Binghamton
Buffalo
Stony Brook
Syracuse University
United States Military Academy
Wagner College

North Carolina

Appalachian State University
Campbell University
Davidson College
Duke University
East Carolina University
Elon University W
Gardner-Webb University
High Point University
North Carolina Agricultural and
Technical State University
North Carolina Central University
North Carolina State University
University of North Carolina
Asheville
Chapel Hill
Charlotte
Greensboro
Wilmington
Wake Forest University
Western Carolina University
Winston-Salem State University

North Dakota

North Dakota State University
University of North Dakota

Ohio

Bowling Green State University
W
Kent State University
Miami University
Oxford Campus
Ohio State University
Columbus Campus
Ohio University W
University of Akron
University of Cincinnati
University of Dayton W
University of Toledo W
Wright State University
Xavier University
Youngstown State University

Oklahoma

Oklahoma State University
Oral Roberts University
University of Oklahoma
University of Tulsa

Oregon

Oregon State University W
Portland State University
University of Oregon
University of Portland

Pennsylvania

Bucknell University
Duquesne University
La Salle University
Lafayette College
Lehigh University
Penn State
University Park
Robert Morris University
St. Francis University
Saint Joseph's University
Temple University
University of Pennsylvania
University of Pittsburgh
Villanova University

Rhode Island

Brown University
Bryant University
Providence College
University of Rhode Island

South Carolina

Charleston Southern University
The Citadel
Clemson University
Coastal Carolina University
College of Charleston W
Furman University
South Carolina State University
University of South Carolina
University of South Carolina
Upstate
Winthrop University
Wofford College

South Dakota

South Dakota State University
University of South Dakota

Tennessee

Austin Peay State University W
Belmont University
East Tennessee State University
Lipscomb University
Middle Tennessee State
University
Tennessee State University
Tennessee Technological
University W
University of Memphis
University of Tennessee
Chattanooga
Knoxville
Vanderbilt University W

Texas

Baylor University
Houston Baptist University
Lamar University
Prairie View A&M University
Rice University
Sam Houston State University
Southern Methodist University W
Stephen F. Austin State University
Texas A&M University
Texas A&M University
Corpus Christi
Texas Christian University
Texas Southern University
Texas State University: San
Marcos
Texas Tech University
University of Houston
University of North Texas
University of Texas
Arlington
Austin
El Paso
Pan American
San Antonio

Utah

Brigham Young University
Southern Utah University
University of Utah W
Utah State University
Utah Valley University
Weber State University

Vermont

University of Vermont

Virginia

College of William and Mary
George Mason University
Hampton University
James Madison University W
Liberty University
Norfolk State University
Radford University
University of Richmond
University of Virginia
Virginia Commonwealth
University
Virginia Military Institute
Virginia Polytechnic Institute and
State University

Washington

Eastern Washington University
Gonzaga University
Seattle University
University of Washington
Washington State University

West Virginia

Marshall University W
West Virginia University W

Wisconsin

Marquette University
University of Wisconsin
Madison
Milwaukee

Wyoming

University of Wyoming

Track, outdoor Division II

Alabama

Miles College
Tuskegee University
University of Alabama
Huntsville

Alaska

University of Alaska
Anchorage

Arkansas

Harding University
Southern Arkansas University

California

California State Polytechnic
University: Pomona
California State University
Chico
Dominguez Hills W
Los Angeles
Stanislaus
Humboldt State University
San Francisco State University W
University of California
San Diego

Colorado

Adams State College
Colorado School of Mines
Mesa State College W
Metropolitan State College of
Denver
University of Colorado
Colorado Springs
Western State College of
Colorado

Connecticut

Southern Connecticut State
University
University of New Haven

District of Columbia

University of the District of
Columbia W

Florida

Florida Southern College
Nova Southeastern University
University of Tampa
University of West Florida W

Georgia

Albany State University
Clark Atlanta University
Clayton State University
Fort Valley State University
Morehouse College M
Paine College

Idaho

Northwest Nazarene University

Illinois
Lewis University

Indiana
Anderson University W
Saint Joseph's College
University of Indianapolis
University of Southern Indiana

Kansas
Emporia State University
Fort Hays State University
Pittsburg State University

Kentucky
Bellarmine University
Kentucky State University
Northern Kentucky University

Maryland
Bowie State University
Columbia Union College

Massachusetts
American International College
Assumption College
Bentley University
Stonehill College
University of Massachusetts
Lowell

Michigan
Ferris State University
Grand Valley State University
Hillsdale College
Lake Superior State University
Michigan Technological University
Northern Michigan University W
Northwood University: Michigan
Saginaw Valley State University

Minnesota
Bemidji State University
Concordia University: St. Paul
Minnesota State University
Mankato
Moorhead
Saint Cloud State University
University of Minnesota
Duluth
Winona State University W

Missouri
Drury University
Lincoln University
Missouri Southern State University
Northwest Missouri State University
Southwest Baptist University
Truman State University
University of Central Missouri
University of Missouri
Missouri University of Science and Technology

Montana
Montana State University
Billings

Nebraska
Chadron State College
University of Nebraska
Kearney
Omaha W
Wayne State College

New Jersey
Georgian Court University W

New Mexico
Eastern New Mexico University
New Mexico Highlands University W

New York
Adelphi University
City University of New York
Queens College
College of Saint Rose
Dominican College of Blauvelt W
Long Island University
C. W. Post Campus
Mercy College
Pace University
St. Thomas Aquinas College

North Carolina
Brevard College
Elizabeth City State University W
Johnson C. Smith University
Lees-McRae College
Lenoir-Rhyne University
Livingstone College
Mars Hill College
Mount Olive College
Queens University of Charlotte
St. Andrews Presbyterian College
St. Augustine's College
Shaw University
University of North Carolina
Pembroke

North Dakota
University of Mary

Ohio
Ashland University
Central State University
Tiffin University
University of Findlay

Oregon
Western Oregon University

Pennsylvania
Bloomsburg University of Pennsylvania
California University of Pennsylvania
Cheyney University of Pennsylvania
Clarion University of Pennsylvania W
East Stroudsburg University of Pennsylvania
Edinboro University of Pennsylvania
Indiana University of Pennsylvania
Kutztown University of Pennsylvania
Lock Haven University of Pennsylvania
Mansfield University of Pennsylvania
Millersville University of Pennsylvania
Seton Hill University
Shippensburg University of Pennsylvania
Slippery Rock University of Pennsylvania
University of Pittsburgh
Johnstown W
West Chester University of Pennsylvania

Puerto Rico
University of Puerto Rico
Bayamon University College
Cayey University College M
Mayaguez
Rio Piedras

South Carolina
Anderson University M
Benedict College
Claflin University
Francis Marion University
Limestone College

South Dakota
Augustana College
Northern State University

Tennessee
Carson-Newman College
Lane College

Texas
Abilene Christian University
Angelo State University
Dallas Baptist University
Tarleton State University
Texas A&M University
Commerce
Kingsville
University of the Incarnate Word
West Texas A&M University

Virginia
St. Paul's College
Virginia State University
Virginia Union University

Washington
Central Washington University
Saint Martin's University
Seattle Pacific University
Western Washington University

West Virginia
Alderson-Broaddus College
Concord University
Glenville State College
University of Charleston
West Liberty State College
West Virginia State University
West Virginia Wesleyan College
Wheeling Jesuit University

Wisconsin
University of Wisconsin
Parkside

Track, outdoor Division III

Alabama
Birmingham-Southern College

Arkansas
Hendrix College

California
California Institute of Technology
California Lutheran University
California State University
East Bay
Chapman University W
Claremont McKenna College
Mills College W
Occidental College
Pitzer College M
Pomona College
University of La Verne
University of Redlands
Whittier College

Colorado
Colorado College

Connecticut
Connecticut College M
Eastern Connecticut State University
Trinity College
United States Coast Guard Academy
Wesleyan University

Delaware
Wesley College

District of Columbia
Catholic University of America
Gallaudet University

Georgia
Emory University
Oglethorpe University

Illinois
Augustana College
Aurora University
Benedictine University
Concordia University Chicago
Elmhurst College
Eureka College
Greenville College
Illinois College
Illinois Wesleyan University
Knox College
Millikin University
Monmouth College
North Central College
North Park University
Principia College
Rockford College
University of Chicago
Wheaton College

Indiana
Anderson University M
DePauw University
Earlham College
Franklin College
Hanover College
Manchester College
Rose-Hulman Institute of Technology
Trine University
Wabash College M

Iowa
Buena Vista University
Central College
Coe College
Cornell College
Grinnell College
Loras College
Luther College
Simpson College
University of Dubuque
Wartburg College

Kentucky
Centre College
Transylvania University

Maine
Bates College
Bowdoin College
Colby College
University of Southern Maine

Maryland
Frostburg State University
Goucher College
Hood College
Johns Hopkins University
McDaniel College
Salisbury University

Massachusetts
Amherst College
Babson College
Brandeis University
Bridgewater State College
Emmanuel College
Fitchburg State College
Gordon College
Massachusetts Institute of Technology
Massachusetts Maritime Academy
Mount Holyoke College W
Regis College W
Salem State College
Smith College W
Springfield College
Tufts University
University of Massachusetts
Boston
Dartmouth
Wellesley College W
Westfield State College
Wheaton College
Williams College
Worcester Polytechnic Institute
Worcester State College

Michigan
Adrian College
Albion College
Alma College
Calvin College
Hope College
Olivet College

Minnesota
Augsburg College
Bethel University
Carleton College
College of St. Benedict W
College of St. Catherine W
College of St. Scholastica
Concordia College: Moorhead
Gustavus Adolphus College
Hamline University
Macalester College
Martin Luther College
Northwestern College
St. John's University M
St. Mary's University of Minnesota
St. Olaf College
University of Minnesota
Morris
University of St. Thomas

Mississippi
Mississippi College
Rust College

Missouri
Fontbonne University
Washington University in St. Louis
Webster University

Nebraska
Nebraska Wesleyan University

New Hampshire
Colby-Sawyer College
Keene State College

New Jersey
The College of New Jersey
Kean University
Montclair State University
New Jersey City University
Ramapo College of New Jersey
Richard Stockton College of New Jersey
Rowan University
Rutgers, The State University of New Jersey
Camden Regional Campus
Newark Regional Campus
Stevens Institute of Technology

New York
Alfred University
Bard College
City University of New York
City College
Hunter College
Lehman College
Medgar Evers College
New York City College of Technology
York College
Hamilton College
Ithaca College
Manhattanville College
Nazareth College of Rochester
New York University
Polytechnic Institute of New York University M
Rensselaer Polytechnic Institute
Rochester Institute of Technology
St. Joseph's College: Suffolk Campus
St. Lawrence University
State University of New York
College at Brockport
College at Buffalo
College at Cortland
College at Fredonia
College at Geneseo
College at Oneonta
College at Plattsburgh
College of Agriculture and Technology at Cobleskill
Farmingdale
Oswego
Union College

United States Merchant Marine Academy
University of Rochester
Vassar College

North Carolina
Methodist University

Ohio
Baldwin-Wallace College
Bluffton University
Capital University
Case Western Reserve University
College of Mount St. Joseph
College of Wooster
Defiance College
Denison University
Franciscan University of Steubenville
Heidelberg University
Hiram College
John Carroll University
Kenyon College
Lake Erie College
Marietta College
Mount Union College
Muskingum College
Oberlin College
Ohio Northern University
Ohio Wesleyan University
Otterbein College
Wilmington College
Wittenberg University

Oregon
George Fox University
Lewis & Clark College
Linfield College
Pacific University
Willamette University

Pennsylvania
Albright College
Allegheny College
Bryn Mawr College W
Cabrini College
Carnegie Mellon University
Delaware Valley College
DeSales University
Dickinson College
Elizabethtown College
Franklin & Marshall College
Geneva College
Gettysburg College
Grove City College
Gwynedd-Mercy College
Haverford College
Juniata College
Keystone College
Lebanon Valley College
Lincoln University
Messiah College
Misericordia University
Moravian College
Muhlenberg College
Penn State
Erie, The Behrend College
St. Vincent College M
Susquehanna University
Swarthmore College
Thiel College
Ursinus College
Washington & Jefferson College
Waynesburg University
Westminster College
Widener University
York College of Pennsylvania

Rhode Island
Rhode Island College
Salve Regina University W

South Carolina
Anderson University W

Tennessee
Rhodes College
University of the South

Texas
Hardin-Simmons University
McMurry University
Southwestern University
Sul Ross State University
Texas Lutheran University W
Trinity University
University of Dallas
University of Texas
Tyler

Vermont
Middlebury College

Virginia
Bridgewater College
Christopher Newport University
Eastern Mennonite University
Lynchburg College
Roanoke College
University of Mary Washington
Virginia Wesleyan College
Washington and Lee University

Washington
Pacific Lutheran University
University of Puget Sound
Whitworth University

West Virginia
Bethany College

Wisconsin
Beloit College
Carroll University
Carthage College
Concordia University Wisconsin
Edgewood College
Lakeland College
Lawrence University
Milwaukee School of Engineering
Ripon College
St. Norbert College
University of Wisconsin
Eau Claire
La Crosse
Oshkosh
Platteville
River Falls
Stevens Point
Stout
Superior
Whitewater
Wisconsin Lutheran College

Volleyball Division I

Alabama
Alabama Agricultural and Mechanical University W
Alabama State University W
Auburn University W
Birmingham-Southern College W
Jacksonville State University W
Samford University W
Troy University W
University of Alabama W
University of Alabama
Birmingham W
University of South Alabama W

Arizona
Arizona State University W
Northern Arizona University W
University of Arizona W

Arkansas
Arkansas State University W
University of Arkansas W
University of Arkansas
Little Rock W
Pine Bluff W
University of Central Arkansas W

California
California Polytechnic State University: San Luis Obispo W
California State University
Bakersfield W
Fresno W
Fullerton W
Long Beach W
Northridge W
Sacramento W
Loyola Marymount University W
Pepperdine University W
St. Mary's College of California W
San Diego State University W
San Jose State University W
Santa Clara University W
Stanford University W
University of California
Berkeley W
Davis W
Irvine W
Los Angeles W
Riverside W
Santa Barbara W
University of San Diego W
University of San Francisco W
University of Southern California W
University of the Pacific W

Colorado
Colorado State University W
United States Air Force Academy W
University of Colorado
Boulder W
University of Denver W
University of Northern Colorado W

Connecticut
Central Connecticut State University W
Fairfield University W
Quinnipiac University W
Sacred Heart University W
University of Connecticut W
University of Hartford W
Yale University W

Delaware
Delaware State University W
University of Delaware W

District of Columbia
American University W
George Washington University W
Georgetown University W
Howard University W

Florida
Bethune-Cookman University W
Florida Agricultural and Mechanical University W
Florida Atlantic University W
Florida Gulf Coast University W
Florida International University W
Florida State University W
Jacksonville University W
Stetson University W
University of Central Florida W
University of Florida W
University of Miami W
University of North Florida W
University of South Florida W

Georgia
Georgia Institute of Technology W
Georgia Southern University W
Georgia State University W
Kennesaw State University W
Mercer University W
Savannah State University W
University of Georgia W

Hawaii
University of Hawaii
Manoa W

Idaho
Boise State University W
Idaho State University W
University of Idaho W

Illinois
Bradley University W
Chicago State University W
DePaul University W
Eastern Illinois University W
Illinois State University W
Loyola University Chicago W
Northern Illinois University W
Northwestern University W
Southern Illinois University
Carbondale W
Southern Illinois University
Edwardsville W
University of Illinois
Chicago W
Urbana-Champaign W
Western Illinois University W

Indiana
Ball State University W
Butler University W
Indiana State University W
Indiana University
Bloomington W
Indiana University-Purdue University Fort Wayne W
Indiana University-Purdue University Indianapolis W
Purdue University W
University of Evansville W
University of Notre Dame W
Valparaiso University W

Iowa
Drake University W
Iowa State University W
University of Iowa W
University of Northern Iowa W

Kansas
Kansas State University W
University of Kansas W
Wichita State University W

Kentucky
Eastern Kentucky University W
Morehead State University W
Murray State University W
University of Kentucky W
University of Louisville W
Western Kentucky University W

Louisiana
Centenary College of Louisiana W
Grambling State University W
Louisiana State University and Agricultural and Mechanical College W
Louisiana Tech University W
McNeese State University W
Nicholls State University W
Northwestern State University W
Southeastern Louisiana University W
Southern University and Agricultural and Mechanical College W
Tulane University W
University of Louisiana at Lafayette W
University of Louisiana at Monroe W
University of New Orleans W

Maine
University of Maine W

Maryland
Coppin State University W
Loyola College in Maryland W
Morgan State University W
Towson University W
United States Naval Academy W
University of Maryland
Baltimore County W
College Park W
Eastern Shore W

Massachusetts
Boston College W
College of the Holy Cross W
Harvard College W
Northeastern University W

Michigan
Central Michigan University W
Eastern Michigan University W
Michigan State University W
Oakland University W
University of Michigan W
Western Michigan University W

Minnesota
University of Minnesota
Twin Cities W

Mississippi
Alcorn State University W
Jackson State University W
Mississippi State University W
Mississippi Valley State University W
University of Mississippi W
University of Southern Mississippi W

Missouri
Missouri State University W
Saint Louis University W
Southeast Missouri State University W
University of Missouri
Columbia W
Kansas City W

Montana
Montana State University
Bozeman W
University of Montana W

Nebraska
Creighton University W
University of Nebraska
Lincoln W

Nevada
University of Nevada
Las Vegas W
Reno W

New Hampshire
Dartmouth College W
University of New Hampshire W

New Jersey
Fairleigh Dickinson University
Metropolitan Campus W
New Jersey Institute of Technology W
Princeton University W
Rider University W
Rutgers, The State University of New Jersey
New Brunswick/Piscataway Campus W
Saint Peter's College W
Seton Hall University W

New Mexico
New Mexico State University W
University of New Mexico W

New York
Barnard College W
Canisius College W
Colgate University W
Cornell University W
Fordham University W
Hofstra University W
Iona College W
Long Island University
Brooklyn Campus W
Manhattan College W
Marist College W

Niagara University W
St. Francis College W
St. John's University W
Siena College W
State University of New York
Albany W
Binghamton W
Buffalo W
Stony Brook W
Syracuse University W
United States Military Academy W

North Carolina
Appalachian State University W
Campbell University W
Davidson College W
Duke University W
East Carolina University W
Elon University W
Gardner-Webb University W
High Point University W
North Carolina Agricultural and Technical State University W
North Carolina Central University W
North Carolina State University W
University of North Carolina
Asheville W
Chapel Hill W
Charlotte W
Greensboro W
Wilmington W
Wake Forest University W
Western Carolina University W
Winston-Salem State University W

North Dakota
North Dakota State University W
University of North Dakota W

Ohio
Bowling Green State University W
Cleveland State University W
Kent State University W
Miami University
Oxford Campus W
Ohio State University
Columbus Campus W
Ohio University W
University of Akron W
University of Cincinnati W
University of Dayton W
University of Toledo W
Wright State University W
Xavier University W
Youngstown State University W

Oklahoma
Oral Roberts University W
University of Oklahoma W
University of Tulsa W

Oregon
Oregon State University W
Portland State University W
University of Oregon W
University of Portland W

Pennsylvania
Bucknell University W
Duquesne University W
La Salle University W
Lafayette College W
Lehigh University W
Penn State
University Park W
Robert Morris University W
St. Francis University W
Temple University W
University of Pennsylvania W
University of Pittsburgh W
Villanova University W

Rhode Island
Brown University W
Bryant University W
Providence College W
University of Rhode Island W

South Carolina
Charleston Southern University W
The Citadel W
Clemson University W
Coastal Carolina University W
College of Charleston W
Furman University W
Presbyterian College W
South Carolina State University W
University of South Carolina W
University of South Carolina
Upstate W
Winthrop University W
Wofford College W

South Dakota
South Dakota State University W
University of South Dakota W

Tennessee
Austin Peay State University W
Belmont University W
East Tennessee State University W
Lipscomb University W
Middle Tennessee State University W
Tennessee State University W
Tennessee Technological University W
University of Memphis W
University of Tennessee
Chattanooga W
Knoxville W
Martin W

Texas
Baylor University W
Houston Baptist University W
Lamar University W
Prairie View A&M University W
Rice University W
Sam Houston State University W
Southern Methodist University W
Stephen F. Austin State University W
Texas A&M University W
Texas A&M University
Corpus Christi W
Texas Christian University W
Texas Southern University W
Texas State University: San Marcos W
Texas Tech University W
University of Houston W
University of North Texas W
University of Texas
Arlington W
Austin W
El Paso W
Pan American W
San Antonio W

Utah
Brigham Young University W
University of Utah W
Utah State University W
Utah Valley University W
Weber State University W

Virginia
College of William and Mary W
George Mason University W
Hampton University W
James Madison University W
Liberty University W
Norfolk State University W
Radford University W
University of Virginia W
Virginia Commonwealth University W
Virginia Polytechnic Institute and State University W

Washington
Eastern Washington University W
Gonzaga University W
Seattle University W
University of Washington W
Washington State University W

West Virginia
Marshall University W
West Virginia University W

Wisconsin
Marquette University W
University of Wisconsin
Green Bay W
Madison W
Milwaukee W

Wyoming
University of Wyoming W

Volleyball Division II

Alabama
Miles College W
Tuskegee University W
University of Alabama
Huntsville W
University of Montevallo W
University of North Alabama W
University of West Alabama W

Alaska
University of Alaska
Anchorage W
Fairbanks W

Arizona
Grand Canyon University W

Arkansas
Arkansas Tech University W
Harding University W
Henderson State University W
Ouachita Baptist University W
Southern Arkansas University W
University of Arkansas
Monticello W

California
California State Polytechnic University: Pomona W
California State University
Chico W
Dominguez Hills W
Los Angeles W
Monterey Bay W
San Bernardino W
Stanislaus W
Humboldt State University W
Notre Dame de Namur University W
San Francisco State University W
Sonoma State University W
University of California
San Diego W

Colorado
Adams State College W
Colorado Christian University W
Colorado School of Mines W
Colorado State University
Pueblo W
Fort Lewis College W
Mesa State College W
Metropolitan State College of Denver W
Regis University W
University of Colorado
Colorado Springs W
Western State College of Colorado W

Connecticut
Post University W
Southern Connecticut State University W
University of Bridgeport W
University of New Haven W

Delaware
Goldey-Beacom College W
Wilmington University W

District of Columbia
University of the District of Columbia W

Florida
Barry University W
Eckerd College W
Flagler College W
Florida Institute of Technology W
Florida Southern College W
Lynn University W
Nova Southeastern University W
Palm Beach Atlantic University W
Rollins College W
St. Leo University W
University of Tampa W
University of West Florida W

Georgia
Albany State University W
Armstrong Atlantic State University W
Augusta State University W
Clark Atlanta University W
Fort Valley State University W
Paine College W
University of West Georgia W
Valdosta State University W

Hawaii
Brigham Young University-Hawaii W
Chaminade University of Honolulu W
Hawaii Pacific University W
University of Hawaii
Hilo W

Idaho
Northwest Nazarene University W

Illinois
Lewis University W
Quincy University W

Indiana
Oakland City University W
Saint Joseph's College W
University of Indianapolis W
University of Southern Indiana W

Iowa
Upper Iowa University W

Kansas
Emporia State University W
Fort Hays State University W
Newman University W
Pittsburg State University W
Washburn University W

Kentucky
Bellarmine University W
Kentucky State University W
Kentucky Wesleyan College W
Northern Kentucky University W

Maryland
Bowie State University W

Massachusetts
American International College W
Assumption College W
Bentley University W
Merrimack College W
Stonehill College W
University of Massachusetts
Lowell W

Michigan
Ferris State University W
Grand Valley State University W
Hillsdale College W
Lake Superior State University W
Michigan Technological University W
Northern Michigan University W
Northwood University: Michigan W
Saginaw Valley State University W
Wayne State University W

Minnesota
Bemidji State University W
Concordia University: St. Paul W
Minnesota State University
Mankato W
Moorhead W
Saint Cloud State University W
Southwest Minnesota State University W
University of Minnesota
Crookston W
Duluth W
Winona State University W

Missouri
Drury University W
Missouri Southern State University W
Missouri Western State University W
Northwest Missouri State University W
Rockhurst University W
Southwest Baptist University W
Truman State University W
University of Central Missouri W
University of Missouri
Missouri University of Science and Technology W
St. Louis W

Montana
Montana State University
Billings W

Nebraska
Chadron State College W
University of Nebraska
Kearney W
Omaha W
Wayne State College W

New Hampshire
Franklin Pierce University W
St. Anselm College W
Southern New Hampshire University W

New Jersey
Bloomfield College W
Caldwell College W
Felician College W
Georgian Court University W

New Mexico
Eastern New Mexico University W
New Mexico Highlands University W
Western New Mexico University W

New York
Adelphi University W
City University of New York
Queens College W
College of Saint Rose W
Concordia College W
Dominican College of Blauvelt W
Dowling College W
Le Moyne College W
Long Island University
C. W. Post Campus W
Mercy College W
Molloy College W
New York Institute of Technology W
Nyack College W
Pace University W

North Carolina
Barton College W
Belmont Abbey College W
Brevard College W
Catawba College W
Elizabeth City State University W
Fayetteville State University W
Johnson C. Smith University W
Lees-McRae College W
Lenoir-Rhyne University W
Livingstone College W
Mars Hill College W
Mount Olive College W
Pfeiffer University W
Queens University of Charlotte W
St. Andrews Presbyterian College W
St. Augustine's College W
Shaw University W
University of North Carolina
Pembroke W
Wingate University W

North Dakota
University of Mary W

Ohio
Ashland University W
Central State University W
Tiffin University W
University of Findlay W

Oklahoma
Cameron University W
East Central University W
Oklahoma Panhandle State University W
Southeastern Oklahoma State University W
Southwestern Oklahoma State University W
University of Central Oklahoma W

Oregon
Western Oregon University W

Pennsylvania
California University of Pennsylvania W
Chestnut Hill College W
Cheyney University of Pennsylvania W
Clarion University of Pennsylvania W
East Stroudsburg University of Pennsylvania W
Edinboro University of Pennsylvania W
Gannon University W
Holy Family University W
Indiana University of Pennsylvania W
Kutztown University of Pennsylvania W
Lock Haven University of Pennsylvania W
Mercyhurst College W
Millersville University of Pennsylvania W
Philadelphia University W
Seton Hill University W
Shippensburg University of Pennsylvania W
Slippery Rock University of Pennsylvania W
University of Pittsburgh
Johnstown W
University of the Sciences in Philadelphia W
West Chester University of Pennsylvania W

Puerto Rico
University of Puerto Rico
Bayamon University College W
Cayey University College W
Mayaguez W
Rio Piedras W

South Carolina
Anderson University W
Benedict College W
Claflin University W
Converse College W
Francis Marion University W
Lander University W
Limestone College W
Newberry College W
North Greenville University W
University of South Carolina
Aiken W

South Dakota
Augustana College W
Northern State University W

Tennessee
Carson-Newman College W
Christian Brothers University W
Lane College W
LeMoyne-Owen College W
Lincoln Memorial University W
Tusculum College W

Texas
Abilene Christian University W
Angelo State University W
Dallas Baptist University W
Midwestern State University W
St. Edward's University W
St. Mary's University W
Tarleton State University W
Texas A&M International University W
Texas A&M University
Commerce W
Kingsville W
Texas Woman's University W
University of Texas
of the Permian Basin W
University of the Incarnate Word W
West Texas A&M University W

Utah
Dixie State College of Utah W

Vermont
St. Michael's College W

Virginia
St. Paul's College W
Virginia State University W
Virginia Union University W

Washington
Central Washington University W
Saint Martin's University W
Seattle Pacific University W
Western Washington University W

West Virginia
Alderson-Broaddus College W
Bluefield State College W
Concord University W
Davis and Elkins College W
Fairmont State University W
Glenville State College W
Ohio Valley University W
Salem International University W
Shepherd University W
University of Charleston W
West Liberty State College W
West Virginia State University W
West Virginia Wesleyan College W
Wheeling Jesuit University W

Wisconsin
University of Wisconsin
Parkside W

Volleyball Division III

Alabama
Huntingdon College W

Arkansas
Hendrix College W

California
California Institute of Technology W
California Lutheran University W
California State University
East Bay W
Chapman University W
Claremont McKenna College W
La Sierra University W
Menlo College W
Mills College W
Occidental College W
Pomona College W
University of California
Santa Cruz W
University of La Verne W
University of Redlands W
Whittier College W

Colorado
Colorado College W

Connecticut
Albertus Magnus College W
Connecticut College W
Eastern Connecticut State University W
Mitchell College W
St. Joseph College W
Trinity College W
United States Coast Guard Academy W
Wesleyan University W
Western Connecticut State University W

Delaware
Wesley College W

District of Columbia
Catholic University of America W
Gallaudet University W
Trinity Washington University W

Georgia
Emory University W
LaGrange College W
Oglethorpe University W
Piedmont College W
Spelman College W

Illinois
Augustana College W
Aurora University W
Benedictine University W
Blackburn College W
Concordia University Chicago W
Dominican University W
Elmhurst College W
Eureka College W
Greenville College W
Illinois College W
Illinois Wesleyan University W
Knox College W
Lake Forest College W
MacMurray College W
Millikin University W
Monmouth College W
North Central College W
North Park University W
Principia College W
Rockford College W
University of Chicago W
Wheaton College W

Indiana
Anderson University W
DePauw University W
Earlham College W
Franklin College W
Hanover College W
Manchester College W
Rose-Hulman Institute of Technology W
Saint Mary's College W
Trine University W

Iowa
Buena Vista University W
Central College W
Coe College W
Cornell College W
Grinnell College W
Loras College W
Luther College W
Simpson College W
University of Dubuque W
Wartburg College W

Kentucky
Centre College W
Spalding University W
Thomas More College W
Transylvania University W

Maine
Bates College W
Bowdoin College W
Colby College W
Husson University W
Maine Maritime Academy W
St. Joseph's College W
Thomas College W
University of Maine
Farmington W
Presque Isle W
University of New England W

Maryland
College of Notre Dame of Maryland W
Frostburg State University W
Goucher College W
Hood College W
Johns Hopkins University W
McDaniel College W
St. Mary's College of Maryland W
Salisbury University W
Stevenson University W
Washington College W

Massachusetts
Amherst College W
Anna Maria College W
Babson College W
Bay Path College W
Becker College W
Brandeis University W
Bridgewater State College W
Clark University W
Elms College W
Emerson College W
Emmanuel College W
Endicott College W
Framingham State College W
Gordon College W
Lasell College W
Lesley University W
Massachusetts College of Liberal Arts W
Massachusetts Institute of Technology W
Massachusetts Maritime Academy W
Mount Holyoke College W
Mount Ida College W
Newbury College W
Pine Manor College W
Regis College W
Salem State College W
Simmons College W
Smith College W
Springfield College W
Suffolk University W
Tufts University W
University of Massachusetts
Boston W
Dartmouth W
Wellesley College W
Wentworth Institute of Technology W
Western New England College W
Westfield State College W
Wheaton College W
Williams College W
Worcester Polytechnic Institute W
Worcester State College W

Michigan
Adrian College W
Albion College W
Alma College W
Calvin College W
Finlandia University W
Hope College W
Kalamazoo College W
Olivet College W

Minnesota
Augsburg College W
Bethany Lutheran College W
Bethel University W
Carleton College W
College of St. Benedict W
College of St. Catherine W
College of St. Scholastica W
Concordia College: Moorhead W
Crown College W
Gustavus Adolphus College W
Hamline University W
Macalester College W
Martin Luther College W
Northwestern College W
St. Mary's University of Minnesota W
St. Olaf College W
University of Minnesota
Morris W
University of St. Thomas W

Mississippi
Millsaps College W
Mississippi College W
Rust College W

Missouri
Fontbonne University W
Maryville University of Saint Louis W
Washington University in St. Louis W
Webster University W
Westminster College W

Nebraska
Nebraska Wesleyan University W

New Hampshire
Colby-Sawyer College W
Daniel Webster College W
Keene State College W
Plymouth State University W
Rivier College W

New Jersey
Centenary College W
College of St. Elizabeth W
Fairleigh Dickinson University
College at Florham W
Kean University W
Montclair State University W
New Jersey City University W
Ramapo College of New Jersey W
Richard Stockton College of New Jersey W
Rowan University W
Rutgers, The State University of New Jersey
Camden Regional Campus W
Newark Regional Campus W

Tables and Indexes

Stevens Institute of Technology W
William Paterson University of New Jersey W

New York
Alfred University W
Bard College W
Cazenovia College W
City University of New York
Baruch College W
Brooklyn College W
City College W
College of Staten Island W
Hunter College W
John Jay College of Criminal Justice W
Lehman College W
Medgar Evers College W
New York City College of Technology W
York College W
Clarkson University W
College of Mount St. Vincent W
College of New Rochelle W
D'Youville College W
Elmira College W
Hamilton College W
Hartwick College W
Hilbert College W
Ithaca College W
Keuka College W
Manhattanville College W
Medaille College W
Mount St. Mary College W
Nazareth College of Rochester W
New York University W
Polytechnic Institute of New York University W
Rochester Institute of Technology W
Russell Sage College W
St. John Fisher College W
St. Joseph's College W
St. Joseph's College: Suffolk Campus W
St. Lawrence University W
Skidmore College W
State University of New York
College at Brockport W
College at Buffalo W
College at Cortland W
College at Fredonia W
College at Geneseo W
College at Old Westbury W
College at Oneonta W
College at Plattsburgh W
College at Potsdam W
College of Agriculture and Technology at Cobleskill W
College of Agriculture and Technology at Morrisville W
Farmingdale W
Institute of Technology at Utica/Rome W
Maritime College W
New Paltz W
Oswego W
Purchase W
Union College W
United States Merchant Marine Academy W
University of Rochester W
Utica College W
Vassar College W
Yeshiva University W

North Carolina
Greensboro College W
Guilford College W
Meredith College W
Methodist University W
North Carolina Wesleyan College W
Peace College W
Salem College W

Ohio
Baldwin-Wallace College W
Bluffton University W
Capital University W
Case Western Reserve University W
College of Mount St. Joseph W
College of Wooster W
Defiance College W
Denison University W
Franciscan University of Steubenville W
Heidelberg University W
Hiram College W
John Carroll University W
Kenyon College W
Lake Erie College W
Marietta College W
Mount Union College W
Muskingum College W
Oberlin College W
Ohio Northern University W
Ohio Wesleyan University W
Otterbein College W
Wilmington College W
Wittenberg University W

Oregon
George Fox University W
Lewis & Clark College W
Linfield College W
Pacific University W
Willamette University W

Pennsylvania
Albright College W
Allegheny College W
Alvernia University W
Arcadia University W
Baptist Bible College of Pennsylvania W
Bryn Mawr College W
Cabrini College W
Carnegie Mellon University W
Cedar Crest College W
Chatham University W
Delaware Valley College W
DeSales University W
Dickinson College W
Eastern University W
Elizabethtown College W
Franklin & Marshall College W
Geneva College W
Gettysburg College W
Grove City College W
Gwynedd-Mercy College W
Haverford College W
Immaculata University W
Juniata College W
King's College W
La Roche College W
Lancaster Bible College W
Lebanon Valley College W
Lincoln University W
Lycoming College W
Marywood University W
Messiah College W
Misericordia University W
Moravian College W
Mount Aloysius College W
Muhlenberg College W
Neumann College W
Penn State
Altoona W
Berks W
Erie, The Behrend College W
Harrisburg W
Philadelphia Biblical University W
Rosemont College W
St. Vincent College W
Susquehanna University W
Swarthmore College W
Thiel College W
University of Pittsburgh
Bradford W
Greensburg W
University of Scranton W
Ursinus College W
Washington & Jefferson College W
Waynesburg University W
Westminster College W
Widener University W
Wilkes University W
York College of Pennsylvania W

Rhode Island
Johnson & Wales University: Providence W
Rhode Island College W
Roger Williams University W
Salve Regina University W

South Dakota
Presentation College W

Tennessee
Maryville College W
Rhodes College W
University of the South W

Texas
Austin College W
Concordia University Texas W
East Texas Baptist University W
Hardin-Simmons University W
Howard Payne University W
LeTourneau University W
McMurry University W
Schreiner University W
Southwestern University W
Sul Ross State University W
Texas Lutheran University W
Trinity University W
University of Dallas W
University of Mary Hardin-Baylor W
University of Texas
Dallas W
Tyler W

Vermont
Castleton State College W
Green Mountain College W
Lyndon State College W
Middlebury College W
Norwich University W
Southern Vermont College W

Virginia
Averett University W
Bridgewater College W
Christopher Newport University W
Eastern Mennonite University W
Emory & Henry College W
Ferrum College W
Lynchburg College W
Mary Baldwin College W
Marymount University W
Randolph College W
Randolph-Macon College W
Roanoke College W
Shenandoah University W
Sweet Briar College W
University of Mary Washington W
Virginia Wesleyan College W
Washington and Lee University W

Washington
Pacific Lutheran University W
University of Puget Sound W
Whitman College W
Whitworth University W

West Virginia
Bethany College W

Wisconsin
Alverno College W
Beloit College W
Carroll University W
Carthage College W
Concordia University Wisconsin W
Edgewood College W
Lakeland College W
Lawrence University W
Maranatha Baptist Bible College W
Marian University W
Milwaukee School of Engineering W
Mount Mary College W
Northland College W
Ripon College W
St. Norbert College W
University of Wisconsin
Eau Claire W
La Crosse W
Oshkosh W
Platteville W
River Falls W
Stevens Point W
Stout W
Superior W
Whitewater W
Wisconsin Lutheran College W

Water polo Division I

Arizona
Arizona State University W

California
California State University
Bakersfield W
Long Beach W
Northridge W
Loyola Marymount University W
Pepperdine University M
San Diego State University W
San Jose State University W
Santa Clara University W
Stanford University W
University of California
Berkeley W
Davis W
Irvine W
Los Angeles W
Santa Barbara W
University of Southern California W
University of the Pacific W

Colorado
Colorado State University W
United States Air Force Academy M

District of Columbia
George Washington University W

Hawaii
University of Hawaii
Manoa W

Indiana
Indiana University
Bloomington W

Maryland
United States Naval Academy M
University of Maryland
College Park W

Massachusetts
Harvard College W

Michigan
University of Michigan W

New Jersey
Princeton University W

New York
Fordham University M
Hartwick College W
Iona College W
Marist College W
St. Francis College W
Siena College W
Wagner College W

Pennsylvania
Bucknell University W
Villanova University W

Rhode Island
Brown University W

Water polo Division II

Arizona
Arizona State University W

California
California State University
Bakersfield W
Long Beach W
Northridge W
Loyola Marymount University W
San Diego State University W
San Jose State University W
Santa Clara University W
Stanford University W
University of California
Berkeley W
Davis W
Irvine W
Los Angeles W
San Diego M
Santa Barbara W
University of Southern California W
University of the Pacific W

Colorado
Colorado State University W

District of Columbia
George Washington University W

Hawaii
University of Hawaii
Manoa W

Indiana
Indiana University
Bloomington W

Maryland
University of Maryland
College Park W

Massachusetts
Harvard College W

Michigan
University of Michigan W

New Jersey
Princeton University W

New York
City University of New York
Queens College M
Hartwick College W
Iona College W
Marist College W
St. Francis College W
Siena College W
Wagner College W

Pennsylvania
Bucknell University W
Gannon University M
Mercyhurst College M
Villanova University W

Rhode Island
Brown University W

West Virginia
Salem International University M

Water polo Division III

Arizona
Arizona State University W

California
California Institute of Technology M
California Lutheran University M
California State University
Bakersfield W
Long Beach W
Northridge W
Chapman University M
Claremont McKenna College M
Loyola Marymount University W
Occidental College M
Pitzer College M
Pomona College M
San Diego State University W
San Jose State University W
Santa Clara University W
Stanford University W
University of California
Berkeley W
Davis W
Irvine W
Los Angeles W
Santa Barbara W
Santa Cruz M
University of La Verne M
University of Redlands M
University of Southern California W
University of the Pacific W
Whittier College M

Colorado
Colorado State University W

Connecticut
Connecticut College M

District of Columbia
George Washington University W

Hawaii
University of Hawaii
Manoa W

Indiana
Indiana University
Bloomington W

Maryland
Johns Hopkins University M
University of Maryland
College Park W

Massachusetts
Harvard College W
Massachusetts Institute of Technology M

Michigan
University of Michigan W

New Jersey
Princeton University W

New York
Hartwick College W
Iona College W
Marist College W
St. Francis College W
Siena College W
Wagner College W

Pennsylvania
Bucknell University W
Penn State
Erie, The Behrend College M
Villanova University W
Washington & Jefferson College M

Rhode Island
Brown University W

Wrestling Division I

Arizona
Arizona State University M

California
California Polytechnic State University: San Luis Obispo M
California State University
Bakersfield M
Fullerton M
Stanford University M
University of California
Davis M

Colorado
United States Air Force Academy M
University of Northern Colorado M

Connecticut
Sacred Heart University M

Delaware
Delaware State University M

District of Columbia
American University M

Idaho
Boise State University M

Illinois
Northern Illinois University M
Northwestern University M
Southern Illinois University
Edwardsville M
University of Illinois
Urbana-Champaign M

Indiana
Indiana University
Bloomington M
Purdue University M

Iowa
Iowa State University M
University of Iowa M
University of Northern Iowa M

Maryland
United States Naval Academy M
University of Maryland
College Park M

Massachusetts
Boston University M
Harvard College M

Michigan
Central Michigan University M
Eastern Michigan University M
Michigan State University M
University of Michigan M

Minnesota
University of Minnesota
Twin Cities M

Missouri
University of Missouri
Columbia M

Nebraska
University of Nebraska
Lincoln M

New Jersey
Princeton University M
Rider University M
Rutgers, The State University of New Jersey
New Brunswick/Piscataway Campus M

New York
Columbia University M
Cornell University M
Hofstra University M
State University of New York
Binghamton M
Buffalo M
United States Military Academy M

North Carolina
Appalachian State University M
Campbell University M
Davidson College M
Duke University M
Gardner-Webb University M
North Carolina State University M
University of North Carolina
Chapel Hill M
Greensboro M

North Dakota
North Dakota State University M

Ohio
Cleveland State University M
Kent State University M
Ohio State University
Columbus Campus M
Ohio University M

Oklahoma
Oklahoma State University M
University of Oklahoma M

Oregon
Oregon State University M
Portland State University M

Pennsylvania
Bloomsburg University of Pennsylvania M
Bucknell University M
Clarion University of Pennsylvania M
Drexel University M
Duquesne University M
East Stroudsburg University of Pennsylvania M
Edinboro University of Pennsylvania M
Franklin & Marshall College M
Lehigh University M
Lock Haven University of Pennsylvania M
Millersville University of Pennsylvania M
Penn State
University Park M
University of Pennsylvania M
University of Pittsburgh M

Rhode Island
Brown University M

South Carolina
The Citadel M

South Dakota
South Dakota State University M

Tennessee
University of Tennessee
Chattanooga M

Utah
Utah Valley University M

Virginia
George Mason University M
Liberty University M
Old Dominion University M
University of Virginia M
Virginia Military Institute M
Virginia Polytechnic Institute and State University M

West Virginia
West Virginia University M

Wisconsin
University of Wisconsin
Madison M

Wyoming
University of Wyoming M

Wrestling Division II

Arizona
Grand Canyon University M

California
San Francisco State University M

Colorado
Adams State College M
Colorado School of Mines M
Colorado State University
Pueblo M
Mesa State College M
Western State College of Colorado M

Indiana
University of Indianapolis M

Iowa
Upper Iowa University M

Kansas
Fort Hays State University M
Newman University M

Massachusetts
American International College M

Minnesota
Minnesota State University
Mankato M
Moorhead M
Saint Cloud State University M
Southwest Minnesota State University M

Missouri
Truman State University M
University of Central Missouri M

Nebraska
Chadron State College M
University of Nebraska
Kearney M
Omaha M

New Mexico
New Mexico Highlands University M

North Carolina
Belmont Abbey College M
St. Andrews Presbyterian College M
University of North Carolina
Pembroke M

North Dakota
University of Mary M

Ohio
Ashland University M
University of Findlay M

Oklahoma
University of Central Oklahoma M

Pennsylvania
Gannon University M
Kutztown University of Pennsylvania M
Mercyhurst College M
Seton Hill University M
Shippensburg University of Pennsylvania M
University of Pittsburgh
Johnstown M

Puerto Rico
University of Puerto Rico
Mayaguez M
Rio Piedras M

South Carolina
Anderson University M
Limestone College M
Newberry College M

South Dakota
Augustana College M
Northern State University M

Tennessee
Carson-Newman College M

West Virginia
West Liberty State College M

Wisconsin
University of Wisconsin
Parkside M

Wrestling Division III

California
Menlo College M

Connecticut
Trinity College M
United States Coast Guard Academy M
Wesleyan University M

Illinois
Augustana College M
Elmhurst College M
Illinois College M
Knox College M
North Central College M
University of Chicago M
Wheaton College M

Indiana
Manchester College M
Rose-Hulman Institute of Technology M
Trine University M
Wabash College M

Iowa
Buena Vista University M
Central College M
Coe College M
Cornell College M
Loras College M
Luther College M
Simpson College M
University of Dubuque M
Wartburg College M

Maine
University of Southern Maine M

Maryland
Johns Hopkins University M
McDaniel College M

Massachusetts
Bridgewater State College M
Massachusetts Institute of Technology M
Springfield College M
Western New England College M
Williams College M
Worcester Polytechnic Institute M

Michigan
Olivet College M

Minnesota
Augsburg College M
Concordia College: Moorhead M
St. John's University M
St. Olaf College M

New Hampshire
Plymouth State University M

New Jersey
Centenary College M
The College of New Jersey M
Stevens Institute of Technology M

New York
City University of New York
Hunter College M
Ithaca College M
New York University M
Rochester Institute of Technology M

State University of New York
College at Brockport M
College at Cortland M
College at Oneonta M
College of Agriculture and Technology at Morrisville M
Oswego M
United States Merchant Marine Academy M
Yeshiva University M

Ohio

Baldwin-Wallace College M
Case Western Reserve University M
College of Mount St. Joseph M
Heidelberg University M
John Carroll University M
Mount Union College M
Muskingum College M
Ohio Northern University M
Wilmington College M

Oregon

Pacific University M

Pennsylvania

Delaware Valley College M
Elizabethtown College M
Gettysburg College M
King's College M
Lycoming College M
Messiah College M
Muhlenberg College M
Thiel College M
University of Scranton M
Ursinus College M
Washington & Jefferson College M
Waynesburg University M
Wilkes University M
York College of Pennsylvania M

Rhode Island

Johnson & Wales University: Providence M
Rhode Island College M
Roger Williams University M

Vermont

Norwich University M

Virginia

Washington and Lee University M

Wisconsin

Concordia University Wisconsin M
Lakeland College M
Lawrence University M
Maranatha Baptist Bible College M
Milwaukee School of Engineering M
University of Wisconsin
Eau Claire M
La Crosse M
Oshkosh M
Platteville M
Stevens Point M
Whitewater M

Alphabetical index of colleges

Abilene Christian University (TX) 1175
Abraham Baldwin Agricultural College (GA) 1521
Academy College (MN) 1688
Academy of Art University (CA) 99
Academy of Court Reporting
  Akron (OH) 1854
  Cincinnati (OH) 1854
  Cleveland (OH) 1854
  Columbus (OH) 1854
Acadia University (FN) 1350
Adams State College (CO) 182
Adelphi University (NY) 753
Adirondack Community College (NY) 1777
Adrian College (MI) 572
Advanced Technology Institute (VA) 2017
Agnes Scott College (GA) 272
AIB College of Business (IA) 1597
Aiken Technical College (SC) 1944
Aims Community College (CO) 1474
Alabama Agricultural and Mechanical University (AL) 49
Alabama Southern Community College (AL) 1365
Alabama State University (AL) 49
Alamance Community College (NC) 1818
Alaska Bible College (AK) 70
Alaska Pacific University (AK) 70
Albany College of Pharmacy and Health Sciences (NY) 753
Albany State University (GA) 272
Albany Technical College (GA) 1521
Albertus Magnus College (CT) 201
Albion College (MI) 572
Albright College (PA) 991
Albuquerque Technical-Vocational Institute *see* Central New Mexico Community College (NM)
Alcorn State University (MS) 638
Alderson-Broaddus College (WV) 1306
Alexandria Technical College (MN) 1688
Alfred University (NY) 754
Alice Lloyd College (KY) 446
Allan Hancock College (CA) 1404
Allegany College of Maryland (MD) 1647
Allegheny College (PA) 991
Allegheny Wesleyan College (OH) 902
Allen College (IA) 402
Allen County Community College (KS) 1610
Allen University (SC) 1113
Alliant International University (CA) 99
Allied Medical and Technical Institute (PA) 1908
Alma College (MI) 573
Alpena Community College (MI) 1672
Alvernia University (PA) 992
Alverno College (WI) 1321
Alvin Community College (TX) 1971
Amarillo College (TX) 1971
Amberton University (TX) 1175
American Academy McAllister Institute of Funeral Service (NY) 1777
American Academy of Art (IL) 317
American Academy of Dramatic Arts (NY) 1777
American Academy of Dramatic Arts West (CA) 1404
American Baptist College of ABT Seminary (TN) 1144
American Indian College of the Assemblies of God (AZ) 74
American InterContinental University (GA) 273
American International College (MA) 521
American Jewish University (CA) 100
American Public University System (WV) 1306
American River College (CA) 1404
American Samoa Community College (AS) 2079
American Sentinel University (CO) 182
American University (DC) 222
American University in Cairo Egypt 1356
American University in Dubai (AE) 1363
American University of Beirut (FN) 1358
American University of Paris (FN) 1357
American University of Puerto Rico (PR) 1085
Amherst College (MA) 521
Amridge University (AL) 50
Ancilla College (IN) 1582
Anderson University (IN) 369
Anderson University (SC) 1113
Andover College (ME) 1642
Andrew College (GA) 1522
Andrew Jackson University (AL) 50
Andrews University (MI) 574
Angelina College (TX) 1971
Angelo State University (TX) 1176
Angley College (FL) 1498
Anna Maria College (MA) 522
Anne Arundel Community College (MD) 1647
Anoka Technical College (MN) 1688
Anoka-Ramsey Community College (MN) 1689
Antelope Valley College (CA) 1405
Anthem College (AZ) 1378
Antioch University Los Angeles (CA) 100
Antioch University McGregor (OH) 902
Antioch University Santa Barbara (CA) 101
Antioch University Seattle (WA) 1287
Antonelli College (OH) 1854
Antonelli College
  Hattiesburg (MS) 1710
  Jackson (MS) 1710
Antonelli Institute of Art and Photography (PA) 1908
Apex School of Theology (NC) 855
Appalachian Bible College (WV) 1307
Appalachian State University (NC) 855
Aquinas College (MI) 575
Aquinas College (TN) 1144
Arapahoe Community College (CO) 1474
Arcadia University (PA) 993
Argosy University (IL) 317
Arizona Automotive Institute (AZ) 1378
Arizona State University (AZ) 74
Arizona Western College (AZ) 1378
Arkansas Baptist College (AR) 84
Arkansas Northeastern College (AR) 1393
Arkansas State University (AR) 84
Arkansas State University
  Beebe (AR) 1393
  Mountain Home (AR) 1393
  Newport (AR) 1394
Arkansas Tech University (AR) 85
Arlington Baptist College (TX) 1176
Armstrong Atlantic State University (GA) 273
Art Academy of Cincinnati (OH) 902
Art Center College of Design (CA) 101
Art Center Design College (AZ) 75
Art Center Design College (NM) 746
Art Institute of Atlanta (GA) 274
Art Institute of Boston at Lesley University (MA) 523
Art Institute of California
  Hollywood (CA) 101
  Inland Empire (CA) 102
  Los Angeles (CA) 1405
  Orange County (CA) 102
  Sacramento (CA) 102
  San Diego (CA) 102
  San Francisco (CA) 103
  Sunnyvale (CA) 1406
Art Institute of Charlotte (NC) 856
Art Institute of Cincinnati (OH) 1854
Art Institute of Colorado (CO) 183
Art Institute of Dallas (TX) 1177
Art Institute of Fort Lauderdale (FL) 230
Art Institute of Houston (TX) 1177
Art Institute of Las Vegas (NV) 706
Art Institute of Michigan (MI) 575
Art Institute of New York City (NY) 1778
Art Institute of Ohio
  Cincinnati (OH) 1855
Art Institute of Philadelphia (PA) 994
Art Institute of Phoenix (AZ) 75
Art Institute of Pittsburgh (PA) 994
Art Institute of Portland (OR) 973
Art Institute of Seattle (WA) 1287
Art Institute of Tucson (AZ) 76
Art Institute of Washington (VA) 1252
Art Institute of York (PA) 1908
Art Institute Online (PA) 994
Art Institutes International Minnesota (MN) 609
ASA Institute of Business and Computer Technology (NY) 1778
Asbury College (KY) 446
Asheville-Buncombe Technical Community College (NC) 1818
Ashford University (IA) 402
Ashland Community and Technical College (KY) 1623
Ashland University (OH) 902
Ashworth University (GA) 1522
Asnuntuck Community College (CT) 1487
Aspen University (CO) 183
Assumption College (MA) 523
Assumption College for Sisters (NJ) 1756
Athens State University (AL) 51
Athens Technical College (GA) 1522
ATI Career Training Center
  Dallas (TX) 1972
  Ft. Lauderdale (FL) 1498
  Oakland Park (FL) 1498
ATI College of Health (FL) 1498
Atlanta Christian College (GA) 274
Atlanta Metropolitan College (GA) 1523
Atlanta Technical College (GA) 1523
Atlantic Cape Community College (NJ) 1756
Atlantic College (PR) 1085
Atlantic Union College (MA) 524
ATS Institute of Technology (OH) 1855
Auburn University (AL) 51
Auburn University at Montgomery (AL) 52
Augsburg College (MN) 609
Augusta State University (GA) 275
Augusta Technical College (GA) 1524
Augustana College (IL) 317
Augustana College (SD) 1135
Aultman College of Nursing and Health Sciences (OH) 1855
Aurora University (IL) 318
Austin College (TX) 1177
Austin Community College (TX) 1972
Austin Graduate School of Theology (TX) 1178
Austin Peay State University (TN) 1144
Ave Maria University (FL) 230
Averett University (VA) 1252
Aviation Institute of Maintenance
  Indianapolis (IN) 1582
  Kansas City (MO) 1719
  Virginia Beach (VA) 2017
Avila University (MO) 650
Azusa Pacific University (CA) 103
Babson College (MA) 524
Bacone College (OK) 955
Bainbridge College (GA) 1524
Baker College of Allen Park (MI) 576
Baker College of Auburn Hills (MI) 576
Baker College of Cadillac (MI) 576
Baker College of Clinton Township (MI) 577
Baker College of Flint (MI) 577
Baker College of Jackson (MI) 577
Baker College of Muskegon (MI) 578
Baker College of Owosso (MI) 578
Baker College of Port Huron (MI) 579
Baker University (KS) 428
Bakersfield College (CA) 1406
Baldwin-Wallace College (OH) 903
Ball State University (IN) 369
Baltimore City Community College (MD) 1648
Baltimore Hebrew University (MD) 499
Baltimore International College (MD) 499
Baptist Bible College (MO) 650
Baptist Bible College of Pennsylvania (PA) 995
Baptist College of Florida (FL) 231
Baptist College of Health Sciences (TN) 1145
Baptist Missionary Association Theological Seminary (TX) 1178
Baptist University of the Americas (TX) 1179
Barclay College (KS) 428
Bard College (NY) 755
Bard College at Simon's Rock (MA) 525
Barnard College (NY) 756

Barnes-Jewish College of Nursing *see* Goldfarb School of Nursing at Barnes-Jewish College (MO)
Barry University (FL) 231
Barstow Community College (CA) 1406
Barton College (NC) 856
Barton County Community College (KS) 1610
Bastyr University (WA) 1287
Bates College (ME) 485
Bates Technical College (WA) 2034
Baton Rouge Community College (LA) 1635
Baton Rouge School of Computers (LA) 1635
Bauder College (GA) 276
Bay de Noc Community College (MI) 1672
Bay Mills Community College (MI) 1673
Bay Path College (MA) 526
Bay State College (MA) 1658
Bayamon Central University (PR) 1085
Baylor University (TX) 1179
Beacon College (FL) 232
Beal College (ME) 1642
Beaufort County Community College (NC) 1819
Becker College (MA) 526
Beckfield College (KY) 447
Beis Medrash Heichal Dovid (NY) 756
Belhaven College (MS) 638
Bellarmine University (KY) 447
Bellevue Community College (WA) 2034
Bellevue University (NE) 692
Bellin College of Nursing (WI) 1321
Bellingham Technical College (WA) 2035
Belmont Abbey College (NC) 857
Belmont Technical College (OH) 1855
Belmont University (TN) 1145
Beloit College (WI) 1321
Bel-Rea Institute of Animal Technology (CO) 1475
Bemidji State University (MN) 610
Benedict College (SC) 1114
Benedictine College (KS) 429
Benedictine University (IL) 319
Benjamin Franklin Institute of Technology (MA) 1658
Bennett College (NC) 857
Bennington College (VT) 1240
Bentley College *see* Bentley University (MA)
Bentley University (MA) 527
Berea College (KY) 448
Bergen Community College (NJ) 1757
Berkeley City College (CA) 1407
Berkeley College (NJ) 723
Berkeley College (NY) 756
Berkeley College of New York City (NY) 757
Berklee College of Music (MA) 528
Berks Technical Institute (PA) 1908
Berkshire Community College (MA) 1658
Bermuda College (FN) 2081
Berry College (GA) 276
Beth Hamedrash Shaarei Yosher Institute (NY) 757
Beth Hatalmud Rabbinical College (NY) 757
Beth Medrash Govoha (NJ) 723
Bethany College (KS) 430
Bethany College (WV) 1307
Bethany Lutheran College (MN) 610
Bethany University (CA) 104
Bethel College (IN) 370
Bethel College (KS) 430
Bethel College (TN) 1146
Bethel University (MN) 611
Bethesda Christian University (CA) 104
Bethune-Cookman University (FL) 232
Beulah Heights University (GA) 277
Bevill State Community College (AL) 1365
Bidwell Training Center (PA) 1909
Big Bend Community College (WA) 2035
Big Sandy Community and Technical College (KY) 1623
Biola University (CA) 105
Birmingham-Southern College (AL) 53
Bishop State Community College (AL) 1366
Bismarck State College (ND) 1849
Black Hawk College (IL) 1550
Black Hawk College
East Campus (IL) 1550
Black Hills State University (SD) 1135
Black River Technical College (AR) 1394
Blackburn College (IL) 319
Blackfeet Community College (MT) 1736
Blackhawk Technical College (WI) 2058
Bladen Community College (NC) 1819
Blessing-Rieman College of Nursing (IL) 320
Blinn College (TX) 1973
Bloomfield College (NJ) 723
Bloomsburg University of Pennsylvania (PA) 995
Blue Cliff College
Gulfport (MS) 1710
Houma (LA) 1635
Lafayette (LA) 1635
Metairie (LA) 1636
Shreveport (LA) 1636
Blue Mountain College (MS) 639
Blue Mountain Community College (OR) 1899
Blue Ridge Community and Technical College (WV) 2052
Blue Ridge Community College (NC) 1820
Blue Ridge Community College (VA) 2017
Bluefield College (VA) 1253
Bluefield State College (WV) 1308
Bluegrass Community and Technical College (KY) 1624
Bluffton University (OH) 904
Bob Jones University (SC) 1114
Bohecker College (OH) 1856
Boise Bible College (ID) 310
Boise State University (ID) 310
Bolivar Technical College (MO) 1719
Boricua College (NY) 757
Bossier Parish Community College (LA) 1636
Boston Architectural College (MA) 528
Boston Baptist College (MA) 529
Boston College (MA) 529
Boston Conservatory (MA) 530
Boston University (MA) 530
Boulder College of Massage Therapy (CO) 1475
Bowdoin College (ME) 485
Bowie State University (MD) 499
Bowling Green State University (OH) 905
Bowling Green State University
Firelands College (OH) 1856
Bradford School (OH) 1857
Bradford School of Business (TX) 1973
Bradford School
Pittsburgh (PA) 1909
Bradley Academy for the Visual Arts *see* Art Institute of York (PA)
Bradley University (IL) 320
Bramson ORT College (NY) 1779
Brandeis University (MA) 531
Brazosport College (TX) 1973
Brenau University (GA) 277
Brescia University (KY) 449
Brevard College (NC) 858
Brevard Community College (FL) 1498
Brewton-Parker College (GA) 278
Briar Cliff University (IA) 403
Briarcliffe College (NY) 758
Briarwood College (CT) 1487
Bridgewater College (VA) 1253
Bridgewater State College (MA) 532
Brigham Young University (UT) 1231
Brigham Young University-Hawaii (HI) 306
Brigham Young University-Idaho (ID) 311
Bristol Community College (MA) 1659
Brookdale Community College (NJ) 1757
Brookhaven College (TX) 1974
Brooks Institute (CA) 106
Brooks Institute
Ventura (CA) 106
Broome Community College (NY) 1779
Broward College (FL) 1499
Broward Community College *see* Broward College (FL)
Brown College (MN) 612
Brown Mackie College
Akron (OH) 1857
Atlanta (GA) 1525
Cincinnati (OH) 1857
Findlay (OH) 1857
Fort Wayne (IN) 1582
Hopkinsville (KY) 1624
Louisville (KY) 1624
Merrillville (IN) 1583
Miami (FL) 1500
Michigan City (IN) 1583
North Canton (OH) 1857
North Kentucky (KY) 1624
Salina (KS) 1611
South Bend (IN) 1583
Tucson (AZ) 76
Brown University (RI) 1105
Brunswick Community College (NC) 1820
Bryan College (TN) 1147
Bryan College
Los Angeles (CA) 1407
Sacramento (CA) 1407
BryanLGH College of Health Sciences (NE) 692
Bryant & Stratton College
Albany (NY) 1780
Amherst (NY) 1780
Buffalo (NY) 1780
Cleveland (OH) 1857
Eastlake (OH) 906
Henrietta (NY) 1780
Milwaukee (WI) 2058
Parma (OH) 906
Richmond (VA) 2017
Rochester (NY) 1781
Southtowns (NY) 1781
Syracuse (NY) 1781
Syracuse North (NY) 1781
Virginia Beach (VA) 2018
Bryant University (RI) 1105
Bryman School (AZ) 1379
Bryn Athyn College of the New Church (PA) 996
Bryn Mawr College (PA) 997
Bucknell University (PA) 997
Bucks County Community College (PA) 1909
Buena Vista University (IA) 403
Bunker Hill Community College (MA) 1660
Burlington College (VT) 1240
Burlington County College (NJ) 1758
Business Informatics Center (NY) 1782
Butler County Community College (KS) 1611
Butler County Community College (PA) 1910
Butler University (IN) 371
Butte College (CA) 1407
Cabarrus College of Health Sciences (NC) 859
Cabrillo College (CA) 1408
Cabrini College (PA) 998
Caldwell College (NJ) 724
Caldwell Community College and Technical Institute (NC) 1821
Calhoun Community College (AL) 1366
California Baptist University (CA) 106
California Christian College (CA) 1408
California Coast University (CA) 107
California College of the Arts (CA) 107
California College San Diego (CA) 108
California Culinary Academy (CA) 1409
California Design College *see* Art Institute of California: Hollywood (CA)
California Institute of Integral Studies (CA) 108
California Institute of Technology (CA) 109
California Institute of the Arts (CA) 109
California Lutheran University (CA) 110
California Maritime Academy (CA) 111
California National University for Advanced Studies (CA) 111
California Polytechnic State University
San Luis Obispo (CA) 111
California School of Culinary Arts (CA) 1409
California State Polytechnic University
Pomona (CA) 112

Tables and Indexes

California State University
Bakersfield (CA) 113
Channel Islands (CA) 114
Chico (CA) 114
Dominguez Hills (CA) 115
East Bay (CA) 116
Fresno (CA) 116
Fullerton (CA) 117
Long Beach (CA) 118
Los Angeles (CA) 119
Monterey Bay (CA) 119
Northridge (CA) 120
Sacramento (CA) 121
San Bernardino (CA) 122
San Marcos (CA) 122
Stanislaus (CA) 123
California University of Management and Sciences (CA) 124
California University of Pennsylvania (PA) 999
Calumet College of St. Joseph (IN) 371
Calvary Bible College and Theological Seminary (MO) 651
Calvin College (MI) 579
Cambria-Rowe Business College (PA) 1910
Cambria-Rowe Business College Indiana (PA) 1910
Cambridge College (CO) 1475
Cambridge College (MA) 533
Camden County College (NJ) 1758
Camelot College (LA) 1637
Cameron University (OK) 955
Campbell University (NC) 859
Campbellsville University (KY) 449
Canada College (CA) 1409
Canisius College (NY) 758
Cankdeska Cikana Community College (ND) 1849
Cape Cod Community College (MA) 1660
Cape Fear Community College (NC) 1821
Capella University (MN) 612
Capital Community College (CT) 1488
Capital University (OH) 906
Capitol College (MD) 500
Cardinal Stritch University (WI) 1322
Career College of Northern Nevada (NV) 1748
Career Training Academy (PA) 1911
Career Training Academy
Monroeville (PA) 1911
Pittsburgh (PA) 1911
Careers Unlimited (UT) 2011
Caribbean University (PR) 1086
Caritas Laboure College (MA) 1661
Carl Albert State College (OK) 1889
Carl Sandburg College (IL) 1551
Carleton College (MN) 613
Carlos Albizu University (FL) 233
Carlos Albizu University
San Juan (PR) 1086
Carlow University (PA) 1000
Carnegie Mellon University (PA) 1000
Carolina Christian College (NC) 860
Carolinas College of Health Sciences (NC) 1822
Carroll College (MT) 685
Carroll Community College (MD) 1648
Carroll University (WI) 1323
Carson-Newman College (TN) 1147
Carteret Community College (NC) 1822
Carthage College (WI) 1323
Carver Bible College (GA) 278
Cascadia Community College (WA) 2035
Case Western Reserve University (OH) 907
Casper College (WY) 2073
Castleton State College (VT) 1241
Catawba College (NC) 860
Catawba Valley Community College (NC) 1823
Catholic Distance University (VA) 1254
Catholic University of America (DC) 222
Cayuga County Community College (NY) 1782
Cazenovia College (NY) 759
Cecil College (MD) 1649
Cedar Crest College (PA) 1001
Cedar Valley College (TX) 1974
Cedarville University (OH) 908
Centenary College (NJ) 724
Centenary College of Louisiana (LA) 467
Central Alabama Community College (AL) 1367
Central Arizona College (AZ) 1379
Central Baptist College (AR) 85
Central Bible College (MO) 651
Central Carolina Community College (NC) 1823
Central Carolina Technical College (SC) 1944
Central Christian College of Kansas (KS) 431
Central Christian College of the Bible (MO) 652
Central College (IA) 404
Central Community College (NE) 1741
Central Connecticut State University (CT) 201
Central Florida College (FL) 1500
Central Florida Community College (FL) 1500
Central Georgia Technical College (GA) 1525
Central Lakes College (MN) 1689
Central Maine Community College (ME) 1642
Central Maine Medical Center College of Nursing and Health Professions (ME) 1643
Central Methodist University (MO) 652
Central Michigan University (MI) 580
Central Missouri State University *see* University of Central Missouri (MO)
Central New Mexico Community College (NM) 1768
Central Ohio Technical College (OH) 1858
Central Oregon Community College (OR) 1899
Central Pennsylvania College (PA) 1002
Central Piedmont Community College (NC) 1824
Central State University (OH) 909
Central Texas College (TX) 1975
Central Virginia Community College (VA) 2018
Central Washington University (WA) 1288
Central Wyoming College (WY) 2073
Central Yeshiva Tomchei Tmimim-Lubavitch (NY) 760
Centralia College (WA) 2036
Centre College (KY) 450
Centro de Estudios Multidisciplinarios (PR) 1941
Centura College
Chesapeake (VA) 2019
Newport News (VA) 2019
Norfolk (VA) 2019
Richmond (VA) 2019
Richmond Westend (VA) 2019
Virginia Beach (VA) 2019
Century Community and Technical College (MN) 1690
Cerritos College (CA) 1409
Cerro Coso Community College (CA) 1410
Chabot College (CA) 1410
Chadron State College (NE) 693
Chaffey College (CA) 1411
Chamberlain College of Nursing (MO) 653
Chaminade University of Honolulu (HI) 306
Champlain College (VT) 1242
Chancellor University (OH) 909
Chandler-Gilbert Community College
Pecos (AZ) 1380
Sun Lakes Education Center (AZ) 1380
Williams Campus (AZ) 1380
Chapman University (CA) 124
Charles R. Drew University of Medicine and Science (CA) 125
Charleston Southern University (SC) 1114
Charter College (AK) 71
Charter Oak State College (CT) 202
Chatfield College (OH) 1858
Chatham University (PA) 1002
Chattahoochee Technical College (GA) 1525
Chattahoochee Valley Community College (AL) 1367
Chattanooga State Technical Community College (TN) 1959
Chemeketa Community College (OR) 1900
Chesapeake College (MD) 1649
Chester College of New England (NH) 712
Chestnut Hill College (PA) 1003
Cheyney University of Pennsylvania (PA) 1004
CHI Institute
Broomall (PA) 1911
Franklin Mills (PA) 1911
Chicago State University (IL) 321
Chief Dull Knife College (MT) 1736
Chipola College (FL) 233
Chippewa Valley Technical College (WI) 2058
Chowan University (NC) 861
Christendom College (VA) 1254
Christian Brothers University (TN) 1147
Christopher Newport University (VA) 1255
Cincinnati Christian University (OH) 909
Cincinnati College of Mortuary Science (OH) 910
Cincinnati State Technical and Community College (OH) 1859
Circleville Bible College *see* Ohio Christian University (OH)
Cisco Junior College (TX) 1975
The Citadel (SC) 1115
Citrus College (CA) 1411
City College
Casselberry (FL) 1500
Fort Lauderdale (FL) 234
Gainesville (FL) 1501
Miami (FL) 1501
City College of San Francisco (CA) 1412
City Colleges of Chicago
Harold Washington College (IL) 1551
Harry S. Truman College (IL) 1552
Kennedy-King College (IL) 1552
Malcolm X College (IL) 1553
Olive-Harvey College (IL) 1553
Richard J. Daley College (IL) 1554
Wright College (IL) 1554
City University of New York
Baruch College (NY) 760
Borough of Manhattan Community College (NY) 1783
Bronx Community College (NY) 1783
Brooklyn College (NY) 760
City College (NY) 761
College of Staten Island (NY) 762
CUNY Online (NY) 763
Hostos Community College (NY) 1784
Hunter College (NY) 763
John Jay College of Criminal Justice (NY) 764
Kingsborough Community College (NY) 1784
LaGuardia Community College (NY) 1785
Lehman College (NY) 764
Medgar Evers College (NY) 765
New York City College of Technology (NY) 766
Queens College (NY) 766
Queensborough Community College (NY) 1786
York College (NY) 767
City University of Seattle (WA) 1289
Clackamas Community College (OR) 1900
Claflin University (SC) 1116
Claremont McKenna College (CA) 125
Clarendon College (TX) 1976
Clarion University of Pennsylvania (PA) 1005
Clark Atlanta University (GA) 279
Clark College (WA) 2036
Clark State Community College (OH) 1859
Clark University (MA) 533
Clarke College (IA) 405
Clarkson College (NE) 693
Clarkson University (NY) 768
Clatsop Community College (OR) 1901
Clayton State University (GA) 279
Clear Creek Baptist Bible College (KY) 451
Clearwater Christian College (FL) 234
Cleary University (MI) 581
Clemens College (CT) 1488
Clemson University (SC) 1116
Cleveland Institute of Art (OH) 910
Cleveland Institute of Electronics (OH) 1860
Cleveland Institute of Music (OH) 911
Cleveland State Community College (TN) 1959
Cleveland State University (OH) 911
Clinton Community College (IA) 1597
Clinton Community College (NY) 1786
Clinton Junior College (SC) 1945
Cloud County Community College (KS) 1611
Clover Park Technical College (WA) 2037
Clovis Community College (NM) 1768
Coahoma Community College (MS) 1710
Coastal Bend College (TX) 1976
Coastal Carolina Community College (NC) 1824
Coastal Carolina University (SC) 1117

Coastal Georgia Community College *see* College of Coastal Georgia (GA)
Coastline Community College (CA) 1413
Cochise College (AZ) 1380
Cochran School of Nursing-St. John's Riverside Hospital (NY) 1787
Coconino County Community College (AZ) 1381
Coe College (IA) 406
Coffeyville Community College (KS) 1612
Cogswell Polytechnical College (CA) 126
Coker College (SC) 1118
Colby College (ME) 486
Colby Community College (KS) 1612
Colby-Sawyer College (NH) 712
Colegio Biblico Pentecostal (PR) 1086
Colegio de las Ciencias Artes y Television (PR) 1941
Colegio Pentecostal Mizpa (PR) 1087
Coleman College *see* Coleman University (CA)
Coleman College
San Marcos (CA) 1413
Coleman University (CA) 126
Colgate University (NY) 768
College for Creative Studies (MI) 581
College of Alameda (CA) 1413
College of Biblical Studies-Houston (TX) 1180
College of Business and Technology
Flagler (FL) 1501
Hialeah (FL) 1501
Kendall (FL) 1501
College of Charleston (SC) 1118
College of Coastal Georgia (GA) 1526
College of Court Reporting (IN) 1583
College of DuPage (IL) 1554
College of Eastern Utah (UT) 2011
College of Idaho (ID) 311
College of Lake County (IL) 1555
College of Marin
Kentfield (CA) 1414
College of Menominee Nation (WI) 2059
College of Micronesia-FSM (FN) 2080
College of Mount St. Joseph (OH) 912
College of Mount St. Vincent (NY) 769
The College of New Jersey (NJ) 725
College of New Rochelle (NY) 770
College of Notre Dame of Maryland (MD) 500
College of Office Technology (IL) 1556
College of St. Benedict (MN) 613
College of St. Catherine (MN) 614
College of St. Elizabeth (NJ) 726
College of St. Joseph in Vermont (VT) 1242
College of Saint Mary (NE) 694
College of Saint Rose (NY) 771
College of St. Scholastica (MN) 615
College of Saint Thomas More (TX) 1180
College of San Mateo (CA) 1414
College of Southern Idaho (ID) 1547
College of Southern Maryland (MD) 1650
College of Southern Nevada (NV) 1748
College of the Albemarle (NC) 1825
College of the Atlantic (ME) 487
College of the Canyons (CA) 1414
College of the Desert (CA) 1415
College of the Holy Cross (MA) 534
College of the Humanities and Sciences (AZ) 76
College of the Mainland (TX) 1977
College of the Marshall Islands (TT) 2080
College of the Ozarks (MO) 653
College of the Redwoods (CA) 1416
College of the Sequoias (CA) 1416
College of the Siskiyous (CA) 1417
College of the Southwest *see* University of the Southwest (NM)
College of Visual Arts (MN) 615
College of Westchester (NY) 1787
College of William and Mary (VA) 1256
College of Wooster (OH) 913
CollegeAmerica
Colorado Springs (CO) 183
Denver (CO) 1475
Fort Collins (CO) 184
Collin County Community College District (TX) 1977
Collins College (AZ) 76
Colorado Christian University (CO) 184
Colorado College (CO) 185
Colorado Mountain College (CO) 1476
Colorado Northwestern Community College (CO) 1476
Colorado School of Healing Arts (CO) 1477
Colorado School of Mines (CO) 185
Colorado School of Trades (CO) 1477
Colorado State University (CO) 186
Colorado State University
Pueblo (CO) 187
Colorado Technical University (CO) 188
Colorado Technical University
North Kansas City (MO) 1719
Columbia Basin College (WA) 2038
Columbia Centro Universitario
Caguas (PR) 1087
Yauco (PR) 1941
Columbia College (CA) 1417
Columbia College (MO) 654
Columbia College (SC) 1119
Columbia College Chicago (IL) 322
Columbia College of Nursing (WI) 1324
Columbia International University (SC) 1120
Columbia Southern University (AL) 53
Columbia State Community College (TN) 1960
Columbia Union College (MD) 501
Columbia University (NY) 771
Columbia University
School of General Studies (NY) 772
Columbia-Greene Community College (NY) 1788
Columbus College of Art and Design (OH) 914
Columbus State Community College (OH) 1860
Columbus State University (GA) 280
Columbus Technical College (GA) 1527
Commonwealth Institute of Funeral Service (TX) 1978
Commonwealth Technical Institute (PA) 1911
Community College of Allegheny County (PA) 1912
Community College of Aurora (CO) 1477
Community College of Baltimore County (MD) 1651
Community College of Beaver County (PA) 1912
Community College of Denver (CO) 1478
Community College of Philadelphia (PA) 1913
Community College of Rhode Island (RI) 1943
Community College of the Air Force (AL) 1367
Community College of Vermont (VT) 2015
Compton Community College *see* El Camino College: Compton Center (CA)
Conception Seminary College (MO) 655
Concord University (WV) 1308
Concorde Career College
Aurora (CO) 1478
Garden Grove (CA) 1418
Kansas City (MO) 1719
North Hollywood (CA) 1418
San Bernardino (CA) 1418
San Diego (CA) 1418
Concordia College (AL) 54
Concordia College (NY) 773
Concordia College
Moorhead (MN) 616
Concordia University (CA) 127
Concordia University (MI) 582
Concordia University (NE) 694
Concordia University (OR) 973
Concordia University Chicago (IL) 323
Concordia University *see* Concordia University Chicago (IL)
Concordia University
St. Paul (MN) 617
Concordia University Texas (TX) 1181
Concordia University Wisconsin (WI) 1325
Connecticut College (CT) 202
Connors State College (OK) 1889
Conservatory of Music of Puerto Rico (PR) 1087
Consolidated School of Business
Lancaster (PA) 1913
York (PA) 1914
Contra Costa College (CA) 1418
Converse College (SC) 1120
Cooking & Hospitality Institute of Chicago (IL) 1556
Cooper Union for the Advancement of Science and Art (NY) 773
Coosa Valley Technical College (GA) 1527
Copiah-Lincoln Community College (MS) 1711
Copper Mountain College (CA) 1419
Coppin State University (MD) 502
Corban College (OR) 974
Corcoran College of Art and Design (DC) 223
Cornell College (IA) 406
Cornell University (NY) 774
Cornerstone University (MI) 583
Corning Community College (NY) 1788
Cornish College of the Arts (WA) 1289
Cossatot Community College of the University of Arkansas (AR) 1395
Cosumnes River College (CA) 1419
Cottey College (MO) 1719
County College of Morris (NJ) 1759
Court Reporting Institute of Dallas (TX) 1978
Court Reporting Institute of Houston (TX) 1979
Covenant College (GA) 281
Cowley County Community College (KS) 1613
Cox College (MO) 655
Crafton Hills College (CA) 1420
Craven Community College (NC) 1826
Creative Center (NE) 695
Creighton University (NE) 695
Crichton College (TN) 1148
Criswell College (TX) 1181
Crossroads College (MN) 617
Crowder College (MO) 1720
Crowley's Ridge College (AR) 1395
Crown College (MN) 618
Cuesta College (CA) 1420
Culinary Institute Alain & Marie LeNotre (TX) 1979
Culinary Institute of America (NY) 775
Culver-Stockton College (MO) 655
Cumberland County College (NJ) 1759
Cumberland University (TN) 1149
Curry College (MA) 534
Curtis Institute of Music (PA) 1005
Cuyahoga Community College
Eastern Campus (OH) 1861
Metropolitan Campus (OH) 1861
Western Campus (OH) 1862
Cuyamaca College (CA) 1420
Cypress College (CA) 1421
Dabney S. Lancaster Community College (VA) 2020
Daemen College (NY) 776
Dakota County Technical College (MN) 1690
Dakota State University (SD) 1136
Dakota Wesleyan University (SD) 1137
Dallas Baptist University (TX) 1181
Dallas Christian College (TX) 1182
Dallas Institute of Funeral Service (TX) 1979
Dalton State College (GA) 281
Dana College (NE) 696
Daniel Webster College (NH) 713
Danville Area Community College (IL) 1556
Danville Community College (VA) 2020
Darkei Noam Rabbinical College (NY) 776
Dartmouth College (NH) 713
Darton College (GA) 1527
Davenport University (MI) 583
David N. Myers University *see* Chancellor University (OH)
Davidson College (NC) 861
Davidson County Community College (NC) 1826
Davis and Elkins College (WV) 1309
Davis College (OH) 1862
Davis College (NY) 777
Dawson Community College (MT) 1736
Daymar College
Louisville (KY) 1624
Owensboro (KY) 1624
Paducah (KY) 1625
Daytona State College (FL) 1502
De Anza College (CA) 1421
Deaconess College of Nursing *see* Chamberlain College of Nursing (MO)
Dean College (MA) 1661
Dean Institute of Technology (PA) 1914
Deep Springs College (NV) 1422
Defiance College (OH) 914

Tables and Indexes

DeKalb Technical College (GA) 1528
Del Mar College (TX) 1979
Delaware College of Art and Design (DE) 1496
Delaware County Community College (PA) 1914
Delaware State University (DE) 218
Delaware Technical and Community College
Owens (DE) 1496
Stanton/Wilmington (DE) 1497
Terry (DE) 1497
Delaware Valley College (PA) 1006
Delgado Community College (LA) 1637
Delta College (MI) 1673
Delta College of Arts & Technology (LA) 1637
Delta School of Business & Technology (LA) 1638
Delta State University (MS) 639
Denison University (OH) 915
Denmark Technical College (SC) 1945
Denver Academy of Court Reporting (CO) 1478
Denver Career College *see* Kaplan College: Denver (CO)
DePaul University (IL) 323
DePauw University (IN) 372
Des Moines Area Community College (IA) 1598
DeSales University (PA) 1006
Design Institute of San Diego (CA) 127
Devry College of New York (NY) 777
DeVry Institute of Technology: New York *see* Devry College of New York (NY)
DeVry University
Addison (IL) 324
Alpharetta (GA) 282
Arlington (VA) 1256
Bethesda (MD) 502
Charlotte (NC) 862
Chicago (IL) 325
Columbus (OH) 915
DeVry University: Crystal City *see* DeVry University: Arlington (VA)
Decatur (GA) 282
Edina (MN) 619
Federal Way (WA) 1290
Fort Washington (PA) 1007
Fremont (CA) 128
Henderson (NV) 706
Houston (TX) 1183
Indianapolis (IN) 373
Irving (TX) 1183
Kansas City (MO) 656
DeVry University: Las Vegas *see* DeVry University: Henderson (NV)
Long Beach (CA) 128
Memphis (TN) 1149
Milwaukee (WI) 1325
Miramar (FL) 235
North Brunswick (NJ) 727
Oklahoma City Center (OK) 956
Online (IL) 325
Orlando (FL) 235
Phoenix (AZ) 76
Pomona (CA) 128
Portland (OR) 974
Sandy (UT) 1231
Sherman Oaks (CA) 129
Tinley Park (IL) 325
Westminster (CO) 188
Diablo Valley College (CA) 1422
Dickinson College (PA) 1008
Dickinson State University (ND) 895
DigiPen Institute of Technology (WA) 1290
Dillard University (LA) 467
Dine College (AZ) 1381
Divine Word College (IA) 407
Dixie State College of Utah (UT) 1232
Doane College (NE) 696
Dodge City Community College (KS) 1614
Dominican College of Blauvelt (NY) 777
Dominican University (IL) 326
Dominican University of California (CA) 129
Dona Ana Community College of New Mexico State University (NM) 1769
Donnelly College (KS) 1614
Dordt College (IA) 408
Douglas Education Center (PA) 1915
Dowling College (NY) 778
Drake University (IA) 408
Draughons Junior College (KY) 1625
Draughons Junior College
Clarksville (TN) 1960
Murfreesboro (TN) 1960
Nashville (TN) 1960
Drew University (NJ) 727
Drexel University (PA) 1008
Drury University (MO) 657
DuBois Business College (PA) 1915
DuBois Business College
Huntingdon (PA) 1915
Oil City (PA) 1915
Duff's Business Institute *see* Everest Institute: Pittsburgh (PA)
Duke University (NC) 862
Duluth Business University (MN) 1691
Dunwoody College of Technology (MN) 1691
Duquesne University (PA) 1009
Durham Technical Community College (NC) 1827
Dutchess Community College (NY) 1789
Dyersburg State Community College (TN) 1961
D'Youville College (NY) 779
Eagle Gate College
Layton (UT) 2011
Murray (UT) 2011
Salt Lake City (UT) 2012
Earlham College (IN) 373
East Arkansas Community College (AR) 1395
East Carolina University (NC) 863
East Central College (MO) 1721
East Central Community College (MS) 1711
East Central University (OK) 956
East Georgia College (GA) 1528
East Los Angeles College (CA) 1423
East Mississippi Community College (MS) 1712
East Stroudsburg University of Pennsylvania (PA) 1010
East Tennessee State University (TN) 1150
East Texas Baptist University (TX) 1183
Eastern Arizona College (AZ) 1382
Eastern Connecticut State University (CT) 203
Eastern Idaho Technical College (ID) 1547
Eastern Illinois University (IL) 327
Eastern Kentucky University (KY) 451
Eastern Maine Community College (ME) 1643
Eastern Mennonite University (VA) 1257
Eastern Michigan University (MI) 584
Eastern Nazarene College (MA) 535
Eastern New Mexico University (NM) 746
Eastern New Mexico University
Roswell Campus (NM) 1769
Eastern Oklahoma State College (OK) 1890
Eastern Oregon University (OR) 975
Eastern Shore Community College (VA) 2021
Eastern University (PA) 1011
Eastern Washington University (WA) 1291
Eastern West Virginia Community and Technical College (WV) 2052
Eastern Wyoming College (WY) 2074
Eastfield College (TX) 1980
Eastman School of Music of the University of Rochester (NY) 779
East-West University (IL) 326
Ecclesia College (AR) 86
Eckerd College (FL) 235
ECPI College of Technology
Newport News (VA) 1257
Virginia Beach (VA) 1258
ECPI Technical College
Glen Allen (VA) 1258
Richmond (VA) 2021
Roanoke (VA) 2021
Edgecombe Community College (NC) 1827
Edgewood College (WI) 1326
EDIC College (PR) 1941
Edinboro University of Pennsylvania (PA) 1011
Edison College *see* Edison State College (FL)
Edison State College (FL) 236
Edison State Community College (OH) 1862
Edmonds Community College (WA) 2038
Edward Waters College (FL) 237
El Camino College (CA) 1424
El Camino College
Compton Center (CA) 1424
El Centro College (TX) 1981
El Paso Community College (TX) 1981
Electronic Computer Programming College (TN) 1961
Electronic Data Processing College of Puerto Rico (PR) 1088
Electronic Data Processing College
San Sebastian (PR) 1088
Elgin Community College (IL) 1557
Elizabeth City State University (NC) 864
Elizabethtown College (PA) 1012
Elizabethtown Community and Technical College (KY) 1625
Ellsworth Community College (IA) 1598
Elmhurst College (IL) 327
Elmira Business Institute (NY) 1789
Elmira Business Institute
Vestal (NY) 1790
Elmira College (NY) 780
Elms College (MA) 535
Elon University (NC) 864
Embry-Riddle Aeronautical University (FL) 237
Embry-Riddle Aeronautical University
Prescott Campus (AZ) 77
Worldwide Campus (FL) 238
Emerson College (MA) 536
Emmanuel College (GA) 283
Emmanuel College (MA) 537
Emmaus Bible College (IA) 409
Emory & Henry College (VA) 1258
Emory University (GA) 283
Empire College (CA) 1425
Emporia State University (KS) 432
Endicott College (MA) 537
Enterprise-Ozark Community College (AL) 1368
Erie Business Center (PA) 1916
Erie Business Center South (PA) 1916
Erie Community College
City Campus (NY) 1790
North Campus (NY) 1791
South Campus (NY) 1791
Erie Institute of Technology (PA) 1916
Erskine College (SC) 1121
Escuela de Artes Plasticas de Puerto Rico (PR) 1088
Essex County College (NJ) 1760
Estrella Mountain Community College (AZ) 1383
ETI Technical College of Niles (OH) 1863
Eugene Bible College (OR) 975
Eugene Lang College The New School for Liberal Arts (NY) 781
Eureka College (IL) 328
Evangel University (MO) 657
Everest College
Arlington (VA) 2021
Arlington (TX) 1982
Aurora (CO) 1479
Colorado Springs (CO) 1479
Dallas (TX) 1982
Denver (CO) 1479
Fort Worth (TX) 1982
Ontario Metro (CA) 130
Phoenix (AZ) 1383
Portland (OR) 1901
Everest College: Rancho Cucamonga *see* Everest College: Ontario Metro (CA)
Rochester (NY) 1792
Salt Lake City (UT) 2012
Springfield (MO) 658
Tysons Corner (VA) 2022
Vancouver (WA) 2039
Everest Institute (GA) 1529
Everest Institute
Cross Lanes (WV) 2052
Pittsburgh (PA) 1916
Everest University
Brandon (FL) 238
Jacksonville (FL) 238
Lakeland (FL) 238
Largo (FL) 239
Melbourne (FL) 239
North Orlando (FL) 239
Orange Park (FL) 239
Pompano Beach (FL) 239
South Orlando (FL) 239
Tampa (FL) 240
Everett Community College (WA) 2039

Everglades University
Boca Raton (FL) 240
Orlando (FL) 240
Evergreen State College (WA) 1291
Evergreen Valley College (CA) 1425
Excelsior College (NY) 781
Ex'pression College for Digital Arts (CA) 130
Fairfield University (CT) 204
Fairleigh Dickinson University
College at Florham (NJ) 728
Metropolitan Campus (NJ) 728
Fairmont State University (WV) 1310
Faith Baptist Bible College and Theological Seminary (IA) 410
Faith Evangelical Seminary (WA) 1292
Family of Faith College (OK) 957
Fashion Careers College (CA) 1425
Fashion Institute of Design and Merchandising
Los Angeles (CA) 1426
San Diego (CA) 1426
San Francisco (CA) 1427
Fashion Institute of Technology (NY) 782
Faulkner State Community College (AL) 1368
Faulkner University (AL) 54
Fayetteville State University (NC) 865
Fayetteville Technical Community College (NC) 1828
Feather River College (CA) 1427
Felician College (NJ) 729
Ferris State University (MI) 585
Ferrum College (VA) 1259
Finger Lakes Community College (NY) 1792
Finlandia University (MI) 586
Fisher College (MA) 1662
Fisk University (TN) 1150
Fitchburg State College (MA) 538
Five Towns College (NY) 782
Flagler College (FL) 240
Flathead Valley Community College (MT) 1736
Florence-Darlington Technical College (SC) 1945
Florida Agricultural and Mechanical University (FL) 241
Florida Atlantic University (FL) 242
Florida Career College
Hialeah (FL) 1502
Lauderdale Lakes (FL) 242
Miami (FL) 1502
Pembroke Pines (FL) 1502
West Palm Beach (FL) 1502
Florida Christian College (FL) 243
Florida College (FL) 243
Florida College of Natural Health
Bradenton (FL) 1503
Maitland (FL) 1503
Miami (FL) 1503
Pompano Beach (FL) 1503
Florida Community College at Jacksonville (FL) 1503
Florida Gulf Coast University (FL) 244
Florida Hospital College of Health Sciences (FL) 244
Florida Institute of Technology (FL) 245
Florida International University (FL) 246
Florida Keys Community College (FL) 1504
Florida Memorial University (FL) 246
Florida National College (FL) 1504
Florida Southern College (FL) 247
Florida State University (FL) 248
Florida Technical College
Auburndale (FL) 1505
Deland (FL) 1505
Jacksonville (FL) 1505
Orlando (FL) 1505
Folsom Lake College (CA) 1428
Fond du Lac Tribal and Community College (MN) 1692
Fontbonne University (MO) 658
Foothill College (CA) 1428
Fordham University (NY) 783
Forrest Junior College (SC) 1946
Forsyth Technical Community College (NC) 1828
Fort Belknap College (MT) 1737
Fort Berthold Community College (ND) 1849
Fort Hays State University (KS) 432
Fort Lewis College (CO) 188
Fort Peck Community College (MT) 1737
Fort Scott Community College (KS) 1615
Fort Valley State University (GA) 284
Fountainhead College of Technology (TN) 1961
Fox College (IL) 1558
Fox Valley Technical College (WI) 2059
Framingham State College (MA) 539
Francis Marion University (SC) 1122
Franciscan University of Steubenville (OH) 916
Frank Phillips College (TX) 1982
Franklin & Marshall College (PA) 1013
Franklin College (IN) 374
Franklin College
Switzerland (CH) 1362
Franklin Pierce University (NH) 714
Franklin University (OH) 917
Franklin W. Olin College of Engineering (MA) 540
Frederick Community College (MD) 1651
Free Will Baptist Bible College (TN) 1151
Freed-Hardeman University (TN) 1151
Fremont College (CA) 1429
Fresno City College (CA) 1429
Fresno Pacific University (CA) 130
Friends University (KS) 433
Front Range Community College (CO) 1479
Frostburg State University (MD) 503
Full Sail University (FL) 1506
Fullerton College (CA) 1430
Fulton-Montgomery Community College (NY) 1793
Furman University (SC) 1122
Gadsden State Community College (AL) 1369
Gainesville State College (GA) 1529
Gallaudet University (DC) 224
Gallipolis Career College (OH) 1863
Galveston College (TX) 1983
Gannon University (PA) 1014
Garden City Community College (KS) 1615
Gardner-Webb University (NC) 866
Garrett College (MD) 1652
Gaston College (NC) 1829
Gateway Community and Technical College (KY) 1626
Gateway Community College (AZ) 1383
Gateway Community College (CT) 1489
Gateway Technical College (WI) 2059
Gavilan College (CA) 1430
Genesee Community College (NY) 1793
Geneva College (PA) 1015
George C. Wallace Community College at Dothan (AL) 1369
George C. Wallace State Community College at Selma (AL) 1370
George Fox University (OR) 976
George Mason University (VA) 1259
George Washington University (DC) 224
Georgetown College (KY) 452
Georgetown University (DC) 225
Georgia College and State University (GA) 285
Georgia Highlands College (GA) 1530
Georgia Institute of Technology (GA) 285
Georgia Military College (GA) 1530
Georgia Perimeter College (GA) 1531
Georgia Southern University (GA) 286
Georgia Southwestern State University (GA) 287
Georgia State University (GA) 288
Georgian Court University (NJ) 730
Germanna Community College (VA) 2022
Gettysburg College (PA) 1015
Glen Oaks Community College (MI) 1673
Glendale Community College (AZ) 1384
Glendale Community College (CA) 1431
Glenville State College (WV) 1311
Global University (MO) 659
Globe Institute of Technology (NY) 784
Globe University (MN) 619
Gloucester County College (NJ) 1761
Goddard College (VT) 1243
God's Bible School and College (OH) 917
Gogebic Community College (MI) 1674
Golden Gate University (CA) 131
Golden West College (CA) 1431
Goldey-Beacom College (DE) 218
Goldfarb School of Nursing at Barnes-Jewish College (MO) 659
Golf Academy of America
Orlando (FL) 1506
Phoenix (AZ) 1384
San Diego (CA) 1432
The Carolinas (SC) 1946
Golf Academy of Arizona *see* Golf Academy of America: Phoenix (AZ)
Golf Academy of San Diego *see* Golf Academy of America: San Diego (CA)
Golf Academy of the Carolinas *see* Golf Academy of America: The Carolinas (SC)
Golf Academy of the South *see* Golf Academy of America: Orlando (FL)
Gonzaga University (WA) 1292
Good Samaritan College of Nursing and Health Science (OH) 1864
Goodwin College (CT) 1489
Gordon College (GA) 1531
Gordon College (MA) 540
Goshen College (IN) 374
Goucher College (MD) 503
Governors State University (IL) 329
Grace Bible College (MI) 586
Grace College (IN) 375
Grace University (NE) 697
Graceland University (IA) 410
Grambling State University (LA) 468
Grand Canyon University (AZ) 78
Grand Rapids Community College (MI) 1674
Grand Valley State University (MI) 587
Grand View College *see* Grand View University (IA)
Grand View University (IA) 411
Granite State College (NH) 715
Grantham University (MO) 659
Gratz College (PA) 1016
Grays Harbor College (WA) 2039
Grayson County College (TX) 1983
Great Basin College (NV) 706
Great Bay Community College (NH) 1752
Great Lakes Christian College (MI) 588
Green Mountain College (VT) 1243
Green River Community College (WA) 2040
Greenfield Community College (MA) 1663
Greensboro College (NC) 867
Greenville College (IL) 329
Greenville Technical College (SC) 1946
Gretna Career College (LA) 1638
Griffin Technical College (GA) 1532
Griggs University (MD) 504
Grinnell College (IA) 412
Grossmont College (CA) 1432
Grove City College (PA) 1016
Guam Community College (GU) 2079
Guilford College (NC) 867
Guilford Technical Community College (NC) 1829
Gulf Coast College (FL) 1506
Gulf Coast Community College (FL) 1506
Gupton Jones College of Funeral Service (GA) 1532
Gustavus Adolphus College (MN) 619
Gutenberg College (OR) 977
Gwinnett College (GA) 1533
Gwinnett Technical College (GA) 1533
Gwynedd-Mercy College (PA) 1017
Hagerstown Community College (MD) 1652
Halifax Community College (NC) 1830
Hallmark College of Aeronautics (TX) 1983
Hallmark College of Technology (TX) 1984
Hamilton College (NY) 784
Hamilton Technical College (IA) 412
Hamline University (MN) 620
Hampden-Sydney College (VA) 1260
Hampshire College (MA) 541
Hampton University (VA) 1261
Hannibal-LaGrange College (MO) 660
Hanover College (IN) 376
Harcum College (PA) 1916
Harding University (AR) 86
Hardin-Simmons University (TX) 1184
Harford Community College (MD) 1653
Harper College (IL) 1558
Harrington College of Design (IL) 330

Harrisburg Area Community College (PA) 1917
Harrisburg University of Science and Technology (PA) 1018
Harris-Stowe State University (MO) 660
Hartnell College (CA) 1432
Hartwick College (NY) 785
Harvard College (MA) 542
Harvey Mudd College (CA) 131
Haskell Indian Nations University (KS) 434
Hastings College (NE) 698
Haverford College (PA) 1018
Hawaii Pacific University (HI) 307
Hawaii Tokai International College (HI) 1542
Hawkeye Community College (IA) 1599
Haywood Community College (NC) 1830
Hazard Community and Technical College (KY) 1626
Heald College
Concord (CA) 1433
Fresno (CA) 1433
Hayward (CA) 1433
Honolulu (HI) 1542
Portland (OR) 1901
Rancho Cordova (CA) 1433
Roseville (CA) 1434
Salinas (CA) 1434
San Francisco (CA) 1434
San Jose (CA) 1435
Stockton (CA) 1435
Heartland Community College (IL) 1558
Hebrew Theological College (IL) 330
Heidelberg College *see* Heidelberg University (OH)
Heidelberg University (OH) 917
Helena College of Technology of the University of Montana (MT) 1738
Helene Fuld College of Nursing (NY) 1794
Hellenic College/Holy Cross (MA) 543
Henderson Community College (KY) 1626
Henderson State University (AR) 87
Hendrix College (AR) 88
Hennepin Technical College (MN) 1692
Henry Ford Community College (MI) 1675
Heritage Christian University (AL) 54
Heritage University (WA) 1293
Herkimer County Community College (NY) 1794
Herzing College (FL) 1507
Herzing College (AL) 55
Herzing College (GA) 288
Herzing College (LA) 469
Herzing College (WI) 1326
Hesser College (NH) 715
Hesston College (KS) 1616
Hibbing Community College (MN) 1693
Hickey College (MO) 661
High Point University (NC) 868
Highland Community College (IL) 1559
Highland Community College (KS) 1616
Highline Community College (WA) 2040
High-Tech Institute (FL) 1507
High-Tech Institute (GA) 1534
High-Tech Institute (MN) 1693
High-Tech Institute (MO) 1721
High-Tech Institute (NV) 1749
High-Tech Institute (TN) 1962
Hilbert College (NY) 785
Hill College (TX) 1984
Hillsborough Community College (FL) 1507
Hillsdale College (MI) 588
Hillsdale Free Will Baptist College (OK) 957
Hinds Community College (MS) 1712
Hiram College (OH) 918
Hobart and William Smith Colleges (NY) 786
Hobe Sound Bible College (FL) 249
Hocking College (OH) 1864
Hodges University (FL) 249
Hofstra University (NY) 787
Hollins University (VA) 1262
Holmes Community College (MS) 1713
Holy Apostles College and Seminary (CT) 205
Holy Cross College (IN) 377
Holy Family University (PA) 1019
Holy Names University (CA) 132
Holy Trinity Orthodox Seminary (NY) 788
Holyoke Community College (MA) 1663
Hondros College (OH) 1865
Hood College (MD) 504
Hope College (MI) 589
Hope International University (CA) 133
Hopkinsville Community College (KY) 1626
Horizon College of San Diego (CA) 133
Horry-Georgetown Technical College (SC) 1947
Houghton College (NY) 788
Housatonic Community College (CT) 1490
Houston Baptist University (TX) 1185
Houston Community College System (TX) 1985
Howard College (TX) 1985
Howard Community College (MD) 1654
Howard Payne University (TX) 1185
Howard University (DC) 226
Hudson County Community College (NJ) 1761
Hudson Valley Community College (NY) 1795
Huertas Junior College (PR) 1941
Humacao Community College (PR) 1942
Humboldt State University (CA) 133
Humphreys College (CA) 134
Huntingdon College (AL) 55
Huntington College of Health Sciences (TN) 1962
Huntington Junior College (WV) 2053
Huntington University (IN) 377
Huntsville Bible College (AL) 56
Hussian School of Art (PA) 1918
Husson College *see* Husson University (ME)
Husson University (ME) 488
Huston-Tillotson University (TX) 1186
Hutchinson Community College (KS) 1617
ICM School of Business & Medical Careers *see* Kaplan Career Institute: Pittsburgh (PA)
ICPR Junior College (PR) 1942
Idaho State University (ID) 312
IIA College
Albuquerque (NM) 1770
Mesa (AZ) 1385
Phoenix (AZ) 1385
Tucson (AZ) 1385
Ilisagvik College (AK) 1377
Illinois Central College (IL) 1560
Illinois College (IL) 330
Illinois Eastern Community Colleges
Frontier Community College (IL) 1560
Lincoln Trail College (IL) 1561
Olney Central College (IL) 1561
Wabash Valley College (IL) 1562
Illinois Institute of Art
Chicago (IL) 331
Schaumburg (IL) 331
Illinois Institute of Art-Schaumburg *see* Illinois Institute of Art: Schaumburg (IL)
Illinois Institute of Technology (IL) 332
Illinois State University (IL) 333
Illinois Valley Community College (IL) 1562
Illinois Wesleyan University (IL) 333
Immaculata University (PA) 1020
Imperial Valley College (CA) 1435
Independence Community College (KS) 1618
Independence University (UT) 1232
Indian Hills Community College (IA) 1600
Indian River State College (FL) 1508
Indiana Business College
Anderson (IN) 1583
Columbus (IN) 1584
Elkhart (IN) 1584
Evansville (IN) 1584
Fort Wayne (IN) 1584
Indianapolis (IN) 1585
Indianapolis Northwest (IN) 1585
Lafayette (IN) 1585
Marion (IN) 1585
Medical (IN) 1586
Muncie (IN) 1586
Terre Haute (IN) 1586
Indiana Institute of Technology (IN) 378
Indiana State University (IN) 379
Indiana University Bloomington (IN) 379
Indiana University East (IN) 380
Indiana University Kokomo (IN) 381
Indiana University Northwest (IN) 381
Indiana University of Pennsylvania (PA) 1020
Indiana University South Bend (IN) 382
Indiana University Southeast (IN) 383
Indiana University-Purdue University Fort Wayne (IN) 383
Indiana University-Purdue University Indianapolis (IN) 384
Indiana Wesleyan University (IN) 385
Institute of American Indian Arts (NM) 747
Institute of Business & Medical Careers (CO) 1480
Institute of Design and Construction (NY) 1795
Instituto Tecnologico Autonomo de Mexico (MX) 1359
Instituto Tecnologico y de Estudios Superiores de Occidente (MX) 1359
IntelliTec College (CO) 1480
IntelliTec College
Grand Junction (CO) 1481
Inter American University of Puerto Rico
Aguadilla Campus (PR) 1088
Arecibo Campus (PR) 1089
Barranquitas Campus (PR) 1089
Bayamon Campus (PR) 1089
Fajardo Campus (PR) 1090
Guayama Campus (PR) 1090
Metropolitan Campus (PR) 1091
Ponce Campus (PR) 1091
San German Campus (PR) 1092
Interior Designers Institute (CA) 135
International Academy of Design and Technology
Chicago (IL) 334
Detroit (MI) 590
Henderson (NV) 707
Nashville (TN) 1152
Orlando (FL) 249
Sacramento (CA) 135
San Antonio (TX) 1986
Schaumburg (IL) 335
Seattle (WA) 1294
Tampa (FL) 250
International Baptist College (AZ) 78
International Business College (IN) 386
International Business College
Indianapolis (IN) 1586
International College *see* Hodges University (FL)
International College of Broadcasting (OH) 1865
International College of Hospitality Management *see* Clemens College (CT)
International Import-Export Institute (AZ) 78
International Institute of the Americas: Albuquerque *see* IIA College: Albuquerque (NM)
International Institute of the Americas: Mesa *see* IIA College: Mesa (AZ)
International Institute of the Americas: Phoenix *see* IIA College: Phoenix (AZ)
International Institute of the Americas: Tucson *see* IIA College: Tucson (AZ)
International University of Monaco
Monaco 1361
Inver Hills Community College (MN) 1693
Iona College (NY) 789
Iowa Central Community College (IA) 1600
Iowa Lakes Community College (IA) 1601
Iowa State University (IA) 413
Iowa Wesleyan College (IA) 414
Iowa Western Community College (IA) 1601
Irvine Valley College (CA) 1436
Island Drafting and Technical Institute (NY) 1796
Isothermal Community College (NC) 1831
Itasca Community College (MN) 1694
Itawamba Community College (MS) 1713
Ithaca College (NY) 790
ITI Technical College (LA) 1638

ITT Technical Institute
Albany (NY) 1796
Albuquerque (NM) 747
Anaheim (CA) 135
Arlington (TX) 1986
Arnold (MO) 661
Austin (TX) 1986
Bensalem (PA) 1918
Birmingham (AL) 56
Boise (ID) 313
Burr Ridge (IL) 335
Canton (MI) 1675
Chantilly (VA) 1262
Dayton (OH) 1865
Duluth (GA) 289
Earth City (MO) 661
Eden Prairie (MN) 1694
Everett (WA) 1294
Fort Wayne (IN) 386
Ft. Lauderdale (FL) 250
Getzville (NY) 1796
Grand Rapids (MI) 1676
Green Bay (WI) 1327
Greenfield (WI) 1327
Greenville (SC) 1123
Henderson (NV) 707
Hilliard (OH) 1865
Houston (TX) 1986
Houston North (TX) 1986
Houston South (TX) 1986
Indianapolis (IN) 386
Jacksonville (FL) 250
Kansas City (MO) 1721
Kennesaw (GA) 1534
King of Prussia (PA) 1918
Knoxville (TN) 1152
Lake Mary (FL) 250
Lathrop (CA) 135
Little Rock (AR) 89
Liverpool (NY) 1796
Louisville (KY) 453
Memphis (TN) 1153
Miami (FL) 250
Monroeville (PA) 1918
Mount Prospect (IL) 335
Murray (UT) 1233
Nashville (TN) 1153
Newburgh (IN) 1587
Norfolk (VA) 1262
Norwood (MA) 1664
Norwood (OH) 1865
Omaha (NE) 698
Owings Mill (MD) 505
Oxnard (CA) 135
Pittsburgh (PA) 1918
Portland (OR) 977
Rancho Cordova (CA) 135
Richardson (TX) 1986
Richmond (VA) 1262
St. Rose (LA) 469
San Antonio (TX) 1986
San Bernardino (CA) 135
San Diego (CA) 135
Seattle (WA) 1294
Spokane (WA) 1294
Springfield (VA) 1263
Strongsville (OH) 1865
Sylmar (CA) 135
Tampa (FL) 250
Tempe (AZ) 79
Thornton (CO) 189
Torrance (CA) 136
Troy (MI) 1676
Tucson (AZ) 79
Tulsa (OK) 957
Woburn (MA) 1664
Youngstown (OH) 1866

Ivy Tech Community College
Bloomington (IN) 1587
Central Indiana (IN) 1587
Columbus (IN) 1588
East Central (IN) 1588
Kokomo (IN) 1589
Lafayette (IN) 1589
North Central (IN) 1590
Northeast (IN) 1590
Northwest (IN) 1591
Richmond (IN) 1591
South Central (IN) 1592
Southeast (IN) 1592
Southwest (IN) 1593
Wabash Valley (IN) 1594
J. Sargeant Reynolds Community College (VA) 2022
Jackson Community College (MI) 1676
Jackson State Community College (TN) 1962
Jackson State University (MS) 640
Jacksonville College (TX) 1986
Jacksonville State University (AL) 56
Jacksonville University (FL) 250
James A. Rhodes State College (OH) 1866
James Madison University (VA) 1263
James Sprunt Community College (NC) 1831
Jamestown Business College (NY) 1796
Jamestown College (ND) 895
Jamestown Community College (NY) 1796
Jarvis Christian College (TX) 1187
Jefferson College (MO) 1721
Jefferson College of Health Sciences (VA) 1263
Jefferson Community and Technical College (KY) 1627
Jefferson Community College (NY) 1797
Jefferson Community College (OH) 1866
Jefferson Davis Community College (AL) 1370
Jefferson State Community College (AL) 1371
Jewish Theological Seminary of America (NY) 790
JNA Institute of Culinary Arts (PA) 1918
John A. Gupton College (TN) 1962
John A. Logan College (IL) 1563
John Brown University (AR) 89
John Carroll University (OH) 919
John F. Kennedy University (CA) 136
John Tyler Community College (VA) 2023
John Wesley College (NC) 869
John Wood Community College (IL) 1563
Johns Hopkins University (MD) 505
Johns Hopkins University
Peabody Conservatory of Music (MD) 506
Johnson & Wales University
Charlotte (NC) 869
Denver (CO) 189
North Miami (FL) 251
Providence (RI) 1106
Johnson Bible College (TN) 1153
Johnson C. Smith University (NC) 870
Johnson College (PA) 1919
Johnson County Community College (KS) 1618
Johnson State College (VT) 1244
Johnston Community College (NC) 1832
Joliet Junior College (IL) 1564
Jones College (FL) 252
Jones College
Miami (FL) 252
Jones County Junior College (MS) 1714
Jones International University (CO) 190
Judson College (AL) 57
Judson University (IL) 335
Juilliard School (NY) 791
Juniata College (PA) 1021
Kalamazoo College (MI) 590
Kalamazoo Valley Community College (MI) 1676
Kankakee Community College (IL) 1564
Kansas City Art Institute (MO) 661
Kansas City Kansas Community College (KS) 1619
Kansas State University (KS) 434
Kansas Wesleyan University (KS) 435
Kaplan Career Institute
Harrisburg (PA) 1919
Pittsburgh (PA) 1919

Kaplan College
Denver (CO) 1481
Hagerstown (MD) 1654
Hammond (IN) 1594
Indianapolis (IN) 1594
Las Vegas (NV) 1749
Merrillville (IN) 1594
Palm Springs (CA) 1436
Panorama City (CA) 1436
Phoenix (AZ) 1386
Sacramento (CA) 1436
Salida (CA) 1437
San Diego (CA) 1437
Vista (CA) 1437
Kaplan University
Cedar Falls (IA) 414
Cedar Rapids (IA) 1602
Davenport (IA) 415
Des Moines (IA) 415
Lincoln (NE) 1741
Mason City (IA) 415
Omaha (NE) 1742
Kaskaskia College (IL) 1565
Katharine Gibbs School
Melville (NY) 1798
Kean University (NJ) 730
Keene State College (NH) 716
Kehilath Yakov Rabbinical Seminary (NY) 792
Keiser Career College
Greenacres (FL) 1508
Miami Lakes (FL) 1509
Keiser University (FL) 1509
Kellogg Community College (MI) 1677
Kendall College (IL) 336
Kendall College of Art and Design of Ferris State University (MI) 591
Kennebec Valley Community College (ME) 1644
Kennesaw State University (GA) 289
Kent State University (OH) 920
Kent State University
Ashtabula (OH) 1867
East Liverpool (OH) 1867
Geauga (OH) 1868
Salem (OH) 1869
Stark (OH) 1869
Trumbull (OH) 1870
Tuscarawas (OH) 1870
Kentucky Christian University (KY) 453
Kentucky Mountain Bible College (KY) 453
Kentucky State University (KY) 454
Kentucky Wesleyan College (KY) 454
Kenyon College (OH) 920
Kettering College of Medical Arts (OH) 921
Kettering University (MI) 591
Keuka College (NY) 792
Key College (FL) 1509
Keystone College (PA) 1022
Keystone Technical Institute (PA) 1920
Kilgore College (TX) 1987
Kilian Community College (SD) 1956
King College (TN) 1153
King's College (NC) 1832
King's College (NY) 792
King's College (PA) 1023
The King's College and Seminary (CA) 136
Kirkwood Community College (IA) 1602
Kirtland Community College (MI) 1677
Kishwaukee College (IL) 1566
Klamath Community College (OR) 1902
Knox College (IL) 336
Kutztown University of Pennsylvania (PA) 1024
Kuyper College (MI) 592
LA College International (CA) 136
La Roche College (PA) 1025
La Salle University (PA) 1025
La Sierra University (CA) 137
Labette Community College (KS) 1619
Laboratory Institute of Merchandising (NY) 793
Lac Courte Oreilles Ojibwa Community College (WI) 2060
Lackawanna College (PA) 1920
Lafayette College (PA) 1026
LaGrange College (GA) 290
Laguna College of Art and Design (CA) 137
Lake Area Technical Institute (SD) 1956
Lake City Community College (FL) 1509

Tables and Indexes

Lake Erie College (OH) 922
Lake Forest College (IL) 337
Lake Land College (IL) 1566
Lake Michigan College (MI) 1678
Lake Region State College (ND) 1850
Lake Superior College (MN) 1695
Lake Superior State University (MI) 592
Lake Tahoe Community College (CA) 1437
Lake Washington Technical College (WA) 2041
Lakeland Academy Division of Herzing College (MN) 1695
Lakeland College (WI) 1327
Lakeland Community College (OH) 1871
Lakes Region Community College (NH) 1752
Lakeshore Technical College (WI) 2060
Lake-Sumter Community College (FL) 1510
Lakeview College of Nursing (IL) 338
Lamar Community College (CO) 1481
Lamar Institute of Technology (TX) 1988
Lamar State College at Orange (TX) 1988
Lamar State College at Port Arthur (TX) 1988
Lamar University (TX) 1187
Lambuth University (TN) 1154
Lamson College (AZ) 1386
Lancaster Bible College (PA) 1027
Lander University (SC) 1123
Landmark College (VT) 2015
Lane College (TN) 1155
Lane Community College (OR) 1902
Laney College (CA) 1437
Langston University (OK) 957
Lansdale School of Business (PA) 1921
Lansing Community College (MI) 1679
Laramie County Community College (WY) 2075
Laredo Community College (TX) 1989
Las Positas College (CA) 1438
Las Vegas College (NV) 1749
Lasell College (MA) 543
Lassen College *see* Lassen Community College (CA)
Lassen Community College (CA) 1438
Laura and Alvin Siegal College of Judaic Studies (OH) 922
Laurel Business Institute (PA) 1921
Laurel Technical Institute (PA) 1921
Lawrence Technological University (MI) 593
Lawrence University (WI) 1328
Lawson State Community College (AL) 1371
LDS Business College (UT) 2012
Le Cordon Bleu College of Culinary Arts (GA) 1534
Le Cordon Bleu College of Culinary Arts (MN) 1695
Le Cordon Bleu College of Culinary Arts (NV) 1749
Le Cordon Bleu College of Culinary Arts Miami (FL) 1510
Le Moyne College (NY) 793
Lebanon College (NH) 1752
Lebanon Valley College (PA) 1027
L'Ecole Culinaire (MO) 1722
Lee College (TX) 1989
Lee University (TN) 1155
Leech Lake Tribal College (MN) 1696
Lees-McRae College (NC) 871
Lehigh Carbon Community College (PA) 1921
Lehigh University (PA) 1028
LeMoyne-Owen College (TN) 1156
Lenoir Community College (NC) 1832
Lenoir-Rhyne University (NC) 871
Lesley University (MA) 544
Lester L. Cox College of Nursing and Health Sciences *see* Cox College (MO)
LeTourneau University (TX) 1188
Lewis & Clark College (OR) 977
Lewis and Clark Community College (IL) 1567
Lewis University (IL) 338
Lewis-Clark State College (ID) 313
Lexington College (IL) 339
Liberty University (VA) 1264
Life Pacific College (CA) 138
LIFE Pacific College *see* Life Pacific College (CA)
Life University (GA) 290
Limestone College (SC) 1124
Lincoln Christian College and Seminary (IL) 339
Lincoln College (IL) 1567
Lincoln College of Technology
Denver (CO) 1482
Grand Prairie (TX) 1990
Indianapolis (IN) 1595
West Palm Beach (FL) 1510
Lincoln Land Community College (IL) 1568
Lincoln Memorial University (TN) 1156
Lincoln Technical Institute
Allentown (PA) 1922
Northeast Philadelphia (PA) 1922
Philadelphia (PA) 1923
Lincoln University (CA) 138
Lincoln University (MO) 662
Lincoln University (PA) 1029
Lindenwood University (MO) 663
Lindsey Wilson College (KY) 455
Linfield College (OR) 978
Linn State Technical College (MO) 1722
Linn-Benton Community College (OR) 1902
Lipscomb University (TN) 1157
Little Big Horn College (MT) 1738
Little Priest Tribal College (NE) 1742
Livingstone College (NC) 872
Lock Haven University of Pennsylvania (PA) 1030
Loma Linda University (CA) 138
Lon Morris College (TX) 1990
Lone Star College System (TX) 1991
Long Beach City College (CA) 1439
Long Island Business Institute (NY) 1798
Long Island Business Institute Flushing (NY) 1798
Long Island College Hospital School of Nursing (NY) 1798
Long Island University
Brooklyn Campus (NY) 794
C. W. Post Campus (NY) 795
Longview Community College *see* Metropolitan Community College: Longview (MO)
Longwood University (VA) 1265
Lorain County Community College (OH) 1871
Loras College (IA) 416
Lord Fairfax Community College (VA) 2023
Los Angeles City College (CA) 1439
Los Angeles County College of Nursing and Allied Health (CA) 1440
Los Angeles Harbor College (CA) 1440
Los Angeles Mission College (CA) 1440
Los Angeles Pierce College (CA) 1441
Los Angeles Southwest College (CA) 1441
Los Angeles Trade and Technical College (CA) 1442
Los Angeles Valley College (CA) 1442
Los Medanos College (CA) 1443
Louisburg College (NC) 1833
Louisiana College (LA) 469
Louisiana State University and Agricultural and Mechanical College (LA) 470
Louisiana State University at Alexandria (LA) 470
Louisiana State University at Eunice (LA) 1638
Louisiana State University Health Sciences Center (LA) 471
Louisiana State University in Shreveport (LA) 471
Louisiana Tech University (LA) 472
Louisville Technical Institute (KY) 1628
Lourdes College (OH) 923
Lower Columbia College (WA) 2041
Loyola College in Maryland (MD) 506
Loyola Marymount University (CA) 139
Loyola University Chicago (IL) 340
Loyola University New Orleans (LA) 473
Loyola University of Chicago *see* Loyola University Chicago (IL)
Lubbock Christian University (TX) 1189
Luna Community College (NM) 1770
Lurleen B. Wallace Community College (AL) 1372
Luther College (IA) 416
Luther Rice University (GA) 291
Luzerne County Community College (PA) 1923
Lycoming College (PA) 1030
Lyme Academy College of Fine Arts (CT) 205
Lynchburg College (VA) 1266
Lyndon State College (VT) 1245
Lynn University (FL) 252
Lyon College (AR) 89
Macalester College (MN) 621
MacCormac College (IL) 1569
Machzikei Hadath Rabbinical College (NY) 795
MacMurray College (IL) 340
Macomb Community College (MI) 1679
Macon State College (GA) 291
Madison Area Technical College (WI) 2060
Madison Media Institute (WI) 2061
Madisonville Community College (KY) 1628
Madonna University (MI) 594
Magdalen College (NH) 716
Magnolia Bible College (MS) 641
Maharishi University of Management (IA) 417
Maine College of Art (ME) 488
Maine Maritime Academy (ME) 489
Malone University (OH) 923
Manatee Community College (FL) 1510
Manchester College (IN) 386
Manchester Community College (NH) 1753
Manchester Community College (CT) 1490
Manhattan Area Technical College (KS) 1620
Manhattan Christian College (KS) 435
Manhattan College (NY) 795
Manhattan School of Music (NY) 796
Manhattanville College (NY) 797
Mannes College The New School for Music (NY) 797
Manor College (PA) 1923
Mansfield University of Pennsylvania (PA) 1031
Maranatha Baptist Bible College (WI) 1328
Maria College (NY) 1798
Marian College (IN) 387
Marian College of Fond du Lac *see* Marian University (WI)
Marian Court College (MA) 1664
Marian University (WI) 1329
Marietta College (OH) 924
Marion Military Institute (AL) 1372
Marion Technical College (OH) 1871
Marist College (NY) 798
Marlboro College (VT) 1246
Marquette University (WI) 1330
Mars Hill College (NC) 872
Marshall University (WV) 1311
Marshalltown Community College (IA) 1603
Martin Community College (NC) 1834
Martin Luther College (MN) 621
Martin Methodist College (TN) 1158
Martin University (IN) 388
Mary Baldwin College (VA) 1266
Marygrove College (MI) 594
Maryland Institute College of Art (MD) 507
Marylhurst University (OR) 978
Marymount College (CA) 1443
Marymount Manhattan College (NY) 799
Marymount University (VA) 1267
Maryville College (TN) 1158
Maryville University of Saint Louis (MO) 663
Marywood University (PA) 1032
Massachusetts Bay Community College (MA) 1664
Massachusetts College of Art and Design (MA) 544
Massachusetts College of Liberal Arts (MA) 545
Massachusetts College of Pharmacy and Health Sciences (MA) 546
Massachusetts Institute of Technology (MA) 546
Massachusetts Maritime Academy (MA) 547
Massasoit Community College (MA) 1665
The Master's College (CA) 140
Mayland Community College (NC) 1834
Maysville Community and Technical College (KY) 1629
Mayville State University (ND) 896
McCann School of Business and Technology
Dickson City (PA) 1924
Hazleton (PA) 1924
Pottsville (PA) 1925
Sunbury (PA) 1925
McDaniel College (MD) 508

McDowell Technical Community
College (NC) 1835
McGill University (FN) 1351
McHenry County College (IL) 1569
McKendree University (IL) 341
McLennan Community College (TX) 1991
McMurry University (TX) 1190
McNeese State University (LA) 473
McPherson College (KS) 436
Medaille College (NY) 799
Medaille College
Amherst (NY) 800
Rochester (NY) 800
Medcenter One College of Nursing (ND) 897
MedCentral College of Nursing (OH) 925
Medical College of Georgia (GA) 291
Medical University of South Carolina (SC) 1125
Memorial University of
Newfoundland (FN) 1352
Memphis College of Art (TN) 1159
Mendocino College (CA) 1444
Menlo College (CA) 140
Merced College (CA) 1444
Mercer County Community College (NJ) 1762
Mercer University (GA) 292
Mercy College (NY) 800
Mercy College of Health Sciences (IA) 418
Mercy College of Northwest Ohio (OH) 925
Mercyhurst College (PA) 1033
Meredith College (NC) 873
Meridian Community College (MS) 1714
Merrimack College (MA) 548
Merritt College (CA) 1445
Mesa Community College (AZ) 1386
Mesa State College (CO) 190
Mesabi Range Community and Technical
College (MN) 1696
Mesalands Community College (NM) 1770
Mesivta Torah Vodaath Seminary (NY) 801
Messiah College (PA) 1033
Methodist University (NC) 874
Metro Business College (MO) 1722
Metro Business College
Jefferson City (MO) 1723
Rolla (MO) 1723
Metropolitan Career Center Computer
Technology Institute (PA) 1925
Metropolitan College of New York (NY) 801
Metropolitan Community College (NE) 1742
Metropolitan Community College
Blue River (MO) 1723
Longview (MO) 1724
Maple Woods (MO) 1724
Penn Valley (MO) 1725
Metropolitan State College of Denver (CO) 191
Metropolitan State University (MN) 622
Miami Dade College (FL) 1511
Miami International University of Art and
Design (FL) 253
Miami University
Hamilton Campus (OH) 1872
Middletown Campus (OH) 1873
Oxford Campus (OH) 926
Miami-Jacobs Career College (OH) 1873
Michigan Jewish Institute (MI) 595
Michigan State University (MI) 595
Michigan Technological University (MI) 596
Michigan Theological Seminary (MI) 597
Mid Michigan Community College (MI) 1680
Mid-America Christian University (OK) 958
Mid-America College of Funeral
Service (IN) 1595
MidAmerica Nazarene University (KS) 436
Mid-Continent University (KY) 456
Middle Georgia College (GA) 1534
Middle Georgia Technical College (GA) 1535
Middle Tennessee State University (TN) 1160
Middlebury College (VT) 1246
Middlesex Community College (CT) 1491
Middlesex Community College (MA) 1665
Middlesex County College (NJ) 1762
Midland College (TX) 1992
Midland Lutheran College (NE) 698
Midlands Technical College (SC) 1947
Mid-Plains Community College Area (NE) 1743
Mid-South Community College (AR) 1396
Midstate College (IL) 342
Mid-State Technical College (WI) 2061
Midway College (KY) 456
Midwest University (MO) 664
Midwestern State University (TX) 1190
Mildred Elley (NY) 1799
Miles College (AL) 57
Miles Community College (MT) 1738
Miller-Motte Technical College (SC) 1948
Miller-Motte Technical College (NC) 875
Miller-Motte Technical College
Cary (NC) 1835
Chattanooga (TN) 1963
Clarksville (TN) 1963
Lynchburg (VA) 2024
Millersville University of
Pennsylvania (PA) 1034
Milligan College (UT) 1161
Millikin University (IL) 342
Mills College (CA) 141
Millsaps College (MS) 641
Milwaukee Area Technical College (WI) 2062
Milwaukee Institute of Art & Design (WI) 1331
Milwaukee School of Engineering (WI) 1331
Mineral Area College (MO) 1725
Minneapolis Business College (MN) 1696
Minneapolis College of Art and
Design (MN) 623
Minneapolis Community and Technical
College (MN) 1697
Minneapolis Drafting School Division of
Herzing College (MN) 1697
Minnesota School of Business (MN) 623
Minnesota School of Business
Blaine (MN) 623
Brooklyn Center (MN) 1697
Plymouth (MN) 624
Rochester (MN) 624
St. Cloud (MN) 624
Shakopee (MN) 624
Minnesota State College
Southeast Technical (MN) 1698
Minnesota State Community and Technical
College (MN) 1698
Minnesota State University
Mankato (MN) 625
Moorhead (MN) 625
Minnesota West Community and Technical
College (MN) 1699
Minot State University (ND) 897
Minot State University
Bottineau Campus (ND) 1850
MiraCosta College (CA) 1445
Mirrer Yeshiva Central Institute (NY) 802
Misericordia University (PA) 1035
Mission College (CA) 1446
Mississippi College (MS) 642
Mississippi Delta Community
College (MS) 1715
Mississippi Gulf Coast Community
College (MS) 1715
Mississippi State University (MS) 643
Mississippi University for Women (MS) 644
Mississippi Valley State University (MS) 644
Missouri Baptist University (MO) 664
Missouri College (MO) 1726
Missouri Southern State University (MO) 665
Missouri State University (MO) 666
Missouri State University
West Plains (MO) 1726
Missouri Technical School (MO) 667
Missouri University of Science and
Technology (MO) 667
Missouri Valley College (MO) 668
Missouri Western State University (MO) 668
Mitchell College (CT) 206
Mitchell Community College (NC) 1835
Mitchell Technical Institute (SD) 1956
Moberly Area Community College (MO) 1726
Modesto Junior College (CA) 1446
Mohave Community College (AZ) 1387
Mohawk Valley Community College (NY) 1799
Molloy College (NY) 802
Monmouth College (IL) 343
Monmouth University (NJ) 731
Monroe College (NY) 802
Monroe Community College (NY) 1800
Monroe County Community College (MI) 1680
Montana State University
Billings (MT) 685
Bozeman (MT) 686
Montana State University College of
Technology
Great Falls (MT) 1739
Montana State University
Northern (MT) 687
Montana Tech of the University of
Montana (MT) 687
Montcalm Community College (MI) 1681
Montclair State University (NJ) 732
Monterey Institute of International
Studies (CA) 142
Monterey Peninsula College (CA) 1447
Montgomery College (MD) 1655
Montgomery Community College (NC) 1836
Montgomery County Community
College (PA) 1925
Montreat College (NC) 875
Montserrat College of Art (MA) 549
Moody Bible Institute (IL) 344
Moore College of Art and Design (PA) 1036
Moorpark College (CA) 1447
Moraine Park Technical College (WI) 2062
Moraine Valley Community College (IL) 1569
Moravian College (PA) 1036
Morehead State University (KY) 457
Morehouse College (GA) 293
Morgan Community College (CO) 1482
Morgan State University (MD) 508
Morningside College (IA) 418
Morris College (SC) 1125
Morrison Institute of Technology (IL) 1570
Morrison University (NV) 707
Morton College (IL) 1571
Motlow State Community College (TN) 1963
Mott Community College (MI) 1681
Mount Aloysius College (PA) 1037
Mount Angel Seminary (OR) 979
Mount Carmel College of Nursing (OH) 927
Mount Holyoke College (MA) 549
Mount Ida College (MA) 550
Mount Marty College (SD) 1137
Mount Mary College (WI) 1332
Mount Mercy College (IA) 419
Mount Olive College (NC) 876
Mount St. Mary College (NY) 803
Mount St. Mary's College (CA) 142
Mount St. Mary's University (MD) 509
Mount San Antonio College (CA) 1448
Mount San Jacinto College (CA) 1448
Mount Union College (OH) 927
Mount Vernon Nazarene University (OH) 928
Mount Wachusett Community
College (MA) 1666
Mountain Empire Community
College (VA) 2024
Mountain State College (WV) 2053
Mountain State University (WV) 1312
Mountain View College (TX) 1992
Mt. Hood Community College (OR) 1903
Mt. Sierra College (CA) 143
MTI College (CA) 1449
Muhlenberg College (PA) 1038
Multnomah University (OR) 979
Murray State College (OK) 1890
Murray State University (KY) 458
Muscatine Community College (IA) 1603
Muskegon Community College (MI) 1682
Muskingum College (OH) 929
Myotherapy Institute (NE) 1744
Napa Valley College (CA) 1449
Naropa University (CO) 192
Nash Community College (NC) 1836
Nashua Community College (NH) 1753
Nashville Auto-Diesel College (TN) 1964
Nashville State Community College (TN) 1964
Nassau Community College (NY) 1801
National American University
Denver (CO) 192
Kansas City (MO) 669
Rapid City (SD) 1138
Rio Rancho (NM) 747
Roseville (MN) 626
St. Paul (MN) 626

Tables and Indexes

Tables and Indexes

National College
- Bartlett (TN) 1964
- Bluefield (VA) 2024
- Bristol (TN) 1965
- Charlottesville (VA) 2025
- Cincinnati (OH) 1873
- Danville (KY) 1629
- Danville (VA) 2025
- Dayton (OH) 1874
- Florence (KY) 1630
- Harrisonburg (VA) 2025
- Indianapolis (IN) 1595
- Knoxville (TN) 1965
- Lexington (KY) 1630
- Louisville (KY) 1630
- Lynchburg (VA) 2026
- Madison (TN) 1965
- Martinsville (VA) 2026
- Memphis (TN) 1965
- Nashville (TN) 1965

National College of Business & Technology: Tri Cities/Bristol *see* National College: Bristol (TN)

National College of Business and Technology
- Arecibo (PR) 1093
- Bayamon (PR) 1093
- Rio Grande (PR) 1093

National College
- Pikeville (KY) 1630
- Richmond (KY) 1631
- Roanoke Valley (VA) 1268
- Stow (OH) 1874
- Youngstown (OH) 1874

National Hispanic University (CA) 143
National Institute of Technology (OH) 1874
National Labor College (MD) 510
National Park Community College (AR) 1396
National Polytechnic College of Science (CA) 1449
National University (CA) 143
National University of Health Sciences (IL) 344
National-Louis University (IL) 345
Naugatuck Valley Community College (CT) 1491
Navajo Technical College (NM) 1771
Navarro College (TX) 1992
Nazarene Bible College (CO) 193
Nazareth College of Rochester (NY) 803
Nebraska Christian College (NE) 698
Nebraska College of Technical Agriculture (NE) 1744
Nebraska Indian Community College (NE) 1744
Nebraska Methodist College of Nursing and Allied Health (NE) 698
Nebraska Wesleyan University (NE) 699
Neosho County Community College (KS) 1620
Ner Israel Rabbinical College (MD) 510
Neumann College (PA) 1039
Neumont University (UT) 1233
Nevada State College (NV) 708
New Castle School of Trades (PA) 1926
New College of Florida (FL) 253
New England College (NH) 717
New England College of Finance (MA) 1667
New England Conservatory of Music (MA) 551
New England Culinary Institute (VT) 2016
New England Culinary Institute
- Essex Junction (VT) 2016

New England Institute of Art (MA) 551
New England Institute of Technology (RI) 1107
New England School of Communications (ME) 490
New Hampshire Community Technical College: Berlin *see* White Mountains Community College (NH)
New Hampshire Community Technical College: Claremont *see* River Valley Community College (NH)
New Hampshire Community Technical College: Laconia *see* Lakes Region Community College (NH)
New Hampshire Community Technical College: Manchester *see* Manchester Community College (NH)
New Hampshire Community Technical College: Nashua *see* Nashua Community College (NH)
New Hampshire Community Technical College: Stratham *see* Great Bay Community College (NH)
New Hampshire Technical Institute *see* NHTI-Concord's Community College (NH)
New Jersey City University (NJ) 733
New Jersey Institute of Technology (NJ) 733
New Mexico Highlands University (NM) 747
New Mexico Institute of Mining and Technology (NM) 748
New Mexico Junior College (NM) 1771
New Mexico Military Institute (NM) 1772
New Mexico State University (NM) 748
New Mexico State University at Alamogordo (NM) 1772
New Mexico State University at Carlsbad (NM) 1773
New Mexico State University at Grants (NM) 1773
New Orleans Baptist Theological Seminary Leavell College (LA) 474
New River Community and Technical College (WV) 2053
New River Community College (VA) 2026
New Saint Andrews College (ID) 314
New York Career Institute (NY) 1802
New York Institute of Technology (NY) 804
New York School of Interior Design (NY) 805
New York University (NY) 806
Newberry College (SC) 1126
Newbury College (MA) 551
Newman University (KS) 437
Newport Business Institute
- Lower Burrell (PA) 1926
- Williamsport (PA) 1927

NewSchool of Architecture & Design (CA) 144
NHTI-Concord's Community College (NH) 1754
Niagara County Community College (NY) 1802
Niagara University (NY) 807
Nicholls State University (LA) 474
Nichols College (MA) 552
Nicolet Area Technical College (WI) 2063
Norfolk State University (VA) 1268
Normandale Community College (MN) 1699
North Arkansas College (AR) 1397
North Carolina Agricultural and Technical State University (NC) 876
North Carolina Central University (NC) 877
North Carolina School of the Arts *see* University of North Carolina School of the Arts (NC)
North Carolina State University (NC) 878
North Carolina Wesleyan College (NC) 879
North Central College (IL) 345
North Central Kansas Technical College (KS) 1621
North Central Michigan College (MI) 1682
North Central Missouri College (MO) 1727
North Central State College (OH) 1874
North Central Texas College (TX) 1993
North Central University (MN) 627
North Country Community College (NY) 1803
North Dakota State College of Science (ND) 1851
North Dakota State University (ND) 898
North Florida Community College (FL) 1512
North Florida Institute
- Orange Park (FL) 1512

North Georgia College & State University (GA) 293
North Georgia Technical College (GA) 1535
North Greenville University (SC) 1126
North Harris Montgomery Community College *see* Lone Star College System (TX)
North Hennepin Community College (MN) 1700
North Idaho College (ID) 1548
North Iowa Area Community College (IA) 1604
North Lake College (TX) 1993
North Metro Technical College (GA) 1536
North Park University (IL) 346
North Seattle Community College (WA) 2042
North Shore Community College (MA) 1667
Northampton Community College (PA) 1927
Northcentral Technical College (WI) 2063
Northcentral University (AZ) 79
Northeast Alabama Community College (AL) 1373
Northeast Community College (NE) 1745
Northeast Iowa Community College (IA) 1605
Northeast Mississippi Community College (MS) 1716
Northeast State Technical Community College (TN) 1966
Northeast Texas Community College (TX) 1994
Northeast Wisconsin Technical College (WI) 2063
Northeastern Illinois University (IL) 347
Northeastern Junior College (CO) 1482
Northeastern Oklahoma Agricultural and Mechanical College (OK) 1891
Northeastern State University (OK) 958
Northeastern Technical College (SC) 1948
Northeastern University (MA) 553
Northern Arizona University (AZ) 79
Northern Essex Community College (MA) 1668
Northern Illinois University (IL) 347
Northern Kentucky University (KY) 459
Northern Maine Community College (ME) 1644
Northern Marianas College Northern Mariana Islands 1350
Northern Michigan University (MI) 597
Northern New Mexico College (NM) 1774
Northern Oklahoma College (OK) 1891
Northern State University (SD) 1138
Northern Virginia Community College (VA) 2027
Northland Baptist Bible College (WI) 1332
Northland College (WI) 1333
Northland Community & Technical College (MN) 1701
Northland Pioneer College (AZ) 1387
Northwest Arkansas Community College (AR) 1398
Northwest Aviation College (WA) 2042
Northwest Christian University (OR) 980
Northwest College (WY) 2075
Northwest College of Art (WA) 1294
Northwest Florida State College (FL) 254
Northwest Indian College (WA) 2043
Northwest Iowa Community College (IA) 1605
Northwest Mississippi Community College (MS) 1716
Northwest Missouri State University (MO) 669
Northwest Nazarene University (ID) 314
Northwest School of Wooden Boatbuilding (WA) 2043
Northwest State Community College (OH) 1875
Northwest Technical College (MN) 1701
Northwest Technical Institute (MN) 1702
Northwest University (WA) 1294
Northwest Vista College (TX) 1994
Northwestern Business College (IL) 1571
Northwestern College (IA) 419
Northwestern College (MN) 627
Northwestern Connecticut Community College (CT) 1492
Northwestern Health Sciences University (MN) 627
Northwestern Michigan College (MI) 1683
Northwestern Oklahoma State University (OK) 959
Northwestern Polytechnic University (CA) 144
Northwestern State University (LA) 475
Northwestern Technical College (GA) 1536
Northwestern University (IL) 348
Northwest-Shoals Community College (AL) 1373
Northwood University
- Florida (FL) 254
- Michigan (MI) 598
- Texas (TX) 1191

Norwalk Community College (CT) 1492
Norwich University (VT) 1247
Nossi College of Art (TN) 1966
Notre Dame College (OH) 929
Notre Dame de Namur University (CA) 145
Nova Southeastern University (FL) 255
Nunez Community College (LA) 1639
Nyack College (NY) 807

Oak Hills Christian College (MN) 628
Oakbridge Academy of Arts (PA) 1928
Oakland City University (IN) 388
Oakland Community College (MI) 1683
Oakland University (MI) 599
Oakton Community College (IL) 1572
Oakwood University (AL) 58
Oberlin College (OH) 930
Occidental College (CA) 145
Ocean County College (NJ) 1763
Odessa College (TX) 1994
Oglala Lakota College (SD) 1139
Oglethorpe University (GA) 294
Ohio Business College (OH) 1875
Ohio Business College
Sandusky (OH) 1875
Ohio Christian University (OH) 931
Ohio College of Massotherapy (OH) 1875
Ohio Dominican University (OH) 931
Ohio Institute of Health Careers
Columbus (OH) 1876
Elyria (OH) 1876
Ohio Institute of Photography and Technology (OH) 1876
Ohio Northern University (OH) 932
Ohio State University Agricultural Technical Institute (OH) 1876
Ohio State University
Columbus Campus (OH) 933
Lima Campus (OH) 934
Mansfield Campus (OH) 934
Marion Campus (OH) 935
Newark Campus (OH) 935
Ohio Technical College (OH) 1877
Ohio University (OH) 936
Ohio University
Chillicothe Campus (OH) 937
Eastern Campus (OH) 937
Lancaster Campus (OH) 938
Southern Campus at Ironton (OH) 938
Zanesville Campus (OH) 938
Ohio Valley College of Technology (OH) 1877
Ohio Valley University (WV) 1313
Ohio Wesleyan University (OH) 939
Ohlone College (CA) 1450
Ohr Somayach Tanenbaum Education Center (NY) 808
Oklahoma Baptist University (OK) 960
Oklahoma Christian University (OK) 960
Oklahoma City Community College (OK) 1892
Oklahoma City University (OK) 961
Oklahoma Panhandle State University (OK) 962
Oklahoma State University (OK) 963
Oklahoma State University Institute of Technology
Okmulgee (OK) 1892
Oklahoma State University
Oklahoma City (OK) 1893
Oklahoma Wesleyan University (OK) 963
Old Dominion University (VA) 1269
Olean Business Institute (NY) 1803
Olivet College (MI) 600
Olivet Nazarene University (IL) 349
Olympic College (WA) 2043
O'More College of Design (TN) 1161
Onondaga Community College (NY) 1804
Oral Roberts University (OK) 964
Orange Coast College (CA) 1450
Orange County Community College (NY) 1804
Orangeburg-Calhoun Technical College (SC) 1949
Oregon College of Art & Craft (OR) 980
Oregon Health & Science University (OR) 981
Oregon Institute of Technology (OR) 981
Oregon State University (OR) 982
Orlando Culinary Academy (FL) 1512
Orleans Technical Institute
Center City Campus (PA) 1928
Otero Junior College (CO) 1483
Otis College of Art and Design (CA) 146
Ottawa University (KS) 438
Otterbein College (OH) 940
Ouachita Baptist University (AR) 90
Ouachita Technical College (AR) 1398
Our Lady of Holy Cross College (LA) 476
Our Lady of the Lake College (LA) 476
Our Lady of the Lake University of San Antonio (TX) 1192
Owens Community College
Toledo (OH) 1877
Owensboro Community and Technical College (KY) 1631
Oxford College of Emory University (GA) 1536
Oxnard College (CA) 1451
Ozark Christian College (MO) 670
Ozarka College (AR) 1399
Ozarks Technical Community College (MO) 1728
Pace Institute (PA) 1928
Pace University (NY) 808
Pace University
Pleasantville/Briarcliff (NY) 809
Pacific Lutheran University (WA) 1295
Pacific Northwest College of Art (OR) 983
Pacific Oaks College (CA) 147
Pacific States University (CA) 147
Pacific Union College (CA) 147
Pacific University (OR) 983
Paier College of Art (CT) 206
Paine College (GA) 295
Palau Community College (TT) 2080
Palm Beach Atlantic University (FL) 256
Palm Beach Community College (FL) 1512
Palo Alto College (TX) 1995
Palo Verde College (CA) 1451
Palomar College (CA) 1452
Pamlico Community College (NC) 1837
Panola College (TX) 1995
Paradise Valley Community College (AZ) 1387
Paralegal Institute (AZ) 1388
Paris Junior College (TX) 1996
Park University (MO) 670
Parkland College (IL) 1572
Parks College: Arlington *see* Everest College: Arlington (VA)
Parks College: Aurora *see* Everest College: Aurora (CO)
Parks College *see* Everest College: Denver (CO)
Parks College: Tysons Corner *see* Everest College: Tysons Corner (VA)
Parsons Paris School of Design (FN) 1357
Parsons The New School for Design (NY) 809
Pasadena City College (CA) 1452
Pasco-Hernando Community College (FL) 1513
Passaic County Community College (NJ) 1763
Patricia Stevens College (MO) 1728
Patrick Henry College (VA) 1270
Patrick Henry Community College (VA) 2027
Patten University (CA) 148
Paul D. Camp Community College (VA) 2027
Paul Quinn College (TX) 1192
Paul Smith's College (NY) 810
Peace College (NC) 879
Pearl River Community College (MS) 1717
Peirce College (PA) 1039
Pellissippi State Technical Community College (TN) 1966
Peninsula College (WA) 2044
Penn Commercial Business and Technical School (PA) 1929
Penn Foster College (AZ) 1388
Penn State Abington (PA) 1040
Penn State Altoona (PA) 1041
Penn State Beaver (PA) 1041
Penn State Berks (PA) 1042
Penn State Brandywine (PA) 1043
Penn State Dubois (PA) 1044
Penn State Erie, The Behrend College (PA) 1045
Penn State Fayette, The Eberly Campus (PA) 1045
Penn State Greater Allegheny (PA) 1046
Penn State Harrisburg (PA) 1047
Penn State Hazleton (PA) 1048
Penn State Lehigh Valley (PA) 1048
Penn State McKeesport *see* Penn State Greater Allegheny (PA)
Penn State Mont Alto (PA) 1049
Penn State New Kensington (PA) 1050
Penn State Schuylkill (PA) 1051
Penn State Shenango (PA) 1052
Penn State University Park (PA) 1052
Penn State Wilkes-Barre (PA) 1053
Penn State Worthington Scranton (PA) 1054
Penn State York (PA) 1055
Penn Valley Community College *see* Metropolitan Community College: Penn Valley (MO)
Pennco Tech (PA) 1929
Pennsylvania College of Art and Design (PA) 1056
Pennsylvania College of Technology (PA) 1056
Pennsylvania Culinary Institute (PA) 1929
Pennsylvania Highlands Community College (PA) 1929
Pennsylvania Institute of Health and Technology (PA) 1930
Pennsylvania Institute of Technology (PA) 1930
Pennsylvania School of Business (PA) 1930
Pensacola Junior College (FL) 1514
Pepperdine University (CA) 148
Peru State College (NE) 700
Pfeiffer University (NC) 880
Philadelphia Biblical University (PA) 1057
Philadelphia University (PA) 1057
Philander Smith College (AR) 91
Phillips Beth Israel School of Nursing (NY) 1805
Phillips Community College of the University of Arkansas (AR) 1399
Phoenix College (AZ) 1388
Piedmont Baptist College (NC) 880
Piedmont College (GA) 295
Piedmont Community College (NC) 1837
Piedmont Technical College (SC) 1949
Piedmont Virginia Community College (VA) 2028
Pierce College (WA) 2044
Pikes Peak Community College (CO) 1483
Pikeville College (KY) 459
Pima Community College (AZ) 1389
Pine Manor College (MA) 553
Pine Technical College (MN) 1702
Pinnacle Career Institute
Kansas City (MO) 1728
Pioneer Pacific College (OR) 1904
Pioneer Pacific College
Springfield (OR) 1904
Pitt Community College (NC) 1837
Pittsburg State University (KS) 438
Pittsburgh Institute of Aeronautics (PA) 1931
Pittsburgh Institute of Mortuary Science (PA) 1931
Pittsburgh Technical Institute (PA) 1931
Pitzer College (CA) 149
PJA School (PA) 1932
Platt College
Aurora (CO) 193
Huntington Beach (CA) 1453
Los Angeles (CA) 1453
Oklahoma City Central (OK) 1893
Ontario (CA) 150
San Diego (CA) 150
Tulsa (OK) 1894
Plaza College (NY) 1805
Plymouth State University (NH) 717
Point Loma Nazarene University (CA) 150
Point Park University (PA) 1058
Polk Community College (FL) 1514
Polytechnic Institute of New York University (NY) 810
Pomona College (CA) 151
Ponce Paramedical College (PR) 1942
Pontifical Catholic University of Puerto Rico (PR) 1094
Pontifical College Josephinum (OH) 940
Porterville College (CA) 1453
Portland Community College (OR) 1904
Portland State University (OR) 984
Post University (CT) 207
Potomac College (DC) 227
Potomac College (VA) 1270
Potomac State College of West Virginia University (WV) 2053
Prairie State College (IL) 1573
Prairie View A&M University (TX) 1192
Pratt Community College (KS) 1621
Pratt Institute (NY) 811
Presbyterian College (SC) 1127
Prescott College (AZ) 80
Presentation College (SD) 1139

Tables and Indexes

Prince George's Community College (MD) 1656
Prince Institute of Professional Studies (AL) 1374
Prince William Sound Community College (AK) 1377
Princeton University (NJ) 734
Principia College (IL) 350
Professional Business College (NY) 1806
Professional Golfers Career College (CA) 1454
Professional Golfers Career College Orlando (FL) 1515
Providence College (RI) 1107
Provo College (UT) 2012
Pueblo Community College (CO) 1484
Pulaski Technical College (AR) 1400
Purdue University (IN) 389
Purdue University Calumet (IN) 389
Purdue University North Central (IN) 390
Queens University of Charlotte (NC) 881
Quincy College (MA) 1668
Quincy University (IL) 350
Quinebaug Valley Community College (CT) 1493
Quinnipiac University (CT) 207
Quinsigamond Community College (MA) 1669
Rabbi Jacob Joseph School (NJ) 735
Rabbinical Academy Mesivta Rabbi Chaim Berlin (NY) 812
Rabbinical College Beth Shraga (NY) 812
Rabbinical College Bobover Yeshiva B'nei Zion (NY) 812
Rabbinical College Ch'san Sofer of New York (NY) 812
Rabbinical College of America (NJ) 735
Rabbinical College of Long Island (NY) 812
Rabbinical College of Ohr Shimon Yisroel (NY) 812
Rabbinical College of Telshe (OH) 941
Rabbinical Seminary Adas Yereim (NY) 812
Rabbinical Seminary of America (NY) 813
Radford University (VA) 1270
Rainy River Community College (MN) 1702
Ramapo College of New Jersey (NJ) 735
Randolph College (VA) 1271
Randolph Community College (NC) 1838
Randolph-Macon College (VA) 1272
Randolph-Macon Woman's College *see* Randolph College (VA)
Ranger College (TX) 1997
Ranken Technical College (MO) 1729
Rappahannock Community College (VA) 2028
Raritan Valley Community College (NJ) 1764
Rasmussen College
- Aurora (IL) 1573
- Bismarck (ND) 1852
- Brooklyn Park (MN) 1703
- Eagan (MN) 1703
- Eden Prairie (MN) 1704
- Fargo (ND) 899
- Fort Myers (FL) 256
- Green Bay (WI) 2064
- Lake Elmo/Woodbury (MN) 628
- Mankato (MN) 1704
- Ocala (FL) 257
- Pasco County (FL) 257
- Rockford (IL) 1573
- St. Cloud (MN) 1704

Reading Area Community College (PA) 1932
Red Rocks Community College (CO) 1484
Redlands Community College (OK) 1894
Redstone College (CO) 1485
Reed College (OR) 985
Reedley College (CA) 1454
Refrigeration School (AZ) 1389
Regent University (VA) 1273
Regions University *see* Amridge University (AL)
Regis College (MA) 554
Regis University (CO) 193
Reinhardt College (GA) 296
Remington College
- Baton Rouge (LA) 1639
- Cleveland (OH) 1878
- Cleveland West (OH) 1878
- Colorado Springs (CO) 1485
- Dallas (TX) 1997
- Fort Worth (TX) 1997
- Honolulu (HI) 1542
- Houston (TX) 1997
- Lafayette (LA) 1640
- Largo (FL) 257
- Little Rock (AR) 1400
- Memphis (TN) 1967
- Mobile (AL) 1374
- Nashville (TN) 1967
- North Houston (TX) 1997
- San Diego (CA) 152
- Shreveport (LA) 1640
- Tampa (FL) 257

Rend Lake College (IL) 1574
Rensselaer Polytechnic Institute (NY) 813
Renton Technical College (WA) 2045
Research College of Nursing (MO) 671
Restaurant School at Walnut Hill College (PA) 1059
RETS Tech Center (OH) 1878
Rhode Island College (RI) 1108
Rhode Island School of Design (RI) 1109
Rhodec International (MA) 555
Rhodes College (TN) 1162
Rice University (TX) 1193
Rich Mountain Community College (AR) 1400
Richard Bland College (VA) 2029
Richard Stockton College of New Jersey (NJ) 736
Richland College (TX) 1997
Richland Community College (IL) 1574
Richmond Community College (NC) 1838
Richmond, The American International University in London (UK) 1363
Rider University (NJ) 737
Ridgewater College (MN) 1705
Ringling College of Art and Design (FL) 258
Rio Hondo College (CA) 1454
Rio Salado College (AZ) 1390
Ripon College (WI) 1333
River Parishes Community College (LA) 1640
River Valley Community College (NH) 1754
Riverland Community College (MN) 1705
Riverside Community College (CA) 1455
Rivier College (NH) 718
Roane State Community College (TN) 1967
Roanoke Bible College (NC) 882
Roanoke College (VA) 1273
Roanoke-Chowan Community College (NC) 1839
Robert Morris College
- Chicago (IL) 351

Robert Morris University (PA) 1059
Roberts Wesleyan College (NY) 813
Robeson Community College (NC) 1839
Rochester Business Institute *see* Everest College: Rochester (NY)
Rochester College (MI) 600
Rochester Community and Technical College (MN) 1706
Rochester Institute of Technology (NY) 814
Rock Valley College (IL) 1575
Rockford Business College (IL) 1575
Rockford College (IL) 352
Rockhurst University (MO) 671
Rockingham Community College (NC) 1839
Rockland Community College (NY) 1806
Rocky Mountain College (MT) 688
Rocky Mountain College of Art & Design (CO) 194
Roger Williams University (RI) 1109
Rogers State University (OK) 965
Rogue Community College (OR) 1905
Rollins College (FL) 258
Roosevelt University (IL) 352
Rosalind Franklin University of Medicine and Science (IL) 353
Rose State College (OK) 1895
Rosedale Bible College (OH) 1879
Rosedale Technical Institute (PA) 1933
Rose-Hulman Institute of Technology (IN) 391
Rosemont College (PA) 1060
Rowan University (NJ) 737
Rowan-Cabarrus Community College (NC) 1840
Roxbury Community College (MA) 1669
Rush University (IL) 353
Russell Sage College (NY) 815
Rust College (MS) 645
Rutgers, The State University of New Jersey
- Camden Regional Campus (NJ) 738
- New Brunswick/Piscataway Campus (NJ) 739
- Newark Regional Campus (NJ) 740

Sacramento City College (CA) 1455
Sacred Heart Major Seminary (MI) 601
Sacred Heart University (CT) 208
Saddleback College (CA) 1456
Sage College (CA) 1456
Sage College of Albany (NY) 816
Saginaw Chippewa Tribal College (MI) 1684
Saginaw Valley State University (MI) 601
St. Ambrose University (IA) 420
St. Andrews Presbyterian College (NC) 882
St. Anselm College (NH) 719
Saint Anthony College of Nursing (IL) 354
St. Augustine College (IL) 354
St. Augustine's College (NC) 883
Saint Bonaventure University (NY) 817
St. Catharine College (KY) 460
St. Charles Borromeo Seminary Overbrook (PA) 1060
St. Charles Community College (MO) 1729
St. Clair County Community College (MI) 1684
Saint Cloud State University (MN) 628
St. Cloud Technical College (MN) 1706
St. Edward's University (TX) 1194
St. Elizabeth College of Nursing (NY) 1806
St. Francis College (NY) 817
St. Francis Medical Center College of Nursing (IL) 354
St. Francis University (PA) 1061
St. Gregory's University (OK) 965
St. John Fisher College (NY) 818
St. John Vianney College Seminary (FL) 259
St. John's College (IL) 355
St. John's College (MD) 510
St. John's College (NM) 749
Saint Johns River Community College (FL) 1515
St. John's University (MN) 629
St. John's University (NY) 819
St. Joseph College (CT) 209
St. Joseph Seminary College (LA) 477
Saint Joseph's College (IN) 391
St. Joseph's College (ME) 490
St. Joseph's College (NY) 820
St. Joseph's College of Nursing (NY) 1807
St. Joseph's College
- Suffolk Campus (NY) 820

Saint Joseph's University (PA) 1062
St. Lawrence University (NY) 821
St. Leo University (FL) 259
St. Louis Christian College (MO) 672
St. Louis Community College (MO) 1730
St. Louis Community College at Florissant Valley (MO) 1730
St. Louis Community College at Meramec (MO) 1731
Saint Louis University (MO) 673
St. Louis University *see* Saint Louis University (MO)
St. Luke's College (IA) 1606
St. Luke's College (MO) 674
Saint Martin's University (WA) 1296
St. Mary-of-the-Woods College (IN) 392
Saint Mary's College (IN) 393
St. Mary's College of California (CA) 152
St. Mary's College of Maryland (MD) 511
St. Mary's University (TX) 1195
St. Mary's University of Minnesota (MN) 630
St. Michael's College (VT) 1248
St. Norbert College (WI) 1334
St. Olaf College (MN) 631
St. Paul College (MN) 1707
St. Paul's College (VA) 1274
Saint Peter's College (NJ) 741
St. Petersburg College (FL) 1515
St. Philip's College (TX) 1998

St. Thomas Aquinas College (NY) 822
Saint Thomas University (FL) 260
St. Vincent Catholic Medical Centers (NY) 1807
St. Vincent College (PA) 1062
St. Vincent's College (CT) 1493
St. Xavier University (IL) 355
Salem College (NC) 884
Salem Community College (NJ) 1765
Salem International University (WV) 1314
Salem State College (MA) 555
Salisbury University (MD) 511
Salish Kootenai College (MT) 689
Salt Lake Community College (UT) 2012
Salvation Army College for Officer
Training at Crestmont (CA) 1457
Salve Regina University (RI) 1110
Sam Houston State University (TX) 1196
Samford University (AL) 58
Sampson Community College (NC) 1840
Samuel Merritt University (CA) 153
Samuel Stephen College (OH) 1879
San Antonio College (TX) 1998
San Bernardino Valley College (CA) 1457
San Diego Christian College (CA) 153
San Diego City College (CA) 1457
San Diego Mesa College (CA) 1458
San Diego Miramar College (CA) 1458
San Diego State University (CA) 154
San Francisco Art Institute (CA) 155
San Francisco Conservatory of Music (CA) 155
San Francisco State University (CA) 156
San Jacinto College (TX) 1999
San Joaquin Delta College (CA) 1459
San Joaquin Valley College (CA) 1459
San Jose City College (CA) 1460
San Jose State University (CA) 156
San Juan College (NM) 1774
Sandhills Community College (NC) 1841
Sanford-Brown College (MO) 1731
Sanford-Brown College
Hazelwood (MO) 1731
Milwaukee (WI) 1335
St. Peters (MO) 1732
Vienna (VA) 1274
Sanford-Brown Institute
Jacksonville (FL) 1516
Monroeville (PA) 1933
Pittsburgh (PA) 1933
Tampa (FL) 1516
Santa Ana College (CA) 1460
Santa Barbara Business College (CA) 1461
Santa Barbara Business College
Bakersfield (CA) 1461
Palm Desert (CA) 1461
Santa Maria (CA) 1461
Ventura (CA) 1462
Santa Barbara City College (CA) 1462
Santa Clara University (CA) 157
Santa Fe College (FL) 1516
Santa Fe Community College (NM) 1775
Santa Fe Community College *see* Santa Fe
College (FL)
Santa Monica College (CA) 1463
Santa Rosa Junior College (CA) 1463
Santiago Canyon College (CA) 1464
Sarah Lawrence College (NY) 822
Sauk Valley Community College (IL) 1576
Savannah College of Art and Design (GA) 297
Savannah River College (GA) 1537
Savannah State University (GA) 297
Savannah Technical College (GA) 1537
Schenectady County Community
College (NY) 1807
Schiller International University (FL) 261
School of Advertising Art (OH) 1879
School of the Art Institute of Chicago (IL) 356
School of the Museum of Fine Arts (MA) 556
School of Urban Missions
New Orleans (LA) 477
Oakland (CA) 158
School of Visual Arts (NY) 823
Schoolcraft College (MI) 1685
Schreiner University (TX) 1196
Scott Community College (IA) 1606
Scottsdale Community College (AZ) 1390
Scottsdale Culinary Institute (AZ) 1391
Scripps College (CA) 158
Seattle Central Community College (WA) 2045
Seattle Pacific University (WA) 1297
Seattle University (WA) 1297
Selma University (AL) 59
Seminole Community College (FL) 1517
Seminole State College (OK) 1895
Seton Hall University (NJ) 741
Seton Hill University (PA) 1063
Seward County Community College (KS) 1622
Shasta Bible College and Graduate
School (CA) 159
Shasta College (CA) 1464
Shaw University (NC) 884
Shawnee Community College (IL) 1576
Shawnee State University (OH) 941
Shelton State Community College (AL) 1374
Shenandoah University (VA) 1274
Shepherd University (WV) 1314
Shepherds Theological Seminary (NC) 1841
Sheridan College (WY) 2076
Shimer College (IL) 356
Shippensburg University of
Pennsylvania (PA) 1064
Shor Yoshuv Rabbinical College (NY) 824
Shoreline Community College (WA) 2045
Shorter College (GA) 298
Siena College (NY) 824
Siena Heights University (MI) 602
Sierra College (CA) 1465
Sierra Nevada College (NV) 708
Silicon Valley University (CA) 159
Silver Lake College (WI) 1335
Simmons College (MA) 556
Simon Fraser University (FN) 1352
Simpson College (IA) 421
Simpson University (CA) 159
Sinclair Community College (OH) 1879
Singapore Management University
Singapore 1362
Sinte Gleska University (SD) 1140
Sisseton Wahpeton College (SD) 1957
Sitting Bull College (ND) 1852
Skagit Valley College (WA) 2046
Skidmore College (NY) 824
Skyline College (CA) 1465
Slippery Rock University of
Pennsylvania (PA) 1065
Smith College (MA) 557
Snead State Community College (AL) 1375
Snow College (UT) 2013
Sojourner-Douglass College (MD) 512
Soka University of America (CA) 160
Solano Community College (CA) 1466
Somerset Christian College (NJ) 742
Somerset Community College (KY) 1632
Sonoma State University (CA) 161
South Arkansas Community College (AR) 1401
South Carolina State University (SC) 1128
South Central College (MN) 1708
South Coast College (CA) 1466
South College (NC) 1842
South College (TN) 1162
South Dakota School of Mines and
Technology (SD) 1140
South Dakota State University (SD) 1141
South Florida Community College (FL) 1517
South Georgia College (GA) 1538
South Hills School of Business &
Technology (PA) 1933
South Hills School of Business &
Technology
Altoona (PA) 1934
South Louisiana Community College (LA) 1640
South Mountain Community College (AZ) 1391
South Piedmont Community College (NC) 1842
South Plains College (TX) 2000
South Puget Sound Community
College (WA) 2046
South Seattle Community College (WA) 2047
South Suburban College of Cook
County (IL) 1577
South Texas College (TX) 2000
South University
Columbia (SC) 1128
Montgomery (AL) 59
Savannah (GA) 299
Tampa (FL) 261
West Palm Beach (FL) 261
Southeast Arkansas College (AR) 1401
Southeast Community College (NE) 1745
Southeast Kentucky Community and
Technical College (KY) 1632
Southeast Missouri Hospital College of
Nursing and Health Sciences (MO) 1732
Southeast Missouri State University (MO) 674
Southeast Technical Institute (SD) 1957
Southeastern Baptist College (MS) 645
Southeastern Baptist Theological
Seminary (NC) 885
Southeastern Bible College (AL) 60
Southeastern Business College *see* Samuel
Stephen College (OH)
Southeastern Business College
Jackson (OH) 1880
Lancaster (OH) 1880
New Boston (OH) 1880
Southeastern College of the Assemblies of
God *see* Southeastern University (FL)
Southeastern Community College (NC) 1842
Southeastern Community College
North Campus (IA) 1607
South Campus (IA) 1607
Southeastern Illinois College (IL) 1577
Southeastern Louisiana University (LA) 478
Southeastern Oklahoma State
University (OK) 966
Southeastern Technical College (GA) 1538
Southeastern University (FL) 261
Southeastern University (DC) 227
Southern Adventist University (TN) 1163
Southern Arkansas University (AR) 91
Southern Arkansas University Tech (AR) 1402
Southern California Institute of
Architecture (CA) 161
Southern California Institute of
Technology (CA) 162
Southern California Seminary (CA) 162
Southern Connecticut State University (CT) 209
Southern Illinois University
Carbondale (IL) 357
Southern Illinois University
Edwardsville (IL) 358
Southern Maine Community College (ME) 1645
Southern Methodist College (SC) 1129
Southern Methodist University (TX) 1197
Southern Nazarene University (OK) 967
Southern New Hampshire University (NH) 720
Southern Oregon University (OR) 985
Southern Polytechnic State
University (GA) 299
Southern State Community College (OH) 1880
Southern Union State Community
College (AL) 1375
Southern University and Agricultural and
Mechanical College (LA) 478
Southern University at New Orleans (LA) 479
Southern University at Shreveport (LA) 1641
Southern Utah University (UT) 1233
Southern Vermont College (VT) 1248
Southern Virginia University (VA) 1275
Southern Wesleyan University (SC) 1129
Southern West Virginia Community and
Technical College (WV) 2054
Southside Virginia Community
College (VA) 2029
Southwest Baptist University (MO) 675
Southwest Florida College (FL) 1518
Southwest Florida College
Tampa (FL) 1518
Southwest Georgia Technical College (GA) 1539
Southwest Institute of Technology (TX) 2001
Southwest Minnesota State
University (MN) 632
Southwest Mississippi Community
College (MS) 1717
Southwest Tennessee Community
College (TN) 1968
Southwest Texas Junior College (TX) 2001
Southwest University (LA) 480

Tables and Indexes

Southwest Virginia Community College (VA) 2030
Southwest Wisconsin Technical College (WI) 2064
Southwestern Adventist University (TX) 1198
Southwestern Assemblies of God University (TX) 1198
Southwestern Baptist Theological Seminary (TX) 1199
Southwestern Christian College (TX) 1199
Southwestern Christian University (OK) 967
Southwestern College (CA) 1467
Southwestern College (AZ) 81
Southwestern College (KS) 439
Southwestern College
- Dayton (OH) 1881
- Florence (KY) 1633
- Franklin (OH) 1881
- Tri-County (OH) 1881
- Vine Street Campus (OH) 1882

Southwestern Community College (IA) 1607
Southwestern Community College (NC) 1843
Southwestern Illinois College (IL) 1578
Southwestern Indian Polytechnic Institute (NM) 1775
Southwestern Michigan College (MI) 1685
Southwestern Oklahoma State University (OK) 968
Southwestern Oregon Community College (OR) 1906
Southwestern University (TX) 1199
Spalding University (KY) 460
Spartan College of Aeronautics and Technology (OK) 969
Spartanburg Community College (SC) 1950
Spartanburg Methodist College (SC) 1950
Spelman College (GA) 300
Spencerian College (KY) 1633
Spencerian College
- Lexington (KY) 1633

Spokane Community College (WA) 2048
Spokane Falls Community College (WA) 2048
Spoon River College (IL) 1578
Spring Arbor University (MI) 602
Spring Hill College (AL) 60
Springfield College (MA) 558
Springfield College in Illinois (IL) 1578
Springfield Technical Community College (MA) 1670
Stanford University (CA) 162
Stanly Community College (NC) 1844
Stark State College of Technology (OH) 1882
State Fair Community College (MO) 1732
State University of New York at Albany (NY) 825
State University of New York at Binghamton (NY) 826
State University of New York at Buffalo (NY) 827
State University of New York at Farmingdale (NY) 828
State University of New York at New Paltz (NY) 828
State University of New York at Oswego (NY) 829
State University of New York at Purchase (NY) 830
State University of New York at Stony Brook (NY) 831
State University of New York College at Brockport (NY) 832
State University of New York College at Buffalo (NY) 833
State University of New York College at Cortland (NY) 833
State University of New York College at Fredonia (NY) 834
State University of New York College at Geneseo (NY) 835
State University of New York College at Old Westbury (NY) 836
State University of New York College at Oneonta (NY) 837
State University of New York College at Plattsburgh (NY) 838
State University of New York College at Potsdam (NY) 838
State University of New York College of Agriculture and Technology at Cobleskill (NY) 1808
State University of New York College of Agriculture and Technology at Morrisville (NY) 1809
State University of New York College of Environmental Science and Forestry (NY) 839
State University of New York College of Technology at Alfred (NY) 1810
State University of New York College of Technology at Canton (NY) 1810
State University of New York College of Technology at Delhi (NY) 1811
State University of New York Downstate Medical Center (NY) 840
State University of New York Empire State College (NY) 841
State University of New York Institute of Technology at Utica/Rome (NY) 841
State University of New York Maritime College (NY) 842
State University of New York Upstate Medical University (NY) 843
Stautzenberger College (OH) 1882
Stautzenberger College
- Strongsville (OH) 1883

Stenotype Institute
- Jacksonville (FL) 1519
- Orlando (FL) 1519

Stephen F. Austin State University (TX) 1200
Stephens College (MO) 675
Sterling College (KS) 440
Sterling College (VT) 1249
Stetson University (FL) 262
Stevens Institute of Technology (NJ) 743
Stevens-Henager College
- Boise (ID) 1548
- Logan (UT) 1234
- Murray (UT) 1234
- Ogden (UT) 1234
- Orem (UT) 1234

Stevenson University (MD) 512
Stillman College (AL) 61
Stone Child College (MT) 1739
Stonehill College (MA) 558
Stratford University
- Falls Church (VA) 1276
- Woodbridge (VA) 1276

Strayer University (DC) 228
Suffolk County Community College (NY) 1812
Suffolk University (MA) 559
Sul Ross State University (TX) 1201
Sullivan County Community College (NY) 1812
Sullivan University (KY) 461
Surry Community College (NC) 1844
Susquehanna University (PA) 1066
Sussex County Community College (NJ) 1765
Swarthmore College (PA) 1067
Swedish Institute (NY) 1813
Sweet Briar College (VA) 1276
Syracuse University (NY) 843
Tabor College (KS) 440
Tacoma Community College (WA) 2049
Taft College (CA) 1467
Talladega College (AL) 61
Tallahassee Community College (FL) 1519
Talmudic College of Florida (FL) 263
Talmudical Academy of New Jersey (NJ) 743
Talmudical Institute of Upstate New York (NY) 844
Talmudical Seminary Oholei Torah (NY) 844
Talmudical Yeshiva of Philadelphia (PA) 1067
Tarleton State University (TX) 1201
Tarrant County College (TX) 2001
Taylor Business Institute (IL) 1579
Taylor University (IN) 394
Technical Career Institutes (NY) 1813
Technical College of the Lowcountry (SC) 1951
Technology Education College (OH) 1883
Teikyo Loretto Heights University (CO) 194
Telshe Yeshiva-Chicago (IL) 359
Temple Baptist College (OH) 942
Temple College (TX) 2002
Temple University (PA) 1068
Tennessee State University (TN) 1163
Tennessee Technological University (TN) 1164
Tennessee Temple University (TN) 1165
Tennessee Wesleyan College (TN) 1165
Terra State Community College (OH) 1883
TESST College of Technology
- Alexandria (VA) 2031
- Baltimore (MD) 1656
- Beltsville (MD) 1656
- Towson (MD) 1656

Texarkana College (TX) 2003
Texas A&M International University (TX) 1202
Texas A&M University (TX) 1203
Texas A&M University-Baylor College of Dentistry (TX) 1203
Texas A&M University-Commerce (TX) 1204
Texas A&M University-Corpus Christi (TX) 1205
Texas A&M University-Galveston (TX) 1205
Texas A&M University-Kingsville (TX) 1206
Texas A&M University-Texarkana (TX) 1206
Texas Christian University (TX) 1207
Texas College (TX) 1208
Texas County Technical Institute (MO) 1733
Texas Culinary Academy (TX) 2003
Texas Lutheran University (TX) 1208
Texas Southern University (TX) 1209
Texas State Technical College
- Harlingen (TX) 2003
- Marshall (TX) 2004

Texas State Technical College: Sweetwater *see* Texas State Technical College: West Texas (TX)
- Waco (TX) 2004
- West Texas (TX) 2004

Texas State University
- San Marcos (TX) 1210

Texas Tech University (TX) 1211
Texas Tech University Health Sciences Center (TX) 1211
Texas Wesleyan University (TX) 1212
Texas Woman's University (TX) 1212
Thaddeus Stevens College of Technology (PA) 1934
Thiel College (PA) 1068
Thomas Aquinas College (CA) 163
Thomas College (ME) 491
Thomas Edison State College (NJ) 743
Thomas Jefferson University
- College of Health Professions (PA) 1069

Thomas More College (KY) 461
Thomas More College of Liberal Arts (NH) 720
Thomas Nelson Community College (VA) 2031
Thomas University (GA) 300
Thompson Institute *see* Kaplan Career Institute: Harrisburg (PA)
Three Rivers Community College (CT) 1494
Three Rivers Community College (MO) 1733
Tidewater Community College (VA) 2031
Tiffin University (OH) 942
Toccoa Falls College (GA) 301
Tohono O'odham Community College (AZ) 1391
Tompkins Cortland Community College (NY) 1813
Torah Temimah Talmudical Seminary (NY) 844
Tougaloo College (MS) 645
Touro College (NY) 844
Towson University (MD) 513
TransPacific Hawaii College (HI) 1542
Transylvania University (KY) 462
Treasure Valley Community College (OR) 1906
Trevecca Nazarene University (TN) 1166
Triangle Tech
- Bethlehem (PA) 1935
- DuBois (PA) 1935
- Erie (PA) 1935
- Greensburg (PA) 1936
- Pittsburgh (PA) 1936
- Sunbury (PA) 1937

Tri-County Community College (NC) 1844
Tri-County Technical College (SC) 1951
Trident Technical College (SC) 1952
Trine University (IN) 395
Trinidad State Junior College (CO) 1486
Trinity Baptist College (FL) 263
Trinity Bible College (ND) 899
Trinity Christian College (IL) 359
Trinity College (CT) 210

Tables and Indexes

Trinity College of Florida (FL) 263
Trinity College of Nursing and Health Sciences (IL) 359
Trinity International University (IL) 360
Trinity Life Bible College (CA) 1468
Trinity Lutheran College (WA) 1298
Trinity University (TX) 1213
Trinity Valley Community College (TX) 2005
Trinity Washington University (DC) 228
Tri-State Bible College (OH) 942
Tri-State Business Institute (PA) 1935
Tri-State College (OH) 1884
Tri-State University *see* Trine University (IN)
Triton College (IL) 1579
Trocaire College (NY) 1814
Troy University (AL) 61
Truckee Meadows Community College (NV) 1750
Truett-McConnell College (GA) 301
Truman State University (MO) 676
Trumbull Business College (OH) 1884
Tucson Design College *see* Art Institute of Tucson (AZ)
Tufts University (MA) 560
Tulane University (LA) 480
Tulsa Community College (OK) 1896
Tulsa Welding School (OK) 1896
Tunxis Community College (CT) 1494
Turabo University (PR) 1095
Turtle Mountain Community College (ND) 1852
Tusculum College (TN) 1167
Tuskegee University (AL) 62
Tyler Junior College (TX) 2005
Ulster County Community College (NY) 1815
Umpqua Community College (OR) 1907
Union College (KY) 463
Union College (NE) 700
Union College (NY) 845
Union County College (NJ) 1766
Union Institute & University (OH) 943
Union University (TN) 1167
United States Air Force Academy (CO) 195
United States Coast Guard Academy (CT) 211
United States Merchant Marine Academy (NY) 846
United States Military Academy (NY) 846
United States Naval Academy (MD) 514
United States Sports Academy (AL) 63
United Talmudical Seminary (NY) 847
United Tribes Technical College (ND) 1852
Unity College (ME) 491
Universal Technical Institute (AZ) 1392
Universal Technology College of Puerto Rico (PR) 1942
Universidad Adventista de las Antillas (PR) 1095
Universidad Anahuac (MX) 1360
Universidad Autonoma de Aguascalientes (MX) 1360
Universidad Autonoma de Coahuila (MX) 1360
Universidad Central del Caribe (PR) 1096
Universidad de Monterrey (MX) 1360
Universidad del Este (PR) 1096
Universidad del Valle de Guatemala Guatemala 1358
Universidad FLET (FL) 264
Universidad Metropolitana (PR) 1096
Universidad Politecnica de Puerto Rico (PR) 1097
Universidad Privada Boliviana (FN) 1350
University College of San Juan (PR) 1097
University of Advancing Technology (AZ) 81
University of Akron (OH) 943
University of Akron
Wayne College (OH) 1884
University of Alabama (AL) 63
University of Alabama at Birmingham (AL) 64
University of Alabama in Huntsville (AL) 65
University of Alaska Anchorage (AK) 71
University of Alaska Fairbanks (AK) 71
University of Alaska Southeast (AK) 72
University of Alberta (FN) 1353
University of Arizona (AZ) 82
University of Arkansas (AR) 92
University of Arkansas at Fort Smith (AR) 93
University of Arkansas at Little Rock (AR) 93
University of Arkansas at Monticello (AR) 94
University of Arkansas at Pine Bluff (AR) 95
University of Arkansas
Community College at Batesville (AR) 1403
Community College at Hope (AR) 1403
University of Arkansas Community College at Morrilton (AR) 1402
University of Arkansas for Medical Sciences (AR) 95
University of Baltimore (MD) 515
University of Bridgeport (CT) 212
University of British Columbia (FN) 1354
University of California
Berkeley (CA) 164
Davis (CA) 164
Irvine (CA) 165
Los Angeles (CA) 166
Merced (CA) 167
Riverside (CA) 168
San Diego (CA) 168
Santa Barbara (CA) 169
Santa Cruz (CA) 170
University of Central Arkansas (AR) 96
University of Central Florida (FL) 264
University of Central Missouri (MO) 677
University of Central Oklahoma (OK) 969
University of Charleston (WV) 1315
University of Chicago (IL) 361
University of Cincinnati (OH) 944
University of Cincinnati
Clermont College (OH) 1885
Raymond Walters College (OH) 1885
University of Colorado at Boulder (CO) 195
University of Colorado at Colorado Springs (CO) 196
University of Colorado at Denver (CO) 197
University of Connecticut (CT) 212
University of Dallas (TX) 1214
University of Dayton (OH) 945
University of Delaware (DE) 219
University of Denver (CO) 198
University of Detroit Mercy (MI) 603
University of Dubuque (IA) 422
University of Evansville (IN) 395
University of Findlay (OH) 946
University of Florida (FL) 265
University of Georgia (GA) 302
University of Great Falls (MT) 689
University of Guam (GU) 1349
University of Hartford (CT) 213
University of Hawaii at Hilo (HI) 308
University of Hawaii at Manoa (HI) 308
University of Hawaii
Hawaii Community College (HI) 1543
Honolulu Community College (HI) 1543
Kapiolani Community College (HI) 1544
Kauai Community College (HI) 1544
Leeward Community College (HI) 1545
Maui Community College (HI) 1545
West Oahu (HI) 309
Windward Community College (HI) 1545
University of Houston (TX) 1215
University of Houston-Clear Lake (TX) 1215
University of Houston-Downtown (TX) 1216
University of Houston-Victoria (TX) 1217
University of Idaho (ID) 315
University of Illinois at Chicago (IL) 361
University of Illinois at Urbana-Champaign (IL) 362
University of Illinois
Springfield (IL) 363
University of Indianapolis (IN) 396
University of Iowa (IA) 422
University of Judaism *see* American Jewish University (CA)
University of Kansas (KS) 441
University of Kansas Medical Center (KS) 442
University of Karlsruhe Germany 1358
University of Kentucky (KY) 464
University of La Verne (CA) 171
University of Louisiana at Lafayette (LA) 481
University of Louisiana at Monroe (LA) 481
University of Louisville (KY) 464
University of Maine (ME) 492
University of Maine at Augusta (ME) 493
University of Maine at Farmington (ME) 493
University of Maine at Fort Kent (ME) 494
University of Maine at Machias (ME) 495
University of Maine at Presque Isle (ME) 496
University of Management and Technology (VA) 1277
University of Manitoba (FN) 1355
University of Mary (ND) 899
University of Mary Hardin-Baylor (TX) 1217
University of Mary Washington (VA) 1277
University of Maryland
Baltimore (MD) 515
Baltimore County (MD) 516
College Park (MD) 516
Eastern Shore (MD) 517
University College (MD) 518
University of Massachusetts Amherst (MA) 561
University of Massachusetts Boston (MA) 562
University of Massachusetts Dartmouth (MA) 562
University of Massachusetts Lowell (MA) 563
University of Medicine and Dentistry of New Jersey
School of Health Related Professions (NJ) 744
School of Nursing (NJ) 744
University of Memphis (TN) 1168
University of Miami (FL) 266
University of Michigan (MI) 604
University of Michigan
Dearborn (MI) 605
Flint (MI) 605
University of Minnesota
Crookston (MN) 632
Duluth (MN) 633
Morris (MN) 634
Twin Cities (MN) 634
University of Mississippi (MS) 646
University of Mississippi Medical Center (MS) 647
University of Missouri
Columbia (MO) 678
Kansas City (MO) 679
University of Missouri: Rolla *see* Missouri University of Science and Technology (MO)
St. Louis (MO) 679
University of Mobile (AL) 65
University of Montana (MT) 690
University of Montana Western (MT) 691
University of Montevallo (AL) 66
University of Nebraska
Kearney (NE) 701
Lincoln (NE) 702
Omaha (NE) 703
University of Nebraska Medical Center (NE) 703
University of Nevada
Las Vegas (NV) 709
Reno (NV) 709
University of New England (ME) 496
University of New Hampshire (NH) 721
University of New Hampshire at Manchester (NH) 722
University of New Haven (CT) 214
University of New Mexico (NM) 750
University of New Orleans (LA) 482
University of North Alabama (AL) 67
University of North Carolina at Asheville (NC) 885
University of North Carolina at Chapel Hill (NC) 886
University of North Carolina at Charlotte (NC) 887
University of North Carolina at Greensboro (NC) 888
University of North Carolina at Pembroke (NC) 888
University of North Carolina at Wilmington (NC) 889
University of North Carolina School of the Arts (NC) 890
University of North Dakota (ND) 900
University of North Florida (FL) 267
University of North Texas (TX) 1218
University of Northern Colorado (CO) 198
University of Northern Iowa (IA) 423
University of Northwestern Ohio (OH) 1886

University of Notre Dame (IN) 397
University of Oklahoma (OK) 970
University of Oregon (OR) 986
University of Pennsylvania (PA) 1070
University of Phoenix (AZ) 82
University of Pittsburgh (PA) 1071
University of Pittsburgh at Bradford (PA) 1071
University of Pittsburgh at Greensburg (PA) 1072
University of Pittsburgh at Johnstown (PA) 1073
University of Pittsburgh at Titusville (PA) 1937
University of Portland (OR) 987
University of Puerto Rico
  Aguadilla (PR) 1098
  Arecibo (PR) 1098
  Bayamon University College (PR) 1098
  Carolina Regional College (PR) 1099
  Cayey University College (PR) 1099
  Humacao (PR) 1100
  Mayaguez (PR) 1101
  Medical Sciences (PR) 1101
  Ponce (PR) 1102
  Rio Piedras (PR) 1102
  Utuado (PR) 1103
University of Puget Sound (WA) 1298
University of Redlands (CA) 171
University of Rhode Island (RI) 1111
University of Richmond (VA) 1278
University of Rio Grande (OH) 946
University of Rochester (NY) 847
University of St. Francis (IL) 364
University of St. Francis (IN) 398
University of St. Mary (KS) 442
University of St. Thomas (MN) 635
University of St. Thomas (TX) 1219
University of San Diego (CA) 172
University of San Francisco (CA) 173
University of Science and Arts of Oklahoma (OK) 971
University of Scranton (PA) 1074
University of Sioux Falls (SD) 1142
University of South Alabama (AL) 67
University of South Carolina (SC) 1129
University of South Carolina at Aiken (SC) 1130
University of South Carolina at Beaufort (SC) 1131
University of South Carolina at Lancaster (SC) 1952
University of South Carolina at Sumter (SC) 1953
University of South Carolina at Union (SC) 1953
University of South Carolina
  Salkehatchie Regional Campus (SC) 1954
University of South Carolina Upstate (SC) 1132
University of South Dakota (SD) 1142
University of South Florida (FL) 267
University of Southern California (CA) 174
University of Southern Indiana (IN) 398
University of Southern Maine (ME) 497
University of Southern Mississippi (MS) 647
University of Southern Nevada (NV) 710
University of Tampa (FL) 268
University of Tennessee
  Chattanooga (TN) 1169
University of Tennessee Health Science Center (TN) 1169
  Knoxville (TN) 1170
  Martin (TN) 1171
University of Texas at Arlington (TX) 1219
University of Texas at Austin (TX) 1220
University of Texas at Brownsville
  Texas Southmost College (TX) 1221
University of Texas at Dallas (TX) 1222
University of Texas at El Paso (TX) 1222
University of Texas at San Antonio (TX) 1223
University of Texas at Tyler (TX) 1224
University of Texas Health Science Center at Houston (TX) 1225
University of Texas Health Science Center at San Antonio (TX) 1225
University of Texas Medical Branch at Galveston (TX) 1225
University of Texas of the Permian Basin (TX) 1226
University of Texas
  Pan American (TX) 1227
University of Texas Southwestern Medical Center at Dallas (TX) 1226
University of the Arts (PA) 1074
University of the Cumberlands (KY) 465
University of the District of Columbia (DC) 229
University of the Incarnate Word (TX) 1227
University of the Ozarks (AR) 96
University of the Pacific (CA) 175
University of the Sacred Heart (PR) 1103
University of the Sciences in Philadelphia (PA) 1075
University of the South (TN) 1172
University of the Southwest (NM) 751
University of the Virgin Islands (VI), U.S. 1349
University of the West (CA) 175
University of Toledo (OH) 947
University of Toronto (FN) 1355
University of Tulsa (OK) 971
University of Utah (UT) 1235
University of Vermont (VT) 1250
University of Virginia (VA) 1278
University of Virginia's College at Wise (VA) 1279
University of Washington (WA) 1299
University of Washington Bothell (WA) 1300
University of Washington Tacoma (WA) 1301
University of West Alabama (AL) 68
University of West Florida (FL) 269
University of West Georgia (GA) 303
University of Wisconsin-Baraboo/Sauk County (WI) 2065
University of Wisconsin-Barron County (WI) 2065
University of Wisconsin-Eau Claire (WI) 1336
University of Wisconsin-Fond du Lac (WI) 2066
University of Wisconsin-Fox Valley (WI) 2066
University of Wisconsin-Green Bay (WI) 1336
University of Wisconsin-La Crosse (WI) 1337
University of Wisconsin-Madison (WI) 1338
University of Wisconsin-Manitowoc (WI) 2066
University of Wisconsin-Marathon County (WI) 2067
University of Wisconsin-Marinette (WI) 2067
University of Wisconsin-Marshfield/Wood County (WI) 2068
University of Wisconsin-Milwaukee (WI) 1339
University of Wisconsin-Oshkosh (WI) 1340
University of Wisconsin-Parkside (WI) 1340
University of Wisconsin-Platteville (WI) 1341
University of Wisconsin-Richland (WI) 2068
University of Wisconsin-River Falls (WI) 1342
University of Wisconsin-Rock County (WI) 2069
University of Wisconsin-Sheboygan (WI) 2069
University of Wisconsin-Stevens Point (WI) 1342
University of Wisconsin-Stout (WI) 1343
University of Wisconsin-Superior (WI) 1344
University of Wisconsin-Washington County (WI) 2070
University of Wisconsin-Waukesha (WI) 2070
University of Wisconsin-Whitewater (WI) 1345
University of Wyoming (WY) 1348
Upper Iowa University (IA) 424
Urban College of Boston (MA) 1670
Urbana University (OH) 948
Ursinus College (PA) 1076
Ursuline College (OH) 949
U.T.A. Mesivta-Kiryas Jocl (NY) 845
Utah Career College (UT) 2014
Utah State University (UT) 1236
Utah Valley State College *see* Utah Valley University (UT)
Utah Valley University (UT) 1236
Utica College (NY) 848
Utica School of Commerce (NY) 1815
Utica School of Commerce
  Canastota (NY) 1816
  Oneonta (NY) 1816
Valdosta State University (GA) 304
Valdosta Technical College (GA) 1539
Valencia Community College (FL) 1519
Valley City State University (ND) 901
Valley College (WV) 2054
Valley Forge Christian College (PA) 1076
Valley Forge Military Academy & College (PA) 1938
Valley Forge Military College *see* Valley Forge Military Academy & College (PA)
Valparaiso University (IN) 399
Vance-Granville Community College (NC) 1845
Vanderbilt University (TN) 1173
VanderCook College of Music (IL) 364
Vanguard University of Southern California (CA) 176
Vassar College (NY) 849
Vatterott College (IA) 1608
Vatterott College (MO) 1733
Vatterott College (OK) 1897
Vatterott College
  Cleveland (OH) 1886
  Joplin (MO) 1734
  Kansas City (MO) 1734
  Memphis (TN) 1968
  O'Fallon (MO) 1734
  Quincy (IL) 1580
  St. Joseph (MO) 1734
  Spring Valley (NE) 1746
  Springfield (MO) 1734
  Sunset Hills (MO) 1735
  Tulsa (OK) 1897
Vaughn College of Aeronautics and Technology (NY) 850
Ventura College (CA) 1468
Vermilion Community College (MN) 1708
Vermont Technical College (VT) 1251
Vernon College (TX) 2006
Vet Tech Institute (PA) 1938
Victor Valley College (CA) 1468
Victoria College (TX) 2006
Villa Maria College of Buffalo (NY) 1816
Villanova University (PA) 1077
Vincennes University (IN) 1595
Virginia Baptist College (VA) 1280
Virginia College (MS) 1717
Virginia College (AL) 69
Virginia College at Austin (TX) 2006
Virginia College at Huntsville (AL) 69
Virginia College at Mobile (AL) 1376
Virginia College at Montgomery (AL) 1376
Virginia College at Pensacola (FL) 1520
Virginia College Gulf Coast (MS) 1718
Virginia Commonwealth University (VA) 1280
Virginia Highlands Community College (VA) 2032
Virginia Intermont College (VA) 1281
Virginia Marti College of Art and Design (OH) 1887
Virginia Military Institute (VA) 1282
Virginia Polytechnic Institute and State University (VA) 1282
Virginia State University (VA) 1283
Virginia Union University (VA) 1284
Virginia University of Lynchburg (VA) 1284
Virginia Wesleyan College (VA) 1285
Virginia Western Community College (VA) 2032
Visible School
  Music and Worship Arts College (TN) 1173
Vista Community College *see* Berkeley City College (CA)
Viterbo University (WI) 1345
Volunteer State Community College (TN) 1968
Voorhees College (SC) 1132
Wabash College (IN) 400
Wade College (TX) 2006
Wagner College (NY) 850
Wake Forest University (NC) 890
Wake Technical Community College (NC) 1845
Walden University (MN) 636
Waldorf College (IA) 425
Walla Walla Community College (WA) 2049
Walla Walla University (WA) 1301
Wallace State Community College at Hanceville (AL) 1376
Walsh College of Accountancy and Business Administration (MI) 606
Walsh University (OH) 949
Walters State Community College (TN) 1969
Warner Pacific College (OR) 988
Warner Southern College *see* Warner University (FL)
Warner University (FL) 270
Warren County Community College (NJ) 1766
Warren Wilson College (NC) 891
Wartburg College (IA) 426
Washburn University (KS) 443

Washington & Jefferson College (PA) 1078
Washington and Lee University (VA) 1285
Washington Bible College (MD) 518
Washington College (MD) 519
Washington County Community College (ME) 1645
Washington State Community College (OH) 1887
Washington State University (WA) 1302
Washington University in St. Louis (MO) 680
Washtenaw Community College (MI) 1686
Watkins College of Art, Design and Film (TN) 1174
Waubonsee Community College (IL) 1580
Waukesha County Technical College (WI) 2071
Waycross College (GA) 1539
Wayland Baptist University (TX) 1228
Wayne Community College (NC) 1846
Wayne County Community College (MI) 1686
Wayne State College (NE) 704
Wayne State University (MI) 607
Waynesburg University (PA) 1079
Weatherford College (TX) 2007
Webb Institute (NY) 851
Webber International University (FL) 270
Weber State University (UT) 1237
Webster University (MO) 681
Wellesley College (MA) 564
Wells College (NY) 852
Wenatchee Valley College (WA) 2050
Wentworth Institute of Technology (MA) 565
Wentworth Military Junior College (MO) 1735
Wesley College (DE) 220
Wesley College (MS) 648
Wesleyan College (GA) 304
Wesleyan University (CT) 215
West Central Technical College (GA) 1540
West Chester University of Pennsylvania (PA) 1079
West Coast University (CA) 176
West Georgia Technical College (GA) 1540
West Hills College
Coalinga (CA) 1469
Lemoore (CA) 1469
West Kentucky Community and Technical College (KY) 1634
West Liberty State College (WV) 1316
West Los Angeles College (CA) 1470
West Shore Community College (MI) 1687
West Suburban College of Nursing (IL) 365
West Tennessee Business College (TN) 1970
West Texas A&M University (TX) 1229
West Valley College (CA) 1470
West Virginia Business College
Nutter Fort (WV) 2055
Wheeling (WV) 2055
West Virginia Career Institute *see* Pennsylvania Institute of Health and Technology (PA)
West Virginia Junior College (WV) 2055
West Virginia Junior College
Bridgeport (WV) 2056
Charleston (WV) 2056
West Virginia Northern Community College (WV) 2056
West Virginia State Community and Technical College (WV) 2056
West Virginia State University (WV) 1316
West Virginia University (WV) 1317
West Virginia University at Parkersburg (WV) 1318
West Virginia University Institute of Technology (WV) 1318
West Virginia Wesleyan College (WV) 1319
Westchester Community College (NY) 1816
Western Career College
Antioch (CA) 1470
Citrus Heights (CA) 1471
Emeryville (CA) 177
Pleasant Hill (CA) 1471
Sacramento (CA) 1471
San Jose (CA) 1471
San Leandro (CA) 1471
Stockton (CA) 1471
Western Carolina University (NC) 892
Western Connecticut State University (CT) 215
Western Culinary Institute (OR) 1907
Western Dakota Technical Institute (SD) 1958
Western Governors University (UT) 1238
Western Illinois University (IL) 365
Western Illinois University
Quad Cities (IL) 366
Western International University (AZ) 83
Western Iowa Tech Community College (IA) 1608
Western Kentucky University (KY) 466
Western Michigan University (MI) 607
Western Nebraska Community College (NE) 1746
Western Nevada College (NV) 1750
Western New England College (MA) 565
Western New Mexico University (NM) 751
Western Oklahoma State College (OK) 1897
Western Oregon University (OR) 988
Western Piedmont Community College (NC) 1846
Western School of Health and Business Careers *see* Sanford-Brown Institute: Pittsburgh (PA)
Western School of Health and Business Careers: Monroeville *see* Sanford-Brown Institute: Monroeville (PA)
Western State College of Colorado (CO) 199
Western Technical College (WI) 2071
Western Technical College (TX) 2007
Western Technical College
Diana Drive (TX) 2008
Western Texas College (TX) 2008
Western Washington University (WA) 1303
Western Wisconsin Technical College *see* Western Technical College (WI)
Western Wyoming Community College (WY) 2077
Westfield State College (MA) 566
Westminster College (MO) 682
Westminster College (PA) 1080
Westminster College (UT) 1238
Westmont College (CA) 177
Westmoreland County Community College (PA) 1938
Westwood College
Anaheim (CA) 178
Atlanta Midtown (GA) 305
Chicago Loop (IL) 366
Dallas (TX) 2008
Denver North (CO) 200
Denver South (CO) 200
DuPage (IL) 366
Fort Worth (TX) 2008
Houston South (TX) 2009
Inland Empire (CA) 178
Los Angeles (CA) 1472
Northlake (GA) 305
Westwood College of Aviation Technology *see* Redstone College (CO)
O'Hare Airport (IL) 367
River Oaks (IL) 367
South Bay (CA) 178
Wharton County Junior College (TX) 2009
Whatcom Community College (WA) 2050
Wheaton College (IL) 367
Wheaton College (MA) 567
Wheeling Jesuit University (WV) 1320
Wheelock College (MA) 568
White Earth Tribal and Community College (MN) 1709
White Mountains Community College (NH) 1755
Whitman College (WA) 1304
Whittier College (CA) 178
Whitworth University (WA) 1305
Wichita State University (KS) 444
Widener University (PA) 1081
Wilberforce University (OH) 950
Wiley College (TX) 1230
Wilkes Community College (NC) 1847
Wilkes University (PA) 1082
Willamette University (OR) 989
William Carey University (MS) 648
William Jessup University (CA) 179
William Jewell College (MO) 682
William Paterson University of New Jersey (NJ) 745
William Penn University (IA) 426
William Rainey Harper College *see* Harper College (IL)
William Woods University (MO) 683
Williams Baptist College (AR) 97
Williams College (MA) 568
Williamsburg Technical College (SC) 1954
Williamson Christian College (TN) 1174
Williamson Free School of Mechanical Trades (PA) 1939
Williston State College (ND) 1853
Wilmington College (OH) 951
Wilmington University (DE) 220
Wilson College (PA) 1082
Wilson Community College (NC) 1847
Wingate University (NC) 893
Winona State University (MN) 636
Winston-Salem Bible College *see* Carolina Christian College (NC)
Winston-Salem State University (NC) 893
Winthrop University (SC) 1133
Wisconsin Indianhead Technical College (WI) 2072
Wisconsin Lutheran College (WI) 1346
Wittenberg University (OH) 951
W.L. Bonner Bible College (SC) 1132
Wofford College (SC) 1133
Wood Tobe-Coburn School (NY) 1817
Woodbury Institute of Champlain College (VT) 1251
Woodbury University (CA) 180
Worcester Polytechnic Institute (MA) 569
Worcester State College (MA) 570
World College (VA) 1286
World Mission University (CA) 180
Wor-Wic Community College (MD) 1657
Wright State University (OH) 952
Wright State University
Lake Campus (OH) 1887
WyoTech
Fremont (CA) 1472
Laramie (WY) 2077
Long Beach (CA) 1472
Wytheville Community College (VA) 2033
Xavier University (OH) 953
Xavier University of Louisiana (LA) 483
Yakima Valley Community College (WA) 2051
Yale University (CT) 216
Yavapai College (AZ) 1392
Yeshiva and Kolel Bais Medrash Elyon (NY) 852
Yeshiva and Kollel Harbotzas Torah (NY) 852
Yeshiva Beth Yehuda-Yeshiva Gedolah of Greater Detroit (MI) 608
Yeshiva College of the Nations Capital (MD) 520
Yeshiva Derech Chaim (NY) 853
Yeshiva D'Monsey Rabbinical College (NY) 853
Yeshiva Gedolah Imrei Yosef D'Spinka (NY) 853
Yeshiva Gedolah Rabbinical College (FL) 271
Yeshiva Gedolah Zichron Moshe (NY) 853
Yeshiva Karlin Stolin (NY) 853
Yeshiva Mikdash Melech (NY) 853
Yeshiva of Nitra (NY) 853
Yeshiva of the Telshe Alumni (NY) 853
Yeshiva Ohr Elchonon Chabad/West Coast Talmudical Seminary (CA) 181
Yeshiva Shaar Hatorah (NY) 854
Yeshiva Shaarei Torah of Rockland (NY) 854
Yeshiva Toras Chaim Talmudical Seminary (CO) 200
Yeshiva University (NY) 854
Yeshivas Novominsk (NY) 854
Yeshivath Beth Moshe (PA) 1083
Yeshivath Viznitz (NY) 854
Yonsei University Republic of Korea 1361
York College (NE) 705
York College of Pennsylvania (PA) 1083
York County Community College (ME) 1646
York Technical College (SC) 1955
Yorktowne Business Institute (PA) 1939
Young Harris College (GA) 1541
Youngstown State University (OH) 954
YTI Career Institute
Lancaster (PA) 1940
York (PA) 1940
Yuba Community College District (CA) 1472
Zane State College (OH) 1888
Zion Bible College (MA) 570